THE SPORT AMERICANA®

Baseball Card PRICE GUIDE

By

DR. JAMES BECKETT

NUMBER 15

EDGEWATER BOOK COMPANY • CLEVELAND

EDGEWATER BOOK COMPANY
P.O. BOX 40238
CLEVELAND, OHIO 44140

BECKETT PUBLICATIONS
DALLAS, TEXAS

Manufactured in the United States of America

First Printing

Library of Congress catalog card number: 79-643474

ISBN 0-937424-65-X

The Sport Americana Baseball Card Price Guide

Table of Contents

About the Author 12
How To Use This Book 12
Introduction 14
How To Collect 14
Obtaining Cards 16
Preserving Your Cards 16
Collecting vs. Investing 16
Terminology 18
Glossary/Legend 18
Understanding Card Values 26
Determining Value 26
Regional Variation 26
Set Prices 30
Scarce Series 30
Grading Your Cards 30
Condition Guide 35
Selling Your Cards 36
Interesting Notes 36
Advertising 37
Additional Reading 37
Prices in This Guide 38
History of Baseball Cards 38
Increasing Popularity 40
Intensified Competition 44
Sharing the Pie 44
Finding Out More 45
Acknowledgments 45, 1052

Vintage

Batter-Up 46
Cracker Jack
1914 47
1915 48
Delong 49
Diamond Stars 50
Double Play 51
Fleischmann Bread 52
Fro Joy 53
Goudey
1933 53
1934 55
1935 Puzzle 56
1936 B/W 57
1938 Heads Up 58
M101-4 Sporting News 58
M101-5 Sporting News 59
M116 Sporting Life 61
N28 Allen and Ginter 63
N29 Allen and Ginter 63
N43 Allen and Ginter 64
N162 Goodwin 65
N172 Old Judge 65
N184 Kimball's 71
N284 Buchner 72
N300 Mayo 74
Play Ball
1939 75
1940 76
1941 77
T3 Turkey Red 78
T200 Fatima 79
T201 Mecca 80
T202 Triple Folders 80
T204 Ramly 82
T205 Gold Border 83
T206 White Border 85
T207 Brown Background 90
W517 92
W572 92
W711-1 Orange/Gray 93
W711-2 Harry Hartman 94
W753 Browns 94
W754 Cardinals 94
Yuenglings 95

Modern

Action Packed
1988 Test 96
1992 ASG Prototypes 96
1992 All-Star Gallery 96
American Tract Society 97
Arena Holograms
1991 98
1992 Kid Griff 98
Astros
1967 Team Issue 98
1989 Lennox HSE 98
1990 Lennox HSE 99
Babe Ruth Story 99
Baseball Wit 100
Bazooka
1988 101
1989 Shining Stars 101
1990 Shining Stars 101
1991 Shining Stars 102
1992 Quadracard '53 Archives 102
Berk Ross
1951 103
1952 104
Best Western Nolan Ryan 104
Big League Chew 104
Bleachers
1991 23K Ken Griffey Jr. 105
1991 23K Frank Thomas 105
1991-92 Promos 105
1992 23K Dave Justice 106
1992 23K Nolan Ryan 106
1993 Promos 106
1993 23K Barry Bonds 107
1993 23K Ryne Sandberg 107
Blue Jays
1991 Score 107
1992 Oh Henry 108
Boardwalk and Baseball 108
Bond Bread 109
Bowman
1948 109
1949 110
1950 111
1951 113
1952 115
1953 Color 117
1953 B/W 118
1954 118
1955 120
1989 122
1989 Reprint Inserts 125
1990 125
1990 Inserts 129
1991 129
1992 133
Braves
1953 Johnston Cookies 137
1953-54 Spic and Span 3x5 138
1953-56 Spic and Span 7x10 138
1954 Johnston Cookies 138
1954 Spic and Span Postcards 139
1955 Johnston Cookies 139
1955 Spic and Span Die-Cut 140
1957 Spic and Span 4x5 140
1960 Lake to Lake 140
1960 Spic and Span 141
1985 Hostess 141
1992 Lykes Perforated 142
Brewers
1970 McDonald's 142
1983 Gardner's 142
1984 Gardner's 143
1985 Gardner's 143
1989 Gardner's 144
1989 Yearbook 144
1990 Miller Brewing 144
1991 Miller Brewing 145
1992 Carlson Travel 145
Burger King
1977 Yankees 146
1978 Astros 146
1978 Rangers 146
1978 Tigers 147
1978 Yankees 147
1979 Phillies 147
1979 Yankees 148
1980 Phillies 148
1980 Pitch/Hit/Run 148
1986 All-Pro 149
1987 All-Pro 149
Cardinals McDonald's/Pacific 150
Chef Boyardee 150
Circle K 151
Classic
1987 Game 151
1987 Update Yellow 152
1988 Blue 152
1988 Red 153
1989 Light Blue 153
1989 Travel Orange 154
1989 Travel Purple 155
1990 Blue 155
1990 Update 156
1990 III 157
1990 Draft Picks 158
1991 Game 200 158
1991 I 159
1991 II 160
1991 III 161
1991 Draft Picks 162
1992 Game 200 162
1992 I 164
1992 II 165
1992 Draft Picks Previews 166
1992 Draft Picks Promos 166
1992 Draft Picks 166
1992 Draft Picks Foil Bonus 167
CMC
1988 Don Mattingly 167
1989 Jose Canseco 168
1989 Mickey Mantle 168
1989 Babe Ruth 169
Coke
1981 Team Sets 169
1991 Don Mattingly 170
Colla
1990 Jose Canseco 171
1990 Will Clark 171
1990 Kevin Maas 172
1990 Don Mattingly 172
1991 Roberto Alomar 172
1991 Barry Bonds 173
1991 Joe Carter 173
1991 Dwight Gooden 174
1991 Ken Griffey Jr. 174
1991 Dave Justice 174
1991 Ryne Sandberg 175
1991 Darryl Strawberry 175
1992 All-Star Game 176
1992 Jeff Bagwell 176
1992 Tony Gwynn 177
1992 Mark McGwire 177
1992 Nolan Ryan 177
1992 Frank Thomas 178
Collect-A-Books
1990 178
1991 179
Conlon
1983 Marketcom 179
1986 Series 1 180
1987 Series 2 180
1988 Series 3 181
1988 Series 4 181
1988 Series 5 182
1988 American All-Stars 182
1988 National All-Stars 182
1988 Negro All-Stars 183
1988 Hardee's/Coke 183
1991 TSN 183
1991-92 TSN Prototypes 186
1992 TSN 13th National 186
1992 TSN 186
1992 TSN All-Star Program 189
1992 TSN Gold Inserts 189
1992-93 TSN Color Inserts 189
1993 TSN 190
Cracker Jack
1982 192
1991 Topps I 192
1991 Topps II 193
1992 Donruss I 193
1992 Donruss II 194
Cubs
1982 Red Lobster 194
1983 Thorn Apple Valley 195
1984 Seven-Up 195
1985 Seven-Up 195
1986 Gatorade 196
1986 Unocal 196
1987 David Berg 197
1988 David Berg 197
1989 Marathon 197
1990 Marathon 198
1991 Marathon 198
1991 Vine Line 199
1992 Marathon 199
Dan Dee 200
Denny's Grand Slam
1991 200
1992 200
Dexter Press 201
Dodgers
1958 Bell Brand 202
1959 Morrell 202
1960 Bell Brand 202
1960 Morrell 203
1961 Bell Brand 203
1961 Morrell 203
1962 Bell Brand 203
1971 Ticketron 204
1985 Coke Postcards 204
1986 Coke Postcards 205
1990 Target 205
Donruss
1981 211
1982 215
1983 220
1983 Action All-Stars 224
1983 HOF Heroes 224
1984 225
1984 Action All-Stars 229
1984 Champions 230
1985 231
1985 Action All-Stars 235
1985 Highlights 235
1985 Super DK's 236
1985 Wax Box Cards 236
1986 237
1986 All-Stars 241
1986 All-Star Box 241
1986 Highlights 242
1986 Pop-Ups 243
1986 Rookies 243
1986 Super DK's 243
1986 Wax Box Cards 244
1987 244
1987 All-Stars 248
1987 All-Star Box 249
1987 Highlights 249
1987 Opening Day 250
1987 Pop-Ups 252
1987 Rookies 252
1987 Super DK's 252
1987 Wax Box Cards 253
1988 253
1988 All-Stars 257
1988 Baseball's Best 258
1988 Pop-Ups 260
1988 Rookies 260
1988 Super DK's 261
1988 Athletics Team Book 261
1988 Cubs Team Book 262
1988 Mets Team Book 262
1988 Red Sox Team Book 263
1988 Yankees Team Book 263
1989 263
1989 All-Stars 268
1989 Baseball's Best 268
1989 Grand Slammers 270
1989 Pop-Ups 271

1989 Rookies 271
1989 Super DK's 272
1989 Traded 272
1990 Previews 272
1990 273
1990 Best AL 278
1990 Best NL 279
1990 Grand Slammers 280
1990 Learning Series 281
1990 Rookies 281
1990 Super DK's 282
1991 Previews 282
1991 282
1991 Elite 288
1991 Grand Slammers 288
1991 Rookies 288
1991 Super DK's 289
1992 Previews 289
1992 290
1992 Diamond Kings 294
1992 Durivage Expos 295
1992 Elite 295
1992 McDonald's 295
1992 Nolan Ryan Coke 296
1992 Phenoms 297
1992 Rookies 297
1992 Triple Play Previews 298
1992 Triple Play 298
1992 Triple Play Gallery 300
1993 Previews 300
1993 301
1993 Diamond Kings 303
1993 Elite 304
1993 Spirit of the Game 304

Dorman's Cheese 304

Drake's

1950 305
1981 305
1982 305
1983 306
1984 306
1985 307
1986 307
1987 308
1988 308

Elite Senior League 309

Fleer

1959 310
1960 311
1961 312
1963 313
1970 World Series 314
1971 World Series 314
1972 Famous Feats 315
1973 Wildest Days 316
1974 Baseball Firsts 316
1975 Pioneers 317
1981 317
1981 Sticker Cards 322
1982 323
1983 327
1984 331
1984 Update 335
1985 336
1985 Limited Edition 341
1985 Update 341
1986 342
1986 All-Star Inserts 346
1986 Future HOF 347
1986 League Leaders 347
1986 Limited Edition 347
1986 Mini 348
1986 Sluggers/Pitchers 349
1986 Slug/Pitch Box Cards 349
1986 Sticker Cards 349
1986 Sticker Wax Box 350
1986 Update 351
1986 Wax Box Cards 352
1987 352
1987 All-Star Inserts 356
1987 Award Winners 356
1987 Baseball All-Stars 357
1987 Exciting Stars 357
1987 Game Winners 358
1987 Headliners 358
1987 Hottest Stars 359
1987 League Leaders 359
1987 Limited Edition 360
1987 Limited Box Cards 360
1987 Mini 360
1987 Record Setters 361
1987 Sluggers/Pitchers 362
1987 Slug/Pitch Box Cards 362
1987 Sticker Cards 362
1987 Sticker Wax Box 363
1987 Update 364
1987 Wax Box Cards 365
1987 World Series 365
1988 365
1988 All-Star Inserts 370
1988 Award Winners 370
1988 Baseball All-Stars 371
1988 Baseball MVP's 371
1988 Exciting Stars 372
1988 Headliners 372
1988 Hottest Stars 372
1988 League Leaders 373
1988 Mini 373
1988 Record Setters 374
1988 Sluggers/Pitchers 375
1988 Slug/Pitch Box Cards 375
1988 Sticker Cards 376
1988 Sticker Box Cards 376
1988 Superstars 377
1988 Superstars Box Cards 377
1988 Team Leaders 378
1988 Update 378
1988 Wax Box Cards 379
1988 World Series 379
1989 380
1989 All-Star Inserts 385
1989 Baseball All-Stars 385
1989 Baseball MVP's 386
1989 Exciting Stars 386
1989 For The Record 387
1989 Heroes of Baseball 387
1989 League Leaders 387
1989 Superstars 388
1989 Update 388
1989 Wax Box Cards 389
1989 World Series 390
1990 390
1990 All-Star Inserts 395
1990 Award Winners 395
1990 Baseball All-Stars 396
1990 Baseball MVP's 396
1990 League Leaders 397
1990 League Standouts 397
1990 Soaring Stars 397
1990 Update 398
1990 Wax Box Cards 399
1990 World Series 399
1991 399
1991 All-Star Inserts 404
1991 Pro-Visions 405
1991 Pro-Visions Factory 405
1991 Update 405
1991 Wax Box Cards 406
1991 World Series 407
1992 407
1992 All-Stars 411
1992 Lumber Company 412
1992 Roger Clemens 412
1992 Rookie Sensations 413
1992 Smoke 'n Heat 413
1992 Team Leaders 413
1992 The Performer 414
1992 Update 414
1993 415
1993 All-Stars 418
1993 Golden Moments 418
1993 Major League Prospects 418
1993 Pro-Visions 419
1993 Tom Glavine 419

French's 419

Front Row

1991 Draft Picks 420
1992 Draft Picks 421
1992 Griffey Club House 422
1992 Griffey Gold 422
1992 Griffey Holograms 422
1992 Frank Thomas 422
1992 Frank Thomas Gold 423

Giants

1958 S.F. Call-Bulletin 423
1971 Ticketron 424
1991 Pacific Gas and Electric 424

Gold Entertainment Babe Ruth 424

Golden Press 425

Granny Goose A's

1981 425
1982 425
1983 426

Greyhound Heroes of Base Paths

1974 426
1975 427
1976 427

Griffey Gazette 427

Hires

1958 427
1958 Test 428

Home Run Derby 428

Homers Cookies Classics 429

Homogenized Bond 429

Hostess

1975 430
1975 Twinkie 431
1976 431
1976 Twinkie 432
1977 433
1978 434
1979 435

Indians

1952 Num Num 436
1956 Carling Black Label 436
1957 Sohio 437
1982 Burger King 437
1982 Wheaties 437
1983 Wheaties 438
1984 Wheaties 438
1985 Polaroid 439
1986 Oh Henry 439
1987 Gatorade 440
1988 Gatorade 440
1991 Fan Club/McDonald's 440

Jimmy Dean

1991 Signature 441
1992 18 441
1992 Living Legends 442
1992 Rookie Stars 442

Kahn's

1955 442
1956 443
1957 443
1958 443
1959 444
1960 444
1961 445
1962 445
1962 Atlanta 446
1963 446
1964 446
1965 447
1966 447
1967 448
1968 449
1969 450
1987 Reds 450
1988 Mets 450
1988 Reds 451
1989 Cooperstown 451
1989 Mets 452
1989 Reds 452
1990 Mets 453
1990 Reds 453
1991 Mets 453
1991 Reds 454
1992 Mets 454
1992 Reds 455

Kay-Bee

1986 455
1987 456
1988 456
1989 456
1990 457

Kellogg's

1970 457
1971 458
1972 459
1972 ATG 460
1973 2D 460
1974 461
1975 461
1976 462
1977 462
1978 463
1979 464
1980 464
1981 465
1982 465
1983 466
1991 Leyendas 467
1991 Stand Ups 467
1991 3D 467
1992 All-Stars 468

K-Mart

1982 468
1987 468
1988 Moments 469
1989 Career Batting Leaders 469
1989 Dream Team 470
1990 Career Batting Leaders 470
1990 Superstars 470

Laughlin

1968 World Series 471
1972 Great Feats 472
1974 All-Star Games 472
1974 Old Time Black Stars 473
1974 Sportslang 473
1975 Batty Baseball 473
1976 Diamond Jubilee 474
1976 Indianapolis Clowns 474
1978 Long Ago Black Stars 475
1980 Famous Feats 475
1980 300/400/500 476

Leaf

1948-49 476
1960 477
1987 Special Olympics 478
1990 Previews 478
1990 479
1991 Previews 482
1991 482
1991 Gold Rookies 485
1992 Previews 486
1992 Gold Previews 486
1992 487
1992 Gold Rookies 490

Lime Rock Griffey Holograms 490

Line Drive

1991 491
1991 Ryne Sandberg 491

Little Sun Writers 492

MacGregor Staff

1960 492
1965 492

Mariners Country Hearth 493

McCallum Ty Cobb 493

McDonald's Ken Griffey Jr. 494

MDA All-Stars 494

Megacards Babe Ruth

1992 Prototypes 494
1992 495

Mets

1984 Fan Club 497
1985 Fan Club 497
1986 Fan Club 497
1987 Fan Club 497
1988 Fan Club 498
1989 Fan Club 498
1990 Fan Club 498
1991 WIZ 499

Milton Bradley 501

MJB Holographics

1992 Prototypes 502
1992 Jeff Bagwell 502
1992 Chuck Knoblauch 502

MnM's Star Lineup 503

MooTown Snackers

1991 503
1992 504

Mother's

1983 Giants 504
1984 A's 504
1984 Astros 505
1984 Giants 505
1984 Mariners 506
1984 Padres 506
1985 A's 507
1985 Astros 507
1985 Giants 507
1985 Mariners 508

1985 Padres....508
1986 A's....509
1986 Astros....509
1986 Giants....509
1986 Mariners....510
1987 A's....510
1987 Astros....511
1987 Dodgers....511
1987 Giants....511
1987 Mariners....512
1987 McGwire....512
1987 Rangers....513
1988 A's....513
1988 Astros....513
1988 Will Clark....514
1988 Dodgers....514
1988 Giants....514
1988 Mariners....515
1988 McGwire....515
1988 Rangers....516
1989 A's....516
1989 A's ROY's....516
1989 Astros....517
1989 Canseco....517
1989 Will Clark....517
1989 Dodgers....518
1989 Giants....518
1989 Griffey Jr.....519
1989 Mariners....519
1989 McGwire....519
1989 Rangers....520
1990 Astros....520
1990 Athletics....520
1990 Canseco....521
1990 Will Clark....521
1990 Dodgers....521
1990 Giants....522
1990 Mariners....522
1990 McGwire....523
1990 Rangers....523
1990 Ryan....524
1990 Matt Williams....524
1991 Astros....524
1991 Athletics....524
1991 Dodgers....525
1991 Giants....525
1991 Griffeys....526
1991 Rangers....526
1991 Nolan Ryan....526
1992 Astros....527
1992 Athletics....527
1992 Jeff Bagwell....528
1992 Dodgers....528
1992 Giants....528
1992 Chuck Knoblauch....529
1992 Mariners....529
1992 Padres....529
1992 Rangers....530
1992 Nolan Ryan 7 No-Hitters....530
Motorola Old Timers....531
Mr. Turkey Superstars....531
MSA
1989 Cereal Superstars....531
1990 AGFA....532
1990 Soda Superstars....532
MTV Rock n' Jock....532
Nabisco Canada....533
Negro League
1986 Fritsch....533
1988 Duquesne....534
1990 Stars....535
1991 Ron Lewis....535
1992 Paul Lee....535
Nestle
1984 Dream Team....536
1984 792....536
1987 Dream Team....536
1988....537
New York Journal American....537
Nissen....538
Nu-Card
1960 Hi-Lites....538
1961 Scoops....539
O-Pee-Chee Premier
1991....540
1992....541
Orioles
1973 Johnny Pro....542
1987 French Bray....543
1988 French Bray....543
1989 French Bray/WWF....543
1991 Crown....544
Pacific
1980-83 Legends....547
1988 Eight Men Out....548
1988 Legends I....549
1989 Legends II....550
1989-90 Senior League....551
1990 Legends....552
1991 Nolan Ryan Texas Exp. I....553
1991 Nolan Ryan Inserts 8....554
1991 Nolan Ryan 7th No-Hitter....554
1991 Senior League....555
1992 Nolan Ryan Texas Exp. II....556
1992 Nolan Ryan Gold....557
1992 Nolan Ryan Limited 6....557
1992 Nolan Ryan Magazine 6....558
1992 Tom Seaver....558
1992 Tom Seaver Inserts 6....559
Packard Bell....560
Padres
1977 Schedule Cards....560
1978 Family Fun....561
1987 Bohemian Hearth Bread....562
1988 Coke....562
1989 Coke....562
1989 Magazine....563
1990 Coke....563
1990 Magazine/Unocal....564
1991 Magazine/Rally's....564
1992 Carl's Jr.....565
Pepsi
1989 McGwire....565
1990 Jose Canseco....565
1991 Ken Griffey Jr.....566
1991 Rickey Henderson....566
1991 Superstar....566
1992 Diet Canada MSA....567
Perma-Graphic
1981 All-Stars....567
1981 Credit Cards....568
1982 All-Stars....568
1982 Credit Cards....568
1983 All-Stars....569
1983 Credit Cards....569
Petro-Canada Standups....570
Phillies
1964 Philadelphia Bulletin....570
1974 Johnny Pro....570
1984 Tastykake....571
1985 CIGNA....571
1985 Tastykake....571
1986 CIGNA....572
1986 Tastykake....572
1987 Champion....573
1987 Tastykake....573
1988 Tastykake....574
1989 Tastykake....574
1990 Tastykake....575
1991 Medford....575
1992 Medford....576
Pinnacle
1992....576
1992 Mickey Mantle....580
1992 Rookie Idols....580
1992 Rookies....581
1992 Slugfest....581
1992 Team Pinnacle....582
1992 Team 2000....582
Pirates
1963 IDL....583
1966 East Hills....583
1968 KDKA....583
1989 Very Fine Juice....584
1990 Homers Cookies....584
1992 Nationwide Insurance....585
Police
1979 Giants....585
1980 Dodgers....585
1980 Giants....586
1981 Braves....586
1981 Dodgers....587
1981 Mariners....587
1981 Royals....587
1982 Braves....588
1982 Brewers....588
1982 Dodgers....589
1983 Braves....589
1983 Brewers....590
1983 Dodgers....590
1983 Royals....590
1984 Braves....591
1984 Brewers....591
1984 Dodgers....592
1985 Braves....592
1985 Brewers....592
1985 Mets/Yankees....593
1986 Astros....593
1986 Braves....594
1986 Brewers....594
1986 Dodgers....594
1987 Astros....595
1987 Brewers....595
1987 Dodgers....596
1988 Astros....596
1988 Brewers....596
1988 Dodgers....597
1988 Tigers....597
1989 Brewers....598
1989 Dodgers....598
1989 Tigers....598
1990 Brewers....599
1990 Dodgers....599
1991 Brewers....600
1991 Cardinals....600
1991 Dodgers....600
1991 Royals....601
1991 Tigers....601
1992 Angels....602
1992 Brewers....602
1992 Cardinals....602
1992 Dodgers....603
1992 Royals....603
Post
1961 Cereal....604
1962 Cereal....606
1963 Cereal....608
1990....609
1991....610
1991 Canada....610
1992....611
1992 Canada....611
Quaker Granola....612
Ralston Purina
1984....612
1987....612
Rangers
1983 Affiliated Food....613
1984 Jarvis Press....613
1985 Performance....614
1986 Performance....614
Red Heart....615
Red Man
1952....615
1953....616
1954....616
1955....617
Red Sox
1982 Coke....617
1990 Pepsi....617
1991 Pepsi....618
1992 Dunkin' Donuts....618
Reds
1957 Sohio....619
1982 Coke....619
1986 Texas Gold....619
1991 Pepsi....620
Rembrandt Ultra-Pro Promos....620
Rodeo Meats
1955....621
1956....621
Royals National Photo....622
S.F. Examiner
1991 Athletics....622
1991 Giants....622
Score
1987-88 Test Samples....623
1988....623
1988 Box Bottoms....627
1988 Rookie/Traded....628
1988 Young Superstars I....628
1988 Young Superstars II....629
1989....629
1989 Hottest 100 Rookies....634
1989 Hottest 100 Stars....634
1989 Rookie/Traded....635
1989 Scoremasters....636
1989 Young Superstars I....637
1989 Young Superstars II....637
1990....637
1990 McDonald's....642
1990 Nolan Ryan Commemorative....643
1990 100 Rising Stars....643
1990 100 Superstars....644
1990 Rookie/Traded....644
1990 Young Superstars I....645
1990 Young Superstars II....646
1991....646
1991 All-Star Fanfest....652
1991 Cooperstown....652
1991 Hot Rookies....653
1991 Mickey Mantle Promos....653
1991 Nolan Ryan Life and Times....653
1991 100 Rising Stars....654
1991 100 Superstars....654
1991 Rookies 40....655
1991 Rookie/Traded....656
1992 Previews....657
1992....657
1992 Joe DiMaggio....662
1992 Factory Inserts....663
1992 Hot Rookies....663
1992 Impact Players....663
1992 100 Rising Stars....664
1992 100 Superstars....665
1992 Proctor and Gamble....666
1992 Rookies....666
1992 Rookie/Traded....667
1992 The Franchise....668
1993 Select Promos....668
1993 Select....668
1993 Select Aces....671
1993 Select Chase Rookies....671
1993 Select Chase Stars....671
1993 Select Triple Crown....672
Sentry Robin Yount....672
7-Eleven....672
SilverStar Holograms....673
Smokey
1984 Angels....673
1984 Dodgers....674
1984 Padres....674
1985 Angels....674
1986 Angels....675
1987 A's Colorgrams....675
1987 American League....675
1987 Angels....676
1987 Braves....676
1987 Cardinals....676
1987 Dodger All-Stars....677
1987 National League....677
1987 Rangers....678
1988 Angels....678
1988 Cardinals....678
1988 Dodgers....679
1988 Padres....679
1988 Rangers....680
1988 Royals....680
1988 Twins Colorgrams....680
1989 Angels All-Stars....681
1989 Cardinals....681
1989 Colt .45s....681
1989 Dodger Greats....682
1989 Rangers....683
1990 Angels....683
1990 Cardinals....683
1990 Southern Cal....684
1991 Angels....684
1992 Padres....684
Socko Orel Hershiser....685
Sportflics
1985-86 Prototypes....685
1985-86 Test....686
1986....686
1986 Decade Greats....688
1986 Rookies....689
1987....690
1987 Dealer Panels....692
1987 Rookie Packs....692
1987 Rookies I....693
1987 Rookies II....693
1987 Team Preview....693

1988 ... 694
1988 Gamewinners ... 695
1989 ... 696
1990 ... 697

Squirt
1981 ... 699
1982 ... 699

SSPC ... 700

Stadium Club
1991 ... 703
1991 Charter Member * ... 707
1991 Members Only * ... 708
1992 ... 709
1992 Dome ... 714
1992 First Draft Picks ... 715
1992 Master Photos ... 716
1992 Members Only ... 716

Stahl Meyer
1953 ... 716
1954 ... 716
1955 ... 717

Starline Long John Silver ... 717

Studio
1991 Previews ... 718
1991 ... 718
1992 Previews ... 720
1992 ... 720
1992 Heritage ... 722

Sugardale
1962 ... 722
1963 ... 723

Sunflower Seeds
1990 ... 723
1991 ... 723
1992 ... 724

Swell
1948 Sport Thrills ... 724
1989 Baseball Greats ... 725
1990 Baseball Greats ... 726
1991 Baseball Greats ... 727

Swifts Franks ... 728

Tigers
1953 Glendale ... 728
1981 Detroit News ... 729
1983 Al Kaline Story ... 730
1985 Wendy's/Coke ... 731
1987 Coke ... 731
1988 Domino's ... 731
1988 Pepsi/Kroger ... 732
1989 Marathon ... 732
1990 Coke/Kroger ... 732
1991 Coke/Kroger ... 733

Tip Top ... 733

T/M
1988 Umpires ... 734
1989 Umpires ... 735
1989-90 Senior League ... 736
1990 Umpires ... 737

Topps
1951 Blue Backs ... 737
1951 Red Backs ... 738
1951 Connie Mack ... 738
1951 Current AS ... 739
1951 Teams ... 739
1952 ... 739
1953 ... 742
1954 ... 744
1955 ... 746
1955 Double Header ... 747
1956 ... 748
1957 ... 750
1958 ... 753
1959 ... 757
1960 ... 761
1961 ... 765
1962 ... 769
1963 ... 774
1964 ... 778
1964 Giants ... 783
1964 Stand Ups ... 783
1965 ... 784
1966 ... 789
1967 ... 793
1968 ... 798
1968 Game ... 802
1969 ... 803
1969 Deckle ... 808
1969 Super ... 809
1970 ... 809
1971 ... 814
1972 ... 820
1973 ... 825
1974 ... 831
1974 Traded ... 836
1975 ... 837
1976 ... 842
1976 Traded ... 846
1977 ... 847
1978 ... 852
1979 ... 857
1980 ... 862
1981 ... 867
1981 Traded ... 872
1982 ... 873
1982 Traded ... 879
1983 ... 880
1983 Gaylord Perry ... 885
1983 Glossy 40 ... 885
1983 Traded ... 885
1984 ... 886
1984 All-Star Glossy 22 ... 892
1984 Cereal ... 892
1984 Glossy 40 ... 893
1984 Traded ... 893
1985 ... 894
1985 All-Star Glossy 22 ... 899
1985 Glossy 40 ... 899
1985 Traded ... 900
1986 ... 901
1986 All-Star Glossy 22 ... 906
1986 Glossy Send-In 60 ... 906
1986 Mini Leaders ... 907
1986 Traded ... 908
1986 Wax Box Cards ... 909
1987 ... 909
1987 All-Star Glossy 22 ... 914
1987 Glossy Send-In 60 ... 915
1987 Jumbo Rookies ... 915
1987 Mini Leaders ... 915
1987 Traded ... 916
1987 Wax Box Cards ... 917
1988 ... 918
1988 All-Star Glossy 22 ... 923
1988 Big ... 923
1988 Glossy Send-In 60 ... 925
1988 Jumbo Rookies ... 925
1988 Mini Leaders ... 926
1988 Revco League Leaders ... 926
1988 Rite-Aid Team MVP's ... 927
1988 Traded ... 927
1988 UK Minis ... 928
1988 Wax Box Cards ... 929
1989 ... 929
1989 All-Star Glossy 22 ... 935
1989 Ames 20/20 Club ... 935
1989 Big ... 936
1989 Cap'n Crunch ... 938
1989 Glossy Send-In 60 ... 938
1989 Hills Team MVP's ... 938
1989 Jumbo Rookies ... 939
1989 Mini Leaders ... 939
1989 Traded ... 940
1989 UK Minis ... 941
1989 Wax Box Cards ... 942
1989 Senior League ... 942
1990 ... 943
1990 All-Star Glossy 22 ... 948
1990 Ames All-Stars ... 948
1990 Big ... 948
1990 Debut '89 ... 950
1990 Glossy Send-In 60 ... 952
1990 Hills Hit Men ... 952
1990 Jumbo Rookies ... 952
1990 Mini Leaders ... 953
1990 Traded ... 954
1990 TV All-Stars ... 955
1990 TV Cardinals ... 955
1990 TV Cubs ... 956
1990 TV Mets ... 956
1990 TV Red Sox ... 957
1990 TV Yankees ... 958
1990 Wax Box Cards ... 958
1991 ... 959
1991 Archive 1953 ... 964
1991 Babe Ruth ... 966
1991 Debut '90 ... 967
1991 Traded ... 968
1991 Wax Box Cards ... 969
1992 Promo Sheet ... 969
1992 Gold Promo Sheet ... 970
1992 ... 970
1992 Debut '91 ... 975
1992 Dairy Queen ... 976
1992 Gold ... 977
1992 Highland Mint Mint-Cards ... 977
1992 McDonald's Best ... 977
1992 Micro Gold Insert ... 978
1992 Kids ... 978
1992 Traded ... 979
1993 Pre-Production Sheet ... 980
1993 Holiday Previews ... 981
1993 ... 981
1993 Black Gold ... 983

Toys'R'Us Rookies
1987 ... 984
1988 ... 984
1989 ... 985
1990 ... 985
1991 ... 985

True Value ... 986

Twins 7-Eleven ... 986

Ultra
1991 ... 987
1991 Gold ... 989
1991 Update ... 990
1992 ... 991
1992 All-Rookies ... 995
1992 All-Stars ... 995
1992 Award Winners ... 995
1992 Tony Gwynn ... 996

Upper Deck
1988 Samples ... 996
1989 ... 996
1990 ... 1002
1990 Reggie Jackson Heroes ... 1008
1991 ... 1008
1991 Hank Aaron Heroes ... 1013
1991 Final Edition ... 1013
1991 HOF Heroes ... 1014
1991 Nolan Ryan Heroes ... 1015
1991 Silver Sluggers ... 1015
1992 ... 1015
1992 All-Star FanFest ... 1021
1992 Bench/Morgan Heroes ... 1021
1992 HOF Heroes ... 1022
1992 Heroes Highlights ... 1022
1992 Home Run Heroes ... 1022
1992 Scouting Report ... 1023
1992 Team MVP Holograms ... 1023
1992 Ted Williams Best ... 1024
1992 Ted Williams Heroes ... 1024
1992 Ted Williams Waxboxes ... 1025
1993 ... 1025
1993 Willie Mays Heroes ... 1028
1993 Then And Now ... 1028
1993 Triple Crown ... 1028

U.S. Playing Cards
1990 All-Stars ... 1029
1991 All-Stars ... 1029
1992 Aces ... 1030
1992 Braves ... 1031
1992 Cubs ... 1031
1992 Red Sox ... 1032
1992 Tigers ... 1033
1992 Twins ... 1033

USPS Legends Stamp Cards ... 1034

White Sox
1983 True Value ... 1034
1984 True Value ... 1034
1985 Coke ... 1035
1986 Coke ... 1035
1987 Coke ... 1036
1988 Coke ... 1036
1988 Kodak ... 1037
1989 Coke ... 1037
1989 Kodak ... 1037
1990 Coke ... 1038
1990 Kodak ... 1038
1991 Kodak ... 1038
1992 Kodak ... 1039

Whitehall Legends to Life ... 1039

Wilson ... 1040

Wonder Bread Stars ... 1040

Woolworth's
1985 ... 1040
1986 ... 1041
1987 Highlights ... 1041
1988 Highlights ... 1042
1989 Highlights ... 1042
1990 Highlights ... 1042
1991 Highlights ... 1043

W576 Callahan HOF ... 1043

W605 Robert Gould ... 1044

Yankees
1989 Score Nat West ... 1045
1990 Score Nat West ... 1045
1992 WIZ All-Stars ... 1045
1992 WIZ HOF ... 1046
1992 WIZ 60s ... 1046
1992 WIZ 70s ... 1048
1992 WIZ 80s ... 1049
Ziploc ... 1050

Index to Advertisers

707 Sportscards Ltd. ... 25
Johnny Adams, Jr. ... 1059
Alex's MVP Cards ... 1063
Always Baseball ... 1062
B&F Sports Cards ... 1063
Baseball Cards & Souvenirs ... 1062
Baseball Cards North ... 1063
Baseball Nostalgia ... 1063
Beverly Hills Baseball Cards ... 1061
Bill Henderson's Cards ... 5, 1055
Bill's Sports Collectibles ... 1057
Bleachers ... 41
BP Sports Investments ... 19
Brewart Coins & Stamps ... 1062
California Sports Card Exchange ... 1060
Card Collectors Company ... 27
Cavalier Cards ... 15
Center Field ... 1063
Champion Sports ... 23
Clayton Pasternack ... 1061
Cleveland Area Sports ... 1061
The Collectors Corporation ... 1062
Collector's World ... 1063
Comics Unlimited Ltd. ... 31,1055
Charles M. Conlon ... 11
Cornell & Finkelmeier ... 1063
Bill Dodge ... 1066,1067
Doubleheaders ... 1057
Dragon's Den ... 21
E Gads ... 1063
Family Coins ... 1060
First Base (Grove) ... 1051
Four C's ... 1062
Larry Fritsch Cards ... 3
Georgia Music & Sports ... 1064
Gordon Sports Collectibles ... 9
House of Cards ... 1060
Mark R. Jordan ... 39
Locker Room Sports Cards ... 1063
Mark Macrae ... 13
Mr. Mint ... 1053
B.A. Murry Cards ... 1061
Neil Z's Baseball Cards & Comics ... 1062
Non-Sports Update ... 1062
One if By Cards, Two if By Comics ... 43
Pat's Coins & Cards ... 1063
Peninsula Sports Cards ... 1062
Porky's Baseball Cards & Stuff ... 1062
Ragtime ... 1062
Roanoke Coin Exchange ... 1063
Sack's Sportscard Warehouse ... 1062
St. Louis Baseball Cards ... 1065
San Diego Sports Collectibles ... 28,29
San Francisco Card Exchange ... 1062
Barry Sloate ... 31
South Bay Sports Cards ... 1062
Sports Fan-Attic ... 1062
Sportscards Plus ... 17
Tarrant Printing ... 1063
Temdee ... 1063
Two Capitals Card Co. ... 1063
University Trading Cards ... 1059
Kit Young ... 7

About the Author

Jim Beckett, the leading authority on sport card values in the United States, maintains a wide range of activities in the world of sports. He possesses one of the finest collections of sports cards and autographs in the world, has made numerous appearances on radio and television, and has been frequently cited in many national publications. He was awarded the first "Special Achievement Award" for Contributions to the Hobby by the National Sports Collectors Convention in 1980, the "Jock-Jaspersen Award" for Hobby Dedication in 1983, and the "Buck Barker, Spirit of the Hobby" Award in 1991.

Dr. Beckett is the author of *The Sport Americana Baseball Card Price Guide, The Official Price Guide to Baseball Cards, The Sport Americana Price Guide to Baseball Collectibles, The Sport Americana Baseball Memorabilia and Autograph Price Guide, The Sport Americana Football Card Price Guide, The Official Price Guide to Football Cards, The Sport Americana Hockey Card Price Guide, The Official Price Guide to Hockey Cards, The Sport Americana Basketball Card Price Guide and Alphabetical Checklist, The Official Price Guide to Basketball Cards*, and *The Sport Americana Baseball Card Alphabetical Checklist*. In addition, he is the founder, publisher, and editor of *Beckett Baseball Card Monthly, Beckett Basketball Monthly, Beckett Football Card Monthly, Beckett Hockey Monthly*, and *Beckett Focus on Future Stars*, magazines dedicated to advancing the card collecting hobby.

Jim Beckett received his Ph.D. in Statistics from Southern Methodist University in 1975. Prior to starting Beckett Publications in 1984, Dr. Beckett served as an Associate Professor of Statistics at Bowling Green State University and as a Vice President of a consulting firm in Dallas, Texas. He currently resides in Dallas with his wife, Patti, and their daughters, Christina, Rebecca, and Melissa.

How To Use This Book

Isn't it great? Every year this book gets bigger and bigger with all the new sets coming out. But even more exciting is that every year there are more collectors, more shows, more stores, and more interest in the cards we love so much. This edition has been enhanced and expanded from the previous edition. The cards you collect — who appears on them, what they look like, where they are from, and (most important to most of you) what their current values are — enumerated within. Many of the features contained in the other Beckett Price Guides have been incorporated into this volume since condition grading, nomenclature, and many other aspects of collecting are common to the card hobby in general. We hope you find the book both interesting and useful in your collecting pursuits.

The Beckett Guide has been successful where other attempts have failed because it is complete, current, and valid. This Price Guide contains not just one, but three prices by condition for all the baseball cards listed. These account for most of the baseball cards in existence. The prices were added to the card lists just prior to printing and reflect not the author's opinions or desires but the going retail prices for each card, based on the marketplace (sports memorabilia conventions and shows, sports card shops, hobby papers, current mail-order catalogs, local club meetings, auction results, and other firsthand reportings of actually realized prices).

What is the best price guide available on the market today? Of course card sellers will prefer the price guide with the highest prices, while card buyers will naturally prefer the one with the lowest prices. Accuracy, however, is the true test. Use the price guide used by more collectors and dealers than all the others combined. Look for the Beckett® name. I won't put my name on anything I won't stake my reputation on. Not the lowest and not the highest — but the most accurate, with integrity.

To facilitate your use of this book, read the complete introductory section on the following pages before going to the pricing pages. Every collectible field has its own terminology; we've tried to capture most of these terms and definitions in our glossary. Please read carefully the section on grading and the condition of your cards, as you will not be able to determine which price column is appropriate for a given card without first knowing its condition.

Welcome to the world of baseball cards.

Jim Beckett

Introduction

Welcome to the exciting world of baseball card collecting, America's fastest-growing avocation. You have made a good choice in buying this book, since it will open up to you the entire panorama of this field in the simplest, most concise way. It is estimated that a third of a million different baseball cards have been issued during the past century. And the number of total cards put out by all manufacturers last year has been estimated at several billion, with an initial wholesale price of more than $500 million. Sales of older cards by dealers may account for a like amount. With all that cardboard available in the marketplace, it should be no surprise that several million sports fans like you collect baseball cards today, and that number is growing by hundreds of thousands each year.

The growth of *Beckett Baseball Card Monthly* is another indication of this rising crescendo of popularity for baseball cards. Founded in 1984 by Dr. James Beckett, the author of this Price Guide, *Beckett Baseball Card Monthly* has grown to the pinnacle of the baseball card hobby with more than a million readers anxiously awaiting each enjoyable issue.

So collecting baseball cards — while still pursued as a hobby with youthful exuberance by kids in the neighborhood — has also taken on the trappings of an industry, with thousands of full- and part-time card dealers, as well as vendors of supplies, clubs and conventions. In fact, each year since 1980 thousands of hobbyists have assembled for a National Sports Collectors Convention, at which hundreds of dealers have displayed their wares, seminars have been conducted, autographs penned by sports notables, and millions of cards changed hands. These colossal affairs have been staged in Los Angeles, Detroit, St. Louis, Chicago, New York, Anaheim, Arlington (Texas), San Francisco, Atlantic City, and Atlanta. So baseball card collecting really is national in scope!

This increasing interest has been reflected in card values. As more collectors compete for available supplies, card prices (especially for premium-grade cards) rise. A national publication indicated a "very strong advance" in baseball card prices during the past decade, and a quick perusal of prices in this book compared to the figures in earlier editions of this Price Guide will quickly confirm this. Which brings us back around again to the book you have in your hands. It is the best annual guide available to this exciting world of baseball cards. Read it and use it. May your enjoyment and your card collection increase in the coming months and years.

How to Collect

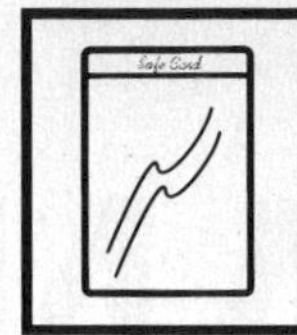

Each collection is personal and reflects the individuality of its owner. There are no set rules on how to collect cards. Since card collecting is a hobby or leisure pastime, what you collect, how much you collect, and how much time and money you spend collecting are entirely up to you. The funds you have available for collecting and your own personal taste should determine how you collect. Information and ideas presented here are intended to help you get the most enjoyment from this hobby.

It is impossible to collect every card ever produced. Therefore, beginners as well as intermediate and advanced collectors usually specialize in some way. One of the reasons this hobby is popular is that individual collectors can define and tailor their collecting methods to match their own tastes. To give you some ideas of the various approaches to collecting, we will list some of the more popular areas of specialization.

Many collectors select complete sets from particular years. For example, they may concentrate on assembling complete sets from all the years since their birth or since they became avid sports fans. They may try to collect a card for every player during that specified period of time. Many others wish to acquire only certain players. Usually such players are the superstars of the sport, but occasionally collectors will specialize in all the cards of players who attended a particular college or came from a certain town. Some collectors are only interested in the first cards or Rookie Cards of certain players. A handy guide for collectors interested in pursuing the hobby this way is the *Sport Americana Baseball Card Alphabetical Checklist No. 5*.

Another fun way to collect cards is by team. Most fans have a favorite team, and it is natural for that loyalty to be translated into a desire for cards of the players on that favorite team. For most of the recent years, team sets (all the cards from a given team for that year) are readily available at a reason-

able price. *The Sport Americana Team Baseball Card Checklist* will open up this field to the collector.

Obtaining Cards

Several avenues are open to card collectors. Cards still can be purchased in the traditional way: by the pack at the local candy, grocery, or drug stores. But there are also thousands of card shops across the country that specialize in selling cards individually or by the pack, box, or set. Another alternative is the thousands of card shows held each month around the country, which feature anywhere from five to 800 tables of sports cards and memorabilia for sale. For many years, it has been possible to purchase complete sets of baseball cards through mail-order advertisers found in traditional sports media publications, such as *The Sporting News, Baseball Digest, Street & Smith* yearbooks, and others. These sets also are advertised in the card collecting periodicals. Many collectors will begin by subscribing to at least one of the hobby periodicals, all with good up-to-date information. In fact, subscription offers can be found in the advertising section of this book.

Most serious card collectors obtain old (and new) cards from one or more of several main sources: (1) trading or buying from other collectors or dealers; (2) responding to sale or auction ads in the hobby publications; (3) buying at a local hobby store; and/or (4) attending sports collectibles shows or conventions. We advise that you try all four methods since each has its own distinct advantages: (1) trading is a great way to make new friends; (2) hobby periodicals help you keep up with what's going on in the hobby (including when and where the conventions are happening); (3) stores provide the opportunity to enjoy personalized service and consider a great diversity of material in a relaxed sports-oriented atmosphere; and (4) shows allow you to choose from multiple dealers and thousands of cards under one roof in a competitive situation.

Preserving Your Cards

Cards are fragile. They must be handled properly in order to retain their value. Careless handling can easily result in creased or bent cards. It is, however, not recommended that tweezers or tongs be used to pick up your cards since such utensils might mar or indent card surfaces and thus reduce those cards' conditions and values. In general, your cards should be handled directly as little as possible. This is sometimes easier to say than to do.

Although there are still many who use custom boxes, storage trays, or even shoe boxes, plastic sheets are the preferred method of many collectors for storing cards. A collection stored in plastic pages in a three-ring album allows you to view your collection at any time without the need to touch the card itself. Cards can also be kept in single holders (of various types and thickness) designed for the enjoyment of each card individually. For a large collection, some collectors may use a combination of the above methods. When purchasing plastic sheets for your cards, be sure that you find the pocket size that fits the cards snugly. Don't put your 1951 Bowmans in a sheet designed to fit 1981 Topps. Most hobby and collectibles shops and virtually all collectors' conventions will have these plastic pages available in quantity for the various sizes offered, or you can purchase them directly from the advertisers in this book. Also, remember that pocket size isn't the only factor to consider when looking for plastic sheets. Other factors such as safety, economy, appearance, availability, or personal preference also may indicate which types of sheets a collector may want to buy.

Damp, sunny and/or hot conditions — no, this is not a weather forecast — are three elements to avoid in extremes if you are interested in preserving your collection. Too much (or too little) humidity can cause gradual deterioration of a card. Direct, bright sun (or fluorescent light) over time will bleach out the color of a card. Extreme heat accelerates the decomposition of the card. On the other hand, many cards have lasted more than 50 years without much scientific intervention. So be cautious, even if the above factors typically present a problem only when present in the extreme. It never hurts to be prudent.

Collecting vs. Investing

Collecting individual players and collecting complete sets are both popular vehicles for investment and speculation. Most investors and speculators stock up on complete sets or on quantities of players they think have good investment potential. There is obviously no guarantee in this book, or anywhere else for that matter, that cards will outperform the stock market or other investment alternatives in the future. After all, baseball cards do not pay quarterly dividends and cards cannot be sold at their "current values" as easily as stocks or bonds. Nevertheless, investors have noticed a favorable long-term trend in the past performance of baseball

and other sports collectibles, and certain cards and sets have outperformed just about any other investment in some years. Many hobbyists maintain that the best investment is and always will be the building of a collection, which traditionally has held up better than outright speculation.

Some of the obvious questions are: Which cards? When to buy? When to sell? The best investment you can make is in your own education. The more you know about your collection and the hobby, the more informed the decisions you will be able to make. We're not selling investment tips. We're selling information about the current value of baseball cards. It's up to you to use that information to your best advantage.

Terminology

Each hobby has its own language to describe its area of interest. The nomenclature traditionally used for trading cards is derived from the *American Card Catalog*, published in 1960 by Nostalgia Press. That catalog, written by Jefferson Burdick (who is called the "Father of Card Collecting" for his pioneering work), uses letter and number designations for each separate set of cards. The letter used in the ACC designation refers to the generic type of card. While both sport and non-sport issues are classified in the ACC, we shall confine ourselves to the sport issues. The following list defines the letters and their meanings as used by the *American Card Catalog*.

(none) or N - 19th Century U.S. Tobacco
B - Blankets
D - Bakery Inserts Including Bread
E - Early Candy and Gum
F - Food Inserts
H - Advertising
M - Periodicals
PC - Postcards
R - Candy and Gum since 1930

Following the letter prefix and an optional hyphen are one-, two-, or three-digit numbers, 1-999. These typically represent the company or entity issuing the cards. In several cases, the ACC number is extended by an additional hyphen and another one- or two-digit numerical suffix. For example, the 1957 Topps regular-series baseball card issue carries an ACC designation of R414-11. The "R" indicates a Candy or Gum card produced since 1930. The "414" is the ACC designation for Topps Chewing Gum baseball card issues, and the "11" is the ACC designation for the 1957 regular issue (Topps' eleventh baseball set). Like other traditional methods of identification, this system provides order to the process of cataloging cards; however, most serious collectors learn the ACC designation of the popular sets by repetition and familiarity, rather than by attempting to "figure out" what they might or should be. From 1948 forward, collectors and dealers commonly refer to all sets by their year, maker, type of issue, and any other distinguishing characteristic. For example, such a characteristic could be an unusual issue or one of several regular issues put out by a specific maker in a single year. Regional issues are usually referred to by year, maker, and sometimes by title or theme of the set.

Glossary/Legend

Our glossary defines terms frequently used in the card collecting hobby. Many of these terms are also common to other types of sports memorabilia collecting. Some terms may have several meanings depending on use.

AAS - Action All-Stars, a postcard-size set issued by Donruss during the mid-1980s.
ACC - Acronym for American Card Catalog.
ALP - Alphabetical checklist.
ANN - Announcer.
AS - All-Star card. A card portraying an All-Star Player of the previous year that says "All-Star" on its face.
ATG - All-Time Great card.
ATL - All-Time Leaders card.
AU - With autograph.
BC - Bonus Card
BL - Blue letters.
BLANKET - A felt square (normally 5 to 6 inches) portraying a baseball player.
BOX - Card issued on a box or a card depicting a Boxer.
BRICK - A group of 50 or more cards having common characteristics that is intended to be bought, sold or traded as a unit.
CABINETS - Popular and highly valuable photographs on thick card stock produced in the 19th and early 20th century.
CH - Community Heroes (Upper Deck).
CHECKLIST - A list of the cards contained in a particular set. The list is always in numerical order if the cards are numbered. Some unnumbered sets are artificially numbered in

REDS
2nd BASE
PETE ROSE

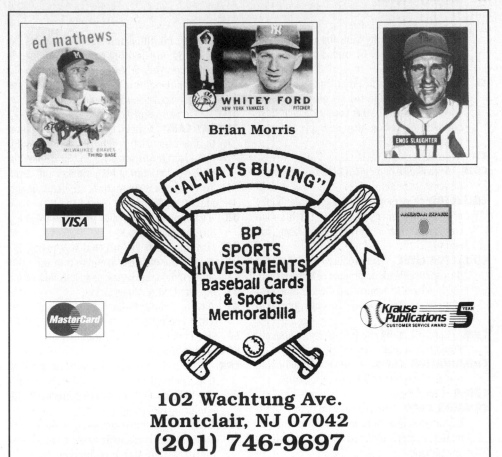

WILLIAMS

alphabetical order, by team and alphabetically within the team, or by uniform number for convenience.

CL - Checklist card. A card that lists in order the cards and players in the set or series. Older checklist cards in Mint condition that have not been marked are very desirable and command premiums.

CO - Abbreviation for Coach.

COIN - A small disc of metal or plastic portraying a player in its center.

COLLECTOR - A person who engages in the hobby of collecting cards primarily for his own enjoyment, with any profit motive being secondary.

COLLECTOR ISSUE - A set produced for the sake of the card itself with no product or service sponsor. It derives its name from the fact that most of these sets are produced for sale directly to the hobby market.

COM - Card issued by the Post Cereal Company through their mail-in offer.

COMBINATION CARD - A single card depicting two or more players (but not a team card).

COMM - Commissioner.

COMMON CARD - The typical card of any set; it has no premium value accruing from subject matter, numerical scarcity, popular demand, or anomaly.

CONVENTION - A gathering of dealers and collectors at a single location for the purpose of buying, selling, and trading sports memorabilia items. Conventions are open to the public and sometimes feature autograph guests, door prizes, contests, seminars, etc. They are frequently referred to simply as "shows."

CONVENTION ISSUE - A set produced in conjunction with a sports collectibles convention to commemorate or promote the show.

COR - Corrected card.

COUPON - See Tab.

CREASE - A wrinkle on the card, usually caused by bending the card. Creases are a common (and serious) defect resulting from careless handling.

CY - Cy Young Award.

DC - Draft Choice.

DD - Diamond Debut (Upper Deck).

DEALER - A person who engages in buying, selling, and trading sports collectibles or supplies. A dealer may also be a collector, but as a dealer, his main goal is to earn a profit.

DIE-CUT - A card with part of its stock partially cut, allowing one or more parts to be folded or removed. After removal or appropriate folding, the remaining part of the card can frequently be made to stand up.

DISC - A circular-shaped card.

DISPLAY CARD - A sheet, usually containing three to nine cards, that is printed and used by the manufacturer to advertise and/or display the packages containing his products and cards. The backs of display cards are blank or contain advertisements.

DK - Diamond King (artwork produced by Perez-Steele for Donruss).

DP - Double Print (a card that was printed in double the quantity compared to the other cards in the same series) or a Draft Pick card.

DS - Diamond Skills (Upper Deck).

DT - Dream Team (produced by Score in 1990, 1991 and 1992).

EP - Elite Performer (1991 Ultra).

ERA - Earned Run Average.

ERR - Error card. A card with erroneous information, spelling, or depiction on either side of the card. Most errors are not corrected by the producing card company.

EXHIBIT - The generic name given to thick-stock, postcard-size cards with single color obverse pictures. The name is derived from the Exhibit Supply Co. of Chicago, the principal manufacturer of this type of card. These also are known as Arcade cards since they were found in many arcades.

FDP - First Draft Pick.

FOIL - Foil embossed stamp on card.

FRAN - The Franchise card (1991 Score).

FS - Father/son card.

FULL SHEET - A complete sheet of cards that has not been cut up into individual cards by the manufacturer. Also called an uncut sheet.

GL - Green letters.

HIGH NUMBER - The cards in the last series of numbers in a year in which such higher-numbered cards were printed or distributed in significantly lesser amounts than the lower-numbered cards. The high-number designation refers to a scarcity of the high-numbered cards. Not all years have high numbers in terms of this definition.

HL - Highlight card.

HOF - Hall of Fame, or a card that portrays a Hall of Famer (HOFer).

HOR - Horizontal pose on card as opposed to the standard vertical orientation found on most cards.

I - Idols.

IA - In Action card.

IF - Infielder.

INSERT - A card of a different type or any other sports collectible (typically a poster or sticker) contained and sold in the same package along with a card or cards of a major set. An insert card is either unnumbered or not numbered in the same sequence as the major set. Sometimes the inserts are randomly distributed and are not found in every pack.

ISSUE - Synonymous with set, but usually used in conjunction with a manufacturer, e.g., a Topps issue.

K - Strikeout.

KM - K-Man (1991 Score).

KP - Kid Picture (a subset issued in the Topps Baseball sets of 1972 and 1973).

LAYERING - The separation or peeling of one or more layers of the card stock, usually at the corner of the card.

LEGITIMATE ISSUE - A set produced to promote or boost sales of a product or service, e.g., bubblegum, cereal, cigarettes, etc. Most collector issues are not legitimate issues in this sense.

LHP - Lefthanded pitcher.

LID - A circular-shaped card (possibly with tab) that forms the top of the container for the product being promoted.

LL - League leaders card or large letters on card.

MAJOR SET - A set produced by a national manufacturer of cards containing a large number of cards. Usually 100 or more different cards comprise a major set.

MB - Master Blaster (1991 Score).

MC - Members Choice (Topps Stadium Club).

MEM - Memorial card. For example, the 1990 Donruss and Topps Bart Giamatti cards.

MG - Manager.

MINI - A small card; for example, a 1975 Topps card of identical design but smaller dimensions than the regular Topps issue of 1975.

ML - Major League.

MVP - Most Valuable Player.

NAU - No autograph on card.

NH - No-Hitter card.

NNOF - No Name on Front (1949 Bowman).

NOF - Name on Front (1949 Bowman).

NON-SPORT CARD - A card from a set whose major theme is a subject other than a sports subject. A card of a sports figure or event that is part of a non-sport set is still a non-sport card, e.g., while the "Look 'N' See" non-sport card set contains a card of Babe Ruth, a sports figure, that card is a non-sport card.

NOTCHING - The grooving of the card, usually caused by fingernails, rubber bands, or bumping card edges against other objects.

OBVERSE - The front, face, or pictured side of the card.

OF - Outfield or Outfielder.

OLY - Olympics (see the 1985 Topps and 1988 Topps Traded sets; the members of the U.S. Olympic Baseball teams were featured subsets in both of these sets).

ORG - Organist.

P - Pitcher or Pitching pose.

P1 - First Printing.

P2 - Second Printing.

P3 - Third Printing.

PANEL - An extended card that is composed of two or more individual cards. Often the panel forms the back part of the container for the product being promoted, e.g., a Hostess panel, a Bazooka panel, an Esskay Meat panel.

PCL - Pacific Coast League.

PLASTIC SHEET - A clear, plastic page that is punched for insertion into a binder (with standard three-ring spacing) containing pockets for displaying cards. Many different styles of sheets exist with pockets of varying sizes to hold the many differing card formats. Also called a display sheet or storage sheet.

PREMIUM - A card, sometimes on photographic stock, that is purchased or obtained in conjunction with, or redemption for, another card or product. The premium is not packaged in the same unit as the primary item.

PRES - President.

PUZZLE CARD - A card whose back contains a part of a picture which, when joined correctly with other puzzle cards, forms the completed picture.

PUZZLE PIECE - A die-cut piece designed to interlock with similar pieces.

PVC - Polyvinyl Chloride, a substance used to make many of the popular card display protective sheets. Non-PVC sheets are considered preferable for long-term storage of cards by many.

RARE - A card or series of cards of very limited

availability. Unfortunately, "rare" is a subjective term frequently used indiscriminately to hype value. "Rare" cards are harder to obtain than "scarce" cards.

RB - Record Breaker card.

REGIONAL - A card or set of cards issued and distributed only in a limited geographical area of the country.

REVERSE - The back or narrative side of the card.

RHP - Righthanded pitcher.

RIF - Rifleman (1991 Score).

ROY - Rookie of the Year.

RP - Relief pitcher.

RR - Rated Rookies (a subset featured in Donruss sets).

SA - Super Action card.

SASE - Self-Addressed, Stamped Envelope.

SB - Stolen Bases.

SCARCE - A card or series of cards of limited availability. This subjective term is sometimes used indiscriminately to hype value. "Scarce" cards are not as difficult to obtain as "rare" cards.

SCR - Script name on back (1949 Bowman).

SEMI-HIGH - A card from the next to last series of a sequentially issued set. It has more value than an average card and generally less value than a high number. A card is not called a semi-high unless the next to last series in which it exists has an additional premium attached to it.

SERIES - The entire set of cards issued by a particular producer in a particular year; e.g., the 1971 Topps series. Also, within a particular set, series can refer to a group of (consecutively numbered) cards printed at the same time; e.g., the first series of the 1957 Topps issue (#'s1-88).

SET - One each of the entire run of cards of the same type produced by a particular manufacturer during a single year. In other words, if you have a complete set of 1976 Topps then you have every card from #1 up to and including #660, i.e., all of the different cards that were produced.

SH - Shades (Score Pinnacle).

SI - Sidelines.

SKIP-NUMBERED - A set that has many unissued card numbers between the lowest number in the set and the highest number in the set; e.g., the 1948 Leaf baseball set contains 98 cards skip-numbered from #1 to #168. A major set in which a few numbers were not printed is not considered to be skip-numbered.

SLUG - Silver Slugger card (1991 Bowman).

SP - Single or Short Print (a card which was printed in lesser quantity compared to the other cards in the same series; see also DP and TP).

SPECIAL CARD - A card that portrays something other than a single player or team; for example, a card that portrays the previous year's statistical leaders or the results from the previous year's World Series.

SR - Star Rookies (Upper Deck).

SS - Shortstop.

STAMP - Adhesive-backed papers depicting a player. The stamp may be individual or in a sheet of many stamps. Moisture must be applied to the adhesive in order for the stamp to be attached to another surface.

STAR CARD - A card that portrays a player of some repute, usually determined by his ability, however, sometimes referring to sheer popularity.

STICKER - A card with a removable layer that can be affixed to (stuck onto) another surface.

STOCK - The cardboard or paper on which the card is printed.

STRIP CARDS - A sheet or strip of cards, particularly popular in the 1920s and 1930s, with the individual cards usually separated by broken or dotted lines.

SUPERSTAR CARD - A card that portrays a superstar; e.g., a Hall of Famer or player with strong Hall of Fame potential.

SV - Super Veteran (see 1982 Topps).

TAB - A card portion set off from the rest of the card, usually with perforations, that may be removed without damaging the central character or event depicted by the card.

TBC - Turn Back the Clock cards.

TC - Team Checklist cards.

TEAM CARD - A card that depicts an entire team.

TEST SET - A set, usually containing a small number of cards, issued by a national card producer and distributed in a limited section or sections of the country. Presumably, the purpose of a test set is to test market appeal for a particular type of card.

TL - Team Leader card.

TP - Triple Print (a card that was printed in triple the quantity compared to the other cards in the same series).

TRIMMED - A card cut down from its original

size. Trimmed cards are undesirable to most collectors.

UER - Uncorrected Error.

UMP - Umpire.

USA - Team USA cards.

VAR - Variation card. One of two or more cards from the same series with the same number (or player with identical pose if the series is unnumbered) differing from one another by some aspect, the different feature stemming from the printing or stock of the card. This can be caused when the manufacturer of the cards notices an error in one or more of the cards, makes the changes, and then resumes the print run. In this case there will be two versions or variations of the same card. Sometimes one of the variations is relatively scarce.

VERT - Vertical pose on card.

WAS - Washington National League (1974 Topps).

WS - World Series card.

YL - Yellow Letters (1958 Topps).

YT - Yellow Team (1958 Topps).

* - to denote multi-sport sets.

Understanding Card Values

Determining Value

Why are some cards more valuable than others? Obviously, the economic laws of supply and demand are applicable to card collecting just as they are to any other field where a commodity is bought, sold or traded in a free, unregulated market.

Supply (the number of cards available on the market) is less than the total number of cards originally produced since attrition diminishes that original quantity. Each year a percentage of cards is typically thrown away, destroyed or otherwise lost to collectors. This percentage is much, much smaller today than it was in the past because more and more people have become increasingly aware of the value of their cards.

For those who collect only Mint condition cards, the supply of older cards can be quite small indeed. Until recently, collectors were not so conscious of the need to preserve the condition of their cards. For this reason, it is difficult to know exactly how many 1953 Topps are currently available, Mint or otherwise. It is generally accepted that there are fewer 1953 Topps available than 1963, 1973 or 1983 Topps cards. If demand were equal for each of these sets, the law of supply and demand would increase the price for the least available sets. Demand, however, is never equal for all sets, so price correlations can be complicated. The demand for a card is influenced by many factors. These include: (1) the age of the card; (2) the number of cards printed; (3) the player(s) portrayed on the card; (4) the attractiveness and popularity of the set; and (5) the physical condition of the card.

In general, (1) the older the card, (2) the fewer the number of the cards printed, (3) the more famous, popular and talented the player, (4) the more attractive and popular the set, and (5) the better the condition of the card, the higher the value of the card will be. There are exceptions to all but one of these factors: the condition of the card. Given two cards similar in all respects except condition, the one in the best condition will always be valued higher.

While those guidelines help to establish the value of a card, the countless exceptions and peculiarities make any simple, direct mathematical formula to determine card values impossible.

Regional Variation

Since the market varies from region to region, card prices of local players may be higher. This is known as a regional premium. How significant the premium is — and if there is any premium at all — depends on the local popularity of the team and the player.

The largest regional premiums usually do not apply to superstars, who often are so well known nationwide that the prices of their key cards are too high for local dealers to realize a premium.

Lesser stars often command the strongest premiums. Their popularity is concentrated in their home region, creating local demand that greatly exceeds overall demand.

Regional premiums can apply to popular retired players and sometimes can be found in the areas where the players grew up or starred in college.

A regional discount is the converse of a regional premium. Regional discounts occur when a player has been so popular in his region for so long that local collectors and dealers have accumulated quantities of his key cards. The abundant supply may make the cards available in that area at the lowest prices anywhere.

THE COLLA COLLECTION
LIMITED EDITION BASEBALL CARD SETS

- ♦ EACH SET IS LIMITED AND NUMBERED
- ♦ EACH SET COMES IN A FULL COLOR COLLECTORS' BOX
- ♦ EACH SET HAS 12 UNIQUELY PHOTOGRAPHED CARDS OF THE FEATURED PLAYER
- ♦ PRINTED WITH A HIGH GLOSS DIAMOND VIEW™ PROCESS

THE COLLA COLLECTION

Barry Colla Photography has issued the following player sets with the first card of each limited edition set numbered to ensure the investment potential. All sets have 12 cards and a limited number of Promo cards. ALL COLLA LIMITED SETS ARE LISTED IN THE ANNUAL BECKETT® GUIDE.

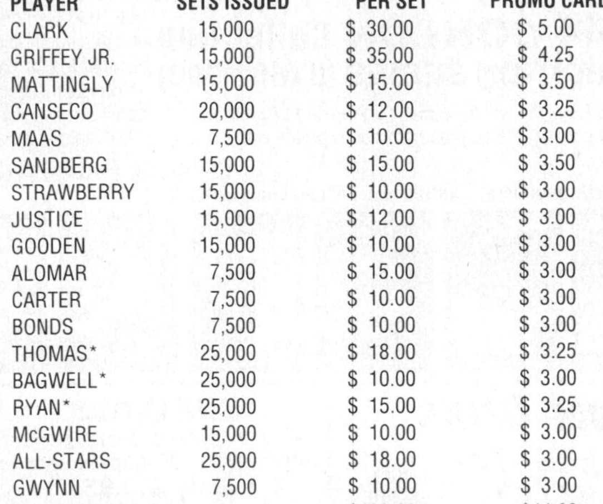

SET PRICES

PLAYER	NUMBER OF SETS ISSUED	PRICE PER SET	PRICE PER PROMO CARD
CLARK	15,000	$ 30.00	$ 5.00
GRIFFEY JR.	15,000	$ 35.00	$ 4.25
MATTINGLY	15,000	$ 15.00	$ 3.50
CANSECO	20,000	$ 12.00	$ 3.25
MAAS	7,500	$ 10.00	$ 3.00
SANDBERG	15,000	$ 15.00	$ 3.50
STRAWBERRY	15,000	$ 10.00	$ 3.00
JUSTICE	15,000	$ 12.00	$ 3.00
GOODEN	15,000	$ 10.00	$ 3.00
ALOMAR	7,500	$ 15.00	$ 3.00
CARTER	7,500	$ 10.00	$ 3.00
BONDS	7,500	$ 10.00	$ 3.00
THOMAS*	25,000	$ 18.00	$ 3.25
BAGWELL*	25,000	$ 10.00	$ 3.00
RYAN*	25,000	$ 15.00	$ 3.25
McGWIRE	15,000	$ 10.00	$ 3.00
ALL-STARS	25,000	$ 18.00	$ 3.00
GWYNN	7,500	$ 10.00	$ 3.00
ALL OF THE ABOVE		$190.00	$44.00

All 18 Colla Sets and Promo Cards: $215.00

***THESE SETS INCLUDE 200 RANDOMLY PACKED AUTOGRAPHED CARDS SIGNED AND NUMBERED BY THE FEATURED PLAYER.**

PREMIER LIMITED EDITION COLLA ALL-STARS SET

OFFICIAL CARD SET OF THE 1992 ALL-STAR GAME

The *PREMIER LIMITED EDITION COLLA ALL-STAR SET* was issued in July, 1992. This *FIRST EVER COLLA ALL-STAR SET* includes 24 All-Stars from the 1992 Game played in San Diego. All sets are numbered and in a full color collectors' box. This is the only set with the All-Star logo on the cards. Price per set is $18.00

New 96-page catalog with every order.

FOUNDING MEMBERS
SCA
SPORTS COLLECTORS ASSOCIATION INTERNATIONAL

CARD COLLECTOR'S CO.

A Division of Nostalgia, Inc.

105 West 77th Street, New York, NY 10024

(212) 873-6999

CALL TOLL FREE FOR ORDERS ONLY: 1(800) 822-0028

FAX: (212) 787-2279

POSTAGE AND HANDLING CHARGE
$3.95 Per Order
New York State Residents Please Add sales Tax

Set Prices

A somewhat paradoxical situation exists in the price of a complete set vs. the combined cost of the individual cards in the set. In nearly every case, the sum of the prices for the individual cards is higher than the cost for the complete set. This is prevalent especially in the cards of the past few years. The reasons for this apparent anomaly stem from the habits of collectors and from the carrying costs to dealers. Today, each card in a set normally is produced in the same quantity as all others in its set.

Many collectors pick up only stars, superstars and particular teams. As a result, the dealer is left with a shortage of certain player cards and an abundance of others. He therefore incurs an expense in simply "carrying" these less desirable cards in stock. On the other hand, if he sells a complete set, he gets rid of large numbers of cards at one time. For this reason, he generally is willing to receive less money for a complete set. By doing this, he recovers all of his costs and also makes a profit.

The disparity between the price of the complete set and the sum of the individual cards also has been influenced by the fact that some of the major manufacturers now are pre-collating card sets. Since "pulling" individual cards from the sets of all three manufacturers involves a specific type of labor (and cost), the singles or star card market is not affected significantly by pre-collation.

Set prices also do not include rare card varieties, unless specifically stated. Of course, the prices for sets do include one example of each type for the given set, but this is the least expensive variety.

Scarce Series

Scarce series occur because cards issued before 1974 were made available to the public each year in several series of finite numbers of cards, rather than all cards of the set being available for purchase at one time. At some point during the year, usually toward the end of the baseball season, interest in current year baseball cards waned. Consequently, the manufacturers produced smaller numbers of these later-series cards.

Nearly all nationwide issues from post-World War II manufacturers (1948 to 1973) exhibit these series variations. In the past, Topps, for example, may have issued series consisting of many different numbers of cards, including 55, 66, 80, 88 and others. Recently, Topps has settled on what is now its standard sheet size of 132 cards, six of which comprise its 792-card set.

While the number of cards within a given series is usually the same as the number of cards on one printed sheet, this is not always the case. For example, Bowman used 36 cards on its standard printed sheets, but in 1948 substituted 12 cards during later print runs of that year's baseball cards. Twelve of the cards from the initial sheet of 36 cards were removed and replaced by 12 different cards giving, in effect, a first series of 36 cards and a second series of 12 new cards. This replacement produced a scarcity of 24 cards — the 12 cards removed from the original sheet and the 12 new cards added to the sheet. A full sheet of 1948 Bowman cards (second printing) shows that card numbers 37 through 48 have replaced 12 of the cards on the first printing sheet.

The Topps Company also has created scarcities and/or excesses of certain cards in many of its sets. Topps, however, has most frequently gone the other direction by double printing some of the cards. Double printing causes an abundance of cards of the players who are on the same sheet more than one time. During the years from 1978 to 1981, Topps double printed 66 cards out of their large 726-card set. The Topps practice of double printing cards in earlier years is the most logical explanation for the known scarcities of particular cards in some of these Topps sets.

From 1988 through 1990, Donruss short printed and double printed certain cards in its major sets. Ostensibly this was because of its addition of bonus team MVP cards in its regular-issue wax packs.

We are always looking for information or photographs of printing sheets of cards for research. Each year, we try to update the hobby's knowledge of distribution anomalies. Please let us know at the address in this book if you have first-hand knowledge that would be helpful in this pursuit.

Grading Your Cards

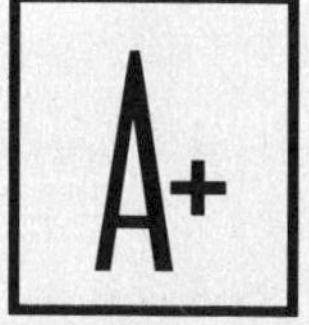

Each hobby has its own grading terminology — stamps, coins, comic books, record collecting, etc. Collectors of sports cards are no exception. The one invariable criterion for determining the value of a card is its condition: the better the condition of the card, the more valuable it is.

Condition grading, however, is subjective. Individual card dealers and collectors differ in the strictness of their grading, but the stated condition of a card should be determined without regard to whether it is being bought or sold.

No allowance is made for age. A 1952 card is judged by the same standards as a 1992 card. But there are specific sets and cards that are condition sensitive (marked with "!" in the Price Guide) because of their border color, consistently poor centering, etc. Such cards and sets sometimes command premiums above the listed percentages in Mint condition.

Centering

Current centering terminology uses numbers representing the percentage of border on either side of the main design. Obviously, centering is diminished in importance for borderless cards such as Stadium Club.

Slightly Off-Center (60/40): A slightly off-center card is one that upon close inspection is found to have one border bigger than the opposite border. This degree once was offensive to only purists, but now some hobbyists try to avoid cards that are anything other than perfectly centered.

Off-Center (70/30): An off-center card has one border that is noticeably more than twice as wide as the opposite border.

Badly Off-Center (80/20 or worse): A badly off-center card has virtually no border on one side of the card.

Miscut: A miscut card actually shows part of the adjacent card in its larger border and consequently a corresponding amount of its card is cut off.

Corner Wear

Corner wear is the most scrutinized grading criteria in the hobby. These are the major categories of corner wear:

Corner with a slight touch of wear: The corner still is sharp, but there is a slight touch of wear showing. On a dark-bordered card, this shows as a dot of white.

Fuzzy corner: The corner still comes to a point, but the point has just begun to fray. A slightly "dinged" corner is considered the same as a fuzzy corner.

Slightly rounded corner: The fraying of the corner has increased to where there is only a hint of a point. Mild layering may be evident. A "dinged" corner is considered the same as a slightly rounded corner.

Rounded corner: The point is completely gone. Some layering is noticeable.

Badly rounded corner: The corner is completely round and rough. Severe layering is evident.

Creases

A third common defect is the crease. The degree of creasing in a card is difficult to show in a drawing or picture. On giving the specific condition of an expensive card for sale, the seller should note any creases additionally. Creases can be categorized as to severity according to the following scale.

Light Crease: A light crease is a crease that is barely noticeable upon close inspection. In fact, when cards are in plastic sheets or holders, a light crease may not be seen (until the card is taken out of the holder). A light crease on the front is much more serious than a light crease on the card back only.

Medium Crease: A medium crease is noticeable when held and studied at arm's length by the naked eye, but does not overly detract from the appearance of the card. It is an obvious crease, but not one that breaks the picture surface of the card.

Heavy Crease: A heavy crease is one that has torn or broken through the card's picture surface, e.g., puts a tear in the photo surface.

Alterations

Deceptive Trimming: This occurs when someone alters the card in order (1) to shave off edge wear, (2) to improve the sharpness of the corners, or (3) to improve centering — obviously their objective is to falsely increase the perceived value of the card to an unsuspecting buyer. The shrinkage usually is evident only if the trimmed card is compared to an adjacent full-sized card or if the trimmed card is itself measured.

Obvious Trimming: Obvious trimming is noticeable and unfortunate. It is usually performed by non-collectors who give no thought to the present or future value of their cards.

Deceptively Retouched Borders: This occurs when the borders (especially on those cards with dark borders) are touched up on the edges and corners with magic marker or crayons of appropriate color in order to make the card appear to be Mint.

Centering

Well-centered

Slightly Off-centered

Off-centered

Badly Off-centered

Miscut

Corner Wear

The partial cards shown at right have been photographed at 300%. This was done in order to magnify each card's corner wear to such a degree that differences could be shown on a printed page.

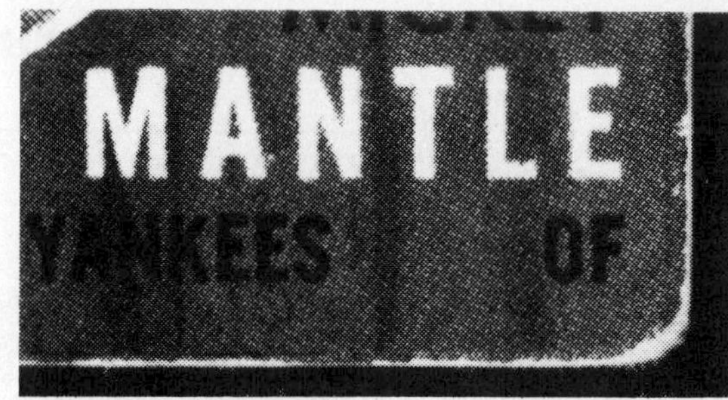

The 1962 Topps Mickey Mantle card definitely has a rounded corner. Some may say that this card is badly rounded, but that is a judgment call.

The 1962 Topps Hank Aaron card has a slightly rounded corner. Note that there is definite corner wear evident by the fraying and that there is no longer a sharp point to which the corner converges.

The 1962 Topps Gil Hodges card has corner wear; it is slightly better than the Aaron card above. Nevertheless, some collectors might classify this Hodges corner as slightly rounded.

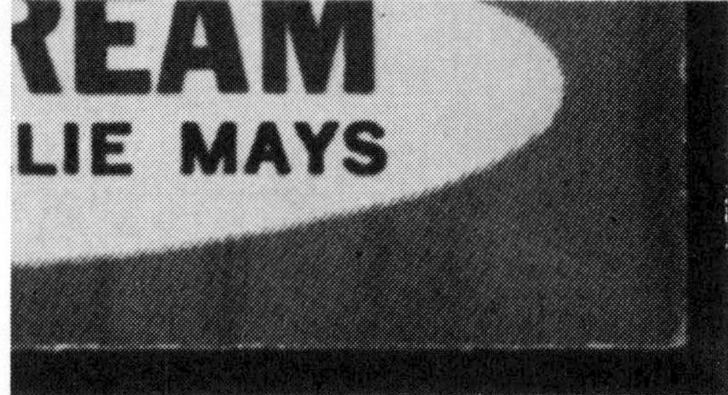

The 1962 Topps Manager's Dream card showing Mantle and Mays has slight corner wear. This is not a fuzzy corner as very slight wear is noticeable on the card's photo surface.

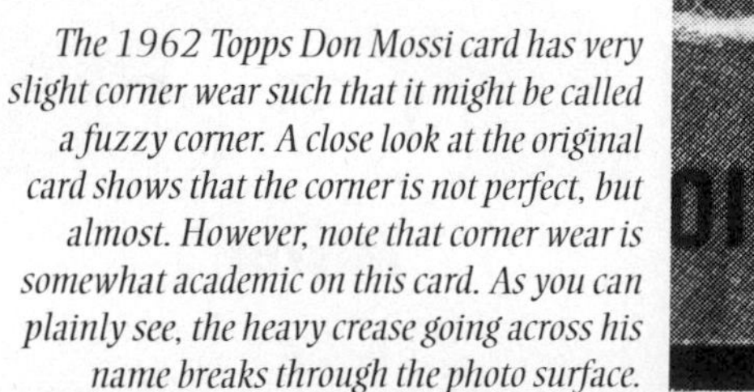

The 1962 Topps Don Mossi card has very slight corner wear such that it might be called a fuzzy corner. A close look at the original card shows that the corner is not perfect, but almost. However, note that corner wear is somewhat academic on this card. As you can plainly see, the heavy crease going across his name breaks through the photo surface.

Categorization of Defects

Miscellaneous Flaws

The following are common minor flaws that, depending on severity, lower a card's condition by one to four grades and often render it no better than Excellent-Mint: bubbles (lumps in surface), gum and wax stains, diamond cutting (slanted borders), notching, off-centered backs, paper wrinkles, scratched-off cartoons or puzzles on back, rubber band marks, scratches, surface impressions and warping.

The following are common serious flaws that, depending on severity, lower a card's condition at least four grades and often render it no better than Good: chemical or sun fading, erasure marks, mildew, miscutting (severe off-centering), holes, bleached or retouched borders, tape marks, tears, trimming, water or coffee stains and writing.

Condition Guide

Grades

Mint (Mt) - A card with no flaws or wear. The card has four perfect corners, 60/40 or better centering from top to bottom and from left to right, original gloss, smooth edges and original color borders. A Mint card does not have print spots, color or focus imperfections.

Near Mint-Mint (NrMt-Mt) - A card with one minor flaw. Any one of the following would lower a Mint card to Near Mint-Mint: one corner with a slight touch of wear, barely noticeable print spots, color or focus imperfections. The card must have 60/40 or better centering in both directions, original gloss, smooth edges and original color borders.

Near Mint (NrMt) - A card with one minor flaw. Any one of the following would lower a Mint card to Near Mint: one fuzzy corner or two to four corners with slight touches of wear, 70/30 to 60/40 centering, slightly rough edges, minor print spots, color or focus imperfections. The card must have original gloss and original color borders.

Excellent-Mint (ExMt) - A card with two or three fuzzy, but not rounded, corners and centering no worse than 80/20. The card may have no more than two of the following: slightly rough edges, very slightly discolored borders, minor print spots, color or focus imperfections. The card must have original gloss.

Excellent (Ex) - A card with four fuzzy but definitely not rounded corners and centering no worse than 80/20. The card may have a small amount of original gloss lost, rough edges, slightly discolored borders and minor print spots, color or focus imperfections.

Very Good (Vg) - A card that has been handled but not abused: slightly rounded corners with slight layering, slight notching on edges, a significant amount of gloss lost from the surface but no scuffing and moderate discoloration of borders. The card may have a few light creases.

Good (G), **Fair** (F), **Poor** (P) - A well-worn, mishandled or abused card: badly rounded and layered corners, scuffing, most or all original gloss missing, seriously discolored borders, moderate or heavy creases, and one or more serious flaws. The grade of Good, Fair or Poor depends on the severity of wear and flaws. Good, Fair and Poor cards generally are used only as fillers.

The most widely used grades are defined above. Obviously, many cards will not perfectly fit one of the definitions.

Therefore, categories between the major grades known as in-between grades are used, such as Good to Very Good (G-Vg), Very Good to Excellent (VgEx), and Excellent-Mint to Near Mint (ExMt-NrMt). Such grades indicate a card with all qualities of the lower category but with at least a few qualities of the higher category.

The *Sport Americana Baseball Card Price Guide* lists each card and set in three grades, with the middle grade valued at about 40-45% of the top grade, and the bottom grade valued at about 10-15% of the top grade.

The value of cards that fall between the listed columns can also be calculated using a percentage of the top grade. For example, a card that falls between the top and middle grades (Ex, ExMt or NrMt in most cases) will generally be valued at anywhere from 50% to 90% of the top grade.

Similarly, a card that falls between the middle and bottom grades (G-Vg, Vg or VgEx in most cases) will generally be valued at anywhere from 20% to 40% of the top grade.

There are also cases where cards are in better condition than the top grade or worse than the bottom grade. Cards that grade worse than the lowest grade are generally valued at 5-10% of the top grade.

When a card exceeds the top grade by one — such as NrMt-Mt when the top grade is NrMt, or

Mint when the top grade is NrMt-Mt — a premium of up to 50% is possible, with 10-20% the usual norm.

When a card exceeds the top grade by two — such as Mint when the top grade is NrMt, or NrMt-Mt when the top grade is ExMt — a premium of 25-50% is the usual norm. But certain condition sensitive cards or sets, particularly those from the pre-war era, can bring premiums of up to 100% or even more.

Unopened packs, boxes and factory-collated sets are considered Mint in their unknown (and presumed perfect) state. Once opened, however, each card can be graded (and valued) in its own right by taking into account any defects that may be present in spite of the fact that the card has never been handled.

Selling Your Cards

Just about every collector sells cards or will sell cards eventually. Someday you may be interested in selling your duplicates or maybe even your whole collection. You may sell to other collectors, friends or dealers. You may even sell cards you purchased from a certain dealer back to that same dealer. In any event, it helps to know some of the mechanics of the typical transaction between buyer and seller.

Dealers will buy cards in order to resell them to other collectors who are interested in the cards. Dealers will always pay a higher percentage for items that (in their opinion) can be resold quickly, and a much lower percentage for those items that are perceived as having low demand and hence are slow moving. In either case, dealers must buy at a price that allows for the expense of doing business and a margin for profit.

If you have cards for sale, the best advice we can give is that you get several offers for your cards — either from card shops or at a card show — and take the best offer, all things considered. Note, the "best" offer may not be the one for the highest amount. And remember, if a dealer really wants your cards, he won't let you get away without making his best competitive offer. Another alternative is to place your cards in an auction as one or several lots.

Many people think nothing of going into a department store and paying $15 for an item of clothing for which the store paid $5. But if you were selling your $15 card to a dealer and he offered you $5 for it, you might think his mark-up unreasonable. To complete the analogy: most department stores (and card dealers) that consistently pay $10 for $15 items eventually go out of business. An exception is when the dealer has lined up a willing buyer for the item(s) you are attempting to sell, or if the cards are so Hot that it's likely he'll have to hold the cards for only a short period of time.

In those cases, an offer of up to 75 percent of book value still will allow the dealer to make a reasonable profit considering the short time he will need to hold the merchandise. In general, however, most cards and collections will bring offers in the range of 25 to 50 percent of retail price. Also consider that most material from the past five to 10 years is plentiful. If that's what you're selling, don't be surprised if your best offer is well below that range.

Interesting Notes

The first card numerically of an issue is the single card most likely to obtain excessive wear. Consequently, you typically will find the price on the #1 card (in NrMt or Mint condition) somewhat higher than might otherwise be the case. Similarly, but to a lesser extent (because normally the less important, reverse side of the card is the one exposed), the last card numerically in an issue also is prone to abnormal wear. This extra wear and tear occurs because the first and last cards are exposed to the elements (human element included) more than any other cards. They are generally end cards in any brick formations, rubber bandings, stackings on wet surfaces, and like activities.

Sports cards have no intrinsic value. The value of a card, like the value of other collectibles, can be determined only by you and your enjoyment in viewing and possessing these cardboard treasures.

Remember, the buyer ultimately determines the price of each baseball card. You are the determining price factor because you have the ability to say "No" to the price of any card by not exchanging your hard-earned money for a given card. When the cost of a trading card exceeds the enjoyment you will receive from it, your answer should be "No." We assess and report the prices. You set them!

We are always interested in receiving the price

input of collectors and dealers from around the country. We happily credit major contributors. We welcome your opinions, since your contributions assist us in ensuring a better guide each year. If you would like to join our survey list for the next editions of this book and others authored by Dr. Beckett, please send your name and address to Dr. James Beckett, 4887 Alpha Road, Suite 200, Dallas, Texas 75244.

Advertising

Within this Price Guide you will find advertisements for sports memorabilia material, mail order, and retail sports collectibles establishments. All advertisements were accepted in good faith based on the reputation of the advertiser; however, neither the author, the publisher, the distributors, nor the other advertisers in this Price Guide accept any responsibility for any particular advertiser not complying with the terms of his or her ad.

Readers also should be aware that prices in advertisements are subject to change over the annual period before a new edition of this volume is issued each spring. When replying to an advertisement late in the baseball year, the reader should take this into account, and contact the dealer by phone or in writing for up-to-date price information. Should you come into contact with any of the advertisers in this guide as a result of their advertisement herein, please mention this source as your contact.

Additional Reading

With the increase in popularity of the hobby in recent years, there has been a corresponding increase in available literature. Below is a list of the books and periodicals that receive our highest recommendation and that we hope will further advance your knowledge and enjoyment of our great hobby.

The Sport Americana Baseball Card Card Price Guide by Dr. James Beckett (Fifteenth Edition, $15.95, released 1993, published by Edgewater Book Company) — the most comprehensive Price Guide and checklist ever issued on baseball cards.

The Official Price Guide to Baseball Cards by Dr. James Beckett (Thirteenth Edition, $5.99, released 1993, published by The House of Collectibles) — an abridgment of the *Sport Americana Price Guide* in a convenient and economical pocket-size format providing Dr. Beckett's pricing of the major baseball sets since 1948.

The Sport Americana Price Guide to Baseball Collectibles by Dr. James Beckett (Second Edition, $12.95, released 1988, published by Edgewater Book Company) — the complete guide and checklist with up-to-date values for box cards, coins, labels, Canadian cards, stamps, stickers, pins, etc.

The Sport Americana Football Card Price Guide by Dr. James Beckett (Ninth Edition, $14.95, released 1992, published by Edgewater Book Company) — the most comprehensive Price Guide and checklist ever issued on football cards. No serious football card hobbyist should be without it.

The Official Price Guide to Football Cards by Dr. James Beckett (Twelfth Edition, $5.99, released 1992, published by The House of Collectibles) — an abridgment of the *Sport Americana Price Guide* listed above in a convenient and economical pocket-size format providing Dr. Beckett's pricing of the major football sets since 1948.

The Sport Americana Hockey Card Price Guide by Dr. James Beckett (Second Edition, $12.95, released 1992, published by Edgewater Book Company) — the most comprehensive Price Guide and checklist ever issued on hockey cards.

The Official Price Guide to Hockey Cards by Dr. James Beckett (Second Edition, $5.99, released 1993, published by The House of Collectibles) — an abridgment of the *Sport Americana Price Guide* listed above in a convenient and economical pocket-size format providing Dr. Beckett's pricing of the major hockey sets since 1951.

The Sport Americana Basketball Card Price Guide and Alphabetical Checklist by Dr. James Beckett (Second Edition, $12.95, released 1992, published by Edgewater Book Company) — the most comprehensive combination Price Guide and alphabetical checklist ever issued on basketball cards.

The Official Price Guide to Basketball Cards by Dr. James Beckett (Second Edition, $5.99, released 1992, published by The House of Collectibles) — an abridgment of the *Sport Americana Price Guide* listed above in a convenient and economical pocket-size format providing Dr. Beckett's pricing of the major basketball sets since 1948.

The Sport Americana Baseball Card Alphabetical Checklist by Dr. James Beckett (Fifth

Edition, $14.95, released 1992, published by Edgewater Book Company) — an alphabetical listing, by the last name of the player portrayed on the card, of virtually all baseball cards (major league and minor league) produced up through the 1992 major sets.

The Sport Americana Price Guide to the Non-Sports Cards 1930-1960 by Christopher Benjamin and Dennis W. Eckes ($14.95, released 1991, published by Edgewater Book Company) — the definitive guide to virtually all popular non-sports American tobacco and bubblegum cards issued between 1930 and 1960. In addition to cards, illustrations and prices for wrappers also are included.

The Sport Americana Price Guide to the Non-Sports Cards by Christopher Benjamin (Fourth Edition, $14.95, released 1992, published by Edgewater Book Company) — the definitive guide to all popular non-sports American cards. In addition to cards, illustrations and prices for wrappers also are included. This volume covers non-sports cards from 1961 to 1992.

The Sport Americana Baseball Address List by Jack Smalling (Seventh Edition, $12.95, released 1992, published by Edgewater Book Company) — the definitive guide for autograph hunters, giving addresses and deceased information for virtually all Major League Baseball players past and present.

The Sport Americana Team Baseball Card Checklist by Jeff Fritsch (Sixth Edition, $12.95, released 1992, published by Edgewater Book Company) — includes all Topps, Bowman, Donruss, Fleer, Score, Play Ball, Goudey, and Upper Deck cards, with the players portrayed on the cards listed with the teams for whom they played. The book is invaluable to the collector who specializes in an individual team because it is the most complete baseball card team checklist available.

The Sport Americana Team Football and Basketball Card Checklist by Jane Fritsch, Jeff Fritsch, and Dennis Eckes (First Edition, $10.95, released 1990, published by Edgewater Book Company) — the book is invaluable to the collector who specializes in an individual team because it is the most complete football and basketball card team checklist available.

The Encyclopedia of Baseball Cards, Volume I: 19th Century Cards by Lew Lipset ($11.95, released 1983, published by the author) — everything you ever wanted to know about 19th century cards.

The Encyclopedia of Baseball Cards, Volume II: Early Gum and Candy Cards by Lew Lipset ($10.95, released 1984, published by the author) — everything you ever wanted to know about early candy and gum cards.

The Encyclopedia of Baseball Cards, Volume III: 20th Century Tobacco Cards, 1909-1932 by Lew Lipset ($12.95, released 1986, published by the author) — everything you ever wanted to know about old tobacco cards.

Beckett Baseball Card Monthly, published and edited by Dr. James Beckett — contains the most extensive and accepted monthly Price Guide, collectible glossy superstar covers, colorful feature articles, "who's Hot and who's Not" section, Convention Calendar, tips for beginners, "Readers Write" letters to and responses from the editor, information on errors and varieties, autograph collecting tips and profiles of the sport's Hottest stars. Published every month, *BBCM* is the hobby's largest paid circulation periodical. *Beckett Football Card Monthly, Beckett Basketball Monthly, Beckett Hockey Monthly* and *Beckett Focus on Future Stars* were built on the success of *BBCM*.

Prices in this Guide

Prices found in this guide reflect current retail rates just prior to the printing of this book. They do not reflect the FOR SALE prices of the author, the publisher, the distributors, the advertisers, or any card dealers associated with this guide. No one is obligated in any way to buy, sell or trade his or her cards based on these prices. The price listings were compiled by the author from actual buy/sell transactions at sports conventions, sports card shops, buy/sell advertisements in the hobby papers, for sale prices from dealer catalogs and price lists, and discussions with leading hobbyists in the U.S. and Canada. All prices are in U.S. dollars.

History of Baseball Cards

Today's version of the baseball card, with its colorful and oft times high-tech fronts and backs, is a far cry from its earliest predecessors. The issue remains cloudy as to which was the very first baseball card ever produced, but the institution

of baseball cards dates from the latter half of the 19th century, more than 100 years ago. Early issues, generally printed on heavy cardboard, were of poor quality, with photographs, drawings, and printing far short of today's standards.

Goodwin & Co., of New York, makers of Gypsy Queen, Old Judge, and other cigarette brands, is considered by many to be the first issuer of baseball and other sports cards. Its issues, predominantly sized 1-1/2 by 2-1/2 inches, generally consisted of photographs of baseball players, boxers, wrestlers, and other subjects mounted on stiff cardboard. More than 2,000 different photos of baseball players alone have been identified. These "Old Judges," a collective name commonly used for the Goodwin & Co. cards, were issued from 1886 to 1890 and are treasured parts of many collections today.

Among the other cigarette companies that issued baseball cards still attracting attention today are Allen & Ginter, D. Buchner & Co. (Gold Coin Chewing Tobacco), and P.H. Mayo & Brother. Cards from the first two companies bore colored line drawings, while the Mayos are sepia photographs on black cardboard.In addition to the small-size cards from this era, several tobacco companies issued cabinet-size baseball cards. These "cabinets" were considerably larger than the small cards, usually about 4-1/4 by 6-1/2 inches, and were printed on heavy stock. Goodwin & Co.'s Old Judge cabinets and the National Tobacco Works' "Newsboy" baseball photos are two that remain popular today.

By 1895, the American Tobacco Company began to dominate its competition. They discontinued baseball card inserts in their cigarette packages (actually slide boxes in those days). The lack of competition in the cigarette market had made these inserts unnecessary. This marked the end of the first era of baseball cards. At the dawn of the 20th century, few baseball cards were being issued. But once again, it was the cigarette companies — particularly, the American Tobacco Company — followed to a lesser extent by the candy and gum makers that revived the practice of including baseball cards with their products. The bulk of these cards, identified in the American Card Catalog (designated hereafter as ACC) as T or E cards for 20th century "Tobacco" or "Early Candy and Gum" issues, respectively, were released from 1909 to 1915.

This romantic and popular era of baseball card collecting produced many desirable items. The most outstanding is the fabled T-206 Honus Wagner card. Other perennial favorites among collectors are the T-206 Eddie Plank card, and the T-206 Magee error card. The former was once the second most valuable card and only recently relinquished that position to a more distinctive and aesthetically pleasing Napoleon Lajoie card from the 1933-34 Goudey Gum series. The latter misspells the player's name as "Magie," the most famous and valuable blooper card.

The ingenuity and distinctiveness of this era has yet to be surpassed. Highlights include the T-202 Hassan triple-folders, one of the best looking and the most distinctive cards ever issued; the durable T-201 Mecca double-folders, one of the first sets with players' records on the reverse; the T-3 Turkey Reds, the hobby's most popular cabinet card; the E-145 Cracker Jacks, the only major set containing Federal League player cards; and the T-204 Ramlys, with their distinctive black-and-white oval photos and ornate gold borders. These are but a few of the varieties issued during this period.

While the American Tobacco Company dominated the field, several other tobacco companies, as well as clothing manufacturers, newspapers and periodicals, game makers, and companies whose identities remain anonymous, also issued cards during this period. In fact, the Collins-McCarthy Candy Company, makers of Zeenuts Pacific Coast League baseball cards, issued cards yearly from 1911 to 1938. Its record for continuous annual card production has been exceeded only by the Topps Chewing Gum Company. The era of the tobacco card issues closed with the onset of World War I, with the exception of the Red Man chewing tobacco sets produced from 1952 to 1955.

Increasing Popularity

The next flurry of card issues broke out in the roaring and prosperous 1920s, the era of the E card. The caramel companies (National Caramel, American Caramel, York Caramel) were the leading distributors of these E cards. In addition, the strip card, a continous strip with several cards divided by dotted lines or other sectioning features, flourished during this time. While the E cards and the strip cards generally are considered less imaginative than the T cards or the recent candy and gum issues, they still are pursued by many advanced collectors.

Another significant event of the 1920s was the introduction of the arcade card. Taking its desig-

nation from its issuer, the Exhibit Supply Company of Chicago, it is usually known as the "Exhibit" card. Once a trademark of the penny arcades, amusement parks and county fairs across the country, Exhibit machines dispensed nearly postcard-size photos on thick stock for one penny. These picture cards bore likenesses of a favorite cowboy, actor, actress or baseball player. Exhibit Supply and its associated companies produced baseball cards during a longer time span, although discontinuous, than any other manufacturer. Its first cards appeared in 1921, while its last issue was in 1966. In 1979, the Exhibit Supply Company was bought and somewhat revived by a collector/dealer who has since reprinted Exhibit photos of the past.

If the T card period, from 1909 to 1915, can be designated the "Golden Age" of baseball card collecting, then perhaps the "Silver Age" commenced with the introduction of the Big League Gum series of 239 cards in 1933 (a 240th card was added in 1934). These are the forerunners of today's baseball gum cards, and the Goudey Gum Company of Boston is responsible for their success. This era spanned the period from the Depression days of 1933 to America's formal involvement in World War II in 1941.

Goudey's attractive designs, with full-color line drawings on thick card stock, greatly influenced other cards being issued at that time. As a result, the most attractive and popular cards in collecting history were produced in this "Silver Age." The 1933 Goudey Big League Gum series also owes its popularity to the more than 40 Hall of Fame players in the set. These include four cards of Babe Ruth and two of Lou Gehrig. Goudey's reign continued in 1934, when it issued a 96-card set in color, together with the single remaining card from the 1933 series, #106, the Napoleon Lajoie card.

In addition to Goudey, several other bubblegum manufacturers issued baseball cards during this era. DeLong Gum Company issued an extremely attractive set in 1933. National Chicle Company's 192-card "Batter-Up" series of 1934-1936 became the largest die-cut set in card history. In addition, that company offered the popular "Diamond Stars" series during the same period. Other popular sets included the "Tattoo Orbit" set of 60 color cards issued in 1933 and Gum Products' 75-card "Double Play" set, featuring sepia depictions of two players per card.

In 1939, Gum Inc., which later became Bowman Gum, replaced Goudey Gum as the leading baseball card producer. In 1939 and the following year, it issued two important sets of black-and-white cards. In 1939, its "Play Ball America" set consisted of 162 cards. The larger, 240-card "Play Ball" set of 1940 still is considered by many to be the most attractive black-and-white cards ever produced. That firm introduced its only color set in 1941, consisting of 72 cards titled "Play Ball Sports Hall of Fame." Many of these were colored repeats of poses from the black-and-white 1940 series.

In addition to regular gum cards, many manufacturers distributed premium issues during the 1930s. These premiums were printed on paper or photographic stock, rather than card stock. They were much larger than the regular cards and were sold for a penny across the counter with gum (which was packaged separately from the premium). They often were redeemed at the store or through the mail in exchange for the wrappers of previously purchased gum cards, a la proof-of-purchase box-top premiums today. The gum premiums are scarcer than the card issues of the 1930s and in most cases no manufacturer's name is present.

World War II brought an end to this popular era of card collecting when paper and rubber shortages curtailed the production of bubblegum baseball cards. They were resurrected again in 1948 by the Bowman Gum Company (the direct descendant of Gum, Inc.). This marked the beginning of the modern era of card collecting.

In 1948, Bowman Gum issued a 48-card set in black and white consisting of one card and one slab of gum in every one-cent pack. That same year, the Leaf Gum Company also issued a set of cards. Although rather poor in quality, these cards were issued in color. A squabble over the rights to use players' pictures developed between Bowman and Leaf. Eventually Leaf dropped out of the card market, but not before it had left a lasting heritage to the hobby by issuing some of the rarest cards now in existence. Leaf's baseball card series of 1948-49 contained 98 cards, skip numbered to #168 (not all numbers were printed). Of these 98 cards, 49 are relatively plentiful; the other 49, however, are rare and quite valuable.

Bowman continued its production of cards in 1949 with a color series of 240 cards. Because there are many scarce "high numbers," this series remains the most difficult Bowman regular issue to complete. Although the set was printed in color and commands great interest due to its scarcity, it is

considered aesthetically inferior to the Goudey and National Chicle issues of the 1930s. In addition to the regular issue of 1949, Bowman also produced a set of 36 Pacific Coast League players. While this was not a regular issue, it still is prized by collectors. In fact, it has become the most valuable Bowman series.

In 1950 (representing Bowman's one-year monopoly of the baseball card market), the company began a string of top quality cards that continued until its demise in 1955. The 1950 series was itself something of an oddity because the low numbers, rather than the traditional high numbers, were the more difficult cards to obtain.

Intensified Competition

The year 1951 marked the beginning of the most competitive and perhaps the highest quality period of baseball card production. In that year, Topps Chewing Gum Company of Brooklyn entered the market. Topps' 1951 series consisted of two sets of 52 cards each, one set with red backs and the other with blue backs. In addition, Topps also issued 31 insert cards, three of which remain the rarest Topps cards ("Current All-Stars" Konstanty, Roberts and Stanky). The 1951 Topps cards were unattractive and paled in comparison to the 1951 Bowman issues. They were successful, however, and Topps has continued to produce cards ever since.

Topps issued a larger and more attractive card set in 1952. This larger size became standard for the next five years. (Bowman followed with larger-size baseball cards in 1953.) This 1952 Topps set has become, like the 1933 Goudey series and the T-206 white border series, the classic set of its era. The 407-card set is a collector's dream of scarcities, rarities, errors and variations. It also contains the first Topps issues of Mickey Mantle and Willie Mays.

As with Bowman and Leaf in the late 1940s, competition over player rights arose. Ensuing court battles occurred between Topps and Bowman. Topps, using the Bowman name, ressurected Bowman as a later label in 1989. The market split due to stiff competition, and in January 1956, Topps bought out Bowman. Topps remained essentially unchallenged as the primary producer of baseball cards through 1980. So, the story of major baseball card sets from 1956 through 1980 is by and large the story of Topps' issues. Notable exceptions include the small sets produced by Fleer Gum in 1959, 1960, 1961 and 1963, and the Kellogg's Cereal and Hostess Cakes baseball cards issued to promote their products.

A court decision in 1980 paved the way for two other large gum companies to enter (or reenter, in Fleer's case) the baseball card arena. Fleer, which had last made photo cards in 1963, and the Donruss Company (then a division of General Mills) secured rights to produce baseball cards of current players, thus breaking Topps' monopoly. Each company issued major card sets in 1981 with bubblegum products.

Then a higher court decision in that year overturned the lower court ruling against Topps. It appeared that Topps had regained its sole position as a producer of baseball cards. Undaunted by the revocation ruling, Fleer and Donruss continued to issue cards in 1982 but without bubblegum or any other edible product. Fleer issued its current player baseball cards with "team logo stickers," while Donruss issued its cards with a piece of a baseball jigsaw puzzle.

Sharing the Pie

Since 1981, these three major baseball card producers have all thrived, sharing relatively equal recognition. Each has steadily increased its involvement in terms of numbers of issues per year. To the delight of collectors, their competition has generated novel, and in some cases exceptional, issues of current major league baseball players. Collectors also eagerly accepted the debut efforts of Score (1988) and Upper Deck (1989), the newest companies to enter the baseball card producing derby.

Upper Deck's successful entry into the market turned out to be very important. The company's card stock, photography, packaging and marketing gave baseball cards a new standard for quality, and began the "premium card" trend that continues today. The second premium baseball card set to be issued was the 1990 Leaf set, named for and issued by the parent company of Donruss. To gauge the significance of the premium card trend, one need only note that the two most valuable post-1986 regular-issue cards in the hobby are the 1989 Upper Deck Ken Griffey Jr. and 1990 Leaf Frank Thomas Rookie Cards. The impressive debut of Leaf in 1990 was followed by Leaf Studio, Fleer Ultra, and Topps Stadium Club in 1991. Of those, Topps Stadium Club made the biggest impact. In 1992, Bowman, Pinnacle, and Score Select joined the premium fray. In 1992, Donruss and Fleer abandoned the traditional 50-cent pack market and instead produced premium sets comparable to (and presumably designed to compete against) Upper Deck's set. Those moves, combined with the almost instantaneous spread of premium cards to the other major team sports cards, serve as strong indicators that premium cards probably are here to stay. Bowman had been a lower-level product from 1989-91.

All current major card producers have become increasingly aware of the organized collecting market. While the drugstores and grocery stores down the street remain major outlets for card sales, an increasing number of issues have been directed to this organized hobby marketplace. In fact, many issues now are distributed exclusively through hobby channels. Although no one can ever say what the future will bring, one only can surmise that the hobby market will play a significant role in future plans of all the major baseball card producers.

Finding Out More

The above has been a thumbnail sketch of card collecting from its inception in the 1880s to the present. It is difficult to tell the whole story in just a few pages — there are several other good sources of information. Serious collectors should subscribe to at least one of the excellent hobby periodicals. We also suggest that collectors visit their local card shop(s) and also attend a sports collectibles show in their area. Card collecting is still a young and informal hobby. You can learn more about it in either place. After all, smart dealers realize that spending a few minutes teaching beginners about the hobby often pays off for them in the long run.

Acknowledgments

A great deal of diligence, hard work, and dedicated effort went into this year's volume. The high standards to which we hold ourselves, however, could not have been met without the expert input and generous amount of time contributed by many people. Our sincere thanks are extended to each and every one of you.

A complete list of these invaluable contributors appears after the Price Guide section.

Vintage Baseball Cards

1887-1946

1934-36 Batter-Up

The 1934-36 Batter-Up set issued by National Chicle contains 192 blank-backed die-cut cards. Numbers 1 to 80 are 2 3/8" by 3 1/4" in size while 81 to 192 are 2 3/8" by 3". The latter are more difficult to find than the former. The pictures come in basic black and white or in tints of blue, brown, green, purple, red, or sepia. There are three combination cards (each featuring two players per card) in the high series (98, 111, and 115). The catalog designation for the set is R318. Cards with the die-cut backing removed are graded fair at best.

	EX-MT	VG-E	GOOD
COMPLETE SET (192)	23500.	10500.	3200.00
COMMON PLAYER (1-80)	50.00	20.00	5.00
COMMON PLAYER (81-192)	100.00	40.00	10.00
☐ 1 Wally Berger	100.00	35.00	7.00
☐ 2 Ed Brandt	50.00	20.00	5.00
☐ 3 Al Lopez	125.00	50.00	12.50
☐ 4 Dick Bartell	50.00	20.00	5.00
☐ 5 Carl Hubbell	180.00	75.00	18.00
☐ 6 Bill Terry	180.00	75.00	18.00
☐ 7 Pepper Martin	75.00	30.00	7.50
☐ 8 Jim Bottomley	125.00	50.00	12.50
☐ 9 Tom Bridges	60.00	24.00	6.00
☐ 10 Rick Ferrell	125.00	50.00	12.50
☐ 11 Ray Benge	50.00	20.00	5.00
☐ 12 Wes Ferrell	60.00	24.00	6.00
☐ 13 Chalmer Cissell	50.00	20.00	5.00
☐ 14 Pie Traynor	180.00	75.00	18.00
☐ 15 Leroy Mahaffey	50.00	20.00	5.00
☐ 16 Chick Hafey	125.00	50.00	12.50
☐ 17 Lloyd Waner	125.00	50.00	12.50
☐ 18 Jack Burns	50.00	20.00	5.00
☐ 19 Buddy Myer	50.00	20.00	5.00
☐ 20 Bob Johnson	60.00	24.00	6.00
☐ 21 Arky Vaughan	125.00	50.00	12.50
☐ 22 Red Rolfe	60.00	24.00	6.00
☐ 23 Lefty Gomez	180.00	75.00	18.00
☐ 24 Earl Averill	125.00	50.00	12.50
☐ 25 Mickey Cochrane	180.00	75.00	18.00
☐ 26 Van Lingle Mungo	60.00	24.00	6.00
☐ 27 Mel Ott	250.00	100.00	25.00
☐ 28 Jimmy Foxx	250.00	100.00	25.00
☐ 29 Jimmy Dykes	60.00	24.00	6.00
☐ 30 Bill Dickey	225.00	90.00	22.00
☐ 31 Lefty Grove	225.00	90.00	22.00
☐ 32 Joe Cronin	180.00	75.00	18.00
☐ 33 Frank Frisch	180.00	75.00	18.00
☐ 34 Al Simmons	150.00	60.00	15.00
☐ 35 Rogers Hornsby	250.00	100.00	25.00
☐ 36 Ted Lyons	125.00	50.00	12.50
☐ 37 Rabbit Maranville	125.00	50.00	12.50
☐ 38 Jimmy Wilson	50.00	20.00	5.00
☐ 39 Willie Kamm	50.00	20.00	5.00
☐ 40 Bill Hallahan	50.00	20.00	5.00
☐ 41 Gus Suhr	50.00	20.00	5.00
☐ 42 Charlie Gehringer	150.00	60.00	15.00
☐ 43 Joe Heving	50.00	20.00	5.00
☐ 44 Adam Comorosky	50.00	20.00	5.00
☐ 45 Tony Lazzeri	150.00	60.00	15.00
☐ 46 Sam Leslie	50.00	20.00	5.00
☐ 47 Bob Smith	50.00	20.00	5.00
☐ 48 Willis Hudlin	50.00	20.00	5.00
☐ 49 Carl Reynolds	50.00	20.00	5.00
☐ 50 Fred Schulte	50.00	20.00	5.00
☐ 51 Cookie Lavagetto	60.00	24.00	6.00
☐ 52 Hal Schumacher	60.00	24.00	6.00
☐ 53 Roger Cramer	60.00	24.00	6.00
☐ 54 Sylvester Johnson	50.00	20.00	5.00
☐ 55 Ollie Bejma	50.00	20.00	5.00
☐ 56 Sam Byrd	50.00	20.00	5.00
☐ 57 Hank Greenberg	225.00	90.00	22.00
☐ 58 Bill Knickerbocker	50.00	20.00	5.00
☐ 59 Bill Urbanski	50.00	20.00	5.00
☐ 60 Eddie Morgan	50.00	20.00	5.00
☐ 61 Rabbit McNair	50.00	20.00	5.00
☐ 62 Ben Chapman	60.00	24.00	6.00
☐ 63 Roy Johnson	50.00	20.00	5.00
☐ 64 Dizzy Dean	400.00	160.00	40.00
☐ 65 Zeke Bonura	50.00	20.00	5.00
☐ 66 Fred Marberry	50.00	20.00	5.00
☐ 67 Gus Mancuso	50.00	20.00	5.00
☐ 68 Joe Vosmik	50.00	20.00	5.00
☐ 69 Earl Grace	50.00	20.00	5.00
☐ 70 Tony Piet	50.00	20.00	5.00
☐ 71 Rollie Hemsley	50.00	20.00	5.00
☐ 72 Fred Fitzsimmons	60.00	24.00	6.00
☐ 73 Hack Wilson	180.00	75.00	18.00
☐ 74 Chick Fullis	50.00	20.00	5.00
☐ 75 Fred Frankhouse	50.00	20.00	5.00
☐ 76 Ethan Allen	50.00	20.00	5.00
☐ 77 Heinie Manush	125.00	50.00	12.50
☐ 78 Rip Collins	50.00	20.00	5.00
☐ 79 Tony Cuccinello	50.00	20.00	5.00
☐ 80 Joe Kuhel	50.00	20.00	5.00
☐ 81 Tom Bridges	110.00	45.00	11.00
☐ 82 Clint Brown	100.00	40.00	10.00
☐ 83 Albert Blanche	100.00	40.00	10.00
☐ 84 Boze Berger	100.00	40.00	10.00
☐ 85 Goose Goslin	225.00	90.00	22.00
☐ 86 Lefty Gomez	350.00	140.00	35.00
☐ 87 Joe Glenn	100.00	40.00	10.00
☐ 88 Cy Blanton	100.00	40.00	10.00
☐ 89 Tom Carey	100.00	40.00	10.00
☐ 90 Ralph Birkofer	100.00	40.00	10.00
☐ 91 Fred Gabler	100.00	40.00	10.00
☐ 92 Dick Coffman	100.00	40.00	10.00
☐ 93 Ollie Bejma	100.00	40.00	10.00
☐ 94 Leroy Parmelee	100.00	40.00	10.00
☐ 95 Carl Reynolds	100.00	40.00	10.00
☐ 96 Ben Cantwell	100.00	40.00	10.00
☐ 97 Curtis Davis	100.00	40.00	10.00
☐ 98 Earl Webb and Wally Moses	120.00	50.00	12.00

☐ 99 Ray Benge	100.00	40.00	10.00
☐ 100 Pie Traynor	250.00	100.00	25.00
☐ 101 Phil Cavarretta	135.00	54.00	13.50
☐ 102 Pep Young	100.00	40.00	10.00
☐ 103 Willis Hudlin	100.00	40.00	10.00
☐ 104 Mickey Haslin	100.00	40.00	10.00
☐ 105 Oswald Bluege	110.00	45.00	11.00
☐ 106 Paul Andrews	100.00	40.00	10.00
☐ 107 Ed Brandt	100.00	40.00	10.00
☐ 108 Don Taylor	100.00	40.00	10.00
☐ 109 Thornton Lee	110.00	45.00	11.00
☐ 110 Hal Schumacher	110.00	45.00	11.00
☐ 111 Hayes and Ted Lyons	180.00	75.00	18.00
☐ 112 Odell Hale	100.00	40.00	10.00
☐ 113 Earl Averill	225.00	90.00	22.00
☐ 114 Italo Chelini	100.00	40.00	10.00
☐ 115 Andrews and Jim Bottomley	180.00	75.00	18.00
☐ 116 Bill Walker	100.00	40.00	10.00
☐ 117 Bill Dickey	400.00	160.00	40.00
☐ 118 Gerald Walker	100.00	40.00	10.00
☐ 119 Ted Lyons	225.00	90.00	22.00
☐ 120 Eldon Auker	100.00	40.00	10.00
☐ 121 Bill Hallahan	100.00	40.00	10.00
☐ 122 Fred Lindstrom	225.00	90.00	22.00
☐ 123 Oral Hildebrand	100.00	40.00	10.00
☐ 124 Luke Appling	300.00	120.00	30.00
☐ 125 Pepper Martin	135.00	54.00	13.50
☐ 126 Rick Ferrell	225.00	90.00	22.00
☐ 127 Ival Goodman	100.00	40.00	10.00
☐ 128 Joe Kuhel	100.00	40.00	10.00
☐ 129 Ernie Lombardi	225.00	90.00	22.00
☐ 130 Charlie Gehringer	300.00	120.00	30.00
☐ 131 Van Lingle Mungo	110.00	45.00	11.00
☐ 132 Larry French	100.00	40.00	10.00
☐ 133 Buddy Myer	100.00	40.00	10.00
☐ 134 Mel Harder	135.00	54.00	13.50
☐ 135 Augie Galan	100.00	40.00	10.00
☐ 136 Gabby Hartnett	225.00	90.00	22.00
☐ 137 Stan Hack	110.00	45.00	11.00
☐ 138 Billy Herman	225.00	90.00	22.00
☐ 139 Bill Jurges	100.00	40.00	10.00
☐ 140 Bill Lee	100.00	40.00	10.00
☐ 141 Zeke Bonura	100.00	40.00	10.00
☐ 142 Tony Piet	100.00	40.00	10.00
☐ 143 Paul Dean	150.00	60.00	15.00
☐ 144 Jimmy Foxx	500.00	200.00	50.00
☐ 145 Joe Medwick	300.00	120.00	30.00
☐ 146 Rip Collins	100.00	40.00	10.00
☐ 147 Mel Almada	100.00	40.00	10.00
☐ 148 Allan Cooke	100.00	40.00	10.00
☐ 149 Moe Berg	200.00	80.00	20.00
☐ 150 Dolph Camilli	110.00	45.00	11.00
☐ 151 Oscar Melillo	100.00	40.00	10.00
☐ 152 Bruce Campbell	100.00	40.00	10.00
☐ 153 Lefty Grove	400.00	160.00	40.00
☐ 154 Johnny Murphy	125.00	50.00	12.50
☐ 155 Luke Sewell	110.00	45.00	11.00
☐ 156 Leo Durocher	300.00	120.00	30.00
☐ 157 Lloyd Waner	225.00	90.00	22.00
☐ 158 Guy Bush	100.00	40.00	10.00
☐ 159 Jimmy Dykes	125.00	50.00	12.50
☐ 160 Steve O'Neill	110.00	45.00	11.00
☐ 161 General Crowder	100.00	40.00	10.00
☐ 162 Joe Cascarella	100.00	40.00	10.00
☐ 163 Daniel(Bud) Hafey	110.00	45.00	11.00
☐ 164 Gilly Campbell	100.00	40.00	10.00
☐ 165 Ray Hayworth	100.00	40.00	10.00
☐ 166 Frank Demaree	100.00	40.00	10.00
☐ 167 John Babich	100.00	40.00	10.00
☐ 168 Marvin Owen	100.00	40.00	10.00
☐ 169 Ralph Kress	100.00	40.00	10.00
☐ 170 Mule Haas	100.00	40.00	10.00
☐ 171 Frank Higgins	110.00	45.00	11.00
☐ 172 Wally Berger	125.00	50.00	12.50
☐ 173 Frank Frisch	300.00	120.00	30.00
☐ 174 Wes Ferrell	125.00	50.00	12.50
☐ 175 Pete Fox	100.00	40.00	10.00
☐ 176 John Vergez	100.00	40.00	10.00
☐ 177 Billy Rogell	100.00	40.00	10.00
☐ 178 Don Brennan	100.00	40.00	10.00
☐ 179 Jim Bottomley	225.00	90.00	22.00
☐ 180 Travis Jackson	225.00	90.00	22.00
☐ 181 Red Rolfe	125.00	50.00	12.50
☐ 182 Frank Crosetti	175.00	70.00	18.00
☐ 183 Joe Cronin	225.00	90.00	22.00
☐ 184 Schoolboy Rowe	135.00	54.00	13.50
☐ 185 Chuck Klein	300.00	120.00	30.00
☐ 186 Lon Warneke	110.00	45.00	11.00
☐ 187 Gus Suhr	100.00	40.00	10.00
☐ 188 Ben Chapman	110.00	45.00	11.00
☐ 189 Clint Brown	100.00	40.00	10.00
☐ 190 Paul Derringer	150.00	60.00	15.00
☐ 191 John Burns	100.00	40.00	10.00
☐ 192 John Broaca	150.00	60.00	12.00

1914 Cracker Jack

42

Albert H. Bridwell, infielder of the St. Louis Federal League team, was born in Portsmouth, Ohio, January 4, 1884, and began playing ball when he was eighteen years old. He was tried out by Columbus, and then loaned to Cincinnati in 1903. He was recalled to Columbus and played with that team in 1904. He was sold to Cincinnati that fall. In 1905 he was traded to Boston, and in 1907 joined the New York Giants. From New York he went to Boston, and from there to the Chicago Cubs, and played with that team until early in 1914, when he joined the Federals.

This is one of a series of colored pictures of famous Ball Players and Managers given Free with Cracker Jack, "The Famous Popcorn Confection," one card in each package. Our first issue is 10,000,000 pictures. Complete set has 144 pictures of Stars in the American, National and Federal Leagues.

RUECKHEIM BROS. & ECKSTEIN
Brooklyn, N. Y. Chicago, Ill.

The cards in this 144-card set measure approximately 2 1/4" by 3". This "Series of colored pictures of Famous Ball Players and Managers" was issued in packages of Cracker Jack in 1914. The cards have tinted photos set against red backgrounds and many are found with caramel stains. The set also contains Federal League players. The company claims to have printed 15 million cards. The 1914 series can be distinguished from the 1915 issue by the advertising found on the back of the cards. The catalog number for this set is E145-1.

	EX-MT	VG-E	GOOD
COMPLETE SET (144)	50000.	21000.	7000.00
COMMON PLAYER (1-144)	165.00	67.50	20.00
☐ 1 Otto Knabe	200.00	80.00	20.00
☐ 2 Frank Baker	400.00	160.00	40.00
☐ 3 Joe Tinker	325.00	130.00	32.00
☐ 4 Larry Doyle	185.00	75.00	24.00
☐ 5 Ward Miller	165.00	67.50	20.00
☐ 6 Eddie Plank (Phila. AL)	450.00	180.00	45.00
☐ 7 Eddie Collins (Phila. AL)	450.00	180.00	45.00
☐ 8 Rube Oldring	165.00	67.50	20.00
☐ 9 Artie Hoffman	165.00	67.50	20.00
☐ 10 John McInnis	165.00	67.50	20.00
☐ 11 George Stovall	165.00	67.50	20.00
☐ 12 Connie Mack	500.00	200.00	50.00
☐ 13 Art Wilson	165.00	67.50	20.00
☐ 14 Sam Crawford	325.00	130.00	32.00
☐ 15 Reb Russell	165.00	67.50	20.00
☐ 16 Howie Camnitz	165.00	67.50	20.00
☐ 17 Roger Bresnahan (Catcher)	375.00	150.00	37.00
☐ 18 Johnny Evers	325.00	130.00	32.00
☐ 19 Chief Bender (Phila. AL)	450.00	180.00	45.00
☐ 20 Cy Falkenberg	165.00	67.50	20.00
☐ 21 Heinie Zimmerman	165.00	67.50	20.00
☐ 22 Joe Wood	250.00	100.00	25.00
☐ 23 Charles Comiskey	375.00	150.00	37.00
☐ 24 George Mullen	165.00	67.50	20.00
☐ 25 Michael Simon	165.00	67.50	20.00
☐ 26 James Scott	165.00	67.50	20.00
☐ 27 Bill Carrigan	165.00	67.50	20.00
☐ 28 Jack Barry	165.00	67.50	20.00
☐ 29 Vean Gregg (Cleveland)	200.00	80.00	20.00
☐ 30 Ty Cobb	6000.00	2500.00	750.00
☐ 31 Heinie Wagner	165.00	67.50	20.00
☐ 32 Mordecai Brown	325.00	130.00	32.00
☐ 33 Amos Strunk	165.00	67.50	20.00
☐ 34 Ira Thomas	165.00	67.50	20.00
☐ 35 Harry Hooper	325.00	130.00	32.00
☐ 36 Ed Walsh	325.00	130.00	32.00
☐ 37 Grover Alexander	750.00	300.00	75.00
☐ 38 Red Dooin (Phila. NL)	200.00	80.00	20.00
☐ 39 Chick Gandil	250.00	100.00	25.00

☐ 40 Jimmy Austin (St.L. AL)	200.00	80.00	20.00
☐ 41 Tommy Leach	165.00	67.50	20.00
☐ 42 Al Bridwell	165.00	67.50	20.00
☐ 43 Rube Marquard (NY NL)	400.00	160.00	40.00
☐ 44 Charles Tesreau	165.00	67.50	20.00
☐ 45 Fred Luderus	165.00	67.50	20.00
☐ 46 Bob Groom	165.00	67.50	20.00
☐ 47 Josh Devore (Phila. NL)	200.00	80.00	20.00
☐ 48 Harry Lord	300.00	120.00	30.00
☐ 49 John Miller	165.00	67.50	20.00
☐ 50 John Hummell	165.00	67.50	20.00
☐ 51 Nap Rucker	185.00	75.00	24.00
☐ 52 Zach Wheat	325.00	130.00	32.00
☐ 53 Otto Miller	165.00	67.50	20.00
☐ 54 Marty O'Toole	165.00	67.50	20.00
☐ 55 Dick Hoblitzel (Cinc.)	200.00	80.00	20.00
☐ 56 Clyde Milan	185.00	75.00	24.00
☐ 57 Walter Johnson	1500.00	600.00	200.00
☐ 58 Wally Schang	185.00	75.00	24.00
☐ 59 Harry Gessler	165.00	67.50	20.00
☐ 60 Rollie Zeider	250.00	100.00	25.00
☐ 61 Ray Schalk	400.00	160.00	40.00
☐ 62 Jay Cashion	300.00	120.00	30.00
☐ 63 Babe Adams	185.00	75.00	24.00
☐ 64 Jimmy Archer	165.00	67.50	20.00
☐ 65 Tris Speaker	750.00	300.00	75.00
☐ 66 Napoleon Lajoie (Cleve.)	900.00	360.00	90.00
☐ 67 Otis Crandall	165.00	67.50	20.00
☐ 68 Honus Wagner	1500.00	600.00	200.00
☐ 69 John McGraw	450.00	180.00	45.00
☐ 70 Fred Clarke	325.00	130.00	32.00
☐ 71 Chief Meyers	165.00	67.50	20.00
☐ 72 John Boehling	165.00	67.50	20.00
☐ 73 Max Carey	325.00	130.00	32.00
☐ 74 Frank Owens	165.00	67.50	20.00
☐ 75 Miller Huggins	325.00	130.00	32.00
☐ 76 Claude Hendrix	165.00	67.50	20.00
☐ 77 Hugh Jennings	325.00	130.00	32.00
☐ 78 Fred Merkle	200.00	80.00	20.00
☐ 79 Ping Bodie	185.00	75.00	24.00
☐ 80 Ed Ruelbach	185.00	75.00	24.00
☐ 81 Jim C. Delehanty	185.00	75.00	24.00
☐ 82 Gavvy Cravath	200.00	80.00	20.00
☐ 83 Russ Ford	165.00	67.50	20.00
☐ 84 Elmer E. Knetzer	165.00	67.50	20.00
☐ 85 Buck Herzog	165.00	67.50	20.00
☐ 86 Burt Shotton	165.00	67.50	20.00
☐ 87 Forrest Cady	165.00	67.50	20.00
☐ 88 Christy Mathewson (Pitching)	1800.00	750.00	250.00
☐ 89 Lawrence Cheney	165.00	67.50	20.00
☐ 90 Frank Smith	165.00	67.50	20.00
☐ 91 Roger Peckinpaugh	165.00	67.50	20.00
☐ 92 Al Demaree (N.Y. NL)	200.00	80.00	20.00
☐ 93 Del Pratt (Throwing)	250.00	100.00	25.00
☐ 94 Eddie Cicotte	250.00	100.00	25.00
☐ 95 Ray Keating	165.00	67.50	20.00
☐ 96 Beals Becker	165.00	67.50	20.00
☐ 97 John(Rube) Benton	165.00	67.50	20.00
☐ 98 Frank LaPorte	165.00	67.50	20.00
☐ 99 Frank Chance	1200.00	500.00	150.00
☐ 100 Thomas Seaton	165.00	67.50	20.00
☐ 101 Frank Schulte	165.00	67.50	20.00
☐ 102 Ray Fisher	165.00	67.50	20.00
☐ 103 Joe Jackson	7500.00	3000.00	900.00
☐ 104 Vic Saier	165.00	67.50	20.00
☐ 105 James Lavender	165.00	67.50	20.00
☐ 106 Joe Birmingham	165.00	67.50	20.00
☐ 107 Tom Downey	165.00	67.50	20.00
☐ 108 Sherwood Magee (Phila. NL)	200.00	80.00	20.00
☐ 109 Fred Blanding	165.00	67.50	20.00
☐ 110 Bob Bescher	165.00	67.50	20.00
☐ 111 Jim Callahan	300.00	120.00	30.00
☐ 112 Ed Sweeney	165.00	67.50	20.00
☐ 113 George Suggs	165.00	67.50	20.00
☐ 114 Geo.J. Moriarty	185.00	75.00	24.00
☐ 115 Addison Brennan	165.00	67.50	20.00
☐ 116 Rollie Zeider	165.00	67.50	20.00
☐ 117 Ted Easterly	165.00	67.50	20.00
☐ 118 Ed Konetchy (Pittsburgh)	200.00	80.00	20.00
☐ 119 George Perring	165.00	67.50	20.00
☐ 120 Mike Doolan	165.00	67.50	20.00
☐ 121 Hub Perdue (Boston NL)	200.00	80.00	20.00
☐ 122 Owen Bush	165.00	67.50	20.00
☐ 123 Slim Sallee	165.00	67.50	20.00
☐ 124 Earl Moore	165.00	67.50	20.00
☐ 125 Bert Niehoff	200.00	80.00	20.00
☐ 126 Walter Blair	165.00	67.50	20.00
☐ 127 Butch Schmidt	165.00	67.50	20.00
☐ 128 Steve Evans	165.00	67.50	20.00
☐ 129 Ray Caldwell	165.00	67.50	20.00
☐ 130 Ivy Wingo	165.00	67.50	20.00
☐ 131 George Baumgardner	165.00	67.50	20.00
☐ 132 Les Nunamaker	165.00	67.50	20.00
☐ 133 Branch Rickey	450.00	180.00	45.00
☐ 134 Armando Marsans (Cincinnati)	200.00	80.00	20.00
☐ 135 Bill Killefer	165.00	67.50	20.00
☐ 136 Rabbit Maranville	325.00	130.00	32.00
☐ 137 William Rariden	165.00	67.50	20.00
☐ 138 Hank Gowdy	165.00	67.50	20.00
☐ 139 Rebel Oakes	165.00	67.50	20.00
☐ 140 Danny Murphy	165.00	67.50	20.00
☐ 141 Cy Barger	165.00	67.50	20.00
☐ 142 Eugene Packard	165.00	67.50	20.00
☐ 143 Jake Daubert	200.00	80.00	20.00
☐ 144 James C. Walsh	200.00	80.00	20.00

1915 Cracker Jack

106

Joseph Birmingham, manager of the Cleveland American League team, was born in Elmira, N. Y., August 6, 1884. He played on local nines in 1901 and with the Mercersburg, Pa., Preparatory School team during 1902 and 1903. In 1906 he played baseball professionally with the A. J. G. Club of the New York State League, and was secured by Cleveland in August of the same year.

This is one of a series of pictures of famous Ball Players and Managers in the American, National and Federal Leagues, given Free with Cracker Jack, "The Famous Popcorn Confection," one card in each package. Send 100 Cracker Jack Coupons, or 1 Coupon and 25c. to CHICAGO OFFICE for complete set of 176 Pictures. Handsome Album to hold full set of pictures sent postpaid for 50 Coupons, or 1 Coupon and 10c. in coin or stamps.

RUECKHEIM BROS. & ECKSTEIN
Brooklyn, N. Y. Chicago, Ill.

The cards in this 176-card set measure approximately 2 1/4" by 3". When turned over in a lateral motion, a 1915 "series of 176" Cracker Jack card shows the back printing upside-down. Cards were available in boxes of Cracker Jack or from the company for "100 Cracker Jack coupons, or one coupon and 25 cents." An album was available for "50 coupons or one coupon and 10 cents." Because of this send-in offer, the 1915 Cracker Jack cards are noticeably easier to find than the 1914 Cracker Jack cards, although obviously neither set is plentiful. The set essentially duplicates E145-1 (1914 Cracker Jack) except for some additional cards and new poses. Players in the Federal League are indicated by FED in the checklist below. The catalog designation for the set is E145-2.

	EX-MT	VG-E	GOOD
COMPLETE SET (176)	37500.	15000.	5000.00
COMMON PLAYER (1-144)	110.00	45.00	11.00
COMMON PLAYER (145-176)	135.00	54.00	13.50
☐ 1 Otto Knabe	150.00	60.00	15.00
☐ 2 Frank Baker	300.00	120.00	30.00
☐ 3 Joe Tinker	225.00	90.00	22.00
☐ 4 Larry Doyle	125.00	50.00	12.50
☐ 5 Ward Miller	110.00	45.00	11.00
☐ 6 Eddie Plank (St.L. FED)	400.00	160.00	40.00
☐ 7 Eddie Collins (Chicago AL)	350.00	140.00	35.00
☐ 8 Rube Oldring	110.00	45.00	11.00
☐ 9 Artie Hoffman	110.00	45.00	11.00
☐ 10 John McInnis	110.00	45.00	11.00
☐ 11 George Stovall	110.00	45.00	11.00
☐ 12 Connie Mack MG	350.00	140.00	35.00
☐ 13 Art Wilson	110.00	45.00	11.00
☐ 14 Sam Crawford	225.00	90.00	22.00
☐ 15 Reb Russell	110.00	45.00	11.00
☐ 16 Howie Camnitz	110.00	45.00	11.00

☐ 17 Roger Bresnahan	250.00	100.00	25.00
☐ 18 Johnny Evers	225.00	90.00	22.00
☐ 19 Chief Bender (Baltimore FED)	400.00	160.00	40.00
☐ 20 Cy Falkenberg	110.00	45.00	11.00
☐ 21 Heinie Zimmerman	110.00	45.00	11.00
☐ 22 Joe Wood	165.00	67.50	20.00
☐ 23 Charles Comiskey	250.00	100.00	25.00
☐ 24 George Mullen	110.00	45.00	11.00
☐ 25 Michael Simon	110.00	45.00	11.00
☐ 26 James Scott	110.00	45.00	11.00
☐ 27 Bill Carrigan	110.00	45.00	11.00
☐ 28 Jack Barry	110.00	45.00	11.00
☐ 29 Vean Gregg (Boston AL)	150.00	60.00	15.00
☐ 30 Ty Cobb	4500.00	2000.00	600.00
☐ 31 Heinie Wagner	110.00	45.00	11.00
☐ 32 Mordecai Brown	225.00	90.00	22.00
☐ 33 Amos Strunk	110.00	45.00	11.00
☐ 34 Ira Thomas	110.00	45.00	11.00
☐ 35 Harry Hooper	225.00	90.00	22.00
☐ 36 Ed Walsh	225.00	90.00	22.00
☐ 37 Grover C. Alexander	500.00	200.00	50.00
☐ 38 Red Dooin (Cincinnati)	150.00	60.00	15.00
☐ 39 Chick Gandil	200.00	80.00	20.00
☐ 40 Jimmy Austin (Pitts. FED)	175.00	70.00	18.00
☐ 41 Tommy Leach	110.00	45.00	11.00
☐ 42 Al Bridwell	110.00	45.00	11.00
☐ 43 Rube Marquard (Brooklyn FED)	400.00	160.00	40.00
☐ 44 Charles(Jeff) Tesreau	110.00	45.00	11.00
☐ 45 Fred Luderus	110.00	45.00	11.00
☐ 46 Bob Groom	110.00	45.00	11.00
☐ 47 Josh Devore (Boston NL)	150.00	60.00	15.00
☐ 48 Steve O'Neill	150.00	60.00	15.00
☐ 49 John Miller	110.00	45.00	11.00
☐ 50 John Hummell	110.00	45.00	11.00
☐ 51 Nap Rucker	125.00	50.00	12.50
☐ 52 Zach Wheat	225.00	90.00	22.00
☐ 53 Otto Miller	110.00	45.00	11.00
☐ 54 Marty O'Toole	110.00	45.00	11.00
☐ 55 Dick Hoblitzel (Boston AL)	150.00	60.00	15.00
☐ 56 Clyde Milan	125.00	50.00	12.50
☐ 57 Walter Johnson	1200.00	500.00	150.00
☐ 58 Wally Schang	125.00	50.00	12.50
☐ 59 Harry Gessler	110.00	45.00	11.00
☐ 60 Oscar Dugey	150.00	60.00	15.00
☐ 61 Ray Schalk	250.00	100.00	25.00
☐ 62 Willie Mitchell	150.00	60.00	15.00
☐ 63 Babe Adams	125.00	50.00	12.50
☐ 64 Jimmy Archer	110.00	45.00	11.00
☐ 65 Tris Speaker	500.00	200.00	50.00
☐ 66 Napoleon Lajoie (Phila. AL)	600.00	240.00	60.00
☐ 67 Otis Crandall	110.00	45.00	11.00
☐ 68 Honus Wagner	1200.00	500.00	150.00
☐ 69 John McGraw	300.00	120.00	30.00
☐ 70 Fred Clarke	225.00	90.00	22.00
☐ 71 Chief Meyers	110.00	45.00	11.00
☐ 72 John Boehling	110.00	45.00	11.00
☐ 73 Max Carey	225.00	90.00	22.00
☐ 74 Frank Owens	110.00	45.00	11.00
☐ 75 Miller Huggins	225.00	90.00	22.00
☐ 76 Claude Hendrix	110.00	45.00	11.00
☐ 77 Hugh Jennings MG	225.00	90.00	22.00
☐ 78 Fred Merkle	150.00	60.00	15.00
☐ 79 Ping Bodie	125.00	50.00	12.50
☐ 80 Ed Ruelbach	125.00	50.00	12.50
☐ 81 Jim C. Delehanty	125.00	50.00	12.50
☐ 82 Gavvy Cravath	150.00	60.00	15.00
☐ 83 Russ Ford	110.00	45.00	11.00
☐ 84 Elmer E. Knetzer	110.00	45.00	11.00
☐ 85 Buck Herzog	110.00	45.00	11.00
☐ 86 Burt Shotton	110.00	45.00	11.00
☐ 87 Forrest Cady	110.00	45.00	11.00
☐ 88 Christy Mathewson (Portrait)	1500.00	600.00	200.00
☐ 89 Lawrence Cheney	110.00	45.00	11.00
☐ 90 Frank Smith	110.00	45.00	11.00
☐ 91 Roger Peckinpaugh	125.00	50.00	12.50
☐ 92 Al Demaree (Phila. NL)	150.00	60.00	15.00
☐ 93 Del Pratt (Portrait)	200.00	80.00	20.00
☐ 94 Eddie Cicotte	175.00	70.00	18.00
☐ 95 Ray Keating	110.00	45.00	11.00
☐ 96 Beals Becker	110.00	45.00	11.00
☐ 97 John(Rube) Benton	110.00	45.00	11.00
☐ 98 Frank LaPorte	110.00	45.00	11.00

☐ 99 Hal Chase	300.00	120.00	30.00
☐ 100 Thomas Seaton	110.00	45.00	11.00
☐ 101 Frank Schulte	110.00	45.00	11.00
☐ 102 Ray Fisher	110.00	45.00	11.00
☐ 103 Joe Jackson	6000.00	2500.00	750.00
☐ 104 Vic Saier	110.00	45.00	11.00
☐ 105 James Lavender	110.00	45.00	11.00
☐ 106 Joe Birmingham	110.00	45.00	11.00
☐ 107 Thomas Downey	110.00	45.00	11.00
☐ 108 Sherwood Magee (Boston NL)	150.00	60.00	15.00
☐ 109 Fred Blanding	110.00	45.00	11.00
☐ 110 Bob Bescher	110.00	45.00	11.00
☐ 111 Herbie Moran	150.00	60.00	15.00
☐ 112 Ed Sweeney	110.00	45.00	11.00
☐ 113 George Suggs	110.00	45.00	11.00
☐ 114 Geo.J. Moriarty	125.00	50.00	12.50
☐ 115 Addison Brennan	110.00	45.00	11.00
☐ 116 Rollie Zeider	110.00	45.00	11.00
☐ 117 Ted Easterly	110.00	45.00	11.00
☐ 118 Ed Konetchy (Pitts. FED)	175.00	70.00	18.00
☐ 119 George Perring	110.00	45.00	11.00
☐ 120 Mike Doolan	110.00	45.00	11.00
☐ 121 Hub Perdue (St. Louis NL)	150.00	60.00	15.00
☐ 122 Owen Bush	110.00	45.00	11.00
☐ 123 Slim Sallee	110.00	45.00	11.00
☐ 124 Earl Moore	110.00	45.00	11.00
☐ 125 Bert Niehoff (Phila. NL)	150.00	60.00	15.00
☐ 126 Walter Blair	110.00	45.00	11.00
☐ 127 Butch Schmidt	110.00	45.00	11.00
☐ 128 Steve Evans	110.00	45.00	11.00
☐ 129 Ray Caldwell	110.00	45.00	11.00
☐ 130 Ivy Wingo	110.00	45.00	11.00
☐ 131 Geo. Baumgardner	110.00	45.00	11.00
☐ 132 Les Nunamaker	110.00	45.00	11.00
☐ 133 Branch Rickey	325.00	130.00	32.00
☐ 134 Armando Marsans (St.L. FED)	175.00	70.00	18.00
☐ 135 William Killefer	110.00	45.00	11.00
☐ 136 Rabbit Maranville	225.00	90.00	22.00
☐ 137 William Rariden	110.00	45.00	11.00
☐ 138 Hank Gowdy	110.00	45.00	11.00
☐ 139 Rebel Oakes	110.00	45.00	11.00
☐ 140 Danny Murphy	110.00	45.00	11.00
☐ 141 Cy Barger	110.00	45.00	11.00
☐ 142 Eugene Packard	110.00	45.00	11.00
☐ 143 Jake Daubert	150.00	60.00	15.00
☐ 144 James C. Walsh	110.00	45.00	11.00
☐ 145 Ted Cather	135.00	54.00	13.50
☐ 146 George Tyler	135.00	54.00	13.50
☐ 147 Lee Magee	135.00	54.00	13.50
☐ 148 Owen Wilson	135.00	54.00	13.50
☐ 149 Hal Janvrin	135.00	54.00	13.50
☐ 150 Doc Johnston	135.00	54.00	13.50
☐ 151 George Whitted	135.00	54.00	13.50
☐ 152 George McQuillen	135.00	54.00	13.50
☐ 153 Bill James	135.00	54.00	13.50
☐ 154 Dick Rudolph	135.00	54.00	13.50
☐ 155 Joe Connolly	135.00	54.00	13.50
☐ 156 Jean Dubuc	135.00	54.00	13.50
☐ 157 George Kaiserling	135.00	54.00	13.50
☐ 158 Fritz Maisel	135.00	54.00	13.50
☐ 159 Heinie Groh	135.00	54.00	13.50
☐ 160 Benny Kauff	135.00	54.00	13.50
☐ 161 Edd Roush	300.00	120.00	30.00
☐ 162 George Stallings MG	135.00	54.00	13.50
☐ 163 Bert Whaling	135.00	54.00	13.50
☐ 164 Bob Shawkey	165.00	67.50	20.00
☐ 165 Eddie Murphy	135.00	54.00	13.50
☐ 166 Joe Bush	165.00	67.50	20.00
☐ 167 Clark Griffith	300.00	120.00	30.00
☐ 168 Vin Campbell	135.00	54.00	13.50
☐ 169 Raymond Collins	135.00	54.00	13.50
☐ 170 Hans Lobert	135.00	54.00	13.50
☐ 171 Earl Hamilton	135.00	54.00	13.50
☐ 172 Erskine Mayer	135.00	54.00	13.50
☐ 173 Tilly Walker	135.00	54.00	13.50
☐ 174 Robert Veach	135.00	54.00	13.50
☐ 175 Joseph Benz	135.00	54.00	13.50
☐ 176 Jim Vaughn	165.00	67.50	20.00

1933 Delong

The cards in this 24-card set measure approximately 2" by 3". The 1933 Delong Gum set of 24 multi-colored cards

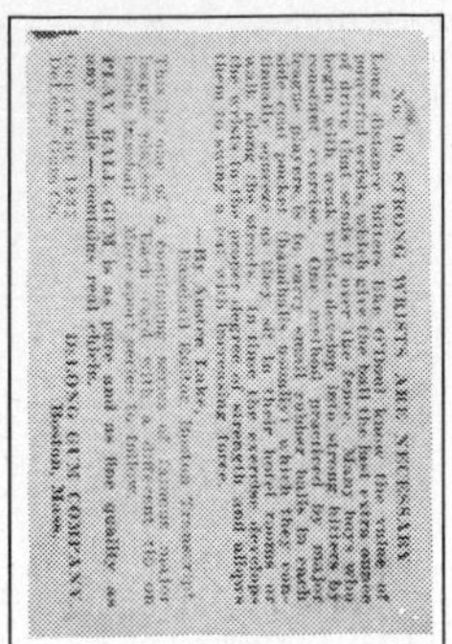

was, along with the 1933 Goudey Big League series, one of the first baseball card sets issued with chewing gum. It was the only card set issued by this company. The reverse text was written by Austen Lake, who also wrote the sports tips found on the Diamond Stars series which began in 1934, leading to speculation that Delong was bought out by National Chicle. The catalog designation for this set is R333.

	EX-MT	VG-E	GOOD
COMPLETE SET (24)	11000.	4750.00	1500.00
COMMON PLAYER (1-24)	200.00	80.00	20.00
☐ 1 Marty McManus	200.00	80.00	20.00
☐ 2 Al Simmons	350.00	140.00	35.00
☐ 3 Oscar Melillo	200.00	80.00	20.00
☐ 4 William Terry	450.00	180.00	45.00
☐ 5 Charlie Gehringer	450.00	180.00	45.00
☐ 6 Mickey Cochrane	450.00	180.00	45.00
☐ 7 Lou Gehrig	3500.00	1500.00	500.00
☐ 8 Kiki Cuyler	350.00	140.00	35.00
☐ 9 Bill Urbanski	200.00	80.00	20.00
☐ 10 Lefty O'Doul	225.00	90.00	22.00
☐ 11 Fred Lindstrom	325.00	130.00	32.00
☐ 12 Pie Traynor	400.00	160.00	40.00
☐ 13 Rabbit Maranville	325.00	130.00	32.00
☐ 14 Lefty Gomez	450.00	180.00	45.00
☐ 15 Riggs Stephenson	225.00	90.00	22.00
☐ 16 Lon Warneke	200.00	80.00	20.00
☐ 17 Pepper Martin	225.00	90.00	22.00
☐ 18 Jimmy Dykes	200.00	80.00	20.00
☐ 19 Chick Hafey	325.00	130.00	32.00
☐ 20 Joe Vosmik	200.00	80.00	20.00
☐ 21 Jimmie Foxx	750.00	300.00	75.00
☐ 22 Chuck Klein	400.00	160.00	40.00
☐ 23 Lefty Grove	550.00	220.00	55.00
☐ 24 Goose Goslin	350.00	140.00	35.00

1934-36 Diamond Stars

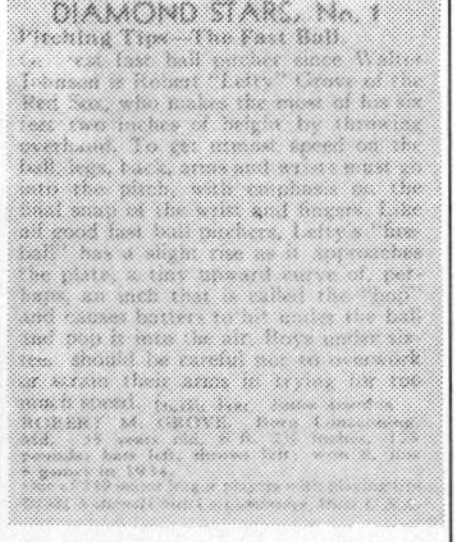
DIAMOND STARS, No. 1
Pitching Tips—The Fast Ball.

The cards in this 108-card set measure approximately 2 3/8" by 2 7/8". The Diamond Stars set produced by National Chicle from 1934-36 is also commonly known by its catalog designation, R327. The year of production can be determined by the statistics contained on the back of the card. There are at least 168 possible front/back combinations counting blue (B) and green (G) backs over all three years. The last twelve cards are repeat players and are quite scarce. The checklist below lists the year(s) and back color(s) for the cards. Cards 32 through 72 were issued only in 1935 with green ink on back. Cards 73 through 84 were issued three ways: 35B, 35G, and 36B. Card numbers 85 through 108 were issued only in 1936 with blue ink on back. The complete set price below refers to the set of all variations listed explicitly below. A blank-backed proof sheet of 12 additional (never-issued) cards was discovered in 1980.

	EX-MT	VG-E	GOOD
COMPLETE SET (119)	18000.	8000.00	2600.00
COMMON PLAYER (1-31)	50.00	20.00	5.00
COMMON PLAYER (32-72)	60.00	24.00	6.00
COMMON PLAYER (73-84)	60.00	24.00	6.00
COMMON PLAYER (85-96)	125.00	50.00	12.50
COMMON PLAYER (97-108)	300.00	120.00	30.00
☐ 1 Lefty Grove (34G, 35G)	1000.00	200.00	40.00
☐ 2A Al Simmons (34G, 35G) (Sox on uniform)	150.00	60.00	15.00
☐ 2B Al Simmons (36B) (No name on uniform)	250.00	100.00	25.00
☐ 3 Rabbit Maranville (34G, 35G)	125.00	50.00	12.50
☐ 4 Buddy Myer (34G, 35G, 36B)	50.00	20.00	5.00
☐ 5 Tommy Bridges (34G, 35G, 36B)	50.00	20.00	5.00
☐ 6 Max Bishop (34G, 35G)	50.00	20.00	5.00
☐ 7 Lew Fonseca (34G, 35G)	50.00	20.00	5.00
☐ 8 Joe Vosmik (34G, 35G, 36B)	50.00	20.00	5.00
☐ 9 Mickey Cochrane (34G, 35G, 36B)	175.00	70.00	18.00
☐ 10A Leroy Mahaffey (34G, 35G) (A's on uniform)	50.00	20.00	5.00
☐ 10B Leroy Mahaffey (36B) (No name on uniform)	100.00	40.00	10.00
☐ 11 Bill Dickey (34G, 35G)	250.00	100.00	25.00
☐ 12A F. Walker (34G) (Ruth retires mentioned on back)	75.00	30.00	7.50
☐ 12B Fred Walker (35G) (Ruth to Boston mentioned on back)	60.00	24.00	6.00
☐ 12C Fred Walker (36B)	100.00	40.00	10.00
☐ 13 George Blaeholder (34G, 35G)	50.00	20.00	5.00
☐ 14 Bill Terry (34G, 35G)	175.00	70.00	18.00
☐ 15A Dick Bartell (34G) (Philadelphia Phillies on card back)	75.00	30.00	7.50
☐ 15B Dick Bartell (35G) (New York Giants on card back)	60.00	24.00	6.00
☐ 16 Lloyd Waner (34G, 35G, 36B)	125.00	50.00	12.50
☐ 17 Frank Frisch (34G, 35G)	175.00	70.00	18.00
☐ 18 Chick Hafey (34G, 35G)	125.00	50.00	12.50
☐ 19 Van Lingle Mungo (34G, 35G)	60.00	24.00	6.00
☐ 20 Frank Hogan (34G, 35G)	50.00	20.00	5.00
☐ 21A Johnny Vergez (34G) (New York Giants on card back)	75.00	30.00	7.50
☐ 21B Johnny Vergez (35G) (Philadelphia Phillies on card back)	60.00	24.00	6.00
☐ 22 Jimmy Wilson (34G, 35G, 36B)	50.00	20.00	5.00
☐ 23 Bill Hallahan (34G, 35G)	50.00	20.00	5.00
☐ 24 Earl Adams	50.00	20.00	5.00

(34G, 35G)			
☐ 25 Wally Berger (35G)	60.00	24.00	6.00
☐ 26 Pepper Martin 35G, 36B)	75.00	30.00	7.50
☐ 27 Pie Traynor (35G)	200.00	80.00	20.00
☐ 28 Al Lopez (35G)	150.00	60.00	15.00
☐ 29 Red Rolfe (35G)	75.00	30.00	7.50
☐ 30A Heinie Manush (35G) (W on sleeve)	150.00	60.00	15.00
☐ 30B Heinie Manush (36B) (No W on sleeve)	250.00	100.00	25.00
☐ 31A Kiki Cuyler (35G) (Chicago Cubs)	125.00	50.00	12.50
☐ 31B Kiki Cuyler (36B) (Cincinnati Reds)	200.00	80.00	20.00
☐ 32 Sam Rice	125.00	50.00	12.50
☐ 33 Schoolboy Rowe	75.00	30.00	7.50
☐ 34 Stan Hack	75.00	30.00	7.50
☐ 35 Earl Averill	125.00	50.00	12.50
☐ 36A "Earnie" Lombardi (Sic, Ernie)	300.00	120.00	30.00
☐ 36B "Ernie" Lombardi	150.00	60.00	15.00
☐ 37 Billy Urbanski	60.00	24.00	6.00
☐ 38 Ben Chapman	75.00	30.00	7.50
☐ 39 Carl Hubbell	175.00	70.00	18.00
☐ 40 Blondy Ryan	60.00	24.00	6.00
☐ 41 Harvey Hendrick	60.00	24.00	6.00
☐ 42 Jimmy Dykes	75.00	30.00	7.50
☐ 43 Ted Lyons	125.00	50.00	12.50
☐ 44 Rogers Hornsby	375.00	150.00	37.00
☐ 45 Jo Jo White	60.00	24.00	6.00
☐ 46 Red Lucas	60.00	24.00	6.00
☐ 47 Bob Bolton	60.00	24.00	6.00
☐ 48 Rick Ferrell	125.00	50.00	12.50
☐ 49 Buck Jordan	60.00	24.00	6.00
☐ 50 Mel Ott	275.00	110.00	27.00
☐ 51 Burgess Whitehead	60.00	24.00	6.00
☐ 52 Tuck Stainback	60.00	24.00	6.00
☐ 53 Oscar Melillo	60.00	24.00	6.00
☐ 54A "Hank" Greenburg (Sic, Greenberg)	600.00	240.00	60.00
☐ 54B "Hank" Greenberg	300.00	120.00	30.00
☐ 55 Tony Cuccinello	60.00	24.00	6.00
☐ 56 Gus Suhr	60.00	24.00	6.00
☐ 57 Cy Blanton	60.00	24.00	6.00
☐ 58 Glenn Myatt	60.00	24.00	6.00
☐ 59 Jim Bottomley	125.00	50.00	12.50
☐ 60 Red Ruffing	150.00	60.00	15.00
☐ 61 Bill Werber	60.00	24.00	6.00
☐ 62 Fred Frankhouse	60.00	24.00	6.00
☐ 63 Travis Jackson	125.00	50.00	12.50
☐ 64 Jimmy Foxx	450.00	180.00	45.00
☐ 65 Zeke Bonura	60.00	24.00	6.00
☐ 66 Ducky Medwick	175.00	70.00	18.00
☐ 67 Marvin Owen	60.00	24.00	6.00
☐ 68 Sam Leslie	60.00	24.00	6.00
☐ 69 Earl Grace	60.00	24.00	6.00
☐ 70 Hal Trosky	75.00	30.00	7.50
☐ 71 Ossie Bluege	75.00	30.00	7.50
☐ 72 Tony Piet	60.00	24.00	6.00
☐ 73 Fritz Ostermueller	60.00	24.00	6.00
☐ 74 Tony Lazzeri	200.00	80.00	20.00
☐ 75 Jack Burns	60.00	24.00	6.00
☐ 76 Billy Rogell	60.00	24.00	6.00
☐ 77 Charlie Gehringer	175.00	70.00	18.00
☐ 78 Joe Kuhel	60.00	24.00	6.00
☐ 79 Willis Hudlin	60.00	24.00	6.00
☐ 80 Lou Chiozza	60.00	24.00	6.00
☐ 81 Bill Delancey	60.00	24.00	6.00
☐ 82A Johnny Babich (Dodgers on uniform; 35G, 35B)	60.00	24.00	6.00
☐ 82B Johnny Babich (No name on uniform; 36B)	125.00	50.00	12.50
☐ 83 Paul Waner	150.00	60.00	15.00
☐ 84 Sam Byrd	60.00	24.00	6.00
☐ 85 Moose Solters	125.00	50.00	12.50
☐ 86 Frank Crosetti	150.00	60.00	15.00
☐ 87 Steve O'Neill MG	125.00	50.00	12.50
☐ 88 George Selkirk	150.00	60.00	15.00
☐ 89 Joe Stripp	125.00	50.00	12.50
☐ 90 Ray Hayworth	125.00	50.00	12.50
☐ 91 Bucky Harris MG	225.00	90.00	22.00
☐ 92 Ethan Allen	125.00	50.00	12.50
☐ 93 General Crowder	125.00	50.00	12.50
☐ 94 Wes Ferrell	150.00	60.00	15.00
☐ 95 Luke Appling	300.00	120.00	30.00
☐ 96 Lew Riggs	125.00	50.00	12.50
☐ 97 Al Lopez	600.00	240.00	60.00
☐ 98 Schoolboy Rowe	325.00	130.00	32.00
☐ 99 Pie Traynor	650.00	260.00	65.00
☐ 100 Earl Averill	600.00	240.00	60.00
☐ 101 Dick Bartell	300.00	120.00	30.00
☐ 102 Van Lingle Mungo	325.00	130.00	32.00
☐ 103 Bill Dickey	900.00	360.00	90.00
☐ 104 Red Rolfe	325.00	130.00	32.00
☐ 105 Ernie Lombardi	600.00	240.00	60.00
☐ 106 Red Lucas	300.00	120.00	30.00
☐ 107 Stan Hack	325.00	130.00	32.00
☐ 108 Wally Berger	400.00	160.00	40.00

1941 Double Play

The cards in this 75-card set measure approximately 2 1/2" by 3 1/8". The 1941 Double Play set, listed as R330 in the American Card Catalog, was a blank-backed issue distributed by Gum Products. It consists of 75 numbered cards (two consecutive numbers per card), each depicting two players in sepia tone photographs. Cards 81-100 contain action poses, and the last 50 numbers of the set are slightly harder to find. Cards that have been cut in half to form "singles" have a greatly reduced value.

	EX-MT	VG-E	GOOD
COMPLETE SET (150)	5000.00	2000.00	650.00
COMMON PAIRS (1-100)	30.00	12.00	3.00
COMMON PAIRS (101-150)	35.00	14.00	3.50
☐ 1 Larry French and 2 Vance Page	50.00	20.00	5.00
☐ 3 Billy Herman and 4 Stan Hack	50.00	20.00	5.00
☐ 5 Lonnie Frey and 6 Johnny VanderMeer	35.00	14.00	3.50
☐ 7 Paul Derringer and 8 Bucky Walters	40.00	16.00	4.00
☐ 9 Frank McCormick and 10 Bill Werber	30.00	12.00	3.00
☐ 11 Jimmy Ripple and 12 Ernie Lombardi	50.00	20.00	5.00
☐ 13 Alex Kampouris and 14 Whitlow Wyatt	30.00	12.00	3.00
☐ 15 Mickey Owen and 16 Paul Waner	50.00	20.00	5.00
☐ 17 Cookie Lavagetto and 18 Pete Reiser	35.00	14.00	3.50
☐ 19 James Wasdell and 20 Dolf Camilli	35.00	14.00	3.50
☐ 21 Dixie Walker and 22 Joe Medwick	50.00	20.00	5.00
☐ 23 Pee Wee Reese and 24 Kirby Higbe	175.00	70.00	18.00
☐ 25 Harry Danning and 26 Cliff Melton	30.00	12.00	3.00
☐ 27 Harry Gumbert and 28 Burgess Whitehead	30.00	12.00	3.00
☐ 29 Joe Orengo and 30 Joe Moore	30.00	12.00	3.00
☐ 31 Mel Ott and 32 Norman Young	100.00	40.00	10.00
☐ 33 Lee Handley and 34 Arky Vaughan	50.00	20.00	5.00

☐ 35 Bob Klinger and 36 Stanley Brown	30.00	12.00	3.00
☐ 37 Terry Moore and 38 Gus Mancuso	30.00	12.00	3.00
☐ 39 Johnny Mize and 40 Enos Slaughter	175.00	70.00	18.00
☐ 41 Johnny Cooney and 42 Sibby Sisti	30.00	12.00	3.00
☐ 43 Max West and 44 Carvel Rowell	30.00	12.00	3.00
☐ 45 Danny Litwhiler and 46 Merrill May	30.00	12.00	3.00
☐ 47 Frank Hayes and 48 Al Brancato	30.00	12.00	3.00
☐ 49 Bob Johnson and 50 Bill Nagel	35.00	14.00	3.50
☐ 51 Buck Newsom and 52 Hank Greenberg	80.00	32.00	8.00
☐ 53 Barney McCosky and 54 Charlie Gehringer	70.00	28.00	7.00
☐ 55 Mike Higgins and 56 Dick Bartell	30.00	12.00	3.00
☐ 57 Ted Williams and 58 Jim Tabor	450.00	180.00	45.00
☐ 59 Joe Cronin and 60 Jimmie Foxx	200.00	80.00	20.00
☐ 61 Lefty Gomez and 62 Phil Rizzuto	250.00	100.00	25.00
☐ 63 Joe DiMaggio and 64 Charlie Keller	750.00	300.00	75.00
☐ 65 Red Rolfe and 66 Bill Dickey	125.00	50.00	12.50
☐ 67 Joe Gordon and 68 Red Ruffing	90.00	36.00	9.00
☐ 69 Mike Tresh and 70 Luke Appling	60.00	24.00	6.00
☐ 71 Moose Solters and 72 Johnny Rigney	30.00	12.00	3.00
☐ 73 Buddy Myer and 74 Ben Chapman	30.00	12.00	3.00
☐ 75 Cecil Travis and 76 George Case	30.00	12.00	3.00
☐ 77 Joe Krakauskas and 78 Bob Feller	125.00	50.00	12.50
☐ 79 Ken Keltner and 80 Hal Trosky	35.00	14.00	3.50
☐ 81 Ted Williams and 82 Joe Cronin	600.00	240.00	60.00
☐ 83 Joe Gordon and 84 Charlie Keller	40.00	16.00	4.00
☐ 85 Hank Greenberg and 86 Red Ruffing	225.00	90.00	22.00
☐ 87 Hal Trosky and 88 George Case	30.00	12.00	3.00
☐ 89 Mel Ott and 90 Burgess Whitehead	100.00	40.00	10.00
☐ 91 Harry Danning and 92 Harry Gumbert	30.00	12.00	3.00
☐ 93 Norman Young and 94 Cliff Melton	30.00	12.00	3.00
☐ 95 Jimmy Ripple and 96 Bucky Walters	30.00	12.00	3.00
☐ 97 Stan Hack and 98 Bob Klinger	30.00	12.00	3.00
☐ 99 Johnny Mize and 100 Dan Litwhiler	65.00	26.00	6.50
☐ 101 Dom Dallesandro and 102 Augie Galan	35.00	14.00	3.50
☐ 103 Bill Lee and 104 Phil Cavarretta	40.00	16.00	4.00
☐ 105 Lefty Grove and 106 Bobby Doerr	225.00	90.00	22.00
☐ 107 Frank Pytlak and 108 Dom DiMaggio	45.00	18.00	4.50
☐ 109 Jerry Priddy and 110 Johnny Murphy	35.00	14.00	3.50
☐ 111 Tommy Henrich and 112 Marius Russo	50.00	20.00	5.00
☐ 113 Frank Crosetti and 114 John Sturm	50.00	20.00	5.00
☐ 115 Ival Goodman and 116 Myron McCormick	35.00	14.00	3.50
☐ 117 Eddie Joost and 118 Ernie Koy	35.00	14.00	3.50
☐ 119 Lloyd Waner and 120 Hank Majeski	55.00	22.00	5.50
☐ 121 Buddy Hassett and 122 Eugene Moore	35.00	14.00	3.50
☐ 123 Nick Etten and 124 John Rizzo	35.00	14.00	3.50
☐ 125 Sam Chapman and 126 Wally Moses	35.00	14.00	3.50
☐ 127 Johnny Babich and 128 Dick Siebert	35.00	14.00	3.50
☐ 129 Nelson Potter and 130 Benny McCoy	35.00	14.00	3.50
☐ 131 Clarence Campbell and 132 Lou Boudreau	65.00	26.00	6.50
☐ 133 Rollie Hemsley and 134 Mel Harder	45.00	18.00	4.50
☐ 135 Gerald Walker and 136 Joe Heving	35.00	14.00	3.50
☐ 137 Johnny Rucker and 138 Ace Adams	35.00	14.00	3.50
☐ 139 Morris Arnovich and 140 Carl Hubbell	100.00	40.00	10.00
☐ 141 Lew Riggs and 142 Leo Durocher	65.00	26.00	6.50
☐ 143 Fred Fitzsimmons and 144 Joe Vosmik	35.00	14.00	3.50
☐ 145 Frank Crespi and 146 Jim Brown	35.00	14.00	3.50
☐ 147 Don Heffner and 148 Harlond Clift	35.00	14.00	3.50
☐ 149 Debs Garms and 150 Elbert Fletcher	35.00	14.00	3.50

1916 Fleischmann Bread

This 103-card set was produced by Fleischmann Breads in 1916. These unnumbered cards are arranged here for convenience in alphabetical order; cards with tabs intact are worth 50 percent more than the prices listed below. The catalog designation for this set is D381. The cards measure approximately 2 3/4" by 5 1/2" (with tab) or 2 3/4" by 4 13/16" (without tab). There is also a similar set issued by Ferguson Bread which is harder to find and is distinguished by having the photo caption written on only one line rather than two as with the Fleischmann cards.

	EX-MT	VG-E	GOOD
COMPLETE SET (103)	5250.00	2250.00	650.00
COMMON PLAYER (1-103)	35.00	14.00	3.50
☐ 1 Charles(Babe) Adams	40.00	16.00	4.00
☐ 2 Grover Alexander	125.00	50.00	12.50
☐ 3 Walt E. Alexander	35.00	14.00	3.50
☐ 4 Frank Allen	35.00	14.00	3.50
☐ 5 Fred Anderson	35.00	14.00	3.50
☐ 6 Dave Bancroft	75.00	30.00	7.50
☐ 7 Jack Barry	35.00	14.00	3.50
☐ 8 Beals Becker	35.00	14.00	3.50
☐ 9 Eddie Burns	35.00	14.00	3.50
☐ 10 George J. Burns	35.00	14.00	3.50
☐ 11 Bobby Byrne	35.00	14.00	3.50
☐ 12 Ray B. Caldwell	35.00	14.00	3.50
☐ 13 James J. Callahan	35.00	14.00	3.50
☐ 14 William Carrigan	35.00	14.00	3.50
☐ 15 Larry Cheney	35.00	14.00	3.50
☐ 16 Tom Clarke	35.00	14.00	3.50
☐ 17 Ty Cobb	1000.00	400.00	125.00
☐ 18 Ray W. Collins	35.00	14.00	3.50
☐ 19 Jack Coombs	45.00	18.00	4.50
☐ 20 A. Wilbur Cooper	35.00	14.00	3.50
☐ 21 George Cutshaw	35.00	14.00	3.50
☐ 22 Jake Daubert	40.00	16.00	4.00
☐ 23 Wm.G. Dell	35.00	14.00	3.50
☐ 24 Wm.E. Donovan	35.00	14.00	3.50
☐ 25 Larry Doyle	40.00	16.00	4.00
☐ 26 R.J. Egan	35.00	14.00	3.50

☐ 27 Johnny Evers 85.00 34.00 8.50
☐ 28 Ray Fisher 35.00 14.00 3.50
☐ 29 Harry Gardner (Sic) 35.00 14.00 3.50
☐ 30 Joe Gedeon 35.00 14.00 3.50
☐ 31 Larry Gilbert 35.00 14.00 3.50
☐ 32 Frank Gilhooley 35.00 14.00 3.50
☐ 33 Hank Gowdy 40.00 16.00 4.00
☐ 34 Sylvanus Gregg 35.00 14.00 3.50
☐ 35 Tom Griffith 35.00 14.00 3.50
☐ 36 Heinie Groh 40.00 16.00 4.00
☐ 37 Robert Harmon 35.00 14.00 3.50
☐ 38 Roy A. Hartzell 35.00 14.00 3.50
☐ 39 Claude Hendriksen 35.00 14.00 3.50
☐ 40 Olaf Hendriksen 35.00 14.00 3.50
☐ 41 Buck Herzog 35.00 14.00 3.50
☐ 42 Hugh High 35.00 14.00 3.50
☐ 43 Dick Hoblitzell 35.00 14.00 3.50
☐ 44 Herb H. Hunter 35.00 14.00 3.50
☐ 45 Harold Janvrin 35.00 14.00 3.50
☐ 46 Hugh Jennings 75.00 30.00 7.50
☐ 47 John Johnston 35.00 14.00 3.50
☐ 48 Erving Kantlehner 35.00 14.00 3.50
☐ 49 Bennie Kauff 35.00 14.00 3.50
☐ 50 Ray H. Keating 35.00 14.00 3.50
☐ 51 Wade Killefer 35.00 14.00 3.50
☐ 52 Elmer Knetzer 35.00 14.00 3.50
☐ 53 Brad W. Kocher 35.00 14.00 3.50
☐ 54 Ed Konetchy 35.00 14.00 3.50
☐ 55 Fred Lauderus (Sic) 35.00 14.00 3.50
☐ 56 H.B.(Dutch) Leonard 40.00 16.00 4.00
☐ 57 Duffy Lewis 40.00 16.00 4.00
☐ 58 E.H.(Slim) Love 35.00 14.00 3.50
☐ 59 Albert L. Mamaux 35.00 14.00 3.50
☐ 60 Rabbit Maranville 75.00 30.00 7.50
☐ 61 Rube Marquard 75.00 30.00 7.50
☐ 62 Christy Mathewson 250.00 100.00 25.00
☐ 63 Bill McKechnie 75.00 30.00 7.50
☐ 64 Chief Meyer (Sic) 35.00 14.00 3.50
☐ 65 Otto Miller 35.00 14.00 3.50
☐ 66 Fred Mollwitz 35.00 14.00 3.50
☐ 67 Herbie Moran 35.00 14.00 3.50
☐ 68 Mike Mowrey 35.00 14.00 3.50
☐ 69 Dan Murphy 35.00 14.00 3.50
☐ 70 Art Nehf 35.00 14.00 3.50
☐ 71 Rube Oldring 35.00 14.00 3.50
☐ 72 Oliver O'Mara 35.00 14.00 3.50
☐ 73 Dode Paskert 35.00 14.00 3.50
☐ 74 D.C.Pat Ragan 35.00 14.00 3.50
☐ 75 Wm.A. Rariden 35.00 14.00 3.50
☐ 76 Davis Robertson 35.00 14.00 3.50
☐ 77 Wm. Rodgers 35.00 14.00 3.50
☐ 78 Edw.F.Rousch (Sic) 85.00 34.00 8.50
☐ 79 Nap Rucker 35.00 14.00 3.50
☐ 80 Dick Rudolph 35.00 14.00 3.50
☐ 81 Walter Schang 40.00 16.00 4.00
☐ 82 A.J.(Rube) Schauer 35.00 14.00 3.50
☐ 83 Pete Schneider 35.00 14.00 3.50
☐ 84 Ferd M. Schupp 35.00 14.00 3.50
☐ 85 Ernie Shore 40.00 16.00 4.00
☐ 86 Red Smith 35.00 14.00 3.50
☐ 87 Fred Snodgrass 40.00 16.00 4.00
☐ 88 Tris Speaker 150.00 60.00 15.00
☐ 89 George Stallings MG 35.00 14.00 3.50
☐ 90 Casey Stengel 200.00 80.00 20.00
☐ 91 R. Stroud 35.00 14.00 3.50
☐ 92 Amos Strunk 35.00 14.00 3.50
☐ 93 Charles D. Thomas 35.00 14.00 3.50
☐ 94 Fred Toney 35.00 14.00 3.50
☐ 95 Walter Tragresser 35.00 14.00 3.50
☐ 96 Chas.(Jeff) Tresreau 35.00 14.00 3.50
☐ 97 Honus Wagner 250.00 100.00 25.00
☐ 98 Carl Weilman 35.00 14.00 3.50
☐ 99 Zack Wheat 75.00 30.00 7.50
☐ 100 George Whitted 35.00 14.00 3.50
☐ 101 Arthur Wilson 35.00 14.00 3.50
☐ 102 Ivy Wingo 35.00 14.00 3.50
☐ 103 Joe Wood 60.00 24.00 6.00

1928 Fro Joy

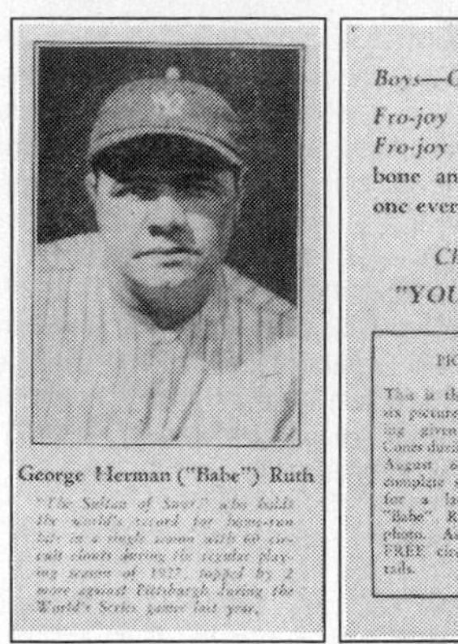

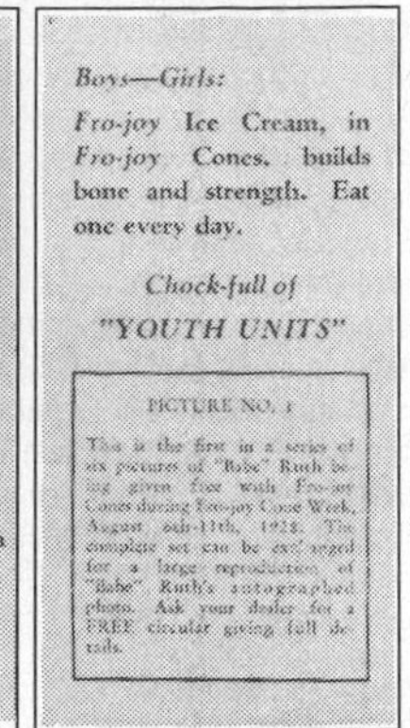

The cards in this six-card set measure approximately 2 1/16" by 4". The Fro Joy set of 1928 was designed to exploit the advertising potential of the mighty Babe Ruth. Six black and white cards explained specific baseball techniques while the reverse advertising extolled the virtues of Fro Joy ice cream and ice cream cones. Unfortunately this small set has been illegally reprinted (several times) and many of these virtually worthless fakes have been introduced into the hobby. The easiest fakes to spot are those cards (or uncut sheets) that are slightly over-sized and blue tinted; however some of the other fakes are more cleverly faithful to the original. Be very careful before purchasing Fro-Joys; obtain a qualified opinion on authenticity from an experienced dealer (preferably one who is unrelated to the dealer trying to sell you his cards). You might also show the cards (before you commit to purchase them) to an experienced printer who can advise you on the true age of the paper stock. More than one dealer has been quoted as saying that 99 percent of the Fro Joys he sees are fakes.

	EX-MT	VG-E	GOOD
COMPLETE SET (6)	600.00	240.00	60.00
COMMON PLAYER (1-6)	100.00	40.00	10.00
☐ 1 George Herman (Babe) Ruth	150.00	60.00	15.00
☐ 2 Look Out, Mr. Pitcher	100.00	40.00	10.00
☐ 3 Bang; The Babe Lines one out	100.00	40.00	10.00
☐ 4 When the Babe Comes Out	100.00	40.00	10.00
☐ 5 Babe Ruth's Grip	100.00	40.00	10.00
☐ 6 Ruth is a Crack Fielder	100.00	40.00	10.00

1933 Goudey

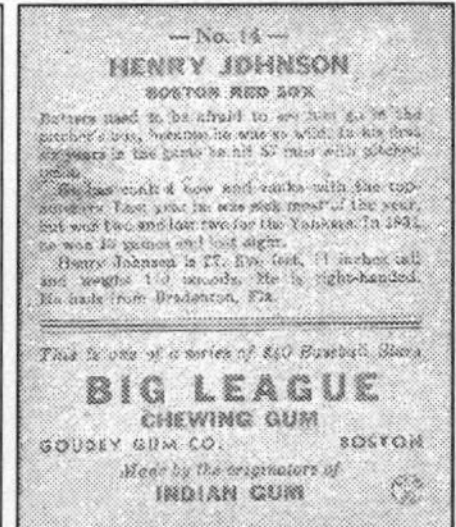

The cards in this 240-card set measure approximately 2 3/8" by 2 7/8". The 1933 Goudey set, designated R319 by the ACC, was that company's first baseball issue. The four Babe Ruth and two Lou Gehrig cards in the set are extremely popular with collectors. Card number 106, Napoleon Lajoie, was not printed in 1933, and was circulated to a limited number of collectors in 1934 upon request (it was printed along with the 1934 Goudey cards). An album was offered to house the 1933 set. Several minor leaguers are depicted. Card number 1 (Bengough) is very rarely found in mint condition; in fact, as a general rule all the first series cards are more difficult to find in Mint condition. Players with more than one card are also sometimes differentiated below by their pose: BAT (Batting), FIELD (Fielding), PIT (Pitching), THROW (Throwing). One of the Babe Ruth cards was double printed (DP) apparently in place of the Lajoie and hence is easier to obtain than the others. Due to the scarcity of the Lajoie card, the set is considered complete at 239 cards and is priced as such below.

	EX-MT	VG-E	GOOD
COMPLETE SET (239)	50000.	20000.	6000.00
COMMON PLAYER (1-40)	100.00	40.00	10.00
COMMON PLAYER (41-44)	60.00	24.00	6.00
COMMON PLAYER (45-52)	100.00	40.00	10.00
COMMON PLAYER (53-240)	60.00	24.00	6.00
☐ 1 Benny Bengough	1500.00	100.00	20.00
☐ 2 Dazzy Vance	200.00	80.00	20.00
☐ 3 Hugh Critz	100.00	40.00	10.00
☐ 4 Heinie Schuble	100.00	40.00	10.00
☐ 5 Babe Herman	125.00	50.00	12.50
☐ 6 Jimmy Dykes	125.00	50.00	12.50
☐ 7 Ted Lyons	200.00	80.00	20.00
☐ 8 Roy Johnson	100.00	40.00	10.00
☐ 9 Dave Harris	100.00	40.00	10.00
☐ 10 Glenn Myatt	100.00	40.00	10.00
☐ 11 Billy Rogell	100.00	40.00	10.00
☐ 12 George Pipgras	100.00	40.00	10.00
☐ 13 Lafayette Thompson	100.00	40.00	10.00
☐ 14 Henry Johnson	100.00	40.00	10.00
☐ 15 Victor Sorrell	100.00	40.00	10.00
☐ 16 George Blaeholder	100.00	40.00	10.00
☐ 17 Watson Clark	100.00	40.00	10.00
☐ 18 Muddy Ruel	100.00	40.00	10.00
☐ 19 Bill Dickey	400.00	160.00	40.00
☐ 20 Bill Terry THROW	300.00	120.00	30.00
☐ 21 Phil Collins	100.00	40.00	10.00
☐ 22 Pie Traynor	250.00	100.00	25.00
☐ 23 Kiki Cuyler	200.00	80.00	20.00
☐ 24 Horace Ford	100.00	40.00	10.00
☐ 25 Paul Waner	200.00	80.00	20.00
☐ 26 Chalmer Cissell	100.00	40.00	10.00
☐ 27 George Connally	100.00	40.00	10.00
☐ 28 Dick Bartell	100.00	40.00	10.00
☐ 29 Jimmy Foxx	500.00	200.00	50.00
☐ 30 Frank Hogan	100.00	40.00	10.00
☐ 31 Tony Lazzeri	350.00	140.00	35.00
☐ 32 Bud Clancy	100.00	40.00	10.00
☐ 33 Ralph Kress	100.00	40.00	10.00
☐ 34 Bob O'Farrell	100.00	40.00	10.00
☐ 35 Al Simmons	350.00	140.00	35.00
☐ 36 Tommy Thevenow	100.00	40.00	10.00
☐ 37 Jimmy Wilson	100.00	40.00	10.00
☐ 38 Fred Brickell	100.00	40.00	10.00
☐ 39 Mark Koenig	100.00	40.00	10.00
☐ 40 Taylor Douthit	100.00	40.00	10.00
☐ 41 Gus Mancuso	60.00	24.00	6.00
☐ 42 Eddie Collins	150.00	60.00	15.00
☐ 43 Lew Fonseca	60.00	24.00	6.00
☐ 44 Jim Bottomley	135.00	54.00	13.50
☐ 45 Larry Benton	100.00	40.00	10.00
☐ 46 Ethan Allen	100.00	40.00	10.00
☐ 47 Heinie Manush BAT	200.00	80.00	20.00
☐ 48 Marty McManus	100.00	40.00	10.00
☐ 49 Frank Frisch	300.00	120.00	30.00
☐ 50 Ed Brandt	100.00	40.00	10.00
☐ 51 Charlie Grimm	125.00	50.00	12.50
☐ 52 Andy Cohen	100.00	40.00	10.00
☐ 53 Babe Ruth	5000.00	2000.00	600.00
☐ 54 Ray Kremer	60.00	24.00	6.00
☐ 55 Pat Malone	60.00	24.00	6.00
☐ 56 Charlie(Red) Ruffing	150.00	60.00	15.00
☐ 57 Earl Clark	60.00	24.00	6.00
☐ 58 Lefty O'Doul	80.00	32.00	8.00
☐ 59 Bing Miller	60.00	24.00	6.00
☐ 60 Waite Hoyt	135.00	54.00	13.50
☐ 61 Max Bishop	60.00	24.00	6.00
☐ 62 Pepper Martin	90.00	36.00	9.00
☐ 63 Joe Cronin BAT	175.00	70.00	18.00
☐ 64 Burleigh Grimes	135.00	54.00	13.50
☐ 65 Milt Gaston	60.00	24.00	6.00
☐ 66 George Grantham	60.00	24.00	6.00
☐ 67 Guy Bush	60.00	24.00	6.00
☐ 68 Horace Lisenbee	60.00	24.00	6.00
☐ 69 Randy Moore	60.00	24.00	6.00
☐ 70 Floyd(Pete) Scott	60.00	24.00	6.00
☐ 71 Robert J. Burke	60.00	24.00	6.00
☐ 72 Owen Carroll	60.00	24.00	6.00
☐ 73 Jess Haines	135.00	54.00	13.50
☐ 74 Eppa Rixey	135.00	54.00	13.50
☐ 75 Willie Kamm	60.00	24.00	6.00
☐ 76 Mickey Cochrane	200.00	80.00	20.00
☐ 77 Adam Comorosky	60.00	24.00	6.00
☐ 78 Jack Quinn	60.00	24.00	6.00
☐ 79 Red Faber	135.00	54.00	13.50
☐ 80 Clyde Manion	60.00	24.00	6.00
☐ 81 Sam Jones	60.00	24.00	6.00
☐ 82 Dibrell Williams	60.00	24.00	6.00
☐ 83 Pete Jablonowski	60.00	24.00	6.00
☐ 84 Glenn Spencer	60.00	24.00	6.00
☐ 85 Heinie Sand	60.00	24.00	6.00
☐ 86 Phil Todt	60.00	24.00	6.00
☐ 87 Frank O'Rourke	60.00	24.00	6.00
☐ 88 Russell Rollings	60.00	24.00	6.00
☐ 89 Tris Speaker RET	400.00	160.00	40.00
☐ 90 Jess Petty	60.00	24.00	6.00
☐ 91 Tom Zachary	60.00	24.00	6.00
☐ 92 Lou Gehrig	3000.00	1200.00	400.00
☐ 93 John Welch	60.00	24.00	6.00
☐ 94 Bill Walker	60.00	24.00	6.00
☐ 95 Alvin Crowder	60.00	24.00	6.00
☐ 96 Willis Hudlin	60.00	24.00	6.00
☐ 97 Joe Morrissey	60.00	24.00	6.00
☐ 98 Walter Berger	80.00	32.00	8.00
☐ 99 Tony Cuccinello	70.00	28.00	7.00
☐ 100 George Uhle	60.00	24.00	6.00
☐ 101 Richard Coffman	60.00	24.00	6.00
☐ 102 Travis Jackson	135.00	54.00	13.50
☐ 103 Earle Combs	135.00	54.00	13.50
☐ 104 Fred Marberry	60.00	24.00	6.00
☐ 105 Bernie Friberg	60.00	24.00	6.00
☐ 106 Napoleon Lajoie SP (Not issued until 1934)	33000.	11000.	4000.00
☐ 107 Heinie Manush	135.00	54.00	13.50
☐ 108 Joe Kuhel	60.00	24.00	6.00
☐ 109 Joe Cronin	175.00	70.00	18.00
☐ 110 Goose Goslin	125.00	50.00	12.50
☐ 111 Monte Weaver	60.00	24.00	6.00
☐ 112 Fred Schulte	60.00	24.00	6.00
☐ 113 Oswald Bluege	70.00	28.00	7.00
☐ 114 Luke Sewell	80.00	32.00	8.00
☐ 115 Cliff Heathcote	60.00	24.00	6.00
☐ 116 Eddie Morgan	60.00	24.00	6.00
☐ 117 Rabbit Maranville	135.00	54.00	13.50
☐ 118 Val Picinich	60.00	24.00	6.00
☐ 119 Rogers Hornsby FIELD	400.00	160.00	40.00
☐ 120 Carl Reynolds	60.00	24.00	6.00
☐ 121 Walter Stewart	60.00	24.00	6.00
☐ 122 Alvin Crowder	60.00	24.00	6.00
☐ 123 Jack Russell	60.00	24.00	6.00
☐ 124 Earl Whitehill	60.00	24.00	6.00
☐ 125 Bill Terry	250.00	100.00	25.00
☐ 126 Joe Moore	60.00	24.00	6.00
☐ 127 Mel Ott	300.00	120.00	30.00
☐ 128 Chuck Klein	200.00	80.00	20.00
☐ 129 Hal Schumacher PIT	70.00	28.00	7.00
☐ 130 Fred Fitzsimmons	70.00	28.00	7.00
☐ 131 Fred Frankhouse	60.00	24.00	6.00
☐ 132 Jim Elliott	60.00	24.00	6.00
☐ 133 Fred Lindstrom	135.00	54.00	13.50
☐ 134 Sam Rice	135.00	54.00	13.50
☐ 135 Woody English	60.00	24.00	6.00
☐ 136 Flint Rhem	60.00	24.00	6.00
☐ 137 Fred(Red) Lucas	60.00	24.00	6.00
☐ 138 Herb Pennock	135.00	54.00	13.50
☐ 139 Ben Cantwell	60.00	24.00	6.00
☐ 140 Bump Hadley	60.00	24.00	6.00
☐ 141 Ray Benge	60.00	24.00	6.00
☐ 142 Paul Richards	80.00	32.00	8.00
☐ 143 Glenn Wright	60.00	24.00	6.00
☐ 144 Babe Ruth BAT DP	4000.00	1600.00	550.00
☐ 145 George Walberg	60.00	24.00	6.00
☐ 146 Walter Stewart PIT	60.00	24.00	6.00
☐ 147 Leo Durocher	200.00	80.00	20.00
☐ 148 Eddie Farrell	60.00	24.00	6.00
☐ 149 Babe Ruth	5000.00	2000.00	600.00
☐ 150 Ray Kolp	60.00	24.00	6.00
☐ 151 Jake Flowers	60.00	24.00	6.00
☐ 152 Zack Taylor	60.00	24.00	6.00
☐ 153 Buddy Myer	60.00	24.00	6.00
☐ 154 Jimmy Foxx	400.00	160.00	40.00
☐ 155 Joe Judge	60.00	24.00	6.00
☐ 156 Danny MacFayden	60.00	24.00	6.00
☐ 157 Sam Byrd	60.00	24.00	6.00
☐ 158 Moe Berg	200.00	80.00	20.00
☐ 159 Oswald Bluege	70.00	28.00	7.00

☐ 160	Lou Gehrig	3000.00	1200.00	400.00
☐ 161	Al Spohrer	60.00	24.00	6.00
☐ 162	Leo Mangum	60.00	24.00	6.00
☐ 163	Luke Sewell	80.00	32.00	8.00
☐ 164	Lloyd Waner	135.00	54.00	13.50
☐ 165	Joe Sewell	135.00	54.00	13.50
☐ 166	Sam West	60.00	24.00	6.00
☐ 167	Jack Russell	60.00	24.00	6.00
☐ 168	Goose Goslin	135.00	54.00	13.50
☐ 169	Al Thomas	60.00	24.00	6.00
☐ 170	Harry McCurdy	60.00	24.00	6.00
☐ 171	Charlie Jamieson	60.00	24.00	6.00
☐ 172	Billy Hargrave	60.00	24.00	6.00
☐ 173	Roscoe Holm	60.00	24.00	6.00
☐ 174	Warren(Curly) Ogden	60.00	24.00	6.00
☐ 175	Dan Howley	60.00	24.00	6.00
☐ 176	John Ogden	60.00	24.00	6.00
☐ 177	Walter French	60.00	24.00	6.00
☐ 178	Jackie Warner	60.00	24.00	6.00
☐ 179	Fred Leach	60.00	24.00	6.00
☐ 180	Eddie Moore	60.00	24.00	6.00
☐ 181	Babe Ruth	5000.00	2000.00	600.00
☐ 182	Andy High	60.00	24.00	6.00
☐ 183	George Walberg	60.00	24.00	6.00
☐ 184	Charley Berry	70.00	28.00	7.00
☐ 185	Bob Smith	60.00	24.00	6.00
☐ 186	John Schulte	60.00	24.00	6.00
☐ 187	Heinie Manush	135.00	54.00	13.50
☐ 188	Rogers Hornsby	400.00	160.00	40.00
☐ 189	Joe Cronin	175.00	70.00	18.00
☐ 190	Fred Schulte	60.00	24.00	6.00
☐ 191	Ben Chapman	80.00	32.00	8.00
☐ 192	Walter Brown	60.00	24.00	6.00
☐ 193	Lynford Lary	60.00	24.00	6.00
☐ 194	Earl Averill	135.00	54.00	13.50
☐ 195	Evar Swanson	60.00	24.00	6.00
☐ 196	Leroy Mahaffey	60.00	24.00	6.00
☐ 197	Rick Ferrell	135.00	54.00	13.50
☐ 198	Jack Burns	60.00	24.00	6.00
☐ 199	Tom Bridges	80.00	32.00	8.00
☐ 200	Bill Hallahan	60.00	24.00	6.00
☐ 201	Ernie Orsatti	60.00	24.00	6.00
☐ 202	Gabby Hartnett	135.00	54.00	13.50
☐ 203	Lon Warneke	80.00	32.00	8.00
☐ 204	Riggs Stephenson	80.00	32.00	8.00
☐ 205	Heinie Meine	60.00	24.00	6.00
☐ 206	Gus Suhr	60.00	24.00	6.00
☐ 207	Mel Ott BAT	350.00	140.00	35.00
☐ 208	Bernie James	60.00	24.00	6.00
☐ 209	Adolfo Luque	70.00	28.00	7.00
☐ 210	Virgil Davis	60.00	24.00	6.00
☐ 211	Hack Wilson	300.00	120.00	30.00
☐ 212	Billy Urbanski	60.00	24.00	6.00
☐ 213	Earl Adams	60.00	24.00	6.00
☐ 214	John Kerr	60.00	24.00	6.00
☐ 215	Russ Van Atta	60.00	24.00	6.00
☐ 216	Vernon(Lefty) Gomez	400.00	160.00	40.00
☐ 217	Frank Crosetti	135.00	54.00	13.50
☐ 218	Wes Ferrell	80.00	32.00	8.00
☐ 219	Mule Haas	60.00	24.00	6.00
☐ 220	Lefty Grove	500.00	200.00	50.00
☐ 221	Dale Alexander	60.00	24.00	6.00
☐ 222	Charley Gehringer	300.00	120.00	30.00
☐ 223	Dizzy Dean	900.00	360.00	90.00
☐ 224	Frank Demaree	60.00	24.00	6.00
☐ 225	Bill Jurges	60.00	24.00	6.00
☐ 226	Charley Root	60.00	24.00	6.00
☐ 227	Billy Herman	135.00	54.00	13.50
☐ 228	Tony Piet	60.00	24.00	6.00
☐ 229	Floyd(Arky) Vaughan	135.00	54.00	13.50
☐ 230	Carl Hubbell PIT	250.00	100.00	25.00
☐ 231	Joe Moore FIELD	60.00	24.00	6.00
☐ 232	Lefty O'Doul	80.00	32.00	8.00
☐ 233	Johnny Vergez	60.00	24.00	6.00
☐ 234	Carl Hubbell	250.00	100.00	25.00
☐ 235	Fred Fitzsimmons	80.00	32.00	8.00
☐ 236	George Davis	60.00	24.00	6.00
☐ 237	Gus Mancuso	60.00	24.00	6.00
☐ 238	Hugh Critz	60.00	24.00	6.00
☐ 239	Leroy Parmelee	60.00	24.00	6.00
☐ 240	Hal Schumacher	135.00	54.00	13.50

1934 Goudey

The cards in this 96-card set measure approximately 2 3/8" by 2 7/8". The 1934 Goudey set of color cards carries the catalog number R320. Cards 1-48 are considered to be the

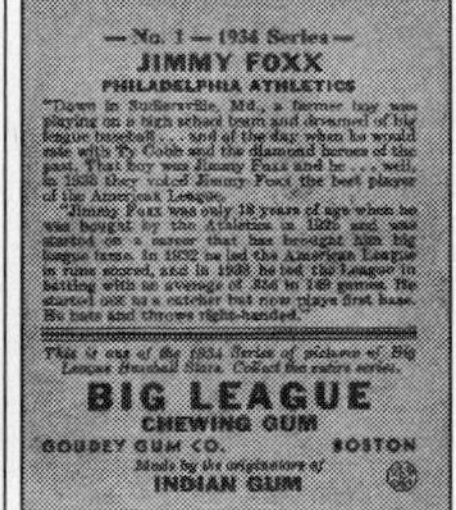

easiest to find (although card number 1, Foxx, is very scarce in mint condition) while 73-96 are much more difficult to find. Cards of this 1934 Goudey series are slightly less abundant than cards of the 1933 Goudey set. Of the 96 cards, 84 contain a "Lou Gehrig Says" line on the front in a blue design, while 12 of the high series (80-91) contain a "Chuck Klein Says" line in a red design. These Chuck Klein cards are indicated in the checklist below by CK and are in fact the 12 National Leaguers in the high series.

		EX-MT	VG-E	GOOD
COMPLETE SET (96)		20000.	8000.00	2500.00
COMMON PLAYER (1-48)		60.00	24.00	6.00
COMMON PLAYER (49-72)		80.00	32.00	8.00
COMMON PLAYER (73-96)		250.00	100.00	25.00
☐ 1	Jimmy Foxx	900.00	175.00	35.00
☐ 2	Mickey Cochrane	200.00	80.00	20.00
☐ 3	Charlie Grimm	80.00	32.00	8.00
☐ 4	Woody English	60.00	24.00	6.00
☐ 5	Ed Brandt	60.00	24.00	6.00
☐ 6	Dizzy Dean	750.00	300.00	75.00
☐ 7	Leo Durocher	150.00	60.00	15.00
☐ 8	Tony Piet	60.00	24.00	6.00
☐ 9	Ben Chapman	80.00	32.00	8.00
☐ 10	Chuck Klein	150.00	60.00	15.00
☐ 11	Paul Waner	135.00	54.00	13.50
☐ 12	Carl Hubbell	200.00	80.00	20.00
☐ 13	Frank Frisch	200.00	80.00	20.00
☐ 14	Willie Kamm	60.00	24.00	6.00
☐ 15	Alvin Crowder	60.00	24.00	6.00
☐ 16	Joe Kuhel	60.00	24.00	6.00
☐ 17	Hugh Critz	60.00	24.00	6.00
☐ 18	Heinie Manush	135.00	54.00	13.50
☐ 19	Lefty Grove	350.00	140.00	35.00
☐ 20	Frank Hogan	60.00	24.00	6.00
☐ 21	Bill Terry	200.00	80.00	20.00
☐ 22	Arky Vaughan	135.00	54.00	13.50
☐ 23	Charlie Gehringer	200.00	80.00	20.00
☐ 24	Ray Benge	60.00	24.00	6.00
☐ 25	Roger Cramer	80.00	32.00	8.00
☐ 26	Gerald Walker	60.00	24.00	6.00
☐ 27	Luke Appling	150.00	60.00	15.00
☐ 28	Ed Coleman	60.00	24.00	6.00
☐ 29	Larry French	60.00	24.00	6.00
☐ 30	Julius Solters	60.00	24.00	6.00
☐ 31	Buck Jordan	60.00	24.00	6.00
☐ 32	Blondy Ryan	60.00	24.00	6.00
☐ 33	Frank Hurst	60.00	24.00	6.00
☐ 34	Chick Hafey	135.00	54.00	13.50
☐ 35	Ernie Lombardi	135.00	54.00	13.50
☐ 36	Walter Betts	60.00	24.00	6.00
☐ 37	Lou Gehrig	3000.00	1200.00	400.00
☐ 38	Oral Hildebrand	60.00	24.00	6.00
☐ 39	Fred Walker	60.00	24.00	6.00
☐ 40	John Stone	60.00	24.00	6.00
☐ 41	George Earnshaw	60.00	24.00	6.00
☐ 42	John Allen	60.00	24.00	6.00
☐ 43	Dick Porter	60.00	24.00	6.00
☐ 44	Tom Bridges	80.00	32.00	8.00
☐ 45	Oscar Melillo	60.00	24.00	6.00
☐ 46	Joe Stripp	60.00	24.00	6.00
☐ 47	John Frederick	60.00	24.00	6.00
☐ 48	Tex Carleton	60.00	24.00	6.00
☐ 49	Sam Leslie	80.00	32.00	8.00
☐ 50	Walter Beck	80.00	32.00	8.00
☐ 51	Rip Collins	80.00	32.00	8.00
☐ 52	Herman Bell	80.00	32.00	8.00
☐ 53	George Watkins	80.00	32.00	8.00
☐ 54	Wesley Schulmerich	80.00	32.00	8.00
☐ 55	Ed Holley	80.00	32.00	8.00
☐ 56	Mark Koenig	100.00	40.00	10.00

☐ 57	Bill Swift	80.00	32.00	8.00
☐ 58	Earl Grace	80.00	32.00	8.00
☐ 59	Joe Mowry	80.00	32.00	8.00
☐ 60	Lynn Nelson	80.00	32.00	8.00
☐ 61	Lou Gehrig	3500.00	1400.00	450.00
☐ 62	Hank Greenberg	400.00	160.00	40.00
☐ 63	Minter Hayes	80.00	32.00	8.00
☐ 64	Frank Grube	80.00	32.00	8.00
☐ 65	Cliff Bolton	80.00	32.00	8.00
☐ 66	Mel Harder	120.00	50.00	12.00
☐ 67	Bob Weiland	80.00	32.00	8.00
☐ 68	Bob Johnson	120.00	50.00	12.00
☐ 69	John Marcum	80.00	32.00	8.00
☐ 70	Pete Fox	80.00	32.00	8.00
☐ 71	Lyle Tinning	80.00	32.00	8.00
☐ 72	Arndt Jorgens	80.00	32.00	8.00
☐ 73	Ed Wells	250.00	100.00	25.00
☐ 74	Bob Boken	250.00	100.00	25.00
☐ 75	Bill Werber	250.00	100.00	25.00
☐ 76	Hal Trosky	275.00	110.00	27.00
☐ 77	Joe Vosmik	250.00	100.00	25.00
☐ 78	Pinky Higgins	275.00	110.00	27.00
☐ 79	Ed Durham	250.00	100.00	25.00
☐ 80	Marty McManus CK	250.00	100.00	25.00
☐ 81	Bob Brown CK	250.00	100.00	25.00
☐ 82	Bill Hallahan CK	250.00	100.00	25.00
☐ 83	Jim Mooney CK	250.00	100.00	25.00
☐ 84	Paul Derringer CK	300.00	120.00	30.00
☐ 85	Adam Comorosky CK	250.00	100.00	25.00
☐ 86	Lloyd Johnson CK	250.00	100.00	25.00
☐ 87	George Darrow CK	250.00	100.00	25.00
☐ 88	Homer Peel CK	250.00	100.00	25.00
☐ 89	Linus Frey CK	250.00	100.00	25.00
☐ 90	Ki-Ki Cuyler CK	500.00	200.00	50.00
☐ 91	Dolph Camilli CK	275.00	110.00	27.00
☐ 92	Steve Larkin	250.00	100.00	25.00
☐ 93	Fred Ostermueller	250.00	100.00	25.00
☐ 94	Red Rolfe	275.00	110.00	27.00
☐ 95	Myril Hoag	250.00	100.00	25.00
☐ 96	James DeShong	350.00	140.00	35.00

1935 Goudey Puzzle

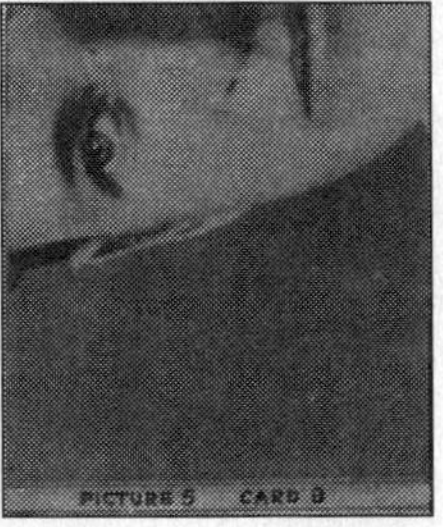

The cards in this 36-card set (the number of different front pictures) measure approximately 2 3/8" by 2 7/8". The 1935 Goudey set is sometimes called the Goudey Puzzle Set, the Goudey 4-in-1's, or R321 (ACC). There are 36 different card fronts but 114 different front/back combinations. The card number in the checklist refers to the back puzzle number, as the backs can be arranged to form a puzzle picturing a player or team. To avoid the confusion caused by two different fronts having the same back number, the rarer cards have been arbitrarily given a "1" prefix. The scarcer puzzle cards are hence all listed at the numerical end of the list below, i.e. rare puzzle 1 is listed as number 11, rare puzzle 2 is listed as 12, etc. The BLUE in the checklist refers to a card with a blue border, as most cards have a red border. The set price below includes all the cards listed. The following is the list of the puzzle back pictures: 1) Detroit Tigers; 2) Chuck Klein; 3) Frankie Frisch; 4) Mickey Cochrane; 5) Joe Cronin; 6) Jimmy Foxx; 7) Al Simmons; 8) Cleveland Indians; and 9) Washington Senators.

		EX-MT	VG-E	GOOD
	COMPLETE SET (114)	17000.	7500.00	2500.00
	COMMON CARDS (1-9)	60.00	24.00	6.00
	COMMON CARDS (11-17)	100.00	40.00	10.00
☐ 1A	F.Frisch/Dizzy Dean E.Orsatti/T.Carleton	175.00	70.00	18.00
☐ 1B	R.Mahaffey/Jimmie Foxx D.Williams/P.Higgins	125.00	50.00	12.50
☐ 1C	Heinie Manush/L.Lary M.Weaver/B.Hadley	75.00	30.00	7.50
☐ 1D	M.Cochrane/C.Gehringer T.Bridges/B.Rogell	125.00	50.00	12.50
☐ 1E	Paul Waner/G.Bush W.Hoyt/Lloyd Waner	125.00	50.00	12.50
☐ 1F	B.Grimes/Chuck Klein K.Cuyler/W.English	125.00	50.00	12.50
☐ 1G	S.Leslie/L.Frey Joe Stripp/W.Clark	60.00	24.00	6.00
☐ 1H	T.Piet/A.Comorosky J.Bottomley/S.Adams	75.00	30.00	7.50
☐ 1I	G.Earnshaw/J.Dykes Luke Sewell/L.Appling	75.00	30.00	7.50
☐ 1J	Babe Ruth/M.McManus E.Brandt/R.Maranville	1000.00	400.00	125.00
☐ 1K	B.Terry/H.Schumacher G.Mancuso/T.Jackson	125.00	50.00	12.50
☐ 1L	W.Kamm/O.Hildebrand E.Averill/H.Trosky	75.00	30.00	7.50
☐ 2A	F.Frisch/Dizzy Dean E.Orsatti/T.Carleton	175.00	70.00	18.00
☐ 2B	R.Mahaffey/Jimmie Foxx D.Williams/P.Higgins	125.00	50.00	12.50
☐ 2C	Heinie Manush/L.Lary M.Weaver/B.Hadley	75.00	30.00	7.50
☐ 2D	M.Cochrane/C.Gehringer T.Bridges/B.Rogell	125.00	50.00	12.50
☐ 2E	W.Kamm/O.Hildebrand Earl Averill/H.Trosky	75.00	30.00	7.50
☐ 2F	G.Earnshaw/J.Dykes Luke Sewell/L.Appling	75.00	30.00	7.50
☐ 3A	Babe Ruth/M.McManus E.Brandt/R.Maranville	1000.00	400.00	125.00
☐ 3B	B.Terry/H.Schumacher G.Mancuso/T.Jackson	125.00	50.00	12.50
☐ 3C	Paul Waner/G.Bush W.Hoyt/Lloyd Waner	125.00	50.00	12.50
☐ 3D	B.Grimes/Chuck Klein K.Cuyler/W.English	125.00	50.00	12.50
☐ 3E	S.Leslie/L.Frey Joe Stripp/W.Clark	60.00	24.00	6.00
☐ 3F	T.Piet/A.Comorosky Jim Bottomley/S.Adams	75.00	30.00	7.50
☐ 4A	H.Critz/D.Bartell BLUE Mel Ott/Mancuso	100.00	40.00	10.00
☐ 4B	P.Traynor/R.Lucas BLUE Tom Thevenow/G.Wright	75.00	30.00	7.50
☐ 4C	C.Berry/B.Burke BLUE R.Kress/Dazzy Vance	75.00	30.00	7.50
☐ 4D	R.Ruffing/P.Malone BLUE T.Lazzeri/Bill Dickey	175.00	70.00	18.00
☐ 4E	R.Moore/S.Hogan BLUE F.Frankhouse/E.Brandt	60.00	24.00	6.00
☐ 4F	P.Martin/O'Farrell BLUE S.Byrd/D.MacFayden	60.00	24.00	6.00
☐ 5A	M.Ruel/Al Simmons W.Kamm/M.Cochrane	125.00	50.00	12.50
☐ 5B	Willis Hudlin/G.Myatt A.Comorosky/J.Bottomley	75.00	30.00	7.50
☐ 5C	Paul Waner/G.Bush W.Hoyt/Lloyd Waner	125.00	50.00	12.50
☐ 5D	S.West/Oscar Melillo G.Blaeholder/D.Coffman	60.00	24.00	6.00
☐ 5E	S.Leslie/L.Frey Joe Stripp/W.Clark	60.00	24.00	6.00
☐ 5F	H.Schuble/F.Marberry Goose Goslin/G.Crowder	75.00	30.00	7.50
☐ 6A	M.Ruel/Al Simmons W.Kamm/M.Cochrane	125.00	50.00	12.50
☐ 6B	Willis Hudlin/G.Myatt A.Comorosky/J.Bottomley	75.00	30.00	7.50
☐ 6C	J.Wilson/E.Allen B.Jonnard/F.Brickell	60.00	24.00	6.00
☐ 6D	S.West/Oscar Melillo G.Blaeholder/D.Coffman	60.00	24.00	6.00
☐ 6E	Joe Cronin/C.Reynolds M.Bishop/C.Cissell	75.00	30.00	7.50
☐ 6F	H.Schuble/F.Marberry Goose Goslin/G.Crowder	75.00	30.00	7.50
☐ 7A	H.Critz/D.Bartell BLUE Mel Ott/G.Mancuso	100.00	40.00	10.00
☐ 7B	P.Traynor/R.Lucas BLUE Tom Thevenow/G.Wright	75.00	30.00	7.50
☐ 7C	C.Berry/B.Burke BLUE	75.00	30.00	7.50

		EX-MT	VG-E	GOOD
	R.Kress/Dazzy Vance			
☐ 7D	R.Ruffing/P.Malone BLUE	175.00	70.00	18.00
	T.Lazzeri/Bill Dickey			
☐ 7E	R.Moore/S.Hogan BLUE	60.00	24.00	6.00
	F.Frankhouse/E.Brandt			
☐ 7F	P.Martin/O'Farrell BLUE	60.00	24.00	6.00
	S.Byrd/D.MacFayden			
☐ 8A	M.Koenig/F.Fitzsimmons	60.00	24.00	6.00
	R.Benge/T.Zachary			
☐ 8B	J.Hayes/Ted Lyons	75.00	30.00	7.50
	M.Haas/Zeke Bonura			
☐ 8C	J.Burns/Rollie Hemsley	60.00	24.00	6.00
	F.Grube/B.Weiland			
☐ 8D	F.Campbell/B.Meyers	60.00	24.00	6.00
	I.Goodman/A.Kampouris			
☐ 8E	J.DeShong/J.Allen	60.00	24.00	6.00
	Red Rolfe/D.Walker			
☐ 8F	P.Fox/Hank Greenberg	100.00	40.00	10.00
	G.Walker/S.Rowe			
☐ 8G	B.Werber/Rick Ferrell	75.00	30.00	7.50
	W.Ferrell/F.Ostermueller			
☐ 8H	Joe Kuhel/E.Whitehill	60.00	24.00	6.00
	B.Myer/J.Stone			
☐ 8I	J.Vosmik/Knickerbocker	60.00	24.00	6.00
	Mel Harder/L.Stewart			
☐ 8J	B.Johnson/E.Coleman	60.00	24.00	6.00
	J.Marcum/D.Cramer			
☐ 8K	B.Herman/G.Suhr	60.00	24.00	6.00
	T.Padden/C.Blanton			
☐ 8L	A.Spohrer/F.Rhem	60.00	24.00	6.00
	B.Cantwell/L.Benton			
☐ 8M	M.Koenig/F.Fitzsimmons	60.00	24.00	6.00
	R.Benge/T.Zachary			
☐ 9B	J.Hayes/Ted Lyons	75.00	30.00	7.50
	M.Haas/Zeke Bonura			
☐ 9C	J.Burns/Rollie Hemsley	60.00	24.00	6.00
	F.Grube/B.Weiland			
☐ 9D	F.Campbell/B.Meyers	60.00	24.00	6.00
	I.Goodman/A.Kampouris			
☐ 9E	J.DeShong/J.Allen	60.00	24.00	6.00
	Red Rolfe/F.Walker			
☐ 9F	P.Fox/Hank Greenberg	100.00	40.00	10.00
	G.Walker/S.Rowe			
☐ 9G	B.Werber/Rick Ferrell	75.00	30.00	7.50
	W.Ferrell/F.Ostermueller			
☐ 9H	Joe Kuhel/E.Whitehill	60.00	24.00	6.00
	B.Myer/J.Stone			
☐ 9I	J.Vosmik/Knickerbocker	60.00	24.00	6.00
	Mel Harder/L.Stewart			
☐ 9J	B.Johnson/E.Coleman	60.00	24.00	6.00
	J.Marcum/D.Cramer			
☐ 9K	B.Herman/G.Suhr	60.00	24.00	6.00
	T.Padden/C.Blanton			
☐ 9L	A.Spohrer/F.Rhem	60.00	24.00	6.00
	B.Cantwell/L.Benton			
☐ 11E	J.Wilson/J.Allen	100.00	40.00	10.00
	B.Jonnard/F.Brickell			
☐ 11F	S.West/O.Melillo	100.00	40.00	10.00
	G.Blaeholder/D.Coffman			
☐ 11G	Joe Cronin/C.Reynolds	150.00	60.00	15.00
	M.Bishop/C.Cissel			
☐ 11H	H.Schuble/F.Marberry	125.00	50.00	12.50
	Goose Goslin/G.Crowder			
☐ 11J	M.Ruel/Al Simmons	180.00	75.00	18.00
	W.Kamm/M.Cochrane			
☐ 11K	W.Hudlin/G.Myatt	125.00	50.00	12.50
	A.Comorosky/J.Bottomley			
☐ 12A	H.Critz/D.Bartell BLUE	150.00	60.00	15.00
	Mel Ott/G.Mancuso			
☐ 12B	P.Traynor/R.Lucas BLUE	125.00	50.00	12.50
	T.Thevenow/G.Wright			
☐ 12C	C.Berry/B.Burke BLUE	125.00	50.00	12.50
	R.Kress/D.Vance			
☐ 12D	Ruffing/P.Malone BLUE	250.00	100.00	25.00
	T.Lazzeri/Bill Dickey			
☐ 12E	R.Moore/S.Hogan BLUE	100.00	40.00	10.00
	F.Frankhouse/E.Brandt			
☐ 12F	Martin/O'Farrell BLUE	100.00	40.00	10.00
	S.Byrd/D.MacFayden			
☐ 13A	M.Ruel/Al Simmons	180.00	75.00	18.00
	W.Kamm/M.Cochrane			
☐ 13B	W.Hudlin/G.Myatt	125.00	50.00	12.50
	A.Comorosky/J.Bottomley			
☐ 13C	J.Wilson/J.Allen	100.00	40.00	10.00
	B.Jonnard/F.Brickell			
☐ 13D	S.West/Oscar Melillo	100.00	40.00	10.00
	G.Blaeholder/D.Coffman			
☐ 13E	Joe Cronin/C.Reynolds	125.00	50.00	12.50
	M.Bishop/C.Cissell			
☐ 13F	H.Schuble/F.Marberry	125.00	50.00	12.50
	Goose Goslin/G.Crowder			
☐ 14A	Babe Ruth/M.McManus	2000.00	800.00	250.00
	E.Brandt/R.Maranville			
☐ 14B	B.Terry/H.Schumacher	165.00	67.50	20.00
	G.Mancuso/T.Jackson			
☐ 14C	Paul Waner/G.Bush	165.00	67.50	20.00
	W.Hoyt/Lloyd Waner			
☐ 14D	B.Grimes/Chuck Klein	165.00	67.50	20.00
	K.Cuyler/W.English			
☐ 14E	S.Leslie/L.Frey	100.00	40.00	10.00
	Joe Stripp/W.Clark			
☐ 14F	T.Piet/A.Comorosky	125.00	50.00	12.50
	Jim Bottomley/S.Adams			
☐ 15A	Babe Ruth/M.McManus	2000.00	800.00	250.00
	E.Brandt/R.Maranville			
☐ 15B	B.Terry/H.Schumacher	165.00	67.50	20.00
	G.Mancuso/T.Jackson			
☐ 15C	J.Wilson/J.Allen	100.00	40.00	10.00
	B.Jonnard/F.Brickell			
☐ 15D	B.Grimes/Chuck Klein	165.00	67.50	20.00
	K.Cuyler/W.English			
☐ 15E	Joe Cronin/C.Reynolds	125.00	50.00	12.50
	M.Bishop/C.Cissell			
☐ 15F	T.Piet/A.Comorosky	125.00	50.00	12.50
	Jim Bottomley/S.Adams			
☐ 16A	F.Frisch/Dizzy Dean	250.00	100.00	25.00
	E.Orsatti/T.Carleton			
☐ 16B	R.Mahaffey/Jimmie Foxx	165.00	67.50	20.00
	D.Williams/P.Higgins			
☐ 16C	Heinie Manush/L.Lary	125.00	50.00	12.50
	M.Weaver/B.Hadley			
☐ 16D	M.Cochrane/C.Gehringer	180.00	75.00	18.00
	Tom Bridges/B.Rogell			
☐ 16E	W.Kamm/O.Hildebrand	125.00	50.00	12.50
	Earl Averill/H.Trosky			
☐ 16F	G.Earnshaw/J.Dykes	125.00	50.00	12.50
	Luke Sewell/L.Appling			
☐ 17A	F.Frisch/Dizzy Dean	250.00	100.00	25.00
	E.Orsatti/T.Carleton			
☐ 17B	R.Mahaffey/Jimmie Foxx	165.00	67.50	20.00
	D.Williams/P.Higgins			
☐ 17C	Heinie Manush/L.Lary	125.00	50.00	12.50
	M.Weaver/B.Hadley			
☐ 17D	M.Cochrane/C.Gehringer	180.00	75.00	18.00
	Tom Bridges/B.Rogell			
☐ 17E	W.Kamm/O.Hildebrand	125.00	50.00	12.50
	Earl Averill/H.Trosky			
☐ 17F	G.Earnshaw/J.Dykes	125.00	50.00	12.50
	Luke Sewell/L.Appling			

1936 Goudey B/W

THREE BAGGER

What a smash down 1st base line!—Too fast for the 1st sacker to even get near it.

Louis (Buck) Newsom — came up with St. Louis in 1934 from the Pacific Coast League. With Los Angeles in 1933 he had won 31 and lost 10. First he was an underhand pitcher; but now he flings overhand. A very colorful player — doing fine work with the Senators.

A line drive to center. The fielder had to move fast to spear this one.

OUT

The cards in this 25-card black and white set measure approximately 2 3/8" by 2 7/8". In contrast to the color artwork of its previous sets, the 1936 Goudey set contained a simple black and white player photograph. A facsimile autograph appeared within the picture area. Each card was issued with a number of different "game situation" backs, and there may be as many as 200 different front/back combinations. The catalog designation for this set is R322. This unnumbered set is checklisted and numbered below in alphabetical order for convenience.

	EX-MT	VG-E	GOOD
COMPLETE SET (25)	2000.00	800.00	250.00
COMMON PLAYER (1-25)	50.00	20.00	5.00
☐ 1 Wally Berger	60.00	24.00	6.00
☐ 2 Zeke Bonura	50.00	20.00	5.00
☐ 3 Frenchy Bordagaray	50.00	20.00	5.00
☐ 4 Bill Brubaker	50.00	20.00	5.00
☐ 5 Dolph Camilli	60.00	24.00	6.00

☐ 6 Clyde Castleman	50.00	20.00	5.00
☐ 7 Mickey Cochrane	200.00	80.00	20.00
☐ 8 Joe Coscarart	50.00	20.00	5.00
☐ 9 Frank Crosetti	75.00	30.00	7.50
☐ 10 Kiki Cuyler	100.00	40.00	10.00
☐ 11 Paul Derringer	60.00	24.00	6.00
☐ 12 Jimmy Dykes	60.00	24.00	6.00
☐ 13 Rick Ferrell	100.00	40.00	10.00
☐ 14 Lefty Gomez	250.00	100.00	25.00
☐ 15 Hank Greenberg	300.00	120.00	30.00
☐ 16 Bucky Harris	100.00	40.00	10.00
☐ 17 Rollie Hemsley	50.00	20.00	5.00
☐ 18 Pinky Higgins	50.00	20.00	5.00
☐ 19 Oral Hildebrand	50 00	20.00	5.00
☐ 20 Chuck Klein	150.00	60.00	15.00
☐ 21 Pepper Martin	75.00	30.00	7.50
☐ 22 Bobo Newsom	60.00	24.00	6.00
☐ 23 Joe Vosmik	50.00	20.00	5.00
☐ 24 Paul Waner	125.00	50.00	12.50
☐ 25 Bill Werber	50.00	20.00	5.00

1938 Goudey Heads Up

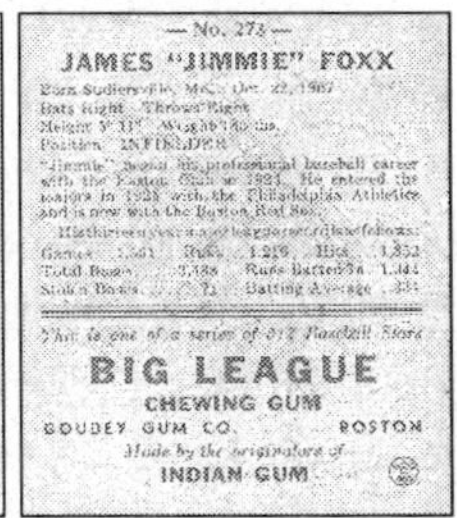

The cards in this 48-card set measure approximately 2 3/8" by 2 7/8". The 1938 Goudey set is commonly referred to as the Heads-Up set, or R323 (ACC). These very popular but difficult to obtain cards came in two series of the same 24 players. The first series, numbers 241-264, is distinguished from the second series, numbers 265-288, in that the second contains etched cartoons and comments surrounding the player picture. Although the set starts with number 241, it is not a continuation of the 1933 Goudey set, but a separate set in its own right.

	EX-MT	VG-E	GOOD
COMPLETE SET (48)	18000.	7000.00	2250.00
COMMON PLAYER (241-264)	100.00	40.00	10.00
COMMON PLAYER (265-288)	125.00	50.00	12.50
☐ 241 Charlie Gehringer	350.00	140.00	35.00
☐ 242 Pete Fox	100.00	40.00	10.00
☐ 243 Joe Kuhel	100.00	40.00	10.00
☐ 244 Frank Demaree	100.00	40.00	10.00
☐ 245 Frank Pytlak	100.00	40.00	10.00
☐ 246 Ernie Lombardi	200.00	80.00	20.00
☐ 247 Joe Vosmik	100.00	40.00	10.00
☐ 248 Dick Bartell	100.00	40.00	10.00
☐ 249 Jimmie Foxx	500.00	200.00	50.00
☐ 250 Joe DiMaggio	4000.00	1600.00	550.00
☐ 251 Bump Hadley	100.00	40.00	10.00
☐ 252 Zeke Bonura	100.00	40.00	10.00
☐ 253 Hank Greenberg	400.00	160.00	40.00
☐ 254 Van Lingle Mungo	125.00	50.00	12.50
☐ 255 Moose Solters	100.00	40.00	10.00
☐ 256 Vernon Kennedy	100.00	40.00	10.00
☐ 257 Al Lopez	200.00	80.00	20.00
☐ 258 Bobby Doerr	350.00	140.00	35.00
☐ 259 Billy Werber	100.00	40.00	10.00
☐ 260 Rudy York	125.00	50.00	12.50
☐ 261 Rip Radcliff	100.00	40.00	10.00
☐ 262 Joe Medwick	300.00	120.00	30.00
☐ 263 Marvin Owen	100.00	40.00	10.00
☐ 264 Bob Feller	750.00	300.00	75.00
☐ 265 Charlie Gehringer	425.00	170.00	42.00
☐ 266 Pete Fox	125.00	50.00	12.50
☐ 267 Joe Kuhel	125.00	50.00	12.50
☐ 268 Frank Demaree	125.00	50.00	12.50
☐ 269 Frank Pytlak	125.00	50.00	12.50
☐ 270 Ernie Lombardi	250.00	100.00	25.00
☐ 271 Joe Vosmik	125.00	50.00	12.50
☐ 272 Dick Bartell	125.00	50.00	12.50
☐ 273 Jimmie Foxx	600.00	240.00	60.00
☐ 274 Joe DiMaggio	5000.00	2000.00	600.00
☐ 275 Bump Hadley	125.00	50.00	12.50
☐ 276 Zeke Bonura	125.00	50.00	12.50
☐ 277 Hank Greenberg	500.00	200.00	50.00
☐ 278 Van Lingle Mungo	150.00	60.00	15.00
☐ 279 Moose Solters	125.00	50.00	12.50
☐ 280 Vernon Kennedy	125.00	50.00	12.50
☐ 281 Al Lopez	250.00	100.00	25.00
☐ 282 Bobby Doerr	450.00	180.00	45.00
☐ 283 Billy Werber	125.00	50.00	12.50
☐ 284 Rudy York	150.00	60.00	15.00
☐ 285 Rip Radcliff	125.00	50.00	12.50
☐ 286 Joe Medwick	375.00	150.00	37.00
☐ 287 Marvin Owen	125.00	50.00	12.50
☐ 288 Bob Feller	900.00	360.00	90.00

1916 M101-4 Sporting News

The cards in this 200-card set measure approximately 1 5/8" by 3". Issued in 1916 as a premium offer, the M101-4 set features black and white photos of current ballplayers. Each card is numbered and the reverse carries Sporting News advertising. The fronts are the same as D329, H801-9 and the unclassified Famous and Barr set. Most of the players in this also appear in the M101-5 set. Those cards which are asterisked in the checklist below are those cards which do not appear in the companion M101-5 set issued the year before.

	EX-MT	VG-E	GOOD
COMPLETE SET (200)	18000.	7500.00	2250.00
COMMON PLAYER (1-200)	35.00	14.00	3.50
☐ 1 Babe Adams	40.00	16.00	4.00
☐ 2 Sam Agnew	35.00	14.00	3.50
☐ 3 Eddie Ainsmith	35.00	14.00	3.50
☐ 4 Grover Alexander	125.00	50.00	12.50
☐ 5 Leon Ames	35.00	14.00	3.50
☐ 6 Jimmy Archer	35.00	14.00	3.50
☐ 7 Jimmy Austin	35.00	14.00	3.50
☐ 8 H.D.(Doug) Baird *	40.00	16.00	4.00
☐ 9 Frank Baker	85.00	34.00	8.50
☐ 10 Dave Bancroft	75.00	30.00	7.50
☐ 11 Jack Barry	35.00	14.00	3.50
☐ 12 Zinn Beck	35.00	14.00	3.50
☐ 13 Chief Bender *	100.00	40.00	10.00
☐ 14 Joe Benz	35.00	14.00	3.50
☐ 15 Bob Bescher	35.00	14.00	3.50
☐ 16 Al Betzel	35.00	14.00	3.50
☐ 17 Mordecai Brown	75.00	30.00	7.50
☐ 18 Eddie Burns	35.00	14.00	3.50
☐ 19 George H. Burns *	40.00	16.00	4.00
☐ 20 George J. Burns	35.00	14.00	3.50
☐ 21 Joe Bush	40.00	16.00	4.00
☐ 22 Donie Bush *	40.00	16.00	4.00
☐ 23 Art Butler	35.00	14.00	3.50
☐ 24 Bobbie Byrne	35.00	14.00	3.50
☐ 25 Forrest Cady *	40.00	16.00	4.00
☐ 26 Jim Callahan	35.00	14.00	3.50
☐ 27 Ray Caldwell	35.00	14.00	3.50

☐ 28 Max Carey	75.00	30.00	7.50
☐ 29 George Chalmers	35.00	14.00	3.50
☐ 30 Ray Chapman	50.00	20.00	5.00
☐ 31 Larry Cheney	35.00	14.00	3.50
☐ 32 Ed Cicotte	60.00	24.00	6.00
☐ 33 Tommy Clarke	35.00	14.00	3.50
☐ 34 Eddie Collins	85.00	34.00	8.50
☐ 35 Shano Collins	35.00	14.00	3.50
☐ 36 Charles Comiskey OWN	85.00	34.00	8.50
☐ 37 Joe Connolly	35.00	14.00	3.50
☐ 38 Ty Cobb *	2000.00	800.00	250.00
☐ 39 Harry Coveleskie	35.00	14.00	3.50
☐ 40 Gavvy Cravath	40.00	16.00	4.00
☐ 41 Sam Crawford	75.00	30.00	7.50
☐ 42 Jean Dale	35.00	14.00	3.50
☐ 43 Jake Daubert	40.00	16.00	4.00
☐ 44 Charles Deal	35.00	14.00	3.50
☐ 45 Frank Demaree	35.00	14.00	3.50
☐ 46 Josh Devore *	40.00	16.00	4.00
☐ 47 William Doak	35.00	14.00	3.50
☐ 48 Bill Donovan	35.00	14.00	3.50
☐ 49 Red Dooin	35.00	14.00	3.50
☐ 50 Mike Doolan	35.00	14.00	3.50
☐ 51 Larry Doyle	40.00	16.00	4.00
☐ 52 Jean Dubuc	35.00	14.00	3.50
☐ 53 Oscar J. Dugey	35.00	14.00	3.50
☐ 54 John Evers	75.00	30.00	7.50
☐ 55 Red Faber	75.00	30.00	7.50
☐ 56 Happy Felsch	75.00	30.00	7.50
☐ 57 Bill Fischer	35.00	14.00	3.50
☐ 58 Ray Fisher	35.00	14.00	3.50
☐ 59 Max Flack	35.00	14.00	3.50
☐ 60 Art Fletcher	35.00	14.00	3.50
☐ 61 Eddie Foster	35.00	14.00	3.50
☐ 62 Jacques Fournier	35.00	14.00	3.50
☐ 63 Del Gainer	35.00	14.00	3.50
☐ 64 Chick Gandil *	100.00	40.00	10.00
☐ 65 Larry Gardner	35.00	14.00	3.50
☐ 66 Joe Gedeon	35.00	14.00	3.50
☐ 67 Gus Getz	35.00	14.00	3.50
☐ 68 George Gibson	35.00	14.00	3.50
☐ 69 Wilbur Good	35.00	14.00	3.50
☐ 70 Hank Gowdy	35.00	14.00	3.50
☐ 71 Jack Graney	35.00	14.00	3.50
☐ 72 Clark Griffith *	100.00	40.00	10.00
☐ 73 Tommy Griffith	35.00	14.00	3.50
☐ 74 Heinie Groh	40.00	16.00	4.00
☐ 75 Earl Hamilton	35.00	14.00	3.50
☐ 76 Bob Harmon	35.00	14.00	3.50
☐ 77 Roy Hartzell	35.00	14.00	3.50
☐ 78 Claude Hendrix	35.00	14.00	3.50
☐ 79 Olaf Henriksen	35.00	14.00	3.50
☐ 80 John Henry	35.00	14.00	3.50
☐ 81 Buck Herzog	35.00	14.00	3.50
☐ 82 Hugh High	35.00	14.00	3.50
☐ 83 Dick Hoblitzell	35.00	14.00	3.50
☐ 84 Harry Hooper	75.00	30.00	7.50
☐ 85 Ivan Howard	35.00	14.00	3.50
☐ 86 Miller Huggins	75.00	30.00	7.50
☐ 87 Joe Jackson	3000.00	1250.00	350.00
☐ 88 William James	35.00	14.00	3.50
☐ 89 Harold Janvrin	35.00	14.00	3.50
☐ 90 Hughie Jennings MG	75.00	30.00	7.50
☐ 91 Walter Johnson	600.00	240.00	60.00
☐ 92 Fielder Jones	35.00	14.00	3.50
☐ 93 Joe Judge *	40.00	16.00	4.00
☐ 94 Benny Kauff	35.00	14.00	3.50
☐ 95 Bill Killifer	35.00	14.00	3.50
☐ 96 Ed Konetchy	35.00	14.00	3.50
☐ 97 Nap Lajoie	250.00	100.00	25.00
☐ 98 Jack Lapp	35.00	14.00	3.50
☐ 99 John Lavan	35.00	14.00	3.50
☐ 100 Jimmy Lavender	35.00	14.00	3.50
☐ 101 Nemo Leibold	35.00	14.00	3.50
☐ 102 Hub Leonard	40.00	16.00	4.00
☐ 103 Duffy Lewis	40.00	16.00	4.00
☐ 104 Hans Lobert	35.00	14.00	3.50
☐ 105 Tom Long	35.00	14.00	3.50
☐ 106 Fred Luderus	35.00	14.00	3.50
☐ 107 Connie Mack MG	200.00	80.00	20.00
☐ 108 Lee Magee	35.00	14.00	3.50
☐ 109 Sherry Magee *	40.00	16.00	4.00
☐ 110 Al Mamaux	35.00	14.00	3.50
☐ 111 Leslie Mann	35.00	14.00	3.50
☐ 112 Rabbit Maranville	75.00	30.00	7.50
☐ 113 Rube Marquard	75.00	30.00	7.50
☐ 114 J.E.(Erskine) Mayer	35.00	14.00	3.50
☐ 115 George McBride	35.00	14.00	3.50
☐ 116 John McGraw MG	125.00	50.00	12.50
☐ 117 Jack McInnis	40.00	16.00	4.00
☐ 118 Fred Merkle	40.00	16.00	4.00
☐ 119 Chief Meyers	35.00	14.00	3.50
☐ 120 Clyde Milan	35.00	14.00	3.50
☐ 121 John Miller *	40.00	16.00	4.00
☐ 122 Otto Miller	35.00	14.00	3.50
☐ 123 Willie Mitchell	35.00	14.00	3.50
☐ 124 Fred Mollwitz	35.00	14.00	3.50
☐ 125 Pat Moran MG	35.00	14.00	3.50
☐ 126 Ray Morgan	35.00	14.00	3.50
☐ 127 George Moriarty	35.00	14.00	3.50
☐ 128 Guy Morton	35.00	14.00	3.50
☐ 129 Mike Mowrey *	40.00	16.00	4.00
☐ 130 Eddie Murphy	35.00	14.00	3.50
☐ 131 Hy Myers	35.00	14.00	3.50
☐ 132 Bert Niehoff	35.00	14.00	3.50
☐ 133 Rube Oldring	35.00	14.00	3.50
☐ 134 Oliver O'Mara	35.00	14.00	3.50
☐ 135 Steve O'Neill	35.00	14.00	3.50
☐ 136 Dode Paskert	35.00	14.00	3.50
☐ 137 Roger Peckinpaugh	40.00	16.00	4.00
☐ 138 Walter Pipp	50.00	20.00	5.00
☐ 139 Del Pratt	35.00	14.00	3.50
☐ 140 Pat Ragan *	40.00	16.00	4.00
☐ 141 Bill Rariden	35.00	14.00	3.50
☐ 142 Eppa Rixey	75.00	30.00	7.50
☐ 143 Davey Robertson	35.00	14.00	3.50
☐ 144 Wilbert Robinson MG	125.00	50.00	12.50
☐ 145 Bob Roth	35.00	14.00	3.50
☐ 146 Eddie Roush	85.00	34.00	8.50
☐ 147 Clarence Rowland MG	35.00	14.00	3.50
☐ 148 Nap Rucker	35.00	14.00	3.50
☐ 149 Dick Rudolph	35.00	14.00	3.50
☐ 150 Reb Russell	35.00	14.00	3.50
☐ 151 Babe Ruth	4500.00	1800.00	550.00
☐ 152 Vic Saier	35.00	14.00	3.50
☐ 153 Slim Sallee	35.00	14.00	3.50
☐ 154 Ray Schalk	75.00	30.00	7.50
☐ 155 Wally Schang	40.00	16.00	4.00
☐ 156 Frank Schulte	35.00	14.00	3.50
☐ 157 Everett Scott	40.00	16.00	4.00
☐ 158 Jim Scott	35.00	14.00	3.50
☐ 159 Tom Seaton	35.00	14.00	3.50
☐ 160 Howard Shanks	35.00	14.00	3.50
☐ 161 Bob Shawkey	40.00	16.00	4.00
☐ 162 Ernie Shore	40.00	16.00	4.00
☐ 163 Burt Shotton	35.00	14.00	3.50
☐ 164 George Sisler	125.00	50.00	12.50
☐ 165 J.C.(Red) Smith	35.00	14.00	3.50
☐ 166 Fred Snodgrass	35.00	14.00	3.50
☐ 167 George Stallings MG	35.00	14.00	3.50
☐ 168 Oscar Stanage	35.00	14.00	3.50
☐ 169 Charles Stengel	600.00	240.00	60.00
☐ 170 Milton Stock	35.00	14.00	3.50
☐ 171 Amos Strunk	35.00	14.00	3.50
☐ 172 Billy Sullivan	40.00	16.00	4.00
☐ 173 Jeff Tesreau	35.00	14.00	3.50
☐ 174 Joe Tinker	75.00	30.00	7.50
☐ 175 Fred Toney	35.00	14.00	3.50
☐ 176 Terry Turner	35.00	14.00	3.50
☐ 177 George Tyler *	40.00	16.00	4.00
☐ 178 Jim Vaughn	35.00	14.00	3.50
☐ 179 Bobby Veach	35.00	14.00	3.50
☐ 180 James Viox	35.00	14.00	3.50
☐ 181 Oscar Vitt	35.00	14.00	3.50
☐ 182 Honus Wagner	600.00	240.00	60.00
☐ 183 Clarence Walker	35.00	14.00	3.50
☐ 184 Ed Walsh	75.00	30.00	7.50
☐ 185 Bill Wambsganss *	50.00	20.00	5.00
☐ 186 Buck Weaver	100.00	40.00	10.00
☐ 187 Carl Weilman	35.00	14.00	3.50
☐ 188 Zack Wheat	75.00	30.00	7.50
☐ 189 George Whitted	35.00	14.00	3.50
☐ 190 Fred Williams	35.00	14.00	3.50
☐ 191 Arthur Wilson	35.00	14.00	3.50
☐ 192 J.O.(Chief) Wilson	35.00	14.00	3.50
☐ 193 Ivy Wingo	35.00	14.00	3.50
☐ 194 Meldon Wolfgang	35.00	14.00	3.50
☐ 195 Joe Wood	60.00	24.00	6.00
☐ 196 Steve Yerkes	35.00	14.00	3.50
☐ 197 Pep Young * (Detroit Tigers)	40.00	16.00	4.00
☐ 198 Rollie Zeider	35.00	14.00	3.50
☐ 199 Heinie Zimmerman	35.00	14.00	3.50
☐ 200 Dutch Zwilling	35.00	14.00	3.50

1915 M101-5 Sporting News

The cards in this 200-card set measure approximately 1 5/8 by 3". The 1915 M101-5 series of black and white, numbered baseball cards is very similar in style to M101-4.

The set was offered as a marketing promotion by C.C. Spink and Son, publishers of The Sporting News ("The Baseball Paper of the World"). Most of the players in this also appear in the M101-4 set. Those cards which are asterisked in the checklist below are those cards which do not appear in the companion M101-4 set issued the next year.

	EX-MT	VG-E	GOOD
COMPLETE SET (200)	24000.	10000.	3000.00
COMMON PLAYER (1-200)	40.00	16.00	4.00

	Player	EX-MT	VG-E	GOOD
1	Babe Adams	40.00	16.00	4.00
2	Sam Agnew	40.00	16.00	4.00
3	Ed Ainsmith	40.00	16.00	4.00
4	Grover Alexander	125.00	50.00	12.50
5	Leon Ames	40.00	16.00	4.00
6	Jimmy Archer	40.00	16.00	4.00
7	Jimmy Austin	40.00	16.00	4.00
8	Frank Baker	90.00	36.00	9.00
9	Dave Bancroft	80.00	32.00	8.00
10	Jack Barry	40.00	16.00	4.00
11	Zinn Beck	40.00	16.00	4.00
12	Luke Boone *	45.00	18.00	4.50
13	Joe Benz	40.00	16.00	4.00
14	Bob Bescher	40.00	16.00	4.00
15	Al Betzel	40.00	16.00	4.00
16	Roger Bresnahan *	90.00	36.00	9.00
17	Eddie Burns	40.00	16.00	4.00
18	George J. Burns	40.00	16.00	4.00
19	Joe Bush	45.00	18.00	4.50
20	Owen Bush *	45.00	18.00	4.50
21	Art Butler	40.00	16.00	4.00
22	Bobby Byrne	40.00	16.00	4.00
23	Mordecai Brown	80.00	32.00	8.00
24	Jimmy Callahan	40.00	16.00	4.00
25	Ray Caldwell	40.00	16.00	4.00
26	Max Carey	80.00	32.00	8.00
27	George Chalmers	40.00	16.00	4.00
28	Frank Chance MG *	125.00	50.00	12.50
29	Ray Chapman	60.00	24.00	6.00
30	Larry Cheney	40.00	16.00	4.00
31	Ed Cicotte	70.00	28.00	7.00
32	Tommy Clarke	40.00	16.00	4.00
33	Eddie Collins	90.00	36.00	9.00
34	Shano Collins	40.00	16.00	4.00
35	Charles Comiskey OWN	90.00	36.00	9.00
36	Joe Connolly	40.00	16.00	4.00
37	L.(Doc) Cook *	45.00	18.00	4.50
38	Jack Coombs *	90.00	36.00	9.00
39	Dan Costello *	45.00	18.00	4.50
40	Harry Coveleskie	45.00	18.00	4.50
41	Gavvy Cravath	45.00	18.00	4.50
42	Sam Crawford	80.00	32.00	8.00
43	Jean Dale	40.00	16.00	4.00
44	Jake Daubert	45.00	18.00	4.50
45	G.A. Davis Jr. *	45.00	18.00	4.50
46	Charles Deal	40.00	16.00	4.00
47	Frank Demaree	40.00	16.00	4.00
48	Bill Doak	40.00	16.00	4.00
49	Bill Donovan	40.00	16.00	4.00
50	Red Dooin	40.00	16.00	4.00
51	Mike Doolan	40.00	16.00	4.00
52	Larry Doyle	45.00	18.00	4.50
53	Jean Dubuc	40.00	16.00	4.00
54	Oscar Dugey	40.00	16.00	4.00
55	John Evers	80.00	32.00	8.00
56	Red Faber	80.00	32.00	8.00
57	Happy Felsch	80.00	32.00	8.00
58	Bill Fischer	40.00	16.00	4.00
59	Ray Fisher	40.00	16.00	4.00
60	Max Flack	40.00	16.00	4.00
61	Art Fletcher	40.00	16.00	4.00
62	Eddie Foster	40.00	16.00	4.00
63	Jacques Fournier	40.00	16.00	4.00
64	Del Gainer	40.00	16.00	4.00
65	Larry Gardner	40.00	16.00	4.00
66	Joe Gedeon	40.00	16.00	4.00
67	Gus Getz	40.00	16.00	4.00
68	George Gibson	40.00	16.00	4.00
69	Wilbur Good	40.00	16.00	4.00
70	Hank Gowdy	40.00	16.00	4.00
71	Jack Graney	40.00	16.00	4.00
72	Tommy Griffith	40.00	16.00	4.00
73	Heinie Groh	45.00	18.00	4.50
74	Earl Hamilton	40.00	16.00	4.00
75	Bob Harmon	40.00	16.00	4.00
76	Roy Hartzell	40.00	16.00	4.00
77	Claude Hendrix	40.00	16.00	4.00
78	Olaf Henriksen	40.00	16.00	4.00
79	John Henry	40.00	16.00	4.00
80	Buck Herzog	40.00	16.00	4.00
81	Hugh High	40.00	16.00	4.00
82	Dick Hoblitzell	40.00	16.00	4.00
83	Harry Hooper	80.00	32.00	8.00
84	Ivan Howard	40.00	16.00	4.00
85	Miller Huggins	80.00	32.00	8.00
86	Joe Jackson	3500.00	1400.00	375.00
87	William James	40.00	16.00	4.00
88	Harold Janvrin	40.00	16.00	4.00
89	Hughie Jennings MG	80.00	32.00	8.00
90	Walter Johnson	600.00	240.00	60.00
91	Fielder Jones	40.00	16.00	4.00
92	Benny Kauff	40.00	16.00	4.00
93	Bill Killefer	40.00	16.00	4.00
94	Ed Konetchy	40.00	16.00	4.00
95	Napoleon Lajoie	250.00	100.00	25.00
96	Jack Lapp	40.00	16.00	4.00
97	John Lavan	40.00	16.00	4.00
98	Jimmy Lavender	40.00	16.00	4.00
99	Nemo Leibold	40.00	16.00	4.00
100	Hub Leonard	45.00	18.00	4.50
101	Duffy Lewis	45.00	18.00	4.50
102	Hans Lobert	40.00	16.00	4.00
103	Tom Long	40.00	16.00	4.00
104	Fred Luderus	40.00	16.00	4.00
105	Connie Mack MG	200.00	80.00	20.00
106	Lee Magee	40.00	16.00	4.00
107	Al Mamaux	40.00	16.00	4.00
108	Leslie Mann	40.00	16.00	4.00
109	Rabbit Maranville	80.00	32.00	8.00
110	Rube Marquard	80.00	32.00	8.00
111	Armando Marsans *	45.00	18.00	4.50
112	J.E.(Erskine) Mayer	40.00	16.00	4.00
113	George McBride	40.00	16.00	4.00
114	John McGraw	125.00	50.00	12.50
115	Jack McInnis	45.00	18.00	4.50
116	Fred Merkle	45.00	18.00	4.50
117	Chief Meyers	40.00	16.00	4.00
118	Clyde Milan	45.00	18.00	4.50
119	Otto Miller	40.00	16.00	4.00
120	Willie Mitchell	40.00	16.00	4.00
121	Fred Mollwitz	40.00	16.00	4.00
122	J.H.(Herbie) Moran *	45.00	18.00	4.50
123	Pat Moran MG	40.00	16.00	4.00
124	Ray Morgan	40.00	16.00	4.00
125	George Moriarty	40.00	16.00	4.00
126	Guy Morton	40.00	16.00	4.00
127	Eddie Murphy	40.00	16.00	4.00
128	Jack Murray *	45.00	18.00	4.50
129	Hy Myers	40.00	16.00	4.00
130	Bert Niehoff	40.00	16.00	4.00
131	Les Nunamaker *	45.00	18.00	4.50
132	Rube Oldring	40.00	16.00	4.00
133	Oliver O'Mara	40.00	16.00	4.00
134	Steve O'Neill	40.00	16.00	4.00
135	Dode Paskert	40.00	16.00	4.00
136	Roger Peckinpaugh	45.00	18.00	4.50
137	E.J.(Jeff) Pfeffer *	45.00	18.00	4.50
138	George Pierce *	45.00	18.00	4.50
139	Walter Pipp	60.00	24.00	6.00
140	Del Pratt	40.00	16.00	4.00
141	Bill Rariden	40.00	16.00	4.00
142	Eppa Rixey	80.00	32.00	8.00
143	Davey Robertson	40.00	16.00	4.00
144	Wilbert Robinson MG	125.00	50.00	12.50
145	Bob Roth	40.00	16.00	4.00
146	Eddie Roush	90.00	36.00	9.00
147	Clarence Rowland MG	40.00	16.00	4.00
148	Nap Rucker	40.00	16.00	4.00
149	Dick Rudolph	40.00	16.00	4.00
150	Reb Russell	40.00	16.00	4.00
151	Babe Ruth	7500.00	3000.00	900.00
152	Vic Saier	40.00	16.00	4.00
153	Slim Sallee	40.00	16.00	4.00
154	Germany Schaefer *	45.00	18.00	4.50

☐ 155 Ray Schalk	80.00	32.00	8.00
☐ 156 Wally Schang	45.00	18.00	4.50
☐ 157 Charles Schmidt *	45.00	18.00	4.50
☐ 158 Frank Schulte	40.00	16.00	4.00
☐ 159 Jim Scott	40.00	16.00	4.00
☐ 160 Everett Scott	45.00	18.00	4.50
☐ 161 Tom Seaton	40.00	16.00	4.00
☐ 162 Howard Shanks	40.00	16.00	4.00
☐ 163 Bob Shawkey	45.00	18.00	4.50
☐ 164 Ernie Shore	45.00	18.00	4.50
☐ 165 Bert Shotton	40.00	16.00	4.00
☐ 166 George Sisler	125.00	50.00	12.50
☐ 167 J.C.(Red) Smith	40.00	16.00	4.00
☐ 168 Fred Snodgrass	45.00	18.00	4.50
☐ 169 George Stallings MG	40.00	16.00	4.00
☐ 170 Oscar Stanage	40.00	16.00	4.00
☐ 171 Charles Stengel	600.00	240.00	60.00
☐ 172 Milton Stock	40.00	16.00	4.00
☐ 173 Amos Strunk	40.00	16.00	4.00
☐ 174 Billy Sullivan	45.00	18.00	4.50
☐ 175 Jeff Tesreau	40.00	16.00	4.00
☐ 176 Jim Thorpe *	3000.00	1200.00	350.00
☐ 177 Joe Tinker	80.00	32.00	8.00
☐ 178 Fred Toney	40.00	16.00	4.00
☐ 179 Terry Turner	40.00	16.00	4.00
☐ 180 Jim Vaughn	40.00	16.00	4.00
☐ 181 Bobby Veach	40.00	16.00	4.00
☐ 182 James Viox	40.00	16.00	4.00
☐ 183 Oscar Vitt	40.00	16.00	4.00
☐ 184 Honus Wagner	600.00	240.00	60.00
☐ 185 Clarence Walker	40.00	16.00	4.00
☐ 186 Zack Wheat	80.00	32.00	8.00
☐ 187 Ed Walsh	80.00	32.00	8.00
☐ 188 Buck Weaver	100.00	40.00	10.00
☐ 189 Carl Weilman	40.00	16.00	4.00
☐ 190 George Whitted	40.00	16.00	4.00
☐ 191 Fred Williams	40.00	16.00	4.00
☐ 192 Arthur Wilson	40.00	16.00	4.00
☐ 193 J.O.(Chief) Wilson	40.00	16.00	4.00
☐ 194 Ivy Wingo	40.00	16.00	4.00
☐ 195 Meldon Wolfgang	40.00	16.00	4.00
☐ 196 Joe Wood	70.00	28.00	7.00
☐ 197 Steve Yerkes	40.00	16.00	4.00
☐ 198 Rollie Zeider	40.00	16.00	4.00
☐ 199 Heinie Zimmerman	40.00	16.00	4.00
☐ 200 Dutch Zwilling	40.00	16.00	4.00

1911 M116 Sporting Life

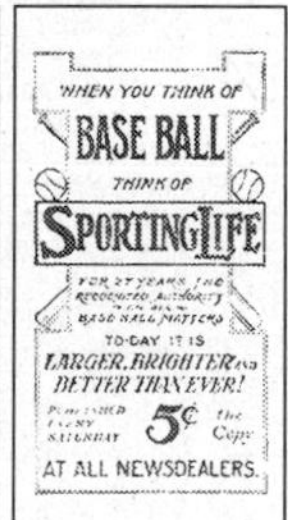

The cards in this 288-card set measure approximately 1 1/2" by 2 5/8". The Sporting Life set was offered as a premium to the publication's subscribers in 1911. Each of the 24 series of 12 cards came in an envelope printed with a list of the players within. Cards marked with an asterisk are also found with a special blue background and are worth double the listed price. McConnell appears with both Boston AL (common) and Chicago White Sox (scarce); McQuillan appears with Phillies (common) and Cincinnati (scarce). Cards are numbered in the checklist below alphabetically within team. Teams are ordered alphabetically within league: Boston AL (1-19), Chicago AL (20-36), Cleveland (37-52), Detroit (53-73), New York AL (74-84), Philadelphia AL (85-105), St. Louis AL (106-120), Washington (121-134), Boston NL (135-147), Brooklyn (148-164), Chicago NL (165-185), Cincinnati (186-203), New York NL (204-223), Philadelphia NL (224-242), Pittsburgh (243-261), and St. Louis (262-279). Cards 280-288 feature minor leaguers and are somewhat more difficult to find since most are from the tougher higher series.

	EX-MT	VG-E	GOOD
COMPLETE SET (290)	25000.	10000.	3000.00
COMMON MAJOR (1-279)	45.00	18.00	4.50
COMMON MINOR (280-288)	60.00	24.00	6.00
COMMON S19-S24	100.00	40.00	10.00
☐ 1 Frank Arellanes	45.00	18.00	4.50
☐ 2 Bill Carrigan	45.00	18.00	4.50
☐ 3 Ed Cicotte	75.00	30.00	7.50
☐ 4 Ray Collins S24	100.00	40.00	10.00
☐ 5 Pat Donahue	45.00	18.00	4.50
☐ 6 Patsy Donovan MG S21	100.00	40.00	10.00
☐ 7 Arthur Engle	45.00	18.00	4.50
☐ 8 Larry Gardner S24	100.00	40.00	10.00
☐ 9 Charles Hall	45.00	18.00	4.50
☐ 10 Harry Hooper S23	250.00	100.00	25.00
☐ 11 Edwin Karger	45.00	18.00	4.50
☐ 12 Harry Lord *	45.00	18.00	4.50
☐ 13 Thomas Madden S24	100.00	40.00	10.00
☐ 14A Amby McConnell (Boston AL)	45.00	18.00	4.50
☐ 14B Amby McConnell (Chicago AL)	1800.00	600.00	200.00
☐ 15 Tris Speaker S23	450.00	180.00	45.00
☐ 16 Jake Stahl	50.00	20.00	5.00
☐ 17 John Thoney	45.00	18.00	4.50
☐ 18 Heinie Wagner	50.00	20.00	5.00
☐ 19 Joe Wood S23	175.00	70.00	18.00
☐ 20 Lena Blackburn UER (Sic, Blackburne)	45.00	18.00	4.50
☐ 21 James J. Block S21	100.00	40.00	10.00
☐ 22 Patsy Dougherty	45.00	18.00	4.50
☐ 23 Hugh Duffy MG	125.00	50.00	12.50
☐ 24 Ed Hahn	45.00	18.00	4.50
☐ 25 Paul Meloan S24	100.00	40.00	10.00
☐ 26 Fred Parent	45.00	18.00	4.50
☐ 27 Frederick Payne S21	100.00	40.00	10.00
☐ 28 William Purtell	45.00	18.00	4.50
☐ 29 James Scott S23	100.00	40.00	10.00
☐ 30 Frank Smith	45.00	18.00	4.50
☐ 31 Billy Sullivan	50.00	20.00	5.00
☐ 32 Lee Tannehill	45.00	18.00	4.50
☐ 33 Ed Walsh	100.00	40.00	10.00
☐ 34 Guy(Doc) White	45.00	18.00	4.50
☐ 35 Irv Young	45.00	18.00	4.50
☐ 36 Dutch Zwilling S24	100.00	40.00	10.00
☐ 37 Harry Bemis	45.00	18.00	4.50
☐ 38 Charles Berger	45.00	18.00	4.50
☐ 39 Joseph Birmingham	45.00	18.00	4.50
☐ 40 Hugh Bradley	45.00	18.00	4.50
☐ 41 Nig Clarke	45.00	18.00	4.50
☐ 42 Cy Falkenberg	45.00	18.00	4.50
☐ 43 Elmer Flick	125.00	50.00	12.50
☐ 44 Addie Joss	150.00	60.00	15.00
☐ 45 Napoleon Lajoie *	250.00	100.00	25.00
☐ 46 Frederick Linke S20	100.00	40.00	10.00
☐ 47 B.(Bris) Lord	45.00	18.00	4.50
☐ 48 Deacon McGuire MG	45.00	18.00	4.50
☐ 49 Harry Niles	45.00	18.00	4.50
☐ 50 George Stovall	45.00	18.00	4.50
☐ 51 Terry Turner	45.00	18.00	4.50
☐ 52 Cy Young	250.00	100.00	25.00
☐ 53 Heine Beckendorf	45.00	18.00	4.50
☐ 54 Donie Bush	45.00	18.00	4.50
☐ 55 Ty Cobb *	2400.00	1000.00	300.00
☐ 56 Sam Crawford *	125.00	50.00	12.50
☐ 57 Jim Delehanty	50.00	20.00	5.00
☐ 58 Bill Donovan	45.00	18.00	4.50
☐ 59 Hugh Jennings MG *	100.00	40.00	10.00
☐ 60 Davy Jones	45.00	18.00	4.50
☐ 61 Tom Jones	45.00	18.00	4.50
☐ 62 Chick Lathers S21	100.00	40.00	10.00
☐ 63 Matty McIntyre	45.00	18.00	4.50
☐ 64 George Moriarty	50.00	20.00	5.00
☐ 65 George Mullin	45.00	18.00	4.50
☐ 66 Charley O'Leary	45.00	18.00	4.50
☐ 67 Hub Pernoll S23	100.00	40.00	10.00
☐ 68 Boss Schmidt	45.00	18.00	4.50
☐ 69 Oscar Stanage	45.00	18.00	4.50
☐ 70 Sailor Stroud S21	100.00	40.00	10.00
☐ 71 Ed Summers	45.00	18.00	4.50
☐ 72 Ed Willett	45.00	18.00	4.50
☐ 73 Ralph Works	45.00	18.00	4.50
☐ 74 Jimmy Austin S19	100.00	40.00	10.00
☐ 75 Hal Chase *	75.00	30.00	7.50
☐ 76 Birdie Cree	45.00	18.00	4.50

☐ 77 Lou Criger	45.00	18.00	4.50
☐ 78 Russ Ford S23	100.00	40.00	10.00
☐ 79 Earle Gardner S23	100.00	40.00	10.00
☐ 80 John Knight S19	100.00	40.00	10.00
☐ 81 Frank LaPorte	45.00	18.00	4.50
☐ 82 George Stallings MG	45.00	18.00	4.50
☐ 83 Jeff Sweeney S19	100.00	40.00	10.00
☐ 84 Harry Wolter	45.00	18.00	4.50
☐ 85 Tommy Atkins S24	100.00	40.00	10.00
☐ 86 Frank Baker	125.00	50.00	12.50
☐ 87 Jack Barry	50.00	20.00	5.00
☐ 88 Chief Bender *	100.00	40.00	10.00
☐ 89 Eddie Collins *	125.00	50.00	12.50
☐ 90 Jack Coombs	60.00	24.00	6.00
☐ 91 Harry Davis *	45.00	18.00	4.50
☐ 92 Jimmy Dygert	45.00	18.00	4.50
☐ 93 Topsy Hartsel	45.00	18.00	4.50
☐ 94 Heinie Heitmuller	45.00	18.00	4.50
☐ 95 Harry Krause	45.00	18.00	4.50
☐ 96 Jack Lapp S24	100.00	40.00	10.00
☐ 97 Paddy Livingstone	45.00	18.00	4.50
☐ 98 Connie Mack MG	175.00	70.00	18.00
☐ 99 Stuffy McInnes S24	100.00	40.00	10.00
(Sic, McInnis)			
☐ 100 Cy Morgan	45.00	18.00	4.50
☐ 101 Danny Murphy	45.00	18.00	4.50
☐ 102 Rube Oldring	45.00	18.00	4.50
☐ 103 Eddie Plank	175.00	70.00	18.00
☐ 104 Amos Strunk S24	100.00	40.00	10.00
☐ 105 Ira Thomas *	45.00	18.00	4.50
☐ 106 Bill Bailey	45.00	18.00	4.50
☐ 107 Dode Criss S19	100.00	40.00	10.00
☐ 108 Bert Graham	45.00	18.00	4.50
☐ 109 Roy Hartzell	45.00	18.00	4.50
☐ 110 Danny Hoffman	45.00	18.00	4.50
☐ 111 Harry Howell	45.00	18.00	4.50
☐ 112 Joe Lake S19	100.00	40.00	10.00
☐ 113 Jack O'Conner	45.00	18.00	4.50
☐ 114 Barney Pelty	45.00	18.00	4.50
☐ 115 Jack Powell	45.00	18.00	4.50
☐ 116 Al Schweitzer	45.00	18.00	4.50
☐ 117 Jim Stephens	45.00	18.00	4.50
☐ 118 George Stone	45.00	18.00	4.50
☐ 119 Rube Waddell	125.00	50.00	12.50
☐ 120 Bobby Wallace	90.00	36.00	9.00
☐ 121 Wid Conroy	45.00	18.00	4.50
☐ 122 Kid Elberfeld	45.00	18.00	4.50
☐ 123 Eddie Foster	45.00	18.00	4.50
☐ 124 Doc Gessler	45.00	18.00	4.50
☐ 125 Walter Johnson	600.00	240.00	60.00
☐ 126 Red Killifer S22	100.00	40.00	10.00
☐ 127 Jimmy McAleer MG	45.00	18.00	4.50
☐ 128 George McBride S21	100.00	40.00	10.00
☐ 129 Clyde Milan	50.00	20.00	5.00
☐ 130 Miller S23	100.00	40.00	10.00
☐ 131 Doc Reisling	45.00	18.00	4.50
☐ 132 Germany Schaefer	50.00	20.00	5.00
☐ 133 Gabby Street	45.00	18.00	4.50
☐ 134 Bob Unglaub	45.00	18.00	4.50
☐ 135 Fred Beck	45.00	18.00	4.50
☐ 136 Buster Brown	45.00	18.00	4.50
☐ 137 Cliff Curtis S23	100.00	40.00	10.00
☐ 138 George Ferguson	45.00	18.00	4.50
☐ 139 Samuel Frock S20	100.00	40.00	10.00
☐ 140 Peaches Graham	45.00	18.00	4.50
☐ 141 Buck Herzog	45.00	18.00	4.50
☐ 142 Fred Lake MG	45.00	18.00	4.50
☐ 143 Bayard Sharpe S23	100.00	40.00	10.00
☐ 144 David Shean S20	100.00	40.00	10.00
☐ 145 Charlie Smith S22	100.00	40.00	10.00
☐ 146 Harry Smith	45.00	18.00	4.50
☐ 147 Bill Sweeney	45.00	18.00	4.50
☐ 148 Cy Barger	45.00	18.00	4.50
☐ 149 George Bell	45.00	18.00	4.50
☐ 150 Bill Bergen	45.00	18.00	4.50
☐ 151 Al Burch	45.00	18.00	4.50
☐ 152 Bill Dahlen MG	50.00	20.00	5.00
☐ 153 William Davidson S21	100.00	40.00	10.00
☐ 154 Frank Dessau S21	100.00	40.00	10.00
☐ 155 Tex Erwin S20	100.00	40.00	10.00
☐ 156 John Hummel	45.00	18.00	4.50
☐ 157 George Hunter	45.00	18.00	4.50
☐ 158 Tim Jordan *	45.00	18.00	4.50
☐ 159 Ed Lennox	45.00	18.00	4.50
☐ 160 Pryor McElveen	45.00	18.00	4.50
☐ 161 Tommy McMillan	45.00	18.00	4.50
☐ 162 Nap Rucker	50.00	20.00	5.00
☐ 163 Doc Scanlon UER	45.00	18.00	4.50
(Sic, Scanlan)			
☐ 164 Kaiser Wilhelm	45.00	18.00	4.50
☐ 165 Jimmy Archer S22	100.00	40.00	10.00
☐ 166 Ginger Beaumont	45.00	18.00	4.50
☐ 167 Mordecai Brown *	125.00	50.00	12.50
☐ 168 Frank Chance *	150.00	60.00	15.00
☐ 169 Johnny Evers	125.00	50.00	12.50
☐ 170 Solly Hofman	45.00	18.00	4.50
☐ 171 John Kane	45.00	18.00	4.50
☐ 172 Johnny Kling	45.00	18.00	4.50
☐ 173 Rube Kroh	45.00	18.00	4.50
☐ 174 Harry McIntire	45.00	18.00	4.50
☐ 175 Tom Needham	45.00	18.00	4.50
☐ 176 Orvie Overall	45.00	18.00	4.50
☐ 177 Big Jeff Pfeffer S23	100.00	40.00	10.00
☐ 178 Jack Pfiester	45.00	18.00	4.50
☐ 179 Ed Reulbach	50.00	20.00	5.00
☐ 180 Lew Richie	45.00	18.00	4.50
☐ 181 Frank Schulte	45.00	18.00	4.50
☐ 182 Jimmy Sheckard	45.00	18.00	4.50
☐ 183 Harry Steinfeldt	60.00	24.00	6.00
☐ 184 Joe Tinker	125.00	50.00	12.50
☐ 185 Heinie Zimmerman S19	100.00	40.00	10.00
☐ 186 Fred Beebe	45.00	18.00	4.50
☐ 187 Bob Bescher	45.00	18.00	4.50
☐ 188 Chappy Charles	45.00	18.00	4.50
☐ 189 Tommy Clarke S20	100.00	40.00	10.00
☐ 190 Tom Downey	45.00	18.00	4.50
☐ 191 Jim Doyle	45.00	18.00	4.50
☐ 192 Dick Eagan UER	45.00	18.00	4.50
(Sic, Egan)			
☐ 193 Art Fromme	45.00	18.00	4.50
☐ 194 Harry Gaspar S19	100.00	40.00	10.00
☐ 195 Clark Griffith MG	100.00	40.00	10.00
☐ 196 Doc Hoblitzel	45.00	18.00	4.50
☐ 197 Hans Lobert	45.00	18.00	4.50
☐ 198 Larry McLean	45.00	18.00	4.50
☐ 199 Mike Mitchell	45.00	18.00	4.50
☐ 200 Art Phelan S23	100.00	40.00	10.00
☐ 201 Jack Rowan	45.00	18.00	4.50
☐ 202 Bob Space UER	45.00	18.00	4.50
(Sic, Spade)			
☐ 203 George Suggs	45.00	18.00	4.50
☐ 204 Red Ames S22	100.00	40.00	10.00
☐ 205 Al Bridwell	45.00	18.00	4.50
☐ 206 Doc Crandall	45.00	18.00	4.50
☐ 207 Art Devlin	45.00	18.00	4.50
☐ 208 Josh Devore S19	100.00	40.00	10.00
☐ 209 Larry Doyle *	45.00	18.00	4.50
☐ 210 Art Fletcher S22	100.00	40.00	10.00
☐ 211 Christy Mathewson	600.00	240.00	60.00
☐ 212 John McGraw MG	175.00	70.00	18.00
☐ 213 Fred Merkle	50.00	20.00	5.00
☐ 214 Red Murray	45.00	18.00	4.50
☐ 215 Chief Myers S23	100.00	40.00	10.00
UER (Sic, Meyers)			
☐ 216 Bugs Raymond	50.00	20.00	5.00
☐ 217 Admiral Schlei	45.00	18.00	4.50
☐ 218 Cy Seymour	45.00	18.00	4.50
☐ 219 Tillie Shafer S19	100.00	40.00	10.00
☐ 220 Fred Snodgrass	45.00	18.00	4.50
☐ 221 Fred Tenney *	45.00	18.00	4.50
☐ 222 Art Wilson S23	100.00	40.00	10.00
☐ 223 Hooks Wiltse	45.00	18.00	4.50
☐ 224 Johnny Bates	45.00	18.00	4.50
☐ 225 Kitty Bransfeld	45.00	18.00	4.50
☐ 226 Red Dooin *	45.00	18.00	4.50
☐ 227 Mickey Doolan	45.00	18.00	4.50
☐ 228 Bob Ewing	45.00	18.00	4.50
☐ 229 Bill Foxen	45.00	18.00	4.50
☐ 230 Eddie Grant	45.00	18.00	4.50
☐ 231 Fred Jacklitsch	45.00	18.00	4.50
☐ 232 Otto Knabe	45.00	18.00	4.50
☐ 233 Sherry Magee	45.00	18.00	4.50
☐ 234A Geo.McQuillan *	45.00	18.00	4.50
(Philadelphia NL)			
☐ 234B Geo.McQuillan	1800.00	600.00	200.00
(Cincinnati NL)			
☐ 235 Earl Moore	45.00	18.00	4.50
☐ 236 Pat Moran	45.00	18.00	4.50
☐ 237 Lew Moren	45.00	18.00	4.50
☐ 238 Dode Paskert S19	100.00	40.00	10.00
☐ 239 Lou Schettler S20	100.00	40.00	10.00
☐ 240 Tully Sparks	45.00	18.00	4.50
☐ 241 John Titus S23	100.00	40.00	10.00
☐ 242A Jimmy Walsh S20	150.00	60.00	15.00
(Dark background)			
☐ 242B Jimmy Walsh S22	150.00	60.00	15.00
(White background)			
☐ 243 Ed Abbaticchio	45.00	18.00	4.50
☐ 244 Babe Adams	50.00	20.00	5.00
☐ 245 Bobby Byrne	45.00	18.00	4.50
☐ 246 Howie Camnitz	45.00	18.00	4.50
☐ 247 Vin Campbell S21	100.00	40.00	10.00
☐ 248 Fred Clarke	125.00	50.00	12.50
☐ 249 John Flynn S20	100.00	40.00	10.00
☐ 250 George Gibson *	45.00	18.00	4.50
☐ 251 Ham Hyatt	45.00	18.00	4.50

		EX-MT	VG-E	GOOD
☐ 252	Fred Leach *	45.00	18.00	4.50
☐ 253	Sam Leever	45.00	18.00	4.50
☐ 254	Lefty Leifield	45.00	18.00	4.50
☐ 255	Nick Maddox	45.00	18.00	4.50
☐ 256	Dots Miller	45.00	18.00	4.50
☐ 257	Paddy O'Conner	45.00	18.00	4.50
☐ 258	Deacon Phillipe	60.00	24.00	6.00
☐ 259	Mike Simon S21	100.00	40.00	10.00
☐ 260	Hans Wagner *	600.00	240.00	60.00
☐ 261	Chief Wilson	45.00	18.00	4.50
☐ 262	Les Bachman UER (Sic, Backman)	45.00	18.00	4.50
☐ 263	Jack Bliss S21	100.00	40.00	10.00
☐ 264	Roger Bresnahan	100.00	40.00	10.00
☐ 265	Frank Corridon	45.00	18.00	4.50
☐ 266	Ray Demmitt S22	100.00	40.00	10.00
☐ 267	Rube Ellis	45.00	18.00	4.50
☐ 268	Steve Evans S23	100.00	40.00	10.00
☐ 269	Bob Harmon S20	100.00	40.00	10.00
☐ 270	Miller Huggins	100.00	40.00	10.00
☐ 271	Rudy Hulswitt	45.00	18.00	4.50
☐ 272	Ed Konetchy	45.00	18.00	4.50
☐ 273	Johnny Lush	45.00	18.00	4.50
☐ 274	Al Mattern	45.00	18.00	4.50
☐ 275	Mike Mowery S21	100.00	40.00	10.00
☐ 276	Rebel Oakes S24	100.00	40.00	10.00
☐ 277	Ed Phelps	45.00	18.00	4.50
☐ 278	Slim Sallee	45.00	18.00	4.50
☐ 279	Vic Willis	60.00	24.00	6.00
☐ 280	Coveleskie: Louisville S22	150.00	60.00	15.00
☐ 281	Foster: Rochester S19	100.00	40.00	10.00
☐ 282	Frill: Jersey City S20	100.00	40.00	10.00
☐ 283	Hughes: Rochester S23	100.00	40.00	10.00
☐ 284	Krueger: Sacramento S20	100.00	40.00	10.00
☐ 285	Mitchell: Rochester S19	100.00	40.00	10.00
☐ 286	O'Hara: Toronto	60.00	24.00	6.00
☐ 287	Perring: Columbus S20	100.00	40.00	10.00
☐ 288	Ray: Western League S24	100.00	40.00	10.00

N28 Allen and Ginter

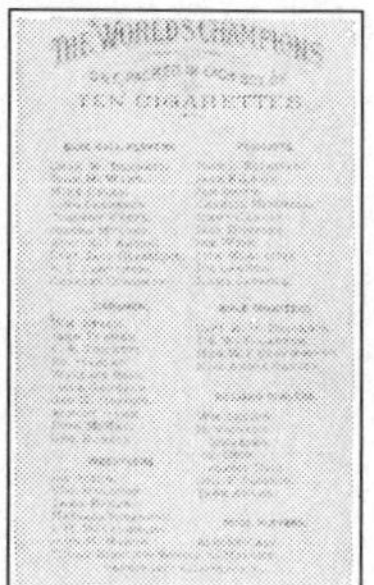

This 50-card set of The World's Champions was marketed by Allen and Ginter in 1887. The cards feature color lithographs of champion athletes from seven categories of sport, with baseball, rowing and boxing each having 10 individuals portrayed. Cards numbered 1 to 10 depict baseball players and cards numbered 11 to 20 depict popular boxers of the era. This set is called the first series although no such title appears on the cards. All 50 cards are checklisted on the reverse, and they are unnumbered. An album (ACC: A16) and an advertising banner (ACC: G20) were also issued in conjunction with this set.

	EX-MT	VG-E	GOOD
COMPLETE SET (50)	9000.00	4000.00	1100.00
COMMON BASEBALL (1-10)	300.00	120.00	30.00
COMMON BOXERS (11-20)	125.00	50.00	12.50
COMMON OTHERS (21-50)	35.00	14.00	3.50

☐ 1	Adrian C. Anson	1600.00	650.00	175.00
☐ 2	Chas. W. Bennett	300.00	120.00	30.00
☐ 3	Robert L. Caruthers	350.00	140.00	35.00
☐ 4	John Clarkson	750.00	300.00	75.00
☐ 5	Charles Comiskey	900.00	360.00	90.00
☐ 6	Capt.Jack Glasscock	350.00	140.00	35.00
☐ 7	Timothy Keefe	750.00	300.00	75.00
☐ 8	Mike Kelly	1100.00	500.00	125.00
☐ 9	Joseph Mulvey	300.00	120.00	30.00
☐ 10	John M. Ward	750.00	300.00	75.00
☐ 11	Jimmy Carney	125.00	50.00	12.50
☐ 12	Jimmy Carroll	125.00	50.00	12.50
☐ 13	Jack Dempsey	200.00	80.00	20.00
☐ 14	Jake Kilrain	150.00	60.00	15.00
☐ 15	Joe Lannon	125.00	50.00	12.50
☐ 16	Jack McAuliffe	125.00	50.00	12.50
☐ 17	Charlie Mitchell	150.00	60.00	15.00
☐ 18	Jem Smith	125.00	50.00	12.50
☐ 19	John L. Sullivan	250.00	100.00	25.00
☐ 20	Ike Weir	125.00	50.00	12.50
☐ 21	Wm. Beach	35.00	14.00	3.50
☐ 22	Geo. Bubear	35.00	14.00	3.50
☐ 23	Jacob Gaudaur	35.00	14.00	3.50
☐ 24	Albert Hamm	35.00	14.00	3.50
☐ 25	Ed. Hanlan	45.00	18.00	4.50
☐ 26	Geo. H. Hosmer	35.00	14.00	3.50
☐ 27	John McKay	35.00	14.00	3.50
☐ 28	Wallace Ross	35.00	14.00	3.50
☐ 29	John Teemer	35.00	14.00	3.50
☐ 30	E.A. Trickett	35.00	14.00	3.50
☐ 31	Joe Acton	35.00	14.00	3.50
☐ 32	Theo. Bauer	35.00	14.00	3.50
☐ 33	Young Bibby (Geo. Mehling)	60.00	24.00	6.00
☐ 34	J.F. McLaughlin	35.00	14.00	3.50
☐ 35	John McMahon	35.00	14.00	3.50
☐ 36	Wm. Muldoon	60.00	24.00	6.00
☐ 37	Matsada Sorakichi	35.00	14.00	3.50
☐ 38	Capt. A.H. Bogardus	35.00	14.00	3.50
☐ 39	Dr. W.F. Carver	35.00	14.00	3.50
☐ 40	Hon. W.F. Cody (Buffalo Bill)	150.00	60.00	15.00
☐ 41	Miss Annie Oakley	100.00	40.00	10.00
☐ 42	Yank Adams	35.00	14.00	3.50
☐ 43	Maurice Daly	35.00	14.00	3.50
☐ 44	Jos. Dion	35.00	14.00	3.50
☐ 45	J. Schaefer	35.00	14.00	3.50
☐ 46	Wm. Sexton	35.00	14.00	3.50
☐ 47	Geo. F. Slosson	35.00	14.00	3.50
☐ 48	M. Vignaux	35.00	14.00	3.50
☐ 49	Albert Frey	35.00	14.00	3.50
☐ 50	J.L. Malone	35.00	14.00	3.50

N29 Allen and Ginter

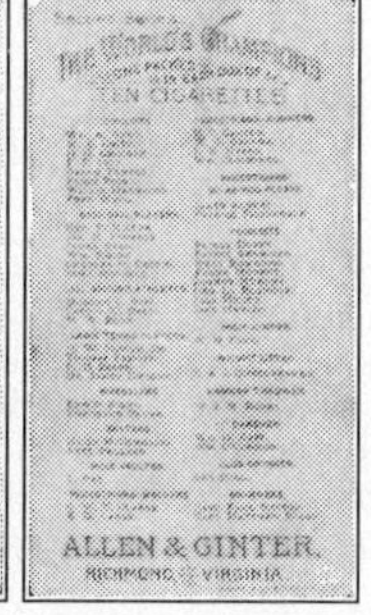

The second series of The World's Champions was probably issued in 1888. Like the first series, the cards are backlisted and unnumbered. However, there are 17 distinct categories of sports represented in this set, with only six baseball players portrayed (as opposed to 10 in the first series). Each card has a color lithograph of the individual set against a white background. An album (ACC: A17) and an advertising banner (ACC: G21) were issued in conjunction with the set.

The numbering below is alphabetical within sport, e.g., baseball players (1-6), boxers (7-14), and other sports (15-50).

	EX-MT	VG-E	GOOD
COMPLETE SET (50)	10500.	4250.00	1250.00
COMMON BASEBALL (1-6)	800.00	320.00	80.00
COMMON BOXERS (7-14)	300.00	120.00	30.00
COMMON OTHERS (15-50)	75.00	30.00	7.50

	EX-MT	VG-E	GOOD
☐ 1 Wm.(Buck) Ewing	1800.00	750.00	225.00
☐ 2 Jas. H. Fogarty	800.00	320.00	80.00
☐ 3 Charles H. Getzien	800.00	320.00	80.00
☐ 4 Geo.F.(Doggie) Miller	800.00	320.00	80.00
☐ 5 John Morrill	800.00	320.00	80.00
☐ 6 James Ryan	850.00	340.00	85.00
☐ 7 Patsey Duffy	300.00	120.00	30.00
☐ 8 Billy Edwards	300.00	120.00	30.00
☐ 9 Jack Havlin	300.00	120.00	30.00
☐ 10 Patsey Kerrigan	300.00	120.00	30.00
☐ 11 Geo. La Blance	300.00	120.00	30.00
☐ 12 Jack McGee	300.00	120.00	30.00
☐ 13 Frank Murphy	300.00	120.00	30.00
☐ 14 Johnny Murphy	300.00	120.00	30.00
☐ 15 Capt. J.C. Daly	75.00	30.00	7.50
☐ 16 M.W. Ford	75.00	30.00	7.50
☐ 17 Duncan C. Ross	75.00	30.00	7.50
☐ 18 W.E. Crist	75.00	30.00	7.50
☐ 19 H.G. Crocken	75.00	30.00	7.50
☐ 20 Willie Harradon	75.00	30.00	7.50
☐ 21 F.F. Ives	75.00	30.00	7.50
☐ 22 Wm. A. Rowe	75.00	30.00	7.50
☐ 23 Percy Stone	75.00	30.00	7.50
☐ 24 Ralph Temple	75.00	30.00	7.50
☐ 25 Fred Wood	75.00	30.00	7.50
☐ 26 Dr. James Dwight	90.00	36.00	9.00
☐ 27 Thomas Pettit	75.00	30.00	7.50
☐ 28 R.D. Sears	90.00	36.00	9.00
☐ 29 H.W. Slocum Jr.	75.00	30.00	7.50
☐ 30 Theobaud Bauer	75.00	30.00	7.50
☐ 31 Edwin Bibby	75.00	30.00	7.50
☐ 32 Hugh McCormack	75.00	30.00	7.50
☐ 33 Axel Paulsen	75.00	30.00	7.50
☐ 34 T. Ray	75.00	30.00	7.50
☐ 35 C.W.V. Clarke	75.00	30.00	7.50
☐ 36 E.D. Lange	75.00	30.00	7.50
☐ 37 E.C. Carter	75.00	30.00	7.50
☐ 38 Wm. Cummings	75.00	30.00	7.50
☐ 39 W.G. George	75.00	30.00	7.50
☐ 40 L.E. Myers	75.00	30.00	7.50
☐ 41 James Albert	75.00	30.00	7.50
☐ 42 Patrick Fitzgerald	75.00	30.00	7.50
☐ 43 W.B. Page	75.00	30.00	7.50
☐ 44 C.A.J. Queckberner	75.00	30.00	7.50
☐ 45 W.J.M. Barry	75.00	30.00	7.50
☐ 46 Wm. G. East	75.00	30.00	7.50
☐ 47 Wm. O'Connor	75.00	30.00	7.50
☐ 48 Gus Hill	75.00	30.00	7.50
☐ 49 Capt. Paul Boyton	75.00	30.00	7.50
☐ 50 Capt. Matthew Webb	90.00	36.00	9.00

N43 Allen and Ginter

The primary designs of this 50-card set are identical to those of N29, but these are placed on a much larger card with extraneous background detail. The set was produced in 1888 by Allen and Ginter as inserts for a larger tobacco package than those in which sets N28 and N29 were marketed. Cards of this set, which is backlisted, are considered to be much scarcer than their counterparts in N29.

	EX-MT	VG-E	GOOD
COMPLETE SET (50)	15000.	6250.00	1800.00
COMMON BASEBALL (1-6)	1350.00	500.00	150.00
COMMON BOXERS (7-14)	450.00	180.00	45.00
COMMON OTHERS (15-50)	125.00	50.00	12.50

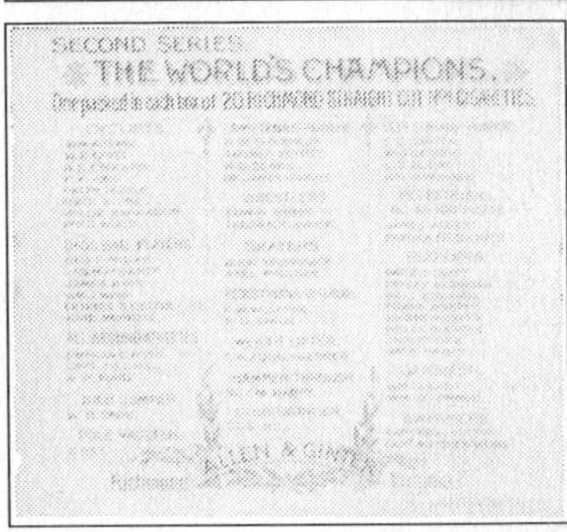
SECOND SERIES

THE WORLD'S CHAMPIONS.

ALLEN & GINTER

	EX-MT	VG-E	GOOD
☐ 1 William(Buck) Ewing	2500.00	1000.00	300.00
☐ 2 Jas. J. Fogarty	1350.00	550.00	175.00
☐ 3 Charles H. Getzien	1350.00	550.00	175.00
☐ 4 Geo.F.(Doggie) Miller	1350.00	550.00	175.00
☐ 5 John Morrill	1350.00	550.00	175.00
☐ 6 James Ryan	1500.00	600.00	200.00
☐ 7 Patsey Duffy	450.00	180.00	45.00
☐ 8 Billy Edwards	450.00	180.00	45.00
☐ 9 Jack Havlin	450.00	180.00	45.00
☐ 10 Patsey Kerrigan	450.00	180.00	45.00
☐ 11 George LaBlanche	450.00	180.00	45.00
☐ 12 Jack McGee	450.00	180.00	45.00
☐ 13 Frank Murphy	450.00	180.00	45.00
☐ 14 Johnny Murphy	450.00	180.00	45.00
☐ 15 James Albert	125.00	50.00	12.50
☐ 16 W.J.M. Barry	125.00	50.00	12.50
☐ 17 Theobaud Bauer	125.00	50.00	12.50
☐ 18 Edwin Bibby	125.00	50.00	12.50
☐ 19 Capt. Paul Boyton	125.00	50.00	12.50
☐ 20 E.C. Carter	125.00	50.00	12.50
☐ 21 C.W.V. Clarke	125.00	50.00	12.50
☐ 22 W.E. Crist	125.00	50.00	12.50
☐ 23 H.G. Crocker	125.00	50.00	12.50
☐ 24 Wm. Cummings	125.00	50.00	12.50
☐ 25 Capt. J.C. Daly	125.00	50.00	12.50
☐ 26 Dr. James Dwight	150.00	60.00	15.00
☐ 27 Wm. G. East	125.00	50.00	12.50
☐ 28 Patrick Fitzgerald	125.00	50.00	12.50
☐ 29 M.W. Ford	125.00	50.00	12.50
☐ 30 W.G. George	125.00	50.00	12.50
☐ 31 Willie Harradon	125.00	50.00	12.50
☐ 32 Gus Hill	125.00	50.00	12.50
☐ 33 F.F. Ives	125.00	50.00	12.50
☐ 34 E.D. Lange	125.00	50.00	12.50
☐ 35 Hugh McCormack	125.00	50.00	12.50
☐ 36 L.E. Myers	125.00	50.00	12.50
☐ 37 Wm. O'Connor	125.00	50.00	12.50
☐ 38 W.B. Page	125.00	50.00	12.50
☐ 39 Axel. Paulsen	125.00	50.00	12.50
☐ 40 Thomas Pettitt	125.00	50.00	12.50
☐ 41 C.A.J. Queckberner	125.00	50.00	12.50
☐ 42 T. Ray	125.00	50.00	12.50
☐ 43 Duncan C. Ross	125.00	50.00	12.50
☐ 44 Wm. A. Rowe	125.00	50.00	12.50
☐ 45 R.D. Sears	150.00	60.00	15.00
☐ 46 H.W. Slocum Jr.	125.00	50.00	12.50
☐ 47 Percy Stone	125.00	50.00	12.50
☐ 48 Ralph Temple	125.00	50.00	12.50
☐ 49 Capt. Matthew Webb	150.00	60.00	15.00
☐ 50 Fred Wood	125.00	50.00	12.50

N162 Goodwin

This 50-card set issued by Goodwin was one of the major competitors to the N28 and N29 sets marketed by Allen and Ginter. It contains individuals representing 18 sports, with eight baseball players pictured. Each color card is backlisted and bears advertising for "Old Judge" and "Gypsy Queen" cigarettes on the front. The set was released to the public in 1888 and an album (ACC: A36) is associated with it as a premium issue.

	EX-MT	VG-E	GOOD
COMPLETE SET (50)	13500.	6000.00	1800.00
COMMON BASEBALL (1-8)	650.00	260.00	65.00
COMMON BOXER	225.00	90.00	22.00
COMMON OTHERS	70.00	28.00	7.00
☐ 1 Ed Andrews: Phila.	650.00	260.00	65.00
☐ 2 Cap Anson: Chicago	2700.00	1100.00	350.00
☐ 3 Dan Brouthers: Detroit	1100.00	450.00	150.00
☐ 4 Bob Caruthers: Brooklyn	700.00	280.00	70.00
☐ 5 Fred Dunlap: Detroit	650.00	260.00	65.00
☐ 6 Jack Glasscock: Indianapolis	700.00	280.00	70.00
☐ 7 Tim Keefe: New York	1100.00	450.00	150.00
☐ 8 King Kelly: Boston	1650.00	700.00	225.00
☐ 9 Acton (Wrestler)	100.00	40.00	10.00
☐ 10 Albert (Pedestrian)	70.00	28.00	7.00
☐ 11 Beach (Oarsman)	70.00	28.00	7.00
☐ 12 Beecher (Football)	750.00	300.00	75.00
☐ 13 Beeckman (Lawn Tennis)	80.00	32.00	8.00
☐ 14 Bogardus (Marksman)	70.00	28.00	7.00
☐ 15 Buffalo Bill (Wild West Hunter)	225.00	90.00	22.00
☐ 16 Daly (Billiards)	70.00	28.00	7.00
☐ 17 Jack Dempsey (Pugilist)	350.00	140.00	35.00
☐ 18 D'oro (Pool)	70.00	28.00	7.00
☐ 19 Dwight (Lawn Tennis)	100.00	40.00	10.00
☐ 20 Fitzgerald (Pedestrian)	70.00	28.00	7.00
☐ 21 Garrison (Jockey)	70.00	28.00	7.00
☐ 22 Gaudaur (Oarsman)	70.00	28.00	7.00
☐ 23 Hanlan (Oarsman)	80.00	32.00	8.00
☐ 24 Jake Kilrain (Pugilist)	300.00	120.00	30.00
☐ 25 MacKenzie (Chess)	70.00	28.00	7.00
☐ 26 McLaughlin (Jockey)	70.00	28.00	7.00
☐ 27 Mitchell (Pugilist)	300.00	120.00	30.00
☐ 28 Muldoon (Wrestler)	100.00	40.00	10.00
☐ 29 Isaac Murphy (Jockey)	80.00	32.00	8.00
☐ 30 Myers (Runner)	70.00	28.00	7.00
☐ 31 Page (High Jumper)	70.00	28.00	7.00
☐ 32 Prince (Bicyclist)	70.00	28.00	7.00
☐ 33 Ross (Broadswordsman)	70.00	28.00	7.00
☐ 34 Rowe (Bicyclist)	70.00	28.00	7.00
☐ 35 Rowell (Pedestrian)	70.00	28.00	7.00
☐ 36 Schaefer (Billiards)	70.00	28.00	7.00
☐ 37 Sears (Lawn Tennis)	100.00	40.00	10.00
☐ 38 Sexton (Billiards)	70.00	28.00	7.00
☐ 39 Slosson (Billiards)	70.00	28.00	7.00
☐ 40 Smith (Pugilist)	225.00	90.00	22.00
☐ 41 Steinitz (Chess)	70.00	28.00	7.00
☐ 42 Stevens (Bicyclist)	70.00	28.00	7.00
☐ 43 John L. Sullivan (Pugilist)	400.00	160.00	40.00
☐ 44 Taylor (Lawn Tennis)	80.00	32.00	8.00
☐ 45 Teemer (Oarsman)	70.00	28.00	7.00
☐ 46 Vignaux (Billiards)	70.00	28.00	7.00
☐ 47 Voss (Strongest Man in the World)	70.00	28.00	7.00
☐ 48 Wood (Bicyclist)	70.00	28.00	7.00
☐ 49 Wood (Jockey)	70.00	28.00	7.00
☐ 50 Zukertort (Chess)	90.00	36.00	9.00

N172 Old Judge

The Goodwin Company's baseball series depicts hundreds of ballplayers from more than 40 major and minor league teams as well as boxers and wrestlers. The cards (approximately 1 1/2" by 2 1/2") are actually photographs from the Hall studio in New York which were pasted onto thick cardboard. The pictures are sepia in color with either a white or pink cast, and the cards are blank backed. They are found either numbered or unnumbered, with or without a copyright date, and with hand printed or machine printed names. All known cards have the name "Goodwin Co., New York" at the base. The cards were marketed during the period 1887-1890 in packs of "Old Judge" and "Gypsy Queen" cigarettes (cards marked with the latter brand are worth double the values listed below). They have been listed alphabetically and assigned numbers in the checklist below for simplicity's sake; the various poses known for some players also have not been listed for the same reason. Some of the players are pictured in horizontal (HOR) poses. In all, more than 2300 different Goodwin cards are known to collectors, with more being discovered every year. Cards from the "Spotted Tie" sub-series are denoted in the checklist below by SPOT.

	EX-MT	VG-E	GOOD
COMPLETE SET	125000.	50000.	15000.
COMMON PLAYER	125.00	50.00	12.50
COMMON PLAYER (DOUBLE)	150.00	60.00	15.00
COMMON BROWNS CHAMP	250.00	100.00	25.00
COMMON PLAYER (PCL)	1250.00	500.00	150.00
COMMON SPOTTED TIE	350.00	140.00	35.00
☐ 1 Gus Albert:	125.00	50.00	12.50

Cleveland-Milwaukee			
☐ 2 Charles Alcott: St. Louis Whites-Mansfield	125.00	50.00	12.50
☐ 3 Alexander: Des Moines	125.00	50.00	12.50
☐ 4 Myron Allen: K.C.	125.00	50.00	12.50
☐ 5 Bob Allen: Pitts.-Phila. N.L.	125.00	50.00	12.50
☐ 6 Uncle Bill Alvord: Toledo-Des Moines	125.00	50.00	12.50
☐ 7 Varney Anderson: St.Paul	125.00	50.00	12.50
☐ 8 Ed Andrews: Phila.	125.00	50.00	12.50
☐ 9 Ed Andrews and Buster Hoover: Philadelphia	150.00	60.00	15.00
☐ 10 Wally Andrews: Omaha	125.00	50.00	12.50
☐ 11 Bill Annis: Omaha-Worchester	125.00	50.00	12.50
☐ 12A Cap Anson: Chicago (In uniform)	12000.	5000.00	1500.00
☐ 12B Cap Anson: Chicago (Not in uniform)	2000.00	800.00	250.00
☐ 13 Old Hoss Ardner: Kansas City-St. Joe	125.00	50.00	12.50
☐ 14 Tug Arundel: Indianapolis-Whites	125.00	50.00	12.50
☐ 15 Jersey Bakley: Cleve.	125.00	50.00	12.50
☐ 16 Clarence Baldwin: Cincinnati	125.00	50.00	12.50
☐ 17 Mark(Fido) Baldwin: Chicago-Columbus	125.00	50.00	12.50
☐ 18 Lady Baldwin: Detroit	125.00	50.00	12.50
☐ 19 James Banning: Wash.	125.00	50.00	12.50
☐ 20 Samuel Barkley: Pittsburgh-K.C.	125.00	50.00	12.50
☐ 21 John Barnes: Mgr. St. Paul	125.00	50.00	12.50
☐ 22 Bald Billy Barnie: Mgr. Baltimore	150.00	60.00	15.00
☐ 23 Charles Bassett: Indianapolis-N.Y.	125.00	50.00	12.50
☐ 24 Charles Bastian: Phila.-Chicago	125.00	50.00	12.50
☐ 25 Charles Bastian and Schriver: Philadelphia	150.00	60.00	15.00
☐ 26 Ollie Beard: Cinc.	125.00	50.00	12.50
☐ 27 Ebenezer Beatin: Cleve.	125.00	50.00	12.50
☐ 28 Jake Beckley: "Eagle Eye" Whites-Pittsburgh	600.00	240.00	60.00
☐ 29 Stephen Behel SPOT	450.00	180.00	45.00
☐ 30 Charles Bennett: Detroit-Boston	125.00	50.00	12.50
☐ 31 Louis Bierbauer: A's	125.00	50.00	12.50
☐ 32 Louis Bierbauer and Robert Gamble: Athletics	150.00	60.00	15.00
☐ 33 Bill Bishop: Pittsburgh-Syracuse	125.00	50.00	12.50
☐ 34 William Blair: A's-Hamiltons	125.00	50.00	12.50
☐ 35 Ned Bligh: Columbus	125.00	50.00	12.50
☐ 36 Bogart: Indianapolis	125.00	50.00	12.50
☐ 37 Boyce: Washington	125.00	50.00	12.50
☐ 38 Jake Boyd: Maroons	150.00	60.00	15.00
☐ 39 Honest John Boyle: St. Louis-Chicago	125.00	50.00	12.50
☐ 40 Handsome Henry Boyle Indianapolis-N.Y.	125.00	50.00	12.50
☐ 41 Nick Bradley: K.C.- Worchester	125.00	50.00	12.50
☐ 42 George(Grin) Bradley Sioux City	125.00	50.00	12.50
☐ 43 Stephen Brady SPOT	450.00	180.00	45.00
☐ 44 Breckinridge: Sacramento PCL	1250.00	500.00	150.00
☐ 45 Jim Brennan: Kansas City- A's	125.00	50.00	12.50
☐ 46 Timothy Brosnan: Minn.-Sioux City	125.00	50.00	12.50
☐ 47 Cal Broughton: St. Paul	125.00	50.00	12.50
☐ 48 Big Dan Brouthers: Detroit-Boston	500.00	200.00	50.00
☐ 49 Thomas Brown: Pittsburgh-Boston	125.00	50.00	12.50
☐ 50 California Brown: New York	125.00	50.00	12.50
☐ 51 Pete Browning: "Gladiator" Louisville	250.00	100.00	25.00
☐ 52 Charles Brynan: Chicago-Des Moines	125.00	50.00	12.50
☐ 53 Al Buckenberger: Mgr. Columbus	125.00	50.00	12.50
☐ 54 Dick Buckley: Indianapolis-N.Y.	125.00	50.00	12.50
☐ 55 Charles Buffington: Philadelphia	125.00	50.00	12.50
☐ 56 Ernest Burch: Brooklyn-Whites	125.00	50.00	12.50
☐ 57 Bill Burdick: Omaha-Indianapolis	125.00	50.00	12.50
☐ 58 Black Jack Burdock: Boston-Brooklyn	125.00	50.00	12.50
☐ 59 Robert Burks: Sioux City	125.00	50.00	12.50
☐ 60 George Burnham "Watch" Mgr. Indianapolis	150.00	60.00	15.00
☐ 61 Burns: Omaha	125.00	50.00	12.50
☐ 62 Jimmy Burns: K.C.	125.00	50.00	12.50
☐ 63 Tommy(Oyster) Burns Baltimore-Brooklyn	125.00	50.00	12.50
☐ 64 Thomas E. Burns: Chicago	125.00	50.00	12.50
☐ 65A Doc Bushong: Brook.	125.00	50.00	12.50
☐ 65B Doc Bushong: Browns Champs	250.00	100.00	25.00
☐ 66 Patsy Cahill: Ind.	125.00	50.00	12.50
☐ 67 Count Campau: Kansas City-Detroit	125.00	50.00	12.50
☐ 68 Jimmy Canavan: Omaha	125.00	50.00	12.50
☐ 69 Bart Cantz: Whites-Baltimore	125.00	50.00	12.50
☐ 70 Handsome Jack Carney Washington	125.00	50.00	12.50
☐ 71 Hick Carpenter Cincinnati	125.00	50.00	12.50
☐ 72 Cliff Carroll: Wash.	125.00	50.00	12.50
☐ 73 Scrappy Carroll: St.Paul-Chicago	125.00	50.00	12.50
☐ 74 Frederick Carroll: Pitts.	125.00	50.00	12.50
☐ 75 Jumbo Cartwright: Kansas City-St. Joe	125.00	50.00	12.50
☐ 76A Bob Caruthers: "Parisian" Brooklyn	150.00	60.00	15.00
☐ 76B Bob Caruthers: "Parisian" Browns Champs	300.00	120.00	30.00
☐ 77 Daniel Casey: Phila.	125.00	50.00	12.50
☐ 78 Icebox Chamberlain: St. Louis	125.00	50.00	12.50
☐ 79 Cupid Childs: Phila.-Syracuse	125.00	50.00	12.50
☐ 80 Bob Clark: Washington	125.00	50.00	12.50
☐ 81 Owen Clark: Washington	125.00	50.00	12.50
☐ 82 Clarke and Mickey Hughes: Brooklyn HOR	150.00	60.00	15.00
☐ 83 William(Dad) Clarke: Chicago-Omaha	125.00	50.00	12.50
☐ 84 John Clarkson: Chicago-Boston	500.00	200.00	50.00
☐ 85 Jack Clements: Philadelphia	125.00	50.00	12.50
☐ 86 Elmer Cleveland: Omaha-New York	125.00	50.00	12.50
☐ 87 Monk Cline: K.C.-Sioux City	125.00	50.00	12.50
☐ 88 Cody: Des Moines	125.00	50.00	12.50
☐ 89 John Coleman: Pittsburgh - A's	125.00	50.00	12.50
☐ 90 Bill Collins: New York-Newark	125.00	50.00	12.50
☐ 91 Hub Collins: Louisville-Brooklyn	125.00	50.00	12.50
☐ 92A Charles Comiskey: Browns Champs	900.00	360.00	90.00
☐ 92B Commy Comiskey: St. Louis-Chicago	600.00	240.00	60.00
☐ 93 Pete Connell: Des Moines	125.00	50.00	12.50
☐ 94A Roger Connor: All-Star	600.00	240.00	60.00
☐ 94B Roger Connor:	600.00	240.00	60.00

	New York			
☐ 95	Richard Conway:	125.00	50.00	12.50
	Boston-Worchester			
☐ 96	Peter Conway:	125.00	50.00	12.50
	Det.-Pitts.-Ind.			
☐ 97	James Conway: K.C.	125.00	50.00	12.50
☐ 98	Paul Cook:	125.00	50.00	12.50
	Louisville			
☐ 99	Jimmy Cooney:	125.00	50.00	12.50
	Omaha-Chicago			
☐ 100	Larry Corcoran:	125.00	50.00	12.50
	Indianapolis-London			
☐ 101	Pop Corkhill:	125.00	50.00	12.50
	Cincinnati-Brooklyn			
☐ 102	Roscoe Coughlin:	150.00	60.00	15.00
	Maroons-Chicago			
☐ 103	Cannon Ball Crane:	125.00	50.00	12.50
	New York			
☐ 104	Samuel Crane: Wash.	125.00	50.00	12.50
☐ 105	Jack Crogan: Maroons	150.00	60.00	15.00
☐ 106	John Crooks:	125.00	50.00	12.50
	Whites-Omaha			
☐ 107	Lave Cross:	125.00	50.00	12.50
	Louisville-A's-Phila.			
☐ 108	Bill Crossley: Milw.	125.00	50.00	12.50
☐ 109A	Joe Crotty SPOT	400.00	160.00	40.00
☐ 109B	Joe Crotty:	125.00	50.00	12.50
	Sioux City			
☐ 110	Billy Crowell:	125.00	50.00	12.50
	Cleveland-St. Joe			
☐ 111	Jim Cudworth:	125.00	50.00	12.50
	St. Louis-Worchester			
☐ 112	Bert Cunningham:	125.00	50.00	12.50
	Baltimore-Phila.			
☐ 113	Tacks Curtis:	125.00	50.00	12.50
	St. Joe			
☐ 114A	Ed Cushman SPOT	450.00	180.00	45.00
☐ 114B	Ed Cushman:	125.00	50.00	12.50
	Toledo			
☐ 115	Tony Cusick: Mil.	125.00	50.00	12.50
☐ 116	Dailey: Oakland PCL	1250.00	500.00	150.00
☐ 117	Edward Dailey:	125.00	50.00	12.50
	Phil.-Wash.-Columbus			
☐ 118	Bill Daley: Boston	125.00	50.00	12.50
☐ 119	Con Daley:	125.00	50.00	12.50
	Boston-Indianapolis			
☐ 120	Abner Dalrymple:	125.00	50.00	12.50
	Pittsburgh-Denver			
☐ 121	Tom Daly:	125.00	50.00	12.50
	Chicago-Wash.-Cleve.			
☐ 122	James Daly: Minn.	125.00	50.00	12.50
☐ 123	Law Daniels: K.C.	125.00	50.00	12.50
☐ 124	Dell Darling:	125.00	50.00	12.50
	Chicago			
☐ 125	Wm. Darnbrough:	125.00	50.00	12.50
	Denver			
☐ 126	D. Davin: Milwaukee	125.00	50.00	12.50
☐ 127	Jumbo Davis: K.C.	125.00	50.00	12.50
☐ 128	Pat Dealey: Wash.	125.00	50.00	12.50
☐ 129	Thomas Deasley:	125.00	50.00	12.50
	New York-Washington			
☐ 130	Edward Decker: Phil.	125.00	50.00	12.50
☐ 131	Big Ed Delahanty:	1000.00	400.00	125.00
	Philadelphia			
☐ 132	Jeremiah Denny:	125.00	50.00	12.50
	Indianapolis-New York			
☐ 133	James Devlin: St.L.	125.00	50.00	12.50
☐ 134	Thomas Dolan:	125.00	50.00	12.50
	Whites-St. Louis-Denver			
☐ 135	Jack Donahue:	1250.00	500.00	150.00
	San Francisco PCL			
☐ 136A	James Donahue SPOT	400.00	160.00	40.00
☐ 136B	James Donahue: K.C.	125.00	50.00	12.50
☐ 137	James Donnelly:	125.00	50.00	12.50
	Washington			
☐ 138	Dooley: Oakland PCL	1250.00	500.00	150.00
☐ 139	J. Doran: Omaha	125.00	50.00	12.50
☐ 140	Michael Dorgan: N.Y.	125.00	50.00	12.50
☐ 141	Doyle: San Fran. PCL	1250.00	500.00	150.00
☐ 142	Homerun Duffe: St.L.	125.00	50.00	12.50
☐ 143	Hugh Duffy: Chicago	600.00	240.00	60.00
☐ 144	Dan Dugdale:	150.00	60.00	15.00
	Maroons-Minneapolis			
☐ 145	Dugrahm: Maroons	150.00	60.00	15.00
☐ 146	Duck Duke: Minn.	125.00	50.00	12.50
☐ 147	Sure Shot Dunlap:	125.00	50.00	12.50
	Pittsburgh			
☐ 148	J. Dunn: Maroons	150.00	60.00	15.00
☐ 149	Jesse(Cyclone)Duryea	125.00	50.00	12.50
	St. Paul-Cinc.			
☐ 150	John Dwyer:	150.00	60.00	15.00
	Chicago-Maroons			
☐ 151	Billy Earle:	125.00	50.00	12.50
	Cincinnati-St.Paul			
☐ 152	Buck Ebright: Wash.	125.00	50.00	12.50
☐ 153	Red Ehret:	125.00	50.00	12.50
	Louisville			
☐ 154	R. Emmerke:	125.00	50.00	12.50
	Des Moines			
☐ 155	Dude Esterbrook:	125.00	50.00	12.50
	Louisville-Ind.-New York-All Star			
☐ 156	Henry Esterday:	125.00	50.00	12.50
	K.C.-Columbus			
☐ 157	Long John Ewing:	125.00	50.00	12.50
	Louisville-N.Y.			
☐ 158	Buck Ewing: New York	500.00	200.00	50.00
☐ 159	Buck Ewing and Mascot:	400.00	160.00	40.00
	New York			
☐ 160	Jay Faatz: Cleveland	125.00	50.00	12.50
☐ 161	Clinkgers Fagan:	125.00	50.00	12.50
	Kansas City-Denver			
☐ 162	William Farmer:	125.00	50.00	12.50
	Pittsburgh-St. Paul			
☐ 163	Sidney Farrar:	150.00	60.00	15.00
	Philadelphia			
☐ 164	John(Moose) Farrell:	125.00	50.00	12.50
	Wash.-Baltimore			
☐ 165	Charles(Duke)Farrell	125.00	50.00	12.50
	Chicago			
☐ 166	Frank Fennelly:	125.00	50.00	12.50
	Cincinnati-A's			
☐ 167	Chas. Ferguson:	125.00	50.00	12.50
	Phila.			
☐ 168	Colonel Ferson:	125.00	50.00	12.50
	Washington			
☐ 169	Wallace Fessenden:	150.00	60.00	15.00
	Umpire National			
☐ 170	Jocko Fields: Pitts.	125.00	50.00	12.50
☐ 171	Fischer: Maroons	150.00	60.00	15.00
☐ 172	Thomas Flanigan:	125.00	50.00	12.50
	Cleve.-Sioux City			
☐ 173	Silver Flint:	125.00	50.00	12.50
	Chicago			
☐ 174	Thomas Flood:	125.00	50.00	12.50
	St. Joe			
☐ 175	Flynn: Omaha	900.00	360.00	90.00
☐ 176	James Fogarty:	125.00	50.00	12.50
	Philadelphia			
☐ 177	Frank(Monkey)Foreman	125.00	50.00	12.50
	Baltimore-Cinc.			
☐ 178	Thomas Forster:	125.00	50.00	12.50
	Milwaukee-Hartford			
☐ 179A	Elmer E. Foster SPOT	400.00	160.00	40.00
☐ 179B	Elmer Foster:	125.00	50.00	12.50
	New York-Chicago			
☐ 180	F.W. Foster SPOT	450.00	180.00	45.00
	T.W. Forster (Sic)			
☐ 181A	Scissors Foutz:	250.00	100.00	25.00
	Browns Champ			
☐ 181B	Scissors Foutz:	125.00	50.00	12.50
	Brooklyn			
☐ 182	Julie Freeman:	125.00	50.00	12.50
	St.L.-Milwaukee			
☐ 183	Will Fry: St. Joe	125.00	50.00	12.50
☐ 184	Fudger: Oakland PCL	1250.00	500.00	150.00
☐ 185	William Fuller:	125.00	50.00	12.50
	Milwaukee			
☐ 186	Shorty Fuller:	125.00	50.00	12.50
	St.Louis			
☐ 187	Christopher Fullmer:	125.00	50.00	12.50
	Baltimore			
☐ 188	Christopher Fullmer and Tom Tucker:	150.00	60.00	15.00
	Baltimore HOR			
☐ 189	Honest John Gaffney:	150.00	60.00	15.00
	Mgr. Washington			
☐ 190	Pud Galvin: Pitts.	600.00	240.00	60.00
☐ 191	Robert Gamble: A's	125.00	50.00	12.50
☐ 192	Charles Ganzel:	125.00	50.00	12.50
	Detroit-Boston			
☐ 193	Frank(Gid) Gardner:	125.00	50.00	12.50
	Phila.-Washington			
☐ 194	Gid Gardner and Miah Murray:	150.00	60.00	15.00
	Washington HOR			
☐ 195	Ed Gastfield: Omaha	125.00	50.00	12.50
☐ 196	Hank Gastreich:	125.00	50.00	12.50
	Columbus			
☐ 197	Emil Geiss: Chicago	125.00	50.00	12.50
☐ 198	Frenchy Genins:	125.00	50.00	12.50
	Sioux City			

☐ 199 William George: N.Y.	125.00	50.00	12.50
☐ 200 Move Up Joe Gerhardt All Star-Jersey City	125.00	50.00	12.50
☐ 201 Pretzels Getzein: Detroit-Ind.	125.00	50.00	12.50
☐ 202 Lee Gibson: A's	125.00	50.00	12.50
☐ 203 Robert Gilks: Cleve.	125.00	50.00	12.50
☐ 204 Pete Gillespie: N.Y.	125.00	50.00	12.50
☐ 205 Barney Gilligan Washington-Detroit	125.00	50.00	12.50
☐ 206 Frank Gilmore: Wash.	125.00	50.00	12.50
☐ 207 Pebbly Jack Glasscock Indianapolis-N.Y.	150.00	60.00	15.00
☐ 208 Kid Gleason: Phila.	150.00	60.00	15.00
☐ 209A Brother Bill Gleason A's-Louisville	125.00	50.00	12.50
☐ 209B William Bill Gleason Browns Champs	250.00	100.00	25.00
☐ 210 Mouse Glenn: Sioux City	125.00	50.00	12.50
☐ 211 Walt Goldsby: Balt.	125.00	50.00	12.50
☐ 212 Michael Goodfellow: Cleveland-Detroit	125.00	50.00	12.50
☐ 213 George Gore (Pianolegs) New York	125.00	50.00	12.50
☐ 214 Frank Graves: Minn.	125.00	50.00	12.50
☐ 215 William Greenwood: Baltimore-Columbus	125.00	50.00	12.50
☐ 216 Michael Greer: Cleveland-Brooklyn	125.00	50.00	12.50
☐ 217 Mike Griffin: Baltimore-Phila NL	125.00	50.00	12.50
☐ 218 Clark Griffith: Milwaukee	600.00	240.00	60.00
☐ 219 Henry Gruber: Cleve.	125.00	50.00	12.50
☐ 220 Addison Gumbert: Chicago-Boston	125.00	50.00	12.50
☐ 221 Thomas Gunning: Philadelphia-A's	125.00	50.00	12.50
☐ 222 Joseph Gunson: K.C.	125.00	50.00	12.50
☐ 223 George Haddock: Washington	125.00	50.00	12.50
☐ 224 William Hafner: K.C.	125.00	50.00	12.50
☐ 225 Willie Hahm: Chicago Mascot	125.00	50.00	12.50
☐ 226 William Hallman: Philadelphia	125.00	50.00	12.50
☐ 227 Charlie Hallstrom: Minn.	125.00	50.00	12.50
☐ 228 Billy Hamilton: Kansas City-Phila.	600.00	240.00	60.00
☐ 229 Willie Hamm and Ned Williamson: Chicago	150.00	60.00	15.00
☐ 230A Frank Hankinson: SPOT	400.00	160.00	40.00
☐ 230B Frank Hankinson: Kansas City	125.00	50.00	12.50
☐ 231 Ned Hanlon: Det.-Boston-Pitts.	150.00	60.00	15.00
☐ 232 William Hanrahan: Maroons-Minn.	150.00	60.00	15.00
☐ 233 Hapeman: Sacramento PCL	1250.00	500.00	150.00
☐ 234 Pa Harkins: Brooklyn-Baltimore	125.00	50.00	12.50
☐ 235 William Hart: Cinc.-Des Moines	125.00	50.00	12.50
☐ 236 Wm. Hasamdear: K.C.	125.00	50.00	12.50
☐ 237 Colonel Hatfield: New York	125.00	50.00	12.50
☐ 238 Egyptian Healey: Wash.-Indianapolis	125.00	50.00	12.50
☐ 239 J.C. Healy: Omaha-Denver	125.00	50.00	12.50
☐ 240 Guy Hecker: Louisville	125.00	50.00	12.50
☐ 241 Tony Hellman: Sioux City	125.00	50.00	12.50
☐ 242 Hardie Henderson: Brook.-Pitts.-Balt.	125.00	50.00	12.50
☐ 243 Hardie Henderson and Michael Greer: Brooklyn	150.00	60.00	15.00
☐ 244 Moxie Hengle: Maroons-Minneapolis	150.00	60.00	15.00
☐ 245 John Henry: Phila.	125.00	50.00	12.50
☐ 246 Edward Herr: Whites-Milwaukee	125.00	50.00	12.50
☐ 247 Hunkey Hines: Whites	125.00	50.00	12.50
☐ 248 Paul Hines: Wash.-Indianapolis	125.00	50.00	12.50
☐ 249 Texas Wonder Hoffman: Denver	125.00	50.00	12.50
☐ 250 Eddie Hogan: Cleve.	125.00	50.00	12.50
☐ 251A William Holbert SPOT	350.00	140.00	35.00
☐ 251B William Holbert: Brooklyn-Mets-Jersey City	125.00	50.00	12.50
☐ 252 James(Bugs) Holliday: Des Moines-Cinc.	125.00	50.00	12.50
☐ 253 Charles Hoover: Maroons-Chi.-K.C.	150.00	60.00	15.00
☐ 254 Buster Hoover: Phila.-Toronto	125.00	50.00	12.50
☐ 255 Jack Horner: Milwaukee-New Haven	125.00	50.00	12.50
☐ 256 Jack Horner and Warner: Milwaukee	150.00	60.00	15.00
☐ 257 Michael Horning: Boston-Balt.-N.Y.	125.00	50.00	12.50
☐ 258 Pete Hotaling: Cleveland	125.00	50.00	12.50
☐ 259 William Howes: Minn..-St. Paul	125.00	50.00	12.50
☐ 260 Dummy Hoy: Washington	350.00	140.00	35.00
☐ 261A Nat Hudson: Browns Champ	250.00	100.00	25.00
☐ 261B Nat Hudson: St. Louis	125.00	50.00	12.50
☐ 262 Mickey Hughes: Brk.	125.00	50.00	12.50
☐ 263 Hungler: Sioux City	125.00	50.00	12.50
☐ 264 Wild Bill Hutchinson: Chicago	125.00	50.00	12.50
☐ 265 John Irwin: Wash.-Wilkes Barre	125.00	50.00	12.50
☐ 266 Cutrate Irwin: Phila.-Boston-Wash.	125.00	50.00	12.50
☐ 267 A.C. Jantzen: Minn.	125.00	50.00	12.50
☐ 268 Frederick Jevne: Minn.-St. Paul	125.00	50.00	12.50
☐ 269 John Johnson: K.C.-Columbus	125.00	50.00	12.50
☐ 270 Richard Johnston: Boston	125.00	50.00	12.50
☐ 271 Jordan: Minneapolis	125.00	50.00	12.50
☐ 272 Heinie Kappell: Columbus-Cincinnati	125.00	50.00	12.50
☐ 273 Keas: Milwaukee	125.00	50.00	12.50
☐ 274 Sir Timothy Keefe: New York	500.00	200.00	50.00
☐ 275 Tim Keefe and Danny Richardson: Stealing 2nd Base New York HOR	400.00	160.00	40.00
☐ 276 George Keefe: Wash.	125.00	50.00	12.50
☐ 277 James Keenan: Cinc.	125.00	50.00	12.50
☐ 278 Mike(King) Kelly "10,000" Chic-Boston	1000.00	400.00	125.00
☐ 279 Honest John Kelly: Mgr. Louisville	150.00	60.00	15.00
☐ 280 Kelly: (Umpire) Western Association	150.00	60.00	15.00
☐ 281 Charles Kelly: Philadelphia	125.00	50.00	12.50
☐ 282 Kelly and Powell: Umpire and Manager Sioux City	150.00	60.00	15.00
☐ 283A Rudolph Kemmler: Browns Champ	250.00	100.00	25.00
☐ 283B Rudolph Kemmler: St. Paul	125.00	50.00	12.50
☐ 284 Theodore Kennedy: Des Moines-Omaha	150.00	60.00	15.00
☐ 285 J.J. Kenyon: Whites-Des Moines	125.00	50.00	12.50
☐ 286 John Kerins: Louisville	125.00	50.00	12.50
☐ 287 Matthew Kilroy: Baltimore-Boston	125.00	50.00	12.50
☐ 288 Charles King: St.L.-Chi.	125.00	50.00	12.50
☐ 289 Aug. Kloff: Minn.-St.Joe	125.00	50.00	12.50
☐ 290 William Klusman: Milwaukee-Denver	125.00	50.00	12.50
☐ 291 Phillip Knell: St. Joe-Phila.	125.00	50.00	12.50
☐ 292 Fred Knouf: St. Louis	125.00	50.00	12.50
☐ 293 Charles Kremmeyer: Sacramento PCL	1250.00	500.00	150.00

☐ 294 William Krieg: Wash.-St. Joe-Minn.	125.00	50.00	12.50
☐ 295 Krieg and Kloff: Minneapolis	150.00	60.00	15.00
☐ 296 Gus Krock: Chicago	125.00	50.00	12.50
☐ 297 Willie Kuehne: Pittsburgh	125.00	50.00	12.50
☐ 298 Frederick Lange: Maroons	150.00	60.00	15.00
☐ 299 Ted Larkin: A's	125.00	50.00	12.50
☐ 300A Arlie Latham: Browns Champ	250.00	100.00	25.00
☐ 300B Arlie Latham: St. Louis-Chicago	150.00	60.00	15.00
☐ 301 John Lauer: Pittsburgh	125.00	50.00	12.50
☐ 302 Lawless: Columbus	125.00	50.00	12.50
☐ 303 John Leighton: Omaha	125.00	50.00	12.50
☐ 304 Levy: San Fran. PCL	1250.00	500.00	150.00
☐ 305 Tom Loftus MG: Whites-Cleveland	125.00	50.00	12.50
☐ 306 Lohbeck: Cleveland	125.00	50.00	12.50
☐ 307 Herman(Germany)Long Maroons-K.C.	200.00	80.00	20.00
☐ 308 Danny Long: Oak. PCL	1250.00	500.00	150.00
☐ 309 Tom Lovett: Omaha-Brooklyn	125.00	50.00	12.50
☐ 310 Bobby(Link) Lowe: Milwaukee	200.00	80.00	20.00
☐ 311A Jack Lynch SPOT	450.00	180.00	45.00
☐ 311B John Lynch: All Stars	125.00	50.00	12.50
☐ 312 Dennis Lyons: A's	125.00	50.00	12.50
☐ 313 Harry Lyons: St. L.	125.00	50.00	12.50
☐ 314 Connie Mack: Wash.	1500.00	600.00	200.00
☐ 315 Joe(Reddie) Mack: Louisville	125.00	50.00	12.50
☐ 316 James(Little Mack) Macullar: Des Moines-Milwaukee	125.00	50.00	12.50
☐ 317 Kid Madden: Boston	125.00	50.00	12.50
☐ 318 Daniel Mahoney: St. Joe	125.00	50.00	12.50
☐ 319 Willard(Grasshopper) Maines: St. Paul	125.00	50.00	12.50
☐ 320 Fred Mann: St.Louis-Hartford	125.00	50.00	12.50
☐ 321 Jimmy Manning: K.C.	125.00	50.00	12.50
☐ 322 Charles(Lefty) Marr: Col.-Cinc.	125.00	50.00	12.50
☐ 323 Mascot(Willie Breslin): New York	150.00	60.00	15.00
☐ 324 Samuel Maskery: Milwaukee-Des Moines	125.00		12.50
☐ 325 Bobby Mathews: A's	125.00	50.00	12.50
☐ 326 Michael Mattimore: New York-A's	125.00	50.00	12.50
☐ 327 Albert Maul: Pitts.	125.00	50.00	12.50
☐ 328A Albert Mays SPOT	350.00	140.00	35.00
☐ 328B Albert Mays: Columbus	125.00	50.00	12.50
☐ 329 James McAleer: Cleveland	125.00	50.00	12.50
☐ 330 Thomas McCarthy: Phila.-St. Louis	500.00	200.00	50.00
☐ 331 John McCarthy: K.C.	125.00	50.00	12.50
☐ 332 James McCauley: Maroons-Phila.	150.00	60.00	15.00
☐ 333 William McClellan: Brooklyn-Denver	125.00	50.00	12.50
☐ 334 John McCormack: Whites	125.00	50.00	12.50
☐ 335 Big Jim McCormick: Chicago-Pittsburgh	125.00	50.00	12.50
☐ 336 McCreachery: Mgr. Indianapolis	150.00	60.00	15.00
☐ 337 Thomas McCullum: Minneapolis	125.00	50.00	12.50
☐ 338 James(Chippy)McGarr: St. Louis-K.C.	125.00	50.00	12.50
☐ 339 Jack McGeachy: Ind.	125.00	50.00	12.50
☐ 340 John McGlone: Cleveland-Detroit	125.00	50.00	12.50
☐ 341 James(Deacon)McGuire Phila.-Toronto	125.00	50.00	12.50
☐ 342 Bill(Gunner) McGunnigle: Mgr. Brooklyn	150.00	60.00	15.00
☐ 343 Ed McKean: Cleveland	125.00	50.00	12.50
☐ 344 Alex McKinnon: Pittsburgh	125.00	50.00	12.50
☐ 345 Thomas McLaughlin SPOT	400.00	160.00	40.00

☐ 346 John(Bid) McPhee: Cincinnati	150.00	60.00	15.00
☐ 347 James McQuaid: Denver	125.00	50.00	12.50
☐ 348 John McQuaid: Umpire Amer. Assoc.	150.00	60.00	15.00
☐ 349 Jame McTamany: Brook.-Col.-K.C.	125.00	50.00	12.50
☐ 350 George McVey: Mil.-Denver-St. Joe	125.00	50.00	12.50
☐ 351 Meegan: San Fran. PCL	1250.00	500.00	150.00
☐ 352 John Messitt: Omaha	125.00	50.00	12.50
☐ 353 George(Doggie)Miller Pittsburgh	125.00	50.00	12.50
☐ 354 Joseph Miller: Omaha-Minneapolis	125.00	50.00	12.50
☐ 355 Jocko Milligan: St. Louis-Phila.	125.00	50.00	12.50
☐ 356 E.L. Mills: Milwaukee	125.00	50.00	12.50
☐ 357 Minnehan: Minneapolis	125.00	50.00	12.50
☐ 358 Samuel Moffet: Ind.	125.00	50.00	12.50
☐ 359 Honest Morrill: Boston-Washington	125.00	50.00	12.50
☐ 360 Ed Morris (Cannonball): Pittsburgh	125.00	50.00	12.50
☐ 361 Morrisey: St. Paul	125.00	50.00	12.50
☐ 362 Tony(Count) Mullane: Cincinnati	150.00	60.00	15.00
☐ 363 Joseph Mulvey: Philadelphia	125.00	50.00	12.50
☐ 364 P.L. Murphy: St. Paul	125.00	50.00	12.50
☐ 365 Pat J. Murphy: New York	125.00	50.00	12.50
☐ 366 Miah Murray: Wash.	125.00	50.00	12.50
☐ 367 James(Truthful) Mutrie: Mgr. N.Y.	125.00	50.00	12.50
☐ 368 George Myers: Indianapolis-Phila.	125.00	50.00	12.50
☐ 369 Al(Cod) Myers: Washington	125.00	50.00	12.50
☐ 370 Thomas Nagle: Omaha-Chi.	125.00	50.00	12.50
☐ 371 Billy Nash: Boston	125.00	50.00	12.50
☐ 372 Jack(Candy) Nelson: SPOT	400.00	160.00	40.00
☐ 373 Kid Nichols: Omaha	750.00	300.00	75.00
☐ 374 Samuel Nichols: Pittsburgh	125.00	50.00	12.50
☐ 375 J.W. Nicholson Maroons-Minn.	150.00	60.00	15.00
☐ 376 Tom Nicholson (Parson) Whites-Cleveland	125.00	50.00	12.50
☐ 377A Nicholls Nicol Browns Champ	250.00	100.00	25.00
☐ 377B Hugh Nicol: Cinc.	125.00	50.00	12.50
☐ 378 Hugh Nicol and Long John Reilly: Cincinnati	150.00	60.00	15.00
☐ 379 Frederick Nyce Whites-Burlington	125.00	50.00	12.50
☐ 380 Doc Oberlander Cleveland-Syracuse	125.00	50.00	12.50
☐ 381 Jack O'Brien Brooklyn-Baltimore	125.00	50.00	12.50
☐ 382 William O'Brien: Washington	125.00	50.00	12.50
☐ 383 William O'Brien and John Irwin: Washington	150.00	60.00	15.00
☐ 384 Darby O'Brien: Brooklyn	125.00	50.00	12.50
☐ 385 John O'Brien: Cleve.	125.00	50.00	12.50
☐ 386 P.J. O'Connell: Omaha-Des Moines	125.00	50.00	12.50
☐ 387 John O'Connor: Cincinnati-Columbus	125.00	50.00	12.50
☐ 388 Hank O'Day: Washington-New York	150.00	60.00	15.00
☐ 389A James O'Neil: St. Louis-Chicago	125.00	50.00	12.50
☐ 389B James O'Neil: Browns Champs	250.00	100.00	25.00
☐ 390 O'Neill: Oakland PCL	1250.00	500.00	150.00
☐ 391 Orator O'Rourke: New York	600.00	240.00	60.00
☐ 392 Thomas O'Rourke: Boston-Jersey City	125.00	50.00	12.50

☐	393A	David Orr SPOT	350.00	140.00	35.00
☐	393B	David Orr: All Star-Brooklyn-Columbus	125.00	50.00	12.50
☐	394	Parsons: Minneapolis	125.00	50.00	12.50
☐	395	Owen Patton: Minn.-Des Moines	125.00	50.00	12.50
☐	396	James Peeples: Brooklyn-Columbus	125.00	50.00	12.50
☐	397	James Peeples and Hardie Henderson: Brooklyn	150.00	60.00	15.00
☐	398	Hip Perrier: San Francisco PCL	1250.00	500.00	150.00
☐	399	Patrick Pettee: Milwaukee-London	125.00	50.00	12.50
☐	400	Patrick Pettee and Bobby Lowe: Milwaukee	150.00	60.00	15.00
☐	401	Bob Pettit: Chicago	125.00	50.00	12.50
☐	402	Dandelion Pfeffer: Chi.	125.00	50.00	12.50
☐	403	Dick Phelan: Des Moines	125.00	50.00	12.50
☐	404	William Phillips: Brooklyn-Kansas City	125.00	50.00	12.50
☐	405	Horace Phillips: Pittsburgh	125.00	50.00	12.50
☐	406	John Pickett: St. Paul-K.C.-Phila.	125.00	50.00	12.50
☐	407	George Pinkney: Brooklyn	125.00	50.00	12.50
☐	408	Thomas Poorman: A's-Milwaukee	125.00	50.00	12.50
☐	409	Henry Porter: Brooklyn-Kansas City	125.00	50.00	12.50
☐	410	James Powell: Sioux City	125.00	50.00	12.50
☐	411	Tom Powers: San Francisco PCL	1250.00	500.00	150.00
☐	412	Bill Purcell: (Blondie) Baltimore-A's	125.00	50.00	12.50
☐	413	Thomas Quinn: Baltimore	125.00	50.00	12.50
☐	414	Joseph Quinn: Des Moines-Boston	125.00	50.00	12.50
☐	415A	Old Hoss Radbourne: Boston (Portrait)	900.00	360.00	90.00
☐	415B	Old Hoss Radbourne: Boston (Non-portrait)	600.00	240.00	60.00
☐	416	Shorty Radford: Brooklyn-Cleveland	125.00	50.00	12.50
☐	417	Tom Ramsey: Louisville	125.00	50.00	12.50
☐	418	Rehse: Minneapolis	125.00	50.00	12.50
☐	419	Long John Reilly: Cincinnati	125.00	50.00	12.50
☐	420	Charles Reilly: (Princeton) St.Paul	125.00	50.00	12.50
☐	421	Charles Reynolds: Kansas City	125.00	50.00	12.50
☐	422	Hardie Richardson Detroit-Boston	125.00	50.00	12.50
☐	423	Danny Richardson: New York	125.00	50.00	12.50
☐	424	Frank Ringo: St. Paul	125.00	50.00	12.50
☐	425	Charles Ripslager SPOT	400.00	160.00	40.00
☐	426	John Roach: New York	125.00	50.00	12.50
☐	427	Wilbert Robinson (Uncle Robbie): A's	600.00	240.00	60.00
☐	428	M.C. Robinson: Minn.	125.00	50.00	12.50
☐	429A	Yank Robinson: St. Louis	125.00	50.00	12.50
☐	429B	Wm.(Yank) Robinson: Browns Champs	250.00	100.00	25.00
☐	430	George Rooks: Maroons-Detroit	150.00	60.00	15.00
☐	431	James(Chief) Roseman SPOT	400.00	160.00	40.00
☐	432	Davis Rowe: Mgr. K.C.-Denver	125.00	50.00	12.50
☐	433	Jack Rowe: Detroit-Pittsburgh	125.00	50.00	12.50
☐	434	Amos(Hoosier Thunderbolt) Rusie: Ind.-New York	900.00	360.00	90.00
☐	435	James Ryan: Chicago	150.00	60.00	15.00
☐	436	Henry Sage: Des Moines-Toledo	125.00	50.00	12.50
☐	437	Henry Sage and William Van Dyke: Des Moines-Toledo	150.00	60.00	15.00
☐	438	Frank Salee Omaha-Boston	125.00	50.00	12.50
☐	439	Sanders: Omaha	125.00	50.00	12.50
☐	440	Al(Ben) Sanders: Philadelphia	125.00	50.00	12.50
☐	441	Frank Scheibeck: Detroit	125.00	50.00	12.50
☐	442	Albert Schellhase: St. Joseph	125.00	50.00	12.50
☐	443	William Schenkle: Milwaukee	125.00	50.00	12.50
☐	444	Bill Schildknecht: Des Moines-Milwaukee	125.00	50.00	12.50
☐	445	Gus(Pink Whiskers) Schmelz Mgr. Cincinnati	125.00	50.00	12.50
☐	446	R. F. Schoch: Wash.	125.00	50.00	12.50
☐	447	Lewis Schoeneck (Jumbo): Maroons-Indianapolis	150.00	60.00	15.00
☐	448	Pop Schriver: Phila.	125.00	50.00	12.50
☐	449	John Seery: Ind.	125.00	50.00	12.50
☐	450	William Serad Cincinnnati-Toronto	125.00	50.00	12.50
☐	451	Edward Seward: A's	125.00	50.00	12.50
☐	452	George(Orator)Shafer Des Moines	125.00	50.00	12.50
☐	453	Frank Shafer: St. Paul	125.00	50.00	12.50
☐	454	Daniel Shannon: Omaha-L'ville-Phila.	125.00	50.00	12.50
☐	455	William Sharsig: Mgr. Athletics	150.00	60.00	15.00
☐	456	Samuel Shaw: Baltimore-Newark	125.00	50.00	12.50
☐	457	John Shaw: Minneapolis	125.00	50.00	12.50
☐	458	William Shindle: Baltimore-Phila.	125.00	50.00	12.50
☐	459	George Shock: Wash.	125.00	50.00	12.50
☐	460	Otto Shomberg: Ind.	125.00	50.00	12.50
☐	461	Lev Shreve: Ind.	125.00	50.00	12.50
☐	462	Ed(Baldy) Silch: Brooklyn-Denver	125.00	50.00	12.50
☐	463	Michael Slattery: New York	125.00	50.00	12.50
☐	464	Sam(Skyrocket)Smith: Louisville	125.00	50.00	12.50
☐	465A	John(Phenomenal) Smith (Portrait)	750.00	300.00	75.00
☐	465B	John(Phenomenal) Smith: Balt.-A's (Non-portrait)	150.00	60.00	15.00
☐	466	Elmer Smith: Cincinnati	125.00	50.00	12.50
☐	467	Fred(Sam) Smith: Des Moines	125.00	50.00	12.50
☐	468	George Smith (Germany) Brooklyn	125.00	50.00	12.50
☐	469	Pop Smith: Pitt.-Bos.-Phila.	125.00	50.00	12.50
☐	470	Nick Smith: St. Joe	125.00	50.00	12.50
☐	471	Pop Snyder: Cleve.	125.00	50.00	12.50
☐	472	P.T. Somers: St. Louis	125.00	50.00	12.50
☐	473	Joe Sommer: Balt.	125.00	50.00	12.50
☐	474	Pete Sommers: Chicago-New York	125.00	50.00	12.50
☐	475	William Sowders: Boston-Pittsburgh	125.00	50.00	12.50
☐	476	John Sowders: St. Paul-Kansas City	125.00	50.00	12.50
☐	477	Charles Sprague: Maroons-Chi.-Cleve.	150.00	60.00	15.00
☐	478	Edward Sproat: Whites	125.00	50.00	12.50
☐	479	Harry Staley: Whites-Pittsburgh	125.00	50.00	12.50
☐	480	Daniel Stearns: Des Moines-K.C.	125.00	50.00	12.50
☐	481	Billy(Cannonball) Stemmyer: Boston-Cleveland	125.00	50.00	12.50
☐	482	Stengel: Columbus	125.00	50.00	12.50
☐	483	B.F. Stephens: Milw.	125.00	50.00	12.50
☐	484	John C. Sterling: Minneapolis	125.00	50.00	12.50
☐	485	Stockwell: S.F. PCL	1250.00	500.00	150.00
☐	486	Harry Stovey:	300.00	120.00	30.00

A's-Boston

☐	487 C. Scott Stratton: Louisville	125.00	50.00	12.50
☐	488 Joseph Straus: Omaha-Milwaukee	125.00	50.00	12.50
☐	489 John(Cub) Stricker: Cleveland	125.00	50.00	12.50
☐	490 J.O. Struck: Milw	125.00	50.00	12.50
☐	491 Marty Sullivan: Chicago-Ind.	125.00	50.00	12.50
☐	492 Michael Sullivan: A's	125.00	50.00	12.50
☐	493 Billy Sunday: Chicago-Pittsburgh	600.00	240.00	60.00
☐	494 Sy Sutcliffe: Cleve.	125.00	50.00	12.50
☐	495 Ezra Sutton: Boston-Milwaukee	125.00	50.00	12.50
☐	496 Ed Cyrus Swartwood: Brook.-D.Moines-Ham.	125.00	50.00	12.50
☐	497 Parke Swartzel: K.C.	125.00	50.00	12.50
☐	498 Peter Sweeney: Wash.	125.00	50.00	12.50
☐	499 Sylvester: Sacra. PCL	1250.00	500.00	150.00
☐	500 Ed(Dimples) Tate: Boston-Baltimore	125.00	50.00	12.50
☐	501 Patsy Tebeau: Chi.-Cleve.-Minn.	125.00	50.00	12.50
☐	502 John Tener: Chicago	150.00	60.00	15.00
☐	503 Bill(Adonis) Terry: Brooklyn	125.00	50.00	12.50
☐	504 Big Sam Thompson: Detroit-Philadelphia	500.00	200.00	50.00
☐	505 Silent Mike Tiernan: New York	125.00	50.00	12.50
☐	506 Ledell Titcomb: N.Y.	125.00	50.00	12.50
☐	507 Phillip Tomney: Louisville	125.00	50.00	12.50
☐	508 Stephen Toole: Brooklyn-K.C.-Rochester	125.00	50.00	12.50
☐	509 George Townsend: A's	125.00	50.00	12.50
☐	510 William Traffley: Des Moines	125.00	50.00	12.50
☐	511 George Treadway: St. Paul-Denver	125.00	50.00	12.50
☐	512 Samuel Trott: Baltimore-Newark	125.00	50.00	12.50
☐	513 Sam Trott and Tommy(Oyster) Burns: Baltimore HOR	150.00	60.00	15.00
☐	514 Tom(Foghorn) Tucker: Baltimore	125.00	50.00	12.50
☐	515 William Tuckerman: St. Paul	125.00	50.00	12.50
☐	516 Turner: Minneapolis	125.00	50.00	12.50
☐	517 Lawrence Twitchell: Detroit-Cleveland	125.00	50.00	12.50
☐	518 James Tyng: Phila.	125.00	50.00	12.50
☐	519 William Van Dyke: Des Moines-Toledo	125.00	50.00	12.50
☐	520 George(Rip) VanHaltren Chicago	125.00	50.00	12.50
☐	521 Harry Vaughn: (Farmer) Louisville-New York	125.00	50.00	12.50
☐	522 Peek-a-Boo Veach: St. Paul	300.00	120.00	30.00
☐	523 Veach: Sacra. PCL	1250.00	500.00	150.00
☐	524 Leon Viau: Cincinnati	125.00	50.00	12.50
☐	525 William Vinton: Minneapolis	125.00	50.00	12.50
☐	526 Joseph Visner: Brooklyn	125.00	50.00	12.50
☐	527 Christian VonDer Ahe Owner Browns Champs	350.00	140.00	35.00
☐	528 Joseph Walsh: Omaha	125.00	50.00	12.50
☐	529 John(Monte) Ward: New York	500.00	200.00	50.00
☐	530 E.H. Warner: Milwaukee	300.00	120.00	30.00
☐	531 William Watkins: Mgr. Detroit-Kansas City	150.00	60.00	15.00
☐	532 Bill Weaver: (Farmer) Louisville	125.00	50.00	12.50
☐	533 Charles Weber: Sioux City	125.00	50.00	12.50
☐	534 George Weidman (Stump): Detroit-New York	125.00	50.00	12.50
☐	535 William Weidner: Columbus	125.00	50.00	12.50
☐	536A Curtis Welch: Browns Champ	250.00	100.00	25.00
☐	536B Curtis Welch: A's	125.00	50.00	12.50
☐	537 Welch and Gleason: Athletics	150.00	60.00	15.00
☐	538 Smilin'Mickey Welch: All Star-New York	600.00	240.00	60.00
☐	539 Jake Wells: K.C.	125.00	50.00	12.50
☐	540 Frank Wells: Des Moines-Mil.	150.00	60.00	15.00
☐	541 Joseph Werrick: Louisville-St. Paul	125.00	50.00	12.50
☐	542 Milton(Buck) West: Minneapolis	125.00	50.00	12.50
☐	543 Gus(Cannonball) Weyhing: A's	125.00	50.00	12.50
☐	544 John Weyhing: Athletics-Columbus	125.00	50.00	12.50
☐	545 Bobby Wheelock: Boston-Detroit	125.00	50.00	12.50
☐	546 Whitacre: A's	125.00	50.00	12.50
☐	547 Pat Whitaker: Balt.	125.00	50.00	12.50
☐	548 Deacon White: Detroit-Pittsburgh	125.00	50.00	12.50
☐	549 William White: Louisville	125.00	50.00	12.50
☐	550 Jim(Grasshopper) Whitney: Wash.-Indianapolis	125.00	50.00	12.50
☐	551 Arthur Whitney: Pittsburgh-New York	125.00	50.00	12.50
☐	552 G. Whitney: St. Joseph	125.00	50.00	12.50
☐	553 James Williams: Mgr. Cleveland	150.00	60.00	15.00
☐	554 Ned Williamson: Chi.	150.00	60.00	15.00
☐	555 Williamson and Mascot	150.00	60.00	15.00
☐	556 C.H. Willis: Omaha	125.00	50.00	12.50
☐	557 Walt Wilmot: Washington-Chicago	125.00	50.00	12.50
☐	558 George Winkleman: Minneapolis-Hartford	125.00	50.00	12.50
☐	559 Samuel Wise: Boston-Washington	125.00	50.00	12.50
☐	560 William Wolf (Chicken) Louisville	125.00	50.00	12.50
☐	561 George(Dandy) Wood: Philadelphia	125.00	50.00	12.50
☐	562 Peter Wood: Phila.	125.00	50.00	12.50
☐	563 Harry Wright: Mgr. Philadelphia	1500.00	600.00	200.00
☐	564 Charles Zimmer (Chief) Cleveland	125.00	50.00	12.50
☐	565 Frank Zinn: Athletics	125.00	50.00	12.50

N184 Kimball's

This set of 50 color pictures of contemporary athletes was Kimball's answer to the sets produced by Allen , Ginter (N28 and N29) and Goodwin (N162). Issued in 1888, the cards are backlisted but are not numbered. The cards are listed below in alphabetical order without regard to sport. There are four baseball players in the set. An album (ACC: A42) was offered as a premium in exchange for coupons found in the tobacco packages. The baseball players are noted in the checklist below by BB after their name; boxers are noted by BOX.

	EX-MT	VG-E	GOOD
COMPLETE SET (50)	5500.00	2250.00	700.00
COMMON BASEBALL	600.00	240.00	60.00
COMMON BOXER	200.00	80.00	20.00
COMMON OTHERS	50.00	20.00	5.00
☐ 1 Wm. Beach	50.00	20.00	5.00
☐ 2 Marve Beardsley	50.00	20.00	5.00
☐ 3 Chas. P. Blatt	50.00	20.00	5.00
☐ 4 Blondin	60.00	24.00	6.00
☐ 5 Paul Boynton	50.00	20.00	5.00
☐ 6 E.A.(Ernie) Burch BB	600.00	240.00	60.00
☐ 7 Patsy Cardiff	50.00	20.00	5.00
☐ 8 Phillip Casey	50.00	20.00	5.00
☐ 9 J.C. Cockburn	50.00	20.00	5.00
☐ 10 Dell Darling BB	600.00	240.00	60.00
☐ 11 Jack Dempsey BOX	300.00	120.00	30.00
☐ 12 Della Ferrell	50.00	20.00	5.00
☐ 13 Clarence Freeman	50.00	20.00	5.00
☐ 14 Louis George	50.00	20.00	5.00
☐ 15 W.G. George	50.00	20.00	5.00
☐ 16 George W. Hamilton	50.00	20.00	5.00
☐ 17 Edward Hanlan	60.00	24.00	6.00
☐ 18 C.H. Heins	50.00	20.00	5.00
☐ 19 Hardie Henderson BB	600.00	240.00	60.00
☐ 20 Thomas H. Hume	50.00	20.00	5.00
☐ 21 J.H. Jordon	50.00	20.00	5.00
☐ 22 Johnny Kane	50.00	20.00	5.00
☐ 23 James McLaughlin	50.00	20.00	5.00
☐ 24 John McPherson	50.00	20.00	5.00
☐ 25 Joseph Morsler	50.00	20.00	5.00
☐ 26 William Muldoon	75.00	30.00	7.50
☐ 27 S. Muller	50.00	20.00	5.00
☐ 28 Isaac Murphy	60.00	24.00	6.00
☐ 29 John Murphy	50.00	20.00	5.00
☐ 30 L.E. Myers	50.00	20.00	5.00
☐ 31 Annie Oakley	150.00	60.00	15.00
☐ 32 Daniel O'Leary	50.00	20.00	5.00
☐ 33 James O'Neil BB	700.00	280.00	70.00
☐ 34 Wm. Byrd Page	50.00	20.00	5.00
☐ 35 Axel Paulsen	50.00	20.00	5.00
☐ 36 Master Ray Perry	50.00	20.00	5.00
☐ 37 Duncan C. Ross	50.00	20.00	5.00
☐ 38 W.A. Rowe	50.00	20.00	5.00
☐ 39 Jacob Schaefer	50.00	20.00	5.00
☐ 40 M. Schloss	50.00	20.00	5.00
☐ 41 Jem Smith	50.00	20.00	5.00
☐ 42 Lillian Smith	50.00	20.00	5.00
☐ 43 Hattie Stewart	50.00	20.00	5.00
☐ 44 John L. Sullivan BOX	350.00	140.00	35.00
☐ 45 Arthur Wallace	50.00	20.00	5.00
☐ 46 Tommy Warren BOX	200.00	80.00	20.00
☐ 47 Ada Webb	50.00	20.00	5.00
☐ 48 John Wessels	50.00	20.00	5.00
☐ 49 Clarence Whistler	50.00	20.00	5.00
☐ 50 Charles Wood	50.00	20.00	5.00

N284 Buchner

The baseball players found in this Buchner set are a part of a larger group of cards portraying policemen, jockeys and actors, all of which were issued with the tobacco brand "Gold Coin." The set is comprised of three major groupings or types. In the first type, nine players from eight teams, plus three Brooklyn players, are all portrayed in identical poses according to position. In the second type, St. Louis has 14 players depicted in poses which are not repeated. The last group contains 53 additional cards which vary according to pose, team change, spelling, etc. These third type cards are indicated in the checklist below by an asterisk. In all, there are 116 individuals portrayed on 142 cards. The existence of an additional player in the set, McClellan of Brooklyn, has never been verified. The set was issued circa 1887. The cards are numbered below in

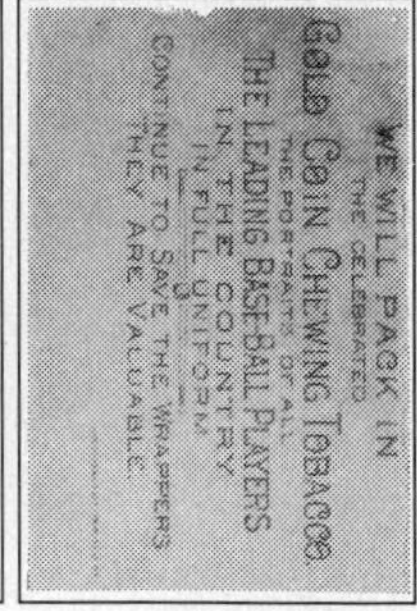

alphabetical order within team with teams themselves listed in alphabetical order: Baltimore (1-4), Boston (5-13), Brooklyn (14-17), Chicago (18-26), Detroit (27-35), Indianapolis (36-47), LaCrosse (48-51), Milwaukee (52-55), New York Mets (56-63), New York (64-73), Philadelphia (74-83), Pittsburg (84-92), St. Louis (93-106), and Washington (107-117).

	EX-MT	VG-E	GOOD
COMPLETE SET (152)	15000.	6000.00	2000.00
COMMON PLAYERS	70.00	28.00	7.00
COMMON ST. LOUIS	90.00	36.00	9.00
COMMON PLAYERS *	90.00	36.00	9.00
☐ 1 Tommy(Oyster) Burns: Baltimore *	90.00	36.00	9.00
☐ 2 Chris Fulmer: Baltimore *	90.00	36.00	9.00
☐ 3 Matt Kilroy: Baltimore *	90.00	36.00	9.00
☐ 4 Blondie Purcell: Baltimore *	90.00	36.00	9.00
☐ 5 John Burdock: Boston	70.00	28.00	7.00
☐ 6 Bill Daley: Boston	70.00	28.00	7.00
☐ 7 Joe Hornung: Boston	70.00	28.00	7.00
☐ 8 Dick Johnston: Boston	70.00	28.00	7.00
☐ 9A King Kelly: Boston (Right field)	200.00	80.00	20.00
☐ 9B King Kelly: Boston (Catcher) *	250.00	100.00	25.00
☐ 10A John Morrill: Boston (Both hands outstretched face high)	70.00	28.00	7.00
☐ 10B John Morrill: Boston * (Hands clasped near chin)	90.00	36.00	9.00
☐ 11A Hoss Radbourn: Boston (Sic, Radbourne)	150.00	60.00	15.00
☐ 11B Hoss Radbourn: Boston * (Sic, Radbourne; hands together above waist)	250.00	100.00	25.00
☐ 12 Ezra Sutton: Boston	70.00	28.00	7.00
☐ 13 Sam Wise: Boston	70.00	28.00	7.00
☐ 14 Bill McClellan: Brooklyn (Never confirmed)	0.00	0.00	0.00
☐ 15 Jimmy Peoples: Brooklyn	70.00	28.00	7.00
☐ 16 Bill Phillips: Brooklyn	70.00	28.00	7.00
☐ 17 Henry Porter: Brooklyn	70.00	28.00	7.00
☐ 18A Adrian Anson: Chicago (Both hands outstretched face high)	325.00	130.00	32.00
☐ 18B Adrian Anson: Chicago * (Left hand on hip, right hand down)	500.00	200.00	50.00
☐ 19 Tom Burns: Chicago	70.00	28.00	7.00
☐ 20A John Clarkson: Chicago	150.00	60.00	15.00
☐ 20B John Clarkson: Chicago *	250.00	100.00	25.00

(Right arm extended, left arm near side)			
☐ 21 Silver Flint: Chicago	70.00	28.00	7.00
☐ 22 Fred Pfeffer: Chicago	70.00	28.00	7.00
☐ 23 Jimmy Ryan: Chicago	90.00	36.00	9.00
☐ 24 Billy Sullivan: Chicago	90.00	36.00	9.00
☐ 25 Billy Sunday: Chicago	175.00	70.00	18.00
☐ 26A Ned Williamson: Chicago (Shortstop)	70.00	28.00	7.00
☐ 26B Ned Williamson: Chicago (Second base) *	90.00	36.00	9.00
☐ 27 Charlie Bennett: Detroit	70.00	28.00	7.00
☐ 28A Dan Brouthers: Detroit (Fielding)	150.00	60.00	15.00
☐ 28B Dan Brouthers: Detroit * (Batting)	250.00	100.00	25.00
☐ 29 Fred Dunlap: Detroit	70.00	28.00	7.00
☐ 30 Charlie Getzien: Detroit	70.00	28.00	7.00
☐ 31 Ned Hanlon: Detroit	80.00	32.00	8.00
☐ 32 Jim Manning: Detoit	70.00	28.00	7.00
☐ 33A Hardy Richardson: Detroit (Hands together in front of chest)	70.00	28.00	7.00
☐ 33B Hardy Richardson: Detroit * (Right hand holding ball above head)	90.00	36.00	9.00
☐ 34A Sam Thompson: Detroit (Looking up with hands at waist)	150.00	60.00	15.00
☐ 34B Sam Thompson: Detroit * (Hands chest high)	250.00	100.00	25.00
☐ 35 Deacon White: Detroit	90.00	36.00	9.00
☐ 36 Tug Arundel: Indianapolis	70.00	28.00	7.00
☐ 37 Charley Bassett: Indianapolis	70.00	28.00	7.00
☐ 38 Henry Boyle: Indianapolis *	70.00	28.00	7.00
☐ 39 John Cahill: Indianapolis *	90.00	36.00	9.00
☐ 40A Jerry Denny: Indianapolis (Hands on knees, legs bent)	70.00	28.00	7.00
☐ 40B Jerry Denny: Indianapolis * (Hands on knees, legs not bent)	90.00	36.00	9.00
☐ 41A Jack Glasscock: Indianapolis (Crouching, catching a grounder)	90.00	36.00	9.00
☐ 41B Jack Glasscock: Indianapolis * (Hands on knees)	125.00	50.00	12.50
☐ 42 John Healy: Indianapolis	70.00	28.00	7.00
☐ 43 George Meyers: Indianapolis *	90.00	36.00	9.00
☐ 44 Jack McGeachy: Indianapolis	70.00	28.00	7.00
☐ 45 Mark Polhemus: Indianapolis	70.00	28.00	7.00
☐ 46A Emmett Seery: Indianapolis (Hands together in front of chest)	70.00	28.00	7.00
☐ 46B Emmett Seery: Indianapolis * (Hands outstretched head high)	90.00	36.00	9.00
☐ 47 Shomberg: Indianapolis	70.00	28.00	7.00
☐ 48 Corbett: LaCrosse *	90.00	36.00	9.00
☐ 49 Crowley: LaCrosse *	90.00	36.00	9.00
☐ 50 Kennedy: LaCrosse *	90.00	36.00	9.00
☐ 51 Rooks: LaCrosse *	90.00	36.00	9.00
☐ 52 Forster: Milwaukee *	90.00	36.00	9.00
☐ 53 Hart: Milwaukee *	90.00	36.00	9.00
☐ 54 Morrissy: Milwaukee *	90.00	36.00	9.00
☐ 55 Strauss: Milwaukee *	90.00	36.00	9.00
☐ 56 Ed Cushmann: NY Mets *	90.00	36.00	9.00
☐ 57 Jim Donohue: NY Mets *	90.00	36.00	9.00
☐ 58 Dude Esterbrooke (Sic): NY Mets *	90.00	36.00	9.00
☐ 59 Joe Gerhardt: NY Mets *	90.00	36.00	9.00
☐ 60 Frank Hankinson: NY Mets *	90.00	36.00	9.00
☐ 61 Jack Nelson: NY Mets *	90.00	36.00	9.00
☐ 62 Dave Orr: NY Mets *	90.00	36.00	9.00
☐ 63 James Rosemann: NY Mets *	90.00	36.00	9.00
☐ 64A Roger Connor: New York (Both hands outstretched face high)	150.00	60.00	15.00
☐ 64B Roger Connor: New York * (Hands outstretched, palms up)	250.00	100.00	25.00
☐ 65 Pat Deasley: New York *	90.00	36.00	9.00
☐ 66A Mike Dorgan: New York (Fielding)	70.00	28.00	7.00
☐ 66B Mike Dorgan: New York (Batting) *	90.00	36.00	9.00
☐ 67A Buck Ewing: New York (Ball in left hand, right arm out shoulder high)	150.00	60.00	15.00
☐ 67B Buck Ewing: New York * (Appears ready to clap)	250.00	100.00	25.00
☐ 68A Pete Gillespie: New York (Fielding)	70.00	28.00	7.00
☐ 68B Pete Gillespie: New York (Batting) *	90.00	36.00	9.00
☐ 69 George Gore: New York	70.00	28.00	7.00
☐ 70A Tim Keefe: New York	150.00	60.00	15.00
☐ 70B Tim Keefe: New York * (Ball just released from right hand)	250.00	100.00	25.00
☐ 71A Jim O'Rourke: New York (Hands cupped in front, thigh high)	150.00	60.00	15.00
☐ 71B Jim O'Rourke: New York * (Hands on knees, looking right)	250.00	100.00	25.00
☐ 72A Danny Richardson: New York (Third base)	70.00	28.00	7.00
☐ 72B Danny Richardson: New York (Second base) *	90.00	36.00	9.00
☐ 73A John M. Ward: New York (Crouching, catching a grounder)	150.00	60.00	15.00
☐ 73B John M. Ward: New York * (Hands by left knee)	250.00	100.00	25.00
☐ 73C John M. Ward: New York * (Hands on knees)	250.00	100.00	25.00
☐ 74A Ed Andrews: Philadelphia (Hands together in front of neck)	70.00	28.00	7.00
☐ 74B Ed Andrews: Philadelphia * (Catching, hands waist high)	90.00	36.00	9.00
☐ 75 Charlie Bastian: Philadelphia	70.00	28.00	7.00
☐ 76 Dan Casey: Philadelphia *	90.00	36.00	9.00
☐ 77 Jack Clements: Philadelphia	70.00	28.00	7.00
☐ 78 Sid Farrar: Philadelphia	90.00	36.00	9.00
☐ 79 Charlie Ferguson: Philadelphia	70.00	28.00	7.00
☐ 80 Jim Fogarty: Philadelphia	70.00	28.00	7.00
☐ 81 Arthur Irwin:	70.00	28.00	7.00

Philadelphia			
☐ 82A Joel Mulvey: Philadelphia (Hands on knees)	70.00	28.00	7.00
☐ 82B Joel Mulvey: Philadelphia * (Hands together above head)	90.00	36.00	9.00
☐ 83A Pete Wood: Philadelphia (Fielding)	70.00	28.00	7.00
☐ 83B Pete Wood: Philadelphia HOR (Stealing a Base) *	90.00	36.00	9.00
☐ 84 Sam Barkley: Pittsburg	70.00	28.00	7.00
☐ 85 Ed Beecher:	70.00	28.00	7.00
☐ 86 Tom Brown:	70.00	28.00	7.00
☐ 87 Fred Carroll:	70.00	28.00	7.00
☐ 88 John Coleman:	70.00	28.00	7.00
☐ 89 Jim McCormick:	70.00	28.00	7.00
☐ 90 Doggie Miller:	70.00	28.00	7.00
☐ 91 Pop Smith:	70.00	28.00	7.00
☐ 92 Art Whitney:	70.00	28.00	7.00
☐ 93 Sam Barkley: St. Louis	90.00	36.00	9.00
☐ 94 Doc Bushong: St. Louis	90.00	36.00	9.00
☐ 95 Bob Carruthers (Sic): St. Louis	100.00	40.00	10.00
☐ 96 Charles Comiskey: St. Louis	300.00	120.00	30.00
☐ 97 Dave Foutz: St. Louis	90.00	36.00	9.00
☐ 98 William Gleason: St. Louis	100.00	40.00	10.00
☐ 99 Arlie Latham: St. Louis	90.00	36.00	9.00
☐ 100 Jumbo McGinnis: St. Louis	90.00	36.00	9.00
☐ 101 Hugh Nicol: St. Louis	90.00	36.00	9.00
☐ 102 James O'Neil: St. Louis	90.00	36.00	9.00
☐ 103 Yank Robinson: St. Louis	90.00	36.00	9.00
☐ 104 Sullivan: St. Louis	90.00	36.00	9.00
☐ 105 Chris Von Der Ahe: St. Louis (Actually a photo, rather than drawing)	300.00	120.00	30.00
☐ 106 Curt Welch: St. Louis	90.00	36.00	9.00
☐ 107 Cliff Carroll: Washington	70.00	28.00	7.00
☐ 108 Craig: Washington *	90.00	36.00	9.00
☐ 109 Sam Crane: Washington *	90.00	36.00	9.00
☐ 110 Ed Dailey: Washington	70.00	28.00	7.00
☐ 111 Jim Donnelly: Washington	70.00	28.00	7.00
☐ 112A Jack Farrell: Washington (Ball in left hand, right arm out shoulder high)	70.00	28.00	7.00
☐ 112B Jack Farrell: Washington * (Ball in hands near right knee)	90.00	36.00	9.00
☐ 113 Barney Gilligan: Washington	70.00	28.00	7.00
☐ 114A Paul Hines: Washington (Fielding)	70.00	28.00	7.00
☐ 114B Paul Hines: Washington * (Batting)	90.00	36.00	9.00
☐ 115 Al Myers: Washington	70.00	28.00	7.00
☐ 116 Billy O'Brien: Washington	70.00	28.00	7.00
☐ 117 Jim Whitney: Washington	70.00	28.00	7.00

N300 Mayo

The Mayo Tobacco Works of Richmond, Va., issued this set of 48 ballplayers about 1895. The cards contain sepia portraits although some pictures appear to be black and white. There are 40 different individuals known in the set; cards 1 to 28 appear in uniform, while the last twelve (29-40) appear in street clothes. Eight of the former also appear with variations in uniform. The player's name appears within the picture area and a "Mayo's Cut Plug" ad is printed in a panel at the base of the card.

	EX-MT	VG-E	GOOD
COMPLETE SET (48)	22000.	9000.00	2750.00
COMMON PLAYERS (1-28)	300.00	120.00	30.00
COMMON PLAYERS (29-40)	300.00	120.00	30.00
☐ 1 Cap Anson: Chicago	1800.00	800.00	250.00
☐ 2 Jimmy Bannon RF: Boston	300.00	120.00	30.00
☐ 3A Dan Brouthers 1B: Baltimore	650.00	260.00	65.00
☐ 3B Dan Brouthers 1B: Louisville	850.00	340.00	85.00
☐ 4 John Clarkson P: St. Louis	650.00	260.00	65.00
☐ 5 Tommy W. Corcoran SS: Brooklyn	300.00	120.00	30.00
☐ 6 Lave Cross 2B: Philadelphia	300.00	120.00	30.00
☐ 7 Hugh Duffy CF: Boston	650.00	260.00	65.00
☐ 8A Buck Ewing RF: Cincinnati	750.00	300.00	75.00
☐ 8B Buck Ewing RF: Cleveland	750.00	300.00	75.00
☐ 9 Dave Foutz 1B: Brooklyn	300.00	120.00	30.00
☐ 10 Charlie Ganzel C: Boston	300.00	120.00	30.00
☐ 11A Jack Glasscock SS: Pittsburgh	350.00	140.00	35.00
☐ 11B Jack Glasscock SS: Louisville	350.00	140.00	35.00
☐ 12 Mike Griffin CF: Brooklyn	300.00	120.00	30.00
☐ 13A George Haddock P: Philadelphia	300.00	120.00	30.00
☐ 13B George Haddock P: no team	300.00	120.00	30.00
☐ 14 Bill Joyce CF: Brooklyn	300.00	120.00	30.00
☐ 15 Wm.(Brickyard) Kennedy P: Brooklyn	300.00	120.00	30.00
☐ 16A Tom F. Kinslow C: Pitts.	300.00	120.00	30.00
☐ 16B Tom F. Kinslow C: no team	300.00	120.00	30.00
☐ 17 Arlie Latham 3B: Cincinnati	300.00	120.00	30.00
☐ 18 Herman Long SS: Boston	350.00	140.00	35.00
☐ 19 Lovett P: Boston	300.00	120.00	30.00
☐ 20 Link Lowe 2B: Boston	350.00	140.00	35.00
☐ 21 Tommy McCarthy LF: Boston	650.00	260.00	65.00
☐ 22 Yale Murphy SS: New York	300.00	120.00	30.00
☐ 23 Billy Nash 3B: Boston	300.00	120.00	30.00
☐ 24 Kid Nicols P: Boston	650.00	260.00	65.00
☐ 25A Fred Pfeffer 2B: Louisville	300.00	120.00	30.00
☐ 25B Fred Pfeffer (Retired)	300.00	120.00	30.00
☐ 26A Amos Rusie P: New York	1000.00	400.00	125.00

☐	26B	Amos Russie (Sic) P: New York	750.00	300.00	75.00
☐	27	Tommy Tucker 1B: Boston	300.00	120.00	30.00
☐	28A	John Ward 2B: New York	650.00	260.00	65.00
☐	28B	John Ward (Retired)	850.00	340.00	85.00
☐	29	Charlie S. Abbey CF: Washington	300.00	120.00	30.00
☐	30	Ed W. Cartwright FB: Washington	300.00	120.00	30.00
☐	31	William F. Dahlen SS: Chicago	350.00	140.00	35.00
☐	32	Tom P. Daly 2B: Brooklyn	300.00	120.00	30.00
☐	33	Ed J. Delehanty LF: Phila.	1000.00	400.00	125.00
☐	34	Bill W. Hallman 2B: Phila.	300.00	120.00	30.00
☐	35	Billy Hamilton CF: Phila.	650.00	260.00	65.00
☐	36	Wilbert Robinson C: Baltimore	650.00	260.00	65.00
☐	37	James Ryan RF: Chicago	350.00	140.00	35.00
☐	38	Billy Shindle 3B: Brooklyn	300.00	120.00	30.00
☐	39	George J. Smith SS: Cinc.	300.00	120.00	30.00
☐	40	Otis H. Stockdale P: Washington	300.00	120.00	30.00

1939 Play Ball

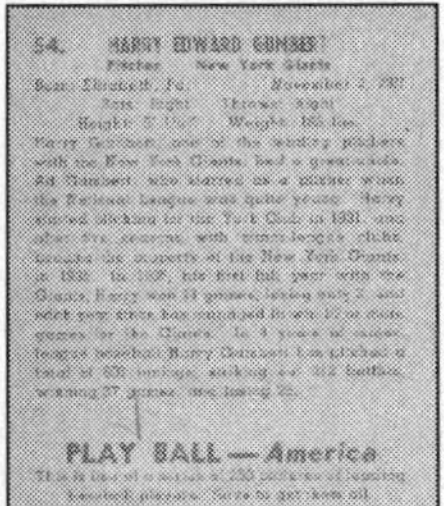

The cards in this 161-card set measure approximately 2 1/2" by 3 1/8". Gum Incorporated introduced a brief (war-shortened) but innovative era of baseball card production with its set of 1939. The combination of actual player photos (black and white), large card size, and extensive biography proved extremely popular. Player names are found either entirely capitalized or with initial caps only, and a "sample card" overprint is not uncommon. The "sample card" overprint variations are valued at double the prices below. Card number 126 was never issued, and cards 116-162 were produced in lesser quantities than cards 1-115. The catalog designation for this set is R334.

	EX-MT	VG-E	GOOD
COMPLETE SET	14000.	6000.00	1750.00
COMMON PLAYER (1-115)	18.00	7.25	1.80
COMMON PLAYER (116-162)	135.00	54.00	13.50

			EX-MT	VG-E	GOOD
☐	1	Jake Powell	90.00	18.00	3.50
☐	2	Lee Grissom	18.00	7.25	1.80
☐	3	Red Ruffing	90.00	36.00	9.00
☐	4	Eldon Auker	18.00	7.25	1.80
☐	5	Luke Sewell	25.00	10.00	2.50
☐	6	Leo Durocher	75.00	30.00	7.50
☐	7	Bobby Doerr	100.00	40.00	10.00
☐	8	Henry Pippen	18.00	7.25	1.80
☐	9	James Tobin	18.00	7.25	1.80
☐	10	James DeShong	18.00	7.25	1.80
☐	11	Johnny Rizzo	18.00	7.25	1.80
☐	12	Hershel Martin	18.00	7.25	1.80
☐	13	Luke Hamlin	18.00	7.25	1.80
☐	14	Jim Tabor	18.00	7.25	1.80
☐	15	Paul Derringer	30.00	12.00	3.00
☐	16	John Peacock	18.00	7.25	1.80
☐	17	Emerson Dickman	18.00	7.25	1.80
☐	18	Harry Danning	18.00	7.25	1.80
☐	19	Paul Dean	30.00	12.00	3.00
☐	20	Joe Heving	18.00	7.25	1.80
☐	21	Dutch Leonard	25.00	10.00	2.50
☐	22	Bucky Walters	25.00	10.00	2.50
☐	23	Burgess Whitehead	18.00	7.25	1.80
☐	24	Richard Coffman	18.00	7.25	1.80
☐	25	George Selkirk	30.00	12.00	3.00
☐	26	Joe DiMaggio	2500.00	1000.00	300.00
☐	27	Fred Ostermueller	18.00	7.25	1.80
☐	28	Sylvester Johnson	18.00	7.25	1.80
☐	29	John(Jack) Wilson	18.00	7.25	1.80
☐	30	Bill Dickey	175.00	70.00	18.00
☐	31	Sam West	18.00	7.25	1.80
☐	32	Bob Seeds	18.00	7.25	1.80
☐	33	Del Young	18.00	7.25	1.80
☐	34	Frank Demaree	18.00	7.25	1.80
☐	35	Bill Jurges	18.00	7.25	1.80
☐	36	Frank McCormick	25.00	10.00	2.50
☐	37	Virgil Davis	18.00	7.25	1.80
☐	38	Billy Myers	18.00	7.25	1.80
☐	39	Rick Ferrell	75.00	30.00	7.50
☐	40	James Bagby Jr.	18.00	7.25	1.80
☐	41	Lon Warneke	18.00	7.25	1.80
☐	42	Arndt Jorgens	18.00	7.25	1.80
☐	43	Melo Almada	18.00	7.25	1.80
☐	44	Don Heffner	18.00	7.25	1.80
☐	45	Merrill May	18.00	7.25	1.80
☐	46	Morris Arnovich	18.00	7.25	1.80
☐	47	Buddy Lewis	18.00	7.25	1.80
☐	48	Lefty Gomez	135.00	54.00	13.50
☐	49	Eddie Miller	18.00	7.25	1.80
☐	50	Charlie Gehringer	135.00	54.00	13.50
☐	51	Mel Ott	175.00	70.00	18.00
☐	52	Tommy Henrich	35.00	14.00	3.50
☐	53	Carl Hubbell	135.00	54.00	13.50
☐	54	Harry Gumpert	18.00	7.25	1.80
☐	55	Arky Vaughan	75.00	30.00	7.50
☐	56	Hank Greenberg	175.00	70.00	18.00
☐	57	Buddy Hassett	18.00	7.25	1.80
☐	58	Lou Chiozza	18.00	7.25	1.80
☐	59	Ken Chase	18.00	7.25	1.80
☐	60	Schoolboy Rowe	25.00	10.00	2.50
☐	61	Tony Cuccinello	18.00	7.25	1.80
☐	62	Tom Carey	18.00	7.25	1.80
☐	63	Emmett Mueller	18.00	7.25	1.80
☐	64	Wally Moses	25.00	10.00	2.50
☐	65	Harry Craft	18.00	7.25	1.80
☐	66	Jimmy Ripple	18.00	7.25	1.80
☐	67	Ed Joost	18.00	7.25	1.80
☐	68	Fred Sington	18.00	7.25	1.80
☐	69	Elbie Fletcher	18.00	7.25	1.80
☐	70	Fred Frankhouse	18.00	7.25	1.80
☐	71	Monte Pearson	25.00	10.00	2.50
☐	72	Debs Garms	18.00	7.25	1.80
☐	73	Hal Schumacher	25.00	10.00	2.50
☐	74	Cookie Lavagetto	25.00	10.00	2.50
☐	75	Stan Bordagaray	18.00	7.25	1.80
☐	76	Goody Rosen	18.00	7.25	1.80
☐	77	Lew Riggs	18.00	7.25	1.80
☐	78	Julius Solters	18.00	7.25	1.80
☐	79	Jo Jo Moore	18.00	7.25	1.80
☐	80	Pete Fox	18.00	7.25	1.80
☐	81	Babe Dahlgren	25.00	10.00	2.50
☐	82	Chuck Klein	135.00	54.00	13.50
☐	83	Gus Suhr	18.00	7.25	1.80
☐	84	Skeeter Newsom	18.00	7.25	1.80
☐	85	Johnny Cooney	18.00	7.25	1.80
☐	86	Dolph Camilli	25.00	10.00	2.50
☐	87	Milburn Shoffner	18.00	7.25	1.80
☐	88	Charlie Keller	30.00	12.50	3.75
☐	89	Lloyd Waner	75.00	30.00	7.50
☐	90	Robert Klinger	18.00	7.25	1.80
☐	91	John Knott	18.00	7.25	1.80
☐	92	Ted Williams	2500.00	1000.00	300.00
☐	93	Charles Gelbert	18.00	7.25	1.80
☐	94	Heinie Manush	75.00	30.00	7.50
☐	95	Whit Wyatt	25.00	10.00	2.50
☐	96	Babe Phelps	18.00	7.25	1.80
☐	97	Bob Johnson	25.00	10.00	2.50
☐	98	Pinky Whitney	18.00	7.25	1.80
☐	99	Wally Berger	25.00	10.00	2.50
☐	100	Charles Myer	18.00	7.25	1.80
☐	101	Roger Cramer	25.00	10.00	2.50
☐	102	Lem Young	18.00	7.25	1.80
☐	103	Moe Berg	60.00	24.00	6.00
☐	104	Tom Bridges	25.00	10.00	2.50
☐	105	Rabbit McNair	18.00	7.25	1.80
☐	106	Dolly Stark	25.00	10.00	2.50
☐	107	Joe Vosmik	18.00	7.25	1.80

☐ 108	Frank Hayes	18.00	7.25	1.80
☐ 109	Myril Hoag	18.00	7.25	1.80
☐ 110	Fred Fitzsimmons	25.00	10.00	2.50
☐ 111	Van Lingle Mungo	25.00	10.00	2.50
☐ 112	Paul Waner	90.00	36.00	9.00
☐ 113	Al Schacht	25.00	10.00	2.50
☐ 114	Cecil Travis	18.00	7.25	1.80
☐ 115	Ralph Kress	18.00	7.25	1.80
☐ 116	Gene Desautels	135.00	54.00	13.50
☐ 117	Wayne Ambler	135.00	54.00	13.50
☐ 118	Lynn Nelson	135.00	54.00	13.50
☐ 119	Will Hershberger	165.00	67.50	20.00
☐ 120	Rabbit Warstler	135.00	54.00	13.50
☐ 121	Bill Posedel	135.00	54.00	13.50
☐ 122	George McQuinn	135.00	54.00	13.50
☐ 123	Ray T. Davis	135.00	54.00	13.50
☐ 124	Walter Brown	135.00	54.00	13.50
☐ 125	Cliff Melton	135.00	54.00	13.50
☐ 126	Not issued	0.00	0.00	0.00
☐ 127	Gil Brack	135.00	54.00	13.50
☐ 128	Joe Bowman	135.00	54.00	13.50
☐ 129	Bill Swift	135.00	54.00	13.50
☐ 130	Bill Brubaker	135.00	54.00	13.50
☐ 131	Mort Cooper	165.00	67.50	20.00
☐ 132	Jim Brown	135.00	54.00	13.50
☐ 133	Lynn Myers	135.00	54.00	13.50
☐ 134	Tot Presnell	135.00	54.00	13.50
☐ 135	Mickey Owen	165.00	67.50	20.00
☐ 136	Roy Bell	135.00	54.00	13.50
☐ 137	Pete Appleton	135.00	54.00	13.50
☐ 138	George Case	165.00	67.50	20.00
☐ 139	Vito Tamulis	135.00	54.00	13.50
☐ 140	Ray Hayworth	135.00	54.00	13.50
☐ 141	Pete Coscarart	135.00	54.00	13.50
☐ 142	Ira Hutchinson	135.00	54.00	13.50
☐ 143	Earl Averill	375.00	150.00	37.00
☐ 144	Zeke Bonura	135.00	54.00	13.50
☐ 145	Hugh Mulcahy	135.00	54.00	13.50
☐ 146	Tom Sunkel	135.00	54.00	13.50
☐ 147	George Coffman	135.00	54.00	13.50
☐ 148	Bill Trotter	135.00	54.00	13.50
☐ 149	Max West	135.00	54.00	13.50
☐ 150	James Walkup	135.00	54.00	13.50
☐ 151	Hugh Casey	165.00	67.50	20.00
☐ 152	Roy Weatherly	135.00	54.00	13.50
☐ 153	Paul Trout	165.00	67.50	20.00
☐ 154	Johnny Hudson	135.00	54.00	13.50
☐ 155	Jimmy Outlaw	135.00	54.00	13.50
☐ 156	Ray Berres	135.00	54.00	13.50
☐ 157	Don Padgett	135.00	54.00	13.50
☐ 158	Bud Thomas	135.00	54.00	13.50
☐ 159	Red Evans	135.00	54.00	13.50
☐ 160	Gene Moore	135.00	54.00	13.50
☐ 161	Lonnie Frey	135.00	54.00	13.50
☐ 162	Whitey Moore	165.00	67.50	20.00

1940 Play Ball

The cards in this 240-card series measure approximately 2 1/2" by 3 1/8". Gum Inc. improved upon its 1939 design by enclosing the 1940 black and white player photo with a frame line and printing the player's name in a panel below the picture (often using a nickname). The set included many Hall of Famers and Old Timers. Cards 181-240 are scarcer than cards 1-180. The backs contain an extensive biography and a dated copyright line. The catalog number for this set is R335.

		EX-MT	VG-E	GOOD
COMPLETE SET (240)		20000.	8000.00	2500.00
COMMON PLAYER (1-120)		18.00	7.25	1.80
COMMON PLAYER (121-180)		20.00	8.00	2.00
COMMON PLAYER (181-240)		75.00	30.00	7.50
☐ 1	Joe DiMaggio	3000.00	900.00	200.00
☐ 2	Art Jorgens	18.00	7.25	1.80
☐ 3	Babe Dahlgren	25.00	10.00	2.50
☐ 4	Tommy Henrich	35.00	14.00	3.50
☐ 5	Monte Pearson	25.00	10.00	2.50
☐ 6	Lefty Gomez	175.00	70.00	18.00
☐ 7	Bill Dickey	200.00	80.00	20.00
☐ 8	George Selkirk	25.00	10.00	2.50
☐ 9	Charlie Keller	30.00	12.00	3.00
☐ 10	Red Ruffing	90.00	36.00	9.00
☐ 11	Jake Powell	18.00	7.25	1.80
☐ 12	Johnny Schulte	18.00	7.25	1.80
☐ 13	Jack Knott	18.00	7.25	1.80
☐ 14	Rabbit McNair	18.00	7.25	1.80
☐ 15	George Case	25.00	10.00	2.50
☐ 16	Cecil Travis	18.00	7.25	1.80
☐ 17	Buddy Myer	18.00	7.25	1.80
☐ 18	Charlie Gelbert	18.00	7.25	1.80
☐ 19	Ken Chase	18.00	7.25	1.80
☐ 20	Buddy Lewis	18.00	7.25	1.80
☐ 21	Rick Ferrell	75.00	30.00	7.50
☐ 22	Sammy West	18.00	7.25	1.80
☐ 23	Dutch Leonard	25.00	10.00	2.50
☐ 24	Frank Hayes	18.00	7.25	1.80
☐ 25	Bob Johnson	25.00	10.00	2.50
☐ 26	Wally Moses	25.00	10.00	2.50
☐ 27	Ted Williams	1750.00	700.00	225.00
☐ 28	Gene Desautels	18.00	7.25	1.80
☐ 29	Doc Cramer	25.00	10.00	2.50
☐ 30	Moe Berg	60.00	24.00	6.00
☐ 31	Jack Wilson	18.00	7.25	1.80
☐ 32	Jim Bagby	18.00	7.25	1.80
☐ 33	Fritz Ostermueller	18.00	7.25	1.80
☐ 34	John Peacock	18.00	7.25	1.80
☐ 35	Joe Heving	18.00	7.25	1.80
☐ 36	Jim Tabor	18.00	7.25	1.80
☐ 37	Emerson Dickman	18.00	7.25	1.80
☐ 38	Bobby Doerr	90.00	36.00	9.00
☐ 39	Tom Carey	18.00	7.25	1.80
☐ 40	Hank Greenberg	200.00	80.00	20.00
☐ 41	Charley Gehringer	175.00	70.00	18.00
☐ 42	Bud Thomas	18.00	7.25	1.80
☐ 43	Pete Fox	18.00	7.25	1.80
☐ 44	Dizzy Trout	25.00	10.00	2.50
☐ 45	Red Kress	18.00	7.25	1.80
☐ 46	Earl Averill	100.00	40.00	10.00
☐ 47	Oscar Vitt	18.00	7.25	1.80
☐ 48	Luke Sewell	25.00	10.00	2.50
☐ 49	Stormy Weatherly	18.00	7.25	1.80
☐ 50	Hal Trosky	25.00	10.00	2.50
☐ 51	Don Heffner	18.00	7.25	1.80
☐ 52	Myril Hoag	18.00	7.25	1.80
☐ 53	George McQuinn	18.00	7.25	1.80
☐ 54	Bill Trotter	18.00	7.25	1.80
☐ 55	Slick Coffman	18.00	7.25	1.80
☐ 56	Eddie Miller	18.00	7.25	1.80
☐ 57	Max West	18.00	7.25	1.80
☐ 58	Bill Posedel	18.00	7.25	1.80
☐ 59	Rabbit Warstler	18.00	7.25	1.80
☐ 60	John Cooney	18.00	7.25	1.80
☐ 61	Tony Cuccinello	18.00	7.25	1.80
☐ 62	Buddy Hassett	18.00	7.25	1.80
☐ 63	Pete Coscarart	18.00	7.25	1.80
☐ 64	Van Lingle Mungo	25.00	10.00	2.50
☐ 65	Fred Fitzsimmons	25.00	10.00	2.50
☐ 66	Babe Phelps	18.00	7.25	1.80
☐ 67	Whit Wyatt	25.00	10.00	2.50
☐ 68	Dolph Camilli	25.00	10.00	2.50
☐ 69	Cookie Lavagetto	18.00	7.25	1.80
☐ 70	Hot Potato Hamlin	18.00	7.25	1.80
☐ 71	Mel Almada	18.00	7.25	1.80
☐ 72	Chuck Dressen	25.00	10.00	2.50
☐ 73	Bucky Walters	25.00	10.00	2.50
☐ 74	Duke Derringer	30.00	12.00	3.00
☐ 75	Buck McCormick	25.00	10.00	2.50
☐ 76	Lonny Frey	18.00	7.25	1.80
☐ 77	Willard Hershberger	25.00	10.00	2.50
☐ 78	Lew Riggs	18.00	7.25	1.80
☐ 79	Harry Craft	18.00	7.25	1.80
☐ 80	Billy Myers	18.00	7.25	1.80
☐ 81	Wally Berger	25.00	10.00	2.50
☐ 82	Hank Gowdy	18.00	7.25	1.80
☐ 83	Cliff Melton	18.00	7.25	1.80
☐ 84	Jo Jo Moore	18.00	7.25	1.80
☐ 85	Hal Schumacher	25.00	10.00	2.50
☐ 86	Harry Gumbert	18.00	7.25	1.80
☐ 87	Carl Hubbell	175.00	70.00	18.00
☐ 88	Mel Ott	200.00	80.00	20.00

☐ 89 Bill Jurges	18.00	7.25	1.80
☐ 90 Frank Demaree	18.00	7.25	1.80
☐ 91 Bob Seeds	18.00	7.25	1.80
☐ 92 Whitey Whitehead	18.00	7.25	1.80
☐ 93 Harry Danning	18.00	7.25	1.80
☐ 94 Gus Suhr	18.00	7.25	1.80
☐ 95 Hugh Mulcahy	18.00	7.25	1.80
☐ 96 Heinie Mueller	18.00	7.25	1.80
☐ 97 Morry Arnovich	18.00	7.25	1.80
☐ 98 Pinky May	18.00	7.25	1.80
☐ 99 Syl Johnson	18.00	7.25	1.80
☐ 100 Hersh Martin	18.00	7.25	1.80
☐ 101 Del Young	18.00	7.25	1.80
☐ 102 Chuck Klein	150.00	60.00	15.00
☐ 103 Elbie Fletcher	18.00	7.25	1.80
☐ 104 Paul Waner	100.00	40.00	10.00
☐ 105 Lloyd Waner	90.00	36.00	9.00
☐ 106 Pep Young	18.00	7.25	1.80
☐ 107 Arky Vaughan	80.00	32.00	8.00
☐ 108 Johnny Rizzo	18.00	7.25	1.80
☐ 109 Don Padgett	18.00	7.25	1.80
☐ 110 Tom Sunkel	18.00	7.25	1.80
☐ 111 Mickey Owen	25.00	10.00	2.50
☐ 112 Jimmy Brown	18.00	7.25	1.80
☐ 113 Mort Cooper	25.00	10.00	2.50
☐ 114 Lon Warneke	25.00	10.00	2.50
☐ 115 Mike Gonzalez	18.00	7.25	1.80
☐ 116 Al Schacht	25.00	10.00	2.50
☐ 117 Dolly Stark	25.00	10.00	2.50
☐ 118 Schoolboy Hoyt	100.00	40.00	10.00
☐ 119 Grover C. Alexander	200.00	80.00	20.00
☐ 120 Walter Johnson	300.00	120.00	30.00
☐ 121 Atley Donald	20.00	8.00	2.00
☐ 122 Sandy Sundra	20.00	8.00	2.00
☐ 123 Hildy Hildebrand	20.00	8.00	2.00
☐ 124 Earle Combs	135.00	54.00	13.50
☐ 125 Art Fletcher	20.00	8.00	2.00
☐ 126 Jake Solters	20.00	8.00	2.00
☐ 127 Muddy Ruel	20.00	8.00	2.00
☐ 128 Pete Appleton	20.00	8.00	2.00
☐ 129 Bucky Harris	80.00	32.00	8.00
☐ 130 Deerfoot Milan	20.00	8.00	2.00
☐ 131 Zeke Bonura	25.00	10.00	2.50
☐ 132 Connie Mack	200.00	80.00	20.00
☐ 133 Jimmie Foxx	300.00	120.00	30.00
☐ 134 Joe Cronin	175.00	70.00	18.00
☐ 135 Line Drive Nelson	20.00	8.00	2.00
☐ 136 Cotton Pippen	20.00	8.00	2.00
☐ 137 Bing Miller	20.00	8.00	2.00
☐ 138 Beau Bell	20.00	8.00	2.00
☐ 139 Elden Auker	20.00	8.00	2.00
☐ 140 Dick Coffman	20.00	8.00	2.00
☐ 141 Casey Stengel	250.00	100.00	25.00
☐ 142 George Kelly	100.00	40.00	10.00
☐ 143 Gene Moore	20.00	8.00	2.00
☐ 144 Joe Vosmik	20.00	8.00	2.00
☐ 145 Vito Tamulis	20.00	8.00	2.00
☐ 146 Tot Pressnell	20.00	8.00	2.00
☐ 147 Johnny Hudson	20.00	8.00	2.00
☐ 148 Hugh Casey	25.00	10.00	2.50
☐ 149 Pinky Shoffner	20.00	8.00	2.00
☐ 150 Whitey Moore	20.00	8.00	2.00
☐ 151 Edwin Joost	20.00	8.00	2.00
☐ 152 Jimmy Wilson	20.00	8.00	2.00
☐ 153 Bill McKechnie	90.00	36.00	9.00
☐ 154 Jumbo Brown	20.00	8.00	2.00
☐ 155 Ray Hayworth	20.00	8.00	2.00
☐ 156 Daffy Dean	35.00	14.00	3.50
☐ 157 Lou Chiozza	20.00	8.00	2.00
☐ 158 Travis Jackson	100.00	40.00	10.00
☐ 159 Pancho Snyder	20.00	8.00	2.00
☐ 160 Hans Lobert	20.00	8.00	2.00
☐ 161 Debs Garms	20.00	8.00	2.00
☐ 162 Joe Bowman	20.00	8.00	2.00
☐ 163 Spud Davis	20.00	8.00	2.00
☐ 164 Ray Berres	20.00	8.00	2.00
☐ 165 Bob Klinger	20.00	8.00	2.00
☐ 166 Bill Brubaker	20.00	8.00	2.00
☐ 167 Frankie Frisch	135.00	54.00	13.50
☐ 168 Honus Wagner	350.00	140.00	35.00
☐ 169 Gabby Street	20.00	8.00	2.00
☐ 170 Tris Speaker	300.00	120.00	30.00
☐ 171 Harry Heilmann	135.00	54.00	13.50
☐ 172 Chief Bender	100.00	40.00	10.00
☐ 173 Larry Lajoie	300.00	120.00	30.00
☐ 174 Johnny Evers	100.00	40.00	10.00
☐ 175 Christy Mathewson	350.00	140.00	35.00
☐ 176 Heinie Manush	100.00	40.00	10.00
☐ 177 Homerun Baker	135.00	54.00	13.50
☐ 178 Max Carey	100.00	40.00	10.00
☐ 179 George Sisler	135.00	54.00	13.50
☐ 180 Mickey Cochrane	200.00	80.00	20.00
☐ 181 Spud Chandler	100.00	40.00	10.00
☐ 182 Knick Knickerbocker	75.00	30.00	7.50
☐ 183 Marvin Breuer	75.00	30.00	7.50
☐ 184 Mule Haas	75.00	30.00	7.50
☐ 185 Joe Kuhel	75.00	30.00	7.50
☐ 186 Taft Wright	75.00	30.00	7.50
☐ 187 Jimmy Dykes	90.00	36.00	9.00
☐ 188 Joe Krakauskas	75.00	30.00	7.50
☐ 189 Jim Bloodworth	75.00	30.00	7.50
☐ 190 Charley Berry	75.00	30.00	7.50
☐ 191 John Babich	75.00	30.00	7.50
☐ 192 Dick Siebert	75.00	30.00	7.50
☐ 193 Chubby Dean	75.00	30.00	7.50
☐ 194 Sam Chapman	75.00	30.00	7.50
☐ 195 Dee Miles	75.00	30.00	7.50
☐ 196 Red(Nonny) Nonnenkamp	75.00	30.00	7.50
☐ 197 Lou Finney	75.00	30.00	7.50
☐ 198 Denny Galehouse	75.00	30.00	7.50
☐ 199 Pinky Higgins	75.00	30.00	7.50
☐ 200 Soup Campbell	75.00	30.00	7.50
☐ 201 Barney McCosky	75.00	30.00	7.50
☐ 202 Al Milnar	75.00	30.00	7.50
☐ 203 Bad News Hale	75.00	30.00	7.50
☐ 204 Harry Eisenstat	75.00	30.00	7.50
☐ 205 Rollie Hemsley	75.00	30.00	7.50
☐ 206 Chet Laabs	75.00	30.00	7.50
☐ 207 Gus Mancuso	75.00	30.00	7.50
☐ 208 Lee Gamble	75.00	30.00	7.50
☐ 209 Hy Vandenberg	75.00	30.00	7.50
☐ 210 Bill Lohrman	75.00	30.00	7.50
☐ 211 Pop Joiner	75.00	30.00	7.50
☐ 212 Babe Young	75.00	30.00	7.50
☐ 213 John Rucker	75.00	30.00	7.50
☐ 214 Ken O'Dea	75.00	30.00	7.50
☐ 215 Johnnie McCarthy	75.00	30.00	7.50
☐ 216 Joe Marty	75.00	30.00	7.50
☐ 217 Walter Beck	75.00	30.00	7.50
☐ 218 Wally Millies	75.00	30.00	7.50
☐ 219 Russ Bauers	75.00	30.00	7.50
☐ 220 Mace Brown	75.00	30.00	7.50
☐ 221 Lee Handley	75.00	30.00	7.50
☐ 222 Max Butcher	75.00	30.00	7.50
☐ 223 Hugh Jennings	150.00	60.00	15.00
☐ 224 Pie Traynor	175.00	70.00	18.00
☐ 225 Shoeless Joe Jackson	2500.00	1000.00	300.00
☐ 226 Harry Hooper	150.00	60.00	15.00
☐ 227 Pop Haines	150.00	60.00	15.00
☐ 228 Charley Grimm	90.00	36.00	9.00
☐ 229 Buck Herzog	75.00	30.00	7.50
☐ 230 Red Faber	150.00	60.00	15.00
☐ 231 Dolf Luque	75.00	30.00	7.50
☐ 232 Goose Goslin	150.00	60.00	15.00
☐ 233 Moose Earnshaw	75.00	30.00	7.50
☐ 234 Frank(Husk) Chance	175.00	70.00	18.00
☐ 235 John J. McGraw	200.00	80.00	20.00
☐ 236 Jim Bottomley	150.00	60.00	15.00
☐ 237 Wee Willie Keeler	250.00	100.00	25.00
☐ 238 Tony Lazzeri	200.00	80.00	20.00
☐ 239 George Uhle	75.00	30.00	7.50
☐ 240 Bill Atwood	100.00	40.00	10.00

1941 Play Ball

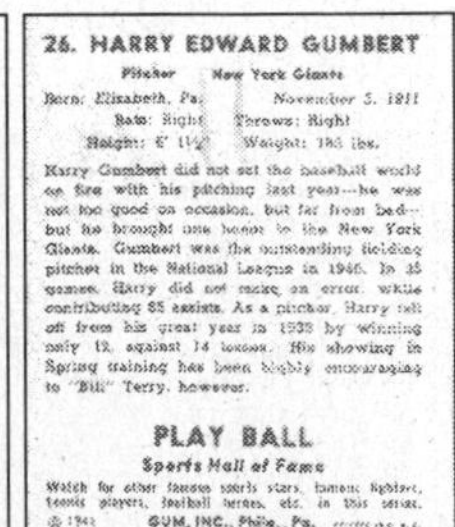

The cards in this 72-card set measure approximately 2 1/2" by 3 1/8". Many of the cards in the 1941 Play Ball series are simply color versions of pictures appearing in the 1940 set. This was the only color baseball card set produced by Gum, Inc., and it carries the catalog designation R336. Card numbers 49-72 are slightly more difficult to obtain as they were not issued until 1942. In 1942, numbers 1-48 were also reissued but without the copyright date. The cards were also printed on paper without a cardboard backing; these are generally encountered in sheets or strips.

	EX-MT	VG-E	GOOD
COMPLETE SET	11000.	4750.00	1350.00
COMMON PLAYER (1-48)	45.00	18.00	4.50
COMMON PLAYER (49-72)	75.00	30.00	7.50
☐ 1 Eddie Miller	135.00	30.00	6.00
☐ 2 Max West	45.00	18.00	4.50
☐ 3 Bucky Walters	50.00	20.00	5.00
☐ 4 Paul Derringer	55.00	22.00	5.50
☐ 5 Buck McCormick	50.00	20.00	5.00
☐ 6 Carl Hubbell	225.00	90.00	22.00
☐ 7 Harry Danning	45.00	18.00	4.50
☐ 8 Mel Ott	300.00	120.00	30.00
☐ 9 Pinky May	45.00	18.00	4.50
☐ 10 Arky Vaughan	100.00	40.00	10.00
☐ 11 Debs Garms	45.00	18.00	4.50
☐ 12 Jimmy Brown	45.00	18.00	4.50
☐ 13 Jimmy Foxx	400.00	160.00	40.00
☐ 14 Ted Williams	1750.00	700.00	225.00
☐ 15 Joe Cronin	135.00	54.00	13.50
☐ 16 Hal Trosky	50.00	20.00	5.00
☐ 17 Roy Weatherly	45.00	18.00	4.50
☐ 18 Hank Greenberg	300.00	120.00	30.00
☐ 19 Charlie Gehringer	225.00	90.00	22.00
☐ 20 Red Ruffing	135.00	54.00	13.50
☐ 21 Charlie Keller	75.00	30.00	7.50
☐ 22 Indian Bob Johnson	55.00	22.00	5.50
☐ 23 George McQuinn	45.00	18.00	4.50
☐ 24 Dutch Leonard	50.00	20.00	5.00
☐ 25 Gene Moore	45.00	18.00	4.50
☐ 26 Harry Gumpert	45.00	18.00	4.50
☐ 27 Babe Young	45.00	18.00	4.50
☐ 28 Joe Marty	45.00	18.00	4.50
☐ 29 Jack Wilson	45.00	18.00	4.50
☐ 30 Lou Finney	45.00	18.00	4.50
☐ 31 Joe Kuhel	45.00	18.00	4.50
☐ 32 Taft Wright	45.00	18.00	4.50
☐ 33 Al Milnar	45.00	18.00	4.50
☐ 34 Rollie Hemsley	45.00	18.00	4.50
☐ 35 Pinky Higgins	45.00	18.00	4.50
☐ 36 Barney McCosky	45.00	18.00	4.50
☐ 37 Bruce Campbell	45.00	18.00	4.50
☐ 38 Atley Donald	45.00	18.00	4.50
☐ 39 Tom Henrich	75.00	30.00	7.50
☐ 40 John Babich	45.00	18.00	4.50
☐ 41 Frank(Blimp) Hayes	45.00	18.00	4.50
☐ 42 Wally Moses	50.00	20.00	5.00
☐ 43 Al Brancato	45.00	18.00	4.50
☐ 44 Sam Chapman	45.00	18.00	4.50
☐ 45 Eldon Auker	45.00	18.00	4.50
☐ 46 Sid Hudson	45.00	18.00	4.50
☐ 47 Buddy Lewis	45.00	18.00	4.50
☐ 48 Cecil Travis	45.00	18.00	4.50
☐ 49 Babe Dahlgren	90.00	36.00	9.00
☐ 50 Johnny Cooney	75.00	30.00	7.50
☐ 51 Dolph Camilli	90.00	36.00	9.00
☐ 52 Kirby Higbe	75.00	30.00	7.50
☐ 53 Luke Hamlin	75.00	30.00	7.50
☐ 54 Pee Wee Reese	900.00	360.00	90.00
☐ 55 Whit Wyatt	90.00	36.00	9.00
☐ 56 Johnny VanderMeer	135.00	54.00	13.50
☐ 57 Moe Arnovich	75.00	30.00	7.50
☐ 58 Frank Demaree	75.00	30.00	7.50
☐ 59 Bill Jurges	75.00	30.00	7.50
☐ 60 Chuck Klein	225.00	90.00	22.00
☐ 61 Vince DiMaggio	300.00	120.00	30.00
☐ 62 Elbie Fletcher	75.00	30.00	7.50
☐ 63 Dom DiMaggio	300.00	120.00	30.00
☐ 64 Bobby Doerr	200.00	80.00	20.00
☐ 65 Tommy Bridges	90.00	36.00	9.00
☐ 66 Harland Clift	75.00	30.00	7.50
☐ 67 Walt Judnich	75.00	30.00	7.50
☐ 68 John Knott	75.00	30.00	7.50
☐ 69 George Case	90.00	36.00	9.00
☐ 70 Bill Dickey	600.00	240.00	60.00
☐ 71 Joe DiMaggio	2500.00	1000.00	300.00
☐ 72 Lefty Gomez	500.00	125.00	25.00

1911 T3 Turkey Red

The cards in this 126-card set measure approximately 5 3/4" by 8". The 1911 "Turkey Red" set of color cabinet style cards, designated T3 in the American Card Catalog, is

named after the brand of cigarettes with which it was offered as a premium. Cards 1-50 and 77-126 depict baseball players while the middle series (51-76) portrays boxers. The cards themselves are not numbered but were assigned numbers for ordering purposes by the manufacturer. This list appears on the backs of cards in the 77-126 sub-series and has been used in the checklist below. The boxers (51-76) were formerly assigned a separate catalog number (T9) but have now been returned to the classification to which they properly belong and are indicated in the checklist below by BOX. This attractive set has been reprinted recently in 2 1/2" by 3 1/2" form.

	EX-MT	VG-E	GOOD
COMPLETE SET (126)	45000.	21000.	5500.00
COMMON BASEBALL (1-50)	250.00	100.00	25.00
COMMON BOXERS (51-76)	150.00	60.00	15.00
COMMON BASEBALL (77-126)	275.00	110.00	27.00
☐ 1 Mordecai Brown: Chicago NL	500.00	200.00	50.00
☐ 2 Bill Bergen: Brooklyn	250.00	100.00	25.00
☐ 3 Fred Leach: Pittsburgh	250.00	100.00	25.00
☐ 4 Roger Bresnahan: St. Louis NL	450.00	180.00	45.00
☐ 5 Sam Crawford: Detroit	500.00	200.00	50.00
☐ 6 Hal Chase: New York AL	300.00	120.00	30.00
☐ 7 Howie Camnitz: Pittsburgh	250.00	100.00	25.00
☐ 8 Fred Clarke: Pittsburgh	450.00	180.00	45.00
☐ 9 Ty Cobb: Detroit	5500.00	2000.00	600.00
☐ 10 Art Devlin: New York NL	250.00	100.00	25.00
☐ 11 Bill Dahlen: Brooklyn	300.00	120.00	30.00
☐ 12 Bill Donovan: Detroit	250.00	100.00	25.00
☐ 13 Larry Doyle: New York NL	275.00	110.00	27.00
☐ 14 Red Dooin: Phila. NL	250.00	100.00	25.00
☐ 15 Kid Elberfeld: Wash.	250.00	100.00	25.00
☐ 16 Johnny Evers: Chicago NL	500.00	200.00	50.00
☐ 17 Clark Griffith: Cinc.	450.00	180.00	45.00
☐ 18 Hugh Jennings: Detroit	450.00	180.00	45.00
☐ 19 Addie Joss: Cleveland	550.00	220.00	55.00
☐ 20 Tim Jordan: Brooklyn	250.00	100.00	25.00
☐ 21 Red Kleinow: New York NL	250.00	100.00	25.00
☐ 22 Harry Krause: Phila. AL	250.00	100.00	25.00
☐ 23 Nap Lajoie: Cleveland	1200.00	500.00	150.00
☐ 24 Mike Mitchell: Cinc.	250.00	100.00	25.00
☐ 25 Matty McIntyre: Detroit	250.00	100.00	25.00
☐ 26 John McGraw: New York NL	650.00	260.00	65.00
☐ 27 Christy Mathewson: New York NL	1600.00	650.00	200.00
☐ 28 Harry McIntire: Brooklyn	250.00	100.00	25.00
☐ 29 Amby McConnell: Boston AL	250.00	100.00	25.00
☐ 30 George Mullin: Detroit	250.00	100.00	25.00

☐ 31 Sherry Magee: Phila. NL ... 250.00 100.00 25.00
☐ 32 Orval Overall: Chicago NL ... 250.00 100.00 25.00
☐ 33 Jack Pfeister: Chicago NL ... 250.00 100.00 25.00
☐ 34 Nap Rucker: Brooklyn ... 250.00 100.00 25.00
☐ 35 Joe Tinker: Chicago NL ... 500.00 200.00 50.00
☐ 36 Tris Speaker: Boston AL ... 1100.00 450.00 125.00
☐ 37 Slim Sallee: St. Louis NL ... 250.00 100.00 25.00
☐ 38 Jake Stahl: Boston AL ... 250.00 100.00 25.00
☐ 39 Rube Waddell: St. Louis AL ... 550.00 220.00 55.00
☐ 40 Vic Willis: St. Louis NL ... 300.00 120.00 30.00
☐ 41 Hooks Wiltse: New York NL ... 250.00 100.00 25.00
☐ 42 Cy Young: Cleveland ... 1350.00 550.00 175.00
☐ 43 Out At Third ... 250.00 100.00 25.00
☐ 44 Trying to Catch Him Napping ... 250.00 100.00 25.00
☐ 45 Jordan and Herzog at First ... 250.00 100.00 25.00
☐ 46 Safe At Third ... 250.00 100.00 25.00
☐ 47 Frank Chance At Bat ... 450.00 180.00 45.00
☐ 48 Jack Murray At Bat ... 250.00 100.00 25.00
☐ 49 Close Play At Second ... 250.00 100.00 25.00
☐ 50 Chief Myers At Bat (Sic, Meyers) ... 250.00 100.00 25.00
☐ 51 Jim Driscoll BOX ... 150.00 60.00 15.00
☐ 52 Abe Attell BOX ... 175.00 70.00 18.00
☐ 53 Ad. Walgast BOX ... 150.00 60.00 15.00
☐ 54 Johnny Coulon BOX ... 150.00 60.00 15.00
☐ 55 James Jeffries BOX ... 300.00 120.00 30.00
☐ 56 Jack Sullivan BOX (Twin) ... 175.00 70.00 18.00
☐ 57 Battling Nelson BOX ... 150.00 60.00 15.00
☐ 58 Packey McFarland BOX ... 150.00 60.00 15.00
☐ 59 Tommy Murphy BOX ... 150.00 60.00 15.00
☐ 60 Owen Moran BOX ... 150.00 60.00 15.00
☐ 61 Johnny Marto BOX ... 150.00 60.00 15.00
☐ 62 Jimmie Gardner BOX ... 150.00 60.00 15.00
☐ 63 Harry Lewis BOX ... 150.00 60.00 15.00
☐ 64 Wm. Papke BOX ... 150.00 60.00 15.00
☐ 65 Sam Langford BOX ... 200.00 80.00 20.00
☐ 66 Knock-out Brown BOX ... 150.00 60.00 15.00
☐ 67 Stanley Ketchel BOX ... 200.00 80.00 20.00
☐ 68 Joe Jeannette BOX ... 175.00 70.00 18.00
☐ 69 Leach Cross BOX ... 150.00 60.00 15.00
☐ 70 Phil. McGovern BOX ... 150.00 60.00 15.00
☐ 71 Battling Hurley BOX ... 150.00 60.00 15.00
☐ 72 Honey Mellody BOX ... 150.00 60.00 15.00
☐ 73 Al Kaufman BOX ... 150.00 60.00 15.00
☐ 74 Willie Lewis BOX ... 150.00 60.00 15.00
☐ 75 Jack O'Brien BOX "Philadelphia" ... 175.00 70.00 18.00
☐ 76 Jack Johnson BOX ... 275.00 110.00 27.00
☐ 77 Red Ames: New York NL ... 275.00 110.00 27.00
☐ 78 Frank Baker: Phila. AL (Picture probably Jack Barry) ... 500.00 200.00 50.00
☐ 79 George Bell: Brooklyn ... 275.00 110.00 27.00
☐ 80 Chief Bender: Phila. AL ... 500.00 200.00 50.00
☐ 81 Bob Bescher: Cinc. ... 275.00 110.00 27.00
☐ 82 Kitty Bransfield: Phila. NL ... 275.00 110.00 27.00
☐ 83 Al Bridwell: Phila. NL ... 275.00 110.00 27.00
☐ 84 George Browne: Wash. and Chicago ... 275.00 110.00 27.00
☐ 85 Bill Burns: Chicago and Cinc. ... 275.00 110.00 27.00
☐ 86 Bill Carrigan: Boston AL ... 275.00 110.00 27.00
☐ 87 Eddie Collins: Phila. AL ... 550.00 220.00 55.00
☐ 88 Harry Coveleski: Cinc. ... 275.00 110.00 27.00
☐ 89 Lou Criger: New York AL ... 275.00 110.00 27.00
☐ 90 Mickey Doolan: Phila. NL ... 275.00 110.00 27.00
☐ 91 Tom Downey: Cinc. ... 275.00 110.00 27.00
☐ 92 Jimmy Dygert: Phila. AL ... 275.00 110.00 27.00
☐ 93 Art Fromme: Cinc. ... 275.00 110.00 27.00
☐ 94 George Gibson: Pittsburgh ... 275.00 110.00 27.00
☐ 95 Peaches Graham: Boston NL ... 275.00 110.00 27.00
☐ 96 Bob Groom: Washington ... 275.00 110.00 27.00
☐ 97 Bob Hoblitzel: Cinc. ... 275.00 110.00 27.00
☐ 98 Doc Hofman: Chicago NL ... 275.00 110.00 27.00
☐ 99 Walter Johnson: Wash. ... 1800.00 750.00 225.00
☐ 100 Davy Jones: Detroit ... 275.00 110.00 27.00
☐ 101 Willie Keeler: New York NL ... 750.00 300.00 75.00
☐ 102 Johnny Kling: Chicago NL ... 275.00 110.00 27.00
☐ 103 Ed Konetchy: St. Louis NL ... 275.00 110.00 27.00
☐ 104 Ed Lennox: Brooklyn ... 275.00 110.00 27.00
☐ 105 Hans Lobert: Cinc. ... 275.00 110.00 27.00
☐ 106 Bris Lord: Boston and Chicago ... 275.00 110.00 27.00
☐ 107 Rube Manning: New York AL ... 275.00 110.00 27.00
☐ 108 Fred Merkle: New York NL ... 300.00 120.00 30.00
☐ 109 Pat Moran: Chicago and Phila. ... 275.00 110.00 27.00
☐ 110 George McBride: Wash. ... 275.00 110.00 27.00
☐ 111 Harry Niles: Boston and Cleveland ... 275.00 110.00 27.00
☐ 112 Dode Paskert: Cinc. ... 275.00 110.00 27.00
☐ 113 Bugs Raymond: New York NL ... 300.00 120.00 30.00
☐ 114 Bob Rhoads: Cleveland ... 350.00 140.00 35.00
☐ 115 Admiral Schlei: New York NL ... 275.00 110.00 27.00
☐ 116 Boss Schmidt: Detroit ... 275.00 110.00 27.00
☐ 117 Frank Schulte: Chicago NL ... 275.00 110.00 27.00
☐ 118 Charlie Smith: Chicago and Boston ... 275.00 110.00 27.00
☐ 119 George Stone: St. Louis AL ... 275.00 110.00 27.00
☐ 120 Gabby Street: Wash. ... 275.00 110.00 27.00
☐ 121 Billy Sullivan: Chicago AL ... 275.00 110.00 27.00
☐ 122 Fred Tenney: New York NL ... 275.00 110.00 27.00
☐ 123 Ira Thomas: Phila. AL ... 275.00 110.00 27.00
☐ 124 Bobby Wallace: St. Louis AL ... 450.00 180.00 45.00
☐ 125 Ed Walsh: Chicago AL ... 500.00 200.00 50.00
☐ 126 Chief Wilson: Pittsburgh ... 275.00 110.00 27.00

1913 T200 Fatima

The cards in this 16-card set measure approximately 2 5/8" by 5 13/16". The 1913 Fatima Cigarettes issue contains unnumbered glossy surface team cards. Both St. Louis team cards are considered difficult to obtain. A large 13" by 21" unnumbered, heavy cardboard premium issue is also known to exist and is quite scarce. These unnumbered team cards are ordered below by team alphabetical order within league.

	EX-MT	VG-E	GOOD
COMPLETE SET (16)	5000.00	2100.00	700.00
COMMON TEAM (1-16)	200.00	80.00	20.00

☐ 1 Boston AL	250.00	100.00	25.00
☐ 2 Chicago AL	200.00	80.00	20.00
☐ 3 Cleveland AL	800.00	320.00	80.00
☐ 4 Detroit AL	500.00	200.00	50.00
☐ 5 New York AL	700.00	280.00	70.00
☐ 6 Philadelphia AL	200.00	80.00	20.00
☐ 7 St. Louis AL	450.00	180.00	45.00
☐ 8 Washington AL	250.00	100.00	25.00
☐ 9 Boston NL	300.00	120.00	30.00
☐ 10 Brooklyn NL	200.00	80.00	20.00
☐ 11 Chicago NL	200.00	80.00	20.00
☐ 12 Cincinnati NL	200.00	80.00	20.00
☐ 13 New York NL	450.00	180.00	45.00
☐ 14 Philadelphia NL	200.00	80.00	20.00
☐ 15 Pittsburg NL	200.00	80.00	20.00
☐ 16 St. Louis NL	300.00	120.00	30.00

1911 T201 Mecca

The cards in this 50-card set measure approximately 2 1/4" by 4 11/16". The 1911 Mecca Double Folder issue contains unnumbered cards. This issue was one of the first to list statistics of players portrayed on the cards. Each card portrays two players, one when the card is folded, another when the card is unfolded. The card of Dougherty and Lord is considered scarce.

	EX-MT	VG-E	GOOD
COMPLETE SET (50)	5500.00	2200.00	700.00
COMMON PAIR (1-50)	50.00	20.00	5.00
☐ 1 F.Baker and Collins	200.00	80.00	20.00
☐ 2 Barry and Lapp	50.00	20.00	5.00
☐ 3 Bergen and Z.Wheat	100.00	40.00	10.00
☐ 4 Blair and Hartzell	50.00	20.00	5.00
☐ 5 Bresnahan and Huggins	175.00	70.00	18.00
☐ 6 Bridwell and Mathewson	400.00	160.00	40.00
☐ 7 Butler and Abstein	50.00	20.00	5.00
☐ 8 Byrne and F.Clarke	100.00	40.00	10.00
☐ 9 Chance and Evers	250.00	100.00	25.00
☐ 10 Clark and Gaspar	50.00	20.00	5.00
☐ 11 Cobb and S.Crawford	1350.00	600.00	175.00
☐ 12 Cole and Kling	50.00	20.00	5.00
☐ 13 Coombs and Thomas	50.00	20.00	5.00
☐ 14 Daubert and Rucker	50.00	20.00	5.00
☐ 15 Dougherty and Lord	350.00	140.00	35.00
☐ 16 Dooin and Titus	50.00	20.00	5.00
☐ 17 Downie and Baker	50.00	20.00	5.00
☐ 18 Dygert and Seymour	50.00	20.00	5.00
☐ 19 Elberfeld and McBride	50.00	20.00	5.00
☐ 20 Falkenberg and Lajoie	150.00	60.00	15.00
☐ 21 Fitzpatrick and Killian	50.00	20.00	5.00
☐ 22 Gardner and Speaker	150.00	60.00	15.00
☐ 23 Gibson and Leach	50.00	20.00	5.00
☐ 24 Graham and Mattern	50.00	20.00	5.00
☐ 25 Hauser and Lush	50.00	20.00	5.00
☐ 26 Herzog and Miller	50.00	20.00	5.00
☐ 27 Hinchman and Hickman	50.00	20.00	5.00
☐ 28 Hofman and M.Brown	100.00	40.00	10.00
☐ 29 Jennings and Summers	100.00	40.00	10.00
☐ 30 Johnson and Ford	50.00	20.00	5.00
☐ 31 McCarty and McGinnity	100.00	40.00	10.00
☐ 32 McGlyn and Barrett	50.00	20.00	5.00
☐ 33 McLean and Grant	50.00	20.00	5.00
☐ 34 Merkle and Wiltse	50.00	20.00	5.00
☐ 35 Meyers and Doyle	50.00	20.00	5.00
☐ 36 Moore and Lobert	50.00	20.00	5.00
☐ 37 Odwell and Downs	50.00	20.00	5.00
☐ 38 Oldring and Bender	100.00	40.00	10.00
☐ 39 Payne and Walsh	100.00	40.00	10.00
☐ 40 Simon and Leifield	50.00	20.00	5.00
☐ 41 Starr and McCabe	50.00	20.00	5.00
☐ 42 Stephens and LaPorte	50.00	20.00	5.00
☐ 43 Stovall and Turner	50.00	20.00	5.00
☐ 44 Street and W.Johnson	400.00	160.00	40.00
☐ 45 Stroud and Donovan	50.00	20.00	5.00
☐ 46 Sweeney and Chase	50.00	20.00	5.00
☐ 47 Thoney and Cicotte	50.00	20.00	5.00
☐ 48 Wallace and Lake	100.00	40.00	10.00
☐ 49 Ward and Foster	50.00	20.00	5.00
☐ 50 Williams and Woodruff	50.00	20.00	5.00

1912 T202 Triple Folders

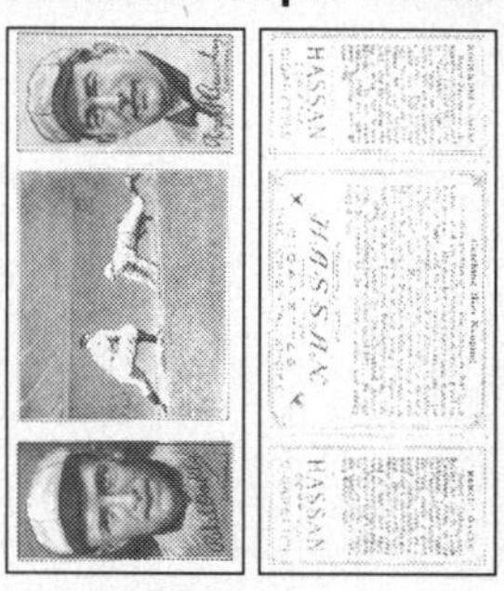

The cards in this 134-card set measure approximately 2 1/4" by 5 1/4". The 1912 T202 Hassan Triple Folder issue is perhaps the most ingenious baseball card ever issued. The two end cards of each panel are full color, T205-like individual cards whereas the black and white center panel pictures an action photo or portrait. The end cards can be folded across the center panel and stored in this manner. Seventy-six different center panels are known to exist; however, many of the center panels contain more than one combination of end cards. The center panel titles are listed below in alphabetical order while the different combinations of end cards are listed below each center panel as they appear left to right on the front of the card. A total of 132 different card fronts exist. The set price below includes all panel and player combinations listed in the checklist. Back color variations (red or black) also exist. The Birmingham's Home Run card is difficult to obtain as are other cards whose center panel exists with but one combination of end cards. The Devlin with Mathewson end panels on numbers 29A and 74C picture Devlin as a Giant. Devlin is pictured as a Rustler on 29B and 74D.

	EX-MT	VG-E	GOOD
COMPLETE SET (132)	35000.	14500.	4750.00
COMMON PANEL (1-76)	150.00	60.00	15.00
☐ 1A A Close Play at Home: Wallace-LaPorte	175.00	70.00	18.00
☐ 1B A Close Play at Home: Wallace-Pelty	175.00	70.00	18.00
☐ 2 A Desperate Slide: O'Leary-Cobb	1250.00	500.00	150.00
☐ 3A A Great Batsman: Barger-Bergen	150.00	60.00	15.00
☐ 3B A Great Batsman: Rucker-Bergen	150.00	60.00	15.00
☐ 4 Ambrose McConnell at Bat: Blair-Quinn	175.00	70.00	18.00
☐ 5 A Wide Throw Saves Crawford: Mullin-Stanage	200.00	80.00	20.00
☐ 6 Baker Gets His Man: Collins-Baker	350.00	140.00	35.00
☐ 7 Birmingham Gets to Third:	450.00	180.00	45.00

Johnson-Street

☐ 8 Birmingham's Home Run: Birmingham-Turner	400.00	160.00	40.00
☐ 9 Bush Just Misses Austin: Moran-Magee	175.00	70.00	18.00
☐ 10A Carrigan Blocks His Man: Gaspar-McLean	150.00	60.00	15.00
☐ 10B Carrigan Blocks His Man: Wagner-Carrigan	150.00	60.00	15.00
☐ 11 Catching Him Napping: Oakes-Bresnahan	200.00	80.00	20.00
☐ 12 Caught Asleep Off First: Bresnahan-Harmon	200.00	80.00	20.00
☐ 13A Chance Beats Out a Hit: Chance-Foxen	250.00	100.00	25.00
☐ 13B Chance Beats Out a Hit: McIntire-Archer	175.00	70.00	18.00
☐ 13C Chance Beats Out a Hit: Overall-Archer	175.00	70.00	18.00
☐ 13D Chance Beats Out a Hit: Rowan-Archer	175.00	70.00	18.00
☐ 13E Chance Beats Out a Hit: Shean-Chance	250.00	100.00	25.00
☐ 14A Chase Dives into Third: Chase-Wolter	150.00	60.00	15.00
☐ 14B Chase Dives into Third: Gibson-Clarke	175.00	70.00	18.00
☐ 14C Chase Dives into Third: Phillippe-Gibson	150.00	60.00	15.00
☐ 15A Chase Gets Ball Too Late: Egan-Mitchell	150.00	60.00	15.00
☐ 15B Chase Gets Ball Too Late: Wolter-Chase	150.00	60.00	15.00
☐ 16A Chase Guarding First: Chase-Wolter	150.00	60.00	15.00
☐ 16B Chase Guarding First: Gibson-Clarke	175.00	70.00	18.00
☐ 16C Chase Guarding First: Leifield-Gibson	150.00	60.00	15.00
☐ 17 Chase Ready Squeeze Play: Paskert-Magee	175.00	70.00	18.00
☐ 18 Chase Safe at Third: Barry-Baker	200.00	80.00	20.00
☐ 19 Chief Bender Waiting: Bender-Thomas	225.00	90.00	22.00
☐ 20 Clarke Hikes for Home: Bridwell-Kling	200.00	80.00	20.00
☐ 21 Close at First: Ball-Stovall	175.00	70.00	18.00
☐ 22A Close at the Plate: Walsh-Payne	175.00	70.00	18.00
☐ 22B Close at the Plate: White-Payne	150.00	60.00	15.00
☐ 23 Close at Third (Speak-er): Wood-Speaker	400.00	160.00	40.00
☐ 24 Close at Third (Wagner): Wagner-Carrigan	175.00	70.00	18.00
☐ 25A Collins Easily Safe: Byrne-Clarke	175.00	70.00	18.00
☐ 25B Collins Easily Safe: Collins-Baker	350.00	140.00	35.00
☐ 25C Collins Easily Safe: Collins-Murphy	250.00	100.00	25.00
☐ 26 Crawford About to Smash: Stanage-Summers	200.00	80.00	20.00
☐ 27 Cree Rolls Home: Daubert-Hummell	175.00	70.00	18.00
☐ 28 Davy Jones' Great Slide: Delahanty-Jones	175.00	70.00	18.00
☐ 29A Devlin Gets His Man: Devlin (Giants)-Mathewson	1250.00	500.00	150.00
☐ 29B Devlin Gets His Man: Devlin (Rustlers)-Mathewson	300.00	120.00	30.00
☐ 29C Devlin Gets His Man: Fletcher-Mathewson	300.00	120.00	30.00
☐ 29D Devlin Gets His Man: Meyers-Mathewson	300.00	120.00	30.00
☐ 30A Donlin Out at First: Camnitz-Gibson	150.00	60.00	15.00
☐ 30B Donlin Out at First: Doyle-Merkle	150.00	60.00	15.00
☐ 30C Donlin Out at First: Leach-Wilson	150.00	60.00	15.00
☐ 30D Donlin Out at First: Magee-Dooin	150.00	60.00	15.00
☐ 30E Donlin Out at First: Phillippe-Gibson	150.00	60.00	15.00
☐ 31A Dooin Gets His Man: Dooin-Doolan	150.00	60.00	15.00
☐ 31B Dooin Gets His Man: Lobert-Dooin	150.00	60.00	15.00
☐ 31C Dooin Gets His Man: Titus-Dooin	150.00	60.00	15.00
☐ 32 Easy for Larry: Doyle-Merkle	175.00	70.00	18.00
☐ 33 Elberfeld Beats: Milan-Elberfeld	175.00	70.00	18.00
☐ 34 Elberfeld Gets His Man: Milan-Elberfeld	175.00	70.00	18.00
☐ 35 Engle in a Close Play: Speaker-Engle	250.00	100.00	25.00
☐ 36A Evers Makes Safe Slide: Archer-Evers	225.00	90.00	22.00
☐ 36B Evers Makes Safe Slide: Evers-Chance	350.00	140.00	35.00
☐ 36C Evers Makes Safe Slide: Overall-Archer	175.00	70.00	18.00
☐ 36D Evers Makes Safe Slide: Reulbach-Archer	175.00	70.00	18.00
☐ 36E Evers Makes Safe Slide: Tinker-Chance	750.00	300.00	75.00
☐ 37 Fast Work at Third: O'Leary-Cobb	1250.00	500.00	150.00
☐ 38A Ford Putting Over Spitter: Ford-Vaughn	150.00	60.00	15.00
☐ 38B Ford Putting Over Spitter: Sweeney-Ford	150.00	60.00	15.00
☐ 39 Good Play at Third: Moriarty-Cobb	1250.00	500.00	150.00
☐ 40 Grant Gets His Man: Hoblitzel-Grant	175.00	70.00	18.00
☐ 41A Hal Chase Too Late: McIntyre-McConnell	150.00	60.00	15.00
☐ 41B Hal Chase Too Late: Suggs-McLean	150.00	60.00	15.00
☐ 42 Harry Lord at Third: Lennox-Tinker	200.00	80.00	20.00
☐ 43 Hartzell Covering: Scanlon-Dahlen	175.00	70.00	18.00
☐ 44 Hartzell Strikes Out: Groom-Gray	175.00	70.00	18.00
☐ 45 Held at Third: Tannehill-Lord	175.00	70.00	18.00
☐ 46 Jake Stahl Guarding: Cicotte-Stahl	175.00	70.00	18.00
☐ 47 Jim Delahanty at Bat: Delahanty-Jones	175.00	70.00	18.00
☐ 48A Just Before the Battle: Ames-Meyers	150.00	60.00	15.00
☐ 48B Just Before the Battle: Bresnahan-McGraw	350.00	140.00	35.00
☐ 48C Just Before the Battle: Crandall-Meyers	150.00	60.00	15.00
☐ 48D Just Before the Battle: Devore-Becker	150.00	60.00	15.00
☐ 48E Just Before the Battle: Fletcher-Mathewson	300.00	120.00	30.00
☐ 48F Just Before the Battle: Marquard-Meyers	175.00	70.00	18.00
☐ 48G Just Before the Battle: McGraw-Jennings	350.00	140.00	35.00
☐ 48H Just Before the Battle: Meyers-Mathewson	300.00	120.00	30.00
☐ 48I Just Before the Battle: Snodgrass-Murray	150.00	60.00	15.00
☐ 48J Just Before the Battle: Wiltse-Meyers	150.00	60.00	15.00
☐ 49 Knight Catches Runner: Knight-Johnson	450.00	180.00	45.00
☐ 50A Lobert Almost Caught: Bridwell-Kling	150.00	60.00	15.00
☐ 50B Lobert Almost Caught: Kling-Young	225.00	90.00	22.00
☐ 50C Lobert Almost Caught:	150.00	60.00	15.00

	EX-MT	VG-E	GOOD
Mattern-Kling			
☐ 50D Lobert Almost Caught: Steinfeldt-Kling	150.00	60.00	15.00
☐ 51 Lobert Gets Tenney: Lobert-Dooin	175.00	70.00	18.00
☐ 52 Lord Catches His Man: Tannehill-Lord	175.00	70.00	18.00
☐ 53 McConnell Caught: Richie-Needham	175.00	70.00	18.00
☐ 54 McIntyre at Bat: McIntrye-McConnell	175.00	70.00	18.00
☐ 55 Moriarty Spiked: Willett-Stanage	175.00	70.00	18.00
☐ 56 Nearly Caught: Bates-Bescher	200.00	80.00	20.00
☐ 57 Oldring Almost Home: Lord-Oldring	175.00	70.00	18.00
☐ 58 Schaefer on First: McBride-Milan	175.00	70.00	18.00
☐ 59 Schaefer Steals Second: McBride-Griffith	200.00	80.00	20.00
☐ 60 Scoring from Second: Lord-Oldring	175.00	70.00	18.00
☐ 61A Scrambling Back: Barger-Bergen	150.00	60.00	15.00
☐ 61B Scrambling Back: Wolter-Chase	150.00	60.00	15.00
☐ 62 Speaker Almost Caught: Miller-Clarke	400.00	160.00	40.00
☐ 63 Speaker Rounding Third: Wood-Speaker	750.00	300.00	75.00
☐ 64 Speaker Scores: Speaker-Engle	400.00	160.00	40.00
☐ 65 Stahl Safe: Stovall-Austin	175.00	70.00	18.00
☐ 66 Stone About to Swing: Sheckard-Schulte	175.00	70.00	18.00
☐ 67A Sullivan Puts Up High One: Evans-Huggins	175.00	70.00	18.00
☐ 67B Sullivan Puts Up High One: Sweeney-Ford	150.00	60.00	15.00
☐ 68A Sweeney Gets Stahl: Ford-Vaughn	150.00	60.00	15.00
☐ 68B Sweeney Gets Stahl: Sweeney-Ford	150.00	60.00	15.00
☐ 69 Tenney Lands Safely: Raymond-Latham	175.00	70.00	18.00
☐ 70A The Athletic Infield: Barry-Baker	175.00	70.00	18.00
☐ 70B The Athletic Infield: Brown-Graham	150.00	60.00	15.00
☐ 70C The Athletic Infield: Hauser-Konetchy	150.00	60.00	15.00
☐ 70D The Athletic Infield: Krause-Thomas	150.00	60.00	15.00
☐ 71 The Pinch Hitter: Hoblitzel-Egan	175.00	70.00	18.00
☐ 72 The Scissors Slide: Birmingham-Turner	175.00	70.00	18.00
☐ 73A Tom Jones at Bat: Fromme-McLean	150.00	60.00	15.00
☐ 73B Tom Jones at Bat: Gaspar-McLean	150.00	60.00	15.00
☐ 74A Too Late for Devlin: Ames-Meyers	150.00	60.00	15.00
☐ 74B Too Late for Devlin: Crandall-Meyers	150.00	60.00	15.00
☐ 74C Too Late for Devlin: Devlin (Giants)-Mathewson	1250.00	500.00	150.00
☐ 74D Too Late for Devlin: Devlin (Rustlers)-Mathewson	300.00	120.00	30.00
☐ 74E Too Late for Devlin: Marquard-Meyers	175.00	70.00	18.00
☐ 74F Too Late for Devlin: Wiltse-Meyers	150.00	60.00	15.00
☐ 75A Ty Cobb Steals Third: Jennings-Cobb	2500.00	1000.00	300.00
☐ 75B Ty Cobb Steals Third: Moriarty-Cobb	2000.00	800.00	250.00
☐ 75C Ty Cobb Steals Third: Stovall-Austin	1600.00	700.00	200.00
☐ 76 Wheat Strikes Out: Dahlen-Wheat	250.00	100.00	25.00

1909 T204 Ramly

The cards in this 121-card set measure approximately 2" by 2 1/2". The Ramly baseball series, designated T204 in the ACC, contains unnumbered cards. This set is one of the most distinguished ever produced, containing ornate gold borders around a black and white portrait of each player. There are spelling errors, and two distinct backs, "Ramly" and "TT", are known. Much of the obverse card detail is actually embossed. The players have been alphabetized and numbered for reference in the checklist below.

	EX-MT	VG-E	GOOD
COMPLETE SET (121)	35000.	14000.	4250.00
COMMON PLAYER (1-121)	200.00	80.00	20.00
☐ 1 Whitey Alperman	200.00	80.00	20.00
☐ 2 John J. Anderson	200.00	80.00	20.00
☐ 3 Jimmy Archer	200.00	80.00	20.00
☐ 4 Frank Arellanes	200.00	80.00	20.00
☐ 5 Jim Ball (Boston NL)	200.00	80.00	20.00
☐ 6 Neal Ball (N.Y. AL)	200.00	80.00	20.00
☐ 7 Dave Bancroft	600.00	240.00	60.00
☐ 8 Johnny Bates	200.00	80.00	20.00
☐ 9 Fred Beebe	200.00	80.00	20.00
☐ 10 George Bell	200.00	80.00	20.00
☐ 11 Chief Bender	600.00	240.00	60.00
☐ 12 Walter Blair	200.00	80.00	20.00
☐ 13 Cliff Blankenship	200.00	80.00	20.00
☐ 14 Frank Bowerman	200.00	80.00	20.00
☐ 15 Kitty Bransfield	200.00	80.00	20.00
☐ 16 Roger Bresnahan	600.00	240.00	60.00
☐ 17 Al Bridwell	200.00	80.00	20.00
☐ 18 Mordecai Brown	600.00	240.00	60.00
☐ 19 Fred Burchell	200.00	80.00	20.00
☐ 20 Jesse Burkett	750.00	300.00	75.00
☐ 21 Robert Byrne	200.00	80.00	20.00
☐ 22 Bill Carrigan	200.00	80.00	20.00
☐ 23 Frank Chance	750.00	300.00	75.00
☐ 24 Charles Chech	200.00	80.00	20.00
☐ 25 Eddie Cicotte	250.00	100.00	25.00
☐ 26 Otis Clymer	200.00	80.00	20.00
☐ 27 Andrew Coakley	200.00	80.00	20.00
☐ 28 Eddie Collins	750.00	300.00	75.00
☐ 29 Jimmy Collins	750.00	300.00	75.00
☐ 30 Wid Conroy	200.00	80.00	20.00
☐ 31 Jack Coombs	250.00	100.00	25.00
☐ 32 Doc Crandall	200.00	80.00	20.00
☐ 33 Lou Criger	200.00	80.00	20.00
☐ 34 Harry(Jasper) Davis	200.00	80.00	20.00
☐ 35 Art Devlin	200.00	80.00	20.00
☐ 36 Bill Dineen	200.00	80.00	20.00
☐ 37 Pat Donahue	200.00	80.00	20.00
☐ 38 Mike Donlin	225.00	90.00	22.00
☐ 39 Wild Bill Donovan	200.00	80.00	20.00
☐ 40 Gus Dorner	200.00	80.00	20.00
☐ 41 Joe Dunn	200.00	80.00	20.00
☐ 42 Norman Elberfield (Sic) Elberfeld	200.00	80.00	20.00
☐ 43 Johnny Evers	750.00	300.00	75.00
☐ 44 George L. Ewing	200.00	80.00	20.00
☐ 45 George Ferguson	200.00	80.00	20.00
☐ 46 Hobe Ferris	200.00	80.00	20.00
☐ 47 James J. Freeman	200.00	80.00	20.00
☐ 48 Art Fromme	200.00	80.00	20.00
☐ 49 Bob Ganley	200.00	80.00	20.00
☐ 50 Harry(Doc) Gessler	200.00	80.00	20.00
☐ 51 George Graham	200.00	80.00	20.00
☐ 52 Clark Griffith	600.00	240.00	60.00

☐	53	Roy Hartzell	200.00	80.00	20.00
☐	54	Charlie Hemphill	200.00	80.00	20.00
☐	55	Dick Hoblitzell	200.00	80.00	20.00
☐	56	George(Del) Howard	200.00	80.00	20.00
☐	57	Harry Howell	200.00	80.00	20.00
☐	58	Miller Huggins	750.00	300.00	75.00
☐	59	John Hummel	200.00	80.00	20.00
☐	60	Walter Johnson	4000.00	1500.00	450.00
☐	61	Charles Jones	200.00	80.00	20.00
☐	62	Michael Kahoe	200.00	80.00	20.00
☐	63	Ed Karger	200.00	80.00	20.00
☐	64	Willie Keeler	750.00	300.00	75.00
☐	65	Ed Kenotchey (Sic) Konetchy	200.00	80.00	20.00
☐	66	John(Red) Kleinow	200.00	80.00	20.00
☐	67	John Knight	200.00	80.00	20.00
☐	68	Vive Lindeman	200.00	80.00	20.00
☐	69	Hans Loebert (Sic) Lobert	200.00	80.00	20.00
☐	70	Harry Lord	200.00	80.00	20.00
☐	71	Harry Lumley	200.00	80.00	20.00
☐	72	Ernie Lush	200.00	80.00	20.00
☐	73	Rube Manning	200.00	80.00	20.00
☐	74	James McAleer	200.00	80.00	20.00
☐	75	Amby McConnell	200.00	80.00	20.00
☐	76	Moose McCormick	200.00	80.00	20.00
☐	77	Matthew McIntyre	200.00	80.00	20.00
☐	78	Larry McLean	200.00	80.00	20.00
☐	79	Fred Merkle	250.00	100.00	25.00
☐	80	Clyde Milan	225.00	90.00	22.00
☐	81	Michael Mitchell	200.00	80.00	20.00
☐	82	Pat Moran	200.00	80.00	20.00
☐	83	Harry(Cy) Morgan	200.00	80.00	20.00
☐	84	Tim Murnane	200.00	80.00	20.00
☐	85	Danny Murphy	200.00	80.00	20.00
☐	86	Red Murray	200.00	80.00	20.00
☐	87	Eustace(Doc) Newton	200.00	80.00	20.00
☐	88	Simon Nichols (Sic) Nicholls	200.00	80.00	20.00
☐	89	Harry Niles	200.00	80.00	20.00
☐	90	Bill O'Hara	200.00	80.00	20.00
☐	91	Charley O'Leary	200.00	80.00	20.00
☐	92	Dode Paskert	200.00	80.00	20.00
☐	93	Barney Pelty	200.00	80.00	20.00
☐	94	Jack Pfeister	200.00	80.00	20.00
☐	95	Eddie Plank	1250.00	500.00	150.00
☐	96	Jack Powell	200.00	80.00	20.00
☐	97	Bugs Raymond	225.00	90.00	22.00
☐	98	Thomas Reilly	200.00	80.00	20.00
☐	99	Lewis Ritchie (Sic) Richie	200.00	80.00	20.00
☐	100	Nap Rucker	225.00	90.00	22.00
☐	101	Ed Ruelbach (Sic) Reulbach	225.00	90.00	22.00
☐	102	Slim Sallee	200.00	80.00	20.00
☐	103	Germany Schaefer	225.00	90.00	22.00
☐	104	Jimmy Schekard (Sic) Sheckard	200.00	80.00	20.00
☐	105	Admiral Schlei	200.00	80.00	20.00
☐	106	Frank Schulte	200.00	80.00	20.00
☐	107	James Sebring	200.00	80.00	20.00
☐	108	Bill Shipke	200.00	80.00	20.00
☐	109	Anthony Smith	200.00	80.00	20.00
☐	110	Tubby Spencer	200.00	80.00	20.00
☐	111	Jake Stahl	250.00	100.00	25.00
☐	112	Harry Steinfeldt	250.00	100.00	25.00
☐	113	Jim Stephens	200.00	80.00	20.00
☐	114	Gabby Street	200.00	80.00	20.00
☐	115	William Sweeney	200.00	80.00	20.00
☐	116	Fred Tenney	200.00	80.00	20.00
☐	117	Ira Thomas	200.00	80.00	20.00
☐	118	Joe Tinker	750.00	300.00	75.00
☐	119	Bob Unglaub	200.00	80.00	20.00
☐	120	Heinie Wagner	200.00	80.00	20.00
☐	121	Bobby Wallace	750.00	300.00	75.00

T205 Gold Border

The cards in this 208-card set measure approximately 1 1/2" by 2 5/8". The T205 set (catalog designation), also known as the "Gold Border" set, was issued in 1911 in packages of the following cigarette brands: American Beauty, Broadleaf, Cycle, Drum, Hassan, Honest Long Cut, Piedmont, Polar Bear, Sovereign and Sweet Caporal. All the above were

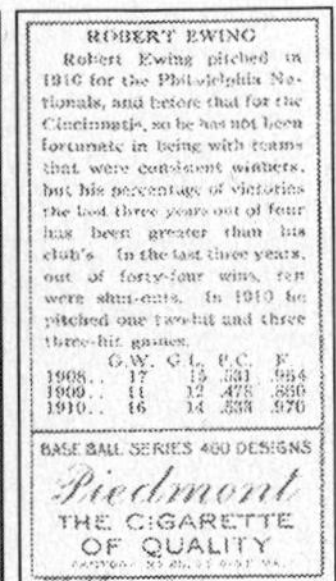
ROBERT EWING

Robert Ewing pitched in 1910 for the Philadelphia Nationals, and before that for the Cincinnatis, so he has not been fortunate in being with teams that were consistent winners, but his percentage of victories the last three years out of four has been greater than his club's. In the last three years, out of forty-four wins, ten were shut-outs. In 1910 he pitched one two-hit and three three-hit games.

	G.W.	G.L.	P.C.	F.
1908..	17	15	.531	.954
1909..	11	12	.478	.860
1910..	16	14	.533	.970

BASE BALL SERIES 460 DESIGNS

Piedmont

THE CIGARETTE OF QUALITY

products of the American Tobacco Company, and the ads for the various brands appear below the biographical section on the back of each card. There are pose variations noted in the checklist (which is alphabetized and numbered for reference) and there are 12 minor league cards of a more ornate design which are somewhat scarce. The numbers below correspond to alphabetical order within category, i.e., major leaguers and minor leaguers are alphabetized separately. The gold borders of T205 cards chip easily and they are hard to find in "Mint" or even "Near Mint" condition; however they (T205) are not appreciably tougher to find than T206 cards for lesser conditions or grades.

			EX-MT	VG-E	GOOD
		COMPLETE SET (208)	33000.	13500.	4250.00
		COMMON MAJORS (1-185)	75.00	30.00	7.50
		COMMON MINORS (186-197)	225.00	90.00	22.00
☐	1	Edward J. Abbaticchio	75.00	30.00	7.50
☐	2	Leon Ames	75.00	30.00	7.50
☐	3	James P. Archer	75.00	30.00	7.50
☐	4	James Austin	75.00	30.00	7.50
☐	5	William Bailey	75.00	30.00	7.50
☐	6	Frank Baker	300.00	120.00	30.00
☐	7	Neal Ball	75.00	30.00	7.50
☐	8A	Edward B. Barger (Full B)	75.00	30.00	7.50
☐	8B	Edward B. Barger (Part B)	300.00	120.00	30.00
☐	9	John J. Barry	75.00	30.00	7.50
☐	10	John W. Bates	75.00	30.00	7.50
☐	11	Frederick T. Beck	75.00	30.00	7.50
☐	12	Beals Becker	75.00	30.00	7.50
☐	13	George G. Bell	75.00	30.00	7.50
☐	14	Charles A. Bender	250.00	100.00	25.00
☐	15	William Bergen	75.00	30.00	7.50
☐	16	Robert H. Bescher	75.00	30.00	7.50
☐	17	Joseph Birmingham	75.00	30.00	7.50
☐	18	Russell Blackburne	75.00	30.00	7.50
☐	19	Wm. E. Bransfield	75.00	30.00	7.50
☐	20A	Roger Bresnahan (Mouth closed)	250.00	100.00	25.00
☐	20B	Roger Bresnahan (Mouth open)	500.00	200.00	50.00
☐	21	Albert Bridwell	75.00	30.00	7.50
☐	22	Mordecai Brown	250.00	100.00	25.00
☐	23	Robert Byrne	75.00	30.00	7.50
☐	24	Howard Camnitz	75.00	30.00	7.50
☐	25	William Carrigan	75.00	30.00	7.50
☐	26	Frank L. Chance	250.00	100.00	25.00
☐	27A	Harold W. Chase (Chase only)	450.00	180.00	45.00
☐	27B	Harold W. Chase (Hal Chase)	150.00	60.00	15.00
☐	28	Edward V. Cicotte	125.00	50.00	12.50
☐	29	Fred Clarke	250.00	100.00	25.00
☐	30	Tyrus Raymond Cobb	3000.00	1200.00	400.00
☐	31A	Edward T. Collins (Mouth closed)	250.00	100.00	25.00
☐	31B	Edward T. Collins (Mouth open)	500.00	200.00	50.00
☐	32	Frank J. Corridon	75.00	30.00	7.50
☐	32	Otis Crandall	75.00	30.00	7.50
☐	33	Louis Criger	75.00	30.00	7.50
☐	34	William Dahlen	300.00	120.00	30.00
☐	35	Jacob Daubert	125.00	50.00	12.50
☐	36	James Delahanty	75.00	30.00	7.50
☐	37	Arthur Devlin	75.00	30.00	7.50

☐	38	Joshua Devore	75.00	30.00	7.50
☐	39	W.R. Dickson	75.00	30.00	7.50
☐	40	J. Donohue	250.00	100.00	25.00
☐	41	Charles S. Dooin	75.00	30.00	7.50
☐	42	Michael Doolan	75.00	30.00	7.50
☐	43A	Patsy Dougherty (White stocking)	250.00	100.00	25.00
☐	43B	Patsy Dougherty (Red stocking)	75.00	30.00	7.50
☐	44	Thomas W. Downey	75.00	30.00	7.50
☐	45	Lawrence Doyle	75.00	30.00	7.50
☐	46	Hugh Duffy	400.00	160.00	40.00
☐	47	James H. Dygert	75.00	30.00	7.50
☐	48	Richard J. Egan	75.00	30.00	7.50
☐	49	Norman Elberfeld	75.00	30.00	7.50
☐	50	Clyde Engle	75.00	30.00	7.50
☐	51	Louis Evans	75.00	30.00	7.50
☐	52	John J. Evers	250.00	100.00	25.00
☐	53	Robert Ewing	75.00	30.00	7.50
☐	54	G.C. Ferguson	75.00	30.00	7.50
☐	55	Ray Fisher	300.00	120.00	30.00
☐	56	Arthur Fletcher	75.00	30.00	7.50
☐	57	John Flynn	75.00	30.00	7.50
☐	58A	Russell Ford (Dark cap)	75.00	30.00	7.50
☐	58B	Russell Ford (Light cap)	300.00	120.00	30.00
☐	59	William A. Foxen	75.00	30.00	7.50
☐	60	Arthur Fromme	75.00	30.00	7.50
☐	61	Earl Gardner	75.00	30.00	7.50
☐	62	Harry L. Gaspar	75.00	30.00	7.50
☐	63	George Gibson	75.00	30.00	7.50
☐	64	Wilbur Good	75.00	30.00	7.50
☐	65A	George F. Graham (Boston Rustlers)	75.00	30.00	7.50
☐	65B	George F. Graham (Chicago Cubs)	500.00	200.00	50.00
☐	66	Edward L. Grant	250.00	100.00	25.00
☐	67	Gray	75.00	30.00	7.50
☐	68	Clark Griffith	250.00	100.00	25.00
☐	69	Robert Groom	75.00	30.00	7.50
☐	70A	Robert Harmon (Both ears)	75.00	30.00	7.50
☐	70B	Robert Harmon (Left ear only)	300.00	120.00	30.00
☐	71	Frederick T. Hartsel	75.00	30.00	7.50
☐	72	Arnold J. Hauser	75.00	30.00	7.50
☐	73	Charles Hemphill	75.00	30.00	7.50
☐	74	Charles L. Herzog	75.00	30.00	7.50
☐	75	Richard Hoblitzell	75.00	30.00	7.50
☐	76	Daniel J. Hoffman	75.00	30.00	7.50
☐	77	Miller Huggins	250.00	100.00	25.00
☐	78	John E. Hummell	75.00	30.00	7.50
☐	79	Fred Jacklitsch	75.00	30.00	7.50
☐	80	Hugh Jennings	250.00	100.00	25.00
☐	81	Walter Johnson	1250.00	500.00	150.00
☐	82	David Jones	75.00	30.00	7.50
☐	83	Thomas Jones	75.00	30.00	7.50
☐	84	Addie Joss	750.00	300.00	75.00
☐	85	Edward Karger	300.00	120.00	30.00
☐	86	Edward Killian	75.00	30.00	7.50
☐	87	John Kleinow	300.00	120.00	30.00
☐	88	John Kling	75.00	30.00	7.50
☐	89	Jack Knight	75.00	30.00	7.50
☐	90	Edward Konetchy	75.00	30.00	7.50
☐	91	Harry Krause	75.00	30.00	7.50
☐	92	Floyd M. Kroh	75.00	30.00	7.50
☐	93	Frank Lang	75.00	30.00	7.50
☐	94	Frank LaPorte	75.00	30.00	7.50
☐	95	W.A. Latham	75.00	30.00	7.50
☐	96	Thomas W. Leach	75.00	30.00	7.50
☐	97	Sam Leever	75.00	30.00	7.50
☐	98	Albert P. Leifield	75.00	30.00	7.50
☐	99	Edgar Lennox	75.00	30.00	7.50
☐	100	Pat'k J. Livingston	75.00	30.00	7.50
☐	101	John Lobert	75.00	30.00	7.50
☐	102	Briscoe Lord	75.00	30.00	7.50
☐	103	Harry D. Lord	75.00	30.00	7.50
☐	104	John Lush	75.00	30.00	7.50
☐	105	Nicholas Maddox	75.00	30.00	7.50
☐	106	Sherwood R. Magee	75.00	30.00	7.50
☐	107	Richard Marquard	250.00	100.00	25.00
☐	108	Christy Mathewson	1000.00	400.00	125.00
☐	109	A.A. Mattern	75.00	30.00	7.50
☐	110	George F. McBride	75.00	30.00	7.50
☐	111	Ambrose McConnell	75.00	30.00	7.50
☐	112	Pryor McElveen	75.00	30.00	7.50
☐	113	John J. McGraw	400.00	160.00	40.00
☐	114	Harry McIntire	75.00	30.00	7.50
☐	115	Matthew McIntyre	75.00	30.00	7.50
☐	116	John B. McLean	75.00	30.00	7.50
☐	117	Fred Merkle	125.00	50.00	12.50
☐	118	John T. Meyers	75.00	30.00	7.50
☐	119	J. Clyde Milan	75.00	30.00	7.50
☐	120	John D. Miller	75.00	30.00	7.50
☐	121	Michael Mitchell	75.00	30.00	7.50
☐	122	Patrick J. Moran	75.00	30.00	7.50
☐	123	George Moriarity	75.00	30.00	7.50
☐	124	George J. Mullin	75.00	30.00	7.50
☐	125	Daniel Murphy	75.00	30.00	7.50
☐	126	John J. Murray	75.00	30.00	7.50
☐	127	Thomas J. Needham	75.00	30.00	7.50
☐	128	Rebel Oakes	75.00	30.00	7.50
☐	129	Reuben N. Oldring	75.00	30.00	7.50
☐	130	Charles O'Leary	75.00	30.00	7.50
☐	131	Frederick Olmstead	75.00	30.00	7.50
☐	132	Orval Overall	75.00	30.00	7.50
☐	133	F. Parent	75.00	30.00	7.50
☐	134	George Paskert	75.00	30.00	7.50
☐	135	Fred Payne	75.00	30.00	7.50
☐	136	B. Pelty	75.00	30.00	7.50
☐	137	John A. Pfiester	75.00	30.00	7.50
☐	138	Edward Phelps	75.00	30.00	7.50
☐	139	Charles Phillippe	125.00	50.00	12.50
☐	140	John Quinn	75.00	30.00	7.50
☐	141	Arthur L. Raymond	300.00	120.00	30.00
☐	142	Edward M. Reulbach	75.00	30.00	7.50
☐	143	Lewis Richie	75.00	30.00	7.50
☐	144	John A. Rowan	300.00	120.00	30.00
☐	145	G.N. Rucker	75.00	30.00	7.50
☐	146	W.D. Scanlan	300.00	120.00	30.00
☐	147	Herman Schaefer	75.00	30.00	7.50
☐	148	George H. Schlei	75.00	30.00	7.50
☐	149	Charles Schmidt	75.00	30.00	7.50
☐	150	Frank M. Schulte	75.00	30.00	7.50
☐	151	James Scott	75.00	30.00	7.50
☐	152	Bayard H. Sharpe	75.00	30.00	7.50
☐	153A	David Shean (Boston Rustlers)	75.00	30.00	7.50
☐	153B	David Shean (Chicago Cubs)	500.00	200.00	50.00
☐	154	James T. Sheckard	75.00	30.00	7.50
☐	155	George Simmons	75.00	30.00	7.50
☐	156	Tony Smith	75.00	30.00	7.50
☐	157	Fred C. Snodgrass	75.00	30.00	7.50
☐	158	Tris Speaker	600.00	240.00	60.00
☐	159	Jacob G. Stahl	100.00	40.00	10.00
☐	160	Oscar Stanage	75.00	30.00	7.50
☐	161	Harry Steinfeldt	75.00	30.00	7.50
☐	162	George Stone	75.00	30.00	7.50
☐	163	George T. Stovall	75.00	30.00	7.50
☐	164	Charles E. Street	75.00	30.00	7.50
☐	165	George Suggs	300.00	120.00	30.00
☐	166	Edgar Summers	75.00	30.00	7.50
☐	167	Edward Sweeney	300.00	120.00	30.00
☐	168	Lee Ford Tannehill	75.00	30.00	7.50
☐	169	Ira Thomas	75.00	30.00	7.50
☐	170	Joseph B. Tinker	250.00	100.00	25.00
☐	171	John Titus	75.00	30.00	7.50
☐	172	Terence Turner	300.00	120.00	30.00
☐	173	James Vaughn	300.00	120.00	30.00
☐	174	Charles Wagner	300.00	120.00	30.00
☐	175A	Roderick J. Wallace (With cap)	250.00	100.00	25.00
☐	175B	Roderick J. Wallace (Without cap)	500.00	200.00	50.00
☐	176	Edward Walsh	450.00	180.00	45.00
☐	177	Zach D. Wheat	250.00	100.00	25.00
☐	178	G.H. White	75.00	30.00	7.50
☐	179	Kirb White	300.00	120.00	30.00
☐	180	Irvin K. Wilhelm	300.00	120.00	30.00
☐	181	Edgar Willett	75.00	30.00	7.50
☐	182A	George Wiltse (Both ears)	75.00	30.00	7.50
☐	182B	George Wiltse (Right ear only)	300.00	120.00	30.00
☐	183	J. Owen Wilson	75.00	30.00	7.50
☐	184	Harry Wolter	75.00	30.00	7.50
☐	185	Denton T. Young	900.00	360.00	90.00
☐	186	Dr.Merle T. Adkins: Baltimore	225.00	90.00	22.00
☐	187	John Dunn: Baltimore	250.00	100.00	25.00
☐	188	George Merritt: Buffalo	225.00	90.00	22.00
☐	189	Charles Hanford: Jersey City	225.00	90.00	22.00
☐	190	Forrest D. Cady: Newark	225.00	90.00	22.00
☐	191	James Frick: Newark	225.00	90.00	22.00
☐	192	Wyatt Lee: Newark	225.00	90.00	22.00
☐	193	Lewis McAllister: Newark	225.00	90.00	22.00
☐	194	John Nee: Newark	225.00	90.00	22.00
☐	195	James Collins: Providence	500.00	200.00	50.00

		EX-MT	VG-E	GOOD
☐	196 James Phelan: Providence	225.00	90.00	22.00
☐	197 Henry Batch: Rochester	225.00	90.00	22.00

T206 White Border

The cards in this 524-card set measure approximately 1 7/16" by 2 5/8". The T206 set was and is the most popular of all the tobacco issues. The set was issued from 1909 to 1911 with sixteen different brands of cigarettes: American Beauty, Broadleaf, Cycle, Carolina Brights, Drum, El Principe de Gales, Hindu, Lenox, Old Mill, Piedmont, Polar Bear, Sovereign, Sweet Caporal, Tolstoi, Ty Cobb and Uzit. The Ty Cobb brand back is very scarce. The minor league cards are supposedly slightly more difficult to obtain than the cards of the major leaguers, with the Southern League player cards being the most difficult. Minor League players were obtained from the American Association and the Eastern league. Southern League players were obtained from a variety of leagues including the following: South Atlantic League, Southern League, Texas League, and Virginia League. The set price below does not include ultra-expensive Wagner, Plank, Magie error, or Doyle variation.

	EX-MT	VG-E	GOOD
COMPLETE SET (520)	75000.	30000.	9000.00
COMMON MAJORS (1-389)	60.00	24.00	6.00
COMMON MINORS (390-475)	50.00	20.00	5.00
COMMON SOUTHERN(476-523)	125.00	50.00	12.50

		EX-MT	VG-E	GOOD
☐	1 Ed Abbaticchio: Pitt., Batting, follow thru	60.00	24.00	6.00
☐	2 Ed Abbaticchio: Pitt., Batting, waiting pitch	75.00	30.00	7.50
☐	3 Bill Abstein: Pitt	60.00	24.00	6.00
☐	4 Whitey Alperman: Brooklyn	75.00	30.00	7.50
☐	5 Red Ames: N.Y. NL, Portrait	75.00	30.00	7.50
☐	6 Red Ames: N.Y. NL, Hands over head	60.00	24.00	6.00
☐	7 Red Ames: N.Y. NL, Hands in front of chest	75.00	30.00	7.50
☐	8 Frank Arellanes: Boston AL	60.00	24.00	6.00
☐	9 Jake Atz: Chicago AL	60.00	24.00	6.00
☐	10 Frank Baker: Phila. AL	250.00	100.00	25.00
☐	11 Neal Ball: N.Y. AL	75.00	30.00	7.50
☐	12 Neal Ball: Cleveland	60.00	24.00	6.00
☐	13 Jap Barbeau: St. Louis NL	60.00	24.00	6.00
☐	14 Jack Barry: Phila. AL	60.00	24.00	6.00
☐	15 Johnny Bates: Boston NL	75.00	30.00	7.50
☐	16 Ginger Beaumont: Boston NL	75.00	30.00	7.50
☐	17 Fred Beck: Boston NL	60.00	24.00	6.00
☐	18 Beals Becker: Boston NL	60.00	24.00	6.00
☐	19 George Bell: Brooklyn, pitching, follow thru	60.00	24.00	6.00
☐	20 George Bell: Brooklyn, Hands over head	75.00	30.00	7.50
☐	21 Chief Bender: Phila. AL, Portrait	300.00	120.00	30.00
☐	22 Chief Bender: Phila. AL, pitching, trees	200.00	80.00	20.00
☐	23 Chief Bender: Phila. AL, pitching, no trees	200.00	80.00	20.00
☐	24 Bill Bergen: Brooklyn, Catching	60.00	24.00	6.00
☐	25 Bill Bergen: Brooklyn, Batting	75.00	30.00	7.50
☐	26 Berger: Cleveland	60.00	24.00	6.00
☐	27 Bob Bescher: Cinc., Catching fly ball	60.00	24.00	6.00
☐	28 Bob Bescher: Cinc. Portrait	60.00	24.00	6.00
☐	29 Joe Birmingham: Cleveland	75.00	30.00	7.50
☐	30 Jack Bliss: St.L. NL	60.00	24.00	6.00
☐	31 Frank Bowerman: Boston NL	75.00	30.00	7.50
☐	32 Bill Bradley: Cleveland, Portrait	75.00	30.00	7.50
☐	33 Bill Bradley: Cleveland, Batting	60.00	24.00	6.00
☐	34 Kitty Bransfield: Phila. NL	75.00	30.00	7.50
☐	35 Roger Bresnahan: St.L. NL, Portrait	300.00	120.00	30.00
☐	36 Roger Bresnahan: St.L. NL, Batting	200.00	80.00	20.00
☐	37 Al Bridwell: N.Y. NL, Portrait	75.00	30.00	7.50
☐	38 Al Bridwell: N.Y. NL, Wearing sweater	60.00	24.00	6.00
☐	39 George Brown: Chicago NL (Sic, Browne)	150.00	60.00	15.00
☐	40 George Brown: Washington (Sic, Browne)	600.00	240.00	60.00
☐	41 Mordecai Brown: Chicago NL, Portrait	325.00	130.00	32.00
☐	42 Mordecai Brown: Chicago NL, Chicago down front of shirt	225.00	90.00	22.00
☐	43 Mordecai Brown: Chicago NL, Cubs across chest	400.00	160.00	40.00
☐	44 Al Burch: Brooklyn, Fielding	60.00	24.00	6.00
☐	45 Al Burch: Brooklyn, Batting	150.00	60.00	15.00
☐	46 Bill Burns: Chicago AL	60.00	24.00	6.00
☐	47 Donie Bush: Detroit	75.00	30.00	7.50
☐	48 Bobby Byrne: St. Louis NL	60.00	24.00	6.00
☐	49 Howie Camnitz: Pitt., Arms folded over chest	75.00	30.00	7.50
☐	50 Howie Camnitz: Pitt., Hands over head	60.00	24.00	6.00
☐	51 Howie Camnitz: Pitt., Throwing	60.00	24.00	6.00
☐	52 Billy Campbell: Cincinnati	60.00	24.00	6.00
☐	53 Bill Carrigan: Boston AL	60.00	24.00	6.00
☐	54 Frank Chance: Chicago NL, Cubs across chest	400.00	160.00	40.00
☐	55 Frank Chance: Chicago NL, Chicago down front of shirt	225.00	90.00	22.00
☐	56 Frank Chance: Chicago NL, Batting	225.00	90.00	22.00
☐	57 Chappy Charles: St. Louis NL	60.00	24.00	6.00
☐	58 Hal Chase: N.Y. AL, Port. blue bkgd.	100.00	40.00	10.00
☐	59 Hal Chase: N.Y. AL, Port., pink bkgd.	300.00	120.00	30.00
☐	60 Hal Chase: N.Y. AL,	90.00	36.00	9.00

	Holding cup			
☐ 61	Hal Chase: N.Y. AL, Throwing, dark cap	90.00	36.00	9.00
☐ 62	Hal Chase: N.Y. AL, Throwing, white cap	250.00	100.00	25.00
☐ 63	Jack Chesbro: New York AL	350.00	140.00	35.00
☐ 64	Eddie Cicotte: Boston AL	150.00	60.00	15.00
☐ 65	Fred Clarke: Pitt., Portrait	300.00	120.00	30.00
☐ 66	Fred Clarke: Pitt.	200.00	80.00	20.00
☐ 67	Josh Clarke: Cleve.	75.00	30.00	7.50
☐ 68	Ty Cobb: Detroit, Port., red bkgd.	2000.00	800.00	250.00
☐ 69	Ty Cobb: Detroit, Port., green background	3500.00	1400.00	450.00
☐ 70	Ty Cobb: Detroit, Bat on shoulder	2000.00	800.00	250.00
☐ 71	Ty Cobb: Detroit, Bat away from shoulder	1600.00	700.00	225.00
☐ 72	Eddie Collins: Phila. AL	225.00	90.00	22.00
☐ 73	Wid Conroy: Washington, Fielding	75.00	30.00	7.50
☐ 74	Wid Conroy: Wash., Bat on shoulder	60.00	24.00	6.00
☐ 75	Harry Covaleski: Phila. NL	75.00	30.00	7.50
☐ 76	Doc Crandall: N.Y. NL, without cap	75.00	30.00	7.50
☐ 77	Doc Crandall: N.Y. NL, sweater and cap	60.00	24.00	6.00
☐ 78	Sam Crawford: Detroit, Batting	200.00	80.00	20.00
☐ 79	Sam Crawford: Detroit, Throwing	250.00	100.00	25.00
☐ 80	Birdie Cree: N.Y. AL	60.00	24.00	6.00
☐ 81	Lou Criger: St.L. AL	75.00	30.00	7.50
☐ 82	Dode Criss: St.L. AL	75.00	30.00	7.50
☐ 83	Bill Dahlen: Boston NL	100.00	40.00	10.00
☐ 84	Bill Dahlen: Brooklyn	350.00	140.00	35.00
☐ 85	George Davis: Chicago AL	75.00	30.00	7.50
☐ 86	Harry Davis: Phila. AL, Davis on card	60.00	24.00	6.00
☐ 87	Harry Davis: Phila. AL, H.Davis on card	75.00	30.00	7.50
☐ 88	Jim Delehanty: Wash.	75.00	30.00	7.50
☐ 89	Ray Demmitt: St.L. AL	4500.00	1800.00	600.00
☐ 90	Ray Demmitt: N.Y. AL	75.00	30.00	7.50
☐ 91	Art Devlin: N.Y. NL	75.00	30.00	7.50
☐ 92	Josh Devore: N.Y. NL	60.00	24.00	6.00
☐ 93	Bill Dineen: St. Louis AL	60.00	24.00	6.00
☐ 94	Mike Donlin: N.Y. NL, Fielding	150.00	60.00	15.00
☐ 95	Mike Donlin: N.Y. NL, Sitting	90.00	36.00	9.00
☐ 96	Mike Donlin: N.Y. NL, Batting	75.00	30.00	7.50
☐ 97	Jiggs Donohue: Chicago AL	75.00	30.00	7.50
☐ 98	Bill Donovan: Detroit, Portrait	75.00	30.00	7.50
☐ 99	Bill Donovan: Detroit, Throwing	60.00	24.00	6.00
☐ 100	Red Dooin: Phila. NL	75.00	30.00	7.50
☐ 101	Mickey Doolan: Phila. NL, Fielding	60.00	24.00	6.00
☐ 102	Mickey Doolan: Phila. NL, Batting	60.00	24.00	6.00
☐ 103	Mickey Doolin (Sic, Doolan): Phila. NL,	75.00	30.00	7.50
☐ 104	Patsy Dougherty: Chicago AL, Portrait	75.00	30.00	7.50
☐ 105	Patsy Dougherty: Chicago AL, Fielding	60.00	24.00	6.00
☐ 106	Tom Downey: Cinc., Batting	60.00	24.00	6.00
☐ 107	Tom Downey: Cinc., Fielding	60.00	24.00	6.00
☐ 108A	Larry Doyle: N.Y. (Hands over head)	90.00	36.00	9.00
☐ 108B	Larry Doyle: N.Y. NAT'L, hands over head)	18000.	7500.00	2250.00
☐ 109	Larry Doyle: N.Y. NL, Sweater	75.00	30.00	7.50
☐ 110	Larry Doyle: N.Y. NL, Throwing	90.00	36.00	9.00
☐ 111	Larry Doyle: N.Y. NL, Bat on shoulder	75.00	30.00	7.50
☐ 112	Jean Dubuc: Cin.	60.00	24.00	6.00
☐ 113	Hugh Duffy: Chicago AL	225.00	90.00	22.00
☐ 114	Joe Dunn: Brooklyn	60.00	24.00	6.00
☐ 115	Bull Durham: N.Y. NL	75.00	30.00	7.50
☐ 116	Jimmy Dygert: Phila. AL	60.00	24.00	6.00
☐ 117	Ted Easterly: Cleveland	60.00	24.00	6.00
☐ 118	Dick Egan: Cinc.	60.00	24.00	6.00
☐ 119	Kid Elberfeld: Wash., Fielding	60.00	24.00	6.00
☐ 120	Kid Elberfeld: Wash., Portrait	1500.00	600.00	200.00
☐ 121	Kid Elberfeld: N.Y. AL, Portrait	75.00	30.00	7.50
☐ 122	Clyde Engle: N.Y. AL	60.00	24.00	6.00
☐ 123	Steve Evans: St. Louis NL	60.00	24.00	6.00
☐ 124	Johnny Evers: Chicago NL, Portrait	325.00	130.00	32.00
☐ 125	Johnny Evers: Chicago NL, Cubs across chest	400.00	160.00	40.00
☐ 126	Johnny Evers: Chicago NL, Chicago down front of shirt	225.00	90.00	22.00
☐ 127	Bob Ewing: Cinc.	75.00	30.00	7.50
☐ 128	George Ferguson: Boston NL	60.00	24.00	6.00
☐ 129	Hobe Ferris: St. Louis AL	75.00	30.00	7.50
☐ 130	Lou Fiene: Chicago AL, Portrait	60.00	24.00	6.00
☐ 131	Lou Fiene: Chicago AL, Throwing	60.00	24.00	6.00
☐ 132	Art Fletcher: New York NL	60.00	24.00	6.00
☐ 133	Elmer Flick: Cleveland	300.00	120.00	30.00
☐ 134	Russ Ford: N.Y. AL	60.00	24.00	6.00
☐ 135	John Frill: N.Y. AL	60.00	24.00	6.00
☐ 136	Art Fromme: Cinc.	60.00	24.00	6.00
☐ 137	Chick Gandil: Chicago AL	200.00	80.00	20.00
☐ 138	Bob Ganley: Washington	75.00	30.00	7.50
☐ 139	Harry Gasper: Cinc. (Sic, Gaspar)	60.00	24.00	6.00
☐ 140	Rube Geyer: St.L. NL	60.00	24.00	6.00
☐ 141	George Gibson: Pitt.	75.00	30.00	7.50
☐ 142	Billy Gilbert: St. Louis NL	75.00	30.00	7.50
☐ 143	Wilbur Goode (Sic, Good): Cleve.	75.00	30.00	7.50
☐ 144	Bill Graham: St. Louis AL	60.00	24.00	6.00
☐ 145	Peaches Graham: Boston NL	60.00	24.00	6.00
☐ 146	Dolly Gray: Washington	75.00	30.00	7.50
☐ 147	Clark Griffith: Cinc., Portrait	300.00	120.00	30.00
☐ 148	Clark Griffith: Cinc., Batting	200.00	80.00	20.00
☐ 149	Bob Groom: Washington	60.00	24.00	6.00
☐ 150	Ed Hahn: Chicago AL	75.00	30.00	7.50
☐ 151	Topsy Hartsel: Phila. AL	60.00	24.00	6.00
☐ 152	Charlie Hemphill: N.Y. AL	75.00	30.00	7.50
☐ 153	Buck Herzog: N.Y. NL	75.00	30.00	7.50
☐ 154	Buck Herzog: Boston NL	60.00	24.00	6.00
☐ 155	Bill Hinchman: Cleveland	75.00	30.00	7.50
☐ 156	Doc Hoblitzell: Cincinnati	60.00	24.00	6.00
☐ 157	Danny Hoffman: St. Louis AL	60.00	24.00	6.00
☐ 158	Solly Hofman: Chicago NL	60.00	24.00	6.00
☐ 159	Del Howard: Chicago NL	60.00	24.00	6.00
☐ 160	Harry Howell: St.L. AL, Portrait	60.00	24.00	6.00
☐ 161	Harry Howell: St.L. AL, Left hand on hip	60.00	24.00	6.00

☐ 162 Miller Huggins: Cinc., Portrait	300.00	120.00	30.00
☐ 163 Miller Huggins: Cinc., Hands to mouth	200.00	80.00	20.00
☐ 164 Rudy Hulswitt: St. Louis NL	60.00	24.00	6.00
☐ 165 John Hummel: Brooklyn	60.00	24.00	6.00
☐ 166 George Hunter: Brooklyn	60.00	24.00	6.00
☐ 167 Frank Isbell: Chicago AL	75.00	30.00	7.50
☐ 168 Fred Jacklitsch: Phila. NL	75.00	30.00	7.50
☐ 169 Hugh Jennings: Detroit, Portrait	300.00	120.00	30.00
☐ 170 Hugh Jennings: Detroit, Yelling	200.00	80.00	20.00
☐ 171 Hugh Jennings: Detroit, Dancing for joy	200.00	80.00	20.00
☐ 172 Walter Johnson: Washington, Portrait	1250.00	500.00	150.00
☐ 173 Walter Johnson: Washington, Ready to pitch	750.00	300.00	75.00
☐ 174 Tom Jones: St.L. AL	75.00	30.00	7.50
☐ 175 Tom Jones: Detroit	60.00	24.00	6.00
☐ 176 Fielder Jones: Chic. AL, Portrait	75.00	30.00	7.50
☐ 177 Fielder Jones: Chic. AL, Hands on hips	75.00	30.00	7.50
☐ 178 Tim Jordan: Brooklyn, Portrait	75.00	30.00	7.50
☐ 179 Tim Jordan: Brooklyn, Batting	60.00	24.00	6.00
☐ 180 Addie Joss: Cleveland, Portrait	450.00	180.00	45.00
☐ 181 Addie Joss: Cleveland, Ready to pitch	250.00	100.00	25.00
☐ 182 Ed Karger: Cinc.	75.00	30.00	7.50
☐ 183 Willie Keeler: N.Y. AL, Portrait	450.00	180.00	45.00
☐ 184 Willie Keeler: N.Y. AL, Batting	300.00	120.00	30.00
☐ 185 Ed Killian: Detroit, Portrait	75.00	30.00	7.50
☐ 186 Ed Killian: Detroit, Pitching	60.00	24.00	6.00
☐ 187 Red Kleinow: N.Y. AL, Batting	75.00	30.00	7.50
☐ 188 Red Kleinow: N.Y. AL, Catching	60.00	24.00	6.00
☐ 189 Red Kleinow: Boston AL, Catching	350.00	140.00	35.00
☐ 190 Johnny Kling: Chicago NL	75.00	30.00	7.50
☐ 191 Otto Knabe: Phila. NL	60.00	24.00	6.00
☐ 192 John Knight: N.Y. AL, Portrait	60.00	24.00	6.00
☐ 193 John Knight: N.Y. AL, Batting	60.00	24.00	6.00
☐ 194 Ed Konetchy: St.L. NL, Awaiting low ball	60.00	24.00	6.00
☐ 195 Ed Konetchy: St.L. NL, Glove above head	75.00	30.00	7.50
☐ 196 Harry Krause: Phila. AL, Portrait	60.00	24.00	6.00
☐ 197 Harry Krause: Phila. AL, Pitching	60.00	24.00	6.00
☐ 198 Rube Kroh: Chicago NL	60.00	24.00	6.00
☐ 199 Nap Lajoie: Cleveland, Portrait	600.00	240.00	60.00
☐ 200 Nap Lajoie: Cleveland, Batting	350.00	140.00	35.00
☐ 201 Nap Lajoie: Cleveland, Throwing	400.00	160.00	40.00
☐ 202 Joe Lake: N.Y. AL	75.00	30.00	7.50
☐ 203 Joe Lake: St.L. AL, Hands over head	60.00	24.00	6.00
☐ 204 Joe Lake: St.L. AL, Throwing	60.00	24.00	6.00
☐ 205 Frank LaPorte: N.Y. AL	60.00	24.00	6.00
☐ 206 Arlie Latham: N.Y. NL	60.00	24.00	6.00
☐ 207 Fred Leach: Pitt., Portrait	75.00	30.00	7.50
☐ 208 Fred Leach: Pitt., In fielding position	60.00	24.00	6.00
☐ 209 Lefty Leifield: Pitt., Batting	60.00	24.00	6.00
☐ 210 Lefty Leifield: Pitt., Hands behind head	75.00	30.00	7.50
☐ 211 Ed Lennox: Brooklyn	60.00	24.00	6.00
☐ 212 Glenn Liebhardt: Cleveland	75.00	30.00	7.50
☐ 213 Vive Lindaman: Boston NL	100.00	40.00	10.00
☐ 214 Paddy Livingstone: Phila. AL	60.00	24.00	6.00
☐ 215 Hans Lobert: Cinc.	75.00	30.00	7.50
☐ 216 Harry Lord: Bost. AL	60.00	24.00	6.00
☐ 217 Harry Lumley: Brooklyn	75.00	30.00	7.50
☐ 218 Carl Lundgren: Chicago NL	400.00	160.00	40.00
☐ 219 Nick Maddox: Pitt.	60.00	24.00	6.00
☐ 220 Sherry Magee: Phila. NL, Portrait	90.00	36.00	9.00
☐ 221 Sherry Magee: Phila. NL, Batting	60.00	24.00	6.00
☐ 222 Sherry Magie: Phila. NL, (Sic, Magee) Portrait, name misspelled	15000.	6000.00	2000.00
☐ 223 Rube Manning: N.Y. AL, Batting	75.00	30.00	7.50
☐ 224 Rube Manning: N.Y. AL, Hands over head	60.00	24.00	6.00
☐ 225 Rube Marquard: N.Y. NL, Portrait	300.00	120.00	30.00
☐ 226 Rube Marquard: N.Y. NL, Pitching	200.00	80.00	20.00
☐ 227 Rube Marquard: N.Y. NL, Standing	250.00	100.00	25.00
☐ 228 Doc Marshall: Brooklyn	60.00	24.00	6.00
☐ 229 Christy Mathewson: N.Y. NL, Portrait	1250.00	500.00	150.00
☐ 230 Christy Mathewson: N.Y. NL, Pitching, white cap	750.00	300.00	75.00
☐ 231 Christy Mathewson: N.Y. NL, Pitching, dark cap	750.00	300.00	75.00
☐ 232 Al Mattern: Boston NL	60.00	24.00	6.00
☐ 233 Jack McAleese: St. Louis AL	60.00	24.00	6.00
☐ 234 George McBride: Washington	60.00	24.00	6.00
☐ 235 Moose McCormick: N.Y. NL	60.00	24.00	6.00
☐ 236 Pryor McElveen: Brooklyn	60.00	24.00	6.00
☐ 237 John McGraw: N.Y. NL, Portrait, no cap	450.00	180.00	45.00
☐ 238 John McGraw: N.Y. NL, Wearing sweater	250.00	100.00	25.00
☐ 239 John McGraw: N.Y. NL, pointing	300.00	120.00	30.00
☐ 240 John McGraw: N.Y. NL, Glove on hip	300.00	120.00	30.00
☐ 241 Matty McIntyre: Brooklyn	75.00	30.00	7.50
☐ 242 Matty McIntyre: Brooklyn and Chicago NL	60.00	24.00	6.00
☐ 243 Mike McIntyre: Detroit	60.00	24.00	6.00
☐ 244 Larry McLean: Cinc.	60.00	24.00	6.00
☐ 245 George McQuillan: Phila. NL, Throwing	75.00	30.00	7.50
☐ 246 George McQuillan: Phila. NL, Batting	60.00	24.00	6.00
☐ 247 Fred Merkle: N.Y. NL, Portrait	75.00	30.00	7.50
☐ 248 Fred Merkle: N.Y. NL, Throwing	90.00	36.00	9.00
☐ 249 Chief Meyers: New York NL	60.00	24.00	6.00
☐ 250 Clyde Milan: Washington	60.00	24.00	6.00
☐ 251 Dots Miller: Pitt.	60.00	24.00	6.00
☐ 252 Mike Mitchell: Cinc.	60.00	24.00	6.00
☐ 253 Pat Moran: Chicago NL	60.00	24.00	6.00
☐ 254 George Moriarty: Detroit	60.00	24.00	6.00
☐ 255 Mike Mowrey: Cinc.	60.00	24.00	6.00
☐ 256 George Mullen:	60.00	24.00	6.00

Detroit (Sic, Mullin)			
☐ 257 George Mullin: Detroit, Throwing	75.00	30.00	7.50
☐ 258 George Mullin: Detroit, Batting	60.00	24.00	6.00
☐ 259 Danny Murphy: Phila AL, Throwing	75.00	30.00	7.50
☐ 260 Danny Murphy: Phila AL, Bat on shoulder	60.00	24.00	6.00
☐ 261 Red Murray: N.Y. NL, Sweater	60.00	24.00	6.00
☐ 262 Red Murray: N.Y. NL, Bat on shoulder	60.00	24.00	6.00
☐ 263 Chief Myers (Sic, Meyers): N.Y. NL, Fielding	60.00	24.00	6.00
☐ 264 Chief Myers (Sic, Meyers): N.Y. NL, Batting	60.00	24.00	6.00
☐ 265 Tom Needham: Chicago NL	60.00	24.00	6.00
☐ 266 Simon Nicholls: Phila. AL	75.00	30.00	7.50
☐ 267 Simon Nichols (Sic, Nicholls): Phila. AL	60.00	24.00	6.00
☐ 268 Harry Niles: Boston AL	75.00	30.00	7.50
☐ 269 Rebel Oakes: Cinc.	60.00	24.00	6.00
☐ 270 Bill O'Hara: N.Y. NL	60.00	24.00	6.00
☐ 271 Bill O'Hara: St. Louis NL	4500.00	1800.00	600.00
☐ 272 Rube Oldring: Phila. AL, Fielding	75.00	30.00	7.50
☐ 273 Rube Oldring: Phila. AL, Bat on shoulder	60.00	24.00	6.00
☐ 274 Charley O'Leary: Detroti, Portrait	75.00	30.00	7.50
☐ 275 Charley O'Leary: Detroit, Hands on knees	60.00	24.00	6.00
☐ 276 Orval Overall: Chicago NL, Portrait	75.00	30.00	7.50
☐ 277 Orval Overall: Chicago NL, Pitching, follow thru	60.00	24.00	6.00
☐ 278 Orval Overall: Chicago NL, Pitching hiding ball in glove	60.00	24.00	6.00
☐ 279 Frank Owen: Chicago AL (Sic, Owens)	75.00	30.00	7.50
☐ 280 Freddy Parent: Chicago AL	75.00	30.00	7.50
☐ 281 Dode Paskert: Cinc.	60.00	24.00	6.00
☐ 282 Jim Pastorius: Brooklyn	75.00	30.00	7.50
☐ 283 Harry Pattee: Brooklyn	125.00	50.00	12.50
☐ 284 Fred Payne: Chicago AL	60.00	24.00	6.00
☐ 285 Barney Pelty: St.L. AL, HOR	125.00	50.00	12.50
☐ 286 Barney Pelty: St.L. AL, VERT	60.00	24.00	6.00
☐ 287 George Perring: Cleveland	60.00	24.00	6.00
☐ 288 Jeff Pfeffer: Chicago NL	60.00	24.00	6.00
☐ 289 Jack Pfeister: Chic. NL, Sitting	60.00	24.00	6.00
☐ 290 Jack Pfeister: Chic. NL, Pitching	60.00	24.00	6.00
☐ 291 Ed Phelps: St.L. NL	60.00	24.00	6.00
☐ 292 Deacon Phillippe: Pitt.	90.00	36.00	9.00
☐ 293 Eddie Plank: Phila. AL	25000.	10000.	3000.00
☐ 294 Jack Powell: St. Louis AL	75.00	30.00	7.50
☐ 295 Mike Powers: Phila. AL	125.00	50.00	12.50
☐ 296 Billy Purtell: Chicago AL	60.00	24.00	6.00
☐ 297 Jack Quinn: N.Y. AL	60.00	24.00	6.00
☐ 298 Bugs Raymond: New York NL	75.00	30.00	7.50
☐ 299 Ed Reulbach: Chicago NL, Pitching	75.00	30.00	7.50
☐ 300 Ed Reulbach: Chicago NL, Hands at side	125.00	50.00	12.50
☐ 301 Bob Rhoades: sic, Rhoads, Cleveland, Hand in air	60.00	24.00	6.00
☐ 302 Bob Rhoades: sic, Rhoads, Cleveland, Ready to pitch	60.00	24.00	6.00
☐ 303 Charlie Rhodes: St. Louis NL	60.00	24.00	6.00
☐ 304 Claude Ritchey: Boston NL	75.00	30.00	7.50
☐ 305 Claude Rossman: Detroit	60.00	24.00	6.00
☐ 306 Nap Rucker: Brooklyn, Portrait	90.00	36.00	9.00
☐ 307 Nap Rucker: Brooklyn, Pitching	75.00	30.00	7.50
☐ 308 Germany Schaefer: Washington	75.00	30.00	7.50
☐ 309 Germany Schaefer: Detroit	90.00	36.00	9.00
☐ 310 Admiral Schlei: N.Y. NL, Sweater	60.00	24.00	6.00
☐ 311 Admiral Schlei: N.Y. NL, Batting	60.00	24.00	6.00
☐ 312 Admiral Schlei: N.Y. NL, Fielding	75.00	30.00	7.50
☐ 313 Boss Schmidt: Detroit, Portrait	60.00	24.00	6.00
☐ 314 Boss Schmidt: Detroit, Throwing	75.00	30.00	7.50
☐ 315 Frank Schulte: Chicago NL, Batting, back turned	60.00	24.00	6.00
☐ 316 Frank Schulte: Chicago NL, Batting, front pose	75.00	30.00	7.50
☐ 317 Jim Scott: Chicago AL	60.00	24.00	6.00
☐ 318 Cy Seymour: N.Y. NL, Portrait	60.00	24.00	6.00
☐ 319 Cy Seymour: N.Y. NL, Throwing	60.00	24.00	6.00
☐ 320 Cy Seymour: N.Y. NL, Batting	75.00	30.00	7.50
☐ 321 Al Shaw: St.L. NL	75.00	30.00	7.50
☐ 322 Jimmy Sheckard: Chicago NL, Throwing	60.00	24.00	6.00
☐ 323 Jimmy Sheckard: Chicago NL, Side view	75.00	30.00	7.50
☐ 324 Bill Shipke: Washington	75.00	30.00	7.50
☐ 325 Frank Smith: Chicago AL, Listed as Smith	60.00	24.00	6.00
☐ 326 Frank Smith: Chicago and Boston AL	450.00	180.00	45.00
☐ 327 Frank Smith: Chicago AL (Listed as F.Smith)	75.00	30.00	7.50
☐ 328 Happy Smith: Brk.	60.00	24.00	6.00
☐ 329 Fred Snodgrass: N.Y. NL, Batting	75.00	30.00	7.50
☐ 330 Fred Snodgrass: N.Y. NL, Catching	75.00	30.00	7.50
☐ 331 Bob Spade: Cinc.	75.00	30.00	7.50
☐ 332 Tris Speaker: Boston AL	500.00	200.00	50.00
☐ 333 Tubby Spencer: Boston AL	75.00	30.00	7.50
☐ 334 Jake Stahl: Boston AL Catching fly ball	75.00	30.00	7.50
☐ 335 Jake Stahl: Boston AL Standing, arms down	75.00	30.00	7.50
☐ 336 Oscar Stanage: Detroit	60.00	24.00	6.00
☐ 337 Charlie Starr: Boston NL	60.00	24.00	6.00
☐ 338 Harry Steinfeldt: Chicago NL, Portrait	90.00	36.00	9.00
☐ 339 Harry Steinfeldt: Chicago NL, Batting	75.00	30.00	7.50
☐ 340 Jim Stephens: St.L. AL	60.00	24.00	6.00
☐ 341 George Stone: St.L. AL	75.00	30.00	7.50
☐ 342 George Stovall: Cleveland, Portrait	75.00	30.00	7.50
☐ 343 George Stovall: Cleveland, Batting	60.00	24.00	6.00
☐ 344 Gabby Street: Washington, Portrait	75.00	30.00	7.50
☐ 345 Gabby Street: Washington, Catching	60.00	24.00	6.00
☐ 346 Billy Sullivan: Chicago AL	75.00	30.00	7.50

☐ 347 Ed Summers: Detroit 60.00 24.00 6.00
☐ 348 Jeff Sweeney: New York AL 60.00 24.00 6.00
☐ 349 Bill Sweeney: Boston NL 60.00 24.00 6.00
☐ 350 Jesse Tannehill: Washington 60.00 24.00 6.00
☐ 351 Lee Tannehill: Chicago AL (Listed as L.Tannehill) 75.00 30.00 7.50
☐ 352 Lee Tannehill: Chicago AL (Listed as Tannehill) 60.00 24.00 6.00
☐ 353 Fred Tenney: N.Y. NL 75.00 30.00 7.50
☐ 354 Ira Thomas: Phila. AL 60.00 24.00 6.00
☐ 355 Joe Tinker: Chicago NL, Ready to hit 225.00 90.00 22.00
☐ 356 Joe Tinker: Chicago NL, Bat on shoulder 225.00 90.00 22.00
☐ 357 Joe Tinker: Chicago NL, Portrait 300.00 120.00 30.00
☐ 358 Joe Tinker: Chicago NL, Hands on knees 300.00 120.00 30.00
☐ 359 John Titus: Phila. NL 60.00 24.00 6.00
☐ 360 Terry Turner: Cleveland 75.00 30.00 7.50
☐ 361 Bob Unglaub: Washington 60.00 24.00 6.00
☐ 362 Rube Waddell: St.L. AL, Portrait 400.00 160.00 40.00
☐ 363 Rube Waddell: St.L. AL, Pitching 250.00 100.00 25.00
☐ 364 Heinie Wagner: Boston AL, Bat on left shoulder 125.00 50.00 12.50
☐ 365 Heinie Wagner: Boston AL, Bat on right shoulder 75.00 30.00 7.50
☐ 366 Honus Wagner: Pitt. 250000. 100000. 33000.
☐ 367 Bobby Wallace: St. Louis AL 225.00 90.00 22.00
☐ 368 Ed Walsh: Chicago AL 250.00 100.00 25.00
☐ 369 Jack Warhop: N.Y. AL 60.00 24.00 6.00
☐ 370 Jake Weimer: N.Y. NL 75.00 30.00 7.50
☐ 371 Zach Wheat: Brooklyn 250.00 100.00 25.00
☐ 372 Doc White: Chicago AL, Portrait 75.00 30.00 7.50
☐ 373 Doc White: Chicago AL, Pitching 60.00 24.00 6.00
☐ 374 Kaiser Wilhelm: Brooklyn, Batting 60.00 24.00 6.00
☐ 375 Kaiser Wilhelm: Brooklyn, Hands to chest 75.00 30.00 7.50
☐ 376 Ed Willett: Detroit, Batting 60.00 24.00 6.00
☐ 377 Ed Willetts (Sic, Willett): Detroit, Pitching 60.00 24.00 6.00
☐ 378 Jimmy Williams: St. Louis AL 75.00 30.00 7.50
☐ 379 Vic Willis: Pitt. 125.00 50.00 12.50
☐ 380 Vic Willis: St.L. NL, Pitching 100.00 40.00 10.00
☐ 381 Vic Willis: St.L. NL, Batting 100.00 40.00 10.00
☐ 382 Chief Wilson: Pitt. 60.00 24.00 6.00
☐ 383 Hooks Wiltse: N.Y. NL, Portrait 75.00 30.00 7.50
☐ 384 Hooks Wiltse: N.Y. NL, Sweater 60.00 24.00 6.00
☐ 385 Hooks Wiltse: N.Y. NL, Pitching 60.00 24.00 6.00
☐ 386 Cy Young: Cleveland, Portrait 1000.00 400.00 125.00
☐ 387 Cy Young: Cleveland, Pitch, front view 650.00 260.00 65.00
☐ 388 Cy Young: Cleveland, Pitch, side view 650.00 260.00 65.00
☐ 389 Heinie Zimmerman: Chicago NL 60.00 24.00 6.00
☐ 390 Fred Abbott: Toledo 50.00 20.00 5.00
☐ 391 Merle(Doc) Adkins: Baltimore 50.00 20.00 5.00
☐ 392 John Anderson: Providence 50.00 20.00 5.00
☐ 393 Herman Armbruster: St. Paul 50.00 20.00 5.00
☐ 394 Harry Arndt: Prov. 50.00 20.00 5.00
☐ 395 Cy Barger: Rochester 60.00 24.00 6.00
☐ 396 John Barry: Milwaukee 50.00 20.00 5.00
☐ 397 Emil H. Batch: Rochester 50.00 20.00 5.00
☐ 398 Jake Beckley: K.C. 250.00 100.00 25.00
☐ 399 Russell Blackburne (Lena): Providence 50.00 20.00 5.00
☐ 400 David Brain: Buffalo 50.00 20.00 5.00
☐ 401 Roy Brashear: K.C. 50.00 20.00 5.00
☐ 402 Fred Burchell: Buffalo 50.00 20.00 5.00
☐ 403 Jimmy Burke: Ind. 50.00 20.00 5.00
☐ 404 John Butler: Roch. 50.00 20.00 5.00
☐ 405 Charles Carr: Ind. 50.00 20.00 5.00
☐ 406 James Peter Casey (Doc): Montreal 50.00 20.00 5.00
☐ 407 Peter Cassidy: Baltimore 50.00 20.00 5.00
☐ 408 Wm. Chappelle: Rochester 50.00 20.00 5.00
☐ 409 Wm. Clancy: Buffalo 50.00 20.00 5.00
☐ 410 Joshua Clark: Col. 50.00 20.00 5.00
☐ 411 William Clymer: Columbus 50.00 20.00 5.00
☐ 412 Jimmy Collins: Minneapolis 300.00 120.00 30.00
☐ 413 Bunk Congalton: Columbus 50.00 20.00 5.00
☐ 414 Gavvy Cravath: Minneapolis 75.00 30.00 7.50
☐ 415 Monte Cross: Ind. 50.00 20.00 5.00
☐ 416 Paul Davidson: Ind. 50.00 20.00 5.00
☐ 417 Frank Delehanty: Louisville 60.00 24.00 6.00
☐ 418 Rube Dessau: Balt. 50.00 20.00 5.00
☐ 419 Gus Dorner: K.C. 50.00 20.00 5.00
☐ 420 Jerome Downs: Minn. 50.00 20.00 5.00
☐ 421 Jack Dunn: Baltimore 60.00 24.00 6.00
☐ 422 James Flanagan: Buffalo 50.00 20.00 5.00
☐ 423 James Freeman: Tol. 50.00 20.00 5.00
☐ 424 John Ganzel: Roch. 50.00 20.00 5.00
☐ 425 Myron Grimshaw: Toronto 50.00 20.00 5.00
☐ 426 Robert Hall: Balt. 50.00 20.00 5.00
☐ 427 William Hallman: Kansas City 50.00 20.00 5.00
☐ 428 John Hannifan: J.C. 50.00 20.00 5.00
☐ 429 Jack Hayden: Ind. 50.00 20.00 5.00
☐ 430 Harry Hinchman: Toledo 50.00 20.00 5.00
☐ 431 Harry C. Hoffman (Izzy): Providence 50.00 20.00 5.00
☐ 432 James B. Jackson: Baltimore 60.00 24.00 6.00
☐ 433 Joe Kelley: Tor. 300.00 120.00 30.00
☐ 434 Rube Kisinger: Buffalo, (Sic) Kissinger 50.00 20.00 5.00
☐ 435 Otto Kruger: Col. (Sic) Krueger 50.00 20.00 5.00
☐ 436 Wm. Lattimore: Tol. 50.00 20.00 5.00
☐ 437 James Lavender: Providence 50.00 20.00 5.00
☐ 438 Carl Lundgren: K.C. 50.00 20.00 5.00
☐ 439 Wm. Malarkey: Buff. 60.00 24.00 6.00
☐ 440 Wm. Maloney: Roch. 50.00 20.00 5.00
☐ 441 Dennis McGann: Milwaukee 50.00 20.00 5.00
☐ 442 James McGinley: Toronto 50.00 20.00 5.00
☐ 443 Joe McGinnity: New. 250.00 100.00 25.00
☐ 444 Ulysses McGlynn: Milwaukee 50.00 20.00 5.00
☐ 445 George Merritt: Jersey City 50.00 20.00 5.00
☐ 446 Wm. Milligan: J.C. 50.00 20.00 5.00
☐ 447 Fred Mitchell: Tor. 50.00 20.00 5.00
☐ 448 Dan Moeller: J.C. 50.00 20.00 5.00
☐ 449 Joseph Herbert Moran: Providence 50.00 20.00 5.00
☐ 450 Wm. Nattress: Buffalo 50.00 20.00 5.00
☐ 451 Frank Oberlin: Minneapolis 50.00 20.00 5.00
☐ 452 Peter O'Brien: St. Paul 50.00 20.00 5.00
☐ 453 Wm. O'Neil: Minn. 50.00 20.00 5.00
☐ 454 James Phelan: Prov. 50.00 20.00 5.00
☐ 455 Oliver Pickering: Minneapolis. 50.00 20.00 5.00

Player	EX-MT	VG-E	GOOD
☐ 456 Philip Poland: Baltimore	50.00	20.00	5.00
☐ 457 Ambrose Puttman: Louisville	50.00	20.00	5.00
☐ 458 Lee Quillen: Minn.	50.00	20.00	5.00
☐ 459 Newton Randall: Milwaukee	50.00	20.00	5.00
☐ 460 Louis Ritter: K.C.	50.00	20.00	5.00
☐ 461 Dick Rudolph: Tor.	50.00	20.00	5.00
☐ 462 George Schirm: Buffalo	50.00	20.00	5.00
☐ 463 Larry Schlafly: Newark	50.00	20.00	5.00
☐ 464 Ossie Schreck: Col. (Sic) Schreckengost	50.00	20.00	5.00
☐ 465 William Shannon: Kansas City	50.00	20.00	5.00
☐ 466 Bayard Sharpe: Newark	50.00	20.00	5.00
☐ 467 Royal Shaw: Prov.	50.00	20.00	5.00
☐ 468 James Slagle: Balt.	50.00	20.00	5.00
☐ 469 George Henry Smith: Buffalo	50.00	20.00	5.00
☐ 470 Samuel Strang: Baltimore	50.00	20.00	5.00
☐ 471 Luther Taylor: (Dummy): Buffalo	90.00	36.00	9.00
☐ 472 John Thielman: Louisville	50.00	20.00	5.00
☐ 473 John F. White: Buffalo	50.00	20.00	5.00
☐ 474 William Wright: Toledo	50.00	20.00	5.00
☐ 475 Irving M. Young: Minneapolis	60.00	24.00	6.00
☐ 476 Jack Bastian: San Antonio	125.00	50.00	12.50
☐ 477 Harry Bay: Nashv.	125.00	50.00	12.50
☐ 478 Wm. Bernhard: Nashville	125.00	50.00	12.50
☐ 479 Ted Breitenstein: New Orleans	125.00	50.00	12.50
☐ 480 George Carey: (Scoops): Memphis	125.00	50.00	12.50
☐ 481 Cad Coles: Augusta	125.00	50.00	12.50
☐ 482 Wm. Cranston: Memphis	125.00	50.00	12.50
☐ 483 Roy Ellam: Nashville	125.00	50.00	12.50
☐ 484 Edward Foster: Charleston	125.00	50.00	12.50
☐ 485 Charles Fritz: N.O.	125.00	50.00	12.50
☐ 486 Ed Greminger: Montgomery	125.00	50.00	12.50
☐ 487 Guiheen: Portsmouth	125.00	50.00	12.50
☐ 488 William F. Hart Little Rock	125.00	50.00	12.50
☐ 489 James Henry Hart: Montgomery	125.00	50.00	12.50
☐ 490 J.R. Helm: Columbus (Georgia)	125.00	50.00	12.50
☐ 491 Gordon Hickman: Mobile	125.00	50.00	12.50
☐ 492 Buck Hooker: Lynchburg	125.00	50.00	12.50
☐ 493 Ernie Howard: Sav.	125.00	50.00	12.50
☐ 494 A.O. Jordan: Atlanta	125.00	50.00	12.50
☐ 495 J.F. Kiernan: Columbia	125.00	50.00	12.50
☐ 496 Frank King: Danville	125.00	50.00	12.50
☐ 497 James LaFitte: Macon	125.00	50.00	12.50
☐ 498 Harry Lentz: Little Rock (Sic) Sentz	125.00	50.00	12.50
☐ 499 Perry Lipe: Richmond	125.00	50.00	12.50
☐ 500 George Manion: Columbia	125.00	50.00	12.50
☐ 501 McCauley: Portsmouth	125.00	50.00	12.50
☐ 502 Charles B. Miller: Dallas	125.00	50.00	12.50
☐ 503 Carlton Molesworth: Birmingham	125.00	50.00	12.50
☐ 504 Dominic Mullaney: Jacksonville	125.00	50.00	12.50
☐ 505 Albert Orth: Lynchburg	125.00	50.00	12.50
☐ 506 William Otey: Norf.	125.00	50.00	12.50
☐ 507 George Paige: Charleston	125.00	50.00	12.50
☐ 508 Hub Perdue: Nashv.	150.00	60.00	15.00
☐ 509 Archie Persons: Montgomery	125.00	50.00	12.50
☐ 510 Edward Reagan: N.O.	125.00	50.00	12.50
☐ 511 R.H. Revelle: Richmond	125.00	50.00	12.50
☐ 512 Isaac Rockenfeld: Montgomery	125.00	50.00	12.50
☐ 513 Ray Ryan: Roanoke	125.00	50.00	12.50
☐ 514 Charles Seitz: Norfolk	125.00	50.00	12.50
☐ 515 Frank Shaughnessy (Shag): Roanoke	150.00	60.00	15.00
☐ 516 Carlos Smith: Shreveport	125.00	50.00	12.50
☐ 517 Sid Smith: Atlanta	125.00	50.00	12.50
☐ 518 M.R.(Dolly) Stark: San Antonio	150.00	60.00	15.00
☐ 519 Tony Thebo: Waco	125.00	50.00	12.50
☐ 520 Woodie Thornton: Mobile	125.00	50.00	12.50
☐ 521 Juan Violat: Jacksonville: (Sic) Viola	125.00	50.00	12.50
☐ 522 James Westlake: Danville	125.00	50.00	12.50
☐ 523 Foley White: Houston	125.00	50.00	12.50

T207 Brown Background

The cards in this 207-card set measure approximately 1 1/2" by 2 5/8". The T207 set, also known as the "Brown Background" set was issued with Broadleaf, Cycle, Napoleon, Recruit and anonymous (Factories no. 2, 3 or 25) backs in 1912. Broadleaf, Cycle and anonymous backs are difficult to obtain. Although many scarcities and cards with varying degrees of difficulty to obtain exist (see prices below), the Loudermilk, Lewis (Boston NL) and Miller (Chicago NL) cards are the rarest, followed by Saier and Tyler. The cards are numbered below for reference in alphabetical order by player's name. The complete set price below does include the Lewis variation missing the Braves patch on the sleeve.

	EX-MT	VG-E	GOOD
COMPLETE SET (208)	32000.	13500.	4000.00
COMMON PLAYER (1-207)	65.00	26.00	6.50
☐ 1 Bert Adams: Cleve	90.00	36.00	9.00
☐ 2 Eddie Ainsmith: Wash	65.00	26.00	6.50
☐ 3 Rafael Almeida: Cinc	90.00	36.00	9.00
☐ 4 Jimmy Austin: StL AL with StL on shirt	65.00	26.00	6.50
☐ 5 Jimmy Austin: StL AL without StL on shirt	180.00	75.00	18.00
☐ 6 Neal Ball: Cleve	65.00	26.00	6.50
☐ 7 Cy Barger: Brk	65.00	26.00	6.50
☐ 8 Jack Barry: Phil AL	65.00	26.00	6.50
☐ 9 Paddy Bauman: Det	180.00	75.00	18.00
☐ 10 Beals Becker: NY NL	65.00	26.00	6.50
☐ 11 Chief Bender: Phil AL	200.00	80.00	20.00
☐ 12 Joe Benz: Chi AL	90.00	36.00	9.00
☐ 13 Bob Bescher: Cinc	65.00	26.00	6.50

☐ 14 Joe Birmingham: Cleve	90.00	36.00	9.00
☐ 15 Lena Blackburne: Chi AL	90.00	36.00	9.00
☐ 16 Fred Blanding: Cleve	90.00	36.00	9.00
☐ 17 Bruno Block: Chi AL	65.00	26.00	6.50
☐ 18 Ping Bodie: Chi AL	65.00	26.00	6.50
☐ 19 Hugh Bradley: Bos AL	65.00	26.00	6.50
☐ 20 Roger Bresnahan: StL NL	200.00	80.00	20.00
☐ 21 Jack Bushelman: Bos AL	90.00	36.00	9.00
☐ 22 Hank Butcher: Cleve	90.00	36.00	9.00
☐ 23 Bobby Byrne: Pitt	65.00	26.00	6.50
☐ 24 Nixey Callahan: Chi AL	65.00	26.00	6.50
☐ 25 Howie Camnitz: Pitt	65.00	26.00	6.50
☐ 26 Max Carey: Pitt	200.00	80.00	20.00
☐ 27 Bill Carrigan: Bos AL correct back	65.00	26.00	6.50
☐ 28 Bill Carrigan: Bos AL Wagner back	225.00	90.00	22.00
☐ 29 George Chalmers: Phil NL	65.00	26.00	6.50
☐ 30 Frank Chance: Chi NL	275.00	110.00	27.00
☐ 31 Eddie Cicotte: Bos AL	125.00	50.00	12.50
☐ 32 Tommy Clarke: Cinc	65.00	26.00	6.50
☐ 33 King Cole: Chi NL	65.00	26.00	6.50
☐ 34 Eddie Collins: Chi AL	325.00	130.00	32.00
☐ 35 Bob Coulson: Brk	65.00	26.00	6.50
☐ 36 Tex Covington: Det	65.00	26.00	6.50
☐ 37 Doc Crandall: NY NL	65.00	26.00	6.50
☐ 38 Bill Cunningham: Wash	90.00	36.00	9.00
☐ 39 Dave Danforth: Phil AL	65.00	26.00	6.50
☐ 40 Bert Daniels: NY AL	65.00	26.00	6.50
☐ 41 Jake Daubert: Brk	90.00	36.00	9.00
☐ 42 Harry Davis: Cleve	65.00	26.00	6.50
☐ 43 Jim Delahanty: Det	75.00	30.00	7.50
☐ 44 Claud Derrick: Phil AL	65.00	26.00	6.50
☐ 45 Art Devlin: Bos NL	65.00	26.00	6.50
☐ 46 Josh Devore: NY NL	65.00	26.00	6.50
☐ 47 Mike Donlin: Pitt	90.00	36.00	9.00
☐ 48 Ed Donnelly: Bos NL	90.00	36.00	9.00
☐ 49 Red Dooin: Phil NL	65.00	26.00	6.50
☐ 50 Tom Downey: Phil NL	90.00	36.00	9.00
☐ 51 Larry Doyle: NY NL	75.00	30.00	7.50
☐ 52 Dellos Drake: Det	65.00	26.00	6.50
☐ 53 Ted Easterly: Cleve	65.00	26.00	6.50
☐ 54 Rube Ellis: StL NL	65.00	26.00	6.50
☐ 55 Clyde Engle: Bos AL	65.00	26.00	6.50
☐ 56 Tex Erwin: Brk	65.00	26.00	6.50
☐ 57 Steve Evans: StL NL	65.00	26.00	6.50
☐ 58 Jack Ferry: Pitt	65.00	26.00	6.50
☐ 59 Ray Fisher: NY AL white cap	180.00	75.00	18.00
☐ 60 Ray Fisher: NY AL blue cap	90.00	36.00	9.00
☐ 61 Art Fletcher: NY NL	65.00	26.00	6.50
☐ 62 Jack Fournier: Chi AL	90.00	36.00	9.00
☐ 63 Art Fromme: Cinc	65.00	26.00	6.50
☐ 64 Del Gainor: Det	65.00	26.00	6.50
☐ 65 Larry Gardner: Bos AL	65.00	26.00	6.50
☐ 66 Lefty George: Cleve	65.00	26.00	6.50
☐ 67 Roy Golden: StL NL	65.00	26.00	6.50
☐ 68 Hank Gowdy: Bos NL	75.00	30.00	7.50
☐ 69 Peaches Graham: Phil NL	90.00	36.00	9.00
☐ 70 Jack Graney: Cleve	65.00	26.00	6.50
☐ 71 Vean Gregg: Cleve	90.00	36.00	9.00
☐ 72 Casey Hageman: Bos AL	65.00	26.00	6.50
☐ 73 Sea Lion Hall: Bos AL	65.00	26.00	6.50
☐ 74 Ed Hallinan: St.L. AL	65.00	26.00	6.50
☐ 75 Earl Hamilton: St.L. AL	65.00	26.00	6.50
☐ 76 Bob Harmon: St.L. NL	65.00	26.00	6.50
☐ 77 Grover Hartley: NY NL	90.00	36.00	9.00
☐ 78 Olaf Henriksen: Bos AL	65.00	26.00	6.50
☐ 79 John Henry: Wash	90.00	36.00	9.00
☐ 80 Buck Herzog: NY NL	90.00	36.00	9.00
☐ 81 Bob Higgins: Brk	65.00	26.00	6.50
☐ 82 Red Hoff: NY AL	90.00	36.00	9.00
☐ 83 Willie Hogan: StL AL	65.00	26.00	6.50
☐ 84 Harry Hooper: Bos AL	500.00	200.00	50.00
☐ 85 Ben Houser: Bos NL	90.00	36.00	9.00
☐ 86 Ham Hyatt: Pitt	90.00	36.00	9.00
☐ 87 Walter Johnson: Wash	1250.00	500.00	150.00
☐ 88 George Kaler: Cleve	65.00	26.00	6.50
☐ 89 Billy Kelly: Pitt	90.00	36.00	9.00
☐ 90 Jay Kirke: Bos NL	90.00	36.00	9.00
☐ 91 Johnny Kling: Bos NL	65.00	26.00	6.50
☐ 92 Otto Knabe: Phil NL	65.00	26.00	6.50
☐ 93 Elmer Knetzer: Brk	65.00	26.00	6.50
☐ 94 Ed Konetchy: StL NL	65.00	26.00	6.50
☐ 95 Harry Krause: Phil AL	65.00	26.00	6.50
☐ 96 Walt Kuhn: Chi AL	90.00	36.00	9.00
☐ 97 Joe Kutina: StL AL	90.00	36.00	9.00
☐ 98 Frank Lange: Chi AL	90.00	36.00	9.00
☐ 99 Jack Lapp: Phil AL	65.00	26.00	6.50
☐ 100 Arlie Latham: NY NL	65.00	26.00	6.50
☐ 101 Tommy Leach: Pitt	65.00	26.00	6.50
☐ 102 Lefty Leifield: Pitt	65.00	26.00	6.50
☐ 103 Ed Lennox: Chi NL	65.00	26.00	6.50
☐ 104 Duffy Lewis: Bos AL	65.00	26.00	6.50
☐ 105A Jack Lewis: Bos NL (Braves patch on sleeve)	2500.00	1000.00	300.00
☐ 105B Jack Lewis: Bos NL (Nothing on sleeve)	3000.00	1200.00	400.00
☐ 106 Otto Lively: Det	65.00	26.00	6.50
☐ 107 Paddy Livingston: Cleve ("A" shirt)	250.00	100.00	25.00
☐ 108 Paddy Livingston: Cleve ("C" shirt)	250.00	100.00	25.00
☐ 109 Paddy Livingston: Cleve ("c" shirt)	90.00	36.00	9.00
☐ 110 Bris Lord: Phil AL	65.00	26.00	6.50
☐ 111 Harry Lord: Chi AL	65.00	26.00	6.50
☐ 112 Louis Loudermilk: StL NL	2500.00	1000.00	300.00
☐ 113 Rube Marquard: NY NL	200.00	80.00	20.00
☐ 114 Armando Marsans: Cinc	65.00	26.00	6.50
☐ 115 George McBride: Wash	65.00	26.00	6.50
☐ 116 Alex McCarthy: Pitt	250.00	100.00	25.00
☐ 117 Ed McDonald: Bos NL	65.00	26.00	6.50
☐ 118 John McGraw: NY NL	275.00	110.00	27.00
☐ 119 Harry McIntire: Chi NL	65.00	26.00	6.50
☐ 120 Matty McIntyre: Chi AL	65.00	26.00	6.50
☐ 121 Bill McKechnie: Pitt	400.00	160.00	40.00
☐ 122 Larry McLean: Cinc	65.00	26.00	6.50
☐ 123 Clyde Milan: Wash	75.00	30.00	7.50
☐ 124 Dots Miller: Pitt	65.00	26.00	6.50
☐ 125 Ward Miller: Chi NL	2000.00	800.00	250.00
☐ 126 Otto Miller: Brk	90.00	36.00	9.00
☐ 127 Doc Miller: Bos NL	90.00	36.00	9.00
☐ 128 Mike Mitchell: Cinc	65.00	26.00	6.50
☐ 129 Willie Mitchell: Cleve	90.00	36.00	9.00
☐ 130 George Mogridge: Chi AL	90.00	36.00	9.00
☐ 131 Earl Moore: Phil NL	90.00	36.00	9.00
☐ 132 Herbie Moran: Phil NL	65.00	26.00	6.50
☐ 133 Cy Morgan: Phil AL	65.00	26.00	6.50
☐ 134 Ray Morgan: Wash	65.00	26.00	6.50
☐ 135 George Moriarity: Det	90.00	36.00	9.00
☐ 136 George Mullin: Det (With "D" on cap)	90.00	36.00	9.00
☐ 137 George Mullin: Det (Without "D" on cap)	250.00	100.00	25.00
☐ 138 Tom Needham: Chi NL	65.00	26.00	6.50
☐ 139 Red Nelson: StL AL	90.00	36.00	9.00
☐ 140 Hub Northen: Brk	65.00	26.00	6.50
☐ 141 Les Nunamaker: Bos AL	65.00	26.00	6.50
☐ 142 Rebel Oakes: StL NL	65.00	26.00	6.50
☐ 143 Buck O'Brien: Bos AL	65.00	26.00	6.50
☐ 144 Rube Oldring: Phil AL	65.00	26.00	6.50
☐ 145 Ivy Olson: Cleve	65.00	26.00	6.50
☐ 146 Marty O'Toole: Pitt	65.00	26.00	6.50
☐ 147 Dode Paskert: Phil NL	65.00	26.00	6.50
☐ 148 Barney Pelty: StL AL	90.00	36.00	9.00
☐ 149 Hub Perdue: Bos NL	75.00	30.00	7.50
☐ 150 Rube Peters: Chi AL	90.00	36.00	9.00
☐ 151 Art Phelan: Cinc	90.00	36.00	9.00
☐ 152 Jack Quinn: NY AL	65.00	26.00	6.50
☐ 153 Pat Ragan: Brk	550.00	220.00	55.00
☐ 154 Rasmussen: Phil NL	450.00	180.00	45.00
☐ 155 Morrie Rath: Chi AL	90.00	36.00	9.00
☐ 156 Ed Reulbach: Chi NL	75.00	30.00	7.50
☐ 157 Nap Rucker: Brk	75.00	30.00	7.50
☐ 158 Ryan: Cleve	90.00	36.00	9.00
☐ 159 Vic Saier: Chi NL	1000.00	400.00	125.00
☐ 160 Scanlon: Phil NL	65.00	26.00	6.50
☐ 161 Germany Schaefer: Wash	65.00	26.00	6.50
☐ 162 Bill Schardt: Brk	65.00	26.00	6.50
☐ 163 Frank Schulte: Chi NL	65.00	26.00	6.50
☐ 164 Jim Scott: Chi AL	65.00	26.00	6.50
☐ 165 Hank Severeid: Cinc	65.00	26.00	6.50
☐ 166 Mike Simon: Pitt NL	65.00	26.00	6.50
☐ 167 Wally Smith: StL NL	65.00	26.00	6.50
☐ 168 Frank Smith: Cinc	65.00	26.00	6.50
☐ 169 Fred Snodgrass: NY NL	90.00	36.00	9.00
☐ 170 Tris Speaker: Bos AL	1100.00	450.00	135.00
☐ 171 Harry Spratt: Bos NL	65.00	26.00	6.50
☐ 172 Eddie Stack: Brk	65.00	26.00	6.50
☐ 173 Oscar Stanage: Det	65.00	26.00	6.50

☐ 174 Bill Steele: StL NL	65.00	26.00	6.50
☐ 175 Harry Steinfeldt: StL NL	75.00	30.00	7.50
☐ 176 George Stovall: StL AL	65.00	26.00	6.50
☐ 177 Gabby Street: NY AL	75.00	30.00	7.50
☐ 178 Amos Strunk: Phil AL	65.00	26.00	6.50
☐ 179 Billy Sullivan: Chi AL	75.00	30.00	7.50
☐ 180 Bill Sweeney: Bos NL	180.00	75.00	18.00
☐ 181 Lee Tannehill: Chi AL	65.00	26.00	6.50
☐ 182 Thomas: Bos AL	65.00	26.00	6.50
☐ 183 Joe Tinker: Chi NL	200.00	80.00	20.00
☐ 184 Bert Tooley: Brk	65.00	26.00	6.50
☐ 185 Terry Turner: Cleve	65.00	26.00	6.50
☐ 186 Lefty Tyler: Bos NL	1000.00	400.00	125.00
☐ 187 Hippo Vaughn: NY AL	65.00	26.00	6.50
☐ 188 Heine Wagner: Bos AL correct back	90.00	36.00	9.00
☐ 189 Heine Wagner: Bos AL Carrigan back	250.00	100.00	25.00
☐ 190 Tilly Walker: Wash	65.00	26.00	6.50
☐ 191 Bobby Wallace: StL AL	200.00	80.00	20.00
☐ 192 Jack Warhop: NY AL	65.00	26.00	6.50
☐ 193 Buck Weaver: Chi AL	400.00	160.00	40.00
☐ 194 Zack Wheat: Brk	200.00	80.00	20.00
☐ 195 Doc White: Chi AL	90.00	36.00	9.00
☐ 196 Dewey Wilie: StL NL	90.00	36.00	9.00
☐ 197 Bob Williams: NY AL	65.00	26.00	6.50
☐ 198 Art Wilson: NY NL	65.00	26.00	6.50
☐ 199 Chief Wilson: Pitt	90.00	36.00	9.00
☐ 200 Hooks Wiltse: NY NL	65.00	26.00	6.50
☐ 201 Ivey Wingo: StL NL	65.00	26.00	6.50
☐ 202 Harry Wolverton: NY AL	65.00	26.00	6.50
☐ 203 Joe Wood: Bos AL	180.00	75.00	18.00
☐ 204 Gene Woodburn: StL NL	90.00	36.00	9.00
☐ 205 Ralph Works: Det	350.00	140.00	35.00
☐ 206 Steve Yerkes: Bos AL	65.00	26.00	6.50
☐ 207 Rollie Zeider: Chi AL	90.00	36.00	9.00

1931 W517

The cards in this 54-card set measure approximately 3" by 4". This 1931 set of numbered, blank-backed cards was placed in the "W" category in the original American Card Catalog because (1) its producer was unknown and (2) it was issued in strips of three. The photo is black and white but the entire obverse of each card is generally found tinted in tones of sepia, blue, green, yellow, rose, black or gray. The cards are numbered in a small circle on the front. A solid dark line at one end of a card entitled the purchaser to another piece of candy as a prize. There are two different cards of both Babe Ruth and Mickey Cochrane.

	EX-MT	VG-E	GOOD
COMPLETE SET (54)	8250.00	3500.00	1000.00
COMMON PLAYER (1-54)	40.00	16.00	4.00
☐ 1 Earle Combs	90.00	36.00	9.00
☐ 2 Pie Traynor	110.00	45.00	11.00
☐ 3 Eddie Roush (Wearing Cincinnati uniform, but listed as a New York Giant)	110.00	45.00	11.00
☐ 4 Babe Ruth (Throwing)	1500.00	600.00	200.00
☐ 5 Chalmer Cissell	40.00	16.00	4.00
☐ 6 Bill Sherdel	40.00	16.00	4.00
☐ 7 Bill Shore	40.00	16.00	4.00
☐ 8 George Earnshaw	40.00	16.00	4.00
☐ 9 Bucky Harris	80.00	32.00	8.00
☐ 10 Chuck Klein	110.00	45.00	11.00
☐ 11 George Kelly	90.00	36.00	9.00
☐ 12 Travis Jackson	90.00	36.00	9.00
☐ 13 Willie Kamm	40.00	16.00	4.00
☐ 14 Harry Heilmann	110.00	45.00	11.00
☐ 15 Grover Alexander	135.00	54.00	13.50
☐ 16 Frank Frisch	110.00	45.00	11.00
☐ 17 Jack Quinn	40.00	16.00	4.00
☐ 18 Cy Williams	40.00	16.00	4.00
☐ 19 Kiki Cuyler	90.00	36.00	9.00
☐ 20 Babe Ruth (Portrait)	1800.00	750.00	225.00
☐ 21 Jimmy Foxx	250.00	100.00	25.00
☐ 22 Jimmy Dykes	50.00	20.00	5.00
☐ 23 Bill Terry	125.00	50.00	12.50
☐ 24 Freddy Lindstrom	90.00	36.00	9.00
☐ 25 Hugh Critz	40.00	16.00	4.00
☐ 26 Pete Donahue	40.00	16.00	4.00
☐ 27 Tony Lazzeri	100.00	40.00	10.00
☐ 28 Heinie Manush	90.00	36.00	9.00
☐ 29 Chick Hafey	90.00	36.00	9.00
☐ 30 Melvin Ott	175.00	70.00	18.00
☐ 31 Bing Miller	40.00	16.00	4.00
☐ 32 Mule Haas	40.00	16.00	4.00
☐ 33 Lefty O'Doul	60.00	24.00	6.00
☐ 34 Paul Waner	90.00	36.00	9.00
☐ 35 Lou Gehrig	900.00	360.00	90.00
☐ 36 Dazzy Vance	90.00	36.00	9.00
☐ 37 Mickey Cochrane (Catching pose)	135.00	54.00	13.50
☐ 38 Rogers Hornsby	250.00	100.00	25.00
☐ 39 Lefty Grove	175.00	70.00	18.00
☐ 40 Al Simmons	110.00	45.00	11.00
☐ 41 Rube Walberg	40.00	16.00	4.00
☐ 42 Hack Wilson	135.00	54.00	13.50
☐ 43 Art Shires	40.00	16.00	4.00
☐ 44 Sammy Hale	40.00	16.00	4.00
☐ 45 Ted Lyons	90.00	36.00	9.00
☐ 46 Joe Sewell	90.00	36.00	9.00
☐ 47 Goose Goslin	90.00	36.00	9.00
☐ 48 Lou Fonseca	50.00	20.00	5.00
☐ 49 Bob Meusel	60.00	24.00	6.00
☐ 50 Lu Blue	40.00	16.00	4.00
☐ 51 Earl Averill	90.00	36.00	9.00
☐ 52 Eddie Collins	110.00	45.00	11.00
☐ 53 Joe Judge	40.00	16.00	4.00
☐ 54 Mickey Cochrane (Portrait)	135.00	54.00	13.50

1922 W572

This 119-card set was issued in 1922 in ten-card strips along with strips of boxer cards. The cards measure approximately 1 5/16" by 2 1/2" and are blank backed. Most of the player photos on the fronts are black and white, although a few photos are sepia-toned. The pictures are the same ones used in the E120 set, but they have been cropped to fit on the smaller format. The player's signature and team appear at the bottom of the pictures, along with an IFS (International Feature Service) copyright notice. The cards are unnumbered and checklisted below in alphabetical order.

	EX-MT	VG-E	GOOD
COMPLETE SET (119)	3250.00	1300.00	400.00
COMMON PLAYER (1-119)	15.00	6.00	1.50
☐ 1 Eddie Ainsmith	15.00	6.00	1.50
☐ 2 Vic Aldridge	15.00	6.00	1.50
☐ 3 Grover C. Alexander	75.00	30.00	7.50
☐ 4 Dave Bancroft	30.00	12.00	3.00
☐ 5 Jesse Barnes	15.00	6.00	1.50
☐ 6 John Bassler	15.00	6.00	1.50
☐ 7 Lu Blue	15.00	6.00	1.50
☐ 8 Norm Boeckel	15.00	6.00	1.50
☐ 9 George Burns	15.00	6.00	1.50
☐ 10 Joe Bush	15.00	6.00	1.50
☐ 11 Leon Cadore	15.00	6.00	1.50
☐ 12 Virgil Cheevers	15.00	6.00	1.50
☐ 13 Ty Cobb	350.00	140.00	35.00
☐ 14 Eddie Collins	40.00	16.00	4.00
☐ 15 John Collins	15.00	6.00	1.50
☐ 16 Wilbur Cooper	15.00	6.00	1.50
☐ 17 Stanley Coveleski	30.00	12.00	3.00
☐ 18 Walton Cruise	15.00	6.00	1.50
☐ 19 Dave Danforth	15.00	6.00	1.50
☐ 20 Jake Daubert	18.00	7.25	1.80
☐ 21 Hank DeBerry	15.00	6.00	1.50
☐ 22 Lou DeVormer	15.00	6.00	1.50
☐ 23 Bill Doak	15.00	6.00	1.50
☐ 24 Pete Donohue	15.00	6.00	1.50
☐ 25 Pat Duncan	15.00	6.00	1.50
☐ 26 Jimmy Dykes	18.00	7.25	1.80
☐ 27 Urban Faber	30.00	12.00	3.00
☐ 28 Bibb Falk	15.00	6.00	1.50
☐ 29 Frank Frisch	45.00	18.00	4.50
☐ 30 Chick Galloway	15.00	6.00	1.50
☐ 31 Ed Gharrity	15.00	6.00	1.50
☐ 32 Charles Glazner	15.00	6.00	1.50
☐ 33 Hank Gowdy	15.00	6.00	1.50
☐ 34 Tom Griffith	15.00	6.00	1.50
☐ 35 Burleigh Grimes	30.00	12.00	3.00
☐ 36 Ray Grimes	15.00	6.00	1.50
☐ 37 Heinie Groh	18.00	7.25	1.80
☐ 38 Joe Harris	15.00	6.00	1.50
☐ 39 Bucky Harris	30.00	12.00	3.00
☐ 40 Joe Hauser	15.00	6.00	1.50
☐ 41 Harry Heilmann	40.00	16.00	4.00
☐ 42 Walter Henline	15.00	6.00	1.50
☐ 43 Charles Hollocher	15.00	6.00	1.50
☐ 44 Harry Hooper	40.00	16.00	4.00
☐ 45 Rogers Hornsby	100.00	40.00	10.00
☐ 46 Waite Hoyt	30.00	12.00	3.00
☐ 47 Wilbur Hubbell	15.00	6.00	1.50
☐ 48 William Jacobson	15.00	6.00	1.50
☐ 49 Charles Jamieson	15.00	6.00	1.50
☐ 50 Syl Johnson	15.00	6.00	1.50
☐ 51 Walter Johnson	150.00	60.00	15.00
☐ 52 Jimmy Johnston	15.00	6.00	1.50
☐ 53 Joe Judge	15.00	6.00	1.50
☐ 54 George Kelly	30.00	12.00	3.00
☐ 55 Lee King	15.00	6.00	1.50
☐ 56 Larry Kopf	15.00	6.00	1.50
☐ 57 George Leverette	15.00	6.00	1.50
☐ 58 Al Mamaux	15.00	6.00	1.50
☐ 59 Rabbit Maranville	30.00	12.00	3.00
☐ 60 Rube Marquard	30.00	12.00	3.00
☐ 61 Martin McManus	15.00	6.00	1.50
☐ 62 Lee Meadows	15.00	6.00	1.50
☐ 63 Mike Menosky	15.00	6.00	1.50
☐ 64 Bob Meusel	20.00	8.00	2.00
☐ 65 Emil Meusel	18.00	7.25	1.80
☐ 66 George Mogridge	15.00	6.00	1.50
☐ 67 John Morrison	15.00	6.00	1.50
☐ 68 Johnny Mostil	15.00	6.00	1.50
☐ 69 Roleine Naylor	15.00	6.00	1.50
☐ 70 Art Nehf	15.00	6.00	1.50
☐ 71 Joe Oeschger	15.00	6.00	1.50
☐ 72 Bob O'Farrell	15.00	6.00	1.50
☐ 73 Steve O'Neill	15.00	6.00	1.50
☐ 74 Frank Parkinson	15.00	6.00	1.50
☐ 75 Ralph Perkins	15.00	6.00	1.50
☐ 76 Herman Pillette	15.00	6.00	1.50
☐ 77 Babe Pinelli	15.00	6.00	1.50
☐ 78 Wallie Pipp	18.00	7.25	1.80
☐ 79 Ray Powell	15.00	6.00	1.50
☐ 80 Jack Quinn	15.00	6.00	1.50
☐ 81 Goldie Rapp	15.00	6.00	1.50
☐ 82 Walt Reuther	15.00	6.00	1.50
☐ 83 Sam Rice	30.00	12.00	3.00
☐ 84 Emory Rigney	15.00	6.00	1.50
☐ 85 Eppa Rixey	30.00	12.00	3.00
☐ 86 Ed Rommel	18.00	7.25	1.80
☐ 87 Eddie Roush	45.00	18.00	4.50
☐ 88 Babe Ruth	600.00	240.00	60.00
☐ 89 Ray Schalk	30.00	12.00	3.00
☐ 90 Wally Schang	18.00	7.25	1.80
☐ 91 Walter Schmidt	15.00	6.00	1.50
☐ 92 Joe Schultz	15.00	6.00	1.50
☐ 93 Hank Severeid	15.00	6.00	1.50
☐ 94 Joe Sewell	30.00	12.00	3.00
☐ 95 Bob Shawkey	18.00	7.25	1.80
☐ 96 Earl Sheely	15.00	6.00	1.50
☐ 97 Will Sherdel	15.00	6.00	1.50
☐ 98 Urban Shocker	18.00	7.25	1.80
☐ 99 George Sisler	60.00	24.00	6.00
☐ 100 Earl Smith	15.00	6.00	1.50
☐ 101 Elmer Smith	15.00	6.00	1.50
☐ 102 Jack Smith	15.00	6.00	1.50
☐ 103 Bill Southworth	18.00	7.25	1.80
☐ 104 Tris Speaker	75.00	30.00	7.50
☐ 105 Milton Stock	15.00	6.00	1.50
☐ 106 Jim Tierney	15.00	6.00	1.50
☐ 107 Harold Traynor	40.00	16.00	4.00
☐ 108 George Uhle	15.00	6.00	1.50
☐ 109 Bob Veach	15.00	6.00	1.50
☐ 110 Clarence Walker	15.00	6.00	1.50
☐ 111 Curtis Walker	15.00	6.00	1.50
☐ 112 Bill Wambsganss	18.00	7.25	1.80
☐ 113 Aaron Ward	15.00	6.00	1.50
☐ 114 Zach Wheat	30.00	12.00	3.00
☐ 115 Fred Williams	15.00	6.00	1.50
☐ 116 Ken Williams	18.00	7.25	1.80
☐ 117 Ivy Wingo	15.00	6.00	1.50
☐ 118 Joe Wood	25.00	10.00	2.50
☐ 119 Tom Zachary	15.00	6.00	1.50

1938-39 W711-1 Orange/Gray

EDDIE JOOST
Infielder

Reserve infielder of the Reds, made the All-Star team of the American Association last season. Came to the Reds as a shortstop three years ago, but is now a second baseman. He can also play third. Joost is one of the many players who learned the rudiments of baseball around San Francisco.

The cards in this 32-card set measure approximately 2" by 3". The 1938-39 Cincinnati Reds Baseball player set was printed in orange and gray tones. Many back variations exist and there are two poses of Vander Meer, portrait (PORT) and an action (ACT) poses. The set was sold at the ballpark and was printed on thin cardboard stock. The cards are unnumbered but have been alphabetized and numbered in the checklist below.

	EX-MT	VG-E	GOOD
COMPLETE SET (32)	700.00	280.00	70.00
COMMON PLAYER (1-32)	14.00	5.75	1.40
☐ 1 Wally Berger (2)	18.00	7.25	1.80
☐ 2 Nino Bongiovanni (39)	50.00	20.00	5.00
☐ 3 Stanley Bordagaray Frenchy (39)	50.00	20.00	5.00
☐ 4 Joe Cascarella (38)	14.00	5.75	1.40
☐ 5 Allen Dusty Cooke (38)	14.00	5.75	1.40
☐ 6 Harry Craft	14.00	5.75	1.40
☐ 7 Ray(Peaches) Davis	14.00	5.75	1.40
☐ 8 Paul Derringer (2)	20.00	8.00	2.00
☐ 9 Linus Frey (2)	14.00	5.75	1.40
☐ 10 Lee Gamble (2)	14.00	5.75	1.40
☐ 11 Ival Goodman (2)	14.00	5.75	1.40
☐ 12 Hank Gowdy CO	14.00	5.75	1.40

☐ 13 Lee Grissom (2)	14.00	5.75	1.40
☐ 14 Willard Hershberger (2)	18.00	7.25	1.80
☐ 15 Eddie Joost (39)	14.00	5.75	1.40
☐ 16 Wes Livengood (39)	100.00	40.00	10.00
☐ 17 Ernie Lombardi (2)	50.00	20.00	5.00
☐ 18 Frank McCormick	18.00	7.25	1.80
☐ 19 Bill McKechnie (2) MG	30.00	12.00	3.00
☐ 20 Lloyd Whitey Moore (2)	14.00	5.75	1.40
☐ 21 Billy Myers (2)	14.00	5.75	1.40
☐ 22 Lew Riggs (2)	14.00	5.75	1.40
☐ 23 Eddie Roush CO (38)	45.00	18.00	4.50
☐ 24 Les Scarsella (39)	14.00	5.75	1.40
☐ 25 Gene Schott (38)	14.00	5.75	1.40
☐ 26 Eugene Thompson	14.00	5.75	1.40
☐ 27 Johnny VanderMeer PORT	30.00	12.00	3.00
☐ 28 Johnny VanderMeer ACT	30.00	12.00	3.00
☐ 29 Wm.(Bucky) Walters (2)	18.00	7.25	1.80
☐ 30 Jim Weaver	14.00	5.75	1.40
☐ 31 Bill Werber (39)	14.00	5.75	1.40
☐ 32 Jimmy Wilson (39)	14.00	5.75	1.40

1941 W711-2 Harry Hartman

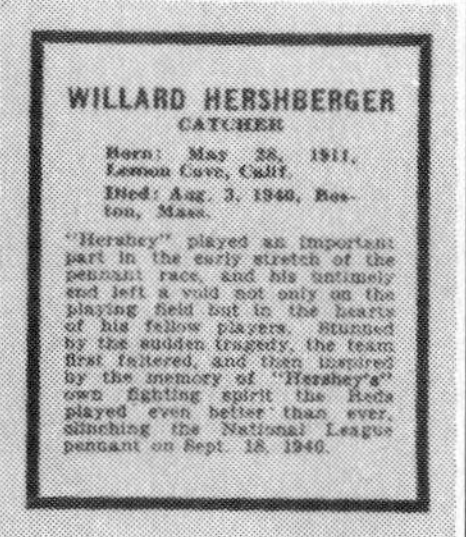

WILLARD HERSHBERGER
CATCHER

Born: May 28, 1911, Lemon Cove, Calif.

Died: Aug. 3, 1940, Boston, Mass.

"Hershey" played an important part in the early stretch of the pennant race, and his untimely end left a void not only on the playing field but in the hearts of his fellow players. Stunned by the sudden tragedy, the team first faltered, and then inspired by the memory of "Hershey's" own fighting spirit the Reds played even better than ever, clinching the National League pennant on Sept. 18, 1940.

The cards in this 34-card set measure approximately 2 1/8" by 2 5/8". The W711-2 Cincinnati Reds set contains unnumbered, black and white cards. This issue is sometimes called the "Harry Hartman" set. The cards are numbered below in alphabetical order by player's name with non-player cards listed at the end.

	EX-MT	VG-E	GOOD
COMPLETE SET (34)	450.00	180.00	45.00
COMMON PLAYER (1-28)	12.00	5.00	1.20
COMMON CARD (29-34)	8.00	3.25	.80
☐ 1 Morris Arnovich	12.00	5.00	1.20
☐ 2 William(Bill) Baker	12.00	5.00	1.20
☐ 3 Joseph Beggs	12.00	5.00	1.20
☐ 4 Harry Craft	12.00	5.00	1.20
☐ 5 Paul Derringer	18.00	7.25	1.80
☐ 6 Linus Frey	12.00	5.00	1.20
☐ 7 Ival Goodman	12.00	5.00	1.20
☐ 8 Hank Gowdy CO	12.00	5.00	1.20
☐ 9 Witt Guise	12.00	5.00	1.20
☐ 10 Willard Hershberger	15.00	6.00	1.50
☐ 11 John Hutchings	12.00	5.00	1.20
☐ 12 Edwin Joost	12.00	5.00	1.20
☐ 13 Ernie Lombardi	50.00	20.00	5.00
☐ 14 Frank McCormick	18.00	7.25	1.80
☐ 15 Myron McCormick	12.00	5.00	1.20
☐ 16 Bill McKechnie MG	30.00	12.00	3.00
☐ 17 Whitey Moore	12.00	5.00	1.20
☐ 18 William(Bill) Myers	12.00	5.00	1.20
☐ 19 Elmer Riddle	12.00	5.00	1.20
☐ 20 Lewis Riggs	12.00	5.00	1.20
☐ 21 James A. Ripple	12.00	5.00	1.20
☐ 22 Milburn Shoffner	12.00	5.00	1.20
☐ 23 Eugene Thompson	12.00	5.00	1.20
☐ 24 James Turner	15.00	6.00	1.50
☐ 25 John VanderMeer	25.00	10.00	2.50
☐ 26 Bucky Walters	18.00	7.25	1.80
☐ 27 Bill Werber	12.00	5.00	1.20
☐ 28 James Wilson	12.00	5.00	1.20
☐ 29 Results 1940 World Series	8.00	3.25	.80
☐ 30 The Cincinati Reds (Title Card)	8.00	3.25	.80
☐ 31 The Cincinnati Reds World's Champions (Title Card)	8.00	3.25	.80
☐ 32 Debt of Gratitude to Wm. Koehl Co.	8.00	3.25	.80
☐ 33 Tell the World About Our Reds	8.00	3.25	.80
☐ 34 Harry Hartman ANN	8.00	3.25	.80

1941 W753 Browns

The cards in this 29-card set measure approximately 2 1/8" by 2 5/8". The 1941 W753 set features unnumbered cards of the St. Louis Browns. The cards are numbered below alphabetically by player's name.

	EX-MT	VG-E	GOOD
COMPLETE SET (29)	400.00	160.00	40.00
COMMON PLAYER (1-29)	12.00	5.00	1.20
☐ 1 Johnny Allen	12.00	5.00	1.20
☐ 2 Elden Auker	12.00	5.00	1.20
☐ 3 Donald L. Barnes OWN	12.00	5.00	1.20
☐ 4 Johnny Berardino	16.00	6.50	1.60
☐ 5 George Caster	12.00	5.00	1.20
☐ 6 Harland Clift	12.00	5.00	1.20
☐ 7 Roy J. Cullenbine	12.00	5.00	1.20
☐ 8 William O. DeWitt GM	12.00	5.00	1.20
☐ 9 Robert Estalella	12.00	5.00	1.20
☐ 10 Rick Ferrell	60.00	24.00	6.00
☐ 11 Dennis W. Galehouse	12.00	5.00	1.20
☐ 12 Joseph L. Grace	12.00	5.00	1.20
☐ 13 Frank Grube	12.00	5.00	1.20
☐ 14 Robert A. Harris	12.00	5.00	1.20
☐ 15 Donald Heffner	12.00	5.00	1.20
☐ 16 Fred Hofmann	12.00	5.00	1.20
☐ 17 Walter F. Judnich	12.00	5.00	1.20
☐ 18 Jack Kramer	12.00	5.00	1.20
☐ 19 Chester(Chet) Laabs	12.00	5.00	1.20
☐ 20 John Lucadello	12.00	5.00	1.20
☐ 21 George H. McQuinn	12.00	5.00	1.20
☐ 22 Robert Muncrief Jr.	12.00	5.00	1.20
☐ 23 John Niggeling	12.00	5.00	1.20
☐ 24 Fritz Ostermueller	12.00	5.00	1.20
☐ 25 James(Luke) Sewell MG	18.00	7.25	1.80
☐ 26 Alan C. Strange	12.00	5.00	1.20
☐ 27 Bob Swift	12.00	5.00	1.20
☐ 28 James(Zack) Taylor CO	12.00	5.00	1.20
☐ 29 Bill Trotter	12.00	5.00	1.20

1941 W754 Cardinals

The cards in this 29-card set measure approximately 2 1/8" by 2 5/8". The 1941 W754 set of unnumbered cards features St. Louis Cardinals. The cards are numbered below alphabetically by player's name.

	EX-MT	VG-E	GOOD
COMPLETE SET (29)	500.00	200.00	50.00
COMMON PLAYER (1-29)	12.00	5.00	1.20

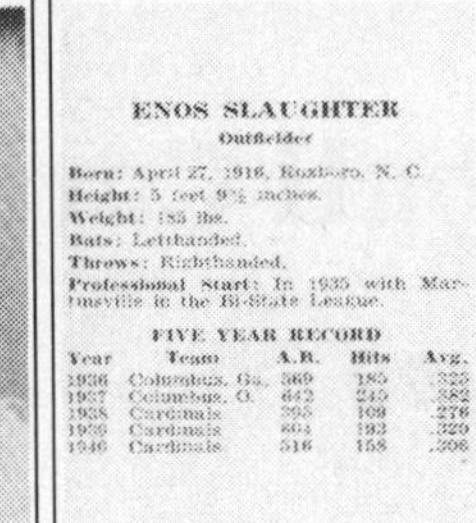

☐ 1 Sam Breadon OWN	12.00	5.00	1.20
☐ 2 Jimmy Brown	12.00	5.00	1.20
☐ 3 Mort Cooper	16.00	6.50	1.60
☐ 4 Walker Cooper	12.00	5.00	1.20
☐ 5 Estel Crabtree	12.00	5.00	1.20
☐ 6 Frank Crespi	12.00	5.00	1.20
☐ 7 Bill Crouch	12.00	5.00	1.20
☐ 8 Mike Gonzalez CO	12.00	5.00	1.20
☐ 9 Harry Gumpert	12.00	5.00	1.20
☐ 10 John Hopp	14.00	5.75	1.40
☐ 11 Ira Hutchinson	12.00	5.00	1.20
☐ 12 Howie Krist	12.00	5.00	1.20
☐ 13 Eddie Lake	12.00	5.00	1.20
☐ 14 Max Lanier	16.00	6.50	1.60
☐ 15 Gus Mancuso	12.00	5.00	1.20
☐ 16 Marty Marion	30.00	12.00	3.00
☐ 17 Steve Mesner	12.00	5.00	1.20
☐ 18 John Mize	60.00	24.00	6.00
☐ 19 Terry Moore	21.00	8.50	2.10
☐ 20 Sam Nahem	12.00	5.00	1.20
☐ 21 Don Padgett	12.00	5.00	1.20
☐ 22 Branch Rickey GM	60.00	24.00	6.00
☐ 23 Clyde Shoun	12.00	5.00	1.20
☐ 24 Enos Slaughter	60.00	24.00	6.00
☐ 25 Billy Southworth MG	12.00	5.00	1.20
☐ 26 Coaker Triplett	12.00	5.00	1.20
☐ 27 Buzzy Wares	12.00	5.00	1.20
☐ 28 Lon Warneke	14.00	5.75	1.40
☐ 29 Ernie White	12.00	5.00	1.20

1928 Yuenglings

The cards in this 60-card set measure approximately 1 3/8" by 2 9/16". This black and white, numbered set contains many Hall of Famers. The obverses are the same as those found in sets of E210 and W502. The Paul Waner card, number 45, actually contains a picture of Clyde Barnhardt. Each back contains an offer to redeem pictures of Babe Ruth for ice cream. The catalog designation for this set is F50.

	EX-MT	VG-E	GOOD
COMPLETE SET (60)	2500.00	1000.00	300.00
COMMON PLAYER (1-60)	12.50	5.00	1.25
☐ 1 Burleigh Grimes	25.00	10.00	2.50
☐ 2 Walter Reuther	12.50	5.00	1.25
☐ 3 Joe Dugan	15.00	6.00	1.50
☐ 4 Red Faber	25.00	10.00	2.50
☐ 5 Gabby Hartnett	30.00	12.00	3.00
☐ 6 Babe Ruth	600.00	240.00	60.00
☐ 7 Bob Meusel	15.00	6.00	1.50
☐ 8 Herb Pennock	25.00	10.00	2.50
☐ 9 George Burns	12.50	5.00	1.25
☐ 10 Joe Sewell	25.00	10.00	2.50
☐ 11 George Uhle	12.50	5.00	1.25
☐ 12 Bob O'Farrell	12.50	5.00	1.25
☐ 13 Rogers Hornsby	80.00	32.00	8.00
☐ 14 Pie Traynor	35.00	14.00	3.50
☐ 15 Clarence Mitchell	12.50	5.00	1.25
☐ 16 Eppa Rixey	25.00	10.00	2.50
☐ 17 Carl Mays	18.00	7.25	1.80
☐ 18 Adolfo Luque	12.50	5.00	1.25
☐ 19 Dave Bancroft	25.00	10.00	2.50
☐ 20 George Kelly	25.00	10.00	2.50
☐ 21 Earle Combs	25.00	10.00	2.50
☐ 22 Harry Heilmann	30.00	12.00	3.00
☐ 23 Ray Schalk	25.00	10.00	2.50
☐ 24 John Mostil	12.50	5.00	1.25
☐ 25 Hack Wilson	40.00	16.00	4.00
☐ 26 Lou Gehrig	300.00	120.00	30.00
☐ 27 Ty Cobb	300.00	120.00	30.00
☐ 28 Tris Speaker	65.00	26.00	6.50
☐ 29 Tony Lazzeri	35.00	14.00	3.50
☐ 30 Waite Hoyt	25.00	10.00	2.50
☐ 31 Sherwood Smith	12.50	5.00	1.25
☐ 32 Max Carey	25.00	10.00	2.50
☐ 33 Gene Hargrave	12.50	5.00	1.25
☐ 34 Miguel Gonzalez	12.50	5.00	1.25
☐ 35 Joe Judge	12.50	5.00	1.25
☐ 36 Sam Rice	25.00	10.00	2.50
☐ 37 Earl Sheely	12.50	5.00	1.25
☐ 38 Sam Jones	12.50	5.00	1.25
☐ 39 Bibb Falk	12.50	5.00	1.25
☐ 40 Willie Kamm	12.50	5.00	1.25
☐ 41 Stan(Bucky) Harris	20.00	8.00	2.00
☐ 42 John McGraw MG	40.00	16.00	4.00
☐ 43 Art Nehf	12.50	5.00	1.25
☐ 44 Grover C. Alexander	65.00	26.00	6.50
☐ 45 Paul Waner	25.00	10.00	2.50
☐ 46 Bill Terry	45.00	18.00	4.50
☐ 47 Glenn Wright	12.50	5.00	1.25
☐ 48 Earl Smith	12.50	5.00	1.25
☐ 49 Goose Goslin	25.00	10.00	2.50
☐ 50 Frank Frisch	40.00	16.00	4.00
☐ 51 Joe Harris	12.50	5.00	1.25
☐ 52 Cy Williams	15.00	6.00	1.50
☐ 53 Eddie Roush	30.00	12.00	3.00
☐ 54 George Sisler	45.00	18.00	4.50
☐ 55 Ed Rommel	15.00	6.00	1.50
☐ 56 Roger Peckinpaugh	12.50	5.00	1.25
☐ 57 Stanley Coveleskie	25.00	10.00	2.50
☐ 58 Lester Bell	12.50	5.00	1.25
☐ 59 Lloyd Waner	25.00	10.00	2.50
☐ 60 John McInnis	15.00	6.00	1.50

Modern Baseball Cards

1947-1993

1988 Action Packed Test

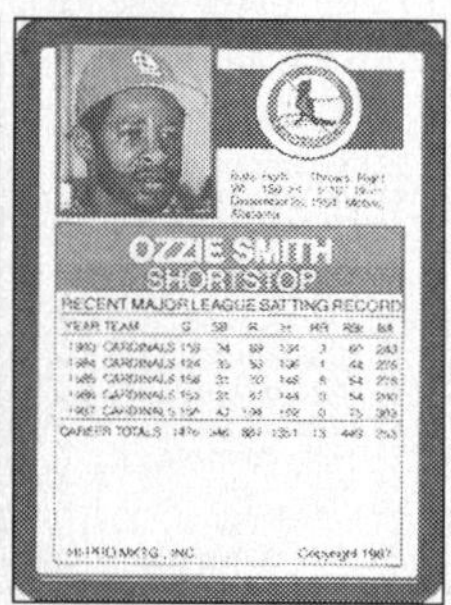

The 1988 Action Packed Test set contains six standard-size (2 1/2" by 3 1/2") cards with slightly rounded corners. This apparently was the set of cards that Action Packed produced to show their technique to Major League Baseball and the Major League Baseball Players Association in their unsuccessful attempt to seek a baseball card license in 1988. The embossed color player photos on the fronts are bordered in gold. In black lettering, the player's name appears on a gold plaque above the picture, and the team name on a gold plaque beneath the picture. The card backs have the same design as Score issues, with a color head shot, team logo, biography, and major league batting or pitching statistics, again inside a gold border. The face on the front photo of the Ozzie Smith card was apparently considered too dark and thus reportedly not submitted. The cards are unnumbered and checklisted below in alphabetical order.

	MT	EX-MT	VG
COMPLETE SET (6)	350.00	160.00	45.00
COMMON PLAYER (1-6)	25.00	11.50	3.10
☐ 1 Wade Boggs	60.00	27.00	7.50
☐ 2 Andre Dawson	60.00	27.00	7.50
☐ 3 Dwight Gooden	45.00	20.00	5.75
☐ 4 Carney Lansford	25.00	11.50	3.10
☐ 5 Don Mattingly	90.00	40.00	11.50
☐ 6 Ozzie Smith	125.00	57.50	15.50

1992 Action Packed ASG Prototypes

This five-card prototype set was issued to show the design of the 1992 Action Packed All-Star Gallery regular issue. The prototypes differ from the regular issue in that they are not numbered on the back, and the phrase "1992 Prototype" is printed diagonally in white lettering across the back. The

cards are standard size, 2 1/2" by 3 1/2". The cards are unnumbered and checklisted below in alphabetical order.

	MT	EX-MT	VG
COMPLETE SET (5)	50.00	23.00	6.25
COMMON PLAYER (1-5)	10.00	4.50	1.25
☐ 1 Yogi Berra	15.00	6.75	1.90
☐ 2 Bob Gibson	10.00	4.50	1.25
☐ 3 Willie Mays	20.00	9.00	2.50
☐ 4 Warren Spahn	10.00	4.50	1.25
☐ 5 Willie Stargell	10.00	4.50	1.25

1992 Action Packed All-Star Gallery

The 1992 Action Packed All-Star Gallery consists of 84 player cards and pays tribute to former greats of baseball. With the exception of Joe Garagiola, all the players represented appeared in at least one All-Star game. The first 18 cards feature Hall of Famers, and Action Packed guaranteed one Hall of Famer card in each seven-card foil pack. Also 24K gold leaf stamped versions of these Hall of Famer cards were randomly inserted into foil packs. These

24K cards are valued approximately from 25 to 50 times the value of the respective regular issue card. The fronts of these standard-size (2 1/2" by 3 1/2") cards feature embossed action player photos framed by inner gold border stripes and a black outer border. Most of the photos are color; 13 of them, however, are sepia-toned that have been converted to black and white. On a gray background, the horizontally oriented backs carry biography, career statistics, and a special career highlight section that lists memorable highlights that spanned the players' career. The cards are numbered on the back.

	MT	EX-MT	VG
COMPLETE SET (84)	24.00	11.00	3.00
COMMON PLAYER (1-18)	.50	.23	.06
COMMON PLAYER (19-84)	.20	.09	.03
☐ 1 Yogi Berra	1.25	.55	.16
☐ 2 Lou Brock	1.00	.45	.13
☐ 3 Bob Gibson	1.00	.45	.13
☐ 4 Ferguson Jenkins	.75	.35	.09
☐ 5 Ralph Kiner	.75	.35	.09
☐ 6 Al Kaline	1.00	.45	.13
☐ 7 Lou Boudreau	.50	.23	.06
☐ 8 Bobby Doerr	.50	.23	.06
☐ 9 Billy Herman	.50	.23	.06
☐ 10 Monte Irvin	.50	.23	.06
☐ 11 George Kell	.50	.23	.06
☐ 12 Robin Roberts	.75	.35	.09
☐ 13 Johnny Mize	.75	.35	.09
☐ 14 Willie Mays	2.50	1.15	.30
☐ 15 Enos Slaughter	.50	.23	.06
☐ 16 Warren Spahn	.75	.35	.09
☐ 17 Willie Stargell	.75	.35	.09
☐ 18 Billy Williams	.75	.35	.09
☐ 19 Vernon Law	.20	.09	.03
☐ 20 Virgil Trucks	.20	.09	.03
☐ 21 Mel Parnell	.20	.09	.03
☐ 22 Wally Moon	.20	.09	.03
☐ 23 Gene Woodling	.20	.09	.03
☐ 24 Richie Ashburn	.75	.35	.09
☐ 25 Mark Fidrych	.25	.11	.03
☐ 26 Elroy Face	.25	.11	.03
☐ 27 Larry Doby	.25	.11	.03
☐ 28 Dick Groat	.25	.11	.03
☐ 29 Cesar Cedeno	.20	.09	.03
☐ 30 Bob Horner	.20	.09	.03
☐ 31 Bobby Richardson	.40	.18	.05
☐ 32 Bobby Murcer	.25	.11	.03
☐ 33 Gil McDougald	.25	.11	.03
☐ 34 Roy White	.20	.09	.03
☐ 35 Bill Skowron	.30	.14	.04
☐ 36 Mickey Lolich	.30	.14	.04
☐ 37 Minnie Minoso	.30	.14	.04
☐ 38 Bill Pierce	.30	.14	.04
☐ 39 Ron Santo	.40	.18	.05
☐ 40 Sal Bando	.30	.14	.04
☐ 41 Ralph Branca	.25	.11	.03
☐ 42 Bert Campaneris	.25	.11	.03
☐ 43 Joe Garagiola	.50	.23	.06
☐ 44 Vida Blue	.25	.11	.03
☐ 45 Frank Crosetti	.25	.11	.03
☐ 46 Luis Tiant	.20	.09	.03
☐ 47 Maury Wills	.40	.18	.05
☐ 48 Sam McDowell	.20	.09	.03
☐ 49 Jimmy Piersall	.30	.14	.04
☐ 50 Jim Lonborg	.25	.11	.03
☐ 51 Don Newcombe	.30	.14	.04
☐ 52 Bobby Thomson	.30	.14	.04
☐ 53 Wilbur Wood	.20	.09	.03
☐ 54 Carl Erskine	.30	.14	.04
☐ 55 Chris Chambliss	.30	.14	.04
☐ 56 Dave Kingman	.30	.14	.04
☐ 57 Ken Holtzman	.20	.09	.03
☐ 58 Bud Harrelson	.20	.09	.03
☐ 59 Clem Labine	.25	.11	.03
☐ 60 Tony Oliva	.40	.18	.05
☐ 61 George Foster	.30	.14	.04
☐ 62 Bobby Bonds	.30	.14	.04
☐ 63 Harvey Haddix	.20	.09	.03
☐ 64 Steve Garvey	.50	.23	.06
☐ 65 Rocky Colavito	.50	.23	.06
☐ 66 Orlando Cepeda	.40	.18	.05
☐ 67 Ed Lopat	.30	.14	.04
☐ 68 Al Oliver	.30	.14	.04
☐ 69 Bill Mazeroski	.40	.18	.05
☐ 70 Al Rosen	.30	.14	.04
☐ 71 Bob Grich	.30	.14	.04
☐ 72 Curt Flood	.30	.14	.04
☐ 73 Willie Horton	.25	.11	.03
☐ 74 Rico Carty	.25	.11	.03
☐ 75 Davey Johnson	.30	.14	.04
☐ 76 Don Kessinger	.25	.11	.03
☐ 77 Frank Thomas	.20	.09	.03
☐ 78 Bobby Shantz	.25	.11	.03
☐ 79 Herb Score	.30	.14	.04
☐ 80 Boog Powell	.30	.14	.04
☐ 81 Rusty Staub	.30	.14	.04
☐ 82 Bill Madlock	.25	.11	.03
☐ 83 Manny Mota	.25	.11	.03
☐ 84 Bill White	.40	.18	.05

1962 American Tract Society

These cards are quite attractive and feature the "pure card" concept that is always popular with collectors, i.e., no borders or anything else on the card front to detract from the color photo. The cards are numbered on the back and the skip-numbering of the cards below is actually due to the fact that these cards are part of a much larger (sport and non-sport) set with a Christian theme. The set features Christian ballplayers giving first-person testimonies on the card backs telling how Jesus Christ has changed their lives. These cards are sometimes referred to as "Tracards." The cards measure approximately 2 3/4" by 3 1/2". The set price below refers to only one of each player, not including any variations.

	NRMT	VG-E	GOOD
COMPLETE SET (4)	21.00	9.50	2.60
COMMON PLAYER	5.00	2.30	.60
☐ 43A Bobby Richardson (black print on back)	10.00	4.50	1.25
☐ 43B Bobby Richardson (blue print on back)	15.00	6.75	1.90
☐ 43C Bobby Richardson (black print on back with Play Ball in red)	15.00	6.75	1.90
☐ 43D Bobby Richardson (black print on back with exclamation point after Play Ball)	15.00	6.75	1.90
☐ 51A Jerry Kindall (portrait from chest up, black print on back)	5.00	2.30	.60
☐ 51B Jerry Kindall (on one knee with bat, blue print on back)	5.00	2.30	.60
☐ 52A Felipe Alou (on one knee looking up, black print on back)	8.00	3.60	1.00
☐ 52B Felipe Alou (on one knee looking up, blue print on back)	8.00	3.60	1.00
☐ 52C Felipe Alou (batting pose)	8.00	3.60	1.00
☐ 66 Al Worthington (black print on back)	5.00	2.30	.60

1991 Arena Holograms

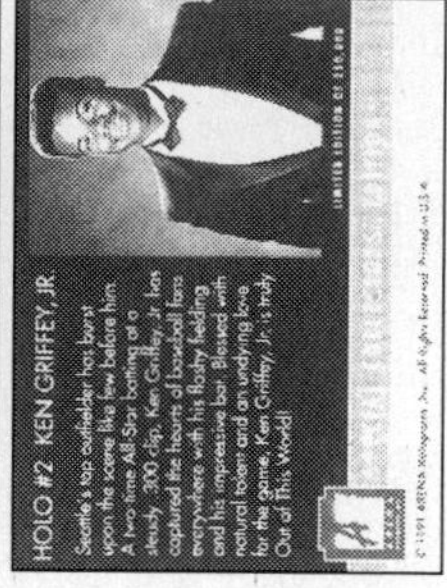

The 1991 Arena hologram cards were distributed through hobby dealers and feature famous football, basketball, and baseball players. According to Arena, production quantities were limited to 250,000 of each card. The cards measure the standard size (2 1/2" by 3 1/2") and display holograms on the fronts. The horizontally oriented backs have a color photo of the player in a tuxedo on the right portion, while the left portion presents player profile in white lettering on black. The cards are numbered on the back.

	MT	EX-MT	VG
COMPLETE SET (5)	7.50	3.40	.95
COMMON PLAYER (1-5)	2.00	.90	.25
☐ 1 Joe Montana	2.00	.90	.25
☐ 2 Ken Griffey Jr.	2.00	.90	.25
☐ 3 Frank Thomas	2.00	.90	.25
☐ 4 Barry Sanders	2.00	.90	.25
☐ 5 David Robinson	2.00	.90	.25

1992 Arena Kid Griff Comic Holograms

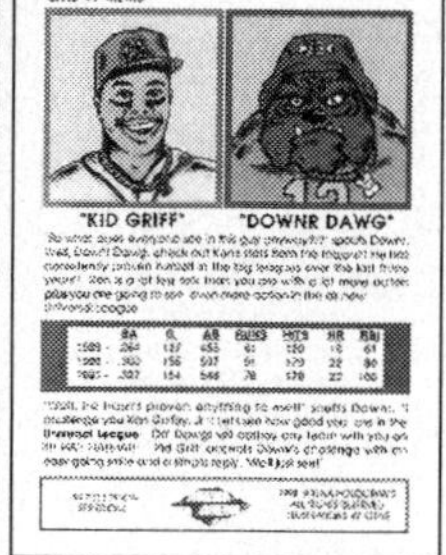

Released in September 1992, this five-card hologram set was produced by Arena Holograms. The production run is reported to be 1,700 individually numbered cases, and premium gold edition cards were randomly inserted throughout. The holograms measure the standard size (2 1/2" by 3 1/2"). Each foil pack contained one card in a card protector, and each protector had a different color border (1-clear, 2-black, 3-red, 4-white, and 5-blue). The fronts feature animated holograms, with the player's name and a subtitle appearing across the card top. The backs are white and present head-to-head situations between Kid Griff and Downr Dawg in the opening game of the Inter-Dimensional Universal League. The cards are numbered on the back.

	MT	EX-MT	VG
COMPLETE SET (5)	6.00	2.70	.75
COMMON PLAYER (1-5)	1.50	.65	.19
☐ 1 Ken Griffey Jr. The Kid	1.50	.65	.19
☐ 2 Ken Griffey Jr. Speed	1.50	.65	.19
☐ 3 Ken Griffey Jr. Power	1.50	.65	.19
☐ 4 Ken Griffey Jr. Defense	1.50	.65	.19
☐ 5 Ken Griffey Jr. Superstar	1.50	.65	.19

1967 Astros Team Issue

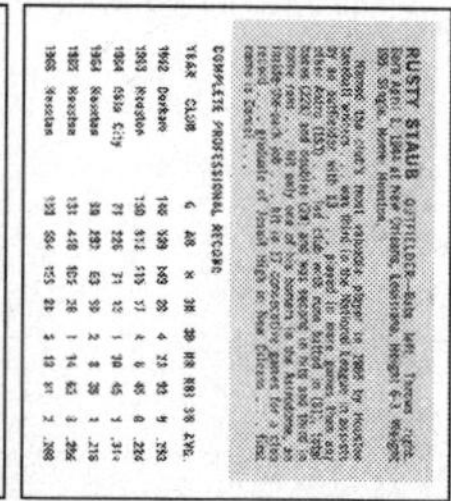

This 12-card team-issued set features the 1967 Houston Astros. The cards measure approximately 2 1/2" by 3" and show signs of perforation on their sides. The posed color player photos have white borders and a facsimile autograph inscribed across them. The horizontally oriented backs have biography and career summary information on a yellow background, and complete statistics. The cards are unnumbered and checklisted below in alphabetical order.

	NRMT	VG-E	GOOD
COMPLETE SET (12)	60.00	27.00	7.50
COMMON PLAYER (1-12)	3.00	1.35	.40
☐ 1 Bob Aspromonte	4.00	1.80	.50
☐ 2 John Bateman	4.00	1.80	.50
☐ 3 Mike Cuellar	4.00	1.80	.50
☐ 4 Larry Dierker	4.00	1.80	.50
☐ 5 Dave Giusti	4.00	1.80	.50
☐ 6 Grady Hatton MG	3.00	1.35	.40
☐ 7 Bill Heath	3.00	1.35	.40
☐ 8 Sonny Jackson	3.00	1.35	.40
☐ 9 Eddie Mathews	20.00	9.00	2.50
☐ 10 Joe Morgan	20.00	9.00	2.50
☐ 11 Rusty Staub	7.50	3.40	.95
☐ 12 Jim Wynn	6.00	2.70	.75

1989 Astros Lennox HSE

The 1989 Lennox HSE Astros set contains 26 cards measuring approximately 2 5/8" by 4 1/8". The fronts have color photos with burnt orange and white borders; the backs feature biographical information and career highlights. The set looks very much like the Police Astros sets of the previous years but is not since it was not sponsored by any Police Department and does not have a safety tip anywhere on the card.

	MT	EX-MT	VG
COMPLETE SET (26)	7.50	3.40	.95
COMMON PLAYER (1-26)	.25	.11	.03
☐ 1 Billy Hatcher	.35	.16	.04
☐ 2 Greg Gross	.25	.11	.03
☐ 3 Rick Rhoden	.25	.11	.03
☐ 4 Mike Scott	.50	.23	.06

☐ 5 Kevin Bass	.35	.16	.04
☐ 6 Alex Trevino	.25	.11	.03
☐ 7 Jim Clancy	.25	.11	.03
☐ 8 Bill Doran	.35	.16	.04
☐ 9 Dan Schatzeder	.25	.11	.03
☐ 10 Bob Knepper	.25	.11	.03
☐ 11 Jim Deshaies	.35	.16	.04
☐ 12 Eric Yelding	.25	.11	.03
☐ 13 Danny Darwin	.25	.11	.03
☐ 14 Astros Coaches Matt Galante Yogi Berra Ed Napoleon Ed Ott Phil Garner Les Moss	.35	.16	.04
☐ 15 Craig Reynolds	.25	.11	.03
☐ 16 Rafael Ramirez	.25	.11	.03
☐ 17 Juan Agosto	.25	.11	.03
☐ 18 Larry Andersen	.25	.11	.03
☐ 19 Dave Smith	.35	.16	.04
☐ 20 Gerald Young	.25	.11	.03
☐ 21 Ken Caminiti	.50	.23	.06
☐ 22 Terry Puhl	.35	.16	.04
☐ 23 Bob Forsch	.35	.16	.04
☐ 24 Craig Biggio	1.00	.45	.13
☐ 25 Art Howe MG	.35	.16	.04
☐ 26 Glenn Davis	.60	.25	.08

1990 Astros Lennox HSE

This 28-card, approximately 3 1/2" by 5", set (of 1990 Houston Astros) was issued in conjunction with HSE Cable Network and Lennox Heating and Air Conditioning as indicated on both the front and back of the cards. The front of the cards have full color portraits of the player while the back gives brief information about the player. The set has been checklisted below in alphabetical order with the player's uniform number noted next to his name.

	MT	EX-MT	VG
COMPLETE SET (28)	10.00	4.50	1.25
COMMON PLAYER (1-28)	.40	.18	.05
☐ 1 Juan Agosto 49	.40	.18	.05
☐ 2 Larry Andersen 47	.40	.18	.05
☐ 3 Eric Anthony 23	1.00	.45	.13
☐ 4 Craig Biggio 7	.90	.40	.11
☐ 5 Ken Caminiti 11	.75	.35	.09
☐ 6 Casey Candaele 1	.40	.18	.05
☐ 7 Jose Cano 39	.40	.18	.05
☐ 8 Jim Clancy 38	.40	.18	.05
☐ 9 Danny Darwin 44	.40	.18	.05
☐ 10 Mark Davidson 22	.40	.18	.05
☐ 11 Glenn Davis 27	.90	.40	.11
☐ 12 Jim Deshaies 43	.40	.18	.05
☐ 13 Bill Doran 19	.50	.23	.06
☐ 14 Bill Gullickson 36	.60	.25	.08
☐ 15 Xavier Hernandez 31	.50	.23	.06
☐ 16 Art Howe MG 18	.50	.23	.06
☐ 17 Mark Portugal 51	.40	.18	.05
☐ 18 Terry Puhl 21	.50	.23	.06
☐ 19 Rafael Ramirez 16	.40	.18	.05
☐ 20 David Rohde 6	.50	.23	.06
☐ 21 Dan Schatzeder 20	.40	.18	.05
☐ 22 Mike Scott 33	.75	.35	.09
☐ 23 Dave Smith 45	.50	.23	.06
☐ 24 Franklin Stubbs 24	.50	.23	.06
☐ 25 Alex Trevino 9	.40	.18	.05
☐ 26 Glenn Wilson 12	.40	.18	.05
☐ 27 Eric Yelding 15	.40	.18	.05
☐ 28 Gerald Young 13	.40	.18	.05

1948 Babe Ruth Story

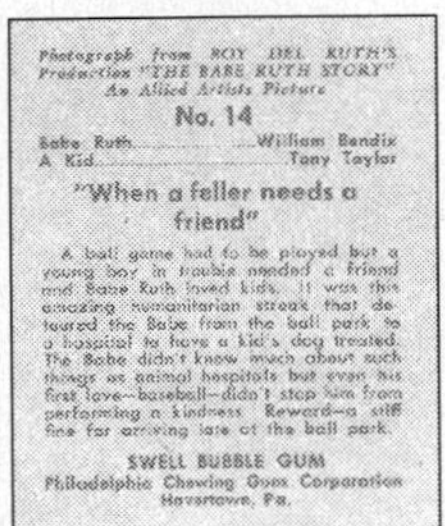

The 1948 Babe Ruth Story set of 28 black and white numbered cards (measuring approximately 2" by 2 1/2") was issued by the Philadelphia Chewing Gum Company to commemorate the 1949 movie of the same name starring William Bendix, Claire Trevor, and Charles Bickford. Babe Ruth himself appears on several cards. The last 12 cards (17 to 28) are more difficult to obtain than other cards in the set and are also more desirable in that most picture actual players as well as actors from the movie. Supposedly these last 12 cards were issued much later after the first 16 cards had already been released and distributed. The last seven cards (22-28) in the set are subtitled "The Babe Ruth Story in the Making" at the top of each reverse. The bottom of every card says "Swell Bubble Gum, Philadelphia Chewing Gum Corporation." The catalog designation for this set is R421.

	NRMT	VG-E	GOOD
COMPLETE SET (28)	1250.00	575.00	160.00
COMMON PLAYER (1-16)	15.00	6.75	1.90
COMMON PLAYER (17-24)	45.00	20.00	5.75
COMMON PLAYER (25-28)	135.00	60.00	17.00
☐ 1 The Babe Ruth Story In the Making (Babe Ruth shown with William Bendix)	150.00	40.00	8.00
☐ 2 Bat Boy Becomes the Babe (Facsimile autographed by William Bendix)	25.00	11.50	3.10
☐ 3 Claire Hodgson played by Claire Trevor	15.00	6.75	1.90
☐ 4 Babe Ruth played by William Bendix; Claire Hodgson played by Claire Trevor	15.00	6.75	1.90

☐ 5 Brother Matthias played by Charles Bickford	15.00	6.75	1.90
☐ 6 Phil Conrad played by Sam Levene	15.00	6.75	1.90
☐ 7 Night Club Singer played by Gertrude Niesen	15.00	6.75	1.90
☐ 8 Baseball's Famous Deal	15.00	6.75	1.90
☐ 9 Babe Ruth played by William Bendix; Mrs.Babe Ruth played by Claire Trevor	15.00	6.75	1.90
☐ 10 Actors for Babe Ruth, Mrs. Babe Ruth, and Brother Matthias	15.00	6.75	1.90
☐ 11 Babe Ruth played by William Bendix; Miller Huggins played by Fred Lightner	15.00	6.75	1.90
☐ 12 Babe Ruth played by William Bendix; Johnny Sylvester played by George Marshall	15.00	6.75	1.90
☐ 13 Actors for Mr., Mrs. and Johnny Sylvester	15.00	6.75	1.90
☐ 14 When A Feller Needs A Friend	15.00	6.75	1.90
☐ 15 Dramatic Home Run	15.00	6.75	1.90
☐ 16 The Homer That Set the Record	15.00	6.75	1.90
☐ 17 The Slap That Started Baseball's Most Famous Career	45.00	20.00	5.75
☐ 18 The Babe Plays Santa Claus	45.00	20.00	5.75
☐ 19 Actors for Ed Barrow, Jacob Ruppert, and Miller Huggins	45.00	20.00	5.75
☐ 20 Broken Window Paid Off	45.00	20.00	5.75
☐ 21 Regardless of the Generation/ Babe Ruth (Bendix shown getting mobbed by crowd)	45.00	20.00	5.75
☐ 22 Ted Lyons and William Bendix	60.00	27.00	7.50
☐ 23 Charley Grimm and William Bendix	45.00	20.00	5.75
☐ 24 Lefty Gomez, William Bendix, and Bucky Harris	75.00	34.00	9.50
☐ 25 Babe Ruth and William Bendix (Babe Ruth pictured with ball)	135.00	60.00	17.00
☐ 26 Babe Ruth and William Bendix (Babe Ruth pictured with bat)	135.00	60.00	17.00
☐ 27 Babe Ruth and Claire Trevor	135.00	60.00	17.00
☐ 28 William Bendix, Babe Ruth, Claire Trevor (Babe Ruth pictured autographing ball)	135.00	60.00	17.00

1990 Baseball Wit

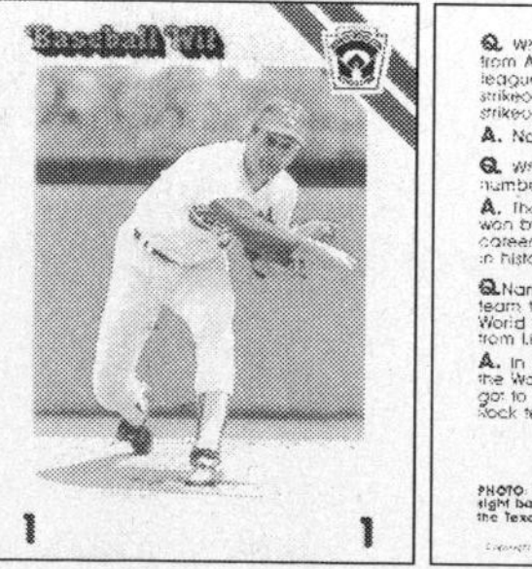

Q. Who is the Little League graduate from Alvin, Texas who has the major league record or most career strikeouts, no hitters, and most strikeouts in a season?

A. Nolan Ryan of the Texas Rangers.

Q. Why is "511" a famous baseball number?

A. That was the number of games won by Hall of Famer Cy Young—more career victories than any other pitcher in history.

Q. Name the only father and son team to ever play in the Little League World Series. (Hint: They both came from Little Rock, Arkansas.)

A. In 1953, James Herring took part in the World Series. In 1979, his son Jay got to the World Series with his Little Rock team.

PHOTO: NOLAN RYAN pitching left handed. A sight batters wouldn't mind seeing. Courtesy of the Texas Rangers.

The 1990 Baseball Wit set was issued in complete set form only. This set was dedicated to and featured several ex-members of the Little Leagues. This 108-card, standard-size (2 1/2" by 3 1/2") set was available primarily in retail and chain outlets. Most of the older (retired) players in the set are shown in black and white. The card backs typically give three trivia questions with answers following. The object of the game is to collect points by correctly answering any one of the questions on the back of each card or identifying the picture on the front. The first printing of 10,000 sets had several errors, and the cards were not numbered. The second printing corrected these errors and numbered the cards.

	MT	EX-MT	VG
COMPLETE SET (108)	10.00	4.50	1.25
COMMON PLAYER (1-108)	.08	.04	.01
☐ 1 Orel Hershiser	.12	.05	.02
☐ 2 Tony Gwynn	.30	.14	.04
☐ 3 Mickey Mantle	.75	.35	.09
☐ 4 Willie Stargell	.15	.07	.02
☐ 5 Don Baylor	.12	.05	.02
☐ 6 Hank Aaron	.30	.14	.04
☐ 7 Don Larsen	.08	.04	.01
☐ 8 Lee Mazzilli	.08	.04	.01
☐ 9 Boog Powell	.12	.05	.02
☐ 10 Little League World Series	.08	.04	.01
☐ 11 Jose Canseco	.40	.18	.05
☐ 12 Mike Scott	.08	.04	.01
☐ 13 Bob Feller	.15	.07	.02
☐ 14 Ron Santo	.08	.04	.01
☐ 15A Mel Stottlemyer ERR (sic, Stottlemyre)	.12	.05	.02
☐ 15B Mel Stottlemyre COR	.12	.05	.02
☐ 16 Shea Stadium	.08	.04	.01
☐ 17 Brooks Robinson	.12	.05	.02
☐ 18 Willie Mays	.30	.14	.04
☐ 19 Ernie Banks	.20	.09	.03
☐ 20 Keith Hernandez	.08	.04	.01
☐ 21 Bret Saberhagen	.12	.05	.02
☐ 22 Baseball Hall of Fame	.08	.04	.01
☐ 23 Luis Aparicio	.12	.05	.02
☐ 24 Yogi Berra	.20	.09	.03
☐ 25 Manny Mota	.08	.04	.01
☐ 26 Steve Garvey	.12	.05	.02
☐ 27 Bill Shea	.08	.04	.01
☐ 28 Fred Lynn	.08	.04	.01
☐ 29 Todd Worrell	.12	.05	.02
☐ 30 Roy Campanella	.20	.09	.03
☐ 31 Bob Gibson	.15	.07	.02
☐ 32 Gary Carter	.12	.05	.02
☐ 33 Jim Palmer	.15	.07	.02
☐ 34 Carl Yastrzemski	.15	.07	.02
☐ 35 Dwight Gooden	.15	.07	.02
☐ 36 Stan Musial	.30	.14	.04
☐ 37 Rickey Henderson	.30	.14	.04
☐ 38 Dale Murphy	.15	.07	.02
☐ 39 Mike Schmidt	.25	.11	.03
☐ 40 Gaylord Perry	.12	.05	.02
☐ 41 Ozzie Smith	.15	.07	.02
☐ 42 Reggie Jackson	.25	.11	.03
☐ 43 Steve Carlton	.15	.07	.02
☐ 44 Jim Perry	.08	.04	.01
☐ 45 Vince Coleman	.12	.05	.02
☐ 46 Tom Seaver	.25	.11	.03
☐ 47 Marty Marion	.08	.04	.01
☐ 48 Frank Robinson	.12	.05	.02
☐ 49 Joe DiMaggio	.50	.23	.06
☐ 50 Ted Williams	.40	.18	.05
☐ 51 Rollie Fingers	.12	.05	.02
☐ 52 Jackie Robinson	.40	.18	.05
☐ 53 Vic Raschi	.08	.04	.01
☐ 54 Johnny Bench	.20	.09	.03
☐ 55 Nolan Ryan	.75	.35	.09
☐ 56 Ty Cobb	.50	.23	.06
☐ 57 Harry Steinfeldt	.08	.04	.01
☐ 58 James O'Rourke	.08	.04	.01
☐ 59 John McGraw	.12	.05	.02
☐ 60 Candy Cummings	.12	.05	.02
☐ 61 Jimmie Foxx	.12	.05	.02
☐ 62 Walter Johnson	.15	.07	.02
☐ 63 1903 World Series	.08	.04	.01
☐ 64 Satchel Paige	.20	.09	.03
☐ 65 Bobby Wallace	.12	.05	.02
☐ 66 Cap Anson	.12	.05	.02
☐ 67 Hugh Duffy	.12	.05	.02
☐ 68 William(Buck) Ewing	.12	.05	.02

☐ 69 Bobo Holloman	.08	.04	.01
☐ 70 Ed Delahanty	.12	.05	.02
☐ 71 Dizzy Dean	.15	.07	.02
☐ 72 Tris Speaker	.12	.05	.02
☐ 73 Lou Gehrig	.50	.23	.06
☐ 74 Wee Willie Keeler	.12	.05	.02
☐ 75 Cal Hubbard	.12	.05	.02
☐ 76 Eddie Collins	.12	.05	.02
☐ 77 Chris Von Der Ahe	.08	.04	.01
☐ 78 Sam Crawford	.12	.05	.02
☐ 79 Cy Young	.15	.07	.02
☐ 80 Johnny Vander Meer	.08	.04	.01
☐ 81 Joey Jay	.08	.04	.01
☐ 82 Zack Wheat	.12	.05	.02
☐ 83 Jim Bottomley	.12	.05	.02
☐ 84 Honus Wagner	.30	.14	.04
☐ 85 Casey Stengel	.20	.09	.03
☐ 86 Babe Ruth	.75	.35	.09
☐ 87 John Lindemuth and Carl Stotz	.08	.04	.01
☐ 88 Max Carey	.12	.05	.02
☐ 89 Mordecai Brown	.12	.05	.02
☐ 90 1869 Cincinnati Red Stockings	.08	.04	.01
☐ 91 Rube Marquard	.12	.05	.02
☐ 92 Charles Radbourne (Horse)	.12	.05	.02
☐ 93 Hack Wilson	.12	.05	.02
☐ 94 Lefty Grove	.12	.05	.02
☐ 95 Carl Hubbell	.12	.05	.02
☐ 96 A.J. Cartwright	.08	.04	.01
☐ 97 Roger Hornsby	.15	.07	.02
☐ 98 Ernest Thayer	.08	.04	.01
☐ 99 Connie Mack	.12	.05	.02
☐ 100 1939 Centennial Celebration	.08	.04	.01
☐ 101 Branch Rickey	.12	.05	.02
☐ 102 Dan Brouthers	.08	.04	.01
☐ 103 First Baseball Uniform	.08	.04	.01
☐ 104 Christy Mathewson	.20	.09	.03
☐ 105 Joe Nuxhall	.08	.04	.01
☐ 106 1939 Centennial Celebration	.08	.04	.01
☐ 107 President William Howard Taft	.12	.05	.02
☐ 108 Abner Doubleday	.08	.04	.01

1988 Bazooka

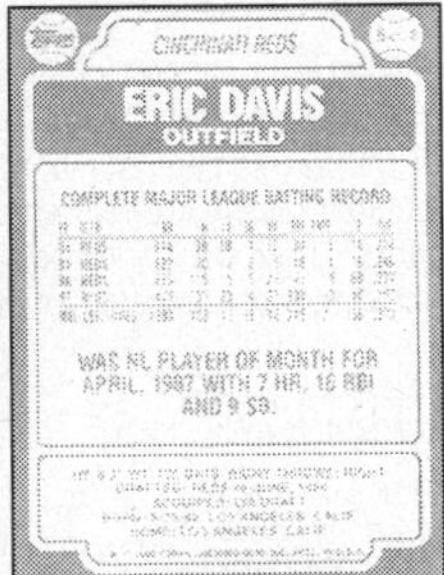

There are 22 standard-size (2 1/2" by 3 1/2") cards in the set. The cards have extra thick white borders. Card backs are printed in blue and red on white card stock. Some sets can also be found with gray backs; these gray backs carry no additional value premium. Cards are numbered on the back; they were numbered by Topps alphabetically. The word "Bazooka" only appears faintly as background for the statistics on the back of the card. Cards were available inside specially marked boxes of Bazooka gum retailing between 59 cents and 99 cents. The emphasis in the player selection for this set is on young stars of baseball.

	MT	EX-MT	VG
COMPLETE SET (22)	10.00	4.50	1.25
COMMON PLAYER (1-22)	.30	.14	.04

☐ 1 George Bell	.30	.14	.04
☐ 2 Wade Boggs	.75	.35	.09
☐ 3 Jose Canseco	1.25	.55	.16
☐ 4 Roger Clemens	1.50	.65	.19
☐ 5 Vince Coleman	.40	.18	.05
☐ 6 Eric Davis	.50	.23	.06
☐ 7 Tony Fernandez	.30	.14	.04
☐ 8 Dwight Gooden	.50	.23	.06
☐ 9 Tony Gwynn	.75	.35	.09
☐ 10 Wally Joyner	.40	.18	.05
☐ 11 Don Mattingly	1.00	.45	.13
☐ 12 Willie McGee	.30	.14	.04
☐ 13 Mark McGwire	1.00	.45	.13
☐ 14 Kirby Puckett	1.25	.55	.16
☐ 15 Tim Raines	.40	.18	.05
☐ 16 Dave Righetti	.30	.14	.04
☐ 17 Cal Ripken	1.50	.65	.19
☐ 18 Juan Samuel	.30	.14	.04
☐ 19 Ryne Sandberg	1.50	.65	.19
☐ 20 Benny Santiago	.40	.18	.05
☐ 21 Darryl Strawberry	.75	.35	.09
☐ 22 Todd Worrell	.30	.14	.04

1989 Bazooka Shining Stars

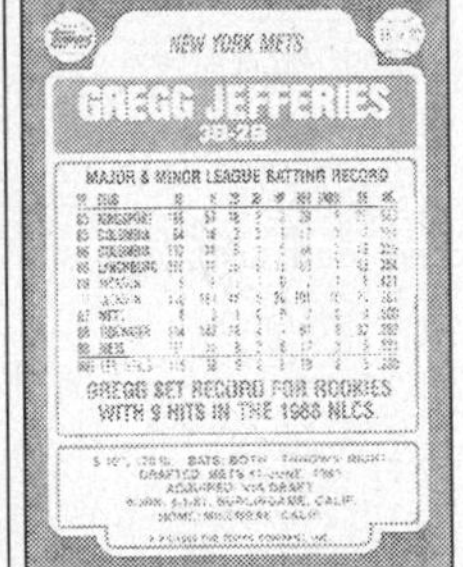

The 1989 Bazooka Shining Stars set contains 22 standard-size (2 1/2" by 3 1/2") cards. The fronts have white borders and a large yellow stripe; the vertically oriented backs are pink, red and white and have career stats. The cards were inserted one per box of Bazooka Gum.

	MT	EX-MT	VG
COMPLETE SET (22)	9.00	4.00	1.15
COMMON PLAYER (1-22)	.30	.14	.04

☐ 1 Tim Belcher	.30	.14	.04
☐ 2 Damon Berryhill	.30	.14	.04
☐ 3 Wade Boggs	.75	.35	.09
☐ 4 Jay Buhner	.40	.18	.05
☐ 5 Jose Canseco	1.25	.55	.16
☐ 6 Vince Coleman	.40	.18	.05
☐ 7 Cecil Espy	.30	.14	.04
☐ 8 Dave Gallagher	.30	.14	.04
☐ 9 Ron Gant	.75	.35	.09
☐ 10 Kirk Gibson	.40	.18	.05
☐ 11 Paul Gibson	.30	.14	.04
☐ 12 Mark Grace	1.00	.45	.13
☐ 13 Tony Gwynn	.75	.35	.09
☐ 14 Rickey Henderson	1.00	.45	.13
☐ 15 Orel Hershiser	.50	.23	.06
☐ 16 Gregg Jefferies	1.00	.45	.13
☐ 17 Ricky Jordan	.40	.18	.05
☐ 18 Chris Sabo	.50	.23	.06
☐ 19 Gary Sheffield	1.25	.55	.16
☐ 20 Darryl Strawberry	.75	.35	.09
☐ 21 Frank Viola	.40	.18	.05
☐ 22 Walt Weiss	.40	.18	.05

1990 Bazooka Shining Stars

The 1990 Bazooka Shining Stars set contains 22 cards with a mix of award winners, league leaders, and young stars. This standard-size (2 1/2" by 3 1/2") set was issued by

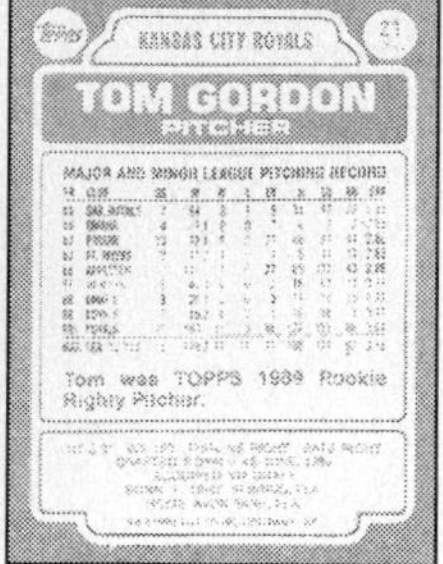

Topps using the Bazooka name. Card backs were printed in blue and red on white card stock. Cards are numbered on the back. The word "Bazooka" appears faintly as background for the statistics on the back of the card as well as appearing prominently on the front of each card.

	MT	EX-MT	VG
COMPLETE SET (22)	8.00	3.60	1.00
COMMON PLAYER (1-22)	.30	.14	.04
☐ 1 Kevin Mitchell	.50	.23	.06
☐ 2 Robin Yount	.75	.35	.09
☐ 3 Mark Davis	.30	.14	.04
☐ 4 Bret Saberhagen	.50	.23	.06
☐ 5 Fred McGriff	.60	.25	.08
☐ 6 Tony Gwynn	.60	.25	.08
☐ 7 Kirby Puckett	1.00	.45	.13
☐ 8 Vince Coleman	.40	.18	.05
☐ 9 Rickey Henderson	.90	.40	.11
☐ 10 Ben McDonald	.75	.35	.09
☐ 11 Gregg Olson	.40	.18	.05
☐ 12 Todd Zeile	.40	.18	.05
☐ 13 Carlos Martinez	.30	.14	.04
☐ 14 Gregg Jefferies	.60	.25	.08
☐ 15 Craig Worthington	.30	.14	.04
☐ 16 Gary Sheffield	1.00	.45	.13
☐ 17 Greg Briley	.30	.14	.04
☐ 18 Ken Griffey Jr.	1.50	.65	.19
☐ 19 Jerome Walton	.30	.14	.04
☐ 20 Bob Geren	.30	.14	.04
☐ 21 Tom Gordon	.30	.14	.04
☐ 22 Jim Abbott	.75	.35	.09

1991 Bazooka Shining Stars

The 1991 Bazooka Shining Stars set contains 22 cards featuring league leaders and rookie sensations. The standard-size (2 1/2" by 3 1/2") cards were produced by Topps for Bazooka. One card was inserted in each box of Bazooka Bubble Gum. The fronts are similar to the Topps regular issue, only that the "Shining Star" emblem appears at the card top and the Bazooka logo overlays the lower right corner of the picture. In a blue and red design on white card stock, the backs have statistics and biography. The cards are numbered on the back.

	MT	EX-MT	VG
COMPLETE SET (22)	12.50	5.75	1.55
COMMON PLAYER (1-22)	.30	.14	.04
☐ 1 Barry Bonds	1.00	.45	.13
☐ 2 Rickey Henderson	1.00	.45	.13
☐ 3 Bob Welch	.30	.14	.04
☐ 4 Doug Drabek	.40	.18	.05
☐ 5 Alex Fernandez	.40	.18	.05
☐ 6 Jose Offerman	.40	.18	.05
☐ 7 Frank Thomas	3.00	1.35	.40
☐ 8 Cecil Fielder	.75	.35	.09
☐ 9 Ryne Sandberg	1.25	.55	.16
☐ 10 George Brett	.75	.35	.09
☐ 11 Willie McGee	.40	.18	.05
☐ 12 Vince Coleman	.40	.18	.05
☐ 13 Hal Morris	.50	.23	.06
☐ 14 Delino DeShields	.75	.35	.09
☐ 15 Robin Ventura	1.00	.45	.13
☐ 16 Jeff Huson	.30	.14	.04
☐ 17 Felix Jose	.50	.23	.06
☐ 18 Dave Justice	1.50	.65	.19
☐ 19 Larry Walker	1.00	.45	.13
☐ 20 Sandy Alomar Jr.	.50	.23	.06
☐ 21 Kevin Appier	.40	.18	.05
☐ 22 Scott Radinsky	.40	.18	.05

1992 Bazooka Quadracard '53 Archives

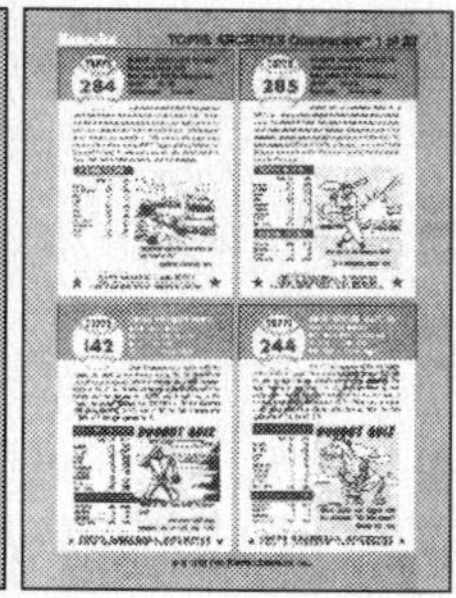

This 22-card set was produced by Topps for Bazooka, and the set is subtitled "Topps Archives Quadracard" on the top of the backs. Each standard-size (2 1/2" by 3 1/2") card features four micro-reproductions of 1953 Topps baseball cards. These front and back borders of the cards are blue. The cards are numbered on the back.

	MT	EX-MT	VG
COMPLETE SET (22)	10.00	4.50	1.25
COMMON PLAYER (1-22)	.35	.16	.04
☐ 1 Joe Adcock Bob Lemon Willie Mays Vic Wertz	1.00	.45	.13
☐ 2 Carl Furillo Don Newcombe Phil Rizzuto Hank Sauer	.35	.16	.04
☐ 3 Ferris Fain John Logan Ed Mathews Bobby Shantz	.35	.16	.04
☐ 4 Yogi Berra Del Crandall Howie Pollet Gene Woodling	.75	.35	.09
☐ 5 Richie Ashburn Leo Durocher Allie Reynolds Early Wynn	.75	.35	.09
☐ 6 Hank Aaron Ray Boone Luke Easter Dick Williams	1.00	.45	.13
☐ 7 Ralph Branca Bob Feller	.75	.35	.09

	Rogers Hornsby			
	Bobby Thomson			
☐ 8	Jim Gilliam	.50	.23	.06
	Billy Martin			
	Minnie Minoso			
	Hal Newhouser			
☐ 9	Smoky Burgess	.50	.23	.06
	John Mize			
	Preacher Roe			
	Warren Spahn			
☐ 10	Monte Irvin	.75	.35	.09
	Bobo Newsom			
	Duke Snider			
	Wes Westrum			
☐ 11	Carl Erskine	.50	.23	.06
	Jackie Jensen			
	George Kell			
	Red Schoendienst			
☐ 12	Bill Bruton	.50	.23	.06
	Whitey Ford			
	Ed Lopat			
	Mickey Vernon			
☐ 13	Joe Black	.35	.16	.04
	Lew Burdette			
	Johnny Pesky			
	Enos Slaughter			
☐ 14	Gus Bell	.75	.35	.09
	Mike Garia			
	Mel Parnell			
	Jackie Robinson			
☐ 15	Alvin Dark	.50	.23	.06
	Dick Groat			
	Pee Wee Reese			
	John Sain			
☐ 16	Gil Hodges	.50	.23	.06
	Sal Maglie			
	Wilmer Mizell			
	Billy Pierce			
☐ 17	Nellie Fox	.50	.23	.06
	Ralph Kiner			
	Ted Kluszewski			
	Eddie Stanky			
☐ 18	Ewell Blackwell	.50	.23	.06
	Vern Law			
	Satchel Paige			
	Jim Wilson			
☐ 19	Lou Boudreau	.35	.16	.04
	Roy Face			
	Harvey Haddix			
	Bill Rigney			
☐ 20	Roy Campanella	.50	.23	.06
	Walt Dropo			
	Harvey Kuenn			
	Al Rosen			
☐ 21	Joe Garagiola	.75	.35	.09
	Robin Roberts			
	Casey Stengel MG			
	Hoyt Wilhelm			
☐ 22	John Antonelli	1.00	.45	.13
	Bob Friend			
	Dixie Walker CO			
	Ted Williams			

1951 Berk Ross

HIT PARADE OF CHAMPIONS
1951
Trade Mark Reg. U.S. Pat. Off.
RICHIE ASHBURN
Outfield, Philadelphia Phillies
Member of Philadelphia Phillies
National League Champions
Born March 19, 1927
Tilden, Nebraska
Height 5-11, Weight 170
Throws Right, Bats Left
1950 Hit .303 in 151 Games
No. 1-9 © Berk Ross Inc., New York, N.Y.

The 1951 Berk Ross set consists of 72 cards (each measuring approximately 2 1/16" by 2 1/2") with tinted photographs, divided evenly into four series (designated in the checklist as A, B, C and D). The cards were marketed in boxes containing two card panels, without gum, and the set includes stars of other sports as well as baseball players. The set is sometimes still found in the original packaging. Intact panels are worth 20 percent more than the sum of the individual cards. The catalog designation for this set is W532-1. In every series the first ten cards are baseball players; the set has a heavy emphasis on Yankees and Phillies players as they were in the World Series the year before.

	NRMT	VG-E	GOOD
COMPLETE SET (72)	1000.00	450.00	125.00
COMMON BASEBALL	9.00	4.00	1.15
COMMON FOOTBALL	9.00	4.00	1.15
COMMON OTHERS	5.00	2.30	.60
☐ A1 Al Rosen	12.00	5.50	1.50
☐ A2 Bob Lemon	18.00	8.00	2.30
☐ A3 Phil Rizzuto	24.00	11.00	3.00
☐ A4 Hank Bauer	13.50	6.00	1.70
☐ A5 Billy Johnson	9.00	4.00	1.15
☐ A6 Jerry Coleman	9.00	4.00	1.15
☐ A7 Johnny Mize	24.00	11.00	3.00
☐ A8 Dom DiMaggio	13.50	6.00	1.70
☐ A9 Richie Ashburn	18.00	8.00	2.30
☐ A10 Del Ennis	9.00	4.00	1.15
☐ A11 Bob Cousy	125.00	57.50	15.50
☐ A12 Dick Schnittker	5.00	2.30	.60
☐ A13 Ezzard Charles	9.00	4.00	1.15
☐ A14 Leon Hart	12.00	5.50	1.50
☐ A15 James Martin	9.00	4.00	1.15
☐ A16 Ben Hogan	25.00	11.50	3.10
☐ A17 Bill Durnan	15.00	6.75	1.90
☐ A18 Bill Quackenbush	10.00	4.50	1.25
☐ B1 Stan Musial	90.00	40.00	11.50
☐ B2 Warren Spahn	30.00	13.50	3.80
☐ B3 Tom Henrich	12.00	5.50	1.50
☐ B4 Yogi Berra	70.00	32.00	8.75
☐ B5 Joe DiMaggio	150.00	70.00	19.00
☐ B6 Bobby Brown	13.50	6.00	1.70
☐ B7 Granny Hamner	9.00	4.00	1.15
☐ B8 Willie Jones	9.00	4.00	1.15
☐ B9 Stan Lopata	9.00	4.00	1.15
☐ B10 Mike Goliat	9.00	4.00	1.15
☐ B11 Sherman White	9.00	4.00	1.15
☐ B12 Joe Maxim	6.00	2.70	.75
☐ B13 Ray Robinson	24.00	11.00	3.00
☐ B14 Doak Walker	18.00	8.00	2.30
☐ B15 Emil Sitko	5.00	2.30	.60
☐ B16 Jack Stewart	5.00	2.30	.60
☐ B17 Dick Button	9.00	4.00	1.15
☐ B18 Melvin Patton	5.00	2.30	.60
☐ C1 Ralph Kiner	24.00	11.00	3.00
☐ C2 Bill Goodman	9.00	4.00	1.15
☐ C3 Allie Reynolds	15.00	6.75	1.90
☐ C4 Vic Raschi	15.00	6.75	1.90
☐ C5 Joe Page	12.00	5.50	1.50
☐ C6 Eddie Lopat	15.00	6.75	1.90
☐ C7 Andy Seminick	9.00	4.00	1.15
☐ C8 Dick Sisler	9.00	4.00	1.15
☐ C9 Eddie Waitkus	9.00	4.00	1.15
☐ C10 Ken Heintzelman	9.00	4.00	1.15
☐ C11 Paul Unruh	5.00	2.30	.60
☐ C12 Jake LaMotta	20.00	9.00	2.50
☐ C13 Ike Williams	5.00	2.30	.60
☐ C14 Wade Walker	5.00	2.30	.60
☐ C15 Rodney Franz	5.00	2.30	.60
☐ C16 Sid Abel	15.00	6.75	1.90
☐ C17 Claire Sherman	5.00	2.30	.60
☐ C18 Jesse Owens	20.00	9.00	2.50
☐ D1 Gene Woodling	12.00	5.50	1.50
☐ D2 Cliff Mapes	9.00	4.00	1.15
☐ D3 Fred Sanford	9.00	4.00	1.15
☐ D4 Tommy Byrne	9.00	4.00	1.15
☐ D5 Whitey Ford	30.00	13.50	3.80
☐ D6 Jim Konstanty	9.00	4.00	1.15
☐ D7 Russ Meyer	9.00	4.00	1.15
☐ D8 Robin Roberts	24.00	11.00	3.00
☐ D9 Curt Simmons	12.00	5.50	1.50
☐ D10 Sam Jethroe	9.00	4.00	1.15
☐ D11 Bill Sharman	25.00	11.50	3.10
☐ D12 Sandy Saddler	5.00	2.30	.60
☐ D13 Margaret DuPont	5.00	2.30	.60
☐ D14 Arnold Galiffa	12.00	5.50	1.50
☐ D15 Charlie Justice	18.00	8.00	2.30
☐ D16 Glen Cunningham	6.00	2.70	.75
☐ D17 Gregory Rice	5.00	2.30	.60
☐ D18 Harrison Dillard	6.00	2.70	.75

1952 Berk Ross

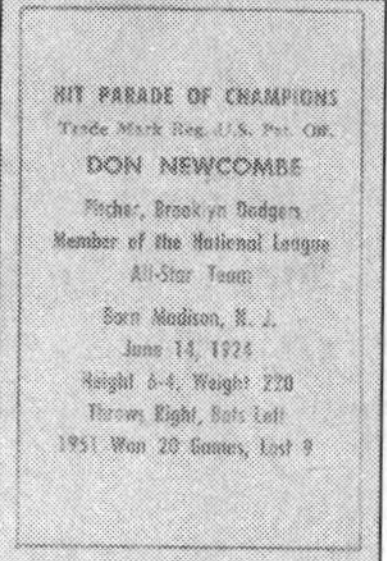

The 1952 Berk Ross set of 72 unnumbered, tinted photocards, each measuring approximately 2" by 3", seems to have been patterned after the highly successful 1951 Bowman set. The reverses of Ewell Blackwell and Nellie Fox are transposed while Phil Rizzuto comes with two different poses. The complete set below includes both poses of Rizzuto. There is a card of Joe DiMaggio even though he retired after the 1951 season. The catalog designation for this set is W532-2, and the cards have been assigned numbers in the alphabetical checklist below.

	NRMT	VG-E	GOOD
COMPLETE SET (72)	5500.00	2500.00	700.00
COMMON PLAYER (1-72)	15.00	6.75	1.90
☐ 1 Richie Ashburn	45.00	15.00	3.00
☐ 2 Hank Bauer	20.00	9.00	2.50
☐ 3 Yogi Berra	150.00	70.00	19.00
☐ 4 Ewell Blackwell UER (photo actually Nellie Fox)	25.00	11.50	3.10
☐ 5 Bobby Brown	22.50	10.00	2.80
☐ 6 Jim Busby	15.00	6.75	1.90
☐ 7 Roy Campanella	150.00	70.00	19.00
☐ 8 Chico Carrasquel	15.00	6.75	1.90
☐ 9 Jerry Coleman	15.00	6.75	1.90
☐ 10 Joe Collins	15.00	6.75	1.90
☐ 11 Alvin Dark	18.00	8.00	2.30
☐ 12 Dom DiMaggio	22.50	10.00	2.80
☐ 13 Joe DiMaggio	1000.00	400.00	125.00
☐ 14 Larry Doby	25.00	11.50	3.10
☐ 15 Bobby Doerr	45.00	20.00	5.75
☐ 16 Bob Elliott	15.00	6.75	1.90
☐ 17 Del Ennis	15.00	6.75	1.90
☐ 18 Ferris Fain	15.00	6.75	1.90
☐ 19 Bob Feller	100.00	45.00	12.50
☐ 20 Nellie Fox UER (photo actually Ewell Blackwell)	25.00	11.50	3.10
☐ 21 Ned Garver	15.00	6.75	1.90
☐ 22 Clint Hartung	15.00	6.75	1.90
☐ 23 Jim Hearn	15.00	6.75	1.90
☐ 24 Gil Hodges	50.00	23.00	6.25
☐ 25 Monte Irvin	45.00	20.00	5.75
☐ 26 Larry Jansen	15.00	6.75	1.90
☐ 27 Sheldon Jones	15.00	6.75	1.90
☐ 28 George Kell	45.00	20.00	5.75
☐ 29 Monte Kennedy	15.00	6.75	1.90
☐ 30 Ralph Kiner	60.00	27.00	7.50
☐ 31 Dave Koslo	15.00	6.75	1.90
☐ 32 Bob Kuzava	15.00	6.75	1.90
☐ 33 Bob Lemon	45.00	20.00	5.75
☐ 34 Whitey Lockman	15.00	6.75	1.90
☐ 35 Ed Lopat	25.00	11.50	3.10
☐ 36 Sal Maglie	20.00	9.00	2.50
☐ 37 Mickey Mantle	1500.00	600.00	200.00
☐ 38 Billy Martin	60.00	27.00	7.50
☐ 39 Willie Mays	500.00	230.00	65.00
☐ 40 Gil McDougald	25.00	11.50	3.10
☐ 41 Minnie Minoso	25.00	11.50	3.10
☐ 42 Johnny Mize	60.00	27.00	7.50
☐ 43 Tom Morgan	15.00	6.75	1.90
☐ 44 Don Mueller	15.00	6.75	1.90
☐ 45 Stan Musial	300.00	135.00	38.00
☐ 46 Don Newcombe	25.00	11.50	3.10
☐ 47 Ray Noble	15.00	6.75	1.90
☐ 48 Joe Ostrowski	15.00	6.75	1.90
☐ 49 Mel Parnell	18.00	8.00	2.30
☐ 50 Vic Raschi	22.50	10.00	2.80
☐ 51 Pee Wee Reese	90.00	40.00	11.50
☐ 52 Allie Reynolds	25.00	11.50	3.10
☐ 53 Bill Rigney	15.00	6.75	1.90
☐ 54A Phil Rizzuto (bunting)	60.00	27.00	7.50
☐ 54B Phil Rizzuto (swinging)	60.00	27.00	7.50
☐ 55 Robin Roberts	50.00	23.00	6.25
☐ 56 Eddie Robinson	15.00	6.75	1.90
☐ 57 Jackie Robinson	300.00	135.00	38.00
☐ 58 Preacher Roe	22.50	10.00	2.80
☐ 59 Johnny Sain	25.00	11.50	3.10
☐ 60 Red Schoendienst	50.00	23.00	6.25
☐ 61 Duke Snider	150.00	70.00	19.00
☐ 62 George Spencer	15.00	6.75	1.90
☐ 63 Eddie Stanky	18.00	8.00	2.30
☐ 64 Hank Thompson	18.00	8.00	2.30
☐ 65 Bobby Thomson	20.00	9.00	2.50
☐ 66 Vic Wertz	15.00	6.75	1.90
☐ 67 Wally Westlake	15.00	6.75	1.90
☐ 68 Wes Westrum	15.00	6.75	1.90
☐ 69 Ted Williams	400.00	180.00	50.00
☐ 70 Gene Woodling	18.00	8.00	2.30
☐ 71 Gus Zernial	15.00	6.75	1.90

1989 Best Western Nolan Ryan

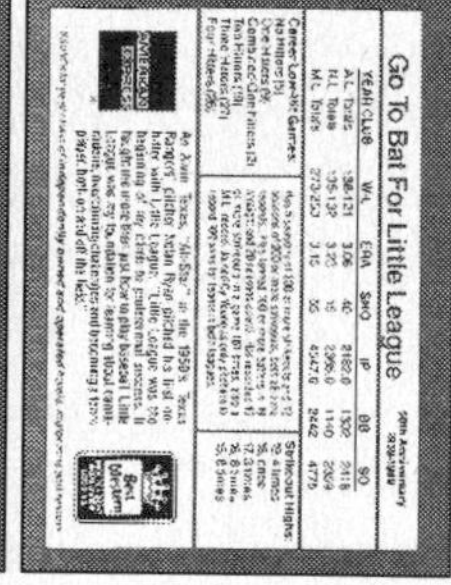

This one-card set was sponsored by Best Western in conjunction with American Express to commemorate the 50th anniversary of Little League Baseball. Supposedly a card was given to each child who stayed at a Best Western motel during the promotion. The standard-size (2 1/2" by 3 1/2") card has a black and white photo of Nolan Ryan in his Little League uniform. The photo is bordered in cherry red, and a 50th Anniversary logo appears in the shape of a baseball on the card face. Noaln Ryan's name and age are given toward the bottom of the card. In a horizontal format, the backs have Major League statistics, career highlights, and a player quote regarding the importance of Little League. The card is unnumbered.

	MT	EX-MT	VG
COMPLETE SET (1)	5.00	2.30	.60
☐ NNO Nolan Ryan (Little League photo)	5.00	2.30	.60

1986 Big League Chew

This 12-card set was produced by Big League Chew and was inserted in with their packages of Big League Chew chewing gum, which were shaped and styled after a pouch of chewing tobacco. The cards were found one per pouch of shredded chewing gum or were available through a mail-in offer of two coupons and $2.00 for a complete set. The players featured are members of the 500 career home run

club. The backs are printed in blue ink on white card stock. The cards are standard size, 2 1/2" by 3 1/2", and are subtitled "Home Run Legends". The front of each card shows a year inside a small flag; the year is the year that player passed 500 homers.

	MT	EX-MT	VG
COMPLETE SET (12)	5.00	2.30	.60
COMMON PLAYER (1-12)	.35	.16	.04
☐ 1 Hank Aaron	1.00	.45	.13
☐ 2 Babe Ruth	2.00	.90	.25
☐ 3 Willie Mays	1.00	.45	.13
☐ 4 Frank Robinson	.50	.23	.06
☐ 5 Harmon Killebrew	.35	.16	.04
☐ 6 Mickey Mantle	1.50	.65	.19
☐ 7 Jimmie Foxx	.35	.16	.04
☐ 8 Ted Williams	1.00	.45	.13
☐ 9 Ernie Banks	.50	.23	.06
☐ 10 Eddie Mathews	.35	.16	.04
☐ 11 Mel Ott	.35	.16	.04
☐ 12 500 HR Members	.35	.16	.04

1991 Bleachers 23K Ken Griffey Jr.

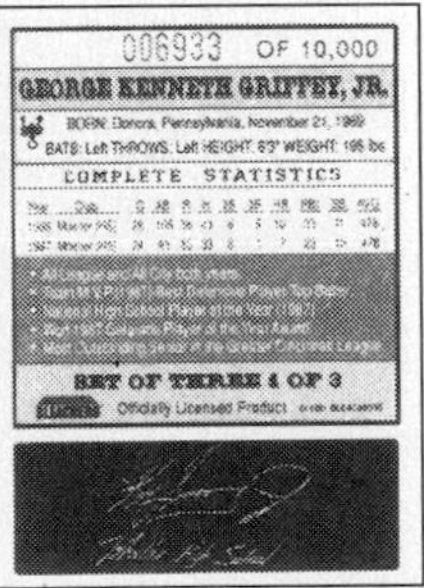

These three 23-karat gold cards were issued by Bleachers and measure the standard size (2 1/2" by 3 1/2"). The production run was reported to be 10,000 numbered sets and 1,500 uncut numbered strips. Extended by a small semi-circle, the color player photos on the fronts capture Griffey in three different phases of his career. Each card has a different color inner border (1-yellow; 2-gray; 3-red) and a gold outer border. On white, green, yellow, and blue bars, the backs carry the player's name, biography, statistics, highlights, and a serial number ("X of 10,000") inside a black border. The player's name and team name are etched in gold at the card bottom. The cards are numbered on the back.

	MT	EX-MT	VG
COMPLETE SET (3)	30.00	13.50	3.80
COMMON PLAYER (1-3)	12.00	5.50	1.50
☐ 1 Ken Griffey Jr. Moeller High	12.00	5.50	1.50
☐ 2 Ken Griffey Jr. Bellingham Mariners	12.00	5.50	1.50
☐ 3 Ken Griffey Jr. San Bernardino Spirit	12.00	5.50	1.50

1991 Bleachers 23K Frank Thomas

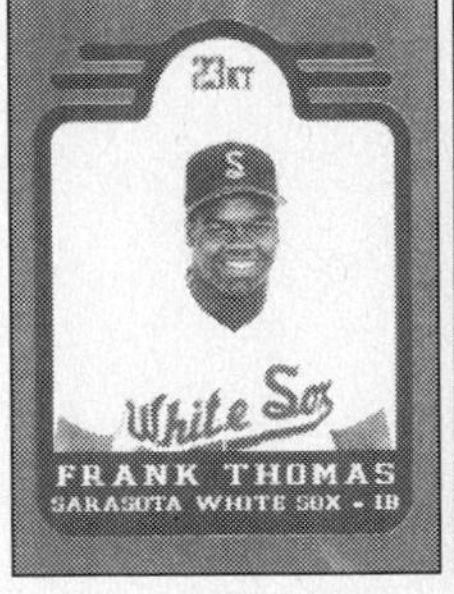

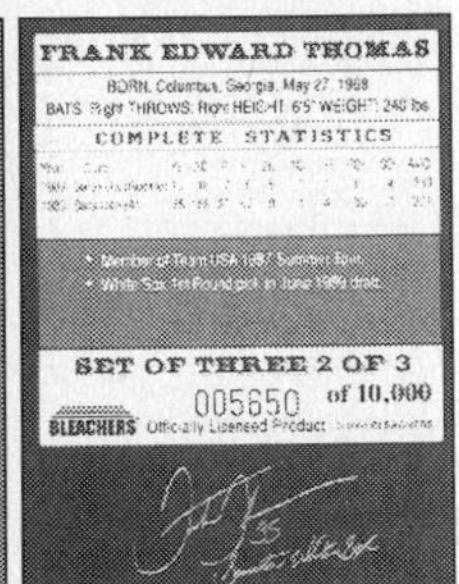

These three 23-karat gold cards were produced by Bleachers and measure the standard size (2 1/2" by 3 1/2"). On a gold card front, posed color player photos are enframed by different color borders (1-blue; 2-black; 3-red). The top of each photo is extended by a small semi-circle that is intersected by two border stripes. The player's name, team name, and position are printed in white lettering in the border beneath the picture. On gray, yellow, white, and red stripes, the back has the player's name, biography, statistics, highlights, and the serial number (1 of 10,000), inside a black border. It is reported that the production run was limited to 10,000 sets and 1,500 uncut numbered strips. The player's signature, team name, and jersey number are written in gold at the bottom of the card. The cards are numbered on the back.

	MT	EX-MT	VG
COMPLETE SET (3)	40.00	18.00	5.00
COMMON PLAYER (1-3)	15.00	6.75	1.90
☐ 1 Frank Thomas Auburn Tigers	15.00	6.75	1.90
☐ 2 Frank Thomas Sarasota White Sox	15.00	6.75	1.90
☐ 3 Frank Thomas Birmingham Barons	15:00	6.75	1.90

1991-92 Bleachers Promos

These promo cards were distributed to dealers to promote the new forthcoming Bleachers 23K card sets. The cards are all standard size, 2 1/2" by 3 1/2". The card backs contain order information as well as information about Bleachers upcoming releases.

	MT	EX-MT	VG
COMPLETE SET (6)	16.00	7.25	2.00
COMMON PLAYER (1-6)	2.00	.90	.25
☐ 1 Ken Griffey Jr. (Spirit jersey; 1991 copyright; Frank Thomas pictured on back)	3.00	1.35	.40
☐ 2 Dave Justice (1992 copyright; wearing Bleachers tee-shirt)	2.00	.90	.25
☐ 2 Nolan Ryan (1992 copyright; wearing tuxedo; green and yellow back, no 800 number in border)	3.00	1.35	.40
☐ 3 Nolan Ryan (1992 copyright; wearing tuxedo; blue and yellow back, 800 number in border)	3.00	1.35	.40
☐ 4 Nolan Ryan (1992 copyright; wearing tuxedo; gold foil stamped "East Coast National '92" on front)	3.00	1.35	.40
☐ 5 Nolan Ryan (1992 copyright; wearing tuxedo; gold foil stamped "SF Sports Collectors Card Expo '92" on front)	3.00	1.35	.40
☐ 6 Nolan Ryan (1992 copyright; wearing tuxedo; gold foil stamped "Tri-Star St. Louis '92" on front)	3.00	1.35	.40

1992 Bleachers 23K Dave Justice

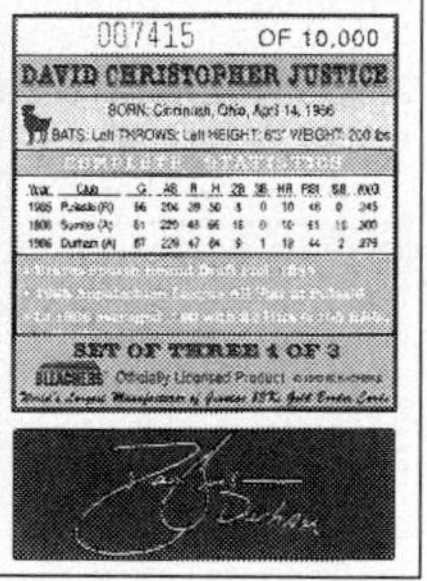

These three 23-karat gold cards were issued by Bleachers and measure the standard size (2 1/2" by 3 1/2"). The production run was reported to be 10,000 numbered sets and 1,500 uncut numbered strips. The color player photos on the fronts capture Justice in three different phases of his career, and the front design differs slightly from that of the previous year's issues. Each card has a different color inner border (1-aqua; 2-black; 3-yellow) and a gold outer border. On white, pink, and orange bars, the backs carry the player's name, biography, statistics, highlights, and a serial number ("X of 10,000") inside a black border. The player's name and team name are etched in gold at the card bottom. The cards are numbered on the back. Prism cards (silver prism border instead of gold) were randomly inserted in sets on a limited basis. These prism versions are valued at double the prices listed below.

	MT	EX-MT	VG
COMPLETE SET (3)	21.00	9.50	2.60
COMMON PLAYER (1-3)	8.00	3.60	1.00
☐ 1 Dave Justice, Durham Bulls	8.00	3.60	1.00
☐ 2 Dave Justice, Greenville Braves	8.00	3.60	1.00
☐ 3 Dave Justice, Richmond Braves	8.00	3.60	1.00

1992 Bleachers 23K Nolan Ryan

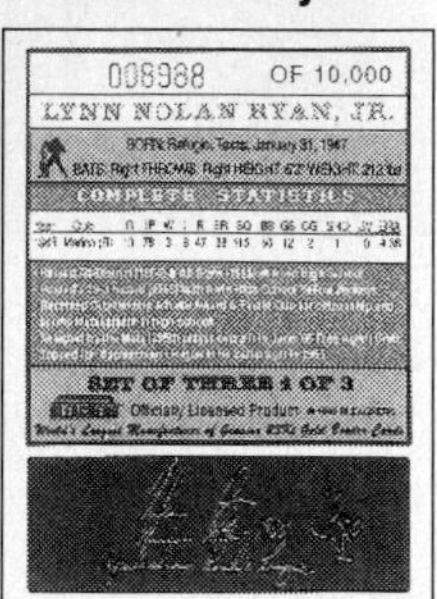

These three 23-karat gold cards were issued by Bleachers and measure the standard size (2 1/2" by 3 1/2"). The sets were packaged in a cardboard sleeve and shrink wrapped; promo cards and prism cards were randomly inserted. The production run is reported to be 10,000 numbered sets and 1,500 uncut numbered strips. The color player photos on the fronts capture Nolan Ryan in three different phases of his career, and the front design differs slightly from that of the previous year's issues. Each card has a different color inner border (1-blue; 2-gray; 3-orange) and a gold outer border. On white, purple, and orange bars, the backs carry the player's name, biography, statistics, highlights, and a serial number ("X of 10,000") inside a black border. The player's name and team name are etched in gold at the card bottom. The cards are numbered on the back. Prism cards (silver prism border instead of gold) were randomly inserted in sets on a limited basis. These prism versions are valued at double the prices listed below.

	MT	EX-MT	VG
COMPLETE SET (3)	27.00	12.00	3.40
COMMON PLAYER (1-3)	10.00	4.50	1.25
☐ 1 Nolan Ryan, Marion Mets	10.00	4.50	1.25
☐ 2 Nolan Ryan, Greenville Mets	10.00	4.50	1.25
☐ 3 Nolan Ryan, Jacksonville Suns	10.00	4.50	1.25

1993 Bleachers Promos

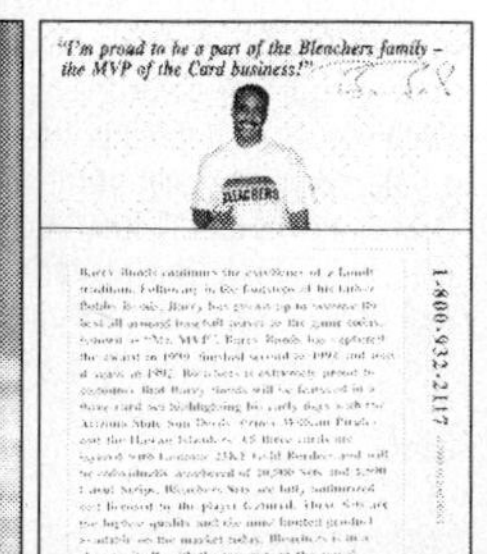

These promo cards were distributed to dealers to promote the new upcoming Bleachers 23K card sets. The cards are all standard size, 2 1/2" by 3 1/2". The card backs contain order information as well as information about Bleachers upcoming releases.

	MT	EX-MT	VG
COMPLETE SET (7)	25.00	11.50	3.10
COMMON PLAYER (1-7)	3.00	1.35	.40
☐ 1 Barry Bonds (1993 copyright)	3.00	1.35	.40
☐ 2 Nolan Ryan (1992 copyright; wearing tuxedo; Tri-Star Houston '93 gold stamped on front)	3.00	1.35	.40
☐ 3 Nolan Ryan (1993 copyright; sitting; western gear)	3.00	1.35	.40
☐ 4 Nolan Ryan (1993 copyright; wearing tuxedo; gold-speckled background)	6.00	2.70	.75
☐ 5 Nolan Ryan (1993 copyright; wearing tuxedo; silver-speckled background)	6.00	2.70	.75
☐ 6 Nolan Ryan (1993 copyright; wearing tuxedo; silver-wavy background)	6.00	2.70	.75
☐ 7 Ryne Sandberg (1993 copyright; three photos, baseball, basketball, and football)	3.00	1.35	.40

1993 Bleachers 23K Barry Bonds

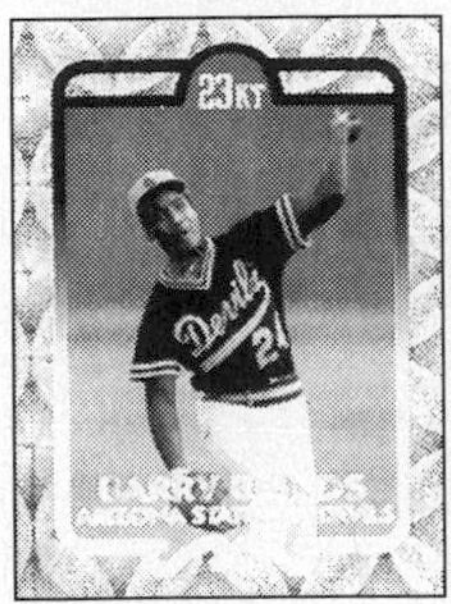

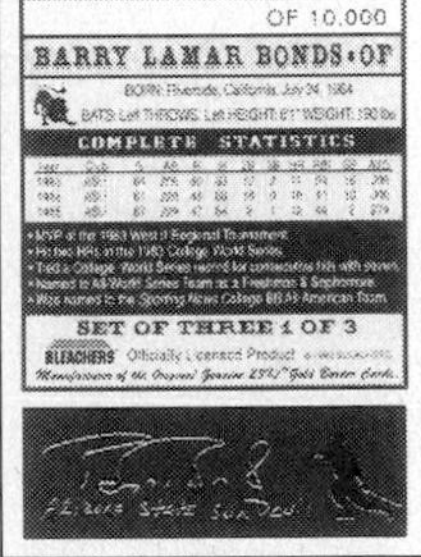

These three 23-karat gold cards were issued by Bleachers and measure the standard size (2 1/2" by 3 1/2"). The sets were packaged in a cardboard sleeve and shrink wrapped; promo cards and prism cards were randomly inserted. The production run was reported to be 10,000 numbered sets and 1,500 uncut numbered strips. The color player photos on the fronts capture Barry Bonds in three different phases of his career. The backs carry the player's name, biography, statistics, highlights, and a serial number ("X of 10,000") inside a black border. The player's name and team name are etched in gold at the card bottom. The cards are numbered on the back. Prism cards (silver prism border instead of gold) were randomly inserted in sets on a limited basis. These prism versions are valued at double the prices listed below.

	MT	EX-MT	VG
COMPLETE SET (3)	27.00	12.00	3.40
COMMON PLAYER (1-3)	10.00	4.50	1.25
☐ 1 Barry Bonds Arizona State Sun Devils	10.00	4.50	1.25
☐ 2 Barry Bonds Prince William Pirates	10.00	4.50	1.25
☐ 3 Barry Bonds Hawaii Islanders	10.00	4.50	1.25

1993 Bleachers 23K Ryne Sandberg

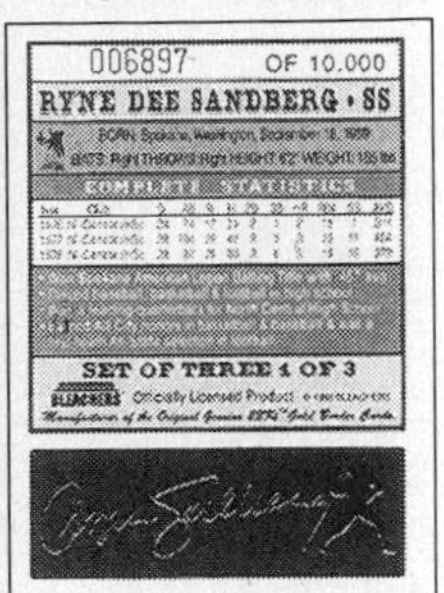

These three 23-karat gold cards were issued by Bleachers and measure the standard size (2 1/2" by 3 1/2"). The sets were packaged in a cardboard sleeve and shrink wrapped; promo cards and prism cards were randomly inserted. The production run was reported to be 10,000 numbered sets and 1,500 uncut numbered strips. The color player photos on the fronts capture Ryne Sandberg in three different phases of his career. The backs carry the player's name, biography, statistics, highlights, and a serial number ("X of 10,000") inside a black border. The player's name and team name are etched in gold at the card bottom. The cards are numbered on the back. Prism cards (silver prism border instead of gold) were randomly inserted in sets on a limited basis. These prism versions are valued at double the prices listed below.

	MT	EX-MT	VG
COMPLETE SET (3)	27.00	12.00	3.40
COMMON PLAYER (1-3)	10.00	4.50	1.25
☐ 1 Ryne Sandberg North Central High School	10.00	4.50	1.25
☐ 2 Ryne Sandberg Helena Phillies	10.00	4.50	1.25
☐ 3 Ryne Sandberg Reading Phillies	10.00	4.50	1.25

1991 Blue Jays Score

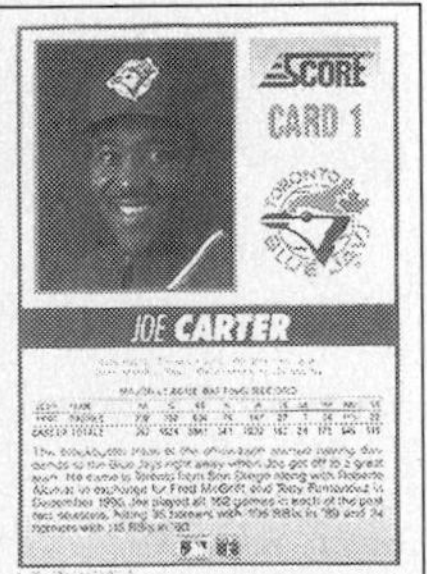

The 1991 Score Toronto Blue Jays set contains 40 player cards plus five magic motion trivia cards. The standard-size (2 1/2" by 3 1/2") cards feature on the fronts glossy color action photos with white borders. The bottom corners of the pictures are cut off by aqua-shaped triangles. The player's name and position appear in an aqua stripe above the picture. The producer's name and the team logo at the bottom round out the card face. The backs have a color head shot of the player, biography, Major League statistics, and a player profile. The cards are numbered on the back.

	MT	EX-MT	VG
COMPLETE SET (40)	16.00	7.25	2.00
COMMON PLAYER (1-40)	.30	.14	.04
☐ 1 Joe Carter	1.50	.65	.19
☐ 2 Tom Henke	.50	.23	.06
☐ 3 Jimmy Key	.50	.23	.06
☐ 4 Al Leiter	.30	.14	.04
☐ 5 Dave Stieb	.40	.18	.05
☐ 6 Todd Stottlemyre	.50	.23	.06
☐ 7 Mike Timlin	.30	.14	.04
☐ 8 Duane Ward	.40	.18	.05
☐ 9 David Wells	.40	.18	.05
☐ 10 Frank Wills	.30	.14	.04
☐ 11 Pat Borders	.50	.23	.06
☐ 12 Greg Myers	.30	.14	.04
☐ 13 Roberto Alomar	2.00	.90	.25
☐ 14 Rene Gonzales	.30	.14	.04
☐ 15 Kelly Gruber	.60	.25	.08
☐ 16 Manny Lee	.40	.18	.05
☐ 17 Rance Mulliniks	.30	.14	.04
☐ 18 John Olerud	1.00	.45	.13
☐ 19 Pat Tabler	.30	.14	.04
☐ 20 Derek Bell	1.00	.45	.13
☐ 21 Jim Acker	.30	.14	.04
☐ 22 Rob Ducey	.30	.14	.04
☐ 23 Devon White	.60	.25	.08
☐ 24 Mookie Wilson	.40	.18	.05
☐ 25 Juan Guzman	2.50	1.15	.30
☐ 26 Ed Sprague	.60	.25	.08
☐ 27 Ken Dayley	.30	.14	.04
☐ 28 Tom Candiotti	.50	.23	.06
☐ 29 Candy Maldonado	.50	.23	.06
☐ 30 Eddie Zosky	.50	.23	.06
☐ 31 Steve Karsay	.60	.25	.08
☐ 32 Bob MacDonald	.40	.18	.05
☐ 33 Ray Giannelli	.40	.18	.05
☐ 34 Jerry Schunk	.40	.18	.05
☐ 35 Dave Weathers	.50	.23	.06
☐ 36 Cito Gaston MG	.40	.18	.05
☐ 37 Joe Carter AS	.75	.35	.09
☐ 38 Jimmy Key AS	.40	.18	.05
☐ 39 Roberto Alomar AS	.75	.35	.09
☐ 40 1991 All-Star Game	.30	.14	.04

1992 Blue Jays Oh Henry

This 36-card set measures the standard size (2 1/2" by 3 1/2") and was jointly sponsored by the Ontario Association of Fire Chiefs, The Ministry of the Solicitor General, Mac's, Mike's Mart, and Oh Henry. The cards are printed on recycled paper and are thinner than most sports cards. Full-bleed color player photos with a torn effect at the bottom enhance the card fronts. The player's name, number, and position appear in a sandy border. The backs feature biographical and statistical player information and fire safety tips. The cards are skip-numbered by jersey number and checklisted below accordingly.

	MT	EX-MT	VG
COMPLETE SET (36)	15.00	6.75	1.90
COMMON PLAYER	.35	.16	.04
☐ 1 Eddie Zosky	.60	.25	.08
☐ 2 Manuel Lee	.35	.16	.04
☐ 3 Bob Bailor CO	.35	.16	.04
☐ 4 Alfredo Griffin	.35	.16	.04
☐ 5 Rance Mulliniks	.35	.16	.04
☐ 7 Rich Hacker CO	.35	.16	.04
☐ 8 John Sullivan CO	.35	.16	.04
☐ 9 John Olerud	1.00	.45	.13
☐ 10 Pat Borders	.45	.20	.06
☐ 12 Roberto Alomar	2.00	.90	.25
☐ 14 Derek Bell	.60	.25	.08
☐ 15 Pat Tabler	.35	.16	.04
☐ 17 Kelly Gruber	.60	.25	.08
☐ 18 Gene Tenace CO	.35	.16	.04
☐ 20 Rob Ducey	.35	.16	.04
☐ 21 Greg Myers	.35	.16	.04
☐ 22 Jimmy Key	.45	.20	.06
☐ 23 Candy Maldonado	.45	.20	.06
☐ 24 Turner Ward	.35	.16	.04
☐ 25 Devon White	.60	.25	.08
☐ 29 Joe Carter	1.50	.65	.19
☐ 30 Todd Stottlemyre	.60	.25	.08
☐ 31 Duane Ward	.60	.25	.08
☐ 32 Dave Winfield	1.00	.45	.13
☐ 36 David Wells	.45	.20	.06
☐ 37 Dave Stieb	.45	.20	.06
☐ 39 Larry Hisle CO	.35	.16	.04
☐ 40 Mike Timlin	.35	.16	.04
☐ 42 Galen Cisco CO	.35	.16	.04
☐ 43 Cito Gaston MG	.45	.20	.06
☐ 45 Bob MacDonald	.35	.16	.04
☐ 46 Ken Dayley	.35	.16	.04
☐ 47 Jack Morris	.75	.35	.09
☐ 50 Tom Henke	.75	.35	.09
☐ 66 Juan Guzman	1.50	.65	.19
☐ NNO Checklist Card	.45	.20	.06

1987 Boardwalk and Baseball

This 33-card set was produced by Topps for distribution by the "Boardwalk and Baseball" Theme Park located near Orlando, Florida. The cards are standard size, 2 1/2" by 3 1/2", and come in a custom blue collector box. The full-color fronts are surrounded by a pink and black frame border. The card backs are printed in pink and black on white card stock. The set is subtitled "Top Run Makers." Hence no pitchers are included in the set. The checklist for the set is given on the back panel of the box.

	MT	EX-MT	VG
COMPLETE SET (33)	4.00	1.80	.50
COMMON PLAYER (1-33)	.10	.05	.01
☐ 1 Mike Schmidt	.60	.25	.08
☐ 2 Eddie Murray	.40	.18	.05
☐ 3 Dale Murphy	.30	.14	.04
☐ 4 Dave Winfield	.50	.23	.06
☐ 5 Jim Rice	.15	.07	.02
☐ 6 Cecil Cooper	.10	.05	.01
☐ 7 Dwight Evans	.10	.05	.01
☐ 8 Rickey Henderson	.60	.25	.08

☐ 9 Robin Yount	.50	.23	.06
☐ 10 Andre Dawson	.50	.23	.06
☐ 11 Gary Carter	.20	.09	.03
☐ 12 Keith Hernandez	.10	.05	.01
☐ 13 George Brett	.50	.23	.06
☐ 14 Bill Buckner	.10	.05	.01
☐ 15 Tony Armas	.10	.05	.01
☐ 16 Harold Baines	.15	.07	.02
☐ 17 Don Baylor	.15	.07	.02
☐ 18 Steve Garvey	.20	.09	.03
☐ 19 Lance Parrish	.10	.05	.01
☐ 20 Dave Parker	.15	.07	.02
☐ 21 Buddy Bell	.10	.05	.01
☐ 22 Cal Ripken	1.00	.45	.13
☐ 23 Bob Horner	.10	.05	.01
☐ 24 Tim Raines	.15	.07	.02
☐ 25 Jack Clark	.10	.05	.01
☐ 26 Leon Durham	.10	.05	.01
☐ 27 Pedro Guerrero	.15	.07	.02
☐ 28 Kent Hrbek	.15	.07	.02
☐ 29 Kirk Gibson	.15	.07	.02
☐ 30 Ryne Sandberg	.90	.40	.11
☐ 31 Wade Boggs	.60	.25	.08
☐ 32 Don Mattingly	.75	.35	.09
☐ 33 Darryl Strawberry	.60	.25	.08

1947 Bond Bread

The 1947 Bond Bread Jackie Robinson set features 13 unnumbered cards of Jackie in different action or portrait poses; each card measures approximately 2 1/4" by 3 1/2". Card number 7, which is the only card in the set to contain a facsimile autograph, was apparently issued in greater quantity than other cards in the set and has been noted as a double print (DP) in the checklist below. Several of the cards have a horizontal format; these are marked in the checklist below by HOR. The catalog designation for this set is D302.

	NRMT	VG-E	GOOD
COMPLETE SET (13)	7000.00	3200.00	900.00
COMMON PLAYER (1-13)	600.00	275.00	75.00
☐ 1 Sliding into base, cap, ump in photo, HOR	600.00	275.00	75.00
☐ 2 Running down 3rd base line	600.00	275.00	75.00
☐ 3 Batting, bat behind head, facing camera	600.00	275.00	75.00
☐ 4 Moving towards second, throw almost to glove, HOR	600.00	275.00	75.00
☐ 5 Taking throw at first, HOR	600.00	275.00	75.00
☐ 6 Jumping high in the air for ball	600.00	275.00	75.00
☐ 7 Profile with glove in front of head; facsimile autograph) DP	300.00	135.00	38.00
☐ 8 Leaping over second base, ready to throw	600.00	275.00	75.00
☐ 9 Portrait, holding glove over head	600.00	275.00	75.00
☐ 10 Portrait, holding bat perpendicular to body	600.00	275.00	75.00
☐ 11 Reaching for throw, glove near ankle	600.00	275.00	75.00
☐ 12 Leaping for throw, no scoreboard in background	600.00	275.00	75.00
☐ 13 Portrait, holding bat parallel to body	600.00	275.00	75.00

1948 Bowman

The 48-card Bowman set of 1948 was the first major set of the post-war period. Each 2 1/16" by 2 1/2" card had a black and white photo of a current player, with his biographical information printed in black ink on a gray back. Due to the printing process and the 36-card sheet size upon which Bowman was then printing, the 12 cards marked with an SP in the checklist are scarcer numerically, as they were removed from the printing sheet in order to make room for the 12 high numbers (37-48). Many cards are found with over-printed, transposed, or blank backs. The set features the Rookie Cards of Hall of Famers Yogi Berra, Ralph Kiner, Stan Musial, Red Schoendienst, and Warren Spahn. Half of the cards in the set feature New York players (Yankees or Giants).

	NRMT	VG-E	GOOD
COMPLETE SET (48)	3600.00	1600.00	450.00
COMMON PLAYER (1-36)	20.00	9.00	2.50
COMMON PLAYER (37-48)	30.00	13.50	3.80
☐ 1 Bob Elliott	100.00	20.00	6.00
☐ 2 Ewell Blackwell	50.00	23.00	6.25
☐ 3 Ralph Kiner	200.00	90.00	25.00
☐ 4 Johnny Mize	110.00	50.00	14.00
☐ 5 Bob Feller	250.00	115.00	31.00
☐ 6 Yogi Berra	575.00	250.00	70.00
☐ 7 Pete Reiser SP	60.00	27.00	7.50
☐ 8 Phil Rizzuto SP	250.00	115.00	31.00
☐ 9 Walker Cooper	20.00	9.00	2.50
☐ 10 Buddy Rosar	20.00	9.00	2.50
☐ 11 Johnny Lindell	23.00	10.50	2.90
☐ 12 Johnny Sain	50.00	23.00	6.25
☐ 13 Willard Marshall SP	38.00	17.00	4.70
☐ 14 Allie Reynolds	50.00	23.00	6.25
☐ 15 Eddie Joost	20.00	9.00	2.50
☐ 16 Jack Lohrke SP	38.00	17.00	4.70
☐ 17 Enos Slaughter	100.00	45.00	12.50
☐ 18 Warren Spahn	325.00	145.00	40.00
☐ 19 Tommy Henrich	30.00	13.50	3.80
☐ 20 Buddy Kerr SP	38.00	17.00	4.70
☐ 21 Ferris Fain	25.00	11.50	3.10
☐ 22 Floyd Bevens SP	40.00	18.00	5.00
☐ 23 Larry Jansen	25.00	11.50	3.10
☐ 24 Dutch Leonard SP	38.00	17.00	4.70
☐ 25 Barney McCosky	20.00	9.00	2.50
☐ 26 Frank Shea SP	38.00	17.00	4.70
☐ 27 Sid Gordon	20.00	9.00	2.50
☐ 28 Emil Verban SP	38.00	17.00	4.70
☐ 29 Joe Page SP	50.00	23.00	6.25
☐ 30 Whitey Lockman SP	45.00	20.00	5.75
☐ 31 Bill McCahan	20.00	9.00	2.50
☐ 32 Bill Rigney	20.00	9.00	2.50

Card	NRMT	VG-E	GOOD
☐ 33 Bill Johnson	23.00	10.50	2.90
☐ 34 Sheldon Jones SP	38.00	17.00	4.70
☐ 35 Snuffy Stirnweiss	25.00	11.50	3.10
☐ 36 Stan Musial	900.00	400.00	115.00
☐ 37 Clint Hartung	35.00	16.00	4.40
☐ 38 Red Schoendienst	175.00	80.00	22.00
☐ 39 Augie Galan	30.00	13.50	3.80
☐ 40 Marty Marion	80.00	36.00	10.00
☐ 41 Rex Barney	35.00	16.00	4.40
☐ 42 Ray Poat	30.00	13.50	3.80
☐ 43 Bruce Edwards	30.00	13.50	3.80
☐ 44 Johnny Wyrostek	30.00	13.50	3.80
☐ 45 Hank Sauer	40.00	18.00	5.00
☐ 46 Herman Wehmeier	30.00	13.50	3.80
☐ 47 Bobby Thomson	80.00	36.00	10.00
☐ 48 Dave Koslo	60.00	27.00	7.50

1949 Bowman

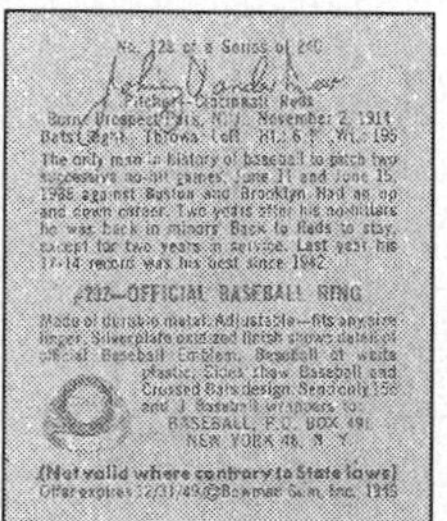

The cards in this 240-card set measure approximately 2 1/16" by 2 1/2". In 1949 Bowman took an intermediate step between black and white and full color with this set of tinted photos on colored backgrounds. Collectors should note the series price variations, which reflect some inconsistencies in the printing process. There are four major varieties in name printing, which are noted in the checklist below: NOF: name on front; NNOF: no name on front; PR: printed name on back; and SCR: script name on back. These variations resulted when Bowman used twelve of the lower numbers to fill out the last press sheet of 36 cards, adding to numbers 217-240. Cards 1-3 and 5-73 can be found with either gray or white backs. The set features the Rookie Cards of Hall of Famers Roy Campanella, Bob Lemon, Robin Roberts, Duke Snider, and Early Wynn as well as Rookie Cards of Richie Ashburn and Gil Hodges.

	NRMT	VG-E	GOOD
COMPLETE SET (240)	16500.00	7400.00	2100.00
COMMON (1-3/5-36/73)	18.00	8.00	2.30
COMMON PLAYER (37-72)	20.00	9.00	2.50
COMMON PLAYER (4/74-108)	17.00	7.75	2.10
COMMON PLAYER (109-144)	15.00	6.75	1.90
COMMON PLAYER (145-180)	90.00	40.00	11.50
COMMON PLAYER (181-240)	80.00	36.00	10.00

Card	NRMT	VG-E	GOOD
☐ 1 Vern Bickford	90.00	18.00	5.50
☐ 2 Whitey Lockman	20.00	9.00	2.50
☐ 3 Bob Porterfield	20.00	9.00	2.50
☐ 4A Jerry Priddy NNOF	42.00	19.00	5.25
☐ 4B Jerry Priddy NOF	44.00	20.00	5.50
☐ 5 Hank Sauer	22.50	10.00	2.80
☐ 6 Phil Cavarretta	22.50	10.00	2.80
☐ 7 Joe Dobson	18.00	8.00	2.30
☐ 8 Murry Dickson	18.00	8.00	2.30
☐ 9 Ferris Fain	20.00	9.00	2.50
☐ 10 Ted Gray	18.00	8.00	2.30
☐ 11 Lou Boudreau	65.00	29.00	8.25
☐ 12 Cass Michaels	18.00	8.00	2.30
☐ 13 Bob Chesnes	18.00	8.00	2.30
☐ 14 Curt Simmons	35.00	16.00	4.40
☐ 15 Ned Garver	18.00	8.00	2.30
☐ 16 Al Kozar	18.00	8.00	2.30
☐ 17 Earl Torgeson	18.00	8.00	2.30
☐ 18 Bobby Thomson	30.00	13.50	3.80
☐ 19 Bobby Brown	55.00	25.00	7.00
☐ 20 Gene Hermanski	18.00	8.00	2.30
☐ 21 Frank Baumholtz	20.00	9.00	2.50
☐ 22 Peanuts Lowrey	18.00	8.00	2.30
☐ 23 Bobby Doerr	65.00	29.00	8.25
☐ 24 Stan Musial	600.00	275.00	75.00
☐ 25 Carl Scheib	18.00	8.00	2.30
☐ 26 George Kell	50.00	23.00	6.25
☐ 27 Bob Feller	175.00	80.00	22.00
☐ 28 Don Kolloway	18.00	8.00	2.30
☐ 29 Ralph Kiner	100.00	45.00	12.50
☐ 30 Andy Seminick	20.00	9.00	2.50
☐ 31 Dick Kokos	18.00	8.00	2.30
☐ 32 Eddie Yost	25.00	11.50	3.10
☐ 33 Warren Spahn	175.00	80.00	22.00
☐ 34 Dave Koslo	18.00	8.00	2.30
☐ 35 Vic Raschi	50.00	23.00	6.25
☐ 36 Pee Wee Reese	210.00	95.00	26.00
☐ 37 Johnny Wyrostek	20.00	9.00	2.50
☐ 38 Emil Verban	20.00	9.00	2.50
☐ 39 Billy Goodman	22.50	10.00	2.80
☐ 40 Red Munger	20.00	9.00	2.50
☐ 41 Lou Brissie	20.00	9.00	2.50
☐ 42 Hoot Evers	20.00	9.00	2.50
☐ 43 Dale Mitchell	22.50	10.00	2.80
☐ 44 Dave Philley	20.00	9.00	2.50
☐ 45 Wally Westlake	20.00	9.00	2.50
☐ 46 Robin Roberts	280.00	125.00	35.00
☐ 47 Johnny Sain	35.00	16.00	4.40
☐ 48 Willard Marshall	20.00	9.00	2.50
☐ 49 Frank Shea	22.00	10.00	2.80
☐ 50 Jackie Robinson	850.00	375.00	105.00
☐ 51 Herman Wehmeier	20.00	9.00	2.50
☐ 52 Johnny Schmitz	20.00	9.00	2.50
☐ 53 Jack Kramer	20.00	9.00	2.50
☐ 54 Marty Marion	30.00	13.50	3.80
☐ 55 Eddie Joost	20.00	9.00	2.50
☐ 56 Pat Mullin	20.00	9.00	2.50
☐ 57 Gene Bearden	22.00	10.00	2.80
☐ 58 Bob Elliott	22.00	10.00	2.80
☐ 59 Jack Lohrke	20.00	9.00	2.50
☐ 60 Yogi Berra	325.00	145.00	40.00
☐ 61 Rex Barney	22.00	10.00	2.80
☐ 62 Grady Hatton	20.00	9.00	2.50
☐ 63 Andy Pafko	22.50	10.00	2.80
☐ 64 Dom DiMaggio	30.00	13.50	3.80
☐ 65 Enos Slaughter	95.00	42.50	12.00
☐ 66 Elmer Valo	22.50	10.00	2.80
☐ 67 Alvin Dark	35.00	16.00	4.40
☐ 68 Sheldon Jones	20.00	9.00	2.50
☐ 69 Tommy Henrich	30.00	13.50	3.80
☐ 70 Carl Furillo	75.00	34.00	9.50
☐ 71 Vern Stephens	22.50	10.00	2.80
☐ 72 Tommy Holmes	22.50	10.00	2.80
☐ 73 Billy Cox	30.00	13.50	3.80
☐ 74 Tom McBride	17.00	7.75	2.10
☐ 75 Eddie Mayo	17.00	7.75	2.10
☐ 76 Bill Nicholson	22.50	10.00	2.80
☐ 77 Ernie Bonham	17.00	7.75	2.10
☐ 78A Sam Zoldak NNOF	42.00	19.00	5.25
☐ 78B Sam Zoldak NOF	17.00	7.75	2.10
☐ 79 Ron Northey	17.00	7.75	2.10
☐ 80 Bill McCahan	17.00	7.75	2.10
☐ 81 Virgil Stallcup	17.00	7.75	2.10
☐ 82 Joe Page	25.00	11.50	3.10
☐ 83A Bob Scheffing NNOF	42.00	19.00	5.25
☐ 83B Bob Scheffing NOF	17.00	7.75	2.10
☐ 84 Roy Campanella	800.00	350.00	100.00
☐ 85A Johnny Mize NNOF	90.00	40.00	11.50
☐ 85B Johnny Mize NOF	150.00	70.00	19.00
☐ 86 Johnny Pesky	25.00	11.50	3.10
☐ 87 Randy Gumpert	17.00	7.75	2.10
☐ 88A Bill Salkeld NNOF	42.00	19.00	5.25
☐ 88B Bill Salkeld NOF	17.00	7.75	2.10
☐ 89 Mizell Platt	17.00	7.75	2.10
☐ 90 Gil Coan	17.00	7.75	2.10
☐ 91 Dick Wakefield	17.00	7.75	2.10
☐ 92 Willie Jones	19.00	8.50	2.40
☐ 93 Ed Stevens	17.00	7.75	2.10
☐ 94 Mickey Vernon	35.00	16.00	4.40
☐ 95 Howie Pollet	20.00	9.00	2.50
☐ 96 Taft Wright	17.00	7.75	2.10
☐ 97 Danny Litwhiler	17.00	7.75	2.10
☐ 98A Phil Rizzuto NNOF	110.00	50.00	14.00
☐ 98B Phil Rizzuto NOF	210.00	95.00	26.00
☐ 99 Frank Gustine	17.00	7.75	2.10
☐ 100 Gil Hodges	250.00	115.00	31.00
☐ 101 Sid Gordon	17.00	7.75	2.10
☐ 102 Stan Spence	17.00	7.75	2.10
☐ 103 Joe Tipton	17.00	7.75	2.10
☐ 104 Eddie Stanky	30.00	13.50	3.80
☐ 105 Bill Kennedy	17.00	7.75	2.10
☐ 106 Jake Early	17.00	7.75	2.10

☐ 107 Eddie Lake	17.00	7.75	2.10
☐ 108 Ken Heintzelman	17.00	7.75	2.10
☐ 109A Ed Fitzgerald SCR	40.00	18.00	5.00
☐ 109B Ed Fitzgerald PR	15.00	6.75	1.90
☐ 110 Early Wynn	130.00	57.50	16.50
☐ 111 Red Schoendienst	80.00	36.00	10.00
☐ 112 Sam Chapman	15.00	6.75	1.90
☐ 113 Ray LaManno	15.00	6.75	1.90
☐ 114 Allie Reynolds	35.00	16.00	4.40
☐ 115 Dutch Leonard	15.00	6.75	1.90
☐ 116 Joe Hatton	15.00	6.75	1.90
☐ 117 Walker Cooper	15.00	6.75	1.90
☐ 118 Sam Mele	15.00	6.75	1.90
☐ 119 Floyd Baker	15.00	6.75	1.90
☐ 120 Cliff Fannin	15.00	6.75	1.90
☐ 121 Mark Christman	15.00	6.75	1.90
☐ 122 George Vico	15.00	6.75	1.90
☐ 123 Johnny Blatnick	15.00	6.75	1.90
☐ 124A Danny Murtaugh SCR	45.00	20.00	5.75
☐ 124B Danny Murtaugh PR	22.00	10.00	2.80
☐ 125 Ken Keltner	17.00	7.75	2.10
☐ 126A Al Brazle SCR	40.00	18.00	5.00
☐ 126B Al Brazle PR	15.00	6.75	1.90
☐ 127A Hank Majeski SCR	40.00	18.00	5.00
☐ 127B Hank Majeski PR	15.00	6.75	1.90
☐ 128 Johnny VanderMeer	25.00	11.50	3.10
☐ 129 Bill Johnson	17.00	7.75	2.10
☐ 130 Harry Walker	15.00	6.75	1.90
☐ 131 Paul Lehner	15.00	6.75	1.90
☐ 132A Al Evans SCR	40.00	18.00	5.00
☐ 132B Al Evans PR	15.00	6.75	1.90
☐ 133 Aaron Robinson	15.00	6.75	1.90
☐ 134 Hank Borowy	15.00	6.75	1.90
☐ 135 Stan Rojek	15.00	6.75	1.90
☐ 136 Hank Edwards	15.00	6.75	1.90
☐ 137 Ted Wilks	15.00	6.75	1.90
☐ 138 Buddy Rosar	15.00	6.75	1.90
☐ 139 Hank Arft	15.00	6.75	1.90
☐ 140 Ray Scarborough	15.00	6.75	1.90
☐ 141 Tony Lupien	15.00	6.75	1.90
☐ 142 Eddie Waitkus	20.00	9.00	2.50
☐ 143A Bob Dillinger SCR	42.00	19.00	5.25
☐ 143B Bob Dillinger PR	20.00	9.00	2.50
☐ 144 Mickey Haefner	15.00	6.75	1.90
☐ 145 Sylvester Donnelly	90.00	40.00	11.50
☐ 146 Mike McCormick	100.00	45.00	12.50
☐ 147 Bert Singleton	90.00	40.00	11.50
☐ 148 Bob Swift	90.00	40.00	11.50
☐ 149 Roy Partee	90.00	40.00	11.50
☐ 150 Allie Clark	90.00	40.00	11.50
☐ 151 Mickey Harris	90.00	40.00	11.50
☐ 152 Clarence Maddern	90.00	40.00	11.50
☐ 153 Phil Masi	90.00	40.00	11.50
☐ 154 Clint Hartung	100.00	45.00	12.50
☐ 155 Mickey Guerra	90.00	40.00	11.50
☐ 156 Al Zarilla	90.00	40.00	11.50
☐ 157 Walt Masterson	90.00	40.00	11.50
☐ 158 Harry Brecheen	105.00	47.50	13.00
☐ 159 Glen Moulder	90.00	40.00	11.50
☐ 160 Jim Blackburn	90.00	40.00	11.50
☐ 161 Jocko Thompson	90.00	40.00	11.50
☐ 162 Preacher Roe	145.00	65.00	18.00
☐ 163 Clyde McCullough	90.00	40.00	11.50
☐ 164 Vic Wertz	110.00	50.00	14.00
☐ 165 Snuffy Stirnweiss	100.00	45.00	12.50
☐ 166 Mike Tresh	90.00	40.00	11.50
☐ 167 Babe Martin	90.00	40.00	11.50
☐ 168 Doyle Lade	90.00	40.00	11.50
☐ 169 Jeff Heath	90.00	40.00	11.50
☐ 170 Bill Rigney	90.00	40.00	11.50
☐ 171 Dick Fowler	90.00	40.00	11.50
☐ 172 Eddie Pellagrini	90.00	40.00	11.50
☐ 173 Eddie Stewart	90.00	40.00	11.50
☐ 174 Terry Moore	125.00	57.50	15.50
☐ 175 Luke Appling	150.00	70.00	19.00
☐ 176 Ken Raffensberger	90.00	40.00	11.50
☐ 177 Stan Lopata	90.00	40.00	11.50
☐ 178 Tom Brown	90.00	40.00	11.50
☐ 179 Hugh Casey	100.00	45.00	12.50
☐ 180 Connie Berry	90.00	40.00	11.50
☐ 181 Gus Niarhos	80.00	36.00	10.00
☐ 182 Hal Peck	80.00	36.00	10.00
☐ 183 Lou Stringer	80.00	36.00	10.00
☐ 184 Bob Chipman	80.00	36.00	10.00
☐ 185 Pete Reiser	105.00	47.50	13.00
☐ 186 Buddy Kerr	80.00	36.00	10.00
☐ 187 Phil Marchildon	80.00	36.00	10.00
☐ 188 Karl Drews	80.00	36.00	10.00
☐ 189 Earl Wooten	80.00	36.00	10.00
☐ 190 Jim Hearn	80.00	36.00	10.00
☐ 191 Joe Haynes	80.00	36.00	10.00
☐ 192 Harry Gumbert	80.00	36.00	10.00
☐ 193 Ken Trinkle	80.00	36.00	10.00
☐ 194 Ralph Branca	110.00	50.00	14.00
☐ 195 Eddie Bockman	80.00	36.00	10.00
☐ 196 Fred Hutchinson	100.00	45.00	12.50
☐ 197 Johnny Lindell	90.00	40.00	11.50
☐ 198 Steve Gromek	80.00	36.00	10.00
☐ 199 Tex Hughson	80.00	36.00	10.00
☐ 200 Jess Dobernic	80.00	36.00	10.00
☐ 201 Sibby Sisti	80.00	36.00	10.00
☐ 202 Larry Jansen	95.00	42.50	12.00
☐ 203 Barney McCosky	80.00	36.00	10.00
☐ 204 Bob Savage	80.00	36.00	10.00
☐ 205 Dick Sisler	90.00	40.00	11.50
☐ 206 Bruce Edwards	80.00	36.00	10.00
☐ 207 Johnny Hopp	95.00	42.50	12.00
☐ 208 Dizzy Trout	95.00	42.50	12.00
☐ 209 Charlie Keller	110.00	50.00	14.00
☐ 210 Joe Gordon	110.00	50.00	14.00
☐ 211 Boo Ferriss	80.00	36.00	10.00
☐ 212 Ralph Hamner	80.00	36.00	10.00
☐ 213 Red Barrett	80.00	36.00	10.00
☐ 214 Richie Ashburn	550.00	250.00	70.00
☐ 215 Kirby Higbe	80.00	36.00	10.00
☐ 216 Schoolboy Rowe	95.00	42.50	12.00
☐ 217 Marino Pieretti	80.00	36.00	10.00
☐ 218 Dick Kryhoski	80.00	36.00	10.00
☐ 219 Virgil Fire Trucks	95.00	42.50	12.00
☐ 220 Johnny McCarthy	80.00	36.00	10.00
☐ 221 Bob Muncrief	80.00	36.00	10.00
☐ 222 Alex Kellner	80.00	36.00	10.00
☐ 223 Bobby Hofman	80.00	36.00	10.00
☐ 224 Satchell Paige	1300.00	575.00	160.00
☐ 225 Jerry Coleman	115.00	52.50	14.50
☐ 226 Duke Snider	1200.00	550.00	150.00
☐ 227 Fritz Ostermueller	80.00	36.00	10.00
☐ 228 Jackie Mayo	80.00	36.00	10.00
☐ 229 Ed Lopat	150.00	70.00	19.00
☐ 230 Augie Galan	80.00	36.00	10.00
☐ 231 Earl Johnson	80.00	36.00	10.00
☐ 232 George McQuinn	80.00	36.00	10.00
☐ 233 Larry Doby	175.00	80.00	22.00
☐ 234 Rip Sewell	80.00	36.00	10.00
☐ 235 Jim Russell	80.00	36.00	10.00
☐ 236 Fred Sanford	80.00	36.00	10.00
☐ 237 Monte Kennedy	80.00	36.00	10.00
☐ 238 Bob Lemon	275.00	125.00	34.00
☐ 239 Frank McCormick	80.00	36.00	10.00
☐ 240 Babe Young UER (Photo actually Bobby Young)	150.00	45.00	15.00

1950 Bowman

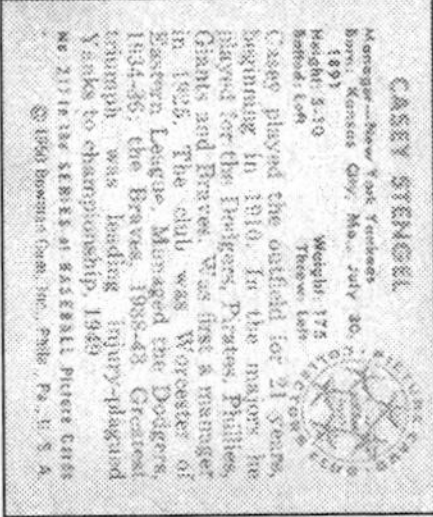

The cards in this 252-card set measure approximately 2 1/16" by 2 1/2". This set, marketed in 1950 by Bowman, represented a major improvement in terms of quality over their previous efforts. Each card was a beautifully colored line drawing developed from a simple photograph. The first 72 cards are the scarcest in the set, while the final 72 cards may be found with or without the copyright line. This was the only Bowman sports set to carry the famous "5-Star" logo. Key rookies in this set are Hank Bauer, Don Newcombe, and Al Rosen.

	NRMT	VG-E	GOOD
COMPLETE SET (252)	10000.00	4500.00	1250.00
COMMON PLAYER (1-36)	55.00	25.00	7.00
COMMON PLAYER (37-72)	55.00	25.00	7.00
COMMON PLAYER (73-108)	18.00	8.00	2.30

COMMON PLAYER (109-144)	18.00	8.00	2.30
COMMON PLAYER (145-180)	18.00	8.00	2.30
COMMON PLAYER (181-216)	18.00	8.00	2.30
COMMON PLAYER (217-252)	20.00	9.00	2.50
☐ 1 Mel Parnell	200.00	40.00	12.00
☐ 2 Vern Stephens	60.00	27.00	7.50
☐ 3 Dom DiMaggio	70.00	32.00	8.75
☐ 4 Gus Zernial	65.00	29.00	8.25
☐ 5 Bob Kuzava	55.00	25.00	7.00
☐ 6 Bob Feller	200.00	90.00	25.00
☐ 7 Jim Hegan	60.00	27.00	7.50
☐ 8 George Kell	100.00	45.00	12.50
☐ 9 Vic Wertz	60.00	27.00	7.50
☐ 10 Tommy Henrich	65.00	29.00	8.25
☐ 11 Phil Rizzuto	175.00	80.00	22.00
☐ 12 Joe Page	65.00	29.00	8.25
☐ 13 Ferris Fain	60.00	27.00	7.50
☐ 14 Alex Kellner	55.00	25.00	7.00
☐ 15 Al Kozar	55.00	25.00	7.00
☐ 16 Roy Sievers	65.00	29.00	8.25
☐ 17 Sid Hudson	55.00	25.00	7.00
☐ 18 Eddie Robinson	55.00	25.00	7.00
☐ 19 Warren Spahn	225.00	100.00	28.00
☐ 20 Bob Elliott	60.00	27.00	7.50
☐ 21 Pee Wee Reese	225.00	100.00	28.00
☐ 22 Jackie Robinson	700.00	325.00	90.00
☐ 23 Don Newcombe	150.00	70.00	19.00
☐ 24 Johnny Schmitz	55.00	25.00	7.00
☐ 25 Hank Sauer	60.00	27.00	7.50
☐ 26 Grady Hatton	55.00	25.00	7.00
☐ 27 Herman Wehmeier	55.00	25.00	7.00
☐ 28 Bobby Thomson	65.00	29.00	8.25
☐ 29 Eddie Stanky	60.00	27.00	7.50
☐ 30 Eddie Waitkus	55.00	25.00	7.00
☐ 31 Del Ennis	70.00	32.00	8.75
☐ 32 Robin Roberts	150.00	70.00	19.00
☐ 33 Ralph Kiner	125.00	57.50	15.50
☐ 34 Murry Dickson	55.00	25.00	7.00
☐ 35 Enos Slaughter	125.00	57.50	15.50
☐ 36 Eddie Kazak	60.00	27.00	7.50
☐ 37 Luke Appling	85.00	38.00	10.50
☐ 38 Bill Wight	55.00	25.00	7.00
☐ 39 Larry Doby	70.00	32.00	8.75
☐ 40 Bob Lemon	110.00	50.00	14.00
☐ 41 Hoot Evers	55.00	25.00	7.00
☐ 42 Art Houtteman	55.00	25.00	7.00
☐ 43 Bobby Doerr	100.00	45.00	12.50
☐ 44 Joe Dobson	55.00	25.00	7.00
☐ 45 Al Zarilla	55.00	25.00	7.00
☐ 46 Yogi Berra	400.00	180.00	50.00
☐ 47 Jerry Coleman	65.00	29.00	8.25
☐ 48 Lou Brissie	55.00	25.00	7.00
☐ 49 Elmer Valo	55.00	25.00	7.00
☐ 50 Dick Kokos	55.00	25.00	7.00
☐ 51 Ned Garver	55.00	25.00	7.00
☐ 52 Sam Mele	55.00	25.00	7.00
☐ 53 Clyde Vollmer	55.00	25.00	7.00
☐ 54 Gil Coan	55.00	25.00	7.00
☐ 55 Buddy Kerr	55.00	25.00	7.00
☐ 56 Del Crandall	70.00	32.00	8.75
☐ 57 Vern Bickford	55.00	25.00	7.00
☐ 58 Carl Furillo	75.00	34.00	9.50
☐ 59 Ralph Branca	65.00	29.00	8.25
☐ 60 Andy Pafko	60.00	27.00	7.50
☐ 61 Bob Rush	55.00	25.00	7.00
☐ 62 Ted Kluszewski	90.00	40.00	11.50
☐ 63 Ewell Blackwell	60.00	27.00	7.50
☐ 64 Alvin Dark	65.00	29.00	8.25
☐ 65 Dave Koslo	55.00	25.00	7.00
☐ 66 Larry Jansen	60.00	27.00	7.50
☐ 67 Willie Jones	55.00	25.00	7.00
☐ 68 Curt Simmons	60.00	27.00	7.50
☐ 69 Wally Westlake	55.00	25.00	7.00
☐ 70 Bob Chesnes	55.00	25.00	7.00
☐ 71 Red Schoendienst	110.00	50.00	14.00
☐ 72 Howie Pollet	55.00	25.00	7.00
☐ 73 Willard Marshall	18.00	8.00	2.30
☐ 74 Johnny Antonelli	35.00	16.00	4.40
☐ 75 Roy Campanella	300.00	135.00	38.00
☐ 76 Rex Barney	20.00	9.00	2.50
☐ 77 Duke Snider	300.00	135.00	38.00
☐ 78 Mickey Owen	20.00	9.00	2.50
☐ 79 Johnny VanderMeer	25.00	11.50	3.10
☐ 80 Howard Fox	18.00	8.00	2.30
☐ 81 Ron Northey	18.00	8.00	2.30
☐ 82 Whitey Lockman	20.00	9.00	2.50
☐ 83 Sheldon Jones	18.00	8.00	2.30
☐ 84 Richie Ashburn	110.00	50.00	14.00
☐ 85 Ken Heintzelman	18.00	8.00	2.30
☐ 86 Stan Rojek	18.00	8.00	2.30
☐ 87 Bill Werle	18.00	8.00	2.30
☐ 88 Marty Marion	25.00	11.50	3.10
☐ 89 Red Munger	18.00	8.00	2.30
☐ 90 Harry Brecheen	20.00	9.00	2.50
☐ 91 Cass Michaels	18.00	8.00	2.30
☐ 92 Hank Majeski	18.00	8.00	2.30
☐ 93 Gene Bearden	20.00	9.00	2.50
☐ 94 Lou Boudreau	50.00	23.00	6.25
☐ 95 Aaron Robinson	18.00	8.00	2.30
☐ 96 Virgil Trucks	20.00	9.00	2.50
☐ 97 Maurice McDermott	18.00	8.00	2.30
☐ 98 Ted Williams	800.00	350.00	100.00
☐ 99 Billy Goodman	20.00	9.00	2.50
☐ 100 Vic Raschi	35.00	16.00	4.40
☐ 101 Bobby Brown	35.00	16.00	4.40
☐ 102 Billy Johnson	20.00	9.00	2.50
☐ 103 Eddie Joost	18.00	8.00	2.30
☐ 104 Sam Chapman	18.00	8.00	2.30
☐ 105 Bob Dillinger	18.00	8.00	2.30
☐ 106 Cliff Fannin	18.00	8.00	2.30
☐ 107 Sam Dente	18.00	8.00	2.30
☐ 108 Ray Scarborough	18.00	8.00	2.30
☐ 109 Sid Gordon	18.00	8.00	2.30
☐ 110 Tommy Holmes	20.00	9.00	2.50
☐ 111 Walker Cooper	18.00	8.00	2.30
☐ 112 Gil Hodges	100.00	45.00	12.50
☐ 113 Gene Hermanski	18.00	8.00	2.30
☐ 114 Wayne Terwilliger	22.50	10.00	2.80
☐ 115 Roy Smalley	18.00	8.00	2.30
☐ 116 Virgil Stallcup	18.00	8.00	2.30
☐ 117 Bill Rigney	18.00	8.00	2.30
☐ 118 Clint Hartung	18.00	8.00	2.30
☐ 119 Dick Sisler	20.00	9.00	2.50
☐ 120 John Thompson	18.00	8.00	2.30
☐ 121 Andy Seminick	18.00	8.00	2.30
☐ 122 Johnny Hopp	20.00	9.00	2.50
☐ 123 Dino Restelli	18.00	8.00	2.30
☐ 124 Clyde McCullough	18.00	8.00	2.30
☐ 125 Del Rice	18.00	8.00	2.30
☐ 126 Al Brazle	18.00	8.00	2.30
☐ 127 Dave Philley	18.00	8.00	2.30
☐ 128 Phil Masi	18.00	8.00	2.30
☐ 129 Joe Gordon	22.50	10.00	2.80
☐ 130 Dale Mitchell	20.00	9.00	2.50
☐ 131 Steve Gromek	18.00	8.00	2.30
☐ 132 Mickey Vernon	22.50	10.00	2.80
☐ 133 Don Kolloway	18.00	8.00	2.30
☐ 134 Paul Trout	18.00	8.00	2.30
☐ 135 Pat Mullin	18.00	8.00	2.30
☐ 136 Warren Rosar	18.00	8.00	2.30
☐ 137 Johnny Pesky	22.00	10.00	2.80
☐ 138 Allie Reynolds	35.00	16.00	4.40
☐ 139 Johnny Mize	75.00	34.00	9.50
☐ 140 Pete Suder	18.00	8.00	2.30
☐ 141 Joe Coleman	18.00	8.00	2.30
☐ 142 Sherm Lollar	25.00	11.50	3.10
☐ 143 Eddie Stewart	18.00	8.00	2.30
☐ 144 Al Evans	18.00	8.00	2.30
☐ 145 Jack Graham	18.00	8.00	2.30
☐ 146 Floyd Baker	18.00	8.00	2.30
☐ 147 Mike Garcia	25.00	11.50	3.10
☐ 148 Early Wynn	65.00	29.00	8.25
☐ 149 Bob Swift	18.00	8.00	2.30
☐ 150 George Vico	18.00	8.00	2.30
☐ 151 Fred Hutchinson	22.50	10.00	2.80
☐ 152 Ellis Kinder	18.00	8.00	2.30
☐ 153 Walt Masterson	18.00	8.00	2.30
☐ 154 Gus Niarhos	18.00	8.00	2.30
☐ 155 Frank Shea	20.00	9.00	2.50
☐ 156 Fred Sanford	20.00	9.00	2.50
☐ 157 Mike Guerra	18.00	8.00	2.30
☐ 158 Paul Lehner	18.00	8.00	2.30
☐ 159 Joe Tipton	18.00	8.00	2.30
☐ 160 Mickey Harris	18.00	8.00	2.30
☐ 161 Sherry Robertson	18.00	8.00	2.30
☐ 162 Eddie Yost	20.00	9.00	2.50
☐ 163 Earl Torgeson	18.00	8.00	2.30
☐ 164 Sibby Sisti	18.00	8.00	2.30
☐ 165 Bruce Edwards	18.00	8.00	2.30
☐ 166 Joe Hatton	18.00	8.00	2.30
☐ 167 Preacher Roe	35.00	16.00	4.40
☐ 168 Bob Scheffing	18.00	8.00	2.30
☐ 169 Hank Edwards	18.00	8.00	2.30
☐ 170 Dutch Leonard	18.00	8.00	2.30
☐ 171 Harry Gumbert	18.00	8.00	2.30
☐ 172 Peanuts Lowrey	18.00	8.00	2.30
☐ 173 Lloyd Merriman	18.00	8.00	2.30
☐ 174 Hank Thompson	25.00	11.50	3.10
☐ 175 Monte Kennedy	18.00	8.00	2.30
☐ 176 Sylvester Donnelly	18.00	8.00	2.30
☐ 177 Hank Borowy	18.00	8.00	2.30
☐ 178 Ed Fitzgerald	18.00	8.00	2.30
☐ 179 Chuck Diering	18.00	8.00	2.30
☐ 180 Harry Walker	18.00	8.00	2.30
☐ 181 Marino Pieretti	18.00	8.00	2.30
☐ 182 Sam Zoldak	18.00	8.00	2.30

☐ 183 Mickey Haefner	18.00	8.00	2.30
☐ 184 Randy Gumpert	18.00	8.00	2.30
☐ 185 Howie Judson	18.00	8.00	2.30
☐ 186 Ken Keltner	20.00	9.00	2.50
☐ 187 Lou Stringer	18.00	8.00	2.30
☐ 188 Earl Johnson	18.00	8.00	2.30
☐ 189 Owen Friend	18.00	8.00	2.30
☐ 190 Ken Wood	18.00	8.00	2.30
☐ 191 Dick Starr	18.00	8.00	2.30
☐ 192 Bob Chipman	18.00	8.00	2.30
☐ 193 Pete Reiser	22.50	10.00	2.80
☐ 194 Billy Cox	22.50	10.00	2.80
☐ 195 Phil Cavarretta	25.00	11.50	3.10
☐ 196 Doyle Lade	18.00	8.00	2.30
☐ 197 Johnny Wyrostek	18.00	8.00	2.30
☐ 198 Danny Litwhiler	18.00	8.00	2.30
☐ 199 Jack Kramer	18.00	8.00	2.30
☐ 200 Kirby Higbe	18.00	8.00	2.30
☐ 201 Pete Castiglione	18.00	8.00	2.30
☐ 202 Cliff Chambers	18.00	8.00	2.30
☐ 203 Danny Murtaugh	20.00	9.00	2.50
☐ 204 Granny Hamner	25.00	11.50	3.10
☐ 205 Mike Goliat	18.00	8.00	2.30
☐ 206 Stan Lopata	18.00	8.00	2.30
☐ 207 Max Lanier	18.00	8.00	2.30
☐ 208 Jim Hearn	18.00	8.00	2.30
☐ 209 Johnny Lindell	18.00	8.00	2.30
☐ 210 Ted Gray	18.00	8.00	2.30
☐ 211 Charlie Keller	20.00	9.00	2.50
☐ 212 Jerry Priddy	18.00	8.00	2.30
☐ 213 Carl Scheib	18.00	8.00	2.30
☐ 214 Dick Fowler	18.00	8.00	2.30
☐ 215 Ed Lopat	35.00	16.00	4.40
☐ 216 Bob Porterfield	20.00	9.00	2.50
☐ 217 Casey Stengel MG	150.00	70.00	19.00
☐ 218 Cliff Mapes	22.00	10.00	2.80
☐ 219 Hank Bauer	85.00	38.00	10.50
☐ 220 Leo Durocher MG	70.00	32.00	8.75
☐ 221 Don Mueller	35.00	16.00	4.40
☐ 222 Bobby Morgan	20.00	9.00	2.50
☐ 223 Jim Russell	20.00	9.00	2.50
☐ 224 Jack Banta	20.00	9.00	2.50
☐ 225 Eddie Sawyer MG	22.00	10.00	2.80
☐ 226 Jim Konstanty	40.00	18.00	5.00
☐ 227 Bob Miller	20.00	9.00	2.50
☐ 228 Bill Nicholson	22.00	10.00	2.80
☐ 229 Frank Frisch MG	45.00	20.00	5.75
☐ 230 Bill Serena	20.00	9.00	2.50
☐ 231 Preston Ward	20.00	9.00	2.50
☐ 232 Al Rosen	70.00	32.00	8.75
☐ 233 Allie Clark	20.00	9.00	2.50
☐ 234 Bobby Shantz	35.00	16.00	4.40
☐ 235 Harold Gilbert	20.00	9.00	2.50
☐ 236 Bob Cain	20.00	9.00	2.50
☐ 237 Bill Salkeld	20.00	9.00	2.50
☐ 238 Nippy Jones	20.00	9.00	2.50
☐ 239 Bill Howerton	20.00	9.00	2.50
☐ 240 Eddie Lake	20.00	9.00	2.50
☐ 241 Neil Berry	20.00	9.00	2.50
☐ 242 Dick Kryhoski	20.00	9.00	2.50
☐ 243 Johnny Groth	20.00	9.00	2.50
☐ 244 Dale Coogan	20.00	9.00	2.50
☐ 245 Al Papai	20.00	9.00	2.50
☐ 246 Walt Dropo	30.00	13.50	3.80
☐ 247 Irv Noren	22.50	10.00	2.80
☐ 248 Sam Jethroe	22.50	10.00	2.80
☐ 249 Snuffy Stirnweiss	22.00	10.00	2.80
☐ 250 Ray Coleman	20.00	9.00	2.50
☐ 251 John Moss	20.00	9.00	2.50
☐ 252 Billy DeMars	75.00	23.00	7.50

1951 Bowman

The cards in this 324-card set measure approximately 2 1/16" by 3 1/8". Many of the obverses of the cards appearing in the 1951 Bowman set are enlargements of those appearing in the previous year. The high number series (253-324) is highly valued and contains the true "Rookie" cards of Mickey Mantle and Willie Mays. Card number 195 depicts Paul Richards in caricature. George Kell's card (number 46) incorrectly lists him as being in the "1941" Bowman series. Player names are found printed in a panel on the front of the card. These cards were supposedly also sold in sheets in variety stores in the Philadelphia area.

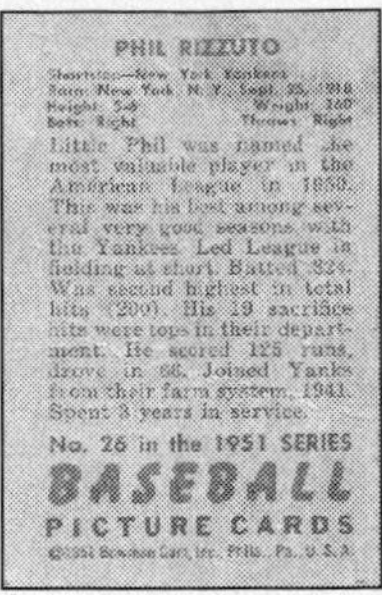

	NRMT	VG-E	GOOD
COMPLETE SET (324)	21000.00	9500.00	2600.00
COMMON PLAYER (1-36)	20.00	9.00	2.50
COMMON PLAYER (37-72)	18.00	8.00	2.30
COMMON PLAYER (73-108)	15.00	6.75	1.90
COMMON PLAYER (109-144)	15.00	6.75	1.90
COMMON PLAYER (145-180)	15.00	6.75	1.90
COMMON PLAYER (181-216)	15.00	6.75	1.90
COMMON PLAYER (217-252)	15.00	6.75	1.90
COMMON PLAYER (253-324)	60.00	27.00	7.50
☐ 1 Whitey Ford	1325.00	325.00	105.00
☐ 2 Yogi Berra	475.00	210.00	60.00
☐ 3 Robin Roberts	80.00	36.00	10.00
☐ 4 Del Ennis	25.00	11.50	3.10
☐ 5 Dale Mitchell	23.00	10.50	2.90
☐ 6 Don Newcombe	45.00	20.00	5.75
☐ 7 Gil Hodges	90.00	40.00	11.50
☐ 8 Paul Lehner	20.00	9.00	2.50
☐ 9 Sam Chapman	20.00	9.00	2.50
☐ 10 Red Schoendienst	80.00	36.00	10.00
☐ 11 Red Munger	20.00	9.00	2.50
☐ 12 Hank Majeski	20.00	9.00	2.50
☐ 13 Eddie Stanky	25.00	11.50	3.10
☐ 14 Alvin Dark	30.00	13.50	3.80
☐ 15 Johnny Pesky	25.00	11.50	3.10
☐ 16 Maurice McDermott	20.00	9.00	2.50
☐ 17 Pete Castiglione	20.00	9.00	2.50
☐ 18 Gil Coan	20.00	9.00	2.50
☐ 19 Sid Gordon	20.00	9.00	2.50
☐ 20 Del Crandall UER (Misspelled Crandell on card)	23.00	10.50	2.90
☐ 21 Snuffy Stirnweiss	22.00	10.00	2.80
☐ 22 Hank Sauer	25.00	11.50	3.10
☐ 23 Hoot Evers	20.00	9.00	2.50
☐ 24 Ewell Blackwell	25.00	11.50	3.10
☐ 25 Vic Raschi	35.00	16.00	4.40
☐ 26 Phil Rizzuto	110.00	50.00	14.00
☐ 27 Jim Konstanty	25.00	11.50	3.10
☐ 28 Eddie Waitkus	20.00	9.00	2.50
☐ 29 Allie Clark	20.00	9.00	2.50
☐ 30 Bob Feller	140.00	65.00	17.50
☐ 31 Roy Campanella	275.00	125.00	34.00
☐ 32 Duke Snider	275.00	125.00	34.00
☐ 33 Bob Hooper	20.00	9.00	2.50
☐ 34 Marty Marion	27.00	12.00	3.40
☐ 35 Al Zarilla	20.00	9.00	2.50
☐ 36 Joe Dobson	20.00	9.00	2.50
☐ 37 Whitey Lockman	20.00	9.00	2.50
☐ 38 Al Evans	18.00	8.00	2.30
☐ 39 Ray Scarborough	18.00	8.00	2.30
☐ 40 Gus Bell	30.00	13.50	3.80
☐ 41 Eddie Yost	20.00	9.00	2.50
☐ 42 Vern Bickford	18.00	8.00	2.30
☐ 43 Billy DeMars	18.00	8.00	2.30
☐ 44 Roy Smalley	18.00	8.00	2.30
☐ 45 Art Houtteman	18.00	8.00	2.30
☐ 46 George Kell 1941 UER	55.00	25.00	7.00
☐ 47 Grady Hatton	18.00	8.00	2.30
☐ 48 Ken Raffensberger	18.00	8.00	2.30
☐ 49 Jerry Coleman	23.00	10.50	2.90
☐ 50 Johnny Mize	60.00	27.00	7.50
☐ 51 Andy Seminick	18.00	8.00	2.30
☐ 52 Dick Sisler	20.00	9.00	2.50
☐ 53 Bob Lemon	50.00	23.00	6.25
☐ 54 Ray Boone	25.00	11.50	3.10
☐ 55 Gene Hermanski	18.00	8.00	2.30
☐ 56 Ralph Branca	30.00	13.50	3.80
☐ 57 Alex Kellner	18.00	8.00	2.30
☐ 58 Enos Slaughter	60.00	27.00	7.50
☐ 59 Randy Gumpert	18.00	8.00	2.30
☐ 60 Chico Carrasquel	25.00	11.50	3.10

☐ 61 Jim Hearn 18.00 8.00 2.30
☐ 62 Lou Boudreau 50.00 23.00 6.25
☐ 63 Bob Dillinger 18.00 8.00 2.30
☐ 64 Bill Werle 18.00 8.00 2.30
☐ 65 Mickey Vernon 20.00 9.00 2.50
☐ 66 Bob Elliott 20.00 9.00 2.50
☐ 67 Roy Sievers 20.00 9.00 2.50
☐ 68 Dick Kokos 18.00 8.00 2.30
☐ 69 Johnny Schmitz 18.00 8.00 2.30
☐ 70 Ron Northey 18.00 8.00 2.30
☐ 71 Jerry Priddy 18.00 8.00 2.30
☐ 72 Lloyd Merriman 18.00 8.00 2.30
☐ 73 Tommy Byrne 15.00 6.75 1.90
☐ 74 Billy Johnson 17.00 7.75 2.10
☐ 75 Russ Meyer 18.00 8.00 2.30
☐ 76 Stan Lopata 15.00 6.75 1.90
☐ 77 Mike Goliat 15.00 6.75 1.90
☐ 78 Early Wynn 50.00 23.00 6.25
☐ 79 Jim Hegan 17.00 7.75 2.10
☐ 80 Pee Wee Reese 150.00 70.00 19.00
☐ 81 Carl Furillo 40.00 18.00 5.00
☐ 82 Joe Tipton 15.00 6.75 1.90
☐ 83 Carl Scheib 15.00 6.75 1.90
☐ 84 Barney McCosky 15.00 6.75 1.90
☐ 85 Eddie Kazak 15.00 6.75 1.90
☐ 86 Harry Brecheen 17.00 7.75 2.10
☐ 87 Floyd Baker 15.00 6.75 1.90
☐ 88 Eddie Robinson 15.00 6.75 1.90
☐ 89 Hank Thompson 17.00 7.75 2.10
☐ 90 Dave Koslo 15.00 6.75 1.90
☐ 91 Clyde Vollmer 15.00 6.75 1.90
☐ 92 Vern Stephens 17.00 7.75 2.10
☐ 93 Danny O'Connell 15.00 6.75 1.90
☐ 94 Clyde McCullough 15.00 6.75 1.90
☐ 95 Sherry Robertson 15.00 6.75 1.90
☐ 96 Sandy Consuegra 15.00 6.75 1.90
☐ 97 Bob Kuzava 15.00 6.75 1.90
☐ 98 Willard Marshall 15.00 6.75 1.90
☐ 99 Earl Torgeson 15.00 6.75 1.90
☐ 100 Sherm Lollar 17.00 7.75 2.10
☐ 101 Owen Friend 15.00 6.75 1.90
☐ 102 Dutch Leonard 15.00 6.75 1.90
☐ 103 Andy Pafko 17.00 7.75 2.10
☐ 104 Virgil Trucks 17.00 7.75 2.10
☐ 105 Don Kolloway 15.00 6.75 1.90
☐ 106 Pat Mullin 15.00 6.75 1.90
☐ 107 Johnny Wyrostek 15.00 6.75 1.90
☐ 108 Virgil Stallcup 15.00 6.75 1.90
☐ 109 Allie Reynolds 30.00 13.50 3.80
☐ 110 Bobby Brown 35.00 16.00 4.40
☐ 111 Curt Simmons 20.00 9.00 2.50
☐ 112 Willie Jones 15.00 6.75 1.90
☐ 113 Bill Nicholson 17.00 7.75 2.10
☐ 114 Sam Zoldak 15.00 6.75 1.90
☐ 115 Steve Gromek 15.00 6.75 1.90
☐ 116 Bruce Edwards 15.00 6.75 1.90
☐ 117 Eddie Miksis 15.00 6.75 1.90
☐ 118 Preacher Roe 30.00 13.50 3.80
☐ 119 Eddie Joost 15.00 6.75 1.90
☐ 120 Joe Coleman 15.00 6.75 1.90
☐ 121 Jerry Staley 15.00 6.75 1.90
☐ 122 Joe Garagiola 150.00 70.00 19.00
☐ 123 Howie Judson 15.00 6.75 1.90
☐ 124 Gus Niarhos 15.00 6.75 1.90
☐ 125 Bill Rigney 15.00 6.75 1.90
☐ 126 Bobby Thomson 30.00 13.50 3.80
☐ 127 Sal Maglie 50.00 23.00 6.25
☐ 128 Ellis Kinder 15.00 6.75 1.90
☐ 129 Matt Batts 15.00 6.75 1.90
☐ 130 Tom Saffell 15.00 6.75 1.90
☐ 131 Cliff Chambers 15.00 6.75 1.90
☐ 132 Cass Michaels 15.00 6.75 1.90
☐ 133 Sam Dente 15.00 6.75 1.90
☐ 134 Warren Spahn 125.00 57.50 15.50
☐ 135 Walker Cooper 15.00 6.75 1.90
☐ 136 Ray Coleman 15.00 6.75 1.90
☐ 137 Dick Starr 15.00 6.75 1.90
☐ 138 Phil Cavarretta 20.00 9.00 2.50
☐ 139 Doyle Lade 15.00 6.75 1.90
☐ 140 Eddie Lake 15.00 6.75 1.90
☐ 141 Fred Hutchinson 20.00 9.00 2.50
☐ 142 Aaron Robinson 15.00 6.75 1.90
☐ 143 Ted Kluszewski 40.00 18.00 5.00
☐ 144 Herman Wehmeier 15.00 6.75 1.90
☐ 145 Fred Sanford 17.00 7.75 2.10
☐ 146 Johnny Hopp 17.00 7.75 2.10
☐ 147 Ken Heintzelman 15.00 6.75 1.90
☐ 148 Granny Hamner 15.00 6.75 1.90
☐ 149 Bubba Church 15.00 6.75 1.90
☐ 150 Mike Garcia 17.00 7.75 2.10
☐ 151 Larry Doby 35.00 16.00 4.40
☐ 152 Cal Abrams 15.00 6.75 1.90
☐ 153 Rex Barney 17.00 7.75 2.10
☐ 154 Pete Suder 15.00 6.75 1.90
☐ 155 Lou Brissie 15.00 6.75 1.90
☐ 156 Del Rice 15.00 6.75 1.90
☐ 157 Al Brazle 15.00 6.75 1.90
☐ 158 Chuck Diering 15.00 6.75 1.90
☐ 159 Eddie Stewart 15.00 6.75 1.90
☐ 160 Phil Masi 15.00 6.75 1.90
☐ 161 Wes Westrum 20.00 9.00 2.50
☐ 162 Larry Jansen 17.00 7.75 2.10
☐ 163 Monte Kennedy 15.00 6.75 1.90
☐ 164 Bill Wight 15.00 6.75 1.90
☐ 165 Ted Williams 675.00 300.00 85.00
☐ 166 Stan Rojek 15.00 6.75 1.90
☐ 167 Murry Dickson 15.00 6.75 1.90
☐ 168 Sam Mele 15.00 6.75 1.90
☐ 169 Sid Hudson 15.00 6.75 1.90
☐ 170 Sibby Sisti 15.00 6.75 1.90
☐ 171 Buddy Kerr 15.00 6.75 1.90
☐ 172 Ned Garver 15.00 6.75 1.90
☐ 173 Hank Arft 15.00 6.75 1.90
☐ 174 Mickey Owen 17.00 7.75 2.10
☐ 175 Wayne Terwilliger 15.00 6.75 1.90
☐ 176 Vic Wertz 17.00 7.75 2.10
☐ 177 Charlie Keller 17.00 7.75 2.10
☐ 178 Ted Gray 15.00 6.75 1.90
☐ 179 Danny Litwhiler 15.00 6.75 1.90
☐ 180 Howie Fox 15.00 6.75 1.90
☐ 181 Casey Stengel MG 100.00 45.00 12.50
☐ 182 Tom Ferrick 15.00 6.75 1.90
☐ 183 Hank Bauer 35.00 16.00 4.40
☐ 184 Eddie Sawyer MG 17.00 7.75 2.10
☐ 185 Jimmy Bloodworth 15.00 6.75 1.90
☐ 186 Richie Ashburn 65.00 29.00 8.25
☐ 187 Al Rosen 30.00 13.50 3.80
☐ 188 Bobby Avila 20.00 9.00 2.50
☐ 189 Erv Palica 15.00 6.75 1.90
☐ 190 Joe Hatton 15.00 6.75 1.90
☐ 191 Billy Hitchcock 15.00 6.75 1.90
☐ 192 Hank Wyse 15.00 6.75 1.90
☐ 193 Ted Wilks 15.00 6.75 1.90
☐ 194 Peanuts Lowrey 15.00 6.75 1.90
☐ 195 Paul Richards MG 20.00 9.00 2.50
(Caricature)
☐ 196 Billy Pierce 30.00 13.50 3.80
☐ 197 Bob Cain 15.00 6.75 1.90
☐ 198 Monte Irvin 110.00 50.00 14.00
☐ 199 Sheldon Jones 15.00 6.75 1.90
☐ 200 Jack Kramer 15.00 6.75 1.90
☐ 201 Steve O'Neill MG 15.00 6.75 1.90
☐ 202 Mike Guerra 15.00 6.75 1.90
☐ 203 Vernon Law 30.00 13.50 3.80
☐ 204 Vic Lombardi 15.00 6.75 1.90
☐ 205 Mickey Grasso 15.00 6.75 1.90
☐ 206 Conrado Marrero 15.00 6.75 1.90
☐ 207 Billy Southworth MG 15.00 6.75 1.90
☐ 208 Blix Donnelly 15.00 6.75 1.90
☐ 209 Ken Wood 15.00 6.75 1.90
☐ 210 Les Moss 15.00 6.75 1.90
☐ 211 Hal Jeffcoat 15.00 6.75 1.90
☐ 212 Bob Rush 15.00 6.75 1.90
☐ 213 Neil Berry 15.00 6.75 1.90
☐ 214 Bob Swift 15.00 6.75 1.90
☐ 215 Ken Peterson 15.00 6.75 1.90
☐ 216 Connie Ryan 15.00 6.75 1.90
☐ 217 Joe Page 20.00 9.00 2.50
☐ 218 Ed Lopat 35.00 16.00 4.40
☐ 219 Gene Woodling 40.00 18.00 5.00
☐ 220 Bob Miller 15.00 6.75 1.90
☐ 221 Dick Whitman 15.00 6.75 1.90
☐ 222 Thurman Tucker 15.00 6.75 1.90
☐ 223 Johnny VanderMeer 25.00 11.50 3.10
☐ 224 Billy Cox 20.00 9.00 2.50
☐ 225 Dan Bankhead 17.00 7.75 2.10
☐ 226 Jimmy Dykes MG 18.00 8.00 2.30
☐ 227 Bobby Schantz UER 20.00 9.00 2.50
(Sic, Shantz)
☐ 228 Cloyd Boyer 17.00 7.75 2.10
☐ 229 Bill Howerton 15.00 6.75 1.90
☐ 230 Max Lanier 15.00 6.75 1.90
☐ 231 Luis Aloma 15.00 6.75 1.90
☐ 232 Nelson Fox 150.00 70.00 19.00
☐ 233 Leo Durocher MG 55.00 25.00 7.00
☐ 234 Clint Hartung 15.00 6.75 1.90
☐ 235 Jack Lohrke 15.00 6.75 1.90
☐ 236 Warren Rosar 15.00 6.75 1.90
☐ 237 Billy Goodman 17.00 7.75 2.10
☐ 238 Pete Reiser 20.00 9.00 2.50
☐ 239 Bill MacDonald 15.00 6.75 1.90
☐ 240 Joe Haynes 15.00 6.75 1.90
☐ 241 Irv Noren 17.00 7.75 2.10
☐ 242 Sam Jethroe 17.00 7.75 2.10
☐ 243 Johnny Antonelli 17.00 7.75 2.10
☐ 244 Cliff Fannin 15.00 6.75 1.90

☐ 245	John Berardino	25.00	11.50	3.10
☐ 246	Bill Serena	15.00	6.75	1.90
☐ 247	Bob Ramazzotti	15.00	6.75	1.90
☐ 248	Johnny Klippstein	15.00	6.75	1.90
☐ 249	Johnny Groth	15.00	6.75	1.90
☐ 250	Hank Borowy	15.00	6.75	1.90
☐ 251	Willard Ramsdell	15.00	6.75	1.90
☐ 252	Dixie Howell	15.00	6.75	1.90
☐ 253	Mickey Mantle	8750.00	3900.00	1100.00
☐ 254	Jackie Jensen	150.00	70.00	19.00
☐ 255	Milo Candini	60.00	27.00	7.50
☐ 256	Ken Sylvestri	60.00	27.00	7.50
☐ 257	Birdie Tebbetts	70.00	32.00	8.75
☐ 258	Luke Easter	70.00	32.00	8.75
☐ 259	Chuck Dressen MG	80.00	36.00	10.00
☐ 260	Carl Erskine	125.00	57.50	15.50
☐ 261	Wally Moses	65.00	29.00	8.25
☐ 262	Gus Zernial	70.00	32.00	8.75
☐ 263	Howie Pollet	65.00	29.00	8.25
☐ 264	Don Richmond	60.00	27.00	7.50
☐ 265	Steve Bilko	65.00	29.00	8.25
☐ 266	Harry Dorish	60.00	27.00	7.50
☐ 267	Ken Holcombe	60.00	27.00	7.50
☐ 268	Don Mueller	70.00	32.00	8.75
☐ 269	Ray Noble	60.00	27.00	7.50
☐ 270	Willard Nixon	60.00	27.00	7.50
☐ 271	Tommy Wright	60.00	27.00	7.50
☐ 272	Billy Meyer MG	60.00	27.00	7.50
☐ 273	Danny Murtaugh	65.00	29.00	8.25
☐ 274	George Metkovich	60.00	27.00	7.50
☐ 275	Bucky Harris MG	80.00	36.00	10.00
☐ 276	Frank Quinn	60.00	27.00	7.50
☐ 277	Roy Hartsfield	60.00	27.00	7.50
☐ 278	Norman Roy	60.00	27.00	7.50
☐ 279	Jim Delsing	60.00	27.00	7.50
☐ 280	Frank Overmire	60.00	27.00	7.50
☐ 281	Al Widmar	60.00	27.00	7.50
☐ 282	Frank Frisch MG	100.00	45.00	12.50
☐ 283	Walt Dubiel	60.00	27.00	7.50
☐ 284	Gene Bearden	65.00	29.00	8.25
☐ 285	Johnny Lipon	60.00	27.00	7.50
☐ 286	Bob Usher	60.00	27.00	7.50
☐ 287	Jim Blackburn	60.00	27.00	7.50
☐ 288	Bobby Adams	60.00	27.00	7.50
☐ 289	Cliff Mapes	65.00	29.00	8.25
☐ 290	Bill Dickey CO	175.00	80.00	22.00
☐ 291	Tommy Henrich CO	75.00	34.00	9.50
☐ 292	Eddie Pellegrini	60.00	27.00	7.50
☐ 293	Ken Johnson	60.00	27.00	7.50
☐ 294	Jocko Thompson	60.00	27.00	7.50
☐ 295	Al Lopez MG	125.00	57.50	15.50
☐ 296	Bob Kennedy	65.00	29.00	8.25
☐ 297	Dave Philley	60.00	27.00	7.50
☐ 298	Joe Astroth	60.00	27.00	7.50
☐ 299	Clyde King	60.00	27.00	7.50
☐ 300	Hal Rice	60.00	27.00	7.50
☐ 301	Tommy Glaviano	60.00	27.00	7.50
☐ 302	Jim Busby	60.00	27.00	7.50
☐ 303	Marv Rotblatt	60.00	27.00	7.50
☐ 304	Al Gettell	60.00	27.00	7.50
☐ 305	Willie Mays	3750.00	1700.00	475.00
☐ 306	Jim Piersall	125.00	57.50	15.50
☐ 307	Walt Masterson	60.00	27.00	7.50
☐ 308	Ted Beard	60.00	27.00	7.50
☐ 309	Mel Queen	60.00	27.00	7.50
☐ 310	Erv Dusak	60.00	27.00	7.50
☐ 311	Mickey Harris	60.00	27.00	7.50
☐ 312	Gene Mauch	80.00	36.00	10.00
☐ 313	Ray Mueller	60.00	27.00	7.50
☐ 314	Johnny Sain	80.00	36.00	10.00
☐ 315	Zack Taylor MG	60.00	27.00	7.50
☐ 316	Duane Pillette	60.00	27.00	7.50
☐ 317	Smoky Burgess	90.00	40.00	11.50
☐ 318	Warren Hacker	60.00	27.00	7.50
☐ 319	Red Rolfe MG	70.00	32.00	8.75
☐ 320	Hal White	60.00	27.00	7.50
☐ 321	Earl Johnson	60.00	27.00	7.50
☐ 322	Luke Sewell MG	65.00	29.00	8.25
☐ 323	Joe Adcock	100.00	45.00	12.50
☐ 324	Johnny Pramesa	125.00	38.00	12.50

1952 Bowman

The cards in this 252-card set measure approximately 2 1/16" by 3 1/8". While the Bowman set of 1952 retained the card size introduced in 1951, it employed a modification of color tones from the two preceding years. The cards also

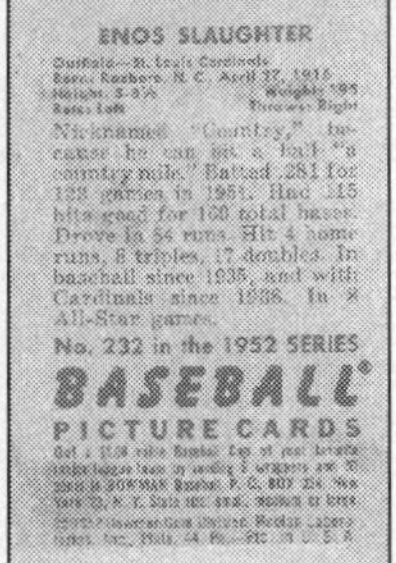

appeared with a facsimile autograph on the front and, for the first time since 1949, premium advertising on the back. The 1952 set was apparently sold in sheets as well as in gum packs. Artwork for 15 cards that were never issued was discovered in the early 1980s. Notable Rookie Cards in this set are Lew Burdette, Gil McDougald, and Minnie Minoso.

	NRMT	VG-E	GOOD
COMPLETE SET (252)	9400.00	4200.00	1200.00
COMMON PLAYER (1-36)	20.00	9.00	2.50
COMMON PLAYER (37-72)	18.00	8.00	2.30
COMMON PLAYER (73-108)	15.00	6.75	1.90
COMMON PLAYER (109-144)	15.00	6.75	1.90
COMMON PLAYER (145-180)	15.00	6.75	1.90
COMMON PLAYER (181-216)	14.00	6.25	1.75
COMMON PLAYER (217-252)	33.00	15.00	4.10

☐ 1	Yogi Berra	600.00	180.00	60.00
☐ 2	Bobby Thomson	35.00	16.00	4.40
☐ 3	Fred Hutchinson	25.00	11.50	3.10
☐ 4	Robin Roberts	70.00	32.00	8.75
☐ 5	Minnie Minoso	100.00	45.00	12.50
☐ 6	Virgil Stallcup	20.00	9.00	2.50
☐ 7	Mike Garcia	22.00	10.00	2.80
☐ 8	Pee Wee Reese	110.00	50.00	14.00
☐ 9	Vern Stephens	22.00	10.00	2.80
☐ 10	Bob Hooper	20.00	9.00	2.50
☐ 11	Ralph Kiner	70.00	32.00	8.75
☐ 12	Max Surkont	20.00	9.00	2.50
☐ 13	Cliff Mapes	20.00	9.00	2.50
☐ 14	Cliff Chambers	20.00	9.00	2.50
☐ 15	Sam Mele	20.00	9.00	2.50
☐ 16	Turk Lown	20.00	9.00	2.50
☐ 17	Ed Lopat	35.00	16.00	4.40
☐ 18	Don Mueller	22.00	10.00	2.80
☐ 19	Bob Cain	20.00	9.00	2.50
☐ 20	Willie Jones	20.00	9.00	2.50
☐ 21	Nellie Fox	50.00	23.00	6.25
☐ 22	Willard Ramsdell	20.00	9.00	2.50
☐ 23	Bob Lemon	60.00	27.00	7.50
☐ 24	Carl Furillo	35.00	16.00	4.40
☐ 25	Mickey McDermott	20.00	9.00	2.50
☐ 26	Eddie Joost	20.00	9.00	2.50
☐ 27	Joe Garagiola	75.00	34.00	9.50
☐ 28	Roy Hartsfield	20.00	9.00	2.50
☐ 29	Ned Garver	20.00	9.00	2.50
☐ 30	Red Schoendienst	65.00	29.00	8.25
☐ 31	Eddie Yost	22.00	10.00	2.80
☐ 32	Eddie Miksis	20.00	9.00	2.50
☐ 33	Gil McDougald	70.00	32.00	8.75
☐ 34	Alvin Dark	25.00	11.50	3.10
☐ 35	Granny Hamner	20.00	9.00	2.50
☐ 36	Cass Michaels	20.00	9.00	2.50
☐ 37	Vic Raschi	25.00	11.50	3.10
☐ 38	Whitey Lockman	20.00	9.00	2.50
☐ 39	Vic Wertz	20.00	9.00	2.50
☐ 40	Bubba Church	18.00	8.00	2.30
☐ 41	Chico Carrasquel	20.00	9.00	2.50
☐ 42	Johnny Wyrostek	18.00	8.00	2.30
☐ 43	Bob Feller	125.00	57.50	15.50
☐ 44	Roy Campanella	225.00	100.00	28.00
☐ 45	Johnny Pesky	25.00	11.50	3.10
☐ 46	Carl Scheib	18.00	8.00	2.30
☐ 47	Pete Castiglione	18.00	8.00	2.30
☐ 48	Vern Bickford	18.00	8.00	2.30
☐ 49	Jim Hearn	18.00	8.00	2.30
☐ 50	Jerry Staley	18.00	8.00	2.30
☐ 51	Gil Coan	18.00	8.00	2.30
☐ 52	Phil Rizzuto	90.00	40.00	11.50
☐ 53	Richie Ashburn	60.00	27.00	7.50
☐ 54	Billy Pierce	25.00	11.50	3.10
☐ 55	Ken Raffensberger	18.00	8.00	2.30

☐ 56 Clyde King	18.00	8.00	2.30
☐ 57 Clyde Vollmer	18.00	8.00	2.30
☐ 58 Hank Majeski	18.00	8.00	2.30
☐ 59 Murry Dickson	18.00	8.00	2.30
☐ 60 Sid Gordon	18.00	8.00	2.30
☐ 61 Tommy Byrne	18.00	8.00	2.30
☐ 62 Joe Presko	18.00	8.00	2.30
☐ 63 Irv Noren	20.00	9.00	2.50
☐ 64 Roy Smalley	18.00	8.00	2.30
☐ 65 Hank Bauer	30.00	13.50	3.80
☐ 66 Sal Maglie	25.00	11.50	3.10
☐ 67 Johnny Groth	18.00	8.00	2.30
☐ 68 Jim Busby	18.00	8.00	2.30
☐ 69 Joe Adcock	25.00	11.50	3.10
☐ 70 Carl Erskine	30.00	13.50	3.80
☐ 71 Vernon Law	25.00	11.50	3.10
☐ 72 Earl Torgeson	18.00	8.00	2.30
☐ 73 Jerry Coleman	20.00	9.00	2.50
☐ 74 Wes Westrum	16.00	7.25	2.00
☐ 75 George Kell	45.00	20.00	5.75
☐ 76 Del Ennis	20.00	9.00	2.50
☐ 77 Eddie Robinson	15.00	6.75	1.90
☐ 78 Lloyd Merriman	15.00	6.75	1.90
☐ 79 Lou Brissie	15.00	6.75	1.90
☐ 80 Gil Hodges	80.00	36.00	10.00
☐ 81 Billy Goodman	16.00	7.25	2.00
☐ 82 Gus Zernial	16.00	7.25	2.00
☐ 83 Howie Pollet	15.00	6.75	1.90
☐ 84 Sam Jethroe	16.00	7.25	2.00
☐ 85 Marty Marion CO	20.00	9.00	2.50
☐ 86 Cal Abrams	15.00	6.75	1.90
☐ 87 Mickey Vernon	17.00	7.75	2.10
☐ 88 Bruce Edwards	15.00	6.75	1.90
☐ 89 Billy Hitchcock	15.00	6.75	1.90
☐ 90 Larry Jansen	16.00	7.25	2.00
☐ 91 Don Kolloway	15.00	6.75	1.90
☐ 92 Eddie Waitkus	15.00	6.75	1.90
☐ 93 Paul Richards MG	16.00	7.25	2.00
☐ 94 Luke Sewell MG	16.00	7.25	2.00
☐ 95 Luke Easter	16.00	7.25	2.00
☐ 96 Ralph Branca	20.00	9.00	2.50
☐ 97 Willard Marshall	15.00	6.75	1.90
☐ 98 Jimmy Dykes MG	20.00	9.00	2.50
☐ 99 Clyde McCullough	15.00	6.75	1.90
☐ 100 Sibby Sisti	15.00	6.75	1.90
☐ 101 Mickey Mantle	2400.00	1100.00	300.00
☐ 102 Peanuts Lowrey	15.00	6.75	1.90
☐ 103 Joe Haynes	15.00	6.75	1.90
☐ 104 Hal Jeffcoat	15.00	6.75	1.90
☐ 105 Bobby Brown	25.00	11.50	3.10
☐ 106 Randy Gumpert	15.00	6.75	1.90
☐ 107 Del Rice	15.00	6.75	1.90
☐ 108 George Metkovich	16.00	7.25	2.00
☐ 109 Tom Morgan	16.00	7.25	2.00
☐ 110 Max Lanier	15.00	6.75	1.90
☐ 111 Hoot Evers	15.00	6.75	1.90
☐ 112 Smoky Burgess	17.00	7.75	2.10
☐ 113 Al Zarilla	15.00	6.75	1.90
☐ 114 Frank Hiller	15.00	6.75	1.90
☐ 115 Larry Doby	25.00	11.50	3.10
☐ 116 Duke Snider	200.00	90.00	25.00
☐ 117 Bill Wight	15.00	6.75	1.90
☐ 118 Ray Murray	15.00	6.75	1.90
☐ 119 Bill Howerton	15.00	6.75	1.90
☐ 120 Chet Nichols	15.00	6.75	1.90
☐ 121 Al Corwin	15.00	6.75	1.90
☐ 122 Billy Johnson	15.00	6.75	1.90
☐ 123 Sid Hudson	15.00	6.75	1.90
☐ 124 Birdie Tebbetts	16.00	7.25	2.00
☐ 125 Howie Fox	15.00	6.75	1.90
☐ 126 Phil Cavarretta	20.00	9.00	2.50
☐ 127 Dick Sisler	15.00	6.75	1.90
☐ 128 Don Newcombe	30.00	13.50	3.80
☐ 129 Gus Niarhos	15.00	6.75	1.90
☐ 130 Allie Clark	15.00	6.75	1.90
☐ 131 Bob Swift	15.00	6.75	1.90
☐ 132 Dave Cole	15.00	6.75	1.90
☐ 133 Dick Kryhoski	15.00	6.75	1.90
☐ 134 Al Brazle	15.00	6.75	1.90
☐ 135 Mickey Harris	15.00	6.75	1.90
☐ 136 Gene Hermanski	15.00	6.75	1.90
☐ 137 Stan Rojek	15.00	6.75	1.90
☐ 138 Ted Wilks	15.00	6.75	1.90
☐ 139 Jerry Priddy	15.00	6.75	1.90
☐ 140 Ray Scarborough	15.00	6.75	1.90
☐ 141 Hank Edwards	15.00	6.75	1.90
☐ 142 Early Wynn	50.00	23.00	6.25
☐ 143 Sandy Consuegra	15.00	6.75	1.90
☐ 144 Joe Hatton	15.00	6.75	1.90
☐ 145 Johnny Mize	60.00	27.00	7.50
☐ 146 Leo Durocher MG	45.00	20.00	5.75
☐ 147 Marlin Stuart	15.00	6.75	1.90
☐ 148 Ken Heintzelman	15.00	6.75	1.90
☐ 149 Howie Judson	15.00	6.75	1.90
☐ 150 Herman Wehmeier	15.00	6.75	1.90
☐ 151 Al Rosen	25.00	11.50	3.10
☐ 152 Billy Cox	18.00	8.00	2.30
☐ 153 Fred Hatfield	15.00	6.75	1.90
☐ 154 Ferris Fain	16.00	7.25	2.00
☐ 155 Billy Meyer MG	15.00	6.75	1.90
☐ 156 Warren Spahn	110.00	50.00	14.00
☐ 157 Jim Delsing	15.00	6.75	1.90
☐ 158 Bucky Harris MG	30.00	13.50	3.80
☐ 159 Dutch Leonard	15.00	6.75	1.90
☐ 160 Eddie Stanky	17.00	7.75	2.10
☐ 161 Jackie Jensen	35.00	16.00	4.40
☐ 162 Monte Irvin	50.00	23.00	6.25
☐ 163 Johnny Lipon	15.00	6.75	1.90
☐ 164 Connie Ryan	15.00	6.75	1.90
☐ 165 Saul Rogovin	15.00	6.75	1.90
☐ 166 Bobby Adams	15.00	6.75	1.90
☐ 167 Bobby Avila	16.00	7.25	2.00
☐ 168 Preacher Roe	28.00	12.50	3.50
☐ 169 Walt Dropo	16.00	7.25	2.00
☐ 170 Joe Astroth	15.00	6.75	1.90
☐ 171 Mel Queen	15.00	6.75	1.90
☐ 172 Ebba St.Claire	15.00	6.75	1.90
☐ 173 Gene Bearden	15.00	6.75	1.90
☐ 174 Mickey Grasso	15.00	6.75	1.90
☐ 175 Randy Jackson	15.00	6.75	1.90
☐ 176 Harry Brecheen	16.00	7.25	2.00
☐ 177 Gene Woodling	20.00	9.00	2.50
☐ 178 Dave Williams	20.00	9.00	2.50
☐ 179 Pete Suder	15.00	6.75	1.90
☐ 180 Ed Fitzgerald	15.00	6.75	1.90
☐ 181 Joe Collins	18.00	8.00	2.30
☐ 182 Dave Koslo	14.00	6.25	1.75
☐ 183 Pat Mullin	14.00	6.25	1.75
☐ 184 Curt Simmons	16.00	7.25	2.00
☐ 185 Eddie Stewart	14.00	6.25	1.75
☐ 186 Frank Smith	14.00	6.25	1.75
☐ 187 Jim Hegan	15.00	6.75	1.90
☐ 188 Charlie Dressen MG	16.00	7.25	2.00
☐ 189 Jim Piersall	20.00	9.00	2.50
☐ 190 Dick Fowler	14.00	6.25	1.75
☐ 191 Bob Friend	25.00	11.50	3.10
☐ 192 John Cusick	14.00	6.25	1.75
☐ 193 Bobby Young	14.00	6.25	1.75
☐ 194 Bob Porterfield	14.00	6.25	1.75
☐ 195 Frank Baumholtz	14.00	6.25	1.75
☐ 196 Stan Musial	525.00	240.00	65.00
☐ 197 Charlie Silvera	18.00	8.00	2.30
☐ 198 Chuck Diering	14.00	6.25	1.75
☐ 199 Ted Gray	14.00	6.25	1.75
☐ 200 Ken Silvestri	14.00	6.25	1.75
☐ 201 Ray Coleman	14.00	6.25	1.75
☐ 202 Harry Perkowski	14.00	6.25	1.75
☐ 203 Steve Gromek	14.00	6.25	1.75
☐ 204 Andy Pafko	15.00	6.75	1.90
☐ 205 Walt Masterson	14.00	6.25	1.75
☐ 206 Elmer Valo	14.00	6.25	1.75
☐ 207 George Strickland	14.00	6.25	1.75
☐ 208 Walker Cooper	14.00	6.25	1.75
☐ 209 Dick Littlefield	14.00	6.25	1.75
☐ 210 Archie Wilson	14.00	6.25	1.75
☐ 211 Paul Minner	14.00	6.25	1.75
☐ 212 Solly Hemus	14.00	6.25	1.75
☐ 213 Monte Kennedy	14.00	6.25	1.75
☐ 214 Ray Boone	15.00	6.75	1.90
☐ 215 Sheldon Jones	14.00	6.25	1.75
☐ 216 Matt Batts	14.00	6.25	1.75
☐ 217 Casey Stengel MG	175.00	80.00	22.00
☐ 218 Willie Mays	1300.00	575.00	160.00
☐ 219 Neil Berry	33.00	15.00	4.10
☐ 220 Russ Meyer	33.00	15.00	4.10
☐ 221 Lou Kretlow	33.00	15.00	4.10
☐ 222 Dixie Howell	33.00	15.00	4.10
☐ 223 Harry Simpson	33.00	15.00	4.10
☐ 224 Johnny Schmitz	33.00	15.00	4.10
☐ 225 Del Wilber	33.00	15.00	4.10
☐ 226 Alex Kellner	33.00	15.00	4.10
☐ 227 Clyde Sukeforth CO	33.00	15.00	4.10
☐ 228 Bob Chipman	33.00	15.00	4.10
☐ 229 Hank Arft	33.00	15.00	4.10
☐ 230 Frank Shea	33.00	15.00	4.10
☐ 231 Dee Fondy	33.00	15.00	4.10
☐ 232 Enos Slaughter	100.00	45.00	12.50
☐ 233 Bob Kuzava	33.00	15.00	4.10
☐ 234 Fred Fitzsimmons CO	35.00	16.00	4.40
☐ 235 Steve Souchock	33.00	15.00	4.10
☐ 236 Tommy Brown	33.00	15.00	4.10
☐ 237 Sherm Lollar	35.00	16.00	4.40
☐ 238 Roy McMillan	35.00	16.00	4.40
☐ 239 Dale Mitchell	35.00	16.00	4.40
☐ 240 Billy Loes	40.00	18.00	5.00
☐ 241 Mel Parnell	35.00	16.00	4.40

☐	242 Everett Kell	33.00	15.00	4.10
☐	243 Red Munger	33.00	15.00	4.10
☐	244 Lew Burdette	65.00	29.00	8.25
☐	245 George Schmees	33.00	15.00	4.10
☐	246 Jerry Snyder	33.00	15.00	4.10
☐	247 Johnny Pramesa	33.00	15.00	4.10
☐	248 Bill Werle	33.00	15.00	4.10
☐	249 Hank Thompson	35.00	16.00	4.40
☐	250 Ike Delock	33.00	15.00	4.10
☐	251 Jack Lohrke	33.00	15.00	4.10
☐	252 Frank Crosetti CO	165.00	42.50	13.00

1953 Bowman Color

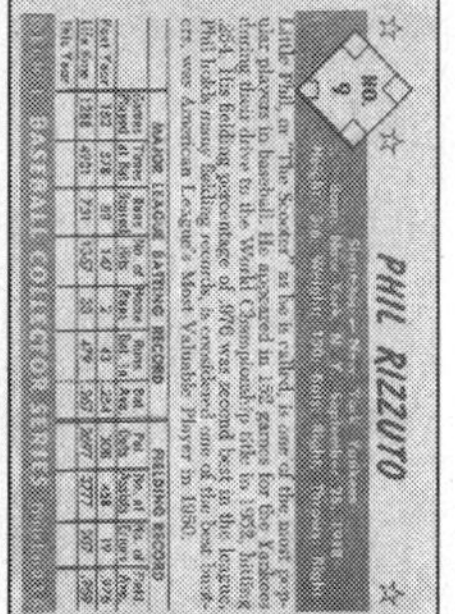

The cards in this 160-card set measure approximately 2 1/2" by 3 3/4". The 1953 Bowman Color set, considered by many to be the best looking set of the modern era, contains Kodachrome photographs with no names or facsimile autographs on the face. Numbers 113 to 160 are somewhat more difficult to obtain, with numbers 113 to 128 being the most difficult. There are two cards of Al Corwin (126 and 149). There are no key Rookie Cards in this set.

		NRMT	VG-E	GOOD
	COMPLETE SET (160)	11000.00	5000.00	1400.00
	COMMON PLAYER (1-96)	30.00	13.50	3.80
	COMMON PLAYER (97-112)	35.00	16.00	4.40
	COMMON PLAYER (113-128)	55.00	25.00	7.00
	COMMON PLAYER (129-160)	42.00	19.00	5.25
☐	1 Dave Williams	90.00	18.00	5.50
☐	2 Vic Wertz	33.00	15.00	4.10
☐	3 Sam Jethroe	33.00	15.00	4.10
☐	4 Art Houtteman	30.00	13.50	3.80
☐	5 Sid Gordon	30.00	13.50	3.80
☐	6 Joe Ginsberg	30.00	13.50	3.80
☐	7 Harry Chiti	30.00	13.50	3.80
☐	8 Al Rosen	50.00	23.00	6.25
☐	9 Phil Rizzuto	115.00	52.50	14.50
☐	10 Richie Ashburn	95.00	42.50	12.00
☐	11 Bobby Shantz	40.00	18.00	5.00
☐	12 Carl Erskine	40.00	18.00	5.00
☐	13 Gus Zernial	33.00	15.00	4.10
☐	14 Billy Loes	35.00	16.00	4.40
☐	15 Jim Busby	30.00	13.50	3.80
☐	16 Bob Friend	33.00	15.00	4.10
☐	17 Gerry Staley	30.00	13.50	3.80
☐	18 Nellie Fox	70.00	32.00	8.75
☐	19 Alvin Dark	40.00	18.00	5.00
☐	20 Don Lenhardt	30.00	13.50	3.80
☐	21 Joe Garagiola	80.00	36.00	10.00
☐	22 Bob Porterfield	30.00	13.50	3.80
☐	23 Herman Wehmeier	30.00	13.50	3.80
☐	24 Jackie Jensen	40.00	18.00	5.00
☐	25 Hoot Evers	30.00	13.50	3.80
☐	26 Roy McMillan	33.00	15.00	4.10
☐	27 Vic Raschi	40.00	18.00	5.00
☐	28 Smoky Burgess	33.00	15.00	4.10
☐	29 Bobby Avila	33.00	15.00	4.10
☐	30 Phil Cavarretta	33.00	15.00	4.10
☐	31 Jimmy Dykes MG	33.00	15.00	4.10
☐	32 Stan Musial	550.00	250.00	70.00
☐	33 Pee Wee Reese HOR	480.00	220.00	60.00
☐	34 Gil Coan	30.00	13.50	3.80
☐	35 Maurice McDermott	30.00	13.50	3.80
☐	36 Minnie Minoso	60.00	27.00	7.50
☐	37 Jim Wilson	30.00	13.50	3.80
☐	38 Harry Byrd	30.00	13.50	3.80
☐	39 Paul Richards MG	33.00	15.00	4.10
☐	40 Larry Doby	45.00	20.00	5.75
☐	41 Sammy White	30.00	13.50	3.80
☐	42 Tommy Brown	30.00	13.50	3.80
☐	43 Mike Garcia	33.00	15.00	4.10
☐	44 Berra/Bauer/Mantle	475.00	210.00	60.00
☐	45 Walt Dropo	33.00	15.00	4.10
☐	46 Roy Campanella	265.00	120.00	33.00
☐	47 Ned Garver	30.00	13.50	3.80
☐	48 Hank Sauer	33.00	15.00	4.10
☐	49 Eddie Stanky MG	33.00	15.00	4.10
☐	50 Lou Kretlow	30.00	13.50	3.80
☐	51 Monte Irvin	60.00	27.00	7.50
☐	52 Marty Marion MG	40.00	18.00	5.00
☐	53 Del Rice	30.00	13.50	3.80
☐	54 Chico Carrasquel	30.00	13.50	3.80
☐	55 Leo Durocher MG	60.00	27.00	7.50
☐	56 Bob Cain	30.00	13.50	3.80
☐	57 Lou Boudreau MG	50.00	23.00	6.25
☐	58 Willard Marshall	30.00	13.50	3.80
☐	59 Mickey Mantle	2500.00	1150.00	325.00
☐	60 Granny Hamner	30.00	13.50	3.80
☐	61 George Kell	65.00	29.00	8.25
☐	62 Ted Kluszewski	60.00	27.00	7.50
☐	63 Gil McDougald	60.00	27.00	7.50
☐	64 Curt Simmons	33.00	15.00	4.10
☐	65 Robin Roberts	80.00	36.00	10.00
☐	66 Mel Parnell	33.00	15.00	4.10
☐	67 Mel Clark	30.00	13.50	3.80
☐	68 Allie Reynolds	50.00	23.00	6.25
☐	69 Charlie Grimm MG	33.00	15.00	4.10
☐	70 Clint Courtney	30.00	13.50	3.80
☐	71 Paul Minner	30.00	13.50	3.80
☐	72 Ted Gray	30.00	13.50	3.80
☐	73 Billy Pierce	40.00	18.00	5.00
☐	74 Don Mueller	33.00	15.00	4.10
☐	75 Saul Rogovin	30.00	13.50	3.80
☐	76 Jim Hearn	30.00	13.50	3.80
☐	77 Mickey Grasso	30.00	13.50	3.80
☐	78 Carl Furillo	50.00	23.00	6.25
☐	79 Ray Boone	33.00	15.00	4.10
☐	80 Ralph Kiner	85.00	38.00	10.50
☐	81 Enos Slaughter	85.00	38.00	10.50
☐	82 Joe Astroth	30.00	13.50	3.80
☐	83 Jack Daniels	33.00	15.00	4.10
☐	84 Hank Bauer	50.00	23.00	6.25
☐	85 Solly Hemus	30.00	13.50	3.80
☐	86 Harry Simpson	30.00	13.50	3.80
☐	87 Harry Perkowski	30.00	13.50	3.80
☐	88 Joe Dobson	30.00	13.50	3.80
☐	89 Sandy Consuegra	30.00	13.50	3.80
☐	90 Joe Nuxhall	40.00	18.00	5.00
☐	91 Steve Souchock	30.00	13.50	3.80
☐	92 Gil Hodges	125.00	57.50	15.50
☐	93 Phil Rizzuto and Billy Martin	240.00	110.00	30.00
☐	94 Bob Addis	30.00	13.50	3.80
☐	95 Wally Moses CO	33.00	15.00	4.10
☐	96 Sal Maglie	45.00	20.00	5.75
☐	97 Eddie Mathews	200.00	90.00	25.00
☐	98 Hector Rodriguez	35.00	16.00	4.40
☐	99 Warren Spahn	200.00	90.00	25.00
☐	100 Bill Wight	35.00	16.00	4.40
☐	101 Red Schoendienst	90.00	40.00	11.50
☐	102 Jim Hegan	38.00	17.00	4.70
☐	103 Del Ennis	40.00	18.00	5.00
☐	104 Luke Easter	38.00	17.00	4.70
☐	105 Eddie Joost	35.00	16.00	4.40
☐	106 Ken Raffensberger	35.00	16.00	4.40
☐	107 Alex Kellner	35.00	16.00	4.40
☐	108 Bobby Adams	35.00	16.00	4.40
☐	109 Ken Wood	35.00	16.00	4.40
☐	110 Bob Rush	35.00	16.00	4.40
☐	111 Jim Dyck	35.00	16.00	4.40
☐	112 Toby Atwell	35.00	16.00	4.40
☐	113 Karl Drews	55.00	25.00	7.00
☐	114 Bob Feller	325.00	145.00	40.00
☐	115 Cloyd Boyer	55.00	25.00	7.00
☐	116 Eddie Yost	60.00	27.00	7.50
☐	117 Duke Snider	600.00	275.00	75.00
☐	118 Billy Martin	325.00	145.00	40.00
☐	119 Dale Mitchell	60.00	27.00	7.50
☐	120 Marlin Stuart	55.00	25.00	7.00
☐	121 Yogi Berra	600.00	275.00	75.00
☐	122 Bill Serena	55.00	25.00	7.00
☐	123 Johnny Lipon	55.00	25.00	7.00
☐	124 Charlie Dressen MG	65.00	29.00	8.25
☐	125 Fred Hatfield	55.00	25.00	7.00
☐	126 Al Corwin	55.00	25.00	7.00
☐	127 Dick Kryhoski	55.00	25.00	7.00
☐	128 Whitey Lockman	60.00	27.00	7.50

☐ 129 Russ Meyer	42.00	19.00	5.25
☐ 130 Cass Michaels	42.00	19.00	5.25
☐ 131 Connie Ryan	42.00	19.00	5.25
☐ 132 Fred Hutchinson	45.00	20.00	5.75
☐ 133 Willie Jones	42.00	19.00	5.25
☐ 134 Johnny Pesky	45.00	20.00	5.75
☐ 135 Bobby Morgan	42.00	19.00	5.25
☐ 136 Jim Bridewe ser	42.00	19.00	5.25
☐ 137 Sam Dente	42.00	19.00	5.25
☐ 138 Bubba Church	42.00	19.00	5.25
☐ 139 Pete Runnels	45.00	20.00	5.75
☐ 140 Al Brazle	42.00	19.00	5.25
☐ 141 Frank Shea	42.00	19.00	5.25
☐ 142 Larry Miggins	42.00	19.00	5.25
☐ 143 Al Lopez MG	65.00	29.00	8.25
☐ 144 Warren Hacker	42.00	19.00	5.25
☐ 145 George Shuba	45.00	20.00	5.75
☐ 146 Early Wynn	125.00	57.50	15.50
☐ 147 Clem Koshorek	42.00	19.00	5.25
☐ 148 Billy Goodman	45.00	20.00	5.75
☐ 149 Al Corwin	42.00	19.00	5.25
☐ 150 Carl Scheib	42.00	19.00	5.25
☐ 151 Joe Adcock	50.00	23.00	6.25
☐ 152 Clyde Vollmer	42.00	19.00	5.25
☐ 153 Whitey Ford	500.00	230.00	65.00
☐ 154 Turk Lown	42.00	19.00	5.25
☐ 155 Allie Clark	42.00	19.00	5.25
☐ 156 Max Surkont	42.00	19.00	5.25
☐ 157 Sherm Lollar	45.00	20.00	5.75
☐ 158 Howard Fox	42.00	19.00	5.25
☐ 159 Mickey Vernon UER (Photo actually Floyd Baker)	50.00	23.00	6.25
☐ 160 Cal Abrams	85.00	26.00	8.50

1953 Bowman B/W

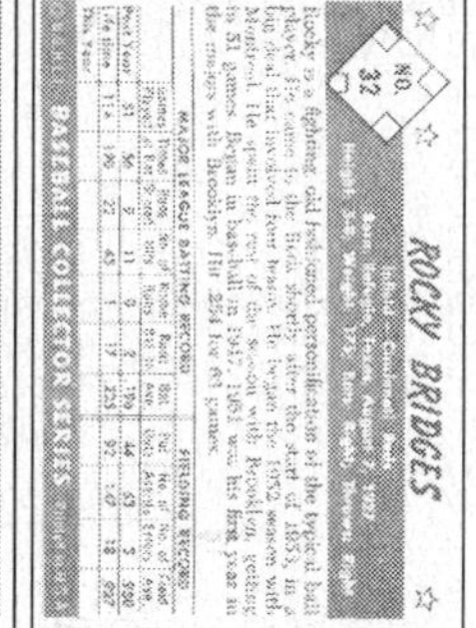

The cards in this 64-card set measure approximately 2 1/2" by 3 3/4". Some collectors believe that the high cost of producing the 1953 color series forced Bowman to issue this set in black and white, since the two sets are identical in design except for the element of color. This set was also produced in fewer numbers than its color counterpart, and is popular among collectors for the challenge involved in completing it. There are no key Rookie Cards in this set.

	NRMT	VG-E	GOOD
COMPLETE SET (64)	2500.00	1150.00	325.00
COMMON PLAYER (1-64)	35.00	16.00	4.40

☐ 1 Gus Bell	125.00	25.00	10.00
☐ 2 Willard Nixon	35.00	16.00	4.40
☐ 3 Bill Rigney	35.00	16.00	4.40
☐ 4 Pat Mullin	35.00	16.00	4.40
☐ 5 Dee Fondy	35.00	16.00	4.40
☐ 6 Ray Murray	35.00	16.00	4.40
☐ 7 Andy Seminick	35.00	16.00	4.40
☐ 8 Pete Suder	35.00	16.00	4.40
☐ 9 Walt Masterson	35.00	16.00	4.40
☐ 10 Dick Sisler	38.00	17.00	4.70
☐ 11 Dick Gernert	35.00	16.00	4.40
☐ 12 Randy Jackson	35.00	16.00	4.40
☐ 13 Joe Tipton	35.00	16.00	4.40
☐ 14 Bill Nicholson	38.00	17.00	4.70
☐ 15 Johnny Mize	125.00	57.50	15.50
☐ 16 Stu Miller	40.00	18.00	5.00
☐ 17 Virgil Trucks	38.00	17.00	4.70
☐ 18 Billy Hoeft	40.00	18.00	5.00
☐ 19 Paul LaPalme	35.00	16.00	4.40
☐ 20 Eddie Robinson	35.00	16.00	4.40
☐ 21 Clarence Podbielan	35.00	16.00	4.40
☐ 22 Matt Batts	35.00	16.00	4.40
☐ 23 Wilmer Mizell	40.00	18.00	5.00
☐ 24 Del Wilber	35.00	16.00	4.40
☐ 25 Johnny Sain	55.00	25.00	7.00
☐ 26 Preacher Roe	55.00	25.00	7.00
☐ 27 Bob Lemon	125.00	57.50	15.50
☐ 28 Hoyt Wilhelm	125.00	57.50	15.50
☐ 29 Sid Hudson	35.00	16.00	4.40
☐ 30 Walker Cooper	35.00	16.00	4.40
☐ 31 Gene Woodling	50.00	23.00	6.25
☐ 32 Rocky Bridges	35.00	16.00	4.40
☐ 33 Bob Kuzava	35.00	16.00	4.40
☐ 34 Ebba St.Claire	35.00	16.00	4.40
☐ 35 Johnny Wyrostek	35.00	16.00	4.40
☐ 36 Jim Piersall	50.00	23.00	6.25
☐ 37 Hal Jeffcoat	35.00	16.00	4.40
☐ 38 Dave Cole	35.00	16.00	4.40
☐ 39 Casey Stengel MG	325.00	145.00	40.00
☐ 40 Larry Jansen	38.00	17.00	4.70
☐ 41 Bob Ramazzotti	35.00	16.00	4.40
☐ 42 Howie Judson	35.00	16.00	4.40
☐ 43 Hal Bevan	35.00	16.00	4.40
☐ 44 Jim Delsing	35.00	16.00	4.40
☐ 45 Irv Noren	38.00	17.00	4.70
☐ 46 Bucky Harris MG	55.00	25.00	7.00
☐ 47 Jack Lohrke	35.00	16.00	4.40
☐ 48 Steve Ridzik	35.00	16.00	4.40
☐ 49 Floyd Baker	35.00	16.00	4.40
☐ 50 Dutch Leonard	35.00	16.00	4.40
☐ 51 Lou Burdette	50.00	23.00	6.25
☐ 52 Ralph Branca	40.00	18.00	5.00
☐ 53 Morrie Martin	35.00	16.00	4.40
☐ 54 Bill Miller	35.00	16.00	4.40
☐ 55 Don Johnson	35.00	16.00	4.40
☐ 56 Roy Smalley	35.00	16.00	4.40
☐ 57 Andy Pafko	38.00	17.00	4.70
☐ 58 Jim Konstanty	40.00	18.00	5.00
☐ 59 Duane Pillette	35.00	16.00	4.40
☐ 60 Billy Cox	40.00	18.00	5.00
☐ 61 Tom Gorman	35.00	16.00	4.40
☐ 62 Keith Thomas	35.00	16.00	4.40
☐ 63 Steve Gromek	35.00	16.00	4.40
☐ 64 Andy Hansen	45.00	20.00	5.75

1954 Bowman

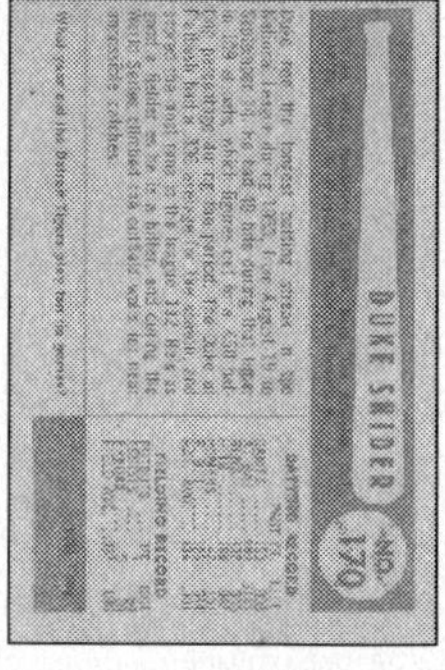

The cards in this 224-card set measure approximately 2 1/2" by 3 3/4". A contractual problem apparently resulted in the deletion of the number 66 Ted Williams card from this Bowman set, thereby creating a scarcity that is highly valued among collectors. The set price below does NOT include number 66 Williams but does include number 66 Jim Piersall, the apparent replacement for Williams in spite of the fact that Piersall was already number 210 to appear later in the set. Many errors in players' statistics exist (and some were corrected) while a few players' names were printed on the front, instead of appearing as a facsimile autograph. The notable Rookie Cards in this set are Harvey Kuenn and Don Larsen.

	NRMT	VG-E	GOOD
COMPLETE SET (224)	4500.00	2000.00	575.00
COMMON PLAYER (1-128)	10.00	4.50	1.25
COMMON PLAYER (129-224)	15.00	6.75	1.90
☐ 1 Phil Rizzuto	135.00	40.00	13.50
☐ 2 Jackie Jensen	15.00	6.75	1.90
☐ 3 Marion Fricano	10.00	4.50	1.25
☐ 4 Bob Hooper	10.00	4.50	1.25
☐ 5 Billy Hunter	10.00	4.50	1.25
☐ 6 Nellie Fox	25.00	11.50	3.10
☐ 7 Walt Dropo	11.00	4.90	1.40
☐ 8 Jim Busby	10.00	4.50	1.25
☐ 9 Dave Williams	10.00	4.50	1.25
☐ 10 Carl Erskine	15.00	6.75	1.90
☐ 11 Sid Gordon	10.00	4.50	1.25
☐ 12 Roy McMillan	11.00	4.90	1.40
☐ 13 Paul Minner	10.00	4.50	1.25
☐ 14 Jerry Staley	10.00	4.50	1.25
☐ 15 Richie Ashburn	35.00	16.00	4.40
☐ 16 Jim Wilson	10.00	4.50	1.25
☐ 17 Tom Gorman	10.00	4.50	1.25
☐ 18 Hoot Evers	10.00	4.50	1.25
☐ 19 Bobby Shantz	12.50	5.75	1.55
☐ 20 Art Houtteman	10.00	4.50	1.25
☐ 21 Vic Wertz	11.00	4.90	1.40
☐ 22 Sam Mele	10.00	4.50	1.25
☐ 23 Harvey Kuenn	33.00	15.00	4.10
☐ 24 Bob Porterfield	10.00	4.50	1.25
☐ 25 Wes Westrum	11.00	4.90	1.40
☐ 26 Billy Cox	12.50	5.75	1.55
☐ 27 Dick Cole	10.00	4.50	1.25
☐ 28 Jim Greengrass	10.00	4.50	1.25
☐ 29 Johnny Klippstein	10.00	4.50	1.25
☐ 30 Del Rice	10.00	4.50	1.25
☐ 31 Smoky Burgess	11.00	4.90	1.40
☐ 32 Del Crandall	11.00	4.90	1.40
☐ 33A Vic Raschi (No mention of trade on back)	20.00	9.00	2.50
☐ 33B Vic Raschi (Traded to St.Louis)	35.00	16.00	4.40
☐ 34 Sammy White	10.00	4.50	1.25
☐ 35 Eddie Joost	10.00	4.50	1.25
☐ 36 George Strickland	10.00	4.50	1.25
☐ 37 Dick Kokos	10.00	4.50	1.25
☐ 38 Minnie Minoso	20.00	9.00	2.50
☐ 39 Ned Garver	10.00	4.50	1.25
☐ 40 Gil Coan	10.00	4.50	1.25
☐ 41 Alvin Dark	13.00	5.75	1.65
☐ 42 Billy Loes	11.00	4.90	1.40
☐ 43 Bob Friend	11.00	4.90	1.40
☐ 44 Harry Perkowski	10.00	4.50	1.25
☐ 45 Ralph Kiner	45.00	20.00	5.75
☐ 46 Rip Repulski	10.00	4.50	1.25
☐ 47 Granny Hamner	10.00	4.50	1.25
☐ 48 Jack Dittmer	10.00	4.50	1.25
☐ 49 Harry Byrd	10.00	4.50	1.25
☐ 50 George Kell	30.00	13.50	3.80
☐ 51 Alex Kellner	10.00	4.50	1.25
☐ 52 Joe Ginsberg	10.00	4.50	1.25
☐ 53 Don Lenhardt	10.00	4.50	1.25
☐ 54 Chico Carrasquel	10.00	4.50	1.25
☐ 55 Jim Delsing	10.00	4.50	1.25
☐ 56 Maurice McDermott	10.00	4.50	1.25
☐ 57 Hoyt Wilhelm	30.00	13.50	3.80
☐ 58 Pee Wee Reese	75.00	34.00	9.50
☐ 59 Bob Schultz	10.00	4.50	1.25
☐ 60 Fred Baczewski	10.00	4.50	1.25
☐ 61 Eddie Miksis	10.00	4.50	1.25
☐ 62 Enos Slaughter	45.00	20.00	5.75
☐ 63 Earl Torgeson	10.00	4.50	1.25
☐ 64 Eddie Mathews	65.00	29.00	8.25
☐ 65 Mickey Mantle	1000.00	450.00	125.00
☐ 66A Ted Williams	5000.00	1500.00	500.00
☐ 66B Jim Piersall	100.00	45.00	12.50
☐ 67 Carl Scheib	10.00	4.50	1.25
☐ 68 Bobby Avila	11.00	4.90	1.40
☐ 69 Clint Courtney	10.00	4.50	1.25
☐ 70 Willard Marshall	10.00	4.50	1.25
☐ 71 Ted Gray	10.00	4.50	1.25
☐ 72 Eddie Yost	11.00	4.90	1.40
☐ 73 Don Mueller	11.00	4.90	1.40
☐ 74 Jim Gilliam	22.00	10.00	2.80
☐ 75 Max Surkont	10.00	4.50	1.25
☐ 76 Joe Nuxhall	11.00	4.90	1.40
☐ 77 Bob Rush	10.00	4.50	1.25
☐ 78 Sal Yvars	10.00	4.50	1.25
☐ 79 Curt Simmons	11.00	4.90	1.40
☐ 80 Johnny Logan	15.00	6.75	1.90
☐ 81 Jerry Coleman	11.00	4.90	1.40
☐ 82 Billy Goodman	11.00	4.90	1.40
☐ 83 Ray Murray	10.00	4.50	1.25
☐ 84 Larry Doby	15.00	6.75	1.90
☐ 85 Jim Dyck	10.00	4.50	1.25
☐ 86 Harry Dorish	10.00	4.50	1.25
☐ 87 Don Lund	10.00	4.50	1.25
☐ 88 Tom Umphlett	10.00	4.50	1.25
☐ 89 Willie Mays	425.00	190.00	52.50
☐ 90 Roy Campanella	150.00	70.00	19.00
☐ 91 Cal Abrams	10.00	4.50	1.25
☐ 92 Ken Raffensberger	10.00	4.50	1.25
☐ 93 Bill Serena	10.00	4.50	1.25
☐ 94 Solly Hemus	10.00	4.50	1.25
☐ 95 Robin Roberts	40.00	18.00	5.00
☐ 96 Joe Adcock	11.00	4.90	1.40
☐ 97 Gil McDougald	20.00	9.00	2.50
☐ 98 Ellis Kinder	10.00	4.50	1.25
☐ 99 Pete Suder	10.00	4.50	1.25
☐ 100 Mike Garcia	11.00	4.90	1.40
☐ 101 Don Larsen	45.00	20.00	5.75
☐ 102 Billy Pierce	12.50	5.75	1.55
☐ 103 Steve Souchock	10.00	4.50	1.25
☐ 104 Frank Shea	10.00	4.50	1.25
☐ 105 Sal Maglie	15.00	6.75	1.90
☐ 106 Clem Labine	12.50	5.75	1.55
☐ 107 Paul LaPalme	10.00	4.50	1.25
☐ 108 Bobby Adams	10.00	4.50	1.25
☐ 109 Roy Smalley	10.00	4.50	1.25
☐ 110 Red Schoendienst	40.00	18.00	5.00
☐ 111 Murry Dickson	10.00	4.50	1.25
☐ 112 Andy Pafko	11.00	4.90	1.40
☐ 113 Allie Reynolds	20.00	9.00	2.50
☐ 114 Willard Nixon	10.00	4.50	1.25
☐ 115 Don Bollweg	10.00	4.50	1.25
☐ 116 Luke Easter	11.00	4.90	1.40
☐ 117 Dick Kryhoski	10.00	4.50	1.25
☐ 118 Bob Boyd	10.00	4.50	1.25
☐ 119 Fred Hatfield	10.00	4.50	1.25
☐ 120 Mel Hoderlein	10.00	4.50	1.25
☐ 121 Ray Katt	10.00	4.50	1.25
☐ 122 Carl Furillo	20.00	9.00	2.50
☐ 123 Toby Atwell	10.00	4.50	1.25
☐ 124 Gus Bell	11.00	4.90	1.40
☐ 125 Warren Hacker	10.00	4.50	1.25
☐ 126 Cliff Chambers	10.00	4.50	1.25
☐ 127 Del Ennis	12.50	5.75	1.55
☐ 128 Ebba St.Claire	10.00	4.50	1.25
☐ 129 Hank Bauer	22.00	10.00	2.80
☐ 130 Milt Bolling	15.00	6.75	1.90
☐ 131 Joe Astroth	15.00	6.75	1.90
☐ 132 Bob Feller	95.00	42.50	12.00
☐ 133 Duane Pillette	15.00	6.75	1.90
☐ 134 Luis Aloma	15.00	6.75	1.90
☐ 135 Johnny Pesky	18.00	8.00	2.30
☐ 136 Clyde Vollmer	15.00	6.75	1.90
☐ 137 Al Corwin	15.00	6.75	1.90
☐ 138 Gil Hodges	70.00	32.00	8.75
☐ 139 Preston Ward	15.00	6.75	1.90
☐ 140 Saul Rogovin	15.00	6.75	1.90
☐ 141 Joe Garagiola	50.00	23.00	6.25
☐ 142 Al Brazle	15.00	6.75	1.90
☐ 143 Willie Jones	15.00	6.75	1.90
☐ 144 Ernie Johnson	20.00	9.00	2.50
☐ 145 Billy Martin	70.00	32.00	8.75
☐ 146 Dick Gernert	15.00	6.75	1.90
☐ 147 Joe DeMaestri	15.00	6.75	1.90
☐ 148 Dale Mitchell	17.00	7.75	2.10
☐ 149 Bob Young	15.00	6.75	1.90
☐ 150 Cass Michaels	15.00	6.75	1.90
☐ 151 Pat Mullin	15.00	6.75	1.90
☐ 152 Mickey Vernon	17.00	7.75	2.10
☐ 153 Whitey Lockman	17.00	7.75	2.10
☐ 154 Don Newcombe	25.00	11.50	3.10
☐ 155 Frank Thomas	20.00	9.00	2.50
☐ 156 Rocky Bridges	15.00	6.75	1.90
☐ 157 Turk Lown	15.00	6.75	1.90
☐ 158 Stu Miller	17.00	7.75	2.10
☐ 159 Johnny Lindell	15.00	6.75	1.90
☐ 160 Danny O'Connell	15.00	6.75	1.90
☐ 161 Yogi Berra	175.00	80.00	22.00
☐ 162 Ted Lepcio	15.00	6.75	1.90
☐ 163A Dave Philley ERR (No mention of trade on back)	20.00	9.00	2.50
☐ 163B Dave Philley COR (Traded to Cleveland)	30.00	13.50	3.80
☐ 164 Early Wynn	50.00	23.00	6.25
☐ 165 Johnny Groth	15.00	6.75	1.90
☐ 166 Sandy Consuegra	15.00	6.75	1.90
☐ 167 Billy Hoeft	15.00	6.75	1.90

☐ 168 Ed Fitzgerald	15.00	6.75	1.90
☐ 169 Larry Jansen	17.00	7.75	2.10
☐ 170 Duke Snider	175.00	80.00	22.00
☐ 171 Carlos Bernier	15.00	6.75	1.90
☐ 172 Andy Seminick	15.00	6.75	1.90
☐ 173 Dee Fondy	15.00	6.75	1.90
☐ 174 Pete Castiglione	15.00	6.75	1.90
☐ 175 Mel Clark	15.00	6.75	1.90
☐ 176 Vern Bickford	15.00	6.75	1.90
☐ 177 Whitey Ford	110.00	50.00	14.00
☐ 178 Del Wilber	15.00	6.75	1.90
☐ 179 Morrie Martin	15.00	6.75	1.90
☐ 180 Joe Tipton	15.00	6.75	1.90
☐ 181 Les Moss	15.00	6.75	1.90
☐ 182 Sherm Lollar	17.00	7.75	2.10
☐ 183 Matt Batts	15.00	6.75	1.90
☐ 184 Mickey Grasso	15.00	6.75	1.90
☐ 185 Daryl Spencer	15.00	6.75	1.90
☐ 186 Russ Meyer	15.00	6.75	1.90
☐ 187 Vernon Law	17.00	7.75	2.10
☐ 188 Frank Smith	15.00	6.75	1.90
☐ 189 Randy Jackson	15.00	6.75	1.90
☐ 190 Joe Presko	15.00	6.75	1.90
☐ 191 Karl Drews	15.00	6.75	1.90
☐ 192 Lou Burdette	20.00	9.00	2.50
☐ 193 Eddie Robinson	15.00	6.75	1.90
☐ 194 Sid Hudson	15.00	6.75	1.90
☐ 195 Bob Cain	15.00	6.75	1.90
☐ 196 Bob Lemon	40.00	18.00	5.00
☐ 197 Lou Kretlow	15.00	6.75	1.90
☐ 198 Virgil Trucks	17.00	7.75	2.10
☐ 199 Steve Gromek	15.00	6.75	1.90
☐ 200 Conrado Marrero	15.00	6.75	1.90
☐ 201 Bobby Thomson	20.00	9.00	2.50
☐ 202 George Shuba	17.00	7.75	2.10
☐ 203 Vic Janowicz	20.00	9.00	2.50
☐ 204 Jack Collum	15.00	6.75	1.90
☐ 205 Hal Jeffcoat	15.00	6.75	1.90
☐ 206 Steve Bilko	15.00	6.75	1.90
☐ 207 Stan Lopata	15.00	6.75	1.90
☐ 208 Johnny Antonelli	20.00	9.00	2.50
☐ 209 Gene Woodling	20.00	9.00	2.50
☐ 210 Jim Piersall	20.00	9.00	2.50
☐ 211 Al Robertson	15.00	6.75	1.90
☐ 212 Owen Friend	15.00	6.75	1.90
☐ 213 Dick Littlefield	15.00	6.75	1.90
☐ 214 Ferris Fain	17.00	7.75	2.10
☐ 215 Johnny Bucha	15.00	6.75	1.90
☐ 216 Jerry Snyder	15.00	6.75	1.90
☐ 217 Hank Thompson	17.00	7.75	2.10
☐ 218 Preacher Roe	20.00	9.00	2.50
☐ 219 Hal Rice	15.00	6.75	1.90
☐ 220 Hobie Landrith	15.00	6.75	1.90
☐ 221 Frank Baumholtz	15.00	6.75	1.90
☐ 222 Memo Luna	15.00	6.75	1.90
☐ 223 Steve Ridzik	15.00	6.75	1.90
☐ 224 Bill Bruton	45.00	9.00	2.70

1955 Bowman

The cards in this 320-card set measure approximately 2 1/2" by 3 3/4". The Bowman set of 1955 is known as the "TV set" because each player photograph is cleverly shown within a television set design. The set contains umpire cards, some transposed pictures (e.g., Johnsons and Bollings), an incorrect spelling for Harvey Kuenn, and a traded line for Palica (all of which are noted in the checklist below). Some three-card advertising strips exist, the backs of these panels contain advertising for Bowman products. Advertising panels seen include Nellie Fox/Carl Furillo/Carl Erskine, Hank Aaron/Johnny Logan/Eddie Miksis, and a panel including Early Wynn and Pee Wee Reese. The notable Rookie Cards in this set are Elston Howard and Don Zimmer.

	NRMT	VG-E	GOOD
COMPLETE SET (320)	5300.00	2400.00	650.00
COMMON PLAYER (1-96)	8.00	3.60	1.00
COMMON PLAYER (97-224)	6.50	2.90	.80
COMMON PLAYER (225-320)	15.00	6.75	1.90
☐ 1 Hoyt Wilhelm	100.00	20.00	6.00
☐ 2 Alvin Dark	12.00	5.50	1.50
☐ 3 Joe Coleman	8.00	3.60	1.00
☐ 4 Eddie Waitkus	8.00	3.60	1.00
☐ 5 Jim Robertson	8.00	3.60	1.00
☐ 6 Pete Suder	8.00	3.60	1.00
☐ 7 Gene Baker	8.00	3.60	1.00
☐ 8 Warren Hacker	8.00	3.60	1.00
☐ 9 Gil McDougald	18.00	8.00	2.30
☐ 10 Phil Rizzuto	55.00	25.00	7.00
☐ 11 Bill Bruton	9.00	4.00	1.15
☐ 12 Andy Pafko	9.00	4.00	1.15
☐ 13 Clyde Vollmer	8.00	3.60	1.00
☐ 14 Gus Keriazakos	8.00	3.60	1.00
☐ 15 Frank Sullivan	8.00	3.60	1.00
☐ 16 Jim Piersall	11.00	4.90	1.40
☐ 17 Del Ennis	9.00	4.00	1.15
☐ 18 Stan Lopata	8.00	3.60	1.00
☐ 19 Bobby Avila	9.00	4.00	1.15
☐ 20 Al Smith	9.00	4.00	1.15
☐ 21 Don Hoak	10.00	4.50	1.25
☐ 22 Roy Campanella	110.00	50.00	14.00
☐ 23 Al Kaline	160.00	70.00	20.00
☐ 24 Al Aber	8.00	3.60	1.00
☐ 25 Minnie Minoso	18.00	8.00	2.30
☐ 26 Virgil Trucks	9.00	4.00	1.15
☐ 27 Preston Ward	8.00	3.60	1.00
☐ 28 Dick Cole	8.00	3.60	1.00
☐ 29 Red Schoendienst	28.00	12.50	3.50
☐ 30 Bill Sarni	8.00	3.60	1.00
☐ 31 Johnny Temple	12.00	5.50	1.50
☐ 32 Wally Post	10.00	4.50	1.25
☐ 33 Nellie Fox	22.50	10.00	2.80
☐ 34 Clint Courtney	8.00	3.60	1.00
☐ 35 Bill Tuttle	8.00	3.60	1.00
☐ 36 Wayne Belardi	8.00	3.60	1.00
☐ 37 Pee Wee Reese	75.00	34.00	9.50
☐ 38 Early Wynn	28.00	12.50	3.50
☐ 39 Bob Darnell	8.00	3.60	1.00
☐ 40 Vic Wertz	9.00	4.00	1.15
☐ 41 Mel Clark	8.00	3.60	1.00
☐ 42 Bob Greenwood	8.00	3.60	1.00
☐ 43 Bob Buhl	9.00	4.00	1.15
☐ 44 Danny O'Connell	8.00	3.60	1.00
☐ 45 Tom Umphlett	8.00	3.60	1.00
☐ 46 Mickey Vernon	9.00	4.00	1.15
☐ 47 Sammy White	8.00	3.60	1.00
☐ 48A Milt Bolling ERR (Name on back is Frank Bolling)	10.00	4.50	1.25
☐ 48B Milt Bolling COR	30.00	13.50	3.80
☐ 49 Jim Greengrass	8.00	3.60	1.00
☐ 50 Hobie Landrith	8.00	3.60	1.00
☐ 51 Elvin Tappe	8.00	3.60	1.00
☐ 52 Hal Rice	8.00	3.60	1.00
☐ 53 Alex Kellner	8.00	3.60	1.00
☐ 54 Don Bollweg	8.00	3.60	1.00
☐ 55 Cal Abrams	8.00	3.60	1.00
☐ 56 Billy Cox	9.00	4.00	1.15
☐ 57 Bob Friend	9.00	4.00	1.15
☐ 58 Frank Thomas	9.00	4.00	1.15
☐ 59 Whitey Ford	75.00	34.00	9.50
☐ 60 Enos Slaughter	30.00	13.50	3.80
☐ 61 Paul LaPalme	8.00	3.60	1.00
☐ 62 Royce Lint	8.00	3.60	1.00
☐ 63 Irv Noren	9.00	4.00	1.15
☐ 64 Curt Simmons	9.00	4.00	1.15
☐ 65 Don Zimmer	30.00	13.50	3.80
☐ 66 George Shuba	9.00	4.00	1.15
☐ 67 Don Larsen	20.00	9.00	2.50
☐ 68 Elston Howard	70.00	32.00	8.75
☐ 69 Billy Hunter	8.00	3.60	1.00
☐ 70 Lou Burdette	11.00	4.90	1.40
☐ 71 Dave Jolly	8.00	3.60	1.00
☐ 72 Chet Nichols	8.00	3.60	1.00
☐ 73 Eddie Yost	9.00	4.00	1.15
☐ 74 Jerry Snyder	8.00	3.60	1.00

☐ 75 Brooks Lawrence	10.00	4.50	1.25
☐ 76 Tom Poholsky	8.00	3.60	1.00
☐ 77 Jim McDonald	8.00	3.60	1.00
☐ 78 Gil Coan	8.00	3.60	1.00
☐ 79 Willie Miranda	8.00	3.60	1.00
☐ 80 Lou Limmer	8.00	3.60	1.00
☐ 81 Bobby Morgan	8.00	3.60	1.00
☐ 82 Lee Walls	8.00	3.60	1.00
☐ 83 Max Surkont	8.00	3.60	1.00
☐ 84 George Freese	8.00	3.60	1.00
☐ 85 Cass Michaels	8.00	3.60	1.00
☐ 86 Ted Gray	8.00	3.60	1.00
☐ 87 Randy Jackson	8.00	3.60	1.00
☐ 88 Steve Bilko	8.00	3.60	1.00
☐ 89 Lou Boudreau MG	25.00	11.50	3.10
☐ 90 Art Ditmar	8.00	3.60	1.00
☐ 91 Dick Marlowe	8.00	3.60	1.00
☐ 92 George Zuverink	8.00	3.60	1.00
☐ 93 Andy Seminick	8.00	3.60	1.00
☐ 94 Hank Thompson	9.00	4.00	1.15
☐ 95 Sal Maglie	12.00	5.50	1.50
☐ 96 Ray Narleski	11.00	4.90	1.40
☐ 97 Johnny Podres	18.00	8.00	2.30
☐ 98 Jim Gilliam	18.00	8.00	2.30
☐ 99 Jerry Coleman	7.50	3.40	.95
☐ 100 Tom Morgan	6.50	2.90	.80
☐ 101A Don Johnson ERR (Photo actually Ernie Johnson)	10.00	4.50	1.25
☐ 101B Don Johnson COR	30.00	13.50	3.80
☐ 102 Bobby Thomson	12.00	5.50	1.50
☐ 103 Eddie Mathews	55.00	25.00	7.00
☐ 104 Bob Porterfield	6.50	2.90	.80
☐ 105 Johnny Schmitz	6.50	2.90	.80
☐ 106 Del Rice	6.50	2.90	.80
☐ 107 Solly Hemus	6.50	2.90	.80
☐ 108 Lou Kretlow	6.50	2.90	.80
☐ 109 Vern Stephens	7.50	3.40	.95
☐ 110 Bob Miller	6.50	2.90	.80
☐ 111 Steve Ridzik	6.50	2.90	.80
☐ 112 Granny Hamner	6.50	2.90	.80
☐ 113 Bob Hall	6.50	2.90	.80
☐ 114 Vic Janowicz	10.00	4.50	1.25
☐ 115 Roger Bowman	6.50	2.90	.80
☐ 116 Sandy Consuegra	6.50	2.90	.80
☐ 117 Johnny Groth	6.50	2.90	.80
☐ 118 Bobby Adams	6.50	2.90	.80
☐ 119 Joe Astroth	6.50	2.90	.80
☐ 120 Ed Burtschy	6.50	2.90	.80
☐ 121 Rufus Crawford	6.50	2.90	.80
☐ 122 Al Corwin	6.50	2.90	.80
☐ 123 Marv Grissom	6.50	2.90	.80
☐ 124 Johnny Antonelli	7.50	3.40	.95
☐ 125 Paul Giel	7.50	3.40	.95
☐ 126 Billy Goodman	7.50	3.40	.95
☐ 127 Hank Majeski	6.50	2.90	.80
☐ 128 Mike Garcia	7.50	3.40	.95
☐ 129 Hal Naragon	6.50	2.90	.80
☐ 130 Richie Ashburn	25.00	11.50	3.10
☐ 131 Wiliard Marshall	6.50	2.90	.80
☐ 132A Harvey Kueen ERR (Sic, Kuenn)	12.50	5.75	1.55
☐ 132B Harvey Kuenn COR	30.00	13.50	3.80
☐ 133 Charles King	6.50	2.90	.80
☐ 134 Bob Feller	65.00	29.00	8.25
☐ 135 Lloyd Merriman	6.50	2.90	.80
☐ 136 Rocky Bridges	6.50	2.90	.80
☐ 137 Bob Talbot	6.50	2.90	.80
☐ 138 Davey Williams	6.50	2.90	.80
☐ 139 Shantz Brothers (Wilmer and Bobby)	10.00	4.50	1.25
☐ 140 Bobby Shantz	7.50	3.40	.95
☐ 141 Wes Westrum	7.50	3.40	.95
☐ 142 Rudy Regalado	6.50	2.90	.80
☐ 143 Don Newcombe	18.00	8.00	2.30
☐ 144 Art Houtteman	6.50	2.90	.80
☐ 145 Bob Nieman	6.50	2.90	.80
☐ 146 Don Liddle	6.50	2.90	.80
☐ 147 Sam Mele	6.50	2.90	.80
☐ 148 Bob Chakales	6.50	2.90	.80
☐ 149 Cloyd Boyer	6.50	2.90	.80
☐ 150 Billy Klaus	6.50	2.90	.80
☐ 151 Jim Brideweser	6.50	2.90	.80
☐ 152 Johnny Klippstein	6.50	2.90	.80
☐ 153 Eddie Robinson	6.50	2.90	.80
☐ 154 Frank Lary	12.50	5.75	1.55
☐ 155 Gerry Staley	6.50	2.90	.80
☐ 156 Jim Hughes	6.50	2.90	.80
☐ 157A Ernie Johnson ERR (Photo actually Don Johnson)	10.00	4.50	1.25
☐ 157B Ernie Johnson COR	30.00	13.50	3.80
☐ 158 Gil Hodges	40.00	18.00	5.00
☐ 159 Harry Byrd	6.50	2.90	.80
☐ 160 Bill Skowron	25.00	11.50	3.10
☐ 161 Matt Batts	6.50	2.90	.80
☐ 162 Charlie Maxwell	7.50	3.40	.95
☐ 163 Sid Gordon	6.50	2.90	.80
☐ 164 Toby Atwell	6.50	2.90	.80
☐ 165 Maurice McDermott	6.50	2.90	.80
☐ 166 Jim Busby	6.50	2.90	.80
☐ 167 Bob Grim	12.00	5.50	1.50
☐ 168 Yogi Berra	110.00	50.00	14.00
☐ 169 Carl Furillo	18.00	8.00	2.30
☐ 170 Carl Erskine	18.00	8.00	2.30
☐ 171 Robin Roberts	30.00	13.50	3.80
☐ 172 Willie Jones	6.50	2.90	.80
☐ 173 Chico Carrasquel	6.50	2.90	.80
☐ 174 Sherm Lollar	7.50	3.40	.95
☐ 175 Wilmer Shantz	6.50	2.90	.80
☐ 176 Joe DeMaestri	6.50	2.90	.80
☐ 177 Willard Nixon	6.50	2.90	.80
☐ 178 Tom Brewer	6.50	2.90	.80
☐ 179 Hank Aaron	250.00	115.00	31.00
☐ 180 Johnny Logan	7.50	3.40	.95
☐ 181 Eddie Miksis	6.50	2.90	.80
☐ 182 Bob Rush	6.50	2.90	.80
☐ 183 Ray Katt	6.50	2.90	.80
☐ 184 Willie Mays	250.00	115.00	31.00
☐ 185 Vic Raschi	10.00	4.50	1.25
☐ 186 Alex Grammas	6.50	2.90	.80
☐ 187 Fred Hatfield	6.50	2.90	.80
☐ 188 Ned Garver	6.50	2.90	.80
☐ 189 Jack Collum	6.50	2.90	.80
☐ 190 Fred Baczewski	6.50	2.90	.80
☐ 191 Bob Lemon	27.00	12.00	3.40
☐ 192 George Strickland	6.50	2.90	.80
☐ 193 Howie Judson	6.50	2.90	.80
☐ 194 Joe Nuxhall	7.50	3.40	.95
☐ 195A Erv Palica (Without trade)	7.50	3.40	.95
☐ 195B Erv Palica (With trade)	30.00	13.50	3.80
☐ 196 Russ Meyer	6.50	2.90	.80
☐ 197 Ralph Kiner	30.00	13.50	3.80
☐ 198 Dave Pope	6.50	2.90	.80
☐ 199 Vernon Law	7.50	3.40	.95
☐ 200 Dick Littlefield	6.50	2.90	.80
☐ 201 Allie Reynolds	17.00	7.75	2.10
☐ 202 Mickey Mantle	575.00	250.00	70.00
☐ 203 Steve Gromek	6.50	2.90	.80
☐ 204A Frank Bolling ERR (Name on back is Milt Bolling)	10.00	4.50	1.25
☐ 204B Frank Bolling COR	30.00	13.50	3.80
☐ 205 Rip Repulski	6.50	2.90	.80
☐ 206 Ralph Beard	6.50	2.90	.80
☐ 207 Frank Shea	6.50	2.90	.80
☐ 208 Ed Fitzgerald	6.50	2.90	.80
☐ 209 Smoky Burgess	7.50	3.40	.95
☐ 210 Earl Torgeson	6.50	2.90	.80
☐ 211 Sonny Dixon	6.50	2.90	.80
☐ 212 Jack Dittmer	6.50	2.90	.80
☐ 213 George Kell	22.00	10.00	2.80
☐ 214 Billy Pierce	10.00	4.50	1.25
☐ 215 Bob Kuzava	6.50	2.90	.80
☐ 216 Preacher Roe	12.00	5.50	1.50
☐ 217 Del Crandall	7.50	3.40	.95
☐ 218 Joe Adcock	7.50	3.40	.95
☐ 219 Whitey Lockman	7.50	3.40	.95
☐ 220 Jim Hearn	6.50	2.90	.80
☐ 221 Hector Brown	6.50	2.90	.80
☐ 222 Russ Kemmerer	6.50	2.90	.80
☐ 223 Hal Jeffcoat	6.50	2.90	.80
☐ 224 Dee Fondy	6.50	2.90	.80
☐ 225 Paul Richards MG	17.50	8.00	2.20
☐ 226 Bill McKinley UMP	25.00	11.50	3.10
☐ 227 Frank Baumholtz	15.00	6.75	1.90
☐ 228 John Phillips	15.00	6.75	1.90
☐ 229 Jim Brosnan	20.00	9.00	2.50
☐ 230 Al Brazle	15.00	6.75	1.90
☐ 231 Jim Konstanty	20.00	9.00	2.50
☐ 232 Birdie Tebbetts MG	17.50	8.00	2.20
☐ 233 Bill Serena	15.00	6.75	1.90
☐ 234 Dick Bartell CO	20.00	9.00	2.50
☐ 235 Joe Paparella UMP	25.00	11.50	3.10
☐ 236 Murry Dickson	15.00	6.75	1.90
☐ 237 Johnny Wyrostek	15.00	6.75	1.90
☐ 238 Eddie Stanky MG	20.00	9.00	2.50
☐ 239 Edwin Rommel UMP	25.00	11.50	3.10
☐ 240 Billy Loes	17.50	8.00	2.20
☐ 241 Johnny Pesky CO	20.00	9.00	2.50
☐ 242 Ernie Banks	400.00	180.00	50.00
☐ 243 Gus Bell	17.50	8.00	2.20
☐ 244 Duane Pillette	15.00	6.75	1.90
☐ 245 Bill Miller	15.00	6.75	1.90

□ 246 Hank Bauer	40.00	18.00	5.00
□ 247 Dutch Leonard CO	15.00	6.75	1.90
□ 248 Harry Dorish	15.00	6.75	1.90
□ 249 Billy Gardner	17.50	8.00	2.20
□ 250 Larry Napp UMP	25.00	11.50	3.10
□ 251 Stan Jok	15.00	6.75	1.90
□ 252 Roy Smalley	15.00	6.75	1.90
□ 253 Jim Wilson	15.00	6.75	1.90
□ 254 Bennett Flowers	15.00	6.75	1.90
□ 255 Pete Runnels	17.50	8.00	2.20
□ 256 Owen Friend	15.00	6.75	1.90
□ 257 Tom Alston	15.00	6.75	1.90
□ 258 John Stevens UMP	25.00	11.50	3.10
□ 259 Don Mossi	25.00	11.50	3.10
□ 260 Edwin Hurley UMP	25.00	11.50	3.10
□ 261 Walt Moryn	15.00	6.75	1.90
□ 262 Jim Lemon	20.00	9.00	2.50
□ 263 Eddie Joost	15.00	6.75	1.90
□ 264 Bill Henry	15.00	6.75	1.90
□ 265 Albert Barlick UMP	85.00	38.00	10.50
□ 266 Mike Fornieles	15.00	6.75	1.90
□ 267 Jim Honochick UMP	80.00	36.00	10.00
□ 268 Roy Lee Hawes	15.00	6.75	1.90
□ 269 Joe Amalfitano	20.00	9.00	2.50
□ 270 Chico Fernandez	15.00	6.75	1.90
□ 271 Bob Hooper	15.00	6.75	1.90
□ 272 John Flaherty UMP	25.00	11.50	3.10
□ 273 Bubba Church	15.00	6.75	1.90
□ 274 Jim Delsing	15.00	6.75	1.90
□ 275 William Grieve UMP	25.00	11.50	3.10
□ 276 Ike Delock	15.00	6.75	1.90
□ 277 Ed Runge UMP	30.00	13.50	3.80
□ 278 Charlie Neal	30.00	13.50	3.80
□ 279 Hank Soar UMP	25.00	11.50	3.10
□ 280 Clyde McCullough	15.00	6.75	1.90
□ 281 Charles Berry UMP	25.00	11.50	3.10
□ 282 Phil Cavarretta	20.00	9.00	2.50
□ 283 Nestor Chylak UMP	25.00	11.50	3.10
□ 284 Bill Jackowski UMP	25.00	11.50	3.10
□ 285 Walt Dropo	17.50	8.00	2.20
□ 286 Frank Secory UMP	25.00	11.50	3.10
□ 287 Ron Mrozinski	15.00	6.75	1.90
□ 288 Dick Smith	15.00	6.75	1.90
□ 289 Arthur Gore UMP	25.00	11.50	3.10
□ 290 Hershell Freeman	15.00	6.75	1.90
□ 291 Frank Dascoli UMP	25.00	11.50	3.10
□ 292 Marv Blaylock	15.00	6.75	1.90
□ 293 Thomas Gorman UMP	30.00	13.50	3.80
□ 294 Wally Moses CO	17.50	8.00	2.20
□ 295 Lee Ballanfant UMP	25.00	11.50	3.10
□ 296 Bill Virdon	35.00	16.00	4.40
□ 297 Dusty Boggess UMP	25.00	11.50	3.10
□ 298 Charlie Grimm MG	20.00	9.00	2.50
□ 299 Lon Warneke UMP	30.00	13.50	3.80
□ 300 Tommy Byrne	15.00	6.75	1.90
□ 301 William Engeln UMP	25.00	11.50	3.10
□ 302 Frank Malzone	30.00	13.50	3.80
□ 303 Jocko Conlan UMP	100.00	45.00	12.50
□ 304 Harry Chiti	15.00	6.75	1.90
□ 305 Frank Umont UMP	25.00	11.50	3.10
□ 306 Bob Cerv	25.00	11.50	3.10
□ 307 Babe Pinelli UMP	30.00	13.50	3.80
□ 308 Al Lopez MG	50.00	23.00	6.25
□ 309 Hal Dixon UMP	25.00	11.50	3.10
□ 310 Ken Lehman	15.00	6.75	1.90
□ 311 Lawrence Goetz UMP	25.00	11.50	3.10
□ 312 Bill Wight	15.00	6.75	1.90
□ 313 Augie Donatelli UMP	40.00	18.00	5.00
□ 314 Dale Mitchell	17.50	8.00	2.20
□ 315 Cal Hubbard UMP	100.00	45.00	12.50
□ 316 Marion Fricano	15.00	6.75	1.90
□ 317 William Summers UMP	30.00	13.50	3.80
□ 318 Sid Hudson	15.00	6.75	1.90
□ 319 Al Schroll	15.00	6.75	1.90
□ 320 George Susce Jr.	50.00	10.00	3.00

1989 Bowman

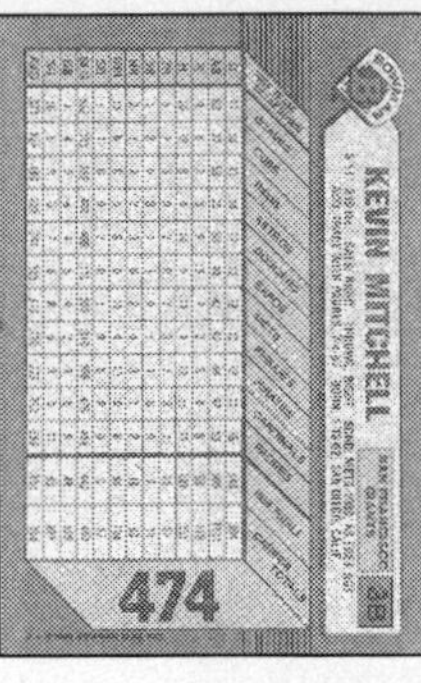

The 1989 Bowman set, which was actually produced by Topps, contains 484 cards measuring approximately 2 1/2" by 3 3/4". The fronts have white-bordered color photos with facsimile autographs and small Bowman logos. The backs are scarlet and feature charts detailing 1988 player performances vs. each team. The cards are checklisted below alphabetically according to teams in the AL and NL as follows: Baltimore Orioles (1-18), Boston Red Sox (19-36), California Angels (37-54), Chicago White Sox (55-72), Cleveland Indians (73-91), Detroit Tigers (92-109), Kansas City Royals (110-128), Milwaukee Brewers (129-146), Minnesota Twins (147-164), New York Yankees (165-183), Oakland Athletics (184-202), Seattle Mariners (203-220), Texas Rangers (221-238), Toronto Blue Jays (239-257), Atlanta Braves (262-279), Chicago Cubs (280-298), Cincinnati Reds (299-316), Houston Astros (317-334), Los Angeles Dodgers (335-352), Montreal Expos (353-370), New York Mets (371-389), Philadelphia Phillies (390-408), Pittsburgh Pirates (409-426), St. Louis Cardinals (427-444), San Diego Padres (445-462), and San Francisco Giants (463-480). Cards 258-261 form a father\son subset. The player selection is concentrated on prospects and "name" players. The cards were released in midseason 1989 in wax, rack, and cello pack formats. The key Rookie Cards in this set are Jim Abbott, Steve Avery, Andy Benes, Royce Clayton, Ken Griffey Jr., Tino Martinez, Gary Sheffield, John Smoltz, Robin Ventura, and Jerome Walton. Topps also produced a limited Bowman "Tiffany" set with supposedly only 6,000 sets being produced. This Tiffany version is valued approximately from five to ten times the values listed below.

	MT	EX-MT	VG
COMPLETE SET (484)	15.00	6.75	1.90
COMPLETE FACT.SET (484)	15.00	6.75	1.90
COMMON PLAYER (1-484)	.04	.02	.01
□ 1 Oswald Peraza	.04	.02	.01
□ 2 Brian Holton	.04	.02	.01
□ 3 Jose Bautista	.04	.02	.01
□ 4 Pete Harnisch	.15	.07	.02
□ 5 Dave Schmidt	.04	.02	.01
□ 6 Gregg Olson	.40	.18	.05
□ 7 Jeff Ballard	.04	.02	.01
□ 8 Bob Melvin	.04	.02	.01
□ 9 Cal Ripken	.50	.23	.06
□ 10 Randy Milligan	.04	.02	.01
□ 11 Juan Bell	.10	.05	.01
□ 12 Billy Ripken	.04	.02	.01
□ 13 Jim Traber	.04	.02	.01
□ 14 Pete Stanicek	.04	.02	.01
□ 15 Steve Finley	.35	.16	.04
□ 16 Larry Sheets	.04	.02	.01
□ 17 Phil Bradley	.04	.02	.01
□ 18 Brady Anderson	.60	.25	.08
□ 19 Lee Smith	.07	.03	.01
□ 20 Tom Fischer	.04	.02	.01
□ 21 Mike Boddicker	.04	.02	.01
□ 22 Rob Murphy	.04	.02	.01
□ 23 Wes Gardner	.04	.02	.01
□ 24 John Dopson	.04	.02	.01
□ 25 Bob Stanley	.04	.02	.01
□ 26 Roger Clemens	.40	.18	.05
□ 27 Rich Gedman	.04	.02	.01
□ 28 Marty Barrett	.04	.02	.01
□ 29 Luis Rivera	.04	.02	.01
□ 30 Jody Reed	.04	.02	.01
□ 31 Nick Esasky	.04	.02	.01
□ 32 Wade Boggs	.25	.11	.03
□ 33 Jim Rice	.07	.03	.01
□ 34 Mike Greenwell	.07	.03	.01
□ 35 Dwight Evans	.07	.03	.01

☐ 36 Ellis Burks	.07	.03	.01
☐ 37 Chuck Finley	.07	.03	.01
☐ 38 Kirk McCaskill	.04	.02	.01
☐ 39 Jim Abbott	1.00	.45	.13
☐ 40 Bryan Harvey	.25	.11	.03
☐ 41 Bert Blyleven	.07	.03	.01
☐ 42 Mike Witt	.04	.02	.01
☐ 43 Bob McClure	.04	.02	.01
☐ 44 Bill Schroeder	.04	.02	.01
☐ 45 Lance Parrish	.07	.03	.01
☐ 46 Dick Schofield	.04	.02	.01
☐ 47 Wally Joyner	.08	.04	.01
☐ 48 Jack Howell	.04	.02	.01
☐ 49 Johnny Ray	.04	.02	.01
☐ 50 Chili Davis	.07	.03	.01
☐ 51 Tony Armas	.04	.02	.01
☐ 52 Claudell Washington	.04	.02	.01
☐ 53 Brian Downing	.04	.02	.01
☐ 54 Devon White	.07	.03	.01
☐ 55 Bobby Thigpen	.04	.02	.01
☐ 56 Bill Long	.04	.02	.01
☐ 57 Jerry Reuss	.04	.02	.01
☐ 58 Shawn Hillegas	.04	.02	.01
☐ 59 Melido Perez	.12	.05	.02
☐ 60 Jeff Bittiger	.04	.02	.01
☐ 61 Jack McDowell	.25	.11	.03
☐ 62 Carlton Fisk	.12	.05	.02
☐ 63 Steve Lyons	.04	.02	.01
☐ 64 Ozzie Guillen	.04	.02	.01
☐ 65 Robin Ventura	1.00	.45	.13
☐ 66 Fred Manrique	.04	.02	.01
☐ 67 Dan Pasqua	.04	.02	.01
☐ 68 Ivan Calderon	.04	.02	.01
☐ 69 Ron Kittle	.04	.02	.01
☐ 70 Daryl Boston	.04	.02	.01
☐ 71 Dave Gallagher	.04	.02	.01
☐ 72 Harold Baines	.07	.03	.01
☐ 73 Charles Nagy	.60	.25	.08
☐ 74 John Farrell	.04	.02	.01
☐ 75 Kevin Wickander	.04	.02	.01
☐ 76 Greg Swindell	.07	.03	.01
☐ 77 Mike Walker	.04	.02	.01
☐ 78 Doug Jones	.07	.03	.01
☐ 79 Rich Yett	.04	.02	.01
☐ 80 Tom Candiotti	.04	.02	.01
☐ 81 Jesse Orosco	.04	.02	.01
☐ 82 Bud Black	.04	.02	.01
☐ 83 Andy Allanson	.04	.02	.01
☐ 84 Pete O'Brien	.04	.02	.01
☐ 85 Jerry Browne	.04	.02	.01
☐ 86 Brook Jacoby	.04	.02	.01
☐ 87 Mark Lewis	.30	.14	.04
☐ 88 Luis Aguayo	.04	.02	.01
☐ 89 Cory Snyder	.04	.02	.01
☐ 90 Oddibe McDowell	.04	.02	.01
☐ 91 Joe Carter	.25	.11	.03
☐ 92 Frank Tanana	.04	.02	.01
☐ 93 Jack Morris	.10	.05	.01
☐ 94 Doyle Alexander	.04	.02	.01
☐ 95 Steve Searcy	.04	.02	.01
☐ 96 Randy Bockus	.04	.02	.01
☐ 97 Jeff M. Robinson	.04	.02	.01
☐ 98 Mike Henneman	.07	.03	.01
☐ 99 Paul Gibson	.04	.02	.01
☐ 100 Frank Williams	.04	.02	.01
☐ 101 Matt Nokes	.07	.03	.01
☐ 102 Rico Brogna UER (Misspelled Ricco on card back)	.20	.09	.03
☐ 103 Lou Whitaker	.07	.03	.01
☐ 104 Al Pedrique	.04	.02	.01
☐ 105 Alan Trammell	.07	.03	.01
☐ 106 Chris Brown	.04	.02	.01
☐ 107 Pat Sheridan	.04	.02	.01
☐ 108 Chet Lemon	.04	.02	.01
☐ 109 Keith Moreland	.04	.02	.01
☐ 110 Mel Stottlemyre Jr.	.07	.03	.01
☐ 111 Bret Saberhagen	.07	.03	.01
☐ 112 Floyd Bannister	.04	.02	.01
☐ 113 Jeff Montgomery	.07	.03	.01
☐ 114 Steve Farr	.04	.02	.01
☐ 115 Tom Gordon UER (Front shows autograph of Don Gordon)	.10	.05	.01
☐ 116 Charlie Leibrandt	.04	.02	.01
☐ 117 Mark Gubicza	.04	.02	.01
☐ 118 Mike Macfarlane	.15	.07	.02
☐ 119 Bob Boone	.07	.03	.01
☐ 120 Kurt Stillwell	.04	.02	.01
☐ 121 George Brett	.20	.09	.03
☐ 122 Frank White	.04	.02	.01
☐ 123 Kevin Seitzer	.07	.03	.01
☐ 124 Willie Wilson	.04	.02	.01
☐ 125 Pat Tabler	.04	.02	.01
☐ 126 Bo Jackson	.20	.09	.03
☐ 127 Hugh Walker	.10	.05	.01
☐ 128 Danny Tartabull	.10	.05	.01
☐ 129 Teddy Higuera	.04	.02	.01
☐ 130 Don August	.04	.02	.01
☐ 131 Juan Nieves	.04	.02	.01
☐ 132 Mike Birkbeck	.04	.02	.01
☐ 133 Dan Plesac	.04	.02	.01
☐ 134 Chris Bosio	.04	.02	.01
☐ 135 Bill Wegman	.04	.02	.01
☐ 136 Chuck Crim	.04	.02	.01
☐ 137 B.J. Surhoff	.04	.02	.01
☐ 138 Joey Meyer	.04	.02	.01
☐ 139 Dale Sveum	.04	.02	.01
☐ 140 Paul Molitor	.10	.05	.01
☐ 141 Jim Gantner	.04	.02	.01
☐ 142 Gary Sheffield	2.00	.90	.25
☐ 143 Greg Brock	.04	.02	.01
☐ 144 Robin Yount	.20	.09	.03
☐ 145 Glenn Braggs	.04	.02	.01
☐ 146 Rob Deer	.07	.03	.01
☐ 147 Fred Toliver	.04	.02	.01
☐ 148 Jeff Reardon	.07	.03	.01
☐ 149 Allan Anderson	.04	.02	.01
☐ 150 Frank Viola	.07	.03	.01
☐ 151 Shane Rawley	.04	.02	.01
☐ 152 Juan Berenguer	.04	.02	.01
☐ 153 Johnny Ard	.10	.05	.01
☐ 154 Tim Laudner	.04	.02	.01
☐ 155 Brian Harper	.07	.03	.01
☐ 156 Al Newman	.04	.02	.01
☐ 157 Kent Hrbek	.07	.03	.01
☐ 158 Gary Gaetti	.04	.02	.01
☐ 159 Wally Backman	.04	.02	.01
☐ 160 Gene Larkin	.04	.02	.01
☐ 161 Greg Gagne	.04	.02	.01
☐ 162 Kirby Puckett	.40	.18	.05
☐ 163 Dan Gladden	.04	.02	.01
☐ 164 Randy Bush	.04	.02	.01
☐ 165 Dave LaPoint	.04	.02	.01
☐ 166 Andy Hawkins	.04	.02	.01
☐ 167 Dave Righetti	.04	.02	.01
☐ 168 Lance McCullers	.04	.02	.01
☐ 169 Jimmy Jones	.04	.02	.01
☐ 170 Al Leiter	.04	.02	.01
☐ 171 John Candelaria	.04	.02	.01
☐ 172 Don Slaught	.04	.02	.01
☐ 173 Jamie Quirk	.04	.02	.01
☐ 174 Rafael Santana	.04	.02	.01
☐ 175 Mike Pagliarulo	.04	.02	.01
☐ 176 Don Mattingly	.25	.11	.03
☐ 177 Ken Phelps	.04	.02	.01
☐ 178 Steve Sax	.07	.03	.01
☐ 179 Dave Winfield	.20	.09	.03
☐ 180 Stan Jefferson	.04	.02	.01
☐ 181 Rickey Henderson	.20	.09	.03
☐ 182 Bob Brower	.04	.02	.01
☐ 183 Roberto Kelly	.15	.07	.02
☐ 184 Curt Young	.04	.02	.01
☐ 185 Gene Nelson	.04	.02	.01
☐ 186 Bob Welch	.07	.03	.01
☐ 187 Rick Honeycutt	.04	.02	.01
☐ 188 Dave Stewart	.07	.03	.01
☐ 189 Mike Moore	.04	.02	.01
☐ 190 Dennis Eckersley	.12	.05	.02
☐ 191 Eric Plunk	.04	.02	.01
☐ 192 Storm Davis	.04	.02	.01
☐ 193 Terry Steinbach	.07	.03	.01
☐ 194 Ron Hassey	.04	.02	.01
☐ 195 Stan Royer	.20	.09	.03
☐ 196 Walt Weiss	.07	.03	.01
☐ 197 Mark McGwire	.35	.16	.04
☐ 198 Carney Lansford	.07	.03	.01
☐ 199 Glenn Hubbard	.04	.02	.01
☐ 200 Dave Henderson	.07	.03	.01
☐ 201 Jose Canseco	.40	.18	.05
☐ 202 Dave Parker	.07	.03	.01
☐ 203 Scott Bankhead	.04	.02	.01
☐ 204 Tom Niedenfuer	.04	.02	.01
☐ 205 Mark Langston	.07	.03	.01
☐ 206 Erik Hanson	.20	.09	.03
☐ 207 Mike Jackson	.04	.02	.01
☐ 208 Dave Valle	.04	.02	.01
☐ 209 Scott Bradley	.04	.02	.01
☐ 210 Harold Reynolds	.04	.02	.01
☐ 211 Tino Martinez	.30	.14	.04
☐ 212 Rich Renteria	.04	.02	.01
☐ 213 Rey Quinones	.04	.02	.01
☐ 214 Jim Presley	.04	.02	.01
☐ 215 Alvin Davis	.04	.02	.01
☐ 216 Edgar Martinez	.25	.11	.03
☐ 217 Darnell Coles	.04	.02	.01

☐ 218	Jeffrey Leonard	.04	.02	.01
☐ 219	Jay Buhner	.10	.05	.01
☐ 220	Ken Griffey Jr.	4.50	2.00	.55
☐ 221	Drew Hall	.04	.02	.01
☐ 222	Bobby Witt	.07	.03	.01
☐ 223	Jamie Moyer	.04	.02	.01
☐ 224	Charlie Hough	.04	.02	.01
☐ 225	Nolan Ryan	.60	.25	.08
☐ 226	Jeff Russell	.04	.02	.01
☐ 227	Jim Sundberg	.04	.02	.01
☐ 228	Julio Franco	.07	.03	.01
☐ 229	Buddy Bell	.07	.03	.01
☐ 230	Scott Fletcher	.04	.02	.01
☐ 231	Jeff Kunkel	.04	.02	.01
☐ 232	Steve Buechele	.04	.02	.01
☐ 233	Monty Fariss	.30	.14	.04
☐ 234	Rick Leach	.04	.02	.01
☐ 235	Ruben Sierra	.30	.14	.04
☐ 236	Cecil Espy	.04	.02	.01
☐ 237	Rafael Palmeiro	.15	.07	.02
☐ 238	Pete Incaviglia	.04	.02	.01
☐ 239	Dave Stieb	.07	.03	.01
☐ 240	Jeff Musselman	.04	.02	.01
☐ 241	Mike Flanagan	.04	.02	.01
☐ 242	Todd Stottlemyre	.10	.05	.01
☐ 243	Jimmy Key	.07	.03	.01
☐ 244	Tony Castillo	.04	.02	.01
☐ 245	Alex Sanchez	.04	.02	.01
☐ 246	Tom Henke	.07	.03	.01
☐ 247	John Cerutti	.04	.02	.01
☐ 248	Ernie Whitt	.04	.02	.01
☐ 249	Bob Brenly	.04	.02	.01
☐ 250	Rance Mulliniks	.04	.02	.01
☐ 251	Kelly Gruber	.07	.03	.01
☐ 252	Ed Sprague	.30	.14	.04
☐ 253	Fred McGriff	.20	.09	.03
☐ 254	Tony Fernandez	.07	.03	.01
☐ 255	Tom Lawless	.04	.02	.01
☐ 256	George Bell	.07	.03	.01
☐ 257	Jesse Barfield	.04	.02	.01
☐ 258	Roberto Alomar w/Dad	.30	.14	.04
☐ 259	Ken Griffey Jr./Sr.	1.00	.45	.13
☐ 260	Cal Ripken Jr./Sr.	.20	.09	.03
☐ 261	M.Stottlemyre Jr./Sr.	.05	.02	.01
☐ 262	Zane Smith	.04	.02	.01
☐ 263	Charlie Puleo	.04	.02	.01
☐ 264	Derek Lilliquist	.10	.05	.01
☐ 265	Paul Assenmacher	.04	.02	.01
☐ 266	John Smoltz	.60	.25	.08
☐ 267	Tom Glavine	.50	.23	.06
☐ 268	Steve Avery	1.00	.45	.13
☐ 269	Pete Smith	.07	.03	.01
☐ 270	Jody Davis	.04	.02	.01
☐ 271	Bruce Benedict	.04	.02	.01
☐ 272	Andres Thomas	.04	.02	.01
☐ 273	Gerald Perry	.04	.02	.01
☐ 274	Ron Gant	.40	.18	.05
☐ 275	Darrell Evans	.07	.03	.01
☐ 276	Dale Murphy	.10	.05	.01
☐ 277	Dion James	.04	.02	.01
☐ 278	Lonnie Smith	.04	.02	.01
☐ 279	Geronimo Berroa	.04	.02	.01
☐ 280	Steve Wilson	.04	.02	.01
☐ 281	Rick Sutcliffe	.07	.03	.01
☐ 282	Kevin Coffman	.04	.02	.01
☐ 283	Mitch Williams	.07	.03	.01
☐ 284	Greg Maddux	.30	.14	.04
☐ 285	Paul Kilgus	.04	.02	.01
☐ 286	Mike Harkey	.12	.05	.02
☐ 287	Lloyd McClendon	.04	.02	.01
☐ 288	Damon Berryhill	.04	.02	.01
☐ 289	Ty Griffin	.08	.04	.01
☐ 290	Ryne Sandberg	.40	.18	.05
☐ 291	Mark Grace	.30	.14	.04
☐ 292	Curt Wilkerson	.04	.02	.01
☐ 293	Vance Law	.04	.02	.01
☐ 294	Shawon Dunston	.07	.03	.01
☐ 295	Jerome Walton	.10	.05	.01
☐ 296	Mitch Webster	.04	.02	.01
☐ 297	Dwight Smith	.10	.05	.01
☐ 298	Andre Dawson	.15	.07	.02
☐ 299	Jeff Sellers	.04	.02	.01
☐ 300	Jose Rijo	.07	.03	.01
☐ 301	John Franco	.07	.03	.01
☐ 302	Rick Mahler	.04	.02	.01
☐ 303	Ron Robinson	.04	.02	.01
☐ 304	Danny Jackson	.04	.02	.01
☐ 305	Rob Dibble	.20	.09	.03
☐ 306	Tom Browning	.07	.03	.01
☐ 307	Bo Diaz	.04	.02	.01
☐ 308	Manny Trillo	.04	.02	.01
☐ 309	Chris Sabo	.25	.11	.03
☐ 310	Ron Oester	.04	.02	.01

☐ 311	Barry Larkin	.15	.07	.02
☐ 312	Todd Benzinger	.04	.02	.01
☐ 313	Paul O'Neill	.07	.03	.01
☐ 314	Kal Daniels	.07	.03	.01
☐ 315	Joel Youngblood	.04	.02	.01
☐ 316	Eric Davis	.10	.05	.01
☐ 317	Dave Smith	.04	.02	.01
☐ 318	Mark Portugal	.04	.02	.01
☐ 319	Brian Meyer	.04	.02	.01
☐ 320	Jim Deshaies	.04	.02	.01
☐ 321	Juan Agosto	.04	.02	.01
☐ 322	Mike Scott	.04	.02	.01
☐ 323	Rick Rhoden	.04	.02	.01
☐ 324	Jim Clancy	.04	.02	.01
☐ 325	Larry Andersen	.04	.02	.01
☐ 326	Alex Trevino	.04	.02	.01
☐ 327	Alan Ashby	.04	.02	.01
☐ 328	Craig Reynolds	.04	.02	.01
☐ 329	Bill Doran	.04	.02	.01
☐ 330	Rafael Ramirez	.04	.02	.01
☐ 331	Glenn Davis	.07	.03	.01
☐ 332	Willie Ansley	.12	.05	.02
☐ 333	Gerald Young	.04	.02	.01
☐ 334	Cameron Drew	.04	.02	.01
☐ 335	Jay Howell	.04	.02	.01
☐ 336	Tim Belcher	.07	.03	.01
☐ 337	Fernando Valenzuela	.07	.03	.01
☐ 338	Ricky Horton	.04	.02	.01
☐ 339	Tim Leary	.04	.02	.01
☐ 340	Bill Bene	.04	.02	.01
☐ 341	Orel Hershiser	.07	.03	.01
☐ 342	Mike Scioscia	.04	.02	.01
☐ 343	Rick Dempsey	.04	.02	.01
☐ 344	Willie Randolph	.07	.03	.01
☐ 345	Alfredo Griffin	.04	.02	.01
☐ 346	Eddie Murray	.12	.05	.02
☐ 347	Mickey Hatcher	.04	.02	.01
☐ 348	Mike Sharperson	.04	.02	.01
☐ 349	John Shelby	.04	.02	.01
☐ 350	Mike Marshall	.04	.02	.01
☐ 351	Kirk Gibson	.07	.03	.01
☐ 352	Mike Davis	.04	.02	.01
☐ 353	Bryn Smith	.04	.02	.01
☐ 354	Pascual Perez	.04	.02	.01
☐ 355	Kevin Gross	.04	.02	.01
☐ 356	Andy McGaffigan	.04	.02	.01
☐ 357	Brian Holman	.10	.05	.01
☐ 358	Dave Wainhouse	.10	.05	.01
☐ 359	Dennis Martinez	.07	.03	.01
☐ 360	Tim Burke	.04	.02	.01
☐ 361	Nelson Santovenia	.04	.02	.01
☐ 362	Tim Wallach	.07	.03	.01
☐ 363	Spike Owen	.04	.02	.01
☐ 364	Rex Hudler	.04	.02	.01
☐ 365	Andres Galarraga	.04	.02	.01
☐ 366	Otis Nixon	.07	.03	.01
☐ 367	Hubie Brooks	.04	.02	.01
☐ 368	Mike Aldrete	.04	.02	.01
☐ 369	Tim Raines	.07	.03	.01
☐ 370	Dave Martinez	.07	.03	.01
☐ 371	Bob Ojeda	.04	.02	.01
☐ 372	Ron Darling	.07	.03	.01
☐ 373	Wally Whitehurst	.10	.05	.01
☐ 374	Randy Myers	.07	.03	.01
☐ 375	David Cone	.15	.07	.02
☐ 376	Dwight Gooden	.12	.05	.02
☐ 377	Sid Fernandez	.07	.03	.01
☐ 378	Dave Proctor	.04	.02	.01
☐ 379	Gary Carter	.07	.03	.01
☐ 380	Keith Miller	.04	.02	.01
☐ 381	Gregg Jefferies	.20	.09	.03
☐ 382	Tim Teufel	.04	.02	.01
☐ 383	Kevin Elster	.04	.02	.01
☐ 384	Dave Magadan	.07	.03	.01
☐ 385	Keith Hernandez	.07	.03	.01
☐ 386	Mookie Wilson	.07	.03	.01
☐ 387	Darryl Strawberry	.25	.11	.03
☐ 388	Kevin McReynolds	.07	.03	.01
☐ 389	Mark Carreon	.04	.02	.01
☐ 390	Jeff Parrett	.04	.02	.01
☐ 391	Mike Maddux	.04	.02	.01
☐ 392	Don Carman	.04	.02	.01
☐ 393	Bruce Ruffin	.04	.02	.01
☐ 394	Ken Howell	.04	.02	.01
☐ 395	Steve Bedrosian	.04	.02	.01
☐ 396	Floyd Youmans	.04	.02	.01
☐ 397	Larry McWilliams	.04	.02	.01
☐ 398	Pat Combs	.10	.05	.01
☐ 399	Steve Lake	.04	.02	.01
☐ 400	Dickie Thon	.04	.02	.01
☐ 401	Ricky Jordan	.10	.05	.01
☐ 402	Mike Schmidt	.35	.16	.04
☐ 403	Tom Herr	.04	.02	.01

Card	Player			
☐	404 Chris James	.04	.02	.01
☐	405 Juan Samuel	.04	.02	.01
☐	406 Von Hayes	.04	.02	.01
☐	407 Ron Jones	.04	.02	.01
☐	408 Curt Ford	.04	.02	.01
☐	409 Bob Walk	.04	.02	.01
☐	410 Jeff D. Robinson	.04	.02	.01
☐	411 Jim Gott	.04	.02	.01
☐	412 Scott Medvin	.04	.02	.01
☐	413 John Smiley	.07	.03	.01
☐	414 Bob Kipper	.04	.02	.01
☐	415 Brian Fisher	.04	.02	.01
☐	416 Doug Drabek	.07	.03	.01
☐	417 Mike LaValliere	.04	.02	.01
☐	418 Ken Oberkfell	.04	.02	.01
☐	419 Sid Bream	.04	.02	.01
☐	420 Austin Manahan	.10	.05	.01
☐	421 Jose Lind	.04	.02	.01
☐	422 Bobby Bonilla	.15	.07	.02
☐	423 Glenn Wilson	.04	.02	.01
☐	424 Andy Van Slyke	.10	.05	.01
☐	425 Gary Redus	.04	.02	.01
☐	426 Barry Bonds	.40	.18	.05
☐	427 Don Heinkel	.04	.02	.01
☐	428 Ken Dayley	.04	.02	.01
☐	429 Todd Worrell	.07	.03	.01
☐	430 Brad DuVall	.04	.02	.01
☐	431 Jose DeLeon	.04	.02	.01
☐	432 Joe Magrane	.04	.02	.01
☐	433 John Ericks	.04	.02	.01
☐	434 Frank DiPino	.04	.02	.01
☐	435 Tony Pena	.04	.02	.01
☐	436 Ozzie Smith	.15	.07	.02
☐	437 Terry Pendleton	.12	.05	.02
☐	438 Jose Oquendo	.04	.02	.01
☐	439 Tim Jones	.04	.02	.01
☐	440 Pedro Guerrero	.07	.03	.01
☐	441 Milt Thompson	.04	.02	.01
☐	442 Willie McGee	.07	.03	.01
☐	443 Vince Coleman	.07	.03	.01
☐	444 Tom Brunansky	.07	.03	.01
☐	445 Walt Terrell	.04	.02	.01
☐	446 Eric Show	.04	.02	.01
☐	447 Mark Davis	.04	.02	.01
☐	448 Andy Benes	.50	.23	.06
☐	449 Ed Whitson	.04	.02	.01
☐	450 Dennis Rasmussen	.04	.02	.01
☐	451 Bruce Hurst	.07	.03	.01
☐	452 Pat Clements	.04	.02	.01
☐	453 Benito Santiago	.07	.03	.01
☐	454 Sandy Alomar Jr.	.25	.11	.03
☐	455 Garry Templeton	.04	.02	.01
☐	456 Jack Clark	.07	.03	.01
☐	457 Tim Flannery	.04	.02	.01
☐	458 Roberto Alomar	.75	.35	.09
☐	459 Carmelo Martinez	.04	.02	.01
☐	460 John Kruk	.07	.03	.01
☐	461 Tony Gwynn	.25	.11	.03
☐	462 Jerald Clark	.15	.07	.02
☐	463 Don Robinson	.04	.02	.01
☐	464 Craig Lefferts	.04	.02	.01
☐	465 Kelly Downs	.04	.02	.01
☐	466 Rick Reuschel	.04	.02	.01
☐	467 Scott Garrelts	.04	.02	.01
☐	468 Wil Tejada	.04	.02	.01
☐	469 Kirt Manwaring	.04	.02	.01
☐	470 Terry Kennedy	.04	.02	.01
☐	471 Jose Uribe	.04	.02	.01
☐	472 Royce Clayton	.40	.18	.05
☐	473 Robby Thompson	.04	.02	.01
☐	474 Kevin Mitchell	.10	.05	.01
☐	475 Ernie Riles	.04	.02	.01
☐	476 Will Clark	.40	.18	.05
☐	477 Donell Nixon	.04	.02	.01
☐	478 Candy Maldonado	.04	.02	.01
☐	479 Tracy Jones	.04	.02	.01
☐	480 Brett Butler	.07	.03	.01
☐	481 Checklist Card	.05	.01	.00
☐	482 Checklist Card	.05	.01	.00
☐	483 Checklist Card	.05	.01	.00
☐	484 Checklist Card	.05	.01	.00

1989 Bowman Reprint Inserts

The 1989 Bowman Reprint Inserts set contains 11 cards measuring approximately 2 1/2" by 3 3/4". The fronts depict reproduced actual size "classic" Bowman cards, which are

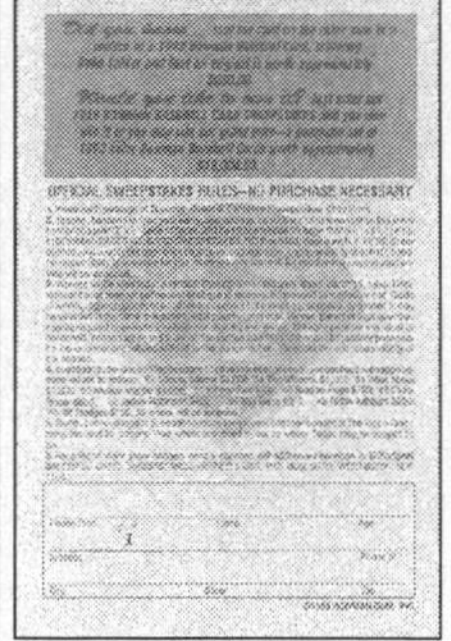

noted as reprints. The backs are devoted to a sweepstakes entry form. One of these reprint cards was included in each 1989 Bowman wax pack thus making these "reprints" quite easy to find. Since the cards are unnumbered, they are ordered below in alphabetical order by player's name and year within player.

	MT	EX-MT	VG
COMPLETE SET (11)	2.00	.90	.25
COMMON PLAYER (1-11)	.15	.07	.02
☐ 1 Richie Ashburn '49	.15	.07	.02
☐ 2 Yogi Berra '48	.25	.11	.03
☐ 3 Whitey Ford '51	.20	.09	.03
☐ 4 Gil Hodges '49	.15	.07	.02
☐ 5 Mickey Mantle '51	.50	.23	.06
☐ 6 Mickey Mantle '53	.40	.18	.05
☐ 7 Willie Mays '51	.30	.14	.04
☐ 8 Satchel Paige '49	.25	.11	.03
☐ 9 Jackie Robinson '50	.25	.11	.03
☐ 10 Duke Snider '49	.20	.09	.03
☐ 11 Ted Williams '54	.30	.14	.04

1990 Bowman

The 1990 Bowman set was issued in the standard card size of 2 1/2" by 3 1/2". This was the second issue by Topps using the Bowman name. The set consists of 528 cards, increased from 1989's edition of 484 cards. The cards feature a white border with the player's photo inside and the Bowman logo on top. Again, the Bowman cards were issued with the backs featuring team by team statistics. The card numbering is in team order with the teams themselves being ordered alphabetically within each league. The set numbering is as follows: Atlanta Braves (1-20), Chicago Cubs (21-40), Cincinnati Reds (41-60), Houston Astros (61-81), Los Angeles Dodgers (82-101), Montreal Expos (102-121), New York Mets (122-142), Philadelphia Phillies (143-162), Pittsburgh Pirates (163-182), St. Louis Cardinals (183-202), San Diego Padres (203-222), San Francisco

Giants (223-242), Baltimore Orioles (243-262), Boston Red Sox (263-282), California Angels (283-302), Chicago White Sox (303-322), Cleveland Indians (323-342), Detroit Tigers (343-362), Kansas City Royals (363-383), Milwaukee Brewers (384-404), Minnesota Twins (405-424), New York Yankees (425-444), Oakland A's (445-464), Seattle Mariners (465-484), Texas Rangers (485-503), and Toronto Blue Jays (504-524). The key Rookie Cards in this set are Carlos Baerga, Delino DeShields, Cal Eldred, Travis Fryman, Leo Gomez, Juan Gonzalez, Marquis Grissom, Chuck Knoblauch, Ray Lankford, Kevin Maas, Ben McDonald, Jose Offerman, John Olerud, Frank Thomas, Mo Vaughn, and Larry Walker. Topps also produced a Bowman Tiffany glossy set. Production of these Tiffany Bowmans was reported to be approximately 3,000 sets. These Tiffany versions are valued at approximately five to ten times the values listed below.

	MT	EX-MT	VG
COMPLETE SET (528)	15.00	6.75	1.90
COMPLETE FACT.SET (528)	15.00	6.75	1.90
COMMON PLAYER (1-528)	.04	.02	.01
☐ 1 Tommy Greene	.12	.05	.02
☐ 2 Tom Glavine	.25	.11	.03
☐ 3 Andy Nezelek	.04	.02	.01
☐ 4 Mike Stanton	.15	.07	.02
☐ 5 Rick Luecken	.04	.02	.01
☐ 6 Kent Mercker	.12	.05	.02
☐ 7 Derek Lilliquist	.04	.02	.01
☐ 8 Charlie Leibrandt	.04	.02	.01
☐ 9 Steve Avery	.60	.25	.08
☐ 10 John Smoltz	.25	.11	.03
☐ 11 Mark Lemke	.07	.03	.01
☐ 12 Lonnie Smith	.04	.02	.01
☐ 13 Oddibe McDowell	.04	.02	.01
☐ 14 Tyler Houston	.10	.05	.01
☐ 15 Jeff Blauser	.07	.03	.01
☐ 16 Ernie Whitt	.04	.02	.01
☐ 17 Alexis Infante	.04	.02	.01
☐ 18 Jim Presley	.04	.02	.01
☐ 19 Dale Murphy	.10	.05	.01
☐ 20 Nick Esasky	.04	.02	.01
☐ 21 Rick Sutcliffe	.07	.03	.01
☐ 22 Mike Bielecki	.04	.02	.01
☐ 23 Steve Wilson	.04	.02	.01
☐ 24 Kevin Blankenship	.04	.02	.01
☐ 25 Mitch Williams	.07	.03	.01
☐ 26 Dean Wilkins	.04	.02	.01
☐ 27 Greg Maddux	.20	.09	.03
☐ 28 Mike Harkey	.07	.03	.01
☐ 29 Mark Grace	.20	.09	.03
☐ 30 Ryne Sandberg	.35	.16	.04
☐ 31 Greg Smith	.10	.05	.01
☐ 32 Dwight Smith	.04	.02	.01
☐ 33 Damon Berryhill	.04	.02	.01
☐ 34 Earl Cunningham UER (Errant * by the word "in")	.12	.05	.02
☐ 35 Jerome Walton	.07	.03	.01
☐ 36 Lloyd McClendon	.04	.02	.01
☐ 37 Ty Griffin	.04	.02	.01
☐ 38 Shawon Dunston	.07	.03	.01
☐ 39 Andre Dawson	.12	.05	.02
☐ 40 Luis Salazar	.04	.02	.01
☐ 41 Tim Layana	.04	.02	.01
☐ 42 Rob Dibble	.07	.03	.01
☐ 43 Tom Browning	.04	.02	.01
☐ 44 Danny Jackson	.04	.02	.01
☐ 45 Jose Rijo	.07	.03	.01
☐ 46 Scott Scudder	.04	.02	.01
☐ 47 Randy Myers UER (Career ERA .274, should be 2.74)	.07	.03	.01
☐ 48 Brian Lane	.10	.05	.01
☐ 49 Paul O'Neill	.07	.03	.01
☐ 50 Barry Larkin	.12	.05	.02
☐ 51 Reggie Jefferson	.25	.11	.03
☐ 52 Jeff Branson	.10	.05	.01
☐ 53 Chris Sabo	.07	.03	.01
☐ 54 Joe Oliver	.10	.05	.01
☐ 55 Todd Benzinger	.04	.02	.01
☐ 56 Rolando Roomes	.04	.02	.01
☐ 57 Hal Morris	.15	.07	.02
☐ 58 Eric Davis	.10	.05	.01
☐ 59 Scott Bryant	.12	.05	.02
☐ 60 Ken Griffey Sr.	.07	.03	.01
☐ 61 Darryl Kile	.15	.07	.02
☐ 62 Dave Smith	.04	.02	.01
☐ 63 Mark Portugal	.04	.02	.01
☐ 64 Jeff Juden	.20	.09	.03
☐ 65 Bill Gullickson	.04	.02	.01
☐ 66 Danny Darwin	.04	.02	.01
☐ 67 Larry Andersen	.04	.02	.01
☐ 68 Jose Cano	.04	.02	.01
☐ 69 Dan Schatzeder	.04	.02	.01
☐ 70 Jim Deshaies	.04	.02	.01
☐ 71 Mike Scott	.04	.02	.01
☐ 72 Gerald Young	.04	.02	.01
☐ 73 Ken Caminiti	.07	.03	.01
☐ 74 Ken Oberkfell	.04	.02	.01
☐ 75 Dave Rohde	.04	.02	.01
☐ 76 Bill Doran	.04	.02	.01
☐ 77 Andujar Cedeno	.20	.09	.03
☐ 78 Craig Biggio	.10	.05	.01
☐ 79 Karl Rhodes	.04	.02	.01
☐ 80 Glenn Davis	.07	.03	.01
☐ 81 Eric Anthony	.30	.14	.04
☐ 82 John Wetteland	.15	.07	.02
☐ 83 Jay Howell	.04	.02	.01
☐ 84 Orel Hershiser	.07	.03	.01
☐ 85 Tim Belcher	.07	.03	.01
☐ 86 Kiki Jones	.10	.05	.01
☐ 87 Mike Hartley	.04	.02	.01
☐ 88 Ramon Martinez	.15	.07	.02
☐ 89 Mike Scioscia	.04	.02	.01
☐ 90 Willie Randolph	.07	.03	.01
☐ 91 Juan Samuel	.04	.02	.01
☐ 92 Jose Offerman	.20	.09	.03
☐ 93 Dave Hansen	.15	.07	.02
☐ 94 Jeff Hamilton	.04	.02	.01
☐ 95 Alfredo Griffin	.04	.02	.01
☐ 96 Tom Goodwin	.15	.07	.02
☐ 97 Kirk Gibson	.07	.03	.01
☐ 98 Jose Vizcaino	.10	.05	.01
☐ 99 Kal Daniels	.04	.02	.01
☐ 100 Hubie Brooks	.04	.02	.01
☐ 101 Eddie Murray	.10	.05	.01
☐ 102 Dennis Boyd	.04	.02	.01
☐ 103 Tim Burke	.04	.02	.01
☐ 104 Bill Sampen	.04	.02	.01
☐ 105 Brett Gideon	.04	.02	.01
☐ 106 Mark Gardner	.12	.05	.02
☐ 107 Howard Farmer	.04	.02	.01
☐ 108 Mel Rojas	.12	.05	.02
☐ 109 Kevin Gross	.04	.02	.01
☐ 110 Dave Schmidt	.04	.02	.01
☐ 111 Denny Martinez	.07	.03	.01
☐ 112 Jerry Goff	.04	.02	.01
☐ 113 Andres Galarraga	.04	.02	.01
☐ 114 Tim Wallach	.07	.03	.01
☐ 115 Marquis Grissom	.60	.25	.08
☐ 116 Spike Owen	.04	.02	.01
☐ 117 Larry Walker	.90	.40	.11
☐ 118 Tim Raines	.07	.03	.01
☐ 119 Delino DeShields	.60	.25	.08
☐ 120 Tom Foley	.04	.02	.01
☐ 121 Dave Martinez	.07	.03	.01
☐ 122 Frank Viola UER (Career ERA .384, should be 3.84)	.07	.03	.01
☐ 123 Julio Valera	.15	.07	.02
☐ 124 Alejandro Pena	.04	.02	.01
☐ 125 David Cone	.12	.05	.02
☐ 126 Dwight Gooden	.10	.05	.01
☐ 127 Kevin D. Brown	.04	.02	.01
☐ 128 John Franco	.07	.03	.01
☐ 129 Terry Bross	.04	.02	.01
☐ 130 Blaine Beatty	.04	.02	.01
☐ 131 Sid Fernandez	.07	.03	.01
☐ 132 Mike Marshall	.04	.02	.01
☐ 133 Howard Johnson	.07	.03	.01
☐ 134 Jaime Roseboro	.07	.03	.01
☐ 135 Alan Zinter	.10	.05	.01
☐ 136 Keith Miller	.04	.02	.01
☐ 137 Kevin Elster	.04	.02	.01
☐ 138 Kevin McReynolds	.07	.03	.01
☐ 139 Barry Lyons	.04	.02	.01
☐ 140 Gregg Jefferies	.12	.05	.02
☐ 141 Darryl Strawberry	.20	.09	.03
☐ 142 Todd Hundley	.15	.07	.02
☐ 143 Scott Service	.04	.02	.01
☐ 144 Chuck Malone	.04	.02	.01
☐ 145 Steve Ontiveros	.04	.02	.01
☐ 146 Roger McDowell	.04	.02	.01
☐ 147 Ken Howell	.04	.02	.01
☐ 148 Pat Combs	.07	.03	.01
☐ 149 Jeff Parrett	.04	.02	.01
☐ 150 Chuck McElroy	.12	.05	.02
☐ 151 Jason Grimsley	.10	.05	.01
☐ 152 Len Dykstra	.07	.03	.01
☐ 153 Mickey Morandini	.25	.11	.03

☐ 154	John Kruk	.07	.03	.01
☐ 155	Dickie Thon	.04	.02	.01
☐ 156	Ricky Jordan	.04	.02	.01
☐ 157	Jeff Jackson	.10	.05	.01
☐ 158	Darren Daulton	.07	.03	.01
☐ 159	Tom Herr	.04	.02	.01
☐ 160	Von Hayes	.04	.02	.01
☐ 161	Dave Hollins	.60	.25	.08
☐ 162	Carmelo Martinez	.04	.02	.01
☐ 163	Bob Walk	.04	.02	.01
☐ 164	Doug Drabek	.07	.03	.01
☐ 165	Walt Terrell	.04	.02	.01
☐ 166	Bill Landrum	.04	.02	.01
☐ 167	Scott Ruskin	.04	.02	.01
☐ 168	Bob Patterson	.04	.02	.01
☐ 169	Bobby Bonilla	.12	.05	.02
☐ 170	Jose Lind	.04	.02	.01
☐ 171	Andy Van Slyke	.10	.05	.01
☐ 172	Mike LaValliere	.04	.02	.01
☐ 173	Willie Greene	.50	.23	.06
☐ 174	Jay Bell	.07	.03	.01
☐ 175	Sid Bream	.04	.02	.01
☐ 176	Tom Prince	.04	.02	.01
☐ 177	Wally Backman	.04	.02	.01
☐ 178	Moises Alou	.50	.23	.06
☐ 179	Steve Carter	.04	.02	.01
☐ 180	Gary Redus	.04	.02	.01
☐ 181	Barry Bonds	.30	.14	.04
☐ 182	Don Slaught UER (Card back shows headings for a pitcher)	.04	.02	.01
☐ 183	Joe Magrane	.04	.02	.01
☐ 184	Bryn Smith	.04	.02	.01
☐ 185	Todd Worrell	.04	.02	.01
☐ 186	Jose DeLeon	.04	.02	.01
☐ 187	Frank DiPino	.04	.02	.01
☐ 188	John Tudor	.04	.02	.01
☐ 189	Howard Hilton	.10	.05	.01
☐ 190	John Ericks	.04	.02	.01
☐ 191	Ken Dayley	.04	.02	.01
☐ 192	Ray Lankford	1.00	.45	.13
☐ 193	Todd Zeile	.15	.07	.02
☐ 194	Willie McGee	.07	.03	.01
☐ 195	Ozzie Smith	.12	.05	.02
☐ 196	Milt Thompson	.04	.02	.01
☐ 197	Terry Pendleton	.10	.05	.01
☐ 198	Vince Coleman	.07	.03	.01
☐ 199	Paul Coleman	.12	.05	.02
☐ 200	Jose Oquendo	.04	.02	.01
☐ 201	Pedro Guerrero	.07	.03	.01
☐ 202	Tom Brunansky	.07	.03	.01
☐ 203	Roger Smithberg	.10	.05	.01
☐ 204	Eddie Whitson	.04	.02	.01
☐ 205	Dennis Rasmussen	.04	.02	.01
☐ 206	Craig Lefferts	.04	.02	.01
☐ 207	Andy Benes	.15	.07	.02
☐ 208	Bruce Hurst	.07	.03	.01
☐ 209	Eric Show	.04	.02	.01
☐ 210	Rafael Valdez	.10	.05	.01
☐ 211	Joey Cora	.04	.02	.01
☐ 212	Thomas Howard	.12	.05	.02
☐ 213	Rob Nelson	.04	.02	.01
☐ 214	Jack Clark	.07	.03	.01
☐ 215	Garry Templeton	.04	.02	.01
☐ 216	Fred Lynn	.07	.03	.01
☐ 217	Tony Gwynn	.20	.09	.03
☐ 218	Benito Santiago	.07	.03	.01
☐ 219	Mike Pagliarulo	.04	.02	.01
☐ 220	Joe Carter	.20	.09	.03
☐ 221	Roberto Alomar	.40	.18	.05
☐ 222	Bip Roberts	.07	.03	.01
☐ 223	Rick Reuschel	.04	.02	.01
☐ 224	Russ Swan	.10	.05	.01
☐ 225	Eric Gunderson	.10	.05	.01
☐ 226	Steve Bedrosian	.04	.02	.01
☐ 227	Mike Remlinger	.10	.05	.01
☐ 228	Scott Garrelts	.04	.02	.01
☐ 229	Ernie Camacho	.04	.02	.01
☐ 230	Andres Santana	.12	.05	.02
☐ 231	Will Clark	.30	.14	.04
☐ 232	Kevin Mitchell	.10	.05	.01
☐ 233	Robby Thompson	.04	.02	.01
☐ 234	Bill Bathe	.04	.02	.01
☐ 235	Tony Perezchica	.04	.02	.01
☐ 236	Gary Carter	.07	.03	.01
☐ 237	Brett Butler	.07	.03	.01
☐ 238	Matt Williams	.10	.05	.01
☐ 239	Earnie Riles	.04	.02	.01
☐ 240	Kevin Bass	.04	.02	.01
☐ 241	Terry Kennedy	.04	.02	.01
☐ 242	Steve Hosey	.50	.23	.06
☐ 243	Ben McDonald	.50	.23	.06
☐ 244	Jeff Ballard	.04	.02	.01
☐ 245	Joe Price	.04	.02	.01
☐ 246	Curt Schilling	.15	.07	.02
☐ 247	Pete Harnisch	.07	.03	.01
☐ 248	Mark Williamson	.04	.02	.01
☐ 249	Gregg Olson	.10	.05	.01
☐ 250	Chris Myers	.10	.05	.01
☐ 251A	David Segui ERR (Missing vital stats at top of card back under name)	.30	.14	.04
☐ 251B	David Segui COR	.10	.05	.01
☐ 252	Joe Orsulak	.04	.02	.01
☐ 253	Craig Worthington	.04	.02	.01
☐ 254	Mickey Tettleton	.07	.03	.01
☐ 255	Cal Ripken	.40	.18	.05
☐ 256	Billy Ripken	.04	.02	.01
☐ 257	Randy Milligan	.04	.02	.01
☐ 258	Brady Anderson	.10	.05	.01
☐ 259	Chris Hoiles	.40	.18	.05
☐ 260	Mike Devereaux	.07	.03	.01
☐ 261	Phil Bradley	.04	.02	.01
☐ 262	Leo Gomez	.50	.23	.06
☐ 263	Lee Smith	.07	.03	.01
☐ 264	Mike Rochford	.04	.02	.01
☐ 265	Jeff Reardon	.07	.03	.01
☐ 266	Wes Gardner	.04	.02	.01
☐ 267	Mike Boddicker	.04	.02	.01
☐ 268	Roger Clemens	.35	.16	.04
☐ 269	Rob Murphy	.04	.02	.01
☐ 270	Mickey Pina	.07	.03	.01
☐ 271	Tony Pena	.04	.02	.01
☐ 272	Jody Reed	.04	.02	.01
☐ 273	Kevin Romine	.04	.02	.01
☐ 274	Mike Greenwell	.07	.03	.01
☐ 275	Maurice Vaughn	.35	.16	.04
☐ 276	Danny Heep	.04	.02	.01
☐ 277	Scott Cooper	.40	.18	.05
☐ 278	Greg Blosser	.20	.09	.03
☐ 279	Dwight Evans UER (* by "1990 Team Breakdown")	.07	.03	.01
☐ 280	Ellis Burks	.07	.03	.01
☐ 281	Wade Boggs	.20	.09	.03
☐ 282	Marty Barrett	.04	.02	.01
☐ 283	Kirk McCaskill	.04	.02	.01
☐ 284	Mark Langston	.07	.03	.01
☐ 285	Bert Blyleven	.07	.03	.01
☐ 286	Mike Fetters	.10	.05	.01
☐ 287	Kyle Abbott	.20	.09	.03
☐ 288	Jim Abbott	.20	.09	.03
☐ 289	Chuck Finley	.07	.03	.01
☐ 290	Gary DiSarcina	.20	.09	.03
☐ 291	Dick Schofield	.04	.02	.01
☐ 292	Devon White	.07	.03	.01
☐ 293	Bobby Rose	.07	.03	.01
☐ 294	Brian Downing	.04	.02	.01
☐ 295	Lance Parrish	.07	.03	.01
☐ 296	Jack Howell	.04	.02	.01
☐ 297	Claudell Washington	.04	.02	.01
☐ 298	John Orton	.10	.05	.01
☐ 299	Wally Joyner	.07	.03	.01
☐ 300	Lee Stevens	.10	.05	.01
☐ 301	Chili Davis	.07	.03	.01
☐ 302	Johnny Ray	.04	.02	.01
☐ 303	Greg Hibbard	.20	.09	.03
☐ 304	Eric King	.04	.02	.01
☐ 305	Jack McDowell	.20	.09	.03
☐ 306	Bobby Thigpen	.04	.02	.01
☐ 307	Adam Peterson	.04	.02	.01
☐ 308	Scott Radinsky	.15	.07	.02
☐ 309	Wayne Edwards	.04	.02	.01
☐ 310	Melido Perez	.04	.02	.01
☐ 311	Robin Ventura	.60	.25	.08
☐ 312	Sammy Sosa	.15	.07	.02
☐ 313	Dan Pasqua	.04	.02	.01
☐ 314	Carlton Fisk	.10	.05	.01
☐ 315	Ozzie Guillen	.04	.02	.01
☐ 316	Ivan Calderon	.04	.02	.01
☐ 317	Daryl Boston	.04	.02	.01
☐ 318	Craig Grebeck	.15	.07	.02
☐ 319	Scott Fletcher	.04	.02	.01
☐ 320	Frank Thomas	4.00	1.80	.50
☐ 321	Steve Lyons	.04	.02	.01
☐ 322	Carlos Martinez	.04	.02	.01
☐ 323	Joe Skalski	.04	.02	.01
☐ 324	Tom Candiotti	.04	.02	.01
☐ 325	Greg Swindell	.07	.03	.01
☐ 326	Steve Olin	.20	.09	.03
☐ 327	Kevin Wickander	.04	.02	.01
☐ 328	Doug Jones	.07	.03	.01
☐ 329	Jeff Shaw	.04	.02	.01
☐ 330	Kevin Bearse	.04	.02	.01
☐ 331	Dion James	.04	.02	.01

□ 332 Jerry Browne	.04	.02	.01
□ 333 Joey Belle	.50	.23	.06
□ 334 Felix Fermin	.04	.02	.01
□ 335 Candy Maldonado	.04	.02	.01
□ 336 Cory Snyder	.04	.02	.01
□ 337 Sandy Alomar Jr.	.10	.05	.01
□ 338 Mark Lewis	.12	.05	.02
□ 339 Carlos Baerga	1.25	.55	.16
□ 340 Chris James	.04	.02	.01
□ 341 Brook Jacoby	.04	.02	.01
□ 342 Keith Hernandez	.07	.03	.01
□ 343 Frank Tanana	.04	.02	.01
□ 344 Scott Aldred	.20	.09	.03
□ 345 Mike Henneman	.04	.02	.01
□ 346 Steve Wapnick	.04	.02	.01
□ 347 Greg Gohr	.15	.07	.02
□ 348 Eric Stone	.10	.05	.01
□ 349 Brian DuBois	.04	.02	.01
□ 350 Kevin Ritz	.10	.05	.01
□ 351 Rico Brogna	.04	.02	.01
□ 352 Mike Heath	.04	.02	.01
□ 353 Alan Trammell	.07	.03	.01
□ 354 Chet Lemon	.04	.02	.01
□ 355 Dave Bergman	.04	.02	.01
□ 356 Lou Whitaker	.07	.03	.01
□ 357 Cecil Fielder UER (* by "1990 Team Breakdown")	.20	.09	.03
□ 358 Milt Cuyler	.20	.09	.03
□ 359 Tony Phillips	.04	.02	.01
□ 360 Travis Fryman	1.50	.65	.19
□ 361 Ed Romero	.04	.02	.01
□ 362 Lloyd Moseby	.04	.02	.01
□ 363 Mark Gubicza	.04	.02	.01
□ 364 Bret Saberhagen	.07	.03	.01
□ 365 Tom Gordon	.07	.03	.01
□ 366 Steve Farr	.04	.02	.01
□ 367 Kevin Appier	.25	.11	.03
□ 368 Storm Davis	.04	.02	.01
□ 369 Mark Davis	.04	.02	.01
□ 370 Jeff Montgomery	.07	.03	.01
□ 371 Frank White	.04	.02	.01
□ 372 Brent Mayne	.15	.07	.02
□ 373 Bob Boone	.07	.03	.01
□ 374 Jim Eisenreich	.04	.02	.01
□ 375 Danny Tartabull	.07	.03	.01
□ 376 Kurt Stillwell	.04	.02	.01
□ 377 Bill Pecota	.04	.02	.01
□ 378 Bo Jackson	.15	.07	.02
□ 379 Bob Hamelin	.12	.05	.02
□ 380 Kevin Seitzer	.07	.03	.01
□ 381 Rey Palacios	.04	.02	.01
□ 382 George Brett	.15	.07	.02
□ 383 Gerald Perry	.04	.02	.01
□ 384 Teddy Higuera	.04	.02	.01
□ 385 Tom Filer	.04	.02	.01
□ 386 Dan Plesac	.04	.02	.01
□ 387 Cal Eldred	1.00	.45	.13
□ 388 Jaime Navarro	.20	.09	.03
□ 389 Chris Bosio	.04	.02	.01
□ 390 Randy Veres	.04	.02	.01
□ 391 Gary Sheffield	.50	.23	.06
□ 392 George Canale	.04	.02	.01
□ 393 B.J. Surhoff	.04	.02	.01
□ 394 Tim McIntosh	.10	.05	.01
□ 395 Greg Brock	.04	.02	.01
□ 396 Greg Vaughn	.15	.07	.02
□ 397 Darryl Hamilton	.12	.05	.02
□ 398 Dave Parker	.07	.03	.01
□ 399 Paul Molitor	.10	.05	.01
□ 400 Jim Gantner	.04	.02	.01
□ 401 Rob Deer	.07	.03	.01
□ 402 Billy Spiers	.04	.02	.01
□ 403 Glenn Braggs	.04	.02	.01
□ 404 Robin Yount	.15	.07	.02
□ 405 Rick Aguilera	.07	.03	.01
□ 406 Johnny Ard	.07	.03	.01
□ 407 Kevin Tapani	.35	.16	.04
□ 408 Park Pittman	.04	.02	.01
□ 409 Allan Anderson	.04	.02	.01
□ 410 Juan Berenguer	.04	.02	.01
□ 411 Willie Banks	.25	.11	.03
□ 412 Rich Yett	.04	.02	.01
□ 413 Dave West	.04	.02	.01
□ 414 Greg Gagne	.04	.02	.01
□ 415 Chuck Knoblauch	1.00	.45	.13
□ 416 Randy Bush	.04	.02	.01
□ 417 Gary Gaetti	.04	.02	.01
□ 418 Kent Hrbek	.07	.03	.01
□ 419 Al Newman	.04	.02	.01
□ 420 Danny Gladden	.04	.02	.01
□ 421 Paul Sorrento	.25	.11	.03
□ 422 Derek Parks	.10	.05	.01
□ 423 Scott Leius	.25	.11	.03
□ 424 Kirby Puckett	.30	.14	.04
□ 425 Willie Smith	.07	.03	.01
□ 426 Dave Righetti	.04	.02	.01
□ 427 Jeff D. Robinson	.04	.02	.01
□ 428 Alan Mills	.12	.05	.02
□ 429 Tim Leary	.04	.02	.01
□ 430 Pascual Perez	.04	.02	.01
□ 431 Alvaro Espinoza	.04	.02	.01
□ 432 Dave Winfield	.15	.07	.02
□ 433 Jesse Barfield	.04	.02	.01
□ 434 Randy Velarde	.04	.02	.01
□ 435 Rick Cerone	.04	.02	.01
□ 436 Steve Balboni	.04	.02	.01
□ 437 Mel Hall	.04	.02	.01
□ 438 Bob Geren	.04	.02	.01
□ 439 Bernie Williams	.30	.14	.04
□ 440 Kevin Maas	.25	.11	.03
□ 441 Mike Blowers	.04	.02	.01
□ 442 Steve Sax	.07	.03	.01
□ 443 Don Mattingly	.20	.09	.03
□ 444 Roberto Kelly	.12	.05	.02
□ 445 Mike Moore	.04	.02	.01
□ 446 Reggie Harris	.10	.05	.01
□ 447 Scott Sanderson	.04	.02	.01
□ 448 Dave Otto	.04	.02	.01
□ 449 Dave Stewart	.07	.03	.01
□ 450 Rick Honeycutt	.04	.02	.01
□ 451 Dennis Eckersley	.12	.05	.02
□ 452 Carney Lansford	.07	.03	.01
□ 453 Scott Hemond	.10	.05	.01
□ 454 Mark McGwire	.30	.14	.04
□ 455 Felix Jose	.20	.09	.03
□ 456 Terry Steinbach	.07	.03	.01
□ 457 Rickey Henderson	.20	.09	.03
□ 458 Dave Henderson	.04	.02	.01
□ 459 Mike Gallego	.04	.02	.01
□ 460 Jose Canseco	.30	.14	.04
□ 461 Walt Weiss	.04	.02	.01
□ 462 Ken Phelps	.04	.02	.01
□ 463 Darren Lewis	.20	.09	.03
□ 464 Ron Hassey	.04	.02	.01
□ 465 Roger Salkeld	.20	.09	.03
□ 466 Scott Bankhead	.04	.02	.01
□ 467 Keith Comstock	.04	.02	.01
□ 468 Randy Johnson	.15	.07	.02
□ 469 Erik Hanson	.07	.03	.01
□ 470 Mike Schooler	.04	.02	.01
□ 471 Gary Eave	.04	.02	.01
□ 472 Jeffrey Leonard	.04	.02	.01
□ 473 Dave Valle	.04	.02	.01
□ 474 Omar Vizquel	.07	.03	.01
□ 475 Pete O'Brien	.04	.02	.01
□ 476 Henry Cotto	.04	.02	.01
□ 477 Jay Buhner	.07	.03	.01
□ 478 Harold Reynolds	.04	.02	.01
□ 479 Alvin Davis	.04	.02	.01
□ 480 Darnell Coles	.04	.02	.01
□ 481 Ken Griffey Jr.	1.25	.55	.16
□ 482 Greg Briley	.04	.02	.01
□ 483 Scott Bradley	.04	.02	.01
□ 484 Tino Martinez	.12	.05	.02
□ 485 Jeff Russell	.04	.02	.01
□ 486 Nolan Ryan	.50	.23	.06
□ 487 Robb Nen	.10	.05	.01
□ 488 Kevin Brown	.10	.05	.01
□ 489 Brian Bohanon	.10	.05	.01
□ 490 Ruben Sierra	.20	.09	.03
□ 491 Pete Incaviglia	.04	.02	.01
□ 492 Juan Gonzalez	2.00	.90	.25
□ 493 Steve Buechele	.04	.02	.01
□ 494 Scott Coolbaugh	.04	.02	.01
□ 495 Geno Petralli	.04	.02	.01
□ 496 Rafael Palmeiro	.12	.05	.02
□ 497 Julio Franco	.07	.03	.01
□ 498 Gary Pettis	.04	.02	.01
□ 499 Donald Harris	.10	.05	.01
□ 500 Monty Fariss	.07	.03	.01
□ 501 Harold Baines	.07	.03	.01
□ 502 Cecil Espy	.04	.02	.01
□ 503 Jack Daugherty	.04	.02	.01
□ 504 Willie Blair	.10	.05	.01
□ 505 Dave Stieb	.07	.03	.01
□ 506 Tom Henke	.07	.03	.01
□ 507 John Cerutti	.04	.02	.01
□ 508 Paul Kilgus	.04	.02	.01
□ 509 Jimmy Key	.07	.03	.01
□ 510 John Olerud	.60	.25	.08
□ 511 Ed Sprague	.07	.03	.01
□ 512 Manny Lee	.04	.02	.01
□ 513 Fred McGriff	.20	.09	.03
□ 514 Glenallen Hill	.07	.03	.01
□ 515 George Bell	.07	.03	.01

☐ 516 Mookie Wilson	.04	.02	.01
☐ 517 Luis Sojo	.15	.07	.02
☐ 518 Nelson Liriano	.04	.02	.01
☐ 519 Kelly Gruber	.07	.03	.01
☐ 520 Greg Myers	.04	.02	.01
☐ 521 Pat Borders	.07	.03	.01
☐ 522 Junior Felix	.07	.03	.01
☐ 523 Eddie Zosky	.15	.07	.02
☐ 524 Tony Fernandez	.07	.03	.01
☐ 525 Checklist 1-132 UER (No copyright mark on the back)	.05	.01	.00
☐ 526 Checklist 133-264	.05	.01	.00
☐ 527 Checklist 265-396	.05	.01	.00
☐ 528 Checklist 397-528	.05	.01	.00

1990 Bowman Inserts

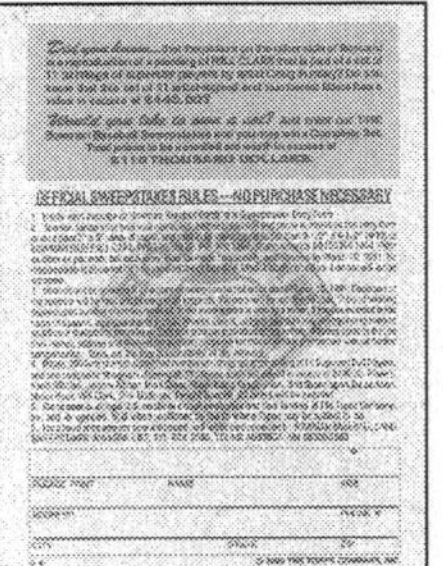

These 2 1/2" by 3 1/2" cards were an insert in every 1990 Bowman pack. This set, which consists of 11 superstars, depicts drawings by Craig Pursley with the backs being descriptions of the 1990 Bowman sweepstakes. We have checklisted the set alphabetically by player. All the cards in this set can be found with either one asterisk or two on the back.

	MT	EX-MT	VG
COMPLETE SET (11)	2.00	.90	.25
COMMON PLAYER (1-11)	.10	.05	.01
☐ 1 Will Clark	.30	.14	.04
☐ 2 Mark Davis	.10	.05	.01
☐ 3 Dwight Gooden	.20	.09	.03
☐ 4 Bo Jackson	.30	.14	.04
☐ 5 Don Mattingly	.30	.14	.04
☐ 6 Kevin Mitchell	.15	.07	.02
☐ 7 Gregg Olson	.15	.07	.02
☐ 8 Nolan Ryan	.60	.25	.08
☐ 9 Bret Saberhagen	.20	.09	.03
☐ 10 Jerome Walton	.10	.05	.01
☐ 11 Robin Yount	.25	.11	.03

1991 Bowman

This 704-card standard size (2 1/2" by 3 1/2") set marked the third straight year that Topps issued a set using the Bowman name. The cards are arranged in team order by division as follows: AL East, AL West, NL East, and NL West. Some of the specials in the set include cards made for all the 1990 MVP's in each minor league, the leader sluggers by position (Silver Sluggers), and special cards commemorating long-time baseball figure Jimmie Reese, General Colin Powell, newly inducted Hall of Famer Rod Carew and Rickey Henderson's 938th Stolen Base. The cards themselves are designed just like the 1990 Bowman set while the backs again feature the innovative team by team breakdown of how the player did the previous year

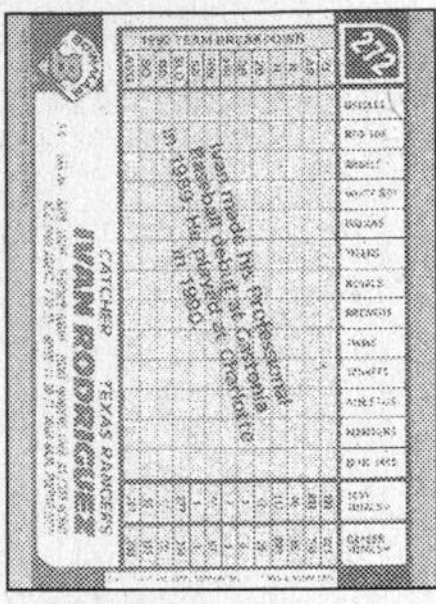

against a green background. The set numbering is as follows: Toronto Blue Jays (6-30), Milwaukee Brewers (31-56), Cleveland Indians (57-82), Baltimore Orioles (83-106), Boston Red Sox (107-130), Detroit Tigers (131-154), New York Yankees (155-179), California Angels (187-211), Oakland Athletics (212-238), Seattle Mariners (239-264), Texas Rangers (265-290), Kansas City Royals (291-316), Minnesota Twins (317-341), Chicago White Sox (342-366), St. Louis Cardinals (385-409), Chicago Cubs (411-433), Montreal Expos (434-459), New York Mets (460-484), Philadelphia Phillies (485-508), Pittsburgh Pirates (509-532), Houston Astros (539-565), Atlanta Braves (566-590), Los Angles Dodgers (591-615), San Fransico Giants (616-641), San Diego Padres (642-665), and Cincinnati Reds (666-691). Special subsets feature AL Silver Sluggers (367-375) and NL Silver Sluggers (376-384). There are two instances of misnumbering in the set; Ken Griffey (should be 255) and Ken Griffey Jr. are both numbered 246 and Donovan Osborne (should be 406) and Thomson/Branca share number 410. The noteworthy Rookie Cards in this set are Jeff Bagwell, Bret Boone, Jeromy Burnitz, Eric Karros, Ryan Klesko, Kenny Lofton, Sam Militello, Mike Mussina, Phil Plantier, Ivan Rodriguez, Tim Salmon, Reggie Sanders, Todd Van Poppel, Bob Wickman.

	MT	EX-MT	VG
COMPLETE SET (704)	15.00	6.75	1.90
COMPLETE FACT.SET (704)	15.00	6.75	1.90
COMMON PLAYER (1-704)	.04	.02	.01
☐ 1 Rod Carew I	.15	.07	.02
☐ 2 Rod Carew II	.15	.07	.02
☐ 3 Rod Carew III	.15	.07	.02
☐ 4 Rod Carew IV	.15	.07	.02
☐ 5 Rod Carew V	.15	.07	.02
☐ 6 Willie Fraser	.04	.02	.01
☐ 7 John Olerud	.15	.07	.02
☐ 8 William Suero	.10	.05	.01
☐ 9 Roberto Alomar	.20	.09	.03
☐ 10 Todd Stottlemyre	.07	.03	.01
☐ 11 Joe Carter	.12	.05	.02
☐ 12 Steve Karsay	.25	.11	.03
☐ 13 Mark Whiten	.12	.05	.02
☐ 14 Pat Borders	.04	.02	.01
☐ 15 Mike Timlin	.10	.05	.01
☐ 16 Tom Henke	.07	.03	.01
☐ 17 Eddie Zosky	.04	.02	.01
☐ 18 Kelly Gruber	.07	.03	.01
☐ 19 Jimmy Key	.04	.02	.01
☐ 20 Jerry Schunk	.10	.05	.01
☐ 21 Manny Lee	.04	.02	.01
☐ 22 Dave Stieb	.04	.02	.01
☐ 23 Pat Hentgen	.15	.07	.02
☐ 24 Glenallen Hill	.04	.02	.01
☐ 25 Rene Gonzales	.04	.02	.01
☐ 26 Ed Sprague	.15	.07	.02
☐ 27 Ken Dayley	.04	.02	.01
☐ 28 Pat Tabler	.04	.02	.01
☐ 29 Denis Boucher	.12	.05	.02
☐ 30 Devon White	.07	.03	.01
☐ 31 Dante Bichette	.04	.02	.01
☐ 32 Paul Molitor	.10	.05	.01
☐ 33 Greg Vaughn	.10	.05	.01
☐ 34 Dan Plesac	.04	.02	.01

☐ 35 Chris George	.10	.05	.01
☐ 36 Tim McIntosh	.04	.02	.01
☐ 37 Franklin Stubbs	.04	.02	.01
☐ 38 Bo Dodson	.15	.07	.02
☐ 39 Ron Robinson	.04	.02	.01
☐ 40 Ed Nunez	.04	.02	.01
☐ 41 Greg Brock	.04	.02	.01
☐ 42 Jaime Navarro	.07	.03	.01
☐ 43 Chris Bosio	.04	.02	.01
☐ 44 B.J. Surhoff	.04	.02	.01
☐ 45 Chris Johnson	.10	.05	.01
☐ 46 Willie Randolph	.07	.03	.01
☐ 47 Narciso Elvira	.10	.05	.01
☐ 48 Jim Gantner	.04	.02	.01
☐ 49 Kevin Brown	.04	.02	.01
☐ 50 Julio Machado	.04	.02	.01
☐ 51 Chuck Crim	.04	.02	.01
☐ 52 Gary Sheffield	.25	.11	.03
☐ 53 Angel Miranda	.12	.05	.02
☐ 54 Teddy Higuera	.04	.02	.01
☐ 55 Robin Yount	.10	.05	.01
☐ 56 Cal Eldred	.35	.16	.04
☐ 57 Sandy Alomar Jr.	.07	.03	.01
☐ 58 Greg Swindell	.07	.03	.01
☐ 59 Brook Jacoby	.04	.02	.01
☐ 60 Efrain Valdez	.04	.02	.01
☐ 61 Ever Magallanes	.10	.05	.01
☐ 62 Tom Candiotti	.04	.02	.01
☐ 63 Eric King	.04	.02	.01
☐ 64 Alex Cole	.04	.02	.01
☐ 65 Charles Nagy	.20	.09	.03
☐ 66 Mitch Webster	.04	.02	.01
☐ 67 Chris James	.04	.02	.01
☐ 68 Jim Thome	.20	.09	.03
☐ 69 Carlos Baerga	.20	.09	.03
☐ 70 Mark Lewis	.10	.05	.01
☐ 71 Jerry Browne	.04	.02	.01
☐ 72 Jesse Orosco	.04	.02	.01
☐ 73 Mike Huff	.04	.02	.01
☐ 74 Jose Escobar	.10	.05	.01
☐ 75 Jeff Manto	.04	.02	.01
☐ 76 Turner Ward	.10	.05	.01
☐ 77 Doug Jones	.04	.02	.01
☐ 78 Bruce Egloff	.10	.05	.01
☐ 79 Tim Costo	.20	.09	.03
☐ 80 Beau Allred	.04	.02	.01
☐ 81 Albert Belle	.12	.05	.02
☐ 82 John Farrell	.04	.02	.01
☐ 83 Glenn Davis	.07	.03	.01
☐ 84 Joe Orsulak	.04	.02	.01
☐ 85 Mark Williamson	.04	.02	.01
☐ 86 Ben McDonald	.10	.05	.01
☐ 87 Billy Ripken	.04	.02	.01
☐ 88 Leo Gomez	.15	.07	.02
☐ 89 Bob Melvin	.04	.02	.01
☐ 90 Jeff M. Robinson	.04	.02	.01
☐ 91 Jose Mesa	.04	.02	.01
☐ 92 Gregg Olson	.07	.03	.01
☐ 93 Mike Devereaux	.07	.03	.01
☐ 94 Luis Mercedes	.20	.09	.03
☐ 95 Arthur Rhodes	.35	.16	.04
☐ 96 Juan Bell	.04	.02	.01
☐ 97 Mike Mussina	1.50	.65	.19
☐ 98 Jeff Ballard	.04	.02	.01
☐ 99 Chris Hoiles	.10	.05	.01
☐ 100 Brady Anderson	.07	.03	.01
☐ 101 Bob Milacki	.04	.02	.01
☐ 102 David Segui	.04	.02	.01
☐ 103 Dwight Evans	.07	.03	.01
☐ 104 Cal Ripken	.30	.14	.04
☐ 105 Mike Linskey	.12	.05	.02
☐ 106 Jeff Tackett	.15	.07	.02
☐ 107 Jeff Reardon	.07	.03	.01
☐ 108 Dana Kiecker	.04	.02	.01
☐ 109 Ellis Burks	.07	.03	.01
☐ 110 Dave Owen	.04	.02	.01
☐ 111 Danny Darwin	.04	.02	.01
☐ 112 Mo Vaughn	.10	.05	.01
☐ 113 Jeff McNeely	.20	.09	.03
☐ 114 Tom Bolton	.04	.02	.01
☐ 115 Greg Blosser	.10	.05	.01
☐ 116 Mike Greenwell	.07	.03	.01
☐ 117 Phil Plantier	.50	.23	.06
☐ 118 Roger Clemens	.25	.11	.03
☐ 119 John Marzano	.04	.02	.01
☐ 120 Jody Reed	.04	.02	.01
☐ 121 Scott Taylor	.10	.05	.01
☐ 122 Jack Clark	.07	.03	.01
☐ 123 Derek Livernois	.10	.05	.01
☐ 124 Tony Pena	.04	.02	.01
☐ 125 Tom Brunansky	.07	.03	.01
☐ 126 Carlos Quintana	.04	.02	.01
☐ 127 Tim Naehring	.07	.03	.01
☐ 128 Matt Young	.04	.02	.01
☐ 129 Wade Boggs	.12	.05	.02
☐ 130 Kevin Morton	.10	.05	.01
☐ 131 Pete Incaviglia	.04	.02	.01
☐ 132 Rob Deer	.07	.03	.01
☐ 133 Bill Gullickson	.04	.02	.01
☐ 134 Rico Brogna	.10	.05	.01
☐ 135 Lloyd Moseby	.04	.02	.01
☐ 136 Cecil Fielder	.12	.05	.02
☐ 137 Tony Phillips	.04	.02	.01
☐ 138 Mark Leiter	.10	.05	.01
☐ 139 John Cerutti	.04	.02	.01
☐ 140 Mickey Tettleton	.07	.03	.01
☐ 141 Milt Cuyler	.07	.03	.01
☐ 142 Greg Gohr	.04	.02	.01
☐ 143 Tony Bernazard	.04	.02	.01
☐ 144 Dan Gakeler	.04	.02	.01
☐ 145 Travis Fryman	.40	.18	.05
☐ 146 Dan Petry	.04	.02	.01
☐ 147 Scott Aldred	.04	.02	.01
☐ 148 John DeSilva	.20	.09	.03
☐ 149 Rusty Meacham	.10	.05	.01
☐ 150 Lou Whitaker	.07	.03	.01
☐ 151 Dave Haas	.10	.05	.01
☐ 152 Luis de los Santos	.04	.02	.01
☐ 153 Ivan Cruz	.15	.07	.02
☐ 154 Alan Trammell	.07	.03	.01
☐ 155 Pat Kelly	.15	.07	.02
☐ 156 Carl Everett	.25	.11	.03
☐ 157 Greg Cadaret	.04	.02	.01
☐ 158 Kevin Maas	.10	.05	.01
☐ 159 Jeff Johnson	.10	.05	.01
☐ 160 Willie Smith	.04	.02	.01
☐ 161 Gerald Williams	.20	.09	.03
☐ 162 Mike Humphreys	.15	.07	.02
☐ 163 Alvaro Espinoza	.04	.02	.01
☐ 164 Matt Nokes	.04	.02	.01
☐ 165 Wade Taylor	.04	.02	.01
☐ 166 Roberto Kelly	.07	.03	.01
☐ 167 John Habyan	.04	.02	.01
☐ 168 Steve Farr	.04	.02	.01
☐ 169 Jesse Barfield	.04	.02	.01
☐ 170 Steve Sax	.07	.03	.01
☐ 171 Jim Leyritz	.04	.02	.01
☐ 172 Robert Eenhoorn	.12	.05	.02
☐ 173 Bernie Williams	.10	.05	.01
☐ 174 Scott Lusader	.04	.02	.01
☐ 175 Torey Lovullo	.04	.02	.01
☐ 176 Chuck Cary	.04	.02	.01
☐ 177 Scott Sanderson	.04	.02	.01
☐ 178 Don Mattingly	.15	.07	.02
☐ 179 Mel Hall	.04	.02	.01
☐ 180 Juan Gonzalez Minor League MVP	.35	.16	.04
☐ 181 Hensley Meulens Minor League MVP	.08	.04	.01
☐ 182 Jose Offerman Minor League MVP	.10	.05	.01
☐ 183 Jeff Bagwell Minor League MVP	1.25	.55	.16
☐ 184 Jeff Conine Minor League MVP	.25	.11	.03
☐ 185 Henry Rodriguez Minor League MVP	.20	.09	.03
☐ 186 Jimmie Reese CO	.07	.03	.01
☐ 187 Kyle Abbott	.07	.03	.01
☐ 188 Lance Parrish	.07	.03	.01
☐ 189 Rafael Montalvo	.10	.05	.01
☐ 190 Floyd Bannister	.04	.02	.01
☐ 191 Dick Schofield	.04	.02	.01
☐ 192 Scott Lewis	.10	.05	.01
☐ 193 Jeff D. Robinson	.04	.02	.01
☐ 194 Kent Anderson	.04	.02	.01
☐ 195 Wally Joyner	.07	.03	.01
☐ 196 Chuck Finley	.07	.03	.01
☐ 197 Luis Sojo	.04	.02	.01
☐ 198 Jeff Richardson	.10	.05	.01
☐ 199 Dave Parker	.07	.03	.01
☐ 200 Jim Abbott	.12	.05	.02
☐ 201 Junior Felix	.04	.02	.01
☐ 202 Mark Langston	.07	.03	.01
☐ 203 Tim Salmon	1.00	.45	.13
☐ 204 Cliff Young	.04	.02	.01
☐ 205 Scott Bailes	.04	.02	.01
☐ 206 Bobby Rose	.04	.02	.01
☐ 207 Gary Gaetti	.04	.02	.01
☐ 208 Ruben Amaro	.12	.05	.02
☐ 209 Luis Polonia	.07	.03	.01
☐ 210 Dave Winfield	.10	.05	.01
☐ 211 Bryan Harvey	.04	.02	.01
☐ 212 Mike Moore	.04	.02	.01
☐ 213 Rickey Henderson	.12	.05	.02
☐ 214 Steve Chitren	.10	.05	.01

☐	215 Bob Welch	.04	.02	.01
☐	216 Terry Steinbach	.07	.03	.01
☐	217 Earnest Riles	.04	.02	.01
☐	218 Todd Van Poppel	.50	.23	.06
☐	219 Mike Gallego	.04	.02	.01
☐	220 Curt Young	.04	.02	.01
☐	221 Todd Burns	.04	.02	.01
☐	222 Vance Law	.04	.02	.01
☐	223 Eric Show	.04	.02	.01
☐	224 Don Peters	.10	.05	.01
☐	225 Dave Stewart	.07	.03	.01
☐	226 Dave Henderson	.04	.02	.01
☐	227 Jose Canseco	.20	.09	.03
☐	228 Walt Weiss	.04	.02	.01
☐	229 Dann Howitt	.04	.02	.01
☐	230 Willie Wilson	.04	.02	.01
☐	231 Harold Baines	.07	.03	.01
☐	232 Scott Hemond	.04	.02	.01
☐	233 Joe Slusarski	.10	.05	.01
☐	234 Mark McGwire	.20	.09	.03
☐	235 Kirk Dressendorfer	.10	.05	.01
☐	236 Craig Paquette	.20	.09	.03
☐	237 Dennis Eckersley	.12	.05	.02
☐	238 Dana Allison	.10	.05	.01
☐	239 Scott Bradley	.04	.02	.01
☐	240 Brian Holman	.04	.02	.01
☐	241 Mike Schooler	.04	.02	.01
☐	242 Rich DeLucia	.04	.02	.01
☐	243 Edgar Martinez	.07	.03	.01
☐	244 Henry Cotto	.04	.02	.01
☐	245 Omar Vizquel	.04	.02	.01
☐	246 Ken Griffey Jr. (See also 255)	.50	.23	.06
☐	247 Jay Buhner	.07	.03	.01
☐	248 Bill Krueger	.04	.02	.01
☐	249 Dave Fleming	1.00	.45	.13
☐	250 Patrick Lennon	.12	.05	.02
☐	251 Dave Valle	.04	.02	.01
☐	252 Harold Reynolds	.04	.02	.01
☐	253 Randy Johnson	.07	.03	.01
☐	254 Scott Bankhead	.04	.02	.01
☐	255 Ken Griffey Sr. UER (Card number is 246)	.07	.03	.01
☐	256 Greg Briley	.04	.02	.01
☐	257 Tino Martinez	.10	.05	.01
☐	258 Alvin Davis	.04	.02	.01
☐	259 Pete O'Brien	.04	.02	.01
☐	260 Erik Hanson	.04	.02	.01
☐	261 Bret Boone	1.00	.45	.13
☐	262 Roger Salkeld	.10	.05	.01
☐	263 Dave Burba	.10	.05	.01
☐	264 Kerry Woodson	.15	.07	.02
☐	265 Julio Franco	.07	.03	.01
☐	266 Dan Peltier	.12	.05	.02
☐	267 Jeff Russell	.04	.02	.01
☐	268 Steve Buechele	.04	.02	.01
☐	269 Donald Harris	.04	.02	.01
☐	270 Robb Nen	.04	.02	.01
☐	271 Rich Gossage	.07	.03	.01
☐	272 Ivan Rodriguez	1.25	.55	.16
☐	273 Jeff Huson	.04	.02	.01
☐	274 Kevin Brown	.07	.03	.01
☐	275 Dan Smith	.20	.09	.03
☐	276 Gary Pettis	.04	.02	.01
☐	277 Jack Daugherty	.04	.02	.01
☐	278 Mike Jeffcoat	.04	.02	.01
☐	279 Brad Arnsberg	.04	.02	.01
☐	280 Nolan Ryan	.40	.18	.05
☐	281 Eric McCray	.10	.05	.01
☐	282 Scott Chiamparino	.07	.03	.01
☐	283 Ruben Sierra	.15	.07	.02
☐	284 Geno Petralli	.04	.02	.01
☐	285 Monty Fariss	.07	.03	.01
☐	286 Rafael Palmeiro	.10	.05	.01
☐	287 Bobby Witt	.04	.02	.01
☐	288 Dean Palmer UER (Photo actually Dan Peltier)	.20	.09	.03
☐	289 Tony Scruggs	.10	.05	.01
☐	290 Kenny Rogers	.04	.02	.01
☐	291 Bret Saberhagen	.07	.03	.01
☐	292 Brian McRae	.20	.09	.03
☐	293 Storm Davis	.04	.02	.01
☐	294 Danny Tartabull	.07	.03	.01
☐	295 David Howard	.10	.05	.01
☐	296 Mike Boddicker	.04	.02	.01
☐	297 Joel Johnston	.10	.05	.01
☐	298 Tim Spehr	.10	.05	.01
☐	299 Hector Wagner	.04	.02	.01
☐	300 George Brett	.10	.05	.01
☐	301 Mike Macfarlane	.04	.02	.01
☐	302 Kirk Gibson	.07	.03	.01
☐	303 Harvey Pulliam	.15	.07	.02
☐	304 Jim Eisenreich	.04	.02	.01
☐	305 Kevin Seitzer	.07	.03	.01
☐	306 Mark Davis	.04	.02	.01
☐	307 Kurt Stillwell	.04	.02	.01
☐	308 Jeff Montgomery	.04	.02	.01
☐	309 Kevin Appier	.07	.03	.01
☐	310 Bob Hamelin	.07	.03	.01
☐	311 Tom Gordon	.07	.03	.01
☐	312 Kerwin Moore	.15	.07	.02
☐	313 Hugh Walker	.04	.02	.01
☐	314 Terry Shumpert	.04	.02	.01
☐	315 Warren Cromartie	.04	.02	.01
☐	316 Gary Thurman	.04	.02	.01
☐	317 Steve Bedrosian	.04	.02	.01
☐	318 Danny Gladden	.04	.02	.01
☐	319 Jack Morris	.10	.05	.01
☐	320 Kirby Puckett	.20	.09	.03
☐	321 Kent Hrbek	.07	.03	.01
☐	322 Kevin Tapani	.07	.03	.01
☐	323 Denny Neagle	.15	.07	.02
☐	324 Rich Garces	.10	.05	.01
☐	325 Larry Casian	.04	.02	.01
☐	326 Shane Mack	.07	.03	.01
☐	327 Allan Anderson	.04	.02	.01
☐	328 Junior Ortiz	.04	.02	.01
☐	329 Paul Abbott	.10	.05	.01
☐	330 Chuck Knoblauch	.30	.14	.04
☐	331 Chili Davis	.07	.03	.01
☐	332 Todd Ritchie	.10	.05	.01
☐	333 Brian Harper	.04	.02	.01
☐	334 Rick Aguilera	.07	.03	.01
☐	335 Scott Erickson	.20	.09	.03
☐	336 Pedro Munoz	.25	.11	.03
☐	337 Scott Leius	.04	.02	.01
☐	338 Greg Gagne	.04	.02	.01
☐	339 Mike Pagliarulo	.04	.02	.01
☐	340 Terry Leach	.04	.02	.01
☐	341 Willie Banks	.10	.05	.01
☐	342 Bobby Thigpen	.04	.02	.01
☐	343 Roberto Hernandez	.20	.09	.03
☐	344 Melido Perez	.07	.03	.01
☐	345 Carlton Fisk	.10	.05	.01
☐	346 Norberto Martin	.10	.05	.01
☐	347 Johnny Ruffin	.15	.07	.02
☐	348 Jeff Carter	.10	.05	.01
☐	349 Lance Johnson	.04	.02	.01
☐	350 Sammy Sosa	.07	.03	.01
☐	351 Alex Fernandez	.15	.07	.02
☐	352 Jack McDowell	.10	.05	.01
☐	353 Bob Wickman	.40	.18	.05
☐	354 Wilson Alvarez	.10	.05	.01
☐	355 Charlie Hough	.04	.02	.01
☐	356 Ozzie Guillen	.04	.02	.01
☐	357 Cory Snyder	.04	.02	.01
☐	358 Robin Ventura	.20	.09	.03
☐	359 Scott Fletcher	.04	.02	.01
☐	360 Cesar Bernhardt	.10	.05	.01
☐	361 Dan Pasqua	.04	.02	.01
☐	362 Tim Raines	.07	.03	.01
☐	363 Brian Drahman	.10	.05	.01
☐	364 Wayne Edwards	.04	.02	.01
☐	365 Scott Radinsky	.04	.02	.01
☐	366 Frank Thomas	1.25	.55	.16
☐	367 Cecil Fielder SLUG	.10	.05	.01
☐	368 Julio Franco SLUG	.05	.02	.01
☐	369 Kelly Gruber SLUG	.05	.02	.01
☐	370 Alan Trammell SLUG	.05	.02	.01
☐	371 Rickey Henderson SLUG	.10	.05	.01
☐	372 Jose Canseco SLUG	.10	.05	.01
☐	373 Ellis Burks SLUG	.05	.02	.01
☐	374 Lance Parrish SLUG	.05	.02	.01
☐	375 Dave Parker SLUG	.05	.02	.01
☐	376 Eddie Murray SLUG	.10	.05	.01
☐	377 Ryne Sandberg SLUG	.12	.05	.02
☐	378 Matt Williams SLUG	.05	.02	.01
☐	379 Barry Larkin SLUG	.05	.02	.01
☐	380 Barry Bonds SLUG	.10	.05	.01
☐	381 Bobby Bonilla SLUG	.08	.04	.01
☐	382 Darryl Strawberry SLUG	.10	.05	.01
☐	383 Benny Santiago SLUG	.05	.02	.01
☐	384 Don Robinson SLUG	.05	.02	.01
☐	385 Paul Coleman	.04	.02	.01
☐	386 Milt Thompson	.04	.02	.01
☐	387 Lee Smith	.07	.03	.01
☐	388 Ray Lankford	.30	.14	.04
☐	389 Tom Pagnozzi	.04	.02	.01
☐	390 Ken Hill	.07	.03	.01
☐	391 Jamie Moyer	.04	.02	.01
☐	392 Greg Carmona	.10	.05	.01
☐	393 John Ericks	.04	.02	.01
☐	394 Bob Tewksbury	.07	.03	.01
☐	395 Jose Oquendo	.04	.02	.01
☐	396 Rheal Cormier	.15	.07	.02

☐ 397 Mike Milchin .12 .05 .02
☐ 398 Ozzie Smith .10 .05 .01
☐ 399 Aaron Holbert .12 .05 .02
☐ 400 Jose DeLeon .04 .02 .01
☐ 401 Felix Jose .07 .03 .01
☐ 402 Juan Agosto .04 .02 .01
☐ 403 Pedro Guerrero .07 .03 .01
☐ 404 Todd Zeile .07 .03 .01
☐ 405 Gerald Perry .04 .02 .01
☐ 406 Donovan Osborne UER .50 .23 .06
(Card number is 410)
☐ 407 Bryn Smith .04 .02 .01
☐ 408 Bernard Gilkey .15 .07 .02
☐ 409 Rex Hudler .04 .02 .01
☐ 410 Thomson/Branca Shot .10 .05 .01
Bobby Thomson
Ralph Branca
(See also 406)
☐ 411 Lance Dickson .10 .05 .01
☐ 412 Danny Jackson .04 .02 .01
☐ 413 Jerome Walton .04 .02 .01
☐ 414 Sean Cheetham .12 .05 .02
☐ 415 Joe Girardi .04 .02 .01
☐ 416 Ryne Sandberg .25 .11 .03
☐ 417 Mike Harkey .07 .03 .01
☐ 418 George Bell .07 .03 .01
☐ 419 Rick Wilkins .10 .05 .01
☐ 420 Earl Cunningham .04 .02 .01
☐ 421 Heathcliff Slocumb .04 .02 .01
☐ 422 Mike Bielecki .04 .02 .01
☐ 423 Jessie Hollins .12 .05 .02
☐ 424 Shawon Dunston .07 .03 .01
☐ 425 Dave Smith .04 .02 .01
☐ 426 Greg Maddux .10 .05 .01
☐ 427 Jose Vizcaino .04 .02 .01
☐ 428 Luis Salazar .04 .02 .01
☐ 429 Andre Dawson .10 .05 .01
☐ 430 Rick Sutcliffe .07 .03 .01
☐ 431 Paul Assenmacher .04 .02 .01
☐ 432 Erik Pappas .04 .02 .01
☐ 433 Mark Grace .10 .05 .01
☐ 434 Dennis Martinez .07 .03 .01
☐ 435 Marquis Grissom .15 .07 .02
☐ 436 Wilfredo Cordero .50 .23 .06
☐ 437 Tim Wallach .07 .03 .01
☐ 438 Brian Barnes .12 .05 .02
☐ 439 Barry Jones .04 .02 .01
☐ 440 Ivan Calderon .04 .02 .01
☐ 441 Stan Spencer .10 .05 .01
☐ 442 Larry Walker .20 .09 .03
☐ 443 Chris Haney .10 .05 .01
☐ 444 Hector Rivera .10 .05 .01
☐ 445 Delino DeShields .15 .07 .02
☐ 446 Andres Galarraga .04 .02 .01
☐ 447 Gilberto Reyes .04 .02 .01
☐ 448 Willie Greene .20 .09 .03
☐ 449 Greg Colbrunn .25 .11 .03
☐ 450 Rondell White .50 .23 .06
☐ 451 Steve Frey .04 .02 .01
☐ 452 Shane Andrews .20 .09 .03
☐ 453 Mike Fitzgerald .04 .02 .01
☐ 454 Spike Owen .04 .02 .01
☐ 455 Dave Martinez .04 .02 .01
☐ 456 Dennis Boyd .04 .02 .01
☐ 457 Eric Bullock .04 .02 .01
☐ 458 Reid Cornelius .12 .05 .02
☐ 459 Chris Nabholz .10 .05 .01
☐ 460 David Cone .10 .05 .01
☐ 461 Hubie Brooks .04 .02 .01
☐ 462 Sid Fernandez .07 .03 .01
☐ 463 Doug Simons .10 .05 .01
☐ 464 Howard Johnson .07 .03 .01
☐ 465 Chris Donnels .12 .05 .02
☐ 466 Anthony Young .12 .05 .02
☐ 467 Todd Hundley .04 .02 .01
☐ 468 Rick Cerone .04 .02 .01
☐ 469 Kevin Elster .04 .02 .01
☐ 470 Wally Whitehurst .04 .02 .01
☐ 471 Vince Coleman .07 .03 .01
☐ 472 Dwight Gooden .07 .03 .01
☐ 473 Charlie O'Brien .04 .02 .01
☐ 474 Jeromy Burnitz .30 .14 .04
☐ 475 John Franco .07 .03 .01
☐ 476 Daryl Boston .04 .02 .01
☐ 477 Frank Viola .07 .03 .01
☐ 478 D.J. Dozier .10 .05 .01
☐ 479 Kevin McReynolds .07 .03 .01
☐ 480 Tom Herr .04 .02 .01
☐ 481 Gregg Jefferies .07 .03 .01
☐ 482 Pete Schourek .12 .05 .02
☐ 483 Ron Darling .07 .03 .01
☐ 484 Dave Magadan .07 .03 .01
☐ 485 Andy Ashby .12 .05 .02
☐ 486 Dale Murphy .07 .03 .01
☐ 487 Von Hayes .04 .02 .01
☐ 488 Kim Batiste .20 .09 .03
☐ 489 Tony Longmire .10 .05 .01
☐ 490 Wally Backman .04 .02 .01
☐ 491 Jeff Jackson .04 .02 .01
☐ 492 Mickey Morandini .10 .05 .01
☐ 493 Darrel Akerfelds .04 .02 .01
☐ 494 Ricky Jordan .04 .02 .01
☐ 495 Randy Ready .04 .02 .01
☐ 496 Darrin Fletcher .04 .02 .01
☐ 497 Chuck Malone .04 .02 .01
☐ 498 Pat Combs .04 .02 .01
☐ 499 Dickie Thon .04 .02 .01
☐ 500 Roger McDowell .04 .02 .01
☐ 501 Len Dykstra .07 .03 .01
☐ 502 Joe Boever .04 .02 .01
☐ 503 John Kruk .07 .03 .01
☐ 504 Terry Mulholland .04 .02 .01
☐ 505 Wes Chamberlain .20 .09 .03
☐ 506 Mike Lieberthal .20 .09 .03
☐ 507 Darren Daulton .07 .03 .01
☐ 508 Charlie Hayes .04 .02 .01
☐ 509 John Smiley .07 .03 .01
☐ 510 Gary Varsho .04 .02 .01
☐ 511 Curt Wilkerson .04 .02 .01
☐ 512 Orlando Merced .20 .09 .03
☐ 513 Barry Bonds .20 .09 .03
☐ 514 Mike LaValliere .04 .02 .01
☐ 515 Doug Drabek .07 .03 .01
☐ 516 Gary Redus .04 .02 .01
☐ 517 William Pennyfeather .15 .07 .02
☐ 518 Randy Tomlin .20 .09 .03
☐ 519 Mike Zimmerman .10 .05 .01
☐ 520 Jeff King .04 .02 .01
☐ 521 Kurt Miller .25 .11 .03
☐ 522 Jay Bell .07 .03 .01
☐ 523 Bill Landrum .04 .02 .01
☐ 524 Zane Smith .04 .02 .01
☐ 525 Bobby Bonilla .10 .05 .01
☐ 526 Bob Walk .04 .02 .01
☐ 527 Austin Manahan .04 .02 .01
☐ 528 Joe Ausanio .10 .05 .01
☐ 529 Andy Van Slyke .07 .03 .01
☐ 530 Jose Lind .04 .02 .01
☐ 531 Carlos Garcia .20 .09 .03
☐ 532 Don Slaught .04 .02 .01
☐ 533 Colin Powell .15 .07 .02
(General)
☐ 534 Frank Bolick .12 .05 .02
☐ 535 Gary Scott .15 .07 .02
☐ 536 Nikco Riesgo .12 .05 .02
☐ 537 Reggie Sanders .75 .35 .09
☐ 538 Tim Howard .10 .05 .01
☐ 539 Ryan Bowen .15 .07 .02
☐ 540 Eric Anthony .07 .03 .01
☐ 541 Jim Deshaies .04 .02 .01
☐ 542 Tom Nevers .12 .05 .02
☐ 543 Ken Caminiti .07 .03 .01
☐ 544 Karl Rhodes .04 .02 .01
☐ 545 Xavier Hernandez .04 .02 .01
☐ 546 Mike Scott .04 .02 .01
☐ 547 Jeff Juden .07 .03 .01
☐ 548 Darryl Kile .07 .03 .01
☐ 549 Willie Ansley .07 .03 .01
☐ 550 Luis Gonzalez .20 .09 .03
☐ 551 Mike Simms .10 .05 .01
☐ 552 Mark Portugal .04 .02 .01
☐ 553 Jimmy Jones .04 .02 .01
☐ 554 Jim Clancy .04 .02 .01
☐ 555 Pete Harnisch .07 .03 .01
☐ 556 Craig Biggio .07 .03 .01
☐ 557 Eric Yelding .04 .02 .01
☐ 558 Dave Rohde .04 .02 .01
☐ 559 Casey Candaele .04 .02 .01
☐ 560 Curt Schilling .07 .03 .01
☐ 561 Steve Finley .07 .03 .01
☐ 562 Javier Ortiz .04 .02 .01
☐ 563 Andujar Cedeno .10 .05 .01
☐ 564 Rafael Ramirez .04 .02 .01
☐ 565 Kenny Lofton 1.00 .45 .13
☐ 566 Steve Avery .20 .09 .03
☐ 567 Lonnie Smith .04 .02 .01
☐ 568 Kent Mercker .07 .03 .01
☐ 569 Chipper Jones .75 .35 .09
☐ 570 Terry Pendleton .10 .05 .01
☐ 571 Otis Nixon .07 .03 .01
☐ 572 Juan Berenguer .04 .02 .01
☐ 573 Charlie Leibrandt .04 .02 .01
☐ 574 David Justice .30 .14 .04
☐ 575 Keith Mitchell .20 .09 .03
☐ 576 Tom Glavine .20 .09 .03
☐ 577 Greg Olson .04 .02 .01

☐ 578 Rafael Belliard .04 .02 .01
☐ 579 Ben Rivera .15 .07 .02
☐ 580 John Smoltz .10 .05 .01
☐ 581 Tyler Houston .04 .02 .01
☐ 582 Mark Wohlers .20 .09 .03
☐ 583 Ron Gant .12 .05 .02
☐ 584 Ramon Caraballo .12 .05 .02
☐ 585 Sid Bream .04 .02 .01
☐ 586 Jeff Treadway .04 .02 .01
☐ 587 Javier Lopez .60 .25 .08
☐ 588 Deion Sanders .20 .09 .03
☐ 589 Mike Heath .04 .02 .01
☐ 590 Ryan Klesko 1.00 .45 .13
☐ 591 Bob Ojeda .04 .02 .01
☐ 592 Alfredo Griffin .04 .02 .01
☐ 593 Raul Mondesi .50 .23 .06
☐ 594 Greg Smith .04 .02 .01
☐ 595 Orel Hershiser .07 .03 .01
☐ 596 Juan Samuel .04 .02 .01
☐ 597 Brett Butler .07 .03 .01
☐ 598 Gary Carter .07 .03 .01
☐ 599 Stan Javier .04 .02 .01
☐ 600 Kal Daniels .04 .02 .01
☐ 601 Jamie McAndrew .15 .07 .02
☐ 602 Mike Sharperson .04 .02 .01
☐ 603 Jay Howell .04 .02 .01
☐ 604 Eric Karros 1.50 .65 .19
☐ 605 Tim Belcher .07 .03 .01
☐ 606 Dan Opperman .10 .05 .01
☐ 607 Lenny Harris .04 .02 .01
☐ 608 Tom Goodwin .07 .03 .01
☐ 609 Darryl Strawberry .12 .05 .02
☐ 610 Ramon Martinez .10 .05 .01
☐ 611 Kevin Gross .04 .02 .01
☐ 612 Zakary Shinall .15 .07 .02
☐ 613 Mike Scioscia .04 .02 .01
☐ 614 Eddie Murray .10 .05 .01
☐ 615 Ronnie Walden .10 .05 .01
☐ 616 Will Clark .20 .09 .03
☐ 617 Adam Hyzdu .15 .07 .02
☐ 618 Matt Williams .07 .03 .01
☐ 619 Don Robinson .04 .02 .01
☐ 620 Jeff Brantley .04 .02 .01
☐ 621 Greg Litton .04 .02 .01
☐ 622 Steve Decker .15 .07 .02
☐ 623 Robby Thompson .04 .02 .01
☐ 624 Mark Leonard .10 .05 .01
☐ 625 Kevin Bass .04 .02 .01
☐ 626 Scott Garrelts .04 .02 .01
☐ 627 Jose Uribe .04 .02 .01
☐ 628 Eric Gunderson .04 .02 .01
☐ 629 Steve Hosey .15 .07 .02
☐ 630 Trevor Wilson .04 .02 .01
☐ 631 Terry Kennedy .04 .02 .01
☐ 632 Dave Righetti .04 .02 .01
☐ 633 Kelly Downs .04 .02 .01
☐ 634 Johnny Ard .04 .02 .01
☐ 635 Eric Christopherson .15 .07 .02
☐ 636 Kevin Mitchell .07 .03 .01
☐ 637 John Burkett .04 .02 .01
☐ 638 Kevin Rogers .15 .07 .02
☐ 639 Bud Black .04 .02 .01
☐ 640 Willie McGee .07 .03 .01
☐ 641 Royce Clayton .15 .07 .02
☐ 642 Tony Fernandez .07 .03 .01
☐ 643 Ricky Bones .20 .09 .03
☐ 644 Thomas Howard .04 .02 .01
☐ 645 Dave Staton .25 .11 .03
☐ 646 Jim Presley .04 .02 .01
☐ 647 Tony Gwynn .12 .05 .02
☐ 648 Marty Barrett .04 .02 .01
☐ 649 Scott Coolbaugh .04 .02 .01
☐ 650 Craig Lefferts .04 .02 .01
☐ 651 Eddie Whitson .04 .02 .01
☐ 652 Oscar Azocar .04 .02 .01
☐ 653 Wes Gardner .04 .02 .01
☐ 654 Bip Roberts .07 .03 .01
☐ 655 Robbie Beckett .12 .05 .02
☐ 656 Benito Santiago .07 .03 .01
☐ 657 Greg W.Harris .04 .02 .01
☐ 658 Jerald Clark .04 .02 .01
☐ 659 Fred McGriff .12 .05 .02
☐ 660 Larry Andersen .04 .02 .01
☐ 661 Bruce Hurst .07 .03 .01
☐ 662 Steve Martin .10 .05 .01
☐ 663 Rafael Valdez .04 .02 .01
☐ 664 Paul Faries .10 .05 .01
☐ 665 Andy Benes .07 .03 .01
☐ 666 Randy Myers .07 .03 .01
☐ 667 Rob Dibble .07 .03 .01
☐ 668 Glenn Sutko .04 .02 .01
☐ 669 Glenn Braggs .04 .02 .01
☐ 670 Billy Hatcher .04 .02 .01
☐ 671 Joe Oliver .04 .02 .01
☐ 672 Freddy Benavides .04 .02 .01
☐ 673 Barry Larkin .10 .05 .01
☐ 674 Chris Sabo .07 .03 .01
☐ 675 Mariano Duncan .04 .02 .01
☐ 676 Chris Jones .04 .02 .01
☐ 677 Gino Minutelli .10 .05 .01
☐ 678 Reggie Jefferson .10 .05 .01
☐ 679 Jack Armstrong .04 .02 .01
☐ 680 Chris Hammond .10 .05 .01
☐ 681 Jose Rijo .07 .03 .01
☐ 682 Bill Doran .04 .02 .01
☐ 683 Terry Lee .10 .05 .01
☐ 684 Tom Browning .04 .02 .01
☐ 685 Paul O'Neill .07 .03 .01
☐ 686 Eric Davis .07 .03 .01
☐ 687 Dan Wilson .15 .07 .02
☐ 688 Ted Power .04 .02 .01
☐ 689 Tim Layana .04 .02 .01
☐ 690 Norm Charlton .07 .03 .01
☐ 691 Hal Morris .07 .03 .01
☐ 692 Rickey Henderson .10 .05 .01
☐ 693 Sam Militello .50 .23 .06
Minor League MVP
☐ 694 Matt Mieske .25 .11 .03
Minor League MVP
☐ 695 Paul Russo .20 .09 .03
Minor League MVP
☐ 696 Domingo Mota .10 .05 .01
Minor League MVP
☐ 697 Todd Guggiana .10 .05 .01
Minor League MVP
☐ 698 Marc Newfield .40 .18 .05
Minor League MVP
☐ 699 Checklist 1 .05 .02 .01
☐ 700 Checklist 2 .05 .02 .01
☐ 701 Checklist 3 .05 .02 .01
☐ 702 Checklist 4 .05 .02 .01
☐ 703 Checklist 5 .05 .02 .01
☐ 704 Checklist 6 .05 .02 .01

1992 Bowman

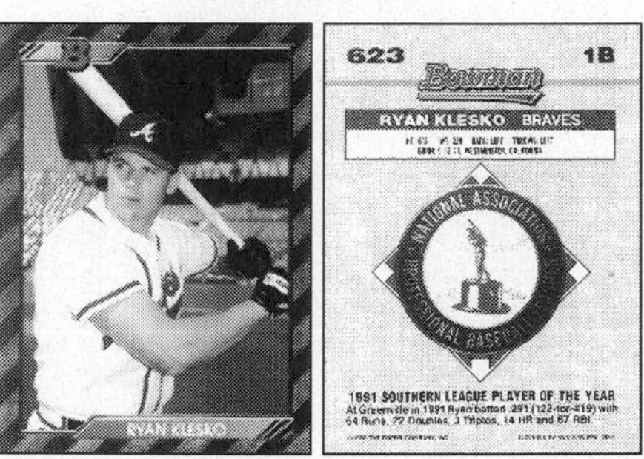

The cards in this 705-card set measure the standard size (2 1/2" by 3 1/2") and feature posed and action color player photos on a UV-coated white card face. A gradated orange bar accented with black diagonal stripes carries the player's name at the bottom right corner. The backs display close-up color photos and biography on a burlap-textured background. Below the photo, statistical information appears in a yellow-and-white grid with the player's name in a red bar at the top of the grid. Interspersed throughout the set are 45 special cards with an identical front design except for a textured gold-foil border. The foil cards were inserted one per wax pack and two per jumbo (23 regular cards) pack. These foil cards feature past and present Team USA players and minor league POY Award winners. Their backs have the same burlap background but display one of three emblems: 1) U.S. Baseball Federation; 2) Topps Team USA 1992; or 3) National Association of Professional Baseball Leagues. The player's name and biography are shown in a blue-and-white box above these emblems. Some of the regular and special cards picture players in civilian clothing who are still in the farm system. The cards are numbered on the back. The key Rookie Cards in this set are Carlos Delgado, Cliff Floyd, Pat Listach, David Nied, Brien Taylor, and Nigel Wilson.

	MT	EX-MT	VG
COMPLETE SET (705)	100.00	45.00	12.50
COMMON PLAYER (1-705)	.08	.04	.01
☐ 1 Ivan Rodriguez	1.00	.45	.13
☐ 2 Kirk McCaskill	.08	.04	.01
☐ 3 Scott Livingstone	.20	.09	.03
☐ 4 Salomon Torres	.50	.23	.06
☐ 5 Carlos Hernandez	.08	.04	.01
☐ 6 Dave Hollins	.25	.11	.03
☐ 7 Scott Fletcher	.08	.04	.01
☐ 8 Jorge Fabregas	.20	.09	.03
☐ 9 Andujar Cedeno	.12	.05	.02
☐ 10 Howard Johnson	.10	.04	.01
☐ 11 Trevor Hoffman	.25	.11	.03
☐ 12 Roberto Kelly	.12	.05	.02
☐ 13 Gregg Jefferies	.10	.04	.01
☐ 14 Marquis Grissom	.25	.11	.03
☐ 15 Mike Ignasiak	.20	.09	.03
☐ 16 Jack Morris	.15	.07	.02
☐ 17 William Pennyfeather	.15	.07	.02
☐ 18 Todd Stottlemyre	.10	.04	.01
☐ 19 Chito Martinez	.08	.04	.01
☐ 20 Roberto Alomar	.60	.25	.08
☐ 21 Sam Militello	.50	.23	.06
☐ 22 Hector Fajardo	.25	.11	.03
☐ 23 Paul Quantrill	.15	.07	.02
☐ 24 Chuck Knoblauch	.50	.23	.06
☐ 25 Reggie Jefferson	.30	.14	.04
☐ 26 Jeremy McGarity	.15	.07	.02
☐ 27 Jerome Walton	.08	.04	.01
☐ 28 Chipper Jones	1.25	.55	.16
☐ 29 Brian Barber	.40	.18	.05
☐ 30 Ron Darling	.10	.04	.01
☐ 31 Roberto Petagine	.30	.14	.04
☐ 32 Chuck Finley	.08	.04	.01
☐ 33 Edgar Martinez	.10	.04	.01
☐ 34 Napoleon Robinson	.15	.07	.02
☐ 35 Andy Van Slyke	.12	.05	.02
☐ 36 Bobby Thigpen	.08	.04	.01
☐ 37 Travis Fryman	1.00	.45	.13
☐ 38 Eric Christopherson	.10	.05	.01
☐ 39 Terry Mulholland	.08	.04	.01
☐ 40 Darryl Strawberry	.35	.16	.04
☐ 41 Manny Alexander	.30	.14	.04
☐ 42 Tracy Sanders	.35	.16	.04
☐ 43 Pete Incaviglia	.08	.04	.01
☐ 44 Kim Batiste	.15	.07	.02
☐ 45 Frank Rodriguez	.50	.23	.06
☐ 46 Greg Swindell	.10	.04	.01
☐ 47 Delino DeShields	.25	.11	.03
☐ 48 John Ericks	.08	.04	.01
☐ 49 Franklin Stubbs	.08	.04	.01
☐ 50 Tony Gwynn	.35	.16	.04
☐ 51 Clifton Garrett	.15	.07	.02
☐ 52 Mike Gardella	.15	.07	.02
☐ 53 Scott Erickson	.15	.07	.02
☐ 54 Gary Caraballo	.15	.07	.02
☐ 55 Jose Oliva	.35	.16	.04
☐ 56 Brook Fordyce	.10	.05	.01
☐ 57 Mark Whiten	.10	.04	.01
☐ 58 Joe Slusarski	.08	.04	.01
☐ 59 J.R. Phillips	.15	.07	.02
☐ 60 Barry Bonds	.60	.25	.08
☐ 61 Bob Milacki	.08	.04	.01
☐ 62 Keith Mitchell	.15	.07	.02
☐ 63 Angel Miranda	.15	.07	.02
☐ 64 Raul Mondesi	.60	.25	.08
☐ 65 Brian Koelling	.15	.07	.02
☐ 66 Brian McRae	.12	.05	.02
☐ 67 John Patterson	.20	.09	.03
☐ 68 John Wetteland	.08	.04	.01
☐ 69 Wilson Alvarez	.08	.04	.01
☐ 70 Wade Boggs	.30	.14	.04
☐ 71 Darryl Ratliff	.15	.07	.02
☐ 72 Jeff Jackson	.08	.04	.01
☐ 73 Jeremy Hernandez	.15	.07	.02
☐ 74 Darryl Hamilton	.10	.04	.01
☐ 75 Rafael Belliard	.08	.04	.01
☐ 76 Rick Trlicek	.20	.09	.03
☐ 77 Felipe Crespo	.20	.09	.03
☐ 78 Carney Lansford	.10	.04	.01
☐ 79 Ryan Long	.20	.09	.03
☐ 80 Kirby Puckett	.75	.35	.09
☐ 81 Earl Cunningham	.10	.05	.01
☐ 82 Pedro Martinez	.75	.35	.09
☐ 83 Scott Hatteberg	.15	.07	.02
☐ 84 Juan Gonzalez	1.25	.55	.16
☐ 85 Robert Nutting	.15	.07	.02
☐ 86 Calvin Reese	.30	.14	.04
☐ 87 Dave Silvestri	.30	.14	.04
☐ 88 Scott Ruffcorn	.60	.25	.08
☐ 89 Rick Aguilera	.10	.04	.01
☐ 90 Cecil Fielder	.35	.16	.04
☐ 91 Kirk Dressendorfer	.08	.04	.01
☐ 92 Jerry DiPoto	.20	.09	.03
☐ 93 Mike Felder	.08	.04	.01
☐ 94 Craig Paquette	.08	.04	.01
☐ 95 Elvin Paulino	.20	.09	.03
☐ 96 Donovan Osborne	.60	.25	.08
☐ 97 Hubie Brooks	.08	.04	.01
☐ 98 Derek Lowe	.25	.11	.03
☐ 99 David Zancanaro	.20	.09	.03
☐ 100 Ken Griffey Jr.	2.00	.90	.25
☐ 101 Todd Hundley	.08	.04	.01
☐ 102 Mike Trombley	.30	.14	.04
☐ 103 Ricky Gutierrez	.15	.07	.02
☐ 104 Braulio Castillo	.25	.11	.03
☐ 105 Craig Lefferts	.08	.04	.01
☐ 106 Rick Sutcliffe	.10	.04	.01
☐ 107 Dean Palmer	.50	.23	.06
☐ 108 Henry Rodriguez	.20	.09	.03
☐ 109 Mark Clark	.15	.07	.02
☐ 110 Kenny Lofton	1.25	.55	.16
☐ 111 Mark Carreon	.08	.04	.01
☐ 112 J.T. Bruett	.15	.07	.02
☐ 113 Gerald Williams	.20	.09	.03
☐ 114 Frank Thomas	4.00	1.80	.50
☐ 115 Kevin Reimer	.08	.04	.01
☐ 116 Sammy Sosa	.08	.04	.01
☐ 117 Mickey Tettleton	.10	.04	.01
☐ 118 Reggie Sanders	.75	.35	.09
☐ 119 Trevor Wilson	.08	.04	.01
☐ 120 Cliff Brantley	.12	.05	.02
☐ 121 Spike Owen	.08	.04	.01
☐ 122 Jeff Montgomery	.08	.04	.01
☐ 123 Alex Sutherland	.15	.07	.02
☐ 124 Brien Taylor	5.00	2.30	.60
☐ 125 Brian Williams	.50	.23	.06
☐ 126 Kevin Seitzer	.10	.04	.01
☐ 127 Carlos Delgado	3.50	1.55	.45
☐ 128 Gary Scott	.10	.04	.01
☐ 129 Scott Cooper	.25	.11	.03
☐ 130 Domingo Jean	.35	.16	.04
☐ 131 Pat Mahomes	.50	.23	.06
☐ 132 Mike Boddicker	.08	.04	.01
☐ 133 Roberto Hernandez	.20	.09	.03
☐ 134 Dave Valle	.08	.04	.01
☐ 135 Kurt Stillwell	.08	.04	.01
☐ 136 Brad Pennington	.35	.16	.04
☐ 137 Jermaine Swinton	.15	.07	.02
☐ 138 Ryan Hawblitzel	.50	.23	.06
☐ 139 Tito Navarro	.25	.11	.03
☐ 140 Sandy Alomar	.10	.04	.01
☐ 141 Todd Benzinger	.08	.04	.01
☐ 142 Danny Jackson	.08	.04	.01
☐ 143 Melvin Nieves	.75	.35	.09
☐ 144 Jim Campanis	.20	.09	.03
☐ 145 Luis Gonzalez	.12	.05	.02
☐ 146 Dave Doorneweerd	.20	.09	.03
☐ 147 Charlie Hayes	.08	.04	.01
☐ 148 Greg Maddux	.20	.09	.03
☐ 149 Brian Harper	.08	.04	.01
☐ 150 Brent Miller	.15	.07	.02
☐ 151 Shawn Estes	.30	.14	.04
☐ 152 Mike Williams	.30	.14	.04
☐ 153 Charlie Hough	.08	.04	.01
☐ 154 Randy Myers	.10	.04	.01
☐ 155 Kevin Young	.75	.35	.09
☐ 156 Rick Wilkins	.08	.04	.01
☐ 157 Terry Shumpert	.08	.04	.01
☐ 158 Steve Karsay	.25	.11	.03
☐ 159 Gary DiSarcina	.10	.04	.01
☐ 160 Deion Sanders	.40	.18	.05
☐ 161 Tom Browning	.08	.04	.01
☐ 162 Dickie Thon	.08	.04	.01
☐ 163 Luis Mercedes	.25	.11	.03
☐ 164 Riccardo Ingram	.25	.11	.03
☐ 165 Tavo Alvarez	.40	.18	.05
☐ 166 Rickey Henderson	.30	.14	.04
☐ 167 Jaime Navarro	.10	.04	.01
☐ 168 Billy Ashley	1.00	.45	.13
☐ 169 Phil Dauphin	.20	.09	.03
☐ 170 Ivan Cruz	.15	.07	.02
☐ 171 Harold Baines	.10	.04	.01
☐ 172 Bryan Harvey	.08	.04	.01
☐ 173 Alex Cole	.08	.04	.01
☐ 174 Curtis Shaw	.20	.09	.03
☐ 175 Matt Williams	.10	.05	.01

☐	176	Felix Jose	.10	.04	.01
☐	177	Sam Horn	.08	.04	.01
☐	178	Randy Johnson	.10	.04	.01
☐	179	Ivan Calderon	.08	.04	.01
☐	180	Steve Avery	.50	.23	.06
☐	181	William Suero	.12	.05	.02
☐	182	Bill Swift	.08	.04	.01
☐	183	Howard Battle	.35	.16	.04
☐	184	Ruben Amaro	.10	.05	.01
☐	185	Jim Abbott	.20	.09	.03
☐	186	Mike Fitzgerald	.08	.04	.01
☐	187	Bruce Hurst	.10	.04	.01
☐	188	Jeff Juden	.15	.07	.02
☐	189	Jeromy Burnitz	.40	.18	.05
☐	190	Dave Burba	.08	.04	.01
☐	191	Kevin Brown	.10	.04	.01
☐	192	Patrick Lennon	.12	.05	.02
☐	193	Jeff McNeely	.20	.09	.03
☐	194	Wilfredo Cordero	.50	.23	.06
☐	195	Chili Davis	.10	.04	.01
☐	196	Milt Cuyler	.08	.04	.01
☐	197	Von Hayes	.08	.04	.01
☐	198	Todd Revenig	.20	.09	.03
☐	199	Joel Johnston	.08	.04	.01
☐	200	Jeff Bagwell	.75	.35	.09
☐	201	Alex Fernandez	.10	.04	.01
☐	202	Todd Jones	.15	.07	.02
☐	203	Charles Nagy	.25	.11	.03
☐	204	Tim Raines	.12	.05	.02
☐	205	Kevin Maas	.12	.05	.02
☐	206	Julio Franco	.10	.04	.01
☐	207	Randy Velarde	.08	.04	.01
☐	208	Lance Johnson	.08	.04	.01
☐	209	Scott Leius	.08	.04	.01
☐	210	Derek Lee	.15	.07	.02
☐	211	Joe Sondrini	.20	.09	.03
☐	212	Royce Clayton	.40	.18	.05
☐	213	Chris George	.10	.05	.01
☐	214	Gary Sheffield	.75	.35	.09
☐	215	Mark Gubicza	.08	.04	.01
☐	216	Mike Moore	.08	.04	.01
☐	217	Rick Huisman	.30	.14	.04
☐	218	Jeff Russell	.08	.04	.01
☐	219	D.J. Dozier	.10	.04	.01
☐	220	Dave Martinez	.08	.04	.01
☐	221	Alan Newman	.20	.09	.03
☐	222	Nolan Ryan	1.50	.65	.19
☐	223	Teddy Higuera	.08	.04	.01
☐	224	Damon Buford	.30	.14	.04
☐	225	Ruben Sierra	.40	.18	.05
☐	226	Tom Nevers	.10	.05	.01
☐	227	Tommy Greene	.08	.04	.01
☐	228	Nigel Wilson	3.50	1.55	.45
☐	229	John DeSilva	.12	.05	.02
☐	230	Bobby Witt	.08	.04	.01
☐	231	Greg Cadaret	.08	.04	.01
☐	232	John Vander Wal	.25	.11	.03
☐	233	Jack Clark	.10	.04	.01
☐	234	Bill Doran	.08	.04	.01
☐	235	Bobby Bonilla	.20	.09	.03
☐	236	Steve Olin	.08	.04	.01
☐	237	Derek Bell	.35	.16	.04
☐	238	David Cone	.10	.05	.01
☐	239	Victor Cole	.30	.14	.04
☐	240	Rod Bolton	.08	.04	.01
☐	241	Tom Pagnozzi	.08	.04	.01
☐	242	Rob Dibble	.10	.04	.01
☐	243	Michael Carter	.15	.07	.02
☐	244	Don Peters	.10	.05	.01
☐	245	Mike LaValliere	.08	.04	.01
☐	246	Joe Perona	.12	.05	.02
☐	247	Mitch Williams	.08	.04	.01
☐	248	Jay Buhner	.10	.04	.01
☐	249	Andy Benes	.12	.05	.02
☐	250	Alex Ochoa	.20	.09	.03
☐	251	Greg Blosser	.15	.07	.02
☐	252	Jack Armstrong	.08	.04	.01
☐	253	Juan Samuel	.08	.04	.01
☐	254	Terry Pendleton	.12	.05	.02
☐	255	Ramon Martinez	.12	.05	.02
☐	256	Rico Brogna	.10	.05	.01
☐	257	John Smiley	.10	.04	.01
☐	258	Carl Everett	.20	.09	.03
☐	259	Tim Salmon	1.25	.55	.16
☐	260	Will Clark	.60	.25	.08
☐	261	Ugueth Urbina	.25	.11	.03
☐	262	Jason Wood	.15	.07	.02
☐	263	Dave Magadan	.10	.04	.01
☐	264	Dante Bichette	.08	.04	.01
☐	265	Jose DeLeon	.08	.04	.01
☐	266	Mike Neill	.75	.35	.09
☐	267	Paul O'Neill	.10	.04	.01
☐	268	Anthony Young	.12	.05	.02

☐	269	Greg W. Harris	.08	.04	.01
☐	270	Todd Van Poppel	.40	.18	.05
☐	271	Pete Castellano	.30	.14	.04
☐	272	Tony Phillips	.15	.07	.02
☐	273	Mike Gallego	.08	.04	.01
☐	274	Steve Cooke	.30	.14	.04
☐	275	Robin Ventura	.50	.23	.06
☐	276	Kevin Mitchell	.12	.05	.02
☐	277	Doug Linton	.12	.05	.02
☐	278	Robert Eenhoorn	.12	.05	.02
☐	279	Gabe White	.25	.11	.03
☐	280	Dave Stewart	.10	.04	.01
☐	281	Mo Sanford	.15	.07	.02
☐	282	Greg Perschke	.15	.07	.02
☐	283	Kevin Flora	.25	.11	.03
☐	284	Jeff Williams	.15	.07	.02
☐	285	Keith Miller	.08	.04	.01
☐	286	Andy Ashby	.15	.07	.02
☐	287	Doug Dascenzo	.08	.04	.01
☐	288	Eric Karros	1.75	.80	.22
☐	289	Glenn Murray	.20	.09	.03
☐	290	Troy Percival	.40	.18	.05
☐	291	Orlando Merced	.12	.05	.02
☐	292	Peter Hoy	.15	.07	.02
☐	293	Tony Fernandez	.10	.04	.01
☐	294	Juan Guzman	2.00	.90	.25
☐	295	Jesse Barfield	.08	.04	.01
☐	296	Sid Fernandez	.10	.04	.01
☐	297	Scott Cepicky	.35	.16	.04
☐	298	Garret Anderson	.15	.07	.02
☐	299	Cal Eldred	1.25	.55	.16
☐	300	Ryne Sandberg	1.00	.45	.13
☐	301	Jim Gantner	.08	.04	.01
☐	302	Mariano Rivera	.20	.09	.03
☐	303	Ron Lockett	.15	.07	.02
☐	304	Jose Offerman	.10	.04	.01
☐	305	Denny Martinez	.10	.04	.01
☐	306	Luis Ortiz	.20	.09	.03
☐	307	David Howard	.08	.04	.01
☐	308	Russ Springer	.35	.16	.04
☐	309	Chris Howard	.15	.07	.02
☐	310	Kyle Abbott	.15	.07	.02
☐	311	Aaron Sele	.75	.35	.09
☐	312	David Justice	.75	.35	.09
☐	313	Pete O'Brien	.08	.04	.01
☐	314	Greg Hansell	.35	.16	.04
☐	315	Dave Winfield	.20	.09	.03
☐	316	Lance Dickson	.08	.04	.01
☐	317	Eric King	.08	.04	.01
☐	318	Vaughn Eshelman	.15	.07	.02
☐	319	Tim Belcher	.10	.04	.01
☐	320	Andres Galarraga	.08	.04	.01
☐	321	Scott Bullett	.20	.09	.03
☐	322	Doug Strange	.08	.04	.01
☐	323	Jerald Clark	.08	.04	.01
☐	324	Dave Righetti	.08	.04	.01
☐	325	Greg Hibbard	.08	.04	.01
☐	326	Eric Hillman	.35	.16	.04
☐	327	Shane Reynolds	.15	.07	.02
☐	328	Chris Hammond	.10	.04	.01
☐	329	Albert Belle	.35	.16	.04
☐	330	Rich Becker	.35	.16	.04
☐	331	Eddie Williams	.15	.07	.02
☐	332	Donald Harris	.08	.04	.01
☐	333	Dave Smith	.08	.04	.01
☐	334	Steve Fireovid	.08	.04	.01
☐	335	Steve Buechele	.08	.04	.01
☐	336	Mike Schooler	.08	.04	.01
☐	337	Kevin McReynolds	.10	.04	.01
☐	338	Hensley Meulens	.08	.04	.01
☐	339	Benji Gil	.40	.18	.05
☐	340	Don Mattingly	.35	.16	.04
☐	341	Alvin Davis	.08	.04	.01
☐	342	Alan Mills	.08	.04	.01
☐	343	Kelly Downs	.08	.04	.01
☐	344	Leo Gomez	.20	.09	.03
☐	345	Tarrik Brock	.15	.07	.02
☐	346	Ryan Turner	.75	.35	.09
☐	347	John Smoltz	.20	.09	.03
☐	348	Bill Sampen	.08	.04	.01
☐	349	Paul Byrd	.25	.11	.03
☐	350	Mike Bordick	.15	.07	.02
☐	351	Jose Lind	.08	.04	.01
☐	352	David Wells	.08	.04	.01
☐	353	Barry Larkin	.20	.09	.03
☐	354	Bruce Ruffin	.08	.04	.01
☐	355	Luis Rivera	.08	.04	.01
☐	356	Sid Bream	.08	.04	.01
☐	357	Julian Vasquez	.15	.07	.02
☐	358	Jason Bere	.35	.16	.04
☐	359	Ben McDonald	.15	.07	.02
☐	360	Scott Stahoviak	.40	.18	.05
☐	361	Kirt Manwaring	.08	.04	.01

☐ 362 Jeff Johnson .08 .04 .01
☐ 363 Rob Deer .10 .04 .01
☐ 364 Tony Pena .08 .04 .01
☐ 365 Melido Perez .10 .04 .01
☐ 366 Clay Parker .08 .04 .01
☐ 367 Dale Sveum .08 .04 .01
☐ 368 Mike Scioscia .08 .04 .01
☐ 369 Roger Salkeld .15 .07 .02
☐ 370 Mike Stanley .08 .04 .01
☐ 371 Jack McDowell .12 .05 .02
☐ 372 Tim Wallach .10 .04 .01
☐ 373 Billy Ripken .08 .04 .01
☐ 374 Mike Christopher .15 .07 .02
☐ 375 Paul Molitor .12 .05 .02
☐ 376 Dave Stieb .08 .04 .01
☐ 377 Pedro Guerrero .10 .04 .01
☐ 378 Russ Swan .08 .04 .01
☐ 379 Bob Ojeda .08 .04 .01
☐ 380 Donn Pall .08 .04 .01
☐ 381 Eddie Zosky .15 .07 .02
☐ 382 Darnell Coles .08 .04 .01
☐ 383 Tom Smith .15 .07 .02
☐ 384 Mark McGwire .50 .23 .06
☐ 385 Gary Carter .10 .04 .01
☐ 386 Rich Amaral .12 .05 .02
☐ 387 Alan Embree .50 .23 .06
☐ 388 Jonathan Hurst .30 .14 .04
☐ 389 Bobby Jones 1.00 .45 .13
☐ 390 Rico Rossy .15 .07 .02
☐ 391 Dan Smith .20 .09 .03
☐ 392 Terry Steinbach .10 .04 .01
☐ 393 Jon Farrell .20 .09 .03
☐ 394 Dave Anderson .08 .04 .01
☐ 395 Benny Santiago .12 .05 .02
☐ 396 Mark Wohlers .20 .09 .03
☐ 397 Mo Vaughn .12 .05 .02
☐ 398 Randy Kramer .08 .04 .01
☐ 399 John Jaha .60 .25 .08
☐ 400 Cal Ripken 1.00 .45 .13
☐ 401 Ryan Bowen .15 .07 .02
☐ 402 Tim McIntosh .08 .04 .01
☐ 403 Bernard Gilkey .10 .05 .01
☐ 404 Junior Felix .08 .04 .01
☐ 405 Cris Colon .20 .09 .03
☐ 406 Marc Newfield .40 .18 .05
☐ 407 Bernie Williams .25 .11 .03
☐ 408 Jay Howell .08 .04 .01
☐ 409 Zane Smith .08 .04 .01
☐ 410 Jeff Shaw .08 .04 .01
☐ 411 Kerry Woodson .20 .09 .03
☐ 412 Wes Chamberlain .12 .05 .02
☐ 413 Dave Mlicki .25 .11 .03
☐ 414 Benny Distefano .08 .04 .01
☐ 415 Kevin Rogers .08 .04 .01
☐ 416 Tim Naehring .10 .04 .01
☐ 417 Clemente Nunez .60 .25 .08
☐ 418 Luis Sojo .08 .04 .01
☐ 419 Kevin Ritz .08 .04 .01
☐ 420 Omar Olivares .08 .04 .01
☐ 421 Manuel Lee .08 .04 .01
☐ 422 Julio Valera .15 .07 .02
☐ 423 Omar Vizquel .08 .04 .01
☐ 424 Darren Burton .20 .09 .03
☐ 425 Mel Hall .08 .04 .01
☐ 426 Dennis Powell .08 .04 .01
☐ 427 Lee Stevens .08 .04 .01
☐ 428 Glenn Davis .10 .04 .01
☐ 429 Willie Greene .50 .23 .06
☐ 430 Kevin Wickander .08 .04 .01
☐ 431 Dennis Eckersley .15 .07 .02
☐ 432 Joe Orsulak .08 .04 .01
☐ 433 Eddie Murray .20 .09 .03
☐ 434 Matt Stairs .30 .14 .04
☐ 435 Wally Joyner .10 .04 .01
☐ 436 Rondell White .50 .23 .06
☐ 437 Rob Maurer .20 .09 .03
☐ 438 Joe Redfield .15 .07 .02
☐ 439 Mark Lewis .10 .04 .01
☐ 440 Darren Daulton .10 .04 .01
☐ 441 Mike Henneman .08 .04 .01
☐ 442 John Cangelosi .08 .04 .01
☐ 443 Vince Moore .15 .07 .02
☐ 444 John Wehner .10 .05 .01
☐ 445 Kent Hrbek .10 .04 .01
☐ 446 Mark McLemore .08 .04 .01
☐ 447 Bill Wegman .08 .04 .01
☐ 448 Robby Thompson .08 .04 .01
☐ 449 Mark Anthony .15 .07 .02
☐ 450 Archi Cianfrocco .20 .09 .03
☐ 451 Johnny Ruffin .15 .07 .02
☐ 452 Javier Lopez .75 .35 .09
☐ 453 Greg Gohr .15 .07 .02
☐ 454 Tim Scott .15 .07 .02
☐ 455 Stan Belinda .08 .04 .01
☐ 456 Darrin Jackson .10 .04 .01
☐ 457 Chris Gardner .15 .07 .02
☐ 458 Esteban Beltre .15 .07 .02
☐ 459 Phil Plantier .30 .14 .04
☐ 460 Jim Thome .30 .14 .04
☐ 461 Mike Piazza 1.00 .45 .13
☐ 462 Matt Sinatro .08 .04 .01
☐ 463 Scott Servais .08 .04 .01
☐ 464 Brian Jordan .60 .25 .08
☐ 465 Doug Drabek .10 .04 .01
☐ 466 Carl Willis .08 .04 .01
☐ 467 Bret Barbarie .12 .05 .02
☐ 468 Hal Morris .10 .04 .01
☐ 469 Steve Sax .10 .04 .01
☐ 470 Jerry Willard .08 .04 .01
☐ 471 Dan Wilson .15 .07 .02
☐ 472 Chris Hoiles .12 .05 .02
☐ 473 Rheal Cormier .15 .07 .02
☐ 474 John Morris .08 .04 .01
☐ 475 Jeff Reardon .12 .05 .02
☐ 476 Mark Leiter .08 .04 .01
☐ 477 Tom Gordon .08 .04 .01
☐ 478 Kent Bottenfield .25 .11 .03
☐ 479 Gene Larkin .08 .04 .01
☐ 480 Dwight Gooden .12 .05 .02
☐ 481 B.J. Surhoff .08 .04 .01
☐ 482 Andy Stankiewicz .25 .11 .03
☐ 483 Tino Martinez .10 .05 .01
☐ 484 Craig Biggio .10 .04 .01
☐ 485 Denny Neagle .12 .05 .02
☐ 486 Rusty Meacham .08 .04 .01
☐ 487 Kal Daniels .08 .04 .01
☐ 488 Dave Henderson .08 .04 .01
☐ 489 Tim Costo .20 .09 .03
☐ 490 Doug Davis .15 .07 .02
☐ 491 Frank Viola .10 .04 .01
☐ 492 Cory Snyder .08 .04 .01
☐ 493 Chris Martin .15 .07 .02
☐ 494 Dion James .08 .04 .01
☐ 495 Randy Tomlin .08 .04 .01
☐ 496 Greg Vaughn .10 .04 .01
☐ 497 Dennis Cook .08 .04 .01
☐ 498 Rosario Rodriguez .10 .05 .01
☐ 499 Dave Staton .20 .09 .03
☐ 500 George Brett .25 .11 .03
☐ 501 Brian Barnes .08 .04 .01
☐ 502 Butch Henry .20 .09 .03
☐ 503 Harold Reynolds .08 .04 .01
☐ 504 David Nied 4.00 1.80 .50
☐ 505 Lee Smith .10 .04 .01
☐ 506 Steve Chitren .08 .04 .01
☐ 507 Ken Hill .08 .04 .01
☐ 508 Robbie Beckett .12 .05 .02
☐ 509 Troy Afenir .08 .04 .01
☐ 510 Kelly Gruber .10 .04 .01
☐ 511 Bret Boone 1.00 .45 .13
☐ 512 Jeff Branson .08 .04 .01
☐ 513 Mike Jackson .08 .04 .01
☐ 514 Pete Harnisch .08 .04 .01
☐ 515 Chad Kreuter .08 .04 .01
☐ 516 Joe Vitko .30 .14 .04
☐ 517 Orel Hershiser .12 .05 .02
☐ 518 John Doherty .20 .09 .03
☐ 519 Jay Bell .08 .04 .01
☐ 520 Mark Langston .10 .04 .01
☐ 521 Dann Howitt .08 .04 .01
☐ 522 Bobby Reed .15 .07 .02
☐ 523 Roberto Munoz .15 .07 .02
☐ 524 Todd Ritchie .10 .05 .01
☐ 525 Bip Roberts .10 .04 .01
☐ 526 Pat Listach 2.50 1.15 .30
☐ 527 Scott Brosius .15 .07 .02
☐ 528 John Roper .40 .18 .05
☐ 529 Phil Hiatt .50 .23 .06
☐ 530 Denny Walling .08 .04 .01
☐ 531 Carlos Baerga .50 .23 .06
☐ 532 Manny Ramirez 1.25 .55 .16
☐ 533 Pat Clements .08 .04 .01
☐ 534 Ron Gant .20 .09 .03
☐ 535 Pat Kelly .10 .05 .01
☐ 536 Billy Spiers .08 .04 .01
☐ 537 Darren Reed .08 .04 .01
☐ 538 Ken Caminiti .10 .04 .01
☐ 539 Butch Huskey .30 .14 .04
☐ 540 Matt Nokes .08 .04 .01
☐ 541 John Kruk .10 .04 .01
☐ 542 John Jaha FOIL .60 .25 .08
☐ 543 Justin Thompson .30 .14 .04
☐ 544 Steve Hosey .60 .25 .08
☐ 545 Joe Kmak .15 .07 .02
☐ 546 John Franco .10 .04 .01
☐ 547 Devon White .10 .04 .01

☐ 548	Elston Hansen FOIL	.30	.14	.04
☐ 549	Ryan Klesko	1.00	.45	.13
☐ 550	Danny Tartabull	.12	.05	.02
☐ 551	Frank Thomas FOIL	8.00	3.60	1.00
☐ 552	Kevin Tapani	.10	.04	.01
☐ 553	Willie Banks	.20	.09	.03
☐ 554	B.J. Wallace FOIL	1.25	.55	.16
☐ 555	Orlando Miller	.15	.07	.02
☐ 556	Mark Smith	.75	.35	.09
☐ 557	Tim Wallach FOIL	.10	.05	.01
☐ 558	Bill Gullickson	.08	.04	.01
☐ 559	Derek Bell FOIL	.50	.23	.06
☐ 560	Joe Randa FOIL	.40	.18	.05
☐ 561	Frank Seminara	.40	.18	.05
☐ 562	Mark Gardner	.08	.04	.01
☐ 563	Rick Greene FOIL	.40	.18	.05
☐ 564	Gary Gaetti	.08	.04	.01
☐ 565	Ozzie Guillen	.08	.04	.01
☐ 566	Charles Nagy FOIL	.35	.16	.04
☐ 567	Mike Milchin	.12	.05	.02
☐ 568	Ben Shelton	.30	.14	.04
☐ 569	Chris Roberts FOIL	1.00	.45	.13
☐ 570	Ellis Burks	.10	.04	.01
☐ 571	Scott Scudder	.08	.04	.01
☐ 572	Jim Abbott FOIL	.40	.18	.05
☐ 573	Joe Carter	.35	.16	.04
☐ 574	Steve Finley	.10	.04	.01
☐ 575	Jim Olander FOIL	.15	.07	.02
☐ 576	Carlos Garcia	.20	.09	.03
☐ 577	Gregg Olson	.10	.04	.01
☐ 578	Greg Swindell FOIL	.12	.05	.02
☐ 579	Matt Williams FOIL	.15	.07	.02
☐ 580	Mark Grace	.15	.07	.02
☐ 581	Howard House FOIL	.30	.14	.04
☐ 582	Luis Polonia	.10	.04	.01
☐ 583	Erik Hanson	.08	.04	.01
☐ 584	Salomon Torres FOIL	.50	.23	.06
☐ 585	Carlton Fisk	.20	.09	.03
☐ 586	Bret Saberhagen	.12	.05	.02
☐ 587	Chad McConnell FOIL	.75	.35	.09
☐ 588	Jimmy Key	.08	.04	.01
☐ 589	Mike Macfarlane	.08	.04	.01
☐ 590	Barry Bonds FOIL	.75	.35	.09
☐ 591	Jamie McAndrew	.12	.05	.02
☐ 592	Shane Mack	.10	.04	.01
☐ 593	Kerwin Moore	.12	.05	.02
☐ 594	Joe Oliver	.08	.04	.01
☐ 595	Chris Sabo	.10	.04	.01
☐ 596	Alex Gonzalez	.30	.14	.04
☐ 597	Brett Butler	.10	.04	.01
☐ 598	Mark Hutton	.40	.18	.05
☐ 599	Andy Benes FOIL	.12	.05	.02
☐ 600	Jose Canseco	.60	.25	.08
☐ 601	Darryl Kile	.15	.07	.02
☐ 602	Matt Stairs FOIL	.40	.18	.05
☐ 603	Robert Butler FOIL	.30	.14	.04
☐ 604	Willie McGee	.10	.04	.01
☐ 605	Jack McDowell FOIL	.20	.09	.03
☐ 606	Tom Candiotti	.08	.04	.01
☐ 607	Ed Martel	.20	.09	.03
☐ 608	Matt Mieske FOIL	.50	.23	.06
☐ 609	Darrin Fletcher	.08	.04	.01
☐ 610	Rafael Palmeiro	.12	.05	.02
☐ 611	Bill Swift FOIL	.10	.05	.01
☐ 612	Mike Mussina	2.00	.90	.25
☐ 613	Vince Coleman	.10	.04	.01
☐ 614	Scott Cepicky FOIL UER (Bats: LEFLT)	.50	.23	.06
☐ 615	Mike Greenwell	.12	.05	.02
☐ 616	Kevin McGehee	.15	.07	.02
☐ 617	Jeffrey Hammonds FOIL	3.50	1.55	.45
☐ 618	Scott Taylor	.10	.05	.01
☐ 619	Dave Otto	.08	.04	.01
☐ 620	Mark McGwire FOIL	.75	.35	.09
☐ 621	Kevin Tatar	.15	.07	.02
☐ 622	Steve Farr	.08	.04	.01
☐ 623	Ryan Klesko FOIL	1.50	.65	.19
☐ 624	Dave Fleming	1.00	.45	.13
☐ 625	Andre Dawson	.20	.09	.03
☐ 626	Tino Martinez FOIL	.12	.05	.02
☐ 627	Chad Curtis	.50	.23	.06
☐ 628	Mickey Morandini	.12	.05	.02
☐ 629	Gregg Olson FOIL	.10	.05	.01
☐ 630	Lou Whitaker	.12	.05	.02
☐ 631	Arthur Rhodes	.40	.18	.05
☐ 632	Brandon Wilson	.15	.07	.02
☐ 633	Lance Jennings	.20	.09	.03
☐ 634	Allen Watson	.60	.25	.08
☐ 635	Len Dykstra	.10	.04	.01
☐ 636	Joe Girardi	.08	.04	.01
☐ 637	Kiki Hernandez FOIL	.40	.18	.05
☐ 638	Mike Hampton	.15	.07	.02
☐ 639	Al Osuna	.08	.04	.01
☐ 640	Kevin Appier	.10	.04	.01
☐ 641	Rick Helling FOIL	.40	.18	.05
☐ 642	Jody Reed	.08	.04	.01
☐ 643	Ray Lankford	.40	.18	.05
☐ 644	John Olerud	.25	.11	.03
☐ 645	Paul Molitor FOIL	.12	.05	.02
☐ 646	Pat Borders	.08	.04	.01
☐ 647	Mike Morgan	.08	.04	.01
☐ 648	Larry Walker	.40	.18	.05
☐ 649	Pete Castellano FOIL	.40	.18	.05
☐ 650	Fred McGriff	.30	.14	.04
☐ 651	Walt Weiss	.08	.04	.01
☐ 652	Calvin Murray FOIL	1.50	.65	.19
☐ 653	Dave Nilsson	.40	.18	.05
☐ 654	Greg Pirkl	.40	.18	.05
☐ 655	Robin Ventura FOIL	1.00	.45	.13
☐ 656	Mark Portugal	.08	.04	.01
☐ 657	Roger McDowell	.08	.04	.01
☐ 658	Rick Hirtensteiner FOIL	.30	.14	.04
☐ 659	Glenallen Hill	.08	.04	.01
☐ 660	Greg Gagne	.08	.04	.01
☐ 661	Charles Johnson FOIL	2.00	.90	.25
☐ 662	Brian Hunter	.20	.09	.03
☐ 663	Mark Lemke	.08	.04	.01
☐ 664	Tim Belcher FOIL	.10	.05	.01
☐ 665	Rich DeLucia	.08	.04	.01
☐ 666	Bob Walk	.08	.04	.01
☐ 667	Joe Carter FOIL	.40	.18	.05
☐ 668	Jose Guzman	.08	.04	.01
☐ 669	Otis Nixon	.08	.04	.01
☐ 670	Phil Nevin FOIL	4.00	1.80	.50
☐ 671	Eric Davis	.12	.05	.02
☐ 672	Damion Easley	.75	.35	.09
☐ 673	Will Clark FOIL	.75	.35	.09
☐ 674	Mark Kiefer	.15	.07	.02
☐ 675	Ozzie Smith	.20	.09	.03
☐ 676	Manny Ramirez FOIL	2.00	.90	.25
☐ 677	Gregg Olson	.10	.04	.01
☐ 678	Cliff Floyd	1.50	.65	.19
☐ 679	Duane Singleton	.15	.07	.02
☐ 680	Jose Rijo	.10	.04	.01
☐ 681	Willie Randolph	.10	.04	.01
☐ 682	Michael Tucker FOIL	2.00	.90	.25
☐ 683	Darren Lewis	.10	.04	.01
☐ 684	Dale Murphy	.10	.04	.01
☐ 685	Mike Pagliarulo	.08	.04	.01
☐ 686	Paul Miller	.15	.07	.02
☐ 687	Mike Robertson	.25	.11	.03
☐ 688	Mike Devereaux	.10	.04	.01
☐ 689	Pedro Astacio	.75	.35	.09
☐ 690	Alan Trammell	.12	.05	.02
☐ 691	Roger Clemens	.75	.35	.09
☐ 692	Bud Black	.08	.04	.01
☐ 693	Turk Wendell	.25	.11	.03
☐ 694	Barry Larkin FOIL	.30	.14	.04
☐ 695	Todd Zeile	.08	.04	.01
☐ 696	Pat Hentgen	.15	.07	.02
☐ 697	Eddie Taubensee	.20	.09	.03
☐ 698	Guillermo Velasquez	.20	.09	.03
☐ 699	Tom Glavine	.30	.14	.04
☐ 700	Robin Yount	.25	.11	.03
☐ 701	Checklist 1	.08	.01	.00
☐ 702	Checklist 2	.08	.01	.00
☐ 703	Checklist 3	.08	.01	.00
☐ 704	Checklist 4	.08	.01	.00
☐ 705	Checklist 5	.08	.01	.00

1953 Braves Johnston Cookies

The cards in this 25-card set measure approximately 2 9/16" by 3 5/8". The 1953 Johnston's Cookies set of numbered cards features Milwaukee Braves players only. This set is the most plentiful of the three Johnston's Cookies sets and no known scarcities exist. The catalog designation for this set is D356-1.

	NRMT	VG-E	GOOD
COMPLETE SET (25)	275.00	125.00	34.00
COMMON PLAYER (1-25)	9.00	4.00	1.15
☐ 1 Charlie Grimm MG	12.00	5.50	1.50
☐ 2 John Antonelli	12.00	5.50	1.50
☐ 3 Vern Bickford	9.00	4.00	1.15
☐ 4 Bob Buhl	12.00	5.50	1.50
☐ 5 Lew Burdette	14.00	6.25	1.75

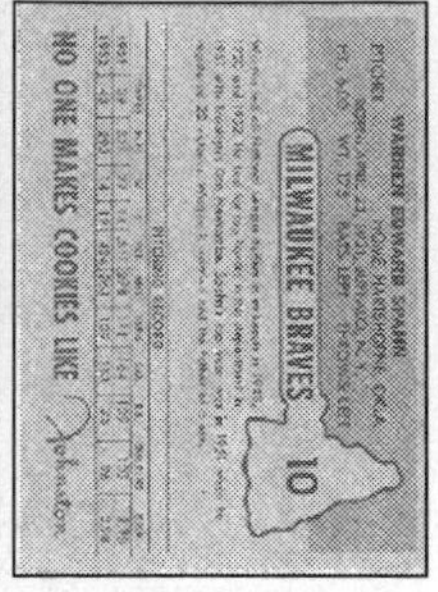

☐ 6 Dave Cole	9.00	4.00	1.15
☐ 7 Ernie Johnson	12.00	5.50	1.50
☐ 8 Dave Jolly	9.00	4.00	1.15
☐ 9 Don Liddle	9.00	4.00	1.15
☐ 10 Warren Spahn	60.00	27.00	7.50
☐ 11 Max Surkont	9.00	4.00	1.15
☐ 12 Jim Wilson	9.00	4.00	1.15
☐ 13 Sibbi Sisti	9.00	4.00	1.15
☐ 14 Walker Cooper	9.00	4.00	1.15
☐ 15 Del Crandall	12.00	5.50	1.50
☐ 16 Ebba St.Claire	9.00	4.00	1.15
☐ 17 Joe Adcock	14.00	6.25	1.75
☐ 18 George Crowe	9.00	4.00	1.15
☐ 19 Jack Dittmer	9.00	4.00	1.15
☐ 20 Johnny Logan	12.00	5.50	1.50
☐ 21 Ed Mathews	60.00	27.00	7.50
☐ 22 Bill Bruton	12.00	5.50	1.50
☐ 23 Sid Gordon	9.00	4.00	1.15
☐ 24 Andy Pafko	12.00	5.50	1.50
☐ 25 Jim Pendleton	9.00	4.00	1.15

1953-54 Braves Spic and Span 3x5

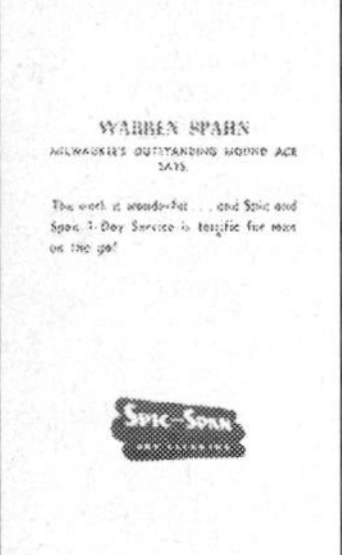

This 27-card set features only members of the Milwaukee Braves. The cards are black and white and approximately 3 1/4" by 5 1/2". Some of the photos in the set are posed against blank backgrounds, but most are posed against seats and a chain link fence, hence the set is sometimes referred to as the "chain link fence" set. There is a facsimile autograph at the bottom of the card. The set was probably issued in 1953 and 1954 since Hank Aaron is not included in the set and Don Liddle, Ebba St.Claire, and Johnny Antonelli were traded from the Braves on February 1, 1954 for Bobby Thomson (who is also in the set). Cards can be found either blank back or with player's name, comment, and logo in blue on the back

	NRMT	VG-E	GOOD
COMPLETE SET (27)	900.00	400.00	115.00
COMMON PLAYER (1-27)	27.00	12.00	3.40
☐ 1 Joe Adcock	35.00	16.00	4.40
☐ 2 Johnny Antonelli	32.00	14.50	4.00
☐ 3 Vern Bickford	27.00	12.00	3.40
☐ 4 Bill Bruton	32.00	14.50	4.00
☐ 5 Bob Buhl	32.00	14.50	4.00
☐ 6 Lew Burdette	40.00	18.00	5.00
☐ 7 Dick Cole	27.00	12.00	3.40
☐ 8 Walker Cooper	27.00	12.00	3.40
☐ 9 Del Crandall	32.00	14.50	4.00
☐ 10 George Crowe	27.00	12.00	3.40
☐ 11 Jack Dittmer	27.00	12.00	3.40
☐ 12 Sid Gordon	27.00	12.00	3.40
☐ 13 Ernie Johnson	32.00	14.50	4.00
☐ 14 Dave Jolly	27.00	12.00	3.40
☐ 15 Don Liddle	27.00	12.00	3.40
☐ 16 John Logan	32.00	14.50	4.00
☐ 17 Ed Mathews	125.00	57.50	15.50
☐ 18 Danny O'Connell	27.00	12.00	3.40
☐ 19 Andy Pafko	27.00	12.00	3.40
☐ 20 Jim Pendleton	27.00	12.00	3.40
☐ 21 Ebba St.Claire	27.00	12.00	3.40
☐ 22 Warren Spahn	125.00	57.50	15.50
☐ 23 Max Surkont	27.00	12.00	3.40
☐ 24 Bob Thomson	36.00	16.00	4.50
☐ 25 Bob Thorpe	27.00	12.00	3.40
☐ 26 Roberto Vargas	27.00	12.00	3.40
☐ 27 Jim Wilson	27.00	12.00	3.40

1953-56 Braves Spic and Span 7x10

This 13-card set features only members of the Milwaukee Braves. The set was issued beginning in 1953 but may have been issued for several years as they seem to be the most common of all the Spic and Span issues. In addition, Danny O'Connell and Bobby Thomson were not on the '53 Braves team. The front of each card shows the logo, "Spic and Span Dry Cleaners ... the Choice of Your Favorite Braves." There is a thick white border around the cards with facsimile autograph in black in the bottom border. The cards have blank backs and are approximately 7" by 10".

	NRMT	VG-E	GOOD
COMPLETE SET (13)	150.00	70.00	19.00
COMMON PLAYER (1-13)	7.50	3.40	.95
☐ 1 Joe Adcock	13.50	6.00	1.70
☐ 2 Billy Bruton	9.00	4.00	1.15
☐ 3 Bob Buhl	9.00	4.00	1.15
☐ 4 Lew Burdette	15.00	6.75	1.90
☐ 5 Del Crandall	10.00	4.50	1.25
☐ 6 Jack Dittmer	7.50	3.40	.95
☐ 7 Johnny Logan	9.00	4.00	1.15
☐ 8 Eddie Mathews	40.00	18.00	5.00
☐ 9 Chet Nichols	7.50	3.40	.95
☐ 10 Danny O'Connell	7.50	3.40	.95
☐ 11 Andy Pafko	7.50	3.40	.95
☐ 12 Warren Spahn	40.00	18.00	5.00
☐ 13 Bob Thomson	13.50	6.00	1.70

1954 Braves Johnston Cookies

The cards in this 35-card set measure approximately 2" by 3 7/8". The 1954 Johnston's Cookies set of color cards of

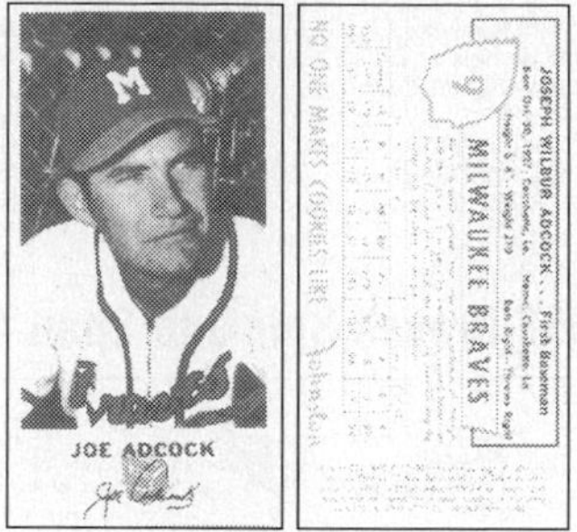

Milwaukee Braves are numbered according to the player's uniform number, except for the non-players, Lacks and Taylor, who are found at the end of the set. The Bobby Thomson card was withdrawn early in the year after his injury and is scarce. The catalog number for this set is D356-2. The Hank Aaron card shows him with uniform number 5, rather than the more familiar 44, that he switched to shortly thereafter.

	NRMT	VG-E	GOOD
COMPLETE SET (35)	1350.00	600.00	170.00
COMMON PLAYER (1-50)	12.00	5.50	1.50
☐ 1 Del Crandall	16.00	7.25	2.00
☐ 3 Jim Pendleton	12.00	5.50	1.50
☐ 4 Danny O'Connell	12.00	5.50	1.50
☐ 5 Hank Aaron	650.00	300.00	80.00
☐ 6 Jack Dittmer	12.00	5.50	1.50
☐ 9 Joe Adcock	18.00	8.00	2.30
☐ 10 Bob Buhl	14.00	6.25	1.75
☐ 11 Phil Paine	12.00	5.50	1.50
☐ 12 Ben Johnson	12.00	5.50	1.50
☐ 13 Sibbi Sisti	12.00	5.50	1.50
☐ 15 Charles Gorin	12.00	5.50	1.50
☐ 16 Chet Nichols	12.00	5.50	1.50
☐ 17 Dave Jolly	12.00	5.50	1.50
☐ 19 Jim Wilson	12.00	5.50	1.50
☐ 20 Ray Crone	12.00	5.50	1.50
☐ 21 Warren Spahn	75.00	34.00	9.50
☐ 22 Gene Conley	12.00	5.50	1.50
☐ 23 Johnny Logan	16.00	7.25	2.00
☐ 24 Charlie White	12.00	5.50	1.50
☐ 27 George Metkovich	12.00	5.50	1.50
☐ 28 Johnny Cooney CO	12.00	5.50	1.50
☐ 29 Paul Burris	12.00	5.50	1.50
☐ 31 Bucky Walters CO	14.00	6.25	1.75
☐ 32 Ernie Johnson	14.00	6.25	1.75
☐ 33 Lou Burdette	25.00	11.50	3.10
☐ 34 Bob Thomson SP	250.00	115.00	31.00
☐ 35 Bob Keely	12.00	5.50	1.50
☐ 38 Bill Bruton	14.00	6.25	1.75
☐ 40 Charlie Grimm MG	16.00	7.25	2.00
☐ 41 Eddie Mathews	75.00	34.00	9.50
☐ 42 Sam Calderone	12.00	5.50	1.50
☐ 47 Joey Jay	14.00	6.25	1.75
☐ 48 Andy Pafko	14.00	6.25	1.75
☐ NNO Dr. Charles Lacks (Unnumbered)	12.00	5.50	1.50
☐ NNO Joseph F. Taylor (Unnumbered)	12.00	5.50	1.50

1954 Braves Spic and Span Postcards

This black and white set features only members of the Milwaukee Braves. The cards have postcard backs and measure approximately 3 11/16" by 6". The postcards were issued beginning in 1954. There is a facsimile autograph on the front in black or white ink. The set apparently was also issued with white borders in a 5" by 7" size. The catalog designation for this set is PC756. The front of each card shows the logo, "Spic and Span Dry Cleaners ... the Choice of Your Favorite Braves."

	NRMT	VG-E	GOOD
COMPLETE SET (18)	500.00	230.00	65.00
COMMON PLAYER (1-18)	15.00	6.75	1.90
☐ 1 Henry Aaron	175.00	80.00	22.00
☐ 2 Joe Adcock	22.00	10.00	2.80
☐ 3 Billy Bruton	18.00	8.00	2.30
☐ 4 Bob Buhl	18.00	8.00	2.30
☐ 5 Lew Burdette	24.00	11.00	3.00
☐ 6 Gene Conley	18.00	8.00	2.30
☐ 7 Del Crandall	20.00	9.00	2.50
☐ 8 Ray Crone	15.00	6.75	1.90
☐ 9 Jack Dittmer	15.00	6.75	1.90
☐ 10 Ernie Johnson	18.00	8.00	2.30
☐ 11 Dave Jolly	15.00	6.75	1.90
☐ 12 Johnny Logan	18.00	8.00	2.30
☐ 13 Eddie Mathews	75.00	34.00	9.50
☐ 14 Chet Nichols	15.00	6.75	1.90
☐ 15 Danny O'Connell	15.00	6.75	1.90
☐ 16 Andy Pafko	15.00	6.75	1.90
☐ 17 Warren Spahn	75.00	34.00	9.50
☐ 18 Bob Thomson	22.00	10.00	2.80

1955 Braves Johnston Cookies

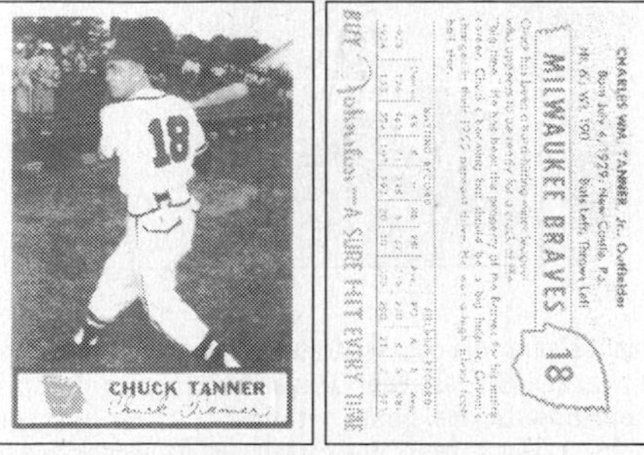

The cards in this 35-card set measure approximately 2 3/4" by 4". This set of Milwaukee Braves issued in 1955 by Johnston Cookies are numbered by the uniform number of the player depicted, except for non-players Lacks, Lewis and Taylor. The cards were issued in strips of six which accounts for the rouletted edges found on single cards. They are larger in size than the two previous sets but are printed on thinner cardboard. Each player in the checklist has been marked to show on which panel or strip he appeared (Pafko appears twice). A complete panel of six cards is worth 25 percent more than the sum of the individual players. The catalog designation for this set is D356-3.

	NRMT	VG-E	GOOD
COMPLETE SET (35)	1200.00	550.00	150.00
COMMON PLAYER (1-51)	20.00	9.00	2.50
☐ 1 Del Crandall P1	24.00	11.00	3.00
☐ 3 Jim Pendleton P3	20.00	9.00	2.50
☐ 4 Danny O'Connell P1	20.00	9.00	2.50
☐ 6 Jack Dittmer P6	20.00	9.00	2.50
☐ 9 Joe Adcock P2	27.00	12.00	3.40
☐ 10 Bob Buhl P6	22.00	10.00	2.80
☐ 11 Phil Paine P5	20.00	9.00	2.50
☐ 12 Ray Crone P5	20.00	9.00	2.50
☐ 15 Charlie Gorin P1	20.00	9.00	2.50
☐ 16 Dave Jolly P4	20.00	9.00	2.50
☐ 17 Chet Nichols P2	20.00	9.00	2.50
☐ 18 Chuck Tanner P5	27.00	12.00	3.40
☐ 19 Jim Wilson P6	20.00	9.00	2.50
☐ 20 Dave Koslo P4	20.00	9.00	2.50
☐ 21 Warren Spahn P3	90.00	40.00	11.50
☐ 22 Gene Conley P3	22.00	10.00	2.80
☐ 23 Johnny Logan P4	24.00	11.00	3.00
☐ 24 Charlie White P2	20.00	9.00	2.50
☐ 28 Johnny Cooney P4 CO	20.00	9.00	2.50
☐ 30 Roy Smalley P3	20.00	9.00	2.50
☐ 31 Bucky Walters P6 CO	22.00	10.00	2.80
☐ 32 Ernie Johnson P5	22.00	10.00	2.80
☐ 33 Lew Burdette P1	36.00	16.00	4.50
☐ 34 Bobby Thomson P6	27.00	12.00	3.40
☐ 35 Bob Keely P1	20.00	9.00	2.50
☐ 38 Bill Bruton P4	22.00	10.00	2.80
☐ 39 George Crowe P3	20.00	9.00	2.50
☐ 40 Charlie Grimm MG P6	24.00	11.00	3.00
☐ 41 Eddie Mathews P5	90.00	40.00	11.50
☐ 44 Hank Aaron P1	350.00	160.00	45.00
☐ 47 Joey Jay P2	22.00	10.00	2.80
☐ 48 Andy Pafko P2 P4	20.00	9.00	2.50
☐ 49 Dr. Charles Leaks P2 (Unnumbered)	20.00	9.00	2.50
☐ NNO Duffy Lewis P5 (Unnumbered)	20.00	9.00	2.50
☐ NNO Joe Taylor P3 (Unnumbered)	20.00	9.00	2.50

1955 Braves Spic and Span Die-Cut

This 18-card, die-cut, set features only members of the Milwaukee Braves. Each player measures differently according to the pose but they are, on average, approximately 8" by 8". The cards could be folded together to stand up. Each card contains a logo in the middle at the bottom and a copyright notice, "1955 Spic and Span Cleaners" in the lower right corner.

	NRMT	VG-E	GOOD
COMPLETE SET (18)	3500.00	1600.00	450.00
COMMON PLAYER (1-18)	125.00	57.50	15.50
☐ 1 Hank Aaron	900.00	400.00	115.00
☐ 2 Joe Adcock	165.00	75.00	21.00
☐ 3 Billy Bruton	135.00	60.00	17.00
☐ 4 Bob Buhl	135.00	60.00	17.00
☐ 5 Lew Burdette	175.00	80.00	22.00
☐ 6 Gene Conley	125.00	57.50	15.50
☐ 7 Del Crandall	150.00	70.00	19.00
☐ 8 Jack Dittmer	125.00	57.50	15.50
☐ 9 Ernie Johnson	135.00	60.00	17.00
☐ 10 Dave Jolly	125.00	57.50	15.50
☐ 11 Johnny Logan	135.00	60.00	17.00
☐ 12 Eddie Mathews	375.00	170.00	47.50
☐ 13 Chet Nichols	125.00	57.50	15.50
☐ 14 Danny O'Connell	125.00	57.50	15.50
☐ 15 Andy Pafko	125.00	57.50	15.50
☐ 16 Warren Spahn	375.00	170.00	47.50
☐ 17 Bob Thomson	165.00	75.00	21.00
☐ 18 Jim Wilson	125.00	57.50	15.50

1957 Braves Spic and Span 4x5

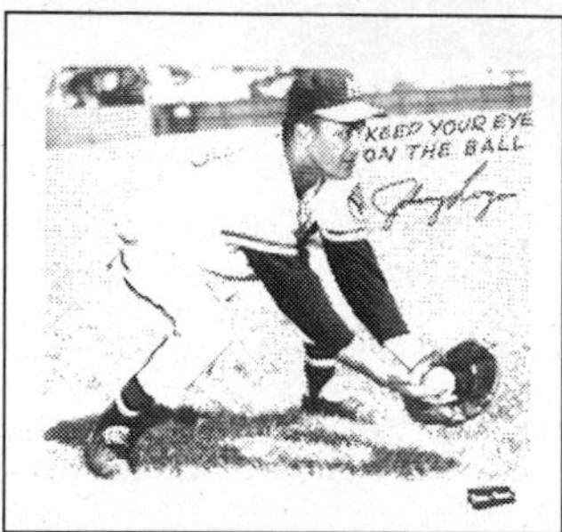

This set contains 20 black and white photos each with a blue-printed message such as "Stay in There and Pitch" and blue facsimile autograph The set features only members of the Milwaukee Braves. Red Schoendienst was traded to the Braves on June 15, 1957 in exchange for Danny O'Connell, Ray Crone, and Bobby Thomson. Wes Covington, Felix Mantilla, and Bob Trowbridge are also listed as shorter-printed (SP) cards as they were apparently mid-season call-ups. The cards are approximately 4 5/16" by 5" with a thick white border and are blank backed. Spic and Span appears in blue in the white border in the lower right corner of the card.

	NRMT	VG-E	GOOD
COMPLETE SET (20)	500.00	230.00	65.00
COMMON PLAYER (1-20)	10.00	4.50	1.25
COMMON PLAYER SP	25.00	11.50	3.10
☐ 1 Henry Aaron	135.00	60.00	17.00
☐ 2 Joe Adcock	16.00	7.25	2.00
☐ 3 Billy Bruton	12.00	5.50	1.50
☐ 4 Bob Buhl	12.00	5.50	1.50
☐ 5 Lew Burdette	18.00	8.00	2.30
☐ 6 Gene Conley	12.00	5.50	1.50
☐ 7 Wes Covington SP	25.00	11.50	3.10
☐ 7 Del Crandall	14.00	6.25	1.75
☐ 8 Ray Crone	10.00	4.50	1.25
☐ 9 Fred Haney MG	10.00	4.50	1.25
☐ 10 Ernie Johnson	12.00	5.50	1.50
☐ 11 Johnny Logan	12.00	5.50	1.50
☐ 12 Felix Mantilla SP	25.00	11.50	3.10
☐ 12 Ed Mathews	60.00	27.00	7.50
☐ 13 Danny O'Connell	10.00	4.50	1.25
☐ 14 Andy Pafko	10.00	4.50	1.25
☐ 15 Red Schoendienst SP	60.00	27.00	7.50
☐ 15 Warren Spahn	60.00	27.00	7.50
☐ 16 Bob Thomson	16.00	7.25	2.00
☐ 16 Bob Trowbridge SP	25.00	11.50	3.10

1960 Braves Lake to Lake

The cards in this 28-card set measure 2 1/2" by 3 1/4". The 1960 Lake to Lake set of unnumbered, blue tinted cards features Milwaukee Braves players only. For some reason, this set of Braves does not include Eddie Mathews. The cards were issued on milk cartons by Lake to Lake Dairy. Most cards have staple holes in the upper right corner. The backs are in red and give details and prizes associated with

the card promotion. Cards with staple holes can be considered very good to excellent at best. The catalog designation for this set is F102-1.

	NRMT	VG-E	GOOD
COMPLETE SET (28)	1300.00	575.00	160.00
COMMON PLAYER (1-28)	16.00	7.25	2.00
☐ 1 Hank Aaron	375.00	170.00	47.50
☐ 2 Joe Adcock	22.50	10.00	2.80
☐ 3 Ray Boone	150.00	70.00	19.00
☐ 4 Bill Bruton	350.00	160.00	45.00
☐ 5 Bob Buhl	18.00	8.00	2.30
☐ 6 Lew Burdette	25.00	11.50	3.10
☐ 7 Chuck Cottier	16.00	7.25	2.00
☐ 8 Wes Covington	18.00	8.00	2.30
☐ 9 Del Crandall	20.00	9.00	2.50
☐ 10 Chuck Dressen MG	16.00	7.25	2.00
☐ 11 Bob Giggie	16.00	7.25	2.00
☐ 12 Joey Jay	16.00	7.25	2.00
☐ 13 Johnny Logan	20.00	9.00	2.50
☐ 14 Felix Mantilla	16.00	7.25	2.00
☐ 15 Lee Maye	16.00	7.25	2.00
☐ 16 Don McMahon	16.00	7.25	2.00
☐ 17 George Myatt CO	16.00	7.25	2.00
☐ 18 Andy Pafko CO	16.00	7.25	2.00
☐ 19 Juan Pizarro	16.00	7.25	2.00
☐ 20 Mel Roach	16.00	7.25	2.00
☐ 21 Bob Rush	16.00	7.25	2.00
☐ 22 Bob Scheffing CO	16.00	7.25	2.00
☐ 23 Red Schoendienst	50.00	23.00	6.25
☐ 24 Warren Spahn	75.00	34.00	9.50
☐ 25 Al Spangler	16.00	7.25	2.00
☐ 26 Frank Torre	18.00	8.00	2.30
☐ 27 Carlton Willey	16.00	7.25	2.00
☐ 28 Whit Wyatt CO	16.00	7.25	2.00

1960 Braves Spic and Span

This 26-card set features only members of the Milwaukee Braves. These small cards each measure approximately 2 13/16" by 3 1/16". The cards have a thin white border around a black and white photo with no other writing or words on the front. The card backs have the Spic and Span logo at the bottom along with "Photographed and Autographed Exclusively for Spic and Span". A message and facsimile autograph from the player is presented inside a square box all in blue on the card back.

	NRMT	VG-E	GOOD
COMPLETE SET (27)	550.00	250.00	70.00
COMMON PLAYER (1-26)	10.00	4.50	1.25
☐ 1 Henry Aaron	135.00	60.00	17.00
☐ 2 Joe Adcock	16.00	7.25	2.00
☐ 3 Billy Bruton	12.00	5.50	1.50
☐ 4 Bob Buhl	12.00	5.50	1.50
☐ 5 Lew Burdette	18.00	8.00	2.30
☐ 6 Chuck Cottier	10.00	4.50	1.25
☐ 7A Del Crandall ERR (Reversed negative)	60.00	27.00	7.50
☐ 7B Del Crandall COR	16.00	7.25	2.00
☐ 8 Charlie Dressen MG	12.00	5.50	1.50
☐ 9 Joey Jay	10.00	4.50	1.25
☐ 10 Johnny Logan	12.00	5.50	1.50
☐ 11 Felix Mantilla	10.00	4.50	1.25
☐ 12 Ed Mathews	60.00	27.00	7.50
☐ 13 Lee Maye	10.00	4.50	1.25
☐ 14 Don McMahon	10.00	4.50	1.25
☐ 15 George Myatt CO	10.00	4.50	1.25
☐ 16 Andy Pafko CO	10.00	4.50	1.25
☐ 17 Juan Pizarro	10.00	4.50	1.25
☐ 18 Mel Roach	10.00	4.50	1.25
☐ 19 Bob Rush	10.00	4.50	1.25
☐ 20 Bob Scheffing CO	10.00	4.50	1.25
☐ 21 Red Schoendienst	40.00	18.00	5.00
☐ 22 Warren Spahn	60.00	27.00	7.50
☐ 23 Al Spangler	10.00	4.50	1.25
☐ 24 Frank Torre	12.00	5.50	1.50
☐ 25 Carl Willey	10.00	4.50	1.25
☐ 26 Whit Wyatt CO	12.00	5.50	1.50

1985 Braves Hostess

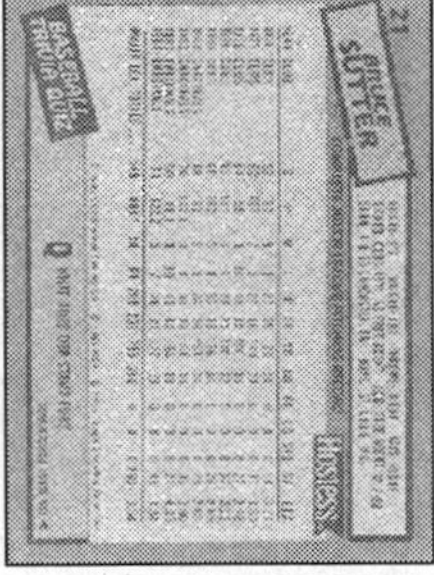

The cards in this 22-card set measure 2 1/2" by 3 1/2" and feature players of the Atlanta Braves. Cards were produced by Topps for Hostess (Continental Baking Co.) and are quite attractive. The card backs are similar in design to the 1985 Topps regular issue; however all photos are different from those that Topps used as these were apparently taken during Spring Training. Cards were available in boxes of Hostess products in packs of four (three players and a contest card). Other than the manager card, the rest of the set is ordered and numbered alphabetically.

	NRMT-MT	EXC	G-VG
COMPLETE SET (22)	8.00	3.60	1.00
COMMON PLAYER (1-22)	.30	.14	.04
☐ 1 Eddie Haas MG	.30	.14	.04
☐ 2 Len Barker	.40	.18	.05
☐ 3 Steve Bedrosian	.60	.25	.08
☐ 4 Bruce Benedict	.30	.14	.04
☐ 5 Rick Camp	.30	.14	.04
☐ 6 Rick Cerone	.30	.14	.04
☐ 7 Chris Chambliss	.60	.25	.08
☐ 8 Terry Forster	.40	.18	.05
☐ 9 Gene Garber	.30	.14	.04
☐ 10 Albert Hall	.30	.14	.04
☐ 11 Bob Horner	.75	.35	.09
☐ 12 Glenn Hubbard	.30	.14	.04
☐ 13 Brad Komminsk	.40	.18	.05

☐ 14 Rick Mahler	.30	.14	.04
☐ 15 Craig McMurtry	.30	.14	.04
☐ 16 Dale Murphy	4.00	1.80	.50
☐ 17 Ken Oberkfell	.30	.14	.04
☐ 18 Pascual Perez	.50	.23	.06
☐ 19 Gerald Perry	.40	.18	.05
☐ 20 Rafael Ramirez	.40	.18	.05
☐ 21 Bruce Sutter	.75	.35	.09
☐ 22 Claudell Washington	.40	.18	.05

1992 Braves Lykes Perforated

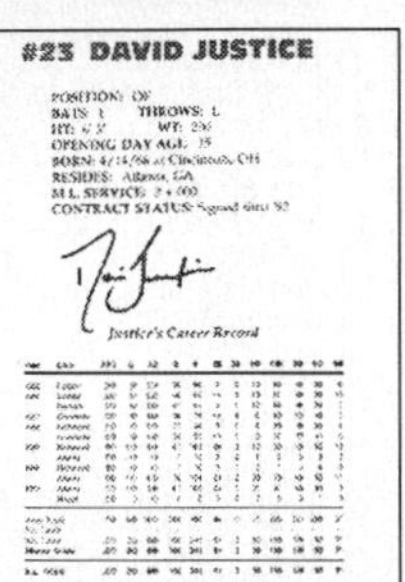

The 1992 Atlanta Braves Team Picture Card set was sponsored by Lykes and distributed as an uncut, perforated sheet before a Braves' home game. It consists of three large sheets (each measuring approximately 10 5/8" by 9 3/8") joined together to form one continuous sheet. The first panel features a team photo, while the second and third panels feature 15 player cards each. After perforation, the cards measure approximately 2 1/8" by 3 1/8". On a white card face, the fronts have posed color player photos with the top corners of the picture rounded off. The player's name appears in a red stripe below the picture with the team and sponsor logos immediately below. In red and blue print on white, the backs have the player's name, jersey number, biography, statistics, and a facsimile autograph. The cards are unnumbered and checklisted below in alphabetical order.

	MT	EX-MT	VG
COMPLETE SET (30)	10.00	4.50	1.25
COMMON PLAYER (1-30)	.25	.11	.03
☐ 1 Steve Avery	1.00	.45	.13
☐ 2 Rafael Belliard	.25	.11	.03
☐ 3 Juan Berenguer	.25	.11	.03
☐ 4 Damon Berryhill	.35	.16	.04
☐ 5 Mike Bielecki	.35	.16	.04
☐ 6 Jeff Blauser	.35	.16	.04
☐ 7 Sid Bream	.35	.16	.04
☐ 8 Francisco Cabrera	.50	.23	.06
☐ 9 Bobby Cox MG	.25	.11	.03
☐ 10 Nick Esasky	.25	.11	.03
☐ 11 Marvin Freeman	.25	.11	.03
☐ 12 Ron Gant	.75	.35	.09
☐ 13 Tom Glavine	1.00	.45	.13
☐ 14 Tommy Gregg	.25	.11	.03
☐ 15 Brian Hunter	.50	.23	.06
☐ 16 David Justice	1.25	.55	.16
☐ 17 Charlie Leibrandt	.35	.16	.04
☐ 18 Mark Lemke	.35	.16	.04
☐ 19 Kent Mercker	.35	.16	.04
☐ 20 Otis Nixon	.35	.16	.04
☐ 21 Greg Olson	.25	.11	.03
☐ 22 Alejandro Pena	.25	.11	.03
☐ 23 Terry Pendleton	.75	.35	.09
☐ 24 Deion Sanders	1.25	.55	.16
☐ 25 Lonnie Smith	.25	.11	.03
☐ 26 John Smoltz	.75	.35	.09
☐ 27 Mike Stanton	.35	.16	.04
☐ 28 Jeff Treadway	.25	.11	.03
☐ 29 Jerry Willard	.25	.11	.03
☐ 30 Mark Wohlers	.35	.16	.04

1970 Brewers McDonald's

This 31-card set features cards measuring approximately 2 15/16" by 4 3/8" and was issued during the Brewers' first year in Milwaukee after moving from Seattle. The cards are drawings of the members of the 1970 Milwaukee Brewers and underneath the drawings there is information about the players. These cards are still often found in uncut sheet form and hence have no extra value in that form. The backs are blank. The set is checklisted alphabetically with the number of the sheet being listed next to the players name. There were six different sheets of six cards each although only one sheet contained six players; the other sheets depicted five players and a Brewers' logo.

	NRMT-MT	EXC	G-VG
COMPLETE SET (31)	7.00	3.10	.85
COMMON PLAYER (1-31)	.30	.14	.04
☐ 1 Max Alvis 6	.30	.14	.04
☐ 2 Bob Bolin 1	.30	.14	.04
☐ 3 Gene Brabender 3	.30	.14	.04
☐ 4 Dave Bristol 5 MG	.40	.18	.05
☐ 5 Wayne Comer 2	.30	.14	.04
☐ 6 Cal Ermer 3 CO	.30	.14	.04
☐ 7 John Gelner 4	.30	.14	.04
☐ 8 Greg Goossen 5	.30	.14	.04
☐ 9 Tommy Harper 5	.40	.18	.05
☐ 10 Mike Hegan 3	.40	.18	.05
☐ 11 Mike Hershberger 3	.30	.14	.04
☐ 12 Steve Hovley 2	.30	.14	.04
☐ 13 John Kennedy 2	.30	.14	.04
☐ 14 Lew Krausse 4	.30	.14	.04
☐ 15 Ted Kubiak 1	.30	.14	.04
☐ 16 George Lauzerique 6	.30	.14	.04
☐ 17 Bob Locker 5	.30	.14	.04
☐ 18 Roy McMillan 4 CO	.40	.18	.05
☐ 19 Jerry McNertney 4	.30	.14	.04
☐ 20 Bob Meyer 2	.30	.14	.04
☐ 21 Jackie Moore 6 CO	.40	.18	.05
☐ 22 John Morris 1	.30	.14	.04
☐ 23 John O'Donoghue 1	.30	.14	.04
☐ 24 Marty Pattin 6	.30	.14	.04
☐ 25 Rich Rollins 4	.40	.18	.05
☐ 26 Phil Roof 5	.30	.14	.04
☐ 27 Ted Savage 1	.30	.14	.04
☐ 28 Russ Snyder 6	.30	.14	.04
☐ 29 Wes Stock 2 CO	.40	.18	.05
☐ 30 Sandy Valdespino 2	.30	.14	.04
☐ 31 Danny Walton 3	.30	.14	.04

1983 Brewers Gardner's

The cards in this 22-card set measure 2 1/2" by 3 1/2". The 1983 Gardner's Brewers set features Milwaukee Brewer players and manager Harvey Kuenn. Topps printed the set for the Madison (Wisconsin) bakery, hence, the backs are identical to the 1983 Topps backs except for the card

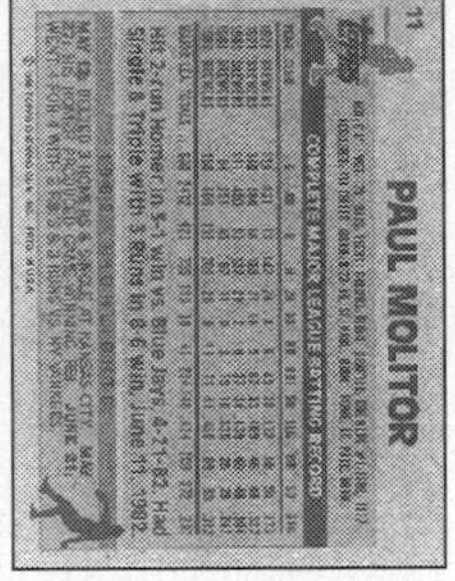

number. The fronts of the cards, however, feature all new photos and include the Gardner's logo and the Brewers' logo. Many of the cards are grease laden, as they were issued with packages of bread and hamburger and hot-dog buns. The card numbering for this set is essentially in alphabetical order by player's name (after the manager is listed first).

	NRMT-MT	EXC	G-VG
COMPLETE SET (22)	27.00	12.00	3.40
COMMON PLAYER (1-22)	.60	.25	.08
☐ 1 Harvey Kuenn MG	1.00	.45	.13
☐ 2 Dwight Bernard	.60	.25	.08
☐ 3 Mark Brouhard	.60	.25	.08
☐ 4 Mike Caldwell	.75	.35	.09
☐ 5 Cecil Cooper	1.50	.65	.19
☐ 6 Marshall Edwards	.60	.25	.08
☐ 7 Rollie Fingers	5.00	2.30	.60
☐ 8 Jim Gantner	1.00	.45	.13
☐ 9 Moose Haas	.75	.35	.09
☐ 10 Bob McClure	.60	.25	.08
☐ 11 Paul Molitor	6.00	2.70	.75
☐ 12 Don Money	.75	.35	.09
☐ 13 Charlie Moore	.75	.35	.09
☐ 14 Ben Oglivie	1.00	.45	.13
☐ 15 Ed Romero	.60	.25	.08
☐ 16 Ted Simmons	2.00	.90	.25
☐ 17 Jim Slaton	.75	.35	.09
☐ 18 Don Sutton	3.00	1.35	.40
☐ 19 Gorman Thomas	1.00	.45	.13
☐ 20 Pete Vuckovich	.75	.35	.09
☐ 21 Ned Yost	.60	.25	.08
☐ 22 Robin Yount	10.00	4.50	1.25

1984 Brewers Gardner's

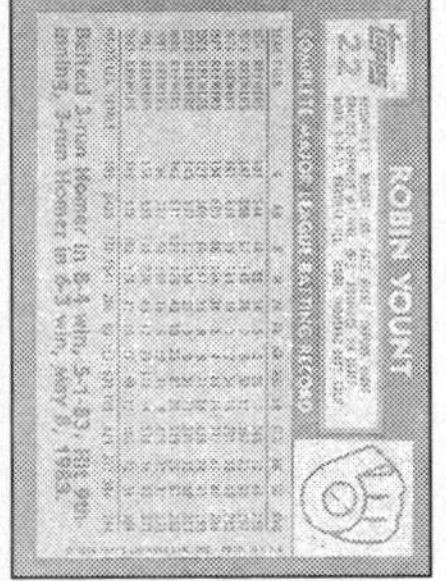

The cards in this 22-card set measure 2 1/2" by 3 1/2". For the second year in a row, the Gardner Bakery Company issued a set of cards available in packages of Gardner Bakery products. The set was manufactured by Topps, and the backs of the cards are identical to the Topps cards of this year except for the numbers. The Gardner logo appears on the fronts of the cards with the player's name, position abbreviation, the name Brewers, and the words 1984 Series II. The card numbering for this set is essentially in alphabetical order by player's name (after the manager is listed first).

	NRMT-MT	EXC	G-VG
COMPLETE SET (22)	10.00	4.50	1.25
COMMON PLAYER (1-22)	.35	.16	.04
☐ 1 Rene Lachemann MG	.45	.20	.06
☐ 2 Mark Brouhard	.35	.16	.04
☐ 3 Mike Caldwell	.45	.20	.06
☐ 4 Bobby Clark	.35	.16	.04
☐ 5 Cecil Cooper	.75	.35	.09
☐ 6 Rollie Fingers	2.00	.90	.25
☐ 7 Jim Gantner	.75	.35	.09
☐ 8 Moose Haas	.45	.20	.06
☐ 9 Roy Howell	.35	.16	.04
☐ 10 Pete Ladd	.35	.16	.04
☐ 11 Rick Manning	.35	.16	.04
☐ 12 Bob McClure	.35	.16	.04
☐ 13 Paul Molitor	2.50	1.15	.30
☐ 14 Charlie Moore	.45	.20	.06
☐ 15 Ben Oglivie	.60	.25	.08
☐ 16 Ed Romero	.35	.16	.04
☐ 17 Ted Simmons	1.00	.45	.13
☐ 18 Jim Sundberg	.45	.20	.06
☐ 19 Don Sutton	1.75	.80	.22
☐ 20 Tom Tellman	.35	.16	.04
☐ 21 Pete Vuckovich	.60	.25	.08
☐ 22 Robin Yount	4.50	2.00	.55

1985 Brewers Gardner's

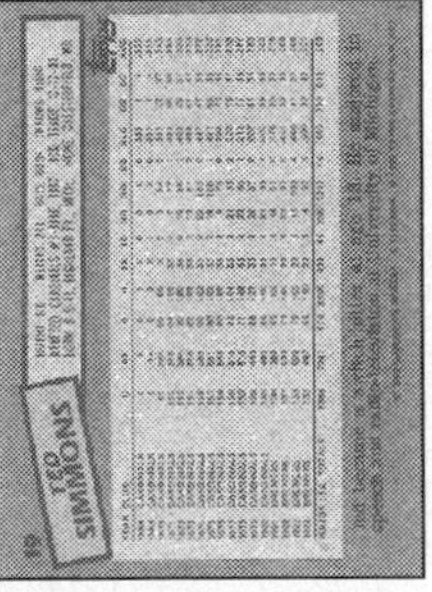

The cards in this 22-card set measure 2 1/2" by 3 1/2". For the third year in a row, the Gardner Bakery Company issued a set of cards available in packages of Gardner Bakery products. The set was manufactured by Topps, and the backs of the cards are identical to the Topps cards of this year except for the card numbers and copyright information. The Gardner logo appears on the fronts of the cards with the player's name, position abbreviation, and the name Brewers. The card numbering for this set is essentially in alphabetical order.

	NRMT-MT	EXC	G-VG
COMPLETE SET (22)	10.00	4.50	1.25
COMMON PLAYER (1-22)	.35	.16	.04
☐ 1 George Bamberger MG	.45	.20	.06
☐ 2 Mark Brouhard	.35	.16	.04
☐ 3 Bobby Clark	.35	.16	.04
☐ 4 Jaime Cocanower	.35	.16	.04
☐ 5 Cecil Cooper	.75	.35	.09
☐ 6 Rollie Fingers	2.00	.90	.25
☐ 7 Jim Gantner	.75	.35	.09
☐ 8 Moose Haas	.45	.20	.06
☐ 9 Dion James	.45	.20	.06
☐ 10 Pete Ladd	.35	.16	.04
☐ 11 Rick Manning	.35	.16	.04
☐ 12 Bob McClure	.35	.16	.04
☐ 13 Paul Molitor	2.50	1.15	.30
☐ 14 Charlie Moore	.45	.20	.06
☐ 15 Ben Oglivie	.60	.25	.08
☐ 16 Chuck Porter	.35	.16	.04
☐ 17 Ed Romero	.35	.16	.04
☐ 18 Bill Schroeder	.45	.20	.06

☐ 19 Ted Simmons	1.00	.45	.13
☐ 20 Tom Tellman	.35	.16	.04
☐ 21 Pete Vuckovich	.60	.25	.08
☐ 22 Robin Yount	4.50	2.00	.55

1989 Brewers Gardner's

The 1989 Gardner's Brewers set contains 15 standard-size (2 1/2" by 3 1/2") cards. The fronts feature airbrushed mugshots with sky blue backgrounds and white borders. The backs are white and feature career stats. One card was distributed in each specially marked Gardner's bakery product. Cards were issued during the middle of the season. For some reason Riles is included in the set even though he had been traded by the Brewers during the 1988 season.

	MT	EX-MT	VG
COMPLETE SET (15)	6.00	2.70	.75
COMMON PLAYER (1-15)	.25	.11	.03
☐ 1 Paul Molitor	1.50	.65	.19
☐ 2 Robin Yount	2.50	1.15	.30
☐ 3 Jim Gantner	.50	.23	.06
☐ 4 Rob Deer	.50	.23	.06
☐ 5 B.J. Surhoff	.50	.23	.06
☐ 6 Dale Sveum	.25	.11	.03
☐ 7 Ted Higuera	.35	.16	.04
☐ 8 Dan Plesac	.35	.16	.04
☐ 9 Bill Wegman	.35	.16	.04
☐ 10 Juan Nieves	.25	.11	.03
☐ 11 Greg Brock	.25	.11	.03
☐ 12 Glenn Braggs	.35	.16	.04
☐ 13 Joey Meyer	.25	.11	.03
☐ 14 Earnest Riles	.25	.11	.03
☐ 15 Don August	.25	.11	.03

1989 Brewers Yearbook

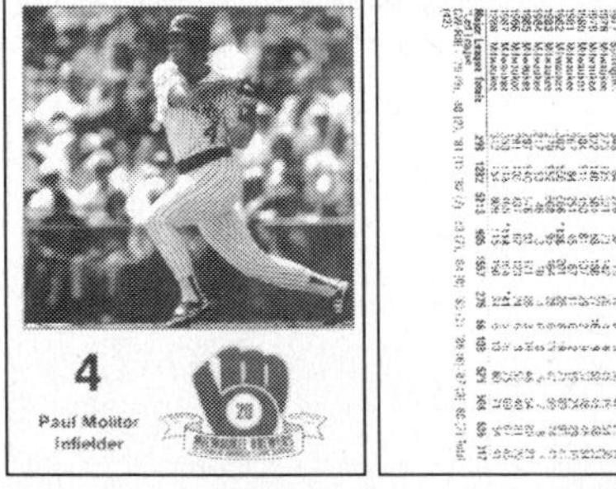

This 18-card standard size, 2 1/2" by 3 1/2" set was issued as an insert in the 1989 Milwaukee Brewer Yearbooks. The yearbook itself had a suggested retail price of $4.95. The card set features 17 of the Brewers and their manager. The cards are dominated by a full-color photo of the player on the top two-thirds of the cards along with the uniform number name and position underneath the player. There is also a large logo on the bottom right of the card commemorating the twentieth anniversary of the Brewers in Milwaukee. The backs only contain the player's name and their career statistics. The set is checklisted below by uniform numbers.

	MT	EX-MT	VG
COMPLETE SET (18)	8.00	3.60	1.00
COMMON PLAYER	.35	.16	.04
☐ 1 Gary Sheffield	1.50	.65	.19
☐ 4 Paul Molitor	1.25	.55	.16
☐ 5 B.J. Surhoff	.45	.20	.06
☐ 7 Dale Sveum	.35	.16	.04
☐ 9 Greg Brock	.35	.16	.04
☐ 17 Jim Gantner	.45	.20	.06
☐ 19 Robin Yount	1.50	.65	.19
☐ 20 Juan Nieves	.35	.16	.04
☐ 26 Glenn Braggs	.35	.16	.04
☐ 29 Chris Bosio	.75	.35	.09
☐ 32 Chuck Crim	.35	.16	.04
☐ 37 Dan Plesac	.45	.20	.06
☐ 38 Don August	.35	.16	.04
☐ 40 Mike Birkbeck	.35	.16	.04
☐ 42 Tom Trebelhorn MG	.35	.16	.04
☐ 45 Rob Deer	.60	.25	.08
☐ 46 Bill Wegman	.45	.20	.06
☐ 49 Ted Higuera	.45	.20	.06

1990 Brewers Miller Brewing

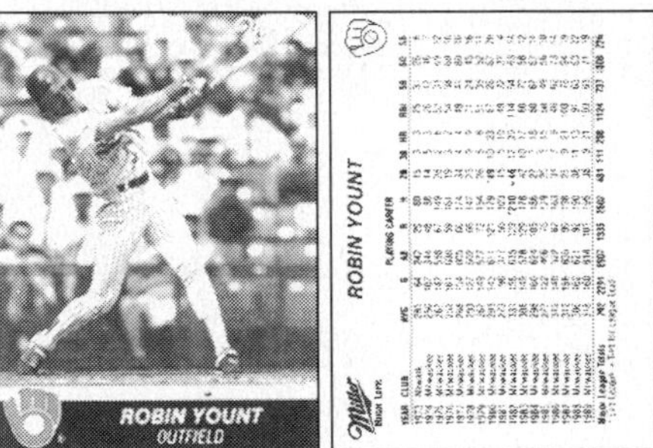

This 32-card set and a plastic binder were sponsored by Miller Brewing Co. and given away to the first 25,000 adults (21 years and older) attending the Brewers' home game against the White Sox on August 4th. The cards measure the standard size (2 1/2" by 3 1/2"). The fronts have either action or posed color player photos, with the player's name and position given in white lettering on a black stripe at the bottom of the card face. The backs have biographical information and player statistics. The cards are unnumbered and checklisted below in alphabetical order. The complete set price below does not include the binder.

	MT	EX-MT	VG
COMPLETE SET (32)	13.50	6.00	1.70
COMMON PLAYER (1-32)	.35	.16	.04
☐ 1 Chris Bosio	.75	.35	.09
☐ 2 Greg Brock	.35	.16	.04
☐ 3 Chuck Crim	.35	.16	.04
☐ 4 Rob Deer	.60	.25	.08
☐ 5 Edgar Diaz	.35	.16	.04
☐ 6 Tom Edens	.35	.16	.04
☐ 7 Mike Felder	.35	.16	.04
☐ 8 Tom Filer	.35	.16	.04
☐ 9 Jim Gantner	.60	.25	.08
☐ 10 Darryl Hamilton	.75	.35	.09
☐ 11 Teddy Higuera	.45	.20	.06
☐ 12 Mark Knudson	.35	.16	.04
☐ 13 Bill Krueger	.35	.16	.04

	MT	EX-MT	VG
☐ 14 Paul Mirabella	.35	.16	.04
☐ 15 Paul Molitor	1.25	.55	.16
☐ 16 Jaime Navarro	1.00	.45	.13
☐ 17 Charlie O'Brien	.35	.16	.04
☐ 18 Dave Parker	.75	.35	.09
☐ 19 Dan Plesac	.45	.20	.06
☐ 20 Dennis Powell	.35	.16	.04
☐ 21 Ron Robinson	.35	.16	.04
☐ 22 Bob Sebra	.35	.16	.04
☐ 23 Gary Sheffield	1.25	.55	.16
☐ 24 Bill Spiers	.45	.20	.06
☐ 25 B.J. Surhoff	.45	.20	.06
☐ 26 Dale Sveum	.35	.16	.04
☐ 27 Tom Trebelhorn MG	.35	.16	.04
☐ 28 Greg Vaughn	.75	.35	.09
☐ 29 Randy Veres	.35	.16	.04
☐ 30 Bill Wegman	.45	.20	.06
☐ 31 Robin Yount	1.75	.80	.22
☐ 32 Coaches Card Don Baylor Ray Burris Duffy Dyer Andy Etchebarren Larry Haney	.35	.16	.04

1991 Brewers Miller Brewing

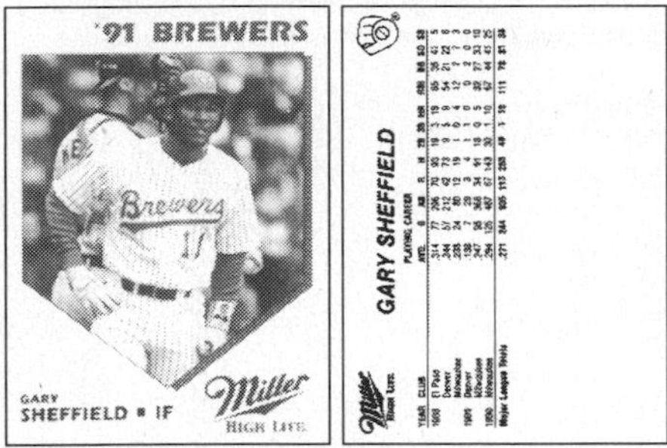

This 32-card set was sponsored by the Miller Brewing Company, and the company logo appears in red lettering at the lower right corner of the front. The sets were given away at the Brewers' home game against the Baltimore Orioles on August 17. The standard size (2 1/2" by 3 1/2") cards feature on the fronts color action player photos inside a pentagonal-shaped design. A black border on the right side of the pentagon creates the impression of a shadow. The words "'91 Brewers" appears in bluish-purple lettering above the photo, with player information given in black lettering in the lower left corner of the card face. The backs are printed in black and present complete Major League statistics. The cards are unnumbered and checklisted below in alphabetical order, with the coaches' card listed at the end.

	MT	EX-MT	VG
COMPLETE SET (32)	12.00	5.50	1.50
COMMON PLAYER (1-32)	.35	.16	.04
☐ 1 Don August	.35	.16	.04
☐ 2 James Austin	.45	.20	.06
☐ 3 Dante Bichette	.60	.25	.08
☐ 4 Chris Bosio	.75	.35	.09
☐ 5 Kevin Brown	.35	.16	.04
☐ 6 Chuck Crim	.35	.16	.04
☐ 7 Rick Dempsey	.45	.20	.06
☐ 8 Jim Gantner	.60	.25	.08
☐ 9 Darryl Hamilton	.60	.25	.08
☐ 10 Teddy Higuera	.45	.20	.06
☐ 11 Darren Holmes	.35	.16	.04
☐ 12 Jim Hunter	.45	.20	.06
☐ 13 Mark Knudson	.45	.20	.06
☐ 14 Mark Lee	.35	.16	.04
☐ 15 Julio Machado	.35	.16	.04
☐ 16 Candy Maldonado	.45	.20	.06
☐ 17 Paul Molitor	1.25	.55	.16

	MT	EX-MT	VG
☐ 18 Jaime Navarro	.75	.35	.09
☐ 19 Edwin Nunez	.35	.16	.04
☐ 20 Dan Plesac	.45	.20	.06
☐ 21 Willie Randolph	.45	.20	.06
☐ 22 Ron Robinson	.35	.16	.04
☐ 23 Gary Sheffield	1.00	.45	.13
☐ 24 Bill Spiers	.45	.20	.06
☐ 25 Franklin Stubbs	.45	.20	.06
☐ 26 B.J. Surhoff	.45	.20	.06
☐ 27 Dale Sveum	.35	.16	.04
☐ 28 Tom Trebelhorn MG	.35	.16	.04
☐ 29 Greg Vaughn	.75	.35	.09
☐ 30 Bill Wegman	.45	.20	.06
☐ 31 Robin Yount	1.75	.80	.22
☐ 32 Coaches Card Don Baylor Fred Stanley Duffy Dyer Larry Haney Andy Etchebarren Ray Burris	.35	.16	.04

1992 Brewers Carlson Travel

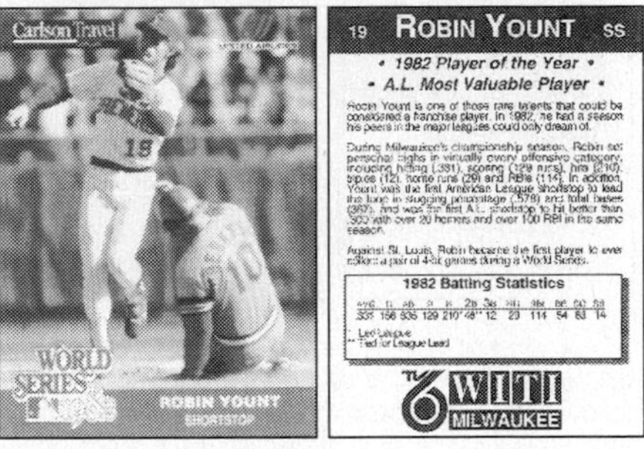

This 31-card set was sponsored by Carlson Travel in conjunction with United Airlines and TV Channel 6 (WITI in Milwaukee). It was issued to commemorate the 1982 Milwaukee Brewers team who played in the World Series. The set included a travel coupon entitling the holder to $50.00 off per couple on the next cruise vacation. The cards measure the standard size (2 1/2" by 3 1/2"). The fronts display color action player photos, with sponsor logos superimposed at the top corners. At the bottom, the player's name and position appear in a blue stripe, which intersects a "World Series 1982" logo in the lower left corner. In blue print on a white background, the backs carry season summary and (batting or pitching) statistics. The cards are unnumbered and checklisted below in alphabetical order.

	MT	EX-MT	VG
COMPLETE SET (31)	8.00	3.60	1.00
COMMON PLAYER (1-31)	.25	.11	.03
☐ 1 Jerry Augustine	.25	.11	.03
☐ 2 Dwight Bernard	.25	.11	.03
☐ 3 Mark Brouhard	.25	.11	.03
☐ 4 Mike Caldwell	.35	.16	.04
☐ 5 Cecil Cooper	.50	.23	.06
☐ 6 Marshall Edwards	.25	.11	.03
☐ 7 Rollie Fingers	.75	.35	.09
☐ 8 Jim Gantner	.50	.23	.06
☐ 9 Moose Haas	.25	.11	.03
☐ 10 Roy Howell	.25	.11	.03
☐ 11 Harvey Kuenn MG	.35	.16	.04
☐ 12 Pete Ladd	.25	.11	.03
☐ 13 Bob McClure	.35	.16	.04
☐ 14 Doc Medich	.25	.11	.03
☐ 15 Paul Molitor	.75	.35	.09
☐ 16 Don Money	.35	.16	.04
☐ 17 Charlie Moore	.25	.11	.03
☐ 18 Ben Oglivie	.35	.16	.04
☐ 19 Ed Romero	.25	.11	.03
☐ 20 Ted Simmons	.50	.23	.06
☐ 21 Jim Slaton	.35	.16	.04
☐ 22 Don Sutton	.75	.35	.09

☐ 23 Gorman Thomas	.50	.23	.06
☐ 24 Pete Vuckovich	.35	.16	.04
☐ 25 Ned Yost	.25	.11	.03
☐ 26 Robin Yount	1.00	.45	.13
☐ xx Bernie Brewer (Team Mascot)	.35	.16	.04
☐ xx Coaches Larry Haney Ron Hansen Harry Warner Cal McLish Pat Dobson	.25	.11	.03
☐ xx Post Season Rally	.25	.11	.03
☐ xx Team Photo	.35	.16	.04
☐ xx Carlson Travel Coupon	.25	.11	.03

1977 Burger King Yankees

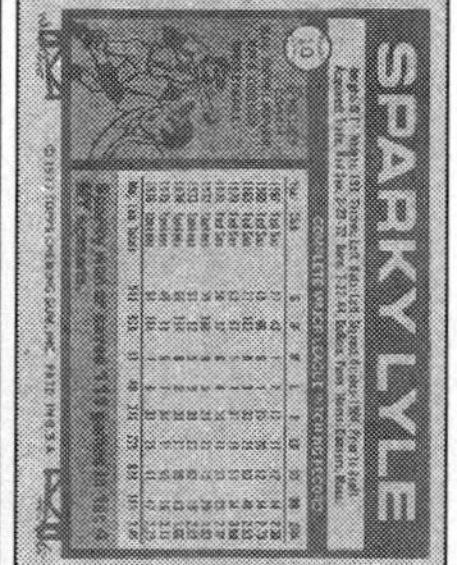

The cards in this 24-card set measure 2 1/2" by 3 1/2". The cards in this set marked with an asterisk have different poses than those cards in the regular 1977 Topps set. The checklist card is unnumbered and the Piniella card was issued subsequent to the original printing. The complete set price below refers to all 24 cards listed, including Piniella.

	NRMT-MT	EXC	G-VG
COMPLETE SET (24)	45.00	20.00	5.75
COMMON PLAYER (1-23)	.40	.18	.05
☐ 1 Yankees Team Billy Martin MG	1.25	.55	.16
☐ 2 Thurman Munson * UER (Facsimile autograph misspelled)	9.00	4.00	1.15
☐ 3 Fran Healy	.40	.18	.05
☐ 4 Jim Hunter	3.00	1.35	.40
☐ 5 Ed Figueroa	.40	.18	.05
☐ 6 Don Gullett * (Mouth closed)	.75	.35	.09
☐ 7 Mike Torrez *	.60	.25	.08
☐ 8 Ken Holtzman	.50	.23	.06
☐ 9 Dick Tidrow	.40	.18	.05
☐ 10 Sparky Lyle	.60	.25	.08
☐ 11 Ron Guidry	2.00	.90	.25
☐ 12 Chris Chambliss	.60	.25	.08
☐ 13 Willie Randolph * (No rookie trophy)	1.50	.65	.19
☐ 14 Bucky Dent * (Shown as White Sox in 1977 Topps)	1.50	.65	.19
☐ 15 Graig Nettles * (Closer photo than in 1977 Topps)	1.50	.65	.19
☐ 16 Fred Stanley	.40	.18	.05
☐ 17 Reggie Jackson * (Looking up with bat)	15.00	6.75	1.90
☐ 18 Mickey Rivers	.50	.23	.06
☐ 19 Roy White	.50	.23	.06
☐ 20 Jim Wynn * (Shown as Brave in 1977 Topps)	.75	.35	.09
☐ 21 Paul Blair * (Shown as Oriole in 1977 Topps)	.75	.35	.09
☐ 22 Carlos May *	.60	.25	.08
☐ 23 Lou Piniella SP	20.00	9.00	2.50
☐ NNO Checklist Card TP	.25	.11	.03

1978 Burger King Astros

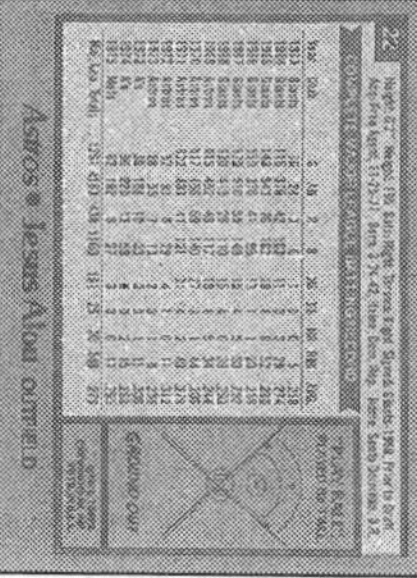

The cards in this 23-card set measure 2 1/2" by 3 1/2". Released in local Houston Burger King outlets during the 1978 season, this Houston Astros series contains the standard 22 numbered player cards and one unnumbered checklist. The player poses found to differ from the regular Topps issue are marked with astericks.

	NRMT-MT	EXC	G-VG
COMPLETE SET (23)	12.00	5.50	1.50
COMMON PLAYER (1-22)	.40	.18	.05
☐ 1 Bill Virdon MG	.60	.25	.08
☐ 2 Joe Ferguson	.50	.23	.06
☐ 3 Ed Herrmann	.40	.18	.05
☐ 4 J.R. Richard	1.00	.45	.13
☐ 5 Joe Niekro	1.00	.45	.13
☐ 6 Floyd Bannister	.90	.40	.11
☐ 7 Joaquin Andujar	1.00	.45	.13
☐ 8 Ken Forsch	.50	.23	.06
☐ 9 Mark Lemongello	.40	.18	.05
☐ 10 Joe Sambito	.50	.23	.06
☐ 11 Gene Pentz	.40	.18	.05
☐ 12 Bob Watson	.75	.35	.09
☐ 13 Julio Gonzales	.40	.18	.05
☐ 14 Enos Cabell	.40	.18	.05
☐ 15 Roger Metzger	.40	.18	.05
☐ 16 Art Howe	.90	.40	.11
☐ 17 Jose Cruz	1.50	.65	.19
☐ 18 Cesar Cedeno	1.00	.45	.13
☐ 19 Terry Puhl	.60	.25	.08
☐ 20 Wilbur Howard	.40	.18	.05
☐ 21 Dave Bergman *	.75	.35	.09
☐ 22 Jesus Alou *	.60	.25	.08
☐ NNO Checklist Card TP	.15	.07	.02

1978 Burger King Rangers

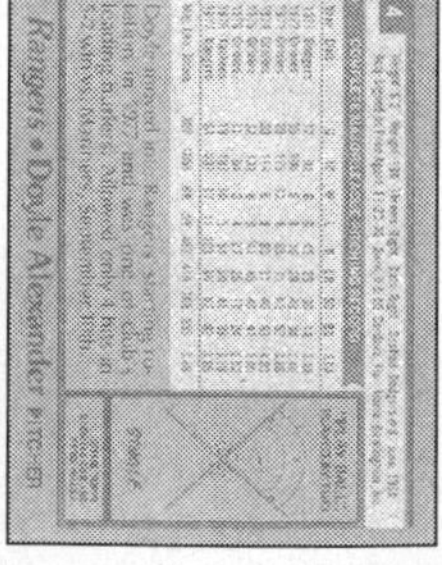

The cards in this 23-card set measure 2 1/2" by 3 1/2". This set of 22 numbered player cards (featuring the Texas Rangers) and one unnumbered checklist was issued regionally by Burger King in 1978. Astericks denote poses different from those found in the regular Topps cards of this year.

	NRMT-MT	EXC	G-VG
COMPLETE SET (23)	12.00	5.50	1.50
COMMON PLAYER (1-22)	.40	.18	.05
☐ 1 Billy Hunter MG	.40	.18	.05
☐ 2 Jim Sundberg	1.00	.45	.13
☐ 3 John Ellis	.40	.18	.05
☐ 4 Doyle Alexander	.60	.25	.08
☐ 5 Jon Matlack *	.75	.35	.09
☐ 6 Dock Ellis	.40	.18	.05
☐ 7 Doc Medich	.50	.23	.06
☐ 8 Fergie Jenkins *	4.00	1.80	.50
☐ 9 Len Barker	.40	.18	.05
☐ 10 Reggie Cleveland *	.50	.23	.06
☐ 11 Mike Hargrove	.75	.35	.09
☐ 12 Bump Wills	.40	.18	.05
☐ 13 Toby Harrah	.75	.35	.09
☐ 14 Bert Campaneris	.60	.25	.08
☐ 15 Sandy Alomar	.50	.23	.06
☐ 16 Kurt Bevacqua	.40	.18	.05
☐ 17 Al Oliver *	1.00	.45	.13
☐ 18 Juan Beniquez	.50	.23	.06
☐ 19 Claudell Washington	.75	.35	.09
☐ 20 Richie Zisk	.50	.23	.06
☐ 21 John Lowenstein *	.50	.23	.06
☐ 22 Bobby Thompson *	.50	.23	.06
☐ NNO Checklist Card TP	.15	.07	.02

1978 Burger King Tigers

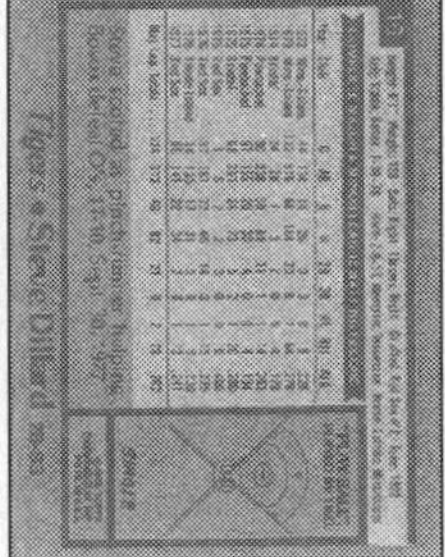

The cards in this 23-card set measure 2 1/2" by 3 1/2". Twenty-three color cards, 22 players and one numbered checklist, comprise the 1978 Burger King Tigers set issued in the Detroit area. The cards marked with an asterisk contain photos different from those appearing on the Topps regular issue cards of that year. For example, Jack Morris, Alan Trammell, and Lou Whitaker (in the 1978 Topps regular issue cards) each appear on rookie prospect cards with three other young players; whereas in this Burger King set, each has his own individual card.

	NRMT-MT	EXC	G-VG
COMPLETE SET (23)	60.00	27.00	7.50
COMMON PLAYER (1-22)	.40	.18	.05
☐ 1 Ralph Houk MG	.60	.25	.08
☐ 2 Milt May	.40	.18	.05
☐ 3 John Wockenfuss	.40	.18	.05
☐ 4 Mark Fidrych	1.50	.65	.19
☐ 5 Dave Rozema	.40	.18	.05
☐ 6 Jack Billingham *	.50	.23	.06
☐ 7 Jim Slaton *	.50	.23	.06
☐ 8 Jack Morris *	18.00	8.00	2.30
☐ 9 John Hiller	.60	.25	.08
☐ 10 Steve Foucault	.40	.18	.05
☐ 11 Milt Wilcox	.50	.23	.06
☐ 12 Jason Thompson	.75	.35	.09
☐ 13 Lou Whitaker *	18.00	8.00	2.30
☐ 14 Aurelio Rodriguez	.50	.23	.06
☐ 15 Alan Trammell *	20.00	9.00	2.50
☐ 16 Steve Dillard *	.50	.23	.06
☐ 17 Phil Mankowski	.40	.18	.05
☐ 18 Steve Kemp	.60	.25	.08
☐ 19 Ron LeFlore	.50	.23	.06
☐ 20 Tim Corcoran	.40	.18	.05
☐ 21 Mickey Stanley	.50	.23	.06
☐ 22 Rusty Staub	1.00	.45	.13
☐ NNO Checklist Card TP	.15	.07	.02

1978 Burger King Yankees

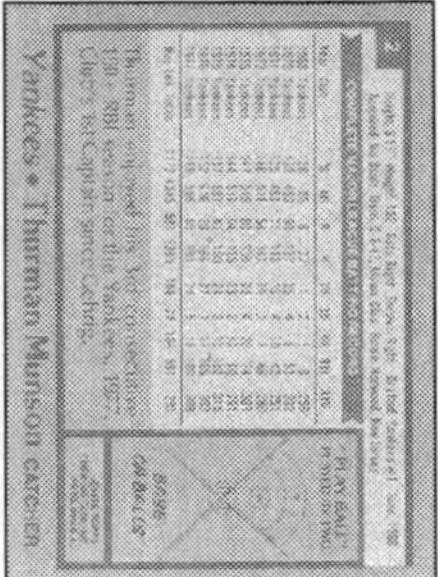

The cards in this 23-card set measure 2 1/2" by 3 1/2". These cards were distributed in packs of three players plus a checklist at Burger King's New York area outlets. Cards with an asterisk have different poses than those in the Topps regular issue.

	NRMT-MT	EXC	G-VG
COMPLETE SET (23)	15.00	6.75	1.90
COMMON PLAYER (1-22)	.25	.11	.03
☐ 1 Billy Martin MG	.75	.35	.09
☐ 2 Thurman Munson	4.00	1.80	.50
☐ 3 Cliff Johnson	.25	.11	.03
☐ 4 Ron Guidry	1.25	.55	.16
☐ 5 Ed Figueroa	.25	.11	.03
☐ 6 Dick Tidrow	.25	.11	.03
☐ 7 Jim Hunter	2.00	.90	.25
☐ 8 Don Gullett	.35	.16	.04
☐ 9 Sparky Lyle	.50	.23	.06
☐ 10 Rich Gossage *	1.50	.65	.19
☐ 11 Rawly Eastwick *	.35	.16	.04
☐ 12 Chris Chambliss	.50	.23	.06
☐ 13 Willie Randolph	.75	.35	.09
☐ 14 Graig Nettles	.75	.35	.09
☐ 15 Bucky Dent	.60	.25	.08
☐ 16 Jim Spencer *	.35	.16	.04
☐ 17 Fred Stanley	.25	.11	.03
☐ 18 Lou Piniella	.75	.35	.09
☐ 19 Roy White	.35	.16	.04
☐ 20 Mickey Rivers	.35	.16	.04
☐ 21 Reggie Jackson	6.00	2.70	.75
☐ 22 Paul Blair	.25	.11	.03
☐ NNO Checklist Card TP	.10	.05	.01

1979 Burger King Phillies

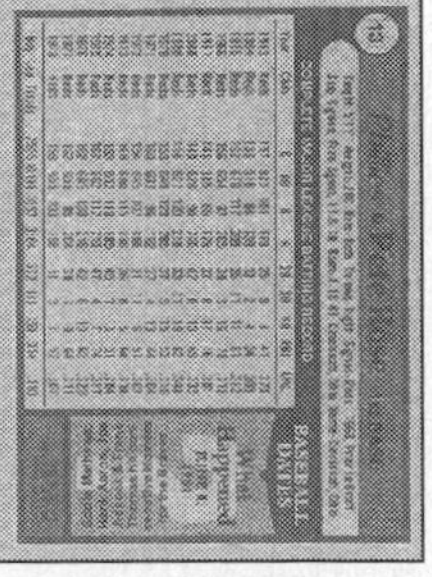

The cards in this 23-card set measure 2 1/2" by 3 1/2". The 1979 Burger King Phillies set follows the regular format of 22 player cards and one unnumbered checklist card. The asterisk indicates where the pose differs from the Topps card of that year. The set features the first card of Pete Rose as a member of the Philadelphia Phillies.

	NRMT-MT	EXC	G-VG
COMPLETE SET (23)	10.00	4.50	1.25
COMMON PLAYER (1-22)	.15	.07	.02
☐ 1 Danny Ozark MG *	.25	.11	.03
☐ 2 Bob Boone	.50	.23	.06
☐ 3 Tim McCarver	.50	.23	.06
☐ 4 Steve Carlton	2.50	1.15	.30
☐ 5 Larry Christenson	.15	.07	.02
☐ 6 Dick Ruthven	.15	.07	.02
☐ 7 Ron Reed	.15	.07	.02
☐ 8 Randy Lerch	.15	.07	.02
☐ 9 Warren Brusstar	.15	.07	.02
☐ 10 Tug McGraw	.35	.16	.04
☐ 11 Nino Espinosa *	.25	.11	.03
☐ 12 Doug Bird *	.25	.11	.03
☐ 13 Pete Rose *	5.00	2.30	.60
☐ 14 Manny Trillo *	.25	.11	.03
☐ 15 Larry Bowa	.35	.16	.04
☐ 16 Mike Schmidt	3.50	1.55	.45
☐ 17 Pete Mackanin *	.25	.11	.03
☐ 18 Jose Cardenal	.15	.07	.02
☐ 19 Greg Luzinski	.35	.16	.04
☐ 20 Garry Maddox	.15	.07	.02
☐ 21 Bake McBride	.15	.07	.02
☐ 22 Greg Gross *	.25	.11	.03
☐ NNO Checklist Card TP	.05	.02	.01

1979 Burger King Yankees

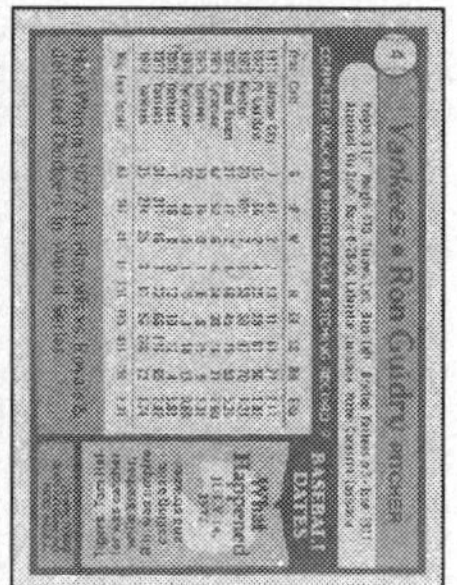

The cards in this 23-card set measure 2 1/2" by 3 1/2". There are 22 numbered cards and one unnumbered checklist in the 1979 Burger King Yankee set. The poses of Guidry, Tiant, John and Beniquez, each marked with an asterisk below, are different from their poses appearing in the regular Topps issue. The team card has a picture of Lemon rather than Martin.

	NRMT-MT	EXC	G-VG
COMPLETE SET (23)	10.00	4.50	1.25
COMMON PLAYER (1-22)	.15	.07	.02
☐ 1 Yankees Team: Bob Lemon MG *	.75	.35	.09
☐ 2 Thurman Munson	3.00	1.35	.40
☐ 3 Cliff Johnson	.15	.07	.02
☐ 4 Ron Guidry *	1.25	.55	.16
☐ 5 Jay Johnstone	.35	.16	.04
☐ 6 Jim Hunter	1.50	.65	.19
☐ 7 Jim Beattie	.15	.07	.02
☐ 8 Luis Tiant *	.35	.16	.04
☐ 9 Tommy John *	1.25	.55	.16
☐ 10 Rich Gossage	.75	.35	.09
☐ 11 Ed Figueroa	.15	.07	.02
☐ 12 Chris Chambliss	.30	.14	.04
☐ 13 Willie Randolph	.50	.23	.06
☐ 14 Bucky Dent	.40	.18	.05
☐ 15 Graig Nettles	.50	.23	.06
☐ 16 Fred Stanley	.15	.07	.02
☐ 17 Jim Spencer	.15	.07	.02
☐ 18 Lou Piniella	.60	.25	.08
☐ 19 Roy White	.25	.11	.03
☐ 20 Mickey Rivers	.25	.11	.03
☐ 21 Reggie Jackson	4.00	1.80	.50
☐ 22 Juan Beniquez *	.25	.11	.03
☐ NNO Checklist Card TP	.05	.02	.01

1980 Burger King Phillies

The cards in this 23-card set measure 2 1/2" by 3 1/2". The 1980 edition of Burger King Phillies follows the established pattern of 22 numbered player cards and one unnumbered checklist. Cards marked with astericks contain poses different from those found in the regular 1980 Topps cards. This was the first Burger King set to carry the Burger King logo and hence does not generate the same confusion that the three previous years do for collectors trying to distinguish Burger King cards from the very similar Topps cards of the same years. Keith Moreland's card predates his Rookie Cards by one year as he did not appear on a regular issue card until 1981.

	NRMT-MT	EXC	G-VG
COMPLETE SET (23)	9.00	4.00	1.15
COMMON PLAYER (1-22)	.15	.07	.02
☐ 1 Dallas Green MG *	.35	.16	.04
☐ 2 Bob Boone	.40	.18	.05
☐ 3 Keith Moreland *	.60	.25	.08
☐ 4 Pete Rose	3.50	1.55	.45
☐ 5 Manny Trillo	.15	.07	.02
☐ 6 Mike Schmidt	3.50	1.55	.45
☐ 7 Larry Bowa	.35	.16	.04
☐ 8 John Vukovich *	.25	.11	.03
☐ 9 Bake McBride	.15	.07	.02
☐ 10 Garry Maddox	.25	.11	.03
☐ 11 Greg Luzinski	.35	.16	.04
☐ 12 Greg Gross	.15	.07	.02
☐ 13 Del Unser	.15	.07	.02
☐ 14 Lonnie Smith *	1.00	.45	.13
☐ 15 Steve Carlton	2.00	.90	.25
☐ 16 Larry Christenson	.15	.07	.02
☐ 17 Nino Espinosa	.15	.07	.02
☐ 18 Randy Lerch	.15	.07	.02
☐ 19 Dick Ruthven	.15	.07	.02
☐ 20 Tug McGraw	.35	.16	.04
☐ 21 Ron Reed	.15	.07	.02
☐ 22 Kevin Saucier *	.25	.11	.03
☐ NNO Checklist Card TP	.05	.02	.01

1980 Burger King Pitch/Hit/Run

The cards in this 34-card set measure 2 1/2" by 3 1/2". The "Pitch, Hit, and Run" set was a promotion introduced by Burger King in 1980. The cards carry a Burger King logo on the front and those marked by an asterisk in the checklist contain a different photo from that found in the regularly issued Topps series. For example, Nolan Ryan was shown as a California Angel and Joe Morgan was a Cincinnati Red in the 1980 Topps regular set. Cards 1-11 are pitchers,

12-22 are hitters, and 23-33 are speedsters. Within each subgroup, the players are numbered corresponding to the alphabetical order of their names. The unnumbered checklist card was triple printed and is the least valuable card in the set.

	NRMT-MT	EXC	G-VG
COMPLETE SET (34)	25.00	11.50	3.10
COMMON PLAYER (1-33)	.15	.07	.02
☐ 1 Vida Blue *	.25	.11	.03
☐ 2 Steve Carlton	2.00	.90	.25
☐ 3 Rollie Fingers	1.25	.55	.16
☐ 4 Ron Guidry *	.50	.23	.06
☐ 5 Jerry Koosman *	.35	.16	.04
☐ 6 Phil Niekro	.75	.35	.09
☐ 7 Jim Palmer *	2.50	1.15	.30
☐ 8 J.R. Richard	.15	.07	.02
☐ 9 Nolan Ryan * Houston Astros	12.50	5.75	1.55
☐ 10 Tom Seaver *	4.50	2.00	.55
☐ 11 Bruce Sutter	.15	.07	.02
☐ 12 Don Baylor	.25	.11	.03
☐ 13 George Brett	3.50	1.55	.45
☐ 14 Rod Carew	1.25	.55	.16
☐ 15 George Foster	.15	.07	.02
☐ 16 Keith Hernandez *	.50	.23	.06
☐ 17 Reggie Jackson *	5.00	2.30	.60
☐ 18 Fred Lynn *	.35	.16	.04
☐ 19 Dave Parker	.35	.16	.04
☐ 20 Jim Rice	.35	.16	.04
☐ 21 Pete Rose	3.00	1.35	.40
☐ 22 Dave Winfield *	4.00	1.80	.50
☐ 23 Bobby Bonds *	.25	.11	.03
☐ 24 Enos Cabell	.15	.07	.02
☐ 25 Cesar Cedeno	.15	.07	.02
☐ 26 Julio Cruz	.15	.07	.02
☐ 27 Ron LeFlore *	.25	.11	.03
☐ 28 Dave Lopes *	.25	.11	.03
☐ 29 Omar Moreno *	.25	.11	.03
☐ 30 Joe Morgan * Houston Astros	2.50	1.15	.30
☐ 31 Bill North	.15	.07	.02
☐ 32 Frank Taveras	.15	.07	.02
☐ 33 Willie Wilson	.25	.11	.03
☐ NNO Checklist Card TP	.05	.02	.01

1986 Burger King All-Pro

This 20-card set was distributed in Burger King restaurants across the country. They were produced as panels of three where the middle card was actually a special discount coupon card. The folded panel was given with the purchase of a Whopper. Each individual card measures 2 1/2" by 3 1/2". The team logos have been airbrushed from the pictures. The cards are numbered on the front at the top.

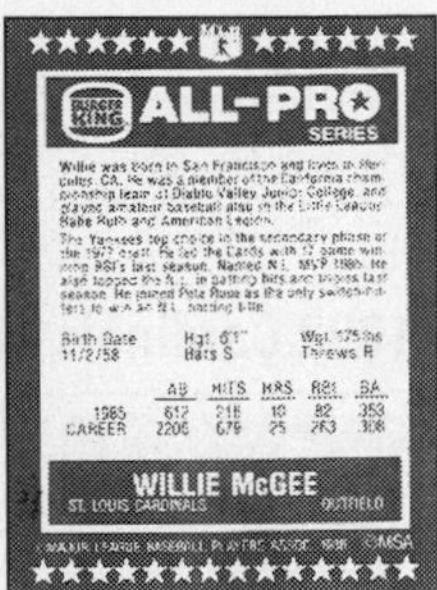

	MT	EX-MT	VG
COMPLETE SET (20)	6.00	2.70	.75
COMMON PLAYER (1-20)	.20	.09	.03
☐ 1 Tony Pena	.20	.09	.03
☐ 2 Dave Winfield	.70	.30	.09
☐ 3 Fernando Valenzuela	.20	.09	.03
☐ 4 Pete Rose	.90	.40	.11
☐ 5 Mike Schmidt	.90	.40	.11
☐ 6 Steve Carlton	.60	.25	.08
☐ 7 Glenn Wilson	.20	.09	.03
☐ 8 Jim Rice	.25	.11	.03
☐ 9 Wade Boggs	.80	.35	.10
☐ 10 Juan Samuel	.20	.09	.03
☐ 11 Dale Murphy	.40	.18	.05
☐ 12 Reggie Jackson	.80	.35	.10
☐ 13 Kirk Gibson	.25	.11	.03
☐ 14 Eddie Murray	.50	.23	.06
☐ 15 Cal Ripken	1.25	.55	.16
☐ 16 Willie McGee	.20	.09	.03
☐ 17 Dwight Gooden	.40	.18	.05
☐ 18 Steve Garvey	.30	.14	.04
☐ 19 Don Mattingly	.80	.35	.10
☐ 20 George Brett	.80	.35	.10

1987 Burger King All-Pro

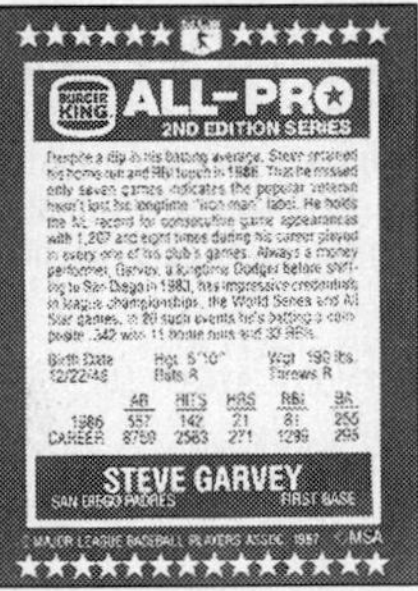

This 20-card set consists of ten panels of two cards each joined together along with a promotional coupon. Individual cards measure 2 1/2" by 3 1/2" whereas the panels measure approximately 3 1/2" by 7 5/8". MSA (Mike Schechter Associates produced the cards for Burger King; there are no Major League logos on the cards. The cards are numbered on the front. The set card numbering is almost (but not quite) in alphabetical order by player's name.

	MT	EX-MT	VG
COMPLETE SET (20)	5.00	2.30	.60
COMMON PLAYER (1-20)	.20	.09	.03
☐ 1 Wade Boggs	.80	.35	.10
☐ 2 Gary Carter	.40	.18	.05
☐ 3 Will Clark	1.00	.45	.13
☐ 4 Roger Clemens	1.00	.45	.13
☐ 5 Steve Garvey	.30	.14	.04
☐ 6 Ron Darling	.30	.14	.04
☐ 7 Pedro Guerrero	.25	.11	.03
☐ 8 Von Hayes	.20	.09	.03
☐ 9 Rickey Henderson	.80	.35	.10
☐ 10 Keith Hernandez	.25	.11	.03
☐ 11 Wally Joyner	.30	.14	.04
☐ 12 Mike Krukow	.20	.09	.03
☐ 13 Don Mattingly	.80	.35	.10
☐ 14 Ozzie Smith	.60	.25	.08

	MT	EX-MT	VG
☐ 15 Tony Pena	.20	.09	.03
☐ 16 Jim Rice	.25	.11	.03
☐ 17 Mike Schmidt	.90	.40	.11
☐ 18 Ryne Sandberg	1.00	.45	.13
☐ 19 Darryl Strawberry	.60	.25	.08
☐ 20 Fernando Valenzuela	.20	.09	.03

1992 Cardinals McDonald's/Pacific

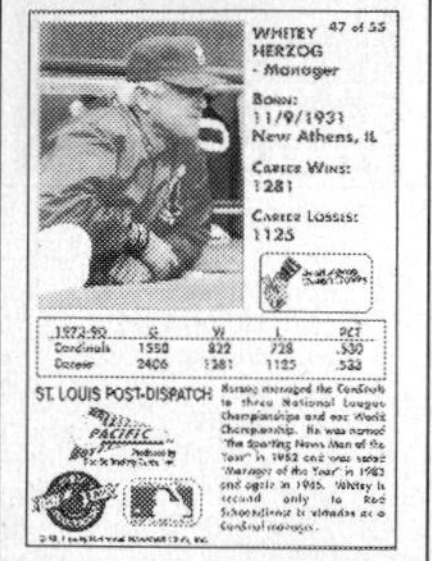

Produced by Pacific, this 55-card set measures the standard size (2 1/2" by 3 1/2") and commemorates the 100th anniversary of the St. Louis Cardinals. The collection was available at McDonald's restaurants in the greater St. Louis area for $1.49 with a purchase, and was distributed to raise money for Ronald McDonald Children's Charities. The set features black-and-white and color action player photos of players throughout Cardinals' history. The pictures are bordered in gold and include the player's name, the Cardinals 100th anniversary logo, and the McDonald's logo. The back design consists of a posed player photo, biographical and statistical information, and a career summary. The cards are numbered on the back.

	MT	EX-MT	VG
COMPLETE SET (55)	35.00	16.00	4.40
COMMON PLAYER (1-55)	.40	.18	.05
☐ 1 Jim Bottomley	.75	.35	.09
☐ 2 Rip Collins	.40	.18	.05
☐ 3 Johnny Mize	1.00	.45	.13
☐ 4 Rogers Hornsby	1.25	.55	.16
☐ 5 Miller Huggins	.75	.35	.09
☐ 6 Marty Marion	.60	.25	.08
☐ 7 Frank Frisch	.75	.35	.09
☐ 8 Whitey Kurowski	.40	.18	.05
☐ 9 Joe Medwick	.75	.35	.09
☐ 10 Terry Moore	.50	.23	.06
☐ 11 Chick Hafey	.75	.35	.09
☐ 12 Pepper Martin	.60	.25	.08
☐ 13 Bob O'Farrell	.40	.18	.05
☐ 14 Walker Cooper	.40	.18	.05
☐ 15 Dizzy Dean	1.25	.55	.16
☐ 16 Grover C. Alexander	1.00	.45	.13
☐ 17 Jesse Haines	.75	.35	.09
☐ 18 Bill Hallahan	.40	.18	.05
☐ 19 Mort Cooper	.40	.18	.05
☐ 20 Burleigh Grimes	.75	.35	.09
☐ 21 Red Schoendienst	1.00	.45	.13
☐ 22 Stan Musial	2.50	1.15	.30
☐ 23 Enos Slaughter	1.00	.45	.13
☐ 24 Keith Hernandez	.75	.35	.09
☐ 25 Bill White	.75	.35	.09
☐ 26 Orlando Cepeda	.75	.35	.09
☐ 27 Julian Javier	.50	.23	.06
☐ 28 Dick Groat	.60	.25	.08
☐ 29 Ken Boyer	.75	.35	.09
☐ 30 Lou Brock	1.00	.45	.13
☐ 31 Mike Shannon	.60	.25	.08
☐ 32 Curt Flood	.60	.25	.08
☐ 33 Joe Cunningham	.40	.18	.05
☐ 34 Reggie Smith	.50	.23	.06
☐ 35 Ted Simmons	.75	.35	.09
☐ 36 Tim McCarver	.75	.35	.09
☐ 37 Tom Herr	.40	.18	.05
☐ 38 Ozzie Smith	2.00	.90	.25
☐ 39 Joe Torre	.75	.35	.09
☐ 40 Terry Pendleton	1.00	.45	.13
☐ 41 Ken Reitz	.40	.18	.05
☐ 42 Vince Coleman	.60	.25	.08
☐ 43 Willie McGee	.60	.25	.08
☐ 44 Bake McBride	.40	.18	.05
☐ 45 George Hendrick	.40	.18	.05
☐ 46 Bob Gibson	1.00	.45	.13
☐ 47 Whitey Herzog MG	.75	.35	.09
☐ 48 Harry Brecheen	.40	.18	.05
☐ 49 Howard Pollet	.40	.18	.05
☐ 50 John Tudor	.50	.23	.06
☐ 51 Bob Forsch	.40	.18	.05
☐ 52 Bruce Sutter	.60	.25	.08
☐ 53 Lee Smith	.75	.35	.09
☐ 54 Todd Worrell	.60	.25	.08
☐ 55 Al Hrabosky	.50	.23	.06

1988 Chef Boyardee

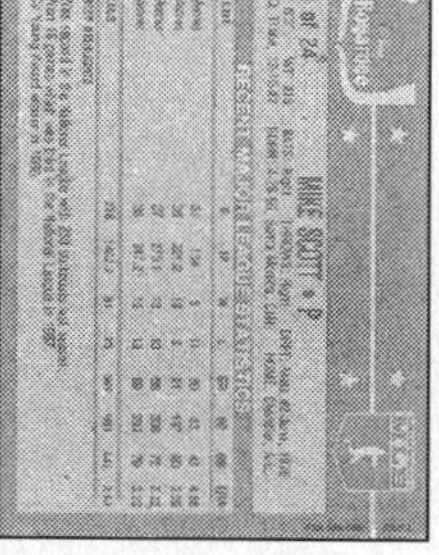

This 24-card set was distributed as a perforated sheet of four rows and six columns of cards in return for ten proofs of purchase of Chef Boyardeee products and $1.50 for postage and handling. The card photos on the fronts are in full color with a light blue border but are not shown with team logos. The card backs are numbered and printed in red and blue on gray card stock. Individual cards measure approximately 2 1/2" by 3 1/2" and show the Chef Boyardee logo in the upper right corner of the obverse. Card backs feature year-by-year season statistics since 1984. There is no additional premium for having the sheet intact as opposed to having individual cards neatly cut.

	MT	EX-MT	VG
COMPLETE SET (24)	10.00	4.50	1.25
COMMON PLAYER (1-24)	.30	.14	.04
☐ 1 Mark McGwire	.90	.40	.11
☐ 2 Eric Davis	.50	.23	.06
☐ 3 Jack Morris	.50	.23	.06
☐ 4 George Bell	.40	.18	.05
☐ 5 Ozzie Smith	.75	.35	.09
☐ 6 Tony Gwynn	.90	.40	.11
☐ 7 Cal Ripken	1.25	.55	.16
☐ 8 Todd Worrell	.30	.14	.04
☐ 9 Larry Parrish	.30	.14	.04
☐ 10 Gary Carter	.40	.18	.05
☐ 11 Ryne Sandberg	1.00	.45	.13
☐ 12 Keith Hernandez	.40	.18	.05
☐ 13 Kirby Puckett	1.00	.45	.13
☐ 14 Mike Schmidt	.90	.40	.11
☐ 15 Frank Viola	.40	.18	.05
☐ 16 Don Mattingly	.90	.40	.11
☐ 17 Dale Murphy	.50	.23	.06
☐ 18 Andre Dawson	.75	.35	.09
☐ 19 Mike Scott	.30	.14	.04
☐ 20 Rickey Henderson	.90	.40	.11
☐ 21 Jim Rice	.40	.18	.05
☐ 22 Wade Boggs	.75	.35	.09
☐ 23 Roger Clemens	1.00	.45	.13
☐ 24 Fernando Valenzuela	.30	.14	.04

1985 Circle K

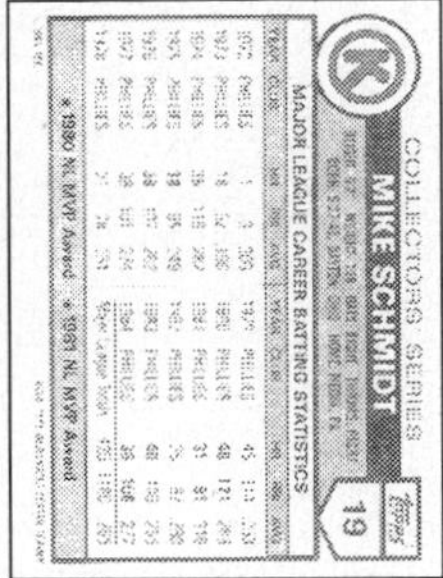

The cards in this 33-card set measure 2 1/2" by 3 1/2" and were issued with an accompanying custom box. In 1985, Topps produced this set for Circle K; cards were printed in Ireland. Cards are numbered on the back according to each player's rank on the all-time career Home Run list. The backs are printed in blue and red on white card stock. The card fronts are glossy and each player is named in the lower left corner. Most of the obverses are in color, although the older vintage players are pictured in black and white. Joe DiMaggio was not included in the set; card number 31 does not exist. It was intended to be DiMaggio but he apparently would not consent to be included in the set.

	NRMT-MT	EXC	G-VG
COMPLETE SET (33)	5.00	2.30	.60
COMMON PLAYER (1-34)	.10	.05	.01
☐ 1 Hank Aaron	.60	.25	.08
☐ 2 Babe Ruth	1.00	.45	.13
☐ 3 Willie Mays	.60	.25	.08
☐ 4 Frank Robinson	.20	.09	.03
☐ 5 Harmon Killebrew	.15	.07	.02
☐ 6 Mickey Mantle	1.00	.45	.13
☐ 7 Jimmie Foxx	.15	.07	.02
☐ 8 Willie McCovey	.20	.09	.03
☐ 9 Ted Williams	.50	.23	.06
☐ 10 Ernie Banks	.20	.09	.03
☐ 11 Eddie Mathews	.15	.07	.02
☐ 12 Mel Ott	.15	.07	.02
☐ 13 Reggie Jackson	.50	.23	.06
☐ 14 Lou Gehrig	.60	.25	.08
☐ 15 Stan Musial	.40	.18	.05
☐ 16 Willie Stargell	.20	.09	.03
☐ 17 Carl Yastrzemski	.30	.14	.04
☐ 18 Billy Williams	.15	.07	.02
☐ 19 Mike Schmidt	.60	.25	.08
☐ 20 Duke Snider	.30	.14	.04
☐ 21 Al Kaline	.25	.11	.03
☐ 22 Johnny Bench	.30	.14	.04
☐ 23 Frank Howard	.10	.05	.01
☐ 24 Orlando Cepeda	.10	.05	.01
☐ 25 Norm Cash	.10	.05	.01
☐ 26 Dave Kingman	.10	.05	.01
☐ 27 Rocky Colavito	.10	.05	.01
☐ 28 Tony Perez	.15	.07	.02
☐ 29 Gil Hodges	.10	.05	.01
☐ 30 Ralph Kiner	.10	.05	.01
☐ 31 Joe DiMaggio (not included in set, card does not exist)	xx	xx	xx
☐ 32 Johnny Mize	.15	.07	.02
☐ 33 Yogi Berra	.30	.14	.04
☐ 34 Lee May	.10	.05	.01

1987 Classic Game

This 100-card set was actually distributed as part of a trivia board game. The card backs contain several trivia questions (and answers) which are used to play the game. A dark green border frames the full-color photo. The games were

produced by Game Time, Ltd. and were available in toy stores as well as from card dealers. According to the producers of this game, only 75,000 sets were distributed. The cards are standard size, 2 1/2" by 3 1/2".

	MT	EX-MT	VG
COMPLETE SET (100)	125.00	57.50	15.50
COMMON PLAYER (1-100)	.30	.14	.04
☐ 1 Pete Rose	4.00	1.80	.50
☐ 2 Len Dykstra	.60	.25	.08
☐ 3 Darryl Strawberry	2.50	1.15	.30
☐ 4 Keith Hernandez	.40	.18	.05
☐ 5 Gary Carter	.60	.25	.08
☐ 6 Wally Joyner	2.00	.90	.25
☐ 7 Andres Thomas	.30	.14	.04
☐ 8 Pat Dodson	.30	.14	.04
☐ 9 Kirk Gibson	.40	.18	.05
☐ 10 Don Mattingly	3.50	1.55	.45
☐ 11 Dave Winfield	1.00	.45	.13
☐ 12 Rickey Henderson	3.50	1.55	.45
☐ 13 Dan Pasqua	.30	.14	.04
☐ 14 Don Baylor	.40	.18	.05
☐ 15 Bo Jackson (Swinging bat in Auburn FB uniform)	30.00	13.50	3.80
☐ 16 Pete Incaviglia	.60	.25	.08
☐ 17 Kevin Bass	.30	.14	.04
☐ 18 Barry Larkin	4.00	1.80	.50
☐ 19 Dave Magadan	.75	.35	.09
☐ 20 Steve Sax	.50	.23	.06
☐ 21 Eric Davis	1.00	.45	.13
☐ 22 Mike Pagliarulo	.30	.14	.04
☐ 23 Fred Lynn	.40	.18	.05
☐ 24 Reggie Jackson	1.50	.65	.19
☐ 25 Larry Parrish	.30	.14	.04
☐ 26 Tony Gwynn	3.00	1.35	.40
☐ 27 Steve Garvey	.75	.35	.09
☐ 28 Glenn Davis	.50	.23	.06
☐ 29 Tim Raines	.50	.23	.06
☐ 30 Vince Coleman	.60	.25	.08
☐ 31 Willie McGee	.40	.18	.05
☐ 32 Ozzie Smith	1.00	.45	.13
☐ 33 Dave Parker	.50	.23	.06
☐ 34 Tony Pena	.30	.14	.04
☐ 35 Ryne Sandberg	6.00	2.70	.75
☐ 36 Brett Butler	.50	.23	.06
☐ 37 Dale Murphy	.75	.35	.09
☐ 38 Bob Horner	.30	.14	.04
☐ 39 Pedro Guerrero	.40	.18	.05
☐ 40 Brook Jacoby	.30	.14	.04
☐ 41 Carlton Fisk	1.00	.45	.13
☐ 42 Harold Baines	.40	.18	.05
☐ 43 Rob Deer	.40	.18	.05
☐ 44 Robin Yount	2.00	.90	.25
☐ 45 Paul Molitor	.75	.35	.09
☐ 46 Jose Canseco	24.00	11.00	3.00
☐ 47 George Brett	2.00	.90	.25
☐ 48 Jim Presley	.30	.14	.04
☐ 49 Rich Gedman	.30	.14	.04
☐ 50 Lance Parrish	.40	.18	.05
☐ 51 Eddie Murray	1.00	.45	.13
☐ 52 Cal Ripken	8.00	3.60	1.00
☐ 53 Kent Hrbek	.50	.23	.06
☐ 54 Gary Gaetti	.40	.18	.05
☐ 55 Kirby Puckett	4.50	2.00	.55
☐ 56 George Bell	.40	.18	.05
☐ 57 Tony Fernandez	.40	.18	.05
☐ 58 Jesse Barfield	.40	.18	.05
☐ 59 Jim Rice	.50	.23	.06
☐ 60 Wade Boggs	2.50	1.15	.30
☐ 61 Marty Barrett	.30	.14	.04

☐ 62 Mike Schmidt	4.00	1.80	.50
☐ 63 Von Hayes	.30	.14	.04
☐ 64 Jeff Leonard	.30	.14	.04
☐ 65 Chris Brown	.30	.14	.04
☐ 66 Dave Smith	.30	.14	.04
☐ 67 Mike Krukow	.30	.14	.04
☐ 68 Ron Guidry	.40	.18	.05
☐ 69 Rob Woodward	.30	.14	.04
☐ 70 Rob Murphy	.30	.14	.04
☐ 71 Andres Galarraga	.60	.25	.08
☐ 72 Dwight Gooden	1.00	.45	.13
☐ 73 Bob Ojeda	.30	.14	.04
☐ 74 Sid Fernandez	.40	.18	.05
☐ 75 Jesse Orosco	.30	.14	.04
☐ 76 Roger McDowell	.30	.14	.04
☐ 77 John Tudor UER (Misspelled Tutor)	.40	.18	.05
☐ 78 Tom Browning	.40	.18	.05
☐ 79 Rick Aguilera	.40	.18	.05
☐ 80 Lance McCullers	.30	.14	.04
☐ 81 Mike Scott	.40	.18	.05
☐ 82 Nolan Ryan	12.00	5.50	1.50
☐ 83 Bruce Hurst	.40	.18	.05
☐ 84 Roger Clemens	7.00	3.10	.85
☐ 85 Dennis Boyd	.30	.14	.04
☐ 86 Dave Righetti	.30	.14	.04
☐ 87 Dennis Rasmussen	.30	.14	.04
☐ 88 Bret Saberhagen	.75	.35	.09
☐ 89 Mark Langston	.50	.23	.06
☐ 90 Jack Morris	.60	.25	.08
☐ 91 Fernando Valenzuela	.40	.18	.05
☐ 92 Orel Hershiser	.75	.35	.09
☐ 93 Rick Honeycutt	.30	.14	.04
☐ 94 Jeff Reardon	.60	.25	.08
☐ 95 John Habyan	.30	.14	.04
☐ 96 Goose Gossage	.50	.23	.06
☐ 97 Todd Worrell	.60	.25	.08
☐ 98 Floyd Youmans	.30	.14	.04
☐ 99 Don Aase	.30	.14	.04
☐ 100 John Franco	.40	.18	.05

1987 Classic Update Yellow

This 50-card set was actually distributed as part of an update to a trivia board game, but (unlike the original Classic game) was sold without the game. The set is sometimes referred to as the "Travel Edition" of the game. The card backs contain several trivia questions (and answers) which are used to play the game. A yellow border frames the full-color photo. The games were produced by Game Time, Ltd. and were available in toy stores as well as from card dealers. Cards are numbered beginning with 101, as they are an extension of the original set. According to the set's producers, supposedly about 1/3 of the 150,000 sets printed were error sets in that they had green backs instead of yellow backs. This "green back" variation/error set is valued at approximately double the prices listed below. The cards are standard size, 2 1/2" by 3 1/2".

	MT	EX-MT	VG
COMPLETE SET (50)	22.50	10.00	2.80
COMMON PLAYER (101-150)	.15	.07	.02
☐ 101 Mike Schmidt	1.75	.80	.22
☐ 102 Eric Davis	.75	.35	.09
☐ 103 Pete Rose	1.50	.65	.19
☐ 104 Don Mattingly	1.50	.65	.19
☐ 105 Wade Boggs	1.25	.55	.16
☐ 106 Dale Murphy	.50	.23	.06
☐ 107 Glenn Davis	.40	.18	.05
☐ 108 Wally Joyner	.75	.35	.09
☐ 109 Bo Jackson	3.00	1.35	.40
☐ 110 Cory Snyder	.25	.11	.03
☐ 111 Jim Lindeman	.15	.07	.02
☐ 112 Kirby Puckett	2.00	.90	.25
☐ 113 Barry Bonds	4.50	2.00	.55
☐ 114 Roger Clemens	2.50	1.15	.30
☐ 115 Oddibe McDowell	.15	.07	.02
☐ 116 Bret Saberhagen	.40	.18	.05
☐ 117 Joe Magrane	.15	.07	.02
☐ 118 Scott Fletcher	.15	.07	.02
☐ 119 Mark McLemore	.15	.07	.02
☐ 120 Who Me (Joe Niekro)	.25	.11	.03
☐ 121 Mark McGwire	2.50	1.15	.30
☐ 122 Darryl Strawberry	1.25	.55	.16
☐ 123 Mike Scott	.25	.11	.03
☐ 124 Andre Dawson	.75	.35	.09
☐ 125 Jose Canseco	3.00	1.35	.40
☐ 126 Kevin McReynolds	.25	.11	.03
☐ 127 Joe Carter	1.25	.55	.16
☐ 128 Casey Candaele	.15	.07	.02
☐ 129 Matt Nokes	.35	.16	.04
☐ 130 Kal Daniels	.25	.11	.03
☐ 131 Pete Incaviglia	.25	.11	.03
☐ 132 Benito Santiago	1.00	.45	.13
☐ 133 Barry Larkin	1.25	.55	.16
☐ 134 Gary Pettis	.15	.07	.02
☐ 135 B.J. Surhoff	.25	.11	.03
☐ 136 Juan Nieves	.15	.07	.02
☐ 137 Jim Deshaies	.15	.07	.02
☐ 138 Pete O'Brien	.15	.07	.02
☐ 139 Kevin Seitzer	.25	.11	.03
☐ 140 Devon White	.25	.11	.03
☐ 141 Rob Deer	.25	.11	.03
☐ 142 Kurt Stillwell	.15	.07	.02
☐ 143 Edwin Correa	.15	.07	.02
☐ 144 Dion James	.15	.07	.02
☐ 145 Danny Tartabull	1.00	.45	.13
☐ 146 Jerry Browne	.15	.07	.02
☐ 147 Ted Higuera	.15	.07	.02
☐ 148 Jack Clark	.25	.11	.03
☐ 149 Ruben Sierra	4.00	1.80	.50
☐ 150 Mark McGwire and Eric Davis	1.00	.45	.13

1988 Classic Blue

This 50-card blue-bordered set was actually distributed as part of an update to a trivia board game, but (unlike the original Classic game) was sold without the game. The card backs contain several trivia questions (and answers) which are used to play the game. A blue border frames the full color photo. The games were produced by Game Time, Ltd. and were available in toy stores as well as from card dealers. Cards are numbered beginning with 201 as they are an extension of the original sets. The cards are standard size, 2 1/2" by 3 1/2".

	MT	EX-MT	VG
COMPLETE SET (50)	15.00	6.75	1.90

COMMON PLAYER (201-250)	.12	.05	.02
☐ 201 Eric Davis and Dale Murphy	.30	.14	.04
☐ 202 B.J. Surhoff	.20	.09	.03
☐ 203 John Kruk	.40	.18	.05
☐ 204 Sam Horn	.12	.05	.02
☐ 205 Jack Clark	.12	.05	.02
☐ 206 Wally Joyner	.25	.11	.03
☐ 207 Matt Nokes	.20	.09	.03
☐ 208 Bo Jackson	2.00	.90	.25
☐ 209 Darryl Strawberry	.75	.35	.09
☐ 210 Ozzie Smith	.60	.25	.08
☐ 211 Don Mattingly	1.00	.45	.13
☐ 212 Mark McGwire	1.00	.45	.13
☐ 213 Eric Davis	.40	.18	.05
☐ 214 Wade Boggs	.90	.40	.11
☐ 215 Dale Murphy	.40	.18	.05
☐ 216 Andre Dawson	.50	.23	.06
☐ 217 Roger Clemens	1.50	.65	.19
☐ 218 Kevin Seitzer	.20	.09	.03
☐ 219 Benito Santiago	.40	.18	.05
☐ 220 Tony Gwynn	1.00	.45	.13
☐ 221 Mike Scott	.20	.09	.03
☐ 222 Steve Bedrosian	.12	.05	.02
☐ 223 Vince Coleman	.25	.11	.03
☐ 224 Rick Sutcliffe	.20	.09	.03
☐ 225 Will Clark	4.00	1.80	.50
☐ 226 Pete Rose	1.25	.55	.16
☐ 227 Mike Greenwell	.50	.23	.06
☐ 228 Ken Caminiti	.30	.14	.04
☐ 229 Ellis Burks	.50	.23	.06
☐ 230 Dave Magadan	.20	.09	.03
☐ 231 Alan Trammell	.30	.14	.04
☐ 232 Paul Molitor	.40	.18	.05
☐ 233 Gary Gaetti	.12	.05	.02
☐ 234 Rickey Henderson	1.25	.55	.16
☐ 235 Danny Tartabull UER (Photo actually Hal McRae)	.60	.25	.08
☐ 236 Bobby Bonilla	1.25	.55	.16
☐ 237 Mike Dunne	.12	.05	.02
☐ 238 Al Leiter	.12	.05	.02
☐ 239 John Farrell	.12	.05	.02
☐ 240 Joe Magrane	.12	.05	.02
☐ 241 Mike Henneman	.20	.09	.03
☐ 242 George Bell	.25	.11	.03
☐ 243 Gregg Jeffries	1.00	.45	.13
☐ 244 Jay Buhner	.35	.16	.04
☐ 245 Todd Benzinger	.20	.09	.03
☐ 246 Matt Williams	1.50	.65	.19
☐ 247 Mark McGwire and Don Mattingly (Unnumbered; game instructions on back)	1.00	.45	.13
☐ 248 George Brett	.90	.40	.11
☐ 249 Jimmy Key	.25	.11	.03
☐ 250 Mark Langston	.20	.09	.03

1988 Classic Red

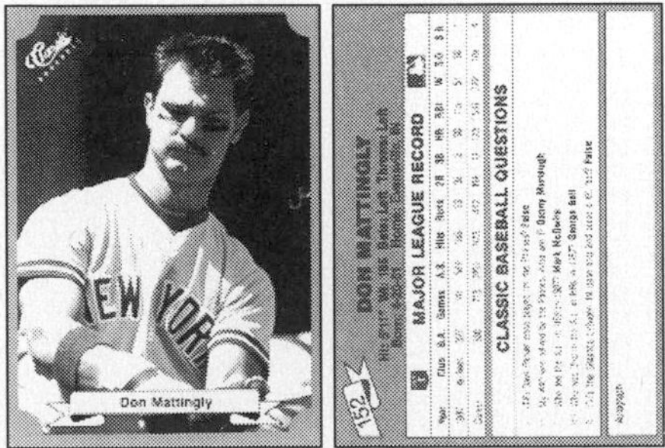

This 50-card red-bordered set was actually distributed as part of an update to a trivia board game, but (unlike the original Classic game) was sold without the game. The card backs contain several trivia questions (and answers) which are used to play the game. A red border frames the full color photo. The games were produced by Game Time, Ltd. and were available in toy stores as well as from card dealers. Cards are numbered beginning with 151 as they are an extension of the original sets. The cards are standard size, 2 1/2" by 3 1/2".

	MT	EX-MT	VG
COMPLETE SET (50)	13.50	6.00	1.70
COMMON PLAYER (151-200)	.12	.05	.02
☐ 151 Mark McGwire and Don Mattingly	1.50	.65	.19
☐ 152 Don Mattingly	1.00	.45	.13
☐ 153 Mark McGwire	1.00	.45	.13
☐ 154 Eric Davis	.50	.23	.06
☐ 155 Wade Boggs	.90	.40	.11
☐ 156 Dale Murphy	.35	.16	.04
☐ 157 Andre Dawson	.50	.23	.06
☐ 158 Roger Clemens	1.50	.65	.19
☐ 159 Kevin Seitzer	.20	.09	.03
☐ 160 Benito Santiago	.50	.23	.06
☐ 161 Kal Daniels	.20	.09	.03
☐ 162 John Kruk	.50	.23	.06
☐ 163 Bill Ripken	.20	.09	.03
☐ 164 Kirby Puckett	1.25	.55	.16
☐ 165 Jose Canseco	1.25	.55	.16
☐ 166 Matt Nokes	.20	.09	.03
☐ 167 Mike Schmidt	1.00	.45	.13
☐ 168 Tim Raines	.25	.11	.03
☐ 169 Ryne Sandberg	1.50	.65	.19
☐ 170 Dave Winfield	.75	.35	.09
☐ 171 Dwight Gooden	.40	.18	.05
☐ 172 Bret Saberhagen	.30	.14	.04
☐ 173 Willie McGee	.20	.09	.03
☐ 174 Jack Morris	.30	.14	.04
☐ 175 Jeff Leonard	.12	.05	.02
☐ 176 Cal Ripken	2.00	.90	.25
☐ 177 Pete Incaviglia	.20	.09	.03
☐ 178 Devon White	.20	.09	.03
☐ 179 Nolan Ryan	4.00	1.80	.50
☐ 180 Ruben Sierra	1.25	.55	.16
☐ 181 Todd Worrell	.20	.09	.03
☐ 182 Glenn Davis	.20	.09	.03
☐ 183 Frank Viola	.20	.09	.03
☐ 184 Cory Snyder	.20	.09	.03
☐ 185 Tracy Jones	.12	.05	.02
☐ 186 Terry Steinbach	.25	.11	.03
☐ 187 Julio Franco	.25	.11	.03
☐ 188 Larry Sheets	.12	.05	.02
☐ 189 John Marzano	.12	.05	.02
☐ 190 Kevin Elster	.12	.05	.02
☐ 191 Vicente Palacios	.12	.05	.02
☐ 192 Kent Hrbek	.20	.09	.03
☐ 193 Eric Bell	.12	.05	.02
☐ 194 Kelly Downs	.12	.05	.02
☐ 195 Jose Lind	.20	.09	.03
☐ 196 Dave Stewart	.20	.09	.03
☐ 197 Mark McGwire and Jose Canseco	1.00	.45	.13
☐ 198 Phil Niekro Cleveland Indians	.20	.09	.03
☐ 199 Phil Niekro Toronto Blue Jays	.20	.09	.03
☐ 200 Phil Niekro Atlanta Braves	.20	.09	.03

1989 Classic Light Blue

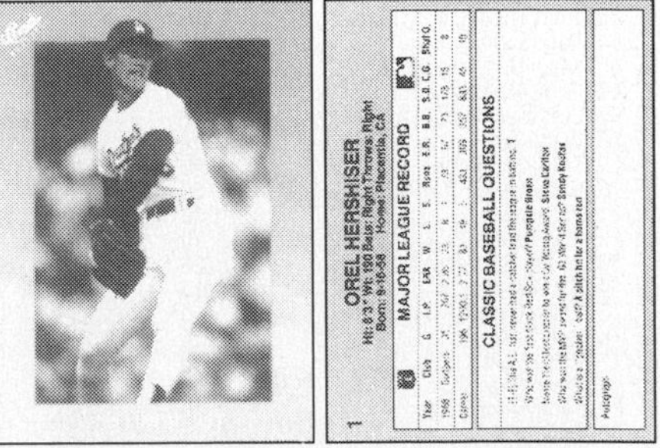

The 1989 Classic set contains 100 standard-size (2 1/2" by 3 1/2") cards. The fronts of these cards have light blue borders. The backs feature 1988 and lifetime stats. The cards were distributed with a baseball boardgame. Supposedly there were 150,000 sets produced.

	MT	EX-MT	VG
COMPLETE SET (100)	27.00	12.00	3.40
COMMON PLAYER (1-100)	.10	.05	.01
☐ 1 Orel Hershiser	.25	.11	.03
☐ 2 Wade Boggs	.75	.35	.09
☐ 3 Jose Canseco	1.25	.55	.16
☐ 4 Mark McGwire	.90	.40	.11
☐ 5 Don Mattingly	1.00	.45	.13
☐ 6 Gregg Jefferies	.75	.35	.09
☐ 7 Dwight Gooden	.40	.18	.05
☐ 8 Darryl Strawberry	.75	.35	.09
☐ 9 Eric Davis	.35	.16	.04
☐ 10 Joey Meyer	.10	.05	.01
☐ 11 Joe Carter	.60	.25	.08
☐ 12 Paul Molitor	.30	.14	.04
☐ 13 Mark Grace	1.50	.65	.19
☐ 14 Kurt Stillwell	.15	.07	.02
☐ 15 Kirby Puckett	1.25	.55	.16
☐ 16 Keith Miller	.10	.05	.01
☐ 17 Glenn Davis	.20	.09	.03
☐ 18 Will Clark	1.25	.55	.16
☐ 19 Cory Snyder	.15	.07	.02
☐ 20 Jose Lind	.10	.05	.01
☐ 21 Andres Thomas	.10	.05	.01
☐ 22 Dave Smith	.10	.05	.01
☐ 23 Mike Scott	.15	.07	.02
☐ 24 Kevin McReynolds	.15	.07	.02
☐ 25 B.J. Surhoff	.15	.07	.02
☐ 26 Mackey Sasser	.15	.07	.02
☐ 27 Chad Kreuter	.10	.05	.01
☐ 28 Hal Morris	.75	.35	.09
☐ 29 Wally Joyner	.25	.11	.03
☐ 30 Tony Gwynn	.75	.35	.09
☐ 31 Kevin Mitchell	.60	.25	.08
☐ 32 Dave Winfield	.50	.23	.06
☐ 33 Billy Bean	.10	.05	.01
☐ 34 Steve Bedrosian	.10	.05	.01
☐ 35 Ron Gant	.90	.40	.11
☐ 36 Len Dykstra	.20	.09	.03
☐ 37 Andre Dawson	.50	.23	.06
☐ 38 Brett Butler	.20	.09	.03
☐ 39 Rob Deer	.15	.07	.02
☐ 40 Tommy John	.20	.09	.03
☐ 41 Gary Gaetti	.10	.05	.01
☐ 42 Tim Raines	.20	.09	.03
☐ 43 George Bell	.20	.09	.03
☐ 44 Dwight Evans	.15	.07	.02
☐ 45 Dennis Martinez	.15	.07	.02
☐ 46 Andres Galarraga	.20	.09	.03
☐ 47 George Brett	.75	.35	.09
☐ 48 Mike Schmidt	1.00	.45	.13
☐ 49 Dave Stieb	.15	.07	.02
☐ 50 Rickey Henderson	.90	.40	.11
☐ 51 Craig Biggio	.40	.18	.05
☐ 52 Mark Lemke	.20	.09	.03
☐ 53 Chris Sabo	.60	.25	.08
☐ 54 Jeff Treadway	.10	.05	.01
☐ 55 Kent Hrbek	.15	.07	.02
☐ 56 Cal Ripken	1.50	.65	.19
☐ 57 Tim Belcher	.15	.07	.02
☐ 58 Ozzie Smith	.45	.20	.06
☐ 59 Keith Hernandez	.15	.07	.02
☐ 60 Pedro Guerrero	.15	.07	.02
☐ 61 Greg Swindell	.20	.09	.03
☐ 62 Bret Saberhagen	.25	.11	.03
☐ 63 John Tudor	.15	.07	.02
☐ 64 Gary Carter	.20	.09	.03
☐ 65 Kevin Seitzer	.10	.05	.01
☐ 66 Jesse Barfield	.10	.05	.01
☐ 67 Luis Medina	.10	.05	.01
☐ 68 Walt Weiss	.15	.07	.02
☐ 69 Terry Steinbach	.20	.09	.03
☐ 70 Barry Larkin	.50	.23	.06
☐ 71 Pete Rose	1.00	.45	.13
☐ 72 Luis Salazar	.10	.05	.01
☐ 73 Benito Santiago	.25	.11	.03
☐ 74 Kal Daniels	.15	.07	.02
☐ 75 Kevin Elster	.10	.05	.01
☐ 76 Rob Dibble	.35	.16	.04
☐ 77 Bobby Witt	.25	.11	.03
☐ 78 Steve Searcy	.10	.05	.01
☐ 79 Sandy Alomar Jr.	.40	.18	.05
☐ 80 Chili Davis	.15	.07	.02
☐ 81 Alvin Davis	.10	.05	.01
☐ 82 Charlie Leibrandt	.10	.05	.01
☐ 83 Robin Yount	.75	.35	.09
☐ 84 Mark Carreon	.10	.05	.01
☐ 85 Pascual Perez	.15	.07	.02
☐ 86 Dennis Rasmussen	.10	.05	.01
☐ 87 Ernie Riles	.10	.05	.01
☐ 88 Melido Perez	.30	.14	.04
☐ 89 Doug Jones	.15	.07	.02
☐ 90 Dennis Eckersley	.30	.14	.04
☐ 91 Bob Welch	.15	.07	.02
☐ 92 Bob Milacki	.15	.07	.02
☐ 93 Jeff Robinson	.10	.05	.01
☐ 94 Mike Henneman	.15	.07	.02
☐ 95 Randy Johnson	.30	.14	.04
☐ 96 Ron Jones	.10	.05	.01
☐ 97 Jack Armstrong	.10	.05	.01
☐ 98 Willie McGee	.15	.07	.02
☐ 99 Ryne Sandberg	1.25	.55	.16
☐ 100 David Cone and Danny Jackson	.30	.14	.04

1989 Classic Travel Orange

The 1989 Classic Travel Orange set contains 50 standard-size (2 1/2" by 3 1/2") cards. The fronts of the cards have orange borders. The backs feature 1988 and lifetime stats. This subset of cards were distributed as a set in blister packs as "Travel Update I" subsets. Supposedly there were 150,000 sets produced.

	MT	EX-MT	VG
COMPLETE SET (50)	14.00	6.25	1.75
COMMON PLAYER (101-150)	.10	.05	.01
☐ 101 Gary Sheffield	1.50	.65	.19
☐ 102 Wade Boggs	.75	.35	.09
☐ 103 Jose Canseco	1.25	.55	.16
☐ 104 Mark McGwire	.90	.40	.11
☐ 105 Orel Hershiser	.20	.09	.03
☐ 106 Don Mattingly	.90	.40	.11
☐ 107 Dwight Gooden	.30	.14	.04
☐ 108 Darryl Strawberry	.75	.35	.09
☐ 109 Eric Davis	.30	.14	.04
☐ 110 Hensley Meulens UER (Listed on card as Bam Bam Muelens)	.35	.16	.04
☐ 111 Andy Van Slyke	.25	.11	.03
☐ 112 Al Leiter	.10	.05	.01
☐ 113 Matt Nokes	.15	.07	.02
☐ 114 Mike Krukow	.10	.05	.01
☐ 115 Tony Fernandez	.15	.07	.02
☐ 116 Fred McGriff	.90	.40	.11
☐ 117 Barry Bonds	.75	.35	.09
☐ 118 Gerald Perry	.10	.05	.01
☐ 119 Roger Clemens	1.25	.55	.16
☐ 120 Kirk Gibson	.20	.09	.03
☐ 121 Greg Maddux	.60	.25	.08
☐ 122 Bo Jackson	1.00	.45	.13
☐ 123 Danny Jackson	.15	.07	.02
☐ 124 Dale Murphy	.30	.14	.04
☐ 125 David Cone	.40	.18	.05
☐ 126 Tom Browning	.15	.07	.02
☐ 127 Roberto Alomar	1.50	.65	.19
☐ 128 Alan Trammell	.20	.09	.03
☐ 129 Ricky Jordan UER (Misspelled Jordon on card back)	.15	.07	.02
☐ 130 Ramon Martinez	.75	.35	.09
☐ 131 Ken Griffey Jr.	7.00	3.10	.85
☐ 132 Gregg Olson	.40	.18	.05
☐ 133 Carlos Quintana	.30	.14	.04
☐ 134 Dave West	.15	.07	.02
☐ 135 Cameron Drew	.10	.05	.01

	MT	EX-MT	VG
☐ 136 Teddy Higuera	.10	.05	.01
☐ 137 Sil Campusano	.10	.05	.01
☐ 138 Mark Gubicza	.10	.05	.01
☐ 139 Mike Boddicker	.10	.05	.01
☐ 140 Paul Gibson	.10	.05	.01
☐ 141 Jose Rijo	.30	.14	.04
☐ 142 John Costello	.10	.05	.01
☐ 143 Cecil Espy	.10	.05	.01
☐ 144 Frank Viola	.15	.07	.02
☐ 145 Erik Hanson	.30	.14	.04
☐ 146 Juan Samuel	.10	.05	.01
☐ 147 Harold Reynolds	.15	.07	.02
☐ 148 Joe Magrane	.10	.05	.01
☐ 149 Mike Greenwell	.25	.11	.03
☐ 150 Darryl Strawberry and Will Clark	.60	.25	.08

1989 Classic Travel Purple

The 1989 Classic "Travel Update II" set contains 50 standard-size (2 1/2" by 3 1/2") cards. The fronts have purple (and gray) borders. The set features "two sport" cards of Bo Jackson and Deion Sanders. The cards were distributed as a set in blister packs.

	MT	EX-MT	VG
COMPLETE SET (50)	12.00	5.50	1.50
COMMON PLAYER (151-200)	.10	.05	.01

	MT	EX-MT	VG
☐ 151 Jim Abbott	1.00	.45	.13
☐ 152 Ellis Burks	.25	.11	.03
☐ 153 Mike Schmidt	.90	.40	.11
☐ 154 Gregg Jefferies	.40	.18	.05
☐ 155 Mark Grace	.40	.18	.05
☐ 156 Jerome Walton	.20	.09	.03
☐ 157 Bo Jackson	1.00	.45	.13
☐ 158 Jack Clark	.10	.05	.01
☐ 159 Tom Glavine	.75	.35	.09
☐ 160 Eddie Murray	.30	.14	.04
☐ 161 John Dopson	.10	.05	.01
☐ 162 Ruben Sierra	.40	.18	.05
☐ 163 Rafael Palmeiro	.30	.14	.04
☐ 164 Nolan Ryan	2.00	.90	.25
☐ 165 Barry Larkin	.35	.16	.04
☐ 166 Tommy Herr	.10	.05	.01
☐ 167 Roberto Kelly	.50	.23	.06
☐ 168 Glenn Davis	.15	.07	.02
☐ 169 Glenn Braggs	.10	.05	.01
☐ 170 Juan Bell	.10	.05	.01
☐ 171 Todd Burns	.10	.05	.01
☐ 172 Derek Lilliquist	.10	.05	.01
☐ 173 Orel Hershiser	.20	.09	.03
☐ 174 John Smoltz	1.00	.45	.13
☐ 175 Ozzie Guillen and Ellis Burks	.20	.09	.03
☐ 176 Kirby Puckett	1.00	.45	.13
☐ 177 Robin Ventura	1.00	.45	.13
☐ 178 Allan Anderson	.10	.05	.01
☐ 179 Steve Sax	.15	.07	.02
☐ 180 Will Clark	.90	.40	.11
☐ 181 Mike Devereaux	.25	.11	.03
☐ 182 Tom Gordon	.15	.07	.02
☐ 183 Rob Murphy	.10	.05	.01
☐ 184 Pete O'Brien	.10	.05	.01
☐ 185 Cris Carpenter	.10	.05	.01
☐ 186 Tom Brunansky	.15	.07	.02
☐ 187 Bob Boone	.15	.07	.02
☐ 188 Lou Whitaker	.15	.07	.02
☐ 189 Dwight Gooden	.25	.11	.03
☐ 190 Mark McGwire	.75	.35	.09
☐ 191 John Smiley	.15	.07	.02
☐ 192 Tommy Gregg	.10	.05	.01
☐ 193 Ken Griffey Jr.	3.50	1.55	.45
☐ 194 Bruce Hurst	.15	.07	.02
☐ 195 Greg Swindell	.20	.09	.03
☐ 196 Nelson Liriano	.10	.05	.01
☐ 197 Randy Myers	.20	.09	.03
☐ 198 Kevin Mitchell	.30	.14	.04
☐ 199 Dante Bichette	.15	.07	.02
☐ 200 Deion Sanders	1.00	.45	.13

1990 Classic Blue

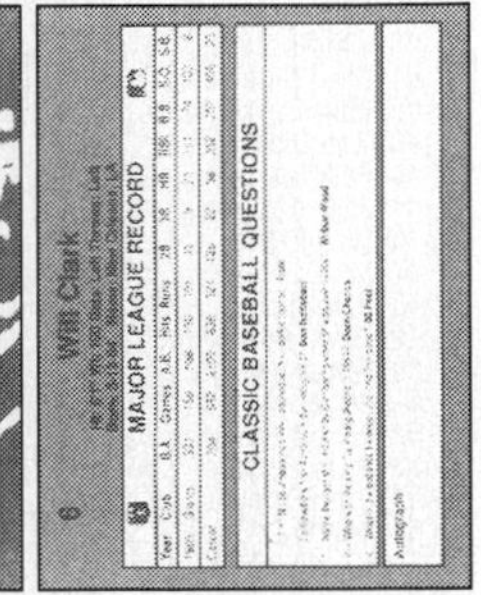

The 1990 Classic Blue (Game) set contains 150 standard-size (2 1/2" by 3 1/2") cards, the largest Classic set to date in terms of player selection. The front borders are blue with magenta splotches. The backs feature 1989 and career total stats. The cards were distributed as a set in blister packs. According to distributors of the set, supposedly there were 200,000 sets produced. Supposedly the Sanders "correction" was made at Sanders own request; less than 10 percent of the sets contain the first version and hence it has the higher value in the checklist below. The complete set price below does not include any of the more difficult variation cards.

	MT	EX-MT	VG
COMPLETE SET (150)	20.00	9.00	2.50
COMMON PLAYER (1-150)	.10	.05	.01

	MT	EX-MT	VG
☐ 1 Nolan Ryan	1.50	.65	.19
☐ 2 Bo Jackson	.90	.40	.11
☐ 3 Gregg Olson	.20	.09	.03
☐ 4 Tom Gordon	.15	.07	.02
☐ 5 Robin Ventura	.60	.25	.08
☐ 6 Will Clark	.90	.40	.11
☐ 7 Ruben Sierra	.40	.18	.05
☐ 8 Mark Grace	.40	.18	.05
☐ 9 Luis DeLosSantos	.10	.05	.01
☐ 10 Bernie Williams	.60	.25	.08
☐ 11 Eric Davis	.25	.11	.03
☐ 12 Carney Lansford	.15	.07	.02
☐ 13 John Smoltz	.35	.16	.04
☐ 14 Gary Sheffield	.75	.35	.09
☐ 15 Kent Mercker	.15	.07	.02
☐ 16 Don Mattingly	.75	.35	.09
☐ 17 Tony Gwynn	.50	.23	.06
☐ 18 Ozzie Smith	.35	.16	.04
☐ 19 Fred McGriff	.40	.18	.05
☐ 20 Ken Griffey Jr.	2.00	.90	.25
☐ 21A Deion Sanders (Identified only as "Prime Time" on front)	9.00	4.00	1.15
☐ 21B Deion Sanders (Identified as Deion "Prime Time" Sanders on front of card)	1.25	.55	.16
☐ 22 Jose Canseco	1.00	.45	.13
☐ 23 Mitch Williams	.15	.07	.02
☐ 24 Cal Ripken UER (Misspelled Ripkin on the card back)	1.25	.55	.16

☐ 25 Bob Geren .10 .05 .01
☐ 26 Wade Boggs .60 .25 .08
☐ 27 Ryne Sandberg 1.00 .45 .13
☐ 28 Kirby Puckett .90 .40 .11
☐ 29 Mike Scott .15 .07 .02
☐ 30 Dwight Smith .10 .05 .01
☐ 31 Craig Worthington .10 .05 .01
☐ 32A Ricky Jordan ERR 4.00 1.80 .50
(Misspelled Jordon on card back)
☐ 32B Ricky Jordan COR .25 .11 .03
☐ 33 Darryl Strawberry .75 .35 .09
☐ 34 Jerome Walton .10 .05 .01
☐ 35 John Olerud 1.00 .45 .13
☐ 36 Tom Glavine .50 .23 .06
☐ 37 Rickey Henderson .90 .40 .11
☐ 38 Rolando Roomes .10 .05 .01
☐ 39 Mickey Tettleton .15 .07 .02
☐ 40 Jim Abbott .40 .18 .05
☐ 41 Dave Righetti .10 .05 .01
☐ 42 Mike LaValliere .10 .05 .01
☐ 43 Rob Dibble .20 .09 .03
☐ 44 Pete Harnisch .15 .07 .02
☐ 45 Jose Offerman .25 .11 .03
☐ 46 Walt Weiss .10 .05 .01
☐ 47 Mike Greenwell .20 .09 .03
☐ 48 Barry Larkin .30 .14 .04
☐ 49 Dave Gallagher .10 .05 .01
☐ 50 Junior Felix .20 .09 .03
☐ 51 Roger Clemens 1.00 .45 .13
☐ 52 Lonnie Smith .10 .05 .01
☐ 53 Jerry Browne .10 .05 .01
☐ 54 Greg Briley .10 .05 .01
☐ 55 Delino DeShields .75 .35 .09
☐ 56 Carmelo Martinez .10 .05 .01
☐ 57 Craig Biggio .20 .09 .03
☐ 58 Dwight Gooden .30 .14 .04
☐ 59A Bo/Rubin/Mark 6.00 2.70 .75
Bo Jackson
Ruben Sierra
Mark McGwire
☐ 59B A.L. Fence Busters 1.00 .45 .13
Bo Jackson
Ruben Sierra
Mark McGwire
☐ 60 Greg Vaughn .60 .25 .08
☐ 61 Roberto Alomar .75 .35 .09
☐ 62 Steve Bedrosian .10 .05 .01
☐ 63 Devon White .15 .07 .02
☐ 64 Kevin Mitchell .25 .11 .03
☐ 65 Marquis Grissom 1.00 .45 .13
☐ 66 Brian Holman .15 .07 .02
☐ 67 Julio Franco .20 .09 .03
☐ 68 Dave West .10 .05 .01
☐ 69 Harold Baines .15 .07 .02
☐ 70 Eric Anthony .35 .16 .04
☐ 71 Glenn Davis .20 .09 .03
☐ 72 Mark Langston .15 .07 .02
☐ 73 Matt Williams .30 .14 .04
☐ 74 Rafael Palmeiro .25 .11 .03
☐ 75 Pete Rose Jr. .25 .11 .03
☐ 76 Ramon Martinez .25 .11 .03
☐ 77 Dwight Evans .15 .07 .02
☐ 78 Mackey Sasser .10 .05 .01
☐ 79 Mike Schooler .10 .05 .01
☐ 80 Dennis Cook .10 .05 .01
☐ 81 Orel Hershiser .20 .09 .03
☐ 82 Barry Bonds .60 .25 .08
☐ 83 Geronimo Berroa .10 .05 .01
☐ 84 George Bell .15 .07 .02
☐ 85 Andre Dawson .35 .16 .04
☐ 86 John Franco .15 .07 .02
☐ 87A Clark/Gwynn 4.00 1.80 .50
Will Clark
Tony Gwynn
☐ 87B N.L. Hit Kings .75 .35 .09
Will Clark
Tony Gwynn
☐ 88 Glenallen Hill .25 .11 .03
☐ 89 Jeff Ballard .10 .05 .01
☐ 90 Todd Zeile .50 .23 .06
☐ 91 Frank Viola .15 .07 .02
☐ 92 Ozzie Guillen .10 .05 .01
☐ 93 Jeffrey Leonard .10 .05 .01
☐ 94 Dave Smith .10 .05 .01
☐ 95 Dave Parker .15 .07 .02
☐ 96 Jose Gonzalez .10 .05 .01
☐ 97 Dave Stieb .15 .07 .02
☐ 98 Charlie Hayes .20 .09 .03
☐ 99 Jesse Barfield .15 .07 .02
☐ 100 Joey Belle .90 .40 .11
☐ 101 Jeff Reardon .20 .09 .03
☐ 102 Bruce Hurst .15 .07 .02
☐ 103 Luis Medina .10 .05 .01
☐ 104 Mike Moore .15 .07 .02
☐ 105 Vince Coleman .20 .09 .03
☐ 106 Alan Trammell .20 .09 .03
☐ 107 Randy Myers .15 .07 .02
☐ 108 Frank Tanana .15 .07 .02
☐ 109 Craig Lefferts .10 .05 .01
☐ 110 John Wetteland .20 .09 .03
☐ 111 Chris Gwynn .10 .05 .01
☐ 112 Mark Carreon .10 .05 .01
☐ 113 Von Hayes .10 .05 .01
☐ 114 Doug Jones .10 .05 .01
☐ 115 Andres Galarraga .20 .09 .03
☐ 116 Carlton Fisk UER .50 .23 .06
(Bellows Falls misspelled as Bellow Falls on back)
☐ 117 Paul O'Neill .20 .09 .03
☐ 118 Tim Raines .15 .07 .02
☐ 119 Tom Brunansky .15 .07 .02
☐ 120 Andy Benes .50 .23 .06
☐ 121 Mark Portugal .10 .05 .01
☐ 122 Willie Randolph .15 .07 .02
☐ 123 Jeff Blauser .15 .07 .02
☐ 124 Don August .10 .05 .01
☐ 125 Chuck Cary .10 .05 .01
☐ 126 John Smiley .20 .09 .03
☐ 127 Terry Mulholland .10 .05 .01
☐ 128 Harold Reynolds .15 .07 .02
☐ 129 Hubie Brooks .10 .05 .01
☐ 130 Ben McDonald .60 .25 .08
☐ 131 Kevin Ritz .15 .07 .02
☐ 132 Luis Quinones .10 .05 .01
☐ 133A Hensley Meulens ERR 10.00 4.50 1.25
(Misspelled Muelens on card front)
☐ 133B Hensley Meulens COR .50 .23 .06
☐ 134 Bill Spiers UER .15 .07 .02
(Orangeburg misspelled as Orangburg on back)
☐ 135 Andy Hawkins .10 .05 .01
☐ 136 Alvin Davis .15 .07 .02
☐ 137 Lee Smith .20 .09 .03
☐ 138 Joe Carter .40 .18 .05
☐ 139 Bret Saberhagen .20 .09 .03
☐ 140 Sammy Sosa .30 .14 .04
☐ 141 Matt Nokes .15 .07 .02
☐ 142 Bert Blyleven .15 .07 .02
☐ 143 Bobby Bonilla .35 .16 .04
☐ 144 Howard Johnson .20 .09 .03
☐ 145 Joe Magrane .10 .05 .01
☐ 146 Pedro Guerrero .15 .07 .02
☐ 147 Robin Yount .60 .25 .08
☐ 148 Dan Gladden .10 .05 .01
☐ 149 Steve Sax .20 .09 .03
☐ 150A Clark/Mitchell 3.00 1.35 .40
Will Clark
Kevin Mitchell
☐ 150B Bay Bombers .50 .23 .06
Will Clark
Kevin Mitchell

1990 Classic Update

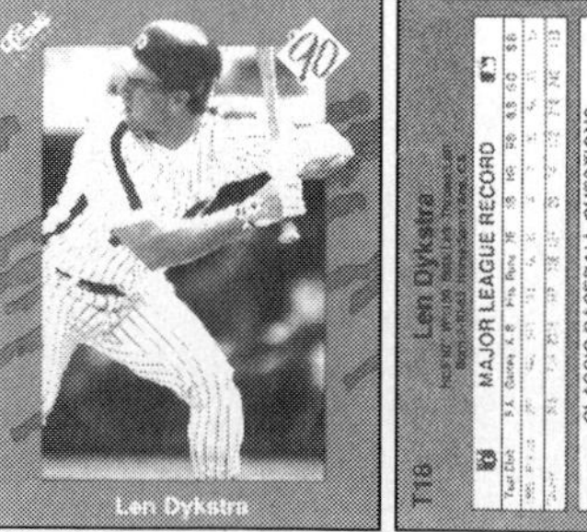

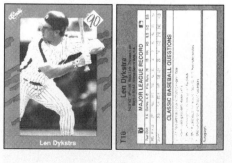

The 1990 Classic Update set was the second set issued by the Classic Game company in 1990. Sometimes referenced as Classic Pink or Red, this set included a Kevin Maas card. This 50-card, standard-size (2 1/2" by 3 1/2") set was issued in late June of 1990. With a few exceptions, the set numbering is in alphabetical order by player's name.

	MT	EX-MT	VG
COMPLETE SET (50)	9.00	4.00	1.15
COMMON PLAYER (T1-T49)	.10	.05	.01
☐ NNO Royal Flush Mark Davis Bret Saberhagen (Unnnumbered; game instructions on back)	.20	.09	.03
☐ T1 Gregg Jefferies	.35	.16	.04
☐ T2 Steve Adkins	.10	.05	.01
☐ T3 Sandy Alomar Jr.	.25	.11	.03
☐ T4 Steve Avery	1.00	.45	.13
☐ T5 Mike Blowers	.15	.07	.02
☐ T6 George Brett	.50	.23	.06
☐ T7 Tom Browning	.15	.07	.02
☐ T8 Ellis Burks	.20	.09	.03
☐ T9 Joe Carter	.35	.16	.04
☐ T10 Jerald Clark	.20	.09	.03
☐ T11 Hot Corners HOR Matt Williams Will Clark	.45	.20	.06
☐ T12 Pat Combs	.15	.07	.02
☐ T13 Scott Cooper	.25	.11	.03
☐ T14 Mark Davis	.10	.05	.01
☐ T15 Storm Davis	.10	.05	.01
☐ T16 Larry Walker	.50	.23	.06
☐ T17 Brian DuBois	.10	.05	.01
☐ T18 Len Dykstra	.15	.07	.02
☐ T19 John Franco	.15	.07	.02
☐ T20 Kirk Gibson	.15	.07	.02
☐ T21 Juan Gonzalez	2.50	1.15	.30
☐ T22 Tommy Greene	.15	.07	.02
☐ T23 Kent Hrbek	.15	.07	.02
☐ T24 Mike Huff	.15	.07	.02
☐ T25 Bo Jackson	.75	.35	.09
☐ T26 Nolan Ryan (Nolan Knows Bo)	2.50	1.15	.30
☐ T27 Roberto Kelly	.20	.09	.03
☐ T28 Mark Langston	.15	.07	.02
☐ T29 Ray Lankford	.75	.35	.09
☐ T30 Kevin Maas	.60	.25	.08
☐ T31 Julio Machado	.10	.05	.01
☐ T32 Greg Maddux	.30	.14	.04
☐ T33 Mark McGwire	.45	.20	.06
☐ T34 Paul Molitor	.20	.09	.03
☐ T35 Hal Morris	.30	.14	.04
☐ T36 Dale Murphy	.25	.11	.03
☐ T37 Eddie Murray	.30	.14	.04
☐ T38 Jaime Navarro	.25	.11	.03
☐ T39 Dean Palmer	.60	.25	.08
☐ T40 Derek Parks	.20	.09	.03
☐ T41 Bobby Rose	.10	.05	.01
☐ T42 Wally Joyner	.20	.09	.03
☐ T43 Chris Sabo	.20	.09	.03
☐ T44 Benito Santiago	.25	.11	.03
☐ T45 Mike Stanton	.15	.07	.02
☐ T46 Terry Steinbach UER (Career BA .725)	.15	.07	.02
☐ T47 Dave Stewart	.20	.09	.03
☐ T48 Greg Swindell	.20	.09	.03
☐ T49 Jose Vizcaino	.15	.07	.02

1990 Classic III

The 1990 Classic III set is also referenced as Classic Yellow. This set also featured number one draft picks of the current year mixed with the other Classic cards. This 100-card set was issued in standard size (2 1/2" by 3 1/2") and also contained a special Nolan Ryan commemorative card, Texas Heat. Card T8 was never issued.

	MT	EX-MT	VG
COMPLETE SET (100)	12.00	5.50	1.50
COMMON PLAYER (T1-T100)	.10	.05	.01
☐ NNO Micro Players Frank Viola Texas Heat Don Mattingly Chipper Jones (Blue blank back)	.35	.16	.04
☐ T1 Ken Griffey Jr.	1.50	.65	.19
☐ T2 John Tudor	.10	.05	.01
☐ T3 John Kruk	.20	.09	.03
☐ T4 Mark Gardner	.15	.07	.02
☐ T5 Scott Radinsky	.20	.09	.03
☐ T6 John Burkett	.15	.07	.02
☐ T7 Will Clark	.75	.35	.09
☐ T8 Not issued	.00	.00	.00
☐ T9 Ted Higuera	.10	.05	.01
☐ T10 Dave Parker	.15	.07	.02
☐ T11 Dante Bichette	.20	.09	.03
☐ T12 Don Mattingly	.50	.23	.06
☐ T13 Greg Harris	.10	.05	.01
☐ T14 Dave Hollins	.50	.23	.06
☐ T15 Matt Nokes	.15	.07	.02
☐ T16 Kevin Tapani	.25	.11	.03
☐ T17 Shane Mack	.30	.14	.04
☐ T18 Randy Myers	.15	.07	.02
☐ T19 Greg Olson	.10	.05	.01
☐ T20 Shawn Abner	.10	.05	.01
☐ T21 Jim Presley	.10	.05	.01
☐ T22 Randy Johnson	.20	.09	.03
☐ T23 Edgar Martinez	.30	.14	.04
☐ T24 Scott Coolbaugh	.10	.05	.01
☐ T25 Jeff Treadway	.10	.05	.01
☐ T26 Joe Klink	.10	.05	.01
☐ T27 Rickey Henderson	.60	.25	.08
☐ T28 Sam Horn	.10	.05	.01
☐ T29 Kurt Stillwell	.10	.05	.01
☐ T30 Andy Van Slyke	.20	.09	.03
☐ T31 Willie Banks	.25	.11	.03
☐ T32 Jose Canseco	.75	.35	.09
☐ T33 Felix Jose	.25	.11	.03
☐ T34 Candy Maldonado	.10	.05	.01
☐ T35 Carlos Baerga	.50	.23	.06
☐ T36 Keith Hernandez	.15	.07	.02
☐ T37 Frank Viola	.15	.07	.02
☐ T38 Pete O'Brien	.10	.05	.01
☐ T39 Pat Borders	.20	.09	.03
☐ T40 Mike Heath	.10	.05	.01
☐ T41 Kevin Brown	.20	.09	.03
☐ T42 Chris Bosio	.20	.09	.03
☐ T43 Shawn Boskie	.10	.05	.01
☐ T44 Carlos Quintana	.15	.07	.02
☐ T45 Juan Samuel	.10	.05	.01
☐ T46 Tim Layana	.10	.05	.01
☐ T47 Mike Harkey	.20	.09	.03
☐ T48 Gerald Perry	.10	.05	.01
☐ T49 Mike Witt	.10	.05	.01
☐ T50 Joe Orsulak	.10	.05	.01
☐ T51 Not issued	.00	.00	.00
☐ T52 Willie Blair	.10	.05	.01
☐ T53 Gene Larkin	.10	.05	.01
☐ T54 Jody Reed	.10	.05	.01
☐ T55 Jeff Reardon	.20	.09	.03
☐ T56 Kevin McReynolds	.15	.07	.02
☐ T57 Mike Marshall (Unnumbered; game instructions on back)	.15	.07	.02
☐ T58 Eric Yelding	.10	.05	.01
☐ T59 Fred Lynn	.15	.07	.02
☐ T60 Jim Leyritz	.10	.05	.01
☐ T61 John Orton	.10	.05	.01
☐ T62 Mike Lieberthal	.30	.14	.04
☐ T63 Mike Hartley	.15	.07	.02
☐ T64 Kal Daniels	.15	.07	.02
☐ T65 Terry Shumpert	.10	.05	.01
☐ T66 Sil Campusano	.10	.05	.01
☐ T67 Tony Pena	.10	.05	.01
☐ T68 Barry Bonds	.45	.20	.06
☐ T69 Roger McDowell	.10	.05	.01
☐ T70 Kelly Gruber	.15	.07	.02
☐ T71 Willie Randolph	.15	.07	.02
☐ T72 Rick Parker	.10	.05	.01

		MT	EX-MT	VG
☐ T73	Bobby Bonilla	.30	.14	.04
☐ T74	Jack Armstrong	.15	.07	.02
☐ T75	Hubie Brooks	.10	.05	.01
☐ T76	Sandy Alomar Jr.	.20	.09	.03
☐ T77	Ruben Sierra	.35	.16	.04
☐ T78	Erik Hanson	.10	.05	.01
☐ T79	Tony Phillips	.15	.07	.02
☐ T80	Rondell White	.75	.35	.09
☐ T81	Bobby Thigpen	.15	.07	.02
☐ T82	Ron Walden	.15	.07	.02
☐ T83	Don Peters	.15	.07	.02
☐ T84	Nolan Ryan 6th	1.25	.55	.16
☐ T85	Lance Dickson	.20	.09	.03
☐ T86	Ryne Sandberg	.75	.35	.09
☐ T87	Eric Christopherson	.30	.14	.04
☐ T88	Shane Andrews	.30	.14	.04
☐ T89	Marc Newfield	1.00	.45	.13
☐ T90	Adam Hyzdu	.35	.16	.04
☐ T91	Texas Heat Nolan Ryan Reid Ryan	2.00	.90	.25
☐ T92	Chipper Jones	.75	.35	.09
☐ T93	Frank Thomas	3.00	1.35	.40
☐ T94	Cecil Fielder	.50	.23	.06
☐ T95	Delino DeShields	.40	.18	.05
☐ T96	John Olerud	.40	.18	.05
☐ T97	Dave Justice	1.25	.55	.16
☐ T98	Joe Oliver	.15	.07	.02
☐ T99	Alex Fernandez	.30	.14	.04
☐ T100	Todd Hundley	.20	.09	.03

1990 Classic Draft Picks

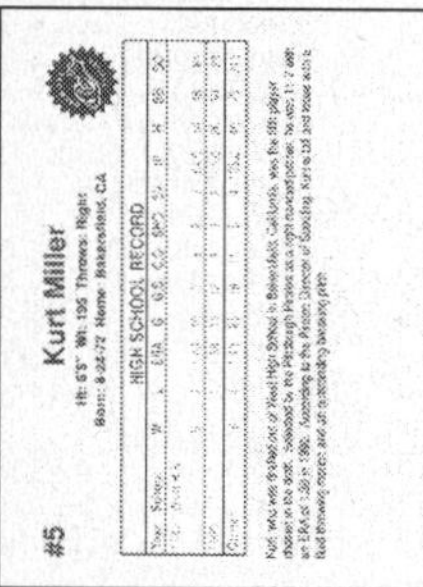

The 1990 Classic Draft Pick set is a standard-size (2 1/2" by 3 1/2"), 26-card set honoring the number one (first round) draft picks of 1990. According to the producer, the printing on this set was limited to 150,000 of each card. This was the first Classic set that was not a game set or trivia set. Card numbers 2 and 22 were not issued.

	MT	EX-MT	VG
COMPLETE SET (25)	15.00	6.75	1.90
COMMON PLAYER (1-26)	.25	.11	.03

		MT	EX-MT	VG
☐ 1	Chipper Jones	2.00	.90	.25
☐ 2	Not issued	.00	.00	.00
☐ 3	Mike Lieberthal	.60	.25	.08
☐ 4	Alex Fernandez	.75	.35	.09
☐ 5	Kurt Miller	.75	.35	.09
☐ 6	Marc Newfield UER	1.50	.65	.19
☐ 7	Dan Wilson	.75	.35	.09
☐ 8	Tim Costo	.60	.25	.08
☐ 9	Ron Walden	.25	.11	.03
☐ 10	Carl Everett UER (Misspelled Evertt on card front)	.90	.40	.11
☐ 11	Shane Andrews	.60	.25	.08
☐ 12	Todd Ritchie	.50	.23	.06
☐ 13	Donovan Osborne	1.00	.45	.13
☐ 14	Todd Van Poppel	2.50	1.15	.30
☐ 15	Adam Hyzdu	.75	.35	.09
☐ 16	Dan Smith	.50	.23	.06
☐ 17	Jeromy Burnitz	1.00	.45	.13
☐ 18	Aaron Holbert	.35	.16	.04
☐ 19	Eric Christopherson	.50	.23	.06
☐ 20	Mike Mussina	3.50	1.55	.45
☐ 21	Tom Nevers	.50	.23	.06
☐ 22	Not issued	.00	.00	.00
☐ 23	Lance Dickson	.60	.25	.08
☐ 24	Rondell White	1.50	.65	.19
☐ 25	Robbie Beckett	.25	.11	.03
☐ 26	Don Peters	.25	.11	.03
☐ NNO	Future Stars HOR Chipper Jones Rondell White (Unnumbered; check- list on back)	.60	.25	.08

1991 Classic Game 200

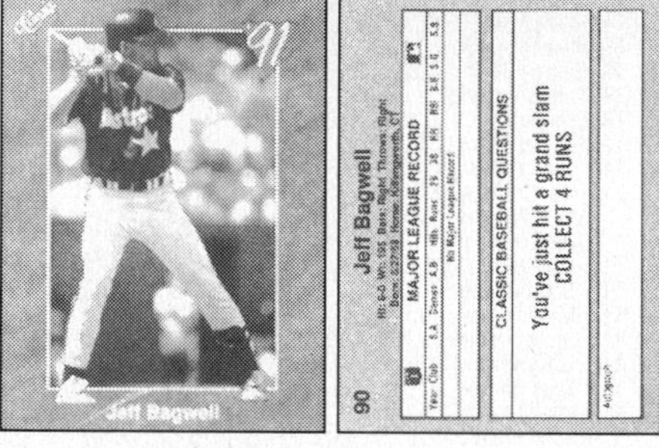

The 1991 Classic Baseball Collector's Edition board game is Classic's first Big Game issue since the 1989 Big Game. Only 100,000 games were produced, and each one included a board game, action spinner, eight stand-up baseball player pieces, action scoreboard, eight-page picture book with tips from five great baseball players (Carew, Spahn, Schmidt, Brock, and Aaron), 200 player cards, and a certificate of limited edition. The standard-size (2 1/2" by 3 1/2") cards have on the fronts glossy color action photos bordered in purple. The backs are purple and white and have biography, statistics, five trivia questions, and an autograph slot. The cards are numbered on the back.

	MT	EX-MT	VG
COMPLETE SET (200)	27.00	12.00	3.40
COMMON PLAYER (1-200)	.10	.05	.01

		MT	EX-MT	VG
☐ 1	Frank Viola	.15	.07	.02
☐ 2	Tim Wallach	.15	.07	.02
☐ 3	Lou Whitaker	.15	.07	.02
☐ 4	Brett Butler	.20	.09	.03
☐ 5	Jim Abbott	.40	.18	.05
☐ 6	Jack Armstrong	.10	.05	.01
☐ 7	Craig Biggio	.15	.07	.02
☐ 8	Brian Barnes	.15	.07	.02
☐ 9	Dennis(Oil Can) Boyd	.10	.05	.01
☐ 10	Tom Browning	.15	.07	.02
☐ 11	Tom Brunansky	.15	.07	.02
☐ 12	Ellis Burks	.20	.09	.03
☐ 13	Harold Baines	.15	.07	.02
☐ 14	Kal Daniels	.15	.07	.02
☐ 15	Mark Davis	.10	.05	.01
☐ 16	Storm Davis	.10	.05	.01
☐ 17	Tom Glavine	.40	.18	.05
☐ 18	Mike Greenwell	.20	.09	.03
☐ 19	Kelly Gruber	.15	.07	.02
☐ 20	Mark Gubicza	.10	.05	.01
☐ 21	Pedro Guerrero	.15	.07	.02
☐ 22	Mike Harkey	.15	.07	.02
☐ 23	Orel Hershiser	.20	.09	.03
☐ 24	Ted Higuera	.10	.05	.01
☐ 25	Von Hayes	.10	.05	.01
☐ 26	Andre Dawson	.35	.16	.04
☐ 27	Shawon Dunston	.15	.07	.02
☐ 28	Roberto Kelly	.20	.09	.03
☐ 29	Joe Magrane	.10	.05	.01
☐ 30	Dennis Martinez	.15	.07	.02
☐ 31	Kevin McReynolds	.15	.07	.02
☐ 32	Matt Nokes	.15	.07	.02
☐ 33	Dan Plesac	.10	.05	.01
☐ 34	Dave Parker	.15	.07	.02
☐ 35	Randy Johnson	.15	.07	.02
☐ 36	Bret Saberhagen	.20	.09	.03

☐ 37 Mackey Sasser .10 .05 .01
☐ 38 Mike Scott .15 .07 .02
☐ 39 Ozzie Smith .30 .14 .04
☐ 40 Kevin Seitzer .15 .07 .02
☐ 41 Ruben Sierra .30 .14 .04
☐ 42 Kevin Tapani .20 .09 .03
☐ 43 Danny Tartabull .30 .14 .04
☐ 44 Robby Thompson .10 .05 .01
☐ 45 Andy Van Slyke .20 .09 .03
☐ 46 Greg Vaughn .20 .09 .03
☐ 47 Harold Reynolds .15 .07 .02
☐ 48 Will Clark .50 .23 .06
☐ 49 Gary Gaetti .10 .05 .01
☐ 50 Joe Grahe .15 .07 .02
☐ 51 Carlton Fisk .25 .11 .03
☐ 52 Robin Ventura .30 .14 .04
☐ 53 Ozzie Guillen .10 .05 .01
☐ 54 Tom Candiotti .15 .07 .02
☐ 55 Doug Jones .10 .05 .01
☐ 56 Eric King .10 .05 .01
☐ 57 Kirk Gibson .15 .07 .02
☐ 58 Tim Costo .30 .14 .04
☐ 59 Robin Yount .40 .18 .05
☐ 60 Sammy Sosa .20 .09 .03
☐ 61 Jesse Barfield .15 .07 .02
☐ 62 Marc Newfield .75 .35 .09
☐ 63 Jimmy Key .15 .07 .02
☐ 64 Felix Jose .20 .09 .03
☐ 65 Mark Whiten .20 .09 .03
☐ 66 Tommy Greene .15 .07 .02
☐ 67 Kent Mercker .15 .07 .02
☐ 68 Greg Maddux .30 .14 .04
☐ 69 Danny Jackson .10 .05 .01
☐ 70 Reggie Sanders .60 .25 .08
☐ 71 Eric Yelding .10 .05 .01
☐ 72 Karl Rhodes .10 .05 .01
☐ 73 Fernando Valenzuela .15 .07 .02
☐ 74 Chris Nabholz .10 .05 .01
☐ 75 Andres Galarraga .15 .07 .02
☐ 76 Howard Johnson .20 .09 .03
☐ 77 Hubie Brooks .10 .05 .01
☐ 78 Terry Mulholland .15 .07 .02
☐ 79 Paul Molitor .25 .11 .03
☐ 80 Roger McDowell .10 .05 .01
☐ 81 Darren Daulton .25 .11 .03
☐ 82 Zane Smith .10 .05 .01
☐ 83 Ray Lankford .40 .18 .05
☐ 84 Bruce Hurst .15 .07 .02
☐ 85 Andy Benes .20 .09 .03
☐ 86 John Burkett .15 .07 .02
☐ 87 Dave Righetti .10 .05 .01
☐ 88 Steve Karsay .25 .11 .03
☐ 89 D.J. Dozier .20 .09 .03
☐ 90 Jeff Bagwell 1.00 .45 .13
☐ 91 Joe Carter .35 .16 .04
☐ 92 Wes Chamberlain .35 .16 .04
☐ 93 Vince Coleman .20 .09 .03
☐ 94 Pat Combs .15 .07 .02
☐ 95 Jerome Walton .15 .07 .02
☐ 96 Jeff Conine .30 .14 .04
☐ 97 Alan Trammell .20 .09 .03
☐ 98 Don Mattingly .50 .23 .06
☐ 99 Ramon Martinez .25 .11 .03
☐ 100 Dave Magadan .15 .07 .02
☐ 101 Greg Swindell UER .20 .09 .03
(Misnumbered as T10)
☐ 102 Dave Stewart .20 .09 .03
☐ 103 Gary Sheffield .50 .23 .06
☐ 104 George Bell .20 .09 .03
☐ 105 Mark Grace .30 .14 .04
☐ 106 Steve Sax .15 .07 .02
☐ 107 Ryne Sandberg .60 .25 .08
☐ 108 Chris Sabo .20 .09 .03
☐ 109 Jose Rijo .15 .07 .02
☐ 110 Cal Ripken .75 .35 .09
☐ 111 Kirby Puckett .50 .23 .06
☐ 112 Eddie Murray .25 .11 .03
☐ 113 Roberto Alomar .50 .23 .06
☐ 114 Randy Myers .15 .07 .02
☐ 115 Rafael Palmeiro .20 .09 .03
☐ 116 John Olerud .35 .16 .04
☐ 117 Gregg Jefferies .30 .14 .04
☐ 118 Kent Hrbek .15 .07 .02
☐ 119 Marquis Grissom .30 .14 .04
☐ 120 Ken Griffey Jr. 1.50 .65 .19
☐ 121 Dwight Gooden .25 .11 .03
☐ 122 Juan Gonzalez .75 .35 .09
☐ 123 Ron Gant .35 .16 .04
☐ 124 Travis Fryman .90 .40 .11
☐ 125 John Franco .15 .07 .02
☐ 126 Dennis Eckersley .25 .11 .03
☐ 127 Cecil Fielder .35 .16 .04
☐ 128 Phil Plantier .75 .35 .09
☐ 129 Kevin Mitchell .25 .11 .03
☐ 130 Kevin Maas .25 .11 .03
☐ 131 Mark McGwire .45 .20 .06
☐ 132 Ben McDonald .30 .14 .04
☐ 133 Len Dykstra .15 .07 .02
☐ 134 Delino DeShields .30 .14 .04
☐ 135 Jose Canseco .50 .23 .06
☐ 136 Eric Davis .20 .09 .03
☐ 137 George Brett .40 .18 .05
☐ 138 Steve Avery .40 .18 .05
☐ 139 Eric Anthony .20 .09 .03
☐ 140 Bobby Thigpen .15 .07 .02
☐ 141 Ken Griffey Sr. .15 .07 .02
☐ 142 Barry Larkin .20 .09 .03
☐ 143 Jeff Brantley .15 .07 .02
☐ 144 Bobby Bonilla .25 .11 .03
☐ 145 Jose Offerman .20 .09 .03
☐ 146 Mike Mussina .75 .35 .09
☐ 147 Erik Hanson .10 .05 .01
☐ 148 Dale Murphy .25 .11 .03
☐ 149 Roger Clemens .60 .25 .08
☐ 150 Tino Martinez .25 .11 .03
☐ 151 Todd Van Poppel .90 .40 .11
☐ 152 Mo Vaughn .35 .16 .04
☐ 153 Derrick May .35 .16 .04
☐ 154 Jack Clark .10 .05 .01
☐ 155 Dave Hansen .15 .07 .02
☐ 156 Tony Gwynn .40 .18 .05
☐ 157 Brian McRae .30 .14 .04
☐ 158 Matt Williams .20 .09 .03
☐ 159 Kirk Dressendorfer .20 .09 .03
☐ 160 Scott Erickson .45 .20 .06
☐ 161 Tony Fernandez .15 .07 .02
☐ 162 Willie McGee .15 .07 .02
☐ 163 Fred McGriff .30 .14 .04
☐ 164 Leo Gomez .40 .18 .05
☐ 165 Bernard Gilkey .30 .14 .04
☐ 166 Bobby Witt .15 .07 .02
☐ 167 Doug Drabek .15 .07 .02
☐ 168 Rob Dibble .15 .07 .02
☐ 169 Glenn Davis .15 .07 .02
☐ 170 Danny Darwin .10 .05 .01
☐ 171 Eric Karros 1.25 .55 .16
☐ 172 Eddie Zosky .20 .09 .03
☐ 173 Todd Zeile .25 .11 .03
☐ 174 Tim Raines .15 .07 .02
☐ 175 Benito Santiago .20 .09 .03
☐ 176 Dan Peltier .20 .09 .03
☐ 177 Darryl Strawberry .45 .20 .06
☐ 178 Hal Morris .20 .09 .03
☐ 179 Hensley Meulens .20 .09 .03
☐ 180 John Smoltz .25 .11 .03
☐ 181 Frank Thomas 1.50 .65 .19
☐ 182 Dave Staton .25 .11 .03
☐ 183 Scott Chiamparino .15 .07 .02
☐ 184 Alex Fernandez .25 .11 .03
☐ 185 Mark Lewis .25 .11 .03
☐ 186 Bo Jackson .75 .35 .09
☐ 187 Mickey Morandini UER .25 .11 .03
(Photo is actually
Darren Daulton)
☐ 188 Cory Snyder .15 .07 .02
☐ 189 Rickey Henderson .50 .23 .06
☐ 190 Junior Felix .15 .07 .02
☐ 191 Milt Cuyler .20 .09 .03
☐ 192 Wade Boggs .40 .18 .05
☐ 193 Dave Justice .75 .35 .09
(Justice Prevails)
☐ 194 Sandy Alomar Jr. .20 .09 .03
☐ 195 Barry Bonds .40 .18 .05
☐ 196 Nolan Ryan 1.00 .45 .13
☐ 197 Rico Brogna .30 .14 .04
☐ 198 Steve Decker .15 .07 .02
☐ 199 Bob Welch .15 .07 .02
☐ 200 Andujar Cedeno .25 .11 .03

1991 Classic I

This 100-card set features many of the most popular players in the game of baseball as well as some of the more exciting prospects. The set measures the standard size, 2 1/2" by 3 1/2", and includes trivia questions on the backs of the cards. For the most part the set is arranged alphabetically by team and then alphabetically by players within that team.

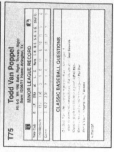

	MT	EX-MT	VG
COMPLETE SET (100)	10.00	4.50	1.25
COMMON PLAYER (T1-T99)	.10	.05	.01
☐ NNO Todd Van Poppel Dave Justice Ryne Sandberg Kevin Maas (Blank back)	.75	.35	.09
☐ T1 John Olerud	.30	.14	.04
☐ T2 Tino Martinez	.20	.09	.03
☐ T3 Ken Griffey Jr.	1.00	.45	.13
☐ T4 Jeromy Burnitz	.60	.25	.08
☐ T5 Ron Gant	.30	.14	.04
☐ T6 Mike Benjamin	.10	.05	.01
☐ T7 Steve Decker	.15	.07	.02
☐ T8 Matt Williams	.20	.09	.03
☐ T9 Rafael Novoa	.15	.07	.02
☐ T10 Kevin Mitchell	.20	.09	.03
☐ T11 Dave Justice	.60	.25	.08
☐ T12 Leo Gomez	.30	.14	.04
☐ T13 Chris Hoiles	.20	.09	.03
☐ T14 Ben McDonald	.20	.09	.03
☐ T15 David Segui	.15	.07	.02
☐ T16 Anthony Telford	.10	.05	.01
☐ T17 Mike Mussina	1.00	.45	.13
☐ T18 Roger Clemens	.50	.23	.06
☐ T19 Wade Boggs	.40	.18	.05
☐ T20 Tim Naehring	.20	.09	.03
☐ T21 Joe Carter	.25	.11	.03
☐ T22 Phil Plantier	.50	.23	.06
☐ T23 Rob Dibble	.15	.07	.02
☐ T24 Maurice Vaughn	.35	.16	.04
☐ T25 Lee Stevens	.20	.09	.03
☐ T26 Chris Sabo	.20	.09	.03
☐ T27 Mark Grace	.25	.11	.03
☐ T28 Derrick May	.35	.16	.04
☐ T29 Ryne Sandberg	.60	.25	.08
☐ T30 Matt Stark	.15	.07	.02
☐ T31 Bobby Thigpen	.15	.07	.02
☐ T32 Frank Thomas	1.25	.55	.16
☐ T33 Don Mattingly	.50	.23	.06
☐ T34 Eric Davis	.25	.11	.03
☐ T35 Reggie Jefferson	.50	.23	.06
☐ T36 Alex Cole	.20	.09	.03
☐ T37 Mark Lewis	.30	.14	.04
☐ T38 Tim Costo	.35	.16	.04
☐ T39 Sandy Alomar Jr.	.20	.09	.03
☐ T40 Travis Fryman	.90	.40	.11
☐ T41 Cecil Fielder	.35	.16	.04
☐ T42 Milt Cuyler	.25	.11	.03
☐ T43 Andujar Cedeno	.25	.11	.03
☐ T44 Danny Darwin	.10	.05	.01
☐ T45 Randy Hennis	.15	.07	.02
☐ T46 George Brett	.40	.18	.05
☐ T47 Jeff Conine	.25	.11	.03
☐ T48 Bo Jackson	.75	.35	.09
☐ T49 Brian McRae	.30	.14	.04
☐ T50 Brent Mayne	.20	.09	.03
☐ T51 Eddie Murray	.20	.09	.03
☐ T52 Ramon Martinez	.25	.11	.03
☐ T53 Jim Neidlinger	.10	.05	.01
☐ T54 Jim Poole	.10	.05	.01
☐ T55 Tim McIntosh	.10	.05	.01
☐ T56 Randy Veres	.10	.05	.01
☐ T57 Kirby Puckett	.50	.23	.06
☐ T58 Todd Ritchie	.20	.09	.03
☐ T59 Rich Garces	.15	.07	.02
☐ T60 Moises Alou	.25	.11	.03
☐ T61 Delino DeShields	.20	.09	.03
☐ T62 Oscar Azocar	.10	.05	.01
☐ T63 Kevin Maas	.25	.11	.03
☐ T64 Alan Mills	.20	.09	.03
☐ T65 John Franco	.15	.07	.02
☐ T66 Chris Jelic	.25	.11	.03
☐ T67 Dave Magadan	.15	.07	.02
☐ T68 Darryl Strawberry	.35	.16	.04
☐ T69 Hensley Meulens	.15	.07	.02
☐ T70 Juan Gonzalez	.75	.35	.09
☐ T71 Reggie Harris	.15	.07	.02
☐ T72 Rickey Henderson	.45	.20	.06
☐ T73 Mark McGwire	.40	.18	.05
☐ T74 Willie McGee	.15	.07	.02
☐ T75 Todd Van Poppel	.75	.35	.09
☐ T76 Bob Welch	.15	.07	.02
☐ T77 Future Aces Todd Van Poppel Don Peters David Zancanaro Kirk Dressendorfer	.75	.35	.09
☐ T78 Len Dykstra	.15	.07	.02
☐ T79 Mickey Morandini	.20	.09	.03
☐ T80 Wes Chamberlain	.25	.11	.03
☐ T81 Barry Bonds	.40	.18	.05
☐ T82 Doug Drabek	.15	.07	.02
☐ T83 Randy Tomlin	.20	.09	.03
☐ T84 Scott Chiamparino	.15	.07	.02
☐ T85 Rafael Palmiero	.20	.09	.03
☐ T86 Nolan Ryan	1.00	.45	.13
☐ T87 Bobby Witt	.15	.07	.02
☐ T88 Fred McGriff	.30	.14	.04
☐ T89 Dave Stieb	.15	.07	.02
☐ T90 Ed Sprague	.30	.14	.04
☐ T91 Vince Coleman	.15	.07	.02
☐ T92 Rod Brewer	.20	.09	.03
☐ T93 Bernard Gilkey	.35	.16	.04
☐ T94 Roberto Alomar	.45	.20	.06
☐ T95 Chuck Finley	.10	.05	.01
☐ T96 Dale Murphy	.20	.09	.03
☐ T97 Jose Rijo	.15	.07	.02
☐ T98 Hal Morris	.20	.09	.03
☐ T99 Friendly Foes Darryl Strawberry Dwight Gooden (Instructions on back)	.25	.11	.03

1991 Classic II

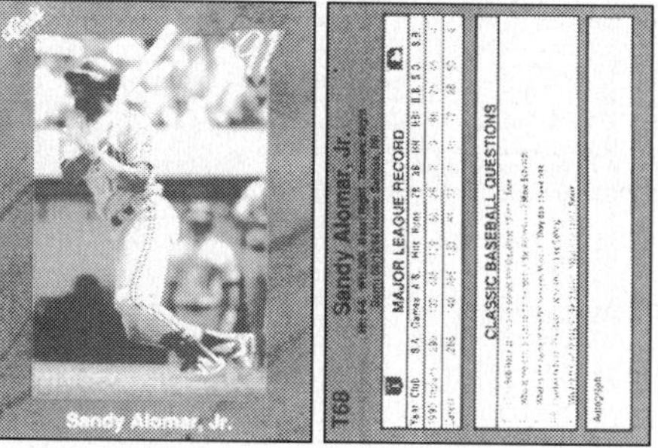

This second issue of the 1991 Classic baseball trivia game contains a small gameboard, accessories, 99 player cards with trivia questions on the backs, and one "4-in-1" micro player card. The cards measure the standard size (2 1/2" by 3 1/2") and have on the fronts glossy color action photos with cranberry red borders. The backs are cranberry and white and have biography, statistics, five trivia questions, and an autograph slot. The cards are numbered on the back.

	MT	EX-MT	VG
COMPLETE SET (100)	10.00	4.50	1.25
COMMON PLAYER (T1-T100)	.10	.05	.01
☐ T0 Greg Swindell	.15	.07	.02
☐ T1 Ken Griffey Jr.	1.00	.45	.13
☐ T2 Wilfredo Cordero	.40	.18	.05
☐ T3 Cal Ripken	.60	.25	.08
☐ T4 D.J. Dozier	.15	.07	.02
☐ T5 Darrin Fletcher	.10	.05	.01
☐ T6 Glenn Davis	.15	.07	.02
☐ T7 Alex Fernandez	.20	.09	.03

□ T8 Cory Snyder	.15	.07	.02
□ T9 Tim Raines	.15	.07	.02
□ T11 Mark Lewis	.25	.11	.03
□ T12 Rico Brogna	.25	.11	.03
□ T13 Gary Sheffield	.45	.20	.06
□ T14 Paul Molitor	.20	.09	.03
□ T15 Kent Hrbek	.15	.07	.02
□ T16 Scott Erickson	.40	.18	.05
□ T17 Steve Sax	.15	.07	.02
□ T18 Dennis Eckersley	.25	.11	.03
□ T19 Jose Canseco	.50	.23	.06
□ T20 Kirk Dressendorfer	.15	.07	.02
□ T21 Ken Griffey Sr.	.15	.07	.02
□ T22 Erik Hanson	.10	.05	.01
□ T23 Dan Peltier	.20	.09	.03
□ T24 John Olerud	.25	.11	.03
□ T25 Eddie Zosky	.15	.07	.02
□ T26 Steve Avery	.35	.16	.04
□ T27 John Smoltz	.25	.11	.03
□ T28 Frank Thomas	1.00	.45	.13
□ T29 Jerome Walton	.10	.05	.01
□ T30 George Bell	.15	.07	.02
□ T31 Jose Rijo	.15	.07	.02
□ T32 Randy Myers	.15	.07	.02
□ T33 Barry Larkin	.20	.09	.03
□ T34 Eric Anthony	.20	.09	.03
□ T35 Dave Hansen	.15	.07	.02
□ T36 Eric Karros	1.00	.45	.13
□ T37 Jose Offerman	.20	.09	.03
□ T38 Marquis Grissom	.25	.11	.03
□ T39 Dwight Gooden	.20	.09	.03
□ T40 Gregg Jefferies	.25	.11	.03
□ T41 Pat Combs	.15	.07	.02
□ T42 Todd Zeile	.15	.07	.02
□ T43 Benito Santiago	.20	.09	.03
□ T44 Dave Staton	.25	.11	.03
□ T45 Tony Fernandez	.15	.07	.02
□ T46 Fred McGriff	.25	.11	.03
□ T47 Jeff Brantley	.10	.05	.01
□ T48 Junior Felix	.15	.07	.02
□ T49 Jack Morris	.20	.09	.03
□ T50 Chris George	.15	.07	.02
□ T51 Henry Rodriguez	.25	.11	.03
□ T52 Paul Marak	.15	.07	.02
□ T53 Ryan Klesko	1.00	.45	.13
□ T54 Darren Lewis	.15	.07	.02
□ T55 Lance Dickson	.15	.07	.02
□ T56 Anthony Young	.20	.09	.03
□ T57 Willie Banks	.15	.07	.02
□ T58 Mike Bordick	.30	.14	.04
□ T59 Roger Salkeld	.25	.11	.03
□ T60 Steve Karsay	.25	.11	.03
□ T61 Bernie Williams	.30	.14	.04
□ T62 Mickey Tettleton	.15	.07	.02
□ T63 Dave Justice	.60	.25	.08
□ T64 Steve Decker	.15	.07	.02
□ T65 Roger Clemens	.60	.25	.08
□ T66 Phil Plantier	.40	.18	.05
□ T67 Ryne Sandberg	.60	.25	.08
□ T68 Sandy Alomar Jr.	.20	.09	.03
□ T69 Cecil Fielder	.35	.16	.04
□ T70 George Brett	.30	.14	.04
□ T71 Delino DeShields	.25	.11	.03
□ T72 Dave Magadan	.10	.05	.01
□ T73 Darryl Strawberry	.45	.20	.06
□ T74 Juan Gonzalez	.60	.25	.08
□ T75 Rickey Henderson	.45	.20	.06
□ T76 Willie McGee	.15	.07	.02
□ T77 Todd Van Poppel	.60	.25	.08
□ T78 Barry Bonds	.35	.16	.04
□ T79 Doug Drabek	.15	.07	.02
□ T80 Nolan Ryan (300 Game Winner)	.90	.40	.11
□ T81 Roberto Alomar	.45	.20	.06
□ T82 Ivan Rodriguez	.90	.40	.11
□ T83 Dan Opperman	.15	.07	.02
□ T84 Jeff Bagwell	.90	.40	.11
□ T85 Braulio Castillo	.25	.11	.03
□ T86 Doug Simons	.15	.07	.02
□ T87 Wade Taylor	.15	.07	.02
□ T88 Gary Scott	.20	.09	.03
□ T89 Dave Stewart	.15	.07	.02
□ T90 Mike Simms	.15	.07	.02
□ T91 Luis Gonzalez	.25	.11	.03
□ T92 Bobby Bonilla	.25	.11	.03
□ T93 Tony Gwynn	.35	.16	.04
□ T94 Will Clark	.45	.20	.06
□ T95 Rich Rowland	.15	.07	.02
□ T96 Alan Trammell	.20	.09	.03
□ T97 Strikeout Kings Nolan Ryan Roger Clemens	.90	.40	.11
□ T98 Joe Carter	.30	.14	.04
□ T99 Jack Clark	.15	.07	.02
□ T100 Steve Decker	.15	.07	.02

1991 Classic III

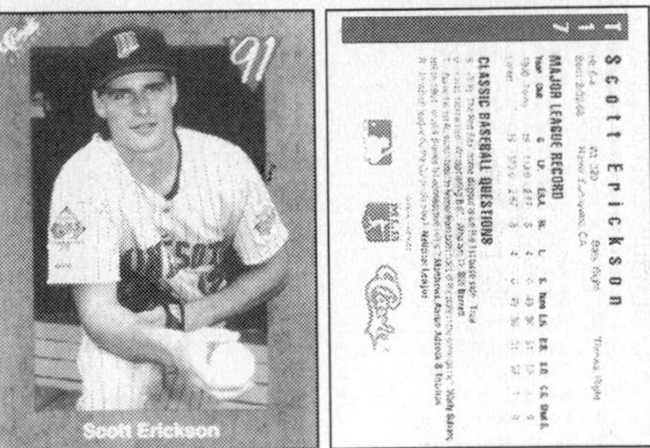

'91
Scott Erickson
Scott Erickson
MAJOR LEAGUE RECORD
CLASSIC BASEBALL QUESTIONS

The third issue of the 1991 Classic baseball trivia game contains a small gameboard, accessories, 99 player cards with trivia questions on the backs, and one "4-in-1" micro player card. The cards measure the standard size (2 1/2" by 3 1/2") and have on the fronts glossy color action photos with grayish-green borders. In a horizontal format, the backs feature biography, statistics, and five trivia questions. This information is superimposed over the team logo. The card numbers on the back appear in a green stripe. With few exceptions, the cards are arranged in alphabetical order.

	MT	EX-MT	VG
COMPLETE SET (100)	10.00	4.50	1.25
COMMON PLAYER (T1-T99)	.10	.05	.01
□ NNO 4-in-1 Card Bobby Bonilla Will Clark Cal Ripken Scott Erickson (Unnumbered)	.50	.23	.06
□ T1 Jim Abbott	.35	.16	.04
□ T2 Craig Biggio	.15	.07	.02
□ T3 Wade Boggs	.40	.18	.05
□ T4 Bobby Bonilla	.30	.14	.04
□ T5 Ivan Calderon	.15	.07	.02
□ T6 Jose Canseco	.45	.20	.06
□ T7 Andy Benes	.20	.09	.03
□ T8 Wes Chamberlain	.20	.09	.03
□ T9 Will Clark	.45	.20	.06
□ T10 Royce Clayton	.30	.14	.04
□ T11 Gerald Alexander	.10	.05	.01
□ T12 Chili Davis	.15	.07	.02
□ T13 Eric Davis	.20	.09	.03
□ T14 Andre Dawson	.25	.11	.03
□ T15 Rob Dibble	.15	.07	.02
□ T16 Chris Donnels	.20	.09	.03
□ T17 Scott Erickson	.30	.14	.04
□ T18 Monty Fariss	.15	.07	.02
□ T19 Ruben Amaro Jr.	.15	.07	.02
□ T20 Chuck Finley	.10	.05	.01
□ T21 Carlton Fisk	.25	.11	.03
□ T22 Carlos Baerga	.50	.23	.06
□ T23 Ron Gant	.25	.11	.03
□ T24 Dave Justice and Ron Gant	.50	.23	.06
□ T25 Mike Gardiner	.15	.07	.02
□ T26 Tom Glavine	.35	.16	.04
□ T27 Joe Grahe	.15	.07	.02
□ T28 Derek Bell	.35	.16	.04
□ T29 Mike Greenwell	.20	.09	.03
□ T30 Ken Griffey Jr.	.90	.40	.11
□ T31 Leo Gomez	.25	.11	.03
□ T32 Tom Goodwin	.20	.09	.03
□ T33 Tony Gwynn	.35	.16	.04
□ T34 Mel Hall	.10	.05	.01
□ T35 Brian Harper	.10	.05	.01
□ T36 Dave Henderson	.10	.05	.01
□ T37 Albert Belle	.25	.11	.03
□ T38 Orel Hershiser	.15	.07	.02
□ T39 Brian Hunter	.35	.16	.04

☐ T40 Howard Johnson	.20	.09	.03
☐ T41 Felix Jose	.20	.09	.03
☐ T42 Wally Joyner	.15	.07	.02
☐ T43 Jeff Juden	.25	.11	.03
☐ T44 Pat Kelly	.25	.11	.03
☐ T45 Jimmy Key	.15	.07	.02
☐ T46 Chuck Knoblauch	.40	.18	.05
☐ T47 John Kruk	.15	.07	.02
☐ T48 Ray Lankford	.35	.16	.04
☐ T49 Ced Landrum	.15	.07	.02
☐ T50 Scott Livingstone	.15	.07	.02
☐ T51 Kevin Maas	.20	.09	.03
☐ T52 Greg Maddux	.25	.11	.03
☐ T53 Dennis Martinez	.15	.07	.02
☐ T54 Edgar Martinez	.20	.09	.03
☐ T55 Pedro Martinez	.75	.35	.09
☐ T56 Don Mattingly	.50	.23	.06
☐ T57 Orlando Merced	.25	.11	.03
☐ T58 Keith Mitchell	.25	.11	.03
☐ T59 Kevin Mitchell	.20	.09	.03
☐ T60 Paul Molitor	.20	.09	.03
☐ T61 Jack Morris	.20	.09	.03
☐ T62 Hal Morris	.20	.09	.03
☐ T63 Kevin Morton	.10	.05	.01
☐ T64 Pedro Munoz	.30	.14	.04
☐ T65 Eddie Murray	.20	.09	.03
☐ T66 Jack McDowell	.20	.09	.03
☐ T67 Jeff McNeely	.30	.14	.04
☐ T68 Brian McRae	.20	.09	.03
☐ T69 Kevin McReynolds	.15	.07	.02
☐ T70 Gregg Olson	.15	.07	.02
☐ T71 Rafael Palmeiro	.20	.09	.03
☐ T72 Dean Palmer	.30	.14	.04
☐ T73 Tony Phillips	.15	.07	.02
☐ T74 Kirby Puckett	.45	.20	.06
☐ T75 Carlos Quintana	.15	.07	.02
☐ T76 Pat Rice	.15	.07	.02
☐ T77 Cal Ripken	.60	.25	.08
☐ T78 Ivan Rodriguez	.75	.35	.09
☐ T79 Nolan Ryan Number 7	.75	.35	.09
☐ T80 Bret Saberhagen	.20	.09	.03
☐ T81 Tim Salmon	.60	.25	.08
☐ T82 Juan Samuel	.10	.05	.01
☐ T83 Ruben Sierra	.30	.14	.04
☐ T84 Heathcliff Slocumb	.10	.05	.01
☐ T85 Joe Slusarski	.15	.07	.02
☐ T86 John Smiley	.15	.07	.02
☐ T87 Dave Smith	.10	.05	.01
☐ T88 Ed Sprague	.15	.07	.02
☐ T89 Todd Stottlemyre	.15	.07	.02
☐ T90 Mike Timlin	.15	.07	.02
☐ T91 Greg Vaughn	.25	.11	.03
☐ T92 Frank Viola	.15	.07	.02
☐ T93 Chico Walker	.15	.07	.02
☐ T94 Devon White	.15	.07	.02
☐ T95 Matt Williams	.25	.11	.03
☐ T96 Rick Wilkins	.15	.07	.02
☐ T97 Bernie Williams	.25	.11	.03
☐ T98 Starter and Stopper Nolan Ryan Goose Gossage	.50	.23	.06
☐ T99 Gerald Williams	.45	.20	.06

1991 Classic Draft Picks

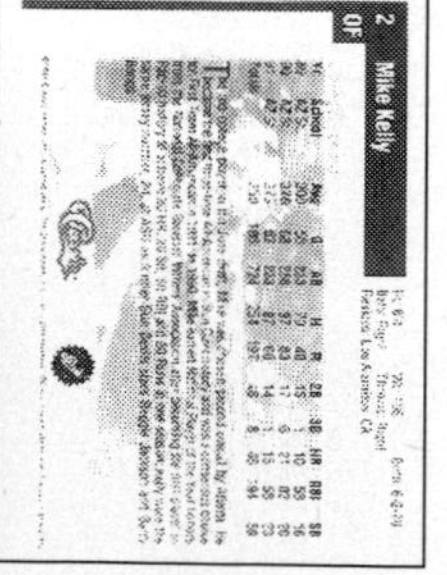

The premier edition of the 1991 Classic Draft Picks set contains 50 standard size (2 1/2" by 3 1/2") cards, plus a bonus card featuring Frankie Rodriguez. The production run was distributed between 330,000 hobby sets, 165,000 non-hobby sets, and 1,500 test sets. Each set includes a certificate of limited edition with a unique set number. The fronts display glossy color player photos, with maroon borders and a gray card face. The draft pick number, player's name, and position appear in the maroon border at the bottom of the picture. The horizontally oriented backs have biography and maroon border stripes intersecting at the upper corner. Also high school or college statistics and player profile are printed over a washed-out picture of a batter and catcher at home plate. The cards are numbered on the back. This set includes Brien Taylor, the first pick of the '91 draft. The Frankie Rodriguez bonus card was only included in hobby sets.

	MT	EX-MT	VG
COMPLETE SET (50)	9.00	4.00	1.15
COMMON PLAYER (1-50)	.10	.05	.01
☐ 1 Brien Taylor	3.00	1.35	.40
☐ 2 Mike Kelly	1.75	.80	.22
☐ 3 David McCarty	1.75	.80	.22
☐ 4 Dmitri Young	1.50	.65	.19
☐ 5 Joe Vitiello	.75	.35	.09
☐ 6 Mark Smith	.75	.35	.09
☐ 7 Tyler Green	.75	.35	.09
☐ 8 Shawn Estes	.50	.23	.06
☐ 9 Doug Glanville	.50	.23	.06
☐ 10 Manny Ramirez	1.00	.45	.13
☐ 11 Cliff Floyd	1.50	.65	.19
☐ 12 Tyrone Hill	.75	.35	.09
☐ 13 Eduardo Perez	1.25	.55	.16
☐ 14 Al Shirley	.75	.35	.09
☐ 15 Benji Gil	.75	.35	.09
☐ 16 Calvin Reese	.50	.23	.06
☐ 17 Allen Watson	.50	.23	.06
☐ 18 Brian Barber	.35	.16	.04
☐ 19 Aaron Sele	.75	.35	.09
☐ 20 Jon Farrell UER (Misspelled John)	.20	.09	.03
☐ 21 Scott Ruffcorn	.50	.23	.06
☐ 22 Brent Gates	.60	.25	.08
☐ 23 Scott Stahoviak	.50	.23	.06
☐ 24 Tom McKinnon	.15	.07	.02
☐ 25 Shawn Livsey	.25	.11	.03
☐ 26 Jason Pruitt	.15	.07	.02
☐ 27 Greg Anthony	.15	.07	.02
☐ 28 Justin Thompson	.15	.07	.02
☐ 29 Steve Whitaker	.10	.05	.01
☐ 30 Jorge Fabregas	.30	.14	.04
☐ 31 Jeff Ware	.40	.18	.05
☐ 32 Bobby Jones	.75	.35	.09
☐ 33 J.J. Johnson	.15	.07	.02
☐ 34 Mike Rossiter	.10	.05	.01
☐ 35 Dan Cholowsky	.75	.35	.09
☐ 36 Jimmy Gonzalez	.10	.05	.01
☐ 37 Trever Miller UER (Misspelled Trevor)	.25	.11	.03
☐ 38 Scott Hatteberg	.30	.14	.04
☐ 39 Mike Groppuso	.15	.07	.02
☐ 40 Ryan Long	.15	.07	.02
☐ 41 Eddie Williams	.40	.18	.05
☐ 42 Mike Durant	.25	.11	.03
☐ 43 Buck McNabb	.10	.05	.01
☐ 44 Jimmy Lewis	.25	.11	.03
☐ 45 Eddie Ramos	.10	.05	.01
☐ 46 Terry Horn	.10	.05	.01
☐ 47 Jon Barnes	.10	.05	.01
☐ 48 Shawn Curran	.10	.05	.01
☐ 49 Tommy Adams	.60	.25	.08
☐ 50 Trevor Mallory	.20	.09	.03
☐ NNO Frankie Rodriguez Bonus card	1.00	.45	.13

1992 Classic Game 200

The 1992 Classic Baseball Collector's Edition game contains 200 cards measuring the standard size (2 1/2" by 3 1/2"). The cards were issued in two boxes labeled "Trivia Cards A" and "Trivia Cards B." The game also included an official Major League Action Spinner, eight stand-up baseball hero player pieces, an action scoreboard, a hand-illustrated game board, and a collectible book featuring tips from a new

group of baseball legends. According to Classic, production has been limited to 125,000 games. The cards measure the standard size (2 1/2" by 3 1/2"). The fronts display glossy color action photos bordered in dark purple. The Classic logo and the year "1992" appear in the top border, while the player's name is given in white lettering in the bottom border. The horizontally oriented backs present biography, statistics (1991 and career), and five baseball trivia questions. The cards are numbered on the back.

	MT	EX-MT	VG
COMPLETE SET (200)	25.00	11.50	3.10
COMMON PLAYER (1-200)	.10	.05	.01
☐ 1 Chuck Finley	.10	.05	.01
☐ 2 Craig Biggio	.15	.07	.02
☐ 3 Luis Gonzalez	.15	.07	.02
☐ 4 Pete Harnisch	.15	.07	.02
☐ 5 Jeff Juden	.15	.07	.02
☐ 6 Harold Baines	.15	.07	.02
☐ 7 Kirk Dressendorfer	.15	.07	.02
☐ 8 Dennis Eckersley	.20	.09	.03
☐ 9 Dave Henderson	.10	.05	.01
☐ 10 Dave Stewart	.15	.07	.02
☐ 11 Joe Carter	.25	.11	.03
☐ 12 Juan Guzman	1.50	.65	.19
☐ 13 Dave Stieb	.15	.07	.02
☐ 14 Todd Stottlemyre	.15	.07	.02
☐ 15 Ron Gant	.25	.11	.03
☐ 16 Brian Hunter	.25	.11	.03
☐ 17 Dave Justice	.45	.20	.06
☐ 18 John Smoltz	.25	.11	.03
☐ 19 Mike Stanton	.15	.07	.02
☐ 20 Chris George	.15	.07	.02
☐ 21 Paul Molitor	.20	.09	.03
☐ 22 Omar Olivares	.10	.05	.01
☐ 23 Lee Smith	.15	.07	.02
☐ 24 Ozzie Smith	.25	.11	.03
☐ 25 Todd Zeile	.15	.07	.02
☐ 26 George Bell	.15	.07	.02
☐ 27 Andre Dawson	.25	.11	.03
☐ 28 Shawon Dunston	.15	.07	.02
☐ 29 Mark Grace	.25	.11	.03
☐ 30 Greg Maddux	.25	.11	.03
☐ 31 Dave Smith	.10	.05	.01
☐ 32 Brett Butler	.15	.07	.02
☐ 33 Orel Hershiser	.20	.09	.03
☐ 34 Eric Karros	.60	.25	.08
☐ 35 Ramon Martinez	.15	.07	.02
☐ 36 Jose Offerman	.15	.07	.02
☐ 37 Juan Samuel	.10	.05	.01
☐ 38 Delino DeShields	.25	.11	.03
☐ 39 Marquis Grissom	.25	.11	.03
☐ 40 Tim Wallach	.15	.07	.02
☐ 41 Eric Gunderson	.15	.07	.02
☐ 42 Willie McGee	.15	.07	.02
☐ 43 Dave Righetti	.10	.05	.01
☐ 44 Robby Thompson	.10	.05	.01
☐ 45 Matt Williams	.15	.07	.02
☐ 46 Sandy Alomar Jr.	.15	.07	.02
☐ 47 Reggie Jefferson	.20	.09	.03
☐ 48 Mark Lewis	.20	.09	.03
☐ 49 Robin Ventura	.30	.14	.04
☐ 50 Tino Martinez	.20	.09	.03
☐ 51 Roberto Kelly	.15	.07	.02
☐ 52 Vince Coleman	.15	.07	.02
☐ 53 Dwight Gooden	.20	.09	.03
☐ 54 Todd Hundley	.15	.07	.02
☐ 55 Kevin Maas	.20	.09	.03
☐ 56 Wade Taylor	.15	.07	.02
☐ 57 Bryan Harvey	.20	.09	.03
☐ 58 Leo Gomez	.25	.11	.03
☐ 59 Ben McDonald	.25	.11	.03
☐ 60 Ricky Bones	.20	.09	.03
☐ 61 Tony Gwynn	.35	.16	.04
☐ 62 Benito Santiago	.20	.09	.03
☐ 63 Wes Chamberlain	.15	.07	.02
☐ 64 Tommy Greene	.10	.05	.01
☐ 65 Dale Murphy	.20	.09	.03
☐ 66 Steve Buechele	.10	.05	.01
☐ 67 Doug Drabek	.15	.07	.02
☐ 68 Joe Grahe	.10	.05	.01
☐ 69 Rafael Palmeiro	.20	.09	.03
☐ 70 Wade Boggs	.30	.14	.04
☐ 71 Ellis Burks	.15	.07	.02
☐ 72 Mike Greenwell	.15	.07	.02
☐ 73 Mo Vaughn	.25	.11	.03
☐ 74 Derek Bell	.35	.16	.04
☐ 75 Rob Dibble	.15	.07	.02
☐ 76 Barry Larkin	.20	.09	.03
☐ 77 Jose Rijo	.15	.07	.02
☐ 78 Doug Henry	.20	.09	.03
☐ 79 Chris Sabo	.15	.07	.02
☐ 80 Pedro Guerrero	.15	.07	.02
☐ 81 George Brett	.25	.11	.03
☐ 82 Tom Gordon	.10	.05	.01
☐ 83 Mark Gubicza	.10	.05	.01
☐ 84 Mark Whiten	.15	.07	.02
☐ 85 Brian McRae	.15	.07	.02
☐ 86 Danny Jackson	.10	.05	.01
☐ 87 Milt Cuyler	.15	.07	.02
☐ 88 Travis Fryman	.50	.23	.06
☐ 89 Mickey Tettleton	.15	.07	.02
☐ 90 Alan Trammell	.15	.07	.02
☐ 91 Lou Whitaker	.15	.07	.02
☐ 92 Chili Davis	.15	.07	.02
☐ 93 Scott Erickson	.20	.09	.03
☐ 94 Kent Hrbek	.15	.07	.02
☐ 95 Alex Fernandez	.15	.07	.02
☐ 96 Carlton Fisk	.20	.09	.03
☐ 97 Ramon Garcia	.15	.07	.02
☐ 98 Ozzie Guillen	.15	.07	.02
☐ 99 Tim Raines	.15	.07	.02
☐ 100 Bobby Thigpen	.15	.07	.02
☐ 101 Kirby Puckett	.40	.18	.05
☐ 102 Bernie Williams	.20	.09	.03
☐ 103 Dave Hansen	.15	.07	.02
☐ 104 Kevin Tapani	.15	.07	.02
☐ 105 Don Mattingly	.30	.14	.04
☐ 106 Frank Thomas	1.00	.45	.13
☐ 107 Monty Fariss	.15	.07	.02
☐ 108 Bo Jackson	.25	.11	.03
☐ 109 Jim Abbott	.20	.09	.03
☐ 110 Jose Canseco	.35	.16	.04
☐ 111 Phil Plantier	.30	.14	.04
☐ 112 Brian Williams	.35	.16	.04
☐ 113 Mark Langston	.15	.07	.02
☐ 114 Wilson Alvarez	.15	.07	.02
☐ 115 Roberto Hernandez	.20	.09	.03
☐ 116 Darryl Kile	.15	.07	.02
☐ 117 Ryan Bowen	.15	.07	.02
☐ 118 Rickey Henderson	.30	.14	.04
☐ 119 Mark McGwire	.30	.14	.04
☐ 120 Devon White	.15	.07	.02
☐ 121 Roberto Alomar	.40	.18	.05
☐ 122 Kelly Gruber	.15	.07	.02
☐ 123 Eddie Zosky	.15	.07	.02
☐ 124 Tom Glavine	.30	.14	.04
☐ 125 Kal Daniels	.10	.05	.01
☐ 126 Cal Eldred	.60	.25	.08
☐ 127 Deion Sanders	.35	.16	.04
☐ 128 Robin Yount	.25	.11	.03
☐ 129 Cecil Fielder	.20	.09	.03
☐ 130 Ray Lankford	.25	.11	.03
☐ 131 Ryne Sandberg	.35	.16	.04
☐ 132 Darryl Strawberry	.25	.11	.03
☐ 133 Chris Haney	.15	.07	.02
☐ 134 Dennis Martinez	.15	.07	.02
☐ 135 Bryan Hickerson	.15	.07	.02
☐ 136 Will Clark	.35	.16	.04
☐ 137 Hal Morris	.15	.07	.02
☐ 138 Charles Nagy	.25	.11	.03
☐ 139 Jim Thome	.30	.14	.04
☐ 140 Albert Belle	.20	.09	.03
☐ 141 Reggie Sanders	.50	.23	.06
☐ 142 Scott Cooper	.20	.09	.03
☐ 143 David Cone	.20	.09	.03
☐ 144 Anthony Young	.20	.09	.03
☐ 145 Howard Johnson	.15	.07	.02
☐ 146 Arthur Rhodes	.30	.14	.04
☐ 147 Scott Aldred	.15	.07	.02
☐ 148 Mike Mussina	.90	.40	.11
☐ 149 Fred McGriff	.20	.09	.03

☐ 150 Andy Benes	.15	.07	.02
☐ 151 Ruben Sierra	.25	.11	.03
☐ 152 Len Dykstra	.15	.07	.02
☐ 153 Andy Van Slyke	.15	.07	.02
☐ 154 Orlando Merced	.15	.07	.02
☐ 155 Barry Bonds	.25	.11	.03
☐ 156 John Smiley	.15	.07	.02
☐ 157 Julio Franco	.15	.07	.02
☐ 158 Juan Gonzalez	.40	.18	.05
☐ 159 Ivan Rodriguez	.60	.25	.08
☐ 160 Willie Banks	.20	.09	.03
☐ 161 Eric Davis	.20	.09	.03
☐ 162 Eddie Murray	.20	.09	.03
☐ 163 Dave Fleming	.75	.35	.09
☐ 164 Wally Joyner	.15	.07	.02
☐ 165 Kevin Mitchell	.15	.07	.02
☐ 166 Ed Taubensee	.15	.07	.02
☐ 167 Danny Tartabull	.20	.09	.03
☐ 168 Ken Hill	.10	.05	.01
☐ 169 Willie Randolph	.15	.07	.02
☐ 170 Kevin McReynolds	.15	.07	.02
☐ 171 Gregg Jefferies	.20	.09	.03
☐ 172 Patrick Lennon	.15	.07	.02
☐ 173 Luis Mercedes	.25	.11	.03
☐ 174 Glenn Davis	.15	.07	.02
☐ 175 Bret Saberhagen	.15	.07	.02
☐ 176 Bobby Bonilla	.20	.09	.03
☐ 177 Kenny Lofton	.50	.23	.06
☐ 178 Jose Lind	.10	.05	.01
☐ 179 Royce Clayton	.25	.11	.03
☐ 180 Scott Scudder	.10	.05	.01
☐ 181 Chuck Knoblauch	.30	.14	.04
☐ 182 Terry Pendleton	.20	.09	.03
☐ 183 Nolan Ryan	.60	.25	.08
☐ 184 Rob Maurer	.30	.14	.04
☐ 185 Brian Bohanon	.10	.05	.01
☐ 186 Ken Griffey Jr.	.75	.35	.09
☐ 187 Jeff Bagwell	.35	.16	.04
☐ 188 Steve Avery	.25	.11	.03
☐ 189 Roger Clemens	.35	.16	.04
☐ 190 Cal Ripken	.45	.20	.06
☐ 191 Kim Batiste	.15	.07	.02
☐ 192 Bip Roberts	.15	.07	.02
☐ 193 Greg Swindell	.15	.07	.02
☐ 194 Dave Winfield	.25	.11	.03
☐ 195 Steve Sax	.15	.07	.02
☐ 196 Frank Viola	.15	.07	.02
☐ 197 Mo Sanford	.15	.07	.02
☐ 198 Kyle Abbott	.10	.05	.01
☐ 199 Jack Morris	.15	.07	.02
☐ 200 Andy Ashby	.15	.07	.02

1992 Classic I

The first issue of the 1992 Classic baseball trivia game contains a small gameboard, accessories, 99 player cards with trivia questions on the backs, one "4-in-1" micro player card, and four micro player pieces. The cards measure the standard size (2 1/2" by 3 1/2") and have on the fronts glossy color action photos bordered in white. A red, gray, and purple stripe with the year "1992" traverses the top of the card. In a horizontal format, the backs feature biography, statistics, and five trivia questions, printed on a ghosted image of the 26 major league city skylines. The cards are numbered on the back and basically arranged in alphabetical order.

	MT	EX-MT	VG
COMPLETE SET (100)	9.00	4.00	1.15
COMMON PLAYER (T1-T99)	.10	.05	.01
☐ NNO 4-in-1 Card Barry Bonds Roger Clemens Steve Avery Nolan Ryan	.50	.23	.06
☐ T1 Jim Abbott	.30	.14	.04
☐ T2 Kyle Abbott	.10	.05	.01
☐ T3 Scott Aldred	.10	.05	.01
☐ T4 Roberto Alomar	.35	.16	.04
☐ T5 Wilson Alvarez	.15	.07	.02
☐ T6 Andy Ashby	.15	.07	.02
☐ T7 Steve Avery	.25	.11	.03
☐ T8 Jeff Bagwell	.40	.18	.05
☐ T9 Bret Barberie	.20	.09	.03
☐ T10 Kim Batiste	.15	.07	.02
☐ T11 Derek Bell	.25	.11	.03
☐ T12 Jay Bell	.10	.05	.01
☐ T13 Albert Belle	.20	.09	.03
☐ T14 Andy Benes	.15	.07	.02
☐ T15 Sean Berry	.15	.07	.02
☐ T16 Barry Bonds	.30	.14	.04
☐ T17 Ryan Bowen	.20	.09	.03
☐ T18 Trifecta Alejandro Pena Mark Wohlers Kent Mercker	.10	.05	.01
☐ T19 Scott Brosius	.15	.07	.02
☐ T20 Jay Buhner	.15	.07	.02
☐ T21 David Burba	.15	.07	.02
☐ T22 Jose Canseco	.35	.16	.04
☐ T23 Andujar Cedeno	.20	.09	.03
☐ T24 Will Clark	.40	.18	.05
☐ T25 Royce Clayton	.20	.09	.03
☐ T26 Roger Clemens	.45	.20	.06
☐ T27 David Cone	.20	.09	.03
☐ T28 Scott Cooper	.20	.09	.03
☐ T29 Chris Cron	.15	.07	.02
☐ T30 Len Dykstra	.15	.07	.02
☐ T31 Cal Eldred	.35	.16	.04
☐ T32 Hector Fajardo	.15	.07	.02
☐ T33 Cecil Fielder	.25	.11	.03
☐ T34 Dave Fleming	.30	.14	.04
☐ T35 Steve Foster	.15	.07	.02
☐ T36 Julio Franco	.15	.07	.02
☐ T37 Carlos Garcia	.25	.11	.03
☐ T38 Tom Glavine	.25	.11	.03
☐ T39 Tom Goodwin	.20	.09	.03
☐ T40 Ken Griffey Jr.	.75	.35	.09
☐ T41 Chris Haney	.15	.07	.02
☐ T42 Bryan Harvey	.15	.07	.02
☐ T43 Rickey Henderson 939	.35	.16	.04
☐ T44 Carlos Hernandez	.15	.07	.02
☐ T45 Roberto Hernandez	.20	.09	.03
☐ T46 Brook Jacoby	.10	.05	.01
☐ T47 Howard Johnson	.20	.09	.03
☐ T48 Pat Kelly	.15	.07	.02
☐ T49 Darryl Kile	.15	.07	.02
☐ T50 Chuck Knoblauch	.25	.11	.03
☐ T51 Ray Lankford	.25	.11	.03
☐ T52 Mark Leiter	.15	.07	.02
☐ T53 Darren Lewis	.15	.07	.02
☐ T54 Scott Livingstone	.10	.05	.01
☐ T55 Shane Mack	.15	.07	.02
☐ T56 Chito Martinez	.20	.09	.03
☐ T57 Dennis Martinez (The Perfect Game)	.10	.05	.01
☐ T58 Don Mattingly	.40	.18	.05
☐ T59 Paul McClellan	.15	.07	.02
☐ T60 Chuck McElroy	.15	.07	.02
☐ T61 Fred McGriff	.20	.09	.03
☐ T62 Orlando Merced	.20	.09	.03
☐ T63 Luis Mercedes	.25	.11	.03
☐ T64 Kevin Mitchell	.20	.09	.03
☐ T65 Hal Morris	.15	.07	.02
☐ T66 Jack Morris	.15	.07	.02
☐ T67 Mike Mussina	.35	.16	.04
☐ T68 Denny Neagle	.20	.09	.03
☐ T69 Tom Pagnozzi	.10	.05	.01
☐ T70 Terry Pendleton	.20	.09	.03
☐ T71 Phil Plantier	.25	.11	.03
☐ T72 Kirby Puckett	.35	.16	.04
☐ T73 Carlos Quintana	.10	.05	.01
☐ T74 Willie Randolph	.10	.05	.01
☐ T75 Arthur Rhodes	.25	.11	.03
☐ T76 Cal Ripken	.45	.20	.06

☐ T77 Ivan Rodriguez	.40	.18	.05
☐ T78 Nolan Ryan	.75	.35	.09
☐ T79 Ryne Sandberg	.45	.20	.06
☐ T80 Deion Sanders (Deion Drops In)	.25	.11	.03
☐ T81 Reggie Sanders	.25	.11	.03
☐ T82 Mo Sanford	.15	.07	.02
☐ T83 Terry Shumpert	.10	.05	.01
☐ T84 Tim Spehr	.15	.07	.02
☐ T85 Lee Stevens	.15	.07	.02
☐ T86 Darryl Strawberry	.30	.14	.04
☐ T87 Kevin Tapani	.15	.07	.02
☐ T88 Danny Tartabull	.20	.09	.03
☐ T89 Frank Thomas	.75	.35	.09
☐ T90 Jim Thome	.30	.14	.04
☐ T91 Todd Van Poppel	.40	.18	.05
☐ T92 Andy Van Slyke	.20	.09	.03
☐ T93 John Wehner	.15	.07	.02
☐ T94 John Wetteland	.15	.07	.02
☐ T95 Devon White	.15	.07	.02
☐ T96 Brian Williams	.20	.09	.03
☐ T97 Mark Wohlers	.20	.09	.03
☐ T98 Robin Yount	.30	.14	.04
☐ T99 Eddie Zosky	.15	.07	.02

1992 Classic II

The 1992 Series II baseball trivia board game features 99 new player trivia cards (each measuring the standard size, 2 1/2" by 3 1/2"), one "4-in-1" micro player card, a gameboard, and a spinner. The standard-size (2 1/2" by 3 1/2") cards display color action player photos on the fronts. The side borders are either red or blue, shading to white as they merge with the top and bottom borders. The player's name appears in a blue stripe at the bottom of the picture. In a horizontal format, the backs have biography, statistics (1991 and career), five trivia questions, and a color drawing of the team's uniform. The cards are numbered on the back. According to Classic, the production run was 175,000 games.

	MT	EX-MT	VG
COMPLETE SET (100)	9.00	4.00	1.15
COMMON PLAYER (T1-T99)	.10	.05	.01
☐ NNO 4-in-1 Card Ryne Sandberg Mike Mussina Reggie Sanders Jose Canseco	.50	.23	.06
☐ T1 Jim Abbott	.20	.09	.03
☐ T2 Jeff Bagwell	.35	.16	.04
☐ T3 Jose Canseco	.35	.16	.04
☐ T4 Julio Valera	.10	.05	.01
☐ T5 Scott Brosius	.15	.07	.02
☐ T6 Mark Langston	.10	.05	.01
☐ T7 Andy Stankiewicz	.25	.11	.03
☐ T8 Gary DiSarcina	.10	.05	.01
☐ T9 Pete Harnisch	.15	.07	.02
☐ T10 Mark McGwire	.35	.16	.04
☐ T11 Ricky Bones	.15	.07	.02
☐ T12 Steve Avery	.25	.11	.03
☐ T13 Deion Sanders	.25	.11	.03
☐ T14 Mike Mussina	.75	.35	.09
☐ T15 Dave Justice	.30	.14	.04
☐ T16 Pat Hentgen	.15	.07	.02
☐ T17 Tom Glavine	.25	.11	.03
☐ T18 Juan Guzman	.90	.40	.11
☐ T19 Ron Gant	.20	.09	.03
☐ T20 Kelly Gruber	.15	.07	.02
☐ T21 Eric Karros	.50	.23	.06
☐ T22 Derrick May	.15	.07	.02
☐ T23 Dave Hansen	.15	.07	.02
☐ T24 Andre Dawson	.20	.09	.03
☐ T25 Eric Davis	.15	.07	.02
☐ T26 Ozzie Smith	.20	.09	.03
☐ T27 Sammy Sosa	.15	.07	.02
☐ T28 Lee Smith	.15	.07	.02
☐ T29 Ryne Sandberg	.35	.16	.04
☐ T30 Robin Yount	.20	.09	.03
☐ T31 Matt Williams	.15	.07	.02
☐ T32 John Vander Wal	.15	.07	.02
☐ T33 Bill Swift	.10	.05	.01
☐ T34 Delino DeShields	.20	.09	.03
☐ T35 Royce Clayton	.25	.11	.03
☐ T36 Moises Alou	.15	.07	.02
☐ T37 Will Clark	.30	.14	.04
☐ T38 Darryl Strawberry	.25	.11	.03
☐ T39 Larry Walker	.25	.11	.03
☐ T40 Ramon Martinez	.15	.07	.02
☐ T41 Howard Johnson	.15	.07	.02
☐ T42 Tino Martinez	.15	.07	.02
☐ T43 Dwight Gooden	.15	.07	.02
☐ T44 Ken Griffey Jr.	.75	.35	.09
☐ T45 David Cone	.15	.07	.02
☐ T46 Kenny Lofton	.35	.16	.04
☐ T47 Bobby Bonilla	.15	.07	.02
☐ T48 Carlos Baerga	.25	.11	.03
☐ T49 Don Mattingly	.25	.11	.03
☐ T50 Sandy Alomar Jr.	.15	.07	.02
☐ T51 Lenny Dykstra	.15	.07	.02
☐ T52 Tony Gwynn	.25	.11	.03
☐ T53 Felix Jose	.15	.07	.02
☐ T54 Rick Sutcliffe	.15	.07	.02
☐ T55 Wes Chamberlain	.15	.07	.02
☐ T56 Cal Ripken	.40	.18	.05
☐ T57 Kyle Abbott	.10	.05	.01
☐ T58 Leo Gomez	.20	.09	.03
☐ T59 Gary Sheffield	.45	.20	.06
☐ T60 Anthony Young	.15	.07	.02
☐ T61 Roger Clemens	.35	.16	.04
☐ T62 Rafael Palmeiro	.20	.09	.03
☐ T63 Wade Boggs	.25	.11	.03
☐ T64 Andy Van Slyke	.15	.07	.02
☐ T65 Ruben Sierra	.25	.11	.03
☐ T66 Denny Neagle	.15	.07	.02
☐ T67 Nolan Ryan	.50	.23	.06
☐ T68 Doug Drabek	.15	.07	.02
☐ T69 Ivan Rodriguez	.35	.16	.04
☐ T70 Barry Bonds	.25	.11	.03
☐ T71 Chuck Knoblauch	.25	.11	.03
☐ T72 Reggie Sanders	.35	.16	.04
☐ T73 Cecil Fielder	.20	.09	.03
☐ T74 Barry Larkin	.20	.09	.03
☐ T75 Scott Aldred	.10	.05	.01
☐ T76 Rob Dibble	.15	.07	.02
☐ T77 Brian McRae	.15	.07	.02
☐ T78 Tim Belcher	.15	.07	.02
☐ T79 George Brett	.20	.09	.03
☐ T80 Frank Viola	.15	.07	.02
☐ T81 Roberto Kelly	.15	.07	.02
☐ T82 Jack McDowell	.15	.07	.02
☐ T83 Mel Hall	.15	.07	.02
☐ T84 Esteban Beltre	.15	.07	.02
☐ T85 Robin Ventura	.25	.11	.03
☐ T86 George Bell	.15	.07	.02
☐ T87 Frank Thomas	1.00	.45	.13
☐ T88 John Smiley	.15	.07	.02
☐ T89 Bobby Thigpen	.15	.07	.02
☐ T90 Kirby Puckett	.35	.16	.04
☐ T91 Kevin Mitchell	.15	.07	.02
☐ T92 Peter Hoy	.15	.07	.02
☐ T93 Russ Springer	.20	.09	.03
☐ T94 Donovan Osborne	.35	.16	.04
☐ T95 Dave Silvestri	.15	.07	.02
☐ T96 Chad Curtis	.40	.18	.05
☐ T97 Pat Mahomes	.25	.11	.03
☐ T98 Danny Tartabull	.15	.07	.02
☐ T99 John Doherty	.15	.07	.02

1992 Classic Draft Picks Previews

These five baseball draft preview cards were inserted into Classic basketball draft pick foil packs and measure the standard size (2 1/2" by 3 1/2"). According to the backs, only 11,200 of each card were produced. The fronts display glossy color action player photos with white borders. The player's name appears in a teal stripe beneath the picture. This stripe intersects the Classic logo at the lower left corner, and the word "Preview" wraps around the top of the logo. The brightly colored backs display a drawing of a batter clad in a red-and-purple uniform with a stadium in the background. This picture is accented by two series of short purple diagonal stripes on the left and right. The picture is overprinted with silver foil lettering. The cards are numbered on the back.

	MT	EX-MT	VG
COMPLETE SET (5)	45.00	20.00	5.75
COMMON PLAYER (1-5)	7.00	3.10	.85
☐ 1 Phil Nevin	15.00	6.75	1.90
☐ 2 Paul Shuey	7.00	3.10	.85
☐ 3 B.J. Wallace	8.00	3.60	1.00
☐ 4 Jeffrey Hammonds	15.00	6.75	1.90
☐ 5 Chad Mottola	9.00	4.00	1.15

1992 Classic Draft Picks Promos

These three standard-size (2 1/2" by 3 1/2") cards were sealed in a cello pack and show the design of the 1992 Classic Draft Picks issues. All three cards have color player photos on the fronts; card numbers 1-2 have white borders while card number 3 has a silver foil border. The player's name appears in a teal stripe beneath the picture with the Classic logo at the lower left corner. On a forest green background, the backs have a second color photo, biography, and player profile. The backs of card numbers 1-2 are glossy while that of number 3 is not. The cards are marked "For Promotional Purposes Only" on the back. The cards are unnumbered and checklisted below in alphabetical order.

	MT	EX-MT	VG
COMPLETE SET (3)	20.00	9.00	2.50
COMMON PLAYER (1-3)	6.00	2.70	.75
☐ 1 Jeffrey Hammonds UER (Misspelled Jeffery on card front)	6.00	2.70	.75
☐ 2 Phil Nevin	6.00	2.70	.75
☐ 3 Brien Taylor	9.00	4.00	1.15

1992 Classic Draft Picks

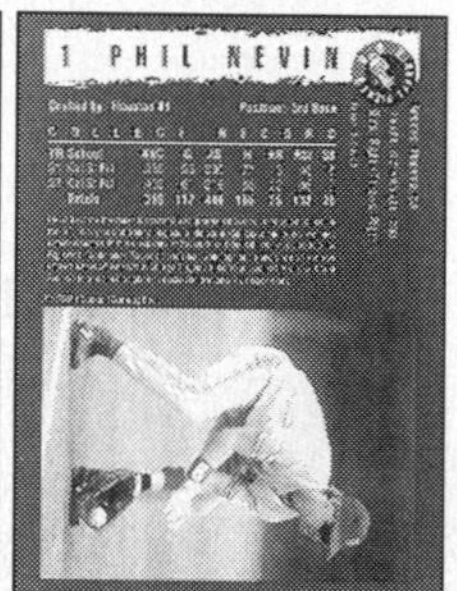

The 1992 Classic Draft Picks set consists of 125 standard-size (2 1/2" by 3 1/2") cards. The set was sold in 16-card jumbo packs only to the hobby and periodical industries. The production run was reported to be 5,000 individually number cases, and no factory sets were produced. The fronts display color action player photos bordered in white. The player's name appears in a forest green stripe beneath the picture, and his position is printed in a small black bar. On a forest green background with white lettering, the backs present 1991 and 1992 college (and/or high school) statistics, player profile, and biography on the upper portion and a second color player photo on the lower portion. A ten-card flashback subset (cards 86-95) features Mike Mussina, Brien Taylor, and Mike Kelly. The cards are numbered on the back.

	MT	EX-MT	VG
COMPLETE SET (125)	11.00	4.90	1.40
COMMON PLAYER (1-125)	.05	.02	.01
☐ 1 Phil Nevin	1.75	.80	.22
☐ 2 Paul Shuey	.50	.23	.06
☐ 3 B.J. Wallace	.75	.35	.09
☐ 4 Jeffrey Hammonds	1.75	.80	.22
☐ 5 Chad Mottola	.75	.35	.09
☐ 6 Derek Jeter	.60	.25	.08
☐ 7 Michael Tucker	1.25	.55	.16
☐ 8 Derek Wallace	.50	.23	.06
☐ 9 Kenny Felder	.40	.18	.05
☐ 10 Chad McConnell	.50	.23	.06
☐ 11 Sean Lowe	.35	.16	.04
☐ 12 Ricky Greene	.35	.16	.04
☐ 13 Chris Roberts	.50	.23	.06
☐ 14 Shannon Stewart	.25	.11	.03
☐ 15 Benji Grigsby	.30	.14	.04
☐ 16 Jamie Arnold	.25	.11	.03
☐ 17 Rick Helling	.40	.18	.05
☐ 18 Jason Kendall	.50	.23	.06
☐ 19 Todd Steverson	.40	.18	.05
☐ 20 Dan Serafini	.20	.09	.03
☐ 21 Jeff Schmidt	.25	.11	.03
☐ 22 Sherard Clinkscales	.25	.11	.03
☐ 23 Ryan Luzinski	.50	.23	.06
☐ 24 Shon Walker	.25	.11	.03
☐ 25 Brandon Cromer	.25	.11	.03
☐ 26 Dave Landaker	.20	.09	.03
☐ 27 Michael Mathews	.25	.11	.03
☐ 28 Brian Sackinsky	.20	.09	.03

☐ 29 Jon Lieber	.20	.09	.03
☐ 30 Jim Rosenbohm	.20	.09	.03
☐ 31 DeShawn Warren	.25	.11	.03
☐ 32 Danny Clyburn	.25	.11	.03
☐ 33 Chris Smith	.25	.11	.03
☐ 34 Dwain Bostic	.20	.09	.03
☐ 35 Bobby Hughes	.25	.11	.03
☐ 36 Rick Magdellano	.20	.09	.03
☐ 37 Bob Wolcott	.20	.09	.03
☐ 38 Mike Gulan	.20	.09	.03
☐ 39 Yuri Sanchez	.20	.09	.03
☐ 40 Tony Sheffield	.30	.14	.04
☐ 41 Dan Melendez	.20	.09	.03
☐ 42 Jason Giambi	.40	.18	.05
☐ 43 Ritchie Moody	.20	.09	.03
☐ 44 Trey Beamon	.30	.14	.04
☐ 45 Tim Crabtree	.25	.11	.03
☐ 46 Chad Roper	.30	.14	.04
☐ 47 Mark Thompson	.25	.11	.03
☐ 48 Marquis Riley	.25	.11	.03
☐ 49 Tom Knauss	.20	.09	.03
☐ 50 Chris Holt	.15	.07	.02
☐ 51 Jonathan Nunnally	.20	.09	.03
☐ 52 Everett Stull	.10	.05	.01
☐ 53 Billy Owens	.20	.09	.03
☐ 54 Todd Etler	.15	.07	.02
☐ 55 Benji Simonton	.20	.09	.03
☐ 56 Dwight Maness	.10	.05	.01
☐ 57 Chris Eddy	.15	.07	.02
☐ 58 Brant Brown	.10	.05	.01
☐ 59 Trevor Humphrey	.15	.07	.02
☐ 60 Chris Widger	.15	.07	.02
☐ 61 Steve Montgomery	.15	.07	.02
☐ 62 Chris Gomez	.10	.05	.01
☐ 63 Jared Baker	.15	.07	.02
☐ 64 Doug Hecker	.15	.07	.02
☐ 65 David Spykstra	.10	.05	.01
☐ 66 Scott Miller	.10	.05	.01
☐ 67 Carey Paige	.15	.07	.02
☐ 68 Dave Manning	.15	.07	.02
☐ 69 James Keith	.15	.07	.02
☐ 70 Levon Largusa	.10	.05	.01
☐ 71 Roger Bailey	.25	.11	.03
☐ 72 Rich Ireland	.15	.07	.02
☐ 73 Matt Williams	.05	.02	.01
☐ 74 Scott Gentile	.05	.02	.01
☐ 75 Hut Smith	.05	.02	.01
☐ 76 Rodney Henderson	.25	.11	.03
☐ 77 Mike Buddie	.05	.02	.01
☐ 78 Stephen Lyons	.05	.02	.01
☐ 79 John Burke	.50	.23	.06
☐ 80 Jim Pittsley	.40	.18	.05
☐ 81 Donnie Leshnock	.20	.09	.03
☐ 82 Cory Pearson	.05	.02	.01
☐ 83 Kurt Ehmann	.05	.02	.01
☐ 84 Bobby Bonds Jr.	.25	.11	.03
☐ 85 Steven Cox	.05	.02	.01
☐ 86 Brien Taylor FLB	.50	.23	.06
☐ 87 Mike Kelly FLB	.25	.11	.03
☐ 88 David McCarty FLB	.25	.11	.03
☐ 89 Dmitri Young FLB	.20	.09	.03
☐ 90 Joey Hamilton FLB	.10	.05	.01
☐ 91 Mark Smith FLB	.15	.07	.02
☐ 92 Doug Glanville FLB	.10	.05	.01
☐ 93 Mike Lieberthal FLB	.10	.05	.01
☐ 94 Joe Vitiello FLB	.10	.05	.01
☐ 95 Mike Mussina FLB	.40	.18	.05
☐ 96 Derek Hacopian	.05	.02	.01
☐ 97 Ted Corbin	.05	.02	.01
☐ 98 Carlton Fleming	.05	.02	.01
☐ 99 Aaron Rounsifer	.05	.02	.01
☐ 100 Chad Fox	.05	.02	.01
☐ 101 Chris Sheff	.05	.02	.01
☐ 102 Ben Jones	.05	.02	.01
☐ 103 David Post	.05	.02	.01
☐ 104 Jonnie Gendron	.05	.02	.01
☐ 105 Bob Juday	.05	.02	.01
☐ 106 David Becker	.05	.02	.01
☐ 107 Brandon Pico	.05	.02	.01
☐ 108 Tom Evans	.05	.02	.01
☐ 109 Jeff Faino	.05	.02	.01
☐ 110 Shawn Wills	.05	.02	.01
☐ 111 Derrick Cantrell	.05	.02	.01
☐ 112 Steve Rodriguez	.20	.09	.03
☐ 113 Ray Suplee	.05	.02	.01
☐ 114 Pat Leahy	.05	.02	.01
☐ 115 Matt Luke	.05	.02	.01
☐ 116 Jon McMullen	.05	.02	.01
☐ 117 Preston Wilson	.50	.23	.06
☐ 118 Gus Gandarillas	.10	.05	.01
☐ 119 Pete Janicki	.50	.23	.06
☐ 120 Byron Mathews	.15	.07	.02
☐ 121 Eric Owens	.05	.02	.01
☐ 122 John Lynch	.25	.11	.03
☐ 123 Mike Hickey	.05	.02	.01
☐ 124 Checklist 1	.05	.02	.01
☐ 125 Checklist 2	.05	.02	.01

1992 Classic Draft Picks Foil Bonus

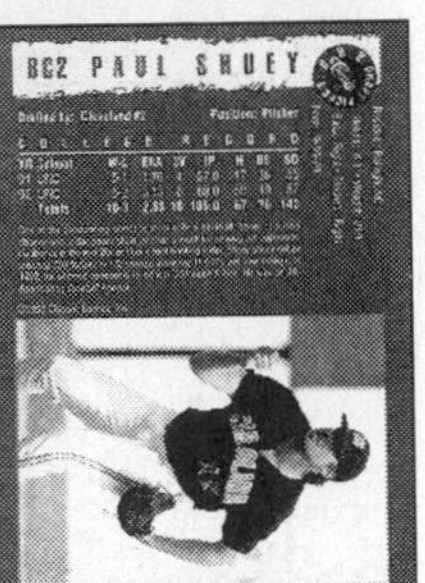

One of these twenty foil bonus cards was inserted in each 1992 Classic Draft Picks jumbo pack. The cards measure the standard size (2 1/2" by 3 1/2"). The photos and text of these bonus cards are identical to the regular issues, except that a silver foil coating has created a metallic sheen on the front, and the forest green backs have a faded look. A three-card flashback subset (cards BC18-BC20) features Brien Taylor, Mike Kelly, and Mike Mussina. The cards are numbered on the back.

	MT	EX-MT	VG
COMPLETE SET (20)	18.00	8.00	2.30
COMMON PLAYER (1-20)	.50	.23	.06

☐ BC1 Phil Nevin	5.00	2.30	.60
☐ BC2 Paul Shuey	1.00	.45	.13
☐ BC3 B.J. Wallace	1.50	.65	.19
☐ BC4 Jeffrey Hammonds	3.50	1.55	.45
☐ BC5 Chad Mottola	1.50	.65	.19
☐ BC6 Derek Jeter	1.25	.55	.16
☐ BC7 Michael Tucker	2.50	1.15	.30
☐ BC8 Derek Wallace	1.00	.45	.13
☐ BC9 Kenny Felder	.75	.35	.09
☐ BC10 Chad McConnell	1.00	.45	.13
☐ BC11 Sean Lowe	.75	.35	.09
☐ BC12 Chris Roberts	1.00	.45	.13
☐ BC13 Shannon Stewart	.60	.25	.08
☐ BC14 Benji Grisby	.60	.25	.08
☐ BC15 Jamie Arnold	.60	.25	.08
☐ BC16 Ryan Luzinski	1.00	.45	.13
☐ BC17 Bobby Bonds Jr.	.50	.23	.06
☐ BC18 Brien Taylor (Flashback)	2.50	1.15	.30
☐ BC19 Mike Kelly (Flashback)	1.25	.55	.16
☐ BC20 Mike Mussina (Flashback)	2.00	.90	.25

1988 CMC Don Mattingly

This 20-card set featuring Don Mattingly was distributed as part of a Collecting Kit produced by Collector's Marketing Corp. The cards themselves measure approximately 2 1/2" by 3 1/2" and have a light blue border. The card backs describe some aspect of Mattingly's career. Also in the kit were plastic sheets, a small album, a record, a booklet, and information on how to join Don's Fan Club. The set price below is for the whole kit as well as the cards.

	MT	EX-MT	VG
COMPLETE SET (20)	9.00	4.00	1.15
COMMON PLAYER (1-20)	.75	.35	.09

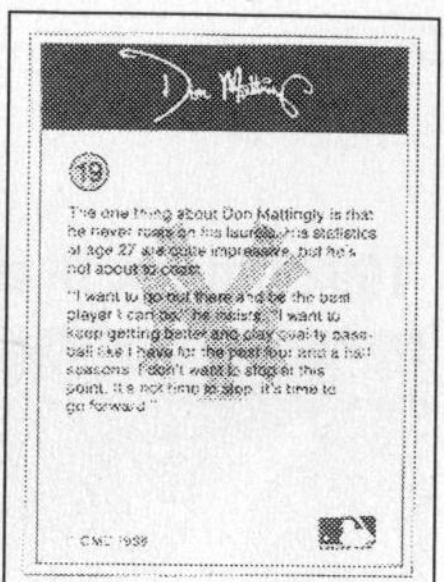

☐ 1 Game Face	.75	.35	.09
☐ 2 Columbus Clippers	.75	.35	.09
☐ 3 1983 Spring Camp	.75	.35	.09
☐ 4 AL Batting Crown	.75	.35	.09
☐ 5 1981 All-Star Outfielder	.75	.35	.09
☐ 6 The Batting Tee	.75	.35	.09
☐ 7 AL MVP Honors	.75	.35	.09
☐ 8 Gold Glove Winner	.75	.35	.09
☐ 9 Batting Practice	.75	.35	.09
☐ 10 Yankee Records	.75	.35	.09
☐ 11 Baseball On His Mind	.75	.35	.09
☐ 12 Big Home Runs	.75	.35	.09
☐ 13 Hustle and Determination	.75	.35	.09
☐ 14 Delivering In The Clutch	.75	.35	.09
☐ 15 A Slick First Baseman	.75	.35	.09
☐ 16 Keep Playing Hard	.75	.35	.09
☐ 17 Mattingly's Eight-Game Streak	.75	.35	.09
☐ 18 The Textbook Swing	.75	.35	.09
☐ 19 It's Time To Go Forward	.75	.35	.09
☐ 20 Surehanded First Baseman	.75	.35	.09

1989 CMC Jose Canseco

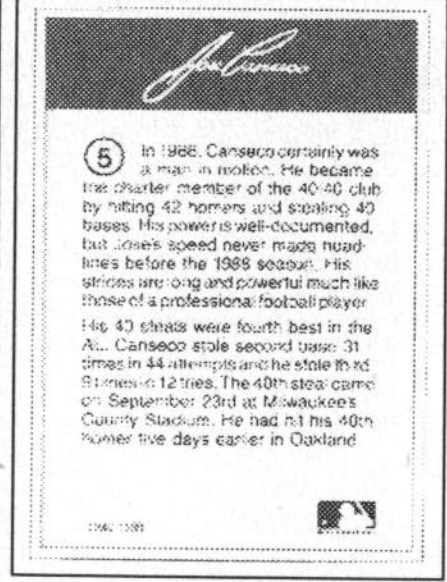

The 1989 CMC Jose Canseco Collector's Kit set contains 20 numbered standard-size (2 1/2" by 3 1/2") cards. The front borders are Oakland A's green and yellow. The backs are green and white, and feature narratives and facsimile signatures. The cards were distributed as a set in a box along with an album and a booklet as well as other elements by CMC, Collectors Marketing Corporation. Since all the cards in the set feature the same player, cards in the checklist below are differentiated by some other characteristic of the particular card.

	MT	EX-MT	VG
COMPLETE SET (20)	9.00	4.00	1.15
COMMON PLAYER (1-20)	.75	.35	.09
☐ 1 Looking up with yellow jersey	.75	.35	.09
☐ 2 Posing with bat from the waist up	.75	.35	.09
☐ 3 Portrait with green cap	.75	.35	.09
☐ 4 Follow-through on swing (catcher visible)	.75	.35	.09
☐ 5 Running the bases	.75	.35	.09
☐ 6 Warming up with bat over head	.75	.35	.09
☐ 7 Sitting in dugout holding bat	.75	.35	.09
☐ 8 Standing in outfield with sunglasses up	.75	.35	.09
☐ 9 Batting stance ready for pitch	.75	.35	.09
☐ 10 Taking a lead off first base	.75	.35	.09
☐ 11 Looking to the side (elephant logo on left shoulder)	.75	.35	.09
☐ 12 Bashing with Mark McGwire after homer	.75	.35	.09
☐ 13 Looking up witrh green batting glove in foreground	.75	.35	.09
☐ 14 Stretching to catch fly ball	.75	.35	.09
☐ 15 Follow through on swing (no catcher visible)	.75	.35	.09
☐ 16 Standing at plate glaring at pitcher	.75	.35	.09
☐ 17 Follow through on swing (stain on pants)	.75	.35	.09
☐ 18 Signing autographs for the fans at the ballpark	.75	.35	.09
☐ 19 Waiting at first base with hands on hips	.75	.35	.09
☐ 20 Admiring his hit at plate with tongue out	.75	.35	.09

1989 CMC Mickey Mantle

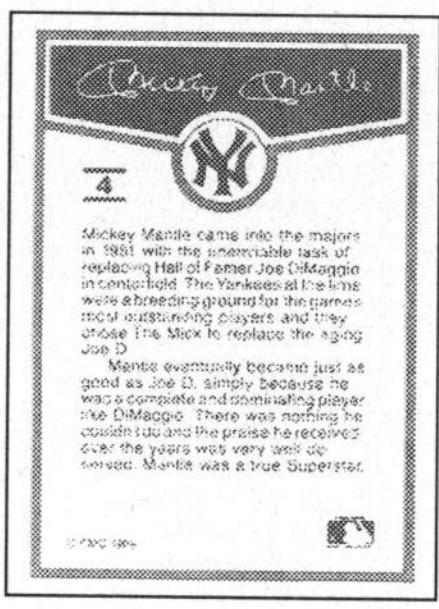

The 1989 CMC Mickey Mantle Collector's Kit set contains 20 numbered standard-size (2 1/2" by 3 1/2") cards. The fronts and backs are white, red and navy. The backs feature narratives and facsimile signatures. The cards were distributed as a set in a box along with an album and a booklet as well as other elements by CMC, Collectors Marketing Corporation. Since all the cards in the set feature the same player, cards in the checklist below are differentiated by some other characteristic of the particular card. Some of the cards in this set are sepia-tone photos as the action predates the widespread use of color film.

	MT	EX-MT	VG
COMPLETE SET (20)	12.00	5.50	1.50
COMMON PLAYER (1-20)	1.00	.45	.13
☐ 1 Standing with bat on left shoulder	1.00	.45	.13
☐ 2 Batting stance lefty (back to camera)	1.00	.45	.13

☐ 3 Looking intense in the field (waist up)	1.00	.45	.13
☐ 4 Follow through on lefty swing	1.00	.45	.13
☐ 5 Half smile (head and shoulders)	1.00	.45	.13
☐ 6 Posing with bat alongside Roger Maris	1.00	.45	.13
☐ 7 Holding up his 1962 contract (wearing suit and tie)	1.00	.45	.13
☐ 8 Receiving 1962 MVP from Joe Cronin	1.00	.45	.13
☐ 9 Batting stance lefty (catcher's glove in picture)	1.00	.45	.13
☐ 10 Posing with Roger Maris and Yogi Berra	1.00	.45	.13
☐ 11 Looking away with eyes closed, holding bat	1.00	.45	.13
☐ 12 Swinging righty at pitch	1.00	.45	.13
☐ 13 Starting to run to first base	1.00	.45	.13
☐ 14 Mickey Mantle Day, September 18, 1965	1.00	.45	.13
☐ 15 Shaking hands with Joe DiMaggio at Yankee Stadium	1.00	.45	.13
☐ 16 Giving speech at Yankee Stadium	1.00	.45	.13
☐ 17 Backing away from plate after pitch	1.00	.45	.13
☐ 18 Getting ready at plate with bat in right hand	1.00	.45	.13
☐ 19 Holding bat in both hands parallel to ground	1.00	.45	.13
☐ 20 Waiting for pitch with bat on shoulder (lefty)	1.00	.45	.13

1989 CMC Babe Ruth

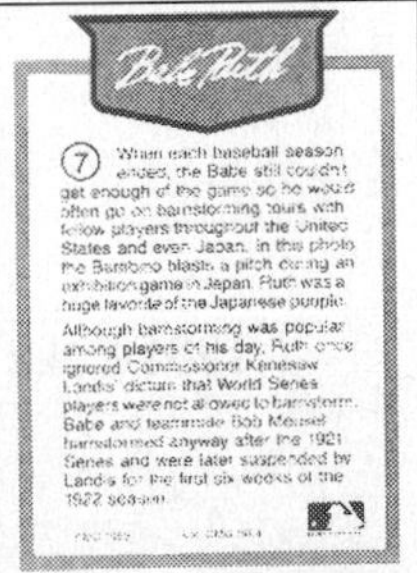

The 1989 CMC Babe Ruth Collector's Kit set contains 20 numbered standard-size (2 1/2" by 3 1/2") cards. The front borders are white, red and navy. The backs are blue and white, and feature narratives and facsimile signatures. The cards were distributed as a set in a box along with an album and a booklet as well as other elements by CMC, Collectors Marketing Corporation. Since all the cards in the set feature the same player, cards in the checklist below are differentiated by some other characteristic of the particular card. All of the cards in this set are sepia-tone photos as the action predates the widespread use of color film.

	MT	EX-MT	VG
COMPLETE SET (20)	9.00	4.00	1.15
COMMON PLAYER (1-20)	.75	.35	.09
☐ 1 Smiling holding three bats	.75	.35	.09
☐ 2 Posing in Red Sox uniform (head and shoulders)	.75	.35	.09
☐ 3 Looking up (waist up)	.75	.35	.09
☐ 4 Holding nine bats in front of him	.75	.35	.09
☐ 5 Golfing swing follow through	.75	.35	.09
☐ 6 Oldtimers' game photo holding two bats	.75	.35	.09
☐ 7 Follow through looking up (in Japan)	.75	.35	.09
☐ 8 Looking dapper in fur coat	.75	.35	.09
☐ 9 Babe Ruth Day, April 27, 1947	.75	.35	.09
☐ 10 Bust photo with no background	.75	.35	.09
☐ 11 Practicing swing (photo from knees up)	.75	.35	.09
☐ 12 Watching his hit after swing (knees up)	.75	.35	.09
☐ 13 Follow through on swing, starting to first base	.75	.35	.09
☐ 14 Practice swing with photographers in background	.75	.35	.09
☐ 15 Posing with Jacob Ruppert	.75	.35	.09
☐ 16 Follow through from waist up	.75	.35	.09
☐ 17 Shaking hands with Miller Huggins	.75	.35	.09
☐ 18 Signing autographs for the kids	.75	.35	.09
☐ 19 Sitting wearing Braves uniform	.75	.35	.09
☐ 20 Hall of Fame Plaque	.75	.35	.09

1981 Coke Team Sets

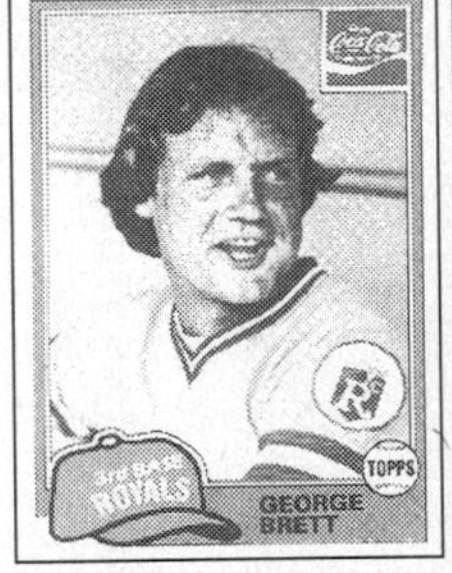

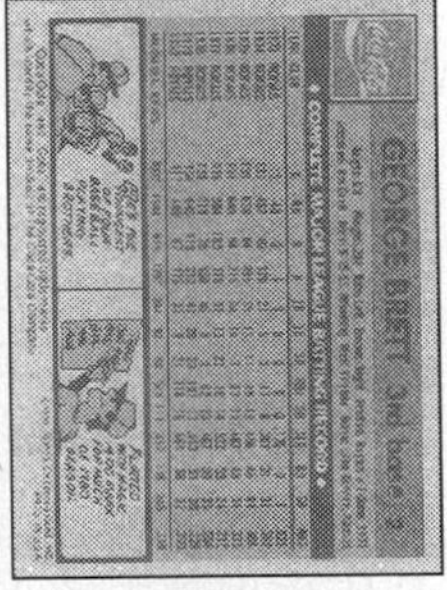

The cards in this 132-card set measure 2 1/2" by 3 1/2". In 1981, Topps produced 11 sets of 12 cards each for the Coca-Cola Company. Each set features 11 star players for a particular team plus an advertising card with the team name on the front. Although the cards are numbered in the upper right corner of the back from 1 to 11, they are re-numbered below within team, i.e., Boston Red Sox (1-12), Chicago Cubs (13-24), Chicago White Sox (25-36), Cincinnati Reds (37-48), Detroit Tigers (49-60), Houston Astros (61-72), Kansas City Royals (73-84), New York Mets (85-96), Philadelphia Phillies (97-108), Pittsburgh Pirates (109-120), and St. Louis Cardinals (121-132). Within each team the player actually numbered number 1 (on the card back) is the first player below and the player numbered number 11 is the last in that team's list. These player cards are quite similar to the 1981 Topps issue but feature a Coca-Cola logo on both the front and the back. The advertising card for each team features, on its back, an offer for obtaining an uncut sheet of 1981 Topps cards. These promotional cards were actually issued by Coke in only a few of the cities, and most of these cards have reached collectors hands through dealers who have purchased the cards through suppliers.

	NRMT-MT	EXC	G-VG
COMPLETE SET (132)	35.00	16.00	4.40
COMMON PLAYER (1-132)	.10	.05	.01
COMMON AD CARD	.05	.02	.01
☐ 1 Tom Burgmeier	.10	.05	.01
☐ 2 Dennis Eckersley	2.00	.90	.25
☐ 3 Dwight Evans	.75	.35	.09
☐ 4 Bob Stanley	.15	.07	.02
☐ 5 Glenn Hoffman	.10	.05	.01
☐ 6 Carney Lansford	.50	.23	.06
☐ 7 Frank Tanana	.25	.11	.03
☐ 8 Tony Perez	1.00	.45	.13
☐ 9 Jim Rice	1.00	.45	.13
☐ 10 Dave Stapleton	.10	.05	.01
☐ 11 Carl Yastrzemski	3.50	1.55	.45
☐ 12 Red Sox Ad Card (Unnumbered)	.05	.02	.01
☐ 13 Tim Blackwell	.10	.05	.01
☐ 14 Bill Buckner	.20	.09	.03
☐ 15 Ivan DeJesus	.10	.05	.01
☐ 16 Leon Durham	.15	.07	.02
☐ 17 Steve Henderson	.10	.05	.01
☐ 18 Mike Krukow	.15	.07	.02
☐ 19 Ken Reitz	.10	.05	.01
☐ 20 Rick Reuschel	.25	.11	.03
☐ 21 Scot Thompson	.10	.05	.01
☐ 22 Dick Tidrow	.10	.05	.01
☐ 23 Mike Tyson	.10	.05	.01
☐ 24 Cubs Ad Card (Unnumbered)	.05	.02	.01
☐ 25 Britt Burns	.15	.07	.02
☐ 26 Todd Cruz	.10	.05	.01
☐ 27 Rich Dotson	.15	.07	.02
☐ 28 Jim Essian	.10	.05	.01
☐ 29 Ed Farmer	.10	.05	.01
☐ 30 Lamar Johnson	.10	.05	.01
☐ 31 Ron LeFlore	.15	.07	.02
☐ 32 Chet Lemon	.15	.07	.02
☐ 33 Bob Molinaro	.10	.05	.01
☐ 34 Jim Morrison	.10	.05	.01
☐ 35 Wayne Nordhagen	.10	.05	.01
☐ 36 White Sox Ad Card (Unnumbered)	.05	.02	.01
☐ 37 Johnny Bench	3.50	1.55	.45
☐ 38 Dave Collins	.15	.07	.02
☐ 39 Dave Concepcion	.40	.18	.05
☐ 40 Dan Driessen	.15	.07	.02
☐ 41 George Foster	.40	.18	.05
☐ 42 Ken Griffey	.40	.18	.05
☐ 43 Tom Hume	.10	.05	.01
☐ 44 Ray Knight	.25	.11	.03
☐ 45 Ron Oester	.15	.07	.02
☐ 46 Tom Seaver	3.50	1.55	.45
☐ 47 Mario Soto	.15	.07	.02
☐ 48 Reds Ad Card (Unnumbered)	.05	.02	.01
☐ 49 Champ Summers	.10	.05	.01
☐ 50 Al Cowens	.10	.05	.01
☐ 51 Rich Hebner	.15	.07	.02
☐ 52 Steve Kemp	.15	.07	.02
☐ 53 Aurelio Lopez	.15	.07	.02
☐ 54 Jack Morris	2.00	.90	.25
☐ 55 Lance Parrish	1.00	.45	.13
☐ 56 Johnny Wockenfuss	.10	.05	.01
☐ 57 Alan Trammell	2.00	.90	.25
☐ 58 Lou Whitaker	1.50	.65	.19
☐ 59 Kirk Gibson	2.50	1.15	.30
☐ 60 Tigers Ad Card (Unnumbered)	.05	.02	.01
☐ 61 Alan Ashby	.10	.05	.01
☐ 62 Cesar Cedeno	.20	.09	.03
☐ 63 Jose Cruz	.20	.09	.03
☐ 64 Art Howe	.20	.09	.03
☐ 65 Rafael Landestoy	.10	.05	.01
☐ 66 Joe Niekro	.20	.09	.03
☐ 67 Terry Puhl	.15	.07	.02
☐ 68 J.R. Richard	.20	.09	.03
☐ 69 Nolan Ryan	8.00	3.60	1.00
☐ 70 Joe Sambito	.15	.07	.02
☐ 71 Don Sutton	1.50	.65	.19
☐ 72 Astros Ad Card (Unnumbered)	.05	.02	.01
☐ 73 Willie Aikens	.15	.07	.02
☐ 74 George Brett	4.00	1.80	.50
☐ 75 Larry Gura	.15	.07	.02
☐ 76 Dennis Leonard	.15	.07	.02
☐ 77 Hal McRae	.30	.14	.04
☐ 78 Amos Otis	.25	.11	.03
☐ 79 Dan Quisenberry	.40	.18	.05
☐ 80 U.L. Washington	.10	.05	.01
☐ 81 John Wathan	.15	.07	.02
☐ 82 Frank White	.25	.11	.03
☐ 83 Willie Wilson	.30	.14	.04
☐ 84 Royals Ad Card (Unnumbered)	.05	.02	.01
☐ 85 Neil Allen	.15	.07	.02
☐ 86 Doug Flynn	.10	.05	.01
☐ 87 Dave Kingman	.30	.14	.04
☐ 88 Randy Jones	.10	.05	.01
☐ 89 Pat Zachry	.10	.05	.01
☐ 90 Lee Mazzilli	.15	.07	.02
☐ 91 Rusty Staub	.30	.14	.04
☐ 92 Craig Swan	.10	.05	.01
☐ 93 Frank Taveras	.10	.05	.01
☐ 94 Alex Trevino	.10	.05	.01
☐ 95 Joel Youngblood	.10	.05	.01
☐ 96 Mets Ad Card (Unnumbered)	.05	.02	.01
☐ 97 Bob Boone	.35	.16	.04
☐ 98 Larry Bowa	.30	.14	.04
☐ 99 Steve Carlton	2.00	.90	.25
☐ 100 Greg Luzinski	.30	.14	.04
☐ 101 Garry Maddox	.15	.07	.02
☐ 102 Bake McBride	.10	.05	.01
☐ 103 Tug McGraw	.30	.14	.04
☐ 104 Pete Rose	2.50	1.15	.30
☐ 105 Mike Schmidt	3.50	1.55	.45
☐ 106 Lonnie Smith	.40	.18	.05
☐ 107 Manny Trillo	.15	.07	.02
☐ 108 Phillies Ad Card (Unnumbered)	.05	.02	.01
☐ 109 Jim Bibby	.10	.05	.01
☐ 110 John Candelaria	.15	.07	.02
☐ 111 Mike Easler	.15	.07	.02
☐ 112 Tim Foli	.10	.05	.01
☐ 113 Phil Garner	.20	.09	.03
☐ 114 Bill Madlock	.25	.11	.03
☐ 115 Omar Moreno	.10	.05	.01
☐ 116 Ed Ott	.10	.05	.01
☐ 117 Dave Parker	1.00	.45	.13
☐ 118 Willie Stargell	1.50	.65	.19
☐ 119 Kent Tekulve	.15	.07	.02
☐ 120 Pirates Ad Card (Unnumbered)	.05	.02	.01
☐ 121 Bob Forsch	.15	.07	.02
☐ 122 George Hendrick	.15	.07	.02
☐ 123 Keith Hernandez	.75	.35	.09
☐ 124 Tom Herr	.20	.09	.03
☐ 125 Sixto Lezcano	.10	.05	.01
☐ 126 Ken Oberkfell	.10	.05	.01
☐ 127 Darrell Porter	.15	.07	.02
☐ 128 Tony Scott	.10	.05	.01
☐ 129 Lary Sorensen	.10	.05	.01
☐ 130 Bruce Sutter	.40	.18	.05
☐ 131 Garry Templeton	.20	.09	.03
☐ 132 Cardinals Ad Card (Unnumbered)	.05	.02	.01

1991 Coke Don Mattingly

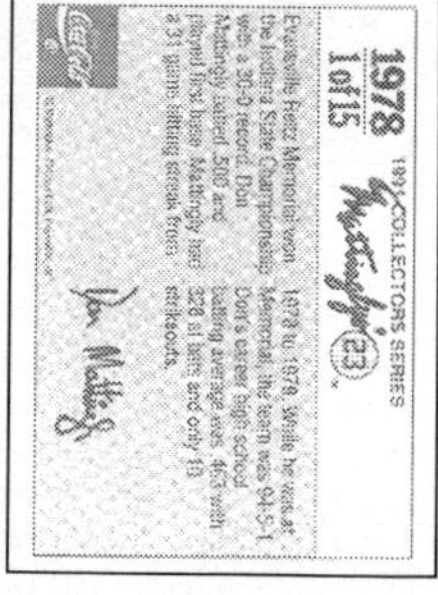

This 15-card set was sponsored by Coca-Cola and measures the standard size (2 1/2" by 3 1/2"). The front design features mostly color action player photos on a white and blue pinstripe card face. Each card has a year number on the top edge of the picture, and the Coke logo is superimposed at the lower left corner. In a horizontal format the backs are printed in blue and red, and present career highlights and statistics. The cards are numbered on the back.

	MT	EX-MT	VG
COMPLETE SET (15)	5.00	2.30	.60
COMMON PLAYER (1-15)	.50	.23	.06
☐ 1 Don Mattingly 1978	.50	.23	.06
☐ 2 Don Mattingly 1979	.50	.23	.06
☐ 3 Don Mattingly 1980	.50	.23	.06
☐ 4 Don Mattingly 1981 (black and white)	.50	.23	.06
☐ 5 Don Mattingly 1982	.50	.23	.06
☐ 6 Don Mattingly 1983	.50	.23	.06
☐ 7 Don Mattingly 1983-84 (black and white)	.50	.23	.06
☐ 8 Don Mattingly 1984	.50	.23	.06
☐ 9 Don Mattingly 1985	.50	.23	.06
☐ 10 Don Mattingly 1986	.50	.23	.06
☐ 11 Don Mattingly 1987	.50	.23	.06
☐ 12 Don Mattingly 1990	.50	.23	.06
☐ 13 Don Mattingly 1991 (Photo)	.50	.23	.06
☐ 14 Don Mattingly 1991 (Drawing)	.50	.23	.06
☐ 15 Don Mattingly 1991 (Career statistics)	.50	.23	.06

1990 Colla Jose Canseco

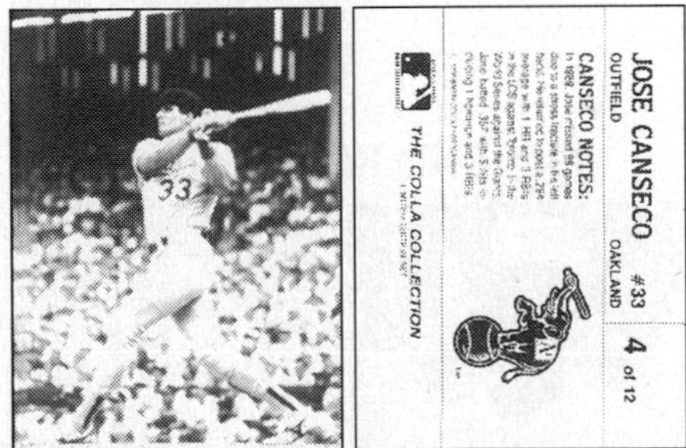

This 12-card set, issued by noted photographer Barry Colla, measures the standard size (2 1/2" by 3 1/2") and features Jose Canseco in various poses. The fronts are beautiful full-color photos while the backs contain notes about Canseco. According to the back of the first card in the set, 20,000 numbered sets were issued.

	MT	EX-MT	VG
COMPLETE SET (12)	9.00	4.00	1.15
COMMON PLAYER (1-12)	1.00	.45	.13
☐ 1 Jose Canseco (Portrait)	1.00	.45	.13
☐ 2 Jose Canseco (Follow-Through, Bat at Waist)	1.00	.45	.13
☐ 3 Jose Canseco (Follow-Through, Bat at Shoulders)	1.00	.45	.13
☐ 4 Jose Canseco (Follow-Through, Helmetless)	1.00	.45	.13
☐ 5 Jose Canseco (Dugout Portrait)	1.00	.45	.13
☐ 6 Jose Canseco (Profile, Bat on Shoulder)	1.00	.45	.13
☐ 7 Jose Canseco (Batting Cage Pose)	1.00	.45	.13
☐ 8 Jose Canseco (Follow-Through, ready to run)	1.00	.45	.13
☐ 9 Jose Canseco (Portrait, Kneeling)	1.00	.45	.13
☐ 10 Jose Canseco (Portrait, bat under shoulder)	1.00	.45	.13
☐ 11 Jose Canseco (At Bat-rack)	1.00	.45	.13
☐ 12 Jose Canseco (Running Bases)	1.00	.45	.13

1990 Colla Will Clark

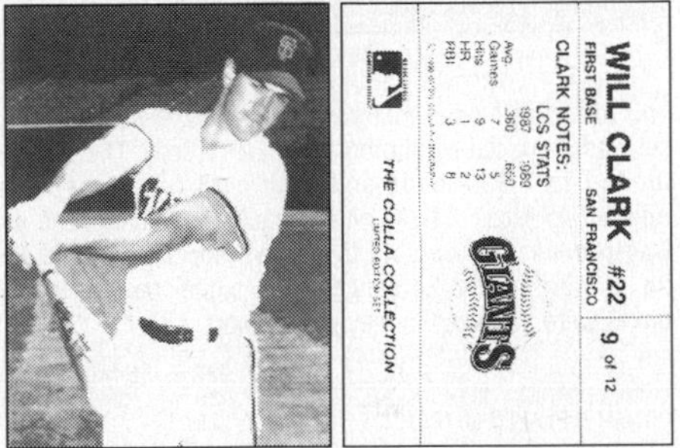

This 12-card set again features the beautiful photography of Barry Colla; this time Will Clark is the featured player. Each card in the set measures the standard size, 2 1/2" by 3 1/2". Again the fronts are borderless photos while the back contains notes about Will Clark. According to card number one, 15,000 numbered sets were produced.

	MT	EX-MT	VG
COMPLETE SET (12)	12.50	5.75	1.55
COMMON PLAYER (1-12)	1.25	.55	.16
☐ 1 Will Clark (Batting Pose, Gray Shirt)	1.25	.55	.16
☐ 2 Will Clark (Bat at Shoulder, Short Sleeves)	1.25	.55	.16
☐ 3 Will Clark (Smiling)	1.25	.55	.16
☐ 4 Will Clark (Ball in Glove)	1.25	.55	.16
☐ 5 Will Clark (Batting Pose, Long Sleeves)	1.25	.55	.16
☐ 6 Will Clark (Follow-Through, bat over head)	1.25	.55	.16
☐ 7 Will Clark (Follow-Through, hand released)	1.25	.55	.16
☐ 8 Will Clark (Standing, bat on ground)	1.25	.55	.16
☐ 9 Will Clark (Pose with bat at waist)	1.25	.55	.16
☐ 10 Will Clark (Portrait with Bat)	1.25	.55	.16
☐ 11 Will Clark (Kneeling with Glove)	1.25	.55	.16
☐ 12 Will Clark (Preparing to Field)	1.25	.55	.16

1990 Colla Kevin Maas

This attractive 12-card standard size (2 1/2" by 3 1/2") card set was produced by photographer Barry Colla. The set was limited to 7,500 made and each card has some facts relevant to Maas' career on the back of the card. The set was produced to be sold in its own special box and the boxes were issued 24 sets to each bigger box. All of the boxes were produced in the team's colors.

	MT	EX-MT	VG
COMPLETE SET (12)	7.50	3.40	.95
COMMON PLAYER (1-12)	.75	.35	.09
☐ 1 Kevin Maas (Batting Pose)	.75	.35	.09
☐ 2 Kevin Maas (Sitting on Dugout Steps)	.75	.35	.09
☐ 3 Kevin Maas (Taking a lead on basepaths)	.75	.35	.09
☐ 4 Kevin Maas (Close-Up)	.75	.35	.09
☐ 5 Kevin Maas (Standing in Dugout)	.75	.35	.09
☐ 6 Kevin Maas (Kneeling with bat)	.75	.35	.09
☐ 7 Kevin Maas (Fielding Pose)	.75	.35	.09
☐ 8 Kevin Maas (Follow Through 24 showing)	.75	.35	.09
☐ 9 Kevin Maas (Portrait with Bat)	.75	.35	.09
☐ 10 Kevin Maas (Follow Through)	.75	.35	.09
☐ 11 Kevin Maas (Side Portrait)	.75	.35	.09
☐ 12 Kevin Maas (Taking Batting Practice)	.75	.35	.09

1990 Colla Don Mattingly

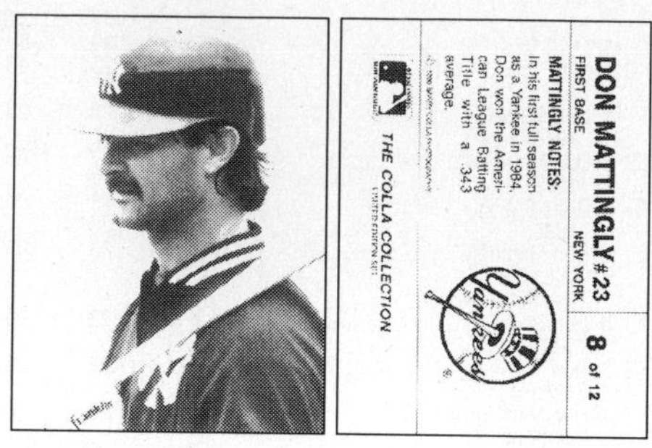

This 12-card set features the photography of Barry Colla as he features Don Mattingly in various poses. Each card in the set measures the standard size, 2 1/2" by 3 1/2". The set was limited to 15,000 numbered sets and feature full-color photographs on the borderless fronts along with notes about Mattingly on the back.

	MT	EX-MT	VG
COMPLETE SET (12)	10.00	4.50	1.25
COMMON PLAYER (1-12)	1.00	.45	.13
☐ 1 Don Mattingly (Head-On Portrait)	1.00	.45	.13
☐ 2 Don Mattingly (Preparing to Swing)	1.00	.45	.13
☐ 3 Don Mattingly (Running Bases)	1.00	.45	.13
☐ 4 Don Mattingly (Portrait with glove in hand)	1.00	.45	.13
☐ 5 Don Mattingly (Backhanding a Ball)	1.00	.45	.13
☐ 6 Don Mattingly (Follow-Through, Bat Pointing Up)	1.00	.45	.13
☐ 7 Don Mattingly (Follow-Through, bat to be released)	1.00	.45	.13
☐ 8 Don Mattingly (Facing left, bat on shoulder)	1.00	.45	.13
☐ 9 Don Mattingly (Portrait, facing right)	1.00	.45	.13
☐ 10 Don Mattingly (Practice Swing, bat at waist)	1.00	.45	.13
☐ 11 Don Mattingly (Preparing to field ball)	1.00	.45	.13
☐ 12 Don Mattingly (Kneeling)	1.00	.45	.13

1991 Colla Roberto Alomar

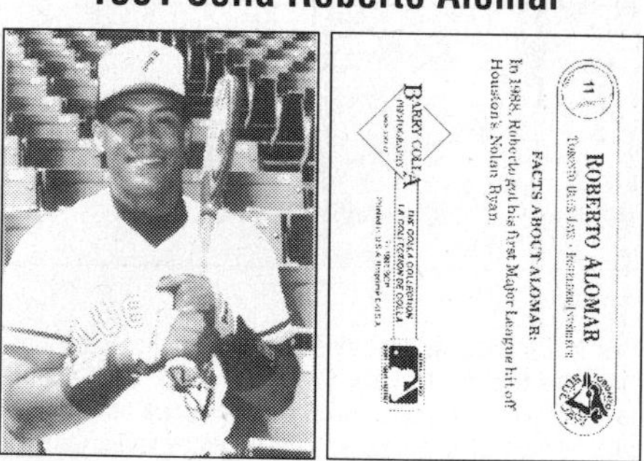

This 13-card standard size (2 1/2" by 3 1/2") set features colorful photos of Roberto Alomar by noted photographer Barry Colla. The high gloss borderless color photos were packed in a full color collector's box. Only 7,500 sets were produced, with 24 sets per display carton. The first card of each set bears the registration number. In black lettering on a light gray background, the horizontally oriented backs feature facts about Alomar. The cards are numbered on the back.

	MT	EX-MT	VG
COMPLETE SET (13)	10.00	4.50	1.25
COMMON PLAYER (1-12)	1.00	.45	.13
☐ 1 Roberto Alomar (Headshot)	1.00	.45	.13
☐ 2 Roberto Alomar (In mid-air at 2nd preparing to throw)	1.00	.45	.13

		MT	EX-MT	VG
☐ 3	Roberto Alomar (In mid-air at 2nd throwing ball)	1.00	.45	.13
☐ 4	Roberto Alomar (Pose showing right shoulder)	1.00	.45	.13
☐ 5	Roberto Alomar (Pose showing left shoulder)	1.00	.45	.13
☐ 6	Roberto Alomar (Watching ball after hit)	1.00	.45	.13
☐ 7	Roberto Alomar (Follow through, hands at waist)	1.00	.45	.13
☐ 8	Roberto Alomar (Headshot, bat on shoulder)	1.00	.45	.13
☐ 9	Roberto Alomar (Posed kneeling)	1.00	.45	.13
☐ 10	Roberto Alomar (Follow through, hands at chest)	1.00	.45	.13
☐ 11	Roberto Alomar (Posed with bat on left shoulder)	1.00	.45	.13
☐ 12	Roberto Alomar (Posed with left shoulder forward and bat on right shoulder)	1.00	.45	.13
☐ xx	Roberto Alomar (Posed with bat on right shoulder)	1.00	.45	.13

1991 Colla Barry Bonds

This 13-card standard size (2 1/2" by 3 1/2") set features colorful photos of Barry Bonds by noted photographer Barry Colla. The high gloss borderless color photos were packed in a full color collector's box. Only 7,500 were produced, with 24 sets per display carton. The first card of each set bears the registration number. In black lettering on a gray background, the horizontally oriented backs feature facts about Bonds. The cards are numbered on the back. This set was issued so late in 1991 that it was actually January 1992 before the set was in general distribution.

		MT	EX-MT	VG
	COMPLETE SET (13)	10.00	4.50	1.25
	COMMON PLAYER (1-12)	1.00	.45	.13
☐ 1	Barry Bonds (Posed with bat behind head)	1.00	.45	.13
☐ 2	Barry Bonds (Kneeling, forearm resting on bat)	1.00	.45	.13
☐ 3	Barry Bonds (Front pose, hand in glove)	1.00	.45	.13
☐ 4	Barry Bonds (Head and shoulders shot)	1.00	.45	.13
☐ 5	Barry Bonds (Warming up in black warm-up jersey)	1.00	.45	.13
☐ 6	Barry Bonds (Follow through, bat behind head)	1.00	.45	.13
☐ 7	Barry Bonds (Crouching posture, ready to field)	1.00	.45	.13
☐ 8	Barry Bonds (Seated in dugout)	1.00	.45	.13
☐ 9	Barry Bonds (Right shoulder forward, bat on shoulder)	1.00	.45	.13
☐ 10	Barry Bonds (Front pose, glove in front of chest)	1.00	.45	.13
☐ 11	Barry Bonds (Right shoulder forward, batting pose)	1.00	.45	.13
☐ 12	Barry Bonds (Front pose, arms crossed)	1.00	.45	.13
☐ xx	Title card (Close-up pose, forearm resting on bat)	1.00	.45	.13

1991 Colla Joe Carter

This 13-card standard size (2 1/2" by 3 1/2") set features colorful photos of Joe Carter by noted photographer Barry Colla. The high gloss borderless color photos were packed in a full color collector's box. Only 7,500 sets were produced, with 24 sets per display carton. The first card of each set bears the registration number. In black lettering on a light gray background, the horizontally oriented backs feature facts about Carter. The cards are numbered on the back.

		MT	EX-MT	VG
	COMPLETE SET (13)	10.00	4.50	1.25
	COMMON PLAYER (1-12)	1.00	.45	.13
☐ 1	Joe Carter (Posed, bat above shoulder)	1.00	.45	.13
☐ 2	Joe Carter (Kneeling pose, arm on bat)	1.00	.45	.13
☐ 3	Joe Carter (Head and shoulders pose)	1.00	.45	.13
☐ 4	Joe Carter (Posed, bat on right shoulder)	1.00	.45	.13
☐ 5	Joe Carter (Kneeling pose, close up)	1.00	.45	.13
☐ 6	Joe Carter (Ready to throw from outfield)	1.00	.45	.13
☐ 7	Joe Carter (After throw from outfield)	1.00	.45	.13
☐ 8	Joe Carter (Watching fly ball after hit)	1.00	.45	.13
☐ 9	Joe Carter (Bat on shoulder in blue uniform)	1.00	.45	.13

		MT	EX-MT	VG
☐ 10	Joe Carter (Batting helmet in hand)	1.00	.45	.13
☐ 11	Joe Carter (Posed in blue uniform and sunglasses)	1.00	.45	.13
☐ 12	Joe Carter (Posed with bat on shoulder, from waist up)	1.00	.45	.13
☐ xx	Joe Carter Title card (Front pose, bat on right shoulder)	1.00	.45	.13

1991 Colla Dwight Gooden

This 13-card standard size (2 1/2" by 3 1/2") set features colorful photos of Dwight Gooden by noted photographer Barry Colla. The high gloss borderless color photos were packed in a full color collector's box. Only 15,000 sets were produced, with 24 sets per display carton. The first card of each set bears the registration number. In black lettering on a light gray background, the horizontally oriented backs feature facts about Gooden. The cards are numbered on the back.

		MT	EX-MT	VG
COMPLETE SET (13)		9.00	4.00	1.15
COMMON PLAYER (1-12)		1.00	.45	.13
☐ 1	Dwight Gooden (Head and shoulders pose)	1.00	.45	.13
☐ 2	Dwight Gooden (Pitching, arm behind back)	1.00	.45	.13
☐ 3	Dwight Gooden (Pitching, arm above head)	1.00	.45	.13
☐ 4	Dwight Gooden (Posed with glove)	1.00	.45	.13
☐ 5	Dwight Gooden (Kneeling, glove on knee)	1.00	.45	.13
☐ 6	Dwight Gooden (Posed, blue uniform)	1.00	.45	.13
☐ 7	Dwight Gooden (Pitching, just after release)	1.00	.45	.13
☐ 8	Dwight Gooden (Pose with glove, left shoulder forward)	1.00	.45	.13
☐ 9	Dwight Gooden (Posed in dugout)	1.00	.45	.13
☐ 10	Dwight Gooden (Head and shoulders pose, blue uniform)	1.00	.45	.13
☐ 11	Dwight Gooden (Kneeling, arms on left knee)	1.00	.45	.13
☐ 12	Dwight Gooden (Left shoulder pose)	1.00	.45	.13
☐ xx	Dwight Gooden Title Card (Front pose)	1.00	.45	.13

1991 Colla Ken Griffey Jr.

This 12-card standard size (2 1/2" by 3 1/2") set features colorful photos of Ken Griffey Jr. by noted photographer Barry Colla. The high gloss borderless color photos were packed in a full color collector's box. Only 15,000 sets were produced, with 24 sets per display carton. The first card of each set bears the registration number. In black lettering on a light gray background, the horizontally oriented backs feature facts about Ken Griffey. The cards are numbered on the back.

		MT	EX-MT	VG
COMPLETE SET (12)		10.00	4.50	1.25
COMMON PLAYER (1-12)		1.00	.45	.13
☐ 1	Ken Griffey Jr. (Bat on shoulder, right side)	1.00	.45	.13
☐ 2	Ken Griffey Jr. (Bat on shoulder, straight on)	1.00	.45	.13
☐ 3	Ken Griffey Jr. (Follow-through)	1.00	.45	.13
☐ 4	Ken Griffey Jr. (Beside batting cage)	1.00	.45	.13
☐ 5	Ken Griffey Jr. (In dugout)	1.00	.45	.13
☐ 6	Ken Griffey Jr. (Batting pose)	1.00	.45	.13
☐ 7	Ken Griffey Jr. (Adjusting hat)	1.00	.45	.13
☐ 8	Ken Griffey Jr. (Swinging bat)	1.00	.45	.13
☐ 9	Ken Griffey Jr. (Pose, middle of swing)	1.00	.45	.13
☐ 10	Ken Griffey Jr. (Bat at waist)	1.00	.45	.13
☐ 11	Ken Griffey Jr. (Middle of swing)	1.00	.45	.13
☐ 12	Ken Griffey Jr. (Hitting fly ball)	1.00	.45	.13

1991 Colla Dave Justice

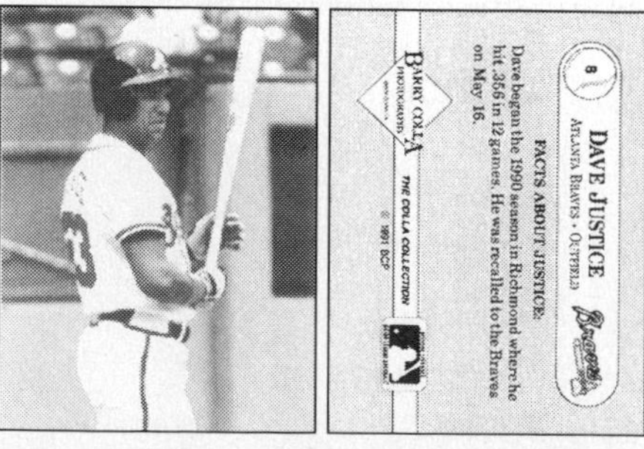

This 13-card standard size (2 1/2" by 3 1/2") set features colorful photos of Dave Justice by noted photographer Barry Colla. The high gloss borderless color photos were packed in a full color collector's box. Only 15,000 sets were produced, with 24 sets per display carton. The first card of each set bears the registration number. In black lettering on a light gray background, the horizontally oriented backs feature facts about Justice. The cards are numbered on the back.

	MT	EX-MT	VG
COMPLETE SET (13)	9.00	4.00	1.15
COMMON PLAYER (1-12)	1.00	.45	.13
☐ 1 Dave Justice (Bat on shoulder, White jersey)	1.00	.45	.13
☐ 2 Dave Justice (Leaning on bat)	1.00	.45	.13
☐ 3 Dave Justice (Running in outfield)	1.00	.45	.13
☐ 4 Dave Justice (Throwing from the outfield)	1.00	.45	.13
☐ 5 Dave Justice (Bat over shoulder)	1.00	.45	.13
☐ 6 Dave Justice (Looking through batting cage)	1.00	.45	.13
☐ 7 Dave Justice (After ball thrown)	1.00	.45	.13
☐ 8 Dave Justice (Just before batting)	1.00	.45	.13
☐ 9 Dave Justice (Watching hit ball)	1.00	.45	.13
☐ 10 Dave Justice (Running to first)	1.00	.45	.13
☐ 11 Dave Justice (Warm-up exercises Stretching)	1.00	.45	.13
☐ 12 Dave Justice (Bat on shoulder, Squatting posture)	1.00	.45	.13
☐ xx Title card (Bat on shoulder, Blue jersey)	1.00	.45	.13

1991 Colla Ryne Sandberg

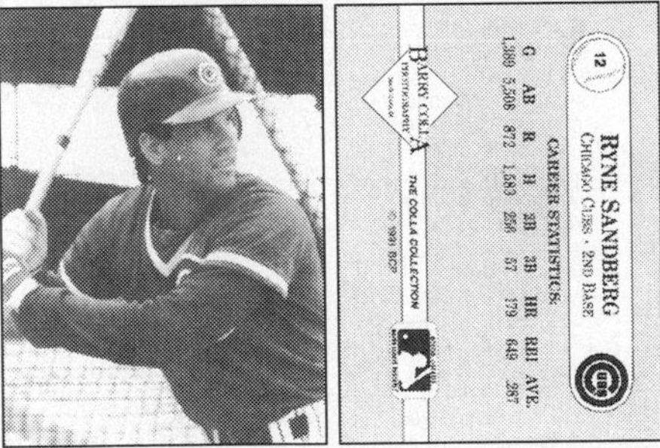

This 13-card standard size (2 1/2" by 3 1/2") set features colorful photos of Ryne Sandberg by noted photographer Barry Colla. The high gloss borderless color photos were packed in a full color collector's box. Only 15,000 sets were produced, with 24 sets per display carton. The first card of each set bears the registration number. In black lettering on a light gray background, the horizontally oriented backs feature facts about Ryne Sandberg. The cards are numbered on the back.

	MT	EX-MT	VG
COMPLETE SET (13)	10.00	4.50	1.25
COMMON PLAYER (1-12)	1.00	.45	.13
☐ 1 Ryne Sandberg (Follow-through, bat in motion)	1.00	.45	.13
☐ 2 Ryne Sandberg (Preparing to field blue uniform)	1.00	.45	.13
☐ 3 Ryne Sandberg (Awaiting throw)	1.00	.45	.13
☐ 4 Ryne Sandberg (Follow-Through facing left close up)	1.00	.45	.13
☐ 5 Ryne Sandberg (Holding bat behind back)	1.00	.45	.13
☐ 6 Ryne Sandberg (Pivoting at second)	1.00	.45	.13
☐ 7 Ryne Sandberg (Ready to throw)	1.00	.45	.13
☐ 8 Ryne Sandberg (Left profile shot)	1.00	.45	.13
☐ 9 Ryne Sandberg (Holding bat at waist)	1.00	.45	.13
☐ 10 Ryne Sandberg (Awaiting pitch)	1.00	.45	.13
☐ 11 Ryne Sandberg (Follow-through, bat at shoulders)	1.00	.45	.13
☐ 12 Ryne Sandberg (Batting Cage Pose)	1.00	.45	.13
☐ xx Ryne Sandberg (Header card)	1.00	.45	.13

1991 Colla Darryl Strawberry

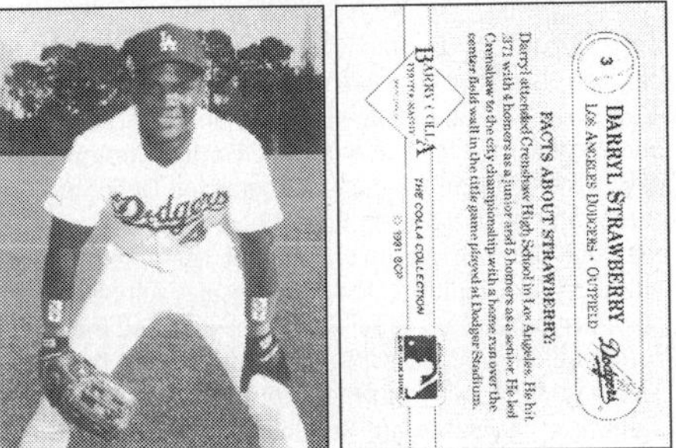

This 13-card standard size (2 1/2" by 3 1/2") set features colorful photos of Darryl Strawberry by noted photographer Barry Colla. The high gloss borderless color photos were packed in a full color collector's box. Only 15,000 sets were produced, with 24 sets per display carton. The first card of each set bears the registration number. In black lettering on a light gray background, the horizontally oriented backs feature facts about Strawberry. The cards are numbered on the back.

	MT	EX-MT	VG
COMPLETE SET (13)	9.00	4.00	1.15
COMMON PLAYER (1-12)	1.00	.45	.13
☐ 1 Darryl Strawberry (Posed follow through)	1.00	.45	.13
☐ 2 Darryl Strawberry (Bat on shoulder)	1.00	.45	.13
☐ 3 Darryl Strawberry (Posed with glove)	1.00	.45	.13
☐ 4 Darryl Strawberry (Kneeling with bat)	1.00	.45	.13
☐ 5 Darryl Strawberry (Head shot with flip-up sunglasses)	1.00	.45	.13
☐ 6 Darryl Strawberry (Ready to run in base path)	1.00	.45	.13
☐ 7 Darryl Strawberry (Awaiting fly ball)	1.00	.45	.13
☐ 8 Darryl Strawberry (Head shot with batting helmet)	1.00	.45	.13

	MT	EX-MT	VG
☐ 9 Darryl Strawberry (Follow through after hit)	1.00	.45	.13
☐ 10 Darryl Strawberry (Watching hit ball)	1.00	.45	.13
☐ 11 Darryl Strawberry (Waiting for at bat)	1.00	.45	.13
☐ 12 Darryl Strawberry (Running bases)	1.00	.45	.13
☐ xx Title card (Two bats on shoulder)	1.00	.45	.13

1992 Colla All-Star Game

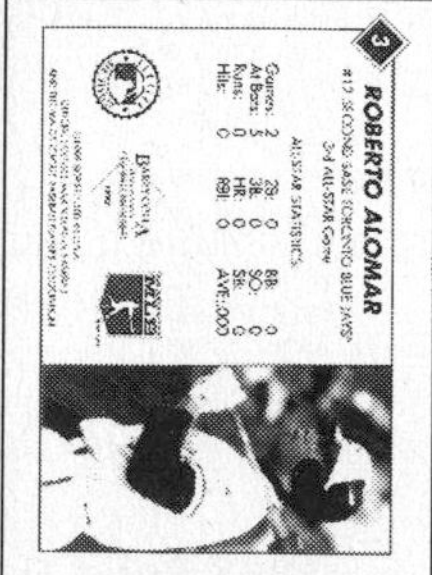

This 24-card set was made available at the 1992 All-Star game in San Diego. The cards measure the standard size (2 1/2" by 3 1/2") and feature 24 All-Stars from the National and American League. Randomly inserted throughout the sets were 200 numbered and autographed Roberto Alomar cards. The production run was limited to 25,000 sets, and the first card (McGwire) of each set bears the set serial number ("X of 25,000"). The fronts display full-bleed glossy color player photos. The All-Star Game logo and the player's name are superimposed across the bottom of the picture. The backs carry a close-up color photo and All-Star statistics. The cards are numbered in a diamond in the upper left corner.

	MT	EX-MT	VG
COMPLETE SET (24)	16.00	7.25	2.00
COMMON PLAYER (1-24)	.25	.11	.03
☐ 1 Mark McGwire	1.25	.55	.16
☐ 2 Will Clark	1.25	.55	.16
☐ 3 Roberto Alomar	1.50	.65	.19
☐ 4 Ryne Sandberg	1.50	.65	.19
☐ 5 Cal Ripken	2.00	.90	.25
☐ 6 Ozzie Smith	.60	.25	.08
☐ 7 Wade Boggs	.75	.35	.09
☐ 8 Terry Pendleton	.40	.18	.05
☐ 9 Kirby Puckett	1.50	.65	.19
☐ 10 Chuck Knoblauch	.75	.35	.09
☐ 11 Ken Griffey Jr.	2.50	1.15	.30
☐ 12 Joe Carter	.75	.35	.09
☐ 13 Sandy Alomar Jr.	.25	.11	.03
☐ 14 Benito Santiago	.25	.11	.03
☐ 15 Mike Mussina	2.50	1.15	.30
☐ 16 Fred McGriff	.75	.35	.09
☐ 17 Dennis Eckersley	.50	.23	.06
☐ 18 Tony Gwynn	.90	.40	.11
☐ 19 Roger Clemens	1.50	.65	.19
☐ 20 Gary Sheffield	1.00	.45	.13
☐ 21 Jose Canseco	1.25	.55	.16
☐ 22 Barry Bonds	1.00	.45	.13
☐ 23 Ivan Rodriguez	1.50	.65	.19
☐ 24 Tony Fernandez	.25	.11	.03

1992 Colla Jeff Bagwell

This 12-card standard-size (2 1/2" by 3 1/2") set features colorful photos of Jeff Bagwell by noted sports photographer Barry Colla. Only 25,000 sets were produced, with 24 sets per display carton. Randomly inserted throughout the sets were 200 numbered and autographed Bagwell cards. Also the set included an Allocation Rights card, which entitled the holder to purchase the Colla Rookie set. The high gloss borderless color photos were packed in a full color collector's box. The first card of each set bears the set serial number. In black lettering on a white background, the horizontally oriented backs feature notes about Bagwell and a baseball cartoon picture. The cards are numbered on the back.

	MT	EX-MT	VG
COMPLETE SET (12)	7.50	3.40	.95
COMMON PLAYER (1-12)	1.00	.45	.13
☐ 1 Jeff Bagwell (Front pose in white jersey with bat on shoulder)	1.00	.45	.13
☐ 2 Jeff Bagwell (Front pose, in shades with two bats on shoulder)	1.00	.45	.13
☐ 3 Jeff Bagwell (Defensive posture, hands on knees)	1.00	.45	.13
☐ 4 Jeff Bagwell (Close-up photo in dark blue jersey with bat on shoulder)	1.00	.45	.13
☐ 5 Jeff Bagwell (Preparing to throw, with shades on)	1.00	.45	.13
☐ 6 Jeff Bagwell (Follow through, watching flight of ball, bat beside body)	1.00	.45	.13
☐ 7 Jeff Bagwell (Follow through, watching flight of ball, bat behind body)	1.00	.45	.13
☐ 8 Jeff Bagwell (Posed action, checking bat swing)	1.00	.45	.13
☐ 9 Jeff Bagwell (Pose from dugout, fore-arms resting on bat)	1.00	.45	.13
☐ 10 Jeff Bagwell (Front pose, holding bat at waist level)	1.00	.45	.13
☐ 11 Jeff Bagwell (Preparing to field ball)	1.00	.45	.13
☐ 12 Jeff Bagwell (Front pose, with ball in glove)	1.00	.45	.13

1992 Colla Tony Gwynn

This 12-card standard size (2 1/2" by 3 1/2") set features colorful photos of Tony Gwynn by noted photographer Barry Colla. The high gloss borderless color photos were packed in a full color collector's box. Only 7,500 sets were produced, with the first card of each set carrying the set number. The "92 The Colla Collection" icon appears in an upper corner and the player's name is printed toward the bottom of the picture. In light black lettering on white, the horizontal backs present biography (1), notes on Gwynn (2-11), or major league statistics (12) on the left portion and baseball cartoons on the right portion. The cards are numbered on the back.

	MT	EX-MT	VG
COMPLETE SET (12)	10.00	4.50	1.25
COMMON PLAYER (1-12)	1.00	.45	.13
☐ 1 Tony Gwynn (Head and shoulders pose; bat on left shoulder)	1.00	.45	.13
☐ 2 Tony Gwynn (Batting posture at plate; awaiting pitch)	1.00	.45	.13
☐ 3 Tony Gwynn (Full body shot; kneeling with forearm resting on bat)	1.00	.45	.13
☐ 4 Tony Gwynn (Shot from waist up with bat on shoulder)	1.00	.45	.13
☐ 5 Tony Gwynn (Full body shot from right side)	1.00	.45	.13
☐ 6 Tony Gwynn (Running to base)	1.00	.45	.13
☐ 7 Tony Gwynn (In dugout with shades raised)	1.00	.45	.13
☐ 8 Tony Gwynn (Carrying baseball equipment bag)	1.00	.45	.13
☐ 9 Tony Gwynn (Bent over at waist; batting weight in hand)	1.00	.45	.13
☐ 10 Tony Gwynn (Outfield catch; ball in glove)	1.00	.45	.13
☐ 11 Tony Gwynn (Front pose from waist up)	1.00	.45	.13
☐ 12 Tony Gwynn (Taking off toward first base; bat extended behind)	1.00	.45	.13

1992 Colla Mark McGwire

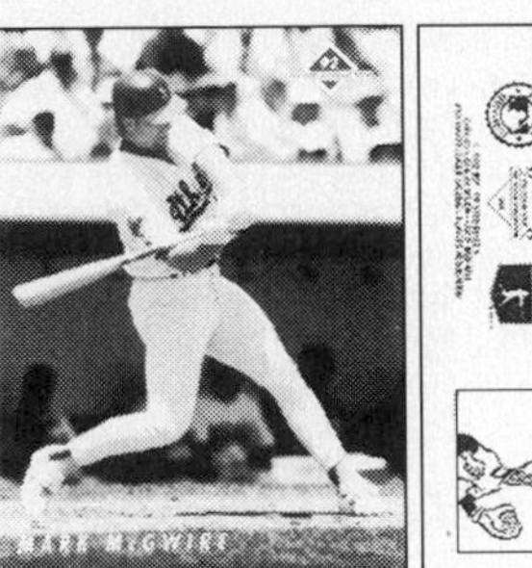

This 12-card standard-size (2 1/2" by 3 1/2") set features colorful photos of Mark McGwire by noted sports photographer Barry Colla. Only 15,000 sets were produced, with 24 sets per display carton. Randomly inserted throughout the sets were 200 numbered and autographed McGwire cards. The high gloss borderless color photos were packed in a full color collector's box. The first card of each set bears the set serial number. In black lettering on a white background, the horizontally oriented backs feature notes about McGwire and a baseball cartoon picture. The cards are numbered on the back.

	MT	EX-MT	VG
COMPLETE SET (12)	10.00	4.50	1.25
COMMON PLAYER (1-12)	1.00	.45	.13
☐ 1 Mark McGwire (Posing without hat)	1.00	.45	.13
☐ 2 Mark McGwire (Swinging-unextended)	1.00	.45	.13
☐ 3 Mark McGwire (Preparing to field)	1.00	.45	.13
☐ 4 Mark McGwire (Leaving batter's box)	1.00	.45	.13
☐ 5 Mark McGwire (Watching flight of ball)	1.00	.45	.13
☐ 6 Mark McGwire (Glaring at umpire)	1.00	.45	.13
☐ 7 Mark McGwire (Sliding)	1.00	.45	.13
☐ 8 Mark McGwire (Front pose, bat on shoulder)	1.00	.45	.13
☐ 9 Mark McGwire (Running to dugout)	1.00	.45	.13
☐ 10 Mark McGwire (Throwing)	1.00	.45	.13
☐ 11 Mark McGwire (Bat on shoulder, in dugout)	1.00	.45	.13
☐ 12 Mark McGwire (Follow through)	1.00	.45	.13

1992 Colla Nolan Ryan

This 12-card standard-size (2 1/2" by 3 1/2") set features colorful photos of Nolan Ryan by noted sports photographer

Barry Colla. Only 25,000 sets were produced, with 24 sets per display carton. Randomly inserted throughout the sets were 200 numbered and autographed Ryan cards. The high-gloss borderless color photos were packed in a full color collector's box. The first card of each set bears the set serial number. In black lettering on a white background, the horizontally oriented backs feature notes about Ryan and a baseball cartoon picture. The cards are numbered on the back.

	MT	EX-MT	VG
COMPLETE SET (12)	10.00	4.50	1.25
COMMON PLAYER (1-12)	1.00	.45	.13
☐ 1 Nolan Ryan (Pitching, ball behind head)	1.00	.45	.13
☐ 2 Nolan Ryan (Close-up photo, from right side)	1.00	.45	.13
☐ 3 Nolan Ryan (Pitching, just after release of ball)	1.00	.45	.13
☐ 4 Nolan Ryan (Close-up photo, pitching with ball behind head)	1.00	.45	.13
☐ 5 Nolan Ryan (Sitting on grass, stretching)	1.00	.45	.13
☐ 6 Nolan Ryan (Wind up, high leg kick)	1.00	.45	.13
☐ 7 Nolan Ryan (Beginning of pitching motion, ball in glove)	1.00	.45	.13
☐ 8 Nolan Ryan (Walking, staring at ground)	1.00	.45	.13
☐ 9 Nolan Ryan (Left side shot, after release of ball)	1.00	.45	.13
☐ 10 Nolan Ryan (Throwing football)	1.00	.45	.13
☐ 11 Nolan Ryan (Close up photo, wind up with leg cocked)	1.00	.45	.13
☐ 12 Nolan Ryan (Walking to batting cage)	1.00	.45	.13

1992 Colla Frank Thomas

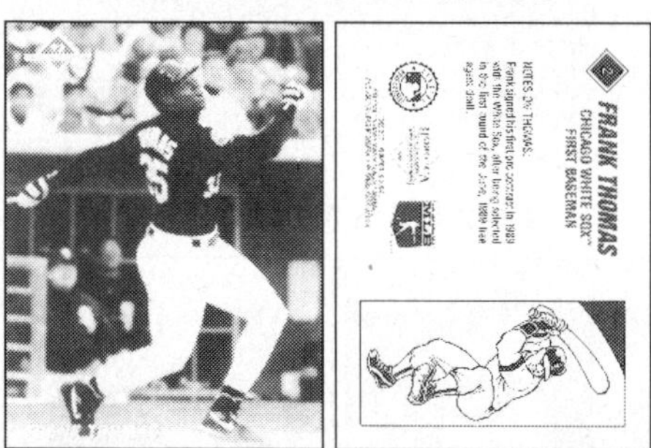

This 12-card standard-size (2 1/2" by 3 1/2") set features colorful photos of Frank Thomas by noted sports photographer Barry Colla. Only 25,000 sets were produced, with 24 sets per display carton. Randomly inserted throughout the sets were 200 numbered and autographed Frank Thomas cards. Also the set included an Allocation Rights card, which entitled the holder to purchase the Colla Rookie set. The high gloss borderless color photos were packed in a full color collector's box. The first card of each set bears the set serial number. In black lettering on a white background, the horizontally oriented backs feature notes about Thomas and a baseball cartoon picture. The cards are numbered on the back.

	MT	EX-MT	VG
COMPLETE SET (12)	10.00	4.50	1.25
COMMON PLAYER (1-12)	1.00	.45	.13
☐ 1 Frank Thomas (Front pose, bat on shoulder)	1.00	.45	.13
☐ 2 Frank Thomas (Follow through, watching flight of ball in black jersey)	1.00	.45	.13
☐ 3 Frank Thomas (Close-up photo, sitting posture)	1.00	.45	.13
☐ 4 Frank Thomas (On deck, lead bat on shoulder)	1.00	.45	.13
☐ 5 Frank Thomas (Eyeing pop-up into glove)	1.00	.45	.13
☐ 6 Frank Thomas (Up close with fans)	1.00	.45	.13
☐ 7 Frank Thomas (Running posture, ball in right hand)	1.00	.45	.13
☐ 8 Frank Thomas (Watching flight of ball, white jersey)	1.00	.45	.13
☐ 9 Frank Thomas (Front pose, kneeling)	1.00	.45	.13
☐ 10 Frank Thomas (Follow through, right hand off bat)	1.00	.45	.13
☐ 11 Frank Thomas (Back and left shoulder shot, glaring)	1.00	.45	.13
☐ 12 Frank Thomas (Front pose, in locker room)	1.00	.45	.13

1990 Collect-A-Books

The 1990 Collect-A-Books set was issued by CMC (Collectors Marketing Corp.) in three different sets (boxes) of 12 players apiece. The sets (boxes) were distinguishable by color, red, yellow, or green. The Collect-A-Books were in the style of the 1970 Topps Comic Book inserts but were much more profesionally made. The cards all fit into a nine-pocket sheet (since they are standard size, 2 1/2" by 3 1/2") even though they can be expanded. The set contains an interesting mixture of retired and current players.

	MT	EX-MT	VG
COMPLETE SET (36)	7.00	3.10	.85
COMMON PLAYER (1-36)	.20	.09	.03
☐ 1 Bo Jackson	.60	.25	.08
☐ 2 Dwight Gooden	.30	.14	.04
☐ 3 Ken Griffey Jr.	1.00	.45	.13
☐ 4 Will Clark	.50	.23	.06

☐ 5 Ozzie Smith	.30	.14	.04
☐ 6 Orel Hershiser	.25	.11	.03
☐ 7 Ruben Sierra	.35	.16	.04
☐ 8 Rickey Henderson	.45	.20	.06
☐ 9 Robin Yount	.40	.18	.05
☐ 10 Babe Ruth	.50	.23	.06
☐ 11 Ernie Banks	.25	.11	.03
☐ 12 Carl Yastrzemski	.30	.14	.04
☐ 13 Don Mattingly	.75	.35	.09
☐ 14 Nolan Ryan	1.00	.45	.13
☐ 15 Jerome Walton	.20	.09	.03
☐ 16 Kevin Mitchell	.25	.11	.03
☐ 17 Tony Gwynn	.35	.16	.04
☐ 18 Dave Stewart	.20	.09	.03
☐ 19 Roger Clemens	.60	.25	.08
☐ 20 Darryl Strawberry	.45	.20	.06
☐ 21 George Brett	.40	.18	.05
☐ 22 Hank Aaron	.40	.18	.05
☐ 23 Ted Williams	.40	.18	.05
☐ 24 Warren Spahn	.20	.09	.03
☐ 25 Jose Canseco	.60	.25	.08
☐ 26 Wade Boggs	.45	.20	.06
☐ 27 Jim Abbott	.35	.16	.04
☐ 28 Eric Davis	.35	.16	.04
☐ 29 Ryne Sandberg	.90	.40	.11
☐ 30 Bret Saberhagen	.25	.11	.03
☐ 31 Mark Grace	.40	.18	.05
☐ 32 Gregg Olson	.25	.11	.03
☐ 33 Kirby Puckett	.50	.23	.06
☐ 34 Lou Gehrig	.50	.23	.06
☐ 35 Roberto Clemente	.35	.16	.04
☐ 36 Bob Feller	.30	.14	.04

1991 Collect-A-Books

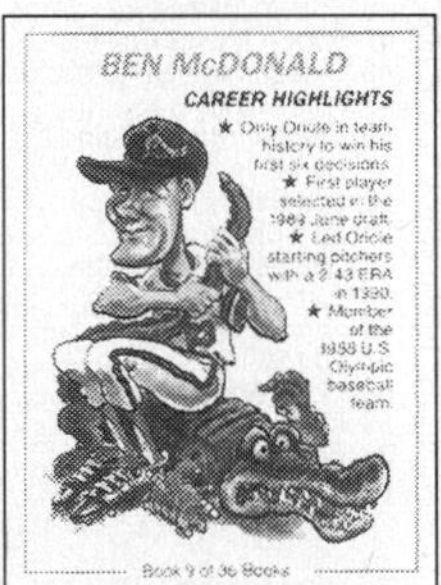

This 36-card set, which measures the standard 2 1/2" by 3 1/2", was issued by Impel for the second consecutive year. Collectors Marketing Corp., the 1990 Collect-a-Book producer, was a division within the Impel Corporation. This 1991 set was issued under Impel's Line Drive brand. Each book consists of eight pages and fits into a standard size plastic sheet. The set features 27 active stars and nine famous retired stars. An action shot of the player is pictured on the first two pages. The next four pages has textual information broken down into biographical information, two pages of more detailed personal information, and a page of statistics. The inside back cover has a quote from the player pictured while the back cover has an attractive drawing of the player. Unlike the 1990 issue, the Collect-A-Books were issued in random packs.

	MT	EX-MT	VG
COMPLETE SET (36)	8.00	3.60	1.00
COMMON PLAYER (1-36)	.20	.09	.03
☐ 1 Roger Clemens	.60	.25	.08
☐ 2 Cal Ripken	.75	.35	.09
☐ 3 Nolan Ryan	1.00	.45	.13
☐ 4 Ken Griffey Jr.	1.00	.45	.13
☐ 5 Bob Welch	.20	.09	.03
☐ 6 Kevin Mitchell	.30	.14	.04
☐ 7 Kirby Puckett	.60	.25	.08
☐ 8 Len Dykstra	.20	.09	.03
☐ 9 Ben McDonald	.30	.14	.04
☐ 10 Don Drysdale	.25	.11	.03
☐ 11 Lou Brock	.25	.11	.03
☐ 12 Ralph Kiner	.25	.11	.03
☐ 13 Jose Canseco	.60	.25	.08
☐ 14 Cecil Fielder	.45	.20	.06
☐ 15 Ryne Sandberg	.75	.35	.09
☐ 16 Wade Boggs	.45	.20	.06
☐ 17 Dwight Gooden	.30	.14	.04
☐ 18 Ramon Martinez	.35	.16	.04
☐ 19 Tony Gwynn	.40	.18	.05
☐ 20 Mark Grace	.35	.16	.04
☐ 21 Kevin Maas	.25	.11	.03
☐ 22 Thurman Munson	.30	.14	.04
☐ 23 Bob Gibson	.30	.14	.04
☐ 24 Bill Mazeroski	.20	.09	.03
☐ 25 Rickey Henderson	.60	.25	.08
☐ 26 Barry Bonds	.45	.20	.06
☐ 27 Jose Rijo	.20	.09	.03
☐ 28 George Brett	.40	.18	.05
☐ 29 Doug Drabek	.20	.09	.03
☐ 30 Matt Williams	.25	.11	.03
☐ 31 Barry Larkin	.25	.11	.03
☐ 32 Dave Stewart	.20	.09	.03
☐ 33 Dave Justice	.45	.20	.06
☐ 34 Harmon Killebrew	.30	.14	.04
☐ 35 Yogi Berra	.35	.16	.04
☐ 36 Billy Williams	.25	.11	.03

1983 Conlon Marketcom

This set of 60 Charles Martin Conlon photo cards was produced by Marketcom in conjunction with The Sporting News. The cards are large size, approximately 4 1/2" by 6 1/8" and are in a sepia tone. The players selected for the set are members of the 1933 American and National League All-Star teams as well as Negro League All-Stars. These cards are numbered at the bottom of each reverse. The set numbering is American League (1-24), National League (25-48), and Negro League (49-60). In the upper right corner of each card's obverse is printed "1933 American (National or Negro League as appropriate) All Stars." Each obverse also features a facsimile autograph of the player pictured.

	NRMT-MT	EXC	G-VG
COMPLETE SET (60)	22.00	10.00	2.80
COMMON PLAYER (1-24)	.30	.14	.04
COMMON PLAYER (25-48)	.30	.14	.04
COMMON PLAYER (49-60)	.40	.18	.05
☐ 1 Jimmy Foxx	.60	.25	.08
☐ 2 Heinie Manush	.40	.18	.05
☐ 3 Lou Gehrig	1.25	.55	.16
☐ 4 Al Simmons	.40	.18	.05
☐ 5 Charlie Gehringer	.40	.18	.05
☐ 6 Luke Appling	.40	.18	.05
☐ 7 Mickey Cochrane	.50	.23	.06
☐ 8 Joe Kuhel	.30	.14	.04
☐ 9 Bill Dickey	.50	.23	.06
☐ 10 Pinky Higgins	.30	.14	.04
☐ 11 Roy Johnson	.30	.14	.04
☐ 12 Ben Chapman	.30	.14	.04
☐ 13 Urban Hodapp	.30	.14	.04
☐ 14 Joe Cronin	.40	.18	.05
☐ 15 Evar Swanson	.30	.14	.04
☐ 16 Earl Averill	.40	.18	.05

☐ 17 Babe Ruth	2.50	1.15	.30
☐ 18 Tony Lazzeri	.40	.18	.05
☐ 19 Alvin Crowder	.30	.14	.04
☐ 20 Lefty Grove	.50	.23	.06
☐ 21 Earl Whitehill	.30	.14	.04
☐ 22 Lefty Gomez	.50	.23	.06
☐ 23 Mel Harder	.30	.14	.04
☐ 24 Tommy Bridges	.30	.14	.04
☐ 25 Chuck Klein	.40	.18	.05
☐ 26 Spud Davis	.30	.14	.04
☐ 27 Riggs Stephenson	.30	.14	.04
☐ 28 Tony Piet	.30	.14	.04
☐ 29 Bill Terry	.40	.18	.05
☐ 30 Wes Schulmerich	.30	.14	.04
☐ 31 Pepper Martin	.30	.14	.04
☐ 32 Arky Vaughan	.40	.18	.05
☐ 33 Wally Berger	.30	.14	.04
☐ 34 Ripper Collins	.30	.14	.04
☐ 35 Fred Lindstrom	.40	.18	.05
☐ 36 Chick Fullis	.30	.14	.04
☐ 37 Paul Waner	.40	.18	.05
☐ 38 Johnny Frederick	.30	.14	.04
☐ 39 Joe Medwick	.40	.18	.05
☐ 40 Pie Traynor	.40	.18	.05
☐ 41 Frankie Frisch	.40	.18	.05
☐ 42 Chick Hafey	.40	.18	.05
☐ 43 Carl Hubbell	.40	.18	.05
☐ 44 Guy Bush	.30	.14	.04
☐ 45 Dizzy Dean	.75	.35	.09
☐ 46 Hal Schumacher	.30	.14	.04
☐ 47 Larry French	.30	.14	.04
☐ 48 Lon Warneke	.30	.14	.04
☐ 49 Cool Papa Bell	.75	.35	.09
☐ 50 Oscar Charleston	.60	.25	.08
☐ 51 Josh Gibson	1.00	.45	.13
☐ 52 Satchel Paige	1.00	.45	.13
☐ 53 Dave Malarcher	.40	.18	.05
☐ 54 John Henry Lloyd	.60	.25	.08
☐ 55 Rube Foster	.60	.25	.08
☐ 56 Buck Leonard	.75	.35	.09
☐ 57 Smoky Joe Williams	.40	.18	.05
☐ 58 Willie Wells	.40	.18	.05
☐ 59 Judy Johnson	.75	.35	.09
☐ 60 Martin DiHigo	.60	.25	.08

1986 Conlon Series 1

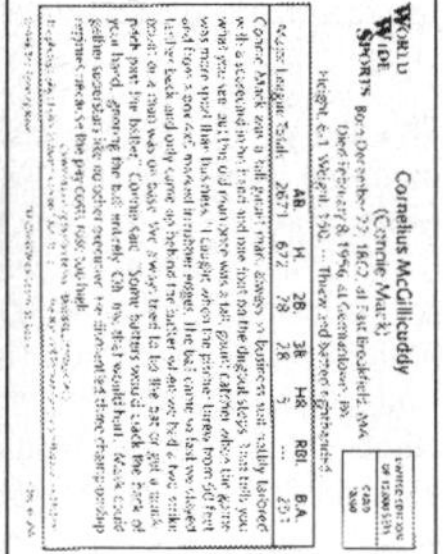

This 60-card set was produced from the black and white photos in the Charles Martin Conlon collection. Each set comes with a special card which contains the number of that set out of the 12,000 sets which were produced. The cards measure 2 1/2" by 3 1/2" and are printed in sepia tones. The cards are individually numbered on the back.

	MT	EX-MT	VG
COMPLETE SET (60)	16.00	7.25	2.00
COMMON PLAYER (1-60)	.25	.11	.03
☐ 1 Lou Gehrig	1.00	.45	.13
☐ 2 Ty Cobb	.90	.40	.11
☐ 3 Grover C. Alexander	.45	.20	.06
☐ 4 Walter Johnson	.60	.25	.08
☐ 5 Bill Klem	.35	.16	.04
☐ 6 Ty Cobb	.90	.40	.11
☐ 7 Gordon S. Cochrane	.35	.16	.04
☐ 8 Paul Waner	.25	.11	.03
☐ 9 Joe Cronin	.25	.11	.03
☐ 10 Jay Hanna Dean	.60	.25	.08
☐ 11 Leo Durocher	.35	.16	.04
☐ 12 Jimmy Foxx	.45	.20	.06
☐ 13 George Herman Ruth	1.50	.65	.19
☐ 14 Mike Gonzalez Frank Frisch Clyde Ellsworth Wares	.25	.11	.03
☐ 15 Carl Hubbell	.35	.16	.04
☐ 16 Miller Huggins	.25	.11	.03
☐ 17 Lou Gehrig	.90	.40	.11
☐ 18 Connie McGillicuddy (Connie Mack)	.35	.16	.04
☐ 19 Heinie Manush	.25	.11	.03
☐ 20 George Herman Ruth	1.50	.65	.19
☐ 22 Pepper Martin	.25	.11	.03
☐ 23 Christy Mathewson	.60	.25	.08
☐ 24 Ty Cobb	.90	.40	.11
☐ 25 Stanley R. Harris	.25	.11	.03
☐ 26 Waite Hoyt	.25	.11	.03
☐ 27 Rube Marquard	.25	.11	.03
☐ 28 Joe McCarthy	.25	.11	.03
☐ 29 John McGraw	.25	.11	.03
☐ 30 Tris Speaker	.35	.16	.04
☐ 31 Bill Terry	.35	.16	.04
☐ 32 Christy Mathewson	.60	.25	.08
☐ 33 Casey Stengel	.60	.25	.08
☐ 34 Robert William Meusel	.25	.11	.03
☐ 35 George Edward Waddell	.25	.11	.03
☐ 36 Mel Ott	.45	.20	.06
☐ 37 Roger Peckinpaugh	.25	.11	.03
☐ 38 Pie Traynor	.25	.11	.03
☐ 39 Chief Bender	.25	.11	.03
☐ 40 John Wesley Coombs	.25	.11	.03
☐ 41 Ty Cobb	.90	.40	.11
☐ 42 Harry Heilmann	.25	.11	.03
☐ 43 Charlie Gehringer	.35	.16	.04
☐ 44 Rogers Hornsby	.60	.25	.08
☐ 45 Vernon Gomez	.45	.20	.06
☐ 46 Christy Mathewson	.60	.25	.08
☐ 47 Robert Moses Grove	.45	.20	.06
☐ 48 George Herman Ruth	1.50	.65	.19
☐ 49 Fred Merkle	.25	.11	.03
☐ 50 George Herman Ruth	1.50	.65	.19
☐ 51 Herb Pennock	.25	.11	.03
☐ 52 Lou Gehrig	.90	.40	.11
☐ 53 Fred Clarke	.25	.11	.03
☐ 54 George Herman Ruth	1.50	.65	.19
☐ 55 John Peter Wagner	.60	.25	.08
☐ 56 Hack Wilson	.35	.16	.04
☐ 57 Lou Gehrig	.90	.40	.11
☐ 58 Lloyd Waner	.25	.11	.03
☐ 59 Charles Martin Conlon	.25	.11	.03
☐ 60 Conlon and Margie	.25	.11	.03
☐ NNO Set Number Card	.25	.11	.03

1987 Conlon Series 2

The second series of 60 Charles Martin Conlon photo cards was produced by World Wide Sports in conjunction with The Sporting News. The cards are standard size, 2 1/2" by 3 1/2" and are in a sepia tone. Supposedly 12,000 sets were produced. The photos were selected and background information written by Paul MacFarlane of The Sporting News. The cards are individually numbered on the back.

	MT	EX-MT	VG
COMPLETE SET (60)	12.00	5.50	1.50
COMMON PLAYER (1-60)	.25	.11	.03

		MT	EX-MT	VG
☐	1 Lou Gehrig	1.00	.45	.13
☐	2 Vernon Gomez	.45	.20	.06
☐	3 Christy Mathewson	.60	.25	.08
☐	4 Grover Alexander	.45	.20	.06
☐	5 Ty Cobb	.90	.40	.11
☐	6 Walter Johnson	.60	.25	.08
☐	7 Charles(Babe) Adams	.30	.14	.04
☐	8 Nick Altrock	.25	.11	.03
☐	9 Al Schacht	.25	.11	.03
☐	10 Hugh Critz	.25	.11	.03
☐	11 Henry Cullop	.25	.11	.03
☐	12 Jacob Daubert	.25	.11	.03
☐	13 William Donovan	.25	.11	.03
☐	14 Chick Hafey	.30	.14	.04
☐	15 Bill Hallahan	.25	.11	.03
☐	16 Fred Haney	.25	.11	.03
☐	17 Charles Hartnett	.35	.16	.04
☐	18 Walter Henline	.25	.11	.03
☐	19 Edwin Rommel	.25	.11	.03
☐	20 Ralph(Babe) Pinelli	.25	.11	.03
☐	21 Robert Meusel	.25	.11	.03
☐	22 Emil Meusel	.25	.11	.03
☐	23 Smead Jolley	.25	.11	.03
☐	24 Ike Boone	.25	.11	.03
☐	25 Earl Webb	.25	.11	.03
☐	26 Charles Comiskey	.35	.16	.04
☐	27 Edward Collins	.35	.16	.04
☐	28 George(Buck) Weaver	.35	.16	.04
☐	29 Eddie Cicotte	.35	.16	.04
☐	30 Sam Crawford	.30	.14	.04
☐	31 Charles Dressen	.25	.11	.03
☐	32 Arthur Fletcher	.25	.11	.03
☐	33 Hugh Duffy	.35	.16	.04
☐	34 Ira Flagstead	.25	.11	.03
☐	35 Harry Hooper	.35	.16	.04
☐	36 George Lewis	.25	.11	.03
☐	37 James Dykes	.25	.11	.03
☐	38 Leon Goslin	.35	.16	.04
☐	39 Henry Gowdy	.25	.11	.03
☐	40 Charles Grimm	.25	.11	.03
☐	41 Mark Koenig	.25	.11	.03
☐	42 James Hogan	.25	.11	.03
☐	43 William Jacobson	.25	.11	.03
☐	44 Fielder Jones	.25	.11	.03
☐	45 George Kelly	.35	.16	.04
☐	46 Adolpho Luque	.25	.11	.03
☐	47 Walter Maranville	.25	.11	.03
☐	48 Carl Mays	.25	.11	.03
☐	49 Edward Plank	.35	.16	.04
☐	50 Hubert Pruett	.25	.11	.03
☐	51 John(Picus) Quinn	.25	.11	.03
☐	52 Charles(Flint) Rhem	.25	.11	.03
☐	53 Amos Rusie	.35	.16	.04
☐	54 Edd Roush	.35	.16	.04
☐	55 Ray Schalk	.35	.16	.04
☐	56 Ernest Shore	.25	.11	.03
☐	57 Joe Wood	.25	.11	.03
☐	58 George Sisler	.45	.20	.06
☐	59 James Thorpe	1.50	.65	.19
☐	60 Earl Whitehill	.25	.11	.03

1988 Conlon Series 3

This third series of 30 Charles Martin Conlon photo cards was produced by World Wide Sports in conjunction with The Sporting News. The cards are standard size, 2 1/2" by 3 1/2" and are in a sepia tone. The photos were selected and background information written by Paul MacFarlane of The Sporting News. These cards are unnumbered and hence are listed below in alphabetical order. Series 3 is indicated in the lower right corner of each card's reverse. A black and white logo for the "Baseball Immortals" and The Conlon Collection is over-printed in the lower left corner of each obverse.

		MT	EX-MT	VG
	COMPLETE SET (30)	6.50	2.90	.80
	COMMON PLAYER (1-30)	.25	.11	.03
☐	1 Ace Adams	.25	.11	.03
☐	2 Grover C. Alexander	.45	.20	.06
☐	3 Elden Auker	.25	.11	.03
☐	4 Jack Barry	.25	.11	.03
☐	5 Wally Berger	.25	.11	.03
☐	6 Ben Chapman	.25	.11	.03
☐	7 Mickey Cochrane	.45	.20	.06
☐	8 Frankie Crosetti	.35	.16	.04
☐	9 Paul Dean	.35	.16	.04
☐	10 Leo Durocher	.45	.20	.06
☐	11 Wes Ferrell	.25	.11	.03
☐	12 Hank Gowdy	.25	.11	.03
☐	13 Andy High	.25	.11	.03
☐	14 Rogers Hornsby	.60	.25	.08
☐	15 Carl Hubbell	.35	.16	.04
☐	16 Joe Judge	.25	.11	.03
☐	17 Tony Lazzeri	.35	.16	.04
☐	18 Pepper Martin	.25	.11	.03
☐	19 Lee Meadows	.25	.11	.03
☐	20 Johnny Murphy	.25	.11	.03
☐	21 Steve O'Neil	.25	.11	.03
☐	22 Ed Plank	.35	.16	.04
☐	23 Jack(Picus) Quinn	.25	.11	.03
☐	24 Charley Root	.25	.11	.03
☐	25 Babe Ruth	1.50	.65	.19
☐	26 Fred Snodgrass	.25	.11	.03
☐	27 Tris Speaker	.45	.20	.06
☐	28 Bill Terry	.35	.16	.04
☐	29 Jeff Tesreau	.25	.11	.03
☐	30 George Toporcer	.25	.11	.03

1988 Conlon Series 4

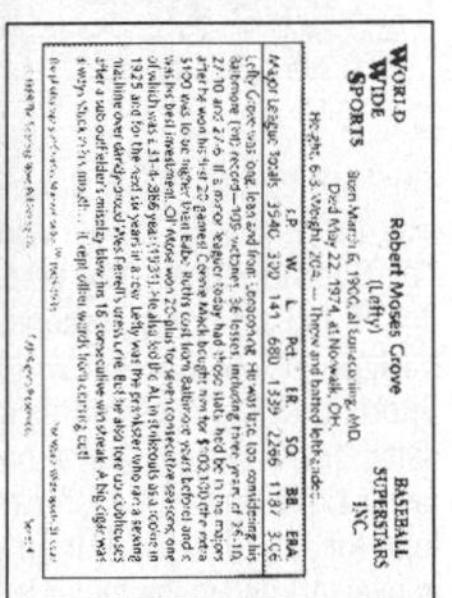

This fourth series of 30 Charles Martin Conlon photo cards was produced by World Wide Sports in conjunction with The Sporting News. The cards are standard size, 2 1/2" by 3 1/2" and are in a sepia tone. The photos were selected and background information written by Paul MacFarlane of The Sporting News. These cards are unnumbered and hence are listed below in alphabetical order. Series 4 is indicated in the lower right corner of each card's reverse. A black and white logo for the "Baseball Immortals" and The Conlon Collection is over-printed in the lower left corner of each obverse.

		MT	EX-MT	VG
	COMPLETE SET (30)	6.50	2.90	.80
	COMMON PLAYER (1-30)	.25	.11	.03
☐	1 Dale Alexander	.25	.11	.03
☐	2 Morris Badgro	.25	.11	.03
☐	3 Dick Bartell	.25	.11	.03
☐	4 Max Bishop	.25	.11	.03
☐	5 Hal Chase	.25	.11	.03
☐	6 Ty Cobb	.90	.40	.11
☐	7 Nick Cullop	.25	.11	.03

	MT	EX-MT	VG
☐ 8 Dizzy Dean	.60	.25	.08
☐ 9 Charlie Dressen	.25	.11	.03
☐ 10 Jimmy Dykes	.25	.11	.03
☐ 11 Art Fletcher	.25	.11	.03
☐ 12 Charlie Grimm	.25	.11	.03
☐ 13 Lefty Grove	.45	.20	.06
☐ 14 Baby Doll Jacobson	.25	.11	.03
☐ 15 Bill Klem	.35	.16	.04
☐ 16 Mark Koenig	.25	.11	.03
☐ 17 Duffy Lewis	.25	.11	.03
☐ 18 Carl Mays	.25	.11	.03
☐ 19 Fred Merkle	.25	.11	.03
☐ 20 Greasy Neale	.25	.11	.03
☐ 21 Mel Ott	.45	.20	.06
☐ 22 Babe Pinelli	.25	.11	.03
☐ 23 Flint Rhem	.25	.11	.03
☐ 24 Slim Sallee UER (Misspelled Salee on card back)	.25	.11	.03
☐ 25 Al Simmons	.35	.16	.04
☐ 26 George Sisler	.45	.20	.06
☐ 27 Riggs Stephenson	.25	.11	.03
☐ 28 Jim Thorpe	1.50	.65	.19
☐ 29 Bill Wambsganss	.25	.11	.03
☐ 30 Cy Young	.45	.20	.06

1988 Conlon Series 5

This fifth series of 30 Charles Martin Conlon photo cards was produced by World Wide Sports in conjunction with The Sporting News. The cards are standard size, 2 1/2" by 3 1/2" and are in a sepia tone. The photos were selected and background information written by Paul MacFarlane of The Sporting News. These cards are unnumbered and hence are listed below in alphabetical order. Series 5 is indicated in the lower right corner of each card's reverse. A black and white logo for the "Baseball Immortals" and The Conlon Collection is over-printed in the lower left corner of each obverse.

	MT	EX-MT	VG
COMPLETE SET (30)	5.50	2.50	.70
COMMON PLAYER (1-30)	.25	.11	.03
☐ 1 Nick Altrock	.25	.11	.03
☐ 2 Del Baker	.25	.11	.03
☐ 3 Moe Berg	.35	.16	.04
☐ 4 Zeke Bonura	.25	.11	.03
☐ 5 Eddie Collins	.35	.16	.04
☐ 6 Hughie Critz	.25	.11	.03
☐ 7 George Dauss	.25	.11	.03
☐ 8 Joe Dugan	.25	.11	.03
☐ 9 Howard Ehmke	.25	.11	.03
☐ 10 James Emory Foxx	.60	.25	.08
☐ 11 Frankie Frisch	.35	.16	.04
☐ 12 Lou Gehrig	.90	.40	.11
☐ 13 Charlie Gehringer	.45	.20	.06
☐ 14 Kid Gleason	.25	.11	.03
☐ 15 Lefty Gomez	.45	.20	.06
☐ 16 Babe Herman	.25	.11	.03
☐ 17 Bill James	.25	.11	.03
☐ 18 Joe Kuhel	.25	.11	.03
☐ 19 Dolf Luque	.25	.11	.03
☐ 20 John McGraw	.35	.16	.04
☐ 21 Stuffy McInnis	.25	.11	.03
☐ 22 Bob Meusel	.25	.11	.03
☐ 23 Lefty O'Doul	.25	.11	.03
☐ 24 Hub Pruett	.25	.11	.03
☐ 25 Paul Richards	.25	.11	.03
☐ 26 Bob Shawkey	.25	.11	.03
☐ 27 Gabby Street	.25	.11	.03
☐ 28 Johnny Tobin	.25	.11	.03
☐ 29 Rube Waddell	.35	.16	.04
☐ 30 Billy Werber	.25	.11	.03

1988 Conlon American All-Stars

This set of 24 Charles Martin Conlon photo cards was produced by World Wide Sports in conjunction with The Sporting News. The cards are standard size, 2 1/2" by 3 1/2" and are in a sepia tone. The photos (members of the 1933 American League All-Star team) were selected and background information written by Paul MacFarlane of The Sporting News. These cards are unnumbered and hence are listed below in alphabetical order. American League is indicated in the lower right corner of each card's reverse. In the upper right corner of each card's obverse is printed "1933 American All Stars."

	MT	EX-MT	VG
COMPLETE SET (24)	5.50	2.50	.70
COMMON PLAYER (1-24)	.25	.11	.03
☐ 1 Luke Appling	.45	.20	.06
☐ 2 Earl Averill	.35	.16	.04
☐ 3 Tommy Bridges	.25	.11	.03
☐ 4 Ben Chapman	.25	.11	.03
☐ 5 Mickey Cochrane	.45	.20	.06
☐ 6 Joe Cronin	.35	.16	.04
☐ 7 Alvin Crowder	.25	.11	.03
☐ 8 Bill Dickey	.45	.20	.06
☐ 9 James Emory Foxx	.60	.25	.08
☐ 10 Lou Gehrig	.90	.40	.11
☐ 11 Charlie Gehringer	.45	.20	.06
☐ 12 Lefty Gomez	.45	.20	.06
☐ 13 Lefty Grove	.45	.20	.06
☐ 14 Mel Harder	.25	.11	.03
☐ 15 Pinky Higgins	.25	.11	.03
☐ 16 Urban Hodapp	.25	.11	.03
☐ 17 Roy Johnson	.25	.11	.03
☐ 18 Joe Kuhel	.25	.11	.03
☐ 19 Tony Lazzeri	.35	.16	.04
☐ 20 Heinie Manush	.45	.20	.06
☐ 21 Babe Ruth	1.50	.65	.19
☐ 22 Al Simmons	.35	.16	.04
☐ 23 Evar Swanson	.25	.11	.03
☐ 24 Earl Whitehill	.25	.11	.03

1988 Conlon National All-Stars

This set of 24 Charles Martin Conlon photo cards was produced by World Wide Sports in conjunction with The Sporting News. The cards are standard size, 2 1/2" by 3 1/2" and are in a sepia tone. The photos (members of the 1933 National League All-Star team) were selected and background information written by Paul MacFarlane of The

Sporting News. These cards are unnumbered and hence are listed below in alphabetical order. American League is indicated in the lower right corner of each card's reverse. In the upper right corner of each card's obverse is printed "1933 National All Stars."

	MT	EX-MT	VG
COMPLETE SET (24)	5.50	2.50	.70
COMMON PLAYER (1-24)	.25	.11	.03
☐ 1 Wally Berger	.25	.11	.03
☐ 2 Guy Bush	.25	.11	.03
☐ 3 Ripper Collins	.25	.11	.03
☐ 4 Spud Davis	.25	.11	.03
☐ 5 Dizzy Dean	.60	.25	.08
☐ 6 Johnny Frederick	.25	.11	.03
☐ 7 Larry French	.25	.11	.03
☐ 8 Frankie Frisch	.35	.16	.04
☐ 9 Chick Fullis	.25	.11	.03
☐ 10 Chick Hafey	.35	.16	.04
☐ 11 Carl Hubbell	.45	.20	.06
☐ 12 Chuck Klein	.35	.16	.04
☐ 13 Fred Lindstrom	.35	.16	.04
☐ 14 Pepper Martin	.25	.11	.03
☐ 15 Joe Medwick	.35	.16	.04
☐ 16 Tony Piet	.25	.11	.03
☐ 17 Wes Schulmerich	.25	.11	.03
☐ 18 Hal Schumacher	.25	.11	.03
☐ 19 Riggs Stephenson	.25	.11	.03
☐ 20 Bill Terry	.45	.20	.06
☐ 21 Pie Traynor	.35	.16	.04
☐ 22 Arky Vaughan	.35	.16	.04
☐ 23 Paul Waner	.35	.16	.04
☐ 24 Lon Warneke	.25	.11	.03

1988 Conlon Negro All-Stars

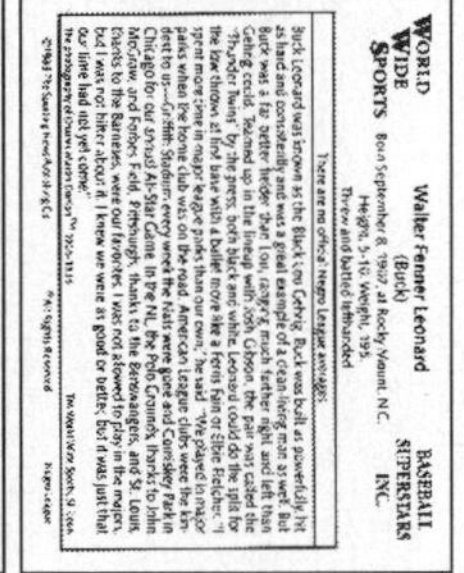

This set of 12 photo cards was produced by World Wide Sports in conjunction with The Sporting News. The cards are standard size, 2 1/2" by 3 1/2" and are in a sepia tone. The photos (Negro League All Stars from 1933) were selected and background information written by Paul MacFarlane of The Sporting News. Despite the stylistic similarity of this set with the other Conlon sets, the photos for this set were not taken by Charles Martin Conlon. These cards are unnumbered and hence are listed below in alphabetical order. Negro League is indicated in the lower right corner of each card's reverse. In the upper right corner of each card's obverse is printed "1933 Negro All Stars." The photo quality on some of the cards is very poor suggesting that the original photo or negative may have been enlarged to an excessive degree.

	MT	EX-MT	VG
COMPLETE SET (12)	5.00	2.30	.60
COMMON PLAYER (1-12)	.40	.18	.05
☐ 1 Cool Papa Bell	.60	.25	.08
☐ 2 Oscar Charleston	.50	.23	.06
☐ 3 Martin DiHigo	.50	.23	.06
☐ 4 Rube Foster	.50	.23	.06
☐ 5 Josh Gibson	.75	.35	.09
☐ 6 Judy Johnson	.50	.23	.06
☐ 7 Buck Leonard	.50	.23	.06
☐ 8 John Henry Lloyd	.50	.23	.06
☐ 9 Dave Malarcher	.40	.18	.05
☐ 10 Satchel Paige	.75	.35	.09
☐ 11 Willie Wells	.40	.18	.05
☐ 12 Smoky Joe Williams	.40	.18	.05

1988 Conlon Hardee's/Coke

This six-card set was issued in 18 central Indiana Hardee's restaurants over a six-week period, a different card per purchase per week. The set features the vintage photography of Charles Martin Conlon, except for the Cool Papa Bell photo which was not shot by Conlon. The cards are sepia tone and are standard size, 2 1/2" by 3 1/2". The card backs contain biographical information, Hardee's logo, and a Coca Cola Classic logo. The cards are also copyrighted by The Sporting News.

	MT	EX-MT	VG
COMPLETE SET (6)	4.00	1.80	.50
COMMON PLAYER (1-6)	.50	.23	.06
☐ 1 James Bell (Cool Papa)	.50	.23	.06
☐ 2 Tyrus Raymond Cobb (Georgia Peach)	1.50	.65	.19
☐ 3 Henry Louis Gehrig (Iron Horse)	1.50	.65	.19
☐ 4 Cornelius McGillicuddy (Connie Mack)	.50	.23	.06
☐ 5 Charles Dillon Stengel (Casey)	.75	.35	.09
☐ 6 George Edward Waddell (Rube)	.50	.23	.06

1991 Conlon TSN

This 330-card set issued in black and white again featured the photography of Charles Conlon. The set was produced by MegaCards in conjunction with The Sporting News. The

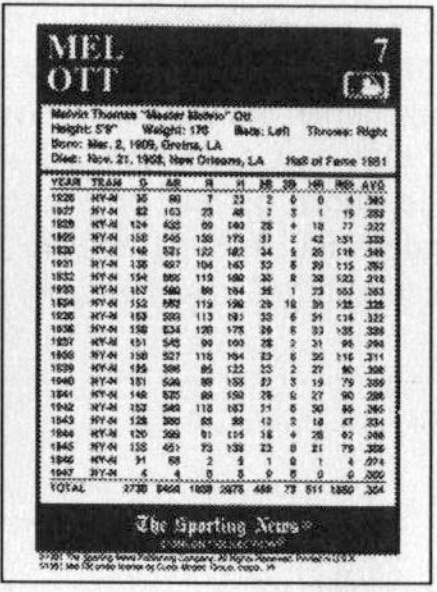

set features standard-size (2 1/2" by 3 1/2") cards with black and white borders surrounded by black borders. The set was available in packs as well as in a factory set. The card backs contain pertinent information relevant to the front of the cards whether it is career statistics or all-time leaders format or the special cards commemorating the great teams of the first part of the twentieth century.

	MT	EX-MT	VG
COMPLETE SET (330)	18.00	8.00	2.30
COMMON PLAYER (1-330)	.08	.04	.01
☐ 1 HOF: Rogers Hornsby	.30	.14	.04
☐ 2 HOF: Jimmy Foxx	.30	.14	.04
☐ 3 HOF: Dizzy Dean	.40	.18	.05
☐ 4 HOF: Rabbit Maranville	.15	.07	.02
☐ 5 HOF: Paul Waner	.15	.07	.02
☐ 6 HOF: Lloyd Waner	.15	.07	.02
☐ 7 HOF: Mel Ott	.30	.14	.04
☐ 8 HOF: Honus Wagner	.40	.18	.05
☐ 9 HOF: Walter Johnson	.30	.14	.04
☐ 10 HOF: Carl Hubbell	.20	.09	.03
☐ 11 HOF: Frank Frisch	.20	.09	.03
☐ 12 HOF: Kiki Cuyler	.15	.07	.02
☐ 13 HOF: Red Ruffing	.15	.07	.02
☐ 14 HOF: Hank Greenberg	.30	.14	.04
☐ 15 HOF: Johnny Evers	.15	.07	.02
☐ 16 HOF: Hugh Jennings	.15	.07	.02
☐ 17 HOF: Dave Bancroft	.15	.07	.02
☐ 18 HOF: Joe Medwick	.20	.09	.03
☐ 19 HOF: Ted Lyons	.15	.07	.02
☐ 20 HOF: Chief Bender	.15	.07	.02
☐ 21 HOF: Eddie Collins	.20	.09	.03
☐ 22 HOF: Jim Bottomley	.15	.07	.02
☐ 23 HOF: Lefty Grove	.30	.14	.04
☐ 24 HOF: Max Carey	.15	.07	.02
☐ 25 HOF: Burleigh Grimes	.15	.07	.02
☐ 26 HOF: Ross Youngs	.20	.09	.03
☐ 27 HOF: Ernie Lombardi	.15	.07	.02
☐ 28 HOF: Joe McCarthy	.15	.07	.02
☐ 29 HOF: Hack Wilson	.25	.11	.03
☐ 30 HOF: Chuck Klein	.15	.07	.02
☐ 31 HOF: Earl Averill	.15	.07	.02
☐ 32 HOF: Grover Alexander	.20	.09	.03
☐ 33 HOF: Chick Hafey	.15	.07	.02
☐ 34 HOF: Bill McKechnie	.15	.07	.02
☐ 35 HOF: Bob Feller	.30	.14	.04
☐ 36 HOF: Pie Traynor	.20	.09	.03
☐ 37 HOF: Casey Stengel	.30	.14	.04
☐ 38 HOF: Arky Vaughan	.15	.07	.02
☐ 39 HOF: Eppa Rixey	.15	.07	.02
☐ 40 HOF: Joe Sewell	.15	.07	.02
☐ 41 HOF: Red Faber	.15	.07	.02
☐ 42 HOF: Travis Jackson	.15	.07	.02
☐ 43 HOF: Jess Haines	.15	.07	.02
☐ 44 HOF: Tris Speaker	.20	.09	.03
☐ 45 HOF: Connie Mack	.20	.09	.03
☐ 46 HOF: Connie Mack	.20	.09	.03
☐ 47 HOF: Connie Mack	.20	.09	.03
☐ 48 HOF: Ray Schalk	.15	.07	.02
☐ 49 HOF: Al Simmons	.15	.07	.02
☐ 50 HOF: Joe Cronin	.20	.09	.03
☐ 51 HOF: Mickey Cochrane	.20	.09	.03
☐ 52 HOF: Harry Heilmann	.20	.09	.03
☐ 53 HOF: Johnny Mize	.20	.09	.03
☐ 54 HOF: Sam Rice	.15	.07	.02
☐ 55 HOF: Edd Roush	.15	.07	.02
☐ 56 HOF: Enos Slaughter	.20	.09	.03
☐ 57 HOF: Christy Mathewson	.35	.16	.04
☐ 58 HOF: Fred Lindstrom	.15	.07	.02
☐ 59 HOF: Gabby Hartnett	.15	.07	.02
☐ 60 HOF: George Kelly	.15	.07	.02
☐ 61 HOF: Bucky Harris	.15	.07	.02
☐ 62 HOF: Goose Goslin	.15	.07	.02
☐ 63 HOF: Heinie Manush	.15	.07	.02
☐ 64 HOF: Bill Terry	.20	.09	.03
☐ 65 HOF: John McGraw	.20	.09	.03
☐ 66 HOF: George Sisler	.20	.09	.03
☐ 67 HOF: Lefty Gomez	.20	.09	.03
☐ 68 Joe Judge	.08	.04	.01
☐ 69 Tommy Thevenow	.08	.04	.01
☐ 70 Charlie Gelbert	.08	.04	.01
☐ 71 Jackie Hayes	.08	.04	.01
☐ 72 Bob Fothergill	.08	.04	.01
☐ 73 Adam Comorosky	.08	.04	.01
☐ 74 Earl Smith	.08	.04	.01
☐ 75 Sam Gray	.08	.04	.01
☐ 76 Pete Appleton	.08	.04	.01
☐ 77 Gene Moore	.08	.04	.01
☐ 78 Art Jorgens	.08	.04	.01
☐ 79 Bill Knickerbocker	.08	.04	.01
☐ 80 Carl Reynolds	.08	.04	.01
☐ 81 Ski Melillo	.08	.04	.01
☐ 82 Johnny Burnett	.08	.04	.01
☐ 83 Jake Powell	.08	.04	.01
☐ 84 Johnny Murphy	.08	.04	.01
☐ 85 Roy Parmelee	.08	.04	.01
☐ 86 Jimmy Ripple	.08	.04	.01
☐ 87 Gee Walker	.08	.04	.01
☐ 88 George Earnshaw	.08	.04	.01
☐ 89 Billy Southworth	.08	.04	.01
☐ 90 Wally Moses	.08	.04	.01
☐ 91 Rube Walberg	.08	.04	.01
☐ 92 Jimmy Dykes	.08	.04	.01
☐ 93 Charlie Root	.08	.04	.01
☐ 94 Johnny Cooney	.08	.04	.01
☐ 95 Charlie Grimm	.08	.04	.01
☐ 96 Bob Johnson	.08	.04	.01
☐ 97 Jack Scott	.08	.04	.01
☐ 98 Rip Radcliff	.08	.04	.01
☐ 99 Fritz Ostermueller	.08	.04	.01
☐ 100 '27NY: Julie Wera	.08	.04	.01
☐ 101 '27NY: Miller Huggins	.20	.09	.03
☐ 102 '27NY: Ray Morehart	.08	.04	.01
☐ 103 '27NY: Benny Bengough	.08	.04	.01
☐ 104 '27NY: Dutch Ruether	.08	.04	.01
☐ 105 '27NY: Earle Combs	.15	.07	.02
☐ 106 '27NY: Myles Thomas	.08	.04	.01
☐ 107 '27NY: Ben Paschal	.08	.04	.01
☐ 108 '27NY: Cedric Durst	.08	.04	.01
☐ 109 '27NY: Wilcy Moore	.08	.04	.01
☐ 110 '27NY: Babe Ruth	.75	.35	.09
☐ 111 '27NY: Lou Gehrig	.50	.23	.06
☐ 112 '27NY: Joe Dugan	.08	.04	.01
☐ 113 '27NY: Tony Lazzeri	.20	.09	.03
☐ 114 '27NY: Urban Shocker	.08	.04	.01
☐ 115 '27NY: Waite Hoyt	.20	.09	.03
☐ 116 '27NY: Charley O'Leary	.08	.04	.01
☐ 117 '27NY: Art Fletcher	.08	.04	.01
☐ 118 '27NY: Pat Collins	.08	.04	.01
☐ 119 '27NY: Joe Giard	.08	.04	.01
☐ 120 '27NY: Herb Pennock	.20	.09	.03
☐ 121 '27NY: Mike Gazella	.08	.04	.01
☐ 122 '27NY: Bob Meusel	.12	.05	.02
☐ 123 '27NY: George Pipgras	.08	.04	.01
☐ 124 '27NY: J.Grabowski	.08	.04	.01
☐ 125 '27NY: Mark Koenig	.08	.04	.01
☐ 126 Stan Hack	.08	.04	.01
☐ 127 Earl Whitehill	.08	.04	.01
☐ 128 Bill Lee	.08	.04	.01
☐ 129 Gus Mancuso	.08	.04	.01
☐ 130 Ray Blades	.08	.04	.01
☐ 131 Jack Burns	.08	.04	.01
☐ 132 Clint Brown	.08	.04	.01
☐ 133 Bill Dietrich	.08	.04	.01
☐ 134 Cy Blanton	.08	.04	.01
☐ 135 Harry Hooper '16 Champs	.20	.09	.03
☐ 136 Chick Shorten '16 Champs	.08	.04	.01
☐ 137 Tilly Walker '16 Champs	.08	.04	.01
☐ 138 Rube Foster '16 Champs	.08	.04	.01
☐ 139 Jack Barry '16 Champs	.08	.04	.01
☐ 140 Sam Jones '16 Champs	.08	.04	.01
☐ 141 Ernie Shore '16 Champs	.08	.04	.01
☐ 142 Dutch Leonard '16 Champs	.08	.04	.01
☐ 143 Herb Pennock '16 Champs	.20	.09	.03

☐	144	Hal Janvrin '16 Champs	.08	.04	.01
☐	145	Babe Ruth '16 Champs	.75	.35	.09
☐	146	Duffy Lewis '16 Champs	.08	.04	.01
☐	147	Larry Gardner '16 Champs	.08	.04	.01
☐	148	Doc Hoblitzel '16 Champs	.08	.04	.01
☐	149	Everett Scott '16 Champs	.08	.04	.01
☐	150	Carl Mays '16 Champs	.08	.04	.01
☐	151	'16LL: Bert Niehoff	.08	.04	.01
☐	152	'16LL: Burt Shotton	.08	.04	.01
☐	153	'16LL: Red Ames	.08	.04	.01
☐	154	'16LL: Cy Williams	.08	.04	.01
☐	155	'16LL: Bill Hinchman	.08	.04	.01
☐	156	'16LL: Bob Shawkey	.08	.04	.01
☐	157	'16LL: Wally Pipp	.15	.07	.02
☐	158	'16LL: George J. Burns	.08	.04	.01
☐	159	'16LL: Bob Veach	.08	.04	.01
☐	160	'16LL: Hal Chase	.08	.04	.01
☐	161	'16LL: Tom Hughes	.08	.04	.01
☐	162	'16LL: Del Pratt	.08	.04	.01
☐	163	'16LL: Heinie Groh	.08	.04	.01
☐	164	'16LL: Zack Wheat	.20	.09	.03
☐	165	Story: Lefty O'Doul	.08	.04	.01
☐	166	Story: Willie Kamm	.08	.04	.01
☐	167	Story: Paul Waner	.20	.09	.03
☐	168	Story: Fred Snodgrass	.08	.04	.01
☐	169	Story: Babe Herman	.20	.09	.03
☐	170	Story: Al Bridwell	.08	.04	.01
☐	171	Story: Chief Meyers	.08	.04	.01
☐	172	Story: Hans Lobert	.08	.04	.01
☐	173	Story: Rube Bressler	.08	.04	.01
☐	174	Story: Sam Jones	.08	.04	.01
☐	175	Story: Bob O'Farrell	.08	.04	.01
☐	176	Story: Specs Toporcer	.08	.04	.01
☐	177	Story: Earl McNeely	.08	.04	.01
☐	178	Story: Jack Knott	.08	.04	.01
☐	179	Heinie Mueller	.08	.04	.01
☐	180	Tommy Bridges	.08	.04	.01
☐	181	Lloyd Brown	.08	.04	.01
☐	182	Larry Benton	.08	.04	.01
☐	183	Max Bishop	.08	.04	.01
☐	184	Moe Berg	.20	.09	.03
☐	185	Cy Perkins	.08	.04	.01
☐	186	Steve O'Neill	.08	.04	.01
☐	187	Glenn Myatt	.08	.04	.01
☐	188	Joe Kuhel	.08	.04	.01
☐	189	Marty McManus	.08	.04	.01
☐	190	Red Lucas	.08	.04	.01
☐	191	Stuffy McInnis	.08	.04	.01
☐	192	Bing Miller	.08	.04	.01
☐	193	Luke Sewell	.08	.04	.01
☐	194	Bill Sherdel	.08	.04	.01
☐	195	Hal Rhyne	.08	.04	.01
☐	196	Guy Bush	.08	.04	.01
☐	197	Pete Fox	.08	.04	.01
☐	198	Wes Ferrell	.08	.04	.01
☐	199	Roy Johnson	.08	.04	.01
☐	200	Bill Wambsganss Triple Play	.08	.04	.01
☐	201	George H. Burns Triple Play	.08	.04	.01
☐	202	Clarence Mitchell Triple Play	.08	.04	.01
☐	203	Neal Ball Triple Play	.08	.04	.01
☐	204	Johnny Neun Triple Play	.08	.04	.01
☐	205	Homer Summa Triple Play	.08	.04	.01
☐	206	Ernie Padgett Triple Play	.08	.04	.01
☐	207	Walter Holke Triple Play	.08	.04	.01
☐	208	Glenn Wright Triple Play	.08	.04	.01
☐	209	Hank Gowdy	.08	.04	.01
☐	210	Zack Taylor	.08	.04	.01
☐	211	Ben Cantwell	.08	.04	.01
☐	212	Frank Demaree	.08	.04	.01
☐	213	Paul Derringer	.08	.04	.01
☐	214	Bill Hallahan	.08	.04	.01
☐	215	Danny MacFayden	.08	.04	.01
☐	216	Harry Rice	.08	.04	.01
☐	217	Bob Smith	.08	.04	.01
☐	218	Riggs Stephenson	.08	.04	.01
☐	219	Pat Malone	.08	.04	.01
☐	220	Bennie Tate	.08	.04	.01

☐	221	Joe Vosmik	.08	.04	.01
☐	222	George Watkins	.08	.04	.01
☐	223	Jimmie Wilson	.08	.04	.01
☐	224	George Uhle	.08	.04	.01
☐	225	Trivia: Mel Ott	.20	.09	.03
☐	226	Trivia: Nick Altrock	.08	.04	.01
☐	227	Trivia: Red Ruffing	.15	.07	.02
☐	228	Trivia: Joe Krakauskas	.08	.04	.01
☐	229	Trivia: Wally Berger	.08	.04	.01
☐	230	Bobo Newsom	.08	.04	.01
☐	231	Lon Warneke	.08	.04	.01
☐	232	Frank Snyder	.08	.04	.01
☐	233	Myril Hoag	.08	.04	.01
☐	234	Mel Almada	.08	.04	.01
☐	235	Ivey Wingo	.08	.04	.01
☐	236	Jimmy Austin	.08	.04	.01
☐	237	Zeke Bonura	.08	.04	.01
☐	238	Russ Wrightstone	.08	.04	.01
☐	239	Al Todd	.08	.04	.01
☐	240	Rabbit Warstler	.08	.04	.01
☐	241	Sammy West	.08	.04	.01
☐	242	Art Reinhart	.08	.04	.01
☐	243	Lefty Stewart	.08	.04	.01
☐	244	Johnny Gooch	.08	.04	.01
☐	245	Bubbles Hargrave	.08	.04	.01
☐	246	George Harper	.08	.04	.01
☐	247	Sarge Connally	.08	.04	.01
☐	248	Garland Braxton	.08	.04	.01
☐	249	Wally Schang	.08	.04	.01
☐	250	ATL: Ty Cobb	.50	.23	.06
☐	251	ATL: Rogers Hornsby	.30	.14	.04
☐	252	ATL: Rube Marquard	.20	.09	.03
☐	253	ATL: Carl Hubbell	.20	.09	.03
☐	254	ATL: Joe Wood	.15	.07	.02
☐	255	ATL: Lefty Grove	.30	.14	.04
☐	256	ATL: Schoolboy Rowe	.08	.04	.01
☐	257	ATL: General Crowder	.08	.04	.01
☐	258	ATL: Walter Johnson	.25	.11	.03
☐	259	ATL: Chick Hafey	.15	.07	.02
☐	260	ATL: Fred Fitzsimmons	.08	.04	.01
☐	261	ATL: Earl Webb	.08	.04	.01
☐	262	ATL: Earle Combs	.15	.07	.02
☐	263	ATL: Ed Konetchy	.08	.04	.01
☐	264	ATL: Taylor Douthit	.08	.04	.01
☐	265	ATL: Lloyd Waner	.15	.07	.02
☐	266	ATL: Mickey Cochrane	.20	.09	.03
☐	267	ATL: Hack Wilson	.20	.09	.03
☐	268	ATL: Pie Traynor	.20	.09	.03
☐	269	ATL: Spud Davis	.08	.04	.01
☐	270	ATL: Heinie Manush	.15	.07	.02
☐	271	ATL: Pinky Higgins	.08	.04	.01
☐	272	ATL: Addie Joss	.20	.09	.03
☐	273	ATL: Ed Walsh	.15	.07	.02
☐	274	ATL: Pepper Martin	.15	.07	.02
☐	275	ATL: Joe Sewell	.15	.07	.02
☐	276	ATL: Dutch Leonard	.08	.04	.01
☐	277	ATL: Gavvy Cravath	.08	.04	.01
☐	278	Oral Hildebrand	.08	.04	.01
☐	279	Ray Kremer	.08	.04	.01
☐	280	Frankie Pytlak	.08	.04	.01
☐	281	Sammy Byrd	.08	.04	.01
☐	282	Curt Davis	.08	.04	.01
☐	283	Lew Fonseca	.08	.04	.01
☐	284	Muddy Ruel	.08	.04	.01
☐	285	Moose Solters	.08	.04	.01
☐	286	Fred Schulte	.08	.04	.01
☐	287	Jack Quinn	.08	.04	.01
☐	288	Pinky Whitney	.08	.04	.01
☐	289	John Stone	.08	.04	.01
☐	290	Hughie Critz	.08	.04	.01
☐	291	Ira Flagstead	.08	.04	.01
☐	292	George Grantham	.08	.04	.01
☐	293	Sammy Hale	.08	.04	.01
☐	294	Shanty Hogan	.08	.04	.01
☐	295	Ossie Bluege	.08	.04	.01
☐	296	Debs Garms	.08	.04	.01
☐	297	Barney Friberg	.08	.04	.01
☐	298	Ed Brandt	.08	.04	.01
☐	299	Rollie Hemsley	.08	.04	.01
☐	300	MVP: Chuck Klein	.20	.09	.03
☐	301	MVP: Mort Cooper	.08	.04	.01
☐	302	MVP: Jim Bottomley	.15	.07	.02
☐	303	MVP: Jimmy Foxx	.30	.14	.04
☐	304	MVP: Fred Schulte	.08	.04	.01
☐	305	MVP: Frank Frisch	.20	.09	.03
☐	306	MVP: Frank McCormick	.08	.04	.01
☐	307	MVP: Jake Daubert	.08	.04	.01
☐	308	MVP: Roger Peckinpaugh	.08	.04	.01
☐	309	MVP: George H. Burns	.08	.04	.01
☐	310	MVP: Lou Gehrig	.50	.23	.06
☐	311	MVP: Al Simmons	.20	.09	.03
☐	312	MVP: Eddie Collins	.20	.09	.03
☐	313	MVP: Gabby Hartnett	.20	.09	.03

	MT	EX-MT	VG
☐ 314 MVP: Joe Cronin	.20	.09	.03
☐ 315 MVP: Paul Waner	.20	.09	.03
☐ 316 MVP: Bob O'Farrell	.08	.04	.01
☐ 317 MVP: Larry Doyle	.12	.05	.02
☐ 318 Lyn Lary	.08	.04	.01
☐ 319 Jakie May	.08	.04	.01
☐ 320 Roy Spencer	.08	.04	.01
☐ 321 Dick Coffman	.08	.04	.01
☐ 322 Pete Donohue	.08	.04	.01
☐ 323 Mule Haas	.08	.04	.01
☐ 324 Doc Farrell	.08	.04	.01
☐ 325 Flint Rhem	.08	.04	.01
☐ 326 Firpo Marberry	.08	.04	.01
☐ 327 Charles Conlon	.08	.04	.01
☐ 328 Checklist 1-110	.08	.04	.01
☐ 329 Checklist 111-220	.08	.04	.01
☐ 330 Checklist 221-330	.08	.04	.01

1991-92 Conlon TSN Prototypes

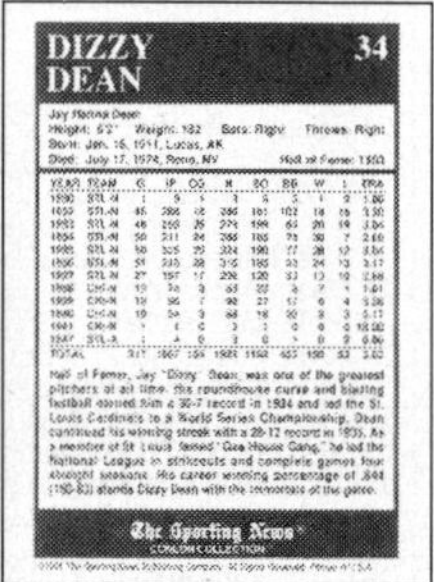

In conjunction with The Sporting News, Megacards issued various prototype cards to preview their soon to be released regular issue sets. All the cards were standard size, 2 1/2" by 3 1/2". The 1991 Conlon prototypes from the first series were not marked as prototypes, and neither did they have the Major League Baseball logo and the Curtis Management logo on their backs. Their numbering was identical with the regular issue cards, with the exception of Dean (number 3 in the regular issue). The production run was reported to be very limited for these first series cards. The 1991 Conlon Color Babe Ruth prototype has the word "prototype" on its reverse. The 50,000 color Ruth prototype cards produced were distributed to collectors and dealers at the 12th National Sports Collectors Convention in Anaheim in July, 1991. Moreover, five prototypes for the second series (1992 Conlon Collection) were distributed at the same time. The production run was announced to be 20,000 for each card, with the exception of Joe Jackson (67,000). All these cards are marked "prototype" on their backs, and with the exception of the Mathewson card, also bear different card numbers from the regular issues. In general, some subtle differences in photos are found with some of the prototype cards. The second series prototypes show a 1992 copyright on the card back. The Cobb and Jackson cards have a computer color-enhanced photo with white and dark blue borders, while the other cards have black and white photos with white and black borders.

	MT	EX-MT	VG
COMPLETE SET (16)	50.00	23.00	6.25
COMMON PLAYER	1.00	.45	.13
☐ 13 Ty Cobb Color (Card 250)	6.00	2.70	.75
☐ 14 Joe Jackson Color (Card 444 in regular set, prototype)	6.00	2.70	.75
☐ 34 Dizzy Dean	10.00	4.50	1.25
☐ 111 Lou Gehrig	10.00	4.50	1.25
☐ 145 Babe Ruth (Color) DP	7.50	3.40	.95
☐ 250 Ty Cobb	10.00	4.50	1.25
☐ 331 Christy Mathewson (Prototype on back)	3.00	1.35	.40
☐ 400 Joe Jackson DP (Prototype on back)	5.00	2.30	.60
☐ 450 Hughie Jennings (Prototype on back)	1.50	.65	.19
☐ 500 Ty Cobb (Prototype on back)	5.00	2.30	.60
☐ 520 Goose Goslin (Prototype on back)	1.50	.65	.19
☐ 661 Bill Terry	2.50	1.15	.30
☐ 662 Lefty Gomez	2.50	1.15	.30
☐ 664 Frank Frisch	1.50	.65	.19
☐ 710 Red Faber	1.50	.65	.19
☐ 905 Lena Blackburne	1.00	.45	.13

1992 Conlon TSN 13th National

In conjunction with The Sporting News, Megacards issued various prototype cards during 1992 to preview their soon to be released regular issue sets. All the cards were standard size, 2 1/2" by 3 1/2". These cards were given away as promotional items at the 13th National Sports Collectors Convention in Atlanta and therefore have "13th National" stamped on their backs.

	MT	EX-MT	VG
COMPLETE SET (4)	7.50	3.40	.95
COMMON PLAYER	1.00	.45	.13
☐ 14 Joe Jackson DP (13th National)	5.00	2.30	.60
☐ 663 Babe Ruth (BW) (13th National)	5.00	2.30	.60
☐ 775 Chief Meyers (13th National)	1.00	.45	.13
☐ 800 Hippo Vaughn (13th National)	1.00	.45	.13

1992 Conlon TSN

This 330-card set is numbered in continuation of the previous year's issue and again features the photography of Charles Conlon. The fronts of these standard-size cards (2 1/2" by 3 1/2") have either posed or action black and white player photos, enframed by a white line on a black card face. A caption in a diagonal stripe cuts across the upper right corner of the picture. The player's name, team, position, and year the photos were taken appear below the pictures in white lettering. The back has biography, statistics, and career summary. The cards are numbered on the back. Special subsets include No-Hitters (331-372), Two Sports (393-407), Great Stories (421-440), Why Not in Hall of Fame (441-450), Hall of Fame (459-474), 75 Years Ago Highlights (483-492), Triple Crown Winners (525-537),

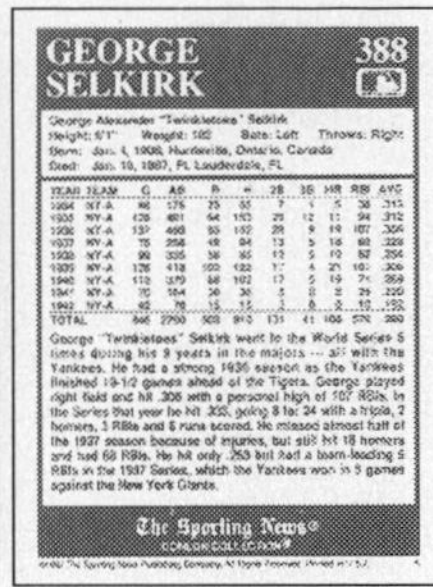

Everyday Heroes (538-550), Nicknames (551-566), Trivia (581-601), and St. Louis Cardinals 1892-1992 (618-657). The set was available in packs as well as in a factory set. Four special gold-border cards previewing the 1993 Conlon Sporting News set were available exclusively in the factory sets. Also randomly inserted in the wax packs were a limited number of personally autographed cards of Bobby Doerr, Bob Feller, Marty Marion, Johnny Mize, Enos Slaughter, and Johnny Vander Meer.

	MT	EX-MT	VG
COMPLETE SET (330)	18.00	8.00	2.30
COMMON PLAYER (331-660)	.08	.04	.01
☐ 331 Christy Mathewson	.35	.16	.04
☐ 332 Hooks Wiltse	.08	.04	.01
☐ 333 Nap Rucker	.08	.04	.01
☐ 334 Red Ames	.08	.04	.01
☐ 335 Chief Bender	.20	.09	.03
☐ 336 Smokey Joe Wood	.15	.07	.02
☐ 337 Ed Walsh	.20	.09	.03
☐ 338 George Mullin	.08	.04	.01
☐ 339 Earl Hamilton	.08	.04	.01
☐ 340 Jeff Tesreau	.08	.04	.01
☐ 341 Jim Scott	.08	.04	.01
☐ 342 Rube Marquard	.20	.09	.03
☐ 343 Claude Hendrix	.08	.04	.01
☐ 344 Jimmy Lavender	.08	.04	.01
☐ 345 Joe Bush	.08	.04	.01
☐ 346 Dutch Leonard	.08	.04	.01
☐ 347 Fred Toney	.08	.04	.01
☐ 348 Hippo Vaughn	.08	.04	.01
☐ 349 Ernie Koob	.08	.04	.01
☐ 350 Bob Groom	.08	.04	.01
☐ 351 Ernie Shore	.08	.04	.01
☐ 352 Hod Eller	.08	.04	.01
☐ 353 Walter Johnson	.35	.16	.04
☐ 354 Charles Robertson	.08	.04	.01
☐ 355 Jesse Barnes	.08	.04	.01
☐ 356 Sad Sam Jones	.08	.04	.01
☐ 357 Howard Ehmke	.08	.04	.01
☐ 358 Jesse Haines	.20	.09	.03
☐ 359 Ted Lyons	.20	.09	.03
☐ 360 Carl Hubbell	.25	.11	.03
☐ 361 Wes Ferrell	.08	.04	.01
☐ 362 Bobby Burke	.08	.04	.01
☐ 363 Daffy Dean	.15	.07	.02
☐ 364 Bobo Newson	.08	.04	.01
☐ 365 Vern Kennedy	.08	.04	.01
☐ 366 Bill Dietrich	.08	.04	.01
☐ 367 Johnny Vander Meer	.15	.07	.02
☐ 368 Johnny Vander Meer	.15	.07	.02
☐ 369 Monte Pearson	.08	.04	.01
☐ 370 Bob Feller	.35	.16	.04
☐ 371 Lon Warneke	.08	.04	.01
☐ 372 Jim Tobin	.08	.04	.01
☐ 373 Earl Moore	.08	.04	.01
☐ 374 Bill Dineen	.08	.04	.01
☐ 375 Mal Eason	.08	.04	.01
☐ 376 George Mogridge	.08	.04	.01
☐ 377 Dazzy Vance	.20	.09	.03
☐ 378 Tex Carleton	.08	.04	.01
☐ 379 Clyde Shoun	.08	.04	.01
☐ 380 Frankie Hayes	.08	.04	.01
☐ 381 Benny Frey	.08	.04	.01
☐ 382 Hank Johnson	.08	.04	.01
☐ 383 Red Kress	.08	.04	.01
☐ 384 Johnny Allen	.08	.04	.01
☐ 385 Hal Trosky	.08	.04	.01
☐ 386 Gene Robertson	.08	.04	.01
☐ 387 Pep Young	.08	.04	.01
☐ 388 George Selkirk	.08	.04	.01
☐ 389 Ed Wells	.08	.04	.01
☐ 390 Jim Weaver	.08	.04	.01
☐ 391 George McQuinn	.08	.04	.01
☐ 392 Hans Lobert	.08	.04	.01
☐ 393 Evar Swanson	.08	.04	.01
☐ 394 Ernie Nevers	.25	.11	.03
☐ 395 Jim Levey	.08	.04	.01
☐ 396 Hugo Bezdek	.08	.04	.01
☐ 397 Walt French	.08	.04	.01
☐ 398 Charlie Berry	.08	.04	.01
☐ 399 Frank Grube	.08	.04	.01
☐ 400 Chuck Dressen	.08	.04	.01
☐ 401 Greasy Neale	.08	.04	.01
☐ 402 Ernie Vick	.08	.04	.01
☐ 403 Jim Thorpe	.75	.35	.09
☐ 404 Wally Gilbert	.08	.04	.01
☐ 405 Luke Urban	.08	.04	.01
☐ 406 Pid Purdy	.08	.04	.01
☐ 407 Ab Wright	.08	.04	.01
☐ 408 Billy Urbanski	.08	.04	.01
☐ 409 Carl Fischer	.08	.04	.01
☐ 410 Jack Warner	.08	.04	.01
☐ 411 Bill Cissell	.08	.04	.01
☐ 412 Merv Shea	.08	.04	.01
☐ 413 Dolf Luque	.08	.04	.01
☐ 414 Johnny Bassler	.08	.04	.01
☐ 415 Odell Hale	.08	.04	.01
☐ 416 Larry French	.08	.04	.01
☐ 417 Curt Walker	.08	.04	.01
☐ 418 Dusty Cooke	.08	.04	.01
☐ 419 Phil Todt	.08	.04	.01
☐ 420 Poison Andrews	.08	.04	.01
☐ 421 Billy Herman	.20	.09	.03
☐ 422 Tris Speaker	.30	.14	.04
☐ 423 Al Simmons	.20	.09	.03
☐ 424 Hack Wilson	.25	.11	.03
☐ 425 Ty Cobb	.50	.23	.06
☐ 426 Babe Ruth	.75	.35	.09
☐ 427 Ernie Lombardi	.20	.09	.03
☐ 428 Dizzy Dean	.40	.18	.05
☐ 429 Lloyd Waner	.20	.09	.03
☐ 430 Hank Greenberg	.30	.14	.04
☐ 431 Lefty Grove	.30	.14	.04
☐ 432 Mickey Cochrane	.25	.11	.03
☐ 433 Burleigh Grimes	.20	.09	.03
☐ 434 Pie Traynor	.20	.09	.03
☐ 435 Johnny Mize	.25	.11	.03
☐ 436 Sam Rice	.20	.09	.03
☐ 437 Goose Goslin	.20	.09	.03
☐ 438 Chuck Klein	.20	.09	.03
☐ 439 Connie Mack	.25	.11	.03
☐ 440 Jim Bottomley	.20	.09	.03
☐ 441 Riggs Stephenson	.08	.04	.01
☐ 442 Ken Williams	.15	.07	.02
☐ 443 Babe Adams	.08	.04	.01
☐ 444 Joe Jackson	.75	.35	.09
☐ 445 Hal Newhouser	.15	.07	.02
☐ 446 Wes Ferrell	.08	.04	.01
☐ 447 Lefty O'Doul	.08	.04	.01
☐ 448 Wally Schang	.08	.04	.01
☐ 449 Sherry Magee	.08	.04	.01
☐ 450 Mike Donlin	.08	.04	.01
☐ 451 Doc Cramer	.08	.04	.01
☐ 452 Dick Bartell	.08	.04	.01
☐ 453 Earle Mack	.08	.04	.01
☐ 454 Jumbo Brown	.08	.04	.01
☐ 455 Johnnie Heving	.08	.04	.01
☐ 456 Percy Jones	.08	.04	.01
☐ 457 Ted Blankenship	.08	.04	.01
☐ 458 Al Wingo	.08	.04	.01
☐ 459 Roger Bresnahan	.20	.09	.03
☐ 460 Bill Klem	.25	.11	.03
☐ 461 Charlie Gehringer	.25	.11	.03
☐ 462 Stan Coveleski	.20	.09	.03
☐ 463 Eddie Plank	.25	.11	.03
☐ 464 Clark Griffith	.20	.09	.03
☐ 465 Herb Pennock	.20	.09	.03
☐ 466 Earle Combs	.20	.09	.03
☐ 467 Bobby Doerr	.25	.11	.03
☐ 468 Waite Hoyt	.20	.09	.03
☐ 469 Tommy Connolly	.08	.04	.01
☐ 470 Harry Hooper	.20	.09	.03
☐ 471 Rick Ferrell	.20	.09	.03
☐ 472 Billy Evans	.08	.04	.01
☐ 473 Billy Herman	.20	.09	.03
☐ 474 Bill Dickey	.30	.14	.04
☐ 475 Luke Appling	.25	.11	.03
☐ 476 Babe Pinelli	.08	.04	.01
☐ 477 Eric McNair	.08	.04	.01
☐ 478 Sherriff Blake	.08	.04	.01
☐ 479 Val Picinich	.08	.04	.01

☐	480	Fred Heimach	.08	.04	.01
☐	481	Jack Graney	.08	.04	.01
☐	482	Reb Russell	.08	.04	.01
☐	483	Red Faber	.20	.09	.03
☐	484	Benny Kauff	.08	.04	.01
☐	485	Pants Rowland	.08	.04	.01
☐	486	Bobby Veach	.08	.04	.01
☐	487	Jim Bagby Sr.	.08	.04	.01
☐	488	Pol Perritt	.08	.04	.01
☐	489	Buck Herzog	.08	.04	.01
☐	490	Art Fletcher	.08	.04	.01
☐	491	Walter Holke	.08	.04	.01
☐	492	Art Nehf	.08	.04	.01
☐	493	Fresco Thompson	.08	.04	.01
☐	494	Jimmy Welsh	.08	.04	.01
☐	495	Ossie Vitt	.08	.04	.01
☐	496	Ownie Carroll	.08	.04	.01
☐	497	Ken O'Dea	.08	.04	.01
☐	498	Fred Frankhouse	.08	.04	.01
☐	499	Jewel Ens	.08	.04	.01
☐	500	Morrie Arnovich	.08	.04	.01
☐	501	Wally Gerber	.08	.04	.01
☐	502	Kiddo Davis	.08	.04	.01
☐	503	Buddy Myer	.08	.04	.01
☐	504	Sam Leslie	.08	.04	.01
☐	505	Cliff Bolton	.08	.04	.01
☐	506	Dixie Walker	.08	.04	.01
☐	507	Jack Smith	.08	.04	.01
☐	508	Bump Hadley	.08	.04	.01
☐	509	Buck Crouse	.08	.04	.01
☐	510	Joe Glenn	.08	.04	.01
☐	511	Chad Kimsey	.08	.04	.01
☐	512	Lou Finney	.08	.04	.01
☐	513	Roxie Lawson	.08	.04	.01
☐	514	Chuck Fullis	.08	.04	.01
☐	515	Earl Sheely	.08	.04	.01
☐	516	George Gibson	.08	.04	.01
☐	517	Johnny Broaca	.08	.04	.01
☐	518	Bibb Falk	.08	.04	.01
☐	519	Don Hurst	.08	.04	.01
☐	520	Grover Hartley	.08	.04	.01
☐	521	Don Heffner	.08	.04	.01
☐	522	Harvey Hendrick	.08	.04	.01
☐	523	Allen Sothoron	.08	.04	.01
☐	524	Tony Piet	.08	.04	.01
☐	525	Ty Cobb	.50	.23	.06
☐	526	Jimmie Foxx	.35	.16	.04
☐	527	Rogers Hornsby	.35	.16	.04
☐	528	Nap Lajoie	.35	.16	.04
☐	529	Lou Gehrig	.50	.23	.06
☐	530	Heinie Zimmerman	.08	.04	.01
☐	531	Chuck Klein	.20	.09	.03
☐	532	Hugh Duffy	.20	.09	.03
☐	533	Lefty Grove	.30	.14	.04
☐	534	Grover C. Alexander	.30	.14	.04
☐	535	Amos Rusie	.20	.09	.03
☐	536	Lefty Gomez	.30	.14	.04
☐	537	Bucky Walters	.08	.04	.01
☐	538	Johnny Hodapp	.08	.04	.01
☐	539	Bruce Campbell	.08	.04	.01
☐	540	Hod Lisenbee	.08	.04	.01
☐	541	Jack Fournier	.08	.04	.01
☐	542	Jim Tabor	.08	.04	.01
☐	543	Johnny Burnett	.08	.04	.01
☐	544	Roy Hartzell	.08	.04	.01
☐	545	Doc Gautreau	.08	.04	.01
☐	546	Emil Yde	.08	.04	.01
☐	547	Bob Johnson	.08	.04	.01
☐	548	Joe Hauser	.08	.04	.01
☐	549	Ed Reulbach	.08	.04	.01
☐	550	Mel Almada	.08	.04	.01
☐	551	Mickey Cochrane	.25	.11	.03
☐	552	Carl Hubbell	.25	.11	.03
☐	553	Charlie Gehringer	.25	.11	.03
☐	554	Al Simmons	.20	.09	.03
☐	555	Mordecai Brown	.20	.09	.03
☐	556	Hughie Jennings	.20	.09	.03
☐	557	Kid Elberfeld	.08	.04	.01
☐	558	Casey Stengel	.30	.14	.04
☐	559	Al Schacht	.15	.07	.02
☐	560	Jimmie Foxx	.35	.16	.04
☐	561	George Kelly	.20	.09	.03
☐	562	Lloyd Waner	.20	.09	.03
☐	563	Paul Waner	.20	.09	.03
☐	564	Walter Johnson	.35	.16	.04
☐	565	Home Run Baker	.20	.09	.03
☐	566	Roy Hughes	.08	.04	.01
☐	567	Lew Riggs	.08	.04	.01
☐	568	John Whitehead	.08	.04	.01
☐	569	Elam Vangilder	.08	.04	.01
☐	570	Billy Zitzmann	.08	.04	.01
☐	571	Walter Schmidt	.08	.04	.01
☐	572	Jackie Tavener	.08	.04	.01
☐	573	Joe Genewich	.08	.04	.01
☐	574	Johnny Marcum	.08	.04	.01
☐	575	Fred Hofmann	.08	.04	.01
☐	576	Red Rolfe	.08	.04	.01
☐	577	Vic Sorrell	.08	.04	.01
☐	578	Pete Scott	.08	.04	.01
☐	579	Tommy Thomas	.08	.04	.01
☐	580	Al Smith	.08	.04	.01
☐	581	Butch Henline	.08	.04	.01
☐	582	Eddie Collins	.20	.09	.03
☐	583	Earle Combs	.20	.09	.03
☐	584	John McGraw	.20	.09	.03
☐	585	Hack Wilson	.20	.09	.03
☐	586	Gabby Hartnett	.20	.09	.03
☐	587	Kiki Cuyler	.20	.09	.03
☐	588	Bill Terry	.25	.11	.03
☐	589	Joe McCarthy	.20	.09	.03
☐	590	Hank Greenberg	.30	.14	.04
☐	591	Tris Speaker	.30	.14	.04
☐	592	Bill McKechnie	.20	.09	.03
☐	593	Bucky Harris	.20	.09	.03
☐	594	Herb Pennock	.20	.09	.03
☐	595	George Sisler	.20	.09	.03
☐	596	Fred Lindstrom	.20	.09	.03
☐	597	Earl Averill	.20	.09	.03
☐	598	Dave Bancroft	.20	.09	.03
☐	599	Connie Mack	.25	.11	.03
☐	600	Joe Cronin	.20	.09	.03
☐	601	Ken Ash	.08	.04	.01
☐	602	Al Spohrer	.08	.04	.01
☐	603	Roy Mahaffey	.08	.04	.01
☐	604	Frank O'Rourke	.08	.04	.01
☐	605	Lil Stoner	.08	.04	.01
☐	606	Frank Gabler	.08	.04	.01
☐	607	Tom Padden	.08	.04	.01
☐	608	Art Shires	.08	.04	.01
☐	609	Sherry Smith	.08	.04	.01
☐	610	Phil Weintraub	.08	.04	.01
☐	611	Russ Van Atta	.08	.04	.01
☐	612	Jo Jo White	.08	.04	.01
☐	613	Cliff Melton	.08	.04	.01
☐	614	Jimmy Ring	.08	.04	.01
☐	615	Heinie Sand	.08	.04	.01
☐	616	Dale Alexander	.08	.04	.01
☐	617	Kent Greenfield	.08	.04	.01
☐	618	Eddie Dyer	.08	.04	.01
☐	619	Bill Sherdel	.08	.04	.01
☐	620	Max Lanier	.08	.04	.01
☐	621	Bob O'Farrell	.08	.04	.01
☐	622	Rogers Hornsby	.30	.14	.04
☐	623	Bill Beckman	.08	.04	.01
☐	624	Mort Cooper	.08	.04	.01
☐	625	Bill DeLancey	.08	.04	.01
☐	626	Marty Marion	.15	.07	.02
☐	627	Billy Southworth	.08	.04	.01
☐	628	Johnny Mize	.25	.11	.03
☐	629	Joe Medwick	.20	.09	.03
☐	630	Grover C. Alexander	.30	.14	.04
☐	631	Daffy Dean	.15	.07	.02
☐	632	Hi Bell	.08	.04	.01
☐	633	Walker Cooper	.08	.04	.01
☐	634	Frankie Frisch	.20	.09	.03
☐	635	Dizzy Dean	.40	.18	.05
☐	636	Don Gutteridge	.08	.04	.01
☐	637	Pepper Martin	.15	.07	.02
☐	638	Ed Konetchy	.08	.04	.01
☐	639	Bill Hallahan	.08	.04	.01
☐	640	Lon Warneke	.08	.04	.01
☐	641	Terry Moore	.08	.04	.01
☐	642	Enos Slaughter	.25	.11	.03
☐	643	Heinie Mueller	.08	.04	.01
☐	644	Specs Toporcer	.08	.04	.01
☐	645	Ed Bottomley	.08	.04	.01
☐	646	Ray Blades	.08	.04	.01
☐	647	Jesse Haines	.20	.09	.03
☐	648	Andy High	.08	.04	.01
☐	649	Miller Huggins	.20	.09	.03
☐	650	Ernie Orsatti	.08	.04	.01
☐	651	Les Bell	.08	.04	.01
☐	652	Gabby Street	.08	.04	.01
☐	653	Wally Roettger	.08	.04	.01
☐	654	Syl Johnson	.08	.04	.01
☐	655	Mike Gonzalez	.08	.04	.01
☐	656	Ripper Collins	.08	.04	.01
☐	657	Chick Hafey	.20	.09	.03
☐	658	Checklist 331-440	.08	.04	.01
☐	659	Checklist 441-550	.08	.04	.01
☐	660	Checklist 551-660	.08	.04	.01

1992 Conlon TSN All-Star Program

In 1992 several gold-foil edition black and white Conlon Collection cards were released to preview the 1993 Conlon Collection. Cards 661G-664G feature four players who played in the first All-Star Game in 1993. Twenty-one thousand of each of these cards were produced exclusively for and inserted (one per program) in the 1992 All-Star Game program. These standard-size (2 1/2" by 3 1/2") cards have the same design typical of other Conlon issues, only that the vintage black and white player photos are framed in gold foil. The cards are numbered on the back.

	MT	EX-MT	VG
COMPLETE SET (4)	18.00	8.00	2.30
COMMON PLAYER (661G-664G)	3.00	1.35	.40
☐ 661G Bill Terry	4.50	2.00	.55
☐ 662G Lefty Gomez	4.50	2.00	.55
☐ 663G Babe Ruth	9.00	4.00	1.15
☐ 664G Frankie Frisch	3.00	1.35	.40

1992 Conlon TSN Gold Inserts

In 1992 several gold-foil edition black and white Conlon Collection cards were released to preview the 1993 Conlon Collection. Card numbers 665, 770, 820, and 880 were included in 1992 Conlon factory sets; reportedly 90,000 of each card were produced. The factory set cases distributed through hobby dealers also included two additional cards (667 and 730) as a bonus (roughly a dozen of each per case), with a stated production run of 20,000 for Appling and 30,000 for Gehringer. Card 1000G, of which 100,000 were produced, was inserted in the 65-card jumbo packs sold only at Toys 'R' Us. The standard-size (2 1/2" by 3 1/2") cards have the same design typical of other Conlon issues, only that the vintage black and white player photos are framed in gold foil. The cards are numbered on the back.

	MT	EX-MT	VG
COMPLETE SET (11)	12.50	5.75	1.55
COMMON PLAYER	1.00	.45	.13
☐ 665 Carl Hubbell	2.00	.90	.25
☐ 667 Charlie Gehringer SP	3.00	1.35	.40
☐ 730 Luke Appling SP (Old Aches and Pains)	3.00	1.35	.40
☐ 770 Tommy Henrich	1.00	.45	.13
☐ 820 John McGraw	2.00	.90	.25
☐ 880 Gabby Hartnett	2.00	.90	.25
☐ 1000G Ty Cobb DP	4.00	1.80	.50

1992-93 Conlon TSN Color Inserts

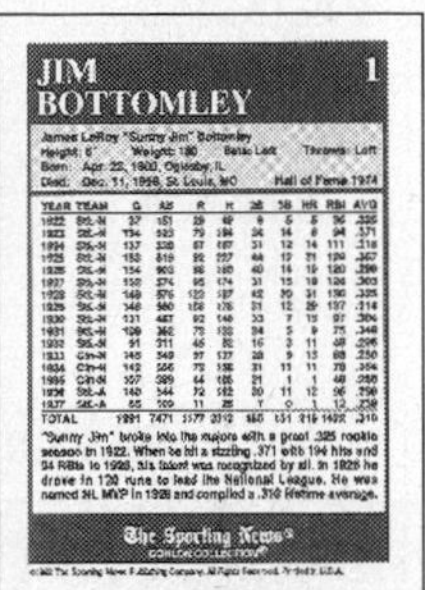

All the cards in this 22-card set were previously released in black and white in the 1991 or 1992 Conlon regular issue sets. Released on two different occasions, cards 1-6 and 7-12 were issued exclusively as a bonus to collectors who purchased Megacards' hobby accessory products (plastic sheets, card frames, and card sleeves) through retail outlets. The announced production figures for cards 1-6 were 250,000 of each card. Cards 13-20 were randomly inserted in 1993 Conlon counter packs and blister packs, with an announced production run of 100,000 of each card. Finally cards 21-22 were available only through a special send-away offer on the backs of Conlon counter packs and blister packs. The cards measure the standard size (2 1/2" by 3 1/2"). The fronts display color player portraits inside a white picture frame on a navy blue card face. A diagonal graphic across the upper right corner of the picture gives the year the player was inducted into the Hall of Fame. The black and white backs are accented in navy blue and provide biography, career statistics, and career summary. The cards are numbered on the back. The corresponding card number of the black and white regular issue card is given on the line after each player's name.

	MT	EX-MT	VG
COMPLETE SET (22)	50.00	23.00	6.25
COMMON PLAYER (1-6)	1.00	.45	.13
COMMON PLAYER (6-12)	1.00	.45	.13
COMMON PLAYER (13-20)	2.00	.90	.25
COMMON PLAYER (21-22)	2.00	.90	.25
☐ 1 Jim Bottomley Card 22	1.00	.45	.13
☐ 2 Lefty Grove Card 23	2.00	.90	.25
☐ 3 Lou Gehrig Card 111	3.00	1.35	.40
☐ 4 Babe Ruth Card 145	5.00	2.30	.60
☐ 5 Casey Stengel Card 37	2.00	.90	.25
☐ 6 Rube Marquard Card 252	1.00	.45	.13
☐ 7 Walter Johnson Card 353	2.00	.90	.25
☐ 8 Lou Gehrig Card 310	3.00	1.35	.40
☐ 9 Christy Mathewson	2.00	.90	.25

Card	Player	MT	EX-MT	VG
	Card 331			
☐ 10	Ty Cobb	3.00	1.35	.40
	Card 250			
☐ 11	Mel Ott	2.00	.90	.25
	Card 225			
☐ 12	Carl Hubbell	1.00	.45	.13
	Card 253			
☐ 13	Al Simmons	2.00	.90	.25
	Card 49			
☐ 14	Connie Mack	3.00	1.35	.40
	Card 47			
☐ 15	Grover C. Alexander	3.00	1.35	.40
	Card 32			
☐ 16	Jimmie Foxx	3.00	1.35	.40
	Card 303			
☐ 17	Lloyd Waner	2.00	.90	.25
	Card 6			
☐ 18	Tris Speaker	3.00	1.35	.40
	Card 422			
☐ 19	Dizzy Dean	4.00	1.80	.50
	Card 3			
☐ 20	Rogers Hornsby	4.00	1.80	.50
	Card 1			
☐ 21	Joe Jackson	4.00	1.80	.50
	Card 444			
☐ 22	Jim Thorpe	4.00	1.80	.50
	Card 403			

1993 Conlon TSN

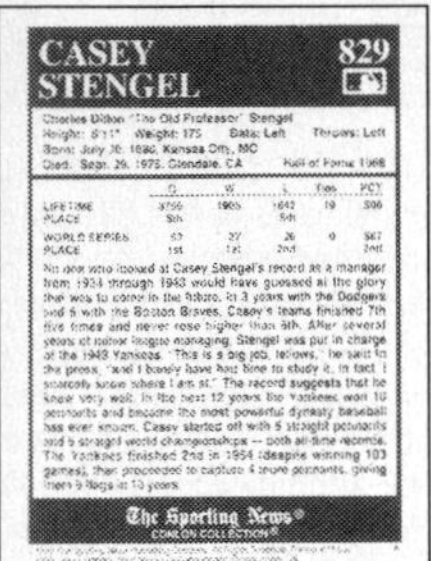

The third 330-card set of The Sporting News Conlon Collection again features turn-of-the-century to World War II-era players photographed by Charles Conlon, including more than 100 cards of Hall of Famers. Cards from a subset displaying computer color-enhanced photos were randomly inserted in the counter box packs and blister packs. The standard-size (2 1/2" by 3 1/2") cards feature a mix of black-and-white vintage player photos inside a white frame on a black card face. Topical subset titles are printed on a diagonal bar at the upper right corner of the pictures. The backs carry biography, statistics, and extended career summary and highlights. The set contains several subsets continuing from last year's issue and some new subsets unique to this year's set: Game of the Century: 1933 All-Star Game (661-689), Spitballers (702-712), Accused Spitballers (717-725), Nicknames (730-741), Great Stories (751-770), Native Americans: American Indians who played big-league ball (771-777), League Leaders (795-798 and 801-805), Great Managers (817-848), Great Backstops (861-880), Against All Odds (881-894), Trivia (905-918), Nolan Ryan: compares eight Hall of Famers to Ryan (928-935), and First Cards: players for whom cards have never been done before (945-987). The set closes with checklist cards (988-990). The cards are numbered on the back.

		MT	EX-MT	VG
COMPLETE SET (330)		18.00	8.00	2.30
COMMON PLAYER (661-990)		.08	.04	.01
☐ 661	Bill Terry	.20	.09	.03
☐ 662	Lefty Gomez	.25	.11	.03
☐ 663	Babe Ruth	.75	.35	.09
☐ 664	Frank Frisch	.20	.09	.03
☐ 665	Carl Hubbell	.20	.09	.03
☐ 666	Al Simmons	.20	.09	.03
☐ 667	Charlie Gehringer	.25	.11	.03
☐ 668	Earl Averill	.20	.09	.03
☐ 669	Lefty Grove	.30	.14	.04
☐ 670	Pie Traynor	.20	.09	.03
☐ 671	Chuck Klein	.20	.09	.03
☐ 672	Paul Waner	.20	.09	.03
☐ 673	Lou Gehrig	.50	.23	.06
☐ 674	Rick Ferrell	.20	.09	.03
☐ 675	Gabby Hartnett	.20	.09	.03
☐ 676	Joe Cronin	.20	.09	.03
☐ 677	Chick Hafey	.20	.09	.03
☐ 678	Jimmy Dykes	.08	.04	.01
☐ 679	Sammy West	.08	.04	.01
☐ 680	Pepper Martin	.15	.07	.02
☐ 681	Lefty O'Doul	.08	.04	.01
☐ 682	General Crowder	.08	.04	.01
☐ 683	Jimmie Wilson	.08	.04	.01
☐ 684	Dick Bartell	.08	.04	.01
☐ 685	Bill Hallahan	.08	.04	.01
☐ 686	Wally Berger	.08	.04	.01
☐ 687	Lon Warneke	.08	.04	.01
☐ 688	Ben Chapman	.08	.04	.01
☐ 689	Woody English	.08	.04	.01
☐ 690	Jimmy Reese	.12	.05	.02
☐ 691	Wattie Holm	.08	.04	.01
☐ 692	Charlie Jamieson	.08	.04	.01
☐ 693	Tom Zachary	.08	.04	.01
☐ 694	Blondy Ryan	.08	.04	.01
☐ 695	Sparky Adams	.08	.04	.01
☐ 696	Bill Hunnefield	.08	.04	.01
☐ 697	Lee Meadows	.08	.04	.01
☐ 698	Tom Carey	.08	.04	.01
☐ 699	Johnny Rawlings	.08	.04	.01
☐ 700	Ken Holloway	.08	.04	.01
☐ 701	Lance Richbourg	.08	.04	.01
☐ 702	Ray Fisher	.08	.04	.01
☐ 703	Ed Walsh	.08	.04	.01
☐ 704	Dick Rudolph	.08	.04	.01
☐ 705	Ray Caldwell	.08	.04	.01
☐ 706	Burleigh Grimes	.20	.09	.03
☐ 707	Stan Coveleski	.20	.09	.03
☐ 708	George Hildebrand	.08	.04	.01
☐ 709	Jack Quinn	.08	.04	.01
☐ 710	Red Faber	.20	.09	.03
☐ 711	Urban Shocker	.08	.04	.01
☐ 712	Dutch Leonard	.08	.04	.01
☐ 713	Lou Koupal	.08	.04	.01
☐ 714	Jimmy Wasdell	.08	.04	.01
☐ 715	Johnny Lindell	.08	.04	.01
☐ 716	Don Padgett	.08	.04	.01
☐ 717	Nelson Potter	.08	.04	.01
☐ 718	Schoolboy Rowe	.08	.04	.01
☐ 719	Dave Danforth	.08	.04	.01
☐ 720	Claude Passeau	.08	.04	.01
☐ 721	Harry Kelley	.08	.04	.01
☐ 722	Johnny Allen	.08	.04	.01
☐ 723	Tommy Bridges	.08	.04	.01
☐ 724	Bill Lee	.08	.04	.01
☐ 725	Fred Frankhouse	.08	.04	.01
☐ 726	Johnny McCarthy	.08	.04	.01
☐ 727	Rip Russell	.08	.04	.01
☐ 728	Emory(Topper) Rigney	.08	.04	.01
☐ 729	Howie Shanks	.08	.04	.01
☐ 730	Luke Appling	.20	.09	.03
☐ 731	Bill Byron UMP	.08	.04	.01
☐ 732	Earle Combs	.20	.09	.03
☐ 733	Hank Greenberg	.30	.14	.04
☐ 734	Walter(Boom Boom) Beck	.08	.04	.01
☐ 735	Sloppy Thurston	.08	.04	.01
☐ 736	Hack Wilson	.25	.11	.03
☐ 737	Bill McGowan	.15	.07	.02
☐ 738	Zeke Bonura	.08	.04	.01
☐ 739	Tom Baker	.08	.04	.01
☐ 740	Bill(Baby Doll) Jacobson	.08	.04	.01
☐ 741	Kiki Cuyler	.20	.09	.03
☐ 742	George Blaeholder	.08	.04	.01
☐ 743	Dee Miles	.08	.04	.01
☐ 744	Lee Handley	.08	.04	.01
☐ 745	Shano Collins	.08	.04	.01
☐ 746	Rosy Ryan	.08	.04	.01
☐ 747	Aaron Ward	.08	.04	.01
☐ 748	Monte Pearson	.08	.04	.01
☐ 749	Jake Early	.08	.04	.01
☐ 750	Bill Atwood	.08	.04	.01
☐ 751	Mark Koenig	.08	.04	.01
☐ 752	Buddy Hassett	.08	.04	.01
☐ 753	Davy Jones	.08	.04	.01

☐ 754 Honus Wagner .35 .16 .04
☐ 755 Bill Dickey .30 .14 .04
☐ 756 Max Butcher .08 .04 .01
☐ 757 Waite Hoyt .20 .09 .03
☐ 758 Walter Johnson .35 .16 .04
☐ 759 Howard Ehmke .08 .04 .01
☐ 760 Bobo Newsom .08 .04 .01
☐ 761 Tony Lazzeri .20 .09 .03
☐ 762 Tony Lazzeri .20 .09 .03
☐ 763 Spud Chandler .08 .04 .01
☐ 764 Kirby Higbe .08 .04 .01
☐ 765 Paul Richards .08 .04 .01
☐ 766 Rogers Hornsby .35 .16 .04
☐ 767 Joe Vosmik .08 .04 .01
☐ 768 Jesse Haines .20 .09 .03
☐ 769 Bucky Walters .08 .04 .01
☐ 770 Tommy Henrich .15 .07 .02
☐ 771 Jim Thorpe .75 .35 .09
☐ 772 Euel Moore .08 .04 .01
☐ 773 Rudy York .15 .07 .02
☐ 774 Chief Bender .20 .09 .03
☐ 775 Chief Meyers .08 .04 .01
☐ 776 Bob Johnson .08 .04 .01
☐ 777 Roy Johnson .08 .04 .01
☐ 778 Dick Porter .08 .04 .01
☐ 779 Ethan Allen .08 .04 .01
☐ 780 Slim Sallee .08 .04 .01
☐ 781 Beau Bell .08 .04 .01
☐ 782 Jigger Statz .08 .04 .01
☐ 783 Dutch Henry .08 .04 .01
☐ 784 Larry Woodall .08 .04 .01
☐ 785 Phil Collins .08 .04 .01
☐ 786 Joe Sewell .20 .09 .03
☐ 787 Billy Herman .20 .09 .03
☐ 788 Rube Oldring .08 .04 .01
☐ 789 Bill Walker .08 .04 .01
☐ 790 Joe Schultz .08 .04 .01
☐ 791 Fred Maguire .08 .04 .01
☐ 792 Claude Willoughby .08 .04 .01
☐ 793 Alex Ferguson .08 .04 .01
☐ 794 Johnny Morrison .08 .04 .01
☐ 795 Tris Speaker .30 .14 .04
☐ 796 Ty Cobb .50 .23 .06
☐ 797 Max Carey .20 .09 .03
☐ 798 George Sisler .25 .11 .03
☐ 799 Charlie Hollocher .08 .04 .01
☐ 800 Hippo Vaughn .08 .04 .01
☐ 801 Sad Sam Jones .08 .04 .01
☐ 802 Harry Hooper .20 .09 .03
☐ 803 Gavvy Cravath .08 .04 .01
☐ 804 Walter Johnson .35 .16 .04
☐ 805 Jake Daubert .08 .04 .01
☐ 806 Clyde Milan .08 .04 .01
☐ 807 Hugh McQuillan .08 .04 .01
☐ 808 Fred Brickell .08 .04 .01
☐ 809 Joe Stripp .08 .04 .01
☐ 810 Johnny Hodapp .08 .04 .01
☐ 811 Johnny Vergez .08 .04 .01
☐ 812 Lonny Frey .08 .04 .01
☐ 813 Bill Regan .08 .04 .01
☐ 814 Babe Young .08 .04 .01
☐ 815 Charlie Robertson .08 .04 .01
☐ 816 Walt Judnich .08 .04 .01
☐ 817 Joe Tinker .20 .09 .03
☐ 818 Johnny Evers .20 .09 .03
☐ 819 Frank Chance .20 .09 .03
☐ 820 John McGraw .20 .09 .03
☐ 821 Charles Grimm .08 .04 .01
☐ 822 Ted Lyons .20 .09 .03
☐ 823 Joe McCarthy .20 .09 .03
☐ 824 Connie Mack .20 .09 .03
☐ 825 George Gibson .08 .04 .01
☐ 826 Steve O'Neill .08 .04 .01
☐ 827 Tris Speaker .25 .11 .03
☐ 828 Bill Carrigan .08 .04 .01
☐ 829 Casey Stengel .30 .14 .04
☐ 830 Miller Huggins .20 .09 .03
☐ 831 Bill McKechnie .20 .09 .03
☐ 832 Chuck Dressen .08 .04 .01
☐ 833 Gabby Street .08 .04 .01
☐ 834 Mel Ott .30 .14 .04
☐ 835 Frank Frisch .20 .09 .03
☐ 836 George Sisler .25 .11 .03
☐ 837 Napoleon Lajoie .30 .14 .04
☐ 838 Ty Cobb .50 .23 .06
☐ 839 Billy Southworth .08 .04 .01
☐ 840 Clark Griffith .20 .09 .03
☐ 841 Bill Terry .25 .11 .03
☐ 842 Rogers Hornsby .30 .14 .04
☐ 843 Joe Cronin .20 .09 .03
☐ 844 Al Lopez .20 .09 .03
☐ 845 Bucky Harris .20 .09 .03
☐ 846 Wilbert Robinson .20 .09 .03

☐ 847 Hughie Jennings .20 .09 .03
☐ 848 Jimmy Dykes .08 .04 .01
☐ 849 Roy Cullenbine .08 .04 .01
☐ 850 Eddie Moore .08 .04 .01
☐ 851 Jack Rothrock .08 .04 .01
☐ 852 Bill Lamar .08 .04 .01
☐ 853 Monte Weaver .08 .04 .01
☐ 854 Ival Goodman .08 .04 .01
☐ 855 Hank Severeid .08 .04 .01
☐ 856 Fred Haney .08 .04 .01
☐ 857 Joe Shaute .08 .04 .01
☐ 858 Smead Jolley .08 .04 .01
☐ 859 Dib Williams .08 .04 .01
☐ 860 Benny Bengough .08 .04 .01
☐ 861 Rick Ferrell .20 .09 .03
☐ 862 Bob O'Farrell .08 .04 .01
☐ 863 Spud Davis .08 .04 .01
☐ 864 Frankie Hayes .08 .04 .01
☐ 865 Muddy Ruel .08 .04 .01
☐ 866 Mickey Cochrane .25 .11 .03
☐ 867 Johnny Kling .08 .04 .01
☐ 868 Ivey Wingo .08 .04 .01
☐ 869 Bill Dickey .30 .14 .04
☐ 870 Frank Snyder .08 .04 .01
☐ 871 Roger Bresnahan .20 .09 .03
☐ 872 Wally Schang .08 .04 .01
☐ 873 Al Lopez .20 .09 .03
☐ 874 Jimmie Wilson .08 .04 .01
☐ 875 Val Picinich .08 .04 .01
☐ 876 Steve O'Neill .08 .04 .01
☐ 877 Ernie Lombardi .20 .09 .03
☐ 878 Johnny Bassler .08 .04 .01
☐ 879 Ray Schalk .08 .04 .01
☐ 880 Gabby Hartnett .20 .09 .03
☐ 881 Bruce Campbell .08 .04 .01
☐ 882 Red Ruffing .20 .09 .03
☐ 883 Mordecai Brown .20 .09 .03
☐ 884 Jimmy Archer .08 .04 .01
☐ 885 Dave Keefe .08 .04 .01
☐ 886 Nate Andrews .08 .04 .01
☐ 887 Sam Rice .20 .09 .03
☐ 888 Babe Ruth .75 .35 .09
☐ 889 Chick Hafey .20 .09 .03
☐ 890 Oscar Melillo .08 .04 .01
☐ 891 Joe Wood .15 .07 .02
☐ 892 Johnny Evers .20 .09 .03
☐ 893 Specs Toporcer .08 .04 .01
☐ 894 Myril Hoag .08 .04 .01
☐ 895 Bob Weiland .08 .04 .01
☐ 896 Joe Marty .08 .04 .01
☐ 897 Sherry Magee .08 .04 .01
☐ 898 Danny Taylor .08 .04 .01
☐ 899 Willie Kamm .08 .04 .01
☐ 900 Jimmy Sheckard .08 .04 .01
☐ 901 Syl Johnson .08 .04 .01
☐ 902 Steve Sundra .08 .04 .01
☐ 903 Doc Cramer .08 .04 .01
☐ 904 Hub Pruett .08 .04 .01
☐ 905 Lena Blackburne .08 .04 .01
☐ 906 Eppa Rixey .20 .09 .03
☐ 907 Goose Goslin .20 .09 .03
☐ 908 George Kelly .20 .09 .03
☐ 909 Jim Bottomley .20 .09 .03
☐ 910 Christy Mathewson .35 .16 .04
☐ 911 Tony Lazzeri .20 .09 .03
☐ 912 Johnny Mostil .08 .04 .01
☐ 913 Bobby Doerr .20 .09 .03
☐ 914 Rabbit Maranville .20 .09 .03
☐ 915 Harry Heilmann .20 .09 .03
☐ 916 Bobby Wallace .20 .09 .03
☐ 917 Jimmie Foxx .30 .14 .04
☐ 918 Johnny Mize .25 .11 .03
☐ 919 Jack Bentley .08 .04 .01
☐ 920 Al Schacht .08 .04 .01
☐ 921 Ed Coleman .08 .04 .01
☐ 922 Dode Paskert .08 .04 .01
☐ 923 Hod Ford .08 .04 .01
☐ 924 Randy Moore .08 .04 .01
☐ 925 Milt Shoffner .08 .04 .01
☐ 926 Dick Siebert .08 .04 .01
☐ 927 Tony Kaufmann .08 .04 .01
☐ 928 Dizzy Dean .40 .18 .05
☐ 929 Dazzy Vance .20 .09 .03
☐ 930 Lefty Grove .30 .14 .04
☐ 931 Rube Waddell .20 .09 .03
☐ 932 Grover C. Alexander .30 .14 .04
☐ 933 Bob Feller .30 .14 .04
☐ 934 Walter Johnson .35 .16 .04
☐ 935 Ted Lyons .20 .09 .03
☐ 936 Jim Bagby Jr. .08 .04 .01
☐ 937 Joe Sugden CO .08 .04 .01
☐ 938 Earl Grace .08 .04 .01
☐ 939 Jeff Heath .08 .04 .01

☐ 940 Ken Williams	.08	.04	.01
☐ 941 Marv Owen	.08	.04	.01
☐ 942 Roy Weatherly	.08	.04	.01
☐ 943 Ed Morgan	.08	.04	.01
☐ 944 Johnny Rizzo	.08	.04	.01
☐ 945 Archie McKain	.08	.04	.01
☐ 946 Bob Garbark	.08	.04	.01
☐ 947 Bob Osborn	.08	.04	.01
☐ 948 Johnny Podgajny	.08	.04	.01
☐ 949 Joe Evans	.08	.04	.01
☐ 950 Tony Rensa	.08	.04	.01
☐ 951 John Humphries	.08	.04	.01
☐ 952 Merritt(Sugar) Cain	.08	.04	.01
☐ 953 Roy(Snipe) Hansen	.08	.04	.01
☐ 954 Johnny Niggeling	.08	.04	.01
☐ 955 Hal Wiltse	.08	.04	.01
☐ 956 Alex Carrasquel	.08	.04	.01
☐ 957 George Grant	.08	.04	.01
☐ 958 Lefty Weinert	.08	.04	.01
☐ 959 Erv Brame	.08	.04	.01
☐ 960 Ray Harrell	.08	.04	.01
☐ 961 Ed Linke	.08	.04	.01
☐ 962 Sam Gibson	.08	.04	.01
☐ 963 Johnny Watwood	.08	.04	.01
☐ 964 Doc Prothro	.08	.04	.01
☐ 965 Julio Bonetti	.08	.04	.01
☐ 966 Lefty Mills	.08	.04	.01
☐ 967 Chick Galloway	.08	.04	.01
☐ 968 Hal Kelleher	.08	.04	.01
☐ 969 Chief Hogsett	.08	.04	.01
☐ 970 Ed Heusser	.08	.04	.01
☐ 971 Ed Baecht	.08	.04	.01
☐ 972 Jack Saltzgaver	.08	.04	.01
☐ 973 Leroy Herrmann	.08	.04	.01
☐ 974 Belve Bean	.08	.04	.01
☐ 975 Harry(Socks) Seibold	.08	.04	.01
☐ 976 Vic Keen	.08	.04	.01
☐ 977 Bill Barrett	.08	.04	.01
☐ 978 Pat McNulty	.08	.04	.01
☐ 979 George Turbeville	.08	.04	.01
☐ 980 Eddie Phillips	.08	.04	.01
☐ 981 Garland Buckeye	.08	.04	.01
☐ 982 Vic Frasier	.08	.04	.01
☐ 983 Gordon Rhodes	.08	.04	.01
☐ 984 Red Barnes	.08	.04	.01
☐ 985 Jim Joe Edwards	.08	.04	.01
☐ 986 Herschel Bennett	.08	.04	.01
☐ 987 Carmen Hill	.08	.04	.01
☐ 988 Checklist 661-770	.08	.04	.01
☐ 989 Checklist 771-880	.08	.04	.01
☐ 990 Checklist 881-990	.08	.04	.01

1982 Cracker Jack

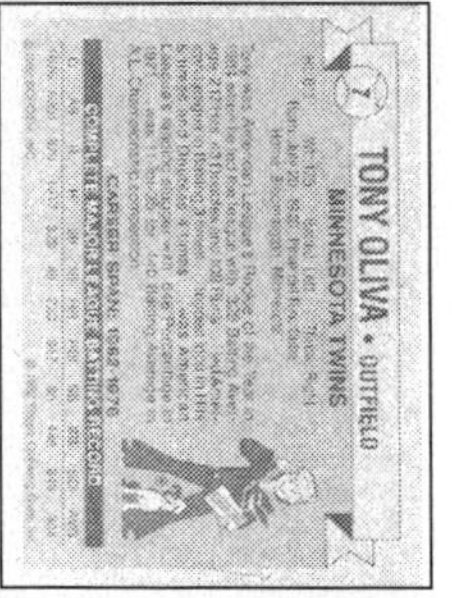

The cards in this 16-card set measure 2 1/2" by 3 1/2"; cards came in two sheets of eight cards, plus an advertising card with a title in the center, which measured approximately 7 1/2" by 10 1/2". Cracker Jack reentered the baseball card market for the first time since 1915 to promote the first "Old Timers Baseball Classic" held July 19, 1982. The color player photos have a Cracker Jack border and have either green (NL) or red (AL) frame lines and name panels. The Cracker Jack logo appears on both sides of each card, with AL players numbered 1-8 and NL players numbered 9-16. Of the 16 ballplayers pictured, five did not appear at the game. At first, the two sheets were available only through the mail but are now commonly found in hobby circles. The set was prepared for Cracker Jack by Topps. The prices below reflect individual card prices; the price for complete panels would be about the same as the sum of the card prices for those players on the panel due to the easy availability of uncut sheets.

	NRMT-MT	EXC	G-VG
COMPLETE SET (16)	10.00	4.50	1.25
COMMON PLAYER (1-16)	.25	.11	.03
☐ 1 Larry Doby	.25	.11	.03
☐ 2 Bob Feller	.75	.35	.09
☐ 3 Whitey Ford	.75	.35	.09
☐ 4 Al Kaline	.90	.40	.11
☐ 5 Harmon Killebrew	.60	.25	.08
☐ 6 Mickey Mantle	2.50	1.15	.30
☐ 7 Tony Oliva	.25	.11	.03
☐ 8 Brooks Robinson	.75	.35	.09
☐ 9 Hank Aaron	1.25	.55	.16
☐ 10 Ernie Banks	.90	.40	.11
☐ 11 Ralph Kiner	.50	.23	.06
☐ 12 Ed Mathews	.50	.23	.06
☐ 13 Willie Mays	1.25	.55	.16
☐ 14 Robin Roberts	.40	.18	.05
☐ 15 Duke Snider	.90	.40	.11
☐ 16 Warren Spahn	.50	.23	.06

1991 Cracker Jack Topps I

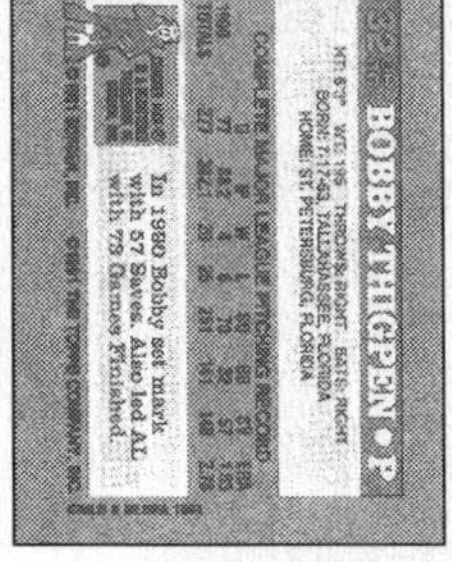

This 36-card set is the first of two 36-card series produced by Topps for Cracker Jack, and the cards were inserted inside specially marked packages of Cracker Jack. These cards were the "toy surprise" inside. The cards measure approximately one-fourth standard-size (1 1/4" by 1 3/4") and are frequently referenced as micro-cards. The micro-cards have color player photos with different color borders but are otherwise identical to the corresponding cards in the Topps regular issue. The horizontally oriented backs are printed in red, blue, and pink, and include biography, complete Major League batting record, career highlights, and the Cracker Jack sailor at the lower left corner. Standard-size (2 1/2" by 3 1/2") cards featuring four micro-cards each were seen at shows but were not inserted inside the product. These were apparently test runs or uncut sheets. Although each mini-card is numbered on the back, the numbering of the four cards on any standard-size card is not consecutive.

	MT	EX-MT	VG
COMPLETE SET (36)	9.00	4.00	1.15
COMMON PLAYER (1-36)	.15	.07	.02
☐ 1 Nolan Ryan	1.25	.55	.16
☐ 2 Paul Molitor	.25	.11	.03
☐ 3 Tim Raines	.25	.11	.03
☐ 4 Frank Viola	.15	.07	.02
☐ 5 Sandy Alomar Jr.	.25	.11	.03
☐ 6 Ryne Sandberg	.75	.35	.09
☐ 7 Don Mattingly	.60	.25	.08

☐ 8 Pedro Guerrero	.15	.07	.02
☐ 9 Jose Rijo	.15	.07	.02
☐ 10 Jose Canseco	.60	.25	.08
☐ 11 Dave Parker	.25	.11	.03
☐ 12 Doug Drabek	.25	.11	.03
☐ 13 Cal Ripken	.75	.35	.09
☐ 14 Dave Justice	.60	.25	.08
☐ 15 George Brett	.45	.20	.06
☐ 16 Eric Davis	.25	.11	.03
☐ 17 Mark Langston	.15	.07	.02
☐ 18 Rickey Henderson	.45	.20	.06
☐ 19 Barry Bonds	.35	.16	.04
☐ 20 Kevin Maas	.25	.11	.03
☐ 21 Len Dykstra	.15	.07	.02
☐ 22 Roger Clemens	.75	.35	.09
☐ 23 Robin Yount	.45	.20	.06
☐ 24 Mark Grace	.35	.16	.04
☐ 25 Bo Jackson	.45	.20	.06
☐ 26 Tony Gwynn	.45	.20	.06
☐ 27 Mark McGwire	.45	.20	.06
☐ 28 Dwight Gooden	.25	.11	.03
☐ 29 Wade Boggs	.45	.20	.06
☐ 30 Kevin Mitchell	.25	.11	.03
☐ 31 Cecil Fielder	.35	.16	.04
☐ 32 Bobby Thigpen	.15	.07	.02
☐ 33 Benito Santiago	.25	.11	.03
☐ 34 Kirby Puckett	.45	.20	.06
☐ 35 Will Clark	.60	.25	.08
☐ 36 Ken Griffey Jr.	1.25	.55	.16

1991 Cracker Jack Topps II

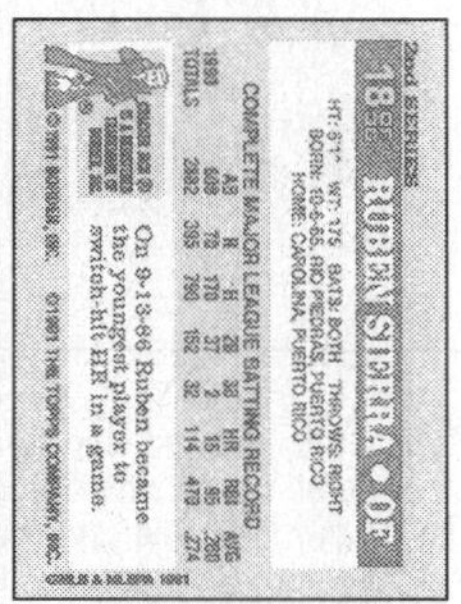

This 36-card set is the second of two different 36-card series produced by Topps for Cracker Jack, and the cards were inserted inside specially marked packages of Cracker Jack. These cards were the "toy surprise" inside. The cards measure approximately one-fourth standard-size (1 1/4" by 1 3/4") and are frequently referenced as micro-cards. The micro-cards have color player photos with different color borders but are otherwise identical to the corresponding cards in the Topps regular issue. The horizontally oriented backs are printed in red, blue, and pink, and include biography, complete Major League batting record, career highlights, and the Cracker Jack sailor at the lower left corner. Standard-size (2 1/2" by 3 1/2") cards featuring four micro-cards each were seen at shows but were not inserted inside the product. These were apparently test runs or uncut sheets. Although each mini-card is numbered on the back, the numbering of the four cards on any standard-size card is not consecutive.

	MT	EX-MT	VG
COMPLETE SET (36)	8.00	3.60	1.00
COMMON PLAYER (1-36)	.15	.07	.02
☐ 1 Eddie Murray	.35	.16	.04
☐ 2 Carlton Fisk	.35	.16	.04
☐ 3 Eric Anthony	.25	.11	.03
☐ 4 Kelly Gruber	.15	.07	.02
☐ 5 Von Hayes	.15	.07	.02
☐ 6 Ben McDonald	.35	.16	.04
☐ 7 Andre Dawson	.35	.16	.04
☐ 8 Ellis Burks	.35	.16	.04
☐ 9 Matt Williams	.35	.16	.04
☐ 10 Dave Stewart	.25	.11	.03
☐ 11 Barry Larkin	.25	.11	.03
☐ 12 Chuck Finley	.15	.07	.02
☐ 13 Shane Andrews	.25	.11	.03
☐ 14 Bret Saberhagen	.25	.11	.03
☐ 15 Bobby Bonilla	.35	.16	.04
☐ 16 Roberto Kelly	.35	.16	.04
☐ 17 Orel Hershiser	.25	.11	.03
☐ 18 Ruben Sierra	.45	.20	.06
☐ 19 Ron Gant	.45	.20	.06
☐ 20 Frank Thomas	2.00	.90	.25
☐ 21 Tim Wallach	.15	.07	.02
☐ 22 Gregg Olson	.25	.11	.03
☐ 23 Shawon Dunston	.15	.07	.02
☐ 24 Kent Hrbek	.15	.07	.02
☐ 25 Ramon Martinez	.45	.20	.06
☐ 26 Alan Trammell	.25	.11	.03
☐ 27 Ozzie Smith	.35	.16	.04
☐ 28 Bob Welch	.15	.07	.02
☐ 29 Chris Sabo	.25	.11	.03
☐ 30 Steve Sax	.15	.07	.02
☐ 31 Bip Roberts	.15	.07	.02
☐ 32 Dave Stieb	.15	.07	.02
☐ 33 Howard Johnson	.25	.11	.03
☐ 34 Mike Greenwell	.25	.11	.03
☐ 35 Delino DeShields	.35	.16	.04
☐ 36 Alex Fernandez	.35	.16	.04

1992 Cracker Jack Donruss I

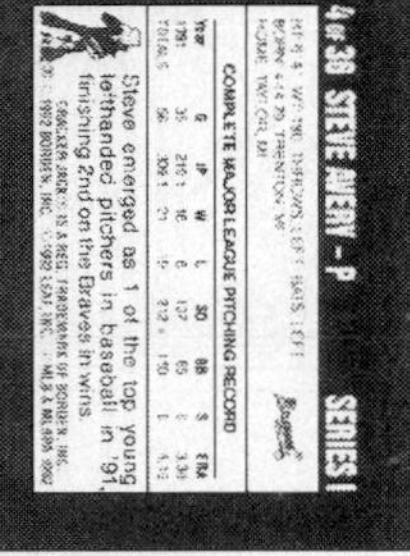

This 36-card set is the first of two series produced by Donruss for Cracker Jack, and the micro cards were protected by a paper sleeve and inserted into specially marked boxes of Cracker Jack. A side panel listed all 36 players in series I. The micro cards measure 1 1/4" by 1 3/4". The front design is the same as the Donruss regular issue cards, only different color player photos are displayed. The backs, however, have a completely different design than the regular issue Donruss cards; they are horizontally oriented and present biography, major league pitching (or batting) record, and brief career summary inside navy blue borders. The cards are numbered on the back. On the paper sleeve was a mail-in offer for a mini card album with six top loading plastic pages for 4.95 per album.

	MT	EX-MT	VG
COMPLETE SET (36)	12.00	5.50	1.50
COMMON PLAYER (1-36)	.15	.07	.02
☐ 1 Jeff Bagwell	.75	.35	.09
☐ 2 Terry Pendleton	.25	.11	.03
☐ 3 Ozzie Smith	.35	.16	.04
☐ 4 Steve Avery	.50	.23	.06
☐ 5 Todd Zeile	.20	.09	.03
☐ 6 Lance Dickson	.15	.07	.02
☐ 7 Ryne Sandberg	.90	.40	.11
☐ 8 Brett Butler	.25	.11	.03
☐ 9 Ramon Martinez	.25	.11	.03
☐ 10 Marquis Grissom	.35	.16	.04
☐ 11 Travis Fryman	.60	.25	.08
☐ 12 Will Clark	.75	.35	.09
☐ 13 Tony Gwynn	.50	.23	.06
☐ 14 Wes Chamberlain	.25	.11	.03
☐ 15 Doug Drabek	.25	.11	.03

☐ 16	Barry Larkin	.25	.11	.03
☐ 17	Hal Morris	.25	.11	.03
☐ 18	Dwight Gooden	.35	.16	.04
☐ 19	Dennis Eckersley	.25	.11	.03
☐ 20	Jose Canseco	.75	.35	.09
☐ 21	Jim Abbott	.35	.16	.04
☐ 22	Kelly Gruber	.15	.07	.02
☐ 23	Robin Yount	.50	.23	.06
☐ 24	Sandy Alomar Jr.	.25	.11	.03
☐ 25	Ken Griffey Jr.	1.50	.65	.19
☐ 26	Cal Ripken	1.25	.55	.16
☐ 27	Nolan Ryan	1.25	.55	.16
☐ 28	Ivan Rodriguez	.75	.35	.09
☐ 29	Roger Clemens	.90	.40	.11
☐ 30	Brian McRae	.25	.11	.03
☐ 31	Kent Hrbek	.15	.07	.02
☐ 32	Cecil Fielder	.50	.23	.06
☐ 33	Chuck Knoblauch	.35	.16	.04
☐ 34	Frank Thomas	1.75	.80	.22
☐ 35	Don Mattingly	.50	.23	.06
☐ 36	Robin Ventura	.50	.23	.06

1992 Cracker Jack Donruss II

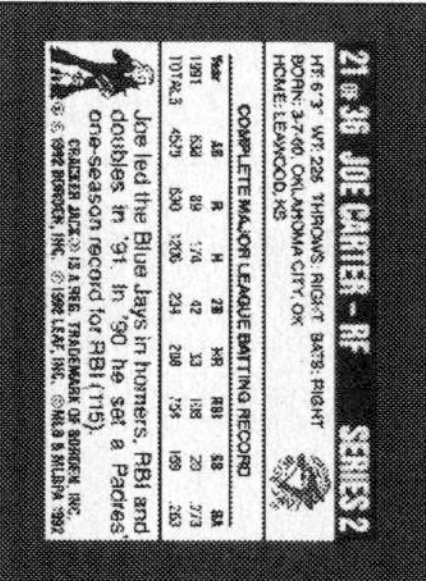

This 36-card set is the second of two series produced by Donruss for Cracker Jack. The mini cards were protected by a paper sleeve and inserted into specially marked boxes of Cracker Jacks. A side panel listed all 36 players in series II. The micro cards measure 1 1/4" by 1 3/4". The front design is the same as the Donruss regular issue cards, only different color player photos are displayed. The backs, however, have a completely different design than the regular issue Donruss cards; they are horizontally oriented and present biography, major league pitching (or batting) record, and brief career summary inside red borders. The cards are numbered on the back. On the paper sleeve was a mail-in offer for a mini card album with six top loading plastic pages for 4.95 per album.

		MT	EX-MT	VG
COMPLETE SET (36)		8.00	3.60	1.00
COMMON PLAYER (1-36)		.15	.07	.02
☐ 1	Craig Biggio	.35	.16	.04
☐ 2	Tom Glavine	.75	.35	.09
☐ 3	David Justice	.90	.40	.11
☐ 4	Lee Smith	.25	.11	.03
☐ 5	Mark Grace	.35	.16	.04
☐ 6	George Bell	.25	.11	.03
☐ 7	Darryl Strawberry	.50	.23	.06
☐ 8	Eric Davis	.25	.11	.03
☐ 9	Ivan Calderon	.15	.07	.02
☐ 10	Royce Clayton	.35	.16	.04
☐ 11	Matt Williams	.25	.11	.03
☐ 12	Fred McGriff	.50	.23	.06
☐ 13	Len Dykstra	.25	.11	.03
☐ 14	Barry Bonds	.60	.25	.08
☐ 15	Reggie Sanders	.50	.23	.06
☐ 16	Chris Sabo	.25	.11	.03
☐ 17	Howard Johnson	.25	.11	.03
☐ 18	Bobby Bonilla	.35	.16	.04
☐ 19	Rickey Henderson	.60	.25	.08
☐ 20	Mark Langston	.25	.11	.03
☐ 21	Joe Carter	.50	.23	.06
☐ 22	Paul Molitor	.35	.16	.04
☐ 23	Glenallen Hill	.25	.11	.03
☐ 24	Edgar Martinez	.35	.16	.04
☐ 25	Gregg Olson	.25	.11	.03
☐ 26	Ruben Sierra	.60	.25	.08
☐ 27	Julio Franco	.25	.11	.03
☐ 28	Phil Plantier	.35	.16	.04
☐ 29	Wade Boggs	.50	.23	.06
☐ 30	George Brett	.50	.23	.06
☐ 31	Alan Trammell	.25	.11	.03
☐ 32	Kirby Puckett	1.00	.45	.13
☐ 33	Scott Erickson	.35	.16	.04
☐ 34	Matt Nokes	.25	.11	.03
☐ 35	Danny Tartabull	.35	.16	.04
☐ 36	Jack McDowell	.35	.16	.04

1982 Cubs Red Lobster

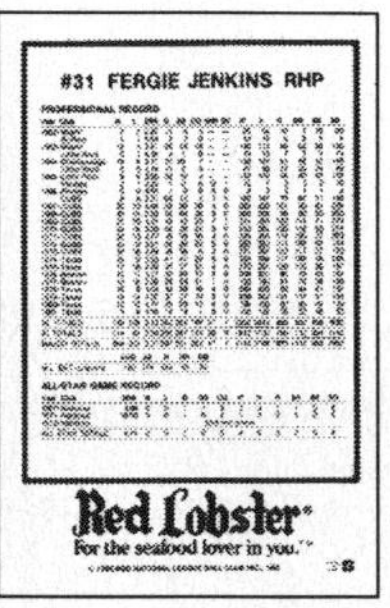

The cards in this 28-card set measure 2 1/4" by 3 1/2". This set of Chicago Cubs players was co-produced by the Cubs and Chicago-area Red Lobster restaurants and was introduced as a promotional giveaway on August 20, 1982, at Wrigley Field. The cards contain borderless color photos of 25 players, manager Lee Elia, the coaching staff, and a team picture. A facsimile autograph appears on the front, and the cards run in sequence by uniform number. While the coaches have a short biographical sketch on back, the player cards simply list the individual's professional record. The key card in the set is obviously Ryne Sandberg's as it predates his Donruss, Fleer, and Topps Rookie Cards by one year.

		NRMT-MT	EXC	G-VG
COMPLETE SET (28)		90.00	40.00	11.50
COMMON PLAYER		.80	.35	.10
☐ 1	Larry Bowa	1.25	.55	.16
☐ 4	Lee Elia MG	.80	.35	.10
☐ 6	Keith Moreland	1.00	.45	.13
☐ 7	Jody Davis	1.00	.45	.13
☐ 10	Leon Durham	1.00	.45	.13
☐ 15	Junior Kennedy	.80	.35	.10
☐ 17	Bump Wills	.80	.35	.10
☐ 18	Scot Thompson	.80	.35	.10
☐ 21	Jay Johnstone	1.25	.55	.16
☐ 22	Bill Buckner	1.50	.65	.19
☐ 23	Ryne Sandberg	60.00	27.00	7.50
☐ 24	Jerry Morales	.80	.35	.10
☐ 25	Gary Woods	.80	.35	.10
☐ 28	Steve Henderson	.80	.35	.10
☐ 29	Bob Molinaro	.80	.35	.10
☐ 31	Fergie Jenkins	4.00	1.80	.50
☐ 33	Al Ripley	.80	.35	.10
☐ 34	Randy Martz	.80	.35	.10
☐ 36	Mike Proly	.80	.35	.10
☐ 37	Ken Kravec	.80	.35	.10
☐ 38	Willie Hernandez	1.25	.55	.16
☐ 39	Bill Campbell	.80	.35	.10
☐ 41	Dick Tidrow	.80	.35	.10
☐ 46	Lee Smith	4.00	1.80	.50
☐ 47	Doug Bird	.80	.35	.10
☐ 48	Dickie Noles	.80	.35	.10

☐ NNO Team Picture	1.25	.55	.16
☐ NNO Coaches Card	1.00	.45	.13
John Vukovich			
Gordy MacKenzie			
Billy Williams			
Billy Connors			
Tom Harmon			

1983 Cubs Thorn Apple Valley

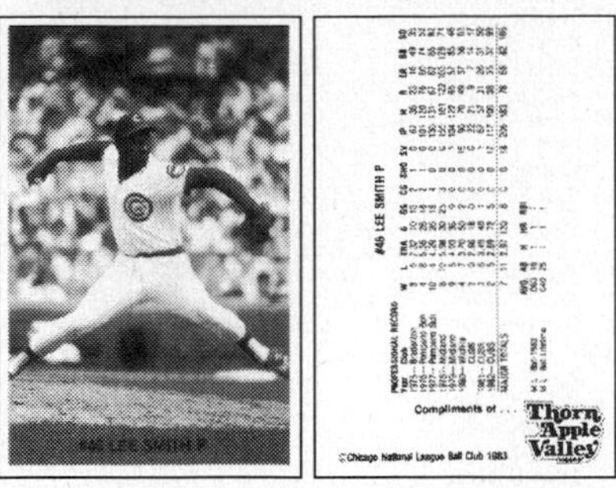

This set of 27 Chicago Cubs features full-color action photos on the front and was sponsored by Thorn Apple Valley. The cards measure approximately 2 1/4" by 3 1/2". The backs provide year-by-year statistics. The cards are unnumbered except for uniform number; they are listed below by uniform with the special cards listed at the end. The card of Joe Carter predates his Donruss Rookie Card by one year.

	NRMT-MT	EXC	G-VG
COMPLETE SET (27)	30.00	13.50	3.80
COMMON PLAYER	.50	.23	.06
☐ 1 Larry Bowa	.75	.35	.09
☐ 6 Keith Moreland	.60	.25	.08
☐ 7 Jody Davis	.60	.25	.08
☐ 10 Leon Durham	.60	.25	.08
☐ 11 Ron Cey	.75	.35	.09
☐ 16 Steve Lake	.50	.23	.06
☐ 20 Thad Bosley	.50	.23	.06
☐ 21 Jay Johnstone	.60	.25	.08
☐ 22 Bill Buckner	.90	.40	.11
☐ 23 Ryne Sandberg	10.00	4.50	1.25
☐ 24 Jerry Morales	.50	.23	.06
☐ 25 Gary Woods	.50	.23	.06
☐ 27 Mel Hall	1.50	.65	.19
☐ 29 Tom Veryzer	.50	.23	.06
☐ 30 Chuck Rainey	.50	.23	.06
☐ 31 Fergie Jenkins	1.50	.65	.19
☐ 32 Craig Lefferts	.75	.35	.09
☐ 33 Joe Carter	15.00	6.75	1.90
☐ 34 Steve Trout	.50	.23	.06
☐ 36 Mike Proly	.50	.23	.06
☐ 39 Bill Campbell	.50	.23	.06
☐ 41 Warren Brusstar	.50	.23	.06
☐ 44 Dick Ruthven	.50	.23	.06
☐ 46 Lee Smith	1.50	.65	.19
☐ 48 Dickie Noles	.50	.23	.06
☐ NNO Manager/Coaches	.50	.23	.06
Lee Elia MG			
Ruben Amaro			
Billy Connors			
Duffy Dyer			
Fred Koenig			
John Vukovich			
☐ NNO Team Photo	.75	.35	.09

1984 Cubs Seven-Up

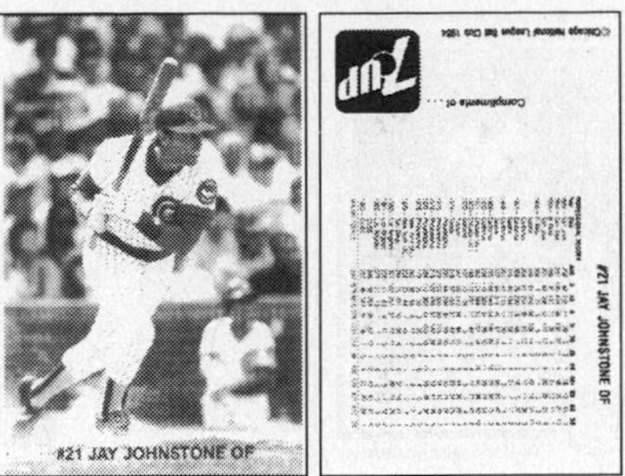

This 28-card set was sponsored by 7-Up. The cards are in full color and measure approximately 2 1/4" by 3 1/2". The card backs are printed in black on white card stock. This set is tougher to find than the other similar Cubs sets since the Cubs were more successful (on the field) in 1984 winning their division, that is, virtually all of the cards printed were distributed during the "Baseball Card Day" promotion (August 12th) which was much better attended that year. There actually were two additional cards produced (in limited quantities) later which some collectors consider part of this set; these late issue cards show four Cubs rookies on each card.

	NRMT-MT	EXC	G-VG
COMPLETE SET (28)	22.00	10.00	2.80
COMMON PLAYER	.60	.25	.08
☐ 1 Larry Bowa	.90	.40	.11
☐ 6 Keith Moreland	.75	.35	.09
☐ 7 Jody Davis	.75	.35	.09
☐ 10 Leon Durham	.75	.35	.09
☐ 11 Ron Cey	.90	.40	.11
☐ 15 Ron Hassey	.60	.25	.08
☐ 18 Richie Hebner	.60	.25	.08
☐ 19 Dave Owen	.60	.25	.08
☐ 20 Bob Dernier	.60	.25	.08
☐ 21 Jay Johnstone	.75	.35	.09
☐ 23 Ryne Sandberg	7.50	3.40	.95
☐ 24 Scott Sanderson	.90	.40	.11
☐ 25 Gary Woods	.60	.25	.08
☐ 27 Thad Bosley	.60	.25	.08
☐ 28 Henry Cotto	.60	.25	.08
☐ 34 Steve Trout	.60	.25	.08
☐ 36 Gary Matthews	.75	.35	.09
☐ 39 George Frazier	.60	.25	.08
☐ 40 Rick Sutcliffe	1.00	.45	.13
☐ 41 Warren Brusstar	.60	.25	.08
☐ 42 Rich Bordi	.60	.25	.08
☐ 43 Dennis Eckersley	2.50	1.15	.30
☐ 44 Dick Ruthven	.60	.25	.08
☐ 46 Lee Smith	1.50	.65	.19
☐ 47 Rick Reuschel	.90	.40	.11
☐ 49 Tim Stoddard	.60	.25	.08
☐ NNO Coaches Card	.60	.25	.08
Ruben Amaro			
Billy Connors			
Johnny Oates			
John Vukovich			
Don Zimmer			
☐ NNO Jim Frey MG	.60	.25	.08

1985 Cubs Seven-Up

This 28-card set was distributed on August 14th at Wrigley Field for the game against the Expos. The cards measure 2 1/2" by 3 1/2" and were distributed wrapped in cellophane. The cards are unnumbered except for uniform number. The card backs are printed in black on white with a 7-Up logo in the upper right hand corner.

	NRMT-MT	EXC	G-VG
COMPLETE SET (28)	10.00	4.50	1.25
COMMON PLAYER	.25	.11	.03
☐ 1 Larry Bowa	.45	.20	.06
☐ 6 Keith Moreland	.35	.16	.04
☐ 7 Jody Davis	.35	.16	.04

☐ 10 Leon Durham	.35	.16	.04
☐ 11 Ron Cey	.45	.20	.06
☐ 15 Davey Lopes	.35	.16	.04
☐ 16 Steve Lake	.25	.11	.03
☐ 18 Rich Hebner	.25	.11	.03
☐ 20 Bob Dernier	.25	.11	.03
☐ 21 Scott Sanderson	.35	.16	.04
☐ 22 Billy Hatcher	.45	.20	.06
☐ 23 Ryne Sandberg	4.00	1.80	.50
☐ 24 Brian Dayett	.25	.11	.03
☐ 25 Gary Woods	.25	.11	.03
☐ 27 Thad Bosley	.25	.11	.03
☐ 28 Chris Speier	.25	.11	.03
☐ 31 Ray Fontenot	.25	.11	.03
☐ 34 Steve Trout	.25	.11	.03
☐ 36 Gary Matthews	.35	.16	.04
☐ 39 George Frazier	.25	.11	.03
☐ 40 Rick Sutcliffe	.60	.25	.08
☐ 41 Warren Brusstar	.25	.11	.03
☐ 42 Lary Sorensen	.25	.11	.03
☐ 43 Dennis Eckersley	1.25	.55	.16
☐ 44 Dick Ruthven	.25	.11	.03
☐ 46 Lee Smith	.75	.35	.09
☐ NNO Jim Frey MG	.25	.11	.03
☐ NNO Cubs Coaching Staff Ruben Amaro Billy Connors Johnny Oates John Vukovich Don Zimmer	.25	.11	.03

1986 Cubs Gatorade

This 28-card set was given out at Wrigley Field on the Cubs' special "baseball card" promotion held July 17th for the game against the Giants. The set was sponsored by Gatorade. The cards are unnumbered except for uniform number. Card backs feature blue print on white card stock. The cards measure approximately 2 7/8" by 4 1/4" and are in full color.

	MT	EX-MT	VG
COMPLETE SET (28)	10.00	4.50	1.25
COMMON PLAYER	.25	.11	.03
☐ 4 Gene Michael MG	.35	.16	.04
☐ 6 Keith Moreland	.35	.16	.04
☐ 7 Jody Davis	.35	.16	.04
☐ 10 Leon Durham	.35	.16	.04
☐ 11 Ron Cey	.45	.20	.06
☐ 12 Shawon Dunston	1.00	.45	.13
☐ 15 Davey Lopes	.35	.16	.04
☐ 16 Terry Francona	.25	.11	.03
☐ 18 Steve Christmas	.25	.11	.03
☐ 19 Manny Trillo	.25	.11	.03
☐ 20 Bob Dernier	.25	.11	.03
☐ 21 Scott Sanderson	.35	.16	.04
☐ 22 Jerry Mumphrey	.25	.11	.03
☐ 23 Ryne Sandberg	3.50	1.55	.45
☐ 27 Thad Bosley	.25	.11	.03
☐ 28 Chris Speier	.25	.11	.03
☐ 29 Steve Lake	.25	.11	.03
☐ 31 Ray Fontenot	.25	.11	.03
☐ 34 Steve Trout	.25	.11	.03
☐ 36 Gary Matthews	.35	.16	.04
☐ 39 George Frazier	.25	.11	.03
☐ 40 Rick Sutcliffe	.50	.23	.06
☐ 43 Dennis Eckersley	1.25	.55	.16
☐ 46 Lee Smith	.75	.35	.09
☐ 48 Jay Baller	.25	.11	.03
☐ 49 Jamie Moyer	.25	.11	.03
☐ 50 Guy Hoffman	.25	.11	.03
☐ NNO Coaches Card Ruben Amaro Billy Connors Johnny Oates John Vukovich Billy Williams	.25	.11	.03

1986 Cubs Unocal

This set of 20 color action player photos was sponsored by Unocal 76. They are bordered in black and are printed on (approximately) 8 1/2" by 11" glossy paper sheets. A color headshot is superimposed on each front. The backs contain extensive player information, including biography, performance in the 1985 season, complete Major League statistics, and career summary. The player photos are unnumbered and checklisted below in alphabetical order.

	MT	EX-MT	VG
COMPLETE SET (20)	8.00	3.60	1.00
COMMON PLAYER (1-20)	.30	.14	.04
☐ 1 Jay Baller	.30	.14	.04
☐ 2 Thad Bosley	.30	.14	.04
☐ 3 Ron Cey	.50	.23	.06
☐ 4 Jody Davis	.40	.18	.05
☐ 5 Bob Dernier	.30	.14	.04
☐ 6 Shawon Dunston	.75	.35	.09
☐ 7 Leon Durham	.40	.18	.05
☐ 8 Dennis Eckersley	1.25	.55	.16
☐ 9 Ray Fontenot	.30	.14	.04
☐ 10 George Frazier	.30	.14	.04
☐ 11 Davey Lopes	.40	.18	.05
☐ 12 Gary Matthews	.40	.18	.05
☐ 13 Keith Moreland	.40	.18	.05
☐ 14 Jerry Mumphrey	.30	.14	.04
☐ 15 Ryne Sandberg	3.50	1.55	.45
☐ 16 Scott Sanderson	.40	.18	.05
☐ 17 Lee Smith	.75	.35	.09
☐ 18 Rick Sutcliffe	.50	.23	.06
☐ 19 Manny Trillo	.30	.14	.04
☐ 20 Steve Trout	.30	.14	.04

1987 Cubs David Berg

This 26-card set was given out at Wrigley Field on the Cubs' special "baseball card" promotion held July 29th. The set was sponsored by David Berg Pure Beef Hot Dogs. The cards are unnumbered except for uniform number. Card backs feature red and blue print on white card stock. The cards measure approximately 2 7/8" by 4 1/4" and are in full color.

	MT	EX-MT	VG
COMPLETE SET (26)	10.00	4.50	1.25
COMMON PLAYER	.25	.11	.03
☐ 1 Dave Martinez	.45	.20	.06
☐ 4 Gene Michael MG	.35	.16	.04
☐ 6 Keith Moreland	.35	.16	.04
☐ 7 Jody Davis	.35	.16	.04
☐ 8 Andre Dawson	1.50	.65	.19
☐ 10 Leon Durham	.35	.16	.04
☐ 11 Jim Sundberg	.35	.16	.04
☐ 12 Shawon Dunston	.75	.35	.09
☐ 19 Manny Trillo	.25	.11	.03
☐ 20 Bob Dernier	.25	.11	.03
☐ 21 Scott Sanderson	.35	.16	.04
☐ 22 Jerry Mumphrey	.25	.11	.03
☐ 23 Ryne Sandberg	2.50	1.15	.30
☐ 24 Brian Dayett	.25	.11	.03
☐ 29 Chico Walker	.35	.16	.04
☐ 31 Greg Maddux	3.00	1.35	.40
☐ 33 Frank DiPino	.25	.11	.03
☐ 34 Steve Trout	.25	.11	.03
☐ 36 Gary Matthews	.35	.16	.04
☐ 37 Ed Lynch	.25	.11	.03
☐ 39 Ron Davis	.25	.11	.03
☐ 40 Rick Sutcliffe	.45	.20	.06
☐ 46 Lee Smith	.60	.25	.08
☐ 47 Dickie Noles	.25	.11	.03
☐ 49 Jamie Moyer	.25	.11	.03
☐ NNO Coaching Staff Johnny Oates Jim Snyder Herm Starrette John Vukovich Billy Williams	.25	.11	.03

1988 Cubs David Berg

This 27-card set was given out at Wrigley Field with every paid admission on the Cubs' special "baseball card" promotion held August 24th. The set was sponsored by David Berg Pure Beef Hot Dogs and the Venture store chain. The cards are unnumbered except for uniform number. Card backs feature primarily black print on white card stock. The cards measure approximately 2 7/8" by 4 1/4" and are in full color.

	MT	EX-MT	VG
COMPLETE SET (27)	9.00	4.00	1.15
COMMON PLAYER	.25	.11	.03

	MT	EX-MT	VG
☐ 2 Vance Law	.35	.16	.04
☐ 4 Don Zimmer MG	.35	.16	.04
☐ 7 Jody Davis	.35	.16	.04
☐ 8 Andre Dawson	1.25	.55	.16
☐ 9 Damon Berryhill	.45	.20	.06
☐ 12 Shawon Dunston	.60	.25	.08
☐ 17 Mark Grace	2.00	.90	.25
☐ 18 Angel Salazar	.25	.11	.03
☐ 19 Manny Trillo	.25	.11	.03
☐ 21 Scott Sanderson	.35	.16	.04
☐ 22 Jerry Mumphrey	.25	.11	.03
☐ 23 Ryne Sandberg	2.00	.90	.25
☐ 24 Gary Varsho	.35	.16	.04
☐ 25 Rafael Palmiero	1.50	.65	.19
☐ 28 Mitch Webster	.35	.16	.04
☐ 30 Darrin Jackson	.75	.35	.09
☐ 31 Greg Maddux	1.25	.55	.16
☐ 32 Calvin Schiraldi	.25	.11	.03
☐ 33 Frank DiPino	.25	.11	.03
☐ 37 Pat Perry	.25	.11	.03
☐ 40 Rick Sutcliffe	.45	.20	.06
☐ 41 Jeff Pico	.25	.11	.03
☐ 45 Al Nipper	.25	.11	.03
☐ 49 Jamie Moyer	.25	.11	.03
☐ 50 Les Lancaster	.25	.11	.03
☐ 54 Rich Gossage	.45	.20	.06
☐ NNO Cubs Coaching Staff Joe Altobelli CO Chuck Cottier CO Larry Cox CO Jose Martinez CO Dick Pole CO	.25	.11	.03

1989 Cubs Marathon

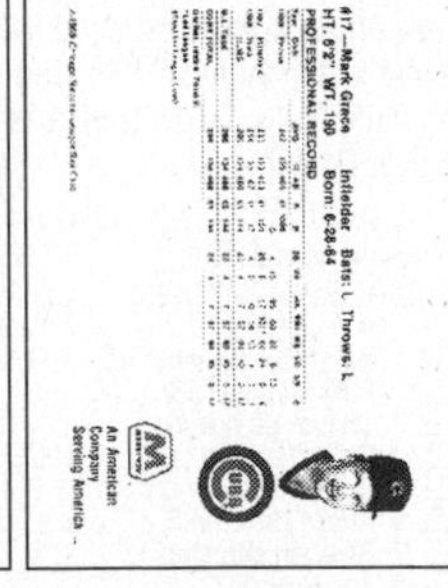

The 1989 Marathon Cubs set features 25 cards measuring approximately 2 3/4" by 4 1/4". The fronts are green and white, and feature facsimile autographs. The backs show black and white mug shots and career stats. The set was given away at the August 10, 1989 Cubs home game. The cards are numbered by the players' uniform numbers.

	MT	EX-MT	VG
COMPLETE SET (25)	12.00	5.50	1.50
COMMON PLAYER	.35	.16	.04

☐ 2 Vance Law	.45	.20	.06
☐ 4 Don Zimmer MG	.45	.20	.06
☐ 7 Joe Girardi	.45	.20	.06
☐ 8 Andre Dawson	1.00	.45	.13
☐ 9 Damon Berryhill	.45	.20	.06
☐ 10 Lloyd McClendon	.35	.16	.04
☐ 12 Shawon Dunston	.75	.35	.09
☐ 15 Domingo Ramos	.35	.16	.04
☐ 17 Mark Grace	1.25	.55	.16
☐ 18 Dwight Smith	.60	.25	.08
☐ 19 Curt Wilkerson	.35	.16	.04
☐ 20 Jerome Walton	.50	.23	.06
☐ 21 Scott Sanderson	.45	.20	.06
☐ 23 Ryne Sandberg	2.00	.90	.25
☐ 28 Mitch Williams	.60	.25	.08
☐ 31 Greg Maddux	1.00	.45	.13
☐ 32 Calvin Schiraldi	.35	.16	.04
☐ 33 Mitch Webster	.35	.16	.04
☐ 36 Mike Bielecki	.45	.20	.06
☐ 39 Paul Kilgus	.35	.16	.04
☐ 40 Rick Sutcliffe	.45	.20	.06
☐ 41 Jeff Pico	.35	.16	.04
☐ 44 Steve Wilson	.45	.20	.06
☐ 50 Les Lancaster	.45	.20	.06
☐ NNO Cubs Coaches Joe Altobelli Chuck Cottier Larry Cox Jose Martinez Dick Pole	.35	.16	.04

1990 Cubs Marathon

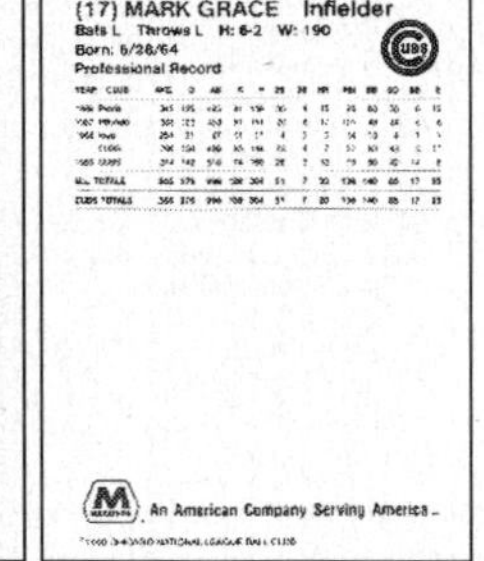

The Marathon Oil Chicago Cubs set contains 28 cards measuring approximately 2 7/8" by 4 1/4" which was given away at the August 17th Cub game. This set is checklisted alphabetically below with the uniform number next to the players name.

	MT	EX-MT	VG
COMPLETE SET (28)	10.00	4.50	1.25
COMMON PLAYER (1-28)	.35	.16	.04
☐ 1 Paul Assenmacher 45	.35	.16	.04
☐ 2 Mike Bielecki 36	.35	.16	.04
☐ 3 Shawn Boskie 47	.45	.20	.06
☐ 4 Dave Clark 30	.35	.16	.04
☐ 5 Doug Dascenzo 29	.35	.16	.04
☐ 6 Andre Dawson 8	1.00	.45	.13
☐ 7 Shawon Dunston 12	.60	.25	.08
☐ 8 Joe Girardi 7	.45	.20	.06
☐ 9 Mark Grace 17	1.00	.45	.13
☐ 10 Mike Harkey 22	.60	.25	.08
☐ 11 Les Lancaster 50	.35	.16	.04
☐ 12 Bill Long 37	.35	.16	.04
☐ 13 Greg Maddux 31	1.00	.45	.13
☐ 14 Lloyd McClendon 10	.35	.16	.04
☐ 15 Jeff Pico 41	.35	.16	.04
☐ 16 Domingo Ramos 15	.35	.16	.04
☐ 17 Luis Salazar 11	.35	.16	.04
☐ 18 Ryne Sandberg 23	1.50	.65	.19
☐ 19 Dwight Smith 18	.45	.20	.06
☐ 20 Rick Sutcliffe 40	.45	.20	.06
☐ 21 Hector Villanueva 32	.45	.20	.06
☐ 22 Jerome Walton 20	.35	.16	.04
☐ 23 Curtis Wilkerson 19	.35	.16	.04
☐ 24 Mitch Williams 28	.45	.20	.06
☐ 25 Steve Wilson 44	.35	.16	.04
☐ 26 Marvell Wynne 25	.35	.16	.04
☐ 27 Don Zimmer 4 MG	.45	.20	.06
☐ 28 Cubs Coaches Joe Altobelli Jose Martinez Phil Roof Chuck Cottier Dick Pole	.35	.16	.04

1991 Cubs Marathon

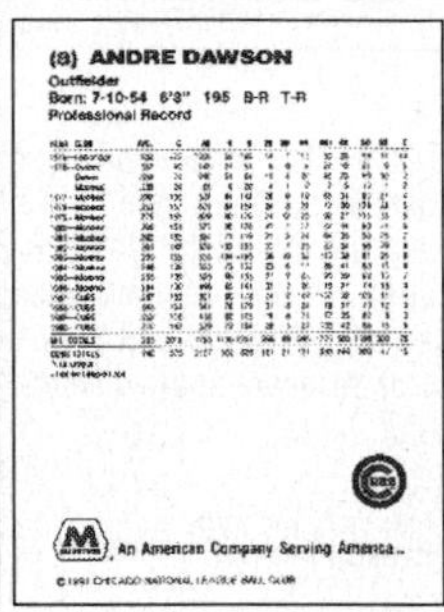

This 28-card set was produced by Marathon Oil, and its company logo appears at the bottom of card back. The cards were given away at the Cubs' home game against Montreal Expos on August 14, 1991. The oversized cards measure approximately 2 7/8" by 4 1/4" and feature on the fronts color action player photos with white borders. The card (uniform) number inside a white diamond and the words "Chicago Cubs" overlay the top portion of the photo. The player's name and position appear in the blue and red stripes traversing the bottom of the card face. The backs are printed in blue, red, and black on a white background and present biographical and statistical information. The set can also be found with blank backs. The cards are skip-numbered by uniform number and checklisted below accordingly.

	MT	EX-MT	VG
COMPLETE SET (28)	9.00	4.00	1.15
COMMON PLAYER	.25	.11	.03
☐ 7 Joe Girardi	.35	.16	.04
☐ 8 Andre Dawson	.90	.40	.11
☐ 9 Damon Berryhill	.35	.16	.04
☐ 10 Luis Salazar	.25	.11	.03
☐ 11 George Bell	.60	.25	.08
☐ 12 Shawon Dunston	.45	.20	.06
☐ 16 Jose Vizcaino	.35	.16	.04
☐ 17 Mark Grace	.90	.40	.11
☐ 18 Dwight Smith	.35	.16	.04
☐ 19 Hector Villanueva	.35	.16	.04
☐ 20 Jerome Walton	.35	.16	.04
☐ 22 Mike Harkey	.45	.20	.06
☐ 23 Ryne Sandberg	1.00	.45	.13
☐ 24 Chico Walker	.35	.16	.04
☐ 29 Doug Dascenzo	.25	.11	.03
☐ 30 Bob Scanlan	.25	.11	.03
☐ 31 Greg Maddux	.90	.40	.11
☐ 32 Danny Jackson	.35	.16	.04
☐ 33 Chuck McElroy	.45	.20	.06
☐ 36 Mike Bielecki	.35	.16	.04
☐ 40 Rick Sutcliffe	.35	.16	.04
☐ 41 Jim Essian MG	.25	.11	.03
☐ 42 Dave Smith	.35	.16	.04
☐ 45 Paul Assenmacher	.25	.11	.03
☐ 47 Shawn Boskie	.35	.16	.04
☐ 50 Les Lancaster	.25	.11	.03
☐ 51 Heathcliff Slocumb	.35	.16	.04

	MT	EX-MT	VG
☐ NNO Coaches Card	.25	.11	.03
Joe Altobelli Chuck Cottier Jose Martinez Billy Connors Phil Roof Richie Zisk			

1991 Cubs Vine Line

This 36-card set was issued as insert sheets in the Cubs' Vine Line fan news magazine. Each sheet measures approximately 7 1/2" by 10 1/2" and features nine different player cards. After perforation, the cards measure the standard size (2 1/2" by 3 1/2"). On a black card face, the photos are framed by a white border stripes, with the words "Vine Line" above and player information beneath the picture. The color action player photos are cut out and superimposed on indistinct, ghosted action scenes. In a horizontal format, the taupe and green backs present biography, career highlights, and statistics (1990 and career). The cards are unnumbered and checklisted below in alphabetical order.

	MT	EX-MT	VG
COMPLETE SET (36)	10.00	4.50	1.25
COMMON PLAYER (1-36)	.25	.11	.03
☐ 1 Paul Assenmacher	.35	.16	.04
☐ 2 Joe Altobelli CO	.25	.11	.03
☐ 3 George Bell	.50	.23	.06
☐ 4 Damon Berryhill	.35	.16	.04
☐ 5 Mike Bielecki	.35	.16	.04
☐ 6 Shawn Boskie	.35	.16	.04
☐ 7 Chuck Cottier CO	.25	.11	.03
☐ 8 Doug Dascenzo	.25	.11	.03
☐ 9 Andre Dawson	.75	.35	.09
☐ 10 Shawon Dunston	.50	.23	.06
☐ 11 Joe Girardi	.35	.16	.04
☐ 12 Mark Grace	.75	.35	.09
☐ 13 Mike Harkey	.60	.25	.08
☐ 14 Danny Jackson	.35	.16	.04
☐ 15 Ferguson Jenkins	.75	.35	.09
☐ 16 Les Lancaster	.25	.11	.03
☐ 17 Greg Maddux	1.00	.45	.13
☐ 18 Jose Martinez CO	.25	.11	.03
☐ 19 Chuck McElroy	.35	.16	.04
☐ 20 Erik Pappas	.25	.11	.03
☐ 21 Dick Pole CO	.25	.11	.03
☐ 22 Phil Roof CO	.25	.11	.03
☐ 23 Ryne Sandberg	1.50	.65	.19
☐ 24 Luis Salazar	.25	.11	.03
☐ 25 Gary Scott	.35	.16	.04
☐ 26 Heathcliff Slocumb	.25	.11	.03
☐ 27 Dave Smith	.25	.11	.03
☐ 28 Dwight Smith	.35	.16	.04
☐ 29 Rick Sutcliffe	.35	.16	.04
☐ 30 Hector Villanueva	.35	.16	.04
☐ 31 Jose Vizcaino	.35	.16	.04
☐ 32 Chico Walker	.35	.16	.04
☐ 33 Jerome Walton	.35	.16	.04
☐ 34 Steve Wilson	.25	.11	.03
☐ 35 Don Zimmer MG	.25	.11	.03
☐ 36 Most Valuable Players	.75	.35	.09
Ryne Sandberg Andre Dawson George Bell			

1992 Cubs Marathon

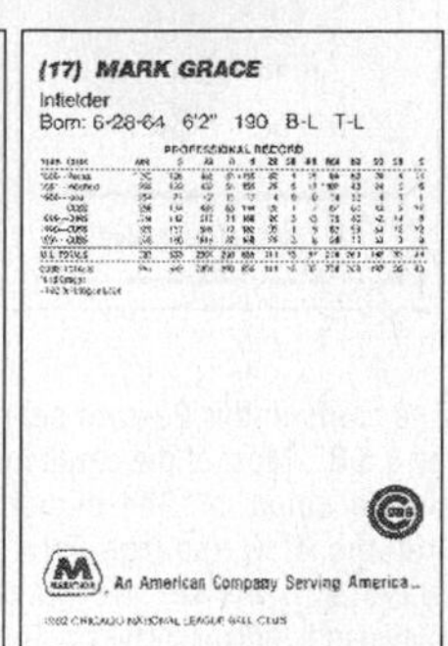

This 28-card set was produced by Marathon Oil, and its company logo appears at the bottom of the card back. The cards measure approximately 2 7/8" by 4 1/4". The fronts display color action player photos bordered in white. The player's name appears in a blue stripe above the picture, while the year is shown in a blue stripe below. The backs are printed in blue, red, and black on a white background and present biographical and statistical information. The cards are skip-numbered on the back by uniform number and checklisted below accordingly.

	MT	EX-MT	VG
COMPLETE SET (28)	8.00	3.60	1.00
COMMON PLAYER	.25	.11	.03
☐ 1 Doug Strange	.25	.11	.03
☐ 5 Jim Lefebvre MG	.25	.11	.03
☐ 6 Rey Sanchez	.35	.16	.04
☐ 7 Joe Girardi	.35	.16	.04
☐ 8 Andre Dawson	.75	.35	.09
☐ 10 Luis Salazar	.25	.11	.03
☐ 12 Shawon Dunston	.45	.20	.06
☐ 16 Jose Vizcaino	.25	.11	.03
☐ 17 Mark Grace	.90	.40	.11
☐ 18 Dwight Smith	.35	.16	.04
☐ 19 Hector Villanueva	.25	.11	.03
☐ 20 Jerome Walton	.25	.11	.03
☐ 21 Sammy Sosa	.35	.16	.04
☐ 23 Ryne Sandberg	1.00	.45	.13
☐ 27 Derrick May	.60	.25	.08
☐ 29 Doug Dascenzo	.25	.11	.03
☐ 30 Bob Scanlan	.25	.11	.03
☐ 31 Greg Maddux	.75	.35	.09
☐ 32 Danny Jackson	.35	.16	.04
☐ 34 Ken Patterson	.25	.11	.03
☐ 35 Chuck McElroy	.35	.16	.04
☐ 36 Mike Morgan	.45	.20	.06
☐ 38 Jeff D. Robinson	.25	.11	.03
☐ 42 Dave Smith	.35	.16	.04
☐ 45 Paul Assenmacher	.25	.11	.03
☐ 47 Shawn Boskie	.25	.11	.03
☐ 49 Frank Castillo	.35	.16	.04
☐ NNO Coaches	.25	.11	.03
Tom Trebelhorn Jose Martinez Billy Williams Sammy Ellis Chuck Cottier Billy Connors			

1954 Dan Dee

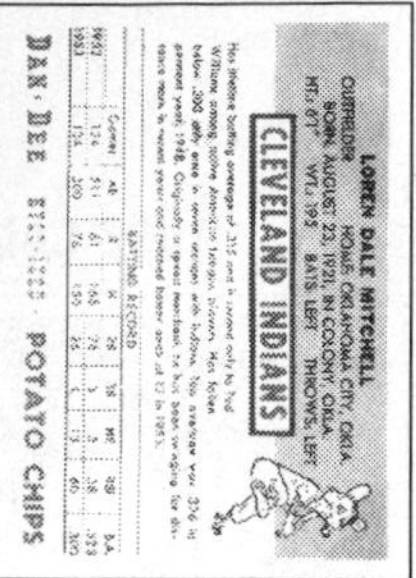

The cards in this 29-card set measure approximately 2 1/2" by 3 5/8". Most of the cards marketed by Dan Dee in bags of potato chips in 1954 depict players from the Cleveland Indians or Pittsburgh Pirates. The Pitttsburgh Pirates players in the set are much tougher to find than the Cleveland Indians players. The pictures used for New York Yankees players were also employed in the Briggs and Stahl-Meyer sets. Dan Dee cards have a waxed surface, but are commonly found with product stains. Paul Smith and Walker Cooper are considered the known scarcities. The catalog designation for this set is F342. These unnumbered cards are listed below in alphabetical order.

	NRMT	VG-E	GOOD
COMPLETE SET (29)	4000.00	1800.00	500.00
COMMON PLAYER (1-29)	50.00	23.00	6.25
COMMON PIRATE PLAYER	75.00	34.00	9.50
☐ 1 Bobby Avila	50.00	23.00	6.25
☐ 2 Hank Bauer	75.00	34.00	9.50
☐ 3 Walker Cooper SP Pittsburgh Pirates	325.00	145.00	40.00
☐ 4 Larry Doby	60.00	27.00	7.50
☐ 5 Luke Easter	50.00	23.00	6.25
☐ 6 Bob Feller	250.00	115.00	31.00
☐ 7 Bob Friend Pittsburgh Pirates	100.00	45.00	12.50
☐ 8 Mike Garcia	60.00	27.00	7.50
☐ 9 Sid Gordon Pittsburgh Pirates	75.00	34.00	9.50
☐ 10 Jim Hegan	50.00	23.00	6.25
☐ 11 Gil Hodges	175.00	80.00	22.00
☐ 12 Art Houtteman	50.00	23.00	6.25
☐ 13 Monte Irvin	110.00	50.00	14.00
☐ 14 Paul LaPalme Pittsburgh Pirates	75.00	34.00	9.50
☐ 15 Bob Lemon	125.00	57.50	15.50
☐ 16 Al Lopez	110.00	50.00	14.00
☐ 17 Mickey Mantle	1200.00	500.00	150.00
☐ 18 Dale Mitchell	50.00	23.00	6.25
☐ 19 Phil Rizzuto	165.00	75.00	21.00
☐ 20 Curt Roberts Pittsburgh Pirates	75.00	34.00	9.50
☐ 21 Al Rosen	75.00	34.00	9.50
☐ 22 Red Schoendienst	165.00	75.00	21.00
☐ 23 Paul Smith SP Pittsburgh Pirates	450.00	200.00	57.50
☐ 24 Duke Snider	225.00	100.00	28.00
☐ 25 George Strickland	50.00	23.00	6.25
☐ 26 Max Surkont Pittsburgh Pirates	75.00	34.00	9.50
☐ 27 Frank Thomas Pittsburgh Pirates	125.00	57.50	15.50
☐ 28 Wally Westlake	50.00	23.00	6.25
☐ 29 Early Wynn	125.00	57.50	15.50

1991 Denny's Grand Slam

The 1991 Denny's Grand Slam hologram baseball card set was produced by Upper Deck. The 26-card set contains one

player from each major league team, who was selected on the basis of the number and circumstances of his grand slam home runs. These standard size (2 1/2" by 3 1/2") cards were available at Denny's only with the purchase of a meal from the restaurant's Grand Slam menu; each card came sealed in a plastic bag that prevents prior identification. It is estimated that two million cards were printed. The 3-D cards alternate between silver and full color, and the player appears to stand apart from a background of exploding fireworks. A stripe at the top of the card has the player's name and team, while the Upper Deck and Denny's logos appear toward the bottom of the card face. The back has a descriptive account of the player's grand slams. The cards are numbered on the front.

	MT	EX-MT	VG
COMPLETE SET (26)	55.00	25.00	7.00
COMMON PLAYER (1-26)	2.00	.90	.25
☐ 1 Ellis Burks	2.00	.90	.25
☐ 2 Cecil Fielder	4.00	1.80	.50
☐ 3 Will Clark	6.00	2.70	.75
☐ 4 Eric Davis	2.50	1.15	.30
☐ 5 Dave Parker	2.00	.90	.25
☐ 6 Kelly Gruber	2.00	.90	.25
☐ 7 Kent Hrbek	2.00	.90	.25
☐ 8 Don Mattingly	4.50	2.00	.55
☐ 9 Brook Jacoby	2.00	.90	.25
☐ 10 Mark McGwire	4.00	1.80	.50
☐ 11 Howard Johnson	2.50	1.15	.30
☐ 12 Tim Wallach	2.00	.90	.25
☐ 13 Ricky Jordan	2.00	.90	.25
☐ 14 Andre Dawson	3.50	1.55	.45
☐ 15 Eddie Murray	3.00	1.35	.40
☐ 16 Danny Tartabull	2.50	1.15	.30
☐ 17 Bobby Bonilla	3.00	1.35	.40
☐ 18 Benito Santiago	2.50	1.15	.30
☐ 19 Alvin Davis	2.00	.90	.25
☐ 20 Cal Ripken	8.00	3.60	1.00
☐ 21 Ruben Sierra	4.00	1.80	.50
☐ 22 Pedro Guerrero	2.00	.90	.25
☐ 23 Wally Joyner	2.50	1.15	.30
☐ 24 Craig Biggio	2.00	.90	.25
☐ 25 Dave Justice	4.50	2.00	.55
☐ 26 Tim Raines	2.00	.90	.25

1992 Denny's Grand Slam

This 26-card set of holographic cards was produced by Upper Deck for Denny's. The set features one player from each major league team, who was selected on the basis of the number and circumstances of his grand slam home runs. With each order of a Grand Slam meal, the customer received one hologram card. The cards measure the standard size (2 1/2" by 3 1/2"). Each hologram shows a cut-out player photo superimposed over a scene from the city in which the team resides. A bar with the words "limited edition" runs along the top of the card, and the words "collector series" run vertically down the right edge. The

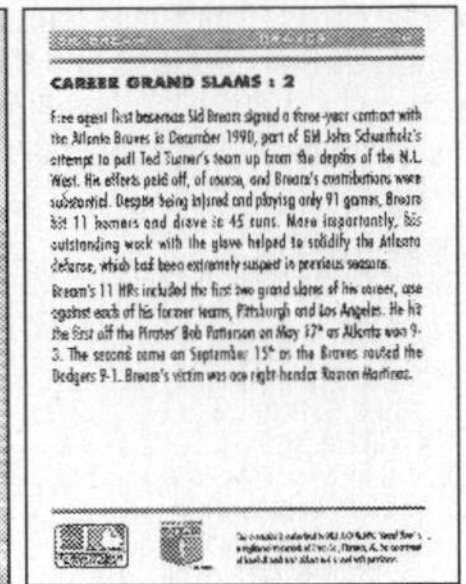

"1992 Grand Slam" insignia appears in the lower left corner, with the player's name in a bar extending to the right. The backs feature a blue stripe with the player's name across the top. Two red stripes border the top and bottom of a career summary printed in black on a white background. The cards are numbered on the back.

	MT	EX-MT	VG
COMPLETE SET (26)	50.00	23.00	6.25
COMMON PLAYER (1-26)	2.00	.90	.25
☐ 1 Marquis Grissom	3.00	1.35	.40
☐ 2 Ken Caminiti	2.00	.90	.25
☐ 3 Fred McGriff	3.00	1.35	.40
☐ 4 Felix Jose	2.50	1.15	.30
☐ 5 Jack Clark	2.00	.90	.25
☐ 6 Albert Belle	2.50	1.15	.30
☐ 7 Sid Bream	2.00	.90	.25
☐ 8 Robin Ventura	3.50	1.55	.45
☐ 9 Cal Ripken	8.00	3.60	1.00
☐ 10 Ryne Sandberg	5.00	2.30	.60
☐ 11 Paul O'Neill	2.00	.90	.25
☐ 12 Luis Polonia	2.00	.90	.25
☐ 13 Cecil Fielder	4.00	1.80	.50
☐ 14 Kal Daniels	2.00	.90	.25
☐ 15 Brian McRae	2.50	1.15	.30
☐ 16 Howard Johnson	2.50	1.15	.30
☐ 17 Greg Vaughn	2.00	.90	.25
☐ 18 Dale Murphy	2.50	1.15	.30
☐ 19 Kent Hrbek	2.00	.90	.25
☐ 20 Barry Bonds	3.50	1.55	.45
☐ 21 Matt Nokes	2.00	.90	.25
☐ 22 Jose Canseco	4.50	2.00	.55
☐ 23 Jay Buhner	2.50	1.15	.30
☐ 24 Will Clark	6.00	2.70	.75
☐ 25 Ruben Sierra	3.50	1.55	.45
☐ 26 Joe Carter	3.50	1.55	.45

1968 Dexter Press

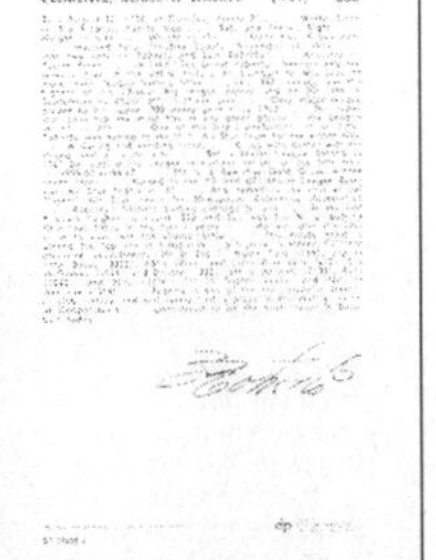

This 77-card set, which measures approximately 3 1/2" by 5 1/2", has beautiful full-color photos on the front of the card with biographical and career information on the back of the card. There are no year by year statistical lines on the back of the card. Dexter Press is another name for cards which the Coca-Cola Company helped to distribute during the mid sixties. The backs of the cards have a facsimile autograph. Dexter Press was located in West Nyack, New York. These unnumbered cards are listed below in alphabetical order.

	NRMT-MT	EXC	G-VG
COMPLETE SET (77)	450.00	200.00	57.50
COMMON PLAYER (1-77)	3.00	1.35	.40
☐ 1 Hank Aaron	45.00	20.00	5.75
☐ 2 Jerry Adair	3.00	1.35	.40
☐ 3 Richie Allen	5.00	2.30	.60
☐ 4 Bob Allison	3.00	1.35	.40
☐ 5 Felipe Alou	4.00	1.80	.50
☐ 6 Jesus Alou	3.00	1.35	.40
☐ 7 Mike Andrews	3.00	1.35	.40
☐ 8 Bob Aspromonte	3.00	1.35	.40
☐ 9 Johnny Bateman	3.00	1.35	.40
☐ 10 Mark Belanger	3.50	1.55	.45
☐ 11 Gary Bell	3.00	1.35	.40
☐ 12 Paul Blair	3.00	1.35	.40
☐ 13 Curt Blefary	3.00	1.35	.40
☐ 14 Bobby Bolin	3.00	1.35	.40
☐ 15 Ken Boswell	3.00	1.35	.40
☐ 16 Clete Boyer	3.50	1.55	.45
☐ 17 Ron Brand	3.00	1.35	.40
☐ 18 Darrell Brandon	3.00	1.35	.40
☐ 19 Don Buford	3.00	1.35	.40
☐ 20 Rod Carew	35.00	16.00	4.40
☐ 21 Clay Carroll	3.00	1.35	.40
☐ 22 Rico Carty	4.00	1.80	.50
☐ 23 Dean Chance	3.50	1.55	.45
☐ 24 Roberto Clemente	40.00	18.00	5.00
☐ 25 Tony Cloninger	3.00	1.35	.40
☐ 26 Mike Cuellar	3.50	1.55	.45
☐ 27 Jim Davenport	3.00	1.35	.40
☐ 28 Ron Davis	3.00	1.35	.40
☐ 29 Moe Drabowsky	3.00	1.35	.40
☐ 30 Dick Ellsworth	3.00	1.35	.40
☐ 31 Andy Etchebarren	3.00	1.35	.40
☐ 32 Joe Foy	3.00	1.35	.40
☐ 33 Bill Freehan	3.50	1.55	.45
☐ 34 Jim Fregosi	3.50	1.55	.45
☐ 35 Julio Gotay	3.00	1.35	.40
☐ 36 Dave Giusti	3.00	1.35	.40
☐ 37 Jim Ray Hart	3.50	1.55	.45
☐ 38 Jack Hiatt	3.00	1.35	.40
☐ 39 Ron Hunt	3.00	1.35	.40
☐ 40 Sonny Jackson	3.00	1.35	.40
☐ 41 Pat Jarvis	3.00	1.35	.40
☐ 42 Dave Johnson	3.50	1.55	.45
☐ 43 Ken Johnson	3.00	1.35	.40
☐ 44 Dalton Jones	3.00	1.35	.40
☐ 45 Jim Kaat	6.00	2.70	.75
☐ 46 Harmon Killebrew	20.00	9.00	2.50
☐ 47 Denny Lemaster	3.00	1.35	.40
☐ 48 Frank Linzy	3.00	1.35	.40
☐ 49 Jim Lonborg	3.50	1.55	.45
☐ 50 Juan Marichal	16.00	7.25	2.00
☐ 51 Willie Mays	45.00	20.00	5.75
☐ 52 Bill Mazeroski	5.00	2.30	.60
☐ 53 Mike McCormick	4.00	1.80	.50
☐ 54 Dave McNally	4.00	1.80	.50
☐ 55 Denis Menke	3.00	1.35	.40
☐ 56 Joe Morgan	18.00	8.00	2.30
☐ 57 Dave Morehead	3.00	1.35	.40
☐ 58 Phil Niekro	16.00	7.25	2.00
☐ 59 Russ Nixon	3.00	1.35	.40
☐ 60 Tony Oliva	7.50	3.40	.95
☐ 61 Gaylord Perry	16.00	7.25	2.00
☐ 62 Rico Petrocelli	4.00	1.80	.50
☐ 63 Tom Phoebus	3.00	1.35	.40
☐ 64 Boog Powell	5.00	2.30	.60
☐ 65 Brooks Robinson	22.00	10.00	2.80
☐ 66 Frank Robinson	20.00	9.00	2.50
☐ 67 Rich Rollins	3.50	1.55	.45
☐ 68 John Roseboro	3.50	1.55	.45
☐ 69 Ray Sadecki	3.00	1.35	.40
☐ 70 George Scott	4.00	1.80	.50
☐ 71 Rusty Staub	6.00	2.70	.75
☐ 72 Cesar Tovar	3.00	1.35	.40
☐ 73 Joe Torre	7.50	3.40	.95
☐ 74 Ted Uhlaender	3.00	1.35	.40
☐ 75 Woody Woodward	3.00	1.35	.40
☐ 76 John Wyatt	3.00	1.35	.40
☐ 77 Jimmy Wynn	4.00	1.80	.50

1958 Dodgers Bell Brand

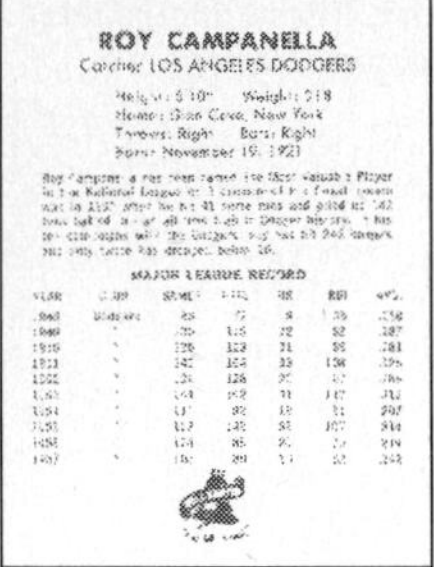

The 1958 Bell Brand Potato Chips set of 10 unnumbered cards features members of the Los Angeles Dodgers exclusively. Each card has a 1/4" green border, and the Gino Cimoli, Johnny Podres, and Duke Snider cards are more difficult to find; they are marked with an SP (short printed) in the checklist below. The cards measure approximately 3" by 4". This set marks the first year for the Dodgers in Los Angeles and includes a Campanella card despite the fact that he never played for the team in California. The catalog designation for this set is F339-1. Cards found still inside the original cellophane wrapper are valued at 50 percent more than the prices below.

	NRMT	VG-E	GOOD
COMPLETE SET (10)	1250.00	575.00	160.00
COMMON PLAYER (1-10)	50.00	23.00	6.25
☐ 1 Roy Campanella	150.00	70.00	19.00
☐ 2 Gino Cimoli SP	150.00	70.00	19.00
☐ 3 Don Drysdale	110.00	50.00	14.00
☐ 4 Jim Gilliam	50.00	23.00	6.25
☐ 5 Gil Hodges	90.00	40.00	11.50
☐ 6 Sandy Koufax	200.00	90.00	25.00
☐ 7 Johnny Podres SP	150.00	70.00	19.00
☐ 8 Pee Wee Reese	110.00	50.00	14.00
☐ 9 Duke Snider SP	300.00	135.00	38.00
☐ 10 Don Zimmer	50.00	23.00	6.25

1959 Dodgers Morrell

The cards in this 12-card set measure 2 1/2" by 3 1/2". The 1959 Morrell Meats set of full color, unnumbered cards features Los Angeles Dodger players only. The photos used are the same as those selected for the Dodger team issue postcards in 1959. The Morrell Meats logo is on the backs of the cards. The Clem Labine card actually features a picture of Stan Williams and the Norm Larker card actually features a picture of Joe Pignatano as indicated in the checklist below. The catalog designation is F172-1.

	NRMT	VG-E	GOOD
COMPLETE SET (12)	1500.00	700.00	190.00
COMMON PLAYER (1-12)	75.00	34.00	9.50
☐ 1 Don Drysdale	150.00	70.00	19.00
☐ 2 Carl Furillo	90.00	40.00	11.50
☐ 3 Jim Gilliam	90.00	40.00	11.50
☐ 4 Gil Hodges	150.00	70.00	19.00
☐ 5 Sandy Koufax	300.00	135.00	38.00
☐ 6 Clem Labine UER (Photo actually Stan Williams)	75.00	34.00	9.50
☐ 7 Norm Larker UER (Photo actually Joe Pignatano)	75.00	34.00	9.50
☐ 8 Charlie Neal	75.00	34.00	9.50
☐ 9 Johnny Podres	90.00	40.00	11.50
☐ 10 John Roseboro	75.00	34.00	9.50
☐ 11 Duke Snider	300.00	135.00	38.00
☐ 12 Don Zimmer	90.00	40.00	11.50

1960 Dodgers Bell Brand

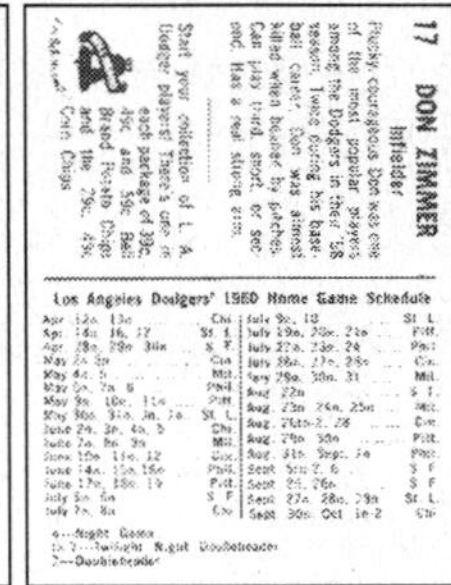

The 1960 Bell Brand Potato Chips set of 20 full color, numbered cards features Los Angeles Dodgers only. Because these cards, measuring approximately 2 1/2" by 3 1/2", were issued in packages of potato chips, many cards suffered from stains. Clem Labine, Johnny Klippstein, and Walter Alston are somewhat more difficult to obtain than other cards in the set; they are marked with SP (short printed) in the checklist below. The catalog designation for this set is F339-2.

	NRMT	VG-E	GOOD
COMPLETE SET (20)	900.00	400.00	115.00
COMMON PLAYER (1-20)	20.00	9.00	2.50
☐ 1 Norm Larker	20.00	9.00	2.50
☐ 2 Duke Snider	90.00	40.00	11.50
☐ 3 Danny McDevitt	20.00	9.00	2.50
☐ 4 Jim Gilliam	24.00	11.00	3.00
☐ 5 Rip Repulski	20.00	9.00	2.50
☐ 6 Clem Labine SP	100.00	45.00	12.50
☐ 7 John Roseboro	22.00	10.00	2.80
☐ 8 Carl Furillo	28.00	12.50	3.50
☐ 9 Sandy Koufax	150.00	70.00	19.00
☐ 10 Joe Pignatano	20.00	9.00	2.50
☐ 11 Chuck Essegian	20.00	9.00	2.50
☐ 12 John Klippstein SP	100.00	45.00	12.50
☐ 13 Ed Roebuck	20.00	9.00	2.50
☐ 14 Don Demeter	20.00	9.00	2.50
☐ 15 Roger Craig	28.00	12.50	3.50
☐ 16 Stan Williams	22.00	10.00	2.80
☐ 17 Don Zimmer	24.00	11.00	3.00
☐ 18 Walt Alston SP MG	150.00	70.00	19.00
☐ 19 Johnny Podres	28.00	12.50	3.50
☐ 20 Maury Wills	50.00	23.00	6.25

1960 Dodgers Morrell

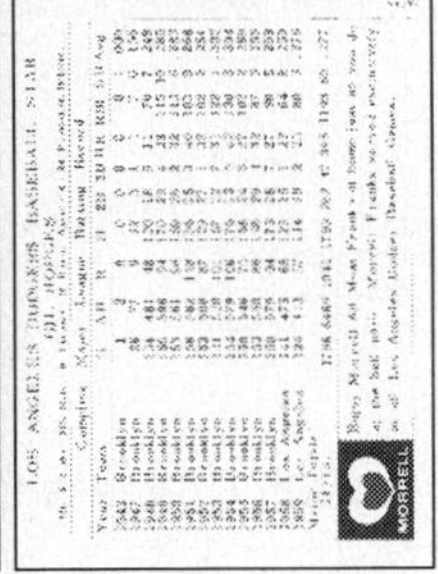

The cards in this 12-card set measure 2 1/2" by 3 1/2". The 1960 Morrell Meats set of full color, unnumbered cards is similar in format to the 1959 Morrell set but can be distinguished from the 1959 set by a red heart which appears in the Morrell logo on the back. The photos used are the same as those selected for the Dodger team issue postcards in 1960. The Furillo, Hodges, and Snider cards received limited distribution and are hence more scarce. The catalog designation is F172-2. The cards were printed in Japan.

	NRMT	VG-E	GOOD
COMPLETE SET (12)	900.00	400.00	115.00
COMMON PLAYER (1-12)	22.00	10.00	2.80
☐ 1 Walt Alston MG	45.00	20.00	5.75
☐ 2 Roger Craig	30.00	13.50	3.80
☐ 3 Don Drysdale	60.00	27.00	7.50
☐ 4 Carl Furillo SP	100.00	45.00	12.50
☐ 5 Gil Hodges SP	150.00	70.00	19.00
☐ 6 Sandy Koufax	150.00	70.00	19.00
☐ 7 Wally Moon	22.00	10.00	2.80
☐ 8 Charlie Neal	22.00	10.00	2.80
☐ 9 Johnny Podres	27.00	12.00	3.40
☐ 10 John Roseboro	22.00	10.00	2.80
☐ 11 Larry Sherry	22.00	10.00	2.80
☐ 12 Duke Snider SP	300.00	135.00	38.00

1961 Dodgers Bell Brand

The 1961 Bell Brand Potato Chips set of 20 full color cards features Los Angeles Dodger players only and is numbered by the uniform numbers of the players. The cards are slightly smaller (approximately 2 7/16" by 3 1/2") than the 1960 Bell Brand cards and are on thinner paper stock. The catalog designation is F339-3.

	NRMT	VG-E	GOOD
COMPLETE SET (20)	500.00	230.00	65.00
COMMON PLAYER	13.50	6.00	1.70
☐ 3 Willie Davis	20.00	9.00	2.50
☐ 4 Duke Snider	70.00	32.00	8.75
☐ 5 Norm Larker	13.50	6.00	1.70
☐ 8 John Roseboro	15.00	6.75	1.90
☐ 9 Wally Moon	13.50	6.00	1.70
☐ 11 Bob Lillis	13.50	6.00	1.70
☐ 12 Tommy Davis	18.00	8.00	2.30
☐ 14 Gil Hodges	30.00	13.50	3.80
☐ 16 Don Demeter	13.50	6.00	1.70
☐ 19 Jim Gilliam	18.00	8.00	2.30
☐ 22 John Podres	18.00	8.00	2.30
☐ 24 Walt Alston MG	27.00	12.00	3.40
☐ 30 Maury Wills	27.00	12.00	3.40
☐ 32 Sandy Koufax	125.00	57.50	15.50
☐ 34 Norm Sherry	13.50	6.00	1.70
☐ 37 Ed Roebuck	13.50	6.00	1.70
☐ 38 Roger Craig	18.00	8.00	2.30
☐ 40 Stan Williams	13.50	6.00	1.70
☐ 43 Charlie Neal	13.50	6.00	1.70
☐ 51 Larry Sherry	15.00	6.75	1.90

1961 Dodgers Morrell

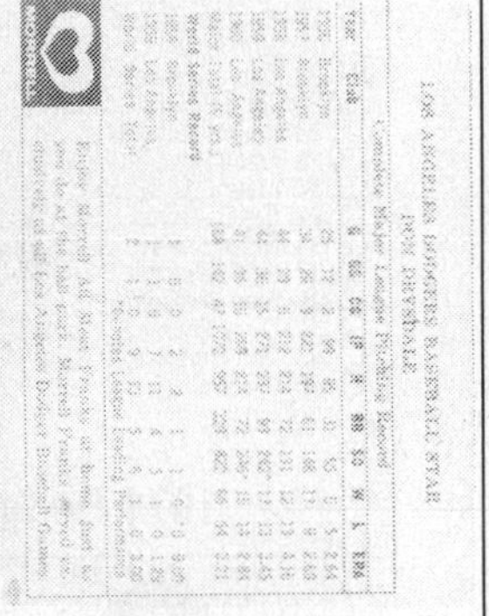

The cards in this six-card set measure 2 1/2" by 3 1/2". The 1961 Morrell Meats set of full color, unnumbered cards features Los Angeles Dodger players only and contains statistical information on the backs of the cards in brown print. The catalog designation is F172-3.

	NRMT	VG-E	GOOD
COMPLETE SET (6)	250.00	115.00	31.00
COMMON PLAYER (1-6)	20.00	9.00	2.50
☐ 1 Tommy Davis	22.00	10.00	2.80
☐ 2 Don Drysdale	55.00	25.00	7.00
☐ 3 Frank Howard	27.00	12.00	3.40
☐ 4 Sandy Koufax	135.00	60.00	17.00
☐ 5 Norm Larker	20.00	9.00	2.50
☐ 6 Maury Wills	40.00	18.00	5.00

1962 Dodgers Bell Brand

The 1962 Bell Brand Potato Chips set of 20 full color cards features Los Angeles Dodger players only and is numbered by the uniform numbers of the players. These cards were printed on a high quality glossy paper, much better than the previous two years, virtually eliminating the grease stains. This set is distinguished by a 1962 Home schedule on the backs of the cards. The cards measure 2 7/16" by 3 1/2", the same size as the year before. The catalog designation is F339-4.

	NRMT	VG-E	GOOD
COMPLETE SET (20)	500.00	230.00	65.00
COMMON PLAYER	13.50	6.00	1.70

☐ 3 Willie Davis	18.00	8.00	2.30
☐ 4 Duke Snider	70.00	32.00	8.75
☐ 6 Ron Fairly	13.50	6.00	1.70
☐ 8 John Roseboro	15.00	6.75	1.90
☐ 9 Wally Moon	13.50	6.00	1.70
☐ 12 Tommy Davis	18.00	8.00	2.30
☐ 16 Ron Perranoski	15.00	6.75	1.90
☐ 19 Jim Gilliam	18.00	8.00	2.30
☐ 20 Daryl Spencer	13.50	6.00	1.70
☐ 22 John Podres	18.00	8.00	2.30
☐ 24 Walt Alston MG	27.00	12.00	3.40
☐ 25 Frank Howard	18.00	8.00	2.30
☐ 30 Maury Wills	27.00	12.00	3.40
☐ 32 Sandy Koufax	125.00	57.50	15.50
☐ 34 Norm Sherry	13.50	6.00	1.70
☐ 37 Ed Roebuck	13.50	6.00	1.70
☐ 40 Stan Williams	13.50	6.00	1.70
☐ 51 Larry Sherry	15.00	6.75	1.90
☐ 53 Don Drysdale	50.00	23.00	6.25
☐ 56 Lee Walls	13.50	6.00	1.70

1971 Dodgers Ticketron

The 1971 Ticketron Los Angeles Dodgers set is a 20-card set with cards measuring approximately 4" by 6". This set has a 1971 Garvey rookie year card as well as 18 other players including Richie Allen in his only year as a Dodger. The fronts are beautiful full-color photos which also have a facsimile autograph on the front and are borderless while the backs contain an advertisement for Ticketron, the 1971 Dodger home schedule and a list of promotional events scheduled for 1971. These unnumbered cards are listed in alphabetical order for convenience.

	NRMT-MT	EXC	G-VG
COMPLETE SET (20)	100.00	45.00	12.50
COMMON PLAYER (1-20)	3.00	1.35	.40
☐ 1 Richie Allen	7.50	3.40	.95
☐ 2 Walter Alston MG	7.50	3.40	.95
☐ 3 Jim Brewer	3.00	1.35	.40
☐ 4 Willie Crawford	3.00	1.35	.40
☐ 5 Willie Davis	4.00	1.80	.50
☐ 6 Steve Garvey	30.00	13.50	3.80
☐ 7 Bill Grabarkewitz	3.00	1.35	.40
☐ 8 Jim Lefebvre	4.00	1.80	.50
☐ 9 Pete Mikkelsen	3.00	1.35	.40
☐ 10 Joe Moeller	3.00	1.35	.40
☐ 11 Manny Mota	4.00	1.80	.50
☐ 12 Claude Osteen	4.00	1.80	.50
☐ 13 Wes Parker	4.00	1.80	.50
☐ 14 Bill Russell	5.00	2.30	.60
☐ 15 Duke Sims	3.00	1.35	.40
☐ 16 Bill Singer	3.00	1.35	.40
☐ 17 Bill Sudakis	3.00	1.35	.40
☐ 18 Don Sutton	10.00	4.50	1.25
☐ 19 Maury Wills	6.00	2.70	.75
☐ 20 Vic Scully and Jerry Doggett (Announcers)	4.00	1.80	.50

1985 Dodgers Coke Postcards

This 34-card set was sponsored by Coke, and the company logo appears on the back of the cards. These oversized cards measure approximately 3 1/2" by 5 1/2". The front design features glossy color player photos, bordered in white and with the player's name below the pictures. Except for the sponsor's logo, the backs are blank. The cards are unnumbered and checklisted below in alphabetical order.

	NRMT-MT	EXC	G-VG
COMPLETE SET (34)	16.00	7.25	2.00
COMMON PLAYER (1-34)	.40	.18	.05
☐ 1 Joe Amalfitano CO	.40	.18	.05
☐ 2 Dave Anderson	.50	.23	.06
☐ 3 Bob Bailor	.40	.18	.05
☐ 4 Monty Basgall CO	.40	.18	.05
☐ 5 Tom Brennan	.40	.18	.05
☐ 6 Greg Brock	.40	.18	.05
☐ 7 Bobby Castillo	.40	.18	.05
☐ 8 Mark Cresse CO	.40	.18	.05
☐ 9 Carlos Diaz	.40	.18	.05
☐ 10 Mariano Duncan	.60	.25	.08
☐ 11 Pedro Guerrero	1.00	.45	.13
☐ 12 Orel Hershiser	2.50	1.15	.30
☐ 13 Rick Honeycutt	.50	.23	.06
☐ 14 Steve Howe	.60	.25	.08
☐ 15 Ken Howell	.40	.18	.05
☐ 16 Jay Johnstone	.60	.25	.08
☐ 17 Ken Landreaux	.50	.23	.06
☐ 18 Tom Lasorda MG	.75	.35	.09
☐ 19 Candy Maldonado	.60	.25	.08
☐ 20 Mike Marshall	.50	.23	.06
☐ 21 Manny Mota CO	.50	.23	.06
☐ 22 Tom Niedenfuer	.40	.18	.05
☐ 23 Al Oliver	.50	.23	.06
☐ 24 Alejandro Pena	.75	.35	.09
☐ 25 Ron Perranoski CO	.50	.23	.06
☐ 26 Jerry Reuss	.50	.23	.06
☐ 27 R.J. Reynolds	.40	.18	.05
☐ 28 Bill Russell	.60	.25	.08
☐ 29 Steve Sax	.75	.35	.09
☐ 30 Mike Scioscia	.60	.25	.08
☐ 31 Fernando Valenzuela	.75	.35	.09
☐ 32 Bob Welch	.75	.35	.09
☐ 33 Terry Whitfield	.40	.18	.05
☐ 34 Steve Yeager	.50	.23	.06

1986 Dodgers Coke Postcards

This 33-card Dodger set was sponsored by Coke, and the company logo appears on the back of the cards. The oversized cards measure approximately 3 1/2" by 5 1/2". The front design features glossy color player photos (mostly action), bordered in white and with the player's name below the picture. The backs are blank. The cards are unnumbered and checklisted below in alphabetical order.

	MT	EX-MT	VG
COMPLETE SET (33)	12.50	5.75	1.55
COMMON PLAYER (1-33)	.40	.18	.05
☐ 1 Joe Amalfitano CO	.40	.18	.05
☐ 2 Dave Anderson	.40	.18	.05
☐ 3 Monty Basgall CO	.40	.18	.05
☐ 4 Greg Brock	.40	.18	.05
☐ 5 Enos Cabell	.40	.18	.05
☐ 6 Cesar Cedeno	.50	.23	.06
☐ 7 Mark Cresse CO	.40	.18	.05
☐ 8 Mariano Duncan	.50	.23	.06
☐ 9 Carlos Diaz	.40	.18	.05
☐ 10 Pedro Guerrero	.75	.35	.09
☐ 11 Orel Hershiser	1.00	.45	.13
☐ 12 Ben Hines TR	.40	.18	.05
☐ 13 Rick Honeycutt	.40	.18	.05
☐ 14 Ken Howell	.40	.18	.05
☐ 15 Ken Landreaux	.50	.23	.06
☐ 16 Tom Lasorda MG	.60	.25	.08
☐ 17 Bill Madlock	.50	.23	.06
☐ 18 Mike Marshall	.50	.23	.06
☐ 19 Len Matuszek	.40	.18	.05
☐ 20 Manny Mota CO	.50	.23	.06
☐ 21 Tom Niedenfuer	.40	.18	.05
☐ 22 Alejandro Pena	.50	.23	.06
☐ 23 Ron Perranoski CO	.50	.23	.06
☐ 24 Dennis Powell	.40	.18	.05
☐ 25 Jerry Reuss	.40	.18	.05
☐ 26 Bill Russell	.50	.23	.06
☐ 27 Steve Sax	.75	.35	.09
☐ 28 Mike Scioscia	.50	.23	.06
☐ 29 Alex Trevino	.40	.18	.05
☐ 30 Fernando Valenzuela	.60	.25	.08
☐ 31 Ed VandeBerg	.40	.18	.05
☐ 32 Bob Welch	.60	.25	.08
☐ 33 Terry Whitfield	.40	.18	.05

1990 Dodgers Target

The 1990 Target Dodgers is one of the largest sets ever made. This (more than) 1000-card set features cards each measuring approximately 2" by 3" individually and was issued in large perforated sheets of 15 cards. Players in the set played at one time or another for one of the Dodgers franchises. As such many of the players in the set are older and relatively unknown to today's younger collectors. The set was apparently intended to be arranged in alphabetical order. There were several numbers not used (408, 458, 463, 792, 902, 907, 969, 996, 1031, 1054, 1061, and 1098) as well as a few instances of duplicated numbers.

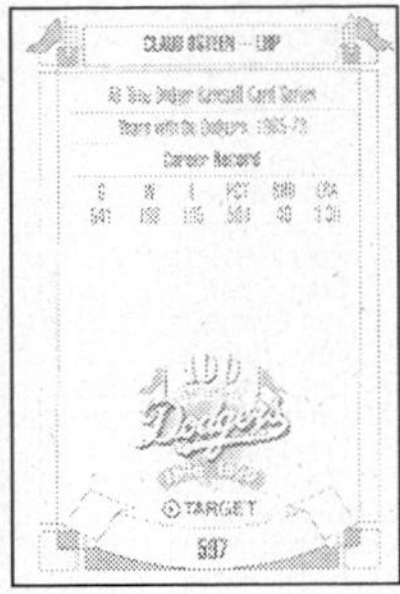

	MT	EX-MT	VG
COMPLETE SET (1106)	125.00	57.50	15.50
COMMON PLAYER	.15	.07	.02
☐ 1 Bert Abbey	.15	.07	.02
☐ 2 Cal Abrams	.15	.07	.02
☐ 3 Hank Aguirre	.15	.07	.02
☐ 4 Eddie Ainsmith	.15	.07	.02
☐ 5 Ed Albosta	.15	.07	.02
☐ 6 Luis Alcaraz	.15	.07	.02
☐ 7 Doyle Alexander	.20	.09	.03
☐ 8 Dick Allen	.30	.14	.04
☐ 9 Frank Allen	.15	.07	.02
☐ 10 Johnny Allen	.15	.07	.02
☐ 11 Mel Almada	.15	.07	.02
☐ 12 Walter Alston	.50	.23	.06
☐ 13 Ed Amelung	.15	.07	.02
☐ 14 Sandy Amoros	.20	.09	.03
☐ 15 Dave Anderson	.15	.07	.02
☐ 16 Ferrell Anderson	.15	.07	.02
☐ 17 John Anderson	.15	.07	.02
☐ 18 Stan Andrews	.15	.07	.02
☐ 19 Bill Antonello	.15	.07	.02
☐ 20 Jimmy Archer	.15	.07	.02
☐ 21 Bob Aspromonte	.15	.07	.02
☐ 22 Rick Auerbach	.15	.07	.02
☐ 23 Charlie Babb	.15	.07	.02
☐ 24 Johnny Babich	.15	.07	.02
☐ 25 Bob Bailey	.15	.07	.02
☐ 26 Bob Bailor	.15	.07	.02
☐ 27 Dusty Baker	.25	.11	.03
☐ 28 Tom Baker	.15	.07	.02
☐ 29 Dave Bancroft	.30	.14	.04
☐ 30 Dan Bankhead	.15	.07	.02
☐ 31 Jack Banta	.15	.07	.02
☐ 32 Jim Barbieri	.15	.07	.02
☐ 33 Red Barkley	.15	.07	.02
☐ 34 Jesse Barnes	.15	.07	.02
☐ 35 Rex Barney	.15	.07	.02
☐ 36 Billy Barnie	.15	.07	.02
☐ 37 Bob Barrett	.15	.07	.02
☐ 38 Jim Baxes	.15	.07	.02
☐ 39 Billy Bean	.15	.07	.02
☐ 40 BoomBoom Beck	.15	.07	.02
☐ 41 Joe Beckwith	.15	.07	.02
☐ 42 Hank Behrman	.15	.07	.02
☐ 43 Mark Belanger	.20	.09	.03
☐ 44 Wayne Belardi	.15	.07	.02
☐ 45 Tim Belcher	.25	.11	.03
☐ 46 George Bell	.15	.07	.02
☐ 47 Ray Benge	.15	.07	.02
☐ 48 Moe Berg	.30	.14	.04
☐ 49 Bill Bergen	.15	.07	.02
☐ 50 Ray Berres	.15	.07	.02
☐ 51 Don Bessent	.15	.07	.02
☐ 52 Steve Bilko	.15	.07	.02
☐ 53 Jack Billingham	.15	.07	.02
☐ 54 Babe Birrer	.15	.07	.02
☐ 55 Del Bissonette	.15	.07	.02
☐ 56 Joe Black	.25	.11	.03
☐ 57 Lu Blue	.15	.07	.02
☐ 58 George Boehler	.15	.07	.02
☐ 59 Sammy Bohne	.15	.07	.02
☐ 60 John Bolling	.15	.07	.02
☐ 61 Ike Boone	.15	.07	.02
☐ 62 Frenchy Bordagaray	.15	.07	.02
☐ 63 Ken Boyer	.25	.11	.03
☐ 64 Buzz Boyle	.15	.07	.02
☐ 65 Mark Bradley	.15	.07	.02
☐ 66 Bobby Bragan	.15	.07	.02
☐ 67 Ralph Branca	.25	.11	.03
☐ 68 Ed Brandt	.15	.07	.02
☐ 69 Sid Bream	.20	.09	.03

☐ 70 Marv Breeding	.15	.07	.02
☐ 71 Tom Brennan	.15	.07	.02
☐ 72 William Brennan	.15	.07	.02
☐ 73 Rube Bressler	.15	.07	.02
☐ 74 Ken Brett	.15	.07	.02
☐ 75 Jim Brewer	.15	.07	.02
☐ 76 Tony Brewer	.15	.07	.02
☐ 77 Rocky Bridges	.15	.07	.02
☐ 78 Greg Brock	.15	.07	.02
☐ 79 Dan Brouthers	.35	.16	.04
☐ 80 Eddie Brown	.15	.07	.02
☐ 81 Elmer Brown	.15	.07	.02
☐ 82 Lindsay Brown	.15	.07	.02
☐ 83 Lloyd Brown	.15	.07	.02
☐ 84 Mace Brown	.15	.07	.02
☐ 85 Tommy Brown	.15	.07	.02
☐ 86 Pete Browning	.25	.11	.03
☐ 87 Ralph Bryant	.15	.07	.02
☐ 88 Jim Bucher	.15	.07	.02
☐ 89 Bill Buckner	.25	.11	.03
☐ 90 Jim Bunning	.30	.14	.04
☐ 91 Jack Burdock	.15	.07	.02
☐ 92 Glenn Burke	.15	.07	.02
☐ 93 Buster Burrell	.15	.07	.02
☐ 94 Larry Burright	.15	.07	.02
☐ 95 Doc Bushong	.15	.07	.02
☐ 96 Max Butcher	.15	.07	.02
☐ 97 Johnny Butler	.15	.07	.02
☐ 98 Enos Cabell	.15	.07	.02
☐ 99 Leon Cadore	.15	.07	.02
☐ 100 Bruce Caldwell	.15	.07	.02
☐ 101 Dick Calmus	.15	.07	.02
☐ 102 Dolf Camilli	.20	.09	.03
☐ 103 Doug Camilli	.15	.07	.02
☐ 104 Roy Campanella	.75	.35	.09
☐ 105 Al Campanis	.30	.14	.04
☐ 106 Jim Campanis	.15	.07	.02
☐ 107A Leo Callahan	.15	.07	.02
☐ 107B Gilly Campbell	.15	.07	.02
☐ 108 Jimmy Canavan	.15	.07	.02
☐ 109 Chris Cannizzaro	.15	.07	.02
☐ 110 Guy Cantrell	.15	.07	.02
☐ 111 Ben Cantwell	.15	.07	.02
☐ 112 Andy Carey	.15	.07	.02
☐ 113 Max Carey	.35	.16	.04
☐ 114 Tex Carleton	.15	.07	.02
☐ 115 Ownie Carroll	.15	.07	.02
☐ 116 Bob Caruthers	.20	.09	.03
☐ 117 Doc Casey	.15	.07	.02
☐ 118 Hugh Casey	.15	.07	.02
☐ 119 Bobby Castillo	.15	.07	.02
☐ 120 Cesar Cedeno	.20	.09	.03
☐ 121 Ron Cey	.25	.11	.03
☐ 122 Ed Chandler	.15	.07	.02
☐ 123 Ben Chapman	.20	.09	.03
☐ 124 Larry Cheney	.15	.07	.02
☐ 125 Bob Chipman	.15	.07	.02
☐ 126 Chuck Churn	.15	.07	.02
☐ 127 Gino Cimoli	.15	.07	.02
☐ 128 Moose Clabaugh	.15	.07	.02
☐ 129 Bud Clancy	.15	.07	.02
☐ 130 Bob Clark	.15	.07	.02
☐ 131 Watty Clark	.15	.07	.02
☐ 132 Alta Cohen	.15	.07	.02
☐ 133 Rocky Colavito	.35	.16	.04
☐ 134 Jackie Collum	.15	.07	.02
☐ 135 Chuck Connors	.40	.18	.05
☐ 136 Jack Coombs	.30	.14	.04
☐ 137 Johnny Cooney	.15	.07	.02
☐ 138 Tommy Corcoran	.15	.07	.02
☐ 139 Pop Corkhill	.15	.07	.02
☐ 140 John Corriden	.15	.07	.02
☐ 141 Pete Coscarart	.15	.07	.02
☐ 142 Wes Covington	.15	.07	.02
☐ 143 Billy Cox	.20	.09	.03
☐ 144 Roger Craig	.25	.11	.03
☐ 146 Willie Crawford	.15	.07	.02
☐ 147 Tim Crews	.15	.07	.02
☐ 148 John Cronin	.15	.07	.02
☐ 149 Lave Cross	.15	.07	.02
☐ 150 Bill Crouch	.15	.07	.02
☐ 151 Don Crow	.15	.07	.02
☐ 152 Henry Cruz	.15	.07	.02
☐ 153 Tony Cuccinello	.15	.07	.02
☐ 154 Roy Cullenbine	.15	.07	.02
☐ 155 George Culver	.15	.07	.02
☐ 156 Nick Cullop	.15	.07	.02
☐ 157 George Cutshaw	.15	.07	.02
☐ 158 Kiki Cuyler	.35	.16	.04
☐ 159 Bill Dahlen	.25	.11	.03
☐ 160 Babe Dahlgren	.20	.09	.03
☐ 161 Jack Dalton	.15	.07	.02
☐ 162 Tom Daly	.15	.07	.02
☐ 163 Cliff Dapper	.15	.07	.02
☐ 164 Bob Darnell	.15	.07	.02
☐ 165 Bobby Darwin	.15	.07	.02
☐ 166 Jake Daubert	.20	.09	.03
☐ 167 Vic Davalillo	.15	.07	.02
☐ 168 Curt Davis	.15	.07	.02
☐ 169 Mike Davis	.15	.07	.02
☐ 170 Ron Davis	.15	.07	.02
☐ 171 Tommy Davis	.25	.11	.03
☐ 172 Willie Davis	.25	.11	.03
☐ 173 Pea Ridge Day	.15	.07	.02
☐ 174 Tommy Dean	.15	.07	.02
☐ 175 Hank DeBerry	.15	.07	.02
☐ 176 Art Decatur	.15	.07	.02
☐ 177 Raoul Dedeaux	.20	.09	.03
☐ 178 Ivan DeJesus	.15	.07	.02
☐ 179 Don Demeter	.15	.07	.02
☐ 180 Gene DeMontreville	.15	.07	.02
☐ 181 Rick Dempsey	.20	.09	.03
☐ 182 Eddie Dent	.15	.07	.02
☐ 183 Mike Devereaux	.25	.11	.03
☐ 184 Carlos Diaz	.15	.07	.02
☐ 185 Dick Dietz	.15	.07	.02
☐ 186 Pop Dillon	.15	.07	.02
☐ 187 Bill Doak	.15	.07	.02
☐ 188 John Dobbs	.15	.07	.02
☐ 189 George Dockins	.15	.07	.02
☐ 190 Cozy Dolan	.15	.07	.02
☐ 191 Patsy Donovan	.15	.07	.02
☐ 192 Wild Bill Donovan	.15	.07	.02
☐ 193 Mickey Doolan	.15	.07	.02
☐ 194 Jack Doscher	.15	.07	.02
☐ 195 Phil Douglas	.15	.07	.02
☐ 196 Snooks Dowd	.15	.07	.02
☐ 197 Al Downing	.20	.09	.03
☐ 198 Red Downs	.15	.07	.02
☐ 199 Jack Doyle	.15	.07	.02
☐ 200 Solly Drake	.15	.07	.02
☐ 201 Tom Drake	.15	.07	.02
☐ 202 Chuck Dressen	.20	.09	.03
☐ 203 Don Drysdale	.40	.18	.05
☐ 204 Clise Dudley	.15	.07	.02
☐ 205 Mariano Duncan	.25	.11	.03
☐ 206 Jack Dunn	.15	.07	.02
☐ 207 Bull Durham	.15	.07	.02
☐ 208 Leo Durocher	.40	.18	.05
☐ 209 Billy Earle	.15	.07	.02
☐ 210 George Earnshaw	.15	.07	.02
☐ 211 Ox Eckhardt	.15	.07	.02
☐ 212 Bruce Edwards	.15	.07	.02
☐ 213 Hank Edwards	.15	.07	.02
☐ 214 Dick W. Egan	.15	.07	.02
☐ 215 Harry Eisenstat	.15	.07	.02
☐ 216 Kid Elberfeld	.15	.07	.02
☐ 217 Jumbo Elliot	.15	.07	.02
☐ 218 Don Elston	.15	.07	.02
☐ 219 Gil English	.15	.07	.02
☐ 220 Johnny Enzmann	.15	.07	.02
☐ 221 Al Epperly	.15	.07	.02
☐ 222 Carl Erskine	.25	.11	.03
☐ 223 Tex Erwin	.15	.07	.02
☐ 224 Cecil Espy	.20	.09	.03
☐ 225 Chuck Essegian	.20	.09	.03
☐ 226 Dude Esterbrook	.15	.07	.02
☐ 227 Red Evans	.15	.07	.02
☐ 228 Bunny Fabrique	.15	.07	.02
☐ 229 Jim Fairey	.15	.07	.02
☐ 230 Ron Fairly	.20	.09	.03
☐ 231 George Fallon	.15	.07	.02
☐ 232 Turk Farrell	.20	.09	.03
☐ 233 Duke Farrel	.15	.07	.02
☐ 234 Jim Faulkner	.15	.07	.02
☐ 235 Alex Ferguson	.15	.07	.02
☐ 236 Joe Ferguson	.20	.09	.03
☐ 237 Chico Fernandez	.15	.07	.02
☐ 238 Sid Fernandez	.25	.11	.03
☐ 239 Al Ferrara	.20	.09	.03
☐ 240 Wes Ferrell	.25	.11	.03
☐ 241 Lou Fette	.15	.07	.02
☐ 242 Chick Fewster	.15	.07	.02
☐ 243 Jack Fimple	.15	.07	.02
☐ 244 Neal Mickey Finn	.15	.07	.02
☐ 245 Bob Fisher	.15	.07	.02
☐ 246 Freddie Fitzsimmons	.20	.09	.03
☐ 247 Tim Flood	.15	.07	.02
☐ 248 Jake Flowers	.15	.07	.02
☐ 249 Hod Ford	.15	.07	.02
☐ 250 Terry Forster	.25	.11	.03
☐ 251 Alan Foster	.15	.07	.02
☐ 252 Jack Fournier	.15	.07	.02
☐ 253 Dave Foutz	.15	.07	.02
☐ 254 Art Fowler	.20	.09	.03
☐ 255 Fred Frankhouse	.15	.07	.02

☐	256	Herman Franks	.15	.07	.02
☐	257	Johnny Frederick	.15	.07	.02
☐	258	Larry French	.15	.07	.02
☐	259	Lonny Frey	.15	.07	.02
☐	260	Pepe Frias	.15	.07	.02
☐	261	Charlie Fuchs	.15	.07	.02
☐	262	Carl Furillo	.25	.11	.03
☐	263	Len Gabrielson	.15	.07	.02
☐	264	Augie Galan	.15	.07	.02
☐	265	Joe Gallagher	.15	.07	.02
☐	266	Phil Gallivan	.15	.07	.02
☐	267	Balvino Galvez	.15	.07	.02
☐	268	Mike Garman	.15	.07	.02
☐	269	Phil Garner	.25	.11	.03
☐	270	Steve Garvey	.35	.16	.04
☐	271	Ned Garvin	.15	.07	.02
☐	272	Hank Gastright	.15	.07	.02
☐	273	Sid Gautreaux	.15	.07	.02
☐	274	Jim Gentile	.25	.11	.03
☐	275	Greek George	.15	.07	.02
☐	276	Ben Geraghty	.15	.07	.02
☐	277	Gus Getz	.15	.07	.02
☐	278	Bob Giallombardo	.15	.07	.02
☐	279	Kirk Gibson	.35	.16	.04
☐	280	Charlie Gilbert	.15	.07	.02
☐	281	Jim Gilliam	.30	.14	.04
☐	282	Al Gionfriddo	.15	.07	.02
☐	283	Tony Giuliani	.15	.07	.02
☐	284	Al Glossop	.15	.07	.02
☐	285	John Gochnaur	.15	.07	.02
☐	286	Jim Golden	.15	.07	.02
☐	287	Dave Goltz	.15	.07	.02
☐	288	Jose Gonzalez	.15	.07	.02
☐	289	Johnny Gooch	.15	.07	.02
☐	290	Ed Goodson	.15	.07	.02
☐	291	Billy Grabarkewitz	.15	.07	.02
☐	292	Jack Graham	.15	.07	.02
☐	293	Mudcat Grant	.20	.09	.03
☐	294	Dick Gray	.15	.07	.02
☐	295	Kent Greenfield	.15	.07	.02
☐	296	Hal Gregg	.15	.07	.02
☐	297	Alfredo Griffin	.15	.07	.02
☐	298	Mike Griffin	.15	.07	.02
☐	299	Derrell Griffith	.15	.07	.02
☐	300	Tommy Griffith	.15	.07	.02
☐	301	Burleigh Grimes	.35	.16	.04
☐	302	Lee Grissom	.15	.07	.02
☐	303	Jerry Grote	.15	.07	.02
☐	304	Pedro Guerrero	.35	.16	.04
☐	305	Brad Gulden	.15	.07	.02
☐	306	Ad Gumbert	.15	.07	.02
☐	307	Chris Gwynn	.25	.11	.03
☐	308	Bert Haas	.15	.07	.02
☐	309	John Hale	.15	.07	.02
☐	310	Tom Haller	.15	.07	.02
☐	311	Bill Hallman	.15	.07	.02
☐	312	Jeff Hamilton	.15	.07	.02
☐	313	Luke Hamlin	.15	.07	.02
☐	314	Ned Hanlon	.20	.09	.03
☐	315	Gerald Hannahs	.15	.07	.02
☐	316	Charlie Hargreaves	.15	.07	.02
☐	317	Tim Harkness	.15	.07	.02
☐	318	Harry Harper	.15	.07	.02
☐	319	Joe Harris	.15	.07	.02
☐	320	Lenny Harris	.25	.11	.03
☐	321	Bill F. Hart	.15	.07	.02
☐	322	Buddy Hassett	.15	.07	.02
☐	323	Mickey Hatcher	.20	.09	.03
☐	324	Joe Hatten	.15	.07	.02
☐	325	Phil Haugstad	.15	.07	.02
☐	326	Brad Havens	.15	.07	.02
☐	327	Ray Hayworth	.15	.07	.02
☐	328	Ed Head	.15	.07	.02
☐	329	Danny Heep	.15	.07	.02
☐	330	Fred Heimach	.15	.07	.02
☐	331	Harvey Hendrick	.15	.07	.02
☐	332	Weldon Henley	.15	.07	.02
☐	333	Butch Henline	.15	.07	.02
☐	334	Dutch Henry	.15	.07	.02
☐	335	Roy Henshaw	.15	.07	.02
☐	336	Babe Herman	.25	.11	.03
☐	337	Billy Herman	.35	.16	.04
☐	338	Gene Hermanski	.15	.07	.02
☐	339	Enzo Hernandez	.15	.07	.02
☐	340	Art Herring	.15	.07	.02
☐	341	Orel Hershiser	.40	.18	.05
☐	342	Dave J. Hickman	.15	.07	.02
☐	343	Jim Hickman	.15	.07	.02
☐	344	Kirby Higbe	.15	.07	.02
☐	345	Andy High	.15	.07	.02
☐	346	George Hildebrand	.15	.07	.02
☐	347	Hunkey Hines	.15	.07	.02
☐	348	Don Hoak	.20	.09	.03
☐	349	Oris Hockett	.15	.07	.02
☐	350	Gil Hodges	.40	.18	.05
☐	351	Glenn Hoffman	.15	.07	.02
☐	352	Al Hollingsworth	.15	.07	.02
☐	353	Tommy Holmes	.25	.11	.03
☐	354	Brian Holton	.15	.07	.02
☐	355	Rick Honeycutt	.15	.07	.02
☐	356	Burt Hooton	.20	.09	.03
☐	357	Gail Hopkins	.15	.07	.02
☐	358	Johnny Hopp	.20	.09	.03
☐	359	Charlie Hough	.25	.11	.03
☐	360	Frank Howard	.30	.14	.04
☐	361	Steve Howe	.20	.09	.03
☐	362	Dixie Howell	.15	.07	.02
☐	363	Harry Howell	.15	.07	.02
☐	364	Jay Howell	.25	.11	.03
☐	365	Ken Howell	.20	.09	.03
☐	366	Waite Hoyt	.35	.16	.04
☐	367	Johnny Hudson	.15	.07	.02
☐	368	Jim J. Hughes	.15	.07	.02
☐	369	Jim R. Hughes	.15	.07	.02
☐	370	Mickey Hughes	.15	.07	.02
☐	371	John Hummel	.15	.07	.02
☐	372	Ron Hunt	.15	.07	.02
☐	373	Willard Hunter	.15	.07	.02
☐	374	Ira Hutchinson	.15	.07	.02
☐	375	Tom Hutton	.15	.07	.02
☐	376	Charlie Irwin	.15	.07	.02
☐	377	Fred Jacklitsch	.15	.07	.02
☐	378	Randy Jackson	.15	.07	.02
☐	379	Merwin Jacobson	.15	.07	.02
☐	380	Cleo James	.15	.07	.02
☐	381	Hal Janvrin	.15	.07	.02
☐	382	Roy Jarvis	.15	.07	.02
☐	383	George Jeffcoat	.15	.07	.02
☐	384	Jack Jenkins	.15	.07	.02
☐	385	Hughie Jennings	.35	.16	.04
☐	386	Tommy John	.30	.14	.04
☐	387	Lou Johnson	.15	.07	.02
☐	388	Fred Ivy Johnston	.15	.07	.02
☐	389	Jimmy Johnston	.15	.07	.02
☐	390	Jay Johnstone	.25	.11	.03
☐	391	Fielder Jones	.15	.07	.02
☐	392	Oscar Jones	.15	.07	.02
☐	393	Tim Jordan	.15	.07	.02
☐	394	Spider Jorgensen	.15	.07	.02
☐	395	Von Joshua	.15	.07	.02
☐	396	Bill Joyce	.15	.07	.02
☐	397	Joe Judge	.15	.07	.02
☐	398	Alex Kampouris	.15	.07	.02
☐	399	Willie Keeler	.40	.18	.05
☐	400	Mike Kekich	.15	.07	.02
☐	401	John Kelleher	.15	.07	.02
☐	402	Frank Kellert	.15	.07	.02
☐	403	Joe Kelley	.40	.18	.05
☐	404	George Kelly	.35	.16	.04
☐	405	Bob Kennedy	.15	.07	.02
☐	406	Brickyard Kennedy	.15	.07	.02
☐	407	John Kennedy	.15	.07	.02
☐	408	Not issued	.00	.00	.00
☐	409	Newt Kimball	.15	.07	.02
☐	410	Clyde King	.15	.07	.02
☐	411	Enos Kirkpatrick	.15	.07	.02
☐	412	Frank Kitson	.15	.07	.02
☐	413	Johnny Klippstein	.15	.07	.02
☐	414	Elmer Klumpp	.15	.07	.02
☐	415	Len Koenecke	.15	.07	.02
☐	416	Ed Konetchy	.15	.07	.02
☐	417	Andy Kosco	.15	.07	.02
☐	418	Sandy Koufax	.75	.35	.09
☐	419	Ernie Koy	.20	.09	.03
☐	420	Charlie Kress	.15	.07	.02
☐	421	Bill Krueger	.20	.09	.03
☐	422	Ernie Krueger	.15	.07	.02
☐	423	Clem Labine	.20	.09	.03
☐	424	Candy LaChance	.15	.07	.02
☐	425	Lee Lacy	.15	.07	.02
☐	426	Lerrin LaGrow	.15	.07	.02
☐	427	Bill Lamar	.15	.07	.02
☐	428	Wayne LaMaster	.15	.07	.02
☐	429	Ray Lamb	.15	.07	.02
☐	430	Rafael Landestoy	.15	.07	.02
☐	431	Ken Landreaux	.20	.09	.03
☐	432	Tito Landrum	.15	.07	.02
☐	433	Norm Larker	.20	.09	.03
☐	434	Lyn Lary	.15	.07	.02
☐	435	Tom Lasorda	.40	.18	.05
☐	436	Cookie Lavagetto	.20	.09	.03
☐	437	Rudy Law	.15	.07	.02
☐	438	Tony Lazzeri	.40	.18	.05
☐	439	Tim Leary	.25	.11	.03
☐	440	Bob Lee	.15	.07	.02
☐	441	Hal Lee	.15	.07	.02

☐ 442	Leron Lee	.15	.07	.02
☐ 443	Jim Lefebvre	.25	.11	.03
☐ 444	Ken Lehman	.15	.07	.02
☐ 445	Don LeJohn	.15	.07	.02
☐ 446	Steve Lembo	.15	.07	.02
☐ 447	Ed Lennox	.15	.07	.02
☐ 448	Dutch Leonard	.25	.11	.03
☐ 449	Jeffery Leonard	.20	.09	.03
☐ 451	Dennis Lewallyn	.15	.07	.02
☐ 452	Bob Lillis	.20	.09	.03
☐ 453	Jim Lindsey	.15	.07	.02
☐ 454	Fred Lindstrom	.35	.16	.04
☐ 455	Billy Loes	.20	.09	.03
☐ 456	Bob Logan	.15	.07	.02
☐ 457	Bill Lohrman	.15	.07	.02
☐ 458	Not issued	.00	.00	.00
☐ 459	Vic Lombardi	.15	.07	.02
☐ 460	Davey Lopes	.25	.11	.03
☐ 461	Al Lopez	.35	.16	.04
☐ 462	Ray Lucas	.15	.07	.02
☐ 463	Not issued	.00	.00	.00
☐ 464	Harry Lumley	.15	.07	.02
☐ 465	Don Lund	.15	.07	.02
☐ 466	Dolf Luque	.20	.09	.03
☐ 467	Jim Lyttle	.15	.07	.02
☐ 468	Max Macon	.15	.07	.02
☐ 469	Bill Madlock	.25	.11	.03
☐ 470	Lee Magee	.15	.07	.02
☐ 471	Sal Maglie	.30	.14	.04
☐ 472	George Magoon	.15	.07	.02
☐ 473	Duster Mails	.15	.07	.02
☐ 474	Candy Maldonado	.25	.11	.03
☐ 475	Tony Malinosky	.15	.07	.02
☐ 476	Lew Malone	.15	.07	.02
☐ 477	Al Mamaux	.15	.07	.02
☐ 478	Gus Mancuso	.15	.07	.02
☐ 479	Charlie Manuel	.15	.07	.02
☐ 480	Heinie Manush	.35	.16	.04
☐ 481	Rabbit Maranville	.35	.16	.04
☐ 482	Juan Marichal	.50	.23	.06
☐ 483	Rube Marquard	.35	.16	.04
☐ 484	Bill Marriott	.20	.09	.03
☐ 485	Buck Marrow	.15	.07	.02
☐ 486	Mike A. Marshall	.25	.11	.03
☐ 487	Mike G. Marshall	.25	.11	.03
☐ 488	Morrie Martin	.15	.07	.02
☐ 489	Ramon Martinez	.50	.23	.06
☐ 490	Teddy Martinez	.15	.07	.02
☐ 491	Earl Mattingly	.15	.07	.02
☐ 492	Len Matuszek	.15	.07	.02
☐ 493	Gene Mauch	.25	.11	.03
☐ 494	Al Maul	.15	.07	.02
☐ 495	Carmen Mauro	.15	.07	.02
☐ 496	Alvin McBean	.15	.07	.02
☐ 497	Bill McCarren	.15	.07	.02
☐ 498	Jack McCarthy	.15	.07	.02
☐ 499	Tommy McCarthy	.20	.09	.03
☐ 500	Lew McCarty	.15	.07	.02
☐ 501	Mike J. McCormick	.15	.07	.02
☐ 502	Judge McCreedie	.15	.07	.02
☐ 503	Tom McCreery	.15	.07	.02
☐ 504	Danny McDevitt	.15	.07	.02
☐ 505	Chappie McFarland	.15	.07	.02
☐ 506	Joe McGinnity	.40	.18	.05
☐ 507	Bob McGraw	.15	.07	.02
☐ 508	Deacon McGuire	.15	.07	.02
☐ 509	Bill McGunnigle	.15	.07	.02
☐ 510	Harry McIntyre	.15	.07	.02
☐ 511	Cal McLish	.15	.07	.02
☐ 512	Ken McMullen	.15	.07	.02
☐ 513	Dough McWeeny	.15	.07	.02
☐ 514	Joe Medwick	.35	.16	.04
☐ 515	Rube Melton	.15	.07	.02
☐ 516	Fred Merkle	.25	.11	.03
☐ 517	Orlando Mercado	.15	.07	.02
☐ 518	Andy Messersmith	.20	.09	.03
☐ 519	Irish Meusel	.20	.09	.03
☐ 520	Benny Meyer	.15	.07	.02
☐ 521	Russ Meyer	.15	.07	.02
☐ 522	Chief Meyers	.15	.07	.02
☐ 523	Gene Michael	.20	.09	.03
☐ 524	Pete Mikkelsen	.15	.07	.02
☐ 525	Eddie Miksis	.15	.07	.02
☐ 526	Johnny Miljus	.15	.07	.02
☐ 527	Bob Miller	.15	.07	.02
☐ 528	Larry Miller	.15	.07	.02
☐ 529	Otto Miller	.15	.07	.02
☐ 530	Ralph Miller	.15	.07	.02
☐ 531	Walt Miller	.15	.07	.02
☐ 532	Wally Millies	.15	.07	.02
☐ 533	Bob Milliken	.15	.07	.02
☐ 534	Buster Mills	.15	.07	.02
☐ 535	Paul Minner	.15	.07	.02
☐ 536	Bobby Mitchell	.15	.07	.02
☐ 537	Clarence Mitchell	.15	.07	.02
☐ 538	Dale Mitchell	.20	.09	.03
☐ 539	Fred Mitchell	.15	.07	.02
☐ 540	Johnny Mitchell	.15	.07	.02
☐ 541	Joe Moeller	.20	.09	.03
☐ 542	Rick Monday	.20	.09	.03
☐ 543	Wally Moon	.20	.09	.03
☐ 544	Cy Moore	.15	.07	.02
☐ 545	Dee Moore	.15	.07	.02
☐ 546	Eddie Moore	.15	.07	.02
☐ 547	Gene Moore	.15	.07	.02
☐ 548	Randy Moore	.15	.07	.02
☐ 549	Ray Moore	.15	.07	.02
☐ 550	Jose Morales	.15	.07	.02
☐ 551	Bobby Morgan	.15	.07	.02
☐ 552	Eddie Morgan	.15	.07	.02
☐ 553	Mike Morgan	.25	.11	.03
☐ 554	Johnny Morrison	.15	.07	.02
☐ 555	Walt Moryn	.15	.07	.02
☐ 556	Ray Moss	.15	.07	.02
☐ 557	Manny Mota	.25	.11	.03
☐ 558	Joe Mulvey	.15	.07	.02
☐ 559	Van Lingle Mungo	.20	.09	.03
☐ 560	Les Munns	.15	.07	.02
☐ 561	Mike Munoz	.20	.09	.03
☐ 562	Simmy Murch	.15	.07	.02
☐ 563	Eddie Murray	.45	.20	.06
☐ 564	Hy Myers	.15	.07	.02
☐ 565	Sam Nahem	.15	.07	.02
☐ 566	Earl Naylor	.15	.07	.02
☐ 567	Charlie Neal	.20	.09	.03
☐ 568	Ron Negray	.15	.07	.02
☐ 569	Bernie Neis	.15	.07	.02
☐ 570	Rocky Nelson	.15	.07	.02
☐ 571	Dick Nen	.15	.07	.02
☐ 572	Don Newcombe	.30	.14	.04
☐ 573	Bobo Newsom	.25	.11	.03
☐ 574	Doc Newton	.15	.07	.02
☐ 575	Tom Niedenfuer	.15	.07	.02
☐ 576	Otho Nitcholas	.15	.07	.02
☐ 577	Al Nixon	.15	.07	.02
☐ 578	Jerry Nops	.15	.07	.02
☐ 579	Irv Noren	.15	.07	.02
☐ 580	Fred Norman	.15	.07	.02
☐ 581	Bill North	.15	.07	.02
☐ 582	Johnny Oates	.25	.11	.03
☐ 583	Bob O'Brien	.15	.07	.02
☐ 584	John O'Brien	.15	.07	.02
☐ 585	Lefty O'Doul	.25	.11	.03
☐ 586	Joe Oeschger	.15	.07	.02
☐ 587	Al Oliver	.25	.11	.03
☐ 588	Nate Oliver	.15	.07	.02
☐ 589	Luis Olmo	.15	.07	.02
☐ 590	Ivy Olson	.15	.07	.02
☐ 591	Mickey O'Neil	.15	.07	.02
☐ 592	Joe Orengo	.15	.07	.02
☐ 593	Jesse Orosco	.15	.07	.02
☐ 594	Frank O'Rourke	.15	.07	.02
☐ 595	Jorge Orta	.15	.07	.02
☐ 596	Phil Ortega	.15	.07	.02
☐ 597	Claude Osteen	.20	.09	.03
☐ 598	Fritz Ostermueller	.15	.07	.02
☐ 599	Mickey Owen	.20	.09	.03
☐ 600	Tom Paciorek	.15	.07	.02
☐ 601	Don Padgett	.15	.07	.02
☐ 602	Andy Pafko	.20	.09	.03
☐ 603	Erv Palica	.15	.07	.02
☐ 604	Ed Palmquist	.15	.07	.02
☐ 605	Wes Parker	.25	.11	.03
☐ 606	Jay Partridge	.15	.07	.02
☐ 607	Camilo Pascual	.20	.09	.03
☐ 608	Kevin Pasley	.15	.07	.02
☐ 609	Dave Patterson	.15	.07	.02
☐ 610	Harley Payne	.15	.07	.02
☐ 611	Johnny Peacock	.15	.07	.02
☐ 612	Hal Peck	.15	.07	.02
☐ 613	Stu Pederson	.15	.07	.02
☐ 614	Alejandro Pena	.25	.11	.03
☐ 615	Jose Pena	.15	.07	.02
☐ 616	Jack Perconte	.15	.07	.02
☐ 617	Charlie Perkins	.15	.07	.02
☐ 618	Ron Perranoski	.25	.11	.03
☐ 619	Jim Peterson	.15	.07	.02
☐ 620	Jesse Petty	.15	.07	.02
☐ 621	Jeff Pfeffer	.15	.07	.02
☐ 622	Babe Phelps	.15	.07	.02
☐ 623	Val Picinich	.15	.07	.02
☐ 624	Joe Pignatano	.15	.07	.02
☐ 625	George Pinckney	.15	.07	.02
☐ 626	Ed Pipgras	.15	.07	.02
☐ 627	Bud Podbielan	.15	.07	.02
☐ 628	Johnny Podres	.25	.11	.03

☐ 629 Boots Poffenberger .15 .07 .02
☐ 630 Nick Polly .15 .07 .02
☐ 631 Paul Popovich .15 .07 .02
☐ 632 Bill Posedel .15 .07 .02
☐ 633 Boog Powell .25 .11 .03
☐ 634 Dennis Powell .15 .07 .02
☐ 635 Paul Ray Powell .15 .07 .02
☐ 636 Ted Power .20 .09 .03
☐ 637 Tot Pressnell .15 .07 .02
☐ 638 John Purdin .15 .07 .02
☐ 639 Jack Quinn .15 .07 .02
☐ 640 Marv Rackley .15 .07 .02
☐ 641 Jack Radtke .15 .07 .02
☐ 642 Pat Ragan .15 .07 .02
☐ 643 Ed Rakow .15 .07 .02
☐ 644 Bob Ramazzotti .15 .07 .02
☐ 645 Willie Ramsdell .15 .07 .02
☐ 646 Mike James Ramsey .15 .07 .02
☐ 647 Mike Jeffery Ramsey .15 .07 .02
☐ 648 Willie Randolph .25 .11 .03
☐ 649 Doug Rau .15 .07 .02
☐ 650 Lance Rautzhan .15 .07 .02
☐ 651 Howie Reed .15 .07 .02
☐ 652 Pee Wee Reese .50 .23 .06
☐ 653 Phil Regan .25 .11 .03
☐ 654 Bill Reidy .15 .07 .02
☐ 655 Bobby Reis .15 .07 .02
☐ 656 Pete Reiser .25 .11 .03
☐ 657 Rip Repulski .15 .07 .02
☐ 658 Ed Reulbach .25 .11 .03
☐ 659 Jerry Reuss .20 .09 .03
☐ 660 R.J. Reynolds .15 .07 .02
☐ 661 Billy Rhiel .15 .07 .02
☐ 662 Rick Rhoden .20 .09 .03
☐ 663 Paul Richards .20 .09 .03
☐ 664 Danny Richardson .15 .07 .02
☐ 665 Pete Richert .15 .07 .02
☐ 666 Harry Riconda .15 .07 .02
☐ 667 Joe Riggert .15 .07 .02
☐ 668 Lew Riggs .15 .07 .02
☐ 669 Jimmy Ripple .15 .07 .02
☐ 670 Lou Ritter .15 .07 .02
☐ 671 German Rivera .15 .07 .02
☐ 672 Johnny Rizzo .15 .07 .02
☐ 673 Jim Roberts .15 .07 .02
☐ 674 Earl Robinson .15 .07 .02
☐ 675 Frank Robinson .50 .23 .06
☐ 676 Jackie Robinson .75 .35 .09
☐ 677A Wilbert Robinson .40 .18 .05
☐ 678 Rich Rodas .15 .07 .02
☐ 678B Sergio Robles .15 .07 .02
☐ 679 Ellie Rodriguez .15 .07 .02
☐ 680 Preacher Roe .25 .11 .03
☐ 681 Ed Roebuck .20 .09 .03
☐ 682 Ron Roenicke .15 .07 .02
☐ 683 Oscar Roettger .20 .09 .03
☐ 684 Lee Rogers .15 .07 .02
☐ 685 Packy Rogers .15 .07 .02
☐ 686 Stan Rojek .15 .07 .02
☐ 687 Vicente Romo .15 .07 .02
☐ 688 Johnny Roseboro .20 .09 .03
☐ 689 Goody Rosen .15 .07 .02
☐ 690 Don Ross .15 .07 .02
☐ 691 Ken Rowe .15 .07 .02
☐ 692 Schoolboy Rowe .25 .11 .03
☐ 693 Luther Roy .15 .07 .02
☐ 694 Jerry Royster .15 .07 .02
☐ 695 Nap Rucker .15 .07 .02
☐ 696 Dutch Ruether .15 .07 .02
☐ 697 Bill Russell .30 .14 .04
☐ 698 Jim Russell .15 .07 .02
☐ 699 John Russell UER .15 .07 .02
(Photo actually
current catcher
John Russell)
☐ 700 Johnny Rutherford .15 .07 .02
☐ 701 John Ryan .15 .07 .02
☐ 702 Rosy Ryan .15 .07 .02
☐ 703 Mike Sandlock .15 .07 .02
☐ 704 Ted Savage .15 .07 .02
☐ 705 Dave Sax .15 .07 .02
☐ 706 Steve Sax .30 .14 .04
☐ 707 Bill Sayles .15 .07 .02
☐ 708 Bill Schardt .15 .07 .02
☐ 709 Johnny Schmitz .15 .07 .02
☐ 710 Dick Schofield .20 .09 .03
☐ 711 Howie Schultz .15 .07 .02
☐ 712 Ferdie Schupp .15 .07 .02
☐ 713 Mike Scioscia .25 .11 .03
☐ 714 Dick Scott .15 .07 .02
☐ 715 Tom Seats .15 .07 .02
☐ 716 Jimmy Sebring .15 .07 .02
☐ 717 Larry See .15 .07 .02
☐ 718 Dave Sells .15 .07 .02
☐ 719 Greg Shanahan .15 .07 .02
☐ 720 Mike Sharperson .20 .09 .03
☐ 721 Joe Shaute .15 .07 .02
☐ 722 Merv Shea .15 .07 .02
☐ 723 Jimmy Sheckhard .15 .07 .02
☐ 724 Jack Sheehan .15 .07 .02
☐ 725 John Shelby .15 .07 .02
☐ 726 Vince Sherlock .15 .07 .02
☐ 727 Larry Sherry .25 .11 .03
☐ 728 Norm Sherry .20 .09 .03
☐ 729 Bill Shindle .15 .07 .02
☐ 730 Craig Shipley .20 .09 .03
☐ 731 Bart Shirley .15 .07 .02
☐ 732 Steve Shirley .15 .07 .02
☐ 733 Burt Shotton .20 .09 .03
☐ 734 George Shuba .20 .09 .03
☐ 735 Dick Siebert .15 .07 .02
☐ 736 Joe Simpson .15 .07 .02
☐ 737 Duke Sims .15 .07 .02
☐ 738 Bill Singer .20 .09 .03
☐ 739 Fred Sington .15 .07 .02
☐ 740 Ted Sizemore .20 .09 .03
☐ 741 Frank Skaff .15 .07 .02
☐ 742 Bill Skowron .25 .11 .03
☐ 743 Gordon Slade .15 .07 .02
☐ 744 Dwain Lefty Sloat .15 .07 .02
☐ 745 Charley Smith .15 .07 .02
☐ 746 Dick Smith .15 .07 .02
☐ 747 George Smith .15 .07 .02
☐ 748 Germany Smith .15 .07 .02
☐ 749 Jack Smith .15 .07 .02
☐ 750 Reggie Smith .25 .11 .03
☐ 751 Sherry Smith .15 .07 .02
☐ 752 Harry Smythe .15 .07 .02
☐ 753 Duke Snider .60 .25 .08
☐ 754 Eddie Solomon .15 .07 .02
☐ 755 Elias Sosa .15 .07 .02
☐ 756 Daryl Spencer .15 .07 .02
☐ 757 Roy Spencer .15 .07 .02
☐ 758 Karl Spooner .15 .07 .02
☐ 759 Eddie Stack .15 .07 .02
☐ 760 Tuck Stainback .15 .07 .02
☐ 761 George Stallings .15 .07 .02
☐ 762 Jerry Standaert .15 .07 .02
☐ 763 Don Stanhouse .20 .09 .03
☐ 764 Eddie Stanky .25 .11 .03
☐ 765 Dolly Stark .20 .09 .03
☐ 766 Jigger Statz .15 .07 .02
☐ 767 Casey Stengel .50 .23 .06
☐ 768 Jerry Stephenson .15 .07 .02
☐ 769 Ed Stevens .15 .07 .02
☐ 770 Dave Stewart .35 .16 .04
☐ 771 Stuffy Stewart .15 .07 .02
☐ 772 Bob Stinson .15 .07 .02
☐ 773 Milt Stock .15 .07 .02
☐ 774 Harry Stovey .25 .11 .03
☐ 775 Mike Strahler .15 .07 .02
☐ 776 Sammy Strang .15 .07 .02
☐ 777 Elmer Stricklett .15 .07 .02
☐ 778 Joe Stripp .15 .07 .02
☐ 779 Dick Stuart .25 .11 .03
☐ 780 Franklin Stubbs .20 .09 .03
☐ 781 Bill Sudakis .15 .07 .02
☐ 782 Clyde Sukeforth .15 .07 .02
☐ 783 Billy Sullivan .25 .11 .03
☐ 784 Tom Sunkel .15 .07 .02
☐ 785 Rick Sutcliffe .25 .11 .03
☐ 786 Don Sutton .35 .16 .04
☐ 787 Bill Swift .20 .09 .03
☐ 788 Vito Tamulis .15 .07 .02
☐ 789 Danny Taylor .15 .07 .02
☐ 790 Harry Taylor .15 .07 .02
☐ 791 Zack Taylor .15 .07 .02
☐ 792 Not issued .00 .00 .00
☐ 793 Chuck Templeton .15 .07 .02
☐ 794 Wayne Terwilliger .15 .07 .02
☐ 795 Derrel Thomas .15 .07 .02
☐ 796 Fay Thomas .15 .07 .02
☐ 797 Gary Thomasson .15 .07 .02
☐ 798 Don Thompson .15 .07 .02
☐ 799 Fresco Thompson .20 .09 .03
☐ 800 Tim Thompson .15 .07 .02
☐ 801 Hank Thormahlen .15 .07 .02
☐ 802 Sloppy Thurston .15 .07 .02
☐ 803 Cotton Tierney .15 .07 .02
☐ 804 Al Todd .15 .07 .02
☐ 805 Bert Tooley .15 .07 .02
☐ 806 Jeff Torborg .25 .11 .03
☐ 807 Dick Tracewski .15 .07 .02
☐ 808 Nick Tremark .15 .07 .02
☐ 809 Alex Trevino .15 .07 .02
☐ 810 Tommy Tucker .15 .07 .02

☐	811	John Tudor	.25	.11	.03
☐	812	Mike Vail	.15	.07	.02
☐	813	Rene Valdes	.15	.07	.02
☐	814	Bobby Valentine	.30	.14	.04
☐	815	Fernando Valenzuela	.35	.16	.04
☐	816	Elmer Valo	.15	.07	.02
☐	817	Dazzy Vance	.35	.16	.04
☐	818	Sandy Vance	.15	.07	.02
☐	819	Chris Van Cuyk	.15	.07	.02
☐	820	Ed VandeBerg	.15	.07	.02
☐	821	Arky Vaughan	.35	.16	.04
☐	822	Zoilo Versalles	.25	.11	.03
☐	823	Joe Vosmik	.15	.07	.02
☐	824	Ben Wade	.15	.07	.02
☐	825	Dixie Walker	.15	.07	.02
☐	826	Rube Walker	.15	.07	.02
☐	827	Stan Wall	.15	.07	.02
☐	828	Lee Walls	.15	.07	.02
☐	829	Danny Walton	.15	.07	.02
☐	830	Lloyd Waner	.35	.16	.04
☐	831	Paul Waner	.35	.16	.04
☐	832	Chuck Ward	.15	.07	.02
☐	833	John Monte Ward	.35	.16	.04
☐	834	Preston Ward	.15	.07	.02
☐	835	Jack Warner	.15	.07	.02
☐	836	Tommy Warren	.15	.07	.02
☐	837	Carl Warwick	.15	.07	.02
☐	838	Jimmy Wasdell	.15	.07	.02
☐	839	Ron Washington	.15	.07	.02
☐	840	George Watkins	.15	.07	.02
☐	841	Hank Webb	.15	.07	.02
☐	842	Les Webber	.15	.07	.02
☐	843	Gary Weiss	.15	.07	.02
☐	844	Bob Welch	.30	.14	.04
☐	845	Brad Wellman	.15	.07	.02
☐	846	John Werhas	.20	.09	.03
☐	847	Max West	.15	.07	.02
☐	848	Gus Weyhing	.15	.07	.02
☐	849	Mack Wheat	.15	.07	.02
☐	850	Zack Wheat	.35	.16	.04
☐	851	Ed Wheeler	.15	.07	.02
☐	852	Larry White	.15	.07	.02
☐	853	Myron White	.15	.07	.02
☐	854	Terry Whitfield	.15	.07	.02
☐	855	Dick Whitman	.15	.07	.02
☐	856	Possum Whitted	.15	.07	.02
☐	857	Kemp Wicker	.15	.07	.02
☐	858	Hoyt Wilhelm	.40	.18	.05
☐	859	Kaiser Wilhelm	.15	.07	.02
☐	860	Nick Willhite	.15	.07	.02
☐	861	Dick Williams	.20	.09	.03
☐	862	Reggie Williams	.15	.07	.02
☐	863	Stan Williams	.20	.09	.03
☐	864	Woody Williams	.15	.07	.02
☐	865	Maury Wills	.35	.16	.04
☐	866	Hack Wilson	.35	.16	.04
☐	867	Robert Wilson	.15	.07	.02
☐	868	Gordon Windhorn	.15	.07	.02
☐	869	Jim Winford	.15	.07	.02
☐	870	Lave Winham	.15	.07	.02
☐	871	Tom Winsett	.15	.07	.02
☐	872	Hank Winston	.15	.07	.02
☐	873	Whitey Witt	.15	.07	.02
☐	874	Pete Wojey	.15	.07	.02
☐	875	Tracy Woodson	.15	.07	.02
☐	876	Clarence Wright	.15	.07	.02
☐	877	Glenn Wright	.15	.07	.02
☐	878	Ricky Wright	.15	.07	.02
☐	879	Whit Wyatt	.20	.09	.03
☐	880	Jimmy Wynn	.20	.09	.03
☐	881	Joe Yeager	.15	.07	.02
☐	882	Steve Yeager	.20	.09	.03
☐	883	Matt Young	.15	.07	.02
☐	884	Tom Zachary	.15	.07	.02
☐	885	Pat Zachry	.20	.09	.03
☐	886	Geoff Zahn	.15	.07	.02
☐	887	Don Zimmer	.25	.11	.03
☐	888	Morrie Aderholt	.15	.07	.02
☐	889	Raleigh Aitchison	.15	.07	.02
☐	890	Whitey Alperman	.15	.07	.02
☐	891	Orlando Alvarez	.15	.07	.02
☐	892	Pat Ankeman	.15	.07	.02
☐	893	Ed Appleton	.15	.07	.02
☐	894	Doug Baird	.15	.07	.02
☐	895	Lady Baldwin	.15	.07	.02
☐	896	Win Ballou	.15	.07	.02
☐	897	Bob Barr	.15	.07	.02
☐	898	Boyd Bartley	.15	.07	.02
☐	899	Eddie Basinski	.15	.07	.02
☐	900	Erve Beck	.15	.07	.02
☐	901	Ralph Birkofer	.15	.07	.02
☐	902	Not issued	.00	.00	.00
☐	903	Joe Bradshaw	.15	.07	.02
☐	904	Bruce Brubaker	.15	.07	.02
☐	905	Oyster Burns	.15	.07	.02
☐	906	John Butler	.15	.07	.02
☐	907	Not issued	.00	.00	.00
☐	908	Kid Carsey	.15	.07	.02
☐	909	Pete Cassidy	.15	.07	.02
☐	910	Tom Catterson	.15	.07	.02
☐	911	Glenn Chapman	.15	.07	.02
☐	912	Paul Chervinko	.15	.07	.02
☐	913	George Cisar	.15	.07	.02
☐	914	Wally Clement	.15	.07	.02
☐	915	Bill Collins	.15	.07	.02
☐	916	Chuck Corgan	.15	.07	.02
☐	917	Dick Cox	.15	.07	.02
☐	918	George Crable	.15	.07	.02
☐	919	Sam Crane	.15	.07	.02
☐	920	Cliff Curtis	.15	.07	.02
☐	921	Fats Dantonio	.15	.07	.02
☐	922	Con Daily	.15	.07	.02
☐	923	Jud Daley	.15	.07	.02
☐	924	Jake Daniel	.15	.07	.02
☐	925	Kal Daniels	.20	.09	.03
☐	926	Dan Daub	.15	.07	.02
☐	927	Lindsay Deal	.15	.07	.02
☐	928	Artie Dede	.15	.07	.02
☐	929	Pat Deisel	.15	.07	.02
☐	930	Bert Delmas	.15	.07	.02
☐	931	Rube Dessau	.15	.07	.02
☐	932	Leo Dickerman	.15	.07	.02
☐	933	John Douglas	.15	.07	.02
☐	934	Red Downey	.15	.07	.02
☐	935	Carl Doyle	.15	.07	.02
☐	936	John Duffie	.15	.07	.02
☐	937	Dick Durning	.15	.07	.02
☐	938	Red Durrett	.15	.07	.02
☐	939	Mal Eason	.15	.07	.02
☐	940	Charlie Ebbetts	.20	.09	.03
☐	941	Rube Ehardt	.15	.07	.02
☐	942	Rowdy Elliot	.15	.07	.02
☐	943	Bones Ely	.15	.07	.02
☐	944	Woody English	.15	.07	.02
☐	945	Roy Evans	.15	.07	.02
☐	946	Gus Felix	.15	.07	.02
☐	947	Bill Fischer	.15	.07	.02
☐	948	Jeff Fischer	.15	.07	.02
☐	949	Chauncey Fisher	.15	.07	.02
☐	950	Tom Fitzsimmons	.15	.07	.02
☐	951	Darrin Fletcher	.20	.09	.03
☐	952	Wes Flowers	.15	.07	.02
☐	953	Howard Freigau	.15	.07	.02
☐	954	Nig Fuller	.15	.07	.02
☐	955	John Gaddy	.15	.07	.02
☐	956	Welcome Gaston	.15	.07	.02
☐	957	Frank Gatins	.15	.07	.02
☐	958	Pete Gilbert	.15	.07	.02
☐	959	Wally Gilbert	.15	.07	.02
☐	960	Carden Gillenwater	.15	.07	.02
☐	961	Roy Gleason	.15	.07	.02
☐	962	Harvey Green	.15	.07	.02
☐	963	Nelson Greene	.15	.07	.02
☐	964	John Grim	.15	.07	.02
☐	965	Dan Griner	.15	.07	.02
☐	967	Bill Hall	.15	.07	.02
☐	968	Johnny Hall	.15	.07	.02
☐	969	Not issued	.00	.00	.00
☐	970	Pat Hanifin	.15	.07	.02
☐	971	Bill Harris	.15	.07	.02
☐	972	Bill W. Hart	.15	.07	.02
☐	973	Chris Hartje	.15	.07	.02
☐	974	Mike Hartley	.15	.07	.02
☐	975	Gil Hatfield	.15	.07	.02
☐	976	Chris Haughey	.15	.07	.02
☐	977	Hugh Hearne	.15	.07	.02
☐	978	Mike Hechinger	.15	.07	.02
☐	979	Jake Hehl	.15	.07	.02
☐	980	Bob Higgins	.15	.07	.02
☐	981	Still Bill Hill	.15	.07	.02
☐	982	Shawn Hillegas	.20	.09	.03
☐	983	Wally Hood	.15	.07	.02
☐	984	Lefty Hopper	.15	.07	.02
☐	985	Ricky Horton	.15	.07	.02
☐	986	Ed Householder	.15	.07	.02
☐	987	Bill Hubbell	.15	.07	.02
☐	988	Al Humphrey	.15	.07	.02
☐	989	Bernie Hungling	.15	.07	.02
☐	990	George Hunter	.15	.07	.02
☐	991	Pat Hurley	.15	.07	.02
☐	992	Joe Hutcheson	.15	.07	.02
☐	993	Roy Hutson	.15	.07	.02
☐	994	Bert Inks	.15	.07	.02
☐	995	Dutch Jordan	.15	.07	.02
☐	996	Not issued	.00	.00	.00
☐	997	Frank Kane	.15	.07	.02

☐ 998 Chet Kehn	.15	.07	.02
☐ 999 Maury Kent	.15	.07	.02
☐ 1000 Tom Kinslow	.15	.07	.02
☐ 1001 Fred Kipp	.15	.07	.02
☐ 1002 Joe Klugman	.15	.07	.02
☐ 1003 Elmer Knetzer	.15	.07	.02
☐ 1004 Barney Koch	.15	.07	.02
☐ 1005 Jim Korwan	.15	.07	.02
☐ 1006 Joe Koukalik	.15	.07	.02
☐ 1007 Lou Koupal	.15	.07	.02
☐ 1008 Joe Kustus	.15	.07	.02
☐ 1009 Frank Lamanske	.15	.07	.02
☐ 1010 Tacks Latimer	.15	.07	.02
☐ 1011 Bill Leard	.15	.07	.02
☐ 1012 Phil Lewis	.15	.07	.02
☐ 1013 Mickey Livingston	.15	.07	.02
☐ 1014 Dick Loftus	.15	.07	.02
☐ 1015 Charlie Loudenslager	.15	.07	.02
☐ 1016 Tom Lovett	.15	.07	.02
☐ 1017 Charlie Malay	.15	.07	.02
☐ 1018 Mal Mallette	.15	.07	.02
☐ 1019 Ralph Mauriello	.15	.07	.02
☐ 1020 Bill McCabe	.15	.07	.02
☐ 1021 Gene McCann	.15	.07	.02
☐ 1022 Mike W. McCormick	.15	.07	.02
☐ 1023 Terry McDermott	.15	.07	.02
☐ 1024 John McDougal	.15	.07	.02
☐ 1025 Pryor McElveen	.15	.07	.02
☐ 1026 Dan McGann	.15	.07	.02
☐ 1027 Pat McGlothin	.15	.07	.02
☐ 1028 Doc McJames	.15	.07	.02
☐ 1029 Kit McKenna	.15	.07	.02
☐ 1030 Sadie McMahon	.15	.07	.02
☐ 1031 Not issued	.00	.00	.00
☐ 1032 Tommy McMillan	.15	.07	.02
☐ 1033 Glenn Mickens	.15	.07	.02
☐ 1034 Don Miles	.15	.07	.02
☐ 1035 Hack Miller	.15	.07	.02
☐ 1036 John Miller	.15	.07	.02
☐ 1037 Lemmie Miller	.15	.07	.02
☐ 1038 George Mohart	.15	.07	.02
☐ 1039 Gary Moore	.15	.07	.02
☐ 1040 Herbie Moran	.15	.07	.02
☐ 1041 Earl Mossor	.15	.07	.02
☐ 1042 Glen Moulder	.15	.07	.02
☐ 1043 Billy Mullen	.15	.07	.02
☐ 1045 Curly Onis	.15	.07	.02
☐ 1046 Tiny Osborne	.15	.07	.02
☐ 1047 Jim Pastorius	.15	.07	.02
☐ 1048 Art Parks	.15	.07	.02
☐ 1049 Chink Outen	.15	.07	.02
☐ 1050 Jimmy Pattison	.15	.07	.02
☐ 1051 Norman Plitt	.15	.07	.02
☐ 1052 Doc Reisling	.15	.07	.02
☐ 1053 Gilberto Reyes	.20	.09	.03
☐ 1054 Not issued	.00	.00	.00
☐ 1055 Lou Rochelli	.15	.07	.02
☐ 1056 Jim Romano	.15	.07	.02
☐ 1057 Max Rosenfeld	.15	.07	.02
☐ 1058 Andy Rush	.15	.07	.02
☐ 1059 Jack Ryan	.15	.07	.02
☐ 1060 Jack Savage	.15	.07	.02
☐ 1061 Not issued	.00	.00	.00
☐ 1062 Ray Schmandt	.15	.07	.02
☐ 1063 Henry Schmidt	.15	.07	.02
☐ 1064 Charlie Schmutz	.15	.07	.02
☐ 1065 Joe Schultz	.15	.07	.02
☐ 1066 Ray Searage	.15	.07	.02
☐ 1067 Elmer Sexauer	.15	.07	.02
☐ 1068 George Sharrott	.15	.07	.02
☐ 1069 Tommy Sheehan	.15	.07	.02
☐ 1071 George Shoch	.15	.07	.02
☐ 1072 Broadway Aleck Smith	.15	.07	.02
☐ 1073 Hap Smith	.15	.07	.02
☐ 1074 Red Smith	.15	.07	.02
☐ 1075 Tony Smith	.15	.07	.02
☐ 1076 Gene Snyder	.15	.07	.02
☐ 1077 Denny Sothern	.15	.07	.02
☐ 1078 Bill Steele	.15	.07	.02
☐ 1080 Farmer Steelman	.15	.07	.02
☐ 1081 Dutch Stryker	.15	.07	.02
☐ 1082 Tommy Tatum	.15	.07	.02
☐ 1084 Adonis Terry	.15	.07	.02
☐ 1085 Ray Thomas	.15	.07	.02
☐ 1086 George Treadway	.15	.07	.02
☐ 1087 Overton Tremper	.15	.07	.02
☐ 1088 Ty Tyson	.15	.07	.02
☐ 1089 Rube Vickers	.15	.07	.02
☐ 1090 Jose Vizcaino	.20	.09	.03
☐ 1091 Bull Wagner	.15	.07	.02
☐ 1092 Butts Wagner	.15	.07	.02
☐ 1093 Rube Ward	.15	.07	.02
☐ 1094 John Wetteland	.25	.11	.03
☐ 1095 Eddie Wilson	.15	.07	.02
☐ 1096 Tex Wilson	.15	.07	.02
☐ 1097 Zeke Wrigley	.15	.07	.02
☐ 1098 Not issued	.00	.00	.00
☐ 1099 Rube Yarrison	.15	.07	.02
☐ 1100 Earl Yingling	.15	.07	.02
☐ 1101 Chink Zachary	.15	.07	.02
☐ 1102 Lefty Davis	.15	.07	.02
☐ 1103 Bob Hall	.15	.07	.02
☐ 1104 Darby O'Brien	.15	.07	.02
☐ 1105 Larry LeJeune	.15	.07	.02
☐ 1144 Hub Northen	.15	.07	.02

1981 Donruss

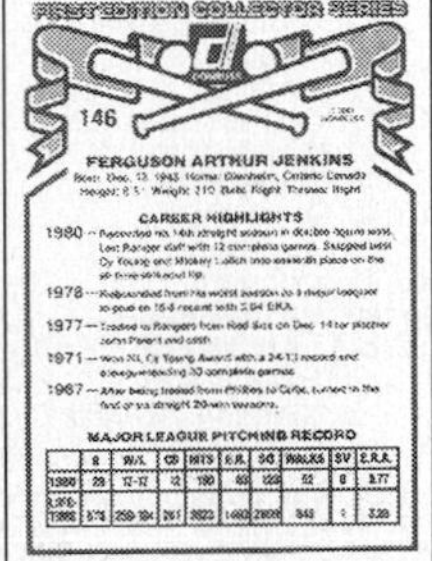

The cards in this 605-card set measure 2 1/2" by 3 1/2". In 1981 Donruss launched itself into the baseball card market with a set containing 600 numbered cards and five unnumbered checklists. Even though the five checklist cards are unnumbered, they are numbered below (601-605) for convenience in reference. The cards are printed on thin stock and more than one pose exists for several popular players. The numerous errors of the first print run were later corrected by the company. These are marked P1 and P2 in the checklist below. The key Rookie Cards in this set are Tim Raines and Jeff Reardon.

	NRMT-MT	EXC	G-VG
COMPLETE SET (605)	60.00	27.00	7.50
COMMON PLAYER (1-605)	.10	.05	.01
☐ 1 Ozzie Smith	3.50	1.55	.45
☐ 2 Rollie Fingers	1.00	.45	.13
☐ 3 Rick Wise	.10	.05	.01
☐ 4 Gene Richards	.10	.05	.01
☐ 5 Alan Trammell	.90	.40	.11
☐ 6 Tom Brookens	.10	.05	.01
☐ 7A Duffy Dyer P1 (1980 batting average has decimal point)	.15	.07	.02
☐ 7B Duffy Dyer P2 (1980 batting average has no decimal point)	.10	.05	.01
☐ 8 Mark Fidrych	.12	.05	.02
☐ 9 Dave Rozema	.10	.05	.01
☐ 10 Ricky Peters	.10	.05	.01
☐ 11 Mike Schmidt	3.00	1.35	.40
☐ 12 Willie Stargell	1.00	.45	.13
☐ 13 Tim Foli	.10	.05	.01
☐ 14 Manny Sanguillen	.12	.05	.02
☐ 15 Grant Jackson	.10	.05	.01
☐ 16 Eddie Solomon	.10	.05	.01
☐ 17 Omar Moreno	.10	.05	.01
☐ 18 Joe Morgan	1.00	.45	.13
☐ 19 Rafael Landestoy	.10	.05	.01
☐ 20 Bruce Bochy	.10	.05	.01
☐ 21 Joe Sambito	.10	.05	.01
☐ 22 Manny Trillo	.10	.05	.01
☐ 23A Dave Smith P1 (Line box around stats is not complete)	.25	.11	.03
☐ 23B Dave Smith P2 (Box totally encloses stats at top)	.25	.11	.03
☐ 24 Terry Puhl	.10	.05	.01
☐ 25 Bump Wills	.10	.05	.01

☐ 26A John Ellis P1 ERR .40 .18 .05
(Photo on front
shows Danny Walton)
☐ 26B John Ellis P2 COR .15 .07 .02
☐ 27 Jim Kern .10 .05 .01
☐ 28 Richie Zisk .10 .05 .01
☐ 29 John Mayberry .10 .05 .01
☐ 30 Bob Davis .10 .05 .01
☐ 31 Jackson Todd .10 .05 .01
☐ 32 Alvis Woods .10 .05 .01
☐ 33 Steve Carlton 2.00 .90 .25
☐ 34 Lee Mazzilli .10 .05 .01
☐ 35 John Stearns .10 .05 .01
☐ 36 Roy Lee Jackson .10 .05 .01
☐ 37 Mike Scott .25 .11 .03
☐ 38 Lamar Johnson .10 .05 .01
☐ 39 Kevin Bell .10 .05 .01
☐ 40 Ed Farmer .10 .05 .01
☐ 41 Ross Baumgarten .10 .05 .01
☐ 42 Leo Sutherland .10 .05 .01
☐ 43 Dan Meyer .10 .05 .01
☐ 44 Ron Reed .10 .05 .01
☐ 45 Mario Mendoza .10 .05 .01
☐ 46 Rick Honeycutt .10 .05 .01
☐ 47 Glenn Abbott .10 .05 .01
☐ 48 Leon Roberts .10 .05 .01
☐ 49 Rod Carew 2.00 .90 .25
☐ 50 Bert Campaneris .12 .05 .02
☐ 51A Tom Donahue P1 ERR .15 .07 .02
(Name on front
misspelled Donahue)
☐ 51B Tom Donohue .10 .05 .01
P2 COR
☐ 52 Dave Frost .10 .05 .01
☐ 53 Ed Halicki .10 .05 .01
☐ 54 Dan Ford .10 .05 .01
☐ 55 Garry Maddox .10 .05 .01
☐ 56A Steve Garvey P1 1.00 .45 .13
("Surpassed 25 HR")
☐ 56B Steve Garvey P2 .75 .35 .09
("Surpassed 21 HR")
☐ 57 Bill Russell .12 .05 .02
☐ 58 Don Sutton .60 .25 .08
☐ 59 Reggie Smith .12 .05 .02
☐ 60 Rick Monday .12 .05 .02
☐ 61 Ray Knight .12 .05 .02
☐ 62 Johnny Bench 2.00 .90 .25
☐ 63 Mario Soto .10 .05 .01
☐ 64 Doug Bair .10 .05 .01
☐ 65 George Foster .20 .09 .03
☐ 66 Jeff Burroughs .10 .05 .01
☐ 67 Keith Hernandez .30 .14 .04
☐ 68 Tom Herr .12 .05 .02
☐ 69 Bob Forsch .10 .05 .01
☐ 70 John Fulgham .10 .05 .01
☐ 71A Bobby Bonds P1 ERR .20 .09 .03
(986 lifetime HR)
☐ 71B Bobby Bonds P2 COR .12 .05 .02
(326 lifetime HR)
☐ 72A Rennie Stennett P1 .15 .07 .02
("Breaking broke leg")
☐ 72B Rennie Stennett P2 .10 .05 .01
(Word "broke" deleted)
☐ 73 Joe Strain .10 .05 .01
☐ 74 Ed Whitson .10 .05 .01
☐ 75 Tom Griffin .10 .05 .01
☐ 76 Billy North .10 .05 .01
☐ 77 Gene Garber .10 .05 .01
☐ 78 Mike Hargrove .12 .05 .02
☐ 79 Dave Rosello .10 .05 .01
☐ 80 Ron Hassey .10 .05 .01
☐ 81 Sid Monge .10 .05 .01
☐ 82A Joe Charboneau P1 .15 .07 .02
('78 highlights,
"For some reason")
☐ 82B Joe Charboneau P2 .12 .05 .02
(Phrase "For some
reason" deleted)
☐ 83 Cecil Cooper .12 .05 .02
☐ 84 Sal Bando .12 .05 .02
☐ 85 Moose Haas .10 .05 .01
☐ 86 Mike Caldwell .10 .05 .01
☐ 87A Larry Hisle P1 .15 .07 .02
('77 highlights, line
ends with "28 RBI")
☐ 87B Larry Hisle P2 .10 .05 .01
(Correct line "28 HR")
☐ 88 Luis Gomez .10 .05 .01
☐ 89 Larry Parrish .10 .05 .01
☐ 90 Gary Carter 1.00 .45 .13
☐ 91 Bill Gullickson 1.00 .45 .13
☐ 92 Fred Norman .10 .05 .01
☐ 93 Tommy Hutton .10 .05 .01
☐ 94 Carl Yastrzemski 2.00 .90 .25
☐ 95 Glenn Hoffman .10 .05 .01
☐ 96 Dennis Eckersley 1.75 .80 .22
☐ 97A Tom Burgmeier P1 .15 .07 .02
ERR (Throws: Right)
☐ 97B Tom Burgmeier P2 .10 .05 .01
COR (Throws: Left)
☐ 98 Win Remmerswaal .10 .05 .01
☐ 99 Bob Horner .12 .05 .02
☐ 100 George Brett 4.00 1.80 .50
☐ 101 Dave Chalk .10 .05 .01
☐ 102 Dennis Leonard .10 .05 .01
☐ 103 Renie Martin .10 .05 .01
☐ 104 Amos Otis .12 .05 .02
☐ 105 Graig Nettles .12 .05 .02
☐ 106 Eric Soderholm .10 .05 .01
☐ 107 Tommy John .20 .09 .03
☐ 108 Tom Underwood .10 .05 .01
☐ 109 Lou Piniella .12 .05 .02
☐ 110 Mickey Klutts .10 .05 .01
☐ 111 Bobby Murcer .12 .05 .02
☐ 112 Eddie Murray 3.00 1.35 .40
☐ 113 Rick Dempsey .12 .05 .02
☐ 114 Scott McGregor .10 .05 .01
☐ 115 Ken Singleton .12 .05 .02
☐ 116 Gary Roenicke .10 .05 .01
☐ 117 Dave Revering .10 .05 .01
☐ 118 Mike Norris .10 .05 .01
☐ 119 Rickey Henderson 13.00 5.75 1.65
☐ 120 Mike Heath .10 .05 .01
☐ 121 Dave Cash .10 .05 .01
☐ 122 Randy Jones .10 .05 .01
☐ 123 Eric Rasmussen .10 .05 .01
☐ 124 Jerry Mumphrey .10 .05 .01
☐ 125 Richie Hebner .10 .05 .01
☐ 126 Mark Wagner .10 .05 .01
☐ 127 Jack Morris 2.00 .90 .25
☐ 128 Dan Petry .12 .05 .02
☐ 129 Bruce Robbins .10 .05 .01
☐ 130 Champ Summers .10 .05 .01
☐ 131A Pete Rose P1 2.00 .90 .25
(Last line ends with
"see card 251")
☐ 131B Pete Rose P2 2.00 .90 .25
(Last line corrected
"see card 371")
☐ 132 Willie Stargell 1.00 .45 .13
☐ 133 Ed Ott .10 .05 .01
☐ 134 Jim Bibby .10 .05 .01
☐ 135 Bert Blyleven .40 .18 .05
☐ 136 Dave Parker .40 .18 .05
☐ 137 Bill Robinson .12 .05 .02
☐ 138 Enos Cabell .10 .05 .01
☐ 139 Dave Bergman .10 .05 .01
☐ 140 J.R. Richard .12 .05 .02
☐ 141 Ken Forsch .10 .05 .01
☐ 142 Larry Bowa UER .12 .05 .02
(Shortshop on front)
☐ 143 Frank LaCorte UER .10 .05 .01
(Photo actually
Randy Niemann)
☐ 144 Denny Walling .10 .05 .01
☐ 145 Buddy Bell .12 .05 .02
☐ 146 Ferguson Jenkins .50 .23 .06
☐ 147 Dannny Darwin .10 .05 .01
☐ 148 John Grubb .10 .05 .01
☐ 149 Alfredo Griffin .10 .05 .01
☐ 150 Jerry Garvin .10 .05 .01
☐ 151 Paul Mirabella .10 .05 .01
☐ 152 Rick Bosetti .10 .05 .01
☐ 153 Dick Ruthven .10 .05 .01
☐ 154 Frank Taveras .10 .05 .01
☐ 155 Craig Swan .10 .05 .01
☐ 156 Jeff Reardon 6.00 2.70 .75
☐ 157 Steve Henderson .10 .05 .01
☐ 158 Jim Morrison .10 .05 .01
☐ 159 Glenn Borgmann .10 .05 .01
☐ 160 LaMarr Hoyt .12 .05 .02
☐ 161 Rich Wortham .10 .05 .01
☐ 162 Thad Bosley .10 .05 .01
☐ 163 Julio Cruz .10 .05 .01
☐ 164A Del Unser P1 .15 .07 .02
(No "3B" heading)
☐ 164B Del Unser P2 .10 .05 .01
(Batting record on back
corrected ("3B")
☐ 165 Jim Anderson .10 .05 .01
☐ 166 Jim Beattie .10 .05 .01
☐ 167 Shane Rawley .10 .05 .01
☐ 168 Joe Simpson .10 .05 .01
☐ 169 Rod Carew 2.00 .90 .25
☐ 170 Fred Patek .10 .05 .01
☐ 171 Frank Tanana .12 .05 .02

☐ 172 Alfredo Martinez .10 .05 .01
☐ 173 Chris Knapp .10 .05 .01
☐ 174 Joe Rudi .12 .05 .02
☐ 175 Greg Luzinski .12 .05 .02
☐ 176 Steve Garvey .75 .35 .09
☐ 177 Joe Ferguson .10 .05 .01
☐ 178 Bob Welch .40 .18 .05
☐ 179 Dusty Baker .12 .05 .02
☐ 180 Rudy Law .10 .05 .01
☐ 181 Dave Concepcion .15 .07 .02
☐ 182 Johnny Bench 2.00 .90 .25
☐ 183 Mike LaCoss .10 .05 .01
☐ 184 Ken Griffey .35 .16 .04
☐ 185 Dave Collins .10 .05 .01
☐ 186 Brian Asselstine .10 .05 .01
☐ 187 Garry Templeton .12 .05 .02
☐ 188 Mike Phillips .10 .05 .01
☐ 189 Pete Vuckovich .12 .05 .02
☐ 190 John Urrea .10 .05 .01
☐ 191 Tony Scott .10 .05 .01
☐ 192 Darrell Evans .12 .05 .02
☐ 193 Milt May .10 .05 .01
☐ 194 Bob Knepper .10 .05 .01
☐ 195 Randy Moffitt .10 .05 .01
☐ 196 Larry Herndon .10 .05 .01
☐ 197 Rick Camp .10 .05 .01
☐ 198 Andre Thornton .12 .05 .02
☐ 199 Tom Veryzer .10 .05 .01
☐ 200 Gary Alexander .10 .05 .01
☐ 201 Rick Waits .10 .05 .01
☐ 202 Rick Manning .10 .05 .01
☐ 203 Paul Molitor 1.25 .55 .16
☐ 204 Jim Gantner .12 .05 .02
☐ 205 Paul Mitchell .10 .05 .01
☐ 206 Reggie Cleveland .10 .05 .01
☐ 207 Sixto Lezcano .10 .05 .01
☐ 208 Bruce Benedict .10 .05 .01
☐ 209 Rodney Scott .10 .05 .01
☐ 210 John Tamargo .10 .05 .01
☐ 211 Bill Lee .10 .05 .01
☐ 212 Andre Dawson UER 2.00 .90 .25
(Middle name Fernando, should be Nolan)
☐ 213 Rowland Office .10 .05 .01
☐ 214 Carl Yastrzemski 2.00 .90 .25
☐ 215 Jerry Remy .10 .05 .01
☐ 216 Mike Torrez .10 .05 .01
☐ 217 Skip Lockwood .10 .05 .01
☐ 218 Fred Lynn .12 .05 .02
☐ 219 Chris Chambliss .12 .05 .02
☐ 220 Willie Aikens .10 .05 .01
☐ 221 John Wathan .10 .05 .01
☐ 222 Dan Quisenberry .25 .11 .03
☐ 223 Willie Wilson .20 .09 .03
☐ 224 Clint Hurdle .10 .05 .01
☐ 225 Bob Watson .12 .05 .02
☐ 226 Jim Spencer .10 .05 .01
☐ 227 Ron Guidry .25 .11 .03
☐ 228 Reggie Jackson 2.50 1.15 .30
☐ 229 Oscar Gamble .10 .05 .01
☐ 230 Jeff Cox .10 .05 .01
☐ 231 Luis Tiant .12 .05 .02
☐ 232 Rich Dauer .10 .05 .01
☐ 233 Dan Graham .10 .05 .01
☐ 234 Mike Flanagan .12 .05 .02
☐ 235 John Lowenstein .10 .05 .01
☐ 236 Benny Ayala .10 .05 .01
☐ 237 Wayne Gross .10 .05 .01
☐ 238 Rick Langford .10 .05 .01
☐ 239 Tony Armas .10 .05 .01
☐ 240A Bob Lacy P1 ERR .20 .09 .03
(Name misspelled Bob "Lacy")
☐ 240B Bob Lacey P2 COR .10 .05 .01
☐ 241 Gene Tenace .10 .05 .01
☐ 242 Bob Shirley .10 .05 .01
☐ 243 Gary Lucas .10 .05 .01
☐ 244 Jerry Turner .10 .05 .01
☐ 245 John Wockenfuss .10 .05 .01
☐ 246 Stan Papi .10 .05 .01
☐ 247 Milt Wilcox .10 .05 .01
☐ 248 Dan Schatzeder .10 .05 .01
☐ 249 Steve Kemp .10 .05 .01
☐ 250 Jim Lentine .10 .05 .01
☐ 251 Pete Rose 2.00 .90 .25
☐ 252 Bill Madlock .12 .05 .02
☐ 253 Dale Berra .10 .05 .01
☐ 254 Kent Tekulve .12 .05 .02
☐ 255 Enrique Romo .10 .05 .01
☐ 256 Mike Easler .10 .05 .01
☐ 257 Chuck Tanner MG .10 .05 .01
☐ 258 Art Howe .12 .05 .02
☐ 259 Alan Ashby .10 .05 .01
☐ 260 Nolan Ryan 8.00 3.60 1.00
☐ 261A Vern Ruhle P1 ERR .40 .18 .05
(Photo on front actually Ken Forsch)
☐ 261B Vern Ruhle P2 COR .15 .07 .02
☐ 262 Bob Boone .12 .05 .02
☐ 263 Cesar Cedeno .12 .05 .02
☐ 264 Jeff Leonard .12 .05 .02
☐ 265 Pat Putnam .10 .05 .01
☐ 266 Jon Matlack .10 .05 .01
☐ 267 Dave Rajsich .10 .05 .01
☐ 268 Billy Sample .10 .05 .01
☐ 269 Damaso Garcia .12 .05 .02
☐ 270 Tom Buskey .10 .05 .01
☐ 271 Joey McLaughlin .10 .05 .01
☐ 272 Barry Bonnell .10 .05 .01
☐ 273 Tug McGraw .12 .05 .02
☐ 274 Mike Jorgensen .10 .05 .01
☐ 275 Pat Zachry .10 .05 .01
☐ 276 Neil Allen .10 .05 .01
☐ 277 Joel Youngblood .10 .05 .01
☐ 278 Greg Pryor .10 .05 .01
☐ 279 Britt Burns .12 .05 .02
☐ 280 Rich Dotson .12 .05 .02
☐ 281 Chet Lemon .12 .05 .02
☐ 282 Rusty Kuntz .10 .05 .01
☐ 283 Ted Cox .10 .05 .01
☐ 284 Sparky Lyle .12 .05 .02
☐ 285 Larry Cox .10 .05 .01
☐ 286 Floyd Bannister .10 .05 .01
☐ 287 Byron McLaughlin .10 .05 .01
☐ 288 Rodney Craig .10 .05 .01
☐ 289 Bobby Grich .12 .05 .02
☐ 290 Dickie Thon .12 .05 .02
☐ 291 Mark Clear .10 .05 .01
☐ 292 Dave Lemanczyk .10 .05 .01
☐ 293 Jason Thompson .12 .05 .02
☐ 294 Rick Miller .10 .05 .01
☐ 295 Lonnie Smith .15 .07 .02
☐ 296 Ron Cey .12 .05 .02
☐ 297 Steve Yeager .10 .05 .01
☐ 298 Bobby Castillo .10 .05 .01
☐ 299 Manny Mota .12 .05 .02
☐ 300 Jay Johnstone .12 .05 .02
☐ 301 Dan Driessen .10 .05 .01
☐ 302 Joe Nolan .10 .05 .01
☐ 303 Paul Householder .10 .05 .01
☐ 304 Harry Spilman .10 .05 .01
☐ 305 Cesar Geronimo .10 .05 .01
☐ 306A Gary Mathews P1 ERR .20 .09 .03
(Name misspelled)
☐ 306B Gary Matthews P2 COR .12 .05 .02
☐ 307 Ken Reitz .10 .05 .01
☐ 308 Ted Simmons .20 .09 .03
☐ 309 John Littlefield .10 .05 .01
☐ 310 George Frazier .10 .05 .01
☐ 311 Dane Iorg .10 .05 .01
☐ 312 Mike Ivie .10 .05 .01
☐ 313 Dennis Littlejohn .10 .05 .01
☐ 314 Gary Lavelle .10 .05 .01
☐ 315 Jack Clark .25 .11 .03
☐ 316 Jim Wohlford .10 .05 .01
☐ 317 Rick Matula .10 .05 .01
☐ 318 Toby Harrah .12 .05 .02
☐ 319A Dwane Kuiper P1 ERR .15 .07 .02
(Name misspelled)
☐ 319B Duane Kuiper P2 COR .10 .05 .01
☐ 320 Len Barker .10 .05 .01
☐ 321 Victor Cruz .10 .05 .01
☐ 322 Dell Alston .10 .05 .01
☐ 323 Robin Yount 4.00 1.80 .50
☐ 324 Charlie Moore .10 .05 .01
☐ 325 Lary Sorensen .10 .05 .01
☐ 326A Gorman Thomas P1 .20 .09 .03
(2nd line on back: "30 HR mark 4th")
☐ 326B Gorman Thomas P2 .12 .05 .02
("30 HR mark 3rd")
☐ 327 Bob Rodgers MG .10 .05 .01
☐ 328 Phil Niekro .60 .25 .08
☐ 329 Chris Speier .10 .05 .01
☐ 330A Steve Rodgers P1 ERR (Name misspelled) .20 .09 .03
☐ 330B Steve Rogers P2 COR .10 .05 .01
☐ 331 Woodie Fryman .10 .05 .01
☐ 332 Warren Cromartie .10 .05 .01
☐ 333 Jerry White .10 .05 .01
☐ 334 Tony Perez .40 .18 .05
☐ 335 Carlton Fisk 2.00 .90 .25
☐ 336 Dick Drago .10 .05 .01
☐ 337 Steve Renko .10 .05 .01
☐ 338 Jim Rice .30 .14 .04

☐ 339 Jerry Royster	.10	.05	.01
☐ 340 Frank White	.12	.05	.02
☐ 341 Jamie Quirk	.10	.05	.01
☐ 342A Paul Spittorff P1 ERR (Name misspelled)	.15	.07	.02
☐ 342B Paul Splittorff P2 COR	.10	.05	.01
☐ 343 Marty Pattin	.10	.05	.01
☐ 344 Pete LaCock	.10	.05	.01
☐ 345 Willie Randolph	.12	.05	.02
☐ 346 Rick Cerone	.10	.05	.01
☐ 347 Rich Gossage	.20	.09	.03
☐ 348 Reggie Jackson	2.50	1.15	.30
☐ 349 Ruppert Jones	.10	.05	.01
☐ 350 Dave McKay	.10	.05	.01
☐ 351 Yogi Berra CO	.40	.18	.05
☐ 352 Doug DeCinces	.12	.05	.02
☐ 353 Jim Palmer	1.75	.80	.22
☐ 354 Tippy Martinez	.10	.05	.01
☐ 355 Al Bumbry	.10	.05	.01
☐ 356 Earl Weaver MG	.12	.05	.02
☐ 357A Bob Picciolo P1 ERR (Name misspelled)	.15	.07	.02
☐ 357B Rob Picciolo P2 COR	.10	.05	.01
☐ 358 Matt Keough	.10	.05	.01
☐ 359 Dwayne Murphy	.10	.05	.01
☐ 360 Brian Kingman	.10	.05	.01
☐ 361 Bill Fahey	.10	.05	.01
☐ 362 Steve Mura	.10	.05	.01
☐ 363 Dennis Kinney	.10	.05	.01
☐ 364 Dave Winfield	3.00	1.35	.40
☐ 365 Lou Whitaker	.90	.40	.11
☐ 366 Lance Parrish	.25	.11	.03
☐ 367 Tim Corcoran	.10	.05	.01
☐ 368 Pat Underwood	.10	.05	.01
☐ 369 Al Cowens	.10	.05	.01
☐ 370 Sparky Anderson MG	.12	.05	.02
☐ 371 Pete Rose	2.00	.90	.25
☐ 372 Phil Garner	.12	.05	.02
☐ 373 Steve Nicosia	.10	.05	.01
☐ 374 John Candelaria	.12	.05	.02
☐ 375 Don Robinson	.10	.05	.01
☐ 376 Lee Lacy	.10	.05	.01
☐ 377 John Milner	.10	.05	.01
☐ 378 Craig Reynolds	.10	.05	.01
☐ 379A Luis Pujois P1 ERR (Name misspelled)	.15	.07	.02
☐ 379B Luis Pujols P2 COR	.10	.05	.01
☐ 380 Joe Niekro	.12	.05	.02
☐ 381 Joaquin Andujar	.12	.05	.02
☐ 382 Keith Moreland	.12	.05	.02
☐ 383 Jose Cruz	.12	.05	.02
☐ 384 Bill Virdon MG	.10	.05	.01
☐ 385 Jim Sundberg	.10	.05	.01
☐ 386 Doc Medich	.10	.05	.01
☐ 387 Al Oliver	.12	.05	.02
☐ 388 Jim Norris	.10	.05	.01
☐ 389 Bob Bailor	.10	.05	.01
☐ 390 Ernie Whitt	.10	.05	.01
☐ 391 Otto Velez	.10	.05	.01
☐ 392 Roy Howell	.10	.05	.01
☐ 393 Bob Walk	.35	.16	.04
☐ 394 Doug Flynn	.10	.05	.01
☐ 395 Pete Falcone	.10	.05	.01
☐ 396 Tom Hausman	.10	.05	.01
☐ 397 Elliott Maddox	.10	.05	.01
☐ 398 Mike Squires	.10	.05	.01
☐ 399 Marvis Foley	.10	.05	.01
☐ 400 Steve Trout	.10	.05	.01
☐ 401 Wayne Nordhagen	.10	.05	.01
☐ 402 Tony LaRussa MG	.12	.05	.02
☐ 403 Bruce Bochte	.10	.05	.01
☐ 404 Bake McBride	.10	.05	.01
☐ 405 Jerry Narron	.10	.05	.01
☐ 406 Rob Dressler	.10	.05	.01
☐ 407 Dave Heaverlo	.10	.05	.01
☐ 408 Tom Paciorek	.12	.05	.02
☐ 409 Carney Lansford	.30	.14	.04
☐ 410 Brian Downing	.12	.05	.02
☐ 411 Don Aase	.10	.05	.01
☐ 412 Jim Barr	.10	.05	.01
☐ 413 Don Baylor	.12	.05	.02
☐ 414 Jim Fregosi MG	.10	.05	.01
☐ 415 Dallas Green MG	.10	.05	.01
☐ 416 Dave Lopes	.12	.05	.02
☐ 417 Jerry Reuss	.12	.05	.02
☐ 418 Rick Sutcliffe	.35	.16	.04
☐ 419 Derrel Thomas	.10	.05	.01
☐ 420 Tom Lasorda MG	.12	.05	.02
☐ 421 Charles Leibrandt	.90	.40	.11
☐ 422 Tom Seaver	2.00	.90	.25
☐ 423 Ron Oester	.10	.05	.01
☐ 424 Junior Kennedy	.10	.05	.01
☐ 425 Tom Seaver	2.00	.90	.25
☐ 426 Bobby Cox MG	.10	.05	.01
☐ 427 Leon Durham	.10	.05	.01
☐ 428 Terry Kennedy	.12	.05	.02
☐ 429 Silvio Martinez	.10	.05	.01
☐ 430 George Hendrick	.12	.05	.02
☐ 431 Red Schoendienst MG	.15	.07	.02
☐ 432 Johnnie LeMaster	.10	.05	.01
☐ 433 Vida Blue	.12	.05	.02
☐ 434 John Montefusco	.10	.05	.01
☐ 435 Terry Whitfield	.10	.05	.01
☐ 436 Dave Bristol MG	.10	.05	.01
☐ 437 Dale Murphy	1.00	.45	.13
☐ 438 Jerry Dybzinski	.10	.05	.01
☐ 439 Jorge Orta	.10	.05	.01
☐ 440 Wayne Garland	.10	.05	.01
☐ 441 Miguel Dilone	.10	.05	.01
☐ 442 Dave Garcia MG	.10	.05	.01
☐ 443 Don Money	.10	.05	.01
☐ 444A Buck Martinez P1 ERR (Reverse negative)	.15	.07	.02
☐ 444B Buck Martinez P2 COR	.10	.05	.01
☐ 445 Jerry Augustine	.10	.05	.01
☐ 446 Ben Oglivie	.12	.05	.02
☐ 447 Jim Slaton	.10	.05	.01
☐ 448 Doyle Alexander	.10	.05	.01
☐ 449 Tony Bernazard	.10	.05	.01
☐ 450 Scott Sanderson	.12	.05	.02
☐ 451 David Palmer	.10	.05	.01
☐ 452 Stan Bahnsen	.10	.05	.01
☐ 453 Dick Williams MG	.10	.05	.01
☐ 454 Rick Burleson	.10	.05	.01
☐ 455 Gary Allenson	.10	.05	.01
☐ 456 Bob Stanley	.10	.05	.01
☐ 457A John Tudor P1 ERR (Lifetime W-L "9.7")	.35	.16	.04
☐ 457B John Tudor P2 COR (Corrected "9-7")	.35	.16	.04
☐ 458 Dwight Evans	.35	.16	.04
☐ 459 Glenn Hubbard	.10	.05	.01
☐ 460 U.L. Washington	.10	.05	.01
☐ 461 Larry Gura	.10	.05	.01
☐ 462 Rich Gale	.10	.05	.01
☐ 463 Hal McRae	.12	.05	.02
☐ 464 Jim Frey MG	.10	.05	.01
☐ 465 Bucky Dent	.12	.05	.02
☐ 466 Dennis Werth	.10	.05	.01
☐ 467 Ron Davis	.10	.05	.01
☐ 468 Reggie Jackson UER (32 HR in 1970, should be 23)	2.50	1.15	.30
☐ 469 Bobby Brown	.10	.05	.01
☐ 470 Mike Davis	.10	.05	.01
☐ 471 Gaylord Perry	.60	.25	.08
☐ 472 Mark Belanger	.12	.05	.02
☐ 473 Jim Palmer	1.75	.80	.22
☐ 474 Sammy Stewart	.10	.05	.01
☐ 475 Tim Stoddard	.10	.05	.01
☐ 476 Steve Stone	.12	.05	.02
☐ 477 Jeff Newman	.10	.05	.01
☐ 478 Steve McCatty	.10	.05	.01
☐ 479 Billy Martin MG	.25	.11	.03
☐ 480 Mitchell Page	.10	.05	.01
☐ 481 Cy Young Winner 1980 Steve Carlton	1.00	.45	.13
☐ 482 Bill Buckner	.12	.05	.02
☐ 483A Ivan DeJesus P1 ERR (Lifetime hits "702")	.15	.07	.02
☐ 483B Ivan DeJesus P2 COR (Lifetime hits "642")	.10	.05	.01
☐ 484 Cliff Johnson	.10	.05	.01
☐ 485 Lenny Randle	.10	.05	.01
☐ 486 Larry Milbourne	.10	.05	.01
☐ 487 Roy Smalley	.10	.05	.01
☐ 488 John Castino	.10	.05	.01
☐ 489 Ron Jackson	.10	.05	.01
☐ 490A Dave Roberts P1 (Career Highlights: "Showed pop in")	.15	.07	.02
☐ 490B Dave Roberts P2 ("Declared himself")	.10	.05	.01
☐ 491 MVP: George Brett	2.00	.90	.25
☐ 492 Mike Cubbage	.10	.05	.01
☐ 493 Rob Wilfong	.10	.05	.01
☐ 494 Danny Goodwin	.10	.05	.01
☐ 495 Jose Morales	.10	.05	.01
☐ 496 Mickey Rivers	.12	.05	.02
☐ 497 Mike Edwards	.10	.05	.01
☐ 498 Mike Sadek	.10	.05	.01
☐ 499 Lenn Sakata	.10	.05	.01
☐ 500 Gene Michael MG	.10	.05	.01
☐ 501 Dave Roberts	.10	.05	.01

☐ 502 Steve Dillard	.10	.05	.01
☐ 503 Jim Essian	.10	.05	.01
☐ 504 Rance Mulliniks	.10	.05	.01
☐ 505 Darrell Porter	.10	.05	.01
☐ 506 Joe Torre MG	.12	.05	.02
☐ 507 Terry Crowley	.10	.05	.01
☐ 508 Bill Travers	.10	.05	.01
☐ 509 Nelson Norman	.10	.05	.01
☐ 510 Bob McClure	.10	.05	.01
☐ 511 Steve Howe	.12	.05	.02
☐ 512 Dave Rader	.10	.05	.01
☐ 513 Mick Kelleher	.10	.05	.01
☐ 514 Kiko Garcia	.10	.05	.01
☐ 515 Larry Biittner	.10	.05	.01
☐ 516A Willie Norwood P1 (Career Highlights "Spent most of")	.15	.07	.02
☐ 516B Willie Norwood P2 ("Traded to Seattle")	.10	.05	.01
☐ 517 Bo Diaz	.10	.05	.01
☐ 518 Juan Beniquez	.10	.05	.01
☐ 519 Scot Thompson	.10	.05	.01
☐ 520 Jim Tracy	.10	.05	.01
☐ 521 Carlos Lezcano	.10	.05	.01
☐ 522 Joe Amalfitano MG	.10	.05	.01
☐ 523 Preston Hanna	.10	.05	.01
☐ 524A Ray Burris P1 (Career Highlights: "Went on ...")	.15	.07	.02
☐ 524B Ray Burris P2 ("Drafted by ...")	.10	.05	.01
☐ 525 Broderick Perkins	.10	.05	.01
☐ 526 Mickey Hatcher	.10	.05	.01
☐ 527 John Goryl MG	.10	.05	.01
☐ 528 Dick Davis	.10	.05	.01
☐ 529 Butch Wynegar	.10	.05	.01
☐ 530 Sal Butera	.10	.05	.01
☐ 531 Jerry Koosman	.12	.05	.02
☐ 532A Geoff Zahn P1 (Career Highlights: "Was 2nd in")	.15	.07	.02
☐ 532B Geoff Zahn P2 ("Signed a 3 year")	.10	.05	.01
☐ 533 Dennis Martinez	.35	.16	.04
☐ 534 Gary Thomasson	.10	.05	.01
☐ 535 Steve Macko	.10	.05	.01
☐ 536 Jim Kaat	.20	.09	.03
☐ 537 Best Hitters George Brett Rod Carew	2.50	1.15	.30
☐ 538 Tim Raines	5.00	2.30	.60
☐ 539 Keith Smith	.10	.05	.01
☐ 540 Ken Macha	.10	.05	.01
☐ 541 Burt Hooton	.10	.05	.01
☐ 542 Butch Hobson	.12	.05	.02
☐ 543 Bill Stein	.10	.05	.01
☐ 544 Dave Stapleton	.10	.05	.01
☐ 545 Bob Pate	.10	.05	.01
☐ 546 Doug Corbett	.10	.05	.01
☐ 547 Darrell Jackson	.10	.05	.01
☐ 548 Pete Redfern	.10	.05	.01
☐ 549 Roger Erickson	.10	.05	.01
☐ 550 Al Hrabosky	.10	.05	.01
☐ 551 Dick Tidrow	.10	.05	.01
☐ 552 Dave Ford	.10	.05	.01
☐ 553 Dave Kingman	.12	.05	.02
☐ 554A Mike Vail P1 (Career Highlights: "After two ...")	.15	.07	.02
☐ 554B Mike Vail P2 ("Traded to ...")	.10	.05	.01
☐ 555A Jerry Martin P1 (Career Highlights: "Overcame a ...")	.15	.07	.02
☐ 555B Jerry Martin P2 ("Traded to ...")	.10	.05	.01
☐ 556A Jesus Figueroa P1 (Career Highlights: "Had an ...")	.15	.07	.02
☐ 556B Jesus Figueroa P2 ("Traded to ...")	.10	.05	.01
☐ 557 Don Stanhouse	.10	.05	.01
☐ 558 Barry Foote	.10	.05	.01
☐ 559 Tim Blackwell	.10	.05	.01
☐ 560 Bruce Sutter	.20	.09	.03
☐ 561 Rick Reuschel	.12	.05	.02
☐ 562 Lynn McGlothen	.10	.05	.01
☐ 563A Bob Owchinko P1 (Career Highlights: "Traded to ...")	.10	.05	.01
☐ 563B Bob Owchinko P2 ("Involved in a ...")	.10	.05	.01
☐ 564 John Verhoeven	.10	.05	.01
☐ 565 Ken Landreaux	.10	.05	.01
☐ 566A Glen Adams P1 ERR (Name misspelled)	.15	.07	.02
☐ 566B Glenn Adams P2 COR	.10	.05	.01
☐ 567 Hosken Powell	.10	.05	.01
☐ 568 Dick Noles	.10	.05	.01
☐ 569 Danny Ainge	2.00	.90	.25
☐ 570 Bobby Mattick MG	.10	.05	.01
☐ 571 Joe Lefebvre	.10	.05	.01
☐ 572 Bobby Clark	.10	.05	.01
☐ 573 Dennis Lamp	.10	.05	.01
☐ 574 Randy Lerch	.10	.05	.01
☐ 575 Mookie Wilson	.50	.23	.06
☐ 576 Ron LeFlore	.12	.05	.02
☐ 577 Jim Dwyer	.10	.05	.01
☐ 578 Bill Castro	.10	.05	.01
☐ 579 Greg Minton	.10	.05	.01
☐ 580 Mark Littell	.10	.05	.01
☐ 581 Andy Hassler	.10	.05	.01
☐ 582 Dave Stieb	.35	.16	.04
☐ 583 Ken Oberkfell	.10	.05	.01
☐ 584 Larry Bradford	.10	.05	.01
☐ 585 Fred Stanley	.10	.05	.01
☐ 586 Bill Caudill	.10	.05	.01
☐ 587 Doug Capilla	.10	.05	.01
☐ 588 George Riley	.10	.05	.01
☐ 589 Willie Hernandez	.12	.05	.02
☐ 590 MVP: Mike Schmidt	1.50	.65	.19
☐ 591 Cy Young Winner 1980: Steve Stone	.10	.05	.01
☐ 592 Rick Sofield	.10	.05	.01
☐ 593 Bombo Rivera	.10	.05	.01
☐ 594 Gary Ward	.10	.05	.01
☐ 595A Dave Edwards P1 (Career Highlights: "Sidelined the")	.15	.07	.02
☐ 595B Dave Edwards P2 ("Traded to ...")	.10	.05	.01
☐ 596 Mike Proly	.10	.05	.01
☐ 597 Tommy Boggs	.10	.05	.01
☐ 598 Greg Gross	.10	.05	.01
☐ 599 Elias Sosa	.10	.05	.01
☐ 600 Pat Kelly	.10	.05	.01
☐ 601A Checklist 1 P1 ERR Unnumbered (51 Donahue)	.15	.02	.00
☐ 601B Checklist 1 P2 COR Unnumbered (51 Donohue)	.75	.08	.02
☐ 602 Checklist 2 Unnumbered	.15	.02	.00
☐ 603A Checklist 3 P1 ERR Unnumbered (306 Mathews)	.15	.02	.00
☐ 603B Checklist 3 P2 COR Unnumbered (306 Matthews)	.15	.02	.00
☐ 604A Checklist 4 P1 ERR Unnumbered (379 Pujois)	.15	.02	.00
☐ 604B Checklist 4 P2 COR Unnumbered (379 Pujols)	.15	.02	.00
☐ 605A Checklist 5 P1 ERR Unnumbered (566 Glen Adams)	.15	.02	.00
☐ 605B Checklist 5 P2 COR Unnumbered (566 Glenn Adams)	.15	.02	.00

1982 Donruss

The 1982 Donruss set contains 653 numbered cards and the seven unnumbered checklists; each card measures 2 1/2" by 3 1/2". The first 26 cards of this set are entitled Donruss Diamond Kings (DK) and feature the artwork of Dick Perez of Perez-Steele Galleries. The set was marketed with puzzle pieces rather than with bubble gum. There are 63 pieces to the puzzle, which, when put together, make a collage of Babe Ruth entitled "Hall of Fame Diamond King." The card stock in this year's Donruss cards is considerably thicker than that of the 1981 cards. The seven unnumbered checklist cards are arbitrarily assigned numbers 654 through 660 and are listed at the end of the list below. The

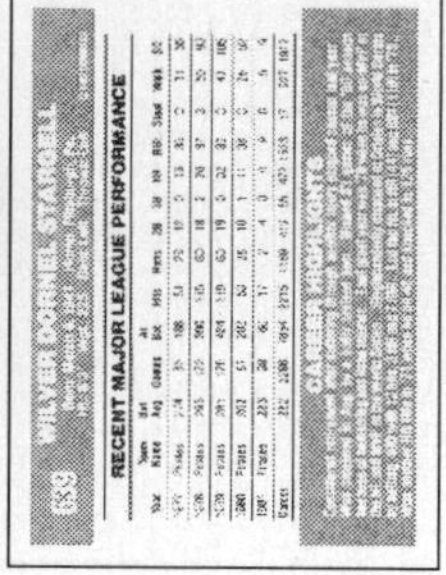

key Rookie Cards in this set are George Bell, Cal Ripken Jr., Steve Sax, Lee Smith, and Dave Stewart.

	NRMT-MT	EXC	G-VG
COMPLETE SET (660)	100.00	45.00	12.50
COMPLETE FACT.SET (660)	100.00	45.00	12.50
COMMON PLAYER (1-660)	.10	.05	.01
□ 1 Pete Rose DK	1.75	.80	.22
□ 2 Gary Carter DK	.50	.23	.06
□ 3 Steve Garvey DK	.30	.14	.04
□ 4 Vida Blue DK	.15	.07	.02
□ 5A Alan Trammel DK ERR	1.00	.45	.13
(Name misspelled)			
□ 5B Alan Trammell DK	.25	.11	.03
COR			
□ 6 Len Barker DK	.15	.07	.02
□ 7 Dwight Evans DK	.15	.07	.02
□ 8 Rod Carew DK	.75	.35	.09
□ 9 George Hendrick DK	.15	.07	.02
□ 10 Phil Niekro DK	.25	.11	.03
□ 11 Richie Zisk DK	.15	.07	.02
□ 12 Dave Parker DK	.15	.07	.02
□ 13 Nolan Ryan DK	3.50	1.55	.45
□ 14 Ivan DeJesus DK	.15	.07	.02
□ 15 George Brett DK	1.50	.65	.19
□ 16 Tom Seaver DK	.75	.35	.09
□ 17 Dave Kingman DK	.15	.07	.02
□ 18 Dave Winfield DK	1.25	.55	.16
□ 19 Mike Norris DK	.15	.07	.02
□ 20 Carlton Fisk DK	.75	.35	.09
□ 21 Ozzie Smith DK	1.00	.45	.13
□ 22 Roy Smalley DK	.15	.07	.02
□ 23 Buddy Bell DK	.15	.07	.02
□ 24 Ken Singleton DK	.15	.07	.02
□ 25 John Mayberry DK	.15	.07	.02
□ 26 Gorman Thomas DK	.15	.07	.02
□ 27 Earl Weaver MG	.12	.05	.02
□ 28 Rollie Fingers	.75	.35	.09
□ 29 Sparky Anderson MG	.12	.05	.02
□ 30 Dennis Eckersley	1.50	.65	.19
□ 31 Dave Winfield	2.50	1.15	.30
□ 32 Burt Hooton	.10	.05	.01
□ 33 Rick Waits	.10	.05	.01
□ 34 George Brett	3.00	1.35	.40
□ 35 Steve McCatty	.10	.05	.01
□ 36 Steve Rogers	.10	.05	.01
□ 37 Bill Stein	.10	.05	.01
□ 38 Steve Renko	.10	.05	.01
□ 39 Mike Squires	.10	.05	.01
□ 40 George Hendrick	.12	.05	.02
□ 41 Bob Knepper	.10	.05	.01
□ 42 Steve Carlton	1.50	.65	.19
□ 43 Larry Biittner	.10	.05	.01
□ 44 Chris Welsh	.10	.05	.01
□ 45 Steve Nicosia	.10	.05	.01
□ 46 Jack Clark	.20	.09	.03
□ 47 Chris Chambliss	.12	.05	.02
□ 48 Ivan DeJesus	.10	.05	.01
□ 49 Lee Mazzilli	.10	.05	.01
□ 50 Julio Cruz	.10	.05	.01
□ 51 Pete Redfern	.10	.05	.01
□ 52 Dave Stieb	.20	.09	.03
□ 53 Doug Corbett	.10	.05	.01
□ 54 Jorge Bell	6.00	2.70	.75
□ 55 Joe Simpson	.10	.05	.01
□ 56 Rusty Staub	.12	.05	.02
□ 57 Hector Cruz	.10	.05	.01
□ 58 Claudell Washington	.10	.05	.01
□ 59 Enrique Romo	.10	.05	.01
□ 60 Gary Lavelle	.10	.05	.01
□ 61 Tim Flannery	.10	.05	.01
□ 62 Joe Nolan	.10	.05	.01
□ 63 Larry Bowa	.12	.05	.02
□ 64 Sixto Lezcano	.10	.05	.01
□ 65 Joe Sambito	.10	.05	.01
□ 66 Bruce Kison	.10	.05	.01
□ 67 Wayne Nordhagen	.10	.05	.01
□ 68 Woodie Fryman	.10	.05	.01
□ 69 Billy Sample	.10	.05	.01
□ 70 Amos Otis	.12	.05	.02
□ 71 Matt Keough	.10	.05	.01
□ 72 Toby Harrah	.12	.05	.02
□ 73 Dave Righetti	.50	.23	.06
□ 74 Carl Yastrzemski	1.50	.65	.19
□ 75 Bob Welch	.30	.14	.04
□ 76A Alan Trammel ERR	1.50	.65	.19
(Name misspelled)			
□ 76B Alan Trammell COR	.60	.25	.08
□ 77 Rick Dempsey	.12	.05	.02
□ 78 Paul Molitor	1.00	.45	.13
□ 79 Dennis Martinez	.25	.11	.03
□ 80 Jim Slaton	.10	.05	.01
□ 81 Champ Summers	.10	.05	.01
□ 82 Carney Lansford	.12	.05	.02
□ 83 Barry Foote	.10	.05	.01
□ 84 Steve Garvey	.60	.25	.08
□ 85 Rick Manning	.10	.05	.01
□ 86 John Wathan	.10	.05	.01
□ 87 Brian Kingman	.10	.05	.01
□ 88 Andre Dawson UER	2.00	.90	.25
(Middle name Fernando,			
should be Nolan)			
□ 89 Jim Kern	.10	.05	.01
□ 90 Bobby Grich	.12	.05	.02
□ 91 Bob Forsch	.10	.05	.01
□ 92 Art Howe	.10	.05	.01
□ 93 Marty Bystrom	.10	.05	.01
□ 94 Ozzie Smith	2.00	.90	.25
□ 95 Dave Parker	.35	.16	.04
□ 96 Doyle Alexander	.10	.05	.01
□ 97 Al Hrabosky	.10	.05	.01
□ 98 Frank Taveras	.10	.05	.01
□ 99 Tim Blackwell	.10	.05	.01
□ 100 Floyd Bannister	.10	.05	.01
□ 101 Alfredo Griffin	.10	.05	.01
□ 102 Dave Engle	.10	.05	.01
□ 103 Mario Soto	.10	.05	.01
□ 104 Ross Baumgarten	.10	.05	.01
□ 105 Ken Singleton	.12	.05	.02
□ 106 Ted Simmons	.12	.05	.02
□ 107 Jack Morris	1.50	.65	.19
□ 108 Bob Watson	.12	.05	.02
□ 109 Dwight Evans	.25	.11	.03
□ 110 Tom Lasorda MG	.12	.05	.02
□ 111 Bert Blyleven	.35	.16	.04
□ 112 Dan Quisenberry	.12	.05	.02
□ 113 Rickey Henderson	4.50	2.00	.55
□ 114 Gary Carter	.90	.40	.11
□ 115 Brian Downing	.12	.05	.02
□ 116 Al Oliver	.12	.05	.02
□ 117 LaMarr Hoyt	.12	.05	.02
□ 118 Cesar Cedeno	.12	.05	.02
□ 119 Keith Moreland	.10	.05	.01
□ 120 Bob Shirley	.10	.05	.01
□ 121 Terry Kennedy	.10	.05	.01
□ 122 Frank Pastore	.10	.05	.01
□ 123 Gene Garber	.10	.05	.01
□ 124 Tony Pena	.20	.09	.03
□ 125 Allen Ripley	.10	.05	.01
□ 126 Randy Martz	.10	.05	.01
□ 127 Richie Zisk	.10	.05	.01
□ 128 Mike Scott	.12	.05	.02
□ 129 Lloyd Moseby	.10	.05	.01
□ 130 Rob Wilfong	.10	.05	.01
□ 131 Tim Stoddard	.10	.05	.01
□ 132 Gorman Thomas	.12	.05	.02
□ 133 Dan Petry	.10	.05	.01
□ 134 Bob Stanley	.10	.05	.01
□ 135 Lou Piniella	.12	.05	.02
□ 136 Pedro Guerrero	.30	.14	.04
□ 137 Len Barker	.10	.05	.01
□ 138 Rich Gale	.10	.05	.01
□ 139 Wayne Gross	.10	.05	.01
□ 140 Tim Wallach	1.00	.45	.13
□ 141 Gene Mauch MG	.10	.05	.01
□ 142 Doc Medich	.10	.05	.01
□ 143 Tony Bernazard	.10	.05	.01
□ 144 Bill Virdon MG	.10	.05	.01
□ 145 John Littlefield	.10	.05	.01
□ 146 Dave Bergman	.10	.05	.01
□ 147 Dick Davis	.10	.05	.01
□ 148 Tom Seaver	1.50	.65	.19
□ 149 Matt Sinatro	.10	.05	.01
□ 150 Chuck Tanner MG	.10	.05	.01
□ 151 Leon Durham	.10	.05	.01

☐ 152	Gene Tenace	.10	.05	.01
☐ 153	Al Bumbry	.10	.05	.01
☐ 154	Mark Brouhard	.10	.05	.01
☐ 155	Rick Peters	.10	.05	.01
☐ 156	Jerry Remy	.10	.05	.01
☐ 157	Rick Reuschel	.12	.05	.02
☐ 158	Steve Howe	.10	.05	.01
☐ 159	Alan Bannister	.10	.05	.01
☐ 160	U.L. Washington	.10	.05	.01
☐ 161	Rick Langford	.10	.05	.01
☐ 162	Bill Gullickson	.25	.11	.03
☐ 163	Mark Wagner	.10	.05	.01
☐ 164	Geoff Zahn	.10	.05	.01
☐ 165	Ron LeFlore	.12	.05	.02
☐ 166	Dane Iorg	.10	.05	.01
☐ 167	Joe Niekro	.12	.05	.02
☐ 168	Pete Rose	1.50	.65	.19
☐ 169	Dave Collins	.10	.05	.01
☐ 170	Rick Wise	.10	.05	.01
☐ 171	Jim Bibby	.10	.05	.01
☐ 172	Larry Herndon	.10	.05	.01
☐ 173	Bob Horner	.12	.05	.02
☐ 174	Steve Dillard	.10	.05	.01
☐ 175	Mookie Wilson	.12	.05	.02
☐ 176	Dan Meyer	.10	.05	.01
☐ 177	Fernando Arroyo	.10	.05	.01
☐ 178	Jackson Todd	.10	.05	.01
☐ 179	Darrell Jackson	.10	.05	.01
☐ 180	Alvis Woods	.10	.05	.01
☐ 181	Jim Anderson	.10	.05	.01
☐ 182	Dave Kingman	.12	.05	.02
☐ 183	Steve Henderson	.10	.05	.01
☐ 184	Brian Asselstine	.10	.05	.01
☐ 185	Rod Scurry	.10	.05	.01
☐ 186	Fred Breining	.10	.05	.01
☐ 187	Danny Boone	.10	.05	.01
☐ 188	Junior Kennedy	.10	.05	.01
☐ 189	Sparky Lyle	.12	.05	.02
☐ 190	Whitey Herzog MG	.12	.05	.02
☐ 191	Dave Smith	.10	.05	.01
☐ 192	Ed Ott	.10	.05	.01
☐ 193	Greg Luzinski	.12	.05	.02
☐ 194	Bill Lee	.10	.05	.01
☐ 195	Don Zimmer MG	.10	.05	.01
☐ 196	Hal McRae	.12	.05	.02
☐ 197	Mike Norris	.10	.05	.01
☐ 198	Duane Kuiper	.10	.05	.01
☐ 199	Rick Cerone	.10	.05	.01
☐ 200	Jim Rice	.25	.11	.03
☐ 201	Steve Yeager	.10	.05	.01
☐ 202	Tom Brookens	.10	.05	.01
☐ 203	Jose Morales	.10	.05	.01
☐ 204	Roy Howell	.10	.05	.01
☐ 205	Tippy Martinez	.10	.05	.01
☐ 206	Moose Haas	.10	.05	.01
☐ 207	Al Cowens	.10	.05	.01
☐ 208	Dave Stapleton	.10	.05	.01
☐ 209	Bucky Dent	.12	.05	.02
☐ 210	Ron Cey	.12	.05	.02
☐ 211	Jorge Orta	.10	.05	.01
☐ 212	Jamie Quirk	.10	.05	.01
☐ 213	Jeff Jones	.10	.05	.01
☐ 214	Tim Raines	1.25	.55	.16
☐ 215	Jon Matlack	.10	.05	.01
☐ 216	Rod Carew	1.50	.65	.19
☐ 217	Jim Kaat	.15	.07	.02
☐ 218	Joe Pittman	.10	.05	.01
☐ 219	Larry Christenson	.10	.05	.01
☐ 220	Juan Bonilla	.10	.05	.01
☐ 221	Mike Easler	.10	.05	.01
☐ 222	Vida Blue	.12	.05	.02
☐ 223	Rick Camp	.10	.05	.01
☐ 224	Mike Jorgensen	.10	.05	.01
☐ 225	Jody Davis	.12	.05	.02
☐ 226	Mike Parrott	.10	.05	.01
☐ 227	Jim Clancy	.10	.05	.01
☐ 228	Hosken Powell	.10	.05	.01
☐ 229	Tom Hume	.10	.05	.01
☐ 230	Britt Burns	.10	.05	.01
☐ 231	Jim Palmer	1.25	.55	.16
☐ 232	Bob Rodgers MG	.10	.05	.01
☐ 233	Milt Wilcox	.10	.05	.01
☐ 234	Dave Revering	.10	.05	.01
☐ 235	Mike Torrez	.10	.05	.01
☐ 236	Robert Castillo	.10	.05	.01
☐ 237	Von Hayes	.30	.14	.04
☐ 238	Renie Martin	.10	.05	.01
☐ 239	Dwayne Murphy	.10	.05	.01
☐ 240	Rodney Scott	.10	.05	.01
☐ 241	Fred Patek	.10	.05	.01
☐ 242	Mickey Rivers	.10	.05	.01
☐ 243	Steve Trout	.10	.05	.01
☐ 244	Jose Cruz	.12	.05	.02
☐ 245	Manny Trillo	.10	.05	.01
☐ 246	Lary Sorensen	.10	.05	.01
☐ 247	Dave Edwards	.10	.05	.01
☐ 248	Dan Driessen	.10	.05	.01
☐ 249	Tommy Boggs	.10	.05	.01
☐ 250	Dale Berra	.10	.05	.01
☐ 251	Ed Whitson	.10	.05	.01
☐ 252	Lee Smith	7.00	3.10	.85
☐ 253	Tom Paciorek	.12	.05	.02
☐ 254	Pat Zachry	.10	.05	.01
☐ 255	Luis Leal	.10	.05	.01
☐ 256	John Castino	.10	.05	.01
☐ 257	Rich Dauer	.10	.05	.01
☐ 258	Cecil Cooper	.12	.05	.02
☐ 259	Dave Rozema	.10	.05	.01
☐ 260	John Tudor	.12	.05	.02
☐ 261	Jerry Mumphrey	.10	.05	.01
☐ 262	Jay Johnstone	.12	.05	.02
☐ 263	Bo Diaz	.10	.05	.01
☐ 264	Dennis Leonard	.10	.05	.01
☐ 265	Jim Spencer	.10	.05	.01
☐ 266	John Milner	.10	.05	.01
☐ 267	Don Aase	.10	.05	.01
☐ 268	Jim Sundberg	.10	.05	.01
☐ 269	Lamar Johnson	.10	.05	.01
☐ 270	Frank LaCorte	.10	.05	.01
☐ 271	Barry Evans	.10	.05	.01
☐ 272	Enos Cabell	.10	.05	.01
☐ 273	Del Unser	.10	.05	.01
☐ 274	George Foster	.12	.05	.02
☐ 275	Brett Butler	2.50	1.15	.30
☐ 276	Lee Lacy	.10	.05	.01
☐ 277	Ken Reitz	.10	.05	.01
☐ 278	Keith Hernandez	.25	.11	.03
☐ 279	Doug DeCinces	.12	.05	.02
☐ 280	Charlie Moore	.10	.05	.01
☐ 281	Lance Parrish	.25	.11	.03
☐ 282	Ralph Houk MG	.10	.05	.01
☐ 283	Rich Gossage	.20	.09	.03
☐ 284	Jerry Reuss	.10	.05	.01
☐ 285	Mike Stanton	.10	.05	.01
☐ 286	Frank White	.12	.05	.02
☐ 287	Bob Owchinko	.10	.05	.01
☐ 288	Scott Sanderson	.10	.05	.01
☐ 289	Bump Wills	.10	.05	.01
☐ 290	Dave Frost	.10	.05	.01
☐ 291	Chet Lemon	.10	.05	.01
☐ 292	Tito Landrum	.10	.05	.01
☐ 293	Vern Ruhle	.10	.05	.01
☐ 294	Mike Schmidt	2.50	1.15	.30
☐ 295	Sam Mejias	.10	.05	.01
☐ 296	Gary Lucas	.10	.05	.01
☐ 297	John Candelaria	.10	.05	.01
☐ 298	Jerry Martin	.10	.05	.01
☐ 299	Dale Murphy	1.00	.45	.13
☐ 300	Mike Lum	.10	.05	.01
☐ 301	Tom Hausman	.10	.05	.01
☐ 302	Glenn Abbott	.10	.05	.01
☐ 303	Roger Erickson	.10	.05	.01
☐ 304	Otto Velez	.10	.05	.01
☐ 305	Danny Goodwin	.10	.05	.01
☐ 306	John Mayberry	.10	.05	.01
☐ 307	Lenny Randle	.10	.05	.01
☐ 308	Bob Bailor	.10	.05	.01
☐ 309	Jerry Morales	.10	.05	.01
☐ 310	Rufino Linares	.10	.05	.01
☐ 311	Kent Tekulve	.12	.05	.02
☐ 312	Joe Morgan	.75	.35	.09
☐ 313	John Urrea	.10	.05	.01
☐ 314	Paul Householder	.10	.05	.01
☐ 315	Garry Maddox	.10	.05	.01
☐ 316	Mike Ramsey	.10	.05	.01
☐ 317	Alan Ashby	.10	.05	.01
☐ 318	Bob Clark	.10	.05	.01
☐ 319	Tony LaRussa MG	.12	.05	.02
☐ 320	Charlie Lea	.10	.05	.01
☐ 321	Danny Darwin	.10	.05	.01
☐ 322	Cesar Geronimo	.10	.05	.01
☐ 323	Tom Underwood	.10	.05	.01
☐ 324	Andre Thornton	.10	.05	.01
☐ 325	Rudy May	.10	.05	.01
☐ 326	Frank Tanana	.12	.05	.02
☐ 327	Dave Lopes	.12	.05	.02
☐ 328	Richie Hebner	.10	.05	.01
☐ 329	Mike Flanagan	.12	.05	.02
☐ 330	Mike Caldwell	.10	.05	.01
☐ 331	Scott McGregor	.10	.05	.01
☐ 332	Jerry Augustine	.10	.05	.01
☐ 333	Stan Papi	.10	.05	.01
☐ 334	Rick Miller	.10	.05	.01
☐ 335	Graig Nettles	.12	.05	.02
☐ 336	Dusty Baker	.12	.05	.02
☐ 337	Dave Garcia MG	.10	.05	.01

☐ 338 Larry Gura	.10	.05	.01
☐ 339 Cliff Johnson	.10	.05	.01
☐ 340 Warren Cromartie	.10	.05	.01
☐ 341 Steve Comer	.10	.05	.01
☐ 342 Rick Burleson	.10	.05	.01
☐ 343 John Martin	.10	.05	.01
☐ 344 Craig Reynolds	.10	.05	.01
☐ 345 Mike Proly	.10	.05	.01
☐ 346 Ruppert Jones	.10	.05	.01
☐ 347 Omar Moreno	.10	.05	.01
☐ 348 Greg Minton	.10	.05	.01
☐ 349 Rick Mahler	.10	.05	.01
☐ 350 Alex Trevino	.10	.05	.01
☐ 351 Mike Krukow	.10	.05	.01
☐ 352A Shane Rawley ERR (Photo actually Jim Anderson)	.75	.35	.09
☐ 352B Shane Rawley COR	.10	.05	.01
☐ 353 Garth Iorg	.10	.05	.01
☐ 354 Pete Mackanin	.10	.05	.01
☐ 355 Paul Moskau	.10	.05	.01
☐ 356 Richard Dotson	.10	.05	.01
☐ 357 Steve Stone	.12	.05	.02
☐ 358 Larry Hisle	.10	.05	.01
☐ 359 Aurelio Lopez	.10	.05	.01
☐ 360 Oscar Gamble	.10	.05	.01
☐ 361 Tom Burgmeier	.10	.05	.01
☐ 362 Terry Forster	.10	.05	.01
☐ 363 Joe Charboneau	.10	.05	.01
☐ 364 Ken Brett	.10	.05	.01
☐ 365 Tony Armas	.10	.05	.01
☐ 366 Chris Speier	.10	.05	.01
☐ 367 Fred Lynn	.12	.05	.02
☐ 368 Buddy Bell	.12	.05	.02
☐ 369 Jim Essian	.10	.05	.01
☐ 370 Terry Puhl	.10	.05	.01
☐ 371 Greg Gross	.10	.05	.01
☐ 372 Bruce Sutter	.20	.09	.03
☐ 373 Joe Lefebvre	.10	.05	.01
☐ 374 Ray Knight	.12	.05	.02
☐ 375 Bruce Benedict	.10	.05	.01
☐ 376 Tim Foli	.10	.05	.01
☐ 377 Al Holland	.10	.05	.01
☐ 378 Ken Kravec	.10	.05	.01
☐ 379 Jeff Burroughs	.10	.05	.01
☐ 380 Pete Falcone	.10	.05	.01
☐ 381 Ernie Whitt	.10	.05	.01
☐ 382 Brad Havens	.10	.05	.01
☐ 383 Terry Crowley	.10	.05	.01
☐ 384 Don Money	.10	.05	.01
☐ 385 Dan Schatzeder	.10	.05	.01
☐ 386 Gary Allenson	.10	.05	.01
☐ 387 Yogi Berra CO	.40	.18	.05
☐ 388 Ken Landreaux	.10	.05	.01
☐ 389 Mike Hargrove	.12	.05	.02
☐ 390 Darryl Motley	.10	.05	.01
☐ 391 Dave McKay	.10	.05	.01
☐ 392 Stan Bahnsen	.10	.05	.01
☐ 393 Ken Forsch	.10	.05	.01
☐ 394 Mario Mendoza	.10	.05	.01
☐ 395 Jim Morrison	.10	.05	.01
☐ 396 Mike Ivie	.10	.05	.01
☐ 397 Broderick Perkins	.10	.05	.01
☐ 398 Darrell Evans	.12	.05	.02
☐ 399 Ron Reed	.10	.05	.01
☐ 400 Johnny Bench	1.50	.65	.19
☐ 401 Steve Bedrosian	.25	.11	.03
☐ 402 Bill Robinson	.12	.05	.02
☐ 403 Bill Buckner	.12	.05	.02
☐ 404 Ken Oberkfell	.10	.05	.01
☐ 405 Cal Ripken Jr.	50.00	23.00	6.25
☐ 406 Jim Gantner	.12	.05	.02
☐ 407 Kirk Gibson	.75	.35	.09
☐ 408 Tony Perez	.35	.16	.04
☐ 409 Tommy John UER (Text says 52-56 as Yankee, should be 52-26)	.20	.09	.03
☐ 410 Dave Stewart	3.00	1.35	.40
☐ 411 Dan Spillner	.10	.05	.01
☐ 412 Willie Aikens	.10	.05	.01
☐ 413 Mike Heath	.10	.05	.01
☐ 414 Ray Burris	.10	.05	.01
☐ 415 Leon Roberts	.10	.05	.01
☐ 416 Mike Witt	.15	.07	.02
☐ 417 Bob Molinaro	.10	.05	.01
☐ 418 Steve Braun	.10	.05	.01
☐ 419 Nolan Ryan UER (Nisnumbering of Nolan's no-hitters on card back)	8.00	3.60	1.00
☐ 420 Tug McGraw	.12	.05	.02
☐ 421 Dave Concepcion	.12	.05	.02
☐ 422A Juan Eichelberger ERR (Photo actually Gary Lucas)	.75	.35	.09
☐ 422B Juan Eichelberger COR	.10	.05	.01
☐ 423 Rick Rhoden	.10	.05	.01
☐ 424 Frank Robinson MG	.30	.14	.04
☐ 425 Eddie Miller	.10	.05	.01
☐ 426 Bill Caudill	.10	.05	.01
☐ 427 Doug Flynn	.10	.05	.01
☐ 428 Larry Andersen UER (Misspelled Anderson on card front)	.10	.05	.01
☐ 429 Al Williams	.10	.05	.01
☐ 430 Jerry Garvin	.10	.05	.01
☐ 431 Glenn Adams	.10	.05	.01
☐ 432 Barry Bonnell	.10	.05	.01
☐ 433 Jerry Narron	.10	.05	.01
☐ 434 John Stearns	.10	.05	.01
☐ 435 Mike Tyson	.10	.05	.01
☐ 436 Glenn Hubbard	.10	.05	.01
☐ 437 Eddie Solomon	.10	.05	.01
☐ 438 Jeff Leonard	.10	.05	.01
☐ 439 Randy Bass	.12	.05	.02
☐ 440 Mike LaCoss	.10	.05	.01
☐ 441 Gary Matthews	.12	.05	.02
☐ 442 Mark Littell	.10	.05	.01
☐ 443 Don Sutton	.40	.18	.05
☐ 444 John Harris	.10	.05	.01
☐ 445 Vada Pinson CO	.12	.05	.02
☐ 446 Elias Sosa	.10	.05	.01
☐ 447 Charlie Hough	.12	.05	.02
☐ 448 Willie Wilson	.12	.05	.02
☐ 449 Fred Stanley	.10	.05	.01
☐ 450 Tom Veryzer	.10	.05	.01
☐ 451 Ron Davis	.10	.05	.01
☐ 452 Mark Clear	.10	.05	.01
☐ 453 Bill Russell	.12	.05	.02
☐ 454 Lou Whitaker	.50	.23	.06
☐ 455 Dan Graham	.10	.05	.01
☐ 456 Reggie Cleveland	.10	.05	.01
☐ 457 Sammy Stewart	.10	.05	.01
☐ 458 Pete Vuckovich	.12	.05	.02
☐ 459 John Wockenfuss	.10	.05	.01
☐ 460 Glenn Hoffman	.10	.05	.01
☐ 461 Willie Randolph	.12	.05	.02
☐ 462 Fernando Valenzuela	.40	.18	.05
☐ 463 Ron Hassey	.10	.05	.01
☐ 464 Paul Splittorff	.10	.05	.01
☐ 465 Rob Picciolo	.10	.05	.01
☐ 466 Larry Parrish	.10	.05	.01
☐ 467 Johnny Grubb	.10	.05	.01
☐ 468 Dan Ford	.10	.05	.01
☐ 469 Silvio Martinez	.10	.05	.01
☐ 470 Kiko Garcia	.10	.05	.01
☐ 4/1 Bob Boone	.12	.05	.02
☐ 472 Luis Salazar	.10	.05	.01
☐ 473 Randy Niemann	.10	.05	.01
☐ 474 Tom Griffin	.10	.05	.01
☐ 475 Phil Niekro	.40	.18	.05
☐ 476 Hubie Brooks	.35	.16	.04
☐ 477 Dick Tidrow	.10	.05	.01
☐ 478 Jim Beattie	.10	.05	.01
☐ 479 Damaso Garcia	.10	.05	.01
☐ 480 Mickey Hatcher	.10	.05	.01
☐ 481 Joe Price	.10	.05	.01
☐ 482 Ed Farmer	.10	.05	.01
☐ 483 Eddie Murray	2.00	.90	.25
☐ 484 Ben Oglivie	.12	.05	.02
☐ 485 Kevin Saucier	.10	.05	.01
☐ 486 Bobby Murcer	.12	.05	.02
☐ 487 Bill Campbell	.10	.05	.01
☐ 488 Reggie Smith	.12	.05	.02
☐ 489 Wayne Garland	.10	.05	.01
☐ 490 Jim Wright	.10	.05	.01
☐ 491 Billy Martin MG	.25	.11	.03
☐ 492 Jim Fanning MG	.10	.05	.01
☐ 493 Don Baylor	.12	.05	.02
☐ 494 Rick Honeycutt	.10	.05	.01
☐ 495 Carlton Fisk	1.50	.65	.19
☐ 496 Denny Walling	.10	.05	.01
☐ 497 Bake McBride	.10	.05	.01
☐ 498 Darrell Porter	.10	.05	.01
☐ 499 Gene Richards	.10	.05	.01
☐ 500 Ron Oester	.10	.05	.01
☐ 501 Ken Dayley	.10	.05	.01
☐ 502 Jason Thompson	.10	.05	.01
☐ 503 Milt May	.10	.05	.01
☐ 504 Doug Bird	.10	.05	.01
☐ 505 Bruce Bochte	.10	.05	.01
☐ 506 Neil Allen	.10	.05	.01
☐ 507 Joey McLaughlin	.10	.05	.01
☐ 508 Butch Wynegar	.10	.05	.01

☐ 509 Gary Roenicke	.10	.05	.01
☐ 510 Robin Yount	3.00	1.35	.40
☐ 511 Dave Tobik	.10	.05	.01
☐ 512 Rich Gedman	.15	.07	.02
☐ 513 Gene Nelson	.10	.05	.01
☐ 514 Rick Monday	.10	.05	.01
☐ 515 Miguel Dilone	.10	.05	.01
☐ 516 Clint Hurdle	.10	.05	.01
☐ 517 Jeff Newman	.10	.05	.01
☐ 518 Grant Jackson	.10	.05	.01
☐ 519 Andy Hassler	.10	.05	.01
☐ 520 Pat Putnam	.10	.05	.01
☐ 521 Greg Pryor	.10	.05	.01
☐ 522 Tony Scott	.10	.05	.01
☐ 523 Steve Mura	.10	.05	.01
☐ 524 Johnnie LeMaster	.10	.05	.01
☐ 525 Dick Ruthven	.10	.05	.01
☐ 526 John McNamara MG	.10	.05	.01
☐ 527 Larry McWilliams	.10	.05	.01
☐ 528 Johnny Ray	.15	.07	.02
☐ 529 Pat Tabler	.20	.09	.03
☐ 530 Tom Herr	.12	.05	.02
☐ 531A San Diego Chicken COR (With TM)	1.50	.65	.19
☐ 531B San Diego Chicken ERR (Without TM)	1.50	.65	.19
☐ 532 Sal Butera	.10	.05	.01
☐ 533 Mike Griffin	.10	.05	.01
☐ 534 Kelvin Moore	.10	.05	.01
☐ 535 Reggie Jackson	2.00	.90	.25
☐ 536 Ed Romero	.10	.05	.01
☐ 537 Derrel Thomas	.10	.05	.01
☐ 538 Mike O'Berry	.10	.05	.01
☐ 539 Jack O'Connor	.10	.05	.01
☐ 540 Bob Ojeda	.40	.18	.05
☐ 541 Roy Lee Jackson	.10	.05	.01
☐ 542 Lynn Jones	.10	.05	.01
☐ 543 Gaylord Perry	.40	.18	.05
☐ 544A Phil Garner ERR (Reverse negative)	.75	.35	.09
☐ 544B Phil Garner COR	.12	.05	.02
☐ 545 Garry Templeton	.12	.05	.02
☐ 546 Rafael Ramirez	.10	.05	.01
☐ 547 Jeff Reardon	2.00	.90	.25
☐ 548 Ron Guidry	.25	.11	.03
☐ 549 Tim Laudner	.10	.05	.01
☐ 550 John Henry Johnson	.10	.05	.01
☐ 551 Chris Bando	.10	.05	.01
☐ 552 Bobby Brown	.10	.05	.01
☐ 553 Larry Bradford	.10	.05	.01
☐ 554 Scott Fletcher	.30	.14	.04
☐ 555 Jerry Royster	.10	.05	.01
☐ 556 Shooty Babitt UER (Spelled Babbitt on front)	.10	.05	.01
☐ 557 Kent Hrbek	2.50	1.15	.30
☐ 558 Yankee Winners Ron Guidry Tommy John	.12	.05	.02
☐ 559 Mark Bomback	.10	.05	.01
☐ 560 Julio Valdez	.10	.05	.01
☐ 561 Buck Martinez	.10	.05	.01
☐ 562 Mike Marshall (Dodger hitter)	.20	.09	.03
☐ 563 Rennie Stennett	.10	.05	.01
☐ 564 Steve Crawford	.10	.05	.01
☐ 565 Bob Babcock	.10	.05	.01
☐ 566 Johnny Podres CO	.12	.05	.02
☐ 567 Paul Serna	.10	.05	.01
☐ 568 Harold Baines	1.00	.45	.13
☐ 569 Dave LaRoche	.10	.05	.01
☐ 570 Lee May	.12	.05	.02
☐ 571 Gary Ward	.10	.05	.01
☐ 572 John Denny	.10	.05	.01
☐ 573 Roy Smalley	.10	.05	.01
☐ 574 Bob Brenly	.10	.05	.01
☐ 575 Bronx Bombers Reggie Jackson Dave Winfield	1.75	.80	.22
☐ 576 Luis Pujols	.10	.05	.01
☐ 577 Butch Hobson	.12	.05	.02
☐ 578 Harvey Kuenn MG	.12	.05	.02
☐ 579 Cal Ripken Sr. CO	.12	.05	.02
☐ 580 Juan Berenguer	.10	.05	.01
☐ 581 Benny Ayala	.10	.05	.01
☐ 582 Vance Law	.10	.05	.01
☐ 583 Rick Leach	.10	.05	.01
☐ 584 George Frazier	.10	.05	.01
☐ 585 Phillies Finest Pete Rose Mike Schmidt	1.50	.65	.19
☐ 586 Joe Rudi	.10	.05	.01
☐ 587 Juan Beniquez	.10	.05	.01
☐ 588 Luis DeLeon	.10	.05	.01
☐ 589 Craig Swan	.10	.05	.01
☐ 590 Dave Chalk	.10	.05	.01
☐ 591 Billy Gardner MG	.10	.05	.01
☐ 592 Sal Bando	.12	.05	.02
☐ 593 Bert Campaneris	.12	.05	.02
☐ 594 Steve Kemp	.10	.05	.01
☐ 595A Randy Lerch ERR (Braves)	.75	.35	.09
☐ 595B Randy Lerch COR (Brewers)	.10	.05	.01
☐ 596 Bryan Clark	.10	.05	.01
☐ 597 Dave Ford	.10	.05	.01
☐ 598 Mike Scioscia	.35	.16	.04
☐ 599 John Lowenstein	.10	.05	.01
☐ 600 Rene Lachemann MG	.10	.05	.01
☐ 601 Mick Kelleher	.10	.05	.01
☐ 602 Ron Jackson	.10	.05	.01
☐ 603 Jerry Koosman	.12	.05	.02
☐ 604 Dave Goltz	.10	.05	.01
☐ 605 Ellis Valentine	.10	.05	.01
☐ 606 Lonnie Smith	.12	.05	.02
☐ 607 Joaquin Andujar	.12	.05	.02
☐ 608 Garry Hancock	.10	.05	.01
☐ 609 Jerry Turner	.10	.05	.01
☐ 610 Bob Bonner	.10	.05	.01
☐ 611 Jim Dwyer	.10	.05	.01
☐ 612 Terry Bulling	.10	.05	.01
☐ 613 Joel Youngblood	.10	.05	.01
☐ 614 Larry Milbourne	.10	.05	.01
☐ 615 Gene Roof UER (Name on front is Phil Roof)	.10	.05	.01
☐ 616 Keith Drumwright	.10	.05	.01
☐ 617 Dave Rosello	.10	.05	.01
☐ 618 Rickey Keeton	.10	.05	.01
☐ 619 Dennis Lamp	.10	.05	.01
☐ 620 Sid Monge	.10	.05	.01
☐ 621 Jerry White	.10	.05	.01
☐ 622 Luis Aguayo	.10	.05	.01
☐ 623 Jamie Easterly	.10	.05	.01
☐ 624 Steve Sax	3.00	1.35	.40
☐ 625 Dave Roberts	.10	.05	.01
☐ 626 Rick Bosetti	.10	.05	.01
☐ 627 Terry Francona	.10	.05	.01
☐ 628 Pride of Reds Tom Seaver Johnny Bench	1.50	.65	.19
☐ 629 Paul Mirabella	.10	.05	.01
☐ 630 Rance Mulliniks	.10	.05	.01
☐ 631 Kevin Hickey	.10	.05	.01
☐ 632 Reid Nichols	.10	.05	.01
☐ 633 Dave Geisel	.10	.05	.01
☐ 634 Ken Griffey	.25	.11	.03
☐ 635 Bob Lemon MG	.15	.07	.02
☐ 636 Orlando Sanchez	.10	.05	.01
☐ 637 Bill Almon	.10	.05	.01
☐ 638 Danny Ainge	.75	.35	.09
☐ 639 Willie Stargell	.75	.35	.09
☐ 640 Bob Sykes	.10	.05	.01
☐ 641 Ed Lynch	.10	.05	.01
☐ 642 John Ellis	.10	.05	.01
☐ 643 Ferguson Jenkins	.40	.18	.05
☐ 644 Lenn Sakata	.10	.05	.01
☐ 645 Julio Gonzalez	.10	.05	.01
☐ 646 Jesse Orosco	.10	.05	.01
☐ 647 Jerry Dybzinski	.10	.05	.01
☐ 648 Tommy Davis CO	.12	.05	.02
☐ 649 Ron Gardenhire	.10	.05	.01
☐ 650 Felipe Alou CO	.12	.05	.02
☐ 651 Harvey Haddix CO	.12	.05	.02
☐ 652 Willie Upshaw	.10	.05	.01
☐ 653 Bill Madlock	.12	.05	.02
☐ 654A DK Checklist ERR (Unnumbered) (With Trammel)	.50	.05	.02
☐ 654B DK Checklist COR (Unnumbered) (With Trammell)	.15	.02	.00
☐ 655 Checklist 1 (Unnumbered)	.15	.02	.00
☐ 656 Checklist 2 (Unnumbered)	.15	.02	.00
☐ 657 Checklist 3 (Unnumbered)	.15	.02	.00
☐ 658 Checklist 4 (Unnumbered)	.15	.02	.00
☐ 659 Checklist 5 (Unnumbered)	.15	.02	.00
☐ 660 Checklist 6 (Unnumbered)	.15	.02	.00

1983 Donruss

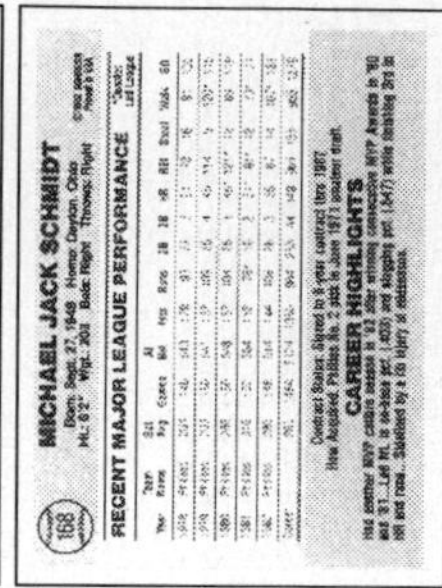

The cards in this 660-card set measure 2 1/2" by 3 1/2". The 1983 Donruss baseball set, issued with a 63-piece Diamond King puzzle, again leads off with a 26-card Diamond Kings (DK) series. Of the remaining 634 cards, two are combination cards, one portrays the San Diego Chicken, one shows the completed Ty Cobb puzzle, and seven are unnumbered checklist cards. The seven unnumbered checklist cards are arbitrarily assigned numbers 654 through 660 and are listed at the end of the list below. The Donruss logo and the year of issue are shown in the upper left corner of the obverse. The card backs have black print on yellow and white and are numbered on a small ball design. The complete set price below includes only the more common of each variation pair. The key Rookie Cards in this set are Wade Boggs, Julio Franco, Tony Gwynn, Howard Johnson, Willie McGee, Ryne Sandberg, and Frank Viola.

	NRMT-MT	EXC	G-VG
COMPLETE SET (660)	130.00	57.50	16.50
COMPLETE FACT.SET (660)	140.00	65.00	17.50
COMMON PLAYER (1-660)	.10	.05	.01
☐ 1 Fernando Valenzuela DK	.30	.14	.04
☐ 2 Rollie Fingers DK	.30	.14	.04
☐ 3 Reggie Jackson DK	.75	.35	.09
☐ 4 Jim Palmer DK	.50	.23	.06
☐ 5 Jack Morris DK	.50	.23	.06
☐ 6 George Foster DK	.15	.07	.02
☐ 7 Jim Sundberg DK	.15	.07	.02
☐ 8 Willie Stargell DK	.30	.14	.04
☐ 9 Dave Stieb DK	.15	.07	.02
☐ 10 Joe Niekro DK	.15	.07	.02
☐ 11 Rickey Henderson DK	2.00	.90	.25
☐ 12 Dale Murphy DK	.40	.18	.05
☐ 13 Toby Harrah DK	.15	.07	.02
☐ 14 Bill Buckner DK	.15	.07	.02
☐ 15 Willie Wilson DK	.15	.07	.02
☐ 16 Steve Carlton DK	.60	.25	.08
☐ 17 Ron Guidry DK	.15	.07	.02
☐ 18 Steve Rogers DK	.15	.07	.02
☐ 19 Kent Hrbek DK	.25	.11	.03
☐ 20 Keith Hernandez DK	.15	.07	.02
☐ 21 Floyd Bannister DK	.15	.07	.02
☐ 22 Johnny Bench DK	.60	.25	.08
☐ 23 Britt Burns DK	.15	.07	.02
☐ 24 Joe Morgan DK	.30	.14	.04
☐ 25 Carl Yastrzemski DK	.60	.25	.08
☐ 26 Terry Kennedy DK	.15	.07	.02
☐ 27 Gary Roenicke	.10	.05	.01
☐ 28 Dwight Bernard	.10	.05	.01
☐ 29 Pat Underwood	.10	.05	.01
☐ 30 Gary Allenson	.10	.05	.01
☐ 31 Ron Guidry	.20	.09	.03
☐ 32 Burt Hooton	.10	.05	.01
☐ 33 Chris Bando	.10	.05	.01
☐ 34 Vida Blue	.12	.05	.02
☐ 35 Rickey Henderson	3.50	1.55	.45
☐ 36 Ray Burris	.10	.05	.01
☐ 37 John Butcher	.10	.05	.01
☐ 38 Don Aase	.10	.05	.01
☐ 39 Jerry Koosman	.12	.05	.02
☐ 40 Bruce Sutter	.20	.09	.03
☐ 41 Jose Cruz	.12	.05	.02
☐ 42 Pete Rose	1.25	.55	.16
☐ 43 Cesar Cedeno	.12	.05	.02
☐ 44 Floyd Chiffer	.10	.05	.01
☐ 45 Larry McWilliams	.10	.05	.01
☐ 46 Alan Fowlkes	.10	.05	.01
☐ 47 Dale Murphy	.75	.35	.09
☐ 48 Doug Bird	.10	.05	.01
☐ 49 Hubie Brooks	.15	.07	.02
☐ 50 Floyd Bannister	.10	.05	.01
☐ 51 Jack O'Connor	.10	.05	.01
☐ 52 Steve Senteney	.10	.05	.01
☐ 53 Gary Gaetti	.40	.18	.05
☐ 54 Damaso Garcia	.10	.05	.01
☐ 55 Gene Nelson	.10	.05	.01
☐ 56 Mookie Wilson	.12	.05	.02
☐ 57 Allen Ripley	.10	.05	.01
☐ 58 Bob Horner	.12	.05	.02
☐ 59 Tony Pena	.12	.05	.02
☐ 60 Gary Lavelle	.10	.05	.01
☐ 61 Tim Lollar	.10	.05	.01
☐ 62 Frank Pastore	.10	.05	.01
☐ 63 Garry Maddox	.10	.05	.01
☐ 64 Bob Forsch	.10	.05	.01
☐ 65 Harry Spilman	.10	.05	.01
☐ 66 Geoff Zahn	.10	.05	.01
☐ 67 Salome Barojas	.10	.05	.01
☐ 68 David Palmer	.10	.05	.01
☐ 69 Charlie Hough	.12	.05	.02
☐ 70 Dan Quisenberry	.12	.05	.02
☐ 71 Tony Armas	.10	.05	.01
☐ 72 Rick Sutcliffe	.25	.11	.03
☐ 73 Steve Balboni	.10	.05	.01
☐ 74 Jerry Remy	.10	.05	.01
☐ 75 Mike Scioscia	.12	.05	.02
☐ 76 John Wockenfuss	.10	.05	.01
☐ 77 Jim Palmer	1.00	.45	.13
☐ 78 Rollie Fingers	.60	.25	.08
☐ 79 Joe Nolan	.10	.05	.01
☐ 80 Pete Vuckovich	.10	.05	.01
☐ 81 Rick Leach	.10	.05	.01
☐ 82 Rick Miller	.10	.05	.01
☐ 83 Graig Nettles	.12	.05	.02
☐ 84 Ron Cey	.12	.05	.02
☐ 85 Miguel Dilone	.10	.05	.01
☐ 86 John Wathan	.10	.05	.01
☐ 87 Kelvin Moore	.10	.05	.01
☐ 88A Byrn Smith ERR (Sic, Bryn)	.15	.07	.02
☐ 88B Bryn Smith COR	.75	.35	.09
☐ 89 Dave Hostetler	.10	.05	.01
☐ 90 Rod Carew	1.25	.55	.16
☐ 91 Lonnie Smith	.12	.05	.02
☐ 92 Bob Knepper	.10	.05	.01
☐ 93 Marty Bystrom	.10	.05	.01
☐ 94 Chris Welsh	.10	.05	.01
☐ 95 Jason Thompson	.10	.05	.01
☐ 96 Tom O'Malley	.10	.05	.01
☐ 97 Phil Niekro	.40	.18	.05
☐ 98 Neil Allen	.10	.05	.01
☐ 99 Bill Buckner	.12	.05	.02
☐ 100 Ed VandeBerg	.10	.05	.01
☐ 101 Jim Clancy	.10	.05	.01
☐ 102 Robert Castillo	.10	.05	.01
☐ 103 Bruce Berenyi	.10	.05	.01
☐ 104 Carlton Fisk	1.25	.55	.16
☐ 105 Mike Flanagan	.12	.05	.02
☐ 106 Cecil Cooper	.12	.05	.02
☐ 107 Jack Morris	1.25	.55	.16
☐ 108 Mike Morgan	.35	.16	.04
☐ 109 Luis Aponte	.10	.05	.01
☐ 110 Pedro Guerrero	.25	.11	.03
☐ 111 Len Barker	.10	.05	.01
☐ 112 Willie Wilson	.12	.05	.02
☐ 113 Dave Beard	.10	.05	.01
☐ 114 Mike Gates	.10	.05	.01
☐ 115 Reggie Jackson	1.50	.65	.19
☐ 116 George Wright	.10	.05	.01
☐ 117 Vance Law	.10	.05	.01
☐ 118 Nolan Ryan	7.00	3.10	.85
☐ 119 Mike Krukow	.10	.05	.01
☐ 120 Ozzie Smith	1.50	.65	.19
☐ 121 Broderick Perkins	.10	.05	.01
☐ 122 Tom Seaver	1.25	.55	.16
☐ 123 Chris Chambliss	.12	.05	.02
☐ 124 Chuck Tanner MG	.10	.05	.01
☐ 125 Johnnie LeMaster	.10	.05	.01
☐ 126 Mel Hall	1.75	.80	.22
☐ 127 Bruce Bochte	.10	.05	.01
☐ 128 Charlie Puleo	.10	.05	.01
☐ 129 Luis Leal	.10	.05	.01
☐ 130 John Pacella	.10	.05	.01
☐ 131 Glenn Gulliver	.10	.05	.01
☐ 132 Don Money	.10	.05	.01
☐ 133 Dave Rozema	.10	.05	.01

☐	134	Bruce Hurst	.50	.23	.06
☐	135	Rudy May	.10	.05	.01
☐	136	Tom Lasorda MG	.12	.05	.02
☐	137	Dan Spillner UER (Photo actually Ed Whitson)	.10	.05	.01
☐	138	Jerry Martin	.10	.05	.01
☐	139	Mike Norris	.10	.05	.01
☐	140	Al Oliver	.12	.05	.02
☐	141	Daryl Sconiers	.10	.05	.01
☐	142	Lamar Johnson	.10	.05	.01
☐	143	Harold Baines	.50	.23	.06
☐	144	Alan Ashby	.10	.05	.01
☐	145	Garry Templeton	.12	.05	.02
☐	146	Al Holland	.10	.05	.01
☐	147	Bo Diaz	.10	.05	.01
☐	148	Dave Concepcion	.12	.05	.02
☐	149	Rick Camp	.10	.05	.01
☐	150	Jim Morrison	.10	.05	.01
☐	151	Randy Martz	.10	.05	.01
☐	152	Keith Hernandez	.20	.09	.03
☐	153	John Lowenstein	.10	.05	.01
☐	154	Mike Caldwell	.10	.05	.01
☐	155	Milt Wilcox	.10	.05	.01
☐	156	Rich Gedman	.10	.05	.01
☐	157	Rich Gossage	.20	.09	.03
☐	158	Jerry Reuss	.10	.05	.01
☐	159	Ron Hassey	.10	.05	.01
☐	160	Larry Gura	.10	.05	.01
☐	161	Dwayne Murphy	.10	.05	.01
☐	162	Woodie Fryman	.10	.05	.01
☐	163	Steve Comer	.10	.05	.01
☐	164	Ken Forsch	.10	.05	.01
☐	165	Dennis Lamp	.10	.05	.01
☐	166	David Green	.10	.05	.01
☐	167	Terry Puhl	.10	.05	.01
☐	168	Mike Schmidt (Wearing 37 rather than 20)	2.00	.90	.25
☐	169	Eddie Milner	.10	.05	.01
☐	170	John Curtis	.10	.05	.01
☐	171	Don Robinson	.10	.05	.01
☐	172	Rich Gale	.10	.05	.01
☐	173	Steve Bedrosian	.10	.05	.01
☐	174	Willie Hernandez	.12	.05	.02
☐	175	Ron Gardenhire	.10	.05	.01
☐	176	Jim Beattie	.10	.05	.01
☐	177	Tim Laudner	.10	.05	.01
☐	178	Buck Martinez	.10	.05	.01
☐	179	Kent Hrbek	.50	.23	.06
☐	180	Alfredo Griffin	.10	.05	.01
☐	181	Larry Andersen	.10	.05	.01
☐	182	Pete Falcone	.10	.05	.01
☐	183	Jody Davis	.10	.05	.01
☐	184	Glenn Hubbard	.10	.05	.01
☐	185	Dale Berra	.10	.05	.01
☐	186	Greg Minton	.10	.05	.01
☐	187	Gary Lucas	.10	.05	.01
☐	188	Dave Van Gorder	.10	.05	.01
☐	189	Bob Dernier	.10	.05	.01
☐	190	Willie McGee	2.50	1.15	.30
☐	191	Dickie Thon	.10	.05	.01
☐	192	Bob Boone	.12	.05	.02
☐	193	Britt Burns	.10	.05	.01
☐	194	Jeff Reardon	1.25	.55	.16
☐	195	Jon Matlack	.10	.05	.01
☐	196	Don Slaught	.50	.23	.06
☐	197	Fred Stanley	.10	.05	.01
☐	198	Rick Manning	.10	.05	.01
☐	199	Dave Righetti	.15	.07	.02
☐	200	Dave Stapleton	.10	.05	.01
☐	201	Steve Yeager	.10	.05	.01
☐	202	Enos Cabell	.10	.05	.01
☐	203	Sammy Stewart	.10	.05	.01
☐	204	Moose Haas	.10	.05	.01
☐	205	Lenn Sakata	.10	.05	.01
☐	206	Charlie Moore	.10	.05	.01
☐	207	Alan Trammell	.50	.23	.06
☐	208	Jim Rice	.20	.09	.03
☐	209	Roy Smalley	.10	.05	.01
☐	210	Bill Russell	.12	.05	.02
☐	211	Andre Thornton	.10	.05	.01
☐	212	Willie Aikens	.10	.05	.01
☐	213	Dave McKay	.10	.05	.01
☐	214	Tim Blackwell	.10	.05	.01
☐	215	Buddy Bell	.12	.05	.02
☐	216	Doug DeCinces	.12	.05	.02
☐	217	Tom Herr	.12	.05	.02
☐	218	Frank LaCorte	.10	.05	.01
☐	219	Steve Carlton	1.25	.55	.16
☐	220	Terry Kennedy	.10	.05	.01
☐	221	Mike Easler	.10	.05	.01
☐	222	Jack Clark	.15	.07	.02
☐	223	Gene Garber	.10	.05	.01
☐	224	Scott Holman	.10	.05	.01
☐	225	Mike Proly	.10	.05	.01
☐	226	Terry Bulling	.10	.05	.01
☐	227	Jerry Garvin	.10	.05	.01
☐	228	Ron Davis	.10	.05	.01
☐	229	Tom Hume	.10	.05	.01
☐	230	Marc Hill	.10	.05	.01
☐	231	Dennis Martinez	.12	.05	.02
☐	232	Jim Gantner	.12	.05	.02
☐	233	Larry Pashnick	.10	.05	.01
☐	234	Dave Collins	.10	.05	.01
☐	235	Tom Burgmeier	.10	.05	.01
☐	236	Ken Landreaux	.10	.05	.01
☐	237	John Denny	.10	.05	.01
☐	238	Hal McRae	.12	.05	.02
☐	239	Matt Keough	.10	.05	.01
☐	240	Doug Flynn	.10	.05	.01
☐	241	Fred Lynn	.12	.05	.02
☐	242	Billy Sample	.10	.05	.01
☐	243	Tom Paciorek	.12	.05	.02
☐	244	Joe Sambito	.10	.05	.01
☐	245	Sid Monge	.10	.05	.01
☐	246	Ken Oberkfell	.10	.05	.01
☐	247	Joe Pittman UER (Photo actually Juan Eichelberger)	.10	.05	.01
☐	248	Mario Soto	.10	.05	.01
☐	249	Claudell Washington	.10	.05	.01
☐	250	Rick Rhoden	.10	.05	.01
☐	251	Darrell Evans	.12	.05	.02
☐	252	Steve Henderson	.10	.05	.01
☐	253	Manny Castillo	.10	.05	.01
☐	254	Craig Swan	.10	.05	.01
☐	255	Joey McLaughlin	.10	.05	.01
☐	256	Pete Redfern	.10	.05	.01
☐	257	Ken Singleton	.12	.05	.02
☐	258	Robin Yount	2.50	1.15	.30
☐	259	Elias Sosa	.10	.05	.01
☐	260	Bob Ojeda	.10	.05	.01
☐	261	Bobby Murcer	.12	.05	.02
☐	262	Candy Maldonado	1.00	.45	.13
☐	263	Rick Waits	.10	.05	.01
☐	264	Greg Pryor	.10	.05	.01
☐	265	Bob Owchinko	.10	.05	.01
☐	266	Chris Speier	.10	.05	.01
☐	267	Bruce Kison	.10	.05	.01
☐	268	Mark Wagner	.10	.05	.01
☐	269	Steve Kemp	.10	.05	.01
☐	270	Phil Garner	.12	.05	.02
☐	271	Gene Richards	.10	.05	.01
☐	272	Renie Martin	.10	.05	.01
☐	273	Dave Roberts	.10	.05	.01
☐	274	Dan Driessen	.10	.05	.01
☐	275	Rufino Linares	.10	.05	.01
☐	276	Lee Lacy	.10	.05	.01
☐	277	Ryne Sandberg	40.00	18.00	5.00
☐	278	Darrell Porter	.10	.05	.01
☐	279	Cal Ripken	18.00	8.00	2.30
☐	280	Jamie Easterly	.10	.05	.01
☐	281	Bill Fahey	.10	.05	.01
☐	282	Glenn Hoffman	.10	.05	.01
☐	283	Willie Randolph	.12	.05	.02
☐	284	Fernando Valenzuela	.15	.07	.02
☐	285	Alan Bannister	.10	.05	.01
☐	286	Paul Splittorff	.10	.05	.01
☐	287	Joe Rudi	.10	.05	.01
☐	288	Bill Gullickson	.20	.09	.03
☐	289	Danny Darwin	.10	.05	.01
☐	290	Andy Hassler	.10	.05	.01
☐	291	Ernesto Escarrega	.10	.05	.01
☐	292	Steve Mura	.10	.05	.01
☐	293	Tony Scott	.10	.05	.01
☐	294	Manny Trillo	.10	.05	.01
☐	295	Greg Harris	.10	.05	.01
☐	296	Luis DeLeon	.10	.05	.01
☐	297	Kent Tekulve	.12	.05	.02
☐	298	Atlee Hammaker	.10	.05	.01
☐	299	Bruce Benedict	.10	.05	.01
☐	300	Fergie Jenkins	.40	.18	.05
☐	301	Dave Kingman	.12	.05	.02
☐	302	Bill Caudill	.10	.05	.01
☐	303	John Castino	.10	.05	.01
☐	304	Ernie Whitt	.10	.05	.01
☐	305	Randy Johnson	.10	.05	.01
☐	306	Garth Iorg	.10	.05	.01
☐	307	Gaylord Perry	.40	.18	.05
☐	308	Ed Lynch	.10	.05	.01
☐	309	Keith Moreland	.10	.05	.01
☐	310	Rafael Ramirez	.10	.05	.01
☐	311	Bill Madlock	.12	.05	.02
☐	312	Milt May	.10	.05	.01
☐	313	John Montefusco	.10	.05	.01

	No.	Player			
☐	314	Wayne Krenchicki	.10	.05	.01
☐	315	George Vukovich	.10	.05	.01
☐	316	Joaquin Andujar	.10	.05	.01
☐	317	Craig Reynolds	.10	.05	.01
☐	318	Rick Burleson	.10	.05	.01
☐	319	Richard Dotson	.10	.05	.01
☐	320	Steve Rogers	.10	.05	.01
☐	321	Dave Schmidt	.10	.05	.01
☐	322	Bud Black	.40	.18	.05
☐	323	Jeff Burroughs	.10	.05	.01
☐	324	Von Hayes	.12	.05	.02
☐	325	Butch Wynegar	.10	.05	.01
☐	326	Carl Yastrzemski	1.25	.55	.16
☐	327	Ron Roenicke	.10	.05	.01
☐	328	Howard Johnson	6.00	2.70	.75
☐	329	Rick Dempsey UER (Posing as a left-handed batter)	.12	.05	.02
☐	330A	Jim Slaton (Bio printed black on white)	.10	.05	.01
☐	330B	Jim Slaton (Bio printed black on yellow)	.15	.07	.02
☐	331	Benny Ayala	.10	.05	.01
☐	332	Ted Simmons	.12	.05	.02
☐	333	Lou Whitaker	.50	.23	.06
☐	334	Chuck Rainey	.10	.05	.01
☐	335	Lou Piniella	.12	.05	.02
☐	336	Steve Sax	.75	.35	.09
☐	337	Toby Harrah	.10	.05	.01
☐	338	George Brett	2.50	1.15	.30
☐	339	Dave Lopes	.12	.05	.02
☐	340	Gary Carter	.75	.35	.09
☐	341	John Grubb	.10	.05	.01
☐	342	Tim Foli	.10	.05	.01
☐	343	Jim Kaat	.15	.07	.02
☐	344	Mike LaCoss	.10	.05	.01
☐	345	Larry Christenson	.10	.05	.01
☐	346	Juan Bonilla	.10	.05	.01
☐	347	Omar Moreno	.10	.05	.01
☐	348	Chili Davis	.50	.23	.06
☐	349	Tommy Boggs	.10	.05	.01
☐	350	Rusty Staub	.12	.05	.02
☐	351	Bump Wills	.10	.05	.01
☐	352	Rick Sweet	.10	.05	.01
☐	353	Jim Gott	.15	.07	.02
☐	354	Terry Felton	.10	.05	.01
☐	355	Jim Kern	.10	.05	.01
☐	356	Bill Almon UER (Expos/Mets in 1983, not Padres/Mets)	.10	.05	.01
☐	357	Tippy Martinez	.10	.05	.01
☐	358	Roy Howell	.10	.05	.01
☐	359	Dan Petry	.10	.05	.01
☐	360	Jerry Mumphrey	.10	.05	.01
☐	361	Mark Clear	.10	.05	.01
☐	362	Mike Marshall	.12	.05	.02
☐	363	Lary Sorensen	.10	.05	.01
☐	364	Amos Otis	.12	.05	.02
☐	365	Rick Langford	.10	.05	.01
☐	366	Brad Mills	.10	.05	.01
☐	367	Brian Downing	.12	.05	.02
☐	368	Mike Richardt	.10	.05	.01
☐	369	Aurelio Rodriguez	.10	.05	.01
☐	370	Dave Smith	.10	.05	.01
☐	371	Tug McGraw	.12	.05	.02
☐	372	Doug Bair	.10	.05	.01
☐	373	Ruppert Jones	.10	.05	.01
☐	374	Alex Trevino	.10	.05	.01
☐	375	Ken Dayley	.10	.05	.01
☐	376	Rod Scurry	.10	.05	.01
☐	377	Bob Brenly	.10	.05	.01
☐	378	Scot Thompson	.10	.05	.01
☐	379	Julio Cruz	.10	.05	.01
☐	380	John Stearns	.10	.05	.01
☐	381	Dale Murray	.10	.05	.01
☐	382	Frank Viola	3.00	1.35	.40
☐	383	Al Bumbry	.10	.05	.01
☐	384	Ben Oglivie	.10	.05	.01
☐	385	Dave Tobik	.10	.05	.01
☐	386	Bob Stanley	.10	.05	.01
☐	387	Andre Robertson	.10	.05	.01
☐	388	Jorge Orta	.10	.05	.01
☐	389	Ed Whitson	.10	.05	.01
☐	390	Don Hood	.10	.05	.01
☐	391	Tom Underwood	.10	.05	.01
☐	392	Tim Wallach	.20	.09	.03
☐	393	Steve Renko	.10	.05	.01
☐	394	Mickey Rivers	.10	.05	.01
☐	395	Greg Luzinski	.12	.05	.02
☐	396	Art Howe	.10	.05	.01
☐	397	Alan Wiggins	.10	.05	.01
☐	398	Jim Barr	.10	.05	.01
☐	399	Ivan DeJesus	.10	.05	.01
☐	400	Tom Lawless	.10	.05	.01
☐	401	Bob Walk	.10	.05	.01
☐	402	Jimmy Smith	.10	.05	.01
☐	403	Lee Smith	2.25	1.00	.30
☐	404	George Hendrick	.12	.05	.02
☐	405	Eddie Murray	1.75	.80	.22
☐	406	Marshall Edwards	.10	.05	.01
☐	407	Lance Parrish	.15	.07	.02
☐	408	Carney Lansford	.12	.05	.02
☐	409	Dave Winfield	2.00	.90	.25
☐	410	Bob Welch	.25	.11	.03
☐	411	Larry Milbourne	.10	.05	.01
☐	412	Dennis Leonard	.10	.05	.01
☐	413	Dan Meyer	.10	.05	.01
☐	414	Charlie Lea	.10	.05	.01
☐	415	Rick Honeycutt	.10	.05	.01
☐	416	Mike Witt	.10	.05	.01
☐	417	Steve Trout	.10	.05	.01
☐	418	Glenn Brummer	.10	.05	.01
☐	419	Denny Walling	.10	.05	.01
☐	420	Gary Matthews	.12	.05	.02
☐	421	Charlie Leibrandt UER (Liebrandt on front of card)	.12	.05	.02
☐	422	Juan Eichelberger UER (Photo actually Joe Pittman)	.10	.05	.01
☐	423	Cecilio Guante UER (Listed as Matt on card)	.12	.05	.02
☐	424	Bill Laskey	.10	.05	.01
☐	425	Jerry Royster	.10	.05	.01
☐	426	Dickie Noles	.10	.05	.01
☐	427	George Foster	.12	.05	.02
☐	428	Mike Moore	1.00	.45	.13
☐	429	Gary Ward	.10	.05	.01
☐	430	Barry Bonnell	.10	.05	.01
☐	431	Ron Washington	.10	.05	.01
☐	432	Rance Mulliniks	.10	.05	.01
☐	433	Mike Stanton	.10	.05	.01
☐	434	Jesse Orosco	.10	.05	.01
☐	435	Larry Bowa	.12	.05	.02
☐	436	Biff Pocoroba	.10	.05	.01
☐	437	Johnny Ray	.10	.05	.01
☐	438	Joe Morgan	.60	.25	.08
☐	439	Eric Show	.10	.05	.01
☐	440	Larry Biittner	.10	.05	.01
☐	441	Greg Gross	.10	.05	.01
☐	442	Gene Tenace	.10	.05	.01
☐	443	Danny Heep	.10	.05	.01
☐	444	Bobby Clark	.10	.05	.01
☐	445	Kevin Hickey	.10	.05	.01
☐	446	Scott Sanderson	.10	.05	.01
☐	447	Frank Tanana	.12	.05	.02
☐	448	Cesar Geronimo	.10	.05	.01
☐	449	Jimmy Sexton	.10	.05	.01
☐	450	Mike Hargrove	.12	.05	.02
☐	451	Doyle Alexander	.10	.05	.01
☐	452	Dwight Evans	.25	.11	.03
☐	453	Terry Forster	.10	.05	.01
☐	454	Tom Brookens	.10	.05	.01
☐	455	Rich Dauer	.10	.05	.01
☐	456	Rob Picciolo	.10	.05	.01
☐	457	Terry Crowley	.10	.05	.01
☐	458	Ned Yost	.10	.05	.01
☐	459	Kirk Gibson	.35	.16	.04
☐	460	Reid Nichols	.10	.05	.01
☐	461	Oscar Gamble	.10	.05	.01
☐	462	Dusty Baker	.12	.05	.02
☐	463	Jack Perconte	.10	.05	.01
☐	464	Frank White	.12	.05	.02
☐	465	Mickey Klutts	.10	.05	.01
☐	466	Warren Cromartie	.10	.05	.01
☐	467	Larry Parrish	.10	.05	.01
☐	468	Bobby Grich	.12	.05	.02
☐	469	Dane Iorg	.10	.05	.01
☐	470	Joe Niekro	.12	.05	.02
☐	471	Ed Farmer	.10	.05	.01
☐	472	Tim Flannery	.10	.05	.01
☐	473	Dave Parker	.35	.16	.04
☐	474	Jeff Leonard	.10	.05	.01
☐	475	Al Hrabosky	.10	.05	.01
☐	476	Ron Hodges	.10	.05	.01
☐	477	Leon Durham	.10	.05	.01
☐	478	Jim Essian	.10	.05	.01
☐	479	Roy Lee Jackson	.10	.05	.01
☐	480	Brad Havens	.10	.05	.01
☐	481	Joe Price	.10	.05	.01
☐	482	Tony Bernazard	.10	.05	.01
☐	483	Scott McGregor	.10	.05	.01
☐	484	Paul Molitor	.75	.35	.09

☐ 485 Mike Ivie .10 .05 .01
☐ 486 Ken Griffey .25 .11 .03
☐ 487 Dennis Eckersley 1.25 .55 .16
☐ 488 Steve Garvey .40 .18 .05
☐ 489 Mike Fischlin .10 .05 .01
☐ 490 U.L. Washington .10 .05 .01
☐ 491 Steve McCatty .10 .05 .01
☐ 492 Roy Johnson .10 .05 .01
☐ 493 Don Baylor .12 .05 .02
☐ 494 Bobby Johnson .10 .05 .01
☐ 495 Mike Squires .10 .05 .01
☐ 496 Bert Roberge .10 .05 .01
☐ 497 Dick Ruthven .10 .05 .01
☐ 498 Tito Landrum .10 .05 .01
☐ 499 Sixto Lezcano .10 .05 .01
☐ 500 Johnny Bench 1.25 .55 .16
☐ 501 Larry Whisenton .10 .05 .01
☐ 502 Manny Sarmiento .10 .05 .01
☐ 503 Fred Breining .10 .05 .01
☐ 504 Bill Campbell .10 .05 .01
☐ 505 Todd Cruz .10 .05 .01
☐ 506 Bob Bailor .10 .05 .01
☐ 507 Dave Stieb .20 .09 .03
☐ 508 Al Williams .10 .05 .01
☐ 509 Dan Ford .10 .05 .01
☐ 510 Gorman Thomas .10 .05 .01
☐ 511 Chet Lemon .10 .05 .01
☐ 512 Mike Torrez .10 .05 .01
☐ 513 Shane Rawley .10 .05 .01
☐ 514 Mark Belanger .10 .05 .01
☐ 515 Rodney Craig .10 .05 .01
☐ 516 Onix Concepcion .10 .05 .01
☐ 517 Mike Heath .10 .05 .01
☐ 518 Andre Dawson UER 1.50 .65 .19
(Middle name Fernando,
should be Nolan)
☐ 519 Luis Sanchez .10 .05 .01
☐ 520 Terry Bogener .10 .05 .01
☐ 521 Rudy Law .10 .05 .01
☐ 522 Ray Knight .12 .05 .02
☐ 523 Joe Lefebvre .10 .05 .01
☐ 524 Jim Wohlford .10 .05 .01
☐ 525 Julio Franco 6.00 2.70 .75
☐ 526 Ron Oester .10 .05 .01
☐ 527 Rick Mahler .10 .05 .01
☐ 528 Steve Nicosia .10 .05 .01
☐ 529 Junior Kennedy .10 .05 .01
☐ 530A Whitey Herzog MG .15 .07 .02
(Bio printed
black on white)
☐ 530B Whitey Herzog MG .15 .07 .02
(Bio printed
black on yellow)
☐ 531A Don Sutton .40 .18 .05
(Blue border
on photo)
☐ 531B Don Sutton .40 .18 .05
(Green border
on photo)
☐ 532 Mark Brouhard .10 .05 .01
☐ 533A Sparky Anderson MG .15 .07 .02
(Bio printed
black on white)
☐ 533B Sparky Anderson MG .15 .07 .02
(Bio printed
black on yellow)
☐ 534 Roger LaFrancois .10 .05 .01
☐ 535 George Frazier .10 .05 .01
☐ 536 Tom Niedenfuer .10 .05 .01
☐ 537 Ed Glynn .10 .05 .01
☐ 538 Lee May .10 .05 .01
☐ 539 Bob Kearney .10 .05 .01
☐ 540 Tim Raines .60 .25 .08
☐ 541 Paul Mirabella .10 .05 .01
☐ 542 Luis Tiant .12 .05 .02
☐ 543 Ron LeFlore .12 .05 .02
☐ 544 Dave LaPoint .12 .05 .02
☐ 545 Randy Moffitt .10 .05 .01
☐ 546 Luis Aguayo .10 .05 .01
☐ 547 Brad Lesley .10 .05 .01
☐ 548 Luis Salazar .10 .05 .01
☐ 549 John Candelaria .10 .05 .01
☐ 550 Dave Bergman .10 .05 .01
☐ 551 Bob Watson .12 .05 .02
☐ 552 Pat Tabler .10 .05 .01
☐ 553 Brent Gaff .10 .05 .01
☐ 554 Al Cowens .10 .05 .01
☐ 555 Tom Brunansky .40 .18 .05
☐ 556 Lloyd Moseby .10 .05 .01
☐ 557A Pascual Perez ERR 2.00 .90 .25
(Twins in glove)
☐ 557B Pascual Perez COR .15 .07 .02
(Braves in glove)
☐ 558 Willie Upshaw .10 .05 .01
☐ 559 Richie Zisk .10 .05 .01
☐ 560 Pat Zachry .10 .05 .01
☐ 561 Jay Johnstone .12 .05 .02
☐ 562 Carlos Diaz .10 .05 .01
☐ 563 John Tudor .12 .05 .02
☐ 564 Frank Robinson MG .30 .14 .04
☐ 565 Dave Edwards .10 .05 .01
☐ 566 Paul Householder .10 .05 .01
☐ 567 Ron Reed .10 .05 .01
☐ 568 Mike Ramsey .10 .05 .01
☐ 569 Kiko Garcia .10 .05 .01
☐ 570 Tommy John .15 .07 .02
☐ 571 Tony LaRussa MG .12 .05 .02
☐ 572 Joel Youngblood .10 .05 .01
☐ 573 Wayne Tolleson .10 .05 .01
☐ 574 Keith Creel .10 .05 .01
☐ 575 Billy Martin MG .15 .07 .02
☐ 576 Jerry Dybzinski .10 .05 .01
☐ 577 Rick Cerone .10 .05 .01
☐ 578 Tony Perez .30 .14 .04
☐ 579 Greg Brock .12 .05 .02
☐ 580 Glenn Wilson .12 .05 .02
☐ 581 Tim Stoddard .10 .05 .01
☐ 582 Bob McClure .10 .05 .01
☐ 583 Jim Dwyer .10 .05 .01
☐ 584 Ed Romero .10 .05 .01
☐ 585 Larry Herndon .10 .05 .01
☐ 586 Wade Boggs 24.00 11.00 3.00
☐ 587 Jay Howell .12 .05 .02
☐ 588 Dave Stewart .75 .35 .09
☐ 589 Bert Blyleven .30 .14 .04
☐ 590 Dick Howser MG .12 .05 .02
☐ 591 Wayne Gross .10 .05 .01
☐ 592 Terry Francona .10 .05 .01
☐ 593 Don Werner .10 .05 .01
☐ 594 Bill Stein .10 .05 .01
☐ 595 Jesse Barfield .20 .09 .03
☐ 596 Bob Molinaro .10 .05 .01
☐ 597 Mike Vail .10 .05 .01
☐ 598 Tony Gwynn 25.00 11.50 3.10
☐ 599 Gary Rajsich .10 .05 .01
☐ 600 Jerry Ujdur .10 .05 .01
☐ 601 Cliff Johnson .10 .05 .01
☐ 602 Jerry White .10 .05 .01
☐ 603 Bryan Clark .10 .05 .01
☐ 604 Joe Ferguson .10 .05 .01
☐ 605 Guy Sularz .10 .05 .01
☐ 606A Ozzie Virgil .15 .07 .02
(Green border
on photo)
☐ 606B Ozzie Virgil .15 .07 .02
(Orange border
on photo)
☐ 607 Terry Harper .10 .05 .01
☐ 608 Harvey Kuenn MG .12 .05 .02
☐ 609 Jim Sundberg .10 .05 .01
☐ 610 Willie Stargell .60 .25 .08
☐ 611 Reggie Smith .12 .05 .02
☐ 612 Rob Wilfong .10 .05 .01
☐ 613 The Niekro Brothers .25 .11 .03
Joe Niekro
Phil Niekro
☐ 614 Lee Elia MG .10 .05 .01
☐ 615 Mickey Hatcher .10 .05 .01
☐ 616 Jerry Hairston .10 .05 .01
☐ 617 John Martin .10 .05 .01
☐ 618 Wally Backman .12 .05 .02
☐ 619 Storm Davis .20 .09 .03
☐ 620 Alan Knicely .10 .05 .01
☐ 621 John Stuper .10 .05 .01
☐ 622 Matt Sinatro .10 .05 .01
☐ 623 Geno Petralli .12 .05 .02
☐ 624 Duane Walker .10 .05 .01
☐ 625 Dick Williams MG .10 .05 .01
☐ 626 Pat Corrales MG .10 .05 .01
☐ 627 Vern Ruhle .10 .05 .01
☐ 628 Joe Torre MG .12 .05 .02
☐ 629 Anthony Johnson .10 .05 .01
☐ 630 Steve Howe .10 .05 .01
☐ 631 Gary Woods .10 .05 .01
☐ 632 LaMarr Hoyt .10 .05 .01
☐ 633 Steve Swisher .10 .05 .01
☐ 634 Terry Leach .12 .05 .02
☐ 635 Jeff Newman .10 .05 .01
☐ 636 Brett Butler .50 .23 .06
☐ 637 Gary Gray .10 .05 .01
☐ 638 Lee Mazzilli .10 .05 .01
☐ 639A Ron Jackson ERR 15.00 6.75 1.90
(A's in glove)
☐ 639B Ron Jackson COR .12 .05 .02
(Angels in glove,
red border

on photo)			
☐ 639C Ron Jackson COR (Angels in glove, green border on photo)	.50	.23	.06
☐ 640 Juan Beniquez	.10	.05	.01
☐ 641 Dave Rucker	.10	.05	.01
☐ 642 Luis Pujols	.10	.05	.01
☐ 643 Rick Monday	.10	.05	.01
☐ 644 Hosken Powell	.10	.05	.01
☐ 645 The Chicken	.30	.14	.04
☐ 646 Dave Engle	.10	.05	.01
☐ 647 Dick Davis	.10	.05	.01
☐ 648 Frank Robinson Vida Blue Joe Morgan	.35	.16	.04
☐ 649 Al Chambers	.10	.05	.01
☐ 650 Jesus Vega	.10	.05	.01
☐ 651 Jeff Jones	.10	.05	.01
☐ 652 Marvis Foley	.10	.05	.01
☐ 653 Ty Cobb Puzzle Card	.15	.07	.02
☐ 654A Dick Perez/Diamond King Checklist (Unnumbered) ERR (Word "checklist" omitted from back)	.25	.03	.01
☐ 654B Dick Perez/Diamond King Checklist (Unnumbered) COR (Word "checklist" is on back)	.25	.03	.01
☐ 655 Checklist 1 (Unnumbered)	.15	.02	.00
☐ 656 Checklist 2 (Unnumbered)	.15	.02	.00
☐ 657 Checklist 3 (Unnumbered)	.15	.02	.00
☐ 658 Checklist 4 (Unnumbered)	.15	.02	.00
☐ 659 Checklist 5 (Unnumbered)	.15	.02	.00
☐ 660 Checklist 6 (Unnumbered)	.15	.02	.00

1983 Donruss Action All-Stars

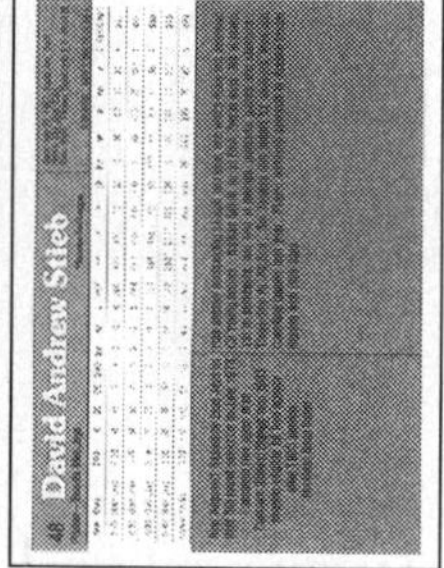

The cards in this 60-card set measure approximately 3 1/2" by 5". The 1983 Action All-Stars series depicts 60 major leaguers in a distinctive new style. Each card contains a large close-up on the left and an action photo on the right. Team affiliations appear as part of the background design, and the cards have cranberry color borders. The backs contain the card number, the player's major league line record, and biographical material. A 63-piece Mickey Mantle puzzle (three pieces on one card per pack) was marketed as an insert premium.

	NRMT-MT	EXC	G-VG
COMPLETE SET (60)	7.50	3.40	.95
COMMON PLAYER (1-60)	.07	.03	.01
☐ 1 Eddie Murray	.45	.20	.06
☐ 2 Dwight Evans	.15	.07	.02
☐ 3A Reggie Jackson ERR (Red screen on back covers some stats)	1.50	.65	.19
☐ 3B Reggie Jackson COR	.75	.35	.09
☐ 4 Greg Luzinski	.10	.05	.01
☐ 5 Larry Herndon	.07	.03	.01
☐ 6 Al Oliver	.10	.05	.01
☐ 7 Bill Buckner	.10	.05	.01
☐ 8 Jason Thompson	.07	.03	.01
☐ 9 Andre Dawson	.50	.23	.06
☐ 10 Greg Minton	.07	.03	.01
☐ 11 Terry Kennedy	.07	.03	.01
☐ 12 Phil Niekro	.25	.11	.03
☐ 13 Willie Wilson	.10	.05	.01
☐ 14 Johnny Bench	.45	.20	.06
☐ 15 Ron Guidry	.10	.05	.01
☐ 16 Hal McRae	.10	.05	.01
☐ 17 Damaso Garcia	.07	.03	.01
☐ 18 Gary Ward	.07	.03	.01
☐ 19 Cecil Cooper	.10	.05	.01
☐ 20 Keith Hernandez	.15	.07	.02
☐ 21 Ron Cey	.07	.03	.01
☐ 22 Rickey Henderson	.90	.40	.11
☐ 23 Nolan Ryan	2.00	.90	.25
☐ 24 Steve Carlton	.35	.16	.04
☐ 25 John Stearns	.07	.03	.01
☐ 26 Jim Sundberg	.07	.03	.01
☐ 27 Joaquin Andujar	.07	.03	.01
☐ 28 Gaylord Perry	.25	.11	.03
☐ 29 Jack Clark	.15	.07	.02
☐ 30 Bill Madlock	.07	.03	.01
☐ 31 Pete Rose	.75	.35	.09
☐ 32 Mookie Wilson	.07	.03	.01
☐ 33 Rollie Fingers	.25	.11	.03
☐ 34 Lonnie Smith	.10	.05	.01
☐ 35 Tony Pena	.07	.03	.01
☐ 36 Dave Winfield	.45	.20	.06
☐ 37 Tim Lollar	.07	.03	.01
☐ 38 Rod Carew	.35	.16	.04
☐ 39 Toby Harrah	.07	.03	.01
☐ 40 Buddy Bell	.07	.03	.01
☐ 41 Bruce Sutter	.10	.05	.01
☐ 42 George Brett	.75	.35	.09
☐ 43 Carlton Fisk	.60	.25	.08
☐ 44 Carl Yastrzemski	.75	.35	.09
☐ 45 Dale Murphy	.35	.16	.04
☐ 46 Bob Horner	.10	.05	.01
☐ 47 Dave Concepcion	.10	.05	.01
☐ 48 Dave Stieb	.15	.07	.02
☐ 49 Kent Hrbek	.15	.07	.02
☐ 50 Lance Parrish	.15	.07	.02
☐ 51 Joe Niekro	.10	.05	.01
☐ 52 Cal Ripken	1.50	.65	.19
☐ 53 Fernando Valenzuela	.15	.07	.02
☐ 54 Richie Zisk	.07	.03	.01
☐ 55 Leon Durham	.07	.03	.01
☐ 56 Robin Yount	.75	.35	.09
☐ 57 Mike Schmidt	1.00	.45	.13
☐ 58 Gary Carter	.35	.16	.04
☐ 59 Fred Lynn	.10	.05	.01
☐ 60 Checklist Card	.07	.03	.01

1983 Donruss HOF Heroes

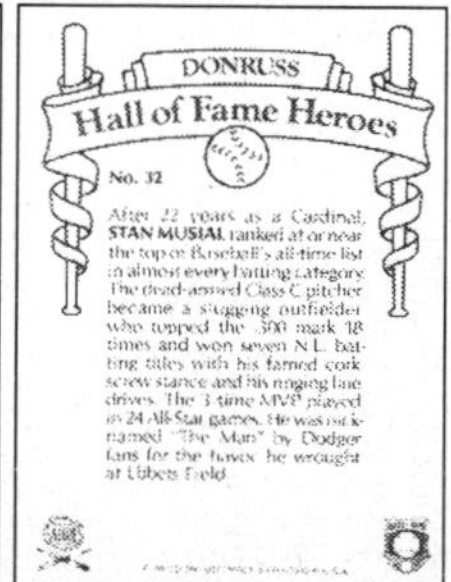

The cards in this 44-card set measure 2 1/2" by 3 1/2". Although it was issued with the same Mantle puzzle as the Action All Stars set, the Donruss Hall of Fame Heroes set is completely different in content and design. Of the 44 cards in the set, 42 are Dick Perez artwork portraying Hall of Fame members, while one card depicts the completed Mantle puzzle and the last card is a checklist. The red, white, and blue backs contain the card number and a short player biography. The cards were packaged eight cards plus one puzzle card (three pieces) for 30 cents in the summer of 1983.

	NRMT-MT	EXC	G-VG
COMPLETE SET (44)	7.50	3.40	.95
COMMON PLAYER (1-44)	.07	.03	.01
☐ 1 Ty Cobb	1.00	.45	.13
☐ 2 Walter Johnson	.35	.16	.04
☐ 3 Christy Mathewson	.35	.16	.04
☐ 4 Josh Gibson	.50	.23	.06
☐ 5 Honus Wagner	.35	.16	.04
☐ 6 Jackie Robinson	.35	.16	.04
☐ 7 Mickey Mantle	2.00	.90	.25
☐ 8 Luke Appling	.07	.03	.01
☐ 9 Ted Williams	.50	.23	.06
☐ 10 Johnny Mize	.15	.07	.02
☐ 11 Satchel Paige	.25	.11	.03
☐ 12 Lou Boudreau	.15	.07	.02
☐ 13 Jimmie Foxx	.15	.07	.02
☐ 14 Duke Snider	.25	.11	.03
☐ 15 Monte Irvin	.15	.07	.02
☐ 16 Hank Greenberg	.15	.07	.02
☐ 17 Roberto Clemente	.25	.11	.03
☐ 18 Al Kaline	.25	.11	.03
☐ 19 Frank Robinson	.25	.11	.03
☐ 20 Joe Cronin	.07	.03	.01
☐ 21 Burleigh Grimes	.07	.03	.01
☐ 22 The Waner Brothers Paul Waner Lloyd Waner	.07	.03	.01
☐ 23 Grover Alexander	.15	.07	.02
☐ 24 Yogi Berra	.25	.11	.03
☐ 25 Cool Papa Bell	.07	.03	.01
☐ 26 Bill Dickey	.15	.07	.02
☐ 27 Cy Young	.25	.11	.03
☐ 28 Charlie Gehringer	.07	.03	.01
☐ 29 Dizzy Dean	.35	.16	.04
☐ 30 Bob Lemon	.15	.07	.02
☐ 31 Red Ruffing	.07	.03	.01
☐ 32 Stan Musial	.35	.16	.04
☐ 33 Carl Hubbell	.15	.07	.02
☐ 34 Hank Aaron	.50	.23	.06
☐ 35 John McGraw	.07	.03	.01
☐ 36 Bob Feller	.35	.16	.04
☐ 37 Casey Stengel	.15	.07	.02
☐ 38 Ralph Kiner	.15	.07	.02
☐ 39 Roy Campanella	.25	.11	.03
☐ 40 Mel Ott	.15	.07	.02
☐ 41 Robin Roberts	.15	.07	.02
☐ 42 Early Wynn	.15	.07	.02
☐ 43 Mantle Puzzle Card	.50	.23	.06
☐ 44 Checklist Card	.07	.03	.01

1984 Donruss

The 1984 Donruss set contains a total of 660 cards, each measuring 2 1/2" by 3 1/2"; however, only 658 are numbered. The first 26 cards in the set are again Diamond Kings (DK), although the drawings this year were styled differently and are easily differentiated from other DK issues. A new feature, Rated Rookies (RR), was introduced with this set with Bill Madden's 20 selections comprising numbers 27 through 46. Two "Living Legend" cards designated A (featuring Gaylord Perry and Rollie Fingers) and B (featuring Johnny Bench and Carl Yastrzemski) were issued as bonus cards in wax packs, but were not issued in the vending sets sold to hobby dealers. The seven unnumbered checklist cards are arbitrarily assigned numbers 652 through 658 and are listed at the end of the list below. The designs on the fronts of the Donruss cards changed considerably from the past two years. The backs contain statistics and are printed in green and black ink. The cards were distributed with a 63-piece puzzle of Duke Snider. There are no extra variation cards included in the complete set price below. The variation cards apparently resulted from a different printing for the factory sets as the Darling and Stenhouse no number variations as well as the Perez-Steel errors were corrected in the factory sets which were released later in the year. The key Rookie Cards in this set are Joe Carter, Ron Darling, Sid Fernandez, Tony Fernandez, Brian Harper, Don Mattingly, Kevin McReynolds, Darryl Strawberry, and Andy Van Slyke.

	NRMT-MT	EXC	G-VG
COMPLETE SET (658)	325.00	145.00	40.00
COMPLETE FACT.SET (658)	400.00	180.00	50.00
COMMON PLAYER (1-658)	.30	.14	.04
☐ 1A Robin Yount DK ERR (Perez Steel)	5.00	2.30	.60
☐ 1B Robin Yount DK COR	5.00	2.30	.60
☐ 2A Dave Concepcion DK ERR (Perez Steel)	.50	.23	.06
☐ 2B Dave Concepcion DK COR	.50	.23	.06
☐ 3A Dwayne Murphy DK ERR (Perez Steel)	.40	.18	.05
☐ 3B Dwayne Murphy DK COR	.40	.18	.05
☐ 4A John Castino DK ERR (Perez Steel)	.40	.18	.05
☐ 4B John Castino DK COR	.40	.18	.05
☐ 5A Leon Durham DK ERR (Perez Steel)	.40	.18	.05
☐ 5B Leon Durham DK COR	.40	.18	.05
☐ 6A Rusty Staub DK ERR (Perez Steel)	.50	.23	.06
☐ 6B Rusty Staub DK COR	.50	.23	.06
☐ 7A Jack Clark DK ERR (Perez Steel)	.50	.23	.06
☐ 7B Jack Clark DK COR	.50	.23	.06
☐ 8A Dave Dravecky DK ERR (Perez Steel)	.50	.23	.06
☐ 8B Dave Dravecky DK COR	.50	.23	.06
☐ 9A Al Oliver DK ERR (Perez Steel)	.40	.18	.05
☐ 9B Al Oliver DK COR	.40	.18	.05
☐ 10A Dave Righetti DK ERR (Perez Steel)	.40	.18	.05
☐ 10B Dave Righetti DK COR	.40	.18	.05
☐ 11A Hal McRae DK ERR (Perez Steel)	.40	.18	.05
☐ 11B Hal McRae DK COR	.40	.18	.05
☐ 12A Ray Knight DK ERR (Perez Steel)	.40	.18	.05
☐ 12B Ray Knight DK COR	.40	.18	.05
☐ 13A Bruce Sutter DK ERR (Perez Steel)	.50	.23	.06
☐ 13B Bruce Sutter DK COR	.50	.23	.06
☐ 14A Bob Horner DK ERR (Perez Steel)	.40	.18	.05
☐ 14B Bob Horner DK COR	.40	.18	.05
☐ 15A Lance Parrish DK ERR (Perez Steel)	.50	.23	.06
☐ 15B Lance Parrish DK COR	.50	.23	.06
☐ 16A Matt Young DK ERR (Perez Steel)	.40	.18	.05
☐ 16B Matt Young DK COR	.40	.18	.05
☐ 17A Fred Lynn DK ERR (Perez Steel) (A's logo on back)	.50	.23	.06
☐ 17B Fred Lynn DK COR	.50	.23	.06
☐ 18A Ron Kittle DK ERR (Perez Steel)	.40	.18	.05
☐ 18B Ron Kittle DK COR	.40	.18	.05
☐ 19A Jim Clancy DK ERR (Perez Steel)	.40	.18	.05
☐ 19B Jim Clancy DK COR	.40	.18	.05

20A	Bill Madlock DK ERR (Perez Steel)	.40	.18	.05
20B	Bill Madlock DK COR	.40	.18	.05
21A	Larry Parrish DK ERR (Perez Steel)	.40	.18	.05
21B	Larry Parrish DK COR	.40	.18	.05
22A	Eddie Murray DK ERR (Perez Steel)	2.00	.90	.25
22B	Eddie Murray DK COR	2.00	.90	.25
23A	Mike Schmidt DK ERR (Perez Steel)	4.00	1.80	.50
23B	Mike Schmidt DK COR	4.00	1.80	.50
24A	Pedro Guerrero DK ERR (Perez Steel)	.50	.23	.06
24B	Pedro Guerrero DK COR	.50	.23	.06
25A	Andre Thornton DK ERR (Perez Steel)	.40	.18	.05
25B	Andre Thornton DK COR	.40	.18	.05
26A	Wade Boggs DK ERR (Perez Steel)	4.50	2.00	.55
26B	Wade Boggs DK COR	4.50	2.00	.55
27	Joel Skinner RR	.35	.16	.04
28	Tommy Dunbar RR	.35	.16	.04
29A	Mike Stenhouse RR ERR (No number on back)	.35	.16	.04
29B	Mike Stenhouse RR COR (Numbered on back)	2.50	1.15	.30
30A	Ron Darling RR ERR (No number on back)	3.00	1.35	.40
30B	Ron Darling RR COR (Numbered on back)	25.00	11.50	3.10
31	Dion James RR	.45	.20	.06
32	Tony Fernandez RR	6.00	2.70	.75
33	Angel Salazar RR	.35	.16	.04
34	Kevin McReynolds RR	3.50	1.55	.45
35	Dick Schofield RR	.50	.23	.06
36	Brad Komminsk RR	.35	.16	.04
37	Tim Teufel RR	.50	.23	.06
38	Doug Frobel RR	.35	.16	.04
39	Greg Gagne RR	1.00	.45	.13
40	Mike Fuentes RR	.35	.16	.04
41	Joe Carter RR	45.00	20.00	5.75
42	Mike Brown RR (Angels OF)	.35	.16	.04
43	Mike Jeffcoat RR	.35	.16	.04
44	Sid Fernandez RR	5.00	2.30	.60
45	Brian Dayett RR	.35	.16	.04
46	Chris Smith RR	.35	.16	.04
47	Eddie Murray	6.50	2.90	.80
48	Robin Yount	10.00	4.50	1.25
49	Lance Parrish	.50	.23	.06
50	Jim Rice	.50	.23	.06
51	Dave Winfield	8.00	3.60	1.00
52	Fernando Valenzuela	.40	.18	.05
53	George Brett	10.00	4.50	1.25
54	Rickey Henderson	14.00	6.25	1.75
55	Gary Carter	2.00	.90	.25
56	Buddy Bell	.40	.18	.05
57	Reggie Jackson	5.00	2.30	.60
58	Harold Baines	1.00	.45	.13
59	Ozzie Smith	6.50	2.90	.80
60	Nolan Ryan	27.00	12.00	3.40
61	Pete Rose	5.00	2.30	.60
62	Ron Oester	.30	.14	.04
63	Steve Garvey	1.50	.65	.19
64	Jason Thompson	.30	.14	.04
65	Jack Clark	.40	.18	.05
66	Dale Murphy	3.00	1.35	.40
67	Leon Durham	.30	.14	.04
68	Darryl Strawberry	45.00	20.00	5.75
69	Richie Zisk	.30	.14	.04
70	Kent Hrbek	1.00	.45	.13
71	Dave Stieb	.40	.18	.05
72	Ken Schrom	.30	.14	.04
73	George Bell	3.00	1.35	.40
74	John Moses	.30	.14	.04
75	Ed Lynch	.30	.14	.04
76	Chuck Rainey	.30	.14	.04
77	Biff Pocoroba	.30	.14	.04
78	Cecilio Guante	.30	.14	.04
79	Jim Barr	.30	.14	.04
80	Kurt Bevacqua	.30	.14	.04
81	Tom Foley	.30	.14	.04
82	Joe Lefebvre	.30	.14	.04
83	Andy Van Slyke	12.00	5.50	1.50
84	Bob Lillis MG	.30	.14	.04
85	Ricky Adams	.30	.14	.04
86	Jerry Hairston	.30	.14	.04
87	Bob James	.30	.14	.04
88	Joe Altobelli MG	.30	.14	.04
89	Ed Romero	.30	.14	.04
90	John Grubb	.30	.14	.04
91	John Henry Johnson	.30	.14	.04
92	Juan Espino	.30	.14	.04
93	Candy Maldonado	.50	.23	.06
94	Andre Thornton	.30	.14	.04
95	Onix Concepcion	.30	.14	.04
96	Donnie Hill UER (Listed as P, should be 2B)	.40	.18	.05
97	Andre Dawson UER (Wrong middle name, should be Nolan)	6.50	2.90	.80
98	Frank Tanana	.40	.18	.05
99	Curt Wilkerson	.30	.14	.04
100	Larry Gura	.30	.14	.04
101	Dwayne Murphy	.30	.14	.04
102	Tom Brennan	.30	.14	.04
103	Dave Righetti	.40	.18	.05
104	Steve Sax	1.25	.55	.16
105	Dan Petry	.30	.14	.04
106	Cal Ripken	30.00	13.50	3.80
107	Paul Molitor UER ('83 stats should say .270 BA, 608 AB, and 164 hits)	3.00	1.35	.40
108	Fred Lynn	.40	.18	.05
109	Neil Allen	.30	.14	.04
110	Joe Niekro	.40	.18	.05
111	Steve Carlton	5.00	2.30	.60
112	Terry Kennedy	.30	.14	.04
113	Bill Madlock	.40	.18	.05
114	Chili Davis	.60	.25	.08
115	Jim Gantner	.40	.18	.05
116	Tom Seaver	7.00	3.10	.85
117	Bill Buckner	.40	.18	.05
118	Bill Caudill	.30	.14	.04
119	Jim Clancy	.30	.14	.04
120	John Castino	.30	.14	.04
121	Dave Concepcion	.40	.18	.05
122	Greg Luzinski	.40	.18	.05
123	Mike Boddicker	.30	.14	.04
124	Pete Ladd	.30	.14	.04
125	Juan Berenguer	.30	.14	.04
126	John Montefusco	.30	.14	.04
127	Ed Jurak	.30	.14	.04
128	Tom Niedenfuer	.30	.14	.04
129	Bert Blyleven	1.00	.45	.13
130	Bud Black	.30	.14	.04
131	Gorman Heimueller	.30	.14	.04
132	Dan Schatzeder	.30	.14	.04
133	Ron Jackson	.30	.14	.04
134	Tom Henke	2.00	.90	.25
135	Kevin Hickey	.30	.14	.04
136	Mike Scott	.40	.18	.05
137	Bo Diaz	.30	.14	.04
138	Glenn Brummer	.30	.14	.04
139	Sid Monge	.30	.14	.04
140	Rich Gale	.30	.14	.04
141	Brett Butler	1.00	.45	.13
142	Brian Harper	2.00	.90	.25
143	John Rabb	.30	.14	.04
144	Gary Woods	.30	.14	.04
145	Pat Putnam	.30	.14	.04
146	Jim Acker	.30	.14	.04
147	Mickey Hatcher	.30	.14	.04
148	Todd Cruz	.30	.14	.04
149	Tom Tellmann	.30	.14	.04
150	John Wockenfuss	.30	.14	.04
151	Wade Boggs	15.00	6.75	1.90
152	Don Baylor	.40	.18	.05
153	Bob Welch	.50	.23	.06
154	Alan Bannister	.30	.14	.04
155	Willie Aikens	.30	.14	.04
156	Jeff Burroughs	.30	.14	.04
157	Bryan Little	.30	.14	.04
158	Bob Boone	.40	.18	.05
159	Dave Hostetler	.30	.14	.04
160	Jerry Dybzinski	.30	.14	.04
161	Mike Madden	.30	.14	.04
162	Luis DeLeon	.30	.14	.04
163	Willie Hernandez	.40	.18	.05
164	Frank Pastore	.30	.14	.04
165	Rick Camp	.30	.14	.04
166	Lee Mazzilli	.30	.14	.04
167	Scot Thompson	.30	.14	.04
168	Bob Forsch	.30	.14	.04
169	Mike Flanagan	.30	.14	.04
170	Rick Manning	.30	.14	.04
171	Chet Lemon	.30	.14	.04
172	Jerry Remy	.30	.14	.04

173 Ron Guidry .40 .18 .05
174 Pedro Guerrero .40 .18 .05
175 Willie Wilson .40 .18 .05
176 Carney Lansford .40 .18 .05
177 Al Oliver .40 .18 .05
178 Jim Sundberg .30 .14 .04
179 Bobby Grich .40 .18 .05
180 Rich Dotson .30 .14 .04
181 Joaquin Andujar .30 .14 .04
182 Jose Cruz .40 .18 .05
183 Mike Schmidt 15.00 6.75 1.90
184 Gary Redus .50 .23 .06
185 Garry Templeton .40 .18 .05
186 Tony Pena .40 .18 .05
187 Greg Minton .30 .14 .04
188 Phil Niekro 1.25 .55 .16
189 Ferguson Jenkins 1.25 .55 .16
190 Mookie Wilson .40 .18 .05
191 Jim Beattie .30 .14 .04
192 Gary Ward .30 .14 .04
193 Jesse Barfield .40 .18 .05
194 Pete Filson .30 .14 .04
195 Roy Lee Jackson .30 .14 .04
196 Rick Sweet .30 .14 .04
197 Jesse Orosco .30 .14 .04
198 Steve Lake .30 .14 .04
199 Ken Dayley .30 .14 .04
200 Manny Sarmiento .30 .14 .04
201 Mark Davis .40 .18 .05
202 Tim Flannery .30 .14 .04
203 Bill Scherrer .30 .14 .04
204 Al Holland .30 .14 .04
205 Dave Von Ohlen .30 .14 .04
206 Mike LaCoss .30 .14 .04
207 Juan Beniquez .30 .14 .04
208 Juan Agosto .30 .14 .04
209 Bobby Ramos .30 .14 .04
210 Al Bumbry .30 .14 .04
211 Mark Brouhard .30 .14 .04
212 Howard Bailey .30 .14 .04
213 Bruce Hurst .40 .18 .05
214 Bob Shirley .30 .14 .04
215 Pat Zachry .30 .14 .04
216 Julio Franco 3.00 1.35 .40
217 Mike Armstrong .30 .14 .04
218 Dave Beard .30 .14 .04
219 Steve Rogers .30 .14 .04
220 John Butcher .30 .14 .04
221 Mike Smithson .30 .14 .04
222 Frank White .40 .18 .05
223 Mike Heath .30 .14 .04
224 Chris Bando .30 .14 .04
225 Roy Smalley .30 .14 .04
226 Dusty Baker .40 .18 .05
227 Lou Whitaker 1.75 .80 .22
228 John Lowenstein .30 .14 .04
229 Ben Oglivie .30 .14 .04
230 Doug DeCinces .30 .14 .04
231 Lonnie Smith .40 .18 .05
232 Ray Knight .40 .18 .05
233 Gary Matthews .40 .18 .05
234 Juan Bonilla .30 .14 .04
235 Rod Scurry .30 .14 .04
236 Atlee Hammaker .30 .14 .04
237 Mike Caldwell .30 .14 .04
238 Keith Hernandez .40 .18 .05
239 Larry Bowa .40 .18 .05
240 Tony Bernazard .30 .14 .04
241 Damaso Garcia .30 .14 .04
242 Tom Brunansky .40 .18 .05
243 Dan Driessen .30 .14 .04
244 Ron Kittle .40 .18 .05
245 Tim Stoddard .30 .14 .04
246 Bob L. Gibson (Brewers Pitcher) .30 .14 .04
247 Marty Castillo .30 .14 .04
248 Don Mattingly UER ("Traiing" on back) 45.00 20.00 5.75
249 Jeff Newman .30 .14 .04
250 Alejandro Pena .75 .35 .09
251 Toby Harrah .30 .14 .04
252 Cesar Geronimo .30 .14 .04
253 Tom Underwood .30 .14 .04
254 Doug Flynn .30 .14 .04
255 Andy Hassler .30 .14 .04
256 Odell Jones .30 .14 .04
257 Rudy Law .30 .14 .04
258 Harry Spilman .30 .14 .04
259 Marty Bystrom .30 .14 .04
260 Dave Rucker .30 .14 .04
261 Ruppert Jones .30 .14 .04
262 Jeff R. Jones (Reds OF) .30 .14 .04
263 Gerald Perry .40 .18 .05
264 Gene Tenace .30 .14 .04
265 Brad Wellman .30 .14 .04
266 Dickie Noles .30 .14 .04
267 Jamie Allen .30 .14 .04
268 Jim Gott .30 .14 .04
269 Ron Davis .30 .14 .04
270 Benny Ayala .30 .14 .04
271 Ned Yost .30 .14 .04
272 Dave Rozema .30 .14 .04
273 Dave Stapleton .30 .14 .04
274 Lou Piniella .40 .18 .05
275 Jose Morales .30 .14 .04
276 Broderick Perkins .30 .14 .04
277 Butch Davis .30 .14 .04
278 Tony Phillips 2.50 1.15 .30
279 Jeff Reardon 2.50 1.15 .30
280 Ken Forsch .30 .14 .04
281 Pete O'Brien .75 .35 .09
282 Tom Paciorek .40 .18 .05
283 Frank LaCorte .30 .14 .04
284 Tim Lollar .30 .14 .04
285 Greg Gross .30 .14 .04
286 Alex Trevino .30 .14 .04
287 Gene Garber .30 .14 .04
288 Dave Parker 1.00 .45 .13
289 Lee Smith 3.00 1.35 .40
290 Dave LaPoint .40 .18 .05
291 John Shelby .30 .14 .04
292 Charlie Moore .30 .14 .04
293 Alan Trammell 1.75 .80 .22
294 Tony Armas .30 .14 .04
295 Shane Rawley .30 .14 .04
296 Greg Brock .30 .14 .04
297 Hal McRae .40 .18 .05
298 Mike Davis .30 .14 .04
299 Tim Raines 1.50 .65 .19
300 Bucky Dent .40 .18 .05
301 Tommy John .40 .18 .05
302 Carlton Fisk 5.00 2.30 .60
303 Darrell Porter .30 .14 .04
304 Dickie Thon .30 .14 .04
305 Garry Maddox .30 .14 .04
306 Cesar Cedeno .40 .18 .05
307 Gary Lucas .30 .14 .04
308 Johnny Ray .30 .14 .04
309 Andy McGaffigan .30 .14 .04
310 Claudell Washington .30 .14 .04
311 Ryne Sandberg 30.00 13.50 3.80
312 George Foster .40 .18 .05
313 Spike Owen .50 .23 .06
314 Gary Gaetti .40 .18 .05
315 Willie Upshaw .30 .14 .04
316 Al Williams .30 .14 .04
317 Jorge Orta .30 .14 .04
318 Orlando Mercado .30 .14 .04
319 Junior Ortiz .30 .14 .04
320 Mike Proly .30 .14 .04
321 Randy Johnson UER ('72-'82 stats are from Twins' Randy Johnson, '83 stats are from Braves' Randy Johnson) .30 .14 .04
322 Jim Morrison .30 .14 .04
323 Max Venable .30 .14 .04
324 Tony Gwynn 20.00 9.00 2.50
325 Duane Walker .30 .14 .04
326 Ozzie Virgil .30 .14 .04
327 Jeff Lahti .30 .14 .04
328 Bill Dawley .30 .14 .04
329 Rob Wilfong .30 .14 .04
330 Marc Hill .30 .14 .04
331 Ray Burris .30 .14 .04
332 Allan Ramirez .30 .14 .04
333 Chuck Porter .30 .14 .04
334 Wayne Krenchicki .30 .14 .04
335 Gary Allenson .30 .14 .04
336 Bobby Meacham .30 .14 .04
337 Joe Beckwith .30 .14 .04
338 Rick Sutcliffe .40 .18 .05
339 Mark Huismann .30 .14 .04
340 Tim Conroy .30 .14 .04
341 Scott Sanderson .30 .14 .04
342 Larry Biittner .30 .14 .04
343 Dave Stewart 1.50 .65 .19
344 Darryl Motley .30 .14 .04
345 Chris Codiroli .30 .14 .04
346 Rich Behenna .30 .14 .04
347 Andre Robertson .30 .14 .04
348 Mike Marshall .40 .18 .05
349 Larry Herndon .30 .14 .04
350 Rich Dauer .30 .14 .04
351 Cecil Cooper .40 .18 .05

☐	352	Rod Carew	5.00	2.30	.60
☐	353	Willie McGee	1.25	.55	.16
☐	354	Phil Garner	.40	.18	.05
☐	355	Joe Morgan	1.50	.65	.19
☐	356	Luis Salazar	.30	.14	.04
☐	357	John Candelaria	.40	.18	.05
☐	358	Bill Laskey	.30	.14	.04
☐	359	Bob McClure	.30	.14	.04
☐	360	Dave Kingman	.40	.18	.05
☐	361	Ron Cey	.40	.18	.05
☐	362	Matt Young	.40	.18	.05
☐	363	Lloyd Moseby	.30	.14	.04
☐	364	Frank Viola	1.75	.80	.22
☐	365	Eddie Milner	.30	.14	.04
☐	366	Floyd Bannister	.30	.14	.04
☐	367	Dan Ford	.30	.14	.04
☐	368	Moose Haas	.30	.14	.04
☐	369	Doug Bair	.30	.14	.04
☐	370	Ray Fontenot	.30	.14	.04
☐	371	Luis Aponte	.30	.14	.04
☐	372	Jack Fimple	.30	.14	.04
☐	373	Neal Heaton	.40	.18	.05
☐	374	Greg Pryor	.30	.14	.04
☐	375	Wayne Gross	.30	.14	.04
☐	376	Charlie Lea	.30	.14	.04
☐	377	Steve Lubratich	.30	.14	.04
☐	378	Jon Matlack	.30	.14	.04
☐	379	Julio Cruz	.30	.14	.04
☐	380	John Mizerock	.30	.14	.04
☐	381	Kevin Gross	.60	.25	.08
☐	382	Mike Ramsey	.30	.14	.04
☐	383	Doug Gwosdz	.30	.14	.04
☐	384	Kelly Paris	.30	.14	.04
☐	385	Pete Falcone	.30	.14	.04
☐	386	Milt May	.30	.14	.04
☐	387	Fred Breining	.30	.14	.04
☐	388	Craig Lefferts	1.00	.45	.13
☐	389	Steve Henderson	.30	.14	.04
☐	390	Randy Moffitt	.30	.14	.04
☐	391	Ron Washington	.30	.14	.04
☐	392	Gary Roenicke	.30	.14	.04
☐	393	Tom Candiotti	1.75	.80	.22
☐	394	Larry Pashnick	.30	.14	.04
☐	395	Dwight Evans	.60	.25	.08
☐	396	Goose Gossage	.40	.18	.05
☐	397	Derrel Thomas	.30	.14	.04
☐	398	Juan Eichelberger	.30	.14	.04
☐	399	Leon Roberts	.30	.14	.04
☐	400	Dave Lopes	.40	.18	.05
☐	401	Bill Gullickson	.40	.18	.05
☐	402	Geoff Zahn	.30	.14	.04
☐	403	Billy Sample	.30	.14	.04
☐	404	Mike Squires	.30	.14	.04
☐	405	Craig Reynolds	.30	.14	.04
☐	406	Eric Show	.30	.14	.04
☐	407	John Denny	.30	.14	.04
☐	408	Dann Bilardello	.30	.14	.04
☐	409	Bruce Benedict	.30	.14	.04
☐	410	Kent Tekulve	.40	.18	.05
☐	411	Mel Hall	.75	.35	.09
☐	412	John Stuper	.30	.14	.04
☐	413	Rick Dempsey	.40	.18	.05
☐	414	Don Sutton	1.25	.55	.16
☐	415	Jack Morris	4.00	1.80	.50
☐	416	John Tudor	.40	.18	.05
☐	417	Willie Randolph	.40	.18	.05
☐	418	Jerry Reuss	.30	.14	.04
☐	419	Don Slaught	.40	.18	.05
☐	420	Steve McCatty	.30	.14	.04
☐	421	Tim Wallach	.40	.18	.05
☐	422	Larry Parrish	.30	.14	.04
☐	423	Brian Downing	.40	.18	.05
☐	424	Britt Burns	.30	.14	.04
☐	425	David Green	.30	.14	.04
☐	426	Jerry Mumphrey	.30	.14	.04
☐	427	Ivan DeJesus	.30	.14	.04
☐	428	Mario Soto	.30	.14	.04
☐	429	Gene Richards	.30	.14	.04
☐	430	Dale Berra	.30	.14	.04
☐	431	Darrell Evans	.40	.18	.05
☐	432	Glenn Hubbard	.30	.14	.04
☐	433	Jody Davis	.30	.14	.04
☐	434	Danny Heep	.30	.14	.04
☐	435	Ed Nunez	.30	.14	.04
☐	436	Bobby Castillo	.30	.14	.04
☐	437	Ernie Whitt	.30	.14	.04
☐	438	Scott Ullger	.30	.14	.04
☐	439	Doyle Alexander	.30	.14	.04
☐	440	Domingo Ramos	.30	.14	.04
☐	441	Craig Swan	.30	.14	.04
☐	442	Warren Brusstar	.30	.14	.04
☐	443	Len Barker	.30	.14	.04
☐	444	Mike Easler	.30	.14	.04
☐	445	Renie Martin	.30	.14	.04
☐	446	Dennis Rasmussen	.40	.18	.05
☐	447	Ted Power	.30	.14	.04
☐	448	Charles Hudson	.30	.14	.04
☐	449	Danny Cox	.40	.18	.05
☐	450	Kevin Bass	.30	.14	.04
☐	451	Daryl Sconiers	.30	.14	.04
☐	452	Scott Fletcher	.30	.14	.04
☐	453	Bryn Smith	.30	.14	.04
☐	454	Jim Dwyer	.30	.14	.04
☐	455	Rob Picciolo	.30	.14	.04
☐	456	Enos Cabell	.30	.14	.04
☐	457	Dennis Boyd	.40	.18	.05
☐	458	Butch Wynegar	.30	.14	.04
☐	459	Burt Hooton	.30	.14	.04
☐	460	Ron Hassey	.30	.14	.04
☐	461	Danny Jackson	.75	.35	.09
☐	462	Bob Kearney	.30	.14	.04
☐	463	Terry Francona	.30	.14	.04
☐	464	Wayne Tolleson	.30	.14	.04
☐	465	Mickey Rivers	.30	.14	.04
☐	466	John Wathan	.30	.14	.04
☐	467	Bill Almon	.30	.14	.04
☐	468	George Vukovich	.30	.14	.04
☐	469	Steve Kemp	.30	.14	.04
☐	470	Ken Landreaux	.30	.14	.04
☐	471	Milt Wilcox	.30	.14	.04
☐	472	Tippy Martinez	.30	.14	.04
☐	473	Ted Simmons	.40	.18	.05
☐	474	Tim Foli	.30	.14	.04
☐	475	George Hendrick	.30	.14	.04
☐	476	Terry Puhl	.30	.14	.04
☐	477	Von Hayes	.40	.18	.05
☐	478	Bobby Brown	.30	.14	.04
☐	479	Lee Lacy	.30	.14	.04
☐	480	Joel Youngblood	.30	.14	.04
☐	481	Jim Slaton	.30	.14	.04
☐	482	Mike Fitzgerald	.30	.14	.04
☐	483	Keith Moreland	.30	.14	.04
☐	484	Ron Roenicke	.30	.14	.04
☐	485	Luis Leal	.30	.14	.04
☐	486	Bryan Oelkers	.30	.14	.04
☐	487	Bruce Berenyi	.30	.14	.04
☐	488	LaMarr Hoyt	.30	.14	.04
☐	489	Joe Nolan	.30	.14	.04
☐	490	Marshall Edwards	.30	.14	.04
☐	491	Mike Laga	.30	.14	.04
☐	492	Rick Cerone	.30	.14	.04
☐	493	Rick Miller UER (Listed as Mike on card front)	.30	.14	.04
☐	494	Rick Honeycutt	.30	.14	.04
☐	495	Mike Hargrove	.40	.18	.05
☐	496	Joe Simpson	.30	.14	.04
☐	497	Keith Atherton	.30	.14	.04
☐	498	Chris Welsh	.30	.14	.04
☐	499	Bruce Kison	.30	.14	.04
☐	500	Bobby Johnson	.30	.14	.04
☐	501	Jerry Koosman	.40	.18	.05
☐	502	Frank DiPino	.30	.14	.04
☐	503	Tony Perez	1.00	.45	.13
☐	504	Ken Oberkfell	.30	.14	.04
☐	505	Mark Thurmond	.30	.14	.04
☐	506	Joe Price	.30	.14	.04
☐	507	Pascual Perez	.30	.14	.04
☐	508	Marvell Wynne	.30	.14	.04
☐	509	Mike Krukow	.30	.14	.04
☐	510	Dick Ruthven	.30	.14	.04
☐	511	Al Cowens	.30	.14	.04
☐	512	Cliff Johnson	.30	.14	.04
☐	513	Randy Bush	.40	.18	.05
☐	514	Sammy Stewart	.30	.14	.04
☐	515	Bill Schroeder	.30	.14	.04
☐	516	Aurelio Lopez	.30	.14	.04
☐	517	Mike G. Brown (Red Sox pitcher)	.30	.14	.04
☐	518	Graig Nettles	.40	.18	.05
☐	519	Dave Sax	.30	.14	.04
☐	520	Jerry Willard	.30	.14	.04
☐	521	Paul Splittorff	.30	.14	.04
☐	522	Tom Burgmeier	.30	.14	.04
☐	523	Chris Speier	.30	.14	.04
☐	524	Bobby Clark	.30	.14	.04
☐	525	George Wright	.30	.14	.04
☐	526	Dennis Lamp	.30	.14	.04
☐	527	Tony Scott	.30	.14	.04
☐	528	Ed Whitson	.30	.14	.04
☐	529	Ron Reed	.30	.14	.04
☐	530	Charlie Puleo	.30	.14	.04
☐	531	Jerry Royster	.30	.14	.04
☐	532	Don Robinson	.30	.14	.04
☐	533	Steve Trout	.30	.14	.04
☐	534	Bruce Sutter	.40	.18	.05

☐ 535 Bob Horner .40 .18 .05
☐ 536 Pat Tabler .30 .14 .04
☐ 537 Chris Chambliss .40 .18 .05
☐ 538 Bob Ojeda .30 .14 .04
☐ 539 Alan Ashby .30 .14 .04
☐ 540 Jay Johnstone .40 .18 .05
☐ 541 Bob Dernier .30 .14 .04
☐ 542 Brook Jacoby .50 .23 .06
☐ 543 U.L. Washington .30 .14 .04
☐ 544 Danny Darwin .30 .14 .04
☐ 545 Kiko Garcia .30 .14 .04
☐ 546 Vance Law UER .30 .14 .04
(Listed as P
on card front)
☐ 547 Tug McGraw .40 .18 .05
☐ 548 Dave Smith .30 .14 .04
☐ 549 Len Matuszek .30 .14 .04
☐ 550 Tom Hume .30 .14 .04
☐ 551 Dave Dravecky .50 .23 .06
☐ 552 Rick Rhoden .30 .14 .04
☐ 553 Duane Kuiper .30 .14 .04
☐ 554 Rusty Staub .40 .18 .05
☐ 555 Bill Campbell .30 .14 .04
☐ 556 Mike Torrez .30 .14 .04
☐ 557 Dave Henderson .60 .25 .08
☐ 558 Len Whitehouse .30 .14 .04
☐ 559 Barry Bonnell .30 .14 .04
☐ 560 Rick Lysander .30 .14 .04
☐ 561 Garth Iorg .30 .14 .04
☐ 562 Bryan Clark .30 .14 .04
☐ 563 Brian Giles .30 .14 .04
☐ 564 Vern Ruhle .30 .14 .04
☐ 565 Steve Bedrosian .40 .18 .05
☐ 566 Larry McWilliams .30 .14 .04
☐ 567 Jeff Leonard UER .30 .14 .04
(Listed as P
on card front)
☐ 568 Alan Wiggins .30 .14 .04
☐ 569 Jeff Russell 1.00 .45 .13
☐ 570 Salome Barojas .30 .14 .04
☐ 571 Dane Iorg .30 .14 .04
☐ 572 Bob Knepper .30 .14 .04
☐ 573 Gary Lavelle .30 .14 .04
☐ 574 Gorman Thomas .30 .14 .04
☐ 575 Manny Trillo .30 .14 .04
☐ 576 Jim Palmer 5.00 2.30 .60
☐ 577 Dale Murray .30 .14 .04
☐ 578 Tom Brookens .30 .14 .04
☐ 579 Rich Gedman .30 .14 .04
☐ 580 Bill Doran .75 .35 .09
☐ 581 Steve Yeager .30 .14 .04
☐ 582 Dan Spillner .30 .14 .04
☐ 583 Dan Quisenberry .40 .18 .05
☐ 584 Rance Mulliniks .30 .14 .04
☐ 585 Storm Davis .40 .18 .05
☐ 586 Dave Schmidt .30 .14 .04
☐ 587 Bill Russell .30 .14 .04
☐ 588 Pat Sheridan .30 .14 .04
☐ 589 Rafael Ramirez .30 .14 .04
UER (A's on front)
☐ 590 Bud Anderson .30 .14 .04
☐ 591 George Frazier .30 .14 .04
☐ 592 Lee Tunnell .30 .14 .04
☐ 593 Kirk Gibson 1.00 .45 .13
☐ 594 Scott McGregor .30 .14 .04
☐ 595 Bob Bailor .30 .14 .04
☐ 596 Tommy Herr .40 .18 .05
☐ 597 Luis Sanchez .30 .14 .04
☐ 598 Dave Engle .30 .14 .04
☐ 599 Craig McMurtry .30 .14 .04
☐ 600 Carlos Diaz .30 .14 .04
☐ 601 Tom O'Malley .30 .14 .04
☐ 602 Nick Esasky .40 .18 .05
☐ 603 Ron Hodges .30 .14 .04
☐ 604 Ed VandeBerg .30 .14 .04
☐ 605 Alfredo Griffin .30 .14 .04
☐ 606 Glenn Hoffman .30 .14 .04
☐ 607 Hubie Brooks .40 .18 .05
☐ 608 Richard Barnes UER .30 .14 .04
(Photo actually
Neal Heaton)
☐ 609 Greg Walker .40 .18 .05
☐ 610 Ken Singleton .40 .18 .05
☐ 611 Mark Clear .30 .14 .04
☐ 612 Buck Martinez .30 .14 .04
☐ 613 Ken Griffey .40 .18 .05
☐ 614 Reid Nichols .30 .14 .04
☐ 615 Doug Sisk .30 .14 .04
☐ 616 Bob Brenly .30 .14 .04
☐ 617 Joey McLaughlin .30 .14 .04
☐ 618 Glenn Wilson .40 .18 .05
☐ 619 Bob Stoddard .30 .14 .04
☐ 620 Lenn Sakata UER .30 .14 .04
(Listed as Len
on card front)
☐ 621 Mike Young .30 .14 .04
☐ 622 John Stefero .30 .14 .04
☐ 623 Carmelo Martinez .40 .18 .05
☐ 624 Dave Bergman .30 .14 .04
☐ 625 Runnin' Reds UER 1.25 .55 .16
(Sic, Redbirds)
David Green
Willie McGee
Lonnie Smith
Ozzie Smith
☐ 626 Rudy May .30 .14 .04
☐ 627 Matt Keough .30 .14 .04
☐ 628 Jose DeLeon .40 .18 .05
☐ 629 Jim Essian .30 .14 .04
☐ 630 Darnell Coles .50 .23 .06
☐ 631 Mike Warren .30 .14 .04
☐ 632 Del Crandall MG .30 .14 .04
☐ 633 Dennis Martinez .40 .18 .05
☐ 634 Mike Moore .50 .23 .06
☐ 635 Lary Sorensen .30 .14 .04
☐ 636 Ricky Nelson .30 .14 .04
☐ 637 Omar Moreno .30 .14 .04
☐ 638 Charlie Hough .40 .18 .05
☐ 639 Dennis Eckersley 5.00 2.30 .60
☐ 640 Walt Terrell .50 .23 .06
☐ 641 Denny Walling .30 .14 .04
☐ 642 Dave Anderson .40 .18 .05
☐ 643 Jose Oquendo .40 .18 .05
☐ 644 Bob Stanley .30 .14 .04
☐ 645 Dave Geisel .30 .14 .04
☐ 646 Scott Garrelts .40 .18 .05
☐ 647 Gary Pettis .40 .18 .05
☐ 648 Duke Snider .40 .18 .05
Puzzle Card
☐ 649 Johnnie LeMaster .30 .14 .04
☐ 650 Dave Collins .30 .14 .04
☐ 651 The Chicken .50 .23 .06
☐ 652 DK Checklist .35 .04 .01
(Unnumbered)
☐ 653 Checklist 1-130 .35 .04 .01
(Unnumbered)
☐ 654 Checklist 131-234 .35 .04 .01
(Unnumbered)
☐ 655 Checklist 235-338 .35 .04 .01
(Unnumbered)
☐ 656 Checklist 339-442 .35 .04 .01
(Unnumbered)
☐ 657 Checklist 443-546 .35 .04 .01
(Unnumbered)
☐ 658 Checklist 547-651 .35 .04 .01
(Unnumbered)
☐ A0 Living Legends A 5.00 2.30 .60
Gaylord Perry
Rollie Fingers
☐ B0 Living Legends B 10.00 4.50 1.25
Carl Yastrzemski
Johnny Bench

1984 Donruss Action All-Stars

The cards in this 60-card set measure approximately 3 1/2" by 5". For the second year in a row, Donruss issued a postcard-size card set. The set was distributed with a 63-piece Ted Williams puzzle. Unlike last year, when the fronts of the cards contained both an action and a portrait shot of the player, the fronts of this year's cards contain only an action photo. On the backs, the top section contains the card number and a full-color portrait of the player pictured on the front. The bottom half features the player's career statistics.

	NRMT-MT	EXC	G-VG
COMPLETE SET (60)	7.50	3.40	.95
COMMON PLAYER (1-60)	.07	.03	.01
☐ 1 Gary Lavelle	.07	.03	.01
☐ 2 Willie McGee	.15	.07	.02
☐ 3 Tony Pena	.07	.03	.01
☐ 4 Lou Whitaker	.25	.11	.03
☐ 5 Robin Yount	.75	.35	.09
☐ 6 Doug DeCinces	.07	.03	.01
☐ 7 John Castino	.07	.03	.01
☐ 8 Terry Kennedy	.07	.03	.01
☐ 9 Rickey Henderson	.90	.40	.11
☐ 10 Bob Horner	.10	.05	.01
☐ 11 Harold Baines	.15	.07	.02
☐ 12 Buddy Bell	.07	.03	.01
☐ 13 Fernando Valenzuela	.10	.05	.01
☐ 14 Nolan Ryan	1.50	.65	.19
☐ 15 Andre Thornton	.07	.03	.01
☐ 16 Gary Redus	.07	.03	.01
☐ 17 Pedro Guerrero	.15	.07	.02
☐ 18 Andre Dawson	.50	.23	.06
☐ 19 Dave Stieb	.10	.05	.01
☐ 20 Cal Ripken	1.25	.55	.16
☐ 21 Ken Griffey	.15	.07	.02
☐ 22 Wade Boggs	.90	.40	.11
☐ 23 Keith Hernandez	.15	.07	.02
☐ 24 Steve Carlton	.35	.16	.04
☐ 25 Hal McRae	.10	.05	.01
☐ 26 John Lowenstein	.07	.03	.01
☐ 27 Fred Lynn	.10	.05	.01
☐ 28 Bill Buckner	.10	.05	.01
☐ 29 Chris Chambliss	.10	.05	.01
☐ 30 Richie Zisk	.07	.03	.01
☐ 31 Jack Clark	.10	.05	.01
☐ 32 George Hendrick	.07	.03	.01
☐ 33 Bill Madlock	.07	.03	.01
☐ 34 Lance Parrish	.15	.07	.02
☐ 35 Paul Molitor	.40	.18	.05
☐ 36 Reggie Jackson	.75	.35	.09
☐ 37 Kent Hrbek	.15	.07	.02
☐ 38 Steve Garvey	.35	.16	.04
☐ 39 Carney Lansford	.10	.05	.01
☐ 40 Dale Murphy	.40	.18	.05
☐ 41 Greg Luzinski	.10	.05	.01
☐ 42 Larry Parrish	.07	.03	.01
☐ 43 Ryne Sandberg	1.25	.55	.16
☐ 44 Dickie Thon	.07	.03	.01
☐ 45 Bert Blyleven	.10	.05	.01
☐ 46 Ron Oester	.07	.03	.01
☐ 47 Dusty Baker	.15	.07	.02
☐ 48 Steve Rogers	.07	.03	.01
☐ 49 Jim Clancy	.07	.03	.01
☐ 50 Eddie Murray	.45	.20	.06
☐ 51 Ron Guidry	.15	.07	.02
☐ 52 Jim Rice	.20	.09	.03
☐ 53 Tom Seaver	.75	.35	.09
☐ 54 Pete Rose	.75	.35	.09
☐ 55 George Brett	.75	.35	.09
☐ 56 Dan Quisenberry	.10	.05	.01
☐ 57 Mike Schmidt	1.00	.45	.13
☐ 58 Ted Simmons	.10	.05	.01
☐ 59 Dave Righetti	.10	.05	.01
☐ 60 Checklist Card	.07	.03	.01

1984 Donruss Champions

The cards in this 60-card set measure approximately 3 1/2" by 5". The 1984 Donruss Champions set is a hybrid photo/artwork issue. Grand Champions, listed GC in the checklist below, feature the artwork of Dick Perez of Perez-Steele Galleries. Current players in the set feature photographs. The theme of this postcard-size set features a Grand Champion and those current players that are directly behind him in a baseball statistical category, for example, Season Home Runs (1-7), Career Home Runs (8-13), Season Batting Average (14-19), Career Batting Average (20-25), Career Hits (26-30), Career Victories (31-36),

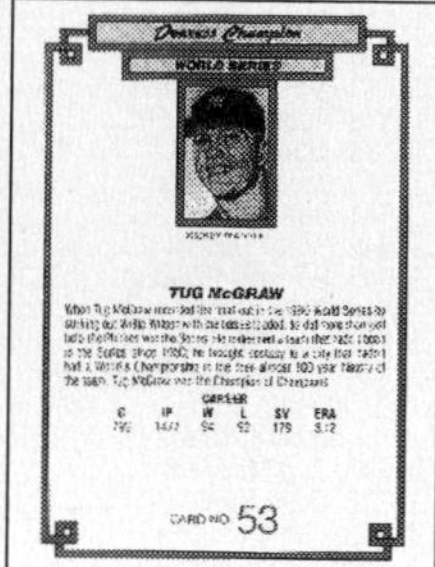

Career Strikeouts (37-42), Most Valuable Players (43-49), World Series stars (50-54), and All-Star heroes (55-59). The cards were issued in cello packs with pieces of the Duke Snider puzzle.

	NRMT-MT	EXC	G-VG
COMPLETE SET (60)	10.00	4.50	1.25
COMMON PLAYER (1-60)	.07	.03	.01
☐ 1 Babe Ruth GC	1.50	.65	.19
☐ 2 George Foster	.10	.05	.01
☐ 3 Dave Kingman	.10	.05	.01
☐ 4 Jim Rice	.15	.07	.02
☐ 5 Gorman Thomas	.07	.03	.01
☐ 6 Ben Oglivie	.07	.03	.01
☐ 7 Jeff Burroughs	.07	.03	.01
☐ 8 Hank Aaron GC	.50	.23	.06
☐ 9 Reggie Jackson	.75	.35	.09
☐ 10 Carl Yastrzemski	.60	.25	.08
☐ 11 Mike Schmidt	1.00	.45	.13
☐ 12 Graig Nettles	.10	.05	.01
☐ 13 Greg Luzinski	.07	.03	.01
☐ 14 Ted Williams GC	.60	.25	.08
☐ 15 George Brett	.75	.35	.09
☐ 16 Wade Boggs	.75	.35	.09
☐ 17 Hal McRae	.10	.05	.01
☐ 18 Bill Buckner	.10	.05	.01
☐ 19 Eddie Murray	.40	.18	.05
☐ 20 Rogers Hornsby GC	.15	.07	.02
☐ 21 Rod Carew	.30	.14	.04
☐ 22 Bill Madlock	.07	.03	.01
☐ 23 Lonnie Smith	.10	.05	.01
☐ 24 Cecil Cooper	.10	.05	.01
☐ 25 Ken Griffey	.10	.05	.01
☐ 26 Ty Cobb GC	.75	.35	.09
☐ 27 Pete Rose	.60	.25	.08
☐ 28 Rusty Staub	.07	.03	.01
☐ 29 Tony Perez	.20	.09	.03
☐ 30 Al Oliver	.10	.05	.01
☐ 31 Cy Young GC	.20	.09	.03
☐ 32 Gaylord Perry	.20	.09	.03
☐ 33 Ferguson Jenkins	.20	.09	.03
☐ 34 Phil Niekro	.20	.09	.03
☐ 35 Jim Palmer	.30	.14	.04
☐ 36 Tommy John	.10	.05	.01
☐ 37 Walter Johnson GC	.25	.11	.03
☐ 38 Steve Carlton	.30	.14	.04
☐ 39 Nolan Ryan	1.50	.65	.19
☐ 40 Tom Seaver	.60	.25	.08
☐ 41 Don Sutton	.15	.07	.02
☐ 42 Bert Blyleven	.10	.05	.01
☐ 43 Frank Robinson GC	.20	.09	.03
☐ 44 Joe Morgan	.25	.11	.03
☐ 45 Rollie Fingers	.25	.11	.03
☐ 46 Keith Hernandez	.15	.07	.02
☐ 47 Robin Yount	.75	.35	.09
☐ 48 Cal Ripken	1.25	.55	.16
☐ 49 Dale Murphy	.35	.16	.04
☐ 50 Mickey Mantle GC	2.00	.90	.25
☐ 51 Johnny Bench	.45	.20	.06
☐ 52 Carlton Fisk	.50	.23	.06
☐ 53 Tug McGraw	.07	.03	.01
☐ 54 Paul Molitor	.25	.11	.03
☐ 55 Carl Hubbell GC	.15	.07	.02
☐ 56 Steve Garvey	.30	.14	.04
☐ 57 Dave Parker	.15	.07	.02
☐ 58 Gary Carter	.25	.11	.03
☐ 59 Fred Lynn	.10	.05	.01
☐ 60 Checklist Card	.07	.03	.01

1985 Donruss

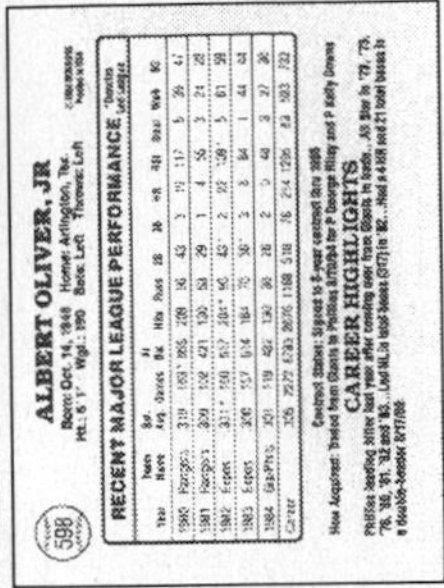

The cards in this 660-card set measure 2 1/2" by 3 1/2". The 1985 Donruss regular issue cards have fronts that feature jet black borders on which orange lines have been placed. The fronts contain the standard team logo, player's name, position, and Donruss logo. The cards were distributed with puzzle pieces from a Dick Perez rendition of Lou Gehrig. The first 26 cards of the set feature Diamond Kings (DK), for the fourth year in a row; the artwork on the Diamond Kings was again produced by the Perez-Steele Galleries. Cards 27-46 feature Rated Rookies (RR). The unnumbered checklist cards are arbitrarily numbered below as numbers 654 through 660. This set is noted for containing the Rookie Cards of Roger Clemens, Alvin Davis, Eric Davis, Shawon Dunston, Dwight Gooden, Orel Hershiser, Jimmy Key, Mark Langston, Terry Pendleton, Kirby Puckett, Jose Rijo, Bret Saberhagen, and Danny Tartabull.

	NRMT-MT	EXC	G-VG
COMPLETE SET (660)	200.00	90.00	25.00
COMPLETE FACT.SET (660)	250.00	115.00	31.00
COMMON PLAYER (1-660)	.10	.05	.01
☐ 1 Ryne Sandberg DK	4.00	1.80	.50
☐ 2 Doug DeCinces DK	.15	.07	.02
☐ 3 Richard Dotson DK	.15	.07	.02
☐ 4 Bert Blyleven DK	.15	.07	.02
☐ 5 Lou Whitaker DK	.25	.11	.03
☐ 6 Dan Quisenberry DK	.15	.07	.02
☐ 7 Don Mattingly DK	2.50	1.15	.30
☐ 8 Carney Lansford DK	.15	.07	.02
☐ 9 Frank Tanana DK	.15	.07	.02
☐ 10 Willie Upshaw DK	.15	.07	.02
☐ 11 Claudell Washington DK	.15	.07	.02
☐ 12 Mike Marshall DK	.15	.07	.02
☐ 13 Joaquin Andujar DK	.15	.07	.02
☐ 14 Cal Ripken DK	4.00	1.80	.50
☐ 15 Jim Rice DK	.15	.07	.02
☐ 16 Don Sutton DK	.20	.09	.03
☐ 17 Frank Viola DK	.25	.11	.03
☐ 18 Alvin Davis DK	.15	.07	.02
☐ 19 Mario Soto DK	.15	.07	.02
☐ 20 Jose Cruz DK	.15	.07	.02
☐ 21 Charlie Lea DK	.15	.07	.02
☐ 22 Jesse Orosco DK	.15	.07	.02
☐ 23 Juan Samuel DK	.15	.07	.02
☐ 24 Tony Pena DK	.15	.07	.02
☐ 25 Tony Gwynn DK	2.25	1.00	.30
☐ 26 Bob Brenly DK	.15	.07	.02
☐ 27 Danny Tartabull RR	10.00	4.50	1.25
☐ 28 Mike Bielecki RR	.40	.18	.05
☐ 29 Steve Lyons RR	.15	.07	.02
☐ 30 Jeff Reed RR	.15	.07	.02
☐ 31 Tony Brewer RR	.15	.07	.02
☐ 32 John Morris RR	.15	.07	.02
☐ 33 Daryl Boston RR	.25	.11	.03
☐ 34 Al Pulido RR	.15	.07	.02
☐ 35 Steve Kiefer RR	.15	.07	.02
☐ 36 Larry Sheets RR	.15	.07	.02
☐ 37 Scott Bradley RR	.15	.07	.02
☐ 38 Calvin Schiraldi RR	.15	.07	.02
☐ 39 Shawon Dunston RR	2.00	.90	.25
☐ 40 Charlie Mitchell RR	.15	.07	.02
☐ 41 Billy Hatcher RR	.35	.16	.04
☐ 42 Russ Stephans RR	.15	.07	.02
☐ 43 Alejandro Sanchez RR	.15	.07	.02
☐ 44 Steve Jeltz RR	.15	.07	.02
☐ 45 Jim Traber RR	.15	.07	.02
☐ 46 Doug Loman RR	.15	.07	.02
☐ 47 Eddie Murray	2.00	.90	.25
☐ 48 Robin Yount	4.00	1.80	.50
☐ 49 Lance Parrish	.12	.05	.02
☐ 50 Jim Rice	.20	.09	.03
☐ 51 Dave Winfield	3.50	1.55	.45
☐ 52 Fernando Valenzuela	.12	.05	.02
☐ 53 George Brett	4.00	1.80	.50
☐ 54 Dave Kingman	.12	.05	.02
☐ 55 Gary Carter	.60	.25	.08
☐ 56 Buddy Bell	.12	.05	.02
☐ 57 Reggie Jackson	2.00	.90	.25
☐ 58 Harold Baines	.35	.16	.04
☐ 59 Ozzie Smith	2.00	.90	.25
☐ 60 Nolan Ryan UER (Set strikeout record in 1973, not 1972)	10.00	4.50	1.25
☐ 61 Mike Schmidt	5.00	2.30	.60
☐ 62 Dave Parker	.40	.18	.05
☐ 63 Tony Gwynn	6.00	2.70	.75
☐ 64 Tony Pena	.12	.05	.02
☐ 65 Jack Clark	.12	.05	.02
☐ 66 Dale Murphy	1.00	.45	.13
☐ 67 Ryne Sandberg	10.00	4.50	1.25
☐ 68 Keith Hernandez	.20	.09	.03
☐ 69 Alvin Davis	.35	.16	.04
☐ 70 Kent Hrbek	.40	.18	.05
☐ 71 Willie Upshaw	.10	.05	.01
☐ 72 Dave Engle	.10	.05	.01
☐ 73 Alfredo Griffin	.10	.05	.01
☐ 74A Jack Perconte (Career Highlights takes four lines)	.10	.05	.01
☐ 74B Jack Perconte (Career Highlights takes three lines)	.10	.05	.01
☐ 75 Jesse Orosco	.10	.05	.01
☐ 76 Jody Davis	.10	.05	.01
☐ 77 Bob Horner	.12	.05	.02
☐ 78 Larry McWilliams	.10	.05	.01
☐ 79 Joel Youngblood	.10	.05	.01
☐ 80 Alan Wiggins	.10	.05	.01
☐ 81 Ron Oester	.10	.05	.01
☐ 82 Ozzie Virgil	.10	.05	.01
☐ 83 Ricky Horton	.10	.05	.01
☐ 84 Bill Doran	.12	.05	.02
☐ 85 Rod Carew	1.75	.80	.22
☐ 86 LaMarr Hoyt	.10	.05	.01
☐ 87 Tim Wallach	.12	.05	.02
☐ 88 Mike Flanagan	.10	.05	.01
☐ 89 Jim Sundberg	.12	.05	.02
☐ 90 Chet Lemon	.10	.05	.01
☐ 91 Bob Stanley	.10	.05	.01
☐ 92 Willie Randolph	.12	.05	.02
☐ 93 Bill Russell	.12	.05	.02
☐ 94 Julio Franco	.90	.40	.11
☐ 95 Dan Quisenberry	.12	.05	.02
☐ 96 Bill Caudill	.10	.05	.01
☐ 97 Bill Gullickson	.12	.05	.02
☐ 98 Danny Darwin	.10	.05	.01
☐ 99 Curtis Wilkerson	.10	.05	.01
☐ 100 Bud Black	.10	.05	.01
☐ 101 Tony Phillips	.12	.05	.02
☐ 102 Tony Bernazard	.10	.05	.01
☐ 103 Jay Howell	.12	.05	.02
☐ 104 Burt Hooton	.10	.05	.01
☐ 105 Milt Wilcox	.10	.05	.01
☐ 106 Rich Dauer	.10	.05	.01
☐ 107 Don Sutton	.50	.23	.06
☐ 108 Mike Witt	.10	.05	.01
☐ 109 Bruce Sutter	.12	.05	.02
☐ 110 Enos Cabell	.10	.05	.01
☐ 111 John Denny	.10	.05	.01
☐ 112 Dave Dravecky	.12	.05	.02
☐ 113 Marvell Wynne	.10	.05	.01
☐ 114 Johnnie LeMaster	.10	.05	.01
☐ 115 Chuck Porter	.10	.05	.01
☐ 116 John Gibbons	.10	.05	.01
☐ 117 Keith Moreland	.10	.05	.01
☐ 118 Darnell Coles	.12	.05	.02
☐ 119 Dennis Lamp	.10	.05	.01
☐ 120 Ron Davis	.10	.05	.01
☐ 121 Nick Esasky	.10	.05	.01
☐ 122 Vance Law	.10	.05	.01
☐ 123 Gary Roenicke	.10	.05	.01
☐ 124 Bill Schroeder	.10	.05	.01
☐ 125 Dave Rozema	.10	.05	.01
☐ 126 Bobby Meacham	.10	.05	.01
☐ 127 Marty Barrett	.10	.05	.01
☐ 128 R.J. Reynolds	.10	.05	.01

☐ 129 Ernie Camacho UER (Photo actually Rich Thompson)	.10	.05	.01
☐ 130 Jorge Orta	.10	.05	.01
☐ 131 Lary Sorensen	.10	.05	.01
☐ 132 Terry Francona	.10	.05	.01
☐ 133 Fred Lynn	.12	.05	.02
☐ 134 Bob Jones	.10	.05	.01
☐ 135 Jerry Hairston	.10	.05	.01
☐ 136 Kevin Bass	.10	.05	.01
☐ 137 Garry Maddox	.10	.05	.01
☐ 138 Dave LaPoint	.10	.05	.01
☐ 139 Kevin McReynolds	.35	.16	.04
☐ 140 Wayne Krenchicki	.10	.05	.01
☐ 141 Rafael Ramirez	.10	.05	.01
☐ 142 Rod Scurry	.10	.05	.01
☐ 143 Greg Minton	.10	.05	.01
☐ 144 Tim Stoddard	.10	.05	.01
☐ 145 Steve Henderson	.10	.05	.01
☐ 146 George Bell	1.00	.45	.13
☐ 147 Dave Meier	.10	.05	.01
☐ 148 Sammy Stewart	.10	.05	.01
☐ 149 Mark Brouhard	.10	.05	.01
☐ 150 Larry Herndon	.10	.05	.01
☐ 151 Oil Can Boyd	.10	.05	.01
☐ 152 Brian Dayett	.10	.05	.01
☐ 153 Tom Niedenfuer	.10	.05	.01
☐ 154 Brook Jacoby	.12	.05	.02
☐ 155 Onix Concepcion	.10	.05	.01
☐ 156 Tim Conroy	.10	.05	.01
☐ 157 Joe Hesketh	.25	.11	.03
☐ 158 Brian Downing	.12	.05	.02
☐ 159 Tommy Dunbar	.10	.05	.01
☐ 160 Marc Hill	.10	.05	.01
☐ 161 Phil Garner	.12	.05	.02
☐ 162 Jerry Davis	.10	.05	.01
☐ 163 Bill Campbell	.10	.05	.01
☐ 164 John Franco	1.50	.65	.19
☐ 165 Len Barker	.10	.05	.01
☐ 166 Benny Distefano	.10	.05	.01
☐ 167 George Frazier	.10	.05	.01
☐ 168 Tito Landrum	.10	.05	.01
☐ 169 Cal Ripken	10.00	4.50	1.25
☐ 170 Cecil Cooper	.12	.05	.02
☐ 171 Alan Trammell	.50	.23	.06
☐ 172 Wade Boggs	5.00	2.30	.60
☐ 173 Don Baylor	.12	.05	.02
☐ 174 Pedro Guerrero	.15	.07	.02
☐ 175 Frank White	.12	.05	.02
☐ 176 Rickey Henderson	4.00	1.80	.50
☐ 177 Charlie Lea	.10	.05	.01
☐ 178 Pete O'Brien	.12	.05	.02
☐ 179 Doug DeCinces	.10	.05	.01
☐ 180 Ron Kittle	.12	.05	.02
☐ 181 George Hendrick	.10	.05	.01
☐ 182 Joe Niekro	.12	.05	.02
☐ 183 Juan Samuel	.25	.11	.03
☐ 184 Mario Soto	.10	.05	.01
☐ 185 Goose Gossage	.15	.07	.02
☐ 186 Johnny Ray	.10	.05	.01
☐ 187 Bob Brenly	.10	.05	.01
☐ 188 Craig McMurtry	.10	.05	.01
☐ 189 Leon Durham	.10	.05	.01
☐ 190 Dwight Gooden	8.00	3.60	1.00
☐ 191 Barry Bonnell	.10	.05	.01
☐ 192 Tim Teufel	.10	.05	.01
☐ 193 Dave Stieb	.12	.05	.02
☐ 194 Mickey Hatcher	.10	.05	.01
☐ 195 Jesse Barfield	.12	.05	.02
☐ 196 Al Cowens	.10	.05	.01
☐ 197 Hubie Brooks	.12	.05	.02
☐ 198 Steve Trout	.10	.05	.01
☐ 199 Glenn Hubbard	.10	.05	.01
☐ 200 Bill Madlock	.12	.05	.02
☐ 201 Jeff D. Robinson (Giants pitcher)	.12	.05	.02
☐ 202 Eric Show	.10	.05	.01
☐ 203 Dave Concepcion	.12	.05	.02
☐ 204 Ivan DeJesus	.10	.05	.01
☐ 205 Neil Allen	.10	.05	.01
☐ 206 Jerry Mumphrey	.10	.05	.01
☐ 207 Mike C. Brown (Angels OF)	.10	.05	.01
☐ 208 Carlton Fisk	1.75	.80	.22
☐ 209 Bryn Smith	.10	.05	.01
☐ 210 Tippy Martinez	.10	.05	.01
☐ 211 Dion James	.10	.05	.01
☐ 212 Willie Hernandez	.10	.05	.01
☐ 213 Mike Easler	.10	.05	.01
☐ 214 Ron Guidry	.12	.05	.02
☐ 215 Rick Honeycutt	.10	.05	.01
☐ 216 Brett Butler	.40	.18	.05
☐ 217 Larry Gura	.10	.05	.01
☐ 218 Ray Burris	.10	.05	.01
☐ 219 Steve Rogers	.10	.05	.01
☐ 220 Frank Tanana UER (Bats Left listed twice on card back)	.12	.05	.02
☐ 221 Ned Yost	.10	.05	.01
☐ 222 Bret Saberhagen UER (18 career IP on back)	5.00	2.30	.60
☐ 223 Mike Davis	.10	.05	.01
☐ 224 Bert Blyleven	.35	.16	.04
☐ 225 Steve Kemp	.10	.05	.01
☐ 226 Jerry Reuss	.10	.05	.01
☐ 227 Darrell Evans UER (80 homers in 1980)	.12	.05	.02
☐ 228 Wayne Gross	.10	.05	.01
☐ 229 Jim Gantner	.10	.05	.01
☐ 230 Bob Boone	.12	.05	.02
☐ 231 Lonnie Smith	.10	.05	.01
☐ 232 Frank DiPino	.10	.05	.01
☐ 233 Jerry Koosman	.12	.05	.02
☐ 234 Graig Nettles	.12	.05	.02
☐ 235 John Tudor	.12	.05	.02
☐ 236 John Rabb	.10	.05	.01
☐ 237 Rick Manning	.10	.05	.01
☐ 238 Mike Fitzgerald	.10	.05	.01
☐ 239 Gary Matthews	.10	.05	.01
☐ 240 Jim Presley	.10	.05	.01
☐ 241 Dave Collins	.10	.05	.01
☐ 242 Gary Gaetti	.12	.05	.02
☐ 243 Dann Bilardello	.10	.05	.01
☐ 244 Rudy Law	.10	.05	.01
☐ 245 John Lowenstein	.10	.05	[illegible]
☐ 246 Tom Tellmann	.10	.05	.01
☐ 247 Howard Johnson	1.50	.65	.19
☐ 248 Ray Fontenot	.10	.05	.01
☐ 249 Tony Armas	.10	.05	.01
☐ 250 Candy Maldonado	.12	.05	.02
☐ 251 Mike Jeffcoat	.10	.05	.01
☐ 252 Dane Iorg	.10	.05	.01
☐ 253 Bruce Bochte	.10	.05	.01
☐ 254 Pete Rose	1.75	.80	.22
☐ 255 Don Aase	.10	.05	.01
☐ 256 George Wright	.10	.05	.01
☐ 257 Britt Burns	.10	.05	.01
☐ 258 Mike Scott	.12	.05	.02
☐ 259 Len Matuszek	.10	.05	.01
☐ 260 Dave Rucker	.10	.05	.01
☐ 261 Craig Lefferts	.12	.05	.02
☐ 262 Jay Tibbs	.10	.05	.01
☐ 263 Bruce Benedict	.10	.05	.01
☐ 264 Don Robinson	.10	.05	.01
☐ 265 Gary Lavelle	.10	.05	.01
☐ 266 Scott Sanderson	.10	.05	.01
☐ 267 Matt Young	.10	.05	.01
☐ 268 Ernie Whitt	.10	.05	.01
☐ 269 Houston Jimenez	.10	.05	.01
☐ 270 Ken Dixon	.10	.05	.01
☐ 271 Pete Ladd	.10	.05	.01
☐ 272 Juan Berenguer	.10	.05	.01
☐ 273 Roger Clemens	60.00	27.00	7.50
☐ 274 Rick Cerone	.10	.05	.01
☐ 275 Dave Anderson	.10	.05	.01
☐ 276 George Vukovich	.10	.05	.01
☐ 277 Greg Pryor	.10	.05	.01
☐ 278 Mike Warren	.10	.05	.01
☐ 279 Bob James	.10	.05	.01
☐ 280 Bobby Grich	.12	.05	.02
☐ 281 Mike Mason	.10	.05	.01
☐ 282 Ron Reed	.10	.05	.01
☐ 283 Alan Ashby	.10	.05	.01
☐ 284 Mark Thurmond	.10	.05	.01
☐ 285 Joe Lefebvre	.10	.05	.01
☐ 286 Ted Power	.10	.05	.01
☐ 287 Chris Chambliss	.12	.05	.02
☐ 288 Lee Tunnell	.10	.05	.01
☐ 289 Rich Bordi	.10	.05	.01
☐ 290 Glenn Brummer	.10	.05	.01
☐ 291 Mike Boddicker	.10	.05	.01
☐ 292 Rollie Fingers	.50	.23	.06
☐ 293 Lou Whitaker	.50	.23	.06
☐ 294 Dwight Evans	.20	.09	.03
☐ 295 Don Mattingly	7.00	3.10	.85
☐ 296 Mike Marshall	.10	.05	.01
☐ 297 Willie Wilson	.12	.05	.02
☐ 298 Mike Heath	.10	.05	.01
☐ 299 Tim Raines	.40	.18	.05
☐ 300 Larry Parrish	.10	.05	.01
☐ 301 Geoff Zahn	.10	.05	.01
☐ 302 Rich Dotson	.10	.05	.01
☐ 303 David Green	.10	.05	.01
☐ 304 Jose Cruz	.12	.05	.02
☐ 305 Steve Carlton	1.75	.80	.22
☐ 306 Gary Redus	.10	.05	.01

307	Steve Garvey	.40	.18	.05
308	Jose DeLeon	.10	.05	.01
309	Randy Lerch	.10	.05	.01
310	Claudell Washington	.10	.05	.01
311	Lee Smith	1.00	.45	.13
312	Darryl Strawberry	7.00	3.10	.85
313	Jim Beattie	.10	.05	.01
314	John Butcher	.10	.05	.01
315	Damaso Garcia	.10	.05	.01
316	Mike Smithson	.10	.05	.01
317	Luis Leal	.10	.05	.01
318	Ken Phelps	.10	.05	.01
319	Wally Backman	.10	.05	.01
320	Ron Cey	.12	.05	.02
321	Brad Komminsk	.10	.05	.01
322	Jason Thompson	.10	.05	.01
323	Frank Williams	.10	.05	.01
324	Tim Lollar	.10	.05	.01
325	Eric Davis	8.00	3.60	1.00
326	Von Hayes	.10	.05	.01
327	Andy Van Slyke	2.00	.90	.25
328	Craig Reynolds	.10	.05	.01
329	Dick Schofield	.10	.05	.01
330	Scott Fletcher	.10	.05	.01
331	Jeff Reardon	.90	.40	.11
332	Rick Dempsey	.10	.05	.01
333	Ben Oglivie	.10	.05	.01
334	Dan Petry	.10	.05	.01
335	Jackie Gutierrez	.10	.05	.01
336	Dave Righetti	.12	.05	.02
337	Alejandro Pena	.12	.05	.02
338	Mel Hall	.25	.11	.03
339	Pat Sheridan	.10	.05	.01
340	Keith Atherton	.10	.05	.01
341	David Palmer	.10	.05	.01
342	Gary Ward	.10	.05	.01
343	Dave Stewart	.50	.23	.06
344	Mark Gubicza	.75	.35	.09
345	Carney Lansford	.12	.05	.02
346	Jerry Willard	.10	.05	.01
347	Ken Griffey	.15	.07	.02
348	Franklin Stubbs	.20	.09	.03
349	Aurelio Lopez	.10	.05	.01
350	Al Bumbry	.10	.05	.01
351	Charlie Moore	.10	.05	.01
352	Luis Sanchez	.10	.05	.01
353	Darrell Porter	.10	.05	.01
354	Bill Dawley	.10	.05	.01
355	Charles Hudson	.10	.05	.01
356	Garry Templeton	.10	.05	.01
357	Cecilio Guante	.10	.05	.01
358	Jeff Leonard	.10	.05	.01
359	Paul Molitor	1.00	.45	.13
360	Ron Gardenhire	.10	.05	.01
361	Larry Bowa	.12	.05	.02
362	Bob Kearney	.10	.05	.01
363	Garth Iorg	.10	.05	.01
364	Tom Brunansky	.12	.05	.02
365	Brad Gulden	.10	.05	.01
366	Greg Walker	.10	.05	.01
367	Mike Young	.10	.05	.01
368	Rick Waits	.10	.05	.01
369	Doug Bair	.10	.05	.01
370	Bob Shirley	.10	.05	.01
371	Bob Ojeda	.10	.05	.01
372	Bob Welch	.20	.09	.03
373	Neal Heaton	.10	.05	.01
374	Danny Jackson UER (Photo actually Frank Wills)	.12	.05	.02
375	Donnie Hill	.10	.05	.01
376	Mike Stenhouse	.10	.05	.01
377	Bruce Kison	.10	.05	.01
378	Wayne Tolleson	.10	.05	.01
379	Floyd Bannister	.10	.05	.01
380	Vern Ruhle	.10	.05	.01
381	Tim Corcoran	.10	.05	.01
382	Kurt Kepshire	.10	.05	.01
383	Bobby Brown	.10	.05	.01
384	Dave Van Gorder	.10	.05	.01
385	Rick Mahler	.10	.05	.01
386	Lee Mazzilli	.10	.05	.01
387	Bill Laskey	.10	.05	.01
388	Thad Bosley	.10	.05	.01
389	Al Chambers	.10	.05	.01
390	Tony Fernandez	.75	.35	.09
391	Ron Washington	.10	.05	.01
392	Bill Swaggerty	.10	.05	.01
393	Bob L. Gibson	.10	.05	.01
394	Marty Castillo	.10	.05	.01
395	Steve Crawford	.10	.05	.01
396	Clay Christiansen	.10	.05	.01
397	Bob Bailor	.10	.05	.01
398	Mike Hargrove	.12	.05	.02
399	Charlie Leibrandt	.12	.05	.02
400	Tom Burgmeier	.10	.05	.01
401	Razor Shines	.10	.05	.01
402	Rob Wilfong	.10	.05	.01
403	Tom Henke	.40	.18	.05
404	Al Jones	.10	.05	.01
405	Mike LaCoss	.10	.05	.01
406	Luis DeLeon	.10	.05	.01
407	Greg Gross	.10	.05	.01
408	Tom Hume	.10	.05	.01
409	Rick Camp	.10	.05	.01
410	Milt May	.10	.05	.01
411	Henry Cotto	.10	.05	.01
412	David Von Ohlen	.10	.05	.01
413	Scott McGregor	.10	.05	.01
414	Ted Simmons	.12	.05	.02
415	Jack Morris	1.25	.55	.16
416	Bill Buckner	.12	.05	.02
417	Butch Wynegar	.10	.05	.01
418	Steve Sax	.50	.23	.06
419	Steve Balboni	.10	.05	.01
420	Dwayne Murphy	.10	.05	.01
421	Andre Dawson	2.00	.90	.25
422	Charlie Hough	.12	.05	.02
423	Tommy John	.20	.09	.03
424A	Tom Seaver ERR (Photo actually Floyd Bannister)	1.75	.80	.22
424B	Tom Seaver COR	30.00	13.50	3.80
425	Tommy Herr	.10	.05	.01
426	Terry Puhl	.10	.05	.01
427	Al Holland	.10	.05	.01
428	Eddie Milner	.10	.05	.01
429	Terry Kennedy	.10	.05	.01
430	John Candelaria	.10	.05	.01
431	Manny Trillo	.10	.05	.01
432	Ken Oberkfell	.10	.05	.01
433	Rick Sutcliffe	.12	.05	.02
434	Ron Darling	.50	.23	.06
435	Spike Owen	.10	.05	.01
436	Frank Viola	.50	.23	.06
437	Lloyd Moseby	.10	.05	.01
438	Kirby Puckett	50.00	23.00	6.25
439	Jim Clancy	.10	.05	.01
440	Mike Moore	.25	.11	.03
441	Doug Sisk	.10	.05	.01
442	Dennis Eckersley	1.25	.55	.16
443	Gerald Perry	.10	.05	.01
444	Dale Berra	.10	.05	.01
445	Dusty Baker	.12	.05	.02
446	Ed Whitson	.10	.05	.01
447	Cesar Cedeno	.12	.05	.02
448	Rick Schu	.10	.05	.01
449	Joaquin Andujar	.10	.05	.01
450	Mark Bailey	.10	.05	.01
451	Ron Romanick	.10	.05	.01
452	Julio Cruz	.10	.05	.01
453	Miguel Dilone	.10	.05	.01
454	Storm Davis	.10	.05	.01
455	Jaime Cocanower	.10	.05	.01
456	Barbaro Garbey	.10	.05	.01
457	Rich Gedman	.10	.05	.01
458	Phil Niekro	.50	.23	.06
459	Mike Scioscia	.12	.05	.02
460	Pat Tabler	.10	.05	.01
461	Darryl Motley	.10	.05	.01
462	Chris Codiroli	.10	.05	.01
463	Doug Flynn	.10	.05	.01
464	Billy Sample	.10	.05	.01
465	Mickey Rivers	.10	.05	.01
466	John Wathan	.10	.05	.01
467	Bill Krueger	.15	.07	.02
468	Andre Thornton	.10	.05	.01
469	Rex Hudler	.20	.09	.03
470	Sid Bream	1.25	.55	.16
471	Kirk Gibson	.30	.14	.04
472	John Shelby	.10	.05	.01
473	Moose Haas	.10	.05	.01
474	Doug Corbett	.10	.05	.01
475	Willie McGee	.40	.18	.05
476	Bob Knepper	.10	.05	.01
477	Kevin Gross	.10	.05	.01
478	Carmelo Martinez	.10	.05	.01
479	Kent Tekulve	.10	.05	.01
480	Chili Davis	.15	.07	.02
481	Bobby Clark	.10	.05	.01
482	Mookie Wilson	.12	.05	.02
483	Dave Owen	.10	.05	.01
484	Ed Nunez	.10	.05	.01
485	Rance Mulliniks	.10	.05	.01
486	Ken Schrom	.10	.05	.01
487	Jeff Russell	.20	.09	.03

□ 488 Tom Paciorek .12 .05 .02
□ 489 Dan Ford .10 .05 .01
□ 490 Mike Caldwell .10 .05 .01
□ 491 Scottie Earl .10 .05 .01
□ 492 Jose Rijo 3.50 1.55 .45
□ 493 Bruce Hurst .12 .05 .02
□ 494 Ken Landreaux .10 .05 .01
□ 495 Mike Fischlin .10 .05 .01
□ 496 Don Slaught .10 .05 .01
□ 497 Steve McCatty .10 .05 .01
□ 498 Gary Lucas .10 .05 .01
□ 499 Gary Pettis .10 .05 .01
□ 500 Marvis Foley .10 .05 .01
□ 501 Mike Squires .10 .05 .01
□ 502 Jim Pankovits .10 .05 .01
□ 503 Luis Aguayo .10 .05 .01
□ 504 Ralph Citarella .10 .05 .01
□ 505 Bruce Bochy .10 .05 .01
□ 506 Bob Owchinko .10 .05 .01
□ 507 Pascual Perez .10 .05 .01
□ 508 Lee Lacy .10 .05 .01
□ 509 Atlee Hammaker .10 .05 .01
□ 510 Bob Dernier .10 .05 .01
□ 511 Ed VandeBerg .10 .05 .01
□ 512 Cliff Johnson .10 .05 .01
□ 513 Len Whitehouse .10 .05 .01
□ 514 Dennis Martinez .12 .05 .02
□ 515 Ed Romero .10 .05 .01
□ 516 Rusty Kuntz .10 .05 .01
□ 517 Rick Miller .10 .05 .01
□ 518 Dennis Rasmussen .10 .05 .01
□ 519 Steve Yeager .10 .05 .01
□ 520 Chris Bando .10 .05 .01
□ 521 U.L. Washington .10 .05 .01
□ 522 Curt Young .10 .05 .01
□ 523 Angel Salazar .10 .05 .01
□ 524 Curt Kaufman .10 .05 .01
□ 525 Odell Jones .10 .05 .01
□ 526 Juan Agosto .10 .05 .01
□ 527 Denny Walling .10 .05 .01
□ 528 Andy Hawkins .10 .05 .01
□ 529 Sixto Lezcano .10 .05 .01
□ 530 Skeeter Barnes .15 .07 .02
□ 531 Randy Johnson .10 .05 .01
□ 532 Jim Morrison .10 .05 .01
□ 533 Warren Brusstar .10 .05 .01
□ 534A Jeff Pendleton ERR 9.00 4.00 1.15
(Wrong first name)
□ 534B Terry Pendleton COR 27.00 12.00 3.40
□ 535 Vic Rodriguez .10 .05 .01
□ 536 Bob McClure .10 .05 .01
□ 537 Dave Bergman .10 .05 .01
□ 538 Mark Clear .10 .05 .01
□ 539 Mike Pagliarulo .20 .09 .03
□ 540 Terry Whitfield .10 .05 .01
□ 541 Joe Beckwith .10 .05 .01
□ 542 Jeff Burroughs .10 .05 .01
□ 543 Dan Schatzeder .10 .05 .01
□ 544 Donnie Scott .10 .05 .01
□ 545 Jim Slaton .10 .05 .01
□ 546 Greg Luzinski .12 .05 .02
□ 547 Mark Salas .10 .05 .01
□ 548 Dave Smith .10 .05 .01
□ 549 John Wockenfuss .10 .05 .01
□ 550 Frank Pastore .10 .05 .01
□ 551 Tim Flannery .10 .05 .01
□ 552 Rick Rhoden .10 .05 .01
□ 553 Mark Davis .12 .05 .02
□ 554 Jeff Dedmon .10 .05 .01
□ 555 Gary Woods .10 .05 .01
□ 556 Danny Heep .10 .05 .01
□ 557 Mark Langston 3.50 1.55 .45
□ 558 Darrell Brown .10 .05 .01
□ 559 Jimmy Key 2.00 .90 .25
□ 560 Rick Lysander .10 .05 .01
□ 561 Doyle Alexander .10 .05 .01
□ 562 Mike Stanton .10 .05 .01
□ 563 Sid Fernandez .50 .23 .06
□ 564 Richie Hebner .10 .05 .01
□ 565 Alex Trevino .10 .05 .01
□ 566 Brian Harper .40 .18 .05
□ 567 Dan Gladden .40 .18 .05
□ 568 Luis Salazar .10 .05 .01
□ 569 Tom Foley .10 .05 .01
□ 570 Larry Andersen .10 .05 .01
□ 571 Danny Cox .10 .05 .01
□ 572 Joe Sambito .10 .05 .01
□ 573 Juan Beniquez .10 .05 .01
□ 574 Joel Skinner .10 .05 .01
□ 575 Randy St.Claire .10 .05 .01
□ 576 Floyd Rayford .10 .05 .01
□ 577 Roy Howell .10 .05 .01
□ 578 John Grubb .10 .05 .01
□ 579 Ed Jurak .10 .05 .01
□ 580 John Montefusco .10 .05 .01
□ 581 Orel Hershiser 3.50 1.55 .45
□ 582 Tom Waddell .10 .05 .01
□ 583 Mark Huismann .10 .05 .01
□ 584 Joe Morgan .60 .25 .08
□ 585 Jim Wohlford .10 .05 .01
□ 586 Dave Schmidt .10 .05 .01
□ 587 Jeff Kunkel .10 .05 .01
□ 588 Hal McRae .12 .05 .02
□ 589 Bill Almon .10 .05 .01
□ 590 Carmen Castillo .10 .05 .01
□ 591 Omar Moreno .10 .05 .01
□ 592 Ken Howell .10 .05 .01
□ 593 Tom Brookens .10 .05 .01
□ 594 Joe Nolan .10 .05 .01
□ 595 Willie Lozado .10 .05 .01
□ 596 Tom Nieto .10 .05 .01
□ 597 Walt Terrell .10 .05 .01
□ 598 Al Oliver .12 .05 .02
□ 599 Shane Rawley .10 .05 .01
□ 600 Denny Gonzalez .10 .05 .01
□ 601 Mark Grant .10 .05 .01
□ 602 Mike Armstrong .10 .05 .01
□ 603 George Foster .12 .05 .02
□ 604 Dave Lopes .12 .05 .02
□ 605 Salome Barojas .10 .05 .01
□ 606 Roy Lee Jackson .10 .05 .01
□ 607 Pete Filson .10 .05 .01
□ 608 Duane Walker .10 .05 .01
□ 609 Glenn Wilson .10 .05 .01
□ 610 Rafael Santana .10 .05 .01
□ 611 Roy Smith .10 .05 .01
□ 612 Ruppert Jones .10 .05 .01
□ 613 Joe Cowley .10 .05 .01
□ 614 Al Nipper UER .10 .05 .01
(Photo actually
Mike Brown)
□ 615 Gene Nelson .10 .05 .01
□ 616 Joe Carter 7.00 3.10 .85
□ 617 Ray Knight .12 .05 .02
□ 618 Chuck Rainey .10 .05 .01
□ 619 Dan Driessen .10 .05 .01
□ 620 Daryl Sconiers .10 .05 .01
□ 621 Bill Stein .10 .05 .01
□ 622 Roy Smalley .10 .05 .01
□ 623 Ed Lynch .10 .05 .01
□ 624 Jeff Stone .10 .05 .01
□ 625 Bruce Berenyi .10 .05 .01
□ 626 Kelvin Chapman .10 .05 .01
□ 627 Joe Price .10 .05 .01
□ 628 Steve Bedrosian .10 .05 .01
□ 629 Vic Mata .10 .05 .01
□ 630 Mike Krukow .10 .05 .01
□ 631 Phil Bradley .12 .05 .02
□ 632 Jim Gott .10 .05 .01
□ 633 Randy Bush .10 .05 .01
□ 634 Tom Browning 1.00 .45 .13
□ 635 Lou Gehrig .20 .09 .03
Puzzle Card
□ 636 Reid Nichols .10 .05 .01
□ 637 Dan Pasqua .40 .18 .05
□ 638 German Rivera .10 .05 .01
□ 639 Don Schulze .10 .05 .01
□ 640A Mike Jones .10 .05 .01
(Career Highlights,
takes five lines)
□ 640B Mike Jones .10 .05 .01
(Career Highlights,
takes four lines)
□ 641 Pete Rose 1.75 .80 .22
□ 642 Wade Rowdon .10 .05 .01
□ 643 Jerry Narron .10 .05 .01
□ 644 Darrell Miller .10 .05 .01
□ 645 Tim Hulett .10 .05 .01
□ 646 Andy McGaffigan .10 .05 .01
□ 647 Kurt Bevacqua .10 .05 .01
□ 648 John Russell .10 .05 .01
□ 649 Ron Robinson .15 .07 .02
□ 650 Donnie Moore .10 .05 .01
□ 651A Two for the Title 3.00 1.35 .40
Dave Winfield
Don Mattingly
(Yellow letters)
□ 651B Two for the Title 10.00 4.50 1.25
Dave Winfield
Don Mattingly
(White letters)
□ 652 Tim Laudner .10 .05 .01
□ 653 Steve Farr .75 .35 .09
□ 654 DK Checklist 1-26 .15 .02 .00
(Unnumbered)
□ 655 Checklist 27-130 .15 .02 .00

(Unnumbered)			
☐ 656 Checklist 131-234	.15	.02	.00
(Unnumbered)			
☐ 657 Checklist 235-338	.15	.02	.00
(Unnumbered)			
☐ 658 Checklist 339-442	.15	.02	.00
(Unnumbered)			
☐ 659 Checklist 443-546	.15	.02	.00
(Unnumbered)			
☐ 660 Checklist 547-653	.15	.02	.00
(Unnumbered)			

1985 Donruss Action All-Stars

The cards in this 60-card set measure approximately 3 1/2" by 5". For the third year in a row, Donruss issued a set of Action All-Stars. This set features action photos on the obverse which also contains a portrait inset of the player. The backs, unlike the year before, do not contain a full color picture of the player but list, if space is available, full statistical data, biographical data, career highlights, and acquisition and contract status. The cards were issued with a Lou Gehrig puzzle card.

	NRMT-MT	EXC	G-VG
COMPLETE SET (60)	7.50	3.40	.95
COMMON PLAYER (1-60)	.07	.03	.01
☐ 1 Tim Raines	.15	.07	.02
☐ 2 Jim Gantner	.07	.03	.01
☐ 3 Mario Soto	.07	.03	.01
☐ 4 Spike Owen	.07	.03	.01
☐ 5 Lloyd Moseby	.07	.03	.01
☐ 6 Damaso Garcia	.07	.03	.01
☐ 7 Cal Ripken	1.25	.55	.16
☐ 8 Dan Quisenberry	.10	.05	.01
☐ 9 Eddie Murray	.35	.16	.04
☐ 10 Tony Pena	.10	.05	.01
☐ 11 Buddy Bell	.10	.05	.01
☐ 12 Dave Winfield	.40	.18	.05
☐ 13 Ron Kittle	.10	.05	.01
☐ 14 Rich Gossage	.15	.07	.02
☐ 15 Dwight Evans	.15	.07	.02
☐ 16 Alvin Davis	.10	.05	.01
☐ 17 Mike Schmidt	.90	.40	.11
☐ 18 Pascual Perez	.07	.03	.01
☐ 19 Tony Gwynn	.75	.35	.09
☐ 20 Nolan Ryan	1.50	.65	.19
☐ 21 Robin Yount	.75	.35	.09
☐ 22 Mike Marshall	.07	.03	.01
☐ 23 Brett Butler	.15	.07	.02
☐ 24 Ryne Sandberg	1.25	.55	.16
☐ 25 Dale Murphy	.40	.18	.05
☐ 26 George Brett	.75	.35	.09
☐ 27 Jim Rice	.20	.09	.03
☐ 28 Ozzie Smith	.45	.20	.06
☐ 29 Larry Parrish	.07	.03	.01
☐ 30 Jack Clark	.10	.05	.01
☐ 31 Manny Trillo	.07	.03	.01
☐ 32 Dave Kingman	.10	.05	.01
☐ 33 Geoff Zahn	.07	.03	.01
☐ 34 Pedro Guerrero	.10	.05	.01
☐ 35 Dave Parker	.15	.07	.02
☐ 36 Rollie Fingers	.20	.09	.03
☐ 37 Fernando Valenzuela	.10	.05	.01
☐ 38 Wade Boggs	.60	.25	.08
☐ 39 Reggie Jackson	.60	.25	.08
☐ 40 Kent Hrbek	.15	.07	.02
☐ 41 Keith Hernandez	.15	.07	.02
☐ 42 Lou Whitaker	.20	.09	.03
☐ 43 Tom Herr	.07	.03	.01
☐ 44 Alan Trammell	.20	.09	.03
☐ 45 Butch Wynegar	.07	.03	.01
☐ 46 Leon Durham	.07	.03	.01
☐ 47 Dwight Gooden	.75	.35	.09
☐ 48 Don Mattingly	1.00	.45	.13
☐ 49 Phil Niekro	.20	.09	.03
☐ 50 Johnny Ray	.07	.03	.01
☐ 51 Doug DeCinces	.07	.03	.01
☐ 52 Willie Upshaw	.07	.03	.01
☐ 53 Lance Parrish	.10	.05	.01
☐ 54 Jody Davis	.07	.03	.01
☐ 55 Steve Carlton	.35	.16	.04
☐ 56 Juan Samuel	.10	.05	.01
☐ 57 Gary Carter	.25	.11	.03
☐ 58 Harold Baines	.10	.05	.01
☐ 59 Eric Show	.07	.03	.01
☐ 60 Checklist Card	.07	.03	.01

1985 Donruss Highlights

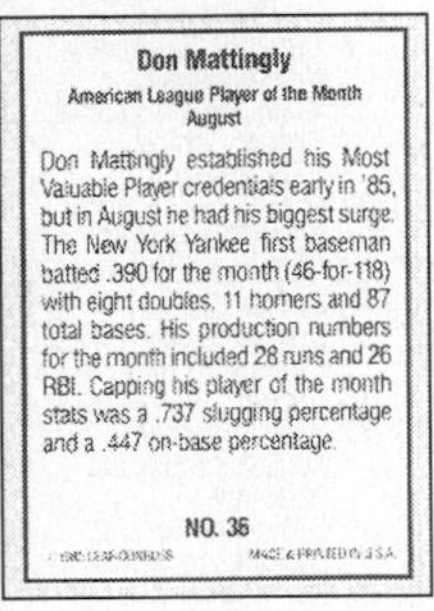

This 56-card set features the players and pitchers of the month for each league as well as a number of highlight cards commemorating the 1985 season. The Donruss Company dedicated the last two cards to their own selections for Rookies of the Year (ROY). This set proved to be more popular than the Donruss Company had predicted, as their first and only print run was exhausted before card dealers' initial orders were filled.

	NRMT-MT	EXC	G-VG
COMPLETE SET (56)	24.00	11.00	3.00
COMMON PLAYER (1-56)	.10	.05	.01
☐ 1 Tom Seaver: Sets Opening Day Record	.75	.35	.09
☐ 2 Rollie Fingers: Sets AL Save Mark	.30	.14	.04
☐ 3 Mike Davis: AL Player April	.10	.05	.01
☐ 4 Charlie Leibrandt: AL Pitcher April	.10	.05	.01
☐ 5 Dale Murphy: NL Player April	.50	.23	.06
☐ 6 Fernando Valenzuela: NL Pitcher April	.15	.07	.02
☐ 7 Larry Bowa: NL Shortstop Record	.10	.05	.01
☐ 8 Dave Concepcion: Joins Reds' 2000 Hit Club	.15	.07	.02
☐ 9 Tony Perez: Eldest Grand Slammer	.25	.11	.03
☐ 10 Pete Rose: NL Career Run Leader	1.00	.45	.13
☐ 11 George Brett: AL Player May	1.00	.45	.13
☐ 12 Dave Stieb: AL Pitcher May	.15	.07	.02
☐ 13 Dave Parker: NL Player May	.15	.07	.02
☐ 14 Andy Hawkins: NL Pitcher May	.10	.05	.01
☐ 15 Andy Hawkins: Records 11th Straight Win	.10	.05	.01

☐ 16 Von Hayes: Two Homers in First Inning	.10	.05	.01
☐ 17 Rickey Henderson: AL Player June	1.00	.45	.13
☐ 18 Jay Howell: AL Pitcher June	.10	.05	.01
☐ 19 Pedro Guerrero: NL Player June	.15	.07	.02
☐ 20 John Tudor: NL Pitcher June	.10	.05	.01
☐ 21 Hernandez/Carter: Marathon Game Iron Men	.25	.11	.03
☐ 22 Nolan Ryan: Records 4000th K	3.00	1.35	.40
☐ 23 LaMarr Hoyt: All-Star Game MVP	.10	.05	.01
☐ 24 Oddibe McDowell: 1st Ranger to Hit for Cycle	.15	.07	.02
☐ 25 George Brett: AL Player July	1.00	.45	.13
☐ 26 Bret Saberhagen: AL Pitcher July	.75	.35	.09
☐ 27 Keith Hernandez: NL Player July	.15	.07	.02
☐ 28 Fernando Valenzuela: NL Pitcher July	.15	.07	.02
☐ 29 W.McGee/V.Coleman: Record Setting Base Stealers	.60	.25	.08
☐ 30 Tom Seaver: Notches 300th Career Win	.50	.23	.06
☐ 31 Rod Carew: Strokes 3000th Hit	.40	.18	.05
☐ 32 Dwight Gooden: Establishes Met Record	1.00	.45	.13
☐ 33 Dwight Gooden: Achieves Strikeout Milestone	1.00	.45	.13
☐ 34 Eddie Murray: Explodes for 9 RBI	.45	.20	.06
☐ 35 Don Baylor: AL Career HBP Leader	.15	.07	.02
☐ 36 Don Mattingly: AL Player August	1.50	.65	.19
☐ 37 Dave Righetti: AL Pitcher August	.10	.05	.01
☐ 38 Willie McGee: NL Player August	.15	.07	.02
☐ 39 Shane Rawley: NL Pitcher August	.10	.05	.01
☐ 40 Pete Rose: Ty-Breaking Hit	1.25	.55	.16
☐ 41 Andre Dawson: Hits 3 HR's Drives in 8 Runs	.45	.20	.06
☐ 42 Rickey Henderson: Sets Yankee Theft Mark	1.00	.45	.13
☐ 43 Tom Browning: 20 Wins in Rookie Season	.15	.07	.02
☐ 44 Don Mattingly: Yankee Milestone for Hits	1.50	.65	.19
☐ 45 Don Mattingly: AL Player September	1.50	.65	.19
☐ 46 Charlie Leibrandt: AL Pitcher September	.10	.05	.01
☐ 47 Gary Carter: NL Player September	.25	.11	.03
☐ 48 Dwight Gooden: NL Pitcher September	1.00	.45	.13
☐ 49 Wade Boggs: Major League Record Setter	1.00	.45	.13
☐ 50 Phil Niekro: Hurls Shutout for 300th Win	.25	.11	.03
☐ 51 Darrell Evans: Venerable HR King	.10	.05	.01
☐ 52 Willie McGee: NL Switch-Hitting Record	.15	.07	.02
☐ 53 Dave Winfield: Equals DiMaggio Feat	.40	.18	.05
☐ 54 Vince Coleman: Donruss NL ROY	1.00	.45	.13
☐ 55 Ozzie Guillen: Donruss AL ROY	.50	.23	.06
☐ 56 Checklist Card (Unnumbered)	.10	.05	.01

1985 Donruss Super DK's

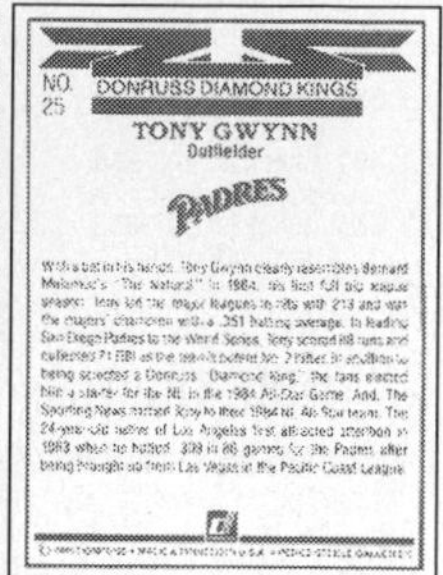

The cards in this 28-card set measure approximately 4 15/16 by 6 3/4". The 1985 Donruss Diamond Kings Supers set contains enlarged cards of the first 26 cards of the Donruss regular set of this year. In addition, the Diamond Kings checklist card, a card of artist Dick Perez, and a Lou Gehrig puzzle card are included in the set. The set was the brain-child of the Perez-Steele Galleries and could be obtained via a write-in offer on the wrappers of the Donruss regular cards of this year. The Gehrig puzzle card is actually a 12-piece jigsaw puzzle. The back of the checklist card is blank; however, the Dick Perez card back gives a short history of Dick Perez and the Perez-Steele Galleries. The offer for obtaining this set was detailed on the wax pack wrappers; three wrappers plus 9.00 was required for this mail-in offer.

	NRMT-MT	EXC	G-VG
COMPLETE SET (28)	12.50	5.75	1.55
COMMON PLAYER (1-28)	.25	.11	.03
☐ 1 Ryne Sandberg	5.00	2.30	.60
☐ 2 Doug DeCinces	.25	.11	.03
☐ 3 Richard Dotson	.25	.11	.03
☐ 4 Bert Blyleven	.35	.16	.04
☐ 5 Lou Whitaker	.50	.23	.06
☐ 6 Dan Quisenberry	.35	.16	.04
☐ 7 Don Mattingly	3.50	1.55	.45
☐ 8 Carney Lansford	.35	.16	.04
☐ 9 Frank Tanana	.35	.16	.04
☐ 10 Willie Upshaw	.25	.11	.03
☐ 11 Claudell Washington	.25	.11	.03
☐ 12 Mike Marshall	.35	.16	.04
☐ 13 Joaquin Andujar	.25	.11	.03
☐ 14 Cal Ripken	5.00	2.30	.60
☐ 15 Jim Rice	.50	.23	.06
☐ 16 Don Sutton	.50	.23	.06
☐ 17 Frank Viola	.50	.23	.06
☐ 18 Alvin Davis	.50	.23	.06
☐ 19 Mario Soto	.25	.11	.03
☐ 20 Jose Cruz	.25	.11	.03
☐ 21 Charlie Lea	.25	.11	.03
☐ 22 Jesse Orosco	.25	.11	.03
☐ 23 Juan Samuel	.35	.16	.04
☐ 24 Tony Pena	.25	.11	.03
☐ 25 Tony Gwynn	3.00	1.35	.40
☐ 26 Bob Brenly	.25	.11	.03
☐ 27 Checklist Card (Unnumbered)	.25	.11	.03
☐ 28 Dick Perez (Unnumbered) (History of DK's)	.25	.11	.03

1985 Donruss Wax Box Cards

The boxes of the 1985 Donruss regular issue baseball cards, in which the wax packs were contained, featured four baseball cards, with backs. The complete set price of the regular issue set does not include these cards; they are

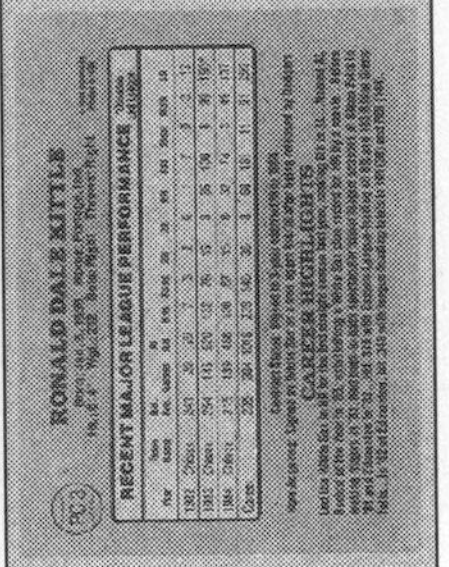

considered a separate set. The cards measure the standard 2 1/2" by 3 1/2" and are styled the same as the regular Donruss cards. The cards are numbered but with the prefix PC before the number. The value of the panel uncut is slightly greater, perhaps by 25 percent greater, than the value of the individual cards cut up carefully.

	NRMT-MT	EXC	G-VG
COMPLETE SET (4)	6.00	2.70	.75
COMMON PLAYER	.15	.07	.02
☐ PC1 Dwight Gooden	3.50	1.55	.45
☐ PC2 Ryne Sandberg	3.50	1.55	.45
☐ PC3 Ron Kittle	.15	.07	.02
☐ PUZ0 Lou Gehrig Puzzle Card	.15	.07	.02

1986 Donruss

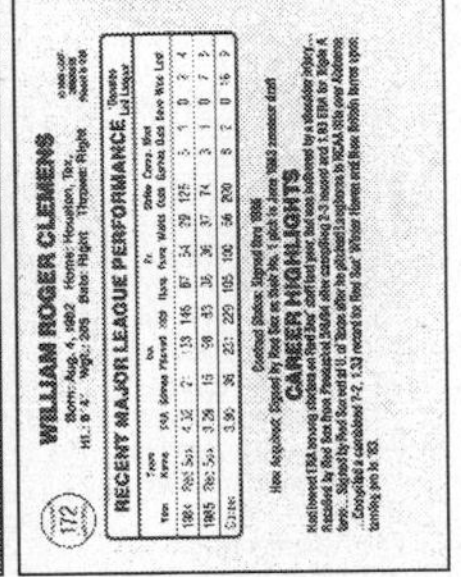

The cards in this 660-card set measure 2 1/2" by 3 1/2". The 1986 Donruss regular issue cards have fronts that feature blue borders. The fronts contain the standard team logo, player's name, position, and Donruss logo. The cards were distributed with puzzle pieces from a Dick Perez rendition of Hank Aaron. The first 26 cards of the set are Diamond Kings (DK), for the fifth year in a row; the artwork on the Diamond Kings was again produced by the Perez-Steele Galleries. Cards 27-46 again feature Rated Rookies (RR); Danny Tartabull is included in this subset for the second year in a row. The unnumbered checklist cards are arbitrarily numbered below as numbers 654 through 660. The key Rookie Cards in this set are Jose Canseco, Vince Coleman, Kal Daniels, Cecil Fielder, Fred McGriff, Paul O'Neill, and Mickey Tettleton.

	MT	EX-MT	VG
COMPLETE SET (660)	140.00	65.00	17.50
COMPLETE FACT.SET (660)	150.00	70.00	19.00
COMMON PLAYER (1-660)	.10	.05	.01
☐ 1 Kirk Gibson DK	.20	.09	.03
☐ 2 Goose Gossage DK	.15	.07	.02
☐ 3 Willie McGee DK	.15	.07	.02
☐ 4 George Bell DK	.20	.09	.03
☐ 5 Tony Armas DK	.15	.07	.02
☐ 6 Chili Davis DK	.15	.07	.02
☐ 7 Cecil Cooper DK	.15	.07	.02
☐ 8 Mike Boddicker DK	.15	.07	.02
☐ 9 Dave Lopes DK	.15	.07	.02
☐ 10 Bill Doran DK	.15	.07	.02
☐ 11 Bret Saberhagen DK	.35	.16	.04
☐ 12 Brett Butler DK	.15	.07	.02
☐ 13 Harold Baines DK	.15	.07	.02
☐ 14 Mike Davis DK	.15	.07	.02
☐ 15 Tony Perez DK	.15	.07	.02
☐ 16 Willie Randolph DK	.15	.07	.02
☐ 17 Bob Boone DK	.15	.07	.02
☐ 18 Orel Hershiser DK	.25	.11	.03
☐ 19 Johnny Ray DK	.15	.07	.02
☐ 20 Gary Ward DK	.15	.07	.02
☐ 21 Rick Mahler DK	.15	.07	.02
☐ 22 Phil Bradley DK	.15	.07	.02
☐ 23 Jerry Koosman DK	.15	.07	.02
☐ 24 Tom Brunansky DK	.15	.07	.02
☐ 25 Andre Dawson DK	.40	.18	.05
☐ 26 Dwight Gooden DK	.40	.18	.05
☐ 27 Kal Daniels RR	1.25	.55	.16
☐ 28 Fred McGriff RR	28.00	12.50	3.50
☐ 29 Cory Snyder RR	.60	.25	.08
☐ 30 Jose Guzman RR	.75	.35	.09
☐ 31 Ty Gainey RR	.12	.05	.02
☐ 32 Johnny Abrego RR	.12	.05	.02
☐ 33A Andres Galarraga RR (No accent)	.60	.25	.08
☐ 33B Andrés Galarraga RR (Accent over e)	1.25	.55	.16
☐ 34 Dave Shipanoff RR	.12	.05	.02
☐ 35 Mark McLemore RR	.20	.09	.03
☐ 36 Marty Clary RR	.12	.05	.02
☐ 37 Paul O'Neill RR	2.50	1.15	.30
☐ 38 Danny Tartabull RR	2.00	.90	.25
☐ 39 Jose Canseco RR	60.00	27.00	7.50
☐ 40 Juan Nieves RR	.12	.05	.02
☐ 41 Lance McCullers RR	.12	.05	.02
☐ 42 Rick Surhoff RR	.12	.05	.02
☐ 43 Todd Worrell RR	.35	.16	.04
☐ 44 Bob Kipper RR	.12	.05	.02
☐ 45 John Habyan RR	.20	.09	.03
☐ 46 Mike Woodard RR	.12	.05	.02
☐ 47 Mike Boddicker	.10	.05	.01
☐ 48 Robin Yount	2.00	.90	.25
☐ 49 Lou Whitaker	.30	.14	.04
☐ 50 Oil Can Boyd	.10	.05	.01
☐ 51 Rickey Henderson	2.00	.90	.25
☐ 52 Mike Marshall	.10	.05	.01
☐ 53 George Brett	2.00	.90	.25
☐ 54 Dave Kingman	.12	.05	.02
☐ 55 Hubie Brooks	.10	.05	.01
☐ 56 Oddibe McDowell	.10	.05	.01
☐ 57 Doug DeCinces	.10	.05	.01
☐ 58 Britt Burns	.10	.05	.01
☐ 59 Ozzie Smith	1.00	.45	.13
☐ 60 Jose Cruz	.10	.05	.01
☐ 61 Mike Schmidt	2.50	1.15	.30
☐ 62 Pete Rose	1.00	.45	.13
☐ 63 Steve Garvey	.35	.16	.04
☐ 64 Tony Pena	.12	.05	.02
☐ 65 Chili Davis	.12	.05	.02
☐ 66 Dale Murphy	.50	.23	.06
☐ 67 Ryne Sandberg	4.50	2.00	.55
☐ 68 Gary Carter	.35	.16	.04
☐ 69 Alvin Davis	.10	.05	.01
☐ 70 Kent Hrbek	.20	.09	.03
☐ 71 George Bell	.50	.23	.06
☐ 72 Kirby Puckett	10.00	4.50	1.25
☐ 73 Lloyd Moseby	.10	.05	.01
☐ 74 Bob Kearney	.10	.05	.01
☐ 75 Dwight Gooden	1.25	.55	.16
☐ 76 Gary Matthews	.10	.05	.01
☐ 77 Rick Mahler	.10	.05	.01
☐ 78 Benny Distefano	.10	.05	.01
☐ 79 Jeff Leonard	.10	.05	.01
☐ 80 Kevin McReynolds	.12	.05	.02
☐ 81 Ron Oester	.10	.05	.01
☐ 82 John Russell	.10	.05	.01
☐ 83 Tommy Herr	.10	.05	.01
☐ 84 Jerry Mumphrey	.10	.05	.01
☐ 85 Ron Romanick	.10	.05	.01
☐ 86 Daryl Boston	.10	.05	.01
☐ 87 Andre Dawson	1.00	.45	.13
☐ 88 Eddie Murray	1.00	.45	.13
☐ 89 Dion James	.10	.05	.01
☐ 90 Chet Lemon	.10	.05	.01
☐ 91 Bob Stanley	.10	.05	.01
☐ 92 Willie Randolph	.12	.05	.02
☐ 93 Mike Scioscia	.10	.05	.01

☐ 94	Tom Waddell	.10	.05	.01
☐ 95	Danny Jackson	.10	.05	.01
☐ 96	Mike Davis	.10	.05	.01
☐ 97	Mike Fitzgerald	.10	.05	.01
☐ 98	Gary Ward	.10	.05	.01
☐ 99	Pete O'Brien	.10	.05	.01
☐ 100	Bret Saberhagen	.75	.35	.09
☐ 101	Alfredo Griffin	.10	.05	.01
☐ 102	Brett Butler	.20	.09	.03
☐ 103	Ron Guidry	.12	.05	.02
☐ 104	Jerry Reuss	.10	.05	.01
☐ 105	Jack Morris	.75	.35	.09
☐ 106	Rick Dempsey	.10	.05	.01
☐ 107	Ray Burris	.10	.05	.01
☐ 108	Brian Downing	.12	.05	.02
☐ 109	Willie McGee	.20	.09	.03
☐ 110	Bill Doran	.10	.05	.01
☐ 111	Kent Tekulve	.10	.05	.01
☐ 112	Tony Gwynn	3.00	1.35	.40
☐ 113	Marvell Wynne	.10	.05	.01
☐ 114	David Green	.10	.05	.01
☐ 115	Jim Gantner	.10	.05	.01
☐ 116	George Foster	.12	.05	.02
☐ 117	Steve Trout	.10	.05	.01
☐ 118	Mark Langston	.50	.23	.06
☐ 119	Tony Fernandez	.25	.11	.03
☐ 120	John Butcher	.10	.05	.01
☐ 121	Ron Robinson	.10	.05	.01
☐ 122	Dan Spillner	.10	.05	.01
☐ 123	Mike Young	.10	.05	.01
☐ 124	Paul Molitor	.40	.18	.05
☐ 125	Kirk Gibson	.15	.07	.02
☐ 126	Ken Griffey	.12	.05	.02
☐ 127	Tony Armas	.10	.05	.01
☐ 128	Mariano Duncan	.60	.25	.08
☐ 129	Pat Tabler	.10	.05	.01
☐ 130	Frank White	.12	.05	.02
☐ 131	Carney Lansford	.12	.05	.02
☐ 132	Vance Law	.10	.05	.01
☐ 133	Dick Schofield	.10	.05	.01
☐ 134	Wayne Tolleson	.10	.05	.01
☐ 135	Greg Walker	.10	.05	.01
☐ 136	Denny Walling	.10	.05	.01
☐ 137	Ozzie Virgil	.10	.05	.01
☐ 138	Ricky Horton	.10	.05	.01
☐ 139	LaMarr Hoyt	.10	.05	.01
☐ 140	Wayne Krenchicki	.10	.05	.01
☐ 141	Glenn Hubbard	.10	.05	.01
☐ 142	Cecilio Guante	.10	.05	.01
☐ 143	Mike Krukow	.10	.05	.01
☐ 144	Lee Smith	.60	.25	.08
☐ 145	Edwin Nunez	.10	.05	.01
☐ 146	Dave Stieb	.12	.05	.02
☐ 147	Mike Smithson	.10	.05	.01
☐ 148	Ken Dixon	.10	.05	.01
☐ 149	Danny Darwin	.10	.05	.01
☐ 150	Chris Pittaro	.10	.05	.01
☐ 151	Bill Buckner	.12	.05	.02
☐ 152	Mike Pagliarulo	.10	.05	.01
☐ 153	Bill Russell	.12	.05	.02
☐ 154	Brook Jacoby	.10	.05	.01
☐ 155	Pat Sheridan	.10	.05	.01
☐ 156	Mike Gallego	.20	.09	.03
☐ 157	Jim Wohlford	.10	.05	.01
☐ 158	Gary Pettis	.10	.05	.01
☐ 159	Toby Harrah	.10	.05	.01
☐ 160	Richard Dotson	.10	.05	.01
☐ 161	Bob Knepper	.10	.05	.01
☐ 162	Dave Dravecky	.12	.05	.02
☐ 163	Greg Gross	.10	.05	.01
☐ 164	Eric Davis	1.25	.55	.16
☐ 165	Gerald Perry	.10	.05	.01
☐ 166	Rick Rhoden	.10	.05	.01
☐ 167	Keith Moreland	.10	.05	.01
☐ 168	Jack Clark	.12	.05	.02
☐ 169	Storm Davis	.10	.05	.01
☐ 170	Cecil Cooper	.12	.05	.02
☐ 171	Alan Trammell	.30	.14	.04
☐ 172	Roger Clemens	12.00	5.50	1.50
☐ 173	Don Mattingly	2.50	1.15	.30
☐ 174	Pedro Guerrero	.12	.05	.02
☐ 175	Willie Wilson	.10	.05	.01
☐ 176	Dwayne Murphy	.10	.05	.01
☐ 177	Tim Raines	.30	.14	.04
☐ 178	Larry Parrish	.10	.05	.01
☐ 179	Mike Witt	.10	.05	.01
☐ 180	Harold Baines	.25	.11	.03
☐ 181	Vince Coleman UER (BA 2.67 on back)	1.75	.80	.22
☐ 182	Jeff Heathcock	.10	.05	.01
☐ 183	Steve Carlton	.90	.40	.11
☐ 184	Mario Soto	.10	.05	.01
☐ 185	Goose Gossage	.15	.07	.02
☐ 186	Johnny Ray	.10	.05	.01
☐ 187	Dan Gladden	.10	.05	.01
☐ 188	Bob Horner	.12	.05	.02
☐ 189	Rick Sutcliffe	.12	.05	.02
☐ 190	Keith Hernandez	.15	.07	.02
☐ 191	Phil Bradley	.10	.05	.01
☐ 192	Tom Brunansky	.12	.05	.02
☐ 193	Jesse Barfield	.12	.05	.02
☐ 194	Frank Viola	.30	.14	.04
☐ 195	Willie Upshaw	.10	.05	.01
☐ 196	Jim Beattie	.10	.05	.01
☐ 197	Darryl Strawberry	2.50	1.15	.30
☐ 198	Ron Cey	.12	.05	.02
☐ 199	Steve Bedrosian	.10	.05	.01
☐ 200	Steve Kemp	.10	.05	.01
☐ 201	Manny Trillo	.10	.05	.01
☐ 202	Garry Templeton	.10	.05	.01
☐ 203	Dave Parker	.20	.09	.03
☐ 204	John Denny	.10	.05	.01
☐ 205	Terry Pendleton	1.50	.65	.19
☐ 206	Terry Puhl	.10	.05	.01
☐ 207	Bobby Grich	.12	.05	.02
☐ 208	Ozzie Guillen	.60	.25	.08
☐ 209	Jeff Reardon	.50	.23	.06
☐ 210	Cal Ripken	5.00	2.30	.60
☐ 211	Bill Schroeder	.10	.05	.01
☐ 212	Dan Petry	.10	.05	.01
☐ 213	Jim Rice	.15	.07	.02
☐ 214	Dave Righetti	.12	.05	.02
☐ 215	Fernando Valenzuela	.12	.05	.02
☐ 216	Julio Franco	.35	.16	.04
☐ 217	Darryl Motley	.10	.05	.01
☐ 218	Dave Collins	.10	.05	.01
☐ 219	Tim Wallach	.12	.05	.02
☐ 220	George Wright	.10	.05	.01
☐ 221	Tommy Dunbar	.10	.05	.01
☐ 222	Steve Balboni	.10	.05	.01
☐ 223	Jay Howell	.12	.05	.02
☐ 224	Joe Carter	2.50	1.15	.30
☐ 225	Ed Whitson	.10	.05	.01
☐ 226	Orel Hershiser	.50	.23	.06
☐ 227	Willie Hernandez	.10	.05	.01
☐ 228	Lee Lacy	.10	.05	.01
☐ 229	Rollie Fingers	.40	.18	.05
☐ 230	Bob Boone	.12	.05	.02
☐ 231	Joaquin Andujar	.10	.05	.01
☐ 232	Craig Reynolds	.10	.05	.01
☐ 233	Shane Rawley	.10	.05	.01
☐ 234	Eric Show	.10	.05	.01
☐ 235	Jose DeLeon	.10	.05	.01
☐ 236	Jose Uribe	.15	.07	.02
☐ 237	Moose Haas	.10	.05	.01
☐ 238	Wally Backman	.10	.05	.01
☐ 239	Dennis Eckersley	.75	.35	.09
☐ 240	Mike Moore	.12	.05	.02
☐ 241	Damaso Garcia	.10	.05	.01
☐ 242	Tim Teufel	.10	.05	.01
☐ 243	Dave Concepcion	.12	.05	.02
☐ 244	Floyd Bannister	.10	.05	.01
☐ 245	Fred Lynn	.12	.05	.02
☐ 246	Charlie Moore	.10	.05	.01
☐ 247	Walt Terrell	.10	.05	.01
☐ 248	Dave Winfield	1.25	.55	.16
☐ 249	Dwight Evans	.12	.05	.02
☐ 250	Dennis Powell	.10	.05	.01
☐ 251	Andre Thornton	.10	.05	.01
☐ 252	Onix Concepcion	.10	.05	.01
☐ 253	Mike Heath	.10	.05	.01
☐ 254A	David Palmer ERR (Position 2B)	.10	.05	.01
☐ 254B	David Palmer COR (Position P)	.60	.25	.08
☐ 255	Donnie Moore	.10	.05	.01
☐ 256	Curtis Wilkerson	.10	.05	.01
☐ 257	Julio Cruz	.10	.05	.01
☐ 258	Nolan Ryan	6.00	2.70	.75
☐ 259	Jeff Stone	.10	.05	.01
☐ 260	John Tudor	.12	.05	.02
☐ 261	Mark Thurmond	.10	.05	.01
☐ 262	Jay Tibbs	.10	.05	.01
☐ 263	Rafael Ramirez	.10	.05	.01
☐ 264	Larry McWilliams	.10	.05	.01
☐ 265	Mark Davis	.12	.05	.02
☐ 266	Bob Dernier	.10	.05	.01
☐ 267	Matt Young	.10	.05	.01
☐ 268	Jim Clancy	.10	.05	.01
☐ 269	Mickey Hatcher	.10	.05	.01
☐ 270	Sammy Stewart	.10	.05	.01
☐ 271	Bob L. Gibson	.10	.05	.01
☐ 272	Nelson Simmons	.10	.05	.01
☐ 273	Rich Gedman	.10	.05	.01
☐ 274	Butch Wynegar	.10	.05	.01
☐ 275	Ken Howell	.10	.05	.01

☐ 276	Mel Hall	.12	.05	.02
☐ 277	Jim Sundberg	.12	.05	.02
☐ 278	Chris Codiroli	.10	.05	.01
☐ 279	Herm Winningham	.20	.09	.03
☐ 280	Rod Carew	.90	.40	.11
☐ 281	Don Slaught	.10	.05	.01
☐ 282	Scott Fletcher	.10	.05	.01
☐ 283	Bill Dawley	.10	.05	.01
☐ 284	Andy Hawkins	.10	.05	.01
☐ 285	Glenn Wilson	.10	.05	.01
☐ 286	Nick Esasky	.10	.05	.01
☐ 287	Claudell Washington	.10	.05	.01
☐ 288	Lee Mazzilli	.10	.05	.01
☐ 289	Jody Davis	.10	.05	.01
☐ 290	Darrell Porter	.10	.05	.01
☐ 291	Scott McGregor	.10	.05	.01
☐ 292	Ted Simmons	.12	.05	.02
☐ 293	Aurelio Lopez	.10	.05	.01
☐ 294	Marty Barrett	.10	.05	.01
☐ 295	Dale Berra	.10	.05	.01
☐ 296	Greg Brock	.10	.05	.01
☐ 297	Charlie Leibrandt	.12	.05	.02
☐ 298	Bill Krueger	.10	.05	.01
☐ 299	Bryn Smith	.10	.05	.01
☐ 300	Burt Hooton	.10	.05	.01
☐ 301	Stu Cliburn	.10	.05	.01
☐ 302	Luis Salazar	.10	.05	.01
☐ 303	Ken Dayley	.10	.05	.01
☐ 304	Frank DiPino	.10	.05	.01
☐ 305	Von Hayes	.10	.05	.01
☐ 306	Gary Redus	.10	.05	.01
☐ 307	Craig Lefferts	.12	.05	.02
☐ 308	Sammy Khalifa	.10	.05	.01
☐ 309	Scott Garrelts	.10	.05	.01
☐ 310	Rick Cerone	.10	.05	.01
☐ 311	Shawon Dunston	.30	.14	.04
☐ 312	Howard Johnson	.60	.25	.08
☐ 313	Jim Presley	.10	.05	.01
☐ 314	Gary Gaetti	.12	.05	.02
☐ 315	Luis Leal	.10	.05	.01
☐ 316	Mark Salas	.10	.05	.01
☐ 317	Bill Caudill	.10	.05	.01
☐ 318	Dave Henderson	.12	.05	.02
☐ 319	Rafael Santana	.10	.05	.01
☐ 320	Leon Durham	.10	.05	.01
☐ 321	Bruce Sutter	.12	.05	.02
☐ 322	Jason Thompson	.10	.05	.01
☐ 323	Bob Brenly	.10	.05	.01
☐ 324	Carmelo Martinez	.10	.05	.01
☐ 325	Eddie Milner	.10	.05	.01
☐ 326	Juan Samuel	.12	.05	.02
☐ 327	Tom Nieto	.10	.05	.01
☐ 328	Dave Smith	.10	.05	.01
☐ 329	Urbano Lugo	.10	.05	.01
☐ 330	Joel Skinner	.10	.05	.01
☐ 331	Bill Gullickson	.12	.05	.02
☐ 332	Floyd Rayford	.10	.05	.01
☐ 333	Ben Oglivie	.10	.05	.01
☐ 334	Lance Parrish	.12	.05	.02
☐ 335	Jackie Gutierrez	.10	.05	.01
☐ 336	Dennis Rasmussen	.10	.05	.01
☐ 337	Terry Whitfield	.10	.05	.01
☐ 338	Neal Heaton	.10	.05	.01
☐ 339	Jorge Orta	.10	.05	.01
☐ 340	Donnie Hill	.10	.05	.01
☐ 341	Joe Hesketh	.10	.05	.01
☐ 342	Charlie Hough	.10	.05	.01
☐ 343	Dave Rozema	.10	.05	.01
☐ 344	Greg Pryor	.10	.05	.01
☐ 345	Mickey Tettleton	2.00	.90	.25
☐ 346	George Vukovich	.10	.05	.01
☐ 347	Don Baylor	.12	.05	.02
☐ 348	Carlos Diaz	.10	.05	.01
☐ 349	Barbaro Garbey	.10	.05	.01
☐ 350	Larry Sheets	.10	.05	.01
☐ 351	Ted Higuera	.20	.09	.03
☐ 352	Juan Beniquez	.10	.05	.01
☐ 353	Bob Forsch	.10	.05	.01
☐ 354	Mark Bailey	.10	.05	.01
☐ 355	Larry Andersen	.10	.05	.01
☐ 356	Terry Kennedy	.10	.05	.01
☐ 357	Don Robinson	.10	.05	.01
☐ 358	Jim Gott	.10	.05	.01
☐ 359	Earnie Riles	.10	.05	.01
☐ 360	John Christensen	.10	.05	.01
☐ 361	Ray Fontenot	.10	.05	.01
☐ 362	Spike Owen	.10	.05	.01
☐ 363	Jim Acker	.10	.05	.01
☐ 364	Ron Davis	.10	.05	.01
☐ 365	Tom Hume	.10	.05	.01
☐ 366	Carlton Fisk	.90	.40	.11
☐ 367	Nate Snell	.10	.05	.01
☐ 368	Rick Manning	.10	.05	.01
☐ 369	Darrell Evans	.12	.05	.02
☐ 370	Ron Hassey	.10	.05	.01
☐ 371	Wade Boggs	2.00	.90	.25
☐ 372	Rick Honeycutt	.10	.05	.01
☐ 373	Chris Bando	.10	.05	.01
☐ 374	Bud Black	.10	.05	.01
☐ 375	Steve Henderson	.10	.05	.01
☐ 376	Charlie Lea	.10	.05	.01
☐ 377	Reggie Jackson	1.00	.45	.13
☐ 378	Dave Schmidt	.10	.05	.01
☐ 379	Bob James	.10	.05	.01
☐ 380	Glenn Davis	1.00	.45	.13
☐ 381	Tim Corcoran	.10	.05	.01
☐ 382	Danny Cox	.10	.05	.01
☐ 383	Tim Flannery	.10	.05	.01
☐ 384	Tom Browning	.25	.11	.03
☐ 385	Rick Camp	.10	.05	.01
☐ 386	Jim Morrison	.10	.05	.01
☐ 387	Dave LaPoint	.10	.05	.01
☐ 388	Dave Lopes	.12	.05	.02
☐ 389	Al Cowens	.10	.05	.01
☐ 390	Doyle Alexander	.10	.05	.01
☐ 391	Tim Laudner	.10	.05	.01
☐ 392	Don Aase	.10	.05	.01
☐ 393	Jaime Cocanower	.10	.05	.01
☐ 394	Randy O'Neal	.10	.05	.01
☐ 395	Mike Easler	.10	.05	.01
☐ 396	Scott Bradley	.10	.05	.01
☐ 397	Tom Niedenfuer	.10	.05	.01
☐ 398	Jerry Willard	.10	.05	.01
☐ 399	Lonnie Smith	.10	.05	.01
☐ 400	Bruce Bochte	.10	.05	.01
☐ 401	Terry Francona	.10	.05	.01
☐ 402	Jim Slaton	.10	.05	.01
☐ 403	Bill Stein	.10	.05	.01
☐ 404	Tim Hulett	.10	.05	.01
☐ 405	Alan Ashby	.10	.05	.01
☐ 406	Tim Stoddard	.10	.05	.01
☐ 407	Garry Maddox	.10	.05	.01
☐ 408	Ted Power	.10	.05	.01
☐ 409	Len Barker	.10	.05	.01
☐ 410	Denny Gonzalez	.10	.05	.01
☐ 411	George Frazier	.10	.05	.01
☐ 412	Andy Van Slyke	.75	.35	.09
☐ 413	Jim Dwyer	.10	.05	.01
☐ 414	Paul Householder	.10	.05	.01
☐ 415	Alejandro Sanchez	.10	.05	.01
☐ 416	Steve Crawford	.10	.05	.01
☐ 417	Dan Pasqua	.12	.05	.02
☐ 418	Enos Cabell	.10	.05	.01
☐ 419	Mike Jones	.10	.05	.01
☐ 420	Steve Kiefer	.10	.05	.01
☐ 421	Tim Burke	.20	.09	.03
☐ 422	Mike Mason	.10	.05	.01
☐ 423	Ruppert Jones	.10	.05	.01
☐ 424	Jerry Hairston	.10	.05	.01
☐ 425	Tito Landrum	.10	.05	.01
☐ 426	Jeff Calhoun	.10	.05	.01
☐ 427	Don Carman	.10	.05	.01
☐ 428	Tony Perez	.30	.14	.04
☐ 429	Jerry Davis	.10	.05	.01
☐ 430	Bob Walk	.10	.05	.01
☐ 431	Brad Wellman	.10	.05	.01
☐ 432	Terry Forster	.10	.05	.01
☐ 433	Billy Hatcher	.12	.05	.02
☐ 434	Clint Hurdle	.10	.05	.01
☐ 435	Ivan Calderon	1.25	.55	.16
☐ 436	Pete Filson	.10	.05	.01
☐ 437	Tom Henke	.30	.14	.04
☐ 438	Dave Engle	.10	.05	.01
☐ 439	Tom Filer	.10	.05	.01
☐ 440	Gorman Thomas	.10	.05	.01
☐ 441	Rick Aguilera	1.75	.80	.22
☐ 442	Scott Sanderson	.10	.05	.01
☐ 443	Jeff Dedmon	.10	.05	.01
☐ 444	Joe Orsulak	.35	.16	.04
☐ 445	Atlee Hammaker	.10	.05	.01
☐ 446	Jerry Royster	.10	.05	.01
☐ 447	Buddy Bell	.12	.05	.02
☐ 448	Dave Rucker	.10	.05	.01
☐ 449	Ivan DeJesus	.10	.05	.01
☐ 450	Jim Pankovits	.10	.05	.01
☐ 451	Jerry Narron	.10	.05	.01
☐ 452	Bryan Little	.10	.05	.01
☐ 453	Gary Lucas	.10	.05	.01
☐ 454	Dennis Martinez	.12	.05	.02
☐ 455	Ed Romero	.10	.05	.01
☐ 456	Bob Melvin	.10	.05	.01
☐ 457	Glenn Hoffman	.10	.05	.01
☐ 458	Bob Shirley	.10	.05	.01
☐ 459	Bob Welch	.15	.07	.02
☐ 460	Carmen Castillo	.10	.05	.01
☐ 461	Dave Leeper OF	.10	.05	.01

☐ 462	Tim Birtsas	.10	.05	.01
☐ 463	Randy St.Claire	.10	.05	.01
☐ 464	Chris Welsh	.10	.05	.01
☐ 465	Greg Harris	.10	.05	.01
☐ 466	Lynn Jones	.10	.05	.01
☐ 467	Dusty Baker	.12	.05	.02
☐ 468	Roy Smith	.10	.05	.01
☐ 469	Andre Robertson	.10	.05	.01
☐ 470	Ken Landreaux	.10	.05	.01
☐ 471	Dave Bergman	.10	.05	.01
☐ 472	Gary Roenicke	.10	.05	.01
☐ 473	Pete Vuckovich	.10	.05	.01
☐ 474	Kirk McCaskill	.30	.14	.04
☐ 475	Jeff Lahti	.10	.05	.01
☐ 476	Mike Scott	.12	.05	.02
☐ 477	Darren Daulton	2.00	.90	.25
☐ 478	Graig Nettles	.12	.05	.02
☐ 479	Bill Almon	.10	.05	.01
☐ 480	Greg Minton	.10	.05	.01
☐ 481	Randy Ready	.10	.05	.01
☐ 482	Len Dykstra	1.75	.80	.22
☐ 483	Thad Bosley	.10	.05	.01
☐ 484	Harold Reynolds	.60	.25	.08
☐ 485	Al Oliver	.12	.05	.02
☐ 486	Roy Smalley	.10	.05	.01
☐ 487	John Franco	.25	.11	.03
☐ 488	Juan Agosto	.10	.05	.01
☐ 489	Al Pardo	.10	.05	.01
☐ 490	Bill Wegman	.50	.23	.06
☐ 491	Frank Tanana	.12	.05	.02
☐ 492	Brian Fisher	.10	.05	.01
☐ 493	Mark Clear	.10	.05	.01
☐ 494	Len Matuszek	.10	.05	.01
☐ 495	Ramon Romero	.10	.05	.01
☐ 496	John Wathan	.10	.05	.01
☐ 497	Rob Picciolo	.10	.05	.01
☐ 498	U.L. Washington	.10	.05	.01
☐ 499	John Candelaria	.10	.05	.01
☐ 500	Duane Walker	.10	.05	.01
☐ 501	Gene Nelson	.10	.05	.01
☐ 502	John Mizerock	.10	.05	.01
☐ 503	Luis Aguayo	.10	.05	.01
☐ 504	Kurt Kepshire	.10	.05	.01
☐ 505	Ed Wojna	.10	.05	.01
☐ 506	Joe Price	.10	.05	.01
☐ 507	Milt Thompson	.20	.09	.03
☐ 508	Junior Ortiz	.10	.05	.01
☐ 509	Vida Blue	.12	.05	.02
☐ 510	Steve Engel	.10	.05	.01
☐ 511	Karl Best	.10	.05	.01
☐ 512	Cecil Fielder	27.00	12.00	3.40
☐ 513	Frank Eufemia	.10	.05	.01
☐ 514	Tippy Martinez	.10	.05	.01
☐ 515	Billy Joe Robidoux	.10	.05	.01
☐ 516	Bill Scherrer	.10	.05	.01
☐ 517	Bruce Hurst	.12	.05	.02
☐ 518	Rich Bordi	.10	.05	.01
☐ 519	Steve Yeager	.10	.05	.01
☐ 520	Tony Bernazard	.10	.05	.01
☐ 521	Hal McRae	.12	.05	.02
☐ 522	Jose Rijo	.60	.25	.08
☐ 523	Mitch Webster	.10	.05	.01
☐ 524	Jack Howell	.10	.05	.01
☐ 525	Alan Bannister	.10	.05	.01
☐ 526	Ron Kittle	.10	.05	.01
☐ 527	Phil Garner	.12	.05	.02
☐ 528	Kurt Bevacqua	.10	.05	.01
☐ 529	Kevin Gross	.10	.05	.01
☐ 530	Bo Diaz	.10	.05	.01
☐ 531	Ken Oberkfell	.10	.05	.01
☐ 532	Rick Reuschel	.10	.05	.01
☐ 533	Ron Meridith	.10	.05	.01
☐ 534	Steve Braun	.10	.05	.01
☐ 535	Wayne Gross	.10	.05	.01
☐ 536	Ray Searage	.10	.05	.01
☐ 537	Tom Brookens	.10	.05	.01
☐ 538	Al Nipper	.10	.05	.01
☐ 539	Billy Sample	.10	.05	.01
☐ 540	Steve Sax	.25	.11	.03
☐ 541	Dan Quisenberry	.12	.05	.02
☐ 542	Tony Phillips	.12	.05	.02
☐ 543	Floyd Youmans	.10	.05	.01
☐ 544	Steve Buechele	1.00	.45	.13
☐ 545	Craig Gerber	.10	.05	.01
☐ 546	Joe DeSa	.10	.05	.01
☐ 547	Brian Harper	.25	.11	.03
☐ 548	Kevin Bass	.10	.05	.01
☐ 549	Tom Foley	.10	.05	.01
☐ 550	Dave Van Gorder	.10	.05	.01
☐ 551	Bruce Bochy	.10	.05	.01
☐ 552	R.J. Reynolds	.10	.05	.01
☐ 553	Chris Brown	.10	.05	.01
☐ 554	Bruce Benedict	.10	.05	.01
☐ 555	Warren Brusstar	.10	.05	.01
☐ 556	Danny Heep	.10	.05	.01
☐ 557	Darnell Coles	.12	.05	.02
☐ 558	Greg Gagne	.12	.05	.02
☐ 559	Ernie Whitt	.10	.05	.01
☐ 560	Ron Washington	.10	.05	.01
☐ 561	Jimmy Key	.25	.11	.03
☐ 562	Billy Swift	.40	.18	.05
☐ 563	Ron Darling	.20	.09	.03
☐ 564	Dick Ruthven	.10	.05	.01
☐ 565	Zane Smith	.25	.11	.03
☐ 566	Sid Bream	.12	.05	.02
☐ 567A	Joel Youngblood ERR (Position P)	.10	.05	.01
☐ 567B	Joel Youngblood COR (Position IF)	.60	.25	.08
☐ 568	Mario Ramirez	.10	.05	.01
☐ 569	Tom Runnells	.12	.05	.02
☐ 570	Rick Schu	.10	.05	.01
☐ 571	Bill Campbell	.10	.05	.01
☐ 572	Dickie Thon	.10	.05	.01
☐ 573	Al Holland	.10	.05	.01
☐ 574	Reid Nichols	.10	.05	.01
☐ 575	Bert Roberge	.10	.05	.01
☐ 576	Mike Flanagan	.10	.05	.01
☐ 577	Tim Leary	.10	.05	.01
☐ 578	Mike Laga	.10	.05	.01
☐ 579	Steve Lyons	.10	.05	.01
☐ 580	Phil Niekro	.30	.14	.04
☐ 581	Gilberto Reyes	.12	.05	.02
☐ 582	Jamie Easterly	.10	.05	.01
☐ 583	Mark Gubicza	.12	.05	.02
☐ 584	Stan Javier	.12	.05	.02
☐ 585	Bill Laskey	.10	.05	.01
☐ 586	Jeff Russell	.12	.05	.02
☐ 587	Dickie Noles	.10	.05	.01
☐ 588	Steve Farr	.12	.05	.02
☐ 589	Steve Ontiveros	.10	.05	.01
☐ 590	Mike Hargrove	.12	.05	.02
☐ 591	Marty Bystrom	.10	.05	.01
☐ 592	Franklin Stubbs	.10	.05	.01
☐ 593	Larry Herndon	.10	.05	.01
☐ 594	Bill Swaggerty	.10	.05	.01
☐ 595	Carlos Ponce	.10	.05	.01
☐ 596	Pat Perry	.10	.05	.01
☐ 597	Ray Knight	.12	.05	.02
☐ 598	Steve Lombardozzi	.10	.05	.01
☐ 599	Brad Havens	.10	.05	.01
☐ 600	Pat Clements	.10	.05	.01
☐ 601	Joe Niekro	.12	.05	.02
☐ 602	Hank Aaron Puzzle Card	.15	.07	.02
☐ 603	Dwayne Henry	.10	.05	.01
☐ 604	Mookie Wilson	.12	.05	.02
☐ 605	Buddy Biancalana	.10	.05	.01
☐ 606	Rance Mulliniks	.10	.05	.01
☐ 607	Alan Wiggins	.10	.05	.01
☐ 608	Joe Cowley	.10	.05	.01
☐ 609A	Tom Seaver (Green borders on name)	1.00	.45	.13
☐ 609B	Tom Seaver (Yellow borders on name)	2.50	1.15	.30
☐ 610	Neil Allen	.10	.05	.01
☐ 611	Don Sutton	.30	.14	.04
☐ 612	Fred Toliver	.10	.05	.01
☐ 613	Jay Baller	.10	.05	.01
☐ 614	Marc Sullivan	.10	.05	.01
☐ 615	John Grubb	.10	.05	.01
☐ 616	Bruce Kison	.10	.05	.01
☐ 617	Bill Madlock	.12	.05	.02
☐ 618	Chris Chambliss	.12	.05	.02
☐ 619	Dave Stewart	.20	.09	.03
☐ 620	Tim Lollar	.10	.05	.01
☐ 621	Gary Lavelle	.10	.05	.01
☐ 622	Charles Hudson	.10	.05	.01
☐ 623	Joel Davis	.10	.05	.01
☐ 624	Joe Johnson	.10	.05	.01
☐ 625	Sid Fernandez	.25	.11	.03
☐ 626	Dennis Lamp	.10	.05	.01
☐ 627	Terry Harper	.10	.05	.01
☐ 628	Jack Lazorko	.10	.05	.01
☐ 629	Roger McDowell	.25	.11	.03
☐ 630	Mark Funderburk	.10	.05	.01
☐ 631	Ed Lynch	.10	.05	.01
☐ 632	Rudy Law	.10	.05	.01
☐ 633	Roger Mason	.20	.09	.03
☐ 634	Mike Felder	.25	.11	.03
☐ 635	Ken Schrom	.10	.05	.01
☐ 636	Bob Ojeda	.10	.05	.01
☐ 637	Ed VandeBerg	.10	.05	.01
☐ 638	Bobby Meacham	.10	.05	.01

☐ 639 Cliff Johnson	.10	.05	.01
☐ 640 Garth Iorg	.10	.05	.01
☐ 641 Dan Driessen	.10	.05	.01
☐ 642 Mike Brown OF	.10	.05	.01
☐ 643 John Shelby	.10	.05	.01
☐ 644 Pete Rose (Ty-Breaking)	.50	.23	.06
☐ 645 The Knuckle Brothers Phil Niekro Joe Niekro	.10	.05	.01
☐ 646 Jesse Orosco	.10	.05	.01
☐ 647 Billy Beane	.10	.05	.01
☐ 648 Cesar Cedeno	.12	.05	.02
☐ 649 Bert Blyleven	.20	.09	.03
☐ 650 Max Venable	.10	.05	.01
☐ 651 Fleet Feet Vince Coleman Willie McGee	.30	.14	.04
☐ 652 Calvin Schiraldi	.10	.05	.01
☐ 653 King of Kings (Pete Rose)	1.00	.45	.13
☐ 654 CL: Diamond Kings (Unnumbered)	.15	.02	.00
☐ 655A CL 1: 27-130 (Unnumbered) (45 Beane ERR)	.15	.02	.00
☐ 655B CL 1: 27-130 (Unnumbered) (45 Habyan COR)	.60	.06	.02
☐ 656 CL 2: 131-234 (Unnumbered)	.15	.02	.00
☐ 657 CL 3: 235-338 (Unnumbered)	.15	.02	.00
☐ 658 CL 4: 339-442 (Unnumbered)	.15	.02	.00
☐ 659 CL 5: 443-546 (Unnumbered)	.15	.02	.00
☐ 660 CL 6: 547-653 (Unnumbered)	.15	.02	.00

1986 Donruss All-Stars

The cards in this 60-card set measure approximately 3 1/2" by 5". Players featured were involved in the 1985 All-Star game played in Minnesota. Cards are very similar in design to the 1986 Donruss regular issue set. The backs give each player's All-Star game statistics and have an orange-yellow border.

	MT	EX-MT	VG
COMPLETE SET (60)	7.50	3.40	.95
COMMON PLAYERS (1-59)	.07	.03	.01
☐ 1 Tony Gwynn	.50	.23	.06
☐ 2 Tommy Herr	.07	.03	.01
☐ 3 Steve Garvey	.30	.14	.04
☐ 4 Dale Murphy	.40	.18	.05
☐ 5 Darryl Strawberry	.60	.25	.08
☐ 6 Graig Nettles	.10	.05	.01
☐ 7 Terry Kennedy	.07	.03	.01
☐ 8 Ozzie Smith	.35	.16	.04
☐ 9 LaMarr Hoyt	.07	.03	.01
☐ 10 Rickey Henderson	.75	.35	.09
☐ 11 Lou Whitaker	.15	.07	.02
☐ 12 George Brett	.60	.25	.08
☐ 13 Eddie Murray	.35	.16	.04
☐ 14 Cal Ripken	1.25	.55	.16
☐ 15 Dave Winfield	.45	.20	.06
☐ 16 Jim Rice	.20	.09	.03
☐ 17 Carlton Fisk	.45	.20	.06
☐ 18 Jack Morris	.25	.11	.03
☐ 19 Jose Cruz	.07	.03	.01
☐ 20 Tim Raines	.15	.07	.02
☐ 21 Nolan Ryan	1.50	.65	.19
☐ 22 Tony Pena	.07	.03	.01
☐ 23 Jack Clark	.10	.05	.01
☐ 24 Dave Parker	.15	.07	.02
☐ 25 Tim Wallach	.07	.03	.01
☐ 26 Ozzie Virgil	.07	.03	.01
☐ 27 Fernando Valenzuela	.10	.05	.01
☐ 28 Dwight Gooden	.50	.23	.06
☐ 29 Glenn Wilson	.07	.03	.01
☐ 30 Garry Templeton	.07	.03	.01
☐ 31 Goose Gossage	.15	.07	.02
☐ 32 Ryne Sandberg	1.25	.55	.16
☐ 33 Jeff Reardon	.20	.09	.03
☐ 34 Pete Rose	.75	.35	.09
☐ 35 Scott Garrelts	.07	.03	.01
☐ 36 Willie McGee	.10	.05	.01
☐ 37 Ron Darling	.15	.07	.02
☐ 38 Dick Williams MG	.07	.03	.01
☐ 39 Paul Molitor	.25	.11	.03
☐ 40 Damaso Garcia	.07	.03	.01
☐ 41 Phil Bradley	.07	.03	.01
☐ 42 Dan Petry	.07	.03	.01
☐ 43 Willie Hernandez	.10	.05	.01
☐ 44 Tom Brunansky	.10	.05	.01
☐ 45 Alan Trammell	.20	.09	.03
☐ 46 Donnie Moore	.07	.03	.01
☐ 47 Wade Boggs	.75	.35	.09
☐ 48 Ernie Whitt	.07	.03	.01
☐ 49 Harold Baines	.10	.05	.01
☐ 50 Don Mattingly	.90	.40	.11
☐ 51 Gary Ward	.07	.03	.01
☐ 52 Bert Blyleven	.10	.05	.01
☐ 53 Jimmy Key	.15	.07	.02
☐ 54 Cecil Cooper	.10	.05	.01
☐ 55 Dave Stieb	.10	.05	.01
☐ 56 Rich Gedman	.07	.03	.01
☐ 57 Jay Howell	.07	.03	.01
☐ 58 Sparky Anderson MG	.07	.03	.01
☐ 59 Minneapolis Metrodome	.07	.03	.01
☐ NNO Checklist Card	.07	.03	.01

1986 Donruss All-Star Box

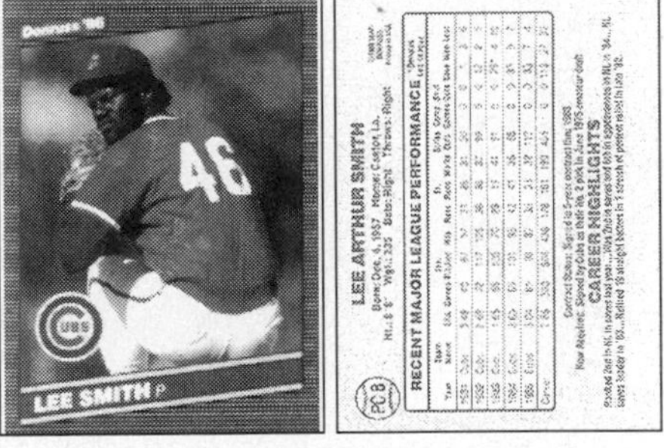

The cards in this four-card set measure the standard 2 1/2" by 3 1/2" in spite of the fact that they form the bottom of the wax pack box for the larger Donruss All-Star cards. These box cards have essentially the same design as the 1986 Donruss regular issue set. The cards were printed on the bottoms of the Donruss All-Star (3 1/2" by 5") wax pack boxes. The four cards (PC7 to PC9 plus a Hank Aaron puzzle card) are considered a separate set in their own right and are not typically included in a complete set of the regular issue 1986 Donruss All-Star (or regular) cards. The value of the panel uncut is slightly greater, perhaps by 25 percent greater, than the value of the individual cards cut up carefully.

	MT	EX-MT	VG
COMPLETE SET (4)	1.50	.65	.19
COMMON PLAYERS	.15	.07	.02

☐ PC7 Wade Boggs	1.25	.55	.16
☐ PC8 Lee Smith	.50	.23	.06
☐ PC9 Cecil Cooper	.15	.07	.02
☐ PUZO Hank Aaron Puzzle Card	.15	.07	.02

1986 Donruss Highlights

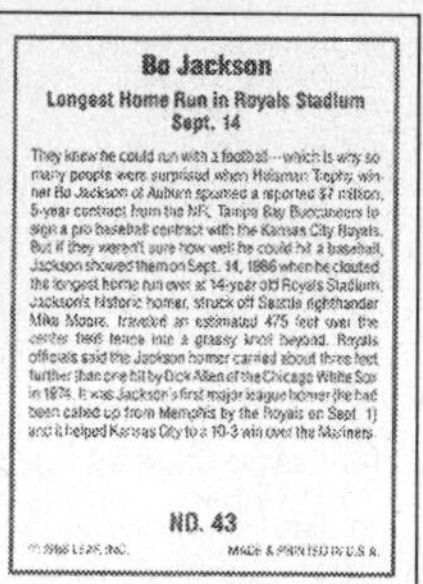

Donruss' second edition of Highlights was released late in 1986. These glossy-coated cards are standard size, measuring 2 1/2" by 3 1/2". Cards commemorate events during the 1986 season, as well as players and pitchers of the month from each league. The set was distributed in its own red, white, blue, and gold box along with a small Hank Aaron puzzle. Card fronts are similar to the regular 1986 Donruss issue except that the Highlights logo is positioned in the lower left-hand corner and the borders are in gold instead of blue. The backs are printed in black and gold on white card stock.

	MT	EX-MT	VG
COMPLETE SET (56)	8.00	3.60	1.00
COMMON PLAYER (1-56)	.06	.03	.01
☐ 1 Will Clark Homers in First At-Bat	1.25	.55	.16
☐ 2 Jose Rijo Oakland Milestone for Strikeouts	.30	.14	.04
☐ 3 George Brett Royals' All-Time Hit Man	.50	.23	.06
☐ 4 Mike Schmidt Phillies RBI Leader	.75	.35	.09
☐ 5 Roger Clemens KKKKKKKKKK KKKKKKKKKK	1.00	.45	.13
☐ 6 Roger Clemens AL Pitcher April	.75	.35	.09
☐ 7 Kirby Puckett AL Player April	.75	.35	.09
☐ 8 Dwight Gooden NL Pitcher April	.30	.14	.04
☐ 9 Johnny Ray NL Player April	.06	.03	.01
☐ 10 Reggie Jackson Eclipses Mantle HR Record	.50	.23	.06
☐ 11 Wade Boggs First Five Hit Game of Career	.50	.23	.06
☐ 12 Don Aase AL Pitcher May	.06	.03	.01
☐ 13 Wade Boggs AL Player May	.50	.23	.06
☐ 14 Jeff Reardon NL Pitcher May	.15	.07	.02
☐ 15 Hubie Brooks NL Player May	.06	.03	.01
☐ 16 Don Sutton Notches 300th	.15	.07	.02
☐ 17 Roger Clemens Starts 14-0	.75	.35	.09
☐ 18 Roger Clemens AL Pitcher June	.75	.35	.09
☐ 19 Kent Hrbek AL Player June	.10	.05	.01
☐ 20 Rick Rhoden NL Pitcher June	.06	.03	.01
☐ 21 Kevin Bass NL Player June	.06	.03	.01
☐ 22 Bob Horner Blasts four HRs in one Game	.10	.05	.01
☐ 23 Wally Joyner Starting All-Star Rookie	.50	.23	.06
☐ 24 Darryl Strawberry Starts Third Straight All-Star Game	.50	.23	.06
☐ 25 Fernando Valenzuela Ties All-Star Game Record	.10	.05	.01
☐ 26 Roger Clemens All-Star Game MVP	.75	.35	.09
☐ 27 Jack Morris AL Pitcher July	.20	.09	.03
☐ 28 Scott Fletcher AL Player July	.06	.03	.01
☐ 29 Todd Worrell NL Pitcher July	.15	.07	.02
☐ 30 Eric Davis NL Player July	.40	.18	.05
☐ 31 Bert Blyleven Records 3000th Strikeout	.10	.05	.01
☐ 32 Bobby Doerr '86 HOF Inductee	.15	.07	.02
☐ 33 Ernie Lombardi '86 HOF Inductee	.15	.07	.02
☐ 34 Willie McCovey '86 HOF Inductee	.25	.11	.03
☐ 35 Steve Carlton Notches 4000th K	.25	.11	.03
☐ 36 Mike Schmidt Surpasses DiMaggio Record	.75	.35	.09
☐ 37 Juan Samuel Records 3rd "Quadruple Double"	.06	.03	.01
☐ 38 Mike Witt AL Pitcher August	.06	.03	.01
☐ 39 Doug DeCinces AL Player August	.06	.03	.01
☐ 40 Bill Gullickson NL Pitcher August	.15	.07	.02
☐ 41 Dale Murphy NL Player August	.30	.14	.04
☐ 42 Joe Carter Sets Tribe Offensive Record	.60	.25	.08
☐ 43 Bo Jackson Longest HR in Royals Stadium	1.00	.45	.13
☐ 44 Joe Cowley Majors 1st No- Hitter in 2 Years	.06	.03	.01
☐ 45 Jim Deshaies Sets ML Strikeout Record	.06	.03	.01
☐ 46 Mike Scott No Hitter Clinches Division	.10	.05	.01
☐ 47 Bruce Hurst AL Pitcher September	.10	.05	.01
☐ 48 Don Mattingly AL Player September	.75	.35	.09
☐ 49 Mike Krukow NL Pitcher September	.06	.03	.01
☐ 50 Steve Sax NL Player September	.15	.07	.02
☐ 51 John Cangelosi AL Rookie Steals Record	.06	.03	.01
☐ 52 Dave Righetti ML Save Mark	.06	.03	.01
☐ 53 Don Mattingly Yankee Record for Hits and Doubles	.75	.35	.09
☐ 54 Todd Worrell Donruss NL ROY	.25	.11	.03
☐ 55 Jose Canseco Donruss AL ROY	1.50	.65	.19
☐ 56 Checklist Card	.06	.03	.01

1986 Donruss Pop-Ups

This set is the companion of the 1986 Donruss All-Star (60) set; as such it features the first 18 cards of that set (the All-Star starting line-ups) in a pop-up, die-cut type of card. These cards (measuring (2 1/2" by 5") can be "popped up" to feature a standing card showing the player in action in front of the Metrodome ballpark background. Although this set is unnumbered it is numbered in the same order as its companion set, presumably according to the respective batting orders of the starting line-ups. The first nine numbers below are National Leaguers and the last nine are American Leaguers. See also the Donruss All-Star checklist card which contains a checklist for the Pop-Ups as well.

	MT	EX-MT	VG
COMPLETE SET (18)	5.00	2.30	.60
COMMON PLAYERS (1-18)	.10	.05	.01
☐ 1 Tony Gwynn	.60	.25	.08
☐ 2 Tommy Herr	.10	.05	.01
☐ 3 Steve Garvey	.35	.16	.04
☐ 4 Dale Murphy	.45	.20	.06
☐ 5 Darryl Strawberry	.75	.35	.09
☐ 6 Graig Nettles	.15	.07	.02
☐ 7 Terry Kennedy	.10	.05	.01
☐ 8 Ozzie Smith	.40	.18	.05
☐ 9 LaMarr Hoyt	.10	.05	.01
☐ 10 Rickey Henderson	.90	.40	.11
☐ 11 Lou Whitaker	.20	.09	.03
☐ 12 George Brett	.75	.35	.09
☐ 13 Eddie Murray	.45	.20	.06
☐ 14 Cal Ripken	1.50	.65	.19
☐ 15 Dave Winfield	.50	.23	.06
☐ 16 Jim Rice	.25	.11	.03
☐ 17 Carlton Fisk	.50	.23	.06
☐ 18 Jack Morris	.30	.14	.04

1986 Donruss Rookies

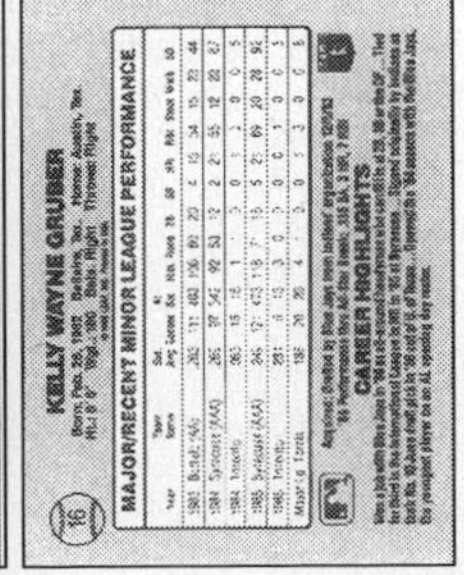

The 1986 Donruss "The Rookies" set features 56 cards plus a 15-piece puzzle of Hank Aaron. Cards are in full color and are standard size, 2 1/2" by 3 1/2". The set was distributed in a small green box with gold lettering. Although the set was wrapped in cellophane, the top card was number 1 Joyner, resulting in a percentage of the Joyner cards arriving in less than perfect condition. Donruss fixed the problem after it was called to their attention and even went so far as to include a customer service phone number in their second printing. Card fronts are similar in design to the 1986 Donruss regular issue except for the presence of "The Rookies" logo in the lower left corner and a bluish green border instead of a blue border. The key (extended) Rookie Cards in this set are Barry Bonds, Bobby Bonilla, Will Clark, Bo Jackson, Wally Joyner, Kevin Mitchell, and Ruben Sierra.

	MT	EX-MT	VG
COMPLETE SET (56)	50.00	23.00	6.25
COMMON PLAYER (1-56)	.10	.05	.01
☐ 1 Wally Joyner	1.75	.80	.22
☐ 2 Tracy Jones	.10	.05	.01
☐ 3 Allan Anderson	.15	.07	.02
☐ 4 Ed Correa	.10	.05	.01
☐ 5 Reggie Williams	.10	.05	.01
☐ 6 Charlie Kerfeld	.15	.07	.02
☐ 7 Andres Galarraga	.30	.14	.04
☐ 8 Bob Tewksbury	.90	.40	.11
☐ 9 Al Newman	.10	.05	.01
☐ 10 Andres Thomas	.10	.05	.01
☐ 11 Barry Bonds	13.00	5.75	1.65
☐ 12 Juan Nieves	.10	.05	.01
☐ 13 Mark Eichhorn	.15	.07	.02
☐ 14 Dan Plesac	.20	.09	.03
☐ 15 Cory Snyder	.40	.18	.05
☐ 16 Kelly Gruber	.90	.40	.11
☐ 17 Kevin Mitchell	2.50	1.15	.30
☐ 18 Steve Lombardozzi	.10	.05	.01
☐ 19 Mitch Williams	.40	.18	.05
☐ 20 John Cerutti	.10	.05	.01
☐ 21 Todd Worrell	.15	.07	.02
☐ 22 Jose Canseco	10.00	4.50	1.25
☐ 23 Pete Incaviglia	.40	.18	.05
☐ 24 Jose Guzman	.30	.14	.04
☐ 25 Scott Bailes	.10	.05	.01
☐ 26 Greg Mathews	.10	.05	.01
☐ 27 Eric King	.10	.05	.01
☐ 28 Paul Assenmacher	.10	.05	.01
☐ 29 Jeff Sellers	.10	.05	.01
☐ 30 Bobby Bonilla	5.00	2.30	.60
☐ 31 Doug Drabek	2.00	.90	.25
☐ 32 Will Clark UER (Listed as throwing right, should be left)	13.00	5.75	1.65
☐ 33 Bip Roberts	1.25	.55	.16
☐ 34 Jim Deshaies	.15	.07	.02
☐ 35 Mike LaValliere	.35	.16	.04
☐ 36 Scott Bankhead	.15	.07	.02
☐ 37 Dale Sveum	.10	.05	.01
☐ 38 Bo Jackson	5.00	2.30	.60
☐ 39 Robby Thompson	.50	.23	.06
☐ 40 Eric Plunk	.10	.05	.01
☐ 41 Bill Bathe	.10	.05	.01
☐ 42 John Kruk	2.00	.90	.25
☐ 43 Andy Allanson	.10	.05	.01
☐ 44 Mark Portugal	.20	.09	.03
☐ 45 Danny Tartabull	2.00	.90	.25
☐ 46 Bob Kipper	.10	.05	.01
☐ 47 Gene Walter	.10	.05	.01
☐ 48 Rey Quinones UER (Misspelled Quinonez)	.10	.05	.01
☐ 49 Bobby Witt	.50	.23	.06
☐ 50 Bill Mooneyham	.10	.05	.01
☐ 51 John Cangelosi	.10	.05	.01
☐ 52 Ruben Sierra	11.00	4.90	1.40
☐ 53 Rob Woodward	.10	.05	.01
☐ 54 Ed Hearn	.10	.05	.01
☐ 55 Joel McKeon	.10	.05	.01
☐ 56 Checklist Card	.15	.02	.00

1986 Donruss Super DK's

This 29-card set of large Diamond Kings features the full-color artwork of Dick Perez. The set could be obtained from Perez-Steele Galleries by sending three Donruss wrappers and 9.00. The cards measure 4 7/8" by 6 13/16" and are

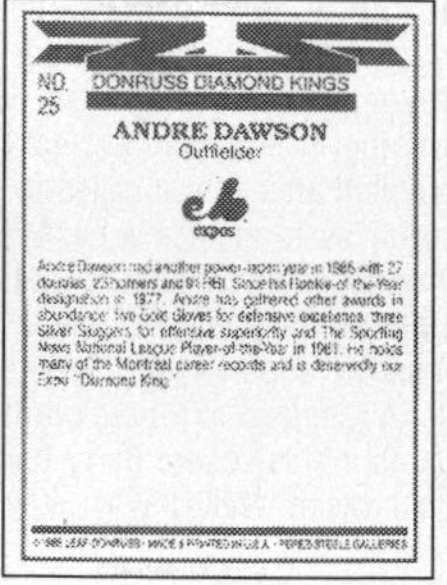

identical in design to the Diamond King cards in the Donruss regular issue.

	MT	EX-MT	VG
COMPLETE SET (29)	9.00	4.00	1.15
COMMON PLAYER (1-29)	.25	.11	.03
☐ 1 Kirk Gibson	.45	.20	.06
☐ 2 Goose Gossage	.45	.20	.06
☐ 3 Willie McGee	.35	.16	.04
☐ 4 George Bell	.45	.20	.06
☐ 5 Tony Armas	.25	.11	.03
☐ 6 Chili Davis	.35	.16	.04
☐ 7 Cecil Cooper	.35	.16	.04
☐ 8 Mike Boddicker	.25	.11	.03
☐ 9 Dave Lopes	.25	.11	.03
☐ 10 Bill Doran	.25	.11	.03
☐ 11 Bret Saberhagen	.60	.25	.08
☐ 12 Brett Butler	.35	.16	.04
☐ 13 Harold Baines	.35	.16	.04
☐ 14 Mike Davis	.25	.11	.03
☐ 15 Tony Perez	.45	.20	.06
☐ 16 Willie Randolph	.35	.16	.04
☐ 17 Bob Boone	.35	.16	.04
☐ 18 Orel Hershiser	.60	.25	.08
☐ 19 Johnny Ray	.25	.11	.03
☐ 20 Gary Ward	.25	.11	.03
☐ 21 Rick Mahler	.25	.11	.03
☐ 22 Phil Bradley	.25	.11	.03
☐ 23 Jerry Koosman	.35	.16	.04
☐ 24 Tom Brunansky	.35	.16	.04
☐ 25 Andre Dawson	.75	.35	.09
☐ 26 Dwight Gooden	1.00	.45	.13
☐ 27 Pete Rose King of Kings	1.00	.45	.13
☐ 28 Checklist Card (unnumbered)	.25	.11	.03
☐ 29 Aaron Large Puzzle (unnumbered)	.60	.25	.08

1986 Donruss Wax Box Cards

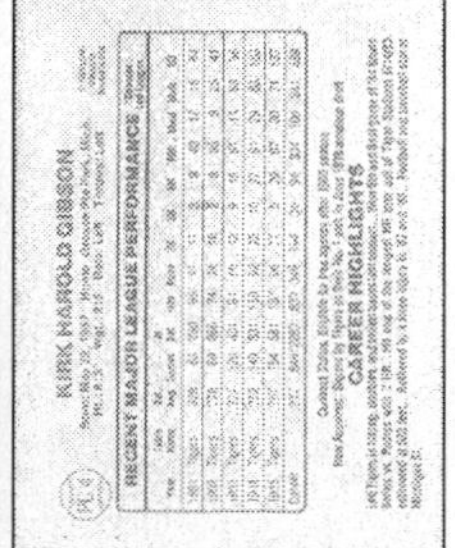

The cards in this four-card set measure the standard 2 1/2" by 3 1/2". Cards have essentially the same design as the 1986 Donruss regular issue set. The cards were printed on the bottoms of the regular issue wax pack boxes. The four cards (PC4 to PC6 plus a Hank Aaron puzzle card) are considered a separate set in their own right and are not typically included in a complete set of the regular issue 1986 Donruss cards. The value of the panel uncut is slightly greater, perhaps by 25 percent greater, than the value of the individual cards cut up carefully.

	MT	EX-MT	VG
COMPLETE SET (4)	.60	.25	.08
COMMON PLAYERS	.15	.07	.02
☐ PC4 Kirk Gibson	.45	.20	.06
☐ PC5 Willie Hernandez	.15	.07	.02
☐ PC6 Doug DeCinces	.15	.07	.02
☐ PUZO Hank Aaron Puzzle Card	.15	.07	.02

1987 Donruss

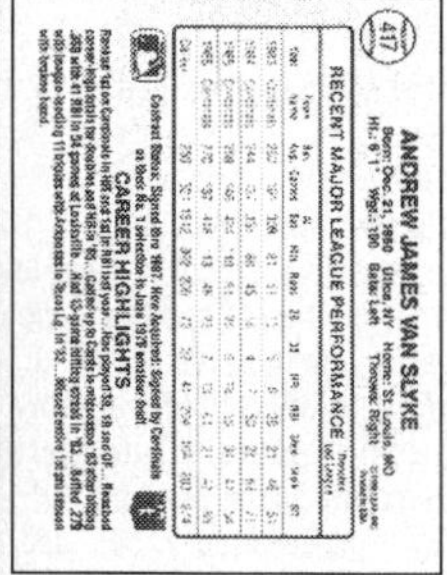

This 660-card set was distributed along with a puzzle of Roberto Clemente. The checklist cards are numbered throughout the set as multiples of 100. The wax pack boxes again contain four separate cards printed on the bottom of the box. Cards measure 2 1/2" by 3 1/2" and feature a black and gold border on the front; the backs are also done in black and gold on white card stock. The popular Diamond King subset returns for the sixth consecutive year. Some of the Diamond King (1-26) selections are repeats from prior years; Perez-Steele Galleries has indicated that a five-year rotation will be maintained in order to avoid depleting the pool of available worthy "kings" on some of the teams. Three of the Diamond Kings have a variation (on the reverse) where the yellow strip behind the words "Donruss Diamond Kings" is not printed and, hence, the background is white. The key Rookie Cards in this set are Barry Bonds, Bobby Bonilla, Kevin Brown, Will Clark, David Cone, Chuck Finley, Mike Greenwell, Bo Jackson, Wally Joyner, Barry Larkin, Greg Maddux, Dave Magadan, Kevin Mitchell, Rafael Palmiero, and Ruben Sierra. The backs of the cards in the factory sets are oriented differently than cards taken from wax packs, giving the appearance that one version or the other is upside down when sorting from the card backs.

	MT	EX-MT	VG
COMPLETE SET (660)	60.00	27.00	7.50
COMPLETE FACT.SET (660)	60.00	27.00	7.50
COMMON PLAYER (1-660)	.05	.02	.01
☐ 1 Wally Joyner DK	.30	.14	.04
☐ 2 Roger Clemens DK	.90	.40	.11
☐ 3 Dale Murphy DK	.15	.07	.02
☐ 4 Darryl Strawberry DK	.35	.16	.04
☐ 5 Ozzie Smith DK	.20	.09	.03
☐ 6 Jose Canseco DK	1.00	.45	.13
☐ 7 Charlie Hough DK	.08	.04	.01
☐ 8 Brook Jacoby DK	.08	.04	.01
☐ 9 Fred Lynn DK	.08	.04	.01
☐ 10 Rick Rhoden DK	.08	.04	.01
☐ 11 Chris Brown DK	.08	.04	.01
☐ 12 Von Hayes DK	.08	.04	.01
☐ 13 Jack Morris DK	.15	.07	.02
☐ 14A Kevin McReynolds DK	.50	.23	.06

Card			
ERR (Yellow strip missing on back)			
☐ 14B Kevin McReynolds DK COR	.08	.04	.01
☐ 15 George Brett DK	.30	.14	.04
☐ 16 Ted Higuera DK	.08	.04	.01
☐ 17 Hubie Brooks DK	.08	.04	.01
☐ 18 Mike Scott DK	.08	.04	.01
☐ 19 Kirby Puckett DK	.75	.35	.09
☐ 20 Dave Winfield DK	.30	.14	.04
☐ 21 Lloyd Moseby DK	.08	.04	.01
☐ 22A Eric Davis DK ERR (Yellow strip missing on back)	.75	.35	.09
☐ 22B Eric Davis DK COR	.20	.09	.03
☐ 23 Jim Presley DK	.08	.04	.01
☐ 24 Keith Moreland DK	.08	.04	.01
☐ 25A Greg Walker DK ERR (Yellow strip missing on back)	.50	.23	.06
☐ 25B Greg Walker DK COR	.08	.04	.01
☐ 26 Steve Sax DK	.08	.04	.01
☐ 27 DK Checklist 1-26	.10	.01	.00
☐ 28 B.J. Surhoff RR	.25	.11	.03
☐ 29 Randy Myers RR	.35	.16	.04
☐ 30 Ken Gerhart RR	.08	.04	.01
☐ 31 Benito Santiago RR	.50	.23	.06
☐ 32 Greg Swindell RR	1.25	.55	.16
☐ 33 Mike Birkbeck RR	.08	.04	.01
☐ 34 Terry Steinbach RR	.40	.18	.05
☐ 35 Bo Jackson RR	3.00	1.35	.40
☐ 36 Greg Maddux RR	6.00	2.70	.75
☐ 37 Jim Lindeman RR	.08	.04	.01
☐ 38 Devon White RR	1.00	.45	.13
☐ 39 Eric Bell RR	.08	.04	.01
☐ 40 Willie Fraser RR	.08	.04	.01
☐ 41 Jerry Browne RR	.20	.09	.03
☐ 42 Chris James RR	.12	.05	.02
☐ 43 Rafael Palmeiro RR	4.00	1.80	.50
☐ 44 Pat Dodson RR	.08	.04	.01
☐ 45 Duane Ward RR	.50	.23	.06
☐ 46 Mark McGwire RR	10.00	4.50	1.25
☐ 47 Bruce Fields RR UER (Photo actually Darnell Coles)	.08	.04	.01
☐ 48 Eddie Murray	.40	.18	.05
☐ 49 Ted Higuera	.05	.02	.01
☐ 50 Kirk Gibson	.10	.05	.01
☐ 51 Oil Can Boyd	.05	.02	.01
☐ 52 Don Mattingly	.90	.40	.11
☐ 53 Pedro Guerrero	.08	.04	.01
☐ 54 George Brett	.75	.35	.09
☐ 55 Jose Rijo	.20	.09	.03
☐ 56 Tim Raines	.15	.07	.02
☐ 57 Ed Correa	.05	.02	.01
☐ 58 Mike Witt	.05	.02	.01
☐ 59 Greg Walker	.05	.02	.01
☐ 60 Ozzie Smith	.40	.18	.05
☐ 61 Glenn Davis	.20	.09	.03
☐ 62 Glenn Wilson	.05	.02	.01
☐ 63 Tom Browning	.08	.04	.01
☐ 64 Tony Gwynn	.90	.40	.11
☐ 65 R.J. Reynolds	.05	.02	.01
☐ 66 Will Clark	8.00	3.60	1.00
☐ 67 Ozzie Virgil	.05	.02	.01
☐ 68 Rick Sutcliffe	.08	.04	.01
☐ 69 Gary Carter	.20	.09	.03
☐ 70 Mike Moore	.05	.02	.01
☐ 71 Bert Blyleven	.12	.05	.02
☐ 72 Tony Fernandez	.12	.05	.02
☐ 73 Kent Hrbek	.15	.07	.02
☐ 74 Lloyd Moseby	.05	.02	.01
☐ 75 Alvin Davis	.05	.02	.01
☐ 76 Keith Hernandez	.08	.04	.01
☐ 77 Ryne Sandberg	1.25	.55	.16
☐ 78 Dale Murphy	.25	.11	.03
☐ 79 Sid Bream	.08	.04	.01
☐ 80 Chris Brown	.05	.02	.01
☐ 81 Steve Garvey	.20	.09	.03
☐ 82 Mario Soto	.05	.02	.01
☐ 83 Shane Rawley	.05	.02	.01
☐ 84 Willie McGee	.08	.04	.01
☐ 85 Jose Cruz	.05	.02	.01
☐ 86 Brian Downing	.05	.02	.01
☐ 87 Ozzie Guillen	.08	.04	.01
☐ 88 Hubie Brooks	.05	.02	.01
☐ 89 Cal Ripken	1.75	.80	.22
☐ 90 Juan Nieves	.05	.02	.01
☐ 91 Lance Parrish	.08	.04	.01
☐ 92 Jim Rice	.12	.05	.02
☐ 93 Ron Guidry	.08	.04	.01
☐ 94 Fernando Valenzuela	.08	.04	.01
☐ 95 Andy Allanson	.05	.02	.01
☐ 96 Willie Wilson	.05	.02	.01
☐ 97 Jose Canseco	5.00	2.30	.60
☐ 98 Jeff Reardon	.20	.09	.03
☐ 99 Bobby Witt	.30	.14	.04
☐ 100 Checklist Card	.10	.01	.00
☐ 101 Jose Guzman	.08	.04	.01
☐ 102 Steve Balboni	.05	.02	.01
☐ 103 Tony Phillips	.08	.04	.01
☐ 104 Brook Jacoby	.05	.02	.01
☐ 105 Dave Winfield	.60	.25	.08
☐ 106 Orel Hershiser	.20	.09	.03
☐ 107 Lou Whitaker	.15	.07	.02
☐ 108 Fred Lynn	.08	.04	.01
☐ 109 Bill Wegman	.05	.02	.01
☐ 110 Donnie Moore	.05	.02	.01
☐ 111 Jack Clark	.08	.04	.01
☐ 112 Bob Knepper	.05	.02	.01
☐ 113 Von Hayes	.05	.02	.01
☐ 114 Bip Roberts	.75	.35	.09
☐ 115 Tony Pena	.05	.02	.01
☐ 116 Scott Garrelts	.05	.02	.01
☐ 117 Paul Molitor	.25	.11	.03
☐ 118 Darryl Strawberry	.75	.35	.09
☐ 119 Shawon Dunston	.08	.04	.01
☐ 120 Jim Presley	.05	.02	.01
☐ 121 Jesse Barfield	.08	.04	.01
☐ 122 Gary Gaetti	.05	.02	.01
☐ 123 Kurt Stillwell	.15	.07	.02
☐ 124 Joel Davis	.05	.02	.01
☐ 125 Mike Boddicker	.05	.02	.01
☐ 126 Robin Yount	.75	.35	.09
☐ 127 Alan Trammell	.15	.07	.02
☐ 128 Dave Righetti	.08	.04	.01
☐ 129 Dwight Evans	.10	.05	.01
☐ 130 Mike Scioscia	.05	.02	.01
☐ 131 Julio Franco	.25	.11	.03
☐ 132 Bret Saberhagen	.25	.11	.03
☐ 133 Mike Davis	.05	.02	.01
☐ 134 Joe Hesketh	.05	.02	.01
☐ 135 Wally Joyner	1.25	.55	.16
☐ 136 Don Slaught	.05	.02	.01
☐ 137 Daryl Boston	.05	.02	.01
☐ 138 Nolan Ryan	2.00	.90	.25
☐ 139 Mike Schmidt	1.00	.45	.13
☐ 140 Tommy Herr	.05	.02	.01
☐ 141 Garry Templeton	.05	.02	.01
☐ 142 Kal Daniels	.10	.05	.01
☐ 143 Billy Sample	.05	.02	.01
☐ 144 Johnny Ray	.05	.02	.01
☐ 145 Rob Thompson	.30	.14	.04
☐ 146 Bob Dernier	.05	.02	.01
☐ 147 Danny Tartabull	.40	.18	.05
☐ 148 Ernie Whitt	.05	.02	.01
☐ 149 Kirby Puckett	2.00	.90	.25
☐ 150 Mike Young	.05	.02	.01
☐ 151 Ernest Riles	.05	.02	.01
☐ 152 Frank Tanana	.05	.02	.01
☐ 153 Rich Gedman	.05	.02	.01
☐ 154 Willie Randolph	.08	.04	.01
☐ 155 Bill Madlock	.08	.04	.01
☐ 156 Joe Carter	.90	.40	.11
☐ 157 Danny Jackson	.05	.02	.01
☐ 158 Carney Lansford	.08	.04	.01
☐ 159 Bryn Smith	.05	.02	.01
☐ 160 Gary Pettis	.05	.02	.01
☐ 161 Oddibe McDowell	.05	.02	.01
☐ 162 John Cangelosi	.05	.02	.01
☐ 163 Mike Scott	.08	.04	.01
☐ 164 Eric Show	.05	.02	.01
☐ 165 Juan Samuel	.05	.02	.01
☐ 166 Nick Esasky	.05	.02	.01
☐ 167 Zane Smith	.08	.04	.01
☐ 168 Mike C. Brown OF	.05	.02	.01
☐ 169 Keith Moreland	.05	.02	.01
☐ 170 John Tudor	.08	.04	.01
☐ 171 Ken Dixon	.05	.02	.01
☐ 172 Jim Gantner	.05	.02	.01
☐ 173 Jack Morris	.30	.14	.04
☐ 174 Bruce Hurst	.08	.04	.01
☐ 175 Dennis Rasmussen	.05	.02	.01
☐ 176 Mike Marshall	.05	.02	.01
☐ 177 Dan Quisenberry	.08	.04	.01
☐ 178 Eric Plunk	.05	.02	.01
☐ 179 Tim Wallach	.08	.04	.01
☐ 180 Steve Buechele	.08	.04	.01
☐ 181 Don Sutton	.15	.07	.02
☐ 182 Dave Schmidt	.05	.02	.01
☐ 183 Terry Pendleton	.40	.18	.05
☐ 184 Jim Deshaies	.12	.05	.02
☐ 185 Steve Bedrosian	.05	.02	.01
☐ 186 Pete Rose	.40	.18	.05
☐ 187 Dave Dravecky	.08	.04	.01
☐ 188 Rick Reuschel	.05	.02	.01
☐ 189 Dan Gladden	.05	.02	.01

190	Rick Mahler	.05	.02	.01
191	Thad Bosley	.05	.02	.01
192	Ron Darling	.08	.04	.01
193	Matt Young	.05	.02	.01
194	Tom Brunansky	.08	.04	.01
195	Dave Stieb	.08	.04	.01
196	Frank Viola	.15	.07	.02
197	Tom Henke	.08	.04	.01
198	Karl Best	.05	.02	.01
199	Dwight Gooden	.35	.16	.04
200	Checklist Card	.10	.01	.00
201	Steve Trout	.05	.02	.01
202	Rafael Ramirez	.05	.02	.01
203	Bob Walk	.05	.02	.01
204	Roger Mason	.08	.04	.01
205	Terry Kennedy	.05	.02	.01
206	Ron Oester	.05	.02	.01
207	John Russell	.05	.02	.01
208	Greg Mathews	.05	.02	.01
209	Charlie Kerfeld	.05	.02	.01
210	Reggie Jackson	.40	.18	.05
211	Floyd Bannister	.05	.02	.01
212	Vance Law	.05	.02	.01
213	Rich Bordi	.05	.02	.01
214	Dan Plesac	.15	.07	.02
215	Dave Collins	.05	.02	.01
216	Bob Stanley	.05	.02	.01
217	Joe Niekro	.08	.04	.01
218	Tom Niedenfuer	.05	.02	.01
219	Brett Butler	.15	.07	.02
220	Charlie Leibrandt	.08	.04	.01
221	Steve Ontiveros	.05	.02	.01
222	Tim Burke	.05	.02	.01
223	Curtis Wilkerson	.05	.02	.01
224	Pete Incaviglia	.25	.11	.03
225	Lonnie Smith	.05	.02	.01
226	Chris Codiroli	.05	.02	.01
227	Scott Bailes	.05	.02	.01
228	Rickey Henderson	.75	.35	.09
229	Ken Howell	.05	.02	.01
230	Darnell Coles	.05	.02	.01
231	Don Aase	.05	.02	.01
232	Tim Leary	.05	.02	.01
233	Bob Boone	.08	.04	.01
234	Ricky Horton	.05	.02	.01
235	Mark Bailey	.05	.02	.01
236	Kevin Gross	.05	.02	.01
237	Lance McCullers	.05	.02	.01
238	Cecilio Guante	.05	.02	.01
239	Bob Melvin	.05	.02	.01
240	Billy Joe Robidoux	.05	.02	.01
241	Roger McDowell	.05	.02	.01
242	Leon Durham	.05	.02	.01
243	Ed Nunez	.05	.02	.01
244	Jimmy Key	.08	.04	.01
245	Mike Smithson	.05	.02	.01
246	Bo Diaz	.05	.02	.01
247	Carlton Fisk	.40	.18	.05
248	Larry Sheets	.05	.02	.01
249	Juan Castillo	.05	.02	.01
250	Eric King	.05	.02	.01
251	Doug Drabek	1.25	.55	.16
252	Wade Boggs	.75	.35	.09
253	Mariano Duncan	.05	.02	.01
254	Pat Tabler	.05	.02	.01
255	Frank White	.05	.02	.01
256	Alfredo Griffin	.05	.02	.01
257	Floyd Youmans	.05	.02	.01
258	Rob Wilfong	.05	.02	.01
259	Pete O'Brien	.05	.02	.01
260	Tim Hulett	.05	.02	.01
261	Dickie Thon	.05	.02	.01
262	Darren Daulton	.30	.14	.04
263	Vince Coleman	.20	.09	.03
264	Andy Hawkins	.05	.02	.01
265	Eric Davis	.35	.16	.04
266	Andres Thomas	.05	.02	.01
267	Mike Diaz	.05	.02	.01
268	Chili Davis	.08	.04	.01
269	Jody Davis	.05	.02	.01
270	Phil Bradley	.05	.02	.01
271	George Bell	.25	.11	.03
272	Keith Atherton	.05	.02	.01
273	Storm Davis	.05	.02	.01
274	Rob Deer	.25	.11	.03
275	Walt Terrell	.05	.02	.01
276	Roger Clemens	2.00	.90	.25
277	Mike Easler	.05	.02	.01
278	Steve Sax	.12	.05	.02
279	Andre Thornton	.05	.02	.01
280	Jim Sundberg	.05	.02	.01
281	Bill Bathe	.05	.02	.01
282	Jay Tibbs	.05	.02	.01
283	Dick Schofield	.05	.02	.01
284	Mike Mason	.05	.02	.01
285	Jerry Hairston	.05	.02	.01
286	Bill Doran	.05	.02	.01
287	Tim Flannery	.05	.02	.01
288	Gary Redus	.05	.02	.01
289	John Franco	.10	.05	.01
290	Paul Assenmacher	.05	.02	.01
291	Joe Orsulak	.05	.02	.01
292	Lee Smith	.25	.11	.03
293	Mike Laga	.05	.02	.01
294	Rick Dempsey	.05	.02	.01
295	Mike Felder	.05	.02	.01
296	Tom Brookens	.05	.02	.01
297	Al Nipper	.05	.02	.01
298	Mike Pagliarulo	.05	.02	.01
299	Franklin Stubbs	.05	.02	.01
300	Checklist Card	.10	.01	.00
301	Steve Farr	.08	.04	.01
302	Bill Mooneyham	.05	.02	.01
303	Andres Galarraga	.08	.04	.01
304	Scott Fletcher	.05	.02	.01
305	Jack Howell	.05	.02	.01
306	Russ Morman	.05	.02	.01
307	Todd Worrell	.08	.04	.01
308	Dave Smith	.05	.02	.01
309	Jeff Stone	.05	.02	.01
310	Ron Robinson	.05	.02	.01
311	Bruce Bochy	.05	.02	.01
312	Jim Winn	.05	.02	.01
313	Mark Davis	.05	.02	.01
314	Jeff Dedmon	.05	.02	.01
315	Jamie Moyer	.05	.02	.01
316	Wally Backman	.05	.02	.01
317	Ken Phelps	.05	.02	.01
318	Steve Lombardozzi	.05	.02	.01
319	Rance Mulliniks	.05	.02	.01
320	Tim Laudner	.05	.02	.01
321	Mark Eichhorn	.08	.04	.01
322	Lee Guetterman	.05	.02	.01
323	Sid Fernandez	.08	.04	.01
324	Jerry Mumphrey	.05	.02	.01
325	David Palmer	.05	.02	.01
326	Bill Almon	.05	.02	.01
327	Candy Maldonado	.08	.04	.01
328	John Kruk	1.25	.55	.16
329	John Denny	.05	.02	.01
330	Milt Thompson	.08	.04	.01
331	Mike LaValliere	.25	.11	.03
332	Alan Ashby	.05	.02	.01
333	Doug Corbett	.05	.02	.01
334	Ron Karkovice	.08	.04	.01
335	Mitch Webster	.05	.02	.01
336	Lee Lacy	.05	.02	.01
337	Glenn Braggs	.15	.07	.02
338	Dwight Lowry	.05	.02	.01
339	Don Baylor	.08	.04	.01
340	Brian Fisher	.05	.02	.01
341	Reggie Williams	.05	.02	.01
342	Tom Candiotti	.08	.04	.01
343	Rudy Law	.05	.02	.01
344	Curt Young	.05	.02	.01
345	Mike Fitzgerald	.05	.02	.01
346	Ruben Sierra	6.00	2.70	.75
347	Mitch Williams	.30	.14	.04
348	Jorge Orta	.05	.02	.01
349	Mickey Tettleton	.25	.11	.03
350	Ernie Camacho	.05	.02	.01
351	Ron Kittle	.05	.02	.01
352	Ken Landreaux	.05	.02	.01
353	Chet Lemon	.05	.02	.01
354	John Shelby	.05	.02	.01
355	Mark Clear	.05	.02	.01
356	Doug DeCinces	.05	.02	.01
357	Ken Dayley	.05	.02	.01
358	Phil Garner	.08	.04	.01
359	Steve Jeltz	.05	.02	.01
360	Ed Whitson	.05	.02	.01
361	Barry Bonds	8.00	3.60	1.00
362	Vida Blue	.08	.04	.01
363	Cecil Cooper	.08	.04	.01
364	Bob Ojeda	.05	.02	.01
365	Dennis Eckersley	.30	.14	.04
366	Mike Morgan	.08	.04	.01
367	Willie Upshaw	.05	.02	.01
368	Allan Anderson	.05	.02	.01
369	Bill Gullickson	.08	.04	.01
370	Bobby Thigpen	.50	.23	.06
371	Juan Beniquez	.05	.02	.01
372	Charlie Moore	.05	.02	.01
373	Dan Petry	.05	.02	.01
374	Rod Scurry	.05	.02	.01
375	Tom Seaver	.40	.18	.05

☐	376	Ed VandeBerg	.05	.02	.01
☐	377	Tony Bernazard	.05	.02	.01
☐	378	Greg Pryor	.05	.02	.01
☐	379	Dwayne Murphy	.05	.02	.01
☐	380	Andy McGaffigan	.05	.02	.01
☐	381	Kirk McCaskill	.05	.02	.01
☐	382	Greg Harris	.05	.02	.01
☐	383	Rich Dotson	.05	.02	.01
☐	384	Craig Reynolds	.05	.02	.01
☐	385	Greg Gross	.05	.02	.01
☐	386	Tito Landrum	.05	.02	.01
☐	387	Craig Lefferts	.08	.04	.01
☐	388	Dave Parker	.12	.05	.02
☐	389	Bob Horner	.08	.04	.01
☐	390	Pat Clements	.05	.02	.01
☐	391	Jeff Leonard	.05	.02	.01
☐	392	Chris Speier	.05	.02	.01
☐	393	John Moses	.05	.02	.01
☐	394	Garth Iorg	.05	.02	.01
☐	395	Greg Gagne	.08	.04	.01
☐	396	Nate Snell	.05	.02	.01
☐	397	Bryan Clutterbuck	.05	.02	.01
☐	398	Darrell Evans	.08	.04	.01
☐	399	Steve Crawford	.05	.02	.01
☐	400	Checklist Card	.10	.01	.00
☐	401	Phil Lombardi	.05	.02	.01
☐	402	Rick Honeycutt	.05	.02	.01
☐	403	Ken Schrom	.05	.02	.01
☐	404	Bud Black	.05	.02	.01
☐	405	Donnie Hill	.05	.02	.01
☐	406	Wayne Krenchicki	.05	.02	.01
☐	407	Chuck Finley	.50	.23	.06
☐	408	Toby Harrah	.05	.02	.01
☐	409	Steve Lyons	.05	.02	.01
☐	410	Kevin Bass	.05	.02	.01
☐	411	Marvell Wynne	.05	.02	.01
☐	412	Ron Roenicke	.05	.02	.01
☐	413	Tracy Jones	.05	.02	.01
☐	414	Gene Garber	.05	.02	.01
☐	415	Mike Bielecki	.05	.02	.01
☐	416	Frank DiPino	.05	.02	.01
☐	417	Andy Van Slyke	.30	.14	.04
☐	418	Jim Dwyer	.05	.02	.01
☐	419	Ben Oglivie	.05	.02	.01
☐	420	Dave Bergman	.05	.02	.01
☐	421	Joe Sambito	.05	.02	.01
☐	422	Bob Tewksbury	.50	.23	.06
☐	423	Len Matuszek	.05	.02	.01
☐	424	Mike Kingery	.05	.02	.01
☐	425	Dave Kingman	.08	.04	.01
☐	426	Al Newman	.05	.02	.01
☐	427	Gary Ward	.05	.02	.01
☐	428	Ruppert Jones	.05	.02	.01
☐	429	Harold Baines	.12	.05	.02
☐	430	Pat Perry	.05	.02	.01
☐	431	Terry Puhl	.05	.02	.01
☐	432	Don Carman	.05	.02	.01
☐	433	Eddie Milner	.05	.02	.01
☐	434	LaMarr Hoyt	.05	.02	.01
☐	435	Rick Rhoden	.05	.02	.01
☐	436	Jose Uribe	.05	.02	.01
☐	437	Ken Oberkfell	.05	.02	.01
☐	438	Ron Davis	.05	.02	.01
☐	439	Jesse Orosco	.05	.02	.01
☐	440	Scott Bradley	.05	.02	.01
☐	441	Randy Bush	.05	.02	.01
☐	442	John Cerutti	.05	.02	.01
☐	443	Roy Smalley	.05	.02	.01
☐	444	Kelly Gruber	.60	.25	.08
☐	445	Bob Kearney	.05	.02	.01
☐	446	Ed Hearn	.05	.02	.01
☐	447	Scott Sanderson	.05	.02	.01
☐	448	Bruce Benedict	.05	.02	.01
☐	449	Junior Ortiz	.05	.02	.01
☐	450	Mike Aldrete	.05	.02	.01
☐	451	Kevin McReynolds	.08	.04	.01
☐	452	Rob Murphy	.05	.02	.01
☐	453	Kent Tekulve	.05	.02	.01
☐	454	Curt Ford	.05	.02	.01
☐	455	Dave Lopes	.08	.04	.01
☐	456	Bob Grich	.08	.04	.01
☐	457	Jose DeLeon	.05	.02	.01
☐	458	Andre Dawson	.50	.23	.06
☐	459	Mike Flanagan	.05	.02	.01
☐	460	Joey Meyer	.05	.02	.01
☐	461	Chuck Cary	.05	.02	.01
☐	462	Bill Buckner	.08	.04	.01
☐	463	Bob Shirley	.05	.02	.01
☐	464	Jeff Hamilton	.05	.02	.01
☐	465	Phil Niekro	.15	.07	.02
☐	466	Mark Gubicza	.05	.02	.01
☐	467	Jerry Willard	.05	.02	.01
☐	468	Bob Sebra	.05	.02	.01
☐	469	Larry Parrish	.05	.02	.01
☐	470	Charlie Hough	.05	.02	.01
☐	471	Hal McRae	.08	.04	.01
☐	472	Dave Leiper	.05	.02	.01
☐	473	Mel Hall	.08	.04	.01
☐	474	Dan Pasqua	.08	.04	.01
☐	475	Bob Welch	.08	.04	.01
☐	476	Johnny Grubb	.05	.02	.01
☐	477	Jim Traber	.05	.02	.01
☐	478	Chris Bosio	.40	.18	.05
☐	479	Mark McLemore	.05	.02	.01
☐	480	John Morris	.05	.02	.01
☐	481	Billy Hatcher	.08	.04	.01
☐	482	Dan Schatzeder	.05	.02	.01
☐	483	Rich Gossage	.10	.05	.01
☐	484	Jim Morrison	.05	.02	.01
☐	485	Bob Brenly	.05	.02	.01
☐	486	Bill Schroeder	.05	.02	.01
☐	487	Mookie Wilson	.08	.04	.01
☐	488	Dave Martinez	.30	.14	.04
☐	489	Harold Reynolds	.05	.02	.01
☐	490	Jeff Hearron	.05	.02	.01
☐	491	Mickey Hatcher	.05	.02	.01
☐	492	Barry Larkin	3.50	1.55	.45
☐	493	Bob James	.05	.02	.01
☐	494	John Habyan	.05	.02	.01
☐	495	Jim Adduci	.05	.02	.01
☐	496	Mike Heath	.05	.02	.01
☐	497	Tim Stoddard	.05	.02	.01
☐	498	Tony Armas	.05	.02	.01
☐	499	Dennis Powell	.05	.02	.01
☐	500	Checklist Card	.10	.01	.00
☐	501	Chris Bando	.05	.02	.01
☐	502	David Cone	3.50	1.55	.45
☐	503	Jay Howell	.08	.04	.01
☐	504	Tom Foley	.05	.02	.01
☐	505	Ray Chadwick	.05	.02	.01
☐	506	Mike Loynd	.05	.02	.01
☐	507	Neil Allen	.05	.02	.01
☐	508	Danny Darwin	.05	.02	.01
☐	509	Rick Schu	.05	.02	.01
☐	510	Jose Oquendo	.05	.02	.01
☐	511	Gene Walter	.05	.02	.01
☐	512	Terry McGriff	.05	.02	.01
☐	513	Ken Griffey	.08	.04	.01
☐	514	Benny Distefano	.05	.02	.01
☐	515	Terry Mulholland	.50	.23	.06
☐	516	Ed Lynch	.05	.02	.01
☐	517	Bill Swift	.12	.05	.02
☐	518	Manny Lee	.08	.04	.01
☐	519	Andre David	.05	.02	.01
☐	520	Scott McGregor	.05	.02	.01
☐	521	Rick Manning	.05	.02	.01
☐	522	Willie Hernandez	.05	.02	.01
☐	523	Marty Barrett	.05	.02	.01
☐	524	Wayne Tolleson	.05	.02	.01
☐	525	Jose Gonzalez	.05	.02	.01
☐	526	Cory Snyder	.15	.07	.02
☐	527	Buddy Biancalana	.05	.02	.01
☐	528	Moose Haas	.05	.02	.01
☐	529	Wilfredo Tejada	.05	.02	.01
☐	530	Stu Cliburn	.05	.02	.01
☐	531	Dale Mohorcic	.05	.02	.01
☐	532	Ron Hassey	.05	.02	.01
☐	533	Ty Gainey	.05	.02	.01
☐	534	Jerry Royster	.05	.02	.01
☐	535	Mike Maddux	.05	.02	.01
☐	536	Ted Power	.05	.02	.01
☐	537	Ted Simmons	.08	.04	.01
☐	538	Rafael Belliard	.20	.09	.03
☐	539	Chico Walker	.08	.04	.01
☐	540	Bob Forsch	.05	.02	.01
☐	541	John Stefero	.05	.02	.01
☐	542	Dale Sveum	.05	.02	.01
☐	543	Mark Thurmond	.05	.02	.01
☐	544	Jeff Sellers	.05	.02	.01
☐	545	Joel Skinner	.05	.02	.01
☐	546	Alex Trevino	.05	.02	.01
☐	547	Randy Kutcher	.05	.02	.01
☐	548	Joaquin Andujar	.05	.02	.01
☐	549	Casey Candaele	.05	.02	.01
☐	550	Jeff Russell	.08	.04	.01
☐	551	John Candelaria	.05	.02	.01
☐	552	Joe Cowley	.05	.02	.01
☐	553	Danny Cox	.05	.02	.01
☐	554	Denny Walling	.05	.02	.01
☐	555	Bruce Ruffin	.05	.02	.01
☐	556	Buddy Bell	.08	.04	.01
☐	557	Jimmy Jones	.20	.09	.03
☐	558	Bobby Bonilla	3.00	1.35	.40
☐	559	Jeff D. Robinson	.05	.02	.01
☐	560	Ed Olwine	.05	.02	.01
☐	561	Glenallen Hill	.30	.14	.04

	Player	MT	EX-MT	VG
☐ 562	Lee Mazzilli	.05	.02	.01
☐ 563	Mike G. Brown P	.05	.02	.01
☐ 564	George Frazier	.05	.02	.01
☐ 565	Mike Sharperson	.15	.07	.02
☐ 566	Mark Portugal	.15	.07	.02
☐ 567	Rick Leach	.05	.02	.01
☐ 568	Mark Langston	.20	.09	.03
☐ 569	Rafael Santana	.05	.02	.01
☐ 570	Manny Trillo	.05	.02	.01
☐ 571	Cliff Speck	.05	.02	.01
☐ 572	Bob Kipper	.05	.02	.01
☐ 573	Kelly Downs	.10	.05	.01
☐ 574	Randy Asadoor	.05	.02	.01
☐ 575	Dave Magadan	.30	.14	.04
☐ 576	Marvin Freeman	.05	.02	.01
☐ 577	Jeff Lahti	.05	.02	.01
☐ 578	Jeff Calhoun	.05	.02	.01
☐ 579	Gus Polidor	.05	.02	.01
☐ 580	Gene Nelson	.05	.02	.01
☐ 581	Tim Teufel	.05	.02	.01
☐ 582	Odell Jones	.05	.02	.01
☐ 583	Mark Ryal	.05	.02	.01
☐ 584	Randy O'Neal	.05	.02	.01
☐ 585	Mike Greenwell	1.00	.45	.13
☐ 586	Ray Knight	.08	.04	.01
☐ 587	Ralph Bryant	.08	.04	.01
☐ 588	Carmen Castillo	.05	.02	.01
☐ 589	Ed Wojna	.05	.02	.01
☐ 590	Stan Javier	.08	.04	.01
☐ 591	Jeff Musselman	.05	.02	.01
☐ 592	Mike Stanley	.05	.02	.01
☐ 593	Darrell Porter	.05	.02	.01
☐ 594	Drew Hall	.05	.02	.01
☐ 595	Rob Nelson	.05	.02	.01
☐ 596	Bryan Oelkers	.05	.02	.01
☐ 597	Scott Nielsen	.05	.02	.01
☐ 598	Brian Holton	.05	.02	.01
☐ 599	Kevin Mitchell	1.50	.65	.19
☐ 600	Checklist Card	.10	.01	.00
☐ 601	Jackie Gutierrez	.05	.02	.01
☐ 602	Barry Jones	.08	.04	.01
☐ 603	Jerry Narron	.05	.02	.01
☐ 604	Steve Lake	.05	.02	.01
☐ 605	Jim Pankovits	.05	.02	.01
☐ 606	Ed Romero	.05	.02	.01
☐ 607	Dave LaPoint	.05	.02	.01
☐ 608	Don Robinson	.05	.02	.01
☐ 609	Mike Krukow	.05	.02	.01
☐ 610	Dave Valle	.05	.02	.01
☐ 611	Len Dykstra	.25	.11	.03
☐ 612	Roberto Clemente PUZ	.15	.07	.02
☐ 613	Mike Trujillo	.05	.02	.01
☐ 614	Damaso Garcia	.05	.02	.01
☐ 615	Neal Heaton	.05	.02	.01
☐ 616	Juan Berenguer	.05	.02	.01
☐ 617	Steve Carlton	.40	.18	.05
☐ 618	Gary Lucas	.05	.02	.01
☐ 619	Geno Petralli	.05	.02	.01
☐ 620	Rick Aguilera	.25	.11	.03
☐ 621	Fred McGriff	3.50	1.55	.45
☐ 622	Dave Henderson	.08	.04	.01
☐ 623	Dave Clark	.05	.02	.01
☐ 624	Angel Salazar	.05	.02	.01
☐ 625	Randy Hunt	.05	.02	.01
☐ 626	John Gibbons	.05	.02	.01
☐ 627	Kevin Brown	2.25	1.00	.30
☐ 628	Bill Dawley	.05	.02	.01
☐ 629	Aurelio Lopez	.05	.02	.01
☐ 630	Charles Hudson	.05	.02	.01
☐ 631	Ray Soff	.05	.02	.01
☐ 632	Ray Hayward	.05	.02	.01
☐ 633	Spike Owen	.05	.02	.01
☐ 634	Glenn Hubbard	.05	.02	.01
☐ 635	Kevin Elster	.10	.05	.01
☐ 636	Mike LaCoss	.05	.02	.01
☐ 637	Dwayne Henry	.05	.02	.01
☐ 638	Rey Quinones	.05	.02	.01
☐ 639	Jim Clancy	.05	.02	.01
☐ 640	Larry Andersen	.05	.02	.01
☐ 641	Calvin Schiraldi	.05	.02	.01
☐ 642	Stan Jefferson	.05	.02	.01
☐ 643	Marc Sullivan	.05	.02	.01
☐ 644	Mark Grant	.05	.02	.01
☐ 645	Cliff Johnson	.05	.02	.01
☐ 646	Howard Johnson	.25	.11	.03
☐ 647	Dave Sax	.05	.02	.01
☐ 648	Dave Stewart	.12	.05	.02
☐ 649	Danny Heep	.05	.02	.01
☐ 650	Joe Johnson	.05	.02	.01
☐ 651	Bob Brower	.05	.02	.01
☐ 652	Rob Woodward	.05	.02	.01
☐ 653	John Mizerock	.05	.02	.01
☐ 654	Tim Pyznarski	.05	.02	.01
☐ 655	Luis Aquino	.05	.02	.01
☐ 656	Mickey Brantley	.05	.02	.01
☐ 657	Doyle Alexander	.05	.02	.01
☐ 658	Sammy Stewart	.05	.02	.01
☐ 659	Jim Acker	.05	.02	.01
☐ 660	Pete Ladd	.05	.02	.01

1987 Donruss All-Stars

This 60-card set features cards measuring approximately 3 1/2" by 5". Card fronts are in full color with a black border. The card backs are printed in black and blue on white card stock. Cards are numbered on the back. Card backs feature statistical information about the player's performance in past All-Star games. The set was distributed in packs which also contained a Pop-Up.

		MT	EX-MT	VG
COMPLETE SET (60)		7.50	3.40	.95
COMMON PLAYER (1-60)		.07	.03	.01
☐ 1	Wally Joyner	.40	.18	.05
☐ 2	Dave Winfield	.40	.18	.05
☐ 3	Lou Whitaker	.15	.07	.02
☐ 4	Kirby Puckett	.90	.40	.11
☐ 5	Cal Ripken	1.25	.55	.16
☐ 6	Rickey Henderson	.75	.35	.09
☐ 7	Wade Boggs	.60	.25	.08
☐ 8	Roger Clemens	1.00	.45	.13
☐ 9	Lance Parrish	.10	.05	.01
☐ 10	Dick Howser MG	.07	.03	.01
☐ 11	Keith Hernandez	.10	.05	.01
☐ 12	Darryl Strawberry	.50	.23	.06
☐ 13	Ryne Sandberg	1.00	.45	.13
☐ 14	Dale Murphy	.35	.16	.04
☐ 15	Ozzie Smith	.35	.16	.04
☐ 16	Tony Gwynn	.45	.20	.06
☐ 17	Mike Schmidt	.75	.35	.09
☐ 18	Dwight Gooden	.35	.16	.04
☐ 19	Gary Carter	.25	.11	.03
☐ 20	Whitey Herzog MG	.07	.03	.01
☐ 21	Jose Canseco	.90	.40	.11
☐ 22	John Franco	.10	.05	.01
☐ 23	Jesse Barfield	.07	.03	.01
☐ 24	Rick Rhoden	.07	.03	.01
☐ 25	Harold Baines	.10	.05	.01
☐ 26	Sid Fernandez	.15	.07	.02
☐ 27	George Brett	.60	.25	.08
☐ 28	Steve Sax	.15	.07	.02
☐ 29	Jim Presley	.07	.03	.01
☐ 30	Dave Smith	.07	.03	.01
☐ 31	Eddie Murray	.30	.14	.04
☐ 32	Mike Scott	.10	.05	.01
☐ 33	Don Mattingly	.75	.35	.09
☐ 34	Dave Parker	.20	.09	.03
☐ 35	Tony Fernandez	.15	.07	.02
☐ 36	Tim Raines	.15	.07	.02
☐ 37	Brook Jacoby	.07	.03	.01
☐ 38	Chili Davis	.10	.05	.01
☐ 39	Rich Gedman	.07	.03	.01
☐ 40	Kevin Bass	.07	.03	.01
☐ 41	Frank White	.07	.03	.01
☐ 42	Glenn Davis	.15	.07	.02
☐ 43	Willie Hernandez	.07	.03	.01
☐ 44	Chris Brown	.07	.03	.01
☐ 45	Jim Rice	.15	.07	.02
☐ 46	Tony Pena	.07	.03	.01

☐ 47 Don Aase	.07	.03	.01
☐ 48 Hubie Brooks	.07	.03	.01
☐ 49 Charlie Hough	.07	.03	.01
☐ 50 Jody Davis	.07	.03	.01
☐ 51 Mike Witt	.07	.03	.01
☐ 52 Jeff Reardon	.25	.11	.03
☐ 53 Ken Schrom	.07	.03	.01
☐ 54 Fernando Valenzuela	.15	.07	.02
☐ 55 Dave Righetti	.10	.05	.01
☐ 56 Shane Rawley	.07	.03	.01
☐ 57 Ted Higuera	.10	.05	.01
☐ 58 Mike Krukow	.07	.03	.01
☐ 59 Lloyd Moseby	.07	.03	.01
☐ 60 Checklist Card	.07	.03	.01

1987 Donruss All-Star Box

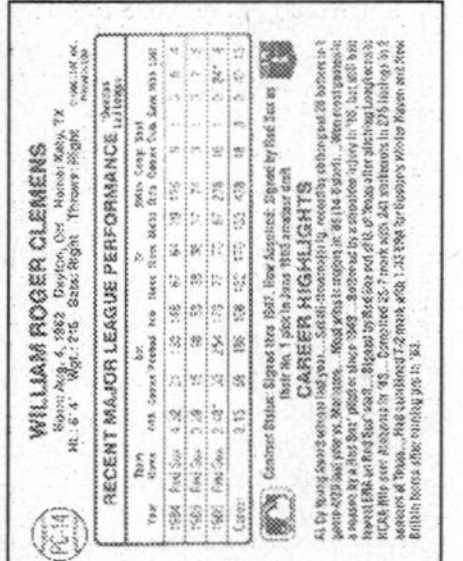

The cards in this four-card set measure the standard 2 1/2" by 3 1/2" in spite of the fact that they form the bottom of the wax pack box for the larger Donruss All-Star cards. These box cards have essentially the same design as the 1987 Donruss regular issue set. The cards were printed on the bottoms of the Donruss All-Star (3 1/2" by 5") wax pack boxes. The four cards (PC13 to PC15 plus a Roberto Clemente puzzle card) are considered a separate set in their own right and are not typically included in a complete set of the 1987 Donruss All-Star (or regular) cards. The value of the panel uncut is slightly greater, perhaps by 25 percent greater, than the value of the individual cards cut up carefully.

	MT	EX-MT	VG
COMPLETE SET (4)	3.00	1.35	.40
COMMON PLAYERS	.15	.07	.02
☐ PC13 Mike Scott	.35	.16	.04
☐ PC14 Roger Clemens	2.50	1.15	.30
☐ PC15 Mike Krukow	.15	.07	.02
☐ PUZO Roberto Clemente Puzzle Card	.15	.07	.02

1987 Donruss Highlights

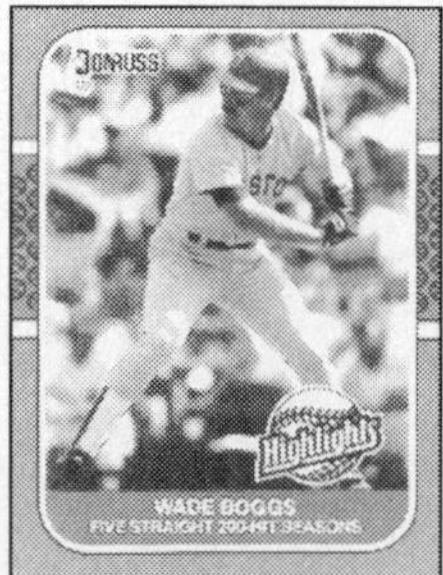

WADE BOGGS
Becomes Only 4th Player in History to Achieve 5 Straight 200-hit Seasons
September 22

NO. 44

Donruss' third (and last) edition of Highlights was released late in 1987. The cards are standard size, measuring 2 1/2" by 3 1/2", and are glossy in appearance. Cards commemorate events during the 1987 season, as well as players and pitchers of the month from each league. The set was distributed in its own red, black, blue, and gold box along with a small Roberto Clemente puzzle. Card fronts are similar to the regular 1987 Donruss issue except that the Highlights logo is positioned in the lower right-hand corner and the borders are in blue instead of black. The backs are printed in black and gold on white card stock.

	MT	EX-MT	VG
COMPLETE SET (56)	7.00	3.10	.85
COMMON PLAYER (1-56)	.06	.03	.01
☐ 1 Juan Nieves First No-Hitter	.06	.03	.01
☐ 2 Mike Schmidt Hits 500th Homer	.50	.23	.06
☐ 3 Eric Davis NL Player April	.25	.11	.03
☐ 4 Sid Fernandez NL Pitcher April	.10	.05	.01
☐ 5 Brian Downing AL Player April	.06	.03	.01
☐ 6 Bret Saberhagen AL Pitcher April	.20	.09	.03
☐ 7 Tim Raines Free Agent Returns	.15	.07	.02
☐ 8 Eric Davis NL Player May	.25	.11	.03
☐ 9 Steve Bedrosian NL Pitcher May	.06	.03	.01
☐ 10 Larry Parrish AL Player May	.06	.03	.01
☐ 11 Jim Clancy AL Pitcher May	.06	.03	.01
☐ 12 Tony Gwynn NL Player June UER (over "20" hits)	.35	.16	.04
☐ 13 Orel Hershiser NL Pitcher June	.20	.09	.03
☐ 14 Wade Boggs AL Player June	.45	.20	.06
☐ 15 Steve Ontiveros AL Pitcher June	.06	.03	.01
☐ 16 Tim Raines All Star Game Hero	.15	.07	.02
☐ 17 Don Mattingly Consecutive Game Homerun Streak	.60	.25	.08
☐ 18 Ray Dandridge 1987 HOF Inductee	.25	.11	.03
☐ 19 Jim"Catfish" Hunter 1987 HOF Inductee	.15	.07	.02
☐ 20 Billy Williams 1987 HOF Inductee	.15	.07	.02
☐ 21 Bo Diaz NL Player July	.06	.03	.01
☐ 22 Floyd Youmans NL Pitcher July	.06	.03	.01
☐ 23 Don Mattingly AL Player July	.60	.25	.08
☐ 24 Frank Viola AL Pitcher July	.15	.07	.02
☐ 25 Bobby Witt Strikes Out Four Batters in One Inning	.15	.07	.02
☐ 26 Kevin Seitzer Ties AL 9-Inning Game Hit Mark	.20	.09	.03
☐ 27 Mark McGwire Sets Rookie HR Record	.90	.40	.11
☐ 28 Andre Dawson Sets Cubs' 1st Year Homer Mark	.35	.16	.04
☐ 29 Paul Molitor Hits in 39 Straight Games	.25	.11	.03
☐ 30 Kirby Puckett Record Weekend	.75	.35	.09
☐ 31 Andre Dawson NL Player August	.35	.16	.04
☐ 32 Doug Drabek NL Pitcher August	.45	.20	.06
☐ 33 Dwight Evans AL Player August	.10	.05	.01
☐ 34 Mark Langston AL Pitcher August	.15	.07	.02

☐ 35 Wally Joyner 100 RBI in 1st Two Major League Seasons	.20	.09	.03
☐ 36 Vince Coleman 100 SB in 1st Three Major League Seasons	.25	.11	.03
☐ 37 Eddie Murray Orioles' All Time Homer King	.25	.11	.03
☐ 38 Cal Ripken Ends Consecutive Innings Streak	1.00	.45	.13
☐ 39 Blue Jays Hit Record 10 Homers In One Game (McGriff/Ducey/Whitt)	.06	.03	.01
☐ 40 McGwire/Canseco Equal A's RBI Marks	.90	.40	.11
☐ 41 Bob Boone Sets All-Time Catching Record	.10	.05	.01
☐ 42 Darryl Strawberry Sets Mets' One-Season Home Run Mark	.40	.18	.05
☐ 43 Howard Johnson NL's All-Time Switchhit HR King	.20	.09	.03
☐ 44 Wade Boggs Five Straight 200 Hit Seasons	.45	.20	.06
☐ 45 Benito Santiago Eclipses Rookie Game Hitting Streak	.30	.14	.04
☐ 46 Mark McGwire Eclipses Jackson's A's HR Record	.90	.40	.11
☐ 47 Kevin Seitzer 13th Rookie to Collect 200 Hits	.20	.09	.03
☐ 48 Don Mattingly Sets Slam Record	.75	.35	.09
☐ 49 Darryl Strawberry NL Player September	.40	.18	.05
☐ 50 Pascual Perez NL Pitcher September	.10	.05	.01
☐ 51 Alan Trammell AL Player September	.15	.07	.02
☐ 52 Doyle Alexander AL Pitcher September	.06	.03	.01
☐ 53 Nolan Ryan Strikeout King Again	1.50	.65	.19
☐ 54 Mark McGwire Donruss AL ROY	1.00	.45	.13
☐ 55 Benito Santiago Donruss NL ROY	.35	.16	.04
☐ 56 Checklist Card	.06	.03	.01

1987 Donruss Opening Day

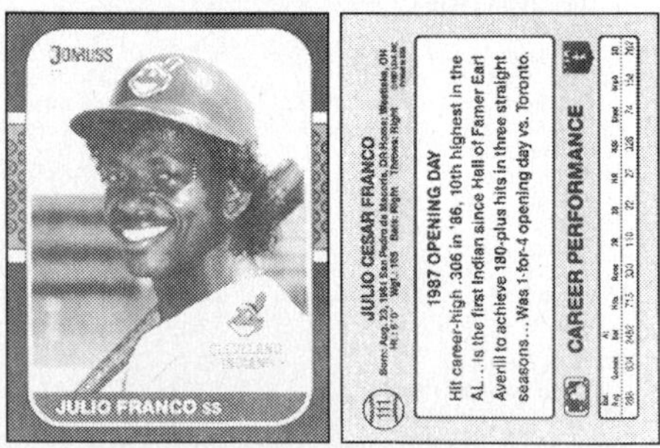

This innovative set of 272 cards features a card for each of the players in the starting line-ups of all the teams on Opening Day 1987. Cards are the standard size, 2 1/2" by 3 1/2", and are packaged as a complete set in a specially designed box. Cards are very similar in design to the 1987 regular Donruss issue except that these "OD" cards have a maroon border instead of a black border. The set features the first card in a Major League uniform of Joey Cora, Mark Davidson, Donell Nixon, Bob Patterson, and Alonzo Powell. Teams in the same city share a checklist card. A 15-piece puzzle of Roberto Clemente is also included with every complete set. The error on Barry Bonds (picturing Johnny Ray by mistake) was corrected very early in the press run; supposedly less than one percent of the sets have the error.

	MT	EX-MT	VG
COMPLETE SET (272)	18.00	8.00	2.30
COMMON PLAYER (1-248)	.05	.02	.01
COMMON LOGO (249-272)	.03	.01	.00

☐ 1 Doug DeCinces	.10	.05	.01
☐ 2 Mike Witt	.05	.02	.01
☐ 3 George Hendrick	.05	.02	.01
☐ 4 Dick Schofield	.05	.02	.01
☐ 5 Devon White	.50	.23	.06
☐ 6 Butch Wynegar	.05	.02	.01
☐ 7 Wally Joyner	.75	.35	.09
☐ 8 Mark McLemore	.05	.02	.01
☐ 9 Brian Downing	.05	.02	.01
☐ 10 Gary Pettis	.05	.02	.01
☐ 11 Bill Doran	.10	.05	.01
☐ 12 Phil Garner	.10	.05	.01
☐ 13 Jose Cruz	.10	.05	.01
☐ 14 Kevin Bass	.05	.02	.01
☐ 15 Mike Scott	.10	.05	.01
☐ 16 Glenn Davis	.20	.09	.03
☐ 17 Alan Ashby	.05	.02	.01
☐ 18 Billy Hatcher	.10	.05	.01
☐ 19 Craig Reynolds	.05	.02	.01
☐ 20 Carney Lansford	.10	.05	.01
☐ 21 Mike Davis	.05	.02	.01
☐ 22 Reggie Jackson	.60	.25	.08
☐ 23 Mickey Tettleton	.25	.11	.03
☐ 24 Jose Canseco	2.50	1.15	.30
☐ 25 Rob Nelson	.05	.02	.01
☐ 26 Tony Phillips	.15	.07	.02
☐ 27 Dwayne Murphy	.05	.02	.01
☐ 28 Alfredo Griffin	.05	.02	.01
☐ 29 Curt Young	.05	.02	.01
☐ 30 Willie Upshaw	.05	.02	.01
☐ 31 Mike Sharperson	.10	.05	.01
☐ 32 Rance Mulliniks	.05	.02	.01
☐ 33 Ernie Whitt	.05	.02	.01
☐ 34 Jesse Barfield	.10	.05	.01
☐ 35 Tony Fernandez	.15	.07	.02
☐ 36 Lloyd Moseby	.05	.02	.01
☐ 37 Jimmy Key	.15	.07	.02
☐ 38 Fred McGriff	2.00	.90	.25
☐ 39 George Bell	.20	.09	.03
☐ 40 Dale Murphy	.25	.11	.03
☐ 41 Rick Mahler	.05	.02	.01
☐ 42 Ken Griffey	.10	.05	.01
☐ 43 Andres Thomas	.05	.02	.01
☐ 44 Dion James	.05	.02	.01
☐ 45 Ozzie Virgil	.05	.02	.01
☐ 46 Ken Oberkfell	.05	.02	.01
☐ 47 Gary Roenicke	.05	.02	.01
☐ 48 Glenn Hubbard	.05	.02	.01
☐ 49 Bill Schroeder	.05	.02	.01
☐ 50 Greg Brock	.05	.02	.01
☐ 51 Billy Joe Robidoux	.05	.02	.01
☐ 52 Glenn Braggs	.10	.05	.01
☐ 53 Jim Gantner	.05	.02	.01
☐ 54 Paul Molitor	.25	.11	.03
☐ 55 Dale Sveum	.05	.02	.01
☐ 56 Ted Higuera	.10	.05	.01
☐ 57 Rob Deer	.15	.07	.02
☐ 58 Robin Yount	.75	.35	.09
☐ 59 Jim Lindeman	.05	.02	.01
☐ 60 Vince Coleman	.25	.11	.03
☐ 61 Tommy Herr	.05	.02	.01
☐ 62 Terry Pendleton	.35	.16	.04
☐ 63 John Tudor	.10	.05	.01
☐ 64 Tony Pena	.05	.02	.01
☐ 65 Ozzie Smith	.40	.18	.05
☐ 66 Tito Landrum	.05	.02	.01
☐ 67 Jack Clark	.10	.05	.01
☐ 68 Bob Dernier	.05	.02	.01
☐ 69 Rick Sutcliffe	.10	.05	.01
☐ 70 Andre Dawson	.35	.16	.04
☐ 71 Keith Moreland	.05	.02	.01
☐ 72 Jody Davis	.05	.02	.01
☐ 73 Brian Dayett	.05	.02	.01
☐ 74 Leon Durham	.05	.02	.01
☐ 75 Ryne Sandberg	1.50	.65	.19
☐ 76 Shawon Dunston	.25	.11	.03
☐ 77 Mike Marshall	.10	.05	.01
☐ 78 Bill Madlock	.05	.02	.01
☐ 79 Orel Hershiser	.30	.14	.04
☐ 80 Mike Ramsey	.10	.05	.01

☐ 81	Ken Landreaux	.05	.02	.01
☐ 82	Mike Scioscia	.05	.02	.01
☐ 83	Franklin Stubbs	.10	.05	.01
☐ 84	Mariano Duncan	.10	.05	.01
☐ 85	Steve Sax	.15	.07	.02
☐ 86	Mitch Webster	.05	.02	.01
☐ 87	Reid Nichols	.05	.02	.01
☐ 88	Tim Wallach	.10	.05	.01
☐ 89	Floyd Youmans	.05	.02	.01
☐ 90	Andres Galarraga	.30	.14	.04
☐ 91	Hubie Brooks	.10	.05	.01
☐ 92	Jeff Reed	.05	.02	.01
☐ 93	Alonzo Powell	.15	.07	.02
☐ 94	Vance Law	.05	.02	.01
☐ 95	Bob Brenly	.05	.02	.01
☐ 96	Will Clark	2.50	1.15	.30
☐ 97	Chili Davis	.10	.05	.01
☐ 98	Mike Krukow	.05	.02	.01
☐ 99	Jose Uribe	.05	.02	.01
☐ 100	Chris Brown	.05	.02	.01
☐ 101	Robby Thompson	.15	.07	.02
☐ 102	Candy Maldonado	.10	.05	.01
☐ 103	Jeff Leonard	.05	.02	.01
☐ 104	Tom Candiotti	.10	.05	.01
☐ 105	Chris Bando	.05	.02	.01
☐ 106	Cory Snyder	.15	.07	.02
☐ 107	Pat Tabler	.05	.02	.01
☐ 108	Andre Thornton	.05	.02	.01
☐ 109	Joe Carter	.90	.40	.11
☐ 110	Tony Bernazard	.05	.02	.01
☐ 111	Julio Franco	.25	.11	.03
☐ 112	Brook Jacoby	.10	.05	.01
☐ 113	Brett Butler	.15	.07	.02
☐ 114	Donell Nixon	.10	.05	.01
☐ 115	Alvin Davis	.10	.05	.01
☐ 116	Mark Langston	.15	.07	.02
☐ 117	Harold Reynolds	.10	.05	.01
☐ 118	Ken Phelps	.05	.02	.01
☐ 119	Mike Kingery	.05	.02	.01
☐ 120	Dave Valle	.05	.02	.01
☐ 121	Rey Quinones	.05	.02	.01
☐ 122	Phil Bradley	.05	.02	.01
☐ 123	Jim Presley	.05	.02	.01
☐ 124	Keith Hernandez	.10	.05	.01
☐ 125	Kevin McReynolds	.15	.07	.02
☐ 126	Rafael Santana	.05	.02	.01
☐ 127	Bob Ojeda	.10	.05	.01
☐ 128	Darryl Strawberry	.75	.35	.09
☐ 129	Mookie Wilson	.05	.02	.01
☐ 130	Gary Carter	.25	.11	.03
☐ 131	Tim Teufel	.05	.02	.01
☐ 132	Howard Johnson	.25	.11	.03
☐ 133	Cal Ripken	1.50	.65	.19
☐ 134	Rick Burleson	.05	.02	.01
☐ 135	Fred Lynn	.10	.05	.01
☐ 136	Eddie Murray	.25	.11	.03
☐ 137	Ray Knight	.10	.05	.01
☐ 138	Alan Wiggins	.05	.02	.01
☐ 139	John Shelby	.05	.02	.01
☐ 140	Mike Boddicker	.05	.02	.01
☐ 141	Ken Gerhart	.05	.02	.01
☐ 142	Terry Kennedy	.05	.02	.01
☐ 143	Steve Garvey	.30	.14	.04
☐ 144	Marvell Wynne	.05	.02	.01
☐ 145	Kevin Mitchell	.90	.40	.11
☐ 146	Tony Gwynn	.75	.35	.09
☐ 147	Joey Cora	.15	.07	.02
☐ 148	Benito Santiago	.75	.35	.09
☐ 149	Eric Show	.05	.02	.01
☐ 150	Garry Templeton	.05	.02	.01
☐ 151	Carmelo Martinez	.05	.02	.01
☐ 152	Von Hayes	.05	.02	.01
☐ 153	Lance Parrish	.10	.05	.01
☐ 154	Milt Thompson	.05	.02	.01
☐ 155	Mike Easler	.05	.02	.01
☐ 156	Juan Samuel	.10	.05	.01
☐ 157	Steve Jeltz	.05	.02	.01
☐ 158	Glenn Wilson	.05	.02	.01
☐ 159	Shane Rawley	.05	.02	.01
☐ 160	Mike Schmidt	1.00	.45	.13
☐ 161	Andy Van Slyke	.35	.16	.04
☐ 162	Johnny Ray	.10	.05	.01
☐ 163A	Barry Bonds ERR (Photo actually Johnny Ray)	200.00	90.00	25.00
☐ 163B	Barry Bonds COR	3.00	1.35	.40
☐ 164	Junior Ortiz	.05	.02	.01
☐ 165	Rafael Belliard	.10	.05	.01
☐ 166	Bob Patterson	.15	.07	.02
☐ 167	Bobby Bonilla	.90	.40	.11
☐ 168	Sid Bream	.10	.05	.01
☐ 169	Jim Morrison	.05	.02	.01
☐ 170	Jerry Browne	.15	.07	.02
☐ 171	Scott Fletcher	.05	.02	.01
☐ 172	Ruben Sierra	2.50	1.15	.30
☐ 173	Larry Parrish	.05	.02	.01
☐ 174	Pete O'Brien	.05	.02	.01
☐ 175	Pete Incaviglia	.15	.07	.02
☐ 176	Don Slaught	.05	.02	.01
☐ 177	Oddibe McDowell	.05	.02	.01
☐ 178	Charlie Hough	.05	.02	.01
☐ 179	Steve Buechele	.10	.05	.01
☐ 180	Bob Stanley	.05	.02	.01
☐ 181	Wade Boggs	.90	.40	.11
☐ 182	Jim Rice	.20	.09	.03
☐ 183	Bill Buckner	.10	.05	.01
☐ 184	Dwight Evans	.15	.07	.02
☐ 185	Spike Owen	.05	.02	.01
☐ 186	Don Baylor	.10	.05	.01
☐ 187	Marc Sullivan	.05	.02	.01
☐ 188	Marty Barrett	.05	.02	.01
☐ 189	Dave Henderson	.10	.05	.01
☐ 190	Bo Diaz	.05	.02	.01
☐ 191	Barry Larkin	1.00	.45	.13
☐ 192	Kal Daniels	.20	.09	.03
☐ 193	Terry Francona	.05	.02	.01
☐ 194	Tom Browning	.15	.07	.02
☐ 195	Ron Oester	.05	.02	.01
☐ 196	Buddy Bell	.10	.05	.01
☐ 197	Eric Davis	.50	.23	.06
☐ 198	Dave Parker	.15	.07	.02
☐ 199	Steve Balboni	.05	.02	.01
☐ 200	Danny Tartabull	.40	.18	.05
☐ 201	Ed Hearn	.05	.02	.01
☐ 202	Buddy Biancalana	.05	.02	.01
☐ 203	Danny Jackson	.10	.05	.01
☐ 204	Frank White	.05	.02	.01
☐ 205	Bo Jackson	1.50	.65	.19
☐ 206	George Brett	.60	.25	.08
☐ 207	Kevin Seitzer	.25	.11	.03
☐ 208	Willie Wilson	.10	.05	.01
☐ 209	Orlando Mercado	.05	.02	.01
☐ 210	Darrell Evans	.10	.05	.01
☐ 211	Larry Herndon	.05	.02	.01
☐ 212	Jack Morris	.25	.11	.03
☐ 213	Chet Lemon	.05	.02	.01
☐ 214	Mike Heath	.05	.02	.01
☐ 215	Darnell Coles	.10	.05	.01
☐ 216	Alan Trammell	.25	.11	.03
☐ 217	Terry Harper	.05	.02	.01
☐ 218	Lou Whitaker	.20	.09	.03
☐ 219	Gary Gaetti	.10	.05	.01
☐ 220	Tom Nieto	.05	.02	.01
☐ 221	Kirby Puckett	1.25	.55	.16
☐ 222	Tom Brunansky	.10	.05	.01
☐ 223	Greg Gagne	.05	.02	.01
☐ 224	Dan Gladden	.05	.02	.01
☐ 225	Mark Davidson	.10	.05	.01
☐ 226	Bert Blyleven	.10	.05	.01
☐ 227	Steve Lombardozzi	.05	.02	.01
☐ 228	Kent Hrbek	.15	.07	.02
☐ 229	Gary Redus	.05	.02	.01
☐ 230	Ivan Calderon	.25	.11	.03
☐ 231	Tim Hulett	.05	.02	.01
☐ 232	Carlton Fisk	.45	.20	.06
☐ 233	Greg Walker	.10	.05	.01
☐ 234	Ron Karkovice	.05	.02	.01
☐ 235	Ozzie Guillen	.15	.07	.02
☐ 236	Harold Baines	.15	.07	.02
☐ 237	Donnie Hill	.05	.02	.01
☐ 238	Rich Dotson	.05	.02	.01
☐ 239	Mike Pagliarulo	.10	.05	.01
☐ 240	Joel Skinner	.05	.02	.01
☐ 241	Don Mattingly	1.00	.45	.13
☐ 242	Gary Ward	.05	.02	.01
☐ 243	Dave Winfield	.40	.18	.05
☐ 244	Dan Pasqua	.15	.07	.02
☐ 245	Wayne Tolleson	.05	.02	.01
☐ 246	Willie Randolph	.10	.05	.01
☐ 247	Dennis Rasmussen	.05	.02	.01
☐ 248	Rickey Henderson	.90	.40	.11
☐ 249	Angels Logo	.03	.01	.00
☐ 250	Astros Logo	.03	.01	.00
☐ 251	A's Logo	.03	.01	.00
☐ 252	Blue Jays Logo	.03	.01	.00
☐ 253	Braves Logo	.03	.01	.00
☐ 254	Brewers Logo	.03	.01	.00
☐ 255	Cardinals Logo	.03	.01	.00
☐ 256	Dodgers Logo	.03	.01	.00
☐ 257	Expos Logo	.03	.01	.00
☐ 258	Giants Logo	.03	.01	.00
☐ 259	Indians Logo	.03	.01	.00
☐ 260	Mariners Logo	.03	.01	.00
☐ 261	Orioles Logo	.03	.01	.00
☐ 262	Padres Logo	.03	.01	.00
☐ 263	Phillies Logo	.03	.01	.00

		MT	EX-MT	VG
☐ 264	Pirates Logo	.03	.01	.00
☐ 265	Rangers Logo	.03	.01	.00
☐ 266	Red Sox Logo	.03	.01	.00
☐ 267	Reds Logo	.03	.01	.00
☐ 268	Royals Logo	.03	.01	.00
☐ 269	Tigers Logo	.03	.01	.00
☐ 270	Twins Logo	.03	.01	.00
☐ 271	Chicago Logos	.03	.01	.00
☐ 272	New York Logos	.03	.01	.00

1987 Donruss Pop-Ups

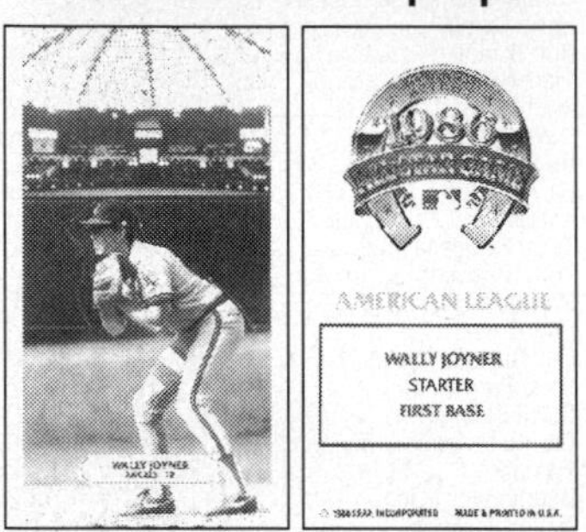

This 20-card set features "fold-out" cards measuring approximately 2 1/2" by 5". Card fronts are in full color. Cards are unnumbered but are listed in the same order as the Donruss All-Stars on the All-Star checklist card. Card backs present essentially no information about the player. The set was distributed in packs which also contained All-Star cards (3 1/2" by 5").

		MT	EX-MT	VG
COMPLETE SET (20)		5.00	2.30	.60
COMMON PLAYER (1-20)		.10	.05	.01
☐ 1	Wally Joyner	.50	.23	.06
☐ 2	Dave Winfield	.50	.23	.06
☐ 3	Lou Whitaker	.20	.09	.03
☐ 4	Kirby Puckett	1.00	.45	.13
☐ 5	Cal Ripken	1.50	.65	.19
☐ 6	Rickey Henderson	.90	.40	.11
☐ 7	Wade Boggs	.75	.35	.09
☐ 8	Roger Clemens	1.25	.55	.16
☐ 9	Lance Parrish	.15	.07	.02
☐ 10	Dick Howser MG	.10	.05	.01
☐ 11	Keith Hernandez	.15	.07	.02
☐ 12	Darryl Strawberry	.60	.25	.08
☐ 13	Ryne Sandberg	1.25	.55	.16
☐ 14	Dale Murphy	.40	.18	.05
☐ 15	Ozzie Smith	.40	.18	.05
☐ 16	Tony Gwynn	.50	.23	.06
☐ 17	Mike Schmidt	.90	.40	.11
☐ 18	Dwight Gooden	.40	.18	.05
☐ 19	Gary Carter	.30	.14	.04
☐ 20	Whitey Herzog MG	.10	.05	.01

1987 Donruss Rookies

The 1987 Donruss "The Rookies" set features 56 cards plus a 15-piece puzzle of Roberto Clemente. Cards are in full color and are standard size, 2 1/2" by 3 1/2". The set was distributed in a small green and black box with gold lettering. Card fronts are similar in design to the 1987 Donruss regular issue except for the presence of "The Rookies" logo in the lower left corner and a green border instead of a black border. The key (extended) Rookie Cards in this set are Ellis Burks, Shane Mack, John Smiley, and Matt Williams.

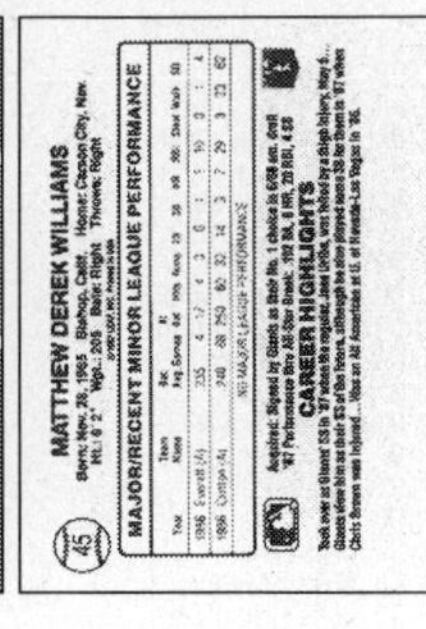

		MT	EX-MT	VG
COMPLETE SET (56)		20.00	9.00	2.50
COMMON PLAYER (1-56)		.08	.04	.01
☐ 1	Mark McGwire	6.00	2.70	.75
☐ 2	Eric Bell	.08	.04	.01
☐ 3	Mark Williamson	.08	.04	.01
☐ 4	Mike Greenwell	.75	.35	.09
☐ 5	Ellis Burks	.75	.35	.09
☐ 6	DeWayne Buice	.08	.04	.01
☐ 7	Mark McLemore	.08	.04	.01
☐ 8	Devon White	.08	.04	.01
☐ 9	Willie Fraser	.08	.04	.01
☐ 10	Les Lancaster	.08	.04	.01
☐ 11	Ken Williams	.08	.04	.01
☐ 12	Matt Nokes	.40	.18	.05
☐ 13	Jeff M. Robinson	.12	.05	.02
☐ 14	Bo Jackson	2.00	.90	.25
☐ 15	Kevin Seitzer	.40	.18	.05
☐ 16	Billy Ripken	.15	.07	.02
☐ 17	B.J. Surhoff	.12	.05	.02
☐ 18	Chuck Crim	.08	.04	.01
☐ 19	Mike Birkbeck	.08	.04	.01
☐ 20	Chris Bosio	.25	.11	.03
☐ 21	Les Straker	.08	.04	.01
☐ 22	Mark Davidson	.08	.04	.01
☐ 23	Gene Larkin	.20	.09	.03
☐ 24	Ken Gerhart	.08	.04	.01
☐ 25	Luis Polonia	.75	.35	.09
☐ 26	Terry Steinbach	.25	.11	.03
☐ 27	Mickey Brantley	.08	.04	.01
☐ 28	Mike Stanley	.08	.04	.01
☐ 29	Jerry Browne	.12	.05	.02
☐ 30	Todd Benzinger	.15	.07	.02
☐ 31	Fred McGriff	3.50	1.55	.45
☐ 32	Mike Henneman	.30	.14	.04
☐ 33	Casey Candaele	.08	.04	.01
☐ 34	Dave Magadan	.15	.07	.02
☐ 35	David Cone	2.50	1.15	.30
☐ 36	Mike Jackson	.20	.09	.03
☐ 37	John Mitchell	.08	.04	.01
☐ 38	Mike Dunne	.08	.04	.01
☐ 39	John Smiley	1.00	.45	.13
☐ 40	Joe Magrane	.15	.07	.02
☐ 41	Jim Lindeman	.08	.04	.01
☐ 42	Shane Mack	1.50	.65	.19
☐ 43	Stan Jefferson	.08	.04	.01
☐ 44	Benito Santiago	.40	.18	.05
☐ 45	Matt Williams	2.50	1.15	.30
☐ 46	Dave Meads	.08	.04	.01
☐ 47	Rafael Palmeiro	2.50	1.15	.30
☐ 48	Bill Long	.08	.04	.01
☐ 49	Bob Brower	.08	.04	.01
☐ 50	James Steels	.08	.04	.01
☐ 51	Paul Noce	.08	.04	.01
☐ 52	Greg Maddux	4.00	1.80	.50
☐ 53	Jeff Musselman	.08	.04	.01
☐ 54	Brian Holton	.08	.04	.01
☐ 55	Chuck Jackson	.08	.04	.01
☐ 56	Checklist Card	.08	.01	.00

1987 Donruss Super DK's

This 28-card set was available through a mail-in offer detailed on the wax packs. The set was sent in return for 8.00 and three wrappers plus 1.50 postage and handling. The set features the popular Diamond King subseries in

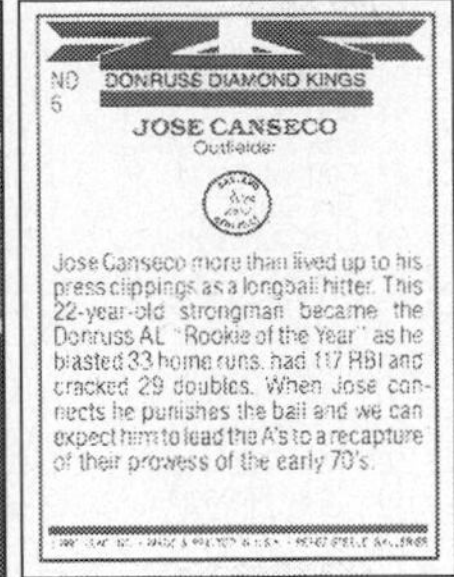

large (approximately 4 7/8" by 6 13/16") form. Dick Perez of Perez-Steele Galleries did another outstanding job on the artwork. The cards are essentially a large version of the Donruss regular issue Diamond Kings.

	MT	EX-MT	VG
COMPLETE SET (28)	11.00	4.90	1.40
COMMON PLAYER (1-28)	.25	.11	.03
☐ 1 Wally Joyner	.75	.35	.09
☐ 2 Roger Clemens	1.75	.80	.22
☐ 3 Dale Murphy	.50	.23	.06
☐ 4 Darryl Strawberry	1.00	.45	.13
☐ 5 Ozzie Smith	.50	.23	.06
☐ 6 Jose Canseco	2.00	.90	.25
☐ 7 Charlie Hough	.25	.11	.03
☐ 8 Brook Jacoby	.25	.11	.03
☐ 9 Fred Lynn	.35	.16	.04
☐ 10 Rick Rhoden	.25	.11	.03
☐ 11 Chris Brown	.25	.11	.03
☐ 12 Von Hayes	.25	.11	.03
☐ 13 Jack Morris	.50	.23	.06
☐ 14 Kevin McReynolds	.35	.16	.04
☐ 15 George Brett	1.00	.45	.13
☐ 16 Ted Higuera	.35	.16	.04
☐ 17 Hubie Brooks	.25	.11	.03
☐ 18 Mike Scott	.35	.16	.04
☐ 19 Kirby Puckett	1.50	.65	.19
☐ 20 Dave Winfield	.60	.25	.08
☐ 21 Lloyd Moseby	.25	.11	.03
☐ 22 Eric Davis	.50	.23	.06
☐ 23 Jim Presley	.25	.11	.03
☐ 24 Keith Moreland	.25	.11	.03
☐ 25 Greg Walker	.25	.11	.03
☐ 26 Steve Sax	.35	.16	.04
☐ 27 DK Checklist 1-26 (Unnumbered)	.25	.11	.03
☐ 28 Roberto Clemente Large Puzzle (Unnumbered)	.50	.23	.06

1987 Donruss Wax Box Cards

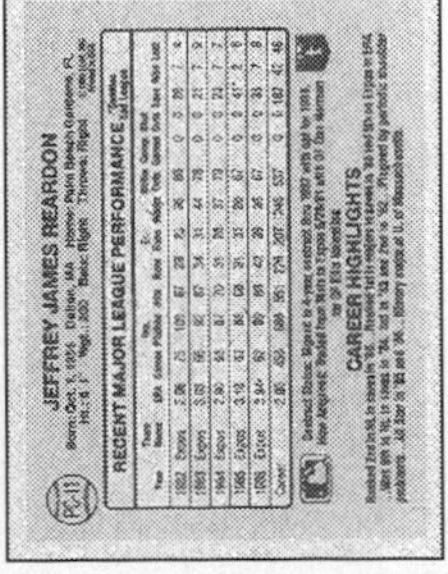

The cards in this four-card set measure the standard 2 1/2" by 3 1/2". Cards have essentially the same design as the 1987 Donruss regular issue set. The cards were printed on the bottoms of the regular issue wax pack boxes. The four cards (PC10 to PC12 plus a Roberto Clemente puzzle card) are considered a separate set in their own right and are not typically included in a complete set of the regular issue 1987 Donruss cards. The value of the panel uncut is slightly greater, perhaps by 25 percent greater, than the value of the individual cards cut up carefully.

	MT	EX-MT	VG
COMPLETE SET (4)	2.50	1.15	.30
COMMON PLAYER	.15	.07	.02
☐ PC10 Dale Murphy	.35	.16	.04
☐ PC11 Jeff Reardon	.35	.16	.04
☐ PC12 Jose Canseco	2.00	.90	.25
☐ PUZO Roberto Clemente (Puzzle Card)	.15	.07	.02

1988 Donruss

This 660-card set was distributed along with a puzzle of Stan Musial. The six regular checklist cards are numbered throughout the set as multiples of 100. Cards measure 2 1/2" by 3 1/2" and feature a distinctive black and blue border on the front. The popular Diamond King subset returns for the seventh consecutive year. Rated Rookies are featured again as cards 28-47. Cards marked as SP (short printed) from 648-660 are more difficult to find than the other 13 SP's in the lower 600s. These 26 cards listed as SP were apparently pulled from the printing sheet to make room for the 26 Bonus MVP cards. Numbered with the prefix "BC" for bonus card, this 26-card set featuring the most valuable player from each of the 26 teams was randomly inserted in the wax and rack packs. The cards are distinguished by the MVP logo in the upper left corner of the obverse, and cards BC14-BC26 are considered to be more difficult to find than cards BC1-BC13. Six of the checklist cards were done two different ways to reflect the inclusion or exclusion of the Bonus MVP cards in the wax packs. In the checklist below, the A variations (for the checklist cards) are from the wax packs and the B variations are from the factory-collated sets. The key Rookie Cards in this set are Roberto Alomar, Ellis Burks, Ron Gant, Tom Glavine, Mark Grace, Gregg Jefferies, Roberto Kelly, Jack McDowell, and Matt Williams. There was also a Kirby Puckett card issued as the package back of Donruss blister packs; it uses a different photo from both of Kirby's regular and Bonus MVP cards and is unnumbered on the back. The design pattern of the factory set card fronts is oriented differently from that of the regular wax pack cards.

	MT	EX-MT	VG
COMPLETE SET (660)	20.00	9.00	2.50
COMPLETE FACT.SET (660)	20.00	9.00	2.50
COMMON PLAYER (1-647)	.04	.02	.01
COMMON PLAYER SP (648-660)	.07	.03	.01
COMPLETE MVP SET (26)	3.50	1.55	.45

COMMON MVP (BC1-BC13)	.05	.02	.01
COMMON MVP SP (BC14-BC26)	.08	.04	.01
☐ 1 Mark McGwire DK	.40	.18	.05
☐ 2 Tim Raines DK	.08	.04	.01
☐ 3 Benito Santiago DK	.08	.04	.01
☐ 4 Alan Trammell DK	.08	.04	.01
☐ 5 Danny Tartabull DK	.10	.05	.01
☐ 6 Ron Darling DK	.05	.02	.01
☐ 7 Paul Molitor DK	.08	.04	.01
☐ 8 Devon White DK	.05	.02	.01
☐ 9 Andre Dawson DK	.10	.05	.01
☐ 10 Julio Franco DK	.05	.02	.01
☐ 11 Scott Fletcher DK	.05	.02	.01
☐ 12 Tony Fernandez DK	.05	.02	.01
☐ 13 Shane Rawley DK	.05	.02	.01
☐ 14 Kal Daniels DK	.05	.02	.01
☐ 15 Jack Clark DK	.05	.02	.01
☐ 16 Dwight Evans DK	.05	.02	.01
☐ 17 Tommy John DK	.05	.02	.01
☐ 18 Andy Van Slyke DK	.08	.04	.01
☐ 19 Gary Gaetti DK	.05	.02	.01
☐ 20 Mark Langston DK	.05	.02	.01
☐ 21 Will Clark DK	.30	.14	.04
☐ 22 Glenn Hubbard DK	.05	.02	.01
☐ 23 Billy Hatcher DK	.05	.02	.01
☐ 24 Bob Welch DK	.05	.02	.01
☐ 25 Ivan Calderon DK	.05	.02	.01
☐ 26 Cal Ripken DK	.30	.14	.04
☐ 27 DK Checklist 1-26	.06	.01	.00
☐ 28 Mackey Sasser RR	.10	.05	.01
☐ 29 Jeff Treadway RR	.10	.05	.01
☐ 30 Mike Campbell RR	.06	.03	.01
☐ 31 Lance Johnson RR	.20	.09	.03
☐ 32 Nelson Liriano RR	.06	.03	.01
☐ 33 Shawn Abner RR	.06	.03	.01
☐ 34 Roberto Alomar RR	5.00	2.30	.60
☐ 35 Shawn Hillegas RR	.06	.03	.01
☐ 36 Joey Meyer RR	.06	.03	.01
☐ 37 Kevin Elster RR	.06	.03	.01
☐ 38 Jose Lind RR	.15	.07	.02
☐ 39 Kirt Manwaring RR	.10	.05	.01
☐ 40 Mark Grace RR	1.25	.55	.16
☐ 41 Jody Reed RR	.25	.11	.03
☐ 42 John Farrell RR	.06	.03	.01
☐ 43 Al Leiter RR	.06	.03	.01
☐ 44 Gary Thurman RR	.06	.03	.01
☐ 45 Vicente Palacios RR	.10	.05	.01
☐ 46 Eddie Williams RR	.06	.03	.01
☐ 47 Jack McDowell RR	1.25	.55	.16
☐ 48 Ken Dixon	.04	.02	.01
☐ 49 Mike Birkbeck	.04	.02	.01
☐ 50 Eric King	.04	.02	.01
☐ 51 Roger Clemens	.50	.23	.06
☐ 52 Pat Clements	.04	.02	.01
☐ 53 Fernando Valenzuela	.07	.03	.01
☐ 54 Mark Gubicza	.04	.02	.01
☐ 55 Jay Howell	.04	.02	.01
☐ 56 Floyd Youmans	.04	.02	.01
☐ 57 Ed Correa	.04	.02	.01
☐ 58 DeWayne Buice	.04	.02	.01
☐ 59 Jose DeLeon	.04	.02	.01
☐ 60 Danny Cox	.04	.02	.01
☐ 61 Nolan Ryan	.75	.35	.09
☐ 62 Steve Bedrosian	.04	.02	.01
☐ 63 Tom Browning	.04	.02	.01
☐ 64 Mark Davis	.04	.02	.01
☐ 65 R.J. Reynolds	.04	.02	.01
☐ 66 Kevin Mitchell	.15	.07	.02
☐ 67 Ken Oberkfell	.04	.02	.01
☐ 68 Rick Sutcliffe	.07	.03	.01
☐ 69 Dwight Gooden	.12	.05	.02
☐ 70 Scott Bankhead	.04	.02	.01
☐ 71 Bert Blyleven	.07	.03	.01
☐ 72 Jimmy Key	.07	.03	.01
☐ 73 Les Straker	.04	.02	.01
☐ 74 Jim Clancy	.04	.02	.01
☐ 75 Mike Moore	.04	.02	.01
☐ 76 Ron Darling	.07	.03	.01
☐ 77 Ed Lynch	.04	.02	.01
☐ 78 Dale Murphy	.10	.05	.01
☐ 79 Doug Drabek	.10	.05	.01
☐ 80 Scott Garrelts	.04	.02	.01
☐ 81 Ed Whitson	.04	.02	.01
☐ 82 Rob Murphy	.04	.02	.01
☐ 83 Shane Rawley	.04	.02	.01
☐ 84 Greg Mathews	.04	.02	.01
☐ 85 Jim Deshaies	.04	.02	.01
☐ 86 Mike Witt	.04	.02	.01
☐ 87 Donnie Hill	.04	.02	.01
☐ 88 Jeff Reed	.04	.02	.01
☐ 89 Mike Boddicker	.04	.02	.01
☐ 90 Ted Higuera	.04	.02	.01
☐ 91 Walt Terrell	.04	.02	.01
☐ 92 Bob Stanley	.04	.02	.01
☐ 93 Dave Righetti	.04	.02	.01
☐ 94 Orel Hershiser	.07	.03	.01
☐ 95 Chris Bando	.04	.02	.01
☐ 96 Bret Saberhagen	.10	.05	.01
☐ 97 Curt Young	.04	.02	.01
☐ 98 Tim Burke	.04	.02	.01
☐ 99 Charlie Hough	.04	.02	.01
☐ 100A Checklist 28-137	.06	.01	.00
☐ 100B Checklist 28-133	.06	.01	.00
☐ 101 Bobby Witt	.07	.03	.01
☐ 102 George Brett	.25	.11	.03
☐ 103 Mickey Tettleton	.12	.05	.02
☐ 104 Scott Bailes	.04	.02	.01
☐ 105 Mike Pagliarulo	.04	.02	.01
☐ 106 Mike Scioscia	.04	.02	.01
☐ 107 Tom Brookens	.04	.02	.01
☐ 108 Ray Knight	.07	.03	.01
☐ 109 Dan Plesac	.04	.02	.01
☐ 110 Wally Joyner	.12	.05	.02
☐ 111 Bob Forsch	.04	.02	.01
☐ 112 Mike Scott	.07	.03	.01
☐ 113 Kevin Gross	.04	.02	.01
☐ 114 Benito Santiago	.10	.05	.01
☐ 115 Bob Kipper	.04	.02	.01
☐ 116 Mike Krukow	.04	.02	.01
☐ 117 Chris Bosio	.07	.03	.01
☐ 118 Sid Fernandez	.07	.03	.01
☐ 119 Jody Davis	.04	.02	.01
☐ 120 Mike Morgan	.07	.03	.01
☐ 121 Mark Eichhorn	.04	.02	.01
☐ 122 Jeff Reardon	.12	.05	.02
☐ 123 John Franco	.04	.02	.01
☐ 124 Richard Dotson	.04	.02	.01
☐ 125 Eric Bell	.04	.02	.01
☐ 126 Juan Nieves	.04	.02	.01
☐ 127 Jack Morris	.12	.05	.02
☐ 128 Rick Rhoden	.04	.02	.01
☐ 129 Rich Gedman	.04	.02	.01
☐ 130 Ken Howell	.04	.02	.01
☐ 131 Brook Jacoby	.04	.02	.01
☐ 132 Danny Jackson	.04	.02	.01
☐ 133 Gene Nelson	.04	.02	.01
☐ 134 Neal Heaton	.04	.02	.01
☐ 135 Willie Fraser	.04	.02	.01
☐ 136 Jose Guzman	.07	.03	.01
☐ 137 Ozzie Guillen	.07	.03	.01
☐ 138 Bob Knepper	.04	.02	.01
☐ 139 Mike Jackson	.10	.05	.01
☐ 140 Joe Magrane	.10	.05	.01
☐ 141 Jimmy Jones	.04	.02	.01
☐ 142 Ted Power	.04	.02	.01
☐ 143 Ozzie Virgil	.04	.02	.01
☐ 144 Felix Fermin	.04	.02	.01
☐ 145 Kelly Downs	.04	.02	.01
☐ 146 Shawon Dunston	.07	.03	.01
☐ 147 Scott Bradley	.04	.02	.01
☐ 148 Dave Stieb	.07	.03	.01
☐ 149 Frank Viola	.07	.03	.01
☐ 150 Terry Kennedy	.04	.02	.01
☐ 151 Bill Wegman	.04	.02	.01
☐ 152 Matt Nokes	.20	.09	.03
☐ 153 Wade Boggs	.30	.14	.04
☐ 154 Wayne Tolleson	.04	.02	.01
☐ 155 Mariano Duncan	.04	.02	.01
☐ 156 Julio Franco	.10	.05	.01
☐ 157 Charlie Leibrandt	.04	.02	.01
☐ 158 Terry Steinbach	.07	.03	.01
☐ 159 Mike Fitzgerald	.04	.02	.01
☐ 160 Jack Lazorko	.04	.02	.01
☐ 161 Mitch Williams	.07	.03	.01
☐ 162 Greg Walker	.04	.02	.01
☐ 163 Alan Ashby	.04	.02	.01
☐ 164 Tony Gwynn	.30	.14	.04
☐ 165 Bruce Ruffin	.04	.02	.01
☐ 166 Ron Robinson	.04	.02	.01
☐ 167 Zane Smith	.04	.02	.01
☐ 168 Junior Ortiz	.04	.02	.01
☐ 169 Jamie Moyer	.04	.02	.01
☐ 170 Tony Pena	.04	.02	.01
☐ 171 Cal Ripken	.60	.25	.08
☐ 172 B.J. Surhoff	.07	.03	.01
☐ 173 Lou Whitaker	.07	.03	.01
☐ 174 Ellis Burks	.25	.11	.03
☐ 175 Ron Guidry	.07	.03	.01
☐ 176 Steve Sax	.07	.03	.01
☐ 177 Danny Tartabull	.15	.07	.02
☐ 178 Carney Lansford	.07	.03	.01
☐ 179 Casey Candaele	.04	.02	.01
☐ 180 Scott Fletcher	.04	.02	.01
☐ 181 Mark McLemore	.04	.02	.01
☐ 182 Ivan Calderon	.07	.03	.01
☐ 183 Jack Clark	.07	.03	.01

☐ 184	Glenn Davis	.07	.03	.01
☐ 185	Luis Aguayo	.04	.02	.01
☐ 186	Bo Diaz	.04	.02	.01
☐ 187	Stan Jefferson	.04	.02	.01
☐ 188	Sid Bream	.07	.03	.01
☐ 189	Bob Brenly	.04	.02	.01
☐ 190	Dion James	.04	.02	.01
☐ 191	Leon Durham	.04	.02	.01
☐ 192	Jesse Orosco	.04	.02	.01
☐ 193	Alvin Davis	.04	.02	.01
☐ 194	Gary Gaetti	.04	.02	.01
☐ 195	Fred McGriff	.40	.18	.05
☐ 196	Steve Lombardozzi	.04	.02	.01
☐ 197	Rance Mulliniks	.04	.02	.01
☐ 198	Rey Quinones	.04	.02	.01
☐ 199	Gary Carter	.10	.05	.01
☐ 200A	Checklist 138-247	.06	.01	.00
☐ 200B	Checklist 134-239	.06	.01	.00
☐ 201	Keith Moreland	.04	.02	.01
☐ 202	Ken Griffey	.07	.03	.01
☐ 203	Tommy Gregg	.04	.02	.01
☐ 204	Will Clark	.60	.25	.08
☐ 205	John Kruk	.15	.07	.02
☐ 206	Buddy Bell	.07	.03	.01
☐ 207	Von Hayes	.04	.02	.01
☐ 208	Tommy Herr	.04	.02	.01
☐ 209	Craig Reynolds	.04	.02	.01
☐ 210	Gary Pettis	.04	.02	.01
☐ 211	Harold Baines	.07	.03	.01
☐ 212	Vance Law	.04	.02	.01
☐ 213	Ken Gerhart	.04	.02	.01
☐ 214	Jim Gantner	.04	.02	.01
☐ 215	Chet Lemon	.04	.02	.01
☐ 216	Dwight Evans	.07	.03	.01
☐ 217	Don Mattingly	.30	.14	.04
☐ 218	Franklin Stubbs	.04	.02	.01
☐ 219	Pat Tabler	.04	.02	.01
☐ 220	Bo Jackson	.30	.14	.04
☐ 221	Tony Phillips	.04	.02	.01
☐ 222	Tim Wallach	.07	.03	.01
☐ 223	Ruben Sierra	.40	.18	.05
☐ 224	Steve Buechele	.04	.02	.01
☐ 225	Frank White	.04	.02	.01
☐ 226	Alfredo Griffin	.04	.02	.01
☐ 227	Greg Swindell	.15	.07	.02
☐ 228	Willie Randolph	.07	.03	.01
☐ 229	Mike Marshall	.04	.02	.01
☐ 230	Alan Trammell	.07	.03	.01
☐ 231	Eddie Murray	.20	.09	.03
☐ 232	Dale Sveum	.04	.02	.01
☐ 233	Dick Schofield	.04	.02	.01
☐ 234	Jose Oquendo	.04	.02	.01
☐ 235	Bill Doran	.04	.02	.01
☐ 236	Milt Thompson	.04	.02	.01
☐ 237	Marvell Wynne	.04	.02	.01
☐ 238	Bobby Bonilla	.25	.11	.03
☐ 239	Chris Speier	.04	.02	.01
☐ 240	Glenn Braggs	.04	.02	.01
☐ 241	Wally Backman	.04	.02	.01
☐ 242	Ryne Sandberg	.50	.23	.06
☐ 243	Phil Bradley	.04	.02	.01
☐ 244	Kelly Gruber	.07	.03	.01
☐ 245	Tom Brunansky	.07	.03	.01
☐ 246	Ron Oester	.04	.02	.01
☐ 247	Bobby Thigpen	.07	.03	.01
☐ 248	Fred Lynn	.07	.03	.01
☐ 249	Paul Molitor	.12	.05	.02
☐ 250	Darrell Evans	.07	.03	.01
☐ 251	Gary Ward	.04	.02	.01
☐ 252	Bruce Hurst	.07	.03	.01
☐ 253	Bob Welch	.07	.03	.01
☐ 254	Joe Carter	.25	.11	.03
☐ 255	Willie Wilson	.04	.02	.01
☐ 256	Mark McGwire	.50	.23	.06
☐ 257	Mitch Webster	.04	.02	.01
☐ 258	Brian Downing	.04	.02	.01
☐ 259	Mike Stanley	.04	.02	.01
☐ 260	Carlton Fisk	.20	.09	.03
☐ 261	Billy Hatcher	.04	.02	.01
☐ 262	Glenn Wilson	.04	.02	.01
☐ 263	Ozzie Smith	.20	.09	.03
☐ 264	Randy Ready	.04	.02	.01
☐ 265	Kurt Stillwell	.04	.02	.01
☐ 266	David Palmer	.04	.02	.01
☐ 267	Mike Diaz	.04	.02	.01
☐ 268	Robby Thompson	.07	.03	.01
☐ 269	Andre Dawson	.20	.09	.03
☐ 270	Lee Guetterman	.04	.02	.01
☐ 271	Willie Upshaw	.04	.02	.01
☐ 272	Randy Bush	.04	.02	.01
☐ 273	Larry Sheets	.04	.02	.01
☐ 274	Rob Deer	.07	.03	.01
☐ 275	Kirk Gibson	.07	.03	.01
☐ 276	Marty Barrett	.04	.02	.01
☐ 277	Rickey Henderson	.30	.14	.04
☐ 278	Pedro Guerrero	.07	.03	.01
☐ 279	Brett Butler	.10	.05	.01
☐ 280	Kevin Seitzer	.07	.03	.01
☐ 281	Mike Davis	.04	.02	.01
☐ 282	Andres Galarraga	.04	.02	.01
☐ 283	Devon White	.10	.05	.01
☐ 284	Pete O'Brien	.04	.02	.01
☐ 285	Jerry Hairston	.04	.02	.01
☐ 286	Kevin Bass	.04	.02	.01
☐ 287	Carmelo Martinez	.04	.02	.01
☐ 288	Juan Samuel	.04	.02	.01
☐ 289	Kal Daniels	.07	.03	.01
☐ 290	Albert Hall	.04	.02	.01
☐ 291	Andy Van Slyke	.10	.05	.01
☐ 292	Lee Smith	.15	.07	.02
☐ 293	Vince Coleman	.07	.03	.01
☐ 294	Tom Niedenfuer	.04	.02	.01
☐ 295	Robin Yount	.25	.11	.03
☐ 296	Jeff M. Robinson	.04	.02	.01
☐ 297	Todd Benzinger	.10	.05	.01
☐ 298	Dave Winfield	.20	.09	.03
☐ 299	Mickey Hatcher	.04	.02	.01
☐ 300A	Checklist 248-357	.06	.01	.00
☐ 300B	Checklist 240-345	.06	.01	.00
☐ 301	Bud Black	.04	.02	.01
☐ 302	Jose Canseco	.60	.25	.08
☐ 303	Tom Foley	.04	.02	.01
☐ 304	Pete Incaviglia	.07	.03	.01
☐ 305	Bob Boone	.07	.03	.01
☐ 306	Bill Long	.04	.02	.01
☐ 307	Willie McGee	.07	.03	.01
☐ 308	Ken Caminiti	.30	.14	.04
☐ 309	Darren Daulton	.07	.03	.01
☐ 310	Tracy Jones	.04	.02	.01
☐ 311	Greg Booker	.04	.02	.01
☐ 312	Mike LaValliere	.04	.02	.01
☐ 313	Chili Davis	.07	.03	.01
☐ 314	Glenn Hubbard	.04	.02	.01
☐ 315	Paul Noce	.04	.02	.01
☐ 316	Keith Hernandez	.07	.03	.01
☐ 317	Mark Langston	.07	.03	.01
☐ 318	Keith Atherton	.04	.02	.01
☐ 319	Tony Fernandez	.07	.03	.01
☐ 320	Kent Hrbek	.07	.03	.01
☐ 321	John Cerutti	.04	.02	.01
☐ 322	Mike Kingery	.04	.02	.01
☐ 323	Dave Magadan	.07	.03	.01
☐ 324	Rafael Palmeiro	.30	.14	.04
☐ 325	Jeff Dedmon	.04	.02	.01
☐ 326	Barry Bonds	.60	.25	.08
☐ 327	Jeffrey Leonard	.04	.02	.01
☐ 328	Tim Flannery	.04	.02	.01
☐ 329	Dave Concepcion	.07	.03	.01
☐ 330	Mike Schmidt	.40	.18	.05
☐ 331	Bill Dawley	.04	.02	.01
☐ 332	Larry Andersen	.04	.02	.01
☐ 333	Jack Howell	.04	.02	.01
☐ 334	Ken Williams	.04	.02	.01
☐ 335	Bryn Smith	.04	.02	.01
☐ 336	Billy Ripken	.10	.05	.01
☐ 337	Greg Brock	.04	.02	.01
☐ 338	Mike Heath	.04	.02	.01
☐ 339	Mike Greenwell	.10	.05	.01
☐ 340	Claudell Washington	.04	.02	.01
☐ 341	Jose Gonzalez	.04	.02	.01
☐ 342	Mel Hall	.04	.02	.01
☐ 343	Jim Eisenreich	.04	.02	.01
☐ 344	Tony Bernazard	.04	.02	.01
☐ 345	Tim Raines	.07	.03	.01
☐ 346	Bob Brower	.04	.02	.01
☐ 347	Larry Parrish	.04	.02	.01
☐ 348	Thad Bosley	.04	.02	.01
☐ 349	Dennis Eckersley	.15	.07	.02
☐ 350	Cory Snyder	.07	.03	.01
☐ 351	Rick Cerone	.04	.02	.01
☐ 352	John Shelby	.04	.02	.01
☐ 353	Larry Herndon	.04	.02	.01
☐ 354	John Habyan	.04	.02	.01
☐ 355	Chuck Crim	.04	.02	.01
☐ 356	Gus Polidor	.04	.02	.01
☐ 357	Ken Dayley	.04	.02	.01
☐ 358	Danny Darwin	.04	.02	.01
☐ 359	Lance Parrish	.07	.03	.01
☐ 360	James Steels	.04	.02	.01
☐ 361	Al Pedrique	.04	.02	.01
☐ 362	Mike Aldrete	.04	.02	.01
☐ 363	Juan Castillo	.04	.02	.01
☐ 364	Len Dykstra	.07	.03	.01
☐ 365	Luis Quinones	.04	.02	.01
☐ 366	Jim Presley	.04	.02	.01
☐ 367	Lloyd Moseby	.04	.02	.01

☐ 368	Kirby Puckett	.40	.18	.05
☐ 369	Eric Davis	.10	.05	.01
☐ 370	Gary Redus	.04	.02	.01
☐ 371	Dave Schmidt	.04	.02	.01
☐ 372	Mark Clear	.04	.02	.01
☐ 373	Dave Bergman	.04	.02	.01
☐ 374	Charles Hudson	.04	.02	.01
☐ 375	Calvin Schiraldi	.04	.02	.01
☐ 376	Alex Trevino	.04	.02	.01
☐ 377	Tom Candiotti	.04	.02	.01
☐ 378	Steve Farr	.04	.02	.01
☐ 379	Mike Gallego	.04	.02	.01
☐ 380	Andy McGaffigan	.04	.02	.01
☐ 381	Kirk McCaskill	.04	.02	.01
☐ 382	Oddibe McDowell	.04	.02	.01
☐ 383	Floyd Bannister	.04	.02	.01
☐ 384	Denny Walling	.04	.02	.01
☐ 385	Don Carman	.04	.02	.01
☐ 386	Todd Worrell	.07	.03	.01
☐ 387	Eric Show	.04	.02	.01
☐ 388	Dave Parker	.07	.03	.01
☐ 389	Rick Mahler	.04	.02	.01
☐ 390	Mike Dunne	.04	.02	.01
☐ 391	Candy Maldonado	.04	.02	.01
☐ 392	Bob Dernier	.04	.02	.01
☐ 393	Dave Valle	.04	.02	.01
☐ 394	Ernie Whitt	.04	.02	.01
☐ 395	Juan Berenguer	.04	.02	.01
☐ 396	Mike Young	.04	.02	.01
☐ 397	Mike Felder	.04	.02	.01
☐ 398	Willie Hernandez	.04	.02	.01
☐ 399	Jim Rice	.07	.03	.01
☐ 400A	Checklist 358-467	.06	.01	.00
☐ 400B	Checklist 346-451	.06	.01	.00
☐ 401	Tommy John	.07	.03	.01
☐ 402	Brian Holton	.04	.02	.01
☐ 403	Carmen Castillo	.04	.02	.01
☐ 404	Jamie Quirk	.04	.02	.01
☐ 405	Dwayne Murphy	.04	.02	.01
☐ 406	Jeff Parrett	.04	.02	.01
☐ 407	Don Sutton	.10	.05	.01
☐ 408	Jerry Browne	.04	.02	.01
☐ 409	Jim Winn	.04	.02	.01
☐ 410	Dave Smith	.04	.02	.01
☐ 411	Shane Mack	.25	.11	.03
☐ 412	Greg Gross	.04	.02	.01
☐ 413	Nick Esasky	.04	.02	.01
☐ 414	Damaso Garcia	.04	.02	.01
☐ 415	Brian Fisher	.04	.02	.01
☐ 416	Brian Dayett	.04	.02	.01
☐ 417	Curt Ford	.04	.02	.01
☐ 418	Mark Williamson	.04	.02	.01
☐ 419	Bill Schroeder	.04	.02	.01
☐ 420	Mike Henneman	.15	.07	.02
☐ 421	John Marzano	.04	.02	.01
☐ 422	Ron Kittle	.04	.02	.01
☐ 423	Matt Young	.04	.02	.01
☐ 424	Steve Balboni	.04	.02	.01
☐ 425	Luis Polonia	.25	.11	.03
☐ 426	Randy St.Claire	.04	.02	.01
☐ 427	Greg Harris	.04	.02	.01
☐ 428	Johnny Ray	.04	.02	.01
☐ 429	Ray Searage	.04	.02	.01
☐ 430	Ricky Horton	.04	.02	.01
☐ 431	Gerald Young	.04	.02	.01
☐ 432	Rick Schu	.04	.02	.01
☐ 433	Paul O'Neill	.10	.05	.01
☐ 434	Rich Gossage	.07	.03	.01
☐ 435	John Cangelosi	.04	.02	.01
☐ 436	Mike LaCoss	.04	.02	.01
☐ 437	Gerald Perry	.04	.02	.01
☐ 438	Dave Martinez	.07	.03	.01
☐ 439	Darryl Strawberry	.30	.14	.04
☐ 440	John Moses	.04	.02	.01
☐ 441	Greg Gagne	.04	.02	.01
☐ 442	Jesse Barfield	.04	.02	.01
☐ 443	George Frazier	.04	.02	.01
☐ 444	Garth Iorg	.04	.02	.01
☐ 445	Ed Nunez	.04	.02	.01
☐ 446	Rick Aguilera	.07	.03	.01
☐ 447	Jerry Mumphrey	.04	.02	.01
☐ 448	Rafael Ramirez	.04	.02	.01
☐ 449	John Smiley	.40	.18	.05
☐ 450	Atlee Hammaker	.04	.02	.01
☐ 451	Lance McCullers	.04	.02	.01
☐ 452	Guy Hoffman	.04	.02	.01
☐ 453	Chris James	.04	.02	.01
☐ 454	Terry Pendleton	.15	.07	.02
☐ 455	Dave Meads	.04	.02	.01
☐ 456	Bill Buckner	.07	.03	.01
☐ 457	John Pawlowski	.04	.02	.01
☐ 458	Bob Sebra	.04	.02	.01
☐ 459	Jim Dwyer	.04	.02	.01
☐ 460	Jay Aldrich	.04	.02	.01
☐ 461	Frank Tanana	.04	.02	.01
☐ 462	Oil Can Boyd	.04	.02	.01
☐ 463	Dan Pasqua	.04	.02	.01
☐ 464	Tim Crews	.04	.02	.01
☐ 465	Andy Allanson	.04	.02	.01
☐ 466	Bill Pecota	.10	.05	.01
☐ 467	Steve Ontiveros	.04	.02	.01
☐ 468	Hubie Brooks	.04	.02	.01
☐ 469	Paul Kilgus	.04	.02	.01
☐ 470	Dale Mohorcic	.04	.02	.01
☐ 471	Dan Quisenberry	.07	.03	.01
☐ 472	Dave Stewart	.07	.03	.01
☐ 473	Dave Clark	.04	.02	.01
☐ 474	Joel Skinner	.04	.02	.01
☐ 475	Dave Anderson	.04	.02	.01
☐ 476	Dan Petry	.04	.02	.01
☐ 477	Carl Nichols	.04	.02	.01
☐ 478	Ernest Riles	.04	.02	.01
☐ 479	George Hendrick	.04	.02	.01
☐ 480	John Morris	.04	.02	.01
☐ 481	Manny Hernandez	.04	.02	.01
☐ 482	Jeff Stone	.04	.02	.01
☐ 483	Chris Brown	.04	.02	.01
☐ 484	Mike Bielecki	.04	.02	.01
☐ 485	Dave Dravecky	.07	.03	.01
☐ 486	Rick Manning	.04	.02	.01
☐ 487	Bill Almon	.04	.02	.01
☐ 488	Jim Sundberg	.04	.02	.01
☐ 489	Ken Phelps	.04	.02	.01
☐ 490	Tom Henke	.07	.03	.01
☐ 491	Dan Gladden	.04	.02	.01
☐ 492	Barry Larkin	.25	.11	.03
☐ 493	Fred Manrique	.04	.02	.01
☐ 494	Mike Griffin	.04	.02	.01
☐ 495	Mark Knudson	.04	.02	.01
☐ 496	Bill Madlock	.07	.03	.01
☐ 497	Tim Stoddard	.04	.02	.01
☐ 498	Sam Horn	.12	.05	.02
☐ 499	Tracy Woodson	.10	.05	.01
☐ 500A	Checklist 468-577	.06	.01	.00
☐ 500B	Checklist 452-557	.06	.01	.00
☐ 501	Ken Schrom	.04	.02	.01
☐ 502	Angel Salazar	.04	.02	.01
☐ 503	Eric Plunk	.04	.02	.01
☐ 504	Joe Hesketh	.04	.02	.01
☐ 505	Greg Minton	.04	.02	.01
☐ 506	Geno Petralli	.04	.02	.01
☐ 507	Bob James	.04	.02	.01
☐ 508	Robbie Wine	.04	.02	.01
☐ 509	Jeff Calhoun	.04	.02	.01
☐ 510	Steve Lake	.04	.02	.01
☐ 511	Mark Grant	.04	.02	.01
☐ 512	Frank Williams	.04	.02	.01
☐ 513	Jeff Blauser	.25	.11	.03
☐ 514	Bob Walk	.04	.02	.01
☐ 515	Craig Lefferts	.04	.02	.01
☐ 516	Manny Trillo	.04	.02	.01
☐ 517	Jerry Reed	.04	.02	.01
☐ 518	Rick Leach	.04	.02	.01
☐ 519	Mark Davidson	.04	.02	.01
☐ 520	Jeff Ballard	.04	.02	.01
☐ 521	Dave Stapleton	.04	.02	.01
☐ 522	Pat Sheridan	.04	.02	.01
☐ 523	Al Nipper	.04	.02	.01
☐ 524	Steve Trout	.04	.02	.01
☐ 525	Jeff Hamilton	.04	.02	.01
☐ 526	Tommy Hinzo	.04	.02	.01
☐ 527	Lonnie Smith	.04	.02	.01
☐ 528	Greg Cadaret	.04	.02	.01
☐ 529	Bob McClure UER ("Rob" on front)	.04	.02	.01
☐ 530	Chuck Finley	.07	.03	.01
☐ 531	Jeff Russell	.04	.02	.01
☐ 532	Steve Lyons	.04	.02	.01
☐ 533	Terry Puhl	.04	.02	.01
☐ 534	Eric Nolte	.04	.02	.01
☐ 535	Kent Tekulve	.04	.02	.01
☐ 536	Pat Pacillo	.04	.02	.01
☐ 537	Charlie Puleo	.04	.02	.01
☐ 538	Tom Prince	.04	.02	.01
☐ 539	Greg Maddux	.40	.18	.05
☐ 540	Jim Lindeman	.04	.02	.01
☐ 541	Pete Stanicek	.04	.02	.01
☐ 542	Steve Kiefer	.04	.02	.01
☐ 543A	Jim Morrison ERR (No decimal before lifetime average)	.30	.14	.04
☐ 543B	Jim Morrison COR	.04	.02	.01
☐ 544	Spike Owen	.04	.02	.01
☐ 545	Jay Buhner	.40	.18	.05
☐ 546	Mike Devereaux	.90	.40	.11
☐ 547	Jerry Don Gleaton	.04	.02	.01

☐ 548 Jose Rijo .10 .05 .01
☐ 549 Dennis Martinez .07 .03 .01
☐ 550 Mike Loynd .04 .02 .01
☐ 551 Darrell Miller .04 .02 .01
☐ 552 Dave LaPoint .04 .02 .01
☐ 553 John Tudor .04 .02 .01
☐ 554 Rocky Childress .04 .02 .01
☐ 555 Wally Ritchie .04 .02 .01
☐ 556 Terry McGriff .04 .02 .01
☐ 557 Dave Leiper .04 .02 .01
☐ 558 Jeff D. Robinson .04 .02 .01
☐ 559 Jose Uribe .04 .02 .01
☐ 560 Ted Simmons .07 .03 .01
☐ 561 Les Lancaster .04 .02 .01
☐ 562 Keith A. Miller .20 .09 .03
☐ 563 Harold Reynolds .04 .02 .01
☐ 564 Gene Larkin .10 .05 .01
☐ 565 Cecil Fielder .30 .14 .04
☐ 566 Roy Smalley .04 .02 .01
☐ 567 Duane Ward .04 .02 .01
☐ 568 Bill Wilkinson .04 .02 .01
☐ 569 Howard Johnson .10 .05 .01
☐ 570 Frank DiPino .04 .02 .01
☐ 571 Pete Smith .40 .18 .05
☐ 572 Darnell Coles .04 .02 .01
☐ 573 Don Robinson .04 .02 .01
☐ 574 Rob Nelson UER .04 .02 .01
(Career 0 RBI,
but 1 RBI in '87)
☐ 575 Dennis Rasmussen .04 .02 .01
☐ 576 Steve Jeltz UER .04 .02 .01
(Photo actually Juan
Samuel; Samuel noted
for one batting glove
and black bat)
☐ 577 Tom Pagnozzi .25 .11 .03
☐ 578 Ty Gainey .04 .02 .01
☐ 579 Gary Lucas .04 .02 .01
☐ 580 Ron Hassey .04 .02 .01
☐ 581 Herm Winningham .04 .02 .01
☐ 582 Rene Gonzales .12 .05 .02
☐ 583 Brad Komminsk .04 .02 .01
☐ 584 Doyle Alexander .04 .02 .01
☐ 585 Jeff Sellers .04 .02 .01
☐ 586 Bill Gullickson .04 .02 .01
☐ 587 Tim Belcher .12 .05 .02
☐ 588 Doug Jones .25 .11 .03
☐ 589 Melido Perez .40 .18 .05
☐ 590 Rick Honeycutt .04 .02 .01
☐ 591 Pascual Perez .04 .02 .01
☐ 592 Curt Wilkerson .04 .02 .01
☐ 593 Steve Howe .04 .02 .01
☐ 594 John Davis .04 .02 .01
☐ 595 Storm Davis .04 .02 .01
☐ 596 Sammy Stewart .04 .02 .01
☐ 597 Neil Allen .04 .02 .01
☐ 598 Alejandro Pena .04 .02 .01
☐ 599 Mark Thurmond .04 .02 .01
☐ 600A Checklist 578-BC26 .06 .01 .00
☐ 600B Checklist 558-660 .06 .01 .00
☐ 601 Jose Mesa .10 .05 .01
☐ 602 Don August .04 .02 .01
☐ 603 Terry Leach SP .07 .03 .01
☐ 604 Tom Newell .04 .02 .01
☐ 605 Randall Byers SP .07 .03 .01
☐ 606 Jim Gott .04 .02 .01
☐ 607 Harry Spilman .04 .02 .01
☐ 608 John Candelaria .04 .02 .01
☐ 609 Mike Brumley .04 .02 .01
☐ 610 Mickey Brantley .04 .02 .01
☐ 611 Jose Nunez SP .04 .02 .01
☐ 612 Tom Nieto .04 .02 .01
☐ 613 Rick Reuschel .04 .02 .01
☐ 614 Lee Mazzilli SP .07 .03 .01
☐ 615 Scott Lusader .04 .02 .01
☐ 616 Bobby Meacham .04 .02 .01
☐ 617 Kevin McReynolds SP .10 .05 .01
☐ 618 Gene Garber .04 .02 .01
☐ 619 Barry Lyons SP .07 .03 .01
☐ 620 Randy Myers .07 .03 .01
☐ 621 Donnie Moore .04 .02 .01
☐ 622 Domingo Ramos .04 .02 .01
☐ 623 Ed Romero .04 .02 .01
☐ 624 Greg Myers .10 .05 .01
☐ 625 Ripken Family .25 .11 .03
Cal Ripken Sr.
Cal Ripken Jr.
Billy Ripken
☐ 626 Pat Perry .04 .02 .01
☐ 627 Andres Thomas SP .07 .03 .01
☐ 628 Matt Williams SP 1.00 .45 .13
☐ 629 Dave Hengel .04 .02 .01
☐ 630 Jeff Musselman SP .07 .03 .01
☐ 631 Tim Laudner .04 .02 .01
☐ 632 Bob Ojeda SP .04 .02 .01
☐ 633 Rafael Santana .04 .02 .01
☐ 634 Wes Gardner .04 .02 .01
☐ 635 Roberto Kelly SP 1.00 .45 .13
☐ 636 Mike Flanagan SP .07 .03 .01
☐ 637 Jay Bell .30 .14 .04
☐ 638 Bob Melvin .04 .02 .01
☐ 639 Damon Berryhill UER .15 .07 .02
(Bats: Swithch)
☐ 640 David Wells SP .15 .07 .02
☐ 641 Stan Musial PUZ .10 .05 .01
☐ 642 Doug Sisk .04 .02 .01
☐ 643 Keith Hughes .04 .02 .01
☐ 644 Tom Glavine 2.25 1.00 .30
☐ 645 Al Newman .04 .02 .01
☐ 646 Scott Sanderson .04 .02 .01
☐ 647 Scott Terry .04 .02 .01
☐ 648 Tim Teufel SP .07 .03 .01
☐ 649 Garry Templeton SP .07 .03 .01
☐ 650 Manny Lee SP .07 .03 .01
☐ 651 Roger McDowell SP .07 .03 .01
☐ 652 Mookie Wilson SP .11 .05 .01
☐ 653 David Cone SP .50 .23 .06
☐ 654 Ron Gant SP 2.25 1.00 .30
☐ 655 Joe Price SP .07 .03 .01
☐ 656 George Bell SP .15 .07 .02
☐ 657 Gregg Jefferies SP 1.25 .55 .16
☐ 658 Todd Stottlemyre SP .35 .16 .04
☐ 659 Geronimo Berroa SP .12 .05 .02
☐ 660 Jerry Royster SP .07 .03 .01
☐ BC1 Cal Ripken .30 .14 .04
☐ BC2 Eric Davis .10 .05 .01
☐ BC3 Paul Molitor .08 .04 .01
☐ BC4 Mike Schmidt .20 .09 .03
☐ BC5 Ivan Calderon .05 .02 .01
☐ BC6 Tony Gwynn .15 .07 .02
☐ BC7 Wade Boggs .15 .07 .02
☐ BC8 Andy Van Slyke .08 .04 .01
☐ BC9 Joe Carter .15 .07 .02
☐ BC10 Andre Dawson .08 .04 .01
☐ BC11 Alan Trammell .08 .04 .01
☐ BC12 Mike Scott .05 .02 .01
☐ BC13 Wally Joyner .10 .05 .01
☐ BC14 Dale Murphy SP .15 .07 .02
☐ BC15 Kirby Puckett SP .40 .18 .05
☐ BC16 Pedro Guerrero SP .08 .04 .01
☐ BC17 Kevin Seitzer SP .08 .04 .01
☐ BC18 Tim Raines SP .08 .04 .01
☐ BC19 George Bell SP .15 .07 .02
☐ BC20 Darryl Strawberry SP .30 .14 .04
☐ BC21 Don Mattingly SP .30 .14 .04
☐ BC22 Ozzie Smith SP .15 .07 .02
☐ BC23 Mark McGwire SP .50 .23 .06
☐ BC24 Will Clark SP .60 .25 .08
☐ BC25 Alvin Davis SP .08 .04 .01
☐ BC26 Ruben Sierra SP .40 .18 .05

1988 Donruss All-Stars

This 64-card set features cards measuring standard size, 2 1/2" by 3 1/2". Card fronts are in full color with a solid blue and black border. The card backs are printed in black and blue on white card stock. Cards are numbered on the back inside a blue star in the upper right hand corner. Card backs feature statistical information about the player's performance in past All-Star games. The set was distributed in packs which also contained a Pop-Up. The AL Checklist card number 32 has two uncorrected errors on it, Wade Boggs is erroneously listed as the AL Leftfielder and Dan Plesac is erroneously listed as being on the Tigers.

	MT	EX-MT	VG
COMPLETE SET (64)	8.00	3.60	1.00
COMMON PLAYER (1-64)	.08	.04	.01
☐ 1 Don Mattingly	.60	.25	.08
☐ 2 Dave Winfield	.40	.18	.05
☐ 3 Willie Randolph	.12	.05	.02
☐ 4 Rickey Henderson	.60	.25	.08
☐ 5 Cal Ripken	1.00	.45	.13
☐ 6 George Bell	.15	.07	.02
☐ 7 Wade Boggs	.50	.23	.06
☐ 8 Bret Saberhagen	.20	.09	.03
☐ 9 Terry Kennedy	.08	.04	.01
☐ 10 John McNamara MG	.08	.04	.01
☐ 11 Jay Howell	.08	.04	.01
☐ 12 Harold Baines	.12	.05	.02
☐ 13 Harold Reynolds	.08	.04	.01
☐ 14 Bruce Hurst	.12	.05	.02
☐ 15 Kirby Puckett	.75	.35	.09
☐ 16 Matt Nokes	.12	.05	.02
☐ 17 Pat Tabler	.08	.04	.01
☐ 18 Dan Plesac	.08	.04	.01
☐ 19 Mark McGwire	.60	.25	.08
☐ 20 Mike Witt	.08	.04	.01
☐ 21 Larry Parrish	.08	.04	.01
☐ 22 Alan Trammell	.20	.09	.03
☐ 23 Dwight Evans	.12	.05	.02
☐ 24 Jack Morris	.25	.11	.03
☐ 25 Tony Fernandez	.15	.07	.02
☐ 26 Mark Langston	.12	.05	.02
☐ 27 Kevin Seitzer	.15	.07	.02
☐ 28 Tom Henke	.15	.07	.02
☐ 29 Dave Righetti	.12	.05	.02
☐ 30 Oakland Stadium	.08	.04	.01
☐ 31 Wade Boggs	.50	.23	.06
☐ 32 AL Checklist UER	.08	.04	.01
☐ 33 Jack Clark	.12	.05	.02
☐ 34 Darryl Strawberry	.40	.18	.05
☐ 35 Ryne Sandberg	.90	.40	.11
☐ 36 Andre Dawson	.40	.18	.05
☐ 37 Ozzie Smith	.35	.16	.04
☐ 38 Eric Davis	.25	.11	.03
☐ 39 Mike Schmidt	.75	.35	.09
☐ 40 Mike Scott	.12	.05	.02
☐ 41 Gary Carter	.20	.09	.03
☐ 42 Davey Johnson MG	.08	.04	.01
☐ 43 Rick Sutcliffe	.08	.04	.01
☐ 44 Willie McGee	.12	.05	.02
☐ 45 Hubie Brooks	.08	.04	.01
☐ 46 Dale Murphy	.25	.11	.03
☐ 47 Bo Diaz	.08	.04	.01
☐ 48 Pedro Guerrero	.12	.05	.02
☐ 49 Keith Hernandez	.15	.07	.02
☐ 50 Ozzie Virgil UER (Phillies logo on card back, wrong birth year)	.08	.04	.01
☐ 51 Tony Gwynn	.45	.20	.06
☐ 52 Rick Reuschel UER (Pirates logo on card back)	.08	.04	.01
☐ 53 John Franco	.12	.05	.02
☐ 54 Jeffrey Leonard	.08	.04	.01
☐ 55 Juan Samuel	.12	.05	.02
☐ 56 Orel Hershiser	.25	.11	.03
☐ 57 Tim Raines	.15	.07	.02
☐ 58 Sid Fernandez	.12	.05	.02
☐ 59 Tim Wallach	.08	.04	.01
☐ 60 Lee Smith	.20	.09	.03
☐ 61 Steve Bedrosian	.08	.04	.01
☐ 62 Tim Raines	.15	.07	.02
☐ 63 Ozzie Smith	.30	.14	.04
☐ 64 NL Checklist	.08	.04	.01

1988 Donruss Baseball's Best

This innovative set of 336 cards was released by Donruss very late in the 1988 season to be sold in large national retail chains as a complete packaged set. Cards are the standard size, 2 1/2" by 3 1/2", and are packaged as a complete set in a specially designed box. Cards are very

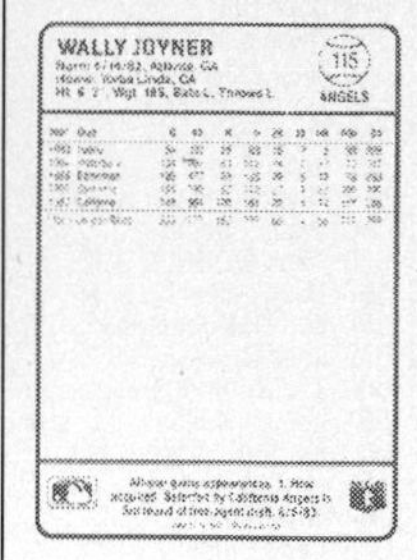

similar in design to the 1988 regular Donruss issue except that these cards have orange and black borders instead of blue and black borders. The set is also sometimes referred to as the Halloween set because of the orange box and design of the cards. Six (2 1/2" by 3 1/2") 15-piece puzzles of Stan Musial are also included with every complete set.

	MT	EX-MT	VG
COMPLETE SET (336)	16.00	7.25	2.00
COMMON PLAYER (1-336)	.04	.02	.01
☐ 1 Don Mattingly	.75	.35	.09
☐ 2 Ron Gant	1.00	.45	.13
☐ 3 Bob Boone	.07	.03	.01
☐ 4 Mark Grace	1.00	.45	.13
☐ 5 Andy Allanson	.04	.02	.01
☐ 6 Kal Daniels	.07	.03	.01
☐ 7 Floyd Bannister	.04	.02	.01
☐ 8 Alan Ashby	.04	.02	.01
☐ 9 Marty Barrett	.04	.02	.01
☐ 10 Tim Belcher	.10	.05	.01
☐ 11 Harold Baines	.10	.05	.01
☐ 12 Hubie Brooks	.04	.02	.01
☐ 13 Doyle Alexander	.04	.02	.01
☐ 14 Gary Carter	.20	.09	.03
☐ 15 Glenn Braggs	.07	.03	.01
☐ 16 Steve Bedrosian	.04	.02	.01
☐ 17 Barry Bonds	.90	.40	.11
☐ 18 Bert Blyleven	.07	.03	.01
☐ 19 Tom Brunansky	.07	.03	.01
☐ 20 John Candelaria	.04	.02	.01
☐ 21 Shawn Abner	.07	.03	.01
☐ 22 Jose Canseco	1.00	.45	.13
☐ 23 Brett Butler	.10	.05	.01
☐ 24 Scott Bradley	.04	.02	.01
☐ 25 Ivan Calderon	.10	.05	.01
☐ 26 Rich Gossage	.10	.05	.01
☐ 27 Brian Downing	.04	.02	.01
☐ 28 Jim Rice	.15	.07	.02
☐ 29 Dion James	.04	.02	.01
☐ 30 Terry Kennedy	.04	.02	.01
☐ 31 George Bell	.15	.07	.02
☐ 32 Scott Fletcher	.04	.02	.01
☐ 33 Bobby Bonilla	.50	.23	.06
☐ 34 Tim Burke	.04	.02	.01
☐ 35 Darrell Evans	.07	.03	.01
☐ 36 Mike Davis	.04	.02	.01
☐ 37 Shawon Dunston	.15	.07	.02
☐ 38 Kevin Bass	.04	.02	.01
☐ 39 George Brett	.40	.18	.05
☐ 40 David Cone	.40	.18	.05
☐ 41 Ron Darling	.15	.07	.02
☐ 42 Roberto Alomar	2.50	1.15	.30
☐ 43 Dennis Eckersley	.25	.11	.03
☐ 44 Vince Coleman	.15	.07	.02
☐ 45 Sid Bream	.04	.02	.01
☐ 46 Gary Gaetti	.07	.03	.01
☐ 47 Phil Bradley	.04	.02	.01
☐ 48 Jim Clancy	.04	.02	.01
☐ 49 Jack Clark	.10	.05	.01
☐ 50 Mike Krukow	.04	.02	.01
☐ 51 Henry Cotto	.04	.02	.01
☐ 52 Rich Dotson	.04	.02	.01
☐ 53 Jim Gantner	.04	.02	.01
☐ 54 John Franco	.07	.03	.01
☐ 55 Pete Incaviglia	.07	.03	.01
☐ 56 Joe Carter	.40	.18	.05
☐ 57 Roger Clemens	.90	.40	.11
☐ 58 Gerald Perry	.04	.02	.01
☐ 59 Jack Howell	.04	.02	.01
☐ 60 Vance Law	.04	.02	.01
☐ 61 Jay Bell	.15	.07	.02

☐ 62 Eric Davis .25 .11 .03
☐ 63 Gene Garber .04 .02 .01
☐ 64 Glenn Davis .15 .07 .02
☐ 65 Wade Boggs .50 .23 .06
☐ 66 Kirk Gibson .10 .05 .01
☐ 67 Carlton Fisk .35 .16 .04
☐ 68 Casey Candaele .04 .02 .01
☐ 69 Mike Heath .04 .02 .01
☐ 70 Kevin Elster .04 .02 .01
☐ 71 Greg Brock .04 .02 .01
☐ 72 Don Carman .04 .02 .01
☐ 73 Doug Drabek .20 .09 .03
☐ 74 Greg Gagne .04 .02 .01
☐ 75 Danny Cox .04 .02 .01
☐ 76 Rickey Henderson .60 .25 .08
☐ 77 Chris Brown .04 .02 .01
☐ 78 Terry Steinbach .07 .03 .01
☐ 79 Will Clark 1.00 .45 .13
☐ 80 Mickey Brantley .04 .02 .01
☐ 81 Ozzie Guillen .07 .03 .01
☐ 82 Greg Maddux .45 .20 .06
☐ 83 Kirk McCaskill .04 .02 .01
☐ 84 Dwight Evans .10 .05 .01
☐ 85 Ozzie Virgil .04 .02 .01
☐ 86 Mike Morgan .10 .05 .01
☐ 87 Tony Fernandez .10 .05 .01
☐ 88 Jose Guzman .10 .05 .01
☐ 89 Mike Dunne .04 .02 .01
☐ 90 Andres Galarraga .10 .05 .01
☐ 91 Mike Henneman .10 .05 .01
☐ 92 Alfredo Griffin .04 .02 .01
☐ 93 Rafael Palmeiro .45 .20 .06
☐ 94 Jim Deshaies .04 .02 .01
☐ 95 Mark Gubicza .07 .03 .01
☐ 96 Dwight Gooden .35 .16 .04
☐ 97 Howard Johnson .20 .09 .03
☐ 98 Mark Davis .10 .05 .01
☐ 99 Dave Stewart .20 .09 .03
☐ 100 Joe Magrane .07 .03 .01
☐ 101 Brian Fisher .04 .02 .01
☐ 102 Kent Hrbek .10 .05 .01
☐ 103 Kevin Gross .07 .03 .01
☐ 104 Tom Henke .15 .07 .02
☐ 105 Mike Pagliarulo .07 .03 .01
☐ 106 Kelly Downs .04 .02 .01
☐ 107 Alvin Davis .07 .03 .01
☐ 108 Willie Randolph .07 .03 .01
☐ 109 Rob Deer .10 .05 .01
☐ 110 Bo Diaz .04 .02 .01
☐ 111 Paul Kilgus .04 .02 .01
☐ 112 Tom Candiotti .07 .03 .01
☐ 113 Dale Murphy .25 .11 .03
☐ 114 Rick Mahler .04 .02 .01
☐ 115 Wally Joyner .25 .11 .03
☐ 116 Ryne Sandberg .90 .40 .11
☐ 117 John Farrell .04 .02 .01
☐ 118 Nick Esasky .04 .02 .01
☐ 119 Bo Jackson .90 .40 .11
☐ 120 Bill Doran .04 .02 .01
☐ 121 Ellis Burks .40 .18 .05
☐ 122 Pedro Guerrero .10 .05 .01
☐ 123 Dave LaPoint .04 .02 .01
☐ 124 Neal Heaton .04 .02 .01
☐ 125 Willie Hernandez .04 .02 .01
☐ 126 Roger McDowell .04 .02 .01
☐ 127 Ted Higuera .04 .02 .01
☐ 128 Von Hayes .04 .02 .01
☐ 129 Mike LaValliere .04 .02 .01
☐ 130 Dan Gladden .04 .02 .01
☐ 131 Willie McGee .10 .05 .01
☐ 132 Al Leiter .04 .02 .01
☐ 133 Mark Grant .04 .02 .01
☐ 134 Bob Welch .10 .05 .01
☐ 135 Dave Dravecky .10 .05 .01
☐ 136 Mark Langston .10 .05 .01
☐ 137 Dan Pasqua .07 .03 .01
☐ 138 Rick Sutcliffe .07 .03 .01
☐ 139 Dan Petry .04 .02 .01
☐ 140 Rich Gedman .04 .02 .01
☐ 141 Ken Griffey Sr. .10 .05 .01
☐ 142 Eddie Murray .25 .11 .03
☐ 143 Jimmy Key .10 .05 .01
☐ 144 Dale Mohorcic .04 .02 .01
☐ 145 Jose Lind .07 .03 .01
☐ 146 Dennis Martinez .10 .05 .01
☐ 147 Chet Lemon .04 .02 .01
☐ 148 Orel Hershiser .20 .09 .03
☐ 149 Dave Martinez .10 .05 .01
☐ 150 Billy Hatcher .07 .03 .01
☐ 151 Charlie Leibrandt .07 .03 .01
☐ 152 Keith Hernandez .10 .05 .01
☐ 153 Kevin McReynolds .15 .07 .02
☐ 154 Tony Gwynn .40 .18 .05
☐ 155 Stan Javier .04 .02 .01
☐ 156 Tony Pena .07 .03 .01
☐ 157 Andy Van Slyke .20 .09 .03
☐ 158 Gene Larkin .07 .03 .01
☐ 159 Chris James .04 .02 .01
☐ 160 Fred McGriff .75 .35 .09
☐ 161 Rick Rhoden .04 .02 .01
☐ 162 Scott Garrelts .04 .02 .01
☐ 163 Mike Campbell .04 .02 .01
☐ 164 Dave Righetti .07 .03 .01
☐ 165 Paul Molitor .20 .09 .03
☐ 166 Danny Jackson .07 .03 .01
☐ 167 Pete O'Brien .04 .02 .01
☐ 168 Julio Franco .20 .09 .03
☐ 169 Mark McGwire .90 .40 .11
☐ 170 Zane Smith .07 .03 .01
☐ 171 Johnny Ray .04 .02 .01
☐ 172 Les Lancaster .04 .02 .01
☐ 173 Mel Hall .07 .03 .01
☐ 174 Tracy Jones .04 .02 .01
☐ 175 Kevin Seitzer .15 .07 .02
☐ 176 Bob Knepper .04 .02 .01
☐ 177 Mike Greenwell .50 .23 .06
☐ 178 Mike Marshall .04 .02 .01
☐ 179 Melido Perez .25 .11 .03
☐ 180 Tim Raines .15 .07 .02
☐ 181 Jack Morris .20 .09 .03
☐ 182 Darryl Strawberry .50 .23 .06
☐ 183 Robin Yount .50 .23 .06
☐ 184 Lance Parrish .07 .03 .01
☐ 185 Darnell Coles .07 .03 .01
☐ 186 Kirby Puckett .75 .35 .09
☐ 187 Terry Pendleton .20 .09 .03
☐ 188 Don Slaught .04 .02 .01
☐ 189 Jimmy Jones .07 .03 .01
☐ 190 Dave Parker .15 .07 .02
☐ 191 Mike Aldrete .04 .02 .01
☐ 192 Mike Moore .10 .05 .01
☐ 193 Greg Walker .07 .03 .01
☐ 194 Calvin Schiraldi .04 .02 .01
☐ 195 Dick Schofield .04 .02 .01
☐ 196 Jody Reed .15 .07 .02
☐ 197 Pete Smith .45 .20 .06
☐ 198 Cal Ripken 1.00 .45 .13
☐ 199 Lloyd Moseby .04 .02 .01
☐ 200 Ruben Sierra .75 .35 .09
☐ 201 R.J. Reynolds .04 .02 .01
☐ 202 Bryn Smith .04 .02 .01
☐ 203 Gary Pettis .04 .02 .01
☐ 204 Steve Sax .15 .07 .02
☐ 205 Frank DiPino .04 .02 .01
☐ 206 Mike Scott UER .10 .05 .01
(1977 Jackson losses say 1.10, should be 1)
☐ 207 Kurt Stillwell .04 .02 .01
☐ 208 Mookie Wilson .07 .03 .01
☐ 209 Lee Mazzilli .04 .02 .01
☐ 210 Lance McCullers .04 .02 .01
☐ 211 Rick Honeycutt .04 .02 .01
☐ 212 John Tudor .07 .03 .01
☐ 213 Jim Gott .04 .02 .01
☐ 214 Frank Viola .10 .05 .01
☐ 215 Juan Samuel .07 .03 .01
☐ 216 Jesse Barfield .07 .03 .01
☐ 217 Claudell Washington .04 .02 .01
☐ 218 Rick Reuschel .07 .03 .01
☐ 219 Jim Presley .04 .02 .01
☐ 220 Tommy John .15 .07 .02
☐ 221 Dan Plesac .04 .02 .01
☐ 222 Barry Larkin .30 .14 .04
☐ 223 Mike Stanley .04 .02 .01
☐ 224 Cory Snyder .07 .03 .01
☐ 225 Andre Dawson .30 .14 .04
☐ 226 Ken Oberkfell .04 .02 .01
☐ 227 Devon White .15 .07 .02
☐ 228 Jamie Moyer .04 .02 .01
☐ 229 Brook Jacoby .04 .02 .01
☐ 230 Rob Murphy .04 .02 .01
☐ 231 Bret Saberhagen .20 .09 .03
☐ 232 Nolan Ryan 1.50 .65 .19
☐ 233 Bruce Hurst .07 .03 .01
☐ 234 Jesse Orosco .04 .02 .01
☐ 235 Bobby Thigpen .10 .05 .01
☐ 236 Pascual Perez .07 .03 .01
☐ 237 Matt Nokes .10 .05 .01
☐ 238 Bob Ojeda .07 .03 .01
☐ 239 Joey Meyer .04 .02 .01
☐ 240 Shane Rawley .04 .02 .01
☐ 241 Jeff Robinson .04 .02 .01
☐ 242 Jeff Reardon .15 .07 .02
☐ 243 Ozzie Smith .30 .14 .04
☐ 244 Dave Winfield .35 .16 .04
☐ 245 John Kruk .20 .09 .03

☐ 246 Carney Lansford	.10	.05	.01
☐ 247 Candy Maldonado	.07	.03	.01
☐ 248 Ken Phelps	.04	.02	.01
☐ 249 Ken Williams	.04	.02	.01
☐ 250 Al Nipper	.04	.02	.01
☐ 251 Mark McLemore	.07	.03	.01
☐ 252 Lee Smith	.15	.07	.02
☐ 253 Albert Hall	.04	.02	.01
☐ 254 Billy Ripken	.07	.03	.01
☐ 255 Kelly Gruber	.15	.07	.02
☐ 256 Charlie Hough	.04	.02	.01
☐ 257 John Smiley	.20	.09	.03
☐ 258 Tim Wallach	.07	.03	.01
☐ 259 Frank Tanana	.07	.03	.01
☐ 260 Mike Scioscia	.04	.02	.01
☐ 261 Damon Berryhill	.10	.05	.01
☐ 262 Dave Smith	.04	.02	.01
☐ 263 Willie Wilson	.07	.03	.01
☐ 264 Len Dykstra	.15	.07	.02
☐ 265 Randy Myers	.10	.05	.01
☐ 266 Keith Moreland	.04	.02	.01
☐ 267 Eric Plunk	.04	.02	.01
☐ 268 Todd Worrell	.10	.05	.01
☐ 269 Bob Walk	.04	.02	.01
☐ 270 Keith Atherton	.04	.02	.01
☐ 271 Mike Schmidt	.60	.25	.08
☐ 272 Mike Flanagan	.07	.03	.01
☐ 273 Rafael Santana	.04	.02	.01
☐ 274 Robby Thompson	.07	.03	.01
☐ 275 Rey Quinones	.04	.02	.01
☐ 276 Cecilio Guante	.04	.02	.01
☐ 277 B.J. Surhoff	.10	.05	.01
☐ 278 Chris Sabo	.60	.25	.08
☐ 279 Mitch Williams	.10	.05	.01
☐ 280 Greg Swindell	.15	.07	.02
☐ 281 Alan Trammell	.15	.07	.02
☐ 282 Storm Davis	.07	.03	.01
☐ 283 Chuck Finley	.15	.07	.02
☐ 284 Dave Stieb	.10	.05	.01
☐ 285 Scott Bailes	.04	.02	.01
☐ 286 Larry Sheets	.04	.02	.01
☐ 287 Danny Tartabull	.25	.11	.03
☐ 288 Checklist Card	.04	.02	.01
☐ 289 Todd Benzinger	.10	.05	.01
☐ 290 John Shelby	.04	.02	.01
☐ 291 Steve Lyons	.04	.02	.01
☐ 292 Mitch Webster	.04	.02	.01
☐ 293 Walt Terrell	.04	.02	.01
☐ 294 Pete Stanicek	.04	.02	.01
☐ 295 Chris Bosio	.20	.09	.03
☐ 296 Milt Thompson	.04	.02	.01
☐ 297 Fred Lynn	.10	.05	.01
☐ 298 Juan Berenguer	.04	.02	.01
☐ 299 Ken Dayley	.04	.02	.01
☐ 300 Joel Skinner	.04	.02	.01
☐ 301 Benito Santiago	.25	.11	.03
☐ 302 Ron Hassey	.04	.02	.01
☐ 303 Jose Uribe	.04	.02	.01
☐ 304 Harold Reynolds	.07	.03	.01
☐ 305 Dale Sveum	.04	.02	.01
☐ 306 Glenn Wilson	.04	.02	.01
☐ 307 Mike Witt	.04	.02	.01
☐ 308 Ron Robinson	.04	.02	.01
☐ 309 Denny Walling	.04	.02	.01
☐ 310 Joe Orsulak	.04	.02	.01
☐ 311 David Wells	.07	.03	.01
☐ 312 Steve Buechele	.07	.03	.01
☐ 313 Jose Oquendo	.04	.02	.01
☐ 314 Floyd Youmans	.04	.02	.01
☐ 315 Lou Whitaker	.15	.07	.02
☐ 316 Fernando Valenzuela	.10	.05	.01
☐ 317 Mike Boddicker	.07	.03	.01
☐ 318 Gerald Young	.07	.03	.01
☐ 319 Frank White	.07	.03	.01
☐ 320 Bill Wegman	.04	.02	.01
☐ 321 Tom Niedenfuer	.04	.02	.01
☐ 322 Ed Whitson	.07	.03	.01
☐ 323 Curt Young	.04	.02	.01
☐ 324 Greg Mathews	.04	.02	.01
☐ 325 Doug Jones	.10	.05	.01
☐ 326 Tommy Herr	.07	.03	.01
☐ 327 Kent Tekulve	.04	.02	.01
☐ 328 Rance Mulliniks	.04	.02	.01
☐ 329 Checklist Card	.04	.02	.01
☐ 330 Craig Lefferts	.10	.05	.01
☐ 331 Franklin Stubbs	.07	.03	.01
☐ 332 Rick Cerone	.04	.02	.01
☐ 333 Dave Schmidt	.04	.02	.01
☐ 334 Larry Parrish	.04	.02	.01
☐ 335 Tom Browning	.10	.05	.01
☐ 336 Checklist Card	.04	.02	.01

1988 Donruss Pop-Ups

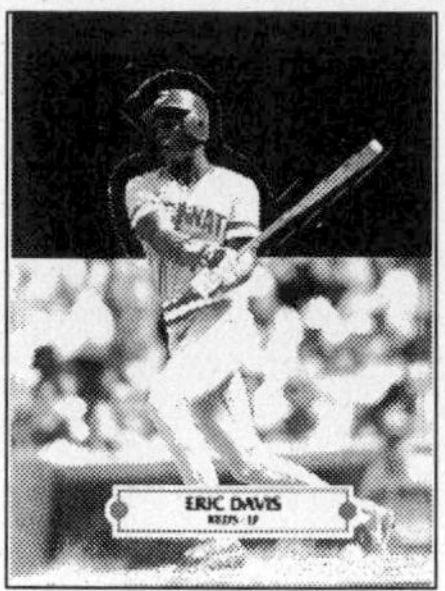

This 20-card set features "fold-out" cards measuring standard size, 2 1/2" by 3 1/2". Card fronts are in full color. Cards are unnumbered but are listed in the same order as the Donruss All-Stars on the All-Star checklist card. Card backs present essentially no information about the player. The set was distributed in packs which also contained All-Star cards. In order to remain in mint condition, the cards should not be popped up.

	MT	EX-MT	VG
COMPLETE SET (20)	5.00	2.30	.60
COMMON PLAYER (1-20)	.10	.05	.01
☐ 1 Don Mattingly	.75	.35	.09
☐ 2 Dave Winfield	.45	.20	.06
☐ 3 Willie Randolph	.15	.07	.02
☐ 4 Rickey Henderson	.75	.35	.09
☐ 5 Cal Ripken	1.25	.55	.16
☐ 6 George Bell	.20	.09	.03
☐ 7 Wade Boggs	.60	.25	.08
☐ 8 Bret Saberhagen	.25	.11	.03
☐ 9 Terry Kennedy	.10	.05	.01
☐ 10 John McNamara MG	.10	.05	.01
☐ 11 Jack Clark	.15	.07	.02
☐ 12 Darryl Strawberry	.45	.20	.06
☐ 13 Ryne Sandberg	1.00	.45	.13
☐ 14 Andre Dawson	.45	.20	.06
☐ 15 Ozzie Smith	.40	.18	.05
☐ 16 Eric Davis	.30	.14	.04
☐ 17 Mike Schmidt	.90	.40	.11
☐ 18 Mike Scott	.15	.07	.02
☐ 19 Gary Carter	.25	.11	.03
☐ 20 Davey Johnson MG	.10	.05	.01

1988 Donruss Rookies

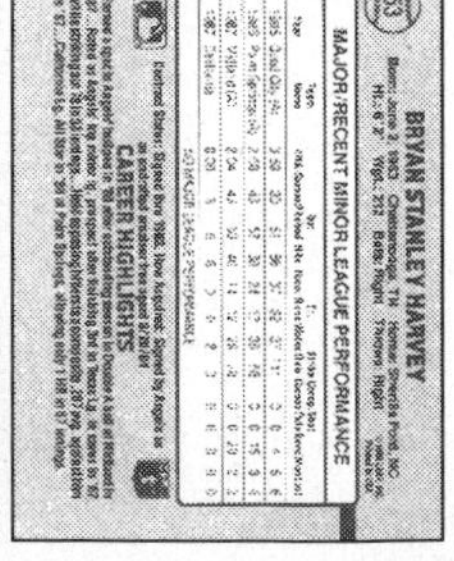

The 1988 Donruss "The Rookies" set features 56 cards plus a 15-piece puzzle of Stan Musial. Cards are in full color and are standard size, 2 1/2" by 3 1/2". The set was distributed in a small green and black box with gold lettering. Card fronts are similar in design to the 1988 Donruss regular issue except for the presence of "The Rookies" logo in the lower right corner and a green and black border instead of a blue and black border on the fronts. The key Rookie Cards in this set are ROY's, Chris Sabo and Walt Weiss. Noteworthy extended Rookie Cards include Brady Anderson and Edgar Martinez.

	MT	EX-MT	VG
COMPLETE SET (56)	20.00	9.00	2.50
COMMON PLAYER (1-56)	.08	.04	.01
☐ 1 Mark Grace	2.00	.90	.25
☐ 2 Mike Campbell	.08	.04	.01
☐ 3 Todd Frohwirth	.08	.04	.01
☐ 4 Dave Stapleton	.08	.04	.01
☐ 5 Shawn Abner	.08	.04	.01
☐ 6 Jose Cecena	.08	.04	.01
☐ 7 Dave Gallagher	.08	.04	.01
☐ 8 Mark Parent	.08	.04	.01
☐ 9 Cecil Espy	.12	.05	.02
☐ 10 Pete Smith	.50	.23	.06
☐ 11 Jay Buhner	.60	.25	.08
☐ 12 Pat Borders	.60	.25	.08
☐ 13 Doug Jennings	.08	.04	.01
☐ 14 Brady Anderson	1.50	.65	.19
☐ 15 Pete Stanicek	.08	.04	.01
☐ 16 Roberto Kelly	1.00	.45	.13
☐ 17 Jeff Treadway	.12	.05	.02
☐ 18 Walt Weiss	.25	.11	.03
☐ 19 Paul Gibson	.08	.04	.01
☐ 20 Tim Crews	.08	.04	.01
☐ 21 Melido Perez	.50	.23	.06
☐ 22 Steve Peters	.08	.04	.01
☐ 23 Craig Worthington	.08	.04	.01
☐ 24 John Trautwein	.08	.04	.01
☐ 25 DeWayne Vaughn	.08	.04	.01
☐ 26 David Wells	.08	.04	.01
☐ 27 Al Leiter	.08	.04	.01
☐ 28 Tim Belcher	.15	.07	.02
☐ 29 Johnny Paredes	.08	.04	.01
☐ 30 Chris Sabo	.75	.35	.09
☐ 31 Damon Berryhill	.12	.05	.02
☐ 32 Randy Milligan	.35	.16	.04
☐ 33 Gary Thurman	.08	.04	.01
☐ 34 Kevin Elster	.08	.04	.01
☐ 35 Roberto Alomar	12.00	5.50	1.50
☐ 36 Edgar Martinez UER (Photo actually Edwin Nunez)	2.00	.90	.25
☐ 37 Todd Stottlemyre	.50	.23	.06
☐ 38 Joey Meyer	.08	.04	.01
☐ 39 Carl Nichols	.08	.04	.01
☐ 40 Jack McDowell	2.00	.90	.25
☐ 41 Jose Bautista	.08	.04	.01
☐ 42 Sil Campusano	.08	.04	.01
☐ 43 John Dopson	.08	.04	.01
☐ 44 Jody Reed	.50	.23	.06
☐ 45 Darrin Jackson	.50	.23	.06
☐ 46 Mike Capel	.08	.04	.01
☐ 47 Ron Gant	2.50	1.15	.30
☐ 48 John Davis	.08	.04	.01
☐ 49 Kevin Coffman	.08	.04	.01
☐ 50 Cris Carpenter	.15	.07	.02
☐ 51 Mackey Sasser	.12	.05	.02
☐ 52 Luis Alicea	.15	.07	.02
☐ 53 Bryan Harvey	.60	.25	.08
☐ 54 Steve Ellsworth	.08	.04	.01
☐ 55 Mike Macfarlane	.40	.18	.05
☐ 56 Checklist Card	.08	.01	.00

1988 Donruss Super DK's

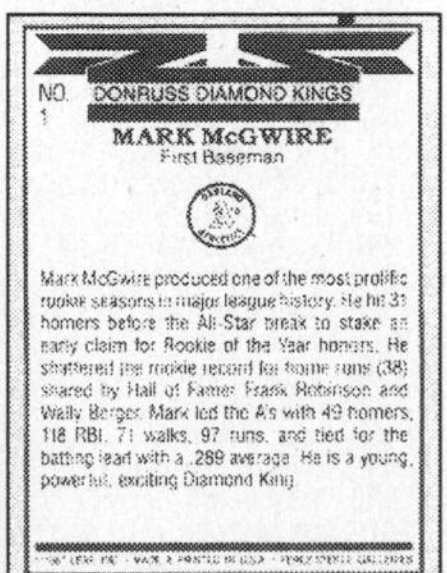

This 26-player card set was available through a mail-in offer detailed on the wax packs. The set was sent in return for 8.00 and three wrappers plus 1.50 postage and handling. The set features the popular Diamond King subseries in large (approximately 4 7/8" by 6 13/16") form. Dick Perez of Perez-Steele Galleries did another outstanding job on the artwork. The cards are essentially a large version of the Donruss regular issue Diamond Kings.

	MT	EX-MT	VG
COMPLETE SET (26)	10.00	4.50	1.25
COMMON PLAYER (1-26)	.25	.11	.03
☐ 1 Mark McGwire	1.25	.55	.16
☐ 2 Tim Raines	.45	.20	.06
☐ 3 Benito Santiago	.45	.20	.06
☐ 4 Alan Trammell	.45	.20	.06
☐ 5 Danny Tartabull	.45	.20	.06
☐ 6 Ron Darling	.35	.16	.04
☐ 7 Paul Molitor	.60	.25	.08
☐ 8 Devon White	.45	.20	.06
☐ 9 Andre Dawson	.60	.25	.08
☐ 10 Julio Franco	.45	.20	.06
☐ 11 Scott Fletcher	.25	.11	.03
☐ 12 Tony Fernandez	.35	.16	.04
☐ 13 Shane Rawley	.25	.11	.03
☐ 14 Kal Daniels	.35	.16	.04
☐ 15 Jack Clark	.35	.16	.04
☐ 16 Dwight Evans	.45	.20	.06
☐ 17 Tommy John	.35	.16	.04
☐ 18 Andy Van Slyke	.60	.25	.08
☐ 19 Gary Gaetti	.35	.16	.04
☐ 20 Mark Langston	.35	.16	.04
☐ 21 Will Clark	1.25	.55	.16
☐ 22 Glenn Hubbard	.25	.11	.03
☐ 23 Billy Hatcher	.25	.11	.03
☐ 24 Bob Welch	.35	.16	.04
☐ 25 Ivan Calderon	.35	.16	.04
☐ 26 Cal Ripken	1.50	.65	.19

1988 Donruss Athletics Team Book

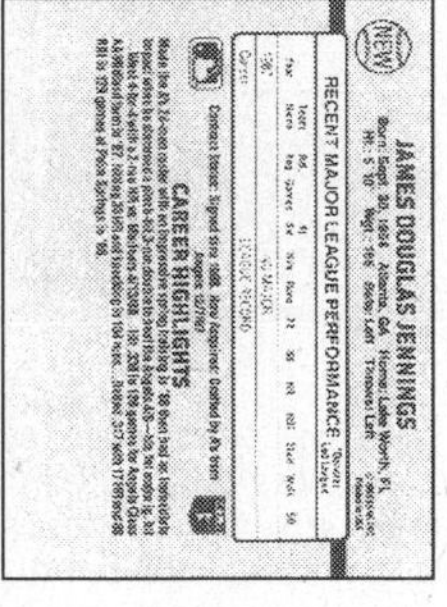

The 1988 Donruss Athletics Team Book set features 27 cards (three pages with nine cards on each page) plus a large full-page puzzle of Stan Musial. Cards are in full color and are standard size, 2 1/2" by 3 1/2". The set was distributed as a four-page book; although the puzzle page was perforated, the card pages were not. The cover of the "Team Collection" book is primarily bright red. Card fronts are very similar in design to the 1988 Donruss regular issue. The card numbers on the backs are the same for those players that are the same as in the regular Donruss set; the new players pictured are numbered on the back as "NEW." In fact 1988 A.L. Rookie of the Year Walt Weiss makes his first Donruss appearance in this set as a "NEW" card. The book is usually sold intact. When cut from the book into individual cards, these cards are distinguishable from the regular 1988 Donruss cards since these have a 1988 copyright on the back whereas the regular issue has a 1987 copyright on the back.

	MT	EX-MT	VG
COMPLETE SET (27)	4.50	2.00	.55
COMMON PLAYER	.08	.04	.01
COMMON NEW PLAYER	.15	.07	.02
☐ 97 Curt Young	.08	.04	.01
☐ 133 Gene Nelson	.08	.04	.01
☐ 158 Terry Steinbach	.20	.09	.03
☐ 178 Carney Lansford	.15	.07	.02
☐ 221 Tony Phillips	.20	.09	.03
☐ 256 Mark McGwire	1.00	.45	.13
☐ 302 Jose Canseco	1.25	.55	.16
☐ 349 Dennis Eckersley	.50	.23	.06
☐ 379 Mike Gallego	.08	.04	.01
☐ 425 Luis Polonia	.08	.04	.01
☐ 467 Steve Ontiveros	.08	.04	.01
☐ 472 Dave Stewart	.40	.18	.05
☐ 503 Eric Plunk	.08	.04	.01
☐ 528 Greg Cadaret	.08	.04	.01
☐ 590 Rick Honeycutt	.08	.04	.01
☐ 595 Storm Davis	.15	.07	.02
☐ NEW Don Baylor UER (Career stats are incorrect)	.30	.14	.04
☐ NEW Ron Hassey	.15	.07	.02
☐ NEW Dave Henderson	.30	.14	.04
☐ NEW Glenn Hubbard	.15	.07	.02
☐ NEW Stan Javier	.15	.07	.02
☐ NEW Doug Jennings	.20	.09	.03
☐ NEW Ed Jurak	.15	.07	.02
☐ NEW Dave Parker	.30	.14	.04
☐ NEW Walt Weiss	.75	.35	.09
☐ NEW Bob Welch	.30	.14	.04
☐ NEW Matt Young	.15	.07	.02

1988 Donruss Cubs Team Book

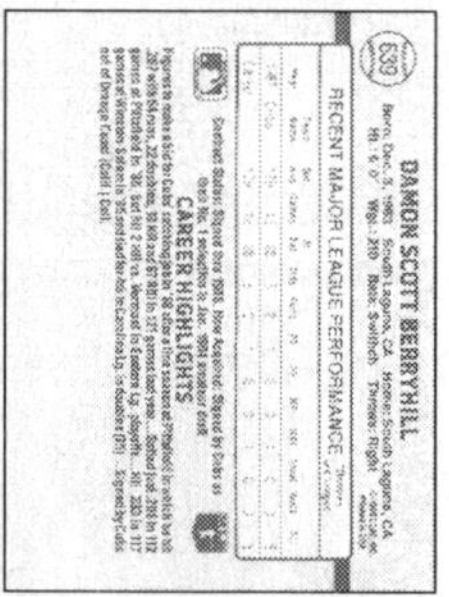

The 1988 Donruss Cubs Team Book set features 27 cards (three pages with nine cards on each page) plus a large full-page puzzle of Stan Musial. Cards are in full color and are standard size, 2 1/2" by 3 1/2". The set was distributed as a four-page book; although the puzzle page was perforated, the card pages were not. The cover of the "Team Collection" book is primarily bright red. Card fronts are very similar in design to the 1988 Donruss regular issue. The card numbers on the backs are the same for those players that are the same as in the regular Donruss set; the new players pictured are numbered on the back as "NEW." The book is usually sold intact. When cut from the book into individual cards, these cards are distinguishable from the regular 1988 Donruss cards since these have a 1988 copyright on the back whereas the regular issue has a 1987 copyright on the back.

	MT	EX-MT	VG
COMPLETE SET (27)	4.50	2.00	.55
COMMON PLAYER	.08	.04	.01
COMMON NEW PLAYER	.15	.07	.02
☐ 40 Mark Grace RR	1.50	.65	.19
☐ 68 Rick Sutcliffe	.15	.07	.02
☐ 119 Jody Davis	.08	.04	.01
☐ 146 Shawon Dunston	.25	.11	.03
☐ 169 Jamie Moyer	.08	.04	.01
☐ 191 Leon Durham	.08	.04	.01
☐ 242 Ryne Sandberg	.90	.40	.11
☐ 269 Andre Dawson	.50	.23	.06
☐ 315 Paul Noce	.15	.07	.02
☐ 324 Rafael Palmeiro	.75	.35	.09
☐ 438 Dave Martinez	.15	.07	.02
☐ 447 Jerry Mumphrey	.08	.04	.01
☐ 488 Jim Sundberg	.12	.05	.02
☐ 516 Manny Trillo	.08	.04	.01
☐ 539 Greg Maddux	.75	.35	.09
☐ 561 Les Lancaster	.08	.04	.01
☐ 570 Frank DiPino	.08	.04	.01
☐ 639 Damon Berryhill	.30	.14	.04
☐ 646 Scott Sanderson	.15	.07	.02
☐ NEW Mike Bielecki	.25	.11	.03
☐ NEW Rich Gossage	.30	.14	.04
☐ NEW Drew Hall	.15	.07	.02
☐ NEW Darrin Jackson	.50	.23	.06
☐ NEW Vance Law	.15	.07	.02
☐ NEW Al Nipper	.15	.07	.02
☐ NEW Angel Salazar	.15	.07	.02
☐ NEW Calvin Schiraldi	.15	.07	.02

1988 Donruss Mets Team Book

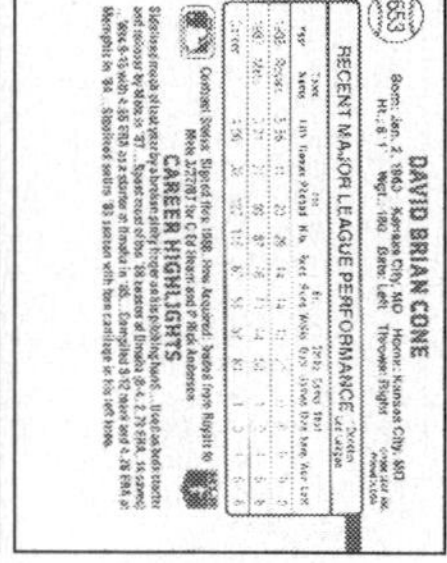

The 1988 Donruss Mets Team Book set features 27 cards (three pages with nine cards on each page) plus a large full-page puzzle of Stan Musial. Cards are in full color and are standard size, 2 1/2" by 3 1/2". The set was distributed as a four-page book; although the puzzle page was perforated, the card pages were not. The cover of the "Team Collection" book is primarily bright red. Card fronts are very similar in design to the 1988 Donruss regular issue. The card numbers on the backs are the same for those players that are the same as in the regular Donruss set; the new players pictured are numbered on the back as "NEW." The book is usually sold intact. When cut from the book into individual cards, these cards are distinguishable from the regular 1988 Donruss cards since these have a 1988 copyright on the back whereas the regular issue has a 1987 copyright on the back.

	MT	EX-MT	VG
COMPLETE SET (27)	4.50	2.00	.55
COMMON PLAYER	.08	.04	.01
COMMON NEW PLAYER	.15	.07	.02
☐ 37 Kevin Elster RR	.08	.04	.01
☐ 69 Dwight Gooden	.35	.16	.04
☐ 76 Ron Darling	.25	.11	.03
☐ 118 Sid Fernandez	.25	.11	.03
☐ 199 Gary Carter	.25	.11	.03
☐ 241 Wally Backman	.08	.04	.01
☐ 316 Keith Hernandez	.20	.09	.03
☐ 323 Dave Magadan	.15	.07	.02
☐ 364 Len Dykstra	.35	.16	.04
☐ 439 Darryl Strawberry	.75	.35	.09
☐ 446 Rick Aguilera	.30	.14	.04
☐ 562 Keith Miller	.20	.09	.03
☐ 569 Howard Johnson	.25	.11	.03
☐ 603 Terry Leach	.08	.04	.01
☐ 614 Lee Mazzilli	.08	.04	.01
☐ 617 Kevin McReynolds	.15	.07	.02
☐ 619 Barry Lyons	.08	.04	.01

		MT	EX-MT	VG
☐ 620	Randy Myers	.30	.14	.04
☐ 632	Bob Ojeda	.15	.07	.02
☐ 648	Tim Teufel	.08	.04	.01
☐ 651	Roger McDowell	.15	.07	.02
☐ 652	Mookie Wilson	.15	.07	.02
☐ 653	David Cone	.75	.35	.09
☐ 657	Gregg Jefferies	1.50	.65	.19
☐ NEW	Jeff Innis	.25	.11	.03
☐ NEW	Mackey Sasser	.35	.16	.04
☐ NEW	Gene Walter	.15	.07	.02

1988 Donruss Red Sox Team Book

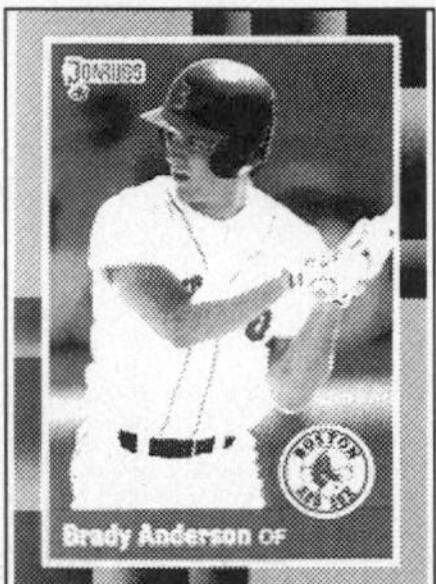

The 1988 Donruss Red Sox Team Book set features 27 cards (three pages with nine cards on each page) plus a large full-page puzzle of Stan Musial. Cards are in full color and are standard size, 2 1/2" by 3 1/2". The set was distributed as a four-page book; although the puzzle page was perforated, the card pages were not. The cover of the "Team Collection" book is primarily bright red. Card fronts are very similar in design to the 1988 Donruss regular issue. The card numbers on the backs are the same for those players that are the same as in the regular Donruss set; the new players pictured are numbered on the back as "NEW." The book is usually sold intact. When cut from the book into individual cards, these cards are distinguishable from the regular 1988 Donruss cards since these have a 1988 copyright on the back whereas the regular issue has a 1987 copyright on the back.

		MT	EX-MT	VG
COMPLETE SET (27)		4.50	2.00	.55
COMMON PLAYER		.08	.04	.01
COMMON NEW PLAYER		.15	.07	.02
☐ 41	Jody Reed RR	.25	.11	.03
☐ 51	Roger Clemens	.90	.40	.11
☐ 92	Bob Stanley	.12	.05	.02
☐ 129	Rich Gedman	.08	.04	.01
☐ 153	Wade Boggs	.75	.35	.09
☐ 174	Ellis Burks	.50	.23	.06
☐ 216	Dwight Evans	.15	.07	.02
☐ 252	Bruce Hurst	.15	.07	.02
☐ 276	Marty Barrett	.08	.04	.01
☐ 297	Todd Benzinger	.20	.09	.03
☐ 339	Mike Greenwell	.60	.25	.08
☐ 399	Jim Rice	.20	.09	.03
☐ 421	John Marzano	.08	.04	.01
☐ 462	Oil Can Boyd	.08	.04	.01
☐ 498	Sam Horn	.15	.07	.02
☐ 544	Spike Owen	.12	.05	.02
☐ 585	Jeff Sellers	.08	.04	.01
☐ 623	Ed Romero	.08	.04	.01
☐ 634	Wes Gardner	.15	.07	.02
☐ NEW	Brady Anderson	.75	.35	.09
☐ NEW	Rick Cerone	.15	.07	.02
☐ NEW	Steve Ellsworth	.25	.11	.03
☐ NEW	Dennis Lamp	.15	.07	.02
☐ NEW	Kevin Romine	.15	.07	.02
☐ NEW	Lee Smith	.35	.16	.04
☐ NEW	Mike Smithson	.15	.07	.02
☐ NEW	John Trautwein	.15	.07	.02

1988 Donruss Yankees Team Book

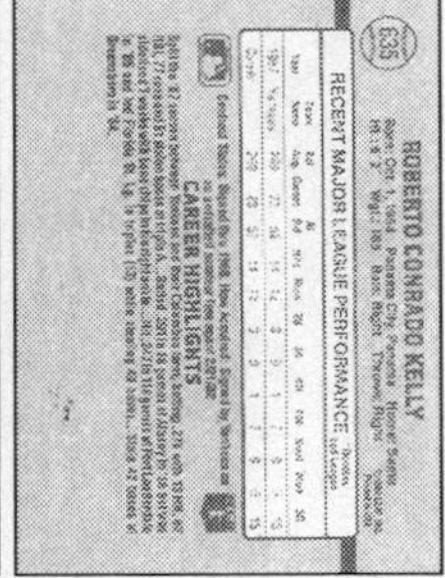

The 1988 Donruss Yankees Team Book set features 27 cards (three pages with nine cards on each page) plus a large full-page puzzle of Stan Musial. Cards are in full color and are standard size, 2 1/2" by 3 1/2". The set was distributed as a four-page book; although the puzzle page was perforated, the card pages were not. The cover of the "Team Collection" book is primarily bright red. Card fronts are very similar in design to the 1988 Donruss regular issue. The card numbers on the backs are the same for those players that are the same as in the regular Donruss set; the new players pictured are numbered on the back as "NEW." The book is usually sold intact. When cut from the book into individual cards, these cards are distinguishable from the regular 1988 Donruss cards since these have a 1988 copyright on the back whereas the regular issue has a 1987 copyright on the back.

		MT	EX-MT	VG
COMPLETE SET (27)		4.50	2.00	.55
COMMON PLAYER		.08	.04	.01
COMMON NEW PLAYER		.15	.07	.02
☐ 43	Al Leiter RR	.15	.07	.02
☐ 93	Dave Righetti	.12	.05	.02
☐ 105	Mike Pagliarulo	.12	.05	.02
☐ 128	Rick Rhoden	.08	.04	.01
☐ 175	Ron Guidry	.25	.11	.03
☐ 217	Don Mattingly	1.00	.45	.13
☐ 228	Willie Randolph	.15	.07	.02
☐ 251	Gary Ward	.08	.04	.01
☐ 277	Rickey Henderson	.90	.40	.11
☐ 278	Dave Winfield	.45	.20	.06
☐ 340	Claudell Washington	.12	.05	.02
☐ 374	Charles Hudson	.08	.04	.01
☐ 401	Tommy John	.20	.09	.03
☐ 474	Joel Skinner	.08	.04	.01
☐ 497	Tim Stoddard	.08	.04	.01
☐ 545	Jay Buhner	.60	.25	.08
☐ 616	Bobby Meacham	.08	.04	.01
☐ 635	Roberto Kelly	1.00	.45	.13
☐ NEW	John Candelaria	.25	.11	.03
☐ NEW	Jack Clark	.35	.16	.04
☐ NEW	Jose Cruz	.25	.11	.03
☐ NEW	Richard Dotson	.15	.07	.02
☐ NEW	Cecilio Guante	.15	.07	.02
☐ NEW	Lee Guetterman	.20	.09	.03
☐ NEW	Rafael Santana	.15	.07	.02
☐ NEW	Steve Shields	.15	.07	.02
☐ NEW	Don Slaught	.25	.11	.03

1989 Donruss

This 660-card set was distributed along with a puzzle of Warren Spahn. The six regular checklist cards are numbered throughout the set as multiples of 100. Cards measure 2 1/2" by 3 1/2" and feature a distinctive black side border with an alternating coating. The popular Diamond King

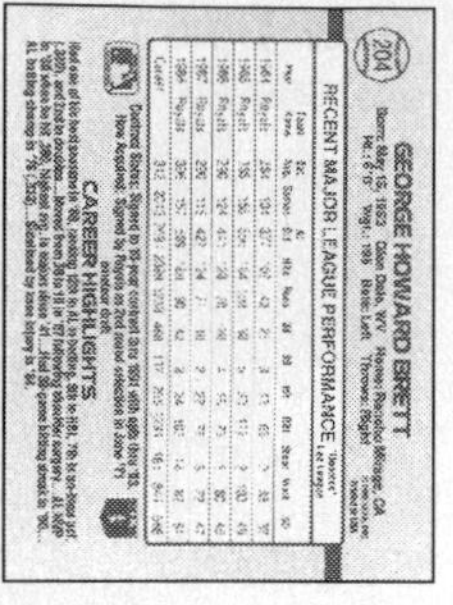

subset returns for the eighth consecutive year. Rated Rookies are featured again as cards 28-47. The Donruss '89 logo appears in the lower left corner of every obverse. There are two variations that occur throughout most of the set. On the card backs "Denotes Led League" can be found with one asterisk to the left or with an asterisk on each side. On the card fronts the horizontal lines on the left and right borders can be glossy or non-glossy. Since both of these variation types are relatively minor and seem equally common, there is no premium value for either type. Rather than short-printing 26 cards in order to make room for printing the Bonus MVP's this year, Donruss apparently chose to double print 106 cards. These double prints are listed below by DP. Numbered with the prefix "BC" for bonus card, the 26-card set featuring the most valuable player from each of the 26 teams was randomly inserted in the wax and rack packs. These cards are distinguished by the bold MVP logo in the upper background of the obverse, and the four doubleprinted cards are denoted by "DP" in the checklist below. The key Rookie Cards in this set are Sandy Alomar Jr., Ken Griffey Jr., Felix Jose, Ramon Martinez, Hal Morris, Gary Sheffield, and John Smoltz.

	MT	EX-MT	VG
COMPLETE SET (660)	20.00	9.00	2.50
COMPLETE FACT.SET (660)	20.00	9.00	2.50
COMMON PLAYER (1-660)	.04	.02	.01
COMMON PLAYER DP	.03	.01	.00
COMPLETE MVP SET (26)	1.25	.55	.16
COMMON MVP (BC1-BC26)	.05	.02	.01
☐ 1 Mike Greenwell DK	.08	.04	.01
☐ 2 Bobby Bonilla DK DP	.08	.04	.01
☐ 3 Pete Incaviglia DK	.05	.02	.01
☐ 4 Chris Sabo DK DP	.08	.04	.01
☐ 5 Robin Yount DK	.10	.05	.01
☐ 6 Tony Gwynn DK DP	.10	.05	.01
☐ 7 Carlton Fisk DK UER (OF on back)	.10	.05	.01
☐ 8 Cory Snyder DK	.05	.02	.01
☐ 9 David Cone DK UER (Sic, "hurdlers")	.08	.04	.01
☐ 10 Kevin Seitzer DK	.05	.02	.01
☐ 11 Rick Reuschel DK	.05	.02	.01
☐ 12 Johnny Ray DK	.05	.02	.01
☐ 13 Dave Schmidt DK	.05	.02	.01
☐ 14 Andres Galarraga DK	.05	.02	.01
☐ 15 Kirk Gibson DK	.05	.02	.01
☐ 16 Fred McGriff DK	.12	.05	.02
☐ 17 Mark Grace DK	.10	.05	.01
☐ 18 Jeff M. Robinson DK	.05	.02	.01
☐ 19 Vince Coleman DK DP	.05	.02	.01
☐ 20 Dave Henderson DK	.05	.02	.01
☐ 21 Harold Reynolds DK	.05	.02	.01
☐ 22 Gerald Perry DK	.05	.02	.01
☐ 23 Frank Viola DK	.05	.02	.01
☐ 24 Steve Bedrosian DK	.05	.02	.01
☐ 25 Glenn Davis DK	.05	.02	.01
☐ 26 Don Mattingly DK UER (Doesn't mention Don's previous DK in 1985)	.12	.05	.02
☐ 27 DK Checklist DP	.05	.01	.00
☐ 28 Sandy Alomar Jr. RR	.25	.11	.03
☐ 29 Steve Searcy RR	.06	.03	.01
☐ 30 Cameron Drew RR	.06	.03	.01
☐ 31 Gary Sheffield RR	2.00	.90	.25
☐ 32 Erik Hanson RR	.20	.09	.03
☐ 33 Ken Griffey Jr. RR	4.50	2.00	.55
☐ 34 Greg W. Harris RR	.10	.05	.01
☐ 35 Gregg Jefferies RR	.20	.09	.03
☐ 36 Luis Medina RR	.06	.03	.01
☐ 37 Carlos Quintana RR	.10	.05	.01
☐ 38 Felix Jose RR	.75	.35	.09
☐ 39 Cris Carpenter RR	.10	.05	.01
☐ 40 Ron Jones RR	.06	.03	.01
☐ 41 Dave West RR	.10	.05	.01
☐ 42 Randy Johnson RR	.35	.16	.04
☐ 43 Mike Harkey RR	.12	.05	.02
☐ 44 Pete Harnisch RR DP	.15	.07	.02
☐ 45 Tom Gordon RR DP	.10	.05	.01
☐ 46 Gregg Olson RR DP	.35	.16	.04
☐ 47 Alex Sanchez RR DP	.06	.03	.01
☐ 48 Ruben Sierra	.30	.14	.04
☐ 49 Rafael Palmeiro	.20	.09	.03
☐ 50 Ron Gant	.40	.18	.05
☐ 51 Cal Ripken	.50	.23	.06
☐ 52 Wally Joyner	.08	.04	.01
☐ 53 Gary Carter	.06	.03	.01
☐ 54 Andy Van Slyke	.10	.05	.01
☐ 55 Robin Yount	.20	.09	.03
☐ 56 Pete Incaviglia	.03	.01	.00
☐ 57 Greg Brock	.03	.01	.00
☐ 58 Melido Perez	.06	.03	.01
☐ 59 Craig Lefferts	.03	.01	.00
☐ 60 Gary Pettis	.03	.01	.00
☐ 61 Danny Tartabull	.12	.05	.02
☐ 62 Guillermo Hernandez	.03	.01	.00
☐ 63 Ozzie Smith	.15	.07	.02
☐ 64 Gary Gaetti	.03	.01	.00
☐ 65 Mark Davis	.03	.01	.00
☐ 66 Lee Smith	.06	.03	.01
☐ 67 Dennis Eckersley	.12	.05	.02
☐ 68 Wade Boggs	.25	.11	.03
☐ 69 Mike Scott	.03	.01	.00
☐ 70 Fred McGriff	.25	.11	.03
☐ 71 Tom Browning	.06	.03	.01
☐ 72 Claudell Washington	.03	.01	.00
☐ 73 Mel Hall	.03	.01	.00
☐ 74 Don Mattingly	.25	.11	.03
☐ 75 Steve Bedrosian	.03	.01	.00
☐ 76 Juan Samuel	.03	.01	.00
☐ 77 Mike Scioscia	.03	.01	.00
☐ 78 Dave Righetti	.03	.01	.00
☐ 79 Alfredo Griffin	.03	.01	.00
☐ 80 Eric Davis UER (165 games in 1988, should be 135)	.12	.05	.02
☐ 81 Juan Berenguer	.03	.01	.00
☐ 82 Todd Worrell	.06	.03	.01
☐ 83 Joe Carter	.25	.11	.03
☐ 84 Steve Sax	.06	.03	.01
☐ 85 Frank White	.03	.01	.00
☐ 86 John Kruk	.06	.03	.01
☐ 87 Rance Mulliniks	.03	.01	.00
☐ 88 Alan Ashby	.03	.01	.00
☐ 89 Charlie Leibrandt	.03	.01	.00
☐ 90 Frank Tanana	.03	.01	.00
☐ 91 Jose Canseco	.40	.18	.05
☐ 92 Barry Bonds	.40	.18	.05
☐ 93 Harold Reynolds	.03	.01	.00
☐ 94 Mark McLemore	.03	.01	.00
☐ 95 Mark McGwire	.35	.16	.04
☐ 96 Eddie Murray	.15	.07	.02
☐ 97 Tim Raines	.06	.03	.01
☐ 98 Robby Thompson	.03	.01	.00
☐ 99 Kevin McReynolds	.06	.03	.01
☐ 100 Checklist Card	.05	.01	.00
☐ 101 Carlton Fisk	.15	.07	.02
☐ 102 Dave Martinez	.06	.03	.01
☐ 103 Glenn Braggs	.03	.01	.00
☐ 104 Dale Murphy	.10	.05	.01
☐ 105 Ryne Sandberg	.40	.18	.05
☐ 106 Dennis Martinez	.06	.03	.01
☐ 107 Pete O'Brien	.03	.01	.00
☐ 108 Dick Schofield	.03	.01	.00
☐ 109 Henry Cotto	.03	.01	.00
☐ 110 Mike Marshall	.03	.01	.00
☐ 111 Keith Moreland	.03	.01	.00
☐ 112 Tom Brunansky	.06	.03	.01
☐ 113 Kelly Gruber UER (Wrong birthdate)	.06	.03	.01
☐ 114 Brook Jacoby	.03	.01	.00
☐ 115 Keith Brown	.03	.01	.00
☐ 116 Matt Nokes	.06	.03	.01
☐ 117 Keith Hernandez	.06	.03	.01
☐ 118 Bob Forsch	.03	.01	.00
☐ 119 Bert Blyleven UER (... 3000 strikeouts in	.06	.03	.01

1987, should be 1986)
☐ 120 Willie Wilson .03 .01 .00
☐ 121 Tommy Gregg .03 .01 .00
☐ 122 Jim Rice .06 .03 .01
☐ 123 Bob Knepper .03 .01 .00
☐ 124 Danny Jackson .03 .01 .00
☐ 125 Eric Plunk .03 .01 .00
☐ 126 Brian Fisher .03 .01 .00
☐ 127 Mike Pagliarulo .03 .01 .00
☐ 128 Tony Gwynn .25 .11 .03
☐ 129 Lance McCullers .03 .01 .00
☐ 130 Andres Galarraga .03 .01 .00
☐ 131 Jose Uribe .03 .01 .00
☐ 132 Kirk Gibson UER .06 .03 .01
(Wrong birthdate)
☐ 133 David Palmer .03 .01 .00
☐ 134 R.J. Reynolds .03 .01 .00
☐ 135 Greg Walker .03 .01 .00
☐ 136 Kirk McCaskill UER .03 .01 .00
(Wrong birthdate)
☐ 137 Shawon Dunston .06 .03 .01
☐ 138 Andy Allanson .03 .01 .00
☐ 139 Rob Murphy .03 .01 .00
☐ 140 Mike Aldrete .03 .01 .00
☐ 141 Terry Kennedy .03 .01 .00
☐ 142 Scott Fletcher .03 .01 .00
☐ 143 Steve Balboni .03 .01 .00
☐ 144 Bret Saberhagen .06 .03 .01
☐ 145 Ozzie Virgil .03 .01 .00
☐ 146 Dale Sveum .03 .01 .00
☐ 147 Darryl Strawberry .25 .11 .03
☐ 148 Harold Baines .06 .03 .01
☐ 149 George Bell .10 .05 .01
☐ 150 Dave Parker .06 .03 .01
☐ 151 Bobby Bonilla .20 .09 .03
☐ 152 Mookie Wilson .06 .03 .01
☐ 153 Ted Power .03 .01 .00
☐ 154 Nolan Ryan .60 .25 .08
☐ 155 Jeff Reardon .06 .03 .01
☐ 156 Tim Wallach .06 .03 .01
☐ 157 Jamie Moyer .03 .01 .00
☐ 158 Rich Gossage .06 .03 .01
☐ 159 Dave Winfield .20 .09 .03
☐ 160 Von Hayes .03 .01 .00
☐ 161 Willie McGee .06 .03 .01
☐ 162 Rich Gedman .03 .01 .00
☐ 163 Tony Pena .03 .01 .00
☐ 164 Mike Morgan .06 .03 .01
☐ 165 Charlie Hough .03 .01 .00
☐ 166 Mike Stanley .03 .01 .00
☐ 167 Andre Dawson .15 .07 .02
☐ 168 Joe Boever .03 .01 .00
☐ 169 Pete Stanicek .03 .01 .00
☐ 170 Bob Boone .06 .03 .01
☐ 171 Ron Darling .06 .03 .01
☐ 172 Bob Walk .03 .01 .00
☐ 173 Rob Deer .06 .03 .01
☐ 174 Steve Buechele .03 .01 .00
☐ 175 Ted Higuera .03 .01 .00
☐ 176 Ozzie Guillen .03 .01 .00
☐ 177 Candy Maldonado .03 .01 .00
☐ 178 Doyle Alexander .03 .01 .00
☐ 179 Mark Gubicza .03 .01 .00
☐ 180 Alan Trammell .06 .03 .01
☐ 181 Vince Coleman .06 .03 .01
☐ 182 Kirby Puckett .40 .18 .05
☐ 183 Chris Brown .03 .01 .00
☐ 184 Marty Barrett .03 .01 .00
☐ 185 Stan Javier .03 .01 .00
☐ 186 Mike Greenwell .06 .03 .01
☐ 187 Billy Hatcher .03 .01 .00
☐ 188 Jimmy Key .06 .03 .01
☐ 189 Nick Esasky .03 .01 .00
☐ 190 Don Slaught .03 .01 .00
☐ 191 Cory Snyder .03 .01 .00
☐ 192 John Candelaria .03 .01 .00
☐ 193 Mike Schmidt .35 .16 .04
☐ 194 Kevin Gross .03 .01 .00
☐ 195 John Tudor .03 .01 .00
☐ 196 Neil Allen .03 .01 .00
☐ 197 Orel Hershiser .06 .03 .01
☐ 198 Kal Daniels .06 .03 .01
☐ 199 Kent Hrbek .06 .03 .01
☐ 200 Checklist Card .05 .01 .00
☐ 201 Joe Magrane .03 .01 .00
☐ 202 Scott Bailes .03 .01 .00
☐ 203 Tim Belcher .06 .03 .01
☐ 204 George Brett .20 .09 .03
☐ 205 Benito Santiago .06 .03 .01
☐ 206 Tony Fernandez .06 .03 .01
☐ 207 Gerald Young .03 .01 .00
☐ 208 Bo Jackson .20 .09 .03
☐ 209 Chet Lemon .03 .01 .00
☐ 210 Storm Davis .03 .01 .00
☐ 211 Doug Drabek .06 .03 .01
☐ 212 Mickey Brantley UER .03 .01 .00
(Photo actually
Nelson Simmons)
☐ 213 Devon White .06 .03 .01
☐ 214 Dave Stewart .06 .03 .01
☐ 215 Dave Schmidt .03 .01 .00
☐ 216 Bryn Smith .03 .01 .00
☐ 217 Brett Butler .06 .03 .01
☐ 218 Bob Ojeda .03 .01 .00
☐ 219 Steve Rosenberg .03 .01 .00
☐ 220 Hubie Brooks .03 .01 .00
☐ 221 B.J. Surhoff .03 .01 .00
☐ 222 Rick Mahler .03 .01 .00
☐ 223 Rick Sutcliffe .06 .03 .01
☐ 224 Neal Heaton .03 .01 .00
☐ 225 Mitch Williams .06 .03 .01
☐ 226 Chuck Finley .06 .03 .01
☐ 227 Mark Langston .06 .03 .01
☐ 228 Jesse Orosco .03 .01 .00
☐ 229 Ed Whitson .03 .01 .00
☐ 230 Terry Pendleton .12 .05 .02
☐ 231 Lloyd Moseby .03 .01 .00
☐ 232 Greg Swindell .06 .03 .01
☐ 233 John Franco .06 .03 .01
☐ 234 Jack Morris .12 .05 .02
☐ 235 Howard Johnson .06 .03 .01
☐ 236 Glenn Davis .06 .03 .01
☐ 237 Frank Viola .06 .03 .01
☐ 238 Kevin Seitzer .06 .03 .01
☐ 239 Gerald Perry .03 .01 .00
☐ 240 Dwight Evans .06 .03 .01
☐ 241 Jim Deshaies .03 .01 .00
☐ 242 Bo Diaz .03 .01 .00
☐ 243 Carney Lansford .06 .03 .01
☐ 244 Mike LaValliere .03 .01 .00
☐ 245 Rickey Henderson .25 .11 .03
☐ 246 Roberto Alomar .75 .35 .09
☐ 247 Jimmy Jones .03 .01 .00
☐ 248 Pascual Perez .03 .01 .00
☐ 249 Will Clark .40 .18 .05
☐ 250 Fernando Valenzuela .06 .03 .01
☐ 251 Shane Rawley .03 .01 .00
☐ 252 Sid Bream .03 .01 .00
☐ 253 Steve Lyons .03 .01 .00
☐ 254 Brian Downing .03 .01 .00
☐ 255 Mark Grace .30 .14 .04
☐ 256 Tom Candiotti .03 .01 .00
☐ 257 Barry Larkin .15 .07 .02
☐ 258 Mike Krukow .03 .01 .00
☐ 259 Billy Ripken .03 .01 .00
☐ 260 Cecilio Guante .03 .01 .00
☐ 261 Scott Bradley .03 .01 .00
☐ 262 Floyd Bannister .03 .01 .00
☐ 263 Pete Smith .06 .03 .01
☐ 264 Jim Gantner UER .03 .01 .00
(Wrong birthdate)
☐ 265 Roger McDowell .03 .01 .00
☐ 266 Bobby Thigpen .03 .01 .00
☐ 267 Jim Clancy .03 .01 .00
☐ 268 Terry Steinbach .06 .03 .01
☐ 269 Mike Dunne .03 .01 .00
☐ 270 Dwight Gooden .12 .05 .02
☐ 271 Mike Heath .03 .01 .00
☐ 272 Dave Smith .03 .01 .00
☐ 273 Keith Atherton .03 .01 .00
☐ 274 Tim Burke .03 .01 .00
☐ 275 Damon Berryhill .03 .01 .00
☐ 276 Vance Law .03 .01 .00
☐ 277 Rich Dotson .03 .01 .00
☐ 278 Lance Parrish .06 .03 .01
☐ 279 Denny Walling .03 .01 .00
☐ 280 Roger Clemens .40 .18 .05
☐ 281 Greg Mathews .03 .01 .00
☐ 282 Tom Niedenfuer .03 .01 .00
☐ 283 Paul Kilgus .03 .01 .00
☐ 284 Jose Guzman .06 .03 .01
☐ 285 Calvin Schiraldi .03 .01 .00
☐ 286 Charlie Puleo UER .03 .01 .00
(Career ERA 4.24,
should be 4.23)
☐ 287 Joe Orsulak .03 .01 .00
☐ 288 Jack Howell .03 .01 .00
☐ 289 Kevin Elster .03 .01 .00
☐ 290 Jose Lind .03 .01 .00
☐ 291 Paul Molitor .10 .05 .01
☐ 292 Cecil Espy .03 .01 .00
☐ 293 Bill Wegman .03 .01 .00
☐ 294 Dan Pasqua .03 .01 .00
☐ 295 Scott Garrelts UER .03 .01 .00
(Wrong birthdate)
☐ 296 Walt Terrell .03 .01 .00
☐ 297 Ed Hearn .03 .01 .00

☐	298 Lou Whitaker	.06	.03	.01
☐	299 Ken Dayley	.03	.01	.00
☐	300 Checklist Card	.05	.01	.00
☐	301 Tommy Herr	.03	.01	.00
☐	302 Mike Brumley	.03	.01	.00
☐	303 Ellis Burks	.06	.03	.01
☐	304 Curt Young UER (Wrong birthdate)	.03	.01	.00
☐	305 Jody Reed	.03	.01	.00
☐	306 Bill Doran	.03	.01	.00
☐	307 David Wells	.03	.01	.00
☐	308 Ron Robinson	.03	.01	.00
☐	309 Rafael Santana	.03	.01	.00
☐	310 Julio Franco	.06	.03	.01
☐	311 Jack Clark	.06	.03	.01
☐	312 Chris James	.03	.01	.00
☐	313 Milt Thompson	.03	.01	.00
☐	314 John Shelby	.03	.01	.00
☐	315 Al Leiter	.03	.01	.00
☐	316 Mike Davis	.03	.01	.00
☐	317 Chris Sabo	.30	.14	.04
☐	318 Greg Gagne	.03	.01	.00
☐	319 Jose Oquendo	.03	.01	.00
☐	320 John Farrell	.03	.01	.00
☐	321 Franklin Stubbs	.03	.01	.00
☐	322 Kurt Stillwell	.03	.01	.00
☐	323 Shawn Abner	.03	.01	.00
☐	324 Mike Flanagan	.03	.01	.00
☐	325 Kevin Bass	.03	.01	.00
☐	326 Pat Tabler	.03	.01	.00
☐	327 Mike Henneman	.06	.03	.01
☐	328 Rick Honeycutt	.03	.01	.00
☐	329 John Smiley	.06	.03	.01
☐	330 Rey Quinones	.03	.01	.00
☐	331 Johnny Ray	.03	.01	.00
☐	332 Bob Welch	.06	.03	.01
☐	333 Larry Sheets	.03	.01	.00
☐	334 Jeff Parrett	.03	.01	.00
☐	335 Rick Reuschel UER (For Don Robinson, should be Jeff)	.03	.01	.00
☐	336 Randy Myers	.06	.03	.01
☐	337 Ken Williams	.03	.01	.00
☐	338 Andy McGaffigan	.03	.01	.00
☐	339 Joey Meyer	.03	.01	.00
☐	340 Dion James	.03	.01	.00
☐	341 Les Lancaster	.03	.01	.00
☐	342 Tom Foley	.03	.01	.00
☐	343 Geno Petralli	.03	.01	.00
☐	344 Dan Petry	.03	.01	.00
☐	345 Alvin Davis	.03	.01	.00
☐	346 Mickey Hatcher	.03	.01	.00
☐	347 Marvell Wynne	.03	.01	.00
☐	348 Danny Cox	.03	.01	.00
☐	349 Dave Stieb	.06	.03	.01
☐	350 Jay Bell	.06	.03	.01
☐	351 Jeff Treadway	.03	.01	.00
☐	352 Luis Salazar	.03	.01	.00
☐	353 Len Dykstra	.06	.03	.01
☐	354 Juan Agosto	.03	.01	.00
☐	355 Gene Larkin	.03	.01	.00
☐	356 Steve Farr	.03	.01	.00
☐	357 Paul Assenmacher	.03	.01	.00
☐	358 Todd Benzinger	.03	.01	.00
☐	359 Larry Andersen	.03	.01	.00
☐	360 Paul O'Neill	.06	.03	.01
☐	361 Ron Hassey	.03	.01	.00
☐	362 Jim Gott	.03	.01	.00
☐	363 Ken Phelps	.03	.01	.00
☐	364 Tim Flannery	.03	.01	.00
☐	365 Randy Ready	.03	.01	.00
☐	366 Nelson Santovenia	.03	.01	.00
☐	367 Kelly Downs	.03	.01	.00
☐	368 Danny Heep	.03	.01	.00
☐	369 Phil Bradley	.03	.01	.00
☐	370 Jeff D. Robinson	.03	.01	.00
☐	371 Ivan Calderon	.03	.01	.00
☐	372 Mike Witt	.03	.01	.00
☐	373 Greg Maddux	.30	.14	.04
☐	374 Carmen Castillo	.03	.01	.00
☐	375 Jose Rijo	.06	.03	.01
☐	376 Joe Price	.03	.01	.00
☐	377 Rene Gonzales	.03	.01	.00
☐	378 Oddibe McDowell	.03	.01	.00
☐	379 Jim Presley	.03	.01	.00
☐	380 Brad Wellman	.03	.01	.00
☐	381 Tom Glavine	.50	.23	.06
☐	382 Dan Plesac	.03	.01	.00
☐	383 Wally Backman	.03	.01	.00
☐	384 Dave Gallagher	.03	.01	.00
☐	385 Tom Henke	.06	.03	.01
☐	386 Luis Polonia	.06	.03	.01
☐	387 Junior Ortiz	.03	.01	.00
☐	388 David Cone	.15	.07	.02
☐	389 Dave Bergman	.03	.01	.00
☐	390 Danny Darwin	.03	.01	.00
☐	391 Dan Gladden	.03	.01	.00
☐	392 John Dopson	.03	.01	.00
☐	393 Frank DiPino	.03	.01	.00
☐	394 Al Nipper	.03	.01	.00
☐	395 Willie Randolph	.06	.03	.01
☐	396 Don Carman	.03	.01	.00
☐	397 Scott Terry	.03	.01	.00
☐	398 Rick Cerone	.03	.01	.00
☐	399 Tom Pagnozzi	.03	.01	.00
☐	400 Checklist Card	.05	.01	.00
☐	401 Mickey Tettleton	.06	.03	.01
☐	402 Curtis Wilkerson	.03	.01	.00
☐	403 Jeff Russell	.03	.01	.00
☐	404 Pat Perry	.03	.01	.00
☐	405 Jose Alvarez	.03	.01	.00
☐	406 Rick Schu	.03	.01	.00
☐	407 Sherman Corbett	.03	.01	.00
☐	408 Dave Magadan	.06	.03	.01
☐	409 Bob Kipper	.03	.01	.00
☐	410 Don August	.03	.01	.00
☐	411 Bob Brower	.03	.01	.00
☐	412 Chris Bosio	.03	.01	.00
☐	413 Jerry Reuss	.03	.01	.00
☐	414 Atlee Hammaker	.03	.01	.00
☐	415 Jim Walewander	.03	.01	.00
☐	416 Mike Macfarlane	.15	.07	.02
☐	417 Pat Sheridan	.03	.01	.00
☐	418 Pedro Guerrero	.06	.03	.01
☐	419 Allan Anderson	.03	.01	.00
☐	420 Mark Parent	.03	.01	.00
☐	421 Bob Stanley	.03	.01	.00
☐	422 Mike Gallego	.03	.01	.00
☐	423 Bruce Hurst	.06	.03	.01
☐	424 Dave Meads	.03	.01	.00
☐	425 Jesse Barfield	.03	.01	.00
☐	426 Rob Dibble	.20	.09	.03
☐	427 Joel Skinner	.03	.01	.00
☐	428 Ron Kittle	.03	.01	.00
☐	429 Rick Rhoden	.03	.01	.00
☐	430 Bob Dernier	.03	.01	.00
☐	431 Steve Jeltz	.03	.01	.00
☐	432 Rick Dempsey	.03	.01	.00
☐	433 Roberto Kelly	.15	.07	.02
☐	434 Dave Anderson	.03	.01	.00
☐	435 Herm Winningham	.03	.01	.00
☐	436 Al Newman	.03	.01	.00
☐	437 Jose DeLeon	.03	.01	.00
☐	438 Doug Jones	.06	.03	.01
☐	439 Brian Holton	.03	.01	.00
☐	440 Jeff Montgomery	.06	.03	.01
☐	441 Dickie Thon	.03	.01	.00
☐	442 Cecil Fielder	.25	.11	.03
☐	443 John Fishel	.03	.01	.00
☐	444 Jerry Don Gleaton	.03	.01	.00
☐	445 Paul Gibson	.03	.01	.00
☐	446 Walt Weiss	.06	.03	.01
☐	447 Glenn Wilson	.03	.01	.00
☐	448 Mike Moore	.03	.01	.00
☐	449 Chili Davis	.06	.03	.01
☐	450 Dave Henderson	.06	.03	.01
☐	451 Jose Bautista	.03	.01	.00
☐	452 Rex Hudler	.03	.01	.00
☐	453 Bob Brenly	.03	.01	.00
☐	454 Mackey Sasser	.03	.01	.00
☐	455 Daryl Boston	.03	.01	.00
☐	456 Mike R. Fitzgerald Montreal Expos	.03	.01	.00
☐	457 Jeffrey Leonard	.03	.01	.00
☐	458 Bruce Sutter	.06	.03	.01
☐	459 Mitch Webster	.03	.01	.00
☐	460 Joe Hesketh	.03	.01	.00
☐	461 Bobby Witt	.06	.03	.01
☐	462 Stew Cliburn	.03	.01	.00
☐	463 Scott Bankhead	.03	.01	.00
☐	464 Ramon Martinez	.50	.23	.06
☐	465 Dave Leiper	.03	.01	.00
☐	466 Luis Alicea	.10	.05	.01
☐	467 John Cerutti	.03	.01	.00
☐	468 Ron Washington	.03	.01	.00
☐	469 Jeff Reed	.03	.01	.00
☐	470 Jeff M. Robinson	.03	.01	.00
☐	471 Sid Fernandez	.06	.03	.01
☐	472 Terry Puhl	.03	.01	.00
☐	473 Charlie Lea	.03	.01	.00
☐	474 Israel Sanchez	.03	.01	.00
☐	475 Bruce Benedict	.03	.01	.00
☐	476 Oil Can Boyd	.03	.01	.00
☐	477 Craig Reynolds	.03	.01	.00
☐	478 Frank Williams	.03	.01	.00
☐	479 Greg Cadaret	.03	.01	.00

Card			
☐ 480 Randy Kramer	.03	.01	.00
☐ 481 Dave Eiland	.03	.01	.00
☐ 482 Eric Show	.03	.01	.00
☐ 483 Garry Templeton	.03	.01	.00
☐ 484 Wallace Johnson	.03	.01	.00
☐ 485 Kevin Mitchell	.10	.05	.01
☐ 486 Tim Crews	.03	.01	.00
☐ 487 Mike Maddux	.03	.01	.00
☐ 488 Dave LaPoint	.03	.01	.00
☐ 489 Fred Manrique	.03	.01	.00
☐ 490 Greg Minton	.03	.01	.00
☐ 491 Doug Dascenzo UER (Photo actually Damon Berryhill)	.03	.01	.00
☐ 492 Willie Upshaw	.03	.01	.00
☐ 493 Jack Armstrong	.12	.05	.02
☐ 494 Kirt Manwaring	.03	.01	.00
☐ 495 Jeff Ballard	.03	.01	.00
☐ 496 Jeff Kunkel	.03	.01	.00
☐ 497 Mike Campbell	.03	.01	.00
☐ 498 Gary Thurman	.03	.01	.00
☐ 499 Zane Smith	.03	.01	.00
☐ 500 Checklist Card DP	.05	.02	.01
☐ 501 Mike Birkbeck	.03	.01	.00
☐ 502 Terry Leach	.03	.01	.00
☐ 503 Shawn Hillegas	.03	.01	.00
☐ 504 Manny Lee	.03	.01	.00
☐ 505 Doug Jennings	.03	.01	.00
☐ 506 Ken Oberkfell	.03	.01	.00
☐ 507 Tim Teufel	.03	.01	.00
☐ 508 Tom Brookens	.03	.01	.00
☐ 509 Rafael Ramirez	.03	.01	.00
☐ 510 Fred Toliver	.03	.01	.00
☐ 511 Brian Holman	.10	.05	.01
☐ 512 Mike Bielecki	.03	.01	.00
☐ 513 Jeff Pico	.03	.01	.00
☐ 514 Charles Hudson	.03	.01	.00
☐ 515 Bruce Ruffin	.03	.01	.00
☐ 516 Larry McWilliams UER (New Richland, should be North Richland)	.03	.01	.00
☐ 517 Jeff Sellers	.03	.01	.00
☐ 518 John Costello	.03	.01	.00
☐ 519 Brady Anderson	.60	.25	.08
☐ 520 Craig McMurtry	.03	.01	.00
☐ 521 Ray Hayward DP	.03	.01	.00
☐ 522 Drew Hall DP	.03	.01	.00
☐ 523 Mark Lemke DP	.12	.05	.02
☐ 524 Oswald Peraza DP	.03	.01	.00
☐ 525 Bryan Harvey DP	.20	.09	.03
☐ 526 Rick Aguilera DP	.03	.01	.00
☐ 527 Tom Prince DP	.03	.01	.00
☐ 528 Mark Clear DP	.03	.01	.00
☐ 529 Jerry Browne DP	.03	.01	.00
☐ 530 Juan Castillo DP	.03	.01	.00
☐ 531 Jack McDowell DP	.25	.11	.03
☐ 532 Chris Speier DP	.03	.01	.00
☐ 533 Darrell Evans DP	.03	.01	.00
☐ 534 Luis Aquino DP	.03	.01	.00
☐ 535 Eric King DP	.03	.01	.00
☐ 536 Ken Hill DP	.35	.16	.04
☐ 537 Randy Bush DP	.03	.01	.00
☐ 538 Shane Mack DP	.06	.03	.01
☐ 539 Tom Bolton DP	.03	.01	.00
☐ 540 Gene Nelson DP	.03	.01	.00
☐ 541 Wes Gardner DP	.03	.01	.00
☐ 542 Ken Caminiti DP	.06	.03	.01
☐ 543 Duane Ward DP	.06	.03	.01
☐ 544 Norm Charlton DP	.15	.07	.02
☐ 545 Hal Morris DP	.30	.14	.04
☐ 546 Rich Yett DP	.03	.01	.00
☐ 547 Hensley Meulens DP	.12	.05	.02
☐ 548 Greg A. Harris DP Philadelphia Phillies	.03	.01	.00
☐ 549 Darren Daulton DP (Posing as right-handed hitter)	.06	.03	.01
☐ 550 Jeff Hamilton DP	.03	.01	.00
☐ 551 Luis Aguayo DP	.03	.01	.00
☐ 552 Tim Leary DP (Resembles M.Marshall)	.03	.01	.00
☐ 553 Ron Oester DP	.03	.01	.00
☐ 554 Steve Lombardozzi DP	.03	.01	.00
☐ 555 Tim Jones DP	.03	.01	.00
☐ 556 Bud Black DP	.03	.01	.00
☐ 557 Alejandro Pena DP	.03	.01	.00
☐ 558 Jose DeJesus DP	.03	.01	.00
☐ 559 Dennis Rasmussen DP	.03	.01	.00
☐ 560 Pat Borders DP	.25	.11	.03
☐ 561 Craig Biggio DP	.30	.14	.04
☐ 562 Luis De Los Santos DP	.03	.01	.00
☐ 563 Fred Lynn DP	.03	.01	.00
☐ 564 Todd Burns DP	.03	.01	.00
☐ 565 Felix Fermin DP	.03	.01	.00
☐ 566 Darnell Coles DP	.03	.01	.00
☐ 567 Willie Fraser DP	.03	.01	.00
☐ 568 Glenn Hubbard DP	.03	.01	.00
☐ 569 Craig Worthington DP	.03	.01	.00
☐ 570 Johnny Paredes DP	.03	.01	.00
☐ 571 Don Robinson DP	.03	.01	.00
☐ 572 Barry Lyons DP	.03	.01	.00
☐ 573 Bill Long DP	.03	.01	.00
☐ 574 Tracy Jones DP	.03	.01	.00
☐ 575 Juan Nieves DP	.03	.01	.00
☐ 576 Andres Thomas DP	.03	.01	.00
☐ 577 Rolando Roomes DP	.03	.01	.00
☐ 578 Luis Rivera UER DP (Wrong birthdate)	.03	.01	.00
☐ 579 Chad Kreuter DP	.03	.01	.00
☐ 580 Tony Armas DP	.03	.01	.00
☐ 581 Jay Buhner	.10	.05	.01
☐ 582 Ricky Horton DP	.03	.01	.00
☐ 583 Andy Hawkins DP	.03	.01	.00
☐ 584 Sil Campusano	.03	.01	.00
☐ 585 Dave Clark	.03	.01	.00
☐ 586 Van Snider DP	.03	.01	.00
☐ 587 Todd Frohwirth DP	.03	.01	.00
☐ 588 Warren Spahn DP PUZ	.08	.04	.01
☐ 589 William Brennan	.03	.01	.00
☐ 590 German Gonzalez	.03	.01	.00
☐ 591 Ernie Whitt DP	.03	.01	.00
☐ 592 Jeff Blauser	.06	.03	.01
☐ 593 Spike Owen DP	.03	.01	.00
☐ 594 Matt Williams	.15	.07	.02
☐ 595 Lloyd McClendon DP	.03	.01	.00
☐ 596 Steve Ontiveros	.03	.01	.00
☐ 597 Scott Medvin	.03	.01	.00
☐ 598 Hipolito Pena DP	.03	.01	.00
☐ 599 Jerald Clark DP	.12	.05	.02
☐ 600A Checklist Card DP (635 Kurt Schilling)	.30	.03	.01
☐ 600B Checklist Card DP (635 Curt Schilling; MVP's not listed on checklist card)	.05	.01	.00
☐ 600C Checklist Card DP (635 Curt Schilling; MVP's listed following 660)	.05	.01	.00
☐ 601 Carmelo Martinez DP	.03	.01	.00
☐ 602 Mike LaCoss	.03	.01	.00
☐ 603 Mike Devereaux	.15	.07	.02
☐ 604 Alex Madrid DP	.03	.01	.00
☐ 605 Gary Redus DP	.03	.01	.00
☐ 606 Lance Johnson	.06	.03	.01
☐ 607 Terry Clark DP	.03	.01	.00
☐ 608 Manny Trillo DP	.03	.01	.00
☐ 609 Scott Jordan	.10	.05	.01
☐ 610 Jay Howell DP	.03	.01	.00
☐ 611 Francisco Melendez	.03	.01	.00
☐ 612 Mike Boddicker	.03	.01	.00
☐ 613 Kevin Brown DP	.25	.11	.03
☐ 614 Dave Valle	.03	.01	.00
☐ 615 Tim Laudner DP	.03	.01	.00
☐ 616 Andy Nezelek UER (Wrong birthdate)	.03	.01	.00
☐ 617 Chuck Crim	.03	.01	.00
☐ 618 Jack Savage DP	.03	.01	.00
☐ 619 Adam Peterson	.03	.01	.00
☐ 620 Todd Stottlemyre	.10	.05	.01
☐ 621 Lance Blankenship	.10	.05	.01
☐ 622 Miguel Garcia DP	.03	.01	.00
☐ 623 Keith A. Miller DP	.03	.01	.00
☐ 624 Ricky Jordan DP	.10	.05	.01
☐ 625 Ernest Riles DP	.03	.01	.00
☐ 626 John Moses DP	.03	.01	.00
☐ 627 Nelson Liriano DP	.03	.01	.00
☐ 628 Mike Smithson DP	.03	.01	.00
☐ 629 Scott Sanderson	.03	.01	.00
☐ 630 Dale Mohorcic	.03	.01	.00
☐ 631 Marvin Freeman DP	.03	.01	.00
☐ 632 Mike Young DP	.03	.01	.00
☐ 633 Dennis Lamp	.03	.01	.00
☐ 634 Dante Bichette DP	.25	.11	.03
☐ 635 Curt Schilling DP	.30	.14	.04
☐ 636 Scott May DP	.03	.01	.00
☐ 637 Mike Schooler	.10	.05	.01
☐ 638 Rick Leach	.03	.01	.00
☐ 639 Tom Lampkin UER (Throws Left, should be Throws Right)	.03	.01	.00
☐ 640 Brian Meyer	.03	.01	.00
☐ 641 Brian Harper	.06	.03	.01
☐ 642 John Smoltz	.60	.25	.08
☐ 643 Jose: 40/40 Club (Jose Canseco)	.20	.09	.03

☐ 644 Bill Schroeder	.03	.01	.00
☐ 645 Edgar Martinez	.40	.18	.05
☐ 646 Dennis Cook	.10	.05	.01
☐ 647 Barry Jones	.03	.01	.00
☐ 648 Orel: 59 and Counting (Orel Hershiser)	.06	.03	.01
☐ 649 Rod Nichols	.03	.01	.00
☐ 650 Jody Davis	.03	.01	.00
☐ 651 Bob Milacki	.10	.05	.01
☐ 652 Mike Jackson	.03	.01	.00
☐ 653 Derek Lilliquist	.10	.05	.01
☐ 654 Paul Mirabella	.03	.01	.00
☐ 655 Mike Diaz	.03	.01	.00
☐ 656 Jeff Musselman	.03	.01	.00
☐ 657 Jerry Reed	.03	.01	.00
☐ 658 Kevin Blankenship	.03	.01	.00
☐ 659 Wayne Tolleson	.03	.01	.00
☐ 660 Eric Hetzel	.03	.01	.00
☐ BC1 Kirby Puckett	.20	.09	.03
☐ BC2 Mike Scott	.05	.02	.01
☐ BC3 Joe Carter	.10	.05	.01
☐ BC4 Orel Hershiser	.05	.02	.01
☐ BC5 Jose Canseco	.20	.09	.03
☐ BC6 Darryl Strawberry	.12	.05	.02
☐ BC7 George Brett	.10	.05	.01
☐ BC8 Andre Dawson	.10	.05	.01
☐ BC9 Paul Molitor UER (Brewers logo missing the word Milwaukee)	.08	.04	.01
☐ BC10 Andy Van Slyke	.08	.04	.01
☐ BC11 Dave Winfield	.10	.05	.01
☐ BC12 Kevin Gross	.05	.02	.01
☐ BC13 Mike Greenwell	.08	.04	.01
☐ BC14 Ozzie Smith	.10	.05	.01
☐ BC15 Cal Ripken	.25	.11	.03
☐ BC16 Andres Galarraga	.05	.02	.01
☐ BC17 Alan Trammell	.08	.04	.01
☐ BC18 Kal Daniels	.05	.02	.01
☐ BC19 Fred McGriff	.12	.05	.02
☐ BC20 Tony Gwynn	.12	.05	.02
☐ BC21 Wally Joyner DP	.08	.04	.01
☐ BC22 Will Clark DP	.15	.07	.02
☐ BC23 Ozzie Guillen	.05	.02	.01
☐ BC24 Gerald Perry DP	.05	.02	.01
☐ BC25 Alvin Davis DP	.05	.02	.01
☐ BC26 Ruben Sierra	.15	.07	.02

1989 Donruss All-Stars

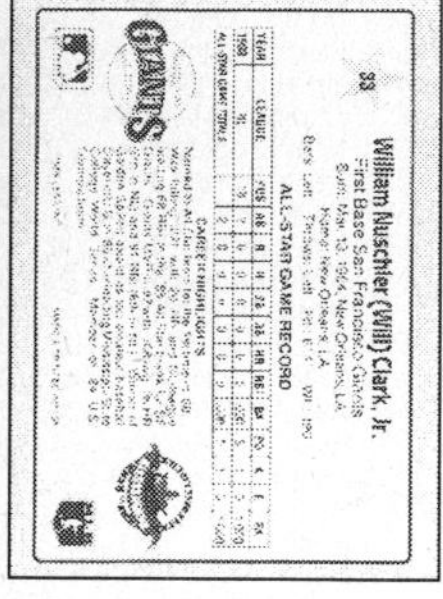

These All-Stars are standard size, 2 1/2" by 3 1/2" and very similar in design to the regular issue of 1989 Donruss. The set is distinguished by the presence of the respective League logos in the lower right corner of each obverse. The cards are numbered on the backs. The players chosen for the set are essentially the participants at the previous year's All-Star Game. Individual wax packs of All Stars (suggested retail price of 35 cents) contained one Pop-Up, five All-Star cards, and a Warren Spahn puzzle card.

	MT	EX-MT	VG
COMPLETE SET (64)	8.00	3.60	1.00
COMMON PLAYER (1-64)	.07	.03	.01
☐ 1 Mark McGwire	.60	.25	.08
☐ 2 Jose Canseco	.75	.35	.09
☐ 3 Paul Molitor	.15	.07	.02
☐ 4 Rickey Henderson	.60	.25	.08
☐ 5 Cal Ripken	1.00	.45	.13
☐ 6 Dave Winfield	.30	.14	.04
☐ 7 Wade Boggs	.50	.23	.06
☐ 8 Frank Viola	.12	.05	.02
☐ 9 Terry Steinbach	.10	.05	.01
☐ 10 Tom Kelly MG	.07	.03	.01
☐ 11 George Brett	.50	.23	.06
☐ 12 Doyle Alexander	.07	.03	.01
☐ 13 Gary Gaetti	.10	.05	.01
☐ 14 Roger Clemens	.90	.40	.11
☐ 15 Mike Greenwell	.30	.14	.04
☐ 16 Dennis Eckersley	.25	.11	.03
☐ 17 Carney Lansford	.10	.05	.01
☐ 18 Mark Gubicza	.07	.03	.01
☐ 19 Tim Laudner	.07	.03	.01
☐ 20 Doug Jones	.10	.05	.01
☐ 21 Don Mattingly	.75	.35	.09
☐ 22 Dan Plesac	.10	.05	.01
☐ 23 Kirby Puckett	.75	.35	.09
☐ 24 Jeff Reardon	.20	.09	.03
☐ 25 Johnny Ray	.07	.03	.01
☐ 26 Jeff Russell	.10	.05	.01
☐ 27 Harold Reynolds	.10	.05	.01
☐ 28 Dave Stieb	.10	.05	.01
☐ 29 Kurt Stillwell	.07	.03	.01
☐ 30 Jose Canseco	.75	.35	.09
☐ 31 Terry Steinbach	.10	.05	.01
☐ 32 AL Checklist	.07	.03	.01
☐ 33 Will Clark	.75	.35	.09
☐ 34 Darryl Strawberry	.60	.25	.08
☐ 35 Ryne Sandberg	.90	.40	.11
☐ 36 Andre Dawson	.35	.16	.04
☐ 37 Ozzie Smith	.35	.16	.04
☐ 38 Vince Coleman	.15	.07	.02
☐ 39 Bobby Bonilla	.35	.16	.04
☐ 40 Dwight Gooden	.30	.14	.04
☐ 41 Gary Carter	.20	.09	.03
☐ 42 Whitey Herzog MG	.07	.03	.01
☐ 43 Shawon Dunston	.15	.07	.02
☐ 44 David Cone	.45	.20	.06
☐ 45 Andres Galarraga	.15	.07	.02
☐ 46 Mark Davis	.07	.03	.01
☐ 47 Barry Larkin	.25	.11	.03
☐ 48 Kevin Gross	.10	.05	.01
☐ 49 Vance Law	.07	.03	.01
☐ 50 Orel Hershiser	.25	.11	.03
☐ 51 Willie McGee	.10	.05	.01
☐ 52 Danny Jackson	.07	.03	.01
☐ 53 Rafael Palmeiro	.35	.16	.04
☐ 54 Bob Knepper	.07	.03	.01
☐ 55 Lance Parrish	.10	.05	.01
☐ 56 Greg Maddux	.35	.16	.04
☐ 57 Gerald Perry	.07	.03	.01
☐ 58 Bob Walk	.07	.03	.01
☐ 59 Chris Sabo	.35	.16	.04
☐ 60 Todd Worrell	.15	.07	.02
☐ 61 Andy Van Slyke	.20	.09	.03
☐ 62 Ozzie Smith	.35	.16	.04
☐ 63 Riverfront Stadium	.07	.03	.01
☐ 64 NL Checklist	.07	.03	.01

1989 Donruss Baseball's Best

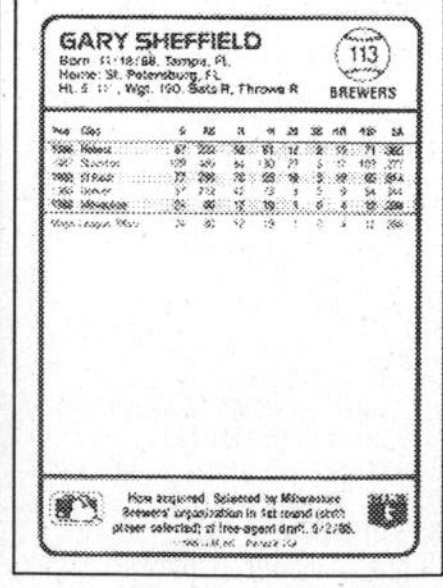

The 1989 Donruss Baseball's Best set contains 336 standard-size (2 1/2" by 3 1/2") glossy cards. The fronts are green and yellow, and the backs feature career highlight information. The backs are green, and feature vertically oriented career stats. The cards were distributed as a set in a blister pack through various retail and department store chains.

	MT	EX-MT	VG
COMPLETE SET (336)	16.00	7.25	2.00
COMMON PLAYER (1-336)	.04	.02	.01
☐ 1 Don Mattingly	.75	.35	.09
☐ 2 Tom Glavine	.75	.35	.09
☐ 3 Bert Blyleven	.10	.05	.01
☐ 4 Andre Dawson	.30	.14	.04
☐ 5 Pete O'Brien	.04	.02	.01
☐ 6 Eric Davis	.20	.09	.03
☐ 7 George Brett	.50	.23	.06
☐ 8 Glenn Davis	.15	.07	.02
☐ 9 Ellis Burks	.20	.09	.03
☐ 10 Kirk Gibson	.10	.05	.01
☐ 11 Carlton Fisk	.35	.16	.04
☐ 12 Andres Galarraga	.10	.05	.01
☐ 13 Alan Trammell	.15	.07	.02
☐ 14 Dwight Gooden	.25	.11	.03
☐ 15 Paul Molitor	.20	.09	.03
☐ 16 Roger McDowell	.04	.02	.01
☐ 17 Doug Drabek	.15	.07	.02
☐ 18 Kent Hrbek	.10	.05	.01
☐ 19 Vince Coleman	.15	.07	.02
☐ 20 Steve Sax	.15	.07	.02
☐ 21 Roberto Alomar	.75	.35	.09
☐ 22 Carney Lansford	.07	.03	.01
☐ 23 Will Clark	.75	.35	.09
☐ 24 Alvin Davis	.04	.02	.01
☐ 25 Bobby Thigpen	.07	.03	.01
☐ 26 Ryne Sandberg	.90	.40	.11
☐ 27 Devon White	.10	.05	.01
☐ 28 Mike Greenwell	.20	.09	.03
☐ 29 Dale Murphy	.25	.11	.03
☐ 30 Jeff Ballard	.04	.02	.01
☐ 31 Kelly Gruber	.07	.03	.01
☐ 32 Julio Franco	.10	.05	.01
☐ 33 Bobby Bonilla	.25	.11	.03
☐ 34 Tim Wallach	.07	.03	.01
☐ 35 Lou Whitaker	.10	.05	.01
☐ 36 Jay Howell	.04	.02	.01
☐ 37 Greg Maddux	.30	.14	.04
☐ 38 Bill Doran	.04	.02	.01
☐ 39 Danny Tartabull	.25	.11	.03
☐ 40 Darryl Strawberry	.45	.20	.06
☐ 41 Ron Darling	.10	.05	.01
☐ 42 Tony Gwynn	.40	.18	.05
☐ 43 Mark McGwire	.60	.25	.08
☐ 44 Ozzie Smith	.30	.14	.04
☐ 45 Andy Van Slyke	.15	.07	.02
☐ 46 Juan Berenguer	.04	.02	.01
☐ 47 Von Hayes	.04	.02	.01
☐ 48 Tony Fernandez	.07	.03	.01
☐ 49 Eric Plunk	.04	.02	.01
☐ 50 Ernest Riles	.04	.02	.01
☐ 51 Harold Reynolds	.04	.02	.01
☐ 52 Andy Hawkins	.04	.02	.01
☐ 53 Robin Yount	.50	.23	.06
☐ 54 Danny Jackson	.07	.03	.01
☐ 55 Nolan Ryan	1.50	.65	.19
☐ 56 Joe Carter	.40	.18	.05
☐ 57 Jose Canseco	.75	.35	.09
☐ 58 Jody Davis	.04	.02	.01
☐ 59 Lance Parrish	.07	.03	.01
☐ 60 Mitch Williams	.07	.03	.01
☐ 61 Brook Jacoby	.04	.02	.01
☐ 62 Tom Browning	.07	.03	.01
☐ 63 Kurt Stillwell	.04	.02	.01
☐ 64 Rafael Ramirez	.04	.02	.01
☐ 65 Roger Clemens	.90	.40	.11
☐ 66 Mike Scioscia	.04	.02	.01
☐ 67 Dave Gallagher	.04	.02	.01
☐ 68 Mark Langston	.10	.05	.01
☐ 69 Chet Lemon	.04	.02	.01
☐ 70 Kevin McReynolds	.10	.05	.01
☐ 71 Rob Deer	.10	.05	.01
☐ 72 Tommy Herr	.04	.02	.01
☐ 73 Barry Bonds	.75	.35	.09
☐ 74 Frank Viola	.10	.05	.01
☐ 75 Pedro Guerrero	.07	.03	.01
☐ 76 Dave Righetti UER (ML total of 7 wins incorrect)	.07	.03	.01
☐ 77 Bruce Hurst	.07	.03	.01
☐ 78 Rickey Henderson	.60	.25	.08
☐ 79 Robby Thompson	.04	.02	.01
☐ 80 Randy Johnson	.15	.07	.02
☐ 81 Harold Baines	.10	.05	.01
☐ 82 Calvin Schiraldi	.04	.02	.01
☐ 83 Kirk McCaskill	.07	.03	.01
☐ 84 Lee Smith	.15	.07	.02
☐ 85 John Smoltz	.60	.25	.08
☐ 86 Mickey Tettleton	.15	.07	.02
☐ 87 Jimmy Key	.10	.05	.01
☐ 88 Rafael Palmeiro	.25	.11	.03
☐ 89 Sid Bream	.04	.02	.01
☐ 90 Dennis Martinez	.07	.03	.01
☐ 91 Frank Tanana	.07	.03	.01
☐ 92 Eddie Murray	.25	.11	.03
☐ 93 Shawon Dunston	.15	.07	.02
☐ 94 Mike Scott	.10	.05	.01
☐ 95 Bret Saberhagen	.20	.09	.03
☐ 96 David Cone	.35	.16	.04
☐ 97 Kevin Elster	.04	.02	.01
☐ 98 Jack Clark	.10	.05	.01
☐ 99 Dave Stewart	.15	.07	.02
☐ 100 Jose Oquendo	.04	.02	.01
☐ 101 Jose Lind	.04	.02	.01
☐ 102 Gary Gaetti	.07	.03	.01
☐ 103 Ricky Jordan	.15	.07	.02
☐ 104 Fred McGriff	.50	.23	.06
☐ 105 Don Slaught	.04	.02	.01
☐ 106 Jose Uribe	.04	.02	.01
☐ 107 Jeffrey Leonard	.04	.02	.01
☐ 108 Lee Guetterman	.04	.02	.01
☐ 109 Chris Bosio	.15	.07	.02
☐ 110 Barry Larkin	.25	.11	.03
☐ 111 Ruben Sierra	.45	.20	.06
☐ 112 Greg Swindell	.10	.05	.01
☐ 113 Gary Sheffield	1.00	.45	.13
☐ 114 Lonnie Smith	.07	.03	.01
☐ 115 Chili Davis	.07	.03	.01
☐ 116 Damon Berryhill	.07	.03	.01
☐ 117 Tom Candiotti	.07	.03	.01
☐ 118 Kal Daniels	.07	.03	.01
☐ 119 Mark Gubicza	.04	.02	.01
☐ 120 Jim Deshaies	.04	.02	.01
☐ 121 Dwight Evans	.10	.05	.01
☐ 122 Mike Morgan	.07	.03	.01
☐ 123 Dan Pasqua	.07	.03	.01
☐ 124 Bryn Smith	.04	.02	.01
☐ 125 Doyle Alexander	.04	.02	.01
☐ 126 Howard Johnson	.15	.07	.02
☐ 127 Chuck Crim	.04	.02	.01
☐ 128 Darren Daulton	.15	.07	.02
☐ 129 Jeff Robinson	.04	.02	.01
☐ 130 Kirby Puckett	.60	.25	.08
☐ 131 Joe Magrane	.04	.02	.01
☐ 132 Jesse Barfield	.07	.03	.01
☐ 133 Mark Davis UER (Photo actually Dave Leiper)	.10	.05	.01
☐ 134 Dennis Eckersley	.25	.11	.03
☐ 135 Mike Krukow	.04	.02	.01
☐ 136 Jay Buhner	.20	.09	.03
☐ 137 Ozzie Guillen	.07	.03	.01
☐ 138 Rick Sutcliffe	.07	.03	.01
☐ 139 Wally Joyner	.15	.07	.02
☐ 140 Wade Boggs	.40	.18	.05
☐ 141 Jeff Treadway	.04	.02	.01
☐ 142 Cal Ripken	.90	.40	.11
☐ 143 Dave Stieb	.07	.03	.01
☐ 144 Pete Incaviglia	.07	.03	.01
☐ 145 Bob Walk	.04	.02	.01
☐ 146 Nelson Santovenia	.04	.02	.01
☐ 147 Mike Heath	.04	.02	.01
☐ 148 Willie Randolph	.07	.03	.01
☐ 149 Paul Kilgus	.04	.02	.01
☐ 150 Billy Hatcher	.07	.03	.01
☐ 151 Steve Farr	.04	.02	.01
☐ 152 Gregg Jefferies	.50	.23	.06
☐ 153 Randy Myers	.10	.05	.01
☐ 154 Garry Templeton	.04	.02	.01
☐ 155 Walt Weiss	.15	.07	.02
☐ 156 Terry Pendleton	.20	.09	.03
☐ 157 John Smiley	.15	.07	.02
☐ 158 Greg Gagne	.04	.02	.01
☐ 159 Len Dykstra	.15	.07	.02
☐ 160 Nelson Liriano	.04	.02	.01
☐ 161 Alvaro Espinoza	.04	.02	.01
☐ 162 Rick Reuschel	.07	.03	.01
☐ 163 Omar Vizquel UER (Photo actually Darnell Coles)	.20	.09	.03
☐ 164 Clay Parker	.04	.02	.01
☐ 165 Dan Plesac	.04	.02	.01
☐ 166 John Franco	.07	.03	.01
☐ 167 Scott Fletcher	.04	.02	.01
☐ 168 Cory Snyder	.07	.03	.01
☐ 169 Bo Jackson	.90	.40	.11
☐ 170 Tommy Gregg	.04	.02	.01
☐ 171 Jim Abbott	.90	.40	.11
☐ 172 Jerome Walton	.10	.05	.01

☐ 173 Doug Jones .04 .02 .01
☐ 174 Todd Benzinger .04 .02 .01
☐ 175 Frank White .04 .02 .01
☐ 176 Craig Biggio .40 .18 .05
☐ 177 John Dopson .04 .02 .01
☐ 178 Alfredo Griffin .04 .02 .01
☐ 179 Melido Perez .15 .07 .02
☐ 180 Tim Burke .04 .02 .01
☐ 181 Matt Nokes .07 .03 .01
☐ 182 Gary Carter .20 .09 .03
☐ 183 Ted Higuera .07 .03 .01
☐ 184 Ken Howell .04 .02 .01
☐ 185 Rey Quinones .04 .02 .01
☐ 186 Wally Backman .04 .02 .01
☐ 187 Tom Brunansky .07 .03 .01
☐ 188 Steve Balboni .04 .02 .01
☐ 189 Marvell Wynne .04 .02 .01
☐ 190 Dave Henderson .07 .03 .01
☐ 191 Don Robinson .04 .02 .01
☐ 192 Ken Griffey Jr. 4.00 1.80 .50
☐ 193 Ivan Calderon .07 .03 .01
☐ 194 Mike Bielecki .07 .03 .01
☐ 195 Johnny Ray .04 .02 .01
☐ 196 Rob Murphy .04 .02 .01
☐ 197 Andres Thomas .04 .02 .01
☐ 198 Phil Bradley .04 .02 .01
☐ 199 Junior Felix .25 .11 .03
☐ 200 Jeff Russell .07 .03 .01
☐ 201 Mike LaValliere .04 .02 .01
☐ 202 Kevin Gross .07 .03 .01
☐ 203 Keith Moreland .04 .02 .01
☐ 204 Mike Marshall .07 .03 .01
☐ 205 Dwight Smith .15 .07 .02
☐ 206 Jim Clancy .04 .02 .01
☐ 207 Kevin Seitzer .07 .03 .01
☐ 208 Keith Hernandez .10 .05 .01
☐ 209 Bob Ojeda .07 .03 .01
☐ 210 Ed Whitson .07 .03 .01
☐ 211 Tony Phillips .07 .03 .01
☐ 212 Milt Thompson .04 .02 .01
☐ 213 Randy Kramer .04 .02 .01
☐ 214 Randy Bush .04 .02 .01
☐ 215 Randy Ready .04 .02 .01
☐ 216 Duane Ward .04 .02 .01
☐ 217 Jimmy Jones .07 .03 .01
☐ 218 Scott Garrelts .04 .02 .01
☐ 219 Scott Bankhead .10 .05 .01
☐ 220 Lance McCullers .04 .02 .01
☐ 221 B.J. Surhoff .07 .03 .01
☐ 222 Chris Sabo .15 .07 .02
☐ 223 Steve Buechele .04 .02 .01
☐ 224 Joel Skinner .04 .02 .01
☐ 225 Orel Hershiser .15 .07 .02
☐ 226 Derek Lilliquist .10 .05 .01
☐ 227 Claudell Washington .04 .02 .01
☐ 228 Lloyd McClendon .04 .02 .01
☐ 229 Felix Fermin .04 .02 .01
☐ 230 Paul O'Neill .15 .07 .02
☐ 231 Charlie Leibrandt .04 .02 .01
☐ 232 Dave Smith .04 .02 .01
☐ 233 Bob Stanley .04 .02 .01
☐ 234 Tim Belcher .10 .05 .01
☐ 235 Eric King .07 .03 .01
☐ 236 Spike Owen .04 .02 .01
☐ 237 Mike Henneman .10 .05 .01
☐ 238 Juan Samuel .07 .03 .01
☐ 239 Greg Brock .04 .02 .01
☐ 240 John Kruk .15 .07 .02
☐ 241 Glenn Wilson .04 .02 .01
☐ 242 Jeff Reardon .15 .07 .02
☐ 243 Todd Worrell .10 .05 .01
☐ 244 Dave LaPoint .04 .02 .01
☐ 245 Walt Terrell .04 .02 .01
☐ 246 Mike Moore .07 .03 .01
☐ 247 Kelly Downs .07 .03 .01
☐ 248 Dave Valle .04 .02 .01
☐ 249 Ron Kittle .10 .05 .01
☐ 250 Steve Wilson .07 .03 .01
☐ 251 Dick Schofield .04 .02 .01
☐ 252 Marty Barrett .04 .02 .01
☐ 253 Dion James .04 .02 .01
☐ 254 Bob Milacki .04 .02 .01
☐ 255 Ernie Whitt .04 .02 .01
☐ 256 Kevin Brown .25 .11 .03
☐ 257 R.J. Reynolds .04 .02 .01
☐ 258 Tim Raines .15 .07 .02
☐ 259 Frank Williams .04 .02 .01
☐ 260 Jose Gonzalez .04 .02 .01
☐ 261 Mitch Webster .04 .02 .01
☐ 262 Ken Caminiti .04 .02 .01
☐ 263 Bob Boone .07 .03 .01
☐ 264 Dave Magadan .07 .03 .01
☐ 265 Rick Aguilera .10 .05 .01
☐ 266 Chris James .04 .02 .01
☐ 267 Bob Welch .10 .05 .01
☐ 268 Ken Dayley .04 .02 .01
☐ 269 Junior Ortiz .04 .02 .01
☐ 270 Allan Anderson .04 .02 .01
☐ 271 Steve Jeltz .04 .02 .01
☐ 272 George Bell .15 .07 .02
☐ 273 Roberto Kelly .30 .14 .04
☐ 274 Brett Butler .10 .05 .01
☐ 275 Mike Schooler .10 .05 .01
☐ 276 Ken Phelps .04 .02 .01
☐ 277 Glenn Braggs .07 .03 .01
☐ 278 Jose Rijo .15 .07 .02
☐ 279 Bobby Witt .10 .05 .01
☐ 280 Jerry Browne .07 .03 .01
☐ 281 Kevin Mitchell .30 .14 .04
☐ 282 Craig Worthington .07 .03 .01
☐ 283 Greg Minton .04 .02 .01
☐ 284 Nick Esasky .04 .02 .01
☐ 285 John Farrell .04 .02 .01
☐ 286 Rick Mahler .04 .02 .01
☐ 287 Tom Gordon .15 .07 .02
☐ 288 Gerald Young .04 .02 .01
☐ 289 Jody Reed .07 .03 .01
☐ 290 Jeff Hamilton .04 .02 .01
☐ 291 Gerald Perry .04 .02 .01
☐ 292 Hubie Brooks .04 .02 .01
☐ 293 Bo Diaz .04 .02 .01
☐ 294 Terry Puhl .04 .02 .01
☐ 295 Jim Gantner .04 .02 .01
☐ 296 Jeff Parrett .04 .02 .01
☐ 297 Mike Boddicker .04 .02 .01
☐ 298 Dan Gladden .04 .02 .01
☐ 299 Tony Pena .04 .02 .01
☐ 300 Checklist Card .04 .02 .01
☐ 301 Tom Henke .10 .05 .01
☐ 302 Pascual Perez .04 .02 .01
☐ 303 Steve Bedrosian .04 .02 .01
☐ 304 Ken Hill .10 .05 .01
☐ 305 Jerry Reuss .04 .02 .01
☐ 306 Jim Eisenreich .07 .03 .01
☐ 307 Jack Howell .04 .02 .01
☐ 308 Rick Cerone .04 .02 .01
☐ 309 Tim Leary .07 .03 .01
☐ 310 Joe Orsulak .07 .03 .01
☐ 311 Jim Dwyer .04 .02 .01
☐ 312 Geno Petralli .04 .02 .01
☐ 313 Rick Honeycutt .04 .02 .01
☐ 314 Tom Foley .04 .02 .01
☐ 315 Kenny Rogers .04 .02 .01
☐ 316 Mike Flanagan .07 .03 .01
☐ 317 Bryan Harvey .30 .14 .04
☐ 318 Billy Ripken .04 .02 .01
☐ 319 Jeff Montgomery .10 .05 .01
☐ 320 Erik Hanson .10 .05 .01
☐ 321 Brian Downing .04 .02 .01
☐ 322 Gregg Olson .35 .16 .04
☐ 323 Terry Steinbach .10 .05 .01
☐ 324 Sammy Sosa .30 .14 .04
☐ 325 Gene Harris .10 .05 .01
☐ 326 Mike Devereaux .15 .07 .02
☐ 327 Dennis Cook .07 .03 .01
☐ 328 David Wells .07 .03 .01
☐ 329 Checklist Card .04 .02 .01
☐ 330 Kirt Manwaring .04 .02 .01
☐ 331 Jim Presley .04 .02 .01
☐ 332 Checklist Card .04 .02 .01
☐ 333 Chuck Finley .10 .05 .01
☐ 334 Rob Dibble .20 .09 .03
☐ 335 Cecil Espy .04 .02 .01
☐ 336 Dave Parker .15 .07 .02

1989 Donruss Grand Slammers

The 1989 Donruss Grand Slammers set contains 12 standard-size (2 1/2" by 3 1/2") cards. Each card in the set can be found with five different colored border combinations, but no color combination of borders appears to be scarcer than any other. The set includes cards for each player who hit one or more grand slams in 1988. The backs detail the players' grand slams. The cards were distributed one per cello pack as well as an insert (complete) set in each factory set.

	MT	EX-MT	VG
COMPLETE SET (12)	2.50	1.15	.30
COMMON PLAYER (1-12)	.10	.05	.01
☐ 1 Jose Canseco	.90	.40	.11
☐ 2 Mike Marshall	.10	.05	.01
☐ 3 Walt Weiss	.15	.07	.02
☐ 4 Kevin McReynolds	.20	.09	.03
☐ 5 Mike Greenwell	.30	.14	.04
☐ 6 Dave Winfield	.40	.18	.05
☐ 7 Mark McGwire	.75	.35	.09
☐ 8 Keith Hernandez	.15	.07	.02
☐ 9 Franklin Stubbs	.10	.05	.01
☐ 10 Danny Tartabull	.35	.16	.04
☐ 11 Jesse Barfield	.15	.07	.02
☐ 12 Ellis Burks	.25	.11	.03

1989 Donruss Pop-Ups

These Pop-Ups are borderless and standard size, 2 1/2" by 3 1/2". The cards are unnumbered; however the All Star checklist card lists the same numbers as the All Star cards. Those numbers are used below for reference. The players chosen for the set are essentially the starting lineups for the previous year's All-Star Game. Individual wax packs of All Stars (suggested retail price of 35 cents) contained one Pop-Up, five All-Star cards, and a puzzle card.

	MT	EX-MT	VG
COMPLETE SET (20)	5.00	2.30	.60
COMMON PLAYER	.10	.05	.01
☐ 1 Mark McGwire	.75	.35	.09
☐ 2 Jose Canseco	.90	.40	.11
☐ 3 Paul Molitor	.20	.09	.03
☐ 4 Rickey Henderson	.75	.35	.09
☐ 5 Cal Ripken	1.25	.55	.16
☐ 6 Dave Winfield	.35	.16	.04
☐ 7 Wade Boggs	.60	.25	.08
☐ 8 Frank Viola	.15	.07	.02
☐ 9 Terry Steinbach	.15	.07	.02
☐ 10 Tom Kelly MG	.10	.05	.01
☐ 33 Will Clark	.90	.40	.11
☐ 34 Darryl Strawberry	.75	.35	.09
☐ 35 Ryne Sandberg	1.00	.45	.13
☐ 36 Andre Dawson	.40	.18	.05
☐ 37 Ozzie Smith	.40	.18	.05
☐ 38 Vince Coleman	.20	.09	.03
☐ 39 Bobby Bonilla	.40	.18	.05
☐ 40 Dwight Gooden	.35	.16	.04
☐ 41 Gary Carter	.25	.11	.03
☐ 42 Whitey Herzog MG	.10	.05	.01

1989 Donruss Rookies

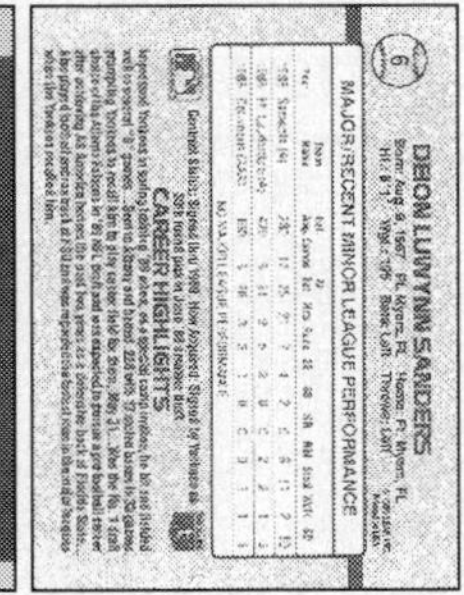

The 1989 Donruss Rookies set contains 56 standard-size (2 1/2" by 3 1/2") cards. The fronts have green and black borders; the backs are green and feature career highlights. The cards were distributed as a boxed set through the Donruss Dealer Network. The key Rookie Cards in this set are Jim Abbott, Junior Felix, Steve Finley, Deion Sanders, and Jerome Walton.

	MT	EX-MT	VG
COMPLETE SET (56)	15.00	6.75	1.90
COMMON PLAYER (1-56)	.05	.02	.01
☐ 1 Gary Sheffield	3.00	1.35	.40
☐ 2 Gregg Jefferies	.35	.16	.04
☐ 3 Ken Griffey Jr.	8.00	3.60	1.00
☐ 4 Tom Gordon	.10	.05	.01
☐ 5 Billy Spiers	.10	.05	.01
☐ 6 Deion Sanders	2.25	1.00	.30
☐ 7 Donn Pall	.05	.02	.01
☐ 8 Steve Carter	.05	.02	.01
☐ 9 Francisco Oliveras	.05	.02	.01
☐ 10 Steve Wilson	.05	.02	.01
☐ 11 Bob Geren	.05	.02	.01
☐ 12 Tony Castillo	.05	.02	.01
☐ 13 Kenny Rogers	.05	.02	.01
☐ 14 Carlos Martinez	.12	.05	.02
☐ 15 Edgar Martinez	.50	.23	.06
☐ 16 Jim Abbott	1.25	.55	.16
☐ 17 Torey Lovullo	.05	.02	.01
☐ 18 Mark Carreon	.05	.02	.01
☐ 19 Geronimo Berroa	.05	.02	.01
☐ 20 Luis Medina	.05	.02	.01
☐ 21 Sandy Alomar Jr.	.25	.11	.03
☐ 22 Bob Milacki	.10	.05	.01
☐ 23 Joe Girardi	.15	.07	.02
☐ 24 German Gonzalez	.05	.02	.01
☐ 25 Craig Worthington	.05	.02	.01
☐ 26 Jerome Walton	.10	.05	.01
☐ 27 Gary Wayne	.05	.02	.01
☐ 28 Tim Jones	.05	.02	.01
☐ 29 Dante Bichette	.08	.04	.01
☐ 30 Alexis Infante	.05	.02	.01
☐ 31 Ken Hill	.40	.18	.05
☐ 32 Dwight Smith	.10	.05	.01
☐ 33 Luis de los Santos	.05	.02	.01
☐ 34 Eric Yelding	.05	.02	.01
☐ 35 Gregg Olson	.50	.23	.06
☐ 36 Phil Stephenson	.05	.02	.01
☐ 37 Ken Patterson	.05	.02	.01
☐ 38 Rick Wrona	.05	.02	.01
☐ 39 Mike Brumley	.05	.02	.01
☐ 40 Cris Carpenter	.10	.05	.01
☐ 41 Jeff Brantley	.10	.05	.01
☐ 42 Ron Jones	.05	.02	.01
☐ 43 Randy Johnson	.15	.07	.02
☐ 44 Kevin Brown	.30	.14	.04
☐ 45 Ramon Martinez	.50	.23	.06
☐ 46 Greg W.Harris	.08	.04	.01

	MT	EX-MT	VG
☐ 47 Steve Finley	.40	.18	.05
☐ 48 Randy Kramer	.05	.02	.01
☐ 49 Erik Hanson	.20	.09	.03
☐ 50 Matt Merullo	.10	.05	.01
☐ 51 Mike Devereaux	.35	.16	.04
☐ 52 Clay Parker	.05	.02	.01
☐ 53 Omar Vizquel	.15	.07	.02
☐ 54 Derek Lilliquist	.10	.05	.01
☐ 55 Junior Felix	.25	.11	.03
☐ 56 Checklist Card	.08	.01	.00

1989 Donruss Super DK's

This 26-player card set was available through a mail-in offer detailed on the wax packs. The set was sent in return for 8.00 and three wrappers plus 2.00 postage and handling. The set features the popular Diamond King subseries in large (approximately 4 7/8" by 6 13/16") form. Dick Perez of Perez-Steele Galleries did another outstanding job on the artwork. The cards are essentially a large version of the Donruss regular issue Diamond Kings.

	MT	EX-MT	VG
COMPLETE SET (26)	10.00	4.50	1.25
COMMON PLAYER (1-26)	.30	.14	.04
☐ 1 Mike Greenwell	.50	.23	.06
☐ 2 Bobby Bonilla	.60	.25	.08
☐ 3 Pete Incaviglia	.40	.18	.05
☐ 4 Chris Sabo	.60	.25	.08
☐ 5 Robin Yount	.75	.35	.09
☐ 6 Tony Gwynn	.75	.35	.09
☐ 7 Carlton Fisk	.60	.25	.08
☐ 8 Cory Snyder	.40	.18	.05
☐ 9 David Cone	.60	.25	.08
☐ 10 Kevin Seitzer	.40	.18	.05
☐ 11 Rick Reuschel	.30	.14	.04
☐ 12 Johnny Ray	.30	.14	.04
☐ 13 Dave Schmidt	.30	.14	.04
☐ 14 Andres Galarraga	.40	.18	.05
☐ 15 Kirk Gibson	.40	.18	.05
☐ 16 Fred McGriff	.75	.35	.09
☐ 17 Mark Grace	1.00	.45	.13
☐ 18 Jeff M. Robinson	.30	.14	.04
☐ 19 Vince Coleman	.40	.18	.05
☐ 20 Dave Henderson	.40	.18	.05
☐ 21 Harold Reynolds	.30	.14	.04
☐ 22 Gerald Perry	.30	.14	.04
☐ 23 Frank Viola	.40	.18	.05
☐ 24 Steve Bedrosian	.30	.14	.04
☐ 25 Glenn Davis	.40	.18	.05
☐ 26 Don Mattingly	1.00	.45	.13

1989 Donruss Traded

The 1989 Donruss Traded set contains 56 standard-size (2 1/2" by 3 1/2") cards. The fronts have yellowish-orange borders; the backs are yellow and feature recent statistics. The cards were distributed as a boxed set. The set was

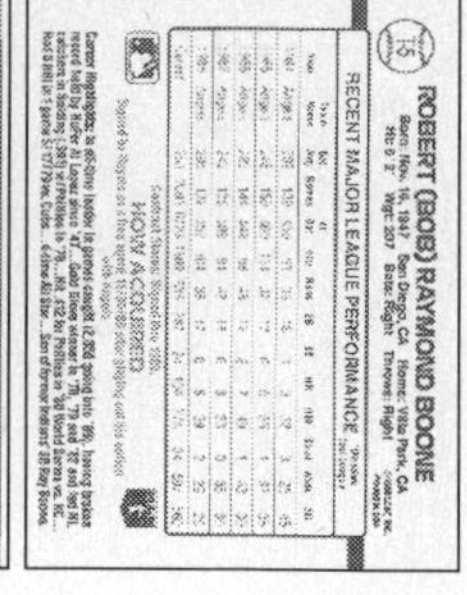

never very popular with collectors since it included (as the name implies) only traded players rather than rookies.

	MT	EX-MT	VG
COMPLETE SET (56)	4.00	1.80	.50
COMMON PLAYER (1-55)	.05	.02	.01
☐ 1 Jeffrey Leonard	.10	.05	.01
☐ 2 Jack Clark	.15	.07	.02
☐ 3 Kevin Gross	.10	.05	.01
☐ 4 Tommy Herr	.10	.05	.01
☐ 5 Bob Boone	.15	.07	.02
☐ 6 Rafael Palmeiro	.45	.20	.06
☐ 7 John Dopson	.05	.02	.01
☐ 8 Willie Randolph	.10	.05	.01
☐ 9 Chris Brown	.05	.02	.01
☐ 10 Wally Backman	.05	.02	.01
☐ 11 Steve Ontiveros	.05	.02	.01
☐ 12 Eddie Murray	.30	.14	.04
☐ 13 Lance McCullers	.05	.02	.01
☐ 14 Spike Owen	.05	.02	.01
☐ 15 Rob Murphy	.05	.02	.01
☐ 16 Pete O'Brien	.05	.02	.01
☐ 17 Ken Williams	.05	.02	.01
☐ 18 Nick Esasky	.05	.02	.01
☐ 19 Nolan Ryan	2.00	.90	.25
☐ 20 Brian Holton	.05	.02	.01
☐ 21 Mike Moore	.15	.07	.02
☐ 22 Joel Skinner	.05	.02	.01
☐ 23 Steve Sax	.15	.07	.02
☐ 24 Rick Mahler	.05	.02	.01
☐ 25 Mike Aldrete	.05	.02	.01
☐ 26 Jesse Orosco	.05	.02	.01
☐ 27 Dave LaPoint	.05	.02	.01
☐ 28 Walt Terrell	.05	.02	.01
☐ 29 Eddie Williams	.05	.02	.01
☐ 30 Mike Devereaux	.25	.11	.03
☐ 31 Julio Franco	.20	.09	.03
☐ 32 Jim Clancy	.05	.02	.01
☐ 33 Felix Fermin	.05	.02	.01
☐ 34 Curt Wilkerson	.05	.02	.01
☐ 35 Bert Blyleven	.15	.07	.02
☐ 36 Mel Hall	.15	.07	.02
☐ 37 Eric King	.05	.02	.01
☐ 38 Mitch Williams	.15	.07	.02
☐ 39 Jamie Moyer	.05	.02	.01
☐ 40 Rick Rhoden	.05	.02	.01
☐ 41 Phil Bradley	.10	.05	.01
☐ 42 Paul Kilgus	.05	.02	.01
☐ 43 Milt Thompson	.05	.02	.01
☐ 44 Jerry Browne	.15	.07	.02
☐ 45 Bruce Hurst	.10	.05	.01
☐ 46 Claudell Washington	.10	.05	.01
☐ 47 Todd Benzinger	.10	.05	.01
☐ 48 Steve Balboni	.05	.02	.01
☐ 49 Oddibe McDowell	.10	.05	.01
☐ 50 Charles Hudson	.05	.02	.01
☐ 51 Ron Kittle	.10	.05	.01
☐ 52 Andy Hawkins	.05	.02	.01
☐ 53 Tom Brookens	.05	.02	.01
☐ 54 Tom Niedenfuer	.05	.02	.01
☐ 55 Jeff Parrett	.05	.02	.01
☐ 56 Checklist Card	.05	.02	.01

1990 Donruss Previews

The 1990 Donruss Previews set contains 12 standard-size (2 1/2" by 3 1/2") cards. The bright red borders are exactly

like the regular 1990 Donruss cards, but many of the photos are different. The horizontally oriented backs are plain white with career highlights in black lettering. Two cards were sent to each dealer in the Donruss dealer network thus making it quite difficult to put together a set.

	MT	EX-MT	VG
COMPLETE SET (12)	900.00	400.00	115.00
COMMON PLAYER (1-12)	30.00	13.50	3.80
☐ 1 Todd Zeile (Not shown as Rated Rookie on front)	50.00	23.00	6.25
☐ 2 Ben McDonald	75.00	34.00	9.50
☐ 3 Bo Jackson	125.00	57.50	15.50
☐ 4 Will Clark	125.00	57.50	15.50
☐ 5 Dave Stewart	30.00	13.50	3.80
☐ 6 Kevin Mitchell	50.00	23.00	6.25
☐ 7 Nolan Ryan	300.00	135.00	38.00
☐ 8 Howard Johnson	40.00	18.00	5.00
☐ 9 Tony Gwynn	100.00	45.00	12.50
☐ 10 Jerome Walton (Shown ready to bunt)	40.00	18.00	5.00
☐ 11 Wade Boggs	100.00	45.00	12.50
☐ 12 Kirby Puckett	125.00	57.50	15.50

1990 Donruss

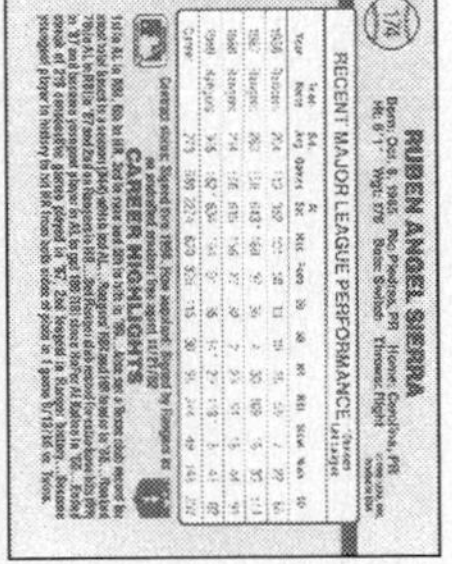

The 1990 Donruss set contains 716 standard-size (2 1/2" by 3 1/2") cards. The front borders are bright red. The horizontally oriented backs are amber. Cards numbered 1-26 are Diamond Kings; cards numbered 28-47 are Rated Rookies (RR). Numbered with the prefix "BC" for bonus card, a 26-card set featuring the most valuable player from each of the 26 teams was randomly inserted in all 1990 Donruss unopened pack formats. Card number 716 was added to the set shortly after the set's initial production, necessitating the checklist variation on card number 700. The set was the largest ever produced by Donruss, unfortunately it also had a large number of errors which were corrected after the cards were released. Every All-Star selection in the set has two versions, the statistical heading on the back is either "Recent Major League Performance" or "All-Star Game Performance." There are a number of cards that have been discovered to have minor printing flaws, which are insignificant variations, that collectors have found unworthy of price differentials. These very minor variations include numbers 1, 18, 154, 168, 206, 270, 321, 347, 405, 408, 425, 583, 585, 619, 637, 639, 699, 701, and 716. The factory sets were distributed without the Bonus Cards; thus there were again new checklist cards printed to reflect the exclusion of the Bonus Cards. These factory set checklist cards are the B variations below (except for 700C). The key Rookie Cards in this set are Delino DeShields, Juan Gonzalez, Marquis Grissom, Dave Justice, Ben McDonald, John Olerud, and Dean Palmer. The unusual number of cards in the set (716 plus 26 BC's, i.e., not divisible by 132) apparently led to 50 double-printed numbers, which are indicated in the checklists below (1990 Donruss and 1990 Donruss Bonus MVP's) by DP.

	MT	EX-MT	VG
COMPLETE SET (716)	15.00	6.75	1.90
COMPLETE FACT.SET (716)	15.00	6.75	1.90
COMMON PLAYER (1-716)	.04	.02	.01
COMPLETE MVP SET (26)	2.00	.90	.25
COMMON MVP (BC1-BC26)	.05	.02	.01
☐ 1 Bo Jackson DK	.12	.05	.02
☐ 2 Steve Sax DK	.05	.02	.01
☐ 3A Ruben Sierra DK ERR (No small line on top border on card back)	.50	.23	.06
☐ 3B Ruben Sierra DK COR	.25	.11	.03
☐ 4 Ken Griffey Jr. DK	.50	.23	.06
☐ 5 Mickey Tettleton DK	.05	.02	.01
☐ 6 Dave Stewart DK	.05	.02	.01
☐ 7 Jim Deshaies DK DP	.05	.02	.01
☐ 8 John Smoltz DK	.12	.05	.02
☐ 9 Mike Bielecki DK	.05	.02	.01
☐ 10A Brian Downing DK ERR (Reverse negative on card front)	.50	.23	.06
☐ 10B Brian Downing DK COR	.05	.02	.01
☐ 11 Kevin Mitchell DK	.08	.04	.01
☐ 12 Kelly Gruber DK	.05	.02	.01
☐ 13 Joe Magrane DK	.05	.02	.01
☐ 14 John Franco DK	.05	.02	.01
☐ 15 Ozzie Guillen DK	.05	.02	.01
☐ 16 Lou Whitaker DK	.05	.02	.01
☐ 17 John Smiley DK	.05	.02	.01
☐ 18 Howard Johnson DK	.05	.02	.01
☐ 19 Willie Randolph DK	.05	.02	.01
☐ 20 Chris Bosio DK	.05	.02	.01
☐ 21 Tommy Herr DK DP	.05	.02	.01
☐ 22 Dan Gladden DK	.05	.02	.01
☐ 23 Ellis Burks DK	.05	.02	.01
☐ 24 Pete O'Brien DK	.05	.02	.01
☐ 25 Bryn Smith DK	.05	.02	.01
☐ 26 Ed Whitson DK DP	.05	.02	.01
☐ 27 DK Checklist DP (Comments on Perez-Steele on back)	.04	.00	.00
☐ 28 Robin Ventura RR	.75	.35	.09
☐ 29 Todd Zeile RR	.15	.07	.02
☐ 30 Sandy Alomar Jr. RR	.10	.05	.01
☐ 31 Kent Mercker RR	.12	.05	.02
☐ 32 Ben McDonald RR UER (Middle name Benard, not Benjamin)	.50	.23	.06
☐ 33A Juan Gonzalez RR ERR (Reverse negative)	3.50	1.55	.45
☐ 33B Juan Gonzalez RR COR	1.75	.80	.22
☐ 34 Eric Anthony RR	.30	.14	.04
☐ 35 Mike Fetters RR	.10	.05	.01
☐ 36 Marquis Grissom RR	.60	.25	.08
☐ 37 Greg Vaughn RR	.15	.07	.02
☐ 38 Brian DuBois RR	.05	.02	.01
☐ 39 Steve Avery RR UER (Born in MI, not NJ)	.75	.35	.09
☐ 40 Mark Gardner RR	.12	.05	.02
☐ 41 Andy Benes RR	.20	.09	.03
☐ 42 Delino DeShields RR	.60	.25	.08
☐ 43 Scott Coolbaugh RR	.05	.02	.01
☐ 44 Pat Combs RR DP	.05	.02	.01
☐ 45 Alex Sanchez RR DP	.05	.02	.01
☐ 46 Kelly Mann RR DP	.05	.02	.01
☐ 47 Julio Machado RR DP	.05	.02	.01
☐ 48 Pete Incaviglia	.04	.02	.01

☐ 49	Shawon Dunston	.07	.03	.01
☐ 50	Jeff Treadway	.04	.02	.01
☐ 51	Jeff Ballard	.04	.02	.01
☐ 52	Claudell Washington	.04	.02	.01
☐ 53	Juan Samuel	.04	.02	.01
☐ 54	John Smiley	.07	.03	.01
☐ 55	Rob Deer	.07	.03	.01
☐ 56	Geno Petralli	.04	.02	.01
☐ 57	Chris Bosio	.04	.02	.01
☐ 58	Carlton Fisk	.10	.05	.01
☐ 59	Kirt Manwaring	.04	.02	.01
☐ 60	Chet Lemon	.04	.02	.01
☐ 61	Bo Jackson	.15	.07	.02
☐ 62	Doyle Alexander	.04	.02	.01
☐ 63	Pedro Guerrero	.07	.03	.01
☐ 64	Allan Anderson	.04	.02	.01
☐ 65	Greg W. Harris	.04	.02	.01
☐ 66	Mike Greenwell	.07	.03	.01
☐ 67	Walt Weiss	.04	.02	.01
☐ 68	Wade Boggs	.20	.09	.03
☐ 69	Jim Clancy	.04	.02	.01
☐ 70	Junior Felix	.07	.03	.01
☐ 71	Barry Larkin	.12	.05	.02
☐ 72	Dave LaPoint	.04	.02	.01
☐ 73	Joel Skinner	.04	.02	.01
☐ 74	Jesse Barfield	.04	.02	.01
☐ 75	Tommy Herr	.04	.02	.01
☐ 76	Ricky Jordan	.04	.02	.01
☐ 77	Eddie Murray	.10	.05	.01
☐ 78	Steve Sax	.07	.03	.01
☐ 79	Tim Belcher	.07	.03	.01
☐ 80	Danny Jackson	.04	.02	.01
☐ 81	Kent Hrbek	.07	.03	.01
☐ 82	Milt Thompson	.04	.02	.01
☐ 83	Brook Jacoby	.04	.02	.01
☐ 84	Mike Marshall	.04	.02	.01
☐ 85	Kevin Seitzer	.07	.03	.01
☐ 86	Tony Gwynn	.20	.09	.03
☐ 87	Dave Stieb	.07	.03	.01
☐ 88	Dave Smith	.04	.02	.01
☐ 89	Bret Saberhagen	.07	.03	.01
☐ 90	Alan Trammell	.07	.03	.01
☐ 91	Tony Phillips	.04	.02	.01
☐ 92	Doug Drabek	.07	.03	.01
☐ 93	Jeffrey Leonard	.04	.02	.01
☐ 94	Wally Joyner	.07	.03	.01
☐ 95	Carney Lansford	.07	.03	.01
☐ 96	Cal Ripken	.40	.18	.05
☐ 97	Andres Galarraga	.04	.02	.01
☐ 98	Kevin Mitchell	.10	.05	.01
☐ 99	Howard Johnson	.07	.03	.01
☐ 100A	Checklist Card (28-129)	.06	.01	.00
☐ 100B	Checklist Card (28-125)	.06	.01	.00
☐ 101	Melido Perez	.07	.03	.01
☐ 102	Spike Owen	.04	.02	.01
☐ 103	Paul Molitor	.10	.05	.01
☐ 104	Geronimo Berroa	.04	.02	.01
☐ 105	Ryne Sandberg	.35	.16	.04
☐ 106	Bryn Smith	.04	.02	.01
☐ 107	Steve Buechele	.04	.02	.01
☐ 108	Jim Abbott	.20	.09	.03
☐ 109	Alvin Davis	.04	.02	.01
☐ 110	Lee Smith	.07	.03	.01
☐ 111	Roberto Alomar	.40	.18	.05
☐ 112	Rick Reuschel	.04	.02	.01
☐ 113A	Kelly Gruber ERR (Born 2/22)	.07	.03	.01
☐ 113B	Kelly Gruber COR (Born 2/26; corrected in factory sets)	.07	.03	.01
☐ 114	Joe Carter	.20	.09	.03
☐ 115	Jose Rijo	.07	.03	.01
☐ 116	Greg Minton	.04	.02	.01
☐ 117	Bob Ojeda	.04	.02	.01
☐ 118	Glenn Davis	.07	.03	.01
☐ 119	Jeff Reardon	.07	.03	.01
☐ 120	Kurt Stillwell	.04	.02	.01
☐ 121	John Smoltz	.25	.11	.03
☐ 122	Dwight Evans	.07	.03	.01
☐ 123	Eric Yelding	.04	.02	.01
☐ 124	John Franco	.07	.03	.01
☐ 125	Jose Canseco	.30	.14	.04
☐ 126	Barry Bonds	.30	.14	.04
☐ 127	Lee Guetterman	.04	.02	.01
☐ 128	Jack Clark	.07	.03	.01
☐ 129	Dave Valle	.04	.02	.01
☐ 130	Hubie Brooks	.04	.02	.01
☐ 131	Ernest Riles	.04	.02	.01
☐ 132	Mike Morgan	.04	.02	.01
☐ 133	Steve Jeltz	.04	.02	.01
☐ 134	Jeff D. Robinson	.04	.02	.01
☐ 135	Ozzie Guillen	.04	.02	.01
☐ 136	Chili Davis	.07	.03	.01
☐ 137	Mitch Webster	.04	.02	.01
☐ 138	Jerry Browne	.04	.02	.01
☐ 139	Bo Diaz	.04	.02	.01
☐ 140	Robby Thompson	.04	.02	.01
☐ 141	Craig Worthington	.04	.02	.01
☐ 142	Julio Franco	.07	.03	.01
☐ 143	Brian Holman	.04	.02	.01
☐ 144	George Brett	.15	.07	.02
☐ 145	Tom Glavine	.25	.11	.03
☐ 146	Robin Yount	.15	.07	.02
☐ 147	Gary Carter	.07	.03	.01
☐ 148	Ron Kittle	.04	.02	.01
☐ 149	Tony Fernandez	.07	.03	.01
☐ 150	Dave Stewart	.07	.03	.01
☐ 151	Gary Gaetti	.04	.02	.01
☐ 152	Kevin Elster	.04	.02	.01
☐ 153	Gerald Perry	.04	.02	.01
☐ 154	Jesse Orosco	.04	.02	.01
☐ 155	Wally Backman	.04	.02	.01
☐ 156	Dennis Martinez	.07	.03	.01
☐ 157	Rick Sutcliffe	.07	.03	.01
☐ 158	Greg Maddux	.20	.09	.03
☐ 159	Andy Hawkins	.04	.02	.01
☐ 160	John Kruk	.07	.03	.01
☐ 161	Jose Oquendo	.04	.02	.01
☐ 162	John Dopson	.04	.02	.01
☐ 163	Joe Magrane	.04	.02	.01
☐ 164	Bill Ripken	.04	.02	.01
☐ 165	Fred Manrique	.04	.02	.01
☐ 166	Nolan Ryan UER (Did not lead NL in K's in '89 as he was in AL in '89)	.50	.23	.06
☐ 167	Damon Berryhill	.04	.02	.01
☐ 168	Dale Murphy	.10	.05	.01
☐ 169	Mickey Tettleton	.07	.03	.01
☐ 170A	Kirk McCaskill ERR (Born 4/19)	.04	.02	.01
☐ 170B	Kirk McCaskill COR (Born 4/9; corrected in factory sets)	.04	.02	.01
☐ 171	Dwight Gooden	.10	.05	.01
☐ 172	Jose Lind	.04	.02	.01
☐ 173	B.J. Surhoff	.04	.02	.01
☐ 174	Ruben Sierra	.20	.09	.03
☐ 175	Dan Plesac	.04	.02	.01
☐ 176	Dan Pasqua	.04	.02	.01
☐ 177	Kelly Downs	.04	.02	.01
☐ 178	Matt Nokes	.04	.02	.01
☐ 179	Luis Aquino	.04	.02	.01
☐ 180	Frank Tanana	.04	.02	.01
☐ 181	Tony Pena	.04	.02	.01
☐ 182	Dan Gladden	.04	.02	.01
☐ 183	Bruce Hurst	.07	.03	.01
☐ 184	Roger Clemens	.35	.16	.04
☐ 185	Mark McGwire	.30	.14	.04
☐ 186	Rob Murphy	.04	.02	.01
☐ 187	Jim Deshaies	.04	.02	.01
☐ 188	Fred McGriff	.20	.09	.03
☐ 189	Rob Dibble	.07	.03	.01
☐ 190	Don Mattingly	.20	.09	.03
☐ 191	Felix Fermin	.04	.02	.01
☐ 192	Roberto Kelly	.10	.05	.01
☐ 193	Dennis Cook	.04	.02	.01
☐ 194	Darren Daulton	.07	.03	.01
☐ 195	Alfredo Griffin	.04	.02	.01
☐ 196	Eric Plunk	.04	.02	.01
☐ 197	Orel Hershiser	.07	.03	.01
☐ 198	Paul O'Neill	.07	.03	.01
☐ 199	Randy Bush	.04	.02	.01
☐ 200A	Checklist Card (130-231)	.06	.01	.00
☐ 200B	Checklist Card (126-223)	.06	.01	.00
☐ 201	Ozzie Smith	.12	.05	.02
☐ 202	Pete O'Brien	.04	.02	.01
☐ 203	Jay Howell	.04	.02	.01
☐ 204	Mark Gubicza	.04	.02	.01
☐ 205	Ed Whitson	.04	.02	.01
☐ 206	George Bell	.07	.03	.01
☐ 207	Mike Scott	.04	.02	.01
☐ 208	Charlie Leibrandt	.04	.02	.01
☐ 209	Mike Heath	.04	.02	.01
☐ 210	Dennis Eckersley	.12	.05	.02
☐ 211	Mike LaValliere	.04	.02	.01
☐ 212	Darnell Coles	.04	.02	.01
☐ 213	Lance Parrish	.07	.03	.01
☐ 214	Mike Moore	.04	.02	.01
☐ 215	Steve Finley	.07	.03	.01
☐ 216	Tim Raines	.07	.03	.01
☐ 217A	Scott Garrelts ERR	.04	.02	.01

(Born 10/20)
☐ 217B Scott Garrelts COR .04 .02 .01
(Born 10/30; corrected in factory sets)
☐ 218 Kevin McReynolds .07 .03 .01
☐ 219 Dave Gallagher .04 .02 .01
☐ 220 Tim Wallach .07 .03 .01
☐ 221 Chuck Crim .04 .02 .01
☐ 222 Lonnie Smith .04 .02 .01
☐ 223 Andre Dawson .12 .05 .02
☐ 224 Nelson Santovenia .04 .02 .01
☐ 225 Rafael Palmeiro .10 .05 .01
☐ 226 Devon White .07 .03 .01
☐ 227 Harold Reynolds .04 .02 .01
☐ 228 Ellis Burks .07 .03 .01
☐ 229 Mark Parent .04 .02 .01
☐ 230 Will Clark .30 .14 .04
☐ 231 Jimmy Key .07 .03 .01
☐ 232 John Farrell .04 .02 .01
☐ 233 Eric Davis .10 .05 .01
☐ 234 Johnny Ray .04 .02 .01
☐ 235 Darryl Strawberry .20 .09 .03
☐ 236 Bill Doran .04 .02 .01
☐ 237 Greg Gagne .04 .02 .01
☐ 238 Jim Eisenreich .04 .02 .01
☐ 239 Tommy Gregg .04 .02 .01
☐ 240 Marty Barrett .04 .02 .01
☐ 241 Rafael Ramirez .04 .02 .01
☐ 242 Chris Sabo .07 .03 .01
☐ 243 Dave Henderson .04 .02 .01
☐ 244 Andy Van Slyke .10 .05 .01
☐ 245 Alvaro Espinoza .04 .02 .01
☐ 246 Garry Templeton .04 .02 .01
☐ 247 Gene Harris .04 .02 .01
☐ 248 Kevin Gross .04 .02 .01
☐ 249 Brett Butler .07 .03 .01
☐ 250 Willie Randolph .07 .03 .01
☐ 251 Roger McDowell .04 .02 .01
☐ 252 Rafael Belliard .04 .02 .01
☐ 253 Steve Rosenberg .04 .02 .01
☐ 254 Jack Howell .04 .02 .01
☐ 255 Marvell Wynne .04 .02 .01
☐ 256 Tom Candiotti .04 .02 .01
☐ 257 Todd Benzinger .04 .02 .01
☐ 258 Don Robinson .04 .02 .01
☐ 259 Phil Bradley .04 .02 .01
☐ 260 Cecil Espy .04 .02 .01
☐ 261 Scott Bankhead .04 .02 .01
☐ 262 Frank White .04 .02 .01
☐ 263 Andres Thomas .04 .02 .01
☐ 264 Glenn Braggs .04 .02 .01
☐ 265 David Cone .12 .05 .02
☐ 266 Bobby Thigpen .04 .02 .01
☐ 267 Nelson Liriano .04 .02 .01
☐ 268 Terry Steinbach .07 .03 .01
☐ 269 Kirby Puckett UER .30 .14 .04
(Back doesn't consider Joe Torre's .363 in '71)
☐ 270 Gregg Jefferies .12 .05 .02
☐ 271 Jeff Blauser .07 .03 .01
☐ 272 Cory Snyder .04 .02 .01
☐ 273 Roy Smith .04 .02 .01
☐ 274 Tom Foley .04 .02 .01
☐ 275 Mitch Williams .07 .03 .01
☐ 276 Paul Kilgus .04 .02 .01
☐ 277 Don Slaught .04 .02 .01
☐ 278 Von Hayes .04 .02 .01
☐ 279 Vince Coleman .07 .03 .01
☐ 280 Mike Boddicker .04 .02 .01
☐ 281 Ken Dayley .04 .02 .01
☐ 282 Mike Devereaux .07 .03 .01
☐ 283 Kenny Rogers .04 .02 .01
☐ 284 Jeff Russell .04 .02 .01
☐ 285 Jerome Walton .07 .03 .01
☐ 286 Derek Lilliquist .04 .02 .01
☐ 287 Joe Orsulak .04 .02 .01
☐ 288 Dick Schofield .04 .02 .01
☐ 289 Ron Darling .07 .03 .01
☐ 290 Bobby Bonilla .12 .05 .02
☐ 291 Jim Gantner .04 .02 .01
☐ 292 Bobby Witt .07 .03 .01
☐ 293 Greg Brock .04 .02 .01
☐ 294 Ivan Calderon .04 .02 .01
☐ 295 Steve Bedrosian .04 .02 .01
☐ 296 Mike Henneman .04 .02 .01
☐ 297 Tom Gordon .07 .03 .01
☐ 298 Lou Whitaker .07 .03 .01
☐ 299 Terry Pendleton .10 .05 .01
☐ 300A Checklist Card .06 .01 .00
(232-333)
☐ 300B Checklist Card .06 .01 .00
(224-321)
☐ 301 Juan Berenguer .04 .02 .01
☐ 302 Mark Davis .04 .02 .01
☐ 303 Nick Esasky .04 .02 .01
☐ 304 Rickey Henderson .20 .09 .03
☐ 305 Rick Cerone .04 .02 .01
☐ 306 Craig Biggio .10 .05 .01
☐ 307 Duane Ward .04 .02 .01
☐ 308 Tom Browning .04 .02 .01
☐ 309 Walt Terrell .04 .02 .01
☐ 310 Greg Swindell .07 .03 .01
☐ 311 Dave Righetti .04 .02 .01
☐ 312 Mike Maddux .04 .02 .01
☐ 313 Len Dykstra .07 .03 .01
☐ 314 Jose Gonzalez .04 .02 .01
☐ 315 Steve Balboni .04 .02 .01
☐ 316 Mike Scioscia .04 .02 .01
☐ 317 Ron Oester .04 .02 .01
☐ 318 Gary Wayne .04 .02 .01
☐ 319 Todd Worrell .04 .02 .01
☐ 320 Doug Jones .07 .03 .01
☐ 321 Jeff Hamilton .04 .02 .01
☐ 322 Danny Tartabull .10 .05 .01
☐ 323 Chris James .04 .02 .01
☐ 324 Mike Flanagan .04 .02 .01
☐ 325 Gerald Young .04 .02 .01
☐ 326 Bob Boone .07 .03 .01
☐ 327 Frank Williams .04 .02 .01
☐ 328 Dave Parker .07 .03 .01
☐ 329 Sid Bream .04 .02 .01
☐ 330 Mike Schooler .04 .02 .01
☐ 331 Bert Blyleven .07 .03 .01
☐ 332 Bob Welch .07 .03 .01
☐ 333 Bob Milacki .04 .02 .01
☐ 334 Tim Burke .04 .02 .01
☐ 335 Jose Uribe .04 .02 .01
☐ 336 Randy Myers .07 .03 .01
☐ 337 Eric King .04 .02 .01
☐ 338 Mark Langston .07 .03 .01
☐ 339 Teddy Higuera .04 .02 .01
☐ 340 Oddibe McDowell .04 .02 .01
☐ 341 Lloyd McClendon .04 .02 .01
☐ 342 Pascual Perez .04 .02 .01
☐ 343 Kevin Brown UER .10 .05 .01
(Signed is misspelled as signeed on back)
☐ 344 Chuck Finley .07 .03 .01
☐ 345 Erik Hanson .07 .03 .01
☐ 346 Rich Gedman .04 .02 .01
☐ 347 Bip Roberts .07 .03 .01
☐ 348 Matt Williams .10 .05 .01
☐ 349 Tom Henke .07 .03 .01
☐ 350 Brad Komminsk .04 .02 .01
☐ 351 Jeff Reed .04 .02 .01
☐ 352 Brian Downing .04 .02 .01
☐ 353 Frank Viola .07 .03 .01
☐ 354 Terry Puhl .04 .02 .01
☐ 355 Brian Harper .07 .03 .01
☐ 356 Steve Farr .04 .02 .01
☐ 357 Joe Boever .04 .02 .01
☐ 358 Danny Heep .04 .02 .01
☐ 359 Larry Andersen .04 .02 .01
☐ 360 Rolando Roomes .04 .02 .01
☐ 361 Mike Gallego .04 .02 .01
☐ 362 Bob Kipper .04 .02 .01
☐ 363 Clay Parker .04 .02 .01
☐ 364 Mike Pagliarulo .04 .02 .01
☐ 365 Ken Griffey Jr. UER 1.25 .55 .16
(Signed through 1990, should be 1991)
☐ 366 Rex Hudler .04 .02 .01
☐ 367 Pat Sheridan .04 .02 .01
☐ 368 Kirk Gibson .07 .03 .01
☐ 369 Jeff Parrett .04 .02 .01
☐ 370 Bob Walk .04 .02 .01
☐ 371 Ken Patterson .04 .02 .01
☐ 372 Bryan Harvey .07 .03 .01
☐ 373 Mike Bielecki .04 .02 .01
☐ 374 Tom Magrann .04 .02 .01
☐ 375 Rick Mahler .04 .02 .01
☐ 376 Craig Lefferts .04 .02 .01
☐ 377 Gregg Olson .10 .05 .01
☐ 378 Jamie Moyer .04 .02 .01
☐ 379 Randy Johnson .07 .03 .01
☐ 380 Jeff Montgomery .07 .03 .01
☐ 381 Marty Clary .04 .02 .01
☐ 382 Bill Spiers .04 .02 .01
☐ 383 Dave Magadan .07 .03 .01
☐ 384 Greg Hibbard .20 .09 .03
☐ 385 Ernie Whitt .04 .02 .01
☐ 386 Rick Honeycutt .04 .02 .01
☐ 387 Dave West .04 .02 .01
☐ 388 Keith Hernandez .07 .03 .01
☐ 389 Jose Alvarez .04 .02 .01
☐ 390 Joey Belle .50 .23 .06
☐ 391 Rick Aguilera .07 .03 .01

☐ 392 Mike Fitzgerald	.04	.02	.01
☐ 393 Dwight Smith	.04	.02	.01
☐ 394 Steve Wilson	.04	.02	.01
☐ 395 Bob Geren	.04	.02	.01
☐ 396 Randy Ready	.04	.02	.01
☐ 397 Ken Hill	.12	.05	.02
☐ 398 Jody Reed	.04	.02	.01
☐ 399 Tom Brunansky	.07	.03	.01
☐ 400A Checklist Card (334-435)	.06	.01	.00
☐ 400B Checklist Card (322-419)	.06	.01	.00
☐ 401 Rene Gonzales	.04	.02	.01
☐ 402 Harold Baines	.07	.03	.01
☐ 403 Cecilio Guante	.04	.02	.01
☐ 404 Joe Girardi	.04	.02	.01
☐ 405A Sergio Valdez ERR (Card front shows black line crossing S in Sergio)	.15	.07	.02
☐ 405B Sergio Valdez COR	.04	.02	.01
☐ 406 Mark Williamson	.04	.02	.01
☐ 407 Glenn Hoffman	.04	.02	.01
☐ 408 Jeff Innis	.04	.02	.01
☐ 409 Randy Kramer	.04	.02	.01
☐ 410 Charlie O'Brien	.04	.02	.01
☐ 411 Charlie Hough	.04	.02	.01
☐ 412 Gus Polidor	.04	.02	.01
☐ 413 Ron Karkovice	.04	.02	.01
☐ 414 Trevor Wilson	.04	.02	.01
☐ 415 Kevin Ritz	.10	.05	.01
☐ 416 Gary Thurman	.04	.02	.01
☐ 417 Jeff M. Robinson	.04	.02	.01
☐ 418 Scott Terry	.04	.02	.01
☐ 419 Tim Laudner	.04	.02	.01
☐ 420 Dennis Rasmussen	.04	.02	.01
☐ 421 Luis Rivera	.04	.02	.01
☐ 422 Jim Corsi	.04	.02	.01
☐ 423 Dennis Lamp	.04	.02	.01
☐ 424 Ken Caminiti	.07	.03	.01
☐ 425 David Wells	.07	.03	.01
☐ 426 Norm Charlton	.07	.03	.01
☐ 427 Deion Sanders	.40	.18	.05
☐ 428 Dion James	.04	.02	.01
☐ 429 Chuck Cary	.04	.02	.01
☐ 430 Ken Howell	.04	.02	.01
☐ 431 Steve Lake	.04	.02	.01
☐ 432 Kal Daniels	.04	.02	.01
☐ 433 Lance McCullers	.04	.02	.01
☐ 434 Lenny Harris	.04	.02	.01
☐ 435 Scott Scudder	.04	.02	.01
☐ 436 Gene Larkin	.04	.02	.01
☐ 437 Dan Quisenberry	.07	.03	.01
☐ 438 Steve Olin	.20	.09	.03
☐ 439 Mickey Hatcher	.04	.02	.01
☐ 440 Willie Wilson	.04	.02	.01
☐ 441 Mark Grant	.04	.02	.01
☐ 442 Mookie Wilson	.04	.02	.01
☐ 443 Alex Trevino	.04	.02	.01
☐ 444 Pat Tabler	.04	.02	.01
☐ 445 Dave Bergman	.04	.02	.01
☐ 446 Todd Burns	.04	.02	.01
☐ 447 R.J. Reynolds	.04	.02	.01
☐ 448 Jay Buhner	.07	.03	.01
☐ 449 Lee Stevens	.10	.05	.01
☐ 450 Ron Hassey	.04	.02	.01
☐ 451 Bob Melvin	.04	.02	.01
☐ 452 Dave Martinez	.07	.03	.01
☐ 453 Greg Litton	.04	.02	.01
☐ 454 Mark Carreon	.04	.02	.01
☐ 455 Scott Fletcher	.04	.02	.01
☐ 456 Otis Nixon	.07	.03	.01
☐ 457 Tony Fossas	.04	.02	.01
☐ 458 John Russell	.04	.02	.01
☐ 459 Paul Assenmacher	.04	.02	.01
☐ 460 Zane Smith	.04	.02	.01
☐ 461 Jack Daugherty	.04	.02	.01
☐ 462 Rich Monteleone	.04	.02	.01
☐ 463 Greg Briley	.04	.02	.01
☐ 464 Mike Smithson	.04	.02	.01
☐ 465 Benito Santiago	.07	.03	.01
☐ 466 Jeff Brantley	.04	.02	.01
☐ 467 Jose Nunez	.04	.02	.01
☐ 468 Scott Bailes	.04	.02	.01
☐ 469 Ken Griffey Sr.	.07	.03	.01
☐ 470 Bob McClure	.04	.02	.01
☐ 471 Mackey Sasser	.04	.02	.01
☐ 472 Glenn Wilson	.04	.02	.01
☐ 473 Kevin Tapani	.35	.16	.04
☐ 474 Bill Buckner	.07	.03	.01
☐ 475 Ron Gant	.25	.11	.03
☐ 476 Kevin Romine	.04	.02	.01
☐ 477 Juan Agosto	.04	.02	.01
☐ 478 Herm Winningham	.04	.02	.01
☐ 479 Storm Davis	.04	.02	.01
☐ 480 Jeff King	.07	.03	.01
☐ 481 Kevin Mmahat	.07	.03	.01
☐ 482 Carmelo Martinez	.04	.02	.01
☐ 483 Omar Vizquel	.07	.03	.01
☐ 484 Jim Dwyer	.04	.02	.01
☐ 485 Bob Knepper	.04	.02	.01
☐ 486 Dave Anderson	.04	.02	.01
☐ 487 Ron Jones	.04	.02	.01
☐ 488 Jay Bell	.07	.03	.01
☐ 489 Sammy Sosa	.15	.07	.02
☐ 490 Kent Anderson	.04	.02	.01
☐ 491 Domingo Ramos	.04	.02	.01
☐ 492 Dave Clark	.04	.02	.01
☐ 493 Tim Birtsas	.04	.02	.01
☐ 494 Ken Oberkfell	.04	.02	.01
☐ 495 Larry Sheets	.04	.02	.01
☐ 496 Jeff Kunkel	.04	.02	.01
☐ 497 Jim Presley	.04	.02	.01
☐ 498 Mike Macfarlane	.04	.02	.01
☐ 499 Pete Smith	.07	.03	.01
☐ 500A Checklist Card DP (436-537)	.06	.01	.00
☐ 500B Checklist Card (420-517)	.06	.01	.00
☐ 501 Gary Sheffield	.50	.23	.06
☐ 502 Terry Bross	.04	.02	.01
☐ 503 Jerry Kutzler	.04	.02	.01
☐ 504 Lloyd Moseby	.04	.02	.01
☐ 505 Curt Young	.04	.02	.01
☐ 506 Al Newman	.04	.02	.01
☐ 507 Keith Miller	.04	.02	.01
☐ 508 Mike Stanton	.15	.07	.02
☐ 509 Rich Yett	.04	.02	.01
☐ 510 Tim Drummond	.04	.02	.01
☐ 511 Joe Hesketh	.04	.02	.01
☐ 512 Rick Wrona	.04	.02	.01
☐ 513 Luis Salazar	.04	.02	.01
☐ 514 Hal Morris	.15	.07	.02
☐ 515 Terry Mulholland	.07	.03	.01
☐ 516 John Morris	.04	.02	.01
☐ 517 Carlos Quintana	.07	.03	.01
☐ 518 Frank DiPino	.04	.02	.01
☐ 519 Randy Milligan	.04	.02	.01
☐ 520 Chad Kreuter	.04	.02	.01
☐ 521 Mike Jeffcoat	.04	.02	.01
☐ 522 Mike Harkey	.07	.03	.01
☐ 523A Andy Nezelek ERR (Wrong birth year)	.04	.02	.01
☐ 523B Andy Nezelek COR (Finally corrected in factory sets)	.15	.07	.02
☐ 524 Dave Schmidt	.04	.02	.01
☐ 525 Tony Armas	.04	.02	.01
☐ 526 Barry Lyons	.04	.02	.01
☐ 527 Rick Reed	.04	.02	.01
☐ 528 Jerry Reuss	.04	.02	.01
☐ 529 Dean Palmer	.60	.25	.08
☐ 530 Jeff Peterek	.10	.05	.01
☐ 531 Carlos Martinez	.07	.03	.01
☐ 532 Atlee Hammaker	.04	.02	.01
☐ 533 Mike Brumley	.04	.02	.01
☐ 534 Terry Leach	.04	.02	.01
☐ 535 Doug Strange	.10	.05	.01
☐ 536 Jose DeLeon	.04	.02	.01
☐ 537 Shane Rawley	.04	.02	.01
☐ 538 Joey Cora	.04	.02	.01
☐ 539 Eric Hetzel	.04	.02	.01
☐ 540 Gene Nelson	.04	.02	.01
☐ 541 Wes Gardner	.04	.02	.01
☐ 542 Mark Portugal	.04	.02	.01
☐ 543 Al Leiter	.04	.02	.01
☐ 544 Jack Armstrong	.07	.03	.01
☐ 545 Greg Cadaret	.04	.02	.01
☐ 546 Rod Nichols	.04	.02	.01
☐ 547 Luis Polonia	.07	.03	.01
☐ 548 Charlie Hayes	.12	.05	.02
☐ 549 Dickie Thon	.04	.02	.01
☐ 550 Tim Crews	.04	.02	.01
☐ 551 Dave Winfield	.15	.07	.02
☐ 552 Mike Davis	.04	.02	.01
☐ 553 Ron Robinson	.04	.02	.01
☐ 554 Carmen Castillo	.04	.02	.01
☐ 555 John Costello	.04	.02	.01
☐ 556 Bud Black	.04	.02	.01
☐ 557 Rick Dempsey	.04	.02	.01
☐ 558 Jim Acker	.04	.02	.01
☐ 559 Eric Show	.04	.02	.01
☐ 560 Pat Borders	.07	.03	.01
☐ 561 Danny Darwin	.04	.02	.01
☐ 562 Rick Luecken	.04	.02	.01
☐ 563 Edwin Nunez	.04	.02	.01

☐ 564 Felix Jose .20 .09 .03
☐ 565 John Cangelosi .04 .02 .01
☐ 566 Bill Swift .07 .03 .01
☐ 567 Bill Schroeder .04 .02 .01
☐ 568 Stan Javier .04 .02 .01
☐ 569 Jim Traber .04 .02 .01
☐ 570 Wallace Johnson .04 .02 .01
☐ 571 Donell Nixon .04 .02 .01
☐ 572 Sid Fernandez .07 .03 .01
☐ 573 Lance Johnson .07 .03 .01
☐ 574 Andy McGaffigan .04 .02 .01
☐ 575 Mark Knudson .04 .02 .01
☐ 576 Tommy Greene .12 .05 .02
☐ 577 Mark Grace .20 .09 .03
☐ 578 Larry Walker .90 .40 .11
☐ 579 Mike Stanley .04 .02 .01
☐ 580 Mike Witt DP .04 .02 .01
☐ 581 Scott Bradley .04 .02 .01
☐ 582 Greg A. Harris .04 .02 .01
☐ 583A Kevin Hickey ERR .15 .07 .02
☐ 583B Kevin Hickey COR .04 .02 .01
☐ 584 Lee Mazzilli .04 .02 .01
☐ 585 Jeff Pico .04 .02 .01
☐ 586 Joe Oliver .10 .05 .01
☐ 587 Willie Fraser DP .04 .02 .01
☐ 588 Carl Yastrzemski .08 .04 .01
Puzzle Card DP
☐ 589 Kevin Bass DP .04 .02 .01
☐ 590 John Moses DP .04 .02 .01
☐ 591 Tom Pagnozzi DP .04 .02 .01
☐ 592 Tony Castillo DP .04 .02 .01
☐ 593 Jerald Clark DP .04 .02 .01
☐ 594 Dan Schatzeder .04 .02 .01
☐ 595 Luis Quinones DP .04 .02 .01
☐ 596 Pete Harnisch DP .07 .03 .01
☐ 597 Gary Redus .04 .02 .01
☐ 598 Mel Hall .04 .02 .01
☐ 599 Rick Schu .04 .02 .01
☐ 600A Checklist Card .06 .01 .00
(538-639)
☐ 600B Checklist Card .06 .01 .00
(518-617)
☐ 601 Mike Kingery DP .04 .02 .01
☐ 602 Terry Kennedy DP .04 .02 .01
☐ 603 Mike Sharperson DP .04 .02 .01
☐ 604 Don Carman DP .04 .02 .01
☐ 605 Jim Gott .04 .02 .01
☐ 606 Donn Pall DP .04 .02 .01
☐ 607 Rance Mulliniks .04 .02 .01
☐ 608 Curt Wilkerson DP .04 .02 .01
☐ 609 Mike Felder DP .04 .02 .01
☐ 610 Guillermo Hernandez DP .04 .02 .01
☐ 611 Candy Maldonado DP .04 .02 .01
☐ 612 Mark Thurmond DP .04 .02 .01
☐ 613 Rick Leach DP .04 .02 .01
☐ 614 Jerry Reed DP .04 .02 .01
☐ 615 Franklin Stubbs .04 .02 .01
☐ 616 Billy Hatcher DP .04 .02 .01
☐ 617 Don August DP .04 .02 .01
☐ 618 Tim Teufel .04 .02 .01
☐ 619 Shawn Hillegas DP .04 .02 .01
☐ 620 Manny Lee .04 .02 .01
☐ 621 Gary Ward DP .04 .02 .01
☐ 622 Mark Guthrie DP .04 .02 .01
☐ 623 Jeff Musselman DP .04 .02 .01
☐ 624 Mark Lemke DP .04 .02 .01
☐ 625 Fernando Valenzuela .07 .03 .01
☐ 626 Paul Sorrento DP .20 .09 .03
☐ 627 Glenallen Hill DP .04 .02 .01
☐ 628 Les Lancaster DP .04 .02 .01
☐ 629 Vance Law DP .04 .02 .01
☐ 630 Randy Velarde DP .04 .02 .01
☐ 631 Todd Frohwirth DP .04 .02 .01
☐ 632 Willie McGee .07 .03 .01
☐ 633 Dennis Boyd DP .04 .02 .01
☐ 634 Cris Carpenter DP .04 .02 .01
☐ 635 Brian Holton .04 .02 .01
☐ 636 Tracy Jones DP .04 .02 .01
☐ 637A Terry Steinbach AS .10 .05 .01
(Recent Major
League Performance)
☐ 637B Terry Steinbach AS .04 .02 .01
(All-Star Game
Performance)
☐ 638 Brady Anderson .12 .05 .02
☐ 639A Jack Morris ERR .20 .09 .03
(Card front shows
black line crossing
J in Jack)
☐ 639B Jack Morris COR .10 .05 .01
☐ 640 Jaime Navarro .20 .09 .03
☐ 641 Darrin Jackson .07 .03 .01
☐ 642 Mike Dyer .04 .02 .01
☐ 643 Mike Schmidt .25 .11 .03
☐ 644 Henry Cotto .04 .02 .01
☐ 645 John Cerutti .04 .02 .01
☐ 646 Francisco Cabrera .10 .05 .01
☐ 647 Scott Sanderson .04 .02 .01
☐ 648 Brian Meyer .04 .02 .01
☐ 649 Ray Searage .04 .02 .01
☐ 650A Bo Jackson AS .20 .09 .03
(Recent Major
League Performance)
☐ 650B Bo Jackson AS .10 .05 .01
(All-Star Game
Performance)
☐ 651 Steve Lyons .04 .02 .01
☐ 652 Mike LaCoss .04 .02 .01
☐ 653 Ted Power .04 .02 .01
☐ 654A Howard Johnson AS .10 .05 .01
(Recent Major
League Performance)
☐ 654B Howard Johnson AS .04 .02 .01
(All-Star Game
Performance)
☐ 655 Mauro Gozzo .04 .02 .01
☐ 656 Mike Blowers .04 .02 .01
☐ 657 Paul Gibson .04 .02 .01
☐ 658 Neal Heaton .04 .02 .01
☐ 659A Nolan Ryan 5000K 3.00 1.35 .40
(665 King of
Kings back) ERR
☐ 659B Nolan Ryan 5000K .40 .18 .05
COR (Still an error as
Ryan did not lead AL
in K's in '75)
☐ 660A Harold Baines AS 2.00 .90 .25
(Black line through
star on front;
Recent Major
League Performance)
☐ 660B Harold Baines AS 4.00 1.80 .50
(Black line through
star on front;
All-Star Game
Performance)
☐ 660C Harold Baines AS 1.00 .45 .13
(Black line behind
star on front;
Recent Major
League Performance)
☐ 660D Harold Baines AS .04 .02 .01
(Black line behind
star on front;
All-Star Game
Performance)
☐ 661 Gary Pettis .04 .02 .01
☐ 662 Clint Zavaras .04 .02 .01
☐ 663A Rick Reuschel AS .10 .05 .01
(Recent Major
League Performance)
☐ 663B Rick Reuschel AS .04 .02 .01
(All-Star Game
Performance)
☐ 664 Alejandro Pena .04 .02 .01
☐ 665A Nolan Ryan KING 2.50 1.15 .30
(659 5000 K
back) ERR
☐ 665B Nolan Ryan KING COR .40 .18 .05
☐ 665C Nolan Ryan KING ERR .90 .40 .11
(No number on back;
in factory sets)
☐ 666 Ricky Horton .04 .02 .01
☐ 667 Curt Schilling .15 .07 .02
☐ 668 Bill Landrum .04 .02 .01
☐ 669 Todd Stottlemyre .07 .03 .01
☐ 670 Tim Leary .04 .02 .01
☐ 671 John Wetteland .15 .07 .02
☐ 672 Calvin Schiraldi .04 .02 .01
☐ 673A Ruben Sierra AS .25 .11 .03
(Recent Major
League Performance)
☐ 673B Ruben Sierra AS .12 .05 .02
(All-Star Game
Performance)
☐ 674A Pedro Guerrero AS .10 .05 .01
(Recent Major
League Performance)
☐ 674B Pedro Guerrero AS .04 .02 .01
(All-Star Game
Performance)
☐ 675 Ken Phelps .04 .02 .01
☐ 676A Cal Ripken AS .40 .18 .05
(Recent Major
League Performance)
☐ 676B Cal Ripken AS .20 .09 .03

(All-Star Game Performance)			
☐ 677 Denny Walling	.04	.02	.01
☐ 678 Goose Gossage	.07	.03	.01
☐ 679 Gary Mielke	.04	.02	.01
☐ 680 Bill Bathe	.04	.02	.01
☐ 681 Tom Lawless	.04	.02	.01
☐ 682 Xavier Hernandez	.12	.05	.02
☐ 683A Kirby Puckett AS (Recent Major League Performance)	.25	.11	.03
☐ 683B Kirby Puckett AS (All-Star Game Performance)	.12	.05	.02
☐ 684 Mariano Duncan	.04	.02	.01
☐ 685 Ramon Martinez	.15	.07	.02
☐ 686 Tim Jones	.04	.02	.01
☐ 687 Tom Filer	.04	.02	.01
☐ 688 Steve Lombardozzi	.04	.02	.01
☐ 689 Bernie Williams	.30	.14	.04
☐ 690 Chip Hale	.04	.02	.01
☐ 691 Beau Allred	.04	.02	.01
☐ 692A Ryne Sandberg AS (Recent Major League Performance)	.35	.16	.04
☐ 692B Ryne Sandberg AS (All-Star Game Performance)	.20	.09	.03
☐ 693 Jeff Huson	.10	.05	.01
☐ 694 Curt Ford	.04	.02	.01
☐ 695A Eric Davis AS (Recent Major League Performance)	.20	.09	.03
☐ 695B Eric Davis AS (All-Star Game Performance)	.10	.05	.01
☐ 696 Scott Lusader	.04	.02	.01
☐ 697A Mark McGwire AS (Recent Major League Performance)	.30	.14	.04
☐ 697B Mark McGwire AS (All-Star Game Performance)	.15	.07	.02
☐ 698 Steve Cummings	.04	.02	.01
☐ 699 George Canale	.04	.02	.01
☐ 700A Checklist Card (640-715/BC1-BC26)	.50	.05	.02
☐ 700B Checklist Card (640-716/BC1-BC26)	.10	.01	.00
☐ 700C Checklist Card (618-716)	.06	.01	.00
☐ 701A Julio Franco AS (Recent Major League Performance)	.10	.05	.01
☐ 701B Julio Franco AS (All-Star Game Performance)	.04	.02	.01
☐ 702 Dave Johnson (P)	.04	.02	.01
☐ 703A Dave Stewart AS (Recent Major League Performance)	.10	.05	.01
☐ 703B Dave Stewart AS (All-Star Game Performance)	.04	.02	.01
☐ 704 Dave Justice	1.25	.55	.16
☐ 705A Tony Gwynn AS (Recent Major League Performance)	.20	.09	.03
☐ 705B Tony Gwynn AS (All-Star Game Performance)	.10	.05	.01
☐ 706 Greg Myers	.04	.02	.01
☐ 707A Will Clark AS (Recent Major League Performance)	.30	.14	.04
☐ 707B Will Clark AS (All-Star Game Performance)	.15	.07	.02
☐ 708A Benito Santiago AS (Recent Major League Performance)	.10	.05	.01
☐ 708B Benito Santiago AS (All-Star Game Performance)	.04	.02	.01
☐ 709 Larry McWilliams	.04	.02	.01
☐ 710A Ozzie Smith AS (Recent Major League Performance)	.10	.05	.01
☐ 710B Ozzie Smith AS (All-Star Game Performance)	.04	.02	.01
☐ 711 John Olerud	.60	.25	.08
☐ 712A Wade Boggs AS (Recent Major League Performance)	.15	.07	.02
☐ 712B Wade Boggs AS (All-Star Game Performance)	.08	.04	.01
☐ 713 Gary Eave	.04	.02	.01
☐ 714 Bob Tewksbury	.07	.03	.01
☐ 715A Kevin Mitchell AS (Recent Major League Performance)	.10	.05	.01
☐ 715B Kevin Mitchell AS (All-Star Game Performance)	.04	.02	.01
☐ 716 Bart Giamatti COMM (In Memoriam)	.20	.09	.03
☐ BC1 Bo Jackson	.10	.05	.01
☐ BC2 Howard Johnson	.05	.02	.01
☐ BC3 Dave Stewart	.05	.02	.01
☐ BC4 Tony Gwynn	.10	.05	.01
☐ BC5 Orel Hershiser	.05	.02	.01
☐ BC6 Pedro Guerrero	.05	.02	.01
☐ BC7 Tim Raines	.08	.04	.01
☐ BC8 Kirby Puckett	.15	.07	.02
☐ BC9 Alvin Davis	.05	.02	.01
☐ BC10 Ryne Sandberg	.20	.09	.03
☐ BC11 Kevin Mitchell	.08	.04	.01
☐ BC12A John Smoltz ERR (Photo actually Tom Glavine)	.40	.18	.05
☐ BC12B John Smoltz COR	1.00	.45	.13
☐ BC13 George Bell	.05	.02	.01
☐ BC14 Julio Franco	.05	.02	.01
☐ BC15 Paul Molitor	.08	.04	.01
☐ BC16 Bobby Bonilla	.08	.04	.01
☐ BC17 Mike Greenwell	.08	.04	.01
☐ BC18 Cal Ripken	.20	.09	.03
☐ BC19 Carlton Fisk	.10	.05	.01
☐ BC20 Chili Davis	.05	.02	.01
☐ BC21 Glenn Davis	.05	.02	.01
☐ BC22 Steve Sax	.05	.02	.01
☐ BC23 Eric Davis DP	.08	.04	.01
☐ BC24 Greg Swindell DP	.05	.02	.01
☐ BC25 Von Hayes DP	.05	.02	.01
☐ BC26 Alan Trammell	.05	.02	.01

1990 Donruss Best AL

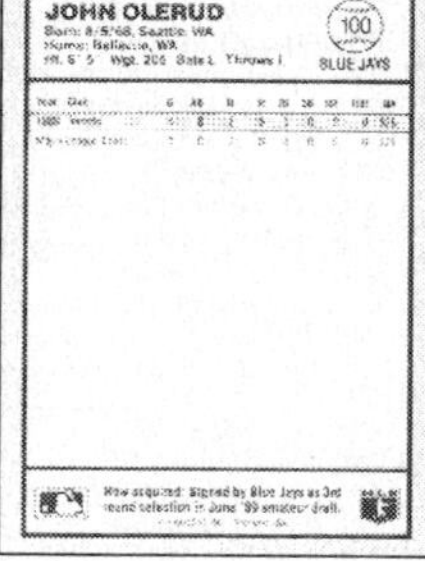

The 1990 Donruss Best of the American League set consists of 144 cards in the standard card size of 2 1/2" by 3 1/2". This was Donruss' latest version of what had been titled the previous two years as Baseball's Best. In 1990, the sets were split into National and American League and marketed separately. The front design was similar to the regular issue Donruss set except for the front borders being blue while the backs have complete major and minor league statistics as compared to the regular Donruss cards which only cover the past five major-league seasons.

	MT	EX-MT	VG
COMPLETE SET (144)	10.00	4.50	1.25
COMMON PLAYER (1-144)	.04	.02	.01
☐ 1 Ken Griffey Jr.	2.50	1.15	.30
☐ 2 Bob Milacki	.04	.02	.01
☐ 3 Mike Boddicker	.04	.02	.01
☐ 4 Bert Blyleven	.07	.03	.01
☐ 5 Carlton Fisk	.25	.11	.03
☐ 6 Greg Swindell	.10	.05	.01

☐ 7 Alan Trammell	.15	.07	.02
☐ 8 Mark Davis	.04	.02	.01
☐ 9 Chris Bosio	.10	.05	.01
☐ 10 Gary Gaetti	.07	.03	.01
☐ 11 Matt Nokes	.07	.03	.01
☐ 12 Dennis Eckersley	.20	.09	.03
☐ 13 Kevin Brown	.15	.07	.02
☐ 14 Tom Henke	.10	.05	.01
☐ 15 Mickey Tettleton	.10	.05	.01
☐ 16 Jody Reed	.07	.03	.01
☐ 17 Mark Langston	.10	.05	.01
☐ 18 Melido Perez UER (Listed as an Expo rather than White Sox)	.20	.09	.03
☐ 19 John Farrell	.04	.02	.01
☐ 20 Tony Phillips	.07	.03	.01
☐ 21 Bret Saberhagen	.15	.07	.02
☐ 22 Robin Yount	.35	.16	.04
☐ 23 Kirby Puckett	.45	.20	.06
☐ 24 Steve Sax	.10	.05	.01
☐ 25 Dave Stewart	.10	.05	.01
☐ 26 Alvin Davis	.04	.02	.01
☐ 27 Geno Petralli	.04	.02	.01
☐ 28 Mookie Wilson	.07	.03	.01
☐ 29 Jeff Ballard	.04	.02	.01
☐ 30 Ellis Burks	.10	.05	.01
☐ 31 Wally Joyner	.15	.07	.02
☐ 32 Bobby Thigpen	.07	.03	.01
☐ 33 Keith Hernandez	.10	.05	.01
☐ 34 Jack Morris	.15	.07	.02
☐ 35 George Brett	.35	.16	.04
☐ 36 Dan Plesac	.04	.02	.01
☐ 37 Brian Harper	.04	.02	.01
☐ 38 Don Mattingly	.60	.25	.08
☐ 39 Dave Henderson	.07	.03	.01
☐ 40 Scott Bankhead UER (Asheboro misspelled as Ashboro on card)	.07	.03	.01
☐ 41 Rafael Palmeiro	.20	.09	.03
☐ 42 Jimmy Key	.07	.03	.01
☐ 43 Gregg Olson	.10	.05	.01
☐ 44 Tony Pena	.04	.02	.01
☐ 45 Jack Howell	.04	.02	.01
☐ 46 Eric King	.04	.02	.01
☐ 47 Cory Snyder	.07	.03	.01
☐ 48 Frank Tanana	.04	.02	.01
☐ 49 Nolan Ryan	1.25	.55	.16
☐ 50 Bob Boone	.07	.03	.01
☐ 51 Dave Parker	.10	.05	.01
☐ 52 Allan Anderson	.04	.02	.01
☐ 53 Tim Leary	.04	.02	.01
☐ 54 Mark McGwire	.45	.20	.06
☐ 55 Dave Valle	.04	.02	.01
☐ 56 Fred McGriff	.35	.16	.04
☐ 57 Cal Ripken	.75	.35	.09
☐ 58 Roger Clemens	.60	.25	.08
☐ 59 Lance Parrish	.07	.03	.01
☐ 60 Robin Ventura	.75	.35	.09
☐ 61 Doug Jones	.07	.03	.01
☐ 62 Lloyd Moseby	.04	.02	.01
☐ 63 Bo Jackson	.75	.35	.09
☐ 64 Paul Molitor	.15	.07	.02
☐ 65 Kent Hrbek	.07	.03	.01
☐ 66 Mel Hall	.07	.03	.01
☐ 67 Bob Welch	.10	.05	.01
☐ 68 Erik Hanson	.10	.05	.01
☐ 69 Harold Baines	.07	.03	.01
☐ 70 Junior Felix	.10	.05	.01
☐ 71 Craig Worthington	.04	.02	.01
☐ 72 Jeff Reardon	.15	.07	.02
☐ 73 Johnny Ray	.04	.02	.01
☐ 74 Ozzie Guillen	.07	.03	.01
☐ 75 Brook Jacoby	.04	.02	.01
☐ 76 Chet Lemon	.04	.02	.01
☐ 77 Mark Gubicza	.04	.02	.01
☐ 78 B.J. Surhoff	.07	.03	.01
☐ 79 Rick Aguilera	.07	.03	.01
☐ 80 Pascual Perez	.07	.03	.01
☐ 81 Jose Canseco	.60	.25	.08
☐ 82 Mike Schooler	.04	.02	.01
☐ 83 Jeff Huson	.04	.02	.01
☐ 84 Kelly Gruber	.10	.05	.01
☐ 85 Randy Milligan	.07	.03	.01
☐ 86 Wade Boggs	.40	.18	.05
☐ 87 Dave Winfield	.30	.14	.04
☐ 88 Scott Fletcher	.04	.02	.01
☐ 89 Tom Candiotti	.07	.03	.01
☐ 90 Mike Heath	.04	.02	.01
☐ 91 Kevin Seitzer	.07	.03	.01
☐ 92 Ted Higuera	.04	.02	.01
☐ 93 Kevin Tapani	.20	.09	.03
☐ 94 Roberto Kelly	.15	.07	.02
☐ 95 Walt Weiss	.07	.03	.01
☐ 96 Checklist Card	.04	.02	.01
☐ 97 Sandy Alomar Jr.	.15	.07	.02
☐ 98 Pete O'Brien	.04	.02	.01
☐ 99 Jeff Russell	.07	.03	.01
☐ 100 John Olerud	1.00	.45	.13
☐ 101 Pete Harnisch	.07	.03	.01
☐ 102 Dwight Evans	.10	.05	.01
☐ 103 Chuck Finley	.07	.03	.01
☐ 104 Sammy Sosa	.25	.11	.03
☐ 105 Mike Henneman	.07	.03	.01
☐ 106 Kurt Stillwell	.04	.02	.01
☐ 107 Greg Vaughn	.25	.11	.03
☐ 108 Dan Gladden	.04	.02	.01
☐ 109 Jesse Barfield	.07	.03	.01
☐ 110 Willie Randolph	.07	.03	.01
☐ 111 Randy Johnson	.10	.05	.01
☐ 112 Julio Franco	.10	.05	.01
☐ 113 Tony Fernandez	.07	.03	.01
☐ 114 Ben McDonald	.45	.20	.06
☐ 115 Mike Greenwell	.15	.07	.02
☐ 116 Luis Polonia	.04	.02	.01
☐ 117 Carney Lansford	.07	.03	.01
☐ 118 Bud Black	.04	.02	.01
☐ 119 Lou Whitaker	.10	.05	.01
☐ 120 Jim Eisenreich	.04	.02	.01
☐ 121 Gary Sheffield	.75	.35	.09
☐ 122 Shane Mack	.10	.05	.01
☐ 123 Alvaro Espinoza	.04	.02	.01
☐ 124 Rickey Henderson	.40	.18	.05
☐ 125 Jeffrey Leonard	.04	.02	.01
☐ 126 Gary Pettis	.04	.02	.01
☐ 127 Dave Stieb	.07	.03	.01
☐ 128 Danny Tartabull	.20	.09	.03
☐ 129 Joe Orsulak	.04	.02	.01
☐ 130 Tom Brunansky	.07	.03	.01
☐ 131 Dick Schofield	.04	.02	.01
☐ 132 Candy Maldonado	.07	.03	.01
☐ 133 Cecil Fielder	.40	.18	.05
☐ 134 Terry Shumpert	.07	.03	.01
☐ 135 Greg Gagne	.04	.02	.01
☐ 136 Dave Righetti	.07	.03	.01
☐ 137 Terry Steinbach	.07	.03	.01
☐ 138 Harold Reynolds	.07	.03	.01
☐ 139 George Bell	.15	.07	.02
☐ 140 Carlos Quintana	.07	.03	.01
☐ 141 Ivan Calderon	.07	.03	.01
☐ 142 Greg Brock	.04	.02	.01
☐ 143 Ruben Sierra	.35	.16	.04
☐ 144 Checklist Card	.04	.02	.01

1990 Donruss Best NL

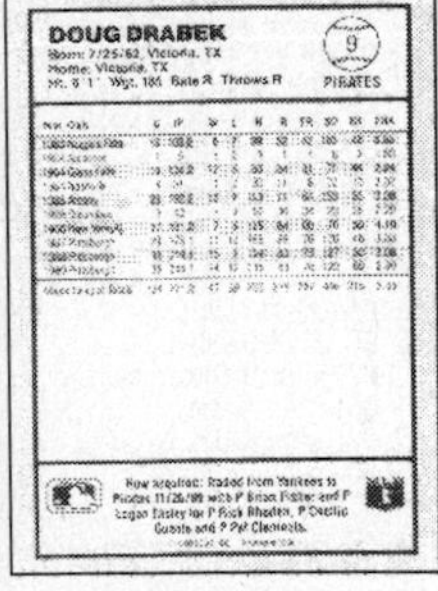

The 1990 Donruss Best of the National League set consists of 144 cards in the standard card size of 2 1/2" by 3 1/2". This was Donruss' latest version of what had been titled the previous two years as Baseball's Best. In 1990, the sets were split into National and American League and marketed separately. The front design was similar to the regular issue Donruss set except for the front borders being blue while the backs have complete major and minor league statistics as compared to the regular Donruss cards which only cover the past five major-league seasons.

	MT	EX-MT	VG
COMPLETE SET (144)	10.00	4.50	1.25
COMMON PLAYER (1-144)	.04	.02	.01

☐ 1 Eric Davis .20 .09 .03
☐ 2 Tom Glavine .40 .18 .05
☐ 3 Mike Bielecki .04 .02 .01
☐ 4 Jim Deshaies .04 .02 .01
☐ 5 Mike Scioscia .04 .02 .01
☐ 6 Spike Owen .04 .02 .01
☐ 7 Dwight Gooden .20 .09 .03
☐ 8 Ricky Jordan .10 .05 .01
☐ 9 Doug Drabek .10 .05 .01
☐ 10 Bryn Smith .04 .02 .01
☐ 11 Tony Gwynn .30 .14 .04
☐ 12 John Burkett .10 .05 .01
☐ 13 Nick Esasky .04 .02 .01
☐ 14 Greg Maddux .30 .14 .04
☐ 15 Joe Oliver .10 .05 .01
☐ 16 Mike Scott .07 .03 .01
☐ 17 Tim Belcher .07 .03 .01
☐ 18 Kevin Gross .07 .03 .01
☐ 19 Howard Johnson .15 .07 .02
☐ 20 Darren Daulton .15 .07 .02
☐ 21 John Smiley .10 .05 .01
☐ 22 Ken Dayley .04 .02 .01
☐ 23 Craig Lefferts .10 .05 .01
☐ 24 Will Clark .60 .25 .08
☐ 25 Greg Olson .10 .05 .01
☐ 26 Ryne Sandberg .75 .35 .09
☐ 27 Tom Browning .07 .03 .01
☐ 28 Eric Anthony .30 .14 .04
☐ 29 Juan Samuel .04 .02 .01
☐ 30 Dennis Martinez .07 .03 .01
☐ 31 Kevin Elster .04 .02 .01
☐ 32 Tom Herr .04 .02 .01
☐ 33 Sid Bream .04 .02 .01
☐ 34 Terry Pendleton .20 .09 .03
☐ 35 Roberto Alomar .75 .35 .09
☐ 36 Kevin Bass .04 .02 .01
☐ 37 Jim Presley .04 .02 .01
☐ 38 Les Lancaster .04 .02 .01
☐ 39 Paul O'Neill .07 .03 .01
☐ 40 Dave Smith .04 .02 .01
☐ 41 Kirk Gibson .07 .03 .01
☐ 42 Tim Burke .04 .02 .01
☐ 43 David Cone .15 .07 .02
☐ 44 Ken Howell .04 .02 .01
☐ 45 Barry Bonds .50 .23 .06
☐ 46 Joe Magrane .04 .02 .01
☐ 47 Andy Benes .15 .07 .02
☐ 48 Gary Carter .10 .05 .01
☐ 49 Pat Combs .07 .03 .01
☐ 50 John Smoltz .25 .11 .03
☐ 51 Mark Grace .30 .14 .04
☐ 52 Barry Larkin .20 .09 .03
☐ 53 Danny Darwin .04 .02 .01
☐ 54 Orel Hershiser .15 .07 .02
☐ 55 Tim Wallach .07 .03 .01
☐ 56 Dave Magadan .07 .03 .01
☐ 57 Roger McDowell .04 .02 .01
☐ 58 Bill Landrum .04 .02 .01
☐ 59 Jose DeLeon .04 .02 .01
☐ 60 Bip Roberts .10 .05 .01
☐ 61 Matt Williams .15 .07 .02
☐ 62 Dale Murphy .15 .07 .02
☐ 63 Dwight Smith .07 .03 .01
☐ 64 Chris Sabo .15 .07 .02
☐ 65 Glenn Davis .10 .05 .01
☐ 66 Jay Howell .04 .02 .01
☐ 67 Andres Galarraga .10 .05 .01
☐ 68 Frank Viola .10 .05 .01
☐ 69 John Kruk .10 .05 .01
☐ 70 Bobby Bonilla .25 .11 .03
☐ 71 Todd Zeile .15 .07 .02
☐ 72 Joe Carter .30 .14 .04
☐ 73 Robby Thompson .04 .02 .01
☐ 74 Jeff Blauser .07 .03 .01
☐ 75 Mitch Williams .07 .03 .01
☐ 76 Rob Dibble .10 .05 .01
☐ 77 Rafael Ramirez .04 .02 .01
☐ 78 Eddie Murray .25 .11 .03
☐ 79 Dave Martinez .04 .02 .01
☐ 80 Darryl Strawberry .40 .18 .05
☐ 81 Dickie Thon .04 .02 .01
☐ 82 Jose Lind .04 .02 .01
☐ 83 Ozzie Smith .25 .11 .03
☐ 84 Bruce Hurst .07 .03 .01
☐ 85 Kevin Mitchell .15 .07 .02
☐ 86 Lonnie Smith .04 .02 .01
☐ 87 Joe Girardi .04 .02 .01
☐ 88 Randy Myers .07 .03 .01
☐ 89 Craig Biggio .15 .07 .02
☐ 90 Fernando Valenzuela .07 .03 .01
☐ 91 Larry Walker .75 .35 .09
☐ 92 John Franco .07 .03 .01
☐ 93 Dennis Cook .07 .03 .01
☐ 94 Bob Walk .04 .02 .01
☐ 95 Pedro Guerrero .07 .03 .01
☐ 96 Checklist Card .04 .02 .01
☐ 97 Andre Dawson .25 .11 .03
☐ 98 Ed Whitson .04 .02 .01
☐ 99 Steve Bedrosian .04 .02 .01
☐ 100 Oddibe McDowell .04 .02 .01
☐ 101 Todd Benzinger .04 .02 .01
☐ 102 Bill Doran .04 .02 .01
☐ 103 Alfredo Griffin .04 .02 .01
☐ 104 Tim Raines .10 .05 .01
☐ 105 Sid Fernandez .07 .03 .01
☐ 106 Charlie Hayes .10 .05 .01
☐ 107 Mike LaValliere .04 .02 .01
☐ 108 Jose Oquendo .04 .02 .01
☐ 109 Jack Clark .07 .03 .01
☐ 110 Scott Garrelts .04 .02 .01
☐ 111 Ron Gant .35 .16 .04
☐ 112 Shawon Dunston .10 .05 .01
☐ 113 Mariano Duncan .07 .03 .01
☐ 114 Eric Yelding .04 .02 .01
☐ 115 Hubie Brooks .04 .02 .01
☐ 116 Delino DeShields .50 .23 .06
☐ 117 Gregg Jefferies .20 .09 .03
☐ 118 Len Dykstra .10 .05 .01
☐ 119 Andy Van Slyke .15 .07 .02
☐ 120 Lee Smith .10 .05 .01
☐ 121 Benito Santiago .15 .07 .02
☐ 122 Jose Uribe .04 .02 .01
☐ 123 Jeff Treadway .04 .02 .01
☐ 124 Jerome Walton .04 .02 .01
☐ 125 Billy Hatcher .04 .02 .01
☐ 126 Ken Caminiti .07 .03 .01
☐ 127 Kal Daniels .07 .03 .01
☐ 128 Marquis Grissom .50 .23 .06
☐ 129 Kevin McReynolds .10 .05 .01
☐ 130 Wally Backman .04 .02 .01
☐ 131 Willie McGee .10 .05 .01
☐ 132 Terry Kennedy .04 .02 .01
☐ 133 Garry Templeton .04 .02 .01
☐ 134 Lloyd McClendon .04 .02 .01
☐ 135 Daryl Boston .04 .02 .01
☐ 136 Jay Bell .07 .03 .01
☐ 137 Mike Pagliarulo .04 .02 .01
☐ 138 Vince Coleman .10 .05 .01
☐ 139 Brett Butler .10 .05 .01
☐ 140 Von Hayes .04 .02 .01
☐ 141 Ramon Martinez .25 .11 .03
☐ 142 Jack Armstrong .10 .05 .01
☐ 143 Franklin Stubbs .07 .03 .01
☐ 144 Checklist Card .04 .02 .01

1990 Donruss Grand Slammers

This 12-card standard size 2 1/2" by 3 1/2" set was in the 1990 Donruss set as a special card deliniating each 55-card section of the 1990 Factory Set. This set honors those players who connected for grand slam homers during the 1989 season. The cards are in the 1990 Donruss design and the back describes the grand slam homer hit by each player.

	MT	EX-MT	VG
COMPLETE SET (12)	2.50	1.15	.30
COMMON PLAYER (1-12)	.10	.05	.01

☐ 1 Matt Williams .30 .14 .04
☐ 2 Jeffrey Leonard .10 .05 .01
☐ 3 Chris James .10 .05 .01

☐ 4 Mark McGwire	.60	.25	.08
☐ 5 Dwight Evans	.15	.07	.02
☐ 6 Will Clark	.75	.35	.09
☐ 7 Mike Scioscia	.10	.05	.01
☐ 8 Todd Benzinger	.10	.05	.01
☐ 9 Fred McGriff	.40	.18	.05
☐ 10 Kevin Bass	.10	.05	.01
☐ 11 Jack Clark	.10	.05	.01
☐ 12 Bo Jackson	.75	.35	.09

1990 Donruss Learning Series

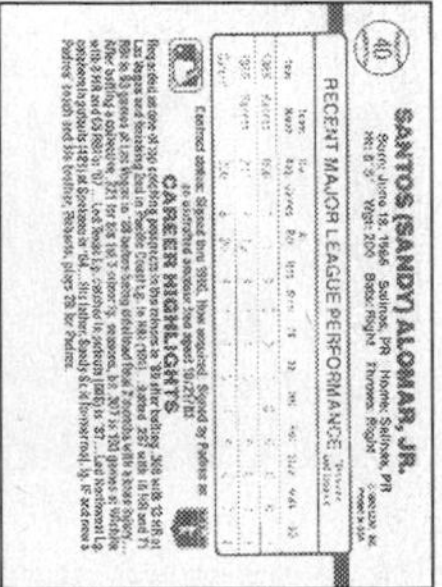

The 1990 Donruss Learning Series consists of 55 standard-size (2 1/2" by 3 1/2") cards that served as part of an educational packet for elementary and middle school students. The cards were issued in two formats. Grades 3 and 4 received the cards, a historical timeline that relates events in baseball to major historical events, additional Donruss cards from wax packs, and a teacher's guide that focused on several academic subjects. Grades 5 through 8 received the cards, a teacher's guide designed for older students, and a 14-minute video shot at Chicago's Wrigley Field. The fronts feature color head shots of the players and bright red borders. The horizontally oriented backs are amber and present biography, statistics, and career highlights. The cards are numbered on the back.

	MT	EX-MT	VG
COMPLETE SET (55)	75.00	34.00	9.50
COMMON PLAYER (1-55)	.50	.23	.06
☐ 1 George Brett DK	4.00	1.80	.50
☐ 2 Kevin Mitchell	2.00	.90	.25
☐ 3 Andy Van Slyke	1.00	.45	.13
☐ 4 Benito Santiago	1.00	.45	.13
☐ 5 Gary Carter	1.00	.45	.13
☐ 6 Jose Canseco	7.50	3.40	.95
☐ 7 Rickey Henderson	7.50	3.40	.95
☐ 8 Ken Griffey Jr.	15.00	6.75	1.90
☐ 9 Ozzie Smith	3.00	1.35	.40
☐ 10 Dwight Gooden	2.50	1.15	.30
☐ 11 Ryne Sandberg DK	7.50	3.40	.95
☐ 12 Don Mattingly	6.00	2.70	.75
☐ 13 Ozzie Guillen	.60	.25	.08
☐ 14 Dave Righetti	.50	.23	.06
☐ 15 Rick Dempsey	.50	.23	.06
☐ 16 Tom Herr	.50	.23	.06
☐ 17 Julio Franco	.75	.35	.09
☐ 18 Von Hayes	.50	.23	.06
☐ 19 Cal Ripken	12.00	5.50	1.50
☐ 20 Alan Trammell	1.50	.65	.19
☐ 21 Wade Boggs	5.00	2.30	.60
☐ 22 Glenn Davis	.90	.40	.11
☐ 23 Will Clark	7.50	3.40	.95
☐ 24 Nolan Ryan	18.00	8.00	2.30
☐ 25 George Bell	.90	.40	.11
☐ 26 Cecil Fielder	4.00	1.80	.50
☐ 27 Gregg Olson	1.00	.45	.13
☐ 28 Tim Wallach	.50	.23	.06
☐ 29 Ron Darling	.60	.25	.08
☐ 30 Kelly Gruber	.75	.35	.09
☐ 31 Shawn Boskie	.50	.23	.06
☐ 32 Mike Greenwell	1.50	.65	.19
☐ 33 Dave Parker	.90	.40	.11
☐ 34 Joe Magrane	.50	.23	.06
☐ 35 Dave Stewart	.90	.40	.11
☐ 36 Kent Hrbek	.60	.25	.08
☐ 37 Robin Yount	4.00	1.80	.50
☐ 38 Bo Jackson	6.00	2.70	.75
☐ 39 Fernando Valenzuela	.60	.25	.08
☐ 40 Sandy Alomar Jr.	.90	.40	.11
☐ 41 Lance Parrish	.60	.25	.08
☐ 42 Candy Maldonado	.60	.25	.08
☐ 43 Mike LaValliere	.50	.23	.06
☐ 44 Jim Abbott	3.00	1.35	.40
☐ 45 Edgar Martinez	1.50	.65	.19
☐ 46 Kirby Puckett	7.50	3.40	.95
☐ 47 Delino DeShields RR	7.50	3.40	.95
☐ 48 Tony Gwynn	5.00	2.30	.60
☐ 49 Carlton Fisk	2.50	1.15	.30
☐ 50 Mike Scott	.60	.25	.08
☐ 51 Barry Larkin	2.50	1.15	.30
☐ 52 Andre Dawson	3.00	1.35	.40
☐ 53 Tom Glavine	3.00	1.35	.40
☐ 54 Tom Browning	.75	.35	.09
☐ 55 Checklist Card	.50	.23	.06

1990 Donruss Rookies

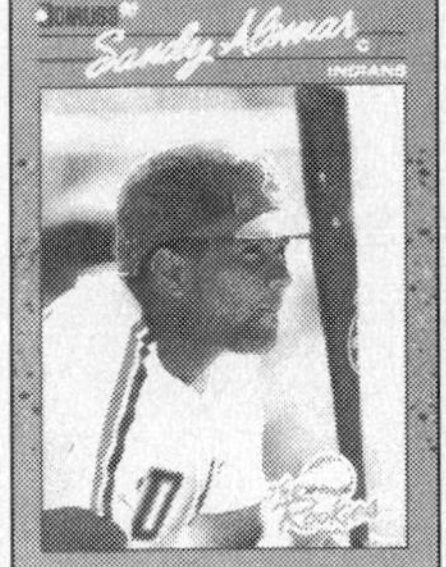
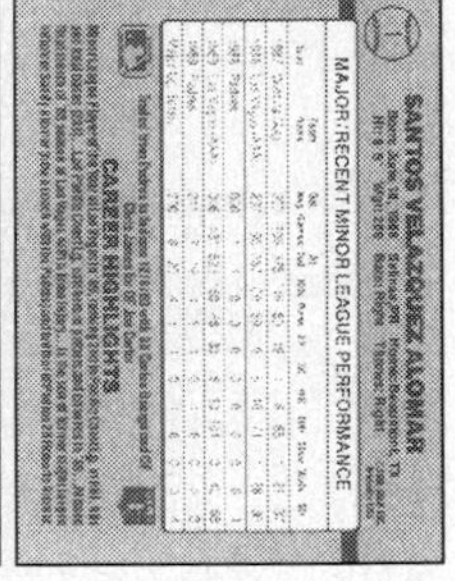

The 1990 Donruss Rookies set marked the fifth consecutive year that Donruss issued a boxed set honoring the best rookies of the season. This set, which used the 1990 Donruss design but featured a green border, was issued exclusively through the Donruss dealer network to hobby dealers. This 56-card, standard size, 2 1/2" by 3 1/2" set came in its own box and the words "The Rookies" are featured prominently on the front of the cards. The key Rookie Cards in this set are Carlos Baerga and Dave Hollins.

	MT	EX-MT	VG
COMPLETE SET (56)	6.00	2.70	.75
COMMON PLAYER (1-56)	.05	.02	.01
☐ 1 Sandy Alomar Jr. UER (No stitches on baseball on Donruss logo on card front)	.10	.05	.01
☐ 2 John Olerud	.60	.25	.08
☐ 3 Pat Combs	.08	.04	.01
☐ 4 Brian DuBois	.05	.02	.01
☐ 5 Felix Jose	.08	.04	.01
☐ 6 Delino DeShields	.60	.25	.08
☐ 7 Mike Stanton	.08	.04	.01
☐ 8 Mike Munoz	.05	.02	.01
☐ 9 Craig Grebeck	.15	.07	.02
☐ 10 Joe Kraemer	.05	.02	.01
☐ 11 Jeff Huson	.05	.02	.01
☐ 12 Bill Sampen	.05	.02	.01
☐ 13 Brian Bohanon	.10	.05	.01
☐ 14 Dave Justice	1.25	.55	.16
☐ 15 Robin Ventura	.60	.25	.08
☐ 16 Greg Vaughn	.20	.09	.03
☐ 17 Wayne Edwards	.05	.02	.01
☐ 18 Shawn Boskie	.10	.05	.01
☐ 19 Carlos Baerga	1.25	.55	.16
☐ 20 Mark Gardner	.12	.05	.02
☐ 21 Kevin Appier	.25	.11	.03
☐ 22 Mike Harkey	.08	.04	.01
☐ 23 Tim Layana	.05	.02	.01
☐ 24 Glenallen Hill	.08	.04	.01
☐ 25 Jerry Kutzler	.05	.02	.01
☐ 26 Mike Blowers	.05	.02	.01

☐ 27 Scott Ruskin	.05	.02	.01
☐ 28 Dana Kiecker	.05	.02	.01
☐ 29 Willie Blair	.10	.05	.01
☐ 30 Ben McDonald	.50	.23	.06
☐ 31 Todd Zeile	.20	.09	.03
☐ 32 Scott Coolbaugh	.05	.02	.01
☐ 33 Xavier Hernandez	.08	.04	.01
☐ 34 Mike Hartley	.05	.02	.01
☐ 35 Kevin Tapani	.35	.16	.04
☐ 36 Kevin Wickander	.05	.02	.01
☐ 37 Carlos Hernandez	.10	.05	.01
☐ 38 Brian Traxler	.10	.05	.01
☐ 39 Marty Brown	.05	.02	.01
☐ 40 Scott Radinsky	.15	.07	.02
☐ 41 Julio Machado	.08	.04	.01
☐ 42 Steve Avery	.60	.25	.08
☐ 43 Mark Lemke	.08	.04	.01
☐ 44 Alan Mills	.12	.05	.02
☐ 45 Marquis Grissom	.60	.25	.08
☐ 46 Greg Olson	.10	.05	.01
☐ 47 Dave Hollins	.60	.25	.08
☐ 48 Jerald Clark	.08	.04	.01
☐ 49 Eric Anthony	.30	.14	.04
☐ 50 Tim Drummond	.05	.02	.01
☐ 51 John Burkett	.10	.05	.01
☐ 52 Brent Knackert	.10	.05	.01
☐ 53 Jeff Shaw	.05	.02	.01
☐ 54 John Orton	.10	.05	.01
☐ 55 Terry Shumpert	.05	.02	.01
☐ 56 Checklist Card	.08	.01	.00

1990 Donruss Super DK's

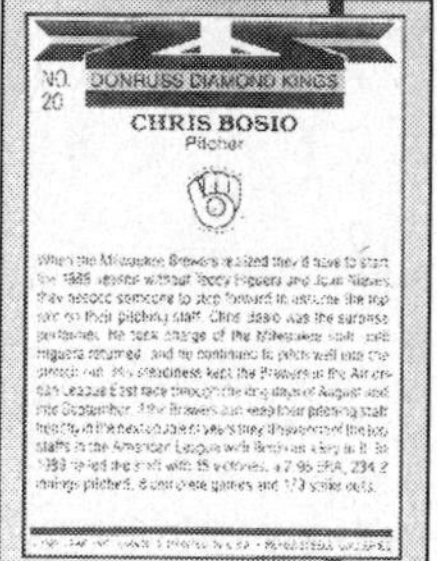

This 26-player card set was available through a mail-in offer detailed on the wax packs. The set was sent in return for 10.00 and three wrappers plus 2.00 postage and handling. The set features the popular Diamond King subseries in large (approximately 4 7/8" by 6 13/16") form. Dick Perez of Perez-Steele Galleries did another outstanding job on the artwork. The cards are essentially a large version of the Donruss regular issue Diamond Kings.

	MT	EX-MT	VG
COMPLETE SET (26)	12.00	5.50	1.50
COMMON PLAYER (1-26)	.35	.16	.04
☐ 1 Bo Jackson	1.00	.45	.13
☐ 2 Steve Sax	.45	.20	.06
☐ 3 Ruben Sierra	.90	.40	.11
☐ 4 Ken Griffey Jr.	4.00	1.80	.50
☐ 5 Mickey Tettleton	.45	.20	.06
☐ 6 Dave Stewart	.45	.20	.06
☐ 7 Jim Deshaies	.35	.16	.04
☐ 8 John Smoltz	.60	.25	.08
☐ 9 Mike Bielecki	.35	.16	.04
☐ 10 Brian Downing	.35	.16	.04
☐ 11 Kevin Mitchell	.60	.25	.08
☐ 12 Kelly Gruber	.45	.20	.06
☐ 13 Joe Magrane	.35	.16	.04
☐ 14 John Franco	.45	.20	.06
☐ 15 Ozzie Guillen	.35	.16	.04
☐ 16 Lou Whitaker	.45	.20	.06
☐ 17 John Smiley	.45	.20	.06
☐ 18 Howard Johnson	.45	.20	.06
☐ 19 Willie Randolph	.45	.20	.06
☐ 20 Chris Bosio	.45	.20	.06
☐ 21 Tommy Herr	.35	.16	.04
☐ 22 Dan Gladden	.35	.16	.04
☐ 23 Ellis Burks	.45	.20	.06
☐ 24 Pete O'Brien	.35	.16	.04
☐ 25 Bryn Smith	.35	.16	.04
☐ 26 Ed Whitson	.35	.16	.04

1991 Donruss Previews

This 12-card set was issued by Donruss for hobby dealers as examples of what the 1991 Donruss cards would look like. This standard size, 2 1/2" by 3 1/2", set had the 1991 Donruss design on the front; the back merely says 1991 Preview card and identifies the player and the team.

	MT	EX-MT	VG
COMPLETE SET (12)	450.00	200.00	57.50
COMMON PLAYER (1-12)	12.00	5.50	1.50
☐ 1 Dave Justice	75.00	34.00	9.50
☐ 2 Doug Drabek	15.00	6.75	1.90
☐ 3 Scott Chiamparino	12.00	5.50	1.50
☐ 4 Ken Griffey Jr.	150.00	70.00	19.00
☐ 5 Bob Welch	12.00	5.50	1.50
☐ 6 Tino Martinez	20.00	9.00	2.50
☐ 7 Nolan Ryan	200.00	90.00	25.00
☐ 8 Dwight Gooden	35.00	16.00	4.40
☐ 9 Ryne Sandberg	90.00	40.00	11.50
☐ 10 Barry Bonds	60.00	27.00	7.50
☐ 11 Jose Canseco	75.00	34.00	9.50
☐ 12 Eddie Murray	30.00	13.50	3.80

1991 Donruss

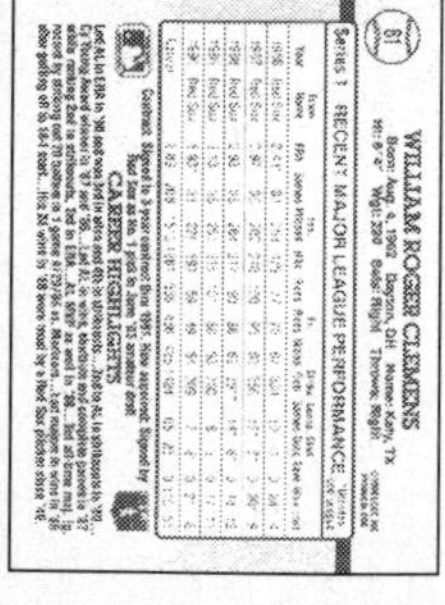

The 1991 Donruss set was issued in two separate series of 396 cards each. This set marked the first time Donruss has issued their cards in series. The cards feature a blue border with some stripes and the players name in white against a red background. The cards measure the standard size of 2 1/2" by 3 1/2". Series I contained 386 cards (numbered 1-386) and another ten cards numbered BC1-BC10. These bonus cards were randomnly inserted in Donruss packs and highlight outstanding player achievements. The first 26 cards again feature the artwork of Dick Perez drawing each team's Diamond King. The first series also contains 20 Rated Rookie (RR) cards and nine All-Star cards (the AS cards are all American Leaguers in this first series). On cards 60, 70, 127, 182, 239, 294, 355, 368, and 377, the border stripes are red and yellow. As a separate promotion wax packs were also given away with six and 12-packs of Coke and Diet Coke. The key Rookie Cards in the set are Wes Chamberlain, Brian McRae, Pedro Munoz, and Phil Plantier. The second series was issued approximately three months after the first series was issued. This series features the 26 MVP cards which Donruss had issued for the three previous years as their Bonus Cards, twenty more rated Rookie Cards and nine All-Star Cards (National Leaguers in this series). There were also special cards to honor the award winners and the heroes of the World Series. Bringing the total to 22, 12 additional Bonus Cards were randomly inserted in packs and pick up in time beginning with Valenzuela's no-hitter and continuing until the end of the season.

	MT	EX-MT	VG
COMPLETE SET (792)	15.00	6.75	1.90
COMPLETE W/4 LEAF PRVWS	25.00	11.50	3.10
COMPLETE W/4 STUDIO PRVWS	20.00	9.00	2.50
COMPLETE BC SET (22)	1.50	.65	.19
COMMON PLAYER (1-386)	.04	.02	.01
COMMON PLAYER (387-770)	.04	.02	.01
COMMON BC (BC1-BC10)	.06	.03	.01
COMMON BC (BC11-BC22)	.06	.03	.01

	MT	EX-MT	VG
☐ 1 Dave Stieb DK	.05	.02	.01
☐ 2 Craig Biggio DK	.05	.02	.01
☐ 3 Cecil Fielder DK	.10	.05	.01
☐ 4 Barry Bonds DK	.10	.05	.01
☐ 5 Barry Larkin DK	.08	.04	.01
☐ 6 Dave Parker DK	.05	.02	.01
☐ 7 Len Dykstra DK	.05	.02	.01
☐ 8 Bobby Thigpen DK	.05	.02	.01
☐ 9 Roger Clemens DK	.12	.05	.02
☐ 10 Ron Gant DK UER (No trademark on team logo on back)	.10	.05	.01
☐ 11 Delino DeShields DK	.10	.05	.01
☐ 12 Roberto Alomar DK UER (No trademark on team logo on back)	.12	.05	.02
☐ 13 Sandy Alomar Jr. DK	.05	.02	.01
☐ 14 Ryne Sandberg DK UER (Was DK in '85, not '83 as shown)	.12	.05	.02
☐ 15 Ramon Martinez DK	.05	.02	.01
☐ 16 Edgar Martinez DK	.05	.02	.01
☐ 17 Dave Magadan DK	.05	.02	.01
☐ 18 Matt Williams DK	.05	.02	.01
☐ 19 Rafael Palmeiro DK UER (No trademark on team logo on back)	.05	.02	.01
☐ 20 Bob Welch DK	.05	.02	.01
☐ 21 Dave Righetti DK	.05	.02	.01
☐ 22 Brian Harper DK	.05	.02	.01
☐ 23 Gregg Olson DK	.05	.02	.01
☐ 24 Kurt Stillwell DK	.05	.02	.01
☐ 25 Pedro Guerrero DK UER (No trademark on team logo on back)	.05	.02	.01
☐ 26 Chuck Finley DK UER (No trademark on team logo on back)	.05	.02	.01
☐ 27 DK Checklist	.05	.01	.00
☐ 28 Tino Martinez RR	.10	.05	.01
☐ 29 Mark Lewis RR	.12	.05	.02
☐ 30 Bernard Gilkey RR	.15	.07	.02
☐ 31 Hensley Meulens RR	.08	.04	.01
☐ 32 Derek Bell RR	.30	.14	.04
☐ 33 Jose Offerman RR	.10	.05	.01
☐ 34 Terry Bross RR	.05	.02	.01
☐ 35 Leo Gomez RR	.25	.11	.03
☐ 36 Derrick May RR	.10	.05	.01
☐ 37 Kevin Morton RR	.10	.05	.01
☐ 38 Moises Alou RR	.25	.11	.03
☐ 39 Julio Valera RR	.15	.07	.02
☐ 40 Milt Cuyler RR	.10	.05	.01
☐ 41 Phil Plantier RR	.50	.23	.06
☐ 42 Scott Chiamparino RR	.08	.04	.01
☐ 43 Ray Lankford RR	.40	.18	.05
☐ 44 Mickey Morandini RR	.12	.05	.02
☐ 45 Dave Hansen RR	.10	.05	.01
☐ 46 Kevin Belcher RR	.10	.05	.01
☐ 47 Darrin Fletcher RR	.05	.02	.01
☐ 48 Steve Sax AS	.05	.02	.01
☐ 49 Ken Griffey Jr. AS	.25	.11	.03
☐ 50A Jose Canseco AS ERR (Team in stat box should be AL, not A's)	.12	.05	.02
☐ 50B Jose Canseco AS COR	1.00	.45	.13
☐ 51 Sandy Alomar Jr. AS	.05	.02	.01
☐ 52 Cal Ripken AS	.15	.07	.02
☐ 53 Rickey Henderson AS	.10	.05	.01
☐ 54 Bob Welch AS	.05	.02	.01
☐ 55 Wade Boggs AS	.10	.05	.01
☐ 56 Mark McGwire AS	.10	.05	.01
☐ 57A Jack McDowell ERR (Career stats do not include 1990)	.10	.05	.01
☐ 57B Jack McDowell COR (Career stats do not include 1990)	.50	.23	.06
☐ 58 Jose Lind	.04	.02	.01
☐ 59 Alex Fernandez	.15	.07	.02
☐ 60 Pat Combs	.04	.02	.01
☐ 61 Mike Walker	.04	.02	.01
☐ 62 Juan Samuel	.04	.02	.01
☐ 63 Mike Blowers UER (Last line has aseball, not baseball)	.04	.02	.01
☐ 64 Mark Guthrie	.04	.02	.01
☐ 65 Mark Salas	.04	.02	.01
☐ 66 Tim Jones	.04	.02	.01
☐ 67 Tim Leary	.04	.02	.01
☐ 68 Andres Galarraga	.04	.02	.01
☐ 69 Bob Milacki	.04	.02	.01
☐ 70 Tim Belcher	.07	.03	.01
☐ 71 Todd Zeile	.07	.03	.01
☐ 72 Jerome Walton	.04	.02	.01
☐ 73 Kevin Seitzer	.07	.03	.01
☐ 74 Jerald Clark	.04	.02	.01
☐ 75 John Smoltz UER (Born in Detroit, not Warren)	.10	.05	.01
☐ 76 Mike Henneman	.04	.02	.01
☐ 77 Ken Griffey Jr.	.50	.23	.06
☐ 78 Jim Abbott	.12	.05	.02
☐ 79 Gregg Jefferies	.07	.03	.01
☐ 80 Kevin Reimer	.10	.05	.01
☐ 81 Roger Clemens	.25	.11	.03
☐ 82 Mike Fitzgerald	.04	.02	.01
☐ 83 Bruce Hurst UER (Middle name is Lee, not Vee)	.07	.03	.01
☐ 84 Eric Davis	.07	.03	.01
☐ 85 Paul Molitor	.10	.05	.01
☐ 86 Will Clark	.20	.09	.03
☐ 87 Mike Bielecki	.04	.02	.01
☐ 88 Bret Saberhagen	.07	.03	.01
☐ 89 Nolan Ryan	.40	.18	.05
☐ 90 Bobby Thigpen	.04	.02	.01
☐ 91 Dickie Thon	.04	.02	.01
☐ 92 Duane Ward	.04	.02	.01
☐ 93 Luis Polonia	.07	.03	.01
☐ 94 Terry Kennedy	.04	.02	.01
☐ 95 Kent Hrbek	.07	.03	.01
☐ 96 Danny Jackson	.04	.02	.01
☐ 97 Sid Fernandez	.07	.03	.01
☐ 98 Jimmy Key	.04	.02	.01
☐ 99 Franklin Stubbs	.04	.02	.01
☐ 100 Checklist Card	.05	.01	.00
☐ 101 R.J. Reynolds	.04	.02	.01
☐ 102 Dave Stewart	.07	.03	.01
☐ 103 Dan Pasqua	.04	.02	.01
☐ 104 Dan Plesac	.04	.02	.01
☐ 105 Mark McGwire	.20	.09	.03
☐ 106 John Farrell	.04	.02	.01
☐ 107 Don Mattingly	.15	.07	.02
☐ 108 Carlton Fisk	.10	.05	.01
☐ 109 Ken Oberkfell	.04	.02	.01
☐ 110 Darrel Akerfelds	.04	.02	.01
☐ 111 Gregg Olson	.07	.03	.01
☐ 112 Mike Scioscia	.04	.02	.01
☐ 113 Bryn Smith	.04	.02	.01
☐ 114 Bob Geren	.04	.02	.01
☐ 115 Tom Candiotti	.04	.02	.01
☐ 116 Kevin Tapani	.07	.03	.01
☐ 117 Jeff Treadway	.04	.02	.01
☐ 118 Alan Trammell	.07	.03	.01
☐ 119 Pete O'Brien (Blue shading goes through stats)	.04	.02	.01
☐ 120 Joel Skinner	.04	.02	.01

☐ 121 Mike LaValliere .04 .02 .01
☐ 122 Dwight Evans .07 .03 .01
☐ 123 Jody Reed .04 .02 .01
☐ 124 Lee Guetterman .04 .02 .01
☐ 125 Tim Burke .04 .02 .01
☐ 126 Dave Johnson .04 .02 .01
☐ 127 Fernando Valenzuela .07 .03 .01
(Lower large stripe in yellow instead of blue) UER
☐ 128 Jose DeLeon .04 .02 .01
☐ 129 Andre Dawson .10 .05 .01
☐ 130 Gerald Perry .04 .02 .01
☐ 131 Greg W. Harris .04 .02 .01
☐ 132 Tom Glavine .20 .09 .03
☐ 133 Lance McCullers .04 .02 .01
☐ 134 Randy Johnson .07 .03 .01
☐ 135 Lance Parrish UER .07 .03 .01
(Born in McKeesport, not Clairton)
☐ 136 Mackey Sasser .04 .02 .01
☐ 137 Geno Petralli .04 .02 .01
☐ 138 Dennis Lamp .04 .02 .01
☐ 139 Dennis Martinez .07 .03 .01
☐ 140 Mike Pagliarulo .04 .02 .01
☐ 141 Hal Morris .07 .03 .01
☐ 142 Dave Parker .07 .03 .01
☐ 143 Brett Butler .07 .03 .01
☐ 144 Paul Assenmacher .04 .02 .01
☐ 145 Mark Gubicza .04 .02 .01
☐ 146 Charlie Hough .04 .02 .01
☐ 147 Sammy Sosa .07 .03 .01
☐ 148 Randy Ready .04 .02 .01
☐ 149 Kelly Gruber .07 .03 .01
☐ 150 Devon White .07 .03 .01
☐ 151 Gary Carter .07 .03 .01
☐ 152 Gene Larkin .04 .02 .01
☐ 153 Chris Sabo .07 .03 .01
☐ 154 David Cone .10 .05 .01
☐ 155 Todd Stottlemyre .07 .03 .01
☐ 156 Glenn Wilson .04 .02 .01
☐ 157 Bob Walk .04 .02 .01
☐ 158 Mike Gallego .04 .02 .01
☐ 159 Greg Hibbard .04 .02 .01
☐ 160 Chris Bosio .04 .02 .01
☐ 161 Mike Moore .04 .02 .01
☐ 162 Jerry Browne UER .04 .02 .01
(Born Christiansted, should be St. Croix)
☐ 163 Steve Sax UER .07 .03 .01
(No asterisk next to his 1989 At Bats)
☐ 164 Melido Perez .07 .03 .01
☐ 165 Danny Darwin .04 .02 .01
☐ 166 Roger McDowell .04 .02 .01
☐ 167 Bill Ripken .04 .02 .01
☐ 168 Mike Sharperson .04 .02 .01
☐ 169 Lee Smith .07 .03 .01
☐ 170 Matt Nokes .04 .02 .01
☐ 171 Jesse Orosco .04 .02 .01
☐ 172 Rick Aguilera .07 .03 .01
☐ 173 Jim Presley .04 .02 .01
☐ 174 Lou Whitaker .07 .03 .01
☐ 175 Harold Reynolds .04 .02 .01
☐ 176 Brook Jacoby .04 .02 .01
☐ 177 Wally Backman .04 .02 .01
☐ 178 Wade Boggs .12 .05 .02
☐ 179 Chuck Cary .04 .02 .01
(Comma after DOB, not on other cards)
☐ 180 Tom Foley .04 .02 .01
☐ 181 Pete Harnisch .07 .03 .01
☐ 182 Mike Morgan .04 .02 .01
☐ 183 Bob Tewksbury .07 .03 .01
☐ 184 Joe Girardi .04 .02 .01
☐ 185 Storm Davis .04 .02 .01
☐ 186 Ed Whitson .04 .02 .01
☐ 187 Steve Avery UER .20 .09 .03
(Born in New Jersey, should be Michigan)
☐ 188 Lloyd Moseby .04 .02 .01
☐ 189 Scott Bankhead .04 .02 .01
☐ 190 Mark Langston .07 .03 .01
☐ 191 Kevin McReynolds .07 .03 .01
☐ 192 Julio Franco .07 .03 .01
☐ 193 John Dopson .04 .02 .01
☐ 194 Dennis Boyd .04 .02 .01
☐ 195 Bip Roberts .07 .03 .01
☐ 196 Billy Hatcher .04 .02 .01
☐ 197 Edgar Diaz .04 .02 .01
☐ 198 Greg Litton .04 .02 .01
☐ 199 Mark Grace .10 .05 .01
☐ 200 Checklist Card .05 .01 .00
☐ 201 George Brett .10 .05 .01
☐ 202 Jeff Russell .04 .02 .01
☐ 203 Ivan Calderon .04 .02 .01
☐ 204 Ken Howell .04 .02 .01
☐ 205 Tom Henke .07 .03 .01
☐ 206 Bryan Harvey .04 .02 .01
☐ 207 Steve Bedrosian .04 .02 .01
☐ 208 Al Newman .04 .02 .01
☐ 209 Randy Myers .07 .03 .01
☐ 210 Daryl Boston .04 .02 .01
☐ 211 Manny Lee .04 .02 .01
☐ 212 Dave Smith .04 .02 .01
☐ 213 Don Slaught .04 .02 .01
☐ 214 Walt Weiss .04 .02 .01
☐ 215 Donn Pall .04 .02 .01
☐ 216 Jaime Navarro .07 .03 .01
☐ 217 Willie Randolph .07 .03 .01
☐ 218 Rudy Seanez .12 .05 .02
☐ 219 Jim Leyritz .04 .02 .01
☐ 220 Ron Karkovice .04 .02 .01
☐ 221 Ken Caminiti .07 .03 .01
☐ 222 Von Hayes .04 .02 .01
☐ 223 Cal Ripken .30 .14 .04
☐ 224 Lenny Harris .04 .02 .01
☐ 225 Milt Thompson .04 .02 .01
☐ 226 Alvaro Espinoza .04 .02 .01
☐ 227 Chris James .04 .02 .01
☐ 228 Dan Gladden .04 .02 .01
☐ 229 Jeff Blauser .04 .02 .01
☐ 230 Mike Heath .04 .02 .01
☐ 231 Omar Vizquel .04 .02 .01
☐ 232 Doug Jones .04 .02 .01
☐ 233 Jeff King .04 .02 .01
☐ 234 Luis Rivera .04 .02 .01
☐ 235 Ellis Burks .07 .03 .01
☐ 236 Greg Cadaret .04 .02 .01
☐ 237 Dave Martinez .04 .02 .01
☐ 238 Mark Williamson .04 .02 .01
☐ 239 Stan Javier .04 .02 .01
☐ 240 Ozzie Smith .10 .05 .01
☐ 241 Shawn Boskie .04 .02 .01
☐ 242 Tom Gordon .07 .03 .01
☐ 243 Tony Gwynn .12 .05 .02
☐ 244 Tommy Gregg .04 .02 .01
☐ 245 Jeff M. Robinson .04 .02 .01
☐ 246 Keith Comstock .04 .02 .01
☐ 247 Jack Howell .04 .02 .01
☐ 248 Keith Miller .04 .02 .01
☐ 249 Bobby Witt .04 .02 .01
☐ 250 Rob Murphy UER .04 .02 .01
(Shown as on Reds in '89 in stats, should be Red Sox)
☐ 251 Spike Owen .04 .02 .01
☐ 252 Garry Templeton .04 .02 .01
☐ 253 Glenn Braggs .04 .02 .01
☐ 254 Ron Robinson .04 .02 .01
☐ 255 Kevin Mitchell .07 .03 .01
☐ 256 Les Lancaster .04 .02 .01
☐ 257 Mel Stottlemyre Jr. .04 .02 .01
☐ 258 Kenny Rogers UER .04 .02 .01
(IP listed as 171, should be 172)
☐ 259 Lance Johnson .04 .02 .01
☐ 260 John Kruk .07 .03 .01
☐ 261 Fred McGriff .12 .05 .02
☐ 262 Dick Schofield .04 .02 .01
☐ 263 Trevor Wilson .04 .02 .01
☐ 264 David West .04 .02 .01
☐ 265 Scott Scudder .04 .02 .01
☐ 266 Dwight Gooden .07 .03 .01
☐ 267 Willie Blair .04 .02 .01
☐ 268 Mark Portugal .04 .02 .01
☐ 269 Doug Drabek .07 .03 .01
☐ 270 Dennis Eckersley .12 .05 .02
☐ 271 Eric King .04 .02 .01
☐ 272 Robin Yount .10 .05 .01
☐ 273 Carney Lansford .07 .03 .01
☐ 274 Carlos Baerga .20 .09 .03
☐ 275 Dave Righetti .04 .02 .01
☐ 276 Scott Fletcher .04 .02 .01
☐ 277 Eric Yelding .04 .02 .01
☐ 278 Charlie Hayes .04 .02 .01
☐ 279 Jeff Ballard .04 .02 .01
☐ 280 Orel Hershiser .07 .03 .01
☐ 281 Jose Oquendo .04 .02 .01
☐ 282 Mike Witt .04 .02 .01
☐ 283 Mitch Webster .04 .02 .01
☐ 284 Greg Gagne .04 .02 .01
☐ 285 Greg Olson .04 .02 .01
☐ 286 Tony Phillips UER .04 .02 .01
(Born 4/15, should be 4/25)

☐ 287 Scott Bradley	.04	.02	.01
☐ 288 Cory Snyder UER (In text, led is repeated and Inglewood is misspelled as Englewood)	.04	.02	.01
☐ 289 Jay Bell UER (Born in Pensacola, not Eglin AFB)	.07	.03	.01
☐ 290 Kevin Romine	.04	.02	.01
☐ 291 Jeff D. Robinson	.04	.02	.01
☐ 292 Steve Frey UER (Bats left, should be right)	.04	.02	.01
☐ 293 Craig Worthington	.04	.02	.01
☐ 294 Tim Crews	.04	.02	.01
☐ 295 Joe Magrane	.04	.02	.01
☐ 296 Hector Villanueva	.04	.02	.01
☐ 297 Terry Shumpert	.04	.02	.01
☐ 298 Joe Carter	.12	.05	.02
☐ 299 Kent Mercker UER (IP listed as 53, should be 52)	.07	.03	.01
☐ 300 Checklist Card	.05	.01	.00
☐ 301 Chet Lemon	.04	.02	.01
☐ 302 Mike Schooler	.04	.02	.01
☐ 303 Dante Bichette	.04	.02	.01
☐ 304 Kevin Elster	.04	.02	.01
☐ 305 Jeff Huson	.04	.02	.01
☐ 306 Greg A. Harris	.04	.02	.01
☐ 307 Marquis Grissom UER (Middle name Deon, should be Dean)	.15	.07	.02
☐ 308 Calvin Schiraldi	.04	.02	.01
☐ 309 Mariano Duncan	.04	.02	.01
☐ 310 Bill Spiers	.04	.02	.01
☐ 311 Scott Garrelts	.04	.02	.01
☐ 312 Mitch Williams	.04	.02	.01
☐ 313 Mike Macfarlane	.04	.02	.01
☐ 314 Kevin Brown	.07	.03	.01
☐ 315 Robin Ventura	.20	.09	.03
☐ 316 Darren Daulton	.07	.03	.01
☐ 317 Pat Borders	.04	.02	.01
☐ 318 Mark Eichhorn	.04	.02	.01
☐ 319 Jeff Brantley	.04	.02	.01
☐ 320 Shane Mack	.07	.03	.01
☐ 321 Rob Dibble	.07	.03	.01
☐ 322 John Franco	.07	.03	.01
☐ 323 Junior Felix	.04	.02	.01
☐ 324 Casey Candaele	.04	.02	.01
☐ 325 Bobby Bonilla	.10	.05	.01
☐ 326 Dave Henderson	.04	.02	.01
☐ 327 Wayne Edwards	.04	.02	.01
☐ 328 Mark Knudson	.04	.02	.01
☐ 329 Terry Steinbach	.07	.03	.01
☐ 330 Colby Ward UER (No comma between city and state)	.04	.02	.01
☐ 331 Oscar Azocar	.04	.02	.01
☐ 332 Scott Radinsky	.04	.02	.01
☐ 333 Eric Anthony	.07	.03	.01
☐ 334 Steve Lake	.04	.02	.01
☐ 335 Bob Melvin	.04	.02	.01
☐ 336 Kal Daniels	.04	.02	.01
☐ 337 Tom Pagnozzi	.04	.02	.01
☐ 338 Alan Mills	.04	.02	.01
☐ 339 Steve Olin	.07	.03	.01
☐ 340 Juan Berenguer	.04	.02	.01
☐ 341 Francisco Cabrera	.04	.02	.01
☐ 342 Dave Bergman	.04	.02	.01
☐ 343 Henry Cotto	.04	.02	.01
☐ 344 Sergio Valdez	.04	.02	.01
☐ 345 Bob Patterson	.04	.02	.01
☐ 346 John Marzano	.04	.02	.01
☐ 347 Dana Kiecker	.04	.02	.01
☐ 348 Dion James	.04	.02	.01
☐ 349 Hubie Brooks	.04	.02	.01
☐ 350 Bill Landrum	.04	.02	.01
☐ 351 Bill Sampen	.04	.02	.01
☐ 352 Greg Briley	.04	.02	.01
☐ 353 Paul Gibson	.04	.02	.01
☐ 354 Dave Eiland	.04	.02	.01
☐ 355 Steve Finley	.07	.03	.01
☐ 356 Bob Boone	.07	.03	.01
☐ 357 Steve Buechele	.04	.02	.01
☐ 358 Chris Hoiles	.15	.07	.02
☐ 359 Larry Walker	.20	.09	.03
☐ 360 Frank DiPino	.04	.02	.01
☐ 361 Mark Grant	.04	.02	.01
☐ 362 Dave Magadan	.07	.03	.01
☐ 363 Robby Thompson	.04	.02	.01
☐ 364 Lonnie Smith	.04	.02	.01
☐ 365 Steve Farr	.04	.02	.01
☐ 366 Dave Valle	.04	.02	.01
☐ 367 Tim Naehring	.07	.03	.01
☐ 368 Jim Acker	.04	.02	.01
☐ 369 Jeff Reardon UER (Born in Pittsfield, not Dalton)	.07	.03	.01
☐ 370 Tim Teufel	.04	.02	.01
☐ 371 Juan Gonzalez	.35	.16	.04
☐ 372 Luis Salazar	.04	.02	.01
☐ 373 Rick Honeycutt	.04	.02	.01
☐ 374 Greg Maddux	.10	.05	.01
☐ 375 Jose Uribe UER (Middle name Elta, should be Alta)	.04	.02	.01
☐ 376 Donnie Hill	.04	.02	.01
☐ 377 Don Carman	.04	.02	.01
☐ 378 Craig Grebeck	.04	.02	.01
☐ 379 Willie Fraser	.04	.02	.01
☐ 380 Glenallen Hill	.04	.02	.01
☐ 381 Joe Oliver	.04	.02	.01
☐ 382 Randy Bush	.04	.02	.01
☐ 383 Alex Cole	.04	.02	.01
☐ 384 Norm Charlton	.07	.03	.01
☐ 385 Gene Nelson	.04	.02	.01
☐ 386 Checklist Card	.05	.01	.00
☐ 387 Rickey Henderson MVP	.10	.05	.01
☐ 388 Lance Parrish MVP	.05	.02	.01
☐ 389 Fred McGriff MVP	.10	.05	.01
☐ 390 Dave Parker MVP	.05	.02	.01
☐ 391 Candy Maldonado MVP	.05	.02	.01
☐ 392 Ken Griffey Jr. MVP	.25	.11	.03
☐ 393 Gregg Olson MVP	.05	.02	.01
☐ 394 Rafael Palmeiro MVP	.08	.04	.01
☐ 395 Roger Clemens MVP	.12	.05	.02
☐ 396 George Brett MVP	.10	.05	.01
☐ 397 Cecil Fielder MVP	.10	.05	.01
☐ 398 Brian Harper MVP UER (Major League Performance, should be Career)	.05	.02	.01
☐ 399 Bobby Thigpen MVP	.05	.02	.01
☐ 400 Roberto Kelly MVP UER (Second Base on front and OF on back)	.05	.02	.01
☐ 401 Danny Darwin MVP	.05	.02	.01
☐ 402 Dave Justice MVP	.15	.07	.02
☐ 403 Lee Smith MVP	.05	.02	.01
☐ 404 Ryne Sandberg MVP	.12	.05	.02
☐ 405 Eddie Murray MVP	.10	.05	.01
☐ 406 Tim Wallach MVP	.05	.02	.01
☐ 407 Kevin Mitchell MVP	.05	.02	.01
☐ 408 Darryl Strawberry MVP	.10	.05	.01
☐ 409 Joe Carter MVP	.08	.04	.01
☐ 410 Len Dykstra MVP	.05	.02	.01
☐ 411 Doug Drabek MVP	.05	.02	.01
☐ 412 Chris Sabo MVP	.05	.02	.01
☐ 413 Paul Marak RR	.05	.02	.01
☐ 414 Tim McIntosh RR	.05	.02	.01
☐ 415 Brian Barnes RR	.12	.05	.02
☐ 416 Eric Gunderson RR	.05	.02	.01
☐ 417 Mike Gardiner RR	.10	.05	.01
☐ 418 Steve Carter RR	.05	.02	.01
☐ 419 Gerald Alexander RR	.10	.05	.01
☐ 420 Rich Garces RR	.10	.05	.01
☐ 421 Chuck Knoblauch RR	.40	.18	.05
☐ 422 Scott Aldred RR	.10	.05	.01
☐ 423 Wes Chamberlain RR	.20	.09	.03
☐ 424 Lance Dickson RR	.10	.05	.01
☐ 425 Greg Colbrunn RR	.25	.11	.03
☐ 426 Rich DeLucia RR UER (Misspelled Delucia on card)	.05	.02	.01
☐ 427 Jeff Conine RR	.25	.11	.03
☐ 428 Steve Decker RR	.15	.07	.02
☐ 429 Turner Ward RR	.10	.05	.01
☐ 430 Mo Vaughn RR	.20	.09	.03
☐ 431 Steve Chitren RR	.10	.05	.01
☐ 432 Mike Benjamin RR	.05	.02	.01
☐ 433 Ryne Sandberg AS	.12	.05	.02
☐ 434 Len Dykstra AS	.05	.02	.01
☐ 435 Andre Dawson AS	.10	.05	.01
☐ 436A Mike Scioscia AS (White star by name)	.05	.02	.01
☐ 436B Mike Scioscia AS (Yellow star by name)	.05	.02	.01
☐ 437 Ozzie Smith AS	.10	.05	.01
☐ 438 Kevin Mitchell AS	.05	.02	.01
☐ 439 Jack Armstrong AS	.05	.02	.01
☐ 440 Chris Sabo AS	.05	.02	.01
☐ 441 Will Clark AS	.10	.05	.01
☐ 442 Mel Hall	.04	.02	.01
☐ 443 Mark Gardner	.04	.02	.01
☐ 444 Mike Devereaux	.07	.03	.01
☐ 445 Kirk Gibson	.07	.03	.01

☐ 446 Terry Pendleton	.10	.05	.01
☐ 447 Mike Harkey	.07	.03	.01
☐ 448 Jim Eisenreich	.04	.02	.01
☐ 449 Benito Santiago	.07	.03	.01
☐ 450 Oddibe McDowell	.04	.02	.01
☐ 451 Cecil Fielder	.12	.05	.02
☐ 452 Ken Griffey Sr.	.07	.03	.01
☐ 453 Bert Blyleven	.07	.03	.01
☐ 454 Howard Johnson	.07	.03	.01
☐ 455 Monty Fariss UER (Misspelled Farris on card)	.15	.07	.02
☐ 456 Tony Pena	.04	.02	.01
☐ 457 Tim Raines	.07	.03	.01
☐ 458 Dennis Rasmussen	.04	.02	.01
☐ 459 Luis Quinones	.04	.02	.01
☐ 460 B.J. Surhoff	.04	.02	.01
☐ 461 Ernest Riles	.04	.02	.01
☐ 462 Rick Sutcliffe	.07	.03	.01
☐ 463 Danny Tartabull	.07	.03	.01
☐ 464 Pete Incaviglia	.04	.02	.01
☐ 465 Carlos Martinez	.04	.02	.01
☐ 466 Ricky Jordan	.04	.02	.01
☐ 467 John Cerutti	.04	.02	.01
☐ 468 Dave Winfield	.10	.05	.01
☐ 469 Francisco Oliveras	.04	.02	.01
☐ 470 Roy Smith	.04	.02	.01
☐ 471 Barry Larkin	.10	.05	.01
☐ 472 Ron Darling	.07	.03	.01
☐ 473 David Wells	.04	.02	.01
☐ 474 Glenn Davis	.07	.03	.01
☐ 475 Neal Heaton	.04	.02	.01
☐ 476 Ron Hassey	.04	.02	.01
☐ 477 Frank Thomas	1.25	.55	.16
☐ 478 Greg Vaughn	.10	.05	.01
☐ 479 Todd Burns	.04	.02	.01
☐ 480 Candy Maldonado	.04	.02	.01
☐ 481 Dave LaPoint	.04	.02	.01
☐ 482 Alvin Davis	.04	.02	.01
☐ 483 Mike Scott	.04	.02	.01
☐ 484 Dale Murphy	.07	.03	.01
☐ 485 Ben McDonald	.10	.05	.01
☐ 486 Jay Howell	.04	.02	.01
☐ 487 Vince Coleman	.07	.03	.01
☐ 488 Alfredo Griffin	.04	.02	.01
☐ 489 Sandy Alomar Jr.	.07	.03	.01
☐ 490 Kirby Puckett	.20	.09	.03
☐ 491 Andres Thomas	.04	.02	.01
☐ 492 Jack Morris	.10	.05	.01
☐ 493 Matt Young	.04	.02	.01
☐ 494 Greg Myers	.04	.02	.01
☐ 495 Barry Bonds	.20	.09	.03
☐ 496 Scott Cooper UER (No BA for 1990 and career)	.25	.11	.03
☐ 497 Dan Schatzeder	.04	.02	.01
☐ 498 Jesse Barfield	.04	.02	.01
☐ 499 Jerry Goff	.04	.02	.01
☐ 500 Checklist Card	.05	.01	.00
☐ 501 Anthony Telford	.04	.02	.01
☐ 502 Eddie Murray	.10	.05	.01
☐ 503 Omar Olivares	.12	.05	.02
☐ 504 Ryne Sandberg	.25	.11	.03
☐ 505 Jeff Montgomery	.04	.02	.01
☐ 506 Mark Parent	.04	.02	.01
☐ 507 Ron Gant	.12	.05	.02
☐ 508 Frank Tanana	.04	.02	.01
☐ 509 Jay Buhner	.07	.03	.01
☐ 510 Max Venable	.04	.02	.01
☐ 511 Wally Whitehurst	.04	.02	.01
☐ 512 Gary Pettis	.04	.02	.01
☐ 513 Tom Brunansky	.07	.03	.01
☐ 514 Tim Wallach	.07	.03	.01
☐ 515 Craig Lefferts	.04	.02	.01
☐ 516 Tim Layana	.04	.02	.01
☐ 517 Darryl Hamilton	.07	.03	.01
☐ 518 Rick Reuschel	.04	.02	.01
☐ 519 Steve Wilson	.04	.02	.01
☐ 520 Kurt Stillwell	.04	.02	.01
☐ 521 Rafael Palmeiro	.10	.05	.01
☐ 522 Ken Patterson	.04	.02	.01
☐ 523 Len Dykstra	.07	.03	.01
☐ 524 Tony Fernandez	.07	.03	.01
☐ 525 Kent Anderson	.04	.02	.01
☐ 526 Mark Leonard	.10	.05	.01
☐ 527 Allan Anderson	.04	.02	.01
☐ 528 Tom Browning	.04	.02	.01
☐ 529 Frank Viola	.07	.03	.01
☐ 530 John Olerud	.15	.07	.02
☐ 531 Juan Agosto	.04	.02	.01
☐ 532 Zane Smith	.04	.02	.01
☐ 533 Scott Sanderson	.04	.02	.01
☐ 534 Barry Jones	.04	.02	.01
☐ 535 Mike Felder	.04	.02	.01
☐ 536 Jose Canseco	.20	.09	.03
☐ 537 Felix Fermin	.04	.02	.01
☐ 538 Roberto Kelly	.07	.03	.01
☐ 539 Brian Holman	.04	.02	.01
☐ 540 Mark Davidson	.04	.02	.01
☐ 541 Terry Mulholland	.04	.02	.01
☐ 542 Randy Milligan	.04	.02	.01
☐ 543 Jose Gonzalez	.04	.02	.01
☐ 544 Craig Wilson	.10	.05	.01
☐ 545 Mike Hartley	.04	.02	.01
☐ 546 Greg Swindell	.07	.03	.01
☐ 547 Gary Gaetti	.04	.02	.01
☐ 548 Dave Justice	.30	.14	.04
☐ 549 Steve Searcy	.04	.02	.01
☐ 550 Erik Hanson	.04	.02	.01
☐ 551 Dave Stieb	.04	.02	.01
☐ 552 Andy Van Slyke	.10	.05	.01
☐ 553 Mike Greenwell	.07	.03	.01
☐ 554 Kevin Maas	.10	.05	.01
☐ 555 Delino DeShields	.15	.07	.02
☐ 556 Curt Schilling	.07	.03	.01
☐ 557 Ramon Martinez	.10	.05	.01
☐ 558 Pedro Guerrero	.07	.03	.01
☐ 559 Dwight Smith	.04	.02	.01
☐ 560 Mark Davis	.04	.02	.01
☐ 561 Shawn Abner	.04	.02	.01
☐ 562 Charlie Leibrandt	.04	.02	.01
☐ 563 John Shelby	.04	.02	.01
☐ 564 Bill Swift	.04	.02	.01
☐ 565 Mike Fetters	.04	.02	.01
☐ 566 Alejandro Pena	.04	.02	.01
☐ 567 Ruben Sierra	.15	.07	.02
☐ 568 Carlos Quintana	.04	.02	.01
☐ 569 Kevin Gross	.04	.02	.01
☐ 570 Derek Lilliquist	.04	.02	.01
☐ 571 Jack Armstrong	.04	.02	.01
☐ 572 Greg Brock	.04	.02	.01
☐ 573 Mike Kingery	.04	.02	.01
☐ 574 Greg Smith	.04	.02	.01
☐ 575 Brian McRae	.20	.09	.03
☐ 576 Jack Daugherty	.04	.02	.01
☐ 577 Ozzie Guillen	.04	.02	.01
☐ 578 Joe Boever	.04	.02	.01
☐ 579 Luis Sojo	.04	.02	.01
☐ 580 Chili Davis	.07	.03	.01
☐ 581 Don Robinson	.04	.02	.01
☐ 582 Brian Harper	.04	.02	.01
☐ 583 Paul O'Neill	.07	.03	.01
☐ 584 Bob Ojeda	.04	.02	.01
☐ 585 Mookie Wilson	.04	.02	.01
☐ 586 Rafael Ramirez	.04	.02	.01
☐ 587 Gary Redus	.04	.02	.01
☐ 588 Jamie Quirk	.04	.02	.01
☐ 589 Shawn Hillegas	.04	.02	.01
☐ 590 Tom Edens	.10	.05	.01
☐ 591 Joe Klink	.04	.02	.01
☐ 592 Charles Nagy	.40	.18	.05
☐ 593 Eric Plunk	.04	.02	.01
☐ 594 Tracy Jones	.04	.02	.01
☐ 595 Craig Biggio	.07	.03	.01
☐ 596 Jose DeJesus	.04	.02	.01
☐ 597 Mickey Tettleton	.07	.03	.01
☐ 598 Chris Gwynn	.04	.02	.01
☐ 599 Rex Hudler	.04	.02	.01
☐ 600 Checklist Card	.05	.01	.00
☐ 601 Jim Gott	.04	.02	.01
☐ 602 Jeff Manto	.04	.02	.01
☐ 603 Nelson Liriano	.04	.02	.01
☐ 604 Mark Lemke	.04	.02	.01
☐ 605 Clay Parker	.04	.02	.01
☐ 606 Edgar Martinez	.07	.03	.01
☐ 607 Mark Whiten	.12	.05	.02
☐ 608 Ted Power	.04	.02	.01
☐ 609 Tom Bolton	.04	.02	.01
☐ 610 Tom Herr	.04	.02	.01
☐ 611 Andy Hawkins UER (Pitched No-Hitter on 7/1, not 7/2)	.04	.02	.01
☐ 612 Scott Ruskin	.04	.02	.01
☐ 613 Ron Kittle	.04	.02	.01
☐ 614 John Wetteland	.07	.03	.01
☐ 615 Mike Perez	.15	.07	.02
☐ 616 Dave Clark	.04	.02	.01
☐ 617 Brent Mayne	.04	.02	.01
☐ 618 Jack Clark	.07	.03	.01
☐ 619 Marvin Freeman	.04	.02	.01
☐ 620 Edwin Nunez	.04	.02	.01
☐ 621 Russ Swan	.04	.02	.01
☐ 622 Johnny Ray	.04	.02	.01
☐ 623 Charlie O'Brien	.04	.02	.01
☐ 624 Joe Bitker	.04	.02	.01
☐ 625 Mike Marshall	.04	.02	.01

626 Otis Nixon	.07	.03	.01
627 Andy Benes	.10	.05	.01
628 Ron Oester	.04	.02	.01
629 Ted Higuera	.04	.02	.01
630 Kevin Bass	.04	.02	.01
631 Damon Berryhill	.04	.02	.01
632 Bo Jackson	.12	.05	.02
633 Brad Arnsberg	.04	.02	.01
634 Jerry Willard	.04	.02	.01
635 Tommy Greene	.04	.02	.01
636 Bob MacDonald	.10	.05	.01
637 Kirk McCaskill	.04	.02	.01
638 John Burkett	.04	.02	.01
639 Paul Abbott	.10	.05	.01
640 Todd Benzinger	.04	.02	.01
641 Todd Hundley	.04	.02	.01
642 George Bell	.07	.03	.01
643 Javier Ortiz	.04	.02	.01
644 Sid Bream	.04	.02	.01
645 Bob Welch	.04	.02	.01
646 Phil Bradley	.04	.02	.01
647 Bill Krueger	.04	.02	.01
648 Rickey Henderson	.12	.05	.02
649 Kevin Wickander	.04	.02	.01
650 Steve Balboni	.04	.02	.01
651 Gene Harris	.04	.02	.01
652 Jim Deshaies	.04	.02	.01
653 Jason Grimsley	.10	.05	.01
654 Joe Orsulak	.04	.02	.01
655 Jim Poole	.04	.02	.01
656 Felix Jose	.07	.03	.01
657 Dennis Cook	.04	.02	.01
658 Tom Brookens	.04	.02	.01
659 Junior Ortiz	.04	.02	.01
660 Jeff Parrett	.04	.02	.01
661 Jerry Don Gleaton	.04	.02	.01
662 Brent Knackert	.07	.03	.01
663 Rance Mulliniks	.04	.02	.01
664 John Smiley	.07	.03	.01
665 Larry Andersen	.04	.02	.01
666 Willie McGee	.07	.03	.01
667 Chris Nabholz	.10	.05	.01
668 Brady Anderson	.07	.03	.01
669 Darren Holmes UER (19 CG's, should be 0)	.15	.07	.02
670 Ken Hill	.07	.03	.01
671 Gary Varsho	.04	.02	.01
672 Bill Pecota	.04	.02	.01
673 Fred Lynn	.07	.03	.01
674 Kevin D. Brown	.04	.02	.01
675 Dan Petry	.04	.02	.01
676 Mike Jackson	.04	.02	.01
677 Wally Joyner	.07	.03	.01
678 Danny Jackson	.04	.02	.01
679 Bill Haselman	.10	.05	.01
680 Mike Boddicker	.04	.02	.01
681 Mel Rojas	.10	.05	.01
682 Roberto Alomar	.20	.09	.03
683 Dave Justice ROY	.15	.07	.02
684 Chuck Crim	.04	.02	.01
685 Matt Williams	.07	.03	.01
686 Shawon Dunston	.07	.03	.01
687 Jeff Schulz	.04	.02	.01
688 John Barfield	.04	.02	.01
689 Gerald Young	.04	.02	.01
690 Luis Gonzalez	.20	.09	.03
691 Frank Wills	.04	.02	.01
692 Chuck Finley	.07	.03	.01
693 Sandy Alomar Jr. ROY	.07	.03	.01
694 Tim Drummond	.04	.02	.01
695 Herm Winningham	.04	.02	.01
696 Darryl Strawberry	.12	.05	.02
697 Al Leiter	.04	.02	.01
698 Karl Rhodes	.04	.02	.01
699 Stan Belinda	.04	.02	.01
700 Checklist Card	.05	.01	.00
701 Lance Blankenship	.04	.02	.01
702 Willie Stargell PUZ	.04	.02	.01
703 Jim Gantner	.04	.02	.01
704 Reggie Harris	.10	.05	.01
705 Rob Ducey	.04	.02	.01
706 Tim Hulett	.04	.02	.01
707 Atlee Hammaker	.04	.02	.01
708 Xavier Hernandez	.04	.02	.01
709 Chuck McElroy	.04	.02	.01
710 John Mitchell	.04	.02	.01
711 Carlos Hernandez	.04	.02	.01
712 Geronimo Pena	.10	.05	.01
713 Jim Neidlinger	.04	.02	.01
714 John Orton	.04	.02	.01
715 Terry Leach	.04	.02	.01
716 Mike Stanton	.04	.02	.01
717 Walt Terrell	.04	.02	.01
718 Luis Aquino	.04	.02	.01
719 Bud Black (Blue Jays uniform, but Giants logo)	.04	.02	.01
720 Bob Kipper	.04	.02	.01
721 Jeff Gray	.04	.02	.01
722 Jose Rijo	.07	.03	.01
723 Curt Young	.04	.02	.01
724 Jose Vizcaino	.04	.02	.01
725 Randy Tomlin	.20	.09	.03
726 Junior Noboa	.04	.02	.01
727 Bob Welch CY	.04	.02	.01
728 Gary Ward	.04	.02	.01
729 Rob Deer (Brewers uniform, but Tigers logo)	.07	.03	.01
730 David Segui	.04	.02	.01
731 Mark Carreon	.04	.02	.01
732 Vicente Palacios	.04	.02	.01
733 Sam Horn	.04	.02	.01
734 Howard Farmer	.04	.02	.01
735 Ken Dayley (Cardinals uniform, but Blue Jays logo)	.04	.02	.01
736 Kelly Mann	.04	.02	.01
737 Joe Grahe	.15	.07	.02
738 Kelly Downs	.04	.02	.01
739 Jimmy Kremers	.04	.02	.01
740 Kevin Appier	.07	.03	.01
741 Jeff Reed	.04	.02	.01
742 Jose Rijo WS	.07	.03	.01
743 Dave Rohde	.04	.02	.01
744 Dr.Dirt/Mr.Clean Len Dykstra Dale Murphy UER (No '91 Donruss logo on card front)	.07	.03	.01
745 Paul Sorrento	.07	.03	.01
746 Thomas Howard	.10	.05	.01
747 Matt Stark	.10	.05	.01
748 Harold Baines	.07	.03	.01
749 Doug Dascenzo	.04	.02	.01
750 Doug Drabek CY	.07	.03	.01
751 Gary Sheffield	.25	.11	.03
752 Terry Lee	.10	.05	.01
753 Jim Vatcher	.04	.02	.01
754 Lee Stevens	.04	.02	.01
755 Randy Veres	.04	.02	.01
756 Bill Doran	.04	.02	.01
757 Gary Wayne	.04	.02	.01
758 Pedro Munoz	.25	.11	.03
759 Chris Hammond	.10	.05	.01
760 Checklist Card	.05	.01	.00
761 Rickey Henderson MVP	.10	.05	.01
762 Barry Bonds MVP	.10	.05	.01
763 Billy Hatcher WS UER (Line 13, on should be one)	.04	.02	.01
764 Julio Machado	.04	.02	.01
765 Jose Mesa	.04	.02	.01
766 Willie Randolph WS	.04	.02	.01
767 Scott Erickson	.20	.09	.03
768 Travis Fryman	.60	.25	.08
769 Rich Rodriguez	.10	.05	.01
770 Checklist Card	.05	.01	.00
BC1 Langston/Witt No-Hits Mariners	.06	.03	.01
BC2 Randy Johnson No-Hits Tigers	.06	.03	.01
BC3 Nolan Ryan No-Hits A's	.35	.16	.04
BC4 Dave Stewart No-Hits Blue Jays	.06	.03	.01
BC5 Cecil Fielder 50 Homer Club	.10	.05	.01
BC6 Carlton Fisk Record Home Run	.10	.05	.01
BC7 Ryne Sandberg Sets Fielding Records	.20	.09	.03
BC8 Gary Carter Breaks Catching Mark	.06	.03	.01
BC9 Mark McGwire Home Run Milestone (Back says First Baseman, others say only base)	.15	.07	.02
BC10 Bo Jackson Four Consecutive HR's	.12	.05	.02
BC11 Fernando Valenzuela No Hits Cardinals	.06	.03	.01
BC12A Andy Hawkins ERR Pitcher	1.00	.45	.13
BC12B Andy Hawkins COR	.06	.03	.01

No Hits White Sox			
☐ BC13 Melido Perez	.06	.03	.01
No Hits Yankees			
☐ BC14 Terry Mulholland	.06	.03	.01
No Hits Giants UER (Charlie Hayes is called Chris Hayes)			
☐ BC15 Nolan Ryan	.35	.16	.04
300th Win			
☐ BC16 Delino DeShields	.15	.07	.02
4 Hits in Debut			
☐ BC17 Cal Ripken	.20	.09	.03
Errorless Games			
☐ BC18 Eddie Murray	.10	.05	.01
Switch Hit Homers			
☐ BC19 George Brett	.10	.05	.01
3 Decade Champ			
☐ BC20 Bobby Thigpen	.06	.03	.01
Shatters Save Mark			
☐ BC21 Dave Stieb	.06	.03	.01
No Hits Indians			
☐ BC22 Willie McGee	.06	.03	.01
NL Batting Champ			

1991 Donruss Elite

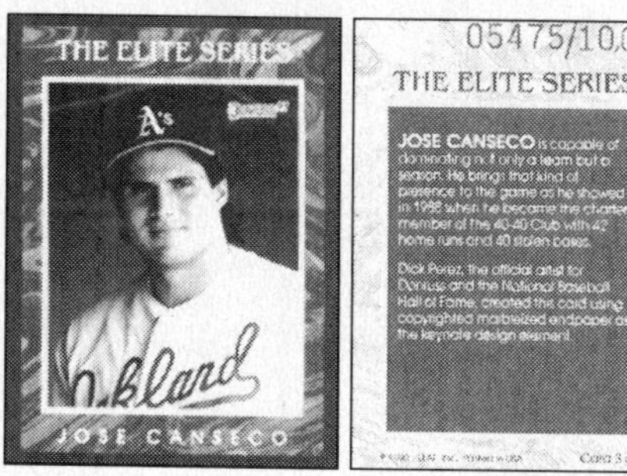

These special cards were inserted in the 1991 Donruss first and second series wax packs. Production was limited to a maximum of 10,000 cards for each card in the Elite series, and lesser production for the Sandberg Signature (5,000) and Ryan Legend (7,500) cards. The regular Elite cards are photos enclosed in a bronze marble borders which surround an evenly squared photo of the players. The Sandberg Signature card has a green marble border and is signed in a blue sharpie. The Nolan Ryan Legend card is a Dick Perez drawing with silver borders. The cards are all numbered on the back, 1 out of 10,000, etc. All of these special cards measure the standard, 2 1/2" by 3 1/2".

	MT	EX-MT	VG
COMPLETE SET (10)	1350.00	600.00	170.00
COMMON ELITE (E1-E8)	45.00	20.00	5.75
☐ E1 Barry Bonds	100.00	45.00	12.50
☐ E2 George Brett	80.00	36.00	10.00
☐ E3 Jose Canseco	100.00	45.00	12.50
☐ E4 Andre Dawson	65.00	29.00	8.25
☐ E5 Doug Drabek	45.00	20.00	5.75
☐ E6 Cecil Fielder	75.00	34.00	9.50
☐ E7 Rickey Henderson	90.00	40.00	11.50
☐ E8 Matt Williams	55.00	25.00	7.00
☐ L1 Nolan Ryan (Legend)	350.00	160.00	45.00
☐ S1 Ryne Sandberg (Signature Series)	400.00	180.00	50.00

1991 Donruss Grand Slammers

This 14-card set commemorates players who hit grand slams in 1990. The cards measure the standard size (2 1/2" by 3 1/2") and feature on the fronts color player photos on a

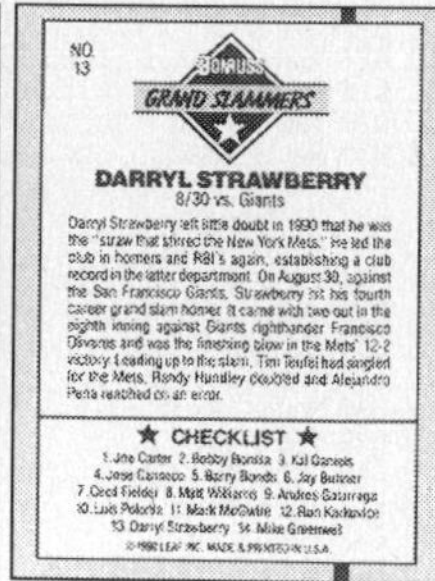

computer-generated background design, enframed by white borders on a green card face crisscrossed by different color diagonal stripes. The player's name is given in a color stripe below the picture. Inside pale green borders, the back recounts grand slam homers by the player. The cards are numbered on the back and include a checklist at the bottom.

	MT	EX-MT	VG
COMPLETE SET (14)	2.50	1.15	.30
COMMON PLAYER (1-14)	.10	.05	.01
☐ 1 Joe Carter	.35	.16	.04
☐ 2 Bobby Bonilla	.20	.09	.03
☐ 3 Kal Daniels	.10	.05	.01
☐ 4 Jose Canseco	.60	.25	.08
☐ 5 Barry Bonds	.50	.23	.06
☐ 6 Jay Buhner	.10	.05	.01
☐ 7 Cecil Fielder	.35	.16	.04
☐ 8 Matt Williams	.15	.07	.02
☐ 9 Andres Galarraga	.10	.05	.01
☐ 10 Luis Polonia	.10	.05	.01
☐ 11 Mark McGwire	.50	.23	.06
☐ 12 Ron Karkovice	.10	.05	.01
☐ 13 Darryl Strawberry UER (Todd Hundley is called Randy)	.35	.16	.04
☐ 14 Mike Greenwell	.10	.05	.01

1991 Donruss Rookies

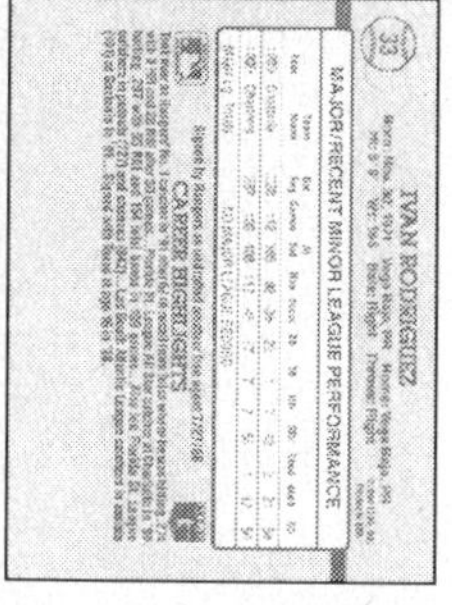

The 1991 Donruss Rookies set is a boxed set issued to honor the best rookies of the season. The cards measure the standard size (2 1/2" by 3 1/2"), and a mini puzzle featuring Hall of Famer Willie Stargell was included with the set. The fronts feature color action player photos, with white and red borders. Yellow and green stripes cut across the bottom of the card face, presenting the player's name and position. The words "The Rookies" and a baseball icon appear in the lower left corner of the picture. The horizontally oriented backs are printed in black on a green and white background, and present biography, statistics, and career highlights. The cards are numbered on the back. Outstanding rookies showcased in the set are Jeff Bagwell, Chito Martinez,

Orlando Merced, Dean Palmer, Ivan Rodriguez, and Todd Van Poppel.

	MT	EX-MT	VG
COMPLETE SET (56)	5.00	2.30	.60
COMMON PLAYER (1-56)	.05	.02	.01
☐ 1 Pat Kelly	.15	.07	.02
☐ 2 Rich DeLucia	.05	.02	.01
☐ 3 Wes Chamberlain	.20	.09	.03
☐ 4 Scott Leius	.10	.05	.01
☐ 5 Darryl Kile	.10	.05	.01
☐ 6 Milt Cuyler	.08	.04	.01
☐ 7 Todd Van Poppel	.50	.23	.06
☐ 8 Ray Lankford	.30	.14	.04
☐ 9 Brian Hunter	.25	.11	.03
☐ 10 Tony Perezchica	.05	.02	.01
☐ 11 Ced Landrum	.10	.05	.01
☐ 12 Dave Burba	.10	.05	.01
☐ 13 Ramon Garcia	.10	.05	.01
☐ 14 Ed Sprague	.20	.09	.03
☐ 15 Warren Newson	.10	.05	.01
☐ 16 Paul Faries	.05	.02	.01
☐ 17 Luis Gonzalez	.20	.09	.03
☐ 18 Charles Nagy	.25	.11	.03
☐ 19 Chris Hammond	.08	.04	.01
☐ 20 Frank Castillo	.15	.07	.02
☐ 21 Pedro Munoz	.25	.11	.03
☐ 22 Orlando Merced	.20	.09	.03
☐ 23 Jose Melendez	.10	.05	.01
☐ 24 Kirk Dressendorfer	.10	.05	.01
☐ 25 Heathcliff Slocumb	.05	.02	.01
☐ 26 Doug Simons	.05	.02	.01
☐ 27 Mike Timlin	.10	.05	.01
☐ 28 Jeff Fassero	.10	.05	.01
☐ 29 Mark Leiter	.10	.05	.01
☐ 30 Jeff Bagwell	1.25	.55	.16
☐ 31 Brian McRae	.20	.09	.03
☐ 32 Mark Whiten	.10	.05	.01
☐ 33 Ivan Rodriguez	1.25	.55	.16
☐ 34 Wade Taylor	.05	.02	.01
☐ 35 Darren Lewis	.10	.05	.01
☐ 36 Mo Vaughn	.20	.09	.03
☐ 37 Mike Remlinger	.05	.02	.01
☐ 38 Rick Wilkins	.10	.05	.01
☐ 39 Chuck Knoblauch	.30	.14	.04
☐ 40 Kevin Morton	.05	.02	.01
☐ 41 Carlos Rodriguez	.10	.05	.01
☐ 42 Mark Lewis	.10	.05	.01
☐ 43 Brent Mayne	.08	.04	.01
☐ 44 Chris Haney	.10	.05	.01
☐ 45 Denis Boucher	.12	.05	.02
☐ 46 Mike Gardiner	.10	.05	.01
☐ 47 Jeff Johnson	.10	.05	.01
☐ 48 Dean Palmer	.20	.09	.03
☐ 49 Chuck McElroy	.05	.02	.01
☐ 50 Chris Jones	.05	.02	.01
☐ 51 Scott Kamieniecki	.10	.05	.01
☐ 52 Al Osuna	.10	.05	.01
☐ 53 Rusty Meacham	.10	.05	.01
☐ 54 Chito Martinez	.10	.05	.01
☐ 55 Reggie Jefferson	.15	.07	.02
☐ 56 Checklist Card	.08	.01	.00

1991 Donruss Super DK's

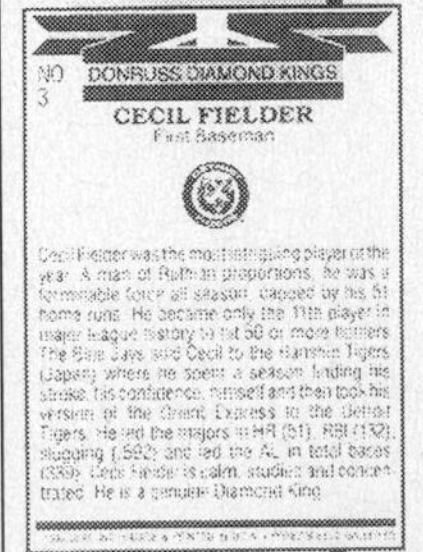

For the seventh consecutive year Donruss has issued a card set featuring the players used in the current year's Diamond King subset in a larger size, approximately 5" by 7". The set again features the art work of famed sports artist Dick Perez and is available through a postpaid mail-in offer detailed on the 1991 Donruss wax packs involving 14.00 and three wax wrappers.

	MT	EX-MT	VG
COMPLETE SET (26)	13.50	6.00	1.70
COMMON PLAYER (1-26)	.40	.18	.05
☐ 1 Dave Stieb	.50	.23	.06
☐ 2 Craig Biggio	.60	.25	.08
☐ 3 Cecil Fielder	1.00	.45	.13
☐ 4 Barry Bonds	1.00	.45	.13
☐ 5 Barry Larkin	.75	.35	.09
☐ 6 Dave Parker	.50	.23	.06
☐ 7 Len Dykstra	.50	.23	.06
☐ 8 Bobby Thigpen	.50	.23	.06
☐ 9 Roger Clemens	1.25	.55	.16
☐ 10 Ron Gant	1.00	.45	.13
☐ 11 Delino DeShields	1.00	.45	.13
☐ 12 Roberto Alomar	1.50	.65	.19
☐ 13 Sandy Alomar Jr.	.60	.25	.08
☐ 14 Ryne Sandberg	1.25	.55	.16
☐ 15 Ramon Martinez	.90	.40	.11
☐ 16 Edgar Martinez	.90	.40	.11
☐ 17 Dave Magadan	.50	.23	.06
☐ 18 Matt Williams	.75	.35	.09
☐ 19 Rafael Palmeiro	.75	.35	.09
☐ 20 Bob Welch	.50	.23	.06
☐ 21 Dave Righetti	.40	.18	.05
☐ 22 Brian Harper	.50	.23	.06
☐ 23 Gregg Olson	.60	.25	.08
☐ 24 Kurt Stillwell	.40	.18	.05
☐ 25 Pedro Guerrero	.50	.23	.06
☐ 26 Chuck Finley	.40	.18	.05

1992 Donruss Previews

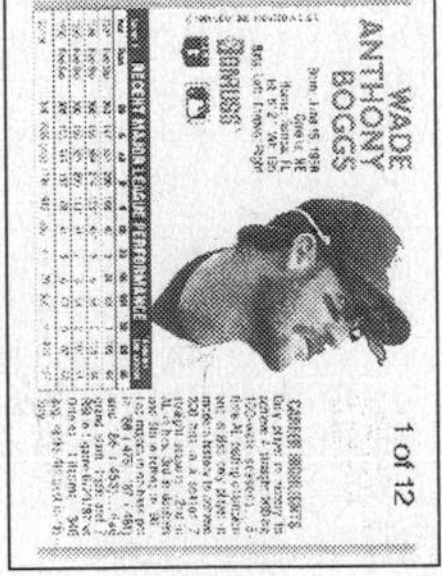

This 12-card preview set was available only to Donruss dealers. The standard-size (2 1/2" by 3 1/2") cards feature the same glossy color player photos on the fronts and player information on the backs as the regular series issue. The statistics only go through the 1990 season. Only the numbering of the cards on the back is different.

	MT	EX-MT	VG
COMPLETE SET (12)	300.00	135.00	38.00
COMMON PLAYER (1-12)	10.00	4.50	1.25
☐ 1 Wade Boggs	35.00	16.00	4.40
☐ 2 Barry Bonds	35.00	16.00	4.40
☐ 3 Will Clark	45.00	20.00	5.75
☐ 4 Andre Dawson	25.00	11.50	3.10
☐ 5 Dennis Eckersley	30.00	13.50	3.80
☐ 6 Robin Ventura	35.00	16.00	4.40
☐ 7 Ken Griffey Jr.	90.00	40.00	11.50
☐ 8 Kelly Gruber	10.00	4.50	1.25
☐ 9 Ryan Klesko	45.00	20.00	5.75
☐ 10 Cal Ripken	75.00	34.00	9.50
☐ 11 Nolan Ryan	100.00	45.00	12.50
☐ 12 Todd Van Poppel	35.00	16.00	4.40

1992 Donruss

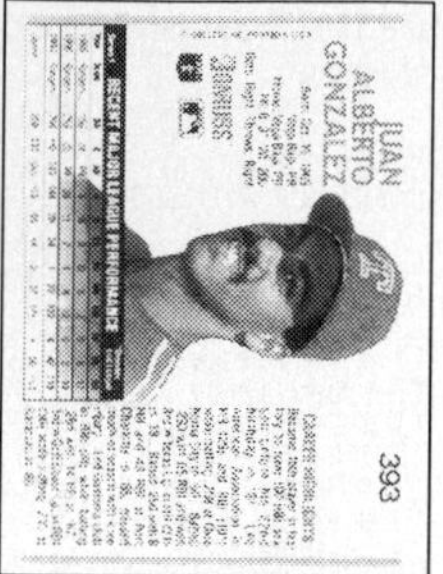

The 1992 Donruss set contains two series each featuring 396 cards, measuring the standard size (2 1/2" by 3 1/2"). The front design features glossy color player photos with white borders. Two-toned blue stripes overlay the top and bottom of the picture, with the player's name printed in silver-and-black lettering above the bottom stripe. The horizontally oriented backs have a color headshot of the player (except on subset cards listed below), biography, career highlights, and recent Major League performance statistics (no earlier than 1987). The set includes Rated Rookies (1-20), AL All-Stars (21-30), Highlights (33, 94, 154, 215, 276), Rated Rookies (397-421), NL All-Stars (422-431), Highlights (434, 495, 555, 616, 677) and a puzzle of Hall of Famer Rod Carew. The cards are numbered on the back and checklisted below accordingly. Thirteen Diamond Kings cards featuring the artwork of Dick Perez were randomly inserted in first series foil packs and 13 more Diamond Kings were randomly inserted in second series foil packs. Inserted in both series foil and rack packs are 5,000 Cal Ripken Signature autographed cards, 7,500 Legend cards of Rickey Henderson, and 10,000 Elite cards each of Wade Boggs, Joe Carter, Will Clark, Dwight Gooden, Ken Griffey Jr., Tony Gwynn, Howard Johnson, Terry Pendleton, Kirby Puckett, and Frank Thomas. Key Rookie Cards in the set are John Jaha, Pat Mahomes, Brian Williams, and Bob Zupcic.

	MT	EX-MT	VG
COMPLETE SET (784)	20.00	9.00	2.50
COMPLETE FACT.SET (788)	30.00	13.50	3.80
COMPLETE SERIES 1 (396)	10.00	4.50	1.25
COMPLETE SERIES 2 (388)	10.00	4.50	1.25
COMPLETE BC SET (8)	1.50	.65	.19
COMMON PLAYER (1-396)	.04	.02	.01
COMMON PLAYER (397-784)	.04	.02	.01
COMMON BC SP (BC1-BC8)	.15	.07	.02

	MT	EX-MT	VG
☐ 1 Mark Wohlers RR	.10	.05	.01
☐ 2 Wilfredo Cordero RR	.15	.07	.02
☐ 3 Kyle Abbott RR	.08	.04	.01
☐ 4 Dave Nilsson RR	.15	.07	.02
☐ 5 Kenny Lofton RR	.40	.18	.05
☐ 6 Luis Mercedes RR	.08	.04	.01
☐ 7 Roger Salkeld RR	.10	.05	.01
☐ 8 Eddie Zosky RR	.08	.04	.01
☐ 9 Todd Van Poppel RR	.20	.09	.03
☐ 10 Frank Seminara RR	.20	.09	.03
☐ 11 Andy Ashby RR	.05	.02	.01
☐ 12 Reggie Jefferson RR	.08	.04	.01
☐ 13 Ryan Klesko RR	.50	.23	.06
☐ 14 Carlos Garcia RR	.08	.04	.01
☐ 15 John Ramos RR	.05	.02	.01
☐ 16 Eric Karros RR	.50	.23	.06
☐ 17 Patrick Lennon RR	.05	.02	.01
☐ 18 Eddie Taubensee RR	.12	.05	.02
☐ 19 Roberto Hernandez RR	.12	.05	.02
☐ 20 D.J. Dozier RR	.08	.04	.01
☐ 21 Dave Henderson AS	.05	.02	.01
☐ 22 Cal Ripken AS	.15	.07	.02
☐ 23 Wade Boggs AS	.10	.05	.01
☐ 24 Ken Griffey Jr. AS	.25	.11	.03
☐ 25 Jack Morris AS	.08	.04	.01
☐ 26 Danny Tartabull AS	.08	.04	.01
☐ 27 Cecil Fielder AS	.10	.05	.01
☐ 28 Roberto Alomar AS	.10	.05	.01
☐ 29 Sandy Alomar Jr. AS	.05	.02	.01
☐ 30 Rickey Henderson AS	.10	.05	.01
☐ 31 Ken Hill	.04	.02	.01
☐ 32 John Habyan	.04	.02	.01
☐ 33 Otis Nixon HL	.05	.02	.01
☐ 34 Tim Wallach	.07	.03	.01
☐ 35 Cal Ripken	.25	.11	.03
☐ 36 Gary Carter	.07	.03	.01
☐ 37 Juan Agosto	.04	.02	.01
☐ 38 Doug Dascenzo	.04	.02	.01
☐ 39 Kirk Gibson	.07	.03	.01
☐ 40 Benito Santiago	.07	.03	.01
☐ 41 Otis Nixon	.04	.02	.01
☐ 42 Andy Allanson	.04	.02	.01
☐ 43 Brian Holman	.04	.02	.01
☐ 44 Dick Schofield	.04	.02	.01
☐ 45 Dave Magadan	.07	.03	.01
☐ 46 Rafael Palmeiro	.07	.03	.01
☐ 47 Jody Reed	.04	.02	.01
☐ 48 Ivan Calderon	.04	.02	.01
☐ 49 Greg W. Harris	.04	.02	.01
☐ 50 Chris Sabo	.07	.03	.01
☐ 51 Paul Molitor	.07	.03	.01
☐ 52 Robby Thompson	.04	.02	.01
☐ 53 Dave Smith	.04	.02	.01
☐ 54 Mark Davis	.04	.02	.01
☐ 55 Kevin Brown	.07	.03	.01
☐ 56 Donn Pall	.04	.02	.01
☐ 57 Len Dykstra	.07	.03	.01
☐ 58 Roberto Alomar	.20	.09	.03
☐ 59 Jeff D. Robinson	.04	.02	.01
☐ 60 Willie McGee	.07	.03	.01
☐ 61 Jay Buhner	.07	.03	.01
☐ 62 Mike Pagliarulo	.04	.02	.01
☐ 63 Paul O'Neill	.07	.03	.01
☐ 64 Hubie Brooks	.04	.02	.01
☐ 65 Kelly Gruber	.07	.03	.01
☐ 66 Ken Caminiti	.07	.03	.01
☐ 67 Gary Redus	.04	.02	.01
☐ 68 Harold Baines	.07	.03	.01
☐ 69 Charlie Hough	.04	.02	.01
☐ 70 B.J. Surhoff	.04	.02	.01
☐ 71 Walt Weiss	.04	.02	.01
☐ 72 Shawn Hillegas	.04	.02	.01
☐ 73 Roberto Kelly	.07	.03	.01
☐ 74 Jeff Ballard	.04	.02	.01
☐ 75 Craig Biggio	.07	.03	.01
☐ 76 Pat Combs	.04	.02	.01
☐ 77 Jeff M. Robinson	.04	.02	.01
☐ 78 Tim Belcher	.07	.03	.01
☐ 79 Cris Carpenter	.04	.02	.01
☐ 80 Checklist Card	.05	.01	.00
☐ 81 Steve Avery	.15	.07	.02
☐ 82 Chris James	.04	.02	.01
☐ 83 Brian Harper	.04	.02	.01
☐ 84 Charlie Leibrandt	.04	.02	.01
☐ 85 Mickey Tettleton	.07	.03	.01
☐ 86 Pete O'Brien	.04	.02	.01
☐ 87 Danny Darwin	.04	.02	.01
☐ 88 Bob Walk	.04	.02	.01
☐ 89 Jeff Reardon	.07	.03	.01
☐ 90 Bobby Rose	.04	.02	.01
☐ 91 Danny Jackson	.04	.02	.01
☐ 92 John Morris	.04	.02	.01
☐ 93 Bud Black	.04	.02	.01
☐ 94 Tommy Greene HL	.05	.02	.01
☐ 95 Rick Aguilera	.07	.03	.01
☐ 96 Gary Gaetti	.04	.02	.01
☐ 97 David Cone	.07	.03	.01
☐ 98 John Olerud	.10	.05	.01
☐ 99 Joel Skinner	.04	.02	.01
☐ 100 Jay Bell	.04	.02	.01
☐ 101 Bob Milacki	.04	.02	.01
☐ 102 Norm Charlton	.07	.03	.01
☐ 103 Chuck Crim	.04	.02	.01
☐ 104 Terry Steinbach	.07	.03	.01
☐ 105 Juan Samuel	.04	.02	.01
☐ 106 Steve Howe	.04	.02	.01
☐ 107 Rafael Belliard	.04	.02	.01
☐ 108 Joey Cora	.04	.02	.01
☐ 109 Tommy Greene	.04	.02	.01
☐ 110 Gregg Olson	.07	.03	.01
☐ 111 Frank Tanana	.04	.02	.01
☐ 112 Lee Smith	.07	.03	.01
☐ 113 Greg A. Harris	.04	.02	.01
☐ 114 Dwayne Henry	.04	.02	.01
☐ 115 Chili Davis	.07	.03	.01
☐ 116 Kent Mercker	.04	.02	.01

☐	117	Brian Barnes	.04	.02	.01
☐	118	Rich DeLucia	.04	.02	.01
☐	119	Andre Dawson	.10	.05	.01
☐	120	Carlos Baerga	.15	.07	.02
☐	121	Mike LaValliere	.04	.02	.01
☐	122	Jeff Gray	.04	.02	.01
☐	123	Bruce Hurst	.07	.03	.01
☐	124	Alvin Davis	.04	.02	.01
☐	125	John Candelaria	.04	.02	.01
☐	126	Matt Nokes	.04	.02	.01
☐	127	George Bell	.07	.03	.01
☐	128	Bret Saberhagen	.07	.03	.01
☐	129	Jeff Russell	.04	.02	.01
☐	130	Jim Abbott	.12	.05	.02
☐	131	Bill Gullickson	.04	.02	.01
☐	132	Todd Zeile	.04	.02	.01
☐	133	Dave Winfield	.10	.05	.01
☐	134	Wally Whitehurst	.04	.02	.01
☐	135	Matt Williams	.07	.03	.01
☐	136	Tom Browning	.04	.02	.01
☐	137	Marquis Grissom	.10	.05	.01
☐	138	Erik Hanson	.04	.02	.01
☐	139	Rob Dibble	.07	.03	.01
☐	140	Don August	.04	.02	.01
☐	141	Tom Henke	.07	.03	.01
☐	142	Dan Pasqua	.04	.02	.01
☐	143	George Brett	.10	.05	.01
☐	144	Jerald Clark	.04	.02	.01
☐	145	Robin Ventura	.15	.07	.02
☐	146	Dale Murphy	.07	.03	.01
☐	147	Dennis Eckersley	.10	.05	.01
☐	148	Eric Yelding	.04	.02	.01
☐	149	Mario Diaz	.04	.02	.01
☐	150	Casey Candaele	.04	.02	.01
☐	151	Steve Olin	.04	.02	.01
☐	152	Luis Salazar	.04	.02	.01
☐	153	Kevin Maas	.07	.03	.01
☐	154	Nolan Ryan HL	.25	.11	.03
☐	155	Barry Jones	.04	.02	.01
☐	156	Chris Hoiles	.07	.03	.01
☐	157	Bobby Ojeda	.04	.02	.01
☐	158	Pedro Guerrero	.07	.03	.01
☐	159	Paul Assenmacher	.04	.02	.01
☐	160	Checklist Card	.05	.01	.00
☐	161	Mike Macfarlane	.04	.02	.01
☐	162	Craig Lefferts	.04	.02	.01
☐	163	Brian Hunter	.10	.05	.01
☐	164	Alan Trammell	.07	.03	.01
☐	165	Ken Griffey Jr.	.50	.23	.06
☐	166	Lance Parrish	.07	.03	.01
☐	167	Brian Downing	.04	.02	.01
☐	168	John Barfield	.04	.02	.01
☐	169	Jack Clark	.07	.03	.01
☐	170	Chris Nabholz	.07	.03	.01
☐	171	Tim Teufel	.04	.02	.01
☐	172	Chris Hammond	.04	.02	.01
☐	173	Robin Yount	.10	.05	.01
☐	174	Dave Righetti	.04	.02	.01
☐	175	Joe Girardi	.04	.02	.01
☐	176	Mike Boddicker	.04	.02	.01
☐	177	Dean Palmer	.12	.05	.02
☐	178	Greg Hibbard	.04	.02	.01
☐	179	Randy Ready	.04	.02	.01
☐	180	Devon White	.07	.03	.01
☐	181	Mark Eichhorn	.04	.02	.01
☐	182	Mike Felder	.04	.02	.01
☐	183	Joe Klink	.04	.02	.01
☐	184	Steve Bedrosian	.04	.02	.01
☐	185	Barry Larkin	.10	.05	.01
☐	186	John Franco	.07	.03	.01
☐	187	Ed Sprague	.07	.03	.01
☐	188	Mark Portugal	.04	.02	.01
☐	189	Jose Lind	.04	.02	.01
☐	190	Bob Welch	.04	.02	.01
☐	191	Alex Fernandez	.07	.03	.01
☐	192	Gary Sheffield	.20	.09	.03
☐	193	Rickey Henderson	.12	.05	.02
☐	194	Rod Nichols	.04	.02	.01
☐	195	Scott Kamieniecki	.04	.02	.01
☐	196	Mike Flanagan	.04	.02	.01
☐	197	Steve Finley	.07	.03	.01
☐	198	Darren Daulton	.07	.03	.01
☐	199	Leo Gomez	.10	.05	.01
☐	200	Mike Morgan	.04	.02	.01
☐	201	Bob Tewksbury	.07	.03	.01
☐	202	Sid Bream	.04	.02	.01
☐	203	Sandy Alomar Jr.	.07	.03	.01
☐	204	Greg Gagne	.04	.02	.01
☐	205	Juan Berenguer	.04	.02	.01
☐	206	Cecil Fielder	.12	.05	.02
☐	207	Randy Johnson	.07	.03	.01
☐	208	Tony Pena	.04	.02	.01
☐	209	Doug Drabek	.07	.03	.01
☐	210	Wade Boggs	.12	.05	.02
☐	211	Bryan Harvey	.04	.02	.01
☐	212	Jose Vizcaino	.04	.02	.01
☐	213	Alonzo Powell	.04	.02	.01
☐	214	Will Clark	.20	.09	.03
☐	215	Rickey Henderson HL	.10	.05	.01
☐	216	Jack Morris	.10	.05	.01
☐	217	Junior Felix	.04	.02	.01
☐	218	Vince Coleman	.07	.03	.01
☐	219	Jimmy Key	.04	.02	.01
☐	220	Alex Cole	.04	.02	.01
☐	221	Bill Landrum	.04	.02	.01
☐	222	Randy Milligan	.04	.02	.01
☐	223	Jose Rijo	.07	.03	.01
☐	224	Greg Vaughn	.07	.03	.01
☐	225	Dave Stewart	.07	.03	.01
☐	226	Lenny Harris	.04	.02	.01
☐	227	Scott Sanderson	.04	.02	.01
☐	228	Jeff Blauser	.04	.02	.01
☐	229	Ozzie Guillen	.04	.02	.01
☐	230	John Kruk	.07	.03	.01
☐	231	Bob Melvin	.04	.02	.01
☐	232	Milt Cuyler	.04	.02	.01
☐	233	Felix Jose	.07	.03	.01
☐	234	Ellis Burks	.07	.03	.01
☐	235	Pete Harnisch	.04	.02	.01
☐	236	Kevin Tapani	.04	.02	.01
☐	237	Terry Pendleton	.10	.05	.01
☐	238	Mark Gardner	.04	.02	.01
☐	239	Harold Reynolds	.04	.02	.01
☐	240	Checklist Card	.05	.01	.00
☐	241	Mike Harkey	.07	.03	.01
☐	242	Felix Fermin	.04	.02	.01
☐	243	Barry Bonds	.15	.07	.02
☐	244	Roger Clemens	.25	.11	.03
☐	245	Dennis Rasmussen	.04	.02	.01
☐	246	Jose DeLeon	.04	.02	.01
☐	247	Orel Hershiser	.07	.03	.01
☐	248	Mel Hall	.04	.02	.01
☐	249	Rick Wilkins	.04	.02	.01
☐	250	Tom Gordon	.04	.02	.01
☐	251	Kevin Reimer	.04	.02	.01
☐	252	Luis Polonia	.07	.03	.01
☐	253	Mike Henneman	.04	.02	.01
☐	254	Tom Pagnozzi	.04	.02	.01
☐	255	Chuck Finley	.04	.02	.01
☐	256	Mackey Sasser	.04	.02	.01
☐	257	John Burkett	.04	.02	.01
☐	258	Hal Morris	.07	.03	.01
☐	259	Larry Walker	.15	.07	.02
☐	260	Billy Swift	.04	.02	.01
☐	261	Joe Oliver	.04	.02	.01
☐	262	Julio Machado	.04	.02	.01
☐	263	Todd Stottlemyre	.07	.03	.01
☐	264	Matt Merullo	.04	.02	.01
☐	265	Brent Mayne	.04	.02	.01
☐	266	Thomas Howard	.04	.02	.01
☐	267	Lance Johnson	.04	.02	.01
☐	268	Terry Mulholland	.04	.02	.01
☐	269	Rick Honeycutt	.04	.02	.01
☐	270	Luis Gonzalez	.07	.03	.01
☐	271	Jose Guzman	.04	.02	.01
☐	272	Jimmy Jones	.04	.02	.01
☐	273	Mark Lewis	.07	.03	.01
☐	274	Rene Gonzales	.04	.02	.01
☐	275	Jeff Johnson	.04	.02	.01
☐	276	Dennis Martinez HL	.05	.02	.01
☐	277	Delino DeShields	.10	.05	.01
☐	278	Sam Horn	.04	.02	.01
☐	279	Kevin Gross	.04	.02	.01
☐	280	Jose Oquendo	.04	.02	.01
☐	281	Mark Grace	.07	.03	.01
☐	282	Mark Gubicza	.04	.02	.01
☐	283	Fred McGriff	.12	.05	.02
☐	284	Ron Gant	.10	.05	.01
☐	285	Lou Whitaker	.07	.03	.01
☐	286	Edgar Martinez	.07	.03	.01
☐	287	Ron Tingley	.04	.02	.01
☐	288	Kevin McReynolds	.07	.03	.01
☐	289	Ivan Rodriguez	.35	.16	.04
☐	290	Mike Gardiner	.04	.02	.01
☐	291	Chris Haney	.04	.02	.01
☐	292	Darrin Jackson	.07	.03	.01
☐	293	Bill Doran	.04	.02	.01
☐	294	Ted Higuera	.04	.02	.01
☐	295	Jeff Brantley	.04	.02	.01
☐	296	Les Lancaster	.04	.02	.01
☐	297	Jim Eisenreich	.04	.02	.01
☐	298	Ruben Sierra	.15	.07	.02
☐	299	Scott Radinsky	.04	.02	.01
☐	300	Jose DeJesus	.04	.02	.01
☐	301	Mike Timlin	.04	.02	.01
☐	302	Luis Sojo	.04	.02	.01

☐ 303 Kelly Downs .04 .02 .01
☐ 304 Scott Bankhead .04 .02 .01
☐ 305 Pedro Munoz .07 .03 .01
☐ 306 Scott Scudder .04 .02 .01
☐ 307 Kevin Elster .04 .02 .01
☐ 308 Duane Ward .04 .02 .01
☐ 309 Darryl Kile .07 .03 .01
☐ 310 Orlando Merced .07 .03 .01
☐ 311 Dave Henderson .04 .02 .01
☐ 312 Tim Raines .07 .03 .01
☐ 313 Mark Lee .04 .02 .01
☐ 314 Mike Gallego .04 .02 .01
☐ 315 Charles Nagy .10 .05 .01
☐ 316 Jesse Barfield .04 .02 .01
☐ 317 Todd Frohwirth .04 .02 .01
☐ 318 Al Osuna .04 .02 .01
☐ 319 Darrin Fletcher .04 .02 .01
☐ 320 Checklist Card .05 .01 .00
☐ 321 David Segui .04 .02 .01
☐ 322 Stan Javier .04 .02 .01
☐ 323 Bryn Smith .04 .02 .01
☐ 324 Jeff Treadway .04 .02 .01
☐ 325 Mark Whiten .07 .03 .01
☐ 326 Kent Hrbek .07 .03 .01
☐ 327 Dave Justice .20 .09 .03
☐ 328 Tony Phillips .04 .02 .01
☐ 329 Rob Murphy .04 .02 .01
☐ 330 Kevin Morton .04 .02 .01
☐ 331 John Smiley .07 .03 .01
☐ 332 Luis Rivera .04 .02 .01
☐ 333 Wally Joyner .07 .03 .01
☐ 334 Heathcliff Slocumb .04 .02 .01
☐ 335 Rick Cerone .04 .02 .01
☐ 336 Mike Remlinger .04 .02 .01
☐ 337 Mike Moore .04 .02 .01
☐ 338 Lloyd McClendon .04 .02 .01
☐ 339 Al Newman .04 .02 .01
☐ 340 Kirk McCaskill .04 .02 .01
☐ 341 Howard Johnson .07 .03 .01
☐ 342 Greg Myers .04 .02 .01
☐ 343 Kal Daniels .04 .02 .01
☐ 344 Bernie Williams .10 .05 .01
☐ 345 Shane Mack .07 .03 .01
☐ 346 Gary Thurman .04 .02 .01
☐ 347 Dante Bichette .04 .02 .01
☐ 348 Mark McGwire .20 .09 .03
☐ 349 Travis Fryman .30 .14 .04
☐ 350 Ray Lankford .15 .07 .02
☐ 351 Mike Jeffcoat .04 .02 .01
☐ 352 Jack McDowell .07 .03 .01
☐ 353 Mitch Williams .04 .02 .01
☐ 354 Mike Devereaux .07 .03 .01
☐ 355 Andres Galarraga .04 .02 .01
☐ 356 Henry Cotto .04 .02 .01
☐ 357 Scott Bailes .04 .02 .01
☐ 358 Jeff Bagwell .25 .11 .03
☐ 359 Scott Leius .04 .02 .01
☐ 360 Zane Smith .04 .02 .01
☐ 361 Bill Pecota .04 .02 .01
☐ 362 Tony Fernandez .07 .03 .01
☐ 363 Glenn Braggs .04 .02 .01
☐ 364 Bill Spiers .04 .02 .01
☐ 365 Vicente Palacios .04 .02 .01
☐ 366 Tim Burke .04 .02 .01
☐ 367 Randy Tomlin .04 .02 .01
☐ 368 Kenny Rogers .04 .02 .01
☐ 369 Brett Butler .07 .03 .01
☐ 370 Pat Kelly .07 .03 .01
☐ 371 Bip Roberts .07 .03 .01
☐ 372 Gregg Jefferies .07 .03 .01
☐ 373 Kevin Bass .04 .02 .01
☐ 374 Ron Karkovice .04 .02 .01
☐ 375 Paul Gibson .04 .02 .01
☐ 376 Bernard Gilkey .07 .03 .01
☐ 377 Dave Gallagher .04 .02 .01
☐ 378 Bill Wegman .04 .02 .01
☐ 379 Pat Borders .04 .02 .01
☐ 380 Ed Whitson .04 .02 .01
☐ 381 Gilberto Reyes .04 .02 .01
☐ 382 Russ Swan .04 .02 .01
☐ 383 Andy Van Slyke .07 .03 .01
☐ 384 Wes Chamberlain .04 .02 .01
☐ 385 Steve Chitren .04 .02 .01
☐ 386 Greg Olson .04 .02 .01
☐ 387 Brian McRae .07 .03 .01
☐ 388 Rich Rodriguez .04 .02 .01
☐ 389 Steve Decker .04 .02 .01
☐ 390 Chuck Knoblauch .20 .09 .03
☐ 391 Bobby Witt .04 .02 .01
☐ 392 Eddie Murray .10 .05 .01
☐ 393 Juan Gonzalez .35 .16 .04
☐ 394 Scott Ruskin .04 .02 .01
☐ 395 Jay Howell .04 .02 .01
☐ 396 Checklist Card .05 .01 .00
☐ 397 Royce Clayton RR .15 .07 .02
☐ 398 John Jaha RR .25 .11 .03
☐ 399 Dan Wilson RR .05 .02 .01
☐ 400 Archie Corbin RR .10 .05 .01
☐ 401 Barry Manuel RR .12 .05 .02
☐ 402 Kim Batiste RR .05 .02 .01
☐ 403 Pat Mahomes RR .25 .11 .03
☐ 404 Dave Fleming RR .50 .23 .06
☐ 405 Jeff Juden RR .10 .05 .01
☐ 406 Jim Thome RR .12 .05 .02
☐ 407 Sam Militello RR .30 .14 .04
☐ 408 Jeff Nelson RR .12 .05 .02
☐ 409 Anthony Young RR .08 .04 .01
☐ 410 Tino Martinez RR .08 .04 .01
☐ 411 Jeff Mutis RR .10 .05 .01
☐ 412 Rey Sanchez RR .12 .05 .02
☐ 413 Chris Gardner RR .10 .05 .01
☐ 414 John VanderWal RR .15 .07 .02
☐ 415 Reggie Sanders RR .25 .11 .03
☐ 416 Brian Williams RR .25 .11 .03
☐ 417 Mo Sanford RR .05 .02 .01
☐ 418 David Weathers RR .20 .09 .03
☐ 419 Hector Fajardo RR .12 .05 .02
☐ 420 Steve Foster RR .10 .05 .01
☐ 421 Lance Dickson RR .05 .02 .01
☐ 422 Andre Dawson AS .10 .05 .01
☐ 423 Ozzie Smith AS .10 .05 .01
☐ 424 Chris Sabo AS .05 .02 .01
☐ 425 Tony Gwynn AS .10 .05 .01
☐ 426 Tom Glavine AS .10 .05 .01
☐ 427 Bobby Bonilla AS .08 .04 .01
☐ 428 Will Clark AS .10 .05 .01
☐ 429 Ryne Sandberg AS .10 .05 .01
☐ 430 Benito Santiago AS .05 .02 .01
☐ 431 Ivan Calderon AS .05 .02 .01
☐ 432 Ozzie Smith .10 .05 .01
☐ 433 Tim Leary .04 .02 .01
☐ 434 Bret Saberhagen HL .07 .03 .01
☐ 435 Mel Rojas .04 .02 .01
☐ 436 Ben McDonald .10 .05 .01
☐ 437 Tim Crews .04 .02 .01
☐ 438 Rex Hudler .04 .02 .01
☐ 439 Chico Walker .04 .02 .01
☐ 440 Kurt Stillwell .04 .02 .01
☐ 441 Tony Gwynn .12 .05 .02
☐ 442 John Smoltz .10 .05 .01
☐ 443 Lloyd Moseby .04 .02 .01
☐ 444 Mike Schooler .04 .02 .01
☐ 445 Joe Grahe .04 .02 .01
☐ 446 Dwight Gooden .07 .03 .01
☐ 447 Oil Can Boyd .04 .02 .01
☐ 448 John Marzano .04 .02 .01
☐ 449 Bret Barberie .07 .03 .01
☐ 450 Mike Maddux .04 .02 .01
☐ 451 Jeff Reed .04 .02 .01
☐ 452 Dale Sveum .04 .02 .01
☐ 453 Jose Uribe .04 .02 .01
☐ 454 Bob Scanlan .04 .02 .01
☐ 455 Kevin Appier .07 .03 .01
☐ 456 Jeff Huson .04 .02 .01
☐ 457 Ken Patterson .04 .02 .01
☐ 458 Ricky Jordan .04 .02 .01
☐ 459 Tom Candiotti .04 .02 .01
☐ 460 Lee Stevens .04 .02 .01
☐ 461 Rod Beck .12 .05 .02
☐ 462 Dave Valle .04 .02 .01
☐ 463 Scott Erickson .10 .05 .01
☐ 464 Chris Jones .04 .02 .01
☐ 465 Mark Carreon .04 .02 .01
☐ 466 Rob Ducey .04 .02 .01
☐ 467 Jim Corsi .04 .02 .01
☐ 468 Jeff King .04 .02 .01
☐ 469 Curt Young .04 .02 .01
☐ 470 Bo Jackson .12 .05 .02
☐ 471 Chris Bosio .04 .02 .01
☐ 472 Jamie Quirk .04 .02 .01
☐ 473 Jesse Orosco .04 .02 .01
☐ 474 Alvaro Espinoza .04 .02 .01
☐ 475 Joe Orsulak .04 .02 .01
☐ 476 Checklist Card .05 .01 .00
☐ 477 Gerald Young .04 .02 .01
☐ 478 Wally Backman .04 .02 .01
☐ 479 Juan Bell .04 .02 .01
☐ 480 Mike Scioscia .04 .02 .01
☐ 481 Omar Olivares .04 .02 .01
☐ 482 Francisco Cabrera .04 .02 .01
☐ 483 Greg Swindell UER .07 .03 .01
(Shown on Indians,
but listed on Reds)
☐ 484 Terry Leach .04 .02 .01
☐ 485 Tommy Gregg .04 .02 .01
☐ 486 Scott Aldred .04 .02 .01

☐	487	Greg Briley	.04	.02	.01
☐	488	Phil Plantier	.15	.07	.02
☐	489	Curtis Wilkerson	.04	.02	.01
☐	490	Tom Brunansky	.07	.03	.01
☐	491	Mike Fetters	.04	.02	.01
☐	492	Frank Castillo	.10	.05	.01
☐	493	Joe Boever	.04	.02	.01
☐	494	Kirt Manwaring	.04	.02	.01
☐	495	Wilson Alvarez HL	.05	.02	.01
☐	496	Gene Larkin	.04	.02	.01
☐	497	Gary DiSarcina	.07	.03	.01
☐	498	Frank Viola	.07	.03	.01
☐	499	Manuel Lee	.04	.02	.01
☐	500	Albert Belle	.12	.05	.02
☐	501	Stan Belinda	.04	.02	.01
☐	502	Dwight Evans	.07	.03	.01
☐	503	Eric Davis	.07	.03	.01
☐	504	Darren Holmes	.04	.02	.01
☐	505	Mike Bordick	.10	.05	.01
☐	506	Dave Hansen	.04	.02	.01
☐	507	Lee Guetterman	.04	.02	.01
☐	508	Keith Mitchell	.07	.03	.01
☐	509	Melido Perez	.07	.03	.01
☐	510	Dickie Thon	.04	.02	.01
☐	511	Mark Williamson	.04	.02	.01
☐	512	Mark Salas	.04	.02	.01
☐	513	Milt Thompson	.04	.02	.01
☐	514	Mo Vaughn	.07	.03	.01
☐	515	Jim Deshaies	.04	.02	.01
☐	516	Rich Garces	.04	.02	.01
☐	517	Lonnie Smith	.04	.02	.01
☐	518	Spike Owen	.04	.02	.01
☐	519	Tracy Jones	.04	.02	.01
☐	520	Greg Maddux	.07	.03	.01
☐	521	Carlos Martinez	.04	.02	.01
☐	522	Neal Heaton	.04	.02	.01
☐	523	Mike Greenwell	.07	.03	.01
☐	524	Andy Benes	.07	.03	.01
☐	525	Jeff Schaefer UER (Photo actually Tino Martinez)	.04	.02	.01
☐	526	Mike Sharperson	.04	.02	.01
☐	527	Wade Taylor	.04	.02	.01
☐	528	Jerome Walton	.04	.02	.01
☐	529	Storm Davis	.04	.02	.01
☐	530	Jose Hernandez	.10	.05	.01
☐	531	Mark Langston	.07	.03	.01
☐	532	Rob Deer	.07	.03	.01
☐	533	Geronimo Pena	.04	.02	.01
☐	534	Juan Guzman	.75	.35	.09
☐	535	Pete Schourek	.07	.03	.01
☐	536	Todd Benzinger	.04	.02	.01
☐	537	Billy Hatcher	.04	.02	.01
☐	538	Tom Foley	.04	.02	.01
☐	539	Dave Cochrane	.04	.02	.01
☐	540	Mariano Duncan	.04	.02	.01
☐	541	Edwin Nunez	.04	.02	.01
☐	542	Rance Mulliniks	.04	.02	.01
☐	543	Carlton Fisk	.10	.05	.01
☐	544	Luis Aquino	.04	.02	.01
☐	545	Ricky Bones	.10	.05	.01
☐	546	Craig Grebeck	.04	.02	.01
☐	547	Charlie Hayes	.04	.02	.01
☐	548	Jose Canseco	.20	.09	.03
☐	549	Andujar Cedeno	.07	.03	.01
☐	550	Geno Petralli	.04	.02	.01
☐	551	Javier Ortiz	.04	.02	.01
☐	552	Rudy Seanez	.04	.02	.01
☐	553	Rich Gedman	.04	.02	.01
☐	554	Eric Plunk	.04	.02	.01
☐	555	Nolan Ryan HL (With Rich Gossage)	.20	.09	.03
☐	556	Checklist Card	.05	.01	.00
☐	557	Greg Colbrunn	.07	.03	.01
☐	558	Chito Martinez	.04	.02	.01
☐	559	Darryl Strawberry	.12	.05	.02
☐	560	Luis Alicea	.04	.02	.01
☐	561	Dwight Smith	.04	.02	.01
☐	562	Terry Shumpert	.04	.02	.01
☐	563	Jim Vatcher	.04	.02	.01
☐	564	Deion Sanders	.15	.07	.02
☐	565	Walt Terrell	.04	.02	.01
☐	566	Dave Burba	.04	.02	.01
☐	567	Dave Howard	.04	.02	.01
☐	568	Todd Hundley	.04	.02	.01
☐	569	Jack Daugherty	.04	.02	.01
☐	570	Scott Cooper	.07	.03	.01
☐	571	Bill Sampen	.04	.02	.01
☐	572	Jose Melendez	.04	.02	.01
☐	573	Freddie Benavides	.04	.02	.01
☐	574	Jim Gantner	.04	.02	.01
☐	575	Trevor Wilson	.04	.02	.01
☐	576	Ryne Sandberg	.25	.11	.03
☐	577	Kevin Seitzer	.07	.03	.01
☐	578	Gerald Alexander	.04	.02	.01
☐	579	Mike Huff	.04	.02	.01
☐	580	Von Hayes	.04	.02	.01
☐	581	Derek Bell	.10	.05	.01
☐	582	Mike Stanley	.04	.02	.01
☐	583	Kevin Mitchell	.07	.03	.01
☐	584	Mike Jackson	.04	.02	.01
☐	585	Dan Gladden	.04	.02	.01
☐	586	Ted Power UER (Wrong year given for signing with Reds)	.04	.02	.01
☐	587	Jeff Innis	.04	.02	.01
☐	588	Bob MacDonald	.04	.02	.01
☐	589	Jose Tolentino	.10	.05	.01
☐	590	Bob Patterson	.04	.02	.01
☐	591	Scott Brosius	.10	.05	.01
☐	592	Frank Thomas	.75	.35	.09
☐	593	Darryl Hamilton	.07	.03	.01
☐	594	Kirk Dressendorfer	.04	.02	.01
☐	595	Jeff Shaw	.04	.02	.01
☐	596	Don Mattingly	.12	.05	.02
☐	597	Glenn Davis	.07	.03	.01
☐	598	Andy Mota	.04	.02	.01
☐	599	Jason Grimsley	.04	.02	.01
☐	600	Jimmy Poole	.04	.02	.01
☐	601	Jim Gott	.04	.02	.01
☐	602	Stan Royer	.04	.02	.01
☐	603	Marvin Freeman	.04	.02	.01
☐	604	Denis Boucher	.07	.03	.01
☐	605	Denny Neagle	.07	.03	.01
☐	606	Mark Lemke	.04	.02	.01
☐	607	Jerry Don Gleaton	.04	.02	.01
☐	608	Brent Knackert	.04	.02	.01
☐	609	Carlos Quintana	.04	.02	.01
☐	610	Bobby Bonilla	.10	.05	.01
☐	611	Joe Hesketh	.04	.02	.01
☐	612	Daryl Boston	.04	.02	.01
☐	613	Shawon Dunston	.07	.03	.01
☐	614	Danny Cox	.04	.02	.01
☐	615	Darren Lewis	.07	.03	.01
☐	616	Braves No-Hitter UER Kent Mercker (Misspelled Merker on card front) Alejandro Pena Mark Wohlers	.05	.02	.01
☐	617	Kirby Puckett	.20	.09	.03
☐	618	Franklin Stubbs	.04	.02	.01
☐	619	Chris Donnels	.04	.02	.01
☐	620	David Wells UER (Career Highlights in black not red)	.04	.02	.01
☐	621	Mike Aldrete	.04	.02	.01
☐	622	Bob Kipper	.04	.02	.01
☐	623	Anthony Telford	.04	.02	.01
☐	624	Randy Myers	.07	.03	.01
☐	625	Willie Randolph	.07	.03	.01
☐	626	Joe Slusarski	.04	.02	.01
☐	627	John Wetteland	.04	.02	.01
☐	628	Greg Cadaret	.04	.02	.01
☐	629	Tom Glavine	.12	.05	.02
☐	630	Wilson Alvarez	.04	.02	.01
☐	631	Wally Ritchie	.04	.02	.01
☐	632	Mike Mussina	.50	.23	.06
☐	633	Mark Leiter	.04	.02	.01
☐	634	Gerald Perry	.04	.02	.01
☐	635	Matt Young	.04	.02	.01
☐	636	Checklist Card	.05	.01	.00
☐	637	Scott Hemond	.04	.02	.01
☐	638	David West	.04	.02	.01
☐	639	Jim Clancy	.04	.02	.01
☐	640	Doug Piatt UER (Not born in 1955 as on card; incorrect info on How Acquired)	.04	.02	.01
☐	641	Omar Vizquel	.04	.02	.01
☐	642	Rick Sutcliffe	.07	.03	.01
☐	643	Glenallen Hill	.04	.02	.01
☐	644	Gary Varsho	.04	.02	.01
☐	645	Tony Fossas	.04	.02	.01
☐	646	Jack Howell	.04	.02	.01
☐	647	Jim Campanis	.10	.05	.01
☐	648	Chris Gwynn	.04	.02	.01
☐	649	Jim Leyritz	.04	.02	.01
☐	650	Chuck McElroy	.04	.02	.01
☐	651	Sean Berry	.04	.02	.01
☐	652	Donald Harris	.04	.02	.01
☐	653	Don Slaught	.04	.02	.01
☐	654	Rusty Meacham	.04	.02	.01
☐	655	Scott Terry	.04	.02	.01
☐	656	Ramon Martinez	.07	.03	.01
☐	657	Keith Miller	.04	.02	.01

Card	Player	MT	EX-MT	VG
☐ 658	Ramon Garcia	.04	.02	.01
☐ 659	Milt Hill	.10	.05	.01
☐ 660	Steve Frey	.04	.02	.01
☐ 661	Bob McClure	.04	.02	.01
☐ 662	Ced Landrum	.04	.02	.01
☐ 663	Doug Henry	.15	.07	.02
☐ 664	Candy Maldonado	.04	.02	.01
☐ 665	Carl Willis	.04	.02	.01
☐ 666	Jeff Montgomery	.04	.02	.01
☐ 667	Craig Shipley	.10	.05	.01
☐ 668	Warren Newson	.04	.02	.01
☐ 669	Mickey Morandini	.07	.03	.01
☐ 670	Brook Jacoby	.04	.02	.01
☐ 671	Ryan Bowen	.07	.03	.01
☐ 672	Bill Krueger	.04	.02	.01
☐ 673	Rob Mallicoat	.04	.02	.01
☐ 674	Doug Jones	.04	.02	.01
☐ 675	Scott Livingstone	.10	.05	.01
☐ 676	Danny Tartabull	.07	.03	.01
☐ 677	Joe Carter HL	.10	.05	.01
☐ 678	Cecil Espy	.04	.02	.01
☐ 679	Randy Velarde	.04	.02	.01
☐ 680	Bruce Ruffin	.04	.02	.01
☐ 681	Ted Wood	.10	.05	.01
☐ 682	Dan Plesac	.04	.02	.01
☐ 683	Eric Bullock	.04	.02	.01
☐ 684	Junior Ortiz	.04	.02	.01
☐ 685	Dave Hollins	.07	.03	.01
☐ 686	Dennis Martinez	.07	.03	.01
☐ 687	Larry Andersen	.04	.02	.01
☐ 688	Doug Simons	.04	.02	.01
☐ 689	Tim Spehr	.04	.02	.01
☐ 690	Calvin Jones	.10	.05	.01
☐ 691	Mark Guthrie	.04	.02	.01
☐ 692	Alfredo Griffin	.04	.02	.01
☐ 693	Joe Carter	.12	.05	.02
☐ 694	Terry Mathews	.10	.05	.01
☐ 695	Pascual Perez	.04	.02	.01
☐ 696	Gene Nelson	.04	.02	.01
☐ 697	Gerald Williams	.10	.05	.01
☐ 698	Chris Cron	.10	.05	.01
☐ 699	Steve Buechele	.04	.02	.01
☐ 700	Paul McClellan	.04	.02	.01
☐ 701	Jim Lindeman	.04	.02	.01
☐ 702	Francisco Oliveras	.04	.02	.01
☐ 703	Rob Maurer	.12	.05	.02
☐ 704	Pat Hentgen	.10	.05	.01
☐ 705	Jaime Navarro	.07	.03	.01
☐ 706	Mike Magnante	.12	.05	.02
☐ 707	Nolan Ryan	.40	.18	.05
☐ 708	Bobby Thigpen	.04	.02	.01
☐ 709	John Cerutti	.04	.02	.01
☐ 710	Steve Wilson	.04	.02	.01
☐ 711	Hensley Meulens	.04	.02	.01
☐ 712	Rheal Cormier	.04	.02	.01
☐ 713	Scott Bradley	.04	.02	.01
☐ 714	Mitch Webster	.04	.02	.01
☐ 715	Roger Mason	.04	.02	.01
☐ 716	Checklist Card	.05	.01	.00
☐ 717	Jeff Fassero	.04	.02	.01
☐ 718	Cal Eldred	.35	.16	.04
☐ 719	Sid Fernandez	.07	.03	.01
☐ 720	Bob Zupcic	.25	.11	.03
☐ 721	Jose Offerman	.07	.03	.01
☐ 722	Cliff Brantley	.10	.05	.01
☐ 723	Ron Darling	.07	.03	.01
☐ 724	Dave Stieb	.04	.02	.01
☐ 725	Hector Villanueva	.04	.02	.01
☐ 726	Mike Hartley	.04	.02	.01
☐ 727	Arthur Rhodes	.15	.07	.02
☐ 728	Randy Bush	.04	.02	.01
☐ 729	Steve Sax	.07	.03	.01
☐ 730	Dave Otto	.04	.02	.01
☐ 731	John Wehner	.07	.03	.01
☐ 732	Dave Martinez	.04	.02	.01
☐ 733	Ruben Amaro	.04	.02	.01
☐ 734	Billy Ripken	.04	.02	.01
☐ 735	Steve Farr	.04	.02	.01
☐ 736	Shawn Abner	.04	.02	.01
☐ 737	Gil Heredia	.10	.05	.01
☐ 738	Ron Jones	.04	.02	.01
☐ 739	Tony Castillo	.04	.02	.01
☐ 740	Sammy Sosa	.04	.02	.01
☐ 741	Julio Franco	.07	.03	.01
☐ 742	Tim Naehring	.07	.03	.01
☐ 743	Steve Wapnick	.04	.02	.01
☐ 744	Craig Wilson	.04	.02	.01
☐ 745	Darrin Chapin	.10	.05	.01
☐ 746	Chris George	.04	.02	.01
☐ 747	Mike Simms	.04	.02	.01
☐ 748	Rosario Rodriguez	.04	.02	.01
☐ 749	Skeeter Barnes	.04	.02	.01
☐ 750	Roger McDowell	.04	.02	.01
☐ 751	Dann Howitt	.04	.02	.01
☐ 752	Paul Sorrento	.07	.03	.01
☐ 753	Braulio Castillo	.15	.07	.02
☐ 754	Yorkis Perez	.15	.07	.02
☐ 755	Willie Fraser	.04	.02	.01
☐ 756	Jeremy Hernandez	.10	.05	.01
☐ 757	Curt Schilling	.07	.03	.01
☐ 758	Steve Lyons	.04	.02	.01
☐ 759	Dave Anderson	.04	.02	.01
☐ 760	Willie Banks	.07	.03	.01
☐ 761	Mark Leonard	.04	.02	.01
☐ 762	Jack Armstrong (Listed on Indians, but shown on Reds)	.04	.02	.01
☐ 763	Scott Servais	.04	.02	.01
☐ 764	Ray Stephens	.04	.02	.01
☐ 765	Junior Noboa	.04	.02	.01
☐ 766	Jim Olander	.10	.05	.01
☐ 767	Joe Magrane	.04	.02	.01
☐ 768	Lance Blankenship	.04	.02	.01
☐ 769	Mike Humphreys	.07	.03	.01
☐ 770	Jarvis Brown	.10	.05	.01
☐ 771	Damon Berryhill	.04	.02	.01
☐ 772	Alejandro Pena	.04	.02	.01
☐ 773	Jose Mesa	.04	.02	.01
☐ 774	Gary Cooper	.10	.05	.01
☐ 775	Carney Lansford	.07	.03	.01
☐ 776	Mike Bielecki (Shown on Cubs, but listed on Braves)	.04	.02	.01
☐ 777	Charlie O'Brien	.04	.02	.01
☐ 778	Carlos Hernandez	.04	.02	.01
☐ 779	Howard Farmer	.04	.02	.01
☐ 780	Mike Stanton	.04	.02	.01
☐ 781	Reggie Harris	.04	.02	.01
☐ 782	Xavier Hernandez	.04	.02	.01
☐ 783	Bryan Hickerson	.10	.05	.01
☐ 784	Checklist Card	.05	.01	.00
☐ BC1	Cal Ripken MVP	.40	.18	.05
☐ BC2	Terry Pendleton MVP	.15	.07	.02
☐ BC3	Roger Clemens CY	.30	.14	.04
☐ BC4	Tom Glavine CY	.20	.09	.03
☐ BC5	Chuck Knoblauch ROY	.30	.14	.04
☐ BC6	Jeff Bagwell ROY	.40	.18	.05
☐ BC7	Colorado Rockies	.50	.23	.06
☐ BC8	Florida Marlins	.50	.23	.06

1992 Donruss Diamond Kings

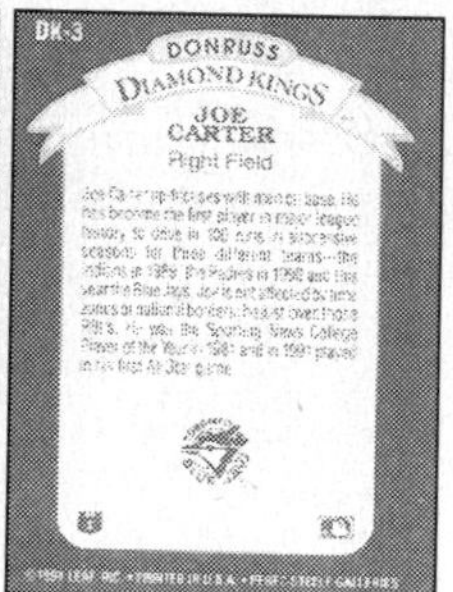

These standard-size (2 1/2" by 3 1/2") cards were randomly inserted in 1992 Donruss I foil packs (cards 1-13 and the checklist only) and in 1992 Donruss II foil packs (cards 14-26). The fronts feature player portraits by noted sports artist Dick Perez. The words "Donruss Diamond Kings" are superimposed at the card top in a gold-trimmed blue and black banner, with the player's name in a similarly designed black stripe at the card bottom. On a white background with a dark blue border, the backs present career summary. The cards are numbered on the back with a DK prefix.

	MT	EX-MT	VG
COMPLETE SET (27)	40.00	18.00	5.00
COMPLETE SERIES 1 (14)	25.00	11.50	3.10
COMPLETE SERIES 2 (13)	15.00	6.75	1.90
COMMON PLAYER (1-13)	1.00	.45	.13
COMMON PLAYER (14-26)	1.00	.45	.13

☐ 1 Paul Molitor	1.25	.55	.16
☐ 2 Will Clark	4.00	1.80	.50
☐ 3 Joe Carter	2.50	1.15	.30
☐ 4 Julio Franco	1.00	.45	.13
☐ 5 Cal Ripken	6.00	2.70	.75
☐ 6 Dave Justice	3.50	1.55	.45
☐ 7 George Bell	1.00	.45	.13
☐ 8 Frank Thomas	12.00	5.50	1.50
☐ 9 Wade Boggs	2.00	.90	.25
☐ 10 Scott Sanderson	1.00	.45	.13
☐ 11 Jeff Bagwell	4.00	1.80	.50
☐ 12 John Kruk	1.00	.45	.13
☐ 13 Felix Jose	1.00	.45	.13
☐ 14 Harold Baines	1.00	.45	.13
☐ 15 Dwight Gooden	1.25	.55	.16
☐ 16 Brian McRae	1.25	.55	.16
☐ 17 Jay Bell	1.00	.45	.13
☐ 18 Brett Butler	1.00	.45	.13
☐ 19 Hal Morris	1.00	.45	.13
☐ 20 Mark Langston	1.00	.45	.13
☐ 21 Scott Erickson	1.25	.55	.16
☐ 22 Randy Johnson	1.00	.45	.13
☐ 23 Greg Swindell	1.00	.45	.13
☐ 24 Dennis Martinez	1.00	.45	.13
☐ 25 Tony Phillips	1.00	.45	.13
☐ 26 Fred McGriff	2.50	1.15	.30
☐ 27 Checklist Card	.60	.25	.08

1992 Donruss Durivage Expos

Featuring the Montreal Expos, the 20-card standard-size (2 1/2" by 3 1/2") set was produced by Donruss for Durivage (a Canadian bread company). The fronts have posed color photos of the players without hats, framed by a gray inner border and a dark green outer border. The team logo, "Durivage" set name, and player information appear at the bottom of card front. In a horizontal format, the bilingual (English and French) backs carry biography and recent major league performance statistics, on a background of gray vertical stripes that fade to white as one moves down the card. The cards are numbered on the back, "No. X de/of 20."

	MT	EX-MT	VG
COMPLETE SET (20)	40.00	18.00	5.00
COMMON PLAYER (1-20)	1.25	.55	.16
☐ 1 Bret Barberie	2.00	.90	.25
☐ 2 Chris Haney	1.50	.65	.19
☐ 3 Bill Sampen	1.25	.55	.16
☐ 4 Ivan Calderon	1.50	.65	.19
☐ 5 Gary Carter	5.00	2.30	.60
☐ 6 Delino DeShields	6.00	2.70	.75
☐ 7 Jeff Fassero	1.25	.55	.16
☐ 8 Darrin Fletcher	1.25	.55	.16
☐ 9 Mark Gardner	1.50	.65	.19
☐ 10 Marquis Grissom	6.00	2.70	.75
☐ 11 Ken Hill	2.00	.90	.25
☐ 12 Dennis Martinez	2.00	.90	.25
☐ 13 Chris Nabholz	1.50	.65	.19
☐ 14 Spike Owen	1.25	.55	.16
☐ 15 Tom Runnells MG	1.25	.55	.16
☐ 16 John Vander Wal	2.00	.90	.25
☐ 17 Bill Landrum	1.25	.55	.16
☐ 18 Larry Walker	7.50	3.40	.95
☐ 19 Tim Wallach	2.00	.90	.25
☐ 20 John Wetteland	2.00	.90	.25

1992 Donruss Elite

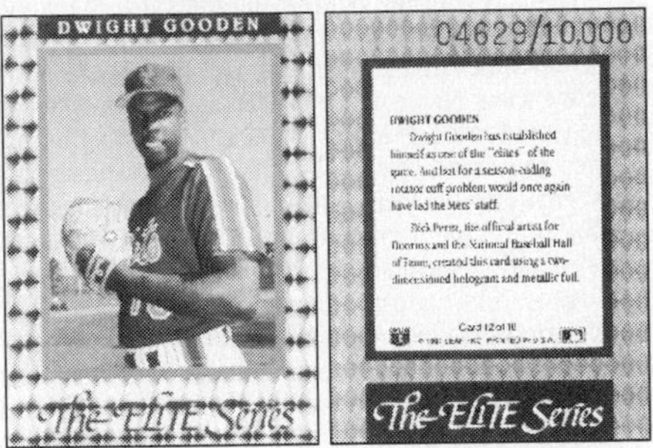

These cards were random inserts in 1992 Donruss foil packs. The numbering on the Elite cards is essentially a continuation of the series started the year before. The Signature Series Cal Ripken card was inserted in 1992 Donruss foil packs. Only 5,000 Ripken Signature Series cards were printed. The Rickey Henderson Legends Series card was inserted in 1992 Donruss foil packs; only 7,500 Henderson Legends cards were printed. All of these special limited cards are standard size, 2 1/2" by 3 1/2".

	MT	EX-MT	VG
COMPLETE SET (12)	1600.00	700.00	200.00
COMMON ELITE (E9-E18)	50.00	23.00	6.25
☐ E9 Wade Boggs	75.00	34.00	9.50
☐ E10 Joe Carter	75.00	34.00	9.50
☐ E11 Will Clark	100.00	45.00	12.50
☐ E12 Dwight Gooden	65.00	29.00	8.25
☐ E13 Ken Griffey Jr.	200.00	90.00	25.00
☐ E14 Tony Gwynn	80.00	36.00	10.00
☐ E15 Howard Johnson	50.00	23.00	6.25
☐ E16 Terry Pendleton	65.00	29.00	8.25
☐ E17 Kirby Puckett	100.00	45.00	12.50
☐ E18 Frank Thomas	250.00	115.00	31.00
☐ L2 Rickey Henderson (Legend Series)	200.00	90.00	25.00
☐ S2 Cal Ripken (Signature Series)	400.00	180.00	50.00

1992 Donruss McDonald's

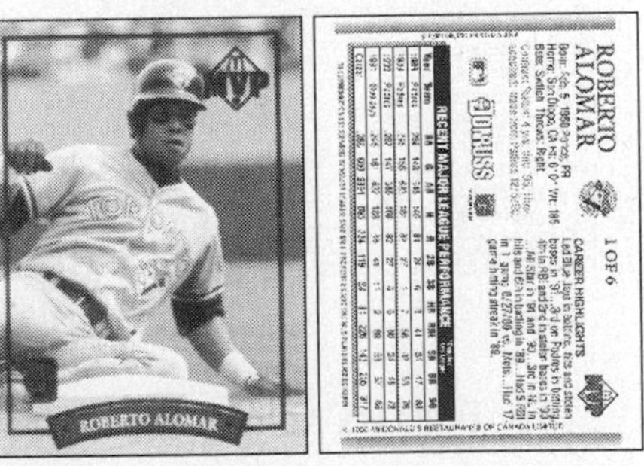

This 33-card set was produced by Donruss for distribution by McDonald's Restaurants in the Toronto area. For 39 cents with the purchase of any sandwich or breakfast entree, the collector received a four-card pack, featuring three cards from the MVP series and one card from the Blue

Jays Gold series. A player from each MLB team is represented in the numbered 26-card MVP subset. Checklist cards were also randomly inserted throughout the foil packs. In addition, 1,000 packs included a randomly inserted prize card. By filling it out, answering the question, and sending it to the address on the card, the winner received one of 1,000 numbered cards autographed by Roberto Alomar. The standard-size (2 1/2" by 3 1/2") cards have the same design as the regular issue cards, with color action photos bordered in white and accented by blue stripes above and below the picture. One difference is an MVP logo with the McDonald's "Golden Arches" trademark on the front. The backs present a head shot, biography, recent major league performance statistics, career highlights, and the card number ("X of 26"). Again, the McDonald's "Golden Arches" trademark appears on the back alongside the other logos. One card from the six-card gold subset (of Toronto Blue Jays) was included in each 1992 Donruss McDonald's MVP four-card foil pack. The gold card fronts feature full-bleed color player photos accented by goil foil stamping. The player's name appears in a dark blue bar that overlays the bottom gold foil border stripe. In a horizontal format, the backs carry biography, contract status information, recent major league performance statistics, and career highlights. As with the MVP series, the McDonald's "Golden Arches" trademark adorns both sides of the card.

	MT	EX-MT	VG
COMPLETE SET (33)	15.00	6.75	1.90
COMMON PLAYER (1-26)	.12	.05	.02
COMMON PLAYER (G1-G6)	.25	.11	.03
☐ 1 Cal Ripken	1.00	.45	.13
☐ 2 Frank Thomas	1.50	.65	.19
☐ 3 George Brett	.35	.16	.04
☐ 4 Roberto Kelly	.20	.09	.03
☐ 5 Nolan Ryan	1.50	.65	.19
☐ 6 Ryne Sandberg	.90	.40	.11
☐ 7 Darryl Strawberry	.40	.18	.05
☐ 8 Len Dykstra	.12	.05	.02
☐ 9 Fred McGriff	.40	.18	.05
☐ 10 Roger Clemens	.90	.40	.11
☐ 11 Sandy Alomar Jr.	.15	.07	.02
☐ 12 Robin Yount	.35	.16	.04
☐ 13 Jose Canseco	.75	.35	.09
☐ 14 Jimmy Key	.12	.05	.02
☐ 15 Barry Larkin	.25	.11	.03
☐ 16 Dennis Martinez	.15	.07	.02
☐ 17 Andy Van Slyke	.20	.09	.03
☐ 18 Will Clark	.75	.35	.09
☐ 19 Mark Langston	.12	.05	.02
☐ 20 Cecil Fielder	.40	.18	.05
☐ 21 Kirby Puckett	.90	.40	.11
☐ 22 Ken Griffey Jr.	1.50	.65	.19
☐ 23 David Justice	.75	.35	.09
☐ 24 Jeff Bagwell	.75	.35	.09
☐ 25 Howard Johnson	.20	.09	.03
☐ 26 Ozzie Smith	.35	.16	.04
☐ G1 Roberto Alomar	2.00	.90	.25
☐ G2 Joe Carter	1.00	.45	.13
☐ G3 Kelly Gruber	.35	.16	.04
☐ G4 Jack Morris	.50	.23	.06
☐ G5 Tom Henke	.35	.16	.04
☐ G6 Devon White	.25	.11	.03
☐ NNO Checklist Card SP	2.00	.90	.25

1992 Donruss Nolan Ryan Coke

This 26-card set was produced by Donruss to commemorate each year of Ryan's professional baseball career. Both sides of the card bear the Coca-Cola logo, and four-card cello packs with one Ryan card and three regular issue 1992 Donruss cards were inserted in 12-can packs of

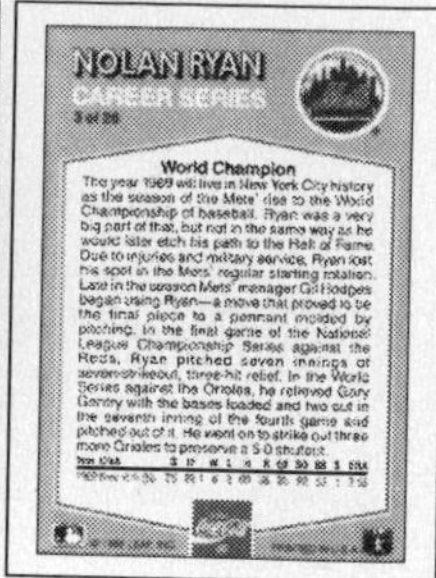

Coca-Cola classic, caffeine-free Coca-Cola classic, diet Coke, caffeine-free diet Coke, Sprite, and diet Sprite. An offer on the back panel of specially marked Coca-Cola multi-packs (and the labels of two-liter bottles) made available boxed factory sets through a mail-in offer for 8.95 and UPC symbols from multi-pack wraps of Coca-Cola products. The promotion ran from April to June and covered nearly 90 percent of the country. The standard-size (2 1/2" by 3 1/2") cards feature on the fronts color player photos enclosed by a gold border. Blue stripes edge the pictures above and below, and in the bottom stripe appears the team name and year that the card captures. The backs are aqua and white and present season summary and statistics. The final card in the set summarizes his career and presents career statistics. The cards are numbered on the back.

	MT	EX-MT	VG
COMPLETE SET (26)	12.00	5.50	1.50
COMMON PLAYER (1-26)	.60	.25	.08
☐ 1 Nolan Ryan Mets 1966	1.00	.45	.13
☐ 2 Nolan Ryan Mets 1968	.75	.35	.09
☐ 3 Nolan Ryan Mets 1969	.60	.25	.08
☐ 4 Nolan Ryan Mets 1970	.60	.25	.08
☐ 5 Nolan Ryan Mets 1971	.60	.25	.08
☐ 6 Nolan Ryan Angels 1972	.60	.25	.08
☐ 7 Nolan Ryan Angels 1973	.60	.25	.08
☐ 8 Nolan Ryan Angels 1974	.60	.25	.08
☐ 9 Nolan Ryan Angels 1975	.60	.25	.08
☐ 10 Nolan Ryan Angels 1976	.60	.25	.08
☐ 11 Nolan Ryan Angels 1977	.60	.25	.08
☐ 12 Nolan Ryan Angels 1978	.60	.25	.08
☐ 13 Nolan Ryan Angels 1979	.60	.25	.08
☐ 14 Nolan Ryan Astros 1980	.60	.25	.08
☐ 15 Nolan Ryan Astros 1981	.60	.25	.08
☐ 16 Nolan Ryan Astros 1982	.60	.25	.08
☐ 17 Nolan Ryan Astros 1983	.60	.25	.08
☐ 18 Nolan Ryan Astros 1984	.60	.25	.08
☐ 19 Nolan Ryan Astros 1985	.60	.25	.08
☐ 20 Nolan Ryan Astros 1986	.60	.25	.08
☐ 21 Nolan Ryan Astros 1987	.60	.25	.08
☐ 22 Nolan Ryan Astros 1988	.60	.25	.08
☐ 23 Nolan Ryan Rangers 1989	.60	.25	.08
☐ 24 Nolan Ryan Rangers 1990	.60	.25	.08

	MT	EX-MT	VG
☐ 25 Nolan Ryan Rangers 1991	.60	.25	.08
☐ 26 Nolan Ryan Rangers 1992	.75	.35	.09

1992 Donruss Phenoms

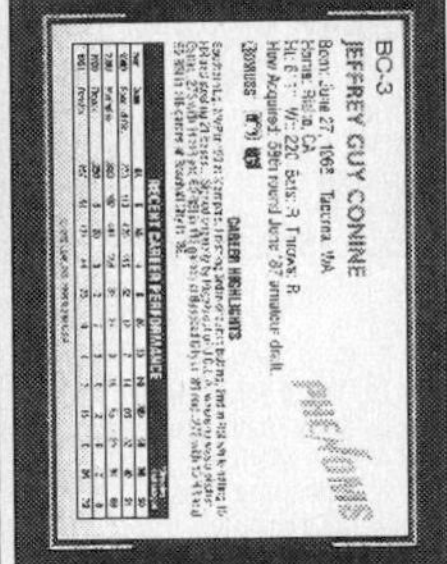

This 20-card set features baseball's most dynamic young prospects. The first 12 Phenom cards (1-12) were randomly inserted into 1992 Donruss The Rookies 12-card foil packs. The last eight Phenom cards (13-20) were randomly inserted in 30-card jumbo packs. The standard-size (2 1/2" by 3 1/2") cards display nonaction color photos that are accented by gold-foil border stripes on a predominantly black card face. The set title "Phenoms" appears in gold foil lettering above the picture, while the player's name is given in the bottom border. In a horizontal format, the backs present biography, career highlights, and recent career performance statistics in a white and gray box enclosed by black and gold borders. The cards are arranged alphabetically and numbered on the back with a BC prefix.

	MT	EX-MT	VG
COMPLETE SET (20)	50.00	23.00	6.25
COMPLETE FOIL SET (12)	35.00	16.00	4.40
COMPLETE JUMBO SET (8)	20.00	9.00	2.50
COMMON PLAYER (1-12)	1.50	.65	.19
COMMON PLAYER (13-20)	2.00	.90	.25
☐ 1 Moises Alou	2.00	.90	.25
☐ 2 Bret Boone	5.00	2.30	.60
☐ 3 Jeff Conine	2.00	.90	.25
☐ 4 Dave Fleming	4.00	1.80	.50
☐ 5 Tyler Green	2.50	1.15	.30
☐ 6 Eric Karros	8.00	3.60	1.00
☐ 7 Pat Listach	8.00	3.60	1.00
☐ 8 Kenny Lofton	6.00	2.70	.75
☐ 9 Mike Piazza	4.50	2.00	.55
☐ 10 Tim Salmon	5.00	2.30	.60
☐ 11 Andy Stankiewicz	1.75	.80	.22
☐ 12 Dan Walters	1.50	.65	.19
☐ 13 Ramon Caraballo	2.00	.90	.25
☐ 14 Brian Jordan	3.00	1.35	.40
☐ 15 Ryan Klesko	6.00	2.70	.75
☐ 16 Sam Militello	4.00	1.80	.50
☐ 17 Frank Seminara	3.00	1.35	.40
☐ 18 Salomon Torres	3.00	1.35	.40
☐ 19 John Valentin	2.00	.90	.25
☐ 20 Wilfredo Cordero	3.50	1.55	.45

1992 Donruss Rookies

After six years of issuing "The Rookies" as a 56-card boxed set, Donruss expanded it to a 132-card set available only as a foil pack product. An additional 20 Phenom cards were randomly inserted in the packs (numbered 1-12 in 12-card foil packs and numbered 13-20 in 30-card jumbo packs). The cards measure the standard size (2 1/2" by 3 1/2"). The

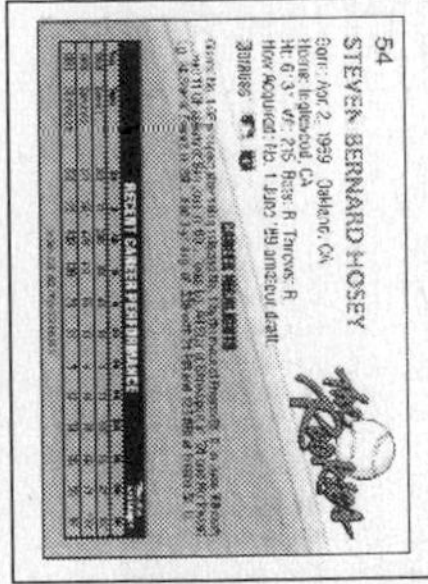

card design is the same as the 1992 Donruss regular issue except that the two-tone blue color bars have been replaced by green, as in the previous six Donruss Rookies sets. The cards are arranged in alphabetical order and numbered on the back. The key Rookie Cards in this set are Billy Ashley, Pedro Astacio, Brent Gates, David Nied, Manny Ramirez, and Tim Wakefield.

	MT	EX-MT	VG
COMPLETE SET (132)	12.00	5.50	1.50
COMMON PLAYER (1-132)	.05	.02	.01
☐ 1 Kyle Abbott	.10	.05	.01
☐ 2 Troy Afenir	.05	.02	.01
☐ 3 Rich Amaral	.10	.05	.01
☐ 4 Ruben Amaro	.05	.02	.01
☐ 5 Billy Ashley	.50	.23	.06
☐ 6 Pedro Astacio	.40	.18	.05
☐ 7 Jim Austin	.10	.05	.01
☐ 8 Robert Ayrault	.10	.05	.01
☐ 9 Kevin Baez	.12	.05	.02
☐ 10 Esteban Beltre	.10	.05	.01
☐ 11 Brian Bohanon	.05	.02	.01
☐ 12 Kent Bottenfield	.15	.07	.02
☐ 13 Jeff Branson	.05	.02	.01
☐ 14 Brad Brink	.10	.05	.01
☐ 15 John Briscoe	.10	.05	.01
☐ 16 Doug Brocail	.10	.05	.01
☐ 17 Rico Brogna	.10	.05	.01
☐ 18 J.T. Bruett	.10	.05	.01
☐ 19 Jacob Brumfield	.10	.05	.01
☐ 20 Jim Bullinger	.10	.05	.01
☐ 21 Kevin Campbell	.10	.05	.01
☐ 22 Pedro Castellano	.15	.07	.02
☐ 23 Mike Christopher	.10	.05	.01
☐ 24 Archi Cianfrocco	.15	.07	.02
☐ 25 Mark Clark	.10	.05	.01
☐ 26 Craig Colbert	.10	.05	.01
☐ 27 Victor Cole	.15	.07	.02
☐ 28 Steve Cooke	.25	.11	.03
☐ 29 Tim Costo	.12	.05	.02
☐ 30 Chad Curtis	.25	.11	.03
☐ 31 Doug Davis	.10	.05	.01
☐ 32 Gary DiSarcina	.08	.04	.01
☐ 33 John Doherty	.15	.07	.02
☐ 34 Mike Draper	.10	.05	.01
☐ 35 Monty Fariss	.10	.05	.01
☐ 36 Bien Figueroa	.10	.05	.01
☐ 37 John Flaherty	.10	.05	.01
☐ 38 Tim Fortugno	.10	.05	.01
☐ 39 Eric Fox	.12	.05	.02
☐ 40 Jeff Frye	.10	.05	.01
☐ 41 Ramon Garcia	.05	.02	.01
☐ 42 Brent Gates	.50	.23	.06
☐ 43 Tom Goodwin	.10	.05	.01
☐ 44 Buddy Groom	.10	.05	.01
☐ 45 Jeff Grotewold	.10	.05	.01
☐ 46 Juan Guerrero	.12	.05	.02
☐ 47 Johnny Guzman	.20	.09	.03
☐ 48 Shawn Hare	.10	.05	.01
☐ 49 Ryan Hawblitzel	.20	.09	.03
☐ 50 Bert Hefferman	.10	.05	.01
☐ 51 Butch Henry	.12	.05	.02
☐ 52 Cesar Hernandez	.10	.05	.01
☐ 53 Vince Horsman	.10	.05	.01
☐ 54 Steve Hosey	.30	.14	.04
☐ 55 Pat Howell	.20	.09	.03
☐ 56 Peter Hoy	.10	.05	.01
☐ 57 Jonathan Hurst	.20	.09	.03
☐ 58 Mark Hutton	.25	.11	.03
☐ 59 Shawn Jeter	.12	.05	.02

		MT	EX-MT	VG
☐	60 Joel Johnston	.05	.02	.01
☐	61 Jeff Kent	.30	.14	.04
☐	62 Kurt Knudsen	.10	.05	.01
☐	63 Kevin Koslofski	.10	.05	.01
☐	64 Danny Leon	.10	.05	.01
☐	65 Jesse Levis	.15	.07	.02
☐	66 Tom Marsh	.10	.05	.01
☐	67 Ed Martel	.15	.07	.02
☐	68 Al Martin	.35	.16	.04
☐	69 Pedro Martinez	.20	.09	.03
☐	70 Derrick May	.08	.04	.01
☐	71 Matt Maysey	.10	.05	.01
☐	72 Russ McGinnis	.10	.05	.01
☐	73 Tim McIntosh	.05	.02	.01
☐	74 Jim McNamara	.10	.05	.01
☐	75 Jeff McNeely	.10	.05	.01
☐	76 Rusty Meacham	.05	.02	.01
☐	77 Tony Menendez	.10	.05	.01
☐	78 Henry Mercedes	.12	.05	.02
☐	79 Paul Miller	.10	.05	.01
☐	80 Joe Millette	.10	.05	.01
☐	81 Blas Minor	.10	.05	.01
☐	82 Dennis Moeller	.10	.05	.01
☐	83 Raul Mondesi	.25	.11	.03
☐	84 Rob Natal	.10	.05	.01
☐	85 Troy Neel	.20	.09	.03
☐	86 David Nied	3.00	1.35	.40
☐	87 Jerry Nielson	.12	.05	.02
☐	88 Donovan Osborne	.30	.14	.04
☐	89 John Patterson	.12	.05	.02
☐	90 Roger Pavlik	.15	.07	.02
☐	91 Dan Peltier	.05	.02	.01
☐	92 Jim Pena	.10	.05	.01
☐	93 William Pennyfeather	.10	.05	.01
☐	94 Mike Perez	.05	.02	.01
☐	95 Hipolito Pichardo	.10	.05	.01
☐	96 Greg Pirkl	.15	.07	.02
☐	97 Harvey Pulliam	.10	.05	.01
☐	98 Manny Ramirez	.60	.25	.08
☐	99 Pat Rapp	.20	.09	.03
☐	100 Jeff Reboulet	.10	.05	.01
☐	101 Darren Reed	.05	.02	.01
☐	102 Shane Reynolds	.10	.05	.01
☐	103 Bill Risley	.10	.05	.01
☐	104 Ben Rivera	.10	.05	.01
☐	105 Henry Rodriguez	.10	.05	.01
☐	106 Rico Rossy	.10	.05	.01
☐	107 Johnny Ruffin	.10	.05	.01
☐	108 Steve Scarsone	.10	.05	.01
☐	109 Tim Scott	.12	.05	.02
☐	110 Steve Shifflett	.10	.05	.01
☐	111 Dave Silvestri	.15	.07	.02
☐	112 Matt Stairs	.15	.07	.02
☐	113 William Suero	.10	.05	.01
☐	114 Jeff Tackett	.10	.05	.01
☐	115 Eddie Taubensee	.10	.05	.01
☐	116 Rick Trlicek	.12	.05	.02
☐	117 Scooter Tucker	.10	.05	.01
☐	118 Shane Turner	.08	.04	.01
☐	119 Julio Valera	.08	.04	.01
☐	120 Paul Wagner	.10	.05	.01
☐	121 Tim Wakefield	3.00	1.35	.40
☐	122 Mike Walker	.10	.05	.01
☐	123 Bruce Walton	.05	.02	.01
☐	124 Lenny Webster	.05	.02	.01
☐	125 Bob Wickman	.30	.14	.04
☐	126 Mike Williams	.15	.07	.02
☐	127 Kerry Woodson	.10	.05	.01
☐	128 Eric Young	.25	.11	.03
☐	129 Kevin Young	.50	.23	.06
☐	130 Pete Young	.10	.05	.01
☐	131 Checklist 1-66	.05	.01	.00
☐	132 Checklist 67-132	.05	.01	.00

1992 Donruss Triple Play Previews

This eight-card set was issued by Donruss to preview the design of the 264-card 1992 Donruss Triple Play set. The front design and player photos are identical to those in the regular issue set; the only difference is the numbering and the word "preview" appearing across the bottom of the backs. The cards are standard size, 2 1/2" by 3 1/2".

	MT	EX-MT	VG
COMPLETE SET (8)	150.00	70.00	19.00
COMMON PLAYER (1-8)	9.00	4.00	1.15

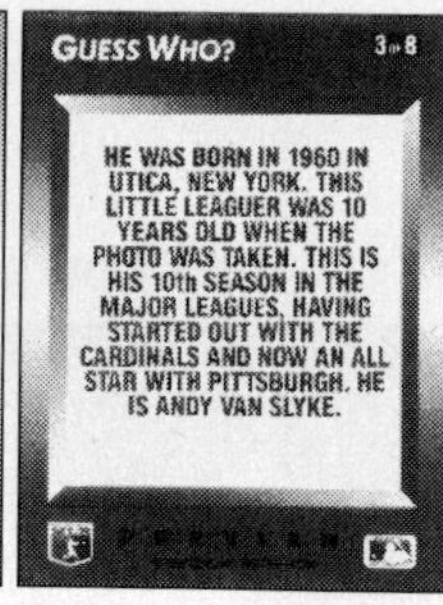

		MT	EX-MT	VG
☐	1 Ken Griffey Jr.	50.00	23.00	6.25
☐	2 Darryl Strawberry	25.00	11.50	3.10
☐	3 Andy Van Slyke	15.00	6.75	1.90
☐	4 Don Mattingly	35.00	16.00	4.40
☐	5 Awesome Action Gary Carter Steve Finley	9.00	4.00	1.15
☐	6 Frank Thomas	60.00	27.00	7.50
☐	7 Kirby Puckett	35.00	16.00	4.40
☐	8 Fun at the Ballpark	9.00	4.00	1.15

1992 Donruss Triple Play

The 1992 Donruss Triple Play set contains 264 cards measuring the standard size (2 1/2" by 3 1/2"). This set was created especially for children ages 5-12, featuring bright color borders, player quotes, fun facts, and a "Little Hotshot" subset (6, 77, 158, 234, 243, 253), picturing some players when they were kids. The Awesome Action subset mostly show more than one player (26, 41, 61, 73, 99, 102, 113, 121, 130, 193, 196). Each 15-card pack included one rub-off game card. Randomly packed Gallery of Stars cards feature the artwork of Dick Perez and capture twelve top players who changed teams in 1992. The color action player photos on the fronts are slightly tilted to the left, and the border alternates shades from red to yellow and back to red again as one moves down the card face. In addition to blue and white print, the backs reflect the same color as the front borders. Player information is displayed inside a home plate or base icon. The cards are numbered on the back and checklisted below accordingly.

	MT	EX-MT	VG
COMPLETE SET (264)	11.00	4.90	1.40
COMMON PLAYER (1-264)	.03	.01	.00

		MT	EX-MT	VG
☐	1 SkyDome	.08	.04	.01
☐	2 Tom Foley	.03	.01	.00
☐	3 Scott Erickson	.10	.05	.01
☐	4 Matt Williams	.06	.03	.01
☐	5 David Valle	.03	.01	.00
☐	6 Andy Van Slyke Little Hotshot 1	.06	.03	.01

☐ 7 Tom Glavine	.15	.07	.02
☐ 8 Kevin Appier	.08	.04	.01
☐ 9 Pedro Guerrero	.06	.03	.01
☐ 10 Terry Steinbach	.06	.03	.01
☐ 11 Terry Mulholland	.03	.01	.00
☐ 12 Mike Boddicker	.03	.01	.00
☐ 13 Gregg Olson	.08	.04	.01
☐ 14 Tim Burke	.03	.01	.00
☐ 15 Candy Maldonado	.06	.03	.01
☐ 16 Orlando Merced	.06	.03	.01
☐ 17 Robin Ventura	.20	.09	.03
☐ 18 Eric Anthony	.10	.05	.01
☐ 19 Greg Maddux	.15	.07	.02
☐ 20 Erik Hanson	.03	.01	.00
☐ 21 Bobby Ojeda	.03	.01	.00
☐ 22 Nolan Ryan	.50	.23	.06
☐ 23 Dave Righetti	.03	.01	.00
☐ 24 Reggie Jefferson	.10	.05	.01
☐ 25 Jody Reed	.03	.01	.00
☐ 26 Awesome Action 1	.06	.03	.01
Steve Finley			
Gary Carter			
☐ 27 Chili Davis	.03	.01	.00
☐ 28 Hector Villanueva	.03	.01	.00
☐ 29 Cecil Fielder	.20	.09	.03
☐ 30 Hal Morris	.08	.04	.01
☐ 31 Barry Larkin	.12	.05	.02
☐ 32 Bobby Thigpen	.06	.03	.01
☐ 33 Andy Benes	.10	.05	.01
☐ 34 Harold Baines	.06	.03	.01
☐ 35 David Cone	.12	.05	.02
☐ 36 Mark Langston	.06	.03	.01
☐ 37 Bryan Harvey	.06	.03	.01
☐ 38 John Kruk	.06	.03	.01
☐ 39 Scott Sanderson	.03	.01	.00
☐ 40 Lonnie Smith	.03	.01	.00
☐ 41 Awesome Action 2	.03	.01	.00
Rex Hudler			
☐ 42 George Bell	.08	.04	.01
☐ 43 Steve Finley	.06	.03	.01
☐ 44 Mickey Tettleton	.10	.05	.01
☐ 45 Robby Thompson	.06	.03	.01
☐ 46 Pat Kelly	.06	.03	.01
☐ 47 Marquis Grissom	.20	.09	.03
☐ 48 Tony Pena	.03	.01	.00
☐ 49 Alex Cole	.03	.01	.00
☐ 50 Steve Buechele	.03	.01	.00
☐ 51 Ivan Rodriguez	.45	.20	.06
☐ 52 John Smiley	.06	.03	.01
☐ 53 Gary Sheffield	.25	.11	.03
☐ 54 Greg Olson	.03	.01	.00
☐ 55 Ramon Martinez	.10	.05	.01
☐ 56 B.J. Surhoff	.06	.03	.01
☐ 57 Bruce Hurst	.06	.03	.01
☐ 58 Todd Stottlemyre	.06	.03	.01
☐ 59 Brett Butler	.06	.03	.01
☐ 60 Glenn Davis	.08	.04	.01
☐ 61 Awesome Action 3	.03	.01	.00
Glenn Braggs			
Kirt Manwaring			
☐ 62 Lee Smith	.08	.04	.01
☐ 63 Rickey Henderson	.20	.09	.03
☐ 64 Fun at the Ballpark	.06	.03	.01
Dave Cone			
Jeff Innis			
John Franco			
☐ 65 Rick Aguilera	.06	.03	.01
☐ 66 Kevin Elster	.03	.01	.00
☐ 67 Dwight Evans	.06	.03	.01
☐ 68 Andujar Cedeno	.08	.04	.01
☐ 69 Brian McRae	.06	.03	.01
☐ 70 Benito Santiago	.10	.05	.01
☐ 71 Randy Johnson	.06	.03	.01
☐ 72 Roberto Kelly	.08	.04	.01
☐ 73 Awesome Action 4	.03	.01	.00
Juan Samuel			
☐ 74 Alex Fernandez	.08	.04	.01
☐ 75 Felix Jose	.08	.04	.01
☐ 76 Brian Harper	.03	.01	.00
☐ 77 Scott Sanderson	.03	.01	.00
Little Hotshot 2			
☐ 78 Ken Caminiti	.06	.03	.01
☐ 79 Mo Vaughn	.12	.05	.02
☐ 80 Roger McDowell	.03	.01	.00
☐ 81 Robin Yount	.15	.07	.02
☐ 82 Dave Magadan	.03	.01	.00
☐ 83 Julio Franco	.08	.04	.01
☐ 84 Roberto Alomar	.30	.14	.04
☐ 85 Steve Avery	.20	.09	.03
☐ 86 Travis Fryman	.25	.11	.03
☐ 87 Fred McGriff	.15	.07	.02
☐ 88 Dave Stewart	.08	.04	.01
☐ 89 Larry Walker	.15	.07	.02
☐ 90 Chris Sabo	.06	.03	.01
☐ 91 Chuck Finley	.06	.03	.01
☐ 92 Dennis Martinez	.06	.03	.01
☐ 93 Jeff Johnson	.03	.01	.00
☐ 94 Len Dykstra	.06	.03	.01
☐ 95 Mark Whiten	.06	.03	.01
☐ 96 Wade Taylor	.06	.03	.01
☐ 97 Lance Dickson	.06	.03	.01
☐ 98 Kevin Tapani	.08	.04	.01
☐ 99 Awesome Action 5	.03	.01	.00
Luis Polonia			
Tony Phillips			
☐ 100 Milt Cuyler	.06	.03	.01
☐ 101 Willie McGee	.06	.03	.01
☐ 102 Awesome Action 6	.06	.03	.01
Tony Fernandez			
☐ 103 Albert Belle	.12	.05	.02
☐ 104 Todd Hundley	.06	.03	.01
☐ 105 Ben McDonald	.12	.05	.02
☐ 106 Doug Drabek	.08	.04	.01
☐ 107 Tim Raines	.08	.04	.01
☐ 108 Joe Carter	.20	.09	.03
☐ 109 Reggie Sanders	.30	.14	.04
☐ 110 John Olerud	.12	.05	.02
☐ 111 Darren Lewis	.06	.03	.01
☐ 112 Juan Gonzalez	.35	.16	.04
☐ 113 Awesome Action 7	.10	.05	.01
Andre Dawson			
☐ 114 Mark Grace	.10	.05	.01
☐ 115 George Brett	.15	.07	.02
☐ 116 Barry Bonds	.20	.09	.03
☐ 117 Lou Whitaker	.06	.03	.01
☐ 118 Jose Oquendo	.03	.01	.00
☐ 119 Lee Stevens	.06	.03	.01
☐ 120 Phil Plantier	.20	.09	.03
☐ 121 Awesome Action 8	.03	.01	.00
Matt Merullo			
☐ 122 Greg Vaughn	.06	.03	.01
☐ 123 Royce Clayton	.15	.07	.02
☐ 124 Bob Welch	.06	.03	.01
☐ 125 Juan Samuel	.03	.01	.00
☐ 126 Ron Gant	.12	.05	.02
☐ 127 Edgar Martinez	.08	.04	.01
☐ 128 Andy Ashby	.06	.03	.01
☐ 129 Jack McDowell	.10	.05	.01
☐ 130 Awesome Action 9	.03	.01	.00
Dave Henderson			
Jerry Browne			
☐ 131 Leo Gomez	.10	.05	.01
☐ 132 Checklist	.03	.01	.00
☐ 133 Phillie Phanatic	.08	.04	.01
☐ 134 Bret Barberie	.06	.03	.01
☐ 135 Kent Hrbek	.06	.03	.01
☐ 136 Hall of Fame	.06	.03	.01
☐ 137 Omar Vizquel	.03	.01	.00
☐ 138 The Famous Chicken	.10	.05	.01
☐ 139 Terry Pendleton	.10	.05	.01
☐ 140 Jim Eisenreich	.03	.01	.00
☐ 141 Todd Zeile	.06	.03	.01
☐ 142 Todd Van Poppel	.25	.11	.03
☐ 143 Darren Daulton	.08	.04	.01
☐ 144 Mike Macfarlane	.03	.01	.00
☐ 145 Luis Mercedes	.08	.04	.01
☐ 146 Trevor Wilson	.06	.03	.01
☐ 147 Dave Stieb	.06	.03	.01
☐ 148 Andy Van Slyke	.10	.05	.01
☐ 149 Carlton Fisk	.15	.07	.02
☐ 150 Craig Biggio	.08	.04	.01
☐ 151 Joe Girardi	.03	.01	.00
☐ 152 Ken Griffey Jr.	.75	.35	.09
☐ 153 Jose Offerman	.08	.04	.01
☐ 154 Bobby Witt	.03	.01	.00
☐ 155 Will Clark	.25	.11	.03
☐ 156 Steve Olin	.03	.01	.00
☐ 157 Greg W. Harris	.03	.01	.00
☐ 158 Dale Murphy	.10	.05	.01
Little Hotshot 3			
☐ 159 Don Mattingly	.20	.09	.03
☐ 160 Shawon Dunston	.06	.03	.01
☐ 161 Bill Gullickson	.06	.03	.01
☐ 162 Paul O'Neill	.06	.03	.01
☐ 163 Norm Charlton	.03	.01	.00
☐ 164 Bo Jackson	.15	.07	.02
☐ 165 Tony Fernandez	.06	.03	.01
☐ 166 Dave Henderson	.03	.01	.00
☐ 167 Dwight Gooden	.12	.05	.02
☐ 168 Junior Felix	.06	.03	.01
☐ 169 Lance Parrish	.06	.03	.01
☐ 170 Pat Combs	.06	.03	.01
☐ 171 Chuck Knoblauch	.25	.11	.03
☐ 172 John Smoltz	.12	.05	.02
☐ 173 Wrigley Field	.10	.05	.01
☐ 174 Andre Dawson	.15	.07	.02

☐ 175 Pete Harnisch .06 .03 .01
☐ 176 Alan Trammell .08 .04 .01
☐ 177 Kirk Dressendorfer .06 .03 .01
☐ 178 Matt Nokes .06 .03 .01
☐ 179 Wilfredo Cordero .15 .07 .02
☐ 180 Scott Cooper .08 .04 .01
☐ 181 Glenallen Hill .06 .03 .01
☐ 182 John Franco .06 .03 .01
☐ 183 Rafael Palmeiro .12 .05 .02
☐ 184 Jay Bell .06 .03 .01
☐ 185 Bill Wegman .03 .01 .00
☐ 186 Deion Sanders .20 .09 .03
☐ 187 Darryl Strawberry .15 .07 .02
☐ 188 Jaime Navarro .08 .04 .01
☐ 189 Darrin Jackson .08 .04 .01
☐ 190 Eddie Zosky .06 .03 .01
☐ 191 Mike Scioscia .03 .01 .00
☐ 192 Chito Martinez .06 .03 .01
☐ 193 Awesome Action 10 .06 .03 .01
Pat Kelly and
Ron Tingley
☐ 194 Ray Lankford .20 .09 .03
☐ 195 Dennis Eckersley .10 .05 .01
☐ 196 Awesome Action 11 .03 .01 .00
Ivan Calderon
Mike Maddux
☐ 197 Shane Mack .08 .04 .01
☐ 198 Checklist .03 .01 .00
☐ 199 Cal Ripken .35 .16 .04
☐ 200 Jeff Bagwell .45 .20 .06
☐ 201 Dave Howard .06 .03 .01
☐ 202 Kirby Puckett .25 .11 .03
☐ 203 Harold Reynolds .03 .01 .00
☐ 204 Jim Abbott .12 .05 .02
☐ 205 Mark Lewis .08 .04 .01
☐ 206 Frank Thomas .75 .35 .09
☐ 207 Rex Hudler .03 .01 .00
☐ 208 Vince Coleman .08 .04 .01
☐ 209 Delino DeShields .15 .07 .02
☐ 210 Luis Gonzalez .06 .03 .01
☐ 211 Wade Boggs .20 .09 .03
☐ 212 Orel Hershiser .08 .04 .01
☐ 213 Cal Eldred .35 .16 .04
☐ 214 Jose Canseco .25 .11 .03
☐ 215 Jose Guzman .06 .03 .01
☐ 216 Roger Clemens .30 .14 .04
☐ 217 David Justice .20 .09 .03
☐ 218 Tony Phillips .06 .03 .01
☐ 219 Tony Gwynn .20 .09 .03
☐ 220 Mitch Williams .06 .03 .01
☐ 221 Bill Sampen .03 .01 .00
☐ 222 Billy Hatcher .03 .01 .00
☐ 223 Gary Gaetti .06 .03 .01
☐ 224 Tim Wallach .06 .03 .01
☐ 225 Kevin Maas .08 .04 .01
☐ 226 Kevin Brown .08 .04 .01
☐ 227 Sandy Alomar Jr. .08 .04 .01
☐ 228 John Habyan .03 .01 .00
☐ 229 Ryne Sandberg .35 .16 .04
☐ 230 Greg Gagne .03 .01 .00
☐ 231 Autographs .15 .07 .02
(Mark McGwire)
☐ 232 Mike LaValliere .03 .01 .00
☐ 233 Mark Gubicza .06 .03 .01
☐ 234 Lance Parrish .06 .03 .01
Little Hotshot 4
☐ 235 Carlos Baerga .20 .09 .03
☐ 236 Howard Johnson .08 .04 .01
☐ 237 Mike Mussina .50 .23 .06
☐ 238 Ruben Sierra .20 .09 .03
☐ 239 Lance Johnson .03 .01 .00
☐ 240 Devon White .06 .03 .01
☐ 241 Dan Wilson .10 .05 .01
☐ 242 Kelly Gruber .06 .03 .01
☐ 243 Brett Butler .06 .03 .01
Little Hotshot 5
☐ 244 Ozzie Smith .15 .07 .02
☐ 245 Chuck McElroy .03 .01 .00
☐ 246 Shawn Boskie .03 .01 .00
☐ 247 Mark Davis .03 .01 .00
☐ 248 Bill Landrum .03 .01 .00
☐ 249 Frank Tanana .03 .01 .00
☐ 250 Darryl Hamilton .06 .03 .01
☐ 251 Gary DiSarcina .06 .03 .01
☐ 252 Mike Greenwell .08 .04 .01
☐ 253 Cal Ripken .30 .14 .04
Little Hotshot 6
☐ 254 Paul Molitor .10 .05 .01
☐ 255 Tim Teufel .03 .01 .00
☐ 256 Chris Hoiles .08 .04 .01
☐ 257 Rob Dibble .06 .03 .01
☐ 258 Sid Bream .03 .01 .00
☐ 259 Tino Martinez .10 .05 .01
☐ 260 Dale Murphy .12 .05 .02
☐ 261 Greg Hibbard .03 .01 .00
☐ 262 Mark McGwire .20 .09 .03
☐ 263 Oriole Park .10 .05 .01
☐ 264 Checklist Card .06 .03 .01

1992 Donruss Triple Play Gallery

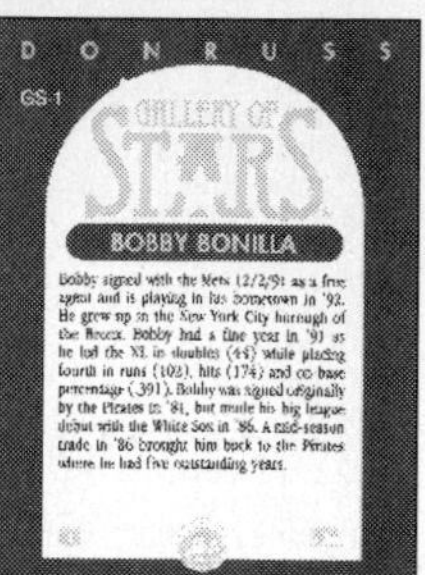

The 1992 Donruss Triple Play Gallery of Stars was an insert subset for the 1992 Donruss Triple Play baseball set. Randomly inserted into foil packs, the first six cards feature six top players who changed teams in 1992 in their new uniforms. The second six cards were randomly inserted into jumbo packs. The cards measure the standard size (2 1/2" by 3 1/2"). On bright-colored backgrounds, the fronts display color player portraits by noted sports artist Dick Perez. The words "Gallery of Stars" appear in a red and silver-foil stamped banner above the portrait, while the player's name appears in a similarly colored bar between two silver foil stars at the card bottom. The backs are red, white, and gray and carry career summary. The cards are numbered on the back with a GS prefix.

	MT	EX-MT	VG
COMPLETE SET (12)	25.00	11.50	3.10
COMMON PLAYER (GS1-GS6)	1.00	.45	.13
COMMON PLAYER (GS7-GS12)	2.00	.90	.25
☐ GS1 Bobby Bonilla	1.50	.65	.19
☐ GS2 Wally Joyner	1.00	.45	.13
☐ GS3 Jack Morris	1.50	.65	.19
☐ GS4 Steve Sax	1.00	.45	.13
☐ GS5 Danny Tartabull	1.50	.65	.19
☐ GS6 Frank Viola	1.00	.45	.13
☐ GS7 Jeff Bagwell	2.00	.90	.25
☐ GS8 Ken Griffey Jr.	6.00	2.70	.75
☐ GS9 Dave Justice	2.50	1.15	.30
☐ GS10 Ryan Klesko	3.00	1.35	.40
☐ GS11 Cal Ripken	4.50	2.00	.55
☐ GS12 Frank Thomas	6.00	2.70	.75

1993 Donruss Previews

This 22-card set was issued by Donruss for hobby dealers to preview the 1993 Donruss regular issue series. The cards measure the standard size (2 1/2" by 3 1/2") and feature glossy color player photos with white borders on the fronts. The team logo appears in a diamond at the lower left corner, while the player's name appears in a bar that extends to the right. Both the diamond and bar are team-color coded. The top half of the back has a color close-up photo; the bottom half presents biography and recent major league statistics. The cards are numbered on the back.

	MT	EX-MT	VG
COMPLETE SET (22)	125.00	57.50	15.50
COMMON PLAYER (1-22)	3.00	1.35	.40
☐ 1 Tom Glavine	6.00	2.70	.75
☐ 2 Ryne Sandberg	10.00	4.50	1.25
☐ 3 Barry Larkin	4.00	1.80	.50
☐ 4 Jeff Bagwell	8.00	3.60	1.00
☐ 5 Eric Karros	8.00	3.60	1.00
☐ 6 Larry Walker	6.00	2.70	.75
☐ 7 Eddie Murray	4.00	1.80	.50
☐ 8 Darren Daulton	3.00	1.35	.40
☐ 9 Andy Van Slyke	4.00	1.80	.50
☐ 10 Gary Sheffield	8.00	3.60	1.00
☐ 11 Will Clark	8.00	3.60	1.00
☐ 12 Cal Ripken	12.00	5.50	1.50
☐ 13 Roger Clemens	10.00	4.50	1.25
☐ 14 Frank Thomas	18.00	8.00	2.30
☐ 15 Cecil Fielder	5.00	2.30	.60
☐ 16 George Brett	5.00	2.30	.60
☐ 17 Robin Yount	5.00	2.30	.60
☐ 18 Don Mattingly	5.00	2.30	.60
☐ 19 Dennis Eckersley	4.00	1.80	.50
☐ 20 Ken Griffey Jr.	15.00	6.75	1.90
☐ 21 Jose Canseco	8.00	3.60	1.00
☐ 22 Roberto Alomar	8.00	3.60	1.00

1993 Donruss

The first series of 1993 Donruss consists of 396 standard-size (2 1/2" by 3 1/2") cards. Fifteen Diamond King cards, featuring the artwork of Dick Perez and gold-foil stamped, were randomly inserted into packs. The ten-card Spirit of the Game random inserts were new in 1993, and they are packed approximately two per box in Series I. Other random inserts featured are the nine-card Elite series, a Will Clark Signature card, and a Legends card honoring Yount. Finally a Rated Rookies subset spotlights 20 top prospects; these Rated Rookies are sprinkled thoughout the set and are designated by RR in the checklist below. The fronts feature glossy color action photos bordered in white. At the bottom of the picture, the team logo appears in a team color-coded diamond with the player's name in a color-coded bar extending to the right. The backs have a second color player photo with biography and recent major league statistics filling up the rest of the card. The cards are numbered in a team color-coded home plate icon at the upper right corner.

	MT	EX-MT	VG
COMPLETE SET (396)	15.00	6.75	1.90
COMMON PLAYER (1-396)	.05	.02	.01
☐ 1 Craig Lefferts	.05	.02	.01
☐ 2 Kent Mercker	.05	.02	.01
☐ 3 Phil Plantier	.07	.03	.01
☐ 4 Alex Arias	.10	.05	.01
☐ 5 Julio Valera	.05	.02	.01
☐ 6 Dan Wilson	.05	.02	.01
☐ 7 Frank Thomas	.75	.35	.09
☐ 8 Eric Anthony	.07	.03	.01
☐ 9 Derek Lilliquist	.05	.02	.01
☐ 10 Rafael Bournigal	.25	.11	.03
☐ 11 Manny Alexander RR	.10	.05	.01
☐ 12 Bret Barberie	.05	.02	.01
☐ 13 Mickey Tettleton	.07	.03	.01
☐ 14 Anthony Young	.07	.03	.01
☐ 15 Tim Spehr	.05	.02	.01
☐ 16 Bob Ayrault	.08	.04	.01
☐ 17 Bill Wegman	.05	.02	.01
☐ 18 Jay Bell	.05	.02	.01
☐ 19 Rick Aguilera	.05	.02	.01
☐ 20 Todd Zeile	.05	.02	.01
☐ 21 Steve Farr	.05	.02	.01
☐ 22 Andy Benes	.07	.03	.01
☐ 23 Lance Blankenship	.05	.02	.01
☐ 24 Ted Wood	.05	.02	.01
☐ 25 Omar Vizquel	.05	.02	.01
☐ 26 Steve Avery	.12	.05	.02
☐ 27 Brian Bohanon	.05	.02	.01
☐ 28 Rick Wilkins	.05	.02	.01
☐ 29 Devon White	.07	.03	.01
☐ 30 Bobby Ayala	.30	.14	.04
☐ 31 Leo Gomez	.07	.03	.01
☐ 32 Mike Simms	.05	.02	.01
☐ 33 Ellis Burks	.07	.03	.01
☐ 34 Steve Wilson	.05	.02	.01
☐ 35 Jim Abbott	.10	.05	.01
☐ 36 Tim Wallach	.07	.03	.01
☐ 37 Wilson Alvarez	.05	.02	.01
☐ 38 Daryl Boston	.05	.02	.01
☐ 39 Sandy Alomar Jr.	.07	.03	.01
☐ 40 Mitch Williams	.05	.02	.01
☐ 41 Rico Brogna	.07	.03	.01
☐ 42 Gary Varsho	.05	.02	.01
☐ 43 Kevin Appier	.07	.03	.01
☐ 44 Eric Wedge RR	.35	.16	.04
☐ 45 Dante Bichette	.05	.02	.01
☐ 46 Jose Oquendo	.05	.02	.01
☐ 47 Mike Trombley	.12	.05	.02
☐ 48 Dan Walters	.08	.04	.01
☐ 49 Gerald Williams	.05	.02	.01
☐ 50 Bud Black	.05	.02	.01
☐ 51 Bobby Witt	.05	.02	.01
☐ 52 Mark Davis	.05	.02	.01
☐ 53 Shawn Barton	.10	.05	.01
☐ 54 Paul Assenmacher	.05	.02	.01
☐ 55 Kevin Reimer	.05	.02	.01
☐ 56 Billy Ashley RR	.20	.09	.03
☐ 57 Eddie Zosky	.05	.02	.01
☐ 58 Chris Sabo	.07	.03	.01
☐ 59 Billy Ripken	.05	.02	.01
☐ 60 Scooter Tucker	.05	.02	.01
☐ 61 Tim Wakefield RR	.60	.25	.08
☐ 62 Mitch Webster	.05	.02	.01
☐ 63 Jack Clark	.07	.03	.01
☐ 64 Mark Gardner	.05	.02	.01
☐ 65 Lee Stevens	.05	.02	.01
☐ 66 Todd Hundley	.05	.02	.01
☐ 67 Bobby Thigpen	.05	.02	.01
☐ 68 Dave Hollins	.07	.03	.01
☐ 69 Jack Armstrong	.05	.02	.01
☐ 70 Alex Cole	.05	.02	.01
☐ 71 Mark Carreon	.05	.02	.01
☐ 72 Todd Worrell	.05	.02	.01
☐ 73 Steve Shifflett	.05	.02	.01
☐ 74 Jerald Clark	.05	.02	.01
☐ 75 Paul Molitor	.07	.03	.01
☐ 76 Larry Carter	.12	.05	.02
☐ 77 Rich Rowland RR	.08	.04	.01
☐ 78 Damon Berryhill	.05	.02	.01
☐ 79 Willie Banks	.07	.03	.01
☐ 80 Hector Villanueva	.05	.02	.01
☐ 81 Mike Gallego	.05	.02	.01
☐ 82 Tim Belcher	.07	.03	.01
☐ 83 Mike Bordick	.05	.02	.01
☐ 84 Craig Biggio	.07	.03	.01
☐ 85 Lance Parrish	.07	.03	.01

☐	86 Brett Butler	.07	.03	.01
☐	87 Mike Timlin	.05	.02	.01
☐	88 Brian Barnes	.05	.02	.01
☐	89 Brady Anderson	.07	.03	.01
☐	90 D.J. Dozier	.07	.03	.01
☐	91 Frank Viola	.07	.03	.01
☐	92 Darren Daulton	.07	.03	.01
☐	93 Chad Curtis	.10	.05	.01
☐	94 Zane Smith	.05	.02	.01
☐	95 George Bell	.07	.03	.01
☐	96 Rex Hudler	.05	.02	.01
☐	97 Mark Whiten	.05	.02	.01
☐	98 Tim Teufel	.05	.02	.01
☐	99 Kevin Ritz	.05	.02	.01
☐	100 Jeff Brantley	.05	.02	.01
☐	101 Jeff Conine	.05	.02	.01
☐	102 Vinny Castilla	.05	.02	.01
☐	103 Greg Vaughn	.07	.03	.01
☐	104 Steve Buechele	.05	.02	.01
☐	105 Darren Reed	.05	.02	.01
☐	106 Bip Roberts	.07	.03	.01
☐	107 John Habyan	.05	.02	.01
☐	108 Scott Servais	.05	.02	.01
☐	109 Walt Weiss	.05	.02	.01
☐	110 J.T. Snow RR	.50	.23	.06
☐	111 Jay Buhner	.07	.03	.01
☐	112 Darryl Strawberry	.12	.05	.02
☐	113 Roger Pavlik	.05	.02	.01
☐	114 Chris Nabholz	.07	.03	.01
☐	115 Pat Borders	.05	.02	.01
☐	116 Pat Howell	.05	.02	.01
☐	117 Gregg Olson	.07	.03	.01
☐	118 Curt Schilling	.05	.02	.01
☐	119 Roger Clemens	.20	.09	.03
☐	120 Victor Cole	.05	.02	.01
☐	121 Gary DiSarcina	.05	.02	.01
☐	122 Checklist 1-80 (Gary Carter and Kirt Manwaring	.06	.02	.01
☐	123 Steve Sax	.07	.03	.01
☐	124 Chuck Carr	.05	.02	.01
☐	125 Mark Lewis	.05	.02	.01
☐	126 Tony Gwynn	.12	.05	.02
☐	127 Travis Fryman	.20	.09	.03
☐	128 Dave Burba	.05	.02	.01
☐	129 Wally Joyner	.07	.03	.01
☐	130 John Smoltz	.10	.05	.01
☐	131 Cal Eldred	.20	.09	.03
☐	132 Checklist 81-159 (Roberto Alomar and Devon White)	.06	.02	.01
☐	133 Arthur Rhodes	.07	.03	.01
☐	134 Jeff Blauser	.05	.02	.01
☐	135 Scott Cooper	.07	.03	.01
☐	136 Doug Strange	.05	.02	.01
☐	137 Luis Sojo	.05	.02	.01
☐	138 Jeff Branson	.05	.02	.01
☐	139 Alex Fernandez	.07	.03	.01
☐	140 Ken Caminiti	.07	.03	.01
☐	141 Charles Nagy	.07	.03	.01
☐	142 Tom Candiotti	.05	.02	.01
☐	143 Willie Greene RR	.15	.07	.02
☐	144 John Vander Wal	.05	.02	.01
☐	145 Kurt Knudsen	.05	.02	.01
☐	146 John Franco	.07	.03	.01
☐	147 Eddie Pierce	.10	.05	.01
☐	148 Kim Batiste	.05	.02	.01
☐	149 Darren Holmes	.05	.02	.01
☐	150 Steve Cooke	.05	.02	.01
☐	151 Terry Jorgensen	.05	.02	.01
☐	152 Mark Clark	.05	.02	.01
☐	153 Randy Velarde	.05	.02	.01
☐	154 Greg W. Harris	.05	.02	.01
☐	155 Kevin Campbell	.05	.02	.01
☐	156 John Burkett	.05	.02	.01
☐	157 Kevin Mitchell	.07	.03	.01
☐	158 Deion Sanders	.12	.05	.02
☐	159 Jose Canseco	.20	.09	.03
☐	160 Jeff Hartsock	.10	.05	.01
☐	161 Tom Quinlan	.12	.05	.02
☐	162 Tim Pugh	.25	.11	.03
☐	163 Glenn Davis	.07	.03	.01
☐	164 Shane Reynolds	.05	.02	.01
☐	165 Jody Reed	.05	.02	.01
☐	166 Mike Sharperson	.05	.02	.01
☐	167 Scott Lewis	.05	.02	.01
☐	168 Dennis Martinez	.07	.03	.01
☐	169 Scott Radinsky	.05	.02	.01
☐	170 Dave Gallagher	.05	.02	.01
☐	171 Jim Thome	.07	.03	.01
☐	172 Terry Mulholland	.05	.02	.01
☐	173 Milt Cuyler	.05	.02	.01
☐	174 Bob Patterson	.05	.02	.01
☐	175 Jeff Montgomery	.05	.02	.01
☐	176 Tim Salmon RR	.25	.11	.03
☐	177 Franklin Stubbs	.05	.02	.01
☐	178 Donovan Osborne	.12	.05	.02
☐	179 Jeff Reboulet	.05	.02	.01
☐	180 Jeremy Hernandez	.05	.02	.01
☐	181 Charlie Hayes	.05	.02	.01
☐	182 Matt Williams	.07	.03	.01
☐	183 Mike Raczka	.10	.05	.01
☐	184 Francisco Cabrera	.05	.02	.01
☐	185 Rich DeLucia	.05	.02	.01
☐	186 Sammy Sosa	.05	.02	.01
☐	187 Ivan Rodriguez	.20	.09	.03
☐	188 Bret Boone RR	.25	.11	.03
☐	189 Juan Guzman	.30	.14	.04
☐	190 Tom Browning	.05	.02	.01
☐	191 Randy Milligan	.05	.02	.01
☐	192 Steve Finley	.05	.02	.01
☐	193 John Patterson RR	.05	.02	.01
☐	194 Kip Gross	.05	.02	.01
☐	195 Tony Fossas	.05	.02	.01
☐	196 Ivan Calderon	.05	.02	.01
☐	197 Junior Felix	.05	.02	.01
☐	198 Pate Schourek	.05	.02	.01
☐	199 Craig Grebeck	.05	.02	.01
☐	200 Juan Bell	.05	.02	.01
☐	201 Glenallen Hill	.05	.02	.01
☐	202 Danny Jackson	.05	.02	.01
☐	203 John Kiely	.05	.02	.01
☐	204 Bob Tewksbury	.05	.02	.01
☐	205 Kevin Koslofski	.05	.02	.01
☐	206 Craig Shipley	.05	.02	.01
☐	207 John Jaha	.10	.05	.01
☐	208 Royce Clayton	.10	.05	.01
☐	209 Mike Piazza RR	.35	.16	.04
☐	210 Ron Gant	.10	.05	.01
☐	211 Scott Erickson	.07	.03	.01
☐	212 Doug Dascenzo	.05	.02	.01
☐	213 Andy Stankiewicz	.05	.02	.01
☐	214 Geronimo Berroa	.05	.02	.01
☐	215 Dennis Eckersley	.10	.05	.01
☐	216 Al Osuna	.05	.02	.01
☐	217 Tino Martinez	.07	.03	.01
☐	218 Henry Rodriguez	.05	.02	.01
☐	219 Ed Sprague	.07	.03	.01
☐	220 Ken Hill	.05	.02	.01
☐	221 Chito Martinez	.05	.02	.01
☐	222 Bret Saberhagen	.07	.03	.01
☐	223 Mike Greenwell	.07	.03	.01
☐	224 Mickey Morandini	.05	.02	.01
☐	225 Chuck Finley	.05	.02	.01
☐	226 Denny Neagle	.05	.02	.01
☐	227 Kirk McCaskill	.05	.02	.01
☐	228 Rheal Cormier	.05	.02	.01
☐	229 Paul Sorrento	.05	.02	.01
☐	230 Darrin Jackson	.05	.02	.01
☐	231 Rob Deer	.07	.03	.01
☐	232 Bill Swift	.05	.02	.01
☐	233 Kevin McReynolds	.07	.03	.01
☐	234 Terry Pendleton	.07	.03	.01
☐	235 Dave Nilsson	.07	.03	.01
☐	236 Chuck McElroy	.05	.02	.01
☐	237 Derek Parks	.05	.02	.01
☐	238 Norm Charlton	.07	.03	.01
☐	239 Matt Nokes	.05	.02	.01
☐	240 Juan Guerrero	.05	.02	.01
☐	241 Jeff Parrett	.05	.02	.01
☐	242 Ryan Thompson RR	.25	.11	.03
☐	243 Dave Fleming	.20	.09	.03
☐	244 Dave Hansen	.05	.02	.01
☐	245 Monty Fariss	.05	.02	.01
☐	246 Archi Cianfrocco	.05	.02	.01
☐	247 Pat Hentgen	.05	.02	.01
☐	248 Bill Pecota	.05	.02	.01
☐	249 Ben McDonald	.07	.03	.01
☐	250 Cliff Brantley	.05	.02	.01
☐	251 John Valentin	.12	.05	.02
☐	252 Jeff King	.05	.02	.01
☐	253 Reggie Williams	.05	.02	.01
☐	254 Checklist 160-238 (Damon Berryhill and Alex Arias)	.06	.02	.01
☐	255 Ozzie Guillen	.05	.02	.01
☐	256 Mike Perez	.05	.02	.01
☐	257 Thomas Howard	.05	.02	.01
☐	258 Kurt Stillwell	.05	.02	.01
☐	259 Mike Henneman	.05	.02	.01
☐	260 Steve Decker	.05	.02	.01
☐	261 Brent Mayne	.05	.02	.01
☐	262 Otis Nixon	.05	.02	.01
☐	263 Mark Kiefer	.10	.05	.01
☐	264 Checklist 239-317 (Don Mattingly	.06	.02	.01

and Mike Bordick)			
☐ 265 Richie Lewis	.15	.07	.02
☐ 266 Pat Gomez	.10	.05	.01
☐ 267 Scott Taylor	.05	.02	.01
☐ 268 Shawon Dunston	.05	.02	.01
☐ 269 Greg Myers	.05	.02	.01
☐ 270 Tim Costo	.07	.03	.01
☐ 271 Greg Hibbard	.05	.02	.01
☐ 272 Pete Harnisch	.05	.02	.01
☐ 273 Dave Mlicki	.10	.05	.01
☐ 274 Orel Hershiser	.07	.03	.01
☐ 275 Sean Berry RR	.05	.02	.01
☐ 276 Doug Simons	.05	.02	.01
☐ 277 John Doherty	.05	.02	.01
☐ 278 Eddie Murray	.10	.05	.01
☐ 279 Chris Haney	.05	.02	.01
☐ 280 Stan Javier	.05	.02	.01
☐ 281 Jaime Navarro	.07	.03	.01
☐ 282 Orlando Merced	.05	.02	.01
☐ 283 Kent Hrbek	.07	.03	.01
☐ 284 Bernard Gilkey	.07	.03	.01
☐ 285 Russ Springer	.12	.05	.02
☐ 286 Mike Maddux	.05	.02	.01
☐ 287 Eric Fox	.05	.02	.01
☐ 288 Mark Leonard	.05	.02	.01
☐ 289 Tim Leary	.05	.02	.01
☐ 290 Brian Hunter	.07	.03	.01
☐ 291 Donald Harris	.05	.02	.01
☐ 292 Bob Scanlan	.05	.02	.01
☐ 293 Turner Ward	.05	.02	.01
☐ 294 Hal Morris	.07	.03	.01
☐ 295 Jimmy Poole	.05	.02	.01
☐ 296 Doug Jones	.05	.02	.01
☐ 297 Tony Pena	.05	.02	.01
☐ 298 Ramon Martinez	.07	.03	.01
☐ 299 Tim Fortugno	.05	.02	.01
☐ 300 Marquis Grissom	.10	.05	.01
☐ 301 Lance Johnson	.05	.02	.01
☐ 302 Jeff Kent	.07	.03	.01
☐ 303 Reggie Jefferson	.07	.03	.01
☐ 304 Wes Chamberlain	.05	.02	.01
☐ 305 Shawn Hare	.05	.02	.01
☐ 306 Mike LaValliere	.05	.02	.01
☐ 307 Gregg Jefferies	.07	.03	.01
☐ 308 Troy Neel RR	.07	.03	.01
☐ 309 Pat Listach	.50	.23	.06
☐ 310 Geronimo Pena	.05	.02	.01
☐ 311 Pedro Munoz	.07	.03	.01
☐ 312 Guillermo Velasquez	.10	.05	.01
☐ 313 Roberto Kelly	.07	.03	.01
☐ 314 Mike Jackson	.05	.02	.01
☐ 315 Rickey Henderson	.12	.05	.02
☐ 316 Mark Lemke	.05	.02	.01
☐ 317 Erik Hanson	.05	.02	.01
☐ 318 Derrick May	.07	.03	.01
☐ 319 Geno Petralli	.05	.02	.01
☐ 320 Melvin Nieves RR	.40	.18	.05
☐ 321 Doug Linton	.10	.05	.01
☐ 322 Rob Dibble	.07	.03	.01
☐ 323 Chris Hoiles	.07	.03	.01
☐ 324 Jimmy Jones	.05	.02	.01
☐ 325 Dave Staton RR	.10	.05	.01
☐ 326 Pedro Martinez	.12	.05	.02
☐ 327 Paul Quantrill	.10	.05	.01
☐ 328 Greg Colbrunn	.07	.03	.01
☐ 329 Hilly Hathaway	.30	.14	.04
☐ 330 Jeff Innis	.05	.02	.01
☐ 331 Ron Karkovice	.05	.02	.01
☐ 332 Keith Shepherd	.20	.09	.03
☐ 333 Alan Embree	.15	.07	.02
☐ 334 Paul Wagner	.05	.02	.01
☐ 335 Dave Haas	.05	.02	.01
☐ 336 Ozzie Canseco	.05	.02	.01
☐ 337 Bill Sampen	.05	.02	.01
☐ 338 Rich Rodriguez	.05	.02	.01
☐ 339 Dean Palmer	.10	.05	.01
☐ 340 Greg Litton	.05	.02	.01
☐ 341 Jim Tatum RR	.20	.09	.03
☐ 342 Todd Haney	.12	.05	.02
☐ 343 Larry Casian	.05	.02	.01
☐ 344 Ryne Sandberg	.20	.09	.03
☐ 345 Sterling Hitchcock	.35	.16	.04
☐ 346 Chris Hammond	.05	.02	.01
☐ 347 Vince Horsman	.05	.02	.01
☐ 348 Butch Henry	.05	.02	.01
☐ 349 Dann Howitt	.05	.02	.01
☐ 350 Roger McDowell	.05	.02	.01
☐ 351 Jack Morris	.10	.05	.01
☐ 352 Bill Krueger	.05	.02	.01
☐ 353 Cris Colon	.10	.05	.01
☐ 354 Joe Vitko	.15	.07	.02
☐ 355 Willie McGee	.07	.03	.01
☐ 356 Jay Baller	.05	.02	.01
☐ 357 Pat Mahomes	.10	.05	.01
☐ 358 Roger Mason	.05	.02	.01
☐ 359 Jerry Nielsen	.05	.02	.01
☐ 360 Tom Pagnozzi	.05	.02	.01
☐ 361 Kevin Baez	.05	.02	.01
☐ 362 Tim Scott	.07	.03	.01
☐ 363 Domingo Martinez	.25	.11	.03
☐ 364 Kirt Manwaring	.05	.02	.01
☐ 365 Rafael Palmeiro	.07	.03	.01
☐ 366 Ray Lankford	.12	.05	.02
☐ 367 Tim McIntosh	.05	.02	.01
☐ 368 Jessie Hollins	.07	.03	.01
☐ 369 Scott Leius	.05	.02	.01
☐ 370 Bill Doran	.05	.02	.01
☐ 371 Sam Militello	.15	.07	.02
☐ 372 Ryan Bowen	.05	.02	.01
☐ 373 Dave Henderson	.05	.02	.01
☐ 374 Dan Smith RR	.07	.03	.01
☐ 375 Steve Reed RR	.12	.05	.02
☐ 376 Jose Offerman	.07	.03	.01
☐ 377 Kevin Brown	.07	.03	.01
☐ 378 Darrin Fletcher	.05	.02	.01
☐ 379 Duane Ward	.05	.02	.01
☐ 380 Wayne Kirby RR	.05	.02	.01
☐ 381 Steve Scarsone	.05	.02	.01
☐ 382 Mariano Duncan	.05	.02	.01
☐ 383 Ken Ryan	.15	.07	.02
☐ 384 Lloyd McClendon	.05	.02	.01
☐ 385 Brian Holman	.05	.02	.01
☐ 386 Braulio Castillo	.05	.02	.01
☐ 387 Danny Leon	.05	.02	.01
☐ 388 Omar Olivares	.05	.02	.01
☐ 389 Kevin Wickander	.05	.02	.01
☐ 390 Fred McGriff	.12	.05	.02
☐ 391 Phil Clark	.05	.02	.01
☐ 392 Darren Lewis	.05	.02	.01
☐ 393 Phil Hiatt	.20	.09	.03
☐ 394 Mike Morgan	.05	.02	.01
☐ 395 Shane Mack	.07	.03	.01
☐ 396 Checklist 318-396	.06	.02	.01
(Dennis Eckersley			
and Art Kusnyer CO)			

1993 Donruss Diamond Kings

These standard-size (2 1/2" by 3 1/2") cards were randomly inserted in 1993 Donruss Series I packs. The cards are gold-foil stamped and feature on the fronts player portraits by noted sports artist Dick Perez. Inside green borders, the backs present career summary. The first 15 cards (1-15) were available in the first series of the 1993 Donruss. Diamond King numbers 27-28 honor the first draft picks of the new Florida Marlins and Colorado Rockies franchises. The cards are numbered on the back.

	MT	EX-MT	VG
COMPLETE SET (15)	40.00	18.00	5.00
COMMON PLAYER (1-15)	1.50	.65	.19
☐ 1 Ken Griffey Jr.	9.00	4.00	1.15
☐ 2 Ryne Sandberg	6.00	2.70	.75
☐ 3 Roger Clemens	6.00	2.70	.75
☐ 4 Kirby Puckett	5.00	2.30	.60
☐ 5 Bill Swift	1.50	.65	.19
☐ 6 Larry Walker	3.00	1.35	.40
☐ 7 Juan Gonzalez	6.00	2.70	.75
☐ 8 Wally Joyner	1.50	.65	.19
☐ 9 Andy Van Slyke	2.00	.90	.25

	MT	EX-MT	VG
☐ 10 Robin Ventura	3.00	1.35	.40
☐ 11 Bip Roberts	1.50	.65	.19
☐ 12 Roberto Kelly	1.50	.65	.19
☐ 13 Carlos Baerga	3.00	1.35	.40
☐ 14 Orel Hershiser	1.50	.65	.19
☐ 15 Cecil Fielder	3.00	1.35	.40

1993 Donruss Elite

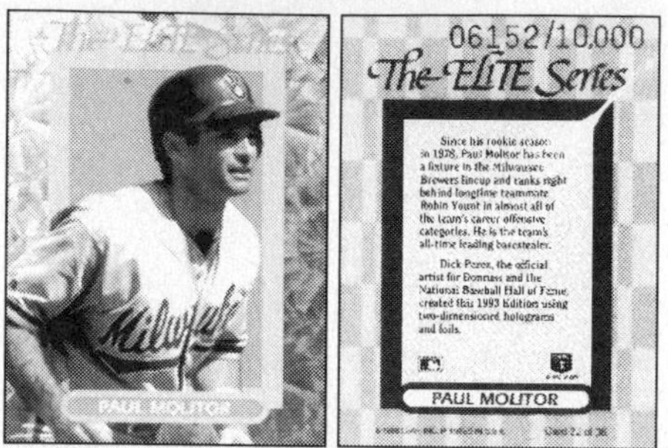

Cards E19-E27 were random inserts in 1993 Donruss series I foil packs while cards 28-36 were inserted in series II packs. The numbering on the 1993 Elite cards follows consecutively after that of the 1992 Elite series cards, and each of the 10,000 Elite cards is serially numbered. The Signature Series Will Clark card was randomly inserted in 1993 Donruss foil packs; he personally autographed 5,000 cards. Featuring a Dick Perez portrait, the ten thousand Legends Series cards honor Robin Yount for his 3,000th hit achievement. All these special cards measure the standard size (2 1/2" by 3 1/2") and are numbered on the back. The front design of the Elite cards features a cutout color player photo superimposed on a neon-colored panel framed by a gray inner border and a variegated silver metallic outer border. The player's name appears in a neon-colored bar toward the bottom of the card. On a gray panel framed by a navy blue inner border and a two-toned blue outer border, the backs present player profile. The backs of the Elite cards also carry the serial number ("X of 10,000) as well as the card number.

	MT	EX-MT	VG
COMPLETE SET (11)	1200.00	550.00	150.00
COMMON ELITE (E19-E27)	50.00	23.00	6.25
☐ E19 Ryne Sandberg	100.00	45.00	12.50
☐ E20 Fred McGriff	80.00	36.00	10.00
☐ E21 Eddie Murray	75.00	34.00	9.50
☐ E22 Paul Molitor	65.00	29.00	8.25
☐ E23 Barry Larkin	65.00	29.00	8.25
☐ E24 Don Mattingly	75.00	34.00	9.50
☐ E25 Dennis Eckersley	65.00	29.00	8.25
☐ E26 Roberto Alomar	100.00	45.00	12.50
☐ E27 Edgar Martinez	50.00	23.00	6.25
☐ L3 Robin Yount (Legend Series)	200.00	90.00	25.00
☐ S3 Will Clark (Signature Series)	400.00	180.00	50.00

1993 Donruss Spirit of the Game

A new subset in 1993, these standard-size (2 1/2" by 3 1/2") cards were randomly inserted in 1993 Donruss Series I packs and packed approximately two per box. The fronts featue full-bleed glossy color action player photos. The set title "Spirit of the Game" is stamped in gold foil script

across the top or bottom of the picture. The backs sport a second full-bleed color player photo; this photo concludes the action portrayed in the front photo. The caption to the second picture is printed in yellow block lettering. The cards are numbered on the back with an SG prefix.

	MT	EX-MT	VG
COMPLETE SET (10)	30.00	13.50	3.80
COMMON PLAYER (1-10)	2.00	.90	.25
☐ 1 Mike Bordick Turning Two	2.50	1.15	.30
☐ 2 Dave Justice Play at the Plate	4.00	1.80	.50
☐ 3 Roberto Alomar In There	5.00	2.30	.60
☐ 4 Dennis Eckersley Pumped	3.00	1.35	.40
☐ 5 Juan Gonzalez and Jose Canseco Dynamic Duo	7.00	3.10	.85
☐ 6 George Bell and Frank Thomas ... Gone	7.00	3.10	.85
☐ 7 Wade Boggs and Luis Polonia Safe or Out	2.50	1.15	.30
☐ 8 Will Clark The Thrill	4.00	1.80	.50
☐ 9 Bip Roberts Safe at Home	2.00	.90	.25
☐ 10 Cecil Fielder Rob Deer Mickey Tettleton Thirty 3	2.50	1.15	.30

1986 Dorman's Cheese

Dorman's
SUPER STAR LIMITED EDITION
REGGIE JACKSON
BORN 5/18/46
Hgt. 6' Wgt. 206
Throws L Bats L
1985
AB 460 HRS 27
HITS 116 RBI 85
BA .252
MSA

This 20-card set was issued in panels of two cards. The individual cards measure approximately 1 1/2" by 2" whereas the panels measure 3" by 2". Team logos have been removed from the photos as these cards were not licensed by Major League Baseball (team owners). The backs contain a minimum of information.

	MT	EX-MT	VG
COMPLETE SET (20)	16.00	7.25	2.00
COMMON PLAYER (1-20)	.75	.35	.09

☐ 1 George Brett	1.50	.65	.19
☐ 2 Jack Morris	.90	.40	.11
☐ 3 Gary Carter	1.00	.45	.13
☐ 4 Cal Ripken	2.50	1.15	.30
☐ 5 Dwight Gooden	1.00	.45	.13
☐ 6 Kent Hrbek	.75	.35	.09
☐ 7 Rickey Henderson	1.25	.55	.16
☐ 8 Mike Schmidt	1.50	.65	.19
☐ 9 Keith Hernandez	.75	.35	.09
☐ 10 Dale Murphy	1.00	.45	.13
☐ 11 Reggie Jackson	1.00	.45	.13
☐ 12 Eddie Murray	.90	.40	.11
☐ 13 Don Mattingly	1.50	.65	.19
☐ 14 Ryne Sandberg	2.00	.90	.25
☐ 15 Willie McGee	.75	.35	.09
☐ 16 Robin Yount	1.50	.65	.19
☐ 17 Rick Sutcliffe	.75	.35	.09
☐ 18 Wade Boggs	1.25	.55	.16
☐ 19 Dave Winfield	1.25	.55	.16
☐ 20 Jim Rice	.90	.40	.11

1950 Drake's

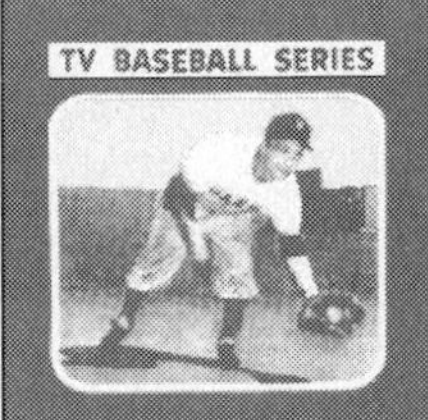

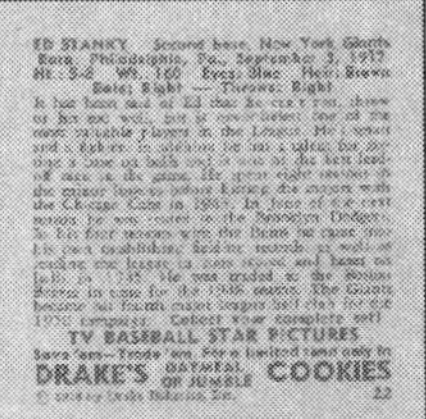

The cards in this 36-card set measure approximately 2 1/2" by 2 1/2". The 1950 Drake's Cookies set contains numbered black and white cards. The players are pictured inside a simulated television screen and the caption "TV Baseball Series" appears on the cards. The players selected for this set show a heavy representation of players from New York teams. The catalog designation for this set is D358.

	NRMT	VG-E	GOOD
COMPLETE SET (36)	4000.00	1800.00	500.00
COMMON PLAYER (1-36)	60.00	27.00	7.50
☐ 1 Preacher Roe	75.00	34.00	9.50
☐ 2 Clint Hartung	60.00	27.00	7.50
☐ 3 Earl Torgeson	60.00	27.00	7.50
☐ 4 Lou Brissie	60.00	27.00	7.50
☐ 5 Duke Snider	350.00	160.00	45.00
☐ 6 Roy Campanella	400.00	180.00	50.00
☐ 7 Sheldon Jones	60.00	27.00	7.50
☐ 8 Whitey Lockman	65.00	29.00	8.25
☐ 9 Bobby Thomson	75.00	34.00	9.50
☐ 10 Dick Sisler	60.00	27.00	7.50
☐ 11 Gil Hodges	175.00	80.00	22.00
☐ 12 Eddie Waitkus	60.00	27.00	7.50
☐ 13 Bobby Doerr	125.00	57.50	15.50
☐ 14 Warren Spahn	250.00	115.00	31.00
☐ 15 Buddy Kerr	60.00	27.00	7.50
☐ 16 Sid Gordon	60.00	27.00	7.50
☐ 17 Willard Marshall	60.00	27.00	7.50
☐ 18 Carl Furillo	90.00	40.00	11.50
☐ 19 Pee Wee Reese	250.00	115.00	31.00
☐ 20 Alvin Dark	70.00	32.00	8.75
☐ 21 Del Ennis	65.00	29.00	8.25
☐ 22 Ed Stanky	70.00	32.00	8.75
☐ 23 Tom Henrich	75.00	34.00	9.50
☐ 24 Yogi Berra	400.00	180.00	50.00
☐ 25 Phil Rizzuto	200.00	90.00	25.00
☐ 26 Jerry Coleman	60.00	27.00	7.50
☐ 27 Joe Page	70.00	32.00	8.75
☐ 28 Allie Reynolds	90.00	40.00	11.50
☐ 29 Ray Scarborough	60.00	27.00	7.50
☐ 30 Birdie Tebbetts	60.00	27.00	7.50
☐ 31 Maurice McDermott	60.00	27.00	7.50
☐ 32 Johnny Pesky	65.00	29.00	8.25
☐ 33 Dom DiMaggio	90.00	40.00	11.50
☐ 34 Vern Stephens	65.00	29.00	8.25
☐ 35 Bob Elliott	65.00	29.00	8.25
☐ 36 Enos Slaughter	200.00	90.00	25.00

1981 Drake's

The cards in this 33-card set measure 2 1/2" by 3 1/2". The 1981 Drake's Bakeries set contains National and American League stars. Produced in conjunction with Topps and released to the public in Drake's Cakes, this set features red frames for American League players and blue frames for National League players. A Drake's Cakes logo with the words "Big Hitters" appears on the lower front of each card. The backs are quite similar to the 1981 Topps backs but contain the Drake's logo, a different card number, and a short paragraph entitled "What Makes a Big Hitter" at the top of the card.

	NRMT-MT	EXC	G-VG
COMPLETE SET (33)	8.00	3.60	1.00
COMMON PLAYER (1-33)	.06	.03	.01
☐ 1 Carl Yastrzemski	1.00	.45	.13
☐ 2 Rod Carew	.75	.35	.09
☐ 3 Pete Rose	1.25	.55	.16
☐ 4 Dave Parker	.35	.16	.04
☐ 5 George Brett	1.00	.45	.13
☐ 6 Eddie Murray	.90	.40	.11
☐ 7 Mike Schmidt	1.25	.55	.16
☐ 8 Jim Rice	.25	.11	.03
☐ 9 Fred Lynn	.15	.07	.02
☐ 10 Reggie Jackson	1.00	.45	.13
☐ 11 Steve Garvey	.30	.14	.04
☐ 12 Ken Singleton	.06	.03	.01
☐ 13 Bill Buckner	.06	.03	.01
☐ 14 Dave Winfield	.75	.35	.09
☐ 15 Jack Clark	.15	.07	.02
☐ 16 Cecil Cooper	.10	.05	.01
☐ 17 Bob Horner	.10	.05	.01
☐ 18 George Foster	.10	.05	.01
☐ 19 Dave Kingman	.10	.05	.01
☐ 20 Cesar Cedeno	.06	.03	.01
☐ 21 Joe Charboneau	.06	.03	.01
☐ 22 George Hendrick	.06	.03	.01
☐ 23 Gary Carter	.30	.14	.04
☐ 24 Al Oliver	.10	.05	.01
☐ 25 Bruce Bochte	.06	.03	.01
☐ 26 Jerry Mumphrey	.06	.03	.01
☐ 27 Steve Kemp	.06	.03	.01
☐ 28 Bob Watson	.06	.03	.01
☐ 29 John Castino	.06	.03	.01
☐ 30 Tony Armas	.06	.03	.01
☐ 31 John Mayberry	.06	.03	.01
☐ 32 Carlton Fisk	.50	.23	.06
☐ 33 Lee Mazzilli	.06	.03	.01

1982 Drake's

The cards in this 33-card set measure 2 1/2" by 3 1/2". The 1982 Drake's Big Hitters series cards each has the title "2nd Annual Collectors' Edition" in a ribbon design at the top of the picture area. Each color player photo has "photo mount" designs in the corners, red for the AL and green for the NL. The reverses are green and blue, the same as the regular 1982 Topps format, and the photos are larger than those of

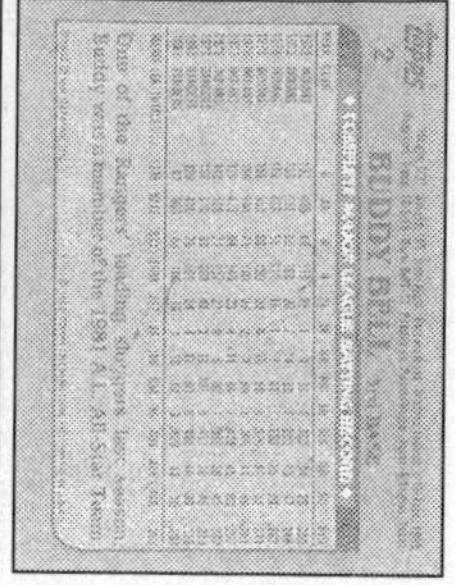

the previous year. Of the 33 hitters featured, 19 represent the National League. There are 21 returnees from the 1981 set and only one photo, that of Kennedy, is the same as that appearing in the regular Topps issue. The Drake's logo appears centered in the bottom border on the obverse. This set's card numbering is essentially in alphabetical order by the player's name.

	NRMT-MT	EXC	G-VG
COMPLETE SET (33)	8.00	3.60	1.00
COMMON PLAYER (1-33)	.06	.03	.01
☐ 1 Tony Armas	.06	.03	.01
☐ 2 Buddy Bell	.10	.05	.01
☐ 3 Johnny Bench	1.00	.45	.13
☐ 4 George Brett	1.00	.45	.13
☐ 5 Bill Buckner	.06	.03	.01
☐ 6 Rod Carew	.75	.35	.09
☐ 7 Gary Carter	.40	.18	.05
☐ 8 Jack Clark	.15	.07	.02
☐ 9 Cecil Cooper	.10	.05	.01
☐ 10 Jose Cruz	.06	.03	.01
☐ 11 Dwight Evans	.15	.07	.02
☐ 12 Carlton Fisk	.50	.23	.06
☐ 13 George Foster	.15	.07	.02
☐ 14 Steve Garvey	.40	.18	.05
☐ 15 Kirk Gibson	.30	.14	.04
☐ 16 Mike Hargrove	.10	.05	.01
☐ 17 George Hendrick	.06	.03	.01
☐ 18 Bob Horner	.10	.05	.01
☐ 19 Reggie Jackson	1.00	.45	.13
☐ 20 Terry Kennedy	.06	.03	.01
☐ 21 Dave Kingman	.10	.05	.01
☐ 22 Greg Luzinski	.10	.05	.01
☐ 23 Bill Madlock	.06	.03	.01
☐ 24 John Mayberry	.06	.03	.01
☐ 25 Eddie Murray	.90	.40	.11
☐ 26 Graig Nettles	.15	.07	.02
☐ 27 Jim Rice	.25	.11	.03
☐ 28 Pete Rose	1.25	.55	.16
☐ 29 Mike Schmidt	1.25	.55	.16
☐ 30 Ken Singleton	.10	.05	.01
☐ 31 Dave Winfield	.75	.35	.09
☐ 32 Butch Wynegar	.06	.03	.01
☐ 33 Richie Zisk	.06	.03	.01

1983 Drake's

The cards in this 33-card series measure 2 1/2" by 3 1/2". For the third year in a row, Drake's Cakes, in conjunction with Topps, issued a set entitled Big Hitters. The fronts appear very similar to those of the previous two years with slight variations on the framelines and player identification sections. The backs are the same as the Topps backs of this year except for the card number and the Drake's logo. This set's card numbering is essentially in alphabetical order by the player's name.

	NRMT-MT	EXC	G-VG
COMPLETE SET (33)	8.00	3.60	1.00
COMMON PLAYER (1-33)	.06	.03	.01
☐ 1 Don Baylor	.15	.07	.02
☐ 2 Bill Buckner	.06	.03	.01
☐ 3 Rod Carew	.75	.35	.09
☐ 4 Gary Carter	.40	.18	.05
☐ 5 Jack Clark	.15	.07	.02
☐ 6 Cecil Cooper	.10	.05	.01
☐ 7 Dwight Evans	.15	.07	.02
☐ 8 George Foster	.15	.07	.02
☐ 9 Pedro Guerrero	.15	.07	.02
☐ 10 George Hendrick	.06	.03	.01
☐ 11 Bob Horner	.10	.05	.01
☐ 12 Reggie Jackson	1.00	.45	.13
☐ 13 Steve Kemp	.06	.03	.01
☐ 14 Dave Kingman	.10	.05	.01
☐ 15 Bill Madlock	.06	.03	.01
☐ 16 Gary Matthews	.06	.03	.01
☐ 17 Hal McRae	.15	.07	.02
☐ 18 Dale Murphy	.75	.35	.09
☐ 19 Eddie Murray	.90	.40	.11
☐ 20 Ben Oglivie	.06	.03	.01
☐ 21 Al Oliver	.10	.05	.01
☐ 22 Jim Rice	.25	.11	.03
☐ 23 Cal Ripken	2.50	1.15	.30
☐ 24 Pete Rose	1.25	.55	.16
☐ 25 Mike Schmidt	1.25	.55	.16
☐ 26 Ken Singleton	.10	.05	.01
☐ 27 Gorman Thomas	.06	.03	.01
☐ 28 Jason Thompson	.06	.03	.01
☐ 29 Mookie Wilson	.10	.05	.01
☐ 30 Willie Wilson	.10	.05	.01
☐ 31 Dave Winfield	.75	.35	.09
☐ 32 Carl Yastrzemski	1.00	.45	.13
☐ 33 Robin Yount	1.00	.45	.13

1984 Drake's

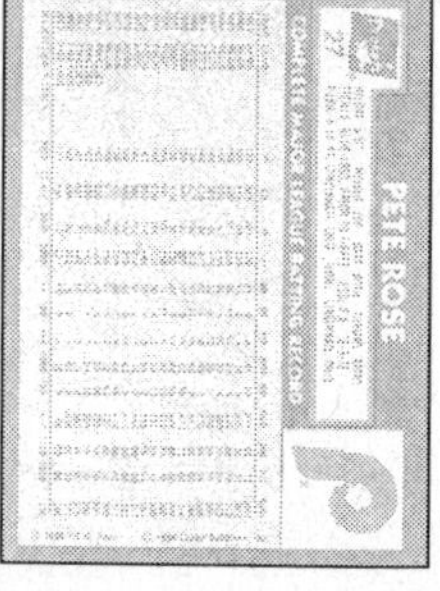

The cards in this 33-card set measure 2 1/2" by 3 1/2". The Fourth Annual Collectors Edition of baseball cards produced by Drake's Cakes in conjunction with Topps continued this now annual set entitled Big Hitters. As in previous years, the front contains a frameline in which the title of the set, the Drake's logo, and the player's name, his team, and position appear. The cards all feature the player in a batting action pose. While the cards fronts are different from the Topps fronts of this year, the backs differ only in the card number and the use of the Drake's logo instead of the Topps logo.

This set's card numbering is essentially in alphabetical order by the player's name.

	NRMT-MT	EXC	G-VG
COMPLETE SET (33)	8.00	3.60	1.00
COMMON PLAYER (1-33)	.06	.03	.01
□ 1 Don Baylor	.15	.07	.02
□ 2 Wade Boggs	1.25	.55	.16
□ 3 George Brett	1.00	.45	.13
□ 4 Bill Buckner	.06	.03	.01
□ 5 Rod Carew	.75	.35	.09
□ 6 Gary Carter	.40	.18	.05
□ 7 Ron Cey	.06	.03	.01
□ 8 Cecil Cooper	.10	.05	.01
□ 9 Andre Dawson	.75	.35	.09
□ 10 Steve Garvey	.40	.18	.05
□ 11 Pedro Guerrero	.15	.07	.02
□ 12 George Hendrick	.06	.03	.01
□ 13 Keith Hernandez	.15	.07	.02
□ 14 Bob Horner	.10	.05	.01
□ 15 Reggie Jackson	1.00	.45	.13
□ 16 Steve Kemp	.06	.03	.01
□ 17 Ron Kittle	.10	.05	.01
□ 18 Greg Luzinski	.10	.05	.01
□ 19 Fred Lynn	.10	.05	.01
□ 20 Bill Madlock	.06	.03	.01
□ 21 Gary Matthews	.06	.03	.01
□ 22 Dale Murphy	.75	.35	.09
□ 23 Eddie Murray	.90	.40	.11
□ 24 Al Oliver	.10	.05	.01
□ 25 Jim Rice	.25	.11	.03
□ 26 Cal Ripken	2.00	.90	.25
□ 27 Pete Rose	1.25	.55	.16
□ 28 Mike Schmidt	1.25	.55	.16
□ 29 Darryl Strawberry	1.50	.65	.19
□ 30 Alan Trammell	.25	.11	.03
□ 31 Mookie Wilson	.06	.03	.01
□ 32 Dave Winfield	.75	.35	.09
□ 33 Robin Yount	1.00	.45	.13

1985 Drake's

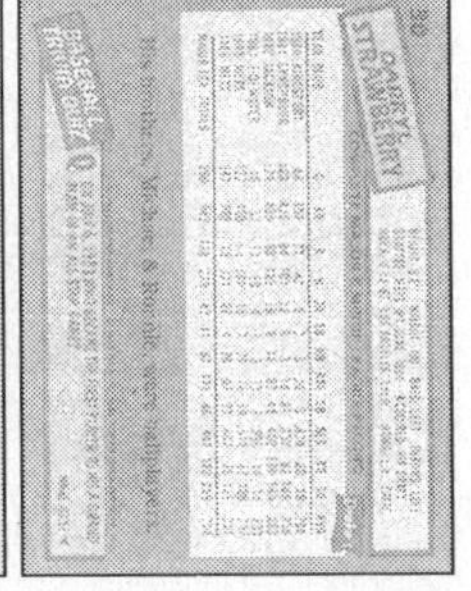

The cards in this 44-card set measure 2 1/2" by 3 1/2". The Fifth Annual Collectors Edition of baseball cards produced by Drake's Cakes in conjunction with Topps continued this apparently annual set with a new twist, for the first time, 11 pitchers were included. The "Big Hitters" are numbered 1-33 and the pitchers are numbered 34-44; each subgroup is ordered alphabetically. The cards are numbered in the upper right corner of the backs of the cards. The complete set could be obtained directly from the company by sending 2.95 with four proofs of purchase.

	NRMT-MT	EXC	G-VG
COMPLETE SET (44)	14.00	6.25	1.75
COMMON PLAYER (1-33)	.06	.03	.01
COMMON PLAYER (34-44)	.10	.05	.01
□ 1 Tony Armas	.06	.03	.01
□ 2 Harold Baines	.10	.05	.01
□ 3 Don Baylor	.15	.07	.02
□ 4 George Brett	1.00	.45	.13
□ 5 Gary Carter	.40	.18	.05
□ 6 Ron Cey	.06	.03	.01
□ 7 Jose Cruz	.06	.03	.01
□ 8 Alvin Davis	.10	.05	.01
□ 9 Chili Davis	.10	.05	.01
□ 10 Dwight Evans	.15	.07	.02
□ 11 Steve Garvey	.40	.18	.05
□ 12 Kirk Gibson	.30	.14	.04
□ 13 Pedro Guerrero	.15	.07	.02
□ 14 Tony Gwynn	.90	.40	.11
□ 15 Keith Hernandez	.15	.07	.02
□ 16 Kent Hrbek	.15	.07	.02
□ 17 Reggie Jackson	1.00	.45	.13
□ 18 Gary Matthews	.06	.03	.01
□ 19 Don Mattingly	1.00	.45	.13
□ 20 Dale Murphy	.75	.35	.09
□ 21 Eddie Murray	.90	.40	.11
□ 22 Dave Parker	.20	.09	.03
□ 23 Lance Parrish	.10	.05	.01
□ 24 Tim Raines	.20	.09	.03
□ 25 Jim Rice	.20	.09	.03
□ 26 Cal Ripken	1.50	.65	.19
□ 27 Juan Samuel	.10	.05	.01
□ 28 Ryne Sandberg	1.25	.55	.16
□ 29 Mike Schmidt	1.25	.55	.16
□ 30 Darryl Strawberry	1.00	.45	.13
□ 31 Alan Trammell	.25	.11	.03
□ 32 Dave Winfield	.75	.35	.09
□ 33 Robin Yount	1.00	.45	.13
□ 34 Mike Boddicker	.10	.05	.01
□ 35 Steve Carlton	.50	.23	.06
□ 36 Dwight Gooden	1.50	.65	.19
□ 37 Willie Hernandez	.10	.05	.01
□ 38 Mark Langston	.50	.23	.06
□ 39 Dan Quisenberry	.15	.07	.02
□ 40 Dave Righetti	.15	.07	.02
□ 41 Tom Seaver	1.00	.45	.13
□ 42 Bob Stanley	.10	.05	.01
□ 43 Rick Sutcliffe	.10	.05	.01
□ 44 Bruce Sutter	.15	.07	.02

1986 Drake's

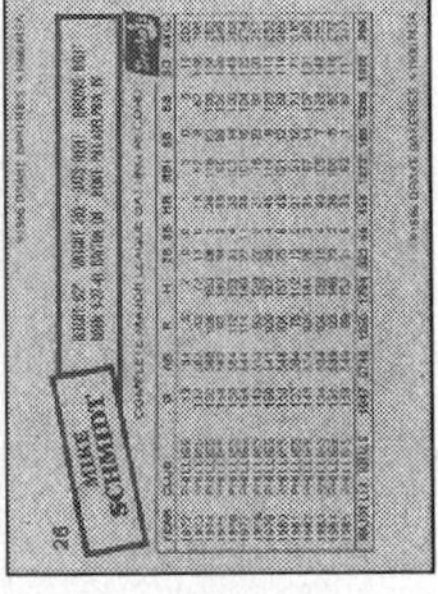

This set of 37 cards was distributed as back panels of various Drake's snack products. Each individual card measures 2 1/2" by 3 1/2". Each specially marked package features two, three, or four cards on the back. The set is easily recognized by the Drake's logo and "6th Annual Collector's Edition" at the top of the obverse. Cards are numbered on the front and the back. Cards below are coded based on the product upon which they appeared, for example, Apple Pies (AP), Cherry Pies (CP), Chocolate Donut Delites (CDD), Coffee Cake Jr. (CCJ), Creme Shortcakes (CS), Devil Dogs (DD), Fudge Brownies (FUD), Funny Bones (FB), Peanut Butter Squares (PBS), Powdered Sugar Donut Delites (PSDD), Ring Ding Jr. (RDJ), Sunny Doodles (SD), Swiss Rolls (SR), Yankee Doodles (YD), and Yodels (Y). The last nine cards are pitchers. Complete panels would be valued approximately 50 percent higher than the individual card prices listed below.

	MT	EX-MT	VG
COMPLETE SET (37)	30.00	13.50	3.80
COMMON PLAYER (1-37)	.35	.16	.04
□ 1 Gary Carter Y	.75	.35	.09

☐ 2 Dwight Evans Y	.45	.20	.06
☐ 3 Reggie Jackson SR	1.50	.65	.19
☐ 4 Dave Parker SR	.60	.25	.08
☐ 5 Rickey Henderson FB	1.50	.65	.19
☐ 6 Pedro Guerrero FB	.45	.20	.06
☐ 7 Don Mattingly YD	2.00	.90	.25
☐ 8 Mike Marshall YD	.35	.16	.04
☐ 9 Keith Moreland YD	.35	.16	.04
☐ 10 Keith Hernandez CS	.50	.23	.06
☐ 11 Cal Ripken CS	3.00	1.35	.40
☐ 12 Dale Murphy RDJ	1.00	.45	.13
☐ 13 Jim Rice RDJ	.45	.20	.06
☐ 14 George Brett CCJ	1.50	.65	.19
☐ 15 Tim Raines CCJ	.60	.25	.08
☐ 16 Darryl Strawberry DD	1.50	.65	.19
☐ 17 Bill Buckner DD	.35	.16	.04
☐ 18 Dave Winfield AP	1.25	.55	.16
☐ 19 Ryne Sandberg AP	2.50	1.15	.30
☐ 20 Steve Balboni AP	.35	.16	.04
☐ 21 Tommy Herr AP	.35	.16	.04
☐ 22 Pete Rose CP	2.00	.90	.25
☐ 23 Willie McGee CP	.45	.20	.06
☐ 24 Harold Baines CP	.45	.20	.06
☐ 25 Eddie Murray CP	1.25	.55	.16
☐ 26 Mike Schmidt SD/FUD	2.00	.90	.25
☐ 27 Wade Boggs SD/FUD	1.50	.65	.19
☐ 28 Kirk Gibson SD/FUD	.45	.20	.06
☐ 29 Bret Saberhagen PBS	.60	.25	.08
☐ 30 John Tudor PBS	.35	.16	.04
☐ 31 Orel Hershiser PBS	.60	.25	.08
☐ 32 Ron Guidry CDD	.45	.20	.06
☐ 33 Nolan Ryan CDD	5.00	2.30	.60
☐ 34 Dave Stieb CDD	.45	.20	.06
☐ 35 Dwight Gooden SDD	.75	.35	.09
☐ 36 Fern.Valenzuela SDD	.45	.20	.06
☐ 37 Tom Browning SDD	.45	.20	.06

1987 Drake's

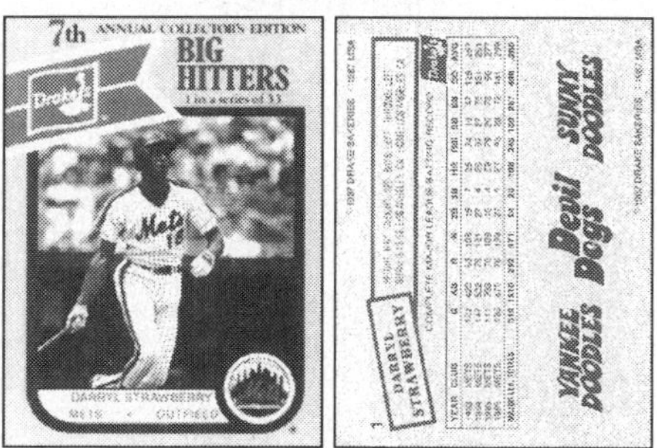

This 33-card set features 25 top hitters and eight top pitchers. Cards were printed in groups of two, three, or four on the backs of Drake's bakery products. Individual cards measure 2 1/2" by 3 1/2" and tout the 7th annual edition. Card backs feature year-by-year season statistics. The cards are numbered such that the pitchers are listed numerically last, e.g., top hitters 1-25 and pitchers 26-33). Complete panels would be valued approximately 50 percent higher than the individual card prices listed below.

	MT	EX-MT	VG
COMPLETE SET (33)	30.00	13.50	3.80
COMMON PLAYER (1-33)	.35	.16	.04
☐ 1 Darryl Strawberry	1.50	.65	.19
☐ 2 Wally Joyner	1.00	.45	.13
☐ 3 Von Hayes	.35	.16	.04
☐ 4 Jose Canseco	3.00	1.35	.40
☐ 5 Dave Winfield	1.25	.55	.16
☐ 6 Cal Ripken	3.00	1.35	.40
☐ 7 Keith Moreland	.35	.16	.04
☐ 8 Don Mattingly	2.00	.90	.25
☐ 9 Willie McGee	.45	.20	.06
☐ 10 Keith Hernandez	.60	.25	.08
☐ 11 Tony Gwynn	1.25	.55	.16
☐ 12 Rickey Henderson	1.50	.65	.19
☐ 13 Dale Murphy	1.00	.45	.13
☐ 14 George Brett	1.25	.55	.16
☐ 15 Jim Rice	.60	.25	.08
☐ 16 Wade Boggs	1.50	.65	.19
☐ 17 Kevin Bass	.35	.16	.04
☐ 18 Dave Parker	.60	.25	.08
☐ 19 Kirby Puckett	2.00	.90	.25
☐ 20 Gary Carter	.75	.35	.09
☐ 21 Ryne Sandberg	2.50	1.15	.30
☐ 22 Harold Baines	.45	.20	.06
☐ 23 Mike Schmidt	2.00	.90	.25
☐ 24 Eddie Murray	1.25	.55	.16
☐ 25 Steve Sax	.45	.20	.06
☐ 26 Dwight Gooden	.75	.35	.09
☐ 27 Jack Morris	.60	.25	.08
☐ 28 Ron Darling	.45	.20	.06
☐ 29 Fernando Valenzuela	.45	.20	.06
☐ 30 John Tudor	.35	.16	.04
☐ 31 Roger Clemens	2.00	.90	.25
☐ 32 Nolan Ryan	3.50	1.55	.45
☐ 33 Mike Scott	.45	.20	.06

1988 Drake's

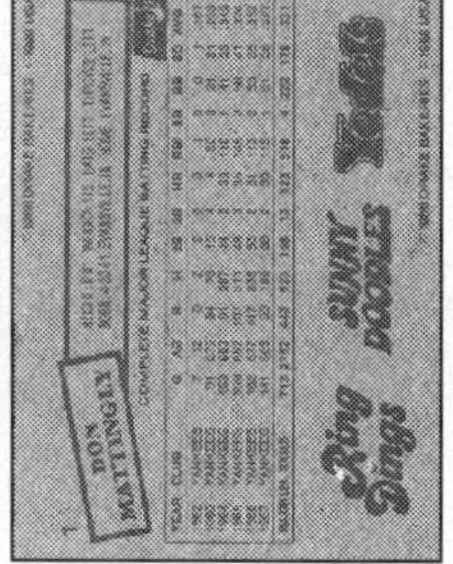

This 33-card set features 27 top hitters and six top pitchers. Cards were printed in groups of two, three, or four on the backs of Drake's bakery products. Individual cards measure approximately 2 1/2" by 3 1/2" and tout the 8th annual edition. Card backs feature year-by-year season statistics. The cards are numbered such that the pitchers are listed numerically last, e.g., top hitters 1-27 and pitchers 28-33). The product affiliations are as follows, 1-2 Ring Dings, 3-4 Devil Dogs, 5-6 Coffee Cakes, 7-9 Yankee Doodles, 10-11 Funny Bones, 12-14 Fudge Brownies, 15-18 Cherry Pies, 19-21 Sunny Doodles, 22-24 Powdered Sugar Donuts, 25-27 Chocolate Donuts, 28-29 Yodels, and 30-33 Apple Pies. Complete panels would be valued approximately 50 percent higher than the individual card prices listed below.

	MT	EX-MT	VG
COMPLETE SET (33)	30.00	13.50	3.80
COMMON PLAYER (1-33)	.35	.16	.04
☐ 1 Don Mattingly	2.00	.90	.25
☐ 2 Tim Raines	.60	.25	.08
☐ 3 Darryl Strawberry	1.50	.65	.19
☐ 4 Wade Boggs	1.50	.65	.19
☐ 5 Keith Hernandez	.60	.25	.08
☐ 6 Mark McGwire	1.50	.65	.19
☐ 7 Rickey Henderson	1.50	.65	.19
☐ 8 Mike Schmidt	2.00	.90	.25
☐ 9 Dwight Evans	.45	.20	.06
☐ 10 Gary Carter	.75	.35	.09
☐ 11 Paul Molitor	.75	.35	.09
☐ 12 Dave Winfield	1.25	.55	.16
☐ 13 Alan Trammell	.60	.25	.08
☐ 14 Tony Gwynn	1.25	.55	.16
☐ 15 Dale Murphy	1.00	.45	.13
☐ 16 Andre Dawson	1.00	.45	.13
☐ 17 Von Hayes	.35	.16	.04
☐ 18 Willie Randolph	.35	.16	.04
☐ 19 Kirby Puckett	2.00	.90	.25
☐ 20 Juan Samuel	.35	.16	.04
☐ 21 Eddie Murray	1.25	.55	.16
☐ 22 George Bell	.75	.35	.09
☐ 23 Larry Sheets	.35	.16	.04
☐ 24 Eric Davis	1.00	.45	.13

	MT	EX-MT	VG
☐ 25 Cal Ripken	3.00	1.35	.40
☐ 26 Pedro Guerrero	.45	.20	.06
☐ 27 Will Clark	2.00	.90	.25
☐ 28 Dwight Gooden	.75	.35	.09
☐ 29 Frank Viola	.60	.25	.08
☐ 30 Roger Clemens	2.00	.90	.25
☐ 31 Rick Sutcliffe	.45	.20	.06
☐ 32 Jack Morris	.60	.25	.08
☐ 33 John Tudor	.35	.16	.04

1990 Elite Senior League

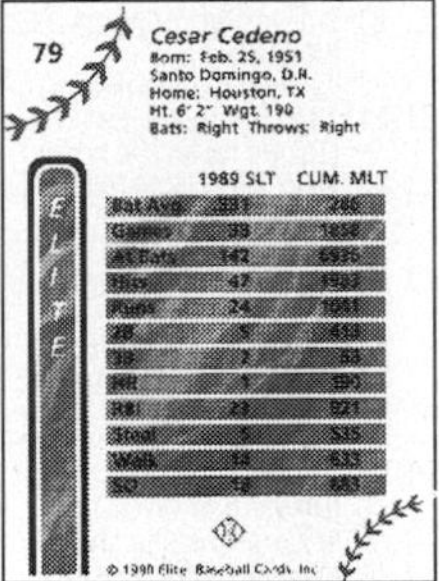

The 1990 Elite Senior Pro League Set was a 126-card set issued after the conclusion of the first Senior League season. The card stock was essentially the same type of card stock used by Upper Deck. The set featured full-color fronts and had complete Senior League stats on the back. This set is standard size, 2 1/2" by 3 1/2". It has been reported that there were 5,000 cases of these cards produced. Prior to the debut of the set, Elite also passed out (to prospective dealers) two promo cards for the set, Earl Weaver (numbered 120 rather than 91) and Mike Easler (numbered 1 rather than 19).

	MT	EX-MT	VG
COMPLETE SET (126)	7.50	3.40	.95
COMMON PLAYER (1-126)	.08	.04	.01
☐ 1 Curt Flood (commissioner)	.40	.18	.05
☐ 2 Bob Tolan	.12	.05	.02
☐ 3 Dick Bosman	.08	.04	.01
☐ 4 Ivan DeJesus	.08	.04	.01
☐ 5 Dock Ellis	.08	.04	.01
☐ 6 Roy Howell	.08	.04	.01
☐ 7 Lamar Johnson	.08	.04	.01
☐ 8 Steve Kemp	.12	.05	.02
☐ 9 Ken Landreaux	.12	.05	.02
☐ 10 Randy Lerch	.08	.04	.01
☐ 11 Jon Matlack	.12	.05	.02
☐ 12 Gary Rajsich	.08	.04	.01
☐ 13 Lenny Randle	.08	.04	.01
☐ 14 Elias Sosa	.08	.04	.01
☐ 15 Ozzie Virgil	.08	.04	.01
☐ 16 Milt Wilcox	.08	.04	.01
☐ 17 Steve Henderson 3X	.12	.05	.02
☐ 18 Ray Burris	.12	.05	.02
☐ 19 Mike Easler	.08	.04	.01
☐ 20 Juan Eichelberger	.08	.04	.01
☐ 21 Rollie Fingers	1.25	.55	.16
☐ 22 Toby Harrah	.15	.07	.02
☐ 23 Randy Johnson	.08	.04	.01
☐ 24 Dave Kingman	.40	.18	.05
☐ 25 Lee Lacy	.08	.04	.01
☐ 26 Tito Landrum	.12	.05	.02
☐ 27 Paul Mirabella	.08	.04	.01
☐ 28 Mickey Rivers	.20	.09	.03
☐ 29 Rodney Scott	.08	.04	.01
☐ 30 Tim Stoddard	.08	.04	.01
☐ 31 Ron Washington	.08	.04	.01
☐ 32 Jerry White	.08	.04	.01
☐ 33 Dick Williams MG	.12	.05	.02
☐ 34 Clete Boyer MG	.12	.05	.02
☐ 35 Steve Dillard	.08	.04	.01
☐ 36 Garth Iorg	.08	.04	.01
☐ 37 Bruce Kison	.08	.04	.01
☐ 38 Wayne Krenchicki	.08	.04	.01
☐ 39 Ron LeFlore	.12	.05	.02
☐ 40 Tippy Martinez	.08	.04	.01
☐ 41 Omar Moreno	.08	.04	.01
☐ 42 Jim Morrison	.08	.04	.01
☐ 43 Graig Nettles	.25	.11	.03
☐ 44 Jim Nettles	.08	.04	.01
☐ 45 Wayne Nordhagen	.08	.04	.01
☐ 46 Al Oliver	.25	.11	.03
☐ 47 Jerry Royster	.08	.04	.01
☐ 48 Sammy Stewart	.08	.04	.01
☐ 49 Randy Bass	.15	.07	.02
☐ 50 Vida Blue	.15	.07	.02
☐ 51 Bruce Bochy	.08	.04	.01
☐ 52 Doug Corbett	.08	.04	.01
☐ 53 Jose Cruz	.15	.07	.02
☐ 54 Jamie Easterly	.08	.04	.01
☐ 55 Pete Falcone	.08	.04	.01
☐ 56 Bob Galasso	.08	.04	.01
☐ 57 Johnny Grubb	.08	.04	.01
☐ 58 Bake McBride	.12	.05	.02
☐ 59 Dyar Miller	.08	.04	.01
☐ 60 Tom Paciorek	.08	.04	.01
☐ 61 Ken Reitz	.08	.04	.01
☐ 62 U.L. Washington	.08	.04	.01
☐ 63 Alan Ashby	.08	.04	.01
☐ 64 Pat Dobson	.12	.05	.02
☐ 65 Doug Bird	.08	.04	.01
☐ 66 Marty Castillo	.08	.04	.01
☐ 67 Dan Driessen	.12	.05	.02
☐ 68 Wayne Garland	.12	.05	.02
☐ 69 Tim Ireland	.08	.04	.01
☐ 70 Ron Jackson	.08	.04	.01
☐ 71 Bobby Jones	.08	.04	.01
☐ 72 Dennis Leonard	.15	.07	.02
☐ 73 Rick Manning	.08	.04	.01
☐ 74 Amos Otis	.20	.09	.03
☐ 75 Pat Putnam	.08	.04	.01
☐ 76 Eric Rasmussen	.08	.04	.01
☐ 77 Paul Blair	.12	.05	.02
☐ 78 Bert Campaneris	.15	.07	.02
☐ 79 Cesar Cedeno	.15	.07	.02
☐ 80 Ed Figueroa	.08	.04	.01
☐ 81 Ross Grimsley	.12	.05	.02
☐ 82 George Hendrick	.12	.05	.02
☐ 83 Cliff Johnson	.12	.05	.02
☐ 84 Mike Kekich	.08	.04	.01
☐ 85 Rafael Landestoy	.08	.04	.01
☐ 86 Larry Milbourne	.08	.04	.01
☐ 87 Bobby Molinaro	.08	.04	.01
☐ 88 Sid Monge	.08	.04	.01
☐ 89 Rennie Stennett	.12	.05	.02
☐ 90 Derrell Thomas	.08	.04	.01
☐ 91 Earl Weaver MG	.25	.11	.03
☐ 92 Gary Allenson	.08	.04	.01
☐ 93 Pedro Borbon	.08	.04	.01
☐ 94 Al Bumbry	.12	.05	.02
☐ 95 Bill Campbell	.08	.04	.01
☐ 96 Bernie Carbo	.08	.04	.01
☐ 97 Fergie Jenkins	1.00	.45	.13
☐ 98 Pete LaCock	.08	.04	.01
☐ 99 Bill Lee	.15	.07	.02
☐ 100 Tommy McMillan	.08	.04	.01
☐ 101 Joe Pittman	.08	.04	.01
☐ 102 Gene Richards	.08	.04	.01
☐ 103 Leon Roberts	.08	.04	.01
☐ 104 Tony Scott	.08	.04	.01
☐ 105 Doug Simunic	.08	.04	.01
☐ 106 Rick Wise	.15	.07	.02
☐ 107 Willie Aikens	.15	.07	.02
☐ 108 Juan Beniquez	.15	.07	.02
☐ 109 Bobby Bonds	.35	.16	.04
☐ 110 Sergio Ferrer	.08	.04	.01
☐ 111 Chuck Ficks	.08	.04	.01
☐ 112 George Foster	.25	.11	.03
☐ 113 Dave Hilton	.08	.04	.01
☐ 114 Al Holland	.08	.04	.01
☐ 115 Clint Hurdle	.12	.05	.02
☐ 116 Bill Madlock	.20	.09	.03
☐ 117 Steve Ontiveros	.08	.04	.01
☐ 118 Roy Thomas	.08	.04	.01
☐ 119 Luis Tiant	.20	.09	.03
☐ 120 Walt Williams	.15	.07	.02
☐ 121 Vida Blue	.15	.07	.02
☐ 122 Bobby Bonds	.35	.16	.04
☐ 123 Rollie Fingers	1.25	.55	.16
☐ 124 George Foster	.40	.18	.05
☐ 125 Fergie Jenkins	1.00	.45	.13
☐ 126 Dave Kingman	.40	.18	.05

1959 Fleer

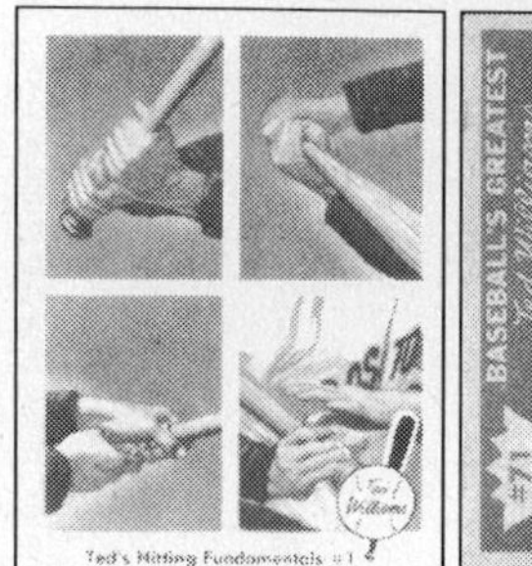

The cards in this 80-card set measure 2 1/2" by 3 1/2". The 1959 Fleer set, with a catalog designation of R418-1, portrays the life of Ted Williams. The wording of the wrapper, "Baseball's Greatest Series," has led to speculation that Fleer contemplated similar sets honoring other baseball immortals, but chose to develop instead the format of the 1960 and 1961 issues. Card number 68, which was withdrawn early in production, is considered scarce and has even been counterfeited; the fake has a rosy coloration and a cross-hatch pattern visible over the picture area. The card numbering is arranged essentially in chronological order.

	NRMT	VG-E	GOOD
COMPLETE SET (80)	1400.00	650.00	180.00
COMMON CARDS (1-80)	7.50	3.40	.95
☐ 1 The Early Years (Choosing up sides on the sandlots)	50.00	7.50	1.50
☐ 2 Ted's Idol Babe Ruth (Meeting boyhood idol, Babe Ruth)	60.00	27.00	7.50
☐ 3 Practice Makes Perfect (At place practicing on the sandlots)	7.50	3.40	.95
☐ 4 Learns Fine Points (Sliding at Herbert Hoover High)	7.50	3.40	.95
☐ 5 Ted's Fame Spreads (At plate at Herbert Hoover High)	7.50	3.40	.95
☐ 6 Ted Turns Pro (Portrait, San Diego Padres, PCL League uniform)	15.00	6.75	1.90
☐ 7 From Mound to Plate (At plate, San Diego Padres, PCL)	7.50	3.40	.95
☐ 8 1937 First Full Season (Making a leaping catch)	9.00	4.00	1.15
☐ 9 First Step to Majors (With Eddie Collins)	12.50	5.75	1.55
☐ 10 Gunning as Pastime (Wearing hunting gear, taking aim)	7.50	3.40	.95
☐ 11 First Spring Training (with Jimmie Foxx)	25.00	11.50	3.10
☐ 12 Burning Up Minors (Pitching for Minneapolis in American Association)	12.50	5.75	1.55
☐ 13 1939 Shows Will Stay (Follow-through)	9.00	4.00	1.15
☐ 14 Outstanding Rookie '39 (Follow-through)	9.00	4.00	1.15
☐ 15 Licks Sophomore Jinx (Sliding into third base for a triple)	9.00	4.00	1.15
☐ 16 1941 Greatest Year (Follow-through at plate)	9.00	4.00	1.15
☐ 17 How Ted Hit .400 (Youthful Williams, as he looked in '41)	25.00	11.50	3.10
☐ 18 1941 All Star Hero (Crossing plate after home run)	9.00	4.00	1.15
☐ 19 Ted Wins Triple Crown (Crossing plate at Fenway Park)	9.00	4.00	1.15
☐ 20 On to Naval Training (In training plane at Amherst College)	7.50	3.40	.95
☐ 21 Honors for Williams (Receiving 1942 Sporting News POY)	9.00	4.00	1.15
☐ 22 1944 Ted Solos (In cockpit at Pensacola, FL Navy Air Station)	7.50	3.40	.95
☐ 23 Williams Wins Wings (Wearing Naval Aviation Cadet uniform)	9.00	4.00	1.15
☐ 24 1945 Sharpshooter (Taking Naval eye test)	7.50	3.40	.95
☐ 25 1945 Ted Discharged (In cockpit, giving the thumbs up)	9.00	4.00	1.15
☐ 26 Off to Flying Start (In batters box, spring training 1946)	9.00	4.00	1.15
☐ 27 7/9/46 One Man Show (Riding "blooper" pitch out of park)	9.00	4.00	1.15
☐ 28 The Williams Shift (Diagram of Cleveland Indians' position shift to defense Williams)	7.50	3.40	.95
☐ 29 Ted Hits for Cycle (Close-up of follow-through)	12.50	5.75	1.55
☐ 30 Beating Williams Shift (Crossing plate after home run)	9.00	4.00	1.15
☐ 31 Sox Lose Series (Sliding across plate, Sept. 14, 1946)	9.00	4.00	1.15
☐ 32 Most Valuable Player (Receiving MVP Award from Joseph Cashman)	9.00	4.00	1.15
☐ 33 Another Triple Crown (Famous "Williams' Grip")	7.50	3.40	.95
☐ 34 Runs Scored Record (Sliding into 2nd base in 1947 AS Game)	7.50	3.40	.95
☐ 35 Sox Miss Pennant (Checking weight on new 36 oz. hickory bat)	7.50	3.40	.95
☐ 36 Banner Year for Ted (Bunting down the 3rd base line)	9.00	4.00	1.15
☐ 37 1949 Sox Miss Again (Two moods: grim and determined, smiling and happy)	9.00	4.00	1.15
☐ 38 1949 Power Rampage (Full shot of his batting follow-through)	9.00	4.00	1.15
☐ 39 1950 Great Start (Signing 125,000 contract, shaking hands with Joe Cronin and Eddie Collins)	12.50	5.75	1.55
☐ 40 Ted Crashes into Wall (Making catch in 1950 A-S game and crashing into wall)	9.00	4.00	1.15
☐ 41 1950 Ted Recovers (Recuperating from elbow operation in hospital)	7.50	3.40	.95
☐ 42 Slowed by Injury (With Tom Yawkey)	9.00	4.00	1.15
☐ 43 Double Play Lead (Leaping high to make great catch)	9.00	4.00	1.15
☐ 44 Back to Marines (Hanging up number 9 prior to leaving for Marines)	9.00	4.00	1.15
☐ 45 Farewell to Baseball (Honored at Fenway Park prior to return to service)	9.00	4.00	1.15
☐ 46 Ready for Combat (Drawing jet pilot equipment	7.50	3.40	.95

		NRMT	VG-E	GOOD
	in Willow Grove)			
☐ 47	Ted Crash Lands Jet (In flying gear and jet he crash landed in)	7.50	3.40	.95
☐ 48	1953 Ted Returns (Throwing out 1st ball at AS Game in Cincinnati; Ford Frick looks on)	12.50	5.75	1.55
☐ 49	Smash Return (Giving his arm whirlpool treatment)	7.50	3.40	.95
☐ 50	1954 Spring Injury (Full batting pose at plate)	12.50	5.75	1.55
☐ 51	Ted is Patched Up (In first workout after fractured collar bone)	7.50	3.40	.95
☐ 52	1954 Ted's Comeback (Hitting a home run against Detroit)	12.50	5.75	1.55
☐ 53	Comeback is Success (Beating catcher's tag at home plate)	9.00	4.00	1.15
☐ 54	Ted Hooks Big One (With prize catch, 1235 lb. black marlin)	9.00	4.00	1.15
☐ 55	Retirement "No Go" (Returning from retirement and signing with Joe Cronin in '55)	12.50	5.75	1.55
☐ 56	2000th Hit (2,000th Major League hit, 8/11/55)	9.00	4.00	1.15
☐ 57	400th Homer (In locker room after hitting 400th homerun)	9.00	4.00	1.15
☐ 58	Williams Hits .388 (Four-picture sequence of his batting swing)	9.00	4.00	1.15
☐ 59	Hot September for Ted (Full shot of follow-through at plate)	9.00	4.00	1.15
☐ 60	More Records for Ted (Swinging and missing)	9.00	4.00	1.15
☐ 61	1957 Outfielder Ted (Warming up prior to ball game)	9.00	4.00	1.15
☐ 62	1958 Sixth Batting Title (Slamming pitch into stands)	7.50	3.40	.95
☐ 63	Ted's All-Star Record (Portrait and facsimile autograph)	45.00	20.00	5.75
☐ 64	Daughter and Daddy (In uniform holding Barbara, his daughter)	7.50	3.40	.95
☐ 65	1958 August 30 (Determination on face; connecting with ball)	9.00	4.00	1.15
☐ 66	1958 Powerhouse (Stance and follow-through in batters box)	7.50	3.40	.95
☐ 67	Two Famous Fishermen (With Sam Snead, testing fishing equipment)	20.00	9.00	2.50
☐ 68	Ted Signs for 1959 SP (With Bucky Harris, signing contract)	750.00	350.00	95.00
☐ 69	A Future Ted Williams (With eager, young newcomer)	9.00	4.00	1.15
☐ 70	Williams and Thorpe (With Jim Thorpe, at Sportsmen's Show)	25.00	11.50	3.10
☐ 71	Hitting Fund. 1 (Proper gripping of a baseball bat)	7.50	3.40	.95
☐ 72	Hitting Fund. 2 (Checking his swing)	7.50	3.40	.95
☐ 73	Hitting Fund. 3 (Stance and follow-through)	7.50	3.40	.95
☐ 74	Here's How (Demonstrating in locker room an aspect of hitting)	7.50	3.40	.95
☐ 75	Williams' Value to Sox (Ed Collins and Babe Ruth)	45.00	20.00	5.75
☐ 76	On Base Record (Awaiting intentional walk to first base)	7.50	3.40	.95
☐ 77	Ted Relaxes (Displaying bone-fish which he caught)	9.00	4.00	1.15
☐ 78	Honors for Williams (With Representative Joe Martin and Chief Justice Earl Warren; Clark Griffith Memorial Award)	9.00	4.00	1.15
☐ 79	Where Ted Stands (Wielding giant eight-foot bat when honored as modern-day Paul Bunyan)	12.50	5.75	1.55
☐ 80	Ted's Goals for 1959 (Admiring his portrait)	25.00	6.00	1.20

1960 Fleer

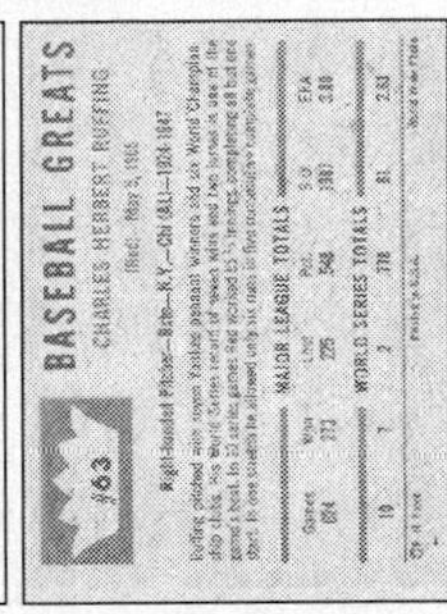

The cards in this 79-card set measure 2 1/2" by 3 1/2". The cards from the 1960 Fleer series of Baseball Greats are sometimes mistaken for 1930s cards by collectors not familiar with this set. The cards each contain a tinted photo of a baseball immortal, and were issued in one series. There are no known scarcities, although a number 80 card (Pepper Martin reverse with either Eddie Collins or Lefty Grove obverse) exists (this is not considered part of the set). The catalog designation for 1960 Fleer is R418-2. The cards were printed on a 96-card sheet with 17 double prints. These are noted in the checklist below by DP. On the sheet the second Eddie Collins card is typically found in the number 80 position.

	NRMT	VG-E	GOOD
COMPLETE SET (79)	500.00	230.00	65.00
COMMON PLAYER (1-79)	3.50	1.55	.45
COMMON PLAYER DP	3.00	1.35	.40
☐ 1 Napoleon Lajoie DP	20.00	5.00	1.00
☐ 2 Christy Mathewson	10.00	4.50	1.25
☐ 3 Babe Ruth	90.00	40.00	11.50
☐ 4 Carl Hubbell	6.00	2.70	.75
☐ 5 Grover Alexander	6.00	2.70	.75
☐ 6 Walter Johnson DP	8.00	3.60	1.00
☐ 7 Chief Bender	3.50	1.55	.45
☐ 8 Roger Bresnahan	3.50	1.55	.45
☐ 9 Mordecai Brown	3.50	1.55	.45
☐ 10 Tris Speaker	6.00	2.70	.75
☐ 11 Arky Vaughan DP	3.00	1.35	.40
☐ 12 Zach Wheat	3.50	1.55	.45
☐ 13 George Sisler	3.50	1.55	.45
☐ 14 Connie Mack	6.00	2.70	.75
☐ 15 Clark Griffith	3.50	1.55	.45
☐ 16 Lou Boudreau DP	6.00	2.70	.75
☐ 17 Ernie Lombardi	3.50	1.55	.45
☐ 18 Heinie Manush	3.50	1.55	.45
☐ 19 Marty Marion	3.50	1.55	.45
☐ 20 Eddie Collins DP	3.00	1.35	.40
☐ 21 Rabbit Maranville DP	3.00	1.35	.40
☐ 22 Joe Medwick	3.50	1.55	.45

☐	23 Ed Barrow	3.50	1.55	.45
☐	24 Mickey Cochrane	4.50	2.00	.55
☐	25 Jimmy Collins	3.50	1.55	.45
☐	26 Bob Feller DP	12.00	5.50	1.50
☐	27 Luke Appling	6.00	2.70	.75
☐	28 Lou Gehrig	50.00	23.00	6.25
☐	29 Gabby Hartnett	3.50	1.55	.45
☐	30 Chuck Klein	3.50	1.55	.45
☐	31 Tony Lazzeri DP	4.50	2.00	.55
☐	32 Al Simmons	3.50	1.55	.45
☐	33 Wilbert Robinson	3.50	1.55	.45
☐	34 Edgar(Sam) Rice	3.50	1.55	.45
☐	35 Herb Pennock	3.50	1.55	.45
☐	36 Mel Ott DP	6.00	2.70	.75
☐	37 Lefty O'Doul	3.50	1.55	.45
☐	38 Johnny Mize	7.00	3.10	.85
☐	39 Edmund(Bing) Miller	3.50	1.55	.45
☐	40 Joe Tinker	3.50	1.55	.45
☐	41 Frank Baker DP	3.00	1.35	.40
☐	42 Ty Cobb	50.00	23.00	6.25
☐	43 Paul Derringer	3.50	1.55	.45
☐	44 Adrian(Cap) Anson	3.50	1.55	.45
☐	45 Jim Bottomley	3.50	1.55	.45
☐	46 Eddie Plank DP	3.50	1.55	.45
☐	47 Denton(Cy) Young	8.00	3.60	1.00
☐	48 Hack Wilson	6.00	2.70	.75
☐	49 Edward Walsh UER (Photo actually Ed Walsh Jr.)	3.50	1.55	.45
☐	50 Frank Chance	3.50	1.55	.45
☐	51 Dazzy Vance DP	3.00	1.35	.40
☐	52 Bill Terry	6.00	2.70	.75
☐	53 Jimmy Foxx	8.00	3.60	1.00
☐	54 Lefty Gomez	7.00	3.10	.85
☐	55 Branch Rickey	3.50	1.55	.45
☐	56 Ray Schalk DP	3.00	1.35	.40
☐	57 Johnny Evers	3.50	1.55	.45
☐	58 Charles Gehringer	6.00	2.70	.75
☐	59 Burleigh Grimes	3.50	1.55	.45
☐	60 Lefty Grove	7.00	3.10	.85
☐	61 Rube Waddell DP	3.00	1.35	.40
☐	62 John(Honus) Wagner	10.00	4.50	1.25
☐	63 Charles(Red) Ruffing	3.50	1.55	.45
☐	64 Kenesaw M. Landis	3.50	1.55	.45
☐	65 Harry Heilmann	3.50	1.55	.45
☐	66 John McGraw DP	3.00	1.35	.40
☐	67 Hugh Jennings	3.50	1.55	.45
☐	68 Hal Newhouser	4.50	2.00	.55
☐	69 Waite Hoyt	3.50	1.55	.45
☐	70 Louis(Bobo) Newsom	3.50	1.55	.45
☐	71 Earl Averill DP	3.00	1.35	.40
☐	72 Ted Williams	75.00	34.00	9.50
☐	73 Warren Giles	3.50	1.55	.45
☐	74 Ford Frick	3.50	1.55	.45
☐	75 Hazen(Kiki) Cuyler	3.50	1.55	.45
☐	76 Paul Waner DP	3.00	1.35	.40
☐	77 Harold(Pie) Traynor	3.50	1.55	.45
☐	78 Lloyd Waner	3.50	1.55	.45
☐	79 Ralph Kiner	9.00	3.00	.75
☐	80A Pepper Martin SP (Eddie Collins pictured on obverse)	1800.00	750.00	250.00
☐	80B Pepper Martin SP (Lefty Grove pictured on obverse)	1200.00	500.00	150.00

1961 Fleer

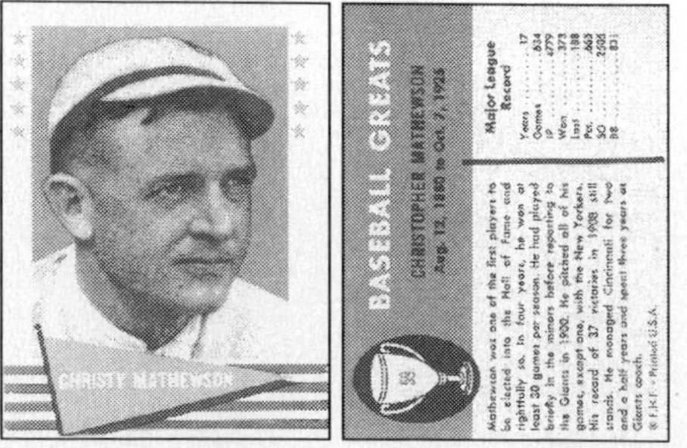

The cards in this 154-card set measure 2 1/2" by 3 1/2". In 1961, Fleer continued its Baseball Greats format by issuing this series of cards. The set was released in two distinct series, 1-88 and 89-154 (of which the latter is more difficult to obtain). The players within each series are conveniently numbered in alphabetical order. It appears that this set continued to be issued the following year by Fleer. The catalog number for this set is F418-3. In each first series pack Fleer inserted a Major League team decal and a pennant sticker honoring past World Series winners.

	NRMT	VG-E	GOOD
COMPLETE SET (154)	1000.00	450.00	125.00
COMMON PLAYER (1-88)	3.00	1.35	.40
COMMON PLAYER (89-154)	6.00	2.70	.75

☐	1 Baker/Cobb/Wheat (Checklist back)	40.00	6.00	1.20
☐	2 Grover C. Alexander	6.00	2.70	.75
☐	3 Nick Altrock	3.00	1.35	.40
☐	4 Cap Anson	3.00	1.35	.40
☐	5 Earl Averill	3.00	1.35	.40
☐	6 Frank Baker	3.00	1.35	.40
☐	7 Dave Bancroft	3.00	1.35	.40
☐	8 Chief Bender	3.00	1.35	.40
☐	9 Jim Bottomley	3.00	1.35	.40
☐	10 Roger Bresnahan	3.00	1.35	.40
☐	11 Mordecai Brown	3.00	1.35	.40
☐	12 Max Carey	3.00	1.35	.40
☐	13 Jack Chesbro	3.00	1.35	.40
☐	14 Ty Cobb	40.00	18.00	5.00
☐	15 Mickey Cochrane	4.00	1.80	.50
☐	16 Eddie Collins	3.00	1.35	.40
☐	17 Earle Combs	3.00	1.35	.40
☐	18 Charles Comiskey	3.00	1.35	.40
☐	19 Kiki Cuyler	3.00	1.35	.40
☐	20 Paul Derringer	3.00	1.35	.40
☐	21 Howard Ehmke	3.00	1.35	.40
☐	22 Billy Evans	3.00	1.35	.40
☐	23 Johnny Evers	3.00	1.35	.40
☐	24 Urban Faber	3.00	1.35	.40
☐	25 Bob Feller	10.00	4.50	1.25
☐	26 Wes Ferrell	3.00	1.35	.40
☐	27 Lew Fonseca	3.00	1.35	.40
☐	28 Jimmy Foxx	7.00	3.10	.85
☐	29 Ford Frick	3.00	1.35	.40
☐	30 Frank Frisch	4.00	1.80	.50
☐	31 Lou Gehrig	40.00	18.00	5.00
☐	32 Charlie Gehringer	5.00	2.30	.60
☐	33 Warren Giles	3.00	1.35	.40
☐	34 Lefty Gomez	5.00	2.30	.60
☐	35 Goose Goslin	3.00	1.35	.40
☐	36 Clark Griffith	3.00	1.35	.40
☐	37 Burleigh Grimes	3.00	1.35	.40
☐	38 Lefty Grove	6.00	2.70	.75
☐	39 Chick Hafey	3.00	1.35	.40
☐	40 Jesse Haines	3.00	1.35	.40
☐	41 Gabby Hartnett	3.00	1.35	.40
☐	42 Harry Heilmann	3.00	1.35	.40
☐	43 Rogers Hornsby	7.00	3.10	.85
☐	44 Waite Hoyt	3.00	1.35	.40
☐	45 Carl Hubbell	5.00	2.30	.60
☐	46 Miller Huggins	3.00	1.35	.40
☐	47 Hugh Jennings	3.00	1.35	.40
☐	48 Ban Johnson	3.00	1.35	.40
☐	49 Walter Johnson	10.00	4.50	1.25
☐	50 Ralph Kiner	7.00	3.10	.85
☐	51 Chuck Klein	3.00	1.35	.40
☐	52 Johnny Kling	3.00	1.35	.40
☐	53 Kenesaw M. Landis	3.00	1.35	.40
☐	54 Tony Lazzeri	4.00	1.80	.50
☐	55 Ernie Lombardi	3.00	1.35	.40
☐	56 Dolf Luque	3.00	1.35	.40
☐	57 Heinie Manush	3.00	1.35	.40
☐	58 Marty Marion	3.00	1.35	.40
☐	59 Christy Mathewson	10.00	4.50	1.25
☐	60 John McGraw	4.00	1.80	.50
☐	61 Joe Medwick	3.00	1.35	.40
☐	62 Edmund(Bing) Miller	3.00	1.35	.40
☐	63 Johnny Mize	6.00	2.70	.75
☐	64 John Mostil	3.00	1.35	.40
☐	65 Art Nehf	3.00	1.35	.40
☐	66 Hal Newhouser	4.00	1.80	.50
☐	67 Bobo Newsom	3.00	1.35	.40
☐	68 Mel Ott	5.00	2.30	.60
☐	69 Allie Reynolds	3.00	1.35	.40
☐	70 Sam Rice	3.00	1.35	.40
☐	71 Eppa Rixey	3.00	1.35	.40
☐	72 Edd Roush	3.00	1.35	.40
☐	73 Schoolboy Rowe	3.00	1.35	.40
☐	74 Red Ruffing	3.00	1.35	.40
☐	75 Babe Ruth	80.00	36.00	10.00
☐	76 Joe Sewell	3.00	1.35	.40

☐ 77 Al Simmons	3.00	1.35	.40
☐ 78 George Sisler	3.00	1.35	.40
☐ 79 Tris Speaker	6.00	2.70	.75
☐ 80 Fred Toney	3.00	1.35	.40
☐ 81 Dazzy Vance	3.00	1.35	.40
☐ 82 Jim Vaughn	3.00	1.35	.40
☐ 83 Ed Walsh	3.00	1.35	.40
☐ 84 Lloyd Waner	3.00	1.35	.40
☐ 85 Paul Waner	3.00	1.35	.40
☐ 86 Zack Wheat	3.00	1.35	.40
☐ 87 Hack Wilson	4.00	1.80	.50
☐ 88 Jimmy Wilson	3.00	1.35	.40
☐ 89 George Sisler and Pie Traynor (Checklist back)	30.00	5.00	1.00
☐ 90 Babe Adams	6.00	2.70	.75
☐ 91 Dale Alexander	6.00	2.70	.75
☐ 92 Jim Bagby	6.00	2.70	.75
☐ 93 Ossie Bluege	6.00	2.70	.75
☐ 94 Lou Boudreau	10.00	4.50	1.25
☐ 95 Tom Bridges	6.00	2.70	.75
☐ 96 Donie Bush	6.00	2.70	.75
☐ 97 Dolph Camilli	6.00	2.70	.75
☐ 98 Frank Chance	8.00	3.60	1.00
☐ 99 Jimmy Collins	8.00	3.60	1.00
☐ 100 Stan Coveleskie	8.00	3.60	1.00
☐ 101 Hugh Critz	6.00	2.70	.75
☐ 102 Alvin Crowder	6.00	2.70	.75
☐ 103 Joe Dugan	6.00	2.70	.75
☐ 104 Bibb Falk	6.00	2.70	.75
☐ 105 Rick Ferrell	8.00	3.60	1.00
☐ 106 Art Fletcher	6.00	2.70	.75
☐ 107 Dennis Galehouse	6.00	2.70	.75
☐ 108 Chick Galloway	6.00	2.70	.75
☐ 109 Mule Haas	6.00	2.70	.75
☐ 110 Stan Hack	6.00	2.70	.75
☐ 111 Bump Hadley	6.00	2.70	.75
☐ 112 Billy Hamilton	8.00	3.60	1.00
☐ 113 Joe Hauser	6.00	2.70	.75
☐ 114 Babe Herman	6.00	2.70	.75
☐ 115 Travis Jackson	10.00	4.50	1.25
☐ 116 Eddie Joost	6.00	2.70	.75
☐ 117 Addie Joss	10.00	4.50	1.25
☐ 118 Joe Judge	6.00	2.70	.75
☐ 119 Joe Kuhel	6.00	2.70	.75
☐ 120 Napoleon Lajoie	15.00	6.75	1.90
☐ 121 Dutch Leonard	6.00	2.70	.75
☐ 122 Ted Lyons	8.00	3.60	1.00
☐ 123 Connie Mack	15.00	6.75	1.90
☐ 124 Rabbit Maranville	8.00	3.60	1.00
☐ 125 Fred Marberry	6.00	2.70	.75
☐ 126 Joe McGinnity	10.00	4.50	1.25
☐ 127 Oscar Melillo	6.00	2.70	.75
☐ 128 Ray Mueller	6.00	2.70	.75
☐ 129 Kid Nichols	8.00	3.60	1.00
☐ 130 Lefty O'Doul	6.00	2.70	.75
☐ 131 Bob O'Farrell	6.00	2.70	.75
☐ 132 Roger Peckinpaugh	6.00	2.70	.75
☐ 133 Herb Pennock	8.00	3.60	1.00
☐ 134 George Pipgras	6.00	2.70	.75
☐ 135 Eddie Plank	10.00	4.50	1.25
☐ 136 Ray Schalk	8.00	3.60	1.00
☐ 137 Hal Schumacher	6.00	2.70	.75
☐ 138 Luke Sewell	6.00	2.70	.75
☐ 139 Bob Shawkey	6.00	2.70	.75
☐ 140 Riggs Stephenson	6.00	2.70	.75
☐ 141 Billy Sullivan	6.00	2.70	.75
☐ 142 Bill Terry	15.00	6.75	1.90
☐ 143 Joe Tinker	8.00	3.60	1.00
☐ 144 Pie Traynor	10.00	4.50	1.25
☐ 145 Hal Trosky	6.00	2.70	.75
☐ 146 George Uhle	6.00	2.70	.75
☐ 147 Johnny VanderMeer	8.00	3.60	1.00
☐ 148 Arky Vaughan	8.00	3.60	1.00
☐ 149 Rube Waddell	8.00	3.60	1.00
☐ 150 Honus Wagner	40.00	18.00	5.00
☐ 151 Dixie Walker	6.00	2.70	.75
☐ 152 Ted Williams	80.00	36.00	10.00
☐ 153 Cy Young	25.00	11.50	3.10
☐ 154 Ross Youngs	20.00	7.50	1.50

1963 Fleer

The cards in this 66-card set measure 2 1/2" by 3 1/2". The Fleer set of current baseball players was marketed in 1963 in a gum card-style waxed wrapper package which contained a cherry cookie instead of gum. The cards were

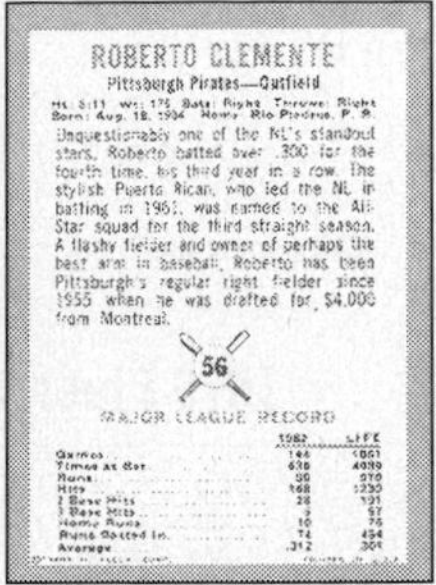

printed in sheets of 66 with the scarce card of Adcock apparently being replaced by the unnumbered checklist card for the final press run. The complete set price includes the checklist card. The catalog designation for this set is R418-4. The key Rookie Card in this set is Maury Wills. The set is basically arranged numerically in alphabetical order by teams which are also in alphabetical order.

	NRMT	VG-E	GOOD
COMPLETE SET (67)	1250.00	575.00	160.00
COMMON PLAYER (1-66)	8.00	3.60	1.00
☐ 1 Steve Barber	16.00	7.25	2.00
☐ 2 Ron Hansen	8.00	3.60	1.00
☐ 3 Milt Pappas	9.00	4.00	1.15
☐ 4 Brooks Robinson	55.00	25.00	7.00
☐ 5 Willie Mays	120.00	55.00	15.00
☐ 6 Lou Clinton	8.00	3.60	1.00
☐ 7 Bill Monbouquette	8.00	3.60	1.00
☐ 8 Carl Yastrzemski	100.00	45.00	12.50
☐ 9 Ray Herbert	8.00	3.60	1.00
☐ 10 Jim Landis	8.00	3.60	1.00
☐ 11 Dick Donovan	8.00	3.60	1.00
☐ 12 Tito Francona	8.00	3.60	1.00
☐ 13 Jerry Kindall	8.00	3.60	1.00
☐ 14 Frank Lary	9.00	4.00	1.15
☐ 15 Dick Howser	9.00	4.00	1.15
☐ 16 Jerry Lumpe	8.00	3.60	1.00
☐ 17 Norm Siebern	8.00	3.60	1.00
☐ 18 Don Lee	8.00	3.60	1.00
☐ 19 Albie Pearson	9.00	4.00	1.15
☐ 20 Bob Rodgers	9.00	4.00	1.15
☐ 21 Leon Wagner	8.00	3.60	1.00
☐ 22 Jim Kaat	15.00	6.75	1.90
☐ 23 Vic Power	9.00	4.00	1.15
☐ 24 Rich Rollins	9.00	4.00	1.15
☐ 25 Bobby Richardson	15.00	6.75	1.90
☐ 26 Ralph Terry	9.00	4.00	1.15
☐ 27 Tom Cheney	8.00	3.60	1.00
☐ 28 Chuck Cottier	8.00	3.60	1.00
☐ 29 Jim Piersall	11.00	4.90	1.40
☐ 30 Dave Stenhouse	8.00	3.60	1.00
☐ 31 Glen Hobbie	8.00	3.60	1.00
☐ 32 Ron Santo	15.00	6.75	1.90
☐ 33 Gene Freese	8.00	3.60	1.00
☐ 34 Vada Pinson	15.00	6.75	1.90
☐ 35 Bob Purkey	8.00	3.60	1.00
☐ 36 Joe Amalfitano	8.00	3.60	1.00
☐ 37 Bob Aspromonte	8.00	3.60	1.00
☐ 38 Dick Farrell	8.00	3.60	1.00
☐ 39 Al Spangler	8.00	3.60	1.00
☐ 40 Tommy Davis	11.00	4.90	1.40
☐ 41 Don Drysdale	40.00	18.00	5.00
☐ 42 Sandy Koufax	135.00	60.00	17.00
☐ 43 Maury Wills	85.00	38.00	10.50
☐ 44 Frank Bolling	8.00	3.60	1.00
☐ 45 Warren Spahn	40.00	18.00	5.00
☐ 46 Joe Adcock SP	165.00	75.00	21.00
☐ 47 Roger Craig	11.00	4.90	1.40
☐ 48 Al Jackson	8.00	3.60	1.00
☐ 49 Rod Kanehl	8.00	3.60	1.00
☐ 50 Ruben Amaro	8.00	3.60	1.00
☐ 51 Johnny Callison	9.00	4.00	1.15
☐ 52 Clay Dalrymple	8.00	3.60	1.00
☐ 53 Don Demeter	8.00	3.60	1.00
☐ 54 Art Mahaffey	8.00	3.60	1.00
☐ 55 Smoky Burgess	9.00	4.00	1.15
☐ 56 Roberto Clemente	130.00	57.50	16.50
☐ 57 Roy Face	11.00	4.90	1.40
☐ 58 Vern Law	9.00	4.00	1.15
☐ 59 Bill Mazeroski	14.00	6.25	1.75

☐ 60 Ken Boyer	15.00	6.75	1.90
☐ 61 Bob Gibson	45.00	20.00	5.75
☐ 62 Gene Oliver	8.00	3.60	1.00
☐ 63 Bill White	15.00	6.75	1.90
☐ 64 Orlando Cepeda	20.00	9.00	2.50
☐ 65 Jim Davenport	8.00	3.60	1.00
☐ 66 Billy O'Dell	16.00	7.25	2.00
☐ NNO Checklist card	450.00	70.00	23.00

1970 Fleer World Series

This set of 66 cards was distributed by Fleer. The cards are standard size, 2 1/2" by 3 1/2", and are in crude color on the front with light blue printing on white card stock on the back. All the years are represented except for 1904 when no World Series was played. In the list below, the winning series team is listed first. The year of the Series on the obverse is inside a white baseball. The original art for the cards in this set was drawn by sports artist, R.G. Laughlin.

	NRMT-MT	EXC	G-VG
COMPLETE SET (66)	50.00	23.00	6.25
COMMON PLAYER (1-66)	.75	.35	.09
☐ 1 1903 Red Sox/Pirates	.75	.35	.09
☐ 2 1905 Giants/A's (Christy Mathewson)	1.25	.55	.16
☐ 3 1906 White Sox/Cubs	.75	.35	.09
☐ 4 1907 Cubs/Tigers	.75	.35	.09
☐ 5 1908 Cubs/Tigers (Tinker/Evers/Chance)	1.25	.55	.16
☐ 6 1909 Pirates/Tigers (Wagner/Cobb)	2.00	.90	.25
☐ 7 1910 A's/Cubs (Bender/Coombs)	1.00	.45	.13
☐ 8 1911 A's/Giants (John McGraw)	1.00	.45	.13
☐ 9 1912 Red Sox/Giants	.75	.35	.09
☐ 10 1913 A's/Giants	.75	.35	.09
☐ 11 1914 Braves/A's	.75	.35	.09
☐ 12 1915 Red Sox/Phillies (Babe Ruth)	2.00	.90	.25
☐ 13 1916 Red Sox/Dodgers (Babe Ruth)	2.00	.90	.25
☐ 14 1917 White Sox/Giants	.75	.35	.09
☐ 15 1918 Red Sox/Cubs	.75	.35	.09
☐ 16 1919 Reds/White Sox	2.00	.90	.25
☐ 17 1920 Indians/Dodgers (Stan Coveleski)	1.00	.45	.13
☐ 18 1921 Giants/Yankees (Commissioner Landis)	.75	.35	.09
☐ 19 1922 Giants/Yankees	.75	.35	.09
☐ 20 1923 Yankees/Giants (Babe Ruth)	2.00	.90	.25
☐ 21 1924 Senators/Giants (John McGraw)	1.00	.45	.13
☐ 22 1925 Pirates/Senators (Walter Johnson)	1.25	.55	.16
☐ 23 1926 Cardinals/Yankees (Alexander/Lazzeri)	1.00	.45	.13
☐ 24 1927 Yankees/Pirates	.75	.35	.09
☐ 25 1928 Yankees/Cardinals (Ruth/Gehrig)	2.00	.90	.25
☐ 26 1929 A's/Cubs	.75	.35	.09
☐ 27 1930 A's/Cardinals	.75	.35	.09
☐ 28 1931 Cardinals/A's (Pepper Martin)	.75	.35	.09
☐ 29 1932 Yankees/Cubs (Ruth/Gehrig)	2.00	.90	.25
☐ 30 1933 Giants/Senators (Mel Ott)	1.00	.45	.13
☐ 31 1934 Cardinals/Tigers	.75	.35	.09
☐ 32 1935 Tigers/Cubs (Gehringer/Bridges)	1.00	.45	.13
☐ 33 1936 Yankees/Giants	.75	.35	.09
☐ 34 1937 Yankees/Giants (Carl Hubbell)	1.00	.45	.13
☐ 35 1938 Yankees/Cubs (Lou Gehrig)	1.50	.65	.19
☐ 36 1939 Yankees/Reds	.75	.35	.09
☐ 37 1940 Reds/Tigers	.75	.35	.09
☐ 38 1941 Yankees/Dodgers	.75	.35	.09
☐ 39 1942 Cardinals/Yankees	.75	.35	.09
☐ 40 1943 Yankees/Cardinals	.75	.35	.09
☐ 41 1944 Cardinals/Browns	.75	.35	.09
☐ 42 1945 Tigers/Cubs (Hank Greenberg)	1.25	.55	.16
☐ 43 1946 Cardinals/Red Sox (Enos Slaughter)	1.00	.45	.13
☐ 44 1947 Yankees/Dodgers (Al Gionfriddo)	.75	.35	.09
☐ 45 1948 Indians/Braves	.75	.35	.09
☐ 46 1949 Yankees/Dodgers (Reynolds/Roe)	.75	.35	.09
☐ 47 1950 Yankees/Phillies	.75	.35	.09
☐ 48 1951 Yankees/Giants	.75	.35	.09
☐ 49 1952 Yankees/Dodgers (Mize/Snider)	1.50	.65	.19
☐ 50 1953 Yankees/Dodgers (Carl Erskine)	.75	.35	.09
☐ 51 1954 Giants/Indians (Johnny Antonelli)	.75	.35	.09
☐ 52 1955 Dodgers/Yankees (Johnny Podres)	.75	.35	.09
☐ 53 1956 Yankees/Dodgers	.75	.35	.09
☐ 54 1957 Braves/Yankees (Lew Burdette)	.75	.35	.09
☐ 55 1958 Yankees/Braves (Bob Turley)	.75	.35	.09
☐ 56 1959 Dodgers/White Sox (Chuck Essegian)	.75	.35	.09
☐ 57 1960 Pirates/Yankees	.75	.35	.09
☐ 58 1961 Yankees/Reds (Whitey Ford)	1.00	.45	.13
☐ 59 1962 Yankees/Giants	.75	.35	.09
☐ 60 1963 Dodgers/Yankees (Moose Skowron)	.75	.35	.09
☐ 61 1964 Cardinals/Yankees (Bobby Richardson)	1.00	.45	.13
☐ 62 1965 Dodgers/Twins	.75	.35	.09
☐ 63 1966 Orioles/Dodgers	.75	.35	.09
☐ 64 1967 Cardinals/Red Sox	.75	.35	.09
☐ 65 1968 Tigers/Cardinals	.75	.35	.09
☐ 66 1969 Mets/Orioles	1.00	.45	.13

1971 Fleer World Series

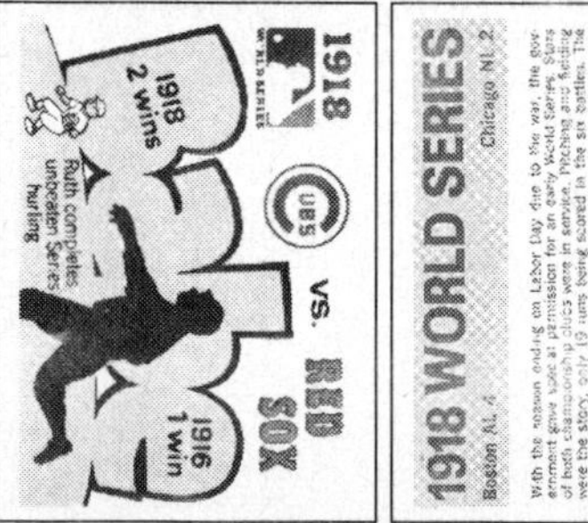

This set of 68 cards was distributed by Fleer. The cards are standard size, 2 1/2" by 3 1/2" and are in crude color on the front with brown printing on white card stock on the back. All the years since 1903 are represented in this set including 1904, when no World Series was played. That year is represented by a card explaining why there was no World Series that year. In the list below, the winning series team is listed first. The year of the Series on the obverse is inside a white square over the official World Series logo.

	NRMT-MT	EXC	G-VG
COMPLETE SET (68)	50.00	23.00	6.25
COMMON PLAYER (1-68)	.75	.35	.09
☐ 1 1903 Red Sox/Pirates (Cy Young)	1.25	.55	.16
☐ 2 1904 NO Series (John McGraw)	1.00	.45	.13
☐ 3 1905 Giants/A's (Mathewson, Bender, and McGinnity)	1.25	.55	.16
☐ 4 1906 White Sox/Cubs	.75	.35	.09
☐ 5 1907 Cubs/Tigers	.75	.35	.09
☐ 6 1908 Cubs/Tigers (Ty Cobb)	1.50	.65	.19
☐ 7 1909 Pirates/Tigers	.75	.35	.09
☐ 8 1910 A's/Cubs (Eddie Collins)	1.00	.45	.13
☐ 9 1911 A's/Giants (Home Run Baker)	1.00	.45	.13
☐ 10 1912 Red Sox/Giants	.75	.35	.09
☐ 11 1913 A's/Giants (Christy Mathewson)	1.25	.55	.16
☐ 12 1914 Braves/A's	.75	.35	.09
☐ 13 1915 Red Sox/Phillies (Grover Alexander)	1.00	.45	.13
☐ 14 1916 Red Sox/Dodgers	.75	.35	.09
☐ 15 1917 White Sox/Giants (Red Faber)	1.00	.45	.13
☐ 16 1918 Red Sox/Cubs (Babe Ruth)	2.00	.90	.25
☐ 17 1919 Reds/White Sox	2.00	.90	.25
☐ 18 1920 Indians/Dodgers	.75	.35	.09
☐ 19 1921 Giants/Yankees (Waite Hoyt)	1.00	.45	.13
☐ 20 1922 Giants/Yankees	.75	.35	.09
☐ 21 1923 Yankees/Giants (Herb Pennock)	1.00	.45	.13
☐ 22 1924 Senators/Giants (Walter Johnson)	1.25	.55	.16
☐ 23 1925 Pirates/Senators (Cuyler/W.Johnson)	1.00	.45	.13
☐ 24 1926 Cardinals/Yankees (Rogers Hornsby)	1.25	.55	.16
☐ 25 1927 Yankees/Pirates	.75	.35	.09
☐ 26 1928 Yankees/Cardinals (Lou Gehrig)	1.50	.65	.19
☐ 27 1929 A's/Cubs	.75	.35	.09
☐ 28 1930 A's/Cardinals (Jimmie Foxx)	1.25	.55	.16
☐ 29 1931 Cardinals/A's (Pepper Martin)	.75	.35	.09
☐ 30 1932 Yankees/Cubs (Babe Ruth)	2.00	.90	.25
☐ 31 1933 Giants/Senators (Carl Hubbell)	1.00	.45	.13
☐ 32 1934 Cardinals/Tigers	.75	.35	.09
☐ 33 1935 Tigers/Cubs (Mickey Cochrane)	1.00	.45	.13
☐ 34 1936 Yankees/Giants (Red Rolfe)	.75	.35	.09
☐ 35 1937 Yankees/Giants (Tony Lazzeri)	1.00	.45	.13
☐ 36 1938 Yankees/Cubs	.75	.35	.09
☐ 37 1939 Yankees/Reds	.75	.35	.09
☐ 38 1940 Reds/Tigers	.75	.35	.09
☐ 39 1941 Yankees/Dodgers	.75	.35	.09
☐ 40 1942 Cardinals/Yankees	.75	.35	.09
☐ 41 1943 Yankees/Cardinals	.75	.35	.09
☐ 42 1944 Cardinals/Browns	.75	.35	.09
☐ 43 1945 Tigers/Cubs (Hank Greenberg)	1.25	.55	.16
☐ 44 1946 Cardinals/Red Sox (Enos Slaughter)	1.00	.45	.13
☐ 45 1947 Yankees/Dodgers	.75	.35	.09
☐ 46 1948 Indians/Braves	.75	.35	.09
☐ 47 1949 Yankees/Dodgers (Preacher Roe)	.75	.35	.09
☐ 48 1950 Yankees/Phillies (Allie Reynolds)	.75	.35	.09
☐ 49 1951 Yankees/Giants (Ed Lopat)	.75	.35	.09
☐ 50 1952 Yankees/Dodgers (Johnny Mize)	1.00	.45	.13
☐ 51 1953 Yankees/Dodgers	.75	.35	.09
☐ 52 1954 Giants/Indians	.75	.35	.09
☐ 53 1955 Dodgers/Yankees (Duke Snider)	1.00	.45	.13
☐ 54 1956 Yankees/Dodgers	.75	.35	.09
☐ 55 1957 Braves/Yankees	.75	.35	.09
☐ 56 1958 Yankees/Braves (Hank Bauer)	.75	.35	.09
☐ 57 1959 Dodgers/Wh.Sox (Duke Snider)	1.00	.45	.13
☐ 58 1960 Pirates/Yankees	.75	.35	.09
☐ 59 1961 Yankees/Reds (Whitey Ford)	1.00	.45	.13
☐ 60 1962 Yankees/Giants	.75	.35	.09
☐ 61 1963 Dodgers/Yankees	.75	.35	.09
☐ 62 1964 Cardinals/Yankees	.75	.35	.09
☐ 63 1965 Dodgers/Twins	.75	.35	.09
☐ 64 1966 Orioles/Dodgers	.75	.35	.09
☐ 65 1967 Cardinals/Red Sox	.75	.35	.09
☐ 66 1968 Tigers/Cardinals	.75	.35	.09
☐ 67 1969 Mets/Orioles	.75	.35	.09
☐ 68 1970 Orioles/Reds	1.00	.45	.13

1972 Fleer Famous Feats

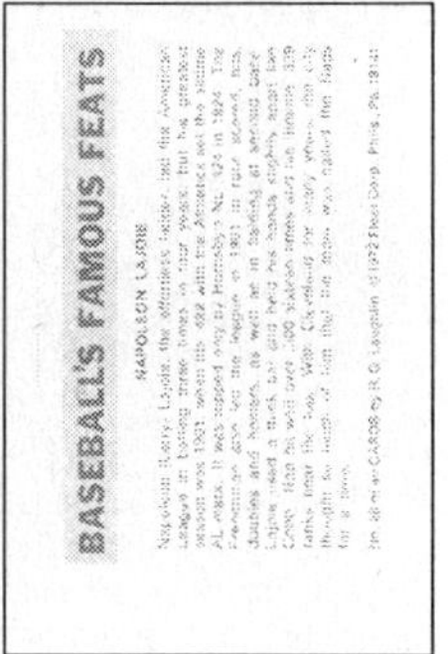

This Fleer set of 40 cards features the artwork of sports artist R.G. Laughlin. The set is titled "Baseball's Famous Feats." The cards are numbered both on the front and back. The backs are printed in light blue on white card stock. The cards measure approximately 2 1/2" by 4". This set was licensed by Major League Baseball.

	NRMT-MT	EXC	G-VG
COMPLETE SET (40)	25.00	11.50	3.10
COMMON PLAYER (1-40)	.50	.23	.06
☐ 1 Joe McGinnity	.60	.25	.08
☐ 2 Rogers Hornsby	1.25	.55	.16
☐ 3 Christy Mathewson	1.25	.55	.16
☐ 4 Dazzy Vance	.60	.25	.08
☐ 5 Lou Gehrig	2.00	.90	.25
☐ 6 Jim Bottomley	.60	.25	.08
☐ 7 Johnny Evers	.60	.25	.08
☐ 8 Walter Johnson	1.25	.55	.16
☐ 9 Hack Wilson	.75	.35	.09
☐ 10 Wilbert Robinson	.60	.25	.08
☐ 11 Cy Young	1.00	.45	.13
☐ 12 Rudy York	.50	.23	.06
☐ 13 Grover C. Alexander	.75	.35	.09
☐ 14 Fred Toney and Hippo Vaughan	.50	.23	.06
☐ 15 Ty Cobb	2.00	.90	.25
☐ 16 Jimmie Foxx	1.25	.55	.16
☐ 17 Hub Leonard	.50	.23	.06
☐ 18 Eddie Collins	.60	.25	.08
☐ 19 Joe Oeschger and Leon Cadore	.50	.23	.06
☐ 20 Babe Ruth	3.00	1.35	.40
☐ 21 Honus Wagner	1.25	.55	.16
☐ 22 Red Rolfe	.50	.23	.06
☐ 23 Ed Walsh	.60	.25	.08
☐ 24 Paul Waner	.60	.25	.08
☐ 25 Mel Ott	1.00	.45	.13
☐ 26 Eddie Plank	.75	.35	.09
☐ 27 Sam Crawford	.60	.25	.08
☐ 28 Napoleon Lajoie	1.00	.45	.13
☐ 29 Ed Reulbach	.50	.23	.06
☐ 30 Pinky Higgins	.50	.23	.06
☐ 31 Bill Klem	.60	.25	.08
☐ 32 Tris Speaker	1.00	.45	.13
☐ 33 Hank Gowdy	.50	.23	.06

☐ 34 Lefty O'Doul	.50	.23	.06
☐ 35 Lloyd Waner	.60	.25	.08
☐ 36 Chuck Klein	.60	.25	.08
☐ 37 Deacon Phillippe	.50	.23	.06
☐ 38 Ed Delahanty	.60	.25	.08
☐ 39 Jack Chesbro	.60	.25	.08
☐ 40 Willie Keeler	.75	.35	.09

1973 Fleer Wildest Days

Baseball's
WILDEST
DAYS
AND PLAYS
Thorpe Homered Into
Three States In One Game!
When "the world's greatest athlete," Jim Thorpe, was stripped of his 1912 Olympic medals because of a few pro baseball games at the Carlisle Indian School, manager John McGraw hurried to sign him for the Giants. McGraw knew he'd be a great attraction. It turned out he was a greater attraction than a baseball player. he did have one fantastic day on a spring exhibition tour, in a game in Texas, at the convergence of the Oklahoma and Arkansas borders. Big Jim homered into three states in the one game. His first drive cleared the leftfield fence into Oklahoma, his second the rightfield fence into Arkansas, and his third was an inside-the-park round-tripper—in Texas!
No. 3 of 42 CARDS by R. G. Laughlin
©1973 Fleer Corp., Phila., Pa. 19141

This Fleer set of 42 cards is titled "Baseball's Wildest Days and Plays" and features the artwork of sports artist R.G. Laughlin. The cards are numbered on the back. The backs are printed in dark red on white card stock. The cards measure approximately 2 1/2" by 4". This set was not licensed by Major League Baseball.

	NRMT-MT	EXC	G-VG
COMPLETE SET (42)	20.00	9.00	2.50
COMMON PLAYER (1-42)	.50	.23	.06
☐ 1 Cubs and Phillies Score 49 Runs in Game	.75	.35	.09
☐ 2 Frank Chance Five HBP's in One Day	.60	.25	.08
☐ 3 Jim Thorpe Homered into 3 States	2.00	.90	.25
☐ 4 Eddie Gaedel Midget in Majors	1.00	.45	.13
☐ 5 Most Tied Game Ever	.50	.23	.06
☐ 6 Seven Errors in One Inning	.50	.23	.06
☐ 7 Four 20-Game Winners But No Pennant	.50	.23	.06
☐ 8 Dummy Hoy Umpires Signal Strikes	1.00	.45	.13
☐ 9 Fourteeen Hits in One Inning	.50	.23	.06
☐ 10 Yankees Not Shut Out For Two Years	.50	.23	.06
☐ 11 Buck Weaver 17 Straight Fouls	1.00	.45	.13
☐ 12 George Sisler Greatest Thrill Was as a Pitcher	.60	.25	.08
☐ 13 Wrong-Way Baserunner	.50	.23	.06
☐ 14 Kiki Cuyler Sits Out Series	.60	.25	.08
☐ 15 Grounder Climbed Wall	.50	.23	.06
☐ 16 Gabby Street Washington Monument	.60	.25	.08
☐ 17 Mel Ott Ejected Twice	1.00	.45	.13
☐ 18 Shortest Pitching Career	.50	.23	.06
☐ 19 Three Homers in One Inning	.50	.23	.06
☐ 20 Bill Byron Singing Umpire	.50	.23	.06
☐ 21 Fred Clarke Walking Steal of Home	.60	.25	.08
☐ 22 Christy Mathewson 373rd Win Discovered	1.00	.45	.13
☐ 23 Hitting Through the Unglaub Arc	.50	.23	.06
☐ 24 Jim O'Rourke Catching at 52	.50	.23	.06
☐ 25 Fired for Striking Out in Series	.50	.23	.06
☐ 26 Eleven Run Inning on One Hit	.50	.23	.06
☐ 27 58 Innings in 3 Days	.50	.23	.06
☐ 28 Homer on Warm-Up Pitch	.50	.23	.06
☐ 29 Giants Win 26 Straight But Finish Fourth	.50	.23	.06
☐ 30 Player Who Stole First Base	.50	.23	.06
☐ 31 Ernie Shore Perfect Game in Relief	.60	.25	.08
☐ 32 Greatest Comeback	.50	.23	.06
☐ 33 All-Time Flash-In-The-Pan	.50	.23	.06
☐ 34 Pruett Fanned Ruth 19 out of 31	1.00	.45	.13
☐ 35 Fixed Batting Race Cobb/Lajoie	1.00	.45	.13
☐ 36 Wild-Pitch Rebound Play	.50	.23	.06
☐ 37 17 Straight Scoring Innings	.50	.23	.06
☐ 38 Wildest Opening Day	.50	.23	.06
☐ 39 Baseball's Strike One	.50	.23	.06
☐ 40 Opening Day No Hitter That Didn't Count	.50	.23	.06
☐ 41 Jimmie Foxx Six Straight Walks in One Game	1.00	.45	.13
☐ 42 Entire Team Hit and Scored in Inning	.75	.35	.09

1974 Fleer Baseball Firsts

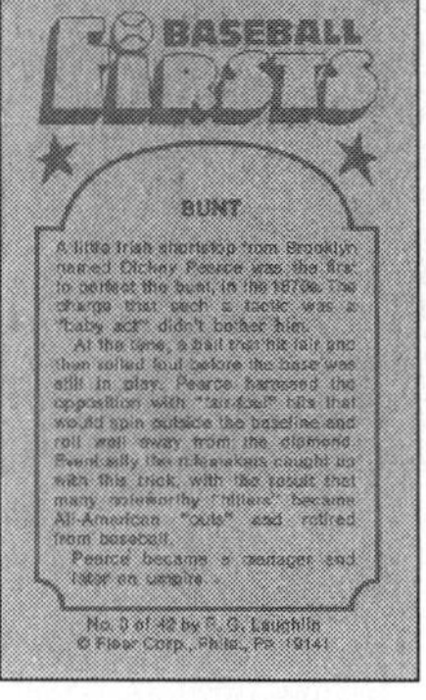

This Fleer set of 42 cards is titled "Baseball Firsts" and features the artwork of sports artist R.G. Laughlin. The cards are numbered on the back. The backs are printed in black on gray card stock. The cards measure approximately 2 1/2" by 4". This set was not licensed by Major League Baseball.

	NRMT-MT	EXC	G-VG
COMPLETE SET (42)	10.00	4.50	1.25
COMMON PLAYER (1-42)	.25	.11	.03
☐ 1 Slide	.50	.23	.06
☐ 2 Spring Training	.25	.11	.03
☐ 3 Bunt	.25	.11	.03
☐ 4 Catcher's Mask	.25	.11	.03
☐ 5 Four Straight Homers (Lou Gehrig)	1.50	.65	.19
☐ 6 Radio Broadcast	.25	.11	.03
☐ 7 Numbered Uniforms	.25	.11	.03
☐ 8 Shin Guards	.25	.11	.03
☐ 9 Players Association	.25	.11	.03
☐ 10 Knuckleball	.25	.11	.03
☐ 11 Player With Glasses	.25	.11	.03
☐ 12 Baseball Cards	2.00	.90	.25
☐ 13 Standardized Rules	.25	.11	.03

☐ 14 Grand Slam	.25	.11	.03
☐ 15 Player Fined	.25	.11	.03
☐ 16 Presidential Opener	.25	.11	.03
☐ 17 Player Transaction	.25	.11	.03
☐ 18 All-Star Game	.25	.11	.03
☐ 19 Scoreboard	.25	.11	.03
☐ 20 Cork Center Ball	.25	.11	.03
☐ 21 Scorekeeping	.25	.11	.03
☐ 22 Domed Stadium	.25	.11	.03
☐ 23 Batting Helmet	.25	.11	.03
☐ 24 Fatality	.25	.11	.03
☐ 25 Unassisted Triple Play	.25	.11	.03
☐ 26 Home Run At Night	.25	.11	.03
☐ 27 Black Major Leaguer	.50	.23	.06
☐ 28 Pinch Hitter	.25	.11	.03
☐ 29 Million-Dollar World Series	.25	.11	.03
☐ 30 Tarpaulin	.25	.11	.03
☐ 31 Team Initials	.25	.11	.03
☐ 32 Pennant Playoff	.25	.11	.03
☐ 33 Glove	.25	.11	.03
☐ 34 Curve Ball	.25	.11	.03
☐ 35 Night Game	.25	.11	.03
☐ 36 Admission Charge	.25	.11	.03
☐ 37 Farm System	.25	.11	.03
☐ 38 Telecast	.25	.11	.03
☐ 39 Commissioner	.25	.11	.03
☐ 40 .400 Hitter	.25	.11	.03
☐ 41 World Series	.25	.11	.03
☐ 42 Player Into Service	.50	.23	.06

1975 Fleer Pioneers

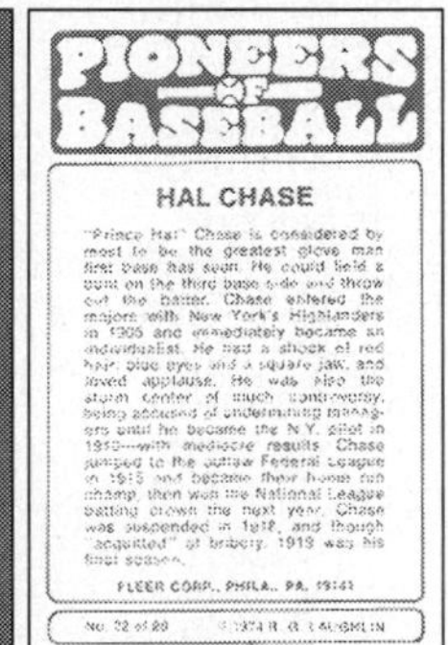

This 28-card set of brown and white sepia-toned photos of old timers is subtitled "Pioneers of Baseball. The graphics artwork was done by R.G. Laughlin. The cards measure approximately 2 1/2" by 4". The card backs are a narrative about the particular player. The cards are numbered on the back at the bottom.

	NRMT-MT	EXC	G-VG
COMPLETE SET (28)	15.00	6.75	1.90
COMMON PLAYER (1-28)	.50	.23	.06
☐ 1 Cap Anson	.75	.35	.09
☐ 2 Harry Wright	.60	.25	.08
☐ 3 Buck Ewing	.60	.25	.08
☐ 4 Al G. Spalding	.60	.25	.08
☐ 5 Old Hoss Radbourn	.60	.25	.08
☐ 6 Dan Brouthers	.60	.25	.08
☐ 7 Roger Bresnahan	.60	.25	.08
☐ 8 Mike Kelly	.60	.25	.08
☐ 9 Ned Hanlon	.50	.23	.06
☐ 10 Ed Delahanty	.60	.25	.08
☐ 11 Pud Galvin	.60	.25	.08
☐ 12 Amos Rusie	.60	.25	.08
☐ 13 Tommy McCarthy	.60	.25	.08
☐ 14 Ty Cobb	2.00	.90	.25
☐ 15 John McGraw	.60	.25	.08
☐ 16 Home Run Baker	.60	.25	.08
☐ 17 Johnny Evers	.60	.25	.08
☐ 18 Nap Lajoie	.75	.35	.09
☐ 19 Cy Young	1.00	.45	.13
☐ 20 Eddie Collins	.60	.25	.08
☐ 21 John Glasscock	.50	.23	.06
☐ 22 Hal Chase	.50	.23	.06
☐ 23 Mordecai Brown	.60	.25	.08
☐ 24 Jake Daubert	.50	.23	.06
☐ 25 Mike Donlin	.50	.23	.06
☐ 26 John Clarkson	.60	.25	.08
☐ 27 Buck Herzog	.50	.23	.06
☐ 28 Art Nehf	.75	.35	.09

1981 Fleer

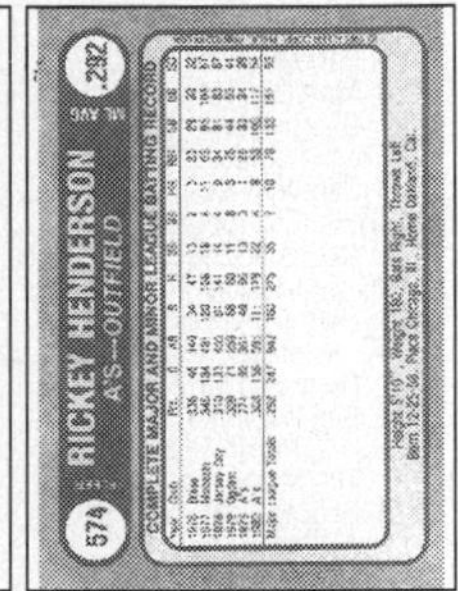

The cards in this 660-card set measure 2 1/2" by 3 1/2". This issue of cards marks Fleer's first entry into the current player baseball card market since 1963. Players from the same team are conveniently grouped together by number in the set. The teams are ordered (by 1980 standings) as follows: Philadelphia (1-27), Kansas City (28-50), Houston (51-78), New York Yankees (79-109), Los Angeles (110-141), Montreal (142-168), Baltimore (169-195), Cincinnati (196-220), Boston (221-241), Atlanta (242-267), California (268-290), Chicago Cubs (291-315), New York Mets (316-338), Chicago White Sox (339-350 and 352-359), Pittsburgh (360-386), Cleveland (387-408), Toronto (409-431), San Francisco (432-458), Detroit (459-483), San Diego (484-506), Milwaukee (507-527), St. Louis (528-550), Minnesota (551-571), Oakland (351 and 572-594), Seattle (595-616), and Texas (617-637). Cards 638-660 feature specials and checklists. The cards of pitchers in this set erroneously show a heading (on the card backs) of "Batting Record" over their career pitching statistics. There were three distinct printings: the two following the primary run were designed to correct numerous errors. The variations caused by these multiple printings are noted in the checklist below (P1, P2, or P3). The C. Nettles variation was corrected before the end of the first printing and thus is not included in the complete set consideration. The key Rookie Cards in this set are Harold Baines, Kirk Gibson, Jeff Reardon, and Fernando Valenzuela, whose first name was erroneously spelled Fernand on the card front.

	NRMT-MT	EXC	G-VG
COMPLETE SET (660)	60.00	27.00	7.50
COMMON PLAYER (1-660)	.10	.05	.01
☐ 1 Pete Rose UER (270 hits in '63, should be 170)	2.50	1.15	.30
☐ 2 Larry Bowa	.12	.05	.02
☐ 3 Manny Trillo	.10	.05	.01
☐ 4 Bob Boone	.12	.05	.02
☐ 5 Mike Schmidt (See also 640A)	3.00	1.35	.40
☐ 6A Steve Carlton P1 UER Pitcher of Year (See also 660A; Back "1066 Cardinals")	2.00	.90	.25
☐ 6B Steve Carlton P2 UER Pitcher of Year (Back "1066 Cardinals")	2.00	.90	.25
☐ 6C Steve Carlton P3	2.00	.90	.25

("1966 Cardinals")
☐ 7 Tug McGraw .12 .05 .02
(See 657A)
☐ 8 Larry Christenson .10 .05 .01
☐ 9 Bake McBride .10 .05 .01
☐ 10 Greg Luzinski .12 .05 .02
☐ 11 Ron Reed .10 .05 .01
☐ 12 Dickie Noles .10 .05 .01
☐ 13 Keith Moreland .12 .05 .02
☐ 14 Bob Walk .35 .16 .04
☐ 15 Lonnie Smith .15 .07 .02
☐ 16 Dick Ruthven .10 .05 .01
☐ 17 Sparky Lyle .12 .05 .02
☐ 18 Greg Gross .10 .05 .01
☐ 19 Garry Maddox .10 .05 .01
☐ 20 Nino Espinosa .10 .05 .01
☐ 21 George Vukovich .10 .05 .01
☐ 22 John Vukovich .10 .05 .01
☐ 23 Ramon Aviles .10 .05 .01
☐ 24A Ken Saucier P1 UER .10 .05 .01
(Name on back "Ken")
☐ 24B Ken Saucier P2 UER .10 .05 .01
(Name on back "Ken")
☐ 24C Kevin Saucier P3 .25 .11 .03
(Name on back "Kevin")
☐ 25 Randy Lerch .10 .05 .01
☐ 26 Del Unser .10 .05 .01
☐ 27 Tim McCarver .12 .05 .02
☐ 28 George Brett 4.00 1.80 .50
(See also 655A)
☐ 29 Willie Wilson .20 .09 .03
(See also 653A)
☐ 30 Paul Splittorff .10 .05 .01
☐ 31 Dan Quisenberry .25 .11 .03
☐ 32A Amos Otis P1 .15 .07 .02
(Batting Pose;
"Outfield";
32 on back)
☐ 32B Amos Otis P2 .15 .07 .02
"Series Starter"
(483 on back)
☐ 33 Steve Busby .10 .05 .01
☐ 34 U.L. Washington .10 .05 .01
☐ 35 Dave Chalk .10 .05 .01
☐ 36 Darrell Porter .10 .05 .01
☐ 37 Marty Pattin .10 .05 .01
☐ 38 Larry Gura .10 .05 .01
☐ 39 Renie Martin .10 .05 .01
☐ 40 Rich Gale .10 .05 .01
☐ 41A Hal McRae P1 .50 .23 .06
("Royals" on front
in black letters)
☐ 41B Hal McRae P2 .15 .07 .02
("Royals" on front
in blue letters)
☐ 42 Dennis Leonard .10 .05 .01
☐ 43 Willie Aikens .10 .05 .01
☐ 44 Frank White .12 .05 .02
☐ 45 Clint Hurdle .10 .05 .01
☐ 46 John Wathan .10 .05 .01
☐ 47 Pete LaCock .10 .05 .01
☐ 48 Rance Mulliniks .10 .05 .01
☐ 49 Jeff Twitty .10 .05 .01
☐ 50 Jamie Quirk .10 .05 .01
☐ 51 Art Howe .12 .05 .02
☐ 52 Ken Forsch .10 .05 .01
☐ 53 Vern Ruhle .10 .05 .01
☐ 54 Joe Niekro .12 .05 .02
☐ 55 Frank LaCorte .10 .05 .01
☐ 56 J.R. Richard .12 .05 .02
☐ 57 Nolan Ryan 8.00 3.60 1.00
☐ 58 Enos Cabell .10 .05 .01
☐ 59 Cesar Cedeno .12 .05 .02
☐ 60 Jose Cruz .12 .05 .02
☐ 61 Bill Virdon MG .10 .05 .01
☐ 62 Terry Puhl .10 .05 .01
☐ 63 Joaquin Andujar .12 .05 .02
☐ 64 Alan Ashby .10 .05 .01
☐ 65 Joe Sambito .10 .05 .01
☐ 66 Denny Walling .10 .05 .01
☐ 67 Jeff Leonard .12 .05 .02
☐ 68 Luis Pujols .10 .05 .01
☐ 69 Bruce Bochy .10 .05 .01
☐ 70 Rafael Landestoy .10 .05 .01
☐ 71 Dave Smith .25 .11 .03
☐ 72 Danny Heep .10 .05 .01
☐ 73 Julio Gonzalez .10 .05 .01
☐ 74 Craig Reynolds .10 .05 .01
☐ 75 Gary Woods .10 .05 .01
☐ 76 Dave Bergman .10 .05 .01
☐ 77 Randy Niemann .10 .05 .01
☐ 78 Joe Morgan 1.00 .45 .13
☐ 79 Reggie Jackson 2.50 1.15 .30
(See also 650A)

☐ 80 Bucky Dent .12 .05 .02
☐ 81 Tommy John .20 .09 .03
☐ 82 Luis Tiant .12 .05 .02
☐ 83 Rick Cerone .10 .05 .01
☐ 84 Dick Howser MG .12 .05 .02
☐ 85 Lou Piniella .12 .05 .02
☐ 86 Ron Davis .10 .05 .01
☐ 87A Craig Nettles P1 ERR 10.00 4.50 1.25
(Name on back
misspelled "Craig")
☐ 87B Graig Nettles P2 COR .25 .11 .03
("Graig")
☐ 88 Ron Guidry .25 .11 .03
☐ 89 Rich Gossage .20 .09 .03
☐ 90 Rudy May .10 .05 .01
☐ 91 Gaylord Perry .60 .25 .08
☐ 92 Eric Soderholm .10 .05 .01
☐ 93 Bob Watson .12 .05 .02
☐ 94 Bobby Murcer .12 .05 .02
☐ 95 Bobby Brown .10 .05 .01
☐ 96 Jim Spencer .10 .05 .01
☐ 97 Tom Underwood .10 .05 .01
☐ 98 Oscar Gamble .10 .05 .01
☐ 99 Johnny Oates .10 .05 .01
☐ 100 Fred Stanley .10 .05 .01
☐ 101 Ruppert Jones .10 .05 .01
☐ 102 Dennis Werth .10 .05 .01
☐ 103 Joe Lefebvre .10 .05 .01
☐ 104 Brian Doyle .10 .05 .01
☐ 105 Aurelio Rodriguez .10 .05 .01
☐ 106 Doug Bird .10 .05 .01
☐ 107 Mike Griffin .10 .05 .01
☐ 108 Tim Lollar .10 .05 .01
☐ 109 Willie Randolph .12 .05 .02
☐ 110 Steve Garvey .75 .35 .09
☐ 111 Reggie Smith .12 .05 .02
☐ 112 Don Sutton .60 .25 .08
☐ 113 Burt Hooton .10 .05 .01
☐ 114A Dave Lopes P1 .50 .23 .06
(Small hand on back)
☐ 114B Dave Lopes P2 .12 .05 .02
(No hand)
☐ 115 Dusty Baker .12 .05 .02
☐ 116 Tom Lasorda MG .12 .05 .02
☐ 117 Bill Russell .12 .05 .02
☐ 118 Jerry Reuss UER .12 .05 .02
("Home:" omitted)
☐ 119 Terry Forster .10 .05 .01
☐ 120A Bob Welch P1 .40 .18 .05
(Name on back
is "Bob")
☐ 120B Bob Welch P2 .40 .18 .05
(Name on back
is "Robert")
☐ 121 Don Stanhouse .10 .05 .01
☐ 122 Rick Monday .12 .05 .02
☐ 123 Derrel Thomas .10 .05 .01
☐ 124 Joe Ferguson .10 .05 .01
☐ 125 Rick Sutcliffe .35 .16 .04
☐ 126A Ron Cey P1 .50 .23 .06
(Small hand on back)
☐ 126B Ron Cey P2 .12 .05 .02
(No hand)
☐ 127 Dave Goltz .10 .05 .01
☐ 128 Jay Johnstone .12 .05 .02
☐ 129 Steve Yeager .10 .05 .01
☐ 130 Gary Weiss .10 .05 .01
☐ 131 Mike Scioscia .75 .35 .09
☐ 132 Vic Davalillo .10 .05 .01
☐ 133 Doug Rau .10 .05 .01
☐ 134 Pepe Frias .10 .05 .01
☐ 135 Mickey Hatcher .10 .05 .01
☐ 136 Steve Howe .12 .05 .02
☐ 137 Robert Castillo .10 .05 .01
☐ 138 Gary Thomasson .10 .05 .01
☐ 139 Rudy Law .10 .05 .01
☐ 140 Fernand Valenzuela UER 2.00 .90 .25
(Sic, Fernando)
☐ 141 Manny Mota .12 .05 .02
☐ 142 Gary Carter 1.00 .45 .13
☐ 143 Steve Rogers .10 .05 .01
☐ 144 Warren Cromartie .10 .05 .01
☐ 145 Andre Dawson 2.00 .90 .25
☐ 146 Larry Parrish .10 .05 .01
☐ 147 Rowland Office .10 .05 .01
☐ 148 Ellis Valentine .10 .05 .01
☐ 149 Dick Williams MG .10 .05 .01
☐ 150 Bill Gullickson 1.00 .45 .13
☐ 151 Elias Sosa .10 .05 .01
☐ 152 John Tamargo .10 .05 .01
☐ 153 Chris Speier .10 .05 .01
☐ 154 Ron LeFlore .12 .05 .02
☐ 155 Rodney Scott .10 .05 .01

☐ 156 Stan Bahnsen	.10	.05	.01
☐ 157 Bill Lee	.10	.05	.01
☐ 158 Fred Norman	.10	.05	.01
☐ 159 Woodie Fryman	.10	.05	.01
☐ 160 David Palmer	.10	.05	.01
☐ 161 Jerry White	.10	.05	.01
☐ 162 Roberto Ramos	.10	.05	.01
☐ 163 John D'Acquisto	.10	.05	.01
☐ 164 Tommy Hutton	.10	.05	.01
☐ 165 Charlie Lea	.10	.05	.01
☐ 166 Scott Sanderson	.12	.05	.02
☐ 167 Ken Macha	.10	.05	.01
☐ 168 Tony Bernazard	.10	.05	.01
☐ 169 Jim Palmer	1.75	.80	.22
☐ 170 Steve Stone	.12	.05	.02
☐ 171 Mike Flanagan	.12	.05	.02
☐ 172 Al Bumbry	.10	.05	.01
☐ 173 Doug DeCinces	.12	.05	.02
☐ 174 Scott McGregor	.10	.05	.01
☐ 175 Mark Belanger	.12	.05	.02
☐ 176 Tim Stoddard	.10	.05	.01
☐ 177A Rick Dempsey P1 (Small hand on front)	.50	.23	.06
☐ 177B Rick Dempsey P2 (No hand)	.12	.05	.02
☐ 178 Earl Weaver MG	.12	.05	.02
☐ 179 Tippy Martinez	.12	.05	.02
☐ 180 Dennis Martinez	.35	.16	.04
☐ 181 Sammy Stewart	.10	.05	.01
☐ 182 Rich Dauer	.10	.05	.01
☐ 183 Lee May	.12	.05	.02
☐ 184 Eddie Murray	3.00	1.35	.40
☐ 185 Benny Ayala	.10	.05	.01
☐ 186 John Lowenstein	.10	.05	.01
☐ 187 Gary Roenicke	.10	.05	.01
☐ 188 Ken Singleton	.12	.05	.02
☐ 189 Dan Graham	.10	.05	.01
☐ 190 Terry Crowley	.10	.05	.01
☐ 191 Kiko Garcia	.10	.05	.01
☐ 192 Dave Ford	.10	.05	.01
☐ 193 Mark Corey	.10	.05	.01
☐ 194 Lenn Sakata	.10	.05	.01
☐ 195 Doug DeCinces	.12	.05	.02
☐ 196 Johnny Bench	2.00	.90	.25
☐ 197 Dave Concepcion	.15	.07	.02
☐ 198 Ray Knight	.12	.05	.02
☐ 199 Ken Griffey	.35	.16	.04
☐ 200 Tom Seaver	2.00	.90	.25
☐ 201 Dave Collins	.10	.05	.01
☐ 202A George Foster P1 Slugger (Number on back 216)	.20	.09	.03
☐ 202B George Foster P2 Slugger (Number on back 202)	.20	.09	.03
☐ 203 Junior Kennedy	.10	.05	.01
☐ 204 Frank Pastore	.10	.05	.01
☐ 205 Dan Driessen	.10	.05	.01
☐ 206 Hector Cruz	.10	.05	.01
☐ 207 Paul Moskau	.10	.05	.01
☐ 208 Charlie Leibrandt	.90	.40	.11
☐ 209 Harry Spilman	.10	.05	.01
☐ 210 Joe Price	.10	.05	.01
☐ 211 Tom Hume	.10	.05	.01
☐ 212 Joe Nolan	.10	.05	.01
☐ 213 Doug Bair	.10	.05	.01
☐ 214 Mario Soto	.10	.05	.01
☐ 215A Bill Bonham P1 (Small hand on back)	.50	.23	.06
☐ 215B Bill Bonham P2 (No hand)	.10	.05	.01
☐ 216 George Foster (See 202)	.20	.09	.03
☐ 217 Paul Householder	.10	.05	.01
☐ 218 Ron Oester	.10	.05	.01
☐ 219 Sam Mejias	.10	.05	.01
☐ 220 Sheldon Burnside	.10	.05	.01
☐ 221 Carl Yastrzemski	2.00	.90	.25
☐ 222 Jim Rice	.30	.14	.04
☐ 223 Fred Lynn	.12	.05	.02
☐ 224 Carlton Fisk	2.00	.90	.25
☐ 225 Rick Burleson	.10	.05	.01
☐ 226 Dennis Eckersley	1.75	.80	.22
☐ 227 Butch Hobson	.12	.05	.02
☐ 228 Tom Burgmeier	.10	.05	.01
☐ 229 Garry Hancock	.10	.05	.01
☐ 230 Don Zimmer MG	.10	.05	.01
☐ 231 Steve Renko	.10	.05	.01
☐ 232 Dwight Evans	.35	.16	.04
☐ 233 Mike Torrez	.10	.05	.01
☐ 234 Bob Stanley	.10	.05	.01
☐ 235 Jim Dwyer	.10	.05	.01
☐ 236 Dave Stapleton	.10	.05	.01
☐ 237 Glenn Hoffman	.10	.05	.01
☐ 238 Jerry Remy	.10	.05	.01
☐ 239 Dick Drago	.10	.05	.01
☐ 240 Bill Campbell	.10	.05	.01
☐ 241 Tony Perez	.40	.18	.05
☐ 242 Phil Niekro	.60	.25	.08
☐ 243 Dale Murphy	1.00	.45	.13
☐ 244 Bob Horner	.12	.05	.02
☐ 245 Jeff Burroughs	.10	.05	.01
☐ 246 Rick Camp	.10	.05	.01
☐ 247 Bobby Cox MG	.10	.05	.01
☐ 248 Bruce Benedict	.10	.05	.01
☐ 249 Gene Garber	.10	.05	.01
☐ 250 Jerry Royster	.10	.05	.01
☐ 251A Gary Matthews P1 (Small hand on back)	.50	.23	.06
☐ 251B Gary Matthews P2 (No hand)	.12	.05	.02
☐ 252 Chris Chambliss	.12	.05	.02
☐ 253 Luis Gomez	.10	.05	.01
☐ 254 Bill Nahorodny	.10	.05	.01
☐ 255 Doyle Alexander	.10	.05	.01
☐ 256 Brian Asselstine	.10	.05	.01
☐ 257 Biff Pocoroba	.10	.05	.01
☐ 258 Mike Lum	.10	.05	.01
☐ 259 Charlie Spikes	.10	.05	.01
☐ 260 Glenn Hubbard	.10	.05	.01
☐ 261 Tommy Boggs	.10	.05	.01
☐ 262 Al Hrabosky	.10	.05	.01
☐ 263 Rick Matula	.10	.05	.01
☐ 264 Preston Hanna	.10	.05	.01
☐ 265 Larry Bradford	.10	.05	.01
☐ 266 Rafael Ramirez	.20	.09	.03
☐ 267 Larry McWilliams	.10	.05	.01
☐ 268 Rod Carew	2.00	.90	.25
☐ 269 Bobby Grich	.12	.05	.02
☐ 270 Carney Lansford	.30	.14	.04
☐ 271 Don Baylor	.12	.05	.02
☐ 272 Joe Rudi	.12	.05	.02
☐ 273 Dan Ford	.10	.05	.01
☐ 274 Jim Fregosi MG	.10	.05	.01
☐ 275 Dave Frost	.10	.05	.01
☐ 276 Frank Tanana	.12	.05	.02
☐ 277 Dickie Thon	.12	.05	.02
☐ 278 Jason Thompson	.10	.05	.01
☐ 279 Rick Miller	.10	.05	.01
☐ 280 Bert Campaneris	.12	.05	.02
☐ 281 Tom Donohue	.10	.05	.01
☐ 282 Brian Downing	.12	.05	.02
☐ 283 Fred Patek	.10	.05	.01
☐ 284 Bruce Kison	.10	.05	.01
☐ 285 Dave LaRoche	.10	.05	.01
☐ 286 Don Aase	.10	.05	.01
☐ 287 Jim Barr	.10	.05	.01
☐ 288 Alfredo Martinez	.10	.05	.01
☐ 289 Larry Harlow	.10	.05	.01
☐ 290 Andy Hassler	.10	.05	.01
☐ 291 Dave Kingman	.12	.05	.02
☐ 292 Bill Buckner	.12	.05	.02
☐ 293 Rick Reuschel	.12	.05	.02
☐ 294 Bruce Sutter	.20	.09	.03
☐ 295 Jerry Martin	.10	.05	.01
☐ 296 Scot Thompson	.10	.05	.01
☐ 297 Ivan DeJesus	.10	.05	.01
☐ 298 Steve Dillard	.10	.05	.01
☐ 299 Dick Tidrow	.10	.05	.01
☐ 300 Randy Martz	.10	.05	.01
☐ 301 Lenny Randle	.10	.05	.01
☐ 302 Lynn McGlothen	.10	.05	.01
☐ 303 Cliff Johnson	.10	.05	.01
☐ 304 Tim Blackwell	.10	.05	.01
☐ 305 Dennis Lamp	.10	.05	.01
☐ 306 Bill Caudill	.10	.05	.01
☐ 307 Carlos Lezcano	.10	.05	.01
☐ 308 Jim Tracy	.10	.05	.01
☐ 309 Doug Capilla UER (Cubs on front but Braves on back)	.10	.05	.01
☐ 310 Willie Hernandez	.12	.05	.02
☐ 311 Mike Vail	.10	.05	.01
☐ 312 Mike Krukow	.10	.05	.01
☐ 313 Barry Foote	.10	.05	.01
☐ 314 Larry Biittner	.10	.05	.01
☐ 315 Mike Tyson	.10	.05	.01
☐ 316 Lee Mazzilli	.10	.05	.01
☐ 317 John Stearns	.10	.05	.01
☐ 318 Alex Trevino	.10	.05	.01
☐ 319 Craig Swan	.10	.05	.01
☐ 320 Frank Taveras	.10	.05	.01
☐ 321 Steve Henderson	.10	.05	.01
☐ 322 Neil Allen	.10	.05	.01
☐ 323 Mark Bomback	.10	.05	.01
☐ 324 Mike Jorgensen	.10	.05	.01

□ 325 Joe Torre MG .12 .05 .02
□ 326 Elliott Maddox .10 .05 .01
□ 327 Pete Falcone .10 .05 .01
□ 328 Ray Burris .10 .05 .01
□ 329 Claudell Washington .10 .05 .01
□ 330 Doug Flynn .10 .05 .01
□ 331 Joel Youngblood .10 .05 .01
□ 332 Bill Almon .10 .05 .01
□ 333 Tom Hausman .10 .05 .01
□ 334 Pat Zachry .10 .05 .01
□ 335 Jeff Reardon 6.00 2.70 .75
□ 336 Wally Backman .15 .07 .02
□ 337 Dan Norman .10 .05 .01
□ 338 Jerry Morales .10 .05 .01
□ 339 Ed Farmer .10 .05 .01
□ 340 Bob Molinaro .10 .05 .01
□ 341 Todd Cruz .10 .05 .01
□ 342A Britt Burns P1 .50 .23 .06
(Small hand on front)
□ 342B Britt Burns P2 .12 .05 .02
(No hand)
□ 343 Kevin Bell .10 .05 .01
□ 344 Tony LaRussa MG .12 .05 .02
□ 345 Steve Trout .10 .05 .01
□ 346 Harold Baines 2.50 1.15 .30
□ 347 Richard Wortham .10 .05 .01
□ 348 Wayne Nordhagen .10 .05 .01
□ 349 Mike Squires .10 .05 .01
□ 350 Lamar Johnson .10 .05 .01
□ 351 Rickey Henderson 8.00 3.60 1.00
(Most Stolen Bases AL)
□ 352 Francisco Barrios .10 .05 .01
□ 353 Thad Bosley .10 .05 .01
□ 354 Chet Lemon .10 .05 .01
□ 355 Bruce Kimm .10 .05 .01
□ 356 Richard Dotson .12 .05 .02
□ 357 Jim Morrison .10 .05 .01
□ 358 Mike Proly .10 .05 .01
□ 359 Greg Pryor .10 .05 .01
□ 360 Dave Parker .40 .18 .05
□ 361 Omar Moreno .10 .05 .01
□ 362A Kent Tekulve P1 ERR .15 .07 .02
(Back "1071 Waterbury"
and "1078 Pirates")
□ 362B Kent Tekulve P2 COR .12 .05 .02
("1971 Waterbury" and
"1978 Pirates")
□ 363 Willie Stargell 1.00 .45 .13
□ 364 Phil Garner .12 .05 .02
□ 365 Ed Ott .10 .05 .01
□ 366 Don Robinson .10 .05 .01
□ 367 Chuck Tanner MG .10 .05 .01
□ 368 Jim Rooker .10 .05 .01
□ 369 Dale Berra .10 .05 .01
□ 370 Jim Bibby .10 .05 .01
□ 371 Steve Nicosia .10 .05 .01
□ 372 Mike Easler .10 .05 .01
□ 373 Bill Robinson .12 .05 .02
□ 374 Lee Lacy .10 .05 .01
□ 375 John Candelaria .12 .05 .02
□ 376 Manny Sanguillen .12 .05 .02
□ 377 Rick Rhoden .10 .05 .01
□ 378 Grant Jackson .10 .05 .01
□ 379 Tim Foli .10 .05 .01
□ 380 Rod Scurry .10 .05 .01
□ 381 Bill Madlock .12 .05 .02
□ 382A Kurt Bevacqua P1 ERR .25 .11 .03
(P on cap backwards)
□ 382B Kurt Bevacqua P2 COR .10 .05 .01
□ 383 Bert Blyleven .40 .18 .05
□ 384 Eddie Solomon .10 .05 .01
□ 385 Enrique Romo .10 .05 .01
□ 386 John Milner .10 .05 .01
□ 387 Mike Hargrove .12 .05 .02
□ 388 Jorge Orta .10 .05 .01
□ 389 Toby Harrah .12 .05 .02
□ 390 Tom Veryzer .10 .05 .01
□ 391 Miguel Dilone .10 .05 .01
□ 392 Dan Spillner .10 .05 .01
□ 393 Jack Brohamer .10 .05 .01
□ 394 Wayne Garland .10 .05 .01
□ 395 Sid Monge .10 .05 .01
□ 396 Rick Waits .10 .05 .01
□ 397 Joe Charboneau .12 .05 .02
□ 398 Gary Alexander .10 .05 .01
□ 399 Jerry Dybzinski .10 .05 .01
□ 400 Mike Stanton .10 .05 .01
□ 401 Mike Paxton .10 .05 .01
□ 402 Gary Gray .10 .05 .01
□ 403 Rick Manning .10 .05 .01
□ 404 Bo Diaz .10 .05 .01
□ 405 Ron Hassey .10 .05 .01
□ 406 Ross Grimsley .10 .05 .01
□ 407 Victor Cruz .10 .05 .01
□ 408 Len Barker .10 .05 .01
□ 409 Bob Bailor .10 .05 .01
□ 410 Otto Velez .10 .05 .01
□ 411 Ernie Whitt .10 .05 .01
□ 412 Jim Clancy .10 .05 .01
□ 413 Barry Bonnell .10 .05 .01
□ 414 Dave Stieb .35 .16 .04
□ 415 Damaso Garcia .12 .05 .02
□ 416 John Mayberry .10 .05 .01
□ 417 Roy Howell .10 .05 .01
□ 418 Danny Ainge 2.00 .90 .25
□ 419A Jesse Jefferson P1 ERR .10 .05 .01
(Back says Pirates)
□ 419B Jesse Jefferson P2 ERR .10 .05 .01
(Back says Pirates)
□ 419C Jesse Jefferson P3 COR .25 .11 .03
(Back says Blue Jays)
□ 420 Joey McLaughlin .10 .05 .01
□ 421 Lloyd Moseby .20 .09 .03
□ 422 Alvis Woods .10 .05 .01
□ 423 Garth Iorg .10 .05 .01
□ 424 Doug Ault .10 .05 .01
□ 425 Ken Schrom .10 .05 .01
□ 426 Mike Willis .10 .05 .01
□ 427 Steve Braun .10 .05 .01
□ 428 Bob Davis .10 .05 .01
□ 429 Jerry Garvin .10 .05 .01
□ 430 Alfredo Griffin .10 .05 .01
□ 431 Bob Mattick MG .10 .05 .01
□ 432 Vida Blue .12 .05 .02
□ 433 Jack Clark .25 .11 .03
□ 434 Willie McCovey 1.00 .45 .13
□ 435 Mike Ivie .10 .05 .01
□ 436A Darrel Evans P1 ERR .25 .11 .03
(Name on front
"Darrel")
□ 436B Darrell Evans P2 COR .15 .07 .02
(Name on front
"Darrell")
□ 437 Terry Whitfield .10 .05 .01
□ 438 Rennie Stennett .10 .05 .01
□ 439 John Montefusco .10 .05 .01
□ 440 Jim Wohlford .10 .05 .01
□ 441 Bill North .10 .05 .01
□ 442 Milt May .10 .05 .01
□ 443 Max Venable .10 .05 .01
□ 444 Ed Whitson .12 .05 .02
□ 445 Al Holland .10 .05 .01
□ 446 Randy Moffitt .10 .05 .01
□ 447 Bob Knepper .10 .05 .01
□ 448 Gary Lavelle .10 .05 .01
□ 449 Greg Minton .10 .05 .01
□ 450 Johnnie LeMaster .10 .05 .01
□ 451 Larry Herndon .10 .05 .01
□ 452 Rich Murray .10 .05 .01
□ 453 Joe Pettini .10 .05 .01
□ 454 Allen Ripley .10 .05 .01
□ 455 Dennis Littlejohn .10 .05 .01
□ 456 Tom Griffin .10 .05 .01
□ 457 Alan Hargesheimer .10 .05 .01
□ 458 Joe Strain .10 .05 .01
□ 459 Steve Kemp .10 .05 .01
□ 460 Sparky Anderson MG .12 .05 .02
□ 461 Alan Trammell .90 .40 .11
□ 462 Mark Fidrych .12 .05 .02
□ 463 Lou Whitaker .90 .40 .11
□ 464 Dave Rozema .10 .05 .01
□ 465 Milt Wilcox .10 .05 .01
□ 466 Champ Summers .10 .05 .01
□ 467 Lance Parrish .25 .11 .03
□ 468 Dan Petry .12 .05 .02
□ 469 Pat Underwood .10 .05 .01
□ 470 Rick Peters .10 .05 .01
□ 471 Al Cowens .10 .05 .01
□ 472 John Wockenfuss .10 .05 .01
□ 473 Tom Brookens .10 .05 .01
□ 474 Richie Hebner .10 .05 .01
□ 475 Jack Morris 2.00 .90 .25
□ 476 Jim Lentine .10 .05 .01
□ 477 Bruce Robbins .10 .05 .01
□ 478 Mark Wagner .10 .05 .01
□ 479 Tim Corcoran .10 .05 .01
□ 480A Stan Papi P1 ERR .15 .07 .02
(Front as Pitcher)
□ 480B Stan Papi P2 COR .10 .05 .01
(Front as Shortstop)
□ 481 Kirk Gibson 2.00 .90 .25
□ 482 Dan Schatzeder .10 .05 .01
□ 483A Amos Otis P1 .15 .07 .02
(See card 32)
□ 483B Amos Otis P2 .15 .07 .02
(See card 32)

☐ 484	Dave Winfield	3.00	1.35	.40
☐ 485	Rollie Fingers	1.00	.45	.13
☐ 486	Gene Richards	.10	.05	.01
☐ 487	Randy Jones	.10	.05	.01
☐ 488	Ozzie Smith	3.00	1.35	.40
☐ 489	Gene Tenace	.10	.05	.01
☐ 490	Bill Fahey	.10	.05	.01
☐ 491	John Curtis	.10	.05	.01
☐ 492	Dave Cash	.10	.05	.01
☐ 493A	Tim Flannery P1 ERR (Batting right)	.15	.07	.02
☐ 493B	Tim Flannery P2 COR (Batting left)	.10	.05	.01
☐ 494	Jerry Mumphrey	.10	.05	.01
☐ 495	Bob Shirley	.10	.05	.01
☐ 496	Steve Mura	.10	.05	.01
☐ 497	Eric Rasmussen	.10	.05	.01
☐ 498	Broderick Perkins	.10	.05	.01
☐ 499	Barry Evans	.10	.05	.01
☐ 500	Chuck Baker	.10	.05	.01
☐ 501	Luis Salazar	.20	.09	.03
☐ 502	Gary Lucas	.10	.05	.01
☐ 503	Mike Armstrong	.10	.05	.01
☐ 504	Jerry Turner	.10	.05	.01
☐ 505	Dennis Kinney	.10	.05	.01
☐ 506	Willie Montanez UER (Misspelled Willy on card front)	.10	.05	.01
☐ 507	Gorman Thomas	.12	.05	.02
☐ 508	Ben Oglivie	.12	.05	.02
☐ 509	Larry Hisle	.10	.05	.01
☐ 510	Sal Bando	.12	.05	.02
☐ 511	Robin Yount	4.00	1.80	.50
☐ 512	Mike Caldwell	.10	.05	.01
☐ 513	Sixto Lezcano	.10	.05	.01
☐ 514A	Bill Travers P1 ERR ("Jerry Augustine" with Augustine back)	.15	.07	.02
☐ 514B	Bill Travers P2 COR	.10	.05	.01
☐ 515	Paul Molitor	1.25	.55	.16
☐ 516	Moose Haas	.10	.05	.01
☐ 517	Bill Castro	.10	.05	.01
☐ 518	Jim Slaton	.10	.05	.01
☐ 519	Lary Sorensen	.10	.05	.01
☐ 520	Bob McClure	.10	.05	.01
☐ 521	Charlie Moore	.10	.05	.01
☐ 522	Jim Gantner	.12	.05	.02
☐ 523	Reggie Cleveland	.10	.05	.01
☐ 524	Don Money	.10	.05	.01
☐ 525	Bill Travers	.10	.05	.01
☐ 526	Buck Martinez	.10	.05	.01
☐ 527	Dick Davis	.10	.05	.01
☐ 528	Ted Simmons	.20	.09	.03
☐ 529	Garry Templeton	.12	.05	.02
☐ 530	Ken Reitz	.10	.05	.01
☐ 531	Tony Scott	.10	.05	.01
☐ 532	Ken Oberkfell	.10	.05	.01
☐ 533	Bob Sykes	.10	.05	.01
☐ 534	Keith Smith	.10	.05	.01
☐ 535	John Littlefield	.10	.05	.01
☐ 536	Jim Kaat	.20	.09	.03
☐ 537	Bob Forsch	.10	.05	.01
☐ 538	Mike Phillips	.10	.05	.01
☐ 539	Terry Landrum	.10	.05	.01
☐ 540	Leon Durham	.12	.05	.02
☐ 541	Terry Kennedy	.12	.05	.02
☐ 542	George Hendrick	.12	.05	.02
☐ 543	Dane Iorg	.10	.05	.01
☐ 544	Mark Littell	.10	.05	.01
☐ 545	Keith Hernandez	.30	.14	.04
☐ 546	Silvio Martinez	.10	.05	.01
☐ 547A	Don Hood P1 ERR ("Pete Vuckovich" with Vuckovich back)	.15	.07	.02
☐ 547B	Don Hood P2 COR	.10	.05	.01
☐ 548	Bobby Bonds	.12	.05	.02
☐ 549	Mike Ramsey	.10	.05	.01
☐ 550	Tom Herr	.12	.05	.02
☐ 551	Roy Smalley	.10	.05	.01
☐ 552	Jerry Koosman	.12	.05	.02
☐ 553	Ken Landreaux	.10	.05	.01
☐ 554	John Castino	.10	.05	.01
☐ 555	Doug Corbett	.10	.05	.01
☐ 556	Bombo Rivera	.10	.05	.01
☐ 557	Ron Jackson	.10	.05	.01
☐ 558	Butch Wynegar	.10	.05	.01
☐ 559	Hosken Powell	.10	.05	.01
☐ 560	Pete Redfern	.10	.05	.01
☐ 561	Roger Erickson	.10	.05	.01
☐ 562	Glenn Adams	.10	.05	.01
☐ 563	Rick Sofield	.10	.05	.01
☐ 564	Geoff Zahn	.10	.05	.01
☐ 565	Pete Mackanin	.10	.05	.01
☐ 566	Mike Cubbage	.10	.05	.01
☐ 567	Darrell Jackson	.10	.05	.01
☐ 568	Dave Edwards	.10	.05	.01
☐ 569	Rob Wilfong	.10	.05	.01
☐ 570	Sal Butera	.10	.05	.01
☐ 571	Jose Morales	.10	.05	.01
☐ 572	Rick Langford	.10	.05	.01
☐ 573	Mike Norris	.10	.05	.01
☐ 574	Rickey Henderson	13.00	5.75	1.65
☐ 575	Tony Armas	.10	.05	.01
☐ 576	Dave Revering	.10	.05	.01
☐ 577	Jeff Newman	.10	.05	.01
☐ 578	Bob Lacey	.10	.05	.01
☐ 579	Brian Kingman	.10	.05	.01
☐ 580	Mitchell Page	.10	.05	.01
☐ 581	Billy Martin MG	.25	.11	.03
☐ 582	Rob Picciolo	.10	.05	.01
☐ 583	Mike Heath	.10	.05	.01
☐ 584	Mickey Klutts	.10	.05	.01
☐ 585	Orlando Gonzalez	.10	.05	.01
☐ 586	Mike Davis	.12	.05	.02
☐ 587	Wayne Gross	.10	.05	.01
☐ 588	Matt Keough	.10	.05	.01
☐ 589	Steve McCatty	.10	.05	.01
☐ 590	Dwayne Murphy	.10	.05	.01
☐ 591	Mario Guerrero	.10	.05	.01
☐ 592	Dave McKay	.10	.05	.01
☐ 593	Jim Essian	.10	.05	.01
☐ 594	Dave Heaverlo	.10	.05	.01
☐ 595	Maury Wills MG	.12	.05	.02
☐ 596	Juan Beniquez	.10	.05	.01
☐ 597	Rodney Craig	.10	.05	.01
☐ 598	Jim Anderson	.10	.05	.01
☐ 599	Floyd Bannister	.10	.05	.01
☐ 600	Bruce Bochte	.10	.05	.01
☐ 601	Julio Cruz	.10	.05	.01
☐ 602	Ted Cox	.10	.05	.01
☐ 603	Dan Meyer	.10	.05	.01
☐ 604	Larry Cox	.10	.05	.01
☐ 605	Bill Stein	.10	.05	.01
☐ 606	Steve Garvey (Most Hits NL)	.75	.35	.09
☐ 607	Dave Roberts	.10	.05	.01
☐ 608	Leon Roberts	.10	.05	.01
☐ 609	Reggie Walton	.10	.05	.01
☐ 610	Dave Edler	.10	.05	.01
☐ 611	Larry Milbourne	.10	.05	.01
☐ 612	Kim Allen	.10	.05	.01
☐ 613	Mario Mendoza	.10	.05	.01
☐ 614	Tom Paciorek	.12	.05	.02
☐ 615	Glenn Abbott	.10	.05	.01
☐ 616	Joe Simpson	.10	.05	.01
☐ 617	Mickey Rivers	.12	.05	.02
☐ 618	Jim Kern	.10	.05	.01
☐ 619	Jim Sundberg	.12	.05	.02
☐ 620	Richie Zisk	.10	.05	.01
☐ 621	Jon Matlack	.10	.05	.01
☐ 622	Ferguson Jenkins	.60	.25	.08
☐ 623	Pat Corrales MG	.10	.05	.01
☐ 624	Ed Figueroa	.10	.05	.01
☐ 625	Buddy Bell	.12	.05	.02
☐ 626	Al Oliver	.12	.05	.02
☐ 627	Doc Medich	.10	.05	.01
☐ 628	Bump Wills	.10	.05	.01
☐ 629	Rusty Staub	.12	.05	.02
☐ 630	Pat Putnam	.10	.05	.01
☐ 631	John Grubb	.10	.05	.01
☐ 632	Danny Darwin	.10	.05	.01
☐ 633	Ken Clay	.10	.05	.01
☐ 634	Jim Norris	.10	.05	.01
☐ 635	John Butcher	.10	.05	.01
☐ 636	Dave Roberts	.10	.05	.01
☐ 637	Billy Sample	.10	.05	.01
☐ 638	Carl Yastrzemski	2.00	.90	.25
☐ 639	Cecil Cooper	.12	.05	.02
☐ 640A	Mike Schmidt P1 (Portrait; "Third Base"; number on back 5)	3.00	1.35	.40
☐ 640B	Mike Schmidt P2 ("1980 Home Run King"; 640 on back)	3.00	1.35	.40
☐ 641A	CL: Phils/Royals P1 41 is Hal McRae	.15	.02	.00
☐ 641B	CL: Phils/Royals P2 (41 is Hal McRae, Double Threat)	.15	.02	.00
☐ 642	CL: Astros/Yankees	.15	.02	.00
☐ 643	CL: Expos/Dodgers	.15	.02	.00
☐ 644A	CL: Reds/Orioles P1 (202 is George Foster; Joe Nolan pitcher, should be catcher)	.15	.02	.00

☐ 644B CL: Reds/Orioles P2 (202 is Foster Slugger; Joe Nolan pitcher, should be catcher)	.15	.02	.00
☐ 645A Rose/Bowa/Schmidt ERR . Triple Threat P1 (No number on back)	2.50	1.15	.30
☐ 645B Rose/Bowa/Schmidt COR . Triple Threat P2 (Back numbered 645)	1.75	.80	.22
☐ 646 CL: Braves/Red Sox	.15	.02	.00
☐ 647 CL: Cubs/Angels	.15	.02	.00
☐ 648 CL: Mets/White Sox	.15	.02	.00
☐ 649 CL: Indians/Pirates	.15	.02	.00
☐ 650A Reggie Jackson Mr. Baseball P1 (Number on back 79)	2.50	1.15	.30
☐ 650B Reggie Jackson Mr. Baseball P2 (Number on back 650)	2.50	1.15	.30
☐ 651 CL: Giants/Blue Jays	.15	.02	.00
☐ 652A CL: Tigers/Padres P1 (483 is listed)	.15	.02	.00
☐ 652B CL: Tigers/Padres P2 (483 is deleted)	.15	.02	.00
☐ 653A Willie Wilson P1 Most Hits Most Runs (Number on back 29)	.15	.07	.02
☐ 653B Willie Wilson P2 Most Hits Most Runs (Number on back 653)	.15	.07	.02
☐ 654A CL:Brewers/Cards P1 ERR (514 Jerry Augustine; 547 Pete Vuckovich)	.15	.02	.00
☐ 654B CL:Brewers/Cards P2 COR (514 Billy Travers; 547 Don Hood)	.15	.02	.00
☐ 655A George Brett P1 .390 Average (Number on back 28)	3.00	1.35	.40
☐ 655B George Brett P2 .390 Average (Number on back 655)	3.00	1.35	.40
☐ 656 CL: Twins/Oakland A's	.15	.02	.00
☐ 657A Tug McGraw P1 Game Saver (Number on back 7)	.12	.05	.02
☐ 657B Tug McGraw P2 Game Saver (Number on back 657)	.12	.05	.02
☐ 658 CL: Rangers/Mariners	.15	.02	.00
☐ 659A Checklist P1 of Special Cards (Last lines on front, Wilson Most Hits)	.15	.02	.00
☐ 659B Checklist P2 of Special Cards (Last lines on front, Otis Series Starter)	.15	.02	.00
☐ 660A Steve Carlton P1 ERR Golden Arm (Back "1066 Cardinals"; Number on back 6)	2.00	.90	.25
☐ 660B Steve Carlton P2 ERR Golden Arm (Number on back 660; Back "1066 Cardinals")	2.00	.90	.25
☐ 660C Steve Carlton P3 COR Golden Arm ("1966 Cardinals")	2.00	.90	.25

1981 Fleer Sticker Cards

The stickers in this 128-sticker set measure 2 1/2" by 3 1/2". The 1981 Fleer Baseball Star Stickers consist of numbered cards with peelable, full-color sticker fronts and three unnumbered checklists. The backs of the numbered player cards are the same as the 1981 Fleer regular issue cards except for the numbers, while the checklist cards (cards 126-128 below) have sticker fronts of Jackson (1-42), Brett (43-83), and Schmidt (84-125).

	NRMT-MT	EXC	G-VG
COMPLETE SET (128)	50.00	23.00	6.25
COMMON PLAYER (1-128)	.15	.07	.02

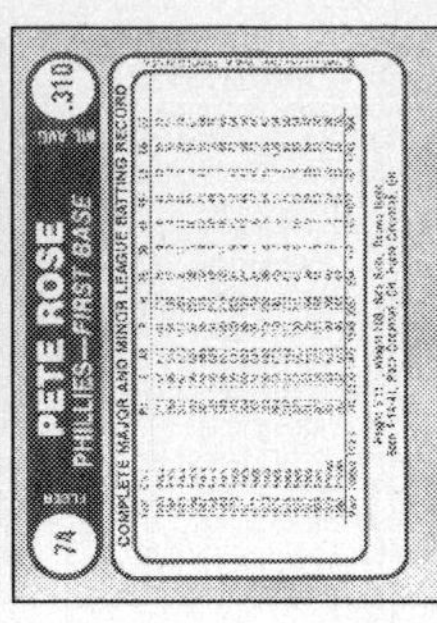

☐ 1 Steve Garvey	2.00	.90	.25
☐ 2 Ron LeFlore	.15	.07	.02
☐ 3 Ron Cey	.15	.07	.02
☐ 4 Dave Revering	.15	.07	.02
☐ 5 Tony Armas	.15	.07	.02
☐ 6 Mike Norris	.15	.07	.02
☐ 7 Steve Kemp	.15	.07	.02
☐ 8 Bruce Bochte	.15	.07	.02
☐ 9 Mike Schmidt	4.50	2.00	.55
☐ 10 Scott McGregor	.15	.07	.02
☐ 11 Buddy Bell	.15	.07	.02
☐ 12 Carney Lansford	.25	.11	.03
☐ 13 Carl Yastrzemski	3.00	1.35	.40
☐ 14 Ben Oglivie	.15	.07	.02
☐ 15 Willie Stargell	1.50	.65	.19
☐ 16 Cecil Cooper	.25	.11	.03
☐ 17 Gene Richards	.15	.07	.02
☐ 18 Jim Kern	.15	.07	.02
☐ 19 Jerry Koosman	.25	.11	.03
☐ 20 Larry Bowa	.25	.11	.03
☐ 21 Kent Tekulve	.15	.07	.02
☐ 22 Dan Driessen	.15	.07	.02
☐ 23 Phil Niekro	1.00	.45	.13
☐ 24 Dan Quisenberry	.25	.11	.03
☐ 25 Dave Winfield	3.00	1.35	.40
☐ 26 Dave Parker	.60	.25	.08
☐ 27 Rick Langford	.15	.07	.02
☐ 28 Amos Otis	.15	.07	.02
☐ 29 Bill Buckner	.25	.11	.03
☐ 30 Al Bumbry	.15	.07	.02
☐ 31 Bake McBride	.15	.07	.02
☐ 32 Mickey Rivers	.15	.07	.02
☐ 33 Rick Burleson	.15	.07	.02
☐ 34 Dennis Eckersley	2.00	.90	.25
☐ 35 Cesar Cedeno	.25	.11	.03
☐ 36 Enos Cabell	.15	.07	.02
☐ 37 Johnny Bench	3.00	1.35	.40
☐ 38 Robin Yount	4.50	2.00	.55
☐ 39 Mark Belanger	.15	.07	.02
☐ 40 Rod Carew	2.50	1.15	.30
☐ 41 George Foster	.50	.23	.06
☐ 42 Lee Mazzilli	.15	.07	.02
☐ 43 Triple Threat: Pete Rose Larry Bowa Mike Schmidt	3.50	1.55	.45
☐ 44 J.R. Richard	.15	.07	.02
☐ 45 Lou Piniella	.35	.16	.04
☐ 46 Ken Landreaux	.15	.07	.02
☐ 47 Rollie Fingers	1.00	.45	.13
☐ 48 Joaquin Andujar	.15	.07	.02
☐ 49 Tom Seaver	3.50	1.55	.45
☐ 50 Bobby Grich	.25	.11	.03
☐ 51 Jon Matlack	.15	.07	.02
☐ 52 Jack Clark	.35	.16	.04
☐ 53 Jim Rice	.60	.25	.08
☐ 54 Rickey Henderson	7.50	3.40	.95
☐ 55 Roy Smalley	.15	.07	.02
☐ 56 Mike Flanagan	.25	.11	.03
☐ 57 Steve Rogers	.15	.07	.02
☐ 58 Carlton Fisk	2.50	1.15	.30
☐ 59 Don Sutton	1.00	.45	.13
☐ 60 Ken Griffey	.35	.16	.04
☐ 61 Burt Hooton	.15	.07	.02
☐ 62 Dusty Baker	.35	.16	.04
☐ 63 Vida Blue	.25	.11	.03
☐ 64 Al Oliver	.25	.11	.03
☐ 65 Jim Bibby	.15	.07	.02
☐ 66 Tony Perez	.90	.40	.11
☐ 67 Davey Lopes	.25	.11	.03
☐ 68 Bill Russell	.25	.11	.03
☐ 69 Larry Parrish	.15	.07	.02
☐ 70 Garry Maddox	.15	.07	.02

71	Phil Garner	.25	.11	.03
72	Graig Nettles	.50	.23	.06
73	Gary Carter	2.00	.90	.25
74	Pete Rose	4.50	2.00	.55
75	Greg Luzinski	.25	.11	.03
76	Ron Guidry	.50	.23	.06
77	Gorman Thomas	.15	.07	.02
78	Jose Cruz	.25	.11	.03
79	Bob Boone	.50	.23	.06
80	Bruce Sutter	.35	.16	.04
81	Chris Chambliss	.25	.11	.03
82	Paul Molitor	1.25	.55	.16
83	Tug McGraw	.25	.11	.03
84	Ferguson Jenkins	1.25	.55	.16
85	Steve Carlton	2.50	1.15	.30
86	Miguel Dilone	.15	.07	.02
87	Reggie Smith	.25	.11	.03
88	Rick Cerone	.15	.07	.02
89	Alan Trammell	1.25	.55	.16
90	Doug DeCinces	.25	.11	.03
91	Sparky Lyle	.35	.16	.04
92	Warren Cromartie	.15	.07	.02
93	Rick Reuschel	.25	.11	.03
94	Larry Hisle	.15	.07	.02
95	Paul Splittorff	.15	.07	.02
96	Manny Trillo	.15	.07	.02
97	Frank White	.15	.07	.02
98	Fred Lynn	.50	.23	.06
99	Bob Horner	.15	.07	.02
100	Omar Moreno	.15	.07	.02
101	Dave Concepcion	.35	.16	.04
102	Larry Gura	.15	.07	.02
103	Ken Singleton	.25	.11	.03
104	Steve Stone	.15	.07	.02
105	Richie Zisk	.15	.07	.02
106	Willie Wilson	.25	.11	.03
107	Willie Randolph	.25	.11	.03
108	Nolan Ryan	10.00	4.50	1.25
109	Joe Morgan	1.75	.80	.22
110	Bucky Dent	.35	.16	.04
111	Dave Kingman	.35	.16	.04
112	John Castino	.15	.07	.02
113	Joe Rudi	.15	.07	.02
114	Ed Farmer	.15	.07	.02
115	Reggie Jackson	3.50	1.55	.45
116	George Brett	4.50	2.00	.55
117	Eddie Murray	3.00	1.35	.40
118	Rich Gossage	.50	.23	.06
119	Dale Murphy	2.50	1.15	.30
120	Ted Simmons	.35	.16	.04
121	Tommy John	.50	.23	.06
122	Don Baylor	.50	.23	.06
123	Andre Dawson	3.00	1.35	.40
124	Jim Palmer	2.00	.90	.25
125	Garry Templeton	.25	.11	.03
126	CL 1: Reggie Jackson (Unnumbered)	2.00	.90	.25
127	CL 2: George Brett (Unnumbered)	3.00	1.35	.40
128	CL 3: Mike Schmidt (Unnumbered)	3.00	1.35	.40

1982 Fleer

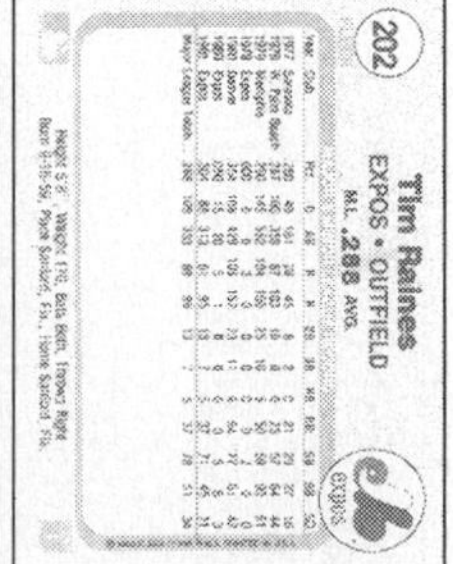

The cards in this 660-card set measure 2 1/2" by 3 1/2". The 1982 Fleer set is again ordered by teams; in fact, the players within each team are listed in alphabetical order. The teams are ordered (by 1981 standings) as follows: Los Angeles (1-29), New York Yankees (30-56), Cincinnati (57-84), Oakland (85-109), St. Louis (110-132), Milwaukee (133-156), Baltimore (157-182), Montreal (183-211), Houston (212-237), Philadelphia (238-262), Detroit (263-286), Boston (287-312), Texas (313-334), Chicago White Sox (335-358), Cleveland (359-382), San Francisco (383-403), Kansas City (404-427), Atlanta (428-449), California (450-474), Pittsburgh (475-501), Seattle (502-519), New York Mets (520-544), Minnesota (545-565), San Diego (566-585), Chicago Cubs (586-607), and Toronto (608-627). Cards numbered 628 through 646 are special cards highlighting some of the stars and leaders of the 1981 season. The last 14 cards in the set (647-660) are checklist cards. The backs feature player statistics and a full-color team logo in the upper right-hand corner of each card. The complete set price below does not include any of the more valuable variation cards listed. The key Rookie Cards in this set are George Bell, Cal Ripken Jr., Steve Sax, Lee Smith, and Dave Stewart.

		NRMT-MT	EXC	G-VG
	COMPLETE SET (660)	100.00	45.00	12.50
	COMMON PLAYER (1-660)	.10	.05	.01
1	Dusty Baker	.12	.05	.02
2	Robert Castillo	.10	.05	.01
3	Ron Cey	.12	.05	.02
4	Terry Forster	.10	.05	.01
5	Steve Garvey	.60	.25	.08
6	Dave Goltz	.10	.05	.01
7	Pedro Guerrero	.30	.14	.04
8	Burt Hooton	.10	.05	.01
9	Steve Howe	.10	.05	.01
10	Jay Johnstone	.12	.05	.02
11	Ken Landreaux	.10	.05	.01
12	Dave Lopes	.12	.05	.02
13	Mike A. Marshall OF	.20	.09	.03
14	Bobby Mitchell	.10	.05	.01
15	Rick Monday	.10	.05	.01
16	Tom Niedenfuer	.10	.05	.01
17	Ted Power	.15	.07	.02
18	Jerry Reuss UER ("Home:" omitted)	.10	.05	.01
19	Ron Roenicke	.10	.05	.01
20	Bill Russell	.12	.05	.02
21	Steve Sax	3.00	1.35	.40
22	Mike Scioscia	.25	.11	.03
23	Reggie Smith	.12	.05	.02
24	Dave Stewart	3.00	1.35	.40
25	Rick Sutcliffe	.30	.14	.04
26	Derrel Thomas	.10	.05	.01
27	Fernando Valenzuela	.25	.11	.03
28	Bob Welch	.30	.14	.04
29	Steve Yeager	.10	.05	.01
30	Bobby Brown	.10	.05	.01
31	Rick Cerone	.10	.05	.01
32	Ron Davis	.10	.05	.01
33	Bucky Dent	.12	.05	.02
34	Barry Foote	.10	.05	.01
35	George Frazier	.10	.05	.01
36	Oscar Gamble	.10	.05	.01
37	Rich Gossage	.20	.09	.03
38	Ron Guidry	.25	.11	.03
39	Reggie Jackson	2.00	.90	.25
40	Tommy John	.20	.09	.03
41	Rudy May	.10	.05	.01
42	Larry Milbourne	.10	.05	.01
43	Jerry Mumphrey	.10	.05	.01
44	Bobby Murcer	.12	.05	.02
45	Gene Nelson	.10	.05	.01
46	Graig Nettles	.12	.05	.02
47	Johnny Oates	.10	.05	.01
48	Lou Piniella	.12	.05	.02
49	Willie Randolph	.12	.05	.02
50	Rick Reuschel	.12	.05	.02
51	Dave Revering	.10	.05	.01
52	Dave Righetti	.50	.23	.06
53	Aurelio Rodriguez	.10	.05	.01
54	Bob Watson	.12	.05	.02
55	Dennis Werth	.10	.05	.01
56	Dave Winfield	2.50	1.15	.30
57	Johnny Bench	1.50	.65	.19
58	Bruce Berenyi	.10	.05	.01
59	Larry Biittner	.10	.05	.01
60	Scott Brown	.10	.05	.01
61	Dave Collins	.10	.05	.01

	Player			
☐ 62	Geoff Combe	.10	.05	.01
☐ 63	Dave Concepcion	.12	.05	.02
☐ 64	Dan Driessen	.10	.05	.01
☐ 65	Joe Edelen	.10	.05	.01
☐ 66	George Foster	.12	.05	.02
☐ 67	Ken Griffey	.25	.11	.03
☐ 68	Paul Householder	.10	.05	.01
☐ 69	Tom Hume	.10	.05	.01
☐ 70	Junior Kennedy	.10	.05	.01
☐ 71	Ray Knight	.12	.05	.02
☐ 72	Mike LaCoss	.10	.05	.01
☐ 73	Rafael Landestoy	.10	.05	.01
☐ 74	Charlie Leibrandt	.10	.05	.01
☐ 75	Sam Mejias	.10	.05	.01
☐ 76	Paul Moskau	.10	.05	.01
☐ 77	Joe Nolan	.10	.05	.01
☐ 78	Mike O'Berry	.10	.05	.01
☐ 79	Ron Oester	.10	.05	.01
☐ 80	Frank Pastore	.10	.05	.01
☐ 81	Joe Price	.10	.05	.01
☐ 82	Tom Seaver	1.50	.65	.19
☐ 83	Mario Soto	.10	.05	.01
☐ 84	Mike Vail	.10	.05	.01
☐ 85	Tony Armas	.10	.05	.01
☐ 86	Shooty Babitt	.10	.05	.01
☐ 87	Dave Beard	.10	.05	.01
☐ 88	Rick Bosetti	.10	.05	.01
☐ 89	Keith Drumwright	.10	.05	.01
☐ 90	Wayne Gross	.10	.05	.01
☐ 91	Mike Heath	.10	.05	.01
☐ 92	Rickey Henderson	4.50	2.00	.55
☐ 93	Cliff Johnson	.10	.05	.01
☐ 94	Jeff Jones	.10	.05	.01
☐ 95	Matt Keough	.10	.05	.01
☐ 96	Brian Kingman	.10	.05	.01
☐ 97	Mickey Klutts	.10	.05	.01
☐ 98	Rick Langford	.10	.05	.01
☐ 99	Steve McCatty	.10	.05	.01
☐ 100	Dave McKay	.10	.05	.01
☐ 101	Dwayne Murphy	.10	.05	.01
☐ 102	Jeff Newman	.10	.05	.01
☐ 103	Mike Norris	.10	.05	.01
☐ 104	Bob Owchinko	.10	.05	.01
☐ 105	Mitchell Page	.10	.05	.01
☐ 106	Rob Picciolo	.10	.05	.01
☐ 107	Jim Spencer	.10	.05	.01
☐ 108	Fred Stanley	.10	.05	.01
☐ 109	Tom Underwood	.10	.05	.01
☐ 110	Joaquin Andujar	.12	.05	.02
☐ 111	Steve Braun	.10	.05	.01
☐ 112	Bob Forsch	.10	.05	.01
☐ 113	George Hendrick	.12	.05	.02
☐ 114	Keith Hernandez	.25	.11	.03
☐ 115	Tom Herr	.12	.05	.02
☐ 116	Dane Iorg	.10	.05	.01
☐ 117	Jim Kaat	.15	.07	.02
☐ 118	Tito Landrum	.10	.05	.01
☐ 119	Sixto Lezcano	.10	.05	.01
☐ 120	Mark Littell	.10	.05	.01
☐ 121	John Martin	.10	.05	.01
☐ 122	Silvio Martinez	.10	.05	.01
☐ 123	Ken Oberkfell	.10	.05	.01
☐ 124	Darrell Porter	.10	.05	.01
☐ 125	Mike Ramsey	.10	.05	.01
☐ 126	Orlando Sanchez	.10	.05	.01
☐ 127	Bob Shirley	.10	.05	.01
☐ 128	Lary Sorensen	.10	.05	.01
☐ 129	Bruce Sutter	.20	.09	.03
☐ 130	Bob Sykes	.10	.05	.01
☐ 131	Garry Templeton	.12	.05	.02
☐ 132	Gene Tenace	.10	.05	.01
☐ 133	Jerry Augustine	.10	.05	.01
☐ 134	Sal Bando	.12	.05	.02
☐ 135	Mark Brouhard	.10	.05	.01
☐ 136	Mike Caldwell	.10	.05	.01
☐ 137	Reggie Cleveland	.10	.05	.01
☐ 138	Cecil Cooper	.12	.05	.02
☐ 139	Jamie Easterly	.10	.05	.01
☐ 140	Marshall Edwards	.10	.05	.01
☐ 141	Rollie Fingers	.75	.35	.09
☐ 142	Jim Gantner	.12	.05	.02
☐ 143	Moose Haas	.10	.05	.01
☐ 144	Larry Hisle	.10	.05	.01
☐ 145	Roy Howell	.10	.05	.01
☐ 146	Rickey Keeton	.10	.05	.01
☐ 147	Randy Lerch	.10	.05	.01
☐ 148	Paul Molitor	1.00	.45	.13
☐ 149	Don Money	.10	.05	.01
☐ 150	Charlie Moore	.10	.05	.01
☐ 151	Ben Oglivie	.10	.05	.01
☐ 152	Ted Simmons	.12	.05	.02
☐ 153	Jim Slaton	.10	.05	.01
☐ 154	Gorman Thomas	.10	.05	.01
☐ 155	Robin Yount	3.00	1.35	.40
☐ 156	Pete Vuckovich (Should precede Yount in the team order)	.12	.05	.02
☐ 157	Benny Ayala	.10	.05	.01
☐ 158	Mark Belanger	.12	.05	.02
☐ 159	Al Bumbry	.10	.05	.01
☐ 160	Terry Crowley	.10	.05	.01
☐ 161	Rich Dauer	.10	.05	.01
☐ 162	Doug DeCinces	.12	.05	.02
☐ 163	Rick Dempsey	.12	.05	.02
☐ 164	Jim Dwyer	.10	.05	.01
☐ 165	Mike Flanagan	.12	.05	.02
☐ 166	Dave Ford	.10	.05	.01
☐ 167	Dan Graham	.10	.05	.01
☐ 168	Wayne Krenchicki	.10	.05	.01
☐ 169	John Lowenstein	.10	.05	.01
☐ 170	Dennis Martinez	.25	.11	.03
☐ 171	Tippy Martinez	.10	.05	.01
☐ 172	Scott McGregor	.10	.05	.01
☐ 173	Jose Morales	.10	.05	.01
☐ 174	Eddie Murray	2.00	.90	.25
☐ 175	Jim Palmer	1.25	.55	.16
☐ 176	Cal Ripken	50.00	23.00	6.25
☐ 177	Gary Roenicke	.10	.05	.01
☐ 178	Lenn Sakata	.10	.05	.01
☐ 179	Ken Singleton	.12	.05	.02
☐ 180	Sammy Stewart	.10	.05	.01
☐ 181	Tim Stoddard	.10	.05	.01
☐ 182	Steve Stone	.12	.05	.02
☐ 183	Stan Bahnsen	.10	.05	.01
☐ 184	Ray Burris	.10	.05	.01
☐ 185	Gary Carter	.90	.40	.11
☐ 186	Warren Cromartie	.10	.05	.01
☐ 187	Andre Dawson	2.00	.90	.25
☐ 188	Terry Francona	.10	.05	.01
☐ 189	Woodie Fryman	.10	.05	.01
☐ 190	Bill Gullickson	.25	.11	.03
☐ 191	Grant Jackson	.10	.05	.01
☐ 192	Wallace Johnson	.10	.05	.01
☐ 193	Charlie Lea	.10	.05	.01
☐ 194	Bill Lee	.10	.05	.01
☐ 195	Jerry Manuel	.10	.05	.01
☐ 196	Brad Mills	.10	.05	.01
☐ 197	John Milner	.10	.05	.01
☐ 198	Rowland Office	.10	.05	.01
☐ 199	David Palmer	.10	.05	.01
☐ 200	Larry Parrish	.10	.05	.01
☐ 201	Mike Phillips	.10	.05	.01
☐ 202	Tim Raines	1.75	.80	.22
☐ 203	Bobby Ramos	.10	.05	.01
☐ 204	Jeff Reardon	2.00	.90	.25
☐ 205	Steve Rogers	.10	.05	.01
☐ 206	Scott Sanderson	.12	.05	.02
☐ 207	Rodney Scott UER (Photo actually Tim Raines)	.20	.09	.03
☐ 208	Elias Sosa	.10	.05	.01
☐ 209	Chris Speier	.10	.05	.01
☐ 210	Tim Wallach	1.00	.45	.13
☐ 211	Jerry White	.10	.05	.01
☐ 212	Alan Ashby	.10	.05	.01
☐ 213	Cesar Cedeno	.12	.05	.02
☐ 214	Jose Cruz	.12	.05	.02
☐ 215	Kiko Garcia	.10	.05	.01
☐ 216	Phil Garner	.12	.05	.02
☐ 217	Danny Heep	.10	.05	.01
☐ 218	Art Howe	.10	.05	.01
☐ 219	Bob Knepper	.10	.05	.01
☐ 220	Frank LaCorte	.10	.05	.01
☐ 221	Joe Niekro	.12	.05	.02
☐ 222	Joe Pittman	.10	.05	.01
☐ 223	Terry Puhl	.10	.05	.01
☐ 224	Luis Pujols	.10	.05	.01
☐ 225	Craig Reynolds	.10	.05	.01
☐ 226	J.R. Richard	.12	.05	.02
☐ 227	Dave Roberts	.10	.05	.01
☐ 228	Vern Ruhle	.10	.05	.01
☐ 229	Nolan Ryan	8.00	3.60	1.00
☐ 230	Joe Sambito	.10	.05	.01
☐ 231	Tony Scott	.10	.05	.01
☐ 232	Dave Smith	.10	.05	.01
☐ 233	Harry Spilman	.10	.05	.01
☐ 234	Don Sutton	.40	.18	.05
☐ 235	Dickie Thon	.10	.05	.01
☐ 236	Denny Walling	.10	.05	.01
☐ 237	Gary Woods	.10	.05	.01
☐ 238	Luis Aguayo	.10	.05	.01
☐ 239	Ramon Aviles	.10	.05	.01
☐ 240	Bob Boone	.12	.05	.02
☐ 241	Larry Bowa	.12	.05	.02
☐ 242	Warren Brusstar	.10	.05	.01
☐ 243	Steve Carlton	1.50	.65	.19

☐	244	Larry Christenson	.10	.05	.01
☐	245	Dick Davis	.10	.05	.01
☐	246	Greg Gross	.10	.05	.01
☐	247	Sparky Lyle	.12	.05	.02
☐	248	Garry Maddox	.10	.05	.01
☐	249	Gary Matthews	.12	.05	.02
☐	250	Bake McBride	.10	.05	.01
☐	251	Tug McGraw	.12	.05	.02
☐	252	Keith Moreland	.10	.05	.01
☐	253	Dickie Noles	.10	.05	.01
☐	254	Mike Proly	.10	.05	.01
☐	255	Ron Reed	.10	.05	.01
☐	256	Pete Rose	1.50	.65	.19
☐	257	Dick Ruthven	.10	.05	.01
☐	258	Mike Schmidt	2.50	1.15	.30
☐	259	Lonnie Smith	.12	.05	.02
☐	260	Manny Trillo	.10	.05	.01
☐	261	Del Unser	.10	.05	.01
☐	262	George Vukovich	.10	.05	.01
☐	263	Tom Brookens	.10	.05	.01
☐	264	George Cappuzzello	.10	.05	.01
☐	265	Marty Castillo	.10	.05	.01
☐	266	Al Cowens	.10	.05	.01
☐	267	Kirk Gibson	.50	.23	.06
☐	268	Richie Hebner	.10	.05	.01
☐	269	Ron Jackson	.10	.05	.01
☐	270	Lynn Jones	.10	.05	.01
☐	271	Steve Kemp	.10	.05	.01
☐	272	Rick Leach	.10	.05	.01
☐	273	Aurelio Lopez	.10	.05	.01
☐	274	Jack Morris	1.50	.65	.19
☐	275	Kevin Saucier	.10	.05	.01
☐	276	Lance Parrish	.25	.11	.03
☐	277	Rick Peters	.10	.05	.01
☐	278	Dan Petry	.10	.05	.01
☐	279	Dave Rozema	.10	.05	.01
☐	280	Stan Papi	.10	.05	.01
☐	281	Dan Schatzeder	.10	.05	.01
☐	282	Champ Summers	.10	.05	.01
☐	283	Alan Trammell	.50	.23	.06
☐	284	Lou Whitaker	.50	.23	.06
☐	285	Milt Wilcox	.10	.05	.01
☐	286	John Wockenfuss	.10	.05	.01
☐	287	Gary Allenson	.10	.05	.01
☐	288	Tom Burgmeier	.10	.05	.01
☐	289	Bill Campbell	.10	.05	.01
☐	290	Mark Clear	.10	.05	.01
☐	291	Steve Crawford	.10	.05	.01
☐	292	Dennis Eckersley	1.50	.65	.19
☐	293	Dwight Evans	.25	.11	.03
☐	294	Rich Gedman	.15	.07	.02
☐	295	Garry Hancock	.10	.05	.01
☐	296	Glenn Hoffman	.10	.05	.01
☐	297	Bruce Hurst	.75	.35	.09
☐	298	Carney Lansford	.12	.05	.02
☐	299	Rick Miller	.10	.05	.01
☐	300	Reid Nichols	.10	.05	.01
☐	301	Bob Ojeda	.40	.18	.05
☐	302	Tony Perez	.35	.16	.04
☐	303	Chuck Rainey	.10	.05	.01
☐	304	Jerry Remy	.10	.05	.01
☐	305	Jim Rice	.25	.11	.03
☐	306	Joe Rudi	.10	.05	.01
☐	307	Bob Stanley	.10	.05	.01
☐	308	Dave Stapleton	.10	.05	.01
☐	309	Frank Tanana	.12	.05	.02
☐	310	Mike Torrez	.10	.05	.01
☐	311	John Tudor	.12	.05	.02
☐	312	Carl Yastrzemski	1.50	.65	.19
☐	313	Buddy Bell	.12	.05	.02
☐	314	Steve Comer	.10	.05	.01
☐	315	Danny Darwin	.10	.05	.01
☐	316	John Ellis	.10	.05	.01
☐	317	John Grubb	.10	.05	.01
☐	318	Rick Honeycutt	.10	.05	.01
☐	319	Charlie Hough	.12	.05	.02
☐	320	Ferguson Jenkins	.40	.18	.05
☐	321	John Henry Johnson	.10	.05	.01
☐	322	Jim Kern	.10	.05	.01
☐	323	Jon Matlack	.10	.05	.01
☐	324	Doc Medich	.10	.05	.01
☐	325	Mario Mendoza	.10	.05	.01
☐	326	Al Oliver	.12	.05	.02
☐	327	Pat Putnam	.10	.05	.01
☐	328	Mickey Rivers	.10	.05	.01
☐	329	Leon Roberts	.10	.05	.01
☐	330	Billy Sample	.10	.05	.01
☐	331	Bill Stein	.10	.05	.01
☐	332	Jim Sundberg	.12	.05	.02
☐	333	Mark Wagner	.10	.05	.01
☐	334	Bump Wills	.10	.05	.01
☐	335	Bill Almon	.10	.05	.01
☐	336	Harold Baines	.60	.25	.08
☐	337	Ross Baumgarten	.10	.05	.01
☐	338	Tony Bernazard	.10	.05	.01
☐	339	Britt Burns	.10	.05	.01
☐	340	Richard Dotson	.10	.05	.01
☐	341	Jim Essian	.10	.05	.01
☐	342	Ed Farmer	.10	.05	.01
☐	343	Carlton Fisk	1.50	.65	.19
☐	344	Kevin Hickey	.10	.05	.01
☐	345	LaMarr Hoyt	.10	.05	.01
☐	346	Lamar Johnson	.10	.05	.01
☐	347	Jerry Koosman	.12	.05	.02
☐	348	Rusty Kuntz	.10	.05	.01
☐	349	Dennis Lamp	.10	.05	.01
☐	350	Ron LeFlore	.12	.05	.02
☐	351	Chet Lemon	.10	.05	.01
☐	352	Greg Luzinski	.12	.05	.02
☐	353	Bob Molinaro	.10	.05	.01
☐	354	Jim Morrison	.10	.05	.01
☐	355	Wayne Nordhagen	.10	.05	.01
☐	356	Greg Pryor	.10	.05	.01
☐	357	Mike Squires	.10	.05	.01
☐	358	Steve Trout	.10	.05	.01
☐	359	Alan Bannister	.10	.05	.01
☐	360	Len Barker	.10	.05	.01
☐	361	Bert Blyleven	.35	.16	.04
☐	362	Joe Charboneau	.10	.05	.01
☐	363	John Denny	.10	.05	.01
☐	364	Bo Diaz	.10	.05	.01
☐	365	Miguel Dilone	.10	.05	.01
☐	366	Jerry Dybzinski	.10	.05	.01
☐	367	Wayne Garland	.10	.05	.01
☐	368	Mike Hargrove	.12	.05	.02
☐	369	Toby Harrah	.12	.05	.02
☐	370	Ron Hassey	.10	.05	.01
☐	371	Von Hayes	.30	.14	.04
☐	372	Pat Kelly	.10	.05	.01
☐	373	Duane Kuiper	.10	.05	.01
☐	374	Rick Manning	.10	.05	.01
☐	375	Sid Monge	.10	.05	.01
☐	376	Jorge Orta	.10	.05	.01
☐	377	Dave Rosello	.10	.05	.01
☐	378	Dan Spillner	.10	.05	.01
☐	379	Mike Stanton	.10	.05	.01
☐	380	Andre Thornton	.12	.05	.02
☐	381	Tom Veryzer	.10	.05	.01
☐	382	Rick Waits	.10	.05	.01
☐	383	Doyle Alexander	.10	.05	.01
☐	384	Vida Blue	.12	.05	.02
☐	385	Fred Breining	.10	.05	.01
☐	386	Enos Cabell	.10	.05	.01
☐	387	Jack Clark	.20	.09	.03
☐	388	Darrell Evans	.12	.05	.02
☐	389	Tom Griffin	.10	.05	.01
☐	390	Larry Herndon	.10	.05	.01
☐	391	Al Holland	.10	.05	.01
☐	392	Gary Lavelle	.10	.05	.01
☐	393	Johnnie LeMaster	.10	.05	.01
☐	394	Jerry Martin	.10	.05	.01
☐	395	Milt May	.10	.05	.01
☐	396	Greg Minton	.10	.05	.01
☐	397	Joe Morgan	.75	.35	.09
☐	398	Joe Pettini	.10	.05	.01
☐	399	Allen Ripley	.10	.05	.01
☐	400	Billy Smith	.10	.05	.01
☐	401	Rennie Stennett	.10	.05	.01
☐	402	Ed Whitson	.10	.05	.01
☐	403	Jim Wohlford	.10	.05	.01
☐	404	Willie Aikens	.10	.05	.01
☐	405	George Brett	3.00	1.35	.40
☐	406	Ken Brett	.10	.05	.01
☐	407	Dave Chalk	.10	.05	.01
☐	408	Rich Gale	.10	.05	.01
☐	409	Cesar Geronimo	.10	.05	.01
☐	410	Larry Gura	.10	.05	.01
☐	411	Clint Hurdle	.10	.05	.01
☐	412	Mike Jones	.10	.05	.01
☐	413	Dennis Leonard	.10	.05	.01
☐	414	Renie Martin	.10	.05	.01
☐	415	Lee May	.10	.05	.01
☐	416	Hal McRae	.12	.05	.02
☐	417	Darryl Motley	.10	.05	.01
☐	418	Rance Mulliniks	.10	.05	.01
☐	419	Amos Otis	.12	.05	.02
☐	420	Ken Phelps	.10	.05	.01
☐	421	Jamie Quirk	.10	.05	.01
☐	422	Dan Quisenberry	.12	.05	.02
☐	423	Paul Splittorff	.10	.05	.01
☐	424	U.L. Washington	.10	.05	.01
☐	425	John Wathan	.10	.05	.01
☐	426	Frank White	.12	.05	.02
☐	427	Willie Wilson	.12	.05	.02
☐	428	Brian Asselstine	.10	.05	.01
☐	429	Bruce Benedict	.10	.05	.01

☐ 430 Tommy Boggs .10 .05 .01
☐ 431 Larry Bradford .10 .05 .01
☐ 432 Rick Camp .10 .05 .01
☐ 433 Chris Chambliss .12 .05 .02
☐ 434 Gene Garber .10 .05 .01
☐ 435 Preston Hanna .10 .05 .01
☐ 436 Bob Horner .12 .05 .02
☐ 437 Glenn Hubbard .10 .05 .01
☐ 438A Al Hrabosky ERR 20.00 9.00 2.50
(Height 5'1", All on reverse)
☐ 438B Al Hrabosky ERR .75 .35 .09
(Height 5'1")
☐ 438C Al Hrabosky COR .12 .05 .02
(Height 5'10")
☐ 439 Rufino Linares .10 .05 .01
☐ 440 Rick Mahler .10 .05 .01
☐ 441 Ed Miller .10 .05 .01
☐ 442 John Montefusco .10 .05 .01
☐ 443 Dale Murphy 1.00 .45 .13
☐ 444 Phil Niekro .40 .18 .05
☐ 445 Gaylord Perry .40 .18 .05
☐ 446 Biff Pocoroba .10 .05 .01
☐ 447 Rafael Ramirez .10 .05 .01
☐ 448 Jerry Royster .10 .05 .01
☐ 449 Claudell Washington .10 .05 .01
☐ 450 Don Aase .10 .05 .01
☐ 451 Don Baylor .12 .05 .02
☐ 452 Juan Beniquez .10 .05 .01
☐ 453 Rick Burleson .10 .05 .01
☐ 454 Bert Campaneris .12 .05 .02
☐ 455 Rod Carew 1.50 .65 .19
☐ 456 Bob Clark .10 .05 .01
☐ 457 Brian Downing .12 .05 .02
☐ 458 Dan Ford .10 .05 .01
☐ 459 Ken Forsch .10 .05 .01
☐ 460A Dave Frost (5 mm space before ERA) .10 .05 .01
☐ 460B Dave Frost .10 .05 .01
(1 mm space)
☐ 461 Bobby Grich .12 .05 .02
☐ 462 Larry Harlow .10 .05 .01
☐ 463 John Harris .10 .05 .01
☐ 464 Andy Hassler .10 .05 .01
☐ 465 Butch Hobson .12 .05 .02
☐ 466 Jesse Jefferson .10 .05 .01
☐ 467 Bruce Kison .10 .05 .01
☐ 468 Fred Lynn .12 .05 .02
☐ 469 Angel Moreno .10 .05 .01
☐ 470 Ed Ott .10 .05 .01
☐ 471 Fred Patek .10 .05 .01
☐ 472 Steve Renko .10 .05 .01
☐ 473 Mike Witt .15 .07 .02
☐ 474 Geoff Zahn .10 .05 .01
☐ 475 Gary Alexander .10 .05 .01
☐ 476 Dale Berra .10 .05 .01
☐ 477 Kurt Bevacqua .10 .05 .01
☐ 478 Jim Bibby .10 .05 .01
☐ 479 John Candelaria .10 .05 .01
☐ 480 Victor Cruz .10 .05 .01
☐ 481 Mike Easler .10 .05 .01
☐ 482 Tim Foli .10 .05 .01
☐ 483 Lee Lacy .10 .05 .01
☐ 484 Vance Law .10 .05 .01
☐ 485 Bill Madlock .12 .05 .02
☐ 486 Willie Montanez .10 .05 .01
☐ 487 Omar Moreno .10 .05 .01
☐ 488 Steve Nicosia .10 .05 .01
☐ 489 Dave Parker .35 .16 .04
☐ 490 Tony Pena .20 .09 .03
☐ 491 Pascual Perez .10 .05 .01
☐ 492 Johnny Ray .15 .07 .02
☐ 493 Rick Rhoden .10 .05 .01
☐ 494 Bill Robinson .12 .05 .02
☐ 495 Don Robinson .10 .05 .01
☐ 496 Enrique Romo .10 .05 .01
☐ 497 Rod Scurry .10 .05 .01
☐ 498 Eddie Solomon .10 .05 .01
☐ 499 Willie Stargell .75 .35 .09
☐ 500 Kent Tekulve .12 .05 .02
☐ 501 Jason Thompson .10 .05 .01
☐ 502 Glenn Abbott .10 .05 .01
☐ 503 Jim Anderson .10 .05 .01
☐ 504 Floyd Bannister .10 .05 .01
☐ 505 Bruce Bochte .10 .05 .01
☐ 506 Jeff Burroughs .10 .05 .01
☐ 507 Bryan Clark .10 .05 .01
☐ 508 Ken Clay .10 .05 .01
☐ 509 Julio Cruz .10 .05 .01
☐ 510 Dick Drago .10 .05 .01
☐ 511 Gary Gray .10 .05 .01
☐ 512 Dan Meyer .10 .05 .01
☐ 513 Jerry Narron .10 .05 .01
☐ 514 Tom Paciorek .12 .05 .02
☐ 515 Casey Parsons .10 .05 .01
☐ 516 Lenny Randle .10 .05 .01
☐ 517 Shane Rawley .10 .05 .01
☐ 518 Joe Simpson .10 .05 .01
☐ 519 Richie Zisk .10 .05 .01
☐ 520 Neil Allen .10 .05 .01
☐ 521 Bob Bailor .10 .05 .01
☐ 522 Hubie Brooks .35 .16 .04
☐ 523 Mike Cubbage .10 .05 .01
☐ 524 Pete Falcone .10 .05 .01
☐ 525 Doug Flynn .10 .05 .01
☐ 526 Tom Hausman .10 .05 .01
☐ 527 Ron Hodges .10 .05 .01
☐ 528 Randy Jones .10 .05 .01
☐ 529 Mike Jorgensen .10 .05 .01
☐ 530 Dave Kingman .12 .05 .02
☐ 531 Ed Lynch .10 .05 .01
☐ 532 Mike G. Marshall P .12 .05 .02
☐ 533 Lee Mazzilli .10 .05 .01
☐ 534 Dyar Miller .10 .05 .01
☐ 535 Mike Scott .12 .05 .02
☐ 536 Rusty Staub .12 .05 .02
☐ 537 John Stearns .10 .05 .01
☐ 538 Craig Swan .10 .05 .01
☐ 539 Frank Taveras .10 .05 .01
☐ 540 Alex Trevino .10 .05 .01
☐ 541 Ellis Valentine .10 .05 .01
☐ 542 Mookie Wilson .12 .05 .02
☐ 543 Joel Youngblood .10 .05 .01
☐ 544 Pat Zachry .10 .05 .01
☐ 545 Glenn Adams .10 .05 .01
☐ 546 Fernando Arroyo .10 .05 .01
☐ 547 John Verhoeven .10 .05 .01
☐ 548 Sal Butera .10 .05 .01
☐ 549 John Castino .10 .05 .01
☐ 550 Don Cooper .10 .05 .01
☐ 551 Doug Corbett .10 .05 .01
☐ 552 Dave Engle .10 .05 .01
☐ 553 Roger Erickson .10 .05 .01
☐ 554 Danny Goodwin .10 .05 .01
☐ 555A Darrell Jackson .75 .35 .09
(Black cap)
☐ 555B Darrell Jackson .12 .05 .02
(Red cap with T)
☐ 555C Darrell Jackson 4.00 1.80 .50
(Red cap, no emblem)
☐ 556 Pete Mackanin .10 .05 .01
☐ 557 Jack O'Connor .10 .05 .01
☐ 558 Hosken Powell .10 .05 .01
☐ 559 Pete Redfern .10 .05 .01
☐ 560 Roy Smalley .12 .05 .02
☐ 561 Chuck Baker UER .10 .05 .01
(Shortshop on front)
☐ 562 Gary Ward .10 .05 .01
☐ 563 Rob Wilfong .10 .05 .01
☐ 564 Al Williams .10 .05 .01
☐ 565 Butch Wynegar .10 .05 .01
☐ 566 Randy Bass .10 .05 .01
☐ 567 Juan Bonilla .10 .05 .01
☐ 568 Danny Boone .10 .05 .01
☐ 569 John Curtis .10 .05 .01
☐ 570 Juan Eichelberger .10 .05 .01
☐ 571 Barry Evans .10 .05 .01
☐ 572 Tim Flannery .10 .05 .01
☐ 573 Ruppert Jones .10 .05 .01
☐ 574 Terry Kennedy .10 .05 .01
☐ 575 Joe Lefebvre .10 .05 .01
☐ 576A John Littlefield ERR 300.00 135.00 38.00
(Left handed; reverse negative)
☐ 576B John Littlefield COR .12 .05 .02
(Right handed)
☐ 577 Gary Lucas .10 .05 .01
☐ 578 Steve Mura .10 .05 .01
☐ 579 Broderick Perkins .10 .05 .01
☐ 580 Gene Richards .10 .05 .01
☐ 581 Luis Salazar .10 .05 .01
☐ 582 Ozzie Smith 2.00 .90 .25
☐ 583 John Urrea .10 .05 .01
☐ 584 Chris Welsh .10 .05 .01
☐ 585 Rick Wise .10 .05 .01
☐ 586 Doug Bird .10 .05 .01
☐ 587 Tim Blackwell .10 .05 .01
☐ 588 Bobby Bonds .12 .05 .02
☐ 589 Bill Buckner .12 .05 .02
☐ 590 Bill Caudill .10 .05 .01
☐ 591 Hector Cruz .10 .05 .01
☐ 592 Jody Davis .12 .05 .02
☐ 593 Ivan DeJesus .10 .05 .01
☐ 594 Steve Dillard .10 .05 .01
☐ 595 Leon Durham .10 .05 .01
☐ 596 Rawly Eastwick .10 .05 .01

☐ 597 Steve Henderson	.10	.05	.01
☐ 598 Mike Krukow	.10	.05	.01
☐ 599 Mike Lum	.10	.05	.01
☐ 600 Randy Martz	.10	.05	.01
☐ 601 Jerry Morales	.10	.05	.01
☐ 602 Ken Reitz	.10	.05	.01
☐ 603A Lee Smith ERR	7.00	3.10	.85
(Cubs logo reversed)			
☐ 603B Lee Smith COR	7.00	3.10	.85
☐ 604 Dick Tidrow	.10	.05	.01
☐ 605 Jim Tracy	.10	.05	.01
☐ 606 Mike Tyson	.10	.05	.01
☐ 607 Ty Waller	.10	.05	.01
☐ 608 Danny Ainge	.75	.35	.09
☐ 609 Jorge Bell	6.00	2.70	.75
☐ 610 Mark Bomback	.10	.05	.01
☐ 611 Barry Bonnell	.10	.05	.01
☐ 612 Jim Clancy	.10	.05	.01
☐ 613 Damaso Garcia	.10	.05	.01
☐ 614 Jerry Garvin	.10	.05	.01
☐ 615 Alfredo Griffin	.10	.05	.01
☐ 616 Garth Iorg	.10	.05	.01
☐ 617 Luis Leal	.10	.05	.01
☐ 618 Ken Macha	.10	.05	.01
☐ 619 John Mayberry	.10	.05	.01
☐ 620 Joey McLaughlin	.10	.05	.01
☐ 621 Lloyd Moseby	.10	.05	.01
☐ 622 Dave Stieb	.20	.09	.03
☐ 623 Jackson Todd	.10	.05	.01
☐ 624 Willie Upshaw	.10	.05	.01
☐ 625 Otto Velez	.10	.05	.01
☐ 626 Ernie Whitt	.10	.05	.01
☐ 627 Alvis Woods	.10	.05	.01
☐ 628 All Star Game	.15	.07	.02
Cleveland, Ohio			
☐ 629 All Star Infielders	.15	.07	.02
Frank White and			
Bucky Dent			
☐ 630 Big Red Machine	.15	.07	.02
Dan Driessen			
Dave Concepcion			
George Foster			
☐ 631 Bruce Sutter	.15	.07	.02
Top NL Relief Pitcher			
☐ 632 "Steve and Carlton"	.75	.35	.09
Steve Carlton and			
Carlton Fisk			
☐ 633 Carl Yastrzemski	.75	.35	.09
3000th Game			
☐ 634 Dynamic Duo	1.50	.65	.19
Johnny Bench and			
Tom Seaver			
☐ 635 West Meets East	.15	.07	.02
Fernando Valenzuela			
and Gary Carter			
☐ 636A Fernando Valenzuela:	.30	.14	.04
NL SO King ("he" NL)			
☐ 636B Fernando Valenzuela:	.15	.07	.02
NL SO King ("the" NL)			
☐ 637 Mike Schmidt	1.25	.55	.16
Home Run King			
☐ 638 NL All Stars	.30	.14	.04
Gary Carter and			
Dave Parker			
☐ 639 Perfect Game UER	.15	.07	.02
Len Barker and			
Bo Diaz			
(Catcher actually			
Ron Hassey)			
☐ 640 Pete and Re-Pete	1.50	.65	.19
Pete Rose and Son			
☐ 641 Phillies Finest	.75	.35	.09
Lonnie Smith			
Mike Schmidt			
Steve Carlton			
☐ 642 Red Sox Reunion	.15	.07	.02
Fred Lynn and			
Dwight Evans			
☐ 643 Rickey Henderson	2.50	1.15	.30
Most Hits and Runs			
☐ 644 Rollie Fingers	.40	.18	.05
Most Saves AL			
☐ 645 Tom Seaver	.75	.35	.09
Most 1981 Wins			
☐ 646A Yankee Powerhouse	1.75	.80	.22
Reggie Jackson and			
Dave Winfield			
(Comma on back			
after outfielder)			
☐ 646B Yankee Powerhouse	1.75	.80	.22
Reggie Jackson and			
Dave Winfield			
(No comma)			

☐ 647 CL: Yankees/Dodgers	.15	.02	.00
☐ 648 CL: A's/Reds	.15	.02	.00
☐ 649 CL: Cards/Brewers	.15	.02	.00
☐ 650 CL: Expos/Orioles	.15	.02	.00
☐ 651 CL: Astros/Phillies	.15	.02	.00
☐ 652 CL: Tigers/Red Sox	.15	.02	.00
☐ 653 CL: Rangers/White Sox	.15	.02	.00
☐ 654 CL: Giants/Indians	.15	.02	.00
☐ 655 CL: Royals/Braves	.15	.02	.00
☐ 656 CL: Angels/Pirates	.15	.02	.00
☐ 657 CL: Mariners/Mets	.15	.02	.00
☐ 658 CL: Padres/Twins	.15	.02	.00
☐ 659 CL: Blue Jays/Cubs	.15	.02	.00
☐ 660 Specials Checklist	.15	.02	.00

1983 Fleer

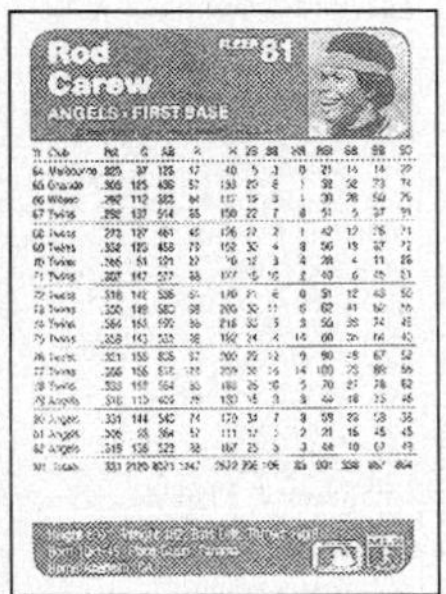

The cards in this 660-card set measure 2 1/2" by 3 1/2". In 1983, for the third straight year, Fleer has produced a baseball series numbering 660 cards. Of these, 1-628 are player cards, 629-646 are special cards, and 647-660 are checklist cards. The player cards are again ordered alphabetically within team. The team order relates back to each team's on-field performance during the previous year, i.e., World Champion Cardinals (1-25), AL Champion Brewers (26-51), Baltimore (52-75), California (76-103), Kansas City (104-128), Atlanta (129-152), Philadelphia (153-176), Boston (177-200), Los Angeles (201-227), Chicago White Sox (228-251), San Francisco (252-276), Montreal (277-301), Pittsburgh (302-326), Detroit (327-351), San Diego (352-375), New York Yankees (376-399), Cleveland (400-423), Toronto (424-444), Houston (445-469), Seattle (470-489), Chicago Cubs (490-512), Oakland (513-535), New York Mets (536-561), Texas (562-583), Cincinnati (584-606), and Minnesota (607-628). The front of each card has a colorful team logo at bottom left and the player's name and position at lower right. The reverses are done in shades of brown on white. The cards are numbered on the back next to a small black and white photo of the player. The key Rookie Cards in this set are Wade Boggs, Tony Gwynn, Howard Johnson, Willie McGee, Ryne Sandberg, and Frank Viola.

	NRMT-MT	EXC	G-VG
COMPLETE SET (660)	130.00	57.50	16.50
COMMON PLAYER (1-660)	.10	.05	.01
☐ 1 Joaquin Andujar	.12	.05	.02
☐ 2 Doug Bair	.10	.05	.01
☐ 3 Steve Braun	.10	.05	.01
☐ 4 Glenn Brummer	.10	.05	.01
☐ 5 Bob Forsch	.10	.05	.01
☐ 6 David Green	.10	.05	.01
☐ 7 George Hendrick	.12	.05	.02
☐ 8 Keith Hernandez	.20	.09	.03
☐ 9 Tom Herr	.12	.05	.02
☐ 10 Dane Iorg	.10	.05	.01
☐ 11 Jim Kaat	.15	.07	.02
☐ 12 Jeff Lahti	.10	.05	.01
☐ 13 Tito Landrum	.10	.05	.01

☐ 14	Dave LaPoint	.12	.05	.02
☐ 15	Willie McGee	2.50	1.15	.30
☐ 16	Steve Mura	.10	.05	.01
☐ 17	Ken Oberkfell	.10	.05	.01
☐ 18	Darrell Porter	.10	.05	.01
☐ 19	Mike Ramsey	.10	.05	.01
☐ 20	Gene Roof	.10	.05	.01
☐ 21	Lonnie Smith	.12	.05	.02
☐ 22	Ozzie Smith	1.50	.65	.19
☐ 23	John Stuper	.10	.05	.01
☐ 24	Bruce Sutter	.20	.09	.03
☐ 25	Gene Tenace	.10	.05	.01
☐ 26	Jerry Augustine	.10	.05	.01
☐ 27	Dwight Bernard	.10	.05	.01
☐ 28	Mark Brouhard	.10	.05	.01
☐ 29	Mike Caldwell	.10	.05	.01
☐ 30	Cecil Cooper	.12	.05	.02
☐ 31	Jamie Easterly	.10	.05	.01
☐ 32	Marshall Edwards	.10	.05	.01
☐ 33	Rollie Fingers	.60	.25	.08
☐ 34	Jim Gantner	.12	.05	.02
☐ 35	Moose Haas	.10	.05	.01
☐ 36	Roy Howell	.10	.05	.01
☐ 37	Pete Ladd	.10	.05	.01
☐ 38	Bob McClure	.10	.05	.01
☐ 39	Doc Medich	.10	.05	.01
☐ 40	Paul Molitor	.90	.40	.11
☐ 41	Don Money	.10	.05	.01
☐ 42	Charlie Moore	.10	.05	.01
☐ 43	Ben Oglivie	.10	.05	.01
☐ 44	Ed Romero	.10	.05	.01
☐ 45	Ted Simmons	.12	.05	.02
☐ 46	Jim Slaton	.10	.05	.01
☐ 47	Don Sutton	.40	.18	.05
☐ 48	Gorman Thomas	.10	.05	.01
☐ 49	Pete Vuckovich	.10	.05	.01
☐ 50	Ned Yost	.10	.05	.01
☐ 51	Robin Yount	2.50	1.15	.30
☐ 52	Benny Ayala	.10	.05	.01
☐ 53	Bob Bonner	.10	.05	.01
☐ 54	Al Bumbry	.10	.05	.01
☐ 55	Terry Crowley	.10	.05	.01
☐ 56	Storm Davis	.20	.09	.03
☐ 57	Rich Dauer	.10	.05	.01
☐ 58	Rick Dempsey UER (Posing batting lefty)	.12	.05	.02
☐ 59	Jim Dwyer	.10	.05	.01
☐ 60	Mike Flanagan	.12	.05	.02
☐ 61	Dan Ford	.10	.05	.01
☐ 62	Glenn Gulliver	.10	.05	.01
☐ 63	John Lowenstein	.10	.05	.01
☐ 64	Dennis Martinez	.12	.05	.02
☐ 65	Tippy Martinez	.10	.05	.01
☐ 66	Scott McGregor	.10	.05	.01
☐ 67	Eddie Murray	1.75	.80	.22
☐ 68	Joe Nolan	.10	.05	.01
☐ 69	Jim Palmer	1.00	.45	.13
☐ 70	Cal Ripken Jr.	18.00	8.00	2.30
☐ 71	Gary Roenicke	.10	.05	.01
☐ 72	Lenn Sakata	.10	.05	.01
☐ 73	Ken Singleton	.12	.05	.02
☐ 74	Sammy Stewart	.10	.05	.01
☐ 75	Tim Stoddard	.10	.05	.01
☐ 76	Don Aase	.10	.05	.01
☐ 77	Don Baylor	.12	.05	.02
☐ 78	Juan Beniquez	.10	.05	.01
☐ 79	Bob Boone	.12	.05	.02
☐ 80	Rick Burleson	.10	.05	.01
☐ 81	Rod Carew	1.25	.55	.16
☐ 82	Bobby Clark	.10	.05	.01
☐ 83	Doug Corbett	.10	.05	.01
☐ 84	John Curtis	.10	.05	.01
☐ 85	Doug DeCinces	.12	.05	.02
☐ 86	Brian Downing	.12	.05	.02
☐ 87	Joe Ferguson	.10	.05	.01
☐ 88	Tim Foli	.10	.05	.01
☐ 89	Ken Forsch	.10	.05	.01
☐ 90	Dave Goltz	.10	.05	.01
☐ 91	Bobby Grich	.12	.05	.02
☐ 92	Andy Hassler	.10	.05	.01
☐ 93	Reggie Jackson	1.50	.65	.19
☐ 94	Ron Jackson	.10	.05	.01
☐ 95	Tommy John	.15	.07	.02
☐ 96	Bruce Kison	.10	.05	.01
☐ 97	Fred Lynn	.12	.05	.02
☐ 98	Ed Ott	.10	.05	.01
☐ 99	Steve Renko	.10	.05	.01
☐ 100	Luis Sanchez	.10	.05	.01
☐ 101	Rob Wilfong	.10	.05	.01
☐ 102	Mike Witt	.10	.05	.01
☐ 103	Geoff Zahn	.10	.05	.01
☐ 104	Willie Aikens	.10	.05	.01
☐ 105	Mike Armstrong	.10	.05	.01
☐ 106	Vida Blue	.12	.05	.02
☐ 107	Bud Black	.40	.18	.05
☐ 108	George Brett	2.50	1.15	.30
☐ 109	Bill Castro	.10	.05	.01
☐ 110	Onix Concepcion	.10	.05	.01
☐ 111	Dave Frost	.10	.05	.01
☐ 112	Cesar Geronimo	.10	.05	.01
☐ 113	Larry Gura	.10	.05	.01
☐ 114	Steve Hammond	.10	.05	.01
☐ 115	Don Hood	.10	.05	.01
☐ 116	Dennis Leonard	.10	.05	.01
☐ 117	Jerry Martin	.10	.05	.01
☐ 118	Lee May	.10	.05	.01
☐ 119	Hal McRae	.12	.05	.02
☐ 120	Amos Otis	.12	.05	.02
☐ 121	Greg Pryor	.10	.05	.01
☐ 122	Dan Quisenberry	.12	.05	.02
☐ 123	Don Slaught	.50	.23	.06
☐ 124	Paul Splittorff	.10	.05	.01
☐ 125	U.L. Washington	.10	.05	.01
☐ 126	John Wathan	.10	.05	.01
☐ 127	Frank White	.12	.05	.02
☐ 128	Willie Wilson	.12	.05	.02
☐ 129	Steve Bedrosian UER (Height 6'33")	.12	.05	.02
☐ 130	Bruce Benedict	.10	.05	.01
☐ 131	Tommy Boggs	.10	.05	.01
☐ 132	Brett Butler	.75	.35	.09
☐ 133	Rick Camp	.10	.05	.01
☐ 134	Chris Chambliss	.12	.05	.02
☐ 135	Ken Dayley	.10	.05	.01
☐ 136	Gene Garber	.10	.05	.01
☐ 137	Terry Harper	.10	.05	.01
☐ 138	Bob Horner	.12	.05	.02
☐ 139	Glenn Hubbard	.10	.05	.01
☐ 140	Rufino Linares	.10	.05	.01
☐ 141	Rick Mahler	.10	.05	.01
☐ 142	Dale Murphy	.75	.35	.09
☐ 143	Phil Niekro	.40	.18	.05
☐ 144	Pascual Perez	.10	.05	.01
☐ 145	Biff Pocoroba	.10	.05	.01
☐ 146	Rafael Ramirez	.10	.05	.01
☐ 147	Jerry Royster	.10	.05	.01
☐ 148	Ken Smith	.10	.05	.01
☐ 149	Bob Walk	.10	.05	.01
☐ 150	Claudell Washington	.10	.05	.01
☐ 151	Bob Watson	.12	.05	.02
☐ 152	Larry Whisenton	.10	.05	.01
☐ 153	Porfirio Altamirano	.10	.05	.01
☐ 154	Marty Bystrom	.10	.05	.01
☐ 155	Steve Carlton	1.25	.55	.16
☐ 156	Larry Christenson	.10	.05	.01
☐ 157	Ivan DeJesus	.10	.05	.01
☐ 158	John Denny	.10	.05	.01
☐ 159	Bob Dernier	.10	.05	.01
☐ 160	Bo Diaz	.10	.05	.01
☐ 161	Ed Farmer	.10	.05	.01
☐ 162	Greg Gross	.10	.05	.01
☐ 163	Mike Krukow	.10	.05	.01
☐ 164	Garry Maddox	.10	.05	.01
☐ 165	Gary Matthews	.12	.05	.02
☐ 166	Tug McGraw	.12	.05	.02
☐ 167	Bob Molinaro	.10	.05	.01
☐ 168	Sid Monge	.10	.05	.01
☐ 169	Ron Reed	.10	.05	.01
☐ 170	Bill Robinson	.12	.05	.02
☐ 171	Pete Rose	1.25	.55	.16
☐ 172	Dick Ruthven	.10	.05	.01
☐ 173	Mike Schmidt	2.00	.90	.25
☐ 174	Manny Trillo	.10	.05	.01
☐ 175	Ozzie Virgil	.10	.05	.01
☐ 176	George Vukovich	.10	.05	.01
☐ 177	Gary Allenson	.10	.05	.01
☐ 178	Luis Aponte	.10	.05	.01
☐ 179	Wade Boggs	24.00	11.00	3.00
☐ 180	Tom Burgmeier	.10	.05	.01
☐ 181	Mark Clear	.10	.05	.01
☐ 182	Dennis Eckersley	1.25	.55	.16
☐ 183	Dwight Evans	.25	.11	.03
☐ 184	Rich Gedman	.10	.05	.01
☐ 185	Glenn Hoffman	.10	.05	.01
☐ 186	Bruce Hurst	.12	.05	.02
☐ 187	Carney Lansford	.12	.05	.02
☐ 188	Rick Miller	.10	.05	.01
☐ 189	Reid Nichols	.10	.05	.01
☐ 190	Bob Ojeda	.12	.05	.02
☐ 191	Tony Perez	.30	.14	.04
☐ 192	Chuck Rainey	.10	.05	.01
☐ 193	Jerry Remy	.10	.05	.01
☐ 194	Jim Rice	.20	.09	.03
☐ 195	Bob Stanley	.10	.05	.01
☐ 196	Dave Stapleton	.10	.05	.01
☐ 197	Mike Torrez	.10	.05	.01

☐	198	John Tudor	.12	.05	.02
☐	199	Julio Valdez	.10	.05	.01
☐	200	Carl Yastrzemski	1.25	.55	.16
☐	201	Dusty Baker	.12	.05	.02
☐	202	Joe Beckwith	.10	.05	.01
☐	203	Greg Brock	.12	.05	.02
☐	204	Ron Cey	.12	.05	.02
☐	205	Terry Forster	.10	.05	.01
☐	206	Steve Garvey	.40	.18	.05
☐	207	Pedro Guerrero	.25	.11	.03
☐	208	Burt Hooton	.10	.05	.01
☐	209	Steve Howe	.10	.05	.01
☐	210	Ken Landreaux	.10	.05	.01
☐	211	Mike Marshall	.12	.05	.02
☐	212	Candy Maldonado	1.00	.45	.13
☐	213	Rick Monday	.10	.05	.01
☐	214	Tom Niedenfuer	.10	.05	.01
☐	215	Jorge Orta	.10	.05	.01
☐	216	Jerry Reuss UER ("Home:" omitted)	.10	.05	.01
☐	217	Ron Roenicke	.10	.05	.01
☐	218	Vicente Romo	.10	.05	.01
☐	219	Bill Russell	.12	.05	.02
☐	220	Steve Sax	.75	.35	.09
☐	221	Mike Scioscia	.12	.05	.02
☐	222	Dave Stewart	.75	.35	.09
☐	223	Derrel Thomas	.10	.05	.01
☐	224	Fernando Valenzuela	.15	.07	.02
☐	225	Bob Welch	.25	.11	.03
☐	226	Ricky Wright	.10	.05	.01
☐	227	Steve Yeager	.10	.05	.01
☐	228	Bill Almon	.10	.05	.01
☐	229	Harold Baines	.50	.23	.06
☐	230	Salome Barojas	.10	.05	.01
☐	231	Tony Bernazard	.10	.05	.01
☐	232	Britt Burns	.10	.05	.01
☐	233	Richard Dotson	.10	.05	.01
☐	234	Ernesto Escarrega	.10	.05	.01
☐	235	Carlton Fisk	1.25	.55	.16
☐	236	Jerry Hairston	.10	.05	.01
☐	237	Kevin Hickey	.10	.05	.01
☐	238	LaMarr Hoyt	.10	.05	.01
☐	239	Steve Kemp	.10	.05	.01
☐	240	Jim Kern	.10	.05	.01
☐	241	Ron Kittle	.25	.11	.03
☐	242	Jerry Koosman	.12	.05	.02
☐	243	Dennis Lamp	.10	.05	.01
☐	244	Rudy Law	.10	.05	.01
☐	245	Vance Law	.10	.05	.01
☐	246	Ron LeFlore	.12	.05	.02
☐	247	Greg Luzinski	.12	.05	.02
☐	248	Tom Paciorek	.12	.05	.02
☐	249	Aurelio Rodriguez	.10	.05	.01
☐	250	Mike Squires	.10	.05	.01
☐	251	Steve Trout	.10	.05	.01
☐	252	Jim Barr	.10	.05	.01
☐	253	Dave Bergman	.10	.05	.01
☐	254	Fred Breining	.10	.05	.01
☐	255	Bob Brenly	.10	.05	.01
☐	256	Jack Clark	.15	.07	.02
☐	257	Chili Davis	.50	.23	.06
☐	258	Darrell Evans	.12	.05	.02
☐	259	Alan Fowlkes	.10	.05	.01
☐	260	Rich Gale	.10	.05	.01
☐	261	Atlee Hammaker	.10	.05	.01
☐	262	Al Holland	.10	.05	.01
☐	263	Duane Kuiper	.10	.05	.01
☐	264	Bill Laskey	.10	.05	.01
☐	265	Gary Lavelle	.10	.05	.01
☐	266	Johnnie LeMaster	.10	.05	.01
☐	267	Renie Martin	.10	.05	.01
☐	268	Milt May	.10	.05	.01
☐	269	Greg Minton	.10	.05	.01
☐	270	Joe Morgan	.60	.25	.08
☐	271	Tom O'Malley	.10	.05	.01
☐	272	Reggie Smith	.12	.05	.02
☐	273	Guy Sularz	.10	.05	.01
☐	274	Champ Summers	.10	.05	.01
☐	275	Max Venable	.10	.05	.01
☐	276	Jim Wohlford	.10	.05	.01
☐	277	Ray Burris	.10	.05	.01
☐	278	Gary Carter	.75	.35	.09
☐	279	Warren Cromartie	.10	.05	.01
☐	280	Andre Dawson	1.50	.65	.19
☐	281	Terry Francona	.10	.05	.01
☐	282	Doug Flynn	.10	.05	.01
☐	283	Woodie Fryman	.10	.05	.01
☐	284	Bill Gullickson	.20	.09	.03
☐	285	Wallace Johnson	.10	.05	.01
☐	286	Charlie Lea	.10	.05	.01
☐	287	Randy Lerch	.10	.05	.01
☐	288	Brad Mills	.10	.05	.01
☐	289	Dan Norman	.10	.05	.01
☐	290	Al Oliver	.12	.05	.02
☐	291	David Palmer	.10	.05	.01
☐	292	Tim Raines	.60	.25	.08
☐	293	Jeff Reardon	1.25	.55	.16
☐	294	Steve Rogers	.10	.05	.01
☐	295	Scott Sanderson	.10	.05	.01
☐	296	Dan Schatzeder	.10	.05	.01
☐	297	Bryn Smith	.12	.05	.02
☐	298	Chris Speier	.10	.05	.01
☐	299	Tim Wallach	.20	.09	.03
☐	300	Jerry White	.10	.05	.01
☐	301	Joel Youngblood	.10	.05	.01
☐	302	Ross Baumgarten	.10	.05	.01
☐	303	Dale Berra	.10	.05	.01
☐	304	John Candelaria	.10	.05	.01
☐	305	Dick Davis	.10	.05	.01
☐	306	Mike Easler	.10	.05	.01
☐	307	Richie Hebner	.10	.05	.01
☐	308	Lee Lacy	.10	.05	.01
☐	309	Bill Madlock	.12	.05	.02
☐	310	Larry McWilliams	.10	.05	.01
☐	311	John Milner	.10	.05	.01
☐	312	Omar Moreno	.10	.05	.01
☐	313	Jim Morrison	.10	.05	.01
☐	314	Steve Nicosia	.10	.05	.01
☐	315	Dave Parker	.35	.16	.04
☐	316	Tony Pena	.12	.05	.02
☐	317	Johnny Ray	.10	.05	.01
☐	318	Rick Rhoden	.10	.05	.01
☐	319	Don Robinson	.10	.05	.01
☐	320	Enrique Romo	.10	.05	.01
☐	321	Manny Sarmiento	.10	.05	.01
☐	322	Rod Scurry	.10	.05	.01
☐	323	Jimmy Smith	.10	.05	.01
☐	324	Willie Stargell	.60	.25	.08
☐	325	Jason Thompson	.10	.05	.01
☐	326	Kent Tekulve	.12	.05	.02
☐	327A	Tom Brookens (Short .375" brown box shaded in on card back)	.10	.05	.01
☐	327B	Tom Brookens (Longer 1.25" brown box shaded in on card back)	.10	.05	.01
☐	328	Enos Cabell	.10	.05	.01
☐	329	Kirk Gibson	.35	.16	.04
☐	330	Larry Herndon	.10	.05	.01
☐	331	Mike Ivie	.10	.05	.01
☐	332	Howard Johnson	6.00	2.70	.75
☐	333	Lynn Jones	.10	.05	.01
☐	334	Rick Leach	.10	.05	.01
☐	335	Chet Lemon	.10	.05	.01
☐	336	Jack Morris	1.25	.55	.16
☐	337	Lance Parrish	.15	.07	.02
☐	338	Larry Pashnick	.10	.05	.01
☐	339	Dan Petry	.10	.05	.01
☐	340	Dave Rozema	.10	.05	.01
☐	341	Dave Rucker	.10	.05	.01
☐	342	Elias Sosa	.10	.05	.01
☐	343	Dave Tobik	.10	.05	.01
☐	344	Alan Trammell	.50	.23	.06
☐	345	Jerry Turner	.10	.05	.01
☐	346	Jerry Ujdur	.10	.05	.01
☐	347	Pat Underwood	.10	.05	.01
☐	348	Lou Whitaker	.50	.23	.06
☐	349	Milt Wilcox	.10	.05	.01
☐	350	Glenn Wilson	.12	.05	.02
☐	351	John Wockenfuss	.10	.05	.01
☐	352	Kurt Bevacqua	.10	.05	.01
☐	353	Juan Bonilla	.10	.05	.01
☐	354	Floyd Chiffer	.10	.05	.01
☐	355	Luis DeLeon	.10	.05	.01
☐	356	Dave Dravecky	.60	.25	.08
☐	357	Dave Edwards	.10	.05	.01
☐	358	Juan Eichelberger	.10	.05	.01
☐	359	Tim Flannery	.10	.05	.01
☐	360	Tony Gwynn	25.00	11.50	3.10
☐	361	Ruppert Jones	.10	.05	.01
☐	362	Terry Kennedy	.10	.05	.01
☐	363	Joe Lefebvre	.10	.05	.01
☐	364	Sixto Lezcano	.10	.05	.01
☐	365	Tim Lollar	.10	.05	.01
☐	366	Gary Lucas	.10	.05	.01
☐	367	John Montefusco	.10	.05	.01
☐	368	Broderick Perkins	.10	.05	.01
☐	369	Joe Pittman	.10	.05	.01
☐	370	Gene Richards	.10	.05	.01
☐	371	Luis Salazar	.10	.05	.01
☐	372	Eric Show	.10	.05	.01
☐	373	Garry Templeton	.12	.05	.02
☐	374	Chris Welsh	.10	.05	.01
☐	375	Alan Wiggins	.10	.05	.01
☐	376	Rick Cerone	.10	.05	.01
☐	377	Dave Collins	.10	.05	.01

☐ 378 Roger Erickson .10 .05 .01
☐ 379 George Frazier .10 .05 .01
☐ 380 Oscar Gamble .10 .05 .01
☐ 381 Rich Gossage .20 .09 .03
☐ 382 Ken Griffey .25 .11 .03
☐ 383 Ron Guidry .20 .09 .03
☐ 384 Dave LaRoche .10 .05 .01
☐ 385 Rudy May .10 .05 .01
☐ 386 John Mayberry .10 .05 .01
☐ 387 Lee Mazzilli .10 .05 .01
☐ 388 Mike Morgan .35 .16 .04
☐ 389 Jerry Mumphrey .10 .05 .01
☐ 390 Bobby Murcer .12 .05 .02
☐ 391 Graig Nettles .12 .05 .02
☐ 392 Lou Piniella .12 .05 .02
☐ 393 Willie Randolph .12 .05 .02
☐ 394 Shane Rawley .10 .05 .01
☐ 395 Dave Righetti .15 .07 .02
☐ 396 Andre Robertson .10 .05 .01
☐ 397 Roy Smalley .10 .05 .01
☐ 398 Dave Winfield 2.00 .90 .25
☐ 399 Butch Wynegar .10 .05 .01
☐ 400 Chris Bando .10 .05 .01
☐ 401 Alan Bannister .10 .05 .01
☐ 402 Len Barker .10 .05 .01
☐ 403 Tom Brennan .10 .05 .01
☐ 404 Carmelo Castillo .10 .05 .01
☐ 405 Miguel Dilone .10 .05 .01
☐ 406 Jerry Dybzinski .10 .05 .01
☐ 407 Mike Fischlin .10 .05 .01
☐ 408 Ed Glynn UER .10 .05 .01
(Photo actually
Bud Anderson)
☐ 409 Mike Hargrove .12 .05 .02
☐ 410 Toby Harrah .10 .05 .01
☐ 411 Ron Hassey .10 .05 .01
☐ 412 Von Hayes .12 .05 .02
☐ 413 Rick Manning .10 .05 .01
☐ 414 Bake McBride .10 .05 .01
☐ 415 Larry Milbourne .10 .05 .01
☐ 416 Bill Nahorodny .10 .05 .01
☐ 417 Jack Perconte .10 .05 .01
☐ 418 Lary Sorensen .10 .05 .01
☐ 419 Dan Spillner .10 .05 .01
☐ 420 Rick Sutcliffe .25 .11 .03
☐ 421 Andre Thornton .10 .05 .01
☐ 422 Rick Waits .10 .05 .01
☐ 423 Eddie Whitson .10 .05 .01
☐ 424 Jesse Barfield .20 .09 .03
☐ 425 Barry Bonnell .10 .05 .01
☐ 426 Jim Clancy .10 .05 .01
☐ 427 Damaso Garcia .10 .05 .01
☐ 428 Jerry Garvin .10 .05 .01
☐ 429 Alfredo Griffin .10 .05 .01
☐ 430 Garth Iorg .10 .05 .01
☐ 431 Roy Lee Jackson .10 .05 .01
☐ 432 Luis Leal .10 .05 .01
☐ 433 Buck Martinez .10 .05 .01
☐ 434 Joey McLaughlin .10 .05 .01
☐ 435 Lloyd Moseby .10 .05 .01
☐ 436 Rance Mulliniks .10 .05 .01
☐ 437 Dale Murray .10 .05 .01
☐ 438 Wayne Nordhagen .10 .05 .01
☐ 439 Geno Petralli .12 .05 .02
☐ 440 Hosken Powell .10 .05 .01
☐ 441 Dave Stieb .20 .09 .03
☐ 442 Willie Upshaw .10 .05 .01
☐ 443 Ernie Whitt .10 .05 .01
☐ 444 Alvis Woods .10 .05 .01
☐ 445 Alan Ashby .10 .05 .01
☐ 446 Jose Cruz .12 .05 .02
☐ 447 Kiko Garcia .10 .05 .01
☐ 448 Phil Garner .12 .05 .02
☐ 449 Danny Heep .10 .05 .01
☐ 450 Art Howe .10 .05 .01
☐ 451 Bob Knepper .10 .05 .01
☐ 452 Alan Knicely .10 .05 .01
☐ 453 Ray Knight .12 .05 .02
☐ 454 Frank LaCorte .10 .05 .01
☐ 455 Mike LaCoss .10 .05 .01
☐ 456 Randy Moffitt .10 .05 .01
☐ 457 Joe Niekro .12 .05 .02
☐ 458 Terry Puhl .10 .05 .01
☐ 459 Luis Pujols .10 .05 .01
☐ 460 Craig Reynolds .10 .05 .01
☐ 461 Bert Roberge .10 .05 .01
☐ 462 Vern Ruhle .10 .05 .01
☐ 463 Nolan Ryan 7.00 3.10 .85
☐ 464 Joe Sambito .10 .05 .01
☐ 465 Tony Scott .10 .05 .01
☐ 466 Dave Smith .10 .05 .01
☐ 467 Harry Spilman .10 .05 .01
☐ 468 Dickie Thon .10 .05 .01
☐ 469 Denny Walling .10 .05 .01
☐ 470 Larry Andersen .10 .05 .01
☐ 471 Floyd Bannister .10 .05 .01
☐ 472 Jim Beattie .10 .05 .01
☐ 473 Bruce Bochte .10 .05 .01
☐ 474 Manny Castillo .10 .05 .01
☐ 475 Bill Caudill .10 .05 .01
☐ 476 Bryan Clark .10 .05 .01
☐ 477 Al Cowens .10 .05 .01
☐ 478 Julio Cruz .10 .05 .01
☐ 479 Todd Cruz .10 .05 .01
☐ 480 Gary Gray .10 .05 .01
☐ 481 Dave Henderson .50 .23 .06
☐ 482 Mike Moore 1.00 .45 .13
☐ 483 Gaylord Perry .40 .18 .05
☐ 484 Dave Revering .10 .05 .01
☐ 485 Joe Simpson .10 .05 .01
☐ 486 Mike Stanton .10 .05 .01
☐ 487 Rick Sweet .10 .05 .01
☐ 488 Ed VandeBerg .10 .05 .01
☐ 489 Richie Zisk .10 .05 .01
☐ 490 Doug Bird .10 .05 .01
☐ 491 Larry Bowa .12 .05 .02
☐ 492 Bill Buckner .12 .05 .02
☐ 493 Bill Campbell .10 .05 .01
☐ 494 Jody Davis .10 .05 .01
☐ 495 Leon Durham .10 .05 .01
☐ 496 Steve Henderson .10 .05 .01
☐ 497 Willie Hernandez .12 .05 .02
☐ 498 Ferguson Jenkins .40 .18 .05
☐ 499 Jay Johnstone .12 .05 .02
☐ 500 Junior Kennedy .10 .05 .01
☐ 501 Randy Martz .10 .05 .01
☐ 502 Jerry Morales .10 .05 .01
☐ 503 Keith Moreland .10 .05 .01
☐ 504 Dickie Noles .10 .05 .01
☐ 505 Mike Proly .10 .05 .01
☐ 506 Allen Ripley .10 .05 .01
☐ 507 Ryne Sandberg UER 40.00 18.00 5.00
(Should say High School
in Spokane, Washington)
☐ 508 Lee Smith 2.25 1.00 .30
☐ 509 Pat Tabler .10 .05 .01
☐ 510 Dick Tidrow .10 .05 .01
☐ 511 Bump Wills .10 .05 .01
☐ 512 Gary Woods .10 .05 .01
☐ 513 Tony Armas .10 .05 .01
☐ 514 Dave Beard .10 .05 .01
☐ 515 Jeff Burroughs .10 .05 .01
☐ 516 John D'Acquisto .10 .05 .01
☐ 517 Wayne Gross .10 .05 .01
☐ 518 Mike Heath .10 .05 .01
☐ 519 Rickey Henderson UER 3.50 1.55 .45
(Brock record listed
as 120 steals)
☐ 520 Cliff Johnson .10 .05 .01
☐ 521 Matt Keough .10 .05 .01
☐ 522 Brian Kingman .10 .05 .01
☐ 523 Rick Langford .10 .05 .01
☐ 524 Dave Lopes .12 .05 .02
☐ 525 Steve McCatty .10 .05 .01
☐ 526 Dave McKay .10 .05 .01
☐ 527 Dan Meyer .10 .05 .01
☐ 528 Dwayne Murphy .10 .05 .01
☐ 529 Jeff Newman .10 .05 .01
☐ 530 Mike Norris .10 .05 .01
☐ 531 Bob Owchinko .10 .05 .01
☐ 532 Joe Rudi .10 .05 .01
☐ 533 Jimmy Sexton .10 .05 .01
☐ 534 Fred Stanley .10 .05 .01
☐ 535 Tom Underwood .10 .05 .01
☐ 536 Neil Allen .10 .05 .01
☐ 537 Wally Backman .12 .05 .02
☐ 538 Bob Bailor .10 .05 .01
☐ 539 Hubie Brooks .15 .07 .02
☐ 540 Carlos Diaz .10 .05 .01
☐ 541 Pete Falcone .10 .05 .01
☐ 542 George Foster .12 .05 .02
☐ 543 Ron Gardenhire .10 .05 .01
☐ 544 Brian Giles .10 .05 .01
☐ 545 Ron Hodges .10 .05 .01
☐ 546 Randy Jones .10 .05 .01
☐ 547 Mike Jorgensen .10 .05 .01
☐ 548 Dave Kingman .12 .05 .02
☐ 549 Ed Lynch .10 .05 .01
☐ 550 Jesse Orosco .10 .05 .01
☐ 551 Rick Ownbey .10 .05 .01
☐ 552 Charlie Puleo .10 .05 .01
☐ 553 Gary Rajsich .10 .05 .01
☐ 554 Mike Scott .12 .05 .02
☐ 555 Rusty Staub .12 .05 .02
☐ 556 John Stearns .10 .05 .01
☐ 557 Craig Swan .10 .05 .01

☐ 558	Ellis Valentine	.10	.05	.01
☐ 559	Tom Veryzer	.10	.05	.01
☐ 560	Mookie Wilson	.12	.05	.02
☐ 561	Pat Zachry	.10	.05	.01
☐ 562	Buddy Bell	.12	.05	.02
☐ 563	John Butcher	.10	.05	.01
☐ 564	Steve Comer	.10	.05	.01
☐ 565	Danny Darwin	.10	.05	.01
☐ 566	Bucky Dent	.12	.05	.02
☐ 567	John Grubb	.10	.05	.01
☐ 568	Rick Honeycutt	.10	.05	.01
☐ 569	Dave Hostetler	.10	.05	.01
☐ 570	Charlie Hough	.12	.05	.02
☐ 571	Lamar Johnson	.10	.05	.01
☐ 572	Jon Matlack	.10	.05	.01
☐ 573	Paul Mirabella	.10	.05	.01
☐ 574	Larry Parrish	.10	.05	.01
☐ 575	Mike Richardt	.10	.05	.01
☐ 576	Mickey Rivers	.10	.05	.01
☐ 577	Billy Sample	.10	.05	.01
☐ 578	Dave Schmidt	.10	.05	.01
☐ 579	Bill Stein	.10	.05	.01
☐ 580	Jim Sundberg	.12	.05	.02
☐ 581	Frank Tanana	.12	.05	.02
☐ 582	Mark Wagner	.10	.05	.01
☐ 583	George Wright	.10	.05	.01
☐ 584	Johnny Bench	1.25	.55	.16
☐ 585	Bruce Berenyi	.10	.05	.01
☐ 586	Larry Biittner	.10	.05	.01
☐ 587	Cesar Cedeno	.12	.05	.02
☐ 588	Dave Concepcion	.12	.05	.02
☐ 589	Dan Driessen	.10	.05	.01
☐ 590	Greg Harris	.10	.05	.01
☐ 591	Ben Hayes	.10	.05	.01
☐ 592	Paul Householder	.10	.05	.01
☐ 593	Tom Hume	.10	.05	.01
☐ 594	Wayne Krenchicki	.10	.05	.01
☐ 595	Rafael Landestoy	.10	.05	.01
☐ 596	Charlie Leibrandt	.12	.05	.02
☐ 597	Eddie Milner	.10	.05	.01
☐ 598	Ron Oester	.10	.05	.01
☐ 599	Frank Pastore	.10	.05	.01
☐ 600	Joe Price	.10	.05	.01
☐ 601	Tom Seaver	1.25	.55	.16
☐ 602	Bob Shirley	.10	.05	.01
☐ 603	Mario Soto	.10	.05	.01
☐ 604	Alex Trevino	.10	.05	.01
☐ 605	Mike Vail	.10	.05	.01
☐ 606	Duane Walker	.10	.05	.01
☐ 607	Tom Brunansky	.40	.18	.05
☐ 608	Bobby Castillo	.10	.05	.01
☐ 609	John Castino	.10	.05	.01
☐ 610	Ron Davis	.10	.05	.01
☐ 611	Lenny Faedo	.10	.05	.01
☐ 612	Terry Felton	.10	.05	.01
☐ 613	Gary Gaetti	.40	.18	.05
☐ 614	Mickey Hatcher	.10	.05	.01
☐ 615	Brad Havens	.10	.05	.01
☐ 616	Kent Hrbek	.75	.35	.09
☐ 617	Randy Johnson	.10	.05	.01
☐ 618	Tim Laudner	.10	.05	.01
☐ 619	Jeff Little	.10	.05	.01
☐ 620	Bobby Mitchell	.10	.05	.01
☐ 621	Jack O'Connor	.10	.05	.01
☐ 622	John Pacella	.10	.05	.01
☐ 623	Pete Redfern	.10	.05	.01
☐ 624	Jesus Vega	.10	.05	.01
☐ 625	Frank Viola	3.00	1.35	.40
☐ 626	Ron Washington	.10	.05	.01
☐ 627	Gary Ward	.10	.05	.01
☐ 628	Al Williams	.10	.05	.01
☐ 629	Red Sox All-Stars Carl Yastrzemski Dennis Eckersley Mark Clear	.75	.35	.09
☐ 630	"300 Career Wins" Gaylord Perry and Terry Bulling 5/6/82	.15	.07	.02
☐ 631	Pride of Venezuela Dave Concepcion and Manny Trillo	.15	.07	.02
☐ 632	All-Star Infielders Robin Yount and Buddy Bell	.60	.25	.08
☐ 633	Mr.Vet and Mr.Rookie Dave Winfield and Kent Hrbek	.60	.25	.08
☐ 634	Fountain of Youth Willie Stargell and Pete Rose	.60	.25	.08
☐ 635	Big Chiefs Toby Harrah and Andre Thornton	.15	.07	.02
☐ 636	Smith Brothers Ozzie and Lonnie	.50	.23	.06
☐ 637	Base Stealers' Threat Bo Diaz and Gary Carter	.15	.07	.02
☐ 638	All-Star Catchers Carlton Fisk and Gary Carter	.25	.11	.03
☐ 639	The Silver Shoe Rickey Henderson	2.00	.90	.25
☐ 640	Home Run Threats Ben Oglivie and Reggie Jackson	.40	.18	.05
☐ 641	Two Teams Same Day Joel Youngblood August 4, 1982	.15	.07	.02
☐ 642	Last Perfect Game Ron Hassey and Len Barker	.15	.07	.02
☐ 643	Black and Blue Vida Blue	.15	.07	.02
☐ 644	Black and Blue Bud Black	.15	.07	.02
☐ 645	Speed and Power Reggie Jackson	.75	.35	.09
☐ 646	Speed and Power Rickey Henderson	1.50	.65	.19
☐ 647	CL: Cards/Brewers	.15	.02	.00
☐ 648	CL: Orioles/Angels	.15	.02	.00
☐ 649	CL: Royals/Braves	.15	.02	.00
☐ 650	CL: Phillies/Red Sox	.15	.02	.00
☐ 651	CL: Dodgers/White Sox	.15	.02	.00
☐ 652	CL: Giants/Expos	.15	.02	.00
☐ 653	CL: Pirates/Tigers	.15	.02	.00
☐ 654	CL: Padres/Yankees	.15	.02	.00
☐ 655	CL: Indians/Blue Jays	.15	.02	.00
☐ 656	CL: Astros/Mariners	.15	.02	.00
☐ 657	CL: Cubs/A's	.15	.02	.00
☐ 658	CL: Mets/Rangers	.15	.02	.00
☐ 659	CL: Reds/Twins	.15	.02	.00
☐ 660	CL: Specials/Teams	.15	.02	.00

1984 Fleer

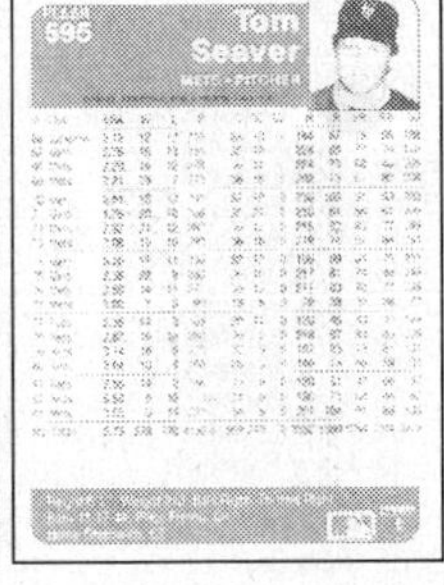

The cards in this 660-card set measure 2 1/2" by 3 1/2". The 1984 Fleer card set featured fronts with full-color team logos along with the player's name and position and the Fleer identification. The set features many imaginative photos, several multi-player cards, and many more action shots than the 1983 card set. The backs are quite similar to the 1983 backs except that blue rather than brown ink is used. The player cards are alphabetized within team and the teams are ordered by their 1983 season finish and won-lost record, e.g., Baltimore (1-23), Philadelphia (24-49), Chicago White Sox (50-73), Detroit (74-95), Los Angeles (96-118), New York Yankees (119-144), Toronto (145-169), Atlanta (170-193), Milwaukee (194-219), Houston (220-244), Pittsburgh (245-269), Montreal (270-293), San Diego (294-317), St. Louis (318-340), Kansas City (341-364), San Francisco (365-387), Boston (388-412), Texas (413-435), Oakland (436-461), Cincinnati (462-485), Chicago (486-507), California (508-532), Cleveland (533-555), Minnesota (556-579), New York Mets (580-603), and Seattle (604-

625). Specials (626-646) and checklist cards (647-660) make up the end of the set. The key Rookie Cards in this set are Tony Fernandez, Don Mattingly, Kevin McReynolds, Juan Samuel, Darryl Strawberry, and Andy Van Slyke.

	NRMT-MT	EXC	G-VG
COMPLETE SET (660)	200.00	90.00	25.00
COMMON PLAYER (1-660)	.15	.07	.02
☐ 1 Mike Boddicker	.20	.09	.03
☐ 2 Al Bumbry	.15	.07	.02
☐ 3 Todd Cruz	.15	.07	.02
☐ 4 Rich Dauer	.15	.07	.02
☐ 5 Storm Davis	.15	.07	.02
☐ 6 Rick Dempsey	.15	.07	.02
☐ 7 Jim Dwyer	.15	.07	.02
☐ 8 Mike Flanagan	.15	.07	.02
☐ 9 Dan Ford	.15	.07	.02
☐ 10 John Lowenstein	.15	.07	.02
☐ 11 Dennis Martinez	.20	.09	.03
☐ 12 Tippy Martinez	.15	.07	.02
☐ 13 Scott McGregor	.15	.07	.02
☐ 14 Eddie Murray	4.00	1.80	.50
☐ 15 Joe Nolan	.15	.07	.02
☐ 16 Jim Palmer	3.00	1.35	.40
☐ 17 Cal Ripken	20.00	9.00	2.50
☐ 18 Gary Roenicke	.15	.07	.02
☐ 19 Lenn Sakata	.15	.07	.02
☐ 20 John Shelby	.15	.07	.02
☐ 21 Ken Singleton	.20	.09	.03
☐ 22 Sammy Stewart	.15	.07	.02
☐ 23 Tim Stoddard	.15	.07	.02
☐ 24 Marty Bystrom	.15	.07	.02
☐ 25 Steve Carlton	3.00	1.35	.40
☐ 26 Ivan DeJesus	.15	.07	.02
☐ 27 John Denny	.15	.07	.02
☐ 28 Bob Dernier	.15	.07	.02
☐ 29 Bo Diaz	.15	.07	.02
☐ 30 Kiko Garcia	.15	.07	.02
☐ 31 Greg Gross	.15	.07	.02
☐ 32 Kevin Gross	.40	.18	.05
☐ 33 Von Hayes	.20	.09	.03
☐ 34 Willie Hernandez	.20	.09	.03
☐ 35 Al Holland	.15	.07	.02
☐ 36 Charles Hudson	.15	.07	.02
☐ 37 Joe Lefebvre	.15	.07	.02
☐ 38 Sixto Lezcano	.15	.07	.02
☐ 39 Garry Maddox	.15	.07	.02
☐ 40 Gary Matthews	.20	.09	.03
☐ 41 Len Matuszek	.15	.07	.02
☐ 42 Tug McGraw	.20	.09	.03
☐ 43 Joe Morgan	1.00	.45	.13
☐ 44 Tony Perez	.75	.35	.09
☐ 45 Ron Reed	.15	.07	.02
☐ 46 Pete Rose	3.00	1.35	.40
☐ 47 Juan Samuel	1.00	.45	.13
☐ 48 Mike Schmidt	9.00	4.00	1.15
☐ 49 Ozzie Virgil	.15	.07	.02
☐ 50 Juan Agosto	.15	.07	.02
☐ 51 Harold Baines	.60	.25	.08
☐ 52 Floyd Bannister	.15	.07	.02
☐ 53 Salome Barojas	.15	.07	.02
☐ 54 Britt Burns	.15	.07	.02
☐ 55 Julio Cruz	.15	.07	.02
☐ 56 Richard Dotson	.15	.07	.02
☐ 57 Jerry Dybzinski	.15	.07	.02
☐ 58 Carlton Fisk	3.00	1.35	.40
☐ 59 Scott Fletcher	.15	.07	.02
☐ 60 Jerry Hairston	.15	.07	.02
☐ 61 Kevin Hickey	.15	.07	.02
☐ 62 Marc Hill	.15	.07	.02
☐ 63 LaMarr Hoyt	.15	.07	.02
☐ 64 Ron Kittle	.20	.09	.03
☐ 65 Jerry Koosman	.20	.09	.03
☐ 66 Dennis Lamp	.15	.07	.02
☐ 67 Rudy Law	.15	.07	.02
☐ 68 Vance Law	.15	.07	.02
☐ 69 Greg Luzinski	.20	.09	.03
☐ 70 Tom Paciorek	.20	.09	.03
☐ 71 Mike Squires	.15	.07	.02
☐ 72 Dick Tidrow	.15	.07	.02
☐ 73 Greg Walker	.20	.09	.03
☐ 74 Glenn Abbott	.15	.07	.02
☐ 75 Howard Bailey	.15	.07	.02
☐ 76 Doug Bair	.15	.07	.02
☐ 77 Juan Berenguer	.15	.07	.02
☐ 78 Tom Brookens	.15	.07	.02
☐ 79 Enos Cabell	.15	.07	.02
☐ 80 Kirk Gibson	.60	.25	.08
☐ 81 John Grubb	.15	.07	.02
☐ 82 Larry Herndon	.15	.07	.02
☐ 83 Wayne Krenchicki	.15	.07	.02
☐ 84 Rick Leach	.15	.07	.02
☐ 85 Chet Lemon	.15	.07	.02
☐ 86 Aurelio Lopez	.15	.07	.02
☐ 87 Jack Morris	2.50	1.15	.30
☐ 88 Lance Parrish	.25	.11	.03
☐ 89 Dan Petry	.15	.07	.02
☐ 90 Dave Rozema	.15	.07	.02
☐ 91 Alan Trammell	1.00	.45	.13
☐ 92 Lou Whitaker	1.00	.45	.13
☐ 93 Milt Wilcox	.15	.07	.02
☐ 94 Glenn Wilson	.15	.07	.02
☐ 95 John Wockenfuss	.15	.07	.02
☐ 96 Dusty Baker	.20	.09	.03
☐ 97 Joe Beckwith	.15	.07	.02
☐ 98 Greg Brock	.15	.07	.02
☐ 99 Jack Fimple	.15	.07	.02
☐ 100 Pedro Guerrero	.25	.11	.03
☐ 101 Rick Honeycutt	.15	.07	.02
☐ 102 Burt Hooton	.15	.07	.02
☐ 103 Steve Howe	.15	.07	.02
☐ 104 Ken Landreaux	.15	.07	.02
☐ 105 Mike Marshall	.20	.09	.03
☐ 106 Rick Monday	.15	.07	.02
☐ 107 Jose Morales	.15	.07	.02
☐ 108 Tom Niedenfuer	.15	.07	.02
☐ 109 Alejandro Pena	.50	.23	.06
☐ 110 Jerry Reuss UER ("Home:" omitted)	.15	.07	.02
☐ 111 Bill Russell	.20	.09	.03
☐ 112 Steve Sax	.75	.35	.09
☐ 113 Mike Scioscia	.20	.09	.03
☐ 114 Derrel Thomas	.15	.07	.02
☐ 115 Fernando Valenzuela	.20	.09	.03
☐ 116 Bob Welch	.30	.14	.04
☐ 117 Steve Yeager	.15	.07	.02
☐ 118 Pat Zachry	.15	.07	.02
☐ 119 Don Baylor	.20	.09	.03
☐ 120 Bert Campaneris	.20	.09	.03
☐ 121 Rick Cerone	.15	.07	.02
☐ 122 Ray Fontenot	.15	.07	.02
☐ 123 George Frazier	.15	.07	.02
☐ 124 Oscar Gamble	.15	.07	.02
☐ 125 Rich Gossage	.25	.11	.03
☐ 126 Ken Griffey	.25	.11	.03
☐ 127 Ron Guidry	.20	.09	.03
☐ 128 Jay Howell	.20	.09	.03
☐ 129 Steve Kemp	.15	.07	.02
☐ 130 Matt Keough	.15	.07	.02
☐ 131 Don Mattingly	25.00	11.50	3.10
☐ 132 John Montefusco	.15	.07	.02
☐ 133 Omar Moreno	.15	.07	.02
☐ 134 Dale Murray	.15	.07	.02
☐ 135 Graig Nettles	.20	.09	.03
☐ 136 Lou Piniella	.20	.09	.03
☐ 137 Willie Randolph	.20	.09	.03
☐ 138 Shane Rawley	.15	.07	.02
☐ 139 Dave Righetti	.20	.09	.03
☐ 140 Andre Robertson	.15	.07	.02
☐ 141 Bob Shirley	.15	.07	.02
☐ 142 Roy Smalley	.15	.07	.02
☐ 143 Dave Winfield	5.00	2.30	.60
☐ 144 Butch Wynegar	.15	.07	.02
☐ 145 Jim Acker	.15	.07	.02
☐ 146 Doyle Alexander	.15	.07	.02
☐ 147 Jesse Barfield	.20	.09	.03
☐ 148 Jorge Bell	1.75	.80	.22
☐ 149 Barry Bonnell	.15	.07	.02
☐ 150 Jim Clancy	.15	.07	.02
☐ 151 Dave Collins	.15	.07	.02
☐ 152 Tony Fernandez	4.00	1.80	.50
☐ 153 Damaso Garcia	.15	.07	.02
☐ 154 Dave Geisel	.15	.07	.02
☐ 155 Jim Gott	.15	.07	.02
☐ 156 Alfredo Griffin	.15	.07	.02
☐ 157 Garth Iorg	.15	.07	.02
☐ 158 Roy Lee Jackson	.15	.07	.02
☐ 159 Cliff Johnson	.15	.07	.02
☐ 160 Luis Leal	.15	.07	.02
☐ 161 Buck Martinez	.15	.07	.02
☐ 162 Joey McLaughlin	.15	.07	.02
☐ 163 Randy Moffitt	.15	.07	.02
☐ 164 Lloyd Moseby	.15	.07	.02
☐ 165 Rance Mulliniks	.15	.07	.02
☐ 166 Jorge Orta	.15	.07	.02
☐ 167 Dave Stieb	.20	.09	.03
☐ 168 Willie Upshaw	.15	.07	.02
☐ 169 Ernie Whitt	.15	.07	.02
☐ 170 Len Barker	.15	.07	.02
☐ 171 Steve Bedrosian	.20	.09	.03
☐ 172 Bruce Benedict	.15	.07	.02
☐ 173 Brett Butler	.60	.25	.08
☐ 174 Rick Camp	.15	.07	.02
☐ 175 Chris Chambliss	.20	.09	.03

☐	176	Ken Dayley	.15	.07	.02
☐	177	Pete Falcone	.15	.07	.02
☐	178	Terry Forster	.15	.07	.02
☐	179	Gene Garber	.15	.07	.02
☐	180	Terry Harper	.15	.07	.02
☐	181	Bob Horner	.20	.09	.03
☐	182	Glenn Hubbard	.15	.07	.02
☐	183	Randy Johnson	.15	.07	.02
☐	184	Craig McMurtry	.15	.07	.02
☐	185	Donnie Moore	.15	.07	.02
☐	186	Dale Murphy	1.75	.80	.22
☐	187	Phil Niekro	.75	.35	.09
☐	188	Pascual Perez	.15	.07	.02
☐	189	Biff Pocoroba	.15	.07	.02
☐	190	Rafael Ramirez	.15	.07	.02
☐	191	Jerry Royster	.15	.07	.02
☐	192	Claudell Washington	.15	.07	.02
☐	193	Bob Watson	.20	.09	.03
☐	194	Jerry Augustine	.15	.07	.02
☐	195	Mark Brouhard	.15	.07	.02
☐	196	Mike Caldwell	.15	.07	.02
☐	197	Tom Candiotti	1.00	.45	.13
☐	198	Cecil Cooper	.20	.09	.03
☐	199	Rollie Fingers	1.00	.45	.13
☐	200	Jim Gantner	.20	.09	.03
☐	201	Bob L. Gibson	.15	.07	.02
☐	202	Moose Haas	.15	.07	.02
☐	203	Roy Howell	.15	.07	.02
☐	204	Pete Ladd	.15	.07	.02
☐	205	Rick Manning	.15	.07	.02
☐	206	Bob McClure	.15	.07	.02
☐	207	Paul Molitor UER ('83 stats should say .270 BA and 608 AB)	1.25	.55	.16
☐	208	Don Money	.15	.07	.02
☐	209	Charlie Moore	.15	.07	.02
☐	210	Ben Oglivie	.15	.07	.02
☐	211	Chuck Porter	.15	.07	.02
☐	212	Ed Romero	.15	.07	.02
☐	213	Ted Simmons	.20	.09	.03
☐	214	Jim Slaton	.15	.07	.02
☐	215	Don Sutton	.75	.35	.09
☐	216	Tom Tellmann	.15	.07	.02
☐	217	Pete Vuckovich	.15	.07	.02
☐	218	Ned Yost	.15	.07	.02
☐	219	Robin Yount	6.00	2.70	.75
☐	220	Alan Ashby	.15	.07	.02
☐	221	Kevin Bass	.15	.07	.02
☐	222	Jose Cruz	.20	.09	.03
☐	223	Bill Dawley	.15	.07	.02
☐	224	Frank DiPino	.15	.07	.02
☐	225	Bill Doran	.50	.23	.06
☐	226	Phil Garner	.20	.09	.03
☐	227	Art Howe	.15	.07	.02
☐	228	Bob Knepper	.15	.07	.02
☐	229	Ray Knight	.20	.09	.03
☐	230	Frank LaCorte	.15	.07	.02
☐	231	Mike LaCoss	.15	.07	.02
☐	232	Mike Madden	.15	.07	.02
☐	233	Jerry Mumphrey	.15	.07	.02
☐	234	Joe Niekro	.20	.09	.03
☐	235	Terry Puhl	.15	.07	.02
☐	236	Luis Pujols	.15	.07	.02
☐	237	Craig Reynolds	.15	.07	.02
☐	238	Vern Ruhle	.15	.07	.02
☐	239	Nolan Ryan	18.00	8.00	2.30
☐	240	Mike Scott	.20	.09	.03
☐	241	Tony Scott	.15	.07	.02
☐	242	Dave Smith	.15	.07	.02
☐	243	Dickie Thon	.15	.07	.02
☐	244	Denny Walling	.15	.07	.02
☐	245	Dale Berra	.15	.07	.02
☐	246	Jim Bibby	.15	.07	.02
☐	247	John Candelaria	.15	.07	.02
☐	248	Jose DeLeon	.20	.09	.03
☐	249	Mike Easler	.15	.07	.02
☐	250	Cecilio Guante	.15	.07	.02
☐	251	Richie Hebner	.15	.07	.02
☐	252	Lee Lacy	.15	.07	.02
☐	253	Bill Madlock	.20	.09	.03
☐	254	Milt May	.15	.07	.02
☐	255	Lee Mazzilli	.15	.07	.02
☐	256	Larry McWilliams	.15	.07	.02
☐	257	Jim Morrison	.15	.07	.02
☐	258	Dave Parker	.60	.25	.08
☐	259	Tony Pena	.20	.09	.03
☐	260	Johnny Ray	.15	.07	.02
☐	261	Rick Rhoden	.15	.07	.02
☐	262	Don Robinson	.15	.07	.02
☐	263	Manny Sarmiento	.15	.07	.02
☐	264	Rod Scurry	.15	.07	.02
☐	265	Kent Tekulve	.20	.09	.03
☐	266	Gene Tenace	.15	.07	.02
☐	267	Jason Thompson	.15	.07	.02
☐	268	Lee Tunnell	.15	.07	.02
☐	269	Marvell Wynne	.15	.07	.02
☐	270	Ray Burris	.15	.07	.02
☐	271	Gary Carter	1.00	.45	.13
☐	272	Warren Cromartie	.15	.07	.02
☐	273	Andre Dawson	4.00	1.80	.50
☐	274	Doug Flynn	.15	.07	.02
☐	275	Terry Francona	.15	.07	.02
☐	276	Bill Gullickson	.20	.09	.03
☐	277	Bob James	.15	.07	.02
☐	278	Charlie Lea	.15	.07	.02
☐	279	Bryan Little	.15	.07	.02
☐	280	Al Oliver	.20	.09	.03
☐	281	Tim Raines	1.00	.45	.13
☐	282	Bobby Ramos	.15	.07	.02
☐	283	Jeff Reardon	1.75	.80	.22
☐	284	Steve Rogers	.15	.07	.02
☐	285	Scott Sanderson	.15	.07	.02
☐	286	Dan Schatzeder	.15	.07	.02
☐	287	Bryn Smith	.15	.07	.02
☐	288	Chris Speier	.15	.07	.02
☐	289	Manny Trillo	.15	.07	.02
☐	290	Mike Vail	.15	.07	.02
☐	291	Tim Wallach	.20	.09	.03
☐	292	Chris Welsh	.15	.07	.02
☐	293	Jim Wohlford	.15	.07	.02
☐	294	Kurt Bevacqua	.15	.07	.02
☐	295	Juan Bonilla	.15	.07	.02
☐	296	Bobby Brown	.15	.07	.02
☐	297	Luis DeLeon	.15	.07	.02
☐	298	Dave Dravecky	.20	.09	.03
☐	299	Tim Flannery	.15	.07	.02
☐	300	Steve Garvey	.90	.40	.11
☐	301	Tony Gwynn	13.00	5.75	1.65
☐	302	Andy Hawkins	.20	.09	.03
☐	303	Ruppert Jones	.15	.07	.02
☐	304	Terry Kennedy	.15	.07	.02
☐	305	Tim Lollar	.15	.07	.02
☐	306	Gary Lucas	.15	.07	.02
☐	307	Kevin McReynolds	2.00	.90	.25
☐	308	Sid Monge	.15	.07	.02
☐	309	Mario Ramirez	.15	.07	.02
☐	310	Gene Richards	.15	.07	.02
☐	311	Luis Salazar	.15	.07	.02
☐	312	Eric Show	.15	.07	.02
☐	313	Elias Sosa	.15	.07	.02
☐	314	Garry Templeton	.20	.09	.03
☐	315	Mark Thurmond	.15	.07	.02
☐	316	Ed Whitson	.15	.07	.02
☐	317	Alan Wiggins	.15	.07	.02
☐	318	Neil Allen	.15	.07	.02
☐	319	Joaquin Andujar	.15	.07	.02
☐	320	Steve Braun	.15	.07	.02
☐	321	Glenn Brummer	.15	.07	.02
☐	322	Bob Forsch	.15	.07	.02
☐	323	David Green	.15	.07	.02
☐	324	George Hendrick	.15	.07	.02
☐	325	Tom Herr	.20	.09	.03
☐	326	Dane Iorg	.15	.07	.02
☐	327	Jeff Lahti	.15	.07	.02
☐	328	Dave LaPoint	.20	.09	.03
☐	329	Willie McGee	.75	.35	.09
☐	330	Ken Oberkfell	.15	.07	.02
☐	331	Darrell Porter	.15	.07	.02
☐	332	Jamie Quirk	.15	.07	.02
☐	333	Mike Ramsey	.15	.07	.02
☐	334	Floyd Rayford	.15	.07	.02
☐	335	Lonnie Smith	.20	.09	.03
☐	336	Ozzie Smith	4.00	1.80	.50
☐	337	John Stuper	.15	.07	.02
☐	338	Bruce Sutter	.25	.11	.03
☐	339	Andy Van Slyke UER (Batting and throwing both wrong on card back)	8.00	3.60	1.00
☐	340	Dave Von Ohlen	.15	.07	.02
☐	341	Willie Aikens	.15	.07	.02
☐	342	Mike Armstrong	.15	.07	.02
☐	343	Bud Black	.15	.07	.02
☐	344	George Brett	6.00	2.70	.75
☐	345	Onix Concepcion	.15	.07	.02
☐	346	Keith Creel	.15	.07	.02
☐	347	Larry Gura	.15	.07	.02
☐	348	Don Hood	.15	.07	.02
☐	349	Dennis Leonard	.15	.07	.02
☐	350	Hal McRae	.20	.09	.03
☐	351	Amos Otis	.20	.09	.03
☐	352	Gaylord Perry	.75	.35	.09
☐	353	Greg Pryor	.15	.07	.02
☐	354	Dan Quisenberry	.20	.09	.03
☐	355	Steve Renko	.15	.07	.02
☐	356	Leon Roberts	.15	.07	.02
☐	357	Pat Sheridan	.15	.07	.02

☐ 358	Joe Simpson	.15	.07	.02
☐ 359	Don Slaught	.20	.09	.03
☐ 360	Paul Splittorff	.15	.07	.02
☐ 361	U.L. Washington	.15	.07	.02
☐ 362	John Wathan	.15	.07	.02
☐ 363	Frank White	.20	.09	.03
☐ 364	Willie Wilson	.20	.09	.03
☐ 365	Jim Barr	.15	.07	.02
☐ 366	Dave Bergman	.15	.07	.02
☐ 367	Fred Breining	.15	.07	.02
☐ 368	Bob Brenly	.15	.07	.02
☐ 369	Jack Clark	.20	.09	.03
☐ 370	Chili Davis	.30	.14	.04
☐ 371	Mark Davis	.20	.09	.03
☐ 372	Darrell Evans	.20	.09	.03
☐ 373	Atlee Hammaker	.15	.07	.02
☐ 374	Mike Krukow	.15	.07	.02
☐ 375	Duane Kuiper	.15	.07	.02
☐ 376	Bill Laskey	.15	.07	.02
☐ 377	Gary Lavelle	.15	.07	.02
☐ 378	Johnnie LeMaster	.15	.07	.02
☐ 379	Jeff Leonard	.15	.07	.02
☐ 380	Randy Lerch	.15	.07	.02
☐ 381	Renie Martin	.15	.07	.02
☐ 382	Andy McGaffigan	.15	.07	.02
☐ 383	Greg Minton	.15	.07	.02
☐ 384	Tom O'Malley	.15	.07	.02
☐ 385	Max Venable	.15	.07	.02
☐ 386	Brad Wellman	.15	.07	.02
☐ 387	Joel Youngblood	.15	.07	.02
☐ 388	Gary Allenson	.15	.07	.02
☐ 389	Luis Aponte	.15	.07	.02
☐ 390	Tony Armas	.15	.07	.02
☐ 391	Doug Bird	.15	.07	.02
☐ 392	Wade Boggs	10.00	4.50	1.25
☐ 393	Dennis Boyd	.20	.09	.03
☐ 394	Mike Brown UER P (shown with record of 31-104)	.15	.07	.02
☐ 395	Mark Clear	.15	.07	.02
☐ 396	Dennis Eckersley	3.50	1.55	.45
☐ 397	Dwight Evans	.35	.16	.04
☐ 398	Rich Gedman	.15	.07	.02
☐ 399	Glenn Hoffman	.15	.07	.02
☐ 400	Bruce Hurst	.20	.09	.03
☐ 401	John Henry Johnson	.15	.07	.02
☐ 402	Ed Jurak	.15	.07	.02
☐ 403	Rick Miller	.15	.07	.02
☐ 404	Jeff Newman	.15	.07	.02
☐ 405	Reid Nichols	.15	.07	.02
☐ 406	Bob Ojeda	.15	.07	.02
☐ 407	Jerry Remy	.15	.07	.02
☐ 408	Jim Rice	.30	.14	.04
☐ 409	Bob Stanley	.15	.07	.02
☐ 410	Dave Stapleton	.15	.07	.02
☐ 411	John Tudor	.20	.09	.03
☐ 412	Carl Yastrzemski	3.00	1.35	.40
☐ 413	Buddy Bell	.20	.09	.03
☐ 414	Larry Biittner	.15	.07	.02
☐ 415	John Butcher	.15	.07	.02
☐ 416	Danny Darwin	.15	.07	.02
☐ 417	Bucky Dent	.20	.09	.03
☐ 418	Dave Hostetler	.15	.07	.02
☐ 419	Charlie Hough	.20	.09	.03
☐ 420	Bobby Johnson	.15	.07	.02
☐ 421	Odell Jones	.15	.07	.02
☐ 422	Jon Matlack	.15	.07	.02
☐ 423	Pete O'Brien	.40	.18	.05
☐ 424	Larry Parrish	.15	.07	.02
☐ 425	Mickey Rivers	.15	.07	.02
☐ 426	Billy Sample	.15	.07	.02
☐ 427	Dave Schmidt	.15	.07	.02
☐ 428	Mike Smithson	.15	.07	.02
☐ 429	Bill Stein	.15	.07	.02
☐ 430	Dave Stewart	.90	.40	.11
☐ 431	Jim Sundberg	.20	.09	.03
☐ 432	Frank Tanana	.20	.09	.03
☐ 433	Dave Tobik	.15	.07	.02
☐ 434	Wayne Tolleson	.15	.07	.02
☐ 435	George Wright	.15	.07	.02
☐ 436	Bill Almon	.15	.07	.02
☐ 437	Keith Atherton	.15	.07	.02
☐ 438	Dave Beard	.15	.07	.02
☐ 439	Tom Burgmeier	.15	.07	.02
☐ 440	Jeff Burroughs	.15	.07	.02
☐ 441	Chris Codiroli	.15	.07	.02
☐ 442	Tim Conroy	.15	.07	.02
☐ 443	Mike Davis	.15	.07	.02
☐ 444	Wayne Gross	.15	.07	.02
☐ 445	Garry Hancock	.15	.07	.02
☐ 446	Mike Heath	.15	.07	.02
☐ 447	Rickey Henderson	9.00	4.00	1.15
☐ 448	Donnie Hill	.15	.07	.02
☐ 449	Bob Kearney	.15	.07	.02
☐ 450	Bill Krueger	.40	.18	.05
☐ 451	Rick Langford	.15	.07	.02
☐ 452	Carney Lansford	.20	.09	.03
☐ 453	Dave Lopes	.20	.09	.03
☐ 454	Steve McCatty	.15	.07	.02
☐ 455	Dan Meyer	.15	.07	.02
☐ 456	Dwayne Murphy	.15	.07	.02
☐ 457	Mike Norris	.15	.07	.02
☐ 458	Ricky Peters	.15	.07	.02
☐ 459	Tony Phillips	1.50	.65	.19
☐ 460	Tom Underwood	.15	.07	.02
☐ 461	Mike Warren	.15	.07	.02
☐ 462	Johnny Bench	3.00	1.35	.40
☐ 463	Bruce Berenyi	.15	.07	.02
☐ 464	Dann Bilardello	.15	.07	.02
☐ 465	Cesar Cedeno	.20	.09	.03
☐ 466	Dave Concepcion	.20	.09	.03
☐ 467	Dan Driessen	.15	.07	.02
☐ 468	Nick Esasky	.20	.09	.03
☐ 469	Rich Gale	.15	.07	.02
☐ 470	Ben Hayes	.15	.07	.02
☐ 471	Paul Householder	.15	.07	.02
☐ 472	Tom Hume	.15	.07	.02
☐ 473	Alan Knicely	.15	.07	.02
☐ 474	Eddie Milner	.15	.07	.02
☐ 475	Ron Oester	.15	.07	.02
☐ 476	Kelly Paris	.15	.07	.02
☐ 477	Frank Pastore	.15	.07	.02
☐ 478	Ted Power	.15	.07	.02
☐ 479	Joe Price	.15	.07	.02
☐ 480	Charlie Puleo	.15	.07	.02
☐ 481	Gary Redus	.30	.14	.04
☐ 482	Bill Scherrer	.15	.07	.02
☐ 483	Mario Soto	.15	.07	.02
☐ 484	Alex Trevino	.15	.07	.02
☐ 485	Duane Walker	.15	.07	.02
☐ 486	Larry Bowa	.20	.09	.03
☐ 487	Warren Brusstar	.15	.07	.02
☐ 488	Bill Buckner	.20	.09	.03
☐ 489	Bill Campbell	.15	.07	.02
☐ 490	Ron Cey	.20	.09	.03
☐ 491	Jody Davis	.15	.07	.02
☐ 492	Leon Durham	.15	.07	.02
☐ 493	Mel Hall	.75	.35	.09
☐ 494	Ferguson Jenkins	.75	.35	.09
☐ 495	Jay Johnstone	.20	.09	.03
☐ 496	Craig Lefferts	.75	.35	.09
☐ 497	Carmelo Martinez	.20	.09	.03
☐ 498	Jerry Morales	.15	.07	.02
☐ 499	Keith Moreland	.15	.07	.02
☐ 500	Dickie Noles	.15	.07	.02
☐ 501	Mike Proly	.15	.07	.02
☐ 502	Chuck Rainey	.15	.07	.02
☐ 503	Dick Ruthven	.15	.07	.02
☐ 504	Ryne Sandberg	20.00	9.00	2.50
☐ 505	Lee Smith	1.75	.80	.22
☐ 506	Steve Trout	.15	.07	.02
☐ 507	Gary Woods	.15	.07	.02
☐ 508	Juan Beniquez	.15	.07	.02
☐ 509	Bob Boone	.20	.09	.03
☐ 510	Rick Burleson	.15	.07	.02
☐ 511	Rod Carew	3.00	1.35	.40
☐ 512	Bobby Clark	.15	.07	.02
☐ 513	John Curtis	.15	.07	.02
☐ 514	Doug DeCinces	.15	.07	.02
☐ 515	Brian Downing	.20	.09	.03
☐ 516	Tim Foli	.15	.07	.02
☐ 517	Ken Forsch	.15	.07	.02
☐ 518	Bobby Grich	.20	.09	.03
☐ 519	Andy Hassler	.15	.07	.02
☐ 520	Reggie Jackson	3.50	1.55	.45
☐ 521	Ron Jackson	.15	.07	.02
☐ 522	Tommy John	.25	.11	.03
☐ 523	Bruce Kison	.15	.07	.02
☐ 524	Steve Lubratich	.15	.07	.02
☐ 525	Fred Lynn	.20	.09	.03
☐ 526	Gary Pettis	.20	.09	.03
☐ 527	Luis Sanchez	.15	.07	.02
☐ 528	Daryl Sconiers	.15	.07	.02
☐ 529	Ellis Valentine	.15	.07	.02
☐ 530	Rob Wilfong	.15	.07	.02
☐ 531	Mike Witt	.15	.07	.02
☐ 532	Geoff Zahn	.15	.07	.02
☐ 533	Bud Anderson	.15	.07	.02
☐ 534	Chris Bando	.15	.07	.02
☐ 535	Alan Bannister	.15	.07	.02
☐ 536	Bert Blyleven	.50	.23	.06
☐ 537	Tom Brennan	.15	.07	.02
☐ 538	Jamie Easterly	.15	.07	.02
☐ 539	Juan Eichelberger	.15	.07	.02
☐ 540	Jim Essian	.15	.07	.02
☐ 541	Mike Fischlin	.15	.07	.02

☐ 542	Julio Franco	2.25	1.00	.30
☐ 543	Mike Hargrove	.20	.09	.03
☐ 544	Toby Harrah	.15	.07	.02
☐ 545	Ron Hassey	.15	.07	.02
☐ 546	Neal Heaton	.20	.09	.03
☐ 547	Bake McBride	.15	.07	.02
☐ 548	Broderick Perkins	.15	.07	.02
☐ 549	Lary Sorensen	.15	.07	.02
☐ 550	Dan Spillner	.15	.07	.02
☐ 551	Rick Sutcliffe	.25	.11	.03
☐ 552	Pat Tabler	.15	.07	.02
☐ 553	Gorman Thomas	.15	.07	.02
☐ 554	Andre Thornton	.15	.07	.02
☐ 555	George Vukovich	.15	.07	.02
☐ 556	Darrell Brown	.15	.07	.02
☐ 557	Tom Brunansky	.25	.11	.03
☐ 558	Randy Bush	.15	.07	.02
☐ 559	Bobby Castillo	.15	.07	.02
☐ 560	John Castino	.15	.07	.02
☐ 561	Ron Davis	.15	.07	.02
☐ 562	Dave Engle	.15	.07	.02
☐ 563	Lenny Faedo	.15	.07	.02
☐ 564	Pete Filson	.15	.07	.02
☐ 565	Gary Gaetti	.20	.09	.03
☐ 566	Mickey Hatcher	.15	.07	.02
☐ 567	Kent Hrbek	.60	.25	.08
☐ 568	Rusty Kuntz	.15	.07	.02
☐ 569	Tim Laudner	.15	.07	.02
☐ 570	Rick Lysander	.15	.07	.02
☐ 571	Bobby Mitchell	.15	.07	.02
☐ 572	Ken Schrom	.15	.07	.02
☐ 573	Ray Smith	.15	.07	.02
☐ 574	Tim Teufel	.30	.14	.04
☐ 575	Frank Viola	1.00	.45	.13
☐ 576	Gary Ward	.15	.07	.02
☐ 577	Ron Washington	.15	.07	.02
☐ 578	Len Whitehouse	.15	.07	.02
☐ 579	Al Williams	.15	.07	.02
☐ 580	Bob Bailor	.15	.07	.02
☐ 581	Mark Bradley	.15	.07	.02
☐ 582	Hubie Brooks	.20	.09	.03
☐ 583	Carlos Diaz	.15	.07	.02
☐ 584	George Foster	.20	.09	.03
☐ 585	Brian Giles	.15	.07	.02
☐ 586	Danny Heep	.15	.07	.02
☐ 587	Keith Hernandez	.25	.11	.03
☐ 588	Ron Hodges	.15	.07	.02
☐ 589	Scott Holman	.15	.07	.02
☐ 590	Dave Kingman	.20	.09	.03
☐ 591	Ed Lynch	.15	.07	.02
☐ 592	Jose Oquendo	.25	.11	.03
☐ 593	Jesse Orosco	.15	.07	.02
☐ 594	Junior Ortiz	.15	.07	.02
☐ 595	Tom Seaver	4.00	1.80	.50
☐ 596	Doug Sisk	.15	.07	.02
☐ 597	Rusty Staub	.20	.09	.03
☐ 598	John Stearns	.15	.07	.02
☐ 599	Darryl Strawberry	25.00	11.50	3.10
☐ 600	Craig Swan	.15	.07	.02
☐ 601	Walt Terrell	.25	.11	.03
☐ 602	Mike Torrez	.15	.07	.02
☐ 603	Mookie Wilson	.20	.09	.03
☐ 604	Jamie Allen	.15	.07	.02
☐ 605	Jim Beattie	.15	.07	.02
☐ 606	Tony Bernazard	.15	.07	.02
☐ 607	Manny Castillo	.15	.07	.02
☐ 608	Bill Caudill	.15	.07	.02
☐ 609	Bryan Clark	.15	.07	.02
☐ 610	Al Cowens	.15	.07	.02
☐ 611	Dave Henderson	.25	.11	.03
☐ 612	Steve Henderson	.15	.07	.02
☐ 613	Orlando Mercado	.15	.07	.02
☐ 614	Mike Moore	.35	.16	.04
☐ 615	Ricky Nelson UER (Jamie Nelson's stats on back)	.15	.07	.02
☐ 616	Spike Owen	.30	.14	.04
☐ 617	Pat Putnam	.15	.07	.02
☐ 618	Ron Roenicke	.15	.07	.02
☐ 619	Mike Stanton	.15	.07	.02
☐ 620	Bob Stoddard	.15	.07	.02
☐ 621	Rick Sweet	.15	.07	.02
☐ 622	Roy Thomas	.15	.07	.02
☐ 623	Ed VandeBerg	.15	.07	.02
☐ 624	Matt Young	.20	.09	.03
☐ 625	Richie Zisk	.15	.07	.02
☐ 626	Fred Lynn 1982 AS Game RB	.20	.09	.03
☐ 627	Manny Trillo 1983 AS Game RB	.20	.09	.03
☐ 628	Steve Garvey NL Iron Man	.40	.18	.05
☐ 629	Rod Carew AL Batting Runner-Up	.60	.25	.08
☐ 630	Wade Boggs AL Batting Champion	2.00	.90	.25
☐ 631	Tim Raines: Letting Go of the Raines	.40	.18	.05
☐ 632	Al Oliver Double Trouble	.20	.09	.03
☐ 633	Steve Sax AS Second Base	.20	.09	.03
☐ 634	Dickie Thon AS Shortstop	.20	.09	.03
☐ 635	Ace Firemen Dan Quisenberry and Tippy Martinez	.20	.09	.03
☐ 636	Reds Reunited Joe Morgan Pete Rose Tony Perez	.75	.35	.09
☐ 637	Backstop Stars Lance Parrish Bob Boone	.20	.09	.03
☐ 638	George Brett and Gaylord Perry Pine Tar 7/24/83	1.25	.55	.16
☐ 639	1983 No Hitters Dave Righetti Mike Warren Bob Forsch	.20	.09	.03
☐ 640	Johnny Bench and Carl Yastrzemski Retiring Superstars	3.00	1.35	.40
☐ 641	Gaylord Perry Going Out In Style	.35	.16	.04
☐ 642	Steve Carlton 300 Club and Strikeout Record	.75	.35	.09
☐ 643	Joe Altobelli and Paul Owens World Series Managers	.20	.09	.03
☐ 644	Rick Dempsey World Series MVP	.20	.09	.03
☐ 645	Mike Boddicker WS Rookie Winner	.20	.09	.03
☐ 646	Scott McGregor WS Clincher	.20	.09	.03
☐ 647	CL: Orioles/Royals	.20	.02	.01
☐ 648	CL: Phillies/Giants	.20	.02	.01
☐ 649	CL: White Sox/Red Sox	.20	.02	.01
☐ 650	CL: Tigers/Rangers	.20	.02	.01
☐ 651	CL: Dodgers/A's	.20	.02	.01
☐ 652	CL: Yankees/Reds	.20	.02	.01
☐ 653	CL: Blue Jays/Cubs	.20	.02	.01
☐ 654	CL: Braves/Angels	.20	.02	.01
☐ 655	CL: Brewers/Indians	.20	.02	.01
☐ 656	CL: Astros/Twins	.20	.02	.01
☐ 657	CL: Pirates/Mets	.20	.02	.01
☐ 658	CL: Expos/Mariners	.20	.02	.01
☐ 659	CL: Padres/Specials	.20	.02	.01
☐ 660	CL: Cardinals/Teams	.20	.02	.01

1984 Fleer Update

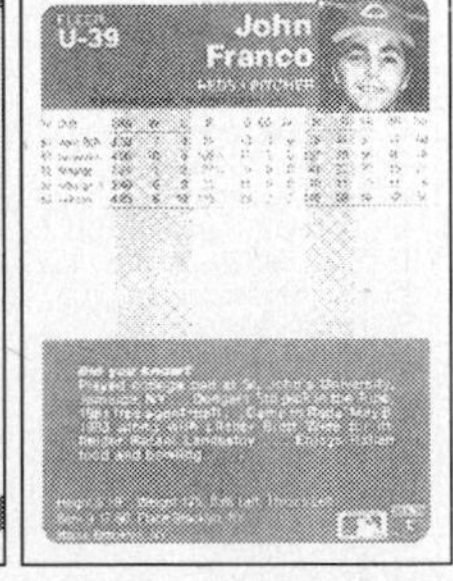

The cards in this 132-card set measure 2 1/2" by 3 1/2". For the first time, the Fleer Gum Company issued a traded, extended, or update set. The purpose of the set was the same as the traded sets issued by Topps over the past four years, i.e., to portray players with their proper team for the current year and to portray rookies who were not in their regular issue. Like the Topps Traded sets of the past four years, the Fleer Update sets were distributed through hobby dealers only. The set was quite popular with collectors, and, apparently, the print run was relatively short, as the set was quickly in short supply and exhibited a rapid and dramatic price increase. The cards are numbered on the back with a U prefix; the order corresponds to the alphabetical order of the subjects' names. The key (extended) Rookie Cards in this set are Roger Clemens, Ron Darling, Alvin Davis, John Franco, Dwight Gooden, Jimmy Key, Mark Langston, Kirby Puckett, Jose Rijo, and Bret Saberhagen. Collectors are urged to be careful if purchasing single cards of Clemens, Darling, Gooden, Puckett, Rose, or Saberhagen as these specific cards have been illegally reprinted. These fakes are blurry when compared to the real thing.

	NRMT-MT	EXC	G-VG
COMPLETE SET (132)	950.00	425.00	120.00
COMMON PLAYER (1-132)	1.00	.45	.13
□ 1 Willie Aikens	1.00	.45	.13
□ 2 Luis Aponte	1.00	.45	.13
□ 3 Mark Bailey	1.00	.45	.13
□ 4 Bob Bailor	1.00	.45	.13
□ 5 Dusty Baker	1.25	.55	.16
□ 6 Steve Balboni	1.00	.45	.13
□ 7 Alan Bannister	1.00	.45	.13
□ 8 Marty Barrett	1.25	.55	.16
□ 9 Dave Beard	1.00	.45	.13
□ 10 Joe Beckwith	1.00	.45	.13
□ 11 Dave Bergman	1.00	.45	.13
□ 12 Tony Bernazard	1.00	.45	.13
□ 13 Bruce Bochte	1.00	.45	.13
□ 14 Barry Bonnell	1.00	.45	.13
□ 15 Phil Bradley	1.25	.55	.16
□ 16 Fred Breining	1.00	.45	.13
□ 17 Mike C. Brown OF	1.00	.45	.13
□ 18 Bill Buckner	1.25	.55	.16
□ 19 Ray Burris	1.00	.45	.13
□ 20 John Butcher	1.00	.45	.13
□ 21 Brett Butler	3.00	1.35	.40
□ 22 Enos Cabell	1.00	.45	.13
□ 23 Bill Campbell	1.00	.45	.13
□ 24 Bill Caudill	1.00	.45	.13
□ 25 Bobby Clark	1.00	.45	.13
□ 26 Bryan Clark	1.00	.45	.13
□ 27 Roger Clemens	450.00	200.00	57.50
□ 28 Jaime Cocanower	1.00	.45	.13
□ 29 Ron Darling	10.00	4.50	1.25
□ 30 Alvin Davis	2.00	.90	.25
□ 31 Bob Dernier	1.00	.45	.13
□ 32 Carlos Diaz	1.00	.45	.13
□ 33 Mike Easler	1.00	.45	.13
□ 34 Dennis Eckersley	20.00	9.00	2.50
□ 35 Jim Essian	1.00	.45	.13
□ 36 Darrell Evans	1.25	.55	.16
□ 37 Mike Fitzgerald	1.00	.45	.13
□ 38 Tim Foli	1.00	.45	.13
□ 39 John Franco	10.00	4.50	1.25
□ 40 George Frazier	1.00	.45	.13
□ 41 Rich Gale	1.00	.45	.13
□ 42 Barbaro Garbey	1.00	.45	.13
□ 43 Dwight Gooden	90.00	40.00	11.50
□ 44 Rich Gossage	1.50	.65	.19
□ 45 Wayne Gross	1.00	.45	.13
□ 46 Mark Gubicza	4.00	1.80	.50
□ 47 Jackie Gutierrez	1.00	.45	.13
□ 48 Toby Harrah	1.00	.45	.13
□ 49 Ron Hassey	1.00	.45	.13
□ 50 Richie Hebner	1.00	.45	.13
□ 51 Willie Hernandez	1.25	.55	.16
□ 52 Ed Hodge	1.00	.45	.13
□ 53 Ricky Horton	1.00	.45	.13
□ 54 Art Howe	1.00	.45	.13
□ 55 Dane Iorg	1.00	.45	.13
□ 56 Brook Jacoby	1.50	.65	.19
□ 57 Dion James	1.25	.55	.16
□ 58 Mike Jeffcoat	1.00	.45	.13
□ 59 Ruppert Jones	1.00	.45	.13
□ 60 Bob Kearney	1.00	.45	.13
□ 61 Jimmy Key	12.00	5.50	1.50
□ 62 Dave Kingman	1.25	.55	.16
□ 63 Brad Komminsk	1.00	.45	.13
□ 64 Jerry Koosman	1.25	.55	.16
□ 65 Wayne Krenchicki	1.00	.45	.13
□ 66 Rusty Kuntz	1.00	.45	.13
□ 67 Frank LaCorte	1.00	.45	.13
□ 68 Dennis Lamp	1.00	.45	.13
□ 69 Tito Landrum	1.00	.45	.13
□ 70 Mark Langston	25.00	11.50	3.10
□ 71 Rick Leach	1.00	.45	.13
□ 72 Craig Lefferts	1.50	.65	.19
□ 73 Gary Lucas	1.00	.45	.13
□ 74 Jerry Martin	1.00	.45	.13
□ 75 Carmelo Martinez	1.25	.55	.16
□ 76 Mike Mason	1.00	.45	.13
□ 77 Gary Matthews	1.25	.55	.16
□ 78 Andy McGaffigan	1.00	.45	.13
□ 79 Joey McLaughlin	1.00	.45	.13
□ 80 Joe Morgan	10.00	4.50	1.25
□ 81 Darryl Motley	1.00	.45	.13
□ 82 Graig Nettles	1.25	.55	.16
□ 83 Phil Niekro	8.00	3.60	1.00
□ 84 Ken Oberkfell	1.00	.45	.13
□ 85 Al Oliver	1.25	.55	.16
□ 86 Jorge Orta	1.00	.45	.13
□ 87 Amos Otis	1.25	.55	.16
□ 88 Bob Owchinko	1.00	.45	.13
□ 89 Dave Parker	5.00	2.30	.60
□ 90 Jack Perconte	1.00	.45	.13
□ 91 Tony Perez	8.00	3.60	1.00
□ 92 Gerald Perry	1.25	.55	.16
□ 93 Kirby Puckett	375.00	170.00	47.50
□ 94 Shane Rawley	1.00	.45	.13
□ 95 Floyd Rayford	1.00	.45	.13
□ 96 Ron Reed	1.00	.45	.13
□ 97 R.J. Reynolds	1.00	.45	.13
□ 98 Gene Richards	1.00	.45	.13
□ 99 Jose Rijo	27.00	12.00	3.40
□ 100 Jeff D. Robinson	1.25	.55	.16
□ 101 Ron Romanick	1.00	.45	.13
□ 102 Pete Rose	25.00	11.50	3.10
□ 103 Bret Saberhagen	35.00	16.00	4.40
□ 104 Scott Sanderson	1.00	.45	.13
□ 105 Dick Schofield	1.50	.65	.19
□ 106 Tom Seaver	25.00	11.50	3.10
□ 107 Jim Slaton	1.00	.45	.13
□ 108 Mike Smithson	1.00	.45	.13
□ 109 Lary Sorensen	1.00	.45	.13
□ 110 Tim Stoddard	1.00	.45	.13
□ 111 Jeff Stone	1.00	.45	.13
□ 112 Champ Summers	1.00	.45	.13
□ 113 Jim Sundberg	1.25	.55	.16
□ 114 Rick Sutcliffe	1.50	.65	.19
□ 115 Craig Swan	1.00	.45	.13
□ 116 Derrel Thomas	1.00	.45	.13
□ 117 Gorman Thomas	1.00	.45	.13
□ 118 Alex Trevino	1.00	.45	.13
□ 119 Manny Trillo	1.00	.45	.13
□ 120 John Tudor	1.25	.55	.16
□ 121 Tom Underwood	1.00	.45	.13
□ 122 Mike Vail	1.00	.45	.13
□ 123 Tom Waddell	1.00	.45	.13
□ 124 Gary Ward	1.00	.45	.13
□ 125 Terry Whitfield	1.00	.45	.13
□ 126 Curtis Wilkerson	1.00	.45	.13
□ 127 Frank Williams	1.00	.45	.13
□ 128 Glenn Wilson	1.00	.45	.13
□ 129 John Wockenfuss	1.00	.45	.13
□ 130 Ned Yost	1.00	.45	.13
□ 131 Mike Young	1.00	.45	.13
□ 132 Checklist: 1-132	1.25	.13	.04

1985 Fleer

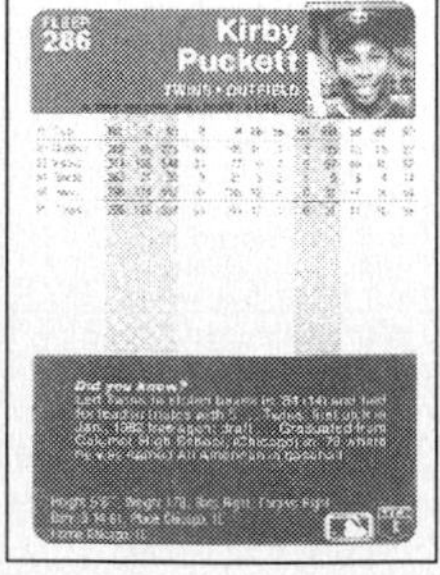

The cards in this 660-card set measure 2 1/2" by 3 1/2". The 1985 Fleer set features fronts that contain the team logo along with the player's name and position. The borders enclosing the photo are color-coded to correspond to the player's team. In each case, the color is one of the standard colors of that team, e.g., orange for Baltimore, red for St. Louis, etc. The backs feature the same name, number, and statistics format that Fleer has been using over the past few years. The cards are ordered alphabetically within team. The teams are ordered based on their respective performance during the prior year, e.g., World Champion Detroit Tigers (1-25), NL Champion San Diego (26-48), Chicago Cubs (49-71), New York Mets (72-95), Toronto (96-119), New York Yankees (120-147), Boston (148-169), Baltimore (170-195), Kansas City (196-218), St. Louis (219-243), Philadelphia (244-269), Minnesota (270-292), California (293-317), Atlanta (318-342), Houston (343-365), Los Angeles (366-391), Montreal (392-413), Oakland (414-436), Cleveland (437-460), Pittsburgh (461-481), Seattle (482-505), Chicago White Sox (506-530), Cincinnati (531-554), Texas (555-575), Milwaukee (576-601), and San Francisco (602-625). Specials (626-643), Major League Prospects (644-653), and checklist cards (654-660) complete the set. The black and white photo on the reverse is included for the third straight year. This set is noted for containing the Rookie Cards of Roger Clemens, Alvin Davis, Eric Davis, Glenn Davis, Rob Deer, Shawon Dunston, Dwight Gooden, Kelly Gruber, Orel Hershiser, Jimmy Key, Mark Langston, Terry Pendleton, Kirby Puckett, Jose Rijo, Bret Saberhagen, and Danny Tartabull.

	NRMT-MT	EXC	G-VG
COMPLETE SET (660)	200.00	90.00	25.00
COMMON PLAYER (1-660)	.10	.05	.01
☐ 1 Doug Bair	.10	.05	.01
☐ 2 Juan Berenguer	.10	.05	.01
☐ 3 Dave Bergman	.10	.05	.01
☐ 4 Tom Brookens	.10	.05	.01
☐ 5 Marty Castillo	.10	.05	.01
☐ 6 Darrell Evans	.12	.05	.02
☐ 7 Barbaro Garbey	.10	.05	.01
☐ 8 Kirk Gibson	.30	.14	.04
☐ 9 John Grubb	.10	.05	.01
☐ 10 Willie Hernandez	.10	.05	.01
☐ 11 Larry Herndon	.10	.05	.01
☐ 12 Howard Johnson	1.50	.65	.19
☐ 13 Ruppert Jones	.10	.05	.01
☐ 14 Rusty Kuntz	.10	.05	.01
☐ 15 Chet Lemon	.10	.05	.01
☐ 16 Aurelio Lopez	.10	.05	.01
☐ 17 Sid Monge	.10	.05	.01
☐ 18 Jack Morris	1.25	.55	.16
☐ 19 Lance Parrish	.12	.05	.02
☐ 20 Dan Petry	.10	.05	.01
☐ 21 Dave Rozema	.10	.05	.01
☐ 22 Bill Scherrer	.10	.05	.01
☐ 23 Alan Trammell	.50	.23	.06
☐ 24 Lou Whitaker	.50	.23	.06
☐ 25 Milt Wilcox	.10	.05	.01
☐ 26 Kurt Bevacqua	.10	.05	.01
☐ 27 Greg Booker	.10	.05	.01
☐ 28 Bobby Brown	.10	.05	.01
☐ 29 Luis DeLeon	.10	.05	.01
☐ 30 Dave Dravecky	.12	.05	.02
☐ 31 Tim Flannery	.10	.05	.01
☐ 32 Steve Garvey	.40	.18	.05
☐ 33 Rich Gossage	.15	.07	.02
☐ 34 Tony Gwynn	6.00	2.70	.75
☐ 35 Greg Harris	.10	.05	.01
☐ 36 Andy Hawkins	.10	.05	.01
☐ 37 Terry Kennedy	.10	.05	.01
☐ 38 Craig Lefferts	.12	.05	.02
☐ 39 Tim Lollar	.10	.05	.01
☐ 40 Carmelo Martinez	.10	.05	.01
☐ 41 Kevin McReynolds	.35	.16	.04
☐ 42 Graig Nettles	.12	.05	.02
☐ 43 Luis Salazar	.10	.05	.01
☐ 44 Eric Show	.10	.05	.01
☐ 45 Garry Templeton	.10	.05	.01
☐ 46 Mark Thurmond	.10	.05	.01
☐ 47 Ed Whitson	.10	.05	.01
☐ 48 Alan Wiggins	.10	.05	.01
☐ 49 Rich Bordi	.10	.05	.01
☐ 50 Larry Bowa	.12	.05	.02
☐ 51 Warren Brusstar	.10	.05	.01
☐ 52 Ron Cey	.12	.05	.02
☐ 53 Henry Cotto	.10	.05	.01
☐ 54 Jody Davis	.10	.05	.01
☐ 55 Bob Dernier	.10	.05	.01
☐ 56 Leon Durham	.10	.05	.01
☐ 57 Dennis Eckersley	1.25	.55	.16
☐ 58 George Frazier	.10	.05	.01
☐ 59 Richie Hebner	.10	.05	.01
☐ 60 Dave Lopes	.12	.05	.02
☐ 61 Gary Matthews	.10	.05	.01
☐ 62 Keith Moreland	.10	.05	.01
☐ 63 Rick Reuschel	.12	.05	.02
☐ 64 Dick Ruthven	.10	.05	.01
☐ 65 Ryne Sandberg	10.00	4.50	1.25
☐ 66 Scott Sanderson	.10	.05	.01
☐ 67 Lee Smith	1.00	.45	.13
☐ 68 Tim Stoddard	.10	.05	.01
☐ 69 Rick Sutcliffe	.12	.05	.02
☐ 70 Steve Trout	.10	.05	.01
☐ 71 Gary Woods	.10	.05	.01
☐ 72 Wally Backman	.10	.05	.01
☐ 73 Bruce Berenyi	.10	.05	.01
☐ 74 Hubie Brooks UER (Kelvin Chapman's stats on card back)	.12	.05	.02
☐ 75 Kelvin Chapman	.10	.05	.01
☐ 76 Ron Darling	.60	.25	.08
☐ 77 Sid Fernandez	.60	.25	.08
☐ 78 Mike Fitzgerald	.10	.05	.01
☐ 79 George Foster	.12	.05	.02
☐ 80 Brent Gaff	.10	.05	.01
☐ 81 Ron Gardenhire	.10	.05	.01
☐ 82 Dwight Gooden	8.00	3.60	1.00
☐ 83 Tom Gorman	.10	.05	.01
☐ 84 Danny Heep	.10	.05	.01
☐ 85 Keith Hernandez	.20	.09	.03
☐ 86 Ray Knight	.12	.05	.02
☐ 87 Ed Lynch	.10	.05	.01
☐ 88 Jose Oquendo	.12	.05	.02
☐ 89 Jesse Orosco	.10	.05	.01
☐ 90 Rafael Santana	.10	.05	.01
☐ 91 Doug Sisk	.10	.05	.01
☐ 92 Rusty Staub	.12	.05	.02
☐ 93 Darryl Strawberry	7.00	3.10	.85
☐ 94 Walt Terrell	.10	.05	.01
☐ 95 Mookie Wilson	.12	.05	.02
☐ 96 Jim Acker	.10	.05	.01
☐ 97 Willie Aikens	.10	.05	.01
☐ 98 Doyle Alexander	.10	.05	.01
☐ 99 Jesse Barfield	.12	.05	.02
☐ 100 George Bell	1.00	.45	.13
☐ 101 Jim Clancy	.10	.05	.01
☐ 102 Dave Collins	.10	.05	.01
☐ 103 Tony Fernandez	.75	.35	.09
☐ 104 Damaso Garcia	.10	.05	.01
☐ 105 Jim Gott	.10	.05	.01
☐ 106 Alfredo Griffin	.10	.05	.01
☐ 107 Garth Iorg	.10	.05	.01
☐ 108 Roy Lee Jackson	.10	.05	.01
☐ 109 Cliff Johnson	.10	.05	.01
☐ 110 Jimmy Key	2.00	.90	.25
☐ 111 Dennis Lamp	.10	.05	.01
☐ 112 Rick Leach	.10	.05	.01
☐ 113 Luis Leal	.10	.05	.01
☐ 114 Buck Martinez	.10	.05	.01
☐ 115 Lloyd Moseby	.10	.05	.01
☐ 116 Rance Mulliniks	.10	.05	.01
☐ 117 Dave Stieb	.12	.05	.02
☐ 118 Willie Upshaw	.10	.05	.01
☐ 119 Ernie Whitt	.10	.05	.01
☐ 120 Mike Armstrong	.10	.05	.01
☐ 121 Don Baylor	.12	.05	.02
☐ 122 Marty Bystrom	.10	.05	.01
☐ 123 Rick Cerone	.10	.05	.01
☐ 124 Joe Cowley	.10	.05	.01
☐ 125 Brian Dayett	.10	.05	.01
☐ 126 Tim Foli	.10	.05	.01
☐ 127 Ray Fontenot	.10	.05	.01
☐ 128 Ken Griffey	.15	.07	.02
☐ 129 Ron Guidry	.12	.05	.02
☐ 130 Toby Harrah	.10	.05	.01
☐ 131 Jay Howell	.12	.05	.02
☐ 132 Steve Kemp	.10	.05	.01
☐ 133 Don Mattingly	7.00	3.10	.85
☐ 134 Bobby Meacham	.10	.05	.01
☐ 135 John Montefusco	.10	.05	.01
☐ 136 Omar Moreno	.10	.05	.01
☐ 137 Dale Murray	.10	.05	.01
☐ 138 Phil Niekro	.50	.23	.06
☐ 139 Mike Pagliarulo	.20	.09	.03
☐ 140 Willie Randolph	.12	.05	.02
☐ 141 Dennis Rasmussen	.10	.05	.01

□ 142 Dave Righetti	.12	.05	.02
□ 143 Jose Rijo	3.50	1.55	.45
□ 144 Andre Robertson	.10	.05	.01
□ 145 Bob Shirley	.10	.05	.01
□ 146 Dave Winfield	3.50	1.55	.45
□ 147 Butch Wynegar	.10	.05	.01
□ 148 Gary Allenson	.10	.05	.01
□ 149 Tony Armas	.10	.05	.01
□ 150 Marty Barrett	.10	.05	.01
□ 151 Wade Boggs	5.00	2.30	.60
□ 152 Dennis Boyd	.10	.05	.01
□ 153 Bill Buckner	.12	.05	.02
□ 154 Mark Clear	.10	.05	.01
□ 155 Roger Clemens	60.00	27.00	7.50
□ 156 Steve Crawford	.10	.05	.01
□ 157 Mike Easler	.10	.05	.01
□ 158 Dwight Evans	.20	.09	.03
□ 159 Rich Gedman	.10	.05	.01
□ 160 Jackie Gutierrez (Wade Boggs shown on deck)	.12	.05	.02
□ 161 Bruce Hurst	.12	.05	.02
□ 162 John Henry Johnson	.10	.05	.01
□ 163 Rick Miller	.10	.05	.01
□ 164 Reid Nichols	.10	.05	.01
□ 165 Al Nipper	.10	.05	.01
□ 166 Bob Ojeda	.10	.05	.01
□ 167 Jerry Remy	.10	.05	.01
□ 168 Jim Rice	.20	.09	.03
□ 169 Bob Stanley	.10	.05	.01
□ 170 Mike Boddicker	.10	.05	.01
□ 171 Al Bumbry	.10	.05	.01
□ 172 Todd Cruz	.10	.05	.01
□ 173 Rich Dauer	.10	.05	.01
□ 174 Storm Davis	.10	.05	.01
□ 175 Rick Dempsey	.10	.05	.01
□ 176 Jim Dwyer	.10	.05	.01
□ 177 Mike Flanagan	.10	.05	.01
□ 178 Dan Ford	.10	.05	.01
□ 179 Wayne Gross	.10	.05	.01
□ 180 John Lowenstein	.10	.05	.01
□ 181 Dennis Martinez	.12	.05	.02
□ 182 Tippy Martinez	.10	.05	.01
□ 183 Scott McGregor	.10	.05	.01
□ 184 Eddie Murray	2.00	.90	.25
□ 185 Joe Nolan	.10	.05	.01
□ 186 Floyd Rayford	.10	.05	.01
□ 187 Cal Ripken	10.00	4.50	1.25
□ 188 Gary Roenicke	.10	.05	.01
□ 189 Lenn Sakata	.10	.05	.01
□ 190 John Shelby	.10	.05	.01
□ 191 Ken Singleton	.12	.05	.02
□ 192 Sammy Stewart	.10	.05	.01
□ 193 Bill Swaggerty	.10	.05	.01
□ 194 Tom Underwood	.10	.05	.01
□ 195 Mike Young	.10	.05	.01
□ 196 Steve Balboni	.10	.05	.01
□ 197 Joe Beckwith	.10	.05	.01
□ 198 Bud Black	.10	.05	.01
□ 199 George Brett	4.00	1.80	.50
□ 200 Onix Concepcion	.10	.05	.01
□ 201 Mark Gubicza	.75	.35	.09
□ 202 Larry Gura	.10	.05	.01
□ 203 Mark Huismann	.10	.05	.01
□ 204 Dane Iorg	.10	.05	.01
□ 205 Danny Jackson	.10	.05	.01
□ 206 Charlie Leibrandt	.12	.05	.02
□ 207 Hal McRae	.12	.05	.02
□ 208 Darryl Motley	.10	.05	.01
□ 209 Jorge Orta	.10	.05	.01
□ 210 Greg Pryor	.10	.05	.01
□ 211 Dan Quisenberry	.12	.05	.02
□ 212 Bret Saberhagen	5.00	2.30	.60
□ 213 Pat Sheridan	.10	.05	.01
□ 214 Don Slaught	.12	.05	.02
□ 215 U.L. Washington	.10	.05	.01
□ 216 John Wathan	.10	.05	.01
□ 217 Frank White	.12	.05	.02
□ 218 Willie Wilson	.12	.05	.02
□ 219 Neil Allen	.10	.05	.01
□ 220 Joaquin Andujar	.10	.05	.01
□ 221 Steve Braun	.10	.05	.01
□ 222 Danny Cox	.10	.05	.01
□ 223 Bob Forsch	.10	.05	.01
□ 224 David Green	.10	.05	.01
□ 225 George Hendrick	.10	.05	.01
□ 226 Tom Herr	.10	.05	.01
□ 227 Ricky Horton	.10	.05	.01
□ 228 Art Howe	.10	.05	.01
□ 229 Mike Jorgensen	.10	.05	.01
□ 230 Kurt Kepshire	.10	.05	.01
□ 231 Jeff Lahti	.10	.05	.01
□ 232 Tito Landrum	.10	.05	.01
□ 233 Dave LaPoint	.10	.05	.01
□ 234 Willie McGee	.40	.18	.05
□ 235 Tom Nieto	.10	.05	.01
□ 236 Terry Pendleton	9.00	4.00	1.15
□ 237 Darrell Porter	.10	.05	.01
□ 238 Dave Rucker	.10	.05	.01
□ 239 Lonnie Smith	.10	.05	.01
□ 240 Ozzie Smith	2.00	.90	.25
□ 241 Bruce Sutter	.12	.05	.02
□ 242 Andy Van Slyke UER (Bats Right, Throws Left)	2.00	.90	.25
□ 243 Dave Von Ohlen	.10	.05	.01
□ 244 Larry Andersen	.10	.05	.01
□ 245 Bill Campbell	.10	.05	.01
□ 246 Steve Carlton	1.75	.80	.22
□ 247 Tim Corcoran	.10	.05	.01
□ 248 Ivan DeJesus	.10	.05	.01
□ 249 John Denny	.10	.05	.01
□ 250 Bo Diaz	.10	.05	.01
□ 251 Greg Gross	.10	.05	.01
□ 252 Kevin Gross	.10	.05	.01
□ 253 Von Hayes	.10	.05	.01
□ 254 Al Holland	.10	.05	.01
□ 255 Charles Hudson	.10	.05	.01
□ 256 Jerry Koosman	.12	.05	.02
□ 257 Joe Lefebvre	.10	.05	.01
□ 258 Sixto Lezcano	.10	.05	.01
□ 259 Garry Maddox	.10	.05	.01
□ 260 Len Matuszek	.10	.05	.01
□ 261 Tug McGraw	.12	.05	.02
□ 262 Al Oliver	.12	.05	.02
□ 263 Shane Rawley	.10	.05	.01
□ 264 Juan Samuel	.20	.09	.03
□ 265 Mike Schmidt	5.00	2.30	.60
□ 266 Jeff Stone	.10	.05	.01
□ 267 Ozzie Virgil	.10	.05	.01
□ 268 Glenn Wilson	.10	.05	.01
□ 269 John Wockenfuss	.10	.05	.01
□ 270 Darrell Brown	.10	.05	.01
□ 271 Tom Brunansky	.12	.05	.02
□ 272 Randy Bush	.10	.05	.01
□ 273 John Butcher	.10	.05	.01
□ 274 Bobby Castillo	.10	.05	.01
□ 275 Ron Davis	.10	.05	.01
□ 276 Dave Engle	.10	.05	.01
□ 277 Pete Filson	.10	.05	.01
□ 278 Gary Gaetti	.12	.05	.02
□ 279 Mickey Hatcher	.10	.05	.01
□ 280 Ed Hodge	.10	.05	.01
□ 281 Kent Hrbek	.40	.18	.05
□ 282 Houston Jimenez	.10	.05	.01
□ 283 Tim Laudner	.10	.05	.01
□ 284 Rick Lysander	.10	.05	.01
□ 285 Dave Meier	.10	.05	.01
□ 286 Kirby Puckett	50.00	23.00	6.25
□ 287 Pat Putnam	.10	.05	.01
□ 288 Ken Schrom	.10	.05	.01
□ 289 Mike Smithson	.10	.05	.01
□ 290 Tim Teufel	.10	.05	.01
□ 291 Frank Viola	.50	.23	.06
□ 292 Ron Washington	.10	.05	.01
□ 293 Don Aase	.10	.05	.01
□ 294 Juan Beniquez	.10	.05	.01
□ 295 Bob Boone	.12	.05	.02
□ 296 Mike C. Brown OF	.10	.05	.01
□ 297 Rod Carew	1.75	.80	.22
□ 298 Doug Corbett	.10	.05	.01
□ 299 Doug DeCinces	.10	.05	.01
□ 300 Brian Downing	.12	.05	.02
□ 301 Ken Forsch	.10	.05	.01
□ 302 Bobby Grich	.12	.05	.02
□ 303 Reggie Jackson	2.00	.90	.25
□ 304 Tommy John	.20	.09	.03
□ 305 Curt Kaufman	.10	.05	.01
□ 306 Bruce Kison	.10	.05	.01
□ 307 Fred Lynn	.12	.05	.02
□ 308 Gary Pettis	.10	.05	.01
□ 309 Ron Romanick	.10	.05	.01
□ 310 Luis Sanchez	.10	.05	.01
□ 311 Dick Schofield	.10	.05	.01
□ 312 Daryl Sconiers	.10	.05	.01
□ 313 Jim Slaton	.10	.05	.01
□ 314 Derrel Thomas	.10	.05	.01
□ 315 Rob Wilfong	.10	.05	.01
□ 316 Mike Witt	.10	.05	.01
□ 317 Geoff Zahn	.10	.05	.01
□ 318 Len Barker	.10	.05	.01
□ 319 Steve Bedrosian	.10	.05	.01
□ 320 Bruce Benedict	.10	.05	.01
□ 321 Rick Camp	.10	.05	.01
□ 322 Chris Chambliss	.12	.05	.02
□ 323 Jeff Dedmon	.10	.05	.01

324	Terry Forster	.10	.05	.01
325	Gene Garber	.10	.05	.01
326	Albert Hall	.10	.05	.01
327	Terry Harper	.10	.05	.01
328	Bob Horner	.12	.05	.02
329	Glenn Hubbard	.10	.05	.01
330	Randy Johnson	.10	.05	.01
331	Brad Komminsk	.10	.05	.01
332	Rick Mahler	.10	.05	.01
333	Craig McMurtry	.10	.05	.01
334	Donnie Moore	.10	.05	.01
335	Dale Murphy	1.00	.45	.13
336	Ken Oberkfell	.10	.05	.01
337	Pascual Perez	.10	.05	.01
338	Gerald Perry	.10	.05	.01
339	Rafael Ramirez	.10	.05	.01
340	Jerry Royster	.10	.05	.01
341	Alex Trevino	.10	.05	.01
342	Claudell Washington	.10	.05	.01
343	Alan Ashby	.10	.05	.01
344	Mark Bailey	.10	.05	.01
345	Kevin Bass	.10	.05	.01
346	Enos Cabell	.10	.05	.01
347	Jose Cruz	.12	.05	.02
348	Bill Dawley	.10	.05	.01
349	Frank DiPino	.10	.05	.01
350	Bill Doran	.12	.05	.02
351	Phil Garner	.12	.05	.02
352	Bob Knepper	.10	.05	.01
353	Mike LaCoss	.10	.05	.01
354	Jerry Mumphrey	.10	.05	.01
355	Joe Niekro	.12	.05	.02
356	Terry Puhl	.10	.05	.01
357	Craig Reynolds	.10	.05	.01
358	Vern Ruhle	.10	.05	.01
359	Nolan Ryan	10.00	4.50	1.25
360	Joe Sambito	.10	.05	.01
361	Mike Scott	.12	.05	.02
362	Dave Smith	.10	.05	.01
363	Julio Solano	.10	.05	.01
364	Dickie Thon	.10	.05	.01
365	Denny Walling	.10	.05	.01
366	Dave Anderson	.10	.05	.01
367	Bob Bailor	.10	.05	.01
368	Greg Brock	.10	.05	.01
369	Carlos Diaz	.10	.05	.01
370	Pedro Guerrero	.15	.07	.02
371	Orel Hershiser	3.50	1.55	.45
372	Rick Honeycutt	.10	.05	.01
373	Burt Hooton	.10	.05	.01
374	Ken Howell	.10	.05	.01
375	Ken Landreaux	.10	.05	.01
376	Candy Maldonado	.12	.05	.02
377	Mike Marshall	.10	.05	.01
378	Tom Niedenfuer	.10	.05	.01
379	Alejandro Pena	.10	.05	.01
380	Jerry Reuss UER ("Home:" omitted)	.10	.05	.01
381	R.J. Reynolds	.10	.05	.01
382	German Rivera	.10	.05	.01
383	Bill Russell	.12	.05	.02
384	Steve Sax	.50	.23	.06
385	Mike Scioscia	.12	.05	.02
386	Franklin Stubbs	.20	.09	.03
387	Fernando Valenzuela	.12	.05	.02
388	Bob Welch	.20	.09	.03
389	Terry Whitfield	.10	.05	.01
390	Steve Yeager	.10	.05	.01
391	Pat Zachry	.10	.05	.01
392	Fred Breining	.10	.05	.01
393	Gary Carter	.60	.25	.08
394	Andre Dawson	2.00	.90	.25
395	Miguel Dilone	.10	.05	.01
396	Dan Driessen	.10	.05	.01
397	Doug Flynn	.10	.05	.01
398	Terry Francona	.10	.05	.01
399	Bill Gullickson	.12	.05	.02
400	Bob James	.10	.05	.01
401	Charlie Lea	.10	.05	.01
402	Bryan Little	.10	.05	.01
403	Gary Lucas	.10	.05	.01
404	David Palmer	.10	.05	.01
405	Tim Raines	.40	.18	.05
406	Mike Ramsey	.10	.05	.01
407	Jeff Reardon	.90	.40	.11
408	Steve Rogers	.10	.05	.01
409	Dan Schatzeder	.10	.05	.01
410	Bryn Smith	.10	.05	.01
411	Mike Stenhouse	.10	.05	.01
412	Tim Wallach	.12	.05	.02
413	Jim Wohlford	.10	.05	.01
414	Bill Almon	.10	.05	.01
415	Keith Atherton	.10	.05	.01
416	Bruce Bochte	.10	.05	.01
417	Tom Burgmeier	.10	.05	.01
418	Ray Burris	.10	.05	.01
419	Bill Caudill	.10	.05	.01
420	Chris Codiroli	.10	.05	.01
421	Tim Conroy	.10	.05	.01
422	Mike Davis	.10	.05	.01
423	Jim Essian	.10	.05	.01
424	Mike Heath	.10	.05	.01
425	Rickey Henderson	4.00	1.80	.50
426	Donnie Hill	.10	.05	.01
427	Dave Kingman	.12	.05	.02
428	Bill Krueger	.12	.05	.02
429	Carney Lansford	.12	.05	.02
430	Steve McCatty	.10	.05	.01
431	Joe Morgan	.60	.25	.08
432	Dwayne Murphy	.10	.05	.01
433	Tony Phillips	.12	.05	.02
434	Lary Sorensen	.10	.05	.01
435	Mike Warren	.10	.05	.01
436	Curt Young	.10	.05	.01
437	Luis Aponte	.10	.05	.01
438	Chris Bando	.10	.05	.01
439	Tony Bernazard	.10	.05	.01
440	Bert Blyleven	.35	.16	.04
441	Brett Butler	.40	.18	.05
442	Ernie Camacho	.10	.05	.01
443	Joe Carter	9.00	4.00	1.15
444	Carmelo Castillo	.10	.05	.01
445	Jamie Easterly	.10	.05	.01
446	Steve Farr	.75	.35	.09
447	Mike Fischlin	.10	.05	.01
448	Julio Franco	.75	.35	.09
449	Mel Hall	.25	.11	.03
450	Mike Hargrove	.12	.05	.02
451	Neal Heaton	.10	.05	.01
452	Brook Jacoby	.10	.05	.01
453	Mike Jeffcoat	.10	.05	.01
454	Don Schulze	.10	.05	.01
455	Roy Smith	.10	.05	.01
456	Pat Tabler	.10	.05	.01
457	Andre Thornton	.10	.05	.01
458	George Vukovich	.10	.05	.01
459	Tom Waddell	.10	.05	.01
460	Jerry Willard	.10	.05	.01
461	Dale Berra	.10	.05	.01
462	John Candelaria	.10	.05	.01
463	Jose DeLeon	.10	.05	.01
464	Doug Frobel	.10	.05	.01
465	Cecilio Guante	.10	.05	.01
466	Brian Harper	.50	.23	.06
467	Lee Lacy	.10	.05	.01
468	Bill Madlock	.12	.05	.02
469	Lee Mazzilli	.10	.05	.01
470	Larry McWilliams	.10	.05	.01
471	Jim Morrison	.10	.05	.01
472	Tony Pena	.12	.05	.02
473	Johnny Ray	.10	.05	.01
474	Rick Rhoden	.10	.05	.01
475	Don Robinson	.10	.05	.01
476	Rod Scurry	.10	.05	.01
477	Kent Tekulve	.10	.05	.01
478	Jason Thompson	.10	.05	.01
479	John Tudor	.12	.05	.02
480	Lee Tunnell	.10	.05	.01
481	Marvell Wynne	.10	.05	.01
482	Salome Barojas	.10	.05	.01
483	Dave Beard	.10	.05	.01
484	Jim Beattie	.10	.05	.01
485	Barry Bonnell	.10	.05	.01
486	Phil Bradley	.12	.05	.02
487	Al Cowens	.10	.05	.01
488	Alvin Davis	.30	.14	.04
489	Dave Henderson	.15	.07	.02
490	Steve Henderson	.10	.05	.01
491	Bob Kearney	.10	.05	.01
492	Mark Langston	3.50	1.55	.45
493	Larry Milbourne	.10	.05	.01
494	Paul Mirabella	.10	.05	.01
495	Mike Moore	.25	.11	.03
496	Edwin Nunez	.10	.05	.01
497	Spike Owen	.10	.05	.01
498	Jack Perconte	.10	.05	.01
499	Ken Phelps	.10	.05	.01
500	Jim Presley	.10	.05	.01
501	Mike Stanton	.10	.05	.01
502	Bob Stoddard	.10	.05	.01
503	Gorman Thomas	.10	.05	.01
504	Ed VandeBerg	.10	.05	.01
505	Matt Young	.10	.05	.01
506	Juan Agosto	.10	.05	.01
507	Harold Baines	.35	.16	.04
508	Floyd Bannister	.10	.05	.01

☐ 509 Britt Burns .10 .05 .01
☐ 510 Julio Cruz .10 .05 .01
☐ 511 Richard Dotson .10 .05 .01
☐ 512 Jerry Dybzinski .10 .05 .01
☐ 513 Carlton Fisk 1.75 .80 .22
☐ 514 Scott Fletcher .10 .05 .01
☐ 515 Jerry Hairston .10 .05 .01
☐ 516 Marc Hill .10 .05 .01
☐ 517 LaMarr Hoyt .10 .05 .01
☐ 518 Ron Kittle .12 .05 .02
☐ 519 Rudy Law .10 .05 .01
☐ 520 Vance Law .10 .05 .01
☐ 521 Greg Luzinski .12 .05 .02
☐ 522 Gene Nelson .10 .05 .01
☐ 523 Tom Paciorek .12 .05 .02
☐ 524 Ron Reed .10 .05 .01
☐ 525 Bert Roberge .10 .05 .01
☐ 526 Tom Seaver 1.75 .80 .22
☐ 527 Roy Smalley .10 .05 .01
☐ 528 Dan Spillner .10 .05 .01
☐ 529 Mike Squires .10 .05 .01
☐ 530 Greg Walker .10 .05 .01
☐ 531 Cesar Cedeno .12 .05 .02
☐ 532 Dave Concepcion .12 .05 .02
☐ 533 Eric Davis 8.00 3.60 1.00
☐ 534 Nick Esasky .10 .05 .01
☐ 535 Tom Foley .10 .05 .01
☐ 536 John Franco UER 1.50 .65 .19
(Koufax misspelled
as Kofax on back)
☐ 537 Brad Gulden .10 .05 .01
☐ 538 Tom Hume .10 .05 .01
☐ 539 Wayne Krenchicki .10 .05 .01
☐ 540 Andy McGaffigan .10 .05 .01
☐ 541 Eddie Milner .10 .05 .01
☐ 542 Ron Oester .10 .05 .01
☐ 543 Bob Owchinko .10 .05 .01
☐ 544 Dave Parker .40 .18 .05
☐ 545 Frank Pastore .10 .05 .01
☐ 546 Tony Perez .40 .18 .05
☐ 547 Ted Power .10 .05 .01
☐ 548 Joe Price .10 .05 .01
☐ 549 Gary Redus .10 .05 .01
☐ 550 Pete Rose 1.75 .80 .22
☐ 551 Jeff Russell .20 .09 .03
☐ 552 Mario Soto .10 .05 .01
☐ 553 Jay Tibbs .10 .05 .01
☐ 554 Duane Walker .10 .05 .01
☐ 555 Alan Bannister .10 .05 .01
☐ 556 Buddy Bell .12 .05 .02
☐ 557 Danny Darwin .10 .05 .01
☐ 558 Charlie Hough .12 .05 .02
☐ 559 Bobby Jones .10 .05 .01
☐ 560 Odell Jones .10 .05 .01
☐ 561 Jeff Kunkel .10 .05 .01
☐ 562 Mike Mason .10 .05 .01
☐ 563 Pete O'Brien .12 .05 .02
☐ 564 Larry Parrish .10 .05 .01
☐ 565 Mickey Rivers .10 .05 .01
☐ 566 Billy Sample .10 .05 .01
☐ 567 Dave Schmidt .10 .05 .01
☐ 568 Donnie Scott .10 .05 .01
☐ 569 Dave Stewart .50 .23 .06
☐ 570 Frank Tanana .12 .05 .02
☐ 571 Wayne Tolleson .10 .05 .01
☐ 572 Gary Ward .10 .05 .01
☐ 573 Curtis Wilkerson .10 .05 .01
☐ 574 George Wright .10 .05 .01
☐ 575 Ned Yost .10 .05 .01
☐ 576 Mark Brouhard .10 .05 .01
☐ 577 Mike Caldwell .10 .05 .01
☐ 578 Bobby Clark .10 .05 .01
☐ 579 Jaime Cocanower .10 .05 .01
☐ 580 Cecil Cooper .12 .05 .02
☐ 581 Rollie Fingers .50 .23 .06
☐ 582 Jim Gantner .10 .05 .01
☐ 583 Moose Haas .10 .05 .01
☐ 584 Dion James .10 .05 .01
☐ 585 Pete Ladd .10 .05 .01
☐ 586 Rick Manning .10 .05 .01
☐ 587 Bob McClure .10 .05 .01
☐ 588 Paul Molitor 1.00 .45 .13
☐ 589 Charlie Moore .10 .05 .01
☐ 590 Ben Oglivie .10 .05 .01
☐ 591 Chuck Porter .10 .05 .01
☐ 592 Randy Ready .15 .07 .02
☐ 593 Ed Romero .10 .05 .01
☐ 594 Bill Schroeder .10 .05 .01
☐ 595 Ray Searage .10 .05 .01
☐ 596 Ted Simmons .12 .05 .02
☐ 597 Jim Sundberg .12 .05 .02
☐ 598 Don Sutton .50 .23 .06
☐ 599 Tom Tellmann .10 .05 .01
☐ 600 Rick Waits .10 .05 .01
☐ 601 Robin Yount 4.00 1.80 .50
☐ 602 Dusty Baker .12 .05 .02
☐ 603 Bob Brenly .10 .05 .01
☐ 604 Jack Clark .12 .05 .02
☐ 605 Chili Davis .15 .07 .02
☐ 606 Mark Davis .12 .05 .02
☐ 607 Dan Gladden .40 .18 .05
☐ 608 Atlee Hammaker .10 .05 .01
☐ 609 Mike Krukow .10 .05 .01
☐ 610 Duane Kuiper .10 .05 .01
☐ 611 Bob Lacey .10 .05 .01
☐ 612 Bill Laskey .10 .05 .01
☐ 613 Gary Lavelle .10 .05 .01
☐ 614 Johnnie LeMaster .10 .05 .01
☐ 615 Jeff Leonard .10 .05 .01
☐ 616 Randy Lerch .10 .05 .01
☐ 617 Greg Minton .10 .05 .01
☐ 618 Steve Nicosia .10 .05 .01
☐ 619 Gene Richards .10 .05 .01
☐ 620 Jeff D. Robinson .12 .05 .02
☐ 621 Scot Thompson .10 .05 .01
☐ 622 Manny Trillo .10 .05 .01
☐ 623 Brad Wellman .10 .05 .01
☐ 624 Frank Williams .10 .05 .01
☐ 625 Joel Youngblood .10 .05 .01
☐ 626 Cal Ripken IA 4.00 1.80 .50
☐ 627 Mike Schmidt IA 2.00 .90 .25
☐ 628 Giving The Signs .15 .07 .02
Sparky Anderson
☐ 629 AL Pitcher's Nightmare 1.75 .80 .22
Dave Winfield
Rickey Henderson
☐ 630 NL Pitcher's Nightmare 2.00 .90 .25
Mike Schmidt
Ryne Sandberg
☐ 631 NL All-Stars 1.00 .45 .13
Darryl Strawberry
Gary Carter
Steve Garvey
Ozzie Smith
☐ 632 A-S Winning Battery .15 .07 .02
Gary Carter
Charlie Lea
☐ 633 NL Pennant Clinchers .15 .07 .02
Steve Garvey
Rich Gossage
☐ 634 NL Rookie Phenoms .50 .23 .06
Dwight Gooden
Juan Samuel
☐ 635 Toronto's Big Guns .15 .07 .02
Willie Upshaw
☐ 636 Toronto's Big Guns .15 .07 .02
Lloyd Moseby
☐ 637 HOLLAND: Al Holland .15 .07 .02
☐ 638 TUNNELL: Lee Tunnell .15 .07 .02
☐ 639 500th Homer .90 .40 .11
Reggie Jackson
☐ 640 4000th Hit .75 .35 .09
Pete Rose
☐ 641 Father and Son 3.50 1.55 .45
Cal Ripken Jr. and Sr.
☐ 642 Cubs: Division Champs .15 .07 .02
☐ 643 Two Perfect Games .15 .07 .02
and One No-Hitter:
Mike Witt
David Palmer
Jack Morris
☐ 644 Willie Lozado and .15 .07 .02
Vic Mata
☐ 645 Kelly Gruber and 4.00 1.80 .50
Randy O'Neal
☐ 646 Jose Roman and .15 .07 .02
Joel Skinner
☐ 647 Steve Kiefer and 9.00 4.00 1.15
Danny Tartabull
☐ 648 Rob Deer and 2.00 .90 .25
Alejandro Sanchez
☐ 649 Billy Hatcher and 2.00 .90 .25
Shawon Dunston
☐ 650 Ron Robinson and .40 .18 .05
Mike Bielecki
☐ 651 Zane Smith and .90 .40 .11
Paul Zuvella
☐ 652 Joe Hesketh and 4.00 1.80 .50
Glenn Davis
☐ 653 John Russell and .15 .07 .02
Steve Jeltz
☐ 654 CL: Tigers/Padres .15 .02 .00
and Cubs/Mets
☐ 655 CL: Blue Jays/Yankees .15 .02 .00
and Red Sox/Orioles
☐ 656 CL: Royals/Cardinals .15 .02 .00

and Phillies/Twins			
☐ 657 CL: Angels/Braves	.15	.02	.00
and Astros/Dodgers			
☐ 658 CL: Expos/A's	.15	.02	.00
and Indians/Pirates			
☐ 659 CL: Mariners/White Sox	.15	.02	.00
and Reds/Rangers			
☐ 660 CL: Brewers/Giants	.15	.02	.00
and Special Cards			

1985 Fleer Limited Edition

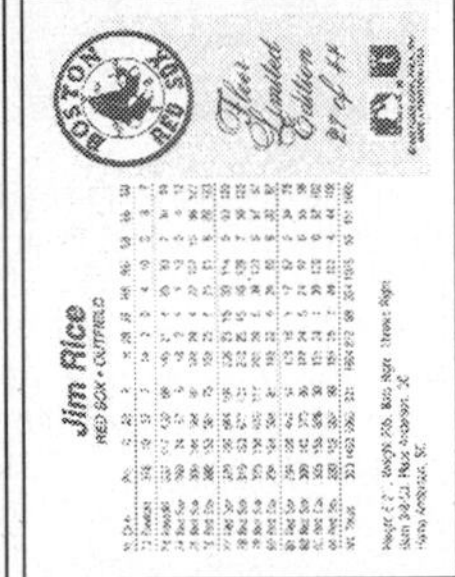

This 44-card set features standard size cards (2 1/2" by 3 1/2") which were distributed in a colorful box as a complete set. The back of the box gives a complete checklist of the cards in the set. The cards are ordered alphabetically by the player's name. Backs of the cards are yellow and white whereas the fronts show a picture of the player inside a red banner-type border.

	NRMT-MT	EXC	G-VG
COMPLETE SET (44)	6.00	2.70	.75
COMMON PLAYER (1-44)	.10	.05	.01
☐ 1 Buddy Bell	.10	.05	.01
☐ 2 Bert Blyleven	.15	.07	.02
☐ 3 Wade Boggs	.75	.35	.09
☐ 4 George Brett	.90	.40	.11
☐ 5 Rod Carew	.60	.25	.08
☐ 6 Steve Carlton	.50	.23	.06
☐ 7 Alvin Davis	.15	.07	.02
☐ 8 Andre Dawson	.50	.23	.06
☐ 9 Steve Garvey	.30	.14	.04
☐ 10 Rich Gossage	.15	.07	.02
☐ 11 Tony Gwynn	.75	.35	.09
☐ 12 Keith Hernandez	.15	.07	.02
☐ 13 Kent Hrbek	.15	.07	.02
☐ 14 Reggie Jackson	.90	.40	.11
☐ 15 Dave Kingman	.10	.05	.01
☐ 16 Ron Kittle	.10	.05	.01
☐ 17 Mark Langston	.25	.11	.03
☐ 18 Jeff Leonard	.10	.05	.01
☐ 19 Bill Madlock	.10	.05	.01
☐ 20 Don Mattingly	.90	.40	.11
☐ 21 Jack Morris	.15	.07	.02
☐ 22 Dale Murphy	.35	.16	.04
☐ 23 Eddie Murray	.50	.23	.06
☐ 24 Tony Pena	.10	.05	.01
☐ 25 Dan Quisenberry	.10	.05	.01
☐ 26 Tim Raines	.20	.09	.03
☐ 27 Jim Rice	.20	.09	.03
☐ 28 Cal Ripken	1.25	.55	.16
☐ 29 Pete Rose	.75	.35	.09
☐ 30 Nolan Ryan	1.50	.65	.19
☐ 31 Ryne Sandberg	1.25	.55	.16
☐ 32 Steve Sax	.15	.07	.02
☐ 33 Mike Schmidt	1.00	.45	.13
☐ 34 Tom Seaver	.75	.35	.09
☐ 35 Ozzie Smith	.50	.23	.06
☐ 36 Mario Soto	.10	.05	.01
☐ 37 Dave Stieb	.10	.05	.01
☐ 38 Darryl Strawberry	.60	.25	.08
☐ 39 Rick Sutcliffe	.10	.05	.01
☐ 40 Alan Trammell	.25	.11	.03
☐ 41 Willie Upshaw	.10	.05	.01
☐ 42 Fernando Valenzuela	.10	.05	.01
☐ 43 Dave Winfield	.50	.23	.06
☐ 44 Robin Yount	.90	.40	.11

1985 Fleer Update

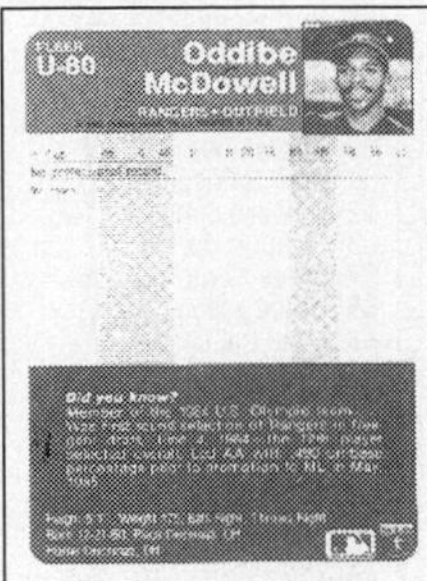

This 132-card set was issued late in the collecting year and features new players and players on new teams compared to the 1985 Fleer regular issue cards. Cards measure 2 1/2" by 3 1/2" and were distributed together as a complete set in a special box. The cards are numbered with a U prefix and are ordered alphabetically by the player's name. This set features the Extended Rookie Cards of Ivan Calderon, Vince Coleman, Darren Daulton, Ozzie Guillen, Teddy Higuera, and Mickey Tettleton.

	NRMT-MT	EXC	G-VG
COMPLETE SET (132)	33.00	15.00	4.10
COMMON PLAYER (1-132)	.15	.07	.02
☐ 1 Don Aase	.15	.07	.02
☐ 2 Bill Almon	.15	.07	.02
☐ 3 Dusty Baker	.25	.11	.03
☐ 4 Dale Berra	.15	.07	.02
☐ 5 Karl Best	.15	.07	.02
☐ 6 Tim Birtsas	.15	.07	.02
☐ 7 Vida Blue	.25	.11	.03
☐ 8 Rich Bordi	.15	.07	.02
☐ 9 Daryl Boston	.25	.11	.03
☐ 10 Hubie Brooks	.25	.11	.03
☐ 11 Chris Brown	.15	.07	.02
☐ 12 Tom Browning	1.00	.45	.13
☐ 13 Al Bumbry	.15	.07	.02
☐ 14 Tim Burke	.25	.11	.03
☐ 15 Ray Burris	.15	.07	.02
☐ 16 Jeff Burroughs	.15	.07	.02
☐ 17 Ivan Calderon	1.75	.80	.22
☐ 18 Jeff Calhoun	.15	.07	.02
☐ 19 Bill Campbell	.15	.07	.02
☐ 20 Don Carman	.15	.07	.02
☐ 21 Gary Carter	1.00	.45	.13
☐ 22 Bobby Castillo	.15	.07	.02
☐ 23 Bill Caudill	.15	.07	.02
☐ 24 Rick Cerone	.15	.07	.02
☐ 25 Jack Clark	.25	.11	.03
☐ 26 Pat Clements	.15	.07	.02
☐ 27 Stewart Cliburn	.15	.07	.02
☐ 28 Vince Coleman	4.00	1.80	.50
☐ 29 Dave Collins	.15	.07	.02
☐ 30 Fritz Connally	.15	.07	.02
☐ 31 Henry Cotto	.15	.07	.02
☐ 32 Danny Darwin	.15	.07	.02
☐ 33 Darren Daulton	5.00	2.30	.60
☐ 34 Jerry Davis	.15	.07	.02
☐ 35 Brian Dayett	.15	.07	.02
☐ 36 Ken Dixon	.15	.07	.02
☐ 37 Tommy Dunbar	.15	.07	.02
☐ 38 Mariano Duncan	1.25	.55	.16
☐ 39 Bob Fallon	.15	.07	.02
☐ 40 Brian Fisher	.15	.07	.02
☐ 41 Mike Fitzgerald	.15	.07	.02
☐ 42 Ray Fontenot	.15	.07	.02
☐ 43 Greg Gagne	.40	.18	.05
☐ 44 Oscar Gamble	.15	.07	.02
☐ 45 Jim Gott	.15	.07	.02
☐ 46 David Green	.15	.07	.02
☐ 47 Alfredo Griffin	.15	.07	.02
☐ 48 Ozzie Guillen	1.25	.55	.16
☐ 49 Toby Harrah	.15	.07	.02
☐ 50 Ron Hassey	.15	.07	.02
☐ 51 Rickey Henderson	5.00	2.30	.60
☐ 52 Steve Henderson	.15	.07	.02
☐ 53 George Hendrick	.15	.07	.02

☐	54 Teddy Higuera	.25	.11	.03
☐	55 Al Holland	.15	.07	.02
☐	56 Burt Hooton	.15	.07	.02
☐	57 Jay Howell	.25	.11	.03
☐	58 LaMarr Hoyt	.15	.07	.02
☐	59 Tim Hulett	.15	.07	.02
☐	60 Bob James	.15	.07	.02
☐	61 Cliff Johnson	.15	.07	.02
☐	62 Howard Johnson	2.00	.90	.25
☐	63 Ruppert Jones	.15	.07	.02
☐	64 Steve Kemp	.15	.07	.02
☐	65 Bruce Kison	.15	.07	.02
☐	66 Mike LaCoss	.15	.07	.02
☐	67 Lee Lacy	.15	.07	.02
☐	68 Dave LaPoint	.15	.07	.02
☐	69 Gary Lavelle	.15	.07	.02
☐	70 Vance Law	.15	.07	.02
☐	71 Manny Lee	.75	.35	.09
☐	72 Sixto Lezcano	.15	.07	.02
☐	73 Tim Lollar	.15	.07	.02
☐	74 Urbano Lugo	.15	.07	.02
☐	75 Fred Lynn	.25	.11	.03
☐	76 Steve Lyons	.25	.11	.03
☐	77 Mickey Mahler	.15	.07	.02
☐	78 Ron Mathis	.15	.07	.02
☐	79 Len Matuszek	.15	.07	.02
☐	80 Oddibe McDowell UER (Part of bio actually Roger's)	.25	.11	.03
☐	81 Roger McDowell UER (Part of bio actually Oddibe's)	.40	.18	.05
☐	82 Donnie Moore	.15	.07	.02
☐	83 Ron Musselman	.15	.07	.02
☐	84 Al Oliver	.25	.11	.03
☐	85 Joe Orsulak	.60	.25	.08
☐	86 Dan Pasqua	.40	.18	.05
☐	87 Chris Pittaro	.15	.07	.02
☐	88 Rick Reuschel	.25	.11	.03
☐	89 Earnie Riles	.15	.07	.02
☐	90 Jerry Royster	.15	.07	.02
☐	91 Dave Rozema	.15	.07	.02
☐	92 Dave Rucker	.15	.07	.02
☐	93 Vern Ruhle	.15	.07	.02
☐	94 Mark Salas	.15	.07	.02
☐	95 Luis Salazar	.15	.07	.02
☐	96 Joe Sambito	.15	.07	.02
☐	97 Billy Sample	.15	.07	.02
☐	98 Alejandro Sanchez	.15	.07	.02
☐	99 Calvin Schiraldi	.15	.07	.02
☐	100 Rick Schu	.15	.07	.02
☐	101 Larry Sheets	.15	.07	.02
☐	102 Ron Shephard	.15	.07	.02
☐	103 Nelson Simmons	.15	.07	.02
☐	104 Don Slaught	.15	.07	.02
☐	105 Roy Smalley	.15	.07	.02
☐	106 Lonnie Smith	.25	.11	.03
☐	107 Nate Snell	.15	.07	.02
☐	108 Lary Sorensen	.15	.07	.02
☐	109 Chris Speier	.15	.07	.02
☐	110 Mike Stenhouse	.15	.07	.02
☐	111 Tim Stoddard	.15	.07	.02
☐	112 John Stuper	.15	.07	.02
☐	113 Jim Sundberg	.25	.11	.03
☐	114 Bruce Sutter	.25	.11	.03
☐	115 Don Sutton	.75	.35	.09
☐	116 Bruce Tanner	.15	.07	.02
☐	117 Kent Tekulve	.15	.07	.02
☐	118 Walt Terrell	.15	.07	.02
☐	119 Mickey Tettleton	5.00	2.30	.60
☐	120 Rich Thompson	.15	.07	.02
☐	121 Louis Thornton	.15	.07	.02
☐	122 Alex Trevino	.15	.07	.02
☐	123 John Tudor	.25	.11	.03
☐	124 Jose Uribe	.25	.11	.03
☐	125 Dave Valle	.15	.07	.02
☐	126 Dave Von Ohlen	.15	.07	.02
☐	127 Curt Wardle	.15	.07	.02
☐	128 U.L. Washington	.15	.07	.02
☐	129 Ed Whitson	.15	.07	.02
☐	130 Herm Winningham	.30	.14	.04
☐	131 Rich Yett	.15	.07	.02
☐	132 Checklist U1-U132	.25	.03	.01

1986 Fleer

The cards in this 660-card set measure 2 1/2" by 3 1/2". The 1986 Fleer set features fronts that contain the team logo

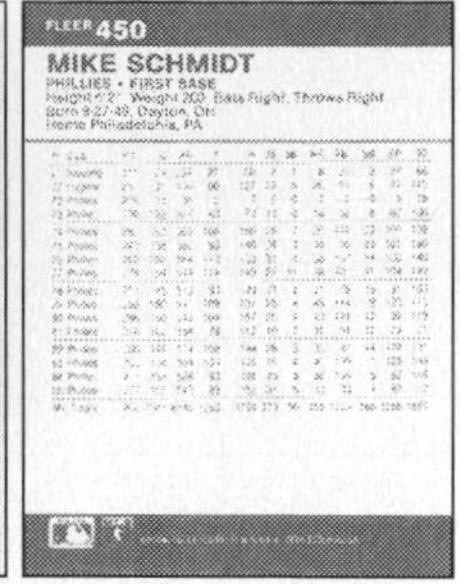

along with the player's name and position. The player cards are alphabetized within team and the teams are ordered by their 1985 season finish and won-lost record, e.g., Kansas City (1-25), St. Louis (26-49), Toronto (50-73), New York Mets (74-97), New York Yankees (98-122), Los Angeles (123-147), California (148-171), Cincinnati (172-196), Chicago White Sox (197-220), Detroit (221-243), Montreal (244-267), Baltimore (268-291), Houston (292-314), San Diego (315-338), Boston (339-360), Chicago Cubs (361-385), Minnesota (386-409), Oakland (410-432), Philadelphia (433-457), Seattle (458-481), Milwaukee (482-506), Atlanta (507-532), San Francisco (533-555), Texas (556-578), Cleveland (579-601), and Pittsburgh (602-625). Specials (626-643), Major League Prospects (644-653), and checklist cards (654-660) complete the set. The border enclosing the photo is dark blue. The backs feature the same name, number, and statistics format that Fleer has been using over the past few years. The Dennis and Tippy Martinez cards were apparently switched in the set numbering, as their adjacent numbers (279 and 280) were reversed on the Orioles checklist card. The set includes the Rookie Cards of Jose Canseco, Vince Coleman, Kal Daniels, Len Dykstra, Cecil Fielder, Benito Santiago, and Mickey Tettleton.

		MT	EX-MT	VG
	COMPLETE SET (660)	125.00	57.50	15.50
	COMPLETE FACT.SET (660)	130.00	57.50	16.50
	COMMON PLAYER (1-660)	.10	.05	.01
☐	1 Steve Balboni	.15	.05	.02
☐	2 Joe Beckwith	.10	.05	.01
☐	3 Buddy Biancalana	.10	.05	.01
☐	4 Bud Black	.10	.05	.01
☐	5 George Brett	2.00	.90	.25
☐	6 Onix Concepcion	.10	.05	.01
☐	7 Steve Farr	.15	.07	.02
☐	8 Mark Gubicza	.15	.07	.02
☐	9 Dane Iorg	.10	.05	.01
☐	10 Danny Jackson	.10	.05	.01
☐	11 Lynn Jones	.10	.05	.01
☐	12 Mike Jones	.10	.05	.01
☐	13 Charlie Leibrandt	.15	.07	.02
☐	14 Hal McRae	.15	.07	.02
☐	15 Omar Moreno	.10	.05	.01
☐	16 Darryl Motley	.10	.05	.01
☐	17 Jorge Orta	.10	.05	.01
☐	18 Dan Quisenberry	.15	.07	.02
☐	19 Bret Saberhagen	.75	.35	.09
☐	20 Pat Sheridan	.10	.05	.01
☐	21 Lonnie Smith	.10	.05	.01
☐	22 Jim Sundberg	.15	.07	.02
☐	23 John Wathan	.10	.05	.01
☐	24 Frank White	.15	.07	.02
☐	25 Willie Wilson	.10	.05	.01
☐	26 Joaquin Andujar	.10	.05	.01
☐	27 Steve Braun	.10	.05	.01
☐	28 Bill Campbell	.10	.05	.01
☐	29 Cesar Cedeno	.15	.07	.02
☐	30 Jack Clark	.15	.07	.02
☐	31 Vince Coleman	1.75	.80	.22
☐	32 Danny Cox	.10	.05	.01
☐	33 Ken Dayley	.10	.05	.01
☐	34 Ivan DeJesus	.10	.05	.01

Card	Player			
☐	35 Bob Forsch	.10	.05	.01
☐	36 Brian Harper	.25	.11	.03
☐	37 Tom Herr	.10	.05	.01
☐	38 Ricky Horton	.10	.05	.01
☐	39 Kurt Kepshire	.10	.05	.01
☐	40 Jeff Lahti	.10	.05	.01
☐	41 Tito Landrum	.10	.05	.01
☐	42 Willie McGee	.20	.09	.03
☐	43 Tom Nieto	.10	.05	.01
☐	44 Terry Pendleton	1.50	.65	.19
☐	45 Darrell Porter	.10	.05	.01
☐	46 Ozzie Smith	1.00	.45	.13
☐	47 John Tudor	.15	.07	.02
☐	48 Andy Van Slyke	.75	.35	.09
☐	49 Todd Worrell	.35	.16	.04
☐	50 Jim Acker	.10	.05	.01
☐	51 Doyle Alexander	.10	.05	.01
☐	52 Jesse Barfield	.15	.07	.02
☐	53 George Bell	.50	.23	.06
☐	54 Jeff Burroughs	.10	.05	.01
☐	55 Bill Caudill	.10	.05	.01
☐	56 Jim Clancy	.10	.05	.01
☐	57 Tony Fernandez	.25	.11	.03
☐	58 Tom Filer	.10	.05	.01
☐	59 Damaso Garcia	.10	.05	.01
☐	60 Tom Henke	.50	.23	.06
☐	61 Garth Iorg	.10	.05	.01
☐	62 Cliff Johnson	.10	.05	.01
☐	63 Jimmy Key	.25	.11	.03
☐	64 Dennis Lamp	.10	.05	.01
☐	65 Gary Lavelle	.10	.05	.01
☐	66 Buck Martinez	.10	.05	.01
☐	67 Lloyd Moseby	.10	.05	.01
☐	68 Rance Mulliniks	.10	.05	.01
☐	69 Al Oliver	.15	.07	.02
☐	70 Dave Stieb	.15	.07	.02
☐	71 Louis Thornton	.10	.05	.01
☐	72 Willie Upshaw	.10	.05	.01
☐	73 Ernie Whitt	.10	.05	.01
☐	74 Rick Aguilera	1.75	.80	.22
☐	75 Wally Backman	.10	.05	.01
☐	76 Gary Carter	.35	.16	.04
☐	77 Ron Darling	.20	.09	.03
☐	78 Len Dykstra	1.75	.80	.22
☐	79 Sid Fernandez	.25	.11	.03
☐	80 George Foster	.15	.07	.02
☐	81 Dwight Gooden	1.25	.55	.16
☐	82 Tom Gorman	.10	.05	.01
☐	83 Danny Heep	.10	.05	.01
☐	84 Keith Hernandez	.15	.07	.02
☐	85 Howard Johnson	.60	.25	.08
☐	86 Ray Knight	.15	.07	.02
☐	87 Terry Leach	.10	.05	.01
☐	88 Ed Lynch	.10	.05	.01
☐	89 Roger McDowell	.25	.11	.03
☐	90 Jesse Orosco	.10	.05	.01
☐	91 Tom Paciorek	.15	.07	.02
☐	92 Ronn Reynolds	.10	.05	.01
☐	93 Rafael Santana	.10	.05	.01
☐	94 Doug Sisk	.10	.05	.01
☐	95 Rusty Staub	.15	.07	.02
☐	96 Darryl Strawberry	2.50	1.15	.30
☐	97 Mookie Wilson	.15	.07	.02
☐	98 Neil Allen	.10	.05	.01
☐	99 Don Baylor	.15	.07	.02
☐	100 Dale Berra	.10	.05	.01
☐	101 Rich Bordi	.10	.05	.01
☐	102 Marty Bystrom	.10	.05	.01
☐	103 Joe Cowley	.10	.05	.01
☐	104 Brian Fisher	.10	.05	.01
☐	105 Ken Griffey	.15	.07	.02
☐	106 Ron Guidry	.15	.07	.02
☐	107 Ron Hassey	.10	.05	.01
☐	108 Rickey Henderson UER (SB Record of 120, sic)	2.00	.90	.25
☐	109 Don Mattingly	2.50	1.15	.30
☐	110 Bobby Meacham	.10	.05	.01
☐	111 John Montefusco	.10	.05	.01
☐	112 Phil Niekro	.30	.14	.04
☐	113 Mike Pagliarulo	.10	.05	.01
☐	114 Dan Pasqua	.15	.07	.02
☐	115 Willie Randolph	.15	.07	.02
☐	116 Dave Righetti	.15	.07	.02
☐	117 Andre Robertson	.10	.05	.01
☐	118 Billy Sample	.10	.05	.01
☐	119 Bob Shirley	.10	.05	.01
☐	120 Ed Whitson	.10	.05	.01
☐	121 Dave Winfield	1.25	.55	.16
☐	122 Butch Wynegar	.10	.05	.01
☐	123 Dave Anderson	.10	.05	.01
☐	124 Bob Bailor	.10	.05	.01
☐	125 Greg Brock	.10	.05	.01
☐	126 Enos Cabell	.10	.05	.01
☐	127 Bobby Castillo	.10	.05	.01
☐	128 Carlos Diaz	.10	.05	.01
☐	129 Mariano Duncan	.60	.25	.08
☐	130 Pedro Guerrero	.12	.05	.02
☐	131 Orel Hershiser	.50	.23	.06
☐	132 Rick Honeycutt	.10	.05	.01
☐	133 Ken Howell	.10	.05	.01
☐	134 Ken Landreaux	.10	.05	.01
☐	135 Bill Madlock	.15	.07	.02
☐	136 Candy Maldonado	.15	.07	.02
☐	137 Mike Marshall	.10	.05	.01
☐	138 Len Matuszek	.10	.05	.01
☐	139 Tom Niedenfuer	.10	.05	.01
☐	140 Alejandro Pena	.10	.05	.01
☐	141 Jerry Reuss	.10	.05	.01
☐	142 Bill Russell	.15	.07	.02
☐	143 Steve Sax	.25	.11	.03
☐	144 Mike Scioscia	.10	.05	.01
☐	145 Fernando Valenzuela	.15	.07	.02
☐	146 Bob Welch	.15	.07	.02
☐	147 Terry Whitfield	.10	.05	.01
☐	148 Juan Beniquez	.10	.05	.01
☐	149 Bob Boone	.15	.07	.02
☐	150 John Candelaria	.10	.05	.01
☐	151 Rod Carew	.90	.40	.11
☐	152 Stewart Cliburn	.10	.05	.01
☐	153 Doug DeCinces	.10	.05	.01
☐	154 Brian Downing	.15	.07	.02
☐	155 Ken Forsch	.10	.05	.01
☐	156 Craig Gerber	.10	.05	.01
☐	157 Bobby Grich	.15	.07	.02
☐	158 George Hendrick	.10	.05	.01
☐	159 Al Holland	.10	.05	.01
☐	160 Reggie Jackson	1.00	.45	.13
☐	161 Ruppert Jones	.10	.05	.01
☐	162 Urbano Lugo	.10	.05	.01
☐	163 Kirk McCaskill	.30	.14	.04
☐	164 Donnie Moore	.10	.05	.01
☐	165 Gary Pettis	.10	.05	.01
☐	166 Ron Romanick	.10	.05	.01
☐	167 Dick Schofield	.10	.05	.01
☐	168 Daryl Sconiers	.10	.05	.01
☐	169 Jim Slaton	.10	.05	.01
☐	170 Don Sutton	.30	.14	.04
☐	171 Mike Witt	.10	.05	.01
☐	172 Buddy Bell	.15	.07	.02
☐	173 Tom Browning	.25	.11	.03
☐	174 Dave Concepcion	.15	.07	.02
☐	175 Eric Davis	1.00	.45	.13
☐	176 Bo Diaz	.10	.05	.01
☐	177 Nick Esasky	.10	.05	.01
☐	178 John Franco	.25	.11	.03
☐	179 Tom Hume	.10	.05	.01
☐	180 Wayne Krenchicki	.10	.05	.01
☐	181 Andy McGaffigan	.10	.05	.01
☐	182 Eddie Milner	.10	.05	.01
☐	183 Ron Oester	.10	.05	.01
☐	184 Dave Parker	.20	.09	.03
☐	185 Frank Pastore	.10	.05	.01
☐	186 Tony Perez	.30	.14	.04
☐	187 Ted Power	.10	.05	.01
☐	188 Joe Price	.10	.05	.01
☐	189 Gary Redus	.10	.05	.01
☐	190 Ron Robinson	.10	.05	.01
☐	191 Pete Rose	1.00	.45	.13
☐	192 Mario Soto	.10	.05	.01
☐	193 John Stuper	.10	.05	.01
☐	194 Jay Tibbs	.10	.05	.01
☐	195 Dave Van Gorder	.10	.05	.01
☐	196 Max Venable	.10	.05	.01
☐	197 Juan Agosto	.10	.05	.01
☐	198 Harold Baines	.25	.11	.03
☐	199 Floyd Bannister	.10	.05	.01
☐	200 Britt Burns	.10	.05	.01
☐	201 Julio Cruz	.10	.05	.01
☐	202 Joel Davis	.10	.05	.01
☐	203 Richard Dotson	.10	.05	.01
☐	204 Carlton Fisk	.90	.40	.11
☐	205 Scott Fletcher	.10	.05	.01
☐	206 Ozzie Guillen	.60	.25	.08
☐	207 Jerry Hairston	.10	.05	.01
☐	208 Tim Hulett	.10	.05	.01
☐	209 Bob James	.10	.05	.01
☐	210 Ron Kittle	.10	.05	.01
☐	211 Rudy Law	.10	.05	.01
☐	212 Bryan Little	.10	.05	.01
☐	213 Gene Nelson	.10	.05	.01
☐	214 Reid Nichols	.10	.05	.01
☐	215 Luis Salazar	.10	.05	.01
☐	216 Tom Seaver	.90	.40	.11
☐	217 Dan Spillner	.10	.05	.01
☐	218 Bruce Tanner	.10	.05	.01
☐	219 Greg Walker	.10	.05	.01

☐ 220 Dave Wehrmeister .10 .05 .01
☐ 221 Juan Berenguer .10 .05 .01
☐ 222 Dave Bergman .10 .05 .01
☐ 223 Tom Brookens .10 .05 .01
☐ 224 Darrell Evans .15 .07 .02
☐ 225 Barbaro Garbey .10 .05 .01
☐ 226 Kirk Gibson .15 .07 .02
☐ 227 John Grubb .10 .05 .01
☐ 228 Willie Hernandez .10 .05 .01
☐ 229 Larry Herndon .10 .05 .01
☐ 230 Chet Lemon .10 .05 .01
☐ 231 Aurelio Lopez .10 .05 .01
☐ 232 Jack Morris .60 .25 .08
☐ 233 Randy O'Neal .10 .05 .01
☐ 234 Lance Parrish .15 .07 .02
☐ 235 Dan Petry .10 .05 .01
☐ 236 Alejandro Sanchez .10 .05 .01
☐ 237 Bill Scherrer .10 .05 .01
☐ 238 Nelson Simmons .10 .05 .01
☐ 239 Frank Tanana .15 .07 .02
☐ 240 Walt Terrell .10 .05 .01
☐ 241 Alan Trammell .30 .14 .04
☐ 242 Lou Whitaker .30 .14 .04
☐ 243 Milt Wilcox .10 .05 .01
☐ 244 Hubie Brooks .10 .05 .01
☐ 245 Tim Burke .20 .09 .03
☐ 246 Andre Dawson 1.00 .45 .13
☐ 247 Mike Fitzgerald .10 .05 .01
☐ 248 Terry Francona .10 .05 .01
☐ 249 Bill Gullickson .15 .07 .02
☐ 250 Joe Hesketh .10 .05 .01
☐ 251 Bill Laskey .10 .05 .01
☐ 252 Vance Law .10 .05 .01
☐ 253 Charlie Lea .10 .05 .01
☐ 254 Gary Lucas .10 .05 .01
☐ 255 David Palmer .10 .05 .01
☐ 256 Tim Raines .30 .14 .04
☐ 257 Jeff Reardon .50 .23 .06
☐ 258 Bert Roberge .10 .05 .01
☐ 259 Dan Schatzeder .10 .05 .01
☐ 260 Bryn Smith .10 .05 .01
☐ 261 Randy St.Claire .10 .05 .01
☐ 262 Scot Thompson .10 .05 .01
☐ 263 Tim Wallach .15 .07 .02
☐ 264 U.L. Washington .10 .05 .01
☐ 265 Mitch Webster .10 .05 .01
☐ 266 Herm Winningham .20 .09 .03
☐ 267 Floyd Youmans .10 .05 .01
☐ 268 Don Aase .10 .05 .01
☐ 269 Mike Boddicker .10 .05 .01
☐ 270 Rich Dauer .10 .05 .01
☐ 271 Storm Davis .10 .05 .01
☐ 272 Rick Dempsey .10 .05 .01
☐ 273 Ken Dixon .10 .05 .01
☐ 274 Jim Dwyer .10 .05 .01
☐ 275 Mike Flanagan .10 .05 .01
☐ 276 Wayne Gross .10 .05 .01
☐ 277 Lee Lacy .10 .05 .01
☐ 278 Fred Lynn .15 .07 .02
☐ 279 Tippy Martinez .10 .05 .01
☐ 280 Dennis Martinez .15 .07 .02
☐ 281 Scott McGregor .10 .05 .01
☐ 282 Eddie Murray 1.00 .45 .13
☐ 283 Floyd Rayford .10 .05 .01
☐ 284 Cal Ripken 5.00 2.30 .60
☐ 285 Gary Roenicke .10 .05 .01
☐ 286 Larry Sheets .10 .05 .01
☐ 287 John Shelby .10 .05 .01
☐ 288 Nate Snell .10 .05 .01
☐ 289 Sammy Stewart .10 .05 .01
☐ 290 Alan Wiggins .10 .05 .01
☐ 291 Mike Young .10 .05 .01
☐ 292 Alan Ashby .10 .05 .01
☐ 293 Mark Bailey .10 .05 .01
☐ 294 Kevin Bass .10 .05 .01
☐ 295 Jeff Calhoun .10 .05 .01
☐ 296 Jose Cruz .10 .05 .01
☐ 297 Glenn Davis .75 .35 .09
☐ 298 Bill Dawley .10 .05 .01
☐ 299 Frank DiPino .10 .05 .01
☐ 300 Bill Doran .10 .05 .01
☐ 301 Phil Garner .15 .07 .02
☐ 302 Jeff Heathcock .10 .05 .01
☐ 303 Charlie Kerfeld .10 .05 .01
☐ 304 Bob Knepper .10 .05 .01
☐ 305 Ron Mathis .10 .05 .01
☐ 306 Jerry Mumphrey .10 .05 .01
☐ 307 Jim Pankovits .10 .05 .01
☐ 308 Terry Puhl .10 .05 .01
☐ 309 Craig Reynolds .10 .05 .01
☐ 310 Nolan Ryan 6.00 2.70 .75
☐ 311 Mike Scott .15 .07 .02
☐ 312 Dave Smith .10 .05 .01
☐ 313 Dickie Thon .10 .05 .01
☐ 314 Denny Walling .10 .05 .01
☐ 315 Kurt Bevacqua .10 .05 .01
☐ 316 Al Bumbry .10 .05 .01
☐ 317 Jerry Davis .10 .05 .01
☐ 318 Luis DeLeon .10 .05 .01
☐ 319 Dave Dravecky .15 .07 .02
☐ 320 Tim Flannery .10 .05 .01
☐ 321 Steve Garvey .35 .16 .04
☐ 322 Rich Gossage .15 .07 .02
☐ 323 Tony Gwynn 3.00 1.35 .40
☐ 324 Andy Hawkins .10 .05 .01
☐ 325 LaMarr Hoyt .10 .05 .01
☐ 326 Roy Lee Jackson .10 .05 .01
☐ 327 Terry Kennedy .10 .05 .01
☐ 328 Craig Lefferts .15 .07 .02
☐ 329 Carmelo Martinez .10 .05 .01
☐ 330 Lance McCullers .10 .05 .01
☐ 331 Kevin McReynolds .12 .05 .02
☐ 332 Graig Nettles .15 .07 .02
☐ 333 Jerry Royster .10 .05 .01
☐ 334 Eric Show .10 .05 .01
☐ 335 Tim Stoddard .10 .05 .01
☐ 336 Garry Templeton .10 .05 .01
☐ 337 Mark Thurmond .10 .05 .01
☐ 338 Ed Wojna .10 .05 .01
☐ 339 Tony Armas .10 .05 .01
☐ 340 Marty Barrett .10 .05 .01
☐ 341 Wade Boggs 2.00 .90 .25
☐ 342 Dennis Boyd .10 .05 .01
☐ 343 Bill Buckner .15 .07 .02
☐ 344 Mark Clear .10 .05 .01
☐ 345 Roger Clemens 12.00 5.50 1.50
☐ 346 Steve Crawford .10 .05 .01
☐ 347 Mike Easler .10 .05 .01
☐ 348 Dwight Evans .12 .05 .02
☐ 349 Rich Gedman .10 .05 .01
☐ 350 Jackie Gutierrez .10 .05 .01
☐ 351 Glenn Hoffman .10 .05 .01
☐ 352 Bruce Hurst .15 .07 .02
☐ 353 Bruce Kison .10 .05 .01
☐ 354 Tim Lollar .10 .05 .01
☐ 355 Steve Lyons .10 .05 .01
☐ 356 Al Nipper .10 .05 .01
☐ 357 Bob Ojeda .10 .05 .01
☐ 358 Jim Rice .15 .07 .02
☐ 359 Bob Stanley .10 .05 .01
☐ 360 Mike Trujillo .10 .05 .01
☐ 361 Thad Bosley .10 .05 .01
☐ 362 Warren Brusstar .10 .05 .01
☐ 363 Ron Cey .15 .07 .02
☐ 364 Jody Davis .10 .05 .01
☐ 365 Bob Dernier .10 .05 .01
☐ 366 Shawon Dunston .30 .14 .04
☐ 367 Leon Durham .10 .05 .01
☐ 368 Dennis Eckersley .75 .35 .09
☐ 369 Ray Fontenot .10 .05 .01
☐ 370 George Frazier .10 .05 .01
☐ 371 Billy Hatcher .15 .07 .02
☐ 372 Dave Lopes .15 .07 .02
☐ 373 Gary Matthews .10 .05 .01
☐ 374 Ron Meridith .10 .05 .01
☐ 375 Keith Moreland .10 .05 .01
☐ 376 Reggie Patterson .10 .05 .01
☐ 377 Dick Ruthven .10 .05 .01
☐ 378 Ryne Sandberg 4.50 2.00 .55
☐ 379 Scott Sanderson .10 .05 .01
☐ 380 Lee Smith .60 .25 .08
☐ 381 Lary Sorensen .10 .05 .01
☐ 382 Chris Speier .10 .05 .01
☐ 383 Rick Sutcliffe .15 .07 .02
☐ 384 Steve Trout .10 .05 .01
☐ 385 Gary Woods .10 .05 .01
☐ 386 Bert Blyleven .20 .09 .03
☐ 387 Tom Brunansky .15 .07 .02
☐ 388 Randy Bush .10 .05 .01
☐ 389 John Butcher .10 .05 .01
☐ 390 Ron Davis .10 .05 .01
☐ 391 Dave Engle .10 .05 .01
☐ 392 Frank Eufemia .10 .05 .01
☐ 393 Pete Filson .10 .05 .01
☐ 394 Gary Gaetti .15 .07 .02
☐ 395 Greg Gagne .15 .07 .02
☐ 396 Mickey Hatcher .10 .05 .01
☐ 397 Kent Hrbek .20 .09 .03
☐ 398 Tim Laudner .10 .05 .01
☐ 399 Rick Lysander .10 .05 .01
☐ 400 Dave Meier .10 .05 .01
☐ 401 Kirby Puckett UER 10.00 4.50 1.25
(Card has him in NL, should be AL)
☐ 402 Mark Salas .10 .05 .01
☐ 403 Ken Schrom .10 .05 .01

☐	404	Roy Smalley	.10	.05	.01
☐	405	Mike Smithson	.10	.05	.01
☐	406	Mike Stenhouse	.10	.05	.01
☐	407	Tim Teufel	.10	.05	.01
☐	408	Frank Viola	.30	.14	.04
☐	409	Ron Washington	.10	.05	.01
☐	410	Keith Atherton	.10	.05	.01
☐	411	Dusty Baker	.15	.07	.02
☐	412	Tim Birtsas	.10	.05	.01
☐	413	Bruce Bochte	.10	.05	.01
☐	414	Chris Codiroli	.10	.05	.01
☐	415	Dave Collins	.10	.05	.01
☐	416	Mike Davis	.10	.05	.01
☐	417	Alfredo Griffin	.10	.05	.01
☐	418	Mike Heath	.10	.05	.01
☐	419	Steve Henderson	.10	.05	.01
☐	420	Donnie Hill	.10	.05	.01
☐	421	Jay Howell	.15	.07	.02
☐	422	Tommy John	.15	.07	.02
☐	423	Dave Kingman	.15	.07	.02
☐	424	Bill Krueger	.10	.05	.01
☐	425	Rick Langford	.10	.05	.01
☐	426	Carney Lansford	.15	.07	.02
☐	427	Steve McCatty	.10	.05	.01
☐	428	Dwayne Murphy	.10	.05	.01
☐	429	Steve Ontiveros	.10	.05	.01
☐	430	Tony Phillips	.15	.07	.02
☐	431	Jose Rijo	.60	.25	.08
☐	432	Mickey Tettleton	2.00	.90	.25
☐	433	Luis Aguayo	.10	.05	.01
☐	434	Larry Andersen	.10	.05	.01
☐	435	Steve Carlton	.90	.40	.11
☐	436	Don Carman	.10	.05	.01
☐	437	Tim Corcoran	.10	.05	.01
☐	438	Darren Daulton	2.00	.90	.25
☐	439	John Denny	.10	.05	.01
☐	440	Tom Foley	.10	.05	.01
☐	441	Greg Gross	.10	.05	.01
☐	442	Kevin Gross	.10	.05	.01
☐	443	Von Hayes	.10	.05	.01
☐	444	Charles Hudson	.10	.05	.01
☐	445	Garry Maddox	.10	.05	.01
☐	446	Shane Rawley	.10	.05	.01
☐	447	Dave Rucker	.10	.05	.01
☐	448	John Russell	.10	.05	.01
☐	449	Juan Samuel	.15	.07	.02
☐	450	Mike Schmidt	2.50	1.15	.30
☐	451	Rick Schu	.10	.05	.01
☐	452	Dave Shipanoff	.10	.05	.01
☐	453	Dave Stewart	.20	.09	.03
☐	454	Jeff Stone	.10	.05	.01
☐	455	Kent Tekulve	.10	.05	.01
☐	456	Ozzie Virgil	.10	.05	.01
☐	457	Glenn Wilson	.10	.05	.01
☐	458	Jim Beattie	.10	.05	.01
☐	459	Karl Best	.10	.05	.01
☐	460	Barry Bonnell	.10	.05	.01
☐	461	Phil Bradley	.10	.05	.01
☐	462	Ivan Calderon	1.25	.55	.16
☐	463	Al Cowens	.10	.05	.01
☐	464	Alvin Davis	.10	.05	.01
☐	465	Dave Henderson	.12	.05	.02
☐	466	Bob Kearney	.10	.05	.01
☐	467	Mark Langston	.50	.23	.06
☐	468	Bob Long	.10	.05	.01
☐	469	Mike Moore	.15	.07	.02
☐	470	Edwin Nunez	.10	.05	.01
☐	471	Spike Owen	.10	.05	.01
☐	472	Jack Perconte	.10	.05	.01
☐	473	Jim Presley	.10	.05	.01
☐	474	Donnie Scott	.10	.05	.01
☐	475	Bill Swift	.40	.18	.05
☐	476	Danny Tartabull	2.00	.90	.25
☐	477	Gorman Thomas	.10	.05	.01
☐	478	Roy Thomas	.10	.05	.01
☐	479	Ed VandeBerg	.10	.05	.01
☐	480	Frank Wills	.10	.05	.01
☐	481	Matt Young	.10	.05	.01
☐	482	Ray Burris	.10	.05	.01
☐	483	Jaime Cocanower	.10	.05	.01
☐	484	Cecil Cooper	.15	.07	.02
☐	485	Danny Darwin	.10	.05	.01
☐	486	Rollie Fingers	.40	.18	.05
☐	487	Jim Gantner	.10	.05	.01
☐	488	Bob L. Gibson	.10	.05	.01
☐	489	Moose Haas	.10	.05	.01
☐	490	Teddy Higuera	.20	.09	.03
☐	491	Paul Householder	.10	.05	.01
☐	492	Pete Ladd	.10	.05	.01
☐	493	Rick Manning	.10	.05	.01
☐	494	Bob McClure	.10	.05	.01
☐	495	Paul Molitor	.40	.18	.05
☐	496	Charlie Moore	.12	.05	.02
☐	497	Ben Oglivie	.10	.05	.01
☐	498	Randy Ready	.10	.05	.01
☐	499	Earnie Riles	.10	.05	.01
☐	500	Ed Romero	.10	.05	.01
☐	501	Bill Schroeder	.10	.05	.01
☐	502	Ray Searage	.10	.05	.01
☐	503	Ted Simmons	.15	.07	.02
☐	504	Pete Vuckovich	.10	.05	.01
☐	505	Rick Waits	.10	.05	.01
☐	506	Robin Yount	2.00	.90	.25
☐	507	Len Barker	.10	.05	.01
☐	508	Steve Bedrosian	.10	.05	.01
☐	509	Bruce Benedict	.10	.05	.01
☐	510	Rick Camp	.10	.05	.01
☐	511	Rick Cerone	.10	.05	.01
☐	512	Chris Chambliss	.15	.07	.02
☐	513	Jeff Dedmon	.10	.05	.01
☐	514	Terry Forster	.10	.05	.01
☐	515	Gene Garber	.10	.05	.01
☐	516	Terry Harper	.10	.05	.01
☐	517	Bob Horner	.15	.07	.02
☐	518	Glenn Hubbard	.10	.05	.01
☐	519	Joe Johnson	.10	.05	.01
☐	520	Brad Komminsk	.10	.05	.01
☐	521	Rick Mahler	.10	.05	.01
☐	522	Dale Murphy	.50	.23	.06
☐	523	Ken Oberkfell	.10	.05	.01
☐	524	Pascual Perez	.10	.05	.01
☐	525	Gerald Perry	.10	.05	.01
☐	526	Rafael Ramirez	.10	.05	.01
☐	527	Steve Shields	.10	.05	.01
☐	528	Zane Smith	.25	.11	.03
☐	529	Bruce Sutter	.15	.07	.02
☐	530	Milt Thompson	.20	.09	.03
☐	531	Claudell Washington	.10	.05	.01
☐	532	Paul Zuvella	.10	.05	.01
☐	533	Vida Blue	.15	.07	.02
☐	534	Bob Brenly	.10	.05	.01
☐	535	Chris Brown	.10	.05	.01
☐	536	Chili Davis	.15	.07	.02
☐	537	Mark Davis	.15	.07	.02
☐	538	Rob Deer	.30	.14	.04
☐	539	Dan Driessen	.10	.05	.01
☐	540	Scott Garrelts	.10	.05	.01
☐	541	Dan Gladden	.10	.05	.01
☐	542	Jim Gott	.10	.05	.01
☐	543	David Green	.10	.05	.01
☐	544	Atlee Hammaker	.10	.05	.01
☐	545	Mike Jeffcoat	.10	.05	.01
☐	546	Mike Krukow	.10	.05	.01
☐	547	Dave LaPoint	.10	.05	.01
☐	548	Jeff Leonard	.10	.05	.01
☐	549	Greg Minton	.10	.05	.01
☐	550	Alex Trevino	.10	.05	.01
☐	551	Manny Trillo	.10	.05	.01
☐	552	Jose Uribe	.15	.07	.02
☐	553	Brad Wellman	.10	.05	.01
☐	554	Frank Williams	.10	.05	.01
☐	555	Joel Youngblood	.10	.05	.01
☐	556	Alan Bannister	.10	.05	.01
☐	557	Glenn Brummer	.10	.05	.01
☐	558	Steve Buechele	1.00	.45	.13
☐	559	Jose Guzman	.75	.35	.09
☐	560	Toby Harrah	.10	.05	.01
☐	561	Greg Harris	.10	.05	.01
☐	562	Dwayne Henry	.10	.05	.01
☐	563	Burt Hooton	.10	.05	.01
☐	564	Charlie Hough	.10	.05	.01
☐	565	Mike Mason	.10	.05	.01
☐	566	Oddibe McDowell	.10	.05	.01
☐	567	Dickie Noles	.10	.05	.01
☐	568	Pete O'Brien	.10	.05	.01
☐	569	Larry Parrish	.10	.05	.01
☐	570	Dave Rozema	.10	.05	.01
☐	571	Dave Schmidt	.10	.05	.01
☐	572	Don Slaught	.10	.05	.01
☐	573	Wayne Tolleson	.10	.05	.01
☐	574	Duane Walker	.10	.05	.01
☐	575	Gary Ward	.10	.05	.01
☐	576	Chris Welsh	.10	.05	.01
☐	577	Curtis Wilkerson	.10	.05	.01
☐	578	George Wright	.10	.05	.01
☐	579	Chris Bando	.10	.05	.01
☐	580	Tony Bernazard	.10	.05	.01
☐	581	Brett Butler	.20	.09	.03
☐	582	Ernie Camacho	.10	.05	.01
☐	583	Joe Carter	2.50	1.15	.30
☐	584	Carmen Castillo	.10	.05	.01
☐	585	Jamie Easterly	.10	.05	.01
☐	586	Julio Franco	.35	.16	.04
☐	587	Mel Hall	.12	.05	.02
☐	588	Mike Hargrove	.15	.07	.02
☐	589	Neal Heaton	.10	.05	.01

☐ 590 Brook Jacoby	.10	.05	.01
☐ 591 Otis Nixon	1.25	.55	.16
☐ 592 Jerry Reed	.10	.05	.01
☐ 593 Vern Ruhle	.10	.05	.01
☐ 594 Pat Tabler	.10	.05	.01
☐ 595 Rich Thompson	.10	.05	.01
☐ 596 Andre Thornton	.10	.05	.01
☐ 597 Dave Von Ohlen	.10	.05	.01
☐ 598 George Vukovich	.10	.05	.01
☐ 599 Tom Waddell	.10	.05	.01
☐ 600 Curt Wardle	.10	.05	.01
☐ 601 Jerry Willard	.10	.05	.01
☐ 602 Bill Almon	.10	.05	.01
☐ 603 Mike Bielecki	.15	.07	.02
☐ 604 Sid Bream	.15	.07	.02
☐ 605 Mike C. Brown OF	.10	.05	.01
☐ 606 Pat Clements	.10	.05	.01
☐ 607 Jose DeLeon	.10	.05	.01
☐ 608 Denny Gonzalez	.10	.05	.01
☐ 609 Cecilio Guante	.10	.05	.01
☐ 610 Steve Kemp	.10	.05	.01
☐ 611 Sammy Khalifa	.10	.05	.01
☐ 612 Lee Mazzilli	.10	.05	.01
☐ 613 Larry McWilliams	.10	.05	.01
☐ 614 Jim Morrison	.10	.05	.01
☐ 615 Joe Orsulak	.35	.16	.04
☐ 616 Tony Pena	.15	.07	.02
☐ 617 Johnny Ray	.10	.05	.01
☐ 618 Rick Reuschel	.10	.05	.01
☐ 619 R.J. Reynolds	.10	.05	.01
☐ 620 Rick Rhoden	.10	.05	.01
☐ 621 Don Robinson	.10	.05	.01
☐ 622 Jason Thompson	.10	.05	.01
☐ 623 Lee Tunnell	.10	.05	.01
☐ 624 Jim Winn	.10	.05	.01
☐ 625 Marvell Wynne	.10	.05	.01
☐ 626 Dwight Gooden IA	.40	.18	.05
☐ 627 Don Mattingly IA	1.25	.55	.16
☐ 628 4192 (Pete Rose)	.60	.25	.08
☐ 629 3000 Career Hits Rod Carew	.45	.20	.06
☐ 630 300 Career Wins Tom Seaver Phil Niekro	.40	.18	.05
☐ 631 Ouch (Don Baylor)	.15	.07	.02
☐ 632 Instant Offense Darryl Strawberry Tim Raines	.50	.23	.06
☐ 633 Shortstops Supreme Cal Ripken Alan Trammell	1.25	.55	.16
☐ 634 Boggs and "Hero" Wade Boggs George Brett	1.00	.45	.13
☐ 635 Braves Dynamic Duo Bob Horner Dale Murphy	.15	.07	.02
☐ 636 Cardinal Ignitors Willie McGee Vince Coleman	.30	.14	.04
☐ 637 Terror on Basepaths Vince Coleman	.30	.14	.04
☐ 638 Charlie Hustle / Dr.K Pete Rose Dwight Gooden	.60	.25	.08
☐ 639 1984 and 1985 AL Batting Champs Wade Boggs Don Mattingly	1.25	.55	.16
☐ 640 NL West Sluggers Dale Murphy Steve Garvey Dave Parker	.30	.14	.04
☐ 641 Staff Aces Fernando Valenzuela Dwight Gooden	.20	.09	.03
☐ 642 Blue Jay Stoppers Jimmy Key Dave Stieb	.15	.07	.02
☐ 643 AL All-Star Backstops Carlton Fisk Rich Gedman	.15	.07	.02
☐ 644 Gene Walter and Benito Santiago	3.50	1.55	.45
☐ 645 Mike Woodard and Colin Ward	.12	.05	.02
☐ 646 Kal Daniels and Paul O'Neill	3.50	1.55	.45
☐ 647 Andres Galarraga and Fred Toliver	.60	.25	.08
☐ 648 Bob Kipper and Curt Ford	.12	.05	.02
☐ 649 Jose Canseco and Eric Plunk	40.00	18.00	5.00
☐ 650 Mark McLemore and Gus Polidor	.20	.09	.03
☐ 651 Rob Woodward and Mickey Brantley	.12	.05	.02
☐ 652 Billy Joe Robidoux and Mark Funderburk	.12	.05	.02
☐ 653 Cecil Fielder and Cory Snyder	20.00	9.00	2.50
☐ 654 CL: Royals/Cardinals Blue Jays/Mets	.12	.01	.00
☐ 655 CL: Yankees/Dodgers Angels/Reds UER (168 Darly Sconiers)	.12	.01	.00
☐ 656 CL: White Sox/Tigers Expos/Orioles (279 Dennis, 280 Tippy)	.12	.01	.00
☐ 657 CL: Astros/Padres Red Sox/Cubs	.12	.01	.00
☐ 658 CL: Twins/A's Phillies/Mariners	.12	.01	.00
☐ 659 CL: Brewers/Braves Giants/Rangers	.12	.01	.00
☐ 660 CL: Indians/Pirates Special Cards	.12	.01	.00

1986 Fleer All-Star Inserts

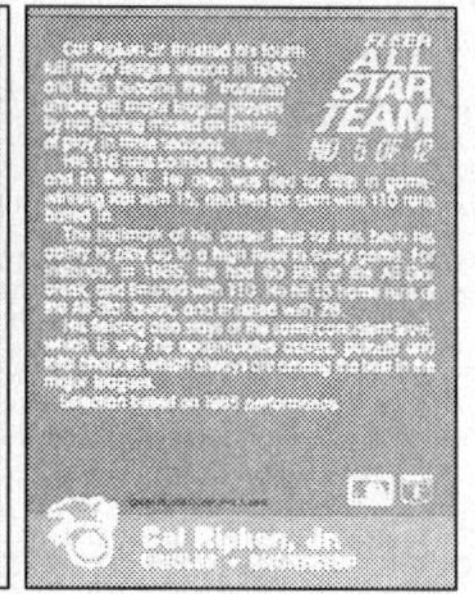

Fleer selected a 12-card (Major League) All-Star team to be included as inserts in their 39 cent wax packs and 59 cent cello packs. However they were randomly inserted in such a way that not all wax packs contain the insert. Cards measure 2 1/2" by 3 1/2" and feature attractive red backgrounds (American Leaguers) and blue backgrounds (National Leaguers). The 12 selections cover each position, left and right-handed starting pitchers, a reliever, and a designated hitter.

	MT	EX-MT	VG
COMPLETE SET (12)	25.00	11.50	3.10
COMMON PLAYER (1-12)	.40	.18	.05
☐ 1 Don Mattingly	6.00	2.70	.75
☐ 2 Tom Herr	.40	.18	.05
☐ 3 George Brett	4.00	1.80	.50
☐ 4 Gary Carter	1.50	.65	.19
☐ 5 Cal Ripken	8.00	3.60	1.00
☐ 6 Dave Parker	.75	.35	.09
☐ 7 Rickey Henderson UER (Misspelled Ricky on card back)	6.00	2.70	.75
☐ 8 Pedro Guerrero	.50	.23	.06
☐ 9 Dan Quisenberry	.40	.18	.05
☐ 10 Dwight Gooden	2.50	1.15	.30
☐ 11 Gorman Thomas	.40	.18	.05
☐ 12 John Tudor	.40	.18	.05

1986 Fleer Future HOF

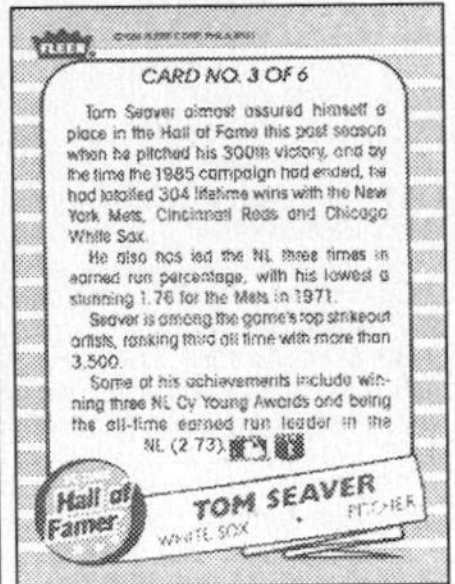

These attractive cards were issued as inserts with the Fleer three-packs. They are the same size as the regular issue (2 1/2" by 3 1/2") and feature players that Fleer predicts will be "Future Hall of Famers." The card backs describe career highlights, records, and honors won by the player. The cards are numbered on the back; Pete Rose is given the honor of being card number 1.

	MT	EX-MT	VG
COMPLETE SET (6)	12.00	5.50	1.50
COMMON PLAYER (1-6)	1.50	.65	.19
☐ 1 Pete Rose	2.50	1.15	.30
☐ 2 Steve Carlton	1.50	.65	.19
☐ 3 Tom Seaver	2.50	1.15	.30
☐ 4 Rod Carew	1.50	.65	.19
☐ 5 Nolan Ryan	6.00	2.70	.75
☐ 6 Reggie Jackson	2.50	1.15	.30

1986 Fleer League Leaders

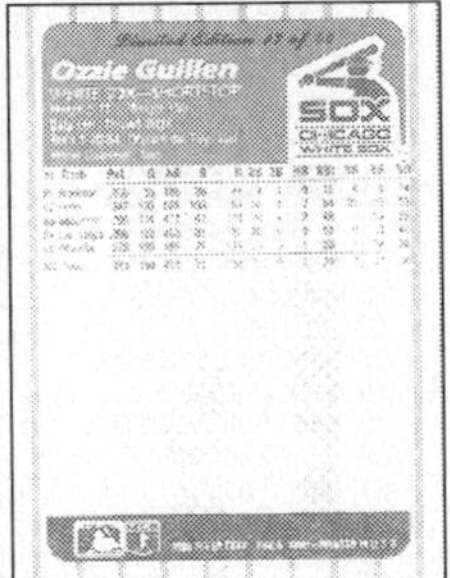

This 44-card set is also sometimes referred to as the Walgreen's set. Although the set was distributed through Walgreen's, there is no mention on the cards or box of that fact. The cards are easily recognizable by the fact that they contain the phrase "Fleer League Leaders" at the top of the obverse. Both sides of the cards are designed with a blue stripe on white pattern. The checklist for the set is given on the outside of the red, white, blue, and gold box in which the set was packaged. Cards are numbered on the back and measure the standard, 2 1/2" by 3 1/2".

	MT	EX-MT	VG
COMPLETE SET (44)	5.00	2.30	.60
COMMON PLAYER (1-44)	.10	.05	.01
☐ 1 Wade Boggs	.75	.35	.09
☐ 2 George Brett	.75	.35	.09
☐ 3 Jose Canseco	1.25	.55	.16
☐ 4 Rod Carew	.50	.23	.06
☐ 5 Gary Carter	.30	.14	.04
☐ 6 Jack Clark	.15	.07	.02
☐ 7 Vince Coleman	.25	.11	.03
☐ 8 Jose Cruz	.10	.05	.01
☐ 9 Alvin Davis	.10	.05	.01
☐ 10 Mariano Duncan	.10	.05	.01
☐ 11 Leon Durham	.10	.05	.01
☐ 12 Carlton Fisk	.50	.23	.06
☐ 13 Julio Franco	.20	.09	.03
☐ 14 Scott Garrelts	.10	.05	.01
☐ 15 Steve Garvey	.30	.14	.04
☐ 16 Dwight Gooden	.35	.16	.04
☐ 17 Ozzie Guillen	.15	.07	.02
☐ 18 Willie Hernandez	.10	.05	.01
☐ 19 Bob Horner	.10	.05	.01
☐ 20 Kent Hrbek	.15	.07	.02
☐ 21 Charlie Leibrandt	.10	.05	.01
☐ 22 Don Mattingly	.75	.35	.09
☐ 23 Oddibe McDowell	.10	.05	.01
☐ 24 Willie McGee	.15	.07	.02
☐ 25 Keith Moreland	.10	.05	.01
☐ 26 Lloyd Moseby	.10	.05	.01
☐ 27 Dale Murphy	.35	.16	.04
☐ 28 Phil Niekro	.25	.11	.03
☐ 29 Joe Orsulak	.10	.05	.01
☐ 30 Dave Parker	.20	.09	.03
☐ 31 Lance Parrish	.15	.07	.02
☐ 32 Kirby Puckett	.75	.35	.09
☐ 33 Tim Raines	.20	.09	.03
☐ 34 Earnie Riles	.10	.05	.01
☐ 35 Cal Ripken	1.00	.45	.13
☐ 36 Pete Rose	.75	.35	.09
☐ 37 Bret Saberhagen	.25	.11	.03
☐ 38 Juan Samuel	.10	.05	.01
☐ 39 Ryne Sandberg	1.00	.45	.13
☐ 40 Tom Seaver	.75	.35	.09
☐ 41 Lee Smith	.20	.09	.03
☐ 42 Ozzie Smith	.35	.16	.04
☐ 43 Dave Stieb	.15	.07	.02
☐ 44 Robin Yount	.75	.35	.09

1986 Fleer Limited Edition

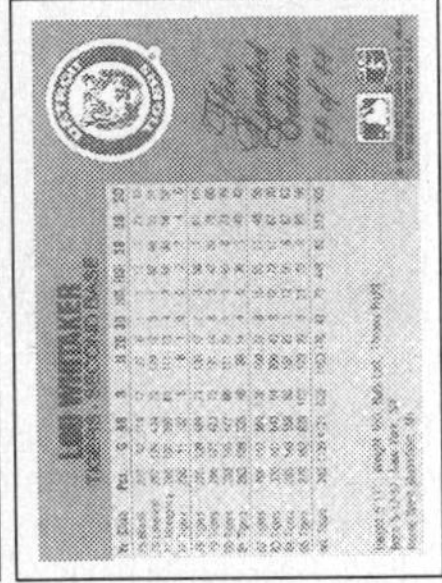

The 44-card boxed set was produced by Fleer for McCrory's. The cards are standard size, 2 1/2" by 3 1/2", and have green and yellow borders. Card backs are printed in red and black on white card stock. Cards are numbered on the back; the back of the original box gives a complete checklist of the players in the set. The set box also contains six logo stickers.

	MT	EX-MT	VG
COMPLETE SET (44)	5.00	2.30	.60
COMMON PLAYER (1-44)	.10	.05	.01
☐ 1 Doyle Alexander	.10	.05	.01
☐ 2 Joaquin Andujar	.10	.05	.01
☐ 3 Harold Baines	.15	.07	.02
☐ 4 Wade Boggs	.60	.25	.08
☐ 5 Phil Bradley	.10	.05	.01
☐ 6 George Brett	.75	.35	.09
☐ 7 Hubie Brooks	.10	.05	.01
☐ 8 Chris Brown	.10	.05	.01
☐ 9 Tom Brunansky	.15	.07	.02
☐ 10 Gary Carter	.40	.18	.05
☐ 11 Vince Coleman	.25	.11	.03
☐ 12 Cecil Cooper	.15	.07	.02
☐ 13 Jose Cruz	.10	.05	.01

☐ 14 Mike Davis	.10	.05	.01
☐ 15 Carlton Fisk	.50	.23	.06
☐ 16 Julio Franco	.20	.09	.03
☐ 17 Damaso Garcia	.10	.05	.01
☐ 18 Rich Gedman	.10	.05	.01
☐ 19 Kirk Gibson	.20	.09	.03
☐ 20 Dwight Gooden	.35	.16	.04
☐ 21 Pedro Guerrero	.15	.07	.02
☐ 22 Tony Gwynn	.60	.25	.08
☐ 23 Rickey Henderson	.60	.25	.08
☐ 24 Orel Hershiser	.25	.11	.03
☐ 25 LaMarr Hoyt	.10	.05	.01
☐ 26 Reggie Jackson	.75	.35	.09
☐ 27 Don Mattingly	.75	.35	.09
☐ 28 Oddibe McDowell	.10	.05	.01
☐ 29 Willie McGee	.15	.07	.02
☐ 30 Paul Molitor	.25	.11	.03
☐ 31 Dale Murphy	.35	.16	.04
☐ 32 Eddie Murray	.40	.18	.05
☐ 33 Dave Parker	.20	.09	.03
☐ 34 Tony Pena	.10	.05	.01
☐ 35 Jeff Reardon	.25	.11	.03
☐ 36 Cal Ripken	1.00	.45	.13
☐ 37 Pete Rose	.75	.35	.09
☐ 38 Bret Saberhagen	.25	.11	.03
☐ 39 Juan Samuel	.10	.05	.01
☐ 40 Ryne Sandberg	1.00	.45	.13
☐ 41 Mike Schmidt	.75	.35	.09
☐ 42 Lee Smith	.20	.09	.03
☐ 43 Don Sutton	.20	.09	.03
☐ 44 Lou Whitaker	.20	.09	.03

1986 Fleer Mini

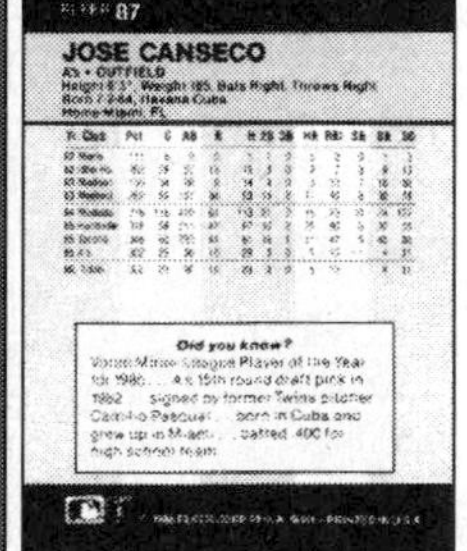

The Fleer "Classic Miniatures" set consists of 120 small cards with all new pictures of the players as compared to the 1986 Fleer regular issue. The cards are only 1 13/16" by 2 9/16", making them one of the smallest (in size) produced in recent memory. Card backs provide career year-by-year statistics. The complete set was distributed in a red, white, and silver box along with 18 logo stickers. The card numbering is done in the same team order as the 1986 Fleer regular set.

	MT	EX-MT	VG
COMPLETE SET (120)	12.50	5.75	1.55
COMMON PLAYER (1-120)	.05	.02	.01
☐ 1 George Brett	.75	.35	.09
☐ 2 Dan Quisenberry	.08	.04	.01
☐ 3 Bret Saberhagen	.25	.11	.03
☐ 4 Lonnie Smith	.08	.04	.01
☐ 5 Willie Wilson	.10	.05	.01
☐ 6 Jack Clark	.10	.05	.01
☐ 7 Vince Coleman	.25	.11	.03
☐ 8 Tom Herr	.05	.02	.01
☐ 9 Willie McGee	.10	.05	.01
☐ 10 Ozzie Smith	.35	.16	.04
☐ 11 John Tudor	.05	.02	.01
☐ 12 Jesse Barfield	.08	.04	.01
☐ 13 George Bell	.20	.09	.03
☐ 14 Tony Fernandez	.10	.05	.01
☐ 15 Damaso Garcia	.05	.02	.01
☐ 16 Dave Stieb	.08	.04	.01
☐ 17 Gary Carter	.20	.09	.03
☐ 18 Ron Darling	.10	.05	.01
☐ 19A Dwight Gooden (R on Mets logo)	1.50	.65	.19
☐ 19B Dwight Gooden (No R on Mets logo)	1.50	.65	.19
☐ 20 Keith Hernandez	.10	.05	.01
☐ 21 Darryl Strawberry	.60	.25	.08
☐ 22 Ron Guidry	.10	.05	.01
☐ 23 Rickey Henderson	.75	.35	.09
☐ 24 Don Mattingly	.75	.35	.09
☐ 25 Dave Righetti	.08	.04	.01
☐ 26 Dave Winfield	.35	.16	.04
☐ 27 Mariano Duncan	.05	.02	.01
☐ 28 Pedro Guerrero	.08	.04	.01
☐ 29 Bill Madlock	.05	.02	.01
☐ 30 Mike Marshall	.05	.02	.01
☐ 31 Fernando Valenzuela	.10	.05	.01
☐ 32 Reggie Jackson	.50	.23	.06
☐ 33 Gary Pettis	.05	.02	.01
☐ 34 Ron Romanick	.05	.02	.01
☐ 35 Don Sutton	.15	.07	.02
☐ 36 Mike Witt	.05	.02	.01
☐ 37 Buddy Bell	.05	.02	.01
☐ 38 Tom Browning	.10	.05	.01
☐ 39 Dave Parker	.15	.07	.02
☐ 40 Pete Rose	.75	.35	.09
☐ 41 Mario Soto	.05	.02	.01
☐ 42 Harold Baines	.10	.05	.01
☐ 43 Carlton Fisk	.35	.16	.04
☐ 44 Ozzie Guillen	.15	.07	.02
☐ 45 Ron Kittle	.08	.04	.01
☐ 46 Tom Seaver	.50	.23	.06
☐ 47 Kirk Gibson	.15	.07	.02
☐ 48 Jack Morris	.20	.09	.03
☐ 49 Lance Parrish	.08	.04	.01
☐ 50 Alan Trammell	.20	.09	.03
☐ 51 Lou Whitaker	.20	.09	.03
☐ 52 Hubie Brooks	.05	.02	.01
☐ 53 Andre Dawson	.35	.16	.04
☐ 54 Tim Raines	.15	.07	.02
☐ 55 Bryn Smith	.05	.02	.01
☐ 56 Tim Wallach	.08	.04	.01
☐ 57 Mike Boddicker	.05	.02	.01
☐ 58 Eddie Murray	.50	.23	.06
☐ 59 Cal Ripken	1.00	.45	.13
☐ 60 John Shelby	.05	.02	.01
☐ 61 Mike Young	.05	.02	.01
☐ 62 Jose Cruz	.08	.04	.01
☐ 63 Glenn Davis	.20	.09	.03
☐ 64 Phil Garner	.10	.05	.01
☐ 65 Nolan Ryan	2.00	.90	.25
☐ 66 Mike Scott	.08	.04	.01
☐ 67 Steve Garvey	.20	.09	.03
☐ 68 Rich Gossage	.12	.05	.02
☐ 69 Tony Gwynn	.50	.23	.06
☐ 70 Andy Hawkins	.05	.02	.01
☐ 71 Garry Templeton	.05	.02	.01
☐ 72 Wade Boggs	.60	.25	.08
☐ 73 Roger Clemens	1.50	.65	.19
☐ 74 Dwight Evans	.10	.05	.01
☐ 75 Rich Gedman	.05	.02	.01
☐ 76 Jim Rice	.15	.07	.02
☐ 77 Shawon Dunston	.15	.07	.02
☐ 78 Leon Durham	.05	.02	.01
☐ 79 Keith Moreland	.05	.02	.01
☐ 80 Ryne Sandberg	1.00	.45	.13
☐ 81 Rick Sutcliffe	.08	.04	.01
☐ 82 Bert Blyleven	.10	.05	.01
☐ 83 Tom Brunansky	.08	.04	.01
☐ 84 Kent Hrbek	.10	.05	.01
☐ 85 Kirby Puckett	1.00	.45	.13
☐ 86 Bruce Bochte	.05	.02	.01
☐ 87 Jose Canseco	2.50	1.15	.30
☐ 88 Mike Davis	.05	.02	.01
☐ 89 Jay Howell	.05	.02	.01
☐ 90 Dwayne Murphy	.05	.02	.01
☐ 91 Steve Carlton	.30	.14	.04
☐ 92 Von Hayes	.05	.02	.01
☐ 93 Juan Samuel	.08	.04	.01
☐ 94 Mike Schmidt	1.00	.45	.13
☐ 95 Glenn Wilson	.05	.02	.01
☐ 96 Phil Bradley	.05	.02	.01
☐ 97 Alvin Davis	.08	.04	.01
☐ 98 Jim Presley	.05	.02	.01
☐ 99 Danny Tartabull	.35	.16	.04
☐ 100 Cecil Cooper	.08	.04	.01
☐ 101 Paul Molitor	.20	.09	.03
☐ 102 Ernie Riles	.05	.02	.01
☐ 103 Robin Yount	.60	.25	.08
☐ 104 Bob Horner	.08	.04	.01
☐ 105 Dale Murphy	.35	.16	.04
☐ 106 Bruce Sutter	.08	.04	.01
☐ 107 Claudell Washington	.05	.02	.01
☐ 108 Chris Brown	.05	.02	.01
☐ 109 Chili Davis	.08	.04	.01
☐ 110 Scott Garrelts	.05	.02	.01

☐ 111 Oddibe McDowell	.05	.02	.01
☐ 112 Pete O'Brien	.05	.02	.01
☐ 113 Gary Ward	.05	.02	.01
☐ 114 Brett Butler	.12	.05	.02
☐ 115 Julio Franco	.15	.07	.02
☐ 116 Brook Jacoby	.05	.02	.01
☐ 117 Mike C. Brown OF	.05	.02	.01
☐ 118 Joe Orsulak	.05	.02	.01
☐ 119 Tony Pena	.08	.04	.01
☐ 120 R.J. Reynolds	.05	.02	.01

1986 Fleer Sluggers/Pitchers

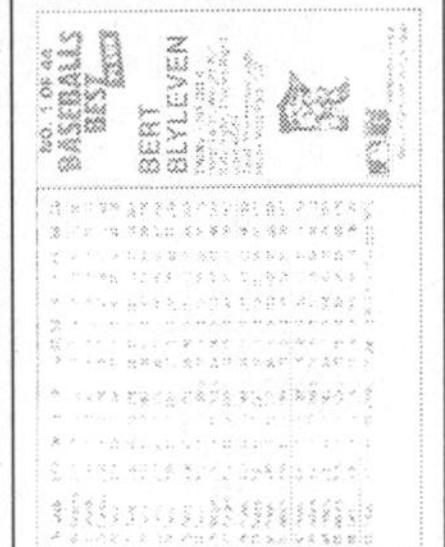

Fleer produced this 44-card boxed set although it was primarily distributed by Kress, McCrory, Newberry, T.G.Y., and other similar stores. The set features 22 sluggers and 22 pitchers and is subtitled "Baseball's Best". Cards are standard-size, 2 1/2" by 3 1/2", and were packaged in a red, white, blue, and yellow custom box along with six logo stickers. The set checklist is given on the back of the box. The card numbering is in alphabetical order by the player's name.

	MT	EX-MT	VG
COMPLETE SET (44)	7.50	3.40	.95
COMMON PLAYER (1-44)	.10	.05	.01
☐ 1 Bert Blyleven	.15	.07	.02
☐ 2 Wade Boggs	.50	.23	.06
☐ 3 George Brett	.60	.25	.08
☐ 4 Tom Browning	.10	.05	.01
☐ 5 Jose Canseco	2.00	.90	.25
☐ 6 Will Clark	2.00	.90	.25
☐ 7 Roger Clemens	1.00	.45	.13
☐ 8 Alvin Davis	.10	.05	.01
☐ 9 Julio Franco	.20	.09	.03
☐ 10 Kirk Gibson	.20	.09	.03
☐ 11 Dwight Gooden	.35	.16	.04
☐ 12 Rich Gossage	.15	.07	.02
☐ 13 Pedro Guerrero	.15	.07	.02
☐ 14 Ron Guidry	.15	.07	.02
☐ 15 Tony Gwynn	.50	.23	.06
☐ 16 Orel Hershiser	.25	.11	.03
☐ 17 Kent Hrbek	.15	.07	.02
☐ 18 Reggie Jackson	.45	.20	.06
☐ 19 Wally Joyner	.50	.23	.06
☐ 20 Charlie Leibrandt	.10	.05	.01
☐ 21 Don Mattingly	.75	.35	.09
☐ 22 Willie McGee	.15	.07	.02
☐ 23 Jack Morris	.20	.09	.03
☐ 24 Dale Murphy	.30	.14	.04
☐ 25 Eddie Murray	.35	.16	.04
☐ 26 Jeff Reardon	.15	.07	.02
☐ 27 Rick Reuschel	.10	.05	.01
☐ 28 Cal Ripken	1.00	.45	.13
☐ 29 Pete Rose	.60	.25	.08
☐ 30 Nolan Ryan	1.50	.65	.19
☐ 31 Bret Saberhagen	.25	.11	.03
☐ 32 Ryne Sandberg	.90	.40	.11
☐ 33 Mike Schmidt	.75	.35	.09
☐ 34 Tom Seaver	.75	.35	.09
☐ 35 Bryn Smith	.10	.05	.01
☐ 36 Mario Soto	.10	.05	.01
☐ 37 Dave Stieb	.15	.07	.02
☐ 38 Darryl Strawberry	.50	.23	.06
☐ 39 Rick Sutcliffe	.15	.07	.02
☐ 40 John Tudor	.10	.05	.01
☐ 41 Fernando Valenzuela	.10	.05	.01
☐ 42 Bobby Witt	.20	.09	.03
☐ 43 Mike Witt	.10	.05	.01
☐ 44 Robin Yount	.50	.23	.06

1986 Fleer Slug/Pitch Box Cards

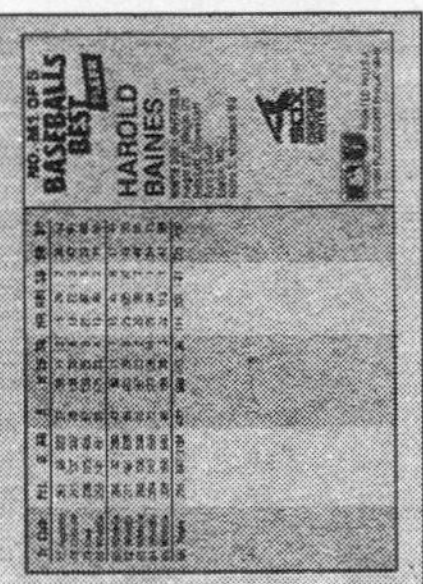

The cards in this six-card set each measure the standard 2 1/2" by 3 1/2". Cards have essentially the same design as the 1986 Fleer Sluggers vs. Pitchers set of Baseball's Best. The cards were printed on the bottom of the counter display box which held 24 small boxed sets; hence theoretically these box cards are 1/24 as plentiful as the regular boxed set cards. These six cards, numbered M1 to M5 with one blank-back (unnumbered) card, are considered a separate set in their own right and are not typically included in a complete set of the 1986 Fleer Sluggers vs. Pitchers set of 44. The value of the panels uncut is slightly greater, perhaps by 25 percent greater, than the value of the individual cards cut up carefully.

	MT	EX-MT	VG
COMPLETE SET (6)	7.00	3.10	.85
COMMON PLAYER	.25	.11	.03
☐ M1 Harold Baines	.35	.16	.04
☐ M2 Steve Carlton	1.25	.55	.16
☐ M3 Gary Carter	.75	.35	.09
☐ M4 Vince Coleman	1.25	.55	.16
☐ M5 Kirby Puckett	4.00	1.80	.50
☐ NNO Team Logo (Blank back)	.25	.11	.03

1986 Fleer Sticker Cards

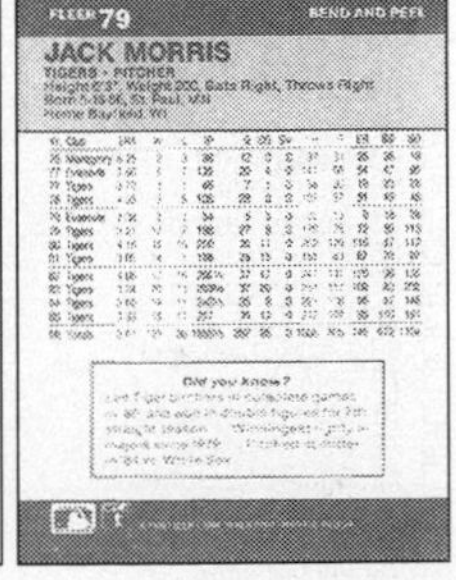

The stickers in this 132-sticker card set are standard card size, 2 1/2" by 3 1/2". The card photo on the front is surrounded by a yellow border and a cranberry frame. The backs are printed in blue and black on white card stock. The backs contain year-by-year statistical information. They are numbered on the back in the upper left-hand corner. The card numbering is in alphabetical order by the player's name.

	MT	EX-MT	VG
COMPLETE SET (132)	28.00	12.50	3.50
COMMON PLAYER (1-132)	.05	.02	.01
☐ 1 Harold Baines	.15	.07	.02
☐ 2 Jesse Barfield	.08	.04	.01
☐ 3 Don Baylor	.12	.05	.02
☐ 4 Juan Beniquez	.05	.02	.01
☐ 5 Tim Birtsas	.05	.02	.01
☐ 6 Bert Blyleven	.10	.05	.01
☐ 7 Bruce Bochte	.05	.02	.01
☐ 8 Wade Boggs	.75	.35	.09
☐ 9 Dennis Boyd	.05	.02	.01
☐ 10 Phil Bradley	.05	.02	.01
☐ 11 George Brett	1.00	.45	.13
☐ 12 Hubie Brooks	.05	.02	.01
☐ 13 Chris Brown	.05	.02	.01
☐ 14 Tom Browning	.10	.05	.01
☐ 15 Tom Brunansky	.10	.05	.01
☐ 16 Bill Buckner	.08	.04	.01
☐ 17 Britt Burns	.05	.02	.01
☐ 18 Brett Butler	.10	.05	.01
☐ 19 Jose Canseco	2.50	1.15	.30
☐ 20 Rod Carew	.60	.25	.08
☐ 21 Steve Carlton	.40	.18	.05
☐ 22 Don Carman	.05	.02	.01
☐ 23 Gary Carter	.30	.14	.04
☐ 24 Jack Clark	.10	.05	.01
☐ 25 Vince Coleman	1.25	.55	.16
☐ 26 Cecil Cooper	.08	.04	.01
☐ 27 Jose Cruz	.08	.04	.01
☐ 28 Ron Darling	.12	.05	.02
☐ 29 Alvin Davis	.05	.02	.01
☐ 30 Jody Davis	.05	.02	.01
☐ 31 Mike Davis	.05	.02	.01
☐ 32 Andre Dawson	.50	.23	.06
☐ 33 Mariano Duncan	.08	.04	.01
☐ 34 Shawon Dunston	.15	.07	.02
☐ 35 Leon Durham	.05	.02	.01
☐ 36 Darrell Evans	.08	.04	.01
☐ 37 Tony Fernandez	.10	.05	.01
☐ 38 Carlton Fisk	.50	.23	.06
☐ 39 John Franco	.12	.05	.02
☐ 40 Julio Franco	.15	.07	.02
☐ 41 Damaso Garcia	.05	.02	.01
☐ 42 Scott Garrelts	.05	.02	.01
☐ 43 Steve Garvey	.40	.18	.05
☐ 44 Rich Gedman	.05	.02	.01
☐ 45 Kirk Gibson	.20	.09	.03
☐ 46 Dwight Gooden	.50	.23	.06
☐ 47 Pedro Guerrero	.10	.05	.01
☐ 48 Ron Guidry	.12	.05	.02
☐ 49 Ozzie Guillen	.20	.09	.03
☐ 50 Tony Gwynn	.75	.35	.09
☐ 51 Andy Hawkins	.05	.02	.01
☐ 52 Von Hayes	.05	.02	.01
☐ 53 Rickey Henderson	1.00	.45	.13
☐ 54 Tom Henke	.12	.05	.02
☐ 55 Keith Hernandez	.10	.05	.01
☐ 56 Willie Hernandez	.05	.02	.01
☐ 57 Tommy Herr	.05	.02	.01
☐ 58 Orel Hershiser	.20	.09	.03
☐ 59 Teddy Higuera	.20	.09	.03
☐ 60 Bob Horner	.08	.04	.01
☐ 61 Charlie Hough	.05	.02	.01
☐ 62 Jay Howell	.05	.02	.01
☐ 63 LaMarr Hoyt	.05	.02	.01
☐ 64 Kent Hrbek	.10	.05	.01
☐ 65 Reggie Jackson	.75	.35	.09
☐ 66 Bob James	.05	.02	.01
☐ 67 Dave Kingman	.10	.05	.01
☐ 68 Ron Kittle	.08	.04	.01
☐ 69 Charlie Leibrandt	.08	.04	.01
☐ 70 Fred Lynn	.10	.05	.01
☐ 71 Mike Marshall	.05	.02	.01
☐ 72 Don Mattingly	1.00	.45	.13
☐ 73 Oddibe McDowell	.05	.02	.01
☐ 74 Willie McGee	.10	.05	.01
☐ 75 Scott McGregor	.05	.02	.01
☐ 76 Paul Molitor	.25	.11	.03
☐ 77 Donnie Moore	.05	.02	.01
☐ 78 Keith Moreland	.05	.02	.01
☐ 79 Jack Morris	.20	.09	.03
☐ 80 Dale Murphy	.50	.23	.06
☐ 81 Eddie Murray	.60	.25	.08
☐ 82 Phil Niekro	.25	.11	.03
☐ 83 Joe Orsulak	.05	.02	.01
☐ 84 Dave Parker	.15	.07	.02
☐ 85 Lance Parrish	.08	.04	.01
☐ 86 Larry Parrish	.05	.02	.01
☐ 87 Tony Pena	.08	.04	.01
☐ 88 Gary Pettis	.05	.02	.01
☐ 89 Jim Presley	.05	.02	.01
☐ 90 Kirby Puckett	1.25	.55	.16
☐ 91 Dan Quisenberry	.10	.05	.01
☐ 92 Tim Raines	.15	.07	.02
☐ 93 Johnny Ray	.05	.02	.01
☐ 94 Jeff Reardon	.15	.07	.02
☐ 95 Rick Reuschel	.05	.02	.01
☐ 96 Jim Rice	.20	.09	.03
☐ 97 Dave Righetti	.08	.04	.01
☐ 98 Earnie Riles	.05	.02	.01
☐ 99 Cal Ripken	1.50	.65	.19
☐ 100 Ron Romanick	.05	.02	.01
☐ 101 Pete Rose	1.00	.45	.13
☐ 102 Nolan Ryan	2.50	1.15	.30
☐ 103 Bret Saberhagen	.30	.14	.04
☐ 104 Mark Salas	.05	.02	.01
☐ 105 Juan Samuel	.08	.04	.01
☐ 106 Ryne Sandberg	1.50	.65	.19
☐ 107 Mike Schmidt	1.25	.55	.16
☐ 108 Mike Scott	.08	.04	.01
☐ 109 Tom Seaver	.50	.23	.06
☐ 110 Bryn Smith	.05	.02	.01
☐ 111 Dave Smith	.05	.02	.01
☐ 112 Lee Smith	.15	.07	.02
☐ 113 Ozzie Smith	.50	.23	.06
☐ 114 Mario Soto	.05	.02	.01
☐ 115 Dave Stieb	.10	.05	.01
☐ 116 Darryl Strawberry	1.00	.45	.13
☐ 117 Bruce Sutter	.10	.05	.01
☐ 118 Garry Templeton	.05	.02	.01
☐ 119 Gorman Thomas	.05	.02	.01
☐ 120 Andre Thornton	.05	.02	.01
☐ 121 Alan Trammell	.20	.09	.03
☐ 122 John Tudor	.08	.04	.01
☐ 123 Fernando Valenzuela	.10	.05	.01
☐ 124 Frank Viola	.15	.07	.02
☐ 125 Gary Ward	.05	.02	.01
☐ 126 Lou Whitaker	.20	.09	.03
☐ 127 Frank White	.08	.04	.01
☐ 128 Glenn Wilson	.05	.02	.01
☐ 129 Willie Wilson	.10	.05	.01
☐ 130 Dave Winfield	.50	.23	.06
☐ 131 Robin Yount	.75	.35	.09
☐ 132 Checklist Card Dwight Gooden Dale Murphy	.50	.23	.06

1986 Fleer Sticker Wax Box

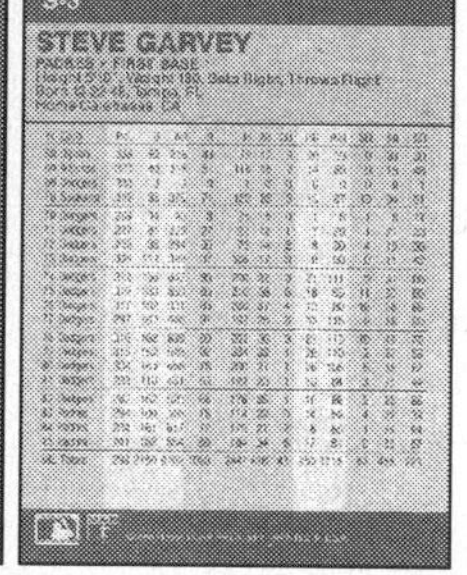

The bottoms of the Star Sticker wax boxes contained a set of four cards done in a similar format to the stickers; these cards (they are not stickers but truly cards) are numbered with the prefix S and are considered a separate set. Each individual card measures 2 1/2" by 3 1/2". The value of the panel uncut is slightly greater, perhaps by 25 percent greater, than the value of the individual cards cut up carefully.

	MT	EX-MT	VG
COMPLETE SET (4)	3.00	1.35	.40
COMMON PLAYER (S1-S4)	.25	.11	.03
☐ S1 Team Logo (Checklist back)	.25	.11	.03

	MT	EX-MT	VG
☐ S2 Wade Boggs	1.50	.65	.19
☐ S3 Steve Garvey	.50	.23	.06
☐ S4 Dave Winfield	1.00	.45	.13

1986 Fleer Update

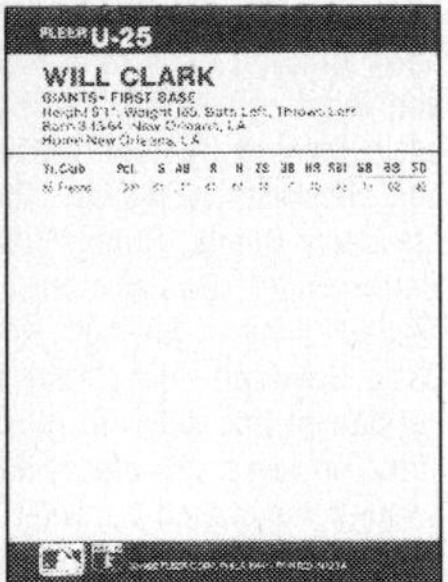

This 132-card set was distributed by Fleer to dealers as a complete set in a custom box. In addition to the complete set of 132 cards, the box also contains 25 Team Logo Stickers.The card fronts look very similar to the 1986 Fleer regular issue. The cards are numbered (with a U prefix) alphabetically according to player's last name. Cards measure the standard size, 2 1/2" by 3 1/2". The key (extended) Rookie Cards in this set are Barry Bonds, Bobby Bonilla, Will Clark, Doug Drabek, Wally Joyner, John Kruk, Kevin Mitchell, and Ruben Sierra.

	MT	EX-MT	VG
COMPLETE SET (132)	30.00	13.50	3.80
COMMON PLAYER (1-132)	.07	.03	.01
☐ 1 Mike Aldrete	.10	.05	.01
☐ 2 Andy Allanson	.07	.03	.01
☐ 3 Neil Allen	.07	.03	.01
☐ 4 Joaquin Andujar	.07	.03	.01
☐ 5 Paul Assenmacher	.07	.03	.01
☐ 6 Scott Bailes	.07	.03	.01
☐ 7 Jay Baller	.07	.03	.01
☐ 8 Scott Bankhead	.10	.05	.01
☐ 9 Bill Bathe	.07	.03	.01
☐ 10 Don Baylor	.10	.05	.01
☐ 11 Billy Beane	.07	.03	.01
☐ 12 Steve Bedrosian	.07	.03	.01
☐ 13 Juan Beniquez	.07	.03	.01
☐ 14 Barry Bonds	9.00	4.00	1.15
☐ 15 Bobby Bonilla UER (Wrong birthday)	4.00	1.80	.50
☐ 16 Rich Bordi	.07	.03	.01
☐ 17 Bill Campbell	.07	.03	.01
☐ 18 Tom Candiotti	.15	.07	.02
☐ 19 John Cangelosi	.07	.03	.01
☐ 20 Jose Canseco UER (Headings on back for a pitcher)	7.00	3.10	.85
☐ 21 Chuck Cary	.07	.03	.01
☐ 22 Juan Castillo	.07	.03	.01
☐ 23 Rick Cerone	.07	.03	.01
☐ 24 John Cerutti	.07	.03	.01
☐ 25 Will Clark	9.00	4.00	1.15
☐ 26 Mark Clear	.07	.03	.01
☐ 27 Darnell Coles	.10	.05	.01
☐ 28 Dave Collins	.07	.03	.01
☐ 29 Tim Conroy	.07	.03	.01
☐ 30 Ed Correa	.07	.03	.01
☐ 31 Joe Cowley	.07	.03	.01
☐ 32 Bill Dawley	.07	.03	.01
☐ 33 Rob Deer	.30	.14	.04
☐ 34 John Denny	.07	.03	.01
☐ 35 Jim Deshaies	.12	.05	.02
☐ 36 Doug Drabek	1.75	.80	.22
☐ 37 Mike Easler	.07	.03	.01
☐ 38 Mark Eichhorn	.10	.05	.01
☐ 39 Dave Engle	.07	.03	.01
☐ 40 Mike Fischlin	.07	.03	.01
☐ 41 Scott Fletcher	.07	.03	.01
☐ 42 Terry Forster	.07	.03	.01
☐ 43 Terry Francona	.07	.03	.01
☐ 44 Andres Galarraga	.20	.09	.03
☐ 45 Lee Guetterman	.07	.03	.01
☐ 46 Bill Gullickson	.10	.05	.01
☐ 47 Jackie Gutierrez	.07	.03	.01
☐ 48 Moose Haas	.07	.03	.01
☐ 49 Billy Hatcher	.10	.05	.01
☐ 50 Mike Heath	.07	.03	.01
☐ 51 Guy Hoffman	.07	.03	.01
☐ 52 Tom Hume	.07	.03	.01
☐ 53 Pete Incaviglia	.30	.14	.04
☐ 54 Dane Iorg	.07	.03	.01
☐ 55 Chris James	.15	.07	.02
☐ 56 Stan Javier	.12	.05	.02
☐ 57 Tommy John	.15	.07	.02
☐ 58 Tracy Jones	.07	.03	.01
☐ 59 Wally Joyner	1.50	.65	.19
☐ 60 Wayne Krenchicki	.07	.03	.01
☐ 61 John Kruk	1.25	.55	.16
☐ 62 Mike LaCoss	.07	.03	.01
☐ 63 Pete Ladd	.07	.03	.01
☐ 64 Dave LaPoint	.07	.03	.01
☐ 65 Mike LaValliere	.30	.14	.04
☐ 66 Rudy Law	.07	.03	.01
☐ 67 Dennis Leonard	.07	.03	.01
☐ 68 Steve Lombardozzi	.07	.03	.01
☐ 69 Aurelio Lopez	.07	.03	.01
☐ 70 Mickey Mahler	.07	.03	.01
☐ 71 Candy Maldonado	.10	.05	.01
☐ 72 Roger Mason	.15	.07	.02
☐ 73 Greg Mathews	.10	.05	.01
☐ 74 Andy McGaffigan	.07	.03	.01
☐ 75 Joel McKeon	.07	.03	.01
☐ 76 Kevin Mitchell	2.00	.90	.25
☐ 77 Bill Mooneyham	.07	.03	.01
☐ 78 Omar Moreno	.07	.03	.01
☐ 79 Jerry Mumphrey	.07	.03	.01
☐ 80 Al Newman	.07	.03	.01
☐ 81 Phil Niekro	.30	.14	.04
☐ 82 Randy Niemann	.07	.03	.01
☐ 83 Juan Nieves	.07	.03	.01
☐ 84 Bob Ojeda	.07	.03	.01
☐ 85 Rick Ownbey	.07	.03	.01
☐ 86 Tom Paciorek	.10	.05	.01
☐ 87 David Palmer	.07	.03	.01
☐ 88 Jeff Parrett	.30	.14	.04
☐ 89 Pat Perry	.07	.03	.01
☐ 90 Dan Plesac	.15	.07	.02
☐ 91 Darrell Porter	.07	.03	.01
☐ 92 Luis Quinones	.07	.03	.01
☐ 93 Rey Quinones UER (Misspelled Quinonez)	.07	.03	.01
☐ 94 Gary Redus	.07	.03	.01
☐ 95 Jeff Reed	.07	.03	.01
☐ 96 Bip Roberts	1.00	.45	.13
☐ 97 Billy Joe Robidoux	.07	.03	.01
☐ 98 Gary Roenicke	.07	.03	.01
☐ 99 Ron Roenicke	.07	.03	.01
☐ 100 Angel Salazar	.07	.03	.01
☐ 101 Joe Sambito	.07	.03	.01
☐ 102 Billy Sample	.07	.03	.01
☐ 103 Dave Schmidt	.07	.03	.01
☐ 104 Ken Schrom	.07	.03	.01
☐ 105 Ruben Sierra	7.00	3.10	.85
☐ 106 Ted Simmons	.10	.05	.01
☐ 107 Sammy Stewart	.07	.03	.01
☐ 108 Kurt Stillwell	.20	.09	.03
☐ 109 Dale Sveum	.07	.03	.01
☐ 110 Tim Teufel	.07	.03	.01
☐ 111 Bob Tewksbury	.60	.25	.08
☐ 112 Andres Thomas	.07	.03	.01
☐ 113 Jason Thompson	.07	.03	.01
☐ 114 Milt Thompson	.10	.05	.01
☐ 115 Robby Thompson	.40	.18	.05
☐ 116 Jay Tibbs	.07	.03	.01
☐ 117 Fred Toliver	.07	.03	.01
☐ 118 Wayne Tolleson	.07	.03	.01
☐ 119 Alex Trevino	.07	.03	.01
☐ 120 Manny Trillo	.07	.03	.01
☐ 121 Ed VandeBerg	.07	.03	.01
☐ 122 Ozzie Virgil	.07	.03	.01
☐ 123 Tony Walker	.07	.03	.01
☐ 124 Gene Walter	.07	.03	.01
☐ 125 Duane Ward	.75	.35	.09
☐ 126 Jerry Willard	.07	.03	.01
☐ 127 Mitch Williams	.35	.16	.04
☐ 128 Reggie Williams	.07	.03	.01
☐ 129 Bobby Witt	.40	.18	.05
☐ 130 Marvell Wynne	.07	.03	.01
☐ 131 Steve Yeager	.07	.03	.01
☐ 132 Checklist 1-132	.10	.01	.00

1986 Fleer Wax Box Cards

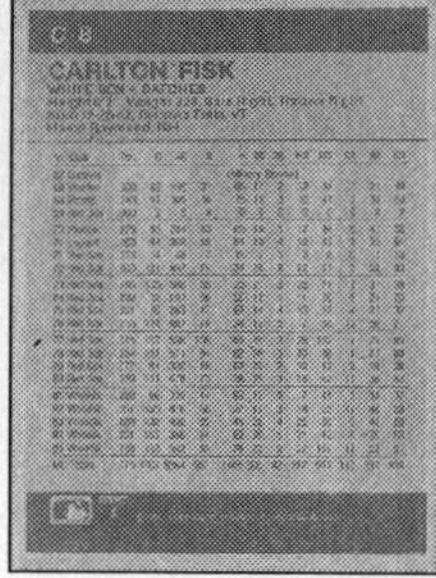

The cards in this eight-card set measure the standard 2 1/2" by 3 1/2" and were found on the bottom of the Fleer regular issue wax pack and cello pack boxes as four-card panel. Cards have essentially the same design as the 1986 Fleer regular issue set. These eight cards (C1 to C8) are considered a separate set in their own right and are not typically included in a complete set of the regular issue 1986 Fleer cards. The value of the panel uncut is slightly greater, perhaps by 25 percent greater, than the value of the individual cards cut up carefully.

	MT	EX-MT	VG
COMPLETE SET (8)	3.00	1.35	.40
COMMON PLAYER (C1-C8)	.15	.07	.02
☐ C1 Royals Logo	.15	.07	.02
☐ C2 George Brett	1.00	.45	.13
☐ C3 Ozzie Guillen	.50	.23	.06
☐ C4 Dale Murphy	.50	.23	.06
☐ C5 Cardinals Logo	.15	.07	.02
☐ C6 Tom Browning	.25	.11	.03
☐ C7 Gary Carter	.50	.23	.06
☐ C8 Carlton Fisk	.75	.35	.09

1987 Fleer

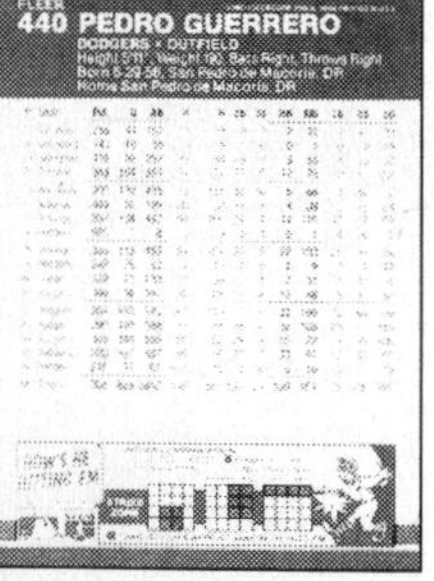

This 660-card set features a distinctive blue border, which fades to white on the card fronts. The backs are printed in blue, red, and pink on white card stock. The bottom of the card back shows an innovative graph of the player's ability, e.g., "He's got the stuff" for pitchers and "How he's hitting 'em," for hitters. Cards are numbered on the back and are again the standard 2 1/2" by 3 1/2". Cards are again organized numerically by teams, i.e., World Champion Mets (1-25), Boston Red Sox (26-48), Houston Astros (49-72), California Angels (73-95), New York Yankees (96-120), Texas Rangers (121-143), Detroit Tigers (144-168), Philadelphia Phillies (169-192), Cincinnati Reds (193-218), Toronto Blue Jays (219-240), Cleveland Indians (241-263), San Francisco Giants (264-288), St. Louis Cardinals (289-312), Montreal Expos (313-337), Milwaukee Brewers (338-361), Kansas City Royals (362-384), Oakland A's (385-410), San Diego Padres (411-435), Los Angeles Dodgers (436-460), Baltimore Orioles (461-483), Chicago White Sox (484-508), Atlanta Braves (509-532), Minnesota Twins (533-554), Chicago Cubs (555-578), Seattle Mariners (579-600), and Pittsburgh Pirates (601-624). The last 36 cards in the set consist of Specials (625-643), Rookie Pairs (644-653), and checklists (654-660). The key Rookie Cards in this set are Barry Bonds, Bobby Bonilla, Will Clark, Doug Drabek, Chuck Finley, Bo Jackson, John Kruk, Barry Larkin, Dave Magadan, Kevin Mitchell, Kevin Seitzer, Ruben Sierra, and Greg Swindell. Fleer also produced a "limited" edition version of this set with glossy coating and packaged in a "tin." However, this glossy tin set was apparently not limited enough (estimated between 75,000 and 100,000 1987 tin sets produced by Fleer), since the values of the "tin" glossy cards are now the same as the values of the regular set cards.

	MT	EX-MT	VG
COMPLETE SET (660)	90.00	40.00	11.50
COMPLETE FACT.SET (672)	90.00	40.00	11.50
COMMON PLAYER (1-660)	.07	.03	.01
COMPLETE WS SET (12)	4.00	1.80	.50
☐ 1 Rick Aguilera	.40	.18	.05
☐ 2 Richard Anderson	.07	.03	.01
☐ 3 Wally Backman	.07	.03	.01
☐ 4 Gary Carter	.30	.14	.04
☐ 5 Ron Darling	.10	.05	.01
☐ 6 Len Dykstra	.35	.16	.04
☐ 7 Kevin Elster	.12	.05	.02
☐ 8 Sid Fernandez	.10	.05	.01
☐ 9 Dwight Gooden	.60	.25	.08
☐ 10 Ed Hearn	.07	.03	.01
☐ 11 Danny Heep	.07	.03	.01
☐ 12 Keith Hernandez	.07	.03	.01
☐ 13 Howard Johnson	.45	.20	.06
☐ 14 Ray Knight	.10	.05	.01
☐ 15 Lee Mazzilli	.07	.03	.01
☐ 16 Roger McDowell	.07	.03	.01
☐ 17 Kevin Mitchell	3.00	1.35	.40
☐ 18 Randy Niemann	.07	.03	.01
☐ 19 Bob Ojeda	.07	.03	.01
☐ 20 Jesse Orosco	.07	.03	.01
☐ 21 Rafael Santana	.07	.03	.01
☐ 22 Doug Sisk	.07	.03	.01
☐ 23 Darryl Strawberry	1.25	.55	.16
☐ 24 Tim Teufel	.07	.03	.01
☐ 25 Mookie Wilson	.10	.05	.01
☐ 26 Tony Armas	.07	.03	.01
☐ 27 Marty Barrett	.07	.03	.01
☐ 28 Don Baylor	.10	.05	.01
☐ 29 Wade Boggs	1.50	.65	.19
☐ 30 Oil Can Boyd	.07	.03	.01
☐ 31 Bill Buckner	.10	.05	.01
☐ 32 Roger Clemens	4.50	2.00	.55
☐ 33 Steve Crawford	.07	.03	.01
☐ 34 Dwight Evans	.12	.05	.02
☐ 35 Rich Gedman	.07	.03	.01
☐ 36 Dave Henderson	.10	.05	.01
☐ 37 Bruce Hurst	.10	.05	.01
☐ 38 Tim Lollar	.07	.03	.01
☐ 39 Al Nipper	.07	.03	.01
☐ 40 Spike Owen	.07	.03	.01
☐ 41 Jim Rice	.15	.07	.02
☐ 42 Ed Romero	.07	.03	.01
☐ 43 Joe Sambito	.07	.03	.01
☐ 44 Calvin Schiraldi	.07	.03	.01
☐ 45 Tom Seaver	.75	.35	.09
☐ 46 Jeff Sellers	.07	.03	.01
☐ 47 Bob Stanley	.07	.03	.01
☐ 48 Sammy Stewart	.07	.03	.01
☐ 49 Larry Andersen	.07	.03	.01
☐ 50 Alan Ashby	.07	.03	.01
☐ 51 Kevin Bass	.07	.03	.01
☐ 52 Jeff Calhoun	.07	.03	.01
☐ 53 Jose Cruz	.07	.03	.01
☐ 54 Danny Darwin	.07	.03	.01
☐ 55 Glenn Davis	.35	.16	.04
☐ 56 Jim Deshaies	.20	.09	.03
☐ 57 Bill Doran	.07	.03	.01
☐ 58 Phil Garner	.10	.05	.01

☐ 59 Billy Hatcher .10 .05 .01
☐ 60 Charlie Kerfeld .07 .03 .01
☐ 61 Bob Knepper .07 .03 .01
☐ 62 Dave Lopes .10 .05 .01
☐ 63 Aurelio Lopez .07 .03 .01
☐ 64 Jim Pankovits .07 .03 .01
☐ 65 Terry Puhl .07 .03 .01
☐ 66 Craig Reynolds .07 .03 .01
☐ 67 Nolan Ryan 4.00 1.80 .50
☐ 68 Mike Scott .10 .05 .01
☐ 69 Dave Smith .07 .03 .01
☐ 70 Dickie Thon .07 .03 .01
☐ 71 Tony Walker .07 .03 .01
☐ 72 Denny Walling .07 .03 .01
☐ 73 Bob Boone .10 .05 .01
☐ 74 Rick Burleson .07 .03 .01
☐ 75 John Candelaria .07 .03 .01
☐ 76 Doug Corbett .07 .03 .01
☐ 77 Doug DeCinces .07 .03 .01
☐ 78 Brian Downing .07 .03 .01
☐ 79 Chuck Finley 1.00 .45 .13
☐ 80 Terry Forster .07 .03 .01
☐ 81 Bob Grich .10 .05 .01
☐ 82 George Hendrick .07 .03 .01
☐ 83 Jack Howell .07 .03 .01
☐ 84 Reggie Jackson .90 .40 .11
☐ 85 Ruppert Jones .07 .03 .01
☐ 86 Wally Joyner 2.00 .90 .25
☐ 87 Gary Lucas .07 .03 .01
☐ 88 Kirk McCaskill .07 .03 .01
☐ 89 Donnie Moore .07 .03 .01
☐ 90 Gary Pettis .07 .03 .01
☐ 91 Vern Ruhle .07 .03 .01
☐ 92 Dick Schofield .07 .03 .01
☐ 93 Don Sutton .25 .11 .03
☐ 94 Rob Wilfong .07 .03 .01
☐ 95 Mike Witt .07 .03 .01
☐ 96 Doug Drabek 2.50 1.15 .30
☐ 97 Mike Easler .07 .03 .01
☐ 98 Mike Fischlin .07 .03 .01
☐ 99 Brian Fisher .07 .03 .01
☐ 100 Ron Guidry .10 .05 .01
☐ 101 Rickey Henderson 1.50 .65 .19
☐ 102 Tommy John .10 .05 .01
☐ 103 Ron Kittle .07 .03 .01
☐ 104 Don Mattingly 1.25 .55 .16
☐ 105 Bobby Meacham .07 .03 .01
☐ 106 Joe Niekro .10 .05 .01
☐ 107 Mike Pagliarulo .07 .03 .01
☐ 108 Dan Pasqua .10 .05 .01
☐ 109 Willie Randolph .10 .05 .01
☐ 110 Dennis Rasmussen .07 .03 .01
☐ 111 Dave Righetti .10 .05 .01
☐ 112 Gary Roenicke .07 .03 .01
☐ 113 Rod Scurry .07 .03 .01
☐ 114 Bob Shirley .07 .03 .01
☐ 115 Joel Skinner .07 .03 .01
☐ 116 Tim Stoddard .07 .03 .01
☐ 117 Bob Tewksbury 1.00 .45 .13
☐ 118 Wayne Tolleson .07 .03 .01
☐ 119 Claudell Washington .07 .03 .01
☐ 120 Dave Winfield 1.00 .45 .13
☐ 121 Steve Buechele .10 .05 .01
☐ 122 Ed Correa .07 .03 .01
☐ 123 Scott Fletcher .07 .03 .01
☐ 124 Jose Guzman .10 .05 .01
☐ 125 Toby Harrah .07 .03 .01
☐ 126 Greg Harris .07 .03 .01
☐ 127 Charlie Hough .07 .03 .01
☐ 128 Pete Incaviglia .50 .23 .06
☐ 129 Mike Mason .07 .03 .01
☐ 130 Oddibe McDowell .07 .03 .01
☐ 131 Dale Mohorcic .07 .03 .01
☐ 132 Pete O'Brien .07 .03 .01
☐ 133 Tom Paciorek .10 .05 .01
☐ 134 Larry Parrish .07 .03 .01
☐ 135 Geno Petralli .07 .03 .01
☐ 136 Darrell Porter .07 .03 .01
☐ 137 Jeff Russell .10 .05 .01
☐ 138 Ruben Sierra 13.00 5.75 1.65
☐ 139 Don Slaught .07 .03 .01
☐ 140 Gary Ward .07 .03 .01
☐ 141 Curtis Wilkerson .07 .03 .01
☐ 142 Mitch Williams .50 .23 .06
☐ 143 Bobby Witt UER .60 .25 .08
(Tulsa misspelled as Tusla; ERA should be 6.43, not .643)
☐ 144 Dave Bergman .07 .03 .01
☐ 145 Tom Brookens .07 .03 .01
☐ 146 Bill Campbell .07 .03 .01
☐ 147 Chuck Cary .07 .03 .01
☐ 148 Darnell Coles .07 .03 .01
☐ 149 Dave Collins .07 .03 .01
☐ 150 Darrell Evans .10 .05 .01
☐ 151 Kirk Gibson .10 .05 .01
☐ 152 John Grubb .07 .03 .01
☐ 153 Willie Hernandez .07 .03 .01
☐ 154 Larry Herndon .07 .03 .01
☐ 155 Eric King .07 .03 .01
☐ 156 Chet Lemon .07 .03 .01
☐ 157 Dwight Lowry .07 .03 .01
☐ 158 Jack Morris .60 .25 .08
☐ 159 Randy O'Neal .07 .03 .01
☐ 160 Lance Parrish .10 .05 .01
☐ 161 Dan Petry .07 .03 .01
☐ 162 Pat Sheridan .07 .03 .01
☐ 163 Jim Slaton .07 .03 .01
☐ 164 Frank Tanana .07 .03 .01
☐ 165 Walt Terrell .07 .03 .01
☐ 166 Mark Thurmond .07 .03 .01
☐ 167 Alan Trammell .25 .11 .03
☐ 168 Lou Whitaker .25 .11 .03
☐ 169 Luis Aguayo .07 .03 .01
☐ 170 Steve Bedrosian .07 .03 .01
☐ 171 Don Carman .07 .03 .01
☐ 172 Darren Daulton .50 .23 .06
☐ 173 Greg Gross .07 .03 .01
☐ 174 Kevin Gross .07 .03 .01
☐ 175 Von Hayes .07 .03 .01
☐ 176 Charles Hudson .07 .03 .01
☐ 177 Tom Hume .07 .03 .01
☐ 178 Steve Jeltz .07 .03 .01
☐ 179 Mike Maddux .07 .03 .01
☐ 180 Shane Rawley .07 .03 .01
☐ 181 Gary Redus .07 .03 .01
☐ 182 Ron Roenicke .07 .03 .01
☐ 183 Bruce Ruffin .07 .03 .01
☐ 184 John Russell .07 .03 .01
☐ 185 Juan Samuel .07 .03 .01
☐ 186 Dan Schatzeder .07 .03 .01
☐ 187 Mike Schmidt 1.75 .80 .22
☐ 188 Rick Schu .07 .03 .01
☐ 189 Jeff Stone .07 .03 .01
☐ 190 Kent Tekulve .07 .03 .01
☐ 191 Milt Thompson .10 .05 .01
☐ 192 Glenn Wilson .07 .03 .01
☐ 193 Buddy Bell .10 .05 .01
☐ 194 Tom Browning .10 .05 .01
☐ 195 Sal Butera .07 .03 .01
☐ 196 Dave Concepcion .10 .05 .01
☐ 197 Kal Daniels .12 .05 .02
☐ 198 Eric Davis .60 .25 .08
☐ 199 John Denny .07 .03 .01
☐ 200 Bo Diaz .07 .03 .01
☐ 201 Nick Esasky .07 .03 .01
☐ 202 John Franco .15 .07 .02
☐ 203 Bill Gullickson .10 .05 .01
☐ 204 Barry Larkin 7.00 3.10 .85
☐ 205 Eddie Milner .07 .03 .01
☐ 206 Rob Murphy .07 .03 .01
☐ 207 Ron Oester .07 .03 .01
☐ 208 Dave Parker .20 .09 .03
☐ 209 Tony Perez .20 .09 .03
☐ 210 Ted Power .07 .03 .01
☐ 211 Joe Price .07 .03 .01
☐ 212 Ron Robinson .07 .03 .01
☐ 213 Pete Rose .75 .35 .09
☐ 214 Mario Soto .07 .03 .01
☐ 215 Kurt Stillwell .30 .14 .04
☐ 216 Max Venable .07 .03 .01
☐ 217 Chris Welsh .07 .03 .01
☐ 218 Carl Willis .15 .07 .02
☐ 219 Jesse Barfield .10 .05 .01
☐ 220 George Bell .50 .23 .06
☐ 221 Bill Caudill .07 .03 .01
☐ 222 John Cerutti .07 .03 .01
☐ 223 Jim Clancy .07 .03 .01
☐ 224 Mark Eichhorn .10 .05 .01
☐ 225 Tony Fernandez .20 .09 .03
☐ 226 Damaso Garcia .07 .03 .01
☐ 227 Kelly Gruber ERR .35 .16 .04
(Wrong birth year)
☐ 228 Tom Henke .10 .05 .01
☐ 229 Garth Iorg .07 .03 .01
☐ 230 Joe Johnson .07 .03 .01
☐ 231 Cliff Johnson .07 .03 .01
☐ 232 Jimmy Key .10 .05 .01
☐ 233 Dennis Lamp .07 .03 .01
☐ 234 Rick Leach .07 .03 .01
☐ 235 Buck Martinez .07 .03 .01
☐ 236 Lloyd Moseby .07 .03 .01
☐ 237 Rance Mulliniks .07 .03 .01
☐ 238 Dave Stieb .10 .05 .01
☐ 239 Willie Upshaw .07 .03 .01
☐ 240 Ernie Whitt .07 .03 .01

☐ 241	Andy Allanson	.07	.03	.01
☐ 242	Scott Bailes	.07	.03	.01
☐ 243	Chris Bando	.07	.03	.01
☐ 244	Tony Bernazard	.07	.03	.01
☐ 245	John Butcher	.07	.03	.01
☐ 246	Brett Butler	.20	.09	.03
☐ 247	Ernie Camacho	.07	.03	.01
☐ 248	Tom Candiotti	.10	.05	.01
☐ 249	Joe Carter	1.50	.65	.19
☐ 250	Carmen Castillo	.07	.03	.01
☐ 251	Julio Franco	.35	.16	.04
☐ 252	Mel Hall	.10	.05	.01
☐ 253	Brook Jacoby	.07	.03	.01
☐ 254	Phil Niekro	.25	.11	.03
☐ 255	Otis Nixon	.35	.16	.04
☐ 256	Dickie Noles	.07	.03	.01
☐ 257	Bryan Oelkers	.07	.03	.01
☐ 258	Ken Schrom	.07	.03	.01
☐ 259	Don Schulze	.07	.03	.01
☐ 260	Cory Snyder	.20	.09	.03
☐ 261	Pat Tabler	.07	.03	.01
☐ 262	Andre Thornton	.07	.03	.01
☐ 263	Rich Yett	.07	.03	.01
☐ 264	Mike Aldrete	.07	.03	.01
☐ 265	Juan Berenguer	.07	.03	.01
☐ 266	Vida Blue	.10	.05	.01
☐ 267	Bob Brenly	.07	.03	.01
☐ 268	Chris Brown	.07	.03	.01
☐ 269	Will Clark	20.00	9.00	2.50
☐ 270	Chili Davis	.10	.05	.01
☐ 271	Mark Davis	.07	.03	.01
☐ 272	Kelly Downs	.12	.05	.02
☐ 273	Scott Garrelts	.07	.03	.01
☐ 274	Dan Gladden	.07	.03	.01
☐ 275	Mike Krukow	.07	.03	.01
☐ 276	Randy Kutcher	.07	.03	.01
☐ 277	Mike LaCoss	.07	.03	.01
☐ 278	Jeff Leonard	.07	.03	.01
☐ 279	Candy Maldonado	.10	.05	.01
☐ 280	Roger Mason	.10	.05	.01
☐ 281	Bob Melvin	.07	.03	.01
☐ 282	Greg Minton	.07	.03	.01
☐ 283	Jeff D. Robinson	.07	.03	.01
☐ 284	Harry Spilman	.07	.03	.01
☐ 285	Robby Thompson	.60	.25	.08
☐ 286	Jose Uribe	.07	.03	.01
☐ 287	Frank Williams	.07	.03	.01
☐ 288	Joel Youngblood	.07	.03	.01
☐ 289	Jack Clark	.10	.05	.01
☐ 290	Vince Coleman	.35	.16	.04
☐ 291	Tim Conroy	.07	.03	.01
☐ 292	Danny Cox	.07	.03	.01
☐ 293	Ken Dayley	.07	.03	.01
☐ 294	Curt Ford	.07	.03	.01
☐ 295	Bob Forsch	.07	.03	.01
☐ 296	Tom Herr	.07	.03	.01
☐ 297	Ricky Horton	.07	.03	.01
☐ 298	Clint Hurdle	.07	.03	.01
☐ 299	Jeff Lahti	.07	.03	.01
☐ 300	Steve Lake	.07	.03	.01
☐ 301	Tito Landrum	.07	.03	.01
☐ 302	Mike LaValliere	.35	.16	.04
☐ 303	Greg Mathews	.07	.03	.01
☐ 304	Willie McGee	.10	.05	.01
☐ 305	Jose Oquendo	.07	.03	.01
☐ 306	Terry Pendleton	.75	.35	.09
☐ 307	Pat Perry	.07	.03	.01
☐ 308	Ozzie Smith	.75	.35	.09
☐ 309	Ray Soff	.07	.03	.01
☐ 310	John Tudor	.10	.05	.01
☐ 311	Andy Van Slyke UER (Bats R, Throws L)	.50	.23	.06
☐ 312	Todd Worrell	.10	.05	.01
☐ 313	Dann Bilardello	.07	.03	.01
☐ 314	Hubie Brooks	.07	.03	.01
☐ 315	Tim Burke	.07	.03	.01
☐ 316	Andre Dawson	.90	.40	.11
☐ 317	Mike Fitzgerald	.07	.03	.01
☐ 318	Tom Foley	.07	.03	.01
☐ 319	Andres Galarraga	.10	.05	.01
☐ 320	Joe Hesketh	.07	.03	.01
☐ 321	Wallace Johnson	.07	.03	.01
☐ 322	Wayne Krenchicki	.07	.03	.01
☐ 323	Vance Law	.07	.03	.01
☐ 324	Dennis Martinez	.10	.05	.01
☐ 325	Bob McClure	.07	.03	.01
☐ 326	Andy McGaffigan	.07	.03	.01
☐ 327	Al Newman	.07	.03	.01
☐ 328	Tim Raines	.25	.11	.03
☐ 329	Jeff Reardon	.40	.18	.05
☐ 330	Luis Rivera	.07	.03	.01
☐ 331	Bob Sebra	.07	.03	.01
☐ 332	Bryn Smith	.07	.03	.01
☐ 333	Jay Tibbs	.07	.03	.01
☐ 334	Tim Wallach	.10	.05	.01
☐ 335	Mitch Webster	.07	.03	.01
☐ 336	Jim Wohlford	.07	.03	.01
☐ 337	Floyd Youmans	.07	.03	.01
☐ 338	Chris Bosio	.75	.35	.09
☐ 339	Glenn Braggs	.25	.11	.03
☐ 340	Rick Cerone	.07	.03	.01
☐ 341	Mark Clear	.07	.03	.01
☐ 342	Bryan Clutterbuck	.07	.03	.01
☐ 343	Cecil Cooper	.10	.05	.01
☐ 344	Rob Deer	.20	.09	.03
☐ 345	Jim Gantner	.07	.03	.01
☐ 346	Ted Higuera	.07	.03	.01
☐ 347	John Henry Johnson	.07	.03	.01
☐ 348	Tim Leary	.07	.03	.01
☐ 349	Rick Manning	.07	.03	.01
☐ 350	Paul Molitor	.40	.18	.05
☐ 351	Charlie Moore	.07	.03	.01
☐ 352	Juan Nieves	.07	.03	.01
☐ 353	Ben Oglivie	.07	.03	.01
☐ 354	Dan Plesac	.20	.09	.03
☐ 355	Ernest Riles	.07	.03	.01
☐ 356	Billy Joe Robidoux	.07	.03	.01
☐ 357	Bill Schroeder	.07	.03	.01
☐ 358	Dale Sveum	.07	.03	.01
☐ 359	Gorman Thomas	.07	.03	.01
☐ 360	Bill Wegman	.20	.09	.03
☐ 361	Robin Yount	1.25	.55	.16
☐ 362	Steve Balboni	.07	.03	.01
☐ 363	Scott Bankhead	.07	.03	.01
☐ 364	Buddy Biancalana	.07	.03	.01
☐ 365	Bud Black	.07	.03	.01
☐ 366	George Brett	1.25	.55	.16
☐ 367	Steve Farr	.10	.05	.01
☐ 368	Mark Gubicza	.07	.03	.01
☐ 369	Bo Jackson	5.00	2.30	.60
☐ 370	Danny Jackson	.07	.03	.01
☐ 371	Mike Kingery	.07	.03	.01
☐ 372	Rudy Law	.07	.03	.01
☐ 373	Charlie Leibrandt	.10	.05	.01
☐ 374	Dennis Leonard	.07	.03	.01
☐ 375	Hal McRae	.10	.05	.01
☐ 376	Jorge Orta	.07	.03	.01
☐ 377	Jamie Quirk	.07	.03	.01
☐ 378	Dan Quisenberry	.10	.05	.01
☐ 379	Bret Saberhagen	.40	.18	.05
☐ 380	Angel Salazar	.07	.03	.01
☐ 381	Lonnie Smith	.07	.03	.01
☐ 382	Jim Sundberg	.07	.03	.01
☐ 383	Frank White	.07	.03	.01
☐ 384	Willie Wilson	.07	.03	.01
☐ 385	Joaquin Andujar	.07	.03	.01
☐ 386	Doug Bair	.07	.03	.01
☐ 387	Dusty Baker	.10	.05	.01
☐ 388	Bruce Bochte	.07	.03	.01
☐ 389	Jose Canseco	10.00	4.50	1.25
☐ 390	Chris Codiroli	.07	.03	.01
☐ 391	Mike Davis	.07	.03	.01
☐ 392	Alfredo Griffin	.07	.03	.01
☐ 393	Moose Haas	.07	.03	.01
☐ 394	Donnie Hill	.07	.03	.01
☐ 395	Jay Howell	.10	.05	.01
☐ 396	Dave Kingman	.10	.05	.01
☐ 397	Carney Lansford	.10	.05	.01
☐ 398	Dave Leiper	.07	.03	.01
☐ 399	Bill Mooneyham	.07	.03	.01
☐ 400	Dwayne Murphy	.07	.03	.01
☐ 401	Steve Ontiveros	.07	.03	.01
☐ 402	Tony Phillips	.10	.05	.01
☐ 403	Eric Plunk	.07	.03	.01
☐ 404	Jose Rijo	.35	.16	.04
☐ 405	Terry Steinbach	.75	.35	.09
☐ 406	Dave Stewart	.25	.11	.03
☐ 407	Mickey Tettleton	.40	.18	.05
☐ 408	Dave Von Ohlen	.07	.03	.01
☐ 409	Jerry Willard	.07	.03	.01
☐ 410	Curt Young	.07	.03	.01
☐ 411	Bruce Bochy	.07	.03	.01
☐ 412	Dave Dravecky	.10	.05	.01
☐ 413	Tim Flannery	.07	.03	.01
☐ 414	Steve Garvey	.35	.16	.04
☐ 415	Rich Gossage	.12	.05	.02
☐ 416	Tony Gwynn	1.75	.80	.22
☐ 417	Andy Hawkins	.07	.03	.01
☐ 418	LaMarr Hoyt	.07	.03	.01
☐ 419	Terry Kennedy	.07	.03	.01
☐ 420	John Kruk	2.50	1.15	.30
☐ 421	Dave LaPoint	.07	.03	.01
☐ 422	Craig Lefferts	.10	.05	.01
☐ 423	Carmelo Martinez	.07	.03	.01
☐ 424	Lance McCullers	.07	.03	.01
☐ 425	Kevin McReynolds	.10	.05	.01

☐ 426 Graig Nettles	.10	.05	.01
☐ 427 Bip Roberts	1.50	.65	.19
☐ 428 Jerry Royster	.07	.03	.01
☐ 429 Benito Santiago	.50	.23	.06
☐ 430 Eric Show	.07	.03	.01
☐ 431 Bob Stoddard	.07	.03	.01
☐ 432 Garry Templeton	.07	.03	.01
☐ 433 Gene Walter	.07	.03	.01
☐ 434 Ed Whitson	.07	.03	.01
☐ 435 Marvell Wynne	.07	.03	.01
☐ 436 Dave Anderson	.07	.03	.01
☐ 437 Greg Brock	.07	.03	.01
☐ 438 Enos Cabell	.07	.03	.01
☐ 439 Mariano Duncan	.07	.03	.01
☐ 440 Pedro Guerrero	.10	.05	.01
☐ 441 Orel Hershiser	.30	.14	.04
☐ 442 Rick Honeycutt	.07	.03	.01
☐ 443 Ken Howell	.07	.03	.01
☐ 444 Ken Landreaux	.07	.03	.01
☐ 445 Bill Madlock	.10	.05	.01
☐ 446 Mike Marshall	.07	.03	.01
☐ 447 Len Matuszek	.07	.03	.01
☐ 448 Tom Niedenfuer	.07	.03	.01
☐ 449 Alejandro Pena	.07	.03	.01
☐ 450 Dennis Powell	.07	.03	.01
☐ 451 Jerry Reuss	.07	.03	.01
☐ 452 Bill Russell	.10	.05	.01
☐ 453 Steve Sax	.20	.09	.03
☐ 454 Mike Scioscia	.07	.03	.01
☐ 455 Franklin Stubbs	.07	.03	.01
☐ 456 Alex Trevino	.07	.03	.01
☐ 457 Fernando Valenzuela	.10	.05	.01
☐ 458 Ed VandeBerg	.07	.03	.01
☐ 459 Bob Welch	.10	.05	.01
☐ 460 Reggie Williams	.07	.03	.01
☐ 461 Don Aase	.07	.03	.01
☐ 462 Juan Beniquez	.07	.03	.01
☐ 463 Mike Boddicker	.07	.03	.01
☐ 464 Juan Bonilla	.07	.03	.01
☐ 465 Rich Bordi	.07	.03	.01
☐ 466 Storm Davis	.07	.03	.01
☐ 467 Rick Dempsey	.07	.03	.01
☐ 468 Ken Dixon	.07	.03	.01
☐ 469 Jim Dwyer	.07	.03	.01
☐ 470 Mike Flanagan	.07	.03	.01
☐ 471 Jackie Gutierrez	.07	.03	.01
☐ 472 Brad Havens	.07	.03	.01
☐ 473 Lee Lacy	.07	.03	.01
☐ 474 Fred Lynn	.10	.05	.01
☐ 475 Scott McGregor	.07	.03	.01
☐ 476 Eddie Murray	.75	.35	.09
☐ 477 Tom O'Malley	.07	.03	.01
☐ 478 Cal Ripken Jr.	3.50	1.55	.45
☐ 479 Larry Sheets	.07	.03	.01
☐ 480 John Shelby	.07	.03	.01
☐ 481 Nate Snell	.07	.03	.01
☐ 482 Jim Traber	.07	.03	.01
☐ 483 Mike Young	.07	.03	.01
☐ 484 Neil Allen	.07	.03	.01
☐ 485 Harold Baines	.15	.07	.02
☐ 486 Floyd Bannister	.07	.03	.01
☐ 487 Daryl Boston	.07	.03	.01
☐ 488 Ivan Calderon	.15	.07	.02
☐ 489 John Cangelosi	.07	.03	.01
☐ 490 Steve Carlton	.75	.35	.09
☐ 491 Joe Cowley	.07	.03	.01
☐ 492 Julio Cruz	.07	.03	.01
☐ 493 Bill Dawley	.07	.03	.01
☐ 494 Jose DeLeon	.07	.03	.01
☐ 495 Richard Dotson	.07	.03	.01
☐ 496 Carlton Fisk	.75	.35	.09
☐ 497 Ozzie Guillen	.10	.05	.01
☐ 498 Jerry Hairston	.07	.03	.01
☐ 499 Ron Hassey	.07	.03	.01
☐ 500 Tim Hulett	.07	.03	.01
☐ 501 Bob James	.07	.03	.01
☐ 502 Steve Lyons	.07	.03	.01
☐ 503 Joel McKeon	.07	.03	.01
☐ 504 Gene Nelson	.07	.03	.01
☐ 505 Dave Schmidt	.07	.03	.01
☐ 506 Ray Searage	.07	.03	.01
☐ 507 Bobby Thigpen	1.00	.45	.13
☐ 508 Greg Walker	.07	.03	.01
☐ 509 Jim Acker	.07	.03	.01
☐ 510 Doyle Alexander	.07	.03	.01
☐ 511 Paul Assenmacher	.07	.03	.01
☐ 512 Bruce Benedict	.07	.03	.01
☐ 513 Chris Chambliss	.10	.05	.01
☐ 514 Jeff Dedmon	.07	.03	.01
☐ 515 Gene Garber	.07	.03	.01
☐ 516 Ken Griffey	.10	.05	.01
☐ 517 Terry Harper	.07	.03	.01
☐ 518 Bob Horner	.10	.05	.01
☐ 519 Glenn Hubbard	.07	.03	.01
☐ 520 Rick Mahler	.07	.03	.01
☐ 521 Omar Moreno	.07	.03	.01
☐ 522 Dale Murphy	.40	.18	.05
☐ 523 Ken Oberkfell	.07	.03	.01
☐ 524 Ed Olwine	.07	.03	.01
☐ 525 David Palmer	.07	.03	.01
☐ 526 Rafael Ramirez	.07	.03	.01
☐ 527 Billy Sample	.07	.03	.01
☐ 528 Ted Simmons	.10	.05	.01
☐ 529 Zane Smith	.10	.05	.01
☐ 530 Bruce Sutter	.10	.05	.01
☐ 531 Andres Thomas	.07	.03	.01
☐ 532 Ozzie Virgil	.07	.03	.01
☐ 533 Allan Anderson	.07	.03	.01
☐ 534 Keith Atherton	.07	.03	.01
☐ 535 Billy Beane	.07	.03	.01
☐ 536 Bert Blyleven	.15	.07	.02
☐ 537 Tom Brunansky	.10	.05	.01
☐ 538 Randy Bush	.07	.03	.01
☐ 539 George Frazier	.07	.03	.01
☐ 540 Gary Gaetti	.07	.03	.01
☐ 541 Greg Gagne	.10	.05	.01
☐ 542 Mickey Hatcher	.07	.03	.01
☐ 543 Neal Heaton	.07	.03	.01
☐ 544 Kent Hrbek	.20	.09	.03
☐ 545 Roy Lee Jackson	.07	.03	.01
☐ 546 Tim Laudner	.07	.03	.01
☐ 547 Steve Lombardozzi	.07	.03	.01
☐ 548 Mark Portugal	.30	.14	.04
☐ 549 Kirby Puckett	4.00	1.80	.50
☐ 550 Jeff Reed	.07	.03	.01
☐ 551 Mark Salas	.07	.03	.01
☐ 552 Roy Smalley	.07	.03	.01
☐ 553 Mike Smithson	.07	.03	.01
☐ 554 Frank Viola	.30	.14	.04
☐ 555 Thad Bosley	.07	.03	.01
☐ 556 Ron Cey	.10	.05	.01
☐ 557 Jody Davis	.07	.03	.01
☐ 558 Ron Davis	.07	.03	.01
☐ 559 Bob Dernier	.07	.03	.01
☐ 560 Frank DiPino	.07	.03	.01
☐ 561 Shawon Dunston UER (Wrong birth year listed on card back)	.10	.05	.01
☐ 562 Leon Durham	.07	.03	.01
☐ 563 Dennis Eckersley	.60	.25	.08
☐ 564 Terry Francona	.07	.03	.01
☐ 565 Dave Gumpert	.07	.03	.01
☐ 566 Guy Hoffman	.07	.03	.01
☐ 567 Ed Lynch	.07	.03	.01
☐ 568 Gary Matthews	.07	.03	.01
☐ 569 Keith Moreland	.07	.03	.01
☐ 570 Jamie Moyer	.07	.03	.01
☐ 571 Jerry Mumphrey	.07	.03	.01
☐ 572 Ryne Sandberg	2.50	1.15	.30
☐ 573 Scott Sanderson	.07	.03	.01
☐ 574 Lee Smith	.40	.18	.05
☐ 575 Chris Speier	.07	.03	.01
☐ 576 Rick Sutcliffe	.10	.05	.01
☐ 577 Manny Trillo	.07	.03	.01
☐ 578 Steve Trout	.07	.03	.01
☐ 579 Karl Best	.07	.03	.01
☐ 580 Scott Bradley	.07	.03	.01
☐ 581 Phil Bradley	.07	.03	.01
☐ 582 Mickey Brantley	.07	.03	.01
☐ 583 Mike G. Brown P	.07	.03	.01
☐ 584 Alvin Davis	.07	.03	.01
☐ 585 Lee Guetterman	.07	.03	.01
☐ 586 Mark Huismann	.07	.03	.01
☐ 587 Bob Kearney	.07	.03	.01
☐ 588 Pete Ladd	.07	.03	.01
☐ 589 Mark Langston	.35	.16	.04
☐ 590 Mike Moore	.07	.03	.01
☐ 591 Mike Morgan	.10	.05	.01
☐ 592 John Moses	.07	.03	.01
☐ 593 Ken Phelps	.07	.03	.01
☐ 594 Jim Presley	.07	.03	.01
☐ 595 Rey Quinones UER (Quinonez on front)	.07	.03	.01
☐ 596 Harold Reynolds	.10	.05	.01
☐ 597 Billy Swift	.12	.05	.02
☐ 598 Danny Tartabull	.75	.35	.09
☐ 599 Steve Yeager	.07	.03	.01
☐ 600 Matt Young	.07	.03	.01
☐ 601 Bill Almon	.07	.03	.01
☐ 602 Rafael Belliard	.35	.16	.04
☐ 603 Mike Bielecki	.07	.03	.01
☐ 604 Barry Bonds	20.00	9.00	2.50
☐ 605 Bobby Bonilla	5.00	2.30	.60
☐ 606 Sid Bream	.10	.05	.01
☐ 607 Mike C. Brown OF	.07	.03	.01
☐ 608 Pat Clements	.07	.03	.01

□ 609 Mike Diaz .07 .03 .01
□ 610 Cecilio Guante .07 .03 .01
□ 611 Barry Jones .10 .05 .01
□ 612 Bob Kipper .07 .03 .01
□ 613 Larry McWilliams .07 .03 .01
□ 614 Jim Morrison .07 .03 .01
□ 615 Joe Orsulak .07 .03 .01
□ 616 Junior Ortiz .07 .03 .01
□ 617 Tony Pena .07 .03 .01
□ 618 Johnny Ray .07 .03 .01
□ 619 Rick Reuschel .07 .03 .01
□ 620 R.J. Reynolds .07 .03 .01
□ 621 Rick Rhoden .07 .03 .01
□ 622 Don Robinson .07 .03 .01
□ 623 Bob Walk .07 .03 .01
□ 624 Jim Winn .07 .03 .01
□ 625 Youthful Power .75 .35 .09
Pete Incaviglia
Jose Canseco
□ 626 300 Game Winners .10 .05 .01
Don Sutton
Phil Niekro
□ 627 AL Firemen .10 .05 .01
Dave Righetti
Don Aase
□ 628 Rookie All-Stars 1.00 .45 .13
Wally Joyner
Jose Canseco
□ 629 Magic Mets .30 .14 .04
Gary Carter
Sid Fernandez
Dwight Gooden
Keith Hernandez
Darryl Strawberry
□ 630 NL Best Righties .10 .05 .01
Mike Scott
Mike Krukow
□ 631 Sensational Southpaws .10 .05 .01
Fernando Valenzuela
John Franco
□ 632 Count'Em .10 .05 .01
Bob Horner
□ 633 AL Pitcher's Nightmare 1.25 .55 .16
Jose Canseco
Jim Rice
Kirby Puckett
□ 634 All-Star Battery .60 .25 .08
Gary Carter
Roger Clemens
□ 635 4000 Strikeouts .15 .07 .02
Steve Carlton
□ 636 Big Bats at First .10 .05 .01
Glenn Davis
Eddie Murray
□ 637 On Base .20 .09 .03
Wade Boggs
Keith Hernandez
□ 638 Sluggers Left Side .75 .35 .09
Don Mattingly
Darryl Strawberry
□ 639 Former MVP's .20 .09 .03
Dave Parker
Ryne Sandberg
□ 640 Dr. K and Super K 1.25 .55 .16
Dwight Gooden
Roger Clemens
□ 641 AL West Stoppers .10 .05 .01
Mike Witt
Charlie Hough
□ 642 Doubles and Triples .10 .05 .01
Juan Samuel
Tim Raines
□ 643 Outfielders with Punch .10 .05 .01
Harold Baines
Jesse Barfield
□ 644 Dave Clark and 3.00 1.35 .40
Greg Swindell
□ 645 Ron Karkovice and .10 .05 .01
Russ Morman
□ 646 Devon White and 1.75 .80 .22
Willie Fraser
□ 647 Mike Stanley and .20 .09 .03
Jerry Browne
□ 648 Dave Magadan and .60 .25 .08
Phil Lombardi
□ 649 Jose Gonzalez and .10 .05 .01
Ralph Bryant
□ 650 Jimmy Jones and .30 .14 .04
Randy Asadoor
□ 651 Tracy Jones and .10 .05 .01
Marvin Freeman
□ 652 John Stefero and 1.00 .45 .13
Kevin Seitzer
□ 653 Rob Nelson and .10 .05 .01
Steve Fireovid
□ 654 CL: Mets/Red Sox .10 .01 .00
Astros/Angels
□ 655 CL: Yankees/Rangers .10 .01 .00
Tigers/Phillies
□ 656 CL: Reds/Blue Jays UER .10 .01 .00
Indians/Giants
(230/231 wrong)
□ 657 CL: Cardinals/Expos .10 .01 .00
Brewers/Royals
□ 658 CL: A's/Padres .10 .01 .00
Dodgers/Orioles
□ 659 CL: White Sox/Braves .10 .01 .00
Twins/Cubs
□ 660 CL: Mariners/Pirates UER .10 .01 .00
Special Cards
(580/581 wrong)

1987 Fleer All-Star Inserts

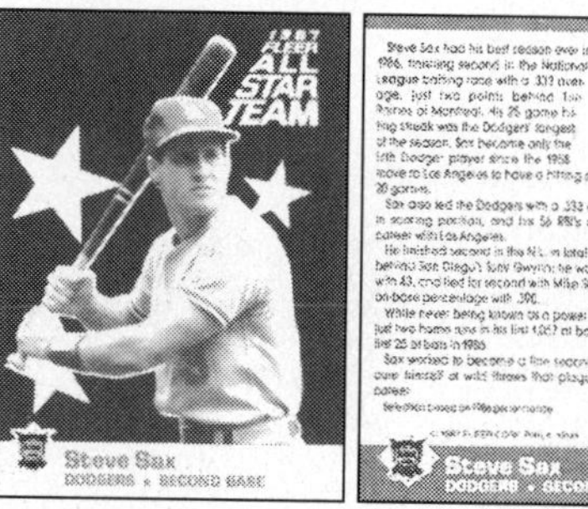

This 12-card set was distributed as an insert in packs of the Fleer regular issue. The cards are 2 1/2" by 3 1/2" and designed with a color player photo superimposed on a gray or black background with yellow stars. The player's name, team, and position are printed in orange on black or gray at the bottom of the obverse. The card backs are done predominantly in gray, red, and black. Cards are numbered on the back in the upper right hand corner.

	MT	EX-MT	VG
COMPLETE SET (12)	16.00	7.25	2.00
COMMON PLAYER (1-12)	.40	.18	.05
□ 1 Don Mattingly	3.50	1.55	.45
□ 2 Gary Carter	1.25	.55	.16
□ 3 Tony Fernandez	.60	.25	.08
□ 4 Steve Sax	.60	.25	.08
□ 5 Kirby Puckett	4.00	1.80	.50
□ 6 Mike Schmidt	3.50	1.55	.45
□ 7 Mike Easler	.40	.18	.05
□ 8 Todd Worrell	.60	.25	.08
□ 9 George Bell	.50	.23	.06
□ 10 Fernando Valenzuela	.50	.23	.06
□ 11 Roger Clemens	4.50	2.00	.55
□ 12 Tim Raines	.75	.35	.09

1987 Fleer Award Winners

This small set of 44 cards was (mass)-produced for 7-Eleven stores by Fleer. The cards measure the standard 2 1/2" by 3 1/2" and feature full color fronts and yellow, white, and black backs. The card fronts are distinguished by their yellow frame around the player's full-color photo. The box for the cards describes the set as the "1987 Limited Edition Baseball's Award Winners." The checklist for the set is given on the back of the set box. The card numbering is in alphabetical order by player's name.

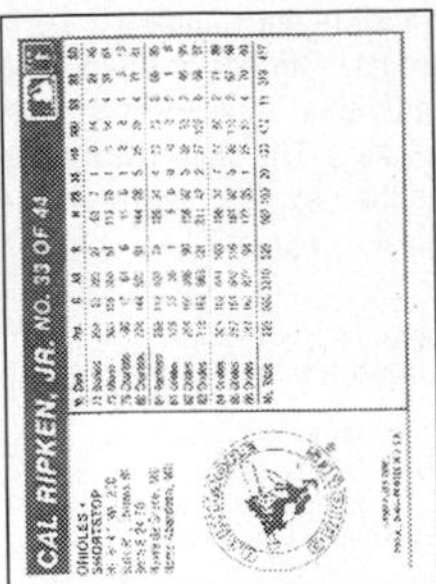

	MT	EX-MT	VG
COMPLETE SET (44)	4.00	1.80	.50
COMMON PLAYER (1-44)	.10	.05	.01
☐ 1 Marty Barrett	.10	.05	.01
☐ 2 George Bell	.15	.07	.02
☐ 3 Bert Blyleven	.15	.07	.02
☐ 4 Bob Boone	.15	.07	.02
☐ 5 John Candelaria	.10	.05	.01
☐ 6 Jose Canseco	.75	.35	.09
☐ 7 Gary Carter	.25	.11	.03
☐ 8 Joe Carter	.40	.18	.05
☐ 9 Roger Clemens	1.00	.45	.13
☐ 10 Cecil Cooper	.10	.05	.01
☐ 11 Eric Davis	.25	.11	.03
☐ 12 Tony Fernandez	.15	.07	.02
☐ 13 Scott Fletcher	.10	.05	.01
☐ 14 Bob Forsch	.10	.05	.01
☐ 15 Dwight Gooden	.25	.11	.03
☐ 16 Ron Guidry	.15	.07	.02
☐ 17 Ozzie Guillen	.15	.07	.02
☐ 18 Bill Gullickson	.15	.07	.02
☐ 19 Tony Gwynn	.75	.35	.09
☐ 20 Bob Knepper	.10	.05	.01
☐ 21 Ray Knight	.15	.07	.02
☐ 22 Mark Langston	.15	.07	.02
☐ 23 Candy Maldonado	.10	.05	.01
☐ 24 Don Mattingly	.75	.35	.09
☐ 25 Roger McDowell	.10	.05	.01
☐ 26 Dale Murphy	.35	.16	.04
☐ 27 Dave Parker	.20	.09	.03
☐ 28 Lance Parrish	.15	.07	.02
☐ 29 Gary Pettis	.10	.05	.01
☐ 30 Kirby Puckett	.75	.35	.09
☐ 31 Johnny Ray	.10	.05	.01
☐ 32 Dave Righetti	.10	.05	.01
☐ 33 Cal Ripken	1.00	.45	.13
☐ 34 Bret Saberhagen	.20	.09	.03
☐ 35 Ryne Sandberg	1.00	.45	.13
☐ 36 Mike Schmidt	.75	.35	.09
☐ 37 Mike Scott	.15	.07	.02
☐ 38 Ozzie Smith	.35	.16	.04
☐ 39 Robby Thompson	.10	.05	.01
☐ 40 Fernando Valenzuela	.15	.07	.02
☐ 41 Mitch Webster UER (Mike on front)	.10	.05	.01
☐ 42 Frank White	.10	.05	.01
☐ 43 Mike Witt	.10	.05	.01
☐ 44 Todd Worrell	.20	.09	.03

1987 Fleer Baseball All-Stars

This small set of 44 cards was produced for Ben Franklin stores by Fleer. The cards measure the standard 2 1/2" by 3 1/2" and feature full color fronts and red, white, and blue backs. The card fronts are easily distinguished by their white vertical stripes over a bright red background. The box for the cards proclaims "Limited Edition Baseball All-Stars" and is styled in the same manner and color scheme as the cards themselves. The checklist for the set is given on the back of the set box. The card numbering is in alphabetical order by player's name.

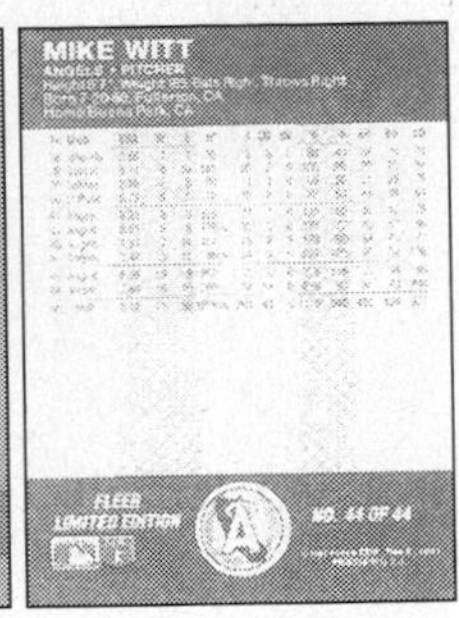

	MT	EX-MT	VG
COMPLETE SET (44)	5.00	2.30	.60
COMMON PLAYER (1-44)	.10	.05	.01
☐ 1 Harold Baines	.15	.07	.02
☐ 2 Jesse Barfield	.10	.05	.01
☐ 3 Wade Boggs	.60	.25	.08
☐ 4 Dennis Boyd	.10	.05	.01
☐ 5 Scott Bradley	.10	.05	.01
☐ 6 Jose Canseco	.75	.35	.09
☐ 7 Gary Carter	.25	.11	.03
☐ 8 Joe Carter	.40	.18	.05
☐ 9 Mark Clear	.10	.05	.01
☐ 10 Roger Clemens	1.00	.45	.13
☐ 11 Jose Cruz	.15	.07	.02
☐ 12 Chili Davis	.15	.07	.02
☐ 13 Jody Davis	.10	.05	.01
☐ 14 Rob Deer	.15	.07	.02
☐ 15 Brian Downing	.10	.05	.01
☐ 16 Sid Fernandez	.15	.07	.02
☐ 17 John Franco	.15	.07	.02
☐ 18 Andres Galarraga	.15	.07	.02
☐ 19 Dwight Gooden	.30	.14	.04
☐ 20 Tony Gwynn	.60	.25	.08
☐ 21 Charlie Hough	.10	.05	.01
☐ 22 Bruce Hurst	.15	.07	.02
☐ 23 Wally Joyner	.25	.11	.03
☐ 24 Carney Lansford	.15	.07	.02
☐ 25 Fred Lynn	.15	.07	.02
☐ 26 Don Mattingly	.75	.35	.09
☐ 27 Willie McGee	.15	.07	.02
☐ 28 Jack Morris	.25	.11	.03
☐ 29 Dale Murphy	.35	.16	.04
☐ 30 Bob Ojeda	.10	.05	.01
☐ 31 Tony Pena	.10	.05	.01
☐ 32 Kirby Puckett	.75	.35	.09
☐ 33 Dan Quisenberry	.15	.07	.02
☐ 34 Tim Raines	.15	.07	.02
☐ 35 Willie Randolph	.15	.07	.02
☐ 36 Cal Ripken	1.00	.45	.13
☐ 37 Pete Rose	.60	.25	.08
☐ 38 Nolan Ryan	1.50	.65	.19
☐ 39 Juan Samuel	.15	.07	.02
☐ 40 Mike Schmidt	.75	.35	.09
☐ 41 Ozzie Smith	.35	.16	.04
☐ 42 Andres Thomas	.10	.05	.01
☐ 43 Fernando Valenzuela	.15	.07	.02
☐ 44 Mike Witt	.10	.05	.01

1987 Fleer Exciting Stars

This small 44-card boxed set was produced by Fleer for distribution by the Cumberland Farm stores. The cards measure the standard 2 1/2" by 3 1/2" and feature full color fronts. The set is titled "Baseball's Exciting Stars." Each individual boxed set includes the 44 cards and six logo stickers. The checklist for the set is found on the back panel of the box. The card numbering is in alphabetical order by player's name.

	MT	EX-MT	VG
COMPLETE SET (44)	5.00	2.30	.60
COMMON PLAYER (1-44)	.10	.05	.01
☐ 1 Don Aase	.10	.05	.01

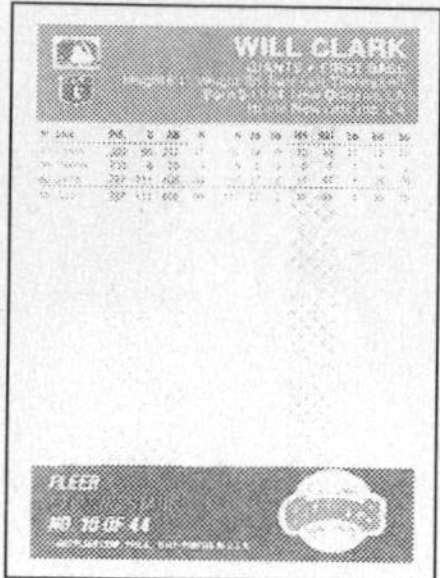

☐ 2 Rick Aguilera	.15	.07	.02
☐ 3 Jesse Barfield	.10	.05	.01
☐ 4 Wade Boggs	.60	.25	.08
☐ 5 Oil Can Boyd	.10	.05	.01
☐ 6 Sid Bream	.10	.05	.01
☐ 7 Jose Canseco	.75	.35	.09
☐ 8 Steve Carlton	.35	.16	.04
☐ 9 Gary Carter	.25	.11	.03
☐ 10 Will Clark	.75	.35	.09
☐ 11 Roger Clemens	1.00	.45	.13
☐ 12 Danny Cox	.10	.05	.01
☐ 13 Alvin Davis	.10	.05	.01
☐ 14 Eric Davis	.25	.11	.03
☐ 15 Rob Deer	.15	.07	.02
☐ 16 Brian Downing	.10	.05	.01
☐ 17 Gene Garber	.10	.05	.01
☐ 18 Steve Garvey	.30	.14	.04
☐ 19 Dwight Gooden	.25	.11	.03
☐ 20 Mark Gubicza	.10	.05	.01
☐ 21 Mel Hall	.15	.07	.02
☐ 22 Terry Harper	.10	.05	.01
☐ 23 Von Hayes	.10	.05	.01
☐ 24 Rickey Henderson	.60	.25	.08
☐ 25 Tom Henke	.15	.07	.02
☐ 26 Willie Hernandez	.10	.05	.01
☐ 27 Ted Higuera	.10	.05	.01
☐ 28 Rick Honeycutt	.10	.05	.01
☐ 29 Kent Hrbek	.15	.07	.02
☐ 30 Wally Joyner	.25	.11	.03
☐ 31 Charlie Kerfeld	.10	.05	.01
☐ 32 Fred Lynn	.15	.07	.02
☐ 33 Don Mattingly	.75	.35	.09
☐ 34 Tim Raines	.20	.09	.03
☐ 35 Dennis Rasmussen	.10	.05	.01
☐ 36 Johnny Ray	.10	.05	.01
☐ 37 Jim Rice	.20	.09	.03
☐ 38 Pete Rose	.60	.25	.08
☐ 39 Lee Smith	.20	.09	.03
☐ 40 Cory Snyder	.15	.07	.02
☐ 41 Darryl Strawberry	.60	.25	.08
☐ 42 Kent Tekulve	.10	.05	.01
☐ 43 Willie Wilson	.15	.07	.02
☐ 44 Bobby Witt	.15	.07	.02

1987 Fleer Game Winners

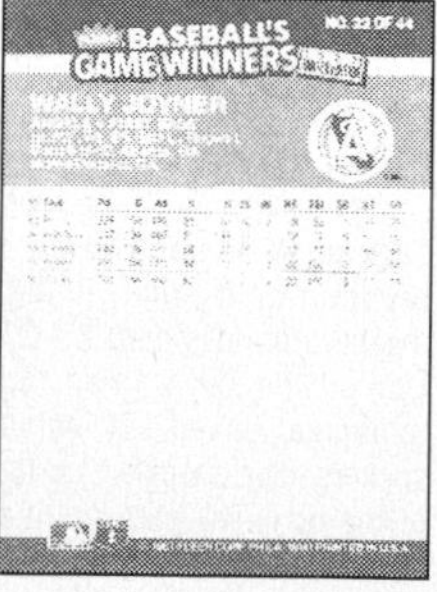

This small 44-card boxed set was produced by Fleer for distribution by several store chains, including Bi-Mart, Pay'n'Save, Mott's, M.E.Moses, and Winn's. The cards measure the standard 2 1/2" by 3 1/2" and feature full color fronts. The set is titled "Baseball's Game Winners." Each individual boxed set includes the 44 cards and six logo stickers. The checklist for the set is found on the back panel of the box. The card numbering is in alphabetical order by player's name.

	MT	EX-MT	VG
COMPLETE SET (44)	4.00	1.80	.50
COMMON PLAYER (1-44)	.10	.05	.01
☐ 1 Harold Baines	.15	.07	.02
☐ 2 Don Baylor	.20	.09	.03
☐ 3 George Bell	.20	.09	.03
☐ 4 Tony Bernazard	.10	.05	.01
☐ 5 Wade Boggs	.60	.25	.08
☐ 6 George Brett	.60	.25	.08
☐ 7 Hubie Brooks	.10	.05	.01
☐ 8 Jose Canseco	.75	.35	.09
☐ 9 Gary Carter	.25	.11	.03
☐ 10 Roger Clemens	1.00	.45	.13
☐ 11 Eric Davis	.25	.11	.03
☐ 12 Glenn Davis	.15	.07	.02
☐ 13 Shawon Dunston	.15	.07	.02
☐ 14 Mark Eichhorn	.10	.05	.01
☐ 15 Gary Gaetti	.10	.05	.01
☐ 16 Steve Garvey	.30	.14	.04
☐ 17 Kirk Gibson	.15	.07	.02
☐ 18 Dwight Gooden	.25	.11	.03
☐ 19 Von Hayes	.10	.05	.01
☐ 20 Willie Hernandez	.10	.05	.01
☐ 21 Ted Higuera	.10	.05	.01
☐ 22 Wally Joyner	.25	.11	.03
☐ 23 Bob Knepper	.10	.05	.01
☐ 24 Mike Krukow	.10	.05	.01
☐ 25 Jeff Leonard	.10	.05	.01
☐ 26 Don Mattingly	.75	.35	.09
☐ 27 Kirk McCaskill	.10	.05	.01
☐ 28 Kevin McReynolds	.15	.07	.02
☐ 29 Jim Morrison	.10	.05	.01
☐ 30 Dale Murphy	.35	.16	.04
☐ 31 Pete O'Brien	.10	.05	.01
☐ 32 Bob Ojeda	.10	.05	.01
☐ 33 Larry Parrish	.10	.05	.01
☐ 34 Ken Phelps	.10	.05	.01
☐ 35 Dennis Rasmussen	.10	.05	.01
☐ 36 Ernest Riles	.10	.05	.01
☐ 37 Cal Ripken	1.00	.45	.13
☐ 38 Ron Robinson	.10	.05	.01
☐ 39 Steve Sax	.20	.09	.03
☐ 40 Mike Schmidt	.75	.35	.09
☐ 41 John Tudor	.10	.05	.01
☐ 42 Fernando Valenzuela	.10	.05	.01
☐ 43 Mike Witt	.10	.05	.01
☐ 44 Curt Young	.10	.05	.01

1987 Fleer Headliners

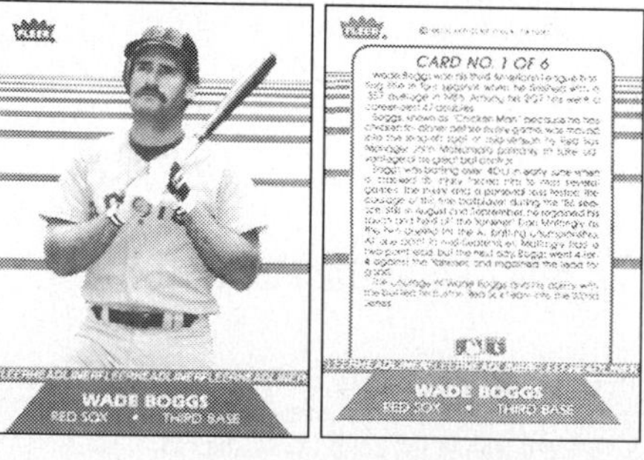

This six-card set was distributed as a special insert in rack packs as well as with three-pack wax pack rack packs. The obverse features the player photo against a beige background with irregular red stripes. The cards measure 2 1/2" by 3 1/2". The cards are numbered on the back. The checklist below also lists each player's team affiliation.

	MT	EX-MT	VG
COMPLETE SET (6)	7.50	3.40	.95
COMMON PLAYER (1-6)	.60	.25	.08
☐ 1 Wade Boggs	1.50	.65	.19
☐ 2 Jose Canseco	2.50	1.15	.30
☐ 3 Dwight Gooden	1.00	.45	.13
☐ 4 Rickey Henderson	2.00	.90	.25
☐ 5 Keith Hernandez	.60	.25	.08
☐ 6 Jim Rice	.60	.25	.08

1987 Fleer Hottest Stars

This 44-card boxed set was produced by Fleer for distribution by Revco stores all over the country. The cards measure the standard 2 1/2" by 3 1/2" and feature full color fronts and red, white, and black backs. The card fronts are easily distinguished by their solid red outside borders and and white and blue inner borders framing the player's picture. The box for the cards proclaims "1987 Limited Edition Baseball's Hottest Stars" and is styled in the same manner and color scheme as the cards themselves. The checklist for the set is given on the back of the set box. The card numbering is in alphabetical order by player's name.

	MT	EX-MT	VG
COMPLETE SET (44)	6.00	2.70	.75
COMMON PLAYER (1-44)	.10	.05	.01
☐ 1 Joaquin Andujar	.10	.05	.01
☐ 2 Harold Baines	.15	.07	.02
☐ 3 Kevin Bass	.10	.05	.01
☐ 4 Don Baylor	.20	.09	.03
☐ 5 Barry Bonds	1.25	.55	.16
☐ 6 George Brett	.60	.25	.08
☐ 7 Tom Brunansky	.15	.07	.02
☐ 8 Brett Butler	.15	.07	.02
☐ 9 Jose Canseco	1.00	.45	.13
☐ 10 Roger Clemens	1.00	.45	.13
☐ 11 Ron Darling	.20	.09	.03
☐ 12 Eric Davis	.25	.11	.03
☐ 13 Andre Dawson	.35	.16	.04
☐ 14 Doug DeCinces	.10	.05	.01
☐ 15 Leon Durham	.10	.05	.01
☐ 16 Mark Eichhorn	.10	.05	.01
☐ 17 Scott Garrelts	.10	.05	.01
☐ 18 Dwight Gooden	.30	.14	.04
☐ 19 Dave Henderson	.10	.05	.01
☐ 20 Rickey Henderson	.75	.35	.09
☐ 21 Keith Hernandez	.15	.07	.02
☐ 22 Ted Higuera	.10	.05	.01
☐ 23 Bob Horner	.10	.05	.01
☐ 24 Pete Incaviglia	.20	.09	.03
☐ 25 Wally Joyner	.35	.16	.04
☐ 26 Mark Langston	.20	.09	.03
☐ 27 Don Mattingly UER (Pirates logo on back)	1.00	.45	.13
☐ 28 Dale Murphy	.35	.16	.04
☐ 29 Kirk McCaskill	.10	.05	.01
☐ 30 Willie McGee	.15	.07	.02
☐ 31 Dave Righetti	.10	.05	.01
☐ 32 Pete Rose	.60	.25	.08
☐ 33 Bruce Ruffin	.10	.05	.01
☐ 34 Steve Sax	.20	.09	.03
☐ 35 Mike Schmidt	.75	.35	.09
☐ 36 Larry Sheets	.10	.05	.01
☐ 37 Eric Show	.10	.05	.01
☐ 38 Dave Smith	.10	.05	.01
☐ 39 Cory Snyder	.15	.07	.02
☐ 40 Frank Tanana	.10	.05	.01
☐ 41 Alan Trammell	.20	.09	.03
☐ 42 Reggie Williams	.10	.05	.01
☐ 43 Mookie Wilson	.10	.05	.01
☐ 44 Todd Worrell	.20	.09	.03

1987 Fleer League Leaders

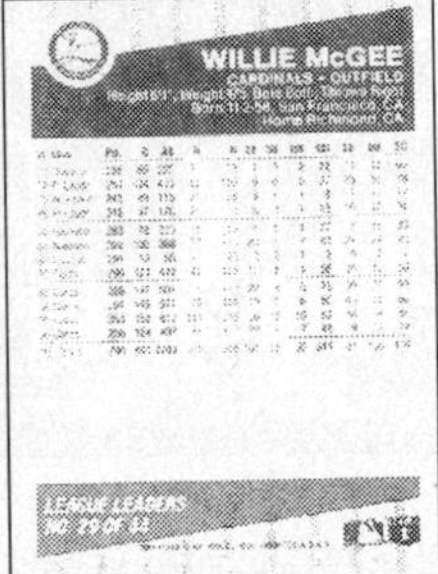

This small set of 44 cards was produced for Walgreens by Fleer. The cards measure the standard 2 1/2" by 3 1/2" and feature full color fronts and red, white, and blue backs. The card fronts are easily distinguished by their light blue vertical stripes over a white background. The box for the cards proclaims a "Walgreens Exclusive" and is styled in the same manner and color scheme as the cards themselves. The checklist for the set is given on the back of the set box. The card numbering is in alphabetical order by player's name.

	MT	EX-MT	VG
COMPLETE SET (44)	5.00	2.30	.60
COMMON PLAYER (1-44)	.10	.05	.01
☐ 1 Jesse Barfield	.10	.05	.01
☐ 2 Mike Boddicker	.10	.05	.01
☐ 3 Wade Boggs	.60	.25	.08
☐ 4 Phil Bradley	.10	.05	.01
☐ 5 George Brett	.60	.25	.08
☐ 6 Hubie Brooks	.10	.05	.01
☐ 7 Chris Brown	.10	.05	.01
☐ 8 Jose Canseco	.75	.35	.09
☐ 9 Joe Carter	.40	.18	.05
☐ 10 Roger Clemens	1.00	.45	.13
☐ 11 Vince Coleman	.25	.11	.03
☐ 12 Joe Cowley	.10	.05	.01
☐ 13 Kal Daniels	.15	.07	.02
☐ 14 Glenn Davis	.20	.09	.03
☐ 15 Jody Davis	.10	.05	.01
☐ 16 Darrell Evans	.10	.05	.01
☐ 17 Dwight Evans	.15	.07	.02
☐ 18 John Franco	.15	.07	.02
☐ 19 Julio Franco	.20	.09	.03
☐ 20 Dwight Gooden	.30	.14	.04
☐ 21 Rich Gossage	.15	.07	.02
☐ 22 Tom Herr	.10	.05	.01
☐ 23 Ted Higuera	.10	.05	.01
☐ 24 Bob Horner	.10	.05	.01
☐ 25 Pete Incaviglia	.20	.09	.03
☐ 26 Wally Joyner	.35	.16	.04
☐ 27 Dave Kingman	.15	.07	.02
☐ 28 Don Mattingly	.75	.35	.09
☐ 29 Willie McGee	.15	.07	.02
☐ 30 Donnie Moore	.10	.05	.01
☐ 31 Keith Moreland	.10	.05	.01
☐ 32 Eddie Murray	.40	.18	.05
☐ 33 Mike Pagliarulo	.10	.05	.01
☐ 34 Larry Parrish	.10	.05	.01
☐ 35 Tony Pena	.10	.05	.01
☐ 36 Kirby Puckett	.75	.35	.09
☐ 37 Pete Rose	.60	.25	.08
☐ 38 Juan Samuel	.15	.07	.02
☐ 39 Ryne Sandberg	.90	.40	.11

		MT	EX-MT	VG
☐ 40	Mike Schmidt	.75	.35	.09
☐ 41	Darryl Strawberry	.50	.23	.06
☐ 42	Greg Walker	.10	.05	.01
☐ 43	Bob Welch	.15	.07	.02
☐ 44	Todd Worrell	.15	.07	.02

1987 Fleer Limited Edition

This 44-card boxed set was (mass) produced by Fleer for distribution by McCrory's and is sometimes referred to as the McCrory's set. The numerical checklist on the back of the box shows that the set is numbered alphabetically. The cards measure 2 1/2" by 3 1/2".

		MT	EX-MT	VG
COMPLETE SET (44)		4.00	1.80	.50
COMMON PLAYER (1-44)		.10	.05	.01
☐ 1	Floyd Bannister	.10	.05	.01
☐ 2	Marty Barrett	.10	.05	.01
☐ 3	Steve Bedrosian	.10	.05	.01
☐ 4	George Bell	.20	.09	.03
☐ 5	George Brett	.60	.25	.08
☐ 6	Jose Canseco	.75	.35	.09
☐ 7	Joe Carter	.40	.18	.05
☐ 8	Will Clark	.75	.35	.09
☐ 9	Roger Clemens	1.00	.45	.13
☐ 10	Vince Coleman	.25	.11	.03
☐ 11	Glenn Davis	.20	.09	.03
☐ 12	Mike Davis	.10	.05	.01
☐ 13	Len Dykstra	.15	.07	.02
☐ 14	John Franco	.15	.07	.02
☐ 15	Julio Franco	.20	.09	.03
☐ 16	Steve Garvey	.30	.14	.04
☐ 17	Kirk Gibson	.15	.07	.02
☐ 18	Dwight Gooden	.30	.14	.04
☐ 19	Tony Gwynn	.60	.25	.08
☐ 20	Keith Hernandez	.15	.07	.02
☐ 21	Teddy Higuera	.10	.05	.01
☐ 22	Kent Hrbek	.15	.07	.02
☐ 23	Wally Joyner	.25	.11	.03
☐ 24	Mike Krukow	.10	.05	.01
☐ 25	Mike Marshall	.10	.05	.01
☐ 26	Don Mattingly	.75	.35	.09
☐ 27	Oddibe McDowell	.10	.05	.01
☐ 28	Jack Morris	.25	.11	.03
☐ 29	Lloyd Moseby	.10	.05	.01
☐ 30	Dale Murphy	.35	.16	.04
☐ 31	Eddie Murray	.40	.18	.05
☐ 32	Tony Pena	.10	.05	.01
☐ 33	Jim Presley	.10	.05	.01
☐ 34	Jeff Reardon	.20	.09	.03
☐ 35	Jim Rice	.20	.09	.03
☐ 36	Pete Rose	.60	.25	.08
☐ 37	Mike Schmidt	.75	.35	.09
☐ 38	Mike Scott	.10	.05	.01
☐ 39	Lee Smith	.20	.09	.03
☐ 40	Lonnie Smith	.10	.05	.01
☐ 41	Gary Ward	.10	.05	.01
☐ 42	Dave Winfield	.50	.23	.06
☐ 43	Todd Worrell	.20	.09	.03
☐ 44	Robin Yount	.60	.25	.08

1987 Fleer Limited Box Cards

The cards in this six-card set each measure the standard 2 1/2" by 3 1/2". Cards have essentially the same design as the 1987 Fleer Limited Edition cards which were distributed by McCrory's. The cards were printed on the bottom of the counter display box which held 24 small boxed sets; hence theoretically these box cards are 1/24 as plentiful as the regular boxed set cards. These six cards, numbered C1 to C6, are considered a separate set in their own right and are not typically included in a complete set of the 1987 Fleer Limited Edition set of 44. The value of the panels uncut is slightly greater, perhaps by 25 percent greater, than the value of the individual cards cut up carefully.

		MT	EX-MT	VG
COMPLETE SET (6)		2.50	1.15	.30
COMMON PLAYERS (C1-C6)		.25	.11	.03
☐ C1	Ron Darling	.50	.23	.06
☐ C2	Bill Buckner	.35	.16	.04
☐ C3	John Candelaria	.25	.11	.03
☐ C4	Jack Clark	.35	.16	.04
☐ C5	Bret Saberhagen	1.00	.45	.13
☐ C6	Team Logo (Checklist back)	.25	.11	.03

1987 Fleer Mini

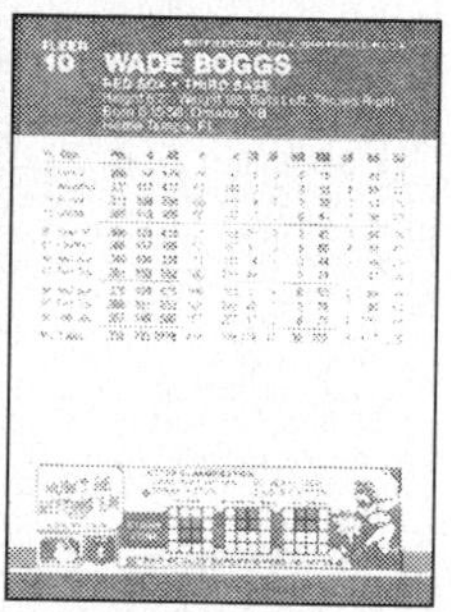

The 1987 Fleer "Classic Miniatures" set consists of 120 small cards with all new pictures of the players as compared to the 1987 Fleer regular issue. The cards are only 1 13/16" by 2 9/16", making them one of the smallest cards available. Card backs provide career year-by-year statistics. The complete set was distributed in a blue, red, white, and silver box along with 18 logo stickers. The card numbering is by alphabetical order.

	MT	EX-MT	VG
COMPLETE SET (120)	7.50	3.40	.95
COMMON PLAYER (1-120)	.05	.02	.01

☐ 1 Don Aase	.05	.02	.01
☐ 2 Joaquin Andujar	.05	.02	.01
☐ 3 Harold Baines	.08	.04	.01
☐ 4 Jesse Barfield	.08	.04	.01
☐ 5 Kevin Bass	.05	.02	.01
☐ 6 Don Baylor	.10	.05	.01
☐ 7 George Bell	.15	.07	.02
☐ 8 Tony Bernazard	.05	.02	.01
☐ 9 Bert Blyleven	.10	.05	.01
☐ 10 Wade Boggs	.60	.25	.08
☐ 11 Phil Bradley	.05	.02	.01
☐ 12 Sid Bream	.05	.02	.01
☐ 13 George Brett	.60	.25	.08
☐ 14 Hubie Brooks	.05	.02	.01
☐ 15 Chris Brown	.05	.02	.01
☐ 16 Tom Candiotti	.08	.04	.01
☐ 17 Jose Canseco	.75	.35	.09
☐ 18 Gary Carter	.20	.09	.03
☐ 19 Joe Carter	.30	.14	.04
☐ 20 Roger Clemens	.90	.40	.11
☐ 21 Vince Coleman	.15	.07	.02
☐ 22 Cecil Cooper	.08	.04	.01
☐ 23 Ron Darling	.10	.05	.01
☐ 24 Alvin Davis	.05	.02	.01
☐ 25 Chili Davis	.08	.04	.01
☐ 26 Eric Davis	.20	.09	.03
☐ 27 Glenn Davis	.15	.07	.02
☐ 28 Mike Davis	.05	.02	.01
☐ 29 Doug DeCinces	.05	.02	.01
☐ 30 Rob Deer	.08	.04	.01
☐ 31 Jim Deshaies	.05	.02	.01
☐ 32 Bo Diaz	.05	.02	.01
☐ 33 Richard Dotson	.05	.02	.01
☐ 34 Brian Downing	.08	.04	.01
☐ 35 Shawon Dunston	.10	.05	.01
☐ 36 Mark Eichhorn	.05	.02	.01
☐ 37 Dwight Evans	.08	.04	.01
☐ 38 Tony Fernandez	.08	.04	.01
☐ 39 Julio Franco	.15	.07	.02
☐ 40 Gary Gaetti	.05	.02	.01
☐ 41 Andres Galarraga	.15	.07	.02
☐ 42 Scott Garrelts	.05	.02	.01
☐ 43 Steve Garvey	.20	.09	.03
☐ 44 Kirk Gibson	.15	.07	.02
☐ 45 Dwight Gooden	.25	.11	.03
☐ 46 Ken Griffey Sr.	.08	.04	.01
☐ 47 Mark Gubicza	.08	.04	.01
☐ 48 Ozzie Guillen	.12	.05	.02
☐ 49 Bill Gullickson	.08	.04	.01
☐ 50 Tony Gwynn	.60	.25	.08
☐ 51 Von Hayes	.05	.02	.01
☐ 52 Rickey Henderson	.60	.25	.08
☐ 53 Keith Hernandez	.12	.05	.02
☐ 54 Willie Hernandez	.05	.02	.01
☐ 55 Ted Higuera	.05	.02	.01
☐ 56 Charlie Hough	.05	.02	.01
☐ 57 Kent Hrbek	.10	.05	.01
☐ 58 Pete Incaviglia	.12	.05	.02
☐ 59 Wally Joyner	.25	.11	.03
☐ 60 Bob Knepper	.05	.02	.01
☐ 61 Mike Krukow	.05	.02	.01
☐ 62 Mark Langston	.12	.05	.02
☐ 63 Carney Lansford	.08	.04	.01
☐ 64 Jim Lindeman	.05	.02	.01
☐ 65 Bill Madlock	.05	.02	.01
☐ 66 Don Mattingly	.75	.35	.09
☐ 67 Kirk McCaskill	.05	.02	.01
☐ 68 Lance McCullers	.05	.02	.01
☐ 69 Keith Moreland	.05	.02	.01
☐ 70 Jack Morris	.15	.07	.02
☐ 71 Jim Morrison	.05	.02	.01
☐ 72 Lloyd Moseby	.05	.02	.01
☐ 73 Jerry Mumphrey	.05	.02	.01
☐ 74 Dale Murphy	.35	.16	.04
☐ 75 Eddie Murray	.40	.18	.05
☐ 76 Pete O'Brien	.05	.02	.01
☐ 77 Bob Ojeda	.05	.02	.01
☐ 78 Jesse Orosco	.05	.02	.01
☐ 79 Dan Pasqua	.05	.02	.01
☐ 80 Dave Parker	.15	.07	.02
☐ 81 Larry Parrish	.05	.02	.01
☐ 82 Jim Presley	.05	.02	.01
☐ 83 Kirby Puckett	.75	.35	.09
☐ 84 Dan Quisenberry	.10	.05	.01
☐ 85 Tim Raines	.15	.07	.02
☐ 86 Dennis Rasmussen	.05	.02	.01
☐ 87 Johnny Ray	.05	.02	.01
☐ 88 Jeff Reardon	.15	.07	.02
☐ 89 Jim Rice	.20	.09	.03
☐ 90 Dave Righetti	.08	.04	.01
☐ 91 Earnest Riles	.05	.02	.01
☐ 92 Cal Ripken	1.00	.45	.13
☐ 93 Ron Robinson	.05	.02	.01
☐ 94 Juan Samuel	.08	.04	.01
☐ 95 Ryne Sandberg	.90	.40	.11
☐ 96 Steve Sax	.12	.05	.02
☐ 97 Mike Schmidt	.75	.35	.09
☐ 98 Ken Schrom	.05	.02	.01
☐ 99 Mike Scott	.05	.02	.01
☐ 100 Ruben Sierra	.75	.35	.09
☐ 101 Lee Smith	.15	.07	.02
☐ 102 Ozzie Smith	.25	.11	.03
☐ 103 Cory Snyder	.08	.04	.01
☐ 104 Kent Tekulve	.05	.02	.01
☐ 105 Andres Thomas	.05	.02	.01
☐ 106 Robby Thompson	.08	.04	.01
☐ 107 Alan Trammell	.15	.07	.02
☐ 108 John Tudor	.08	.04	.01
☐ 109 Fernando Valenzuela	.10	.05	.01
☐ 110 Greg Walker	.05	.02	.01
☐ 111 Mitch Webster	.05	.02	.01
☐ 112 Lou Whitaker	.15	.07	.02
☐ 113 Frank White	.05	.02	.01
☐ 114 Reggie Williams	.05	.02	.01
☐ 115 Glenn Wilson	.05	.02	.01
☐ 116 Willie Wilson	.08	.04	.01
☐ 117 Dave Winfield	.40	.18	.05
☐ 118 Mike Witt	.05	.02	.01
☐ 119 Todd Worrell	.10	.05	.01
☐ 120 Floyd Youmans	.05	.02	.01

1987 Fleer Record Setters

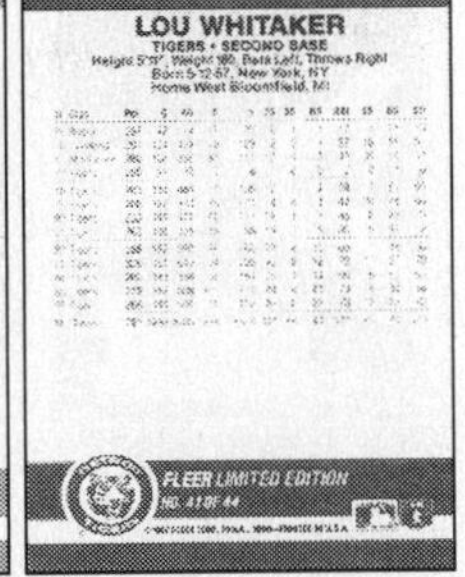

This 44-card boxed set was produced by Fleer for distribution by Eckerd's Drug Stores and is sometimes referred to as the Eckerd's set. Six team logo stickers are included in the box with the complete set. The numerical checklist on the back of the box shows that the set is numbered alphabetically. The cards measure 2 1/2" by 3 1/2".

	MT	EX-MT	VG
COMPLETE SET (44)	5.00	2.30	.60
COMMON PLAYER (1-44)	.10	.05	.01
☐ 1 George Brett	.60	.25	.08
☐ 2 Chris Brown	.10	.05	.01
☐ 3 Jose Canseco UER (3 of 444 on back)	.75	.35	.09
☐ 4 Roger Clemens	.90	.40	.11
☐ 5 Alvin Davis UER (5 of 441 on back, upside down one)	.10	.05	.01
☐ 6 Shawon Dunston	.15	.07	.02
☐ 7 Tony Fernandez	.15	.07	.02
☐ 8 Carlton Fisk UER (8 of 44' on back)	.40	.18	.05
☐ 9 Gary Gaetti UER (9 of 444 on back)	.15	.07	.02
☐ 10 Gene Garber	.10	.05	.01
☐ 11 Rich Gedman	.10	.05	.01
☐ 12 Dwight Gooden	.30	.14	.04
☐ 13 Ozzie Guillen	.15	.07	.02
☐ 14 Bill Gullickson	.15	.07	.02
☐ 15 Billy Hatcher	.10	.05	.01
☐ 16 Orel Hershiser	.25	.11	.03
☐ 17 Wally Joyner	.25	.11	.03
☐ 18 Ray Knight	.15	.07	.02
☐ 19 Craig Lefferts	.15	.07	.02
☐ 20 Don Mattingly	.75	.35	.09

		MT	EX-MT	VG
☐ 21	Kevin Mitchell	.50	.23	.06
☐ 22	Lloyd Moseby	.10	.05	.01
☐ 23	Dale Murphy	.35	.16	.04
☐ 24	Eddie Murray	.40	.18	.05
☐ 25	Phil Niekro	.20	.09	.03
☐ 26	Ben Oglivie	.10	.05	.01
☐ 27	Jesse Orosco	.10	.05	.01
☐ 28	Joe Orsulak	.10	.05	.01
☐ 29	Larry Parrish	.10	.05	.01
☐ 30	Tim Raines	.20	.09	.03
☐ 31	Shane Rawley	.10	.05	.01
☐ 32	Dave Righetti	.10	.05	.01
☐ 33	Pete Rose	.60	.25	.08
☐ 34	Steve Sax	.15	.07	.02
☐ 35	Mike Schmidt	.75	.35	.09
☐ 36	Mike Scott	.10	.05	.01
☐ 37	Don Sutton	.20	.09	.03
☐ 38	Alan Trammell	.20	.09	.03
☐ 39	John Tudor	.10	.05	.01
☐ 40	Gary Ward	.10	.05	.01
☐ 41	Lou Whitaker	.20	.09	.03
☐ 42	Willie Wilson	.15	.07	.02
☐ 43	Todd Worrell	.15	.07	.02
☐ 44	Floyd Youmans	.10	.05	.01

1987 Fleer Sluggers/Pitchers

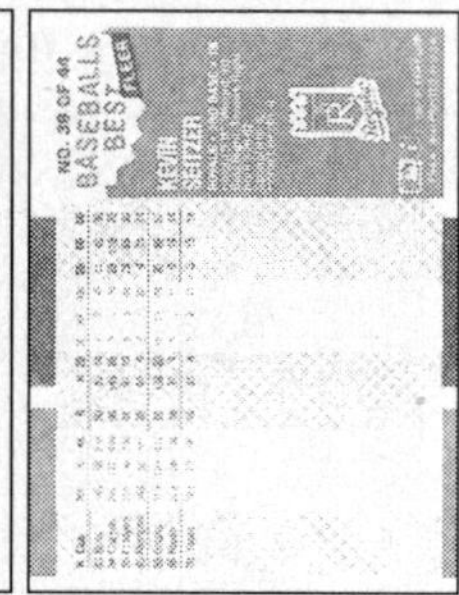

Fleer produced this 44-card boxed set although it was primarily distributed by McCrory, McLellan, Newberry, H.L.Green, T.G.Y., and other similar stores. The set features 28 sluggers and 16 pitchers and is subtitled "Baseball's Best". Cards are standard-size, 2 1/2" by 3 1/2", and were packaged in a red, white, blue, and yellow custom box along with six logo stickers. The set checklist is given on the back of the box. The checklist on the back of the set box misspells McGwire as McGuire. The card numbering is in alphabetical order by player's name.

		MT	EX-MT	VG
COMPLETE SET (44)		5.00	2.30	.60
COMMON PLAYER (1-44)		.10	.05	.01
☐ 1	Kevin Bass	.10	.05	.01
☐ 2	Jesse Barfield	.10	.05	.01
☐ 3	George Bell	.20	.09	.03
☐ 4	Wade Boggs	.60	.25	.08
☐ 5	Sid Bream	.10	.05	.01
☐ 6	George Brett	.60	.25	.08
☐ 7	Ivan Calderon	.15	.07	.02
☐ 8	Jose Canseco	.75	.35	.09
☐ 9	Jack Clark	.10	.05	.01
☐ 10	Roger Clemens	.90	.40	.11
☐ 11	Eric Davis	.25	.11	.03
☐ 12	Andre Dawson	.35	.16	.04
☐ 13	Sid Fernandez	.15	.07	.02
☐ 14	John Franco	.15	.07	.02
☐ 15	Dwight Gooden	.25	.11	.03
☐ 16	Pedro Guerrero	.15	.07	.02
☐ 17	Tony Gwynn	.50	.23	.06
☐ 18	Rickey Henderson	.60	.25	.08
☐ 19	Tom Henke	.20	.09	.03
☐ 20	Ted Higuera	.10	.05	.01
☐ 21	Pete Incaviglia	.20	.09	.03
☐ 22	Wally Joyner	.35	.16	.04
☐ 23	Jeff Leonard	.10	.05	.01
☐ 24	Joe Magrane	.10	.05	.01
☐ 25	Don Mattingly	.75	.35	.09
☐ 26	Mark McGwire	.75	.35	.09
☐ 27	Jack Morris	.20	.09	.03
☐ 28	Dale Murphy	.35	.16	.04
☐ 29	Dave Parker	.15	.07	.02
☐ 30	Ken Phelps	.10	.05	.01
☐ 31	Kirby Puckett	.75	.35	.09
☐ 32	Tim Raines	.20	.09	.03
☐ 33	Jeff Reardon	.20	.09	.03
☐ 34	Dave Righetti	.10	.05	.01
☐ 35	Cal Ripken	1.00	.45	.13
☐ 36	Bret Saberhagen	.25	.11	.03
☐ 37	Mike Schmidt	.75	.35	.09
☐ 38	Mike Scott	.10	.05	.01
☐ 39	Kevin Seitzer	.20	.09	.03
☐ 40	Darryl Strawberry	.60	.25	.08
☐ 41	Rick Sutcliffe	.15	.07	.02
☐ 42	Pat Tabler	.10	.05	.01
☐ 43	Fernando Valenzuela	.10	.05	.01
☐ 44	Mike Witt	.10	.05	.01

1987 Fleer Slug/Pitch Box Cards

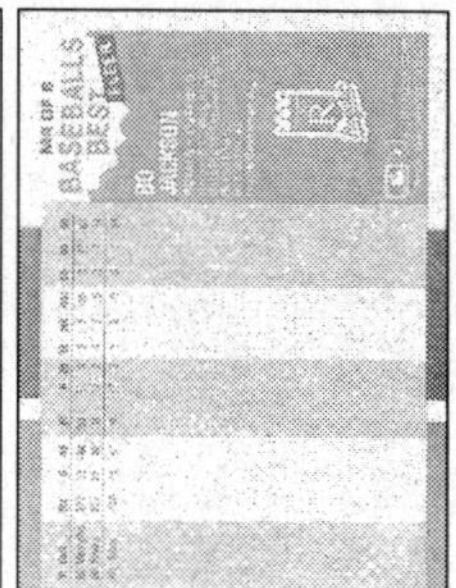

The cards in this six-card set each measure the standard 2 1/2" by 3 1/2". Cards have essentially the same design as the 1987 Fleer Sluggers vs. Pitchers set of Baseball's Best. The cards were printed on the bottom of the counter display box which held 24 small boxed sets; hence theoretically these box cards are 1/24 as plentiful as the regular boxed set cards. These six cards, numbered M1 to M5 with one blank-back (unnumbered) card, are considered a separate set in their own right and are not typically included in a complete set of the 1987 Fleer Sluggers vs. Pitchers set of 44. The value of the panels uncut is slightly greater, perhaps by 25 percent greater, than the value of the individual cards cut up carefully.

		MT	EX-MT	VG
COMPLETE SET (6)		7.00	3.10	.85
COMMON PLAYER		.25	.11	.03
☐ M1	Steve Bedrosian	.25	.11	.03
☐ M2	Will Clark	3.50	1.55	.45
☐ M3	Vince Coleman	.60	.25	.08
☐ M4	Bo Jackson	3.00	1.35	.40
☐ M5	Cory Snyder	.25	.11	.03
☐ NNO	Team Logo (Blank back)	.25	.11	.03

1987 Fleer Sticker Cards

These Star Stickers were distributed as a separate issue by Fleer with five star stickers and a logo sticker in each wax pack. The 132-card (sticker) set features 2 1/2" by 3 1/2" full-color fronts and even statistics on the sticker back, which is an indication that the Fleer Company understands that these stickers are rarely used as stickers but more like traditional cards. The card fronts are surrounded by a green

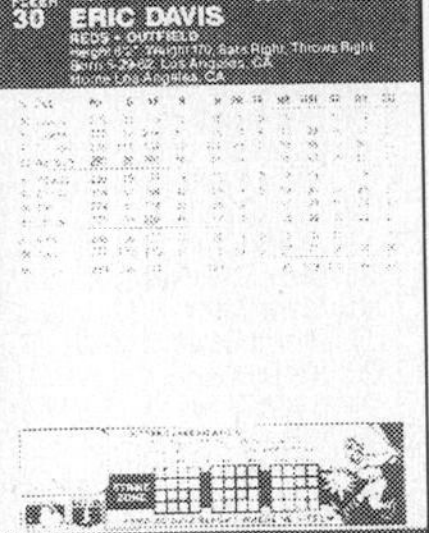

border and the backs are printed in green and yellow on white card stock. The card numbering is in alphabetical order by player's name.

	MT	EX-MT	VG
COMPLETE SET (132)	28.00	12.50	3.50
COMMON PLAYER (1-132)	.05	.02	.01
□ 1 Don Aase	.05	.02	.01
□ 2 Harold Baines	.08	.04	.01
□ 3 Floyd Bannister	.05	.02	.01
□ 4 Jesse Barfield	.05	.02	.01
□ 5 Marty Barrett	.05	.02	.01
□ 6 Kevin Bass	.05	.02	.01
□ 7 Don Baylor	.10	.05	.01
□ 8 Steve Bedrosian	.08	.04	.01
□ 9 George Bell	.15	.07	.02
□ 10 Bert Blyleven	.10	.05	.01
□ 11 Mike Boddicker	.08	.04	.01
□ 12 Wade Boggs	.90	.40	.11
□ 13 Phil Bradley	.05	.02	.01
□ 14 Sid Bream	.05	.02	.01
□ 15 George Brett	1.00	.45	.13
□ 16 Hubie Brooks	.05	.02	.01
□ 17 Tom Brunansky	.08	.04	.01
□ 18 Tom Candiotti	.08	.04	.01
□ 19 Jose Canseco	2.00	.90	.25
□ 20 Gary Carter	.35	.16	.04
□ 21 Joe Carter	.60	.25	.08
□ 22 Will Clark	2.00	.90	.25
□ 23 Mark Clear	.05	.02	.01
□ 24 Roger Clemens	1.50	.65	.19
□ 25 Vince Coleman	.25	.11	.03
□ 26 Jose Cruz	.08	.04	.01
□ 27 Ron Darling	.10	.05	.01
□ 28 Alvin Davis	.05	.02	.01
□ 29 Chili Davis	.08	.04	.01
□ 30 Eric Davis	.50	.23	.06
□ 31 Glenn Davis	.20	.09	.03
□ 32 Mike Davis	.05	.02	.01
□ 33 Andre Dawson	.40	.18	.05
□ 34 Doug DeCinces	.05	.02	.01
□ 35 Brian Downing	.05	.02	.01
□ 36 Shawon Dunston	.10	.05	.01
□ 37 Mark Eichhorn	.05	.02	.01
□ 38 Dwight Evans	.10	.05	.01
□ 39 Tony Fernandez	.10	.05	.01
□ 40 Bob Forsch	.05	.02	.01
□ 41 John Franco	.10	.05	.01
□ 42 Julio Franco	.15	.07	.02
□ 43 Gary Gaetti	.08	.04	.01
□ 44 Gene Garber	.05	.02	.01
□ 45 Scott Garrelts	.05	.02	.01
□ 46 Steve Garvey	.40	.18	.05
□ 47 Kirk Gibson	.15	.07	.02
□ 48 Dwight Gooden	.50	.23	.06
□ 49 Ken Griffey Sr.	.12	.05	.02
□ 50 Ozzie Guillen	.15	.07	.02
□ 51 Bill Gullickson	.08	.04	.01
□ 52 Tony Gwynn	.75	.35	.09
□ 53 Mel Hall	.10	.05	.01
□ 54 Greg A. Harris	.05	.02	.01
□ 55 Von Hayes	.05	.02	.01
□ 56 Rickey Henderson	1.25	.55	.16
□ 57 Tom Henke	.12	.05	.02
□ 58 Keith Hernandez	.12	.05	.02
□ 59 Willie Hernandez	.05	.02	.01
□ 60 Ted Higuera	.05	.02	.01
□ 61 Bob Horner	.08	.04	.01
□ 62 Charlie Hough	.05	.02	.01
□ 63 Jay Howell	.05	.02	.01
□ 64 Kent Hrbek	.10	.05	.01
□ 65 Bruce Hurst	.08	.04	.01
□ 66 Pete Incaviglia	.15	.07	.02
□ 67 Bob James	.05	.02	.01
□ 68 Wally Joyner	.75	.35	.09
□ 69 Mike Krukow	.05	.02	.01
□ 70 Mark Langston	.12	.05	.02
□ 71 Carney Lansford	.10	.05	.01
□ 72 Fred Lynn	.10	.05	.01
□ 73 Bill Madlock	.05	.02	.01
□ 74 Don Mattingly	1.25	.55	.16
□ 75 Kirk McCaskill	.05	.02	.01
□ 76 Lance McCullers	.05	.02	.01
□ 77 Oddibe McDowell	.05	.02	.01
□ 78 Paul Molitor	.25	.11	.03
□ 79 Keith Moreland	.05	.02	.01
□ 80 Jack Morris	.20	.09	.03
□ 81 Jim Morrison	.05	.02	.01
□ 82 Jerry Mumphrey	.05	.02	.01
□ 83 Dale Murphy	.40	.18	.05
□ 84 Eddie Murray	.50	.23	.06
□ 85 Ben Oglivie	.05	.02	.01
□ 86 Bob Ojeda	.08	.04	.01
□ 87 Jesse Orosco	.05	.02	.01
□ 88 Dave Parker	.12	.05	.02
□ 89 Larry Parrish	.05	.02	.01
□ 90 Tony Pena	.05	.02	.01
□ 91 Jim Presley	.08	.04	.01
□ 92 Kirby Puckett	1.50	.65	.19
□ 93 Dan Quisenberry	.10	.05	.01
□ 94 Tim Raines	.15	.07	.02
□ 95 Dennis Rasmussen	.05	.02	.01
□ 96 Shane Rawley	.05	.02	.01
□ 97 Johnny Ray	.05	.02	.01
□ 98 Jeff Reardon	.15	.07	.02
□ 99 Jim Rice	.20	.09	.03
□ 100 Dave Righetti	.08	.04	.01
□ 101 Cal Ripken Jr.	1.50	.65	.19
□ 102 Pete Rose	1.00	.45	.13
□ 103 Nolan Ryan	2.50	1.15	.30
□ 104 Juan Samuel	.08	.04	.01
□ 105 Ryne Sandberg	1.50	.65	.19
□ 106 Steve Sax	.12	.05	.02
□ 107 Mike Schmidt	1.25	.55	.16
□ 108 Mike Scott	.08	.04	.01
□ 109 Dave Smith	.05	.02	.01
□ 110 Lee Smith	.15	.07	.02
□ 111 Lonnie Smith	.08	.04	.01
□ 112 Ozzie Smith	.35	.16	.04
□ 113 Cory Snyder	.10	.05	.01
□ 114 Darryl Strawberry	.75	.35	.09
□ 115 Don Sutton	.20	.09	.03
□ 116 Kent Tekulve	.05	.02	.01
□ 117 Andres Thomas	.05	.02	.01
□ 118 Alan Trammell	.20	.09	.03
□ 119 John Tudor	.05	.02	.01
□ 120 Fernando Valenzuela	.08	.04	.01
□ 121 Bob Welch	.10	.05	.01
□ 122 Lou Whitaker	.15	.07	.02
□ 123 Frank White	.05	.02	.01
□ 124 Reggie Williams	.05	.02	.01
□ 125 Willie Wilson	.08	.04	.01
□ 126 Dave Winfield	.40	.18	.05
□ 127 Mike Witt	.05	.02	.01
□ 128 Todd Worrell	.10	.05	.01
□ 129 Curt Young	.05	.02	.01
□ 130 Robin Yount	1.00	.45	.13
□ 131 Checklist Jose Canseco Don Mattingly	1.50	.65	.19
□ 132 Checklist Bo Jackson Eric Davis	1.50	.65	.19

1987 Fleer Sticker Wax Box

The bottoms of the Star Sticker wax boxes contained two different sets of four cards done in a similar format to the stickers; these cards (they are not stickers but truly cards) are numbered with the prefix S and are considered a separate set. The value of the panels uncut is slightly greater, perhaps by 25 percent greater, than the value of the individual cards cut up carefully. When cut properly, the individual cards measure standard size, 2 1/2" by 3 1/2".

	MT	EX-MT	VG
COMPLETE SET (8)	5.00	2.30	.60
COMMON PLAYER (S1-S8)	.25	.11	.03

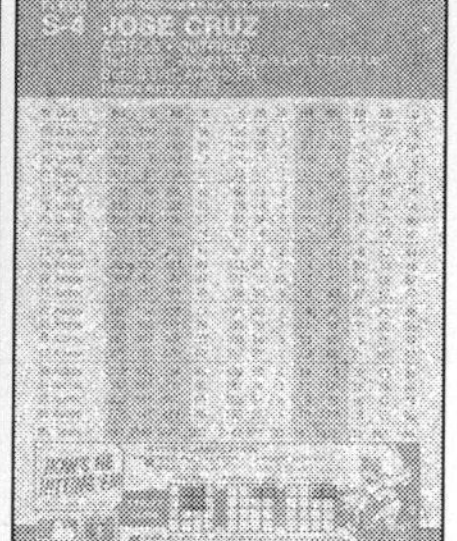

☐ S1	Detroit Logo	.25	.11	.03
☐ S2	Wade Boggs	1.50	.65	.19
☐ S3	Bert Blyleven	.45	.20	.06
☐ S4	Jose Cruz	.35	.16	.04
☐ S5	Glenn Davis	.45	.20	.06
☐ S6	Phillies Logo	.25	.11	.03
☐ S7	Bob Horner	.35	.16	.04
☐ S8	Don Mattingly	2.00	.90	.25

1987 Fleer Update

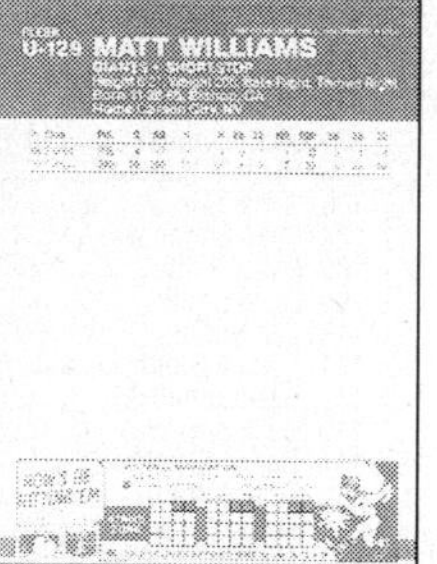

This 132-card set was distributed by Fleer to dealers as a complete set in a custom box. In addition to the complete set of 132 cards, the box also contains 25 Team Logo stickers.The card fronts look very similar to the 1987 Fleer regular issue. The cards are numbered (with a U prefix) alphabetically according to player's last name. Cards measure the standard size, 2 1/2" by 3 1/2". Fleer misalphabetized Jim Winn in their set numbering by putting him ahead of the next four players listed. The key (extended) Rookie Cards in this set are Ellis Burks, Mike Greenwell, Fred McGriff, Mark McGwire and Matt Williams. Fleer also produced a "limited" edition version of this set with glossy coating and packaged in a "tin." However, this glossy tin set was apparently not limited enough (estimated between 75,000 and 100,000 1987 Update tin sets produced by Fleer), since the values of the "tin" glossy cards are now the same as the values of the cards in the regular set.

		MT	EX-MT	VG
COMPLETE SET (132)		14.00	6.25	1.75
COMMON PLAYER (1-132)		.05	.02	.01
☐ 1	Scott Bankhead	.05	.02	.01
☐ 2	Eric Bell	.05	.02	.01
☐ 3	Juan Beniquez	.05	.02	.01
☐ 4	Juan Berenguer	.05	.02	.01
☐ 5	Mike Birkbeck	.05	.02	.01
☐ 6	Randy Bockus	.05	.02	.01
☐ 7	Rod Booker	.05	.02	.01
☐ 8	Thad Bosley	.05	.02	.01
☐ 9	Greg Brock	.05	.02	.01
☐ 10	Bob Brower	.05	.02	.01
☐ 11	Chris Brown	.05	.02	.01
☐ 12	Jerry Browne	.08	.04	.01
☐ 13	Ralph Bryant	.08	.04	.01
☐ 14	DeWayne Buice	.05	.02	.01
☐ 15	Ellis Burks	.75	.35	.09
☐ 16	Casey Candaele	.05	.02	.01
☐ 17	Steve Carlton	.40	.18	.05
☐ 18	Juan Castillo	.05	.02	.01
☐ 19	Chuck Crim	.05	.02	.01
☐ 20	Mark Davidson	.05	.02	.01
☐ 21	Mark Davis	.05	.02	.01
☐ 22	Storm Davis	.05	.02	.01
☐ 23	Bill Dawley	.05	.02	.01
☐ 24	Andre Dawson	.40	.18	.05
☐ 25	Brian Dayett	.05	.02	.01
☐ 26	Rick Dempsey	.05	.02	.01
☐ 27	Ken Dowell	.05	.02	.01
☐ 28	Dave Dravecky	.08	.04	.01
☐ 29	Mike Dunne	.05	.02	.01
☐ 30	Dennis Eckersley	.35	.16	.04
☐ 31	Cecil Fielder	1.50	.65	.19
☐ 32	Brian Fisher	.05	.02	.01
☐ 33	Willie Fraser	.05	.02	.01
☐ 34	Ken Gerhart	.05	.02	.01
☐ 35	Jim Gott	.05	.02	.01
☐ 36	Dan Gladden	.05	.02	.01
☐ 37	Mike Greenwell	.75	.35	.09
☐ 38	Cecilio Guante	.05	.02	.01
☐ 39	Albert Hall	.05	.02	.01
☐ 40	Atlee Hammaker	.05	.02	.01
☐ 41	Mickey Hatcher	.05	.02	.01
☐ 42	Mike Heath	.05	.02	.01
☐ 43	Neal Heaton	.05	.02	.01
☐ 44	Mike Henneman	.30	.14	.04
☐ 45	Guy Hoffman	.05	.02	.01
☐ 46	Charles Hudson	.05	.02	.01
☐ 47	Chuck Jackson	.05	.02	.01
☐ 48	Mike Jackson	.20	.09	.03
☐ 49	Reggie Jackson	.50	.23	.06
☐ 50	Chris James	.05	.02	.01
☐ 51	Dion James	.05	.02	.01
☐ 52	Stan Javier	.05	.02	.01
☐ 53	Stan Jefferson	.05	.02	.01
☐ 54	Jimmy Jones	.05	.02	.01
☐ 55	Tracy Jones	.05	.02	.01
☐ 56	Terry Kennedy	.05	.02	.01
☐ 57	Mike Kingery	.05	.02	.01
☐ 58	Ray Knight	.08	.04	.01
☐ 59	Gene Larkin	.20	.09	.03
☐ 60	Mike LaValliere	.08	.04	.01
☐ 61	Jack Lazorko	.05	.02	.01
☐ 62	Terry Leach	.05	.02	.01
☐ 63	Rick Leach	.05	.02	.01
☐ 64	Craig Lefferts	.05	.02	.01
☐ 65	Jim Lindeman	.05	.02	.01
☐ 66	Bill Long	.05	.02	.01
☐ 67	Mike Loynd	.05	.02	.01
☐ 68	Greg Maddux	4.00	1.80	.50
☐ 69	Bill Madlock	.08	.04	.01
☐ 70	Dave Magadan	.15	.07	.02
☐ 71	Joe Magrane	.15	.07	.02
☐ 72	Fred Manrique	.05	.02	.01
☐ 73	Mike Mason	.05	.02	.01
☐ 74	Lloyd McClendon	.05	.02	.01
☐ 75	Fred McGriff	3.50	1.55	.45
☐ 76	Mark McGwire	6.00	2.70	.75
☐ 77	Mark McLemore	.05	.02	.01
☐ 78	Kevin McReynolds	.08	.04	.01
☐ 79	Dave Meads	.05	.02	.01
☐ 80	Greg Minton	.05	.02	.01
☐ 81	John Mitchell	.05	.02	.01
☐ 82	Kevin Mitchell	.75	.35	.09
☐ 83	John Morris	.05	.02	.01
☐ 84	Jeff Musselman	.05	.02	.01
☐ 85	Randy Myers	.30	.14	.04
☐ 86	Gene Nelson	.05	.02	.01
☐ 87	Joe Niekro	.08	.04	.01
☐ 88	Tom Nieto	.05	.02	.01
☐ 89	Reid Nichols	.05	.02	.01
☐ 90	Matt Nokes	.35	.16	.04
☐ 91	Dickie Noles	.05	.02	.01
☐ 92	Edwin Nunez	.05	.02	.01
☐ 93	Jose Nunez	.05	.02	.01
☐ 94	Paul O'Neill	.30	.14	.04
☐ 95	Jim Paciorek	.05	.02	.01
☐ 96	Lance Parrish	.08	.04	.01
☐ 97	Bill Pecota	.12	.05	.02
☐ 98	Tony Pena	.05	.02	.01
☐ 99	Luis Polonia	.50	.23	.06
☐ 100	Randy Ready	.05	.02	.01
☐ 101	Jeff Reardon	.20	.09	.03
☐ 102	Gary Redus	.05	.02	.01
☐ 103	Rick Rhoden	.05	.02	.01

		MT	EX-MT	VG
☐ 104	Wally Ritchie	.05	.02	.01
☐ 105	Jeff Robinson UER (Wrong Jeff's stats on back)	.08	.04	.01
☐ 106	Mark Salas	.05	.02	.01
☐ 107	Dave Schmidt	.05	.02	.01
☐ 108	Kevin Seitzer UER (Wrong birth year)	.25	.11	.03
☐ 109	John Shelby	.05	.02	.01
☐ 110	John Smiley	1.00	.45	.13
☐ 111	Lary Sorensen	.05	.02	.01
☐ 112	Chris Speier	.05	.02	.01
☐ 113	Randy St.Claire	.05	.02	.01
☐ 114	Jim Sundberg	.05	.02	.01
☐ 115	B.J. Surhoff	.20	.09	.03
☐ 116	Greg Swindell	.75	.35	.09
☐ 117	Danny Tartabull	.40	.18	.05
☐ 118	Dorn Taylor	.05	.02	.01
☐ 119	Lee Tunnell	.05	.02	.01
☐ 120	Ed VandeBerg	.05	.02	.01
☐ 121	Andy Van Slyke	.30	.14	.04
☐ 122	Gary Ward	.05	.02	.01
☐ 123	Devon White	.35	.16	.04
☐ 124	Alan Wiggins	.05	.02	.01
☐ 125	Bill Wilkinson	.05	.02	.01
☐ 126	Jim Winn	.05	.02	.01
☐ 127	Frank Williams	.05	.02	.01
☐ 128	Ken Williams	.05	.02	.01
☐ 129	Matt Williams	2.25	1.00	.30
☐ 130	Herm Willingham	.05	.02	.01
☐ 131	Matt Young	.05	.02	.01
☐ 132	Checklist Card	.08	.01	.00

1987 Fleer Wax Box Cards

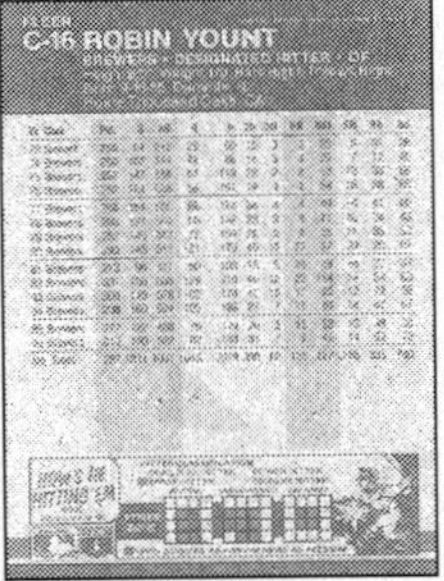

The cards in this 16-card set measure the standard, 2 1/2" by 3 1/2". Cards have essentially the same design as the 1987 Fleer regular issue set. The cards were printed on the bottoms of the regular issue wax pack boxes. These 16 cards (C1 to C16) are considered a separate set in their own right and are not typically included in a complete set of the regular issue 1987 Fleer cards. The value of the panel uncut is slightly greater, perhaps by 25 percent greater, than the value of the individual cards cut up carefully.

		MT	EX-MT	VG
COMPLETE SET (16)		9.00	4.00	1.15
COMMON CARDS (C1-C16)		.15	.07	.02
☐ C1	Mets Logo	.15	.07	.02
☐ C2	Jesse Barfield	.15	.07	.02
☐ C3	George Brett	1.25	.55	.16
☐ C4	Dwight Gooden	.75	.35	.09
☐ C5	Boston Logo	.15	.07	.02
☐ C6	Keith Hernandez	.25	.11	.03
☐ C7	Wally Joyner	1.00	.45	.13
☐ C8	Dale Murphy	.75	.35	.09
☐ C9	Astros Logo	.15	.07	.02
☐ C10	Dave Parker	.35	.16	.04
☐ C11	Kirby Puckett	1.50	.65	.19
☐ C12	Dave Righetti	.25	.11	.03
☐ C13	Angels Logo	.15	.07	.02
☐ C14	Ryne Sandberg	1.50	.65	.19
☐ C15	Mike Schmidt	1.25	.55	.16
☐ C16	Robin Yount	1.25	.55	.16

1987 Fleer World Series

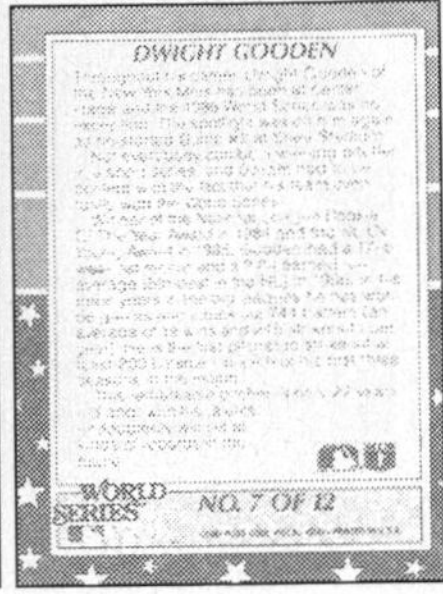

This 12-card set of 2 1/2" by 3 1/2" cards features highlights of the previous year's World Series between the Mets and the Red Sox. The sets were packaged as a complete set insert with the collated sets (of the 1987 Fleer regular issue) which were sold by Fleer directly to hobby card dealers; they were not available in the general retail candy store outlets. The set was also available in a glossy version packaged with the "tin" sets; no extra value is associated with these glossy World Series cards.

		MT	EX-MT	VG
COMPLETE SET (12)		4.00	1.80	.50
COMMON PLAYER (1-12)		.25	.11	.03
☐ 1	Bruce Hurst Left Hand Finesse Beats Mets	.35	.16	.04
☐ 2	Keith Hernandez and Wade Boggs	.50	.23	.06
☐ 3	Roger Clemens HOR	1.50	.65	.19
☐ 4	Clutch Hitting (Gary Carter)	.50	.23	.06
☐ 5	Ron Darling Picks Up Slack	.35	.16	.04
☐ 6	Marty Barrett .433 Series BA	.25	.11	.03
☐ 7	Dwight Gooden	.50	.23	.06
☐ 8	Strategy at Work (Mets Conference)	.25	.11	.03
☐ 9	Dewey Evans (Congratulated by Rich Gedman)	.35	.16	.04
☐ 10	One Strike From Boston Victory (Dave Henderson)	.35	.16	.04
☐ 11	Series Home Run Duo (Ray Knight and Darryl Strawberry)	.60	.25	.08
☐ 12	Ray Knight (Series MVP)	.35	.16	.04

1988 Fleer

This 660-card set features a distinctive white background with red and blue diagonal stripes across the card. The backs are printed in gray and red on white card stock. The bottom of the card back shows an innovative breakdown of the player's demonstrated ability with respect to day, night, home, and road games. Cards are numbered on the back and are again the standard 2 1/2" by 3 1/2". Cards are again organized numerically by teams, i.e., World Champion Twins (1-25), St. Louis Cardinals (26-50), Detroit Tigers (51-75), San Francisco Giants (76-101), Toronto Blue Jays (102-126), New York Mets (127-154), Milwaukee Brewers (155-178), Montreal Expos (179-201), New York Yankees (202-226), Cincinnati Reds (227-250), Kansas City Royals (251-274), Oakland A's (275-296), Philadelphia Phillies (297-

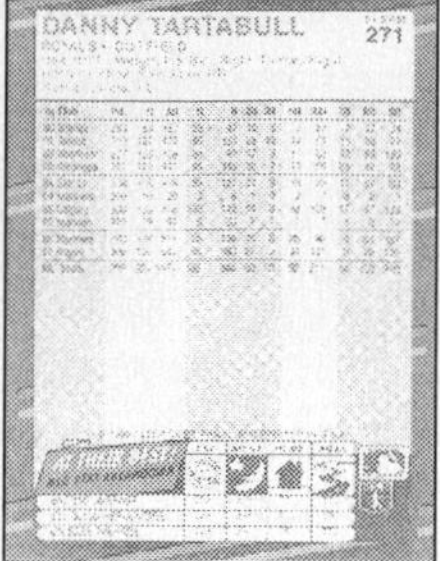

320), Pittsburgh Pirates (321-342), Boston Red Sox (343-367), Seattle Mariners (368-390), Chicago White Sox (391-413), Chicago Cubs (414-436), Houston Astros (437-460), Texas Rangers (461-483), California Angels (484-507), Los Angeles Dodgers (508-530), Atlanta Braves (531-552), Baltimore Orioles (553-575), San Diego Padres (576-599), and Cleveland Indians (600-621). The last 39 cards in the set consist of Specials (622-640), Rookie Pairs (641-653), and checklists (654-660). Cards 90 and 91 are incorrectly numbered on the checklist card number 654. The key Rookie Cards in this set are Ellis Burks, Ron Gant, Tom Glavine, Mark Grace, Gregg Jefferies, Roberto Kelly, Edgar Martinez, Jack McDowell, and Matt Williams. A subset of "Stadium Cards" was randomly inserted throughout the packs. These cards pictured all 26 stadiums used by Major League Baseball and presented facts about these ballparks. Fleer also produced a "limited" edition version of this set with glossy coating and packaged in a "tin." However, this tin set was apparently not limited enough (estimated between 40,000 and 60,000 1988 tin sets produced by Fleer), since the values of the "tin" glossy cards are now only double the values of the respective cards in the regular set.

	MT	EX-MT	VG
COMPLETE SET (660)	33.00	15.00	4.10
COMPLETE FACT.SET (672)	35.00	16.00	4.40
COMMON PLAYER (1-660)	.05	.02	.01
COMPLETE WS SET (12)	2.50	1.15	.30

	MT	EX-MT	VG
☐ 1 Keith Atherton	.05	.02	.01
☐ 2 Don Baylor	.08	.04	.01
☐ 3 Juan Berenguer	.05	.02	.01
☐ 4 Bert Blyleven	.08	.04	.01
☐ 5 Tom Brunansky	.08	.04	.01
☐ 6 Randy Bush	.05	.02	.01
☐ 7 Steve Carlton	.30	.14	.04
☐ 8 Mark Davidson	.05	.02	.01
☐ 9 George Frazier	.05	.02	.01
☐ 10 Gary Gaetti	.05	.02	.01
☐ 11 Greg Gagne	.05	.02	.01
☐ 12 Dan Gladden	.05	.02	.01
☐ 13 Kent Hrbek	.08	.04	.01
☐ 14 Gene Larkin	.12	.05	.02
☐ 15 Tim Laudner	.05	.02	.01
☐ 16 Steve Lombardozzi	.05	.02	.01
☐ 17 Al Newman	.05	.02	.01
☐ 18 Joe Niekro	.08	.04	.01
☐ 19 Kirby Puckett	1.00	.45	.13
☐ 20 Jeff Reardon	.20	.09	.03
☐ 21A Dan Schatzeder ERR (Misspelled Schatzader on card front)	.10	.05	.01
☐ 21B Dan Schatzeder COR	.05	.02	.01
☐ 22 Roy Smalley	.05	.02	.01
☐ 23 Mike Smithson	.05	.02	.01
☐ 24 Les Straker	.05	.02	.01
☐ 25 Frank Viola	.08	.04	.01
☐ 26 Jack Clark	.08	.04	.01
☐ 27 Vince Coleman	.08	.04	.01
☐ 28 Danny Cox	.05	.02	.01
☐ 29 Bill Dawley	.05	.02	.01
☐ 30 Ken Dayley	.05	.02	.01
☐ 31 Doug DeCinces	.05	.02	.01
☐ 32 Curt Ford	.05	.02	.01
☐ 33 Bob Forsch	.05	.02	.01
☐ 34 David Green	.05	.02	.01
☐ 35 Tom Herr	.05	.02	.01
☐ 36 Ricky Horton	.05	.02	.01
☐ 37 Lance Johnson	.40	.18	.05
☐ 38 Steve Lake	.05	.02	.01
☐ 39 Jim Lindeman	.05	.02	.01
☐ 40 Joe Magrane	.15	.07	.02
☐ 41 Greg Mathews	.05	.02	.01
☐ 42 Willie McGee	.08	.04	.01
☐ 43 John Morris	.05	.02	.01
☐ 44 Jose Oquendo	.05	.02	.01
☐ 45 Tony Pena	.05	.02	.01
☐ 46 Terry Pendleton	.25	.11	.03
☐ 47 Ozzie Smith	.40	.18	.05
☐ 48 John Tudor	.05	.02	.01
☐ 49 Lee Tunnell	.05	.02	.01
☐ 50 Todd Worrell	.08	.04	.01
☐ 51 Doyle Alexander	.05	.02	.01
☐ 52 Dave Bergman	.05	.02	.01
☐ 53 Tom Brookens	.05	.02	.01
☐ 54 Darrell Evans	.08	.04	.01
☐ 55 Kirk Gibson	.08	.04	.01
☐ 56 Mike Heath	.05	.02	.01
☐ 57 Mike Henneman	.30	.14	.04
☐ 58 Willie Hernandez	.05	.02	.01
☐ 59 Larry Herndon	.05	.02	.01
☐ 60 Eric King	.05	.02	.01
☐ 61 Chet Lemon	.05	.02	.01
☐ 62 Scott Lusader	.05	.02	.01
☐ 63 Bill Madlock	.05	.02	.01
☐ 64 Jack Morris	.15	.07	.02
☐ 65 Jim Morrison	.05	.02	.01
☐ 66 Matt Nokes	.40	.18	.05
☐ 67 Dan Petry	.05	.02	.01
☐ 68A Jeff M. Robinson ERR (Stats for Jeff D. Robinson on card back, Born 12-13-60)	.25	.11	.03
☐ 68B Jeff M. Robinson COR (Born 12-14-61)	.08	.04	.01
☐ 69 Pat Sheridan	.05	.02	.01
☐ 70 Nate Snell	.05	.02	.01
☐ 71 Frank Tanana	.05	.02	.01
☐ 72 Walt Terrell	.05	.02	.01
☐ 73 Mark Thurmond	.05	.02	.01
☐ 74 Alan Trammell	.08	.04	.01
☐ 75 Lou Whitaker	.08	.04	.01
☐ 76 Mike Aldrete	.05	.02	.01
☐ 77 Bob Brenly	.05	.02	.01
☐ 78 Will Clark	1.50	.65	.19
☐ 79 Chili Davis	.08	.04	.01
☐ 80 Kelly Downs	.05	.02	.01
☐ 81 Dave Dravecky	.08	.04	.01
☐ 82 Scott Garrelts	.05	.02	.01
☐ 83 Atlee Hammaker	.05	.02	.01
☐ 84 Dave Henderson	.08	.04	.01
☐ 85 Mike Krukow	.05	.02	.01
☐ 86 Mike LaCoss	.05	.02	.01
☐ 87 Craig Lefferts	.05	.02	.01
☐ 88 Jeff Leonard	.05	.02	.01
☐ 89 Candy Maldonado	.05	.02	.01
☐ 90 Eddie Milner	.05	.02	.01
☐ 91 Bob Melvin	.05	.02	.01
☐ 92 Kevin Mitchell	.25	.11	.03
☐ 93 Jon Perlman	.05	.02	.01
☐ 94 Rick Reuschel	.05	.02	.01
☐ 95 Don Robinson	.05	.02	.01
☐ 96 Chris Speier	.05	.02	.01
☐ 97 Harry Spilman	.05	.02	.01
☐ 98 Robby Thompson	.08	.04	.01
☐ 99 Jose Uribe	.05	.02	.01
☐ 100 Mark Wasinger	.05	.02	.01
☐ 101 Matt Williams	2.00	.90	.25
☐ 102 Jesse Barfield	.05	.02	.01
☐ 103 George Bell	.15	.07	.02
☐ 104 Juan Beniquez	.05	.02	.01
☐ 105 John Cerutti	.05	.02	.01
☐ 106 Jim Clancy	.05	.02	.01
☐ 107 Rob Ducey	.05	.02	.01
☐ 108 Mark Eichhorn	.05	.02	.01
☐ 109 Tony Fernandez	.08	.04	.01
☐ 110 Cecil Fielder	.60	.25	.08
☐ 111 Kelly Gruber	.08	.04	.01
☐ 112 Tom Henke	.08	.04	.01
☐ 113A Garth Iorg ERR (Misspelled Iorq on card front)	.25	.11	.03
☐ 113B Garth Iorg COR	.05	.02	.01
☐ 114 Jimmy Key	.08	.04	.01
☐ 115 Rick Leach	.05	.02	.01
☐ 116 Manny Lee	.05	.02	.01
☐ 117 Nelson Liriano	.05	.02	.01

Card			
☐ 118 Fred McGriff	1.50	.65	.19
☐ 119 Lloyd Moseby	.05	.02	.01
☐ 120 Rance Mulliniks	.05	.02	.01
☐ 121 Jeff Musselman	.05	.02	.01
☐ 122 Jose Nunez	.05	.02	.01
☐ 123 Dave Stieb	.08	.04	.01
☐ 124 Willie Upshaw	.05	.02	.01
☐ 125 Duane Ward	.25	.11	.03
☐ 126 Ernie Whitt	.05	.02	.01
☐ 127 Rick Aguilera	.08	.04	.01
☐ 128 Wally Backman	.05	.02	.01
☐ 129 Mark Carreon	.15	.07	.02
☐ 130 Gary Carter	.10	.05	.01
☐ 131 David Cone	1.25	.55	.16
☐ 132 Ron Darling	.08	.04	.01
☐ 133 Len Dykstra	.08	.04	.01
☐ 134 Sid Fernandez	.08	.04	.01
☐ 135 Dwight Gooden	.15	.07	.02
☐ 136 Keith Hernandez	.08	.04	.01
☐ 137 Gregg Jefferies	2.00	.90	.25
☐ 138 Howard Johnson	.15	.07	.02
☐ 139 Terry Leach	.05	.02	.01
☐ 140 Barry Lyons	.05	.02	.01
☐ 141 Dave Magadan	.08	.04	.01
☐ 142 Roger McDowell	.05	.02	.01
☐ 143 Kevin McReynolds	.08	.04	.01
☐ 144 Keith A. Miller	.35	.16	.04
☐ 145 John Mitchell	.05	.02	.01
☐ 146 Randy Myers	.12	.05	.02
☐ 147 Bob Ojeda	.05	.02	.01
☐ 148 Jesse Orosco	.05	.02	.01
☐ 149 Rafael Santana	.05	.02	.01
☐ 150 Doug Sisk	.05	.02	.01
☐ 151 Darryl Strawberry	.60	.25	.08
☐ 152 Tim Teufel	.05	.02	.01
☐ 153 Gene Walter	.05	.02	.01
☐ 154 Mookie Wilson	.08	.04	.01
☐ 155 Jay Aldrich	.05	.02	.01
☐ 156 Chris Bosio	.08	.04	.01
☐ 157 Glenn Braggs	.05	.02	.01
☐ 158 Greg Brock	.05	.02	.01
☐ 159 Juan Castillo	.05	.02	.01
☐ 160 Mark Clear	.05	.02	.01
☐ 161 Cecil Cooper	.08	.04	.01
☐ 162 Chuck Crim	.05	.02	.01
☐ 163 Rob Deer	.08	.04	.01
☐ 164 Mike Felder	.05	.02	.01
☐ 165 Jim Gantner	.05	.02	.01
☐ 166 Ted Higuera	.05	.02	.01
☐ 167 Steve Kiefer	.05	.02	.01
☐ 168 Rick Manning	.05	.02	.01
☐ 169 Paul Molitor	.25	.11	.03
☐ 170 Juan Nieves	.05	.02	.01
☐ 171 Dan Plesac	.05	.02	.01
☐ 172 Earnest Riles	.05	.02	.01
☐ 173 Bill Schroeder	.05	.02	.01
☐ 174 Steve Stanicek	.05	.02	.01
☐ 175 B.J. Surhoff	.05	.02	.01
☐ 176 Dale Sveum	.05	.02	.01
☐ 177 Bill Wegman	.05	.02	.01
☐ 178 Robin Yount	.50	.23	.06
☐ 179 Hubie Brooks	.05	.02	.01
☐ 180 Tim Burke	.05	.02	.01
☐ 181 Casey Candaele	.05	.02	.01
☐ 182 Mike Fitzgerald	.05	.02	.01
☐ 183 Tom Foley	.05	.02	.01
☐ 184 Andres Galarraga	.05	.02	.01
☐ 185 Neal Heaton	.05	.02	.01
☐ 186 Wallace Johnson	.05	.02	.01
☐ 187 Vance Law	.05	.02	.01
☐ 188 Dennis Martinez	.08	.04	.01
☐ 189 Bob McClure	.05	.02	.01
☐ 190 Andy McGaffigan	.05	.02	.01
☐ 191 Reid Nichols	.05	.02	.01
☐ 192 Pascual Perez	.05	.02	.01
☐ 193 Tim Raines	.08	.04	.01
☐ 194 Jeff Reed	.05	.02	.01
☐ 195 Bob Sebra	.05	.02	.01
☐ 196 Bryn Smith	.05	.02	.01
☐ 197 Randy St.Claire	.05	.02	.01
☐ 198 Tim Wallach	.08	.04	.01
☐ 199 Mitch Webster	.05	.02	.01
☐ 200 Herm Winningham	.05	.02	.01
☐ 201 Floyd Youmans	.05	.02	.01
☐ 202 Brad Arnsberg	.05	.02	.01
☐ 203 Rick Cerone	.05	.02	.01
☐ 204 Pat Clements	.05	.02	.01
☐ 205 Henry Cotto	.05	.02	.01
☐ 206 Mike Easler	.05	.02	.01
☐ 207 Ron Guidry	.08	.04	.01
☐ 208 Bill Gullickson	.05	.02	.01
☐ 209 Rickey Henderson	.60	.25	.08
☐ 210 Charles Hudson	.05	.02	.01

Card			
☐ 211 Tommy John	.08	.04	.01
☐ 212 Roberto Kelly	2.00	.90	.25
☐ 213 Ron Kittle	.05	.02	.01
☐ 214 Don Mattingly	.60	.25	.08
☐ 215 Bobby Meacham	.05	.02	.01
☐ 216 Mike Pagliarulo	.05	.02	.01
☐ 217 Dan Pasqua	.05	.02	.01
☐ 218 Willie Randolph	.08	.04	.01
☐ 219 Rick Rhoden	.05	.02	.01
☐ 220 Dave Righetti	.05	.02	.01
☐ 221 Jerry Royster	.05	.02	.01
☐ 222 Tim Stoddard	.05	.02	.01
☐ 223 Wayne Tolleson	.05	.02	.01
☐ 224 Gary Ward	.05	.02	.01
☐ 225 Claudell Washington	.05	.02	.01
☐ 226 Dave Winfield	.40	.18	.05
☐ 227 Buddy Bell	.08	.04	.01
☐ 228 Tom Browning	.05	.02	.01
☐ 229 Dave Concepcion	.08	.04	.01
☐ 230 Kal Daniels	.08	.04	.01
☐ 231 Eric Davis	.15	.07	.02
☐ 232 Bo Diaz	.05	.02	.01
☐ 233 Nick Esasky UER (Has a dollar sign before '87 SB totals)	.05	.02	.01
☐ 234 John Franco	.08	.04	.01
☐ 235 Guy Hoffman	.05	.02	.01
☐ 236 Tom Hume	.05	.02	.01
☐ 237 Tracy Jones	.05	.02	.01
☐ 238 Bill Landrum	.08	.04	.01
☐ 239 Barry Larkin	.35	.16	.04
☐ 240 Terry McGriff	.05	.02	.01
☐ 241 Rob Murphy	.05	.02	.01
☐ 242 Ron Oester	.05	.02	.01
☐ 243 Dave Parker	.08	.04	.01
☐ 244 Pat Perry	.05	.02	.01
☐ 245 Ted Power	.05	.02	.01
☐ 246 Dennis Rasmussen	.05	.02	.01
☐ 247 Ron Robinson	.05	.02	.01
☐ 248 Kurt Stillwell	.05	.02	.01
☐ 249 Jeff Treadway	.12	.05	.02
☐ 250 Frank Williams	.05	.02	.01
☐ 251 Steve Balboni	.05	.02	.01
☐ 252 Bud Black	.05	.02	.01
☐ 253 Thad Bosley	.05	.02	.01
☐ 254 George Brett	.50	.23	.06
☐ 255 John Davis	.05	.02	.01
☐ 256 Steve Farr	.05	.02	.01
☐ 257 Gene Garber	.05	.02	.01
☐ 258 Jerry Don Gleaton	.05	.02	.01
☐ 259 Mark Gubicza	.05	.02	.01
☐ 260 Bo Jackson	.75	.35	.09
☐ 261 Danny Jackson	.05	.02	.01
☐ 262 Ross Jones	.05	.02	.01
☐ 263 Charlie Leibrandt	.05	.02	.01
☐ 264 Bill Pecota	.15	.07	.02
☐ 265 Melido Perez	.75	.35	.09
☐ 266 Jamie Quirk	.05	.02	.01
☐ 267 Dan Quisenberry	.08	.04	.01
☐ 268 Bret Saberhagen	.12	.05	.02
☐ 269 Angel Salazar	.05	.02	.01
☐ 270 Kevin Seitzer UER (Wrong birth year)	.08	.04	.01
☐ 271 Danny Tartabull	.25	.11	.03
☐ 272 Gary Thurman	.05	.02	.01
☐ 273 Frank White	.05	.02	.01
☐ 274 Willie Wilson	.05	.02	.01
☐ 275 Tony Bernazard	.05	.02	.01
☐ 276 Jose Canseco	1.50	.65	.19
☐ 277 Mike Davis	.05	.02	.01
☐ 278 Storm Davis	.05	.02	.01
☐ 279 Dennis Eckersley	.30	.14	.04
☐ 280 Alfredo Griffin	.05	.02	.01
☐ 281 Rick Honeycutt	.05	.02	.01
☐ 282 Jay Howell	.05	.02	.01
☐ 283 Reggie Jackson	.50	.23	.06
☐ 284 Dennis Lamp	.05	.02	.01
☐ 285 Carney Lansford	.08	.04	.01
☐ 286 Mark McGwire	2.00	.90	.25
☐ 287 Dwayne Murphy	.05	.02	.01
☐ 288 Gene Nelson	.05	.02	.01
☐ 289 Steve Ontiveros	.05	.02	.01
☐ 290 Tony Phillips	.05	.02	.01
☐ 291 Eric Plunk	.05	.02	.01
☐ 292 Luis Polonia	.60	.25	.08
☐ 293 Rick Rodriguez	.05	.02	.01
☐ 294 Terry Steinbach	.08	.04	.01
☐ 295 Dave Stewart	.08	.04	.01
☐ 296 Curt Young	.05	.02	.01
☐ 297 Luis Aguayo	.05	.02	.01
☐ 298 Steve Bedrosian	.05	.02	.01
☐ 299 Jeff Calhoun	.05	.02	.01
☐ 300 Don Carman	.05	.02	.01

☐ 301 Todd Frohwirth .05 .02 .01
☐ 302 Greg Gross .05 .02 .01
☐ 303 Kevin Gross .05 .02 .01
☐ 304 Von Hayes .05 .02 .01
☐ 305 Keith Hughes .05 .02 .01
☐ 306 Mike Jackson .15 .07 .02
☐ 307 Chris James .05 .02 .01
☐ 308 Steve Jeltz .05 .02 .01
☐ 309 Mike Maddux .05 .02 .01
☐ 310 Lance Parrish .08 .04 .01
☐ 311 Shane Rawley .05 .02 .01
☐ 312 Wally Ritchie .05 .02 .01
☐ 313 Bruce Ruffin .05 .02 .01
☐ 314 Juan Samuel .05 .02 .01
☐ 315 Mike Schmidt .90 .40 .11
☐ 316 Rick Schu .05 .02 .01
☐ 317 Jeff Stone .05 .02 .01
☐ 318 Kent Tekulve .05 .02 .01
☐ 319 Milt Thompson .05 .02 .01
☐ 320 Glenn Wilson .05 .02 .01
☐ 321 Rafael Belliard .05 .02 .01
☐ 322 Barry Bonds 1.50 .65 .19
☐ 323 Bobby Bonilla UER .50 .23 .06
(Wrong birth year)
☐ 324 Sid Bream .08 .04 .01
☐ 325 John Cangelosi .05 .02 .01
☐ 326 Mike Diaz .05 .02 .01
☐ 327 Doug Drabek .20 .09 .03
☐ 328 Mike Dunne .05 .02 .01
☐ 329 Brian Fisher .05 .02 .01
☐ 330 Brett Gideon .05 .02 .01
☐ 331 Terry Harper .05 .02 .01
☐ 332 Bob Kipper .05 .02 .01
☐ 333 Mike LaValliere .05 .02 .01
☐ 334 Jose Lind .30 .14 .04
☐ 335 Junior Ortiz .05 .02 .01
☐ 336 Vicente Palacios .12 .05 .02
☐ 337 Bob Patterson .05 .02 .01
☐ 338 Al Pedrique .05 .02 .01
☐ 339 R.J. Reynolds .05 .02 .01
☐ 340 John Smiley 1.00 .45 .13
☐ 341 Andy Van Slyke UER .20 .09 .03
(Wrong batting and throwing listed)
☐ 342 Bob Walk .05 .02 .01
☐ 343 Marty Barrett .05 .02 .01
☐ 344 Todd Benzinger .15 .07 .02
☐ 345 Wade Boggs .50 .23 .06
☐ 346 Tom Bolton .05 .02 .01
☐ 347 Oil Can Boyd .05 .02 .01
☐ 348 Ellis Burks .75 .35 .09
☐ 349 Roger Clemens 1.00 .45 .13
☐ 350 Steve Crawford .05 .02 .01
☐ 351 Dwight Evans .08 .04 .01
☐ 352 Wes Gardner .05 .02 .01
☐ 353 Rich Gedman .05 .02 .01
☐ 354 Mike Greenwell .30 .14 .04
☐ 355 Sam Horn .20 .09 .03
☐ 356 Bruce Hurst .08 .04 .01
☐ 357 John Marzano .05 .02 .01
☐ 358 Al Nipper .05 .02 .01
☐ 359 Spike Owen .05 .02 .01
☐ 360 Jody Reed .60 .25 .08
☐ 361 Jim Rice .05 .02 .01
☐ 362 Ed Romero .05 .02 .01
☐ 363 Kevin Romine .05 .02 .01
☐ 364 Joe Sambito .05 .02 .01
☐ 365 Calvin Schiraldi .05 .02 .01
☐ 366 Jeff Sellers .05 .02 .01
☐ 367 Bob Stanley .05 .02 .01
☐ 368 Scott Bankhead .05 .02 .01
☐ 369 Phil Bradley .05 .02 .01
☐ 370 Scott Bradley .05 .02 .01
☐ 371 Mickey Brantley .05 .02 .01
☐ 372 Mike Campbell .05 .02 .01
☐ 373 Alvin Davis .05 .02 .01
☐ 374 Lee Guetterman .05 .02 .01
☐ 375 Dave Hengel .05 .02 .01
☐ 376 Mike Kingery .05 .02 .01
☐ 377 Mark Langston .08 .04 .01
☐ 378 Edgar Martinez 3.50 1.55 .45
☐ 379 Mike Moore .05 .02 .01
☐ 380 Mike Morgan .08 .04 .01
☐ 381 John Moses .05 .02 .01
☐ 382 Donell Nixon .05 .02 .01
☐ 383 Edwin Nunez .05 .02 .01
☐ 384 Ken Phelps .05 .02 .01
☐ 385 Jim Presley .05 .02 .01
☐ 386 Rey Quinones .05 .02 .01
☐ 387 Jerry Reed .05 .02 .01
☐ 388 Harold Reynolds .05 .02 .01
☐ 389 Dave Valle .05 .02 .01
☐ 390 Bill Wilkinson .05 .02 .01
☐ 391 Harold Baines .08 .04 .01
☐ 392 Floyd Bannister .05 .02 .01
☐ 393 Daryl Boston .05 .02 .01
☐ 394 Ivan Calderon .08 .04 .01
☐ 395 Jose DeLeon .05 .02 .01
☐ 396 Richard Dotson .05 .02 .01
☐ 397 Carlton Fisk .35 .16 .04
☐ 398 Ozzie Guillen .08 .04 .01
☐ 399 Ron Hassey .05 .02 .01
☐ 400 Donnie Hill .05 .02 .01
☐ 401 Bob James .05 .02 .01
☐ 402 Dave LaPoint .05 .02 .01
☐ 403 Bill Lindsey .05 .02 .01
☐ 404 Bill Long .05 .02 .01
☐ 405 Steve Lyons .05 .02 .01
☐ 406 Fred Manrique .05 .02 .01
☐ 407 Jack McDowell 3.50 1.55 .45
☐ 408 Gary Redus .05 .02 .01
☐ 409 Ray Searage .05 .02 .01
☐ 410 Bobby Thigpen .08 .04 .01
☐ 411 Greg Walker .05 .02 .01
☐ 412 Ken Williams .05 .02 .01
☐ 413 Jim Winn .05 .02 .01
☐ 414 Jody Davis .05 .02 .01
☐ 415 Andre Dawson .40 .18 .05
☐ 416 Brian Dayett .05 .02 .01
☐ 417 Bob Dernier .05 .02 .01
☐ 418 Frank DiPino .05 .02 .01
☐ 419 Shawon Dunston .08 .04 .01
☐ 420 Leon Durham .05 .02 .01
☐ 421 Les Lancaster .05 .02 .01
☐ 422 Ed Lynch .05 .02 .01
☐ 423 Greg Maddux 1.50 .65 .19
☐ 424 Dave Martinez .12 .05 .02
☐ 425A Keith Moreland ERR 1.50 .65 .19
(Photo actually Jody Davis)
☐ 425B Keith Moreland COR .12 .05 .02
(Bat on shoulder)
☐ 426 Jamie Moyer .05 .02 .01
☐ 427 Jerry Mumphrey .05 .02 .01
☐ 428 Paul Noce .05 .02 .01
☐ 429 Rafael Palmeiro 1.00 .45 .13
☐ 430 Wade Rowdon .05 .02 .01
☐ 431 Ryne Sandberg 1.00 .45 .13
☐ 432 Scott Sanderson .05 .02 .01
☐ 433 Lee Smith .25 .11 .03
☐ 434 Jim Sundberg .05 .02 .01
☐ 435 Rick Sutcliffe .08 .04 .01
☐ 436 Manny Trillo .05 .02 .01
☐ 437 Juan Agosto .05 .02 .01
☐ 438 Larry Andersen .05 .02 .01
☐ 439 Alan Ashby .05 .02 .01
☐ 440 Kevin Bass .05 .02 .01
☐ 441 Ken Caminiti .60 .25 .08
☐ 442 Rocky Childress .05 .02 .01
☐ 443 Jose Cruz .05 .02 .01
☐ 444 Danny Darwin .05 .02 .01
☐ 445 Glenn Davis .08 .04 .01
☐ 446 Jim Deshaies .05 .02 .01
☐ 447 Bill Doran .05 .02 .01
☐ 448 Ty Gainey .05 .02 .01
☐ 449 Billy Hatcher .05 .02 .01
☐ 450 Jeff Heathcock .05 .02 .01
☐ 451 Bob Knepper .05 .02 .01
☐ 452 Rob Mallicoat .05 .02 .01
☐ 453 Dave Meads .05 .02 .01
☐ 454 Craig Reynolds .05 .02 .01
☐ 455 Nolan Ryan 1.50 .65 .19
☐ 456 Mike Scott .08 .04 .01
☐ 457 Dave Smith .05 .02 .01
☐ 458 Denny Walling .05 .02 .01
☐ 459 Robbie Wine .05 .02 .01
☐ 460 Gerald Young .05 .02 .01
☐ 461 Bob Brower .05 .02 .01
☐ 462A Jerry Browne ERR 1.50 .65 .19
(Photo actually Bob Brower, white player)
☐ 462B Jerry Browne COR .12 .05 .02
(Black player)
☐ 463 Steve Buechele .05 .02 .01
☐ 464 Edwin Correa .05 .02 .01
☐ 465 Cecil Espy .10 .05 .01
☐ 466 Scott Fletcher .05 .02 .01
☐ 467 Jose Guzman .08 .04 .01
☐ 468 Greg Harris .05 .02 .01
☐ 469 Charlie Hough .05 .02 .01
☐ 470 Pete Incaviglia .08 .04 .01
☐ 471 Paul Kilgus .05 .02 .01
☐ 472 Mike Loynd .05 .02 .01
☐ 473 Oddibe McDowell .05 .02 .01
☐ 474 Dale Mohorcic .05 .02 .01

☐ 475 Pete O'Brien	.05	.02	.01
☐ 476 Larry Parrish	.05	.02	.01
☐ 477 Geno Petralli	.05	.02	.01
☐ 478 Jeff Russell	.05	.02	.01
☐ 479 Ruben Sierra	1.00	.45	.13
☐ 480 Mike Stanley	.05	.02	.01
☐ 481 Curtis Wilkerson	.05	.02	.01
☐ 482 Mitch Williams	.08	.04	.01
☐ 483 Bobby Witt	.08	.04	.01
☐ 484 Tony Armas	.05	.02	.01
☐ 485 Bob Boone	.08	.04	.01
☐ 486 Bill Buckner	.08	.04	.01
☐ 487 DeWayne Buice	.05	.02	.01
☐ 488 Brian Downing	.05	.02	.01
☐ 489 Chuck Finley	.08	.04	.01
☐ 490 Willie Fraser UER	.05	.02	.01
(Wrong bio stats,			
for George Hendrick)			
☐ 491 Jack Howell	.05	.02	.01
☐ 492 Ruppert Jones	.05	.02	.01
☐ 493 Wally Joyner	.20	.09	.03
☐ 494 Jack Lazorko	.05	.02	.01
☐ 495 Gary Lucas	.05	.02	.01
☐ 496 Kirk McCaskill	.05	.02	.01
☐ 497 Mark McLemore	.05	.02	.01
☐ 498 Darrell Miller	.05	.02	.01
☐ 499 Greg Minton	.05	.02	.01
☐ 500 Donnie Moore	.05	.02	.01
☐ 501 Gus Polidor	.05	.02	.01
☐ 502 Johnny Ray	.05	.02	.01
☐ 503 Mark Ryal	.05	.02	.01
☐ 504 Dick Schofield	.05	.02	.01
☐ 505 Don Sutton	.15	.07	.02
☐ 506 Devon White	.12	.05	.02
☐ 507 Mike Witt	.05	.02	.01
☐ 508 Dave Anderson	.05	.02	.01
☐ 509 Tim Belcher	.25	.11	.03
☐ 510 Ralph Bryant	.05	.02	.01
☐ 511 Tim Crews	.05	.02	.01
☐ 512 Mike Devereaux	2.00	.90	.25
☐ 513 Mariano Duncan	.05	.02	.01
☐ 514 Pedro Guerrero	.08	.04	.01
☐ 515 Jeff Hamilton	.05	.02	.01
☐ 516 Mickey Hatcher	.05	.02	.01
☐ 517 Brad Havens	.05	.02	.01
☐ 518 Orel Hershiser	.08	.04	.01
☐ 519 Shawn Hillegas	.05	.02	.01
☐ 520 Ken Howell	.05	.02	.01
☐ 521 Tim Leary	.05	.02	.01
☐ 522 Mike Marshall	.05	.02	.01
☐ 523 Steve Sax	.08	.04	.01
☐ 524 Mike Scioscia	.05	.02	.01
☐ 525 Mike Sharperson	.05	.02	.01
☐ 526 John Shelby	.05	.02	.01
☐ 527 Franklin Stubbs	.05	.02	.01
☐ 528 Fernando Valenzuela	.08	.04	.01
☐ 529 Bob Welch	.08	.04	.01
☐ 530 Matt Young	.05	.02	.01
☐ 531 Jim Acker	.05	.02	.01
☐ 532 Paul Assenmacher	.05	.02	.01
☐ 533 Jeff Blauser	.60	.25	.08
☐ 534 Joe Boever	.05	.02	.01
☐ 535 Martin Clary	.05	.02	.01
☐ 536 Kevin Coffman	.05	.02	.01
☐ 537 Jeff Dedmon	.05	.02	.01
☐ 538 Ron Gant	5.00	2.30	.60
☐ 539 Tom Glavine	9.00	4.00	1.15
☐ 540 Ken Griffey	.08	.04	.01
☐ 541 Albert Hall	.05	.02	.01
☐ 542 Glenn Hubbard	.05	.02	.01
☐ 543 Dion James	.05	.02	.01
☐ 544 Dale Murphy	.15	.07	.02
☐ 545 Ken Oberkfell	.05	.02	.01
☐ 546 David Palmer	.05	.02	.01
☐ 547 Gerald Perry	.05	.02	.01
☐ 548 Charlie Puleo	.05	.02	.01
☐ 549 Ted Simmons	.08	.04	.01
☐ 550 Zane Smith	.05	.02	.01
☐ 551 Andres Thomas	.05	.02	.01
☐ 552 Ozzie Virgil	.05	.02	.01
☐ 553 Don Aase	.05	.02	.01
☐ 554 Jeff Ballard	.05	.02	.01
☐ 555 Eric Bell	.05	.02	.01
☐ 556 Mike Boddicker	.05	.02	.01
☐ 557 Ken Dixon	.05	.02	.01
☐ 558 Jim Dwyer	.05	.02	.01
☐ 559 Ken Gerhart	.05	.02	.01
☐ 560 Rene Gonzales	.20	.09	.03
☐ 561 Mike Griffin	.05	.02	.01
☐ 562 John Habyan UER	.05	.02	.01
(Misspelled Hayban on			
both sides of card)			
☐ 563 Terry Kennedy	.05	.02	.01
☐ 564 Ray Knight	.08	.04	.01
☐ 565 Lee Lacy	.05	.02	.01
☐ 566 Fred Lynn	.08	.04	.01
☐ 567 Eddie Murray	.35	.16	.04
☐ 568 Tom Niedenfuer	.05	.02	.01
☐ 569 Bill Ripken	.15	.07	.02
☐ 570 Cal Ripken	1.25	.55	.16
☐ 571 Dave Schmidt	.05	.02	.01
☐ 572 Larry Sheets	.05	.02	.01
☐ 573 Pete Stanicek	.05	.02	.01
☐ 574 Mark Williamson	.05	.02	.01
☐ 575 Mike Young	.05	.02	.01
☐ 576 Shawn Abner	.05	.02	.01
☐ 577 Greg Booker	.05	.02	.01
☐ 578 Chris Brown	.05	.02	.01
☐ 579 Keith Comstock	.05	.02	.01
☐ 580 Joey Cora	.08	.04	.01
☐ 581 Mark Davis	.05	.02	.01
☐ 582 Tim Flannery	.08	.04	.01
(With surfboard)			
☐ 583 Goose Gossage	.08	.04	.01
☐ 584 Mark Grant	.05	.02	.01
☐ 585 Tony Gwynn	.60	.25	.08
☐ 586 Andy Hawkins	.05	.02	.01
☐ 587 Stan Jefferson	.05	.02	.01
☐ 588 Jimmy Jones	.05	.02	.01
☐ 589 John Kruk	.25	.11	.03
☐ 590 Shane Mack	1.00	.45	.13
☐ 591 Carmelo Martinez	.05	.02	.01
☐ 592 Lance McCullers UER	.05	.02	.01
(6'11" tall)			
☐ 593 Eric Nolte	.05	.02	.01
☐ 594 Randy Ready	.05	.02	.01
☐ 595 Luis Salazar	.05	.02	.01
☐ 596 Benito Santiago	.15	.07	.02
☐ 597 Eric Show	.05	.02	.01
☐ 598 Garry Templeton	.05	.02	.01
☐ 599 Ed Whitson	.05	.02	.01
☐ 600 Scott Bailes	.05	.02	.01
☐ 601 Chris Bando	.05	.02	.01
☐ 602 Jay Bell	.75	.35	.09
☐ 603 Brett Butler	.12	.05	.02
☐ 604 Tom Candiotti	.05	.02	.01
☐ 605 Joe Carter	.60	.25	.08
☐ 606 Carmen Castillo	.05	.02	.01
☐ 607 Brian Dorsett	.05	.02	.01
☐ 608 John Farrell	.05	.02	.01
☐ 609 Julio Franco	.12	.05	.02
☐ 610 Mel Hall	.05	.02	.01
☐ 611 Tommy Hinzo	.05	.02	.01
☐ 612 Brook Jacoby	.05	.02	.01
☐ 613 Doug Jones	.50	.23	.06
☐ 614 Ken Schrom	.05	.02	.01
☐ 615 Cory Snyder	.08	.04	.01
☐ 616 Sammy Stewart	.05	.02	.01
☐ 617 Greg Swindell	.25	.11	.03
☐ 618 Pat Tabler	.05	.02	.01
☐ 619 Ed VandeBerg	.05	.02	.01
☐ 620 Eddie Williams	.05	.02	.01
☐ 621 Rich Yett	.05	.02	.01
☐ 622 Slugging Sophomores	.05	.02	.01
Wally Joyner			
Cory Snyder			
☐ 623 Dominican Dynamite	.05	.02	.01
George Bell			
Pedro Guerrero			
☐ 624 Oakland's Power Team	1.00	.45	.13
Mark McGwire			
Jose Canseco			
☐ 625 Classic Relief	.05	.02	.01
Dave Righetti			
Dan Plesac			
☐ 626 All Star Righties	.05	.02	.01
Bret Saberhagen			
Mike Witt			
Jack Morris			
☐ 627 Game Closers	.05	.02	.01
John Franco			
Steve Bedrosian			
☐ 628 Masters/Double Play	.40	.18	.05
Ozzie Smith			
Ryne Sandberg			
☐ 629 Rookie Record Setter	.60	.25	.08
Mark McGwire			
☐ 630 Changing the Guard	.15	.07	.02
Mike Greenwell			
Ellis Burks			
Todd Benzinger			
☐ 631 NL Batting Champs	.20	.09	.03
Tony Gwynn			
Tim Raines			
☐ 632 Pitching Magic	.05	.02	.01
Mike Scott			

Orel Hershiser			
☐ 633 Big Bats at First	.30	.14	.04
Pat Tabler			
Mark McGwire			
☐ 634 Hitting King/Thief	.20	.09	.03
Tony Gwynn			
Vince Coleman			
☐ 635 Slugging Shortstops	.35	.16	.04
Tony Fernandez			
Cal Ripken			
Alan Trammell			
☐ 636 Tried/True Sluggers	.30	.14	.04
Mike Schmidt			
Gary Carter			
☐ 637 Crunch Time	.25	.11	.03
Darryl Strawberry			
Eric Davis			
☐ 638 AL All-Stars	.25	.11	.03
Matt Nokes			
Kirby Puckett			
☐ 639 NL All-Stars	.05	.02	.01
Keith Hernandez			
Dale Murphy			
☐ 640 The O's Brothers	.50	.23	.06
Billy Ripken			
Cal Ripken			
☐ 641 Mark Grace and	4.00	1.80	.50
Darrin Jackson			
☐ 642 Damon Berryhill and	.75	.35	.09
Jeff Montgomery			
☐ 643 Felix Fermin and	.08	.04	.01
Jesse Reid			
☐ 644 Greg Myers and	.15	.07	.02
Greg Tabor			
☐ 645 Joey Meyer and	.08	.04	.01
Jim Eppard			
☐ 646 Adam Peterson and	.08	.04	.01
Randy Velarde			
☐ 647 Peter Smith and	.75	.35	.09
Chris Gwynn			
☐ 648 Tom Newell and	.08	.04	.01
Greg Jelks			
☐ 649 Mario Diaz and	.08	.04	.01
Clay Parker			
☐ 650 Jack Savage and	.08	.04	.01
Todd Simmons			
☐ 651 John Burkett and	.35	.16	.04
Kirt Manwaring			
☐ 652 Dave Otto and	.35	.16	.04
Walt Weiss			
☐ 653 Jeff King and	.40	.18	.05
Randell Byers			
☐ 654 CL: Twins/Cards	.06	.01	.00
Tigers/Giants UER			
(90 Bob Melvin,			
91 Eddie Milner)			
☐ 655 CL: Blue Jays/Mets	.06	.01	.00
Brewers/Expos UER			
(Mets listed before			
Blue Jays on card)			
☐ 656 CL: Yankees/Reds	.06	.01	.00
Royals/A's			
☐ 657 CL: Phillies/Pirates	.06	.01	.00
Red Sox/Mariners			
☐ 658 CL: White Sox/Cubs	.06	.01	.00
Astros/Rangers			
☐ 659 CL: Angels/Dodgers	.06	.01	.00
Braves/Orioles			
☐ 660 CL: Padres/Indians	.06	.01	.00
Rookies/Specials			

1988 Fleer All-Star Inserts

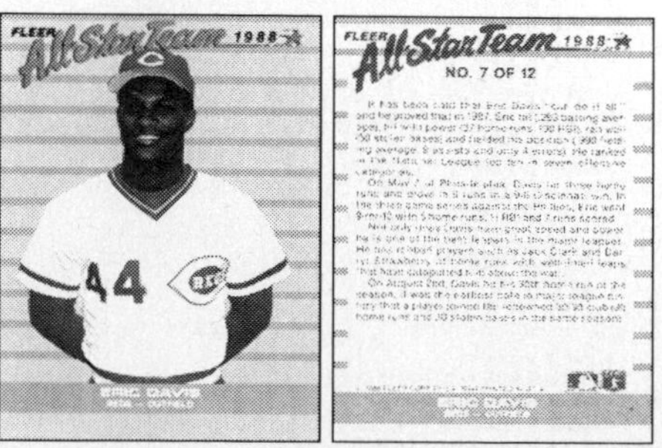

The cards in this 12-card set measure the standard 2 1/2" by 3 1/2". These cards were inserted (randomly) in wax and cello packs of the 1988 Fleer regular issue set. The cards show the player silhouetted against a light green background with dark green stripes. The player's name, team, and position are printed in yellow at the bottom of the obverse. The card backs are done predominantly in green, white, and black. Cards are numbered on the back. These 12 cards are considered a separate set in their own right and are not typically included in a complete set of the regular issue 1988 Fleer cards. The players are the "best" at each position, three pitchers, eight position players, and a designated hitter.

	MT	EX-MT	VG
COMPLETE SET (12)	12.00	5.50	1.50
COMMON PLAYERS (1-12)	.40	.18	.05
☐ 1 Matt Nokes	.60	.25	.08
☐ 2 Tom Henke	.60	.25	.08
☐ 3 Ted Higuera	.40	.18	.05
☐ 4 Roger Clemens	4.50	2.00	.55
☐ 5 George Bell	.75	.35	.09
☐ 6 Andre Dawson	1.00	.45	.13
☐ 7 Eric Davis	1.25	.55	.16
☐ 8 Wade Boggs	2.00	.90	.25
☐ 9 Alan Trammell	.75	.35	.09
☐ 10 Juan Samuel	.40	.18	.05
☐ 11 Jack Clark	.50	.23	.06
☐ 12 Paul Molitor	1.00	.45	.13

1988 Fleer Award Winners

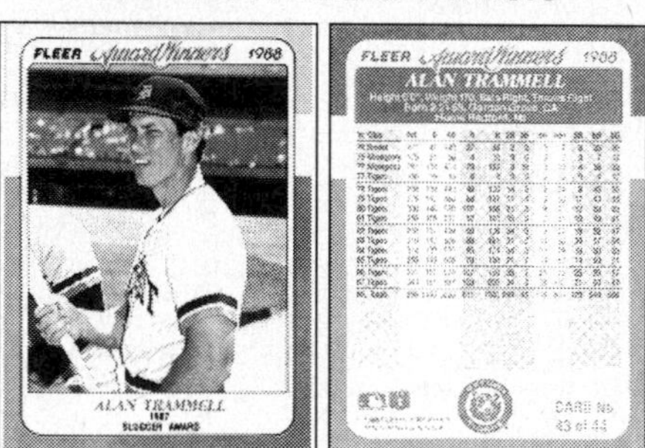

This small set of 44 cards was produced for 7-Eleven stores by Fleer. The cards measure the standard 2 1/2" by 3 1/2" and feature full color fronts and red, white, and blue backs. The card fronts are distinguished by the red, white, and blue frame around the player's full-color photo. The box for the cards describes the set as the "1988 Limited Edition Baseball Award Winners." The checklist for the set is given on the back of the set box. The card numbering is in alphabetical order by player's name.

	MT	EX-MT	VG
COMPLETE SET (44)	4.00	1.80	.50
COMMON PLAYER (1-44)	.10	.05	.01
☐ 1 Steve Bedrosian	.10	.05	.01
☐ 2 George Bell	.20	.09	.03
☐ 3 Wade Boggs	.50	.23	.06
☐ 4 Jose Canseco	.75	.35	.09
☐ 5 Will Clark	.75	.35	.09
☐ 6 Roger Clemens	1.00	.45	.13
☐ 7 Kal Daniels	.15	.07	.02
☐ 8 Eric Davis	.25	.11	.03
☐ 9 Andre Dawson	.35	.16	.04
☐ 10 Mike Dunne	.10	.05	.01
☐ 11 Dwight Evans	.15	.07	.02
☐ 12 Carlton Fisk	.35	.16	.04
☐ 13 Julio Franco	.15	.07	.02
☐ 14 Dwight Gooden	.25	.11	.03
☐ 15 Pedro Guerrero	.15	.07	.02

☐ 16 Tony Gwynn	.50	.23	.06
☐ 17 Orel Hershiser	.15	.07	.02
☐ 18 Tom Henke	.15	.07	.02
☐ 19 Ted Higuera	.10	.05	.01
☐ 20 Charlie Hough	.10	.05	.01
☐ 21 Wally Joyner	.20	.09	.03
☐ 22 Jimmy Key	.15	.07	.02
☐ 23 Don Mattingly	.75	.35	.09
☐ 24 Mark McGwire	.60	.25	.08
☐ 25 Paul Molitor	.20	.09	.03
☐ 26 Jack Morris	.20	.09	.03
☐ 27 Dale Murphy	.30	.14	.04
☐ 28 Terry Pendleton	.25	.11	.03
☐ 29 Kirby Puckett	.75	.35	.09
☐ 30 Tim Raines	.20	.09	.03
☐ 31 Jeff Reardon	.20	.09	.03
☐ 32 Harold Reynolds	.10	.05	.01
☐ 33 Dave Righetti	.10	.05	.01
☐ 34 Benito Santiago	.25	.11	.03
☐ 35 Mike Schmidt	.60	.25	.08
☐ 36 Mike Scott	.15	.07	.02
☐ 37 Kevin Seitzer	.10	.05	.01
☐ 38 Larry Sheets	.10	.05	.01
☐ 39 Ozzie Smith	.30	.14	.04
☐ 40 Darryl Strawberry	.50	.23	.06
☐ 41 Rick Sutcliffe	.10	.05	.01
☐ 42 Danny Tartabull	.30	.14	.04
☐ 43 Alan Trammell	.20	.09	.03
☐ 44 Tim Wallach	.15	.07	.02

1988 Fleer Baseball All-Stars

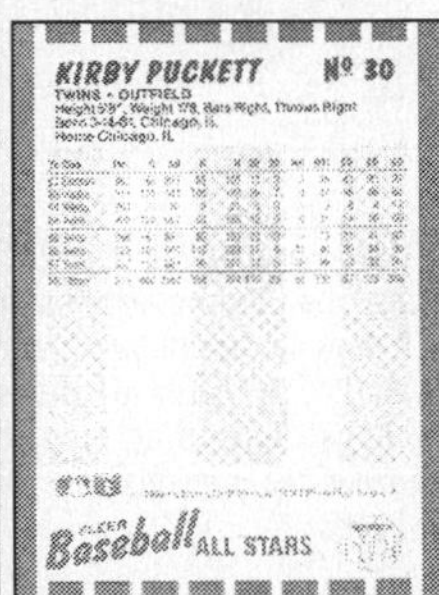

This small boxed set of 44 cards was produced exclusively for Ben Franklin Stores. The cards measure the standard 2 1/2" by 3 1/2" and feature full color fronts and white and blue backs. The card fronts are distinguished by the yellow and blue striped background behind the player's full-color photo. The box for the cards describes the set as the "1988 Fleer Baseball All-Stars." The checklist for the set is given on the back of the set box. The card numbering is in alphabetical order by player's name.

	MT	EX-MT	VG
COMPLETE SET (44)	5.00	2.30	.60
COMMON PLAYER (1-44)	.10	.05	.01
☐ 1 George Bell	.20	.09	.03
☐ 2 Wade Boggs	.50	.23	.06
☐ 3 Bobby Bonilla	.35	.16	.04
☐ 4 George Brett	.50	.23	.06
☐ 5 Jose Canseco	.75	.35	.09
☐ 6 Jack Clark	.15	.07	.02
☐ 7 Will Clark	.75	.35	.09
☐ 8 Roger Clemens	.90	.40	.11
☐ 9 Eric Davis	.25	.11	.03
☐ 10 Andre Dawson	.35	.16	.04
☐ 11 Julio Franco	.20	.09	.03
☐ 12 Dwight Gooden	.25	.11	.03
☐ 13 Tony Gwynn	.50	.23	.06
☐ 14 Orel Hershiser	.15	.07	.02
☐ 15 Teddy Higuera	.10	.05	.01
☐ 16 Charlie Hough	.10	.05	.01
☐ 17 Kent Hrbek	.15	.07	.02
☐ 18 Bruce Hurst	.15	.07	.02
☐ 19 Wally Joyner	.20	.09	.03
☐ 20 Mark Langston	.15	.07	.02
☐ 21 Dave LaPoint	.10	.05	.01
☐ 22 Candy Maldonado	.10	.05	.01
☐ 23 Don Mattingly	.75	.35	.09
☐ 24 Roger McDowell	.10	.05	.01
☐ 25 Mark McGwire	.60	.25	.08
☐ 26 Jack Morris	.20	.09	.03
☐ 27 Dale Murphy	.30	.14	.04
☐ 28 Eddie Murray	.35	.16	.04
☐ 29 Matt Nokes	.20	.09	.03
☐ 30 Kirby Puckett	.75	.35	.09
☐ 31 Tim Raines	.20	.09	.03
☐ 32 Willie Randolph	.15	.07	.02
☐ 33 Jeff Reardon	.20	.09	.03
☐ 34 Nolan Ryan	1.25	.55	.16
☐ 35 Juan Samuel	.15	.07	.02
☐ 36 Mike Schmidt	.75	.35	.09
☐ 37 Mike Scott	.15	.07	.02
☐ 38 Kevin Seitzer	.15	.07	.02
☐ 39 Ozzie Smith	.25	.11	.03
☐ 40 Darryl Strawberry	.50	.23	.06
☐ 41 Rick Sutcliffe	.10	.05	.01
☐ 42 Alan Trammell	.20	.09	.03
☐ 43 Tim Wallach	.15	.07	.02
☐ 44 Dave Winfield	.35	.16	.04

1988 Fleer Baseball MVP's

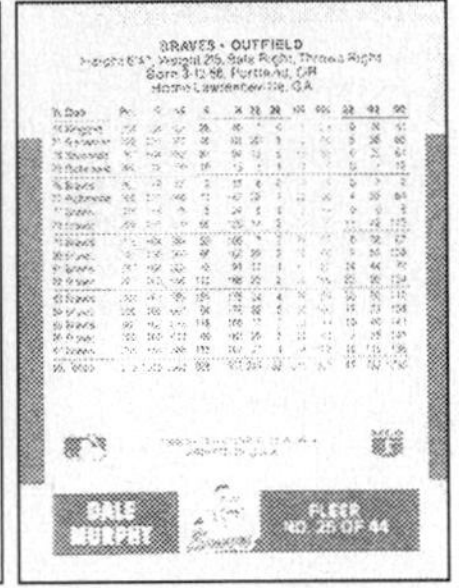

This small 44-card boxed set was produced by Fleer for distribution by the Toys'R'Us stores. The cards measure the standard 2 1/2" by 3 1/2" and feature full color fronts. The set is titled "Baseball MVP." Each individual boxed set includes the 44 cards and six logo stickers. The checklist for the set is found on the back panel of the box. The card fronts have a vanilla-yellow and blue border. The box refers to Toys'R'Us but there is no mention of Toys'R'Us anywhere on the cards themselves. The card numbering is in alphabetical order by player's name.

	MT	EX-MT	VG
COMPLETE SET (44)	5.00	2.30	.60
COMMON PLAYER (1-44)	.10	.05	.01
☐ 1 George Bell	.20	.09	.03
☐ 2 Wade Boggs	.50	.23	.06
☐ 3 Jose Canseco	.75	.35	.09
☐ 4 Ivan Calderon	.15	.07	.02
☐ 5 Will Clark	.75	.35	.09
☐ 6 Roger Clemens	1.00	.45	.13
☐ 7 Vince Coleman	.20	.09	.03
☐ 8 Eric Davis	.25	.11	.03
☐ 9 Andre Dawson	.35	.16	.04
☐ 10 Dave Dravecky	.20	.09	.03
☐ 11 Mike Dunne	.10	.05	.01
☐ 12 Dwight Evans	.15	.07	.02
☐ 13 Sid Fernandez	.15	.07	.02
☐ 14 Tony Fernandez	.15	.07	.02
☐ 15 Julio Franco	.20	.09	.03
☐ 16 Dwight Gooden	.25	.11	.03
☐ 17 Tony Gwynn	.50	.23	.06
☐ 18 Ted Higuera	.10	.05	.01
☐ 19 Charlie Hough	.10	.05	.01
☐ 20 Wally Joyner	.20	.09	.03
☐ 21 Mark Langston	.15	.07	.02
☐ 22 Don Mattingly	.75	.35	.09
☐ 23 Mark McGwire	.60	.25	.08
☐ 24 Jack Morris	.20	.09	.03
☐ 25 Dale Murphy	.30	.14	.04

☐ 26 Kirby Puckett	.75	.35	.09
☐ 27 Tim Raines	.20	.09	.03
☐ 28 Willie Randolph	.15	.07	.02
☐ 29 Ryne Sandberg	.75	.35	.09
☐ 30 Benito Santiago	.25	.11	.03
☐ 31 Mike Schmidt	.60	.25	.08
☐ 32 Mike Scott	.15	.07	.02
☐ 33 Kevin Seitzer	.10	.05	.01
☐ 34 Larry Sheets	.10	.05	.01
☐ 35 Ozzie Smith	.25	.11	.03
☐ 36 Dave Stewart	.15	.07	.02
☐ 37 Darryl Strawberry	.50	.23	.06
☐ 38 Rick Sutcliffe	.15	.07	.02
☐ 39 Alan Trammell	.20	.09	.03
☐ 40 Fernando Valenzuela	.15	.07	.02
☐ 41 Frank Viola	.15	.07	.02
☐ 42 Tim Wallach	.10	.05	.01
☐ 43 Dave Winfield	.35	.16	.04
☐ 44 Robin Yount	.50	.23	.06

1988 Fleer Exciting Stars

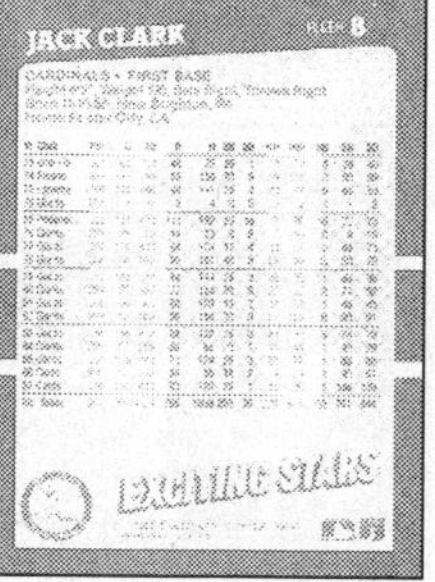

This small boxed set of 44 cards was produced exclusively for Cumberland Farm Stores. The cards measure the standard 2 1/2" by 3 1/2" and feature full color fronts and red, white, and blue backs. The card fronts are distinguished by the framing of the player's full-color photo with a blue border with a red and white bar stripe across the middle. The box for the cards describes the set as the "1988 Fleer Baseball's Exciting Stars." The checklist for the set is given on the back of the set box. The card numbering is in alphabetical order by player's name.

	MT	EX-MT	VG
COMPLETE SET (44)	5.00	2.30	.60
COMMON PLAYER (1-44)	.10	.05	.01

☐ 1 Harold Baines	.15	.07	.02
☐ 2 Kevin Bass	.10	.05	.01
☐ 3 George Bell	.20	.09	.03
☐ 4 Wade Boggs	.50	.23	.06
☐ 5 Mickey Brantley	.10	.05	.01
☐ 6 Sid Bream	.10	.05	.01
☐ 7 Jose Canseco	.75	.35	.09
☐ 8 Jack Clark	.15	.07	.02
☐ 9 Will Clark	.75	.35	.09
☐ 10 Roger Clemens	1.00	.45	.13
☐ 11 Vince Coleman	.20	.09	.03
☐ 12 Eric Davis	.25	.11	.03
☐ 13 Andre Dawson	.35	.16	.04
☐ 14 Julio Franco	.20	.09	.03
☐ 15 Dwight Gooden	.25	.11	.03
☐ 16 Mike Greenwell	.25	.11	.03
☐ 17 Tony Gwynn	.50	.23	.06
☐ 18 Von Hayes	.10	.05	.01
☐ 19 Tom Henke	.15	.07	.02
☐ 20 Orel Hershiser	.20	.09	.03
☐ 21 Teddy Higuera	.10	.05	.01
☐ 22 Brook Jacoby	.10	.05	.01
☐ 23 Wally Joyner	.20	.09	.03
☐ 24 Jimmy Key	.15	.07	.02
☐ 25 Don Mattingly	.75	.35	.09
☐ 26 Mark McGwire	.60	.25	.08
☐ 27 Jack Morris	.20	.09	.03
☐ 28 Dale Murphy	.30	.14	.04
☐ 29 Matt Nokes	.20	.09	.03

☐ 30 Kirby Puckett	.75	.35	.09
☐ 31 Tim Raines	.20	.09	.03
☐ 32 Ryne Sandberg	.75	.35	.09
☐ 33 Benito Santiago	.20	.09	.03
☐ 34 Mike Schmidt	.60	.25	.08
☐ 35 Mike Scott	.15	.07	.02
☐ 36 Kevin Seitzer	.10	.05	.01
☐ 37 Larry Sheets	.10	.05	.01
☐ 38 Ruben Sierra	.75	.35	.09
☐ 39 Darryl Strawberry	.50	.23	.06
☐ 40 Rick Sutcliffe	.15	.07	.02
☐ 41 Danny Tartabull	.25	.11	.03
☐ 42 Alan Trammell	.20	.09	.03
☐ 43 Fernando Valenzuela	.10	.05	.01
☐ 44 Devon White	.20	.09	.03

1988 Fleer Headliners

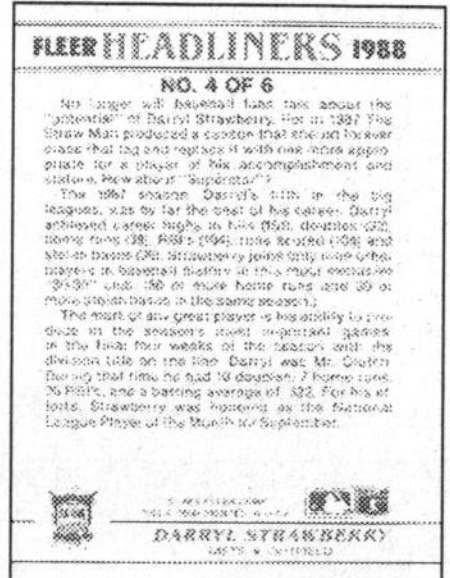

This six-card set was distributed as a special insert in rack packs. The obverse features the player photo superimposed on a gray newsprint background. The cards measure 2 1/2" by 3 1/2". The cards are printed in red, black, and white on the back describing why that particular player made headlines the previous season. The cards are numbered on the back.

	MT	EX-MT	VG
COMPLETE SET (6)	7.00	3.10	.85
COMMON PLAYER (1-6)	.75	.35	.09

☐ 1 Don Mattingly	2.00	.90	.25
☐ 2 Mark McGwire	2.00	.90	.25
☐ 3 Jack Morris	1.00	.45	.13
☐ 4 Darryl Strawberry	1.50	.65	.19
☐ 5 Dwight Gooden	1.00	.45	.13
☐ 6 Tim Raines	.75	.35	.09

1988 Fleer Hottest Stars

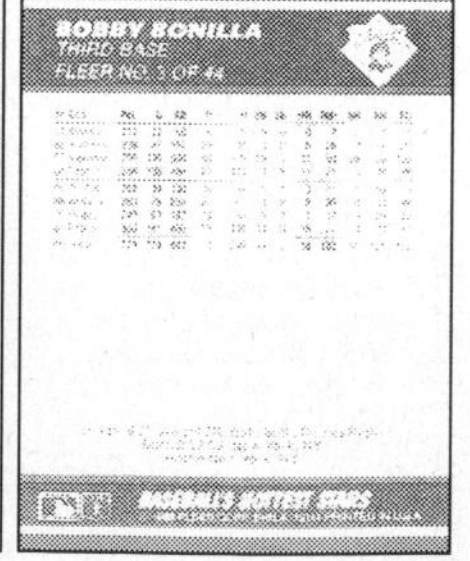

BOBBY BONILLA
THIRD BASE
FLEER NO. 1 OF 44
BASEBALL'S HOTTEST STARS

This 44-card boxed set was produced by Fleer for exclusive distribution by Revco Discount Drug stores all over the country. The cards measure the standard 2 1/2" by 3 1/2" and feature full color fronts and red, white, and blue backs.

The card fronts are easily distinguished by the flaming baseball in the lower right corner which says "Fleer Baseball's Hottest Stars." The player's picture is framed in red fading from orange down to yellow. The box for the cards proclaims "1988 Limited Edition Baseball's Hottest Stars" and is styled in blue, red, and yellow. The checklist for the set is given on the back of the set box. The box refers to Revco but there is no mention of Revco anywhere on the cards themselves. The card numbering is in alphabetical order by player's name.

	MT	EX-MT	VG
COMPLETE SET (44)	5.00	2.30	.60
COMMON PLAYER (1-44)	.10	.05	.01
☐ 1 George Bell	.20	.09	.03
☐ 2 Wade Boggs	.50	.23	.06
☐ 3 Bobby Bonilla	.35	.16	.04
☐ 4 George Brett	.50	.23	.06
☐ 5 Jose Canseco	.75	.35	.09
☐ 6 Will Clark	.75	.35	.09
☐ 7 Roger Clemens	1.00	.45	.13
☐ 8 Eric Davis	.25	.11	.03
☐ 9 Andre Dawson	.35	.16	.04
☐ 10 Tony Fernandez	.15	.07	.02
☐ 11 Julio Franco	.15	.07	.02
☐ 12 Gary Gaetti	.10	.05	.01
☐ 13 Dwight Gooden	.25	.11	.03
☐ 14 Mike Greenwell	.25	.11	.03
☐ 15 Tony Gwynn	.50	.23	.06
☐ 16 Rickey Henderson	.60	.25	.08
☐ 17 Keith Hernandez	.15	.07	.02
☐ 18 Tom Herr	.10	.05	.01
☐ 19 Orel Hershiser	.15	.07	.02
☐ 20 Ted Higuera	.10	.05	.01
☐ 21 Wally Joyner	.20	.09	.03
☐ 22 Jimmy Key	.15	.07	.02
☐ 23 Mark Langston	.15	.07	.02
☐ 24 Don Mattingly	.75	.35	.09
☐ 25 Jack McDowell	.75	.35	.09
☐ 26 Mark McGwire	.60	.25	.08
☐ 27 Kevin Mitchell	.25	.11	.03
☐ 28 Jack Morris	.20	.09	.03
☐ 29 Dale Murphy	.30	.14	.04
☐ 30 Kirby Puckett	.75	.35	.09
☐ 31 Tim Raines	.20	.09	.03
☐ 32 Shane Rawley	.10	.05	.01
☐ 33 Benito Santiago	.20	.09	.03
☐ 34 Mike Schmidt	.60	.25	.08
☐ 35 Mike Scott	.15	.07	.02
☐ 36 Kevin Seitzer	.10	.05	.01
☐ 37 Larry Sheets	.10	.05	.01
☐ 38 Ruben Sierra	.50	.23	.06
☐ 39 Dave Smith	.10	.05	.01
☐ 40 Ozzie Smith	.30	.14	.04
☐ 41 Darryl Strawberry	.50	.23	.06
☐ 42 Rick Sutcliffe	.15	.07	.02
☐ 43 Pat Tabler	.10	.05	.01
☐ 44 Alan Trammell	.20	.09	.03

1988 Fleer League Leaders

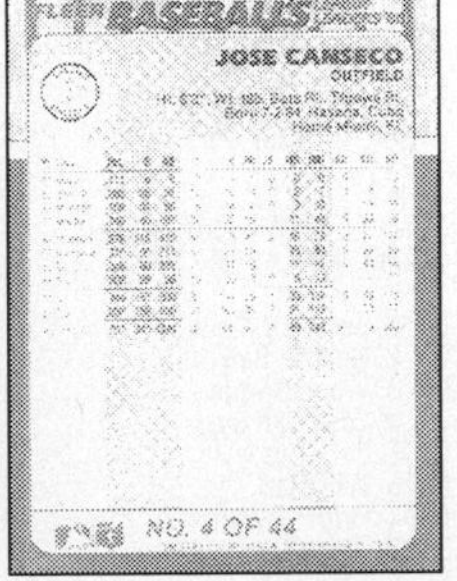

This small boxed set of 44 cards was produced exclusively for Walgreen Drug Stores. The cards measure the standard 2 1/2" by 3 1/2" and feature full color fronts and pink, white, and blue backs. The card fronts are distinguished by the blue solid and striped background behind the player's full-color photo. The box for the cards describes the set as the "1988 Fleer Baseball's League Leaders." The checklist for the set is given on the back of the set box. The card numbering is in alphabetical order by player's name.

	MT	EX-MT	VG
COMPLETE SET (44)	5.00	2.30	.60
COMMON PLAYER (1-44)	.10	.05	.01
☐ 1 George Bell	.20	.09	.03
☐ 2 Wade Boggs	.50	.23	.06
☐ 3 Ivan Calderon	.10	.05	.01
☐ 4 Jose Canseco	.75	.35	.09
☐ 5 Will Clark	.75	.35	.09
☐ 6 Roger Clemens	1.00	.45	.13
☐ 7 Vince Coleman	.20	.09	.03
☐ 8 Eric Davis	.25	.11	.03
☐ 9 Andre Dawson	.35	.16	.04
☐ 10 Bill Doran	.10	.05	.01
☐ 11 Dwight Evans	.15	.07	.02
☐ 12 Julio Franco	.15	.07	.02
☐ 13 Gary Gaetti	.10	.05	.01
☐ 14 Andres Galarraga	.15	.07	.02
☐ 15 Dwight Gooden	.25	.11	.03
☐ 16 Tony Gwynn	.50	.23	.06
☐ 17 Tom Henke	.15	.07	.02
☐ 18 Keith Hernandez	.15	.07	.02
☐ 19 Orel Hershiser	.15	.07	.02
☐ 20 Ted Higuera	.10	.05	.01
☐ 21 Kent Hrbek	.15	.07	.02
☐ 22 Wally Joyner	.15	.07	.02
☐ 23 Jimmy Key	.15	.07	.02
☐ 24 Mark Langston	.15	.07	.02
☐ 25 Don Mattingly	.75	.35	.09
☐ 26 Mark McGwire	.60	.25	.08
☐ 27 Paul Molitor	.25	.11	.03
☐ 28 Jack Morris	.20	.09	.03
☐ 29 Dale Murphy	.30	.14	.04
☐ 30 Kirby Puckett	.75	.35	.09
☐ 31 Tim Raines	.20	.09	.03
☐ 32 Rick Reuschel	.10	.05	.01
☐ 33 Bret Saberhagen	.20	.09	.03
☐ 34 Benito Santiago	.15	.07	.02
☐ 35 Mike Schmidt	.60	.25	.08
☐ 36 Mike Scott	.15	.07	.02
☐ 37 Kevin Seitzer	.10	.05	.01
☐ 38 Larry Sheets	.10	.05	.01
☐ 39 Ruben Sierra	.50	.23	.06
☐ 40 Darryl Strawberry	.50	.23	.06
☐ 41 Rick Sutcliffe	.15	.07	.02
☐ 42 Alan Trammell	.20	.09	.03
☐ 43 Andy Van Slyke	.25	.11	.03
☐ 44 Todd Worrell	.15	.07	.02

1988 Fleer Mini

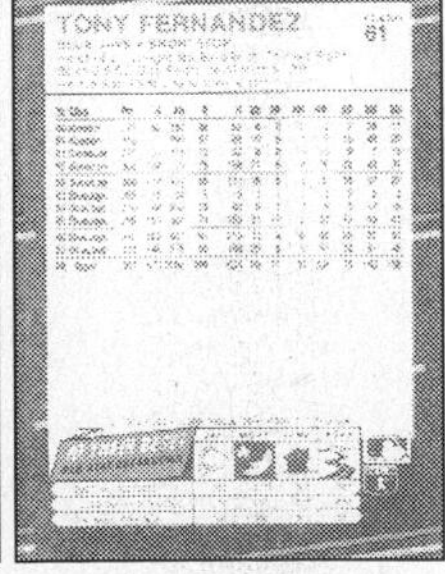

The 1988 Fleer "Classic Miniatures" set consists of 120 small cards with all new pictures of the players as compared to the 1988 Fleer regular issue. The cards are only 1 13/16" by 2 9/16", making them one of the smallest cards available. Card backs provide career year-by-year statistics. The complete set was distributed in a green, red, white, and silver box along with 18 logo stickers. The card numbering is by alphabetical team order within league and alphabetically within each team.

	MT	EX-MT	VG
COMPLETE SET (120)	12.50	5.75	1.55
COMMON PLAYER (1-120)	.05	.02	.01
☐ 1 Eddie Murray	.25	.11	.03
☐ 2 Dave Schmidt	.05	.02	.01
☐ 3 Larry Sheets	.05	.02	.01
☐ 4 Wade Boggs	.75	.35	.09
☐ 5 Roger Clemens	1.25	.55	.16
☐ 6 Dwight Evans	.10	.05	.01
☐ 7 Mike Greenwell	.25	.11	.03
☐ 8 Sam Horn	.05	.02	.01
☐ 9 Lee Smith	.12	.05	.02
☐ 10 Brian Downing	.05	.02	.01
☐ 11 Wally Joyner	.20	.09	.03
☐ 12 Devon White	.15	.07	.02
☐ 13 Mike Witt	.05	.02	.01
☐ 14 Ivan Calderon	.10	.05	.01
☐ 15 Ozzie Guillen	.12	.05	.02
☐ 16 Jack McDowell	.75	.35	.09
☐ 17 Kenny Williams	.05	.02	.01
☐ 18 Joe Carter	.35	.16	.04
☐ 19 Julio Franco	.12	.05	.02
☐ 20 Pat Tabler	.05	.02	.01
☐ 21 Doyle Alexander	.05	.02	.01
☐ 22 Jack Morris	.15	.07	.02
☐ 23 Matt Nokes	.15	.07	.02
☐ 24 Walt Terrell	.05	.02	.01
☐ 25 Alan Trammell	.20	.09	.03
☐ 26 Bret Saberhagen	.20	.09	.03
☐ 27 Kevin Seitzer	.08	.04	.01
☐ 28 Danny Tartabull	.25	.11	.03
☐ 29 Gary Thurman	.05	.02	.01
☐ 30 Ted Higuera	.05	.02	.01
☐ 31 Paul Molitor	.15	.07	.02
☐ 32 Dan Plesac	.05	.02	.01
☐ 33 Robin Yount	.75	.35	.09
☐ 34 Gary Gaetti	.08	.04	.01
☐ 35 Kent Hrbek	.10	.05	.01
☐ 36 Kirby Puckett	.75	.35	.09
☐ 37 Jeff Reardon	.15	.07	.02
☐ 38 Frank Viola	.10	.05	.01
☐ 39 Jack Clark	.08	.04	.01
☐ 40 Rickey Henderson	.75	.35	.09
☐ 41 Don Mattingly	.75	.35	.09
☐ 42 Willie Randolph	.08	.04	.01
☐ 43 Dave Righetti	.05	.02	.01
☐ 44 Dave Winfield	.40	.18	.05
☐ 45 Jose Canseco	.75	.35	.09
☐ 46 Mark McGwire	.60	.25	.08
☐ 47 Dave Parker	.15	.07	.02
☐ 48 Dave Stewart	.10	.05	.01
☐ 49 Walt Weiss	.25	.11	.03
☐ 50 Bob Welch	.08	.04	.01
☐ 51 Mickey Brantley	.05	.02	.01
☐ 52 Mark Langston	.10	.05	.01
☐ 53 Harold Reynolds	.05	.02	.01
☐ 54 Scott Fletcher	.05	.02	.01
☐ 55 Charlie Hough	.05	.02	.01
☐ 56 Pete Incaviglia	.10	.05	.01
☐ 57 Larry Parrish	.05	.02	.01
☐ 58 Ruben Sierra	.50	.23	.06
☐ 59 George Bell	.15	.07	.02
☐ 60 Mark Eichhorn	.05	.02	.01
☐ 61 Tony Fernandez	.08	.04	.01
☐ 62 Tom Henke	.10	.05	.01
☐ 63 Jimmy Key	.10	.05	.01
☐ 64 Dion James	.05	.02	.01
☐ 65 Dale Murphy	.25	.11	.03
☐ 66 Zane Smith	.05	.02	.01
☐ 67 Andre Dawson	.30	.14	.04
☐ 68 Mark Grace	1.00	.45	.13
☐ 69 Jerry Mumphrey	.05	.02	.01
☐ 70 Ryne Sandberg	1.00	.45	.13
☐ 71 Rick Sutcliffe	.08	.04	.01
☐ 72 Kal Daniels	.10	.05	.01
☐ 73 Eric Davis	.25	.11	.03
☐ 74 John Franco	.08	.04	.01
☐ 75 Ron Robinson	.05	.02	.01
☐ 76 Jeff Treadway	.08	.04	.01
☐ 77 Kevin Bass	.05	.02	.01
☐ 78 Glenn Davis	.12	.05	.02
☐ 79 Nolan Ryan	1.50	.65	.19
☐ 80 Mike Scott	.08	.04	.01
☐ 81 Dave Smith	.05	.02	.01
☐ 82 Kirk Gibson	.10	.05	.01
☐ 83 Pedro Guerrero	.10	.05	.01
☐ 84 Orel Hershiser	.15	.07	.02
☐ 85 Steve Sax	.15	.07	.02
☐ 86 Fernando Valenzuela	.10	.05	.01
☐ 87 Tim Burke	.05	.02	.01
☐ 88 Andres Galarraga	.12	.05	.02
☐ 89 Neal Heaton	.05	.02	.01
☐ 90 Tim Raines	.15	.07	.02
☐ 91 Tim Wallach	.08	.04	.01
☐ 92 Dwight Gooden	.25	.11	.03
☐ 93 Keith Hernandez	.10	.05	.01
☐ 94 Gregg Jefferies	1.00	.45	.13
☐ 95 Howard Johnson	.12	.05	.02
☐ 96 Roger McDowell	.05	.02	.01
☐ 97 Darryl Strawberry	.40	.18	.05
☐ 98 Steve Bedrosian	.05	.02	.01
☐ 99 Von Hayes	.05	.02	.01
☐ 100 Shane Rawley	.05	.02	.01
☐ 101 Juan Samuel	.08	.04	.01
☐ 102 Mike Schmidt	.75	.35	.09
☐ 103 Bobby Bonilla	.35	.16	.04
☐ 104 Mike Dunne	.05	.02	.01
☐ 105 Andy Van Slyke	.15	.07	.02
☐ 106 Vince Coleman	.15	.07	.02
☐ 107 Bob Horner	.08	.04	.01
☐ 108 Willie McGee	.12	.05	.02
☐ 109 Ozzie Smith	.30	.14	.04
☐ 110 John Tudor	.08	.04	.01
☐ 111 Todd Worrell	.15	.07	.02
☐ 112 Tony Gwynn	.50	.23	.06
☐ 113 John Kruk	.12	.05	.02
☐ 114 Lance McCullers	.05	.02	.01
☐ 115 Benito Santiago	.20	.09	.03
☐ 116 Will Clark	.75	.35	.09
☐ 117 Jeff Leonard	.05	.02	.01
☐ 118 Candy Maldonado	.05	.02	.01
☐ 119 Kirt Manwaring	.05	.02	.01
☐ 120 Don Robinson	.05	.02	.01

1988 Fleer Record Setters

This small boxed set of 44 cards was produced exclusively for Eckerd's Drug Stores. The cards measure the standard 2 1/2" by 3 1/2" and feature full color fronts and red, white, and blue backs. The card fronts are distinguished by the red and blue frame around the player's full-color photo. The box for the cards describes the set as the "1988 Baseball Record Setters." The checklist for the set is given on the back of the set box. The card numbering is in alphabetical order by player's name.

	MT	EX-MT	VG
COMPLETE SET (44)	5.00	2.30	.60
COMMON PLAYER (1-44)	.10	.05	.01
☐ 1 Jesse Barfield	.10	.05	.01
☐ 2 George Bell	.20	.09	.03
☐ 3 Wade Boggs	.50	.23	.06
☐ 4 Jose Canseco	.75	.35	.09
☐ 5 Jack Clark	.10	.05	.01
☐ 6 Will Clark	.75	.35	.09
☐ 7 Roger Clemens	1.00	.45	.13
☐ 8 Alvin Davis	.10	.05	.01
☐ 9 Eric Davis	.25	.11	.03
☐ 10 Andre Dawson	.35	.16	.04
☐ 11 Mike Dunne	.10	.05	.01
☐ 12 John Franco	.10	.05	.01
☐ 13 Julio Franco	.15	.07	.02
☐ 14 Dwight Gooden	.25	.11	.03
☐ 15 Mark Gubicza (Listed as Gubiczo	.15	.07	.02

		MT	EX-MT	VG
	on box checklist)			
☐ 16	Ozzie Guillen	.15	.07	.02
☐ 17	Tony Gwynn	.50	.23	.06
☐ 18	Orel Hershiser	.20	.09	.03
☐ 19	Teddy Higuera	.10	.05	.01
☐ 20	Howard Johnson UER (Missing '87 stats on card back)	.20	.09	.03
☐ 21	Wally Joyner	.20	.09	.03
☐ 22	Jimmy Key	.15	.07	.02
☐ 23	Jeff Leonard	.10	.05	.01
☐ 24	Don Mattingly	.75	.35	.09
☐ 25	Mark McGwire	.60	.25	.08
☐ 26	Jack Morris	.20	.09	.03
☐ 27	Dale Murphy	.30	.14	.04
☐ 28	Larry Parrish	.10	.05	.01
☐ 29	Kirby Puckett	.75	.35	.09
☐ 30	Tim Raines	.20	.09	.03
☐ 31	Harold Reynolds	.10	.05	.01
☐ 32	Dave Righetti	.10	.05	.01
☐ 33	Cal Ripken	1.00	.45	.13
☐ 34	Benito Santiago	.20	.09	.03
☐ 35	Mike Schmidt	.60	.25	.08
☐ 36	Mike Scott	.15	.07	.02
☐ 37	Kevin Seitzer	.10	.05	.01
☐ 38	Ozzie Smith	.25	.11	.03
☐ 39	Darryl Strawberry	.50	.23	.06
☐ 40	Rick Sutcliffe	.15	.07	.02
☐ 41	Alan Trammell	.20	.09	.03
☐ 42	Frank Viola	.15	.07	.02
☐ 43	Mitch Williams	.15	.07	.02
☐ 44	Todd Worrell	.20	.09	.03

1988 Fleer Sluggers/Pitchers

Fleer produced this 44-card boxed set although it was primarily distributed by McCrory, McLellan, J.J Newberry, H.L.Green, T.G.Y., and other similar stores. The set is subtitled "Baseball's Best". Cards are standard-size, 2 1/2" by 3 1/2", and were packaged in a green custom box along with six logo stickers. The set checklist is given on the back of the box. The bottoms of the boxes which held the individual set boxes also contained a panel of six cards; these box bottom cards were numbered C1 through C6. The card numbering is in alphabetical order by player's name.

		MT	EX-MT	VG
COMPLETE SET (44)		5.00	2.30	.60
COMMON PLAYER (1-44)		.10	.05	.01
☐ 1	George Bell	.20	.09	.03
☐ 2	Wade Boggs	.50	.23	.06
☐ 3	Bobby Bonilla	.35	.16	.04
☐ 4	Tom Brunansky	.15	.07	.02
☐ 5	Ellis Burks	.35	.16	.04
☐ 6	Jose Canseco	.75	.35	.09
☐ 7	Joe Carter	.35	.16	.04
☐ 8	Will Clark	.75	.35	.09
☐ 9	Roger Clemens	1.00	.45	.13
☐ 10	Eric Davis	.25	.11	.03
☐ 11	Glenn Davis	.20	.09	.03
☐ 12	Andre Dawson	.35	.16	.04
☐ 13	Dennis Eckersley	.30	.14	.04
☐ 14	Andres Galarraga	.15	.07	.02
☐ 15	Dwight Gooden	.25	.11	.03
☐ 16	Pedro Guerrero	.15	.07	.02
☐ 17	Tony Gwynn	.50	.23	.06

		MT	EX-MT	VG
☐ 18	Orel Hershiser	.20	.09	.03
☐ 19	Ted Higuera	.10	.05	.01
☐ 20	Pete Incaviglia	.15	.07	.02
☐ 21	Danny Jackson	.10	.05	.01
☐ 22	Doug Jennings	.10	.05	.01
☐ 23	Mark Langston	.15	.07	.02
☐ 24	Dave LaPoint	.10	.05	.01
☐ 25	Mike LaValliere	.10	.05	.01
☐ 26	Don Mattingly	.75	.35	.09
☐ 27	Mark McGwire	.60	.25	.08
☐ 28	Dale Murphy	.30	.14	.04
☐ 29	Ken Phelps	.10	.05	.01
☐ 30	Kirby Puckett	.75	.35	.09
☐ 31	Johnny Ray	.10	.05	.01
☐ 32	Jeff Reardon	.15	.07	.02
☐ 33	Dave Righetti	.10	.05	.01
☐ 34	Cal Ripken UER (Misspelled Ripkin on card front)	1.00	.45	.13
☐ 35	Chris Sabo	.35	.16	.04
☐ 36	Mike Schmidt	.60	.25	.08
☐ 37	Mike Scott	.15	.07	.02
☐ 38	Kevin Seitzer	.10	.05	.01
☐ 39	Dave Stewart	.15	.07	.02
☐ 40	Darryl Strawberry	.50	.23	.06
☐ 41	Greg Swindell	.20	.09	.03
☐ 42	Frank Tanana	.10	.05	.01
☐ 43	Dave Winfield	.35	.16	.04
☐ 44	Todd Worrell	.20	.09	.03

1988 Fleer Slug/Pitch Box Cards

The cards in this six-card set each measure the standard 2 1/2" by 3 1/2". Cards have essentially the same design as the 1988 Fleer Sluggers vs. Pitchers set of Baseball's Best. The cards were printed on the bottom of the counter display box which held 24 small boxed sets; hence theoretically these box cards are 1/24 as plentiful as the regular boxed set cards. These six cards, numbered C1 to C6 are considered a separate set in their own right and are not typically included in a complete set of the 1988 Fleer Sluggers vs. Pitchers set of 44. The value of the panels uncut is slightly greater, perhaps by 25 percent greater, than the value of the individual cards cut up carefully.

		MT	EX-MT	VG
COMPLETE SET (6)		4.50	2.00	.55
COMMON PLAYERS (C1-C6)		.25	.11	.03
☐ C1	Ron Darling	.50	.23	.06
☐ C2	Rickey Henderson	2.00	.90	.25
☐ C3	Carney Lansford	.50	.23	.06
☐ C4	Rafael Palmeiro	1.00	.45	.13
☐ C5	Frank Viola	.50	.23	.06
☐ C6	Twins Logo (Checklist back)	.25	.11	.03

1988 Fleer Sticker Cards

These Star Stickers were distributed as a separate issue by Fleer, with five star stickers and a logo sticker in each wax pack. The 132-card (sticker) set features 2 1/2" by 3 1/2" full-color fronts and even statistics on the sticker back, which is an indication that the Fleer Company understands that these stickers are rarely used as stickers but more like traditional cards. The card fronts are surrounded by a silver-gray border and the backs are printed in red and black on white card stock. The set numbering is in alphabetical order within team and alphabetically by team within each league.

	MT	EX-MT	VG
COMPLETE SET (132)	20.00	9.00	2.50
COMMON PLAYER (1-132)	.05	.02	.01
□ 1 Mike Boddicker	.08	.04	.01
□ 2 Eddie Murray	.25	.11	.03
□ 3 Cal Ripken	1.50	.65	.19
□ 4 Larry Sheets	.05	.02	.01
□ 5 Wade Boggs	.60	.25	.08
□ 6 Ellis Burks	.35	.16	.04
□ 7 Roger Clemens	1.25	.55	.16
□ 8 Dwight Evans	.12	.05	.02
□ 9 Mike Greenwell	.35	.16	.04
□ 10 Bruce Hurst	.08	.04	.01
□ 11 Brian Downing	.05	.02	.01
□ 12 Wally Joyner	.20	.09	.03
□ 13 Mike Witt	.05	.02	.01
□ 14 Ivan Calderon	.08	.04	.01
□ 15 Jose DeLeon	.05	.02	.01
□ 16 Ozzie Guillen	.10	.05	.01
□ 17 Bobby Thigpen	.12	.05	.02
□ 18 Joe Carter	.35	.16	.04
□ 19 Julio Franco	.15	.07	.02
□ 20 Brook Jacoby	.05	.02	.01
□ 21 Cory Snyder	.10	.05	.01
□ 22 Pat Tabler	.05	.02	.01
□ 23 Doyle Alexander	.05	.02	.01
□ 24 Kirk Gibson	.12	.05	.02
□ 25 Mike Henneman	.10	.05	.01
□ 26 Jack Morris	.20	.09	.03
□ 27 Matt Nokes	.15	.07	.02
□ 28 Walt Terrell	.05	.02	.01
□ 29 Alan Trammell	.20	.09	.03
□ 30 George Brett	.60	.25	.08
□ 31 Charlie Leibrandt	.08	.04	.01
□ 32 Bret Saberhagen	.20	.09	.03
□ 33 Kevin Seitzer	.10	.05	.01
□ 34 Danny Tartabull	.30	.14	.04
□ 35 Frank White	.05	.02	.01
□ 36 Rob Deer	.08	.04	.01
□ 37 Ted Higuera	.08	.04	.01
□ 38 Paul Molitor	.20	.09	.03
□ 39 Dan Plesac	.05	.02	.01
□ 40 Robin Yount	.60	.25	.08
□ 41 Bert Blyleven	.10	.05	.01
□ 42 Tom Brunansky	.08	.04	.01
□ 43 Gary Gaetti	.08	.04	.01
□ 44 Kent Hrbek	.10	.05	.01
□ 45 Kirby Puckett	1.25	.55	.16
□ 46 Jeff Reardon	.12	.05	.02
□ 47 Frank Viola	.10	.05	.01
□ 48 Don Mattingly	1.00	.45	.13
□ 49 Mike Pagliarulo	.05	.02	.01
□ 50 Willie Randolph	.08	.04	.01
□ 51 Rick Rhoden	.05	.02	.01
□ 52 Dave Righetti	.08	.04	.01
□ 53 Dave Winfield	.35	.16	.04
□ 54 Jose Canseco	1.00	.45	.13
□ 55 Carney Lansford	.10	.05	.01
□ 56 Mark McGwire	.75	.35	.09
□ 57 Dave Stewart	.12	.05	.02
□ 58 Curt Young	.05	.02	.01
□ 59 Alvin Davis	.08	.04	.01
□ 60 Mark Langston	.10	.05	.01
□ 61 Ken Phelps	.05	.02	.01
□ 62 Harold Reynolds	.05	.02	.01
□ 63 Scott Fletcher	.05	.02	.01
□ 64 Charlie Hough	.05	.02	.01
□ 65 Pete Incaviglia	.10	.05	.01
□ 66 Oddibe McDowell	.05	.02	.01
□ 67 Pete O'Brien	.05	.02	.01
□ 68 Larry Parrish	.05	.02	.01
□ 69 Ruben Sierra	.60	.25	.08
□ 70 Jesse Barfield	.08	.04	.01
□ 71 George Bell	.15	.07	.02
□ 72 Tony Fernandez	.10	.05	.01
□ 73 Tom Henke	.10	.05	.01
□ 74 Jimmy Key	.10	.05	.01
□ 75 Lloyd Moseby	.05	.02	.01
□ 76 Dion James	.05	.02	.01
□ 77 Dale Murphy	.35	.16	.04
□ 78 Zane Smith	.05	.02	.01
□ 79 Andre Dawson	.35	.16	.04
□ 80 Ryne Sandberg	1.50	.65	.19
□ 81 Rick Sutcliffe	.08	.04	.01
□ 82 Kal Daniels	.10	.05	.01
□ 83 Eric Davis	.35	.16	.04
□ 84 John Franco	.05	.02	.01
□ 85 Kevin Bass	.05	.02	.01
□ 86 Glenn Davis	.12	.05	.02
□ 87 Bill Doran	.05	.02	.01
□ 88 Nolan Ryan	3.00	1.35	.40
□ 89 Mike Scott	.08	.04	.01
□ 90 Dave Smith	.05	.02	.01
□ 91 Pedro Guerrero	.08	.04	.01
□ 92 Orel Hershiser	.15	.07	.02
□ 93 Steve Sax	.12	.05	.02
□ 94 Fernando Valenzuela	.08	.04	.01
□ 95 Tim Burke	.05	.02	.01
□ 96 Andres Galarraga	.10	.05	.01
□ 97 Tim Raines	.15	.07	.02
□ 98 Tim Wallach	.08	.04	.01
□ 99 Mitch Webster	.05	.02	.01
□ 100 Ron Darling	.10	.05	.01
□ 101 Sid Fernandez	.10	.05	.01
□ 102 Dwight Gooden	.30	.14	.04
□ 103 Keith Hernandez	.10	.05	.01
□ 104 Howard Johnson	.15	.07	.02
□ 105 Roger McDowell	.05	.02	.01
□ 106 Darryl Strawberry	.75	.35	.09
□ 107 Steve Bedrosian	.05	.02	.01
□ 108 Von Hayes	.05	.02	.01
□ 109 Shane Rawley	.05	.02	.01
□ 110 Juan Samuel	.08	.04	.01
□ 111 Mike Schmidt	1.00	.45	.13
□ 112 Milt Thompson	.05	.02	.01
□ 113 Sid Bream	.05	.02	.01
□ 114 Bobby Bonilla	.40	.18	.05
□ 115 Mike Dunne	.05	.02	.01
□ 116 Andy Van Slyke	.15	.07	.02
□ 117 Vince Coleman	.15	.07	.02
□ 118 Willie McGee	.10	.05	.01
□ 119 Terry Pendleton	.30	.14	.04
□ 120 Ozzie Smith	.35	.16	.04
□ 121 John Tudor	.08	.04	.01
□ 122 Todd Worrell	.10	.05	.01
□ 123 Tony Gwynn	.60	.25	.08
□ 124 John Kruk	.12	.05	.02
□ 125 Benito Santiago	.30	.14	.04
□ 126 Will Clark	1.00	.45	.13
□ 127 Dave Dravecky	.15	.07	.02
□ 128 Jeff Leonard	.05	.02	.01
□ 129 Candy Maldonado	.05	.02	.01
□ 130 Rick Reuschel	.08	.04	.01
□ 131 Don Robinson	.05	.02	.01
□ 132 Checklist Card	.05	.02	.01

1988 Fleer Sticker Box Cards

The bottoms of the Star Sticker wax boxes contained two different sets of four cards done in a similar format to the stickers; these cards (they are not stickers but truly cards) are numbered with the prefix S and are considered a

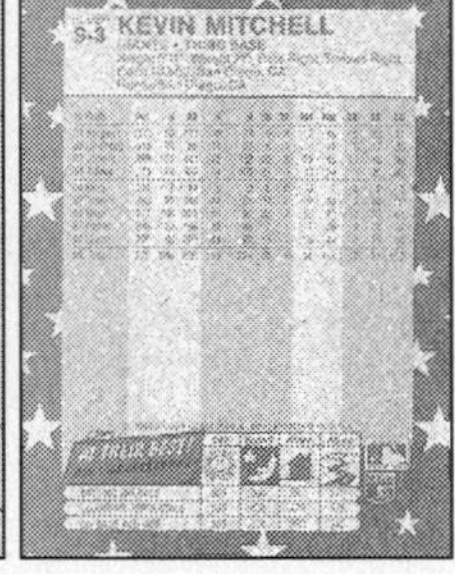

separate set. The value of the panels uncut is slightly greater, perhaps by 25 percent greater, than the value of the individual cards cut up carefully.

	MT	EX-MT	VG
COMPLETE SET (8)	6.00	2.70	.75
COMMON PLAYER (S1-S8)	.25	.11	.03
☐ S1 Don Baylor	.35	.16	.04
☐ S2 Gary Carter	.60	.25	.08
☐ S3 Ron Guidry	.35	.16	.04
☐ S4 Rickey Henderson	2.00	.90	.25
☐ S5 Kevin Mitchell	.75	.35	.09
☐ S6 Mark McGwire and Eric Davis	1.50	.65	.19
☐ S7 Giants Logo	.25	.11	.03
☐ S8 Detroit Logo	.25	.11	.03

1988 Fleer Superstars

Fleer produced this 44-card boxed set although it was primarily distributed by McCrory, McLellan, J.J Newberry, H.L.Green, T.G.Y., and other similar stores. The set is subtitled "Fleer Superstars." Cards are standard-size, 2 1/2" by 3 1/2", and were packaged in a red, white, blue, and yellow custom box along with six logo stickers. The set checklist is given on the back of the box. The bottoms of the boxes which held the individual set boxes also contained a panel of six cards; these box bottom cards were numbered C1 through C6. The card numbering is in alphabetical order by player's name.

	MT	EX-MT	VG
COMPLETE SET (44)	5.00	2.30	.60
COMMON PLAYER (1-44)	.10	.05	.01
☐ 1 Steve Bedrosian	.10	.05	.01
☐ 2 George Bell	.20	.09	.03
☐ 3 Wade Boggs	.50	.23	.06
☐ 4 Barry Bonds	.60	.25	.08
☐ 5 Jose Canseco	.75	.35	.09
☐ 6 Joe Carter	.35	.16	.04
☐ 7 Jack Clark	.10	.05	.01
☐ 8 Will Clark	.75	.35	.09
☐ 9 Roger Clemens	1.00	.45	.13
☐ 10 Alvin Davis	.10	.05	.01
☐ 11 Eric Davis	.25	.11	.03
☐ 12 Glenn Davis	.15	.07	.02
☐ 13 Andre Dawson	.35	.16	.04
☐ 14 Dwight Gooden	.25	.11	.03
☐ 15 Orel Hershiser	.20	.09	.03
☐ 16 Teddy Higuera	.10	.05	.01
☐ 17 Kent Hrbek	.15	.07	.02
☐ 18 Wally Joyner	.20	.09	.03
☐ 19 Jimmy Key	.15	.07	.02
☐ 20 John Kruk	.20	.09	.03
☐ 21 Jeff Leonard	.10	.05	.01
☐ 22 Don Mattingly	.75	.35	.09
☐ 23 Mark McGwire	.60	.25	.08
☐ 24 Kevin McReynolds	.15	.07	.02
☐ 25 Dale Murphy	.30	.14	.04
☐ 26 Matt Nokes	.15	.07	.02
☐ 27 Terry Pendleton	.25	.11	.03
☐ 28 Kirby Puckett	.75	.35	.09
☐ 29 Tim Raines	.20	.09	.03
☐ 30 Rick Rhoden	.10	.05	.01
☐ 31 Cal Ripken	1.00	.45	.13
☐ 32 Benito Santiago	.20	.09	.03
☐ 33 Mike Schmidt	.60	.25	.08
☐ 34 Mike Scott	.15	.07	.02
☐ 35 Kevin Seitzer	.10	.05	.01
☐ 36 Ruben Sierra	.50	.23	.06
☐ 37 Cory Snyder	.15	.07	.02
☐ 38 Darryl Strawberry	.50	.23	.06
☐ 39 Rick Sutcliffe	.10	.05	.01
☐ 40 Danny Tartabull	.25	.11	.03
☐ 41 Alan Trammell	.20	.09	.03
☐ 42 Kenny Williams	.10	.05	.01
☐ 43 Mike Witt	.10	.05	.01
☐ 44 Robin Yount	.60	.25	.08

1988 Fleer Superstars Box Cards

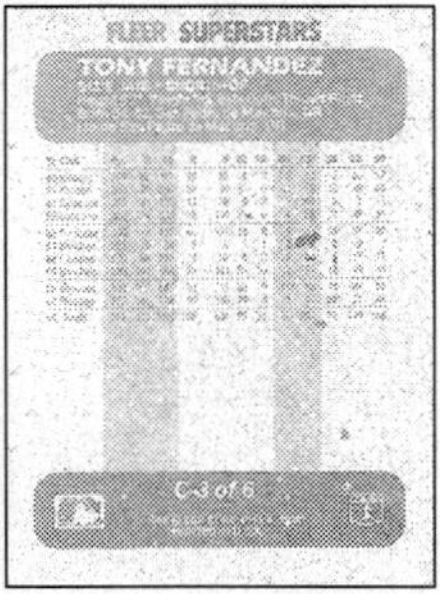

The cards in this six-card set each measure the standard 2 1/2" by 3 1/2". Cards have essentially the same design as the 1988 Fleer Superstars set. The cards were printed on the bottom of the counter display box which held 24 small boxed sets; hence theoretically these box cards are 1/24 as plentiful as the regular boxed set cards. These six cards, numbered C1 to C6 are considered a separate set in their own right and are not typically included in a complete set of the 1988 Fleer Superstars set of 44. The value of the panels uncut is slightly greater, perhaps by 25 percent greater, than the value of the individual cards cut up carefully.

	MT	EX-MT	VG
COMPLETE SET (6)	6.00	2.70	.75
COMMON PLAYER (C1-C6)	.25	.11	.03
☐ C1 Pete Incaviglia	.35	.16	.04
☐ C2 Rickey Henderson	2.00	.90	.25
☐ C3 Tony Fernandez	.35	.16	.04
☐ C4 Shane Rawley	.25	.11	.03
☐ C5 Ryne Sandberg	3.00	1.35	.40
☐ C6 Cardinals Logo (Checklist back)	.25	.11	.03

1988 Fleer Team Leaders

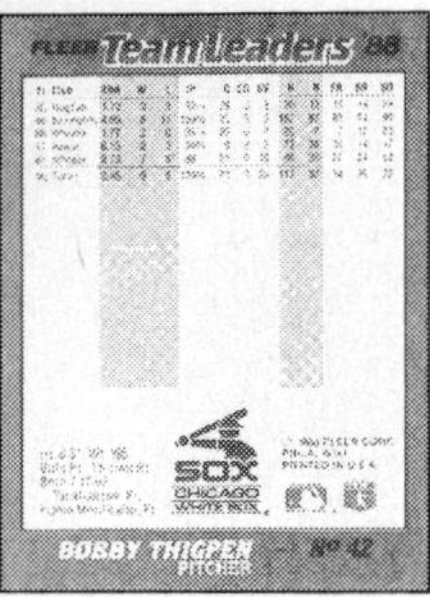

This 44-card boxed set was produced by Fleer for exclusive distribution by Kay Bee Toys and is sometimes referred to as the Fleer Kay Bee set. Six team logo stickers are included in the box with the complete set. The numerical checklist on the back of the box shows that the set is numbered alphabetically. The cards measure 2 1/2" by 3 1/2" and have a distinctive red border on the fronts. The Kay Bee logo is printed in the lower right corner of the obverse of each card.

	MT	EX-MT	VG
COMPLETE SET (44)	5.00	2.30	.60
COMMON PLAYER (1-44)	.10	.05	.01

	MT	EX-MT	VG
☐ 1 George Bell	.20	.09	.03
☐ 2 Wade Boggs	.50	.23	.06
☐ 3 Jose Canseco	.75	.35	.09
☐ 4 Will Clark	.75	.35	.09
☐ 5 Roger Clemens	1.00	.45	.13
☐ 6 Eric Davis	.25	.11	.03
☐ 7 Andre Dawson	.35	.16	.04
☐ 8 Julio Franco	.20	.09	.03
☐ 9 Andres Galarraga	.15	.07	.02
☐ 10 Dwight Gooden	.25	.11	.03
☐ 11 Tony Gwynn	.50	.23	.06
☐ 12 Tom Henke	.15	.07	.02
☐ 13 Orel Hershiser	.20	.09	.03
☐ 14 Kent Hrbek	.15	.07	.02
☐ 15 Ted Higuera	.10	.05	.01
☐ 16 Wally Joyner	.15	.07	.02
☐ 17 Jimmy Key	.15	.07	.02
☐ 18 Mark Langston	.15	.07	.02
☐ 19 Don Mattingly	.75	.35	.09
☐ 20 Willie McGee	.15	.07	.02
☐ 21 Mark McGwire	.60	.25	.08
☐ 22 Paul Molitor	.25	.11	.03
☐ 23 Jack Morris	.20	.09	.03
☐ 24 Dale Murphy	.30	.14	.04
☐ 25 Larry Parrish	.10	.05	.01
☐ 26 Kirby Puckett	.75	.35	.09
☐ 27 Tim Raines	.20	.09	.03
☐ 28 Jeff Reardon	.20	.09	.03
☐ 29 Dave Righetti	.10	.05	.01
☐ 30 Cal Ripken	1.00	.45	.13
☐ 31 Don Robinson	.10	.05	.01
☐ 32 Bret Saberhagen	.20	.09	.03
☐ 33 Juan Samuel	.15	.07	.02
☐ 34 Mike Schmidt	.60	.25	.08
☐ 35 Mike Scott	.15	.07	.02
☐ 36 Kevin Seitzer	.10	.05	.01
☐ 37 Dave Smith	.10	.05	.01
☐ 38 Ozzie Smith	.25	.11	.03
☐ 39 Zane Smith	.10	.05	.01
☐ 40 Darryl Strawberry	.50	.23	.06
☐ 41 Rick Sutcliffe	.15	.07	.02
☐ 42 Bobby Thigpen	.15	.07	.02
☐ 43 Alan Trammell	.20	.09	.03
☐ 44 Andy Van Slyke	.20	.09	.03

1988 Fleer Update

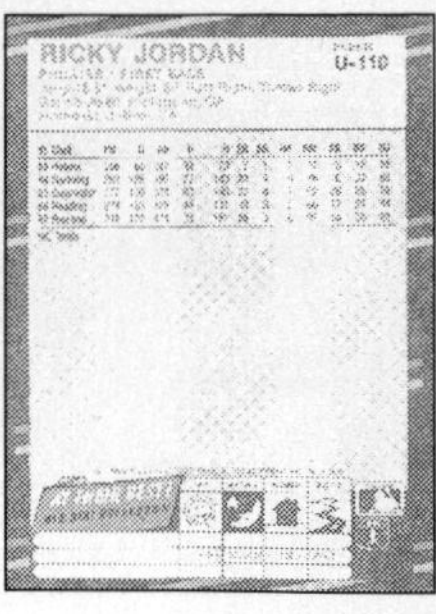

This 132-card set was distributed by Fleer to dealers as a complete set in a custom box. In addition to the complete set of 132 cards, the box also contains 25 Team Logo stickers.The card fronts look very similar to the 1988 Fleer regular issue. The cards are numbered (with a U prefix) alphabetically according to player's last name. Cards measure the standard size, 2 1/2" by 3 1/2". This was the first Fleer Update set to adopt the Fleer "alphabetical within team" numbering system. The key (extended) Rookie Cards in this set are Roberto Alomar, Craig Biggio, Chris Sabo, and John Smoltz. Fleer also produced a "limited" edition version of this set with glossy coating and packaged in a "tin." However, this tin set was apparently not limited enough (estimated between 40,000 and 60,000 1988 Update tin sets produced by Fleer), since the values of the "tin" glossy cards are now only double the values of the respective cards in the regular set.

	MT	EX-MT	VG
COMPLETE SET (132)	18.00	8.00	2.30
COMMON PLAYER (1-132)	.06	.03	.01

	MT	EX-MT	VG
☐ 1 Jose Bautista	.06	.03	.01
☐ 2 Joe Orsulak	.06	.03	.01
☐ 3 Doug Sisk	.06	.03	.01
☐ 4 Craig Worthington	.06	.03	.01
☐ 5 Mike Boddicker	.06	.03	.01
☐ 6 Rick Cerone	.06	.03	.01
☐ 7 Larry Parrish	.06	.03	.01
☐ 8 Lee Smith	.20	.09	.03
☐ 9 Mike Smithson	.06	.03	.01
☐ 10 John Trautwein	.06	.03	.01
☐ 11 Sherman Corbett	.06	.03	.01
☐ 12 Chili Davis	.10	.04	.01
☐ 13 Jim Eppard	.06	.03	.01
☐ 14 Bryan Harvey	.60	.25	.08
☐ 15 John Davis	.06	.03	.01
☐ 16 Dave Gallagher	.06	.03	.01
☐ 17 Ricky Horton	.06	.03	.01
☐ 18 Dan Pasqua	.06	.03	.01
☐ 19 Melido Perez	.40	.18	.05
☐ 20 Jose Segura	.06	.03	.01
☐ 21 Andy Allanson	.06	.03	.01
☐ 22 Jon Perlman	.06	.03	.01
☐ 23 Domingo Ramos	.06	.03	.01
☐ 24 Rick Rodriguez	.06	.03	.01
☐ 25 Willie Upshaw	.06	.03	.01
☐ 26 Paul Gibson	.06	.03	.01
☐ 27 Don Heinkel	.06	.03	.01
☐ 28 Ray Knight	.10	.04	.01
☐ 29 Gary Pettis	.06	.03	.01
☐ 30 Luis Salazar	.06	.03	.01
☐ 31 Mike Macfarlane	.40	.18	.05
☐ 32 Jeff Montgomery	.25	.11	.03
☐ 33 Ted Power	.06	.03	.01
☐ 34 Israel Sanchez	.06	.03	.01
☐ 35 Kurt Stillwell	.06	.03	.01
☐ 36 Pat Tabler	.06	.03	.01
☐ 37 Don August	.06	.03	.01
☐ 38 Darryl Hamilton	.40	.18	.05
☐ 39 Jeff Leonard	.06	.03	.01
☐ 40 Joey Meyer	.06	.03	.01
☐ 41 Allan Anderson	.06	.03	.01
☐ 42 Brian Harper	.10	.04	.01
☐ 43 Tom Herr	.06	.03	.01
☐ 44 Charlie Lea	.06	.03	.01
☐ 45 John Moses (Listed as Hohn on checklist card)	.06	.03	.01
☐ 46 John Candelaria	.06	.03	.01

Card	MT	EX-MT	VG
☐ 47 Jack Clark	.10	.04	.01
☐ 48 Richard Dotson	.06	.03	.01
☐ 49 Al Leiter	.06	.03	.01
☐ 50 Rafael Santana	.06	.03	.01
☐ 51 Don Slaught	.06	.03	.01
☐ 52 Todd Burns	.06	.03	.01
☐ 53 Dave Henderson	.10	.04	.01
☐ 54 Doug Jennings	.06	.03	.01
☐ 55 Dave Parker	.10	.04	.01
☐ 56 Walt Weiss	.25	.11	.03
☐ 57 Bob Welch	.10	.04	.01
☐ 58 Henry Cotto	.06	.03	.01
☐ 59 Mario Diaz UER (Listed as Marion on card front)	.06	.03	.01
☐ 60 Mike Jackson	.06	.03	.01
☐ 61 Bill Swift	.10	.05	.01
☐ 62 Jose Cecena	.06	.03	.01
☐ 63 Ray Hayward	.06	.03	.01
☐ 64 Jim Steels UER (Listed as Jim Steele on card back)	.06	.03	.01
☐ 65 Pat Borders	.60	.25	.08
☐ 66 Sil Campusano	.06	.03	.01
☐ 67 Mike Flanagan	.06	.03	.01
☐ 68 Todd Stottlemyre	.50	.23	.06
☐ 69 David Wells	.20	.09	.03
☐ 70 Jose Alvarez	.06	.03	.01
☐ 71 Paul Runge	.06	.03	.01
☐ 72 Cesar Jimenez UER (Card was intended for German Jiminez, it's his photo)	.06	.03	.01
☐ 73 Pete Smith	.50	.23	.06
☐ 74 John Smoltz	5.00	2.30	.60
☐ 75 Damon Berryhill	.15	.07	.02
☐ 76 Goose Gossage	.10	.04	.01
☐ 77 Mark Grace	2.00	.90	.25
☐ 78 Darrin Jackson	.10	.04	.01
☐ 79 Vance Law	.06	.03	.01
☐ 80 Jeff Pico	.06	.03	.01
☐ 81 Gary Varsho	.06	.03	.01
☐ 82 Tim Birtsas	.06	.03	.01
☐ 83 Rob Dibble	.60	.25	.08
☐ 84 Danny Jackson	.06	.03	.01
☐ 85 Paul O'Neill	.15	.07	.02
☐ 86 Jose Rijo	.15	.07	.02
☐ 87 Chris Sabo	.75	.35	.09
☐ 88 John Fishel	.06	.03	.01
☐ 89 Craig Biggio	1.25	.55	.16
☐ 90 Terry Puhl	.06	.03	.01
☐ 91 Rafael Ramirez	.06	.03	.01
☐ 92 Louie Meadows	.06	.03	.01
☐ 93 Kirk Gibson	.10	.04	.01
☐ 94 Alfredo Griffin	.06	.03	.01
☐ 95 Jay Howell	.06	.03	.01
☐ 96 Jesse Orosco	.06	.03	.01
☐ 97 Alejandro Pena	.06	.03	.01
☐ 98 Tracy Woodson	.12	.05	.02
☐ 99 John Dopson	.06	.03	.01
☐ 100 Brian Holman	.15	.07	.02
☐ 101 Rex Hudler	.06	.03	.01
☐ 102 Jeff Parrett	.06	.03	.01
☐ 103 Nelson Santovenia	.06	.03	.01
☐ 104 Kevin Elster	.06	.03	.01
☐ 105 Jeff Innis	.06	.03	.01
☐ 106 Mackey Sasser	.10	.05	.01
☐ 107 Phil Bradley	.06	.03	.01
☐ 108 Danny Clay	.06	.03	.01
☐ 109 Greg Harris	.06	.03	.01
☐ 110 Ricky Jordan	.20	.09	.03
☐ 111 David Palmer	.06	.03	.01
☐ 112 Jim Gott	.06	.03	.01
☐ 113 Tommy Gregg UER (Photo actually Randy Milligan)	.10	.04	.01
☐ 114 Barry Jones	.06	.03	.01
☐ 115 Randy Milligan	.30	.14	.04
☐ 116 Luis Alicea	.15	.07	.02
☐ 117 Tom Brunansky	.10	.04	.01
☐ 118 John Costello	.06	.03	.01
☐ 119 Jose DeLeon	.06	.03	.01
☐ 120 Bob Horner	.10	.04	.01
☐ 121 Scott Terry	.06	.03	.01
☐ 122 Roberto Alomar	11.00	4.90	1.40
☐ 123 Dave Leiper	.06	.03	.01
☐ 124 Keith Moreland	.06	.03	.01
☐ 125 Mark Parent	.06	.03	.01
☐ 126 Dennis Rasmussen	.06	.03	.01
☐ 127 Randy Bockus	.06	.03	.01
☐ 128 Brett Butler	.10	.05	.01
☐ 129 Donell Nixon	.06	.03	.01
☐ 130 Earnest Riles	.06	.03	.01
☐ 131 Roger Samuels	.06	.03	.01
☐ 132 Checklist U1-U132	.10	.01	.00

1988 Fleer Wax Box Cards

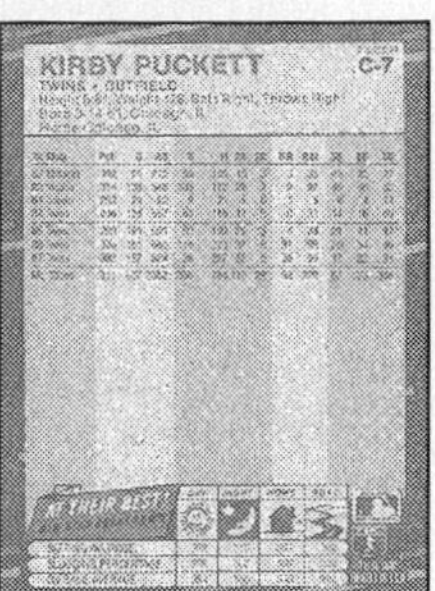

The cards in this 16-card set measure the standard 2 1/2" by 3 1/2". Cards have essentially the same design as the 1988 Fleer regular issue set. The cards were printed on the bottoms of the regular issue wax pack boxes. These 16 cards (C1 to C16) are considered a separate set in their own right and are not typically included in a complete set of the regular issue 1988 Fleer cards. The value of the panel uncut is slightly greater, perhaps by 25 percent greater, than the value of the individual cards cut up carefully.

	MT	EX-MT	VG
COMPLETE SET (16)	6.00	2.70	.75
COMMON PLAYER (C1-C16)	.15	.07	.02
☐ C1 Cardinals Logo	.15	.07	.02
☐ C2 Dwight Evans	.25	.11	.03
☐ C3 Andres Galarraga	.25	.11	.03
☐ C4 Wally Joyner	.40	.18	.05
☐ C5 Twins Logo	.15	.07	.02
☐ C6 Dale Murphy	.40	.18	.05
☐ C7 Kirby Puckett	1.25	.55	.16
☐ C8 Shane Rawley	.15	.07	.02
☐ C9 Giants Logo	.15	.07	.02
☐ C10 Ryne Sandberg	1.25	.55	.16
☐ C11 Mike Schmidt	1.00	.45	.13
☐ C12 Kevin Seitzer	.25	.11	.03
☐ C13 Tigers Logo	.15	.07	.02
☐ C14 Dave Stewart	.25	.11	.03
☐ C15 Tim Wallach	.15	.07	.02
☐ C16 Todd Worrell	.25	.11	.03

1988 Fleer World Series

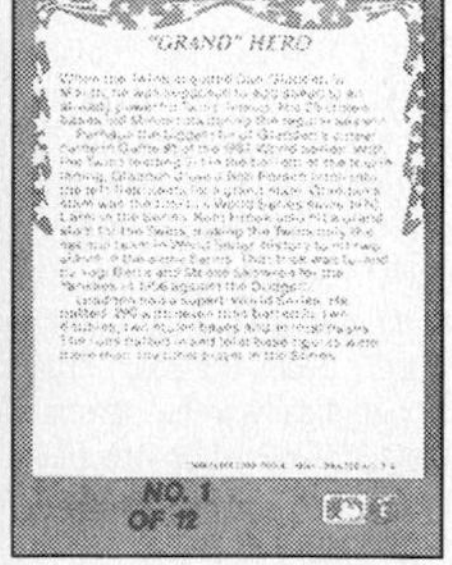

This 12-card set of 2 1/2" by 3 1/2" cards features highlights of the previous year's World Series between the Minnesota Twins and the St. Louis Cardinals. The sets were packaged as a complete set insert with the collated sets (of the 1988 Fleer regular issue) which were sold by Fleer directly to hobby card dealers; they were not available in the general retail candy store outlets. The set numbering is essentially in chronological order of the events from the immediate past World Series. The set was also released in a glossy version along with Fleer's "tin" factory sets.

	MT	EX-MT	VG
COMPLETE SET (12)	2.50	1.15	.30
COMMON PLAYER (1-12)	.20	.09	.03
☐ 1 Dan Gladden Grand Hero Game 1	.20	.09	.03
☐ 2 Randy Bush Cardinals "Bush" Wacked	.20	.09	.03
☐ 3 John Tudor Masterful Performance in Game 3	.30	.14	.04
☐ 4 Ozzie Smith The Wizard	.75	.35	.09
☐ 5 Todd Worrell and Tony Pena Throw Smoke	.30	.14	.04
☐ 6 Vince Coleman Cardinal Attack	.40	.18	.05
☐ 7 Tom Herr/Dan Driessen Herr's Wallop	.20	.09	.03
☐ 8 Kirby Puckett Kirby's Bat Comes Alive	1.00	.45	.13
☐ 9 Kent Hrbek Hrbek's Slam Forces Game 7	.40	.18	.05
☐ 10 Tom Herr Out at First	.20	.09	.03
☐ 11 Don Baylor Game 7's Play At The Plate	.30	.14	.04
☐ 12 Frank Viola Series MVP, 16 K's	.50	.23	.06

1989 Fleer

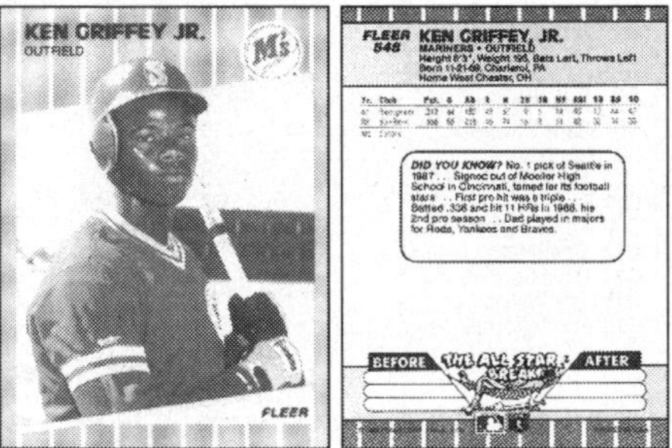

This 660-card set features a distinctive gray border background with white and yellow trim. The backs are printed in gray, black, and yellow on white card stock. The bottom of the card back shows an innovative breakdown of the player's demonstrated ability with respect to his performance before and after the All-Star break. Cards are numbered on the back and are again the standard 2 1/2" by 3 1/2". Cards are again organized numerically by teams and alphabetically within teams: Oakland A's (1-26), New York Mets (27-52), Los Angeles Dodgers (53-77), Boston Red Sox (78-101), Minnesota Twins (102-127), Detroit Tigers (128-151), Cincinnati Reds (152-175), Milwaukee Brewers (176-200), Pittsburgh Pirates (201-224), Toronto Blue Jays (225-248), New York Yankees (249-274), Kansas City Royals (275-298), San Diego Padres (299-322), San Francisco Giants (323-347), Houston Astros (348-370), Montreal Expos (371-395), Cleveland Indians (396-417), Chicago Cubs (418-442), St. Louis Cardinals (443-466), California Angels (467-490), Chicago White Sox (491-513), Texas Rangers (514-537), Seattle Mariners (538-561), Philadelphia Phillies (562-584), Atlanta Braves (585-605), and Baltimore Orioles (606-627). However, pairs 148/149, 153/154, 272/273, 283/284, and 367/368 were apparently mis-alphabetized by Fleer. The last 33 cards in the set consist of Specials (628-639), Rookie Pairs (640-653), and checklists (654-660). Due to the early beginning of production of this set, it seemed Fleer "presumed" that the A's would win the World Series, since they are listed as the first team in the numerical order; in fact, Fleer had the Mets over the underdog (but eventual World Champion) Dodgers as well. Fleer later reported that they merely arranged the teams according to team record due to the early printing date. Approximately half of the California Angels players have white rather than yellow halos. Certain Oakland A's player cards have red instead of green lines for front photo borders. Checklist cards are available either with or without positions listed for each player. The key rookies in this set are Sandy Alomar Jr., Ken Griffey Jr., Felix Jose, Ramon Martinez, Hal Morris, and Gary Sheffield. Fleer also produced the last of their three-year run of "limited" edition glossy, tin sets. This tin set was limited, but only compared to the previous year, as collector and dealer interest in the tin sets was apparently waning. It has been estimated that approximately 30,000 1989 tin sets were produced by Fleer; as a result, the price of the "tin" glossy cards now ranges from double to triple the price of the regular set cards.

	MT	EX-MT	VG
COMPLETE SET (660)	20.00	9.00	2.50
COMPLETE FACT.SET (660)	20.00	9.00	2.50
COMPLETE FACT.SET (672)	22.00	10.00	2.80
COMMON PLAYER (1-660)	.04	.02	.01
COMPLETE WS SET (12)	2.00	.90	.25
☐ 1 Don Baylor	.07	.03	.01
☐ 2 Lance Blankenship	.10	.05	.01
☐ 3 Todd Burns UER (Wrong birthdate; before/after All-Star stats missing)	.04	.02	.01
☐ 4 Greg Cadaret UER (All-Star Break stats show 3 losses, should be 2)	.04	.02	.01
☐ 5 Jose Canseco	.40	.18	.05
☐ 6 Storm Davis	.04	.02	.01
☐ 7 Dennis Eckersley	.12	.05	.02
☐ 8 Mike Gallego	.04	.02	.01
☐ 9 Ron Hassey	.04	.02	.01
☐ 10 Dave Henderson	.07	.03	.01
☐ 11 Rick Honeycutt	.04	.02	.01
☐ 12 Glenn Hubbard	.04	.02	.01
☐ 13 Stan Javier	.04	.02	.01
☐ 14 Doug Jennings	.04	.02	.01
☐ 15 Felix Jose	.75	.35	.09
☐ 16 Carney Lansford	.07	.03	.01
☐ 17 Mark McGwire	.40	.18	.05
☐ 18 Gene Nelson	.04	.02	.01
☐ 19 Dave Parker	.07	.03	.01
☐ 20 Eric Plunk	.04	.02	.01
☐ 21 Luis Polonia	.07	.03	.01
☐ 22 Terry Steinbach	.07	.03	.01
☐ 23 Dave Stewart	.07	.03	.01
☐ 24 Walt Weiss	.07	.03	.01
☐ 25 Bob Welch	.07	.03	.01
☐ 26 Curt Young	.04	.02	.01
☐ 27 Rick Aguilera	.07	.03	.01
☐ 28 Wally Backman	.04	.02	.01
☐ 29 Mark Carreon UER (After All-Star Break batting 7.14)	.04	.02	.01
☐ 30 Gary Carter	.07	.03	.01
☐ 31 David Cone	.15	.07	.02
☐ 32 Ron Darling	.07	.03	.01
☐ 33 Len Dykstra	.07	.03	.01
☐ 34 Kevin Elster	.04	.02	.01
☐ 35 Sid Fernandez	.07	.03	.01
☐ 36 Dwight Gooden	.12	.05	.02
☐ 37 Keith Hernandez	.07	.03	.01

Card			
☐ 38 Gregg Jefferies	.20	.09	.03
☐ 39 Howard Johnson	.07	.03	.01
☐ 40 Terry Leach	.04	.02	.01
☐ 41 Dave Magadan UER (Bio says 15 doubles, should be 13)	.07	.03	.01
☐ 42 Bob McClure	.04	.02	.01
☐ 43 Roger McDowell UER (Led Mets with 58, should be 62)	.04	.02	.01
☐ 44 Kevin McReynolds	.07	.03	.01
☐ 45 Keith A. Miller	.04	.02	.01
☐ 46 Randy Myers	.07	.03	.01
☐ 47 Bob Ojeda	.04	.02	.01
☐ 48 Mackey Sasser	.04	.02	.01
☐ 49 Darryl Strawberry	.25	.11	.03
☐ 50 Tim Teufel	.04	.02	.01
☐ 51 Dave West	.10	.05	.01
☐ 52 Mookie Wilson	.07	.03	.01
☐ 53 Dave Anderson	.04	.02	.01
☐ 54 Tim Belcher	.07	.03	.01
☐ 55 Mike Davis	.04	.02	.01
☐ 56 Mike Devereaux	.15	.07	.02
☐ 57 Kirk Gibson	.07	.03	.01
☐ 58 Alfredo Griffin	.04	.02	.01
☐ 59 Chris Gwynn	.04	.02	.01
☐ 60 Jeff Hamilton	.04	.02	.01
☐ 61A Danny Heep ERR (Home: Lake Hills)	.40	.18	.05
☐ 61B Danny Heep COR (Home: San Antonio)	.10	.05	.01
☐ 62 Orel Hershiser	.07	.03	.01
☐ 63 Brian Holton	.04	.02	.01
☐ 64 Jay Howell	.04	.02	.01
☐ 65 Tim Leary	.04	.02	.01
☐ 66 Mike Marshall	.04	.02	.01
☐ 67 Ramon Martinez	.50	.23	.06
☐ 68 Jesse Orosco	.04	.02	.01
☐ 69 Alejandro Pena	.04	.02	.01
☐ 70 Steve Sax	.07	.03	.01
☐ 71 Mike Scioscia	.04	.02	.01
☐ 72 Mike Sharperson	.04	.02	.01
☐ 73 John Shelby	.04	.02	.01
☐ 74 Franklin Stubbs	.04	.02	.01
☐ 75 John Tudor	.04	.02	.01
☐ 76 Fernando Valenzuela	.07	.03	.01
☐ 77 Tracy Woodson	.04	.02	.01
☐ 78 Marty Barrett	.04	.02	.01
☐ 79 Todd Benzinger	.04	.02	.01
☐ 80 Mike Boddicker UER (Rochester in '76, should be '78)	.04	.02	.01
☐ 81 Wade Boggs	.25	.11	.03
☐ 82 Oil Can Boyd	.04	.02	.01
☐ 83 Ellis Burks	.07	.03	.01
☐ 84 Rick Cerone	.04	.02	.01
☐ 85 Roger Clemens	.40	.18	.05
☐ 86 Steve Curry	.04	.02	.01
☐ 87 Dwight Evans	.07	.03	.01
☐ 88 Wes Gardner	.04	.02	.01
☐ 89 Rich Gedman	.04	.02	.01
☐ 90 Mike Greenwell	.07	.03	.01
☐ 91 Bruce Hurst	.07	.03	.01
☐ 92 Dennis Lamp	.04	.02	.01
☐ 93 Spike Owen	.04	.02	.01
☐ 94 Larry Parrish UER (Before All-Star Break batting 1.90)	.04	.02	.01
☐ 95 Carlos Quintana	.10	.05	.01
☐ 96 Jody Reed	.04	.02	.01
☐ 97 Jim Rice	.07	.03	.01
☐ 98A Kevin Romine ERR (Photo actually Randy Kutcher batting)	.40	.18	.05
☐ 98B Kevin Romine COR (Arms folded)	.10	.05	.01
☐ 99 Lee Smith	.07	.03	.01
☐ 100 Mike Smithson	.04	.02	.01
☐ 101 Bob Stanley	.04	.02	.01
☐ 102 Allan Anderson	.04	.02	.01
☐ 103 Keith Atherton	.04	.02	.01
☐ 104 Juan Berenguer	.04	.02	.01
☐ 105 Bert Blyleven	.07	.03	.01
☐ 106 Eric Bullock UER (Bats/Throws Right, should be Left)	.04	.02	.01
☐ 107 Randy Bush	.04	.02	.01
☐ 108 John Christensen	.04	.02	.01
☐ 109 Mark Davidson	.04	.02	.01
☐ 110 Gary Gaetti	.04	.02	.01
☐ 111 Greg Gagne	.04	.02	.01
☐ 112 Dan Gladden	.04	.02	.01
☐ 113 German Gonzalez	.04	.02	.01
☐ 114 Brian Harper	.07	.03	.01
☐ 115 Tom Herr	.04	.02	.01
☐ 116 Kent Hrbek	.07	.03	.01
☐ 117 Gene Larkin	.04	.02	.01
☐ 118 Tim Laudner	.04	.02	.01
☐ 119 Charlie Lea	.04	.02	.01
☐ 120 Steve Lombardozzi	.04	.02	.01
☐ 121A John Moses (Home: Tempe)	.40	.18	.05
☐ 121B John Moses (Home: Phoenix)	.10	.05	.01
☐ 122 Al Newman	.04	.02	.01
☐ 123 Mark Portugal	.04	.02	.01
☐ 124 Kirby Puckett	.40	.18	.05
☐ 125 Jeff Reardon	.07	.03	.01
☐ 126 Fred Toliver	.04	.02	.01
☐ 127 Frank Viola	.07	.03	.01
☐ 128 Doyle Alexander	.04	.02	.01
☐ 129 Dave Bergman	.04	.02	.01
☐ 130A Tom Brookens ERR (Mike Heath back)	.75	.35	.09
☐ 130B Tom Brookens COR	.10	.05	.01
☐ 131 Paul Gibson	.04	.02	.01
☐ 132A Mike Heath ERR (Tom Brookens back)	.75	.35	.09
☐ 132B Mike Heath COR	.10	.05	.01
☐ 133 Don Heinkel	.04	.02	.01
☐ 134 Mike Henneman	.07	.03	.01
☐ 135 Guillermo Hernandez	.04	.02	.01
☐ 136 Eric King	.04	.02	.01
☐ 137 Chet Lemon	.04	.02	.01
☐ 138 Fred Lynn UER ('74, '75 stats missing)	.07	.03	.01
☐ 139 Jack Morris	.12	.05	.02
☐ 140 Matt Nokes	.07	.03	.01
☐ 141 Gary Pettis	.04	.02	.01
☐ 142 Ted Power	.04	.02	.01
☐ 143 Jeff M. Robinson	.04	.02	.01
☐ 144 Luis Salazar	.04	.02	.01
☐ 145 Steve Searcy	.04	.02	.01
☐ 146 Pat Sheridan	.04	.02	.01
☐ 147 Frank Tanana	.04	.02	.01
☐ 148 Alan Trammell	.07	.03	.01
☐ 149 Walt Terrell	.04	.02	.01
☐ 150 Jim Walewander	.04	.02	.01
☐ 151 Lou Whitaker	.07	.03	.01
☐ 152 Tim Birtsas	.04	.02	.01
☐ 153 Tom Browning	.04	.02	.01
☐ 154 Keith Brown	.04	.02	.01
☐ 155 Norm Charlton	.20	.09	.03
☐ 156 Dave Concepcion	.07	.03	.01
☐ 157 Kal Daniels	.07	.03	.01
☐ 158 Eric Davis	.12	.05	.02
☐ 159 Bo Diaz	.04	.02	.01
☐ 160 Rob Dibble	.20	.09	.03
☐ 161 Nick Esasky	.04	.02	.01
☐ 162 John Franco	.07	.03	.01
☐ 163 Danny Jackson	.04	.02	.01
☐ 164 Barry Larkin	.15	.07	.02
☐ 165 Rob Murphy	.04	.02	.01
☐ 166 Paul O'Neill	.07	.03	.01
☐ 167 Jeff Reed	.04	.02	.01
☐ 168 Jose Rijo	.07	.03	.01
☐ 169 Ron Robinson	.04	.02	.01
☐ 170 Chris Sabo	.30	.14	.04
☐ 171 Candy Sierra	.04	.02	.01
☐ 172 Van Snider	.04	.02	.01
☐ 173A Jeff Treadway UER (Target registration mark above head on front in light blue)	9.00	4.00	1.15
☐ 173B Jeff Treadway COR (No target on front)	.04	.02	.01
☐ 174 Frank Williams UER (After All-Star Break stats are jumbled)	.04	.02	.01
☐ 175 Herm Winningham	.04	.02	.01
☐ 176 Jim Adduci	.04	.02	.01
☐ 177 Don August	.04	.02	.01
☐ 178 Mike Birkbeck	.04	.02	.01
☐ 179 Chris Bosio	.04	.02	.01
☐ 180 Glenn Braggs	.04	.02	.01
☐ 181 Greg Brock	.04	.02	.01
☐ 182 Mark Clear	.04	.02	.01
☐ 183 Chuck Crim	.04	.02	.01
☐ 184 Rob Deer	.07	.03	.01
☐ 185 Tom Filer	.04	.02	.01
☐ 186 Jim Gantner	.04	.02	.01
☐ 187 Darryl Hamilton	.20	.09	.03
☐ 188 Ted Higuera	.04	.02	.01
☐ 189 Odell Jones	.04	.02	.01

☐ 190 Jeffrey Leonard .04 .02 .01
☐ 191 Joey Meyer .04 .02 .01
☐ 192 Paul Mirabella .04 .02 .01
☐ 193 Paul Molitor .10 .05 .01
☐ 194 Charlie O'Brien .04 .02 .01
☐ 195 Dan Plesac .04 .02 .01
☐ 196 Gary Sheffield 2.50 1.15 .30
☐ 197 B.J. Surhoff .04 .02 .01
☐ 198 Dale Sveum .04 .02 .01
☐ 199 Bill Wegman .04 .02 .01
☐ 200 Robin Yount .20 .09 .03
☐ 201 Rafael Belliard .04 .02 .01
☐ 202 Barry Bonds .40 .18 .05
☐ 203 Bobby Bonilla .20 .09 .03
☐ 204 Sid Bream .04 .02 .01
☐ 205 Benny Distefano .04 .02 .01
☐ 206 Doug Drabek .07 .03 .01
☐ 207 Mike Dunne .04 .02 .01
☐ 208 Felix Fermin .04 .02 .01
☐ 209 Brian Fisher .04 .02 .01
☐ 210 Jim Gott .04 .02 .01
☐ 211 Bob Kipper .04 .02 .01
☐ 212 Dave LaPoint .04 .02 .01
☐ 213 Mike LaValliere .04 .02 .01
☐ 214 Jose Lind .04 .02 .01
☐ 215 Junior Ortiz .04 .02 .01
☐ 216 Vicente Palacios .04 .02 .01
☐ 217 Tom Prince .04 .02 .01
☐ 218 Gary Redus .04 .02 .01
☐ 219 R.J. Reynolds .04 .02 .01
☐ 220 Jeff D. Robinson .04 .02 .01
☐ 221 John Smiley .07 .03 .01
☐ 222 Andy Van Slyke .10 .05 .01
☐ 223 Bob Walk .04 .02 .01
☐ 224 Glenn Wilson .04 .02 .01
☐ 225 Jesse Barfield .04 .02 .01
☐ 226 George Bell .10 .05 .01
☐ 227 Pat Borders .30 .14 .04
☐ 228 John Cerutti .04 .02 .01
☐ 229 Jim Clancy .04 .02 .01
☐ 230 Mark Eichhorn .04 .02 .01
☐ 231 Tony Fernandez .07 .03 .01
☐ 232 Cecil Fielder .25 .11 .03
☐ 233 Mike Flanagan .04 .02 .01
☐ 234 Kelly Gruber .07 .03 .01
☐ 235 Tom Henke .07 .03 .01
☐ 236 Jimmy Key .07 .03 .01
☐ 237 Rick Leach .04 .02 .01
☐ 238 Manny Lee UER .04 .02 .01
(Bio says regular
shortstop, sic,
Tony Fernandez)
☐ 239 Nelson Liriano .04 .02 .01
☐ 240 Fred McGriff .25 .11 .03
☐ 241 Lloyd Moseby .04 .02 .01
☐ 242 Rance Mulliniks .04 .02 .01
☐ 243 Jeff Musselman .04 .02 .01
☐ 244 Dave Stieb .07 .03 .01
☐ 245 Todd Stottlemyre .10 .05 .01
☐ 246 Duane Ward .07 .03 .01
☐ 247 David Wells .10 .05 .01
☐ 248 Ernie Whitt UER .04 .02 .01
(HR total 21,
should be 121)
☐ 249 Luis Aguayo .04 .02 .01
☐ 250A Neil Allen .75 .35 .09
(Home: Sarasota, FL)
☐ 250B Neil Allen .10 .05 .01
(Home: Syosset, NY)
☐ 251 John Candelaria .04 .02 .01
☐ 252 Jack Clark .07 .03 .01
☐ 253 Richard Dotson .04 .02 .01
☐ 254 Rickey Henderson .25 .11 .03
☐ 255 Tommy John .07 .03 .01
☐ 256 Roberto Kelly .15 .07 .02
☐ 257 Al Leiter .04 .02 .01
☐ 258 Don Mattingly .25 .11 .03
☐ 259 Dale Mohorcic .04 .02 .01
☐ 260 Hal Morris .60 .25 .08
☐ 261 Scott Nielsen .04 .02 .01
☐ 262 Mike Pagliarulo UER .04 .02 .01
(Wrong birthdate)
☐ 263 Hipolito Pena .04 .02 .01
☐ 264 Ken Phelps .04 .02 .01
☐ 265 Willie Randolph .07 .03 .01
☐ 266 Rick Rhoden .04 .02 .01
☐ 267 Dave Righetti .04 .02 .01
☐ 268 Rafael Santana .04 .02 .01
☐ 269 Steve Shields .04 .02 .01
☐ 270 Joel Skinner .04 .02 .01
☐ 271 Don Slaught .04 .02 .01
☐ 272 Claudell Washington .04 .02 .01
☐ 273 Gary Ward .04 .02 .01
☐ 274 Dave Winfield .20 .09 .03
☐ 275 Luis Aquino .04 .02 .01
☐ 276 Floyd Bannister .04 .02 .01
☐ 277 George Brett .20 .09 .03
☐ 278 Bill Buckner .07 .03 .01
☐ 279 Nick Capra .04 .02 .01
☐ 280 Jose DeJesus .04 .02 .01
☐ 281 Steve Farr .04 .02 .01
☐ 282 Jerry Don Gleaton .04 .02 .01
☐ 283 Mark Gubicza .04 .02 .01
☐ 284 Tom Gordon UER .10 .05 .01
(16.2 innings in '88,
should be 15.2)
☐ 285 Bo Jackson .20 .09 .03
☐ 286 Charlie Leibrandt .04 .02 .01
☐ 287 Mike Macfarlane .15 .07 .02
☐ 288 Jeff Montgomery .07 .03 .01
☐ 289 Bill Pecota UER .04 .02 .01
(Photo actually
Brad Wellman)
☐ 290 Jamie Quirk .04 .02 .01
☐ 291 Bret Saberhagen .07 .03 .01
☐ 292 Kevin Seitzer .07 .03 .01
☐ 293 Kurt Stillwell .04 .02 .01
☐ 294 Pat Tabler .04 .02 .01
☐ 295 Danny Tartabull .12 .05 .02
☐ 296 Gary Thurman .04 .02 .01
☐ 297 Frank White .04 .02 .01
☐ 298 Willie Wilson .04 .02 .01
☐ 299 Roberto Alomar .75 .35 .09
☐ 300 Sandy Alomar Jr. UER .25 .11 .03
(Wrong birthdate, says
6/16/66, should say
6/18/66)
☐ 301 Chris Brown .04 .02 .01
☐ 302 Mike Brumley UER .04 .02 .01
(133 hits in '88,
should be 134)
☐ 303 Mark Davis .04 .02 .01
☐ 304 Mark Grant .04 .02 .01
☐ 305 Tony Gwynn .25 .11 .03
☐ 306 Greg W. Harris .10 .05 .01
☐ 307 Andy Hawkins .04 .02 .01
☐ 308 Jimmy Jones .04 .02 .01
☐ 309 John Kruk .07 .03 .01
☐ 310 Dave Leiper .04 .02 .01
☐ 311 Carmelo Martinez .04 .02 .01
☐ 312 Lance McCullers .04 .02 .01
☐ 313 Keith Moreland .04 .02 .01
☐ 314 Dennis Rasmussen .04 .02 .01
☐ 315 Randy Ready UER .04 .02 .01
(1214 games in '88,
should be 114)
☐ 316 Benito Santiago .07 .03 .01
☐ 317 Eric Show .04 .02 .01
☐ 318 Todd Simmons .04 .02 .01
☐ 319 Garry Templeton .04 .02 .01
☐ 320 Dickie Thon .04 .02 .01
☐ 321 Ed Whitson .04 .02 .01
☐ 322 Marvell Wynne .04 .02 .01
☐ 323 Mike Aldrete .04 .02 .01
☐ 324 Brett Butler .07 .03 .01
☐ 325 Will Clark UER .40 .18 .05
(Three consecutive
100 RBI seasons)
☐ 326 Kelly Downs UER .04 .02 .01
('88 stats missing)
☐ 327 Dave Dravecky .07 .03 .01
☐ 328 Scott Garrelts .04 .02 .01
☐ 329 Atlee Hammaker .04 .02 .01
☐ 330 Charlie Hayes .25 .11 .03
☐ 331 Mike Krukow .04 .02 .01
☐ 332 Craig Lefferts .04 .02 .01
☐ 333 Candy Maldonado .04 .02 .01
☐ 334 Kirt Manwaring UER .04 .02 .01
(Bats Rights)
☐ 335 Bob Melvin .04 .02 .01
☐ 336 Kevin Mitchell .10 .05 .01
☐ 337 Donell Nixon .04 .02 .01
☐ 338 Tony Perezchica .04 .02 .01
☐ 339 Joe Price .04 .02 .01
☐ 340 Rick Reuschel .04 .02 .01
☐ 341 Earnest Riles .04 .02 .01
☐ 342 Don Robinson .04 .02 .01
☐ 343 Chris Speier .04 .02 .01
☐ 344 Robby Thompson UER .04 .02 .01
(West Plam Beach)
☐ 345 Jose Uribe .04 .02 .01
☐ 346 Matt Williams .15 .07 .02
☐ 347 Trevor Wilson .12 .05 .02
☐ 348 Juan Agosto .04 .02 .01
☐ 349 Larry Andersen .04 .02 .01
☐ 350A Alan Ashby ERR 3.00 1.35 .40

(Throws Rig)
☐ 350B Alan Ashby COR .04 .02 .01
☐ 351 Kevin Bass .04 .02 .01
☐ 352 Buddy Bell .07 .03 .01
☐ 353 Craig Biggio .40 .18 .05
☐ 354 Danny Darwin .04 .02 .01
☐ 355 Glenn Davis .07 .03 .01
☐ 356 Jim Deshaies .04 .02 .01
☐ 357 Bill Doran .04 .02 .01
☐ 358 John Fishel .04 .02 .01
☐ 359 Billy Hatcher .04 .02 .01
☐ 360 Bob Knepper .04 .02 .01
☐ 361 Louie Meadows UER .04 .02 .01
(Bio says 10 EBH's and 6 SB's in '88, should be 3 and 4)
☐ 362 Dave Meads .04 .02 .01
☐ 363 Jim Pankovits .04 .02 .01
☐ 364 Terry Puhl .04 .02 .01
☐ 365 Rafael Ramirez .04 .02 .01
☐ 366 Craig Reynolds .04 .02 .01
☐ 367 Mike Scott .04 .02 .01
(Card number listed as 368 on Astros CL)
☐ 368 Nolan Ryan .60 .25 .08
(Card number listed as 367 on Astros CL)
☐ 369 Dave Smith .04 .02 .01
☐ 370 Gerald Young .04 .02 .01
☐ 371 Hubie Brooks .04 .02 .01
☐ 372 Tim Burke .04 .02 .01
☐ 373 John Dopson .04 .02 .01
☐ 374 Mike R. Fitzgerald .04 .02 .01
Montreal Expos
☐ 375 Tom Foley .04 .02 .01
☐ 376 Andres Galarraga UER .04 .02 .01
(Home: Caracus)
☐ 377 Neal Heaton .04 .02 .01
☐ 378 Joe Hesketh .04 .02 .01
☐ 379 Brian Holman .10 .05 .01
☐ 380 Rex Hudler .04 .02 .01
☐ 381 Randy Johnson UER .35 .16 .04
(Innings for '85 and '86 shown as 27 and 120, should be 27.1 and 119.2)
☐ 382 Wallace Johnson .04 .02 .01
☐ 383 Tracy Jones .04 .02 .01
☐ 384 Dave Martinez .07 .03 .01
☐ 385 Dennis Martinez .07 .03 .01
☐ 386 Andy McGaffigan .04 .02 .01
☐ 387 Otis Nixon .07 .03 .01
☐ 388 Johnny Paredes .04 .02 .01
☐ 389 Jeff Parrett .04 .02 .01
☐ 390 Pascual Perez .04 .02 .01
☐ 391 Tim Raines .07 .03 .01
☐ 392 Luis Rivera .04 .02 .01
☐ 393 Nelson Santovenia .04 .02 .01
☐ 394 Bryn Smith .04 .02 .01
☐ 395 Tim Wallach .07 .03 .01
☐ 396 Andy Allanson UER .04 .02 .01
(1214 hits in '88, should be 114)
☐ 397 Rod Allen .04 .02 .01
☐ 398 Scott Bailes .04 .02 .01
☐ 399 Tom Candiotti .04 .02 .01
☐ 400 Joe Carter .25 .11 .03
☐ 401 Carmen Castillo UER .04 .02 .01
(After All-Star Break batting 2.50)
☐ 402 Dave Clark UER .04 .02 .01
(Card front shows position as Rookie; after All-Star Break batting 3.14)
☐ 403 John Farrell UER .04 .02 .01
(Typo in runs allowed in '88)
☐ 404 Julio Franco .07 .03 .01
☐ 405 Don Gordon .04 .02 .01
☐ 406 Mel Hall .04 .02 .01
☐ 407 Brad Havens .04 .02 .01
☐ 408 Brook Jacoby .04 .02 .01
☐ 409 Doug Jones .07 .03 .01
☐ 410 Jeff Kaiser .04 .02 .01
☐ 411 Luis Medina .04 .02 .01
☐ 412 Cory Snyder .04 .02 .01
☐ 413 Greg Swindell .07 .03 .01
☐ 414 Ron Tingley UER .04 .02 .01
(Hit HR in first ML at-bat, should be first AL at-bat)
☐ 415 Willie Upshaw .04 .02 .01
☐ 416 Ron Washington .04 .02 .01
☐ 417 Rich Yett .04 .02 .01
☐ 418 Damon Berryhill .04 .02 .01
☐ 419 Mike Bielecki .04 .02 .01
☐ 420 Doug Dascenzo .04 .02 .01
☐ 421 Jody Davis UER .04 .02 .01
(Braves stats for '88 missing)
☐ 422 Andre Dawson .15 .07 .02
☐ 423 Frank DiPino .04 .02 .01
☐ 424 Shawon Dunston .07 .03 .01
☐ 425 Rich Gossage .07 .03 .01
☐ 426 Mark Grace UER .30 .14 .04
(Minor League stats for '88 missing)
☐ 427 Mike Harkey .12 .05 .02
☐ 428 Darrin Jackson .15 .07 .02
☐ 429 Les Lancaster .04 .02 .01
☐ 430 Vance Law .04 .02 .01
☐ 431 Greg Maddux .30 .14 .04
☐ 432 Jamie Moyer .04 .02 .01
☐ 433 Al Nipper .04 .02 .01
☐ 434 Rafael Palmeiro UER .20 .09 .03
(170 hits in '88, should be 178)
☐ 435 Pat Perry .04 .02 .01
☐ 436 Jeff Pico .04 .02 .01
☐ 437 Ryne Sandberg .40 .18 .05
☐ 438 Calvin Schiraldi .04 .02 .01
☐ 439 Rick Sutcliffe .07 .03 .01
☐ 440A Manny Trillo ERR 3.00 1.35 .40
(Throws Rig)
☐ 440B Manny Trillo COR .04 .02 .01
☐ 441 Gary Varsho UER .04 .02 .01
(Wrong birthdate; .303 should be .302; 11/28 should be 9/19)
☐ 442 Mitch Webster .04 .02 .01
☐ 443 Luis Alicea .10 .05 .01
☐ 444 Tom Brunansky .07 .03 .01
☐ 445 Vince Coleman UER .07 .03 .01
(Third straight with 83, should be fourth straight with 81)
☐ 446 John Costello UER .04 .02 .01
(Home California, should be New York)
☐ 447 Danny Cox .04 .02 .01
☐ 448 Ken Dayley .04 .02 .01
☐ 449 Jose DeLeon .04 .02 .01
☐ 450 Curt Ford .04 .02 .01
☐ 451 Pedro Guerrero .07 .03 .01
☐ 452 Bob Horner .04 .02 .01
☐ 453 Tim Jones .04 .02 .01
☐ 454 Steve Lake .04 .02 .01
☐ 455 Joe Magrane UER .04 .02 .01
(Des Moines, IO)
☐ 456 Greg Mathews .04 .02 .01
☐ 457 Willie McGee .07 .03 .01
☐ 458 Larry McWilliams .04 .02 .01
☐ 459 Jose Oquendo .04 .02 .01
☐ 460 Tony Pena .04 .02 .01
☐ 461 Terry Pendleton .12 .05 .02
☐ 462 Steve Peters UER .04 .02 .01
(Lives in Harrah, not Harah)
☐ 463 Ozzie Smith .15 .07 .02
☐ 464 Scott Terry .04 .02 .01
☐ 465 Denny Walling .04 .02 .01
☐ 466 Todd Worrell .07 .03 .01
☐ 467 Tony Armas UER .04 .02 .01
(Before All-Star Break batting 2.39)
☐ 468 Dante Bichette .25 .11 .03
☐ 469 Bob Boone .07 .03 .01
☐ 470 Terry Clark .04 .02 .01
☐ 471 Stew Cliburn .04 .02 .01
☐ 472 Mike Cook UER .04 .02 .01
(TM near Angels logo missing from front)
☐ 473 Sherman Corbett .04 .02 .01
☐ 474 Chili Davis .07 .03 .01
☐ 475 Brian Downing .04 .02 .01
☐ 476 Jim Eppard .04 .02 .01
☐ 477 Chuck Finley .07 .03 .01
☐ 478 Willie Fraser .04 .02 .01
☐ 479 Bryan Harvey UER .25 .11 .03
(ML record shows 0-0, should be 7-5)
☐ 480 Jack Howell .04 .02 .01
☐ 481 Wally Joyner UER .10 .05 .01
(Yorba Linda, GA)
☐ 482 Jack Lazorko .04 .02 .01
☐ 483 Kirk McCaskill .04 .02 .01

Card			
☐ 484 Mark McLemore	.04	.02	.01
☐ 485 Greg Minton	.04	.02	.01
☐ 486 Dan Petry	.04	.02	.01
☐ 487 Johnny Ray	.04	.02	.01
☐ 488 Dick Schofield	.04	.02	.01
☐ 489 Devon White	.07	.03	.01
☐ 490 Mike Witt	.04	.02	.01
☐ 491 Harold Baines	.07	.03	.01
☐ 492 Daryl Boston	.04	.02	.01
☐ 493 Ivan Calderon UER ('80 stats shifted)	.04	.02	.01
☐ 494 Mike Diaz	.04	.02	.01
☐ 495 Carlton Fisk	.15	.07	.02
☐ 496 Dave Gallagher	.04	.02	.01
☐ 497 Ozzie Guillen	.04	.02	.01
☐ 498 Shawn Hillegas	.04	.02	.01
☐ 499 Lance Johnson	.07	.03	.01
☐ 500 Barry Jones	.04	.02	.01
☐ 501 Bill Long	.04	.02	.01
☐ 502 Steve Lyons	.04	.02	.01
☐ 503 Fred Manrique	.04	.02	.01
☐ 504 Jack McDowell	.30	.14	.04
☐ 505 Donn Pall	.04	.02	.01
☐ 506 Kelly Paris	.04	.02	.01
☐ 507 Dan Pasqua	.04	.02	.01
☐ 508 Ken Patterson	.04	.02	.01
☐ 509 Melido Perez	.07	.03	.01
☐ 510 Jerry Reuss	.04	.02	.01
☐ 511 Mark Salas	.04	.02	.01
☐ 512 Bobby Thigpen UER ('86 ERA 4.69, should be 4.68)	.04	.02	.01
☐ 513 Mike Woodard	.04	.02	.01
☐ 514 Bob Brower	.04	.02	.01
☐ 515 Steve Buechele	.04	.02	.01
☐ 516 Jose Cecena	.04	.02	.01
☐ 517 Cecil Espy	.04	.02	.01
☐ 518 Scott Fletcher	.04	.02	.01
☐ 519 Cecilio Guante ('87 Yankee stats are off-centered)	.04	.02	.01
☐ 520 Jose Guzman	.07	.03	.01
☐ 521 Ray Hayward	.04	.02	.01
☐ 522 Charlie Hough	.04	.02	.01
☐ 523 Pete Incaviglia	.04	.02	.01
☐ 524 Mike Jeffcoat	.04	.02	.01
☐ 525 Paul Kilgus	.04	.02	.01
☐ 526 Chad Kreuter	.04	.02	.01
☐ 527 Jeff Kunkel	.04	.02	.01
☐ 528 Oddibe McDowell	.04	.02	.01
☐ 529 Pete O'Brien	.04	.02	.01
☐ 530 Geno Petralli	.04	.02	.01
☐ 531 Jeff Russell	.04	.02	.01
☐ 532 Ruben Sierra	.30	.14	.04
☐ 533 Mike Stanley	.04	.02	.01
☐ 534A Ed VandeBerg ERR (Throws Lef)	3.00	1.35	.40
☐ 534B Ed VandeBerg COR	.04	.02	.01
☐ 535 Curtis Wilkerson ERR (Pitcher headings at bottom)	.04	.02	.01
☐ 536 Mitch Williams	.07	.03	.01
☐ 537 Bobby Witt UER ('85 ERA .643, should be 6.43)	.07	.03	.01
☐ 538 Steve Balboni	.04	.02	.01
☐ 539 Scott Bankhead	.04	.02	.01
☐ 540 Scott Bradley	.04	.02	.01
☐ 541 Mickey Brantley	.04	.02	.01
☐ 542 Jay Buhner	.10	.05	.01
☐ 543 Mike Campbell	.04	.02	.01
☐ 544 Darnell Coles	.04	.02	.01
☐ 545 Henry Cotto	.04	.02	.01
☐ 546 Alvin Davis	.04	.02	.01
☐ 547 Mario Diaz	.04	.02	.01
☐ 548 Ken Griffey Jr.	6.00	2.70	.75
☐ 549 Erik Hanson	.20	.09	.03
☐ 550 Mike Jackson UER (Lifetime ERA 3.345, should be 3.45)	.04	.02	.01
☐ 551 Mark Langston	.07	.03	.01
☐ 552 Edgar Martinez	.35	.16	.04
☐ 553 Bill McGuire	.04	.02	.01
☐ 554 Mike Moore	.04	.02	.01
☐ 555 Jim Presley	.04	.02	.01
☐ 556 Rey Quinones	.04	.02	.01
☐ 557 Jerry Reed	.04	.02	.01
☐ 558 Harold Reynolds	.04	.02	.01
☐ 559 Mike Schooler	.10	.05	.01
☐ 560 Bill Swift	.07	.03	.01
☐ 561 Dave Valle	.04	.02	.01
☐ 562 Steve Bedrosian	.04	.02	.01
☐ 563 Phil Bradley	.04	.02	.01
☐ 564 Don Carman	.04	.02	.01
☐ 565 Bob Dernier	.04	.02	.01
☐ 566 Marvin Freeman	.04	.02	.01
☐ 567 Todd Frohwirth	.04	.02	.01
☐ 568 Greg Gross	.04	.02	.01
☐ 569 Kevin Gross	.04	.02	.01
☐ 570 Greg A. Harris	.04	.02	.01
☐ 571 Von Hayes	.04	.02	.01
☐ 572 Chris James	.04	.02	.01
☐ 573 Steve Jeltz	.04	.02	.01
☐ 574 Ron Jones UER (Led IL in '88 with 85, should be 75)	.04	.02	.01
☐ 575 Ricky Jordan	.10	.05	.01
☐ 576 Mike Maddux	.04	.02	.01
☐ 577 David Palmer	.04	.02	.01
☐ 578 Lance Parrish	.07	.03	.01
☐ 579 Shane Rawley	.04	.02	.01
☐ 580 Bruce Ruffin	.04	.02	.01
☐ 581 Juan Samuel	.04	.02	.01
☐ 582 Mike Schmidt	.40	.18	.05
☐ 583 Kent Tekulve	.04	.02	.01
☐ 584 Milt Thompson UER (19 hits in '88, should be 109)	.04	.02	.01
☐ 585 Jose Alvarez	.04	.02	.01
☐ 586 Paul Assenmacher	.04	.02	.01
☐ 587 Bruce Benedict	.04	.02	.01
☐ 588 Jeff Blauser	.07	.03	.01
☐ 589 Terry Blocker	.04	.02	.01
☐ 590 Ron Gant	.40	.18	.05
☐ 591 Tom Glavine	.50	.23	.06
☐ 592 Tommy Gregg	.04	.02	.01
☐ 593 Albert Hall	.04	.02	.01
☐ 594 Dion James	.04	.02	.01
☐ 595 Rick Mahler	.04	.02	.01
☐ 596 Dale Murphy	.10	.05	.01
☐ 597 Gerald Perry	.04	.02	.01
☐ 598 Charlie Puleo	.04	.02	.01
☐ 599 Ted Simmons	.07	.03	.01
☐ 600 Pete Smith	.07	.03	.01
☐ 601 Zane Smith	.04	.02	.01
☐ 602 John Smoltz	.75	.35	.09
☐ 603 Bruce Sutter	.07	.03	.01
☐ 604 Andres Thomas	.04	.02	.01
☐ 605 Ozzie Virgil	.04	.02	.01
☐ 606 Brady Anderson	.60	.25	.08
☐ 607 Jeff Ballard	.04	.02	.01
☐ 608 Jose Bautista	.04	.02	.01
☐ 609 Ken Gerhart	.04	.02	.01
☐ 610 Terry Kennedy	.04	.02	.01
☐ 611 Eddie Murray	.15	.07	.02
☐ 612 Carl Nichols UER (Before All-Star Break batting 1.88)	.04	.02	.01
☐ 613 Tom Niedenfuer	.04	.02	.01
☐ 614 Joe Orsulak	.04	.02	.01
☐ 615 Oswald Peraza UER (Shown as Oswaldo)	.04	.02	.01
☐ 616A Bill Ripken ERR (Rick Face written on knob of bat)	10.00	4.50	1.25
☐ 616B Bill Ripken (Bat knob whited out)	40.00	18.00	5.00
☐ 616C Bill Ripken (Words on bat knob scribbled out)	10.00	4.50	1.25
☐ 616D Bill Ripken DP (Black box covering bat knob)	.10	.05	.01
☐ 617 Cal Ripken	.50	.23	.06
☐ 618 Dave Schmidt	.04	.02	.01
☐ 619 Rick Schu	.04	.02	.01
☐ 620 Larry Sheets	.04	.02	.01
☐ 621 Doug Sisk	.04	.02	.01
☐ 622 Pete Stanicek	.04	.02	.01
☐ 623 Mickey Tettleton	.07	.03	.01
☐ 624 Jay Tibbs	.04	.02	.01
☐ 625 Jim Traber	.04	.02	.01
☐ 626 Mark Williamson	.04	.02	.01
☐ 627 Craig Worthington	.04	.02	.01
☐ 628 Speed/Power Jose Canseco	.20	.09	.03
☐ 629 Pitcher Perfect Tom Browning	.06	.03	.01
☐ 630 Like Father/Like Sons UER Roberto Alomar Sandy Alomar Jr. (Names on card listed in wrong order)	.40	.18	.05
☐ 631 NL All Stars UER Will Clark	.20	.09	.03

Card			
Rafael Palmeiro (Gallaraga, sic; Clark 3 consecutive 100 RBI seasons; third with 102 RBI's)			
☐ 632 Homeruns - Coast to Coast UER Darryl Strawberry Will Clark (Homeruns should be two words)	.20	.09	.03
☐ 633 Hot Corners - Hot Hitters UER Wade Boggs Carney Lansford (Boggs hit .366 in '86, should be '88)	.10	.05	.01
☐ 634 Triple A's Jose Canseco Terry Steinbach Mark McGwire	.30	.14	.04
☐ 635 Dual Heat Mark Davis Dwight Gooden	.06	.03	.01
☐ 636 NL Pitching Power UER Danny Jackson David Cone (Hersheiser, sic)	.06	.03	.01
☐ 637 Cannon Arms UER Chris Sabo Bobby Bonilla (Bobby Bonds, sic)	.10	.05	.01
☐ 638 Double Trouble UER Andres Galarraga (Misspelled Gallaraga on card back) Gerald Perry	.06	.03	.01
☐ 639 Power Center Kirby Puckett Eric Davis	.15	.07	.02
☐ 640 Steve Wilson and Cameron Drew	.06	.03	.01
☐ 641 Kevin Brown and Kevin Reimer	.90	.40	.11
☐ 642 Brad Pounders and Jerald Clark	.12	.05	.02
☐ 643 Mike Capel and Drew Hall	.06	.03	.01
☐ 644 Joe Girardi and Rolando Roomes	.12	.05	.02
☐ 645 Lenny Harris and Marty Brown	.12	.05	.02
☐ 646 Luis De Los Santos and Jim Campbell	.06	.03	.01
☐ 647 Randy Kramer and Miguel Garcia	.06	.03	.01
☐ 648 Torey Lovullo and Robert Palacios	.06	.03	.01
☐ 649 Jim Corsi and Bob Milacki	.12	.05	.02
☐ 650 Grady Hall and Mike Rochford	.06	.03	.01
☐ 651 Terry Taylor and Vance Lovelace	.06	.03	.01
☐ 652 Ken Hill and Dennis Cook	.50	.23	.06
☐ 653 Scott Service and Shane Turner	.06	.03	.01
☐ 654 CL: Oakland/Mets Dodgers/Red Sox (10 Hendersor; 68 Jess Orosco)	.05	.01	.00
☐ 655A CL: Twins/Tigers ERR Reds/Brewers (179 Boslo and Twins/Tigers positions listed)	.10	.01	.00
☐ 655B CL: Twins/Tigers COR Reds/Brewers (179 Boslo but Twins/Tigers positions not listed)	.10	.01	.00
☐ 656 CL: Pirates/Blue Jays Yankees/Royals (225 Jess Barfield)	.05	.01	.00
☐ 657 CL: Padres/Giants Astros/Expos (367/368 wrong)	.05	.01	.00
☐ 658 CL: Indians/Cubs Cardinals/Angels (449 Deleon)	.05	.01	.00
☐ 659 CL: White Sox/Rangers Mariners/Phillies	.05	.01	.00
☐ 660 CL: Braves/Orioles UER Specials/Checklists (632 hyphenated differently and 650 Hali; 595 Rich Mahler; 619 Rich Schu)	.05	.01	.00

1989 Fleer All-Star Inserts

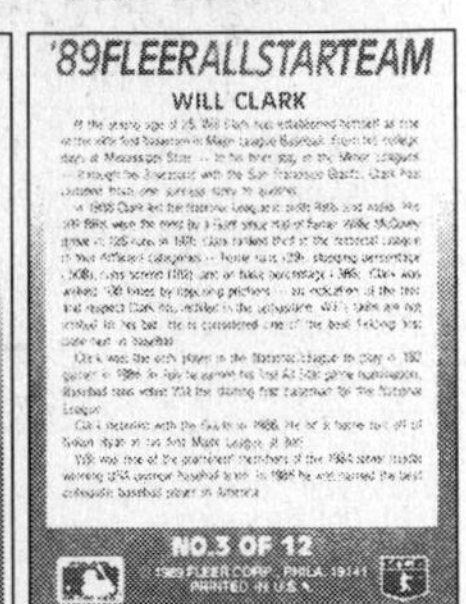

This twelve-card subset was randomly inserted in Fleer wax packs (15 regular cards) and Fleer value packs (36 regular cards). The players selected are the 1989 Fleer Major League All-Star team. One player has been selected for each position along with a DH and three pitchers. The cards are attractively designed and are standard size, 2 1/2" by 3 1/2". The cards are numbered on the backs and feature a distinctive green background on the card fronts.

	MT	EX-MT	VG
COMPLETE SET (12)	10.00	4.50	1.25
COMMON PLAYER (1-12)	.35	.16	.04
☐ 1 Bobby Bonilla	1.00	.45	.13
☐ 2 Jose Canseco	2.50	1.15	.30
☐ 3 Will Clark	2.50	1.15	.30
☐ 4 Dennis Eckersley	1.00	.45	.13
☐ 5 Julio Franco	.50	.23	.06
☐ 6 Mike Greenwell	.75	.35	.09
☐ 7 Orel Hershiser	.75	.35	.09
☐ 8 Paul Molitor	.75	.35	.09
☐ 9 Mike Scioscia	.35	.16	.04
☐ 10 Darryl Strawberry	1.00	.45	.13
☐ 11 Alan Trammell	.75	.35	.09
☐ 12 Frank Viola	.50	.23	.06

1989 Fleer Baseball All-Stars

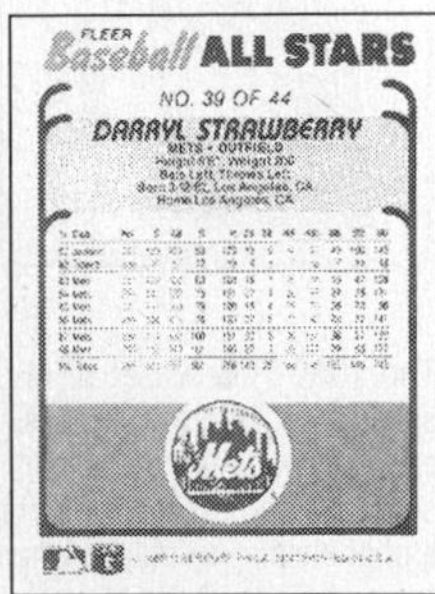

The 1989 Fleer Baseball All-Stars set contains 44 standard-size (2 1/2" by 3 1/2") cards. The fronts are yellowish beige with salmon pinstripes; the vertically oriented backs are red, white and pink and feature career stats. The card numbering of this set is ordered alphabetically by player's name. The cards were distributed through Ben Franklin stores as a boxed set.

	MT	EX-MT	VG
COMPLETE SET (44)	5.00	2.30	.60
COMMON PLAYER (1-44)	.10	.05	.01
☐ 1 Doyle Alexander	.10	.05	.01
☐ 2 George Bell	.15	.07	.02
☐ 3 Wade Boggs	.50	.23	.06
☐ 4 Bobby Bonilla	.35	.16	.04
☐ 5 Jose Canseco	.75	.35	.09
☐ 6 Will Clark	.75	.35	.09
☐ 7 Roger Clemens	1.00	.45	.13
☐ 8 Vince Coleman	.20	.09	.03
☐ 9 David Cone	.25	.11	.03
☐ 10 Mark Davis	.10	.05	.01
☐ 11 Andre Dawson	.30	.14	.04
☐ 12 Dennis Eckersley	.25	.11	.03
☐ 13 Andres Galarraga	.15	.07	.02
☐ 14 Kirk Gibson	.15	.07	.02
☐ 15 Dwight Gooden	.25	.11	.03
☐ 16 Mike Greenwell	.15	.07	.02
☐ 17 Mark Gubicza	.10	.05	.01
☐ 18 Ozzie Guillen	.15	.07	.02
☐ 19 Tony Gwynn	.50	.23	.06
☐ 20 Rickey Henderson	.60	.25	.08
☐ 21 Orel Hershiser	.15	.07	.02
☐ 22 Danny Jackson	.10	.05	.01
☐ 23 Doug Jones	.10	.05	.01
☐ 24 Ricky Jordan	.15	.07	.02
☐ 25 Bob Knepper	.10	.05	.01
☐ 26 Barry Larkin	.20	.09	.03
☐ 27 Vance Law	.10	.05	.01
☐ 28 Don Mattingly	.75	.35	.09
☐ 29 Mark McGwire	.60	.25	.08
☐ 30 Paul Molitor	.25	.11	.03
☐ 31 Gerald Perry	.10	.05	.01
☐ 32 Kirby Puckett	.75	.35	.09
☐ 33 Johnny Ray	.10	.05	.01
☐ 34 Harold Reynolds	.10	.05	.01
☐ 35 Cal Ripken	1.00	.45	.13
☐ 36 Don Robinson	.10	.05	.01
☐ 37 Ruben Sierra	.50	.23	.06
☐ 38 Dave Smith	.10	.05	.01
☐ 39 Darryl Strawberry	.50	.23	.06
☐ 40 Dave Stieb	.10	.05	.01
☐ 41 Alan Trammell	.20	.09	.03
☐ 42 Andy Van Slyke	.20	.09	.03
☐ 43 Frank Viola	.15	.07	.02
☐ 44 Dave Winfield	.35	.16	.04

1989 Fleer Baseball MVP's

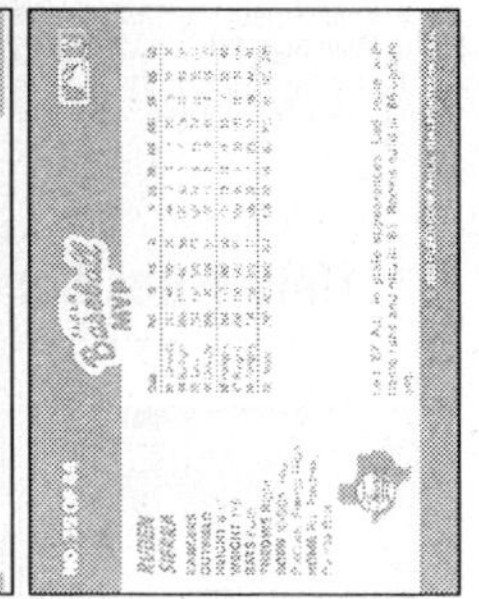

The 1989 Fleer Baseball MVP's set contains 44 standard-size (2 1/2" by 3 1/2") cards. The fronts and backs are green and yellow. The horizontally oriented backs feature career stats. The card numbering of this set is ordered alphabetically by player's name. The cards were distributed through Toys `R' Us stores as a boxed set.

	MT	EX-MT	VG
COMPLETE SET (44)	5.00	2.30	.60
COMMON PLAYER (1-44)	.10	.05	.01
☐ 1 Steve Bedrosian	.10	.05	.01
☐ 2 George Bell	.15	.07	.02
☐ 3 Wade Boggs	.50	.23	.06
☐ 4 George Brett	.50	.23	.06
☐ 5 Hubie Brooks	.10	.05	.01
☐ 6 Jose Canseco	.75	.35	.09
☐ 7 Will Clark	.75	.35	.09
☐ 8 Roger Clemens	1.00	.45	.13
☐ 9 Eric Davis	.25	.11	.03
☐ 10 Glenn Davis	.15	.07	.02
☐ 11 Andre Dawson	.30	.14	.04
☐ 12 Andres Galarraga	.10	.05	.01
☐ 13 Kirk Gibson	.15	.07	.02
☐ 14 Dwight Gooden	.25	.11	.03
☐ 15 Mark Grace	.75	.35	.09
☐ 16 Mike Greenwell	.30	.14	.04
☐ 17 Tony Gwynn	.50	.23	.06
☐ 18 Bryan Harvey	.25	.11	.03
☐ 19 Orel Hershiser	.20	.09	.03
☐ 20 Ted Higuera	.10	.05	.01
☐ 21 Danny Jackson	.10	.05	.01
☐ 22 Mike Jackson	.10	.05	.01
☐ 23 Doug Jones	.10	.05	.01
☐ 24 Greg Maddux	.35	.16	.04
☐ 25 Mike Marshall	.10	.05	.01
☐ 26 Don Mattingly	.75	.35	.09
☐ 27 Fred McGriff	.35	.16	.04
☐ 28 Mark McGwire	.60	.25	.08
☐ 29 Kevin McReynolds	.15	.07	.02
☐ 30 Jack Morris	.20	.09	.03
☐ 31 Gerald Perry	.10	.05	.01
☐ 32 Kirby Puckett	.75	.35	.09
☐ 33 Chris Sabo	.25	.11	.03
☐ 34 Mike Scott	.15	.07	.02
☐ 35 Ruben Sierra	.50	.23	.06
☐ 36 Darryl Strawberry	.50	.23	.06
☐ 37 Danny Tartabull	.25	.11	.03
☐ 38 Bobby Thigpen	.15	.07	.02
☐ 39 Alan Trammell	.20	.09	.03
☐ 40 Andy Van Slyke	.20	.09	.03
☐ 41 Frank Viola	.15	.07	.02
☐ 42 Walt Weiss	.15	.07	.02
☐ 43 Dave Winfield	.35	.16	.04
☐ 44 Todd Worrell	.15	.07	.02

1989 Fleer Exciting Stars

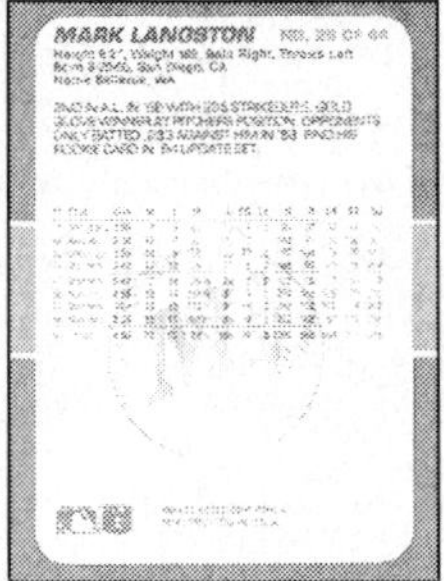

The 1989 Fleer Exciting Stars set contains 44 standard-size (2 1/2" by 3 1/2") cards. The fronts have baby blue borders; the backs are pink and blue. The vertically oriented backs feature career stats. The card numbering of this set is ordered alphabetically by player's name. The cards were distributed as a boxed set.

	MT	EX-MT	VG
COMPLETE SET (44)	5.00	2.30	.60
COMMON PLAYER (1-44)	.10	.05	.01
☐ 1 Harold Baines	.15	.07	.02
☐ 2 Wade Boggs	.50	.23	.06
☐ 3 Jose Canseco	.75	.35	.09
☐ 4 Joe Carter	.35	.16	.04
☐ 5 Will Clark	.75	.35	.09
☐ 6 Roger Clemens	1.00	.45	.13
☐ 7 Vince Coleman	.20	.09	.03
☐ 8 David Cone	.25	.11	.03
☐ 9 Eric Davis	.25	.11	.03
☐ 10 Glenn Davis	.15	.07	.02
☐ 11 Andre Dawson	.30	.14	.04
☐ 12 Dwight Evans	.15	.07	.02
☐ 13 Andres Galarraga	.10	.05	.01
☐ 14 Kirk Gibson	.15	.07	.02
☐ 15 Dwight Gooden	.25	.11	.03
☐ 16 Jim Gott	.10	.05	.01

☐ 17 Mark Grace	.75	.35	.09
☐ 18 Mike Greenwell	.30	.14	.04
☐ 19 Mark Gubicza	.10	.05	.01
☐ 20 Tony Gwynn	.50	.23	.06
☐ 21 Rickey Henderson	.60	.25	.08
☐ 22 Tom Henke	.15	.07	.02
☐ 23 Mike Henneman	.15	.07	.02
☐ 24 Orel Hershiser	.20	.09	.03
☐ 25 Danny Jackson	.10	.05	.01
☐ 26 Gregg Jefferies	.60	.25	.08
☐ 27 Ricky Jordan	.15	.07	.02
☐ 28 Wally Joyner	.15	.07	.02
☐ 29 Mark Langston	.15	.07	.02
☐ 30 Tim Leary	.10	.05	.01
☐ 31 Don Mattingly	.75	.35	.09
☐ 32 Mark McGwire	.60	.25	.08
☐ 33 Dale Murphy	.30	.14	.04
☐ 34 Kirby Puckett	.75	.35	.09
☐ 35 Chris Sabo	.35	.16	.04
☐ 36 Kevin Seitzer	.10	.05	.01
☐ 37 Ruben Sierra	.50	.23	.06
☐ 38 Ozzie Smith	.25	.11	.03
☐ 39 Dave Stewart	.15	.07	.02
☐ 40 Darryl Strawberry	.50	.23	.06
☐ 41 Alan Trammell	.20	.09	.03
☐ 42 Frank Viola	.15	.07	.02
☐ 43 Dave Winfield	.35	.16	.04
☐ 44 Robin Yount	.50	.23	.06

1989 Fleer For The Record

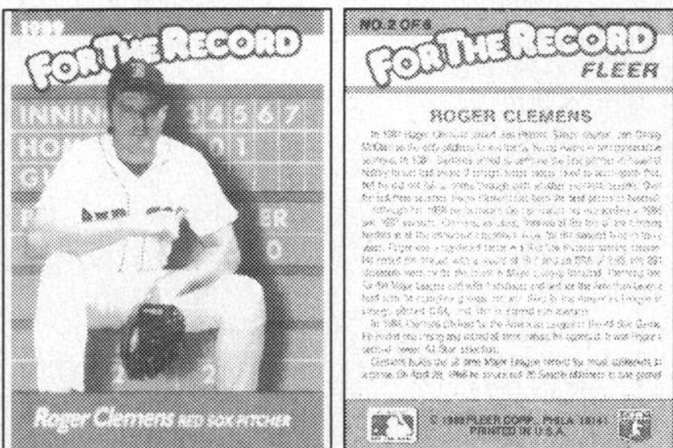

This six-card subset was distributed randomly (as an insert) in Fleer rack packs. These cards are standard size, 2 1/2" by 3 1/2" and are quite attractive. The set is subtitled "For The Record" and commemorates record-breaking events for those players from the previous season. The cards are numbered on the backs. The card backs are printed in red, black, and gray on white card stock.

	MT	EX-MT	VG
COMPLETE SET (6)	6.00	2.70	.75
COMMON PLAYER (1-6)	.50	.23	.06
☐ 1 Wade Boggs	1.25	.55	.16
☐ 2 Roger Clemens	2.50	1.15	.30
☐ 3 Andres Galarraga	.50	.23	.06
☐ 4 Kirk Gibson	.60	.25	.08
☐ 5 Greg Maddux	1.25	.55	.16
☐ 6 Don Mattingly UER (Won batting title '83, should say '84)	1.50	.65	.19

1989 Fleer Heroes of Baseball

The 1989 Fleer Heroes of Baseball set contains 44 standard-size (2 1/2" by 3 1/2") cards. The fronts and backs are red, white and blue. The vertically oriented backs feature career stats. The card numbering of this set is ordered alphabetically by player's name. The cards were distributed through Woolworth stores as a boxed set.

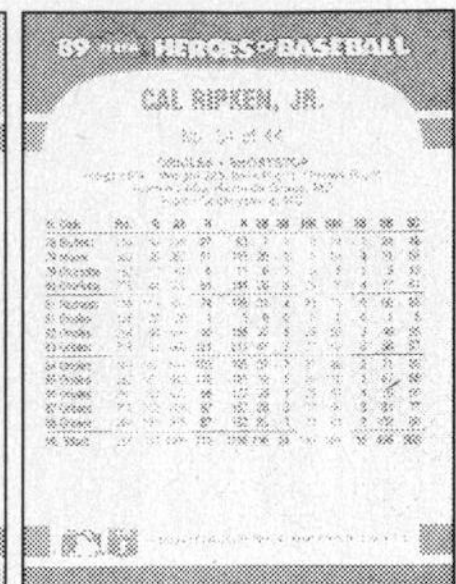

	MT	EX-MT	VG
COMPLETE SET (44)	5.00	2.30	.60
COMMON PLAYER (1-44)	.10	.05	.01
☐ 1 George Bell	.15	.07	.02
☐ 2 Wade Boggs	.50	.23	.06
☐ 3 Barry Bonds	.50	.23	.06
☐ 4 Tom Brunansky	.10	.05	.01
☐ 5 Jose Canseco	.75	.35	.09
☐ 6 Joe Carter	.35	.16	.04
☐ 7 Will Clark	.75	.35	.09
☐ 8 Roger Clemens	1.00	.45	.13
☐ 9 David Cone	.25	.11	.03
☐ 10 Eric Davis	.25	.11	.03
☐ 11 Glenn Davis	.15	.07	.02
☐ 12 Andre Dawson	.30	.14	.04
☐ 13 Dennis Eckersley	.25	.11	.03
☐ 14 John Franco	.10	.05	.01
☐ 15 Gary Gaetti	.10	.05	.01
☐ 16 Andres Galarraga	.10	.05	.01
☐ 17 Kirk Gibson	.15	.07	.02
☐ 18 Dwight Gooden	.25	.11	.03
☐ 19 Mike Greenwell	.25	.11	.03
☐ 20 Tony Gwynn	.50	.23	.06
☐ 21 Bryan Harvey	.20	.09	.03
☐ 22 Orel Hershiser	.20	.09	.03
☐ 23 Ted Higuera	.10	.05	.01
☐ 24 Danny Jackson	.10	.05	.01
☐ 25 Ricky Jordan	.15	.07	.02
☐ 26 Don Mattingly	.75	.35	.09
☐ 27 Fred McGriff	.35	.16	.04
☐ 28 Mark McGwire	.60	.25	.08
☐ 29 Kevin McReynolds	.15	.07	.02
☐ 30 Gerald Perry	.10	.05	.01
☐ 31 Kirby Puckett	.75	.35	.09
☐ 32 Johnny Ray	.10	.05	.01
☐ 33 Harold Reynolds	.10	.05	.01
☐ 34 Cal Ripken	1.00	.45	.13
☐ 35 Ryne Sandberg	.90	.40	.11
☐ 36 Kevin Seitzer	.10	.05	.01
☐ 37 Ruben Sierra	.50	.23	.06
☐ 38 Darryl Strawberry	.50	.23	.06
☐ 39 Bobby Thigpen	.15	.07	.02
☐ 40 Alan Trammell	.20	.09	.03
☐ 41 Andy Van Slyke	.20	.09	.03
☐ 42 Frank Viola	.15	.07	.02
☐ 43 Dave Winfield	.35	.16	.04
☐ 44 Robin Yount	.50	.23	.06

1989 Fleer League Leaders

The 1989 Fleer League Leaders set contains 44 standard-size (2 1/2" by 3 1/2") cards. The fronts are red and yellow; the horizontally oriented backs are light blue and red, and feature career stats. The card numbering of this set is ordered alphabetically by player's name. The cards were distributed through Woolworth stores as a boxed set.

	MT	EX-MT	VG
COMPLETE SET (44)	5.00	2.30	.60
COMMON PLAYER (1-44)	.10	.05	.01
☐ 1 Allan Anderson	.10	.05	.01
☐ 2 Wade Boggs	.50	.23	.06
☐ 3 Jose Canseco	.75	.35	.09
☐ 4 Will Clark	.75	.35	.09

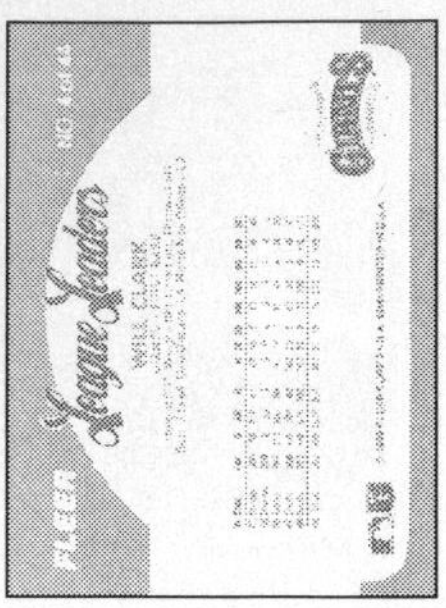

☐ 5 Roger Clemens	1.00	.45	.13
☐ 6 Vince Coleman	.20	.09	.03
☐ 7 David Cone	.25	.11	.03
☐ 8 Kal Daniels	.10	.05	.01
☐ 9 Chili Davis	.10	.05	.01
☐ 10 Eric Davis	.25	.11	.03
☐ 11 Glenn Davis	.15	.07	.02
☐ 12 Andre Dawson	.30	.14	.04
☐ 13 John Franco	.10	.05	.01
☐ 14 Andres Galarraga	.15	.07	.02
☐ 15 Kirk Gibson	.15	.07	.02
☐ 16 Dwight Gooden	.25	.11	.03
☐ 17 Mark Grace	.75	.35	.09
☐ 18 Mike Greenwell	.20	.09	.03
☐ 19 Tony Gwynn	.50	.23	.06
☐ 20 Orel Hershiser	.15	.07	.02
☐ 21 Pete Incaviglia	.15	.07	.02
☐ 22 Danny Jackson	.10	.05	.01
☐ 23 Gregg Jefferies	.75	.35	.09
☐ 24 Joe Magrane	.10	.05	.01
☐ 25 Don Mattingly	.75	.35	.09
☐ 26 Fred McGriff	.35	.16	.04
☐ 27 Mark McGwire	.60	.25	.08
☐ 28 Dale Murphy	.30	.14	.04
☐ 29 Dan Plesac	.10	.05	.01
☐ 30 Kirby Puckett	.75	.35	.09
☐ 31 Harold Reynolds	.10	.05	.01
☐ 32 Cal Ripken	1.00	.45	.13
☐ 33 Jeff Robinson	.10	.05	.01
☐ 34 Mike Scott	.15	.07	.02
☐ 35 Ozzie Smith	.25	.11	.03
☐ 36 Dave Stewart	.15	.07	.02
☐ 37 Darryl Strawberry	.50	.23	.06
☐ 38 Greg Swindell	.15	.07	.02
☐ 39 Bobby Thigpen	.15	.07	.02
☐ 40 Alan Trammell	.20	.09	.03
☐ 41 Andy Van Slyke	.20	.09	.03
☐ 42 Frank Viola	.15	.07	.02
☐ 43 Dave Winfield	.35	.16	.04
☐ 44 Robin Yount	.50	.23	.06

1989 Fleer Superstars

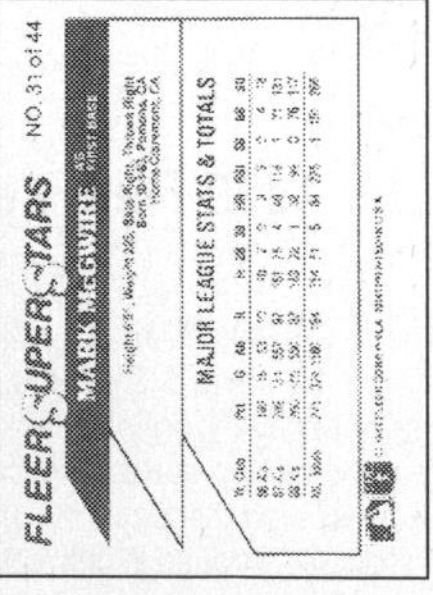

The 1989 Fleer Superstars set contains 44 standard-size (2 1/2" by 3 1/2") cards. The fronts are red and beige; the horizontally oriented backs are yellow, and feature career stats. The card numbering of this set is ordered alphabetically by player's name. The cards were distributed as a boxed set. The back panel of the box contains the complete set checklist.

	MT	EX-MT	VG
COMPLETE SET (44)	6.00	2.70	.75
COMMON PLAYER (1-44)	.10	.05	.01
☐ 1 Roberto Alomar	1.00	.45	.13
☐ 2 Harold Baines	.15	.07	.02
☐ 3 Tim Belcher	.10	.05	.01
☐ 4 Wade Boggs	.50	.23	.06
☐ 5 George Brett	.50	.23	.06
☐ 6 Jose Canseco	.75	.35	.09
☐ 7 Gary Carter	.20	.09	.03
☐ 8 Will Clark	.75	.35	.09
☐ 9 Roger Clemens	1.00	.45	.13
☐ 10 Kal Daniels UER (Reverse negative photo on front)	.15	.07	.02
☐ 11 Eric Davis	.25	.11	.03
☐ 12 Andre Dawson	.30	.14	.04
☐ 13 Tony Fernandez	.15	.07	.02
☐ 14 Scott Fletcher	.10	.05	.01
☐ 15 Andres Galarraga	.10	.05	.01
☐ 16 Kirk Gibson	.15	.07	.02
☐ 17 Dwight Gooden	.25	.11	.03
☐ 18 Jim Gott	.10	.05	.01
☐ 19 Mark Grace	.75	.35	.09
☐ 20 Mike Greenwell	.25	.11	.03
☐ 21 Tony Gwynn	.50	.23	.06
☐ 22 Rickey Henderson	.60	.25	.08
☐ 23 Orel Hershiser	.15	.07	.02
☐ 24 Ted Higuera	.10	.05	.01
☐ 25 Gregg Jefferies	.75	.35	.09
☐ 26 Wally Joyner	.15	.07	.02
☐ 27 Mark Langston	.15	.07	.02
☐ 28 Greg Maddux	.35	.16	.04
☐ 29 Don Mattingly	.75	.35	.09
☐ 30 Fred McGriff	.35	.16	.04
☐ 31 Mark McGwire	.60	.25	.08
☐ 32 Dan Plesac	.10	.05	.01
☐ 33 Kirby Puckett	.75	.35	.09
☐ 34 Jeff Reardon	.15	.07	.02
☐ 35 Chris Sabo	.25	.11	.03
☐ 36 Mike Schmidt	.60	.25	.08
☐ 37 Mike Scott	.15	.07	.02
☐ 38 Cory Snyder	.15	.07	.02
☐ 39 Darryl Strawberry	.50	.23	.06
☐ 40 Alan Trammell	.20	.09	.03
☐ 41 Frank Viola	.15	.07	.02
☐ 42 Walt Weiss	.15	.07	.02
☐ 43 Dave Winfield	.35	.16	.04
☐ 44 Todd Worrell UER (Statistical headings on back for hitter)	.15	.07	.02

1989 Fleer Update

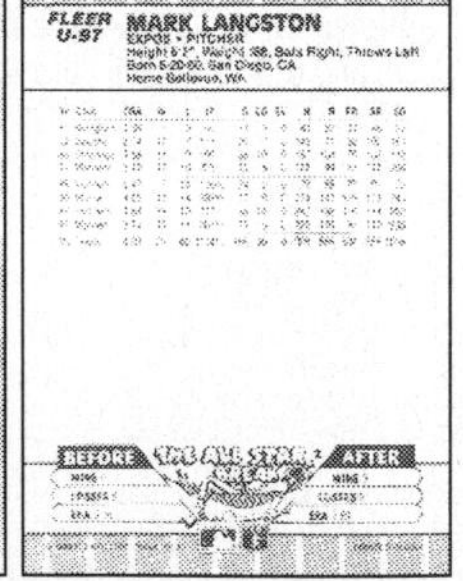

The 1989 Fleer Update set contains 132 standard-size (2 1/2" by 3 1/2") cards. The fronts are gray with white pinstripes. The vertically oriented backs show lifetime stats and performance "Before and After the All-Star Break". The set numbering is in team order with players within teams ordered alphabetically. The set does not include a card of 1989 AL Rookie of the Year Gregg Olson, but contains the first major card of Greg Vaughn and special cards for Nolan Ryan's 5,000th strikeout and Mike Schmidt's retirement.

Other key rookies in this set are Kevin Appier, Joey (Albert) Belle, Junior Felix, Jaime Navarro, Deion Sanders, Robin Ventura, Jerome Walton and Todd Zeile. Fleer did NOT produce a limited (tin) edition version of this set with glossy coating. The card numbering is in alphabetical order within teams with the teams themselves alphabetized within league. Cards are numbered with a U prefix.

	MT	EX-MT	VG
COMPLETE SET (132)	10.00	4.50	1.25
COMMON PLAYER (1-132)	.05	.02	.01
□ 1 Phil Bradley	.05	.02	.01
□ 2 Mike Devereaux	.20	.09	.03
□ 3 Steve Finley	.40	.18	.05
□ 4 Kevin Hickey	.05	.02	.01
□ 5 Brian Holton	.05	.02	.01
□ 6 Bob Milacki	.10	.05	.01
□ 7 Randy Milligan	.05	.02	.01
□ 8 John Dopson	.05	.02	.01
□ 9 Nick Esasky	.05	.02	.01
□ 10 Rob Murphy	.05	.02	.01
□ 11 Jim Abbott	1.25	.55	.16
□ 12 Bert Blyleven	.08	.04	.01
□ 13 Jeff Manto	.10	.05	.01
□ 14 Bob McClure	.05	.02	.01
□ 15 Lance Parrish	.08	.04	.01
□ 16 Lee Stevens	.20	.09	.03
□ 17 Claudell Washington	.05	.02	.01
□ 18 Mark Davis	.05	.02	.01
□ 19 Eric King	.05	.02	.01
□ 20 Ron Kittle	.05	.02	.01
□ 21 Matt Merullo	.05	.02	.01
□ 22 Steve Rosenberg	.05	.02	.01
□ 23 Robin Ventura	2.50	1.15	.30
□ 24 Keith Atherton	.05	.02	.01
□ 25 Joey Belle	2.00	.90	.25
□ 26 Jerry Browne	.05	.02	.01
□ 27 Felix Fermin	.05	.02	.01
□ 28 Brad Komminsk	.05	.02	.01
□ 29 Pete O'Brien	.05	.02	.01
□ 30 Mike Brumley	.05	.02	.01
□ 31 Tracy Jones	.05	.02	.01
□ 32 Mike Schwabe	.05	.02	.01
□ 33 Gary Ward	.05	.02	.01
□ 34 Frank Williams	.05	.02	.01
□ 35 Kevin Appier	1.00	.45	.13
□ 36 Bob Boone	.08	.04	.01
□ 37 Luis de los Santos	.05	.02	.01
□ 38 Jim Eisenreich	.05	.02	.01
□ 39 Jaime Navarro	.75	.35	.09
□ 40 Bill Spiers	.10	.05	.01
□ 41 Greg Vaughn	.75	.35	.09
□ 42 Randy Veres	.05	.02	.01
□ 43 Wally Backman	.05	.02	.01
□ 44 Shane Rawley	.05	.02	.01
□ 45 Steve Balboni	.05	.02	.01
□ 46 Jesse Barfield	.05	.02	.01
□ 47 Alvaro Espinoza	.05	.02	.01
□ 48 Bob Geren	.05	.02	.01
□ 49 Mel Hall	.05	.02	.01
□ 50 Andy Hawkins	.05	.02	.01
□ 51 Hensley Meulens	.12	.05	.02
□ 52 Steve Sax	.08	.04	.01
□ 53 Deion Sanders	2.25	1.00	.30
□ 54 Rickey Henderson	.25	.11	.03
□ 55 Mike Moore	.05	.02	.01
□ 56 Tony Phillips	.05	.02	.01
□ 57 Greg Briley	.10	.05	.01
□ 58 Gene Harris	.10	.05	.01
□ 59 Randy Johnson	.15	.07	.02
□ 60 Jeffrey Leonard	.05	.02	.01
□ 61 Dennis Powell	.05	.02	.01
□ 62 Omar Vizquel	.15	.07	.02
□ 63 Kevin Brown	.25	.11	.03
□ 64 Julio Franco	.08	.04	.01
□ 65 Jamie Moyer	.05	.02	.01
□ 66 Rafael Palmeiro	.20	.09	.03
□ 67 Nolan Ryan	1.50	.65	.19
□ 68 Francisco Cabrera	.30	.14	.04
□ 69 Junior Felix	.25	.11	.03
□ 70 Al Leiter	.05	.02	.01
□ 71 Alex Sanchez	.05	.02	.01
□ 72 Geronimo Berroa	.05	.02	.01
□ 73 Derek Lilliquist	.10	.05	.01
□ 74 Lonnie Smith	.05	.02	.01
□ 75 Jeff Treadway	.08	.04	.01
□ 76 Paul Kilgus	.05	.02	.01
□ 77 Lloyd McClendon	.05	.02	.01
□ 78 Scott Sanderson	.05	.02	.01
□ 79 Dwight Smith	.10	.05	.01
□ 80 Jerome Walton	.10	.05	.01
□ 81 Mitch Williams	.08	.04	.01
□ 82 Steve Wilson	.05	.02	.01
□ 83 Todd Benzinger	.05	.02	.01
□ 84 Ken Griffey Sr.	.08	.04	.01
□ 85 Rick Mahler	.05	.02	.01
□ 86 Rolando Roomes	.05	.02	.01
□ 87 Scott Scudder	.12	.05	.02
□ 88 Jim Clancy	.05	.02	.01
□ 89 Rick Rhoden	.05	.02	.01
□ 90 Dan Schatzeder	.05	.02	.01
□ 91 Mike Morgan	.08	.04	.01
□ 92 Eddie Murray	.15	.07	.02
□ 93 Willie Randolph	.08	.04	.01
□ 94 Ray Searage	.05	.02	.01
□ 95 Mike Aldrete	.05	.02	.01
□ 96 Kevin Gross	.05	.02	.01
□ 97 Mark Langston	.08	.04	.01
□ 98 Spike Owen	.05	.02	.01
□ 99 Zane Smith	.05	.02	.01
□ 100 Don Aase	.05	.02	.01
□ 101 Barry Lyons	.05	.02	.01
□ 102 Juan Samuel	.05	.02	.01
□ 103 Wally Whitehurst	.10	.05	.01
□ 104 Dennis Cook	.08	.04	.01
□ 105 Len Dykstra	.08	.04	.01
□ 106 Charlie Hayes	.20	.09	.03
□ 107 Tommy Herr	.05	.02	.01
□ 108 Ken Howell	.05	.02	.01
□ 109 John Kruk	.08	.04	.01
□ 110 Roger McDowell	.05	.02	.01
□ 111 Terry Mulholland	.10	.05	.01
□ 112 Jeff Parrett	.05	.02	.01
□ 113 Neal Heaton	.05	.02	.01
□ 114 Jeff King	.08	.04	.01
□ 115 Randy Kramer	.05	.02	.01
□ 116 Bill Landrum	.05	.02	.01
□ 117 Cris Carpenter	.10	.05	.01
□ 118 Frank DiPino	.05	.02	.01
□ 119 Ken Hill	.25	.11	.03
□ 120 Dan Quisenberry	.08	.04	.01
□ 121 Milt Thompson	.05	.02	.01
□ 122 Todd Zeile	.60	.25	.08
□ 123 Jack Clark	.08	.04	.01
□ 124 Bruce Hurst	.08	.04	.01
□ 125 Mark Parent	.05	.02	.01
□ 126 Bip Roberts	.08	.04	.01
□ 127 Jeff Brantley UER (Photo actually Joe Kmak)	.10	.05	.01
□ 128 Terry Kennedy	.05	.02	.01
□ 129 Mike LaCoss	.05	.02	.01
□ 130 Greg Litton	.05	.02	.01
□ 131 Mike Schmidt	.50	.23	.06
□ 132 Checklist 1-132	.08	.01	.00

1989 Fleer Wax Box Cards

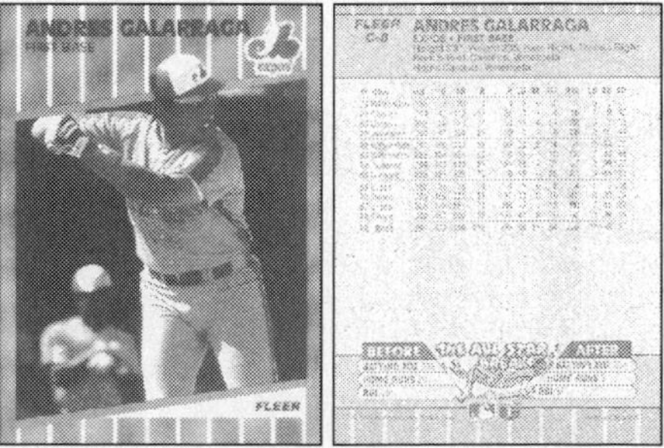

The cards in this 28-card set measure the standard 2 1/2" by 3 1/2". Cards have essentially the same design as the 1989 Fleer regular issue set. The cards were printed on the bottoms of the regular issue wax pack boxes. These 28 cards (C1 to C28) are considered a separate set in their own right and are not typically included in a complete set of the regular issue 1989 Fleer cards. The value of the panel uncut is slightly greater, perhaps by 25 percent greater, than the value of the individual cards cut up carefully. The wax box cards are further distinguished by the gray card stock used.

	MT	EX-MT	VG
COMPLETE SET (28)	10.00	4.50	1.25
COMMON PLAYER (C1-C28)	.15	.07	.02
☐ C1 Mets Logo	.15	.07	.02
☐ C2 Wade Boggs	.75	.35	.09
☐ C3 George Brett	1.00	.45	.13
☐ C4 Jose Canseco UER ('88 strikeouts 121 and career strike-outs 49, should be 128 and 491)	1.25	.55	.16
☐ C5 A's Logo	.15	.07	.02
☐ C6 Will Clark	1.25	.55	.16
☐ C7 David Cone	.50	.23	.06
☐ C8 Andres Galarraga UER (Career average .289 should be .269)	.25	.11	.03
☐ C9 Dodgers Logo	.15	.07	.02
☐ C10 Kirk Gibson	.25	.11	.03
☐ C11 Mike Greenwell	.25	.11	.03
☐ C12 Tony Gwynn	.75	.35	.09
☐ C13 Tigers Logo	.15	.07	.02
☐ C14 Orel Hershiser	.25	.11	.03
☐ C15 Danny Jackson	.15	.07	.02
☐ C16 Wally Joyner	.25	.11	.03
☐ C17 Red Sox Logo	.15	.07	.02
☐ C18 Yankees Logo	.15	.07	.02
☐ C19 Fred McGriff UER (Career BA of .289 should be .269)	.50	.23	.06
☐ C20 Kirby Puckett	1.25	.55	.16
☐ C21 Chris Sabo	.35	.16	.04
☐ C22 Kevin Seitzer	.25	.11	.03
☐ C23 Pirates Logo	.15	.07	.02
☐ C24 Astros Logo	.15	.07	.02
☐ C25 Darryl Strawberry	.75	.35	.09
☐ C26 Alan Trammell	.35	.16	.04
☐ C27 Andy Van Slyke	.35	.16	.04
☐ C28 Frank Viola	.25	.11	.03

1989 Fleer World Series

This 12-card set of 2 1/2" by 3 1/2" cards features highlights of the previous year's World Series between the Dodgers and the Athletics. The sets were packaged as a complete set insert with the collated sets (of the 1989 Fleer regular issue) which were sold by Fleer directly to hobby card dealers; they were not available in the general retail candy store outlets. The set was also produced in a glossy version for inclusion with the Fleer "tin" factory sets.

	MT	EX-MT	VG
COMPLETE SET (12)	2.00	.90	.25
COMMON PLAYER (1-12)	.20	.09	.03
☐ 1 Mickey Hatcher Dodgers' Secret Weapon	.20	.09	.03
☐ 2 Tim Belcher Rookie Starts Series	.20	.09	.03
☐ 3 Jose Canseco Canseco Slams L.A.	.75	.35	.09
☐ 4 Mike Scioscia Dramatic Comeback	.20	.09	.03
☐ 5 Kirk Gibson Gibson Steals The Show	.40	.18	.05
☐ 6 Orel Hershiser Bulldog	.40	.18	.05
☐ 7 Mike Marshall One Swing, Three RBI's	.20	.09	.03
☐ 8 Mark McGwire Game-Winning Homer	.50	.23	.06
☐ 9 Steve Sax UER Sax's Speed Wins Game 4 (actually stole 42 bases in '88)	.30	.14	.04
☐ 10 Walt Weiss Series Caps Award-Winning Year	.20	.09	.03
☐ 11 Orel Hershiser Series MVP Uses Shutout Magic	.40	.18	.05
☐ 12 Dodger Blue, World Champs	.20	.09	.03

1990 Fleer

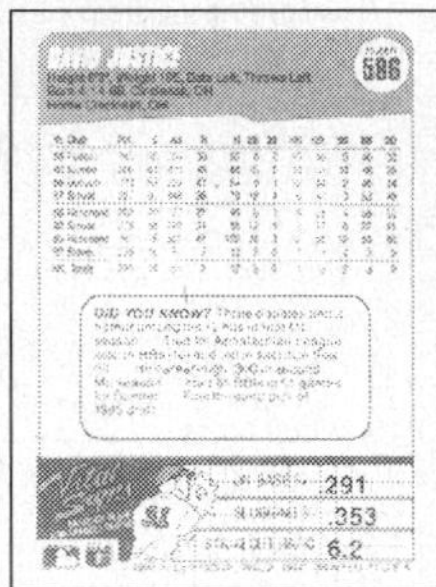

The 1990 Fleer set contains 660 standard-size (2 1/2" by 3 1/2") cards. The outer front borders are white; the inner, ribbon-like borders are different depending on the team. The vertically oriented backs are white, red, pink, and navy. The set is again ordered numerically by teams, followed by combination cards, rookie prospect pairs, and checklists. Just as with the 1989 set, Fleer incorrectly anticipated the outcome of the 1989 Playoffs according to the team ordering. The A's, listed first, did win the World Series, but their opponents were the Giants, not the Cubs. Fleer later reported that they merely arranged the teams according to regular season team record due to the early printing date. The complete team ordering is as follows: Oakland A's (1-24), Chicago Cubs (25-49), San Francisco Giants (50-75), Toronto Blue Jays (76-99), Kansas City Royals (100-124), California Angels (125-148), San Diego Padres (149-171), Baltimore Orioles (172-195), New York Mets (196-219), Houston Astros (220-241), St. Louis Cardinals (242-265), Boston Red Sox (266-289), Texas Rangers (290-315), Milwaukee Brewers (316-340), Montreal Expos (341-364), Minnesota Twins (365-388), Los Angeles Dodgers (389-411), Cincinnati Reds (412-435), New York Yankees (436-458), Pittsburgh Pirates (459-482), Cleveland Indians (483-504), Seattle Mariners (505-528), Chicago White Sox (529-551), Philadelphia Phillies (552-573), Atlanta Braves (574-598), and Detroit Tigers (599-620). The key Rookie Cards in this set are Alex Cole, Delino DeShields, Juan Gonzalez, Marquis Grissom, Dave Justice, Kevin Maas, Ben McDonald, and Larry Walker. The following five cards have minor printing differences, 6, 162, 260, 469, and 550; these differences are so minor that collectors have deemed them not significant enough to effect a price differential. Fleer also produced a separate set for Canada. The Canadian set only differs from the regular set in that it shows copyright "FLEER LTD./LTEE PTD. IN CANADA" on the card backs. Although these Canadian cards were undoubtedly produced in much lesser quantities compared to the U.S. issue, the fact that the versions are so similar has kept the demand (and the price differential) for the Canadian cards down.

	MT	EX-MT	VG
COMPLETE SET (660)	15.00	6.75	1.90
COMPLETE FACT.SET (672)	15.00	6.75	1.90
COMMON PLAYER (1-660)	.04	.02	.01
☐ 1 Lance Blankenship	.04	.02	.01
☐ 2 Todd Burns	.04	.02	.01
☐ 3 Jose Canseco	.30	.14	.04
☐ 4 Jim Corsi	.04	.02	.01
☐ 5 Storm Davis	.04	.02	.01
☐ 6 Dennis Eckersley	.12	.05	.02
☐ 7 Mike Gallego	.04	.02	.01
☐ 8 Ron Hassey	.04	.02	.01
☐ 9 Dave Henderson	.04	.02	.01
☐ 10 Rickey Henderson	.20	.09	.03
☐ 11 Rick Honeycutt	.04	.02	.01
☐ 12 Stan Javier	.04	.02	.01
☐ 13 Felix Jose	.20	.09	.03
☐ 14 Carney Lansford	.07	.03	.01
☐ 15 Mark McGwire UER (1989 runs listed as 4, should be 74)	.30	.14	.04
☐ 16 Mike Moore	.04	.02	.01
☐ 17 Gene Nelson	.04	.02	.01
☐ 18 Dave Parker	.07	.03	.01
☐ 19 Tony Phillips	.04	.02	.01
☐ 20 Terry Steinbach	.07	.03	.01
☐ 21 Dave Stewart	.07	.03	.01
☐ 22 Walt Weiss	.04	.02	.01
☐ 23 Bob Welch	.07	.03	.01
☐ 24 Curt Young	.04	.02	.01
☐ 25 Paul Assenmacher	.04	.02	.01
☐ 26 Damon Berryhill	.04	.02	.01
☐ 27 Mike Bielecki	.04	.02	.01
☐ 28 Kevin Blankenship	.04	.02	.01
☐ 29 Andre Dawson	.12	.05	.02
☐ 30 Shawon Dunston	.07	.03	.01
☐ 31 Joe Girardi	.04	.02	.01
☐ 32 Mark Grace	.20	.09	.03
☐ 33 Mike Harkey	.07	.03	.01
☐ 34 Paul Kilgus	.04	.02	.01
☐ 35 Les Lancaster	.04	.02	.01
☐ 36 Vance Law	.04	.02	.01
☐ 37 Greg Maddux	.20	.09	.03
☐ 38 Lloyd McClendon	.04	.02	.01
☐ 39 Jeff Pico	.04	.02	.01
☐ 40 Ryne Sandberg	.35	.16	.04
☐ 41 Scott Sanderson	.04	.02	.01
☐ 42 Dwight Smith	.04	.02	.01
☐ 43 Rick Sutcliffe	.07	.03	.01
☐ 44 Jerome Walton	.07	.03	.01
☐ 45 Mitch Webster	.04	.02	.01
☐ 46 Curt Wilkerson	.04	.02	.01
☐ 47 Dean Wilkins	.04	.02	.01
☐ 48 Mitch Williams	.07	.03	.01
☐ 49 Steve Wilson	.04	.02	.01
☐ 50 Steve Bedrosian	.04	.02	.01
☐ 51 Mike Benjamin	.10	.05	.01
☐ 52 Jeff Brantley	.04	.02	.01
☐ 53 Brett Butler	.07	.03	.01
☐ 54 Will Clark UER ("Did You Know" says first in runs, should say tied for first)	.30	.14	.04
☐ 55 Kelly Downs	.04	.02	.01
☐ 56 Scott Garrelts	.04	.02	.01
☐ 57 Atlee Hammaker	.04	.02	.01
☐ 58 Terry Kennedy	.04	.02	.01
☐ 59 Mike LaCoss	.04	.02	.01
☐ 60 Craig Lefferts	.04	.02	.01
☐ 61 Greg Litton	.04	.02	.01
☐ 62 Candy Maldonado	.04	.02	.01
☐ 63 Kirt Manwaring UER (No '88 Phoenix stats as noted in box)	.04	.02	.01
☐ 64 Randy McCament	.04	.02	.01
☐ 65 Kevin Mitchell	.10	.05	.01
☐ 66 Donell Nixon	.04	.02	.01
☐ 67 Ken Oberkfell	.04	.02	.01
☐ 68 Rick Reuschel	.04	.02	.01
☐ 69 Ernest Riles	.04	.02	.01
☐ 70 Don Robinson	.04	.02	.01
☐ 71 Pat Sheridan	.04	.02	.01
☐ 72 Chris Speier	.04	.02	.01
☐ 73 Robby Thompson	.04	.02	.01
☐ 74 Jose Uribe	.04	.02	.01
☐ 75 Matt Williams	.10	.05	.01
☐ 76 George Bell	.07	.03	.01
☐ 77 Pat Borders	.07	.03	.01
☐ 78 John Cerutti	.04	.02	.01
☐ 79 Junior Felix	.07	.03	.01
☐ 80 Tony Fernandez	.07	.03	.01
☐ 81 Mike Flanagan	.04	.02	.01
☐ 82 Mauro Gozzo	.04	.02	.01
☐ 83 Kelly Gruber	.07	.03	.01
☐ 84 Tom Henke	.07	.03	.01
☐ 85 Jimmy Key	.07	.03	.01
☐ 86 Manny Lee	.04	.02	.01
☐ 87 Nelson Liriano UER (Should say "led the IL" instead of "led the TL")	.04	.02	.01
☐ 88 Lee Mazzilli	.04	.02	.01
☐ 89 Fred McGriff	.20	.09	.03
☐ 90 Lloyd Moseby	.04	.02	.01
☐ 91 Rance Mulliniks	.04	.02	.01
☐ 92 Alex Sanchez	.04	.02	.01
☐ 93 Dave Stieb	.07	.03	.01
☐ 94 Todd Stottlemyre	.07	.03	.01
☐ 95 Duane Ward UER (Double line of '87 Syracuse stats)	.04	.02	.01
☐ 96 David Wells	.07	.03	.01
☐ 97 Ernie Whitt	.04	.02	.01
☐ 98 Frank Wills	.04	.02	.01
☐ 99 Mookie Wilson	.04	.02	.01
☐ 100 Kevin Appier	.25	.11	.03
☐ 101 Luis Aquino	.04	.02	.01
☐ 102 Bob Boone	.07	.03	.01
☐ 103 George Brett	.15	.07	.02
☐ 104 Jose DeJesus	.04	.02	.01
☐ 105 Luis De Los Santos	.04	.02	.01
☐ 106 Jim Eisenreich	.04	.02	.01
☐ 107 Steve Farr	.04	.02	.01
☐ 108 Tom Gordon	.07	.03	.01
☐ 109 Mark Gubicza	.04	.02	.01
☐ 110 Bo Jackson	.15	.07	.02
☐ 111 Terry Leach	.04	.02	.01
☐ 112 Charlie Leibrandt	.04	.02	.01
☐ 113 Rick Luecken	.04	.02	.01
☐ 114 Mike Macfarlane	.04	.02	.01
☐ 115 Jeff Montgomery	.07	.03	.01
☐ 116 Bret Saberhagen	.07	.03	.01
☐ 117 Kevin Seitzer	.07	.03	.01
☐ 118 Kurt Stillwell	.04	.02	.01
☐ 119 Pat Tabler	.04	.02	.01
☐ 120 Danny Tartabull	.10	.05	.01
☐ 121 Gary Thurman	.04	.02	.01
☐ 122 Frank White	.04	.02	.01
☐ 123 Willie Wilson	.04	.02	.01
☐ 124 Matt Winters	.04	.02	.01
☐ 125 Jim Abbott	.20	.09	.03
☐ 126 Tony Armas	.04	.02	.01
☐ 127 Dante Bichette	.07	.03	.01
☐ 128 Bert Blyleven	.07	.03	.01
☐ 129 Chili Davis	.07	.03	.01
☐ 130 Brian Downing	.04	.02	.01
☐ 131 Mike Fetters	.10	.05	.01
☐ 132 Chuck Finley	.07	.03	.01
☐ 133 Willie Fraser	.04	.02	.01
☐ 134 Bryan Harvey	.07	.03	.01
☐ 135 Jack Howell	.04	.02	.01
☐ 136 Wally Joyner	.07	.03	.01
☐ 137 Jeff Manto	.04	.02	.01
☐ 138 Kirk McCaskill	.04	.02	.01
☐ 139 Bob McClure	.04	.02	.01
☐ 140 Greg Minton	.04	.02	.01
☐ 141 Lance Parrish	.07	.03	.01
☐ 142 Dan Petry	.04	.02	.01
☐ 143 Johnny Ray	.04	.02	.01
☐ 144 Dick Schofield	.04	.02	.01
☐ 145 Lee Stevens	.08	.04	.01
☐ 146 Claudell Washington	.04	.02	.01
☐ 147 Devon White	.07	.03	.01
☐ 148 Mike Witt	.04	.02	.01
☐ 149 Roberto Alomar	.40	.18	.05
☐ 150 Sandy Alomar Jr.	.10	.05	.01
☐ 151 Andy Benes	.20	.09	.03
☐ 152 Jack Clark	.07	.03	.01
☐ 153 Pat Clements	.04	.02	.01
☐ 154 Joey Cora	.04	.02	.01
☐ 155 Mark Davis	.04	.02	.01

☐	156	Mark Grant	.04	.02	.01
☐	157	Tony Gwynn	.20	.09	.03
☐	158	Greg W. Harris	.04	.02	.01
☐	159	Bruce Hurst	.07	.03	.01
☐	160	Darrin Jackson	.07	.03	.01
☐	161	Chris James	.04	.02	.01
☐	162	Carmelo Martinez	.04	.02	.01
☐	163	Mike Pagliarulo	.04	.02	.01
☐	164	Mark Parent	.04	.02	.01
☐	165	Dennis Rasmussen	.04	.02	.01
☐	166	Bip Roberts	.07	.03	.01
☐	167	Benito Santiago	.07	.03	.01
☐	168	Calvin Schiraldi	.04	.02	.01
☐	169	Eric Show	.04	.02	.01
☐	170	Garry Templeton	.04	.02	.01
☐	171	Ed Whitson	.04	.02	.01
☐	172	Brady Anderson	.12	.05	.02
☐	173	Jeff Ballard	.04	.02	.01
☐	174	Phil Bradley	.04	.02	.01
☐	175	Mike Devereaux	.07	.03	.01
☐	176	Steve Finley	.07	.03	.01
☐	177	Pete Harnisch	.10	.05	.01
☐	178	Kevin Hickey	.04	.02	.01
☐	179	Brian Holton	.04	.02	.01
☐	180	Ben McDonald	.50	.23	.06
☐	181	Bob Melvin	.04	.02	.01
☐	182	Bob Milacki	.04	.02	.01
☐	183	Randy Milligan UER (Double line of '87 stats)	.04	.02	.01
☐	184	Gregg Olson	.10	.05	.01
☐	185	Joe Orsulak	.04	.02	.01
☐	186	Bill Ripken	.04	.02	.01
☐	187	Cal Ripken	.40	.18	.05
☐	188	Dave Schmidt	.04	.02	.01
☐	189	Larry Sheets	.04	.02	.01
☐	190	Mickey Tettleton	.07	.03	.01
☐	191	Mark Thurmond	.04	.02	.01
☐	192	Jay Tibbs	.04	.02	.01
☐	193	Jim Traber	.04	.02	.01
☐	194	Mark Williamson	.04	.02	.01
☐	195	Craig Worthington	.04	.02	.01
☐	196	Don Aase	.04	.02	.01
☐	197	Blaine Beatty	.04	.02	.01
☐	198	Mark Carreon	.04	.02	.01
☐	199	Gary Carter	.07	.03	.01
☐	200	David Cone	.12	.05	.02
☐	201	Ron Darling	.07	.03	.01
☐	202	Kevin Elster	.04	.02	.01
☐	203	Sid Fernandez	.07	.03	.01
☐	204	Dwight Gooden	.10	.05	.01
☐	205	Keith Hernandez	.07	.03	.01
☐	206	Jeff Innis	.04	.02	.01
☐	207	Gregg Jefferies	.12	.05	.02
☐	208	Howard Johnson	.07	.03	.01
☐	209	Barry Lyons UER (Double line of '87 stats)	.04	.02	.01
☐	210	Dave Magadan	.07	.03	.01
☐	211	Kevin McReynolds	.07	.03	.01
☐	212	Jeff Musselman	.04	.02	.01
☐	213	Randy Myers	.07	.03	.01
☐	214	Bob Ojeda	.04	.02	.01
☐	215	Juan Samuel	.04	.02	.01
☐	216	Mackey Sasser	.04	.02	.01
☐	217	Darryl Strawberry	.20	.09	.03
☐	218	Tim Teufel	.04	.02	.01
☐	219	Frank Viola	.07	.03	.01
☐	220	Juan Agosto	.04	.02	.01
☐	221	Larry Andersen	.04	.02	.01
☐	222	Eric Anthony	.30	.14	.04
☐	223	Kevin Bass	.04	.02	.01
☐	224	Craig Biggio	.10	.05	.01
☐	225	Ken Caminiti	.07	.03	.01
☐	226	Jim Clancy	.04	.02	.01
☐	227	Danny Darwin	.04	.02	.01
☐	228	Glenn Davis	.07	.03	.01
☐	229	Jim Deshaies	.04	.02	.01
☐	230	Bill Doran	.04	.02	.01
☐	231	Bob Forsch	.04	.02	.01
☐	232	Brian Meyer	.04	.02	.01
☐	233	Terry Puhl	.04	.02	.01
☐	234	Rafael Ramirez	.04	.02	.01
☐	235	Rick Rhoden	.04	.02	.01
☐	236	Dan Schatzeder	.04	.02	.01
☐	237	Mike Scott	.04	.02	.01
☐	238	Dave Smith	.04	.02	.01
☐	239	Alex Trevino	.04	.02	.01
☐	240	Glenn Wilson	.04	.02	.01
☐	241	Gerald Young	.04	.02	.01
☐	242	Tom Brunansky	.07	.03	.01
☐	243	Cris Carpenter	.04	.02	.01
☐	244	Alex Cole	.15	.07	.02
☐	245	Vince Coleman	.07	.03	.01
☐	246	John Costello	.04	.02	.01
☐	247	Ken Dayley	.04	.02	.01
☐	248	Jose DeLeon	.04	.02	.01
☐	249	Frank DiPino	.04	.02	.01
☐	250	Pedro Guerrero	.07	.03	.01
☐	251	Ken Hill	.12	.05	.02
☐	252	Joe Magrane	.04	.02	.01
☐	253	Willie McGee UER (No decimal point before 353)	.07	.03	.01
☐	254	John Morris	.04	.02	.01
☐	255	Jose Oquendo	.04	.02	.01
☐	256	Tony Pena	.04	.02	.01
☐	257	Terry Pendleton	.10	.05	.01
☐	258	Ted Power	.04	.02	.01
☐	259	Dan Quisenberry	.07	.03	.01
☐	260	Ozzie Smith	.12	.05	.02
☐	261	Scott Terry	.04	.02	.01
☐	262	Milt Thompson	.04	.02	.01
☐	263	Denny Walling	.04	.02	.01
☐	264	Todd Worrell	.04	.02	.01
☐	265	Todd Zeile	.15	.07	.02
☐	266	Marty Barrett	.04	.02	.01
☐	267	Mike Boddicker	.04	.02	.01
☐	268	Wade Boggs	.20	.09	.03
☐	269	Ellis Burks	.07	.03	.01
☐	270	Rick Cerone	.04	.02	.01
☐	271	Roger Clemens	.35	.16	.04
☐	272	John Dopson	.04	.02	.01
☐	273	Nick Esasky	.04	.02	.01
☐	274	Dwight Evans	.07	.03	.01
☐	275	Wes Gardner	.04	.02	.01
☐	276	Rich Gedman	.04	.02	.01
☐	277	Mike Greenwell	.07	.03	.01
☐	278	Danny Heep	.04	.02	.01
☐	279	Eric Hetzel	.04	.02	.01
☐	280	Dennis Lamp	.04	.02	.01
☐	281	Rob Murphy UER ('89 stats say Reds, should say Red Sox)	.04	.02	.01
☐	282	Joe Price	.04	.02	.01
☐	283	Carlos Quintana	.07	.03	.01
☐	284	Jody Reed	.04	.02	.01
☐	285	Luis Rivera	.04	.02	.01
☐	286	Kevin Romine	.04	.02	.01
☐	287	Lee Smith	.07	.03	.01
☐	288	Mike Smithson	.04	.02	.01
☐	289	Bob Stanley	.04	.02	.01
☐	290	Harold Baines	.07	.03	.01
☐	291	Kevin Brown	.10	.05	.01
☐	292	Steve Buechele	.04	.02	.01
☐	293	Scott Coolbaugh	.04	.02	.01
☐	294	Jack Daugherty	.04	.02	.01
☐	295	Cecil Espy	.04	.02	.01
☐	296	Julio Franco	.07	.03	.01
☐	297	Juan Gonzalez	2.00	.90	.25
☐	298	Cecilio Guante	.04	.02	.01
☐	299	Drew Hall	.04	.02	.01
☐	300	Charlie Hough	.04	.02	.01
☐	301	Pete Incaviglia	.04	.02	.01
☐	302	Mike Jeffcoat	.04	.02	.01
☐	303	Chad Kreuter	.04	.02	.01
☐	304	Jeff Kunkel	.04	.02	.01
☐	305	Rick Leach	.04	.02	.01
☐	306	Fred Manrique	.04	.02	.01
☐	307	Jamie Moyer	.04	.02	.01
☐	308	Rafael Palmeiro	.10	.05	.01
☐	309	Geno Petralli	.04	.02	.01
☐	310	Kevin Reimer	.04	.02	.01
☐	311	Kenny Rogers	.04	.02	.01
☐	312	Jeff Russell	.04	.02	.01
☐	313	Nolan Ryan	.50	.23	.06
☐	314	Ruben Sierra	.20	.09	.03
☐	315	Bobby Witt	.07	.03	.01
☐	316	Chris Bosio	.04	.02	.01
☐	317	Glenn Braggs UER (Stats say 111 K's, but bio says 117 K's)	.04	.02	.01
☐	318	Greg Brock	.04	.02	.01
☐	319	Chuck Crim	.04	.02	.01
☐	320	Rob Deer	.07	.03	.01
☐	321	Mike Felder	.04	.02	.01
☐	322	Tom Filer	.04	.02	.01
☐	323	Tony Fossas	.04	.02	.01
☐	324	Jim Gantner	.04	.02	.01
☐	325	Darryl Hamilton	.07	.03	.01
☐	326	Teddy Higuera	.04	.02	.01
☐	327	Mark Knudson	.04	.02	.01
☐	328	Bill Krueger UER ('86 stats missing)	.04	.02	.01
☐	329	Tim McIntosh	.10	.05	.01
☐	330	Paul Molitor	.10	.05	.01

☐	331	Jaime Navarro	.07	.03	.01
☐	332	Charlie O'Brien	.04	.02	.01
☐	333	Jeff Peterek	.10	.05	.01
☐	334	Dan Plesac	.04	.02	.01
☐	335	Jerry Reuss	.04	.02	.01
☐	336	Gary Sheffield UER (Bio says played for 3 teams in '87, but stats say in '88)	.50	.23	.06
☐	337	Bill Spiers	.04	.02	.01
☐	338	B.J. Surhoff	.04	.02	.01
☐	339	Greg Vaughn	.20	.09	.03
☐	340	Robin Yount	.15	.07	.02
☐	341	Hubie Brooks	.04	.02	.01
☐	342	Tim Burke	.04	.02	.01
☐	343	Mike Fitzgerald	.04	.02	.01
☐	344	Tom Foley	.04	.02	.01
☐	345	Andres Galarraga	.04	.02	.01
☐	346	Damaso Garcia	.04	.02	.01
☐	347	Marquis Grissom	.60	.25	.08
☐	348	Kevin Gross	.04	.02	.01
☐	349	Joe Hesketh	.04	.02	.01
☐	350	Jeff Huson	.10	.05	.01
☐	351	Wallace Johnson	.04	.02	.01
☐	352	Mark Langston	.07	.03	.01
☐	353A	Dave Martinez (Yellow on front)	3.00	1.35	.40
☐	353B	Dave Martinez (Red on front)	.07	.03	.01
☐	354	Dennis Martinez UER ('87 ERA is 616, should be 6.16)	.07	.03	.01
☐	355	Andy McGaffigan	.04	.02	.01
☐	356	Otis Nixon	.07	.03	.01
☐	357	Spike Owen	.04	.02	.01
☐	358	Pascual Perez	.04	.02	.01
☐	359	Tim Raines	.07	.03	.01
☐	360	Nelson Santovenia	.04	.02	.01
☐	361	Bryn Smith	.04	.02	.01
☐	362	Zane Smith	.04	.02	.01
☐	363	Larry Walker	.90	.40	.11
☐	364	Tim Wallach	.07	.03	.01
☐	365	Rick Aguilera	.07	.03	.01
☐	366	Allan Anderson	.04	.02	.01
☐	367	Wally Backman	.04	.02	.01
☐	368	Doug Baker	.04	.02	.01
☐	369	Juan Berenguer	.04	.02	.01
☐	370	Randy Bush	.04	.02	.01
☐	371	Carmen Castillo	.04	.02	.01
☐	372	Mike Dyer	.04	.02	.01
☐	373	Gary Gaetti	.04	.02	.01
☐	374	Greg Gagne	.04	.02	.01
☐	375	Dan Gladden	.04	.02	.01
☐	376	German Gonzalez UER (Bio says 31 saves in '88, but stats say 30)	.04	.02	.01
☐	377	Brian Harper	.07	.03	.01
☐	378	Kent Hrbek	.07	.03	.01
☐	379	Gene Larkin	.04	.02	.01
☐	380	Tim Laudner UER (No decimal point before '85 BA of 238)	.04	.02	.01
☐	381	John Moses	.04	.02	.01
☐	382	Al Newman	.04	.02	.01
☐	383	Kirby Puckett	.30	.14	.04
☐	384	Shane Rawley	.04	.02	.01
☐	385	Jeff Reardon	.07	.03	.01
☐	386	Roy Smith	.04	.02	.01
☐	387	Gary Wayne	.04	.02	.01
☐	388	Dave West	.04	.02	.01
☐	389	Tim Belcher	.07	.03	.01
☐	390	Tim Crews UER (Stats say 163 IP for '83, but bio says 136)	.04	.02	.01
☐	391	Mike Davis	.04	.02	.01
☐	392	Rick Dempsey	.04	.02	.01
☐	393	Kirk Gibson	.07	.03	.01
☐	394	Jose Gonzalez	.04	.02	.01
☐	395	Alfredo Griffin	.04	.02	.01
☐	396	Jeff Hamilton	.04	.02	.01
☐	397	Lenny Harris	.04	.02	.01
☐	398	Mickey Hatcher	.04	.02	.01
☐	399	Orel Hershiser	.07	.03	.01
☐	400	Jay Howell	.04	.02	.01
☐	401	Mike Marshall	.04	.02	.01
☐	402	Ramon Martinez	.15	.07	.02
☐	403	Mike Morgan	.04	.02	.01
☐	404	Eddie Murray	.10	.05	.01
☐	405	Alejandro Pena	.04	.02	.01
☐	406	Willie Randolph	.07	.03	.01
☐	407	Mike Scioscia	.04	.02	.01
☐	408	Ray Searage	.04	.02	.01
☐	409	Fernando Valenzuela	.07	.03	.01
☐	410	Jose Vizcaino	.10	.05	.01
☐	411	John Wetteland	.07	.03	.01
☐	412	Jack Armstrong	.07	.03	.01
☐	413	Todd Benzinger UER (Bio says .323 at Pawtucket, but stats say .321)	.04	.02	.01
☐	414	Tim Birtsas	.04	.02	.01
☐	415	Tom Browning	.04	.02	.01
☐	416	Norm Charlton	.07	.03	.01
☐	417	Eric Davis	.10	.05	.01
☐	418	Rob Dibble	.07	.03	.01
☐	419	John Franco	.07	.03	.01
☐	420	Ken Griffey Sr.	.07	.03	.01
☐	421	Chris Hammond (No 1989 used for "Did Not Play" stat, actually did play for Nashville in 1989)	.20	.09	.03
☐	422	Danny Jackson	.04	.02	.01
☐	423	Barry Larkin	.12	.05	.02
☐	424	Tim Leary	.04	.02	.01
☐	425	Rick Mahler	.04	.02	.01
☐	426	Joe Oliver	.10	.05	.01
☐	427	Paul O'Neill	.07	.03	.01
☐	428	Luis Quinones UER ('86-'88 stats are omitted from card but included in totals)	.04	.02	.01
☐	429	Jeff Reed	.04	.02	.01
☐	430	Jose Rijo	.07	.03	.01
☐	431	Ron Robinson	.04	.02	.01
☐	432	Rolando Roomes	.04	.02	.01
☐	433	Chris Sabo	.07	.03	.01
☐	434	Scott Scudder	.04	.02	.01
☐	435	Herm Winningham	.04	.02	.01
☐	436	Steve Balboni	.04	.02	.01
☐	437	Jesse Barfield	.04	.02	.01
☐	438	Mike Blowers	.04	.02	.01
☐	439	Tom Brookens	.04	.02	.01
☐	440	Greg Cadaret	.04	.02	.01
☐	441	Alvaro Espinoza UER (Career games say 218, should be 219)	.04	.02	.01
☐	442	Bob Geren	.04	.02	.01
☐	443	Lee Guetterman	.04	.02	.01
☐	444	Mel Hall	.04	.02	.01
☐	445	Andy Hawkins	.04	.02	.01
☐	446	Roberto Kelly	.10	.05	.01
☐	447	Don Mattingly	.20	.09	.03
☐	448	Lance McCullers	.04	.02	.01
☐	449	Hensley Meulens	.07	.03	.01
☐	450	Dale Mohorcic	.04	.02	.01
☐	451	Clay Parker	.04	.02	.01
☐	452	Eric Plunk	.04	.02	.01
☐	453	Dave Righetti	.04	.02	.01
☐	454	Deion Sanders	.40	.18	.05
☐	455	Steve Sax	.07	.03	.01
☐	456	Don Slaught	.04	.02	.01
☐	457	Walt Terrell	.04	.02	.01
☐	458	Dave Winfield	.15	.07	.02
☐	459	Jay Bell	.07	.03	.01
☐	460	Rafael Belliard	.04	.02	.01
☐	461	Barry Bonds	.30	.14	.04
☐	462	Bobby Bonilla	.12	.05	.02
☐	463	Sid Bream	.04	.02	.01
☐	464	Benny Distefano	.04	.02	.01
☐	465	Doug Drabek	.07	.03	.01
☐	466	Jim Gott	.04	.02	.01
☐	467	Billy Hatcher UER (.1 hits for Cubs in 1984)	.04	.02	.01
☐	468	Neal Heaton	.04	.02	.01
☐	469	Jeff King	.07	.03	.01
☐	470	Bob Kipper	.04	.02	.01
☐	471	Randy Kramer	.04	.02	.01
☐	472	Bill Landrum	.04	.02	.01
☐	473	Mike LaValliere	.04	.02	.01
☐	474	Jose Lind	.04	.02	.01
☐	475	Junior Ortiz	.04	.02	.01
☐	476	Gary Redus	.04	.02	.01
☐	477	Rick Reed	.04	.02	.01
☐	478	R.J. Reynolds	.04	.02	.01
☐	479	Jeff D. Robinson	.04	.02	.01
☐	480	John Smiley	.07	.03	.01
☐	481	Andy Van Slyke	.10	.05	.01
☐	482	Bob Walk	.04	.02	.01
☐	483	Andy Allanson	.04	.02	.01
☐	484	Scott Bailes	.04	.02	.01
☐	485	Joey Belle UER (Has Jay Bell "Did You Know")	.50	.23	.06
☐	486	Bud Black	.04	.02	.01

Card			
☐ 487 Jerry Browne	.04	.02	.01
☐ 488 Tom Candiotti	.04	.02	.01
☐ 489 Joe Carter	.20	.09	.03
☐ 490 Dave Clark (No '84 stats)	.04	.02	.01
☐ 491 John Farrell	.04	.02	.01
☐ 492 Felix Fermin	.04	.02	.01
☐ 493 Brook Jacoby	.04	.02	.01
☐ 494 Dion James	.04	.02	.01
☐ 495 Doug Jones	.07	.03	.01
☐ 496 Brad Komminsk	.04	.02	.01
☐ 497 Rod Nichols	.04	.02	.01
☐ 498 Pete O'Brien	.04	.02	.01
☐ 499 Steve Olin	.20	.09	.03
☐ 500 Jesse Orosco	.04	.02	.01
☐ 501 Joel Skinner	.04	.02	.01
☐ 502 Cory Snyder	.04	.02	.01
☐ 503 Greg Swindell	.07	.03	.01
☐ 504 Rich Yett	.04	.02	.01
☐ 505 Scott Bankhead	.04	.02	.01
☐ 506 Scott Bradley	.04	.02	.01
☐ 507 Greg Briley UER (28 SB's in bio, but 27 in stats)	.04	.02	.01
☐ 508 Jay Buhner	.07	.03	.01
☐ 509 Darnell Coles	.04	.02	.01
☐ 510 Keith Comstock	.04	.02	.01
☐ 511 Henry Cotto	.04	.02	.01
☐ 512 Alvin Davis	.04	.02	.01
☐ 513 Ken Griffey Jr.	1.25	.55	.16
☐ 514 Erik Hanson	.07	.03	.01
☐ 515 Gene Harris	.04	.02	.01
☐ 516 Brian Holman	.04	.02	.01
☐ 517 Mike Jackson	.04	.02	.01
☐ 518 Randy Johnson	.07	.03	.01
☐ 519 Jeffrey Leonard	.04	.02	.01
☐ 520 Edgar Martinez	.20	.09	.03
☐ 521 Dennis Powell	.04	.02	.01
☐ 522 Jim Presley	.04	.02	.01
☐ 523 Jerry Reed	.04	.02	.01
☐ 524 Harold Reynolds	.04	.02	.01
☐ 525 Mike Schooler	.04	.02	.01
☐ 526 Bill Swift	.07	.03	.01
☐ 527 Dave Valle	.04	.02	.01
☐ 528 Omar Vizquel	.07	.03	.01
☐ 529 Ivan Calderon	.04	.02	.01
☐ 530 Carlton Fisk UER (Bellow Falls, should be Bellows Falls)	.10	.05	.01
☐ 531 Scott Fletcher	.04	.02	.01
☐ 532 Dave Gallagher	.04	.02	.01
☐ 533 Ozzie Guillen	.04	.02	.01
☐ 534 Greg Hibbard	.20	.09	.03
☐ 535 Shawn Hillegas	.04	.02	.01
☐ 536 Lance Johnson	.07	.03	.01
☐ 537 Eric King	.04	.02	.01
☐ 538 Ron Kittle	.04	.02	.01
☐ 539 Steve Lyons	.04	.02	.01
☐ 540 Carlos Martinez	.04	.02	.01
☐ 541 Tom McCarthy	.04	.02	.01
☐ 542 Matt Merullo (Had 5 ML runs scored entering '90, not 6)	.04	.02	.01
☐ 543 Donn Pall UER (Stats say pro career began in '85, bio says '88)	.04	.02	.01
☐ 544 Dan Pasqua	.04	.02	.01
☐ 545 Ken Patterson	.04	.02	.01
☐ 546 Melido Perez	.07	.03	.01
☐ 547 Steve Rosenberg	.04	.02	.01
☐ 548 Sammy Sosa	.15	.07	.02
☐ 549 Bobby Thigpen	.04	.02	.01
☐ 550 Robin Ventura	.60	.25	.08
☐ 551 Greg Walker	.04	.02	.01
☐ 552 Don Carman	.04	.02	.01
☐ 553 Pat Combs (6 walks for Phillies in '89 in stats, brief bio says 4)	.07	.03	.01
☐ 554 Dennis Cook	.04	.02	.01
☐ 555 Darren Daulton	.07	.03	.01
☐ 556 Len Dykstra	.07	.03	.01
☐ 557 Curt Ford	.04	.02	.01
☐ 558 Charlie Hayes	.07	.03	.01
☐ 559 Von Hayes	.04	.02	.01
☐ 560 Tommy Herr	.04	.02	.01
☐ 561 Ken Howell	.04	.02	.01
☐ 562 Steve Jeltz	.04	.02	.01
☐ 563 Ron Jones	.04	.02	.01
☐ 564 Ricky Jordan UER (Duplicate line of statistics on back)	.04	.02	.01
☐ 565 John Kruk	.07	.03	.01
☐ 566 Steve Lake	.04	.02	.01
☐ 567 Roger McDowell	.04	.02	.01
☐ 568 Terry Mulholland UER ("Did You Know" refers to Dave Magadan)	.07	.03	.01
☐ 569 Dwayne Murphy	.04	.02	.01
☐ 570 Jeff Parrett	.04	.02	.01
☐ 571 Randy Ready	.04	.02	.01
☐ 572 Bruce Ruffin	.04	.02	.01
☐ 573 Dickie Thon	.04	.02	.01
☐ 574 Jose Alvarez UER ('78 and '79 stats are reversed)	.04	.02	.01
☐ 575 Geronimo Berroa	.04	.02	.01
☐ 576 Jeff Blauser	.07	.03	.01
☐ 577 Joe Boever	.04	.02	.01
☐ 578 Marty Clary UER (No comma between city and state)	.04	.02	.01
☐ 579 Jody Davis	.04	.02	.01
☐ 580 Mark Eichhorn	.04	.02	.01
☐ 581 Darrell Evans	.07	.03	.01
☐ 582 Ron Gant	.25	.11	.03
☐ 583 Tom Glavine	.25	.11	.03
☐ 584 Tommy Greene	.12	.05	.02
☐ 585 Tommy Gregg	.04	.02	.01
☐ 586 Dave Justice UER (Actually had 16 doubles in Sumter in '86)	1.25	.55	.16
☐ 587 Mark Lemke	.07	.03	.01
☐ 588 Derek Lilliquist	.04	.02	.01
☐ 589 Oddibe McDowell	.04	.02	.01
☐ 590 Kent Mercker ERA (Bio says 2.75 ERA, stats say 2.68 ERA)	.12	.05	.02
☐ 591 Dale Murphy	.10	.05	.01
☐ 592 Gerald Perry	.04	.02	.01
☐ 593 Lonnie Smith	.04	.02	.01
☐ 594 Pete Smith	.07	.03	.01
☐ 595 John Smoltz	.25	.11	.03
☐ 596 Mike Stanton UER (No comma between city and state)	.15	.07	.02
☐ 597 Andres Thomas	.04	.02	.01
☐ 598 Jeff Treadway	.04	.02	.01
☐ 599 Doyle Alexander	.04	.02	.01
☐ 600 Dave Bergman	.04	.02	.01
☐ 601 Brian DuBois	.04	.02	.01
☐ 602 Paul Gibson	.04	.02	.01
☐ 603 Mike Heath	.04	.02	.01
☐ 604 Mike Henneman	.04	.02	.01
☐ 605 Guillermo Hernandez	.04	.02	.01
☐ 606 Shawn Holman	.04	.02	.01
☐ 607 Tracy Jones	.04	.02	.01
☐ 608 Chet Lemon	.04	.02	.01
☐ 609 Fred Lynn	.07	.03	.01
☐ 610 Jack Morris	.10	.05	.01
☐ 611 Matt Nokes	.04	.02	.01
☐ 612 Gary Pettis	.04	.02	.01
☐ 613 Kevin Ritz	.10	.05	.01
☐ 614 Jeff M. Robinson ('88 stats are not in line)	.04	.02	.01
☐ 615 Steve Searcy	.04	.02	.01
☐ 616 Frank Tanana	.04	.02	.01
☐ 617 Alan Trammell	.07	.03	.01
☐ 618 Gary Ward	.04	.02	.01
☐ 619 Lou Whitaker	.07	.03	.01
☐ 620 Frank Williams	.04	.02	.01
☐ 621A George Brett '80 ERR (Had 10 .390 hitting seasons)	1.25	.55	.16
☐ 621B George Brett '80 COR	.10	.05	.01
☐ 622 Fern.Valenzuela '81	.05	.02	.01
☐ 623 Dale Murphy '82	.10	.05	.01
☐ 624A Cal Ripken '83 ERR (Misspelled Ripkin on card back)	3.50	1.55	.45
☐ 624B Cal Ripken '83 COR	.20	.09	.03
☐ 625 Ryne Sandberg '84	.20	.09	.03
☐ 626 Don Mattingly '85	.10	.05	.01
☐ 627 Roger Clemens '86	.20	.09	.03
☐ 628 George Bell '87	.05	.02	.01
☐ 629 Jose Canseco '88 UER (Reggie won MVP in '83, should say '73)	.15	.07	.02
☐ 630A Will Clark '89 ERR (32 total bases on card back)	1.25	.55	.16
☐ 630B Will Clark '89 COR (321 total bases;	.15	.07	.02

technically still an error, listing only 24 runs)			
☐ 631 Game Savers	.05	.02	.01
Mark Davis Mitch Williams			
☐ 632 Boston Igniters	.10	.05	.01
Wade Boggs Mike Greenwell			
☐ 633 Starter and Stopper	.05	.02	.01
Mark Gubicza Jeff Russell			
☐ 634 League's Best Shortstops	.15	.07	.02
Tony Fernandez Cal Ripken			
☐ 635 Human Dynamos	.15	.07	.02
Kirby Puckett Bo Jackson			
☐ 636 300 Strikeout Club	.20	.09	.03
Nolan Ryan Mike Scott			
☐ 637 The Dynamic Duo	.10	.05	.01
Will Clark Kevin Mitchell			
☐ 638 AL All-Stars	.15	.07	.02
Don Mattingly Mark McGwire			
☐ 639 NL East Rivals	.10	.05	.01
Howard Johnson Ryne Sandberg			
☐ 640 Rudy Seanez	.15	.07	.02
Colin Charland			
☐ 641 George Canale	.30	.14	.04
Kevin Maas UER (Canale listed as INF on front, 1B on back)			
☐ 642 Kelly Mann and Dave Hansen	.15	.07	.02
☐ 643 Greg Smith and Stu Tate	.05	.02	.01
☐ 644 Tom Drees and Dann Howitt	.05	.02	.01
☐ 645 Mike Roesler and Derrick May	.30	.14	.04
☐ 646 Scott Hemond and Mark Gardner	.15	.07	.02
☐ 647 John Orton and Scott Leius	.25	.11	.03
☐ 648 Rich Monteleone and Dana Williams	.05	.02	.01
☐ 649 Mike Huff and Steve Frey	.05	.02	.01
☐ 650 Chuck McElroy and Moises Alou	.50	.23	.06
☐ 651 Bobby Rose and Mike Hartley	.05	.02	.01
☐ 652 Matt Kinzer and Wayne Edwards	.05	.02	.01
☐ 653 Delino DeShields and Jason Grimsley	.60	.25	.08
☐ 654 CL: A's/Cubs Giants/Blue Jays	.05	.01	.00
☐ 655 CL: Royals/Angels Padres/Orioles	.05	.01	.00
☐ 656 CL: Mets/Astros Cards/Red Sox	.05	.01	.00
☐ 657 CL: Rangers/Brewers Expos/Twins	.05	.01	.00
☐ 658 CL: Dodgers/Reds Yankees/Pirates	.05	.01	.00
☐ 659 CL: Indians/Mariners White Sox/Phillies	.05	.01	.00
☐ 660A CL: Braves/Tigers Specials/Checklists (Checklist-660 in smaller print on card front)	.10	.01	.00
☐ 660B CL: Braves/Tigers Specials/Checklists (Checklist-660 in normal print on card front)	.10	.01	.00

1990 Fleer All-Star Inserts

The 1990 Fleer All-Star insert set includes 12 standard-size (2 1/2" by 3 1/2") cards. The fronts are white with a light gray screen and bright red stripes. The vertically oriented backs are red, pink and white. The player selection for the

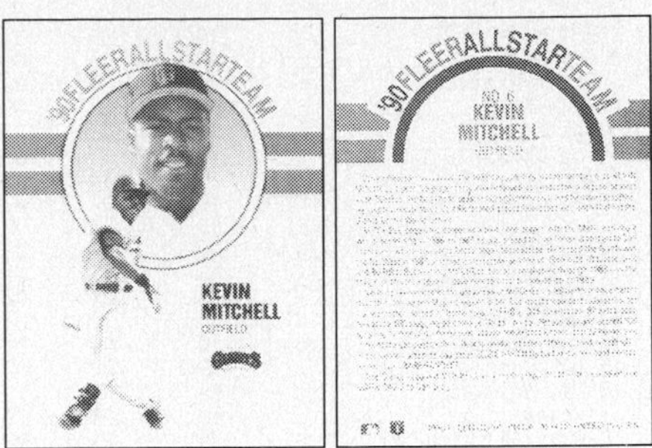

set is Fleer's opinion of the best Major Leaguer at each position. Cards were individually distributed as an insert in 33-card cellos and random wax packs.

	MT	EX-MT	VG
COMPLETE SET (12)	10.00	4.50	1.25
COMMON PLAYER (1-12)	.35	.16	.04
☐ 1 Harold Baines	.45	.20	.06
☐ 2 Will Clark	2.00	.90	.25
☐ 3 Mark Davis	.35	.16	.04
☐ 4 Howard Johnson UER (In middle of 5th line, the is misspelled th)	.60	.25	.08
☐ 5 Joe Magrane	.35	.16	.04
☐ 6 Kevin Mitchell	.75	.35	.09
☐ 7 Kirby Puckett	1.50	.65	.19
☐ 8 Cal Ripken	2.50	1.15	.30
☐ 9 Ryne Sandberg	2.50	1.15	.30
☐ 10 Mike Scott	.35	.16	.04
☐ 11 Ruben Sierra	1.25	.55	.16
☐ 12 Mickey Tettleton	.45	.20	.06

1990 Fleer Award Winners

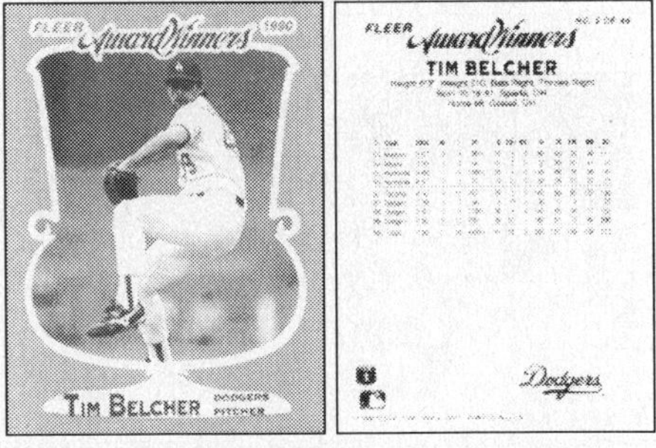

The 1990 Fleer Award Winners set was printed by Fleer for Hills stores (as well as for some 7/Eleven's) and released early in the summer of 1990. The set features an unattractive design of a trophy inside solid blue borders with the players photo within the caricature. This 44-card, standard-size (2 1/2" by 3 1/2") set is numbered in alphabetical order, although Will Clark erroneously precedes Jack Clark. Card number 10 is listed on the box checklist as being Ron Darling, but Darling is not in the set. Consequently the numbers on the box checklist between 10 and 37 are off by one. Darryl Strawberry (38) is not listed on the box, but is included in the set. The box also includes six peel-off team logo stickers. The original suggested retail price for the set at Hills was 2.49.

	MT	EX-MT	VG
COMPLETE SET (44)	5.00	2.30	.60
COMMON PLAYER (1-44)	.10	.05	.01

☐ 1 Jeff Ballard	.10	.05	.01
☐ 2 Tim Belcher	.10	.05	.01
☐ 3 Bert Blyleven	.15	.07	.02
☐ 4 Wade Boggs	.50	.23	.06
☐ 5 Bob Boone	.15	.07	.02
☐ 6 Jose Canseco	.75	.35	.09
☐ 7 Will Clark	.75	.35	.09
☐ 8 Jack Clark	.15	.07	.02
☐ 9 Vince Coleman	.15	.07	.02
☐ 10 Eric Davis	.20	.09	.03
☐ 11 Jose DeLeon	.10	.05	.01
☐ 12 Tony Fernandez	.15	.07	.02
☐ 13 Carlton Fisk	.30	.14	.04
☐ 14 Scott Garrelts	.10	.05	.01
☐ 15 Tom Gordon	.15	.07	.02
☐ 16 Ken Griffey Jr.	1.25	.55	.16
☐ 17 Von Hayes	.10	.05	.01
☐ 18 Rickey Henderson	.60	.25	.08
☐ 19 Bo Jackson	.75	.35	.09
☐ 20 Howard Johnson	.15	.07	.02
☐ 21 Don Mattingly	.75	.35	.09
☐ 22 Fred McGriff	.30	.14	.04
☐ 23 Kevin Mitchell	.25	.11	.03
☐ 24 Gregg Olson	.15	.07	.02
☐ 25 Gary Pettis	.10	.05	.01
☐ 26 Kirby Puckett	.60	.25	.08
☐ 27 Harold Reynolds	.10	.05	.01
☐ 28 Jeff Russell	.10	.05	.01
☐ 29 Nolan Ryan	1.00	.45	.13
☐ 30 Bret Saberhagen	.20	.09	.03
☐ 31 Ryne Sandberg	1.00	.45	.13
☐ 32 Benito Santiago	.20	.09	.03
☐ 33 Mike Scott	.15	.07	.02
☐ 34 Ruben Sierra	.40	.18	.05
☐ 35 Lonnie Smith	.10	.05	.01
☐ 36 Ozzie Smith	.25	.11	.03
☐ 37 Dave Stewart	.15	.07	.02
☐ 38 Darryl Strawberry	.50	.23	.06
☐ 39 Greg Swindell	.15	.07	.02
☐ 40 Andy Van Slyke	.20	.09	.03
☐ 41 Tim Wallach	.10	.05	.01
☐ 42 Jerome Walton	.15	.07	.02
☐ 43 Mitch Williams	.10	.05	.01
☐ 44 Robin Yount	.50	.23	.06

1990 Fleer Baseball All-Stars

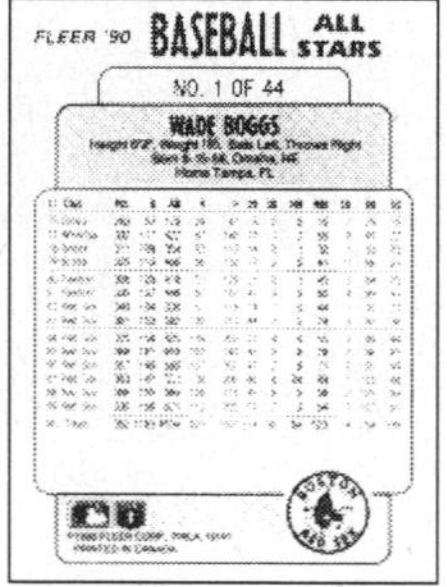

The 1990 Fleer Baseball All-Stars Set was produced by Fleer for the Ben Franklin chain and released early in the summer of 1990. This standard-size (2 1/2" by 3 1/2"), 44-card set features some of the best of today's players in alphabetical order. The design of the cards has vertical stripes on the front of the card. The set's custom box gives the set checklist on the back panel. The box also includes six peel-off team logo stickers each with a trivia quiz on back.

	MT	EX-MT	VG
COMPLETE SET (44)	5.00	2.30	.60
COMMON PLAYER (1-44)	.10	.05	.01
☐ 1 Wade Boggs	.50	.23	.06
☐ 2 Bobby Bonilla	.25	.11	.03
☐ 3 Tim Burke	.10	.05	.01
☐ 4 Jose Canseco	.75	.35	.09
☐ 5 Will Clark	.75	.35	.09
☐ 6 Eric Davis	.20	.09	.03
☐ 7 Glenn Davis	.15	.07	.02
☐ 8 Julio Franco	.15	.07	.02
☐ 9 Tony Fernandez	.15	.07	.02
☐ 10 Gary Gaetti	.10	.05	.01
☐ 11 Scott Garrelts	.10	.05	.01
☐ 12 Mark Grace	.30	.14	.04
☐ 13 Mike Greenwell	.25	.11	.03
☐ 14 Ken Griffey Jr.	1.25	.55	.16
☐ 15 Mark Gubicza	.10	.05	.01
☐ 16 Pedro Guerrero	.15	.07	.02
☐ 17 Von Hayes	.10	.05	.01
☐ 18 Orel Hershiser	.15	.07	.02
☐ 19 Bruce Hurst	.10	.05	.01
☐ 20 Bo Jackson	.75	.35	.09
☐ 21 Howard Johnson	.15	.07	.02
☐ 22 Doug Jones	.10	.05	.01
☐ 23 Barry Larkin	.20	.09	.03
☐ 24 Don Mattingly	.75	.35	.09
☐ 25 Mark McGwire	.60	.25	.08
☐ 26 Kevin McReynolds	.15	.07	.02
☐ 27 Kevin Mitchell	.20	.09	.03
☐ 28 Dan Plesac	.10	.05	.01
☐ 29 Kirby Puckett	.60	.25	.08
☐ 30 Cal Ripken	1.00	.45	.13
☐ 31 Bret Saberhagen	.15	.07	.02
☐ 32 Ryne Sandberg	1.00	.45	.13
☐ 33 Steve Sax	.15	.07	.02
☐ 34 Ruben Sierra	.35	.16	.04
☐ 35 Ozzie Smith	.25	.11	.03
☐ 36 John Smoltz	.25	.11	.03
☐ 37 Daryl Strawberry	.50	.23	.06
☐ 38 Terry Steinbach	.15	.07	.02
☐ 39 Dave Stewart	.15	.07	.02
☐ 40 Bobby Thigpen	.15	.07	.02
☐ 41 Alan Trammell	.15	.07	.02
☐ 42 Devon White	.15	.07	.02
☐ 43 Mitch Williams	.10	.05	.01
☐ 44 Robin Yount	.50	.23	.06

1990 Fleer Baseball MVP's

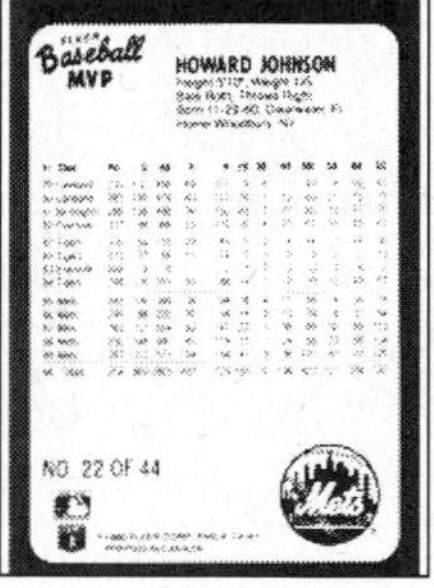

The 1990 Fleer Baseball MVP's were produced by Fleer exclusively for the Toys'R'Us chain and released early in the summer of 1990. This set has a multi-colored border, is standard size, 2 1/2" by 3 1/2", and has 44 players arranged in alphabetical order. The set's custom box gives the set checklist on the back panel. The box also includes six peel-off team logo stickers.

	MT	EX-MT	VG
COMPLETE SET (44)	5.00	2.30	.60
COMMON PLAYER (1-44)	.10	.05	.01
☐ 1 George Bell	.15	.07	.02
☐ 2 Bert Blyleven	.15	.07	.02
☐ 3 Wade Boggs	.50	.23	.06
☐ 4 Bobby Bonilla	.25	.11	.03
☐ 5 George Brett	.50	.23	.06
☐ 6 Jose Canseco	.75	.35	.09
☐ 7 Will Clark	.75	.35	.09
☐ 8 Roger Clemens	.75	.35	.09
☐ 9 Eric Davis	.20	.09	.03
☐ 10 Glenn Davis	.15	.07	.02
☐ 11 Tony Fernandez	.15	.07	.02
☐ 12 Dwight Gooden	.20	.09	.03
☐ 13 Mike Greenwell	.20	.09	.03
☐ 14 Ken Griffey Jr.	1.25	.55	.16
☐ 15 Pedro Guerrero	.15	.07	.02

☐ 16 Tony Gwynn	.50	.23	.06
☐ 17 Rickey Henderson	.60	.25	.08
☐ 18 Tom Herr	.10	.05	.01
☐ 19 Orel Hershiser	.15	.07	.02
☐ 20 Kent Hrbek	.15	.07	.02
☐ 21 Bo Jackson	.75	.35	.09
☐ 22 Howard Johnson	.15	.07	.02
☐ 23 Don Mattingly	.75	.35	.09
☐ 24 Fred McGriff	.30	.14	.04
☐ 25 Mark McGwire	.60	.25	.08
☐ 26 Kevin Mitchell	.25	.11	.03
☐ 27 Paul Molitor	.25	.11	.03
☐ 28 Dale Murphy	.25	.11	.03
☐ 29 Kirby Puckett	.60	.25	.08
☐ 30 Tim Raines	.15	.07	.02
☐ 31 Cal Ripken	.75	.35	.09
☐ 32 Bret Saberhagen	.15	.07	.02
☐ 33 Ryne Sandberg	.75	.35	.09
☐ 34 Ruben Sierra	.50	.23	.06
☐ 35 Dwight Smith	.15	.07	.02
☐ 36 Ozzie Smith	.25	.11	.03
☐ 37 Darryl Strawberry	.45	.20	.06
☐ 38 Dave Stewart	.15	.07	.02
☐ 39 Greg Swindell	.15	.07	.02
☐ 40 Bobby Thigpen	.15	.07	.02
☐ 41 Alan Trammell	.15	.07	.02
☐ 42 Jerome Walton	.15	.07	.02
☐ 43 Mitch Williams	.10	.05	.01
☐ 44 Robin Yount	.50	.23	.06

1990 Fleer League Leaders

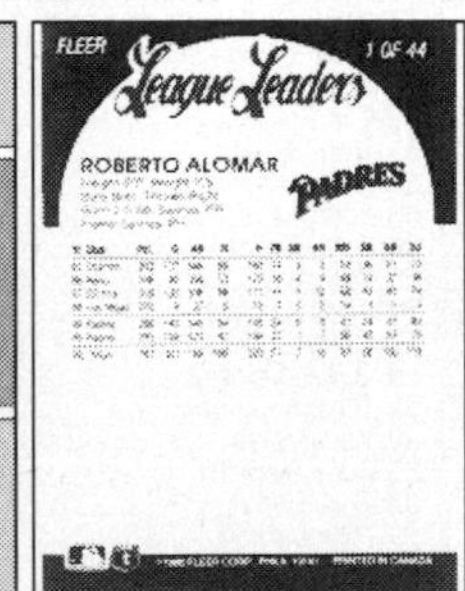

The 1990 Fleer League Leader set was issued by Fleer for Walgreen stores. This set design features solid blue borders with the players photo inset within the middle of the card. This 44-card, standard-size (2 1/2" by 3 1/2") set is numbered in alphabetical order. The set's custom box gives the set checklist on the back panel. The box also includes six peel-off team logo stickers. The original suggested retail price for the set at Walgreen's was 2.49.

	MT	EX-MT	VG
COMPLETE SET (44)	5.00	2.30	.60
COMMON PLAYER (1-44)	.10	.05	.01
☐ 1 Roberto Alomar	1.00	.45	.13
☐ 2 Tim Belcher	.10	.05	.01
☐ 3 George Bell	.15	.07	.02
☐ 4 Wade Boggs	.50	.23	.06
☐ 5 Jose Canseco	.75	.35	.09
☐ 6 Will Clark	.75	.35	.09
☐ 7 David Cone	.25	.11	.03
☐ 8 Eric Davis	.20	.09	.03
☐ 9 Glenn Davis	.15	.07	.02
☐ 10 Nick Esasky	.10	.05	.01
☐ 11 Dennis Eckersley	.20	.09	.03
☐ 12 Mark Grace	.50	.23	.06
☐ 13 Mike Greenwell	.25	.11	.03
☐ 14 Ken Griffey Jr.	1.25	.55	.16
☐ 15 Mark Gubicza	.10	.05	.01
☐ 16 Pedro Guerrero	.15	.07	.02
☐ 17 Tony Gwynn	.50	.23	.06
☐ 18 Rickey Henderson	.60	.25	.08
☐ 19 Bo Jackson	.75	.35	.09
☐ 20 Doug Jones	.10	.05	.01
☐ 21 Ricky Jordan	.15	.07	.02
☐ 22 Barry Larkin	.20	.09	.03
☐ 23 Don Mattingly	.75	.35	.09
☐ 24 Fred McGriff	.30	.14	.04
☐ 25 Mark McGwire	.60	.25	.08
☐ 26 Kevin Mitchell	.25	.11	.03
☐ 27 Jack Morris	.15	.07	.02
☐ 28 Gregg Olson	.15	.07	.02
☐ 29 Dan Plesac	.10	.05	.01
☐ 30 Kirby Puckett	.60	.25	.08
☐ 31 Nolan Ryan	1.00	.45	.13
☐ 32 Bret Saberhagen	.15	.07	.02
☐ 33 Ryne Sandberg	.75	.35	.09
☐ 34 Steve Sax	.15	.07	.02
☐ 35 Mike Scott	.15	.07	.02
☐ 36 Ruben Sierra	.35	.16	.04
☐ 37 Lonnie Smith	.10	.05	.01
☐ 38 Darryl Strawberry	.40	.18	.05
☐ 39 Bobby Thigpen	.15	.07	.02
☐ 40 Andy Van Slyke	.20	.09	.03
☐ 41 Tim Wallach	.15	.07	.02
☐ 42 Jerome Walton UER (Photo actually Eric Yelding)	.15	.07	.02
☐ 43 Devon White	.15	.07	.02
☐ 44 Robin Yount	.45	.20	.06

1990 Fleer League Standouts

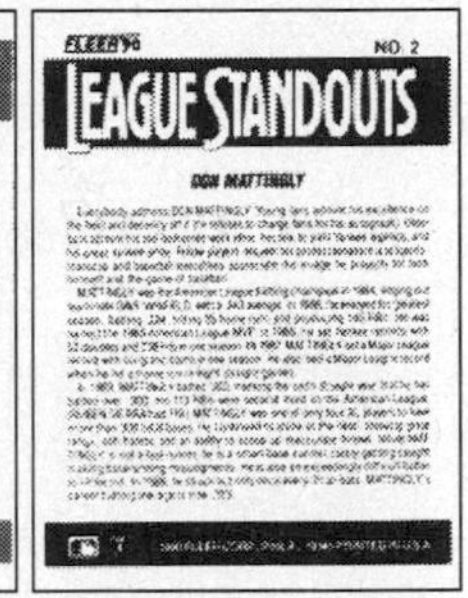

This six-card subset was distributed randomly (as an insert) in Fleer's 45-card rack packs. These cards are standard size, 2 1/2" by 3 1/2" and are quite attractive. The set is subtitled "Standouts" and commemorates outstanding events for those players from the previous season. The cards are numbered on the backs. The card backs are printed on white card stock.

	MT	EX-MT	VG
COMPLETE SET (6)	5.00	2.30	.60
COMMON PLAYER (1-6)	.60	.25	.08
☐ 1 Barry Larkin	.60	.25	.08
☐ 2 Don Mattingly	1.25	.55	.16
☐ 3 Darryl Strawberry	1.00	.45	.13
☐ 4 Jose Canseco	1.25	.55	.16
☐ 5 Wade Boggs	1.00	.45	.13
☐ 6 Mark Grace UER (Chris Sabo misspelled as Cris)	1.00	.45	.13

1990 Fleer Soaring Stars

The 1990 Fleer Soaring Stars set was issued by Fleer in their jumbo cello packs. This 12-card, standard-size (2 1/2" by 3 1/2") set featured 12 of the most popular young players entering the 1990 season. The set gives the visual impression of rockets exploding in the air to honor these young players.

	MT	EX-MT	VG
COMPLETE SET (12)	12.50	5.75	1.55
COMMON PLAYER (1-12)	.35	.16	.04

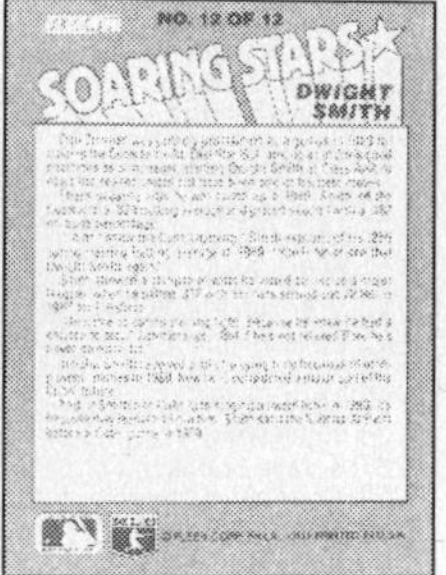

☐ 1 Todd Zeile	.75	.35	.09
☐ 2 Mike Stanton	.35	.16	.04
☐ 3 Larry Walker	1.25	.55	.16
☐ 4 Robin Ventura	2.00	.90	.25
☐ 5 Scott Coolbaugh	.35	.16	.04
☐ 6 Ken Griffey Jr.	6.00	2.70	.75
☐ 7 Tom Gordon	.35	.16	.04
☐ 8 Jerome Walton	.45	.20	.06
☐ 9 Junior Felix	.60	.25	.08
☐ 10 Jim Abbott	2.00	.90	.25
☐ 11 Ricky Jordan	.45	.20	.06
☐ 12 Dwight Smith	.35	.16	.04

1990 Fleer Update

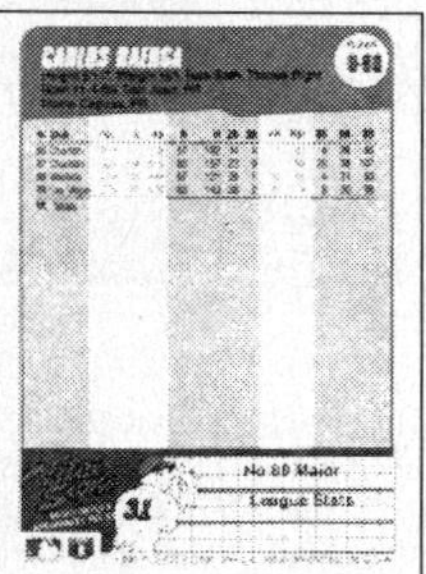

The 1990 Fleer Update set contains 132 standard-size (2 1/2" by 3 1/2") cards. This set marked the seventh consecutive year Fleer issued an end of season Update set. The set was issued exclusively as a boxed set through hobby dealers. The set is checklisted alphabetically by team for each league and then alphabetically within each team. The fronts are styled the same as the 1990 Fleer regular issue set. The backs are numbered with the prefix U for Update. The key rookies in this set are Carlos Baerga, Alex Fernandez, Travis Fryman, Dave Hollins, Jose Offerman, John Olerud, Frank Thomas, and Mark Whiten.

	MT	EX-MT	VG
COMPLETE SET (132)	7.00	3.10	.85
COMMON PLAYER (1-132)	.05	.02	.01
☐ 1 Steve Avery	.75	.35	.09
☐ 2 Francisco Cabrera	.10	.05	.01
☐ 3 Nick Esasky	.05	.02	.01
☐ 4 Jim Kremers	.05	.02	.01
☐ 5 Greg Olson	.10	.05	.01
☐ 6 Jim Presley	.05	.02	.01
☐ 7 Shawn Boskie	.10	.05	.01
☐ 8 Joe Kraemer	.05	.02	.01
☐ 9 Luis Salazar	.05	.02	.01
☐ 10 Hector Villanueva	.10	.05	.01
☐ 11 Glenn Braggs	.05	.02	.01
☐ 12 Mariano Duncan	.05	.02	.01
☐ 13 Billy Hatcher	.05	.02	.01
☐ 14 Tim Layana	.05	.02	.01
☐ 15 Hal Morris	.15	.07	.02
☐ 16 Javier Ortiz	.10	.05	.01
☐ 17 Dave Rohde	.05	.02	.01
☐ 18 Eric Yelding	.05	.02	.01
☐ 19 Hubie Brooks	.05	.02	.01
☐ 20 Kal Daniels	.05	.02	.01
☐ 21 Dave Hansen	.15	.07	.02
☐ 22 Mike Hartley	.05	.02	.01
☐ 23 Stan Javier	.05	.02	.01
☐ 24 Jose Offerman	.20	.09	.03
☐ 25 Juan Samuel	.05	.02	.01
☐ 26 Dennis Boyd	.05	.02	.01
☐ 27 Delino DeShields	.60	.25	.08
☐ 28 Steve Frey	.05	.02	.01
☐ 29 Mark Gardner	.08	.04	.01
☐ 30 Chris Nabholz	.20	.09	.03
☐ 31 Bill Sampen	.05	.02	.01
☐ 32 Dave Schmidt	.05	.02	.01
☐ 33 Daryl Boston	.05	.02	.01
☐ 34 Chuck Carr	.12	.05	.02
☐ 35 John Franco	.08	.04	.01
☐ 36 Todd Hundley	.15	.07	.02
☐ 37 Julio Machado	.08	.04	.01
☐ 38 Alejandro Pena	.05	.02	.01
☐ 39 Darren Reed	.10	.05	.01
☐ 40 Kelvin Torve	.05	.02	.01
☐ 41 Darrel Akerfelds	.05	.02	.01
☐ 42 Jose DeJesus	.05	.02	.01
☐ 43 Dave Hollins (Misspelled Dane on card back)	.60	.25	.08
☐ 44 Carmelo Martinez	.05	.02	.01
☐ 45 Brad Moore	.05	.02	.01
☐ 46 Dale Murphy	.10	.05	.01
☐ 47 Wally Backman	.05	.02	.01
☐ 48 Stan Belinda	.15	.07	.02
☐ 49 Bob Patterson	.05	.02	.01
☐ 50 Ted Power	.05	.02	.01
☐ 51 Don Slaught	.05	.02	.01
☐ 52 Geronimo Pena	.15	.07	.02
☐ 53 Lee Smith	.08	.04	.01
☐ 54 John Tudor	.05	.02	.01
☐ 55 Joe Carter	.20	.09	.03
☐ 56 Thomas Howard	.12	.05	.02
☐ 57 Craig Lefferts	.05	.02	.01
☐ 58 Rafael Valdez	.10	.05	.01
☐ 59 Dave Anderson	.05	.02	.01
☐ 60 Kevin Bass	.05	.02	.01
☐ 61 John Burkett	.10	.05	.01
☐ 62 Gary Carter	.08	.04	.01
☐ 63 Rick Parker	.05	.02	.01
☐ 64 Trevor Wilson	.05	.02	.01
☐ 65 Chris Hoiles	.40	.18	.05
☐ 66 Tim Hulett	.05	.02	.01
☐ 67 Dave Johnson	.05	.02	.01
☐ 68 Curt Schilling	.15	.07	.02
☐ 69 David Segui	.10	.05	.01
☐ 70 Tom Brunansky	.08	.04	.01
☐ 71 Greg A. Harris	.05	.02	.01
☐ 72 Dana Kiecker	.05	.02	.01
☐ 73 Tim Naehring	.15	.07	.02
☐ 74 Tony Pena	.05	.02	.01
☐ 75 Jeff Reardon	.08	.04	.01
☐ 76 Jerry Reed	.05	.02	.01
☐ 77 Mark Eichhorn	.05	.02	.01
☐ 78 Mark Langston	.08	.04	.01
☐ 79 John Orton	.05	.02	.01
☐ 80 Luis Polonia	.08	.04	.01
☐ 81 Dave Winfield	.15	.07	.02
☐ 82 Cliff Young	.10	.05	.01
☐ 83 Wayne Edwards	.05	.02	.01
☐ 84 Alex Fernandez	.40	.18	.05
☐ 85 Craig Grebeck	.15	.07	.02
☐ 86 Scott Radinsky	.15	.07	.02
☐ 87 Frank Thomas	4.00	1.80	.50
☐ 88 Beau Allred	.05	.02	.01
☐ 89 Sandy Alomar Jr.	.10	.05	.01
☐ 90 Carlos Baerga	1.25	.55	.16
☐ 91 Kevin Bearse	.05	.02	.01
☐ 92 Chris James	.05	.02	.01
☐ 93 Candy Maldonado	.05	.02	.01
☐ 94 Jeff Manto	.05	.02	.01
☐ 95 Cecil Fielder	.20	.09	.03
☐ 96 Travis Fryman	1.50	.65	.19
☐ 97 Lloyd Moseby	.05	.02	.01
☐ 98 Edwin Nunez	.05	.02	.01
☐ 99 Tony Phillips	.05	.02	.01
☐ 100 Larry Sheets	.05	.02	.01
☐ 101 Mark Davis	.05	.02	.01
☐ 102 Storm Davis	.05	.02	.01
☐ 103 Gerald Perry	.05	.02	.01
☐ 104 Terry Shumpert	.05	.02	.01
☐ 105 Edgar Diaz	.05	.02	.01

		MT	EX-MT	VG
☐ 106	Dave Parker	.08	.04	.01
☐ 107	Tim Drummond	.05	.02	.01
☐ 108	Junior Ortiz	.05	.02	.01
☐ 109	Park Pittman	.05	.02	.01
☐ 110	Kevin Tapani	.35	.16	.04
☐ 111	Oscar Azocar	.10	.05	.01
☐ 112	Jim Leyritz	.10	.05	.01
☐ 113	Kevin Maas	.25	.11	.03
☐ 114	Alan Mills	.12	.05	.02
☐ 115	Matt Nokes	.05	.02	.01
☐ 116	Pascual Perez	.05	.02	.01
☐ 117	Ozzie Canseco	.10	.05	.01
☐ 118	Scott Sanderson	.05	.02	.01
☐ 119	Tino Martinez	.15	.07	.02
☐ 120	Jeff Schaefer	.05	.02	.01
☐ 121	Matt Young	.05	.02	.01
☐ 122	Brian Bohanon	.10	.05	.01
☐ 123	Jeff Huson	.05	.02	.01
☐ 124	Ramon Manon	.05	.02	.01
☐ 125	Gary Mielke UER (Shown as Blue Jay on front)	.05	.02	.01
☐ 126	Willie Blair	.10	.05	.01
☐ 127	Glenallen Hill	.08	.04	.01
☐ 128	John Olerud	.60	.25	.08
☐ 129	Luis Sojo	.15	.07	.02
☐ 130	Mark Whiten	.35	.16	.04
☐ 131	Nolan Ryan	.60	.25	.08
☐ 132	Checklist 1-132	.08	.01	.00

1990 Fleer Wax Box Cards

The 1990 Fleer wax box cards comprise seven different box bottoms with four cards each, for a total of 28 standard-size (2 1/2" by 3 1/2") cards. The outer front borders are white; the inner, ribbon-like borders are different depending on the team. The vertically oriented backs are gray. The cards are numbered with a C prefix.

		MT	EX-MT	VG
COMPLETE SET (28)		12.50	5.75	1.55
COMMON PLAYER (C1-C28)		.15	.07	.02
☐ C1	Giants Logo	.15	.07	.02
☐ C2	Tim Belcher	.15	.07	.02
☐ C3	Roger Clemens	1.25	.55	.16
☐ C4	Eric Davis	.50	.23	.06
☐ C5	Glenn Davis	.35	.16	.04
☐ C6	Cubs Logo	.15	.07	.02
☐ C7	John Franco	.25	.11	.03
☐ C8	Mike Greenwell	.25	.11	.03
☐ C9	A's Logo	.15	.07	.02
☐ C10	Ken Griffey Jr.	2.50	1.15	.30
☐ C11	Pedro Guerrero	.25	.11	.03
☐ C12	Tony Gwynn	.75	.35	.09
☐ C13	Blue Jays Logo	.15	.07	.02
☐ C14	Orel Hershiser	.25	.11	.03
☐ C15	Bo Jackson	1.00	.45	.13
☐ C16	Howard Johnson	.35	.16	.04
☐ C17	Mets Logo	.15	.07	.02
☐ C18	Cardinals Logo	.15	.07	.02
☐ C19	Don Mattingly	1.00	.45	.13
☐ C20	Mark McGwire	1.00	.45	.13
☐ C21	Kevin Mitchell	.50	.23	.06
☐ C22	Kirby Puckett	1.00	.45	.13
☐ C23	Royals Logo	.15	.07	.02
☐ C24	Orioles Logo	.15	.07	.02
☐ C25	Ruben Sierra	1.00	.45	.13
☐ C26	Dave Stewart	.25	.11	.03
☐ C27	Jerome Walton	.25	.11	.03
☐ C28	Robin Yount	1.00	.45	.13

1990 Fleer World Series

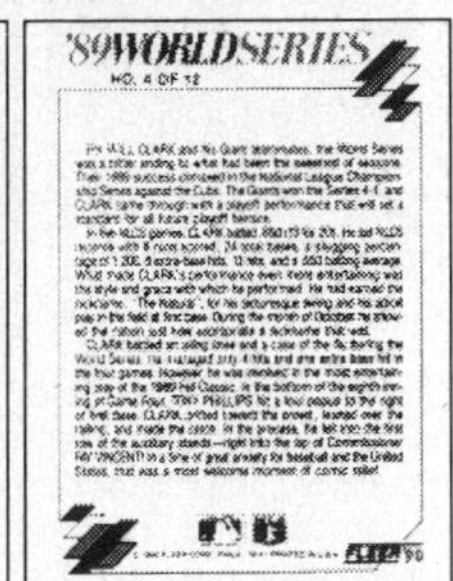

This 12-card standard size, 2 1/2" by 3 1/2" set was issued as an insert in with the Fleer factory sets, celebrating the 1989 World Series. This set marked the fourth year that Fleer issued a special World Series set in their factory (or vend) set. The design of these cards are different from the regular Fleer issue as the photo is framed by a white border with red and blue World Series cards and the player description in black.

		MT	EX-MT	VG
COMPLETE SET (12)		2.00	.90	.25
COMMON PLAYER (1-12)		.20	.09	.03
☐ 1	Mike Moore The final piece of the puzzle	.20	.09	.03
☐ 2	Kevin Mitchell NL MVP	.40	.18	.05
☐ 3	Terry Steinbach Game Two's Crushing Blow	.20	.09	.03
☐ 4	Will Clark Clark Powers Giants into the Series	.60	.25	.08
☐ 5	Jose Canseco Canseco Crushed World Series Slump	.60	.25	.08
☐ 6	Walt Weiss Great Leather in the field	.20	.09	.03
☐ 7	Terry Steinbach Game One and A's Break Out on Top	.20	.09	.03
☐ 8	Dave Stewart Oakland's MVP	.20	.09	.03
☐ 9	Dave Parker Parker's Bat Produces Power	.30	.14	.04
☐ 10	Dave Parker, Jose Canseco, and Will Clark: World Series Record Book Game 3	.50	.23	.06
☐ 11	Rickey Henderson Henderson Swipes Championship Series Records	.50	.23	.06
☐ 12	Oakland A's Celebrate Oakland A's: Baseball's Best in 89	.20	.09	.03

1991 Fleer

The 1991 Fleer set consists of 720 cards which measure the now standard size of 2 1/2" by 3 1/2". This set marks Fleer's eleventh consecutive year of issuing sets of current players.

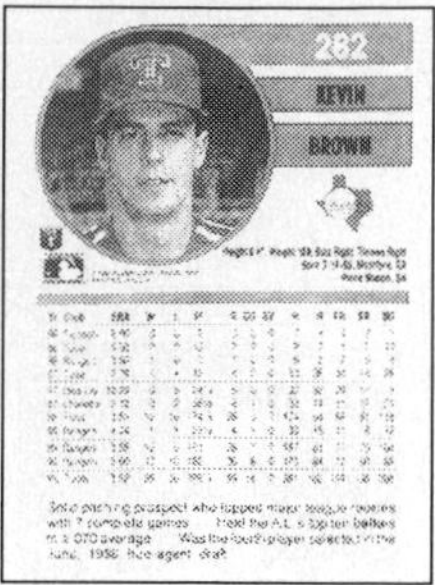

This set does not have what has been a Fleer tradition in recent years, the two-player Rookie Cards and there are less two-player special cards than in prior years. Apparently this was an attempt by Fleer to increase the number of single player cards in the set. The design features solid yellow borders with the information in black indicating name, position, and team. The backs feature beautiful full-color photos along with the career statistics and a biography for those players where there is room. The set is again ordered numerically by teams, followed by combination cards, rookie prospect pairs, and checklists. Again Fleer incorrectly anticipated the outcome of the 1990 Playoffs according to the team ordering. The A's, listed first, did not win the World Series and their opponents (and Series winners) were the Reds, not the Pirates. Fleer later reported that they merely arranged the teams according to regular season team record due to the early printing date. The complete team ordering is as follows: Oakland A's (1-28), Pittsburgh Pirates (29-54), Cincinnati Reds (55-82), Boston Red Sox (83-113), Chicago White Sox (114-139), New York Mets (140-166), Toronto Blue Jays (167-192), Los Angeles Dodgers (193-223), Montreal Expos (224-251), San Francisco Giants (252-277), Texas Rangers (278-304), California Angels (305-330), Detroit Tigers (331-357), Cleveland Indians (358-385), Philadelphia Phillies (386-412), Chicago Cubs (413-441), Seattle Mariners (442-465), Baltimore Orioles (466-496), Houston Astros (497-522) San Diego Padres (523-548), Kansas City Royals (549-575), Milwaukee Brewers (576-601), Minnesota Twins (602-627), St. Louis Cardinals (628-654), New York Yankees (655-680), and Atlanta Braves (681-708). A number of the cards in the set can be found with photos cropped (very slightly) differently as Fleer used two separate printers in their attempt to maximize production. The key Rookie Cards in this set are Wes Chamberlain, Luis Gonzalez, Brian McRae, Pedro Munoz, Phil Plantier, and Randy Tomlin.

	MT	EX-MT	VG
COMPLETE SET (720)	15.00	6.75	1.90
COMPLETE FACT.SET (724)	18.00	8.00	2.30
COMMON PLAYER (1-720)	.04	.02	.01
□ 1 Troy Afenir	.10	.05	.01
□ 2 Harold Baines	.07	.03	.01
□ 3 Lance Blankenship	.04	.02	.01
□ 4 Todd Burns	.04	.02	.01
□ 5 Jose Canseco	.20	.09	.03
□ 6 Dennis Eckersley	.12	.05	.02
□ 7 Mike Gallego	.04	.02	.01
□ 8 Ron Hassey	.04	.02	.01
□ 9 Dave Henderson	.04	.02	.01
□ 10 Rickey Henderson	.12	.05	.02
□ 11 Rick Honeycutt	.04	.02	.01
□ 12 Doug Jennings	.04	.02	.01
□ 13 Joe Klink	.04	.02	.01
□ 14 Carney Lansford	.07	.03	.01
□ 15 Darren Lewis	.10	.05	.01
□ 16 Willie McGee UER (Height 6'11")	.07	.03	.01
□ 17 Mark McGwire UER (183 extra base hits in 1987)	.20	.09	.03
□ 18 Mike Moore	.04	.02	.01
□ 19 Gene Nelson	.04	.02	.01
□ 20 Dave Otto	.04	.02	.01
□ 21 Jamie Quirk	.04	.02	.01
□ 22 Willie Randolph	.07	.03	.01
□ 23 Scott Sanderson	.04	.02	.01
□ 24 Terry Steinbach	.07	.03	.01
□ 25 Dave Stewart	.07	.03	.01
□ 26 Walt Weiss	.04	.02	.01
□ 27 Bob Welch	.04	.02	.01
□ 28 Curt Young	.04	.02	.01
□ 29 Wally Backman	.04	.02	.01
□ 30 Stan Belinda UER (Born in Huntington, should be State College)	.04	.02	.01
□ 31 Jay Bell	.07	.03	.01
□ 32 Rafael Belliard	.04	.02	.01
□ 33 Barry Bonds	.20	.09	.03
□ 34 Bobby Bonilla	.10	.05	.01
□ 35 Sid Bream	.04	.02	.01
□ 36 Doug Drabek	.07	.03	.01
□ 37 Carlos Garcia	.20	.09	.03
□ 38 Neal Heaton	.04	.02	.01
□ 39 Jeff King	.04	.02	.01
□ 40 Bob Kipper	.04	.02	.01
□ 41 Bill Landrum	.04	.02	.01
□ 42 Mike LaValliere	.04	.02	.01
□ 43 Jose Lind	.04	.02	.01
□ 44 Carmelo Martinez	.04	.02	.01
□ 45 Bob Patterson	.04	.02	.01
□ 46 Ted Power	.04	.02	.01
□ 47 Gary Redus	.04	.02	.01
□ 48 R.J. Reynolds	.04	.02	.01
□ 49 Don Slaught	.04	.02	.01
□ 50 John Smiley	.07	.03	.01
□ 51 Zane Smith	.04	.02	.01
□ 52 Randy Tomlin	.20	.09	.03
□ 53 Andy Van Slyke	.10	.05	.01
□ 54 Bob Walk	.04	.02	.01
□ 55 Jack Armstrong	.04	.02	.01
□ 56 Todd Benzinger	.04	.02	.01
□ 57 Glenn Braggs	.04	.02	.01
□ 58 Keith Brown	.04	.02	.01
□ 59 Tom Browning	.04	.02	.01
□ 60 Norm Charlton	.07	.03	.01
□ 61 Eric Davis	.07	.03	.01
□ 62 Rob Dibble	.07	.03	.01
□ 63 Bill Doran	.04	.02	.01
□ 64 Mariano Duncan	.04	.02	.01
□ 65 Chris Hammond	.10	.05	.01
□ 66 Billy Hatcher	.04	.02	.01
□ 67 Danny Jackson	.04	.02	.01
□ 68 Barry Larkin	.10	.05	.01
□ 69 Tim Layana (Black line over made in first text line)	.04	.02	.01
□ 70 Terry Lee	.10	.05	.01
□ 71 Rick Mahler	.04	.02	.01
□ 72 Hal Morris	.07	.03	.01
□ 73 Randy Myers	.07	.03	.01
□ 74 Ron Oester	.04	.02	.01
□ 75 Joe Oliver	.04	.02	.01
□ 76 Paul O'Neill	.07	.03	.01
□ 77 Luis Quinones	.04	.02	.01
□ 78 Jeff Reed	.04	.02	.01
□ 79 Jose Rijo	.07	.03	.01
□ 80 Chris Sabo	.07	.03	.01
□ 81 Scott Scudder	.04	.02	.01
□ 82 Herm Winningham	.04	.02	.01
□ 83 Larry Andersen	.04	.02	.01
□ 84 Marty Barrett	.04	.02	.01
□ 85 Mike Boddicker	.04	.02	.01
□ 86 Wade Boggs	.12	.05	.02
□ 87 Tom Bolton	.04	.02	.01
□ 88 Tom Brunansky	.07	.03	.01
□ 89 Ellis Burks	.07	.03	.01
□ 90 Roger Clemens	.25	.11	.03
□ 91 Scott Cooper	.25	.11	.03
□ 92 John Dopson	.04	.02	.01
□ 93 Dwight Evans	.07	.03	.01
□ 94 Wes Gardner	.04	.02	.01
□ 95 Jeff Gray	.04	.02	.01
□ 96 Mike Greenwell	.07	.03	.01
□ 97 Greg A. Harris	.04	.02	.01
□ 98 Daryl Irvine	.04	.02	.01
□ 99 Dana Kiecker	.04	.02	.01
□ 100 Randy Kutcher	.04	.02	.01
□ 101 Dennis Lamp	.04	.02	.01
□ 102 Mike Marshall	.04	.02	.01
□ 103 John Marzano	.04	.02	.01
□ 104 Rob Murphy	.04	.02	.01
□ 105 Tim Naehring	.07	.03	.01

	Player			
☐ 106	Tony Pena	.04	.02	.01
☐ 107	Phil Plantier	.50	.23	.06
☐ 108	Carlos Quintana	.04	.02	.01
☐ 109	Jeff Reardon	.07	.03	.01
☐ 110	Jerry Reed	.04	.02	.01
☐ 111	Jody Reed	.04	.02	.01
☐ 112	Luis Rivera UER	.04	.02	.01
	(Born 1/3/84)			
☐ 113	Kevin Romine	.04	.02	.01
☐ 114	Phil Bradley	.04	.02	.01
☐ 115	Ivan Calderon	.04	.02	.01
☐ 116	Wayne Edwards	.04	.02	.01
☐ 117	Alex Fernandez	.12	.05	.02
☐ 118	Carlton Fisk	.10	.05	.01
☐ 119	Scott Fletcher	.04	.02	.01
☐ 120	Craig Grebeck	.04	.02	.01
☐ 121	Ozzie Guillen	.04	.02	.01
☐ 122	Greg Hibbard	.04	.02	.01
☐ 123	Lance Johnson UER	.04	.02	.01
	(Born Cincinnati, should be Lincoln Heights)			
☐ 124	Barry Jones	.04	.02	.01
☐ 125	Ron Karkovice	.04	.02	.01
☐ 126	Eric King	.04	.02	.01
☐ 127	Steve Lyons	.04	.02	.01
☐ 128	Carlos Martinez	.04	.02	.01
☐ 129	Jack McDowell UER	.10	.05	.01
	(Stanford misspelled as Standford on back)			
☐ 130	Donn Pall	.04	.02	.01
	(No dots over any i's in text)			
☐ 131	Dan Pasqua	.04	.02	.01
☐ 132	Ken Patterson	.04	.02	.01
☐ 133	Melido Perez	.07	.03	.01
☐ 134	Adam Peterson	.04	.02	.01
☐ 135	Scott Radinsky	.04	.02	.01
☐ 136	Sammy Sosa	.07	.03	.01
☐ 137	Bobby Thigpen	.04	.02	.01
☐ 138	Frank Thomas	1.25	.55	.16
☐ 139	Robin Ventura	.20	.09	.03
☐ 140	Daryl Boston	.04	.02	.01
☐ 141	Chuck Carr	.04	.02	.01
☐ 142	Mark Carreon	.04	.02	.01
☐ 143	David Cone	.10	.05	.01
☐ 144	Ron Darling	.07	.03	.01
☐ 145	Kevin Elster	.04	.02	.01
☐ 146	Sid Fernandez	.07	.03	.01
☐ 147	John Franco	.07	.03	.01
☐ 148	Dwight Gooden	.07	.03	.01
☐ 149	Tom Herr	.04	.02	.01
☐ 150	Todd Hundley	.04	.02	.01
☐ 151	Gregg Jefferies	.07	.03	.01
☐ 152	Howard Johnson	.07	.03	.01
☐ 153	Dave Magadan	.07	.03	.01
☐ 154	Kevin McReynolds	.07	.03	.01
☐ 155	Keith Miller UER	.04	.02	.01
	(Text says Rochester in '87, stats say Tidewater, mixed up with other Keith Miller)			
☐ 156	Bob Ojeda	.04	.02	.01
☐ 157	Tom O'Malley	.04	.02	.01
☐ 158	Alejandro Pena	.04	.02	.01
☐ 159	Darren Reed	.04	.02	.01
☐ 160	Mackey Sasser	.04	.02	.01
☐ 161	Darryl Strawberry	.12	.05	.02
☐ 162	Tim Teufel	.04	.02	.01
☐ 163	Kelvin Torve	.04	.02	.01
☐ 164	Julio Valera	.15	.07	.02
☐ 165	Frank Viola	.07	.03	.01
☐ 166	Wally Whitehurst	.04	.02	.01
☐ 167	Jim Acker	.04	.02	.01
☐ 168	Derek Bell	.30	.14	.04
☐ 169	George Bell	.07	.03	.01
☐ 170	Willie Blair	.04	.02	.01
☐ 171	Pat Borders	.04	.02	.01
☐ 172	John Cerutti	.04	.02	.01
☐ 173	Junior Felix	.04	.02	.01
☐ 174	Tony Fernandez	.07	.03	.01
☐ 175	Kelly Gruber UER	.07	.03	.01
	(Born in Houston, should be Bellaire)			
☐ 176	Tom Henke	.07	.03	.01
☐ 177	Glenallen Hill	.04	.02	.01
☐ 178	Jimmy Key	.04	.02	.01
☐ 179	Manny Lee	.04	.02	.01
☐ 180	Fred McGriff	.12	.05	.02
☐ 181	Rance Mulliniks	.04	.02	.01
☐ 182	Greg Myers	.04	.02	.01
☐ 183	John Olerud	.15	.07	.02
☐ 184	Luis Sojo	.04	.02	.01
☐ 185	Dave Stieb	.04	.02	.01
☐ 186	Todd Stottlemyre	.07	.03	.01
☐ 187	Duane Ward	.04	.02	.01
☐ 188	David Wells	.04	.02	.01
☐ 189	Mark Whiten	.10	.05	.01
☐ 190	Ken Williams	.04	.02	.01
☐ 191	Frank Wills	.04	.02	.01
☐ 192	Mookie Wilson	.04	.02	.01
☐ 193	Don Aase	.04	.02	.01
☐ 194	Tim Belcher UER	.07	.03	.01
	(Born Sparta, Ohio, should say Mt. Gilead)			
☐ 195	Hubie Brooks	.04	.02	.01
☐ 196	Dennis Cook	.04	.02	.01
☐ 197	Tim Crews	.04	.02	.01
☐ 198	Kal Daniels	.04	.02	.01
☐ 199	Kirk Gibson	.07	.03	.01
☐ 200	Jim Gott	.04	.02	.01
☐ 201	Alfredo Griffin	.04	.02	.01
☐ 202	Chris Gwynn	.04	.02	.01
☐ 203	Dave Hansen	.04	.02	.01
☐ 204	Lenny Harris	.04	.02	.01
☐ 205	Mike Hartley	.04	.02	.01
☐ 206	Mickey Hatcher	.04	.02	.01
☐ 207	Carlos Hernandez	.10	.05	.01
☐ 208	Orel Hershiser	.07	.03	.01
☐ 209	Jay Howell UER	.04	.02	.01
	(No 1982 Yankee stats)			
☐ 210	Mike Huff	.04	.02	.01
☐ 211	Stan Javier	.04	.02	.01
☐ 212	Ramon Martinez	.10	.05	.01
☐ 213	Mike Morgan	.04	.02	.01
☐ 214	Eddie Murray	.10	.05	.01
☐ 215	Jim Neidlinger	.04	.02	.01
☐ 216	Jose Offerman	.10	.05	.01
☐ 217	Jim Poole	.04	.02	.01
☐ 218	Juan Samuel	.04	.02	.01
☐ 219	Mike Scioscia	.04	.02	.01
☐ 220	Ray Searage	.04	.02	.01
☐ 221	Mike Sharperson	.04	.02	.01
☐ 222	Fernando Valenzuela	.07	.03	.01
☐ 223	Jose Vizcaino	.04	.02	.01
☐ 224	Mike Aldrete	.04	.02	.01
☐ 225	Scott Anderson	.10	.05	.01
☐ 226	Dennis Boyd	.04	.02	.01
☐ 227	Tim Burke	.04	.02	.01
☐ 228	Delino DeShields	.15	.07	.02
☐ 229	Mike Fitzgerald	.04	.02	.01
☐ 230	Tom Foley	.04	.02	.01
☐ 231	Steve Frey	.04	.02	.01
☐ 232	Andres Galarraga	.04	.02	.01
☐ 233	Mark Gardner	.04	.02	.01
☐ 234	Marquis Grissom	.15	.07	.02
☐ 235	Kevin Gross UER	.04	.02	.01
	(No date given for first Expos win)			
☐ 236	Drew Hall	.04	.02	.01
☐ 237	Dave Martinez	.04	.02	.01
☐ 238	Dennis Martinez	.07	.03	.01
☐ 239	Dale Mohorcic	.04	.02	.01
☐ 240	Chris Nabholz	.07	.03	.01
☐ 241	Otis Nixon	.07	.03	.01
☐ 242	Junior Noboa	.04	.02	.01
☐ 243	Spike Owen	.04	.02	.01
☐ 244	Tim Raines	.07	.03	.01
☐ 245	Mel Rojas UER	.10	.05	.01
	(Stats show 3.60 ERA, bio says 3.19 ERA)			
☐ 246	Scott Ruskin	.04	.02	.01
☐ 247	Bill Sampen	.04	.02	.01
☐ 248	Nelson Santovenia	.04	.02	.01
☐ 249	Dave Schmidt	.04	.02	.01
☐ 250	Larry Walker	.20	.09	.03
☐ 251	Tim Wallach	.07	.03	.01
☐ 252	Dave Anderson	.04	.02	.01
☐ 253	Kevin Bass	.04	.02	.01
☐ 254	Steve Bedrosian	.04	.02	.01
☐ 255	Jeff Brantley	.04	.02	.01
☐ 256	John Burkett	.04	.02	.01
☐ 257	Brett Butler	.07	.03	.01
☐ 258	Gary Carter	.07	.03	.01
☐ 259	Will Clark	.20	.09	.03
☐ 260	Steve Decker	.15	.07	.02
☐ 261	Kelly Downs	.04	.02	.01
☐ 262	Scott Garrelts	.04	.02	.01
☐ 263	Terry Kennedy	.04	.02	.01
☐ 264	Mike LaCoss	.04	.02	.01
☐ 265	Mark Leonard	.10	.05	.01
☐ 266	Greg Litton	.04	.02	.01
☐ 267	Kevin Mitchell	.07	.03	.01
☐ 268	Randy O'Neal	.04	.02	.01
☐ 269	Rick Parker	.04	.02	.01
☐ 270	Rick Reuschel	.04	.02	.01
☐ 271	Ernest Riles	.04	.02	.01

	No.	Player			
□	272	Don Robinson	.04	.02	.01
□	273	Robby Thompson	.04	.02	.01
□	274	Mark Thurmond	.04	.02	.01
□	275	Jose Uribe	.04	.02	.01
□	276	Matt Williams	.07	.03	.01
□	277	Trevor Wilson	.04	.02	.01
□	278	Gerald Alexander	.10	.05	.01
□	279	Brad Arnsberg	.04	.02	.01
□	280	Kevin Belcher	.10	.05	.01
□	281	Joe Bitker	.04	.02	.01
□	282	Kevin Brown	.07	.03	.01
□	283	Steve Buechele	.04	.02	.01
□	284	Jack Daugherty	.04	.02	.01
□	285	Julio Franco	.07	.03	.01
□	286	Juan Gonzalez	.35	.16	.04
□	287	Bill Haselman	.10	.05	.01
□	288	Charlie Hough	.04	.02	.01
□	289	Jeff Huson	.04	.02	.01
□	290	Pete Incaviglia	.04	.02	.01
□	291	Mike Jeffcoat	.04	.02	.01
□	292	Jeff Kunkel	.04	.02	.01
□	293	Gary Mielke	.04	.02	.01
□	294	Jamie Moyer	.04	.02	.01
□	295	Rafael Palmeiro	.10	.05	.01
□	296	Geno Petralli	.04	.02	.01
□	297	Gary Pettis	.04	.02	.01
□	298	Kevin Reimer	.10	.05	.01
□	299	Kenny Rogers	.04	.02	.01
□	300	Jeff Russell	.04	.02	.01
□	301	John Russell	.04	.02	.01
□	302	Nolan Ryan	.40	.18	.05
□	303	Ruben Sierra	.15	.07	.02
□	304	Bobby Witt	.04	.02	.01
□	305	Jim Abbott	.12	.05	.02
□	306	Kent Anderson	.04	.02	.01
□	307	Dante Bichette	.04	.02	.01
□	308	Bert Blyleven	.07	.03	.01
□	309	Chili Davis	.07	.03	.01
□	310	Brian Downing	.04	.02	.01
□	311	Mark Eichhorn	.04	.02	.01
□	312	Mike Fetters	.04	.02	.01
□	313	Chuck Finley	.07	.03	.01
□	314	Willie Fraser	.04	.02	.01
□	315	Bryan Harvey	.04	.02	.01
□	316	Donnie Hill	.04	.02	.01
□	317	Wally Joyner	.07	.03	.01
□	318	Mark Langston	.07	.03	.01
□	319	Kirk McCaskill	.04	.02	.01
□	320	John Orton	.04	.02	.01
□	321	Lance Parrish	.07	.03	.01
□	322	Luis Polonia UER (1984 Madfison, should be Madison)	.07	.03	.01
□	323	Johnny Ray	.04	.02	.01
□	324	Bobby Rose	.04	.02	.01
□	325	Dick Schofield	.04	.02	.01
□	326	Rick Schu	.04	.02	.01
□	327	Lee Stevens	.04	.02	.01
□	328	Devon White	.07	.03	.01
□	329	Dave Winfield	.10	.05	.01
□	330	Cliff Young	.04	.02	.01
□	331	Dave Bergman	.04	.02	.01
□	332	Phil Clark	.15	.07	.02
□	333	Darnell Coles	.04	.02	.01
□	334	Milt Cuyler	.10	.05	.01
□	335	Cecil Fielder	.12	.05	.02
□	336	Travis Fryman	.50	.23	.06
□	337	Paul Gibson	.04	.02	.01
□	338	Jerry Don Gleaton	.04	.02	.01
□	339	Mike Heath	.04	.02	.01
□	340	Mike Henneman	.04	.02	.01
□	341	Chet Lemon	.04	.02	.01
□	342	Lance McCullers	.04	.02	.01
□	343	Jack Morris	.10	.05	.01
□	344	Lloyd Moseby	.04	.02	.01
□	345	Edwin Nunez	.04	.02	.01
□	346	Clay Parker	.04	.02	.01
□	347	Dan Petry	.04	.02	.01
□	348	Tony Phillips	.04	.02	.01
□	349	Jeff M. Robinson	.04	.02	.01
□	350	Mark Salas	.04	.02	.01
□	351	Mike Schwabe	.04	.02	.01
□	352	Larry Sheets	.04	.02	.01
□	353	John Shelby	.04	.02	.01
□	354	Frank Tanana	.04	.02	.01
□	355	Alan Trammell	.07	.03	.01
□	356	Gary Ward	.04	.02	.01
□	357	Lou Whitaker	.07	.03	.01
□	358	Beau Allred	.04	.02	.01
□	359	Sandy Alomar Jr.	.07	.03	.01
□	360	Carlos Baerga	.20	.09	.03
□	361	Kevin Bearse	.04	.02	.01
□	362	Tom Brookens	.04	.02	.01
□	363	Jerry Browne UER (No dot over i in first text line)	.04	.02	.01
□	364	Tom Candiotti	.04	.02	.01
□	365	Alex Cole	.04	.02	.01
□	366	John Farrell UER (Born in Neptune, should be Monmouth)	.04	.02	.01
□	367	Felix Fermin	.04	.02	.01
□	368	Keith Hernandez	.07	.03	.01
□	369	Brook Jacoby	.04	.02	.01
□	370	Chris James	.04	.02	.01
□	371	Dion James	.04	.02	.01
□	372	Doug Jones	.04	.02	.01
□	373	Candy Maldonado	.04	.02	.01
□	374	Steve Olin	.07	.03	.01
□	375	Jesse Orosco	.04	.02	.01
□	376	Rudy Seanez	.07	.03	.01
□	377	Joel Skinner	.04	.02	.01
□	378	Cory Snyder	.04	.02	.01
□	379	Greg Swindell	.07	.03	.01
□	380	Sergio Valdez	.04	.02	.01
□	381	Mike Walker	.04	.02	.01
□	382	Colby Ward	.04	.02	.01
□	383	Turner Ward	.10	.05	.01
□	384	Mitch Webster	.04	.02	.01
□	385	Kevin Wickander	.04	.02	.01
□	386	Darrel Akerfelds	.04	.02	.01
□	387	Joe Boever	.04	.02	.01
□	388	Rod Booker	.04	.02	.01
□	389	Sil Campusano	.04	.02	.01
□	390	Don Carman	.04	.02	.01
□	391	Wes Chamberlain	.20	.09	.03
□	392	Pat Combs	.04	.02	.01
□	393	Darren Daulton	.07	.03	.01
□	394	Jose DeJesus	.04	.02	.01
□	395	Len Dykstra	.07	.03	.01
□	396	Jason Grimsley	.04	.02	.01
□	397	Charlie Hayes	.04	.02	.01
□	398	Von Hayes	.04	.02	.01
□	399	David Hollins UER (Atl-bats, should say at-bats)	.12	.05	.02
□	400	Ken Howell	.04	.02	.01
□	401	Ricky Jordan	.04	.02	.01
□	402	John Kruk	.07	.03	.01
□	403	Steve Lake	.04	.02	.01
□	404	Chuck Malone	.04	.02	.01
□	405	Roger McDowell UER (Says Phillies is saves, should say in)	.04	.02	.01
□	406	Chuck McElroy	.04	.02	.01
□	407	Mickey Morandini	.12	.05	.02
□	408	Terry Mulholland	.04	.02	.01
□	409	Dale Murphy	.07	.03	.01
□	410A	Randy Ready ERR (No Brewers stats listed for 1983)	.04	.02	.01
□	410B	Randy Ready COR	.04	.02	.01
□	411	Bruce Ruffin	.04	.02	.01
□	412	Dickie Thon	.04	.02	.01
□	413	Paul Assenmacher	.04	.02	.01
□	414	Damon Berryhill	.04	.02	.01
□	415	Mike Bielecki	.04	.02	.01
□	416	Shawn Boskie	.04	.02	.01
□	417	Dave Clark	.04	.02	.01
□	418	Doug Dascenzo	.04	.02	.01
□	419A	Andre Dawson ERR (No stats for 1976)	.10	.05	.01
□	419B	Andre Dawson COR	.10	.05	.01
□	420	Shawon Dunston	.07	.03	.01
□	421	Joe Girardi	.04	.02	.01
□	422	Mark Grace	.10	.05	.01
□	423	Mike Harkey	.07	.03	.01
□	424	Les Lancaster	.04	.02	.01
□	425	Bill Long	.04	.02	.01
□	426	Greg Maddux	.10	.05	.01
□	427	Derrick May	.07	.03	.01
□	428	Jeff Pico	.04	.02	.01
□	429	Domingo Ramos	.04	.02	.01
□	430	Luis Salazar	.04	.02	.01
□	431	Ryne Sandberg	.25	.11	.03
□	432	Dwight Smith	.04	.02	.01
□	433	Greg Smith	.04	.02	.01
□	434	Rick Sutcliffe	.07	.03	.01
□	435	Gary Varsho	.04	.02	.01
□	436	Hector Villanueva	.04	.02	.01
□	437	Jerome Walton	.04	.02	.01
□	438	Curtis Wilkerson	.04	.02	.01
□	439	Mitch Williams	.04	.02	.01
□	440	Steve Wilson	.04	.02	.01
□	441	Marvell Wynne	.04	.02	.01
□	442	Scott Bankhead	.04	.02	.01

☐ 443 Scott Bradley .04 .02 .01
☐ 444 Greg Briley .04 .02 .01
☐ 445 Mike Brumley UER .04 .02 .01
(Text 40 SB's in 1988, stats say 41)
☐ 446 Jay Buhner .07 .03 .01
☐ 447 Dave Burba .10 .05 .01
☐ 448 Henry Cotto .04 .02 .01
☐ 449 Alvin Davis .04 .02 .01
☐ 450A Ken Griffey Jr ERR .50 .23 .06
(Bat .300)
☐ 450B Ken Griffey Jr COR .50 .23 .06
(Bat around .300)
☐ 451 Erik Hanson .04 .02 .01
☐ 452 Gene Harris UER .04 .02 .01
(63 career runs, should be 73)
☐ 453 Brian Holman .04 .02 .01
☐ 454 Mike Jackson .04 .02 .01
☐ 455 Randy Johnson .07 .03 .01
☐ 456 Jeffrey Leonard .04 .02 .01
☐ 457 Edgar Martinez .07 .03 .01
☐ 458 Tino Martinez .10 .05 .01
☐ 459 Pete O'Brien UER .04 .02 .01
(1987 BA .266, should be .286)
☐ 460 Harold Reynolds .04 .02 .01
☐ 461 Mike Schooler .04 .02 .01
☐ 462 Bill Swift .04 .02 .01
☐ 463 David Valle .04 .02 .01
☐ 464 Omar Vizquel .04 .02 .01
☐ 465 Matt Young .04 .02 .01
☐ 466 Brady Anderson .07 .03 .01
☐ 467 Jeff Ballard UER .04 .02 .01
(Missing top of right parenthesis after Saberhagen in last text line)
☐ 468 Juan Bell .04 .02 .01
☐ 469A Mike Devereaux ERR .07 .03 .01
(First line of text ends with six)
☐ 469B Mike Devereaux COR .07 .03 .01
(First line of text ends with runs)
☐ 470 Steve Finley .07 .03 .01
☐ 471 Dave Gallagher .04 .02 .01
☐ 472 Leo Gomez .25 .11 .03
☐ 473 Rene Gonzales .04 .02 .01
☐ 474 Pete Harnisch .07 .03 .01
☐ 475 Kevin Hickey .04 .02 .01
☐ 476 Chris Hoiles .10 .05 .01
☐ 477 Sam Horn .04 .02 .01
☐ 478 Tim Hulett .04 .02 .01
(Photo shows National Leaguer sliding into second base)
☐ 479 Dave Johnson .04 .02 .01
☐ 480 Ron Kittle UER .04 .02 .01
(Edmonton misspelled as Edmundton)
☐ 481 Ben McDonald .10 .05 .01
☐ 482 Bob Melvin .04 .02 .01
☐ 483 Bob Milacki .04 .02 .01
☐ 484 Randy Milligan .04 .02 .01
☐ 485 John Mitchell .04 .02 .01
☐ 486 Gregg Olson .07 .03 .01
☐ 487 Joe Orsulak .04 .02 .01
☐ 488 Joe Price .04 .02 .01
☐ 489 Bill Ripken .04 .02 .01
☐ 490 Cal Ripken .30 .14 .04
☐ 491 Curt Schilling .07 .03 .01
☐ 492 David Segui .04 .02 .01
☐ 493 Anthony Telford .04 .02 .01
☐ 494 Mickey Tettleton .07 .03 .01
☐ 495 Mark Williamson .04 .02 .01
☐ 496 Craig Worthington .04 .02 .01
☐ 497 Juan Agosto .04 .02 .01
☐ 498 Eric Anthony .07 .03 .01
☐ 499 Craig Biggio .07 .03 .01
☐ 500 Ken Caminiti UER .07 .03 .01
(Born 4/4, should be 4/21)
☐ 501 Casey Candaele .04 .02 .01
☐ 502 Andujar Cedeno .12 .05 .02
☐ 503 Danny Darwin .04 .02 .01
☐ 504 Mark Davidson .04 .02 .01
☐ 505 Glenn Davis .07 .03 .01
☐ 506 Jim Deshaies .04 .02 .01
☐ 507 Luis Gonzalez .20 .09 .03
☐ 508 Bill Gullickson .04 .02 .01
☐ 509 Xavier Hernandez .04 .02 .01
☐ 510 Brian Meyer .04 .02 .01
☐ 511 Ken Oberkfell .04 .02 .01
☐ 512 Mark Portugal .04 .02 .01
☐ 513 Rafael Ramirez .04 .02 .01
☐ 514 Karl Rhodes .04 .02 .01
☐ 515 Mike Scott .04 .02 .01
☐ 516 Mike Simms .10 .05 .01
☐ 517 Dave Smith .04 .02 .01
☐ 518 Franklin Stubbs .04 .02 .01
☐ 519 Glenn Wilson .04 .02 .01
☐ 520 Eric Yelding UER .04 .02 .01
(Text has 63 steals, stats have 64, which is correct)
☐ 521 Gerald Young .04 .02 .01
☐ 522 Shawn Abner .04 .02 .01
☐ 523 Roberto Alomar .20 .09 .03
☐ 524 Andy Benes .10 .05 .01
☐ 525 Joe Carter .12 .05 .02
☐ 526 Jack Clark .07 .03 .01
☐ 527 Joey Cora .04 .02 .01
☐ 528 Paul Faries .04 .02 .01
☐ 529 Tony Gwynn .12 .05 .02
☐ 530 Atlee Hammaker .04 .02 .01
☐ 531 Greg W. Harris .04 .02 .01
☐ 532 Thomas Howard .04 .02 .01
☐ 533 Bruce Hurst .07 .03 .01
☐ 534 Craig Lefferts .04 .02 .01
☐ 535 Derek Lilliquist .04 .02 .01
☐ 536 Fred Lynn .07 .03 .01
☐ 537 Mike Pagliarulo .04 .02 .01
☐ 538 Mark Parent .04 .02 .01
☐ 539 Dennis Rasmussen .04 .02 .01
☐ 540 Bip Roberts .07 .03 .01
☐ 541 Richard Rodriguez .04 .02 .01
☐ 542 Benito Santiago .07 .03 .01
☐ 543 Calvin Schiraldi .04 .02 .01
☐ 544 Eric Show .04 .02 .01
☐ 545 Phil Stephenson .04 .02 .01
☐ 546 Garry Templeton UER .04 .02 .01
(Born 3/24/57, should be 3/24/56)
☐ 547 Ed Whitson .04 .02 .01
☐ 548 Eddie Williams .04 .02 .01
☐ 549 Kevin Appier .07 .03 .01
☐ 550 Luis Aquino .04 .02 .01
☐ 551 Bob Boone .07 .03 .01
☐ 552 George Brett .10 .05 .01
☐ 553 Jeff Conine .25 .11 .03
☐ 554 Steve Crawford .04 .02 .01
☐ 555 Mark Davis .04 .02 .01
☐ 556 Storm Davis .04 .02 .01
☐ 557 Jim Eisenreich .04 .02 .01
☐ 558 Steve Farr .04 .02 .01
☐ 559 Tom Gordon .07 .03 .01
☐ 560 Mark Gubicza .04 .02 .01
☐ 561 Bo Jackson .12 .05 .02
☐ 562 Mike Macfarlane .04 .02 .01
☐ 563 Brian McRae .20 .09 .03
☐ 564 Jeff Montgomery .04 .02 .01
☐ 565 Bill Pecota .04 .02 .01
☐ 566 Gerald Perry .04 .02 .01
☐ 567 Bret Saberhagen .07 .03 .01
☐ 568 Jeff Schulz .04 .02 .01
☐ 569 Kevin Seitzer .07 .03 .01
☐ 570 Terry Shumpert .04 .02 .01
☐ 571 Kurt Stillwell .04 .02 .01
☐ 572 Danny Tartabull .07 .03 .01
☐ 573 Gary Thurman .04 .02 .01
☐ 574 Frank White .04 .02 .01
☐ 575 Willie Wilson .04 .02 .01
☐ 576 Chris Bosio .04 .02 .01
☐ 577 Greg Brock .04 .02 .01
☐ 578 George Canale .04 .02 .01
☐ 579 Chuck Crim .04 .02 .01
☐ 580 Rob Deer .07 .03 .01
☐ 581 Edgar Diaz .04 .02 .01
☐ 582 Tom Edens .10 .05 .01
☐ 583 Mike Felder .04 .02 .01
☐ 584 Jim Gantner .04 .02 .01
☐ 585 Darryl Hamilton .07 .03 .01
☐ 586 Ted Higuera .04 .02 .01
☐ 587 Mark Knudson .04 .02 .01
☐ 588 Bill Krueger .04 .02 .01
☐ 589 Tim McIntosh .04 .02 .01
☐ 590 Paul Mirabella .04 .02 .01
☐ 591 Paul Molitor .10 .05 .01
☐ 592 Jaime Navarro .07 .03 .01
☐ 593 Dave Parker .07 .03 .01
☐ 594 Dan Plesac .04 .02 .01
☐ 595 Ron Robinson .04 .02 .01
☐ 596 Gary Sheffield .25 .11 .03
☐ 597 Bill Spiers .04 .02 .01
☐ 598 B.J. Surhoff .04 .02 .01

☐	599 Greg Vaughn	.10	.05	.01
☐	600 Randy Veres	.04	.02	.01
☐	601 Robin Yount	.10	.05	.01
☐	602 Rick Aguilera	.07	.03	.01
☐	603 Allan Anderson	.04	.02	.01
☐	604 Juan Berenguer	.04	.02	.01
☐	605 Randy Bush	.04	.02	.01
☐	606 Carmen Castillo	.04	.02	.01
☐	607 Tim Drummond	.04	.02	.01
☐	608 Scott Erickson	.20	.09	.03
☐	609 Gary Gaetti	.04	.02	.01
☐	610 Greg Gagne	.04	.02	.01
☐	611 Dan Gladden	.04	.02	.01
☐	612 Mark Guthrie	.04	.02	.01
☐	613 Brian Harper	.04	.02	.01
☐	614 Kent Hrbek	.07	.03	.01
☐	615 Gene Larkin	.04	.02	.01
☐	616 Terry Leach	.04	.02	.01
☐	617 Nelson Liriano	.04	.02	.01
☐	618 Shane Mack	.07	.03	.01
☐	619 John Moses	.04	.02	.01
☐	620 Pedro Munoz	.25	.11	.03
☐	621 Al Newman	.04	.02	.01
☐	622 Junior Ortiz	.04	.02	.01
☐	623 Kirby Puckett	.20	.09	.03
☐	624 Roy Smith	.04	.02	.01
☐	625 Kevin Tapani	.07	.03	.01
☐	626 Gary Wayne	.04	.02	.01
☐	627 David West	.04	.02	.01
☐	628 Cris Carpenter	.04	.02	.01
☐	629 Vince Coleman	.07	.03	.01
☐	630 Ken Dayley	.04	.02	.01
☐	631 Jose DeLeon	.04	.02	.01
☐	632 Frank DiPino	.04	.02	.01
☐	633 Bernard Gilkey	.15	.07	.02
☐	634 Pedro Guerrero	.07	.03	.01
☐	635 Ken Hill	.07	.03	.01
☐	636 Felix Jose	.07	.03	.01
☐	637 Ray Lankford	.40	.18	.05
☐	638 Joe Magrane	.04	.02	.01
☐	639 Tom Niedenfuer	.04	.02	.01
☐	640 Jose Oquendo	.04	.02	.01
☐	641 Tom Pagnozzi	.04	.02	.01
☐	642 Terry Pendleton	.10	.05	.01
☐	643 Mike Perez	.15	.07	.02
☐	644 Bryn Smith	.04	.02	.01
☐	645 Lee Smith	.07	.03	.01
☐	646 Ozzie Smith	.10	.05	.01
☐	647 Scott Terry	.04	.02	.01
☐	648 Bob Tewksbury	.07	.03	.01
☐	649 Milt Thompson	.04	.02	.01
☐	650 John Tudor	.04	.02	.01
☐	651 Denny Walling	.04	.02	.01
☐	652 Craig Wilson	.10	.05	.01
☐	653 Todd Worrell	.04	.02	.01
☐	654 Todd Zeile	.07	.03	.01
☐	655 Oscar Azocar	.04	.02	.01
☐	656 Steve Balboni UER (Born 1/5/57, should be 1/16)	.04	.02	.01
☐	657 Jesse Barfield	.04	.02	.01
☐	658 Greg Cadaret	.04	.02	.01
☐	659 Chuck Cary	.04	.02	.01
☐	660 Rick Cerone	.04	.02	.01
☐	661 Dave Eiland	.04	.02	.01
☐	662 Alvaro Espinoza	.04	.02	.01
☐	663 Bob Geren	.04	.02	.01
☐	664 Lee Guetterman	.04	.02	.01
☐	665 Mel Hall	.04	.02	.01
☐	666 Andy Hawkins	.04	.02	.01
☐	667 Jimmy Jones	.04	.02	.01
☐	668 Roberto Kelly	.07	.03	.01
☐	669 Dave LaPoint UER (No '81 Brewers stats, totals also are wrong)	.04	.02	.01
☐	670 Tim Leary	.04	.02	.01
☐	671 Jim Leyritz	.04	.02	.01
☐	672 Kevin Maas	.10	.05	.01
☐	673 Don Mattingly	.15	.07	.02
☐	674 Matt Nokes	.04	.02	.01
☐	675 Pascual Perez	.04	.02	.01
☐	676 Eric Plunk	.04	.02	.01
☐	677 Dave Righetti	.04	.02	.01
☐	678 Jeff D. Robinson	.04	.02	.01
☐	679 Steve Sax	.07	.03	.01
☐	680 Mike Witt	.04	.02	.01
☐	681 Steve Avery UER (Born in New Jersey, should say Michigan)	.20	.09	.03
☐	682 Mike Bell	.10	.05	.01
☐	683 Jeff Blauser	.04	.02	.01
☐	684 Francisco Cabrera UER (Born 10/16, should say 10/10)	.04	.02	.01
☐	685 Tony Castillo	.04	.02	.01
☐	686 Marty Clary UER (Shown pitching righty, but bio has left)	.04	.02	.01
☐	687 Nick Esasky	.04	.02	.01
☐	688 Ron Gant	.12	.05	.02
☐	689 Tom Glavine	.20	.09	.03
☐	690 Mark Grant	.04	.02	.01
☐	691 Tommy Gregg	.04	.02	.01
☐	692 Dwayne Henry	.04	.02	.01
☐	693 Dave Justice	.30	.14	.04
☐	694 Jimmy Kremers	.04	.02	.01
☐	695 Charlie Leibrandt	.04	.02	.01
☐	696 Mark Lemke	.04	.02	.01
☐	697 Oddibe McDowell	.04	.02	.01
☐	698 Greg Olson	.04	.02	.01
☐	699 Jeff Parrett	.04	.02	.01
☐	700 Jim Presley	.04	.02	.01
☐	701 Victor Rosario	.10	.05	.01
☐	702 Lonnie Smith	.04	.02	.01
☐	703 Pete Smith	.07	.03	.01
☐	704 John Smoltz	.10	.05	.01
☐	705 Mike Stanton	.04	.02	.01
☐	706 Andres Thomas	.04	.02	.01
☐	707 Jeff Treadway	.04	.02	.01
☐	708 Jim Vatcher	.04	.02	.01
☐	709 Home Run Kings Ryne Sandberg Cecil Fielder	.12	.05	.02
☐	710 2nd Generation Stars Barry Bonds Ken Griffey Jr.	.25	.11	.03
☐	711 NLCS Team Leaders Bobby Bonilla Barry Larkin	.08	.04	.01
☐	712 Top Game Savers Bobby Thigpen John Franco	.05	.02	.01
☐	713 Chicago's 100 Club Andre Dawson Ryne Sandberg UER (Ryno misspelled Rhino)	.10	.05	.01
☐	714 CL:A's/Pirates Reds/Red Sox	.05	.01	.00
☐	715 CL:White Sox/Mets Blue Jays/Dodgers	.05	.01	.00
☐	716 CL:Expos/Giants Rangers/Angels	.05	.01	.00
☐	717 CL:Tigers/Indians Phillies/Cubs	.05	.01	.00
☐	718 CL:Mariners/Orioles Astros/Padres	.05	.01	.00
☐	719 CL:Royals/Brewers Twins/Cardinals	.05	.01	.00
☐	720 CL:Yankees/Braves Superstars/Specials	.05	.01	.00

1991 Fleer All-Star Inserts

For the sixth consecutive year Fleer issued an All-Star insert set. This year the cards were only available in Fleer cello packs. This ten-card set measures the standard size of 2 1/2" by 3 1/2" and is reminiscent of the 1971 Topps Greatest Moments set with two pictures on the (black-bordered) front as well as a photo on the back.

	MT	EX-MT	VG
COMPLETE SET (10)	16.00	7.25	2.00
COMMON PLAYER (1-10)	.40	.18	.05
☐ 1 Ryne Sandberg	2.50	1.15	.30
☐ 2 Barry Larkin	.75	.35	.09
☐ 3 Matt Williams	.50	.23	.06
☐ 4 Cecil Fielder	1.25	.55	.16
☐ 5 Barry Bonds	2.00	.90	.25
☐ 6 Rickey Henderson	1.50	.65	.19
☐ 7 Ken Griffey Jr.	6.00	2.70	.75
☐ 8 Jose Canseco	2.00	.90	.25
☐ 9 Benito Santiago	.40	.18	.05
☐ 10 Roger Clemens	2.50	1.15	.30

1991 Fleer Pro-Visions

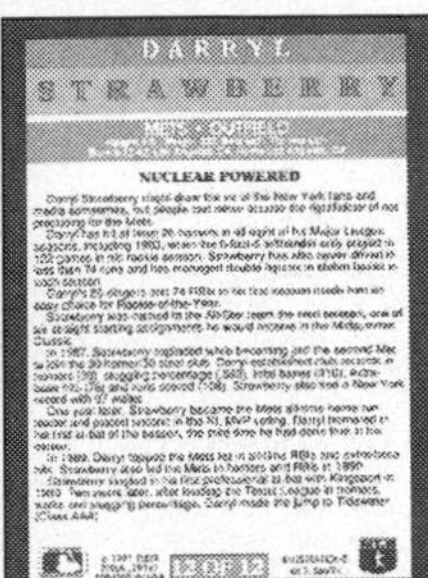

This 12-card subset is in the standard size of 2 1/2" by 3 1/2" and features drawings by talented artist Terry Smith on the front of the card with a description on the back explaining why the card is painted in that way. These cards were only available in Fleer wax and Rak packs. The formal description of this set is the 1991 Fleer Pro-Visions TM Sports Art Cards. The cards have distinctive black borders.

	MT	EX-MT	VG
COMPLETE SET (12)	4.00	1.80	.50
COMMON PLAYER (1-12)	.20	.09	.03
☐ 1 Kirby Puckett UER (.326 average, should be .328)	.60	.25	.08
☐ 2 Will Clark UER (On tenth line, pennant misspelled pennent)	.60	.25	.08
☐ 3 Ruben Sierra UER (No apostrophe in hasn't)	.40	.18	.05
☐ 4 Mark McGwire UER (Fisk won ROY in '72, not '82)	.50	.23	.06
☐ 5 Bo Jackson (Bio says 6', others have him at 6'1")	.40	.18	.05
☐ 6 Jose Canseco UER (Bio 6'3", 230, text has 6'4", 240)	.60	.25	.08
☐ 7 Dwight Gooden UER (2.80 ERA in Lynchburg, should be 2.50)	.20	.09	.03
☐ 8 Mike Greenwell UER (.328 BA and 87 RBI, should be .325 and 95)	.20	.09	.03
☐ 9 Roger Clemens	.60	.25	.08
☐ 10 Eric Davis	.20	.09	.03
☐ 11 Don Mattingly	.40	.18	.05
☐ 12 Darryl Strawberry	.40	.18	.05

1991 Fleer Pro-Visions Factory

This four-card set was inserted only into factory sets. The standard-size (2 1/2" by 3 1/2") cards feature on the fronts colorful player portraits by artist Terry Smith. The pictures are bordered in white, with the player's name immediately below in red lettering. The backs of each card have different colors as well as biography and career highlights. The cards are numbered on the back.

	MT	EX-MT	VG
COMPLETE SET (4)	3.00	1.35	.40
COMMON PLAYER (1F-4F)	.25	.11	.03
☐ 1F Barry Bonds Pittsburgh Pirates	1.25	.55	.16
☐ 2F Rickey Henderson Oakland Athletics	.75	.35	.09
☐ 3F Ryne Sandberg Chicago Cubs	1.50	.65	.19
☐ 4F Dave Stewart Oakland Athletics	.25	.11	.03

1991 Fleer Update

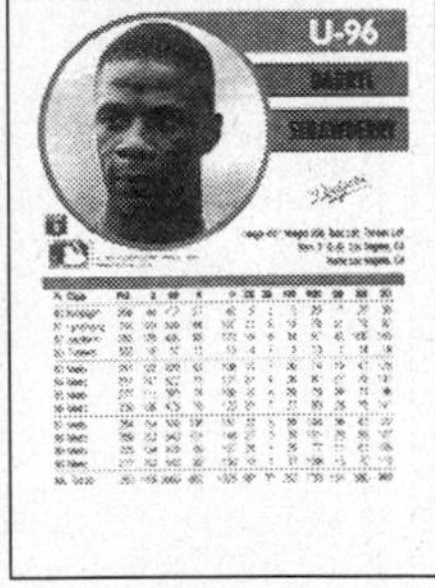

The 1991 Fleer Update set contains 132 cards measuring the standard size (2 1/2" by 3 1/2"). The glossy color action photos on the fronts are placed on a yellow card face and accentuated by black lines above and below. The backs have a head shot (circular format), biography, and complete Major League statistics. The cards are checklisted below alphabetically within and according to teams for each league as follows: Baltimore Orioles (1-3), Boston Red Sox (4-7), California Angels (8-10), Chicago White Sox (11-15), Cleveland Indians (16-21), Detroit Tigers (22-24), Kansas City Royals (25-28), Milwaukee Brewers (29-35), Minnesota Twins (36-41), New York Yankees (42-49), Oakland Athletics (50-51), Seattle Mariners (52-57), Texas Rangers (58-62), Toronto Blue Jays (63-69), Atlanta Braves (70-76), Chicago Cubs (77-83), Cincinnati Reds (84-86), Houston Astros (87-90), Los Angeles Dodgers (91-96), Montreal Expos (97-99), New York Mets (100-104), Philadelphia

Phillies (105-110), Pittsburgh Pirates (111-115), St. Louis Cardinals (116-119), San Diego Padres (120-127), and San Francisco Giants (128-131). The key Rookie Cards in this set are Jeff Bagwell and Ivan Rodriguez. Cards are numbered with a U prefix.

	MT	EX-MT	VG
COMPLETE SET (132)	6.00	2.70	.75
COMMON PLAYER (1-132)	.05	.02	.01
☐ 1 Glenn Davis	.08	.04	.01
☐ 2 Dwight Evans	.08	.04	.01
☐ 3 Jose Mesa	.05	.02	.01
☐ 4 Jack Clark	.08	.04	.01
☐ 5 Danny Darwin	.05	.02	.01
☐ 6 Steve Lyons	.05	.02	.01
☐ 7 Mo Vaughn	.20	.09	.03
☐ 8 Floyd Bannister	.05	.02	.01
☐ 9 Gary Gaetti	.05	.02	.01
☐ 10 Dave Parker	.08	.04	.01
☐ 11 Joey Cora	.05	.02	.01
☐ 12 Charlie Hough	.05	.02	.01
☐ 13 Matt Merullo	.05	.02	.01
☐ 14 Warren Newson	.10	.05	.01
☐ 15 Tim Raines	.08	.04	.01
☐ 16 Albert Belle	.15	.07	.02
☐ 17 Glenallen Hill	.05	.02	.01
☐ 18 Shawn Hillegas	.05	.02	.01
☐ 19 Mark Lewis	.12	.05	.02
☐ 20 Charles Nagy	.40	.18	.05
☐ 21 Mark Whiten	.10	.05	.01
☐ 22 John Cerutti	.05	.02	.01
☐ 23 Rob Deer	.08	.04	.01
☐ 24 Mickey Tettleton	.08	.04	.01
☐ 25 Warren Cromartie	.05	.02	.01
☐ 26 Kirk Gibson	.08	.04	.01
☐ 27 David Howard	.10	.05	.01
☐ 28 Brent Mayne	.05	.02	.01
☐ 29 Dante Bichette	.05	.02	.01
☐ 30 Mark Lee	.10	.05	.01
☐ 31 Julio Machado	.05	.02	.01
☐ 32 Edwin Nunez	.05	.02	.01
☐ 33 Willie Randolph	.08	.04	.01
☐ 34 Franklin Stubbs	.05	.02	.01
☐ 35 Bill Wegman	.05	.02	.01
☐ 36 Chili Davis	.08	.04	.01
☐ 37 Chuck Knoblauch	.40	.18	.05
☐ 38 Scott Leius	.10	.05	.01
☐ 39 Jack Morris	.10	.05	.01
☐ 40 Mike Pagliarulo	.05	.02	.01
☐ 41 Lenny Webster	.05	.02	.01
☐ 42 John Habyan	.05	.02	.01
☐ 43 Steve Howe	.05	.02	.01
☐ 44 Jeff Johnson	.10	.05	.01
☐ 45 Scott Kamieniecki	.10	.05	.01
☐ 46 Pat Kelly	.15	.07	.02
☐ 47 Hensley Meulens	.08	.04	.01
☐ 48 Wade Taylor	.05	.02	.01
☐ 49 Bernie Williams	.20	.09	.03
☐ 50 Kirk Dressendorfer	.10	.05	.01
☐ 51 Ernest Riles	.05	.02	.01
☐ 52 Rich DeLucia	.05	.02	.01
☐ 53 Tracy Jones	.05	.02	.01
☐ 54 Bill Krueger	.05	.02	.01
☐ 55 Alonzo Powell	.10	.05	.01
☐ 56 Jeff Schaefer	.05	.02	.01
☐ 57 Russ Swan	.05	.02	.01
☐ 58 John Barfield	.05	.02	.01
☐ 59 Rich Gossage	.08	.04	.01
☐ 60 Jose Guzman	.05	.02	.01
☐ 61 Dean Palmer	.20	.09	.03
☐ 62 Ivan Rodriguez	1.25	.55	.16
☐ 63 Roberto Alomar	.20	.09	.03
☐ 64 Tom Candiotti	.05	.02	.01
☐ 65 Joe Carter	.12	.05	.02
☐ 66 Ed Sprague	.20	.09	.03
☐ 67 Pat Tabler	.05	.02	.01
☐ 68 Mike Timlin	.10	.05	.01
☐ 69 Devon White	.08	.04	.01
☐ 70 Rafael Belliard	.05	.02	.01
☐ 71 Juan Berenguer	.05	.02	.01
☐ 72 Sid Bream	.05	.02	.01
☐ 73 Marvin Freeman	.05	.02	.01
☐ 74 Kent Mercker	.08	.04	.01
☐ 75 Otis Nixon	.08	.04	.01
☐ 76 Terry Pendleton	.10	.05	.01
☐ 77 George Bell	.08	.04	.01
☐ 78 Danny Jackson	.05	.02	.01
☐ 79 Chuck McElroy	.05	.02	.01
☐ 80 Gary Scott	.15	.07	.02
☐ 81 Heathcliff Slocumb	.05	.02	.01
☐ 82 Dave Smith	.05	.02	.01
☐ 83 Rick Wilkins	.10	.05	.01
☐ 84 Freddie Benavides	.05	.02	.01
☐ 85 Ted Power	.05	.02	.01
☐ 86 Mo Sanford	.15	.07	.02
☐ 87 Jeff Bagwell	1.25	.55	.16
☐ 88 Steve Finley	.08	.04	.01
☐ 89 Pete Harnisch	.08	.04	.01
☐ 90 Darryl Kile	.10	.05	.01
☐ 91 Brett Butler	.08	.04	.01
☐ 92 John Candelaria	.05	.02	.01
☐ 93 Gary Carter	.08	.04	.01
☐ 94 Kevin Gross	.05	.02	.01
☐ 95 Bob Ojeda	.05	.02	.01
☐ 96 Darryl Strawberry	.12	.05	.02
☐ 97 Ivan Calderon	.05	.02	.01
☐ 98 Ron Hassey	.05	.02	.01
☐ 99 Gilberto Reyes	.05	.02	.01
☐ 100 Hubie Brooks	.05	.02	.01
☐ 101 Rick Cerone	.05	.02	.01
☐ 102 Vince Coleman	.08	.04	.01
☐ 103 Jeff Innis	.05	.02	.01
☐ 104 Pete Schourek	.12	.05	.02
☐ 105 Andy Ashby	.12	.05	.02
☐ 106 Wally Backman	.05	.02	.01
☐ 107 Darrin Fletcher	.05	.02	.01
☐ 108 Tommy Greene	.05	.02	.01
☐ 109 John Morris	.05	.02	.01
☐ 110 Mitch Williams	.05	.02	.01
☐ 111 Lloyd McClendon	.05	.02	.01
☐ 112 Orlando Merced	.20	.09	.03
☐ 113 Vicente Palacios	.05	.02	.01
☐ 114 Gary Varsho	.05	.02	.01
☐ 115 John Wehner	.10	.05	.01
☐ 116 Rex Hudler	.05	.02	.01
☐ 117 Tim Jones	.05	.02	.01
☐ 118 Geronimo Pena	.05	.02	.01
☐ 119 Gerald Perry	.05	.02	.01
☐ 120 Larry Andersen	.05	.02	.01
☐ 121 Jerald Clark	.05	.02	.01
☐ 122 Scott Coolbaugh	.05	.02	.01
☐ 123 Tony Fernandez	.08	.04	.01
☐ 124 Darrin Jackson	.08	.04	.01
☐ 125 Fred McGriff	.12	.05	.02
☐ 126 Jose Mota	.10	.05	.01
☐ 127 Tim Teufel	.05	.02	.01
☐ 128 Bud Black	.05	.02	.01
☐ 129 Mike Felder	.05	.02	.01
☐ 130 Willie McGee	.08	.04	.01
☐ 131 Dave Righetti	.05	.02	.01
☐ 132 Checklist Card	.08	.01	.00

1991 Fleer Wax Box Cards

These cards were issued on the bottom of 1991 Fleer wax boxes. This set celebrated the spate of no-hitters in 1990 and were printed on three different boxes. These standard size cards, 2 1/2" by 3 1/2", come four to a box, three about the no-hitters and one team logo card on each box. The cards are blank backed and are numbered on the front in a subtle way. They are ordered below as they are numbered, which is by chronological order of their no-hitters. Only the player cards are listed below since there was a different team logo card on each box.

	MT	EX-MT	VG
COMPLETE SET (9)	2.50	1.15	.30

		MT	EX-MT	VG
	COMMON PLAYER (1-9)	.15	.07	.02
☐ 1	Mark Langston and Mike Witt	.15	.07	.02
☐ 2	Randy Johnson	.25	.11	.03
☐ 3	Nolan Ryan	1.00	.45	.13
☐ 4	Dave Stewart	.25	.11	.03
☐ 5	Fernando Valenzuela	.25	.11	.03
☐ 6	Andy Hawkins	.15	.07	.02
☐ 7	Melido Perez	.25	.11	.03
☐ 8	Terry Mulholland	.15	.07	.02
☐ 9	Dave Stieb	.25	.11	.03

1991 Fleer World Series

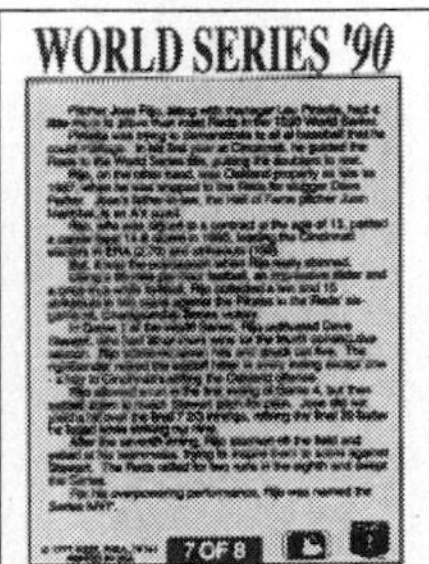

This eight-card set captures highlights from the 1990 World Series between the Cincinnati Reds and the Oakland Athletics. The set was only available as an insert with the 1991 Fleer factory sets. The standard-size (2 1/2" by 3 1/2") cards have on the fronts color action photos, bordered in blue on a white card face. The words "World Series '90" appears in red and blue lettering above the pictures. The backs have a similar design, only with a summary of an aspect of the Series on a yellow background. The cards are numbered on the back.

		MT	EX-MT	VG
	COMPLETE SET (8)	2.00	.90	.25
	COMMON PLAYER (1-8)	.25	.11	.03
☐ 1	Eric Davis	.40	.18	.05
☐ 2	Billy Hatcher	.25	.11	.03
☐ 3	Jose Canseco	.75	.35	.09
☐ 4	Rickey Henderson	.50	.23	.06
☐ 5	Chris Sabo	.25	.11	.03
☐ 6	Dave Stewart	.25	.11	.03
☐ 7	Jose Rijo	.25	.11	.03
☐ 8	Reds Celebrate	.25	.11	.03

1992 Fleer

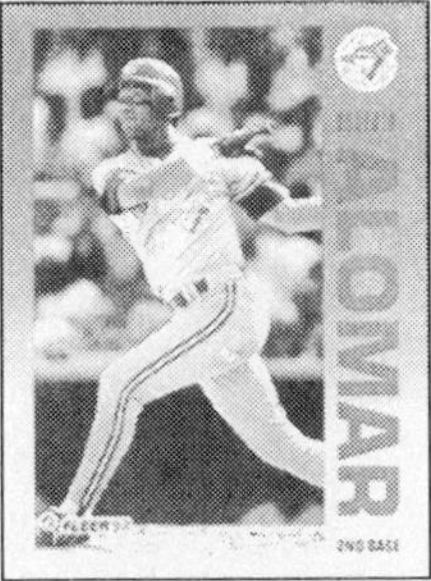

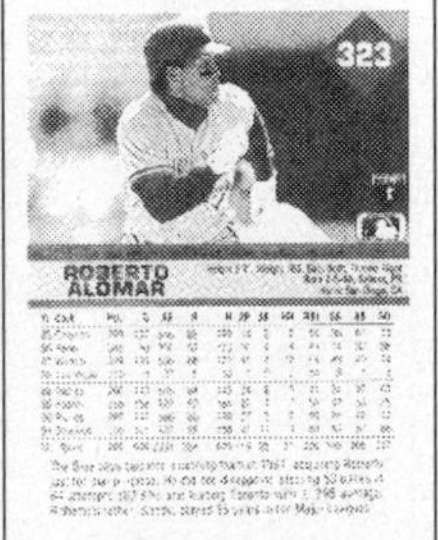

The 1992 Fleer set contains 720 cards measuring the standard size (2 1/2" by 3 1/2"). The card fronts shade from metallic pale green to white as one moves down the face. The team logo and player's name appear to the right of the picture, running the length of the card. The top portion of the backs has a different color player photo and biography, while the bottom portion includes statistics and player profile. The cards are checklisted below alphabetically within and according to teams for each league as follows: Baltimore Orioles (1-31), Boston Red Sox (32-49), California Angels (50-73), Chicago White Sox (74-101), Cleveland Indians (102-126), Detroit Tigers (127-149), Kansas City Royals (150-172), Milwaukee Brewers (173-194), Minnesota Twins (195-220), New York Yankees (221-247), Oakland Athletics (248-272), Seattle Mariners (273-296), Texas Rangers (297-321), Toronto Blue Jays (322-348), Atlanta Braves (349-374), Chicago Cubs (375-397), Cincinnati Reds (398-423), Houston Astros (424-446), Los Angeles Dodgers (447-471), Montreal Expos (472-494), New York Mets (495-520), Philadelphia Phillies (521-547), Pittsburgh Pirates (548-573), St. Louis Cardinals (574-596), San Diego Padres (597-624), and San Francisco Giants (625-651). Topical subsets feature Major League Prospects (652-680), Record Setters (681-687), League Leaders (688-697), Super Star Specials (698-707), Pro Visions (708-713), and Checklists (714-720). The only noteworthy Rookie Card in the set is Rob Maurer.

		MT	EX-MT	VG
	COMPLETE SET (720)	20.00	9.00	2.50
	COMPLETE HOBBY SET (732)	40.00	18.00	5.00
	COMPLETE RETAIL SET (732)	30.00	13.50	3.80
	COMMON PLAYER (1-720)	.04	.02	.01
☐ 1	Brady Anderson	.07	.03	.01
☐ 2	Jose Bautista	.04	.02	.01
☐ 3	Juan Bell	.04	.02	.01
☐ 4	Glenn Davis	.07	.03	.01
☐ 5	Mike Devereaux	.07	.03	.01
☐ 6	Dwight Evans	.07	.03	.01
☐ 7	Mike Flanagan	.04	.02	.01
☐ 8	Leo Gomez	.10	.05	.01
☐ 9	Chris Hoiles	.07	.03	.01
☐ 10	Sam Horn	.04	.02	.01
☐ 11	Tim Hulett	.04	.02	.01
☐ 12	Dave Johnson	.04	.02	.01
☐ 13	Chito Martinez	.04	.02	.01
☐ 14	Ben McDonald	.10	.05	.01
☐ 15	Bob Melvin	.04	.02	.01
☐ 16	Luis Mercedes	.04	.02	.01
☐ 17	Jose Mesa	.04	.02	.01
☐ 18	Bob Milacki	.04	.02	.01
☐ 19	Randy Milligan	.04	.02	.01
☐ 20	Mike Mussina UER (Card back refers to him as Jeff)	.50	.23	.06
☐ 21	Gregg Olson	.07	.03	.01
☐ 22	Joe Orsulak	.04	.02	.01
☐ 23	Jim Poole	.04	.02	.01
☐ 24	Arthur Rhodes	.15	.07	.02
☐ 25	Billy Ripken	.04	.02	.01
☐ 26	Cal Ripken	.25	.11	.03
☐ 27	David Segui	.04	.02	.01
☐ 28	Roy Smith	.04	.02	.01
☐ 29	Anthony Telford	.04	.02	.01
☐ 30	Mark Williamson	.04	.02	.01
☐ 31	Craig Worthington	.04	.02	.01
☐ 32	Wade Boggs	.12	.05	.02
☐ 33	Tom Bolton	.04	.02	.01
☐ 34	Tom Brunansky	.07	.03	.01
☐ 35	Ellis Burks	.07	.03	.01
☐ 36	Jack Clark	.07	.03	.01
☐ 37	Roger Clemens	.25	.11	.03
☐ 38	Danny Darwin	.04	.02	.01
☐ 39	Mike Greenwell	.07	.03	.01
☐ 40	Joe Hesketh	.04	.02	.01
☐ 41	Daryl Irvine	.04	.02	.01
☐ 42	Dennis Lamp	.04	.02	.01
☐ 43	Tony Pena	.04	.02	.01
☐ 44	Phil Plantier	.15	.07	.02
☐ 45	Carlos Quintana	.04	.02	.01
☐ 46	Jeff Reardon	.07	.03	.01
☐ 47	Jody Reed	.04	.02	.01
☐ 48	Luis Rivera	.04	.02	.01
☐ 49	Mo Vaughn	.07	.03	.01
☐ 50	Jim Abbott	.12	.05	.02

☐ 51 Kyle Abbott	.07	.03	.01
☐ 52 Ruben Amaro Jr.	.04	.02	.01
☐ 53 Scott Bailes	.04	.02	.01
☐ 54 Chris Beasley	.10	.05	.01
☐ 55 Mark Eichhorn	.04	.02	.01
☐ 56 Mike Fetters	.04	.02	.01
☐ 57 Chuck Finley	.04	.02	.01
☐ 58 Gary Gaetti	.04	.02	.01
☐ 59 Dave Gallagher	.04	.02	.01
☐ 60 Donnie Hill	.04	.02	.01
☐ 61 Bryan Harvey UER (Lee Smith led the Majors with 47 saves)	.04	.02	.01
☐ 62 Wally Joyner	.07	.03	.01
☐ 63 Mark Langston	.07	.03	.01
☐ 64 Kirk McCaskill	.04	.02	.01
☐ 65 John Orton	.04	.02	.01
☐ 66 Lance Parrish	.07	.03	.01
☐ 67 Luis Polonia	.07	.03	.01
☐ 68 Bobby Rose	.04	.02	.01
☐ 69 Dick Schofield	.04	.02	.01
☐ 70 Luis Sojo	.04	.02	.01
☐ 71 Lee Stevens	.04	.02	.01
☐ 72 Dave Winfield	.10	.05	.01
☐ 73 Cliff Young	.04	.02	.01
☐ 74 Wilson Alvarez	.04	.02	.01
☐ 75 Esteban Beltre	.10	.05	.01
☐ 76 Joey Cora	.04	.02	.01
☐ 77 Brian Drahman	.04	.02	.01
☐ 78 Alex Fernandez	.07	.03	.01
☐ 79 Carlton Fisk	.10	.05	.01
☐ 80 Scott Fletcher	.04	.02	.01
☐ 81 Craig Grebeck	.04	.02	.01
☐ 82 Ozzie Guillen	.04	.02	.01
☐ 83 Greg Hibbard	.04	.02	.01
☐ 84 Charlie Hough	.04	.02	.01
☐ 85 Mike Huff	.04	.02	.01
☐ 86 Bo Jackson	.12	.05	.02
☐ 87 Lance Johnson	.04	.02	.01
☐ 88 Ron Karkovice	.04	.02	.01
☐ 89 Jack McDowell	.07	.03	.01
☐ 90 Matt Merullo	.04	.02	.01
☐ 91 Warren Newson	.04	.02	.01
☐ 92 Donn Pall UER (Called Dunn on card back)	.04	.02	.01
☐ 93 Dan Pasqua	.04	.02	.01
☐ 94 Ken Patterson	.04	.02	.01
☐ 95 Melido Perez	.07	.03	.01
☐ 96 Scott Radinsky	.04	.02	.01
☐ 97 Tim Raines	.07	.03	.01
☐ 98 Sammy Sosa	.04	.02	.01
☐ 99 Bobby Thigpen	.04	.02	.01
☐ 100 Frank Thomas	.75	.35	.09
☐ 101 Robin Ventura	.15	.07	.02
☐ 102 Mike Aldrete	.04	.02	.01
☐ 103 Sandy Alomar Jr.	.07	.03	.01
☐ 104 Carlos Baerga	.15	.07	.02
☐ 105 Albert Belle	.12	.05	.02
☐ 106 Willie Blair	.04	.02	.01
☐ 107 Jerry Browne	.04	.02	.01
☐ 108 Alex Cole	.04	.02	.01
☐ 109 Felix Fermin	.04	.02	.01
☐ 110 Glenallen Hill	.04	.02	.01
☐ 111 Shawn Hillegas	.04	.02	.01
☐ 112 Chris James	.04	.02	.01
☐ 113 Reggie Jefferson	.07	.03	.01
☐ 114 Doug Jones	.04	.02	.01
☐ 115 Eric King	.04	.02	.01
☐ 116 Mark Lewis	.07	.03	.01
☐ 117 Carlos Martinez	.04	.02	.01
☐ 118 Charles Nagy UER (Throws right, but card says left)	.10	.05	.01
☐ 119 Rod Nichols	.04	.02	.01
☐ 120 Steve Olin	.04	.02	.01
☐ 121 Jesse Orosco	.04	.02	.01
☐ 122 Rudy Seanez	.04	.02	.01
☐ 123 Joel Skinner	.04	.02	.01
☐ 124 Greg Swindell	.07	.03	.01
☐ 125 Jim Thome	.12	.05	.02
☐ 126 Mark Whiten	.07	.03	.01
☐ 127 Scott Aldred	.04	.02	.01
☐ 128 Andy Allanson	.04	.02	.01
☐ 129 John Cerutti	.04	.02	.01
☐ 130 Milt Cuyler	.04	.02	.01
☐ 131 Mike Dalton	.10	.05	.01
☐ 132 Rob Deer	.07	.03	.01
☐ 133 Cecil Fielder	.12	.05	.02
☐ 134 Travis Fryman	.30	.14	.04
☐ 135 Dan Gakeler	.04	.02	.01
☐ 136 Paul Gibson	.04	.02	.01
☐ 137 Bill Gullickson	.04	.02	.01
☐ 138 Mike Henneman	.04	.02	.01
☐ 139 Pete Incaviglia	.04	.02	.01
☐ 140 Mark Leiter	.04	.02	.01
☐ 141 Scott Livingstone	.10	.05	.01
☐ 142 Lloyd Moseby	.04	.02	.01
☐ 143 Tony Phillips	.04	.02	.01
☐ 144 Mark Salas	.04	.02	.01
☐ 145 Frank Tanana	.04	.02	.01
☐ 146 Walt Terrell	.04	.02	.01
☐ 147 Mickey Tettleton	.07	.03	.01
☐ 148 Alan Trammell	.07	.03	.01
☐ 149 Lou Whitaker	.07	.03	.01
☐ 150 Kevin Appier	.07	.03	.01
☐ 151 Luis Aquino	.04	.02	.01
☐ 152 Todd Benzinger	.04	.02	.01
☐ 153 Mike Boddicker	.04	.02	.01
☐ 154 George Brett	.10	.05	.01
☐ 155 Storm Davis	.04	.02	.01
☐ 156 Jim Eisenreich	.04	.02	.01
☐ 157 Kirk Gibson	.07	.03	.01
☐ 158 Tom Gordon	.04	.02	.01
☐ 159 Mark Gubicza	.04	.02	.01
☐ 160 David Howard	.04	.02	.01
☐ 161 Mike Macfarlane	.04	.02	.01
☐ 162 Brent Mayne	.04	.02	.01
☐ 163 Brian McRae	.07	.03	.01
☐ 164 Jeff Montgomery	.04	.02	.01
☐ 165 Bill Pecota	.04	.02	.01
☐ 166 Harvey Pulliam	.10	.05	.01
☐ 167 Bret Saberhagen	.07	.03	.01
☐ 168 Kevin Seitzer	.07	.03	.01
☐ 169 Terry Shumpert	.04	.02	.01
☐ 170 Kurt Stillwell	.04	.02	.01
☐ 171 Danny Tartabull	.07	.03	.01
☐ 172 Gary Thurman	.04	.02	.01
☐ 173 Dante Bichette	.04	.02	.01
☐ 174 Kevin D. Brown	.04	.02	.01
☐ 175 Chuck Crim	.04	.02	.01
☐ 176 Jim Gantner	.04	.02	.01
☐ 177 Darryl Hamilton	.07	.03	.01
☐ 178 Ted Higuera	.04	.02	.01
☐ 179 Darren Holmes	.04	.02	.01
☐ 180 Mark Lee	.04	.02	.01
☐ 181 Julio Machado	.04	.02	.01
☐ 182 Paul Molitor	.07	.03	.01
☐ 183 Jaime Navarro	.07	.03	.01
☐ 184 Edwin Nunez	.04	.02	.01
☐ 185 Dan Plesac	.04	.02	.01
☐ 186 Willie Randolph	.07	.03	.01
☐ 187 Ron Robinson	.04	.02	.01
☐ 188 Gary Sheffield	.20	.09	.03
☐ 189 Bill Spiers	.04	.02	.01
☐ 190 B.J. Surhoff	.04	.02	.01
☐ 191 Dale Sveum	.04	.02	.01
☐ 192 Greg Vaughn	.07	.03	.01
☐ 193 Bill Wegman	.04	.02	.01
☐ 194 Robin Yount	.10	.05	.01
☐ 195 Rick Aguilera	.07	.03	.01
☐ 196 Allan Anderson	.04	.02	.01
☐ 197 Steve Bedrosian	.04	.02	.01
☐ 198 Randy Bush	.04	.02	.01
☐ 199 Larry Casian	.04	.02	.01
☐ 200 Chili Davis	.07	.03	.01
☐ 201 Scott Erickson	.10	.05	.01
☐ 202 Greg Gagne	.04	.02	.01
☐ 203 Dan Gladden	.04	.02	.01
☐ 204 Brian Harper	.04	.02	.01
☐ 205 Kent Hrbek	.07	.03	.01
☐ 206 Chuck Knoblauch UER (Career hit total of 59 is wrong)	.20	.09	.03
☐ 207 Gene Larkin	.04	.02	.01
☐ 208 Terry Leach	.04	.02	.01
☐ 209 Scott Leius	.04	.02	.01
☐ 210 Shane Mack	.07	.03	.01
☐ 211 Jack Morris	.10	.05	.01
☐ 212 Pedro Munoz	.07	.03	.01
☐ 213 Denny Neagle	.07	.03	.01
☐ 214 Al Newman	.04	.02	.01
☐ 215 Junior Ortiz	.04	.02	.01
☐ 216 Mike Pagliarulo	.04	.02	.01
☐ 217 Kirby Puckett	.20	.09	.03
☐ 218 Paul Sorrento	.07	.03	.01
☐ 219 Kevin Tapani	.07	.03	.01
☐ 220 Lenny Webster	.04	.02	.01
☐ 221 Jesse Barfield	.04	.02	.01
☐ 222 Greg Cadaret	.04	.02	.01
☐ 223 Dave Eiland	.04	.02	.01
☐ 224 Alvaro Espinoza	.04	.02	.01
☐ 225 Steve Farr	.04	.02	.01
☐ 226 Bob Geren	.04	.02	.01
☐ 227 Lee Guetterman	.04	.02	.01
☐ 228 John Habyan	.04	.02	.01

☐	229	Mel Hall	.04	.02	.01
☐	230	Steve Howe	.04	.02	.01
☐	231	Mike Humphreys	.07	.03	.01
☐	232	Scott Kamieniecki	.04	.02	.01
☐	233	Pat Kelly	.07	.03	.01
☐	234	Roberto Kelly	.07	.03	.01
☐	235	Tim Leary	.04	.02	.01
☐	236	Kevin Maas	.07	.03	.01
☐	237	Don Mattingly	.12	.05	.02
☐	238	Hensley Meulens	.04	.02	.01
☐	239	Matt Nokes	.04	.02	.01
☐	240	Pascual Perez	.04	.02	.01
☐	241	Eric Plunk	.04	.02	.01
☐	242	John Ramos	.04	.02	.01
☐	243	Scott Sanderson	.04	.02	.01
☐	244	Steve Sax	.07	.03	.01
☐	245	Wade Taylor	.04	.02	.01
☐	246	Randy Velarde	.04	.02	.01
☐	247	Bernie Williams	.10	.05	.01
☐	248	Troy Afenir	.04	.02	.01
☐	249	Harold Baines	.07	.03	.01
☐	250	Lance Blankenship	.04	.02	.01
☐	251	Mike Bordick	.10	.05	.01
☐	252	Jose Canseco	.20	.09	.03
☐	253	Steve Chitren	.04	.02	.01
☐	254	Ron Darling	.07	.03	.01
☐	255	Dennis Eckersley	.10	.05	.01
☐	256	Mike Gallego	.04	.02	.01
☐	257	Dave Henderson	.04	.02	.01
☐	258	Rickey Henderson UER (Wearing 24 on front and 22 on back)	.12	.05	.02
☐	259	Rick Honeycutt	.04	.02	.01
☐	260	Brook Jacoby	.04	.02	.01
☐	261	Carney Lansford	.07	.03	.01
☐	262	Mark McGwire	.20	.09	.03
☐	263	Mike Moore	.04	.02	.01
☐	264	Gene Nelson	.04	.02	.01
☐	265	Jamie Quirk	.04	.02	.01
☐	266	Joe Slusarski	.04	.02	.01
☐	267	Terry Steinbach	.07	.03	.01
☐	268	Dave Stewart	.07	.03	.01
☐	269	Todd Van Poppel	.20	.09	.03
☐	270	Walt Weiss	.04	.02	.01
☐	271	Bob Welch	.04	.02	.01
☐	272	Curt Young	.04	.02	.01
☐	273	Scott Bradley	.04	.02	.01
☐	274	Greg Briley	.04	.02	.01
☐	275	Jay Buhner	.07	.03	.01
☐	276	Henry Cotto	.04	.02	.01
☐	277	Alvin Davis	.04	.02	.01
☐	278	Rich DeLucia	.04	.02	.01
☐	279	Ken Griffey Jr.	.50	.23	.06
☐	280	Erik Hanson	.04	.02	.01
☐	281	Brian Holman	.04	.02	.01
☐	282	Mike Jackson	.04	.02	.01
☐	283	Randy Johnson	.07	.03	.01
☐	284	Tracy Jones	.04	.02	.01
☐	285	Bill Krueger	.04	.02	.01
☐	286	Edgar Martinez	.07	.03	.01
☐	287	Tino Martinez	.07	.03	.01
☐	288	Rob Murphy	.04	.02	.01
☐	289	Pete O'Brien	.04	.02	.01
☐	290	Alonzo Powell	.04	.02	.01
☐	291	Harold Reynolds	.04	.02	.01
☐	292	Mike Schooler	.04	.02	.01
☐	293	Russ Swan	.04	.02	.01
☐	294	Bill Swift	.04	.02	.01
☐	295	Dave Valle	.04	.02	.01
☐	296	Omar Vizquel	.04	.02	.01
☐	297	Gerald Alexander	.04	.02	.01
☐	298	Brad Arnsberg	.04	.02	.01
☐	299	Kevin Brown	.07	.03	.01
☐	300	Jack Daugherty	.04	.02	.01
☐	301	Mario Diaz	.04	.02	.01
☐	302	Brian Downing	.04	.02	.01
☐	303	Julio Franco	.07	.03	.01
☐	304	Juan Gonzalez	.35	.16	.04
☐	305	Rich Gossage	.07	.03	.01
☐	306	Jose Guzman	.04	.02	.01
☐	307	Jose Hernandez	.10	.05	.01
☐	308	Jeff Huson	.04	.02	.01
☐	309	Mike Jeffcoat	.04	.02	.01
☐	310	Terry Mathews	.10	.05	.01
☐	311	Rafael Palmeiro	.07	.03	.01
☐	312	Dean Palmer	.12	.05	.02
☐	313	Geno Petralli	.04	.02	.01
☐	314	Gary Pettis	.04	.02	.01
☐	315	Kevin Reimer	.07	.03	.01
☐	316	Ivan Rodriguez	.30	.14	.04
☐	317	Kenny Rogers	.04	.02	.01
☐	318	Wayne Rosenthal	.10	.05	.01
☐	319	Jeff Russell	.04	.02	.01
☐	320	Nolan Ryan	.40	.18	.05
☐	321	Ruben Sierra	.15	.07	.02
☐	322	Jim Acker	.04	.02	.01
☐	323	Roberto Alomar	.20	.09	.03
☐	324	Derek Bell	.10	.05	.01
☐	325	Pat Borders	.04	.02	.01
☐	326	Tom Candiotti	.04	.02	.01
☐	327	Joe Carter	.12	.05	.02
☐	328	Rob Ducey	.04	.02	.01
☐	329	Kelly Gruber	.07	.03	.01
☐	330	Juan Guzman	.75	.35	.09
☐	331	Tom Henke	.07	.03	.01
☐	332	Jimmy Key	.04	.02	.01
☐	333	Manny Lee	.04	.02	.01
☐	334	Al Leiter	.04	.02	.01
☐	335	Bob MacDonald	.04	.02	.01
☐	336	Candy Maldonado	.04	.02	.01
☐	337	Rance Mulliniks	.04	.02	.01
☐	338	Greg Myers	.04	.02	.01
☐	339	John Olerud UER (1991 BA has .256, but text says .258)	.10	.05	.01
☐	340	Ed Sprague	.07	.03	.01
☐	341	Dave Stieb	.04	.02	.01
☐	342	Todd Stottlemyre	.07	.03	.01
☐	343	Mike Timlin	.04	.02	.01
☐	344	Duane Ward	.04	.02	.01
☐	345	David Wells	.04	.02	.01
☐	346	Devon White	.07	.03	.01
☐	347	Mookie Wilson	.04	.02	.01
☐	348	Eddie Zosky	.07	.03	.01
☐	349	Steve Avery	.15	.07	.02
☐	350	Mike Bell	.04	.02	.01
☐	351	Rafael Belliard	.04	.02	.01
☐	352	Juan Berenguer	.04	.02	.01
☐	353	Jeff Blauser	.04	.02	.01
☐	354	Sid Bream	.04	.02	.01
☐	355	Francisco Cabrera	.04	.02	.01
☐	356	Marvin Freeman	.04	.02	.01
☐	357	Ron Gant	.10	.05	.01
☐	358	Tom Glavine	.12	.05	.02
☐	359	Brian Hunter	.10	.05	.01
☐	360	Dave Justice	.20	.09	.03
☐	361	Charlie Leibrandt	.04	.02	.01
☐	362	Mark Lemke	.04	.02	.01
☐	363	Kent Mercker	.04	.02	.01
☐	364	Keith Mitchell	.07	.03	.01
☐	365	Greg Olson	.04	.02	.01
☐	366	Terry Pendleton	.10	.05	.01
☐	367	Armando Reynoso	.10	.05	.01
☐	368	Deion Sanders	.15	.07	.02
☐	369	Lonnie Smith	.07	.03	.01
☐	370	Pete Smith	.07	.03	.01
☐	371	John Smoltz	.10	.05	.01
☐	372	Mike Stanton	.04	.02	.01
☐	373	Jeff Treadway	.04	.02	.01
☐	374	Mark Wohlers	.10	.05	.01
☐	375	Paul Assenmacher	.04	.02	.01
☐	376	George Bell	.07	.03	.01
☐	377	Shawn Boskie	.04	.02	.01
☐	378	Frank Castillo	.04	.02	.01
☐	379	Andre Dawson	.10	.05	.01
☐	380	Shawon Dunston	.07	.03	.01
☐	381	Mark Grace	.07	.03	.01
☐	382	Mike Harkey	.07	.03	.01
☐	383	Danny Jackson	.04	.02	.01
☐	384	Les Lancaster	.04	.02	.01
☐	385	Ced Landrum	.04	.02	.01
☐	386	Greg Maddux	.07	.03	.01
☐	387	Derrick May	.07	.03	.01
☐	388	Chuck McElroy	.04	.02	.01
☐	389	Ryne Sandberg	.20	.09	.03
☐	390	Heathcliff Slocumb	.04	.02	.01
☐	391	Dave Smith	.04	.02	.01
☐	392	Dwight Smith	.04	.02	.01
☐	393	Rick Sutcliffe	.07	.03	.01
☐	394	Hector Villanueva	.04	.02	.01
☐	395	Chico Walker	.04	.02	.01
☐	396	Jerome Walton	.04	.02	.01
☐	397	Rick Wilkins	.04	.02	.01
☐	398	Jack Armstrong	.04	.02	.01
☐	399	Freddie Benavides	.04	.02	.01
☐	400	Glenn Braggs	.04	.02	.01
☐	401	Tom Browning	.04	.02	.01
☐	402	Norm Charlton	.07	.03	.01
☐	403	Eric Davis	.07	.03	.01
☐	404	Rob Dibble	.07	.03	.01
☐	405	Bill Doran	.04	.02	.01
☐	406	Mariano Duncan	.04	.02	.01
☐	407	Kip Gross	.10	.05	.01
☐	408	Chris Hammond	.04	.02	.01
☐	409	Billy Hatcher	.04	.02	.01
☐	410	Chris Jones	.04	.02	.01

	Player			
☐ 411	Barry Larkin	.10	.05	.01
☐ 412	Hal Morris	.07	.03	.01
☐ 413	Randy Myers	.07	.03	.01
☐ 414	Joe Oliver	.04	.02	.01
☐ 415	Paul O'Neill	.07	.03	.01
☐ 416	Ted Power	.04	.02	.01
☐ 417	Luis Quinones	.04	.02	.01
☐ 418	Jeff Reed	.04	.02	.01
☐ 419	Jose Rijo	.07	.03	.01
☐ 420	Chris Sabo	.07	.03	.01
☐ 421	Reggie Sanders	.25	.11	.03
☐ 422	Scott Scudder	.04	.02	.01
☐ 423	Glenn Sutko	.04	.02	.01
☐ 424	Eric Anthony	.07	.03	.01
☐ 425	Jeff Bagwell	.25	.11	.03
☐ 426	Craig Biggio	.07	.03	.01
☐ 427	Ken Caminiti	.07	.03	.01
☐ 428	Casey Candaele	.04	.02	.01
☐ 429	Mike Capel	.04	.02	.01
☐ 430	Andujar Cedeno	.07	.03	.01
☐ 431	Jim Corsi	.04	.02	.01
☐ 432	Mark Davidson	.04	.02	.01
☐ 433	Steve Finley	.07	.03	.01
☐ 434	Luis Gonzalez	.07	.03	.01
☐ 435	Pete Harnisch	.04	.02	.01
☐ 436	Dwayne Henry	.04	.02	.01
☐ 437	Xavier Hernandez	.04	.02	.01
☐ 438	Jimmy Jones	.04	.02	.01
☐ 439	Darryl Kile	.07	.03	.01
☐ 440	Rob Mallicoat	.04	.02	.01
☐ 441	Andy Mota	.04	.02	.01
☐ 442	Al Osuna	.04	.02	.01
☐ 443	Mark Portugal	.04	.02	.01
☐ 444	Scott Servais	.04	.02	.01
☐ 445	Mike Simms	.04	.02	.01
☐ 446	Gerald Young	.04	.02	.01
☐ 447	Tim Belcher	.07	.03	.01
☐ 448	Brett Butler	.07	.03	.01
☐ 449	John Candelaria	.04	.02	.01
☐ 450	Gary Carter	.07	.03	.01
☐ 451	Dennis Cook	.04	.02	.01
☐ 452	Tim Crews	.04	.02	.01
☐ 453	Kal Daniels	.04	.02	.01
☐ 454	Jim Gott	.04	.02	.01
☐ 455	Alfredo Griffin	.04	.02	.01
☐ 456	Kevin Gross	.04	.02	.01
☐ 457	Chris Gwynn	.04	.02	.01
☐ 458	Lenny Harris	.04	.02	.01
☐ 459	Orel Hershiser	.07	.03	.01
☐ 460	Jay Howell	.04	.02	.01
☐ 461	Stan Javier	.04	.02	.01
☐ 462	Eric Karros	.50	.23	.06
☐ 463	Ramon Martinez UER (Card says bats right, should be left)	.07	.03	.01
☐ 464	Roger McDowell UER (Wins add up to 54, totals have 51)	.04	.02	.01
☐ 465	Mike Morgan	.04	.02	.01
☐ 466	Eddie Murray	.10	.05	.01
☐ 467	Jose Offerman	.07	.03	.01
☐ 468	Bob Ojeda	.04	.02	.01
☐ 469	Juan Samuel	.04	.02	.01
☐ 470	Mike Scioscia	.04	.02	.01
☐ 471	Darryl Strawberry	.12	.05	.02
☐ 472	Bret Barberie	.04	.02	.01
☐ 473	Brian Barnes	.04	.02	.01
☐ 474	Eric Bullock	.04	.02	.01
☐ 475	Ivan Calderon	.04	.02	.01
☐ 476	Delino DeShields	.10	.05	.01
☐ 477	Jeff Fassero	.04	.02	.01
☐ 478	Mike Fitzgerald	.04	.02	.01
☐ 479	Steve Frey	.04	.02	.01
☐ 480	Andres Galarraga	.04	.02	.01
☐ 481	Mark Gardner	.04	.02	.01
☐ 482	Marquis Grissom	.10	.05	.01
☐ 483	Chris Haney	.04	.02	.01
☐ 484	Barry Jones	.04	.02	.01
☐ 485	Dave Martinez	.04	.02	.01
☐ 486	Dennis Martinez	.07	.03	.01
☐ 487	Chris Nabholz	.07	.03	.01
☐ 488	Spike Owen	.04	.02	.01
☐ 489	Gilberto Reyes	.04	.02	.01
☐ 490	Mel Rojas	.04	.02	.01
☐ 491	Scott Ruskin	.04	.02	.01
☐ 492	Bill Sampen	.04	.02	.01
☐ 493	Larry Walker	.15	.07	.02
☐ 494	Tim Wallach	.07	.03	.01
☐ 495	Daryl Boston	.04	.02	.01
☐ 496	Hubie Brooks	.04	.02	.01
☐ 497	Tim Burke	.04	.02	.01
☐ 498	Mark Carreon	.04	.02	.01
☐ 499	Tony Castillo	.04	.02	.01
☐ 500	Vince Coleman	.07	.03	.01
☐ 501	David Cone	.07	.03	.01
☐ 502	Kevin Elster	.04	.02	.01
☐ 503	Sid Fernandez	.07	.03	.01
☐ 504	John Franco	.07	.03	.01
☐ 505	Dwight Gooden	.07	.03	.01
☐ 506	Todd Hundley	.04	.02	.01
☐ 507	Jeff Innis	.04	.02	.01
☐ 508	Gregg Jefferies	.07	.03	.01
☐ 509	Howard Johnson	.07	.03	.01
☐ 510	Dave Magadan	.07	.03	.01
☐ 511	Terry McDaniel	.10	.05	.01
☐ 512	Kevin McReynolds	.07	.03	.01
☐ 513	Keith Miller	.04	.02	.01
☐ 514	Charlie O'Brien	.04	.02	.01
☐ 515	Mackey Sasser	.04	.02	.01
☐ 516	Pete Schourek	.07	.03	.01
☐ 517	Julio Valera	.04	.02	.01
☐ 518	Frank Viola	.07	.03	.01
☐ 519	Wally Whitehurst	.04	.02	.01
☐ 520	Anthony Young	.07	.03	.01
☐ 521	Andy Ashby	.04	.02	.01
☐ 522	Kim Batiste	.04	.02	.01
☐ 523	Joe Boever	.04	.02	.01
☐ 524	Wes Chamberlain	.04	.02	.01
☐ 525	Pat Combs	.04	.02	.01
☐ 526	Danny Cox	.04	.02	.01
☐ 527	Darren Daulton	.07	.03	.01
☐ 528	Jose DeJesus	.04	.02	.01
☐ 529	Len Dykstra	.07	.03	.01
☐ 530	Darrin Fletcher	.04	.02	.01
☐ 531	Tommy Greene	.04	.02	.01
☐ 532	Jason Grimsley	.04	.02	.01
☐ 533	Charlie Hayes	.04	.02	.01
☐ 534	Von Hayes	.04	.02	.01
☐ 535	Dave Hollins	.07	.03	.01
☐ 536	Ricky Jordan	.04	.02	.01
☐ 537	John Kruk	.07	.03	.01
☐ 538	Jim Lindeman	.04	.02	.01
☐ 539	Mickey Morandini	.07	.03	.01
☐ 540	Terry Mulholland	.04	.02	.01
☐ 541	Dale Murphy	.07	.03	.01
☐ 542	Randy Ready	.04	.02	.01
☐ 543	Wally Ritchie UER (Letters in data are cut off on card)	.04	.02	.01
☐ 544	Bruce Ruffin	.04	.02	.01
☐ 545	Steve Searcy	.04	.02	.01
☐ 546	Dickie Thon	.04	.02	.01
☐ 547	Mitch Williams	.04	.02	.01
☐ 548	Stan Belinda	.04	.02	.01
☐ 549	Jay Bell	.04	.02	.01
☐ 550	Barry Bonds	.15	.07	.02
☐ 551	Bobby Bonilla	.10	.05	.01
☐ 552	Steve Buechele	.04	.02	.01
☐ 553	Doug Drabek	.07	.03	.01
☐ 554	Neal Heaton	.04	.02	.01
☐ 555	Jeff King	.04	.02	.01
☐ 556	Bob Kipper	.04	.02	.01
☐ 557	Bill Landrum	.04	.02	.01
☐ 558	Mike LaValliere	.04	.02	.01
☐ 559	Jose Lind	.04	.02	.01
☐ 560	Lloyd McClendon	.04	.02	.01
☐ 561	Orlando Merced	.07	.03	.01
☐ 562	Bob Patterson	.04	.02	.01
☐ 563	Joe Redfield	.10	.05	.01
☐ 564	Gary Redus	.04	.02	.01
☐ 565	Rosario Rodriguez	.04	.02	.01
☐ 566	Don Slaught	.04	.02	.01
☐ 567	John Smiley	.07	.03	.01
☐ 568	Zane Smith	.04	.02	.01
☐ 569	Randy Tomlin	.04	.02	.01
☐ 570	Andy Van Slyke	.07	.03	.01
☐ 571	Gary Varsho	.04	.02	.01
☐ 572	Bob Walk	.04	.02	.01
☐ 573	John Wehner UER (Actually played for Carolina in 1991, not Cards)	.07	.03	.01
☐ 574	Juan Agosto	.04	.02	.01
☐ 575	Cris Carpenter	.04	.02	.01
☐ 576	Jose DeLeon	.04	.02	.01
☐ 577	Rich Gedman	.04	.02	.01
☐ 578	Bernard Gilkey	.07	.03	.01
☐ 579	Pedro Guerrero	.07	.03	.01
☐ 580	Ken Hill	.07	.03	.01
☐ 581	Rex Hudler	.04	.02	.01
☐ 582	Felix Jose	.07	.03	.01
☐ 583	Ray Lankford	.15	.07	.02
☐ 584	Omar Olivares	.04	.02	.01
☐ 585	Jose Oquendo	.04	.02	.01
☐ 586	Tom Pagnozzi	.04	.02	.01
☐ 587	Geronimo Pena	.04	.02	.01

	Card			
☐	588 Mike Perez	.04	.02	.01
☐	589 Gerald Perry	.04	.02	.01
☐	590 Bryn Smith	.04	.02	.01
☐	591 Lee Smith	.07	.03	.01
☐	592 Ozzie Smith	.10	.05	.01
☐	593 Scott Terry	.04	.02	.01
☐	594 Bob Tewksbury	.07	.03	.01
☐	595 Milt Thompson	.04	.02	.01
☐	596 Todd Zeile	.04	.02	.01
☐	597 Larry Andersen	.04	.02	.01
☐	598 Oscar Azocar	.04	.02	.01
☐	599 Andy Benes	.07	.03	.01
☐	600 Ricky Bones	.10	.05	.01
☐	601 Jerald Clark	.04	.02	.01
☐	602 Pat Clements	.04	.02	.01
☐	603 Paul Faries	.04	.02	.01
☐	604 Tony Fernandez	.07	.03	.01
☐	605 Tony Gwynn	.12	.05	.02
☐	606 Greg W. Harris	.04	.02	.01
☐	607 Thomas Howard	.04	.02	.01
☐	608 Bruce Hurst	.07	.03	.01
☐	609 Darrin Jackson	.07	.03	.01
☐	610 Tom Lampkin	.04	.02	.01
☐	611 Craig Lefferts	.04	.02	.01
☐	612 Jim Lewis	.10	.05	.01
☐	613 Mike Maddux	.04	.02	.01
☐	614 Fred McGriff	.12	.05	.02
☐	615 Jose Melendez	.04	.02	.01
☐	616 Jose Mota	.04	.02	.01
☐	617 Dennis Rasmussen	.04	.02	.01
☐	618 Bip Roberts	.07	.03	.01
☐	619 Rich Rodriguez	.04	.02	.01
☐	620 Benito Santiago	.07	.03	.01
☐	621 Craig Shipley	.10	.05	.01
☐	622 Tim Teufel	.04	.02	.01
☐	623 Kevin Ward	.10	.05	.01
☐	624 Ed Whitson	.04	.02	.01
☐	625 Dave Anderson	.04	.02	.01
☐	626 Kevin Bass	.04	.02	.01
☐	627 Rod Beck	.12	.05	.02
☐	628 Bud Black	.04	.02	.01
☐	629 Jeff Brantley	.04	.02	.01
☐	630 John Burkett	.04	.02	.01
☐	631 Will Clark	.20	.09	.03
☐	632 Royce Clayton	.15	.07	.02
☐	633 Steve Decker	.04	.02	.01
☐	634 Kelly Downs	.04	.02	.01
☐	635 Mike Felder	.04	.02	.01
☐	636 Scott Garrelts	.04	.02	.01
☐	637 Eric Gunderson	.04	.02	.01
☐	638 Bryan Hickerson	.10	.05	.01
☐	639 Darren Lewis	.07	.03	.01
☐	640 Greg Litton	.04	.02	.01
☐	641 Kirt Manwaring	.04	.02	.01
☐	642 Paul McClellan	.04	.02	.01
☐	643 Willie McGee	.07	.03	.01
☐	644 Kevin Mitchell	.07	.03	.01
☐	645 Francisco Oliveras	.04	.02	.01
☐	646 Mike Remlinger	.04	.02	.01
☐	647 Dave Righetti	.04	.02	.01
☐	648 Robby Thompson	.04	.02	.01
☐	649 Jose Uribe	.04	.02	.01
☐	650 Matt Williams	.07	.03	.01
☐	651 Trevor Wilson	.04	.02	.01
☐	652 Tom Goodwin MLP UER	.05	.02	.01
	(Timed in 3.5, should be be timed)			
☐	653 Terry Bross MLP	.05	.02	.01
☐	654 Mike Christopher MLP	.10	.05	.01
☐	655 Kenny Lofton MLP	.40	.18	.05
☐	656 Chris Cron MLP	.10	.05	.01
☐	657 Willie Banks MLP	.08	.04	.01
☐	658 Pat Rice MLP	.10	.05	.01
☐	659A Rob Maurer MLP ERR	.75	.35	.09
	(Name misspelled as Mauer on card front)			
☐	659B Rob Maurer MLP COR	.15	.07	.02
☐	660 Don Harris MLP	.05	.02	.01
☐	661 Henry Rodriguez MLP	.10	.05	.01
☐	662 Cliff Brantley MLP	.10	.05	.01
☐	663 Mike Linskey MLP UER	.05	.02	.01
	(220 pounds in data, 200 in text)			
☐	664 Gary DiSarcina MLP	.08	.04	.01
☐	665 Gil Heredia MLP	.10	.05	.01
☐	666 Vinny Castilla MLP	.10	.05	.01
☐	667 Paul Abbott MLP	.05	.02	.01
☐	668 Monty Fariss MLP UER	.10	.05	.01
	(Called Paul on back)			
☐	669 Jarvis Brown MLP	.10	.05	.01
☐	670 Wayne Kirby MLP	.10	.05	.01
☐	671 Scott Brosius MLP	.10	.05	.01
☐	672 Bob Hamelin MLP	.08	.04	.01
☐	673 Joel Johnston MLP	.05	.02	.01
☐	674 Tim Spehr MLP	.05	.02	.01
☐	675A Jeff Gardner MLP ERR	.10	.05	.01
	(Shortstop on back, should say Pitcher)			
☐	675B Jeff Gardner MLP COR	.10	.05	.01
☐	676 Rico Rossy MLP	.10	.05	.01
☐	677 Roberto Hernandez MLP	.12	.05	.02
☐	678 Ted Wood MLP	.10	.05	.01
☐	679 Cal Eldred MLP	.35	.16	.04
☐	680 Sean Berry MLP	.08	.04	.01
☐	681 Rickey Henderson RS	.10	.05	.01
☐	682 Nolan Ryan RS	.25	.11	.03
☐	683 Dennis Martinez RS	.05	.02	.01
☐	684 Wilson Alvarez RS	.05	.02	.01
☐	685 Joe Carter RS	.10	.05	.01
☐	686 Dave Winfield RS	.10	.05	.01
☐	687 David Cone RS	.08	.04	.01
☐	688 Jose Canseco LL	.12	.05	.02
☐	689 Howard Johnson LL	.05	.02	.01
☐	690 Julio Franco LL	.05	.02	.01
☐	691 Terry Pendleton LL	.10	.05	.01
☐	692 Cecil Fielder LL	.10	.05	.01
☐	693 Scott Erickson LL	.10	.05	.01
☐	694 Tom Glavine LL	.10	.05	.01
☐	695 Dennis Martinez LL	.05	.02	.01
☐	696 Bryan Harvey LL	.05	.02	.01
☐	697 Lee Smith LL	.05	.02	.01
☐	698 Super Siblings	.15	.07	.02
	Roberto Alomar Sandy Alomar Jr.			
☐	699 The Indispensables	.12	.05	.02
	Bobby Bonilla Will Clark			
☐	700 Teamwork	.05	.02	.01
	Mark Wohlers Kent Mercker Alejandro Pena			
☐	701 Tiger Tandems	.20	.09	.03
	Stacy Jones Bo Jackson Gregg Olson Frank Thomas			
☐	702 The Ignitors	.05	.02	.01
	Paul Molitor Brett Butler			
☐	703 Indispensables II	.15	.07	.02
	Cal Ripken Joe Carter			
☐	704 Power Packs	.10	.05	.01
	Barry Larkin Kirby Puckett			
☐	705 Today and Tomorrow	.10	.05	.01
	Mo Vaughn Cecil Fielder			
☐	706 Teenage Sensations	.05	.02	.01
	Ramon Martinez Ozzie Guillen			
☐	707 Designated Hitters	.05	.02	.01
	Harold Baines Wade Boggs			
☐	708 Robin Yount PV	.15	.07	.02
☐	709 Ken Griffey Jr. PV UER	.75	.35	.09
	(Missing quotations on back; BA has .322, but was actually .327)			
☐	710 Nolan Ryan PV	.60	.25	.08
☐	711 Cal Ripken PV	.50	.23	.06
☐	712 Frank Thomas PV	.75	.35	.09
☐	713 Dave Justice PV	.35	.16	.04
☐	714 Checklist Card	.05	.01	.00
☐	715 Checklist Card	.05	.01	.00
☐	716 Checklist Card	.05	.01	.00
☐	717 Checklist Card	.05	.01	.00
☐	718 Checklist Card	.05	.01	.00
☐	719 Checklist Card	.05	.01	.00
☐	720A Checklist Card ERR	.05	.01	.00
	(659 Rob Mauer)			
☐	720B Checklist Card COR	.05	.01	.00
	(659 Rob Maurer)			

1992 Fleer All-Stars

The 24-card All-Stars series was randomly inserted in 1992 Fleer wax packs (fin-sealed single packs). The cards measure the standard size (2 1/2" by 3 1/2"). The glossy color photos on the fronts are bordered in black and

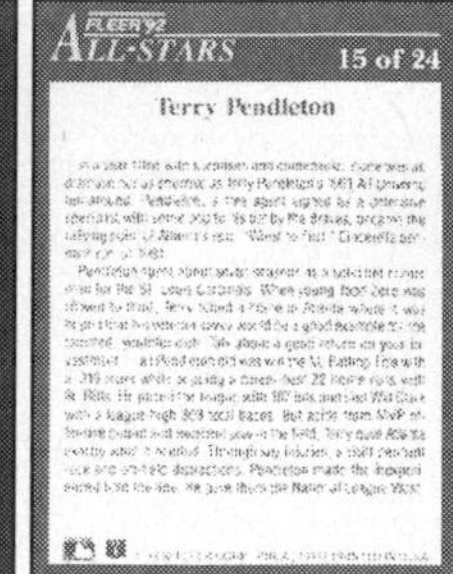

accented above and below with gold stripes and lettering. A diamond with a color head shot of the player is superimposed at the lower right corner of the picture. The player's name and the words "Fleer '92 All-Stars" appear above and below the picture respectively in gold foil lettering. On a white background with black borders, the back has career highlights with the words "Fleer '92 All-Stars" appearing at the top in yellow lettering. The cards are numbered on the back.

	MT	EX-MT	VG
COMPLETE SET (24)	40.00	18.00	5.00
COMMON PLAYER (1-24)	1.00	.45	.13
□ 1 Felix Jose	1.25	.55	.16
□ 2 Tony Gwynn	2.00	.90	.25
□ 3 Barry Bonds	3.00	1.35	.40
□ 4 Bobby Bonilla	1.25	.55	.16
□ 5 Mike LaValliere	1.00	.45	.13
□ 6 Tom Glavine	2.00	.90	.25
□ 7 Ramon Martinez	1.25	.55	.16
□ 8 Lee Smith	1.00	.45	.13
□ 9 Mickey Tettleton	1.00	.45	.13
□ 10 Scott Erickson	1.25	.55	.16
□ 11 Frank Thomas	10.00	4.50	1.25
□ 12 Danny Tartabull	1.25	.55	.16
□ 13 Will Clark	3.00	1.35	.40
□ 14 Ryne Sandberg	3.50	1.55	.45
□ 15 Terry Pendleton	1.00	.45	.13
□ 16 Barry Larkin	1.50	.65	.19
□ 17 Rafael Palmeiro	1.25	.55	.16
□ 18 Julio Franco	1.00	.45	.13
□ 19 Robin Ventura	3.00	1.35	.40
□ 20 Cal Ripken UER (Candidte; total bases misspelled as based)	5.00	2.30	.60
□ 21 Joe Carter	2.00	.90	.25
□ 22 Kirby Puckett	3.00	1.35	.40
□ 23 Ken Griffey Jr.	7.00	3.10	.85
□ 24 Jose Canseco	3.00	1.35	.40

1992 Fleer Lumber Company

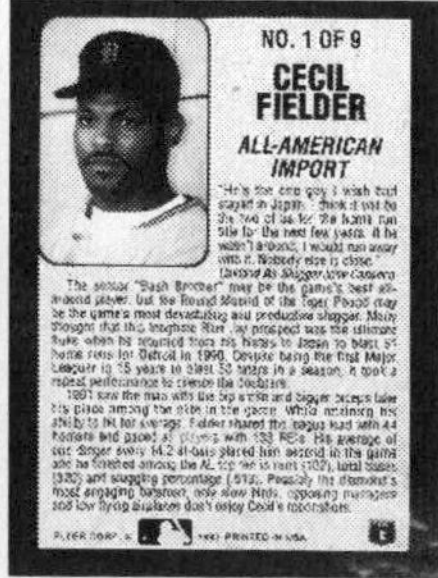

The 1992 Fleer Lumber Company set features nine outstanding hitters in Major League Baseball. The cards measure the standard size (2 1/2" by 3 1/2"). Inside a black glossy frame, the fronts display color action player photos, with the player's name printed in black in a gold foil bar beneath the picture. The wider right border contains the catch phrase "The Lumber Co." in the shape of a baseball bat, complete with woodgrain streaks. The backs carry a color head shot and, on a tan panel, a summary of the player's hitting performance and records. The cards are numbered on the back with an L prefix.

	MT	EX-MT	VG
COMPLETE SET (9)	20.00	9.00	2.50
COMMON PLAYER (L1-L9)	1.50	.65	.19
□ L1 Cecil Fielder	2.50	1.15	.30
□ L2 Mickey Tettleton	1.50	.65	.19
□ L3 Darryl Strawberry	2.50	1.15	.30
□ L4 Ryne Sandberg	4.50	2.00	.55
□ L5 Jose Canseco	4.00	1.80	.50
□ L6 Matt Williams	1.50	.65	.19
□ L7 Cal Ripken	7.00	3.10	.85
□ L8 Barry Bonds	4.00	1.80	.50
□ L9 Ron Gant	2.00	.90	.25

1992 Fleer Roger Clemens

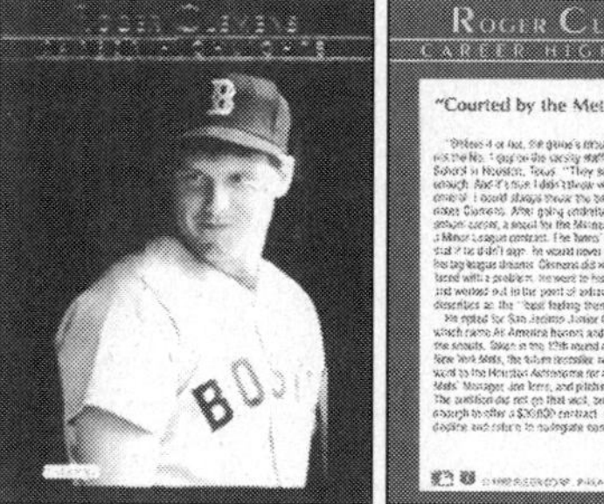

Roger Clemens served as a spokesperson for Fleer during 1992 and was the exclusive subject of this 15-card set. The first 12-card Roger Clemens "Career Highlights" subseries was randomly inserted in 1992 Fleer wax packs. Some signed cards were inserted and one could be won by entering a drawing. Moreover, a three-card Clemens subset (13-15) was available through a special mail-in offer. The cards measure the standard size (2 1/2" by 3 1/2"). The glossy color photos on the fronts are bordered in black and accented with gold stripes and lettering on the top of the card. On a pale yellow background with black borders, the back has player profile and career highlights. The cards are numbered on the back.

	MT	EX-MT	VG
COMPLETE SET (15)	16.00	7.25	2.00
COMMON CLEMENS (1-12)	1.50	.65	.19
COMMON SEND-OFF (13-15)	1.50	.65	.19
□ 1 Quiet Storm	1.50	.65	.19
□ 2 Courted By Mets and Twins	1.50	.65	.19
□ 3 The Show	1.50	.65	.19
□ 4 Rocket Launched	1.50	.65	.19
□ 5 Time Of Trial	1.50	.65	.19
□ 6 Break Through	1.50	.65	.19
□ 7 Play It Again Roger	1.50	.65	.19
□ 8 Business As Usual	1.50	.65	.19
□ 9 Heeee's Back	1.50	.65	.19
□ 10 Blood, Sweat, and Tears	1.50	.65	.19
□ 11 Prime Of Life	1.50	.65	.19
□ 12 Man For Every Season	1.50	.65	.19
□ 13 Cooperstown Bound	1.50	.65	.19
□ 14 The Heat of the Moment	1.50	.65	.19

	MT	EX-MT	VG
☐ 15 Final Words ƒ Q and A with "The Rocket"	1.50	.65	.19
☐ AU0 Roger Clemens (Certified signature)	150.00	70.00	19.00

1992 Fleer Rookie Sensations

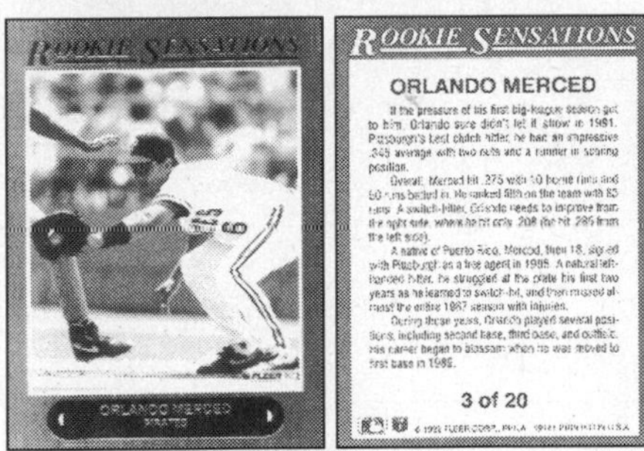

The 20-card Fleer Rookie Sensations series was randomly inserted in 1992 Fleer 35-card cello packs. The cards measure the standard size (2 1/2" by 3 1/2"). The glossy color photos on the fronts have a white border on a royal blue card face. The words "Rookie Sensations" appear above the picture in gold foil lettering, while the player's name appears on a gold foil plaque beneath the picture. On a light blue background with royal blue borders, the backs have career summary. The cards are numbered on the back. Through a mail-in offer for ten Fleer baseball card wrappers and 1.00 for postage and handling, Fleer offered an uncut 8 1/2" by 11" numbered promo sheet picturing ten of the 20-card set on each side in a reduced-size front-only format. The offer indicated an expiration date of July 31, 1992, or whenever the production quantity of 250,000 sheets was exhausted.

	MT	EX-MT	VG
COMPLETE SET (20)	100.00	45.00	12.50
COMMON PLAYER (1-20)	2.00	.90	.25
☐ 1 Frank Thomas	50.00	23.00	6.25
☐ 2 Todd Van Poppel	7.00	3.10	.85
☐ 3 Orlando Merced	3.00	1.35	.40
☐ 4 Jeff Bagwell	16.00	7.25	2.00
☐ 5 Jeff Fassero	2.00	.90	.25
☐ 6 Darren Lewis	2.50	1.15	.30
☐ 7 Milt Cuyler	2.00	.90	.25
☐ 8 Mike Timlin	2.00	.90	.25
☐ 9 Brian McRae	3.00	1.35	.40
☐ 10 Chuck Knoblauch	12.00	5.50	1.50
☐ 11 Rich DeLucia	2.00	.90	.25
☐ 12 Ivan Rodriguez	16.00	7.25	2.00
☐ 13 Juan Guzman	20.00	9.00	2.50
☐ 14 Steve Chitren	2.00	.90	.25
☐ 15 Mark Wohlers	3.00	1.35	.40
☐ 16 Wes Chamberlain	3.00	1.35	.40
☐ 17 Ray Lankford	11.00	4.90	1.40
☐ 18 Chito Martinez	2.00	.90	.25
☐ 19 Phil Plantier	10.00	4.50	1.25
☐ 20 Scott Leius UER (Misspelled Lieus on card front)	2.00	.90	.25

1992 Fleer Smoke 'n Heat

This 12-card set features outstanding major league pitchers, especially the premier fastball pitchers in both leagues. The cards were randomly inserted in Fleer's 1992 Christmas baseball set. The cards measure the standard size (2 1/2" by 3 1/2"). The front design features color action player photos

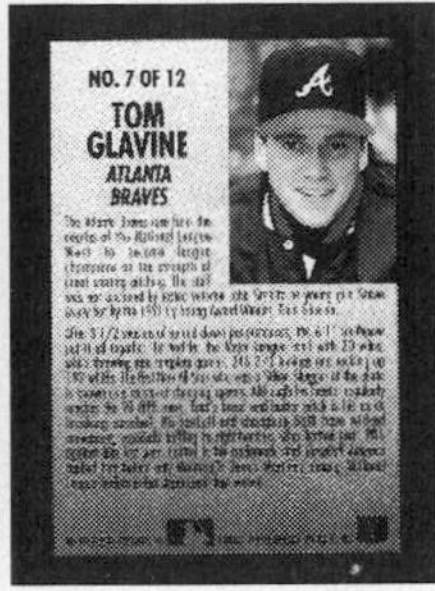

bordered in black. The player's name appears in a gold foil bar beneath the picture, and the words "Smoke 'n Heat" are printed vertically in the wider right border. Within black borders and on a background of yellow shading to orange, the backs carry a color head shot and player profile. The cards are numbered on the back.

	MT	EX-MT	VG
COMPLETE SET (12)	10.00	4.50	1.25
COMMON PLAYER (S1-S12)	.75	.35	.09
☐ S1 Lee Smith	.75	.35	.09
☐ S2 Jack McDowell	1.00	.45	.13
☐ S3 David Cone	1.00	.45	.13
☐ S4 Roger Clemens	3.00	1.35	.40
☐ S5 Nolan Ryan	5.00	2.30	.60
☐ S6 Scott Erickson	1.00	.45	.13
☐ S7 Tom Glavine	1.25	.55	.16
☐ S8 Dwight Gooden	1.00	.45	.13
☐ S9 Andy Benes	1.00	.45	.13
☐ S10 Steve Avery	1.50	.65	.19
☐ S11 Randy Johnson	.75	.35	.09
☐ S12 Jim Abbott	1.00	.45	.13

1992 Fleer Team Leaders

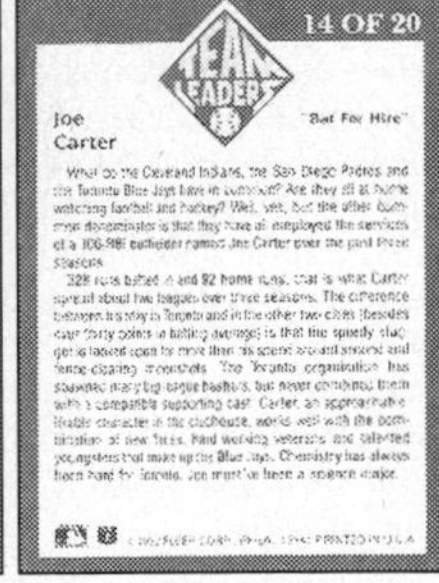

The 20-card Fleer Team Leaders series was randomly inserted in 1992 Fleer 42-card rack packs. The cards measure the standard size (2 1/2" by 3 1/2"). The glossy color photos on the fronts are bordered in white and green. Two gold foil stripes below the picture intersect a diamond-shaped "Team Leaders" emblem. On a pale green background with green borders, the backs have career summary. The cards are numbered on the back.

	MT	EX-MT	VG
COMPLETE SET (20)	30.00	13.50	3.80
COMMON PLAYER (1-20)	1.00	.45	.13
☐ 1 Don Mattingly	2.00	.90	.25
☐ 2 Howard Johnson	1.00	.45	.13
☐ 3 Chris Sabo UER (Where he it, should be Where he hit)	1.00	.45	.13
☐ 4 Carlton Fisk	1.25	.55	.16

	MT	EX-MT	VG
☐ 5 Kirby Puckett	3.00	1.35	.40
☐ 6 Cecil Fielder	2.00	.90	.25
☐ 7 Tony Gwynn	2.00	.90	.25
☐ 8 Will Clark	3.00	1.35	.40
☐ 9 Bobby Bonilla	1.25	.55	.16
☐ 10 Len Dykstra	1.00	.45	.13
☐ 11 Tom Glavine	2.00	.90	.25
☐ 12 Rafael Palmeiro	1.25	.55	.16
☐ 13 Wade Boggs	2.00	.90	.25
☐ 14 Joe Carter	2.00	.90	.25
☐ 15 Ken Griffey Jr.	7.00	3.10	.85
☐ 16 Darryl Strawberry	2.00	.90	.25
☐ 17 Cal Ripken	5.00	2.30	.60
☐ 18 Danny Tartabull	1.25	.55	.16
☐ 19 Jose Canseco	3.00	1.35	.40
☐ 20 Andre Dawson	1.25	.55	.16
☐ 23 Barry Bonds	.50	.23	.06
☐ 24 Roberto Alomar	.60	.25	.08

1992 Fleer The Performer

This 24-card standard-size (2 1/2" by 3 1/2") set was produced by Fleer for 7-Eleven. During April and May at any of the 1,600 participating 7-Eleven stores, customers who purchased eight gallons or more of mid-grade or premium Citgo-brand gasoline received a packet of five trading cards. During June or while supplies last, customers who wanted additional cards could receive three trading cards of their choice per eight gallon or more fill-up by sending in a self-addressed envelope with 1.00 to cover postage and handling. The front design has color action player photos, with a metallic blue-green border that fades to white as one moves down the card face. The card front prominently features "The Performer". The team logo, player's name, and his position appear in the wider right border. The top half of the backs have close-up photos, while the bottom half carry biography and complete career statistics. The cards are numbered on the back.

	MT	EX-MT	VG
COMPLETE SET (24)	9.00	4.00	1.15
COMMON PLAYER (1-24)	.25	.11	.03
☐ 1 Nolan Ryan	1.00	.45	.13
☐ 2 Frank Thomas	1.25	.55	.16
☐ 3 Ryne Sandberg	.75	.35	.09
☐ 4 Ken Griffey Jr.	1.00	.45	.13
☐ 5 Cal Ripken	1.00	.45	.13
☐ 6 Roger Clemens	.75	.35	.09
☐ 7 Cecil Fielder	.35	.16	.04
☐ 8 Dave Justice	.50	.23	.06
☐ 9 Wade Boggs	.50	.23	.06
☐ 10 Tony Gwynn	.50	.23	.06
☐ 11 Kirby Puckett	.60	.25	.08
☐ 12 Darryl Strawberry	.50	.23	.06
☐ 13 Jose Canseco	.60	.25	.08
☐ 14 Barry Larkin	.25	.11	.03
☐ 15 Terry Pendleton	.25	.11	.03
☐ 16 Don Mattingly	.50	.23	.06
☐ 17 Rickey Henderson	.50	.23	.06
☐ 18 Ruben Sierra	.50	.23	.06
☐ 19 Jeff Bagwell	.50	.23	.06
☐ 20 Tom Glavine	.35	.16	.04
☐ 21 Ramon Martinez	.25	.11	.03
☐ 22 Will Clark	.60	.25	.08

1992 Fleer Update

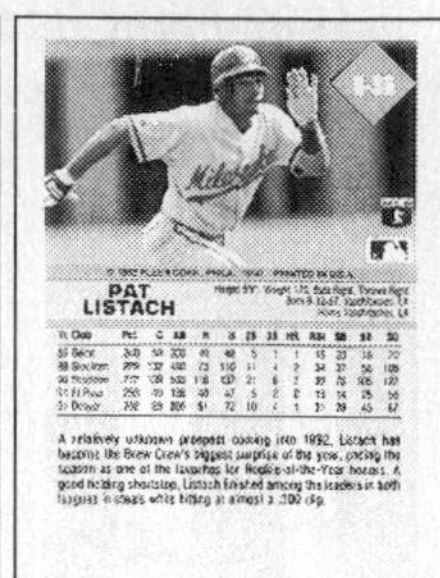

The 1992 Fleer Update set contains 132 cards measuring the standard size (2 1/2" by 3 1/2"). This year's set, which was available only through hobby dealers, included a four-card, black-bordered "92 Headliners" insert subset. For the Headliners the lettering above the photos and stripe carrying the player's name at the card bottom are both in gold foil. The front design of the regular cards in the update set has color action player photos, with a metallic blue-green border that fades to white as one moves down the card face. The team logo, player's name, and his position appear in the wider right border. The top half of the backs has a close-up photo, while the bottom half carry biography and complete career statistics. The cards are checklisted below alphabetically within and according to teams for each league as follows: Baltimore Orioles (1-3), Boston Red Sox (4-6), California Angels (7-11), Chicago White Sox (12-14), Cleveland Indians (15-18), Detroit Tigers (19-25), Kansas City Royals (26-32), Milwaukee Brewers (33-38), Minnesota Twins (39-41), New York Yankees (42-46), Oakland Athletics (47-53), Seattle Mariners (54-58), Texas Rangers (59-62), Toronto Blue Jays (63-67), Atlanta Braves (68-71), Chicago Cubs (72-77), Cincinnati Reds (78-84), Houston Astros (85-88), Los Angeles Dodgers (89-94), Montreal Expos (95-100), New York Mets (101-107), Philadelphia Phillies (108-112), Pittsburgh Pirates (113-117), St. Louis Cardinals (118-121), San Diego Padres (122-126), and San Francisco Giants (127-132). The cards are numbered on the back with a U prefix. The key Rookie Cards in this set are Pat Listach, David Nied, Mike Piazza, and Tim Wakefield.

	MT	EX-MT	VG
COMPLETE FACT.SET (136)	27.00	12.00	3.40
COMPLETE SET (132)	17.00	7.75	2.10
COMMON PLAYER (1-132)	.05	.02	.01
COMPLETE HEADLINERS SET (4)	10.00	4.50	1.25
COMMON HEADLINERS (H1-H4)	.50	.23	.06
☐ 1 Todd Frohwirth	.05	.02	.01
☐ 2 Alan Mills	.05	.02	.01
☐ 3 Rick Sutcliffe	.08	.04	.01
☐ 4 John Valentin	.25	.11	.03
☐ 5 Frank Viola	.08	.04	.01
☐ 6 Bob Zupcic	.25	.11	.03
☐ 7 Mike Butcher	.10	.05	.01
☐ 8 Chad Curtis	.30	.14	.04
☐ 9 Damion Easley	.40	.18	.05
☐ 10 Tim Salmon	.60	.25	.08
☐ 11 Julio Valera	.08	.04	.01
☐ 12 George Bell	.08	.04	.01
☐ 13 Roberto Hernandez	.12	.05	.02
☐ 14 Shawn Jeter	.15	.07	.02
☐ 15 Thomas Howard	.05	.02	.01
☐ 16 Jesse Levis	.15	.07	.02
☐ 17 Kenny Lofton	.40	.18	.05

☐ 18 Paul Sorrento .08 .04 .01
☐ 19 Rico Brogna .10 .05 .01
☐ 20 John Doherty .15 .07 .02
☐ 21 Dan Gladden .05 .02 .01
☐ 22 Buddy Groom .10 .05 .01
☐ 23 Shawn Hare .10 .05 .01
☐ 24 John Kiely .10 .05 .01
☐ 25 Kurt Knudsen .10 .05 .01
☐ 26 Gregg Jefferies .08 .04 .01
☐ 27 Wally Joyner .08 .04 .01
☐ 28 Kevin Koslofski .10 .05 .01
☐ 29 Kevin McReynolds .08 .04 .01
☐ 30 Rusty Meacham .05 .02 .01
☐ 31 Keith Miller .05 .02 .01
☐ 32 Hipolito Pichardo .10 .05 .01
☐ 33 James Austin .10 .05 .01
☐ 34 Scott Fletcher .05 .02 .01
☐ 35 John Jaha .30 .14 .04
☐ 36 Pat Listach 1.50 .65 .19
☐ 37 Dave Nilsson .15 .07 .02
☐ 38 Kevin Seitzer .08 .04 .01
☐ 39 Tom Edens .05 .02 .01
☐ 40 Pat Mahomes .25 .11 .03
☐ 41 John Smiley .08 .04 .01
☐ 42 Charlie Hayes .05 .02 .01
☐ 43 Sam Militello .30 .14 .04
☐ 44 Andy Stankiewicz .15 .07 .02
☐ 45 Danny Tartabull .08 .04 .01
☐ 46 Bob Wickman .30 .14 .04
☐ 47 Jerry Browne .05 .02 .01
☐ 48 Kevin Campbell .10 .05 .01
☐ 49 Vince Horsman .10 .05 .01
☐ 50 Troy Neel .25 .11 .03
☐ 51 Ruben Sierra .15 .07 .02
☐ 52 Bruce Walton .05 .02 .01
☐ 53 Willie Wilson .05 .02 .01
☐ 54 Bret Boone .50 .23 .06
☐ 55 Dave Fleming .50 .23 .06
☐ 56 Kevin Mitchell .08 .04 .01
☐ 57 Jeff Nelson .12 .05 .02
☐ 58 Shane Turner .05 .02 .01
☐ 59 Jose Canseco .25 .11 .03
☐ 60 Jeff Frye .10 .05 .01
☐ 61 Danny Leon .10 .05 .01
☐ 62 Roger Pavlik .15 .07 .02
☐ 63 David Cone .10 .05 .01
☐ 64 Pat Hentgen .10 .05 .01
☐ 65 Randy Knorr .10 .05 .01
☐ 66 Jack Morris .10 .05 .01
☐ 67 Dave Winfield .10 .05 .01
☐ 68 David Nied 3.00 1.35 .40
☐ 69 Otis Nixon .08 .04 .01
☐ 70 Alejandro Pena .05 .02 .01
☐ 71 Jeff Reardon .08 .04 .01
☐ 72 Alex Arias .20 .09 .03
☐ 73 Jim Bullinger .10 .05 .01
☐ 74 Mike Morgan .05 .02 .01
☐ 75 Rey Sanchez .12 .05 .02
☐ 76 Bob Scanlan .05 .02 .01
☐ 77 Sammy Sosa .05 .02 .01
☐ 78 Scott Bankhead .05 .02 .01
☐ 79 Tim Belcher .08 .04 .01
☐ 80 Steve Foster .10 .05 .01
☐ 81 Willie Greene .40 .18 .05
☐ 82 Bip Roberts .08 .04 .01
☐ 83 Scott Ruskin .05 .02 .01
☐ 84 Greg Swindell .08 .04 .01
☐ 85 Juan Guerrero .12 .05 .02
☐ 86 Butch Henry .12 .05 .02
☐ 87 Doug Jones .05 .02 .01
☐ 88 Brian Williams .25 .11 .03
☐ 89 Tom Candiotti .05 .02 .01
☐ 90 Eric Davis .08 .04 .01
☐ 91 Carlos Hernandez .05 .02 .01
☐ 92 Mike Piazza .60 .25 .08
☐ 93 Mike Sharperson .05 .02 .01
☐ 94 Eric Young .25 .11 .03
☐ 95 Moises Alou .10 .05 .01
☐ 96 Greg Colbrunn .10 .05 .01
☐ 97 Wilfredo Cordero .15 .07 .02
☐ 98 Ken Hill .08 .04 .01
☐ 99 John Vander Wal .15 .07 .02
☐ 100 John Wetteland .05 .02 .01
☐ 101 Bobby Bonilla .10 .05 .01
☐ 102 Eric Hillman .20 .09 .03
☐ 103 Pat Howell .20 .09 .03
☐ 104 Jeff Kent .30 .14 .04
☐ 105 Dick Schofield .05 .02 .01
☐ 106 Ryan Thompson .60 .25 .08
☐ 107 Chico Walker .05 .02 .01
☐ 108 Juan Bell .05 .02 .01
☐ 109 Mariano Duncan .05 .02 .01
☐ 110 Jeff Grotewold .10 .05 .01
☐ 111 Ben Rivera .10 .05 .01
☐ 112 Curt Schilling .08 .04 .01
☐ 113 Victor Cole .15 .07 .02
☐ 114 Albert Martin .35 .16 .04
☐ 115 Roger Mason .05 .02 .01
☐ 116 Blas Minor .10 .05 .01
☐ 117 Tim Wakefield 3.00 1.35 .40
☐ 118 Mark Clark .10 .05 .01
☐ 119 Rheal Cormier .10 .05 .01
☐ 120 Donovan Osborne .30 .14 .04
☐ 121 Todd Worrell .05 .02 .01
☐ 122 Jeremy Hernandez .10 .05 .01
☐ 123 Randy Myers .08 .04 .01
☐ 124 Frank Seminara .20 .09 .03
☐ 125 Gary Sheffield .25 .11 .03
☐ 126 Dan Walters .15 .07 .02
☐ 127 Steve Hosey .30 .14 .04
☐ 128 Mike Jackson .05 .02 .01
☐ 129 Jim Pena .10 .05 .01
☐ 130 Cory Snyder .05 .02 .01
☐ 131 Bill Swift .05 .02 .01
☐ 132 Checklist 1-132 .08 .01 .00
☐ H1 Ken Griffey Jr. 7.00 3.10 .85
1992 All-Star Game MVP
☐ H2 Robin Yount 2.00 .90 .25
3000 Career Hits
☐ H3 Jeff Reardon .50 .23 .06
ML Career Saves Record
☐ H4 Cecil Fielder 2.00 .90 .25
Record RBI Performance

1993 Fleer

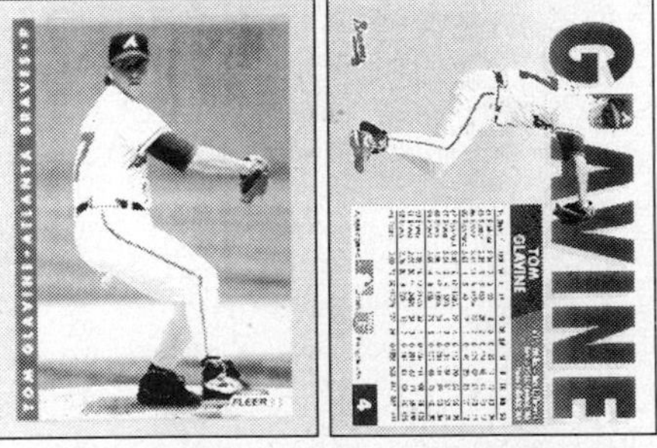

The first series of the 1993 Fleer baseball set comprises 360 cards measuring the standard size (2 1/2" by 3 1/2"). Randomly inserted in the wax packs were a three-card Golden Moments subset, a 12-card NL All-Stars subset, an 18-card Major League Prospects subset, and three Pro-Visions cards. The fronts show glossy color action player photos bordered in silver. A team color-coded stripe edges the left side of the picture and carries the player's name and team name. On a background that shades from white to silver, the horizontally oriented backs have the player's last name in team-color coded block lettering, a cut out color player photo, and a box displaying biographical and statistical information. The cards are checklisted below alphabetically within and according to teams for each league as follows: Atlanta Braves (1-16), Chicago Cubs (17-28), Cincinnati Reds (29-44), Houston Astros (45-56), Los Angeles Dodgers (57-69), Montreal Expos (70-83), New York Mets (84-96), Philadelphia Phillies (97-109), Pittsburgh Pirates (110-123), St. Louis Cardinals (124-136), San Diego Padres (137-149), San Francisco Giants (150-162), Baltimore Orioles (163-175), Boston Red Sox (176-186), California Angels (187-198), Chicago White Sox (199-211), Cleveland Indians (212-223), Detroit Tigers (224-234), Kansas City Royals (235-246), Milwaukee Brewers (247-260), Minnesota Twins (261-275), New York Yankees (276-289), Oakland Athletics (290-303), Seattle Mariners (304-

316), Texas Rangers (317-329), and Toronto Blue Jays (330-343). Topical subsets featured include League Leaders (344-348), NL Round Trippers (349-353), and Super Star Specials (354-357). The set concludes with checklists (358-360).

	MT	EX-MT	VG
COMPLETE SET (360)	15.00	6.75	1.90
COMMON PLAYER (1-360)	.04	.02	.01
☐ 1 Steve Avery	.15	.07	.02
☐ 2 Sid Bream	.04	.02	.01
☐ 3 Ron Gant	.06	.03	.01
☐ 4 Tom Glavine	.12	.05	.02
☐ 5 Brian Hunter	.06	.03	.01
☐ 6 Ryan Klesko	.30	.14	.04
☐ 7 Charlie Leibrandt	.04	.02	.01
☐ 8 Kent Mercker	.04	.02	.01
☐ 9 David Nied	1.00	.45	.13
☐ 10 Otis Nixon	.04	.02	.01
☐ 11 Greg Olson	.04	.02	.01
☐ 12 Terry Pendleton	.06	.03	.01
☐ 13 Deion Sanders	.12	.05	.02
☐ 14 John Smoltz	.10	.05	.01
☐ 15 Mike Stanton	.04	.02	.01
☐ 16 Mark Wohlers	.06	.03	.01
☐ 17 Paul Assenmacher	.04	.02	.01
☐ 18 Steve Buechele	.04	.02	.01
☐ 19 Shawon Dunston	.06	.03	.01
☐ 20 Mark Grace	.06	.03	.01
☐ 21 Derrick May	.06	.03	.01
☐ 22 Chuck McElroy	.04	.02	.01
☐ 23 Mike Morgan	.04	.02	.01
☐ 24 Rey Sanchez	.04	.02	.01
☐ 25 Ryne Sandberg	.20	.09	.03
☐ 26 Bob Scanlan	.04	.02	.01
☐ 27 Sammy Sosa	.04	.02	.01
☐ 28 Rick Wilkins	.04	.02	.01
☐ 29 Bobby Ayala	.20	.09	.03
☐ 30 Tim Belcher	.06	.03	.01
☐ 31 Jeff Branson	.04	.02	.01
☐ 32 Norm Charlton	.04	.02	.01
☐ 33 Steve Foster	.04	.02	.01
☐ 34 Willie Greene	.08	.04	.01
☐ 35 Chris Hammond	.04	.02	.01
☐ 36 Milt Hill	.04	.02	.01
☐ 37 Hal Morris	.06	.03	.01
☐ 38 Joe Oliver	.04	.02	.01
☐ 39 Paul O'Neill	.06	.03	.01
☐ 40 Tim Pugh	.25	.11	.03
☐ 41 Jose Rijo	.06	.03	.01
☐ 42 Bip Roberts	.06	.03	.01
☐ 43 Chris Sabo	.06	.03	.01
☐ 44 Reggie Sanders	.12	.05	.02
☐ 45 Eric Anthony	.06	.03	.01
☐ 46 Jeff Bagwell	.20	.09	.03
☐ 47 Craig Biggio	.06	.03	.01
☐ 48 Joe Boever	.04	.02	.01
☐ 49 Casey Candaele	.04	.02	.01
☐ 50 Steve Finley	.04	.02	.01
☐ 51 Luis Gonzalez	.06	.03	.01
☐ 52 Pete Harnisch	.04	.02	.01
☐ 53 Xavier Hernandez	.04	.02	.01
☐ 54 Doug Jones	.04	.02	.01
☐ 55 Eddie Taubensee	.06	.03	.01
☐ 56 Brian Williams	.06	.03	.01
☐ 57 Pedro Astacio	.20	.09	.03
☐ 58 Todd Benzinger	.04	.02	.01
☐ 59 Brett Butler	.06	.03	.01
☐ 60 Tom Candiotti	.04	.02	.01
☐ 61 Lenny Harris	.04	.02	.01
☐ 62 Carlos Hernandez	.06	.03	.01
☐ 63 Orel Hershiser	.06	.03	.01
☐ 64 Eric Karros	.35	.16	.04
☐ 65 Ramon Martinez	.06	.03	.01
☐ 66 Jose Offerman	.06	.03	.01
☐ 67 Mike Scioscia	.04	.02	.01
☐ 68 Mike Sharperson	.04	.02	.01
☐ 69 Eric Young	.12	.05	.02
☐ 70 Moises Alou	.06	.03	.01
☐ 71 Ivan Calderon	.04	.02	.01
☐ 72 Archi Cianfrocco	.06	.03	.01
☐ 73 Wilfredo Cordero	.10	.05	.01
☐ 74 Delino DeShields	.10	.05	.01
☐ 75 Mark Gardner	.04	.02	.01
☐ 76 Ken Hill	.06	.03	.01
☐ 77 Tim Laker	.12	.05	.02
☐ 78 Chris Nabholz	.06	.03	.01
☐ 79 Mel Rojas	.04	.02	.01
☐ 80 John Vander Wal	.04	.02	.01
☐ 81 Larry Walker	.12	.05	.02
☐ 82 Tim Wallach	.06	.03	.01
☐ 83 John Wetteland	.04	.02	.01
☐ 84 Bobby Bonilla	.10	.05	.01
☐ 85 Daryl Boston	.04	.02	.01
☐ 86 Sid Fernandez	.06	.03	.01
☐ 87 Eric Hillman	.15	.07	.02
☐ 88 Todd Hundley	.04	.02	.01
☐ 89 Howard Johnson	.06	.03	.01
☐ 90 Jeff Kent	.12	.05	.02
☐ 91 Eddie Murray	.10	.05	.01
☐ 92 Bill Pecota	.04	.02	.01
☐ 93 Bret Saberhagen	.06	.03	.01
☐ 94 Dick Schofield	.04	.02	.01
☐ 95 Pete Schourek	.06	.03	.01
☐ 96 Anthony Young	.06	.03	.01
☐ 97 Ruben Amaro Jr.	.04	.02	.01
☐ 98 Juan Bell	.04	.02	.01
☐ 99 Wes Chamberlain	.04	.02	.01
☐ 100 Darren Daulton	.06	.03	.01
☐ 101 Mariano Duncan	.04	.02	.01
☐ 102 Mike Hartley	.04	.02	.01
☐ 103 Ricky Jordan	.04	.02	.01
☐ 104 John Kruk	.06	.03	.01
☐ 105 Mickey Morandini	.06	.03	.01
☐ 106 Terry Mulholland	.04	.02	.01
☐ 107 Ben Rivera	.06	.03	.01
☐ 108 Curt Schilling	.04	.02	.01
☐ 109 Keith Shepherd	.20	.09	.03
☐ 110 Stan Belinda	.04	.02	.01
☐ 111 Jay Bell	.04	.02	.01
☐ 112 Barry Bonds	.20	.09	.03
☐ 113 Jeff King	.04	.02	.01
☐ 114 Mike LaValliere	.04	.02	.01
☐ 115 Jose Lind	.04	.02	.01
☐ 116 Roger Mason	.04	.02	.01
☐ 117 Orlando Merced	.06	.03	.01
☐ 118 Bob Patterson	.04	.02	.01
☐ 119 Don Slaught	.04	.02	.01
☐ 120 Zane Smith	.04	.02	.01
☐ 121 Randy Tomlin	.04	.02	.01
☐ 122 Andy Van Slyke	.06	.03	.01
☐ 123 Tim Wakefield	.60	.25	.08
☐ 124 Rheal Cormier	.04	.02	.01
☐ 125 Bernard Gilkey	.06	.03	.01
☐ 126 Felix Jose	.06	.03	.01
☐ 127 Ray Lankford	.10	.05	.01
☐ 128 Bob McClure	.04	.02	.01
☐ 129 Donovan Osborne	.12	.05	.02
☐ 130 Tom Pagnozzi	.04	.02	.01
☐ 131 Geronimo Pena	.04	.02	.01
☐ 132 Mike Perez	.06	.03	.01
☐ 133 Lee Smith	.06	.03	.01
☐ 134 Bob Tewksbury	.06	.03	.01
☐ 135 Todd Worrell	.04	.02	.01
☐ 136 Todd Zeile	.06	.03	.01
☐ 137 Jerald Clark	.04	.02	.01
☐ 138 Tony Gwynn	.12	.05	.02
☐ 139 Greg W. Harris	.04	.02	.01
☐ 140 Jeremy Hernandez	.04	.02	.01
☐ 141 Darrin Jackson	.04	.02	.01
☐ 142 Mike Maddux	.04	.02	.01
☐ 143 Fred McGriff	.12	.05	.02
☐ 144 Jose Melendez	.04	.02	.01
☐ 145 Rich Rodriguez	.04	.02	.01
☐ 146 Frank Seminara	.04	.02	.01
☐ 147 Gary Sheffield	.20	.09	.03
☐ 148 Kurt Stillwell	.04	.02	.01
☐ 149 Dan Walters	.04	.02	.01
☐ 150 Rod Beck	.06	.03	.01
☐ 151 Bud Black	.04	.02	.01
☐ 152 Jeff Brantley	.04	.02	.01
☐ 153 John Burkett	.04	.02	.01
☐ 154 Will Clark	.20	.09	.03
☐ 155 Royce Clayton	.06	.03	.01
☐ 156 Mike Jackson	.04	.02	.01
☐ 157 Darren Lewis	.04	.02	.01
☐ 158 Kirt Manwaring	.04	.02	.01
☐ 159 Willie McGee	.06	.03	.01
☐ 160 Cory Snyder	.04	.02	.01
☐ 161 Bill Swift	.04	.02	.01
☐ 162 Trevor Wilson	.04	.02	.01
☐ 163 Brady Anderson	.06	.03	.01
☐ 164 Glenn Davis	.06	.03	.01
☐ 165 Mike Devereaux	.06	.03	.01
☐ 166 Todd Frohwirth	.04	.02	.01
☐ 167 Leo Gomez	.06	.03	.01
☐ 168 Chris Hoiles	.06	.03	.01
☐ 169 Ben McDonald	.06	.03	.01
☐ 170 Randy Milligan	.04	.02	.01
☐ 171 Alan Mills	.04	.02	.01
☐ 172 Mike Mussina	.30	.14	.04
☐ 173 Gregg Olson	.06	.03	.01
☐ 174 Arthur Rhodes	.10	.05	.01
☐ 175 David Segui	.04	.02	.01

☐ 176	Ellis Burks	.04	.02	.01
☐ 177	Roger Clemens	.20	.09	.03
☐ 178	Scott Cooper	.06	.03	.01
☐ 179	Danny Darwin	.04	.02	.01
☐ 180	Tony Fossas	.04	.02	.01
☐ 181	Paul Quantrill	.10	.05	.01
☐ 182	Jody Reed	.04	.02	.01
☐ 183	John Valentin	.12	.05	.02
☐ 184	Mo Vaughn	.06	.03	.01
☐ 185	Frank Viola	.06	.03	.01
☐ 186	Bob Zupcic	.06	.03	.01
☐ 187	Jim Abbott	.10	.05	.01
☐ 188	Gary DiSarcina	.06	.03	.01
☐ 189	Damion Easley	.15	.07	.02
☐ 190	Junior Felix	.04	.02	.01
☐ 191	Chuck Finley	.04	.02	.01
☐ 192	Joe Grahe	.04	.02	.01
☐ 193	Bryan Harvey	.04	.02	.01
☐ 194	Mark Langston	.06	.03	.01
☐ 195	John Orton	.04	.02	.01
☐ 196	Luis Polonia	.04	.02	.01
☐ 197	Tim Salmon	.30	.14	.04
☐ 198	Luis Sojo	.04	.02	.01
☐ 199	Wilson Alvarez	.04	.02	.01
☐ 200	George Bell	.06	.03	.01
☐ 201	Alex Fernandez	.06	.03	.01
☐ 202	Craig Grebeck	.04	.02	.01
☐ 203	Ozzie Guillen	.04	.02	.01
☐ 204	Lance Johnson	.04	.02	.01
☐ 205	Ron Karkovice	.04	.02	.01
☐ 206	Kirk McCaskill	.04	.02	.01
☐ 207	Jack McDowell	.06	.03	.01
☐ 208	Scott Radinsky	.04	.02	.01
☐ 209	Tim Raines	.06	.03	.01
☐ 210	Frank Thomas	.75	.35	.09
☐ 211	Robin Ventura	.15	.07	.02
☐ 212	Sandy Alomar Jr.	.06	.03	.01
☐ 213	Carlos Baerga	.15	.07	.02
☐ 214	Dennis Cook	.04	.02	.01
☐ 215	Thomas Howard	.04	.02	.01
☐ 216	Mark Lewis	.06	.03	.01
☐ 217	Derek Lilliquist	.04	.02	.01
☐ 218	Kenny Lofton	.20	.09	.03
☐ 219	Charles Nagy	.06	.03	.01
☐ 220	Steve Olin	.04	.02	.01
☐ 221	Paul Sorrento	.04	.02	.01
☐ 222	Jim Thome	.06	.03	.01
☐ 223	Mark Whiten	.06	.03	.01
☐ 224	Milt Cuyler	.04	.02	.01
☐ 225	Rob Deer	.06	.03	.01
☐ 226	John Doherty	.04	.02	.01
☐ 227	Cecil Fielder	.12	.05	.02
☐ 228	Travis Fryman	.20	.09	.03
☐ 229	Mike Henneman	.04	.02	.01
☐ 230	John Kiely	.04	.02	.01
☐ 231	Kurt Knudsen	.04	.02	.01
☐ 232	Scott Livingstone	.06	.03	.01
☐ 233	Tony Phillips	.04	.02	.01
☐ 234	Mickey Tettleton	.06	.03	.01
☐ 235	Kevin Appier	.06	.03	.01
☐ 236	George Brett	.10	.05	.01
☐ 237	Tom Gordon	.04	.02	.01
☐ 238	Gregg Jefferies	.06	.03	.01
☐ 239	Wally Joyner	.06	.03	.01
☐ 240	Kevin Koslofski	.04	.02	.01
☐ 241	Mike Macfarlane	.04	.02	.01
☐ 242	Brian McRae	.04	.02	.01
☐ 243	Rusty Meacham	.04	.02	.01
☐ 244	Keith Miller	.04	.02	.01
☐ 245	Jeff Montgomery	.04	.02	.01
☐ 246	Hipolito Pichardo	.04	.02	.01
☐ 247	Ricky Bones	.04	.02	.01
☐ 248	Cal Eldred	.20	.09	.03
☐ 249	Mike Fetters	.04	.02	.01
☐ 250	Darryl Hamilton	.06	.03	.01
☐ 251	Doug Henry	.04	.02	.01
☐ 252	John Jaha	.15	.07	.02
☐ 253	Pat Listach	.50	.23	.06
☐ 254	Paul Molitor	.06	.03	.01
☐ 255	Jaime Navarro	.06	.03	.01
☐ 256	Kevin Seitzer	.06	.03	.01
☐ 257	B.J. Surhoff	.04	.02	.01
☐ 258	Greg Vaughn	.06	.03	.01
☐ 259	Bill Wegman	.04	.02	.01
☐ 260	Robin Yount	.10	.05	.01
☐ 261	Rick Aguilera	.06	.03	.01
☐ 262	Chili Davis	.06	.03	.01
☐ 263	Scott Erickson	.04	.02	.01
☐ 264	Greg Gagne	.04	.02	.01
☐ 265	Mark Guthrie	.04	.02	.01
☐ 266	Brian Harper	.04	.02	.01
☐ 267	Kent Hrbek	.06	.03	.01
☐ 268	Terry Jorgensen	.04	.02	.01
☐ 269	Gene Larkin	.04	.02	.01
☐ 270	Scott Leius	.04	.02	.01
☐ 271	Pat Mahomes	.06	.03	.01
☐ 272	Pedro Munoz	.06	.03	.01
☐ 273	Kirby Puckett	.20	.09	.03
☐ 274	Kevin Tapani	.06	.03	.01
☐ 275	Carl Willis	.04	.02	.01
☐ 276	Steve Farr	.04	.02	.01
☐ 277	John Habyan	.04	.02	.01
☐ 278	Mel Hall	.04	.02	.01
☐ 279	Charlie Hayes	.04	.02	.01
☐ 280	Pat Kelly	.06	.03	.01
☐ 281	Don Mattingly	.12	.05	.02
☐ 282	Sam Militello	.15	.07	.02
☐ 283	Matt Nokes	.04	.02	.01
☐ 284	Melido Perez	.04	.02	.01
☐ 285	Andy Stankiewicz	.06	.03	.01
☐ 286	Danny Tartabull	.06	.03	.01
☐ 287	Randy Velarde	.04	.02	.01
☐ 288	Bob Wickman	.20	.09	.03
☐ 289	Bernie Williams	.06	.03	.01
☐ 290	Lance Blankenship	.04	.02	.01
☐ 291	Mike Bordick	.06	.03	.01
☐ 292	Jerry Browne	.04	.02	.01
☐ 293	Dennis Eckersley	.10	.05	.01
☐ 294	Rickey Henderson	.12	.05	.02
☐ 295	Vince Horsman	.04	.02	.01
☐ 296	Mark McGwire	.20	.09	.03
☐ 297	Jeff Parrett	.04	.02	.01
☐ 298	Ruben Sierra	.15	.07	.02
☐ 299	Terry Steinbach	.06	.03	.01
☐ 300	Walt Weiss	.06	.03	.01
☐ 301	Bob Welch	.04	.02	.01
☐ 302	Willie Wilson	.04	.02	.01
☐ 303	Bobby Witt	.04	.02	.01
☐ 304	Bret Boone	.25	.11	.03
☐ 305	Jay Buhner	.06	.03	.01
☐ 306	Dave Fleming	.20	.09	.03
☐ 307	Ken Griffey Jr.	.50	.23	.06
☐ 308	Erik Hanson	.04	.02	.01
☐ 309	Edgar Martinez	.06	.03	.01
☐ 310	Tino Martinez	.06	.03	.01
☐ 311	Jeff Nelson	.04	.02	.01
☐ 312	Dennis Powell	.04	.02	.01
☐ 313	Mike Schooler	.04	.02	.01
☐ 314	Russ Swan	.04	.02	.01
☐ 315	Dave Valle	.04	.02	.01
☐ 316	Omar Vizquel	.04	.02	.01
☐ 317	Kevin Brown	.06	.03	.01
☐ 318	Todd Burns	.04	.02	.01
☐ 319	Jose Canseco	.20	.09	.03
☐ 320	Julio Franco	.06	.03	.01
☐ 321	Jeff Frye	.04	.02	.01
☐ 322	Juan Gonzalez	.30	.14	.04
☐ 323	Jose Guzman	.04	.02	.01
☐ 324	Jeff Huson	.04	.02	.01
☐ 325	Dean Palmer	.06	.03	.01
☐ 326	Kevin Reimer	.06	.03	.01
☐ 327	Ivan Rodriguez	.20	.09	.03
☐ 328	Kenny Rogers	.04	.02	.01
☐ 329	Dan Smith	.12	.05	.02
☐ 330	Roberto Alomar	.20	.09	.03
☐ 331	Derek Bell	.06	.03	.01
☐ 332	Pat Borders	.04	.02	.01
☐ 333	Joe Carter	.12	.05	.02
☐ 334	Kelly Gruber	.06	.03	.01
☐ 335	Tom Henke	.06	.03	.01
☐ 336	Jimmy Key	.04	.02	.01
☐ 337	Manuel Lee	.04	.02	.01
☐ 338	Candy Maldonado	.04	.02	.01
☐ 339	John Olerud	.10	.05	.01
☐ 340	Todd Stottlemyre	.06	.03	.01
☐ 341	Duane Ward	.04	.02	.01
☐ 342	Devon White	.06	.03	.01
☐ 343	Dave Winfield	.10	.05	.01
☐ 344	Edgar Martinez LL	.05	.02	.01
☐ 345	Cecil Fielder LL	.10	.05	.01
☐ 346	Kenny Lofton LL	.10	.05	.01
☐ 347	Jack Morris LL	.10	.05	.01
☐ 348	Roger Clemens LL	.12	.05	.02
☐ 349	Fred McGriff RT	.10	.05	.01
☐ 350	Barry Bonds RT	.10	.05	.01
☐ 351	Gary Sheffield RT	.10	.05	.01
☐ 352	Darren Daulton RT	.05	.02	.01
☐ 353	Dave Hollins RT	.05	.02	.01
☐ 354	Brothers in Blue Pedro Martinez Ramon Martinez	.10	.05	.01
☐ 355	Power Packs Ivan Rodriguez Kirby Puckett	.15	.07	.02
☐ 356	Triple Threats Ryne Sandberg	.15	.07	.02

Gary Sheffield			
☐ 357 Infield Trifecta	.15	.07	.02
Roberto Alomar			
Chuck Knoblauch			
Carlos Baerga			
☐ 358 Checklist 1-120	.05	.01	.00
☐ 359 Checklist 121-240	.05	.01	.00
☐ 360 Checklist 241-360	.05	.01	.00

1993 Fleer All-Stars

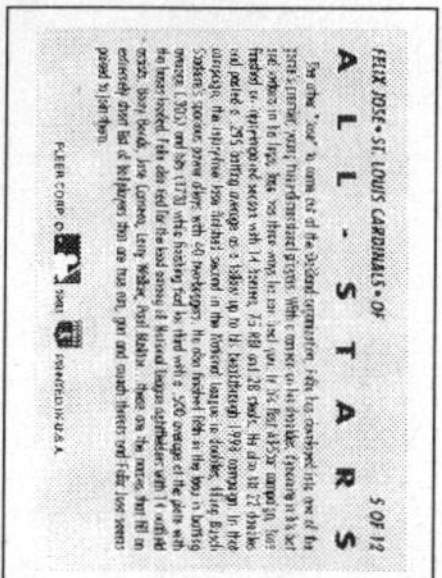

This 12-card standard-size (2 1/2" by 3 1/2") set was randomly inserted in 1993 Fleer series I wax packs. Cards 1-12 feature National League All-Stars. The horizontal fronts feature a color close-up photo cut out and superimposed on a black-and-white action scene framed by white borders. The player's name and the word "All-Stars" are printed in gold foil lettering across the bottom of the picture. On a pastel yellow panel, the horizontal backs carry career summary. The cards are numbered on the back "No. X of 12."

	MT	EX-MT	VG
COMPLETE SET (12)	20.00	9.00	2.50
COMMON PLAYER (1-12)	1.00	.45	.13
☐ 1 Fred McGriff	2.50	1.15	.30
☐ 2 Delino DeShields	2.00	.90	.25
☐ 3 Gary Sheffield	3.50	1.55	.45
☐ 4 Barry Larkin	2.00	.90	.25
☐ 5 Felix Jose	1.00	.45	.13
☐ 6 Larry Walker	2.00	.90	.25
☐ 7 Barry Bonds	4.00	1.80	.50
☐ 8 Andy Van Slyke	1.50	.65	.19
☐ 9 Darren Daulton	1.00	.45	.13
☐ 10 Greg Maddux	2.50	1.15	.30
☐ 11 Tom Glavine	2.50	1.15	.30
☐ 12 Lee Smith	1.00	.45	.13

1993 Fleer Golden Moments

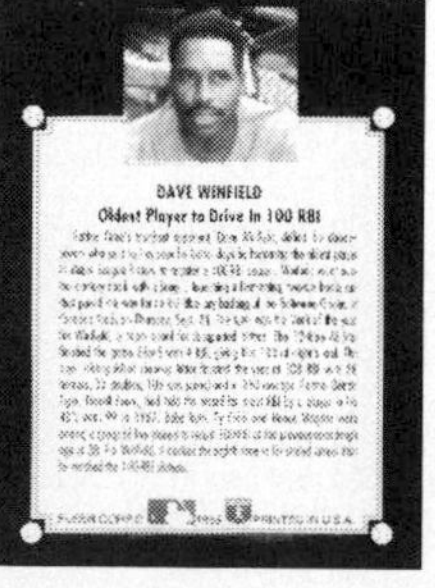

This three-card standard-size (2 1/2" by 3 1/2") set was randomly inserted in 1993 Fleer series I wax packs. The fronts feature glossy color action photos framed by thin aqua and white lines and a black outer border. A gold foil baseball icon appears at each corner of the picture, and the player's name and the set title "Golden Moments" appears in a gold foil bar toward the bottom of the picture. The backs have a similar design to that on the fronts, only with a small color head shot and a summary of the player's outstanding achievement on a white panel. The cards are unnumbered and checklisted below in alphabetical order.

	MT	EX-MT	VG
COMPLETE SET (3)	6.00	2.70	.75
COMMON PLAYER (1-3)	1.00	.45	.13
☐ 1 George Brett	3.50	1.55	.45
3,000 Hits			
☐ 2 Mickey Morandini	1.00	.45	.13
Unassisted Triple Play			
☐ 3 Dave Winfield	3.00	1.35	.40
Oldest Player with 100 RBI Season			

1993 Fleer Major League Prospects

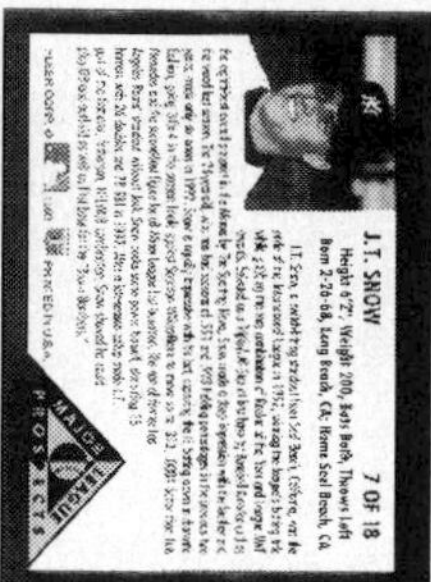

This 18-card standard-size (2 1/2" by 3 1/2") set was randomly inserted in 1993 Fleer series I wax packs. The fronts display glossy color action photos bordered in black. The player's name is printed in gold foil lettering across the top of the picture. At the bottom center, a black and gold foil triangle carries a baseball icon and the words "Major League Prospects." Inside black borders on a white panel, the backs show a color close-up photo, biography, and player profile. The cards are numbered on the back "X of 18."

	MT	EX-MT	VG
COMPLETE SET (18)	25.00	11.50	3.10
COMMON PLAYER (1-18)	1.00	.45	.13
☐ 1 Melvin Nieves	4.00	1.80	.50
☐ 2 Sterling Hitchcock	3.00	1.35	.40
☐ 3 Tim Costo	1.25	.55	.16
☐ 4 Manny Alexander	1.25	.55	.16
☐ 5 Alan Embree	3.00	1.35	.40
☐ 6 Kevin Young	3.00	1.35	.40
☐ 7 J.T. Snow	4.00	1.80	.50
☐ 8 Russ Springer	1.50	.65	.19
☐ 9 Billy Ashley	3.00	1.35	.40
☐ 10 Kevin Rogers	1.00	.45	.13
☐ 11 Steve Hosey	2.00	.90	.25
☐ 12 Eric Wedge	3.00	1.35	.40
☐ 13 Mike Piazza	3.50	1.55	.45
☐ 14 Jesse Levis	1.00	.45	.13
☐ 15 Rico Brogna	1.00	.45	.13
☐ 16 Alex Arias	1.00	.45	.13
☐ 17 Rod Brewer	1.25	.55	.16
☐ 18 Troy Neel	1.25	.55	.16

1993 Fleer Pro-Visions

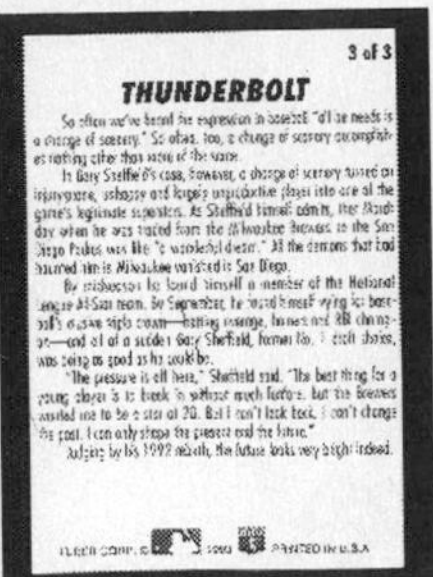

This three-card standard-size (2 1/2" by 3 1/2") set was randomly inserted in 1993 Fleer series I wax packs. Inside a black border, the fronts display surrealistic artistic drawings of the featured player. His name is printed in gold foil block lettering in the wider bottom black border. Inside black borders on a white panel, the backs give the player a nickname illustrated by the front drawing and describes the player's career. The cards are numbered on the back "X of 3."

	MT	EX-MT	VG
COMPLETE SET (3)	7.00	3.10	.85
COMMON PLAYER (1-3)	1.25	.55	.16
☐ 1 Roberto Alomar	4.00	1.80	.50
☐ 2 Dennis Eckersley	1.25	.55	.16
☐ 3 Gary Sheffield	3.00	1.35	.40

1993 Fleer Tom Glavine

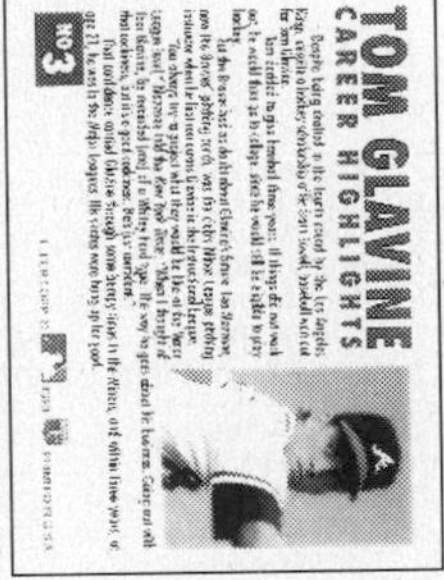

As part of the Signature Series, this 12-card set spotlights Tom Glavine. The cards measure the standard size (2 1/2" by 3 1/2"). The fronts feature glossy color action photos with white borders. The player's name and the words "Career Highlights" appear in gold foil block lettering across the bottom of the picture. The horizontal backs carry a small close-up color photo and summarize chapters of Glavine's career. The cards are numbered on the back at the lower left corner. There are eight variations that appeared only in the first series of wax packs; they are distinguished by the first words of text appearing on the card backs.

	MT	EX-MT	VG
COMPLETE SET (12)	20.00	9.00	2.50
COMMON GLAVINE (1-12)	2.00	.90	.25
☐ 1A Tom Glavine The Glavine family ... (Throwing to first)	3.00	1.35	.40
☐ 1B Tom Glavine Tom Glavine's dream ... (Throwing to first)	2.00	.90	.25
☐ 2A Tom Glavine High School baseball ... (Pitching, with arm behind head, shot from left side)	3.00	1.35	.40
☐ 2B Tom Glavine After Winning ... (Pitching, with arm behind head, shot from left side)	2.00	.90	.25
☐ 3A Tom Glavine Despite being drafted ... (Pitching, close-up shot from left side)	3.00	1.35	.40
☐ 3B Tom Glavine Little Leaguers ... (Pitching, close-up shot from left side)	2.00	.90	.25
☐ 4A Tom Glavine Unflappable is ... (Pitching, shot from almost directly in front)	3.00	1.35	.40
☐ 4B Tom Glavine Will success spoil ... (Pitching, shot from almost directly in front)	2.00	.90	.25
☐ 5 Tom Glavine In 1989 Tom ... (Pitching, shot from right angle)	2.00	.90	.25
☐ 6 Tom Glavine Tom Glavine had ... (Pitching, with ball below waist)	2.00	.90	.25
☐ 7A Tom Glavine Tom Glavine's dream ... (Pitching, close-up shot with ball behind head)	3.00	1.35	.40
☐ 7B Tom Glavine The Glavine family ... (Pitching, close-up shot with ball behind head)	2.00	.90	.25
☐ 8A Tom Glavine After Winning ... (Pitching, shot from directly in front)	3.00	1.35	.40
☐ 8B Tom Glavine High School baseball ... (Pitching, shot from directly in front)	2.00	.90	.25
☐ 9A Tom Glavine Little Leaguers ... (Pitching, just after release with left leg in air)	3.00	1.35	.40
☐ 9B Tom Glavine Despite being drafted ... (Pitching, just after release with left leg in air)	2.00	.90	.25
☐ 10A Tom Glavine Will success spoil ... (Pitching, ball below waist and right leg slightly raised)	3.00	1.35	.40
☐ 10B Tom Glavine Unflappable is ... (Pitching, ball below waist and right leg slightly raised)	2.00	.90	.25
☐ 11 Tom Glavine What makes Tom ... (Batting)	2.00	.90	.25
☐ 12 Tom Glavine It was a day ... (Pitching, close-up shot wearing dark blue top)	2.00	.90	.25
☐ AU0 Tom Glavine (Certified signature)	150.00	70.00	19.00

1992 French's

The 1992 French's Special Edition Combo Series consists of 18 two-player cards and a title/checklist card. The cards measure the standard size (2 1/2" by 3 1/2"). Each card features one player from the American League and one

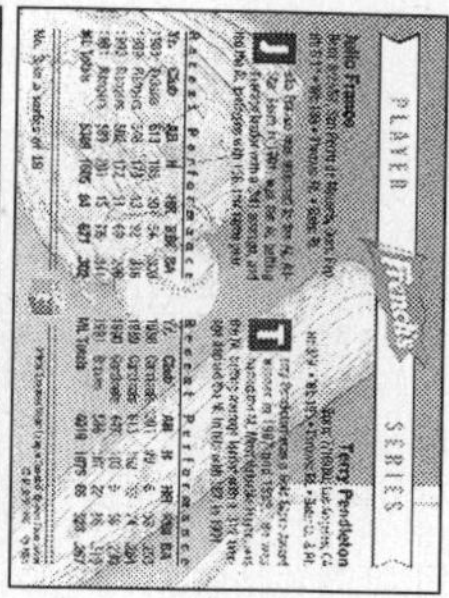

player from the National League. The cards were licensed by the MLBPA and produced by MSA (Michael Schechter Associates). Collectors could obtain the title/checklist card and three free player cards through an on-pack promotion by purchasing a 16 oz. size of French's Classic Yellow Mustard (the cards were enclosed in a plastic hangtag). Alternatively, collectors could collect all 18 player cards in the series by sending in 3.00 plus 75 cents for postage and handling along with one quality seal from the 16 oz. size of French's Classic Yellow Mustard. The released production figures were 43,000 18-card sets and 4,800,000 three-card hangtags. Both sides of the card are vertically oriented; the two color action player photos on the front are bordered in green. A white stripe with the words "Player Series" cuts across the top and intersects the French's trademark logo. Two baseball bats and a ball edge the pictures at the bottom. On a green background that features a glove, ball, bat, and home plate, the backs carry biography, player profile, and recent performance statistics for each player. The cards are numbered on the back.

	MT	EX-MT	VG
COMPLETE SET (19)	10.00	4.50	1.25
COMMON PLAYER (1-18)	.40	.18	.05
☐ 1 Chuck Knoblauch and Jeff Bagwell	1.00	.45	.13
☐ 2 Rogers Clemens and Tom Glavine	.90	.40	.11
☐ 3 Julio Franco and Terry Pendleton	.50	.23	.06
☐ 4 Jose Canseco and Howard Johnson	.75	.35	.09
☐ 5 Scott Erickson and John Smiley	.40	.18	.05
☐ 6 Bryan Harvey and Lee Smith	.50	.23	.06
☐ 7 Kirby Puckett and Barry Bonds	1.00	.45	.13
☐ 8 Robin Ventura and Matt Williams	.60	.25	.08
☐ 9 Tony Pena and Tom Pagnozzi	.40	.18	.05
☐ 10 Sandy Alomar Jr. and Benito Santiago	.50	.23	.06
☐ 11 Don Mattingly and Will Clark	.75	.35	.09
☐ 12 Roberto Alomar and Ryne Sandberg	1.00	.45	.13
☐ 13 Cal Ripken and Ozzie Smith	1.00	.45	.13
☐ 14 Wade Boggs and Chris Sabo	.75	.35	.09
☐ 15 Ken Griffey Jr. and Dave Justice	1.50	.65	.19
☐ 16 Joe Carter and Tony Gwynn	.75	.35	.09
☐ 17 Rickey Henderson and Darryl Strawberry	.75	.35	.09
☐ 18 Jack Morris and Steve Avery	.60	.25	.08
☐ NNO Title/Checklist Card	.40	.18	.05

1991 Front Row Draft Picks

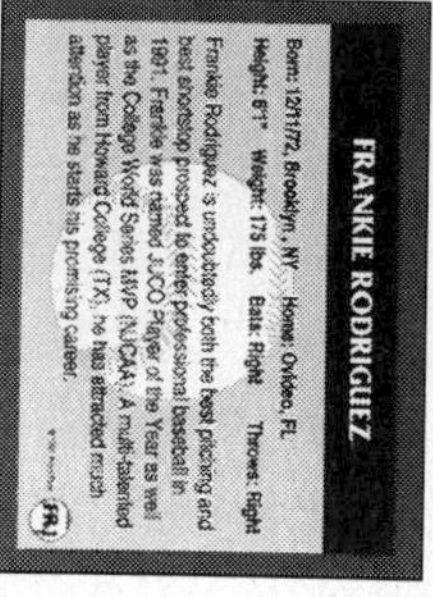

This 50-card premier edition set includes 27 of the top 40 eligible players from the 1991 Baseball Draft. The cards measure the standard size (2 1/2" by 3 1/2"), and only 240,000 sets were produced. Each set contains a numbered card registering the set and one card from a limited Draft Pick subset as a bonus card. In exchange for returning the bonus card, the collector received card number 50 (Benji Gil), a mini-update set (51-54; sent to the first 120,000 respondents), and one card from a five-card Frankie Rodriguez subset. The photos on both sides of the card are highlighted with an ultra violet finish. The obverse has glossy color player photos bordered in gray, with the player's name in black lettering below the picture. The words "Front Row" appear in a baseball in the upper right corner, while the words "'91 Draft Pick" appear in a diamond in the lower left corner. The reverse has a color photo of the player in little league, biography, statistics, and career achievements. The cards are numbered on the back.

	MT	EX-MT	VG
COMPLETE SET (50)	7.00	3.10	.85
COMMON PLAYER (1-50)	.07	.03	.01
COMMON PLAYER (51-54)	.20	.09	.03
☐ 1 Frankie Rodriguez	1.00	.45	.13
☐ 2 Aaron Sele	.60	.25	.08
☐ 3 Chad Schoenvogel	.10	.05	.01
☐ 4 Scott Ruffcorn	.40	.18	.05
☐ 5 Dan Cholowski UER (Name should be spelled Cholowsky)	.60	.25	.08
☐ 6 Gene Schall	.10	.05	.01
☐ 7 Trever Miller	.20	.09	.03
☐ 8 Chris Durkin	.25	.11	.03
☐ 9 Mike Neill	.40	.18	.05
☐ 10 Kevin Stocker	.10	.05	.01
☐ 11 Bobby Jones	.60	.25	.08
☐ 12 Jon Farrell	.15	.07	.02
☐ 13 Ronnie Allen	.10	.05	.01
☐ 14 Mike Rossiter	.10	.05	.01
☐ 15 Scott Hatteberg	.30	.14	.04
☐ 16 Rodney Pedraza	.15	.07	.02
☐ 17 Mike Durant	.25	.11	.03
☐ 18 Ryan Long	.15	.07	.02
☐ 19 Greg Anthony	.15	.07	.02
☐ 20 Jon Barnes	.10	.05	.01
☐ 21 Brian Barber	.30	.14	.04
☐ 22 Brent Gates	.60	.25	.08
☐ 23 Calvin Reese	.40	.18	.05
☐ 24 Terry Horn	.10	.05	.01
☐ 25 Scott Stahoviak	.50	.23	.06
☐ 26 Jason Pruitt	.15	.07	.02
☐ 27 Shawn Curran	.10	.05	.01
☐ 28 Jimmy Lewis	.25	.11	.03
☐ 29 Alex Ochoa	.10	.05	.01
☐ 30 Joe DeBerry	.10	.05	.01
☐ 31 Justin Thompson	.15	.07	.02
☐ 32 Jimmy Gonzalez	.10	.05	.01
☐ 33 Eddie Ramos	.10	.05	.01
☐ 34 Tyler Green	.60	.25	.08
☐ 35 Toby Rumfield	.15	.07	.02
☐ 36 Dave Doornenweerd	.10	.05	.01
☐ 37 Jeff Hostetler	.10	.05	.01

☐ 38 Shawn Livsey	.25	.11	.03
☐ 39 Mike Gropusso	.15	.07	.02
☐ 40 Steve Whitaker	.10	.05	.01
☐ 41 Tom McKinnon	.15	.07	.02
☐ 42 Buck McNabb	.10	.05	.01
☐ 43 Al Shirley	.50	.23	.06
☐ 44 Allen Watson	.35	.16	.04
☐ 45 Bill Bliss	.10	.05	.01
☐ 46 Todd Hollandsworth	.15	.07	.02
☐ 47 Manny Ramirez	.90	.40	.11
☐ 48 J.J. Johnson	.15	.07	.02
☐ 49 Cliff Floyd	1.25	.55	.16
☐ 50A Bonus Card	2.00	.90	.25
☐ 50B Benji Gil	.60	.25	.08
☐ 51 Herb Perry	.25	.11	.03
☐ 52 Tarrik Brock	.25	.11	.03
☐ 53 Trevor Mallory	.20	.09	.03
☐ 54 Chris Pritchett	.20	.09	.03
☐ FR1 Frankie Rodriguez Pitching (Just after release, forward knee bent)	1.00	.45	.13
☐ FR2 Frankie Rodriguez Pitching (Ball in hand behind body, in wind up)	1.00	.45	.13
☐ FR3 Frankie Rodriguez Batting stance (Almost at middle of swing)	1.00	.45	.13
☐ FR4 Frankie Rodriguez Pitching (Just after release, forward leg straight)	1.00	.45	.13
☐ FR5 Frankie Rodriguez Batting stance (Bat cocked above shoulder, waiting for pitch)	1.00	.45	.13

1992 Front Row Draft Picks

This 100-card set measures the standard size (2 1/2" by 3 1/2") and features color action player photos. According to Front Row, the production run was 10,000 wax cases and 2,500 30-set factory cases (both were individually numbered). Gold and silver foil stamped cards were randomly inserted into wax packs. Also randomly inserted were pure gold cards of Ken Griffey Jr. and Frank Thomas and HOFer signature cards of Brooks Robinson, Yogi Berra, Whitey Ford and others. The fronts feature color action player photos with blue borders that fade as one moves down the card face. The words "Draft Pick '92" appear in a yellow stripe that cuts across the card top, intersecting the Front Row logo at the upper right corner. The player's name in a yellow bar toward the bottom complete the front. On a tan panel featuring the Front Row logo, the horizontally oriented backs carry a color photo of the player in little league, biography, complete amateur statistics, and career achievements. The cards are numbered on the back.

	MT	EX-MT	VG
COMPLETE SET (100)	9.00	4.00	1.15
COMMON PLAYER (1-100)	.05	.02	.01

☐ 1 Dan Melendez	.20	.09	.03
☐ 2 Billy Owens	.20	.09	.03
☐ 3 Sherard Clinkscales	.30	.14	.04
☐ 4 Tim Moore	.10	.05	.01
☐ 5 Michael Hickey	.05	.02	.01
☐ 6 Kenny Carlyle	.10	.05	.01
☐ 7 Todd Steverson	.40	.18	.05
☐ 8 Ted Corbin	.05	.02	.01
☐ 9 Tim Crabtree	.25	.11	.03
☐ 10 Jason Angel	.10	.05	.01
☐ 11 Mike Gulan	.20	.09	.03
☐ 12 Jared Baker	.15	.07	.02
☐ 13 Mike Buddie	.05	.02	.01
☐ 14 Brandon Pico	.05	.02	.01
☐ 15 Jonathan Nunnally	.20	.09	.03
☐ 16 Scott Patton	.10	.05	.01
☐ 17 Tony Sheffield	.30	.14	.04
☐ 18 Danny Clyburn	.25	.11	.03
☐ 19 Tom Knauss	.20	.09	.03
☐ 20 Carey Paige	.15	.07	.02
☐ 21 Keith Johnson	.10	.05	.01
☐ 22 Larry Mitchell	.10	.05	.01
☐ 23 Tim Leger	.10	.05	.01
☐ 24 Doug Hecker	.15	.07	.02
☐ 25 Aaron Thatcher	.10	.05	.01
☐ 26 Marquis Riley	.25	.11	.03
☐ 27 Jamie Taylor	.10	.05	.01
☐ 28 Don Wengert	.10	.05	.01
☐ 29 Jason Moler	.10	.05	.01
☐ 30 Kevin Kloek	.10	.05	.01
☐ 31 Kevin Pearson	.05	.02	.01
☐ 32 David Mysel	.10	.05	.01
☐ 33 Chris Holt	.15	.07	.02
☐ 34 Chris Gomez	.10	.05	.01
☐ 35 Joe Hamilton	.10	.05	.01
☐ 36 Brandon Cromer	.25	.11	.03
☐ 37 Lloyd Peever	.10	.05	.01
☐ 38 Gordon Sanchez	.05	.02	.01
☐ 39 Bonus Card	1.50	.65	.19
☐ 40 Jason Giambi	.40	.18	.05
☐ 41 Sean Runyan	.10	.05	.01
☐ 42 Jamie Keefe	.15	.07	.02
☐ 43 Scott Gentile	.05	.02	.01
☐ 44 Michael Tucker	1.25	.55	.16
☐ 45 Scott Klingenbeck	.10	.05	.01
☐ 46 Ed Christian	.05	.02	.01
☐ 47 Scott Miller	.10	.05	.01
☐ 48 Rick Navarro	.05	.02	.01
☐ 49 Bill Selby	.05	.02	.01
☐ 50 Chris Roberts	.50	.23	.06
☐ 51 John Dillinger	.05	.02	.01
☐ 52 Keith Johns	.05	.02	.01
☐ 53 Matt Williams	.05	.02	.01
☐ 54 Garvin Alston	.05	.02	.01
☐ 55 Derek Jeter	.60	.25	.08
☐ 56 Chris Eddy	.15	.07	.02
☐ 57 Jeff Schmidt	.25	.11	.03
☐ 58 Chris Petersen	.05	.02	.01
☐ 59 Chris Sheff	.05	.02	.01
☐ 60 Chad Roper	.30	.14	.04
☐ 61 Rich Ireland	.15	.07	.02
☐ 62 Tibor Brown	.05	.02	.01
☐ 63 Todd Etler	.15	.07	.02
☐ 64 John Turlais	.05	.02	.01
☐ 65 Shawn Holcomb	.10	.05	.01
☐ 66 Ben Jones	.05	.02	.01
☐ 67 Marcel Galligani	.05	.02	.01
☐ 68 Troy Penix	.10	.05	.01
☐ 69 Matt Luke	.05	.02	.01
☐ 70 David Post	.05	.02	.01
☐ 71 Michael Warner	.05	.02	.01
☐ 72 Alexis Aranzamendi	.10	.05	.01
☐ 73 Larry Hingle	.05	.02	.01
☐ 74 Shon Walker	.25	.11	.03
☐ 75 Mark Thompson	.25	.11	.03
☐ 76 John Lieber	.20	.09	.03
☐ 77 Wes Weger	.05	.02	.01
☐ 78 Mike Smith	.10	.05	.01
☐ 79 Ritchie Moody	.20	.09	.03
☐ 80 B.J. Wallace	.75	.35	.09
☐ 81 Rick Helling	.40	.18	.05
☐ 82 Chad Mottola	.75	.35	.09
☐ 83 Brant Brown	.10	.05	.01
☐ 84 Steve Rodriguez	.20	.09	.03
☐ 85 John Vanhof	.10	.05	.01
☐ 86 Brian Wolf	.10	.05	.01
☐ 87 Steve Montgomery	.15	.07	.02
☐ 88 Eric Owens	.05	.02	.01
☐ 89 Jason Kendall	.50	.23	.06
☐ 90 Bob Bennett	.05	.02	.01
☐ 91 Joe Petcka	.10	.05	.01
☐ 92 Jim Rosenbohm	.20	.09	.03
☐ 93 David Manning	.15	.07	.02

☐ 94 Davie Landaker	.20	.09	.03
☐ 95 Dan Kyslinger	.10	.05	.01
☐ 96 Roger Bailey	.25	.11	.03
☐ 97 Jon Zuber	.10	.05	.01
☐ 98 Steve Cox	.05	.02	.01
☐ 99 Chris Widger	.15	.07	.02
☐ 100 Checklist 1-100	.05	.02	.01

1992 Front Row Griffey Club House

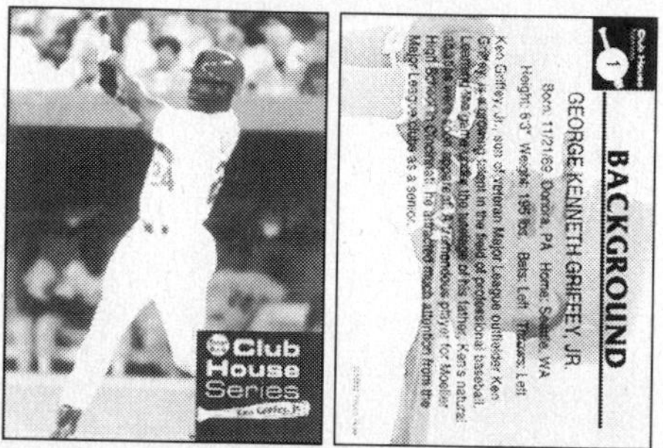

This ten-card standard-size (2 1/2" 3 1/2") set features on the front full-bleed color player photos. The only text on the front appears in a black square at the lower right corner, which reads "Club House Series, Ken Griffey Jr." On the background of a ghosted color close-up photo, the backs carry biography, highlights, or statistics. According to Front Row, 25,000 sets were produced. The cards are numbered on the back.

	MT	EX-MT	VG
COMPLETE SET (10)	7.00	3.10	.85
COMMON PLAYER (1-10)	1.00	.45	.13
☐ 1 Ken Griffey Jr. Background	1.00	.45	.13
☐ 2 Ken Griffey Jr. Drafted	1.00	.45	.13
☐ 3 Ken Griffey Jr. The Majors	1.00	.45	.13
☐ 4 Ken Griffey Jr. The Breakdown	1.00	.45	.13
☐ 5 Ken Griffey Jr. The American League	1.00	.45	.13
☐ 6 Ken Griffey Jr. All-Star	1.00	.45	.13
☐ 7 Ken Griffey Jr. Gold Glove	1.00	.45	.13
☐ 8 Ken Griffey Jr. Homers	1.00	.45	.13
☐ 9 Ken Griffey Jr. Career Highlights	1.00	.45	.13
☐ 10 Ken Griffey Jr. A Closer Look	1.00	.45	.13

1992 Front Row Griffey Gold

This three-card standard-size (2 1/2" by 3 1/2") set features color player photos on the fronts bordered by 23K gold dust stamping. The player's name appears in a blue bar beneath the picture. The backs are bordered in white and have a navy blue stripe at the top and the card's subtitle in a green bar, with text relating to the subtitle on a pastel yellow panel. Each set was accompanied by a certificate of authenticity carrying the production run (20,000) and the set serial number. Five thousand uncut strips of the three-card set were also produced. The cards are numbered on the back.

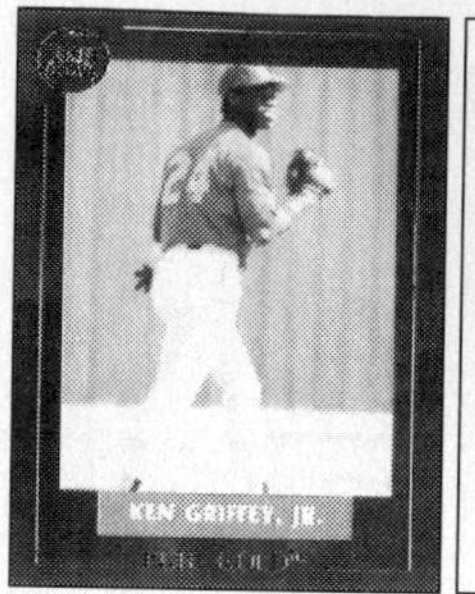

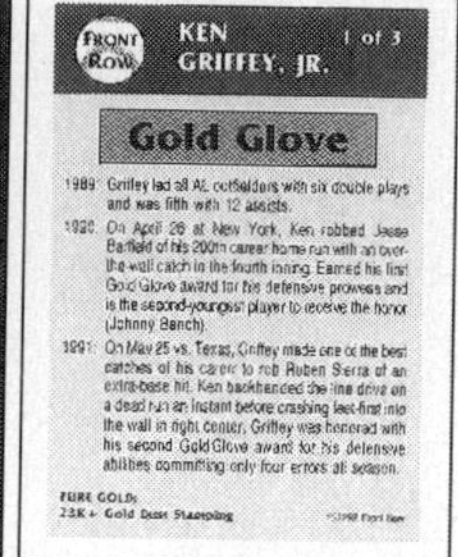

	MT	EX-MT	VG
COMPLETE SET (3)	15.00	6.75	1.90
COMMON PLAYER (1-3)	6.00	2.70	.75
☐ 1 Ken Griffey Jr. Gold Glove	6.00	2.70	.75
☐ 2 Ken Griffey Jr. Background	6.00	2.70	.75
☐ 3 Ken Griffey Jr. Drafted	6.00	2.70	.75

1992 Front Row Griffey Holograms

This three-card hologram set features three-dimensional shots of Ken Griffey Jr. Each set includes an official certificate of authenticity giving the set serial number and production run (50,000). The hologram cards measure the standard size (2 1/2" by 3 1/2"). Cards 1-2 have horizontally oriented backs. The white-bordered backs display color photos of Griffey along with career highlights in a blue-gray box. The cards are numbered on the back. All Seattle Mariner logos have been airbrushed off the cards as they were not licensed by the league or team.

	MT	EX-MT	VG
COMPLETE SET (3)	5.00	2.30	.60
COMMON PLAYER (1-3)	2.50	1.15	.30
☐ 1 Ken Griffey Jr. Making History	2.50	1.15	.30
☐ 2 Ken Griffey Jr. Rewriting the Record Book	2.50	1.15	.30
☐ 3 Ken Griffey Jr. Turning Up Gold	2.50	1.15	.30

1992 Front Row Frank Thomas

This seven-card standard-size (2 1/2" 3 1/2") set features on the front color player photos bordered in white. The player's

name appears in white lettering in a black stripe above the picture. In a horizontal format, the backs have a second player photo as well as biography, statistics (major and minor leagues), career summary, and highlights. Each set includes an official certificate of authenticity that gives the production run (30,000) and the set serial number. The cards are numbered on the back.

	MT	EX-MT	VG
COMPLETE SET (7)	6.00	2.70	.75
COMMON PLAYER (1-7)	1.25	.55	.16
☐ 1 Frank Thomas A Good Start	1.25	.55	.16
☐ 2 Frank Thomas Multi-Talented	1.25	.55	.16
☐ 3 Frank Thomas Auburn Career Statistics	1.25	.55	.16
☐ 4 Frank Thomas Accomplishments	1.25	.55	.16
☐ 5 Frank Thomas Individual Honors	1.25	.55	.16
☐ 6 Frank Thomas Minor League Statistics	1.25	.55	.16
☐ 7 Frank Thomas Major League Statistics	1.25	.55	.16

1992 Front Row Frank Thomas Gold

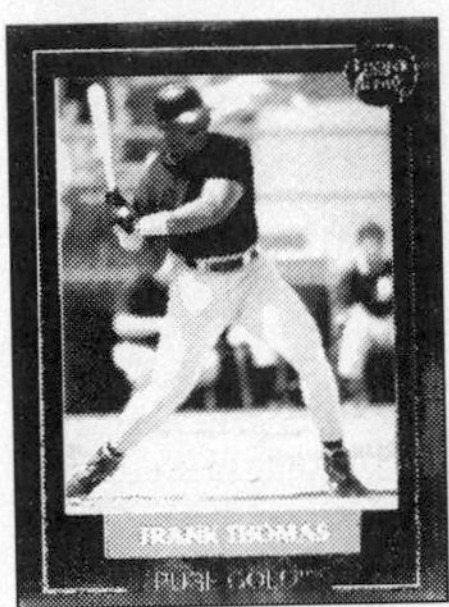

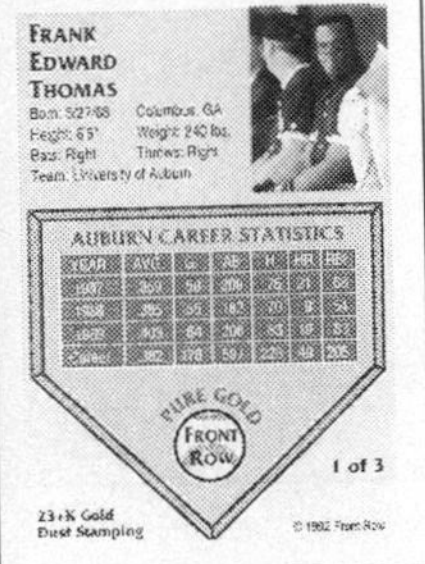

This three-card standard-size (2 1/2" by 3 1/2") set features color player photos on the fronts bordered by 23K gold dust stamping. The player's name appears in a green bar beneath the picture. On a mint green background bordered in white, the backs have biography, a close-up color photo, and statistics presented inside a home plate icon. Each set was accompanied by a certificate of authenticity carrying the production run (20,000) and the set serial number. Five thousand uncut strips of the three-card set were also produced. The cards are numbered on the back.

	MT	EX-MT	VG
COMPLETE SET (3)	15.00	6.75	1.90
COMMON PLAYER (1-3)	6.00	2.70	.75
☐ 1 Frank Thomas Auburn Career Statistics	6.00	2.70	.75
☐ 2 Frank Thomas Minor League Statistics	6.00	2.70	.75
☐ 3 Frank Thomas Major League Statistics	6.00	2.70	.75

1958 Giants S.F. Call-Bulletin

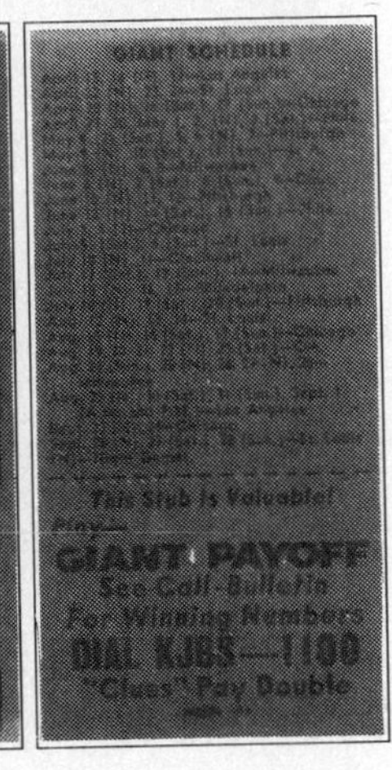

The cards in this 25-card set measure 2" by 4". The 1958 San Francisco Call-Bulletin set of unnumbered cards features black print on orange paper. These cards were given away as inserts in the San Francisco Call-Bulletin newspaper. The backs of the cards list the Giants home schedule and a radio station ad. The cards are entitled "Giant Payoff" and feature San Francisco Giant players only. The bottom part of the card (tab) could be detached as a ticket stub; hence, cards with the tab intact are worth approximately double the prices listed below. The catalog designation for this set is M126. The Tom Bowers card was issued in very short supply; also Bressoud, Jablonski, and Kirkland are tougher to find than the others. All of these tougher cards are asterisked in the checklist below.

	NRMT	VG-E	GOOD
COMPLETE SET (25)	1500.00	700.00	190.00
COMMON PLAYER (1-25)	7.50	3.40	.95
☐ 1 John Antonelli	9.00	4.00	1.15
☐ 2 Curt Barclay	7.50	3.40	.95
☐ 3 Tom Bowers *	750.00	350.00	95.00
☐ 4 Ed Bressoud *	125.00	57.50	15.50
☐ 5 Orlando Cepeda	60.00	27.00	7.50
☐ 6 Ray Crone	7.50	3.40	.95
☐ 7 Jim Davenport	9.00	4.00	1.15
☐ 8 Paul Giel	25.00	11.50	3.10
☐ 9 Ruben Gomez	7.50	3.40	.95
☐ 10 Marv Grissom	7.50	3.40	.95
☐ 11 Ray Jablonski *	125.00	57.50	15.50
☐ 12 Willie Kirkland *	150.00	70.00	19.00
☐ 13 Whitey Lockman	7.50	3.40	.95
☐ 14 Willie Mays	200.00	90.00	25.00
☐ 15 Mike McCormick	10.00	4.50	1.25
☐ 16 Stu Miller	9.00	4.00	1.15
☐ 17 Ray Monzant	7.50	3.40	.95
☐ 18 Danny O'Connell	7.50	3.40	.95
☐ 19 Bill Rigney MG	9.00	4.00	1.15
☐ 20 Hank Sauer	9.00	4.00	1.15
☐ 21 Bob Schmidt	7.50	3.40	.95
☐ 22 Daryl Spencer	7.50	3.40	.95

☐ 23 Valmy Thomas	7.50	3.40	.95
☐ 24 Bobby Thomson	25.00	11.50	3.10
☐ 25 Al Worthington	7.50	3.40	.95

1971 Giants Ticketron

The 1971 Ticketron San Francisco Giants set is a 10-card set featuring members of the division-winning 1971 San Francisco Giants. The set measures approximately 3 7/8" by 6" and features an attractive full-color photo framed by white borders on the front along with a facsimile autograph. The back contains an ad for Ticketron as well as the 1971 Giants home schedule. These unnumbered cards are listed in alphabetical order for convenience.

	NRMT-MT	EXC	G-VG
COMPLETE SET (10)	80.00	36.00	10.00
COMMON PLAYER (1-10)	3.00	1.35	.40
☐ 1 Bobby Bonds	7.50	3.40	.95
☐ 2 Dick Dietz	3.00	1.35	.40
☐ 3 Charles Fox MG	3.00	1.35	.40
☐ 4 Tito Fuentes	3.00	1.35	.40
☐ 5 Ken Henderson	3.00	1.35	.40
☐ 6 Juan Marichal	12.50	5.75	1.55
☐ 7 Willie Mays	40.00	18.00	5.00
☐ 8 Willie McCovey	16.00	7.25	2.00
☐ 9 Don McMahon	3.00	1.35	.40
☐ 10 Gaylord Perry	12.50	5.75	1.55

1991 Giants Pacific Gas and Electric

These cards were issued on six-card sheets; after perforation they measure approximately 2 1/2" by 3 1/2". One sheet was inserted in each of the first five 1991 San Francisco Giants Magazines, which were published by Woodford. The front design has color action player photos, with gray borders on a white card face. Toward the bottom of the picture are the words "San Francisco Giants," two bats, and a red banner with player information. The horizontally oriented backs are printed in black on white and include biography, Major League statistics, and various PGE (Pacific Gas and Electric) advertisements. The cards are numbered on the back in the upper right corner.

	MT	EX-MT	VG
COMPLETE SET (30)	12.00	5.50	1.50
COMMON PLAYER (1-30)	.35	.16	.04
☐ 1 Kevin Mitchell	.75	.35	.09
☐ 2 Robby Thompson	.60	.25	.08
☐ 3 John Burkett	.50	.23	.06
☐ 4 Kelly Downs	.50	.23	.06
☐ 5 Terry Kennedy	.35	.16	.04
☐ 6 Roger Craig MG	.50	.23	.06
☐ 7 Jeff Brantley	.50	.23	.06
☐ 8 Greg Litton	.35	.16	.04
☐ 9 Trevor Wilson	.50	.23	.06
☐ 10 Kevin Bass	.35	.16	.04
☐ 11 Matt Williams	.75	.35	.09
☐ 12 Jose Uribe	.35	.16	.04
☐ 13 Steve Decker	.50	.23	.06
☐ 14 Will Clark	2.00	.90	.25
☐ 15 Dave Righetti	.50	.23	.06
☐ 16 Mike Kingery	.35	.16	.04
☐ 17 Mike LaCoss	.35	.16	.04
☐ 18 Dave Anderson	.35	.16	.04
☐ 19 Bud Black	.35	.16	.04
☐ 20 Mike Benjamin	.35	.16	.04
☐ 21 Don Robinson	.35	.16	.04
☐ 22 Mark Leonard	.35	.16	.04
☐ 23 Willie McGee	.60	.25	.08
☐ 24 Francisco Oliveras	.35	.16	.04
☐ 25 Kirt Manwaring	.35	.16	.04
☐ 26 Rick Parker	.35	.16	.04
☐ 27 Mike Remlinger	.35	.16	.04
☐ 28 Mike Felder	.35	.16	.04
☐ 29 Scott Garrelts	.35	.16	.04
☐ 30 Tony Perezchica	.35	.16	.04

1992 Gold Entertainment Babe Ruth

Gold Entertainment produced this five-card holographic set celebrating the life and legend of Babe Ruth, along with Lou Gehrig and Roger Maris. The artwork for these cards was created by Hollywood artists Mike Butkus and Alan Hunter. This standard-size (2 1/2" by 3 1/2") set was sold in box cases containing 20 five-card sets (16 in silver and four in gold) and four bonus holograms (of a surprise player). The gold sets are valued at one and a half times the (silver) values listed below. The production run is reported to be 12,500 boxes, with each box carrying a numbered holographic seal. Each set features two double-sided full-bleed holograms and three full-color backs presenting biography, statistics, and quotes. The cards are numbered on the front in a diamond in the upper left corner (the cards with the color backs also carry a number on the back).

	MT	EX-MT	VG
COMPLETE SET (5)	8.00	3.60	1.00
COMMON PLAYER (1-5)	2.00	.90	.25
☐ 1 Babe Ruth 1914-1919 (Portrait, batting, and hitting poses)	2.00	.90	.25
☐ 2 Babe Ruth (Two-sided hologram; Ruth's stats on front Gehrig's stats on back)	2.50	1.15	.30
☐ 3 Babe Ruth The Called Shot (Bat extended, point- ing toward outfield)	2.00	.90	.25
☐ 4 Babe Ruth 61 in 1961 - 60 in 1927 (Two-sided hologram; Ruth shown with Maris on front)	2.50	1.15	.30
☐ 5 Babe Ruth 1914-1935 (Portrait, and standing poses)	2.00	.90	.25

1961 Golden Press

9
Joseph Paul DiMaggio
"Joltin' Joe" "The Yankee Clipper"
1936-1951 New York AL
Joe DiMaggio was one of the best center fielders ever to play in the major leagues. As a fielder, he covered the vast center field of Yankee Stadium with ease, making even the most difficult plays look easy. In 1941, DiMaggio hit safely in 56 consecutive games—a major league record. He led the American League in batting in 1939 and 1940, in home runs in 1937 and 1948, and in runs batted in in 1941 and 1948. He appeared in ten World Series, setting many Series records.
Lifetime Record 13 yrs.
G AB R H HR RBI SB PCT
1736 6821 1390 2214 361 1537 30 .325
Elected to Hall of Fame 1955

The cards in this 33-card set measure 2 1/2" by 3 1/2". The 1961 Golden Press set of full color cards features members of Baseball's Hall of Fame. The cards came in a booklet with perforations for punching the cards out of the book. The catalog designation for this set is W524. The price for the full book intact is 50 percent higher than the complete set price listed.

	NRMT	VG-E	GOOD
COMPLETE SET (33)	100.00	45.00	12.50
COMMON PLAYER (1-33)	1.00	.45	.13
☐ 1 Mel Ott	3.00	1.35	.40
☐ 2 Grover C. Alexander	2.00	.90	.25
☐ 3 Babe Ruth	30.00	13.50	3.80
☐ 4 Hank Greenberg	2.00	.90	.25
☐ 5 Bill Terry	1.25	.55	.16
☐ 6 Carl Hubbell	1.25	.55	.16
☐ 7 Rogers Hornsby	4.00	1.80	.50
☐ 8 Dizzy Dean	7.50	3.40	.95
☐ 9 Joe DiMaggio	25.00	11.50	3.10
☐ 10 Charlie Gehringer	1.25	.55	.16
☐ 11 Gabby Hartnett	1.00	.45	.13
☐ 12 Mickey Cochrane	1.00	.45	.13
☐ 13 George Sisler	1.00	.45	.13
☐ 14 Joe Cronin	1.00	.45	.13
☐ 15 Pie Traynor	1.00	.45	.13
☐ 16 Lou Gehrig	20.00	9.00	2.50
☐ 17 Lefty Grove	2.50	1.15	.30
☐ 18 Chief Bender	1.00	.45	.13
☐ 19 Frankie Frisch	1.00	.45	.13
☐ 20 Al Simmons	1.00	.45	.13
☐ 21 Home Run Baker	1.00	.45	.13
☐ 22 Jimmy Foxx	4.00	1.80	.50
☐ 23 John McGraw	1.25	.55	.16
☐ 24 Christy Mathewson	6.00	2.70	.75
☐ 25 Ty Cobb	20.00	9.00	2.50
☐ 26 Dazzy Vance	1.00	.45	.13
☐ 27 Bill Dickey	2.00	.90	.25
☐ 28 Eddie Collins	1.00	.45	.13
☐ 29 Walter Johnson	6.00	2.70	.75
☐ 30 Tris Speaker	3.00	1.35	.40
☐ 31 Nap Lajoie	3.00	1.35	.40
☐ 32 Honus Wagner	6.00	2.70	.75
☐ 33 Cy Young	4.00	1.80	.50

1981 Granny Goose A's

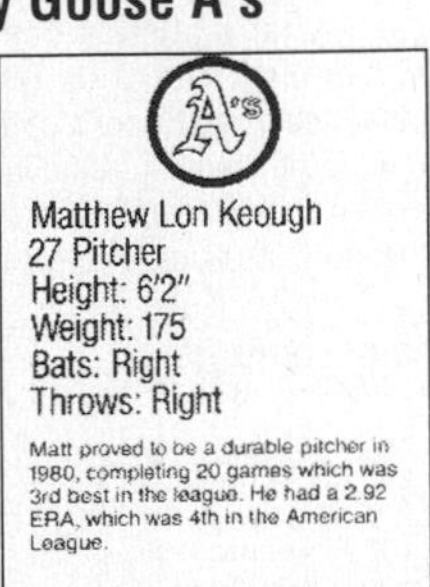

Matthew Lon Keough
27 Pitcher
Height: 6'2"
Weight: 175
Bats: Right
Throws: Right
Matt proved to be a durable pitcher in 1980, completing 20 games which was 3rd best in the league. He had a 2.92 ERA, which was 4th in the American League.

This set is the hardest to obtain of the three years Granny Goose issued cards of the Oakland A's. The Revering card was supposedly destroyed by the printer soon after he was traded away and hence is in shorter supply than the other 14 cards in the set. Wayne Gross is also supposedly available in lesser quantity compared to the other players. Cards are standard size (2 1/2" by 3 1/2") and were issued in bags of potato chips. Cards are numbered on the front and back by the player's uniform number.

	NRMT-MT	EXC	G-VG
COMPLETE SET (15)	80.00	36.00	10.00
COMMON PLAYER	1.50	.65	.19
☐ 1 Billy Martin MG	10.00	4.50	1.25
☐ 2 Mike Heath	1.50	.65	.19
☐ 5 Jeff Newman	1.50	.65	.19
☐ 6 Mitchell Page	1.50	.65	.19
☐ 8 Rob Picciolo	1.50	.65	.19
☐ 10 Wayne Gross SP	6.00	2.70	.75
☐ 13 Dave Revering SP	35.00	16.00	4.40
☐ 17 Mike Norris	1.50	.65	.19
☐ 20 Tony Armas	2.00	.90	.25
☐ 21 Dwayne Murphy	1.50	.65	.19
☐ 22 Rick Langford	1.50	.65	.19
☐ 27 Matt Keough	1.50	.65	.19
☐ 35 Rickey Henderson	35.00	16.00	4.40
☐ 39 Dave McKay	1.50	.65	.19
☐ 54 Steve McCatty	1.50	.65	.19

1982 Granny Goose A's

Billy Martin
1 Manager
Billy was named winner of the 1981 AP, UPI and Sporting News Manager of the Year Award for his performance in 1981. Billy has won 963 games, losing only 768, a .556 percentage, trailing only Weaver, Anderson and Lasorda among active managers.

The cards in this 15-card set measure 2 1/2" by 3 1/2". Granny Goose Foods, Inc., a California based company, repeated its successful promotional idea of 1981 by issuing a new set of Oakland A's baseball cards for 1982. Each color player picture is surrounded by white borders and has trim and lettering done in Oakland's green and yellow colors. The cards are, in a sense, numbered according to the uniform number of the player; the card numbering below is according to alphabetical order by name. The card backs carry vital statistics done in black print on a white background. The cards were distributed in packages of potato chips and were also handed out on Fan Appreciation Day at the stadium. Although Picciolo was traded, his card was not withdrawn (as was Revering in 1981) and, therefore, its value is no greater than other cards in the set.

	NRMT-MT	EXC	G-VG
COMPLETE SET (15)	20.00	9.00	2.50
COMMON PLAYER (1-15)	.60	.25	.08
☐ 1 Tony Armas	.75	.35	.09
☐ 2 Wayne Gross	.60	.25	.08
☐ 3 Mike Heath	.60	.25	.08
☐ 4 Rickey Henderson	12.50	5.75	1.55
☐ 5 Cliff Johnson	.75	.35	.09
☐ 6 Matt Keough	.60	.25	.08
☐ 7 Rick Langford	.75	.35	.09
☐ 8 Davey Lopes	1.00	.45	.13
☐ 9 Billy Martin MG	3.00	1.35	.40
☐ 10 Steve McCatty	.60	.25	.08
☐ 11 Dwayne Murphy	.60	.25	.08
☐ 12 Jeff Newman	.60	.25	.08
☐ 13 Mike Norris	.60	.25	.08
☐ 14 Rob Picciolo	.60	.25	.08
☐ 15 Fred Stanley	.60	.25	.08

1983 Granny Goose A's

The cards in this 15-card set measure 2 1/2" by 4 1/4". The 1983 Granny Goose Potato Chips set again features Oakland A's players. The cards that were issued in bags of potato chips have a tear off coupon on the bottom with a scratch off section featuring prizes. In addition to their release in bags of potato chips, the Granny Goose cards were also given away to fans attending the Oakland game of July 3, 1983. These give away cards did not contain the coupon on the bottom. Prices listed below are for cards without the detachable tabs that came on the bottom of the cards; cards with tabs intact are valued 50 percent higher than the prices below. The card numbering below is according to uniform number.

	NRMT-MT	EXC	G-VG
COMPLETE SET (15)	15.00	6.75	1.90
COMMON PLAYER	.60	.25	.08
☐ 2 Mike Heath	.60	.25	.08
☐ 4 Carney Lansford	2.00	.90	.25
☐ 10 Wayne Gross	.60	.25	.08
☐ 14 Steve Boros MG	.60	.25	.08
☐ 15 Davey Lopes	1.00	.45	.13
☐ 16 Mike Davis	.60	.25	.08
☐ 17 Mike Norris	.60	.25	.08
☐ 21 Dwayne Murphy	.60	.25	.08
☐ 22 Rick Langford	.60	.25	.08
☐ 27 Matt Keough	.60	.25	.08
☐ 31 Tom Underwood	.60	.25	.08
☐ 33 Dave Beard	.60	.25	.08
☐ 35 Rickey Henderson	8.00	3.60	1.00
☐ 39 Tom Burgmeier	.60	.25	.08
☐ 54 Steve McCatty	.60	.25	.08

1974 Greyhound Heroes of Base Paths

Beginning in 1965, the Greyhound Award for Stolen Bases was given to the champions in each league and the second-place finishers. The 1974 Heroes of the Base Paths pamphlet unfolds to reveal five 4" by 9" panels. The first panel is the title page and features on the back a picture of Maury Wills holding the trophy. The second and third panels have on the fronts the history of the award and major league statistics pertaining to stolen bases, while the backs have an essay on the art of base stealing. Finally, the fourth and fifth panels display six player cards; after perforation, the cards measure approximately 4" by 3". Cards 1-4 feature the AL and NL winners, and the runner-ups for each league, in that order. The player cards display a black and white head shot of the player on the left half, with player information and number of stolen bases on the right half. The backs have statistics. Both sides of the cards are framed by thin brown border stripes. Cards 5-6 display black and white player photos of past winners in the AL and NL respectively. The cards are unnumbered.

	NRMT-MT	EXC	G-VG
COMPLETE SET (6)	10.00	4.50	1.25
COMMON PLAYER (1-6)	1.25	.55	.16
☐ 1 Bill North	1.25	.55	.16
☐ 2 Lou Brock	4.00	1.80	.50
☐ 3 Rod Carew	4.00	1.80	.50
☐ 4 Davey Lopes	1.50	.65	.19
☐ 5 American League Dagoberto Campaneris Tommy Harper Amos Otis Dave Nelson Billy North Don Buford Fred Patek Rod Carew	1.25	.55	.16
☐ 6 National League Lou Brock Maury Wills Bobby Tolan Joe Morgan Sonny Jackson Jose Cardenal Davey Lopes	1.50	.65	.19

1975 Greyhound Heroes of Base Paths

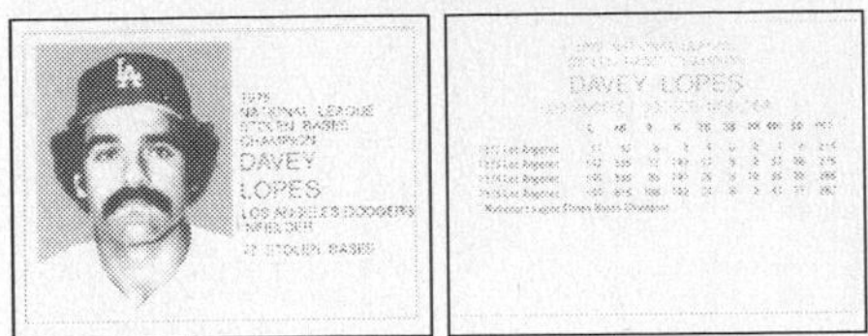

The Greyhound Award for Stolen Bases was given to the champions in each league and the second-place finishers. The 1975 Heroes of the Base Paths pamphlet unfolds to reveal five 4" by 9" panels. The first panel is the title page and features on the back a picture of Maury Wills holding the trophy. The second and third panels have on the fronts the history of the award and major league statistics pertaining to stolen bases, while the backs have an essay on the art of base stealing. Finally, the fourth and fifth panels display six player cards; after perforation, the cards measure approximately 4" by 3". Cards 1-4 feature the AL and NL winners, and the runner-ups for each league, in that order. The player cards display a black and white head shot of the player on the left half, with player information and number of stolen bases on the right half. The backs have statistics. Both sides of the cards are framed by thin powder blue border stripes. Cards 5-6 display black and white player photos of Billy North and Davey Lopes. The cards are unnumbered.

	NRMT-MT	EXC	G-VG
COMPLETE SET (6)	7.50	3.40	.95
COMMON PLAYER (1-6)	1.00	.45	.13
☐ 1 Mickey Rivers	1.00	.45	.13
☐ 2 Davey Lopes	1.25	.55	.16
☐ 3 Claudell Washington	1.00	.45	.13
☐ 4 Joe Morgan	4.00	1.80	.50
☐ 5 Billy North	1.00	.45	.13
☐ 6 Davey Lopes	1.25	.55	.16

1976 Greyhound Heroes of Base Paths

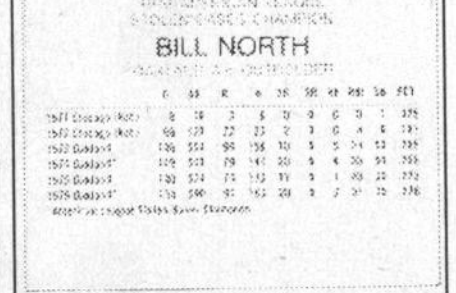

The Greyhound Award for Stolen Bases was given to the champions in each league and the second-place finishers. The 1976 Heroes of the Base Paths pamphlet unfolds to reveal five 4" by 9" panels. The first panel is the title page and features on the back a picture of Maury Wills holding the trophy. The second and third panels have on the fronts the history of the award and major league statistics pertaining to stolen bases, while the backs have an essay on the art of base stealing. Finally, the fourth and fifth panels display six player cards; after perforation, the cards measure approximately 4" by 3". Cards 1-4 feature the AL and NL winners, and the runner-ups for each league, in that order. The player cards display a black and white head shot of the player on the left half, with player information and number of stolen bases on the right half. The backs have statistics. Both sides of the cards are framed by thin powder reddish-brown stripes. Cards 5-6 display black and white player photos of Billy North and Davey Lopes. The cards are unnumbered.

	NRMT-MT	EXC	G-VG
COMPLETE SET (6)	7.50	3.40	.95
COMMON PLAYER (1-6)	1.00	.45	.13
☐ 1 Bill North	1.00	.45	.13
☐ 2 Davey Lopes	1.25	.55	.16
☐ 3 Ron LeFlore	1.00	.45	.13
☐ 4 Joe Morgan	4.00	1.80	.50
☐ 5 Billy North	1.00	.45	.13
☐ 6 Davey Lopes	1.25	.55	.16

1991 Griffey Gazette

These standard-size (2 1/2" by 3 1/2") cards were issued in honor of Ken Griffey Jr. The high gloss color photos on the fronts have gold borders. The horizontally oriented backs have dark blue print on a light blue background and captions to the front pictures. The cards are numbered on the back.

	MT	EX-MT	VG
COMPLETE SET (4)	5.00	2.30	.60
COMMON PLAYER (1-4)	1.75	.80	.22
☐ 1 Crowd Pleaser	1.75	.80	.22
☐ 2 Holdin' On	1.75	.80	.22
☐ 3 A 24ct. Gold Moment	1.75	.80	.22
☐ 4 Next of Ken Ken Griffey Sr. Ken Griffey Jr.	1.75	.80	.22

1958 Hires

The cards in this 66-card set measure approximately 2 5/16" by 3 1/2" or 2 5/16" by 7" with tabs. The 1958 Hires Root Beer set of numbered, colored cards was issued with detachable coupons as inserts with Hires Root Beer cartons. Cards with the coupon still intact are worth double the prices listed below. The card front picture is surrounded by a wood grain effect which makes it look like the player is seen through a knot hole. The numbering of this set is rather strange in that it begins with 10 and skips 69.

	NRMT	VG-E	GOOD
COMPLETE SET (66)	1400.00	650.00	180.00
COMMON PLAYER (10-76)	10.00	4.50	1.25
☐ 10 Richie Ashburn	35.00	16.00	4.40
☐ 11 Chico Carrasquel	10.00	4.50	1.25
☐ 12 Dave Philley	10.00	4.50	1.25
☐ 13 Don Newcombe	18.00	8.00	2.30

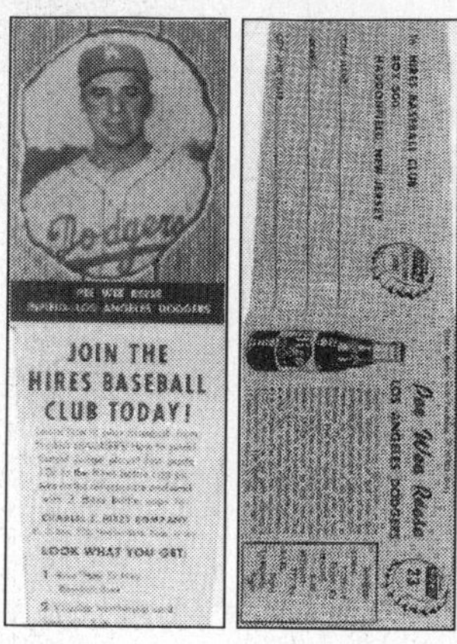

☐ 14 Wally Post	10.00	4.50	1.25
☐ 15 Rip Repulski	10.00	4.50	1.25
☐ 16 Chico Fernandez	10.00	4.50	1.25
☐ 17 Larry Doby	16.00	7.25	2.00
☐ 18 Hector Brown	10.00	4.50	1.25
☐ 19 Danny O'Connell	10.00	4.50	1.25
☐ 20 Granny Hamner	10.00	4.50	1.25
☐ 21 Dick Groat	14.00	6.25	1.75
☐ 22 Ray Narleski	10.00	4.50	1.25
☐ 23 Pee Wee Reese	70.00	32.00	8.75
☐ 24 Bob Friend	12.00	5.50	1.50
☐ 25 Willie Mays	250.00	115.00	31.00
☐ 26 Bob Nieman	10.00	4.50	1.25
☐ 27 Frank Thomas	15.00	6.75	1.90
☐ 28 Curt Simmons	12.00	5.50	1.50
☐ 29 Stan Lopata	10.00	4.50	1.25
☐ 30 Bob Skinner	12.00	5.50	1.50
☐ 31 Ron Kline	10.00	4.50	1.25
☐ 32 Willie Miranda	10.00	4.50	1.25
☐ 33 Bobby Avila	10.00	4.50	1.25
☐ 34 Clem Labine	12.00	5.50	1.50
☐ 35 Ray Jablonski	10.00	4.50	1.25
☐ 36 Bill Mazeroski	22.00	10.00	2.80
☐ 37 Billy Gardner	10.00	4.50	1.25
☐ 38 Pete Runnels	12.00	5.50	1.50
☐ 39 Jack Sanford	10.00	4.50	1.25
☐ 40 Dave Sisler	10.00	4.50	1.25
☐ 41 Don Zimmer	15.00	6.75	1.90
☐ 42 Johnny Podres	16.00	7.25	2.00
☐ 43 Dick Farrell	10.00	4.50	1.25
☐ 44 Hank Aaron	250.00	115.00	31.00
☐ 45 Bill Virdon	15.00	6.75	1.90
☐ 46 Bobby Thomson	15.00	6.75	1.90
☐ 47 Willard Nixon	10.00	4.50	1.25
☐ 48 Billy Loes	10.00	4.50	1.25
☐ 49 Hank Sauer	12.00	5.50	1.50
☐ 50 Johnny Antonelli	12.00	5.50	1.50
☐ 51 Daryl Spencer	10.00	4.50	1.25
☐ 52 Ken Lehman	10.00	4.50	1.25
☐ 53 Sammy White	10.00	4.50	1.25
☐ 54 Charley Neal	12.00	5.50	1.50
☐ 55 Don Drysdale	50.00	23.00	6.25
☐ 56 Jackie Jensen	25.00	11.50	3.10
☐ 57 Ray Katt	10.00	4.50	1.25
☐ 58 Frank Sullivan	10.00	4.50	1.25
☐ 59 Roy Face	15.00	6.75	1.90
☐ 60 Willie Jones	10.00	4.50	1.25
☐ 61 Duke Snider	110.00	50.00	14.00
☐ 62 Whitey Lockman	10.00	4.50	1.25
☐ 63 Gino Cimoli	10.00	4.50	1.25
☐ 64 Marv Grissom	10.00	4.50	1.25
☐ 65 Gene Baker	10.00	4.50	1.25
☐ 66 George Zuverink	10.00	4.50	1.25
☐ 67 Ted Kluszewski	22.00	10.00	2.80
☐ 68 Jim Busby	10.00	4.50	1.25
☐ 69 Not Issued	.00	.00	.00
☐ 70 Curt Barclay	10.00	4.50	1.25
☐ 71 Hank Foiles	10.00	4.50	1.25
☐ 72 Gene Stephens	10.00	4.50	1.25
☐ 73 Al Worthington	10.00	4.50	1.25
☐ 74 Al Walker	10.00	4.50	1.25
☐ 75 Bob Boyd	10.00	4.50	1.25
☐ 76 Al Pilarcik	10.00	4.50	1.25

1958 Hires Test

The cards in this eight-card test set measure approximately 2 5/16" by 3 1/2" or 2 5/16" by 7" with tabs. The 1958 Hires Root Beer test set features unnumbered, color cards. The card front photos are shown on a yellow or orange back ground instead of the wood grain background used in the Hires regular set. The cards contain a detachable coupon just as the regular Hires issue does. Cards were test marketed on a very limited basis in a few cities. Cards with the coupon still intact are especially tough to find and are worth triple the prices in the checklist below. The checklist below is ordered alphabetically.

	NRMT	VG-E	GOOD
COMPLETE SET (8)	1400.00	650.00	180.00
COMMON PLAYER (1-8)	125.00	57.50	15.50
☐ 1 Johnny Antonelli	150.00	70.00	19.00
☐ 2 Jim Busby	125.00	57.50	15.50
☐ 3 Chico Fernandez	125.00	57.50	15.50
☐ 4 Bob Friend	150.00	70.00	19.00
☐ 5 Vern Law	150.00	70.00	19.00
☐ 6 Stan Lopata	125.00	57.50	15.50
☐ 7 Willie Mays	600.00	275.00	75.00
☐ 8 Al Pilarcik	125.00	57.50	15.50

1959 Home Run Derby

This 20-card set was produced in 1959 by American Motors to publicize a TV program. The cards are black and white and blank backed. The cards measure approximately 3 1/8" by 5 1/4". The cards are unnumbered and are ordered alphabetically below for convenience. During 1988, the 19 player cards in this set were publicly reprinted.

	NRMT	VG-E	GOOD
COMPLETE SET (20)	3000.00	1350.00	375.00
COMMON PLAYER (1-20)	50.00	23.00	6.25
☐ 1 Hank Aaron	400.00	180.00	50.00
☐ 2 Bob Allison	50.00	23.00	6.25
☐ 3 Ernie Banks	175.00	80.00	22.00
☐ 4 Ken Boyer	60.00	27.00	7.50
☐ 5 Bob Cerv	50.00	23.00	6.25
☐ 6 Rocky Colavito	100.00	45.00	12.50
☐ 7 Gil Hodges	100.00	45.00	12.50
☐ 8 Jackie Jensen	60.00	27.00	7.50
☐ 9 Al Kaline	175.00	80.00	22.00
☐ 10 Harmon Killebrew	150.00	70.00	19.00
☐ 11 Jim Lemon	50.00	23.00	6.25
☐ 12 Mickey Mantle	1000.00	400.00	125.00
☐ 13 Ed Mathews	150.00	70.00	19.00
☐ 14 Willie Mays	400.00	180.00	50.00
☐ 15 Wally Post	50.00	23.00	6.25
☐ 16 Frank Robinson	150.00	70.00	19.00
☐ 17 Mark Scott ANN	50.00	23.00	6.25
☐ 18 Duke Snider	200.00	90.00	25.00
☐ 19 Dick Stuart	50.00	23.00	6.25
☐ 20 Gus Triandos	50.00	23.00	6.25

1991 Homers Cookies Classics

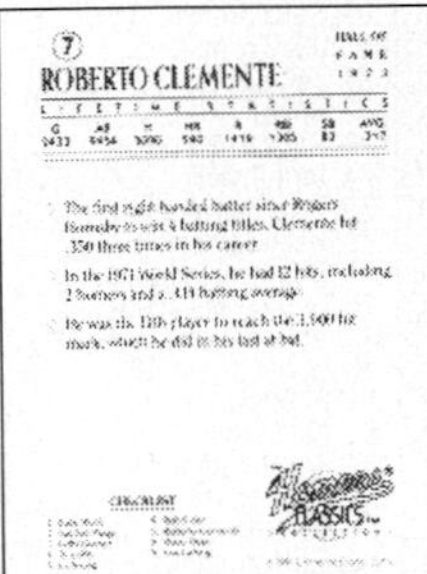

This nine-card set was sponsored by Legend Food Products in honor of Hall of Famers in baseball history. One free card was randomly inserted in each box of Homers Baseball Cookies. The standard-size (2 1/2" by 3 1/2") cards have vintage sepia-toned player photos, with bronze borders on a white card face. The player's name appears in a bronze stripe overlaying the bottom edge of the picture. In black print on white, the back presents lifetime statistics, career highlights, and a checklist for the set. The cards are numbered on the back.

	MT	EX-MT	VG
COMPLETE SET (9)	7.50	3.40	.95
COMMON PLAYER (1-9)	1.00	.45	.13
☐ 1 Babe Ruth	3.00	1.35	.40
☐ 2 Satchel Paige	1.25	.55	.16
☐ 3 Lefty Gomez	1.00	.45	.13
☐ 4 Ty Cobb	1.50	.65	.19
☐ 5 Cy Young	1.25	.55	.16
☐ 6 Bob Feller	1.25	.55	.16
☐ 7 Roberto Clemente	1.50	.65	.19
☐ 8 Dizzy Dean	1.50	.65	.19
☐ 9 Lou Gehrig	1.50	.65	.19

1947 Homogenized Bond

The cards in this 48-card set measure approximately 2 1/4" by 3 1/2". The 1947 W571/D305 Homogenized Bread are sets of unnumbered cards containing 44 baseball players and four boxers. The W571 set exists in two styles. Style one is identical to the D305 set except for the back printing while style two has perforated edges and movie stars

depicted on the backs. The second style of W571 cards contains only 13 cards. The four boxers in the checklist below are indicated by BOX. The checklist below is ordered alphabetically. There are 24 cards in the set which were definitely produced in greater supply. These 24 (marked by DP below) are quite a bit more common than the other 24 cards in the set.

	NRMT	VG-E	GOOD
COMPLETE SET	800.00	350.00	100.00
COMMON PLAYER (1-48)	10.00	4.50	1.25
COMMON BOXER	5.00	2.30	.60
COMMON DP BASEBALL	2.00	.90	.25
COMMON DP BOXER	1.50	.65	.19
☐ 1 Rex Barney	10.00	4.50	1.25
☐ 2 Larry(Yogi) Berra	125.00	57.50	15.50
☐ 3 Ewell Blackwell DP	2.00	.90	.25
☐ 4 Lou Boudreau DP	5.00	2.30	.60
☐ 5 Ralph Branca	11.00	4.90	1.40
☐ 6 Harry Brecheen DP	2.00	.90	.25
☐ 7 Primo Carnera BOX DP	1.50	.65	.19
☐ 8 Marcel Cerdan BOX	5.00	2.30	.60
☐ 9 Dom DiMaggio	12.50	5.75	1.55
☐ 10 Joe DiMaggio	200.00	90.00	25.00
☐ 11 Bobby Doerr DP	6.00	2.70	.75
☐ 12 Bruce Edwards	10.00	4.50	1.25
☐ 13 Bob Elliott DP	2.00	.90	.25
☐ 14 Del Ennis DP	2.00	.90	.25
☐ 15 Bob Feller DP	12.00	5.50	1.50
☐ 16 Carl Furillo	20.00	9.00	2.50
☐ 17 Joe Gordon DP	2.00	.90	.25
☐ 18 Sid Gordon	10.00	4.50	1.25
☐ 19 Joe Hatten	10.00	4.50	1.25
☐ 20 Gil Hodges	60.00	27.00	7.50
☐ 21 Tommy Holmes DP	2.00	.90	.25
☐ 22 Larry Jansen	10.00	4.50	1.25
☐ 23 Sheldon Jones	10.00	4.50	1.25
☐ 24 Edwin Joost	10.00	4.50	1.25
☐ 25 Charlie Keller	12.50	5.75	1.55
☐ 26 Ken Keltner DP	2.00	.90	.25
☐ 27 Buddy Kerr	10.00	4.50	1.25
☐ 28 Ralph Kiner DP	8.00	3.60	1.00
☐ 29 Jake LaMotta BOX	12.50	5.75	1.55
☐ 30 John Lindell	10.00	4.50	1.25
☐ 31 Whitey Lockman	10.00	4.50	1.25
☐ 32 Joe Louis BOX DP	6.00	2.70	.75
☐ 33 Willard Marshall	10.00	4.50	1.25
☐ 34 Johnny Mize DP	7.50	3.40	.95
☐ 35 Stan Musial DP	40.00	18.00	5.00
☐ 36 Andy Pafko DP	2.00	.90	.25
☐ 37 Johnny Pesky DP	2.00	.90	.25
☐ 38 Pee Wee Reese	60.00	27.00	7.50
☐ 39 Phil Rizzuto DP	10.00	4.50	1.25
☐ 40 Aaron Robinson DP	2.00	.90	.25
☐ 41 Jackie Robinson DP	50.00	23.00	6.25
☐ 42 John Sain DP	4.00	1.80	.50
☐ 43 Enos Slaughter DP	7.50	3.40	.95
☐ 44 Vern Stephens DP	2.00	.90	.25
☐ 45 George Tebbetts	10.00	4.50	1.25
☐ 46 Bobby Thomson	12.50	5.75	1.55
☐ 47 Johnny VanderMeer	12.50	5.75	1.55
☐ 48 Ted Williams DP	45.00	20.00	5.75

1975 Hostess

The cards in this 150-card set measure approximately 2 1/4" by 3 1/4" individually or 3 1/4" by 7 1/4" as panels of three. The 1975 Hostess set was issued in panels of three cards each on the backs of family-size packages of Hostess cakes. Card number 125, Bill Madlock, was listed correctly as an infielder and incorrectly as a pitcher. Number 11, Burt Hooton, and number 89, Doug Rader, are spelled two different ways. Some panels are more difficult to find than others as they were issued only on the backs of less popular Hostess products. These scarcer panels are shown with SP in the checklist. Although complete panel prices are not explicitly listed, they would generally have a value 25 percent greater than the sum of the values of the individual players on that panel. One of the more interesting cards in the set is that of Robin Yount; Hostess issued one of the few Yount cards available in 1975, his rookie year for cards.

	NRMT-MT	EXC	G-VG
COMPLETE INDIV.SET (150)	240.00	110.00	30.00
COMMON PLAYER (1-150)	.60	.25	.08
□ 1 Bob Tolan	.60	.25	.08
□ 2 Cookie Rojas	.60	.25	.08
□ 3 Darrell Evans	.90	.40	.11
□ 4 Sal Bando	.90	.40	.11
□ 5 Joe Morgan	5.00	2.30	.60
□ 6 Mickey Lolich	.90	.40	.11
□ 7 Don Sutton	3.50	1.55	.45
□ 8 Bill Melton	.60	.25	.08
□ 9 Tim Foli	.60	.25	.08
□ 10 Joe Lahoud	.60	.25	.08
□ 11A Bert Hooten (Sic)	1.25	.55	.16
□ 11B Burt Hooton COR	1.25	.55	.16
□ 12 Paul Blair	.75	.35	.09
□ 13 Jim Barr	.60	.25	.08
□ 14 Toby Harrah	.90	.40	.11
□ 15 John Milner	.60	.25	.08
□ 16 Ken Holtzman	.75	.35	.09
□ 17 Cesar Cedeno	.90	.40	.11
□ 18 Dwight Evans	2.00	.90	.25
□ 19 Willie McCovey	3.50	1.55	.45
□ 20 Tony Oliva	1.50	.65	.19
□ 21 Manny Sanguillen	.75	.35	.09
□ 22 Mickey Rivers	.75	.35	.09
□ 23 Lou Brock	4.00	1.80	.50
□ 24 Graig Nettles UER (Craig on front)	1.50	.65	.19
□ 25 Jim Wynn	.90	.40	.11
□ 26 George Scott	.75	.35	.09
□ 27 Greg Luzinski	.90	.40	.11
□ 28 Bert Campaneris	.90	.40	.11
□ 29 Pete Rose	10.00	4.50	1.25
□ 30 Buddy Bell	.90	.40	.11
□ 31 Gary Matthews	.75	.35	.09
□ 32 Freddie Patek	.60	.25	.08
□ 33 Mike Lum	.60	.25	.08
□ 34 Ellie Rodriguez	.60	.25	.08
□ 35 Milt May UER (Photo actually Lee May)	.75	.35	.09
□ 36 Willie Horton	.90	.40	.11
□ 37 Dave Winfield	15.00	6.75	1.90
□ 38 Tom Grieve	.75	.35	.09
□ 39 Barry Foote	.60	.25	.08
□ 40 Joe Rudi	.90	.40	.11
□ 41 Bake McBride	.60	.25	.08
□ 42 Mike Cuellar	.75	.35	.09
□ 43 Garry Maddox	.75	.35	.09
□ 44 Carlos May	.60	.25	.08
□ 45 Bud Harrelson	.75	.35	.09
□ 46 Dave Chalk	.60	.25	.08
□ 47 Dave Concepcion	1.00	.45	.13
□ 48 Carl Yastrzemski	8.00	3.60	1.00
□ 49 Steve Garvey	4.00	1.80	.50
□ 50 Amos Otis	.75	.35	.09
□ 51 Rick Reuschel	.75	.35	.09
□ 52 Rollie Fingers	3.50	1.55	.45
□ 53 Bob Watson	.75	.35	.09
□ 54 John Ellis	.60	.25	.08
□ 55 Bob Bailey	.60	.25	.08
□ 56 Rod Carew	6.00	2.70	.75
□ 57 Rich Hebner	.60	.25	.08
□ 58 Nolan Ryan	25.00	11.50	3.10
□ 59 Reggie Smith	.75	.35	.09
□ 60 Joe Coleman	.60	.25	.08
□ 61 Ron Cey	.90	.40	.11
□ 62 Darrell Porter	.60	.25	.08
□ 63 Steve Carlton	5.00	2.30	.60
□ 64 Gene Tenace	.75	.35	.09
□ 65 Jose Cardenal	.60	.25	.08
□ 66 Bill Lee	.75	.35	.09
□ 67 Dave Lopes	.90	.40	.11
□ 68 Wilbur Wood	.75	.35	.09
□ 69 Steve Renko	.60	.25	.08
□ 70 Joe Torre	1.00	.45	.13
□ 71 Ted Sizemore	.60	.25	.08
□ 72 Bobby Grich	.90	.40	.11
□ 73 Chris Speier	.60	.25	.08
□ 74 Bert Blyleven	1.25	.55	.16
□ 75 Tom Seaver	8.00	3.60	1.00
□ 76 Nate Colbert	.60	.25	.08
□ 77 Don Kessinger	.75	.35	.09
□ 78 George Medich	.60	.25	.08
□ 79 Andy Messersmith SP	.75	.35	.09
□ 80 Robin Yount SP	40.00	18.00	5.00
□ 81 Al Oliver SP	1.00	.45	.13
□ 82 Bill Singer SP	.75	.35	.09
□ 83 Johnny Bench SP	10.00	4.50	1.25
□ 84 Gaylord Perry SP	4.00	1.80	.50
□ 85 Dave Kingman SP	1.00	.45	.13
□ 86 Ed Herrmann SP	.75	.35	.09
□ 87 Ralph Garr SP	.75	.35	.09
□ 88 Reggie Jackson SP	10.00	4.50	1.25
□ 89A Doug Radar ERR SP (Sic, Rader)	1.25	.55	.16
□ 89B Doug Rader COR SP	5.00	2.30	.60
□ 90 Elliott Maddox SP	.75	.35	.09
□ 91 Bill Russell SP	.90	.40	.11
□ 92 John Mayberry SP	.90	.40	.11
□ 93 Dave Cash SP	.75	.35	.09
□ 94 Jeff Burroughs SP	.90	.40	.11
□ 95 Ted Simmons SP	2.00	.90	.25
□ 96 Joe Decker SP	.75	.35	.09
□ 97 Bill Buckner SP	1.25	.55	.16
□ 98 Bobby Darwin SP	.75	.35	.09
□ 99 Phil Niekro SP	4.00	1.80	.50
□ 100 Jim Sundberg	1.00	.45	.13
□ 101 Greg Gross	.60	.25	.08
□ 102 Luis Tiant	.90	.40	.11
□ 103 Glenn Beckert	.60	.25	.08
□ 104 Hal McRae	1.25	.55	.16
□ 105 Mike Jorgensen	.60	.25	.08
□ 106 Mike Hargrove	1.00	.45	.13
□ 107 Don Gullett	.75	.35	.09
□ 108 Tito Fuentes	.60	.25	.08
□ 109 John Grubb	.60	.25	.08
□ 110 Jim Kaat	1.50	.65	.19
□ 111 Felix Millan	.60	.25	.08
□ 112 Don Money	.60	.25	.08
□ 113 Rick Monday	.75	.35	.09
□ 114 Dick Bosman	.60	.25	.08
□ 115 Roger Metzger	.60	.25	.08
□ 116 Fergie Jenkins	3.50	1.55	.45
□ 117 Dusty Baker	1.00	.45	.13
□ 118 Billy Champion SP	.75	.35	.09
□ 119 Bob Gibson SP	5.00	2.30	.60
□ 120 Bill Freehan SP	.90	.40	.11
□ 121 Cesar Geronimo	.60	.25	.08
□ 122 Jorge Orta	.60	.25	.08
□ 123 Cleon Jones	.60	.25	.08
□ 124 Steve Busby	.75	.35	.09
□ 125A Bill Madlock ERR (Pitcher)	1.50	.65	.19
□ 125B Bill Madlock COR (Infielder)	1.50	.65	.19
□ 126 Jim Palmer	4.00	1.80	.50
□ 127 Tony Perez	2.50	1.15	.30

Card	NRMT-MT	EXC	G-VG
☐ 128 Larry Hisle	.75	.35	.09
☐ 129 Rusty Staub	.90	.40	.11
☐ 130 Hank Aaron SP	12.00	5.50	1.50
☐ 131 Rennie Stennett SP	.75	.35	.09
☐ 132 Rico Petrocelli SP	.75	.35	.09
☐ 133 Mike Schmidt	12.00	5.50	1.50
☐ 134 Sparky Lyle	1.00	.45	.13
☐ 135 Willie Stargell	4.00	1.80	.50
☐ 136 Ken Henderson	.60	.25	.08
☐ 137 Willie Montanez	.60	.25	.08
☐ 138 Thurman Munson	6.00	2.70	.75
☐ 139 Richie Zisk	.75	.35	.09
☐ 140 George Hendrick	.75	.35	.09
☐ 141 Bobby Murcer	1.00	.45	.13
☐ 142 Lee May	.75	.35	.09
☐ 143 Carlton Fisk	4.00	1.80	.50
☐ 144 Brooks Robinson	4.00	1.80	.50
☐ 145 Bobby Bonds	1.25	.55	.16
☐ 146 Gary Sutherland	.60	.25	.08
☐ 147 Oscar Gamble	.75	.35	.09
☐ 148 Jim Hunter	3.50	1.55	.45
☐ 149 Tug McGraw	1.00	.45	.13
☐ 150 Dave McNally	.75	.35	.09

1975 Hostess Twinkie

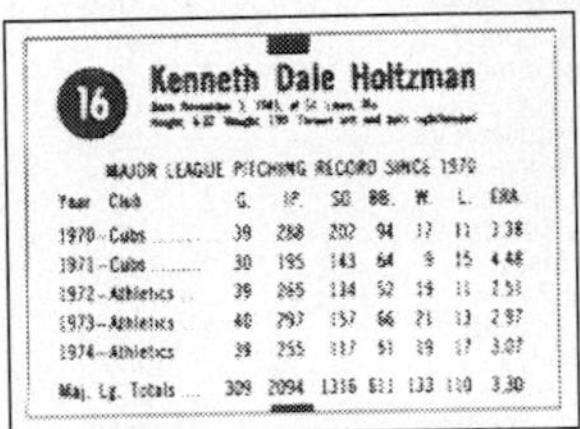

The cards in this 60-card set measure approximately 2 1/4" by 3 1/4". The 1975 Hostess Twinkie set was issued on a limited basis in the far western part of the country. The set contains the same numbers as the regular set to number 36; however, the set is skip numbered after number 36. The cards were issued as the backs for 25-cent Twinkies packs. The fronts are indistinguishable from the regular Hostess cards; however the card backs are different in that the Twinkie cards have a thick black bar in the middle of the reverse. One of the more interesting cards in the set is that of Robin Yount; Hostess issued one of the few Yount cards available in 1975, his rookie year for cards.

	NRMT-MT	EXC	G-VG
COMPLETE SET (60)	120.00	55.00	15.00
COMMON PLAYER	1.00	.45	.13
☐ 1 Bob Tolan	1.00	.45	.13
☐ 2 Cookie Rojas	1.00	.45	.13
☐ 3 Darrell Evans	1.25	.55	.16
☐ 4 Sal Bando	1.25	.55	.16
☐ 5 Joe Morgan	5.00	2.30	.60
☐ 6 Mickey Lolich	1.25	.55	.16
☐ 7 Don Sutton	3.50	1.55	.45
☐ 8 Bill Melton	1.00	.45	.13
☐ 9 Tim Foli	1.00	.45	.13
☐ 10 Joe Lahoud	1.00	.45	.13
☐ 11 Bert Hooten (Sic)	1.25	.55	.16
☐ 12 Paul Blair	1.00	.45	.13
☐ 13 Jim Barr	1.00	.45	.13
☐ 14 Toby Harrah	1.25	.55	.16
☐ 15 John Milner	1.00	.45	.13
☐ 16 Ken Holtzman	1.00	.45	.13
☐ 17 Cesar Cedeno	1.25	.55	.16
☐ 18 Dwight Evans	2.00	.90	.25
☐ 19 Willie McCovey	3.50	1.55	.45
☐ 20 Tony Oliva	1.50	.65	.19
☐ 21 Manny Sanguillen	1.00	.45	.13
☐ 22 Mickey Rivers	1.00	.45	.13
☐ 23 Lou Brock	4.00	1.80	.50
☐ 24 Graig Nettles UER (Craig on front)	1.50	.65	.19
☐ 25 Jim Wynn	1.25	.55	.16
☐ 26 George Scott	1.00	.45	.13
☐ 27 Greg Luzinski	1.25	.55	.16
☐ 28 Bert Campaneris	1.25	.55	.16
☐ 29 Pete Rose	10.00	4.50	1.25
☐ 30 Buddy Bell	1.25	.55	.16
☐ 31 Gary Matthews	1.00	.45	.13
☐ 32 Freddie Patek	1.00	.45	.13
☐ 33 Mike Lum	1.00	.45	.13
☐ 34 Ellie Rodriguez	1.00	.45	.13
☐ 35 Milt May UER (Lee May picture)	1.00	.45	.13
☐ 36 Willie Horton	1.25	.55	.16
☐ 40 Joe Rudi	1.25	.55	.16
☐ 43 Garry Maddox	1.00	.45	.13
☐ 46 Dave Chalk	1.00	.45	.13
☐ 49 Steve Garvey	4.00	1.80	.50
☐ 52 Rollie Fingers	3.50	1.55	.45
☐ 58 Nolan Ryan	25.00	11.50	3.10
☐ 61 Ron Cey	1.25	.55	.16
☐ 64 Gene Tenace	1.00	.45	.13
☐ 65 Jose Cardenal	1.00	.45	.13
☐ 67 Dave Lopes	1.25	.55	.16
☐ 68 Wilbur Wood	1.00	.45	.13
☐ 73 Chris Speier	1.00	.45	.13
☐ 77 Don Kessinger	1.00	.45	.13
☐ 79 Andy Messersmith	1.00	.45	.13
☐ 80 Robin Yount	40.00	18.00	5.00
☐ 82 Bill Singer	1.00	.45	.13
☐ 103 Glenn Beckert	1.00	.45	.13
☐ 110 Jim Kaat	1.50	.65	.19
☐ 112 Don Money	1.00	.45	.13
☐ 113 Rick Monday	1.00	.45	.13
☐ 122 Jorge Orta	1.00	.45	.13
☐ 125 Bill Madlock	1.50	.65	.19
☐ 130 Hank Aaron	12.00	5.50	1.50
☐ 136 Ken Henderson	1.00	.45	.13

1976 Hostess

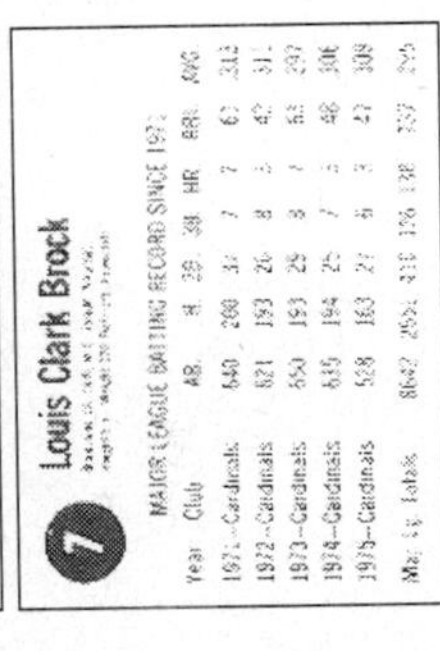

The cards in this 150-card set measure approximately 2 1/4" by 3 1/4" individually or 3 1/4" by 7 1/4" as panels of three. The 1976 Hostess set contains full-color, numbered cards issued in panels of three cards each on family-size packages of Hostess cakes. Scarcer panels (those only found on less popular Hostess products) are listed in the checklist below with SP. Complete panels of three have a value 25 percent more than the sum of the individual cards on the panel. Nine additional numbers (151-159) were apparently planned but never actually issued. These exist as proof cards and are quite scarce, e.g., 151 Ferguson Jenkins (even though he already appears in the set as card number 138), 152 Mike Cuellar, 153 Tom Murphy, 154 Al Cowens, 155 Barry Foote, 156 Steve Carlton, 157 Richie Zisk, 158 Ken Holtzman, and 159 Cliff Johnson. One of the more interesting cards in the set is that of Dennis Eckersley; Hostess issued one of the few Eckersley cards available in 1976, his rookie year for cards.

	NRMT-MT	EXC	G-VG
COMPLETE INDIV.SET (150)	240.00	110.00	30.00
COMMON PLAYER (1-150)	.60	.25	.08
☐ 1 Fred Lynn	1.25	.55	.16
☐ 2 Joe Morgan	5.00	2.30	.60

☐ 3 Phil Niekro 3.50 1.55 .45
☐ 4 Gaylord Perry 3.50 1.55 .45
☐ 5 Bob Watson .75 .35 .09
☐ 6 Bill Freehan .90 .40 .11
☐ 7 Lou Brock 4.00 1.80 .50
☐ 8 Al Fitzmorris .60 .25 .08
☐ 9 Rennie Stennett .60 .25 .08
☐ 10 Tony Oliva 1.25 .55 .16
☐ 11 Robin Yount 16.00 7.25 2.00
☐ 12 Rick Manning .60 .25 .08
☐ 13 Bobby Grich .90 .40 .11
☐ 14 Terry Forster .75 .35 .09
☐ 15 Dave Kingman .90 .40 .11
☐ 16 Thurman Munson 6.00 2.70 .75
☐ 17 Rick Reuschel .90 .40 .11
☐ 18 Bobby Bonds 1.25 .55 .16
☐ 19 Steve Garvey 4.00 1.80 .50
☐ 20 Vida Blue .90 .40 .11
☐ 21 Dave Rader .60 .25 .08
☐ 22 Johnny Bench 7.50 3.40 .95
☐ 23 Luis Tiant .90 .40 .11
☐ 24 Darrell Evans .90 .40 .11
☐ 25 Larry Dierker .60 .25 .08
☐ 26 Willie Horton .90 .40 .11
☐ 27 John Ellis .60 .25 .08
☐ 28 Al Cowens .60 .25 .08
☐ 29 Jerry Reuss .60 .25 .08
☐ 30 Reggie Smith .90 .40 .11
☐ 31 Bobby Darwin SP .75 .35 .09
☐ 32 Fritz Peterson SP .75 .35 .09
☐ 33 Rod Carew SP 6.00 2.70 .75
☐ 34 Carlos May SP .75 .35 .09
☐ 35 Tom Seaver SP 9.00 4.00 1.15
☐ 36 Brooks Robinson SP 6.00 2.70 .75
☐ 37 Jose Cardenal .60 .25 .08
☐ 38 Ron Blomberg .60 .25 .08
☐ 39 Leroy Stanton .60 .25 .08
☐ 40 Dave Cash .60 .25 .08
☐ 41 John Montefusco .75 .35 .09
☐ 42 Bob Tolan .60 .25 .08
☐ 43 Carl Morton .60 .25 .08
☐ 44 Rick Burleson .90 .40 .11
☐ 45 Don Gullett .75 .35 .09
☐ 46 Vern Ruhle .60 .25 .08
☐ 47 Cesar Cedeno .90 .40 .11
☐ 48 Toby Harrah .75 .35 .09
☐ 49 Willie Stargell 4.00 1.80 .50
☐ 50 Al Hrabosky .75 .35 .09
☐ 51 Amos Otis .90 .40 .11
☐ 52 Bud Harrelson .90 .40 .11
☐ 53 Jim Hughes .60 .25 .08
☐ 54 George Scott .75 .35 .09
☐ 55 Mike Vail SP .75 .35 .09
☐ 56 Jim Palmer SP 5.00 2.30 .60
☐ 57 Jorge Orta SP .75 .35 .09
☐ 58 Chris Chambliss SP 1.00 .45 .13
☐ 59 Dave Chalk SP .75 .35 .09
☐ 60 Ray Burris SP .75 .35 .09
☐ 61 Bert Campaneris SP .90 .40 .11
☐ 62 Gary Carter SP 9.00 4.00 1.15
☐ 63 Ron Cey SP 1.00 .45 .13
☐ 64 Carlton Fisk SP 4.00 1.80 .50
☐ 65 Marty Perez SP .75 .35 .09
☐ 66 Pete Rose SP 10.00 4.50 1.25
☐ 67 Roger Metzger SP .75 .35 .09
☐ 68 Jim Sundberg SP .75 .35 .09
☐ 69 Ron LeFlore SP .90 .40 .11
☐ 70 Ted Sizemore SP .75 .35 .09
☐ 71 Steve Busby SP .90 .40 .11
☐ 72 Manny Sanguillen SP .90 .40 .11
☐ 73 Larry Hisle SP .75 .35 .09
☐ 74 Pete Broberg SP .75 .35 .09
☐ 75 Boog Powell SP 1.00 .45 .13
☐ 76 Ken Singleton SP .90 .40 .11
☐ 77 Rich Gossage SP 1.50 .65 .19
☐ 78 Jerry Grote SP .75 .35 .09
☐ 79 Nolan Ryan SP 25.00 11.50 3.10
☐ 80 Rick Monday SP .90 .40 .11
☐ 81 Graig Nettles SP 1.25 .55 .16
☐ 82 Chris Speier .60 .25 .08
☐ 83 Dave Winfield 10.00 4.50 1.25
☐ 84 Mike Schmidt 10.00 4.50 1.25
☐ 85 Buzz Capra .60 .25 .08
☐ 86 Tony Perez 1.75 .80 .22
☐ 87 Dwight Evans 1.25 .55 .16
☐ 88 Mike Hargrove .75 .35 .09
☐ 89 Joe Coleman .60 .25 .08
☐ 90 Greg Gross .60 .25 .08
☐ 91 John Mayberry .75 .35 .09
☐ 92 John Candelaria .75 .35 .09
☐ 93 Bake McBride .60 .25 .08
☐ 94 Hank Aaron 9.00 4.00 1.15
☐ 95 Buddy Bell .75 .35 .09
☐ 96 Steve Braun .60 .25 .08
☐ 97 Jon Matlack .75 .35 .09
☐ 98 Lee May .75 .35 .09
☐ 99 Wilbur Wood .75 .35 .09
☐ 100 Bill Madlock .90 .40 .11
☐ 101 Frank Tanana .90 .40 .11
☐ 102 Mickey Rivers .60 .25 .08
☐ 103 Mike Ivie .60 .25 .08
☐ 104 Rollie Fingers 3.50 1.55 .45
☐ 105 Dave Lopes .75 .35 .09
☐ 106 George Foster 1.25 .55 .16
☐ 107 Denny Doyle .60 .25 .08
☐ 108 Earl Williams .60 .25 .08
☐ 109 Tom Veryzer .60 .25 .08
☐ 110 J.R. Richard .75 .35 .09
☐ 111 Jeff Burroughs .75 .35 .09
☐ 112 Al Oliver .90 .40 .11
☐ 113 Ted Simmons 1.25 .55 .16
☐ 114 George Brett 18.00 8.00 2.30
☐ 115 Frank Duffy .60 .25 .08
☐ 116 Bert Blyleven 1.25 .55 .16
☐ 117 Darrell Porter .75 .35 .09
☐ 118 Don Baylor 1.25 .55 .16
☐ 119 Bucky Dent .90 .40 .11
☐ 120 Felix Millan .60 .25 .08
☐ 121 Mike Cuellar .75 .35 .09
☐ 122 Gene Tenace .75 .35 .09
☐ 123 Bobby Murcer .90 .40 .11
☐ 124 Willie McCovey 3.50 1.55 .45
☐ 125 Greg Luzinski .90 .40 .11
☐ 126 Larry Parrish .75 .35 .09
☐ 127 Jim Rice 4.00 1.80 .50
☐ 128 Dave Concepcion 1.25 .55 .16
☐ 129 Jim Wynn .75 .35 .09
☐ 130 Tom Grieve .75 .35 .09
☐ 131 Mike Cosgrove .60 .25 .08
☐ 132 Dan Meyer .60 .25 .08
☐ 133 Dave Parker 3.00 1.35 .40
☐ 134 Don Kessinger .75 .35 .09
☐ 135 Hal McRae 1.00 .45 .13
☐ 136 Don Money .60 .25 .08
☐ 137 Dennis Eckersley 20.00 9.00 2.50
☐ 138 Fergie Jenkins 3.50 1.55 .45
☐ 139 Mike Torrez .75 .35 .09
☐ 140 Jerry Morales .60 .25 .08
☐ 141 Jim Hunter 3.50 1.55 .45
☐ 142 Gary Matthews .75 .35 .09
☐ 143 Randy Jones .75 .35 .09
☐ 144 Mike Jorgensen .60 .25 .08
☐ 145 Larry Bowa .90 .40 .11
☐ 146 Reggie Jackson 7.50 3.40 .95
☐ 147 Steve Yeager .60 .25 .08
☐ 148 Dave May .60 .25 .08
☐ 149 Carl Yastrzemski 7.50 3.40 .95
☐ 150 Cesar Geronimo .60 .25 .08

1976 Hostess Twinkie

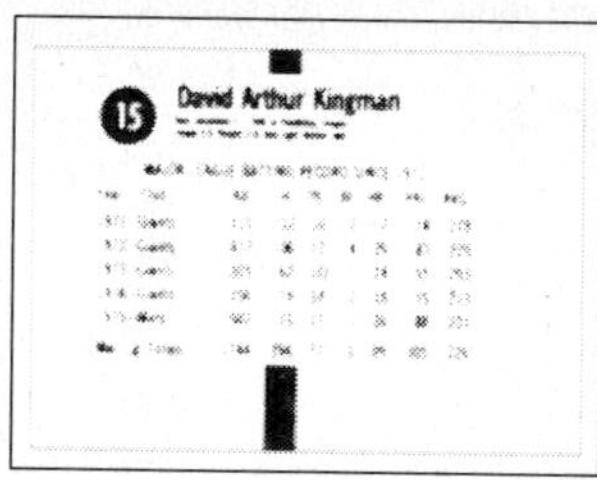

The cards in this 60-card set measure approximately 2 1/4" by 3 1/4". The 1976 Hostess Twinkies set contains the first 60 cards of the 1976 Hostess set. These cards were issued as backs on 25-cent Twinkie packages as in the 1975 Twinkies set. The fronts are indistinguishable from the regular Hostess cards; however the card backs are different in that the Twinkie cards have a thick black bar in the middle of the reverse.

	NRMT-MT	EXC	G-VG
COMPLETE SET (60)	120.00	55.00	15.00
COMMON PLAYER (1-60)	1.00	.45	.13

☐ 1 Fred Lynn	1.25	.55	.16
☐ 2 Joe Morgan	5.00	2.30	.60
☐ 3 Phil Niekro	3.50	1.55	.45
☐ 4 Gaylord Perry	3.50	1.55	.45
☐ 5 Bob Watson	1.00	.45	.13
☐ 6 Bill Freehan	1.25	.55	.16
☐ 7 Lou Brock	4.00	1.80	.50
☐ 8 Al Fitzmorris	1.00	.45	.13
☐ 9 Rennie Stennett	1.00	.45	.13
☐ 10 Tony Oliva	1.50	.65	.19
☐ 11 Robin Yount	16.00	7.25	2.00
☐ 12 Rick Manning	1.00	.45	.13
☐ 13 Bobby Grich	1.25	.55	.16
☐ 14 Terry Forster	1.00	.45	.13
☐ 15 Dave Kingman	1.25	.55	.16
☐ 16 Thurman Munson	6.00	2.70	.75
☐ 17 Rick Reuschel	1.25	.55	.16
☐ 18 Bobby Bonds	1.50	.65	.19
☐ 19 Steve Garvey	4.00	1.80	.50
☐ 20 Vida Blue	1.25	.55	.16
☐ 21 Dave Rader	1.00	.45	.13
☐ 22 Johnny Bench	7.50	3.40	.95
☐ 23 Luis Tiant	1.25	.55	.16
☐ 24 Darrell Evans	1.25	.55	.16
☐ 25 Larry Dierker	1.00	.45	.13
☐ 26 Willie Horton	1.25	.55	.16
☐ 27 John Ellis	1.00	.45	.13
☐ 28 Al Cowens	1.00	.45	.13
☐ 29 Jerry Reuss	1.00	.45	.13
☐ 30 Reggie Smith	1.25	.55	.16
☐ 31 Bobby Darwin	1.00	.45	.13
☐ 32 Fritz Peterson	1.00	.45	.13
☐ 33 Rod Carew	6.00	2.70	.75
☐ 34 Carlos May	1.00	.45	.13
☐ 35 Tom Seaver	9.00	4.00	1.15
☐ 36 Brooks Robinson	6.00	2.70	.75
☐ 37 Jose Cardenal	1.00	.45	.13
☐ 38 Ron Blomberg	1.00	.45	.13
☐ 39 Leroy Stanton	1.00	.45	.13
☐ 40 Dave Cash	1.00	.45	.13
☐ 41 John Montefusco	1.00	.45	.13
☐ 42 Bob Tolan	1.00	.45	.13
☐ 43 Carl Morton	1.00	.45	.13
☐ 44 Rick Burleson	1.25	.55	.16
☐ 45 Don Gullett	1.00	.45	.13
☐ 46 Vern Ruhle	1.00	.45	.13
☐ 47 Cesar Cedeno	1.25	.55	.16
☐ 48 Toby Harrah	1.00	.45	.13
☐ 49 Willie Stargell	4.00	1.80	.50
☐ 50 Al Hrabosky	1.00	.45	.13
☐ 51 Amos Otis	1.25	.55	.16
☐ 52 Bud Harrelson	1.25	.55	.16
☐ 53 Jim Hughes	1.00	.45	.13
☐ 54 George Scott	1.00	.45	.13
☐ 55 Mike Vail	1.00	.45	.13
☐ 56 Jim Palmer	5.00	2.30	.60
☐ 57 Jorge Orta	1.00	.45	.13
☐ 58 Chris Chambliss	1.25	.55	.16
☐ 59 Dave Chalk	1.00	.45	.13
☐ 60 Ray Burris	1.00	.45	.13

1977 Hostess

DAVE WINFIELD
San Diego PADRES
OUTFIELD
44
David Mark Winfield

The cards in this 150-card set measure approximately 2 1/4" by 3 1/4" individually or 3 1/4" by 7 1/4" as panels of three. The 1977 Hostess set contains full-color, numbered cards issued in panels of three cards each with Hostess family-size cake products. Scarcer panels are listed in the checklist below with SP. Although complete panel prices are not explicitly listed below, they would generally have a value 25 percent greater than the sum of the individual players on the panel. There were 10 additional cards proofed, but not produced or distributed; they are 151 Ed Kranepool, 152 Ross Grimsley, 153 Ken Brett, 154 Rowland Office, 155 Rick Wise, 156 Paul Splittorff, 157 Gerald Augustine, 158 Ken Forsch, 159 Jerry Reuss (Reuss is also number 119 in the set), and 160 Nelson Briles. There is also a complete variation set that was available one card per Twinkie package. Common cards in this Twinkie set are worth double the prices listed below, although the stars are only worth about 20 percent more. The Twinkie cards are distinguished by the thick printing bar or band printed on the card backs just below the statistics.

	NRMT-MT	EXC	G-VG
COMPLETE INDIV.SET (150)	225.00	100.00	28.00
COMMON PLAYER (1-150)	.60	.25	.08
☐ 1 Jim Palmer	4.00	1.80	.50
☐ 2 Joe Morgan	4.00	1.80	.50
☐ 3 Reggie Jackson	7.50	3.40	.95
☐ 4 Carl Yastrzemski	7.50	3.40	.95
☐ 5 Thurman Munson	5.00	2.30	.60
☐ 6 Johnny Bench	7.50	3.40	.95
☐ 7 Tom Seaver	7.50	3.40	.95
☐ 8 Pete Rose	9.00	4.00	1.15
☐ 9 Rod Carew	5.00	2.30	.60
☐ 10 Luis Tiant	.90	.40	.11
☐ 11 Phil Garner	.90	.40	.11
☐ 12 Sixto Lezcano	.60	.25	.08
☐ 13 Mike Torrez	.60	.25	.08
☐ 14 Dave Lopes	.75	.35	.09
☐ 15 Doug DeCinces	.75	.35	.09
☐ 16 Jim Spencer	.60	.25	.08
☐ 17 Hal McRae	1.00	.45	.13
☐ 18 Mike Hargrove	.75	.35	.09
☐ 19 Willie Montanez SP	.75	.35	.09
☐ 20 Roger Metzger SP	.75	.35	.09
☐ 21 Dwight Evans SP	1.50	.65	.19
☐ 22 Steve Rogers SP	.75	.35	.09
☐ 23 Jim Rice SP	4.00	1.80	.50
☐ 24 Pete Falcone SP	.75	.35	.09
☐ 25 Greg Luzinski SP	1.00	.45	.13
☐ 26 Randy Jones SP	.90	.40	.11
☐ 27 Willie Stargell SP	4.00	1.80	.50
☐ 28 John Hiller SP	.90	.40	.11
☐ 29 Bobby Murcer SP	1.00	.45	.13
☐ 30 Rick Monday SP	.90	.40	.11
☐ 31 John Montefusco SP	.75	.35	.09
☐ 32 Lou Brock SP	4.00	1.80	.50
☐ 33 Bill North SP	.75	.35	.09
☐ 34 Robin Yount SP	12.00	5.50	1.50
☐ 35 Steve Garvey SP	5.00	2.30	.60
☐ 36 George Brett SP	12.00	5.50	1.50
☐ 37 Toby Harrah SP	.90	.40	.11
☐ 38 Jerry Royster SP	.75	.35	.09
☐ 39 Bob Watson SP	.90	.40	.11
☐ 40 George Foster	1.00	.45	.13
☐ 41 Gary Carter	4.50	2.00	.55
☐ 42 John Denny	.75	.35	.09
☐ 43 Mike Schmidt	9.00	4.00	1.15
☐ 44 Dave Winfield	7.50	3.40	.95
☐ 45 Al Oliver	.90	.40	.11
☐ 46 Mark Fidrych	1.00	.45	.13
☐ 47 Larry Herndon	.60	.25	.08
☐ 48 Dave Goltz	.60	.25	.08
☐ 49 Jerry Morales	.60	.25	.08
☐ 50 Ron LeFlore	.75	.35	.09
☐ 51 Fred Lynn	1.25	.55	.16
☐ 52 Vida Blue	.75	.35	.09
☐ 53 Rick Manning	.60	.25	.08
☐ 54 Bill Buckner	.90	.40	.11
☐ 55 Lee May	.75	.35	.09
☐ 56 John Mayberry	.75	.35	.09
☐ 57 Darrel Chaney	.60	.25	.08
☐ 58 Cesar Cedeno	.75	.35	.09
☐ 59 Ken Griffey	1.25	.55	.16
☐ 60 Dave Kingman	.90	.40	.11
☐ 61 Ted Simmons	1.25	.55	.16
☐ 62 Larry Bowa	.75	.35	.09
☐ 63 Frank Tanana	.90	.40	.11
☐ 64 Jason Thompson	.75	.35	.09
☐ 65 Ken Brett	.60	.25	.08
☐ 66 Roy Smalley	.75	.35	.09
☐ 67 Ray Burris	.60	.25	.08
☐ 68 Rick Burleson	.75	.35	.09

☐ 69 Buddy Bell	.90	.40	.11
☐ 70 Don Sutton	3.50	1.55	.45
☐ 71 Mark Belanger	.75	.35	.09
☐ 72 Dennis Leonard	.75	.35	.09
☐ 73 Gaylord Perry	3.50	1.55	.45
☐ 74 Dick Ruthven	.60	.25	.08
☐ 75 Jose Cruz	.75	.35	.09
☐ 76 Cesar Geronimo	.60	.25	.08
☐ 77 Jerry Koosman	.90	.40	.11
☐ 78 Garry Templeton	1.00	.45	.13
☐ 79 Jim Hunter	3.50	1.55	.45
☐ 80 John Candelaria	.75	.35	.09
☐ 81 Nolan Ryan	25.00	11.50	3.10
☐ 82 Rusty Staub	.90	.40	.11
☐ 83 Jim Barr	.60	.25	.08
☐ 84 Butch Wynegar	.60	.25	.08
☐ 85 Jose Cardenal	.60	.25	.08
☐ 86 Claudell Washington	.75	.35	.09
☐ 87 Bill Travers	.60	.25	.08
☐ 88 Rick Waits	.60	.25	.08
☐ 89 Ron Cey	.90	.40	.11
☐ 90 Al Bumbry	.60	.25	.08
☐ 91 Bucky Dent	.90	.40	.11
☐ 92 Amos Otis	.75	.35	.09
☐ 93 Tom Grieve	.75	.35	.09
☐ 94 Enos Cabell	.60	.25	.08
☐ 95 Dave Concepcion	1.25	.55	.16
☐ 96 Felix Millan	.60	.25	.08
☐ 97 Bake McBride	.60	.25	.08
☐ 98 Chris Chambliss	.75	.35	.09
☐ 99 Butch Metzger	.60	.25	.08
☐ 100 Rennie Stennett	.60	.25	.08
☐ 101 Dave Roberts	.60	.25	.08
☐ 102 Lyman Bostock	.75	.35	.09
☐ 103 Rick Reuschel	.75	.35	.09
☐ 104 Carlton Fisk	4.00	1.80	.50
☐ 105 Jim Slaton	.60	.25	.08
☐ 106 Dennis Eckersley	6.00	2.70	.75
☐ 107 Ken Singleton	.75	.35	.09
☐ 108 Ralph Garr	.75	.35	.09
☐ 109 Freddie Patek SP	.75	.35	.09
☐ 110 Jim Sundberg SP	.75	.35	.09
☐ 111 Phil Niekro SP	3.50	1.55	.45
☐ 112 J.R. Richard SP	.90	.40	.11
☐ 113 Gary Nolan SP	.75	.35	.09
☐ 114 Jon Matlack SP	.75	.35	.09
☐ 115 Keith Hernandez SP	4.00	1.80	.50
☐ 116 Graig Nettles SP	1.00	.45	.13
☐ 117 Steve Carlton SP	5.00	2.30	.60
☐ 118 Bill Madlock SP	1.25	.55	.16
☐ 119 Jerry Reuss SP	.75	.35	.09
☐ 120 Aurelio Rodriguez SP	.75	.35	.09
☐ 121 Dan Ford SP	.75	.35	.09
☐ 122 Ray Fosse SP	.75	.35	.09
☐ 123 George Hendrick SP	.75	.35	.09
☐ 124 Alan Ashby	.60	.25	.08
☐ 125 Joe Lis	.60	.25	.08
☐ 126 Sal Bando	.75	.35	.09
☐ 127 Richie Zisk	.75	.35	.09
☐ 128 Rich Gossage	1.25	.55	.16
☐ 129 Don Baylor	1.00	.45	.13
☐ 130 Dave McKay	.60	.25	.08
☐ 131 Bob Grich	.90	.40	.11
☐ 132 Dave Pagan	.60	.25	.08
☐ 133 Dave Cash	.60	.25	.08
☐ 134 Steve Braun	.60	.25	.08
☐ 135 Dan Meyer	.60	.25	.08
☐ 136 Bill Stein	.60	.25	.08
☐ 137 Rollie Fingers	3.50	1.55	.45
☐ 138 Brian Downing	.90	.40	.11
☐ 139 Bill Singer	.60	.25	.08
☐ 140 Doyle Alexander	.75	.35	.09
☐ 141 Gene Tenace	.75	.35	.09
☐ 142 Gary Matthews	.75	.35	.09
☐ 143 Don Gullett	.75	.35	.09
☐ 144 Wayne Garland	.60	.25	.08
☐ 145 Pete Broberg	.60	.25	.08
☐ 146 Joe Rudi	.75	.35	.09
☐ 147 Glenn Abbott	.60	.25	.08
☐ 148 George Scott	.75	.35	.09
☐ 149 Bert Campaneris	.75	.35	.09
☐ 150 Andy Messersmith	.75	.35	.09

1978 Hostess

The cards in this 150-card set measure approximately 2 1/4" by 3 1/4" individually or 3 1/4" by 7 1/4" as panels of three. The 1978 Hostess set contains full-color, numbered cards

issued in panels of three cards each on family packages of Hostess cake products. Scarcer panels are listed in the checklist with SP. The 1978 Hostess panels are considered by some collectors to be somewhat more difficult to obtain than Hostess panels of other years. Although complete panel prices are not explicitly listed below, they would generally have a value 25 percent greater than the sum of the individual players on the panel. There is additional interest in Eddie Murray number 31, since this card corresponds to his "rookie" year in cards.

	NRMT-MT	EXC	G-VG
COMPLETE INDIV.SET (150)	225.00	100.00	28.00
COMMON PLAYER (1-150)	.60	.25	.08
☐ 1 Butch Hobson	1.00	.45	.13
☐ 2 George Foster	1.25	.55	.16
☐ 3 Bob Forsch	.75	.35	.09
☐ 4 Tony Perez	1.50	.65	.19
☐ 5 Bruce Sutter	1.25	.55	.16
☐ 6 Hal McRae	1.00	.45	.13
☐ 7 Tommy John	1.50	.65	.19
☐ 8 Greg Luzinski	.90	.40	.11
☐ 9 Enos Cabell	.60	.25	.08
☐ 10 Doug DeCinces	.75	.35	.09
☐ 11 Willie Stargell	3.50	1.55	.45
☐ 12 Ed Halicki	.60	.25	.08
☐ 13 Larry Hisle	.60	.25	.08
☐ 14 Jim Slaton	.60	.25	.08
☐ 15 Buddy Bell	.75	.35	.09
☐ 16 Earl Williams	.60	.25	.08
☐ 17 Glenn Abbott	.60	.25	.08
☐ 18 Dan Ford	.60	.25	.08
☐ 19 Gary Matthews	.75	.35	.09
☐ 20 Eric Soderholm	.60	.25	.08
☐ 21 Bump Wills	.60	.25	.08
☐ 22 Keith Hernandez	2.50	1.15	.30
☐ 23 Dave Cash	.60	.25	.08
☐ 24 George Scott	.75	.35	.09
☐ 25 Ron Guidry	2.00	.90	.25
☐ 26 Dave Kingman	.90	.40	.11
☐ 27 George Brett	12.00	5.50	1.50
☐ 28 Bob Watson SP	.75	.35	.09
☐ 29 Bob Boone SP	1.50	.65	.19
☐ 30 Reggie Smith SP	.90	.40	.11
☐ 31 Eddie Murray SP	25.00	11.50	3.10
☐ 32 Gary Lavelle SP	.75	.35	.09
☐ 33 Rennie Stennett SP	.75	.35	.09
☐ 34 Duane Kuiper SP	.75	.35	.09
☐ 35 Sixto Lezcano SP	.75	.35	.09
☐ 36 Dave Rozema SP	.75	.35	.09
☐ 37 Butch Wynegar SP	.75	.35	.09
☐ 38 Mitchell Page SP	.75	.35	.09
☐ 39 Bill Stein SP	.75	.35	.09
☐ 40 Elliott Maddox	.60	.25	.08
☐ 41 Mike Hargrove	.75	.35	.09
☐ 42 Bobby Bonds	1.25	.55	.16
☐ 43 Garry Templeton	.75	.35	.09
☐ 44 Johnny Bench	6.50	2.90	.80
☐ 45 Jim Rice	3.00	1.35	.40
☐ 46 Bill Buckner	.90	.40	.11
☐ 47 Reggie Jackson	6.50	2.90	.80
☐ 48 Freddie Patek	.60	.25	.08
☐ 49 Steve Carlton	4.00	1.80	.50
☐ 50 Cesar Cedeno	.75	.35	.09
☐ 51 Steve Yeager	.60	.25	.08
☐ 52 Phil Garner	.75	.35	.09
☐ 53 Lee May	.75	.35	.09
☐ 54 Darrell Evans	.75	.35	.09
☐ 55 Steve Kemp	.60	.25	.08

☐ 56 Dusty Baker	.90	.40	.11
☐ 57 Ray Fosse	.60	.25	.08
☐ 58 Manny Sanguillen	.75	.35	.09
☐ 59 Tom Johnson	.60	.25	.08
☐ 60 Lee Stanton	.60	.25	.08
☐ 61 Jeff Burroughs	.60	.25	.08
☐ 62 Bobby Grich	.90	.40	.11
☐ 63 Dave Winfield	6.50	2.90	.80
☐ 64 Dan Driessen	.60	.25	.08
☐ 65 Ted Simmons	1.25	.55	.16
☐ 66 Jerry Remy	.60	.25	.08
☐ 67 Al Cowens	.60	.25	.08
☐ 68 Sparky Lyle	.90	.40	.11
☐ 69 Manny Trillo	.75	.35	.09
☐ 70 Don Sutton	3.00	1.35	.40
☐ 71 Larry Bowa	.90	.40	.11
☐ 72 Jose Cruz	.90	.40	.11
☐ 73 Willie McCovey	3.50	1.55	.45
☐ 74 Bert Blyleven	1.25	.55	.16
☐ 75 Ken Singleton	.75	.35	.09
☐ 76 Bill North	.60	.25	.08
☐ 77 Jason Thompson	.60	.25	.08
☐ 78 Dennis Eckersley	3.00	1.35	.40
☐ 79 Jim Sundberg	.75	.35	.09
☐ 80 Jerry Koosman	.90	.40	.11
☐ 81 Bruce Bochte	.60	.25	.08
☐ 82 George Hendrick	.75	.35	.09
☐ 83 Nolan Ryan	25.00	11.50	3.10
☐ 84 Roy Howell	.60	.25	.08
☐ 85 Roger Metzger	.60	.25	.08
☐ 86 Doc Medich	.60	.25	.08
☐ 87 Joe Morgan	4.00	1.80	.50
☐ 88 Dennis Leonard	.75	.35	.09
☐ 89 Willie Randolph	.90	.40	.11
☐ 90 Bobby Murcer	.90	.40	.11
☐ 91 Rick Manning	.60	.25	.08
☐ 92 J.R. Richard	.75	.35	.09
☐ 93 Ron Cey	.90	.40	.11
☐ 94 Sal Bando	.75	.35	.09
☐ 95 Ron LeFlore	.75	.35	.09
☐ 96 Dave Goltz	.60	.25	.08
☐ 97 Dan Meyer	.60	.25	.08
☐ 98 Chris Chambliss	.75	.35	.09
☐ 99 Biff Pocoroba	.60	.25	.08
☐ 100 Oscar Gamble	.75	.35	.09
☐ 101 Frank Tanana	.90	.40	.11
☐ 102 Len Randle	.60	.25	.08
☐ 103 Tommy Hutton	.60	.25	.08
☐ 104 John Candelaria	.75	.35	.09
☐ 105 Jorge Orta	.60	.25	.08
☐ 106 Ken Reitz	.60	.25	.08
☐ 107 Bill Campbell	.60	.25	.08
☐ 108 Dave Concepcion	1.25	.55	.16
☐ 109 Joe Ferguson	.60	.25	.08
☐ 110 Mickey Rivers	.75	.35	.09
☐ 111 Paul Splittorff	.60	.25	.08
☐ 112 Dave Lopes	.75	.35	.09
☐ 113 Mike Schmidt	9.00	4.00	1.15
☐ 114 Joe Rudi	.75	.35	.09
☐ 115 Milt May	.60	.25	.08
☐ 116 Jim Palmer	4.00	1.80	.50
☐ 117 Bill Madlock	1.00	.45	.13
☐ 118 Roy Smalley	.75	.35	.09
☐ 119 Cecil Cooper	1.25	.55	.16
☐ 120 Rick Langford	.60	.25	.08
☐ 121 Ruppert Jones	.75	.35	.09
☐ 122 Phil Niekro	3.00	1.35	.40
☐ 123 Toby Harrah	.75	.35	.09
☐ 124 Chet Lemon	.75	.35	.09
☐ 125 Gene Tenace	.75	.35	.09
☐ 126 Steve Henderson	.60	.25	.08
☐ 127 Mike Torrez	.60	.25	.08
☐ 128 Pete Rose	9.00	4.00	1.15
☐ 129 John Denny	.75	.35	.09
☐ 130 Darrell Porter	.75	.35	.09
☐ 131 Rick Reuschel	.75	.35	.09
☐ 132 Graig Nettles	1.00	.45	.13
☐ 133 Garry Maddox	.60	.25	.08
☐ 134 Mike Flanagan	.75	.35	.09
☐ 135 Dave Parker	2.50	1.15	.30
☐ 136 Terry Whitfield	.60	.25	.08
☐ 137 Wayne Garland	.60	.25	.08
☐ 138 Robin Yount	12.00	5.50	1.50
☐ 139 Gaylord Perry	3.00	1.35	.40
☐ 140 Rod Carew	5.00	2.30	.60
☐ 141 Wayne Gross	.60	.25	.08
☐ 142 Barry Bonnell	.60	.25	.08
☐ 143 Willie Montanez	.60	.25	.08
☐ 144 Rollie Fingers	3.00	1.35	.40
☐ 145 Lyman Bostock	.75	.35	.09
☐ 146 Gary Carter	4.00	1.80	.50
☐ 147 Ron Blomberg	.60	.25	.08
☐ 148 Bob Bailor	.60	.25	.08
☐ 149 Tom Seaver	6.50	2.90	.80
☐ 150 Thurman Munson	5.00	2.30	.60

1979 Hostess

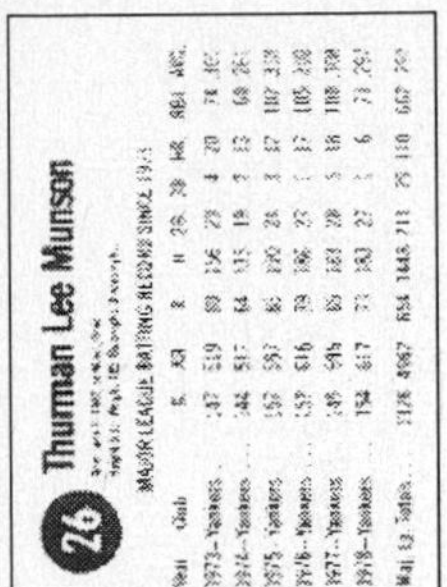

The cards in this 150-card set measure approximately 2 1/4" by 3 1/4" individually or 3 1/4" by 7 1/4" as panels of three. The 1979 Hostess set contains full color, numbered cards issued in panels of three cards each on the backs of family sized Hostess cake products. Scarcer panels are listed in the checklist below with SP. Although complete panel prices are not explicitly listed below they would generally have a value 25 percent greater than the sum of the individual players on the panel. There is additional interest in Ozzie Smith (102) since this card corresponds to his rookie year in cards.

	NRMT-MT	EXC	G-VG
COMPLETE INDIV.SET (150)	225.00	100.00	28.00
COMMON PLAYER (1-150)	.60	.25	.08
☐ 1 John Denny	.75	.35	.09
☐ 2 Jim Rice	3.00	1.35	.40
☐ 3 Doug Bair	.60	.25	.08
☐ 4 Darrell Porter	.60	.25	.08
☐ 5 Ross Grimsley	.60	.25	.08
☐ 6 Bobby Murcer	.90	.40	.11
☐ 7 Lee Mazzilli	.60	.25	.08
☐ 8 Steve Garvey	3.50	1.55	.45
☐ 9 Mike Schmidt	9.00	4.00	1.15
☐ 10 Terry Whitfield	.60	.25	.08
☐ 11 Jim Palmer	3.50	1.55	.45
☐ 12 Omar Moreno	.60	.25	.08
☐ 13 Duane Kuiper	.60	.25	.08
☐ 14 Mike Caldwell	.60	.25	.08
☐ 15 Steve Kemp	.60	.25	.08
☐ 16 Dave Goltz	.60	.25	.08
☐ 17 Mitchell Page	.60	.25	.08
☐ 18 Bill Stein	.60	.25	.08
☐ 19 Gene Tenace	.75	.35	.09
☐ 20 Jeff Burroughs	.60	.25	.08
☐ 21 Francisco Barrios	.60	.25	.08
☐ 22 Mike Torrez	.60	.25	.08
☐ 23 Ken Reitz	.60	.25	.08
☐ 24 Gary Carter	3.50	1.55	.45
☐ 25 Al Hrabosky	.75	.35	.09
☐ 26 Thurman Munson	4.50	2.00	.55
☐ 27 Bill Buckner	1.00	.45	.13
☐ 28 Ron Cey SP	1.00	.45	.13
☐ 29 J.R. Richard SP	.90	.40	.11
☐ 30 Greg Luzinski SP	1.00	.45	.13
☐ 31 Ed Ott SP	.75	.35	.09
☐ 32 Dennis Martinez SP	1.50	.65	.19
☐ 33 Darrell Evans SP	.90	.40	.11
☐ 34 Ron LeFlore	.75	.35	.09
☐ 35 Rick Waits	.60	.25	.08
☐ 36 Cecil Cooper	1.00	.45	.13
☐ 37 Leon Roberts	.60	.25	.08
☐ 38 Rod Carew	5.00	2.30	.60
☐ 39 John Henry Johnson	.60	.25	.08
☐ 40 Chet Lemon	.75	.35	.09
☐ 41 Craig Swan	.60	.25	.08
☐ 42 Gary Matthews	.75	.35	.09
☐ 43 Lamar Johnson	.60	.25	.08
☐ 44 Ted Simmons	1.25	.55	.16
☐ 45 Ken Griffey	1.25	.55	.16
☐ 46 Fred Patek	.60	.25	.08

☐ 47 Frank Tanana .90 .40 .11
☐ 48 Goose Gossage 1.25 .55 .16
☐ 49 Burt Hooton .60 .25 .08
☐ 50 Ellis Valentine .60 .25 .08
☐ 51 Ken Forsch .60 .25 .08
☐ 52 Bob Knepper .60 .25 .08
☐ 53 Dave Parker 2.50 1.15 .30
☐ 54 Doug DeCinces .75 .35 .09
☐ 55 Robin Yount 10.00 4.50 1.25
☐ 56 Rusty Staub .90 .40 .11
☐ 57 Gary Alexander .60 .25 .08
☐ 58 Julio Cruz .60 .25 .08
☐ 59 Matt Keough .60 .25 .08
☐ 60 Roy Smalley .60 .25 .08
☐ 61 Joe Morgan 3.50 1.55 .45
☐ 62 Phil Niekro 2.50 1.15 .30
☐ 63 Don Baylor 1.25 .55 .16
☐ 64 Dwight Evans 1.25 .55 .16
☐ 65 Tom Seaver 6.50 2.90 .80
☐ 66 George Hendrick .60 .25 .08
☐ 67 Rick Reuschel .75 .35 .09
☐ 68 George Brett 10.00 4.50 1.25
☐ 69 Lou Piniella 1.25 .55 .16
☐ 70 Enos Cabell .60 .25 .08
☐ 71 Steve Carlton 4.00 1.80 .50
☐ 72 Reggie Smith .75 .35 .09
☐ 73 Rick Dempsey SP .75 .35 .09
☐ 74 Vida Blue SP .90 .40 .11
☐ 75 Phil Garner SP .90 .40 .11
☐ 76 Rick Manning SP .75 .35 .09
☐ 77 Mark Fidrych SP 1.00 .45 .13
☐ 78 Mario Guerrero SP .75 .35 .09
☐ 79 Bob Stinson SP .75 .35 .09
☐ 80 Al Oliver SP 1.00 .45 .13
☐ 81 Doug Flynn SP .75 .35 .09
☐ 82 John Mayberry .75 .35 .09
☐ 83 Gaylord Perry 2.50 1.15 .30
☐ 84 Joe Rudi .75 .35 .09
☐ 85 Dave Concepcion 1.25 .55 .16
☐ 86 John Candelaria .75 .35 .09
☐ 87 Pete Vuckovich .75 .35 .09
☐ 88 Ivan DeJesus .60 .25 .08
☐ 89 Ron Guidry 1.50 .65 .19
☐ 90 Hal McRae 1.00 .45 .13
☐ 91 Cesar Cedeno .75 .35 .09
☐ 92 Don Sutton 2.50 1.15 .30
☐ 93 Andre Thornton .75 .35 .09
☐ 94 Roger Erickson .60 .25 .08
☐ 95 Larry Hisle .75 .35 .09
☐ 96 Jason Thompson .60 .25 .08
☐ 97 Jim Sundberg .75 .35 .09
☐ 98 Bob Horner 1.25 .55 .16
☐ 99 Ruppert Jones .60 .25 .08
☐ 100 Willie Montanez .60 .25 .08
☐ 101 Nolan Ryan 25.00 11.50 3.10
☐ 102 Ozzie Smith 30.00 13.50 3.80
☐ 103 Eric Soderholm .60 .25 .08
☐ 104 Willie Stargell 3.50 1.55 .45
☐ 105A Bob Bailor ERR .75 .35 .09
(Reverse negative)
☐ 105B Bob Bailor COR 1.50 .65 .19
☐ 106 Carlton Fisk 3.50 1.55 .45
☐ 107 George Foster 1.25 .55 .16
☐ 108 Keith Hernandez 2.50 1.15 .30
☐ 109 Dennis Leonard .75 .35 .09
☐ 110 Graig Nettles .90 .40 .11
☐ 111 Jose Cruz .75 .35 .09
☐ 112 Bobby Grich .75 .35 .09
☐ 113 Bob Boone 1.00 .45 .13
☐ 114 Dave Lopes .75 .35 .09
☐ 115 Eddie Murray 10.00 4.50 1.25
☐ 116 Jack Clark 2.00 .90 .25
☐ 117 Lou Whitaker 2.50 1.15 .30
☐ 118 Miguel Dilone .60 .25 .08
☐ 119 Sal Bando .75 .35 .09
☐ 120 Reggie Jackson 6.50 2.90 .80
☐ 121 Dale Murphy 8.00 3.60 1.00
☐ 122 Jon Matlack .60 .25 .08
☐ 123 Bruce Bochte .60 .25 .08
☐ 124 John Stearns .60 .25 .08
☐ 125 Dave Winfield 5.50 2.50 .70
☐ 126 Jorge Orta .60 .25 .08
☐ 127 Garry Templeton .75 .35 .09
☐ 128 Johnny Bench 5.50 2.50 .70
☐ 129 Butch Hobson .75 .35 .09
☐ 130 Bruce Sutter 1.25 .55 .16
☐ 131 Bucky Dent .90 .40 .11
☐ 132 Amos Otis .75 .35 .09
☐ 133 Bert Blyleven 1.25 .55 .16
☐ 134 Larry Bowa .90 .40 .11
☐ 135 Ken Singleton .75 .35 .09
☐ 136 Sixto Lezcano .60 .25 .08
☐ 137 Roy Howell .60 .25 .08
☐ 138 Bill Madlock 1.00 .45 .13
☐ 139 Dave Revering .60 .25 .08
☐ 140 Richie Zisk .75 .35 .09
☐ 141 Butch Wynegar .60 .25 .08
☐ 142 Alan Ashby .60 .25 .08
☐ 143 Sparky Lyle .90 .40 .11
☐ 144 Pete Rose 9.00 4.00 1.15
☐ 145 Dennis Eckersley 2.50 1.15 .30
☐ 146 Dave Kingman .90 .40 .11
☐ 147 Buddy Bell .75 .35 .09
☐ 148 Mike Hargrove .75 .35 .09
☐ 149 Jerry Koosman .90 .40 .11
☐ 150 Toby Harrah .75 .35 .09

1952 Indians Num Num

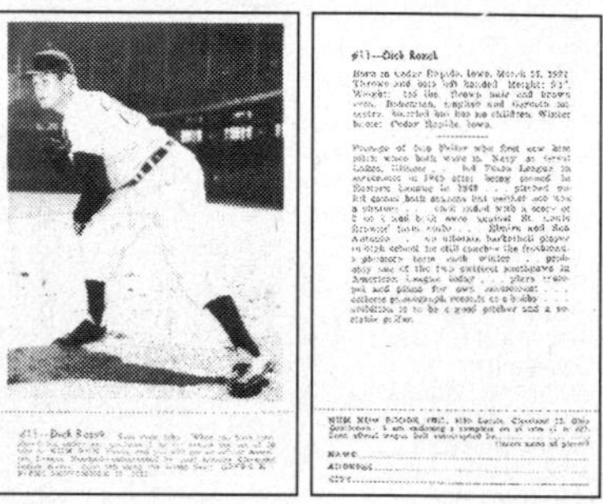

The cards in this 20-card set measure approximately 3 1/2" by 4 1/2". The 1952 Num Num Potato Chips issue features black and white, numbered cards of the Cleveland Indians. Cards came with and without coupons (tabs). The cards were issued without coupons directly by the Cleveland baseball club. When the complete set was obtained the tabs were cut off and exchanged for an autographed baseball. Card Number 16, Kennedy, is rather scarce. Cards with the tabs still intact are worth approximately 25 percent more than the values listed below. The catalog designation for this set is F337-2.

	NRMT	VG-E	GOOD
COMPLETE SET (20)	1000.00	450.00	125.00
COMMON PLAYER (1-20)	25.00	11.50	3.10
☐ 1 Lou Brissie	25.00	11.50	3.10
☐ 2 Jim Hegan	30.00	13.50	3.80
☐ 3 Birdie Tebbetts	25.00	11.50	3.10
☐ 4 Bob Lemon	75.00	34.00	9.50
☐ 5 Bob Feller	125.00	57.50	15.50
☐ 6 Early Wynn	75.00	34.00	9.50
☐ 7 Mike Garcia	35.00	16.00	4.40
☐ 8 Steve Gromek	25.00	11.50	3.10
☐ 9 Bob Chakales	25.00	11.50	3.10
☐ 10 Al Rosen	45.00	20.00	5.75
☐ 11 Dick Rozek	25.00	11.50	3.10
☐ 12 Luke Easter	25.00	11.50	3.10
☐ 13 Ray Boone	25.00	11.50	3.10
☐ 14 Bobby Avila	30.00	13.50	3.80
☐ 15 Dale Mitchell	25.00	11.50	3.10
☐ 16 Bob Kennedy SP	400.00	180.00	50.00
☐ 17 Harry Simpson	25.00	11.50	3.10
☐ 18 Larry Doby	45.00	20.00	5.75
☐ 19 Sam Jones	25.00	11.50	3.10
☐ 20 Al Lopez MG	65.00	29.00	8.25

1956 Indians Carling Black Label

This ten-card, approximately 8 1/2" by 12", set was issued by Carling Beer and celebrated members of the (then) perennial contending Cleveland Indians. These cards feature a black and white photo with the printed name of the player

inserted in the photo. Underneath the photo is a joint advertisement for Carling Black Label Beer and The Cleveland Indians. The set looks like it could be easily replicated and may indeed have been reprinted. The checklist for this unnumbered set is ordered alphabetically.

	NRMT	VG-E	GOOD
COMPLETE SET (10)	75.00	34.00	9.50
COMMON PLAYER (1-10)	5.00	2.30	.60
☐ 1 Bob Feller	30.00	13.50	3.80
☐ 2 Mike Garcia	7.00	3.10	.85
☐ 3 Jim Hegan	6.00	2.70	.75
☐ 4 Art Houtteman	5.00	2.30	.60
☐ 5 Bob Lemon	15.00	6.75	1.90
☐ 6 Al Rosen	10.00	4.50	1.25
☐ 7 Herb Score	10.00	4.50	1.25
☐ 8 Al Smith	5.00	2.30	.60
☐ 9 George Strickland	5.00	2.30	.60
☐ 10 Early Wynn	15.00	6.75	1.90

1957 Indians Sohio

The 1957 Sohio Cleveland Indians set consists of 18 perforated photos, approximately 5" by 7", in black and white with facsimile autographs on the front which were designed to be pasted into a special photo album issued by SOHIO (Standard Oil of Ohio). The set features one of the earliest Roger Maris cards which even predates his 1958 Topps Rookie Card. In addition, the Rocky Colavito card is popular as well as 1957 was Rocky's rookie year for cards. These unnumbered cards are listed below in alphabetical order for convenience. It has been alleged that counterfeits of this set have been recently produced.

	NRMT	VG-E	GOOD
COMPLETE SET (18)	200.00	90.00	25.00
COMMON PLAYER (1-18)	5.00	2.30	.60
☐ 1 Bob Avila	6.00	2.70	.75
☐ 2 Jim Busby	5.00	2.30	.60
☐ 3 Chico Carrasquel	5.00	2.30	.60
☐ 4 Rocky Colavito	30.00	13.50	3.80
☐ 5 Mike Garcia	7.00	3.10	.85
☐ 6 Jim Hegan	6.00	2.70	.75
☐ 7 Bob Lemon	16.00	7.25	2.00
☐ 8 Roger Maris	125.00	57.50	15.50
☐ 9 Don Mossi	7.00	3.10	.85
☐ 10 Ray Narleski	5.00	2.30	.60
☐ 11 Russ Nixon	5.00	2.30	.60
☐ 12 Herb Score	9.00	4.00	1.15
☐ 13 Al Smith	5.00	2.30	.60
☐ 14 George Strickland	5.00	2.30	.60
☐ 15 Bob Usher	5.00	2.30	.60
☐ 16 Vic Wertz	6.00	2.70	.75
☐ 17 Gene Woodling	6.00	2.70	.75
☐ 18 Early Wynn	16.00	7.25	2.00

1982 Indians Burger King

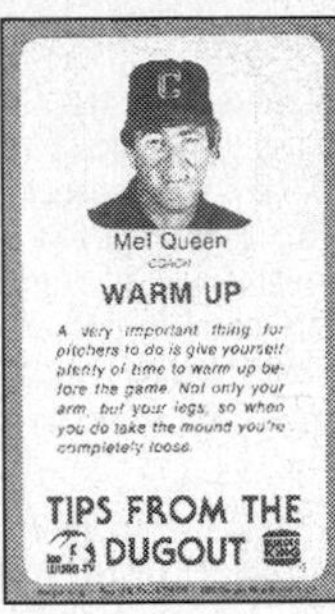

The cards in this 12-card set measure approximately 3" by 5". Tips From The Dugout is the series title of this set issued on a one card per week basis by the Burger King chain in the Cleveland area. Each card contains a black and white photo of manager Dave Garcia or coaches Goryl, McCraw, Queen and Sommers, under whom appears a paragraph explaining some aspect of inside baseball. The photo and "Tip" are set upon a large yellow area surrounded by green borders. The cards are not numbered and are blank-backed. The logos of Burger King and WUAB-TV appear at the base of the card.

	NRMT-MT	EXC	G-VG
COMPLETE SET (12)	5.00	2.30	.60
COMMON PLAYER (1-12)	.50	.23	.06
☐ 1 Dave Garcia: Be in the Game	.50	.23	.06
☐ 2 Dave Garcia: Sportsmanship	.50	.23	.06
☐ 3 Johnny Goryl: Rounding Bases	.50	.23	.06
☐ 4 Johnny Goryl: 3B Running	.50	.23	.06
☐ 5 Tom McCraw: Follow Thru	.50	.23	.06
☐ 6 Tom McCraw: Selecting a Bat	.50	.23	.06
☐ 7 Tom McCraw: Watch the Ball	.50	.23	.06
☐ 8 Mel Queen: Master One Pitch	.50	.23	.06
☐ 9 Mel Queen: Warm Up	.50	.23	.06
☐ 10 Dennis Sommers: Protect Fingers	.50	.23	.06
☐ 11 Dennis Sommers: Tagging 1st Base	.50	.23	.06
☐ 12 Dennis Sommers	.50	.23	.06

1982 Indians Wheaties

The cards in this 30-card set measure approximately 2 13/16" by 4 1/8". This set of Cleveland Indians baseball players was co-produced by the indians baseball club and Wheaties, whose respective logos appear on the front of

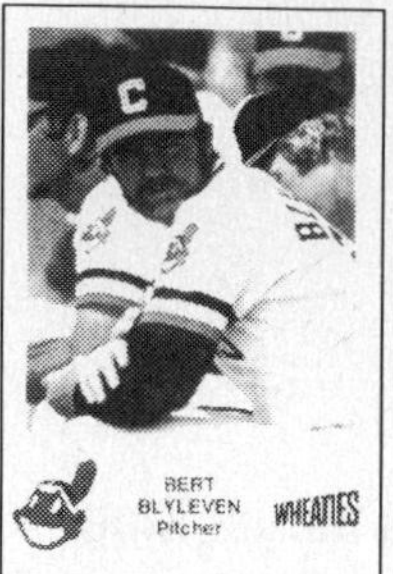

every card. The cards were given away in groups of 10 as a promotion during games on May 30 (1-10), June 19 (11-20) and July 16, 1982 (21-30). The manager (MG), four coaches (CO), and 25 players are featured in a simple format of a color picture, player name and position. The cards are not numbered and the backs contain a Wheaties ad. The set was later sold at the Cleveland Indians gift shop. The cards are ordered below alphabetically within groups of ten as they were issued.

	NRMT-MT	EXC	G-VG
COMPLETE SET (30)	15.00	6.75	1.90
COMMON PLAYER (1-30)	.50	.23	.06
☐ 1 Bert Blyleven	1.50	.65	.19
☐ 2 Joe Charboneau	.75	.35	.09
☐ 3 Jerry Dybzinski	.50	.23	.06
☐ 4 Dave Garcia MG	.50	.23	.06
☐ 5 Toby Harrah	.75	.35	.09
☐ 6 Ron Hassey	.60	.25	.08
☐ 7 Dennis Lewallyn	.50	.23	.06
☐ 8 Rick Manning	.60	.25	.08
☐ 9 Tommy McCraw CO	.50	.23	.06
☐ 10 Rick Waits	.50	.23	.06
☐ 11 Chris Bando	.50	.23	.06
☐ 12 Len Barker	.60	.25	.08
☐ 13 Tom Brennan	.50	.23	.06
☐ 14 Rodney Craig	.50	.23	.06
☐ 15 Mike Fischlin	.50	.23	.06
☐ 16 Johnny Goryl CO	.50	.23	.06
☐ 17 Mel Queen CO	.50	.23	.06
☐ 18 Lary Sorensen	.50	.23	.06
☐ 19 Andre Thornton	.75	.35	.09
☐ 20 Eddie Whitson	.50	.23	.06
☐ 21 Alan Bannister	.50	.23	.06
☐ 22 John Denny	.60	.25	.08
☐ 23 Miguel Dilone	.50	.23	.06
☐ 24 Mike Hargrove	.75	.35	.09
☐ 25 Von Hayes	.90	.40	.11
☐ 26 Bake McBride	.60	.25	.08
☐ 27 Jack Perconte	.50	.23	.06
☐ 28 Dennis Sommers CO	.50	.23	.06
☐ 29 Dan Spillner	.50	.23	.06
☐ 30 Rick Sutcliffe	.90	.40	.11

1983 Indians Wheaties

The cards in this 32-card set measure approximately 2 13/16" by 4 1/8". The full color set of 1983 Wheaties Indians is quite similar to the Wheaties set of 1982. The backs, however, are significantly different. They contain complete career playing records of the players. The complete sets were given away at the ball park on May 15, 1983. The set was later made available at the Indians Gift Shop. The manager (MG) and several coaches (CO) are included in the set. The cards below are ordered alphabetically by the subject's name.

	NRMT-MT	EXC	G-VG
COMPLETE SET (32)	7.50	3.40	.95
COMMON PLAYER (1-32)	.25	.11	.03
☐ 1 Bud Anderson	.25	.11	.03
☐ 2 Jay Baller	.25	.11	.03
☐ 3 Chris Bando	.25	.11	.03
☐ 4 Alan Bannister	.25	.11	.03
☐ 5 Len Barker	.35	.16	.04
☐ 6 Bert Blyleven	.75	.35	.09
☐ 7 Wil Culmer	.25	.11	.03
☐ 8 Miguel Dilone	.25	.11	.03
☐ 9 Juan Eichelberger	.25	.11	.03
☐ 10 Jim Essian	.35	.16	.04
☐ 11 Mike Ferraro MG	.25	.11	.03
☐ 12 Mike Fischlin	.25	.11	.03
☐ 13 Julio Franco	1.50	.65	.19
☐ 14 Ed Glynn	.25	.11	.03
☐ 15 Johnny Goryl CO	.25	.11	.03
☐ 16 Mike Hargrove	.45	.20	.06
☐ 17 Toby Harrah	.35	.16	.04
☐ 18 Ron Hassey	.35	.16	.04
☐ 19 Neal Heaton	.25	.11	.03
☐ 20 Rick Manning	.35	.16	.04
☐ 21 Bake McBride	.35	.16	.04
☐ 22 Don McMahon CO	.25	.11	.03
☐ 23 Ed Napoleon CO	.25	.11	.03
☐ 24 Broderick Perkins	.25	.11	.03
☐ 25 Dennis Sommers CO	.25	.11	.03
☐ 26 Lary Sorensen	.25	.11	.03
☐ 27 Dan Spillner	.25	.11	.03
☐ 28 Rick Sutcliffe	.75	.35	.09
☐ 29 Andre Thornton	.45	.20	.06
☐ 30 Manny Trillo	.35	.16	.04
☐ 31 George Vukovich	.25	.11	.03
☐ 32 Rick Waits	.25	.11	.03

1984 Indians Wheaties

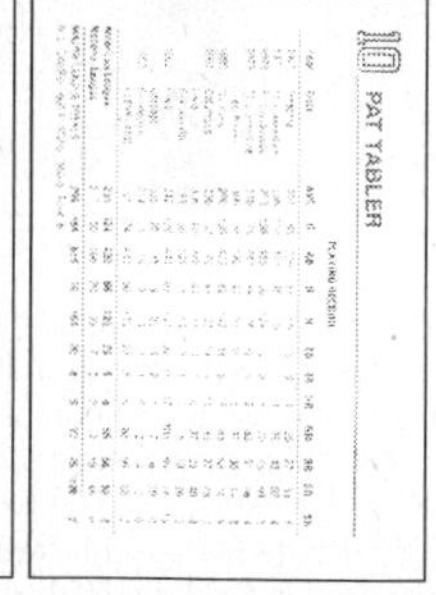

The cards in this 29-card set measure approximately 2 13/16" by 4 1/8". For the third straight year, Wheaties distributed a set of Cleveland Indians baseball cards. These over-sized cards were passed out at a Baseball Card Day at the Cleveland Stadium. Similar in appearance to the cards of the past two years, both the Indians and the Wheaties logos appear on the obverse, along with the name, team and position. Cards are numbered on the back by the player's uniform number.

	NRMT-MT	EXC	G-VG
COMPLETE SET (29)	7.50	3.40	.95
COMMON PLAYER	.25	.11	.03
☐ 2 Brett Butler	.60	.25	.08
☐ 4 Tony Bernazard	.35	.16	.04
☐ 8 Carmelo Castillo	.25	.11	.03
☐ 10 Pat Tabler	.35	.16	.04
☐ 13 Ernie Camacho	.25	.11	.03
☐ 14 Julio Franco	.75	.35	.09
☐ 15 Broderick Perkins	.25	.11	.03
☐ 16 Jerry Willard	.25	.11	.03
☐ 18 Pat Corrales MG	.35	.16	.04
☐ 21 Mike Hargrove	.45	.20	.06
☐ 22 Mike Fischlin	.25	.11	.03
☐ 23 Chris Bando	.25	.11	.03
☐ 24 George Vukovich	.25	.11	.03
☐ 26 Brook Jacoby	.35	.16	.04
☐ 27 Steve Farr	.75	.35	.09
☐ 28 Bert Blyleven	.60	.25	.08
☐ 29 Andre Thornton	.45	.20	.06
☐ 30 Joe Carter	2.50	1.15	.30
☐ 31 Steve Comer	.25	.11	.03
☐ 33 Roy Smith	.25	.11	.03
☐ 34 Mel Hall	.75	.35	.09
☐ 36 Jamie Easterly	.25	.11	.03
☐ 37 Don Schulze	.25	.11	.03
☐ 38 Luis Aponte	.25	.11	.03
☐ 44 Neal Heaton	.25	.11	.03
☐ 46 Mike Jeffcoat	.25	.11	.03
☐ 54 Tom Waddell	.25	.11	.03
☐ NNO Indians Coaches John Goryl Dennis Sommers Ed Napoleon Bobby Bonds Don McMahon	.25	.11	.03
☐ NNO Tom-E-Hawk (Mascot)	.25	.11	.03

1985 Indians Polaroid

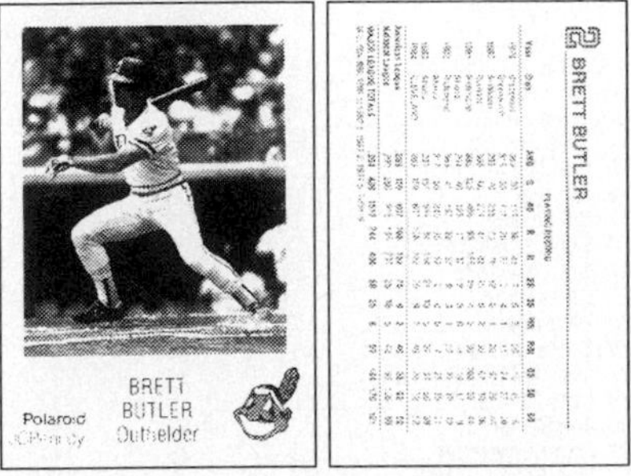

This 32-card set features cards (each measuring approximately 2 13/16" by 4 1/8") of the Cleveland Indians. The cards are unnumbered except for uniform number, as they are listed below. The set was also sponsored by J.C. Penney and was distributed at the stadium to fans in attendance on Baseball Card Day.

	NRMT-MT	EXC	G-VG
COMPLETE SET (32)	20.00	9.00	2.50
COMMON PLAYER	.50	.23	.06
☐ 2 Brett Butler	1.25	.55	.16
☐ 4 Tony Bernazard	.60	.25	.08
☐ 8 Carmen Castillo	.50	.23	.06
☐ 10 Pat Tabler	.60	.25	.08
☐ 12 Benny Ayala	.50	.23	.06
☐ 13 Ernie Camacho	.50	.23	.06
☐ 14 Julio Franco	2.00	.90	.25
☐ 16 Jerry Willard	.50	.23	.06
☐ 18 Pat Corrales MG	.60	.25	.08
☐ 20 Otis Nixon	1.50	.65	.19
☐ 21 Mike Hargrove	.75	.35	.09
☐ 22 Mike Fischlin	.50	.23	.06
☐ 23 Chris Bando	.50	.23	.06
☐ 24 George Vukovich	.50	.23	.06
☐ 26 Brook Jacoby	.75	.35	.09
☐ 27 Mel Hall	.90	.40	.11
☐ 28 Bert Blyleven	1.25	.55	.16
☐ 29 Andre Thornton	.90	.40	.11
☐ 30 Joe Carter	3.50	1.55	.45
☐ 32 Rick Behenna	.50	.23	.06
☐ 33 Roy Smith	.50	.23	.06
☐ 35 Jerry Reed	.50	.23	.06
☐ 36 Jamie Easterly	.50	.23	.06
☐ 38 Dave Von Ohlen	.50	.23	.06
☐ 41 Rich Thompson	.50	.23	.06
☐ 43 Bryan Clark	.50	.23	.06
☐ 44 Neal Heaton	.60	.25	.08
☐ 48 Vern Ruhle	.50	.23	.06
☐ 49 Jeff Barkley	.50	.23	.06
☐ 50 Ramon Romero	.50	.23	.06
☐ 54 Tom Waddell	.50	.23	.06
☐ NNO Coaching Staff Bobby Bonds John Goryl Don McMahon Ed Napoleon Dennis Sommers	.60	.25	.08

1986 Indians Oh Henry

This 30-card set features Cleveland Indians and was distributed at the stadium to fans in attendance on Baseball Card Day. The cards were printed in one folded sheet which was perforated for easy separation into individual cards. The cards have white borders with a blue frame around each photo. The card backs include detailed career year-by-year statistics. The individual cards measure approximately 2 1/4" by 3 1/8" and have full-color fronts.

	MT	EX-MT	VG
COMPLETE SET (30)	15.00	6.75	1.90
COMMON PLAYER	.40	.18	.05
☐ 2 Brett Butler	1.00	.45	.13
☐ 4 Tony Bernazard	.50	.23	.06
☐ 6 Andy Allanson	.40	.18	.05
☐ 7 Pat Corrales MG	.40	.18	.05
☐ 8 Carmen Castillo	.40	.18	.05
☐ 10 Pat Tabler	.50	.23	.06
☐ 13 Ernie Camacho	.40	.18	.05
☐ 14 Julio Franco	1.50	.65	.19
☐ 15 Dan Rohn	.40	.18	.05
☐ 18 Ken Schrom	.40	.18	.05
☐ 20 Otis Nixon	1.25	.55	.16
☐ 22 Fran Mullins	.40	.18	.05
☐ 23 Chris Bando	.40	.18	.05
☐ 24 Ed Williams	.40	.18	.05
☐ 26 Brook Jacoby	.50	.23	.06
☐ 27 Mel Hall	.75	.35	.09
☐ 29 Andre Thornton	.75	.35	.09
☐ 30 Joe Carter	3.00	1.35	.40
☐ 35 Phil Niekro	1.50	.65	.19
☐ 36 Jamie Easterly	.40	.18	.05
☐ 37 Don Schulze	.40	.18	.05
☐ 42 Rick Yett	.40	.18	.05
☐ 43 Scott Bailes	.40	.18	.05
☐ 44 Neal Heaton	.40	.18	.05
☐ 46 Jim Kern	.40	.18	.05
☐ 48 Dickie Noles	.40	.18	.05

	MT	EX-MT	VG
☐ 49 Tom Candiotti	.75	.35	.09
☐ 53 Reggie Ritter	.40	.18	.05
☐ 54 Tom Waddell	.40	.18	.05
☐ NNO Coaching Staff Jack Aker Bobby Bonds Doc Edwards John Goryl	.40	.18	.05

1987 Indians Gatorade

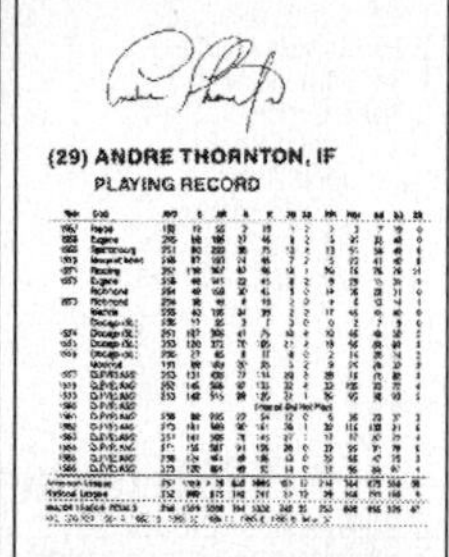

Gatorade sponsored this perforated set of 30 full-color cards of the Cleveland Indians. The cards measure approximately 2 1/8" by 3" (or 3 1/8") and feature the Gatorade logo prominently on the fronts of the cards. The cards were distributed as a tri-folded sheet (each part approximately 9 5/8" by 11 3/16") on April 25th at the stadium during the game against the Yankees. The large team photo is approximately 11 3/16" by 9 5/8". Card backs for the individual players contain year-by-year stats for that player. The cards are referenced and listed below by uniform number.

	MT	EX-MT	VG
COMPLETE SET (30)	12.00	5.50	1.50
COMMON PLAYER	.25	.11	.03
☐ 2 Brett Butler	.75	.35	.09
☐ 4 Tony Bernazard	.35	.16	.04
☐ 6 Andy Allanson	.25	.11	.03
☐ 7 Pat Corrales MG	.25	.11	.03
☐ 8 Carmen Castillo	.25	.11	.03
☐ 10 Pat Tabler	.35	.16	.04
☐ 11 Jamie Easterly	.25	.11	.03
☐ 12 Dave Clark	.25	.11	.03
☐ 13 Ernie Camacho	.25	.11	.03
☐ 14 Julio Franco	.90	.40	.11
☐ 17 Junior Noboa	.35	.16	.04
☐ 18 Ken Schrom	.25	.11	.03
☐ 20 Otis Nixon	1.00	.45	.13
☐ 21 Greg Swindell	1.50	.65	.19
☐ 22 Frank Wills	.25	.11	.03
☐ 23 Chris Bando	.25	.11	.03
☐ 24 Rick Dempsey	.35	.16	.04
☐ 26 Brook Jacoby	.50	.23	.06
☐ 27 Mel Hall	.50	.23	.06
☐ 28 Cory Snyder	.75	.35	.09
☐ 29 Andre Thornton	.35	.16	.04
☐ 30 Joe Carter	2.00	.90	.25
☐ 35 Phil Niekro	1.00	.45	.13
☐ 36 Ed VandeBerg	.25	.11	.03
☐ 42 Rich Yett	.25	.11	.03
☐ 43 Scott Bailes	.25	.11	.03
☐ 46 Doug Jones	.60	.25	.08
☐ 49 Tom Candiotti	.50	.23	.06
☐ 54 Tom Waddell	.25	.11	.03
☐ NNO Indians MG/Coaches Bobby Bonds 25 Johnny Goryl 45 Pat Corrales MG 7 Doc Edwards 32 Jack Aker 1	.35	.16	.04
☐ NNO Team Photo (large size)	1.50	.65	.19

1988 Indians Gatorade

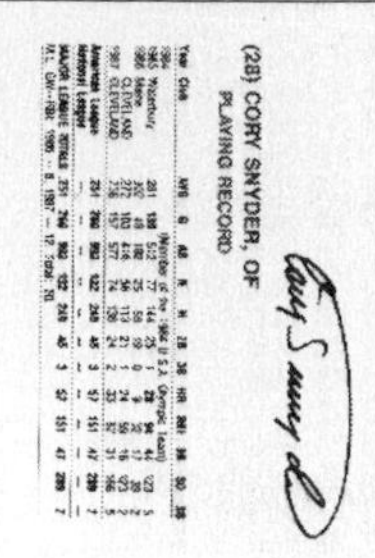

This set was distributed as 30 perforated player cards attached to a large team photo of the Cleveland Indians. The cards measure approximately 2 1/4" by 3". Card backs are oriented either horizontally or vertically. Card backs are printed in red, blue, and black on white card stock. Card backs contain a facsimile autograph of the player. Cards are not arranged on the sheet in any order. The cards are unnumbered except for uniform number, which is given on the front and back of each card. The cards are referenced and listed below by uniform number. The Gatorade logo is on the front of every card in the lower right corner.

	MT	EX-MT	VG
COMPLETE SET (30)	9.00	4.00	1.15
COMMON PLAYER	.25	.11	.03
☐ 2 Tom Spencer CO	.25	.11	.03
☐ 6 Andy Allanson	.25	.11	.03
☐ 7 Luis Isaac CO	.25	.11	.03
☐ 8 Carmen Castillo	.25	.11	.03
☐ 9 Charlie Manuel CO	.25	.11	.03
☐ 10 Pat Tabler	.35	.16	.04
☐ 11 Doug Jones	.50	.23	.06
☐ 14 Julio Franco	.75	.35	.09
☐ 15 Ron Washington	.25	.11	.03
☐ 16 Jay Bell	1.00	.45	.13
☐ 17 Bill Laskey	.25	.11	.03
☐ 20 Willie Upshaw	.25	.11	.03
☐ 21 Greg Swindell	.75	.35	.09
☐ 23 Chris Bando	.25	.11	.03
☐ 25 Dave Clark	.35	.16	.04
☐ 26 Brook Jacoby	.35	.16	.04
☐ 27 Mel Hall	.50	.23	.06
☐ 28 Cory Snyder	.50	.23	.06
☐ 30 Joe Carter	1.50	.65	.19
☐ 31 Dan Schatzeder	.25	.11	.03
☐ 32 Doc Edwards MG	.25	.11	.03
☐ 33 Ron Kittle	.35	.16	.04
☐ 35 Mark Wiley CO	.25	.11	.03
☐ 42 Rich Yett	.25	.11	.03
☐ 43 Scott Bailes	.35	.16	.04
☐ 45 John Goryl CO	.25	.11	.03
☐ 47 Jeff Kaiser	.25	.11	.03
☐ 49 Tom Candiotti	.50	.23	.06
☐ 50 Jeff Dedmon	.25	.11	.03
☐ 52 John Farrell	.35	.16	.04
☐ NNO Team Photo (large size)	1.50	.65	.19

1991 Indians Fan Club/McDonald's

This 30-card set was sponsored by McDonald's and Channel 43 (WUAB). The cards are printed on thin card stock and measure approximately 2 7/8" by 4 1/4". On a white card face, the fronts feature a mix of posed and action color player photos that are framed by red border stripes. The "Tribe Kids Fan Club" emblem appears at the upper left corner. Player information and the sponsor logo appear in the bottom white border. The horizontally oriented backs

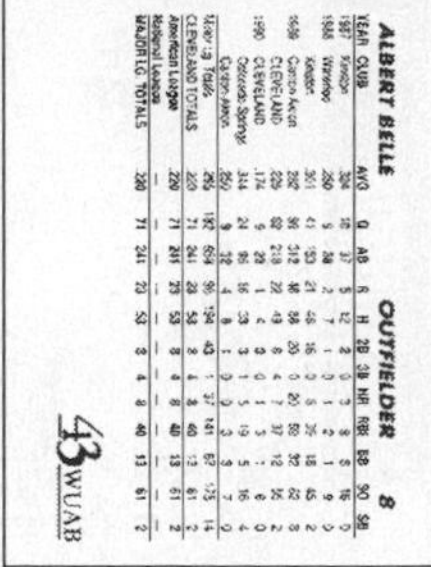

present minor and major league statistics. The cards are unnumbered and checklisted below in alphabetical order.

	MT	EX-MT	VG
COMPLETE SET (30)	10.00	4.50	1.25
COMMON PLAYER (1-30)	.30	.14	.04

	MT	EX-MT	VG
☐ 1 Beau Allred	.30	.14	.04
☐ 2 Sandy Alomar	.60	.25	.08
☐ 3 Carlos Baerga	1.00	.45	.13
☐ 4 Albert Belle	1.00	.45	.13
☐ 5 Jerry Browne	.40	.18	.05
☐ 6 Tom Candiotti	.50	.23	.06
☐ 7 Alex Cole	.50	.23	.06
☐ 8 Bruce Egloff	.30	.14	.04
☐ 9 Jose Escobar	.30	.14	.04
☐ 10 Felix Fermin	.40	.18	.05
☐ 11 Brook Jacoby	.40	.18	.05
☐ 12 John Farrell	.30	.14	.04
☐ 13 Shawn Hillegas	.40	.18	.05
☐ 14 Mike Huff	.30	.14	.04
☐ 15 Chris James	.40	.18	.05
☐ 16 Doug Jones	.50	.23	.06
☐ 17 Eric King	.30	.14	.04
☐ 18 Jeff Manto	.40	.18	.05
☐ 19 John McNamara MG	.30	.14	.04
☐ 20 Charles Nagy	1.00	.45	.13
☐ 21 Rod Nichols	.30	.14	.04
☐ 22 Steve Olin	.40	.18	.05
☐ 23 Jesse Orosco	.40	.18	.05
☐ 24 Dave Otto	.30	.14	.04
☐ 25 Joel Skinner	.30	.14	.04
☐ 26 Greg Swindell	.75	.35	.09
☐ 27 Mike Walker	.30	.14	.04
☐ 28 Turner Ward	.40	.18	.05
☐ 29 Mitch Webster	.30	.14	.04
☐ 30 Coaches Card Billy Williams Jose Morales Rich Dauer Mike Hargrove Luis Isaac Mark Wiley	.40	.18	.05

1991 Jimmy Dean Signature

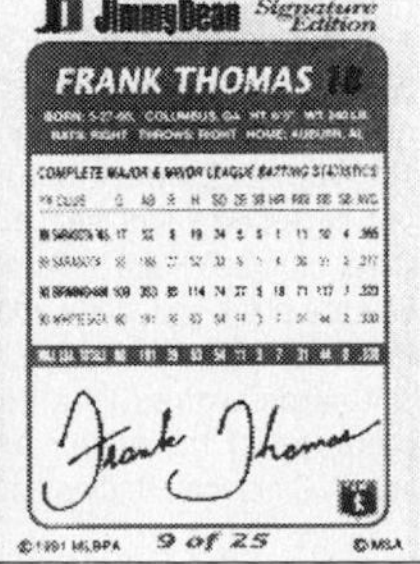

Michael Schechter Associates (MSA) produced this 25-card set on behalf of Jimmy Dean Sausage. These standard-size (2 1/2" by 3 1/2") cards feature an obverse with a color player photo, enframed by yellow and red borders. Since these player photos were not expressly licensed by Major League Baseball, the team logos have been airbrushed out. In a red and white panel with yellow borders, the back has biographical information, complete major (and minor where appropriate) league statistics, and the player's facsimile autograph. The cards are numbered on the back. During the promotion, uncut sheets were offered by the company through a mail-in offer involving Jimmy Dean proofs of purchase.

	MT	EX-MT	VG
COMPLETE SET (25)	15.00	6.75	1.90
COMMON PLAYER (1-25)	.40	.18	.05

	MT	EX-MT	VG
☐ 1 Will Clark	1.00	.45	.13
☐ 2 Ken Griffey Jr.	2.00	.90	.25
☐ 3 Dale Murphy	.50	.23	.06
☐ 4 Barry Bonds	.75	.35	.09
☐ 5 Darryl Strawberry	.75	.35	.09
☐ 6 Ryne Sandberg	1.50	.65	.19
☐ 7 Gary Sheffield	1.50	.65	.19
☐ 8 Sandy Alomar Jr.	.40	.18	.05
☐ 9 Frank Thomas	2.50	1.15	.30
☐ 10 Barry Larkin	.50	.23	.06
☐ 11 Kirby Puckett	1.00	.45	.13
☐ 12 George Brett	.75	.35	.09
☐ 13 Kevin Mitchell	.40	.18	.05
☐ 14 Dave Justice	1.00	.45	.13
☐ 15 Cal Ripken	1.50	.65	.19
☐ 16 Craig Biggio	.50	.23	.06
☐ 17 Rickey Henderson	.75	.35	.09
☐ 18 Roger Clemens	1.50	.65	.19
☐ 19 Jose Canseco	1.00	.45	.13
☐ 20 Ozzie Smith	.60	.25	.08
☐ 21 Cecil Fielder	.75	.35	.09
☐ 22 Dave Winfield	.75	.35	.09
☐ 23 Kevin Maas	.40	.18	.05
☐ 24 Nolan Ryan	2.00	.90	.25
☐ 25 Dwight Gooden	.50	.23	.06

1992 Jimmy Dean 18

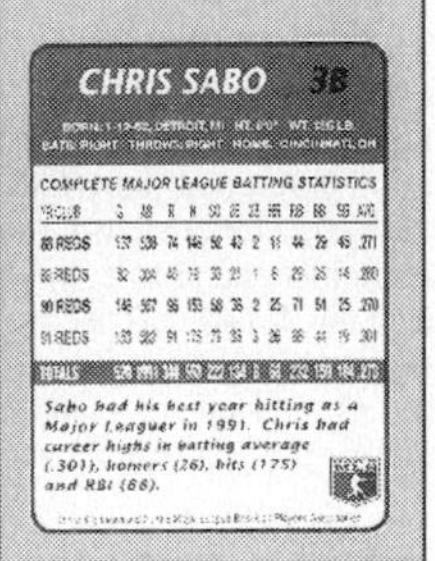

Michael Schechter Associates (MSA) produced this 18-card set for Jimmy Dean. In a cello pack, three free cards were included in any Jimmy Dean Sandwich, Flapsticks, or Links/Patties Breakfast Sausage. The cards measure the standard size (2 1/2" by 3 1/2"). The fronts feature glossy color player photos with team logos airbrushed out. These pictures are bordered on the left by a black bar that includes player information printed vertically. Another bar juts out from the right at the bottom of the picture and has the company logo with the words "Jimmy Dean '92." Inside a blue border, the backs are red, white, and blue and present biography, statistics, and brief career summary. The cards are numbered on the back.

	MT	EX-MT	VG
COMPLETE SET (18)	13.50	6.00	1.70
COMMON PLAYER (1-18)	.35	.16	.04

	MT	EX-MT	VG
☐ 1 Jim Abbott	.50	.23	.06

☐ 2 Barry Bonds	.75	.35	.09
☐ 3 Jeff Bagwell	1.00	.45	.13
☐ 4 Frank Thomas	2.50	1.15	.30
☐ 5 Steve Avery	.75	.35	.09
☐ 6 Chris Sabo	.35	.16	.04
☐ 7 Will Clark	1.00	.45	.13
☐ 8 Don Mattingly	1.00	.45	.13
☐ 9 Darryl Strawberry	.75	.35	.09
☐ 10 Roger Clemens	1.50	.65	.19
☐ 11 Ken Griffey Jr.	2.00	.90	.25
☐ 12 Chuck Knoblauch	.60	.25	.08
☐ 13 Tony Gwynn	.75	.35	.09
☐ 14 Juan Gonzalez	1.25	.55	.16
☐ 15 Cecil Fielder	.75	.35	.09
☐ 16 Bobby Bonilla	.60	.25	.08
☐ 17 Wes Chamberlain	.35	.16	.04
☐ 18 Ryne Sandberg	1.50	.65	.19

1992 Jimmy Dean Living Legends

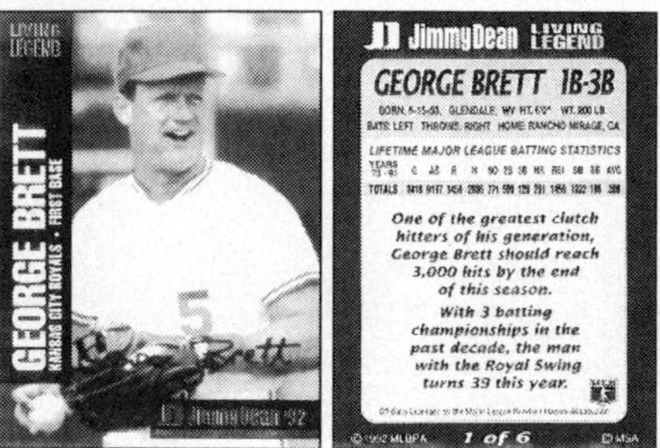

This six-card set was produced by MSA (Michael Schechter Associates) and features future candidates for the Hall of Fame. Collectors could obtain the complete set through a mail-in offer detailed on packages of Jimmy Dean Breakfast Sausage or Smoked Sausage. The standard-size (2 1/2" by 3 1/2") cards feature on the fronts glossy color player photos with team logos airbrushed out. These pictures are bordered on the left by a black bar that includes player information and the words "Living Legend" in gold-foil stamping. Another black bar juts out from the right at the bottom of the picture and has "Jimmy Dean '92" also in gold foil. Finally, inscribed across each photo is the player's signature in gold foil. The backs are black, yellow, and white and carry biography, statistics, and a brief career summary. The cards are numbered on the back.

	MT	EX-MT	VG
COMPLETE SET (6)	6.00	2.70	.75
COMMON PLAYER (1-6)	.75	.35	.09
☐ 1 George Brett	1.00	.45	.13
☐ 2 Carlton Fisk	.75	.35	.09
☐ 3 Ozzie Smith	.75	.35	.09
☐ 4 Robin Yount	1.00	.45	.13
☐ 5 Cal Ripken	2.00	.90	.25
☐ 6 Nolan Ryan	2.50	1.15	.30

1992 Jimmy Dean Rookie Stars

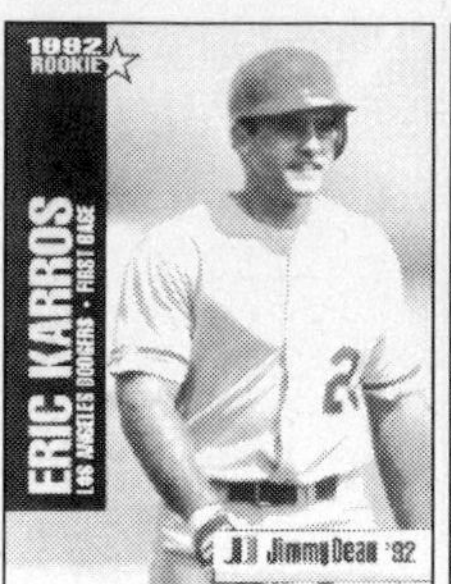

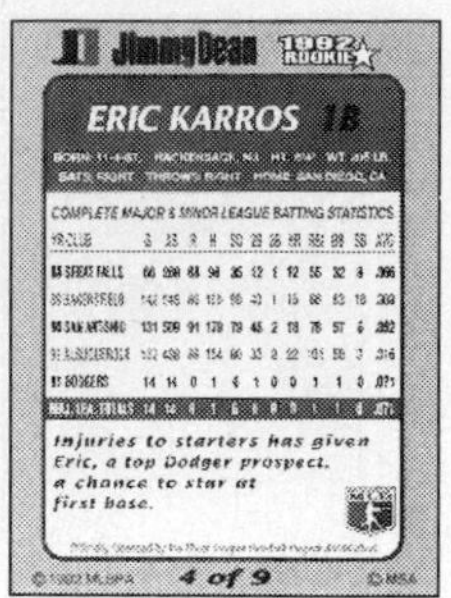

The players in this nine-card set were chosen based on actual 1992 first-half performance. Three free cards were included in specially marked packages of Jimmy Dean Sausage, Chicken Biscuits, Steak Biscuits, and MiniBurgers. The standard-size (2 1/2" by 3 1/2") cards feature on the fronts glossy color player photos with team logos airbrushed out. These pictures are bordered on the left by a black bar that includes the player's name printed vertically in either red or blue lettering. Another bar juts out from the right at the bottom of the picture and has "Jimmy Dean '92" in black lettering. Inside light blue borders, a red and white panel displays biography, statistics, and a brief career summary. The cards are numbered on the back. Oversized 7" by 9 3/4" versions of the cards, featuring a Rookie Star front on one side and a Living Legend front on the other, were placed at point of purchase for promotional purchases.

	MT	EX-MT	VG
COMPLETE SET (9)	9.00	4.00	1.15
COMMON PLAYER (1-9)	.50	.23	.06
☐ 1 Andy Stankiewicz	.50	.23	.06
☐ 2 Pat Listach	3.00	1.35	.40
☐ 3 Brian Jordan	.90	.40	.11
☐ 4 Eric Karros	3.00	1.35	.40
☐ 5 Reggie Sanders	1.00	.45	.13
☐ 6 Dave Fleming	1.50	.65	.19
☐ 7 Donovan Osborne	.90	.40	.11
☐ 8 Kenny Lofton	1.50	.65	.19
☐ 9 Moises Alou	.90	.40	.11

1955 Kahn's

The cards in this six-card set measure 3 1/4" by 4". The 1955 Kahn's Wieners set received very limited distribution. The cards were supposedly given away at an amusement park. The set portrays the players in street clothes rather than in uniform and hence are sometimes referred to as "street clothes" Kahn's. All Kahn's sets from 1955 through 1963 are black and white and contain a 1/2" tab. Cards with the tab still intact are worth approximately 50 percent more than cards without the tab. Cards feature a facsimile autograph of the player on the front. Cards are blank-backed. Cincinnati Redlegs players only are featured.

	NRMT	VG-E	GOOD
COMPLETE SET (6)	3200.00	1450.00	400.00
COMMON PLAYER (1-6)	450.00	200.00	57.50
☐ 1 Gus Bell	750.00	350.00	95.00
☐ 2 Ted Kluszewski	750.00	350.00	95.00
☐ 3 Roy McMillan	450.00	200.00	57.50
☐ 4 Joe Nuxhall	500.00	230.00	65.00

☐ 5 Wally Post	450.00	200.00	57.50
☐ 6 Johnny Temple	450.00	200.00	57.50

1956 Kahn's

The cards in this 15-card set measure 3 1/4" by 4". The 1956 Kahn's set was the first set to be issued with Kahn's meat products. The cards are blank backed. The set is distinguished by the old style, short sleeve shirts on the players and the existence of backgounds (Kahn's cards of later years utilize a blank background). Cards which have the tab still intact are worth approximately 50 percent more than cards without the tab. Cincinnati Redlegs players only are featured. The cards are listed and numbered below in alphabetical order by the subject's name.

	NRMT	VG-E	GOOD
COMPLETE SET (15)	1700.00	750.00	210.00
COMMON PLAYER (1-15)	80.00	36.00	10.00
☐ 1 Ed Bailey	80.00	36.00	10.00
☐ 2 Gus Bell	90.00	40.00	11.50
☐ 3 Joe Black	90.00	40.00	11.50
☐ 4 Smoky Burgess	90.00	40.00	11.50
☐ 5 Art Fowler	80.00	36.00	10.00
☐ 6 Herschel Freeman	80.00	36.00	10.00
☐ 7 Ray Jablonski	80.00	36.00	10.00
☐ 8 John Klippstein	80.00	36.00	10.00
☐ 9 Ted Kluszewski	175.00	80.00	22.00
☐ 10 Brooks Lawrence	80.00	36.00	10.00
☐ 11 Roy McMillan	90.00	40.00	11.50
☐ 12 Joe Nuxhall	90.00	40.00	11.50
☐ 13 Wally Post	90.00	40.00	11.50
☐ 14 Frank Robinson	500.00	230.00	65.00
☐ 15 Johnny Temple	90.00	40.00	11.50

1957 Kahn's

The cards in this 29-card set measure 3 1/4" by 4". The 1957 Kahn's Wieners set contains black and white, blank backed, unnumbered cards. The set features the Cincinnati Redlegs and Pittsburgh Pirates only. The cards feature a light background. Each card features a facsimile autograph of the player on the front. The Groat card exists with a "Richard Groat" autograph and also exists with the printed name "Dick Groat" on the card. The catalog designation is F155-3. The cards are listed and numbered below in alphabetical order by the subject's name.

	NRMT	VG-E	GOOD
COMPLETE SET (29)	2800.00	1250.00	350.00
COMMON PLAYER (1-29)	60.00	27.00	7.50
☐ 1 Tom Acker	60.00	27.00	7.50
☐ 2 Ed Bailey	60.00	27.00	7.50
☐ 3 Gus Bell	75.00	34.00	9.50
☐ 4 Smoky Burgess	75.00	34.00	9.50
☐ 5 Roberto Clemente	750.00	350.00	95.00
☐ 6 George Crowe	60.00	27.00	7.50
☐ 7 Elroy Face	90.00	40.00	11.50
☐ 8 Herschel Freeman	60.00	27.00	7.50
☐ 9 Bob Friend	75.00	34.00	9.50
☐ 10 Dick Groat	90.00	40.00	11.50
☐ 11 Richard Groat	175.00	80.00	22.00
☐ 12 Don Gross	60.00	27.00	7.50
☐ 13 Warren Hacker	60.00	27.00	7.50
☐ 14 Don Hoak	65.00	29.00	8.25
☐ 15 Hal Jeffcoat	60.00	27.00	7.50
☐ 16 Ron Kline	60.00	27.00	7.50
☐ 17 John Klippstein	60.00	27.00	7.50
☐ 18 Ted Kluszewski	135.00	60.00	17.00
☐ 19 Brooks Lawrence	60.00	27.00	7.50
☐ 20 Dale Long	75.00	34.00	9.50
☐ 21 Bill Mazeroski	150.00	70.00	19.00
☐ 22 Roy McMillan	65.00	29.00	8.25
☐ 23 Joe Nuxhall	75.00	34.00	9.50
☐ 24 Wally Post	65.00	29.00	8.25
☐ 25 Frank Robinson	250.00	115.00	31.00
☐ 26 John Temple	65.00	29.00	8.25
☐ 27 Frank Thomas	75.00	34.00	9.50
☐ 28 Bob Thurman	60.00	27.00	7.50
☐ 29 Lee Walls	60.00	27.00	7.50

1958 Kahn's

The cards in this 29-card set measure approximately 3 1/4" by 4". The 1958 Kahn's Wieners set of unnumbered, black and white cards features Cincinnati Redlegs, Philadelphia Phillies, and Pittsburgh Pirates. The backs present a story for each player entitled "My Greatest Thrill in Baseball". A method of distinguishing 1958 Kahn's from 1959 Kahn's is that the word Wieners is found on the front of the 1958 but not on the front of the 1959 cards. Cards of Wally Post, Charlie Rabe, and Frank Thomas are somewhat more difficult to find and are designated SP in the checklist below. The cards are listed and numbered below in alphabetical order by the subject's name.

	NRMT	VG-E	GOOD
COMPLETE SET (29)	3000.00	1350.00	375.00
COMMON PLAYER (1-29)	50.00	23.00	6.25
☐ 1 Ed Bailey	50.00	23.00	6.25
☐ 2 Gene Baker	50.00	23.00	6.25
☐ 3 Gus Bell	60.00	27.00	7.50
☐ 4 Smoky Burgess	60.00	27.00	7.50
☐ 5 Roberto Clemente	600.00	275.00	75.00
☐ 6 George Crowe	50.00	23.00	6.25

	NRMT	VG-E	GOOD
☐ 7 Elroy Face	75.00	34.00	9.50
☐ 8 Hank Foiles	50.00	23.00	6.25
☐ 9 Dee Fondy	50.00	23.00	6.25
☐ 10 Bob Friend	60.00	27.00	7.50
☐ 11 Dick Groat	75.00	34.00	9.50
☐ 12 Harvey Haddix	60.00	27.00	7.50
☐ 13 Don Hoak	50.00	23.00	6.25
☐ 14 Hal Jeffcoat	50.00	23.00	6.25
☐ 15 Ron Kline	50.00	23.00	6.25
☐ 16 Ted Kluszewski	110.00	50.00	14.00
☐ 17 Vernon Law	60.00	27.00	7.50
☐ 18 Brooks Lawrence	50.00	23.00	6.25
☐ 19 Bill Mazeroski	90.00	40.00	11.50
☐ 20 Roy McMillan	50.00	23.00	6.25
☐ 21 Joe Nuxhall	60.00	27.00	7.50
☐ 22 Wally Post SP	350.00	160.00	45.00
☐ 23 John Powers	50.00	23.00	6.25
☐ 24 Bob Purkey	50.00	23.00	6.25
☐ 25 Charlie Rabe SP	350.00	160.00	45.00
☐ 26 Frank Robinson	225.00	100.00	28.00
☐ 27 Bob Skinner	50.00	23.00	6.25
☐ 28 Johnny Temple	60.00	27.00	7.50
☐ 29 Frank Thomas SP	350.00	160.00	45.00

1959 Kahn's

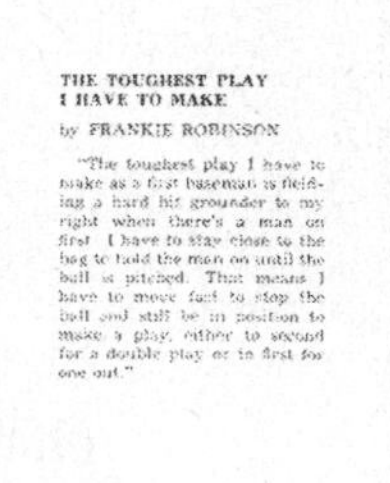

THE TOUGHEST PLAY
I HAVE TO MAKE

by FRANKIE ROBINSON

"The toughest play I have to make as a first baseman is fielding a hard hit grounder to my right when there's a man on first. I have to stay close to the bag to hold the man on until the ball is pitched. That means I have to move fast to stop the ball and still be in position to make a play, either to second for a double play or to first for one out."

The cards in this 38-card set measure approximately 3 1/4" by 4". The 1959 Kahn's set features members of the Cincinnati Reds, Cleveland Indians, and Pittsburgh Pirates. The backs feature stories entitled "The Toughest Play I Have to Make," or "The Toughest Batter I Have To Face." The Brodowski card is very scarce while Haddix, Held and McLish are considered quite difficult to obtain; these scarcities are designated SP in the checklist below. The cards are listed and numbered below in alphabetical order by the subject's name.

	NRMT	VG-E	GOOD
COMPLETE SET (38)	4500.00	2000.00	575.00
COMMON PLAYER (1-38)	50.00	23.00	6.25
☐ 1 Ed Bailey	50.00	23.00	6.25
☐ 2 Gary Bell	50.00	23.00	6.25
☐ 3 Gus Bell	60.00	27.00	7.50
☐ 4 Dick Brodowski SP	600.00	275.00	75.00
☐ 5 Smoky Burgess	60.00	27.00	7.50
☐ 6 Roberto Clemente	500.00	230.00	65.00
☐ 7 Rocky Colavito	110.00	50.00	14.00
☐ 8 Elroy Face	75.00	34.00	9.50
☐ 9 Bob Friend	60.00	27.00	7.50
☐ 10 Joe Gordon MG	60.00	27.00	7.50
☐ 11 Jim Grant	60.00	27.00	7.50
☐ 12 Dick Groat	75.00	34.00	9.50
☐ 13 Harvey Haddix SP (Blank back)	400.00	180.00	50.00
☐ 14 Woodie Held SP	400.00	180.00	50.00
☐ 15 Don Hoak	50.00	23.00	6.25
☐ 16 Ron Kline	50.00	23.00	6.25
☐ 17 Ted Kluszewski	100.00	45.00	12.50
☐ 18 Vernon Law	60.00	27.00	7.50
☐ 19 Jerry Lynch	50.00	23.00	6.25
☐ 20 Billy Martin	125.00	57.50	15.50
☐ 21 Bill Mazeroski	90.00	40.00	11.50
☐ 22 Cal McLish SP	400.00	180.00	50.00
☐ 23 Roy McMillan	50.00	23.00	6.25
☐ 24 Minnie Minoso	90.00	40.00	11.50
☐ 25 Russ Nixon	50.00	23.00	6.25
☐ 26 Joe Nuxhall	60.00	27.00	7.50
☐ 27 Jim Perry	75.00	34.00	9.50
☐ 28 Vada Pinson	90.00	40.00	11.50
☐ 29 Vic Power	50.00	23.00	6.25
☐ 30 Bob Purkey	50.00	23.00	6.25
☐ 31 Frank Robinson	200.00	90.00	25.00
☐ 32 Herb Score	75.00	34.00	9.50
☐ 33 Bob Skinner	50.00	23.00	6.25
☐ 34 George Strickland	50.00	23.00	6.25
☐ 35 Dick Stuart	60.00	27.00	7.50
☐ 36 Johnny Temple	50.00	23.00	6.25
☐ 37 Frank Thomas	60.00	27.00	7.50
☐ 38 George Witt	50.00	23.00	6.25

1960 Kahn's

The cards in this 42-card set measure 3 1/4" by 4". The 1960 Kahn's set features players of the Chicago Cubs, Chicago White Sox, Cincinnati Redlegs, Cleveland Indians, Pittsburgh Pirates, and St. Louis Cardinals. The backs give vital player information and records through the 1959 season. Kline appears with either St. Louis or Pittsburgh. The Harvey Kuenn card (asterisked below) appears with a blank back, and is scarce. The cards are listed and numbered below in alphabetical order by the subject's name.

	NRMT	VG-E	GOOD
COMPLETE SET (43)	2000.00	900.00	250.00
COMMON PLAYER (1-42)	25.00	11.50	3.10
☐ 1 Ed Bailey	25.00	11.50	3.10
☐ 2 Gary Bell	25.00	11.50	3.10
☐ 3 Gus Bell	30.00	13.50	3.80
☐ 4 Smoky Burgess	30.00	13.50	3.80
☐ 5 Gino Cimoli	25.00	11.50	3.10
☐ 6 Roberto Clemente	350.00	160.00	45.00
☐ 7 Roy Face	35.00	16.00	4.40
☐ 8 Tito Francona	25.00	11.50	3.10
☐ 9 Bob Friend	30.00	13.50	3.80
☐ 10 Jim Grant	25.00	11.50	3.10
☐ 11 Dick Groat	35.00	16.00	4.40
☐ 12 Harvey Haddix	30.00	13.50	3.80
☐ 13 Woodie Held	25.00	11.50	3.10
☐ 14 Bill Henry	25.00	11.50	3.10
☐ 15 Don Hoak	25.00	11.50	3.10
☐ 16 Jay Hook	25.00	11.50	3.10
☐ 17 Eddie Kasko	25.00	11.50	3.10
☐ 18A Ron Kline (Pittsburgh)	45.00	20.00	5.75
☐ 18B Ron Kline (St. Louis)	45.00	20.00	5.75
☐ 19 Ted Kluszewski	55.00	25.00	7.00
☐ 20 Harvey Kuenn SP (Blank back)	350.00	160.00	45.00
☐ 21 Vernon Law	30.00	13.50	3.80
☐ 22 Brooks Lawrence	25.00	11.50	3.10
☐ 23 Jerry Lynch	25.00	11.50	3.10
☐ 24 Billy Martin	60.00	27.00	7.50
☐ 25 Bill Mazeroski	40.00	18.00	5.00
☐ 26 Cal McLish	25.00	11.50	3.10
☐ 27 Roy McMillan	25.00	11.50	3.10
☐ 28 Don Newcombe	35.00	16.00	4.40
☐ 29 Russ Nixon	25.00	11.50	3.10
☐ 30 Joe Nuxhall	30.00	13.50	3.80
☐ 31 Jim O'Toole	25.00	11.50	3.10
☐ 32 Jim Perry	30.00	13.50	3.80
☐ 33 Vada Pinson	40.00	18.00	5.00
☐ 34 Vic Power	25.00	11.50	3.10

	NRMT	VG-E	GOOD
☐ 35 Bob Purkey	25.00	11.50	3.10
☐ 36 Frank Robinson	150.00	70.00	19.00
☐ 37 Herb Score	35.00	16.00	4.40
☐ 38 Bob Skinner	25.00	11.50	3.10
☐ 39 Dick Stuart	30.00	13.50	3.80
☐ 40 Johnny Temple	30.00	13.50	3.80
☐ 41 Frank Thomas	30.00	13.50	3.80
☐ 42 Lee Walls	25.00	11.50	3.10

1961 Kahn's

The cards in this 43-card set measure approximately 3 1/4" by 4". The 1961 Kahn's Wieners set of black and white, unnumbered cards features members of the Cincinnati Reds, Cleveland Indians, and Pittsburgh Pirates. This year was the first year Kahn's made complete sets available to the public; hence they are more available, especially in the better condition grades, than the Kahn's of the previous years. The backs give vital player information and year by year career statistics through 1960. The catalog designation is F155-7. The cards are listed and numbered below in alphabetical order by the subject's name.

	NRMT	VG-E	GOOD
COMPLETE SET (43)	850.00	375.00	105.00
COMMON PLAYER (1-43)	12.50	5.75	1.55
☐ 1 John Antonelli	14.00	6.25	1.75
☐ 2 Ed Bailey	12.50	5.75	1.55
☐ 3 Gary Bell	12.50	5.75	1.55
☐ 4 Gus Bell	14.00	6.25	1.75
☐ 5 Jim Brosnan	14.00	6.25	1.75
☐ 6 Smoky Burgess	16.00	7.25	2.00
☐ 7 Gino Cimoli	12.50	5.75	1.55
☐ 8 Roberto Clemente	250.00	115.00	31.00
☐ 9 Gordie Coleman	12.50	5.75	1.55
☐ 10 Jimmy Dykes MG	14.00	6.25	1.75
☐ 11 Roy Face	16.00	7.25	2.00
☐ 12 Tito Francona	12.50	5.75	1.55
☐ 13 Gene Freese	12.50	5.75	1.55
☐ 14 Bob Friend	14.00	6.25	1.75
☐ 15 Jim Grant	12.50	5.75	1.55
☐ 16 Dick Groat	18.00	8.00	2.30
☐ 17 Harvey Haddix	14.00	6.25	1.75
☐ 18 Woodie Held	12.50	5.75	1.55
☐ 19 Don Hoak	12.50	5.75	1.55
☐ 20 Jay Hook	12.50	5.75	1.55
☐ 21 Joey Jay	12.50	5.75	1.55
☐ 22 Eddie Kasko	12.50	5.75	1.55
☐ 23 Willie Kirkland	12.50	5.75	1.55
☐ 24 Vernon Law	14.00	6.25	1.75
☐ 25 Jerry Lynch	12.50	5.75	1.55
☐ 26 Jim Maloney	18.00	8.00	2.30
☐ 27 Bill Mazeroski	20.00	9.00	2.50
☐ 28 Wilmer Mizell	12.50	5.75	1.55
☐ 29 Rocky Nelson	12.50	5.75	1.55
☐ 30 Jim O'Toole	12.50	5.75	1.55
☐ 31 Jim Perry	16.00	7.25	2.00
☐ 32 Bubba Phillips	12.50	5.75	1.55
☐ 33 Vada Pinson	18.00	8.00	2.30
☐ 34 Wally Post	12.50	5.75	1.55
☐ 35 Vic Power	12.50	5.75	1.55
☐ 36 Bob Purkey	12.50	5.75	1.55
☐ 37 Frank Robinson	100.00	45.00	12.50
☐ 38 John Romano	12.50	5.75	1.55
☐ 39 Dick Schofield	12.50	5.75	1.55
☐ 40 Bob Skinner	12.50	5.75	1.55
☐ 41 Hal Smith	12.50	5.75	1.55
☐ 42 Dick Stuart	16.00	7.25	2.00
☐ 43 Johnny Temple	12.50	5.75	1.55

1962 Kahn's

The cards in this 38-card set measure approximately 3 1/4" by 4". The 1962 Kahn's Wieners set of black and white, unnumbered cards features Cincinnati, Cleveland, Minnesota, and Pittsburgh players. Card numbers 1 Bell, 33 Power, and 34 Purkey exist in two different forms; these variations are listed in the checklist below. The backs of the cards contain career information. The catalog designation is F155-8. The set price below includes the set with all variation cards. The cards are listed and numbered below in alphabetical order by the subject's name.

	NRMT	VG-E	GOOD
COMPLETE SET (41)	1100.00	500.00	140.00
COMMON PLAYER (1-38)	11.00	4.90	1.40
☐ 1A Gary Bell (With fat man)	100.00	45.00	12.50
☐ 1B Gary Bell (No fat man)	35.00	16.00	4.40
☐ 2 Jim Brosnan	12.50	5.75	1.55
☐ 3 Smoky Burgess	12.50	5.75	1.55
☐ 4 Chico Cardenas	12.50	5.75	1.55
☐ 5 Roberto Clemente	200.00	90.00	25.00
☐ 6 Ty Cline	11.00	4.90	1.40
☐ 7 Gordon Coleman	12.50	5.75	1.55
☐ 8 Dick Donovan	11.00	4.90	1.40
☐ 9 John Edwards	11.00	4.90	1.40
☐ 10 Tito Francona	12.50	5.75	1.55
☐ 11 Gene Freese	11.00	4.90	1.40
☐ 12 Bob Friend	12.50	5.75	1.55
☐ 13 Joe Gibbon	100.00	45.00	12.50
☐ 14 Jim Grant	11.00	4.90	1.40
☐ 15 Dick Groat	15.00	6.75	1.90
☐ 16 Harvey Haddix	12.50	5.75	1.55
☐ 17 Woodie Held	11.00	4.90	1.40
☐ 18 Bill Henry	11.00	4.90	1.40
☐ 19 Don Hoak	11.00	4.90	1.40
☐ 20 Ken Hunt	11.00	4.90	1.40
☐ 21 Joey Jay	11.00	4.90	1.40
☐ 22 Eddie Kasko	11.00	4.90	1.40
☐ 23 Willie Kirkland	11.00	4.90	1.40
☐ 24 Barry Latman	11.00	4.90	1.40
☐ 25 Jerry Lynch	11.00	4.90	1.40
☐ 26 Jim Maloney	14.00	6.25	1.75
☐ 27 Bill Mazeroski	16.00	7.25	2.00
☐ 28 Jim O'Toole	11.00	4.90	1.40
☐ 29 Jim Perry	12.50	5.75	1.55
☐ 30 Bubba Phillips	11.00	4.90	1.40
☐ 31 Vada Pinson	15.00	6.75	1.90
☐ 32 Wally Post	11.00	4.90	1.40
☐ 33A Vic Power (Indians)	35.00	16.00	4.40
☐ 33B Vic Power (Twins)	100.00	45.00	12.50
☐ 34A Bob Purkey (With autograph)	35.00	16.00	4.40
☐ 34B Bob Purkey (No autograph)	100.00	45.00	12.50
☐ 35 Frank Robinson	85.00	38.00	10.50
☐ 36 John Romano	11.00	4.90	1.40
☐ 37 Dick Stuart	12.50	5.75	1.55
☐ 38 Bill Virdon	15.00	6.75	1.90

1962 Kahn's Atlanta

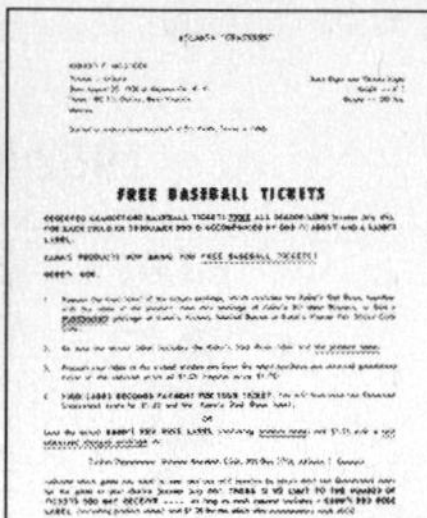
FREE BASEBALL TICKETS

The cards in this 24-card set measure approximately 3 1/4" by 4". The 1962 Kahn's Wieners Atlanta set features unnumbered, black and white cards of the Atlanta Crackers of the International League. The backs contain player statistical information as well as instructions on how to obtain free tickets. The catalog designation is F155-9. The cards are listed and numbered below in alphabetical order by the subject's name.

	NRMT	VG-E	GOOD
COMPLETE SET (24)	375.00	170.00	47.50
COMMON PLAYER (1-24)	12.50	5.75	1.55
☐ 1 Jim Beauchamp	15.00	6.75	1.90
☐ 2 Gerry Buchek	12.50	5.75	1.55
☐ 3 Bob Burda	12.50	5.75	1.55
☐ 4 Dick Dietz	15.00	6.75	1.90
☐ 5 Bob Duliba	12.50	5.75	1.55
☐ 6 Harry Fanok	12.50	5.75	1.55
☐ 7 Phil Gagliano	15.00	6.75	1.90
☐ 8 John Glenn	12.50	5.75	1.55
☐ 9 Leroy Gregory	12.50	5.75	1.55
☐ 10 Dick Hughes	12.50	5.75	1.55
☐ 11 Johnny Kucks	15.00	6.75	1.90
☐ 12 Johnny Lewis	12.50	5.75	1.55
☐ 13 Tim McCarver	75.00	34.00	9.50
☐ 14 Bob Milliken	12.50	5.75	1.55
☐ 15 Joe M. Morgan	15.00	6.75	1.90
☐ 16 Ron Plaza	12.50	5.75	1.55
☐ 17 Bob Sadowski	12.50	5.75	1.55
☐ 18 Jim Saul	12.50	5.75	1.55
☐ 19 Willard Schmidt	12.50	5.75	1.55
☐ 20 Joe Schultz MG	15.00	6.75	1.90
☐ 21 Mike Shannon	30.00	13.50	3.80
☐ 22 Paul Toth	12.50	5.75	1.55
☐ 23 Lou Vickery	12.50	5.75	1.55
☐ 24 Fred Whitfield	15.00	6.75	1.90

1963 Kahn's

The cards in this 30-card set measure approximately 3 1/4" by 4". The 1963 Kahn's Wieners set of black and white, unnumbered cards features players from Cincinnati, Cleveland, St. Louis, Pittsburgh and the New York Yankees. The cards feature a white border around the picture of the players. The backs contain career information. The catalog designation for this set is F155-10. The cards are listed and numbered below in alphabetical order by the subject's name.

	NRMT	VG-E	GOOD
COMPLETE SET (30)	600.00	275.00	75.00
COMMON PLAYER (1-30)	11.00	4.90	1.40
☐ 1 Bob Bailey	11.00	4.90	1.40
☐ 2 Don Blasingame	11.00	4.90	1.40
☐ 3 Clete Boyer	14.00	6.25	1.75
☐ 4 Smoky Burgess	12.00	5.50	1.50
☐ 5 Chico Cardenas	12.00	5.50	1.50
☐ 6 Roberto Clemente	200.00	90.00	25.00
☐ 7 Donn Clendenon	14.00	6.25	1.75
☐ 8 Gordon Coleman	12.00	5.50	1.50
☐ 9 John Edwards	11.00	4.90	1.40
☐ 10 Gene Freese	11.00	4.90	1.40
☐ 11 Bob Friend	12.00	5.50	1.50
☐ 12 Joe Gibbon	11.00	4.90	1.40
☐ 13 Dick Groat	15.00	6.75	1.90
☐ 14 Harvey Haddix	12.00	5.50	1.50
☐ 15 Elston Howard	20.00	9.00	2.50
☐ 16 Joey Jay	11.00	4.90	1.40
☐ 17 Eddie Kasko	11.00	4.90	1.40
☐ 18 Tony Kubek	25.00	11.50	3.10
☐ 19 Jerry Lynch	11.00	4.90	1.40
☐ 20 Jim Maloney	14.00	6.25	1.75
☐ 21 Bill Mazeroski	16.00	7.25	2.00
☐ 22 Joe Nuxhall	12.00	5.50	1.50
☐ 23 Jim O'Toole	11.00	4.90	1.40
☐ 24 Vada Pinson	16.00	7.25	2.00
☐ 25 Bob Purkey	11.00	4.90	1.40
☐ 26 Bobby Richardson	25.00	11.50	3.10
☐ 27 Frank Robinson	85.00	38.00	10.50
☐ 28 Bill Stafford	11.00	4.90	1.40
☐ 29 Ralph Terry	12.00	5.50	1.50
☐ 30 Bill Virdon	12.00	5.50	1.50

1964 Kahn's

Compliments of Kahn's
"THE WIENER THE WORLD AWAITED"

The cards in this 31-card set measure approximately 3" by 3 1/2". The 1964 Kahn's set marks the beginning of the full color cards and the elimination of the tabs which existed on previous Kahn's cards. The set of unnumbered cards contains player information through the 1963 season on the backs. The set features Cincinnati, Cleveland and Pittsburgh players. The cards are listed and numbered below in alphabetical order by the subject's name.

	NRMT	VG-E	GOOD
COMPLETE SET (31)	900.00	400.00	115.00
COMMON PLAYER (1-31)	11.00	4.90	1.40
☐ 1 Max Alvis	11.00	4.90	1.40
☐ 2 Bob Bailey	11.00	4.90	1.40
☐ 3 Chico Cardenas	12.00	5.50	1.50
☐ 4 Roberto Clemente	200.00	90.00	25.00
☐ 5 Donn Clendenon	12.00	5.50	1.50
☐ 6 Vic Davalillo	11.00	4.90	1.40
☐ 7 Dick Donovan	11.00	4.90	1.40
☐ 8 John Edwards	11.00	4.90	1.40
☐ 9 Bob Friend	12.00	5.50	1.50
☐ 10 Jim Grant	11.00	4.90	1.40

☐ 11 Tommy Harper	12.00	5.50	1.50
☐ 12 Woodie Held	11.00	4.90	1.40
☐ 13 Joey Jay	11.00	4.90	1.40
☐ 14 Jack Kralick	11.00	4.90	1.40
☐ 15 Jerry Lynch	11.00	4.90	1.40
☐ 16 Jim Maloney	14.00	6.25	1.75
☐ 17 Bill Mazeroski	16.00	7.25	2.00
☐ 18 Alvin McBean	11.00	4.90	1.40
☐ 19 Joe Nuxhall	12.00	5.50	1.50
☐ 20 Jim Pagliaroni	11.00	4.90	1.40
☐ 21 Vada Pinson	15.00	6.75	1.90
☐ 22 Bob Purkey	11.00	4.90	1.40
☐ 23 Pedro Ramos	11.00	4.90	1.40
☐ 24 Frank Robinson	85.00	38.00	10.50
☐ 25 John Romano	11.00	4.90	1.40
☐ 26 Pete Rose	350.00	160.00	45.00
☐ 27 John Tsitouris	11.00	4.90	1.40
☐ 28 Bob Veale	12.00	5.50	1.50
☐ 29 Bill Virdon	12.00	5.50	1.50
☐ 30 Leon Wagner	11.00	4.90	1.40
☐ 31 Fred Whitfield	11.00	4.90	1.40

1965 Kahn's

Compliments of Kahn's
"THE WIENER THE WORLD AWAITED"

The cards in this 45-card set measure approximately 3" by 3 1/2". The 1965 Kahn's set contains full color, unnumbered cards. The set features Cincinnati, Cleveland, Pittsburgh, and Milwaukee players. Backs contain statistical information through the 1964 season. The cards are listed and numbered below in alphabetical order by the subject's name.

	NRMT	VG-E	GOOD
COMPLETE SET (45)	1000.00	450.00	125.00
COMMON PLAYER (1-45)	11.00	4.90	1.40
☐ 1 Henry Aaron	150.00	70.00	19.00
☐ 2 Max Alvis	11.00	4.90	1.40
☐ 3 Joe Azcue	11.00	4.90	1.40
☐ 4 Bob Bailey	11.00	4.90	1.40
☐ 5 Frank Bolling	11.00	4.90	1.40
☐ 6 Chico Cardenas	12.00	5.50	1.50
☐ 7 Rico Carty	16.00	7.25	2.00
☐ 8 Donn Clendenon	12.00	5.50	1.50
☐ 9 Tony Cloninger	12.00	5.50	1.50
☐ 10 Gordon Coleman	11.00	4.90	1.40
☐ 11 Vic Davalillo	11.00	4.90	1.40
☐ 12 John Edwards	11.00	4.90	1.40
☐ 13 Sammy Ellis	11.00	4.90	1.40
☐ 14 Bob Friend	12.00	5.50	1.50
☐ 15 Tommy Harper	12.00	5.50	1.50
☐ 16 Chuck Hinton	11.00	4.90	1.40
☐ 17 Dick Howser	15.00	6.75	1.90
☐ 18 Joey Jay	11.00	4.90	1.40
☐ 19 Deron Johnson	12.00	5.50	1.50
☐ 20 Jack Kralick	11.00	4.90	1.40
☐ 21 Denver LeMaster	11.00	4.90	1.40
☐ 22 Jerry Lynch	11.00	4.90	1.40
☐ 23 Jim Maloney	14.00	6.25	1.75
☐ 24 Lee Maye	11.00	4.90	1.40
☐ 25 Bill Mazeroski	16.00	7.25	2.00
☐ 26 Alvin McBean	11.00	4.90	1.40
☐ 27 Bill McCool	11.00	4.90	1.40
☐ 28 Sam McDowell	14.00	6.25	1.75
☐ 29 Don McMahon	11.00	4.90	1.40
☐ 30 Denis Menke	11.00	4.90	1.40
☐ 31 Joe Nuxhall	12.00	5.50	1.50
☐ 32 Gene Oliver	11.00	4.90	1.40
☐ 33 Jim O'Toole	11.00	4.90	1.40
☐ 34 Jim Pagliaroni	11.00	4.90	1.40
☐ 35 Vada Pinson	15.00	6.75	1.90
☐ 36 Frank Robinson	85.00	38.00	10.50
☐ 37 Pete Rose	225.00	100.00	28.00
☐ 38 Willie Stargell	100.00	45.00	12.50
☐ 39 Ralph Terry	12.00	5.50	1.50
☐ 40 Luis Tiant	15.00	6.75	1.90
☐ 41 Joe Torre	18.00	8.00	2.30
☐ 42 John Tsitouris	11.00	4.90	1.40
☐ 43 Bob Veale	12.00	5.50	1.50
☐ 44 Bill Virdon	12.00	5.50	1.50
☐ 45 Leon Wagner	11.00	4.90	1.40

1966 Kahn's

The cards in this 32-card set measure approximately 2 13/16" by 4". 1966 Kahn's full color, unnumbered set features players from Atlanta, Cincinnati, Cleveland, and Pittsburgh. The set is identified by yellow and white vertical stripes and the name Kahn's written in red across a red rose at the top. The cards contain a 1 5/16" ad in the form of a tab. Cards with the ad (tab) are worth twice as much as cards without the ad, i.e., double the prices below. The cards are listed and numbered below in alphabetical order by the subject's name.

	NRMT	VG-E	GOOD
COMPLETE SET (32)	600.00	275.00	75.00
COMMON PLAYER (1-32)	9.00	4.00	1.15
☐ 1 Henry Aaron (Portrait, no wind-breaker under jersey	100.00	45.00	12.50
☐ 2 Felipe Alou: Braves (Full pose, batting screen in background)	15.00	6.75	1.90
☐ 3 Max Alvis: Indians (Kneeling, full pose, with bat, no patch on jersey)	9.00	4.00	1.15
☐ 4 Bob Bailey	9.00	4.00	1.15
☐ 5 Wade Blasingame	9.00	4.00	1.15
☐ 6 Frank Bolling	9.00	4.00	1.15
☐ 7 Chico Cardenas: Reds (Fielding, feet at base)	10.00	4.50	1.25
☐ 8 Roberto Clemente	100.00	45.00	12.50
☐ 9 Tony Cloninger: Braves (Pitching, foulpole in background)	10.00	4.50	1.25
☐ 10 Vic Davalillo	9.00	4.00	1.15
☐ 11 John Edwards: Reds (Catching)	9.00	4.00	1.15
☐ 12 Sam Ellis: Reds (White hat)	9.00	4.00	1.15
☐ 13 Pedro Gonzalez	9.00	4.00	1.15
☐ 14 Tommy Harper: Reds (Arm cocked)	10.00	4.50	1.25
☐ 15 Deron Johnson: Reds (Batting with batting cage in background)	10.00	4.50	1.25
☐ 16 Mack Jones	9.00	4.00	1.15
☐ 17 Denver Lemaster	9.00	4.00	1.15
☐ 18 Jim Maloney: Reds	12.00	5.50	1.50

(Pitching, white hat)
☐ 19 Bill Mazeroski: Pirates (Throwing) 14.00 6.25 1.75
☐ 20 Bill McCool: Reds (White hat) 9.00 4.00 1.15
☐ 21 Sam McDowell: Indians (Kneeling) 10.00 4.50 1.25
☐ 22 Denis Menke: Braves (White windbreaker under jersey) 9.00 4.00 1.15
☐ 23 Joe Nuxhall 10.00 4.50 1.25
☐ 24 Jim Pagliaroni: Pirates (Catching) 9.00 4.00 1.15
☐ 25 Milt Pappas 10.00 4.50 1.25
☐ 26 Vada Pinson: Reds (Fielding, ball on ground) 12.00 5.50 1.50
☐ 27 Pete Rose: Reds (With glove) 125.00 57.50 15.50
☐ 28 Sonny Siebert: Indians (Pitching, signature at feet) 10.00 4.50 1.25
☐ 29 Willie Stargell: Pirates (Batting, clouds in sky) 40.00 18.00 5.00
☐ 30 Joe Torre: Braves (Catching with hand on mask) 14.00 6.25 1.75
☐ 31 Bob Veale: Pirates (Hands at knee with glasses) 10.00 4.50 1.25
☐ 32 Fred Whitfield 9.00 4.00 1.15

1967 Kahn's

The cards in this 41-player set measure approximately 2 13/16" by 4". The 1967 Kahn's set of full color, unnumbered cards is almost identical in style to the 1966 issue. Different meat products had different background colors (yellow and white stripes, red and white stripes, etc.). The set features players from Atlanta, Cincinnati, Cleveland, New York Mets and Pittsburgh. Cards with the ads (see 1966 set) are worth twice as much as cards without the ad, i.e., double the prices below. The complete set price below includes all variations. The cards are listed and numbered below in alphabetical order by the subject's name.

	NRMT	VG-E	GOOD
COMPLETE SET (51)	800.00	350.00	100.00
COMMON PLAYER (1-41)	9.00	4.00	1.15

☐ 1A Henry Aaron: Braves (Swinging pose, batting glove, ball, and hat on ground) 100.00 45.00 12.50
☐ 1B Henry Aaron: Braves (Swinging pose, batting glove, ball, and hat on ground; Cut Along Dotted Lines printed on lower tab) 125.00 57.50 15.50
☐ 2 Gene Alley: Pirates (Portrait) 10.00 4.50 1.25
☐ 3 Felipe Alou: Braves (Full pose, bat on shoulder) 15.00 6.75 1.90
☐ 4A Matty Alou: Pirates (Portrait with bat, "Matio Rojas Alou"; yellow stripes) 10.00 4.50 1.25
☐ 4B Matty Alou: Pirates (Portrait with bat, "Matio Rojas Alou"; red stripes) 12.00 5.50 1.50
☐ 5 Max Alvis: Indians (Fielding, hands on knees) 9.00 4.00 1.15
☐ 6A Ken Boyer (Batting righthanded; autograph at waist) 12.00 5.50 1.50
☐ 6B Ken Boyer (Batting righthanded; autograph at shoulders; Cut Along Dotted Lines printed on lower tab) 16.00 7.25 2.00
☐ 7 Chico Cardenas: Reds (Fielding, hand on knee) 10.00 4.50 1.25
☐ 8 Rico Carty 12.00 5.50 1.50
☐ 9 Tony Cloninger: Braves (Pitching, no foul-pole in background) 10.00 4.50 1.25
☐ 10 Tommy Davis 10.00 4.50 1.25
☐ 11 John Edwards: Reds (Kneeling with bat) 9.00 4.00 1.15
☐ 12A Sam Ellis: Reds (All red hat) 9.00 4.00 1.15
☐ 12B Sam Ellis: Reds (All red hat; Cut Along Dotted Lines printed on lower tab) 10.00 4.50 1.25
☐ 13 Jack Fisher 9.00 4.00 1.15
☐ 14 Steve Hargan: Indians (Pitching, no clouds, blue sky) 9.00 4.00 1.15
☐ 15 Tommy Harper: Reds (Fielding, glove on ground) 10.00 4.50 1.25
☐ 16A Tommy Helms (Batting righthanded; top of bat visible) 10.00 4.50 1.25
☐ 16B Tommy Helms (Batting righthanded; bat chopped above hat; Cut Along Dotted Lines printed on lower tab) 12.00 5.50 1.50
☐ 17 Deron Johnson: Reds (Batting, blue sky) 10.00 4.50 1.25
☐ 18 Ken Johnson 9.00 4.00 1.15
☐ 19 Cleon Jones 12.00 5.50 1.50
☐ 20A Ed Kranepool (Ready for throw; yellow stripes) 10.00 4.50 1.25
☐ 20B Ed Kranepool (Ready for throw; red stripes) 12.00 5.50 1.50
☐ 21A Jim Maloney: Reds (Pitching, red hat, follow thru delivery; yellow stripes) 10.00 4.50 1.25
☐ 21B Jim Maloney: Reds (Pitching, red hat, follow thru delivery; red stripes) 12.00 5.50 1.50
☐ 22 Lee May: Reds (Hands on knee) 10.00 4.50 1.25
☐ 23A Bill Mazeroski: Pirates (Portrait; autograph below waist) 12.00 5.50 1.50
☐ 23B Bill Mazeroski: Pirates (Portrait; autograph above waist; Cut Along Dotted Lines printed on lower tab) 16.00 7.25 2.00
☐ 24 Bill McCool: Reds (Red hat, left hand out) 9.00 4.00 1.15
☐ 25 Sam McDowell: Indians (Pitching, left hand under glove) 10.00 4.50 1.25
☐ 26 Denis Menke: Braves (Blue sleeves) 9.00 4.00 1.15
☐ 27 Jim Pagliaroni: Pirates (Catching, no chest protector) 9.00 4.00 1.15
☐ 28 Don Pavletich 9.00 4.00 1.15
☐ 29 Tony Perez: Reds (Throwing) 30.00 13.50 3.80
☐ 30 Vada Pinson: Reds (Ready to throw) 12.00 5.50 1.50

☐ 31 Dennis Ribant	9.00	4.00	1.15
☐ 32 Pete Rose: Reds (Batting)	125.00	57.50	15.50
☐ 33 Art Shamsky: Reds	9.00	4.00	1.15
☐ 34 Bob Shaw	9.00	4.00	1.15
☐ 35 Sonny Siebert: Indians (Pitching, signature at knees)	9.00	4.00	1.15
☐ 36 Willie Stargell: Pirates (Batting, no clouds)	40.00	18.00	5.00
☐ 37A Joe Torre: Braves (Catching, mask on ground)	12.00	5.50	1.50
☐ 37B Joe Torre: Braves (Catching, mask on ground; Cut Along Dotted Lines printed on lower tab)	16.00	7.25	2.00
☐ 38 Bob Veale: Pirates (Portrait, hands not shown)	10.00	4.50	1.25
☐ 39 Leon Wagner: Indians (Fielding)	9.00	4.00	1.15
☐ 40A Fred Whitfield (Batting lefthanded)	9.00	4.00	1.15
☐ 40B Fred Whitfield (Batting lefthanded; Cut Along Dotted Lines printed on lower tab)	10.00	4.50	1.25
☐ 41 Woody Woodward	10.00	4.50	1.25

1968 Kahn's

The cards in this 50-card set contain two different sizes. The smaller of the two sizes, which contains 12 cards, is 2 13/16" by 3 1/4" with the ad tab and 2 13/16" by 1 7/8" without the ad tab. The larger size, which contains 38 cards, measures 2 13/16" by 3 7/8" with the ad tab and 2 13/16" by 2 11/16" without the ad tab. The 1968 Kahn's set of full color, blank backed, unnumbered cards features players from Atlanta, Chicago Cubs, Chicago White Sox, Cincinnati, Cleveland, Detroit, New York Mets, and Pittsburgh. In the set of 12, listed with the letter A in the checklist, Maloney exists with either yellow or yellow and green stripes at the top of the card. The large set of 38, listed with a letter B in the checklist, contains five cards which exist in two variations. The variations in this large set have either yellow or red stripes at the top of the cards, with Maloney being an exception. Maloney has either a yellow stripe or a Blue Mountain ad at the top. Cards with the ad tabs (see other Kahn's sets) are worth twice as much as cards without the ad, i.e., double the prices below. The cards are listed and numbered below in alphabetical order (within each subset) by the subject's name.

	NRMT-MT	EXC	G-VG
COMPLETE SET (50)	1100.00	500.00	140.00
COMMON PLAYER	9.00	4.00	1.15
☐ A1 Hank Aaron	100.00	45.00	12.50
☐ A2 Gene Alley	10.00	4.50	1.25
☐ A3 Max Alvis	9.00	4.00	1.15
☐ A4 Clete Boyer	12.00	5.50	1.50
☐ A5 Chico Cardenas	10.00	4.50	1.25
☐ A6 Bill Freehan	12.00	5.50	1.50
☐ A7 Jim Maloney (2)	12.00	5.50	1.50
☐ A8 Lee May	10.00	4.50	1.25
☐ A9 Bill Mazeroski	12.00	5.50	1.50
☐ A10 Vada Pinson	12.00	5.50	1.50
☐ A11 Joe Torre	12.00	5.50	1.50
☐ A12 Bob Veale	10.00	4.50	1.25
☐ B1 Hank Aaron: Braves (Full pose, batting bat cocked)	100.00	45.00	12.50
☐ B2 Tommy Agee	10.00	4.50	1.25
☐ B3 Gene Alley: Pirates (Fielding, full pose)	10.00	4.50	1.25
☐ B4 Felipe Alou (Full pose, batting, swinging, player in background)	14.00	6.25	1.75
☐ B5 Matty Alou: Pirates (Portrait with bat, "Matio Alou" (2)	10.00	4.50	1.25
☐ B6 Max Alvis (Fielding, glove on ground)	9.00	4.00	1.15
☐ B7 Gerry Arrigo: Reds (Pitching, follow thru delivery)	9.00	4.00	1.15
☐ B8 John Bench	350.00	160.00	45.00
☐ B9 Clete Boyer	12.00	5.50	1.50
☐ B10 Larry Brown	9.00	4.00	1.15
☐ B11 Leo Cardenas: Reds (Leaping in the air)	10.00	4.50	1.25
☐ B12 Bill Freehan	12.00	5.50	1.50
☐ B13 Steve Hargan: Indians (Pitching, clouds in background)	9.00	4.00	1.15
☐ B14 Joel Horlen: White Sox (Portrait)	10.00	4.50	1.25
☐ B15 Tony Horton: Indians (Portrait, signed Anthony)	10.00	4.50	1.25
☐ B16 Willie Horton	12.00	5.50	1.50
☐ B17 Ferguson Jenkins	40.00	18.00	5.00
☐ B18 Deron Johnson: Braves	10.00	4.50	1.25
☐ B19 Mack Jones: Reds	9.00	4.00	1.15
☐ B20 Bob Lee	9.00	4.00	1.15
☐ B21 Jim Maloney: Reds (Red hat, pitching hands up) (2)	12.00	5.50	1.50
☐ B22 Lee May: Reds (Batting)	10.00	4.50	1.25
☐ B23 Bill Mazeroski: Pirates (Fielding, hands in front of body)	12.00	5.50	1.50
☐ B24 Dick McAuliffe	10.00	4.50	1.25
☐ B25 Bill McCool (Red hat, left hand down)	9.00	4.00	1.15
☐ B26 Sam McDowell: Indians (Pitching, left hand over glove (2)	10.00	4.50	1.25
☐ B27 Tony Perez (Fielding ball in glove (2)	25.00	11.50	3.10
☐ B28 Gary Peters: White Sox (Portrait)	9.00	4.00	1.15
☐ B29 Vada Pinson: Reds (Batting)	12.00	5.50	1.50
☐ B30 Chico Ruiz	9.00	4.00	1.15
☐ B31 Ron Santo: Cubs (Batting, follow thru (2)	16.00	7.25	2.00
☐ B32 Art Shamsky: Mets	9.00	4.00	1.15
☐ B33 Luis Tiant: Indians (Hands over head)	12.00	5.50	1.50
☐ B34 Joe Torre: Braves (Batting)	12.00	5.50	1.50
☐ B35 Bob Veale: Pirates (Hands chest high)	10.00	4.50	1.25
☐ B36 Leon Wagner: Indians (Batting)	9.00	4.00	1.15
☐ B37 Billy Williams: Cubs (Bat behind back)	35.00	16.00	4.40
☐ B38 Earl Wilson	10.00	4.50	1.25

1969 Kahn's

The cards in this 25-card set contain two different sizes. The three small cards (see 1968 description) measure 2 13/16" by 3 1/4" and the 22 large cards (see 1968 description) measure 2 13/16" by 3 15/16". The 1969 Kahn's Wieners set of full color, unnumbered cards features players from Atlanta, Chicago Cubs, Chicago White Sox, Cincinnati, Cleveland, Pittsburgh, and St. Louis. The small cards have the letter A in the checklist while the large cards have the letter B in the checklist. Four of the larger cards exist in two variations (red or yellow color stripes at the top of the card). These variations are identified in the checklist below. Cards with the ad tabs (see other Kahn's sets) are worth twice as much as cards without the ad, i.e., double the prices below. The cards are listed and numbered below in alphabetical order (within each subset) by the subject's name.

	NRMT-MT	EXC	G-VG
COMPLETE SET (25)	450.00	200.00	57.50
COMMON PLAYER	9.00	4.00	1.15
☐ A1 Hank Aaron (Portrait)	100.00	45.00	12.50
☐ A2 Jim Maloney (Pitching, hands at side)	10.00	4.50	1.25
☐ A3 Tony Perez (Glove on)	25.00	11.50	3.10
☐ B1 Hank Aaron	100.00	45.00	12.50
☐ B2 Matty Alou (Batting)	10.00	4.50	1.25
☐ B3 Max Alvis ('69 patch)	9.00	4.00	1.15
☐ B4 Gerry Arrigo (Leg up)	9.00	4.00	1.15
☐ B5 Steve Blass	10.00	4.50	1.25
☐ B6 Clay Carroll	9.00	4.00	1.15
☐ B7 Tony Cloninger: Reds	9.00	4.00	1.15
☐ B8 George Culver	9.00	4.00	1.15
☐ B9 Joel Horlen (Pitching)	10.00	4.50	1.25
☐ B10 Tony Horton (Batting)	10.00	4.50	1.25
☐ B11 Alex Johnson	10.00	4.50	1.25
☐ B12 Jim Maloney	10.00	4.50	1.25
☐ B13 Lee May (Foot on bag) (2)	10.00	4.50	1.25
☐ B14 Bill Mazeroski (Hands on knees) (2)	12.00	5.50	1.50
☐ B15 Sam McDowell (Leg up) (2)	10.00	4.50	1.25
☐ B16 Tony Perez	25.00	11.50	3.10
☐ B17 Gary Peters (Pitching)	9.00	4.00	1.15
☐ B18 Ron Santo (Emblem) (2)	13.50	6.00	1.70
☐ B19 Luis Tiant (Glove at knee)	12.00	5.50	1.50
☐ B20 Joe Torre: Cardinals	12.00	5.50	1.50
☐ B21 Bob Veale (Hands at knees, no glasses)	10.00	4.50	1.25
☐ B22 Billy Williams (Bat behind head)	35.00	16.00	4.40

1987 Kahn's Reds

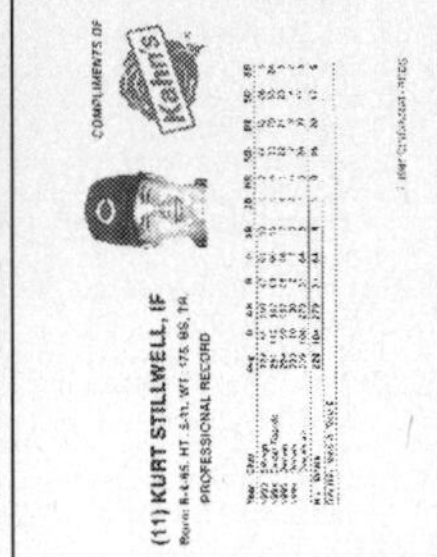

This 28-card set was issued to the first 20,000 fans at the August 2nd game between the Reds and the San Francisco Giants at Riverfront Stadium by Kahn's Wieners. Cards are standard size, 2 1/2" by 3 1/2". The cards are unnumbered except for uniform number and feature full-color photos bordered in red and white on the front. The Kahn's logo is printed in red in the corner of the reverse.

	MT	EX-MT	VG
COMPLETE SET (28)	20.00	9.00	2.50
COMMON PLAYER	.50	.23	.06
☐ 6 Bo Diaz	.50	.23	.06
☐ 10 Terry Francona	.50	.23	.06
☐ 11 Kurt Stillwell	.75	.35	.09
☐ 12 Nick Esasky	.60	.25	.08
☐ 13 Dave Concepcion	1.25	.55	.16
☐ 15 Barry Larkin	6.00	2.70	.75
☐ 16 Ron Oester	.50	.23	.06
☐ 21 Paul O'Neill	1.50	.65	.19
☐ 23 Lloyd McClendon	.50	.23	.06
☐ 25 Buddy Bell	.60	.25	.08
☐ 28 Kal Daniels	1.25	.55	.16
☐ 29 Tracy Jones	.60	.25	.08
☐ 30 Guy Hoffman	.50	.23	.06
☐ 31 John Franco	1.00	.45	.13
☐ 32 Tom Browning	.75	.35	.09
☐ 33 Ron Robinson	.75	.35	.09
☐ 34 Bill Gullickson	.75	.35	.09
☐ 35 Pat Pacillo	.50	.23	.06
☐ 39 Dave Parker	1.25	.55	.16
☐ 43 Bill Landrum	.60	.25	.08
☐ 44 Eric Davis	4.00	1.80	.50
☐ 46 Rob Murphy	.50	.23	.06
☐ 47 Frank Williams	.50	.23	.06
☐ 48 Ted Power	.50	.23	.06
☐ xx Pete Rose MG	1.50	.65	.19
☐ xx Coaches Card Scott Breeden Billy DeMars Tommy Helms Bruce Kimm Jim Lett Tony Perez	.75	.35	.09
☐ xx Ad Card Save 25 cents on Corn Dogs	.50	.23	.06
☐ xx Ad Card Save 30 cents on Smokeys	.50	.23	.06

1988 Kahn's Mets

These 32-card sets were issued to the first 48,000 fans at the June 30th game between the New York Mets and the Houston Astros at Shea Stadium. The set includes 30 players, a team card, and a discount coupon card (to be redeemed at the grocery store). Cards are standard size, 2 1/2" by 3 1/2". The cards are unnumbered except for uniform number and feature full-color photos bordered in

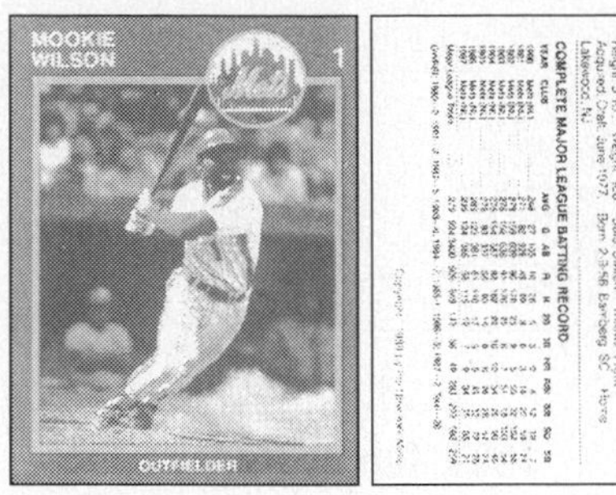

blue and orange on the front. The Kahn's logo is printed in red in the corner of the reverse.

	MT	EX-MT	VG
COMPLETE SET (32)	15.00	6.75	1.90
COMMON PLAYER	.40	.18	.05
☐ 1 Mookie Wilson	.50	.23	.06
☐ 2 Mackey Sasser	.50	.23	.06
☐ 3 Bud Harrelson CO	.50	.23	.06
☐ 4 Len Dykstra	.75	.35	.09
☐ 5 Davey Johnson MG	.60	.25	.08
☐ 6 Wally Backman	.40	.18	.05
☐ 8 Gary Carter	1.00	.45	.13
☐ 11 Tim Teufel	.40	.18	.05
☐ 12 Ron Darling	.75	.35	.09
☐ 13 Lee Mazzilli	.40	.18	.05
☐ 15 Rick Aguilera	.75	.35	.09
☐ 16 Dwight Gooden	1.25	.55	.16
☐ 17 Keith Hernandez	.75	.35	.09
☐ 18 Darryl Strawberry	1.50	.65	.19
☐ 19 Bob Ojeda	.50	.23	.06
☐ 20 Howard Johnson	.90	.40	.11
☐ 21 Kevin Elster	.40	.18	.05
☐ 22 Kevin McReynolds	.75	.35	.09
☐ 26 Terry Leach	.40	.18	.05
☐ 28 Bill Robinson CO	.60	.25	.08
☐ 29 Dave Magadan	.60	.25	.08
☐ 30 Mel Stottlemyre CO	.60	.25	.08
☐ 31 Gene Walter	.40	.18	.05
☐ 33 Barry Lyons	.40	.18	.05
☐ 34 Sam Perlozzo CO	.40	.18	.05
☐ 42 Roger McDowell	.50	.23	.06
☐ 44 David Cone	1.50	.65	.19
☐ 48 Randy Myers	.75	.35	.09
☐ 50 Sid Fernandez	.75	.35	.09
☐ 52 Greg Pavlick CO	.40	.18	.05
☐ NNO Team Photo Card	.50	.23	.06
☐ NNO Discount Coupon	.40	.18	.05

1988 Kahn's Reds

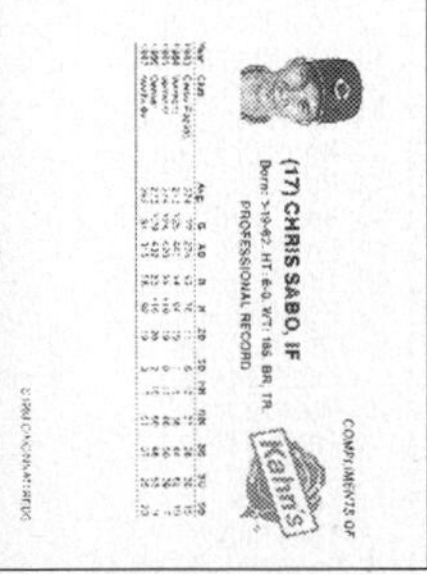

These 26-card sets were issued to fans at the August 14th game between the Cincinnati Reds and the Atlanta Braves at Riverfront Stadium. Cards are standard size, 2 1/2" by 3 1/2". The cards are unnumbered except for uniform number and feature full-color photos bordered in red and white on the front. The Kahn's logo is printed in red in the corner of the reverse. The cards are numbered below by uniform number which is listed parenthetically on the front of the cards.

	MT	EX-MT	VG
COMPLETE SET (26)	15.00	6.75	1.90
COMMON PLAYER	.40	.18	.05
☐ 6 Bo Diaz	.40	.18	.05
☐ 8 Terry McGriff	.40	.18	.05
☐ 9 Eddie Milner	.40	.18	.05
☐ 10 Leon Durham	.40	.18	.05
☐ 11 Barry Larkin	1.75	.80	.22
☐ 12 Nick Esasky	.40	.18	.05
☐ 13 Dave Concepcion	.90	.40	.11
☐ 14 Pete Rose MG	1.00	.45	.13
☐ 15 Jeff Treadway	.50	.23	.06
☐ 17 Chris Sabo	2.00	.90	.25
☐ 20 Danny Jackson	.50	.23	.06
☐ 21 Paul O'Neill	.90	.40	.11
☐ 22 Dave Collins	.40	.18	.05
☐ 27 Jose Rijo	1.00	.45	.13
☐ 28 Kal Daniels	.60	.25	.08
☐ 29 Tracy Jones	.40	.18	.05
☐ 30 Lloyd McClendon	.40	.18	.05
☐ 31 John Franco	.60	.25	.08
☐ 32 Tom Browning	.60	.25	.08
☐ 33 Ron Robinson	.50	.23	.06
☐ 40 Jack Armstrong	.60	.25	.08
☐ 44 Eric Davis	1.25	.55	.16
☐ 46 Rob Murphy	.40	.18	.05
☐ 47 Frank Williams	.40	.18	.05
☐ 48 Tim Birtsas	.40	.18	.05
☐ NNO Reds Coaches Lee May CO Tony Perez CO Bruce Kimm CO Tommy Helms CO Jim Lett CO Scott Breeden CO	.50	.23	.06

1989 Kahn's Cooperstown

The 1989 Kahn's Cooperstown set contains 11 standard-size (2 1/2" by 3 1/2") cards. This set is sometimes referenced as Hillshire Farms or Kahn's Cooperstown Collection. All players included in the set are members (for the most part they are recent inductees) of the Hall of Fame. The pictures are actually paintings and are surrounded by gold borders. The fronts resemble plaques and also have facsimile autographs. The cards were available from the company via a send-in offer. A set of cards was available in return for three proofs of purchase (and 1.00 postage and handling) from Hillshire Farms. The last card in the set is actually a coupon card for Kahn's products; this card is not even considered part of the set by some collectors. A related promotion offered two coin cards (coins laminated on cards) featuring Johnny Bench and Carl Yastrzemski. These coin cards are approximately 5 1/2" by 3 3/4" and are blank backed.

	MT	EX-MT	VG
COMPLETE SET (12)	6.00	2.70	.75
COMMON PLAYER (1-11)	.50	.23	.06
☐ 1 Cool Papa Bell	.50	.23	.06
☐ 2 Johnny Bench	1.00	.45	.13
☐ 3 Lou Brock	.75	.35	.09
☐ 4 Whitey Ford	.75	.35	.09
☐ 5 Bob Gibson	.75	.35	.09
☐ 6 Billy Herman	.50	.23	.06
☐ 7 Harmon Killebrew	.75	.35	.09
☐ 8 Eddie Mathews	.90	.40	.11
☐ 9 Brooks Robinson	1.00	.45	.13
☐ 10 Willie Stargell	1.00	.45	.13
☐ 11 Carl Yastrzemski	1.25	.55	.16
☐ 12 Coupon Card	.50	.23	.06

1989 Kahn's Mets

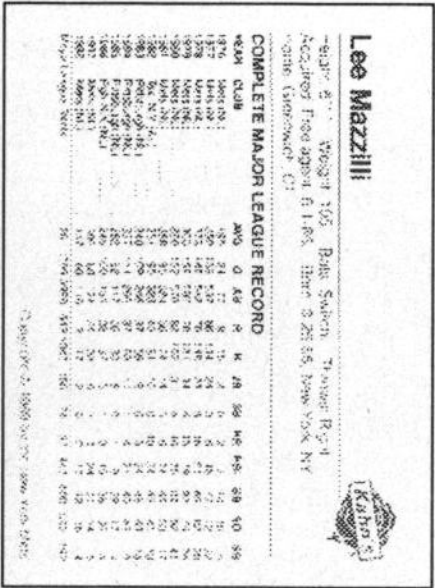

The 1989 Kahn's Mets set contains 36 (32 original and four update) standard-size (2 1/2" by 3 1/2") cards. The fronts have color photos with Mets' colored borders (blue, orange and white). The horizontally oriented backs have career stats. The cards were available from Kahn's by sending three UPC symbols from Kahn's products and a coupon appearing in certain local newspapers. There was also a small late-season update set of Kahn's Mets showing new Mets players arriving in mid-season trades, e.g., Jeff Innis, Keith Miller, Jeff Musselman, and Frank Viola. This "Update" subset was distributed at a different Mets Baseball Card Night game than the main set. The main set is referenced below by uniform number. The update cards are given the prefix U in the checklist below.

	MT	EX-MT	VG
COMPLETE SET (32)	10.00	4.50	1.25
COMPLETE UPDATE SET (4)	2.50	1.15	.30
COMMON PLAYER	.30	.14	.04
COMMON UPDATE (U1-U4)	.60	.25	.08
☐ 1 Mookie Wilson	.40	.18	.05
☐ 2 Mackey Sasser	.40	.18	.05
☐ 3 Bud Harrelson CO	.40	.18	.05
☐ 5 Davey Johnson MG	.40	.18	.05
☐ 7 Juan Samuel	.40	.18	.05
☐ 8 Gary Carter	.75	.35	.09
☐ 9 Gregg Jefferies	1.00	.45	.13
☐ 11 Tim Teufel	.30	.14	.04
☐ 12 Ron Darling	.50	.23	.06
☐ 13 Lee Mazzilli	.30	.14	.04
☐ 16 Dwight Gooden	.90	.40	.11
☐ 17 Keith Hernandez	.50	.23	.06
☐ 18 Darryl Strawberry	1.25	.55	.16
☐ 19 Bob Ojeda	.40	.18	.05
☐ 20 Howard Johnson	.90	.40	.11
☐ 21 Kevin Elster	.30	.14	.04
☐ 22 Kevin McReynolds	.40	.18	.05
☐ 28 Bill Robinson CO	.40	.18	.05
☐ 29 Dave Magadan	.40	.18	.05
☐ 30 Mel Stottlemyre CO	.40	.18	.05
☐ 32 Mark Carreon	.40	.18	.05
☐ 33 Barry Lyons	.30	.14	.04
☐ 34 Sam Perlozzo CO	.30	.14	.04
☐ 38 Rick Aguilera	.50	.23	.06
☐ 44 David Cone	.90	.40	.11
☐ 46 Dave West	.30	.14	.04
☐ 48 Randy Myers	.50	.23	.06
☐ 49 Don Aase	.30	.14	.04
☐ 50 Sid Fernandez	.50	.23	.06
☐ 52 Greg Pavlick CO	.30	.14	.04
☐ NNO Mets Team Photo	.50	.23	.06
☐ NNO Sponsors Card	.30	.14	.04
☐ U1 Jeff Innis	.60	.25	.08
☐ U2 Keith Miller	.75	.35	.09
☐ U3 Jeff Musselman	.60	.25	.08
☐ U4 Frank Viola	1.50	.65	.19

1989 Kahn's Reds

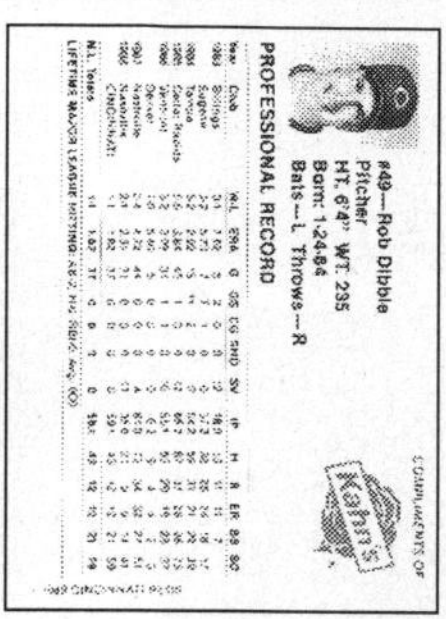

The 1989 Kahn's Reds set contains 28 standard-size (2 1/2" by 3 1/2") cards; each card features a member of the Cincinnati Reds. The fronts have color photos with red borders. The horizontally oriented backs have career stats. The card numbering below is according to uniform number.

	MT	EX-MT	VG
COMPLETE SET (28)	12.00	5.50	1.50
COMMON PLAYER	.35	.16	.04
☐ 6 Bo Diaz	.35	.16	.04
☐ 7 Lenny Harris	.60	.25	.08
☐ 11 Barry Larkin	1.50	.65	.19
☐ 12 Joel Youngblood	.35	.16	.04
☐ 14 Pete Rose MG	1.00	.45	.13
☐ 16 Ron Oester	.35	.16	.04
☐ 17 Chris Sabo	.75	.35	.09
☐ 20 Danny Jackson	.45	.20	.06
☐ 21 Paul O'Neill	.75	.35	.09
☐ 25 Todd Benzinger	.35	.16	.04
☐ 27 Jose Rijo	.90	.40	.11
☐ 28 Kal Daniels	.60	.25	.08
☐ 29 Herm Winningham	.35	.16	.04
☐ 30 Ken Griffey Sr.	.75	.35	.09
☐ 31 John Franco	.60	.25	.08
☐ 32 Tom Browning	.50	.23	.06
☐ 33 Ron Robinson	.35	.16	.04
☐ 34 Jeff Reed	.35	.16	.04
☐ 36 Rolando Roomes	.35	.16	.04
☐ 37 Norm Charlton	.75	.35	.09
☐ 42 Rick Mahler	.35	.16	.04
☐ 43 Kent Tekulve	.35	.16	.04
☐ 44 Eric Davis	1.00	.45	.13
☐ 48 Tim Birtsas	.35	.16	.04
☐ 49 Rob Dibble	.75	.35	.09
☐ xx Coaches Card Scott Breeden Dave Bristol Tommy Helms Jim Lett Lee May Tony Perez	.50	.23	.06
☐ xx Sponsor Coupon Kahn's Corndogs	.35	.16	.04
☐ xx Sponsor Coupon Kahn's Wieners	.35	.16	.04

1990 Kahn's Mets

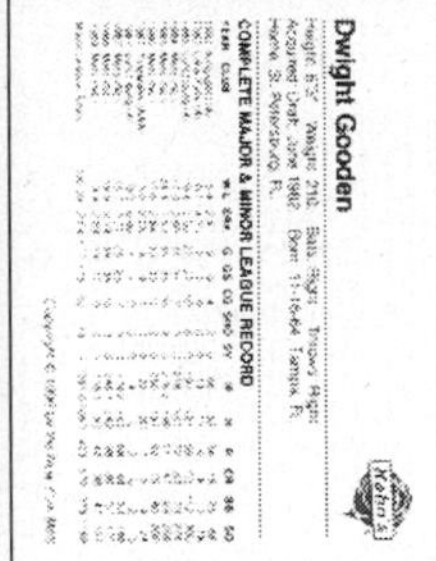

The 1990 Kahn's Mets set was given away as a New York Mets stadium promotion. This standard-size (2 1/2" by 3 1/2") set is skip-numbered by uniform number within the set and features 34 cards and two Kahn's coupon cards. Three players, Thornton, Magadan, and Mercado are wearing different uniform numbers than listed on the front of their cards. In addition to the Shea Stadium promotion, the complete set was also available in specially marked three-packs of Kahn's Wieners.

	MT	EX-MT	VG
COMPLETE SET (34)	7.00	3.10	.85
COMMON PLAYER	.25	.11	.03
☐ 1 Lou Thornton	.25	.11	.03
☐ 2 Mackey Sasser	.35	.16	.04
☐ 3 Bud Harrelson CO	.35	.16	.04
☐ 4 Mike Cubbage CO	.25	.11	.03
☐ 5 Davey Johnson MG	.35	.16	.04
☐ 6 Mike Marshall	.25	.11	.03
☐ 9 Gregg Jefferies	.75	.35	.09
☐ 10 Dave Magadan	.35	.16	.04
☐ 11 Tim Teufel	.25	.11	.03
☐ 13 Jeff Musselman	.25	.11	.03
☐ 15 Ron Darling	.45	.20	.06
☐ 16 Dwight Gooden	.75	.35	.09
☐ 18 Darryl Strawberry	1.00	.45	.13
☐ 19 Bob Ojeda	.35	.16	.04
☐ 20 Howard Johnson	.75	.35	.09
☐ 21 Kevin Elster	.25	.11	.03
☐ 22 Kevin McReynolds	.45	.20	.06
☐ 25 Keith Miller	.35	.16	.04
☐ 26 Alejandro Pena	.35	.16	.04
☐ 27 Tom O'Malley	.25	.11	.03
☐ 29 Frank Viola	.45	.20	.06
☐ 30 Mel Stottlemyre CO	.35	.16	.04
☐ 31 John Franco	.35	.16	.04
☐ 32 Doc Edwards CO	.25	.11	.03
☐ 33 Barry Lyons	.25	.11	.03
☐ 35 Orlando Mercado	.25	.11	.03
☐ 40 Jeff Innis	.25	.11	.03
☐ 44 David Cone	.75	.35	.09
☐ 45 Mark Carreon	.35	.16	.04
☐ 47 Wally Whitehurst	.25	.11	.03
☐ 48 Julio Machado	.35	.16	.04
☐ 50 Sid Fernandez	.35	.16	.04
☐ 52 Greg Pavlick CO	.25	.11	.03
☐ NNO Team Photo	.45	.20	.06

1990 Kahn's Reds

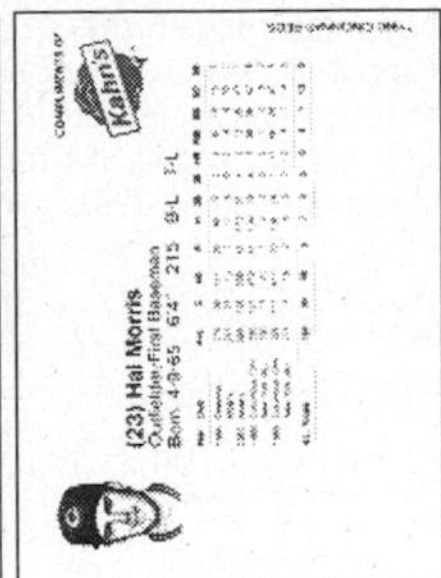

This 27-card, standard size, 2 1/2" by 3 1/2", set of Cincinnati Reds was issued by Kahn's Meats. This set which continued a more than 30-year tradition of Kahn's issuing Cincinnati Reds cards had the player's photos framed by red and white borders. The front have full-color photos while the back have a small black and white photo in the upper left hand corner and complete career statistics on the back of the card. The set is checklisted alphabetically since the cards are unnumbered except for uniform numbers. The number next to the player represents his uniform number.

	MT	EX-MT	VG
COMPLETE SET (27)	10.00	4.50	1.25
COMMON PLAYER (1-27)	.35	.16	.04
☐ 1 Jack Armstrong 40	.45	.20	.06
☐ 2 Todd Benzinger 25	.45	.20	.06
☐ 3 Tim Birtsas 48	.35	.16	.04
☐ 4 Glenn Braggs 15	.35	.16	.04
☐ 5 Tom Browning 32	.60	.25	.08
☐ 6 Norm Charlton 37	.75	.35	.09
☐ 7 Eric Davis 44	1.25	.55	.16
☐ 8 Rob Dibble 49	.75	.35	.09
☐ 9 Mariano Duncan 7	.45	.20	.06
☐ 10 Ken Griffey 30	.75	.35	.09
☐ 11 Billy Hatcher 22	.45	.20	.06
☐ 12 Barry Larkin 11	1.25	.55	.16
☐ 13 Danny Jackson 20	.45	.20	.06
☐ 14 Tim Layana 43	.35	.16	.04
☐ 15 Rick Mahler 42	.35	.16	.04
☐ 16 Hal Morris 23	1.25	.55	.16
☐ 17 Randy Myers 28	.75	.35	.09
☐ 18 Ron Oester 16	.45	.20	.06
☐ 19 Joe Oliver 9	.60	.25	.08
☐ 20 Paul O'Neill 21	.60	.25	.08
☐ 21 Lou Piniella MG 41	.60	.25	.08
☐ 22 Luis Quinones 10	.35	.16	.04
☐ 23 Jeff Reed 34	.35	.16	.04
☐ 24 Jose Rijo 27	.75	.35	.09
☐ 25 Chris Sabo 17	.75	.35	.09
☐ 26 Herm Winningham 29	.35	.16	.04
☐ 27 Reds Coaches Jackie Moore Tony Perez Sam Perlozzo Larry Rothschild Stan Williams	.45	.20	.06

1991 Kahn's Mets

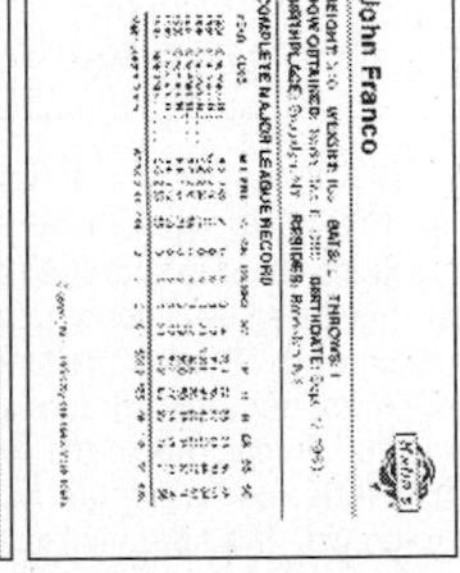

The 1991 Kahn's Mets set contains 33 cards measuring the standard size (2 1/2" by 3 1/2"). The set is skip-numbered on the card fronts by uniform number and includes two Kahn's coupon cards. The front features color action player photos, on a white and blue pinstripe pattern. The player's name is given in an orange stripe below the picture. In a horizontal format the back presents biographical information, major league statistics, and minor league statistics where appropriate. A complete set was given away to each fan attending the New York Mets game at Shea Stadium on June 17, 1991.

	MT	EX-MT	VG
COMPLETE SET (33)	7.00	3.10	.85
COMMON PLAYER	.25	.11	.03
☐ 1 Vince Coleman	.60	.25	.08
☐ 2 Mackey Sasser	.35	.16	.04
☐ 3 Bud Harrelson MG	.35	.16	.04
☐ 4 Mike Cubbage CO	.25	.11	.03
☐ 5 Charlie O'Brien	.25	.11	.03
☐ 7 Hubie Brooks	.35	.16	.04
☐ 8 Daryl Boston	.35	.16	.04
☐ 9 Gregg Jefferies	.75	.35	.09
☐ 10 Dave Magadan	.35	.16	.04
☐ 11 Tim Teufel	.25	.11	.03
☐ 13 Rick Cerone	.25	.11	.03
☐ 15 Ron Darling	.45	.20	.06
☐ 16 Dwight Gooden	.75	.35	.09
☐ 17 David Cone	.60	.25	.08
☐ 20 Howard Johnson	.60	.25	.08
☐ 21 Kevin Elster	.25	.11	.03
☐ 22 Kevin McReynolds	.45	.20	.06
☐ 25 Keith Miller	.35	.16	.04
☐ 26 Alejandro Pena	.35	.16	.04
☐ 28 Tom Herr	.25	.11	.03
☐ 29 Frank Viola	.45	.20	.06
☐ 30 Mel Stottlemyre CO	.35	.16	.04
☐ 31 John Franco	.35	.16	.04
☐ 32 Doc Edwards CO	.25	.11	.03
☐ 40 Jeff Innis	.25	.11	.03
☐ 43 Doug Simons	.25	.11	.03
☐ 45 Mark Carreon	.25	.11	.03
☐ 47 Wally Whitehurst	.25	.11	.03
☐ 48 Pete Schourek	.35	.16	.04
☐ 50 Sid Fernandez	.35	.16	.04
☐ 51 Tom Spencer CO	.25	.11	.03
☐ 52 Greg Pavlick CO	.25	.11	.03
☐ NNO 1991 New York Mets Team photo	.60	.25	.08

1991 Kahn's Reds

The 1991 Kahn's Cincinnati Reds set contains 28 cards measuring the standard size (2 1/2" by 3 1/2"). The set is skip-numbered by uniform number and includes two Kahn's coupon cards. The front features color action player photos which are mounted diagonally on the card face. Red pinstripe borders frame the picture above and below. The front lettering is printed in red and black on a white background. In a horizontal format the back is printed in red and black, and presents complete statistical information. The Kahn's logo in the lower right corner rounds out the back.

	MT	EX-MT	VG
COMPLETE SET (28)	7.00	3.10	.85
COMMON PLAYER	.25	.11	.03
☐ 0 Schottzie Mascot	.35	.16	.04
☐ 7 Mariano Duncan	.35	.16	.04
☐ 9 Joe Oliver	.35	.16	.04
☐ 10 Luis Quinones	.25	.11	.03
☐ 11 Barry Larkin	1.00	.45	.13
☐ 15 Glenn Braggs	.35	.16	.04
☐ 17 Chris Sabo	.50	.23	.06
☐ 19 Bill Doran	.35	.16	.04
☐ 21 Paul O'Neill	.35	.16	.04
☐ 22 Billy Hatcher	.35	.16	.04
☐ 23 Hal Morris	.75	.35	.09
☐ 25 Todd Benzinger	.35	.16	.04
☐ 27 Jose Rijo	.50	.23	.06
☐ 28 Randy Myers	.35	.16	.04
☐ 29 Herm Winningham	.25	.11	.03
☐ 32 Tom Browning	.35	.16	.04
☐ 34 Jeff Reed	.25	.11	.03
☐ 36 Don Carman	.25	.11	.03
☐ 37 Norm Charlton	.50	.23	.06
☐ 40 Jack Armstrong	.35	.16	.04
☐ 41 Lou Piniella MG	.35	.16	.04
☐ 44 Eric Davis	.90	.40	.11
☐ 45 Chris Hammond	.50	.23	.06
☐ 47 Scott Scudder	.35	.16	.04
☐ 48 Ted Power	.25	.11	.03
☐ 49 Rob Dibble	.50	.23	.06
☐ 57 Freddie Benavides	.25	.11	.03
☐ NNO Coaches Card Jackie Moore Tony Perez Sam Perlozzo Larry Rothschild Stan Williams	.35	.16	.04

1992 Kahn's Mets

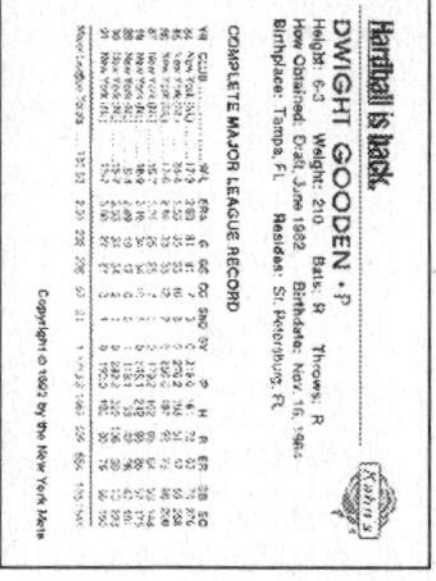

The 1992 Kahn's New York Mets set consists of 35 cards measuring the standard size (2 1/2" by 3 1/2"). The set included two manufacturer's coupons (one for 50 cents off Kahn's Beef Franks and another for the same amount off Kahn's Corn Dogs). The fronts feature color action player photos with a white inner border on a royal blue card face. The upper left corner of the picture is cut off to create space for the team name. An orange stripe bearing the player's name appears beneath the picture and intersects at the lower right corner a baseball with the player's uniform number. In a horizontal format, the backs carry the motto "Hardball is back," biography, and complete major league statistics. The Kahn's logo in red rounds out the back. The cards are skip-numbered by uniform number on the front and checklisted below accordingly.

	MT	EX-MT	VG
COMPLETE SET (35)	7.00	3.10	.85
COMMON PLAYER	.25	.11	.03
☐ 1 Vince Coleman	.50	.23	.06
☐ 2 Mackey Sasser	.25	.11	.03
☐ 3 Junior Noboa	.25	.11	.03
☐ 4 Mike Cubbage CO	.25	.11	.03
☐ 6 Daryl Boston	.25	.11	.03
☐ 8 Dave Gallagher	.25	.11	.03
☐ 9 Todd Hundley	.50	.23	.06
☐ 10 Jeff Torborg MG	.35	.16	.04
☐ 11 Dick Schofield	.25	.11	.03

☐ 12 Willie Randolph	.35	.16	.04
☐ 15 Kevin Elster	.25	.11	.03
☐ 16 Dwight Gooden	.60	.25	.08
☐ 17 David Cone	.60	.25	.08
☐ 18 Bret Saberhagen	.50	.23	.06
☐ 19 Anthony Young	.50	.23	.06
☐ 20 Howard Johnson	.50	.23	.06
☐ 22 Charlie O'Brien	.25	.11	.03
☐ 25 Bobby Bonilla	.75	.35	.09
☐ 26 Barry Foote CO	.25	.11	.03
☐ 27 Tom McCraw CO	.25	.11	.03
☐ 28 Dave LaRoche CO	.25	.11	.03
☐ 29 Dave Magadan	.25	.11	.03
☐ 30 Mel Stottlemyre CO	.35	.16	.04
☐ 31 John Franco	.35	.16	.04
☐ 32 Bill Pecota	.25	.11	.03
☐ 33 Eddie Murray	.60	.25	.08
☐ 40 Jeff Innis	.25	.11	.03
☐ 44 Tim Burke	.25	.11	.03
☐ 45 Paul Gibson	.25	.11	.03
☐ 47 Wally Whitehurst	.25	.11	.03
☐ 50 Sid Fernandez	.35	.16	.04
☐ 51 John Stephenson CO	.25	.11	.03
☐ NNO Team Photo	.35	.16	.04
☐ NNO Manufacturer's Coupon Kahn's Beef Franks	.25	.11	.03
☐ NNO Manufacturer's Coupon Kahn's Corn Dogs	.25	.11	.03

1992 Kahn's Reds

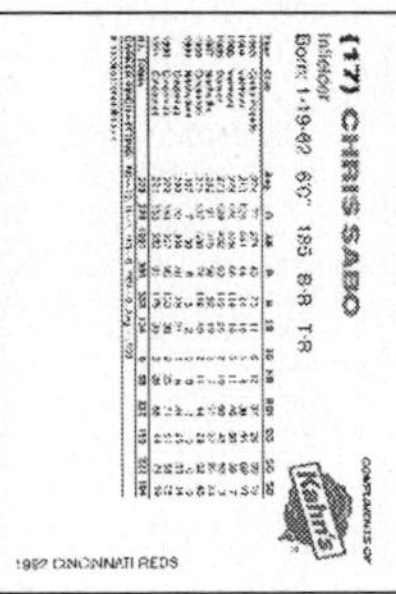

The 1992 Kahn's Cincinnati Reds set consists of 29 cards measuring the standard size (2 1/2" by 3 1/2"). The set included two manufacturer's coupons (one for 50 cents off Kahn's Wieners and another for the same amount off Kahn's Corn Dogs). The fronts feature color action player photos bordered in red. The team name and the player's name appear in white lettering above and below the picture respectively. The team logo overlays the picture at its lower left corner. The horizontally oriented backs have the player's name and sponsor logo in red, while biographical and complete statistical information are printed in black. The cards are skip-numbered by uniform number on both sides and checklisted below accordingly.

	MT	EX-MT	VG
COMPLETE SET (29)	7.00	3.10	.85
COMMON PLAYER	.25	.11	.03
☐ 2 Schottzie (Mascot)	.35	.16	.04
☐ 9 Joe Oliver	.35	.16	.04
☐ 10 Bip Roberts	.50	.23	.06
☐ 11 Barry Larkin	.90	.40	.11
☐ 12 Freddie Benavides	.25	.11	.03
☐ 15 Glenn Braggs	.25	.11	.03
☐ 16 Reggie Sanders	1.00	.45	.13
☐ 17 Chris Sabo	.50	.23	.06
☐ 19 Bill Doran	.25	.11	.03
☐ 21 Paul O'Neill	.35	.16	.04
☐ 23 Hal Morris	.50	.23	.06
☐ 25 Scott Bankhead	.35	.16	.04
☐ 26 Darnell Coles	.25	.11	.03
☐ 27 Jose Rijo	.50	.23	.06
☐ 28 Scott Ruskin	.25	.11	.03
☐ 29 Greg Swindell	.35	.16	.04
☐ 30 Dave Martinez	.35	.16	.04
☐ 31 Tim Belcher	.35	.16	.04
☐ 32 Tom Browning	.35	.16	.04
☐ 34 Jeff Reed	.25	.11	.03
☐ 37 Norm Charlton	.50	.23	.06
☐ 38 Troy Afenir	.25	.11	.03
☐ 41 Lou Piniella MG	.35	.16	.04
☐ 45 Chris Hammond	.35	.16	.04
☐ 48 Dwayne Henry	.25	.11	.03
☐ 49 Rob Dibble	.50	.23	.06
☐ xx Coaches Jackie Moore John McLaren Sam Perlozzo Tony Perez Larry Rothschild	.35	.16	.04
☐ xx Manufacturer's Coupon Kahn's Corn Dogs	.25	.11	.03
☐ xx Manufacturer's Coupon Kahn's Beef Franks	.25	.11	.03

1986 Kay-Bee

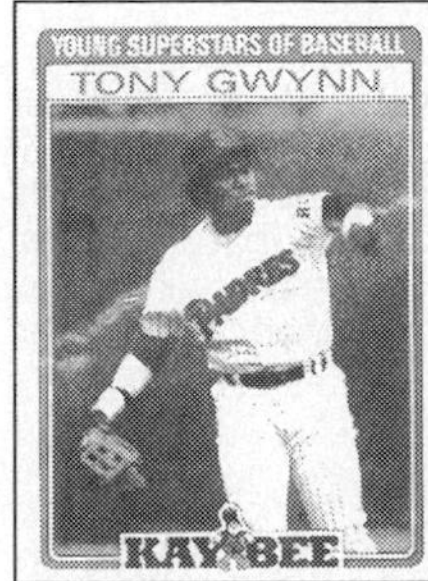

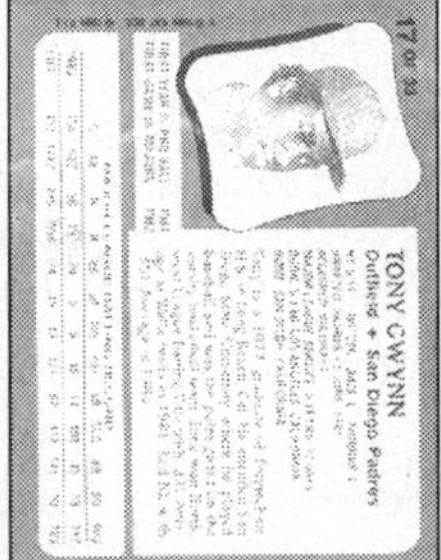

This 33-card, standard-sized (2 1/2" by 3 1/2") set was produced by Topps, although manufactured in Northern Ireland. This boxed set retailed in Kay-Bee stores for 1.99; the checklist was listed on the back of the box. The set is subtitled "Young Superstars of Baseball" and does indeed feature many young players. The cards are numbered on the back; the set card numbering is in alphabetical order by player's name.

	MT	EX-MT	VG
COMPLETE SET (33)	4.00	1.80	.50
COMMON PLAYER (1-33)	.10	.05	.01
☐ 1 Rick Aguilera	.30	.14	.04
☐ 2 Chris Brown	.10	.05	.01
☐ 3 Tom Browning	.15	.07	.02
☐ 4 Tom Brunansky	.10	.05	.01
☐ 5 Vince Coleman	.25	.11	.03
☐ 6 Ron Darling	.15	.07	.02
☐ 7 Alvin Davis	.10	.05	.01
☐ 8 Mariano Duncan	.15	.07	.02
☐ 9 Shawon Dunston	.20	.09	.03
☐ 10 Sid Fernandez	.15	.07	.02
☐ 11 Tony Fernandez	.15	.07	.02
☐ 12 Brian Fisher	.10	.05	.01
☐ 13 John Franco	.15	.07	.02
☐ 14 Julio Franco	.20	.09	.03
☐ 15 Dwight Gooden	.50	.23	.06
☐ 16 Ozzie Guillen	.20	.09	.03
☐ 17 Tony Gwynn	.75	.35	.09
☐ 18 Jimmy Key	.15	.07	.02
☐ 19 Don Mattingly	.75	.35	.09
☐ 20 Oddibe McDowell	.10	.05	.01
☐ 21 Roger McDowell	.15	.07	.02
☐ 22 Dan Pasqua	.10	.05	.01
☐ 23 Terry Pendleton	.50	.23	.06
☐ 24 Jim Presley	.10	.05	.01
☐ 25 Kirby Puckett	1.00	.45	.13
☐ 26 Earnie Riles	.10	.05	.01
☐ 27 Bret Saberhagen	.25	.11	.03
☐ 28 Mark Salas	.10	.05	.01
☐ 29 Juan Samuel	.10	.05	.01
☐ 30 Jeff Stone	.10	.05	.01

☐ 31 Darryl Strawberry	.75	.35	.09
☐ 32 Andy Van Slyke	.30	.14	.04
☐ 33 Frank Viola	.20	.09	.03

1987 Kay-Bee

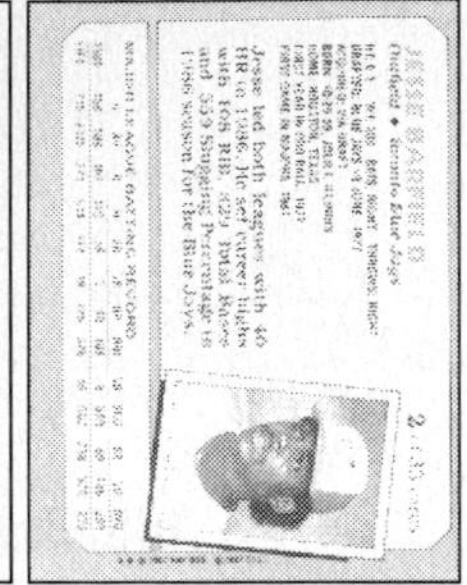

This small 33-card boxed set was produced by Topps for Kay-Bee Toy Stores. The set is subtitled "Super Stars of Baseball" and measures the standard 2 1/2" by 3 1/2" with full-color fronts. The card backs are printed in blue and black on white card stock. The checklist for the set is printed on the back panel of the yellow box. The set card numbering is alphabetical by player's name.

	MT	EX-MT	VG
COMPLETE SET (33)	4.00	1.80	.50
COMMON PLAYER (1-33)	.10	.05	.01
☐ 1 Harold Baines	.10	.05	.01
☐ 2 Jesse Barfield	.10	.05	.01
☐ 3 Don Baylor	.10	.05	.01
☐ 4 Wade Boggs	.60	.25	.08
☐ 5 George Brett	.60	.25	.08
☐ 6 Hubie Brooks	.10	.05	.01
☐ 7 Jose Canseco	.75	.35	.09
☐ 8 Gary Carter	.25	.11	.03
☐ 9 Joe Carter	.35	.16	.04
☐ 10 Roger Clemens	1.00	.45	.13
☐ 11 Vince Coleman	.20	.09	.03
☐ 12 Glenn Davis	.15	.07	.02
☐ 13 Dwight Gooden	.30	.14	.04
☐ 14 Pedro Guerrero	.10	.05	.01
☐ 15 Tony Gwynn	.60	.25	.08
☐ 16 Rickey Henderson	.60	.25	.08
☐ 17 Keith Hernandez	.15	.07	.02
☐ 18 Wally Joyner	.25	.11	.03
☐ 19 Don Mattingly	.75	.35	.09
☐ 20 Jack Morris	.20	.09	.03
☐ 21 Dale Murphy	.25	.11	.03
☐ 22 Eddie Murray	.30	.14	.04
☐ 23 Dave Parker	.15	.07	.02
☐ 24 Kirby Puckett	.75	.35	.09
☐ 25 Tim Raines	.15	.07	.02
☐ 26 Jim Rice	.15	.07	.02
☐ 27 Dave Righetti	.10	.05	.01
☐ 28 Ryne Sandberg	1.00	.45	.13
☐ 29 Mike Schmidt	.75	.35	.09
☐ 30 Mike Scott	.10	.05	.01
☐ 31 Darryl Strawberry	.60	.25	.08
☐ 32 Fernando Valenzuela	.15	.07	.02
☐ 33 Dave Winfield	.40	.18	.05

1988 Kay-Bee

This small 33-card boxed set was produced by Topps for Kay-Bee Toy Stores. The set is subtitled "Superstars of Baseball" and measures the standard 2 1/2" by 3 1/2" with full-color fronts. The card backs are printed in blue and green on white card stock. The checklist for the set is printed on the back panel of the box. These cards are

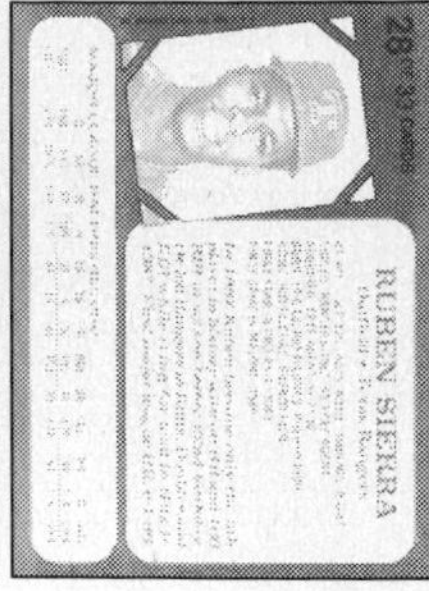

numbered on the back. The set card numbering is alphabetical by player's name.

	MT	EX-MT	VG
COMPLETE SET (33)	4.00	1.80	.50
COMMON PLAYER (1-33)	.10	.05	.01
☐ 1 George Bell	.15	.07	.02
☐ 2 Wade Boggs	.50	.23	.06
☐ 3 Jose Canseco	.75	.35	.09
☐ 4 Joe Carter	.30	.14	.04
☐ 5 Jack Clark	.10	.05	.01
☐ 6 Alvin Davis	.10	.05	.01
☐ 7 Eric Davis	.20	.09	.03
☐ 8 Andre Dawson	.25	.11	.03
☐ 9 Darrell Evans	.10	.05	.01
☐ 10 Dwight Evans	.10	.05	.01
☐ 11 Gary Gaetti	.10	.05	.01
☐ 12 Pedro Guerrero	.10	.05	.01
☐ 13 Tony Gwynn	.50	.23	.06
☐ 14 Howard Johnson	.15	.07	.02
☐ 15 Wally Joyner	.15	.07	.02
☐ 16 Don Mattingly	.60	.25	.08
☐ 17 Willie McGee	.10	.05	.01
☐ 18 Mark McGwire	.60	.25	.08
☐ 19 Paul Molitor	.20	.09	.03
☐ 20 Dale Murphy	.25	.11	.03
☐ 21 Dave Parker	.15	.07	.02
☐ 22 Lance Parrish	.10	.05	.01
☐ 23 Kirby Puckett	.60	.25	.08
☐ 24 Tim Raines	.15	.07	.02
☐ 25 Cal Ripken	1.00	.45	.13
☐ 26 Juan Samuel	.10	.05	.01
☐ 27 Mike Schmidt	.60	.25	.08
☐ 28 Ruben Sierra	.50	.23	.06
☐ 29 Darryl Strawberry	.50	.23	.06
☐ 30 Danny Tartabull	.30	.14	.04
☐ 31 Alan Trammell	.15	.07	.02
☐ 32 Tim Wallach	.10	.05	.01
☐ 33 Dave Winfield	.30	.14	.04

1989 Kay-Bee

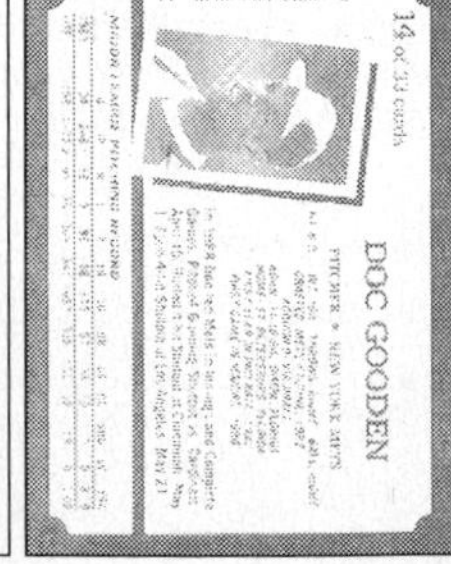

The 1989 Kay-Bee set contains 33 standard-size (2 1/2" by 3 1/2") glossy cards. The fronts have magenta and yellow borders. The horizontally oriented backs are brown and yellow. The cards were distributed as boxed sets through

Kay-Bee toy stores. The set card numbering is alphabetical by player's name.

	MT	EX-MT	VG
COMPLETE SET (33)	4.00	1.80	.50
COMMON PLAYER (1-33)	.10	.05	.01
☐ 1 Wade Boggs	.50	.23	.06
☐ 2 George Brett	.50	.23	.06
☐ 3 Jose Canseco	.75	.35	.09
☐ 4 Gary Carter	.20	.09	.03
☐ 5 Jack Clark	.10	.05	.01
☐ 6 Will Clark	.75	.35	.09
☐ 7 Roger Clemens	.75	.35	.09
☐ 8 Eric Davis	.20	.09	.03
☐ 9 Andre Dawson	.25	.11	.03
☐ 10 Dwight Evans	.10	.05	.01
☐ 11 Carlton Fisk	.25	.11	.03
☐ 12 Andres Galarraga	.10	.05	.01
☐ 13 Kirk Gibson	.10	.05	.01
☐ 14 Dwight Gooden	.25	.11	.03
☐ 15 Mike Greenwell	.20	.09	.03
☐ 16 Pedro Guerrero	.10	.05	.01
☐ 17 Tony Gwynn	.50	.23	.06
☐ 18 Rickey Henderson	.60	.25	.08
☐ 19 Orel Hershiser	.15	.07	.02
☐ 20 Don Mattingly	.60	.25	.08
☐ 21 Mark McGwire	.50	.23	.06
☐ 22 Dale Murphy	.20	.09	.03
☐ 23 Eddie Murray	.25	.11	.03
☐ 24 Kirby Puckett	.60	.25	.08
☐ 25 Tim Raines	.15	.07	.02
☐ 26 Ryne Sandberg	.75	.35	.09
☐ 27 Mike Schmidt	.60	.25	.08
☐ 28 Ozzie Smith	.25	.11	.03
☐ 29 Darryl Strawberry	.50	.23	.06
☐ 30 Alan Trammell	.15	.07	.02
☐ 31 Frank Viola	.10	.05	.01
☐ 32 Dave Winfield	.25	.11	.03
☐ 33 Robin Yount	.50	.23	.06

1990 Kay-Bee

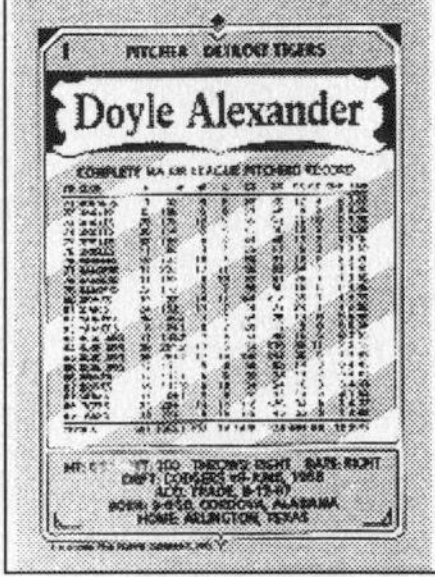

The 1990 Kay-Bee Kings of Baseball set is a standard-size (2 1/2" by 3 1/2"), 33-card set sequenced alphabetically that Topps produced for the Kay-Bee toy store chain. A solid red border inside a purple white striped box is the major design feature of this set. The set card numbering is alphabetical by player's name.

	MT	EX-MT	VG
COMPLETE SET (33)	4.00	1.80	.50
COMMON PLAYER (1-33)	.10	.05	.01
☐ 1 Doyle Alexander	.10	.05	.01
☐ 2 Bert Blyleven	.15	.07	.02
☐ 3 Wade Boggs	.50	.23	.06
☐ 4 George Brett	.50	.23	.06
☐ 5 John Candelaria	.10	.05	.01
☐ 6 Gary Carter	.20	.09	.03
☐ 7 Vince Coleman	.15	.07	.02
☐ 8 Andre Dawson	.25	.11	.03
☐ 9 Dennis Eckersley	.20	.09	.03
☐ 10 Darrell Evans	.10	.05	.01
☐ 11 Dwight Evans	.10	.05	.01
☐ 12 Carlton Fisk	.25	.11	.03
☐ 13 Ken Griffey Sr.	.15	.07	.02
☐ 14 Tony Gwynn	.50	.23	.06
☐ 15 Rickey Henderson	.50	.23	.06
☐ 16 Keith Hernandez	.10	.05	.01
☐ 17 Charlie Hough	.10	.05	.01
☐ 18 Don Mattingly	.60	.25	.08
☐ 19 Jack Morris	.15	.07	.02
☐ 20 Dale Murphy	.20	.09	.03
☐ 21 Eddie Murray	.25	.11	.03
☐ 22 Dave Parker	.15	.07	.02
☐ 23 Kirby Puckett	.60	.25	.08
☐ 24 Tim Raines	.15	.07	.02
☐ 25 Rick Reuschel	.10	.05	.01
☐ 26 Jerry Reuss	.10	.05	.01
☐ 27 Jim Rice	.15	.07	.02
☐ 28 Nolan Ryan	1.00	.45	.13
☐ 29 Ozzie Smith	.25	.11	.03
☐ 30 Frank Tanana	.10	.05	.01
☐ 31 Willie Wilson	.10	.05	.01
☐ 32 Dave Winfield	.25	.11	.03
☐ 33 Robin Yount	.50	.23	.06

1970 Kellogg's

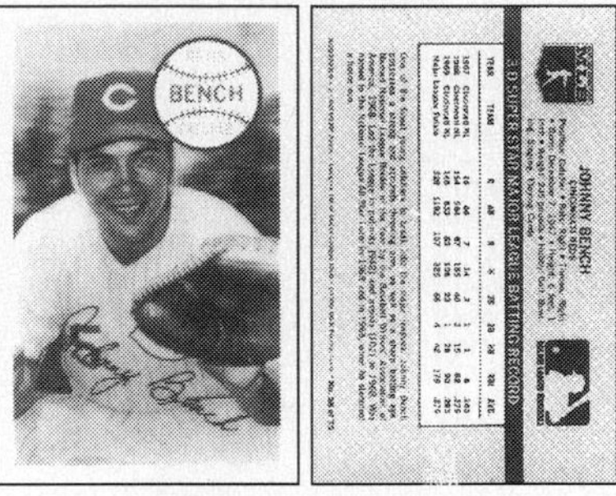

The cards in this 75-card set measure approximately 2 1/4" by 3 1/2". The 1970 Kellogg's set was Kellogg's first venture into the baseball card producing field. The design incorporates a brilliant color photo of the player set against an indistinct background, which is then covered with a layer of plastic to simulate a 3-D look. Some veteran card dealers consider cards 16-30 to be in shorter supply than the other cards in the set.

	NRMT-MT	EXC	G-VG
COMPLETE SET (75)	175.00	80.00	22.00
COMMON PLAYER (1-15)	1.00	.45	.13
COMMON PLAYER (16-30)	1.00	.45	.13
COMMON PLAYER (31-75)	1.00	.45	.13
☐ 1 Ed Kranepool	1.00	.45	.13
☐ 2 Pete Rose	20.00	9.00	2.50
☐ 3 Cleon Jones	1.00	.45	.13
☐ 4 Willie McCovey	7.50	3.40	.95
☐ 5 Mel Stottlemyre	1.50	.65	.19
☐ 6 Frank Howard	1.50	.65	.19
☐ 7 Tom Seaver	16.00	7.25	2.00
☐ 8 Don Sutton	4.00	1.80	.50
☐ 9 Jim Wynn	1.50	.65	.19
☐ 10 Jim Maloney	1.50	.65	.19
☐ 11 Tommie Agee	1.00	.45	.13
☐ 12 Willie Mays	18.00	8.00	2.30
☐ 13 Juan Marichal	5.00	2.30	.60
☐ 14 Dave McNally	1.50	.65	.19
☐ 15 Frank Robinson	6.00	2.70	.75
☐ 16 Carlos May	1.00	.45	.13
☐ 17 Bill Singer	1.00	.45	.13
☐ 18 Rick Reichardt	1.00	.45	.13
☐ 19 Boog Powell	2.00	.90	.25
☐ 20 Gaylord Perry	5.00	2.30	.60
☐ 21 Brooks Robinson	7.50	3.40	.95
☐ 22 Luis Aparicio	4.00	1.80	.50
☐ 23 Joel Horlen	1.00	.45	.13
☐ 24 Mike Epstein	1.00	.45	.13
☐ 25 Tom Haller	1.00	.45	.13
☐ 26 Willie Crawford	1.00	.45	.13
☐ 27 Roberto Clemente	18.00	8.00	2.30
☐ 28 Matty Alou	1.00	.45	.13
☐ 29 Willie Stargell	6.00	2.70	.75
☐ 30 Tim Cullen	1.00	.45	.13

□ 31 Randy Hundley	1.00	.45	.13
□ 32 Reggie Jackson	25.00	11.50	3.10
□ 33 Rich Allen	2.00	.90	.25
□ 34 Tim McCarver	1.50	.65	.19
□ 35 Ray Culp	1.00	.45	.13
□ 36 Jim Fregosi	1.50	.65	.19
□ 37 Billy Williams	4.00	1.80	.50
□ 38 Johnny Odom	1.00	.45	.13
□ 39 Bert Campaneris	1.50	.65	.19
□ 40 Ernie Banks	9.00	4.00	1.15
□ 41 Chris Short	1.00	.45	.13
□ 42 Ron Santo	1.50	.65	.19
□ 43 Glenn Beckert	1.00	.45	.13
□ 44 Lou Brock	5.00	2.30	.60
□ 45 Larry Hisle	1.00	.45	.13
□ 46 Reggie Smith	1.50	.65	.19
□ 47 Rod Carew	7.50	3.40	.95
□ 48 Curt Flood	1.50	.65	.19
□ 49 Jim Lonborg	1.50	.65	.19
□ 50 Sam McDowell	1.50	.65	.19
□ 51 Sal Bando	1.50	.65	.19
□ 52 Al Kaline	9.00	4.00	1.15
□ 53 Gary Nolan	1.00	.45	.13
□ 54 Rico Petrocelli	1.00	.45	.13
□ 55 Ollie Brown	1.00	.45	.13
□ 56 Luis Tiant	1.50	.65	.19
□ 57 Bill Freehan	1.50	.65	.19
□ 58 Johnny Bench	18.00	8.00	2.30
□ 59 Joe Pepitone	1.50	.65	.19
□ 60 Bobby Murcer	1.50	.65	.19
□ 61 Harmon Killebrew	5.00	2.30	.60
□ 62 Don Wilson	1.00	.45	.13
□ 63 Tony Oliva	2.00	.90	.25
□ 64 Jim Perry	1.50	.65	.19
□ 65 Mickey Lolich	1.50	.65	.19
□ 66 Jose Laboy	1.00	.45	.13
□ 67 Dean Chance	1.00	.45	.13
□ 68 Ken Harrelson	1.50	.65	.19
□ 69 Willie Horton	1.00	.45	.13
□ 70 Wally Bunker	1.00	.45	.13
□ 71A Bob Gibson ERR (1959 innings pitched is blank)	6.00	2.70	.75
□ 71B Bob Gibson COR (1959 innings is 76)	6.00	2.70	.75
□ 72 Joe Morgan	5.00	2.30	.60
□ 73 Denny McLain	1.50	.65	.19
□ 74 Tommy Harper	1.00	.45	.13
□ 75 Don Mincher	1.00	.45	.13

1971 Kellogg's

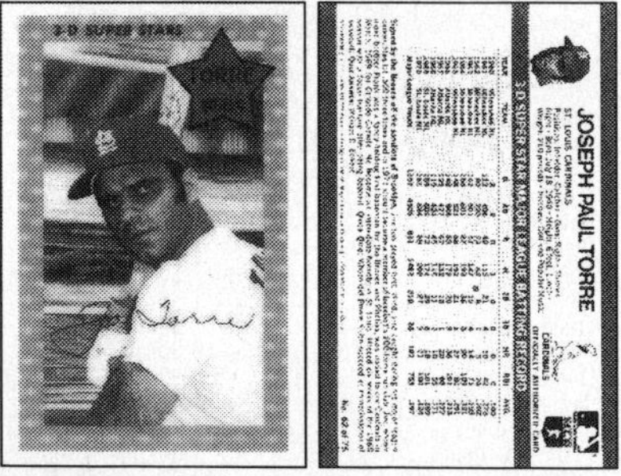

The cards in this 75-card set measure approximately 2 1/4" by 3 1/2". The 1971 set of 3-D cards marketed by the Kellogg Company is the scarcest of all that company's issues. It was distributed as single cards, one in each package of cereal, without the usual complete set mail-in offer. In addition, card dealers were unable to obtain this set in quantity, as they have in other years. All the cards are available with and without the year 1970 before XOGRAPH on the back in the lower left corner; the version without carries a slight premium for most numbers. Prices listed below are for the more common variety with the year 1970.

	NRMT-MT	EXC	G-VG
COMPLETE SET (75)	850.00	375.00	105.00
COMMON PLAYER (1-75)	6.50	2.90	.80
□ 1 Wayne Simpson	6.50	2.90	.80
□ 2 Tom Seaver	40.00	18.00	5.00
□ 3 Jim Perry	7.50	3.40	.95
□ 4 Bob Robertson	6.50	2.90	.80
□ 5 Roberto Clemente	40.00	18.00	5.00
□ 6 Gaylord Perry	21.00	9.50	2.60
□ 7 Felipe Alou	8.50	3.80	1.05
□ 8 Denis Menke	6.50	2.90	.80
□ 9A Don Kessinger (No 1970 date)	8.50	3.80	1.05
□ 9B Don Kessinger ERR (Dated, 1970 hits 167, avg. .265)	8.50	3.80	1.05
□ 9C Don Kessinger COR (Dated, 1970 hits 168, avg. .266)	8.50	3.80	1.05
□ 10 Willie Mays	45.00	20.00	5.75
□ 11 Jim Hickman	6.50	2.90	.80
□ 12 Tony Oliva	10.00	4.50	1.25
□ 13 Manny Sanguillen	7.50	3.40	.95
□ 14 Frank Howard	8.50	3.80	1.05
□ 15 Frank Robinson	25.00	11.50	3.10
□ 16 Willie Davis	8.50	3.80	1.05
□ 17 Lou Brock	25.00	11.50	3.10
□ 18 Cesar Tovar	6.50	2.90	.80
□ 19 Luis Aparicio	16.00	7.25	2.00
□ 20 Boog Powell	10.00	4.50	1.25
□ 21 Dick Selma	6.50	2.90	.80
□ 22 Danny Walton	6.50	2.90	.80
□ 23 Carl Morton	6.50	2.90	.80
□ 24 Sonny Siebert	6.50	2.90	.80
□ 25 Jim Merritt	6.50	2.90	.80
□ 26 Jose Cardenal	6.50	2.90	.80
□ 27 Don Mincher	6.50	2.90	.80
□ 28A Clyde Wright (No 1970 date, team logo is Angels crest)	10.00	4.50	1.25
□ 28B Clyde Wright (No 1970 date, team logo is California outline with Angels written inside)	10.00	4.50	1.25
□ 28C Clyde Wright (Dated 1970, team logo is California state outline)	7.50	3.40	.95
□ 29 Les Cain	6.50	2.90	.80
□ 30 Danny Cater	6.50	2.90	.80
□ 31 Don Sutton	20.00	9.00	2.50
□ 32 Chuck Dobson	6.50	2.90	.80
□ 33 Willie McCovey	25.00	11.50	3.10
□ 34 Mike Epstein	6.50	2.90	.80
□ 35 Paul Blair	6.50	2.90	.80
□ 36A Gary Nolan (No 1970 date)	7.50	3.40	.95
□ 36B Gary Nolan (Dated 1970, 1970 BB 95, SO 177)	7.50	3.40	.95
□ 36C Gary Nolan (Dated 1970, 1970 BB 96, SO 181)	7.50	3.40	.95
□ 37 Sam McDowell	7.50	3.40	.95
□ 38 Amos Otis	7.50	3.40	.95
□ 39 Ray Fosse	6.50	2.90	.80
□ 40 Mel Stottlemyre	8.50	3.80	1.05
□ 41 Clarence Gaston	8.50	3.80	1.05
□ 42 Dick Dietz	6.50	2.90	.80
□ 43 Roy White	7.50	3.40	.95
□ 44 Al Kaline	30.00	13.50	3.80
□ 45 Carlos May	6.50	2.90	.80
□ 46 Tommie Agee	6.50	2.90	.80
□ 47 Tommy Harper	6.50	2.90	.80
□ 48 Larry Dierker	6.50	2.90	.80
□ 49 Mike Cuellar	7.50	3.40	.95
□ 50 Ernie Banks	30.00	13.50	3.80
□ 51 Bob Gibson	25.00	11.50	3.10
□ 52 Reggie Smith	7.50	3.40	.95
□ 53 Matty Alou	7.50	3.40	.95
□ 54A Alex Johnson (No 1970 date, team logo is Angels crest)	10.00	4.50	1.25
□ 54B Alex Johnson (No 1970 date, team logo is California state outline)	10.00	4.50	1.25
□ 54C Alex Johnson (Dated 1970, team logo is California state outline)	7.50	3.40	.95
□ 55 Harmon Killebrew	25.00	11.50	3.10

Card	NRMT-MT	EXC	G-VG
☐ 56 Bill Grabarkewitz	6.50	2.90	.80
☐ 57 Richie Allen	11.00	4.90	1.40
☐ 58 Tony Perez	15.00	6.75	1.90
☐ 59 Dave McNally	7.50	3.40	.95
☐ 60 Jim Palmer	30.00	13.50	3.80
☐ 61 Billy Williams	21.00	9.50	2.60
☐ 62 Joe Torre	11.00	4.90	1.40
☐ 63 Jim Northrup	7.50	3.40	.95
☐ 64A Jim Fregosi (No 1970 date, team logo is Angels crest)	10.00	4.50	1.25
☐ 64B Jim Fregosi (No 1970 date, team logo is California state outline	10.00	4.50	1.25
☐ 64C Jim Fregosi (Dated1970, 1970 Hits 166, avg. .276)	8.50	3.80	1.05
☐ 64D Jim Fregosi (Dated1970, 1970 Hits 167, avg. .278)	8.50	3.80	1.05
☐ 65 Pete Rose	60.00	27.00	7.50
☐ 66A Bud Harrelson (No 1970 date)	8.50	3.80	1.05
☐ 66B Bud Harrelson ERR (Dated 1970, 1970 RBI 43)	8.50	3.80	1.05
☐ 66C Bud Harrelson COR (Dated 1970, 1970 RBI 42)	8.50	3.80	1.05
☐ 67 Tony Taylor	7.50	3.40	.95
☐ 68 Willie Stargell	25.00	11.50	3.10
☐ 69 Tony Horton	7.50	3.40	.95
☐ 70A Claude Osteen ERR (No 1970 date, card number missing)	10.00	4.50	1.25
☐ 70B Claude Osteen COR (No 1970 date, card number present)	10.00	4.50	1.25
☐ 70C Claude Osteen COR (Dated 1970)	7.50	3.40	.95
☐ 71 Glenn Beckert	6.50	2.90	.80
☐ 72 Nate Colbert	6.50	2.90	.80
☐ 73A Rick Monday (No 1970 date)	8.50	3.80	1.05
☐ 73B Rick Monday ERR (Dated 1970, 1970 AB 377, avg. .289)	8.50	3.80	1.05
☐ 73C Rick Monday COR (Dated 1970, 1970 AB 376, avg. .290)	8.50	3.80	1.05
☐ 74 Tommy John	12.50	5.75	1.55
☐ 75 Chris Short	6.50	2.90	.80

1972 Kellogg's

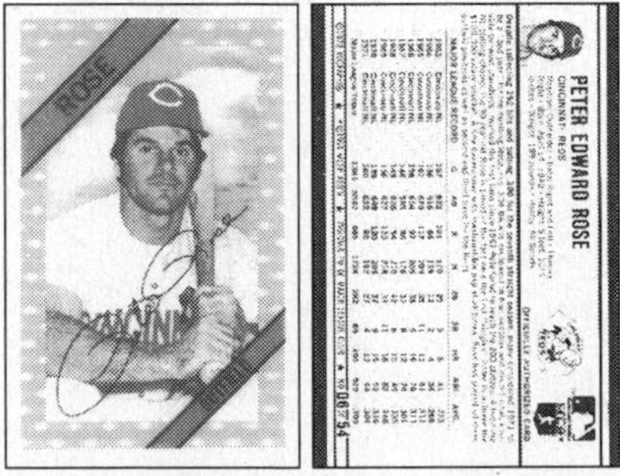

The cards in this 54-card set measure approximately 2 1/8" by 3 1/4". The dimensions of the cards in the 1972 Kellogg's set were reduced in comparison to those of the 1971 series. In addition, the length of the set was set at 54 cards rather than the 75 of the previous year. The cards of this Kellogg's set are characterized by the diagonal bands found on the obverse.

	NRMT-MT	EXC	G-VG
COMPLETE SET (54)	75.00	34.00	9.50
COMMON PLAYER (1-54)	.75	.35	.09

Card	NRMT-MT	EXC	G-VG
☐ 1A Tom Seaver ERR (1970 ERA 2.85)	12.00	5.50	1.50
☐ 1B Tom Seaver COR (1970 ERA 2.81)	24.00	11.00	3.00
☐ 2 Amos Otis	.90	.40	.11
☐ 3A Willie Davis ERR (Lifetime runs 842)	1.50	.65	.19
☐ 3B Willie Davis COR (Lifetime runs 841)	.75	.35	.09
☐ 4 Wilbur Wood	.75	.35	.09
☐ 5 Bill Parsons	.75	.35	.09
☐ 6 Pete Rose	16.00	7.25	2.00
☐ 7A Willie McCovey ERR (Lifetime HR 360)	4.00	1.80	.50
☐ 7B Willie McCovey COR (Lifetime HR 370)	8.00	3.60	1.00
☐ 8 Ferguson Jenkins	3.50	1.55	.45
☐ 9A Vida Blue ERR (Lifetime ERA 2.35)	1.50	.65	.19
☐ 9B Vida Blue COR (Lifetime ERA 2.31)	.75	.35	.09
☐ 10 Joe Torre	1.25	.55	.16
☐ 11 Merv Rettenmund	.75	.35	.09
☐ 12 Bill Melton	.75	.35	.09
☐ 13A Jim Palmer ERR (Lifetime games 170)	5.00	2.30	.60
☐ 13B Jim Palmer COR (Lifetime games 168)	10.00	4.50	1.25
☐ 14 Doug Rader	.75	.35	.09
☐ 15A Dave Roberts ERR ("NL" missing in bio)	.75	.35	.09
☐ 15B Dave Roberts COR ("NL" in bio, line 2)	1.50	.65	.19
☐ 16 Bobby Murcer	.90	.40	.11
☐ 17 Wes Parker	.90	.40	.11
☐ 18A Joe Coleman ERR (Lifetime BB 294)	1.50	.65	.19
☐ 18B Joe Coleman COR (Lifetime BB 393)	.75	.35	.09
☐ 19 Manny Sanguillen	.90	.40	.11
☐ 20 Reggie Jackson	15.00	6.75	1.90
☐ 21 Ralph Garr	.75	.35	.09
☐ 22 Jim Hunter	3.00	1.35	.40
☐ 23 Rick Wise	.75	.35	.09
☐ 24 Glenn Beckert	.75	.35	.09
☐ 25 Tony Oliva	1.50	.65	.19
☐ 26A Bob Gibson ERR (Lifetime SO 2577)	9.00	4.00	1.15
☐ 26B Bob Gibson COR (Lifetime SO 2578)	4.50	2.00	.55
☐ 27A Mike Cuellar ERR (1971 ERA 3.80)	1.50	.65	.19
☐ 27B Mike Cuellar COR (1971 ERA 3.08)	.75	.35	.09
☐ 28 Chris Speier	.75	.35	.09
☐ 29A Dave McNally ERR (Lifetime ERA 3.18)	1.50	.65	.19
☐ 29B Dave McNally COR (Lifetime ERA 3.15)	.75	.35	.09
☐ 30 Leo Cardenas	.75	.35	.09
☐ 31A Bill Freehan ERR (Lifetime runs 497)	.75	.35	.09
☐ 31B Bill Freehan COR (Lifetime runs 500)	1.50	.65	.19
☐ 32A Bud Harrelson ERR (Lifetime hits 634)	1.50	.65	.19
☐ 32B Bud Harrelson COR (Lifetime hits 624)	.75	.35	.09
☐ 33A Sam McDowell ERR (Bio line 3 has "less than 200")	.75	.35	.09
☐ 33B Sam McDowell COR (Bio line 3 has "less than 225")	1.50	.65	.19
☐ 34A Claude Osteen ERR (1971 ERA 3.25)	.75	.35	.09
☐ 34B Claude Osteen COR (1971 ERA 3.51)	1.50	.65	.19
☐ 35 Reggie Smith	.90	.40	.11
☐ 36 Sonny Siebert	.75	.35	.09
☐ 37 Lee May	.90	.40	.11
☐ 38 Mickey Lolich	1.25	.55	.16
☐ 39A Cookie Rojas ERR (Lifetime 2B 149)	1.50	.65	.19
☐ 39B Cookie Rojas COR (Lifetime 2B 150)	.75	.35	.09
☐ 40A Dick Drago ERR (Bio line 3 has Poyals)	1.50	.65	.19
☐ 40B Dick Drago COR (Bio line 3	.75	.35	.09

has Royals)			
☐ 41 Nate Colbert	.75	.35	.09
☐ 42 Andy Messersmith	.75	.35	.09
☐ 43A Dave Johnson ERR (Lifetime AB 3110, avg. .262)	2.00	.90	.25
☐ 43B Dave Johnson COR (Lifetime AB 3113, avg. .264)	1.00	.45	.13
☐ 44 Steve Blass	.75	.35	.09
☐ 45 Bob Robertson	.75	.35	.09
☐ 46A Billy Williams ERR (Bio has "missed only one game")	4.00	1.80	.50
☐ 46B Billy Williams COR (Bio has that line eliminated)	8.00	3.60	1.00
☐ 47 Juan Marichal	3.50	1.55	.45
☐ 48 Lou Brock	4.00	1.80	.50
☐ 49 Roberto Clemente	12.00	5.50	1.50
☐ 50 Mel Stottlemyre	.90	.40	.11
☐ 51 Don Wilson	.75	.35	.09
☐ 52A Sal Bando ERR (Lifetime RBI 355)	.75	.35	.09
☐ 52B Sal Bando COR (Lifetime RBI 356)	1.50	.65	.19
☐ 53A Willie Stargell ERR (Lifetime 2B 197)	9.00	4.00	1.15
☐ 53B Willie Stargell COR (Lifetime 2B 196)	4.50	2.00	.55
☐ 54A Willie Mays ERR (Lifetime RBI 1855)	24.00	11.00	3.00
☐ 54B Willie Mays COR (Lifetime RBI 1856)	12.00	5.50	1.50

1972 Kellogg's ATG

The cards in this 15-card set measure 2 1/4" by 3 1/2". The 1972 All-Time Greats 3-D set was issued with Kellogg's Danish Go Rounds. The set contains two different cards of Babe Ruth. The set is a reissue of a 1970 set issued by Rold Gold Pretzels to commemorate baseball's first 100 years. The Rold Gold cards are copyrighted 1970 on the reverse and are valued at approximately double the prices listed below.

	NRMT-MT	EXC	G-VG
COMPLETE SET (15)	18.00	8.00	2.30
COMMON PLAYER (1-15)	.75	.35	.09
☐ 1 Walter Johnson	1.50	.65	.19
☐ 2 Rogers Hornsby	1.00	.45	.13
☐ 3 John McGraw	.75	.35	.09
☐ 4 Mickey Cochrane	.90	.40	.11
☐ 5 George Sisler	.90	.40	.11
☐ 6 Babe Ruth	5.00	2.30	.60
☐ 7 Lefty Grove	1.00	.45	.13
☐ 8 Pie Traynor	.75	.35	.09
☐ 9 Honus Wagner	1.50	.65	.19
☐ 10 Eddie Collins	.75	.35	.09
☐ 11 Tris Speaker	.90	.40	.11
☐ 12 Cy Young	1.50	.65	.19
☐ 13 Lou Gehrig	3.00	1.35	.40
☐ 14 Babe Ruth	5.00	2.30	.60
☐ 15 Ty Cobb	3.00	1.35	.40

1973 Kellogg's 2D

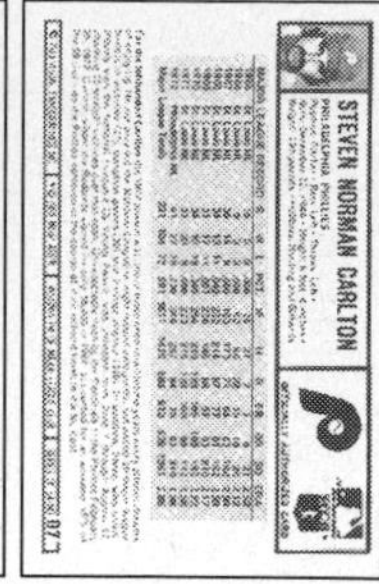

The cards in this 54-card set measure approximately 2 1/4" by 3 1/2". The 1973 Kellogg's set is the only non-3D set produced by the Kellogg Company. Apparently Kellogg's decided to have the cards produced through Visual Panographics rather than by Xograph, as in the other years. The complete set could be obtained from the company through a box-top redemption procedure. The card size is slightly larger than the previous year.

	NRMT-MT	EXC	G-VG
COMPLETE SET (54)	75.00	34.00	9.50
COMMON PLAYER (1-54)	.75	.35	.09
☐ 1 Amos Otis	.90	.40	.11
☐ 2 Ellie Rodriguez	.75	.35	.09
☐ 3 Mickey Lolich	1.25	.55	.16
☐ 4 Tony Oliva	1.50	.65	.19
☐ 5 Don Sutton	3.00	1.35	.40
☐ 6 Pete Rose	16.00	7.25	2.00
☐ 7 Steve Carlton	6.00	2.70	.75
☐ 8 Bobby Bonds	1.25	.55	.16
☐ 9 Wilbur Wood	.75	.35	.09
☐ 10 Billy Williams	3.50	1.55	.45
☐ 11 Steve Blass	.75	.35	.09
☐ 12 Jon Matlack	.75	.35	.09
☐ 13 Cesar Cedeno	.90	.40	.11
☐ 14 Bob Gibson	3.50	1.55	.45
☐ 15 Sparky Lyle	1.25	.55	.16
☐ 16 Nolan Ryan	30.00	13.50	3.80
☐ 17 Jim Palmer	5.00	2.30	.60
☐ 18 Ray Fosse	.75	.35	.09
☐ 19 Bobby Murcer	1.00	.45	.13
☐ 20 Jim Hunter	3.00	1.35	.40
☐ 21 Tom McCraw	.75	.35	.09
☐ 22 Reggie Jackson	10.00	4.50	1.25
☐ 23 Bill Stoneman	.75	.35	.09
☐ 24 Lou Piniella	1.25	.55	.16
☐ 25 Willie Stargell	4.00	1.80	.50
☐ 26 Dick Allen	1.00	.45	.13
☐ 27 Carlton Fisk	7.50	3.40	.95
☐ 28 Ferguson Jenkins	3.00	1.35	.40
☐ 29 Phil Niekro	3.00	1.35	.40
☐ 30 Gary Nolan	.75	.35	.09
☐ 31 Joe Torre	1.25	.55	.16
☐ 32 Bobby Tolan	.75	.35	.09
☐ 33 Nate Colbert	.75	.35	.09
☐ 34 Joe Morgan	4.00	1.80	.50
☐ 35 Bert Blyleven	1.25	.55	.16
☐ 36 Joe Rudi	.90	.40	.11
☐ 37 Ralph Garr	.75	.35	.09
☐ 38 Gaylord Perry	3.00	1.35	.40
☐ 39 Bobby Grich	.90	.40	.11
☐ 40 Lou Brock	3.50	1.55	.45
☐ 41 Pete Broberg	.75	.35	.09
☐ 42 Manny Sanguillen	.75	.35	.09
☐ 43 Willie Davis	.90	.40	.11
☐ 44 Dave Kingman	1.00	.45	.13
☐ 45 Carlos May	.75	.35	.09
☐ 46 Tom Seaver	9.00	4.00	1.15
☐ 47 Mike Cuellar	.75	.35	.09
☐ 48 Joe Coleman	.75	.35	.09
☐ 49 Claude Osteen	.75	.35	.09
☐ 50 Steve Kline	.75	.35	.09
☐ 51 Rod Carew	6.00	2.70	.75
☐ 52 Al Kaline	6.00	2.70	.75
☐ 53 Larry Dierker	.75	.35	.09
☐ 54 Ron Santo	1.25	.55	.16

1974 Kellogg's

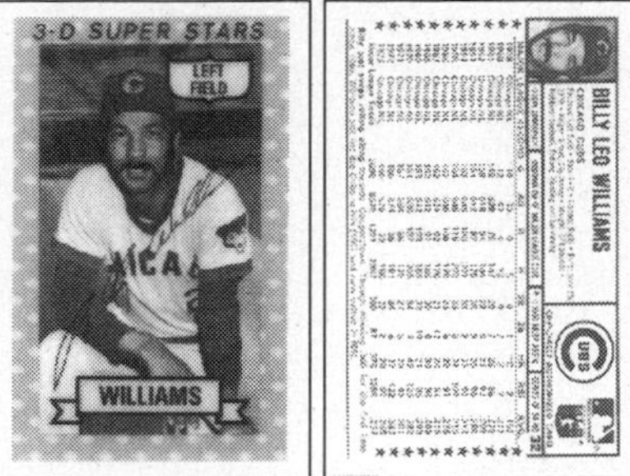

The cards in this 54-card set measure 2 1/8" by 3 1/4". In 1974 the Kellogg's set returned to its 3-D format; it also returned to the smaller-size card. Complete sets could be obtained from the company through a box-top offer. The cards are numbered on the back.

	NRMT-MT	EXC	G-VG
COMPLETE SET (54)	75.00	34.00	9.50
COMMON PLAYER (1-54)	.75	.35	.09
□ 1 Bob Gibson	3.50	1.55	.45
□ 2 Rick Monday	.90	.40	.11
□ 3 Joe Coleman	.75	.35	.09
□ 4 Bert Campaneris	.90	.40	.11
□ 5 Carlton Fisk	4.00	1.80	.50
□ 6 Jim Palmer	3.50	1.55	.45
□ 7A Ron Santo ERR Chicago Cubs	5.00	2.30	.60
□ 7B Ron Santo COR Chicago White Sox	1.00	.45	.13
□ 8 Nolan Ryan	24.00	11.00	3.00
□ 9 Greg Luzinski	1.00	.45	.13
□ 10 Buddy Bell	.90	.40	.11
□ 11 Bob Watson	.90	.40	.11
□ 12 Bill Singer	.75	.35	.09
□ 13 Dave May	.75	.35	.09
□ 14 Jim Brewer	.75	.35	.09
□ 15 Manny Sanguillen	.90	.40	.11
□ 16 Jeff Burroughs	.90	.40	.11
□ 17 Amos Otis	.90	.40	.11
□ 18 Ed Goodson	.75	.35	.09
□ 19 Nate Colbert	.75	.35	.09
□ 20 Reggie Jackson	10.00	4.50	1.25
□ 21 Ted Simmons	1.25	.55	.16
□ 22 Bobby Murcer	1.00	.45	.13
□ 23 Willie Horton	.90	.40	.11
□ 24 Orlando Cepeda	1.50	.65	.19
□ 25 Ron Hunt	.75	.35	.09
□ 26 Wayne Twitchell	.75	.35	.09
□ 27 Ron Fairly	.75	.35	.09
□ 28 Johnny Bench	7.50	3.40	.95
□ 29 John Mayberry	.90	.40	.11
□ 30 Rod Carew	6.00	2.70	.75
□ 31 Ken Holtzman	.75	.35	.09
□ 32 Billy Williams	3.00	1.35	.40
□ 33 Dick Allen	1.25	.55	.16
□ 34A Wilbur Wood ERR (1973 K 198)	3.00	1.35	.40
□ 34B Wilbur Wood COR (1973 K 199)	.75	.35	.09
□ 35 Danny Thompson	.75	.35	.09
□ 36 Joe Morgan	3.50	1.55	.45
□ 37 Willie Stargell	3.50	1.55	.45
□ 38 Pete Rose	12.00	5.50	1.50
□ 39 Bobby Bonds	1.25	.55	.16
□ 40 Chris Speier	.75	.35	.09
□ 41 Sparky Lyle	1.00	.45	.13
□ 42 Cookie Rojas	.75	.35	.09
□ 43 Tommy Davis	.90	.40	.11
□ 44 Jim Hunter	3.00	1.35	.40
□ 45 Willie Davis	.90	.40	.11
□ 46 Bert Blyleven	1.25	.55	.16
□ 47 Pat Kelly	.75	.35	.09
□ 48 Ken Singleton	.90	.40	.11
□ 49 Manny Mota	.90	.40	.11
□ 50 Dave Johnson	1.00	.45	.13
□ 51 Sal Bando	.90	.40	.11
□ 52 Tom Seaver	7.50	3.40	.95
□ 53 Felix Millan	.75	.35	.09
□ 54 Ron Blomberg	.75	.35	.09

1975 Kellogg's

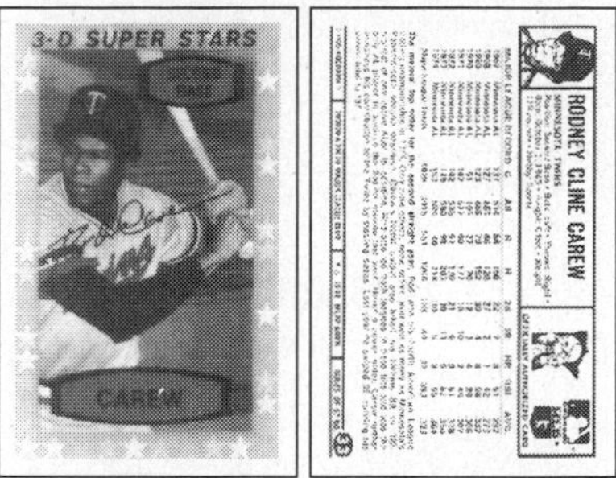

The cards in this 57-card set measure approximately 2 1/8" by 3 1/4". The 1975 Kellogg's 3-D set could be obtained card by card in cereal boxes or as a set from a box-top offer from the company. Card number 44, Jim Hunter, exists with the A's emblem or the Yankees emblem on the back of the card.

	NRMT-MT	EXC	G-VG
COMPLETE SET (57)	165.00	75.00	21.00
COMMON PLAYER (1-57)	1.00	.45	.13
□ 1 Roy White	1.00	.45	.13
□ 2 Ross Grimsley	1.00	.45	.13
□ 3 Reggie Smith	1.25	.55	.16
□ 4A Bob Grich ERR (Bio last line begins "1973 work")	1.25	.55	.16
□ 4B Bob Grich COR (Bio last line begins "because his fielding")	2.50	1.15	.30
□ 5 Greg Gross	1.00	.45	.13
□ 6 Bob Watson	1.25	.55	.16
□ 7 Johnny Bench	12.50	5.75	1.55
□ 8 Jeff Burroughs	1.25	.55	.16
□ 9 Elliott Maddox	1.00	.45	.13
□ 10 Jon Matlack	1.00	.45	.13
□ 11 Pete Rose	18.00	8.00	2.30
□ 12 Lee Stanton	1.00	.45	.13
□ 13 Bake McBride	1.00	.45	.13
□ 14 Jorge Orta	1.00	.45	.13
□ 15 Al Oliver	1.25	.55	.16
□ 16 John Briggs	1.00	.45	.13
□ 17 Steve Garvey	6.00	2.70	.75
□ 18 Brooks Robinson	6.00	2.70	.75
□ 19 John Hiller	1.00	.45	.13
□ 20 Lynn McGlothen	1.00	.45	.13
□ 21 Cleon Jones	1.00	.45	.13
□ 22 Fergie Jenkins	3.50	1.55	.45
□ 23 Bill North	1.00	.45	.13
□ 24 Steve Busby	1.00	.45	.13
□ 25 Richie Zisk	1.00	.45	.13
□ 26 Nolan Ryan	30.00	13.50	3.80
□ 27 Joe Morgan	5.00	2.30	.60
□ 28 Joe Rudi	1.25	.55	.16
□ 29 Jose Cardenal	1.00	.45	.13
□ 30 Andy Messersmith	1.00	.45	.13
□ 31 Willie Montanez	1.00	.45	.13
□ 32 Bill Buckner	1.50	.65	.19
□ 33 Rod Carew	7.50	3.40	.95
□ 34 Lou Piniella	1.50	.65	.19
□ 35 Ralph Garr	1.00	.45	.13
□ 36 Mike Marshall	1.25	.55	.16
□ 37 Garry Maddox	1.00	.45	.13
□ 38 Dwight Evans	2.00	.90	.25
□ 39 Lou Brock	6.00	2.70	.75
□ 40 Ken Singleton	1.25	.55	.16
□ 41 Steve Braun	1.00	.45	.13
□ 42 Rich Allen	1.50	.65	.19
□ 43 John Grubb	1.00	.45	.13
□ 44A Jim Hunter (Oakland A's team logo on back)	4.00	1.80	.50
□ 44B Jim Hunter	12.00	5.50	1.50

	NRMT-MT	EXC	G-VG
(New York Yankees team logo on back)			
☐ 45 Gaylord Perry	4.00	1.80	.50
☐ 46 George Hendrick	1.00	.45	.13
☐ 47 Sparky Lyle	1.25	.55	.16
☐ 48 Dave Cash	1.00	.45	.13
☐ 49 Luis Tiant	1.25	.55	.16
☐ 50 Cesar Geronimo	1.00	.45	.13
☐ 51 Carl Yastrzemski	15.00	6.75	1.90
☐ 52 Ken Brett	1.00	.45	.13
☐ 53 Hal McRae	1.50	.65	.19
☐ 54 Reggie Jackson	18.00	8.00	2.30
☐ 55 Rollie Fingers	4.00	1.80	.50
☐ 56 Mike Schmidt	20.00	9.00	2.50
☐ 57 Richie Hebner	1.00	.45	.13

1976 Kellogg's

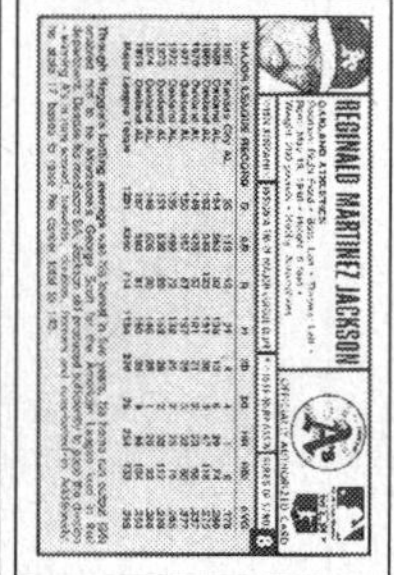

The cards in this 57-card set measure approximately 2 1/8" by 3 1/4". The 1976 Kellogg's 3-D set could be obtained card by card in cereal boxes or as a set from the company for box-tops. Card numbers 1-3 (marked in the checklist below with SP) were apparently printed apart from the other 54 and are in shorter supply.

	NRMT-MT	EXC	G-VG
COMPLETE SET	90.00	40.00	11.50
COMMON PLAYER (1-3) SP	9.00	4.00	1.15
COMMON PLAYER (4-57)	.50	.23	.06
☐ 1 Steve Hargan SP	9.00	4.00	1.15
☐ 2 Claudell Washington SP	9.00	4.00	1.15
☐ 3 Don Gullett SP	9.00	4.00	1.15
☐ 4 Randy Jones	.60	.25	.08
☐ 5 Jim Hunter	2.50	1.15	.30
☐ 6A Clay Carroll (Team logo Cincinnati Reds on back)	2.00	.90	.25
☐ 6B Clay Carroll (Team logo Chicago White Sox on back)	1.00	.45	.13
☐ 7 Joe Rudi	.60	.25	.08
☐ 8 Reggie Jackson	7.50	3.40	.95
☐ 9 Felix Millan	.50	.23	.06
☐ 10 Jim Rice	3.00	1.35	.40
☐ 11 Bert Blyleven	.90	.40	.11
☐ 12 Ken Singleton	.60	.25	.08
☐ 13 Don Sutton	2.50	1.15	.30
☐ 14 Joe Morgan	3.50	1.55	.45
☐ 15 Dave Parker	2.50	1.15	.30
☐ 16 Dave Cash	.50	.23	.06
☐ 17 Ron LeFlore	.60	.25	.08
☐ 18 Greg Luzinski	1.00	.45	.13
☐ 19 Dennis Eckersley	12.00	5.50	1.50
☐ 20 Bill Madlock	.75	.35	.09
☐ 21 George Scott	.50	.23	.06
☐ 22 Willie Stargell	3.00	1.35	.40
☐ 23 Al Hrabosky	.60	.25	.08
☐ 24 Carl Yastrzemski	7.50	3.40	.95
☐ 25A Jim Kaat (Team logo Chicago White Sox on back)	1.50	.65	.19
☐ 25B Jim Kaat (Team logo Philadelphia Phillies on back)	1.50	.65	.19
☐ 26 Marty Perez	.50	.23	.06
☐ 27 Bob Watson	.60	.25	.08
☐ 28 Eric Soderholm	.50	.23	.06
☐ 29 Bill Lee	.60	.25	.08
☐ 30A Frank Tanana ERR (1975 ERA 2.63)	1.00	.45	.13
☐ 30B Frank Tanana COR (1975 ERA 2.62)	1.00	.45	.13
☐ 31 Fred Lynn	1.50	.65	.19
☐ 32A Tom Seaver ERR (1967 Pct. 552 with no decimal point)	7.50	3.40	.95
☐ 32B Tom Seaver COR (1967 Pct. .552)	7.50	3.40	.95
☐ 33 Steve Busby	.60	.25	.08
☐ 34 Gary Carter	5.00	2.30	.60
☐ 35 Rick Wise	.60	.25	.08
☐ 36 Johnny Bench	6.00	2.70	.75
☐ 37 Jim Palmer	3.00	1.35	.40
☐ 38 Bobby Murcer	.75	.35	.09
☐ 39 Von Joshua	.50	.23	.06
☐ 40 Lou Brock	3.50	1.55	.45
☐ 41A Mickey Rivers (Missing line in bio about Yankees)	1.00	.45	.13
☐ 41B Mickey Rivers (Bio has "Yankees obtained ...")	1.00	.45	.13
☐ 42 Manny Sanguillen	.60	.25	.08
☐ 43 Jerry Reuss	.50	.23	.06
☐ 44 Ken Griffey	1.25	.55	.16
☐ 45A Jorge Orta ERR (Lifetime AB 1615)	.60	.25	.08
☐ 45B Jorge Orta COR (Lifetime AB 1616)	.60	.25	.08
☐ 46 John Mayberry	.60	.25	.08
☐ 47A Vida Blue (Bio "struck out more batters")	.75	.35	.09
☐ 47B Vida Blue (Bio "pitched more innings")	.75	.35	.09
☐ 48 Rod Carew	5.00	2.30	.60
☐ 49A Jon Matlack ERR (1975 ER 87)	.75	.35	.09
☐ 49B Jon Matlack COR (1975 ER 86)	.75	.35	.09
☐ 50 Boog Powell	.90	.40	.11
☐ 51A Mike Hargrove ERR (Lifetime AB 935)	1.00	.45	.13
☐ 51B Mike Hargrove COR (Lifetime AB 934)	1.00	.45	.13
☐ 52A Paul Lindblad ERR (1975 ERA 2.43)	.60	.25	.08
☐ 52B Paul Lindblad COR (1975 ERA 2.72)	.60	.25	.08
☐ 53 Thurman Munson	5.00	2.30	.60
☐ 54 Steve Garvey	3.50	1.55	.45
☐ 55 Pete Rose	12.00	5.50	1.50
☐ 56A Greg Gross ERR (Lifetime games 334)	.60	.25	.08
☐ 56B Greg Gross COR (Lifetime games 302)	.60	.25	.08
☐ 57 Ted Simmons	1.00	.45	.13

1977 Kellogg's

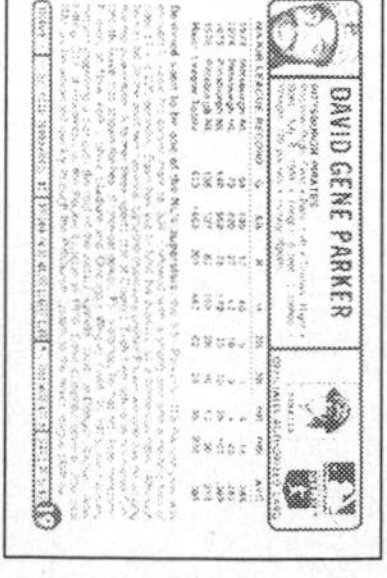

The cards in this 57-card set measure approximately 2 1/8" by 3 1/4". The 1977 Kellogg's series of 3-D baseball player cards could be obtained card by card from cereal boxes or by sending in box-tops and money. Each player's picture appears in miniature form on the reverse, an idea begun in 1971 and replaced in subsequent years by the use of a picture of the Kellogg's mascot.

	NRMT-MT	EXC	G-VG
COMPLETE SET (57)	60.00	27.00	7.50
COMMON PLAYER (1-57)	.40	.18	.05
☐ 1 George Foster	1.00	.45	.13
☐ 2 Bert Campaneris	.50	.23	.06
☐ 3 Fergie Jenkins	2.50	1.15	.30
☐ 4 Dock Ellis	.40	.18	.05
☐ 5 John Montefusco	.40	.18	.05
☐ 6 George Brett	10.00	4.50	1.25
☐ 7 John Candelaria	.50	.23	.06
☐ 8 Fred Norman	.40	.18	.05
☐ 9 Bill Travers	.40	.18	.05
☐ 10 Hal McRae	.75	.35	.09
☐ 11 Doug Rau	.40	.18	.05
☐ 12 Greg Luzinski	.60	.25	.08
☐ 13 Ralph Garr	.50	.23	.06
☐ 14 Steve Garvey	3.50	1.55	.45
☐ 15 Rick Manning	.40	.18	.05
☐ 16A Lyman Bostock ERR (Dock Ellis photo on back)	2.00	.90	.25
☐ 16B Lyman Bostock COR	.50	.23	.06
☐ 17 Randy Jones	.40	.18	.05
☐ 18 Ron Cey	.60	.25	.08
☐ 19 Dave Parker	1.50	.65	.19
☐ 20 Pete Rose	9.00	4.00	1.15
☐ 21A Wayne Garland (No trade to Cleveland is mentioned)	.50	.23	.06
☐ 21B Wayne Garland (Trade mentioned, bio ends "now flip for Cleveland)	1.50	.65	.19
☐ 22 Bill North	.40	.18	.05
☐ 23 Thurman Munson	3.50	1.55	.45
☐ 24 Tom Poquette	.40	.18	.05
☐ 25 Ron LeFlore	.50	.23	.06
☐ 26 Mark Fidrych	.90	.40	.11
☐ 27 Sixto Lezcano	.40	.18	.05
☐ 28 Dave Winfield	6.00	2.70	.75
☐ 29 Jerry Koosman	.60	.25	.08
☐ 30 Mike Hargrove	.50	.23	.06
☐ 31 Willie Montanez	.40	.18	.05
☐ 32 Don Stanhouse	.40	.18	.05
☐ 33 Jay Johnstone	.50	.23	.06
☐ 34 Bake McBride	.40	.18	.05
☐ 35 Dave Kingman	.75	.35	.09
☐ 36 Fred Patek	.40	.18	.05
☐ 37 Garry Maddox	.40	.18	.05
☐ 38A Ken Reitz (No trade mentioned)	.50	.23	.06
☐ 38B Ken Reitz (Trade mentioned)	1.50	.65	.19
☐ 39 Bobby Grich	.60	.25	.08
☐ 40 Cesar Geronimo	.40	.18	.05
☐ 41 Jim Lonborg	.50	.23	.06
☐ 42 Ed Figueroa	.40	.18	.05
☐ 43 Bill Madlock	.75	.35	.09
☐ 44 Jerry Remy	.40	.18	.05
☐ 45 Frank Tanana	.60	.25	.08
☐ 46 Al Oliver	.75	.35	.09
☐ 47 Charlie Hough	.60	.25	.08
☐ 48 Lou Piniella	1.00	.45	.13
☐ 49 Ken Griffey	.90	.40	.11
☐ 50 Jose Cruz	.50	.23	.06
☐ 51 Rollie Fingers	3.00	1.35	.40
☐ 52 Chris Chambliss	.60	.25	.08
☐ 53 Rod Carew	4.50	2.00	.55
☐ 54 Andy Messersmith	.50	.23	.06
☐ 55 Mickey Rivers	.50	.23	.06
☐ 56 Butch Wynegar	.40	.18	.05
☐ 57 Steve Carlton	4.50	2.00	.55

1978 Kellogg's

The cards in this 57-card set measure 2 1/8" by 3 1/4". This 1978 3-D Kellogg's series marks the first year in which Tony the Tiger appears on the reverse of each card next to the team and MLB logos. Once again the set could be obtained as individually wrapped cards in cereal boxes or as a set via a mail-in offer. The key card in the set is Eddie Murray, as it was one of Murray's few card issues in 1978, the year of his Topps Rookie Card.

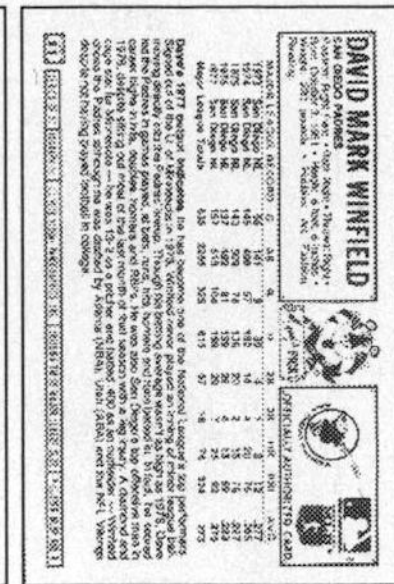

	NRMT-MT	EXC	G-VG
COMPLETE SET (57)	60.00	27.00	7.50
COMMON PLAYER (1-57)	.40	.18	.05
☐ 1 Steve Carlton	4.50	2.00	.55
☐ 2 Bucky Dent	.60	.25	.08
☐ 3 Mike Schmidt	8.00	3.60	1.00
☐ 4 Ken Griffey	.90	.40	.11
☐ 5 Al Cowens	.40	.18	.05
☐ 6 George Brett	9.00	4.00	1.15
☐ 7 Lou Brock	3.00	1.35	.40
☐ 8 Rich Gossage	1.00	.45	.13
☐ 9 Tom Johnson	.40	.18	.05
☐ 10 George Foster	.90	.40	.11
☐ 11 Dave Winfield	4.50	2.00	.55
☐ 12 Dan Meyer	.40	.18	.05
☐ 13 Chris Chambliss	.60	.25	.08
☐ 14 Paul Dade	.40	.18	.05
☐ 15 Jeff Burroughs	.40	.18	.05
☐ 16 Jose Cruz	.50	.23	.06
☐ 17 Mickey Rivers	.50	.23	.06
☐ 18 John Candelaria	.50	.23	.06
☐ 19 Ellis Valentine	.40	.18	.05
☐ 20 Hal McRae	.60	.25	.08
☐ 21 Dave Rozema	.40	.18	.05
☐ 22 Lenny Randle	.40	.18	.05
☐ 23 Willie McCovey	3.00	1.35	.40
☐ 24 Ron Cey	.60	.25	.08
☐ 25 Eddie Murray	24.00	11.00	3.00
☐ 26 Larry Bowa	.60	.25	.08
☐ 27 Tom Seaver	6.00	2.70	.75
☐ 28 Garry Maddox	.50	.23	.06
☐ 29 Rod Carew	4.50	2.00	.55
☐ 30 Thurman Munson	4.50	2.00	.55
☐ 31 Garry Templeton	.50	.23	.06
☐ 32 Eric Soderholm	.40	.18	.05
☐ 33 Greg Luzinski	.60	.25	.08
☐ 34 Reggie Smith	.50	.23	.06
☐ 35 Dave Goltz	.40	.18	.05
☐ 36 Tommy John	.75	.35	.09
☐ 37 Ralph Garr	.40	.18	.05
☐ 38 Alan Bannister	.40	.18	.05
☐ 39 Bob Bailor	.40	.18	.05
☐ 40 Reggie Jackson	6.00	2.70	.75
☐ 41 Cecil Cooper	.60	.25	.08
☐ 42 Burt Hooton	.40	.18	.05
☐ 43 Sparky Lyle	.50	.23	.06
☐ 44 Steve Ontiveros	.40	.18	.05
☐ 45 Rick Reuschel	.60	.25	.08
☐ 46 Lyman Bostock	.50	.23	.06
☐ 47 Mitchell Page	.40	.18	.05
☐ 48 Bruce Sutter	.75	.35	.09
☐ 49 Jim Rice	2.00	.90	.25
☐ 50 Ken Forsch	.40	.18	.05
☐ 51 Nolan Ryan	15.00	6.75	1.90
☐ 52 Dave Parker	1.75	.80	.22
☐ 53 Bert Blyleven	.90	.40	.11
☐ 54 Frank Tanana	.60	.25	.08
☐ 55 Ken Singleton	.50	.23	.06
☐ 56 Mike Hargrove	.50	.23	.06
☐ 57 Don Sutton	2.00	.90	.25

1979 Kellogg's

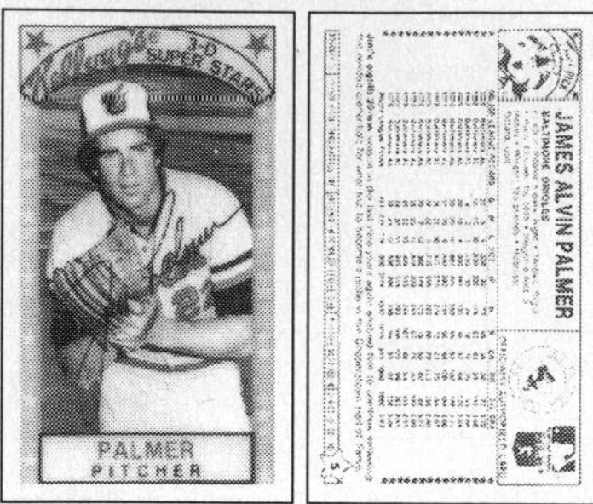

The cards in this 60-card set measure approximately 1 15/16" by 3 1/4". The 1979 edition of Kellogg's 3-D baseball cards have a 3/16" reduced width from the previous year; a nicely designed curved panel above the picture gives this set a distinctive appearance. The set contains the largest number of cards issued in a Kellogg's set since the 1971 series. Three different press runs produced numerous variations in this set. The first two printings were included in cereal boxes, while the third printing was for the complete set mail-in offer. Forty-seven cards have three variations, while thirteen cards (4, 6, 9, 15, 19, 20, 30, 33, 41, 43, 45, 51, and 54) are unchanged from the second and third printings. The three printings may be distinguished by the placement of the registered symbol by Tony the Tiger and by team logos. In the third printing, four cards (16, 18, 22, 44) show the "P" team logo (no registered symbol), and card numbers 56 and 57 omit the registered symbol by Tony.

	NRMT-MT	EXC	G-VG
COMPLETE SET (60)	35.00	16.00	4.40
COMMON PLAYER (1-60)	.25	.11	.03
☐ 1 Bruce Sutter	.50	.23	.06
☐ 2 Ted Simmons	.60	.25	.08
☐ 3 Ross Grimsley	.25	.11	.03
☐ 4 Wayne Nordhagen	.25	.11	.03
☐ 5 Jim Palmer	2.50	1.15	.30
☐ 6 John Henry Johnson	.25	.11	.03
☐ 7 Jason Thompson	.25	.11	.03
☐ 8 Pat Zachry	.25	.11	.03
☐ 9 Dennis Eckersley	2.50	1.15	.30
☐ 10 Paul Splittorff	.25	.11	.03
☐ 11 Ron Guidry	1.25	.55	.16
☐ 12 Jeff Burroughs	.25	.11	.03
☐ 13 Rod Carew	3.00	1.35	.40
☐ 14A Buddy Bell (No trade mentioned)	1.50	.65	.19
☐ 14B Buddy Bell (Traded to Rangers)	.35	.16	.04
☐ 15 Jim Rice	1.75	.80	.22
☐ 16 Garry Maddox	.25	.11	.03
☐ 17 Willie McCovey	2.00	.90	.25
☐ 18 Steve Carlton	2.50	1.15	.30
☐ 19 J.R. Richard	.35	.16	.04
☐ 20 Paul Molitor	2.50	1.15	.30
☐ 21 Dave Parker	1.50	.65	.19
☐ 22 Pete Rose	7.00	3.10	.85
☐ 23 Vida Blue	.35	.16	.04
☐ 24 Richie Zisk	.25	.11	.03
☐ 25 Darrell Porter	.25	.11	.03
☐ 26 Dan Driessen	.25	.11	.03
☐ 27 Geoff Zahn	.25	.11	.03
☐ 28 Phil Niekro	1.50	.65	.19
☐ 29 Tom Seaver	5.00	2.30	.60
☐ 30 Fred Lynn	.75	.35	.09
☐ 31 Bill Bonham	.25	.11	.03
☐ 32 George Foster	.60	.25	.08
☐ 33 Terry Puhl	.35	.16	.04
☐ 34 John Candelaria	.35	.16	.04
☐ 35 Bob Knepper	.25	.11	.03
☐ 36 Fred Patek	.25	.11	.03
☐ 37 Chris Chambliss	.35	.16	.04
☐ 38 Bob Forsch	.25	.11	.03
☐ 39 Ken Griffey	.60	.25	.08
☐ 40 Jack Clark	.90	.40	.11
☐ 41 Dwight Evans	1.00	.45	.13
☐ 42 Lee Mazzilli	.25	.11	.03
☐ 43 Mario Guerrero	.25	.11	.03
☐ 44 Larry Bowa	.35	.16	.04
☐ 45 Carl Yastrzemski	4.50	2.00	.55
☐ 46 Reggie Jackson	6.00	2.70	.75
☐ 47 Rick Reuschel	.35	.16	.04
☐ 48 Mike Flanagan	.35	.16	.04
☐ 49 Gaylord Perry	2.50	1.15	.30
☐ 50 George Brett	6.00	2.70	.75
☐ 51 Craig Reynolds	.25	.11	.03
☐ 52 Dave Lopes	.35	.16	.04
☐ 53 Bill Almon	.25	.11	.03
☐ 54 Roy Howell	.25	.11	.03
☐ 55 Frank Tanana	.35	.16	.04
☐ 56 Doug Rau	.25	.11	.03
☐ 57 Rick Monday	.35	.16	.04
☐ 58 Jon Matlack	.25	.11	.03
☐ 59 Ron Jackson	.25	.11	.03
☐ 60 Jim Sundberg	.25	.11	.03

1980 Kellogg's

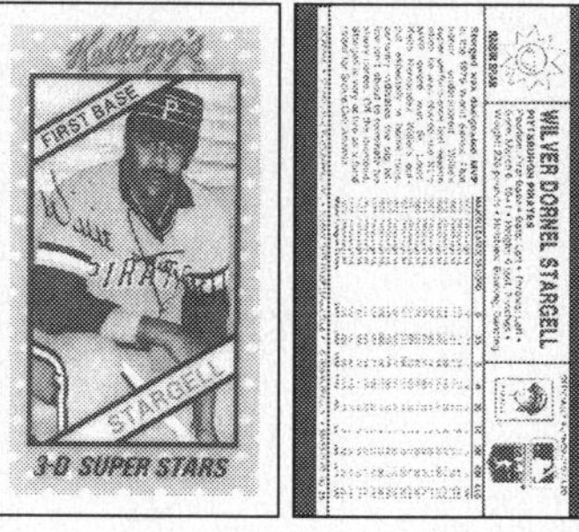

The cards in this 60-card set measure approximately 1 7/8" by 3 1/4". The 1980 Kellogg's 3-D set is quite similar to, but smaller (narrower) than, the other recent Kellogg's issues. Sets could be obtained card by card from cereal boxes or as a set from a box-top offer from the company.

	NRMT-MT	EXC	G-VG
COMPLETE SET (60)	30.00	13.50	3.80
COMMON PLAYER (1-60)	.25	.11	.03
☐ 1 Ross Grimsley	.25	.11	.03
☐ 2 Mike Schmidt	5.00	2.30	.60
☐ 3 Mike Flanagan	.35	.16	.04
☐ 4 Ron Guidry	.75	.35	.09
☐ 5 Bert Blyleven	.75	.35	.09
☐ 6 Dave Kingman	.50	.23	.06
☐ 7 Jeff Newman	.25	.11	.03
☐ 8 Steve Rogers	.25	.11	.03
☐ 9 George Brett	5.00	2.30	.60
☐ 10 Bruce Sutter	.60	.25	.08
☐ 11 Gorman Thomas	.35	.16	.04
☐ 12 Darrell Porter	.25	.11	.03
☐ 13 Roy Smalley	.25	.11	.03
☐ 14 Steve Carlton	3.00	1.35	.40
☐ 15 Jim Palmer	3.00	1.35	.40
☐ 16 Bob Bailor	.25	.11	.03
☐ 17 Jason Thompson	.25	.11	.03
☐ 18 Graig Nettles	.35	.16	.04
☐ 19 Ron Cey	.35	.16	.04
☐ 20 Nolan Ryan	10.00	4.50	1.25
☐ 21 Ellis Valentine	.25	.11	.03
☐ 22 Larry Hisle	.25	.11	.03
☐ 23 Dave Parker	1.00	.45	.13
☐ 24 Eddie Murray	4.00	1.80	.50
☐ 25 Willie Stargell	2.00	.90	.25
☐ 26 Reggie Jackson	4.50	2.00	.55
☐ 27 Carl Yastrzemski	3.50	1.55	.45
☐ 28 Andre Thornton	.25	.11	.03
☐ 29 Dave Lopes	.35	.16	.04
☐ 30 Ken Singleton	.35	.16	.04
☐ 31 Steve Garvey	2.00	.90	.25
☐ 32 Dave Winfield	3.50	1.55	.45

	NRMT-MT	EXC	G-VG
☐ 33 Steve Kemp	.35	.16	.04
☐ 34 Claudell Washington	.35	.16	.04
☐ 35 Pete Rose	5.00	2.30	.60
☐ 36 Cesar Cedeno	.35	.16	.04
☐ 37 John Stearns	.25	.11	.03
☐ 38 Lee Mazzilli	.25	.11	.03
☐ 39 Larry Bowa	.35	.16	.04
☐ 40 Fred Lynn	.60	.25	.08
☐ 41 Carlton Fisk	2.00	.90	.25
☐ 42 Vida Blue	.35	.16	.04
☐ 43 Keith Hernandez	.90	.40	.11
☐ 44 Jim Rice	1.50	.65	.19
☐ 45 Ted Simmons	.60	.25	.08
☐ 46 Chet Lemon	.35	.16	.04
☐ 47 Ferguson Jenkins	2.00	.90	.25
☐ 48 Gary Matthews	.35	.16	.04
☐ 49 Tom Seaver	4.50	2.00	.55
☐ 50 George Foster	.60	.25	.08
☐ 51 Phil Niekro	1.50	.65	.19
☐ 52 Johnny Bench	3.50	1.55	.45
☐ 53 Buddy Bell	.45	.20	.06
☐ 54 Lance Parrish	.90	.40	.11
☐ 55 Joaquin Andujar	.35	.16	.04
☐ 56 Don Baylor	.50	.23	.06
☐ 57 Jack Clark	.60	.25	.08
☐ 58 J.R. Richard	.35	.16	.04
☐ 59 Bruce Bochte	.25	.11	.03
☐ 60 Rod Carew	3.50	1.55	.45

1981 Kellogg's

The cards in this 66-card set measure 2 1/2" by 3 1/2". The 1981 Kellogg's set witnessed an increase in both the size of the card and the size of the set. For the first time, cards were not packed in cereal sizes but available only by mail-in procedure. The offer for the card set was advertised on boxes of Kellogg's Corn Flakes. The cards were printed on a different stock than in previous years, presumably to prevent the cracking problem which has plagued all Kellogg's 3-D issues. At the end of the promotion, the remainder of the sets not distributed (to cereal-eaters), were "sold" into the organized hobby, thus creating a situation where the set is relatively plentiful compared to other years of Kellogg's.

	NRMT-MT	EXC	G-VG
COMPLETE SET (66)	11.00	4.90	1.40
COMMON PLAYER (1-66)	.10	.05	.01
☐ 1 George Foster	.20	.09	.03
☐ 2 Jim Palmer	.60	.25	.08
☐ 3 Reggie Jackson	1.50	.65	.19
☐ 4 Al Oliver	.10	.05	.01
☐ 5 Mike Schmidt	2.00	.90	.25
☐ 6 Nolan Ryan	4.00	1.80	.50
☐ 7 Bucky Dent	.15	.07	.02
☐ 8 George Brett	2.00	.90	.25
☐ 9 Jim Rice	.30	.14	.04
☐ 10 Steve Garvey	.40	.18	.05
☐ 11 Willie Stargell	.60	.25	.08
☐ 12 Phil Niekro	.50	.23	.06
☐ 13 Dave Parker	.20	.09	.03
☐ 14 Cesar Cedeno	.10	.05	.01
☐ 15 Don Baylor	.15	.07	.02
☐ 16 J.R. Richard	.10	.05	.01
☐ 17 Tony Perez	.30	.14	.04
☐ 18 Eddie Murray	1.25	.55	.16
☐ 19 Chet Lemon	.10	.05	.01
☐ 20 Ben Oglivie	.10	.05	.01
☐ 21 Dave Winfield	1.25	.55	.16
☐ 22 Joe Morgan	.60	.25	.08
☐ 23 Vida Blue	.10	.05	.01
☐ 24 Willie Wilson	.15	.07	.02
☐ 25 Steve Henderson	.10	.05	.01
☐ 26 Rod Carew	1.00	.45	.13
☐ 27 Garry Templeton	.10	.05	.01
☐ 28 Dave Concepcion	.20	.09	.03
☐ 29 Dave Lopes	.10	.05	.01
☐ 30 Ken Landreaux	.10	.05	.01
☐ 31 Keith Hernandez	.25	.11	.03
☐ 32 Cecil Cooper	.15	.07	.02
☐ 33 Rickey Henderson	1.50	.65	.19
☐ 34 Frank White	.10	.05	.01
☐ 35 George Hendrick	.10	.05	.01
☐ 36 Reggie Smith	.10	.05	.01
☐ 37 Tug McGraw	.15	.07	.02
☐ 38 Tom Seaver	1.50	.65	.19
☐ 39 Ken Singleton	.10	.05	.01
☐ 40 Fred Lynn	.15	.07	.02
☐ 41 Rich Gossage	.20	.09	.03
☐ 42 Terry Puhl	.10	.05	.01
☐ 43 Larry Bowa	.15	.07	.02
☐ 44 Phil Garner	.15	.07	.02
☐ 45 Ron Guidry	.20	.09	.03
☐ 46 Lee Mazzilli	.10	.05	.01
☐ 47 Dave Kingman	.15	.07	.02
☐ 48 Carl Yastrzemski	.90	.40	.11
☐ 49 Rick Burleson	.10	.05	.01
☐ 50 Steve Carlton	.75	.35	.09
☐ 51 Alan Trammell	.25	.11	.03
☐ 52 Tommy John	.15	.07	.02
☐ 53 Paul Molitor	.40	.18	.05
☐ 54 Joe Charboneau	.10	.05	.01
☐ 55 Rick Langford	.10	.05	.01
☐ 56 Bruce Sutter	.15	.07	.02
☐ 57 Robin Yount	2.00	.90	.25
☐ 58 Steve Stone	.10	.05	.01
☐ 59 Larry Gura	.10	.05	.01
☐ 60 Mike Flanagan	.15	.07	.02
☐ 61 Bob Horner	.15	.07	.02
☐ 62 Bruce Bochte	.10	.05	.01
☐ 63 Pete Rose	1.00	.45	.13
☐ 64 Buddy Bell	.10	.05	.01
☐ 65 Johnny Bench	1.00	.45	.13
☐ 66 Mike Hargrove	.10	.05	.01

1982 Kellogg's

The cards in this 64-card set measure 2 1/8" by 3 1/4". The 1982 version of 3-D cards prepared for the Kellogg Company by Visual Panographics, Inc., is not only smaller in physical dimensions from the 1981 series (which was standard card size at 2 1/2" by 3 1/2") but is also two cards shorter in length (64 in '82 and 66 in '81). In addition, while retaining the policy of not inserting single cards into cereal packages and offering the sets through box-top mail-ins only, the Kellogg Company accepted box tops from four types of cereals, as opposed to only one type the previous year. Each card features a color 3-D ballplayer picture with a vertical line of white stars on each side set upon a blue background. The player's name and the word Kellogg's are printed in red on the obverse, and the card number is found on the bottom right of the reverse. Every card in the set has a statistical procedural error that was never corrected. All seasonal averages were added up and then divided by the number of seasons played.

	NRMT-MT	EXC	G-VG
COMPLETE SET (64)	16.00	7.25	2.00
COMMON PLAYER (1-64)	.15	.07	.02
☐ 1 Richie Zisk	.15	.07	.02
☐ 2 Bill Buckner	.25	.11	.03
☐ 3 George Brett	2.00	.90	.25
☐ 4 Rickey Henderson	2.00	.90	.25
☐ 5 Jack Morris	.35	.16	.04
☐ 6 Ozzie Smith	1.25	.55	.16
☐ 7 Rollie Fingers	.60	.25	.08
☐ 8 Tom Seaver	1.50	.65	.19
☐ 9 Fernando Valuenzuela	.25	.11	.03
☐ 10 Hubie Brooks	.15	.07	.02
☐ 11 Nolan Ryan	3.00	1.35	.40
☐ 12 Dave Winfield	1.00	.45	.13
☐ 13 Bob Horner	.20	.09	.03
☐ 14 Reggie Jackson	1.25	.55	.16
☐ 15 Burt Hooton	.15	.07	.02
☐ 16 Mike Schmidt	2.00	.90	.25
☐ 17 Bruce Sutter	.25	.11	.03
☐ 18 Pete Rose	1.00	.45	.13
☐ 19 Dave Kingman	.25	.11	.03
☐ 20 Neil Allen	.15	.07	.02
☐ 21 Don Sutton	.50	.23	.06
☐ 22 Dave Concepcion	.25	.11	.03
☐ 23 Keith Hernandez	.25	.11	.03
☐ 24 Gary Carter	.50	.23	.06
☐ 25 Carlton Fisk	.75	.35	.09
☐ 26 Ron Guidry	.25	.11	.03
☐ 27 Steve Carlton	.75	.35	.09
☐ 28 Robin Yount	2.00	.90	.25
☐ 29 John Castino	.15	.07	.02
☐ 30 Johnny Bench	1.00	.45	.13
☐ 31 Bob Knepper	.15	.07	.02
☐ 32 Rich Gossage	.25	.11	.03
☐ 33 Buddy Bell	.15	.07	.02
☐ 34 Art Howe	.15	.07	.02
☐ 35 Tony Armas	.15	.07	.02
☐ 36 Phil Niekro	.35	.16	.04
☐ 37 Len Barker	.15	.07	.02
☐ 38 Bob Grich	.25	.11	.03
☐ 39 Steve Kemp	.15	.07	.02
☐ 40 Kirk Gibson	.35	.16	.04
☐ 41 Carney Lansford	.25	.11	.03
☐ 42 Jim Palmer	.75	.35	.09
☐ 43 Carl Yastrzemski	.90	.40	.11
☐ 44 Rick Burleson	.15	.07	.02
☐ 45 Dwight Evans	.25	.11	.03
☐ 46 Ron Cey	.25	.11	.03
☐ 47 Steve Garvey	.35	.16	.04
☐ 48 Dave Parker	.35	.16	.04
☐ 49 Mike Easler	.15	.07	.02
☐ 50 Dusty Baker	.25	.11	.03
☐ 51 Rod Carew	1.00	.45	.13
☐ 52 Chris Chambliss	.25	.11	.03
☐ 53 Tim Raines	.35	.16	.04
☐ 54 Chet Lemon	.15	.07	.02
☐ 55 Bill Madlock	.25	.11	.03
☐ 56 George Foster	.25	.11	.03
☐ 57 Dwayne Murphy	.15	.07	.02
☐ 58 Ken Singleton	.25	.11	.03
☐ 59 Mike Norris	.15	.07	.02
☐ 60 Cecil Cooper	.25	.11	.03
☐ 61 Al Oliver	.25	.11	.03
☐ 62 Willie Wilson	.25	.11	.03
☐ 63 Vida Blue	.25	.11	.03
☐ 64 Eddie Murray	1.00	.45	.13

1983 Kellogg's

The cards in this 60-card set measure approximately 1 7/8" by 3 1/4". For the 14th year in a row, the Kellogg Company issued a card set of Major League players. The set of 3-D cards contains the photo, player's autograph, Kellogg's logo, and name and position of the player on the front of the card. The backs feature the player's team logo, career

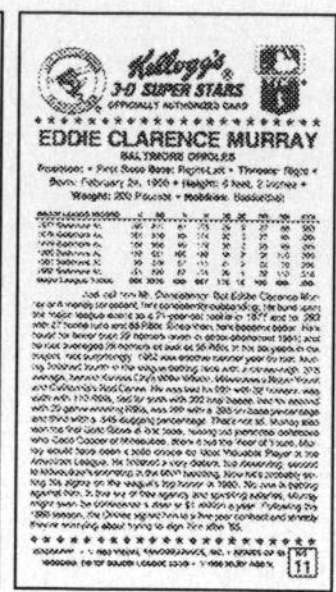

statistics, player biography, and a narrative on the player's career. Every card in the set has a statistical procedural error that was never corrected. All seasonal averages were added up and then divided by the number of seasons played.

	NRMT-MT	EXC	G-VG
COMPLETE SET (60)	15.00	6.75	1.90
COMMON PLAYER (1-60)	.15	.07	.02
☐ 1 Rod Carew	.90	.40	.11
☐ 2 Rollie Fingers	.60	.25	.08
☐ 3 Reggie Jackson	1.25	.55	.16
☐ 4 George Brett	1.50	.65	.19
☐ 5 Hal McRae	.25	.11	.03
☐ 6 Pete Rose	1.00	.45	.13
☐ 7 Fernando Valenzuela	.25	.11	.03
☐ 8 Rickey Henderson	1.25	.55	.16
☐ 9 Carl Yastrzemski	.90	.40	.11
☐ 10 Rich Gossage	.25	.11	.03
☐ 11 Eddie Murray	.90	.40	.11
☐ 12 Buddy Bell	.25	.11	.03
☐ 13 Jim Rice	.35	.16	.04
☐ 14 Robin Yount	1.50	.65	.19
☐ 15 Dave Winfield	.75	.35	.09
☐ 16 Harold Baines	.25	.11	.03
☐ 17 Garry Templeton	.15	.07	.02
☐ 18 Bill Madlock	.25	.11	.03
☐ 19 Pete Vuckovich	.15	.07	.02
☐ 20 Pedro Guerrero	.25	.11	.03
☐ 21 Ozzie Smith	.75	.35	.09
☐ 22 George Foster	.25	.11	.03
☐ 23 Willie Wilson	.25	.11	.03
☐ 24 Johnny Ray	.15	.07	.02
☐ 25 George Hendrick	.25	.11	.03
☐ 26 Andre Thornton	.15	.07	.02
☐ 27 Leon Durham	.15	.07	.02
☐ 28 Cecil Cooper	.25	.11	.03
☐ 29 Don Baylor	.35	.16	.04
☐ 30 Lonnie Smith	.25	.11	.03
☐ 31 Nolan Ryan	3.00	1.35	.40
☐ 32 Dan Quisenberry	.25	.11	.03
☐ 33 Len Barker	.15	.07	.02
☐ 34 Neil Allen	.15	.07	.02
☐ 35 Jack Morris	.35	.16	.04
☐ 36 Dave Stieb	.25	.11	.03
☐ 37 Bruce Sutter	.25	.11	.03
☐ 38 Jim Sundberg	.15	.07	.02
☐ 39 Jim Palmer	.75	.35	.09
☐ 40 Lance Parrish	.25	.11	.03
☐ 41 Floyd Bannister	.15	.07	.02
☐ 42 Larry Gura	.15	.07	.02
☐ 43 Britt Burns	.15	.07	.02
☐ 44 Toby Harrah	.15	.07	.02
☐ 45 Steve Carlton	.75	.35	.09
☐ 46 Greg Minton	.15	.07	.02
☐ 47 Gorman Thomas	.15	.07	.02
☐ 48 Jack Clark	.25	.11	.03
☐ 49 Keith Hernandez	.25	.11	.03
☐ 50 Greg Luzinski	.25	.11	.03
☐ 51 Fred Lynn	.25	.11	.03
☐ 52 Dale Murphy	.60	.25	.08
☐ 53 Kent Hrbek	.35	.16	.04
☐ 54 Bob Horner	.15	.07	.02
☐ 55 Gary Carter	.35	.16	.04
☐ 56 Carlton Fisk	.75	.35	.09
☐ 57 Dave Concepcion	.25	.11	.03
☐ 58 Mike Schmidt	1.50	.65	.19
☐ 59 Bill Buckner	.25	.11	.03
☐ 60 Bob Grich	.25	.11	.03

1991 Kellogg's Leyendas

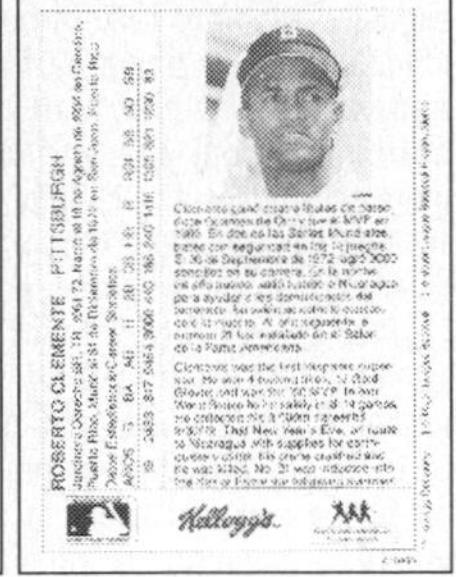

This 11-card "Hispanic Legends of Baseball" set was sponsored by Kellogg's and celebrates ten Hispanic greats from Major League Baseball. The cards were inserted in boxes of Kellogg's Corn Flakes, Frosted Flakes, and Froot Loops in selected geographic areas. The cards measure the standard size (2 1/2" by 3 1/2"). The fronts feature color player photos bordered in white. The pictures are accented above and on the left by red, orange, and yellow border stripes. The set name appears on a home plate icon at the upper left corner, while the player's name appears in a white bar that cuts across the picture. On the bilingual (Spanish and English) backs, the biographical and statistical information are vertically oriented on the left portion, while a black and white head shot and player profile fill out the remainder of the back. The cards are unnumbered and checklisted below in alphabetical order.

	MT	EX-MT	VG
COMPLETE SET (11)	10.00	4.50	1.25
COMMON PLAYER (1-10)	.50	.23	.06
☐ 1 Bert Campaneris	.60	.25	.08
☐ 2 Rod Carew	2.00	.90	.25
☐ 3 Rico Carty	.75	.35	.09
☐ 4 Cesar Cedeno	.60	.25	.08
☐ 5 Orlando Cepeda	1.00	.45	.13
☐ 6 Roberto Clemente	4.00	1.80	.50
☐ 7 Mike Cuellar	.50	.23	.06
☐ 8 Ed Figueroa	.50	.23	.06
☐ 9 Minnie Minoso	.75	.35	.09
☐ 10 Manny Sanguillen	.60	.25	.08
☐ NNO Title Card	.50	.23	.06

1991 Kellogg's Stand Ups

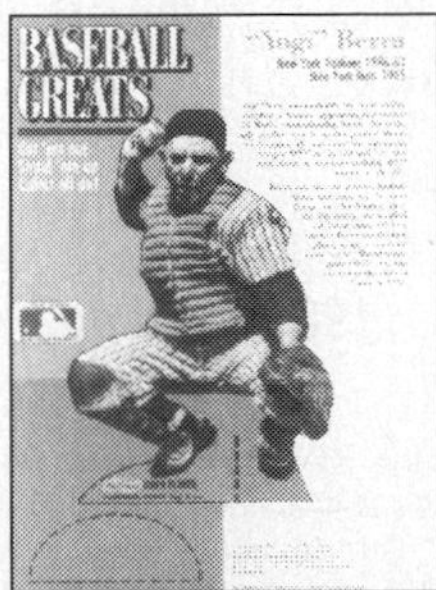

This set was sponsored by Kellogg's in honor of six retired baseball stars as part of a promotion entitled "Baseball Greats." Six different stars are featured on the backs of (specially marked 7 oz. and 12 oz.) Kellogg's Corn Flakes boxes. Since there were two different size boxes, there are two sizes of each card, the larger is approximately 9 1/4" by 6" coming from the 12 oz. box. The color action portraits can be cut out and stood up for display, and career highlights appear to the right of the stand up. The boxes are unnumbered and checklisted below in alphabetical order. All six of these players were also included in the 15-card Kellogg's 3D Baseball Greats set. The complete set price below includes either the small or the large package cards but not both.

	MT	EX-MT	VG
COMPLETE SET (6)	9.00	4.00	1.15
COMMON PLAYER (1-6)	2.00	.90	.25
☐ 1 Hank Aaron	3.00	1.35	.40
☐ 2 Ernie Banks	2.50	1.15	.30
☐ 3 Yogi Berra	2.50	1.15	.30
☐ 4 Lou Brock	2.00	.90	.25
☐ 5 Steve Carlton	2.00	.90	.25
☐ 6 Bob Gibson	2.00	.90	.25

1991 Kellogg's 3D

Sportflics/Optigraphics produced this 15-card set for Kellogg's, and the cards measure approximately 2 1/2" by 3 5/16". The fronts have a three-dimensional image that alternates between a posed or action color shot and a head and shoulders close-up. The card face is aqua blue, with white stripes (that turn pink) and white borders. In red and dark blue print, the horizontally oriented backs have a facial drawing of the player on the left half, and career summary on the right half. The cards are numbered on the back. The cards were inserted in specially marked boxes (18 oz. and 24 oz. only) of Kellogg's Corn Flakes. In addition, the complete set and a blue display rack were available through a mail-in offer for 4.95 and two UPC symbols.

	MT	EX-MT	VG
COMPLETE SET (15)	7.50	3.40	.95
COMMON PLAYER (1-15)	.50	.23	.06
☐ 1 Gaylord Perry	.60	.25	.08
☐ 2 Hank Aaron	1.25	.55	.16
☐ 3 Willie Mays	1.25	.55	.16
☐ 4 Ernie Banks	.90	.40	.11
☐ 5 Bob Gibson	.60	.25	.08
☐ 6 Harmon Killebrew	.60	.25	.08
☐ 7 Rollie Fingers	.60	.25	.08
☐ 8 Steve Carlton	.75	.35	.09
☐ 9 Billy Williams	.60	.25	.08
☐ 10 Lou Brock	.75	.35	.09
☐ 11 Yogi Berra	.90	.40	.11
☐ 12 Warren Spahn	.75	.35	.09
☐ 13 Boog Powell	.50	.23	.06
☐ 14 Don Baylor	.50	.23	.06
☐ 15 Ralph Kiner	.75	.35	.09

1992 Kellogg's All-Stars

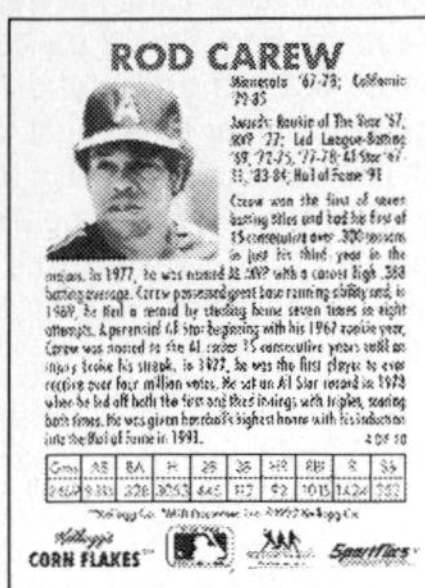

This ten-card set was produced by Optigraphics Corp. (Grand Prairie, TX) for Kellogg's and features retired baseball stars. One card was protected by a cello pack and inserted into Kellogg's cereal boxes. In the U.S., the cards were inserted in boxes of Corn Flakes, while in Canada they were inserted in Frosted Flakes and some other cereals. The complete set and a baseball display board to hold the collection were available through a mail-in offer for 4.75 and two UPC symbols from the side panel of Corn Flakes boxes (in Canada, for 7.99 and three tokens; one token was found on the side panel of each cereal box). The cards measure the standard size (2 1/2" by 3 1/2"). The front of the "Double Action" cards have a three-dimensional image that alternates between two action shots and gives the impression of a batter or pitcher in motion. The pictures are bordered in red, white, and blue. The backs carry a black and white close-up photo, summary of the player's career (teams and years he played for them), awards, and career highlights. The cards are numbered on the back.

	MT	EX-MT	VG
COMPLETE SET (10)	8.00	3.60	1.00
COMMON PLAYER (1-10)	.50	.23	.06
☐ 1 Willie Stargell	1.00	.45	.13
☐ 2 Tony Perez	.75	.35	.09
☐ 3 Jim Palmer	1.25	.55	.16
☐ 4 Rod Carew	1.25	.55	.16
☐ 5 Tom Seaver	2.00	.90	.25
☐ 6 Phil Niekro	.90	.40	.11
☐ 7 Bill Madlock	.50	.23	.06
☐ 8 Jim Rice	.60	.25	.08
☐ 9 Dan Quisenberry	.50	.23	.06
☐ 10 Mike Schmidt	2.50	1.15	.30

1982 K-Mart

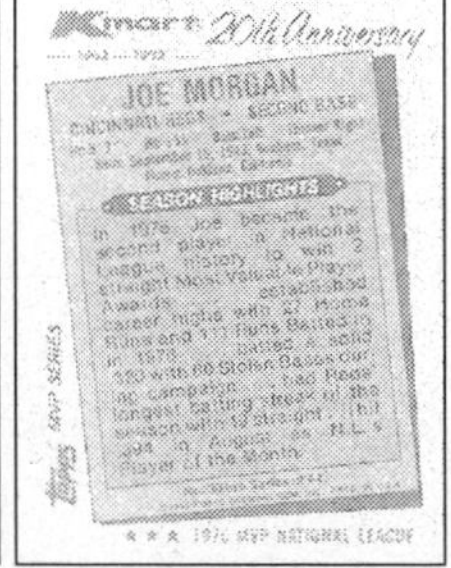

The cards in this 44-card set measure 2 1/2" by 3 1/2". This set was mass produced by Topps for K-Mart's 20th Anniversary Celebration and distributed in a custom box. The set features Topps cards of National and American League MVP's from 1962 through 1981. The backs highlight individual MVP winning performances. The dual National League MVP winners of 1979 and special cards commemorating the accomplishments of Drysdale (scoreless consecutive innings pitched streak), Aaron (home run record), and Rose (National League most hits lifetime record) round out the set. The 1975 Fred Lynn card is an original construction from the multi-player "Rookie Outfielders" card of Lynn of 1975. The Maury Wills card number 2, similarly, was created after the fact as Maury was not originally included in the 1962 Topps set. Topps had solved the same problem in essentially the same way in their 1975 set on card number 200.

	NRMT-MT	EXC	G-VG
COMPLETE SET (44)	1.75	.80	.22
COMMON PLAYER (1-44)	.03	.01	.00
☐ 1 Mickey Mantle: 62AL	.50	.23	.06
☐ 2 Maury Wills: 62NL	.05	.02	.01
☐ 3 Elston Howard: 63AL	.03	.01	.00
☐ 4 Sandy Koufax: 63NL	.15	.07	.02
☐ 5 Brooks Robinson: 64AL	.08	.04	.01
☐ 6 Ken Boyer: 64NL	.03	.01	.00
☐ 7 Zoilo Versalles: 65AL	.03	.01	.00
☐ 8 Willie Mays: 65NL	.20	.09	.03
☐ 9 Frank Robinson: 66AL	.06	.03	.01
☐ 10 Bob Clemente: 66NL	.15	.07	.02
☐ 11 Carl Yastrzemski: 67AL	.12	.05	.02
☐ 12 Orlando Cepeda: 67NL	.03	.01	.00
☐ 13 Denny McLain: 68AL	.03	.01	.00
☐ 14 Bob Gibson: 68NL	.06	.03	.01
☐ 15 Harmon Killebrew: 69AL	.06	.03	.01
☐ 16 Willie McCovey: 69NL	.06	.03	.01
☐ 17 Boog Powell: 70AL	.03	.01	.00
☐ 18 Johnny Bench: 70NL	.10	.05	.01
☐ 19 Vida Blue: 71AL	.03	.01	.00
☐ 20 Joe Torre: 71NL	.03	.01	.00
☐ 21 Rich Allen: 72AL	.03	.01	.00
☐ 22 Johnny Bench: 72NL	.10	.05	.01
☐ 23 Reggie Jackson: 73AL	.12	.05	.02
☐ 24 Pete Rose: 73NL	.10	.05	.01
☐ 25 Jeff Burroughs: 74AL	.03	.01	.00
☐ 26 Steve Garvey: 74NL	.03	.01	.00
☐ 27 Fred Lynn: 75AL	.03	.01	.00
☐ 28 Joe Morgan: 75NL	.06	.03	.01
☐ 29 Thurman Munson: 76AL	.06	.03	.01
☐ 30 Joe Morgan: 76NL	.06	.03	.01
☐ 31 Rod Carew: 77AL	.06	.03	.01
☐ 32 George Foster: 77NL	.03	.01	.00
☐ 33 Jim Rice: 78AL	.03	.01	.00
☐ 34 Dave Parker: 78NL	.03	.01	.00
☐ 35 Don Baylor: 79AL	.03	.01	.00
☐ 36 Keith Hernandez: 79NL	.03	.01	.00
☐ 37 Willie Stargell: 79NL	.06	.03	.01
☐ 38 George Brett: 80AL	.15	.07	.02
☐ 39 Mike Schmidt: 80NL	.10	.05	.01
☐ 40 Rollie Fingers: 81AL	.05	.02	.01
☐ 41 Mike Schmidt: 81NL	.10	.05	.01
☐ 42 '68 HL: Don Drysdale (Scoreless innings)	.06	.03	.01
☐ 43 '74 HL: Hank Aaron (Home run record)	.20	.09	.03
☐ 44 '81 HL: Pete Rose (NL most hits)	.15	.07	.02

1987 K-Mart

Topps produced this 33-card boxed set for K-Mart. The set celebrates K-Mart's 25th anniversary and is subtitled, "Stars of the Decades." Card fronts feature a color photo of the player oriented diagonally. Cards measure 2 1/2" by 3 1/2" and are numbered on the back. Card backs provide statistics for the player's best decade. The set numbering is arranged alphabetically within decade groups: 1960s (1-11), 1970s (12-22), and 1980s (23-33).

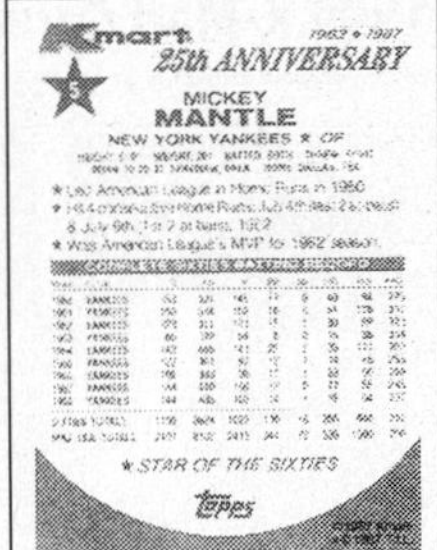

	MT	EX-MT	VG
COMPLETE SET (33)	5.00	2.30	.60
COMMON PLAYER (1-33)	.10	.05	.01
☐ 1 Hank Aaron	.50	.23	.06
☐ 2 Roberto Clemente	.40	.18	.05
☐ 3 Bob Gibson	.15	.07	.02
☐ 4 Harmon Killebrew	.15	.07	.02
☐ 5 Mickey Mantle	1.50	.65	.19
☐ 6 Juan Marichal	.15	.07	.02
☐ 7 Roger Maris	.35	.16	.04
☐ 8 Willie Mays	.50	.23	.06
☐ 9 Brooks Robinson	.20	.09	.03
☐ 10 Frank Robinson	.15	.07	.02
☐ 11 Carl Yastrzemski	.30	.14	.04
☐ 12 Johnny Bench	.30	.14	.04
☐ 13 Lou Brock	.20	.09	.03
☐ 14 Rod Carew	.20	.09	.03
☐ 15 Steve Carlton	.25	.11	.03
☐ 16 Reggie Jackson	.35	.16	.04
☐ 17 Jim Palmer	.25	.11	.03
☐ 18 Jim Rice	.10	.05	.01
☐ 19 Pete Rose	.50	.23	.06
☐ 20 Nolan Ryan	1.50	.65	.19
☐ 21 Tom Seaver	.50	.23	.06
☐ 22 Willie Stargell	.20	.09	.03
☐ 23 Wade Boggs	.40	.18	.05
☐ 24 George Brett	.50	.23	.06
☐ 25 Gary Carter	.20	.09	.03
☐ 26 Dwight Gooden	.25	.11	.03
☐ 27 Rickey Henderson	.50	.23	.06
☐ 28 Don Mattingly	.50	.23	.06
☐ 29 Dale Murphy	.20	.09	.03
☐ 30 Eddie Murray	.25	.11	.03
☐ 31 Mike Schmidt	.50	.23	.06
☐ 32 Darryl Strawberry	.40	.18	.05
☐ 33 Fernando Valenzuela	.10	.05	.01

1988 K-Mart Moments

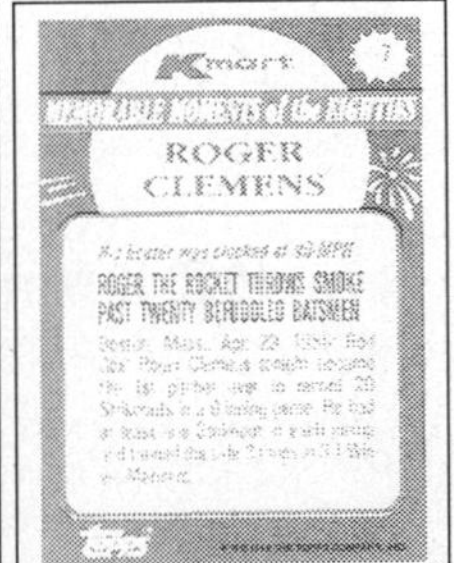

Topps produced this 33-card boxed set exclusively for K-Mart. The set is subtitled, "Memorable Moments." Card fronts feature a color photo of the player with the K-Mart logo in lower right corner. Cards measure 2 1/2" by 3 1/2" and are numbered on the back. Card backs provide details for that player's "memorable moment." The set is packaged in a bright yellow and green box with a checklist on the back panel of the box. The cards in the set were numbered by K-Mart essentially in alphabetical order.

	MT	EX-MT	VG
COMPLETE SET (33)	4.00	1.80	.50
COMMON PLAYER (1-33)	.10	.05	.01
☐ 1 George Bell	.15	.07	.02
☐ 2 Wade Boggs	.50	.23	.06
☐ 3 George Brett	.50	.23	.06
☐ 4 Jose Canseco	.75	.35	.09
☐ 5 Jack Clark	.10	.05	.01
☐ 6 Will Clark	.75	.35	.09
☐ 7 Roger Clemens	1.00	.45	.13
☐ 8 Vince Coleman	.20	.09	.03
☐ 9 Andre Dawson	.30	.14	.04
☐ 10 Dwight Gooden	.25	.11	.03
☐ 11 Pedro Guerrero	.10	.05	.01
☐ 12 Tony Gywnn	.50	.23	.06
☐ 13 Rickey Henderson	.60	.25	.08
☐ 14 Keith Hernandez	.15	.07	.02
☐ 15 Don Mattingly	.60	.25	.08
☐ 16 Mark McGwire	.60	.25	.08
☐ 17 Paul Molitor	.20	.09	.03
☐ 18 Dale Murphy	.20	.09	.03
☐ 19 Tim Raines	.15	.07	.02
☐ 20 Dave Righetti	.10	.05	.01
☐ 21 Cal Ripken	1.00	.45	.13
☐ 22 Pete Rose	.60	.25	.08
☐ 23 Nolan Ryan	1.50	.65	.19
☐ 24 Benito Santiago	.20	.09	.03
☐ 25 Mike Schmidt	.75	.35	.09
☐ 26 Mike Scott	.10	.05	.01
☐ 27 Kevin Seitzer	.10	.05	.01
☐ 28 Ozzie Smith	.30	.14	.04
☐ 29 Darryl Strawberry	.50	.23	.06
☐ 30 Rick Sutcliffe	.10	.05	.01
☐ 31 Fernando Valenzuela	.10	.05	.01
☐ 32 Todd Worrell	.15	.07	.02
☐ 33 Robin Yount	.50	.23	.06

1989 K-Mart Career Batting Leaders

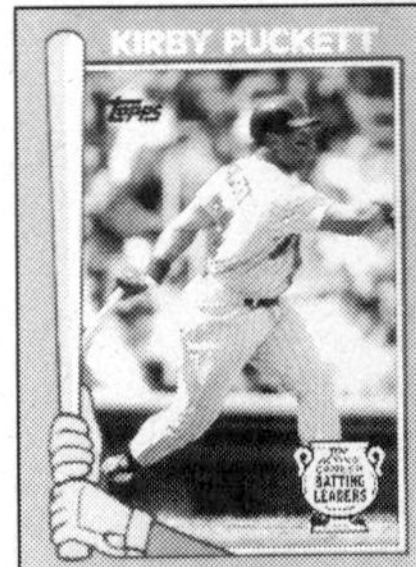

The 1989 K-Mart Career Batting Leaders set contains 22 standard-size (2 1/2" by 3 1/2") glossy cards. The fronts are bright red. The set depicts the 22 veterans with the highest lifetime batting averages. The cards were distributed one per Topps blister pack. These blister packs were sold exclusively through K-Mart stores. The cards in the set were numbered by K-Mart essentially in order of highest active career batting average entering the 1989 season.

	MT	EX-MT	VG
COMPLETE SET (22)	10.00	4.50	1.25
COMMON PLAYER (1-22)	.35	.16	.04
☐ 1 Wade Boggs	1.00	.45	.13
☐ 2 Tony Gwynn	1.00	.45	.13
☐ 3 Don Mattingly	1.00	.45	.13
☐ 4 Kirby Puckett	1.25	.55	.16
☐ 5 George Brett	1.00	.45	.13
☐ 6 Pedro Guerrero	.35	.16	.04
☐ 7 Tim Raines	.45	.20	.06
☐ 8 Keith Hernandez	.45	.20	.06
☐ 9 Jim Rice	.45	.20	.06
☐ 10 Paul Molitor	.60	.25	.08
☐ 11 Eddie Murray	.75	.35	.09

☐ 12 Willie McGee	.35	.16	.04
☐ 13 Dave Parker	.45	.20	.06
☐ 14 Julio Franco	.45	.20	.06
☐ 15 Rickey Henderson	1.00	.45	.13
☐ 16 Kent Hrbek	.45	.20	.06
☐ 17 Willie Wilson	.35	.16	.04
☐ 18 Johnny Ray	.35	.16	.04
☐ 19 Pat Tabler	.35	.16	.04
☐ 20 Carney Lansford	.35	.16	.04
☐ 21 Robin Yount	1.00	.45	.13
☐ 22 Alan Trammell	.45	.20	.06

1989 K-Mart Dream Team

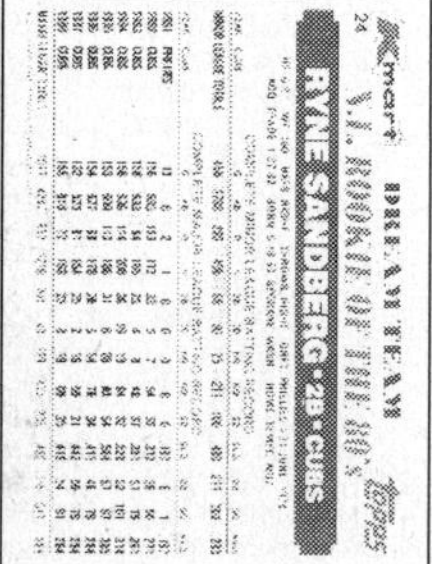

The 1989 K-Mart Dream Team set contains 33 standard-size (2 1/2" by 3 1/2") glossy cards. The fronts are blue. The cards were distributed as a boxed set through K-Mart stores. The set features 11 major league rookies of 1988 plus 11 "American League Rookies of the '80s" and 11 "National League Rookies of the '80s". The complete subject list for the set is provided on the back panel of the custom box.

	MT	EX-MT	VG
COMPLETE SET (33)	3.50	1.55	.45
COMMON PLAYER (1-33)	.10	.05	.01
☐ 1 Mark Grace	.50	.23	.06
☐ 2 Ron Gant	.50	.23	.06
☐ 3 Chris Sabo	.25	.11	.03
☐ 4 Walt Weiss	.15	.07	.02
☐ 5 Jay Buhner	.20	.09	.03
☐ 6 Cecil Espy	.10	.05	.01
☐ 7 Dave Gallagher	.10	.05	.01
☐ 8 Damon Berryhill	.10	.05	.01
☐ 9 Tim Belcher	.10	.05	.01
☐ 10 Paul Gibson	.10	.05	.01
☐ 11 Gregg Jefferies	.50	.23	.06
☐ 12 Don Mattingly	.50	.23	.06
☐ 13 Harold Reynolds	.10	.05	.01
☐ 14 Wade Boggs	.40	.18	.05
☐ 15 Cal Ripken	.75	.35	.09
☐ 16 Kirby Puckett	.50	.23	.06
☐ 17 George Bell	.15	.07	.02
☐ 18 Jose Canseco	.60	.25	.08
☐ 19 Terry Steinbach	.10	.05	.01
☐ 20 Roger Clemens	.75	.35	.09
☐ 21 Mark Langston	.10	.05	.01
☐ 22 Harold Baines	.10	.05	.01
☐ 23 Will Clark	.60	.25	.08
☐ 24 Ryne Sandberg	.75	.35	.09
☐ 25 Tim Wallach	.10	.05	.01
☐ 26 Shawon Dunston	.10	.05	.01
☐ 27 Tim Raines	.15	.07	.02
☐ 28 Darryl Strawberry	.40	.18	.05
☐ 29 Tony Gwynn	.40	.18	.05
☐ 30 Tony Pena	.10	.05	.01
☐ 31 Dwight Gooden	.20	.09	.03
☐ 32 Fernando Valenzuela	.10	.05	.01
☐ 33 Pedro Guerrero	.10	.05	.01

1990 K-Mart Career Batting Leaders

The 1990 K-Mart Career Batting Leaders set contains 22 standard-size (2 1/2" by 3 1/2") cards. The front borders are emerald green, and the backs are white, blue and evergreen. This set, like the 1989 set of the same name, depicts the 22 major leaguers with the highest lifetime batting averages (minimum 765 games). The card numbers correspond to the player's rank in terms of career batting average. Many of the photos are the same as those from the 1989 set. The cards were distributed one per special Topps blister pack available only at K-Mart stores and were produced by Topps. The K-Mart logo does not appear anywhere on the cards themselves, although there is a Topps logo on the front and back of each card.

	MT	EX-MT	VG
COMPLETE SET (22)	9.00	4.00	1.15
COMMON PLAYER (1-22)	.35	.16	.04
☐ 1 Wade Boggs	1.00	.45	.13
☐ 2 Tony Gwynn	1.00	.45	.13
☐ 3 Kirby Puckett	1.25	.55	.16
☐ 4 Don Mattingly	1.00	.45	.13
☐ 5 George Brett	1.00	.45	.13
☐ 6 Pedro Guerrero	.35	.16	.04
☐ 7 Tim Raines	.45	.20	.06
☐ 8 Paul Molitor	.60	.25	.08
☐ 9 Jim Rice	.45	.20	.06
☐ 10 Keith Hernandez	.45	.20	.06
☐ 11 Julio Franco	.45	.20	.06
☐ 12 Carney Lansford	.35	.16	.04
☐ 13 Dave Parker	.45	.20	.06
☐ 14 Willie McGee	.35	.16	.04
☐ 15 Robin Yount	1.00	.45	.13
☐ 16 Tony Fernandez	.35	.16	.04
☐ 17 Eddie Murray	.75	.35	.09
☐ 18 Johnny Ray	.35	.16	.04
☐ 19 Lonnie Smith	.35	.16	.04
☐ 20 Phil Bradley	.35	.16	.04
☐ 21 Rickey Henderson	1.00	.45	.13
☐ 22 Kent Hrbek	.45	.20	.06

1990 K-Mart Superstars

The 1990 K-Mart Superstars set is a 33-card, standard-size (2 1/2" by 3 1/2") set issued for the K-Mart chain by the Topps Company. This set was issued with a piece of gum in the custom set box.

	MT	EX-MT	VG
COMPLETE SET (33)	3.50	1.55	.45
COMMON PLAYER (1-33)	.10	.05	.01
☐ 1 Will Clark	.50	.23	.06
☐ 2 Ryne Sandberg	.75	.35	.09
☐ 3 Howard Johnson	.15	.07	.02
☐ 4 Ozzie Smith	.25	.11	.03
☐ 5 Tony Gwynn	.40	.18	.05
☐ 6 Kevin Mitchell	.20	.09	.03
☐ 7 Jerome Walton	.10	.05	.01

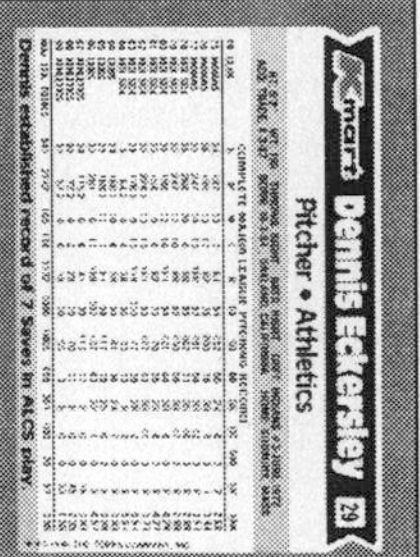

☐ 8 Craig Biggio	.15	.07	.02
☐ 9 Mike Scott	.10	.05	.01
☐ 10 Dwight Gooden	.20	.09	.03
☐ 11 Sid Fernandez	.10	.05	.01
☐ 12 Joe Magrane	.10	.05	.01
☐ 13 Jay Howell	.10	.05	.01
☐ 14 Mark Davis	.10	.05	.01
☐ 15 Pedro Guerrero	.10	.05	.01
☐ 16 Glenn Davis	.15	.07	.02
☐ 17 Don Mattingly	.50	.23	.06
☐ 18 Julio Franco	.15	.07	.02
☐ 19 Wade Boggs	.40	.18	.05
☐ 20 Cal Ripken	.75	.35	.09
☐ 21 Jose Canseco	.50	.23	.06
☐ 22 Kirby Puckett	.50	.23	.06
☐ 23 Rickey Henderson	.50	.23	.06
☐ 24 Mickey Tettleton	.10	.05	.01
☐ 25 Nolan Ryan	1.00	.45	.13
☐ 26 Bret Saberhagen	.15	.07	.02
☐ 27 Jeff Ballard	.10	.05	.01
☐ 28 Chuck Finley	.10	.05	.01
☐ 29 Dennis Eckersley	.20	.09	.03
☐ 30 Dan Plesac	.10	.05	.01
☐ 31 Fred McGriff	.25	.11	.03
☐ 32 Mark McGwire	.50	.23	.06
☐ 33 Tony LaRussa MG and Roger Craig MG	.10	.05	.01

1968 Laughlin World Series

This set of 64 cards was apparently a limited test issue by sports artist R.G. Laughlin for the World Series set concept that was mass marketed by Fleer two and three years later. The cards are slightly oversized, 2 3/4" by 3 1/2" and are black and white on the front and red and white on the back. All the years are represented except for 1904 when no World Series was played. In the list below, the winning series team is listed first.

	NRMT-MT	EXC	G-VG
COMPLETE SET (64)	125.00	57.50	15.50
COMMON PLAYER (1-64)	2.00	.90	.25
☐ 1 1903 Red Sox/Pirates	2.00	.90	.25
☐ 2 1905 Giants/A's (Christy Mathewson)	3.00	1.35	.40
☐ 3 1906 White Sox/Cubs	2.00	.90	.25
☐ 4 1907 Cubs/Tigers	2.00	.90	.25
☐ 5 1908 Cubs/Tigers (Tinker/Evers/Chance)	4.00	1.80	.50
☐ 6 1909 Pirates/Tigers (Wagner/Cobb)	5.00	2.30	.60
☐ 7 1910 A's/Cubs	2.00	.90	.25
☐ 8 1911 A's/Giants (John McGraw)	3.00	1.35	.40
☐ 9 1912 Red Sox/Giants	2.00	.90	.25
☐ 10 1913 A's/Giants	2.00	.90	.25
☐ 11 1914 Braves/A's	2.00	.90	.25
☐ 12 1915 Red Sox/Phillies (Babe Ruth)	6.00	2.70	.75
☐ 13 1916 Red Sox/Dodgers (Babe Ruth)	6.00	2.70	.75
☐ 14 1917 White Sox/Giants	2.00	.90	.25
☐ 15 1918 Red Sox/Cubs	2.00	.90	.25
☐ 16 1919 Reds/White Sox	4.00	1.80	.50
☐ 17 1920 Indians/Dodgers	2.00	.90	.25
☐ 18 1921 Giants/Yankees (Waite Hoyt)	2.50	1.15	.30
☐ 19 1922 Giants/Yankees (Frisch/Groh)	2.50	1.15	.30
☐ 20 1923 Yankees/Giants (Babe Ruth)	6.00	2.70	.75
☐ 21 1924 Senators/Giants	2.00	.90	.25
☐ 22 1925 Pirates/Senators (Walter Johnson)	4.00	1.80	.50
☐ 23 1926 Cardinals/Yankees (Alexander/Lazzeri)	3.00	1.35	.40
☐ 24 1927 Yankees/Pirates	2.00	.90	.25
☐ 25 1928 Yankees/Cardinals (Ruth/Gehrig)	6.00	2.70	.75
☐ 26 1929 A's/Cubs	2.00	.90	.25
☐ 27 1930 A's/Cardinals	2.00	.90	.25
☐ 28 1931 Cardinals/A's (Pepper Martin)	2.50	1.15	.30
☐ 29 1932 Yankees/Cubs (Babe Ruth)	6.00	2.70	.75
☐ 30 1933 Giants/Senators (Mel Ott)	3.00	1.35	.40
☐ 31 1934 Cardinals/Tigers (Dizzy/Paul Dean)	4.00	1.80	.50
☐ 32 1935 Tigers/Cubs	2.00	.90	.25
☐ 33 1936 Yankees/Giants	2.00	.90	.25
☐ 34 1937 Yankees/Giants (Carl Hubbell)	3.00	1.35	.40
☐ 35 1938 Yankees/Cubs	2.00	.90	.25
☐ 36 1939 Yankees/Reds (Joe DiMaggio)	5.00	2.30	.60
☐ 37 1940 Reds/Tigers	2.00	.90	.25
☐ 38 1941 Yankees/Dodgers (Mickey Owen)	2.50	1.15	.30
☐ 39 1942 Cardinals/Yankees	2.00	.90	.25
☐ 40 1943 Yankees/Cardinals (Joe McCarthy)	2.50	1.15	.30
☐ 41 1944 Cardinals/Browns	2.00	.90	.25
☐ 42 1945 Tigers/Cubs (Hank Greenberg)	3.00	1.35	.40
☐ 43 1946 Cardinals/Red Sox (Enos Slaughter)	3.00	1.35	.40
☐ 44 1947 Yankees/Dodgers (Al Gionfriddo)	2.00	.90	.25
☐ 45 1948 Indians/Braves (Bob Feller)	3.00	1.35	.40
☐ 46 1949 Yankees/Dodgers (Reynolds/Roe)	2.50	1.15	.30
☐ 47 1950 Yankees/Phillies	2.00	.90	.25
☐ 48 1951 Yankees/Giants	2.00	.90	.25
☐ 49 1952 Yankees/Dodgers (Mize/Snider)	3.00	1.35	.40
☐ 50 1953 Yankees/Dodgers (Casey Stengel)	3.00	1.35	.40
☐ 51 1954 Giants/Indians (Dusty Rhodes)	2.00	.90	.25
☐ 52 1955 Dodgers/Yankees (Johnny Podres)	2.50	1.15	.30
☐ 53 1956 Yankees/Dodgers (Don Larsen)	2.50	1.15	.30
☐ 54 1957 Braves/Yankees (Lew Burdette)	2.00	.90	.25
☐ 55 1958 Yankees/Braves (Hank Bauer)	2.00	.90	.25
☐ 56 1959 Dodgers/Wh.Sox (Larry Sherry)	2.00	.90	.25
☐ 57 1960 Pirates/Yankees	2.50	1.15	.30
☐ 58 1961 Yankees/Reds (Whitey Ford)	3.00	1.35	.40
☐ 59 1962 Yankees/Giants	2.00	.90	.25
☐ 60 1963 Dodgers/Yankees (Sandy Koufax)	3.00	1.35	.40
☐ 61 1964 Cardinals/Yankees (Mickey Mantle)	6.00	2.70	.75

☐ 62 1965 Dodgers/Twins	2.00	.90	.25
☐ 63 1966 Orioles/Dodgers	2.00	.90	.25
☐ 64 1967 Cardinals/Red Sox (Bob Gibson)	3.00	1.35	.40

1972 Laughlin Great Feats

This set of 51 cards is printed on white card stock. Sports artist R.G. Laughlin 1972 is copyrighted only on the unnumbered title card but not on each card. The obverses are line drawings in black and white inside a red border. The cards measure approximately 2 9/16" by 3 9/16". The set features "Great Feats" from baseball's past. The cards are blank backed and hence are numbered and captioned on the front. There is a variation set with a blue border and colored in flesh tones in the players pictured; this variation is a little more attractive and hence is valued a little higher. The blue-bordered variation set has larger type in the captions; in fact, the type has been reset and there are some minor wording differences. The blue-bordered set is also 1/16" wider.

	NRMT-MT	EXC	G-VG
COMPLETE SET (51)	30.00	13.50	3.80
COMMON PLAYER (1-50)	.50	.23	.06
☐ 1 Joe DiMaggio	4.00	1.80	.50
☐ 2 Walter Johnson	1.25	.55	.16
☐ 3 Rudy York	.50	.23	.06
☐ 4 Sandy Koufax	1.25	.55	.16
☐ 5 George Sisler	.60	.25	.08
☐ 6 Iron Man McGinnity	.50	.23	.06
☐ 7 Johnny VanderMeer	.50	.23	.06
☐ 8 Lou Gehrig	2.00	.90	.25
☐ 9 Max Carey	.50	.23	.06
☐ 10 Ed Delahanty	.50	.23	.06
☐ 11 Pinky Higgins	.50	.23	.06
☐ 12 Jack Chesbro	.50	.23	.06
☐ 13 Jim Bottomley	.50	.23	.06
☐ 14 Rube Marquard	.50	.23	.06
☐ 15 Rogers Hornsby	.75	.35	.09
☐ 16 Lefty Grove	.60	.25	.08
☐ 17 Johnny Mize	.75	.35	.09
☐ 18 Lefty Gomez	.60	.25	.08
☐ 19 Jimmie Foxx	.75	.35	.09
☐ 20 Casey Stengel	1.00	.45	.13
☐ 21 Dazzy Vance	.50	.23	.06
☐ 22 Jerry Lynch	.50	.23	.06
☐ 23 Hughie Jennings	.50	.23	.06
☐ 24 Stan Musial	1.25	.55	.16
☐ 25 Christy Mathewson	1.25	.55	.16
☐ 26 Elroy Face	.50	.23	.06
☐ 27 Hack Wilson	.60	.25	.08
☐ 28 Smoky Burgess	.50	.23	.06
☐ 29 Cy Young	1.00	.45	.13
☐ 30 Wilbert Robinson	.60	.25	.08
☐ 31 Wee Willie Keeler	.60	.25	.08
☐ 32 Babe Ruth	4.00	1.80	.50
☐ 33 Mickey Mantle	4.00	1.80	.50
☐ 34 Hub Leonard	.50	.23	.06
☐ 35 Ty Cobb	2.00	.90	.25
☐ 36 Carl Hubbell	.60	.25	.08
☐ 37 Joe Oeschger and Leon Cadore	.50	.23	.06
☐ 38 Don Drysdale	.60	.25	.08
☐ 39 Fred Toney and Hippo Vaughn	.50	.23	.06
☐ 40 Joe Sewell	.60	.25	.08
☐ 41 Grover C. Alexander	.60	.25	.08
☐ 42 Joe Adcock	.50	.23	.06
☐ 43 Eddie Collins	.60	.25	.08
☐ 44 Bob Feller	1.00	.45	.13
☐ 45 Don Larsen	.50	.23	.06
☐ 46 Dave Philley	.50	.23	.06
☐ 47 Bill Fischer	.50	.23	.06
☐ 48 Dale Long	.50	.23	.06
☐ 49 Bill Wambsganss	.50	.23	.06
☐ 50 Roger Maris	1.00	.45	.13
☐ NNO Title Card	1.00	.45	.13

1974 Laughlin All-Star Games

This set of 40 cards is printed on white card stock. Sports artist R.G. Laughlin 1974 is copyrighted at the bottom of the reverse of each card. The obverses are line drawings primarily in red, light blue, black, and white inside a white border. The cards measure approximately 2 11/16" by 3 3/8". The set features memorable moments from each year's All-Star Game(s). The cards are numbered on the back according to the last two digits of the year and captioned on the front. The backs are printed in blue on white stock. There is no card number 45 in the set as there was no All-Star Game played in 1945 because of World War II.

	NRMT-MT	EXC	G-VG
COMPLETE SET (40)	35.00	16.00	4.40
COMMON PLAYER (33-73)	.50	.23	.06
☐ 33 Babe's Homer	5.00	2.30	.60
☐ 34 Hubbell Fans Five	.75	.35	.09
☐ 35 Foxx Smashes Homer	.75	.35	.09
☐ 36 Ol' Diz Fogs 'Em	1.00	.45	.13
☐ 37 Four Hits for Ducky	.60	.25	.08
☐ 38 No-Hit Vandy	.50	.23	.06
☐ 39 DiMaggio Homers	3.00	1.35	.40
☐ 40 West's 3-Run Shot	.50	.23	.06
☐ 41 Vaughan Busts Two	.60	.25	.08
☐ 42 York's 2-Run Smash	.50	.23	.06
☐ 43 Doerr 3-Run Blast	.60	.25	.08
☐ 44 Cavarretta Reaches	.50	.23	.06
☐ 46 Field Day for Ted	2.00	.90	.25
☐ 47 Big Cat Plants One	1.00	.45	.13
☐ 48 Raschi Pitches	.60	.25	.08
☐ 49 Jackie Scores	1.50	.65	.19
☐ 50 Schoendienst Breaks	.75	.35	.09
☐ 51 Kiner Homers	.75	.35	.09
☐ 52 Sauer's Shot	.50	.23	.06
☐ 53 Slaughter Hustles	.75	.35	.09
☐ 54 Rosen Hits	.50	.23	.06
☐ 55 Stan the Man's Homer	1.25	.55	.16
☐ 56 Ken Boyer Super	.50	.23	.06
☐ 57 Kaline Hits	1.00	.45	.13
☐ 58 Only Nellie Gets Two	.60	.25	.08
☐ 59 F.Robbie Perfect	.75	.35	.09
☐ 60 Willie 3-for-4	1.50	.65	.19
☐ 61 Bunning Hitless	.60	.25	.08
☐ 62 Roberto Perfect	1.50	.65	.19
☐ 63 Monster Strikeouts	.50	.23	.06
☐ 64 Callison's Homer	.50	.23	.06

☐ 65 Stargell Big Day	.75	.35	.09
☐ 66 Brooks Hits	1.00	.45	.13
☐ 67 Fergie Fans Six	.75	.35	.09
☐ 68 Tom Terrific	1.50	.65	.19
☐ 69 Stretch Belts Two	.75	.35	.09
☐ 70 Yaz Four Hits	1.00	.45	.13
☐ 71 Reggie Unloads	1.50	.65	.19
☐ 72 Henry Hammers	1.50	.65	.19
☐ 73 Bonds Perfect	.60	.25	.08

1974 Laughlin Old Time Black Stars

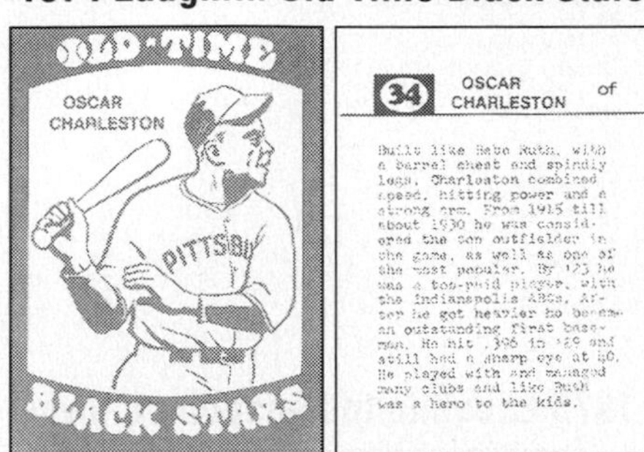

This set of 36 cards is printed on flat (non-glossy) white card stock. Sports artist R.G. Laughlin's work is evident but there are no copyright notices or any mention of him anywhere on any of the cards in this set. The obverses are line drawings in tan and brown. The cards measure approximately 2 5/8" by 3 1/2". The set features outstanding black players form the past. The cards are numbered on the back. The backs are printed in brown on white stock.

	NRMT-MT	EXC	G-VG
COMPLETE SET (36)	50.00	23.00	6.25
COMMON PLAYER (1-36)	1.00	.45	.13
☐ 1 Smokey Joe Williams	3.00	1.35	.40
☐ 2 Rap Dixon	1.00	.45	.13
☐ 3 Oliver Marcelle	1.00	.45	.13
☐ 4 Bingo DeMoss	1.50	.65	.19
☐ 5 Willie Foster	1.50	.65	.19
☐ 6 John Beckwith	1.00	.45	.13
☐ 7 Floyd(Jelly) Gardner	1.00	.45	.13
☐ 8 Josh Gibson	6.00	2.70	.75
☐ 9 Jose Mendez	1.00	.45	.13
☐ 10 Pete Hill	1.00	.45	.13
☐ 11 Buck Leonard	4.00	1.80	.50
☐ 12 Jud Wilson	1.00	.45	.13
☐ 13 Willie Wells	2.00	.90	.25
☐ 14 Jimmie Lyons	1.00	.45	.13
☐ 15 Satchel Paige	6.00	2.70	.75
☐ 16 Louis Santop	1.00	.45	.13
☐ 17 Frank Grant	1.00	.45	.13
☐ 18 Christobel Torrienti	1.50	.65	.19
☐ 19 Bullet Rogon	1.00	.45	.13
☐ 20 Dave Malarcher	1.50	.65	.19
☐ 21 Spot Poles	1.00	.45	.13
☐ 22 Home Run Johnson	1.50	.65	.19
☐ 23 Charlie Grant	1.00	.45	.13
☐ 24 Cool Papa Bell	4.00	1.80	.50
☐ 25 Cannonball Dick Redding	1.00	.45	.13
☐ 26 Ray Dandridge	4.00	1.80	.50
☐ 27 Biz Mackey	2.00	.90	.25
☐ 28 Fats Jenkins	1.00	.45	.13
☐ 29 Martin Dihigo	3.00	1.35	.40
☐ 30 Mule Suttles	1.00	.45	.13
☐ 31 Bill Monroe	1.00	.45	.13
☐ 32 Dan McClellan	1.00	.45	.13
☐ 33 John Henry Lloyd	3.00	1.35	.40
☐ 34 Oscar Charleston	3.00	1.35	.40
☐ 35 Andrew(Rube) Foster	3.00	1.35	.40
☐ 36 William(Judy) Johnson	3.00	1.35	.40

1974 Laughlin Sportslang

This set of 41 cards is printed on white card stock. Sports artist R.G. Laughlin 1974 is copyrighted at the bottom of every reverse. The obverses are drawings in red and blue on a white enamel card stock. The cards measure approximately 2 3/4" by 3 3/8". The set actually features the slang of several sports, not just baseball. The cards are numbered on the back and captioned on the front. The card back also provides an explanation of the slang term pictured on the card front.

	NRMT-MT	EXC	G-VG
COMPLETE SET (41)	8.00	3.60	1.00
COMMON PLAYER (1-41)	.25	.11	.03
☐ 1 Bull Pen	.25	.11	.03
☐ 2 Charley Horse	.25	.11	.03
☐ 3 Derby	.25	.11	.03
☐ 4 Anchor Man	.25	.11	.03
☐ 5 Mascot	.25	.11	.03
☐ 6 Annie Oakley	.35	.16	.04
☐ 7 Taxi Squad	.25	.11	.03
☐ 8 Dukes	.25	.11	.03
☐ 9 Rookie	.25	.11	.03
☐ 10 Jinx	.25	.11	.03
☐ 11 Dark Horse	.25	.11	.03
☐ 12 Hat Trick	.25	.11	.03
☐ 13 Bell Wether	.25	.11	.03
☐ 14 Love	.25	.11	.03
☐ 15 Red Dog	.25	.11	.03
☐ 16 Barnstorm	.25	.11	.03
☐ 17 Bull's Eye	.25	.11	.03
☐ 18 Rabbit Punch	.25	.11	.03
☐ 19 The Upper Hand	.25	.11	.03
☐ 20 Handi Cap	.25	.11	.03
☐ 21 Marathon	.25	.11	.03
☐ 22 Southpaw	.25	.11	.03
☐ 23 Boner	.25	.11	.03
☐ 24 Gridiron	.25	.11	.03
☐ 25 Fan	.25	.11	.03
☐ 26 Moxie	.25	.11	.03
☐ 27 Birdie	.25	.11	.03
☐ 28 Sulky	.25	.11	.03
☐ 29 Dribble	.25	.11	.03
☐ 30 Donnybrook	.25	.11	.03
☐ 31 The Real McCoy	.25	.11	.03
☐ 32 Even Stephen	.25	.11	.03
☐ 33 Chinese Homer	.25	.11	.03
☐ 34 English	.25	.11	.03
☐ 35 Garrison Finish	.25	.11	.03
☐ 36 Foot in the Bucket	.25	.11	.03
☐ 37 Steeple Chase	.25	.11	.03
☐ 38 Long Shot	.25	.11	.03
☐ 39 Nip and Tuck	.25	.11	.03
☐ 40 Battery	.25	.11	.03
☐ xx Title Card (Unnumbered)	.35	.16	.04

1975 Laughlin Batty Baseball

This set of 25 cards is printed on white card stock. Sports artist R.G. Laughlin 1975 is copyrighted on the title card. The obverses are line drawings primarily in orange, black, and white. The cards measure approximately 2 9/16" by 3 7/16". The set features a card for each team with a depiction of a fractured nickname for the team. The cards are

numbered on the front. The backs are blank, but on white stock.

	NRMT-MT	EXC	G-VG
COMPLETE SET (25)	7.50	3.40	.95
COMMON PLAYER (1-24)	.35	.16	.04
☐ 1 Oakland Daze	.35	.16	.04
☐ 2 Boston Wet Sox	.35	.16	.04
☐ 3 Cincinnati Dreads	.35	.16	.04
☐ 4 Chicago Wide Sox	.35	.16	.04
☐ 5 Milwaukee Boozers	.35	.16	.04
☐ 6 Philadelphia Fillies	.35	.16	.04
☐ 7 Cleveland Engines	.35	.16	.04
☐ 8 New York Mitts	.35	.16	.04
☐ 9 Texas Ranchers	.35	.16	.04
☐ 10 San Francisco Gents	.35	.16	.04
☐ 11 Houston Disastros	.35	.16	.04
☐ 12 Chicago Clubs	.35	.16	.04
☐ 13 Minnesota Wins	.35	.16	.04
☐ 14 St. Louis Gardeners	.35	.16	.04
☐ 15 New York Yankers	.35	.16	.04
☐ 16 California Angles	.35	.16	.04
☐ 17 Pittsburgh Irates	.35	.16	.04
☐ 18 Los Angeles Smoggers	.35	.16	.04
☐ 19 Baltimore Oreos	.35	.16	.04
☐ 20 Montreal Expose	.35	.16	.04
☐ 21 San Diego Parties	.35	.16	.04
☐ 22 Detroit Taggers	.35	.16	.04
☐ 23 Kansas City Broils	.35	.16	.04
☐ 24 Atlanta Briefs	.35	.16	.04
☐ xx Title Card (Unnumbered)	.45	.20	.06

1976 Laughlin Diamond Jubilee

Koufax pitches perfect game 4th no-hitter

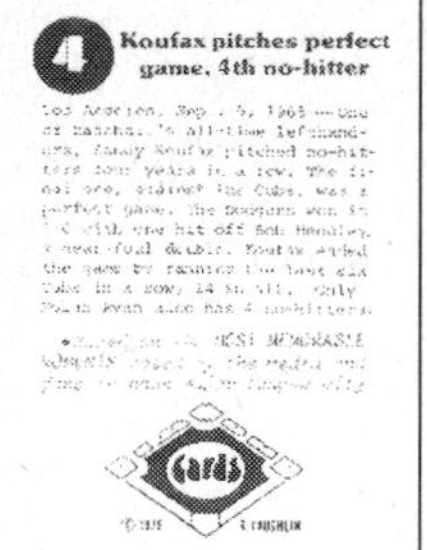

This set of 32 cards is printed on flat (non-glossy) white card stock. Sports artist R.Laughlin 1976 is copyrighted at the bottom of the reverse of each card. The obverses are line drawings primarily in red, blue, black, and white inside a red border. The cards measure approximately 2 13/16" by 3 15/16". The set features memorable moments voted by the media and fans in each major league city. The cards are numbered on the back and captioned on the front and the back. The backs are printed in dark blue on white stock.

	NRMT-MT	EXC	G-VG
COMPLETE SET (32)	45.00	20.00	5.75
COMMON PLAYER (1-32)	.75	.35	.09
☐ 1 Nolan Ryan	7.50	3.40	.95
☐ 2 Ernie Banks	1.50	.65	.19
☐ 3 Mickey Lolich	.75	.35	.09
☐ 4 Sandy Koufax	2.50	1.15	.30
☐ 5 Frank Robinson	1.50	.65	.19
☐ 6 Bill Mazeroski	.75	.35	.09
☐ 7 Jim Hunter	1.00	.45	.13
☐ 8 Hank Aaron	2.50	1.15	.30
☐ 9 Carl Yastrzemski	1.50	.65	.19
☐ 10 Jim Bunning	.90	.40	.11
☐ 11 Brooks Robinson	1.50	.65	.19
☐ 12 John VanderMeer	.75	.35	.09
☐ 13 Harmon Killebrew	1.25	.55	.16
☐ 14 Lou Brock	1.25	.55	.16
☐ 15 Steve Busby	.75	.35	.09
☐ 16 Nate Colbert	.75	.35	.09
☐ 17 Don Larsen	.90	.40	.11
☐ 18 Willie Mays	2.50	1.15	.30
☐ 19 David Clyde	.75	.35	.09
☐ 20 Mack Jones	.75	.35	.09
☐ 21 Mike Hegan	.75	.35	.09
☐ 22 Jerry Koosman	.75	.35	.09
☐ 23 Early Wynn	1.00	.45	.13
☐ 24 Nellie Fox	.90	.40	.11
☐ 25 Joe DiMaggio	5.00	2.30	.60
☐ 26 Jackie Robinson	3.00	1.35	.40
☐ 27 Ted Williams	2.50	1.15	.30
☐ 28 Lou Gehrig	4.00	1.80	.50
☐ 29 Bobby Thomson	.75	.35	.09
☐ 30 Roger Maris	1.25	.55	.16
☐ 31 Harvey Haddix	.75	.35	.09
☐ 32 Babe Ruth	7.50	3.40	.95

1976 Laughlin Indianapolis Clowns

This 42-card set was issued to commemorate the Indianapolis Clowns, a black team that began touring in 1929 and played many games for charity. The cards measure 2 5/8" by 4 1/4". The front design has black , white player photos, inside a white frame against a light blue card face. The team name is printed in red and white above the picture. In red courier-style print on white, the backs present extended captions. The cards are numbered on the front.

	NRMT-MT	EXC	G-VG
COMPLETE SET (42)	40.00	18.00	5.00
COMMON PLAYER (1-40)	1.00	.45	.13
☐ 1 Ed Hamman Ed the Clown	1.50	.65	.19
☐ 2 Dero Austin	1.00	.45	.13
☐ 3 James Williams Nickname Natureboy	1.00	.45	.13
☐ 4 Sam Brison Nickname Birmingham	1.00	.45	.13
☐ 5 Richard King Nickname King Tut	1.00	.45	.13
☐ 6 Syd Pollock Founder	1.00	.45	.13
☐ 7 Nataniel(Lefty) Small	1.00	.45	.13
☐ 8 Grant Greene Nickname Double Duty	1.00	.45	.13
☐ 9 Nancy Miller Lady umpire	1.50	.65	.19
☐ 10 Billy Vaughn	1.00	.45	.13
☐ 11 Sam Brison Putout for Sam	1.00	.45	.13
☐ 12 Ed Hamman	1.00	.45	.13
☐ 13 Dero Austin Home delivery	1.00	.45	.13
☐ 14 Steve(Nub) Anderson	1.00	.45	.13
☐ 15 Joe Cherry	1.00	.45	.13

☐ 16 Reece(Goose) Tatum	4.00	1.80	.50
☐ 17 James Williams Natureboy	1.00	.45	.13
☐ 18 Byron Purnell	1.00	.45	.13
☐ 19 Bat boy	1.00	.45	.13
☐ 20 Spec BeBop	1.00	.45	.13
☐ 21 Satchel Paige	4.00	1.80	.50
☐ 22 Prince Jo Henry	1.00	.45	.13
☐ 23 Ed Hamman Syd Pollock	1.00	.45	.13
☐ 24 Paul Casanova	1.50	.65	.19
☐ 25 Steve(Nub) Anderson Nub singles	1.00	.45	.13
☐ 26 Comiskey Park	1.00	.45	.13
☐ 27 Toni Stone Second basewoman	1.00	.45	.13
☐ 28 Dero Austin Small target	1.00	.45	.13
☐ 29 Sam Brison and Natureboy Williams Calling Dr. Kildare	1.00	.45	.13
☐ 30 Oscar Charleston	2.50	1.15	.30
☐ 31 Richard King King Tut	1.00	.45	.13
☐ 32 Ed Hamman Joe Cherry Hal King Ed and prospects	1.00	.45	.13
☐ 33 In style Team bus	1.00	.45	.13
☐ 34 Hank Aaron	5.00	2.30	.60
☐ 35 The Great Yogi	4.00	1.80	.50
☐ 36 W.H.(Chauff) Wilson	1.00	.45	.13
☐ 37 Sam Brison Sonny Jackson Doin' their thing	1.00	.45	.13
☐ 38 Billy Vaughn The hard way	1.00	.45	.13
☐ 39 James Williams 1B the easy way	1.00	.45	.13
☐ 40 Ed Hamman Casey Stengel Casey and Ed	2.00	.90	.25
☐ xx Title Card	1.50	.65	.19
☐ xx Baseball Laff Book	1.00	.45	.13

1978 Laughlin Long Ago Black Stars

This set of 36 cards is printed on flat (non-glossy) white card stock. Sports artist R.G. Laughlin's work is evident and the reverse of each card indicates copyright by R.G. Laughlin 1978. The obverses are line drawings in light and dark green. The cards measure approximately 2 5/8" by 3 1/2". The set features outstanding black players form the past. The cards are numbered on the back. The backs are printed in black on white stock. This is not a reissue of the similar Laughlin set from 1974 Old Time Black Stars but is actually in effect a second series with all new players.

	NRMT-MT	EXC	G-VG
COMPLETE SET (36)	30.00	13.50	3.80
COMMON PLAYER (1-36)	.75	.35	.09
☐ 1 Ted Trent	1.00	.45	.13
☐ 2 Larry Brown	.75	.35	.09
☐ 3 Newt Allen	1.00	.45	.13
☐ 4 Norman Stearns	.75	.35	.09
☐ 5 Leon Day	2.00	.90	.25
☐ 6 Dick Lundy	.75	.35	.09
☐ 7 Bruce Petway	1.00	.45	.13
☐ 8 Bill Drake	.75	.35	.09
☐ 9 Chaney White	.75	.35	.09
☐ 10 Webster McDonald	.75	.35	.09
☐ 11 Tommy Butts	.75	.35	.09
☐ 12 Ben Taylor	.75	.35	.09
☐ 13 James(Joe) Greene	.75	.35	.09
☐ 14 Dick Seay	.75	.35	.09
☐ 15 Sammy Hughes	.75	.35	.09
☐ 16 Ted Page	1.50	.65	.19
☐ 17 Willie Cornelius	.75	.35	.09
☐ 18 Pat Patterson	.75	.35	.09
☐ 19 Frank Wickware	.75	.35	.09
☐ 20 Albert Haywood	.75	.35	.09
☐ 21 Bill Holland	.75	.35	.09
☐ 22 Sol White	.75	.35	.09
☐ 23 Chet Brewer	1.50	.65	.19
☐ 24 Crush Holloway	.75	.35	.09
☐ 25 George Johnson	.75	.35	.09
☐ 26 George Scales	.75	.35	.09
☐ 27 Dave Brown	.75	.35	.09
☐ 28 John Donaldson	.75	.35	.09
☐ 29 William Johnson	1.25	.55	.16
☐ 30 Bill Yancey	1.00	.45	.13
☐ 31 Sam Bankhead	1.00	.45	.13
☐ 32 Leroy Matlock	.75	.35	.09
☐ 33 Quincy Troupe	.75	.35	.09
☐ 34 Hilton Smith	.75	.35	.09
☐ 35 Jim Crutchfield	1.25	.55	.16
☐ 36 Ted Radcliffe	1.25	.55	.16

1980 Laughlin Famous Feats

This set of 40 cards is printed on white card stock. Sports artist R.G. Laughlin 1980 is copyrighted at the bottom of every obverse. The obverses are line drawings primarily in many colors. The cards measure approximately 2 1/2" by 3 1/2". The set is subtitled as the "Second Series" of Famous Feats. The cards are numbered on the front. The backs are blank, but on white stock.

	NRMT-MT	EXC	G-VG
COMPLETE SET (40)	12.00	5.50	1.50
COMMON PLAYER (1-40)	.20	.09	.03
☐ 1 Honus Wagner	.60	.25	.08
☐ 2 Herb Pennock	.25	.11	.03
☐ 3 Al Simmons	.25	.11	.03
☐ 4 Hack Wilson	.25	.11	.03
☐ 5 Dizzy Dean	.40	.18	.05
☐ 6 Chuck Klein	.25	.11	.03
☐ 7 Nellie Fox	.20	.09	.03
☐ 8 Lefty Grove	.35	.16	.04
☐ 9 George Sisler	.25	.11	.03
☐ 10 Lou Gehrig	1.00	.45	.13
☐ 11 Rube Waddell	.25	.11	.03
☐ 12 Max Carey	.25	.11	.03
☐ 13 Thurman Munson	.40	.18	.05
☐ 14 Mel Ott	.35	.16	.04
☐ 15 Doc White	.20	.09	.03
☐ 16 Babe Ruth	1.50	.65	.19
☐ 17 Schoolboy Rowe	.20	.09	.03
☐ 18 Jackie Robinson	.60	.25	.08
☐ 19 Joe Medwick	.25	.11	.03

☐ 20 Casey Stengel	.40	.18	.05
☐ 21 Roberto Clemente	.50	.23	.06
☐ 22 Christy Mathewson	.50	.23	.06
☐ 23 Jimmie Foxx	.35	.16	.04
☐ 24 Joe Jackson	1.50	.65	.19
☐ 25 Walter Johnson	.50	.23	.06
☐ 26 Tony Lazzeri	.25	.11	.03
☐ 27 Hugh Casey	.20	.09	.03
☐ 28 Ty Cobb	1.00	.45	.13
☐ 29 Stuffy McInnis	.20	.09	.03
☐ 30 Cy Young	.40	.18	.05
☐ 31 Lefty O'Doul	.20	.09	.03
☐ 32 Eddie Collins	.25	.11	.03
☐ 33 Joe McCarthy	.25	.11	.03
☐ 34 Ed Walsh	.25	.11	.03
☐ 35 George Burns	.20	.09	.03
☐ 36 Walt Dropo	.20	.09	.03
☐ 37 Connie Mack	.30	.14	.04
☐ 38 Babe Adams	.20	.09	.03
☐ 39 Rogers Hornsby	.40	.18	.05
☐ 40 Grover C. Alexander	.30	.14	.04

1980 Laughlin 300/400/500

This square (approximately 3 1/4" square) set of 30 players features members of the 300/400/500 club, namely, 300 pitching wins, batting .400 or better, or hitting 500 homers since 1900. Cards are blank backed but are numbered on the front. The cards feature the artwork of R.G. Laughlin for the player's body connected to an out of proportion head shot stock photo. This creates an effect faintly reminiscent of the Goudey Heads Up cards.

	NRMT-MT	EXC	G-VG
COMPLETE SET (30)	20.00	9.00	2.50
COMMON PLAYER (1-30)	.60	.25	.08
☐ 1 Title Card	1.00	.45	.13
☐ 2 Babe Ruth	3.00	1.35	.40
☐ 3 Walter Johnson	1.00	.45	.13
☐ 4 Ty Cobb	1.50	.65	.19
☐ 5 Christy Mathewson	1.00	.45	.13
☐ 6 Ted Williams	1.50	.65	.19
☐ 7 Bill Terry	.75	.35	.09
☐ 8 Grover C. Alexander	.75	.35	.09
☐ 9 Napoleon Lajoie	.75	.35	.09
☐ 10 Willie Mays	1.25	.55	.16
☐ 11 Cy Young	.90	.40	.11
☐ 12 Mel Ott	.90	.40	.11
☐ 13 Joe Jackson	2.50	1.15	.30
☐ 14 Harmon Killebrew	.75	.35	.09
☐ 15 Warren Spahn	.75	.35	.09
☐ 16 Hank Aaron	1.25	.55	.16
☐ 17 Rogers Hornsby	.90	.40	.11
☐ 18 Mickey Mantle	3.00	1.35	.40
☐ 19 Lefty Grove	.75	.35	.09
☐ 20 Ted Williams	1.50	.65	.19
☐ 21 Jimmie Foxx	.90	.40	.11
☐ 22 Eddie Plank	.60	.25	.08
☐ 23 Frank Robinson	.75	.35	.09
☐ 24 George Sisler	.60	.25	.08
☐ 25 Eddie Mathews	.75	.35	.09
☐ 26 Early Wynn	.60	.25	.08
☐ 27 Ernie Banks	.90	.40	.11
☐ 28 Harry Heilmann	.60	.25	.08
☐ 29 Lou Gehrig	1.50	.65	.19
☐ 30 Willie McCovey	.75	.35	.09

1948-49 Leaf

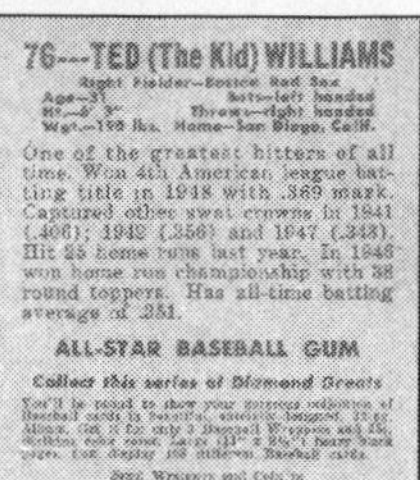

The cards in this 98-card set measure 2 3/8" by 2 7/8". The 1948-49 Leaf set was the first post-war baseball series issued in color. This effort was not entirely successful due to a lack of refinement which resulted in many color variations and cards out of register. In addition, the set was skip numbered from 1-168, with 49 of the 98 cards printed in limited quantities (marked with SP in the checklist). Cards 102 and 136 have variations, and cards are sometimes found with overprinted or incorrect backs. The notable Rookie Cards in this set include Stan Musial, Satchel Paige, and Jackie Robinson.

	NRMT	VG-E	GOOD
COMPLETE SET (98)	28000.	12600.	3500.
COMMON PLAYER (1-168)	25.00	11.50	3.10
☐ 1 Joe DiMaggio	2150.00	950.00	275.00
☐ 3 Babe Ruth	2400.00	1100.00	300.00
☐ 4 Stan Musial	800.00	350.00	100.00
☐ 5 Virgil Trucks SP	425.00	190.00	52.50
☐ 8 Satchel Paige SP	2250.00	1000.00	275.00
☐ 10 Dizzy Trout	28.00	12.50	3.50
☐ 11 Phil Rizzuto	210.00	95.00	26.00
☐ 13 Cass Michaels SP	350.00	160.00	45.00
☐ 14 Billy Johnson	28.00	12.50	3.50
☐ 17 Frank Overmire	25.00	11.50	3.10
☐ 19 Johnny Wyrostek SP	350.00	160.00	45.00
☐ 20 Hank Sauer SP	450.00	200.00	57.50
☐ 22 Al Evans	25.00	11.50	3.10
☐ 26 Sam Chapman	25.00	11.50	3.10
☐ 27 Mickey Harris	25.00	11.50	3.10
☐ 28 Jim Hegan	30.00	13.50	3.80
☐ 29 Elmer Valo	30.00	13.50	3.80
☐ 30 Billy Goodman SP	400.00	180.00	50.00
☐ 31 Lou Brissie	25.00	11.50	3.10
☐ 32 Warren Spahn	275.00	125.00	34.00
☐ 33 Peanuts Lowrey SP	350.00	160.00	45.00
☐ 36 Al Zarilla SP	350.00	160.00	45.00
☐ 38 Ted Kluszewski	95.00	42.50	12.00
☐ 39 Ewell Blackwell	55.00	25.00	7.00
☐ 42 Kent Peterson	25.00	11.50	3.10
☐ 43 Ed Stevens SP	350.00	160.00	45.00
☐ 45 Ken Keltner SP	350.00	160.00	45.00
☐ 46 Johnny Mize	110.00	50.00	14.00
☐ 47 George Vico	25.00	11.50	3.10
☐ 48 Johnny Schmitz SP	350.00	160.00	45.00
☐ 49 Del Ennis	40.00	18.00	5.00
☐ 50 Dick Wakefield	25.00	11.50	3.10
☐ 51 Al Dark SP	450.00	200.00	57.50
☐ 53 Johnny VanderMeer	45.00	20.00	5.75
☐ 54 Bobby Adams SP	350.00	160.00	45.00
☐ 55 Tommy Henrich SP	450.00	200.00	57.50
☐ 56 Larry Jansen	30.00	13.50	3.80
☐ 57 Bob McCall	25.00	11.50	3.10
☐ 59 Luke Appling	90.00	40.00	11.50
☐ 61 Jake Early	25.00	11.50	3.10
☐ 62 Eddie Joost SP	350.00	160.00	45.00
☐ 63 Barney McCosky SP	350.00	160.00	45.00
☐ 65 Robert Elliott UER (Misspelled Elliot on card front)	40.00	18.00	5.00
☐ 66 Orval Grove SP	350.00	160.00	45.00
☐ 68 Eddie Miller SP	350.00	160.00	45.00
☐ 70 Honus Wagner	300.00	135.00	38.00
☐ 72 Hank Edwards	25.00	11.50	3.10
☐ 73 Pat Seerey	25.00	11.50	3.10
☐ 75 Dom DiMaggio SP	575.00	250.00	70.00
☐ 76 Ted Williams	750.00	350.00	95.00

☐ 77 Roy Smalley	30.00	13.50	3.80
☐ 78 Hoot Evers SP	350.00	160.00	45.00
☐ 79 Jackie Robinson	825.00	375.00	105.00
☐ 81 Whitey Kurowski SP	350.00	160.00	45.00
☐ 82 Johnny Lindell	28.00	12.50	3.50
☐ 83 Bobby Doerr	125.00	57.50	15.50
☐ 84 Sid Hudson	25.00	11.50	3.10
☐ 85 Dave Philley SP	400.00	180.00	50.00
☐ 86 Ralph Weigel	25.00	11.50	3.10
☐ 88 Frank Gustine SP	350.00	160.00	45.00
☐ 91 Ralph Kiner	200.00	90.00	25.00
☐ 93 Bob Feller SP	1500.00	700.00	190.00
☐ 95 George Stirnweiss	30.00	13.50	3.80
☐ 97 Marty Marion	55.00	25.00	7.00
☐ 98 Hal Newhouser SP	675.00	300.00	85.00
☐ 102A Gene Hermansk ERR	300.00	135.00	38.00
☐ 102B Gene Hermanski COR	28.00	12.50	3.50
☐ 104 Eddie Stewart SP	350.00	160.00	45.00
☐ 106 Lou Boudreau	110.00	50.00	14.00
☐ 108 Matt Batts SP	350.00	160.00	45.00
☐ 111 Jerry Priddy	25.00	11.50	3.10
☐ 113 Dutch Leonard SP	350.00	160.00	45.00
☐ 117 Joe Gordon	40.00	18.00	5.00
☐ 120 George Kell SP	650.00	300.00	80.00
☐ 121 Johnny Pesky SP	425.00	190.00	52.50
☐ 123 Cliff Fannin SP	350.00	160.00	45.00
☐ 125 Andy Pafko	30.00	13.50	3.80
☐ 127 Enos Slaughter SP	775.00	350.00	95.00
☐ 128 Buddy Rosar	25.00	11.50	3.10
☐ 129 Kirby Higbe SP	350.00	160.00	45.00
☐ 131 Sid Gordon SP	350.00	160.00	45.00
☐ 133 Tommy Holmes SP	425.00	190.00	52.50
☐ 136A Cliff Aberson (Full sleeve)	25.00	11.50	3.10
☐ 136B Cliff Aberson (Short sleeve)	300.00	135.00	38.00
☐ 137 Harry Walker SP	350.00	160.00	45.00
☐ 138 Larry Doby SP	550.00	250.00	70.00
☐ 139 Johnny Hopp	30.00	13.50	3.80
☐ 142 Danny Murtaugh SP	425.00	190.00	52.50
☐ 143 Dick Sisler SP	350.00	160.00	45.00
☐ 144 Bob Dillinger SP	350.00	160.00	45.00
☐ 146 Pete Reiser SP	450.00	200.00	57.50
☐ 149 Hank Majeski SP	350.00	160.00	45.00
☐ 153 Floyd Baker SP	350.00	160.00	45.00
☐ 158 Harry Brecheen SP	425.00	190.00	52.50
☐ 159 Mizell Platt	25.00	11.50	3.10
☐ 160 Bob Scheffing SP	350.00	160.00	45.00
☐ 161 Vern Stephens SP	425.00	190.00	52.50
☐ 163 Fred Hutchinson SP	450.00	200.00	57.50
☐ 165 Dale Mitchell SP	425.00	190.00	52.50
☐ 168 Phil Cavarretta SP	450.00	200.00	57.50

1960 Leaf

The cards in this 144-card set measure 2 1/2" by 3 1/2". The 1960 Leaf set was issued in a regular gum package style but with a marble instead of gum. The series was a joint production by Sports Novelties, Inc., and Leaf, two Chicago-based companies. Cards 73-144 are more difficult to find than the lower numbers. Photo variations exist (probably proof cards) for the seven cards listed with an asterisk and there is a well-known error card, number 25 showing Brooks Lawrence (in a Reds uniform) with Jim Grant's name on front, and Grant's biography and record on back. The corrected version with Grant's photo is the more difficult variety. The only notable Rookie Card in this set is Dallas Green. The complete set price below includes both versions of Jim Grant.

	NRMT	VG-E	GOOD
COMPLETE SET (145)	1200.00	550.00	150.00
COMMON PLAYER (1-72)	2.50	1.15	.30
COMMON PLAYER (73-144)	14.00	6.25	1.75
☐ 1 Luis Aparicio *	20.00	5.00	1.60
☐ 2 Woody Held	2.50	1.15	.30
☐ 3 Frank Lary	3.00	1.35	.40
☐ 4 Camilo Pascual	3.00	1.35	.40
☐ 5 Pancho Herrera	2.50	1.15	.30
☐ 6 Felipe Alou	6.50	2.90	.80
☐ 7 Benjamin Daniels	2.50	1.15	.30
☐ 8 Roger Craig	5.50	2.50	.70
☐ 9 Eddie Kasko	2.50	1.15	.30
☐ 10 Bob Grim	3.00	1.35	.40
☐ 11 Jim Busby	2.50	1.15	.30
☐ 12 Ken Boyer	8.00	3.60	1.00
☐ 13 Bob Boyd	2.50	1.15	.30
☐ 14 Sam Jones	3.00	1.35	.40
☐ 15 Larry Jackson	3.00	1.35	.40
☐ 16 Elroy Face	4.50	2.00	.55
☐ 17 Walt Moryn *	2.50	1.15	.30
☐ 18 Jim Gilliam	4.50	2.00	.55
☐ 19 Don Newcombe	4.50	2.00	.55
☐ 20 Glen Hobbie	2.50	1.15	.30
☐ 21 Pedro Ramos	2.50	1.15	.30
☐ 22 Ryne Duren	4.50	2.00	.55
☐ 23 Joey Jay *	3.00	1.35	.40
☐ 24 Lou Berberet	2.50	1.15	.30
☐ 25A Jim Grant ERR (Photo actually Brooks Lawrence)	13.50	6.00	1.70
☐ 25B Jim Grant COR	20.00	9.00	2.50
☐ 26 Tom Borland	2.50	1.15	.30
☐ 27 Brooks Robinson	35.00	16.00	4.40
☐ 28 Jerry Adair	2.50	1.15	.30
☐ 29 Ron Jackson	2.50	1.15	.30
☐ 30 George Strickland	2.50	1.15	.30
☐ 31 Rocky Bridges	2.50	1.15	.30
☐ 32 Bill Tuttle	2.50	1.15	.30
☐ 33 Ken Hunt	2.50	1.15	.30
☐ 34 Hal Griggs	2.50	1.15	.30
☐ 35 Jim Coates *	2.50	1.15	.30
☐ 36 Brooks Lawrence	2.50	1.15	.30
☐ 37 Duke Snider	48.00	22.00	6.00
☐ 38 Al Spangler	2.50	1.15	.30
☐ 39 Jim Owens	2.50	1.15	.30
☐ 40 Bill Virdon	4.50	2.00	.55
☐ 41 Ernie Broglio	3.00	1.35	.40
☐ 42 Andre Rodgers	2.50	1.15	.30
☐ 43 Julio Becquer	2.50	1.15	.30
☐ 44 Tony Taylor	3.00	1.35	.40
☐ 45 Jerry Lynch	3.00	1.35	.40
☐ 46 Cletis Boyer	4.50	2.00	.55
☐ 47 Jerry Lumpe	2.50	1.15	.30
☐ 48 Charlie Maxwell	3.00	1.35	.40
☐ 49 Jim Perry	4.50	2.00	.55
☐ 50 Danny McDevitt	2.50	1.15	.30
☐ 51 Juan Pizarro	2.50	1.15	.30
☐ 52 Dallas Green	6.50	2.90	.80
☐ 53 Bob Friend	3.00	1.35	.40
☐ 54 Jack Sanford	3.00	1.35	.40
☐ 55 Jim Rivera	2.50	1.15	.30
☐ 56 Ted Wills	2.50	1.15	.30
☐ 57 Milt Pappas	3.00	1.35	.40
☐ 58 Hal Smith *	2.50	1.15	.30
☐ 59 Bobby Avila	2.50	1.15	.30
☐ 60 Clem Labine	3.00	1.35	.40
☐ 61 Norman Rehm *	2.50	1.15	.30
☐ 62 John Gabler	2.50	1.15	.30
☐ 63 John Tsitouris	2.50	1.15	.30
☐ 64 Dave Sisler	2.50	1.15	.30
☐ 65 Vic Power	3.00	1.35	.40
☐ 66 Earl Battey	2.50	1.15	.30
☐ 67 Bob Purkey	2.50	1.15	.30
☐ 68 Moe Drabowsky	3.00	1.35	.40
☐ 69 Hoyt Wilhelm	15.00	6.75	1.90
☐ 70 Humberto Robinson	2.50	1.15	.30
☐ 71 Whitey Herzog	6.00	2.70	.75
☐ 72 Dick Donovan *	2.50	1.15	.30
☐ 73 Gordon Jones	16.00	7.25	2.00
☐ 74 Joe Hicks	14.00	6.25	1.75
☐ 75 Ray Culp	18.00	8.00	2.30
☐ 76 Dick Drott	14.00	6.25	1.75
☐ 77 Bob Duliba	14.00	6.25	1.75
☐ 78 Art Ditmar	14.00	6.25	1.75
☐ 79 Steve Korcheck	14.00	6.25	1.75
☐ 80 Henry Mason	14.00	6.25	1.75
☐ 81 Harry Simpson	14.00	6.25	1.75

☐ 82 Gene Green	14.00	6.25	1.75
☐ 83 Bob Shaw	14.00	6.25	1.75
☐ 84 Howard Reed	14.00	6.25	1.75
☐ 85 Dick Stigman	14.00	6.25	1.75
☐ 86 Rip Repulski	14.00	6.25	1.75
☐ 87 Seth Morehead	14.00	6.25	1.75
☐ 88 Camilo Carreon	14.00	6.25	1.75
☐ 89 John Blanchard	18.00	8.00	2.30
☐ 90 Billy Hoeft	14.00	6.25	1.75
☐ 91 Fred Hopke	14.00	6.25	1.75
☐ 92 Joe Martin	14.00	6.25	1.75
☐ 93 Wally Shannon	14.00	6.25	1.75
☐ 94 Two Hal Smith's Hal R. Smith Hal W. Smith	20.00	9.00	2.50
☐ 95 Al Schroll	14.00	6.25	1.75
☐ 96 John Kucks	14.00	6.25	1.75
☐ 97 Tom Morgan	14.00	6.25	1.75
☐ 98 Willie Jones	14.00	6.25	1.75
☐ 99 Marshall Renfroe	14.00	6.25	1.75
☐ 100 Willie Tasby	14.00	6.25	1.75
☐ 101 Irv Noren	14.00	6.25	1.75
☐ 102 Russ Snyder	14.00	6.25	1.75
☐ 103 Bob Turley	16.50	7.50	2.10
☐ 104 Jim Woods	14.00	6.25	1.75
☐ 105 Ronnie Kline	14.00	6.25	1.75
☐ 106 Steve Bilko	14.00	6.25	1.75
☐ 107 Elmer Valo	14.00	6.25	1.75
☐ 108 Tom McAvoy	14.00	6.25	1.75
☐ 109 Stan Williams	16.00	7.25	2.00
☐ 110 Earl Averill Jr.	14.00	6.25	1.75
☐ 111 Lee Walls	14.00	6.25	1.75
☐ 112 Paul Richards MG	16.00	7.25	2.00
☐ 113 Ed Sadowski	14.00	6.25	1.75
☐ 114 Stover McIlwain	14.00	6.25	1.75
☐ 115 Chuck Tanner UER (Photo actually Ken Kuhn)	16.50	7.50	2.10
☐ 116 Lou Klimchock	14.00	6.25	1.75
☐ 117 Neil Chrisley	14.00	6.25	1.75
☐ 118 John Callison	16.50	7.50	2.10
☐ 119 Hal Smith	14.00	6.25	1.75
☐ 120 Carl Sawatski	14.00	6.25	1.75
☐ 121 Frank Leja	14.00	6.25	1.75
☐ 122 Earl Torgeson	14.00	6.25	1.75
☐ 123 Art Schult	14.00	6.25	1.75
☐ 124 Jim Brosnan	16.00	7.25	2.00
☐ 125 Sparky Anderson	40.00	18.00	5.00
☐ 126 Joe Pignatano	14.00	6.25	1.75
☐ 127 Rocky Nelson	14.00	6.25	1.75
☐ 128 Orlando Cepeda	50.00	23.00	6.25
☐ 129 Daryl Spencer	14.00	6.25	1.75
☐ 130 Ralph Lumenti	14.00	6.25	1.75
☐ 131 Sam Taylor	14.00	6.25	1.75
☐ 132 Harry Brecheen CO	16.00	7.25	2.00
☐ 133 Johnny Groth	14.00	6.25	1.75
☐ 134 Wayne Terwilliger	14.00	6.25	1.75
☐ 135 Kent Hadley	14.00	6.25	1.75
☐ 136 Faye Throneberry	14.00	6.25	1.75
☐ 137 Jack Meyer	14.00	6.25	1.75
☐ 138 Chuck Cottier	16.50	7.50	2.10
☐ 139 Joe DeMaestri	14.00	6.25	1.75
☐ 140 Gene Freese	14.00	6.25	1.75
☐ 141 Curt Flood	25.00	11.50	3.10
☐ 142 Gino Cimoli	14.00	6.25	1.75
☐ 143 Clay Dalrymple	14.00	6.25	1.75
☐ 144 Jim Bunning	50.00	23.00	6.25

1987 Leaf Special Olympics

This set is also known as the Candy City team as that is the logo which appears on the front of the card. This set was issued for the proceeds of the set to go to the Special Olympics. The set was in the style of the 1983 Donruss Hall of Fame Heroes set and the only additions were generic cards about various sports. The cards are standard size, 2 1/2" by 3 1/2".

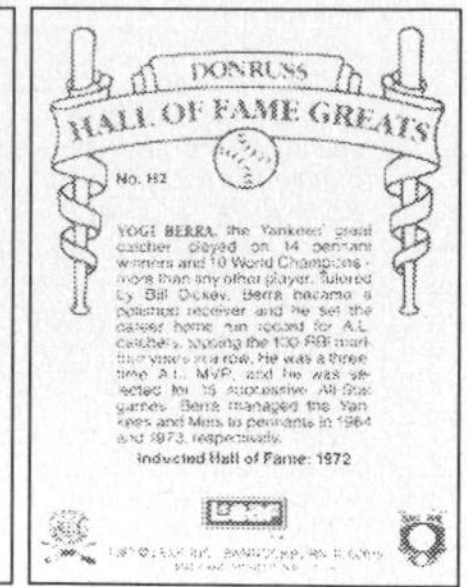

	MT	EX-MT	VG
COMPLETE SET (18)	4.00	1.80	.50
COMMON PLAYER (H1-H12)	.30	.14	.04
COMMON PLAYER (S1-S6)	.10	.05	.01
☐ H1 Mickey Mantle	1.50	.65	.19
☐ H2 Yogi Berra	.50	.23	.06
☐ H3 Roy Campanella	.50	.23	.06
☐ H4 Stan Musial	.50	.23	.06
☐ H5 Ted Williams	.50	.23	.06
☐ H6 Duke Snider	.40	.18	.05
☐ H7 Hank Aaron	.50	.23	.06
☐ H8 Pee Wee Reese	.30	.14	.04
☐ H9 Brooks Robinson	.30	.14	.04
☐ H10 Al Kaline	.30	.14	.04
☐ H11 Willie McCovey	.30	.14	.04
☐ H12 Cool Papa Bell	.30	.14	.04
☐ S1 Basketball	.20	.09	.03
☐ S2 Softball	.10	.05	.01
☐ S3 Track And Field	.10	.05	.01
☐ S4 Soccer	.20	.09	.03
☐ S5 Gymnastics	.10	.05	.01
☐ S6 VII International Summer Games	.10	.05	.01

1990 Leaf Previews

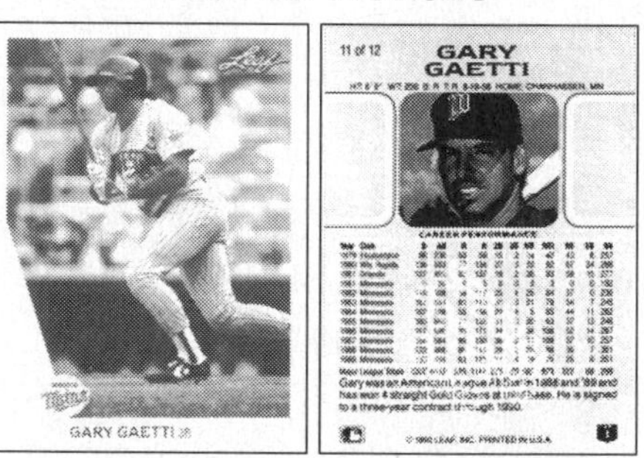

The 1990 Leaf Previews set contains standard-size (2 1/2" by 3 1/2") cards which were mailed to dealers to announce the 1990 version of Donruss' second major set of the year marketed as an upscale alternative under their Leaf name. This 12-card set was presented in the same style as the other Leaf cards were done in except that "Special Preview" was imprinted in white on the back. The cards were released in two series of 264 and the first series was not released until mid-season.

	MT	EX-MT	VG
COMPLETE SET (12)	600.00	275.00	75.00
COMMON PLAYER (1-12)	25.00	11.50	3.10
☐ 1 Steve Sax	25.00	11.50	3.10
☐ 2 Joe Carter	75.00	34.00	9.50
☐ 3 Dennis Eckersley	75.00	34.00	9.50
☐ 4 Ken Griffey Jr.	200.00	90.00	25.00
☐ 5 Barry Larkin	50.00	23.00	6.25
☐ 6 Mark Langston	30.00	13.50	3.80
☐ 7 Eric Anthony	75.00	34.00	9.50
☐ 8 Robin Ventura	100.00	45.00	12.50
☐ 9 Greg Vaughn	35.00	16.00	4.40
☐ 10 Bobby Bonilla	75.00	34.00	9.50
☐ 11 Gary Gaetti	25.00	11.50	3.10
☐ 12 Ozzie Smith	75.00	34.00	9.50

1990 Leaf

The 1990 Leaf set was another major, premium set introduced by Donruss in 1990. This set, which was produced on high quality paper stock, was issued in two separate series of 264 cards each. The second series was issued approximately six weeks after the release of the first series. The cards are in the standard size of 2 1/2" by 3 1/2" and have full-color photos on both the front and the back of the cards. The first card of the set includes a brief history of the Leaf company and the checklists feature player photos in a style very reminiscent to the Topps checklists of the late 1960s. The card style is very similar to Upper Deck, but the Leaf sets were only distributed through hobby channels and were not available in factory sets. The key Rookie Cards in the first series are Eric Anthony, Delino DeShields, Marquis Grissom, Ben McDonald, John Olerud, and Sammy Sosa. The key Rookie Cards in the second series are Carlos Baerga, Chris Hoiles, Dave Justice, Kevin Maas, Jose Offerman, Kevin Tapani, Frank Thomas, Larry Walker, and Mark Whiten. Each pack contained 15 cards and one three-piece puzzle card of a 63-piece Yogi Berra "Donruss Hall of Fame Diamond King" puzzle.

	MT	EX-MT	VG
COMPLETE SET (528)	250.00	115.00	31.00
COMPLETE SERIES 1 (264)	120.00	55.00	15.00
COMPLETE SERIES 2 (264)	130.00	57.50	16.50
COMMON PLAYER (1-264)	.25	.11	.03
COMMON PLAYER (265-528)	.25	.11	.03

	MT	EX-MT	VG
☐ 1 Introductory Card	.25	.11	.03
☐ 2 Mike Henneman	.25	.11	.03
☐ 3 Steve Bedrosian	.25	.11	.03
☐ 4 Mike Scott	.25	.11	.03
☐ 5 Allan Anderson	.25	.11	.03
☐ 6 Rick Sutcliffe	.30	.14	.04
☐ 7 Gregg Olson	1.50	.65	.19
☐ 8 Kevin Elster	.25	.11	.03
☐ 9 Pete O'Brien	.25	.11	.03
☐ 10 Carlton Fisk	1.00	.45	.13
☐ 11 Joe Magrane	.25	.11	.03
☐ 12 Roger Clemens	4.00	1.80	.50
☐ 13 Tom Glavine	9.00	4.00	1.15
☐ 14 Tom Gordon	.30	.14	.04
☐ 15 Todd Benzinger	.25	.11	.03
☐ 16 Hubie Brooks	.25	.11	.03
☐ 17 Roberto Kelly	1.00	.45	.13
☐ 18 Barry Larkin	1.50	.65	.19
☐ 19 Mike Boddicker	.25	.11	.03
☐ 20 Roger McDowell	.25	.11	.03
☐ 21 Nolan Ryan	7.00	3.10	.85
☐ 22 John Farrell	.25	.11	.03
☐ 23 Bruce Hurst	.30	.14	.04
☐ 24 Wally Joyner	.35	.16	.04
☐ 25 Greg Maddux	4.00	1.80	.50
☐ 26 Chris Bosio	.25	.11	.03
☐ 27 John Cerutti	.25	.11	.03
☐ 28 Tim Burke	.25	.11	.03
☐ 29 Dennis Eckersley	.90	.40	.11
☐ 30 Glenn Davis	.30	.14	.04
☐ 31 Jim Abbott	4.00	1.80	.50
☐ 32 Mike LaValliere	.25	.11	.03
☐ 33 Andres Thomas	.25	.11	.03
☐ 34 Lou Whitaker	.30	.14	.04
☐ 35 Alvin Davis	.25	.11	.03
☐ 36 Melido Perez	.30	.14	.04
☐ 37 Craig Biggio	.75	.35	.09
☐ 38 Rick Aguilera	.30	.14	.04
☐ 39 Pete Harnisch	.40	.18	.05
☐ 40 David Cone	1.75	.80	.22
☐ 41 Scott Garrelts	.25	.11	.03
☐ 42 Jay Howell	.25	.11	.03
☐ 43 Eric King	.25	.11	.03
☐ 44 Pedro Guerrero	.30	.14	.04
☐ 45 Mike Bielecki	.25	.11	.03
☐ 46 Bob Boone	.30	.14	.04
☐ 47 Kevin Brown	1.25	.55	.16
☐ 48 Jerry Browne	.25	.11	.03
☐ 49 Mike Scioscia	.25	.11	.03
☐ 50 Chuck Cary	.25	.11	.03
☐ 51 Wade Boggs	1.75	.80	.22
☐ 52 Von Hayes	.25	.11	.03
☐ 53 Tony Fernandez	.30	.14	.04
☐ 54 Dennis Martinez	.30	.14	.04
☐ 55 Tom Candiotti	.25	.11	.03
☐ 56 Andy Benes	3.00	1.35	.40
☐ 57 Rob Dibble	.50	.23	.06
☐ 58 Chuck Crim	.25	.11	.03
☐ 59 John Smoltz	5.00	2.30	.60
☐ 60 Mike Heath	.25	.11	.03
☐ 61 Kevin Gross	.25	.11	.03
☐ 62 Mark McGwire	3.50	1.55	.45
☐ 63 Bert Blyleven	.30	.14	.04
☐ 64 Bob Walk	.25	.11	.03
☐ 65 Mickey Tettleton	.40	.18	.05
☐ 66 Sid Fernandez	.30	.14	.04
☐ 67 Terry Kennedy	.25	.11	.03
☐ 68 Fernando Valenzuela	.30	.14	.04
☐ 69 Don Mattingly	2.00	.90	.25
☐ 70 Paul O'Neill	.30	.14	.04
☐ 71 Robin Yount	1.75	.80	.22
☐ 72 Bret Saberhagen	.30	.14	.04
☐ 73 Geno Petralli	.25	.11	.03
☐ 74 Brook Jacoby	.25	.11	.03
☐ 75 Roberto Alomar	7.00	3.10	.85
☐ 76 Devon White	.30	.14	.04
☐ 77 Jose Lind	.25	.11	.03
☐ 78 Pat Combs	.30	.14	.04
☐ 79 Dave Stieb	.30	.14	.04
☐ 80 Tim Wallach	.30	.14	.04
☐ 81 Dave Stewart	.30	.14	.04
☐ 82 Eric Anthony	2.00	.90	.25
☐ 83 Randy Bush	.25	.11	.03
☐ 84 Checklist Card (Rickey Henderson)	.35	.16	.04
☐ 85 Jaime Navarro	2.00	.90	.25
☐ 86 Tommy Gregg	.25	.11	.03
☐ 87 Frank Tanana	.25	.11	.03
☐ 88 Omar Vizquel	.40	.18	.05
☐ 89 Ivan Calderon	.25	.11	.03
☐ 90 Vince Coleman	.30	.14	.04
☐ 91 Barry Bonds	3.50	1.55	.45
☐ 92 Randy Milligan	.25	.11	.03
☐ 93 Frank Viola	.30	.14	.04
☐ 94 Matt Williams	1.00	.45	.13
☐ 95 Alfredo Griffin	.25	.11	.03
☐ 96 Steve Sax	.30	.14	.04
☐ 97 Gary Gaetti	.25	.11	.03
☐ 98 Ryne Sandberg	4.00	1.80	.50
☐ 99 Danny Tartabull	.75	.35	.09
☐ 100 Rafael Palmeiro	1.25	.55	.16
☐ 101 Jesse Orosco	.25	.11	.03
☐ 102 Garry Templeton	.25	.11	.03
☐ 103 Frank DiPino	.25	.11	.03
☐ 104 Tony Pena	.25	.11	.03
☐ 105 Dickie Thon	.25	.11	.03
☐ 106 Kelly Gruber	.30	.14	.04
☐ 107 Marquis Grissom	6.00	2.70	.75
☐ 108 Jose Canseco	3.50	1.55	.45
☐ 109 Mike Blowers	.25	.11	.03
☐ 110 Tom Browning	.25	.11	.03
☐ 111 Greg Vaughn	1.50	.65	.19
☐ 112 Oddibe McDowell	.25	.11	.03
☐ 113 Gary Ward	.25	.11	.03
☐ 114 Jay Buhner	.35	.16	.04
☐ 115 Eric Show	.25	.11	.03
☐ 116 Bryan Harvey	.35	.16	.04
☐ 117 Andy Van Slyke	.50	.23	.06
☐ 118 Jeff Ballard	.25	.11	.03
☐ 119 Barry Lyons	.25	.11	.03
☐ 120 Kevin Mitchell	.50	.23	.06
☐ 121 Mike Gallego	.25	.11	.03
☐ 122 Dave Smith	.25	.11	.03
☐ 123 Kirby Puckett	3.50	1.55	.45
☐ 124 Jerome Walton	.30	.14	.04
☐ 125 Bo Jackson	1.25	.55	.16

☐ 126 Harold Baines .30 .14 .04
☐ 127 Scott Bankhead .25 .11 .03
☐ 128 Ozzie Guillen .25 .11 .03
☐ 129 Jose Oquendo UER .25 .11 .03
(League misspelled as Legue)
☐ 130 John Dopson .25 .11 .03
☐ 131 Charlie Hayes .50 .23 .06
☐ 132 Fred McGriff 2.00 .90 .25
☐ 133 Chet Lemon .25 .11 .03
☐ 134 Gary Carter .35 .16 .04
☐ 135 Rafael Ramirez .25 .11 .03
☐ 136 Shane Mack 1.00 .45 .13
☐ 137 Mark Grace UER 2.00 .90 .25
(Card back has OB:L, should be B:L)
☐ 138 Phil Bradley .25 .11 .03
☐ 139 Dwight Gooden .50 .23 .06
☐ 140 Harold Reynolds .25 .11 .03
☐ 141 Scott Fletcher .25 .11 .03
☐ 142 Ozzie Smith 1.00 .45 .13
☐ 143 Mike Greenwell .30 .14 .04
☐ 144 Pete Smith .75 .35 .09
☐ 145 Mark Gubicza .25 .11 .03
☐ 146 Chris Sabo .40 .18 .05
☐ 147 Ramon Martinez 1.75 .80 .22
☐ 148 Tim Leary .25 .11 .03
☐ 149 Randy Myers .30 .14 .04
☐ 150 Jody Reed .25 .11 .03
☐ 151 Bruce Ruffin .25 .11 .03
☐ 152 Jeff Russell .25 .11 .03
☐ 153 Doug Jones .30 .14 .04
☐ 154 Tony Gwynn 2.00 .90 .25
☐ 155 Mark Langston .30 .14 .04
☐ 156 Mitch Williams .30 .14 .04
☐ 157 Gary Sheffield 15.00 6.75 1.90
☐ 158 Tom Henke .30 .14 .04
☐ 159 Oil Can Boyd .25 .11 .03
☐ 160 Rickey Henderson 2.00 .90 .25
☐ 161 Bill Doran .25 .11 .03
☐ 162 Chuck Finley .30 .14 .04
☐ 163 Jeff King .30 .14 .04
☐ 164 Nick Esasky .25 .11 .03
☐ 165 Cecil Fielder 2.00 .90 .25
☐ 166 Dave Valle .25 .11 .03
☐ 167 Robin Ventura 11.00 4.90 1.40
☐ 168 Jim Deshaies .25 .11 .03
☐ 169 Juan Berenguer .25 .11 .03
☐ 170 Craig Worthington .25 .11 .03
☐ 171 Gregg Jeffries 1.25 .55 .16
☐ 172 Will Clark 3.50 1.55 .45
☐ 173 Kirk Gibson .30 .14 .04
☐ 174 Checklist Card .30 .14 .04
(Carlton Fisk)
☐ 175 Bobby Thigpen .25 .11 .03
☐ 176 John Tudor .25 .11 .03
☐ 177 Andre Dawson 1.00 .45 .13
☐ 178 George Brett 1.75 .80 .22
☐ 179 Steve Buechele .25 .11 .03
☐ 180 Joey Belle 8.00 3.60 1.00
☐ 181 Eddie Murray 1.00 .45 .13
☐ 182 Bob Geren .25 .11 .03
☐ 183 Rob Murphy .25 .11 .03
☐ 184 Tom Herr .25 .11 .03
☐ 185 George Bell .30 .14 .04
☐ 186 Spike Owen .25 .11 .03
☐ 187 Cory Snyder .25 .11 .03
☐ 188 Fred Lynn .30 .14 .04
☐ 189 Eric Davis .50 .23 .06
☐ 190 Dave Parker .30 .14 .04
☐ 191 Jeff Blauser .30 .14 .04
☐ 192 Matt Nokes .25 .11 .03
☐ 193 Delino DeShields 6.00 2.70 .75
☐ 194 Scott Sanderson .25 .11 .03
☐ 195 Lance Parrish .30 .14 .04
☐ 196 Bobby Bonilla 1.25 .55 .16
☐ 197 Cal Ripken UER 5.00 2.30 .60
(Reistertown, should be Reisterstown)
☐ 198 Kevin McReynolds .30 .14 .04
☐ 199 Robby Thompson .25 .11 .03
☐ 200 Tim Belcher .30 .14 .04
☐ 201 Jesse Barfield .25 .11 .03
☐ 202 Mariano Duncan .25 .11 .03
☐ 203 Bill Spiers .25 .11 .03
☐ 204 Frank White .25 .11 .03
☐ 205 Julio Franco .30 .14 .04
☐ 206 Greg Swindell .50 .23 .06
☐ 207 Benito Santiago .30 .14 .04
☐ 208 Johnny Ray .25 .11 .03
☐ 209 Gary Redus .25 .11 .03
☐ 210 Jeff Parrett .25 .11 .03
☐ 211 Jimmy Key .30 .14 .04
☐ 212 Tim Raines .30 .14 .04
☐ 213 Carney Lansford .30 .14 .04
☐ 214 Gerald Young .25 .11 .03
☐ 215 Gene Larkin .25 .11 .03
☐ 216 Dan Plesac .25 .11 .03
☐ 217 Lonnie Smith .30 .14 .04
☐ 218 Alan Trammell .30 .14 .04
☐ 219 Jeffrey Leonard .25 .11 .03
☐ 220 Sammy Sosa .75 .35 .09
☐ 221 Todd Zeile 1.00 .45 .13
☐ 222 Bill Landrum .25 .11 .03
☐ 223 Mike Devereaux 1.00 .45 .13
☐ 224 Mike Marshall .25 .11 .03
☐ 225 Jose Uribe .25 .11 .03
☐ 226 Juan Samuel .25 .11 .03
☐ 227 Mel Hall .25 .11 .03
☐ 228 Kent Hrbek .30 .14 .04
☐ 229 Shawon Dunston .30 .14 .04
☐ 230 Kevin Seitzer .30 .14 .04
☐ 231 Pete Incaviglia .25 .11 .03
☐ 232 Sandy Alomar Jr. .50 .23 .06
☐ 233 Bip Roberts .30 .14 .04
☐ 234 Scott Terry .25 .11 .03
☐ 235 Dwight Evans .30 .14 .04
☐ 236 Ricky Jordan .30 .14 .04
☐ 237 John Olerud 6.00 2.70 .75
☐ 238 Zane Smith .25 .11 .03
☐ 239 Walt Weiss .25 .11 .03
☐ 240 Alvaro Espinoza .25 .11 .03
☐ 241 Billy Hatcher .25 .11 .03
☐ 242 Paul Molitor .50 .23 .06
☐ 243 Dale Murphy .50 .23 .06
☐ 244 Dave Bergman .25 .11 .03
☐ 245 Ken Griffey Jr. 24.00 11.00 3.00
☐ 246 Ed Whitson .25 .11 .03
☐ 247 Kirk McCaskill .25 .11 .03
☐ 248 Jay Bell .30 .14 .04
☐ 249 Ben McDonald 4.00 1.80 .50
☐ 250 Darryl Strawberry 2.00 .90 .25
☐ 251 Brett Butler .30 .14 .04
☐ 252 Terry Steinbach .30 .14 .04
☐ 253 Ken Caminiti .30 .14 .04
☐ 254 Dan Gladden .25 .11 .03
☐ 255 Dwight Smith .25 .11 .03
☐ 256 Kurt Stillwell .25 .11 .03
☐ 257 Ruben Sierra 2.00 .90 .25
☐ 258 Mike Schooler .25 .11 .03
☐ 259 Lance Johnson .30 .14 .04
☐ 260 Terry Pendleton .60 .25 .08
☐ 261 Ellis Burks .30 .14 .04
☐ 262 Len Dykstra .30 .14 .04
☐ 263 Mookie Wilson .25 .11 .03
☐ 264 Checklist Card .50 .23 .06
(Nolan Ryan) UER
(No TM after Ranger logo)
☐ 265 No Hit King 5.00 2.30 .60
(Nolan Ryan)
☐ 266 Brian DuBois .25 .11 .03
☐ 267 Don Robinson .25 .11 .03
☐ 268 Glenn Wilson .25 .11 .03
☐ 269 Kevin Tapani 2.50 1.15 .30
☐ 270 Marvell Wynne .25 .11 .03
☐ 271 Billy Ripken .25 .11 .03
☐ 272 Howard Johnson .30 .14 .04
☐ 273 Brian Holman .25 .11 .03
☐ 274 Dan Pasqua .25 .11 .03
☐ 275 Ken Dayley .25 .11 .03
☐ 276 Jeff Reardon .40 .18 .05
☐ 277 Jim Presley .25 .11 .03
☐ 278 Jim Eisenreich .25 .11 .03
☐ 279 Danny Jackson .25 .11 .03
☐ 280 Orel Hershiser .30 .14 .04
☐ 281 Andy Hawkins .25 .11 .03
☐ 282 Jose Rijo .35 .16 .04
☐ 283 Luis Rivera .25 .11 .03
☐ 284 John Kruk .40 .18 .05
☐ 285 Jeff Huson .35 .16 .04
☐ 286 Joel Skinner .25 .11 .03
☐ 287 Jack Clark .30 .14 .04
☐ 288 Chili Davis .30 .14 .04
☐ 289 Joe Girardi .25 .11 .03
☐ 290 B.J. Surhoff .25 .11 .03
☐ 291 Luis Sojo .50 .23 .06
☐ 292 Tom Foley .25 .11 .03
☐ 293 Mike Moore .25 .11 .03
☐ 294 Ken Oberkfell .25 .11 .03
☐ 295 Luis Polonia .30 .14 .04
☐ 296 Doug Drabek .35 .16 .04
☐ 297 Dave Justice 20.00 9.00 2.50
☐ 298 Paul Gibson .25 .11 .03
☐ 299 Edgar Martinez 2.50 1.15 .30
☐ 300 Frank Thomas UER 60.00 27.00 7.50

	Card			
	(No B in front of birthdate)			
☐	301 Eric Yelding	.25	.11	.03
☐	302 Greg Gagne	.25	.11	.03
☐	303 Brad Komminsk	.25	.11	.03
☐	304 Ron Darling	.30	.14	.04
☐	305 Kevin Bass	.25	.11	.03
☐	306 Jeff Hamilton	.25	.11	.03
☐	307 Ron Karkovice	.25	.11	.03
☐	308 Milt Thompson UER (Ray Lankford pictured on card back)	.40	.18	.05
☐	309 Mike Harkey	.30	.14	.04
☐	310 Mel Stottlemyre Jr.	.25	.11	.03
☐	311 Kenny Rogers	.25	.11	.03
☐	312 Mitch Webster	.25	.11	.03
☐	313 Kal Daniels	.25	.11	.03
☐	314 Matt Nokes	.30	.14	.04
☐	315 Dennis Lamp	.25	.11	.03
☐	316 Ken Howell	.25	.11	.03
☐	317 Glenallen Hill	.30	.14	.04
☐	318 Dave Martinez	.30	.14	.04
☐	319 Chris James	.25	.11	.03
☐	320 Mike Pagliarulo	.25	.11	.03
☐	321 Hal Morris	1.50	.65	.19
☐	322 Rob Deer	.30	.14	.04
☐	323 Greg Olson	.35	.16	.04
☐	324 Tony Phillips	.25	.11	.03
☐	325 Larry Walker	10.00	4.50	1.25
☐	326 Ron Hassey	.25	.11	.03
☐	327 Jack Howell	.25	.11	.03
☐	328 John Smiley	.30	.14	.04
☐	329 Steve Finley	.60	.25	.08
☐	330 Dave Magadan	.30	.14	.04
☐	331 Greg Litton	.25	.11	.03
☐	332 Mickey Hatcher	.25	.11	.03
☐	333 Lee Guetterman	.25	.11	.03
☐	334 Norm Charlton	.40	.18	.05
☐	335 Edgar Diaz	.25	.11	.03
☐	336 Willie Wilson	.25	.11	.03
☐	337 Bobby Witt	.30	.14	.04
☐	338 Candy Maldonado	.25	.11	.03
☐	339 Craig Lefferts	.25	.11	.03
☐	340 Dante Bichette	.50	.23	.06
☐	341 Wally Backman	.25	.11	.03
☐	342 Dennis Cook	.25	.11	.03
☐	343 Pat Borders	.60	.25	.08
☐	344 Wallace Johnson	.25	.11	.03
☐	345 Willie Randolph	.30	.14	.04
☐	346 Danny Darwin	.25	.11	.03
☐	347 Al Newman	.25	.11	.03
☐	348 Mark Knudson	.25	.11	.03
☐	349 Joe Boever	.25	.11	.03
☐	350 Larry Sheets	.25	.11	.03
☐	351 Mike Jackson	.25	.11	.03
☐	352 Wayne Edwards	.25	.11	.03
☐	353 Bernard Gilkey	1.50	.65	.19
☐	354 Don Slaught	.25	.11	.03
☐	355 Joe Orsulak	.25	.11	.03
☐	356 John Franco	.30	.14	.04
☐	357 Jeff Brantley	.25	.11	.03
☐	358 Mike Morgan	.30	.14	.04
☐	359 Deion Sanders	8.00	3.60	1.00
☐	360 Terry Leach	.25	.11	.03
☐	361 Les Lancaster	.25	.11	.03
☐	362 Storm Davis	.25	.11	.03
☐	363 Scott Coolbaugh	.25	.11	.03
☐	364 Checklist Card (Ozzie Smith)	.30	.14	.04
☐	365 Cecilio Guante	.25	.11	.03
☐	366 Joey Cora	.25	.11	.03
☐	367 Willie McGee	.30	.14	.04
☐	368 Jerry Reed	.25	.11	.03
☐	369 Darren Daulton	.50	.23	.06
☐	370 Manny Lee	.25	.11	.03
☐	371 Mark Gardner	.60	.25	.08
☐	372 Rick Honeycutt	.25	.11	.03
☐	373 Steve Balboni	.25	.11	.03
☐	374 Jack Armstrong	.30	.14	.04
☐	375 Charlie O'Brien	.25	.11	.03
☐	376 Ron Gant	3.00	1.35	.40
☐	377 Lloyd Moseby	.25	.11	.03
☐	378 Gene Harris	.25	.11	.03
☐	379 Joe Carter	2.00	.90	.25
☐	380 Scott Bailes	.25	.11	.03
☐	381 R.J. Reynolds	.25	.11	.03
☐	382 Bob Melvin	.25	.11	.03
☐	383 Tim Teufel	.25	.11	.03
☐	384 John Burkett	.35	.16	.04
☐	385 Felix Jose	1.75	.80	.22
☐	386 Larry Andersen	.25	.11	.03
☐	387 David West	.25	.11	.03
☐	388 Luis Salazar	.25	.11	.03
☐	389 Mike Macfarlane	.35	.16	.04
☐	390 Charlie Hough	.25	.11	.03
☐	391 Greg Briley	.30	.14	.04
☐	392 Donn Pall	.25	.11	.03
☐	393 Bryn Smith	.25	.11	.03
☐	394 Carlos Quintana	.30	.14	.04
☐	395 Steve Lake	.25	.11	.03
☐	396 Mark Whiten	1.50	.65	.19
☐	397 Edwin Nunez	.25	.11	.03
☐	398 Rick Parker	.25	.11	.03
☐	399 Mark Portugal	.25	.11	.03
☐	400 Roy Smith	.25	.11	.03
☐	401 Hector Villanueva	.35	.16	.04
☐	402 Bob Milacki	.25	.11	.03
☐	403 Alejandro Pena	.25	.11	.03
☐	404 Scott Bradley	.25	.11	.03
☐	405 Ron Kittle	.25	.11	.03
☐	406 Bob Tewksbury	.30	.14	.04
☐	407 Wes Gardner	.25	.11	.03
☐	408 Ernie Whitt	.25	.11	.03
☐	409 Terry Shumpert	.25	.11	.03
☐	410 Tim Layana	.25	.11	.03
☐	411 Chris Gwynn	.30	.14	.04
☐	412 Jeff Robinson	.25	.11	.03
☐	413 Scott Scudder	.35	.16	.04
☐	414 Kevin Romine	.25	.11	.03
☐	415 Jose DeJesus	.25	.11	.03
☐	416 Mike Jeffcoat	.25	.11	.03
☐	417 Rudy Seanez	.40	.18	.05
☐	418 Mike Dunne	.25	.11	.03
☐	419 Dick Schofield	.25	.11	.03
☐	420 Steve Wilson	.25	.11	.03
☐	421 Bill Krueger	.25	.11	.03
☐	422 Junior Felix	.50	.23	.06
☐	423 Drew Hall	.25	.11	.03
☐	424 Curt Young	.25	.11	.03
☐	425 Franklin Stubbs	.25	.11	.03
☐	426 Dave Winfield	1.50	.65	.19
☐	427 Rick Reed	.25	.11	.03
☐	428 Charlie Leibrandt	.25	.11	.03
☐	429 Jeff Robinson	.25	.11	.03
☐	430 Erik Hanson	.30	.14	.04
☐	431 Barry Jones	.25	.11	.03
☐	432 Alex Trevino	.25	.11	.03
☐	433 John Moses	.25	.11	.03
☐	434 Dave Johnson	.25	.11	.03
☐	435 Mackey Sasser	.25	.11	.03
☐	436 Rick Leach	.25	.11	.03
☐	437 Lenny Harris	.30	.14	.04
☐	438 Carlos Martinez	.30	.14	.04
☐	439 Rex Hudler	.25	.11	.03
☐	440 Domingo Ramos	.25	.11	.03
☐	441 Gerald Perry	.25	.11	.03
☐	442 Jeff Russell	.25	.11	.03
☐	443 Carlos Baerga	11.00	4.90	1.40
☐	444 Checklist Card (Will Clark)	.35	.16	.04
☐	445 Stan Javier	.25	.11	.03
☐	446 Kevin Maas	1.50	.65	.19
☐	447 Tom Brunansky	.30	.14	.04
☐	448 Carmelo Martinez	.25	.11	.03
☐	449 Willie Blair	.35	.16	.04
☐	450 Andres Galarraga	.30	.14	.04
☐	451 Bud Black	.25	.11	.03
☐	452 Greg W. Harris	.30	.14	.04
☐	453 Joe Oliver	.35	.16	.04
☐	454 Greg Brock	.25	.11	.03
☐	455 Jeff Treadway	.25	.11	.03
☐	456 Lance McCullers	.25	.11	.03
☐	457 Dave Schmidt	.25	.11	.03
☐	458 Todd Burns	.25	.11	.03
☐	459 Max Venable	.25	.11	.03
☐	460 Neal Heaton	.25	.11	.03
☐	461 Mark Williamson	.25	.11	.03
☐	462 Keith Miller	.25	.11	.03
☐	463 Mike LaCoss	.25	.11	.03
☐	464 Jose Offerman	.90	.40	.11
☐	465 Jim Leyritz	.35	.16	.04
☐	466 Glenn Braggs	.25	.11	.03
☐	467 Ron Robinson	.25	.11	.03
☐	468 Mark Davis	.25	.11	.03
☐	469 Gary Pettis	.25	.11	.03
☐	470 Keith Hernandez	.30	.14	.04
☐	471 Dennis Rasmussen	.25	.11	.03
☐	472 Mark Eichhorn	.25	.11	.03
☐	473 Ted Power	.25	.11	.03
☐	474 Terry Mulholland	.30	.14	.04
☐	475 Todd Stottlemyre	.40	.18	.05
☐	476 Jerry Goff	.25	.11	.03
☐	477 Gene Nelson	.25	.11	.03
☐	478 Rich Gedman	.25	.11	.03
☐	479 Brian Harper	.30	.14	.04
☐	480 Mike Felder	.25	.11	.03
☐	481 Steve Avery	11.00	4.90	1.40

☐ 482 Jack Morris	.75	.35	.09
☐ 483 Randy Johnson	1.00	.45	.13
☐ 484 Scott Radinsky	.75	.35	.09
☐ 485 Jose DeLeon	.25	.11	.03
☐ 486 Stan Belinda	.60	.25	.08
☐ 487 Brian Holton	.25	.11	.03
☐ 488 Mark Carreon	.25	.11	.03
☐ 489 Trevor Wilson	.25	.11	.03
☐ 490 Mike Sharperson	.25	.11	.03
☐ 491 Alan Mills	.50	.23	.06
☐ 492 John Candelaria	.25	.11	.03
☐ 493 Paul Assenmacher	.25	.11	.03
☐ 494 Steve Crawford	.25	.11	.03
☐ 495 Brad Arnsberg	.25	.11	.03
☐ 496 Sergio Valdez	.25	.11	.03
☐ 497 Mark Parent	.25	.11	.03
☐ 498 Tom Pagnozzi	.30	.14	.04
☐ 499 Greg A. Harris	.25	.11	.03
☐ 500 Randy Ready	.25	.11	.03
☐ 501 Duane Ward	.25	.11	.03
☐ 502 Nelson Santovenia	.25	.11	.03
☐ 503 Joe Klink	.25	.11	.03
☐ 504 Eric Plunk	.25	.11	.03
☐ 505 Jeff Reed	.25	.11	.03
☐ 506 Ted Higuera	.25	.11	.03
☐ 507 Joe Hesketh	.25	.11	.03
☐ 508 Dan Petry	.25	.11	.03
☐ 509 Matt Young	.25	.11	.03
☐ 510 Jerald Clark	.35	.16	.04
☐ 511 John Orton	.35	.16	.04
☐ 512 Scott Ruskin	.25	.11	.03
☐ 513 Chris Hoiles	3.00	1.35	.40
☐ 514 Daryl Boston	.25	.11	.03
☐ 515 Francisco Oliveras	.25	.11	.03
☐ 516 Ozzie Canseco	.40	.18	.05
☐ 517 Xavier Hernandez	.35	.16	.04
☐ 518 Fred Manrique	.25	.11	.03
☐ 519 Shawn Boskie	.40	.18	.05
☐ 520 Jeff Montgomery	.30	.14	.04
☐ 521 Jack Daugherty	.25	.11	.03
☐ 522 Keith Comstock	.25	.11	.03
☐ 523 Greg Hibbard	.75	.35	.09
☐ 524 Lee Smith	.50	.23	.06
☐ 525 Dana Kiecker	.25	.11	.03
☐ 526 Darrel Akerfelds	.25	.11	.03
☐ 527 Greg Myers	.25	.11	.03
☐ 528 Checklist Card (Ryne Sandberg)	.35	.16	.04

1991 Leaf Previews

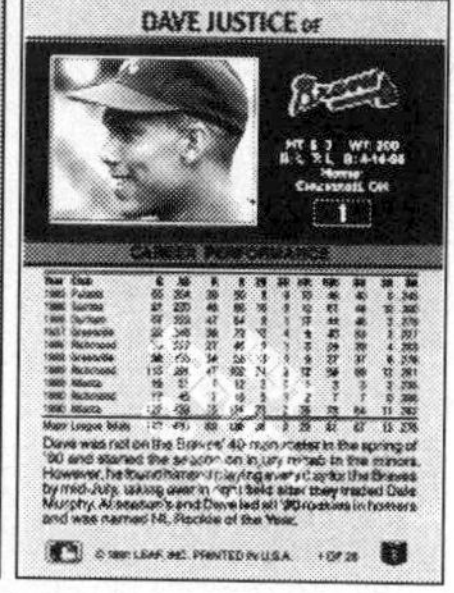

The 1991 Leaf Previews set consists of 26 cards measuring the standard size (2 1/2" by 3 1/2"). The front design has color action player photos, with white and silver borders. Black photo mounts are drawn in at the corners of the pictures, just as one would find in an old-fashioned photo album. The back has a color head shot and biography in the top portion on a black background. A red stripe cuts across the card, and career statistics are given below it on a silver background. The words "1991 Preview Card" appear in white block lettering beneath the statistics. The cards are numbered on the back. Cards from this set were issued as inserts (four at a time) inside specially marked 1991 Donruss hobby factory sets.

	MT	EX-MT	VG
COMPLETE SET (26)	90.00	40.00	11.50
COMMON PLAYER (1-26)	1.50	.65	.19
☐ 1 Dave Justice	9.00	4.00	1.15
☐ 2 Ryne Sandberg	9.00	4.00	1.15
☐ 3 Barry Larkin	2.50	1.15	.30
☐ 4 Craig Biggio	1.50	.65	.19
☐ 5 Ramon Martinez	2.00	.90	.25
☐ 6 Tim Wallach	1.50	.65	.19
☐ 7 Dwight Gooden	2.00	.90	.25
☐ 8 Len Dykstra	1.50	.65	.19
☐ 9 Barry Bonds	6.00	2.70	.75
☐ 10 Ray Lankford	5.00	2.30	.60
☐ 11 Tony Gwynn	5.00	2.30	.60
☐ 12 Will Clark	6.00	2.70	.75
☐ 13 Leo Gomez	2.50	1.15	.30
☐ 14 Wade Boggs	4.50	2.00	.55
☐ 15 Chuck Finley UER (Position on card back is First Base)	1.50	.65	.19
☐ 16 Carlton Fisk	3.00	1.35	.40
☐ 17 Sandy Alomar Jr.	2.00	.90	.25
☐ 18 Cecil Fielder	4.50	2.00	.55
☐ 19 Bo Jackson	4.50	2.00	.55
☐ 20 Paul Molitor	2.50	1.15	.30
☐ 21 Kirby Puckett	6.00	2.70	.75
☐ 22 Don Mattingly	4.50	2.00	.55
☐ 23 Rickey Henderson	4.50	2.00	.55
☐ 24 Tino Martinez	2.00	.90	.25
☐ 25 Nolan Ryan	15.00	6.75	1.90
☐ 26 Dave Stieb	1.50	.65	.19

1991 Leaf

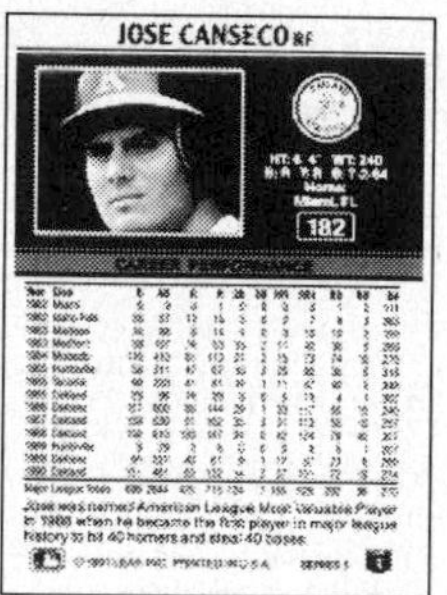

This 528-card standard size 2 1/2" by 3 1/2" set marks the second year Donruss has produced a two-series premium set using the Leaf name. This set features a photo of the player which is surrounded by black and white borders. The whole card is framed in gray borders. The Leaf logo is in the upper right corner of the card. The back of the card features a gray, red and black back with white lettering on the black background and black lettering on the gray and red backgrounds. The backs of the cards also features biographical and statistical information along with a write-up when room is provided. The set was issued using the Donruss dealer distribution network with very little Leaf product being released in other fashions. The cards are numbered on the back. The key Rookie Cards in the first series are Wes Chamberlain, Brian McRae, and Randy Tomlin. The key Rookie Cards in the second series are Orlando Merced and Denny Neagle.

	MT	EX-MT	VG
COMPLETE SET (528)	45.00	20.00	5.75
COMPLETE SERIES 1 (264)	22.50	10.00	2.80
COMPLETE SERIES 2 (264)	22.50	10.00	2.80
COMMON PLAYER (1-264)	.08	.04	.01
COMMON PLAYER (265-528)	.08	.04	.01
☐ 1 The Leaf Card	.10	.04	.01
☐ 2 Kurt Stillwell	.08	.04	.01
☐ 3 Bobby Witt	.08	.04	.01
☐ 4 Tony Phillips	.08	.04	.01

Card			
☐ 5 Scott Garrelts	.08	.04	.01
☐ 6 Greg Swindell	.10	.04	.01
☐ 7 Billy Ripken	.08	.04	.01
☐ 8 Dave Martinez	.08	.04	.01
☐ 9 Kelly Gruber	.10	.04	.01
☐ 10 Juan Samuel	.08	.04	.01
☐ 11 Brian Holman	.08	.04	.01
☐ 12 Craig Biggio	.15	.07	.02
☐ 13 Lonnie Smith	.08	.04	.01
☐ 14 Ron Robinson	.08	.04	.01
☐ 15 Mike LaValliere	.08	.04	.01
☐ 16 Mark Davis	.08	.04	.01
☐ 17 Jack Daugherty	.08	.04	.01
☐ 18 Mike Henneman	.08	.04	.01
☐ 19 Mike Greenwell	.12	.05	.02
☐ 20 Dave Magadan	.10	.04	.01
☐ 21 Mark Williamson	.08	.04	.01
☐ 22 Marquis Grissom	.50	.23	.06
☐ 23 Pat Borders	.08	.04	.01
☐ 24 Mike Scioscia	.08	.04	.01
☐ 25 Shawon Dunston	.10	.04	.01
☐ 26 Randy Bush	.08	.04	.01
☐ 27 John Smoltz	.40	.18	.05
☐ 28 Chuck Crim	.08	.04	.01
☐ 29 Don Slaught	.08	.04	.01
☐ 30 Mike Macfarlane	.08	.04	.01
☐ 31 Wally Joyner	.10	.04	.01
☐ 32 Pat Combs	.08	.04	.01
☐ 33 Tony Pena	.08	.04	.01
☐ 34 Howard Johnson	.10	.04	.01
☐ 35 Leo Gomez	.75	.35	.09
☐ 36 Spike Owen	.08	.04	.01
☐ 37 Eric Davis	.15	.07	.02
☐ 38 Roberto Kelly	.12	.05	.02
☐ 39 Jerome Walton	.08	.04	.01
☐ 40 Shane Mack	.10	.04	.01
☐ 41 Kent Mercker	.08	.04	.01
☐ 42 B.J. Surhoff	.08	.04	.01
☐ 43 Jerry Browne	.08	.04	.01
☐ 44 Lee Smith	.10	.04	.01
☐ 45 Chuck Finley	.10	.04	.01
☐ 46 Terry Mulholland	.08	.04	.01
☐ 47 Tom Bolton	.08	.04	.01
☐ 48 Tom Herr	.08	.04	.01
☐ 49 Jim Deshaies	.08	.04	.01
☐ 50 Walt Weiss	.08	.04	.01
☐ 51 Hal Morris	.10	.04	.01
☐ 52 Lee Guetterman	.08	.04	.01
☐ 53 Paul Assenmacher	.08	.04	.01
☐ 54 Brian Harper	.08	.04	.01
☐ 55 Paul Gibson	.08	.04	.01
☐ 56 John Burkett	.08	.04	.01
☐ 57 Doug Jones	.08	.04	.01
☐ 58 Jose Oquendo	.08	.04	.01
☐ 59 Dick Schofield	.08	.04	.01
☐ 60 Dickie Thon	.08	.04	.01
☐ 61 Ramon Martinez	.15	.07	.02
☐ 62 Jay Buhner	.10	.04	.01
☐ 63 Mark Portugal	.08	.04	.01
☐ 64 Bob Welch	.08	.04	.01
☐ 65 Chris Sabo	.10	.04	.01
☐ 66 Chuck Cary	.08	.04	.01
☐ 67 Mark Langston	.10	.04	.01
☐ 68 Joe Boever	.08	.04	.01
☐ 69 Jody Reed	.08	.04	.01
☐ 70 Alejandro Pena	.08	.04	.01
☐ 71 Jeff King	.08	.04	.01
☐ 72 Tom Pagnozzi	.08	.04	.01
☐ 73 Joe Oliver	.08	.04	.01
☐ 74 Mike Witt	.08	.04	.01
☐ 75 Hector Villanueva	.08	.04	.01
☐ 76 Dan Gladden	.08	.04	.01
☐ 77 Dave Justice	2.00	.90	.25
☐ 78 Mike Gallego	.08	.04	.01
☐ 79 Tom Candiotti	.08	.04	.01
☐ 80 Ozzie Smith	.25	.11	.03
☐ 81 Luis Polonia	.10	.04	.01
☐ 82 Randy Ready	.08	.04	.01
☐ 83 Greg A. Harris	.08	.04	.01
☐ 84 Checklist Card Dave Justice	.15	.07	.02
☐ 85 Kevin Mitchell	.12	.05	.02
☐ 86 Mark McLemore	.08	.04	.01
☐ 87 Terry Steinbach	.10	.04	.01
☐ 88 Tom Browning	.08	.04	.01
☐ 89 Matt Nokes	.08	.04	.01
☐ 90 Mike Harkey	.10	.04	.01
☐ 91 Omar Vizquel	.08	.04	.01
☐ 92 Dave Bergman	.08	.04	.01
☐ 93 Matt Williams	.12	.05	.02
☐ 94 Steve Olin	.10	.04	.01
☐ 95 Craig Wilson	.15	.07	.02
☐ 96 Dave Stieb	.08	.04	.01
☐ 97 Ruben Sierra	.50	.23	.06
☐ 98 Jay Howell	.08	.04	.01
☐ 99 Scott Bradley	.08	.04	.01
☐ 100 Eric Yelding	.08	.04	.01
☐ 101 Rickey Henderson	.40	.18	.05
☐ 102 Jeff Reed	.08	.04	.01
☐ 103 Jimmy Key	.08	.04	.01
☐ 104 Terry Shumpert	.08	.04	.01
☐ 105 Kenny Rogers	.08	.04	.01
☐ 106 Cecil Fielder	.40	.18	.05
☐ 107 Robby Thompson	.08	.04	.01
☐ 108 Alex Cole	.08	.04	.01
☐ 109 Randy Milligan	.08	.04	.01
☐ 110 Andres Galarraga	.08	.04	.01
☐ 111 Bill Spiers	.08	.04	.01
☐ 112 Kal Daniels	.08	.04	.01
☐ 113 Henry Cotto	.08	.04	.01
☐ 114 Casey Candaele	.08	.04	.01
☐ 115 Jeff Blauser	.08	.04	.01
☐ 116 Robin Yount	.35	.16	.04
☐ 117 Ben McDonald	.25	.11	.03
☐ 118 Bret Saberhagen	.10	.04	.01
☐ 119 Juan Gonzalez	4.00	1.80	.50
☐ 120 Lou Whitaker	.10	.04	.01
☐ 121 Ellis Burks	.10	.04	.01
☐ 122 Charlie O'Brien	.08	.04	.01
☐ 123 John Smiley	.10	.04	.01
☐ 124 Tim Burke	.08	.04	.01
☐ 125 John Olerud	.50	.23	.06
☐ 126 Eddie Murray	.25	.11	.03
☐ 127 Greg Maddux	.30	.14	.04
☐ 128 Kevin Tapani	.25	.11	.03
☐ 129 Ron Gant	.40	.18	.05
☐ 130 Jay Bell	.10	.04	.01
☐ 131 Chris Hoiles	.30	.14	.04
☐ 132 Tom Gordon	.10	.04	.01
☐ 133 Kevin Seitzer	.10	.04	.01
☐ 134 Jeff Huson	.08	.04	.01
☐ 135 Jerry Don Gleaton	.08	.04	.01
☐ 136 Jeff Brantley UER (Photo actually Rick Leach on back)	.08	.04	.01
☐ 137 Felix Fermin	.08	.04	.01
☐ 138 Mike Devereaux	.10	.04	.01
☐ 139 Delino DeShields	.50	.23	.06
☐ 140 David Wells	.08	.04	.01
☐ 141 Tim Crews	.08	.04	.01
☐ 142 Erik Hanson	.08	.04	.01
☐ 143 Mark Davidson	.08	.04	.01
☐ 144 Tommy Gregg	.08	.04	.01
☐ 145 Jim Gantner	.08	.04	.01
☐ 146 Jose Lind	.08	.04	.01
☐ 147 Danny Tartabull	.15	.07	.02
☐ 148 Geno Petralli	.08	.04	.01
☐ 149 Travis Fryman	3.50	1.55	.45
☐ 150 Tim Naehring	.15	.07	.02
☐ 151 Kevin McReynolds	.10	.04	.01
☐ 152 Joe Orsulak	.08	.04	.01
☐ 153 Steve Frey	.08	.04	.01
☐ 154 Duane Ward	.08	.04	.01
☐ 155 Stan Javier	.08	.04	.01
☐ 156 Damon Berryhill	.08	.04	.01
☐ 157 Gene Larkin	.08	.04	.01
☐ 158 Greg Olson	.08	.04	.01
☐ 159 Mark Knudson	.08	.04	.01
☐ 160 Carmelo Martinez	.08	.04	.01
☐ 161 Storm Davis	.08	.04	.01
☐ 162 Jim Abbott	.35	.16	.04
☐ 163 Len Dykstra	.10	.04	.01
☐ 164 Tom Brunansky	.10	.04	.01
☐ 165 Dwight Gooden	.15	.07	.02
☐ 166 Jose Mesa	.08	.04	.01
☐ 167 Oil Can Boyd	.08	.04	.01
☐ 168 Barry Larkin	.25	.11	.03
☐ 169 Scott Sanderson	.08	.04	.01
☐ 170 Mark Grace	.30	.14	.04
☐ 171 Mark Guthrie	.08	.04	.01
☐ 172 Tom Glavine	.75	.35	.09
☐ 173 Gary Sheffield	1.25	.55	.16
☐ 174 Checklist Card Roger Clemens	.15	.07	.02
☐ 175 Chris James	.08	.04	.01
☐ 176 Milt Thompson	.08	.04	.01
☐ 177 Donnie Hill	.08	.04	.01
☐ 178 Wes Chamberlain	.60	.25	.08
☐ 179 John Marzano	.08	.04	.01
☐ 180 Frank Viola	.10	.04	.01
☐ 181 Eric Anthony	.12	.05	.02
☐ 182 Jose Canseco	.75	.35	.09
☐ 183 Scott Scudder	.08	.04	.01
☐ 184 Dave Eiland	.08	.04	.01
☐ 185 Luis Salazar	.08	.04	.01
☐ 186 Pedro Munoz	.75	.35	.09

☐ 187 Steve Searcy .08 .04 .01
☐ 188 Don Robinson .08 .04 .01
☐ 189 Sandy Alomar Jr. .10 .04 .01
☐ 190 Jose DeLeon .08 .04 .01
☐ 191 John Orton .08 .04 .01
☐ 192 Darren Daulton .10 .04 .01
☐ 193 Mike Morgan .08 .04 .01
☐ 194 Greg Briley .08 .04 .01
☐ 195 Karl Rhodes .08 .04 .01
☐ 196 Harold Baines .10 .04 .01
☐ 197 Bill Doran .08 .04 .01
☐ 198 Alvaro Espinoza .08 .04 .01
☐ 199 Kirk McCaskill .08 .04 .01
☐ 200 Jose DeJesus .08 .04 .01
☐ 201 Jack Clark .10 .04 .01
☐ 202 Daryl Boston .08 .04 .01
☐ 203 Randy Tomlin .50 .23 .06
☐ 204 Pedro Guerrero .10 .04 .01
☐ 205 Billy Hatcher .08 .04 .01
☐ 206 Tim Leary .08 .04 .01
☐ 207 Ryne Sandberg .90 .40 .11
☐ 208 Kirby Puckett .75 .35 .09
☐ 209 Charlie Leibrandt .08 .04 .01
☐ 210 Rick Honeycutt .08 .04 .01
☐ 211 Joel Skinner .08 .04 .01
☐ 212 Rex Hudler .08 .04 .01
☐ 213 Bryan Harvey .08 .04 .01
☐ 214 Charlie Hayes .08 .04 .01
☐ 215 Matt Young .08 .04 .01
☐ 216 Terry Kennedy .08 .04 .01
☐ 217 Carl Nichols .08 .04 .01
☐ 218 Mike Moore .08 .04 .01
☐ 219 Paul O'Neill .10 .04 .01
☐ 220 Steve Sax .10 .04 .01
☐ 221 Shawn Boskie .08 .04 .01
☐ 222 Rich DeLucia .08 .04 .01
☐ 223 Lloyd Moseby .08 .04 .01
☐ 224 Mike Kingery .08 .04 .01
☐ 225 Carlos Baerga .90 .40 .11
☐ 226 Bryn Smith .08 .04 .01
☐ 227 Todd Stottlemyre .10 .04 .01
☐ 228 Julio Franco .10 .04 .01
☐ 229 Jim Gott .08 .04 .01
☐ 230 Mike Schooler .08 .04 .01
☐ 231 Steve Finley .10 .04 .01
☐ 232 Dave Henderson .08 .04 .01
☐ 233 Luis Quinones .08 .04 .01
☐ 234 Mark Whiten .20 .09 .03
☐ 235 Brian McRae .60 .25 .08
☐ 236 Rich Gossage .10 .04 .01
☐ 237 Rob Deer .10 .04 .01
☐ 238 Will Clark .75 .35 .09
☐ 239 Albert Belle .75 .35 .09
☐ 240 Bob Melvin .08 .04 .01
☐ 241 Larry Walker .75 .35 .09
☐ 242 Dante Bichette .08 .04 .01
☐ 243 Orel Hershiser .12 .05 .02
☐ 244 Pete O'Brien .08 .04 .01
☐ 245 Pete Harnisch .10 .04 .01
☐ 246 Jeff Treadway .08 .04 .01
☐ 247 Julio Machado .08 .04 .01
☐ 248 Dave Johnson .08 .04 .01
☐ 249 Kirk Gibson .10 .04 .01
☐ 250 Kevin Brown .10 .04 .01
☐ 251 Milt Cuyler .15 .07 .02
☐ 252 Jeff Reardon .12 .05 .02
☐ 253 David Cone .20 .09 .03
☐ 254 Gary Redus .08 .04 .01
☐ 255 Junior Noboa .08 .04 .01
☐ 256 Greg Myers .08 .04 .01
☐ 257 Dennis Cook .08 .04 .01
☐ 258 Joe Girardi .08 .04 .01
☐ 259 Allan Anderson .08 .04 .01
☐ 260 Paul Marak .08 .04 .01
☐ 261 Barry Bonds .60 .25 .08
☐ 262 Juan Bell .08 .04 .01
☐ 263 Russ Morman .08 .04 .01
☐ 264 Checklist Card .15 .07 .02
George Brett
☐ 265 Jerald Clark .08 .04 .01
☐ 266 Dwight Evans .10 .04 .01
☐ 267 Roberto Alomar 1.00 .45 .13
☐ 268 Danny Jackson .08 .04 .01
☐ 269 Brian Downing .08 .04 .01
☐ 270 John Cerutti .08 .04 .01
☐ 271 Robin Ventura .90 .40 .11
☐ 272 Gerald Perry .08 .04 .01
☐ 273 Wade Boggs .40 .18 .05
☐ 274 Dennis Martinez .10 .04 .01
☐ 275 Andy Benes .30 .14 .04
☐ 276 Tony Fossas .08 .04 .01
☐ 277 Franklin Stubbs .08 .04 .01
☐ 278 John Kruk .10 .04 .01
☐ 279 Kevin Gross .08 .04 .01
☐ 280 Von Hayes .08 .04 .01
☐ 281 Frank Thomas 6.00 2.70 .75
☐ 282 Rob Dibble .10 .04 .01
☐ 283 Mel Hall .08 .04 .01
☐ 284 Rick Mahler .08 .04 .01
☐ 285 Dennis Eckersley .15 .07 .02
☐ 286 Bernard Gilkey .30 .14 .04
☐ 287 Dan Plesac .08 .04 .01
☐ 288 Jason Grimsley .15 .07 .02
☐ 289 Mark Lewis .30 .14 .04
☐ 290 Tony Gwynn .40 .18 .05
☐ 291 Jeff Russell .08 .04 .01
☐ 292 Curt Schilling .10 .04 .01
☐ 293 Pascual Perez .08 .04 .01
☐ 294 Jack Morris .20 .09 .03
☐ 295 Hubie Brooks .08 .04 .01
☐ 296 Alex Fernandez .30 .14 .04
☐ 297 Harold Reynolds .08 .04 .01
☐ 298 Craig Worthington .08 .04 .01
☐ 299 Willie Wilson .08 .04 .01
☐ 300 Mike Maddux .08 .04 .01
☐ 301 Dave Righetti .08 .04 .01
☐ 302 Paul Molitor .15 .07 .02
☐ 303 Gary Gaetti .08 .04 .01
☐ 304 Terry Pendleton .15 .07 .02
☐ 305 Kevin Elster .08 .04 .01
☐ 306 Scott Fletcher .08 .04 .01
☐ 307 Jeff Robinson .08 .04 .01
☐ 308 Jesse Barfield .08 .04 .01
☐ 309 Mike LaCoss .08 .04 .01
☐ 310 Andy Van Slyke .20 .09 .03
☐ 311 Glenallen Hill .08 .04 .01
☐ 312 Bud Black .08 .04 .01
☐ 313 Kent Hrbek .10 .04 .01
☐ 314 Tim Teufel .08 .04 .01
☐ 315 Tony Fernandez .10 .04 .01
☐ 316 Beau Allred .08 .04 .01
☐ 317 Curtis Wilkerson .08 .04 .01
☐ 318 Bill Sampen .08 .04 .01
☐ 319 Randy Johnson .10 .04 .01
☐ 320 Mike Heath .08 .04 .01
☐ 321 Sammy Sosa .10 .04 .01
☐ 322 Mickey Tettleton .10 .04 .01
☐ 323 Jose Vizcaino .08 .04 .01
☐ 324 John Candelaria .08 .04 .01
☐ 325 Dave Howard .15 .07 .02
☐ 326 Jose Rijo .10 .04 .01
☐ 327 Todd Zeile .15 .07 .02
☐ 328 Gene Nelson .08 .04 .01
☐ 329 Dwayne Henry .08 .04 .01
☐ 330 Mike Boddicker .08 .04 .01
☐ 331 Ozzie Guillen .08 .04 .01
☐ 332 Sam Horn .08 .04 .01
☐ 333 Wally Whitehurst .08 .04 .01
☐ 334 Dave Parker .10 .04 .01
☐ 335 George Brett .35 .16 .04
☐ 336 Bobby Thigpen .08 .04 .01
☐ 337 Ed Whitson .08 .04 .01
☐ 338 Ivan Calderon .08 .04 .01
☐ 339 Mike Pagliarulo .08 .04 .01
☐ 340 Jack McDowell .30 .14 .04
☐ 341 Dana Kiecker .08 .04 .01
☐ 342 Fred McGriff .40 .18 .05
☐ 343 Mark Lee .15 .07 .02
☐ 344 Alfredo Griffin .08 .04 .01
☐ 345 Scott Bankhead .08 .04 .01
☐ 346 Darrin Jackson .10 .04 .01
☐ 347 Rafael Palmeiro .20 .09 .03
☐ 348 Steve Farr .08 .04 .01
☐ 349 Hensley Meulens .10 .04 .01
☐ 350 Danny Cox .08 .04 .01
☐ 351 Alan Trammell .10 .04 .01
☐ 352 Edwin Nunez .08 .04 .01
☐ 353 Joe Carter .40 .18 .05
☐ 354 Eric Show .08 .04 .01
☐ 355 Vance Law .08 .04 .01
☐ 356 Jeff Gray .08 .04 .01
☐ 357 Bobby Bonilla .25 .11 .03
☐ 358 Ernest Riles .08 .04 .01
☐ 359 Ron Hassey .08 .04 .01
☐ 360 Willie McGee .10 .04 .01
☐ 361 Mackey Sasser .08 .04 .01
☐ 362 Glenn Braggs .08 .04 .01
☐ 363 Mario Diaz .08 .04 .01
☐ 364 Checklist Card .12 .05 .02
Barry Bonds
☐ 365 Kevin Bass .08 .04 .01
☐ 366 Pete Incaviglia .08 .04 .01
☐ 367 Luis Sojo UER .08 .04 .01
(1989 stats interspersed with 1990's)
☐ 368 Lance Parrish .10 .04 .01

☐ 369 Mark Leonard .20 .09 .03
☐ 370 Heathcliff Slocumb .08 .04 .01
☐ 371 Jimmy Jones .08 .04 .01
☐ 372 Ken Griffey Jr. 2.00 .90 .25
☐ 373 Chris Hammond .20 .09 .03
☐ 374 Chili Davis .10 .04 .01
☐ 375 Joey Cora .08 .04 .01
☐ 376 Ken Hill .10 .04 .01
☐ 377 Darryl Strawberry .40 .18 .05
☐ 378 Ron Darling .10 .04 .01
☐ 379 Sid Bream .08 .04 .01
☐ 380 Bill Swift .08 .04 .01
☐ 381 Shawn Abner .08 .04 .01
☐ 382 Eric King .08 .04 .01
☐ 383 Mickey Morandini .25 .11 .03
☐ 384 Carlton Fisk .30 .14 .04
☐ 385 Steve Lake .08 .04 .01
☐ 386 Mike Jeffcoat .08 .04 .01
☐ 387 Darren Holmes .30 .14 .04
☐ 388 Tim Wallach .10 .04 .01
☐ 389 George Bell .10 .04 .01
☐ 390 Craig Lefferts .08 .04 .01
☐ 391 Ernie Whitt .08 .04 .01
☐ 392 Felix Jose .15 .07 .02
☐ 393 Kevin Maas .15 .07 .02
☐ 394 Devon White .10 .04 .01
☐ 395 Otis Nixon .10 .04 .01
☐ 396 Chuck Knoblauch 1.75 .80 .22
☐ 397 Scott Coolbaugh .08 .04 .01
☐ 398 Glenn Davis .10 .04 .01
☐ 399 Manny Lee .08 .04 .01
☐ 400 Andre Dawson .25 .11 .03
☐ 401 Scott Chiamparino .10 .04 .01
☐ 402 Bill Gullickson .08 .04 .01
☐ 403 Lance Johnson .08 .04 .01
☐ 404 Juan Agosto .08 .04 .01
☐ 405 Danny Darwin .08 .04 .01
☐ 406 Barry Jones .08 .04 .01
☐ 407 Larry Andersen .08 .04 .01
☐ 408 Luis Rivera .08 .04 .01
☐ 409 Jaime Navarro .10 .04 .01
☐ 410 Roger McDowell .08 .04 .01
☐ 411 Brett Butler .08 .04 .01
☐ 412 Dale Murphy .12 .05 .02
☐ 413 Tim Raines UER .12 .05 .02
(Listed as hitting .500
in 1980, should be .050)
☐ 414 Norm Charlton .10 .04 .01
☐ 415 Greg Cadaret .08 .04 .01
☐ 416 Chris Nabholz .20 .09 .03
☐ 417 Dave Stewart .10 .04 .01
☐ 418 Rich Gedman .08 .04 .01
☐ 419 Willie Randolph .10 .04 .01
☐ 420 Mitch Williams .08 .04 .01
☐ 421 Brook Jacoby .08 .04 .01
☐ 422 Greg W. Harris .08 .04 .01
☐ 423 Nolan Ryan 2.00 .90 .25
☐ 424 Dave Rohde .08 .04 .01
☐ 425 Don Mattingly .40 .18 .05
☐ 426 Greg Gagne .08 .04 .01
☐ 427 Vince Coleman .10 .04 .01
☐ 428 Dan Pasqua .08 .04 .01
☐ 429 Alvin Davis .08 .04 .01
☐ 430 Cal Ripken 1.25 .55 .16
☐ 431 Jamie Quirk .08 .04 .01
☐ 432 Benito Santiago .10 .04 .01
☐ 433 Jose Uribe .08 .04 .01
☐ 434 Candy Maldonado .08 .04 .01
☐ 435 Junior Felix .08 .04 .01
☐ 436 Deion Sanders .75 .35 .09
☐ 437 John Franco .10 .04 .01
☐ 438 Greg Hibbard .08 .04 .01
☐ 439 Floyd Bannister .08 .04 .01
☐ 440 Steve Howe .08 .04 .01
☐ 441 Steve Decker .35 .16 .04
☐ 442 Vicente Palacios .08 .04 .01
☐ 443 Pat Tabler .08 .04 .01
☐ 444 Checklist Card .12 .05 .02
Darryl Strawberry
☐ 445 Mike Felder .08 .04 .01
☐ 446 Al Newman .08 .04 .01
☐ 447 Chris Donnels .20 .09 .03
☐ 448 Rich Rodriguez .12 .05 .02
☐ 449 Turner Ward .15 .07 .02
☐ 450 Bob Walk .08 .04 .01
☐ 451 Gilberto Reyes .08 .04 .01
☐ 452 Mike Jackson .08 .04 .01
☐ 453 Rafael Belliard .08 .04 .01
☐ 454 Wayne Edwards .08 .04 .01
☐ 455 Andy Allanson .08 .04 .01
☐ 456 Dave Smith .08 .04 .01
☐ 457 Gary Carter .10 .04 .01
☐ 458 Warren Cromartie .08 .04 .01
☐ 459 Jack Armstrong .08 .04 .01
☐ 460 Bob Tewksbury .10 .04 .01
☐ 461 Joe Klink .08 .04 .01
☐ 462 Xavier Hernandez .08 .04 .01
☐ 463 Scott Radinsky .08 .04 .01
☐ 464 Jeff Robinson .08 .04 .01
☐ 465 Gregg Jefferies .20 .09 .03
☐ 466 Denny Neagle .40 .18 .05
☐ 467 Carmelo Martinez .08 .04 .01
☐ 468 Donn Pall .08 .04 .01
☐ 469 Bruce Hurst .10 .04 .01
☐ 470 Eric Bullock .08 .04 .01
☐ 471 Rick Aguilera .10 .04 .01
☐ 472 Charlie Hough .08 .04 .01
☐ 473 Carlos Quintana .08 .04 .01
☐ 474 Marty Barrett .08 .04 .01
☐ 475 Kevin D. Brown .08 .04 .01
☐ 476 Bobby Ojeda .08 .04 .01
☐ 477 Edgar Martinez .25 .11 .03
☐ 478 Bip Roberts .10 .04 .01
☐ 479 Mike Flanagan .08 .04 .01
☐ 480 John Habyan .08 .04 .01
☐ 481 Larry Casian .08 .04 .01
☐ 482 Wally Backman .08 .04 .01
☐ 483 Doug Dascenzo .08 .04 .01
☐ 484 Rick Dempsey .08 .04 .01
☐ 485 Ed Sprague .35 .16 .04
☐ 486 Steve Chitren .12 .05 .02
☐ 487 Mark McGwire .75 .35 .09
☐ 488 Roger Clemens 1.00 .45 .13
☐ 489 Orlando Merced .50 .23 .06
☐ 490 Rene Gonzales .08 .04 .01
☐ 491 Mike Stanton .08 .04 .01
☐ 492 Al Osuna .15 .07 .02
☐ 493 Rick Cerone .08 .04 .01
☐ 494 Mariano Duncan .08 .04 .01
☐ 495 Zane Smith .08 .04 .01
☐ 496 John Morris .08 .04 .01
☐ 497 Frank Tanana .08 .04 .01
☐ 498 Junior Ortiz .08 .04 .01
☐ 499 Dave Winfield .25 .11 .03
☐ 500 Gary Varsho .08 .04 .01
☐ 501 Chico Walker .08 .04 .01
☐ 502 Ken Caminiti .10 .04 .01
☐ 503 Ken Griffey Sr. .10 .04 .01
☐ 504 Randy Myers .10 .04 .01
☐ 505 Steve Bedrosian .08 .04 .01
☐ 506 Cory Snyder .08 .04 .01
☐ 507 Cris Carpenter .08 .04 .01
☐ 508 Tim Belcher .10 .04 .01
☐ 509 Jeff Hamilton .08 .04 .01
☐ 510 Steve Avery .90 .40 .11
☐ 511 Dave Valle .08 .04 .01
☐ 512 Tom Lampkin .08 .04 .01
☐ 513 Shawn Hillegas .08 .04 .01
☐ 514 Reggie Jefferson .50 .23 .06
☐ 515 Ron Karkovice .08 .04 .01
☐ 516 Doug Drabek .10 .04 .01
☐ 517 Tom Henke .10 .04 .01
☐ 518 Chris Bosio .08 .04 .01
☐ 519 Gregg Olson .10 .04 .01
☐ 520 Bob Scanlan .20 .09 .03
☐ 521 Alonzo Powell .12 .05 .02
☐ 522 Jeff Ballard .08 .04 .01
☐ 523 Ray Lankford 1.50 .65 .19
☐ 524 Tommy Greene .08 .04 .01
☐ 525 Mike Timlin .25 .11 .03
☐ 526 Juan Berenguer .08 .04 .01
☐ 527 Scott Erickson .60 .25 .08
☐ 528 Checklist Card .12 .05 .02
Sandy Alomar Jr.

1991 Leaf Gold Rookies

This 26-card standard size (2 1/2" by 3 1/2") set was issued by Leaf as an adjunct (inserted in packs) to their 1991 Leaf regular issue. The set features some of the most popular prospects active in baseball. This set marks the first time Leaf Inc. and/or Donruss had produced a card utilizing any of the first 24 young players. The first twelve cards were issued as random inserts in with the first series of 1991 Leaf foil packs. The rest were issued as random inserts in with the second series. The card numbers have a BC prefix. The earliest Leaf Gold Rookie cards issued with the first series can sometimes be found with erroneous regular numbered

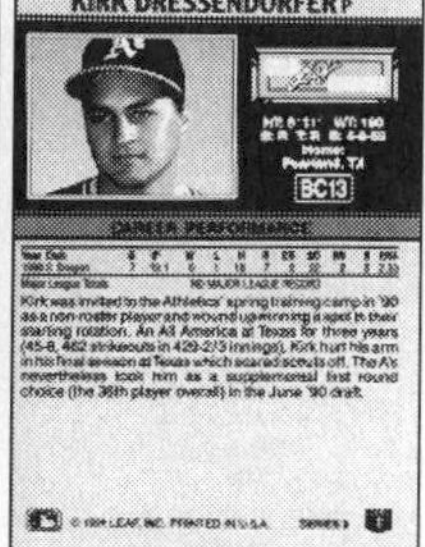

backs 265 through 276 instead of the correct BC1 through BC12. These numbered variations are very tough to find and are valued at ten times the values listed below.

	MT	EX-MT	VG
COMPLETE SET (26)	50.00	23.00	6.25
COMMON PLAYER (1-12)	1.00	.45	.13
COMMON PLAYER (13-26)	1.00	.45	.13
☐ 1 Scott Leius	1.00	.45	.13
☐ 2 Luis Gonzalez	2.00	.90	.25
☐ 3 Wilfredo Cordero	5.00	2.30	.60
☐ 4 Gary Scott	2.00	.90	.25
☐ 5 Willie Banks	2.50	1.15	.30
☐ 6 Arthur Rhodes	4.50	2.00	.55
☐ 7 Mo Vaughn	2.50	1.15	.30
☐ 8 Henry Rodriguez	2.00	.90	.25
☐ 9 Todd Van Poppel	5.00	2.30	.60
☐ 10 Reggie Sanders	7.00	3.10	.85
☐ 11 Rico Brogna	2.00	.90	.25
☐ 12 Mike Mussina	13.00	5.75	1.65
☐ 13 Kirk Dressendorfer	1.00	.45	.13
☐ 14 Jeff Bagwell	10.00	4.50	1.25
☐ 15 Pete Schourek	1.50	.65	.19
☐ 16 Wade Taylor	1.00	.45	.13
☐ 17 Pat Kelly	1.50	.65	.19
☐ 18 Tim Costo	2.50	1.15	.30
☐ 19 Roger Salkeld	2.50	1.15	.30
☐ 20 Andujar Cedeno	2.00	.90	.25
☐ 21 Ryan Klesko UER (1990 Sumter BA .289; should be .368)	10.00	4.50	1.25
☐ 22 Mike Huff	1.00	.45	.13
☐ 23 Anthony Young	2.00	.90	.25
☐ 24 Eddie Zosky	1.50	.65	.19
☐ 25 Nolan Ryan UER No Hitter 7 (Word other repeated in 7th line)	5.00	2.30	.60
☐ 26 Rickey Henderson Record Steal	1.75	.80	.22

1992 Leaf Previews

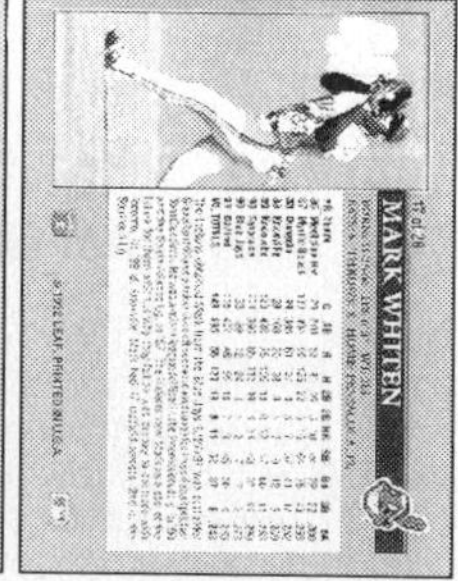

Four Leaf Preview cards were included in each 1992 Donruss hobby factory set. The cards are standard size, 2 1/2" by 3 1/2". The cards were intended to show collectors and dealers the style of the 1992 Leaf set. The fronts carry glossy color player photos framed by silver borders. The player's name, position, and the team logo appear in a black stripe beneath the picture. The horizontal backs have a second color photo, with biography, statistics (on a white panel), and player profile filling out the rest of the card. The cards are numbered on the back.

	MT	EX-MT	VG
COMPLETE SET (26)	90.00	40.00	11.50
COMMON PLAYER (1-26)	1.50	.65	.19
☐ 1 Steve Avery	4.00	1.80	.50
☐ 2 Ryne Sandberg	8.00	3.60	1.00
☐ 3 Chris Sabo	1.50	.65	.19
☐ 4 Jeff Bagwell	6.00	2.70	.75
☐ 5 Darryl Strawberry	4.00	1.80	.50
☐ 6 Bret Barberie	2.00	.90	.25
☐ 7 Howard Johnson	2.00	.90	.25
☐ 8 John Kruk	1.50	.65	.19
☐ 9 Andy Van Slyke	2.50	1.15	.30
☐ 10 Felix Jose	2.00	.90	.25
☐ 11 Fred McGriff	4.00	1.80	.50
☐ 12 Will Clark	7.00	3.10	.85
☐ 13 Cal Ripken	10.00	4.50	1.25
☐ 14 Phil Plantier	3.00	1.35	.40
☐ 15 Lee Stevens	1.50	.65	.19
☐ 16 Frank Thomas	15.00	6.75	1.90
☐ 17 Mark Whiten	2.00	.90	.25
☐ 18 Cecil Fielder	4.00	1.80	.50
☐ 19 George Brett	4.00	1.80	.50
☐ 20 Robin Yount	4.00	1.80	.50
☐ 21 Scott Erickson	2.50	1.15	.30
☐ 22 Don Mattingly	4.00	1.80	.50
☐ 23 Jose Canseco	7.00	3.10	.85
☐ 24 Ken Griffey Jr.	12.00	5.50	1.50
☐ 25 Nolan Ryan	12.00	5.50	1.50
☐ 26 Joe Carter	4.00	1.80	.50

1992 Leaf Gold Previews

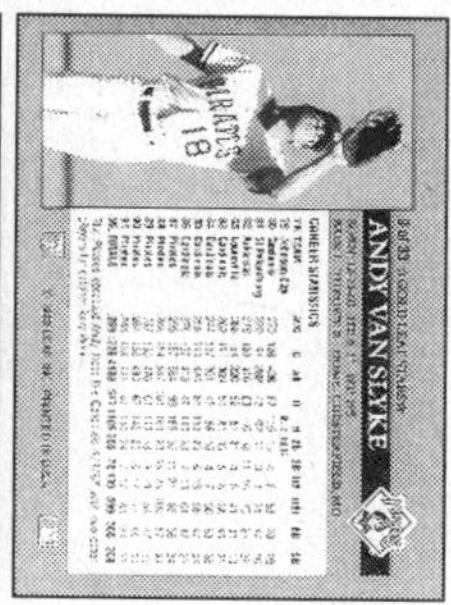

These Leaf Gold Preview cards were sent to members of the Donruss/Leaf Dealer Network to show them the style of the new 1992 Leaf Gold cards which would be included one per pack in the forthcoming set. The cards measure standard size, 2 1/2" by 3 1/2". The fronts feature color action player photos inside a gold foil picture frame and a black outer border. The player's name, position, and a gold foil baseball icon appear inside a gold foil box beneath the picture. On a gold background, the backs carry a second color player photo, biography, and career statistics. The cards are numbered on the back "X of 33."

	MT	EX-MT	VG
COMPLETE SET (33)	200.00	90.00	25.00
COMMON PLAYER (1-33)	3.00	1.35	.40
☐ 1 Steve Avery	8.00	3.60	1.00
☐ 2 Ryne Sandberg	16.00	7.25	2.00
☐ 3 Chris Sabo	3.00	1.35	.40
☐ 4 Jeff Bagwell	10.00	4.50	1.25
☐ 5 Darryl Strawberry	8.00	3.60	1.00
☐ 6 Bret Barberie	4.00	1.80	.50
☐ 7 Howard Johnson	4.00	1.80	.50
☐ 8 John Kruk	3.00	1.35	.40

☐ 9 Andy Van Slyke	6.00	2.70	.75
☐ 10 Felix Jose	4.00	1.80	.50
☐ 11 Fred McGriff	8.00	3.60	1.00
☐ 12 Will Clark	12.00	5.50	1.50
☐ 13 Cal Ripken	16.00	7.25	2.00
☐ 14 Phil Plantier	8.00	3.60	1.00
☐ 15 Lee Stevens	4.00	1.80	.50
☐ 16 Frank Thomas	20.00	9.00	2.50
☐ 17 Mark Whiten	4.00	1.80	.50
☐ 18 Cecil Fielder	8.00	3.60	1.00
☐ 19 George Brett	10.00	4.50	1.25
☐ 20 Robin Yount	10.00	4.50	1.25
☐ 21 Scott Erickson	4.00	1.80	.50
☐ 22 Don Mattingly	12.00	5.50	1.50
☐ 23 Jose Canseco	12.00	5.50	1.50
☐ 24 Ken Griffey Jr.	20.00	9.00	2.50
☐ 25 Nolan Ryan	20.00	9.00	2.50
☐ 26 Joe Carter	8.00	3.60	1.00
☐ 27 Deion Sanders	8.00	3.60	1.00
☐ 28 Dean Palmer	6.00	2.70	.75
☐ 29 Andy Benes	4.00	1.80	.50
☐ 30 Gary DiSarcina	3.00	1.35	.40
☐ 31 Chris Hoiles	3.00	1.35	.40
☐ 32 Mark McGwire	12.00	5.50	1.50
☐ 33 Reggie Sanders	8.00	3.60	1.00

1992 Leaf

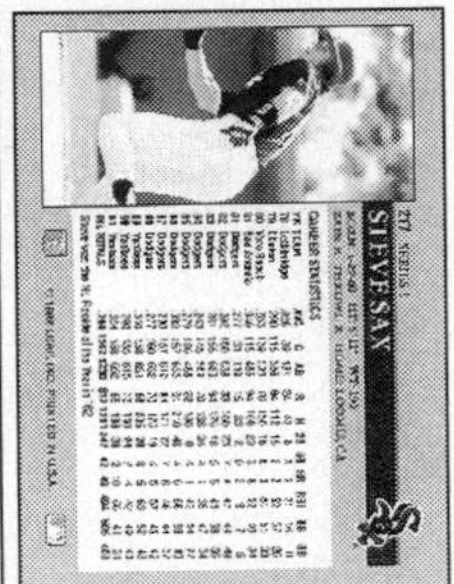

The 1992 Leaf set consists of 528 cards, issued in two series each with 264 cards measuring the standard size (2 1/2" by 3 1/2"). The fronts feature color action player photos on a silver card face. The player's name appears in a black bar edged at the bottom by a thin red stripe. The team logo overlaps the bar at the right corner. The horizontally oriented backs have color action player photos on left portion of the card. The right portion carries the player's name and team logo in a black bar as well as career statistics and career highlights in a white box. The card backs have a silver background. The cards are numbered on the back. Leaf also produced a Gold Foil Version of the complete set (series I and II), featuring gold metallic ink and gold foil highlights instead of the traditional silver. One of these "black gold inserts" was included in each 15-card foil pack. Twelve "Gold Leaf Rookie" bonus cards, numbered BC1-BC12, were randomly inserted in first series foil packs and twelve, numbered BC13-24, were randomly inserted in second series foil packs. The most noteworthy Rookie Card in the first series is Chris Gardner. The most noteworthy Rookie Cards in the second series are Archi Cianfrocco and Pat Listach.

	MT	EX-MT	VG
COMPLETE SET (528)	40.00	18.00	5.00
COMPLETE SERIES 1 (264)	20.00	9.00	2.50
COMPLETE SERIES 2 (264)	20.00	9.00	2.50
COMMON PLAYER (1-264)	.07	.03	.01
COMMON PLAYER (265-528)	.07	.03	.01
☐ 1 Jim Abbott	.20	.09	.03
☐ 2 Cal Eldred	1.00	.45	.13
☐ 3 Bud Black	.07	.03	.01
☐ 4 Dave Howard	.07	.03	.01
☐ 5 Luis Sojo	.07	.03	.01
☐ 6 Gary Scott	.10	.05	.01
☐ 7 Joe Oliver	.07	.03	.01
☐ 8 Chris Gardner	.15	.07	.02
☐ 9 Sandy Alomar Jr.	.10	.05	.01
☐ 10 Greg W. Harris	.07	.03	.01
☐ 11 Doug Drabek	.10	.05	.01
☐ 12 Darryl Hamilton	.10	.05	.01
☐ 13 Mike Mussina	1.75	.80	.22
☐ 14 Kevin Tapani	.10	.05	.01
☐ 15 Ron Gant	.20	.09	.03
☐ 16 Mark McGwire	.50	.23	.06
☐ 17 Robin Ventura	.50	.23	.06
☐ 18 Pedro Guerrero	.10	.05	.01
☐ 19 Roger Clemens	.60	.25	.08
☐ 20 Steve Farr	.07	.03	.01
☐ 21 Frank Tanana	.07	.03	.01
☐ 22 Joe Hesketh	.07	.03	.01
☐ 23 Erik Hanson	.07	.03	.01
☐ 24 Greg Cadaret	.07	.03	.01
☐ 25 Rex Hudler	.07	.03	.01
☐ 26 Mark Grace	.12	.05	.02
☐ 27 Kelly Gruber	.10	.05	.01
☐ 28 Jeff Bagwell	.75	.35	.09
☐ 29 Darryl Strawberry	.30	.14	.04
☐ 30 Dave Smith	.07	.03	.01
☐ 31 Kevin Appier	.10	.05	.01
☐ 32 Steve Chitren	.07	.03	.01
☐ 33 Kevin Gross	.07	.03	.01
☐ 34 Rick Aguilera	.10	.05	.01
☐ 35 Juan Guzman	1.75	.80	.22
☐ 36 Joe Orsulak	.07	.03	.01
☐ 37 Tim Raines	.12	.05	.02
☐ 38 Harold Reynolds	.07	.03	.01
☐ 39 Charlie Hough	.07	.03	.01
☐ 40 Tony Phillips	.07	.03	.01
☐ 41 Nolan Ryan	1.50	.65	.19
☐ 42 Vince Coleman	.10	.05	.01
☐ 43 Andy Van Slyke	.12	.05	.02
☐ 44 Tim Burke	.07	.03	.01
☐ 45 Luis Polonia	.10	.05	.01
☐ 46 Tom Browning	.07	.03	.01
☐ 47 Willie McGee	.10	.05	.01
☐ 48 Gary DiSarcina	.10	.05	.01
☐ 49 Mark Lewis	.10	.05	.01
☐ 50 Phil Plantier	.30	.14	.04
☐ 51 Doug Dascenzo	.07	.03	.01
☐ 52 Cal Ripken	.75	.35	.09
☐ 53 Pedro Munoz	.12	.05	.02
☐ 54 Carlos Hernandez	.07	.03	.01
☐ 55 Jerald Clark	.07	.03	.01
☐ 56 Jeff Brantley	.07	.03	.01
☐ 57 Don Mattingly	.30	.14	.04
☐ 58 Roger McDowell	.07	.03	.01
☐ 59 Steve Avery	.50	.23	.06
☐ 60 John Olerud	.25	.11	.03
☐ 61 Bill Gullickson	.07	.03	.01
☐ 62 Juan Gonzalez	1.25	.55	.16
☐ 63 Felix Jose	.10	.05	.01
☐ 64 Robin Yount	.25	.11	.03
☐ 65 Greg Briley	.07	.03	.01
☐ 66 Steve Finley	.10	.05	.01
☐ 67 Checklist	.10	.01	.00
☐ 68 Tom Gordon	.07	.03	.01
☐ 69 Rob Dibble	.10	.05	.01
☐ 70 Glenallen Hill	.07	.03	.01
☐ 71 Calvin Jones	.12	.05	.02
☐ 72 Joe Girardi	.07	.03	.01
☐ 73 Barry Larkin	.20	.09	.03
☐ 74 Andy Benes	.12	.05	.02
☐ 75 Milt Cuyler	.07	.03	.01
☐ 76 Kevin Bass	.07	.03	.01
☐ 77 Pete Harnisch	.07	.03	.01
☐ 78 Wilson Alvarez	.07	.03	.01
☐ 79 Mike Devereaux	.10	.05	.01
☐ 80 Doug Henry	.30	.14	.04
☐ 81 Orel Hershiser	.12	.05	.02
☐ 82 Shane Mack	.10	.05	.01
☐ 83 Mike Macfarlane	.07	.03	.01
☐ 84 Thomas Howard	.07	.03	.01
☐ 85 Alex Fernandez	.10	.05	.01
☐ 86 Reggie Jefferson	.15	.07	.02
☐ 87 Leo Gomez	.20	.09	.03
☐ 88 Mel Hall	.07	.03	.01
☐ 89 Mike Greenwell	.12	.05	.02
☐ 90 Jeff Russell	.07	.03	.01
☐ 91 Steve Buechele	.07	.03	.01
☐ 92 David Cone	.12	.05	.02
☐ 93 Kevin Reimer	.10	.05	.01
☐ 94 Mark Lemke	.07	.03	.01
☐ 95 Bob Tewksbury	.10	.05	.01
☐ 96 Zane Smith	.07	.03	.01

☐ 97 Mark Eichhorn	.07	.03	.01
☐ 98 Kirby Puckett	.50	.23	.06
☐ 99 Paul O'Neill	.10	.05	.01
☐ 100 Dennis Eckersley	.15	.07	.02
☐ 101 Duane Ward	.07	.03	.01
☐ 102 Matt Nokes	.07	.03	.01
☐ 103 Mo Vaughn	.12	.05	.02
☐ 104 Pat Kelly	.12	.05	.02
☐ 105 Ron Karkovice	.07	.03	.01
☐ 106 Bill Spiers	.07	.03	.01
☐ 107 Gary Gaetti	.07	.03	.01
☐ 108 Mackey Sasser	.07	.03	.01
☐ 109 Robby Thompson	.07	.03	.01
☐ 110 Marvin Freeman	.07	.03	.01
☐ 111 Jimmy Key	.07	.03	.01
☐ 112 Dwight Gooden	.12	.05	.02
☐ 113 Charlie Leibrandt	.07	.03	.01
☐ 114 Devon White	.10	.05	.01
☐ 115 Charles Nagy	.25	.11	.03
☐ 116 Rickey Henderson	.25	.11	.03
☐ 117 Paul Assenmacher	.07	.03	.01
☐ 118 Junior Felix	.07	.03	.01
☐ 119 Julio Franco	.10	.05	.01
☐ 120 Norm Charlton	.10	.05	.01
☐ 121 Scott Servais	.07	.03	.01
☐ 122 Gerald Perry	.07	.03	.01
☐ 123 Brian McRae	.12	.05	.02
☐ 124 Don Slaught	.07	.03	.01
☐ 125 Juan Samuel	.07	.03	.01
☐ 126 Harold Baines	.10	.05	.01
☐ 127 Scott Livingstone	.20	.09	.03
☐ 128 Jay Buhner	.10	.05	.01
☐ 129 Darrin Jackson	.10	.05	.01
☐ 130 Luis Mercedes	.25	.11	.03
☐ 131 Brian Harper	.07	.03	.01
☐ 132 Howard Johnson	.10	.05	.01
☐ 133 Checklist	.10	.01	.00
☐ 134 Dante Bichette	.07	.03	.01
☐ 135 Dave Righetti	.07	.03	.01
☐ 136 Jeff Montgomery	.07	.03	.01
☐ 137 Joe Grahe	.07	.03	.01
☐ 138 Delino DeShields	.25	.11	.03
☐ 139 Jose Rijo	.10	.05	.01
☐ 140 Ken Caminiti	.10	.05	.01
☐ 141 Steve Olin	.07	.03	.01
☐ 142 Kurt Stillwell	.07	.03	.01
☐ 143 Jay Bell	.07	.03	.01
☐ 144 Jaime Navarro	.10	.05	.01
☐ 145 Ben McDonald	.15	.07	.02
☐ 146 Greg Gagne	.07	.03	.01
☐ 147 Jeff Blauser	.07	.03	.01
☐ 148 Carney Lansford	.10	.05	.01
☐ 149 Ozzie Guillen	.07	.03	.01
☐ 150 Milt Thompson	.07	.03	.01
☐ 151 Jeff Reardon	.12	.05	.02
☐ 152 Scott Sanderson	.07	.03	.01
☐ 153 Cecil Fielder	.30	.14	.04
☐ 154 Greg A. Harris	.07	.03	.01
☐ 155 Rich DeLucia	.07	.03	.01
☐ 156 Roberto Kelly	.12	.05	.02
☐ 157 Bryn Smith	.07	.03	.01
☐ 158 Chuck McElroy	.07	.03	.01
☐ 159 Tom Henke	.10	.05	.01
☐ 160 Luis Gonzalez	.12	.05	.02
☐ 161 Steve Wilson	.07	.03	.01
☐ 162 Shawn Boskie	.07	.03	.01
☐ 163 Mark Davis	.07	.03	.01
☐ 164 Mike Moore	.07	.03	.01
☐ 165 Mike Scioscia	.07	.03	.01
☐ 166 Scott Erickson	.15	.07	.02
☐ 167 Todd Stottlemyre	.10	.05	.01
☐ 168 Alvin Davis	.07	.03	.01
☐ 169 Greg Hibbard	.07	.03	.01
☐ 170 David Valle	.07	.03	.01
☐ 171 Dave Winfield	.20	.09	.03
☐ 172 Alan Trammell	.12	.05	.02
☐ 173 Kenny Rogers	.07	.03	.01
☐ 174 John Franco	.10	.05	.01
☐ 175 Jose Lind	.07	.03	.01
☐ 176 Pete Schourek	.10	.05	.01
☐ 177 Von Hayes	.07	.03	.01
☐ 178 Chris Hammond	.07	.03	.01
☐ 179 John Burkett	.07	.03	.01
☐ 180 Dickie Thon	.07	.03	.01
☐ 181 Joel Skinner	.07	.03	.01
☐ 182 Scott Cooper	.25	.11	.03
☐ 183 Andre Dawson	.15	.07	.02
☐ 184 Billy Ripken	.07	.03	.01
☐ 185 Kevin Mitchell	.12	.05	.02
☐ 186 Brett Butler	.10	.05	.01
☐ 187 Tony Fernandez	.10	.05	.01
☐ 188 Cory Snyder	.07	.03	.01
☐ 189 John Habyan	.07	.03	.01

☐ 190 Dennis Martinez	.10	.05	.01
☐ 191 John Smoltz	.20	.09	.03
☐ 192 Greg Myers	.07	.03	.01
☐ 193 Rob Deer	.10	.05	.01
☐ 194 Ivan Rodriguez	1.00	.45	.13
☐ 195 Ray Lankford	.40	.18	.05
☐ 196 Bill Wegman	.07	.03	.01
☐ 197 Edgar Martinez	.10	.05	.01
☐ 198 Darryl Kile	.10	.05	.01
☐ 199 Checklist	.10	.01	.00
☐ 200 Brent Mayne	.07	.03	.01
☐ 201 Larry Walker	.35	.16	.04
☐ 202 Carlos Baerga	.40	.18	.05
☐ 203 Russ Swan	.07	.03	.01
☐ 204 Mike Morgan	.07	.03	.01
☐ 205 Hal Morris	.10	.05	.01
☐ 206 Tony Gwynn	.30	.14	.04
☐ 207 Mark Leiter	.07	.03	.01
☐ 208 Kirt Manwaring	.07	.03	.01
☐ 209 Al Osuna	.07	.03	.01
☐ 210 Bobby Thigpen	.07	.03	.01
☐ 211 Chris Hoiles	.12	.05	.02
☐ 212 B.J. Surhoff	.07	.03	.01
☐ 213 Lenny Harris	.07	.03	.01
☐ 214 Scott Leius	.07	.03	.01
☐ 215 Gregg Jefferies	.10	.05	.01
☐ 216 Bruce Hurst	.10	.05	.01
☐ 217 Steve Sax	.10	.05	.01
☐ 218 Dave Otto	.07	.03	.01
☐ 219 Sam Horn	.07	.03	.01
☐ 220 Charlie Hayes	.07	.03	.01
☐ 221 Frank Viola	.10	.05	.01
☐ 222 Jose Guzman	.07	.03	.01
☐ 223 Gary Redus	.07	.03	.01
☐ 224 Dave Gallagher	.07	.03	.01
☐ 225 Dean Palmer	.40	.18	.05
☐ 226 Greg Olson	.07	.03	.01
☐ 227 Jose DeLeon	.07	.03	.01
☐ 228 Mike LaValliere	.07	.03	.01
☐ 229 Mark Langston	.10	.05	.01
☐ 230 Chuck Knoblauch	.40	.18	.05
☐ 231 Bill Doran	.07	.03	.01
☐ 232 Dave Henderson	.07	.03	.01
☐ 233 Roberto Alomar	.50	.23	.06
☐ 234 Scott Fletcher	.07	.03	.01
☐ 235 Tim Naehring	.07	.03	.01
☐ 236 Mike Gallego	.07	.03	.01
☐ 237 Lance Johnson	.07	.03	.01
☐ 238 Paul Molitor	.12	.05	.02
☐ 239 Dan Gladden	.07	.03	.01
☐ 240 Willie Randolph	.10	.05	.01
☐ 241 Will Clark	.50	.23	.06
☐ 242 Sid Bream	.07	.03	.01
☐ 243 Derek Bell	.30	.14	.04
☐ 244 Bill Pecota	.07	.03	.01
☐ 245 Terry Pendleton	.12	.05	.02
☐ 246 Randy Ready	.07	.03	.01
☐ 247 Jack Armstrong	.07	.03	.01
☐ 248 Todd Van Poppel	.40	.18	.05
☐ 249 Shawon Dunston	.10	.05	.01
☐ 250 Bobby Rose	.07	.03	.01
☐ 251 Jeff Huson	.07	.03	.01
☐ 252 Bip Roberts	.10	.05	.01
☐ 253 Doug Jones	.07	.03	.01
☐ 254 Lee Smith	.10	.05	.01
☐ 255 George Brett	.25	.11	.03
☐ 256 Randy Tomlin	.12	.05	.02
☐ 257 Todd Benzinger	.07	.03	.01
☐ 258 Dave Stewart	.10	.05	.01
☐ 259 Mark Carreon	.07	.03	.01
☐ 260 Pete O'Brien	.07	.03	.01
☐ 261 Tim Teufel	.07	.03	.01
☐ 262 Bob Milacki	.07	.03	.01
☐ 263 Mark Guthrie	.07	.03	.01
☐ 264 Darrin Fletcher	.07	.03	.01
☐ 265 Omar Vizquel	.07	.03	.01
☐ 266 Chris Bosio	.07	.03	.01
☐ 267 Jose Canseco	.50	.23	.06
☐ 268 Mike Boddicker	.07	.03	.01
☐ 269 Lance Parrish	.10	.05	.01
☐ 270 Jose Vizcaino	.07	.03	.01
☐ 271 Chris Sabo	.10	.05	.01
☐ 272 Royce Clayton	.40	.18	.05
☐ 273 Marquis Grissom	.25	.11	.03
☐ 274 Fred McGriff	.30	.14	.04
☐ 275 Barry Bonds	.50	.23	.06
☐ 276 Greg Vaughn	.10	.05	.01
☐ 277 Gregg Olson	.10	.05	.01
☐ 278 Dave Hollins	.25	.11	.03
☐ 279 Tom Glavine	.30	.14	.04
☐ 280 Bryan Hickerson	.07	.03	.01
☐ 281 Scott Radinsky	.07	.03	.01
☐ 282 Omar Olivares	.07	.03	.01

☐ 283	Ivan Calderon	.07	.03	.01
☐ 284	Kevin Maas	.10	.05	.01
☐ 285	Mickey Tettleton	.10	.05	.01
☐ 286	Wade Boggs	.30	.14	.04
☐ 287	Stan Belinda	.07	.03	.01
☐ 288	Bret Barberie	.12	.05	.02
☐ 289	Jose Oquendo	.07	.03	.01
☐ 290	Frank Castillo	.15	.07	.02
☐ 291	Dave Stieb	.07	.03	.01
☐ 292	Tommy Greene	.07	.03	.01
☐ 293	Eric Karros	1.75	.80	.22
☐ 294	Greg Maddux	.15	.07	.02
☐ 295	Jim Eisenreich	.07	.03	.01
☐ 296	Rafael Palmeiro	.12	.05	.02
☐ 297	Ramon Martinez	.12	.05	.02
☐ 298	Tim Wallach	.10	.05	.01
☐ 299	Jim Thome	.25	.11	.03
☐ 300	Chito Martinez	.07	.03	.01
☐ 301	Mitch Williams	.07	.03	.01
☐ 302	Randy Johnson	.10	.05	.01
☐ 303	Carlton Fisk	.20	.09	.03
☐ 304	Travis Fryman	1.00	.45	.13
☐ 305	Bobby Witt	.07	.03	.01
☐ 306	Dave Magadan	.10	.05	.01
☐ 307	Alex Cole	.07	.03	.01
☐ 308	Bobby Bonilla	.15	.07	.02
☐ 309	Bryan Harvey	.07	.03	.01
☐ 310	Rafael Belliard	.07	.03	.01
☐ 311	Mariano Duncan	.07	.03	.01
☐ 312	Chuck Crim	.07	.03	.01
☐ 313	John Kruk	.10	.05	.01
☐ 314	Ellis Burks	.10	.05	.01
☐ 315	Craig Biggio	.10	.05	.01
☐ 316	Glenn Davis	.10	.05	.01
☐ 317	Ryne Sandberg	.60	.25	.08
☐ 318	Mike Sharperson	.07	.03	.01
☐ 319	Rich Rodriguez	.07	.03	.01
☐ 320	Lee Guetterman	.07	.03	.01
☐ 321	Benito Santiago	.12	.05	.02
☐ 322	Jose Offerman	.10	.05	.01
☐ 323	Tony Pena	.07	.03	.01
☐ 324	Pat Borders	.07	.03	.01
☐ 325	Mike Henneman	.07	.03	.01
☐ 326	Kevin Brown	.10	.05	.01
☐ 327	Chris Nabholz	.07	.03	.01
☐ 328	Franklin Stubbs	.07	.03	.01
☐ 329	Tino Martinez	.12	.05	.02
☐ 330	Mickey Morandini	.07	.03	.01
☐ 331	Checklist	.10	.01	.00
☐ 332	Mark Gubicza	.07	.03	.01
☐ 333	Bill Landrum	.07	.03	.01
☐ 334	Mark Whiten	.07	.03	.01
☐ 335	Darren Daulton	.10	.05	.01
☐ 336	Rick Wilkins	.07	.03	.01
☐ 337	Brian Jordan	.40	.18	.05
☐ 338	Kevin Ward	.12	.05	.02
☐ 339	Ruben Amaro	.12	.05	.02
☐ 340	Trevor Wilson	.07	.03	.01
☐ 341	Andujar Cedeno	.12	.05	.02
☐ 342	Michael Huff	.07	.03	.01
☐ 343	Brady Anderson	.10	.05	.01
☐ 344	Craig Grebeck	.07	.03	.01
☐ 345	Bobby Ojeda	.07	.03	.01
☐ 346	Mike Pagliarulo	.07	.03	.01
☐ 347	Terry Shumpert	.07	.03	.01
☐ 348	Dann Bilardello	.07	.03	.01
☐ 349	Frank Thomas	3.00	1.35	.40
☐ 350	Albert Belle	.30	.14	.04
☐ 351	Jose Mesa	.07	.03	.01
☐ 352	Rich Monteleone	.07	.03	.01
☐ 353	Bob Walk	.07	.03	.01
☐ 354	Monty Fariss	.15	.07	.02
☐ 355	Luis Rivera	.07	.03	.01
☐ 356	Anthony Young	.12	.05	.02
☐ 357	Geno Petralli	.07	.03	.01
☐ 358	Otis Nixon	.10	.05	.01
☐ 359	Tom Pagnozzi	.07	.03	.01
☐ 360	Reggie Sanders	.75	.35	.09
☐ 361	Lee Stevens	.07	.03	.01
☐ 362	Kent Hrbek	.10	.05	.01
☐ 363	Orlando Merced	.12	.05	.02
☐ 364	Mike Bordick	.15	.07	.02
☐ 365	Dion James UER (Blue Jays logo on card back)	.07	.03	.01
☐ 366	Jack Clark	.10	.05	.01
☐ 367	Mike Stanley	.07	.03	.01
☐ 368	Randy Velarde	.07	.03	.01
☐ 369	Dan Pasqua	.07	.03	.01
☐ 370	Pat Listach	2.50	1.15	.30
☐ 371	Mike Fitzgerald	.07	.03	.01
☐ 372	Tom Foley	.07	.03	.01
☐ 373	Matt Williams	.12	.05	.02

☐ 374	Brian Hunter	.20	.09	.03
☐ 375	Joe Carter	.30	.14	.04
☐ 376	Bret Saberhagen	.12	.05	.02
☐ 377	Mike Stanton	.07	.03	.01
☐ 378	Hubie Brooks	.07	.03	.01
☐ 379	Eric Bell	.07	.03	.01
☐ 380	Walt Weiss	.07	.03	.01
☐ 381	Danny Jackson	.07	.03	.01
☐ 382	Manuel Lee	.07	.03	.01
☐ 383	Ruben Sierra	.40	.18	.05
☐ 384	Greg Swindell	.10	.05	.01
☐ 385	Ryan Bowen	.15	.07	.02
☐ 386	Kevin Ritz	.07	.03	.01
☐ 387	Curtis Wilkerson	.07	.03	.01
☐ 388	Gary Varsho	.07	.03	.01
☐ 389	Dave Hansen	.12	.05	.02
☐ 390	Bob Welch	.07	.03	.01
☐ 391	Lou Whitaker	.12	.05	.02
☐ 392	Ken Griffey Jr.	2.00	.90	.25
☐ 393	Mike Maddux	.07	.03	.01
☐ 394	Arthur Rhodes	.40	.18	.05
☐ 395	Chili Davis	.10	.05	.01
☐ 396	Eddie Murray	.20	.09	.03
☐ 397	Checklist	.10	.01	.00
☐ 398	Dave Cochrane	.07	.03	.01
☐ 399	Kevin Seitzer	.10	.05	.01
☐ 400	Ozzie Smith	.20	.09	.03
☐ 401	Paul Sorrento	.10	.05	.01
☐ 402	Les Lancaster	.07	.03	.01
☐ 403	Junior Noboa	.07	.03	.01
☐ 404	David Justice	.75	.35	.09
☐ 405	Andy Ashby	.15	.07	.02
☐ 406	Danny Tartabull	.12	.05	.02
☐ 407	Bill Swift	.07	.03	.01
☐ 408	Craig Lefferts	.07	.03	.01
☐ 409	Tom Candiotti	.07	.03	.01
☐ 410	Lance Blankenship	.07	.03	.01
☐ 411	Jeff Tackett	.12	.05	.02
☐ 412	Sammy Sosa	.07	.03	.01
☐ 413	Jody Reed	.07	.03	.01
☐ 414	Bruce Ruffin	.07	.03	.01
☐ 415	Gene Larkin	.07	.03	.01
☐ 416	John Vander Wal	.25	.11	.03
☐ 417	Tim Belcher	.10	.05	.01
☐ 418	Steve Frey	.07	.03	.01
☐ 419	Dick Schofield	.07	.03	.01
☐ 420	Jeff King	.07	.03	.01
☐ 421	Kim Batiste	.15	.07	.02
☐ 422	Jack McDowell	.12	.05	.02
☐ 423	Damon Berryhill	.07	.03	.01
☐ 424	Gary Wayne	.07	.03	.01
☐ 425	Jack Morris	.15	.07	.02
☐ 426	Moises Alou	.20	.09	.03
☐ 427	Mark McLemore	.07	.03	.01
☐ 428	Juan Guerrero	.20	.09	.03
☐ 429	Scott Scudder	.07	.03	.01
☐ 430	Eric Davis	.12	.05	.02
☐ 431	Joe Slusarski	.07	.03	.01
☐ 432	Todd Zeile	.07	.03	.01
☐ 433	Dwayne Henry	.07	.03	.01
☐ 434	Cliff Brantley	.12	.05	.02
☐ 435	Butch Henry	.20	.09	.03
☐ 436	Todd Worrell	.07	.03	.01
☐ 437	Bob Scanlan	.07	.03	.01
☐ 438	Wally Joyner	.10	.05	.01
☐ 439	John Flaherty	.12	.05	.02
☐ 440	Brian Downing	.07	.03	.01
☐ 441	Darren Lewis	.10	.05	.01
☐ 442	Gary Carter	.10	.05	.01
☐ 443	Wally Ritchie	.07	.03	.01
☐ 444	Chris Jones	.07	.03	.01
☐ 445	Jeff Kent	.50	.23	.06
☐ 446	Gary Sheffield	.75	.35	.09
☐ 447	Ron Darling	.10	.05	.01
☐ 448	Deion Sanders	.40	.18	.05
☐ 449	Andres Galarraga	.07	.03	.01
☐ 450	Chuck Finley	.07	.03	.01
☐ 451	Derek Lilliquist	.07	.03	.01
☐ 452	Carl Willis	.07	.03	.01
☐ 453	Wes Chamberlain	.12	.05	.02
☐ 454	Roger Mason	.07	.03	.01
☐ 455	Spike Owen	.07	.03	.01
☐ 456	Thomas Howard	.07	.03	.01
☐ 457	Dave Martinez	.07	.03	.01
☐ 458	Pete Incaviglia	.07	.03	.01
☐ 459	Keith A. Miller	.07	.03	.01
☐ 460	Mike Fetters	.07	.03	.01
☐ 461	Paul Gibson	.07	.03	.01
☐ 462	George Bell	.10	.05	.01
☐ 463	Checklist	.10	.01	.00
☐ 464	Terry Mulholland	.07	.03	.01
☐ 465	Storm Davis	.07	.03	.01
☐ 466	Gary Pettis	.07	.03	.01

☐ 467 Randy Bush	.07	.03	.01
☐ 468 Ken Hill	.07	.03	.01
☐ 469 Rheal Cormier	.15	.07	.02
☐ 470 Andy Stankiewicz	.25	.11	.03
☐ 471 Dave Burba	.07	.03	.01
☐ 472 Henry Cotto	.07	.03	.01
☐ 473 Dale Sveum	.07	.03	.01
☐ 474 Rich Gossage	.10	.05	.01
☐ 475 William Suero	.12	.05	.02
☐ 476 Doug Strange	.07	.03	.01
☐ 477 Bill Krueger	.07	.03	.01
☐ 478 John Wetteland	.07	.03	.01
☐ 479 Melido Perez	.10	.05	.01
☐ 480 Lonnie Smith	.07	.03	.01
☐ 481 Mike Jackson	.07	.03	.01
☐ 482 Mike Gardiner	.07	.03	.01
☐ 483 David Wells	.07	.03	.01
☐ 484 Barry Jones	.07	.03	.01
☐ 485 Scott Bankhead	.07	.03	.01
☐ 486 Terry Leach	.07	.03	.01
☐ 487 Vince Horsman	.12	.05	.02
☐ 488 Dave Eiland	.07	.03	.01
☐ 489 Alejandro Pena	.07	.03	.01
☐ 490 Julio Valera	.15	.07	.02
☐ 491 Joe Boever	.07	.03	.01
☐ 492 Paul Miller	.15	.07	.02
☐ 493 Archi Cianfrocco	.25	.11	.03
☐ 494 Dave Fleming	1.00	.45	.13
☐ 495 Kyle Abbott	.15	.07	.02
☐ 496 Chad Kreuter	.07	.03	.01
☐ 497 Chris James	.07	.03	.01
☐ 498 Donnie Hill	.07	.03	.01
☐ 499 Jacob Brumfield	.12	.05	.02
☐ 500 Ricky Bones	.15	.07	.02
☐ 501 Terry Steinbach	.10	.05	.01
☐ 502 Bernard Gilkey	.12	.05	.02
☐ 503 Dennis Cook	.07	.03	.01
☐ 504 Len Dykstra	.10	.05	.01
☐ 505 Mike Bielecki	.07	.03	.01
☐ 506 Bob Kipper	.07	.03	.01
☐ 507 Jose Melendez	.12	.05	.02
☐ 508 Rick Sutcliffe	.10	.05	.01
☐ 509 Ken Patterson	.07	.03	.01
☐ 510 Andy Allanson	.07	.03	.01
☐ 511 Al Newman	.07	.03	.01
☐ 512 Mark Gardner	.07	.03	.01
☐ 513 Jeff Schaefer	.07	.03	.01
☐ 514 Jim McNamara	.12	.05	.02
☐ 515 Peter Hoy	.12	.05	.02
☐ 516 Curt Schilling	.10	.05	.01
☐ 517 Kirk McCaskill	.07	.03	.01
☐ 518 Chris Gwynn	.07	.03	.01
☐ 519 Sid Fernandez	.10	.05	.01
☐ 520 Jeff Parrett	.07	.03	.01
☐ 521 Scott Ruskin	.07	.03	.01
☐ 522 Kevin McReynolds	.10	.05	.01
☐ 523 Rick Cerone	.07	.03	.01
☐ 524 Jesse Orosco	.07	.03	.01
☐ 525 Troy Afenir	.07	.03	.01
☐ 526 John Smiley	.10	.05	.01
☐ 527 Dale Murphy	.12	.05	.02
☐ 528 Leaf Set Card	.15	.07	.02

1992 Leaf Gold Rookies

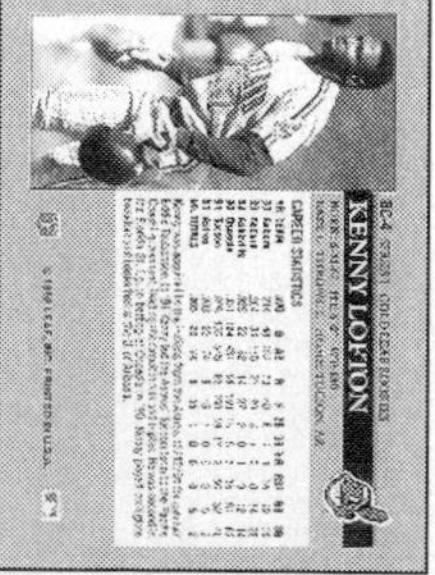

This 24-card standard-size (2 1/2" by 3 1/2") set honors 1992's most promising newcomers. The first 12 cards were randomly inserted in Leaf series I foil packs, while the second 12 cards were featured only in series II packs. The card numbers show a BC prefix. The fronts display full-bleed color action photos highlighted by gold foil border stripes. A gold foil diamond appears at the corners of the picture frame, and the player's name appears in a black bar that extends between the bottom two diamonds. On a gold background, the horizontally oriented backs feature a second color player photo, biography, and, on a white panel, career statistics and career summary. The cards are numbered on the back.

	MT	EX-MT	VG
COMPLETE SET (24)	60.00	27.00	7.50
COMPLETE SERIES 1 (12)	30.00	13.50	3.80
COMPLETE SERIES 2 (12)	30.00	13.50	3.80
COMMON PLAYER (1-12)	1.50	.65	.19
COMMON PLAYER (13-24)	1.50	.65	.19
☐ 1 Chad Curtis	4.00	1.80	.50
☐ 2 Brent Gates	4.50	2.00	.55
☐ 3 Pedro Martinez	4.00	1.80	.50
☐ 4 Kenny Lofton	6.00	2.70	.75
☐ 5 Turk Wendell	1.75	.80	.22
☐ 6 Mark Hutton	2.50	1.15	.30
☐ 7 Todd Hundley	1.50	.65	.19
☐ 8 Matt Stairs	2.00	.90	.25
☐ 9 Eddie Taubensee	2.00	.90	.25
☐ 10 David Nied	10.00	4.50	1.25
☐ 11 Salomon Torres	3.00	1.35	.40
☐ 12 Bret Boone	5.00	2.30	.60
☐ 13 Johnny Ruffin	2.00	.90	.25
☐ 14 Ed Martel	1.75	.80	.22
☐ 15 Rick Trlicek	2.00	.90	.25
☐ 16 Raul Mondesi	4.00	1.80	.50
☐ 17 Pat Mahomes	3.00	1.35	.40
☐ 18 Dan Wilson	2.00	.90	.25
☐ 19 Donovan Osborne	4.00	1.80	.50
☐ 20 Dave Silvestri	2.50	1.15	.30
☐ 21 Gary DiSarcina	1.50	.65	.19
☐ 22 Denny Neagle	1.50	.65	.19
☐ 23 Steve Hosey	4.00	1.80	.50
☐ 24 John Doherty	2.00	.90	.25

1992 Lime Rock Griffey Holograms

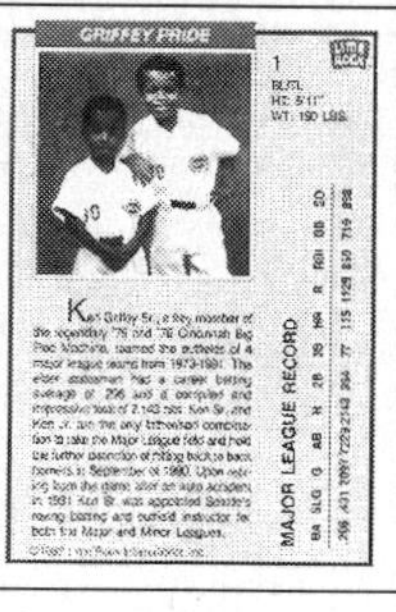

This three-card set was produced by Lime Rock and features baseball's "first family," the Griffeys. Included with each set was a serially numbered coupon that entitled the holder to a free issue of Lime Rock's Inside Trader Club Quarterly News. The sets were sold in a box and included a gold-embossed folder for displaying the cards. According to Lime Rock, 250,000 sets and 5,000 strips were produced. Moreover, 2,500 cards were personally autographed and randomly inserted. Members of Lime Rock's Inside Trader Club had the exclusive right to purchase the same cards as a strip. Also 750 promo sets were produced and distributed at the National Sports Collectors Convention in Atlanta (the promo cards are blank backed). Each standard-size (2 1/2" by 3 1/2") full-bleed hologram captures Ken Sr., Ken Jr., and Craig in game action. At the top of each front appear the words "Griffey Baseball" in the background. Also the player's autograph is inscribed across the holograms. On a pastel green background, the backs carry a color close-up photo, career summary, and statistics. The cards are numbered on the back.

	MT	EX-MT	VG
COMPLETE SET (3)	4.50	2.00	.55
COMMON PLAYER (1-3)	.50	.23	.06
☐ 1 Ken Griffey Sr.	.50	.23	.06
☐ 2 Ken Griffey Jr.	3.50	1.55	.45
☐ 3 Craig Griffey	1.00	.45	.13

1991 Line Drive

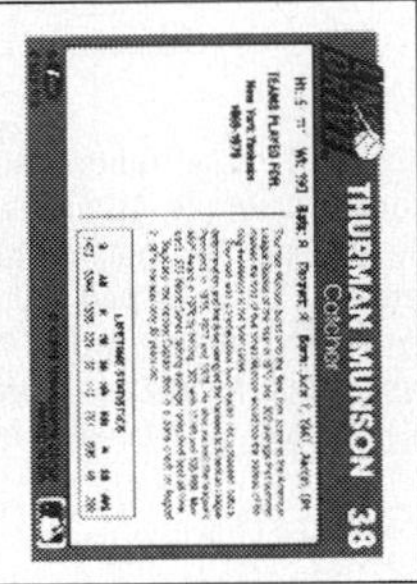

This 50-card set features notable retired players and managers. The cards measure the standard size (2 1/2" by 3 1/2"). The fronts of card numbers 1-42 have color player photos, with blue borders on a white card face. Card numbers 43-50 are similar in design but have sepia-toned photos. The backs of all cards are horizontally oriented and feature biography, career highlights, and lifetime statistics, all inside a red border. The cards are numbered on the back.

	MT	EX-MT	VG
COMPLETE SET (50)	7.00	3.10	.85
COMMON PLAYER (1-50)	.10	.05	.01
☐ 1 Don Drysdale	.35	.16	.04
☐ 2 Joe Torre	.15	.07	.02
☐ 3 Bob Gibson	.40	.18	.05
☐ 4 Bobby Richardson	.20	.09	.03
☐ 5 Ron Santo	.20	.09	.03
☐ 6 Eric Soderholm	.10	.05	.01
☐ 7 Yogi Berra	.50	.23	.06
☐ 8 Steve Garvey	.35	.16	.04
☐ 9 Steve Carlton	.50	.23	.06
☐ 10 Toby Harrah	.10	.05	.01
☐ 11 Luis Tiant	.10	.05	.01
☐ 12 Earl Weaver MG	.10	.05	.01
☐ 13 Bill Mazeroski	.15	.07	.02
☐ 14 Don Baylor	.15	.07	.02
☐ 15 Lew Burdette	.10	.05	.01
☐ 16 Jim Lonborg	.10	.05	.01
☐ 17 Jerry Grote	.10	.05	.01
☐ 18 Ernie Banks	.50	.23	.06
☐ 19 Doug DeCinces	.10	.05	.01
☐ 20 Jimmy Piersall	.15	.07	.02
☐ 21 Ken Holtzman	.10	.05	.01
☐ 22 Manny Mota	.10	.05	.01
☐ 23 Alvin Dark	.10	.05	.01
☐ 24 Lou Brock	.40	.18	.05
☐ 25 Ralph Houk	.10	.05	.01
☐ 26 Graig Nettles	.15	.07	.02
☐ 27 Bill White	.15	.07	.02
☐ 28 Billy Williams	.30	.14	.04
☐ 29 Willie Horton	.15	.07	.02
☐ 30 Tommie Agee	.10	.05	.01
☐ 31 Rico Petrocelli	.10	.05	.01
☐ 32 Julio Cruz	.10	.05	.01
☐ 33 Robin Roberts	.30	.14	.04
☐ 34 Dave Johnson	.10	.05	.01
☐ 35 Wilbur Wood	.10	.05	.01
☐ 36 Cesar Cedeno	.15	.07	.02
☐ 37 George Foster	.15	.07	.02
☐ 38 Thurman Munson	.40	.18	.05
☐ 39 Roberto Clemente	.50	.23	.06
☐ 40 Eddie Mathews	.40	.18	.05
☐ 41 Harmon Killebrew	.35	.16	.04
☐ 42 Monte Irvin	.25	.11	.03
☐ 43 Bob Feller	.35	.16	.04
☐ 44 Jimmie Foxx	.20	.09	.03
☐ 45 Walter Johnson	.25	.11	.03
☐ 46 Casey Stengel	.25	.11	.03
☐ 47 Satchel Paige	.35	.16	.04
☐ 48 Ty Cobb	.50	.23	.06
☐ 49 Mickey Cochrane	.15	.07	.02
☐ 50 Dizzy Dean	.40	.18	.05

1991 Line Drive Ryne Sandberg

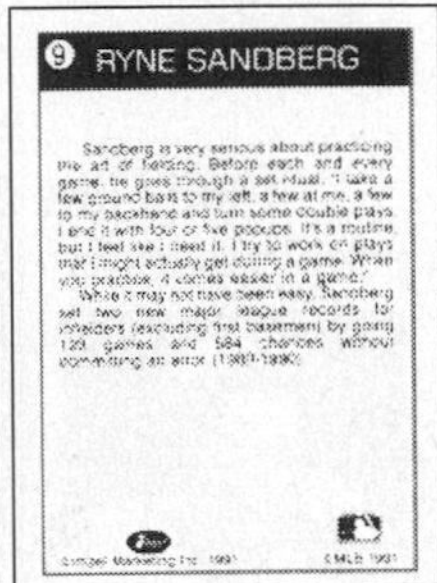

This 20-card set was sold as part of a boxed Ryne Sandberg Baseball Card Kit that included a personalized collector's album, the Ryne Sandberg Story, and a free mail-in offer to receive an 8" by 10" color photo of a top baseball star. The standard-size (2 1/2" by 3 1/2") cards feature color action photos, with blue borders on the left half of the card and red on the right half, on a white card face. In blue and red lettering, the player's name appears above the picture. In dark blue lettering and red borders, the back presents assorted information on Sandberg. The cards are numbered on the back.

	MT	EX-MT	VG
COMPLETE SET (20)	10.00	4.50	1.25
COMMON PLAYER (1-20)	.75	.35	.09
☐ 1 Ryne Sandberg (Catching pop up)	.75	.35	.09
☐ 2 Ryne Sandberg (Running to 1st, Dodger in background)	.75	.35	.09
☐ 3 Ryne Sandberg (Ready to release bat)	.75	.35	.09
☐ 4 Ryne Sandberg (Glove on ground, Waiting for ball)	.75	.35	.09
☐ 5 Ryne Sandberg (Follow through, Hands crossed, Blue uniform)	.75	.35	.09
☐ 6 Ryne Sandberg (Blue uniform, Glove at waist)	.75	.35	.09
☐ 7 Ryne Sandberg (Bat just below waist)	.75	.35	.09
☐ 8 Ryne Sandberg (Posed ready to swing)	.75	.35	.09
☐ 9 Ryne Sandberg (Portrait shot with moustache)	.75	.35	.09
☐ 10 Ryne Sandberg (Transferring ball from glove to hand)	.75	.35	.09
☐ 11 Ryne Sandberg (Dropping bat running to first)	.75	.35	.09
☐ 12 Ryne Sandberg (Running the bases)	.75	.35	.09
☐ 13 Ryne Sandberg (Following through, end of swing,	.75	.35	.09

White uniform)			
☐ 14 Ryne Sandberg (Following through, end of swing, Blue uniform)	.75	.35	.09
☐ 15 Ryne Sandberg (Leading off base)	.75	.35	.09
☐ 16 Ryne Sandberg (Bat behind body)	.75	.35	.09
☐ 17 Ryne Sandberg (Throwing)	.75	.35	.09
☐ 18 Ryne Sandberg (Follow through, hands crossed, white uniform)	.75	.35	.09
☐ 19 Ryne Sandberg (Glove at waist, White uniform)	.75	.35	.09
☐ 20 Ryne Sandberg (Beginning of swing)	.75	.35	.09

1990 Little Sun Writers

This 24-card set honors some of the more influential writers in baseball history, i.e., "major league writers." Cards measure the standard, 2 1/2" by 3 1/2", and have yellow and green borders surrounding black and white photos of the writers pictured. The writer's name is given in black lettering below the picture. The backs have brief biographies of the writers along with "Did you know" features usually about writers not in the set. The cards are numbered on the back in the upper left corner.

	MT	EX-MT	VG
COMPLETE SET (24)	5.00	2.30	.60
COMMON PLAYER (1-24)	.25	.11	.03
☐ 1 Checklist Card	.35	.16	.04
☐ 2 Henry Chadwick	.35	.16	.04
☐ 3 Jacob C. Morse	.25	.11	.03
☐ 4 Francis C. Richter	.25	.11	.03
☐ 5 Grantland Rice	.35	.16	.04
☐ 6 Lee Allen	.25	.11	.03
☐ 7 Joe Reichler	.25	.11	.03
☐ 8 Red Smith	.35	.16	.04
☐ 9 Dick Young	.35	.16	.04
☐ 10 Jim Brosnan	.35	.16	.04
☐ 11 Charles Einstein	.45	.20	.06
☐ 12 Lawrence Ritter	.35	.16	.04
☐ 13 Roger Kahn	.35	.16	.04
☐ 14 Robert Creamer	.35	.16	.04
☐ 15 W.P. Kinsella	.35	.16	.04
☐ 16 Harold Seymour	.25	.11	.03
☐ 17 Ron Shelton	.25	.11	.03
☐ 18 Tom Clark	.25	.11	.03
☐ 19 Mark Harris	.25	.11	.03
☐ 20 John Holway	.25	.11	.03
☐ 21 Peter Golenbock	.35	.16	.04
☐ 22 Jim Bouton	.60	.25	.08
☐ 23 John Thorn	.35	.16	.04
☐ 24 Mike Shannon (Not the ex-Cardinal player)	.25	.11	.03

1960 MacGregor Staff

This 25-card set represents members of the MacGregor Sporting Goods Advisory Staff. Since the cards are unnumbered they ordered below in alphabetical order. The cards are blank backed and measure approximately 3 3/4" by 5". The photos are in black and white. The catalog designation for the set is H825-1. Cards have a facsimile autograph in white lettering on the front.

	NRMT	VG-E	GOOD
COMPLETE SET (25)	550.00	250.00	70.00
COMMON PLAYER (1-25)	10.00	4.50	1.25
☐ 1 Hank Aaron	125.00	57.50	15.50
☐ 2 Richie Ashburn	20.00	9.00	2.50
☐ 3 Gus Bell	12.00	5.50	1.50
☐ 4 Lou Berberet	10.00	4.50	1.25
☐ 5 Jerry Casale	10.00	4.50	1.25
☐ 6 Del Crandall	12.00	5.50	1.50
☐ 7 Art Ditmar	10.00	4.50	1.25
☐ 8 Gene Freese	10.00	4.50	1.25
☐ 9 James Gilliam	14.00	6.25	1.75
☐ 10 Ted Kluszewski	18.00	8.00	2.30
☐ 11 Jim Landis	10.00	4.50	1.25
☐ 12 Al Lopez MG	16.00	7.25	2.00
☐ 13 Willie Mays	125.00	57.50	15.50
☐ 14 Bill Mazeroski	16.00	7.25	2.00
☐ 15 Mike McCormick	10.00	4.50	1.25
☐ 16 Gil McDougald	14.00	6.25	1.75
☐ 17 Russ Nixon	10.00	4.50	1.25
☐ 18 Bill Rigney	10.00	4.50	1.25
☐ 19 Robin Roberts	22.50	10.00	2.80
☐ 20 Frank Robinson	40.00	18.00	5.00
☐ 21 John Roseboro	12.00	5.50	1.50
☐ 22 Red Schoendienst	22.50	10.00	2.80
☐ 23 Bill Skowron	14.00	6.25	1.75
☐ 24 Daryl Spencer	10.00	4.50	1.25
☐ 25 Johnny Temple	10.00	4.50	1.25

1965 MacGregor Staff

This ten-card set represents members of the MacGregor Sporting Goods Advisory Staff. Since the cards are unnumbered they ordered below in alphabetical order. The cards are blank backed and measure approximately 3 9/16" by 5 1/8". The photos are in black and white. The catalog designation for the set is H825-2.

	NRMT	VG-E	GOOD
COMPLETE SET (10)	250.00	115.00	31.00
COMMON PLAYER (1-10)	8.00	3.60	1.00
☐ 1 Roberto Clemente	100.00	45.00	12.50
☐ 2 Al Downing	8.00	3.60	1.00
☐ 3 Johnny Edwards	8.00	3.60	1.00
☐ 4 Ron Hansen	8.00	3.60	1.00
☐ 5 Deron Johnson	8.00	3.60	1.00
☐ 6 Willie Mays	110.00	50.00	14.00
☐ 7 Tony Oliva	16.00	7.25	2.00
☐ 8 Claude Osteen	8.00	3.60	1.00
☐ 9 Bobby Richardson	16.00	7.25	2.00
☐ 10 Zoilo Versalles	8.00	3.60	1.00

1991 Mariners Country Hearth

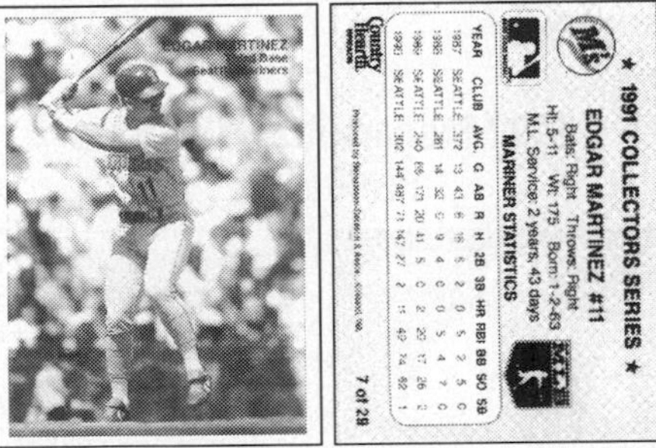

This 29-card set was sponsored and produced by the Country Hearth Breads and Langendorf Baking Company, and individual cards were inserted unprotected in specially marked loaves of Country Hearth. In addition, the cards (ten at a time) were given away to fans attending the Mariners home game at the Seattle Kingdome on August 17th. The cards measure the standard size (2 1/2" by 3 1/2"). The fronts have either a horizontal or vertical orientation and feature glossy color player photos with thin white borders. The player's name and team appear in small white lettering toward the top of the card face. In black print on a light gray background, the horizontally oriented backs present biography, statistics, or career highlights. The cards are numbered on the back. According to sources, only 20,000 sets were produced, and all cards were produced in equal quantities.

	MT	EX-MT	VG
COMPLETE SET (29)	20.00	9.00	2.50
COMMON PLAYER (1-29)	.50	.23	.06
☐ 1 Jim Lefebvre MG	.50	.23	.06
☐ 2 Jeff Schaefer	.50	.23	.06
☐ 3 Harold Reynolds	.60	.25	.08
☐ 4 Greg Briley	.50	.23	.06
☐ 5 Scott Bradley	.50	.23	.06
☐ 6 Dave Valle	.50	.23	.06
☐ 7 Edgar Martinez	1.50	.65	.19
☐ 8 Pete O'Brien	.60	.25	.08
☐ 9 Omar Vizquel	.75	.35	.09
☐ 10 Tino Martinez	1.25	.55	.16
☐ 11 Scott Bankhead	.60	.25	.08
☐ 12 Bill Swift	.75	.35	.09
☐ 13 Jay Buhner	1.00	.45	.13
☐ 14 Alvin Davis	.60	.25	.08
☐ 15 Ken Griffey Jr. (Ready to swing)	5.00	2.30	.60
☐ 16 Tracy Jones	.50	.23	.06
☐ 17 Brent Knackert	.60	.25	.08
☐ 18 Henry Cotto	.50	.23	.06
☐ 19 Ken Griffey Sr. (Watching ball after hit)	.75	.35	.09
☐ 20 Keith Comstock	.50	.23	.06
☐ 21 Brian Holman	.60	.25	.08
☐ 22 Russ Swan	.50	.23	.06
☐ 23 Mike Jackson	.50	.23	.06
☐ 24 Erik Hanson	.75	.35	.09
☐ 25 Mike Schooler	.60	.25	.08
☐ 26 Randy Johnson	.75	.35	.09
☐ 27 Rich DeLucia	.50	.23	.06
☐ 28 Ken Griffey Jr./Sr. (Both on same card)	2.50	1.15	.30
☐ 29 Mariner Moose Mascot	.60	.25	.08

1975 McCallum Ty Cobb

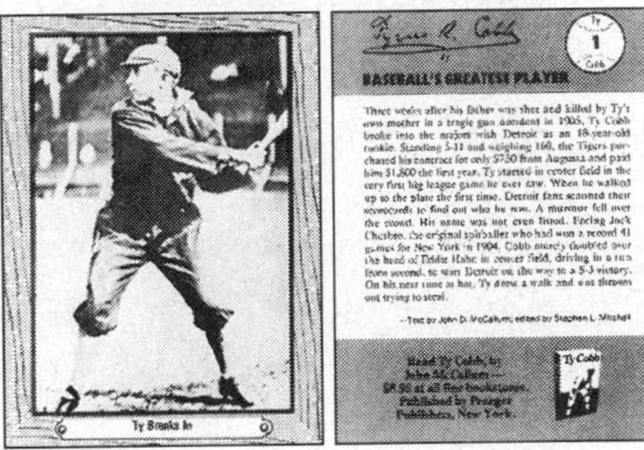

This 20-card set was produced to promote John McCallum's biography on Ty Cobb. The cards measure approximately 2 1/2" by 3 1/2" and feature on the fronts vintage black and white photos, with a hand-drawn artificial wood grain picture frame border. The title to each picture appears in a plaque below the picture. The back has a facsimile autograph and extended caption. The cards are numbered on the back in a baseball icon in the upper right corner.

	NRMT-MT	EXC	G-VG
COMPLETE SET (20)	15.00	6.75	1.90
COMMON PLAYER (1-20)	.75	.35	.09
☐ 1 Ty Breaks In	1.00	.45	.13
☐ 2 Four Inches of the Plate	.75	.35	.09
☐ 3 Slashing into Third	.75	.35	.09
☐ 4 Inking Another Contract	.75	.35	.09
☐ 5 Captain Tyrus R. Cobb	.75	.35	.09
☐ 6 Ty with "The Big Train"	1.50	.65	.19
☐ 7 The End of an Era	.75	.35	.09
☐ 8 All-Time Centerfielder	.75	.35	.09
☐ 9 Ty Could "Walk 'em Down"	.75	.35	.09
☐ 10 Menacing Batsman	.75	.35	.09
☐ 11 With Brother Paul	.75	.35	.09
☐ 12 Thomas Edison, Cobb Fan	1.50	.65	.19
☐ 13 Ty Tangles with Muggsy McGraw	1.25	.55	.16
☐ 14 Author McCallum with Cy Young	1.00	.45	.13
☐ 15 Tris Speaker, Joe DiMaggio, and Ty Cobb	2.50	1.15	.30
☐ 16 Ted Gets a Lesson	1.50	.65	.19
☐ 17 Five for Five	.75	.35	.09
☐ 18 "I have but one regret"	.75	.35	.09
☐ 19 Excellence: The Cobb Standard	.75	.35	.09
☐ 20 His Favorite Photo	1.00	.45	.13

1992 McDonald's Ken Griffey Jr.

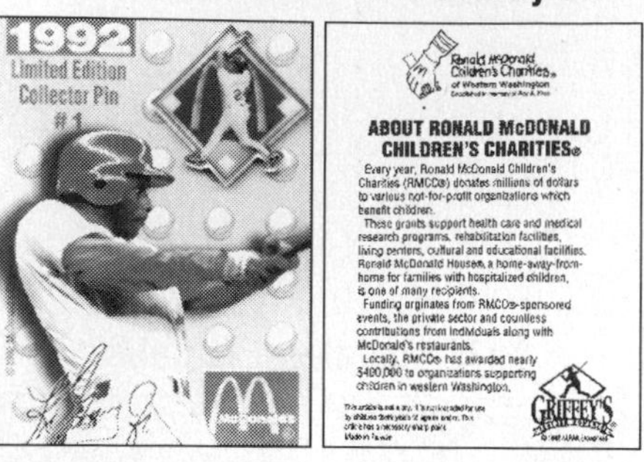

This set, sponsored by McDonald's, contains three card and pin combinations. The cards are numbered on the front and measure 2 1/2" by 3 1/2". The card back describes the Ronald McDonald Children's Charities program in Western Washington.

	MT	EX-MT	VG
COMPLETE SET (3)	10.00	4.50	1.25
COMMON PLAYER (1-3)	4.00	1.80	.50
☐ 1 Ken Griffey Jr. (Yellow background)	4.00	1.80	.50
☐ 2 Ken Griffey Jr. (Black and red background)	4.00	1.80	.50
☐ 3 Ken Griffey Jr. (Black and blue background)	4.00	1.80	.50

1991 MDA All-Stars

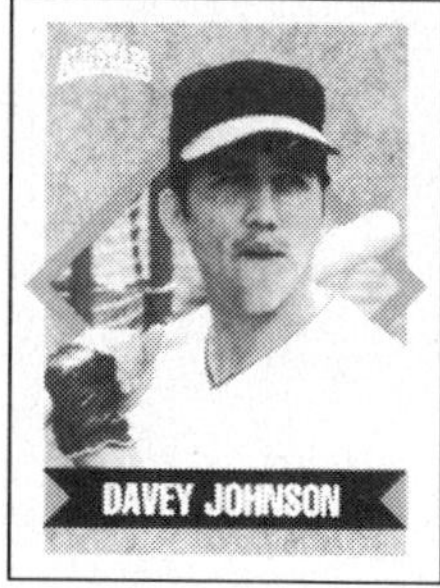

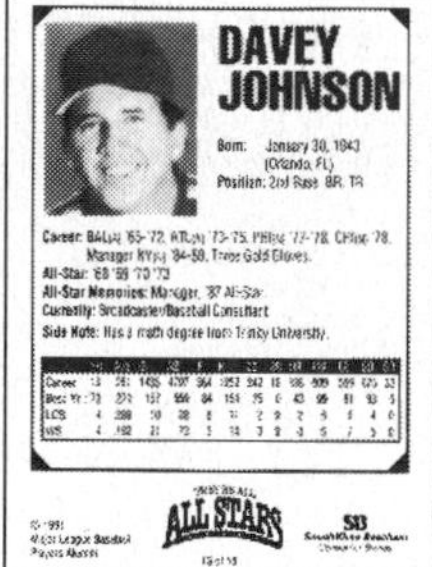

This 20-card set was produced by SmithKline Beecham for the Muscular Dystrophy Association. It includes 18 All-Star Alumni cards that feature retired baseball All-Stars. A vinyl album designed to house the cards was also issued. The cards measure the standard size (2 1/2" by 3 1/2"). The front design includes white borders and a sandy background. Color action player photos are cut out and superimposed on diamonds framed by various color borders. The slogan for the set, "They're All All-Stars," appears in one of the upper corners, while the player's name appears in white lettering in a color stripe cutting across the bottom of the picture. Since the set was licensed by the Major League Baseball Players Alumni, all team logos have been airbrushed out. In black on white, the backs carry a head shot of the player (in retirement), biographical information, and statistics. The cards are numbered on the back.

	MT	EX-MT	VG
COMPLETE SET (20)	12.50	5.75	1.55
COMMON PLAYER (1-18)	.50	.23	.06
☐ 1 Steve Carlton	.75	.35	.09
☐ 2 Ted Simmons	.60	.25	.08
☐ 3 Willie Stargell	.75	.35	.09
☐ 4 Bill Mazeroski	.60	.25	.08
☐ 5 Ron Santo	.60	.25	.08
☐ 6 Dave Concepcion	.60	.25	.08
☐ 7 Bobby Bonds	.60	.25	.08
☐ 8 George Foster	.60	.25	.08
☐ 9 Billy Williams	.75	.35	.09
☐ 10 Whitey Ford	.75	.35	.09
☐ 11 Yogi Berra	1.00	.45	.13
☐ 12 Boog Powell	.60	.25	.08
☐ 13 Davey Johnson	.50	.23	.06
☐ 14 Brooks Robinson	.75	.35	.09
☐ 15 Jim Fregosi	.50	.23	.06
☐ 16 Harmon Killebrew	.75	.35	.09
☐ 17 Ted Williams	1.50	.65	.19
☐ 18 Al Kaline	.75	.35	.09
☐ NNO MDA Fact Card Brooks Robinson Tommy	.75	.35	.09
☐ NNO Title Card	.75	.35	.09

1992 Megacards Babe Ruth Prototypes

Nine prototypes were produced to preview Megacards 1992 Babe Ruth Collection. The cards are very similar to the Conlon sets produced in conjunction with The Sporting News. The cards are standard size, 2 1/2" by 3 1/2". These cards were clearly marked as prototypes, and the bulk of the 12,000 cards produced were included in mailings to hobby dealers. In general, some subtle differences in photos are found with some of the prototype cards. The cards are numbered on the back.

	MT	EX-MT	VG
COMPLETE SET (9)	25.00	11.50	3.10
COMMON PLAYER	3.00	1.35	.40
☐ 14 Year in Review-1921 Best year any batter ever had	3.00	1.35	.40
☐ 31 World Series-1916 Red Sox defeat Dodgers 4 games to 1	3.00	1.35	.40
☐ 75 Place in History-1928 .342 lifetime batting average	3.00	1.35	.40
☐ 106 Career Highlights-1927 Babe's 60th home run September 30th	3.00	1.35	.40
☐ 124 Trivia-1926 He "did something rash"	3.00	1.35	.40
☐ 129 Sultan of Swat-1925 First to hit 30, 40, 50 and 60 home runs	3.00	1.35	.40
☐ 134 Being Remembered-1948 by George Bush	3.00	1.35	.40
☐ 138 Being Remembered-1923 by Grantland Rice	3.00	1.35	.40

		MT	EX-MT	VG
☐ 154	The Bambino-The Man........ Lou Gehrig Appreciation Day: July 4th Lou Gehrig Babe Ruth	3.00	1.35	.40

1992 Megacards Babe Ruth

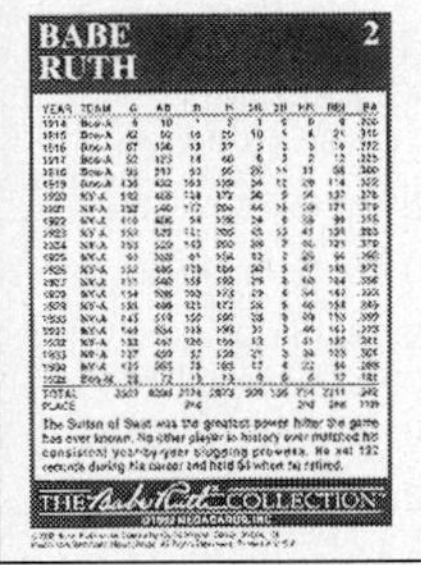

Released by Megacards, the 1992 Babe Ruth Collection consists of 165 standard-size (2 1/2" by 3 1/2") cards, including a card for every year of his career. The cards are very similar to the Conlon sets produced in conjunction with The Sporting News. The cards were sold in both ten-card packs and 22-card blister packs. Complete sets were also available in a commemorative tin. The fronts display glossy black and white, action and portrait shots inside a white picture frame on a black card face. Captions to the pictures and the year appear in the bottom black border. The backs carry biography, statistics, highlights, or career summary. The set is arranged as follows: Babe Ruth (1-4), Year in Review (5-29), World Series (30-39), Place in History (40-70), Career Highlights (71-97), Trivia (98-104), Sultan of SWAT (105-115), The Bambino-The Man (116-142), and Being Remembered (143-163). The set concludes with checklist cards (164-165). The cards are numbered on the back. The set could also be purchased in a special commemorative tin.

		MT	EX-MT	VG
	COMPLETE SET (165)......................	18.00	8.00	2.30
	COMMON PLAYER (1-165)..............	.15	.07	.02
☐ 1	Lifetime Pitching.................... Statistics 1916	.25	.11	.03
☐ 2	Lifetime Batting...................... Statistics 1925	.15	.07	.02
☐ 3	Lifetime-World Series .... Pitching 1916	.15	.07	.02
☐ 4	Lifetime World Series............. Batting 1926	.15	.07	.02
☐ 5	22-9 Record in the .... Minors 1914	.15	.07	.02
☐ 6	2-1 Record First Year............. in Majors 1914	.15	.07	.02
☐ 7	Won 17 of His Last .... 21 Decisions 1915	.15	.07	.02
☐ 8	Led League with 1.75 ERA...... and 9 Shutouts 1916	.15	.07	.02
☐ 9	Defeats Walter......................... Johnson for 6th Time 1917	.25	.11	.03
☐ 10	Doubles as Pitcher.............. and a Regular 1918	.15	.07	.02
☐ 11	First Season in the .... Outfield 1919	.15	.07	.02
☐ 12	Sold to Yankees for............... Sold to Yankees for 100,000 1920	.15	.07	.02
☐ 13	The Best Year Any................ Batter Ever Had 1921	.15	.07	.02
☐ 14	Suspended for First.............. 38 Games 1922	.15	.07	.02
☐ 15	Wins American League .... MVP 1923	.15	.07	.02
☐ 16	Wins Only Batting Title-.378 1924	.15	.07	.02
☐ 17	The Million Dollar.................. Stomach Ache 1925	.15	.07	.02
☐ 18	Bats .372 With a .737............. Slugging Average 1926	.15	.07	.02
☐ 19	The Best Baseball.................. Team in History 1927	.15	.07	.02
☐ 20	Tops 50 Home Runs-4th....... Time 1928	.15	.07	.02
☐ 21	Clubs 500th Home Run......... 1929	.15	.07	.02
☐ 22	Bam Bams Nine in a............. Week 1930	.15	.07	.02
☐ 23	.700 Slugging Average.......... for 9th Time 1931	.15	.07	.02
☐ 24	Blasts Over 40 Homers .... for 11th Time 1932	.15	.07	.02
☐ 25	Over 100 RBIs for .... 13th Time 1933	.15	.07	.02
☐ 26	Tops 2,000 Career................ Walks 1934	.15	.07	.02
☐ 27	Babe Retires 1935.................	.15	.07	.02
☐ 28	Babe Coaches the.................. Dodgers 1938	.15	.07	.02
☐ 29	The Babe in .... Retirement 1942	.15	.07	.02
☐ 30	Warms Bench after .... 18-8 Season 1915	.15	.07	.02
☐ 31	Hurls 14 Inning .... Complete Game Gem 1916	.15	.07	.02
☐ 32	Scoreless Inning .... Streak Soars 1918	.15	.07	.02
☐ 33	Yankees Play in Their........... First World Series 1921	.15	.07	.02
☐ 34	Goes Back to the Farm 1922	.15	.07	.02
☐ 35	Yanks Win First World .... Championship 1923	.15	.07	.02
☐ 36	Belts 4 Home Runs in .... Losing Cause 1926	.15	.07	.02
☐ 37	Yanks Destroy Bucs in .... Four Games 1927	.15	.07	.02
☐ 38	.625 Batting and..................... 1.375 Slugging Avg. 1928	.15	.07	.02
☐ 39	Yanks Sweep Cubs................ 1932	.15	.07	.02
☐ 40	Lifetime-2,056 Walks 1923	.15	.07	.02
☐ 41	First to Fan 1,000.................. Times 1929	.15	.07	.02
☐ 42	Lifetime-2,174 Runs .... Scored 1928	.15	.07	.02
☐ 43	Lifetime-5,793 Total............. Bases 1942	.15	.07	.02
☐ 44	Lifetime-1,356 Extra............. Base Hits 1928	.15	.07	.02
☐ 45	Lifetime-714 Home .... Runs 1935	.15	.07	.02
☐ 46	Lifetime-16 Grand .... Slams 1926	.15	.07	.02
☐ 47	Lifetime-8.5 Home Run......... Percentage 1934	.15	.07	.02
☐ 48	Lifetime-Most Games,........... 2 or More Home Runs 1927	.15	.07	.02
☐ 49	Lifetime-11 Seasons .... with 40 or more HRs 1924	.15	.07	.02
☐ 50	Lifetime-2,211 RBIs..............	.15	.07	.02
☐ 51	Lifetime-.342 Batting .... Average 1928	.15	.07	.02
☐ 52	Lifetime-.690......................... Slugging Average 1934	.15	.07	.02
☐ 53	Season-9 Shutouts 1916	.15	.07	.02
☐ 54	Season-170 Walks 1930.......	.15	.07	.02
☐ 55	Season-177 Runs .... Score 1939	.15	.07	.02
☐ 56	Season-.545 On-Base .... Percentage 1926	.15	.07	.02
☐ 57	Season-457 Total.................. Bases 1926	.15	.07	.02
☐ 58	Season-119 Extra.................. Base Hits 1947	.15	.07	.02
☐ 59	Season-171 Runs .... Batted In 1934	.15	.07	.02
☐ 60	Season-60 Home Runs 1927	.15	.07	.02
☐ 61	Season-11.8 Home Run........ Percentage 1921	.15	.07	.02
☐ 62	Season-.847 Slugging........... Average 1920	.15	.07	.02

	Card			
☐ 63	World Series-3.0 Record 1915	.15	.07	.02
☐ 64	World Series-0.87 ERA 1918	.15	.07	.02
☐ 65	World Series-33 Walks 1928	.15	.07	.02
☐ 66	World Series-37 Runs 1928	.15	.07	.02
☐ 67	World Series-96 Total Bases 1923	.15	.07	.02
☐ 68	World Series-15 Home Runs 1923	.15	.07	.02
☐ 69	World Series-33 RBIs 1929	.15	.07	.02
☐ 70	World Series- .744 Slugging Average 1927	.15	.07	.02
☐ 71	First Major League Victory: July 11, 1914	.15	.07	.02
☐ 72	First Major League Home Run: May 6, 1915	.15	.07	.02
☐ 73	Babe Derails Big Train 1942	.15	.07	.02
☐ 74	Leads American League in Fielding 1928	.15	.07	.02
☐ 75	Babe's First Home Run Record-29 1919	.15	.07	.02
☐ 76	Babe Becomes a Yankee 1920	.15	.07	.02
☐ 77	First Home Run in Yankee Stadium 1923	.15	.07	.02
☐ 78	Wins American League MVP 1923	.15	.07	.02
☐ 79	Wins Only Batting Title 1924	.15	.07	.02
☐ 80	Babe Hits 3 Home Runs in Series Game: October 6, 1926	.15	.07	.02
☐ 81	Babe and Lou Smack 107 Home Runs	.25	.11	.03
☐ 82	The Babe's 60th Home Run: September 30, 1927	.25	.11	.03
☐ 83	3 Home Runs in World Series Game 1928	.15	.07	.02
☐ 84	Early Called Shots by The Bambino 1932	.15	.07	.02
☐ 85	The Called Shot - The Legend 1932	.15	.07	.02
☐ 86	The Called Shot - The Believers 1932	.15	.07	.02
☐ 87	The Called Shot - The Doubters 1948	.15	.07	.02
☐ 88	The Called Shot - Babe's View 1936	.15	.07	.02
☐ 89	Slams First HR in First AS Game 1933	.15	.07	.02
☐ 90	Last Time on the Mound 1933	.15	.07	.02
☐ 91	Babe Hits His 700th Home Run 1934	.15	.07	.02
☐ 92	Banzai Beibu Russu- The Babe in Japan 1934	.25	.11	.03
☐ 93	Last Major League Homers 1935	.15	.07	.02
☐ 94	Inaugurated Into Hall of Fame 1939	.15	.07	.02
☐ 95	Faces Johnson Again: August 23, 1942	.25	.11	.03
☐ 96	Babe Ruth Day: April 27, 1947	.25	.11	.03
☐ 97	Babe's Farewell 1948	.25	.11	.03
☐ 98	A Perfect Punch 1915	.15	.07	.02
☐ 99	Yankees Best Base Thief 1920	.15	.07	.02
☐ 100	Hub Pruett: Babe Buster 1929	.15	.07	.02
☐ 101	Babe Caught Stealing to End Series 1926	.15	.07	.02
☐ 102	Never Won a Triple Crown 1926	.15	.07	.02
☐ 103	Babe Used a 54-Ounce Bat 1926	.15	.07	.02
☐ 104	Babe Bats Righty 1923	.15	.07	.02
☐ 105	Babe's Greatness 1921	.15	.07	.02
☐ 106	The Babe's Best 1942	.15	.07	.02
☐ 107	Outslugged Entire Teams 1923	.15	.07	.02
☐ 108	First to Hit 30, 40, 50 and 60 Home Runs 1923	.15	.07	.02
☐ 109	The Pitkin Study 1926	.15	.07	.02
☐ 110	First to Put the Ball into Orbit 1926	.15	.07	.02
☐ 111	Afraid to Kill Somebody 1926	.15	.07	.02
☐ 112	The Wonder Years, 1926-1931 1927	.15	.07	.02
☐ 113	Hit .422 with 7 Homers on Opening Days 1931	.15	.07	.02
☐ 114	Babe at Bat 1932	.15	.07	.02
☐ 115	Greatest Ballplayer the Game Has Known 1942	.15	.07	.02
☐ 116	The Babe's Early Childhood	.15	.07	.02
☐ 117	St. Mary's Industrial School 1911	.15	.07	.02
☐ 118	Babe and Brother Matthias	.15	.07	.02
☐ 119	The Babe's Nicknames	.15	.07	.02
☐ 120	Babe's First Wife Helen	.15	.07	.02
☐ 121	Babes Second Wife, Claire	.15	.07	.02
☐ 122	Lou Gehrig Appreciation Day: July 4, 1939	.35	.16	.04
☐ 123	Babe's Friendship with Herb Pennock 1921	.25	.11	.03
☐ 124	The Babe and Miller Huggins	.25	.11	.03
☐ 125	The Babe and Ty Cobb	.35	.16	.04
☐ 126	Babe and Walter Johnson 1942	.25	.11	.03
☐ 127	Baseball's Greatest Drawing Card 1923	.15	.07	.02
☐ 128	Babe's Barnstorming	.15	.07	.02
☐ 129	Costly Confrontations 1925	.15	.07	.02
☐ 130	He Often Played Hurt	.15	.07	.02
☐ 131	Babe's Big Bucks 1927	.15	.07	.02
☐ 132	Wanted to be a Manager	.15	.07	.02
☐ 133	The Babe on the Links	.15	.07	.02
☐ 134	Babe in the Movies	.15	.07	.02
☐ 135	Babe Contributes to War Effort	.15	.07	.02
☐ 136	The Babe - Peace Negotiator	.15	.07	.02
☐ 137	Everyone Loved the Babe	.15	.07	.02
☐ 138	He Brought Children Joy 1929	.15	.07	.02
☐ 139	He Always Had Time for Kids	.15	.07	.02
☐ 140	The Johnny Sylvester Story	.15	.07	.02
☐ 141	Moving with the Great 1923	.15	.07	.02
☐ 142	Babe Ruth and The American Dream 1923	.15	.07	.02
☐ 143	Being Remembered by Bill James 1928	.15	.07	.02
☐ 144	Being Remembered by Bill James 1929	.15	.07	.02
☐ 145	Being Remembered by Bill James 1920	.15	.07	.02
☐ 146	Being Remembered by Mel Allen 1923	.15	.07	.02
☐ 147	Being Remembered by Mel Allen 1928	.15	.07	.02
☐ 148	Being Remembered by Wes Ferrell 1930	.15	.07	.02
☐ 149	Being Remembered by George Bush 1948	.35	.16	.04
☐ 150	Being Remembered by Ethan Allan 1948	.15	.07	.02
☐ 151	Being Remembered by Daughter Dorothy 1926	.15	.07	.02
☐ 152	Being Remembered by Daughter Julia 1947	.15	.07	.02
☐ 153	Being Remembered by Daughter Julia 1938	.15	.07	.02
☐ 154	Being Remembered by Mark Koenig 1927	.15	.07	.02
☐ 155	Being Remembered by Donald Honig 1927	.15	.07	.02
☐ 156	Being Remembered by Lloyd Waner and Waite Hoyt 1948	.15	.07	.02
☐ 157	Being Remembered by Waite Hoyt 1938	.15	.07	.02
☐ 158	Being Remembered by Bill Dickey 1938	.20	.09	.03
☐ 159	Being Remembered by Bob Meusel 1922	.15	.07	.02
☐ 160	Being Remembered by	.15	.07	.02

Jim Chapman 1941			
☐ 161 Being Remembered by........ Christy Walsh 1926	.15	.07	.02
☐ 162 Being Remembered............. Heading for Home The Babe Passes Away	.15	.07	.02
☐ 163 Being Remembered by........ Grantland Rice 1923	.15	.07	.02
☐ 164 Checklist 1-83.....................	.15	.07	.02
☐ 165 Checklist 84-165.................	.15	.07	.02

1984 Mets Fan Club

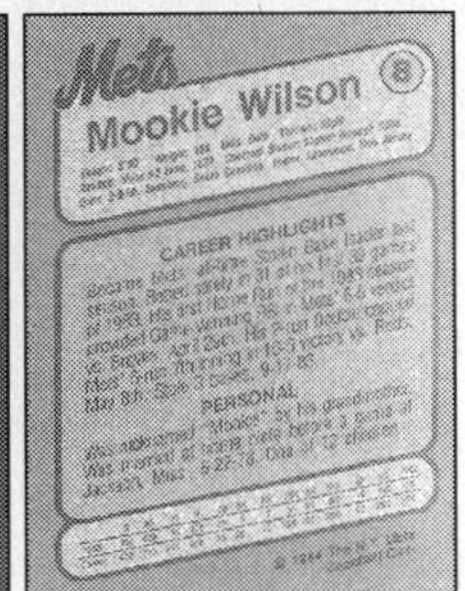

The cards in this eight-player set measure 2 1/2" by 3 1/2". The sheets were produced by Topps for the New York Mets and feature only Mets. The full sheet measures 7 1/2" by 10 1/2". Cards are together on the sheet but are perforated for those collectors who want to separate the individual player cards. The middle (ninth) card is a Mets Fan club membership card which details various promotional days at Shea Stadium on the back. The cards are numbered on the back and printed in orange and blue.

	NRMT-MT	EXC	G-VG
COMPLETE SET (8)..........................	12.00	5.50	1.50
COMMON PLAYER...........................	.50	.23	.06
☐ 1 Dave Johnson MG...................	.60	.25	.08
☐ 2 Ron Darling............................	2.50	1.15	.30
☐ 3 George Foster	1.00	.45	.13
☐ 4 Keith Hernandez......................	1.25	.55	.16
☐ 5 Jesse Orosco	.50	.23	.06
☐ 6 Rusty Staub	1.00	.45	.13
☐ 7 Darryl Strawberry....................	9.00	4.00	1.15
☐ 8 Mookie Wilson	.75	.35	.09
☐ NNO Membership Card	.50	.23	.06

1985 Mets Fan Club

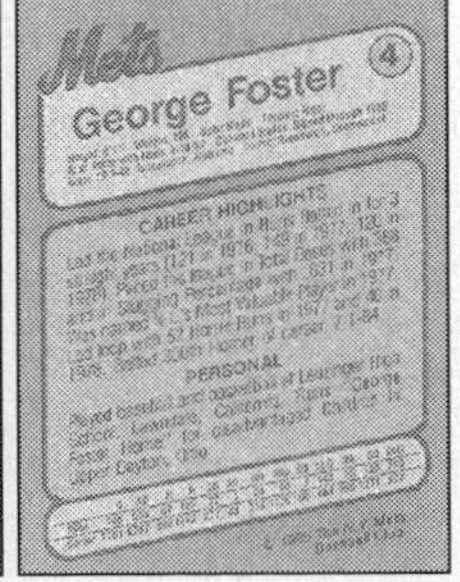

The cards in this eight-player set measure 2 1/2" by 3 1/2". The sheets were produced by Topps for the New York Mets and feature only Mets players. The full sheet measures approximately 7 1/2" by 10 1/2". Cards are together on the sheet but are perforated for those collectors who want to separate the individual player cards. The middle (ninth) card is a Mets Fan club membership card. The set was available as a membership premium for joining the Junior Mets Fan Club for 4.00. The cards are listed below in alphabetical order for convenience.

	NRMT-MT	EXC	G-VG
COMPLETE SET (8)..........................	18.00	8.00	2.30
COMMON PLAYER...........................	.50	.23	.06
☐ 1 Wally Backman	.50	.23	.06
☐ 2 Bruce Berenyi..........................	.50	.23	.06
☐ 3 Gary Carter.............................	1.50	.65	.19
☐ 4 George Foster	1.00	.45	.13
☐ 5 Dwight Gooden	9.00	4.00	1.15
☐ 6 Keith Hernandez......................	1.25	.55	.16
☐ 7 Doug Sisk	.50	.23	.06
☐ 8 Darryl Strawberry....................	6.00	2.70	.75
☐ NNO Membership Card	.50	.23	.06

1986 Mets Fan Club

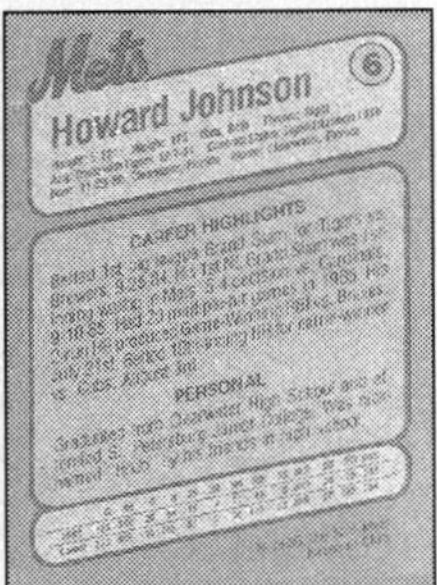

The cards in this eight-player set measure 2 1/2" by 3 1/2". The sheets were produced by Topps for the New York Mets and feature only Mets. The full sheet measures approximately 7 1/2" by 10 1/2". Cards are together on the sheet but are perforated for those collectors who want to separate the individual player cards. The middle (ninth) card is a Mets Fan club membership card. The set was available as a membership premium for joining the Junior Mets Fan Club for 5.00. The cards are listed below in alphabetical order for convenience.

	MT	EX-MT	VG
COMPLETE SET (8)..........................	14.00	6.25	1.75
COMMON PLAYER...........................	.50	.23	.06
☐ 1 Wally Backman	.50	.23	.06
☐ 2 Gary Carter.............................	1.50	.65	.19
☐ 3 Ron Darling.............................	1.00	.45	.13
☐ 4 Dwight Gooden	4.00	1.80	.50
☐ 5 Keith Hernandez......................	1.25	.55	.16
☐ 6 Howard Johnson......................	1.50	.65	.19
☐ 7 Roger McDowell	.75	.35	.09
☐ 8 Darryl Strawberry....................	5.00	2.30	.60
☐ NNO Membership Card	.50	.23	.06

1987 Mets Fan Club

The cards in this eight-player set measure 2 1/2" by 3 1/2". The sheets were produced by Topps for the New York Mets and feature only Mets. The full sheet measures approximately 7 1/2" by 10 1/2". Cards are together on the sheet but are perforated for those collectors who want to separate the individual player cards. The cards have an outer

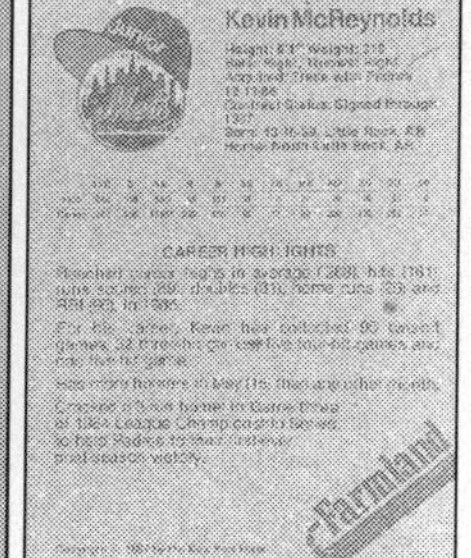

orange border. The set was available as a membership premium for joining the Junior Mets Fan Club for 6.00. The set and club were also sponsored by Farmland Dairies Milk. The cards are unnumbered on the back although they do contain the player's uniform number on the front.

	MT	EX-MT	VG
COMPLETE SET (9)	9.00	4.00	1.15
COMMON PLAYER	.50	.23	.06
☐ 1 Gary Carter 8	1.50	.65	.19
☐ 2 Ron Darling 12	1.00	.45	.13
☐ 3 Len Dykstra 4	1.00	.45	.13
☐ 4 Roger McDowell 42	.60	.25	.08
☐ 5 Kevin McReynolds 22	1.50	.65	.19
☐ 6 Bob Ojeda 19	.75	.35	.09
☐ 7 Darryl Strawberry 18	4.50	2.00	.55
☐ 8 Mookie Wilson 1	.60	.25	.08
☐ 9 Mets Team Card (1986 World Champs)	.50	.23	.06

1988 Mets Fan Club

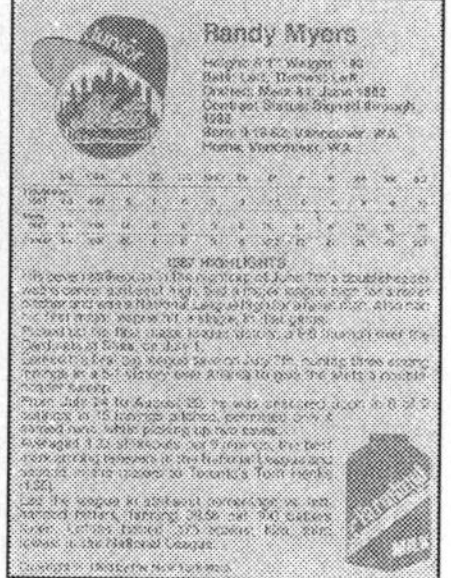

The cards in this nine-player set measure 2 1/2" by 3 1/2". The sheets were produced by Topps for the New York Mets and feature only Mets. The full sheet measures 7 1/2" by 10 1/2". Cards are together on the sheet but are perforated for those collectors who want to separate the individual player cards. The cards have an outer orange border and an inner dark blue border. The set was available as a membership premium for joining the Junior Mets Fan Club for 6.00. The set and club were also sponsored by Farmland Dairies Milk. The cards are unnumbered on the back although they do contain the player's uniform number on the front.

	MT	EX-MT	VG
COMPLETE SET (9)	6.00	2.70	.75
COMMON PLAYER	.40	.18	.05
☐ 8 Gary Carter	1.00	.45	.13
☐ 16 Dwight Gooden	.90	.40	.11
☐ 17 Keith Hernandez	.75	.35	.09
☐ 18 Darryl Strawberry	2.00	.90	.25
☐ 20 Howard Johnson	1.00	.45	.13
☐ 21 Kevin Elster	.40	.18	.05
☐ 42 Roger McDowell	.40	.18	.05
☐ 48 Randy Myers	.60	.25	.08
☐ 50 Sid Fernandez	.60	.25	.08

1989 Mets Fan Club

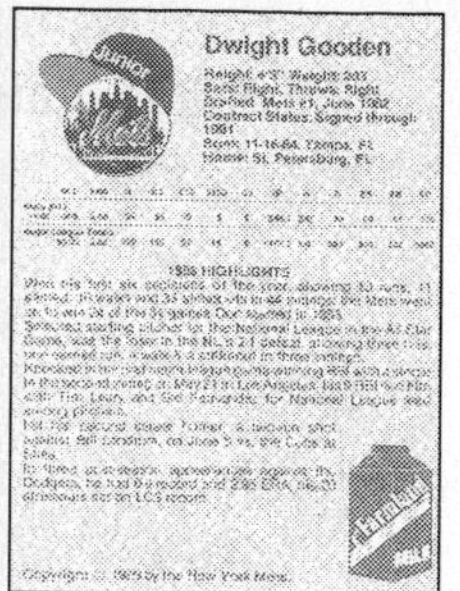

This set was produced by Topps for the Mets Fan Club as a sheet of nine cards each featuring a member of the New York Mets. The individual cards are standard size, 2 1/2" by 3 1/2"; however the set is typically traded as a sheet rather than as individual cards.

	MT	EX-MT	VG
COMPLETE SET (9)	6.00	2.70	.75
COMMON PLAYER	.40	.18	.05
☐ 8 Gary Carter	.90	.40	.11
☐ 9 Gregg Jefferies	1.25	.55	.16
☐ 16 Dwight Gooden	.90	.40	.11
☐ 18 Darryl Strawberry	1.25	.55	.16
☐ 22 Kevin McReynolds	.60	.25	.08
☐ 25 Keith Miller	.50	.23	.06
☐ 42 Roger McDowell	.40	.18	.05
☐ 44 David Cone	1.25	.55	.16
☐ NNO Mets Team Card Eastern Div. Champs	.50	.23	.06

1990 Mets Fan Club

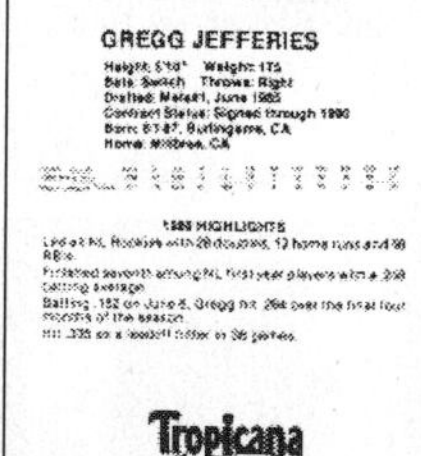

The 1990 Mets Fan Club Tropicana set was issued by the New York Mets fan club in association with the Tropicana Juice Company. For the seventh year, the Mets issued a perforated card sheet in conjunction with their fan clubs. This nine-card, standard-size (2 1/2" by 3 1/2") set is skip-numbered and arranged by uniform numbers.

	MT	EX-MT	VG
COMPLETE SET (9)	5.00	2.30	.60
COMMON PLAYER	.40	.18	.05
☐ 9 Gregg Jefferies	.75	.35	.09

□ 16 Dwight Gooden	.75	.35	.09
□ 18 Darryl Strawberry	.90	.40	.11
□ 20 Howard Johnson	.75	.35	.09
□ 21 Kevin Elster	.40	.18	.05
□ 25 Keith Miller	.50	.23	.06
□ 29 Frank Viola	.60	.25	.08
□ 44 David Cone	.75	.35	.09
□ 50 Sid Fernandez	.50	.23	.06

1991 Mets WIZ

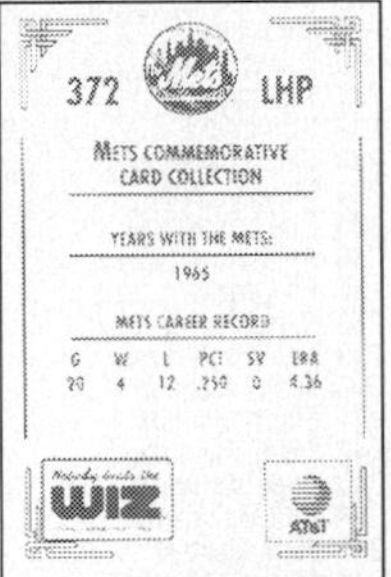

This 450-card commemorative New York Mets set was sponsored by WIZ Home Entertainment Centers and ATT. The set was issued on 30 (approximately) 10" by 9" perforated sheets (15 cards per sheet); after perforation, the cards measure approximately 2" by 3". The fronts have black and white head shots of the players on a white card face decorated with a blue picture frame design. The player's name and position are written vertically alongside the pictures. The team logo above the picture and the Wiz logo below round out the card face. In black lettering on white, the backs have the player's position, years (and stats) with the Mets, and career record. The team and sponsors' logos also appear on the back. The cards are numbered on the back and listed in alphabetical order. The set purports to show every player who ever played for the New York Mets. The set was issued in three series to be distributed at three home games during the year, e.g., the first series was issued to all fans attending the Mets home game on May 25, 1991.

	MT	EX-MT	VG
COMPLETE SET (450)	45.00	20.00	5.75
COMMON PLAYER (1-439)	.15	.07	.02
□ 1 Don Aase	.20	.09	.03
□ 2 Tommie Agee	.20	.09	.03
□ 3 Rick Aguilera	.25	.11	.03
□ 4 Jack Aker	.15	.07	.02
□ 5 Neil Allen	.20	.09	.03
□ 6 Bill Almon	.20	.09	.03
□ 7 Sandy Alomar Sr.	.20	.09	.03
□ 8 Jesus Alou	.20	.09	.03
□ 9 George Altman	.15	.07	.02
□ 10 Luis Alvarado	.15	.07	.02
□ 11 Craig Anderson	.15	.07	.02
□ 12 Rick Anderson	.15	.07	.02
□ 13 Bob Apodaca	.15	.07	.02
□ 14 Gerry Arrigo	.15	.07	.02
□ 15 Richie Ashburn	.40	.18	.05
□ 16 Tucker Ashford	.15	.07	.02
□ 17 Bob Aspromonte	.15	.07	.02
□ 18 Benny Ayala	.15	.07	.02
□ 19 Wally Backman	.20	.09	.03
□ 20 Kevin Baez	.15	.07	.02
□ 21 Bob Bailor	.15	.07	.02
□ 22 Rick Baldwin	.15	.07	.02
□ 23 Billy Baldwin	.15	.07	.02
□ 24 Lute Barnes	.15	.07	.02
□ 25 Ed Bauta	.15	.07	.02
□ 26 Billy Beane	.15	.07	.02
□ 27 Larry Bearnarth	.15	.07	.02
□ 28 Blaine Beatty	.15	.07	.02
□ 29 Jim Beauchamp	.15	.07	.02
□ 30 Gus Bell	.20	.09	.03
□ 31 Dennis Bennett	.15	.07	.02
□ 32 Butch Benton	.15	.07	.02
□ 33 Juan Berenguer	.15	.07	.02
□ 34 Bruce Berenyi	.15	.07	.02
□ 35 Dwight Bernard	.15	.07	.02
□ 36 Yogi Berra	.75	.35	.09
□ 37 Jim Bethke	.15	.07	.02
□ 38 Mike Bishop	.15	.07	.02
□ 39 Terry Blocker	.15	.07	.02
□ 40 Bruce Bochy	.15	.07	.02
□ 41 Bruce Boisclair	.15	.07	.02
□ 42 Dan Boitano	.15	.07	.02
□ 43 Mark Bomback	.15	.07	.02
□ 44 Don Bosch	.15	.07	.02
□ 45 Daryl Boston	.20	.09	.03
□ 46 Ken Boswell	.15	.07	.02
□ 47 Ed Bouchee	.15	.07	.02
□ 48 Larry Bowa	.25	.11	.03
□ 49 Ken Boyer	.25	.11	.03
□ 50 Mark Bradley	.15	.07	.02
□ 51 Eddie Bressoud	.15	.07	.02
□ 52 Hubie Brooks	.25	.11	.03
□ 53 Kevin Brown	.20	.09	.03
□ 54 Leon Brown	.15	.07	.02
□ 55 Mike Bruhert	.15	.07	.02
□ 56 Jerry Buchek	.15	.07	.02
□ 57 Larry Burright	.15	.07	.02
□ 58 Ray Burris	.20	.09	.03
□ 59 John Candelaria	.20	.09	.03
□ 60 Chris Cannizzaro	.15	.07	.02
□ 61 Buzz Capra	.15	.07	.02
□ 62 Jose Cardenal	.15	.07	.02
□ 63 Don Cardwell	.15	.07	.02
□ 64 Duke Carmel	.15	.07	.02
□ 65 Chuck Carr	.25	.11	.03
□ 66 Mark Carreon	.20	.09	.03
□ 67 Gary Carter	.40	.18	.05
□ 68 Elio Chacon	.15	.07	.02
□ 69 Dean Chance	.20	.09	.03
□ 70 Kelvin Chapman	.15	.07	.02
□ 71 Ed Charles	.15	.07	.02
□ 72 Rich Chiles	.15	.07	.02
□ 73 Harry Chiti	.15	.07	.02
□ 74 John Christensen	.15	.07	.02
□ 75 Joe Christopher	.15	.07	.02
□ 76 Galen Cisco	.15	.07	.02
□ 77 Donn Clendenon	.20	.09	.03
□ 78 Gene Clines	.15	.07	.02
□ 79 Choo Choo Coleman	.20	.09	.03
□ 80 Kevin Collins	.15	.07	.02
□ 81 David Cone	.40	.18	.05
□ 82 Bill Connors	.15	.07	.02
□ 83 Cliff Cook	.15	.07	.02
□ 84 Tim Corcoran	.15	.07	.02
□ 85 Mardie Cornejo	.15	.07	.02
□ 86 Billy Cowan	.15	.07	.02
□ 87 Roger Craig	.20	.09	.03
□ 88 Jerry Cram	.15	.07	.02
□ 89 Mike Cubbage	.25	.11	.03
□ 90 Ron Darling	.25	.11	.03
□ 91 Ray Daviault	.15	.07	.02
□ 92 Tommy Davis	.25	.11	.03
□ 93 John DeMerit	.15	.07	.02
□ 94 Bill Denehy	.15	.07	.02
□ 95 Jack DiLauro	.15	.07	.02
□ 96 Carlos Diaz	.15	.07	.02
□ 97 Mario Diaz	.20	.09	.03
□ 98 Steve Dillon	.15	.07	.02
□ 99 Sammy Drake	.15	.07	.02
□ 100 Jim Dwyer	.15	.07	.02
□ 101 Duffy Dyer	.15	.07	.02
□ 102 Len Dykstra	.30	.14	.04
□ 103 Tom Edens	.15	.07	.02
□ 104 Dave Eilers	.15	.07	.02
□ 105 Larry Elliot	.15	.07	.02
□ 106 Dock Ellis	.15	.07	.02
□ 107 Kevin Elster	.20	.09	.03
□ 108 Nino Espinosa	.15	.07	.02
□ 109 Chuck Estrada	.20	.09	.03
□ 110 Francisco Estrada	.15	.07	.02
□ 111 Pete Falcone	.15	.07	.02
□ 112 Sid Fernandez	.25	.11	.03
□ 113 Chico Fernandez	.15	.07	.02
□ 114 Sergio Ferrer	.15	.07	.02
□ 115 Jack Fisher	.15	.07	.02
□ 116 Mike Fitzgerald	.15	.07	.02
□ 117 Shaun Fitzmaurice	.15	.07	.02
□ 118 Gil Flores	.15	.07	.02
□ 119 Doug Flynn	.15	.07	.02
□ 120 Tim Foli	.15	.07	.02
□ 121 Rich Folkers	.15	.07	.02

☐ 122 Larry Foss .15 .07 .02
☐ 123 George Foster .30 .14 .04
☐ 124 Leo Foster .15 .07 .02
☐ 125 Joe Foy .15 .07 .02
☐ 126 John Franco .25 .11 .03
☐ 127 Jim Fregosi .25 .11 .03
☐ 128 Bob Friend .20 .09 .03
☐ 129 Danny Frisella .15 .07 .02
☐ 130 Brent Gaff .15 .07 .02
☐ 131 Bob Gallagher .15 .07 .02
☐ 132 Ron Gardenhire .15 .07 .02
☐ 133 Rob Gardner .15 .07 .02
☐ 134 Wes Gardner .15 .07 .02
☐ 135 Wayne Garrett .15 .07 .02
☐ 136 Rod Gaspar .15 .07 .02
☐ 137 Gary Gentry .20 .09 .03
☐ 138 John Gibbons .15 .07 .02
☐ 139 Bob Gibson .25 .11 .03
☐ 140 Brian Giles .15 .07 .02
☐ 141 Joe Ginsberg .20 .09 .03
☐ 142 Ed Glynn .15 .07 .02
☐ 143 Jesse Gonder .15 .07 .02
☐ 144 Dwight Gooden .75 .35 .09
☐ 145 Greg Goossen .15 .07 .02
☐ 146 Tom Gorman .15 .07 .02
☐ 147 Jim Gosger .15 .07 .02
☐ 148 Bill Graham .15 .07 .02
☐ 149 Wayne Graham .15 .07 .02
☐ 150 Dallas Green .20 .09 .03
☐ 151 Pumpsie Green .15 .07 .02
☐ 152 Tom Grieve .20 .09 .03
☐ 153 Jerry Grote .20 .09 .03
☐ 154 Joe Grzenda .15 .07 .02
☐ 155 Don Hahn .15 .07 .02
☐ 156 Tom Hall .15 .07 .02
☐ 157 Jack Hamilton .15 .07 .02
☐ 158 Ike Hampton .15 .07 .02
☐ 159 Tim Harkness .15 .07 .02
☐ 160 Bud Harrelson .25 .11 .03
☐ 161 Greg A. Harris .20 .09 .03
☐ 162 Greg Harts .15 .07 .02
☐ 163 Andy Hassler .15 .07 .02
☐ 164 Tom Hausman .15 .07 .02
☐ 165 Ed Hearn .15 .07 .02
☐ 166 Richie Hebner .20 .09 .03
☐ 167 Danny Heep .15 .07 .02
☐ 168 Jack Heidemann .15 .07 .02
☐ 169 Bob Heise .15 .07 .02
☐ 170 Ken Henderson .15 .07 .02
☐ 171 Steve Henderson .15 .07 .02
☐ 172 Bob Hendley .15 .07 .02
☐ 173 Phil Hennigan .15 .07 .02
☐ 174 Bill Hepler .15 .07 .02
☐ 175 Ron Herbel .15 .07 .02
☐ 176 Manny Hernandez .15 .07 .02
☐ 177 Keith Hernandez .30 .14 .04
☐ 178 Tommy Herr .20 .09 .03
☐ 179 Rick Herrscher .20 .09 .03
☐ 180 Jim Hickman .15 .07 .02
☐ 181 Joe Hicks .15 .07 .02
☐ 182 Chuck Hiller .15 .07 .02
☐ 183 Dave Hillman .15 .07 .02
☐ 184 Jerry Hinsley .15 .07 .02
☐ 185 Gil Hodges .40 .18 .05
☐ 186 Ron Hodges .15 .07 .02
☐ 187 Scott Holman .15 .07 .02
☐ 188 Jay Hook .15 .07 .02
☐ 189 Mike Howard .15 .07 .02
☐ 190 Jesse Hudson .15 .07 .02
☐ 191 Keith Hughes .20 .09 .03
☐ 192 Todd Hundley .25 .11 .03
☐ 193 Ron Hunt .20 .09 .03
☐ 194 Willard Hunter .15 .07 .02
☐ 195 Clint Hurdle .20 .09 .03
☐ 196 Jeff Innis .20 .09 .03
☐ 197 Al Jackson .15 .07 .02
☐ 198 Roy Lee Jackson .15 .07 .02
☐ 199 Gregg Jefferies .40 .18 .05
☐ 200 Stan Jefferson .15 .07 .02
☐ 201 Chris Jelic .20 .09 .03
☐ 202 Bob D. Johnson .15 .07 .02
☐ 203 Howard Johnson .35 .16 .04
☐ 204 Bob W. Johnson .15 .07 .02
☐ 205 Randy Jones .20 .09 .03
☐ 206 Sherman Jones .15 .07 .02
☐ 207 Cleon Jones .25 .11 .03
☐ 208 Ross Jones .15 .07 .02
☐ 209 Mike Jorgensen .15 .07 .02
☐ 210 Rod Kanehl .15 .07 .02
☐ 211 Dave Kingman .25 .11 .03
☐ 212 Bobby Klaus .15 .07 .02
☐ 213 Jay Kleven .15 .07 .02
☐ 214 Lou Klimchock .15 .07 .02
☐ 215 Ray Knight .25 .11 .03
☐ 216 Kevin Kobel .15 .07 .02
☐ 217 Gary Kolb .15 .07 .02
☐ 218 Cal Koonce .15 .07 .02
☐ 219 Jerry Koosman .30 .14 .04
☐ 220 Ed Kranepool .30 .14 .04
☐ 221 Gary Kroll .15 .07 .02
☐ 222 Clem Labine .20 .09 .03
☐ 223 Jack Lamabe .15 .07 .02
☐ 224 Hobie Landrith .15 .07 .02
☐ 225 Frank Lary .20 .09 .03
☐ 226 Bill Latham .15 .07 .02
☐ 227 Terry Leach .20 .09 .03
☐ 228 Tim Leary .20 .09 .03
☐ 229 John Lewis .15 .07 .02
☐ 230 David Liddell .15 .07 .02
☐ 231 Phil Linz .20 .09 .03
☐ 232 Ron Locke .15 .07 .02
☐ 233 Skip Lockwood .15 .07 .02
☐ 234 Mickey Lolich .25 .11 .03
☐ 235 Phil Lombardi .15 .07 .02
☐ 236 Al Luplow .15 .07 .02
☐ 237 Ed Lynch .15 .07 .02
☐ 238 Barry Lyons .15 .07 .02
☐ 239 Ken MacKenzie .15 .07 .02
☐ 240 Julio Machado .20 .09 .03
☐ 241 Elliott Maddox .15 .07 .02
☐ 242 Dave Magadan .25 .11 .03
☐ 243 Pepe Mangual .15 .07 .02
☐ 244 Phil Mankowski .15 .07 .02
☐ 245 Felix Mantilla .15 .07 .02
☐ 246 Mike G. Marshall .20 .09 .03
(RH Pitcher)
☐ 247 Dave Marshall .15 .07 .02
☐ 248 Jim Marshall .15 .07 .02
☐ 249 Mike A. Marshall .20 .09 .03
(1B/OF)
☐ 250 J.C. Martin .15 .07 .02
☐ 251 Jerry Martin .15 .07 .02
☐ 252 Teddy Martinez .15 .07 .02
☐ 253 Jon Matlack .25 .11 .03
☐ 254 Jerry May .15 .07 .02
☐ 255 Willie Mays .75 .35 .09
☐ 256 Lee Mazzilli .20 .09 .03
☐ 257 Jim McAndrew .15 .07 .02
☐ 258 Bob McClure .15 .07 .02
☐ 259 Roger McDowell .20 .09 .03
☐ 260 Tug McGraw .30 .14 .04
☐ 261 Jeff McKnight .15 .07 .02
☐ 262 Roy McMillan .20 .09 .03
☐ 263 Kevin McReynolds .25 .11 .03
☐ 264 George Medich .15 .07 .02
☐ 265 Orlando Mercado .15 .07 .02
☐ 266 Butch Metzger .15 .07 .02
☐ 267 Felix Millan .20 .09 .03
☐ 268 Bob G. Miller .15 .07 .02
LH Pitcher
☐ 269 Bob L. Miller .15 .07 .02
RH Pitcher
☐ 270 Dyar Miller .15 .07 .02
☐ 271 Larry Miller .15 .07 .02
☐ 272 Keith Miller .20 .09 .03
☐ 273 Randy Milligan .15 .07 .02
☐ 274 John Milner .15 .07 .02
☐ 275 John Mitchell .15 .07 .02
☐ 276 Kevin Mitchell .35 .16 .04
☐ 277 Wilmer Mizell .20 .09 .03
☐ 278 Herb Moford .15 .07 .02
☐ 279 Willie Montanez .20 .09 .03
☐ 280 Joe Moock .15 .07 .02
☐ 281 Tommy Moore .15 .07 .02
☐ 282 Bob Moorhead .15 .07 .02
☐ 283 Jerry Morales .15 .07 .02
☐ 284 Al Moran .15 .07 .02
☐ 285 Jose Moreno .15 .07 .02
☐ 286 Bill Murphy .15 .07 .02
☐ 287 Dale Murray .15 .07 .02
☐ 288 Dennis Musgraves .15 .07 .02
☐ 289 Jeff Musselman .15 .07 .02
☐ 290 Randy Myers .30 .14 .04
☐ 291 Bob Myrick .15 .07 .02
☐ 292 Danny Napoleon .15 .07 .02
☐ 293 Charlie Neal .20 .09 .03
☐ 294 Randy Niemann .15 .07 .02
☐ 295 Joe Nolan .15 .07 .02
☐ 296 Dan Norman .15 .07 .02
☐ 297 Ed Nunez .15 .07 .02
☐ 298 Charlie O'Brien .15 .07 .02
☐ 299 Tom O'Malley .15 .07 .02
☐ 300 Bob Ojeda .25 .11 .03
☐ 301 Jose Oquendo .20 .09 .03
☐ 302 Jesse Orosco .20 .09 .03
☐ 303 Junior Ortiz .15 .07 .02

☐ 304	Brian Ostrosser	.15	.07	.02
☐ 305	Amos Otis	.25	.11	.03
☐ 306	Rick Ownbey	.15	.07	.02
☐ 307	John Pacella	.15	.07	.02
☐ 308	Tom Paciorek	.20	.09	.03
☐ 309	Harry Parker	.15	.07	.02
☐ 310	Tom Parsons	.15	.07	.02
☐ 311	Al Pedrique	.15	.07	.02
☐ 312	Brock Pemberton	.15	.07	.02
☐ 313	Alejandro Pena	.20	.09	.03
☐ 314	Bobby Pfeil	.15	.07	.02
☐ 315	Mike Phillips	.15	.07	.02
☐ 316	Jim Piersall	.25	.11	.03
☐ 317	Joe Pignatano	.20	.09	.03
☐ 318	Grover Powell	.15	.07	.02
☐ 319	Rich Puig	.15	.07	.02
☐ 320	Charlie Puleo	.15	.07	.02
☐ 321	Gary Rajsich	.15	.07	.02
☐ 322	Mario Ramirez	.15	.07	.02
☐ 323	Lenny Randle	.15	.07	.02
☐ 324	Bob Rauch	.15	.07	.02
☐ 325	Jeff Reardon	.30	.14	.04
☐ 326	Darren Reed	.15	.07	.02
☐ 327	Hal Reniff	.15	.07	.02
☐ 328	Ronn Reynolds	.15	.07	.02
☐ 329	Tom Reynolds	.15	.07	.02
☐ 330	Dennis Ribant	.15	.07	.02
☐ 331	Gordie Richardson	.15	.07	.02
☐ 332	Dave Roberts	.15	.07	.02
☐ 333	Les Rohr	.15	.07	.02
☐ 334	Luis Rosado	.15	.07	.02
☐ 335	Don Rose	.15	.07	.02
☐ 336	Don Rowe	.15	.07	.02
☐ 337	Dick Rusteck	.15	.07	.02
☐ 338	Nolan Ryan	1.50	.65	.19
☐ 339	Ray Sadecki	.15	.07	.02
☐ 340	Joe Sambito	.20	.09	.03
☐ 341	Amado Samuel	.15	.07	.02
☐ 342	Juan Samuel	.20	.09	.03
☐ 343	Ken Sanders	.15	.07	.02
☐ 344	Rafael Santana	.15	.07	.02
☐ 345	Mackey Sasser	.20	.09	.03
☐ 346	Mac Scarce	.15	.07	.02
☐ 347	Jim Schaffer	.15	.07	.02
☐ 348	Dan Schatzeder	.15	.07	.02
☐ 349	Calvin Schiraldi	.15	.07	.02
☐ 350	Al Schmelz	.15	.07	.02
☐ 351	Dave Schneck	.15	.07	.02
☐ 352	Ted Schreiber	.15	.07	.02
☐ 353	Don Schulze	.15	.07	.02
☐ 354	Mike Scott	.20	.09	.03
☐ 355	Ray Searage	.15	.07	.02
☐ 356	Tom Seaver	.75	.35	.09
☐ 357	Dick Selma	.15	.07	.02
☐ 358	Art Shamsky	.15	.07	.02
☐ 359	Bob Shaw	.15	.07	.02
☐ 360	Don Shaw	.15	.07	.02
☐ 361	Norm Sherry	.20	.09	.03
☐ 362	Craig Shipley	.20	.09	.03
☐ 363	Bart Shirley	.15	.07	.02
☐ 364	Bill Short	.15	.07	.02
☐ 365	Paul Siebert	.15	.07	.02
☐ 366	Ken Singleton	.25	.11	.03
☐ 367	Doug Sisk	.15	.07	.02
☐ 368	Bobby Gene Smith	.15	.07	.02
☐ 369	Charley Smith	.15	.07	.02
☐ 370	Dick Smith	.15	.07	.02
☐ 371	Duke Snider	.60	.25	.08
☐ 372	Warren Spahn	.50	.23	.06
☐ 373	Larry Stahl	.15	.07	.02
☐ 374	Roy Staiger	.15	.07	.02
☐ 375	Tracy Stallard	.15	.07	.02
☐ 376	Leroy Stanton	.15	.07	.02
☐ 377	Rusty Staub	.30	.14	.04
☐ 378	John Stearns	.20	.09	.03
☐ 379	John Stephenson	.15	.07	.02
☐ 380	Randy Sterling	.15	.07	.02
☐ 381	George Stone	.15	.07	.02
☐ 382	Darryl Strawberry	.75	.35	.09
☐ 383	John Strohmayer	.15	.07	.02
☐ 384	Brent Strom	.15	.07	.02
☐ 385	Dick Stuart	.20	.09	.03
☐ 386	Tom Sturdivant	.15	.07	.02
☐ 387	Bill Sudakis	.15	.07	.02
☐ 388	John Sullivan	.15	.07	.02
☐ 389	Darrell Sutherland	.15	.07	.02
☐ 390	Ron Swoboda	.25	.11	.03
☐ 391	Craig Swan	.20	.09	.03
☐ 392	Rick Sweet	.15	.07	.02
☐ 393	Pat Tabler	.20	.09	.03
☐ 394	Kevin Tapani	.30	.14	.04
☐ 395	Randy Tate	.15	.07	.02
☐ 396	Frank Taveras	.15	.07	.02
☐ 397	Chuck Taylor	.15	.07	.02
☐ 398	Ron Taylor	.15	.07	.02
☐ 399	Bob Taylor	.15	.07	.02
☐ 400	Sammy Taylor	.15	.07	.02
☐ 401	Walt Terrell	.20	.09	.03
☐ 402	Ralph Terry	.20	.09	.03
☐ 403	Tim Teufel	.20	.09	.03
☐ 404	George Theodore	.15	.07	.02
☐ 405	Frank J. Thomas	.20	.09	.03
☐ 406	Lou Thornton	.15	.07	.02
☐ 407	Marv Throneberry	.30	.14	.04
☐ 408	Dick Tidrow	.15	.07	.02
☐ 409	Rusty Tillman	.15	.07	.02
☐ 410	Jackson Todd	.15	.07	.02
☐ 411	Joe Torre	.30	.14	.04
☐ 412	Mike Torrez	.20	.09	.03
☐ 413	Kelvin Torve	.15	.07	.02
☐ 414	Alex Trevino	.15	.07	.02
☐ 415	Wayne Twitchell	.15	.07	.02
☐ 416	Del Unser	.15	.07	.02
☐ 417	Mike Vail	.15	.07	.02
☐ 418	Bobby Valentine	.25	.11	.03
☐ 419	Ellis Valentine	.20	.09	.03
☐ 420	Julio Valera	.25	.11	.03
☐ 421	Tom Veryzer	.15	.07	.02
☐ 422	Frank Viola	.30	.14	.04
☐ 423	Bill Wakefield	.15	.07	.02
☐ 424	Gene Walter	.15	.07	.02
☐ 425	Claudell Washington	.20	.09	.03
☐ 426	Hank Webb	.15	.07	.02
☐ 427	Al Weis	.20	.09	.03
☐ 428	Dave West	.20	.09	.03
☐ 429	Wally Whitehurst	.20	.09	.03
☐ 430	Carl Willey	.15	.07	.02
☐ 431	Nick Willhite	.15	.07	.02
☐ 432	Charlie Williams	.15	.07	.02
☐ 433	Mookie Wilson	.25	.11	.03
☐ 434	Herm Winningham	.15	.07	.02
☐ 435	Gene Woodling	.20	.09	.03
☐ 436	Billy Wynne	.15	.07	.02
☐ 437	Joel Youngblood	.15	.07	.02
☐ 438	Pat Zachry	.15	.07	.02
☐ 439	Don Zimmer	.20	.09	.03
☐ NNO	Checklist 1-20	.15	.07	.02
☐ NNO	Checklist 41-60	.15	.07	.02
☐ NNO	Checklist 81-100	.15	.07	.02
☐ NNO	Checklist 121-140	.15	.07	.02
☐ NNO	Checklist 161-180	.15	.07	.02
☐ NNO	Checklist 201-220	.15	.07	.02
☐ NNO	Checklist 241-260	.15	.07	.02
☐ NNO	Checklist 281-300	.15	.07	.02
☐ NNO	Checklist 321-340	.15	.07	.02
☐ NNO	Checklist 361-380	.15	.07	.02
☐ NNO	Checklist 401-420	.20	.09	.03

1984 Milton Bradley

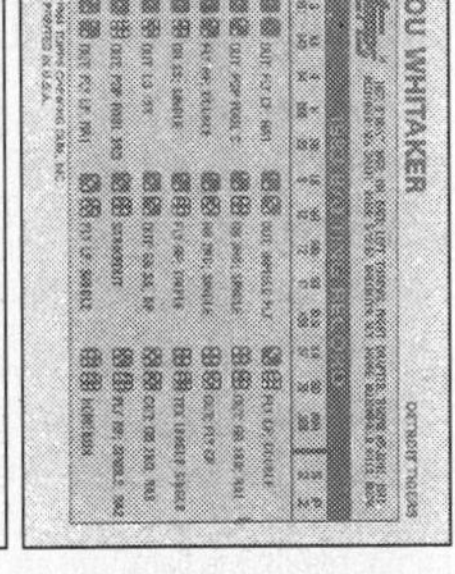

The cards in this 30-card set measure 2 1/2" by 3 1/2". This set of full color cards was produced by Topps for the Milton Bradley Co. The set was included in a board game entitled Championship Baseball. The fronts feature portraits of the players and the name, Championship Baseball, by Milton Bradley. The backs feature the Topps logo, statistics for the past year (pitchers' cards have career statistics), and dice rolls which are part of the board game. Pitcher cards have no dice roll charts. There are 15 players from each league.

These unnumbered cards are listed below in alphabetical order. The cap logos and uniforms have been air-brushed to remove all team references.

	NRMT-MT	EXC	G-VG
COMPLETE SET (30)	12.00	5.50	1.50
COMMON PLAYER (1-30)	.15	.07	.02
☐ 1 Wade Boggs	1.00	.45	.13
☐ 2 George Brett	1.00	.45	.13
☐ 3 Rod Carew	.75	.35	.09
☐ 4 Steve Carlton	.75	.35	.09
☐ 5 Gary Carter	.40	.18	.05
☐ 6 Dave Concepcion	.25	.11	.03
☐ 7 Cecil Cooper	.15	.07	.02
☐ 8 Andre Dawson	.75	.35	.09
☐ 9 Carlton Fisk	.75	.35	.09
☐ 10 Steve Garvey	.35	.16	.04
☐ 11 Pedro Guerrero	.25	.11	.03
☐ 12 Ron Guidry	.25	.11	.03
☐ 13 Rickey Henderson	1.00	.45	.13
☐ 14 Reggie Jackson	1.00	.45	.13
☐ 15 Ron Kittle	.15	.07	.02
☐ 16 Bill Madlock	.15	.07	.02
☐ 17 Dale Murphy	.50	.23	.06
☐ 18 Al Oliver	.15	.07	.02
☐ 19 Darrell Porter	.15	.07	.02
☐ 20 Cal Ripken	1.25	.55	.16
☐ 21 Pete Rose	1.00	.45	.13
☐ 22 Steve Sax	.25	.11	.03
☐ 23 Mike Schmidt	1.00	.45	.13
☐ 24 Ted Simmons	.25	.11	.03
☐ 25 Ozzie Smith	.75	.35	.09
☐ 26 Dave Stieb	.25	.11	.03
☐ 27 Fernando Valenzuela	.25	.11	.03
☐ 28 Lou Whitaker	.35	.16	.04
☐ 29 Dave Winfield	.75	.35	.09
☐ 30 Robin Yount	1.00	.45	.13

1992 MJB Holographics Prototypes

The premier edition of Holoprism 1991 Rookies of the Year presented Chuck Knoblauch, the American League Rookie of the Year, and Jeff Bagwell, the National League Rookie of the Year. MJB Holographics issued a prototype card which corresponded to the first card of each set. The fronts of the standard-size (2 1/2" by 3 1/2") display a holographic action image against nongame backgrounds, while the horizontally oriented backs carry color close-up photos and background information on a pastel purple panel. The cards are numbered on the back and are marked "Prototype."

	MT	EX-MT	VG
COMPLETE SET (2)	5.00	2.30	.60
COMMON PLAYER	3.00	1.35	.40
☐ R1 Jeff Bagwell	3.00	1.35	.40
☐ R1 Chuck Knoblauch	3.00	1.35	.40

1992 MJB Holographics Jeff Bagwell

The premier edition of Holoprism 1991 Rookies of the Year presented Chuck Knoblauch, the American League Rookie of the Year, and Jeff Bagwell, the National League Rookie of the Year. Each four-card holographic set was issued in a plastic "jewel box," similar to that used for storing and protecting audio compact disks. The top has a window through which the consumer can view the top card, while the back of the case displays a certificate of authenticity with the serial number of the set and the production run (250,000 sets). Also Bagwell and Knoblauch each autographed 500 cards that were randomly inserted throughout the sets. The fronts of the standard-size (2 1/2" by 3 1/2") display a holographic action image against nongame backgrounds, while the horizontally oriented backs carry color close-up photos and background information on a pastel purple panel. The cards are numbered on the back.

	MT	EX-MT	VG
COMPLETE SET (4)	3.00	1.35	.40
COMMON PLAYER (1-4)	1.00	.45	.13
☐ R1 Jeff Bagwell (Batting Pose, front view)	1.00	.45	.13
☐ R2 Jeff Bagwell (Crouching posture, ready to field)	1.00	.45	.13
☐ R3 Jeff Bagwell (Follow through)	1.00	.45	.13
☐ R4 Jeff Bagwell (Batting pose, back view)	1.00	.45	.13

1992 MJB Holographics Chuck Knoblauch

The premier edition of Holoprism 1991 Rookies of the Year presented Chuck Knoblauch, the American League Rookie of the Year, and Jeff Bagwell, the National League Rookie of the Year. Each four-card holographic set was issued in a plastic "jewel box," similar to that used for storing and protecting audio compact disks. The top has a window through which the consumer can view the top card, while the back of the case displays a certificate of authenticity with the serial number of the set and the production run (250,000 sets). Also Bagwell and Knoblauch each autographed 500 cards that were randomly inserted throughout the sets. The fronts of the standard-size (2 1/2" by 3 1/2") display a holographic action image against non-game backgrounds, while the horizontally oriented backs carry color close-up photos and background information on a pastel purple panel. The cards are numbered on the back.

	MT	EX-MT	VG
COMPLETE SET (4)	3.00	1.35	.40
COMMON PLAYER (1-4)	1.00	.45	.13
☐ R1 Chuck Knoblauch (Follow through, looking up)	1.00	.45	.13
☐ R2 Chuck Knoblauch (Awaiting throw)	1.00	.45	.13
☐ R3 Chuck Knoblauch (Follow through, ready to run)	1.00	.45	.13
☐ R4 Chuck Knoblauch (Batting pose)	1.00	.45	.13

1987 MnM's Star Lineup

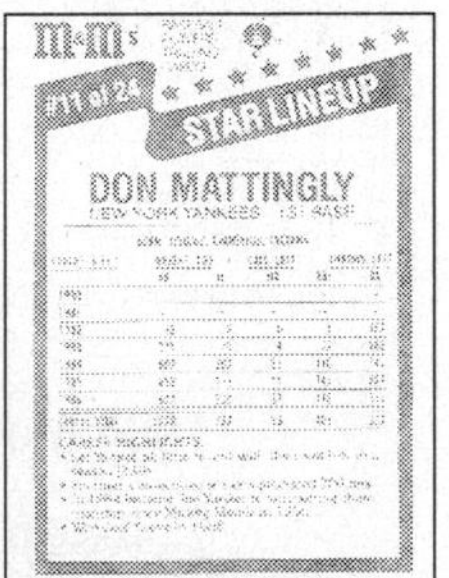

The Mars Candy Company is the sponsor of this 24-card set of cards. The cards were printed in perforated pairs. The pairs measure approximately 5" by 3 1/2" whereas the individual cards measure the standard 2 1/2" by 3 1/2". The players are shown without team logos. The cards were designed and produced by MSA, Mike Schechter Associates. The cards are numbered on the front and back. The backs show statistics for every year since 1980 even if the player was not even playing during those earlier years. The values below are for individual players; panels intact would be valued at 25 percent more than the sum of the two individual players.

	MT	EX-MT	VG
COMPLETE SET (24)	9.00	4.00	1.15
COMMON PLAYER (1-24)	.30	.14	.04
☐ 1 Wally Joyner	.60	.25	.08
☐ 2 Tony Pena	.30	.14	.04
☐ 3 Mike Schmidt	1.00	.45	.13
☐ 4 Ryne Sandberg	1.25	.55	.16
☐ 5 Wade Boggs	1.00	.45	.13
☐ 6 Jack Morris	.50	.23	.06
☐ 7 Roger Clemens	1.25	.55	.16
☐ 8 Harold Baines	.30	.14	.04
☐ 9 Dale Murphy	.50	.23	.06
☐ 10 Jose Canseco	1.00	.45	.13
☐ 11 Don Mattingly	1.00	.45	.13
☐ 12 Gary Carter	.60	.25	.08
☐ 13 Cal Ripken	1.25	.55	.16
☐ 14 George Brett	1.00	.45	.13
☐ 15 Kirby Puckett	1.00	.45	.13
☐ 16 Joe Carter	.75	.35	.09
☐ 17 Mike Witt	.30	.14	.04
☐ 18 Mike Scott	.30	.14	.04
☐ 19 Fernando Valenzuela	.30	.14	.04
☐ 20 Steve Garvey	.50	.23	.06
☐ 21 Steve Sax	.40	.18	.05
☐ 22 Nolan Ryan	1.75	.80	.22
☐ 23 Tony Gwynn	1.00	.45	.13
☐ 24 Ozzie Smith	.75	.35	.09

1991 MooTown Snackers

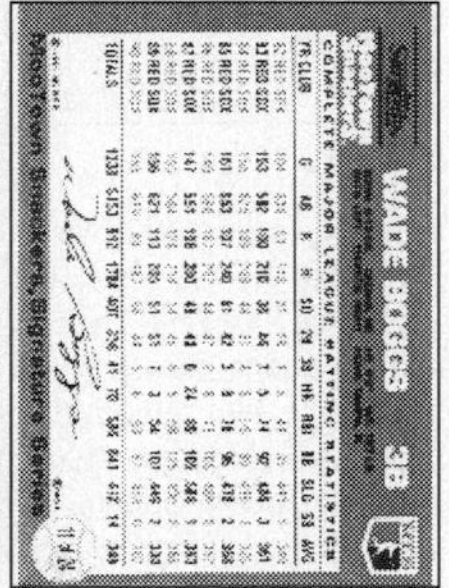

This 24-card standard size (2 1/2" by 3 1/2") set was sponsored by MooTown Snackers. One player card and an attached mail-in certificate (with checklist on back) were included in five-ounce packages of MooTown Snackers cheese snacks. The complete set could be purchased through the mail by sending in the mail-in certificate, three MooTown Snackers UPC codes, and 5.95. The mail-in sets did not come with the attached mail-in tab; cards with tabs are valued approximately 50 percent higher than the prices listed in the checklist below. The card front features a high gloss color action player photo, which is mounted diagonally on the card face. White and yellow stripes border the picture above and below. At the card top appears the company logo on a red triangle, while the words "Signature Series" appears in an aqua blue oval in the upper right corner. The player's name appears in the red triangle below the picture. The backs present statistical information in red, white, and black. On the bottom of the card a facsimile autograph and a card number round out the back.

	MT	EX-MT	VG
COMPLETE SET (24)	15.00	6.75	1.90
COMMON PLAYER (1-24)	.35	.16	.04
☐ 1 Jose Canseco	1.00	.45	.13
☐ 2 Kirby Puckett	1.25	.55	.16
☐ 3 Barry Bonds	.90	.40	.11
☐ 4 Ken Griffey Jr.	2.50	1.15	.30
☐ 5 Ryne Sandberg	1.50	.65	.19
☐ 6 Tony Gwynn	.90	.40	.11
☐ 7 Kal Daniels	.35	.16	.04
☐ 8 Ozzie Smith	.60	.25	.08
☐ 9 Dave Justice	1.00	.45	.13
☐ 10 Sandy Alomar Jr.	.35	.16	.04
☐ 11 Wade Boggs	.90	.40	.11
☐ 12 Ozzie Guillen	.35	.16	.04
☐ 13 Dave Magadan	.35	.16	.04
☐ 14 Cal Ripken	1.50	.65	.19
☐ 15 Don Mattingly	1.00	.45	.13
☐ 16 Ruben Sierra	.75	.35	.09
☐ 17 Robin Yount	1.00	.45	.13
☐ 18 Len Dykstra	.35	.16	.04
☐ 19 George Brett	1.00	.45	.13
☐ 20 Lance Parrish	.35	.16	.04
☐ 21 Chris Sabo	.35	.16	.04
☐ 22 Craig Biggio	.45	.20	.06
☐ 23 Kevin Mitchell	.45	.20	.06
☐ 24 Cecil Fielder	.75	.35	.09

1992 MooTown Snackers

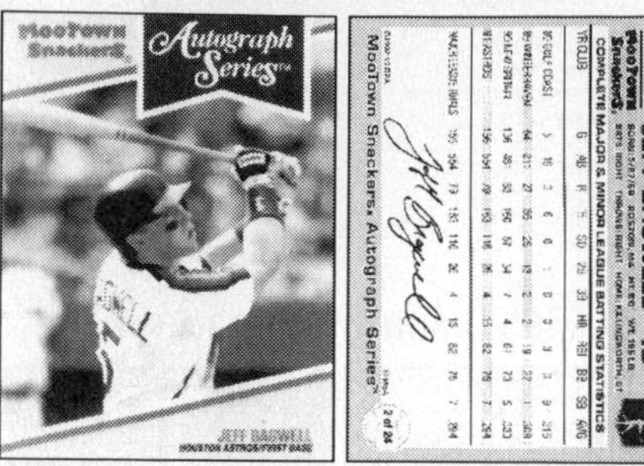

This 24-card standard-size (2 1/2" by 3 1/2") set was produced by MSA (Michael Schechter Associates) for MooTown Snackers. The cards were inserted inside 5 ounce and 10 ounce cheese snack packages. It is reported that more than two million cards were produced. Collectors could also obtain the complete set through a mail-in offer. The color player photos on the fronts are bordered above and below by diagonal white and red stripes that edge a yellow border. Team logos were airbrushed out of the photos. In black print on a yellow and white background, the backs present biography, complete batting or pitching statistics, and facsimile autograph. The cards are numbered on the back.

	MT	EX-MT	VG
COMPLETE SET (24)	15.00	6.75	1.90
COMMON PLAYER (1-24)	.35	.16	.04
☐ 1 Albert Belle	.60	.25	.08
☐ 2 Jeff Bagwell	.75	.35	.09
☐ 3 Jose Rijo	.35	.16	.04
☐ 4 Roger Clemens	1.25	.55	.16
☐ 5 Kevin Maas	.35	.16	.04
☐ 6 Kirby Puckett	1.00	.45	.13
☐ 7 Ken Griffey Jr.	2.50	1.15	.30
☐ 8 Will Clark	1.00	.45	.13
☐ 9 Felix Jose	.45	.20	.06
☐ 10 Cecil Fielder	.75	.35	.09
☐ 11 Darryl Strawberry	.75	.35	.09
☐ 12 John Smiley	.35	.16	.04
☐ 13 Roberto Alomar	1.50	.65	.19
☐ 14 Paul Molitor	.60	.25	.08
☐ 15 Andre Dawson	.60	.25	.08
☐ 16 Terry Mulholland	.35	.16	.04
☐ 17 Fred McGriff	.75	.35	.09
☐ 18 Dwight Gooden	.45	.20	.06
☐ 19 Rickey Henderson	.75	.35	.09
☐ 20 Nolan Ryan	2.50	1.15	.30
☐ 21 George Brett	.90	.40	.11
☐ 22 Tom Glavine	.75	.35	.09
☐ 23 Cal Ripken	1.50	.65	.19
☐ 24 Frank Thomas	3.50	1.55	.45

1983 Mother's Giants

The cards in this 20-card set measure 2 1/2" by 3 1/2". For the first time in 30 years, Mother's Cookies issued a baseball card set. The full color set, produced by hobbyist Barry Colla, features San Francisco Giants players only. Fifteen cards were issued at the Houston Astros vs. San Francisco Giants game of August 7, 1983. Five of the cards were redeemable by sending in a coupon. The five additional cards received from redemption of the coupon were not guaranteed to be the five needed to complete the set. The fronts feature the player's photo, his name, and the Giants' logo, while the backs feature player biographies and the

Mother's Cookies logo. The backs also contain a space in which to obtain the player's autograph.

	NRMT-MT	EXC	G-VG
COMPLETE SET (20)	15.00	6.75	1.90
COMMON PLAYER (1-20)	.60	.25	.08
☐ 1 Frank Robinson MG	3.00	1.35	.40
☐ 2 Jack Clark	1.50	.65	.19
☐ 3 Chili Davis	1.00	.45	.13
☐ 4 Johnnie LeMaster	.60	.25	.08
☐ 5 Greg Minton	.75	.35	.09
☐ 6 Bob Brenly	.60	.25	.08
☐ 7 Fred Breining	.60	.25	.08
☐ 8 Jeff Leonard	.75	.35	.09
☐ 9 Darrell Evans	1.25	.55	.16
☐ 10 Tom O'Malley	.60	.25	.08
☐ 11 Duane Kuiper	.60	.25	.08
☐ 12 Mike Krukow	.75	.35	.09
☐ 13 Atlee Hammaker	.75	.35	.09
☐ 14 Gary Lavelle	.60	.25	.08
☐ 15 Bill Laskey	.60	.25	.08
☐ 16 Max Venable	.60	.25	.08
☐ 17 Joel Youngblood	.60	.25	.08
☐ 18 Dave Bergman	.60	.25	.08
☐ 19 Mike Vail	.60	.25	.08
☐ 20 Andy McGaffigan	.60	.25	.08

1984 Mother's A's

The cards in this 28-card set measure 2 1/2" by 3 1/2". In 1984, the Los Angeles based Mother's Cookies Co. issued five sets of cards featuring players from major league teams. The Oakland A's set features current players depicted by photos. Similar to their 1952 and 1953 issues, the cards have rounded corners. The backs of the cards contain the Mother's Cookies logo. The cards were distributed in partial sets to fans at the respective stadiums of the teams involved. Whereas 20 cards were given to each patron, a redemption card, redeemable for eight more cards was included. Unfortunately, the eight cards received by redeeming the coupon were not necessarily the eight needed to complete a set. Hobbyist Barry Colla was involved in the production of these sets.

	NRMT-MT	EXC	G-VG
COMPLETE SET (28)	15.00	6.75	1.90
COMMON PLAYER (1-28)	.40	.18	.05
☐ 1 Steve Boros MG	.40	.18	.05
☐ 2 Rickey Henderson	5.00	2.30	.60
☐ 3 Joe Morgan	2.25	1.00	.30
☐ 4 Dwayne Murphy	.50	.23	.06
☐ 5 Mike Davis	.40	.18	.05
☐ 6 Bruce Bochte	.40	.18	.05
☐ 7 Carney Lansford	.90	.40	.11
☐ 8 Steve McCatty	.40	.18	.05
☐ 9 Mike Heath	.40	.18	.05
☐ 10 Chris Codiroli	.40	.18	.05
☐ 11 Bill Almon	.40	.18	.05
☐ 12 Bill Caudill	.40	.18	.05
☐ 13 Donnie Hill	.40	.18	.05
☐ 14 Lary Sorensen	.40	.18	.05
☐ 15 Dave Kingman	.80	.35	.10
☐ 16 Garry Hancock	.40	.18	.05
☐ 17 Jeff Burroughs	.50	.23	.06
☐ 18 Tom Burgmeier	.40	.18	.05
☐ 19 Jim Essian	.50	.23	.06
☐ 20 Mike Warren	.40	.18	.05
☐ 21 Davey Lopes	.60	.25	.08
☐ 22 Ray Burris	.40	.18	.05
☐ 23 Tony Phillips	1.25	.55	.16
☐ 24 Tim Conroy	.40	.18	.05
☐ 25 Jeff Bettendorf	.40	.18	.05
☐ 26 Keith Atherton	.40	.18	.05
☐ 27 A's Coaches	.60	.25	.08
Ron Schueler			
Billy Williams			
Clete Boyer			
Jackie Moore			
Bob Didier			
☐ 28 A's Checklist	.50	.23	.06
Oakland Coliseum			

1984 Mother's Astros

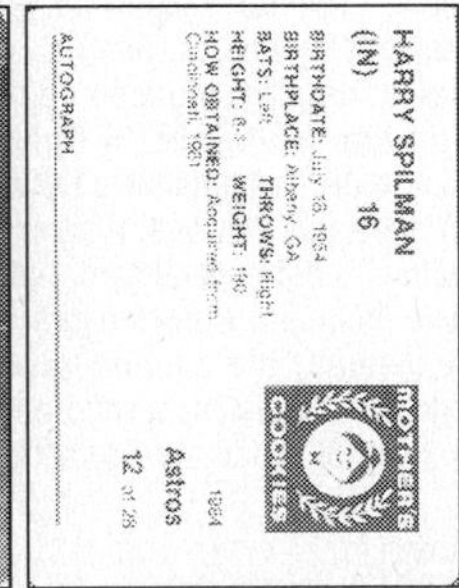

The cards in this 28-card set measure 2 1/2" by 3 1/2". In 1984, the Los Angeles based Mother's Cookies Co. issued five sets of cards featuring players from major league teams. The Houston Astros set features current players depicted by photos. Similar to their 1952 and 1953 issues, the cards have rounded corners. The backs of the cards contain the Mother's Cookies logo. The cards were distributed in partial sets to fans at the respective stadiums of the teams involved. Whereas 20 cards were given to each patron, a redemption card, redeemable for eight more cards was included. Unfortunately, the eight cards received by redeeming the coupon were not necessarily the eight needed to complete a set. Hobbyist Barry Colla was involved in the production of these sets.

	NRMT-MT	EXC	G-VG
COMPLETE SET (28)	16.00	7.25	2.00
COMMON PLAYER (1-28)	.35	.16	.04
☐ 1 Nolan Ryan	9.00	4.00	1.15
☐ 2 Joe Niekro	.75	.35	.09
☐ 3 Alan Ashby	.45	.20	.06
☐ 4 Bill Doran	.75	.35	.09
☐ 5 Phil Garner	.60	.25	.08
☐ 6 Ray Knight	.60	.25	.08
☐ 7 Dickie Thon	.45	.20	.06
☐ 8 Jose Cruz	.60	.25	.08
☐ 9 Jerry Mumphrey	.35	.16	.04
☐ 10 Terry Puhl	.45	.20	.06
☐ 11 Enos Cabell	.35	.16	.04
☐ 12 Harry Spilman	.35	.16	.04
☐ 13 Dave Smith	.60	.25	.08
☐ 14 Mike Scott	1.00	.45	.13
☐ 15 Bob Lillis MG	.35	.16	.04
☐ 16 Bob Knepper	.35	.16	.04
☐ 17 Frank DiPino	.35	.16	.04
☐ 18 Tom Wieghaus	.35	.16	.04
☐ 19 Denny Walling	.35	.16	.04
☐ 20 Tony Scott	.35	.16	.04
☐ 21 Alan Bannister	.35	.16	.04
☐ 22 Bill Dawley	.35	.16	.04
☐ 23 Vern Ruhle	.35	.16	.04
☐ 24 Mike LaCoss	.35	.16	.04
☐ 25 Mike Madden	.35	.16	.04
☐ 26 Craig Reynolds	.45	.20	.06
☐ 27 Astros' Coaches	.35	.16	.04
Cot Deal			
Don Leppert			
Denis Menke			
Les Moss			
Jerry Walker			
☐ 28 Astros' Checklist	.35	.16	.04
Astros Logo			

1984 Mother's Giants

The cards in this 28-card set measure 2 1/2" by 3 1/2". In 1984, the Los Angeles based Mother's Cookies Co. issued five sets of cards featuring players from major league teams. The San Francisco Giants set features previous Giant All-Star selections depicted by drawings. Similar to their 1952 and 1953 issues, the cards have rounded corners. The backs of the cards contain the Mother's Cookies logo. The cards were distributed in partial sets to fans at the respective stadiums of the teams involved. Whereas 20 cards were given to each patron, a redemption card, redeemable for eight more cards was included. Unfortunately, the eight cards received by redeeming the coupon were not necessarily the eight needed to complete a set. Hobbyist Barry Colla was involved in the production of these sets.

	NRMT-MT	EXC	G-VG
COMPLETE SET (28)	15.00	6.75	1.90
COMMON PLAYER (1-28)	.40	.18	.05
☐ 1 Willie Mays	4.00	1.80	.50
☐ 2 Willie McCovey	2.50	1.15	.30
☐ 3 Juan Marichal	2.00	.90	.25
☐ 4 Gaylord Perry	2.00	.90	.25
☐ 5 Tom Haller	.40	.18	.05
☐ 6 Jim Davenport	.40	.18	.05
☐ 7 Jack Clark	.75	.35	.09
☐ 8 Greg Minton	.40	.18	.05
☐ 9 Atlee Hammaker	.40	.18	.05
☐ 10 Gary Lavelle	.40	.18	.05
☐ 11 Orlando Cepeda	1.25	.55	.16
☐ 12 Bobby Bonds	1.00	.45	.13

Card	NRMT-MT	EXC	G-VG
☐ 13 John Antonelli	.40	.18	.05
☐ 14 Bob Schmidt UER (Photo actually Wes Westrum)	.40	.18	.05
☐ 15 Sam Jones	.40	.18	.05
☐ 16 Mike McCormick	.50	.23	.06
☐ 17 Ed Bailey	.40	.18	.05
☐ 18 Stu Miller	.40	.18	.05
☐ 19 Felipe Alou	.75	.35	.09
☐ 20 Jim Ray Hart	.50	.23	.06
☐ 21 Dick Dietz	.40	.18	.05
☐ 22 Chris Speier	.40	.18	.05
☐ 23 Bobby Murcer	.75	.35	.09
☐ 24 John Montefusco	.40	.18	.05
☐ 25 Vida Blue	.60	.25	.08
☐ 26 Ed Whitson	.40	.18	.05
☐ 27 Darrell Evans	.75	.35	.09
☐ 28 Giants Checklist Card All-Star Game Logo	.50	.23	.06

1984 Mother's Mariners

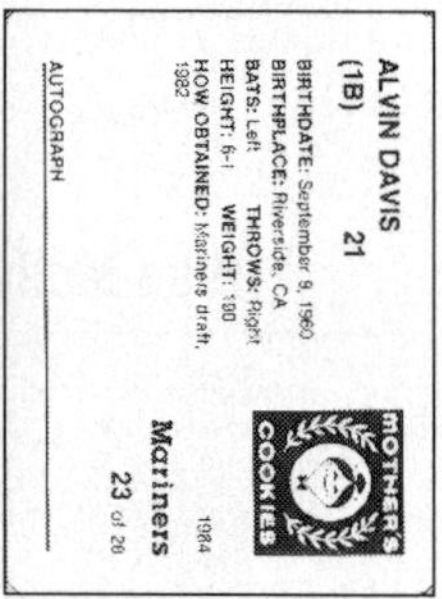

The cards in this 28-card set measure 2 1/2" by 3 1/2". In 1984, The Los Angeles-based Mother's Cookies Co. issued five sets of cards featuring players from major league teams. The Seattle Mariners set features current players depicted by photos. Similar to their 1952 and 1953 issues, the cards have rounded corners. The backs of the cards contain the Mother's Cookies logo. The cards were distributed in partial sets to fans at the respective stadiums of the teams involved. Whereas 20 cards were given to each patron, a redemption card, redeemable for eight more cards was included. Unfortunately, the eight cards received by redeeming the coupon were not necessarily the eight needed to complete a set. Hobbyist Barry Colla was involved in the production of these sets. The key card in the set is Mark Langston, one of his earliest cards issued.

	NRMT-MT	EXC	G-VG
COMPLETE SET (28)	15.00	6.75	1.90
COMMON PLAYER (1-28)	.40	.18	.05
☐ 1 Del Crandall MG	.50	.23	.06
☐ 2 Barry Bonnell	.40	.18	.05
☐ 3 Dave Henderson	.75	.35	.09
☐ 4 Bob Kearney	.40	.18	.05
☐ 5 Mike Moore	1.00	.45	.13
☐ 6 Spike Owen	.60	.25	.08
☐ 7 Gorman Thomas	.60	.25	.08
☐ 8 Ed VandeBerg	.40	.18	.05
☐ 9 Matt Young	.50	.23	.06
☐ 10 Larry Milbourne	.40	.18	.05
☐ 11 Dave Beard	.40	.18	.05
☐ 12 Jim Beattie	.40	.18	.05
☐ 13 Mark Langston	4.00	1.80	.50
☐ 14 Orlando Mercado	.40	.18	.05
☐ 15 Jack Perconte	.40	.18	.05
☐ 16 Pat Putnam	.40	.18	.05
☐ 17 Paul Mirabella	.40	.18	.05
☐ 18 Domingo Ramos	.40	.18	.05
☐ 19 Al Cowens	.40	.18	.05
☐ 20 Mike Stanton	.40	.18	.05
☐ 21 Steve Henderson	.40	.18	.05
☐ 22 Bob Stoddard	.40	.18	.05
☐ 23 Alvin Davis	1.25	.55	.16
☐ 24 Phil Bradley	.75	.35	.09
☐ 25 Roy Thomas	.40	.18	.05
☐ 26 Darnell Coles	.75	.35	.09
☐ 27 Mariners' Coaches Rick Sweet Frank Funk Ben Hines Chuck Cottier Phil Roof	.40	.18	.05
☐ 28 Mariners' Checklist Seattle Kingdome	.50	.23	.06

1984 Mother's Padres

The cards in this 28-card set measure 2 1/2" by 3 1/2". In 1984, the Los Angeles based Mother's Cookies Co. issued five sets of cards featuring players from major league teams. The San Diego Padres set features current players depicted by photos. Similar to their 1952 and 1953 issues, the cards have rounded corners. The backs of the cards contain the Mother's Cookies logo. The cards were distributed in partial sets to fans at the respective stadiums of the teams involved. Whereas 20 cards were given to each patron, a redemption card, redeemable for eight more cards was included. Unfortunately, the eight cards received by redeeming the coupon were not necessarily the eight needed to complete a set. Hobbyist Barry Colla was involved in the production of these sets.

	NRMT-MT	EXC	G-VG
COMPLETE SET (28)	20.00	9.00	2.50
COMMON PLAYER (1-28)	.50	.23	.06
☐ 1 Dick Williams MG	.60	.25	.08
☐ 2 Rich Gossage	1.00	.45	.13
☐ 3 Tim Lollar	.50	.23	.06
☐ 4 Eric Show	.75	.35	.09
☐ 5 Terry Kennedy	.60	.25	.08
☐ 6 Kurt Bevacqua	.50	.23	.06
☐ 7 Steve Garvey	2.00	.90	.25
☐ 8 Garry Templeton	.60	.25	.08
☐ 9 Tony Gwynn	6.00	2.70	.75
☐ 10 Alan Wiggins	.50	.23	.06
☐ 11 Dave Dravecky	1.50	.65	.19
☐ 12 Tim Flannery	.50	.23	.06
☐ 13 Kevin McReynolds	2.50	1.15	.30
☐ 14 Bobby Brown	.50	.23	.06
☐ 15 Ed Whitson	.75	.35	.09
☐ 16 Doug Gwosdz	.50	.23	.06
☐ 17 Luis DeLeon	.50	.23	.06
☐ 18 Andy Hawkins	.75	.35	.09
☐ 19 Craig Lefferts	.90	.40	.11
☐ 20 Carmelo Martinez	.60	.25	.08
☐ 21 Sid Monge	.50	.23	.06
☐ 22 Graig Nettles	.75	.35	.09
☐ 23 Mario Ramirez	.50	.23	.06
☐ 24 Luis Salazar	.60	.25	.08
☐ 25 Champ Summers	.50	.23	.06
☐ 26 Mark Thurmond	.50	.23	.06
☐ 27 Padres' Coaches Harry Dunlop Jack Krol Ozzie Virgil Norm Sherry	.50	.23	.06

	NRMT-MT	EXC	G-VG
Deacon Jones			
☐ 28 Padres' Checklist	.60	.25	.08

1985 Mother's A's

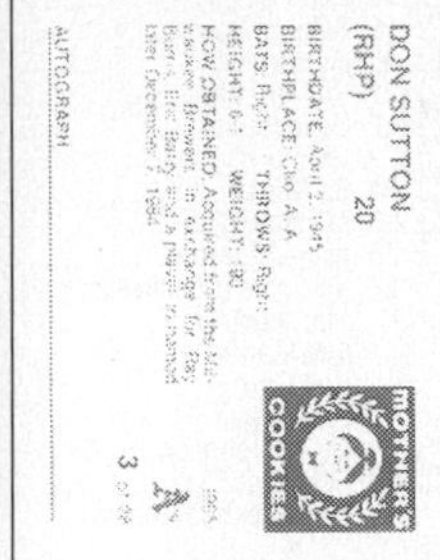

The cards in this 28-card set measure 2 1/2" by 3 1/2". In 1985, the Los Angeles based Mother's Cookies Co. again issued five sets of cards featuring players from major league teams. The Oakland A's set features current players depicted by photos on cards with rounded corners. The backs of the cards contain the Mother's Cookies logo. Cards were passed out at the stadium on July 6.

	NRMT-MT	EXC	G-VG
COMPLETE SET (28)	12.00	5.50	1.50
COMMON PLAYER (1-28)	.35	.16	.04
☐ 1 Jackie Moore MG	.35	.16	.04
☐ 2 Dave Kingman	.75	.35	.09
☐ 3 Don Sutton	1.25	.55	.16
☐ 4 Mike Heath	.35	.16	.04
☐ 5 Alfredo Griffin	.45	.20	.06
☐ 6 Dwayne Murphy	.45	.20	.06
☐ 7 Mike Davis	.35	.16	.04
☐ 8 Carney Lansford	.75	.35	.09
☐ 9 Chris Codiroli	.35	.16	.04
☐ 10 Bruce Bochte	.35	.16	.04
☐ 11 Mickey Tettleton	1.50	.65	.19
☐ 12 Donnie Hill	.35	.16	.04
☐ 13 Rob Picciolo	.35	.16	.04
☐ 14 Dave Collins	.35	.16	.04
☐ 15 Dusty Baker	.75	.35	.09
☐ 16 Tim Conroy	.35	.16	.04
☐ 17 Keith Atherton	.35	.16	.04
☐ 18 Jay Howell	.60	.25	.08
☐ 19 Mike Warren	.35	.16	.04
☐ 20 Steve McCatty	.35	.16	.04
☐ 21 Bill Krueger	.45	.20	.06
☐ 22 Curt Young	.45	.20	.06
☐ 23 Dan Meyer	.35	.16	.04
☐ 24 Mike Gallego	.45	.20	.06
☐ 25 Jeff Kaiser	.35	.16	.04
☐ 26 Steve Henderson	.35	.16	.04
☐ 27 A's Coaches	.45	.20	.06
Clete Boyer			
Bob Didier			
Dave McKay			
Wes Stock			
Billy Williams			
☐ 28 A's Checklist	.45	.20	.06
Oakland Stadium			

1985 Mother's Astros

The cards in this 28-card set measure 2 1/2" by 3 1/2". In 1985, the Los Angeles-based Mother's Cookies Co. again issued five sets of cards featuring players from major league teams. The Houston Astros set features current players depicted by photos on cards with rounded corners. The backs of the cards contain the Mother's Cookies logo. Cards

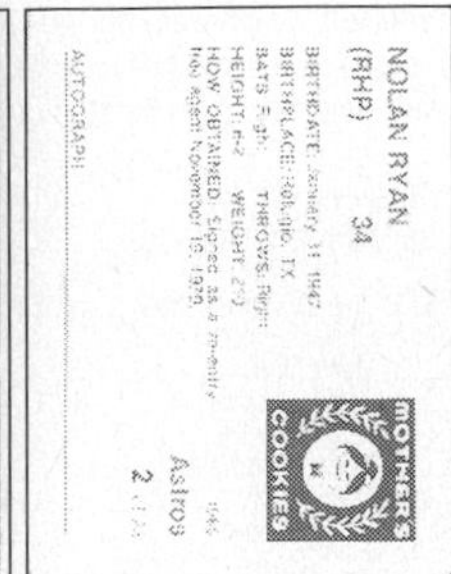

were passed out at the stadium on July 13. The checklist card features the Astros logo on the obverse.

	NRMT-MT	EXC	G-VG
COMPLETE SET (28)	14.00	6.25	1.75
COMMON PLAYER (1-28)	.35	.16	.04
☐ 1 Bob Lillis MG	.35	.16	.04
☐ 2 Nolan Ryan	7.50	3.40	.95
☐ 3 Phil Garner	.60	.25	.08
☐ 4 Jose Cruz	.60	.25	.08
☐ 5 Denny Walling	.35	.16	.04
☐ 6 Joe Niekro	.75	.35	.09
☐ 7 Terry Puhl	.45	.20	.06
☐ 8 Bill Doran	.60	.25	.08
☐ 9 Dickie Thon	.45	.20	.06
☐ 10 Enos Cabell	.35	.16	.04
☐ 11 Frank DiPino	.35	.16	.04
☐ 12 Julio Solano	.35	.16	.04
☐ 13 Alan Ashby	.35	.16	.04
☐ 14 Craig Reynolds	.35	.16	.04
☐ 15 Jerry Mumphrey	.35	.16	.04
☐ 16 Bill Dawley	.35	.16	.04
☐ 17 Mark Bailey	.35	.16	.04
☐ 18 Mike Scott	.75	.35	.09
☐ 19 Harry Spilman	.35	.16	.04
☐ 20 Bob Knepper	.35	.16	.04
☐ 21 Dave Smith	.45	.20	.06
☐ 22 Kevin Bass	.45	.20	.06
☐ 23 Tim Tolman	.35	.16	.04
☐ 24 Jeff Calhoun	.35	.16	.04
☐ 25 Jim Pankovits	.35	.16	.04
☐ 26 Ron Mathis	.35	.16	.04
☐ 27 Astros' Coaches	.35	.16	.04
Cot Deal			
Matt Galante			
Don Leppert			
Denis Menke			
Jerry Walker			
☐ 28 Astros' Checklist	.45	.20	.06
Astros Logo			

1985 Mother's Giants

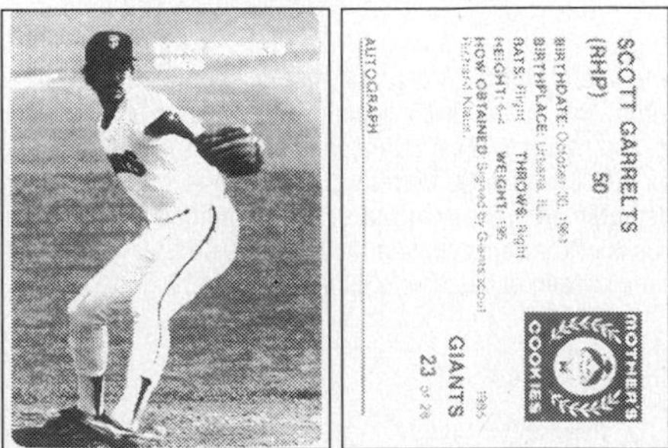

The cards in this 28-card set measure 2 1/2" by 3 1/2". In 1985, the Los Angeles based Mother's Cookies Co. again issued five sets of cards featuring players from major league teams. The San Francisco Giants set features current players depicted by photos on cards with rounded corners. The backs of the cards contain the Mother's Cookies logo. Cards were passed out at the stadium on June 30.

	NRMT-MT	EXC	G-VG
COMPLETE SET (28)	11.00	4.90	1.40
COMMON PLAYER (1-28)	.35	.16	.04
☐ 1 Jim Davenport MG	.35	.16	.04
☐ 2 Chili Davis	.75	.35	.09
☐ 3 Dan Gladden	.75	.35	.09
☐ 4 Jeff Leonard	.45	.20	.06
☐ 5 Manny Trillo	.35	.16	.04
☐ 6 Atlee Hammaker	.45	.20	.06
☐ 7 Bob Brenly	.35	.16	.04
☐ 8 Greg Minton	.35	.16	.04
☐ 9 Bill Laskey	.35	.16	.04
☐ 10 Vida Blue	.45	.20	.06
☐ 11 Mike Krukow	.35	.16	.04
☐ 12 Frank Williams	.35	.16	.04
☐ 13 Jose Uribe	.45	.20	.06
☐ 14 Johnnie LeMaster	.35	.16	.04
☐ 15 Scot Thompson	.35	.16	.04
☐ 16 Dave LaPoint	.35	.16	.04
☐ 17 David Green	.35	.16	.04
☐ 18 Chris Brown	.35	.16	.04
☐ 19 Joel Youngblood	.35	.16	.04
☐ 20 Mark Davis	.60	.25	.08
☐ 21 Jim Gott	.45	.20	.06
☐ 22 Doug Gwosdz	.35	.16	.04
☐ 23 Scott Garrelts	.45	.20	.06
☐ 24 Gary Rajsich	.35	.16	.04
☐ 25 Rob Deer	1.00	.45	.13
☐ 26 Brad Wellman	.35	.16	.04
☐ 27 Giants' Coaches Rocky Bridges Chuck Hiller Tom McCraw Bob Miller Jack Mull	.35	.16	.04
☐ 28 Giants' Checklist Candlestick Park	.45	.20	.06

1985 Mother's Mariners

The cards in this 28-card set measure 2 1/2" by 3 1/2". In 1985, the Los Angeles based Mother's Cookies Co. again issued five sets of cards featuring players from major league teams. The Seattle Mariners set features current players depicted by photos on cards with rounded corners. The backs of the cards contain the Mother's Cookies logo. Cards were passed out at the stadium on August 10.

	NRMT-MT	EXC	G-VG
COMPLETE SET (28)	12.00	5.50	1.50
COMMON PLAYER (1-28)	.35	.16	.04
☐ 1 Chuck Cottier MG	.35	.16	.04
☐ 2 Alvin Davis	.75	.35	.09
☐ 3 Mark Langston	1.50	.65	.19
☐ 4 Dave Henderson	.75	.35	.09
☐ 5 Ed VandeBerg	.35	.16	.04
☐ 6 Al Cowens	.35	.16	.04
☐ 7 Spike Owen	.45	.20	.06
☐ 8 Mike Moore	.75	.35	.09
☐ 9 Gorman Thomas	.60	.25	.08
☐ 10 Barry Bonnell	.35	.16	.04
☐ 11 Jack Perconte	.35	.16	.04
☐ 12 Domingo Ramos	.35	.16	.04
☐ 13 Bob Kearney	.35	.16	.04
☐ 14 Matt Young	.35	.16	.04
☐ 15 Jim Beattie	.35	.16	.04
☐ 16 Mike Stanton	.35	.16	.04
☐ 17 David Valle	.35	.16	.04
☐ 18 Ken Phelps	.45	.20	.06
☐ 19 Salome Barojas	.35	.16	.04
☐ 20 Jim Presley	.45	.20	.06
☐ 21 Phil Bradley	.60	.25	.08
☐ 22 Dave Geisel	.35	.16	.04
☐ 23 Harold Reynolds	1.00	.45	.13
☐ 24 Ed Nunez	.45	.20	.06
☐ 25 Mike Morgan	.75	.35	.09
☐ 26 Ivan Calderon	.90	.40	.11
☐ 27 Mariners' Coaches Marty Martinez Jim Mahoney Phil Roof Phil Regan Deron Johnson	.35	.16	.04
☐ 28 Checklist Card Seattle Kingdome	.45	.20	.06

1985 Mother's Padres

The cards in this 28-card set measure 2 1/2" by 3 1/2". In 1985, the Los Angeles based Mother's Cookies Co. again issued five sets of cards featuring players from major league teams. The San Diego Padres set features current players depicted by photos on cards with rounded corners. The backs of the cards contain the Mother's Cookies logo. Cards were passed out at the stadium on August 11.

	NRMT-MT	EXC	G-VG
COMPLETE SET (28)	12.50	5.75	1.55
COMMON PLAYER (1-28)	.35	.16	.04
☐ 1 Dick Williams MG	.35	.16	.04
☐ 2 Tony Gwynn	3.50	1.55	.45
☐ 3 Kevin McReynolds	1.25	.55	.16
☐ 4 Graig Nettles	.75	.35	.09
☐ 5 Rich Gossage	.90	.40	.11
☐ 6 Steve Garvey	1.50	.65	.19
☐ 7 Garry Templeton	.45	.20	.06
☐ 8 Dave Dravecky	.75	.35	.09
☐ 9 Eric Show	.35	.16	.04
☐ 10 Terry Kennedy	.35	.16	.04
☐ 11 Luis DeLeon	.35	.16	.04
☐ 12 Bruce Bochy	.35	.16	.04
☐ 13 Andy Hawkins	.45	.20	.06
☐ 14 Kurt Bevacqua	.35	.16	.04
☐ 15 Craig Lefferts	.60	.25	.08
☐ 16 Mario Ramirez	.35	.16	.04
☐ 17 LaMarr Hoyt	.35	.16	.04
☐ 18 Jerry Royster	.35	.16	.04
☐ 19 Tim Stoddard	.35	.16	.04
☐ 20 Tim Flannery	.35	.16	.04
☐ 21 Mark Thurmond	.35	.16	.04
☐ 22 Greg Booker	.35	.16	.04
☐ 23 Bobby Brown	.35	.16	.04
☐ 24 Carmelo Martinez	.45	.20	.06
☐ 25 Al Bumbry	.35	.16	.04
☐ 26 Jerry Davis	.35	.16	.04
☐ 27 Padres' Coaches Jack Krol Harry Dunlop	.35	.16	.04

	MT	EX-MT	VG
Deacon Jones			
☐ 28 Padres' Checklist	.45	.20	.06
Jack Murphy Stadium			

1986 Mother's A's

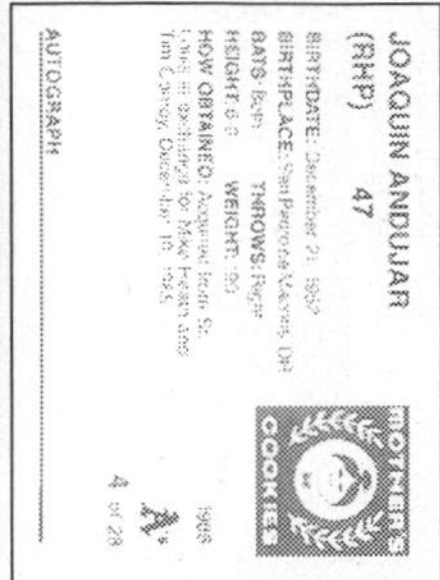

This set consists of 28 full-color, rounded-corner cards each measuring 2 1/2" by 3 1/2". Starter sets (only 20 cards but also including a certificate for eight more cards) were given out at the ballpark and collectors were encouraged to trade to fill in the rest of their set. The cards were originally given away on July 20th at Oakland Coliseum.

	MT	EX-MT	VG
COMPLETE SET (28)	28.00	12.50	3.50
COMMON PLAYER (1-28)	.40	.18	.05
☐ 1 Jackie Moore MG	.40	.18	.05
☐ 2 Dave Kingman	.75	.35	.09
☐ 3 Dusty Baker	.75	.35	.09
☐ 4 Joaquin Andujar	.50	.23	.06
☐ 5 Alfredo Griffin	.50	.23	.06
☐ 6 Dwayne Murphy	.50	.23	.06
☐ 7 Mike Davis	.40	.18	.05
☐ 8 Carney Lansford	.75	.35	.09
☐ 9 Jose Canseco	18.00	8.00	2.30
☐ 10 Bruce Bochte	.40	.18	.05
☐ 11 Mickey Tettleton	1.00	.45	.13
☐ 12 Donnie Hill	.40	.18	.05
☐ 13 Jose Rijo	1.50	.65	.19
☐ 14 Rick Langford	.50	.23	.06
☐ 15 Chris Codiroli	.40	.18	.05
☐ 16 Moose Haas	.40	.18	.05
☐ 17 Keith Atherton	.40	.18	.05
☐ 18 Jay Howell	.60	.25	.08
☐ 19 Tony Phillips	.75	.35	.09
☐ 20 Steve Henderson	.40	.18	.05
☐ 21 Bill Krueger	.50	.23	.06
☐ 22 Steve Ontiveros	.40	.18	.05
☐ 23 Bill Bathe	.40	.18	.05
☐ 24 Ricky Peters	.40	.18	.05
☐ 25 Tim Birtsas	.40	.18	.05
☐ 26 A's Trainers and	.40	.18	.05
Equipment Managers			
Frank Ciensczyk			
Steve Vucinich			
Barry Weinberg			
Larry Davis			
☐ 27 A's Coaches	.40	.18	.05
Bob Didier			
Dave McKay			
Jeff Newman			
Ron Plaza			
Wes Stock			
Bob Watson			
☐ 28 A's Checklist Card	.50	.23	.06
Oakland Coliseum			

1986 Mother's Astros

This set consists of 28 full-color, rounded-corner cards each measuring 2 1/2" by 3 1/2". Starter sets (only 20 cards but also including a certificate for eight more cards) were given

out at the ballpark and collectors were encouraged to trade to fill in the rest of their set. Cards were originally given out at the Astrodome on July 10th. Since the 1986 All-Star Game was held in Houston, the set features Astro All-Stars since 1962 as painted by artist Richard Wallich. The set numbering is essentially chronological according to when each player was selected for the All-Star Game as an Astro.

	MT	EX-MT	VG
COMPLETE SET (28)	12.00	5.50	1.50
COMMON PLAYER (1-28)	.35	.16	.04
☐ 1 Dick Farrell	.35	.16	.04
☐ 2 Hal Woodeshick	.35	.16	.04
☐ 3 Joe Morgan	1.50	.65	.19
☐ 4 Claude Raymond	.35	.16	.04
☐ 5 Mike Cuellar	.45	.20	.06
☐ 6 Rusty Staub	.75	.35	.09
☐ 7 Jimmy Wynn	.60	.25	.08
☐ 8 Larry Dierker	.45	.20	.06
☐ 9 Denis Menke	.35	.16	.04
☐ 10 Don Wilson	.45	.20	.06
☐ 11 Cesar Cedeno	.60	.25	.08
☐ 12 Lee May	.60	.25	.08
☐ 13 Bob Watson	.60	.25	.08
☐ 14 Ken Forsch	.35	.16	.04
☐ 15 Joaquin Andujar	.60	.25	.08
☐ 16 Terry Puhl	.45	.20	.06
☐ 17 Joe Niekro	.60	.25	.08
☐ 18 Craig Reynolds	.35	.16	.04
☐ 19 Joe Sambito	.35	.16	.04
☐ 20 Jose Cruz	.75	.35	.09
☐ 21 J.R. Richard	.60	.25	.08
☐ 22 Bob Knepper	.35	.16	.04
☐ 23 Nolan Ryan	6.00	2.70	.75
☐ 24 Ray Knight	.60	.25	.08
☐ 25 Bill Dawley	.35	.16	.04
☐ 26 Dickie Thon	.45	.20	.06
☐ 27 Jerry Mumphrey	.35	.16	.04
☐ 28 Checklist Card	.45	.20	.06
Astros' A-S Logo			

1986 Mother's Giants

This set consists of 28 full-color, rounded-corner cards each measuring 2 1/2" by 3 1/2". Starter sets (only 20 cards but also including a certificate for eight more cards) were given out at the ballpark and collectors were encouraged to trade to fill in the rest of their set. Cards were originally given out at Candlestick Park on July 13th.

	MT	EX-MT	VG
COMPLETE SET (28)	25.00	11.50	3.10
COMMON PLAYER (1-28)	.40	.18	.05
☐ 1 Roger Craig MG	.60	.25	.08
☐ 2 Chili Davis	.60	.25	.08
☐ 3 Dan Gladden	.50	.23	.06
☐ 4 Jeff Leonard	.50	.23	.06
☐ 5 Bob Brenly	.40	.18	.05
☐ 6 Atlee Hammaker	.50	.23	.06
☐ 7 Will Clark	18.00	8.00	2.30
☐ 8 Greg Minton	.40	.18	.05
☐ 9 Candy Maldonado	.60	.25	.08
☐ 10 Vida Blue	.50	.23	.06
☐ 11 Mike Krukow	.50	.23	.06
☐ 12 Bob Melvin	.40	.18	.05
☐ 13 Jose Uribe	.50	.23	.06
☐ 14 Dan Driessen	.40	.18	.05
☐ 15 Jeff D. Robinson	.40	.18	.05
☐ 16 Robby Thompson	.75	.35	.09
☐ 17 Mike LaCoss	.40	.18	.05
☐ 18 Chris Brown	.40	.18	.05
☐ 19 Scott Garrelts	.50	.23	.06
☐ 20 Mark Davis	.50	.23	.06
☐ 21 Jim Gott	.50	.23	.06
☐ 22 Brad Wellman	.40	.18	.05
☐ 23 Roger Mason	.40	.18	.05
☐ 24 Bill Laskey	.40	.18	.05
☐ 25 Brad Gulden	.40	.18	.05
☐ 26 Joel Youngblood	.40	.18	.05
☐ 27 Juan Berenguer	.40	.18	.05
☐ 28 Checklist Card Bob Lillis CO Gordy MacKenzie CO Bill Fahey CO Norm Sherry CO Jose Morales CO	.50	.23	.06

1986 Mother's Mariners

This set consists of 28 full-color, rounded-corner cards each measuring 2 1/2" by 3 1/2". Starter sets (only 20 cards but also including a certificate for eight more cards) were given out at the ballpark and collectors were encouraged to trade to fill in the rest of their set. Cards were originally given out on July 27th at the Seattle Kingdome.

	MT	EX-MT	VG
COMPLETE SET (28)	12.00	5.50	1.50
COMMON PLAYER (1-28)	.35	.16	.04
☐ 1 Dick Williams MG	.45	.20	.06
☐ 2 Alvin Davis	.60	.25	.08
☐ 3 Mark Langston	1.25	.55	.16
☐ 4 Dave Henderson	.60	.25	.08
☐ 5 Steve Yeager	.45	.20	.06
☐ 6 Al Cowens	.35	.16	.04
☐ 7 Jim Presley	.45	.20	.06
☐ 8 Phil Bradley	.45	.20	.06
☐ 9 Gorman Thomas	.45	.20	.06
☐ 10 Barry Bonnell	.35	.16	.04
☐ 11 Milt Wilcox	.35	.16	.04
☐ 12 Domingo Ramos	.35	.16	.04
☐ 13 Paul Mirabella	.35	.16	.04
☐ 14 Matt Young	.45	.20	.06
☐ 15 Ivan Calderon	1.00	.45	.13
☐ 16 Bill Swift	.75	.35	.09
☐ 17 Pete Ladd	.35	.16	.04
☐ 18 Ken Phelps	.45	.20	.06
☐ 19 Karl Best	.35	.16	.04
☐ 20 Spike Owen	.45	.20	.06
☐ 21 Mike Moore	.60	.25	.08
☐ 22 Danny Tartabull	2.50	1.15	.30
☐ 23 Bob Kearney	.35	.16	.04
☐ 24 Edwin Nunez	.35	.16	.04
☐ 25 Mike Morgan	.60	.25	.08
☐ 26 Roy Thomas	.35	.16	.04
☐ 27 Jim Beattie	.35	.16	.04
☐ 28 Checklist Card Deron Johnson CO Marty Martinez CO Phil Roof CO Phil Regan CO Ozzie Virgil CO	.45	.20	.06

1987 Mother's A's

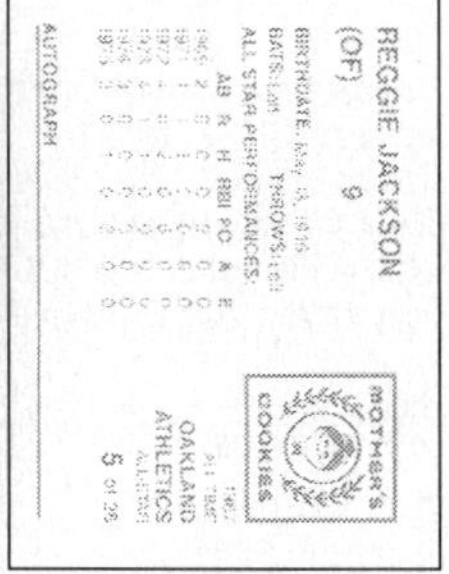

This set consists of 28 full-color, rounded-corner cards each measuring 2 1/2" by 3 1/2". Starter sets (only 20 cards but also including a certificate for eight more cards) were given out at the ballpark and collectors were encouraged to trade to fill in the rest of their set. The cards were originally given away on July 5th at Oakland Coliseum during a game against the Boston Red Sox. This set is actually an All-Time All-Star set including every A's All-Star player since 1968 (when the franchise moved to Oakland). The vintage photos (each shot during the year of All-Star appearance) were taken from the collection of Doug McWilliams. The set is sequenced by what year the player first made the All-Star team. The sets were supposedly given out free to the first 25,000 paid admissions at the game.

	MT	EX-MT	VG
COMPLETE SET (28)	20.00	9.00	2.50
COMMON PLAYER (1-28)	.40	.18	.05
☐ 1 Bert Campaneris	.50	.23	.06
☐ 2 Rick Monday	.50	.23	.06
☐ 3 John Odom	.40	.18	.05
☐ 4 Sal Bando	.60	.25	.08
☐ 5 Reggie Jackson	2.50	1.15	.30
☐ 6 Jim Hunter	1.25	.55	.16
☐ 7 Vida Blue	.60	.25	.08
☐ 8 Dave Duncan	.40	.18	.05
☐ 9 Joe Rudi	.60	.25	.08
☐ 10 Rollie Fingers	1.50	.65	.19
☐ 11 Ken Holtzman	.40	.18	.05
☐ 12 Dick Williams MG	.40	.18	.05
☐ 13 Alvin Dark MG	.40	.18	.05
☐ 14 Gene Tenace	.50	.23	.06
☐ 15 Claudell Washington	.40	.18	.05
☐ 16 Phil Garner	.50	.23	.06
☐ 17 Wayne Gross	.40	.18	.05
☐ 18 Matt Keough	.40	.18	.05
☐ 19 Jeff Newman	.40	.18	.05
☐ 20 Rickey Henderson	3.50	1.55	.45
☐ 21 Tony Armas	.50	.23	.06
☐ 22 Mike Norris	.40	.18	.05

	MT	EX-MT	VG
☐ 23 Billy Martin MG	1.00	.45	.13
☐ 24 Bill Caudill	.40	.18	.05
☐ 25 Jay Howell	.50	.23	.06
☐ 26 Jose Canseco	4.50	2.00	.55
☐ 27 Jose and Reggie (Canseco and Jackson)	3.00	1.35	.40
☐ 28 Checklist Card A's Logo	.50	.23	.06

1987 Mother's Astros

This set consists of 28 full-color, rounded-corner cards each measuring 2 1/2" by 3 1/2". Starter sets (only 20 cards but also including a certificate for eight more cards) were given out at the ballpark and collectors were encouraged to trade to fill in the rest of their set. Cards were originally given out at the Astrodome on July 17th during a game against the Phillies. Photos were taken by Barry Colla. The sets were supposedly given out free to the first 25,000 paid admissions at the game.

	MT	EX-MT	VG
COMPLETE SET (28)	12.00	5.50	1.50
COMMON PLAYER (1-28)	.35	.16	.04
☐ 1 Hal Lanier MG	.45	.20	.06
☐ 2 Mike Scott	.75	.35	.09
☐ 3 Jose Cruz	.60	.25	.08
☐ 4 Bill Doran	.60	.25	.08
☐ 5 Bob Knepper	.35	.16	.04
☐ 6 Phil Garner	.45	.20	.06
☐ 7 Terry Puhl	.45	.20	.06
☐ 8 Nolan Ryan	6.00	2.70	.75
☐ 9 Kevin Bass	.45	.20	.06
☐ 10 Glenn Davis	1.00	.45	.13
☐ 11 Alan Ashby	.35	.16	.04
☐ 12 Charlie Kerfeld	.35	.16	.04
☐ 13 Denny Walling	.35	.16	.04
☐ 14 Danny Darwin	.35	.16	.04
☐ 15 Mark Bailey	.35	.16	.04
☐ 16 Davey Lopes	.45	.20	.06
☐ 17 Dave Meads	.35	.16	.04
☐ 18 Aurelio Lopez	.35	.16	.04
☐ 19 Craig Reynolds	.35	.16	.04
☐ 20 Dave Smith	.45	.20	.06
☐ 21 Larry Andersen	.35	.16	.04
☐ 22 Jim Pankovits	.35	.16	.04
☐ 23 Jim Deshaies	.45	.20	.06
☐ 24 Bert Pena	.35	.16	.04
☐ 25 Dickie Thon	.45	.20	.06
☐ 26 Billy Hatcher	.45	.20	.06
☐ 27 Astros' Coaches Yogi Berra Denis Menke Gene Tenace Matt Galante Les Moss	.60	.25	.08
☐ 28 Checklist Card Astrodome	.45	.20	.06

1987 Mother's Dodgers

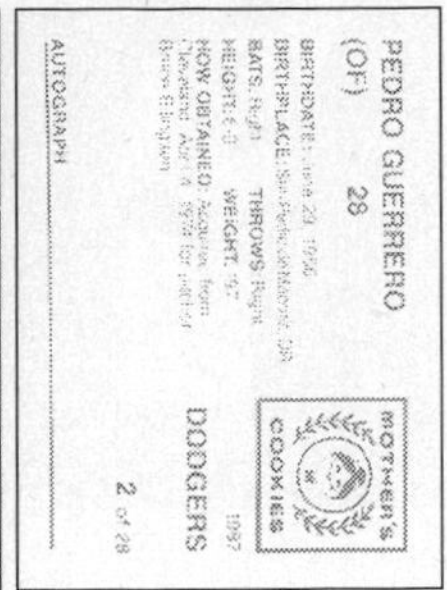

This set consists of 28 full-color, rounded-corner cards each measuring 2 1/2" by 3 1/2". Starter sets (only 20 cards but also including a certificate for eight more cards) were given out at the ballpark and collectors were encouraged to trade to fill in the rest of their set. Cards were originally given out at Dodger Stadium on August 9th. Photos were taken by Barry Colla. The sets were supposedly given out free to all game attendees 14 years of age and under.

	MT	EX-MT	VG
COMPLETE SET (28)	11.00	4.90	1.40
COMMON PLAYER (1-28)	.35	.16	.04
☐ 1 Tom Lasorda MG	.75	.35	.09
☐ 2 Pedro Guerrero	.75	.35	.09
☐ 3 Steve Sax	.60	.25	.08
☐ 4 Fernando Valenzuela	.75	.35	.09
☐ 5 Mike Marshall	.45	.20	.06
☐ 6 Orel Hershiser	1.25	.55	.16
☐ 7 Mariano Duncan	.60	.25	.08
☐ 8 Bill Madlock	.45	.20	.06
☐ 9 Bob Welch	.75	.35	.09
☐ 10 Mike Scioscia	.45	.20	.06
☐ 11 Mike Ramsey	.35	.16	.04
☐ 12 Matt Young	.35	.16	.04
☐ 13 Franklin Stubbs	.45	.20	.06
☐ 14 Tom Niedenfuer	.35	.16	.04
☐ 15 Reggie Williams	.35	.16	.04
☐ 16 Rick Honeycutt	.35	.16	.04
☐ 17 Dave Anderson	.35	.16	.04
☐ 18 Alejandro Pena	.60	.25	.08
☐ 19 Ken Howell	.35	.16	.04
☐ 20 Len Matuszek	.35	.16	.04
☐ 21 Tim Leary	.45	.20	.06
☐ 22 Tracy Woodson	.45	.20	.06
☐ 23 Alex Trevino	.35	.16	.04
☐ 24 Ken Landreaux	.35	.16	.04
☐ 25 Mickey Hatcher	.35	.16	.04
☐ 26 Brian Holton	.35	.16	.04
☐ 27 Dodgers' Coaches	.35	.16	.04
☐ 28 Checklist Card	.45	.20	.06

1987 Mother's Giants

This set consists of 28 full-color, rounded-corner cards each measuring 2 1/2" by 3 1/2". Starter sets (only 20 cards but also including a certificate for eight more cards) were given out at the ballpark and collectors were encouraged to trade to fill in the rest of their set. Cards were originally given out at Candlestick Park on June 27th during a game against the Astros. Photos were taken by Dennis Desprois. The sets were supposedly given out free to the first 25,000 paid admissions at the game.

	MT	EX-MT	VG
COMPLETE SET (28)	16.00	7.25	2.00
COMMON PLAYER (1-28)	.40	.18	.05
☐ 1 Roger Craig MG	.60	.25	.08

	MT	EX-MT	VG
☐ 2 Will Clark	5.00	2.30	.60
☐ 3 Chili Davis	.50	.23	.06
☐ 4 Bob Brenly	.40	.18	.05
☐ 5 Chris Brown	.40	.18	.05
☐ 6 Mike Krukow	.40	.18	.05
☐ 7 Candy Maldonado	.60	.25	.08
☐ 8 Jeffrey Leonard	.50	.23	.06
☐ 9 Greg Minton	.40	.18	.05
☐ 10 Robby Thompson	.50	.23	.06
☐ 11 Scott Garrelts	.40	.18	.05
☐ 12 Bob Melvin	.40	.18	.05
☐ 13 Jose Uribe	.50	.23	.06
☐ 14 Mark Davis	.50	.23	.06
☐ 15 Eddie Milner	.40	.18	.05
☐ 16 Harry Spilman	.40	.18	.05
☐ 17 Kelly Downs	.60	.25	.08
☐ 18 Chris Speier	.40	.18	.05
☐ 19 Jim Gott	.50	.23	.06
☐ 20 Joel Youngblood	.40	.18	.05
☐ 21 Mike LaCoss	.40	.18	.05
☐ 22 Matt Williams	4.00	1.80	.50
☐ 23 Roger Mason	.40	.18	.05
☐ 24 Mike Aldrete	.40	.18	.05
☐ 25 Jeff D. Robinson	.50	.23	.06
☐ 26 Mark Grant	.40	.18	.05
☐ 27 Giants' Coaches Don Zimmer Bob Lillis Jose Morales Norm Sherry Bill Fahey Gordon MacKenzie	.40	.18	.05
☐ 28 Checklist Card Candlestick Park	.50	.23	.06

1987 Mother's Mariners

This set consists of 28 full-color, rounded-corner cards each measuring 2 1/2" by 3 1/2". Starter sets (only 20 cards but also including a certificate for eight more cards) were given out at the ballpark and collectors were encouraged to trade to fill in the rest of their set. Cards were originally given out on August 9th at the Seattle Kingdome. Photos were taken by Barry Colla. The sets were supposedly given out free to the first 20,000 paid admissions at the game.

	MT	EX-MT	VG
COMPLETE SET (28)	10.00	4.50	1.25
COMMON PLAYER (1-28)	.40	.18	.05
☐ 1 Dick Williams MG	.50	.23	.06
☐ 2 Alvin Davis	.60	.25	.08
☐ 3 Mike Moore	.60	.25	.08
☐ 4 Jim Presley	.50	.23	.06
☐ 5 Mark Langston	1.00	.45	.13
☐ 6 Phil Bradley	.50	.23	.06
☐ 7 Ken Phelps	.50	.23	.06
☐ 8 Mike Morgan	.60	.25	.08
☐ 9 David Valle	.40	.18	.05
☐ 10 Harold Reynolds	.60	.25	.08
☐ 11 Edwin Nunez	.40	.18	.05
☐ 12 Bob Kearney	.40	.18	.05
☐ 13 Scott Bankhead	.60	.25	.08
☐ 14 Scott Bradley	.40	.18	.05
☐ 15 Mickey Brantley	.40	.18	.05
☐ 16 Mark Huismann	.40	.18	.05
☐ 17 Mike Kingery	.40	.18	.05
☐ 18 John Moses	.40	.18	.05
☐ 19 Donell Nixon	.40	.18	.05
☐ 20 Rey Quinones	.40	.18	.05
☐ 21 Domingo Ramos	.40	.18	.05
☐ 22 Jerry Reed	.40	.18	.05
☐ 23 Rich Renteria	.40	.18	.05
☐ 24 Rich Monteleone	.40	.18	.05
☐ 25 Mike Trujillo	.40	.18	.05
☐ 26 Bill Wilkinson	.40	.18	.05
☐ 27 John Christensen	.40	.18	.05
☐ 28 Checklist Card Billy Connors CO Frank Howard CO Bobby Tolan CO Ozzie Virgil CO Phil Roof CO	.50	.23	.06

1987 Mother's McGwire

This set consists of 4 full-color, rounded-corner cards each measuring 2 1/2" by 3 1/2" and showing a different pose of A's slugging rookie Mark McGwire. Cards were originally given out at the national Card Collectors Convention in San Francisco. Later they were available through a mail-in offer involving collectors sending in two proofs-of-purchase from any Mother's Cookies products to get one free card. Photos were taken by Doug McWilliams. The cards are numbered on the back.

	MT	EX-MT	VG
COMPLETE SET (4)	15.00	6.75	1.90
COMMON PLAYER (1-4)	4.00	1.80	.50
☐ 1 Mark McGwire (Close-up shot, head and shoulders)	4.00	1.80	.50
☐ 2 Mark McGwire (Waist up, holding bat)	4.50	2.00	.55
☐ 3 Mark McGwire (Batting stance, ready to swing)	4.50	2.00	.55
☐ 4 Mark McGwire (Home run swing, follow through)	5.00	2.30	.60

1987 Mother's Rangers

This set consists of 28 full-color, rounded-corner cards each measuring 2 1/2" by 3 1/2". Starter sets (only 20 cards but also including a certificate for eight more cards) were given out at the ballpark and collectors were encouraged to trade to fill in the rest of their set. Cards were originally given out on July 17th during the game against the Yankees. Photos were taken by Barry Colla. The sets were supposedly given out free to the first 25,000 paid admissions at the game.

	MT	EX-MT	VG
COMPLETE SET (28)	12.00	5.50	1.50
COMMON PLAYER (1-28)	.40	.18	.05
☐ 1 Bobby Valentine MG	.50	.23	.06
☐ 2 Pete Incaviglia	.75	.35	.09
☐ 3 Charlie Hough	.50	.23	.06
☐ 4 Oddibe McDowell	.50	.23	.06
☐ 5 Larry Parrish	.50	.23	.06
☐ 6 Scott Fletcher	.40	.18	.05
☐ 7 Steve Buechele	.60	.25	.08
☐ 8 Tom Paciorek	.40	.18	.05
☐ 9 Pete O'Brien	.50	.23	.06
☐ 10 Darrell Porter	.40	.18	.05
☐ 11 Greg A. Harris	.40	.18	.05
☐ 12 Don Slaught	.40	.18	.05
☐ 13 Ruben Sierra	5.00	2.30	.60
☐ 14 Curtis Wilkerson	.40	.18	.05
☐ 15 Dale Mohorcic	.40	.18	.05
☐ 16 Ron Meredith	.40	.18	.05
☐ 17 Mitch Williams	.75	.35	.09
☐ 18 Bob Brower	.40	.18	.05
☐ 19 Edwin Correa	.40	.18	.05
☐ 20 Geno Petralli	.40	.18	.05
☐ 21 Mike Loynd	.40	.18	.05
☐ 22 Jerry Browne	.75	.35	.09
☐ 23 Jose Guzman	.75	.35	.09
☐ 24 Jeff Kunkel	.40	.18	.05
☐ 25 Bobby Witt	1.00	.45	.13
☐ 26 Jeff Russell	.60	.25	.08
☐ 27 Rangers' Trainers Bill Zeigler Danny Wheat	.40	.18	.05
☐ 28 Checklist Card Tom Robson CO Art Howe CO Joe Ferguson CO Tim Foli CO Tom House CO Dave Oliver CO	.50	.23	.06

1988 Mother's A's

This set consists of 28 full-color, rounded-corner cards each measuring 2 1/2" by 3 1/2". Starter sets (only 20 cards but also including a certificate for eight more cards) were given out at the ballpark and collectors were encouraged to trade to fill in the rest of their set. The cards were originally given away on July 23rd at Oakland Coliseum during a game. Short sets (20 cards plus certificate) were supposedly given out free to the first 35,000 paid admissions at the game.

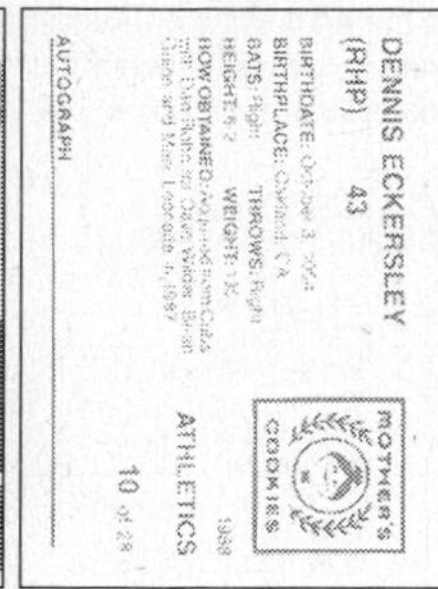

	MT	EX-MT	VG
COMPLETE SET (28)	18.00	8.00	2.30
COMMON PLAYER (1-28)	.40	.18	.05
☐ 1 Tony LaRussa MG	.75	.35	.09
☐ 2 Mark McGwire	3.50	1.55	.45
☐ 3 Dave Stewart	1.00	.45	.13
☐ 4 Terry Steinbach	.75	.35	.09
☐ 5 Dave Parker	.75	.35	.09
☐ 6 Carney Lansford	.75	.35	.09
☐ 7 Jose Canseco	3.50	1.55	.45
☐ 8 Don Baylor	.60	.25	.08
☐ 9 Bob Welch	.75	.35	.09
☐ 10 Dennis Eckersley	2.00	.90	.25
☐ 11 Walt Weiss	1.00	.45	.13
☐ 12 Tony Phillips	.60	.25	.08
☐ 13 Steve Ontiveros	.40	.18	.05
☐ 14 Dave Henderson	.60	.25	.08
☐ 15 Stan Javier	.50	.23	.06
☐ 16 Ron Hassey	.40	.18	.05
☐ 17 Curt Young	.40	.18	.05
☐ 18 Glenn Hubbard	.40	.18	.05
☐ 19 Storm Davis	.50	.23	.06
☐ 20 Eric Plunk	.40	.18	.05
☐ 21 Matt Young	.40	.18	.05
☐ 22 Mike Gallego	.50	.23	.06
☐ 23 Rick Honeycutt	.40	.18	.05
☐ 24 Doug Jennings	.40	.18	.05
☐ 25 Gene Nelson	.40	.18	.05
☐ 26 Greg Cadaret	.40	.18	.05
☐ 27 Athletics Coaches Dave Duncan Rene Lacheman Jim Lefebvre Dave McKay Mike Paul Bob Watson	.40	.18	.05
☐ 28 Checklist Card Jose Canseco Mark McGwire	1.50	.65	.19

1988 Mother's Astros

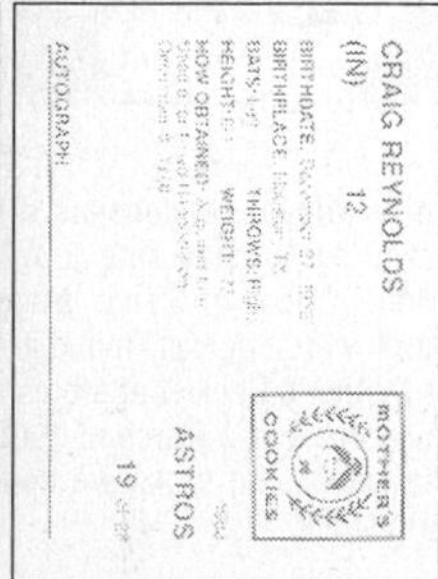

This set consists of 28 full-color, rounded-corner cards each measuring 2 1/2" by 3 1/2". Starter sets (only 20 cards but also including a certificate for eight more cards) were given out at the ballpark and collectors were encouraged to trade to fill in the rest of their set. Cards were originally given out at the Astrodome on August 26th during a game. The sets were supposedly given out free to the first 25,000 paid admissions at the game.

	MT	EX-MT	VG
COMPLETE SET (28)	11.00	4.90	1.40
COMMON PLAYER (1-28)	.40	.18	.05
☐ 1 Hal Lanier MG	.40	.18	.05
☐ 2 Mike Scott	.75	.35	.09
☐ 3 Gerald Young	.40	.18	.05
☐ 4 Bill Doran	.50	.23	.06
☐ 5 Bob Knepper	.40	.18	.05
☐ 6 Billy Hatcher	.50	.23	.06
☐ 7 Terry Puhl	.50	.23	.06
☐ 8 Nolan Ryan	4.50	2.00	.55
☐ 9 Kevin Bass	.50	.23	.06
☐ 10 Glenn Davis	.75	.35	.09
☐ 11 Alan Ashby	.40	.18	.05
☐ 12 Steve Henderson	.40	.18	.05
☐ 13 Denny Walling	.40	.18	.05
☐ 14 Danny Darwin	.40	.18	.05
☐ 15 Mark Bailey	.40	.18	.05
☐ 16 Ernie Camacho	.40	.18	.05
☐ 17 Rafael Ramirez	.40	.18	.05
☐ 18 Jeff Heathcock	.40	.18	.05
☐ 19 Craig Reynolds	.40	.18	.05
☐ 20 Dave Smith	.50	.23	.06
☐ 21 Larry Andersen	.40	.18	.05
☐ 22 Jim Pankovits	.40	.18	.05
☐ 23 Jim Deshaies	.40	.18	.05
☐ 24 Juan Agosto	.40	.18	.05
☐ 25 Chuck Jackson	.40	.18	.05
☐ 26 Joaquin Andujar	.50	.23	.06
☐ 27 Astros' Coaches Yogi Berra Gene Clines Matt Galante Marc Hill Dennis Menke Les Moss	.50	.23	.06
☐ 28 Checklist Card Dave Labossiere TR Dennis Liborio EQMG Doc Ewell TR	.40	.18	.05

1988 Mother's Will Clark

WILL CLARK
San Francisco Giants
WILL CLARK
(1B)
22
MOTHER'S
COOKIES
AUTOGRAPH

This regional set consists of 4 full-color, rounded-corner cards each measuring 2 1/2" by 3 1/2" and showing a different pose of Giants' slugging first baseman Will Clark. Cards were originally found in 18 oz. packages of "Big Bags" of Mother's Cookies at stores in the Northern California area in February and March of 1988. The cards are numbered on the back. Card backs are done in red and purple on white card stock.

	MT	EX-MT	VG
COMPLETE SET (4)	15.00	6.75	1.90
COMMON PLAYER (1-4)	4.00	1.80	.50
☐ 1 Will Clark (Batting Pose, Waist Up)	4.50	2.00	.55
☐ 2 Will Clark (Kneeling In On Deck Circle)	4.00	1.80	.50
☐ 3 Will Clark (Follow Through Swing)	4.00	1.80	.50
☐ 4 Will Clark (Starting Toward First Base)	4.50	2.00	.55

1988 Mother's Dodgers

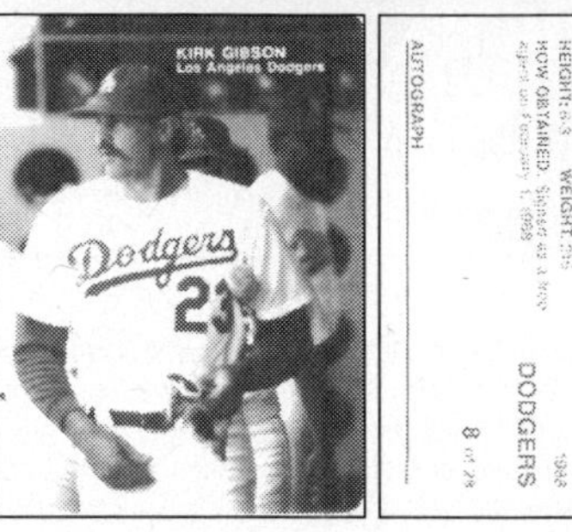

This set consists of 28 full-color, rounded-corner cards each measuring 2 1/2" by 3 1/2". Starter sets (only 20 cards but also including a certificate for eight more cards) were given out at the ballpark and collectors were encouraged to trade to fill in the rest of their set. Cards were originally given out at Dodger Stadium on July 31st. Photos were taken by Barry Colla. The sets were supposedly given out free to the first 25,000 game attendees 14 years of age and under.

	MT	EX-MT	VG
COMPLETE SET (28)	11.00	4.90	1.40
COMMON PLAYER (1-28)	.40	.18	.05
☐ 1 Tom Lasorda MG	.75	.35	.09
☐ 2 Pedro Guerrero	.60	.25	.08
☐ 3 Steve Sax	.60	.25	.08
☐ 4 Fernando Valenzuela	.60	.25	.08
☐ 5 Mike Marshall	.50	.23	.06
☐ 6 Orel Hershiser	1.00	.45	.13
☐ 7 Alfredo Griffin	.40	.18	.05
☐ 8 Kirk Gibson	.90	.40	.11
☐ 9 Don Sutton	.90	.40	.11
☐ 10 Mike Scioscia	.50	.23	.06
☐ 11 Franklin Stubbs	.50	.23	.06
☐ 12 Mike Davis	.40	.18	.05
☐ 13 Jesse Orosco	.40	.18	.05
☐ 14 John Shelby	.40	.18	.05
☐ 15 Rick Dempsey	.50	.23	.06
☐ 16 Jay Howell	.60	.25	.08
☐ 17 Dave Anderson	.40	.18	.05
☐ 18 Alejandro Pena	.60	.25	.08
☐ 19 Jeff Hamilton	.40	.18	.05
☐ 20 Danny Heep	.40	.18	.05
☐ 21 Tim Leary	.50	.23	.06
☐ 22 Brad Havens	.40	.18	.05
☐ 23 Tim Belcher	.75	.35	.09
☐ 24 Ken Howell	.40	.18	.05
☐ 25 Mickey Hatcher	.40	.18	.05
☐ 26 Brian Holton	.40	.18	.05
☐ 27 Mike Devereaux	.75	.35	.09
☐ 28 Checklist Card Joe Ferguson CO Mark Cresse CO Ron Perranoski CO Bill Russell CO Joe Amalfitano CO Manny Mota CO Ben Hines CO	.50	.23	.06

1988 Mother's Giants

This set consists of 28 full-color, rounded-corner cards each measuring 2 1/2" by 3 1/2". Starter sets (only 20 cards but

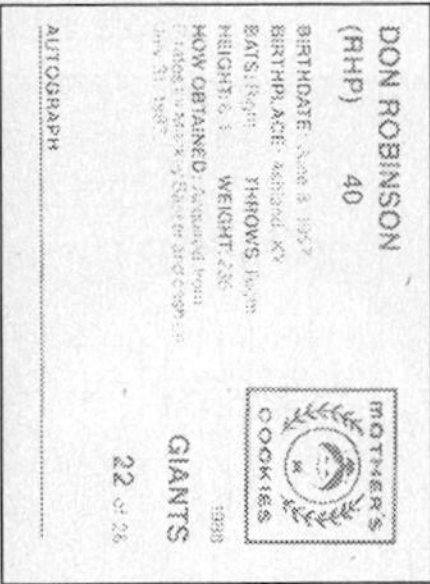

also including a certificate for eight more cards) were given out at the ballpark and collectors were encouraged to trade to fill in the rest of their set. Cards were originally given out at Candlestick Park on July 30th during a game. Photos were taken by Dennis Desprois. The sets were supposedly given out free to the first 35,000 paid admissions at the game.

	MT	EX-MT	VG
COMPLETE SET (28)	11.00	4.90	1.40
COMMON PLAYER (1-28)	.35	.16	.04
☐ 1 Roger Craig MG	.45	.20	.06
☐ 2 Will Clark	3.50	1.55	.45
☐ 3 Kevin Mitchell	1.00	.45	.13
☐ 4 Bob Brenly	.35	.16	.04
☐ 5 Mike Aldrete	.35	.16	.04
☐ 6 Mike Krukow	.35	.16	.04
☐ 7 Candy Maldonado	.60	.25	.08
☐ 8 Jeffrey Leonard	.45	.20	.06
☐ 9 Dave Dravecky	.60	.25	.08
☐ 10 Robby Thompson	.60	.25	.08
☐ 11 Scott Garrelts	.35	.16	.04
☐ 12 Bob Melvin	.35	.16	.04
☐ 13 Jose Uribe	.35	.16	.04
☐ 14 Brett Butler	.75	.35	.09
☐ 15 Rick Reuschel	.45	.20	.06
☐ 16 Harry Spilman	.35	.16	.04
☐ 17 Kelly Downs	.35	.16	.04
☐ 18 Chris Speier	.35	.16	.04
☐ 19 Atlee Hammaker	.35	.16	.04
☐ 20 Joel Youngblood	.35	.16	.04
☐ 21 Mike LaCoss	.35	.16	.04
☐ 22 Don Robinson	.35	.16	.04
☐ 23 Mark Wasinger	.35	.16	.04
☐ 24 Craig Lefferts	.60	.25	.08
☐ 25 Phil Garner	.45	.20	.06
☐ 26 Joe Price	.35	.16	.04
☐ 27 Giants' Coaches Dusty Baker Bill Fahey Bob Lillis Jose Morales Gordie MacKenzie Norm Sherry	.45	.20	.06
☐ 28 Checklist Card Giants NL Champs Logo	.45	.20	.06

1988 Mother's Mariners

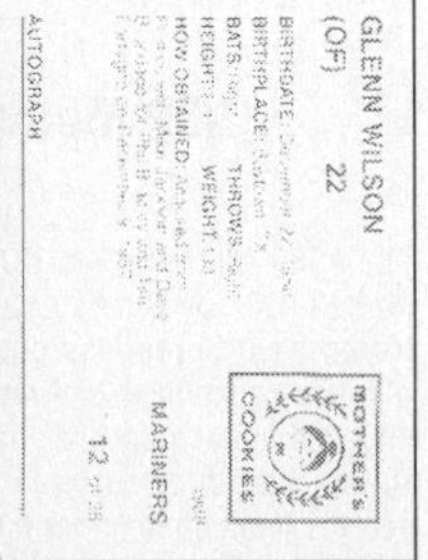

This set consists of 28 full-color, rounded-corner cards each measuring 2 1/2" by 3 1/2". Starter sets (only 20 cards but also including a certificate for eight more cards) were given out at the ballpark and collectors were encouraged to trade to fill in the rest of their set. Cards were originally given out on August 14th at the Seattle Kingdome. Photos were taken by Barry Colla. The sets were supposedly given out free to the first 20,000 paid admissions at the game.

	MT	EX-MT	VG
COMPLETE SET (28)	10.00	4.50	1.25
COMMON PLAYER (1-28)	.40	.18	.05
☐ 1 Dick Williams MG	.40	.18	.05
☐ 2 Alvin Davis	.60	.25	.08
☐ 3 Mike Moore	.60	.25	.08
☐ 4 Jim Presley	.40	.18	.05
☐ 5 Mark Langston	.90	.40	.11
☐ 6 Henry Cotto	.40	.18	.05
☐ 7 Ken Phelps	.50	.23	.06
☐ 8 Steve Trout	.40	.18	.05
☐ 9 David Valle	.40	.18	.05
☐ 10 Harold Reynolds	.60	.25	.08
☐ 11 Edwin Nunez	.40	.18	.05
☐ 12 Glenn Wilson	.40	.18	.05
☐ 13 Scott Bankhead	.60	.25	.08
☐ 14 Scott Bradley	.40	.18	.05
☐ 15 Mickey Brantley	.40	.18	.05
☐ 16 Bruce Fields	.40	.18	.05
☐ 17 Mike Kingery	.40	.18	.05
☐ 18 Mike Campbell	.40	.18	.05
☐ 19 Mike Jackson	.60	.25	.08
☐ 20 Rey Quinones	.40	.18	.05
☐ 21 Mario Diaz	.40	.18	.05
☐ 22 Jerry Reed	.40	.18	.05
☐ 23 Rich Renteria	.40	.18	.05
☐ 24 Julio Solano	.40	.18	.05
☐ 25 Bill Swift	.60	.25	.08
☐ 26 Bill Wilkinson	.40	.18	.05
☐ 27 Mariners Coaches	.40	.18	.05
☐ 28 Checklist Card Henry Genzale EQMG Rick Griffin TR	.50	.23	.06

1988 Mother's McGwire

This regional set consists of 4 full-color, rounded-corner cards each measuring 2 1/2" by 3 1/2" and showing a different pose of Athletics' slugging first baseman Mark McGwire. Cards were originally found in 18 oz. packages of "Big Bags" of Mother's Cookies at stores in the Northern California area in February and March of 1988. The cards are numbered on the back. Card backs are done in red and purple on white card stock.

	MT	EX-MT	VG
COMPLETE SET (4)	12.00	5.50	1.50
COMMON PLAYER (1-4)	4.00	1.80	.50
☐ 1 Mark McGwire (Holding Big Bat)	4.00	1.80	.50
☐ 2 Mark McGwire (Fielding at First Base)	4.00	1.80	.50

	MT	EX-MT	VG
☐ 3 Mark McGwire (Kneeling In On Deck Circle)	4.00	1.80	.50
☐ 4 Mark McGwire (Batting Pose, Waist Up)	4.00	1.80	.50

1988 Mother's Rangers

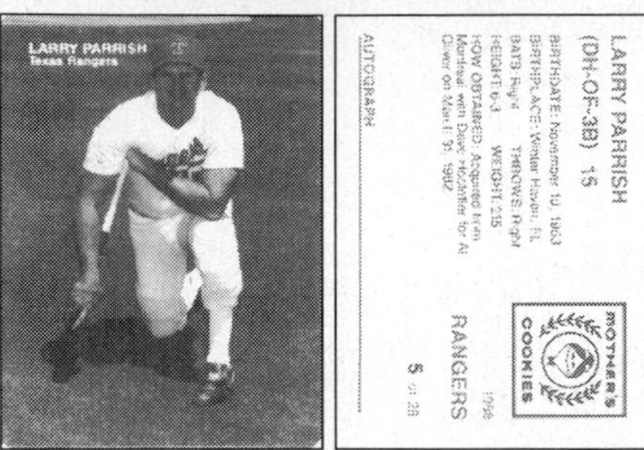

This set consists of 28 full-color, rounded-corner cards each measuring 2 1/2" by 3 1/2". Starter sets (only 20 cards but also including a certificate for eight more cards) were given out at the ballpark and collectors were encouraged to trade to fill in the rest of their set. Cards were originally given out on August 7th. Photos were taken by Barry Colla. The sets were supposedly given out free to the first 25,000 paid admissions at the game.

	MT	EX-MT	VG
COMPLETE SET (28)	10.00	4.50	1.25
COMMON PLAYER (1-28)	.35	.16	.04
☐ 1 Bobby Valentine MG	.45	.20	.06
☐ 2 Pete Incaviglia	.60	.25	.08
☐ 3 Charlie Hough	.45	.20	.06
☐ 4 Oddibe McDowell	.45	.20	.06
☐ 5 Larry Parrish	.45	.20	.06
☐ 6 Scott Fletcher	.35	.16	.04
☐ 7 Steve Buechele	.45	.20	.06
☐ 8 Steve Kemp	.35	.16	.04
☐ 9 Pete O'Brien	.45	.20	.06
☐ 10 Ruben Sierra	1.50	.65	.19
☐ 11 Mike Stanley	.35	.16	.04
☐ 12 Jose Cecena	.35	.16	.04
☐ 13 Cecil Espy	.35	.16	.04
☐ 14 Curtis Wilkerson	.35	.16	.04
☐ 15 Dale Mohorcic	.35	.16	.04
☐ 16 Ray Hayward	.35	.16	.04
☐ 17 Mitch Williams	.45	.20	.06
☐ 18 Bob Brower	.35	.16	.04
☐ 19 Paul Kilgus	.35	.16	.04
☐ 20 Geno Petralli	.35	.16	.04
☐ 21 James Steels	.35	.16	.04
☐ 22 Jerry Browne	.45	.20	.06
☐ 23 Jose Guzman	.60	.25	.08
☐ 24 DeWayne Vaughn	.35	.16	.04
☐ 25 Bobby Witt	.60	.25	.08
☐ 26 Jeff Russell	.50	.23	.06
☐ 27 Rangers' Coaches Richard Egan Tom House Art Howe Davey Lopes David Oliver Tom Robson	.35	.16	.04
☐ 28 Checklist Card Danny Wheat TR Bill Zeigler TR	.35	.16	.04

1989 Mother's A's

The 1989 Mother's Cookies Oakland A's set contains 28 standard-size (2 1/2" by 3 1/2") cards with rounded corners. The fronts have borderless color photos, and the horizontally oriented backs have biographical information. Starter sets containing 20 of these cards were given away at an A's home game during the 1989 season.

	MT	EX-MT	VG
COMPLETE SET (28)	15.00	6.75	1.90
COMMON PLAYER (1-28)	.40	.18	.05
☐ 1 Tony LaRussa MG	.60	.25	.08
☐ 2 Mark McGwire	2.00	.90	.25
☐ 3 Terry Steinbach	.60	.25	.08
☐ 4 Dave Parker	.75	.35	.09
☐ 5 Carney Lansford	.75	.35	.09
☐ 6 Dave Stewart	.75	.35	.09
☐ 7 Jose Canseco	2.50	1.15	.30
☐ 8 Walt Weiss	.60	.25	.08
☐ 9 Bob Welch	.60	.25	.08
☐ 10 Dennis Eckersley	1.25	.55	.16
☐ 11 Tony Phillips	.60	.25	.08
☐ 12 Mike Moore	.60	.25	.08
☐ 13 Dave Henderson	.50	.23	.06
☐ 14 Curt Young	.40	.18	.05
☐ 15 Ron Hassey	.40	.18	.05
☐ 16 Eric Plunk	.40	.18	.05
☐ 17 Luis Polonia	.75	.35	.09
☐ 18 Storm Davis	.50	.23	.06
☐ 19 Glenn Hubbard	.40	.18	.05
☐ 20 Greg Cadaret	.40	.18	.05
☐ 21 Stan Javier	.40	.18	.05
☐ 22 Felix Jose	1.00	.45	.13
☐ 23 Mike Gallego	.40	.18	.05
☐ 24 Todd Burns	.40	.18	.05
☐ 25 Rick Honeycutt	.40	.18	.05
☐ 26 Gene Nelson	.40	.18	.05
☐ 27 A's Coaches Dave Duncan Rene Lachemann Art Kusnyer Dave McKay Tommie Reynolds Merv Rettenmund	.40	.18	.05
☐ 28 Checklist Card Walt Weiss Mark McGwire Jose Canseco	1.25	.55	.16

1989 Mother's A's ROY's

The 1989 Mother's A's ROY's set contains four standard-size (2 1/2" by 3 1/2") cards with rounded corners. The fronts have borderless color photos, and the horizontally oriented backs have biographical information. One card was included in each specially marked box of Mother's Cookies. On the first three cards in the set Rookie of the Year (and year) is mentioned under the player's name.

	MT	EX-MT	VG
COMPLETE SET (4)	12.00	5.50	1.50
COMMON PLAYER (1-4)	2.00	.90	.25
☐ 1 Jose Canseco 1986 ROY	5.00	2.30	.60
☐ 2 Mark McGwire 1987 ROY	4.00	1.80	.50
☐ 3 Walt Weiss 1988 ROY	2.00	.90	.25
☐ 4 Walt Weiss, Mark McGwire, and Jose Canseco	3.00	1.35	.40

1989 Mother's Astros

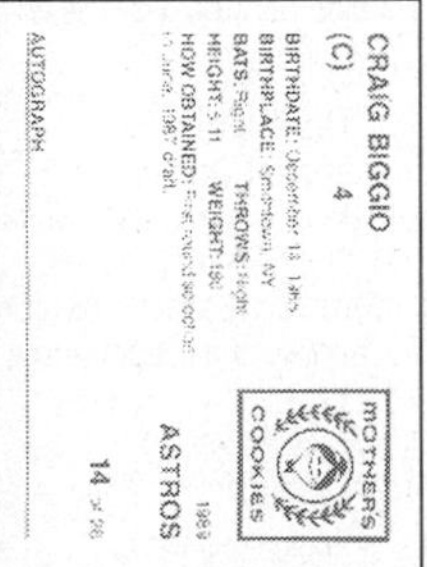

The 1989 Mother's Cookies Houston Astros set contains 28 standard-size (2 1/2" by 3 1/2") cards with rounded corners. The fronts have borderless color photos, and the horizontally oriented backs have biographical information. Starter sets containing 20 of these cards were given away at an Astros home game during the 1989 season.

	MT	EX-MT	VG
COMPLETE SET (28)	10.00	4.50	1.25
COMMON PLAYER (1-28)	.40	.18	.05
☐ 1 Art Howe MG	.50	.23	.06
☐ 2 Mike Scott	.60	.25	.08
☐ 3 Gerald Young	.40	.18	.05
☐ 4 Bill Doran	.50	.23	.06
☐ 5 Billy Hatcher	.40	.18	.05
☐ 6 Terry Puhl	.50	.23	.06
☐ 7 Bob Knepper	.40	.18	.05
☐ 8 Kevin Bass	.50	.23	.06
☐ 9 Glenn Davis	.75	.35	.09
☐ 10 Alan Ashby	.40	.18	.05
☐ 11 Bob Forsch	.40	.18	.05
☐ 12 Greg Gross	.40	.18	.05
☐ 13 Danny Darwin	.40	.18	.05
☐ 14 Craig Biggio	1.25	.55	.16
☐ 15 Jim Clancy	.40	.18	.05
☐ 16 Rafael Ramirez	.40	.18	.05
☐ 17 Alex Trevino	.40	.18	.05
☐ 18 Craig Reynolds	.40	.18	.05
☐ 19 Dave Smith	.50	.23	.06
☐ 20 Larry Andersen	.40	.18	.05
☐ 21 Eric Yelding	.40	.18	.05
☐ 22 Jim Deshaies	.40	.18	.05
☐ 23 Juan Agosto	.40	.18	.05
☐ 24 Rick Rhoden	.40	.18	.05
☐ 25 Ken Caminiti	.75	.35	.09
☐ 26 Dave Meads	.40	.18	.05
☐ 27 Astros Coaches Yogi Berra Ed Napoleon Matt Galante Ed Ott Phil Garner Les Moss	.50	.23	.06
☐ 28 Checklist Card Dave Labossiere TR Doc Ewell TR Dennis Liborio EQMG	.40	.18	.05

1989 Mother's Canseco

The 1989 Mother's Jose Canseco set contains four standard-size (2 1/2" by 3 1/2") cards with rounded corners. The fronts have borderless color photos, and the horizontally oriented backs have biographical information. One card was included in each specially marked box of Mother's Cookies. Since all four cards picture Jose Canseco, the pose is identified parenthetically in the checklist below in order to distinguish the card fronts.

	MT	EX-MT	VG
COMPLETE SET (4)	10.00	4.50	1.25
COMMON PLAYER (1-4)	3.50	1.55	.45
☐ 1 Jose Canseco (Holding ball in hand)	3.50	1.55	.45
☐ 2 Jose Canseco (On one knee with bat)	3.50	1.55	.45
☐ 3 Jose Canseco (Swinging at pitch)	3.50	1.55	.45
☐ 4 Jose Canseco (Running toward second)	3.50	1.55	.45

1989 Mother's Will Clark

The 1989 Mother's Cookies Will Clark set contains four standard-size (2 1/2" by 3 1/2") cards with rounded corners. The fronts have borderless color photos, and the horizontally oriented backs have biographical information. One card was included in each specially marked box of Mother's Cookies. Since all four cards picture Will Clark, the pose is identified parenthetically in the checklist below in order to distinguish the card fronts.

	MT	EX-MT	VG
COMPLETE SET (4)	10.00	4.50	1.25
COMMON PLAYER (1-4)	3.50	1.55	.45

	MT	EX-MT	VG
☐ 1 Will Clark (Ball in glove)	3.50	1.55	.45
☐ 2 Will Clark (Batting stance posed)	3.50	1.55	.45
☐ 3 Will Clark (Swing follow through)	3.50	1.55	.45
☐ 4 Will Clark (Starting toward first after hit, still holding bat)	3.50	1.55	.45

1989 Mother's Dodgers

The 1989 Mother's Los Angeles Dodgers set contains 28 standard-size (2 1/2" by 3 1/2") cards with rounded corners. The fronts have borderless color photos, and the horizontally oriented backs have biographical information. Starter sets containing 20 of these cards were given away at a Dodgers home game during the 1989 season.

	MT	EX-MT	VG
COMPLETE SET (28)	10.00	4.50	1.25
COMMON PLAYER (1-28)	.40	.18	.05
☐ 1 Tom Lasorda MG	.60	.25	.08
☐ 2 Eddie Murray	.90	.40	.11
☐ 3 Mike Scioscia	.50	.23	.06
☐ 4 Fernando Valenzuela	.60	.25	.08
☐ 5 Mike Marshall	.50	.23	.06
☐ 6 Orel Hershiser	.90	.40	.11
☐ 7 Alfredo Griffin	.40	.18	.05
☐ 8 Kirk Gibson	.60	.25	.08
☐ 9 John Tudor	.50	.23	.06
☐ 10 Willie Randolph	.50	.23	.06
☐ 11 Franklin Stubbs	.40	.18	.05
☐ 12 Mike Davis	.40	.18	.05
☐ 13 Mike Morgan	.60	.25	.08
☐ 14 John Shelby	.40	.18	.05
☐ 15 Rick Dempsey	.50	.23	.06
☐ 16 Jay Howell	.50	.23	.06
☐ 17 Dave Anderson	.40	.18	.05
☐ 18 Alejandro Pena	.50	.23	.06
☐ 19 Jeff Hamilton	.40	.18	.05
☐ 20 Ricky Horton	.40	.18	.05
☐ 21 Tim Leary	.40	.18	.05
☐ 22 Ray Searage	.40	.18	.05
☐ 23 Tim Belcher	.75	.35	.09
☐ 24 Tim Crews	.40	.18	.05
☐ 25 Mickey Hatcher	.40	.18	.05
☐ 26 Mariano Duncan	.50	.23	.06
☐ 27 Dodgers Coaches Joe Amalfitano Manny Mota Joe Ferguson Ron Perranoski Bill Russell Mark Cresse Ben Hines	.40	.18	.05
☐ 28 Checklist Card World Championship Trophy	.50	.23	.06

1989 Mother's Giants

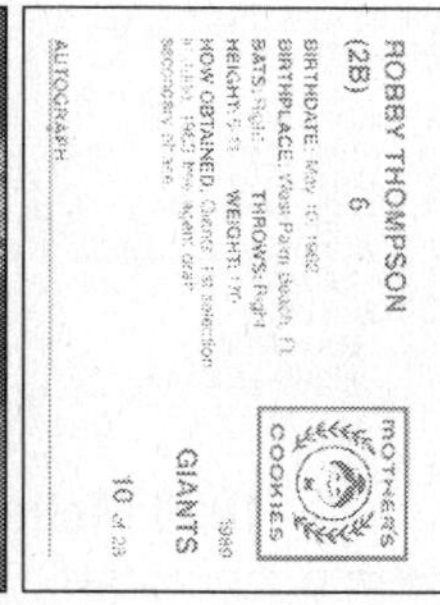

The 1989 Mother's Cookies San Francisco Giants set contains 28 standard-size (2 1/2" by 3 1/2") cards with rounded corners. The fronts have borderless color photos, and the horizontally oriented backs have biographical information. Starter sets containing 20 of these cards were given away at a Giants home game during the 1989 season.

	MT	EX-MT	VG
COMPLETE SET (28)	12.50	5.75	1.55
COMMON PLAYER (1-28)	.40	.18	.05
☐ 1 Roger Craig MG	.50	.23	.06
☐ 2 Will Clark	2.50	1.15	.30
☐ 3 Kevin Mitchell	.90	.40	.11
☐ 4 Kelly Downs	.50	.23	.06
☐ 5 Brett Butler	.75	.35	.09
☐ 6 Mike Krukow	.40	.18	.05
☐ 7 Candy Maldonado	.60	.25	.08
☐ 8 Terry Kennedy	.40	.18	.05
☐ 9 Dave Dravecky	.60	.25	.08
☐ 10 Robby Thompson	.60	.25	.08
☐ 11 Scott Garrelts	.40	.18	.05
☐ 12 Matt Williams	1.25	.55	.16
☐ 13 Jose Uribe	.40	.18	.05
☐ 14 Tracy Jones	.40	.18	.05
☐ 15 Rick Reuschel	.50	.23	.06
☐ 16 Ernest Riles	.40	.18	.05
☐ 17 Jeff Brantley	.50	.23	.06
☐ 18 Chris Speier	.40	.18	.05
☐ 19 Atlee Hammaker	.40	.18	.05
☐ 20 Ed Jurak	.40	.18	.05
☐ 21 Mike LaCoss	.40	.18	.05
☐ 22 Don Robinson	.40	.18	.05
☐ 23 Kirt Manwaring	.40	.18	.05
☐ 24 Craig Lefferts	.60	.25	.08
☐ 25 Donell Nixon	.40	.18	.05
☐ 26 Joe Price	.40	.18	.05
☐ 27 Rich Gossage	.60	.25	.08
☐ 28 Checklist Card Bill Fahey CO Dusty Baker CO Bob Lillis CO Wendell Kim CO Norm Sherry CO	.50	.23	.06

1989 Mother's Griffey Jr.

The 1989 Mother's Cookies Ken Griffey Jr. set contains four standard-size (2 1/2" by 3 1/2") cards with rounded corners. The fronts have borderless color photos, and the horizontally oriented backs have biographical information. One card was included in each specially marked box of Mother's Cookies. Since all four cards picture Ken Griffey Jr., the pose is identified parenthetically in the checklist below in order to distinguish the card fronts. Each card back provides a different aspect or background on Ken and his career. The photos were shot by noted sports photographer Barry Colla.

	MT	EX-MT	VG
COMPLETE SET (4)	16.00	7.25	2.00
COMMON PLAYER (1-4)	4.50	2.00	.55
☐ 1 Ken Griffey Jr. (Arms folded)	4.50	2.00	.55
☐ 2 Ken Griffey Jr. (Baseball in hand)	4.50	2.00	.55
☐ 3 Ken Griffey Jr. (Looking straight ahead with bat)	4.50	2.00	.55
☐ 4 Ken Griffey Jr. (Looking over shoulder with bat)	4.50	2.00	.55

1989 Mother's Mariners

The 1989 Mother's Cookies Seattle Mariners set contains 28 standard-size (2 1/2" by 3 1/2") cards with rounded corners. The fronts have borderless color photos, and the horizontally oriented backs have biographical information. Starter sets containing 20 of these cards were given away at a Mariners home game during the 1989 season.

	MT	EX-MT	VG
COMPLETE SET (28)	18.00	8.00	2.30
COMMON PLAYER (1-28)	.35	.16	.04
☐ 1 Jim Lefebvre MG	.35	.16	.04
☐ 2 Alvin Davis	.60	.25	.08
☐ 3 Ken Griffey Jr.	9.00	4.00	1.15
☐ 4 Jim Presley	.45	.20	.06
☐ 5 Mark Langston	.75	.35	.09
☐ 6 Henry Cotto	.35	.16	.04
☐ 7 Mickey Brantley	.35	.16	.04
☐ 8 Jeffrey Leonard	.45	.20	.06
☐ 9 Dave Valle	.35	.16	.04
☐ 10 Harold Reynolds	.60	.25	.08
☐ 11 Edgar Martinez	2.50	1.15	.30
☐ 12 Tom Niedenfuer	.35	.16	.04
☐ 13 Scott Bankhead	.60	.25	.08
☐ 14 Scott Bradley	.35	.16	.04
☐ 15 Omar Vizquel	.75	.35	.09
☐ 16 Erik Hanson	.90	.40	.11
☐ 17 Bill Swift	.60	.25	.08
☐ 18 Mike Campbell	.35	.16	.04
☐ 19 Mike Jackson	.45	.20	.06
☐ 20 Rich Renteria	.35	.16	.04
☐ 21 Mario Diaz	.35	.16	.04
☐ 22 Jerry Reed	.35	.16	.04
☐ 23 Darnell Coles	.45	.20	.06
☐ 24 Steve Trout	.35	.16	.04
☐ 25 Mike Schooler	.60	.25	.08
☐ 26 Julio Solano	.35	.16	.04
☐ 27 Mariners Coaches Mike Paul Gene Clines Bill Plummer Bob Didier Rusty Kuntz	.35	.16	.04
☐ 28 Checklist Card Henry Genzale EQMG Rick Griffin TR	.35	.16	.04

1989 Mother's McGwire

The 1989 Mother's Cookies Mark McGwire set contains four standard-size (2 1/2" by 3 1/2") cards with rounded corners. The fronts have borderless color photos, and the horizontally oriented backs have biographical information. One card was included in each specially marked box of Mother's Cookies. Since all four cards picture Mark McGwire, the pose is identified parenthetically in the checklist below in order to distinguish the card fronts.

	MT	EX-MT	VG
COMPLETE SET (4)	10.00	4.50	1.25
COMMON PLAYER (1-4)	3.00	1.35	.40
☐ 1 Mark McGwire (Bat on shoulder)	3.00	1.35	.40
☐ 2 Mark McGwire (Batting stance)	3.00	1.35	.40
☐ 3 Mark McGwire (Holding bat in front)	3.00	1.35	.40
☐ 4 Mark McGwire (Batting, follow through)	3.00	1.35	.40

1989 Mother's Rangers

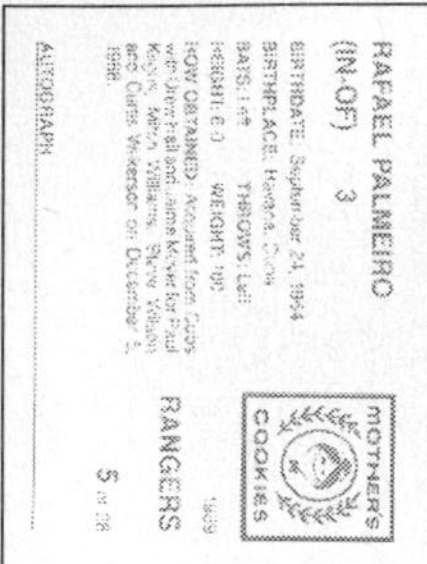

RAFAEL PALMEIRO
(IN-OF) 3
MOTHER'S
COOKIES
RANGERS

The 1989 Mother's Cookies Texas Rangers set contains 28 standard-size (2 1/2" by 3 1/2") cards with rounded corners. The fronts have borderless color photos, and the horizontally oriented backs have biographical information. Starter sets containing 20 of these cards were given away at a Rangers home game during the 1989 season.

	MT	EX-MT	VG
COMPLETE SET (28)	12.50	5.75	1.55
COMMON PLAYER (1-28)	.35	.16	.04
☐ 1 Bobby Valentine MG	.45	.20	.06
☐ 2 Nolan Ryan	5.00	2.30	.60
☐ 3 Julio Franco	1.00	.45	.13
☐ 4 Charlie Hough	.45	.20	.06
☐ 5 Rafael Palmeiro	1.50	.65	.19
☐ 6 Jeff Russell	.45	.20	.06
☐ 7 Ruben Sierra	1.50	.65	.19
☐ 8 Steve Buechele	.45	.20	.06
☐ 9 Buddy Bell	.45	.20	.06
☐ 10 Pete Incaviglia	.45	.20	.06
☐ 11 Geno Petralli	.35	.16	.04
☐ 12 Cecil Espy	.35	.16	.04
☐ 13 Scott Fletcher	.35	.16	.04
☐ 14 Bobby Witt	.60	.25	.08
☐ 15 Brad Arnsberg	.35	.16	.04
☐ 16 Rick Leach	.35	.16	.04
☐ 17 Jamie Moyer	.35	.16	.04
☐ 18 Kevin Brown	1.00	.45	.13
☐ 19 Jeff Kunkel	.35	.16	.04
☐ 20 Craig McMurtry	.35	.16	.04
☐ 21 Kenny Rogers	.45	.20	.06
☐ 22 Mike Stanley	.35	.16	.04
☐ 23 Cecilio Guante	.35	.16	.04
☐ 24 Jim Sundberg	.45	.20	.06
☐ 25 Jose Guzman	.60	.25	.08
☐ 26 Jeff Stone	.35	.16	.04
☐ 27 Rangers' Coaches Dick Egan Tom House Toby Harrah Davey Lopes Dave Oliver Tom Robson	.35	.16	.04
☐ 28 Checklist Card Danny Wheat TR Bill Ziegler TR	.35	.16	.04

1990 Mother's Astros

GLENN DAVIS
(INF) 27
MOTHER'S
COOKIES
ASTROS
2 of 28

This standard-size, 2 1/2" by 3 1/2", 28-card set features members of the 1990 Houston Astros. This set features the traditional rounded corners and has biographical information about each player on the back. These Astros cards were given away on July 15th to the first 25,000 fans at the Astrodome. They were distributed in 20 card random packets at the game and eight more at the redemption booths. However, both groups of cards were random and there was no guarantee of getting a complete set in the cards. The promotional idea was that the only way one could finish the set was to trade for them. The certificates of redemption for eight were redeemable at the major card show at the AstroArena on August 24-26, 1990.

	MT	EX-MT	VG
COMPLETE SET (28)	10.00	4.50	1.25
COMMON PLAYER (1-28)	.35	.16	.04
☐ 1 Art Howe MG	.45	.20	.06
☐ 2 Glenn Davis	.75	.35	.09
☐ 3 Eric Anthony	1.00	.45	.13
☐ 4 Mike Scott	.60	.25	.08
☐ 5 Craig Biggio	.75	.35	.09
☐ 6 Ken Caminiti	.60	.25	.08
☐ 7 Bill Doran	.45	.20	.06
☐ 8 Gerald Young	.35	.16	.04
☐ 9 Terry Puhl	.45	.20	.06
☐ 10 Mark Portugal	.35	.16	.04
☐ 11 Mark Davidson	.35	.16	.04
☐ 12 Jim Deshaies	.35	.16	.04
☐ 13 Bill Gullickson	.45	.20	.06
☐ 14 Franklin Stubbs	.45	.20	.06
☐ 15 Danny Darwin	.35	.16	.04
☐ 16 Ken Oberkfell	.35	.16	.04
☐ 17 Dave Smith	.45	.20	.06
☐ 18 Dan Schatzeder	.35	.16	.04
☐ 19 Rafael Ramirez	.35	.16	.04
☐ 20 Larry Andersen	.35	.16	.04
☐ 21 Alex Trevino	.35	.16	.04
☐ 22 Glenn Wilson	.35	.16	.04
☐ 23 Jim Clancy	.35	.16	.04
☐ 24 Eric Yelding	.35	.16	.04
☐ 25 Casey Candaele	.35	.16	.04
☐ 26 Juan Agosto	.35	.16	.04
☐ 27 Coaches Card Billy Bowman Bob Cluck Phil Garner Matt Galante Ed Napoleon Rudy Jaramillo	.35	.16	.04
☐ 28 Personnel Card Dave Labossiere TR Dennis Liborio EQ.MG Doc Ewell TR	.35	.16	.04

1990 Mother's Athletics

1990 Mother's Cookies Oakland Athletics set contains 28 cards measuring standard size, 2 1/2" by 3 1/2", with rounded corners. The envelope containing the cards honors the 1989 World Championship Oakland Athletics. The A's cards were released at the July 22nd game to the first 35,000 fans to walk through the gates. They were distributed in 20-card random packets at the game and eight more at the redemption booths. However, both groups of cards were random and there was no guarantee of getting a complete set in the cards. The promotional idea was that the only way one could finish the set was to trade for them. The redemption certificates were to be used at the Labor Day San Francisco card show. In addition to this the Mother's Giants cards were also redeemable at that show.

	MT	EX-MT	VG
COMPLETE SET (28)	12.50	5.75	1.55
COMMON PLAYER (1-28)	.35	.16	.04
☐ 1 Tony LaRussa MG	.60	.25	.08
☐ 2 Mark McGwire	1.50	.65	.19
☐ 3 Terry Steinbach	.45	.20	.06
☐ 4 Rickey Henderson	1.50	.65	.19
☐ 5 Dave Stewart	.75	.35	.09
☐ 6 Jose Canseco	2.00	.90	.25
☐ 7 Dennis Eckersley	1.00	.45	.13
☐ 8 Carney Lansford	.60	.25	.08
☐ 9 Mike Moore	.60	.25	.08
☐ 10 Walt Weiss	.60	.25	.08
☐ 11 Scott Sanderson	.45	.20	.06
☐ 12 Ron Hassey	.35	.16	.04
☐ 13 Rick Honeycutt	.35	.16	.04
☐ 14 Ken Phelps	.35	.16	.04
☐ 15 Jamie Quirk	.35	.16	.04
☐ 16 Bob Welch	.60	.25	.08
☐ 17 Felix Jose	.75	.35	.09
☐ 18 Dave Henderson	.45	.20	.06
☐ 19 Mike Norris	.35	.16	.04
☐ 20 Todd Burns	.35	.16	.04
☐ 21 Lance Blankenship	.35	.16	.04
☐ 22 Gene Nelson	.35	.16	.04
☐ 23 Stan Javier	.35	.16	.04
☐ 24 Curt Young	.35	.16	.04
☐ 25 Mike Gallego	.35	.16	.04
☐ 26 Joe Klink	.35	.16	.04
☐ 27 A's Coaches Rene Lachemann Dave Duncan Merv Rettenmund Tommie Reynolds Art Kusnyer Dave McKay	.35	.16	.04
☐ 28 Checklist Card A's Personnel Larry Davis, TR Steve Vuchinch, Visiting Club Mgr. Frank Cienscyk, Equipment Mgr. Barry Weinberg, TR	.35	.16	.04

1990 Mother's Canseco

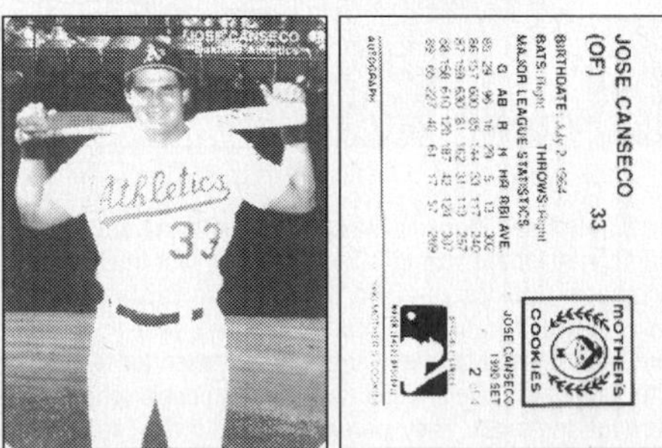

This is a standard Mother's Cookies set with four cards each measuring 2 1/2" by 3 1/2" with rounded corners issued to capitalize on Jose Canseco's popularity. This four-card set features Canseco in various batting poses.

	MT	EX-MT	VG
COMPLETE SET (4)	10.00	4.50	1.25
COMMON PLAYER (1-4)	3.50	1.55	.45
☐ 1 Jose Canseco (Sitting with bat over shoulders)	3.50	1.55	.45
☐ 2 Jose Canseco (Standing with bat behind shoulders)	3.50	1.55	.45
☐ 3 Jose Canseco (Batting Pose)	3.50	1.55	.45
☐ 4 Jose Canseco (Sitting on dugout steps)	3.50	1.55	.45

1990 Mother's Will Clark

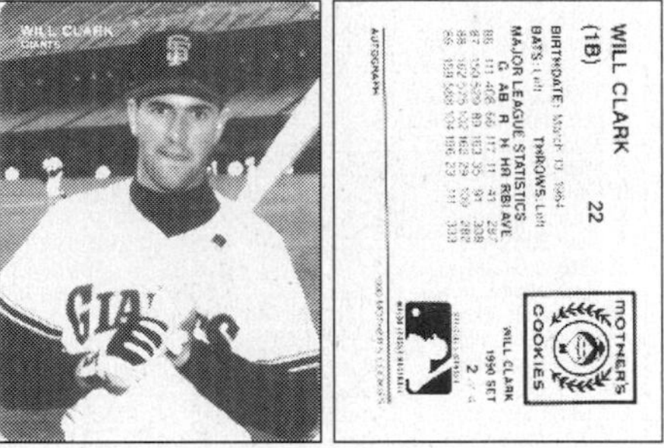

This is a standard Mother's Cookies set with four cards each measuring 2 1/2" by 3 1/2" with rounded corners issued to capitalize on Will Clark's popularity. This four-card set features Clark in various poses as indicated in the checklist below.

	MT	EX-MT	VG
COMPLETE SET (4)	10.00	4.50	1.25
COMMON PLAYER (1-4)	3.50	1.55	.45
☐ 1 Will Clark (Batting pose looking over right shoulder)	3.50	1.55	.45
☐ 2 Will Clark (Holding bat on left shoulder)	3.50	1.55	.45
☐ 3 Will Clark (Holding bat ready to swing)	3.50	1.55	.45
☐ 4 Will Clark (Standing with bat behind shoulders)	3.50	1.55	.45

1990 Mother's Dodgers

The 1990 Mother's Cookies Los Angeles Dodgers set contains 28 cards (2 1/2" by 3 1/2") issued with rounded corners and beautiful full color fronts with biographical information on the back. These Dodgers cards were given away at Chavez Ravine to all fans fourteen and under at the August 19th game. They were distributed in 20-card random packets at the game and eight more at the redemption booths. However, both groups of cards were random and there was no guarantee of getting a complete set in the cards. The promotional idea was that the only way one could

finish the set was to trade for them. The redemption for eight more cards was done at the 22nd Annual Labor Day card show at the Anaheim Convention Center.

	MT	EX-MT	VG
COMPLETE SET (28)	10.00	4.50	1.25
COMMON PLAYER (1-28)	.35	.16	.04
☐ 1 Tom Lasorda MG	.60	.25	.08
☐ 2 Fernando Valenzuela	.60	.25	.08
☐ 3 Kal Daniels	.45	.20	.06
☐ 4 Mike Scioscia	.45	.20	.06
☐ 5 Eddie Murray	.75	.35	.09
☐ 6 Mickey Hatcher	.35	.16	.04
☐ 7 Juan Samuel	.45	.20	.06
☐ 8 Alfredo Griffin	.35	.16	.04
☐ 9 Tim Belcher	.60	.25	.08
☐ 10 Hubie Brooks	.45	.20	.06
☐ 11 Jose Gonzalez	.35	.16	.04
☐ 12 Orel Hershiser	.90	.40	.11
☐ 13 Kirk Gibson	.60	.25	.08
☐ 14 Chris Gwynn	.45	.20	.06
☐ 15 Jay Howell	.45	.20	.06
☐ 16 Rick Dempsey	.35	.16	.04
☐ 17 Ramon Martinez	1.25	.55	.16
☐ 18 Lenny Harris	.45	.20	.06
☐ 19 John Wetteland	.60	.25	.08
☐ 20 Mike Sharperson	.45	.20	.06
☐ 21 Mike Morgan	.45	.20	.06
☐ 22 Ray Searage	.35	.16	.04
☐ 23 Jeff Hamilton	.35	.16	.04
☐ 24 Jim Gott	.35	.16	.04
☐ 25 John Shelby	.35	.16	.04
☐ 26 Tim Crews	.35	.16	.04
☐ 27 Don Aase	.35	.16	.04
☐ 28 Dodger Coaches	.35	.16	.04
Joe Ferguson			
Ron Perranoski			
Mark Cresse			
Ben Hines			
Joe Amalfitano			
Bill Russell			
Manny Mota			

1990 Mother's Giants

The 1990 Mother's Cookies San Francisco Giants set features cards with rounded corners measuring 2 1/2" by 3 1/2". The cards have full-color fronts and biographical information with no stats on the back. The Giants cards were given away at the July 29th game to the first 25,000 children 14 and under. They were distributed in 20-card random packets at the game and eight more at the redemption booths. However, both groups of cards were random and there was no guarantee of getting a complete set in the cards. The promotional idea was that the only way one could finish the set was to trade for them. The redemption certificates were to be used at the Labor Day San Francisco card show. In addition to this the Mother's A's cards were also redeemable at that show.

	MT	EX-MT	VG
COMPLETE SET (28)	11.00	4.90	1.40
COMMON PLAYER (1-28)	.35	.16	.04
☐ 1 Roger Craig MG	.45	.20	.06
☐ 2 Will Clark	2.00	.90	.25
☐ 3 Gary Carter	.75	.35	.09
☐ 4 Kelly Downs	.35	.16	.04
☐ 5 Kevin Mitchell	.90	.40	.11
☐ 6 Steve Bedrosian	.35	.16	.04
☐ 7 Brett Butler	.60	.25	.08
☐ 8 Rick Reuschel	.45	.20	.06
☐ 9 Matt Williams	1.00	.45	.13
☐ 10 Robby Thompson	.45	.20	.06
☐ 11 Mike LaCoss	.35	.16	.04
☐ 12 Terry Kennedy	.35	.16	.04
☐ 13 Atlee Hammaker	.35	.16	.04
☐ 14 Rick Leach	.35	.16	.04
☐ 15 Ernest Riles	.35	.16	.04
☐ 16 Scott Garrelts	.45	.20	.06
☐ 17 Jose Uribe	.35	.16	.04
☐ 18 Greg Litton	.35	.16	.04
☐ 19 Dave Anderson	.35	.16	.04
☐ 20 Don Robinson	.35	.16	.04
☐ 21 Giants Coaches	.45	.20	.06
Dusty Baker			
Bob Lillis			
Bill Fahey			
Norm Sherry			
Wendall Kim			
☐ 22 Bill Bathe	.35	.16	.04
☐ 23 Randy O'Neal	.35	.16	.04
☐ 24 Kevin Bass	.45	.20	.06
☐ 25 Jeff Brantley	.45	.20	.06
☐ 26 John Burkett	.75	.35	.09
☐ 27 Ernie Camacho	.35	.16	.04
☐ 28 Checklist Card	.45	.20	.06

1990 Mother's Mariners

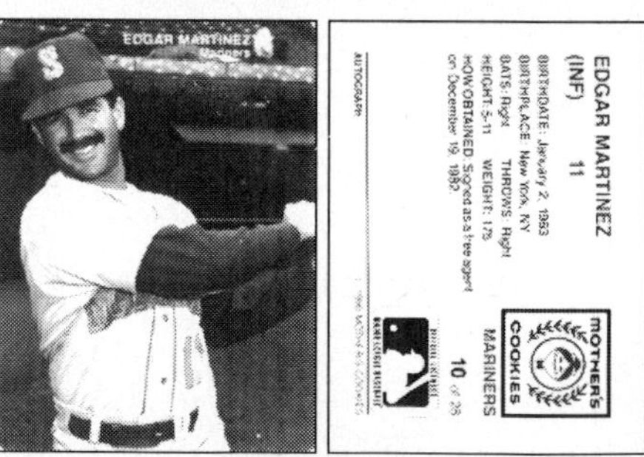

1990 Mother's Cookies Seattle Mariners set contains 28 cards in standard size (2 1/2" by 3 1/2") with the traditional Mother's Cookies rounded corners. The cards have full-color fronts and biographical information with no stats on the back. These Mariners cards were released for the August 5th game and given to the first 25,000 people who passed through the gates. They were distributed in 20-card random packets at the game and eight more at the redemption booths. However, both groups of cards were random and there was no guarantee of getting a complete set in the cards. The promotional idea was that the only way one could finish the set was to trade for them. The redemption for eight more cards were available at the Kingdome Card Show on August 12, 1990.

	MT	EX-MT	VG
COMPLETE SET (28)	11.00	4.90	1.40
COMMON PLAYER (1-28)	.35	.16	.04
☐ 1 Jim Lefebvre MG	.45	.20	.06
☐ 2 Alvin Davis	.60	.25	.08
☐ 3 Ken Griffey Jr.	5.00	2.30	.60
☐ 4 Jeffrey Leonard	.45	.20	.06
☐ 5 David Valle	.35	.16	.04
☐ 6 Harold Reynolds	.60	.25	.08
☐ 7 Jay Buhner	.75	.35	.09
☐ 8 Erik Hanson	.60	.25	.08
☐ 9 Henry Cotto	.35	.16	.04
☐ 10 Edgar Martinez	1.25	.55	.16
☐ 11 Bill Swift	.60	.25	.08
☐ 12 Omar Vizquel	.60	.25	.08
☐ 13 Randy Johnson	.75	.35	.09
☐ 14 Greg Briley	.45	.20	.06
☐ 15 Gene Harris	.35	.16	.04
☐ 16 Matt Young	.35	.16	.04
☐ 17 Pete O'Brien	.45	.20	.06
☐ 18 Brent Knackert	.45	.20	.06
☐ 19 Mike Jackson	.45	.20	.06
☐ 20 Brian Holman	.60	.25	.08
☐ 21 Mike Schooler	.60	.25	.08
☐ 22 Darnell Coles	.45	.20	.06
☐ 23 Keith Comstock	.35	.16	.04
☐ 24 Scott Bankhead	.45	.20	.06
☐ 25 Scott Bradley	.35	.16	.04
☐ 26 Mike Brumley	.35	.16	.04
☐ 27 Mariners Coaches Rusty Kuntz Gene Clines Bill Plummer Mike Paul Bob Didier	.35	.16	.04
☐ 28 Checklist Card Mariners Personnel Henry Genzale EQ.MG Tom Newberg ATR Rick Griffin TR	.35	.16	.04

1990 Mother's McGwire

This is a standard Mother's Cookies set with four cards each measuring 2 1/2" by 3 1/2" with rounded corners issued to capitalize on Mark McGwire's popularity. This four-card set features McGwire in various poses as indicated in the checklist below.

	MT	EX-MT	VG
COMPLETE SET (4)	10.00	4.50	1.25
COMMON PLAYER (1-4)	3.00	1.35	.40
☐ 1 Mark McGwire (Standing with bat on right shoulder)	3.00	1.35	.40
☐ 2 Mark McGwire (Standing in dugout with bat in front)	3.00	1.35	.40
☐ 3 Mark McGwire (Fielding pose)	3.00	1.35	.40
☐ 4 Mark McGwire (Sitting on dugout steps)	3.00	1.35	.40

1990 Mother's Rangers

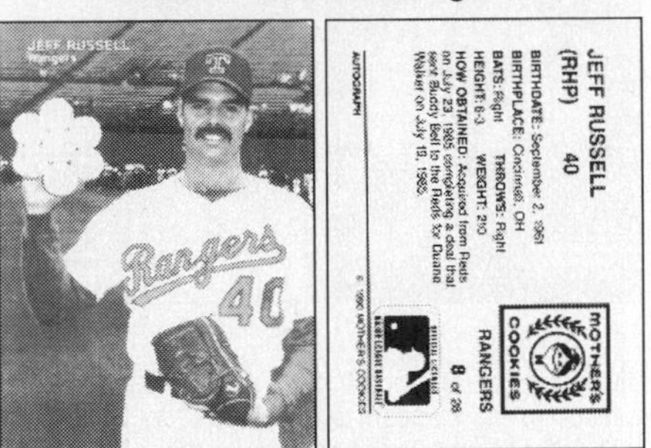

This 28-card, standard-size, 2 1/2" by 3 1/2", set features members of the 1990 Texas Rangers. The set has beautiful full-color photos on the front along with biographical information on the back. The set also features the now traditional Mother's Cookies rounded corners. The Rangers cards were distributed on July 22nd to the first 25,000 game attendees in Arlington. They were distributed in 20-card random packets at the game and eight more at the redemption booths. However, both groups of cards were random and there was no guarantee of getting a complete set in the cards. The promotional idea was that the only way one could finish the set was to trade for them. The certificates to redeem the cards for eigth more cards were able to be redeemed at the 17th annual Dallas Card Convention on August 18-19, 1990.

	MT	EX-MT	VG
COMPLETE SET (28)	11.00	4.90	1.40
COMMON PLAYER (1-28)	.35	.16	.04
☐ 1 Bobby Valentine MG	.45	.20	.06
☐ 2 Nolan Ryan	3.50	1.55	.45
☐ 3 Ruben Sierra	1.25	.55	.16
☐ 4 Pete Incaviglia	.45	.20	.06
☐ 5 Charlie Hough	.45	.20	.06
☐ 6 Harold Baines	.45	.20	.06
☐ 7 Gino Petralli	.35	.16	.04
☐ 8 Jeff Russell	.45	.20	.06
☐ 9 Rafael Palmiero	.90	.40	.11
☐ 10 Julio Franco	.75	.35	.09
☐ 11 Jack Daugherty	.35	.16	.04
☐ 12 Gary Pettis	.35	.16	.04
☐ 13 Brian Bohanon	.45	.20	.06
☐ 14 Steve Buechele	.45	.20	.06
☐ 15 Bobby Witt	.60	.25	.08
☐ 16 Thad Bosley	.35	.16	.04
☐ 17 Gary Mielke	.35	.16	.04
☐ 18 Jeff Kunkel	.35	.16	.04
☐ 19 Mike Jeffcoat	.35	.16	.04
☐ 20 Mike Stanley	.35	.16	.04
☐ 21 Kevin Brown	.75	.35	.09
☐ 22 Kenny Rogers	.35	.16	.04
☐ 23 Jeff Huson	.35	.16	.04
☐ 24 Jamie Moyer	.35	.16	.04
☐ 25 Cecil Espy	.35	.16	.04
☐ 26 John Russell	.35	.16	.04
☐ 27 Coaches Card Dave Oliver Davey Lopes Tom Robson Tom House Toby Harrah	.35	.16	.04
☐ 28 Trainers Card Bill Zeigler TR Joe Macko EQ.MG. Marty Stajduhar, Strength and Cond. Danny Wheat ATR	.35	.16	.04

1990 Mother's Ryan

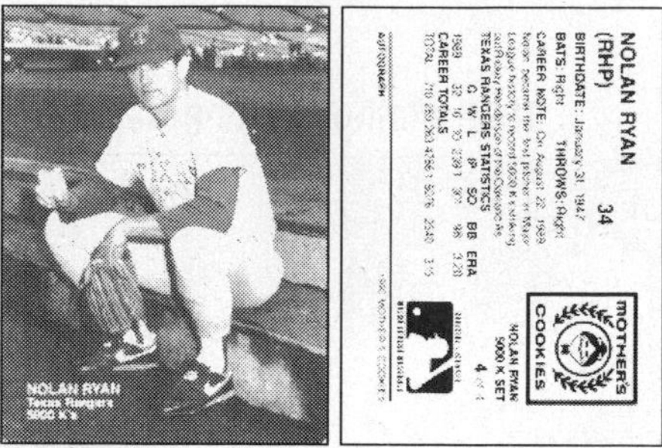

This is a typical Mother's Cookies set with four cards each measuring the standard size of 2 1/2" by 3 1/2" with rounded corners honoring Ryan's more than 5,000 strikeouts over his career. This four-card set features Ryan in various pitching poses. The second card in the set is considered tougher to find than the other three in the set.

	MT	EX-MT	VG
COMPLETE SET (4)	12.50	5.75	1.55
COMMON PLAYER (1-4)	3.50	1.55	.45
☐ 1 Nolan Ryan (Holding ball)	3.50	1.55	.45
☐ 2 Nolan Ryan (Dugout pose)	5.00	2.30	.60
☐ 3 Nolan Ryan (Holding ball behind waist)	3.50	1.55	.45
☐ 4 Nolan Ryan (Holding ball with 5,000 K's)	3.50	1.55	.45

1990 Mother's Matt Williams

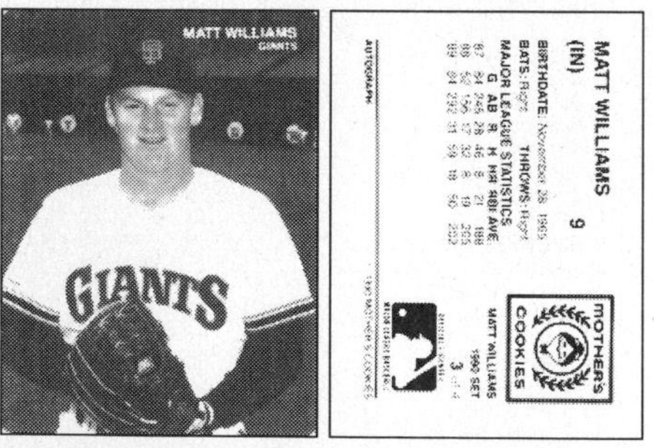

This is a standard Mother's Cookies set with four cards each measuring 2 1/2" by 3 1/2" with rounded corners issued to capitalize on Matt Williams' popularity. This four-card set features Williams in various poses as indicated in the checklist below.

	MT	EX-MT	VG
COMPLETE SET (4)	9.00	4.00	1.15
COMMON PLAYER (1-4)	3.00	1.35	.40
☐ 1 Matt Williams (Standing with bat on right shoulder)	3.00	1.35	.40
☐ 2 Matt Williams (Smiling batting pose)	3.00	1.35	.40
☐ 3 Matt Williams (Posing with glove)	3.00	1.35	.40
☐ 4 Matt Williams (Fielding pose with glove between legs)	3.00	1.35	.40

1991 Mother's Astros

The 1991 Mother's Cookies Houston Astros set contains 28 cards with rounded corners measuring the standard size (2 1/2" by 3 1/2"). The front design has borderless glossy color player photos from the waist up. The horizontally oriented backs are printed in red and purple, present biographical information, and have blank slots for player autographs. The cards are numbered on the back.

	MT	EX-MT	VG
COMPLETE SET (28)	10.00	4.50	1.25
COMMON PLAYER (1-28)	.35	.16	.04
☐ 1 Art Howe MG	.45	.20	.06
☐ 2 Steve Finley	.60	.25	.08
☐ 3 Pete Harnisch	.60	.25	.08
☐ 4 Mike Scott	.60	.25	.08
☐ 5 Craig Biggio	.75	.35	.09
☐ 6 Ken Caminiti	.60	.25	.08
☐ 7 Eric Yelding	.35	.16	.04
☐ 8 Jeff Bagwell	2.50	1.15	.30
☐ 9 Jim Deshaies	.35	.16	.04
☐ 10 Mark Portugal	.35	.16	.04
☐ 11 Mark Davidson	.35	.16	.04
☐ 12 Jimmy Jones	.35	.16	.04
☐ 13 Luis Gonzalez	1.00	.45	.13
☐ 14 Karl Rhodes	.35	.16	.04
☐ 15 Curt Schilling	.60	.25	.08
☐ 16 Ken Oberkfell	.35	.16	.04
☐ 17 Mark McLemore	.45	.20	.06
☐ 18 Dave Rohde	.35	.16	.04
☐ 19 Rafael Ramirez	.35	.16	.04
☐ 20 Al Osuna	.45	.20	.06
☐ 21 Jim Corsi	.35	.16	.04
☐ 22 Carl Nichols	.35	.16	.04
☐ 23 Jim Clancy	.35	.16	.04
☐ 24 Dwayne Henry	.45	.20	.06
☐ 25 Casey Candaele	.35	.16	.04
☐ 26 Xavier Hernandez	.45	.20	.06
☐ 27 Darryl Kile	.60	.25	.08
☐ 28 Checklist Card Phil Garner CO Bob Cluck CO Ed Ott CO Matt Galante CO Rudy Jaramillo CO	.45	.20	.06

1991 Mother's Athletics

The 1991 Mother's Cookies Oakland Athletics set contains 28 cards with rounded corners measuring the standard size (2 1/2" by 3 1/2"). The set includes an additional card advertising a trading card collectors album. The front design has borderless glossy color player photos from the waist up. The horizontally oriented backs are printed in red and

purple, present biographical information, and have blank slots for player autographs. The cards are numbered on the back.

	MT	EX-MT	VG
COMPLETE SET (28)	11.00	4.90	1.40
COMMON PLAYER (1-28)	.35	.16	.04
☐ 1 Tony LaRussa MG	.60	.25	.08
☐ 2 Mark McGwire	1.50	.65	.19
☐ 3 Terry Steinbach	.45	.20	.06
☐ 4 Rickey Henderson	1.50	.65	.19
☐ 5 Dave Stewart	.60	.25	.08
☐ 6 Jose Canseco	2.00	.90	.25
☐ 7 Dennis Eckersley	.75	.35	.09
☐ 8 Carney Lansford	.45	.20	.06
☐ 9 Bob Welch	.45	.20	.06
☐ 10 Walt Weiss	.45	.20	.06
☐ 11 Mike Moore	.45	.20	.06
☐ 12 Vance Law	.35	.16	.04
☐ 13 Rick Honeycutt	.35	.16	.04
☐ 14 Harold Baines	.45	.20	.06
☐ 15 Jamie Quirk	.35	.16	.04
☐ 16 Ernest Riles	.35	.16	.04
☐ 17 Willie Wilson	.45	.20	.06
☐ 18 Dave Henderson	.45	.20	.06
☐ 19 Kirk Dressendorfer	.45	.20	.06
☐ 20 Todd Burns	.35	.16	.04
☐ 21 Lance Blankenship	.35	.16	.04
☐ 22 Gene Nelson	.35	.16	.04
☐ 23 Eric Show	.35	.16	.04
☐ 24 Curt Young	.35	.16	.04
☐ 25 Mike Gallego	.35	.16	.04
☐ 26 Joe Klink	.35	.16	.04
☐ 27 Steve Chitren	.35	.16	.04
☐ 28 Checklist Card Tommie Reynolds CO Art Kusnyer CO Reggie Jackson CO Rick Burleson CO Rene Lachemann CO Dave Duncan CO Dave McKay CO	.45	.20	.06

1991 Mother's Dodgers

The 1991 Mother's Cookies Los Angeles Dodgers set contains 28 cards with rounded corners measuring the standard size (2 1/2" by 3 1/2"). The front design has borderless glossy color player photos. The horizontally oriented backs are printed in red and purple, present biographical information, and have blank slots for player autographs. The cards are numbered on the back.

	MT	EX-MT	VG
COMPLETE SET (28)	10.00	4.50	1.25
COMMON PLAYER (1-28)	.35	.16	.04
☐ 1 Tom Lasorda MG	.60	.25	.08
☐ 2 Darryl Strawberry	1.25	.55	.16
☐ 3 Kal Daniels	.45	.20	.06
☐ 4 Mike Scioscia	.45	.20	.06
☐ 5 Eddie Murray	.75	.35	.09
☐ 6 Brett Butler	.60	.25	.08
☐ 7 Juan Samuel	.45	.20	.06
☐ 8 Alfredo Griffin	.35	.16	.04
☐ 9 Tim Belcher	.45	.20	.06
☐ 10 Ramon Martinez	.75	.35	.09
☐ 11 Jose Gonzalez	.35	.16	.04
☐ 12 Orel Hershiser	.75	.35	.09
☐ 13 Bob Ojeda	.45	.20	.06
☐ 14 Chris Gwynn	.35	.16	.04
☐ 15 Jay Howell	.45	.20	.06
☐ 16 Gary Carter	.60	.25	.08
☐ 17 Kevin Gross	.35	.16	.04
☐ 18 Lenny Harris	.45	.20	.06
☐ 19 Mike Hartley	.35	.16	.04
☐ 20 Mike Sharperson	.45	.20	.06
☐ 21 Mike Morgan	.45	.20	.06
☐ 22 John Candelaria	.35	.16	.04
☐ 23 Jeff Hamilton	.35	.16	.04
☐ 24 Jim Gott	.35	.16	.04
☐ 25 Barry Lyons	.35	.16	.04
☐ 26 Tim Crews	.35	.16	.04
☐ 27 Stan Javier	.35	.16	.04
☐ 28 Checklist Card Joe Ferguson CO Ben Hines CO Mark Cresse CO Joe Amalfitano CO Ron Perranoski CO Manny Mota CO Bill Russell CO	.35	.16	.04

1991 Mother's Giants

The 1991 Mother's Cookies San Francisco Giants set contains 28 cards with rounded corners measuring the standard size (2 1/2" by 3 1/2"). The set includes an additional card advertising a trading card collectors album. The front design has borderless glossy color player photos from the waist up. The horizontally oriented backs are printed in red and purple, present biographical information, and have blank slots for player autographs. The cards are numbered on the back.

	MT	EX-MT	VG
COMPLETE SET (28)	10.00	4.50	1.25
COMMON PLAYER (1-28)	.35	.16	.04
☐ 1 Roger Craig MG	.45	.20	.06
☐ 2 Will Clark	2.00	.90	.25
☐ 3 Steve Decker	.60	.25	.08
☐ 4 Kelly Downs	.35	.16	.04
☐ 5 Kevin Mitchell	.75	.35	.09

☐ 6 Willie McGee	.45	.20	.06
☐ 7 Bud Black	.35	.16	.04
☐ 8 Dave Righetti	.35	.16	.04
☐ 9 Matt Williams	.75	.35	.09
☐ 10 Robby Thompson	.45	.20	.06
☐ 11 Mike LaCoss	.35	.16	.04
☐ 12 Terry Kennedy	.35	.16	.04
☐ 13 Mark Leonard	.35	.16	.04
☐ 14 Rick Reuschel	.45	.20	.06
☐ 15 Mike Felder	.35	.16	.04
☐ 16 Scott Garrelts	.35	.16	.04
☐ 17 Jose Uribe	.35	.16	.04
☐ 18 Greg Litton	.35	.16	.04
☐ 19 Dave Anderson	.35	.16	.04
☐ 20 Don Robinson	.35	.16	.04
☐ 21 Mike Kingery	.35	.16	.04
☐ 22 Trevor Wilson	.45	.20	.06
☐ 23 Kirt Manwaring	.35	.16	.04
☐ 24 Kevin Bass	.45	.20	.06
☐ 25 Jeff Brantley	.35	.16	.04
☐ 26 John Burkett	.45	.20	.06
☐ 27 Giant's Coaches Dusty Baker Bill Fahey Wendell Kim Bob Lillis Norm Sherry	.45	.20	.06
☐ 28 Checklist Card Mark Letendre TR Greg Lynn TR	.35	.16	.04

1991 Mother's Griffeys

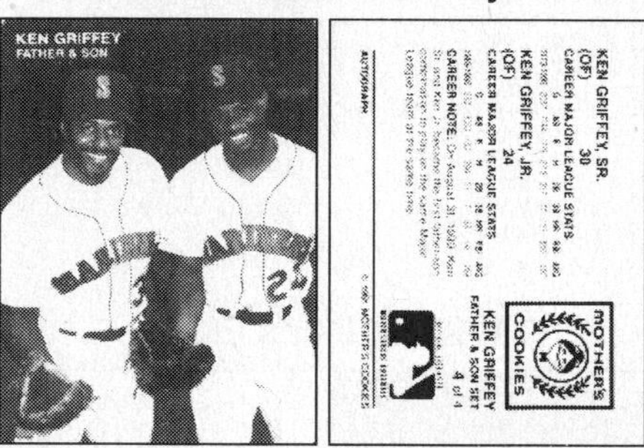

The 1991 Mother's Cookies Father and Son set contains 4 cards with rounded corners measuring the standard size (2 1/2" by 3 1/2"). The front design has borderless glossy color player photos. The horizontally oriented backs are printed in red and purple, and present biographical information as well as career notes. A blank slot for the player's autograph appears at the bottom of each card. The cards are numbered on the back.

	MT	EX-MT	VG
COMPLETE SET (4)	6.00	2.70	.75
COMMON PLAYER (1-4)	.75	.35	.09
☐ 1 Ken Griffey Jr. (Holding bat)	3.00	1.35	.40
☐ 2 Ken Griffey Sr (Holding glove)	.75	.35	.09
☐ 3 Ken Griffey Sr. and Ken Griffey Jr. (Pose with gloves)	2.00	.90	.25
☐ 4 Ken Griffey Sr. and Ken Griffey Jr. (Looking over shoulder)	2.00	.90	.25

1991 Mother's Rangers

The 1991 Mother's Cookies Texas Rangers set contains 28 cards with rounded corners measuring the standard size

(2 1/2" by 3 1/2"). The front design has borderless glossy color player photos, with the locker room as the background. The horizontally oriented backs are printed in red and purple, present biographical information, and have blank slots for player autographs. The cards are numbered on the back.

	MT	EX-MT	VG
COMPLETE SET (28)	11.00	4.90	1.40
COMMON PLAYER (1-28)	.35	.16	.04
☐ 1 Bobby Valentine MG	.45	.20	.06
☐ 2 Nolan Ryan	3.50	1.55	.45
☐ 3 Ruben Sierra	1.25	.55	.16
☐ 4 Juan Gonzalez	2.00	.90	.25
☐ 5 Steve Buechele	.45	.20	.06
☐ 6 Bobby Witt	.45	.20	.06
☐ 7 Geno Petralli	.35	.16	.04
☐ 8 Jeff Russell	.45	.20	.06
☐ 9 Rafael Palmeiro	.90	.40	.11
☐ 10 Julio Franco	.60	.25	.08
☐ 11 Jack Daugherty	.35	.16	.04
☐ 12 Gary Pettis	.35	.16	.04
☐ 13 John Barfield	.35	.16	.04
☐ 14 Scott Chiamparino	.45	.20	.06
☐ 15 Kevin Reimer	.45	.20	.06
☐ 16 Rich Gossage	.60	.25	.08
☐ 17 Brian Downing	.45	.20	.06
☐ 18 Denny Walling	.35	.16	.04
☐ 19 Mike Jeffcoat	.35	.16	.04
☐ 20 Mike Stanley	.35	.16	.04
☐ 21 Kevin Brown	.60	.25	.08
☐ 22 Kenny Rogers	.45	.20	.06
☐ 23 Jeff Huson	.35	.16	.04
☐ 24 Mario Diaz	.35	.16	.04
☐ 25 Brad Arnsberg	.35	.16	.04
☐ 26 John Russell	.35	.16	.04
☐ 27 Gerald Alexander	.35	.16	.04
☐ 28 Checklist Card Tom Robson CO Toby Harrah CO Orlando Gomez CO Tom House CO Dave Oliver CO Davey Lopes CO	.45	.20	.06

1991 Mother's Nolan Ryan

This four-card set was sponsored by Mother's Cookies in honor of Nolan Ryan, baseball's latest 300-game winner. One card was packaged in each box of Mother's Cookies 18-ounce family size bags of five different flavored cookies (Chocolate Chip, Cookie Parade, Oatmeal Raisin, Fudge'N Chips, and Costadas). Also collectors could purchase an uncut strip of the four cards for 7.95 with four proof-of-purchase seals, and a protective sleeve for 1.00. The standard-size (2 1/2" by 3 1/2") cards have on the fronts full-bleed color posed photos with rounded corners. In red and purple print, the horizontally oriented backs have biographical information, career notes, statistics, and space for an autograph. The cards are numbered on the back.

	MT	EX-MT	VG
COMPLETE SET (4)	7.50	3.40	.95
COMMON PLAYER (1-4)	2.50	1.15	.30

	MT	EX-MT	VG
☐ 1 Nolan Ryan (Front pose Hand in glove)	2.50	1.15	.30
☐ 2 Nolan Ryan (Kneeling on one knee)	2.50	1.15	.30
☐ 3 Nolan Ryan (Side pose)	2.50	1.15	.30
☐ 4 Nolan Ryan (Front pose, Ball in hand)	2.50	1.15	.30

1992 Mother's Astros

The 1992 Mother's Cookies Astros set contains 28 cards with rounded corners measuring the standard size (2 1/2" by 3 1/2"). The front design has borderless glossy color player photos in which the players are posed with either their glove or a bat. The player's name and team name appear in the upper right corner. The horizontal backs are printed in red and purple, and present biography and a "how obtained" remark where appropriate. A blank slot for the player's autograph rounds out the back. The cards are numbered on the back.

	MT	EX-MT	VG
COMPLETE SET (28)	10.00	4.50	1.25
COMMON PLAYER (1-28)	.35	.16	.04

	MT	EX-MT	VG
☐ 1 Art Howe MG	.45	.20	.06
☐ 2 Steve Finley	.60	.25	.08
☐ 3 Pete Harnisch	.60	.25	.08
☐ 4 Pete Incaviglia	.45	.20	.06
☐ 5 Craig Biggio	.75	.35	.09
☐ 6 Ken Caminiti	.60	.25	.08
☐ 7 Eric Anthony	.75	.35	.09
☐ 8 Jeff Bagwell	1.00	.45	.13
☐ 9 Andujar Cedeno	.75	.35	.09
☐ 10 Mark Portugal	.35	.16	.04
☐ 11 Eddie Taubensee	.45	.20	.06
☐ 12 Jimmy Jones	.35	.16	.04
☐ 13 Joe Boever	.35	.16	.04
☐ 14 Benny Distefano	.35	.16	.04
☐ 15 Juan Guerrero	.45	.20	.06
☐ 16 Doug Jones	.45	.20	.06
☐ 17 Scott Servais	.35	.16	.04
☐ 18 Butch Henry	.45	.20	.06
☐ 19 Rafael Ramirez	.35	.16	.04
☐ 20 Al Osuna	.45	.20	.06
☐ 21 Rob Murphy Jr.	.35	.16	.04
☐ 22 Chris Jones	.45	.20	.06
☐ 23 Rob Mallicoat	.35	.16	.04
☐ 24 Darryl Kile	.60	.25	.08
☐ 25 Casey Candaele	.35	.16	.04
☐ 26 Xavier Hernandez	.45	.20	.06
☐ 27 Coaches Rudy Jaramillo Ed Ott Matt Galante Bob Cluck Tom Spencer	.35	.16	.04
☐ 28 Checklist Dennis Liborio EQMG Dave Labossiere TR Doc Ewell TR	.35	.16	.04

1992 Mother's Athletics

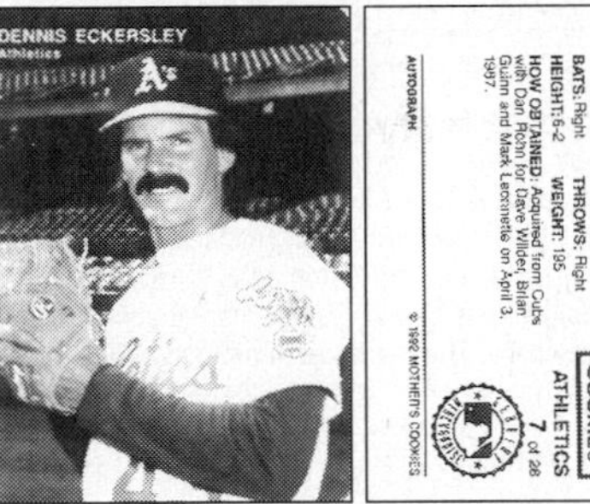

This 28-card set, sponsored by Mother's Cookies, contains borderless posed color player photos of the Oakland Athletics team. The cards measure the standard size (2 1/2" by 3 1/2") and have rounded corners. The red and purple backs include biographical information. The set also includes an order-form card for a Mother's Cookies Oakland Athletics collectors album. The album was available for 3.95. The cards are numbered on the back.

	MT	EX-MT	VG
COMPLETE SET (28)	10.00	4.50	1.25
COMMON PLAYER (1-28)	.35	.16	.04

	MT	EX-MT	VG
☐ 1 Tony LaRussa MG	.60	.25	.08
☐ 2 Mark McGwire	1.25	.55	.16
☐ 3 Terry Steinbach	.45	.20	.06
☐ 4 Rickey Henderson	.75	.35	.09
☐ 5 Dave Stewart	.60	.25	.08
☐ 6 Jose Canseco	1.50	.65	.19
☐ 7 Dennis Eckersley	.75	.35	.09
☐ 8 Carney Lansford	.45	.20	.06
☐ 9 Bob Welch	.45	.20	.06
☐ 10 Walt Weiss	.45	.20	.06
☐ 11 Mike Moore	.45	.20	.06
☐ 12 Goose Gossage	.45	.20	.06
☐ 13 Rick Honeycutt	.35	.16	.04
☐ 14 Harold Baines	.45	.20	.06
☐ 15 Jamie Quirk	.35	.16	.04
☐ 16 Jeff Parrett	.45	.20	.06
☐ 17 Willie Wilson	.45	.20	.06
☐ 18 Dave Henderson	.45	.20	.06
☐ 19 Joe Slusarski	.35	.16	.04
☐ 20 Mike Bordick	.75	.35	.09
☐ 21 Lance Blankenship	.35	.16	.04
☐ 22 Gene Nelson	.35	.16	.04
☐ 23 Vince Horsman	.35	.16	.04
☐ 24 Ron Darling	.45	.20	.06
☐ 25 Randy Ready	.35	.16	.04
☐ 26 Scott Hemond	.35	.16	.04
☐ 27 Scott Brosius	.35	.16	.04

	MT	EX-MT	VG
☐ 28 Checklist Rene Lachemann CO Art Kusnyer CO Dave McKay CO Tommie Reynolds CO Dave Duncan CO Doug Rader CO	.35	.16	.04

1992 Mother's Jeff Bagwell

This four-card standard size (2 1/2" by 3 1/2") set was sponsored by Mother's Cookies. The fronts have rounded corners and feature posed color full-bleed photos of Jeff Bagwell, the 1991 National League Rookie of the Year. The horizontally oriented backs are printed in purple and red and have biographical information, statistics, career notes, and an autograph space. The cards are numbered on the back.

	MT	EX-MT	VG
COMPLETE SET (4)	6.00	2.70	.75
COMMON PLAYER (1-4)	2.00	.90	.25
☐ 1 Jeff Bagwell (Close-up photo, head and shoulders)	2.00	.90	.25
☐ 2 Jeff Bagwell (Close-up photo, bat on shoulder)	2.00	.90	.25
☐ 3 Jeff Bagwell (Close-up photo, from waist up)	2.00	.90	.25
☐ 4 Jeff Bagwell (Close-up photo, ball in glove)	2.00	.90	.25

1992 Mother's Dodgers

The 1992 Mother's Cookies Los Angeles Dodgers set contains 28 standard size (2 1/2" by 3 1/2") cards with rounded corners. The front design features borderless color player photos with the baseball stadium as the background. The horizontally oriented backs display biographical information printed in purple and red. The cards are numbered on the back.

	MT	EX-MT	VG
COMPLETE SET (28)	10.00	4.50	1.25
COMMON PLAYER (1-28)	.35	.16	.04
☐ 1 Tom Lasorda MG	.60	.25	.08
☐ 2 Brett Butler	.60	.25	.08
☐ 3 Tom Candiotti	.45	.20	.06
☐ 4 Eric Davis	.75	.35	.09
☐ 5 Lenny Harris	.45	.20	.06
☐ 6 Orel Hershiser	.75	.35	.09
☐ 7 Ramon Martinez	.75	.35	.09
☐ 8 Jose Offerman	.60	.25	.08
☐ 9 Mike Scioscia	.45	.20	.06
☐ 10 Darryl Strawberry	.75	.35	.09
☐ 11 Todd Benzinger	.35	.16	.04
☐ 12 John Candelaria	.35	.16	.04
☐ 13 Tim Crews	.35	.16	.04
☐ 14 Kal Daniels	.45	.20	.06
☐ 15 Jim Gott	.35	.16	.04
☐ 16 Kevin Gross	.45	.20	.06
☐ 17 Dave Hansen	.45	.20	.06
☐ 18 Carlos Hernandez	.45	.20	.06
☐ 19 Jay Howell	.45	.20	.06
☐ 20 Stan Javier	.35	.16	.04
☐ 21 Eric Karros	2.00	.90	.25
☐ 22 Roger McDowell	.35	.16	.04
☐ 23 Bob Ojeda	.45	.20	.06
☐ 24 Juan Samuel	.35	.16	.04
☐ 25 Mike Sharperson	.45	.20	.06
☐ 26 Mitch Webster	.35	.16	.04
☐ 27 Steve Wilson	.35	.16	.04
☐ 28 Checklist Card Mark Cresse CO Ron Perranoski CO Ben Hines CO Manny Mota CO Joe Amalfitano CO Joe Ferguson CO Ron Roenicke CO	.35	.16	.04

1992 Mother's Giants

The set was sponsored by Mother's Cookies and features full-bleed color player photos of the San Francisco Giants. The 28 cards in this set have rounded corners and measure the standard size (2 1/2" by 3 1/2"). The backs, printed in purple and red, have biographical information. The set included two coupons: one featured a mail-in offer to obtain a trading card collectors album for 3.95, while the second featured a mail-in offer to obtain an additional eight trading cards. The cards are numbered on the back.

	MT	EX-MT	VG
COMPLETE SET (28)	10.00	4.50	1.25
COMMON PLAYER (1-28)	.35	.16	.04
☐ 1 Roger Craig MG	.45	.20	.06
☐ 2 Will Clark	1.50	.65	.19
☐ 3 Bill Swift	.60	.25	.08
☐ 4 Royce Clayton	.90	.40	.11
☐ 5 John Burkett	.45	.20	.06
☐ 6 Willie McGee	.45	.20	.06
☐ 7 Bud Black	.35	.16	.04

☐ 8 Dave Righetti	.35	.16	.04
☐ 9 Matt Williams	.75	.35	.09
☐ 10 Robby Thompson	.45	.20	.06
☐ 11 Darren Lewis	.60	.25	.08
☐ 12 Mike Jackson	.45	.20	.06
☐ 13 Mark Leonard	.35	.16	.04
☐ 14 Rod Beck	.60	.25	.08
☐ 15 Mike Felder	.35	.16	.04
☐ 16 Bryan Hickerson	.45	.20	.06
☐ 17 Jose Uribe	.35	.16	.04
☐ 18 Greg Litton	.35	.16	.04
☐ 19 Cory Snyder	.45	.20	.06
☐ 20 Jim McNamara	.45	.20	.06
☐ 21 Kelly Downs	.35	.16	.04
☐ 22 Trevor Wilson	.35	.16	.04
☐ 23 Kirt Manwaring	.35	.16	.04
☐ 24 Kevin Bass	.45	.20	.06
☐ 25 Jeff Brantley	.35	.16	.04
☐ 26 Dave Burba	.35	.16	.04
☐ 27 Chris James	.45	.20	.06
☐ 28 Checklist Card Carlos Alfonso CO Dusty Baker CO Wendell Kim CO Bob Brenly CO Bob Lillis CO	.45	.20	.06

1992 Mother's Chuck Knoblauch

This four-card set measures the standard size (2 1/2" by 3 1/2") and was sponsored by Mother's Cookies in honor of the 1991 American League Rookie of the Year, Chuck Knoblauch. The fronts feature borderless color photos with rounded corners. The backs are printed in red and purple and contain biographical information, career notes, and statistics. The cards are numbered on the back.

	MT	EX-MT	VG
COMPLETE SET (4)	6.00	2.70	.75
COMMON PLAYER (1-4)	2.00	.90	.25
☐ 1 Chuck Knoblauch (Close-up photo, head and shoulders)	2.00	.90	.25
☐ 2 Chuck Knoblauch (Close-up photo, bat on shoulder)	2.00	.90	.25
☐ 3 Chuck Knoblauch (Close-up photo, from waist up)	2.00	.90	.25
☐ 4 Chuck Knoblauch (Posed action shot, straddling base)	2.00	.90	.25

1992 Mother's Mariners

The 1992 Mother's Cookies Mariners set contains 28 cards with rounded corners measuring the standard size (2 1/2" by 3 1/2"). The front design has borderless glossy color player photos. The player's name and team name appear in one of the upper corners. The horizontal backs are printed in

red and purple, and present biography and a "how obtained" remark where appropriate. A blank slot for the player's autograph rounds out the back. The cards are numbered on the back.

	MT	EX-MT	VG
COMPLETE SET (28)	12.00	5.50	1.50
COMMON PLAYER (1-28)	.35	.16	.04
☐ 1 Bill Plummer MG	.35	.16	.04
☐ 2 Ken Griffey Jr.	3.50	1.55	.45
☐ 3 Harold Reynolds	.45	.20	.06
☐ 4 Kevin Mitchell	.60	.25	.08
☐ 5 David Valle	.35	.16	.04
☐ 6 Jay Buhner	.60	.25	.08
☐ 7 Eric Hanson	.45	.20	.06
☐ 8 Pete O'Brien	.45	.20	.06
☐ 9 Henry Cotto	.35	.16	.04
☐ 10 Mike Schooler	.45	.20	.06
☐ 11 Tino Martinez	.60	.25	.08
☐ 12 Dennis Powell	.35	.16	.04
☐ 13 Randy Johnson	.60	.25	.08
☐ 14 Dave Cochrane	.35	.16	.04
☐ 15 Greg Briley	.35	.16	.04
☐ 16 Omar Vizquel	.45	.20	.06
☐ 17 Dave Fleming	.75	.35	.09
☐ 18 Matt Sinatro	.35	.16	.04
☐ 19 Jeff Nelson	.45	.20	.06
☐ 20 Edgar Martinez	.75	.35	.09
☐ 21 Calvin Jones	.35	.16	.04
☐ 22 Russ Swan	.45	.20	.06
☐ 23 Jim Acker	.35	.16	.04
☐ 24 Jeff Schaefer	.35	.16	.04
☐ 25 Clay Parker	.35	.16	.04
☐ 26 Brian Holman	.35	.16	.04
☐ 27 Coaches Dan Warthen Russ Nixon Rusty Kuntz Marty Martinez Gene Clines Roger Hansen	.35	.16	.04
☐ 28 Checklist	.45	.20	.06

1992 Mother's Padres

The 1992 Mother's Cookies Padres set contains 28 cards with rounded corners measuring the standard size (2 1/2"

by 3 1/2"). The front design has borderless glossy color player photos. The player's name and team name appear in one of the upper corners. The horizontal backs are printed in red and purple, and present biography and a "how obtained" remark where appropriate. A blank slot for the player's autograph rounds out the back. The cards are numbered on the back.

	MT	EX-MT	VG
COMPLETE SET (28)	12.00	5.50	1.50
COMMON PLAYER (1-28)	.35	.16	.04
☐ 1 Greg Riddoch MG	.35	.16	.04
☐ 2 Greg W. Harris	.45	.20	.06
☐ 3 Gary Sheffield	1.50	.65	.19
☐ 4 Fred McGriff	1.25	.55	.16
☐ 5 Kurt Stillwell	.35	.16	.04
☐ 6 Benito Santiago	.60	.25	.08
☐ 7 Tony Gwynn	1.75	.80	.22
☐ 8 Tony Fernandez	.45	.20	.06
☐ 9 Jerald Clark	.45	.20	.06
☐ 10 Dave Eiland	.35	.16	.04
☐ 11 Randy Myers	.45	.20	.06
☐ 12 Oscar Azocar	.35	.16	.04
☐ 13 Dann Bilardello	.35	.16	.04
☐ 14 Jose Melendez	.45	.20	.06
☐ 15 Darrin Jackson	.60	.25	.08
☐ 16 Andy Benes	.75	.35	.09
☐ 17 Tim Teufel	.35	.16	.04
☐ 18 Jeremy Hernandez	.45	.20	.06
☐ 19 Kevin Ward	.45	.20	.06
☐ 20 Bruce Hurst	.45	.20	.06
☐ 21 Larry Andersen	.35	.16	.04
☐ 22 Rich Rodriguez	.35	.16	.04
☐ 23 Pat Clements	.35	.16	.04
☐ 24 Craig Lefferts	.45	.20	.06
☐ 25 Craig Shipley	.35	.16	.04
☐ 26 Mike Maddux	.35	.16	.04
☐ 27 Coaches Jim Snyder Mike Roarke Rob Picciolo Merv Rettenmund Bruce Kimm	.35	.16	.04
☐ 28 Checklist	.35	.16	.04

1992 Mother's Rangers

The 1992 Mother's Cookies Rangers set contains 28 cards with rounded corners measuring the standard size (2 1/2" by 3 1/2"). The front design has borderless glossy color player photos in which the players are posed against a blue background. The player's name and team name appear at one of the upper corners. The horizontal backs are printed in red and purple, and present biography and a "how obtained" remark. A blank slot for the player's autograph rounds out the back. The cards are numbered on the back.

	MT	EX-MT	VG
COMPLETE SET (28)	12.00	5.50	1.50
COMMON PLAYER (1-28)	.35	.16	.04
☐ 1 Bobby Valentine MG	.45	.20	.06
☐ 2 Nolan Ryan	3.00	1.35	.40
☐ 3 Ruben Sierra	1.25	.55	.16
☐ 4 Juan Gonzalez	1.50	.65	.19
☐ 5 Ivan Rodriguez	1.00	.45	.13
☐ 6 Bobby Witt	.45	.20	.06
☐ 7 Geno Petralli	.35	.16	.04
☐ 8 Jeff Russell	.45	.20	.06
☐ 9 Rafael Palmeiro	.90	.40	.11
☐ 10 Julio Franco	.60	.25	.08
☐ 11 Jack Daugherty	.35	.16	.04
☐ 12 Dickie Thon	.45	.20	.06
☐ 13 Floyd Bannister	.35	.16	.04
☐ 14 Scott Chiamparino	.45	.20	.06
☐ 15 Kevin Reimer	.45	.20	.06
☐ 16 Jeff M. Robinson	.35	.16	.04
☐ 17 Brian Downing	.45	.20	.06
☐ 18 Brian Bohanon	.45	.20	.06
☐ 19 Jose Guzman	.60	.25	.08
☐ 20 Terry Mathews	.35	.16	.04
☐ 21 Kevin Brown	.75	.35	.09
☐ 22 Kenny Rogers	.45	.20	.06
☐ 23 Jeff Huson	.35	.16	.04
☐ 24 Monty Fariss	.45	.20	.06
☐ 25 Al Newman	.35	.16	.04
☐ 26 Dean Palmer	.75	.35	.09
☐ 27 John Cangelosi	.35	.16	.04
☐ 28 Coaches/Checklist Tom Robson Ray Burris Toby Harrah Dave Oliver Tom House Orlando Gomez	.35	.16	.04

1992 Mother's Nolan Ryan 7 No-Hitters

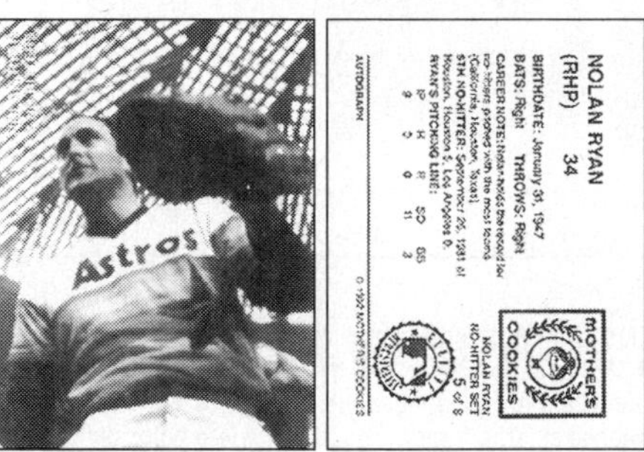

The 1992 Mother's Nolan Ryan Seven No-Hitters set contains eight standard size (2 1/2" by 3 1/2") cards with rounded corners and glossy full-bleed color photos. Card numbers 1-4 were included in 18-ounce Mother's Cookies family size "Big Bag" cookies. Card numbers 5-8 were in 16-ounce packages of "sandwich" cookies. The set was also available as an uncut sheet through a mail-in offer on specially marked packages for 7.95 plus four proofs of purchase. The horizontally oriented backs are printed in red and purple and feature biographical information, career notes, highlights, and statistics for each of his no-hitters (except card number 8). The cards are numbered on the back.

	MT	EX-MT	VG
COMPLETE SET (8)	10.00	4.50	1.25
COMMON PLAYER (1-8)	1.50	.65	.19
☐ 1 Nolan Ryan 1st No-hitter	1.50	.65	.19
☐ 2 Nolan Ryan 2nd No-hitter	1.50	.65	.19
☐ 3 Nolan Ryan 3rd No-hitter	1.50	.65	.19
☐ 4 Nolan Ryan 4th No-hitter (Holding four balls with zeroes on them)	1.50	.65	.19

☐ 5 Nolan Ryan 5th No-hitter (Astros uniform)	1.50	.65	.19
☐ 6 Nolan Ryan 6th No-hitter	1.50	.65	.19
☐ 7 Nolan Ryan 7th No-hitter	1.50	.65	.19
☐ 8 Nolan Ryan 8th No-hitter	1.50	.65	.19

1976 Motorola Old Timers

This 11-card, standard size, 2 1/2" by 3 1/2", set was issued by Motorola in 1976 and honored some of Baseball's all-time greats. The front of the cards were about the player while the backs of the cards talked in technical terms about Motorola products. The cards are also made on a thin (paper-like) card stock and are very flimsy.

	NRMT-MT	EXC	G-VG
COMPLETE SET (11)	22.50	10.00	2.80
COMMON PLAYER (1-11)	1.00	.45	.13
☐ 1 Honus Wagner	4.50	2.00	.55
☐ 2 Nap Lajoie	3.00	1.35	.40
☐ 3 Ty Cobb	6.00	2.70	.75
☐ 4 William Wambsganss	1.00	.45	.13
☐ 5 Mordecai Brown	1.50	.65	.19
☐ 6 Ray Schalk	1.50	.65	.19
☐ 7 Frank Frisch	2.00	.90	.25
☐ 8 Pud Galvin	1.50	.65	.19
☐ 9 Babe Ruth	9.00	4.00	1.15
☐ 10 Grover C. Alexander	2.50	1.15	.30
☐ 11 Frank L. Chance	2.00	.90	.25

1992 Mr. Turkey Superstars

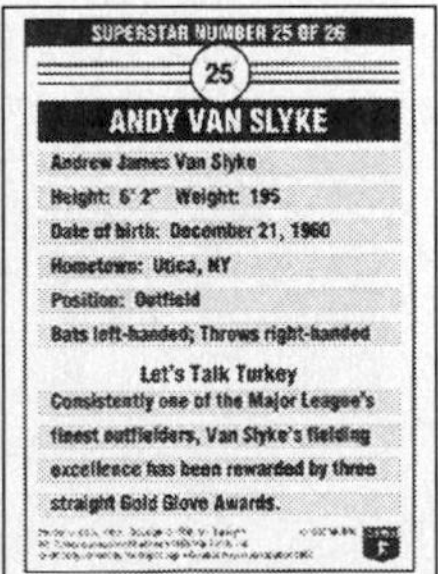

This 26-card set was sponsored by Mr. Turkey. One card was found on the back panel of Mr. Turkey products, such as Hardwood Smoked Turkey Pastrami. The standard-size (2 1/2" by 3 1/2") player card is not perforated. On a pinstripe background whose color is team color-coded, the front design has a color action player photo cut out to fit a circular format. The extreme right portion of the circle extends off the right edge of the card. Team logos have been airbrushed out of the photos. The player's name and team name appear in a colored banner above the player photo. At the lower left corner appears the Mr. Turkey 1992 Superstar emblem, which is designed like a baseball diamond. The backs are printed in blue and carry biography and a "Let's Talk Turkey" trivia fact about the player. The cards are numbered on the back; the card numbering is actually alphabetical by player's name.

	MT	EX-MT	VG
COMPLETE SET (26)	15.00	6.75	1.90
COMMON PLAYER (1-26)	.35	.16	.04
☐ 1 Jim Abbott	.60	.25	.08
☐ 2 Roberto Alomar	1.50	.65	.19
☐ 3 Sandy Alomar Jr.	.35	.16	.04
☐ 4 Craig Biggio	.45	.20	.06
☐ 5 George Brett	.75	.35	.09
☐ 6 Will Clark	1.00	.45	.13
☐ 7 Roger Clemens	1.25	.55	.16
☐ 8 Cecil Fielder	.75	.35	.09
☐ 9 Carlton Fisk	.60	.25	.08
☐ 10 Andres Galarraga	.35	.16	.04
☐ 11 Dwight Gooden	.45	.20	.06
☐ 12 Ken Griffey Jr.	2.50	1.15	.30
☐ 13 Tony Gwynn	.75	.35	.09
☐ 14 Rickey Henderson	.75	.35	.09
☐ 15 Dave Justice	1.00	.45	.13
☐ 16 Don Mattingly	.75	.35	.09
☐ 17 Dale Murphy	.45	.20	.06
☐ 18 Kirby Puckett	1.25	.55	.16
☐ 19 Cal Ripken	1.75	.80	.22
☐ 20 Nolan Ryan	2.50	1.15	.30
☐ 21 Chris Sabo	.35	.16	.04
☐ 22 Ryne Sandberg	1.50	.65	.19
☐ 23 Ozzie Smith	.60	.25	.08
☐ 24 Darryl Strawberry	.75	.35	.09
☐ 25 Andy Van Slyke	.45	.20	.06
☐ 26 Robin Yount	.75	.35	.09

1989 MSA Cereal Superstars

This 12-card, standard size, 2 1/2" by 3 1/2", set was issued by MSA (Michael Schechter Associates) and celebrated 12 of the leading players in the game as of 1989. The sets have an attractive design of stars in each of the front corners with the word Superstars on the top of the card and players name, team, and position underneath the full color photo of the player. Like most of the MSA sets there are no team logos used. The vertically oriented backs show career statistics. Supposedly two cards were included in each specially marked Ralston Purina cereal box.

	MT	EX-MT	VG
COMPLETE SET (12)	7.00	3.10	.85
COMMON PLAYER (1-12)	.45	.20	.06
☐ 1 Ozzie Smith	.60	.25	.08
☐ 2 Andre Dawson	.60	.25	.08

☐ 3 Darryl Strawberry	.75	.35	.09
☐ 4 Mike Schmidt	.90	.40	.11
☐ 5 Orel Hershiser	.45	.20	.06
☐ 6 Tim Raines	.45	.20	.06
☐ 7 Roger Clemens	1.00	.45	.13
☐ 8 Kirby Puckett	1.00	.45	.13
☐ 9 George Brett	.75	.35	.09
☐ 10 Alan Trammell	.45	.20	.06
☐ 11 Don Mattingly	.75	.35	.09
☐ 12 Jose Canseco	.90	.40	.11

1990 MSA AGFA

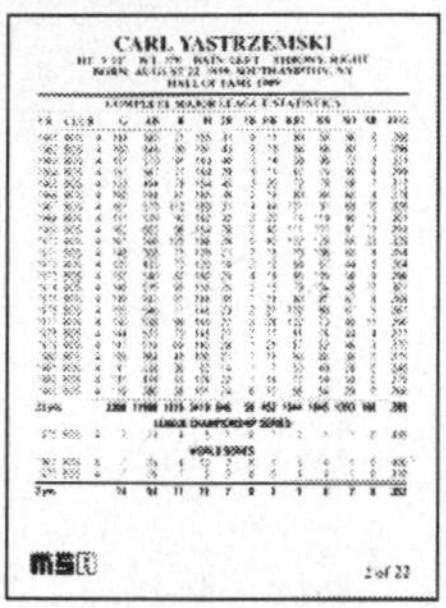

This 22-card set was issued by MSA (Michael Schechter Associates) for AGFA. The cards measure the standard size (2 1/2" by 3 1/2"). The fronts display color head and shoulders shots, with a thin red border on a white card face. In turquoise lettering, the words "Limited Edition Series" appear above the pictures; the player's name is given below the pictures. In black on white, the backs present complete year by year major league statistics. The cards are numbered on the back. The promotion supposedly consisted of a three-card pack of these cards given away with any purchase of a three-pack of AGFA film.

	MT	EX-MT	VG
COMPLETE SET (22)	20.00	9.00	2.50
COMMON PLAYER (1-22)	.45	.20	.06
☐ 1 Willie Mays	2.00	.90	.25
☐ 2 Carl Yastrzemski	1.25	.55	.16
☐ 3 Harmon Killebrew	.75	.35	.09
☐ 4 Joe Torre	.45	.20	.06
☐ 5 Al Kaline	1.00	.45	.13
☐ 6 Hank Aaron	2.00	.90	.25
☐ 7 Rod Carew	1.00	.45	.13
☐ 8 Roberto Clemente	1.50	.65	.19
☐ 9 Luis Aparicio	.60	.25	.08
☐ 10 Roger Maris	1.00	.45	.13
☐ 11 Joe Morgan	.75	.35	.09
☐ 12 Maury Wills	.45	.20	.06
☐ 13 Brooks Robinson	1.00	.45	.13
☐ 14 Tom Seaver	1.50	.65	.19
☐ 15 Steve Carlton	1.00	.45	.13
☐ 16 Whitey Ford	.90	.40	.11
☐ 17 Jim Palmer	.90	.40	.11
☐ 18 Rollie Fingers	.90	.40	.11
☐ 19 Bruce Sutter	.45	.20	.06
☐ 20 Willie McCovey	1.00	.45	.13
☐ 21 Mike Schmidt	1.50	.65	.19
☐ 22 Yogi Berra	1.25	.55	.16

1990 MSA Soda Superstars

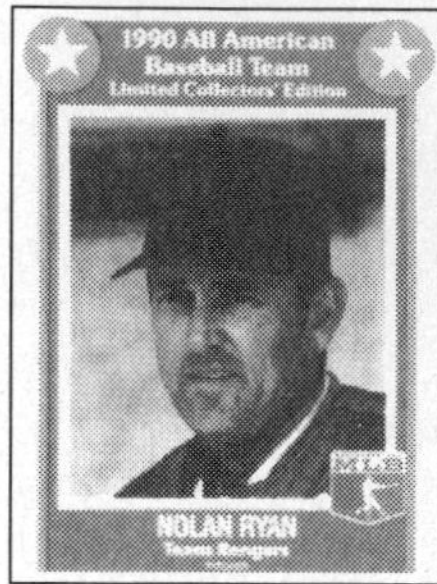

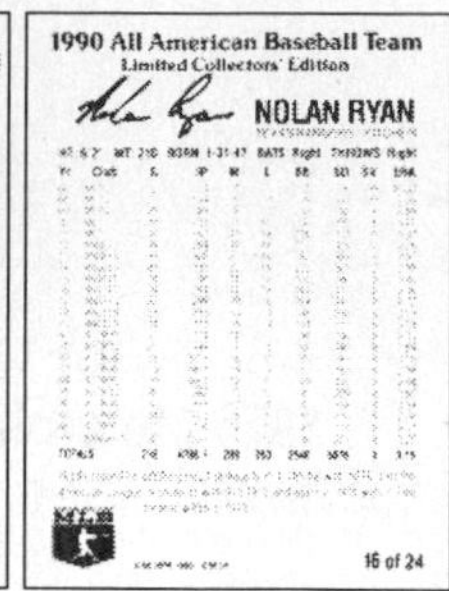

This 24-card, standard size, 2 1/2" by 3 1/2", set was issued by MSA (Michael Schechter Associates) for 7/11, Squirt, and Dr. Pepper, and other carbonated beverages (but there are no markings on the cards whatsoever to indicate who sponsored the set other than MSA). These cards were distributed and issued inside 12-packs of sodas. The 12-packs included a checklist on one panel, and the cards themselves were glued on the inside of the pack so that it was difficult to remove a card without damaging it. The fronts feature a red-white and blue design framing the players photos while the back has major league career statistics and a sentence of career highlights. The back also has a fascimile autograph of the player on the back. Like many of the sets sponsored by MSA there are no team logos on the cards as they have been airbrushed away.

	MT	EX-MT	VG
COMPLETE SET (24)	30.00	13.50	3.80
COMMON PLAYER (1-24)	.50	.23	.06
☐ 1 George Brett	1.25	.55	.16
☐ 2 Mark McGwire	1.25	.55	.16
☐ 3 Wade Boggs	1.25	.55	.16
☐ 4 Cal Ripken	2.00	.90	.25
☐ 5 Rickey Henderson	1.50	.65	.19
☐ 6 Dwight Gooden	.75	.35	.09
☐ 7 Bo Jackson	1.75	.80	.22
☐ 8 Roger Clemens	2.00	.90	.25
☐ 9 Orel Hershiser	.60	.25	.08
☐ 10 Ozzie Smith	.90	.40	.11
☐ 11 Don Mattingly	1.25	.55	.16
☐ 12 Kirby Puckett	1.50	.65	.19
☐ 13 Robin Yount	1.25	.55	.16
☐ 14 Tony Gwynn	1.25	.55	.16
☐ 15 Jose Canseco	1.75	.80	.22
☐ 16 Nolan Ryan	3.50	1.55	.45
☐ 17 Ken Griffey Jr.	4.50	2.00	.55
☐ 18 Will Clark	1.75	.80	.22
☐ 19 Ryne Sandberg	2.00	.90	.25
☐ 20 Kent Hrbek	.50	.23	.06
☐ 21 Carlton Fisk	1.00	.45	.13
☐ 22 Paul Molitor	.75	.35	.09
☐ 23 Dave Winfield	1.00	.45	.13
☐ 24 Andre Dawson	.90	.40	.11

1992 MTV Rock n' Jock

This three-card set was sponsored by MTV to promote the 3rd Annual Rock n' Jock Softball Challenge held January 11, 1992, in Los Angeles. According to the card backs, 20,000

sets were produced. The cards measure the standard size (2 1/2" by 3 1/2"). The fronts feature color player photos, and each card has a different color inner border (1-brick red; 2-kelly green; 3-blue). The outer border of all cards consists of yellow, orange, and purple stars on a white background. The backs have a black and white version of the outer border of the fronts and present an advertisement for the softball challenge. The cards are numbered on the back.

	MT	EX-MT	VG
COMPLETE SET (3)	3.50	1.55	.45
COMMON PLAYER (1-3)	.75	.35	.09
☐ 1 Hammer	.75	.35	.09
☐ 2 Frank Thomas	2.00	.90	.25
☐ 3 Ken Griffey Jr.	1.50	.65	.19

1992 Nabisco Canada

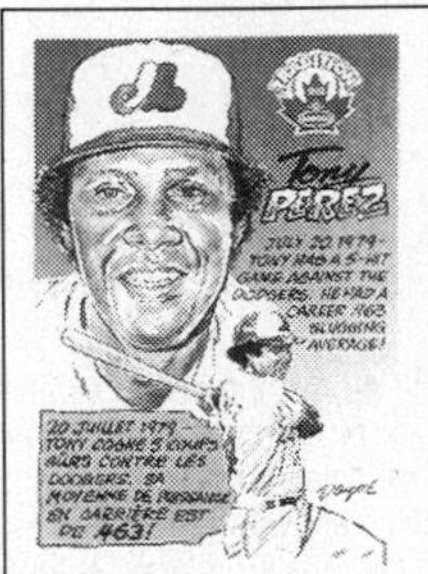

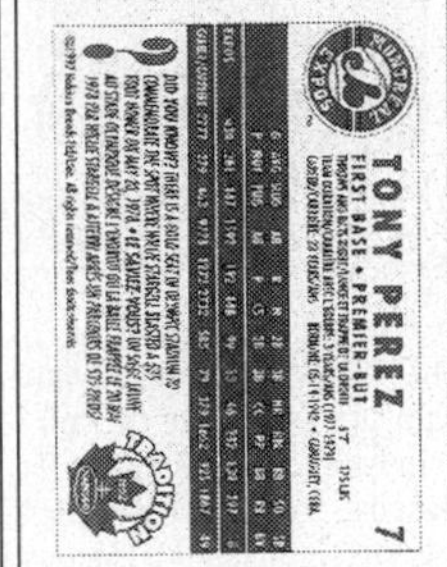

This 36-card set was sponsored by Nabisco and inserted in Shreddies cereal boxes and other Nabisco products in Canada. Three collector cards were protected by a cardboard sleeve that included two Bingo game symbols and a checklist on its back. The inside of each cereal box featured a Baseball Bingo Game Board. The collector became eligible to win prizes when he completed one vertical row, which consists of two required symbols and two correctly answered trivia questions. The odd number cards are Montreal Expos, while the even number cards are Toronto Blue Jays. Each card commemorates an outstanding achievement in the history of these two baseball franchises. The cards measure the standard size (2 1/2" by 3 1/2"). The fronts display a color close-up and an action portrait, and the text narrating the career highlight is neatly handwritten in both English and French. In a horizontal format, the bilingual backs carry biography, statistics (on a blue panel), and trivia questions. The team logo appears in the upper left corner, while the card number is printed in red in the upper right corner.

	MT	EX-MT	VG
COMPLETE SET (36)	18.00	8.00	2.30
COMMON PLAYER (1-36)	.50	.23	.06
☐ 1 Bill Lee	.60	.25	.08
☐ 2 Cliff Johnson	.50	.23	.06
☐ 3 Ken Singleton	.75	.35	.09
☐ 4 Al Woods	.50	.23	.06
☐ 5 Ron Hunt	.50	.23	.06
☐ 6 Barry Bonnell	.50	.23	.06
☐ 7 Tony Perez	1.00	.45	.13
☐ 8 Willie Upshaw	.50	.23	.06
☐ 9 Coco Laboy	.50	.23	.06
☐ 10 Famous Moments 1 October 5, 1985 Blue Jays win AL East	.60	.25	.08
☐ 11 Bob Bailey	.50	.23	.06
☐ 12 Dave McKay	.50	.23	.06
☐ 13 Rodney Scott	.50	.23	.06
☐ 14 Jerry Garvin	.50	.23	.06
☐ 15 Famous Moments 2 October 11, 1981 Expos win NL East	.60	.25	.08
☐ 16 Rick Bosetti	.50	.23	.06
☐ 17 Larry Parrish	.60	.25	.08
☐ 18 Bill Singer	.50	.23	.06
☐ 19 Ron Fairly	.50	.23	.06
☐ 20 Damaso Garcia	.60	.25	.08
☐ 21 Al Oliver	.75	.35	.09
☐ 22 Famous Moments 3 September 30, 1989 Blue Jays capture Divisional Championship	.60	.25	.08
☐ 23 Claude Raymond	.50	.23	.06
☐ 24 Buck Martinez	.50	.23	.06
☐ 25 Rusty Staub	.75	.35	.09
☐ 26 Otto Velez	.50	.23	.06
☐ 27 Mack Jones	.50	.23	.06
☐ 28 Garth Iorg	.50	.23	.06
☐ 29 Bill Stoneman	.50	.23	.06
☐ 30 Doug Ault	.50	.23	.06
☐ 31 Famous Moments 4 July 6, 1982 Expos hosts 1st AS Game played outside US	.60	.25	.08
☐ 32 Jesse Jefferson	.50	.23	.06
☐ 33 Steve Rogers	.60	.25	.08
☐ 34 Ernie Whitt	.50	.23	.06
☐ 35 John Boccabella	.50	.23	.06
☐ 36 Bob Bailor	.50	.23	.06

1986 Negro League Fritsch

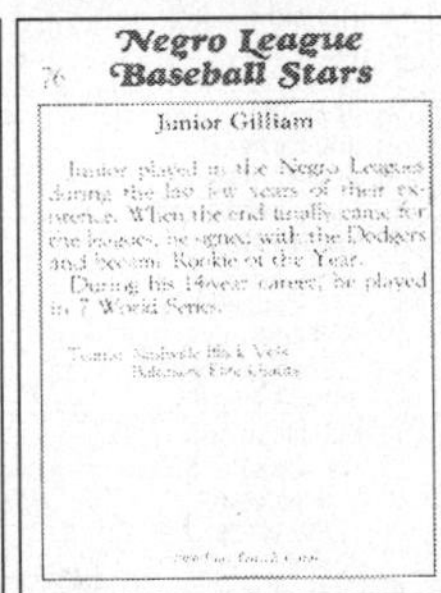

This 119-card set of Negro League stars was issued in the standard size of 2 1/2" by 3 1/2". The set features black and white photos framed by the title "Negro League Baseball Stars" in red above the player's name and the player's name in red below the photo. Each card back features a brief biography of the player pictured on the front of the card. The set was produced by long time Wisconsin card hobbyist Larry Fritsch and featured most of the great players of the old Negro Leagues.

	MT	EX-MT	VG
COMPLETE SET (119)	12.50	5.75	1.55
COMMON PLAYER (1-119)	.10	.05	.01
☐ 1 Buck Leonard	.75	.35	.09
☐ 2 Ted Page	.30	.14	.04
☐ 3 Cool Papa Bell	.75	.35	.09
☐ 4 Charleston/Gibson/ Page/Johnson	.60	.25	.08
☐ 5 Judy Johnson	.60	.25	.08
☐ 6 Monte Irvin	.60	.25	.08
☐ 7 Ray Dandridge	.60	.25	.08
☐ 8 Oscar Charleston	.60	.25	.08
☐ 9 Josh Gibson	1.00	.45	.13
☐ 10 Satchel Paige	1.00	.45	.13
☐ 11 Jackie Robinson	1.00	.45	.13
☐ 12 Lorenzo Piper Davis	.20	.09	.03
☐ 13 Josh Johnson	.10	.05	.01
☐ 14 Lou Dials	.50	.23	.06
☐ 15 Andy Porter	.10	.05	.01
☐ 16 John Henry Lloyd	.60	.25	.08
☐ 17 Andy Watts	.10	.05	.01
☐ 18 Rube Foster	.60	.25	.08
☐ 19 Martin DiHigo	.60	.25	.08

☐ 20 Lou Dials	.50	.23	.06
☐ 21 Satchel Paige	1.00	.45	.13
☐ 22 Crush Holloway	.10	.05	.01
☐ 23 Josh Gibson	1.00	.45	.13
☐ 24 Oscar Charleston	.60	.25	.08
☐ 25 Jackie Robinson	1.00	.45	.13
☐ 26 Larry Brown	.10	.05	.01
☐ 27 Hilton Smith	.10	.05	.01
☐ 28 Moses F. Walker	.25	.11	.03
☐ 29 Jimmie Crutchfield	.20	.09	.03
☐ 30 Josh Gibson	1.00	.45	.13
☐ 31 Josh Gibson	1.00	.45	.13
☐ 32 Bullet Rogan	.20	.09	.03
☐ 33 Clint Thomas	.10	.05	.01
☐ 34 Rats Henderson	.10	.05	.01
☐ 35 Pat Scantlebury	.10	.05	.01
☐ 36 Sydney Sy Morton	.10	.05	.01
☐ 37 Larry Kimbrough	.10	.05	.01
☐ 38 Sam Jethroe	.20	.09	.03
☐ 39 Normal(Tweed) Webb	.10	.05	.01
☐ 40 Mahlon Duckett	.10	.05	.01
☐ 41 Andy Anderson	.10	.05	.01
☐ 42 Buster Haywood	.10	.05	.01
☐ 43 Bob Trice	.10	.05	.01
☐ 44 Buster Clarkson	.10	.05	.01
☐ 45 Buck O'Neil	.10	.05	.01
☐ 46 Jim Zapp	.10	.05	.01
☐ 47 Lorenzo(Piper) Davis	.10	.05	.01
☐ 48 Ed Steel	.10	.05	.01
☐ 49 Bob Boyd	.20	.09	.03
☐ 50 Marlin Carter	.10	.05	.01
☐ 51 George Giles	.10	.05	.01
☐ 52 Bill Byrd	.10	.05	.01
☐ 53 Art Pennington	.10	.05	.01
☐ 54 Max Manning	.10	.05	.01
☐ 55 Ronald Teasley	.10	.05	.01
☐ 56 Ziggy Marcell	.10	.05	.01
☐ 57 Bill Cash	.10	.05	.01
☐ 58 Joe Scott	.10	.05	.01
☐ 59 Joe Fillmore	.10	.05	.01
☐ 60 Bob Thurman	.10	.05	.01
☐ 61 Larry Kimbrough	.10	.05	.01
☐ 62 Verdell Mathis	.10	.05	.01
☐ 63 Josh Johnson	.20	.09	.03
☐ 64 Ted Radcliffe	.20	.09	.03
☐ 65 William Bobby Robinson	.15	.07	.02
☐ 66 Bingo DeMoss	.20	.09	.03
☐ 67 John Beckwith	.10	.05	.01
☐ 68 Bill Jackman	.10	.05	.01
☐ 69 Bill Drake	.10	.05	.01
☐ 70 Charlie Grant	.10	.05	.01
☐ 71 Willie Wells	.30	.14	.04
☐ 72 Jose Fernandez	.10	.05	.01
☐ 73 Isidro Fabri	.10	.05	.01
☐ 74 Frank Austin	.10	.05	.01
☐ 75 Dick Lundy	.10	.05	.01
☐ 76 Junior Gilliam	.30	.14	.04
☐ 77 John Donaldson	.10	.05	.01
☐ 78 Rap Dixon	.10	.05	.01
☐ 79 Slim Jones	.10	.05	.01
☐ 80 Sam Jones	.20	.09	.03
☐ 81 Dave Hoskins	.10	.05	.01
☐ 82 Jerry Benjamin	.10	.05	.01
☐ 83 Luke Easter	.20	.09	.03
☐ 84 Ramon Herrera	.10	.05	.01
☐ 85 Matthew Carlisle	.10	.05	.01
☐ 86 Smokey Joe Williams	.30	.14	.04
☐ 87 Marvin Williams	.10	.05	.01
☐ 88 William Yancey	.10	.05	.01
☐ 89 Monte Irvin	.60	.25	.08
☐ 90 Cool Papa Bell	.75	.35	.09
☐ 91 Biz Mackey	.50	.23	.06
☐ 92 Harry Simpson	.20	.09	.03
☐ 93 Lazerio Salazar	.10	.05	.01
☐ 94 Bill Perkins	.10	.05	.01
☐ 95 Johnny Davis	.10	.05	.01
☐ 96 Jelly Jackson	.20	.09	.03
☐ 97 Sam Bankhead	.10	.05	.01
☐ 98 Hank Thompson	.20	.09	.03
☐ 99 William Bell	.10	.05	.01
☐ 100 Cliff Bell	.10	.05	.01
☐ 101 Dave Barnhill	.10	.05	.01
☐ 102 Dan Bankhead	.10	.05	.01
☐ 103 Pepper Bassett	.10	.05	.01
☐ 104 Newt Allen	.20	.09	.03
☐ 105 George Jefferson	.10	.05	.01
☐ 106 Pat Paterson	.10	.05	.01
☐ 107 Goose Tatum	.75	.35	.09
☐ 108 Dave Malarcher	.20	.09	.03
☐ 109 Home Run Johnson	.20	.09	.03
☐ 110 Bill Monroe	.10	.05	.01
☐ 111 Sammy Hughes	.10	.05	.01
☐ 112 Dick Redding	.20	.09	.03
☐ 113 Fats Jenkins	.10	.05	.01
☐ 114 Jimmie Lyons	.10	.05	.01
☐ 115 Mule Suttles	.20	.09	.03
☐ 116 Ted Trent	.10	.05	.01
☐ 117 George Sweatt	.10	.05	.01
☐ 118 Frank Duncan	.10	.05	.01
☐ 119 Checklist Card	.20	.09	.03

1988 Negro League Duquesne

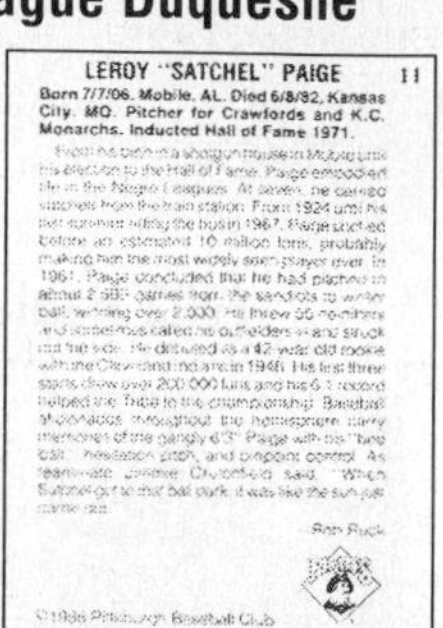

This 20-card set was sponsored by the Pittsburgh Pirates with the assistance of Rob Ruck of Chatham College and Duquesne Light Company. The set celebrates Negro League Baseball by depicting major black stars who played or were involved in the negro leagues in the Pittsburgh area. The set was given away at the Pittsburgh Pirates' home game on September 10, 1988. The set was issued in a sheet with five rows of four cards each; after perforation, the cards measure the standard size (2 1/2" by 3 1/2"). The fronts have sepia-toned player photos, with thin black borders on a white card face. A mustard-colored banner above the pictures reads "Negro League Stars." Also a mustard-colored baseball field logo appears in the lower right corner of the card face. The backs are printed in black on white and have biography as well as career summary. The Pirates' logo appears in the lower right corner, and the cards are numbered on the back.

	MT	EX-MT	VG
COMPLETE SET (20)	18.00	8.00	2.30
COMMON PLAYER (1-20)	.75	.35	.09
☐ 1 Andrew(Rube) Foster	2.00	.90	.25
☐ 2 1913 Homestead Grays	.75	.35	.09
☐ 3 Cum Posey	.75	.35	.09
☐ 4 1926 Pittsburgh Crawfords	.75	.35	.09
☐ 5 Gus Greenlee OWN	.75	.35	.09
☐ 6 John Henry(Pop) Lloyd	2.00	.90	.25
☐ 7 Oscar Charleston	2.00	.90	.25
☐ 8 Smokey Joe Williams	1.25	.55	.16
☐ 9 William(Judy) Johnson	2.00	.90	.25
☐ 10 Martin Dihigo	2.00	.90	.25
☐ 11 LeRoy(Satchel) Paige	3.00	1.35	.40
☐ 12 Josh Gibson	3.00	1.35	.40
☐ 13 Sam Streeter	.75	.35	.09
☐ 14 James(Cool Papa) Bell	2.50	1.15	.30
☐ 15 Ted Page	1.50	.65	.19
☐ 16 Walter(Buck) Leonard	2.00	.90	.25
☐ 17 Ray(Hooks) Dandridge	2.00	.90	.25
☐ 18 Willis Moody and Ralph(Lefty) Mellix	.75	.35	.09
☐ 19 Harold Tinker	.75	.35	.09
☐ 20 Monte Irvin	2.00	.90	.25

1990 Negro League Stars

JOSH GIBSON 2

The exclusion of black and Latino players from Major League Baseball from 1889 to 1947 resulted in these same players forming their own teams and leagues, and this 36-card set pays tribute to these men. These standard size (2 1/2" by 3 1/2") cards feature beautiful water color portraits of the players, painted by Mark Chiarello. The left side of the picture has a white border, while the bottom has a black border. The intersection of the two borders in the lower left corner is red in color. The player's name appears in the bottom black border. The backs are printed in black on white and summarize the player's career. The cards are numbered on the back.

	MT	EX-MT	VG
COMPLETE SET (36)	12.00	5.50	1.50
COMMON PLAYER (1-36)	.35	.16	.04
☐ 1 Title Card	.45	.20	.06
☐ 2 Josh Gibson	1.25	.55	.16
☐ 3 Cannonball Redding	.60	.25	.08
☐ 4 Biz Mackey	.60	.25	.08
☐ 5 Pop Lloyd	.90	.40	.11
☐ 6 Bingo Demoss	.60	.25	.08
☐ 7 Willard Brown	.35	.16	.04
☐ 8 John Donaldson	.35	.16	.04
☐ 9 Monte Irvin	.90	.40	.11
☐ 10 Ben Taylor	.35	.16	.04
☐ 11 Willie Wells	.60	.25	.08
☐ 12 Dave Brown	.35	.16	.04
☐ 13 Leon Day	.75	.35	.09
☐ 14 Ray Dandridge	.90	.40	.11
☐ 15 Turkey Stearnes	.35	.16	.04
☐ 16 Rube Foster	.90	.40	.11
☐ 17 Oliver Marcelle	.35	.16	.04
☐ 18 Judy Johnson	.90	.40	.11
☐ 19 Christobel Torrienti	.60	.25	.08
☐ 20 Satchel Paige	1.25	.55	.16
☐ 21 Mule Suttles	.45	.20	.06
☐ 22 John Beckwith	.35	.16	.04
☐ 23 Martin Dihigo	.90	.40	.11
☐ 24 Willie Foster	.35	.16	.04
☐ 25 Dick Lundy	.35	.16	.04
☐ 26 Buck Leonard	.90	.40	.11
☐ 27 Smokey Joe Williams	.45	.20	.06
☐ 28 Cool Papa Bell	.90	.40	.11
☐ 29 Bullet Rogan	.45	.20	.06
☐ 30 Newt Allen	.45	.20	.06
☐ 31 Bruce Petway	.45	.20	.06
☐ 32 Jose Mendez	.35	.16	.04
☐ 33 Louis Santop	.35	.16	.04
☐ 34 Jud Wilson	.35	.16	.04
☐ 35 Sammy T. Hughes	.35	.16	.04
☐ 36 Oscar Charleston	.90	.40	.11

1991 Negro League Ron Lewis

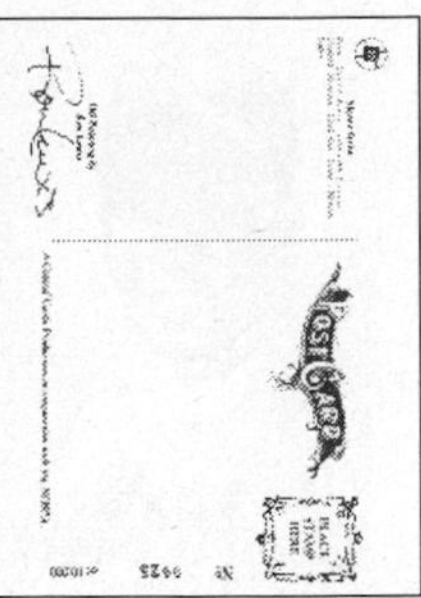

This 26-card boxed set was produced by the Negro League Baseball Players Association and noted sports artist Ron Lewis and was subtitled Living Legends. Production quantities were limited to 10,000 sets, and each card of the set bears a unique serial number on the back. Also 200 uncut sheets were printed. The cards were issued in the postcard format and measure approximately 3 1/2" by 5 1/4". The front design features a full color painting of the player by Ron Lewis. The paintings are bordered in white, and the player's name appears at the bottom of the front. The backs have brief biographical information and the card number in the upper left corner.

	MT	EX-MT	VG
COMPLETE SET (30)	30.00	13.50	3.80
COMMON PLAYER (1-30)	1.00	.45	.13
☐ 1 George Giles	1.00	.45	.13
☐ 2 Bill Cash	1.00	.45	.13
☐ 3 Bob Harvey	1.00	.45	.13
☐ 4 Lyman Bostock Sr.	1.50	.65	.19
☐ 5 Ray Dandridge	3.00	1.35	.40
☐ 6 Leon Day	1.50	.65	.19
☐ 7 Lefty Mathis	1.00	.45	.13
☐ 8 Jimmie Crutchfield	1.50	.65	.19
☐ 9 Clyde McNeal	1.00	.45	.13
☐ 10 Bill Wright	1.00	.45	.13
☐ 11 Mahlon Duckett	1.00	.45	.13
☐ 12 Bobby Robinson	1.50	.65	.19
☐ 13 Max Manning	1.00	.45	.13
☐ 14 Armando Vazquez	1.00	.45	.13
☐ 15 Jehosie Heard	1.00	.45	.13
☐ 16 Quincy Trouppe	1.00	.45	.13
☐ 17 Wilmer Fields	1.00	.45	.13
☐ 18 Lonnie Blair	1.00	.45	.13
☐ 19 Garnett Blair	1.00	.45	.13
☐ 20 Monte Irvin	3.00	1.35	.40
☐ 21 Willie Mays	6.00	2.70	.75
☐ 22 Buck Leonard	3.00	1.35	.40
☐ 23 Frank Evans	1.00	.45	.13
☐ 24 Josh Gibson Jr.	2.00	.90	.25
☐ 25 Ted Radcliffe	1.50	.65	.19
☐ 26 Josh Johnson	1.00	.45	.13
☐ 27 Gene Benson	1.00	.45	.13
☐ 28 Lester Lockett	1.50	.65	.19
☐ 29 Bubba Hyde	1.00	.45	.13
☐ 30 Rufus Lewis	1.00	.45	.13

1992 Negro League Paul Lee

On June 2, 1992 at Shea Stadium, Eclipse Enterprises Inc. sponsored the Negro League Baseball Players Association Night. This four-card set was created especially for this event by Eclipse artist Paul Lee, and they were given out to the first 50,000 fans in attendance. Each set included an insert outlining the goals of the association. The standard-size (2 1/2" by 3 1/2") cards feature on the fronts water color portraits inside white borders. The player's name and position appear in a brick-red stripe overlaying the bottom edge of the picture. The backs carry biography and career summary between two black bars. The cards are numbered on the back.

	MT	EX-MT	VG
COMPLETE SET (4)	5.00	2.30	.60
COMMON PLAYER (1-4)	1.50	.65	.19

1 MONTE IRVIN

Monford Merrill (Monte) Irvin, an outstanding athlete, had power, speed, and a strong arm. He played his entire Negro League career with the Newark Eagles, having joined them from Lincoln University in 1938. He compiled a .346 career league average and hit a league-leading .403 in 1941 and .394 in 1946. He appeared in four East-West All-Star games and helped bring the Eagles to the 1946 World Series. Playing winter ball in Mexico, Monte led the league in hitting and HRs in 1942. He spent the 1943 season in Mexico, then left baseball for the Army. Upon his discharge, he rejoined the Negro Leagues. After the 1948 season, he was signed by the New York Giants. During a successful eight-year Major League career, he starred in two World Series. In 1973, Monte was elected to the National Baseball Hall of Fame. He is the President of the Negro League Baseball Players Association.

THE NEGRO LEAGUE BASEBALL PLAYERS ASSOCIATION

Shea Stadium June 2, 1992
Sponsored by Eclipse Enterprises

☐ 1 Monte Irvin	1.50	.65	.19
☐ 2 Walter(Buck) Leonard	1.50	.65	.19
☐ 3 Josh Gibson	2.00	.90	.25
☐ 4 Ray Dandridge	1.50	.65	.19

1984 Nestle Dream Team

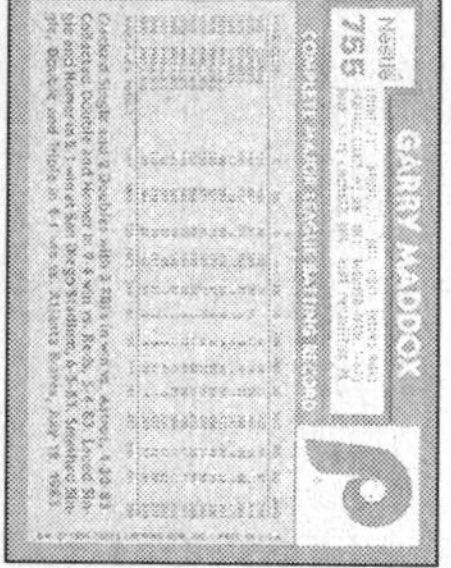

The cards in this 22-card set measure 2 1/2" by 3 1/2". In conjunction with Topps, the Nestle Company issued this set entitled the Dream Team. The fronts have the Nestle trademark in the upper frameline, and the backs are identical to the Topps cards of this year except for the number and the Nestle's logo. Cards 1-11 feature stars of the American League while cards 12-22 show National League stars. Each league's "Dream Team" consists of eight position players and three pitchers. The cards were included with the Nestle chocolate bars as a pack of four (three player cards and a checklist header card. This set should not be confused with the Nestle 792-card (same player-number correspondence as 1984 Topps 792) set.

	NRMT-MT	EXC	G-VG
COMPLETE SET (22)	25.00	11.50	3.10
COMMON PLAYER (1-22)	.50	.23	.06
☐ 1 Eddie Murray	2.00	.90	.25
☐ 2 Lou Whitaker	.75	.35	.09
☐ 3 George Brett	3.50	1.55	.45
☐ 4 Cal Ripken	5.00	2.30	.60
☐ 5 Jim Rice	.90	.40	.11
☐ 6 Dave Winfield	2.00	.90	.25
☐ 7 Lloyd Moseby	.50	.23	.06
☐ 8 Lance Parrish	.60	.25	.08
☐ 9 LaMarr Hoyt	.50	.23	.06
☐ 10 Ron Guidry	.60	.25	.08
☐ 11 Dan Quisenberry	.60	.25	.08
☐ 12 Steve Garvey	1.00	.45	.13
☐ 13 Johnny Ray	.50	.23	.06
☐ 14 Mike Schmidt	4.00	1.80	.50
☐ 15 Ozzie Smith	2.00	.90	.25
☐ 16 Andre Dawson	2.00	.90	.25
☐ 17 Tim Raines	.90	.40	.11
☐ 18 Dale Murphy	2.00	.90	.25
☐ 19 Tony Pena	.50	.23	.06
☐ 20 John Denny	.50	.23	.06
☐ 21 Steve Carlton	1.50	.65	.19
☐ 22 Al Holland	.50	.23	.06
☐ NNO Checklist card	.60	.25	.08

1984 Nestle 792

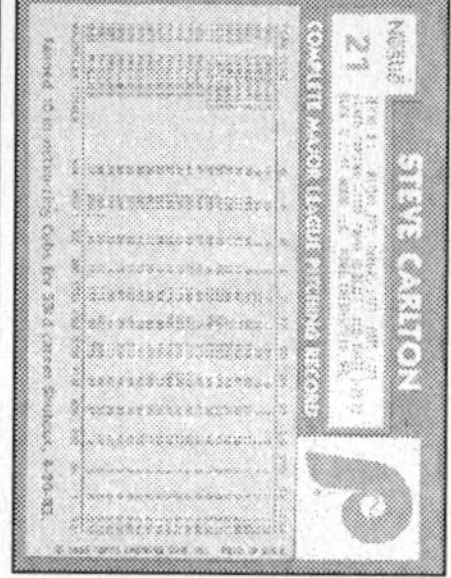

The cards in this 792-card set measure 2 1/2" by 3 1/2" and are extremely similar to the 1984 Topps regular issue (except for the Nestle logo instead of Topps logo on the front). In conjunction with Topps, the Nestle Company issued this set as six sheets available as a premium. The set was (as detailed on the back of the checklist card for the Nestle Dream Team cards) originally available from the Nestle Company in full sheets of 132 cards, 24" by 48", for 4.95 plus five Nestle candy wrappers per sheet. The backs are virtually identical to the Topps cards of this year, i.e., same player-number correspondence. These sheets have been cut up into individual cards and are available from a few dealers around the country. This is one of the few instances in this hobby where the complete uncut sheet is worth considerably less than the sum of the individual cards due to the expense required in having the sheet cut professionally (and precisely) into individual cards. Supposedly less than 5000 sets were printed. Since the checklist is exactly the same as that of the 1984 Topps, these Nestle cards are generally priced as a multiple of the corresponding Topps card. Individual Nestle cards are priced at approximately five times the corresponding 1984 Topps price. Beware also on this set to look for fakes and forgeries. Cards billed as Nestle proofs in black and white are fakes; there are even a few counterfeits in color.

	NRMT-MT	EXC	G-VG
COMPLETE CUT SET (792)	375.00	170.00	47.50
COMMON PLAYER (1-792)	.25	.11	.03

1987 Nestle Dream Team

This 33-card set is, in a sense, three sets: Golden Era (1-11 gold), AL Modern Era (12-22 red), and NL Modern Era (23-33 blue). Cards are 2 1/2" by 3 1/2" and have color coded borders by era. The first 11 card photos are in black and white. The Nestle set was apparently not licensed by Major League Baseball and hence the team logos are not shown in the photos. Six-packs of certain Nestle candy bars contained three cards; cards were also available through a send-in offer.

	MT	EX-MT	VG
COMPLETE SET (33)	8.00	3.60	1.00
COMMON PLAYER (1-33)	.15	.07	.02

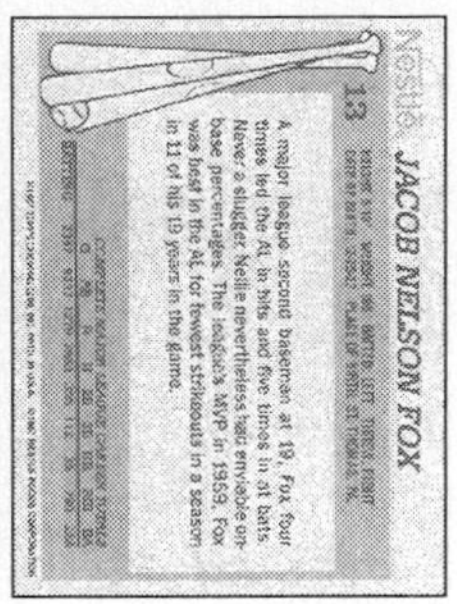

☐ 1 Lou Gehrig	.75	.35	.09
☐ 2 Rogers Hornsby	.25	.11	.03
☐ 3 Pie Traynor	.15	.07	.02
☐ 4 Honus Wagner	.45	.20	.06
☐ 5 Babe Ruth	1.25	.55	.16
☐ 6 Tris Speaker	.25	.11	.03
☐ 7 Ty Cobb	.75	.35	.09
☐ 8 Mickey Cochrane	.25	.11	.03
☐ 9 Walter Johnson	.45	.20	.06
☐ 10 Carl Hubbell	.25	.11	.03
☐ 11 Jimmy Foxx	.35	.16	.04
☐ 12 Rod Carew	.35	.16	.04
☐ 13 Nellie Fox	.15	.07	.02
☐ 14 Brooks Robinson	.35	.16	.04
☐ 15 Luis Aparicio	.15	.07	.02
☐ 16 Frank Robinson	.25	.11	.03
☐ 17 Mickey Mantle	1.25	.55	.16
☐ 18 Ted Williams	.75	.35	.09
☐ 19 Yogi Berra	.45	.20	.06
☐ 20 Bob Feller	.35	.16	.04
☐ 21 Whitey Ford	.35	.16	.04
☐ 22 Harmon Killebrew	.25	.11	.03
☐ 23 Stan Musial	.45	.20	.06
☐ 24 Jackie Robinson	.65	.30	.08
☐ 25 Eddie Mathews	.25	.11	.03
☐ 26 Ernie Banks	.35	.16	.04
☐ 27 Roberto Clemente	.65	.30	.08
☐ 28 Willie Mays	.65	.30	.08
☐ 29 Hank Aaron	.65	.30	.08
☐ 30 Johnny Bench	.35	.16	.04
☐ 31 Bob Gibson	.35	.16	.04
☐ 32 Warren Spahn	.25	.11	.03
☐ 33 Duke Snider	.35	.16	.04
☐ NNO Checklist card	.45	.20	.06

1988 Nestle

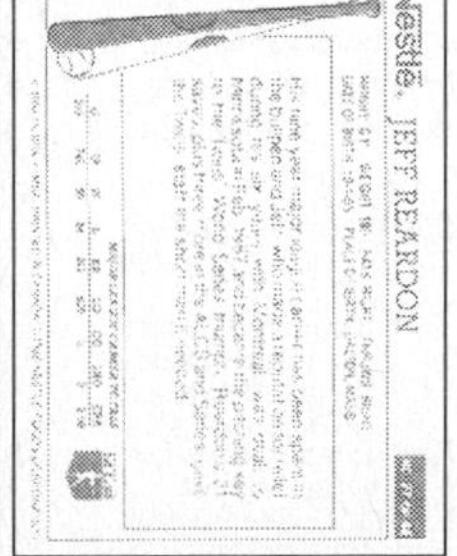

This 44-card set was produced for Nestle by Mike Schechter Associates and was printed in Canada. Cards are 2 1/2" by 3 1/2" and have yellow borders. The Nestle set was apparently not licensed by Major League Baseball and hence the team logos are not shown in the photos. The cards are numbered on the back. The backs are printed in red and blue on white card stock.

	MT	EX-MT	VG
COMPLETE SET (44)	22.50	10.00	2.80
COMMON PLAYER (1-44)	.35	.16	.04
☐ 1 Roger Clemens	2.00	.90	.25
☐ 2 Dale Murphy	.75	.35	.09
☐ 3 Eric Davis	.75	.35	.09
☐ 4 Gary Gaetti	.35	.16	.04
☐ 5 Ozzie Smith	.90	.40	.11
☐ 6 Mike Schmidt	1.50	.65	.19
☐ 7 Ozzie Guillen	.35	.16	.04
☐ 8 John Franco	.35	.16	.04
☐ 9 Andre Dawson	.90	.40	.11
☐ 10 Mark McGwire	1.25	.55	.16
☐ 11 Bret Saberhagen	.60	.25	.08
☐ 12 Benito Santiago	.60	.25	.08
☐ 13 Jose Uribe	.35	.16	.04
☐ 14 Will Clark	1.50	.65	.19
☐ 15 Don Mattingly	1.25	.55	.16
☐ 16 Juan Samuel	.35	.16	.04
☐ 17 Jack Clark	.35	.16	.04
☐ 18 Darryl Strawberry	1.00	.45	.13
☐ 19 Bill Doran	.35	.16	.04
☐ 20 Pete Incaviglia	.45	.20	.06
☐ 21 Dwight Gooden	.60	.25	.08
☐ 22 Willie Randolph	.35	.16	.04
☐ 23 Tim Wallach	.35	.16	.04
☐ 24 Pedro Guerrero	.35	.16	.04
☐ 25 Steve Bedrosian	.35	.16	.04
☐ 26 Gary Carter	.60	.25	.08
☐ 27 Jeff Reardon	.45	.20	.06
☐ 28 Dave Righetti	.35	.16	.04
☐ 29 Frank White	.35	.16	.04
☐ 30 Buddy Bell	.35	.16	.04
☐ 31 Tim Raines	.45	.20	.06
☐ 32 Wade Boggs	1.00	.45	.13
☐ 33 Dave Winfield	.90	.40	.11
☐ 34 George Bell	.45	.20	.06
☐ 35 Alan Trammell	.45	.20	.06
☐ 36 Joe Carter	.75	.35	.09
☐ 37 Jose Canseco	1.50	.65	.19
☐ 38 Carlton Fisk	1.00	.45	.13
☐ 39 Kirby Puckett	1.50	.65	.19
☐ 40 Tony Gwynn	1.00	.45	.13
☐ 41 Matt Nokes	.35	.16	.04
☐ 42 Keith Hernandez	.35	.16	.04
☐ 43 Nolan Ryan	3.00	1.35	.40
☐ 44 Wally Joyner	.60	.25	.08

1954 New York Journal American

The cards in this 59-card set measure approximately 2" by 4". The 1954 New York Journal American set contains black and white, unnumbered cards issued in conjunction with the newspaper. News stands were given boxes of cards to be distributed with purchases and each card had a serial number for redemption in the contest. The set spotlights New York teams only and carries game schedules on the reverse. The cards have been assigned numbers in the listing below alphabetically within team so that Brooklyn Dodgers are 1-19, New York Giants are 20-39, and New York Yankees are 40-59. There is speculation that a 20th Dodger card may exist. The catalog designation for this set is M127.

	NRMT	VG-E	GOOD
COMPLETE SET (59)	2000.00	900.00	250.00
COMMON PLAYER (1-59)	12.00	5.50	1.50
☐ 1 Joe Black	13.50	6.00	1.70
☐ 2 Roy Campanella	125.00	57.50	15.50
☐ 3 Billy Cox	12.00	5.50	1.50
☐ 4 Carl Erskine	16.00	7.25	2.00
☐ 5 Carl Furillo	20.00	9.00	2.50
☐ 6 Junior Gilliam	18.00	8.00	2.30
☐ 7 Gil Hodges	50.00	23.00	6.25
☐ 8 Jim Hughes	12.00	5.50	1.50
☐ 9 Clem Labine	13.50	6.00	1.70
☐ 10 Billy Loes	12.00	5.50	1.50
☐ 11 Russ Meyer	12.00	5.50	1.50
☐ 12 Don Newcombe	20.00	9.00	2.50
☐ 13 Ervin Palica	12.00	5.50	1.50
☐ 14 Pee Wee Reese	75.00	34.00	9.50
☐ 15 Jackie Robinson	150.00	70.00	19.00
☐ 16 Preacher Roe	20.00	9.00	2.50
☐ 17 George Shuba	12.00	5.50	1.50
☐ 18 Duke Snider	125.00	57.50	15.50
☐ 19 Dick Williams	16.00	7.25	2.00
☐ 20 John Antonelli	13.50	6.00	1.70
☐ 21 Alvin Dark	16.00	7.25	2.00
☐ 22 Marv Grissom	12.00	5.50	1.50
☐ 23 Ruben Gomez	12.00	5.50	1.50
☐ 24 Jim Hearn	12.00	5.50	1.50
☐ 25 Bobby Hofman	12.00	5.50	1.50
☐ 26 Monte Irvin	40.00	18.00	5.00
☐ 27 Larry Jansen	12.00	5.50	1.50
☐ 28 Ray Katt	12.00	5.50	1.50
☐ 29 Don Liddle	12.00	5.50	1.50
☐ 30 Whitey Lockman	12.00	5.50	1.50
☐ 31 Sal Maglie	18.00	8.00	2.30
☐ 32 Willie Mays	250.00	115.00	31.00
☐ 33 Don Mueller	13.50	6.00	1.70
☐ 34 Dusty Rhodes	13.50	6.00	1.70
☐ 35 Hank Thompson	13.50	6.00	1.70
☐ 36 Wes Westrum	12.00	5.50	1.50
☐ 37 Hoyt Wilhelm	50.00	23.00	6.25
☐ 38 Davey Williams	12.00	5.50	1.50
☐ 39 Al Worthington	12.00	5.50	1.50
☐ 40 Hank Bauer	18.00	8.00	2.30
☐ 41 Yogi Berra	125.00	57.50	15.50
☐ 42 Harry Byrd	12.00	5.50	1.50
☐ 43 Andy Carey	12.00	5.50	1.50
☐ 44 Jerry Coleman	13.50	6.00	1.70
☐ 45 Joe Collins	12.00	5.50	1.50
☐ 46 Whitey Ford	75.00	34.00	9.50
☐ 47 Steve Kraly	12.00	5.50	1.50
☐ 48 Bob Kuzava	12.00	5.50	1.50
☐ 49 Frank Leja	12.00	5.50	1.50
☐ 50 Ed Lopat	20.00	9.00	2.50
☐ 51 Mickey Mantle	500.00	230.00	65.00
☐ 52 Gil McDougald	18.00	8.00	2.30
☐ 53 Bill Miller	12.00	5.50	1.50
☐ 54 Tom Morgan	12.00	5.50	1.50
☐ 55 Irv Noren	12.00	5.50	1.50
☐ 56 Allie Reynolds	20.00	9.00	2.50
☐ 57 Phil Rizzuto	50.00	23.00	6.25
☐ 58 Eddie Robinson	12.00	5.50	1.50
☐ 59 Gene Woodling	13.50	6.00	1.70

1989 Nissen

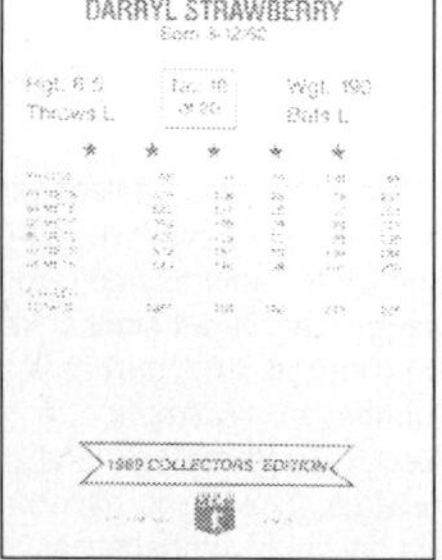

The 1989 J.J. Nissen set contains 20 standard-size (2 1/2" by 3 1/2") cards. The fronts have airbrushed facial photos with white and yellow borders and orange trim. The backs are white and feature career stats. The complete set price below does not include the error version of Mark Grace.

	MT	EX-MT	VG
COMPLETE SET (20)	12.00	5.50	1.50
COMMON PLAYER (1-20)	.35	.16	.04
☐ 1 Wally Joyner	.60	.25	.08
☐ 2 Wade Boggs	1.00	.45	.13
☐ 3 Ellis Burks	.60	.25	.08
☐ 4 Don Mattingly	1.00	.45	.13
☐ 5 Jose Canseco	1.25	.55	.16
☐ 6 Mike Greenwell	.45	.20	.06
☐ 7 Eric Davis	.45	.20	.06
☐ 8 Kirby Puckett	1.25	.55	.16
☐ 9 Kevin Seitzer	.35	.16	.04
☐ 10 Darryl Strawberry	1.00	.45	.13
☐ 11 Gregg Jefferies	1.00	.45	.13
☐ 12A Mark Grace ERR (Photo actually Vance Law)	12.00	5.50	1.50
☐ 12B Mark Grace COR	1.25	.55	.16
☐ 13 Matt Nokes	.35	.16	.04
☐ 14 Mark McGwire	1.00	.45	.13
☐ 15 Bobby Bonilla	.60	.25	.08
☐ 16 Roger Clemens	1.50	.65	.19
☐ 17 Frank Viola	.45	.20	.06
☐ 18 Orel Hershiser	.45	.20	.06
☐ 19 David Cone	.60	.25	.08
☐ 20 Ted Williams	1.25	.55	.16

1960 Nu-Card Hi-Lites

The cards in this 72-card set measure approximately 3 1/4" by 5 3/8". In 1960, the Nu-Card Company introduced its Baseball Hi-Lites set of newspaper style cards. Each card singled out an individual baseball achievement with a picture and story. The reverses contain a baseball quiz. Cards 1-18 are more valuable if found printed totally in black on the front; these are copy-righted CVC as opposed to the NCI designation found on the red and black printed fronts.

	NRMT	VG-E	GOOD
COMPLETE SET (72)	250.00	115.00	31.00
COMMON PLAYER (1-72)	2.50	1.15	.30
☐ 1 Babe Hits 3 Homers In A Series Game	20.00	9.00	2.50
☐ 2 Podres Pitching Wins Series	2.50	1.15	.30
☐ 3 Bevans Pitches No Hitter, Almost	2.50	1.15	.30
☐ 4 Box Score Devised By Reporter	2.50	1.15	.30
☐ 5 VanderMeer Pitches Two No Hitters	2.50	1.15	.30
☐ 6 Indians Take Bums	2.50	1.15	.30
☐ 7 DiMag Comes Thru	15.00	6.75	1.90
☐ 8 Mathewson Pitches Three WS Shutouts	3.50	1.55	.45
☐ 9 Haddix Pitches 12 Perfect Innings	2.50	1.15	.30
☐ 10 Thomson's Homer Sinks Dodgers	3.00	1.35	.40
☐ 11 Hubbell Strikes Out Five A.L. Stars	3.00	1.35	.40
☐ 12 Pickoff Ends Series	3.50	1.55	.45

☐ 13 Cards Take Series From Yanks	2.50	1.15	.30
☐ 14 Dizzy And Daffy Dean Win Series	3.50	1.55	.45
☐ 15 Owen Drops 3rd Strike	2.50	1.15	.30
☐ 16 Ruth Calls Shot	20.00	9.00	2.50
☐ 17 Merkle Pulls Boner	3.50	1.55	.45
☐ 18 Larsen Hurls Perfect World Series Game	3.50	1.55	.45
☐ 19 Bean Ball Ends Career of Mickey Cochrane	3.00	1.35	.40
☐ 20 Banks Belts 47 Homers Earns MVP	5.00	2.30	.60
☐ 21 Stan Musial Hits Five Homers in One Day	7.50	3.40	.95
☐ 22 Mickey Mantle Hits Longest Homer	20.00	9.00	2.50
☐ 23 Sievers Captures Home Run Title	2.50	1.15	.30
☐ 24 Gehrig 2130 Consecutive Game Record Ends	12.00	5.50	1.50
☐ 25 Red Schoendienst Key Player Braves Pennant	3.00	1.35	.40
☐ 26 Midget Pinch-Hits For St. Louis	5.00	2.30	.60
☐ 27 Willie Mays Makes Greatest Catch	12.00	5.50	1.50
☐ 28 Homer by Yogi Berra Puts Yanks In 1st	6.00	2.70	.75
☐ 29 Campy NL MVP	6.00	2.70	.75
☐ 30 Bob Turley Hurls Yankees To WS Champions	2.50	1.15	.30
☐ 31 Dodgers Take Series From Sox in Six	2.50	1.15	.30
☐ 32 Furillo Hero as Dodgers Beat Chicago in 3rd WS Game	3.00	1.35	.40
☐ 33 Adcock Gets 4 Homers And A Double	2.50	1.15	.30
☐ 34 Dickey Chosen All-Star Catcher	3.00	1.35	.40
☐ 35 Burdette Beats Yanks In Three WS Games	2.50	1.15	.30
☐ 36 Umpires Clear White Sox Bench	2.50	1.15	.30
☐ 37 Reese Honored As Greatest Dodger SS	4.00	1.80	.50
☐ 38 Joe DiMaggio Hits In 56 Straight	15.00	6.75	1.90
☐ 39 Ted Williams Hits .406 For Season	12.00	5.50	1.50
☐ 40 Walter Johnson Pitches 56 Straight	3.50	1.55	.45
☐ 41 Hodges Hits 4 Home Runs In Nite Game	3.00	1.35	.40
☐ 42 Greenberg Returns to Tigers From Army	3.50	1.55	.45
☐ 43 Ty Cobb Named Best Player Of All Time	12.00	5.50	1.50
☐ 44 Robin Roberts Wins 28 Games	3.50	1.55	.45
☐ 45 Rizzuto's Two Runs Save 1st Place	3.50	1.55	.45
☐ 46 Tigers Beat Out Senators For Pennant	2.50	1.15	.30
☐ 47 Babe Ruth Hits 60th Home Run	20.00	9.00	2.50
☐ 48 Cy Young Honored	3.50	1.55	.45
☐ 49 Killebrew Starts Spring Training	4.00	1.80	.50
☐ 50 Mantle Hits Longest Homer at Stadium	20.00	9.00	2.50
☐ 51 Braves Take Pennant	2.50	1.15	.30
☐ 52 Ted Williams Hero Of All-Star Game	12.00	5.50	1.50
☐ 53 Robinson Saves Dodgers For Play-off Series	9.00	4.00	1.15
☐ 54 Snodgrass Muffs Fly	2.50	1.15	.30
☐ 55 Snider Belts 2 Homers Ties Homer Record	5.00	2.30	.60
☐ 56 Giants Win 26 Straight	2.50	1.15	.30
☐ 57 Ted Kluszewski Stars In 1st Series Win	3.00	1.35	.40
☐ 58 Ott Walks 5 Times In Single Game	3.50	1.55	.45
☐ 59 Harvey Kuenn Takes A.L. Batting Title	2.50	1.15	.30
☐ 60 Bob Feller Hurls 3rd No-Hitter of Career	4.50	2.00	.55
☐ 61 Yanks Champs Again	2.50	1.15	.30
☐ 62 Aaron's Bat Beats Yankees In Series	12.00	5.50	1.50
☐ 63 Warren Spahn Beats Yanks in W.S.	5.00	2.30	.60
☐ 64 Ump's Wrong Call Helps Dodgers Beat Yanks	2.50	1.15	.30
☐ 65 Kaline Hits 3 Homers Two In Same Inning	4.00	1.80	.50
☐ 66 Bob Allison Named AL Rookie of the Year	2.50	1.15	.30
☐ 67 McCovey Blasts Way Into Giant Lineup	4.00	1.80	.50
☐ 68 Colavito Hits Four Homers in One Game	3.50	1.55	.45
☐ 69 Erskine Sets Strike Out Record in World Series	2.50	1.15	.30
☐ 70 Sal Maglie Pitches No-Hit Game	2.50	1.15	.30
☐ 71 Early Wynn Victory Crushes Yanks	3.00	1.35	.40
☐ 72 Nellie Fox AL MVP	3.00	1.35	.40

1961 Nu-Card Scoops

The cards in this 80-card set measure 2 1/2" by 3 1/2". This series depicts great moments in the history of individual ballplayers. Each card is designed as a miniature newspaper front-page, complete with data and picture. Both the number (401-480) and title are printed in red on the obverse, and the story is found on the back. An album was issued to hold the set. The set has been illegally reprinted, which has served to suppress the demand for the originals as well as the reprints.

	NRMT	VG-E	GOOD
COMPLETE SET (80)	150.00	70.00	19.00
COMMON PLAYER (401-480)	.75	.35	.09
☐ 401 Jim Gentile	.75	.35	.09
☐ 402 Warren Spahn (No-hitter)	3.00	1.35	.40
☐ 403 Bill Mazeroski	1.00	.45	.13
☐ 404 Willie Mays: (Three triples)	7.50	3.40	.95
☐ 405 Woodie Held	.75	.35	.09
☐ 406 Vern Law	1.00	.45	.13
☐ 407 Pete Runnels	.75	.35	.09
☐ 408 Lew Burdette (No-hitter)	1.00	.45	.13
☐ 409 Dick Stuart	.75	.35	.09
☐ 410 Don Cardwell	.75	.35	.09
☐ 411 Camilo Pascual	.75	.35	.09
☐ 412 Ed Mathews	3.00	1.35	.40
☐ 413 Dick Groat	1.00	.45	.13
☐ 414 Gene Autry OWN	3.00	1.35	.40
☐ 415 Bobby Richardson	1.50	.65	.19
☐ 416 Roger Maris	7.50	3.40	.95
☐ 417 Fred Merkle	.75	.35	.09
☐ 418 Don Larsen	1.00	.45	.13
☐ 419 Mickey Cochrane	1.00	.45	.13
☐ 420 Ernie Banks	3.50	1.55	.45
☐ 421 Stan Musial	6.00	2.70	.75
☐ 422 Mickey Mantle (Longest homer)	15.00	6.75	1.90
☐ 423 Roy Sievers	.75	.35	.09
☐ 424 Lou Gehrig	9.00	4.00	1.15

☐ 425 Red Schoendienst	2.00	.90	.25
☐ 426 Eddie Gaedel	2.00	.90	.25
☐ 427 Willie Mays	7.50	3.40	.95
(Greatest catch)			
☐ 428 Jackie Robinson	6.00	2.70	.75
☐ 429 Roy Campanella	6.00	2.70	.75
☐ 430 Bob Turley	.75	.35	.09
☐ 431 Larry Sherry	.75	.35	.09
☐ 432 Carl Furillo	1.00	.45	.13
☐ 433 Joe Adcock	.75	.35	.09
☐ 434 Bill Dickey	1.00	.45	.13
☐ 435 Lew Burdette 3 wins	.75	.35	.09
☐ 436 Umpire Clears Bench	.75	.35	.09
☐ 437 Pee Wee Reese	3.50	1.55	.45
☐ 438 Joe DiMaggio	12.50	5.75	1.55
(56 Game Hit Streak)			
☐ 439 Ted Williams	9.00	4.00	1.15
(Hits .406)			
☐ 440 Walter Johnson	3.50	1.55	.45
☐ 441 Gil Hodges	2.00	.90	.25
☐ 442 Hank Greenberg	2.50	1.15	.30
☐ 443 Ty Cobb	9.00	4.00	1.15
☐ 444 Robin Roberts	3.00	1.35	.40
☐ 445 Phil Rizzuto	2.50	1.15	.30
☐ 446 Hal Newhouser	2.00	.90	.25
☐ 447 Babe Ruth 60th Homer	15.00	6.75	1.90
☐ 448 Cy Young	3.50	1.55	.45
☐ 449 Harmon Killebrew	3.50	1.55	.45
☐ 450 Mickey Mantle	15.00	6.75	1.90
(Longest homer)			
☐ 451 Braves Take Pennant	.75	.35	.09
☐ 452 Ted Williams	9.00	4.00	1.15
(All-Star Hero)			
☐ 453 Yogi Berra	6.00	2.70	.75
☐ 454 Fred Snodgrass	.75	.35	.09
☐ 455 Ruth 3 Homers	15.00	6.75	1.90
☐ 456 Giants 26 Game Streak	.75	.35	.09
☐ 457 Ted Kluszewski	1.25	.55	.16
☐ 458 Mel Ott	2.00	.90	.25
☐ 459 Harvey Kuenn	1.00	.45	.13
☐ 460 Bob Feller	3.50	1.55	.45
☐ 461 Casey Stengel	3.00	1.35	.40
☐ 462 Hank Aaron	7.50	3.40	.95
☐ 463 Spahn Beats Yanks	2.50	1.15	.30
☐ 464 Ump's Wrong Call	.75	.35	.09
☐ 465 Al Kaline	3.50	1.55	.45
☐ 466 Bob Allison	.75	.35	.09
☐ 467 Joe DiMaggio	12.50	5.75	1.55
(Four Homers)			
☐ 468 Rocky Colavito	1.25	.55	.16
☐ 469 Carl Erskine	1.00	.45	.13
☐ 470 Sal Maglie	1.00	.45	.13
☐ 471 Early Wynn	2.00	.90	.25
☐ 472 Nellie Fox	1.50	.65	.19
☐ 473 Marty Marion	1.00	.45	.13
☐ 474 Johnny Podres	.75	.35	.09
☐ 475 Mickey Owen	.75	.35	.09
☐ 476 Dean Brothers	2.50	1.15	.30
(Dizzy and Daffy)			
☐ 477 Christy Mathewson	3.00	1.35	.40
☐ 478 Harvey Haddix	.75	.35	.09
☐ 479 Carl Hubbell	1.00	.45	.13
☐ 480 Bobby Thomson	1.00	.45	.13

1991 O-Pee-Chee Premier

The 1991 O-Pee-Chee Premier set contains 132 standard-size (2 1/2" by 3 1/2") cards. The fronts feature color action player photos on a white card face. All the pictures are bordered in gold above, while the color of the border stripes on the other three sides varies from card to card. The player's name, team name, and position (the last item in English and French) appear below the picture. In a horizontal format, the backs have a color head shot and the team logo in a circular format. Biography and statistics (1990 and career) are presented on an orange and yellow striped background. The cards are arranged in alphabetical order and numbered on the back. Small packs of these cards were given out at the Fan Fest to commemorate the 1991 All-Star Game in Canada. The key Rookie Cards in this set are Lance Dickson, Kirk Dressendorfer, and Gary Scott.

	MT	EX-MT	VG
COMPLETE SET (132)	18.00	8.00	2.30
COMMON PLAYER (1-132)	.05	.02	.01
☐ 1 Roberto Alomar	.50	.23	.06
☐ 2 Sandy Alomar Jr.	.08	.04	.01
☐ 3 Moises Alou	.15	.07	.02
☐ 4 Brian Barnes	.20	.09	.03
☐ 5 Steve Bedrosian	.05	.02	.01
☐ 6 George Bell	.08	.04	.01
☐ 7 Juan Bell	.05	.02	.01
☐ 8 Albert Belle	.40	.18	.05
☐ 9 Bud Black	.05	.02	.01
☐ 10 Mike Boddicker	.05	.02	.01
☐ 11 Wade Boggs	.35	.16	.04
☐ 12 Barry Bonds	.35	.16	.04
☐ 13 Denis Boucher	.10	.05	.01
☐ 14 George Brett	.30	.14	.04
☐ 15 Hubie Brooks	.05	.02	.01
☐ 16 Brett Butler	.08	.04	.01
☐ 17 Ivan Calderon	.05	.02	.01
☐ 18 Jose Canseco	.60	.25	.08
☐ 19 Gary Carter	.10	.05	.01
☐ 20 Joe Carter	.20	.09	.03
☐ 21 Jack Clark	.08	.04	.01
☐ 22 Will Clark	.60	.25	.08
☐ 23 Roger Clemens	.75	.35	.09
☐ 24 Alex Cole	.08	.04	.01
☐ 25 Vince Coleman	.10	.05	.01
☐ 26 Jeff Conine	.45	.20	.06
☐ 27 Milt Cuyler	.20	.09	.03
☐ 28 Danny Darwin	.05	.02	.01
☐ 29 Eric Davis	.15	.07	.02
☐ 30 Glenn Davis	.10	.05	.01
☐ 31 Andre Dawson	.20	.09	.03
☐ 32 Ken Dayley	.05	.02	.01
☐ 33 Steve Decker	.25	.11	.03
☐ 34 Delino DeShields	.25	.11	.03
☐ 35 Lance Dickson	.25	.11	.03
☐ 36 Kirk Dressendorfer	.10	.05	.01
☐ 37 Shawon Dunston	.08	.04	.01
☐ 38 Dennis Eckersley	.12	.05	.02
☐ 39 Dwight Evans	.08	.04	.01
☐ 40 Howard Farmer	.08	.04	.01
☐ 41 Junior Felix	.08	.04	.01
☐ 42 Alex Fernandez	.20	.09	.03
☐ 43 Tony Fernandez	.08	.04	.01
☐ 44 Cecil Fielder	.40	.18	.05
☐ 45 Carlton Fisk	.20	.09	.03
☐ 46 Willie Fraser	.05	.02	.01
☐ 47 Gary Gaetti	.05	.02	.01
☐ 48 Andres Galarraga	.05	.02	.01
☐ 49 Ron Gant	.25	.11	.03
☐ 50 Kirk Gibson	.08	.04	.01
☐ 51 Bernard Gilkey	.20	.09	.03
☐ 52 Leo Gomez	.45	.20	.06
☐ 53 Rene Gonzales	.05	.02	.01
☐ 54 Juan Gonzalez	3.00	1.35	.40
☐ 55 Dwight Gooden	.15	.07	.02
☐ 56 Ken Griffey Jr.	3.00	1.35	.40
☐ 57 Kelly Gruber	.08	.04	.01
☐ 58 Pedro Guerrero	.08	.04	.01
☐ 59 Tony Gwynn	.35	.16	.04
☐ 60 Chris Hammond	.12	.05	.02
☐ 61 Ron Hassey	.05	.02	.01
☐ 62 Rickey Henderson	.40	.18	.05
☐ 63 Tom Henke	.08	.04	.01
☐ 64 Orel Hershiser	.12	.05	.02
☐ 65 Chris Hoiles	.25	.11	.03
☐ 66 Todd Hundley	.15	.07	.02
☐ 67 Pete Incaviglia	.08	.04	.01
☐ 68 Danny Jackson	.05	.02	.01
☐ 69 Barry Jones	.05	.02	.01
☐ 70 Dave Justice	1.50	.65	.19
☐ 71 Jimmy Key	.08	.04	.01
☐ 72 Ray Lankford	.60	.25	.08

	MT	EX-MT	VG
☐ 73 Darren Lewis	.15	.07	.02
☐ 74 Kevin Maas	.20	.09	.03
☐ 75 Denny Martinez	.08	.04	.01
☐ 76 Tino Martinez	.20	.09	.03
☐ 77 Don Mattingly	.40	.18	.05
☐ 78 Willie McGee	.08	.04	.01
☐ 79 Fred McGriff	.25	.11	.03
☐ 80 Hensley Meulens	.08	.04	.01
☐ 81 Kevin Mitchell	.12	.05	.02
☐ 82 Paul Molitor	.12	.05	.02
☐ 83 Mickey Morandini	.15	.07	.02
☐ 84 Jack Morris	.12	.05	.02
☐ 85 Dale Murphy	.12	.05	.02
☐ 86 Eddie Murray	.15	.07	.02
☐ 87 Chris Nabholz	.12	.05	.02
☐ 88 Tim Naehring	.15	.07	.02
☐ 89 Otis Nixon	.08	.04	.01
☐ 90 Jose Offerman	.10	.05	.01
☐ 91 Bob Ojeda	.05	.02	.01
☐ 92 John Olerud	.30	.14	.04
☐ 93 Gregg Olson	.10	.05	.01
☐ 94 Dave Parker	.08	.04	.01
☐ 95 Terry Pendleton	.15	.07	.02
☐ 96 Kirby Puckett	.40	.18	.05
☐ 97 Tim Raines	.10	.05	.01
☐ 98 Jeff Reardon	.10	.05	.01
☐ 99 Dave Righetti	.05	.02	.01
☐ 100 Cal Ripken	.90	.40	.11
☐ 101 Mel Rojas	.08	.04	.01
☐ 102 Nolan Ryan	2.50	1.15	.30
☐ 103 Ryne Sandberg	.75	.35	.09
☐ 104 Scott Sanderson	.05	.02	.01
☐ 105 Benny Santiago	.10	.05	.01
☐ 106 Pete Schourek	.15	.07	.02
☐ 107 Gary Scott	.25	.11	.03
☐ 108 Terry Shumpert	.05	.02	.01
☐ 109 Ruben Sierra	.35	.16	.04
☐ 110 Doug Simons	.10	.05	.01
☐ 111 Dave Smith	.05	.02	.01
☐ 112 Ozzie Smith	.15	.07	.02
☐ 113 Cory Snyder	.08	.04	.01
☐ 114 Luis Sojo	.08	.04	.01
☐ 115 Dave Stewart	.08	.04	.01
☐ 116 Dave Stieb	.08	.04	.01
☐ 117 Darryl Strawberry	.40	.18	.05
☐ 118 Pat Tabler	.05	.02	.01
☐ 119 Wade Taylor	.12	.05	.02
☐ 120 Bobby Thigpen	.08	.04	.01
☐ 121 Frank Thomas	6.00	2.70	.75
☐ 122 Mike Timlin	.12	.05	.02
☐ 123 Alan Trammell	.10	.05	.01
☐ 124 Mo Vaughn	.40	.18	.05
☐ 125 Tim Wallach	.08	.04	.01
☐ 126 Devon White	.08	.04	.01
☐ 127 Mark Whiten	.25	.11	.03
☐ 128 Bernie Williams	.50	.23	.06
☐ 129 Willie Wilson	.08	.04	.01
☐ 130 Dave Winfield	.30	.14	.04
☐ 131 Robin Yount	.30	.14	.04
☐ 132 Checklist Card	.08	.04	.01

1992 O-Pee-Chee Premier

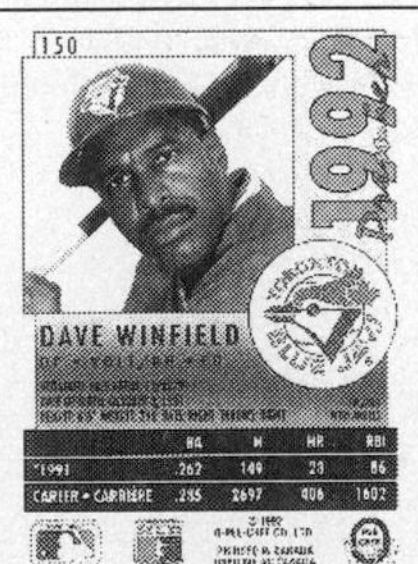

The 1992 O-Pee-Chee Premier baseball set consists of 198 cards, each measuring the standard-size (2 1/2" by 3 1/2"). The fronts feature a mix of color action and posed player photos bordered in white. Gold stripes edge the picture on top and below, while colored stripes edge the pictures on the left and right sides. The player's name, position, and team appear in the bottom white border. In addition to a color head shot, the backs carry biography and the team logo on a panel that shades from green to blue as well as statistics on a black panel. The cards are numbered on the back.

	MT	EX-MT	VG
COMPLETE SET (198)	14.00	6.25	1.75
COMMON PLAYER (1-198)	.05	.02	.01
☐ 1 Wade Boggs	.25	.11	.03
☐ 2 John Smiley	.08	.04	.01
☐ 3 Checklist	.08	.04	.01
☐ 4 Ron Gant	.12	.05	.02
☐ 5 Mike Bordick	.15	.07	.02
☐ 6 Charlie Hayes	.08	.04	.01
☐ 7 Kevin Morton	.08	.04	.01
☐ 8 Checklist	.05	.02	.01
☐ 9 Chris Gwynn	.05	.02	.01
☐ 10 Melido Perez	.08	.04	.01
☐ 11 Dan Gladden	.05	.02	.01
☐ 12 Brian McRae	.08	.04	.01
☐ 13 Dennis Martinez	.08	.04	.01
☐ 14 Bob Scanlan	.08	.04	.01
☐ 15 Julio Franco	.10	.05	.01
☐ 16 Ruben Amaro	.08	.04	.01
☐ 17 Mo Sanford	.10	.05	.01
☐ 18 Scott Bankhead	.05	.02	.01
☐ 19 Dickie Thon	.05	.02	.01
☐ 20 Chris James	.05	.02	.01
☐ 21 Mike Huff	.05	.02	.01
☐ 22 Orlando Merced	.10	.05	.01
☐ 23 Chris Sabo	.08	.04	.01
☐ 24 Jose Canseco	.35	.16	.04
☐ 25 Reggie Sanders	.45	.20	.06
☐ 26 Chris Nabholz	.08	.04	.01
☐ 27 Kevin Seitzer	.05	.02	.01
☐ 28 Ryan Bowen	.10	.05	.01
☐ 29 Gary Carter	.10	.05	.01
☐ 30 Wayne Rosenthal	.05	.02	.01
☐ 31 Alan Trammell	.08	.04	.01
☐ 32 Doug Drabek	.08	.04	.01
☐ 33 Craig Shipley	.05	.02	.01
☐ 34 Ryne Sandberg	.45	.20	.06
☐ 35 Chuck Knoblauch	.25	.11	.03
☐ 36 Bret Barberie	.10	.05	.01
☐ 37 Tim Naehring	.08	.04	.01
☐ 38 Omar Olivares	.05	.02	.01
☐ 39 Royce Clayton	.20	.09	.03
☐ 40 Brent Mayne	.08	.04	.01
☐ 41 Darrin Fletcher	.05	.02	.01
☐ 42 Howard Johnson	.08	.04	.01
☐ 43 Steve Sax	.08	.04	.01
☐ 44 Greg Swindell	.08	.04	.01
☐ 45 Andre Dawson	.15	.07	.02
☐ 46 Kent Hrbek	.08	.04	.01
☐ 47 Dwight Gooden	.10	.05	.01
☐ 48 Mark Leiter	.05	.02	.01
☐ 49 Tom Glavine	.20	.09	.03
☐ 50 Mo Vaughn	.12	.05	.02
☐ 51 Doug Jones	.05	.02	.01
☐ 52 Brian Barnes	.08	.04	.01
☐ 53 Rob Dibble	.08	.04	.01
☐ 54 Kevin McReynolds	.08	.04	.01
☐ 55 Ivan Rodriguez	.60	.25	.08
☐ 56 Scott Livingstone	.10	.05	.01
☐ 57 Mike Magnante	.08	.04	.01
☐ 58 Pete Schourek	.05	.02	.01
☐ 59 Frank Thomas	1.00	.45	.13
☐ 60 Kirk McCaskill	.05	.02	.01
☐ 61 Wally Joyner	.08	.04	.01
☐ 62 Rick Aguilera	.05	.02	.01
☐ 63 Eric Karros	.60	.25	.08
☐ 64 Tino Martinez	.10	.05	.01
☐ 65 Bryan Hickerson	.10	.05	.01
☐ 66 Ruben Sierra	.20	.09	.03
☐ 67 Willie Randolph	.05	.02	.01
☐ 68 Bill Landrum	.05	.02	.01
☐ 69 Bip Roberts	.08	.04	.01
☐ 70 Cecil Fielder	.25	.11	.03
☐ 71 Pat Kelly	.10	.05	.01
☐ 72 Kenny Lofton	.35	.16	.04
☐ 73 John Franco	.08	.04	.01
☐ 74 Phil Plantier	.25	.11	.03
☐ 75 Dave Martinez	.08	.04	.01
☐ 76 Warren Newson	.05	.02	.01
☐ 77 Chito Martinez	.08	.04	.01
☐ 78 Brian Hunter	.15	.07	.02
☐ 79 Jack Morris	.10	.05	.01
☐ 80 Eric King	.05	.02	.01
☐ 81 Nolan Ryan	.60	.25	.08

☐ 82 Bret Saberhagen	.08	.04	.01
☐ 83 Roberto Kelly	.10	.05	.01
☐ 84 Ozzie Smith	.15	.07	.02
☐ 85 Chuck McElroy	.05	.02	.01
☐ 86 Carlton Fisk	.15	.07	.02
☐ 87 Mike Mussina	.60	.25	.08
☐ 88 Mark Carreon	.05	.02	.01
☐ 89 Ken Hill	.08	.04	.01
☐ 90 Rick Cerone	.05	.02	.01
☐ 91 Deion Sanders	.25	.11	.03
☐ 92 Don Mattingly	.25	.11	.03
☐ 93 Danny Tartabull	.10	.05	.01
☐ 94 Keith Miller	.05	.02	.01
☐ 95 Gregg Jefferies	.10	.05	.01
☐ 96 Barry Larkin	.10	.05	.01
☐ 97 Kevin Mitchell	.10	.05	.01
☐ 98 Rick Sutcliffe	.08	.04	.01
☐ 99 Mark McGwire	.25	.11	.03
☐ 100 Albert Belle	.12	.05	.02
☐ 101 Gregg Olson	.10	.05	.01
☐ 102 Kirby Puckett	.35	.16	.04
☐ 103 Luis Gonzalez	.08	.04	.01
☐ 104 Randy Myers	.08	.04	.01
☐ 105 Roger Clemens	.35	.16	.04
☐ 106 Tony Gwynn	.25	.11	.03
☐ 107 Jeff Bagwell	.60	.25	.08
☐ 108 John Wetteland	.10	.05	.01
☐ 109 Bernie Williams	.15	.07	.02
☐ 110 Scott Kamieniecki	.08	.04	.01
☐ 111 Robin Yount	.25	.11	.03
☐ 112 Dean Palmer	.25	.11	.03
☐ 113 Tim Belcher	.08	.04	.01
☐ 114 George Brett	.25	.11	.03
☐ 115 Frank Viola	.10	.05	.01
☐ 116 Kelly Gruber	.08	.04	.01
☐ 117 David Justice	.30	.14	.04
☐ 118 Scott Leius	.05	.02	.01
☐ 119 Jeff Fassero	.05	.02	.01
☐ 120 Sammy Sosa	.08	.04	.01
☐ 121 Al Osuna	.05	.02	.01
☐ 122 Wilson Alvarez	.08	.04	.01
☐ 123 Jose Offerman	.10	.05	.01
☐ 124 Mel Rojas	.08	.04	.01
☐ 125 Shawon Dunston	.08	.04	.01
☐ 126 Pete Incaviglia	.05	.02	.01
☐ 127 Von Hayes	.05	.02	.01
☐ 128 Dave Gallagher	.05	.02	.01
☐ 129 Eric Davis	.10	.05	.01
☐ 130 Roberto Alomar	.35	.16	.04
☐ 131 Mike Gallego	.05	.02	.01
☐ 132 Robin Ventura	.25	.11	.03
☐ 133 Bill Swift	.08	.04	.01
☐ 134 John Kruk	.08	.04	.01
☐ 135 Craig Biggio	.10	.05	.01
☐ 136 Eddie Taubensee	.08	.04	.01
☐ 137 Cal Ripken	.50	.23	.06
☐ 138 Charles Nagy	.15	.07	.02
☐ 139 Jose Melendez	.05	.02	.01
☐ 140 Jim Abbott	.12	.05	.02
☐ 141 Paul Molitor	.10	.05	.01
☐ 142 Tom Candiotti	.08	.04	.01
☐ 143 Bobby Bonilla	.15	.07	.02
☐ 144 Matt Williams	.10	.05	.01
☐ 145 Brett Butler	.08	.04	.01
☐ 146 Will Clark	.35	.16	.04
☐ 147 Rickey Henderson	.35	.16	.04
☐ 148 Ray Lankford	.20	.09	.03
☐ 149 Bill Pecota	.05	.02	.01
☐ 150 Dave Winfield	.20	.09	.03
☐ 151 Darren Lewis	.10	.05	.01
☐ 152 Bob MacDonald	.05	.02	.01
☐ 153 David Segui	.08	.04	.01
☐ 154 Benny Santiago	.10	.05	.01
☐ 155 Chuck Finley	.05	.02	.01
☐ 156 Andujar Cedeno	.10	.05	.01
☐ 157 Barry Bonds	.25	.11	.03
☐ 158 Joe Grahe	.10	.05	.01
☐ 159 Frank Castillo	.12	.05	.02
☐ 160 Dave Burba	.08	.04	.01
☐ 161 Leo Gomez	.12	.05	.02
☐ 162 Orel Hershiser	.10	.05	.01
☐ 163 Delino DeShields	.15	.07	.02
☐ 164 Sandy Alomar Jr.	.10	.05	.01
☐ 165 Denny Neagle	.08	.04	.01
☐ 166 Fred McGriff	.20	.09	.03
☐ 167 Ken Griffey Jr.	.90	.40	.11
☐ 168 Juan Guzman	.75	.35	.09
☐ 169 Bobby Rose	.05	.02	.01
☐ 170 Steve Avery	.25	.11	.03
☐ 171 Rich DeLucia	.05	.02	.01
☐ 172 Mike Timlin	.08	.04	.01
☐ 173 Randy Johnson	.08	.04	.01
☐ 174 Paul Gibson	.05	.02	.01
☐ 175 David Cone	.10	.05	.01
☐ 176 Marquis Grissom	.15	.07	.02
☐ 177 Kurt Stillwell	.05	.02	.01
☐ 178 Mark Whiten	.10	.05	.01
☐ 179 Darryl Strawberry	.25	.11	.03
☐ 180 Mike Morgan	.08	.04	.01
☐ 181 Scott Scudder	.05	.02	.01
☐ 182 George Bell	.08	.04	.01
☐ 183 Alvin Davis	.05	.02	.01
☐ 184 Len Dykstra	.08	.04	.01
☐ 185 Kyle Abbott	.05	.02	.01
☐ 186 Chris Haney	.08	.04	.01
☐ 187 Junior Noboa	.05	.02	.01
☐ 188 Dennis Eckersley	.12	.05	.02
☐ 189 Derek Bell	.20	.09	.03
☐ 190 Lee Smith	.08	.04	.01
☐ 191 Andres Galarraga	.05	.02	.01
☐ 192 Jack Armstrong	.05	.02	.01
☐ 193 Eddie Murray	.15	.07	.02
☐ 194 Joe Carter	.20	.09	.03
☐ 195 Terry Pendleton	.12	.05	.02
☐ 196 Darryl Kile	.10	.05	.01
☐ 197 Rod Beck	.10	.05	.01
☐ 198 Hubie Brooks	.05	.02	.01

1973 Orioles Johnny Pro

This 25-card set measures approximately 4 1/4" by 7 1/4" and features members of the 1973 Baltimore Orioles. The cards were designed to be pushed-out in a style similar to the 1964 Topps Stand Ups. The sides of the cards have a small advertisement for Johnny Pro Enterprises and even gives a phone number where they could have been reached. Oddly, the Orlando Pena card was not available in a die-cut version. The cards have the player's photo against a distinctive solid green background. The cards are blank backed. There are several variations within the set; the complete set price below does not include the any of the variation cards. The set is checklisted in order by uniform number. According to informed sources, there were 15,000 sets produced.

	NRMT-MT	EXC	G-VG
COMPLETE SET (25)	200.00	90.00	25.00
COMMON PLAYER	4.00	1.80	.50
☐ 1 Al Bumbry OF	4.00	1.80	.50
☐ 2 Rich Coggins OF	4.00	1.80	.50
☐ 3A Bobby Grich 2B (Fielding)	8.00	3.60	1.00
☐ 3B Bobby Grich 2B (Batting)	16.00	7.25	2.00
☐ 4 Earl Weaver MG	8.00	3.60	1.00
☐ 5A Brooks Robinson 3B (Fielding)	20.00	9.00	2.50
☐ 5B Brooks Robinson 3B (Batting)	40.00	18.00	5.00
☐ 6 Paul Blair OF	6.00	2.70	.75
☐ 7 Mark Belanger SS	6.00	2.70	.75
☐ 8 Andy Etchebarren C	4.00	1.80	.50
☐ 10 Elrod Hendricks C	4.00	1.80	.50
☐ 11 Terry Crowley OF	4.00	1.80	.50
☐ 12 Tommy Davis OF	6.00	2.70	.75
☐ 13 Doyle Alexander P	6.00	2.70	.75
☐ 14 Merv Rettenmund OF	4.00	1.80	.50

	MT	EX-MT	VG
☐ 15 Frank Baker IF	4.00	1.80	.50
☐ 19 Dave McNally P	6.00	2.70	.75
☐ 21 Larry Brown IF	4.00	1.80	.50
☐ 22A Jim Palmer P	20.00	9.00	2.50
☐ 22B Jim Palmer P (Pitching)	40.00	18.00	5.00
☐ 23 Grant Jackson P	4.00	1.80	.50
☐ 25 Don Baylor OF	8.00	3.60	1.00
☐ 26 John(Boog) Powell 1B	10.00	4.50	1.25
☐ 27 Orlando Pena P (NOT die-cut)	12.00	5.50	1.50
☐ 32 Earl Williams C	4.00	1.80	.50
☐ 34 Bob Reynolds P	4.00	1.80	.50
☐ 35 Mike Cuellar P	6.00	2.70	.75
☐ 39 Eddie Watt P	4.00	1.80	.50

1987 Orioles French Bray

16 SCOTT McGREGOR, P
Compliments of
FRENCH/BRAY, INC.

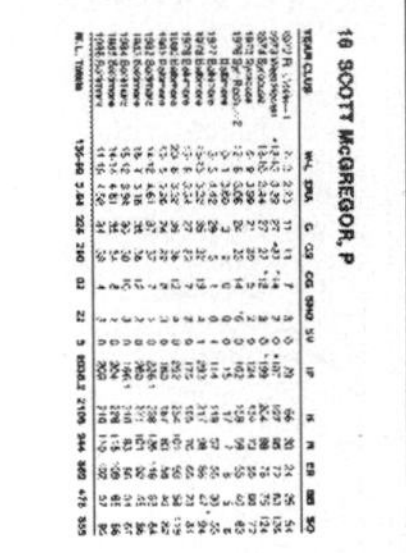

The 1987 French Bray set contains 30 cards (featuring members of the Baltimore Orioles) measuring approximately 2 1/4" by 3". The fronts have facial photos with white and orange borders; the horizontally oriented backs are white and feature career stats. The cards were given away in perforated sheet form on Photo Card Day at the Orioles home game on July 26, 1987. A large team photo was also included as one of the three panels in this perforated card set. The cards are unnumbered except for uniform number.

	MT	EX-MT	VG
COMPLETE SET (30)	12.50	5.75	1.55
COMMON PLAYER	.35	.16	.04
☐ 2 Alan Wiggins	.35	.16	.04
☐ 3 Bill Ripken	.60	.25	.08
☐ 6 Floyd Rayford	.35	.16	.04
☐ 7 Cal Ripken Sr. MG	.45	.20	.06
☐ 8 Cal Ripken Jr.	5.00	2.30	.60
☐ 9 Jim Dwyer	.35	.16	.04
☐ 10 Terry Crowley CO	.35	.16	.04
☐ 15 Terry Kennedy	.45	.20	.06
☐ 16 Scott McGregor	.45	.20	.06
☐ 18 Larry Sheets	.45	.20	.06
☐ 19 Fred Lynn	.60	.25	.08
☐ 20 Frank Robinson CO	1.50	.65	.19
☐ 24 Dave Schmidt	.35	.16	.04
☐ 25 Ray Knight	.45	.20	.06
☐ 27 Lee Lacy	.35	.16	.04
☐ 31 Mark Wiley CO	.35	.16	.04
☐ 32 Mark Williamson	.35	.16	.04
☐ 33 Eddie Murray	1.50	.65	.19
☐ 38 Ken Gerhart	.35	.16	.04
☐ 39 Ken Dixon	.35	.16	.04
☐ 40 Jimmy Williams CO	.35	.16	.04
☐ 42 Mike Griffin	.35	.16	.04
☐ 43 Mike Young	.35	.16	.04
☐ 44 Elrod Hendricks CO	.35	.16	.04
☐ 45 Eric Bell	.35	.16	.04
☐ 46 Mike Flanagan	.45	.20	.06
☐ 49 Tom Niedenfuer	.35	.16	.04
☐ 52 Mike Boddicker	.45	.20	.06
☐ 54 John Habyan	.35	.16	.04
☐ 57 Tony Arnold	.35	.16	.04

1988 Orioles French Bray

20 FRANK ROBINSON, Manager
Compliments of
FRENCH BRAY, INC.

This set was distributed as a perforated set of 30 full-color cards attached to a large team photo on July 31, 1988, the Baltimore Orioles' Photo Card Day. The cards measure approximately 2 1/4" by 3 1/16". Card backs are simply done in black and white with statistics but no narrative or any personal information. Cards are unnumbered except for uniform number. Card front have a thin orange inner border and have the French Bray (Printing and Graphic Communication) logo in the lower right corner.

	MT	EX-MT	VG
COMPLETE SET (30)	10.00	4.50	1.25
COMMON PLAYER	.35	.16	.04
☐ 2 Don Buford CO	.35	.16	.04
☐ 6 Joe Orsulak	.45	.20	.06
☐ 7 Bill Ripken	.45	.20	.06
☐ 8 Cal Ripken	4.00	1.80	.50
☐ 9 Jim Dwyer	.35	.16	.04
☐ 10 Terry Crowley CO	.35	.16	.04
☐ 12 Mike Morgan	.60	.25	.08
☐ 14 Mickey Tettleton	.75	.35	.09
☐ 15 Terry Kennedy	.45	.20	.06
☐ 17 Pete Stanicek	.35	.16	.04
☐ 18 Larry Sheets	.45	.20	.06
☐ 19 Fred Lynn	.60	.25	.08
☐ 20 Frank Robinson MG	1.25	.55	.16
☐ 23 Ozzie Peraza	.35	.16	.04
☐ 24 Dave Schmidt	.35	.16	.04
☐ 25 Rick Schu	.35	.16	.04
☐ 28 Jim Traber	.35	.16	.04
☐ 31 Herm Starrette CO	.35	.16	.04
☐ 33 Eddie Murray	1.25	.55	.16
☐ 34 Jeff Ballard	.35	.16	.04
☐ 38 Ken Gerhart	.35	.16	.04
☐ 40 Minnie Mendoza CO	.35	.16	.04
☐ 41 Don Aase	.35	.16	.04
☐ 44 Elrod Hendricks CO	.35	.16	.04
☐ 47 John Hart CO	.35	.16	.04
☐ 48 Jose Bautista	.35	.16	.04
☐ 49 Tom Niedenfuer	.35	.16	.04
☐ 52 Mike Boddicker	.45	.20	.06
☐ 53 Jay Tibbs	.35	.16	.04
☐ 88 Rene Gonzales	.45	.20	.06

1989 Orioles French Bray/WWF

The 1989 French Bray/WWF Orioles set contains 31 cards measuring approximately 2 1/4" by 3". The fronts have facial photos with orange and white borders; the backs are white and feature career stats. The set was given away at a Baltimore home game on May 12, 1989. The cards are numbered by the players' uniform numbers.

	MT	EX-MT	VG
COMPLETE SET (32)	10.00	4.50	1.25
COMMON PLAYER	.35	.16	.04
☐ 3 Bill Ripken	.45	.20	.06
☐ 6 Joe Orsulak	.45	.20	.06

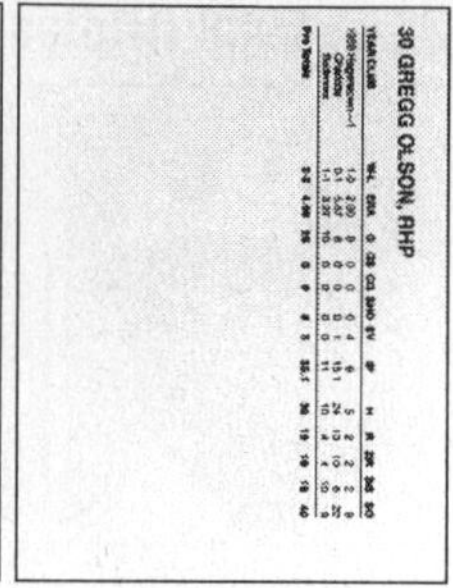

☐ 7 Cal Ripken Sr. CO	.45	.20	.06
☐ 8 Cal Ripken Jr.	3.00	1.35	.40
☐ 9 Brady Anderson	1.25	.55	.16
☐ 10 Steve Finley	.75	.35	.09
☐ 11 Craig Worthington	.45	.20	.06
☐ 12 Mike Devereaux	1.00	.45	.13
☐ 14 Mickey Tettleton	.75	.35	.09
☐ 15 Randy Milligan	.75	.35	.09
☐ 16 Phil Bradley	.45	.20	.06
☐ 18 Bob Milacki	.60	.25	.08
☐ 19 Larry Sheets	.45	.20	.06
☐ 20 Frank Robinson MG	1.00	.45	.13
☐ 21 Mark Thurmond	.35	.16	.04
☐ 23 Kevin Hickey	.35	.16	.04
☐ 24 Dave Schmidt	.45	.20	.06
☐ 28 Jim Traber	.35	.16	.04
☐ 29 Jeff Ballard	.45	.20	.06
☐ 30 Gregg Olson	1.25	.55	.16
☐ 31 Al Jackson CO	.35	.16	.04
☐ 32 Mark Williamson	.35	.16	.04
☐ 36 Bob Melvin	.35	.16	.04
☐ 37 Brian Holton	.35	.16	.04
☐ 40 Tom McCraw CO	.35	.16	.04
☐ 42 Pete Harnisch	.75	.35	.09
☐ 43 Francisco Melendez	.35	.16	.04
☐ 44 Elrod Hendricks CO	.35	.16	.04
☐ 46 Johnny Oates CO	.45	.20	.06
☐ 48 Jose Bautista	.35	.16	.04
☐ 88 Rene Gonzales	.45	.20	.06
☐ NNO Sponsor ad	.35	.16	.04

1991 Orioles Crown

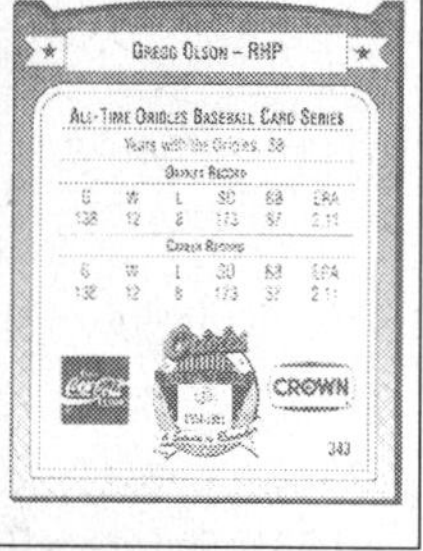

This 501-card set was produced by the Baltimore Orioles in conjunction with Crown Gasoline Stations and Coca-Cola. The cards measure approximately 2 1/2" by 3 1/8" and feature every Oriole player in the team's modern history (1954-1991). The cards were issued in four series, with ten twelve-card sheets per set. The front features a black and white head shot of the player, with a green border and an orange picture frame. The player's name and position appear above the picture, while the Orioles' team logo is superimposed at the lower left corner. In a similar design to the front, the back is printed in black and gray, and presents the player's Orioles statistics and Major League statistics. The sponsors' logos adorn the bottom of the card back, with the card number in the lower right hand corner. The first set was given away at the Orioles May 17th game against the California Angels, and the following day the set went on sale at Baltimore area Crown gasoline stations for 1.99 with an eight gallon fill-up. The second set was given away at the Orioles June 28th game against the Boston Red Sox, and again it went on sale the following day at Crown gasoline stations. The third set was given away at the Orioles August 11th game against the Chicago White Sox and went on sale on the same day. The fourth set went on sale at Crown gasoline stations on September 16. The cards are arranged alphabetically by player and checklisted below accordingly.

	MT	EX-MT	VG
COMPLETE SET (501)	40.00	18.00	5.00
COMMON PLAYER (1-360)	.10	.05	.01
COMMON PLAYER (361-501)	.10	.05	.01
☐ 1 Don Aase	.15	.07	.02
☐ 2 Cal Abrams	.10	.05	.01
☐ 3 Jerry Adair	.10	.05	.01
☐ 4 Bobby Adams	.10	.05	.01
☐ 5 Mike Adamson	.10	.05	.01
☐ 6 Jay Aldrich	.10	.05	.01
☐ 7 Bob Alexander	.10	.05	.01
☐ 8 Doyle Alexander	.15	.07	.02
☐ 9 Brady Anderson	.35	.16	.04
☐ 10 John Anderson	.10	.05	.01
☐ 11 Mike Anderson	.10	.05	.01
☐ 12 Luis Aparicio	.50	.23	.06
☐ 13 Tony Arnold	.10	.05	.01
☐ 14 Bobby Avila	.10	.05	.01
☐ 15 Benny Ayala	.10	.05	.01
☐ 16 Bob Bailor	.10	.05	.01
☐ 17 Frank Baker	.10	.05	.01
☐ 18 Jeff Ballard	.10	.05	.01
☐ 19 George Bamberger	.10	.05	.01
☐ 20 Steve Barber	.10	.05	.01
☐ 21 Ray(Buddy) Barker	.10	.05	.01
☐ 22 Ed Barnowski	.10	.05	.01
☐ 23 Jose Bautista	.10	.05	.01
☐ 24 Don Baylor	.25	.11	.03
☐ 25 Charlie Beamon	.10	.05	.01
☐ 26 Fred Beene	.10	.05	.01
☐ 27 Mark Belanger	.20	.09	.03
☐ 28 Eric Bell	.10	.05	.01
☐ 29 Juan Bell	.10	.05	.01
☐ 30 Juan Beniquez	.10	.05	.01
☐ 31 Neil Berry	.10	.05	.01
☐ 32 Frank Bertaina	.10	.05	.01
☐ 33 Fred Besana	.10	.05	.01
☐ 34 Vern Bickford	.10	.05	.01
☐ 35 Babe Birrer	.10	.05	.01
☐ 36 Paul Blair	.20	.09	.03
☐ 37 Curt Blefary	.15	.07	.02
☐ 38 Mike Blyzka	.10	.05	.01
☐ 39 Mike Boddicker	.15	.07	.02
☐ 40 Juan Bonilla	.10	.05	.01
☐ 41 Bob Bonner	.10	.05	.01
☐ 42 Dan Boone	.10	.05	.01
☐ 43 Rich Bordi	.10	.05	.01
☐ 44 Dave Boswell	.10	.05	.01
☐ 45 Sam Bowens	.10	.05	.01
☐ 46 Bob Boyd	.10	.05	.01
☐ 47 Gene Brabender	.10	.05	.01
☐ 48 Phil Bradley	.15	.07	.02
☐ 49 Jackie Brandt	.10	.05	.01
☐ 50 Marv Breeding	.10	.05	.01
☐ 51 Jim Bridewester	.10	.05	.01
☐ 52 Nellie Briles	.15	.07	.02
☐ 53 Dick Brown	.10	.05	.01
☐ 54 Hal Brown	.10	.05	.01
☐ 55 Larry Brown	.10	.05	.01
☐ 56 Mark Brown	.10	.05	.01
☐ 57 Marty Brown	.10	.05	.01
☐ 58 George Brunet	.10	.05	.01
☐ 59 Don Buford	.15	.07	.02
☐ 60 Al Bumbry	.10	.05	.01
☐ 61 Wally Bunker	.15	.07	.02
☐ 62 Leo Burke	.10	.05	.01
☐ 63 Rick Burleson	.15	.07	.02
☐ 64 Pete Burnside	.10	.05	.01
☐ 65 Jim Busby	.10	.05	.01
☐ 66 John Buzhardt	.10	.05	.01
☐ 67 Harry Byrd	.10	.05	.01
☐ 68 Enos Cabell	.10	.05	.01
☐ 69 Chico Carrasquel	.10	.05	.01
☐ 70 Camilo Carreon	.10	.05	.01

Card			
☐ 71 Foster Castleman	.10	.05	.01
☐ 72 Wayne Causey	.10	.05	.01
☐ 73 Art Ceccarelli	.10	.05	.01
☐ 74 Bob Chakales	.10	.05	.01
☐ 75 Tony Chevez	.10	.05	.01
☐ 76 Tom Chism	.10	.05	.01
☐ 77 Gino Cimoli	.10	.05	.01
☐ 78 Gil Coan	.10	.05	.01
☐ 79 Rich Coggins	.10	.05	.01
☐ 80 Joe Coleman	.10	.05	.01
☐ 81 Rip Coleman	.10	.05	.01
☐ 82 Fritz Connally	.10	.05	.01
☐ 83 Sandy Consuegra	.10	.05	.01
☐ 84 Doug Corbett	.10	.05	.01
☐ 85 Mark Corey	.10	.05	.01
☐ 86 Clint Courtney	.10	.05	.01
☐ 87 Billy Cox	.15	.07	.02
☐ 88 Dave Criscione	.10	.05	.01
☐ 89 Terry Crowley	.10	.05	.01
☐ 90 Todd Cruz	.10	.05	.01
☐ 91 Mike Cuellar	.20	.09	.03
☐ 92 Angie Dagres	.10	.05	.01
☐ 93 Clay Dalrymple	.10	.05	.01
☐ 94 Rich Dauer	.10	.05	.01
☐ 95 Jerry DaVanon	.10	.05	.01
☐ 96 Butch Davis	.10	.05	.01
☐ 97 Storm Davis	.15	.07	.02
☐ 98 Tommy Davis	.15	.07	.02
☐ 99 Doug DeCinces	.25	.11	.03
☐ 100 Luis DeLeon	.10	.05	.01
☐ 101 Ike Delock	.10	.05	.01
☐ 102 Rick Dempsey	.20	.09	.03
☐ 103 Mike Devereaux	.25	.11	.03
☐ 104 Chuck Diering	.10	.05	.01
☐ 105 Gordon Dillard	.10	.05	.01
☐ 106 Bill Dillman	.10	.05	.01
☐ 107 Mike Dimmel	.10	.05	.01
☐ 108 Ken Dixon	.10	.05	.01
☐ 109 Pat Dobson	.15	.07	.02
☐ 110 Tom Dodd	.10	.05	.01
☐ 111 Harry Dorish	.10	.05	.01
☐ 112 Moe Drabowsky	.15	.07	.02
☐ 113 Dick Drago	.10	.05	.01
☐ 114 Walt Dropo	.15	.07	.02
☐ 115 Tom Dukes	.10	.05	.01
☐ 116 Dave Duncan	.10	.05	.01
☐ 117 Ryne Duren	.20	.09	.03
☐ 118 Joe Durham	.10	.05	.01
☐ 119 Jim Dwyer	.10	.05	.01
☐ 120 Jim Dyck	.10	.05	.01
☐ 121 Mike Epstein	.15	.07	.02
☐ 122 Chuck Essegian	.10	.05	.01
☐ 123 Chuck Estrada	.15	.07	.02
☐ 124 Andy Etchebarren	.15	.07	.02
☐ 125 Hoot Evers	.10	.05	.01
☐ 126 Ed Farmer	.10	.05	.01
☐ 127 Chico Fernandez	.10	.05	.01
☐ 128 Don Ferrarese	.10	.05	.01
☐ 129 Jim Finigan	.10	.05	.01
☐ 130 Steve Finley	.20	.09	.03
☐ 131 Mike Fiore	.10	.05	.01
☐ 132 Eddie Fisher	.10	.05	.01
☐ 133 Jack Fisher	.10	.05	.01
☐ 134 Tom Fisher	.10	.05	.01
☐ 135 Mike Flanagan	.20	.09	.03
☐ 136 John Flinn	.10	.05	.01
☐ 137 Bobby Floyd	.10	.05	.01
☐ 138 Hank Foiles	.10	.05	.01
☐ 139 Dan Ford	.10	.05	.01
☐ 140 Dave Ford	.10	.05	.01
☐ 141 Mike Fornieles	.10	.05	.01
☐ 142 Howie Fox	.10	.05	.01
☐ 143 Tito Francona	.15	.07	.02
☐ 144 Joe Frazier	.10	.05	.01
☐ 145 Roger Freed	.10	.05	.01
☐ 146 Jim Fridley	.10	.05	.01
☐ 147 Jim Fuller	.10	.05	.01
☐ 148 Joe Gaines	.10	.05	.01
☐ 149 Vinicio(Chico) Garcia	.10	.05	.01
☐ 150 Kiko Garcia	.10	.05	.01
☐ 151 Billy Gardner	.10	.05	.01
☐ 152 Wayne Garland	.10	.05	.01
☐ 153 Tommy Gastall	.10	.05	.01
☐ 154 Jim Gentile	.20	.09	.03
☐ 155 Ken Gerhart	.10	.05	.01
☐ 156 Paul Gilliford	.10	.05	.01
☐ 157 Joe Ginsberg	.10	.05	.01
☐ 158 Leo Gomez	.25	.11	.03
☐ 159 Rene Gonzales	.15	.07	.02
☐ 160 Billy Goodman	.15	.07	.02
☐ 161 Dan Graham	.10	.05	.01
☐ 162 Ted Gray	.10	.05	.01
☐ 163 Gene Green	.10	.05	.01
☐ 164 Lenny Green	.10	.05	.01
☐ 165 Bobby Grich	.25	.11	.03
☐ 166 Nuje Griffin	.10	.05	.01
☐ 167 Ross Grimsley	.10	.05	.01
☐ 168 Wayne Gross	.10	.05	.01
☐ 169 Glenn Gulliver	.10	.05	.01
☐ 170 Jackie Guttierrez	.10	.05	.01
☐ 171 John Habyan	.10	.05	.01
☐ 172 Harvey Haddix	.15	.07	.02
☐ 173 Bob Hale	.10	.05	.01
☐ 174 Dick Hall	.10	.05	.01
☐ 175 Bert Hamric	.10	.05	.01
☐ 176 Larry Haney	.10	.05	.01
☐ 177 Ron Hansen	.15	.07	.02
☐ 178 Jim Hardin	.10	.05	.01
☐ 179 Larry Harlow	.10	.05	.01
☐ 180 Pete Harnisch	.20	.09	.03
☐ 181 Tommy Harper	.15	.07	.02
☐ 182 Bob Harrison	.10	.05	.01
☐ 183 Roric Harrison	.10	.05	.01
☐ 184 Jack Harshman	.10	.05	.01
☐ 185 Mike Hart	.10	.05	.01
☐ 186 Pete Hartzell	.10	.05	.01
☐ 187 Grady Hatton	.10	.05	.01
☐ 188 Brad Havens	.10	.05	.01
☐ 189 Drungo Hazewood	.10	.05	.01
☐ 190 Jehosie Heard	.10	.05	.01
☐ 191 Mel Held	.10	.05	.01
☐ 192 Woodie Held	.15	.07	.02
☐ 193 Ellie Hendricks	.15	.07	.02
☐ 194 Leo Hernandez	.10	.05	.01
☐ 195 Whitey Herzog	.25	.11	.03
☐ 196 Kevin Hickey	.10	.05	.01
☐ 197 Billy Hoeft	.15	.07	.02
☐ 198 Chris Hoiles	.25	.11	.03
☐ 199 Fred Holdsworth	.10	.05	.01
☐ 200 Brian Holton	.10	.05	.01
☐ 201 Ken Holtzman	.15	.07	.02
☐ 202 Don Hood	.10	.05	.01
☐ 203 Sam Horn	.20	.09	.03
☐ 204 Art Houtteman	.10	.05	.01
☐ 205 Bruce Howard	.10	.05	.01
☐ 206 Rex Hudler	.15	.07	.02
☐ 207 Phil Huffman	.10	.05	.01
☐ 208 Keith Hughes	.10	.05	.01
☐ 209 Mark Huismann	.10	.05	.01
☐ 210 Tim Hulett	.10	.05	.01
☐ 211 Billy Hunter	.15	.07	.02
☐ 212 Dave Huppert	.10	.05	.01
☐ 213 Jim Hutto	.10	.05	.01
☐ 214 Dick Hyde	.10	.05	.01
☐ 215 Grant Jackson	.15	.07	.02
☐ 216 Lou Jackson	.15	.07	.02
☐ 217 Reggie Jackson	1.00	.45	.13
☐ 218 Ron Jackson	.10	.05	.01
☐ 219 Jesse Jefferson	.10	.05	.01
☐ 220 Stan Jefferson	.10	.05	.01
☐ 221 Bob Johnson	.10	.05	.01
☐ 222 Connie Johnson	.10	.05	.01
☐ 223 Darrell Johnson	.10	.05	.01
☐ 224 Dave Johnson	.10	.05	.01
☐ 225 Davey Johnson	.25	.11	.03
☐ 226 David Johnson	.10	.05	.01
☐ 227 Don Johnson	.10	.05	.01
☐ 228 Ernie Johnson	.15	.07	.02
☐ 229 Gordon Jones	.10	.05	.01
☐ 230 Ricky Jones	.10	.05	.01
☐ 231 O'Dell Jones	.10	.05	.01
☐ 232 Sam Jones	.15	.07	.02
☐ 233 George Kell	.40	.18	.05
☐ 234 Frank Kellert	.10	.05	.01
☐ 235 Pat Kelly	.15	.07	.02
☐ 236 Bob Kennedy	.15	.07	.02
☐ 237 Terry Kennedy	.15	.07	.02
☐ 238 Joe Kerrigan	.10	.05	.01
☐ 239 Mike Kinnunen	.10	.05	.01
☐ 240 Willie Kirkland	.15	.07	.02
☐ 241 Ron Kittle	.15	.07	.02
☐ 242 Billy Klaus	.10	.05	.01
☐ 243 Ray Knight	.20	.09	.03
☐ 244 Darold Knowles	.10	.05	.01
☐ 245 Dick Kokos	.10	.05	.01
☐ 246 Brad Komminsk	.10	.05	.01
☐ 247 Dave Koslo	.10	.05	.01
☐ 248 Wayne Krenchicki	.10	.05	.01
☐ 249 Lou Kretlow	.10	.05	.01
☐ 250 Dick Kryhoski	.10	.05	.01
☐ 251 Bob Kuzava	.10	.05	.01
☐ 252 Lee Lacy	.10	.05	.01
☐ 253 Hobie Landrith	.10	.05	.01
☐ 254 Tito Landrum	.10	.05	.01
☐ 255 Don Larsen	.25	.11	.03
☐ 256 Charlie Lau	.15	.07	.02

□ 257 Jim Lehew .10 .05 .01
□ 258 Ken Lehman .10 .05 .01
□ 259 Don Lenhardt .10 .05 .01
□ 260 Dave Leonard .10 .05 .01
□ 261 Don Leppert .10 .05 .01
□ 262 Dick Littlefield .10 .05 .01
□ 263 Charlie Locke .10 .05 .01
□ 264 Whitey Lockman .15 .07 .02
□ 265 Billy Loes .15 .07 .02
□ 266 Ed Lopat .20 .09 .03
□ 267 Carlos Lopez .10 .05 .01
□ 268 Marcelino Lopez .10 .05 .01
□ 269 John Lowenstein .10 .05 .01
□ 270 Steve Luebber .10 .05 .01
□ 271 Dick Luebke .10 .05 .01
□ 272 Fred Lynn .20 .09 .03
□ 273 Bobby Mabe .10 .05 .01
□ 274 Elliott Maddox .10 .05 .01
□ 275 Hank Majeski .10 .05 .01
□ 276 Roger Marquis .10 .05 .01
□ 277 Freddie Marsh .10 .05 .01
□ 278 Jim Marshall .10 .05 .01
□ 279 Morrie Martin .10 .05 .01
□ 280 Dennis Martinez .25 .11 .03
□ 281 Tippy Martinez .10 .05 .01
□ 282 Tom Matchick .10 .05 .01
□ 283 Charlie Maxwell .15 .07 .02
□ 284 Dave May .10 .05 .01
□ 285 Lee May .15 .07 .02
□ 286 Rudy May .10 .05 .01
□ 287 Mike McCormick .15 .07 .02
□ 288 Ben McDonald .35 .16 .04
□ 289 Jim McDonald .10 .05 .01
□ 290 Scott McGregor .15 .07 .02
□ 291 Mickey McGuire .10 .05 .01
□ 292 Jeff McKnight .10 .05 .01
□ 293 Dave McNally .25 .11 .03
□ 294 Sam Mele .10 .05 .01
□ 295 Francisco Melendez .10 .05 .01
□ 296 Bob Melvin .10 .05 .01
□ 297 Jose Mesa .10 .05 .01
□ 298 Eddie Miksis .10 .05 .01
□ 299 Bob Milacki .15 .07 .02
□ 300 Bill Miller .10 .05 .01
□ 301 Dyar Miller .10 .05 .01
□ 302 John Miller .10 .05 .01
□ 303 Randy Miller .10 .05 .01
□ 304 Stu Miller .15 .07 .02
□ 305 Randy Milligan .20 .09 .03
□ 306 Paul Mirabella .10 .05 .01
□ 307 Willie Miranda .10 .05 .01
□ 308 John Mitchell .10 .05 .01
□ 309 Paul Mitchell .10 .05 .01
□ 310 Ron Moeller .10 .05 .01
□ 311 Bob Molinaro .10 .05 .01
□ 312 Ray Moore .10 .05 .01
□ 313 Andres Mora .10 .05 .01
□ 314 Jose Morales .10 .05 .01
□ 315 Keith Moreland .10 .05 .01
□ 316 Mike Morgan .20 .09 .03
□ 317 Dan Morogiello .10 .05 .01
□ 318 John Morris .10 .05 .01
□ 319 Les Moss .10 .05 .01
□ 320 Curt Motton .10 .05 .01
□ 321 Eddie Murray .50 .23 .06
□ 322 Ray Murray .10 .05 .01
□ 323 Tony Muser .10 .05 .01
□ 324 Buster Narum .10 .05 .01
□ 325 Bob Nelson .10 .05 .01
□ 326 Roger Nelson .10 .05 .01
□ 327 Carl Nichols .10 .05 .01
□ 328 Dave Nicholson .10 .05 .01
□ 329 Tim Niedenfuer .10 .05 .01
□ 330 Bob Nieman .10 .05 .01
□ 331 Donell Nixon .10 .05 .01
□ 332 Joe Nolan .10 .05 .01
□ 333 Dickie Noles .10 .05 .01
□ 334 Tim Nordbrook .10 .05 .01
□ 335 Jim Northrup .15 .07 .02
□ 336 Jack O'Connor .10 .05 .01
□ 337 Billy O'Dell .10 .05 .01
□ 338 John O'Donoghue .10 .05 .01
□ 339 Tom O'Malley .10 .05 .01
□ 340 Johnny Oates .20 .09 .03
□ 341 Chuck Oertel .10 .05 .01
□ 342 Bob Oliver .10 .05 .01
□ 343 Gregg Olson .35 .16 .04
□ 344 John Orsino .10 .05 .01
□ 345 Joe Orsulak .15 .07 .02
□ 346 John Pacella .10 .05 .01
□ 347 Dave Pagan .10 .05 .01
□ 348 Erv Palica .10 .05 .01
□ 349 Jim Palmer .75 .35 .09
□ 350 John Papa .10 .05 .01
□ 351 Milt Pappas .20 .09 .03
□ 352 Al Pardo .10 .05 .01
□ 353 Kelly Paris .10 .05 .01
□ 354 Mike Parrott .10 .05 .01
□ 355 Tom Patton .10 .05 .01
□ 356 Albie Pearson .10 .05 .01
□ 357 Orlando Pena .10 .05 .01
□ 358 Oswaldo Peraza .10 .05 .01
□ 359 Buddy Peterson .10 .05 .01
□ 360 Dave Philley .10 .05 .01
□ 361 Tom Phoebus .10 .05 .01
□ 362 Al Pilarcik .10 .05 .01
□ 363 Duane Pillette .10 .05 .01
□ 364 Lou Piniella .25 .11 .03
(Pictured wearing
a KC Royals cap)
□ 365 Dave Pope .10 .05 .01
□ 366 Arnie Portocarrero .10 .05 .01
□ 367 Boog Powell .30 .14 .04
□ 368 Johnny Powers .10 .05 .01
□ 369 Carl Powis .10 .05 .01
□ 370 Joe Price .10 .05 .01
□ 371 Jim Pyburn .10 .05 .01
□ 372 Art Quirk .10 .05 .01
□ 373 Jamie Quirk .10 .05 .01
□ 374 Allan Ramirez .10 .05 .01
□ 375 Floyd Rayford .10 .05 .01
□ 376 Mike Reinbach .10 .05 .01
□ 377 Merv Rettenmund .15 .07 .02
□ 378 Bob Reynolds .10 .05 .01
□ 379 Del Rice .10 .05 .01
(Wearing St. Louis
Cardinals cap)
□ 380 Pete Richert .10 .05 .01
□ 381 Jeff Rineer .10 .05 .01
□ 382 Bill Ripken .20 .09 .03
□ 383 Cal Ripken 1.50 .65 .19
□ 384 Robin Roberts .50 .23 .06
□ 385 Brooks Robinson 1.00 .45 .13
□ 386 Earl Robinson .10 .05 .01
□ 387 Eddie Robinson .10 .05 .01
□ 388 Frank Robinson .75 .35 .09
□ 389 Sergio Robles .10 .05 .01
□ 390 Aurelio Rodriguez .10 .05 .01
□ 391 Vic Rodriquez .10 .05 .01
□ 392 Gary Roenicke .15 .07 .02
□ 393 Saul Rogovin .10 .05 .01
(Wearing Philadelphia
Phillies cap)
□ 394 Wade Rowdon .10 .05 .01
□ 395 Ken Rowe .10 .05 .01
□ 396 Willie Royster .10 .05 .01
□ 397 Vic Roznovsky .10 .05 .01
□ 398 Ken Rudolph .10 .05 .01
□ 399 Lenn Sakata .10 .05 .01
□ 400 Chico Salmon .10 .05 .01
□ 401 Orlando Sanchez .10 .05 .01
(Pictured wearing St.
Louis Cardinals cap)
□ 402 Bob Saverine .10 .05 .01
□ 403 Art Schallock .10 .05 .01
□ 404 Bill Scherrer .10 .05 .01
(Wearing Detroit
Tigers cap)
□ 405 Curt Schilling .20 .09 .03
□ 406 Dave Schmidt .15 .07 .02
□ 407 Johnny Schmitz .10 .05 .01
□ 408 Jeff Schneider .10 .05 .01
□ 409 Rick Schu .10 .05 .01
□ 410 Mickey Scott .10 .05 .01
□ 411 Kal Segrist .10 .05 .01
□ 412 David Segui .15 .07 .02
□ 413 Al Severinsen .10 .05 .01
□ 414 Larry Sheets .15 .07 .02
□ 415 John Shelby .10 .05 .01
□ 416 Barry Shetrone .10 .05 .01
□ 417 Tom Shopay .10 .05 .01
□ 418 Bill Short .10 .05 .01
□ 419 Norm Siebern .15 .07 .02
□ 420 Nelson Simmons .10 .05 .01
□ 421 Ken Singleton .25 .11 .03
□ 422 Doug Sisk .10 .05 .01
□ 423 Dave Skaggs .10 .05 .01
□ 424 Lou Sleater .10 .05 .01
□ 425 Al Smith .15 .07 .02
□ 426 Billy Smith .10 .05 .01
□ 427 Hal Smith .10 .05 .01
□ 428 Mike(Texas) Smith .10 .05 .01
□ 429 Nate Smith .10 .05 .01
□ 430 Nate Snell .10 .05 .01
□ 431 Russ Snyder .10 .05 .01
□ 432 Don Stanhouse .15 .07 .02

□ 433 Pete Stanicek	.10	.05	.01
□ 434 Herm Starrette	.10	.05	.01
□ 435 John Stefero	.10	.05	.01
□ 436 Gene Stephens	.10	.05	.01
□ 437 Vern Stephens	.15	.07	.02
□ 438 Earl Stephenson	.10	.05	.01
□ 439 Sammy Stewart	.15	.07	.02
□ 440 Royle Stillman	.10	.05	.01
□ 441 Wes Stock	.15	.07	.02
□ 442 Tim Stoddard	.15	.07	.02
□ 443 Dean Stone	.10	.05	.01
□ 444 Jeff Stone	.10	.05	.01
□ 445 Steve Stone	.15	.07	.02
□ 446 Marlin Stuart	.10	.05	.01
□ 447 Gordie Sundin	.10	.05	.01
□ 448 Bill Swaggerty	.10	.05	.01
□ 449 Willie Tasby	.10	.05	.01
□ 450 Joe Taylor	.10	.05	.01
□ 451 Dorn Taylor	.10	.05	.01
□ 452 Anthony Telford	.15	.07	.02
□ 453 Johnny Temple	.15	.07	.02
□ 454 Mickey Tettleton	.25	.11	.03
□ 455 Valmy Thomas (Wearing Philadelphia Phillies cap)	.10	.05	.01
□ 456 Bobby Thomson (Wearing Boston Red Sox cap)	.15	.07	.02
□ 457 Marv Throneberry	.20	.09	.03
□ 458 Mark Thurmond	.10	.05	.01
□ 459 Jay Tibbs	.10	.05	.01
□ 460 Mike Torrez	.15	.07	.02
□ 461 Jim Traber	.10	.05	.01
□ 462 Gus Triandos	.20	.09	.03
□ 463 Paul(Dizzy) Trout (Wearing Detroit Tigers cap)	.15	.07	.02
□ 464 Bob Turley	.20	.09	.03
□ 465 Tom Underwood	.10	.05	.01
□ 466 Fred Valentine	.10	.05	.01
□ 467 Dave Van Gorder	.10	.05	.01
□ 468 Dave Vineyard	.10	.05	.01
□ 469 Ozzie Virgil	.15	.07	.02
□ 470 Eddie Waitkus	.15	.07	.02
□ 471 Greg Walker	.15	.07	.02
□ 472 Jerry Walker	.10	.05	.01
□ 473 Pete Ward	.10	.05	.01
□ 474 Carl Warwick	.10	.05	.01
□ 475 Ron Washington	.10	.05	.01
□ 476 Eddie Watt	.10	.05	.01
□ 477 Don Welchel	.10	.05	.01
□ 478 George Werley	.10	.05	.01
□ 479 Vic Wertz	.15	.07	.02
□ 480 Wally Westlake (Wearing a Pittsburgh Pirates cap)	.10	.05	.01
□ 481 Mickey Weston	.10	.05	.01
□ 482 Alan Wiggins	.10	.05	.01
□ 483 Bill Wight	.10	.05	.01
□ 484 Hoyt Wilhelm	.45	.20	.06
□ 485 Dallas Williams	.10	.05	.01
□ 486 Dick Williams	.15	.07	.02
□ 487 Earl Williams	.10	.05	.01
□ 488 Mark Williamson	.10	.05	.01
□ 489 Jim Wilson	.10	.05	.01
□ 490 Gene Woodling	.15	.07	.02
□ 491 Craig Worthington	.10	.05	.01
□ 492 Bobby Young	.10	.05	.01
□ 493 Mike Young	.10	.05	.01
□ 494 Frank Zupo	.10	.05	.01
□ 495 George Zuverink	.10	.05	.01
□ 496 Glenn Davis	.30	.14	.04
□ 497 Dwight Evans	.20	.09	.03
□ 498 Dave Gallagher	.10	.05	.01
□ 499 Paul Kilgus	.10	.05	.01
□ 500 Jeff Robinson	.10	.05	.01
□ 501 Ernie Whitt	.10	.05	.01

1980-83 Pacific Legends

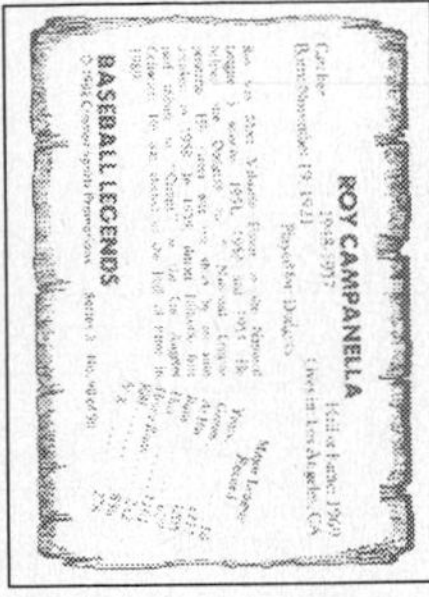

This 124-card set is actually four 30-card subsets plus a four-card wax box bottom panel. The set was distributed by series over several years beginning in 1980 with the first 30 cards. The set was produced by Pacific Trading Cards and is frequently referred to as Cramer Legends, for the founder of Pacific Trading cards, Mike Cramer. Cards are standard size, 2 1/2" by 3 1/2" and are golden-toned. Even though the wax box cards are numbered from 121-124 and called "series 5," the set is considered complete without them.

	NRMT-MT	EXC	G-VG
COMPLETE SET (120)	30.00	13.50	3.80
COMMON PLAYER (1-120)	.15	.07	.02
COMMON PLAYER (121-124)	.35	.16	.04
□ 1 Babe Ruth	3.00	1.35	.40
□ 2 Heinie Manush	.15	.07	.02
□ 3 Rabbit Maranville	.15	.07	.02
□ 4 Earl Averill	.15	.07	.02
□ 5 Joe DiMaggio	2.00	.90	.25
□ 6 Mickey Mantle	3.00	1.35	.40
□ 7 Hank Aaron	1.25	.55	.16
□ 8 Stan Musial	.75	.35	.09
□ 9 Bill Terry	.15	.07	.02
□ 10 Sandy Koufax	.75	.35	.09
□ 11 Ernie Lombardi	.15	.07	.02
□ 12 Dizzy Dean	.60	.25	.08
□ 13 Lou Gehrig	1.50	.65	.19
□ 14 Walter Alston	.15	.07	.02
□ 15 Jackie Robinson	.75	.35	.09
□ 16 Jimmie Foxx	.35	.16	.04
□ 17 Billy Southworth	.15	.07	.02
□ 18 Honus Wagner	.60	.25	.08
□ 19 Duke Snider	.60	.25	.08
□ 20 Rogers Hornsby UER (At bat total of 1873 is incorrect)	.50	.23	.06
□ 21 Paul Waner	.15	.07	.02
□ 22 Luke Appling	.15	.07	.02
□ 23 Billy Herman	.15	.07	.02
□ 24 Lloyd Waner	.15	.07	.02
□ 25 Fred Hutchinson	.15	.07	.02
□ 26 Eddie Collins	.15	.07	.02
□ 27 Lefty Grove	.35	.16	.04
□ 28 Chuck Connors	.50	.23	.06
□ 29 Lefty O'Doul	.15	.07	.02
□ 30 Hank Greenberg	.50	.23	.06
□ 31 Ty Cobb	1.50	.65	.19
□ 32 Enos Slaughter	.25	.11	.03
□ 33 Ernie Banks	.50	.23	.06
□ 34 Christy Mathewson	.50	.23	.06
□ 35 Mel Ott	.35	.16	.04
□ 36 Pie Traynor	.15	.07	.02
□ 37 Clark Griffith	.15	.07	.02
□ 38 Mickey Cochrane	.15	.07	.02
□ 39 Joe Cronin	.15	.07	.02
□ 40 Leo Durocher	.25	.11	.03
□ 41 Home Run Baker	.15	.07	.02
□ 42 Joe Tinker	.15	.07	.02
□ 43 John McGraw	.15	.07	.02
□ 44 Bill Dickey	.25	.11	.03
□ 45 Walter Johnson	.50	.23	.06
□ 46 Frankie Frisch	.15	.07	.02
□ 47 Casey Stengel	.50	.23	.06
□ 48 Willie Mays	1.25	.55	.16
□ 49 Johnny Mize	.25	.11	.03
□ 50 Roberto Clemente	.75	.35	.09
□ 51 Burleigh Grimes	.15	.07	.02
□ 52 Pee Wee Reese	.50	.23	.06
□ 53 Bob Feller	.50	.23	.06
□ 54 Brooks Robinson	.50	.23	.06
□ 55 Sam Crawford	.15	.07	.02
□ 56 Robin Roberts	.25	.11	.03
□ 57 Warren Spahn	.35	.16	.04
□ 58 Joe McCarthy	.15	.07	.02
□ 59 Jocko Conlan	.15	.07	.02
□ 60 Satchel Paige	.75	.35	.09
□ 61 Ted Williams	1.00	.45	.13
□ 62 George Kelly	.15	.07	.02

☐ 63 Gil Hodges	.25	.11	.03
☐ 64 Jim Bottomley	.15	.07	.02
☐ 65 Al Kaline	.50	.23	.06
☐ 66 Harvey Kuenn	.15	.07	.02
☐ 67 Yogi Berra	.75	.35	.09
☐ 68 Nellie Fox	.15	.07	.02
☐ 69 Harmon Killebrew	.35	.16	.04
☐ 70 Edd Roush	.15	.07	.02
☐ 71 Mordecai Brown	.15	.07	.02
☐ 72 Gabby Hartnett	.15	.07	.02
☐ 73 Early Wynn	.25	.11	.03
☐ 74 Nap Lajoie	.35	.16	.04
☐ 75 Charlie Grimm	.15	.07	.02
☐ 76 Joe Garagiola	.35	.16	.04
☐ 77 Ted Lyons	.15	.07	.02
☐ 78 Mickey Vernon	.15	.07	.02
☐ 79 Lou Boudreau	.25	.11	.03
☐ 80 Al Dark	.15	.07	.02
☐ 81 Ralph Kiner	.35	.16	.04
☐ 82 Phil Rizzuto	.35	.16	.04
☐ 83 Stan Hack	.15	.07	.02
☐ 84 Frank Chance	.15	.07	.02
☐ 85 Ray Schalk	.15	.07	.02
☐ 86 Bill McKechnie	.15	.07	.02
☐ 87 Travis Jackson	.15	.07	.02
☐ 88 Pete Reiser	.15	.07	.02
☐ 89 Carl Hubbell	.35	.16	.04
☐ 90 Roy Campanella	.60	.25	.08
☐ 91 Cy Young	.35	.16	.04
☐ 92 Kiki Cuyler	.15	.07	.02
☐ 93 Chief Bender	.15	.07	.02
☐ 94 Richie Ashburn	.35	.16	.04
☐ 95 Riggs Stephenson	.15	.07	.02
☐ 96 Minnie Minoso	.15	.07	.02
☐ 97 Hack Wilson	.25	.11	.03
☐ 98 Al Lopez	.15	.07	.02
☐ 99 Willie Keeler	.15	.07	.02
☐ 100 Fred Lindstrom	.15	.07	.02
☐ 101 Roger Maris	.50	.23	.06
☐ 102 Roger Bresnahan	.15	.07	.02
☐ 103 Monty Stratton	.25	.11	.03
☐ 104 Goose Goslin	.15	.07	.02
☐ 105 Earle Combs	.15	.07	.02
☐ 106 Pepper Martin	.15	.07	.02
☐ 107 Joe Jackson	2.00	.90	.25
☐ 108 George Sisler	.25	.11	.03
☐ 109 Red Ruffing	.15	.07	.02
☐ 110 Johnny Vander Meer	.15	.07	.02
☐ 111 Herb Pennock	.15	.07	.02
☐ 112 Chuck Klein	.25	.11	.03
☐ 113 Paul Derringer	.15	.07	.02
☐ 114 Addie Joss	.15	.07	.02
☐ 115 Bobby Thomson	.15	.07	.02
☐ 116 Chick Hafey	.15	.07	.02
☐ 117 Lefty Gomez	.35	.16	.04
☐ 118 George Kell	.15	.07	.02
☐ 119 Al Simmons	.15	.07	.02
☐ 120 Bob Lemon	.15	.07	.02
☐ 121 Hoyt Wilhelm (Wax box card)	.75	.35	.09
☐ 122 Arky Vaughan (Wax box card)	.35	.16	.04
☐ 123 Frank Robinson (Wax box card)	1.00	.45	.13
☐ 124 Grover Alexander (Wax box card)	.75	.35	.09

1988 Pacific Eight Men Out

This set was produced by Mike Cramer's Pacific Trading Cards of Edmonds, Washington. The set was released in conjunction with the popular movie of the same name, which told the story of the "fix" of the 1919 World Series between the Cincinnati Reds and the Chicago "Black" Sox. The cards are standard size, 2 1/2" by 3 1/2" and have a raspberry-colored border on the card fronts as well as raspberry-colored print on the white card stock backs. The cards were available either as wax packs or as collated sets. Generally the cards relating to the movie (showing actors) are in full-color whereas the vintage photography showing the actual players involved is in a sepia tone.

	MT	EX-MT	VG
COMPLETE SET (110)	7.50	3.40	.95
COMMON PLAYER (1-110)	.10	.05	.01
☐ 1 We're Going To See The Sox	.20	.09	.03
☐ 2 White Sox Win The Pennant	.10	.05	.01
☐ 3 The Series	.10	.05	.01
☐ 4 1919 Chicago White Sox	.10	.05	.01
☐ 5 The Black Sox Scandal	.10	.05	.01
☐ 6 Eddie Cicotte 29-7 in 1919	.15	.07	.02
☐ 7 "Buck's Their Favorite"	.15	.07	.02
☐ 8 Eddie Collins	.25	.11	.03
☐ 9 Michael Rooker as Chick Gandil	.10	.05	.01
☐ 10 Charlie Sheen as Hap Felsch	.35	.16	.04
☐ 11 James Read as Lefty Williams	.10	.05	.01
☐ 12 John Cusack as Buck Weaver	.15	.07	.02
☐ 13 D.B. Sweeney as Joe Jackson	.25	.11	.03
☐ 14 David Strathairn as Eddie Cicotte	.10	.05	.01
☐ 15 Perry Lang as Fred McMullin	.10	.05	.01
☐ 16 Don Harvey as Swede Risberg	.10	.05	.01
☐ 17 The Gambler Burns And Maharg	.10	.05	.01
☐ 18 "Sleepy"Bill Burns	.10	.05	.01
☐ 19 The Key is Cicotte	.10	.05	.01
☐ 20 C'mon Betsy	.10	.05	.01
☐ 21 The Fix	.10	.05	.01
☐ 22 Chick Approaches Cicotte	.10	.05	.01
☐ 23 Kid Gleason	.10	.05	.01
☐ 24 Charles Comiskey Owner	.10	.05	.01
☐ 25 Chick Gandil 1st Baseman	.15	.07	.02
☐ 26 Swede Risberg	.10	.05	.01
☐ 27 Sport Sullivan	.10	.05	.01
☐ 28 Abe Attell And Arnold Rothstein	.10	.05	.01
☐ 29 Hugh Fullerton Sportswriter	.10	.05	.01
☐ 30 Ring Lardner Sportswriter	.10	.05	.01
☐ 31 "Shoeless"Joe His Batting Eye	.25	.11	.03
☐ 32 "Shoeless Joe"	.35	.16	.04
☐ 33 Buck Can't Sleep	.10	.05	.01
☐ 34 George"Buck" Weaver	.10	.05	.01
☐ 35 Hugh and Ring Confront Kid	.10	.05	.01
☐ 36 Joe Doesn't Want To Play	.15	.07	.02
☐ 37 "Shoeless" Joe Jackson	.35	.16	.04
☐ 38 "Sore Arm, Cicotte," "Old Man Cicotte"	.10	.05	.01
☐ 39 The Fix Is On	.10	.05	.01
☐ 40 Buck Plays To Win	.10	.05	.01
☐ 41 Hap Makes A Great Catch	.10	.05	.01
☐ 42 Hugh and Ring Suspect	.10	.05	.01
☐ 43 Ray Gets Things Going	.10	.05	.01

☐ 44	Lefty Loses Game Two	.10	.05	.01
☐ 45	Lefty Crosses Up Catcher Ray Schalk	.10	.05	.01
☐ 46	Chick's RBI Wins Game Three	.10	.05	.01
☐ 47	Dickie Kerr Wins Game Three	.10	.05	.01
☐ 48	Chick Leaves Buck At Third	.10	.05	.01
☐ 49	Williams Loses Game Five	.10	.05	.01
☐ 50	Ray Schalk	.10	.05	.01
☐ 51	Schalk Blocks The Plate	.10	.05	.01
☐ 52	Schalk Is Thrown Out	.10	.05	.01
☐ 53	Chicago Stickball Game	.10	.05	.01
☐ 54	I'm Forever Blowing Ball Games	.10	.05	.01
☐ 55	Felsch Scores Jackson	.25	.11	.03
☐ 56	Kerr Wins Game Six	.10	.05	.01
☐ 57	Where's The Money	.10	.05	.01
☐ 58	Cicotte Wins Game Seven	.10	.05	.01
☐ 59	Kid Watches Eddie	.10	.05	.01
☐ 60	Lefty Is Threatened	.10	.05	.01
☐ 61	James, Get Your Arm Ready, Fast	.10	.05	.01
☐ 62	Shoeless Joe's Home Run	.35	.16	.04
☐ 63	Buck Played His Best	.10	.05	.01
☐ 64	Hugh Exposes The Fix	.10	.05	.01
☐ 65	"Sign The Petition"	.10	.05	.01
☐ 66	Baseball Owners Hire A Commissioner	.10	.05	.01
☐ 67	Judge Kenesaw Mountain Landis	.10	.05	.01
☐ 68	Grand Jury Summoned	.10	.05	.01
☐ 69	"Say It Ain't So, Joe"	.25	.11	.03
☐ 70	The Swede's A Hard Guy	.10	.05	.01
☐ 71	Buck Loves The Game	.10	.05	.01
☐ 72	The Trial	.10	.05	.01
☐ 73	Kid Gleason Takes The Stand	.10	.05	.01
☐ 74	The Verdict	.10	.05	.01
☐ 75	Eight Men Out	.10	.05	.01
☐ 76	Oscar(Happy) Felsch	.20	.09	.03
☐ 77	Who's Joe Jackson	.35	.16	.04
☐ 78	Ban Johnson PRES	.10	.05	.01
☐ 79	Judge Landis COMM	.10	.05	.01
☐ 80	Charles Comiskey OWN	.10	.05	.01
☐ 81	Heinie Groh	.10	.05	.01
☐ 82	Slim Sallee	.10	.05	.01
☐ 83	Dutch Ruether	.10	.05	.01
☐ 84	Edd Roush	.25	.11	.03
☐ 85	Morrie Rath	.10	.05	.01
☐ 86	Bill Rariden	.10	.05	.01
☐ 87	Jimmy Ring	.10	.05	.01
☐ 88	Greasy Neale	.15	.07	.02
☐ 89	Pat Moran MG	.10	.05	.01
☐ 90	Adolfo Luque	.10	.05	.01
☐ 91	Larry Kopf	.10	.05	.01
☐ 92	Ray Fisher	.10	.05	.01
☐ 93	Hod Eller	.10	.05	.01
☐ 94	Pat Duncan	.10	.05	.01
☐ 95	Jake Daubert	.10	.05	.01
☐ 96	Red Faber	.25	.11	.03
☐ 97	Dickie Kerr	.10	.05	.01
☐ 98	Shano Collins	.10	.05	.01
☐ 99	Eddie Collins	.25	.11	.03
☐ 100	Ray Schalk	.25	.11	.03
☐ 101	Nemo Leibold	.10	.05	.01
☐ 102	Kid Gleason	.10	.05	.01
☐ 103	Swede Risberg	.15	.07	.02
☐ 104	Eddie Cicotte	.15	.07	.02
☐ 105	Fred McMullin	.10	.05	.01
☐ 106	Chick Gandil	.15	.07	.02
☐ 107	Buck Weaver	.15	.07	.02
☐ 108	Lefty Williams	.15	.07	.02
☐ 109	Happy Felsch	.15	.07	.02
☐ 110	Joe Jackson	.75	.35	.09

1988 Pacific Legends I

This attractive set of 110 full-color cards was produced by Mike Cramer's Pacific Trading Cards of Edmonds,

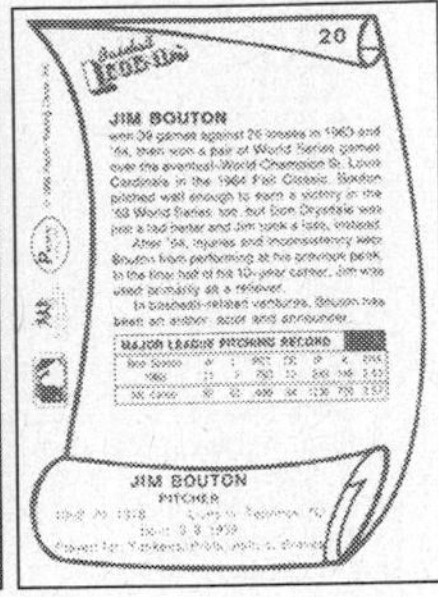

Washington. The cards are silver bordered and are standard size, 2 1/2" by 3 1/2". Card backs are printed in yellow, black, and gray on white card stock. The cards were available either as wax packs or as collated sets. The players pictured in the set had retired many years before, but most are still well remembered. The statistics on the card backs give the player's career and "best season" statistics. The set was licensed by Major League Baseball Players Alumni.

		MT	EX-MT	VG
	COMPLETE SET (110)	11.00	4.90	1.40
	COMMON PLAYER (1-110)	.05	.02	.01
☐ 1	Hank Aaron	.75	.35	.09
☐ 2	Red Schoendienst	.25	.11	.03
☐ 3	Brooks Robinson	.35	.16	.04
☐ 4	Luke Appling	.20	.09	.03
☐ 5	Gene Woodling	.05	.02	.01
☐ 6	Stan Musial	.60	.25	.08
☐ 7	Mickey Mantle	1.50	.65	.19
☐ 8	Richie Ashburn	.20	.09	.03
☐ 9	Ralph Kiner	.25	.11	.03
☐ 10	Phil Rizzuto	.20	.09	.03
☐ 11	Harvey Haddix	.05	.02	.01
☐ 12	Ken Boyer	.10	.05	.01
☐ 13	Clete Boyer	.05	.02	.01
☐ 14	Ken Harrelson	.10	.05	.01
☐ 15	Robin Roberts	.20	.09	.03
☐ 16	Catfish Hunter	.20	.09	.03
☐ 17	Frank Howard	.10	.05	.01
☐ 18	Jim Perry	.05	.02	.01
☐ 19A	Elston Howard ERR (Reversed negative)	.15	.07	.02
☐ 19B	Elston Howard COR	.15	.07	.02
☐ 20	Jim Bouton	.10	.05	.01
☐ 21	Pee Wee Reese	.25	.11	.03
☐ 22A	Mel Stottlemyre ERR (Spelled Stottlemyer on card front)	.15	.07	.02
☐ 22B	Mel Stottlemyre COR	.15	.07	.02
☐ 23	Hank Sauer	.05	.02	.01
☐ 24	Willie Mays	.75	.35	.09
☐ 25	Tom Tresh	.10	.05	.01
☐ 26	Roy Sievers	.05	.02	.01
☐ 27	Leo Durocher	.20	.09	.03
☐ 28	Al Dark	.05	.02	.01
☐ 29	Tony Kubek	.15	.07	.02
☐ 30	Johnny VanderMeer	.10	.05	.01
☐ 31	Joe Adcock	.05	.02	.01
☐ 32	Bob Lemon	.15	.07	.02
☐ 33	Don Newcombe	.10	.05	.01
☐ 34	Thurman Munson	.30	.14	.04
☐ 35	Earl Battey	.05	.02	.01
☐ 36	Ernie Banks	.35	.16	.04
☐ 37	Matty Alou	.05	.02	.01
☐ 38	Dave McNally	.05	.02	.01
☐ 39	Mickey Lolich	.10	.05	.01
☐ 40	Jackie Robinson	.60	.25	.08
☐ 41	Allie Reynolds	.10	.05	.01
☐ 42A	Don Larsen ERR (Misspelled Larson on card front)	.15	.07	.02
☐ 42B	Don Larsen COR	.15	.07	.02
☐ 43	Fergie Jenkins	.30	.14	.04
☐ 44	Jim Gilliam	.10	.05	.01
☐ 45	Bobby Thomson	.10	.05	.01
☐ 46	Sparky Anderson	.10	.05	.01
☐ 47	Roy Campanella	.40	.18	.05
☐ 48	Marv Throneberry	.10	.05	.01
☐ 49	Bill Virdon	.05	.02	.01
☐ 50	Ted Williams	.60	.25	.08

☐	51	Minnie Minoso	.10	.05	.01
☐	52	Bob Turley	.05	.02	.01
☐	53	Yogi Berra	.40	.18	.05
☐	54	Juan Marichal	.20	.09	.03
☐	55	Duke Snider	.40	.18	.05
☐	56	Harvey Kuenn	.10	.05	.01
☐	57	Nellie Fox	.15	.07	.02
☐	58	Felipe Alou	.10	.05	.01
☐	59	Tony Oliva	.10	.05	.01
☐	60	Bill Mazeroski	.15	.07	.02
☐	61	Bobby Shantz	.05	.02	.01
☐	62	Mark Fidrych	.10	.05	.01
☐	63	Johnny Mize	.20	.09	.03
☐	64	Ralph Terry	.05	.02	.01
☐	65	Gus Bell	.05	.02	.01
☐	66	Jerry Koosman	.10	.05	.01
☐	67	Mike McCormick	.05	.02	.01
☐	68	Lou Burdette	.10	.05	.01
☐	69	George Kell	.20	.09	.03
☐	70	Vic Raschi	.10	.05	.01
☐	71	Chuck Connors	.50	.23	.06
☐	72	Ted Kluszewski	.20	.09	.03
☐	73	Bobby Doerr	.20	.09	.03
☐	74	Bobby Richardson	.15	.07	.02
☐	75	Carl Erskine	.10	.05	.01
☐	76	Hoyt Wilhelm	.20	.09	.03
☐	77	Bob Purkey	.05	.02	.01
☐	78	Bob Friend	.05	.02	.01
☐	79	Monte Irvin	.20	.09	.03
☐	80A	Jim Lonborg ERR (Misspelled Longborg on card front)	.15	.07	.02
☐	80B	Jim Lonborg COR	.15	.07	.02
☐	81	Wally Moon	.05	.02	.01
☐	82	Moose Skowron	.10	.05	.01
☐	83	Tommy Davis	.10	.05	.01
☐	84	Enos Slaughter	.20	.09	.03
☐	85	Sal Maglie UER (1945-1917 on back)	.10	.05	.01
☐	86	Harmon Killebrew	.20	.09	.03
☐	87	Gil Hodges	.20	.09	.03
☐	88	Jim Kaat	.10	.05	.01
☐	89	Roger Maris	.40	.18	.05
☐	90	Billy Williams	.20	.09	.03
☐	91	Luis Aparicio	.20	.09	.03
☐	92	Jim Bunning	.15	.07	.02
☐	93	Bill Freehan	.10	.05	.01
☐	94	Orlando Cepeda	.15	.07	.02
☐	95	Early Wynn	.20	.09	.03
☐	96	Tug McGraw	.10	.05	.01
☐	97	Ron Santo	.10	.05	.01
☐	98	Del Crandall	.05	.02	.01
☐	99	Sal Bando	.05	.02	.01
☐	100	Joe DiMaggio	1.00	.45	.13
☐	101	Bob Feller	.35	.16	.04
☐	102	Larry Doby	.10	.05	.01
☐	103	Rollie Fingers	.25	.11	.03
☐	104	Al Kaline	.30	.14	.04
☐	105	Johnny Podres	.10	.05	.01
☐	106	Lou Boudreau	.20	.09	.03
☐	107	Zoilo Versalles	.05	.02	.01
☐	108	Dick Groat	.10	.05	.01
☐	109	Warren Spahn	.30	.14	.04
☐	110	Johnny Bench	.40	.18	.05

1989 Pacific Legends II

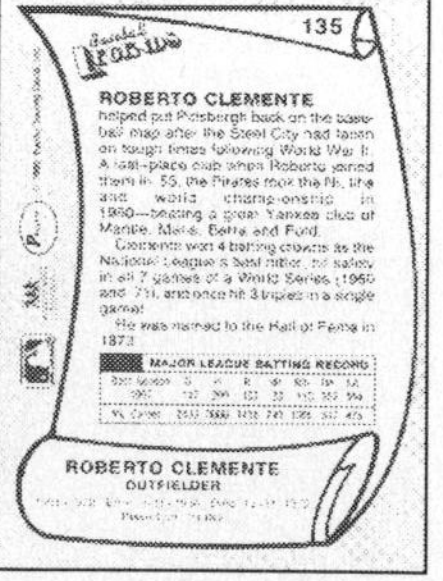

The 1989 Pacific Legends Series II set contains 110 standard-size (2 1/2" by 3 1/2") cards. The fronts have vintage color photos with silver borders. The backs are gray and feature career highlights and lifetime statistics. The cards were distributed as sets and in ten-card wax packs.

	MT	EX-MT	VG
COMPLETE SET (110)	10.00	4.50	1.25
COMMON PLAYER (111-220)	.05	.02	.01

			MT	EX-MT	VG
☐	111	Reggie Jackson	.90	.40	.11
☐	112	Rich Reese	.05	.02	.01
☐	113	Frankie Frisch	.10	.05	.01
☐	114	Ed Kranepool	.05	.02	.01
☐	115	Al Hrabosky	.05	.02	.01
☐	116	Eddie Mathews	.25	.11	.03
☐	117	Ty Cobb	.75	.35	.09
☐	118	Jim Davenport	.05	.02	.01
☐	119	Buddy Lewis	.05	.02	.01
☐	120	Virgil Trucks	.05	.02	.01
☐	121	Del Ennis	.05	.02	.01
☐	122	Dick Radatz	.05	.02	.01
☐	123	Andy Pafko	.05	.02	.01
☐	124	Wilbur Wood	.05	.02	.01
☐	125	Joe Sewell	.10	.05	.01
☐	126	Herb Score	.05	.02	.01
☐	127	Paul Waner	.10	.05	.01
☐	128	Lloyd Waner	.10	.05	.01
☐	129	Brooks Robinson	.35	.16	.04
☐	130	Bo Belinsky	.05	.02	.01
☐	131	Phil Cavarretta	.05	.02	.01
☐	132	Claude Osteen	.05	.02	.01
☐	133	Tito Francona	.05	.02	.01
☐	134	Billy Pierce	.05	.02	.01
☐	135	Roberto Clemente	.50	.23	.06
☐	136	Spud Chandler	.05	.02	.01
☐	137	Enos Slaughter	.20	.09	.03
☐	138	Ken Holtzman	.05	.02	.01
☐	139	John Hopp	.05	.02	.01
☐	140	Tony LaRussa	.15	.07	.02
☐	141	Ryne Duren	.05	.02	.01
☐	142	Glenn Beckert UER (Misspelled Glen on card front)	.05	.02	.01
☐	143	Ken Keltner	.05	.02	.01
☐	144	Hank Bauer	.05	.02	.01
☐	145	Roger Craig	.10	.05	.01
☐	146	Frank Baker	.10	.05	.01
☐	147	Jim O'Toole	.05	.02	.01
☐	148	Rogers Hornsby	.25	.11	.03
☐	149	Jose Cardenal	.05	.02	.01
☐	150	Bobby Doerr	.20	.09	.03
☐	151	Mickey Cochrane	.15	.07	.02
☐	152	Gaylord Perry	.25	.11	.03
☐	153	Frank Thomas	.05	.02	.01
☐	154	Ted Williams	.60	.25	.08
☐	155	Sam McDowell	.05	.02	.01
☐	156	Bob Feller	.40	.18	.05
☐	157	Bert Campaneris	.05	.02	.01
☐	158	Thornton Lee UER (Misspelled Thorton on card front)	.05	.02	.01
☐	159	Gary Peters	.05	.02	.01
☐	160	Joe Medwick	.15	.07	.02
☐	161	Joe Nuxhall	.05	.02	.01
☐	162	Joe Schultz	.15	.07	.02
☐	163	Harmon Killebrew	.30	.14	.04
☐	164	Bucky Walters	.05	.02	.01
☐	165	Bob Allison	.05	.02	.01
☐	166	Lou Boudreau	.15	.07	.02
☐	167	Joe Cronin	.15	.07	.02
☐	168	Mike Torrez	.05	.02	.01
☐	169	Rich Rollins	.05	.02	.01
☐	170	Tony Cuccinello	.05	.02	.01
☐	171	Hoyt Wilhelm	.20	.09	.03
☐	172	Ernie Harwell ANN	.15	.07	.02
☐	173	George Foster	.10	.05	.01
☐	174	Lou Gehrig	.75	.35	.09
☐	175	Dave Kingman	.10	.05	.01
☐	176	Babe Ruth	1.50	.65	.19
☐	177	Joe Black	.05	.02	.01
☐	178	Roy Face	.05	.02	.01
☐	179	Earl Weaver MG	.10	.05	.01
☐	180	Johnny Mize	.20	.09	.03
☐	181	Roger Cramer	.05	.02	.01
☐	182	Jim Piersall	.10	.05	.01
☐	183	Ned Garver	.05	.02	.01
☐	184	Billy Williams	.15	.07	.02
☐	185	Lefty Grove	.20	.09	.03
☐	186	Jim Grant	.05	.02	.01
☐	187	Elmer Valo	.05	.02	.01
☐	188	Ewell Blackwell	.05	.02	.01
☐	189	Mel Ott	.20	.09	.03
☐	190	Harry Walker	.05	.02	.01
☐	191	Bill Campbell	.05	.02	.01

□ 192 Walter Johnson	.30	.14	.04
□ 193 Catfish Hunter	.20	.09	.03
□ 194 Charlie Keller	.05	.02	.01
□ 195 Hank Greenberg	.25	.11	.03
□ 196 Bobby Murcer	.10	.05	.01
□ 197 Al Lopez	.15	.07	.02
□ 198 Vida Blue	.05	.02	.01
□ 199 Shag Crawford UMP	.05	.02	.01
□ 200 Arky Vaughan	.15	.07	.02
□ 201 Smoky Burgess	.05	.02	.01
□ 202 Rip Sewell	.05	.02	.01
□ 203 Earl Averill	.10	.05	.01
□ 204 Milt Pappas	.05	.02	.01
□ 205 Mel Harder	.05	.02	.01
□ 206 Sam Jethroe	.05	.02	.01
□ 207 Randy Hundley	.05	.02	.01
□ 208 Jesse Haines	.05	.02	.01
□ 209 Jack Brickhouse ANN	.05	.02	.01
□ 210 Whitey Ford	.25	.11	.03
□ 211 Honus Wagner	.40	.18	.05
□ 212 Phil Niekro	.20	.09	.03
□ 213 Gary Bell	.05	.02	.01
□ 214 Jon Matlack	.05	.02	.01
□ 215 Moe Drabowsky	.05	.02	.01
□ 216 Edd Roush	.15	.07	.02
□ 217 Joel Horlen	.05	.02	.01
□ 218 Casey Stengel	.25	.11	.03
□ 219 Burt Hooton	.05	.02	.01
□ 220 Joe Jackson	1.00	.45	.13

1989-90 Pacific Senior League

The 1989-90 Pacific Trading Cards Senior League set contains 220 standard-size (2 1/2" by 3 1/2") cards. The fronts feature color photos with silver borders and player names and positions at the bottom. The horizontally oriented backs are red, white, and blue, and show vital statistics and career highlights. The cards were distributed as a boxed set with 15 card-sized logo stickers/puzzle pieces as well as in wax packs. There are several In Action cards in the set, designated by IA in the checklist below. The Nettles card was corrected very late according to the set's producer.

	MT	EX-MT	VG
COMPLETE SET (220)	10.00	4.50	1.25
COMMON PLAYER (1-220)	.05	.02	.01

	MT	EX-MT	VG
□ 1 Bobby Tolan MG	.15	.07	.02
□ 2 Sergio Ferrer	.05	.02	.01
□ 3 David Rajsich	.05	.02	.01
□ 4 Ron LeFlore	.10	.05	.01
□ 5 Steve Henderson	.05	.02	.01
□ 6 Jerry Martin	.05	.02	.01
□ 7 Gary Rajsich	.05	.02	.01
□ 8 Elias Sosa	.05	.02	.01
□ 9 Jon Matlack	.10	.05	.01
□ 10 Steve Kemp	.10	.05	.01
□ 11 Lenny Randle	.05	.02	.01
□ 12 Roy Howell	.05	.02	.01
□ 13 Milt Wilcox	.05	.02	.01
□ 14 Alan Bannister	.05	.02	.01
□ 15 Dock Ellis	.05	.02	.01
□ 16 Mike Williams	.05	.02	.01
□ 17 Luis Gomez	.05	.02	.01
□ 18 Joe Sambito	.05	.02	.01
□ 19 Bake McBride	.05	.02	.01
□ 20 Pat Zachry UER (Photo actually Dick Bosman)	.05	.02	.01
□ 21 Dwight Lowry	.05	.02	.01
□ 22 Ozzie Virgil Sr. CO	.05	.02	.01
□ 23 Randy Lerch	.05	.02	.01
□ 24 Butch Benton	.05	.02	.01
□ 25 Tom Zimmer CO UER (No bio information)	.05	.02	.01
□ 26 Al Holland UER (Photo actually Nardi Contreras)	.10	.05	.01
□ 27 Sammy Stewart	.05	.02	.01
□ 28 Bill Lee	.10	.05	.01
□ 29 Ferguson Jenkins	1.25	.55	.16
□ 30 Leon Roberts	.05	.02	.01
□ 31 Rick Wise	.10	.05	.01
□ 32 Butch Hobson	.15	.07	.02
□ 33 Pete LaCock	.05	.02	.01
□ 34 Bill Campbell	.05	.02	.01
□ 35 Doug Simunic	.05	.02	.01
□ 36 Mario Guerrero	.05	.02	.01
□ 37 Jim Willoughby	.05	.02	.01
□ 38 Joe Pittman	.05	.02	.01
□ 39 Mark Bomback	.05	.02	.01
□ 40 Tommy McMillian	.05	.02	.01
□ 41 Gary Allanson	.05	.02	.01
□ 42 Cecil Cooper	.15	.07	.02
□ 43 John LaRosa	.05	.02	.01
□ 44 Darrell Brandon	.05	.02	.01
□ 45 Bernie Carbo	.05	.02	.01
□ 46 Mike Cuellar	.10	.05	.01
□ 47 Al Bumbry	.05	.02	.01
□ 48 Gene Richards	.05	.02	.01
□ 49 Pedro Borbon	.05	.02	.01
□ 50 Julio Solo	.05	.02	.01
□ 51 Ed Nottle MG	.05	.02	.01
□ 52 Jim Bibby	.05	.02	.01
□ 53 Doug Griffin CO	.05	.02	.01
□ 54 Ed Clements	.05	.02	.01
□ 55 Dalton Jones	.05	.02	.01
□ 56 Earl Weaver MG	.50	.23	.06
□ 57 Jesus De La Rosa	.05	.02	.01
□ 58 Paul Casanova	.05	.02	.01
□ 59 Frank Riccelli	.05	.02	.01
□ 60 Rafael Landestoy UER (Misspelled Raphael on card back)	.05	.02	.01
□ 61 George Hendrick	.10	.05	.01
□ 62 Cesar Cedeno	.15	.07	.02
□ 63 Bert Campaneris	.15	.07	.02
□ 64 Derrel Thomas	.05	.02	.01
□ 65 Bobby Ramos	.05	.02	.01
□ 66 Grant Jackson	.05	.02	.01
□ 67 Steve Whitaker	.05	.02	.01
□ 68 Pedro Ramos	.05	.02	.01
□ 69 Joe Hicks UER (No height or weight information)	.05	.02	.01
□ 70 Taylor Duncan	.05	.02	.01
□ 71 Tom Shopay	.05	.02	.01
□ 72 Ken Clay	.05	.02	.01
□ 73 Mike Kekich	.05	.02	.01
□ 74 Ed Halicki	.05	.02	.01
□ 75 Ed Figueroa	.10	.05	.01
□ 76 Paul Blair	.10	.05	.01
□ 77 Luis Tiant	.20	.09	.03
□ 78 Stan Bahnsen	.05	.02	.01
□ 79 Rennie Stennett	.05	.02	.01
□ 80 Bobby Molinaro	.05	.02	.01
□ 81 Jim Gideon	.05	.02	.01
□ 82 Orlando Gonzalez	.05	.02	.01
□ 83 Amos Otis	.15	.07	.02
□ 84 Dennis Leonard	.10	.05	.01
□ 85 Pat Putman	.05	.02	.01
□ 86 Rick Manning	.05	.02	.01
□ 87 Pat Dobson MG	.10	.05	.01
□ 88 Marty Castillo	.05	.02	.01
□ 89 Steve McCatty	.05	.02	.01
□ 90 Doug Bird	.05	.02	.01
□ 91 Rick Waits	.05	.02	.01
□ 92 Ron Jackson	.05	.02	.01
□ 93 Tim Hosley	.05	.02	.01
□ 94 Steve Luebber	.05	.02	.01
□ 95 Rich Gale	.05	.02	.01
□ 96 Champ Summers	.05	.02	.01
□ 97 Dave LaRoche	.05	.02	.01
□ 98 Bobby Jones	.05	.02	.01
□ 99 Kim Allen	.05	.02	.01
□ 100 Wayne Garland	.05	.02	.01
□ 101 Tom Spencer	.05	.02	.01
□ 102 Dan Driessen	.10	.05	.01
□ 103 Ron Pruitt	.05	.02	.01

Card	MT	EX-MT	VG
☐ 104 Tim Ireland	.05	.02	.01
☐ 105 Dan Driessen IA	.10	.05	.01
☐ 106 Pepe Frias UER (Misspelled Pepi on card front)	.05	.02	.01
☐ 107 Eric Rasmussen	.05	.02	.01
☐ 108 Don Hood	.05	.02	.01
☐ 109 Joe Coleman CO UER (Photo actually Tony Torchia)	.05	.02	.01
☐ 110 Jim Slaton	.05	.02	.01
☐ 111 Clint Hurdle	.10	.05	.01
☐ 112 Larry Milbourne	.05	.02	.01
☐ 113 Al Holland	.05	.02	.01
☐ 114 George Foster	.15	.07	.02
☐ 115 Graig Nettles MG	.15	.07	.02
☐ 116 Oscar Gamble	.10	.05	.01
☐ 117 Ross Grimsley	.10	.05	.01
☐ 118 Bill Travers	.05	.02	.01
☐ 119 Jose Beniquez	.10	.05	.01
☐ 120 Jerry Grote IA	.05	.02	.01
☐ 121 John D'Acquisto	.05	.02	.01
☐ 122 Tom Murphy	.05	.02	.01
☐ 123 Walt Williams UER (Listed as pitcher)	.10	.05	.01
☐ 124 Roy Thomas	.05	.02	.01
☐ 125 Jerry Grote	.05	.02	.01
☐ 126A Jim Nettles ERR (Writing on bat knob)	.50	.23	.06
☐ 126B Jim Nettles COR	5.00	2.30	.60
☐ 127 Randy Niemann	.05	.02	.01
☐ 128 Bobby Bonds	.50	.23	.06
☐ 129 Ed Glynn	.05	.02	.01
☐ 130 Ed Hicks	.05	.02	.01
☐ 131 Ivan Murrell	.05	.02	.01
☐ 132 Graig Nettles MG	.25	.11	.03
☐ 133 Hal McRae	.25	.11	.03
☐ 134 Pat Kelly	.10	.05	.01
☐ 135 Sammy Stewart	.05	.02	.01
☐ 136 Bruce Kison	.10	.05	.01
☐ 137 Jim Morrison	.05	.02	.01
☐ 138 Omar Moreno	.05	.02	.01
☐ 139 Tom Brown	.05	.02	.01
☐ 140 Steve Dillard	.05	.02	.01
☐ 141 Gary Alexander	.05	.02	.01
☐ 142 Al Oliver	.25	.11	.03
☐ 143 Rick Lysander	.05	.02	.01
☐ 144 Tippy Martinez	.10	.05	.01
☐ 145 Al Cowens	.10	.05	.01
☐ 146 Gene Clines	.05	.02	.01
☐ 147 Willie Aikens	.10	.05	.01
☐ 148 Tommy Moore	.05	.02	.01
☐ 149 Clete Boyer MG	.10	.05	.01
☐ 150 Stan Cliburn	.05	.02	.01
☐ 151 Ken Kravec	.05	.02	.01
☐ 152 Garth Iorg	.05	.02	.01
☐ 153 Rick Peterson	.05	.02	.01
☐ 154 Wayne Nordhagen UER (Misspelled Nordgahen on card back)	.05	.02	.01
☐ 155 Danny Meyer	.05	.02	.01
☐ 156 Wayne Garrett	.05	.02	.01
☐ 157 Wayne Krenchicki	.05	.02	.01
☐ 158 Graig Nettles	.25	.11	.03
☐ 159 Earl Stephenson	.05	.02	.01
☐ 160 Carl Taylor	.05	.02	.01
☐ 161 Rollie Fingers	1.25	.55	.16
☐ 162 Toby Harrah	.10	.05	.01
☐ 163 Mickey Rivers	.10	.05	.01
☐ 164 Dave Kingman	.15	.07	.02
☐ 165 Paul Mirabella	.05	.02	.01
☐ 166 Dick Williams MG	.10	.05	.01
☐ 167 Luis Pujols	.05	.02	.01
☐ 168 Tito Landrum	.10	.05	.01
☐ 169 Tom Underwood	.05	.02	.01
☐ 170 Mark Wagner	.05	.02	.01
☐ 171 Odell Jones	.05	.02	.01
☐ 172 Doug Capilla	.05	.02	.01
☐ 173 Alfie Rondon	.05	.02	.01
☐ 174 Lowell Palmer	.05	.02	.01
☐ 175 Juan Eichelberger	.05	.02	.01
☐ 176 Wes Clements	.05	.02	.01
☐ 177 Rodney Scott	.05	.02	.01
☐ 178 Ron Washington	.05	.02	.01
☐ 179 Al Hrabosky	.10	.05	.01
☐ 180 Sid Monge	.05	.02	.01
☐ 181 Randy Johnson	.05	.02	.01
☐ 182 Tim Stoddard	.05	.02	.01
☐ 183 Dick Williams MG	.10	.05	.01
☐ 184 Lee Lacy	.10	.05	.01
☐ 185 Jerry White	.05	.02	.01
☐ 186 Dave Kingman	.15	.07	.02
☐ 187 Checklist 1-110	.05	.02	.01
☐ 188 Jose Cruz	.15	.07	.02
☐ 189 Jamie Easterly	.05	.02	.01
☐ 190 Ike Blessit	.05	.02	.01
☐ 191 Johnny Grubb	.05	.02	.01
☐ 192 Dave Cash	.05	.02	.01
☐ 193 Doug Corbett	.05	.02	.01
☐ 194 Bruce Bochy	.05	.02	.01
☐ 195 Mark Corey	.05	.02	.01
☐ 196 Gil Rondon	.05	.02	.01
☐ 197 Jerry Martin	.05	.02	.01
☐ 198 Gerry Pirtle	.05	.02	.01
☐ 199 Gates Brown MG	.10	.05	.01
☐ 200 Bob Galasso	.05	.02	.01
☐ 201 Bake McBride	.05	.02	.01
☐ 202 Wayne Granger	.05	.02	.01
☐ 203 Larry Milbourne	.05	.02	.01
☐ 204 Tom Paciorek	.05	.02	.01
☐ 205 U.L. Washington	.05	.02	.01
☐ 206 Larvell Blanks	.05	.02	.01
☐ 207 Bob Shirley	.05	.02	.01
☐ 208 Pete Falcone	.05	.02	.01
☐ 209 Sal Butera	.05	.02	.01
☐ 210 Roy Branch	.05	.02	.01
☐ 211 Dyar Miller	.05	.02	.01
☐ 212 Paul Siebert	.05	.02	.01
☐ 213 Ken Reitz	.05	.02	.01
☐ 214 Bill Madlock	.20	.09	.03
☐ 215 Vida Blue	.15	.07	.02
☐ 216 Dave Hilton	.05	.02	.01
☐ 217 Pedro Ramos CO and Charlie Bree CO	.05	.02	.01
☐ 218 Checklist 111-220	.05	.02	.01
☐ 219 Pat Dobson MG and Earl Weaver MG	.20	.09	.03
☐ 220 Curt Flood COMM	.25	.11	.03

1990 Pacific Legends

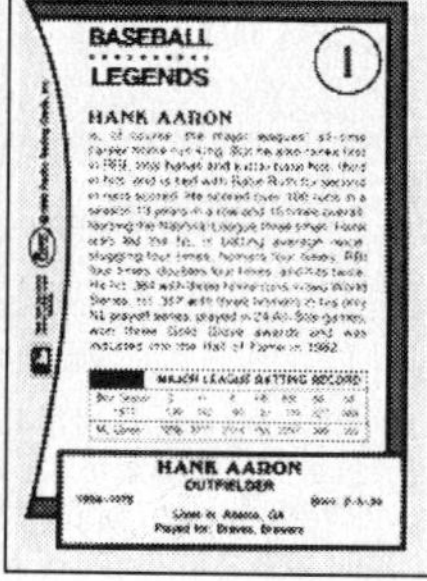

The 1990 Pacific Legends set was a 110-card set issued by Pacific Trading Cards. The set numbering is basically arranged in two alphabetical sequences. This is a standard size (2 1/2" by 3 1/2") set which was available as factory set as well as in wax packs. The set does include some active players, Willie Wilson and Jesse Barfield, the last two players in the set.

	MT	EX-MT	VG
COMPLETE SET (110)	9.00	4.00	1.15
COMMON PLAYER (1-110)	.05	.02	.01
☐ 1 Hank Aaron	.60	.25	.08
☐ 2 Tommie Agee	.05	.02	.01
☐ 3 Luke Appling	.15	.07	.02
☐ 4 Sal Bando	.05	.02	.01
☐ 5 Ernie Banks	.35	.16	.04
☐ 6 Don Baylor	.10	.05	.01
☐ 7 Yogi Berra	.40	.18	.05
☐ 8 Vida Blue	.05	.02	.01
☐ 9 Lou Boudreau	.15	.07	.02
☐ 10 Clete Boyer	.05	.02	.01
☐ 11 George Bamberger	.05	.02	.01
☐ 12 Lou Brock	.25	.11	.03
☐ 13 Ralph Branca	.05	.02	.01
☐ 14 Carl Erskine	.05	.02	.01
☐ 15 Bert Campaneris	.05	.02	.01

☐ 16 Steve Carlton	.25	.11	.03
☐ 17 Rod Carew	.35	.16	.04
☐ 18 Rocky Colavito	.15	.07	.02
☐ 19 Frankie Crosetti	.10	.05	.01
☐ 20 Larry Doby	.10	.05	.01
☐ 21 Bobby Doerr	.15	.07	.02
☐ 22 Walt Dropo	.05	.02	.01
☐ 23 Rick Ferrell	.15	.07	.02
☐ 24 Joe Garagiola	.20	.09	.03
☐ 25 Ralph Garr	.05	.02	.01
☐ 26 Dick Groat	.05	.02	.01
☐ 27 Steve Garvey	.15	.07	.02
☐ 28 Bob Gibson	.25	.11	.03
☐ 29 Don Drysdale	.20	.09	.03
☐ 30 Billy Herman	.15	.07	.02
☐ 31 Bobby Grich	.05	.02	.01
☐ 32 Monte Irvin	.15	.07	.02
☐ 33 Dave Johnson	.05	.02	.01
☐ 34 Don Kessinger	.05	.02	.01
☐ 35 Harmon Killebrew	.20	.09	.03
☐ 36 Ralph Kiner	.20	.09	.03
☐ 37 Vern Law	.05	.02	.01
☐ 38 Ed Lopat	.10	.05	.01
☐ 39 Bill Mazeroski	.10	.05	.01
☐ 40 Rick Monday	.05	.02	.01
☐ 41 Manny Mota	.05	.02	.01
☐ 42 Don Newcombe	.10	.05	.01
☐ 43 Gaylord Perry	.20	.09	.03
☐ 44 Jim Piersall	.10	.05	.01
☐ 45 Johnny Podres	.10	.05	.01
☐ 46 Boog Powell	.10	.05	.01
☐ 47 Robin Roberts	.20	.09	.03
☐ 48 Ron Santo	.10	.05	.01
☐ 49 Herb Score	.10	.05	.01
☐ 50 Enos Slaughter	.20	.09	.03
☐ 51 Warren Spahn	.25	.11	.03
☐ 52 Rusty Staub	.10	.05	.01
☐ 53 Frank Torre	.05	.02	.01
☐ 54 Bob Horner	.05	.02	.01
☐ 55 Lee May	.05	.02	.01
☐ 56 Bill White	.10	.05	.01
☐ 57 Hoyt Wilhelm	.15	.07	.02
☐ 58 Billy Williams	.20	.09	.03
☐ 59 Ted Williams	.50	.23	.06
☐ 60 Tom Seaver	.50	.23	.06
☐ 61 Carl Yastrzemski	.40	.18	.05
☐ 62 Marv Throneberry	.05	.02	.01
☐ 63 Steve Stone	.05	.02	.01
☐ 64 Rico Petrocelli	.05	.02	.01
☐ 65 Orlando Cepeda	.15	.07	.02
☐ 66 Eddie Mathews	.20	.09	.03
☐ 67 Joe Sewell	.15	.07	.02
☐ 68 Catfish Hunter	.20	.09	.03
☐ 69 Alvin Dark	.10	.05	.01
☐ 70 Richie Ashburn	.15	.07	.02
☐ 71 Dusty Baker	.10	.05	.01
☐ 72 George Foster	.10	.05	.01
☐ 73 Eddie Yost	.05	.02	.01
☐ 74 Buddy Bell	.05	.02	.01
☐ 75 Manny Sanguillen	.05	.02	.01
☐ 76 Jim Bunning	.10	.05	.01
☐ 77 Smoky Burgess	.05	.02	.01
☐ 78 Al Rosen	.10	.05	.01
☐ 79 Gene Conley	.05	.02	.01
☐ 80 Dave Dravecky	.10	.05	.01
☐ 81 Charlie Gehringer	.15	.07	.02
☐ 82 Billy Pierce	.05	.02	.01
☐ 83 Willie Horton	.05	.02	.01
☐ 84 Ron Hunt	.05	.02	.01
☐ 85 Bob Feller	.25	.11	.03
☐ 86 George Kell	.15	.07	.02
☐ 87 Dave Kingman	.10	.05	.01
☐ 88 Jerry Koosman	.10	.05	.01
☐ 89 Clem Labine	.05	.02	.01
☐ 90 Tony LaRussa	.15	.07	.02
☐ 91 Dennis Leonard	.05	.02	.01
☐ 92 Dale Long	.05	.02	.01
☐ 93 Sparky Lyle	.10	.05	.01
☐ 94 Gil McDougald	.10	.05	.01
☐ 95 Don Mossi	.05	.02	.01
☐ 96 Phil Niekro	.25	.11	.03
☐ 97 Tom Paciorek	.05	.02	.01
☐ 98 Mel Parnell	.05	.02	.01
☐ 99 Lou Piniella	.15	.07	.02
☐ 100 Bobby Richardson	.15	.07	.02
☐ 101 Phil Rizzuto	.20	.09	.03
☐ 102 Brooks Robinson	.25	.11	.03
☐ 103 Pete Runnels	.05	.02	.01
☐ 104 Diego Segui	.05	.02	.01
☐ 105 Bobby Shantz	.05	.02	.01
☐ 106 Bobby Thomson	.10	.05	.01
☐ 107 Joe Torre	.20	.09	.03
☐ 108 Earl Weaver MG	.15	.07	.02
☐ 109 Willie Wilson	.10	.05	.01
☐ 110 Jesse Barfield	.10	.05	.01

1991 Pacific Nolan Ryan Texas Exp. I

This 110-card set measures the standard 2 1/2" by 3 1/2" and traces the career of Nolan Ryan from the start of his career into the 1991 season as well as his personal life with his family on his ranch in Alvin, Texas. This set features glossy full-color photos on the front and either biographical information or an action shot of Ryan on the back which is framed by a fireball. The backs are printed in purple and red on a white background. Inside a flaming baseball design, one finds biography, career highlights, player quote, or an extended caption to the front picture. The cards are numbered on the back. This set was issued by Pacific Trading cards and was the first set featuring an individual baseball player to be sold in wax packs since the 1959 Fleer Ted Williams issue. The cards were available in 12-card foil packs and factory sets. Moreover, eight unnumbered bonus cards (1-6 No Hitters, 1991 25th Season, and Rookie year with the Mets) were produced in quantities of 1,000 of each card in gold foil and 10,000 of each card in silver foil; these bonus cards were randomly inserted in foil packs only.

	MT	EX-MT	VG
COMPLETE SET (110)	10.00	4.50	1.25
COMMON PLAYER (1-110)	.15	.07	.02
☐ 1 Future Hall of Famer	.30	.14	.04
☐ 2 From Little League to the Major Leagues	.15	.07	.02
☐ 3 A Dream Come True	.15	.07	.02
☐ 4 Signed by the Mets	.15	.07	.02
☐ 5 Fireball Pitcher	.15	.07	.02
☐ 6 New York Mets Rookie Pitcher	.15	.07	.02
☐ 7 First Major League Win	.15	.07	.02
☐ 8 Early in 1969	.15	.07	.02
☐ 9 Tensions of a Pennant Race	.15	.07	.02
☐ 10 Mets Clinch NL East	.15	.07	.02
☐ 11 Keep the Ball Down	.15	.07	.02
☐ 12 Playoff Victory for Ryan	.15	.07	.02
☐ 13 World Series Victory	.15	.07	.02
☐ 14 The Amazin' Mets	.15	.07	.02
☐ 15 Nolan Sets Met Record for Strikeouts	.15	.07	.02
☐ 16 One of the Worst Trades in Baseball	.15	.07	.02
☐ 17 Slow Start with Mets	.15	.07	.02
☐ 18 Pitcher New York Mets	.15	.07	.02
☐ 19 Traded to the Angels	.15	.07	.02
☐ 20 Meeting New Friends	.15	.07	.02
☐ 21 Throwing Fast Balls	.15	.07	.02
☐ 22 Move the Ball Around	.15	.07	.02
☐ 23 Nolan Heat	.15	.07	.02
☐ 24 No-Hitter Number 1	.15	.07	.02
☐ 25 Looking Back on Number 1	.15	.07	.02
☐ 26 No-Hitter Number 2	.15	.07	.02

☐ 27 Single Season Strikeout Record	.15	.07	.02
☐ 28 21 Wins in 1973	.15	.07	.02
☐ 29 Fastest Pitch Ever Thrown Clocked at 100.9 MPH	.20	.09	.03
☐ 30 No-Hitter Number 3	.20	.09	.03
☐ 31 No-Hitter Number 4	.20	.09	.03
☐ 32 Ryan and Tanana	.20	.09	.03
☐ 33 Learning Change-Up	.15	.07	.02
☐ 34 Pitcher California Angels	.15	.07	.02
☐ 35 Nolan Joins Astros	.15	.07	.02
☐ 36 Starting Pitcher Nolan Ryan	.20	.09	.03
☐ 37 Taking Batting Practice	.15	.07	.02
☐ 38 The Game's Greatest Power Pitcher	.15	.07	.02
☐ 39 3000 Career Strikeout	.15	.07	.02
☐ 40 A Ryan Home Run	.20	.09	.03
☐ 41 The Fast Ball Grip	.15	.07	.02
☐ 42 Record 5th No-Hitter	.20	.09	.03
☐ 43 No-Hitter Number 5	.20	.09	.03
☐ 44 A Dream Fulfilled	.15	.07	.02
☐ 45 Nolan passes Walter Johnson	.20	.09	.03
☐ 46 Strikeout 4000	.20	.09	.03
☐ 47 Astros win Western Division Title	.15	.07	.02
☐ 48 Pitcher Houston Astros	.15	.07	.02
☐ 49 Milestone Strikeouts	.15	.07	.02
☐ 50 Post Season Participant	.15	.07	.02
☐ 51 Hurling for Houston	.15	.07	.02
☐ 52 135 NL Wins	.15	.07	.02
☐ 53 Through with Chew	.15	.07	.02
☐ 54 Signed by Rangers 1989	.15	.07	.02
☐ 55 Pleasant Change for Nolan	.15	.07	.02
☐ 56 Real Special Moment	.15	.07	.02
☐ 57 Nolan Enters 1989 All-Star Game	.15	.07	.02
☐ 58 Pitching in 1989 All-Star Game	.15	.07	.02
☐ 59 5000 Strikeouts; A Standing Ovation	.20	.09	.03
☐ 60 Great Moments in 1989	.15	.07	.02
☐ 61 Nolan with Dan Smith, Rangers First Draft Pick	.20	.09	.03
☐ 62 Ranger Club Record, 16 Strikeouts	.15	.07	.02
☐ 63 Last Pitch No-Hitter Number 6	.20	.09	.03
☐ 64 Sweet Number 6	.20	.09	.03
☐ 65 Oldest To Throw No-Hitter	.15	.07	.02
☐ 66 Another Ryan Win	.15	.07	.02
☐ 67 20th Pitcher to Win 300, Acknowledging the Fans	.15	.07	.02
☐ 68 300 Game Win Battery, Arnsberg/Ryan/Petralli	.15	.07	.02
☐ 69 A 300 Game Winner	.15	.07	.02
☐ 70 Perfect Mechanics	.15	.07	.02
☐ 71 22 Seasons with 100 or more Strikeouts	.15	.07	.02
☐ 72 11th Strikeout Title	.15	.07	.02
☐ 73 232 Strikeouts, 1990	.15	.07	.02
☐ 74 The 1990 Season	.15	.07	.02
☐ 75 Pitcher Texas Rangers	.20	.09	.03
☐ 76 1991, Nolan's 25th Season	.15	.07	.02
☐ 77 Throwing Spirals	.20	.09	.03
☐ 78 Running the Steps	.15	.07	.02
☐ 79 Hard Work and Conditioning	.15	.07	.02
☐ 80 The Rigid Workout	.15	.07	.02
☐ 81 Ryan's Routine	.15	.07	.02
☐ 82 Ryan's Routine Between Starts	.15	.07	.02
☐ 83 Running in Outfield Before the Big Game	.15	.07	.02
☐ 84 B.P. in Texas	.15	.07	.02
☐ 85 18 Career Low-Hitters	.15	.07	.02
☐ 86 My Job is to Give My Team a Chance to Win	.15	.07	.02
☐ 87 The Spring Workout	.15	.07	.02
☐ 88 Power versus Power	.15	.07	.02
☐ 89 Awesome Power	.15	.07	.02
☐ 90 Blazing Speed	.15	.07	.02
☐ 91 The Pick Off	.15	.07	.02
☐ 92 Nolan's a Real Gamer (Bloody lip and blood all over jersey)	.90	.40	.11
☐ 93 Ranger Battery Mates	.15	.07	.02
☐ 94 The Glare	.15	.07	.02
☐ 95 The High Leg Kick	.15	.07	.02
☐ 96 Day Off from Pitcher	.15	.07	.02
☐ 97 A New Ball for Nolan	.15	.07	.02
☐ 98 Going to Rosin Bag	.15	.07	.02
☐ 99 Time for Relief	.15	.07	.02
☐ 100 A Lone Star Legend	.15	.07	.02
☐ 101 Fans' Favorite	.15	.07	.02
☐ 102 Watching Nolan Pitch	.15	.07	.02
☐ 103 Our Family of Five	.15	.07	.02
☐ 104 Texas Beefmaster	.15	.07	.02
☐ 105 Gentleman Rancher	.15	.07	.02
☐ 106 Texas Cowboy Life	.15	.07	.02
☐ 107 The Ryan Family	.15	.07	.02
☐ 108 Participating in Cutting Horse Contest	.15	.07	.02
☐ 109 Nolan Interviews	.15	.07	.02
☐ 110 Lynn Nolan Ryan	.30	.14	.04

1991 Pacific Nolan Ryan Inserts

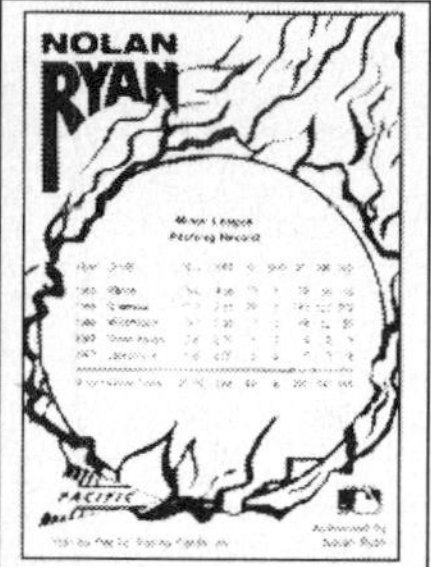

These eight standard-size (2 1/2" by 3 1/2") cards were inserts in 1991 Pacific Nolan Ryan Texas Express foil packs. As with the regular issue, the fronts display glossy color photos that are bordered in silver foil and either purple/red or red/orange border stripes. Inside a flaming baseball design, the back presents either a player photo, statistics, or career highlights. The cards are unnumbered and checklisted below in chronological order. Besides the silver cards, they were also issued on a much more limited basis in gold. The gold versions are valued at quadruple the prices listed below.

	MT	EX-MT	VG
COMPLETE SET (8)	150.00	70.00	19.00
COMMON PLAYER (1-8)	25.00	11.50	3.10
☐ 1 New York Mets Rookie Pitcher	25.00	11.50	3.10
☐ 2 No-Hitter 1	25.00	11.50	3.10
☐ 3 No-Hitter 2	25.00	11.50	3.10
☐ 4 No-Hitter 3	25.00	11.50	3.10
☐ 5 No-Hitter 4	25.00	11.50	3.10
☐ 6 No-Hitter 5	25.00	11.50	3.10
☐ 7 Sweet 6	25.00	11.50	3.10
☐ 8 1991: Nolan's 25th Season	25.00	11.50	3.10

1991 Pacific Nolan Ryan 7th No-Hitter

This seven-card set was produced by Pacific Trading Cards Inc. to capture various moments of Nolan Ryan's 7th no-

hitter. These cards were produced in the following numbers: 1,000 of each card in gold foil and 10,000 of each card in silver foil. The cards measure the standard size (2 1/2" by 3 1/2") and they were randomly inserted in foil packs only. The fronts feature glossy color photos, with silver or gold borders on the sides and faded red borders above and below the picture. In addition, the player's name is written vertically in a multi-colored stripe on the left side of the picture. A flaming baseball in the lower left corner completes the card face. The backs are printed in purple and red on a white background. Inside a flaming baseball design, one finds an extended caption to the front picture. The cards are numbered on the back in the lower left corner. Supposedly as many as half of the cards were destroyed and never released. The prices below refer to the silver versions; the gold versions would be valued at quadruple the prices below.

	MT	EX-MT	VG
COMPLETE SET (7)	150.00	70.00	19.00
COMMON PLAYER (1-7)	25.00	11.50	3.10
☐ 1 Last Pitch 7th No-Hitter	25.00	11.50	3.10
☐ 2 No-Hitter Number 7	25.00	11.50	3.10
☐ 3 Number 7 Was The Best	25.00	11.50	3.10
☐ 4 Time to Celebrate	25.00	11.50	3.10
☐ 5 Congratulations from Ranger Fans	25.00	11.50	3.10
☐ 6 Catcher Mike Stanley and Nolan hold the No-Hitter Ball UER (Back reads Bryan, should read Ryan)	25.00	11.50	3.10
☐ 7 All in a Day's Work	25.00	11.50	3.10

1991 Pacific Senior League

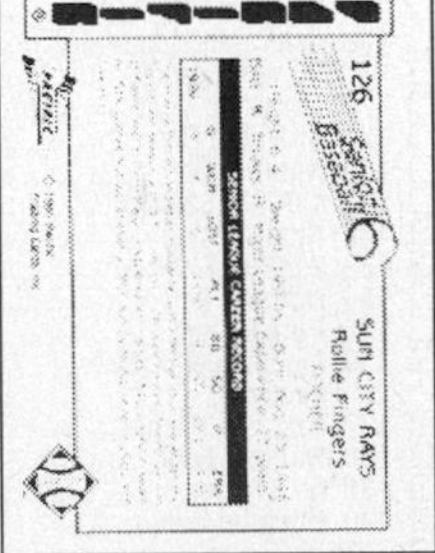

Pacific Trading Cards released this 160-card set just after the Senior League suspended operations. The standard size (2 1/2" by 3 1/2") cards were sold in wax packs and as complete sets. The fronts have glossy color player photos, with white borders and the team name written vertically in a stripe running down the left side of the picture. The backs are mint-colored and feature career highlights. Apparently there are two different versions of cards for the following players: Jim Rice, Rollie Fingers, Vida Blue, Dave Cash, Dan Norman, Ron LeFlore, Cesar Cedeno, Rafael Landestoy, and Dan Driessen. The cards are numbered on the back.

	MT	EX-MT	VG
COMPLETE SET (160)	9.00	4.00	1.15
COMMON PLAYER (1-160)	.05	.02	.01
☐ 1 Dan Driessen	.10	.05	.01
☐ 2 Marty Castillo	.05	.02	.01
☐ 3 Jerry White	.05	.02	.01
☐ 4 Bud Anderson	.05	.02	.01
☐ 5 Ron Jackson	.05	.02	.01
☐ 6 Fred Stanley CO	.10	.05	.01
☐ 7 Steve Luebber	.05	.02	.01
☐ 8 Jerry Terrell CO	.05	.02	.01
☐ 9 Pat Dobson	.10	.05	.01
☐ 10 Ken Kravec	.05	.02	.01
☐ 11 Gil Rondon	.05	.02	.01
☐ 12 Dyar Miller CO	.05	.02	.01
☐ 13 Bobby Molinaro	.05	.02	.01
☐ 14 Jerry Martin	.05	.02	.01
☐ 15 Rick Waits	.10	.05	.01
☐ 16 Steve McCatty	.10	.05	.01
☐ 17 Roger Slagle	.05	.02	.01
☐ 18 Mike Ramsey	.10	.05	.01
☐ 19 Rich Gale	.10	.05	.01
☐ 20 Larry Harlow	.05	.02	.01
☐ 21 Dan Rohn	.05	.02	.01
☐ 22 Don Cooper	.05	.02	.01
☐ 23 Marv Foley	.05	.02	.01
☐ 24 Rafael Landestoy	.05	.02	.01
☐ 25 Eddie Milner	.05	.02	.01
☐ 26 Amos Otis	.10	.05	.01
☐ 27 Odell Jones	.05	.02	.01
☐ 28 Tippy Martinez	.10	.05	.01
☐ 29 Stu Cliburn	.05	.02	.01
☐ 30 Stan Cliburn	.05	.02	.01
☐ 31 Tony Cloninger CO	.05	.02	.01
☐ 32 Jeff Jones	.05	.02	.01
☐ 33 Ken Reitz	.05	.02	.01
☐ 34 Dave Sax	.05	.02	.01
☐ 35 Orlando Gonzalez	.05	.02	.01
☐ 36 Jose Cruz	.10	.05	.01
☐ 37 Mickey Mahler	.05	.02	.01
☐ 38 Derek Botelho	.05	.02	.01
☐ 39 Rick Lysander	.05	.02	.01
☐ 40 Cesar Cedeno	.15	.07	.02
☐ 41 Garth Iorg	.05	.02	.01
☐ 42 Wayne Krenchicki	.05	.02	.01
☐ 43 Clete Boyer CO	.10	.05	.01
☐ 44 Dan Boone	.10	.05	.01
☐ 45 George Vukovich	.05	.02	.01
☐ 46 Omar Moreno	.05	.02	.01
☐ 47 Ron Washington	.05	.02	.01
☐ 48 Ron Washington Most Valuable Player	.05	.02	.01
☐ 49 Rick Peterson	.05	.02	.01
☐ 50 Tack Wilson	.10	.05	.01
☐ 51 Stan and Stu Cliburn	.10	.05	.01
☐ 52 Rick Lysander Player of the Year	.10	.05	.01
☐ 53 Cesar Cedeno and Pete LaCock	.10	.05	.01
☐ 54 Jim Marshall MG and Cleet Boyer MG	.10	.05	.01
☐ 55 Doug Simunic	.05	.02	.01
☐ 56 Pat Kelly	.10	.05	.01
☐ 57 Roy Branch	.05	.02	.01
☐ 58 Dave Cash	.10	.05	.01
☐ 59 Bobby Jones	.10	.05	.01
☐ 60 Hector Cruz	.05	.02	.01
☐ 61 Reggie Cleveland	.05	.02	.01
☐ 62 Gary Lance	.05	.02	.01
☐ 63 Ron LeFlore	.10	.05	.01
☐ 64 Dan Norman	.05	.02	.01
☐ 65 Renie Martin	.05	.02	.01
☐ 66 Pete Mackanin MG	.05	.02	.01
☐ 67 Frank Riccelli	.05	.02	.01
☐ 68 Alfie Rondon	.05	.02	.01
☐ 69 Rodney Scott	.05	.02	.01
☐ 70 Jim Tracy	.05	.02	.01
☐ 71 Ed Dennis	.05	.02	.01
☐ 72 Rick Lindell	.05	.02	.01
☐ 73 Stu Pepper	.05	.02	.01
☐ 74 Jeff Youngbauer	.05	.02	.01
☐ 75 Russ Foster	.05	.02	.01

☐ 76 Jeff Capriati	.10	.05	.01
☐ 77 Art DeFreites	.05	.02	.01
☐ 78 Alfie Rondon	.05	.02	.01
☐ 79 Reggie Cleveland IA	.05	.02	.01
☐ 80 Dave Cash	.10	.05	.01
☐ 81 Vida Blue	.15	.07	.02
☐ 82 Ed Glynn	.05	.02	.01
☐ 83 Bob Owchinko	.05	.02	.01
☐ 84 Bill Fleming	.05	.02	.01
☐ 85 Ron and Gary Roenicke	.10	.05	.01
☐ 86 Tom Thompson CO	.05	.02	.01
☐ 87 Derrel Thomas UER (Name misspelled Derrell)	.10	.05	.01
☐ 88 Jim Willoughby	.05	.02	.01
☐ 89 Jim Pankovits	.05	.02	.01
☐ 90 Jack Cooley CO	.05	.02	.01
☐ 91 Lenn Sakata	.05	.02	.01
☐ 92 Mike Brocki	.05	.02	.01
☐ 93 Chuck Fick	.05	.02	.01
☐ 94 Tom Benedict	.05	.02	.01
☐ 95 Anthony Davis	.50	.23	.06
☐ 96 Cardell Camper	.05	.02	.01
☐ 97 Leon Roberts	.05	.02	.01
☐ 98 Roger Erickson	.05	.02	.01
☐ 99 Kim Allen	.05	.02	.01
☐ 100 Dave Skaggs	.05	.02	.01
☐ 101 Joe Decker	.05	.02	.01
☐ 102 U.L. Washington	.05	.02	.01
☐ 103 Don Fletcher	.05	.02	.01
☐ 104 Gary Roenicke	.10	.05	.01
☐ 105 Rich Dauer MG	.10	.05	.01
☐ 106 Ron Roenicke	.10	.05	.01
☐ 107 Mike Norris	.10	.05	.01
☐ 108 Ferguson Jenkins	.75	.35	.09
☐ 109 Ronn Reynolds	.05	.02	.01
☐ 110 Pete Falcone	.05	.02	.01
☐ 111 Gary Allenson	.05	.02	.01
☐ 112 Mark Wagner	.05	.02	.01
☐ 113 Jack Lazorko	.05	.02	.01
☐ 114 Bob Galasso	.05	.02	.01
☐ 115 Ron Davis	.05	.02	.01
☐ 116 Lenny Randle	.05	.02	.01
☐ 117 Ricky Peters	.05	.02	.01
☐ 118 Jim Dwyer	.05	.02	.01
☐ 119 Juan Eichelberger	.05	.02	.01
☐ 120 Pete LaCock	.10	.05	.01
☐ 121 Tony Scott	.10	.05	.01
☐ 122 Rick Lancellotti	.05	.02	.01
☐ 123 Barry Bonnell	.10	.05	.01
☐ 124 Dave Hilton	.05	.02	.01
☐ 125 Bill Campbell	.10	.05	.01
☐ 126 Rollie Fingers	.75	.35	.09
☐ 127 Jim Marshall MG	.05	.02	.01
☐ 128 Razor Shines	.05	.02	.01
☐ 129 Guy Sularz	.05	.02	.01
☐ 130 Roy Thomas	.05	.02	.01
☐ 131 Joel Youngblood	.05	.02	.01
☐ 132 Ernie Camacho	.10	.05	.01
☐ 133 Dave Hilton CO, Jim Marshall MG, and Fred Stanley CO	.10	.05	.01
☐ 134 Ken Landreaux	.10	.05	.01
☐ 135 Dave Rozema	.10	.05	.01
☐ 136 Tom Zimmer CO	.05	.02	.01
☐ 137 Elias Sosa	.05	.02	.01
☐ 138 Ossie Virgil Sr. CO	.05	.02	.01
☐ 139 Al Holland	.05	.02	.01
☐ 140 Milt Wilcox	.10	.05	.01
☐ 141 Jerry Reed	.05	.02	.01
☐ 142 Chris Welsh	.05	.02	.01
☐ 143 Luis Gomez	.05	.02	.01
☐ 144 Steve Henderson	.05	.02	.01
☐ 145 Butch Benton	.05	.02	.01
☐ 146 Bill Lee	.10	.05	.01
☐ 147 Todd Cruz	.05	.02	.01
☐ 148 Jim Rice	.30	.14	.04
☐ 149 Tito Landrum	.10	.05	.01
☐ 150 Ozzie Virgil Jr.	.10	.05	.01
☐ 151 Joe Pittman	.05	.02	.01
☐ 152 Bobby Tolan MG	.10	.05	.01
☐ 153 Len Barker	.10	.05	.01
☐ 154 Dave Rajsich	.05	.02	.01
☐ 155 Glenn Gulliver	.05	.02	.01
☐ 156 Gary Rajsich	.05	.02	.01
☐ 157 Joe Sambito	.10	.05	.01
☐ 158 Frank Vito	.05	.02	.01
☐ 159 Ozzie Virgil Jr./Sr.	.10	.05	.01
☐ 160 Dave and Gary Rajsich	.10	.05	.01

1992 Pacific Nolan Ryan Texas Exp. II

This 110-card set measures the standard size (2 1/2" by 3 1/2"). A six-card insert set was randomly inserted in foil packs, with 1,000 autographed and numbered of card number 1. The fronts feature glossy posed and action photos (some color, some black-and-white) of Ryan in various stages of his life and career. The pictures are bordered at the top and bottom in varying shades of red, orange and purple. His name is printed in silver vertically down the left edge of the card on either red, orange or purple. A fiery baseball overlaps the border and photo at the bottom. The backs show the fiery baseball with either statistics, career highlights, pictures, or quotes about Nolan printed in blue on the baseball. The cards are numbered on the back. This set is essentially an extension or second series of the 1991 Pacific Nolan Ryan set and is numbered that way.

	MT	EX-MT	VG
COMPLETE SET (110)	9.00	4.00	1.15
COMMON PLAYER (111-220)	.15	.07	.02
☐ 111 The Golden Arm	.25	.11	.03
☐ 112 Little League All-Star	.15	.07	.02
☐ 113 All-State Pitcher	.15	.07	.02
☐ 114 Nolan Ryan Field	.15	.07	.02
☐ 115 Nolan at Age 20	.15	.07	.02
☐ 116 Nolan Ryan Jacksonville Suns	.15	.07	.02
☐ 117 Surrounded By Friends	.15	.07	.02
☐ 118 Nolan the Cowboy	.20	.09	.03
☐ 119 The Simple Life	.15	.07	.02
☐ 120 Nolan Loves Animals	.15	.07	.02
☐ 121 Growing Up in New York	.15	.07	.02
☐ 122 New York Strikeout Record	.20	.09	.03
☐ 123 Traded	.15	.07	.02
☐ 124 Hall of Fame Victims	.20	.09	.03
☐ 125 Number 500	.15	.07	.02
☐ 126 California Victory	.15	.07	.02
☐ 127 20 Win Season	.15	.07	.02
☐ 128 Throwing Heat	.15	.07	.02
☐ 129 Strikeout Record	.20	.09	.03
☐ 130 Number One	.20	.09	.03
☐ 131 1,000th Strikeout	.15	.07	.02
☐ 132 Number Two	.20	.09	.03
☐ 133 2,000th Strikeout	.15	.07	.02
☐ 134 Number Three	.20	.09	.03
☐ 135 Pure Speed	.15	.07	.02
☐ 136 Independence Day Fireworks	.15	.07	.02
☐ 137 Fast Ball Pitcher	.15	.07	.02
☐ 138 Number Four	.20	.09	.03
☐ 139 Free Agent	.15	.07	.02
☐ 140 Houston Bound	.15	.07	.02
☐ 141 Big Dollars	.15	.07	.02
☐ 142 Strong Houston Staff	.20	.09	.03
☐ 143 Number Five	.20	.09	.03
☐ 144 Astro MVP	.15	.07	.02
☐ 145 Western Division Game	.15	.07	.02
☐ 146 National League All-Star	.15	.07	.02
☐ 147 Major League Record	.15	.07	.02

☐ 148 Nolan Breaks Johnson's Record	.20	.09	.03
☐ 149 Reese and Nolan	.25	.11	.03
☐ 150 100th National League Win	.15	.07	.02
☐ 151 4,000th Strikeout	.15	.07	.02
☐ 152 League Leader	.15	.07	.02
☐ 153 250th Career Win	.15	.07	.02
☐ 154 The Seldom of Swat	.15	.07	.02
☐ 155 4,500th Strikeout	.15	.07	.02
☐ 156 Like Father Like Son	.20	.09	.03
☐ 157 Spoiled in the Ninth	.15	.07	.02
☐ 158 Leaving Houston in Style	.15	.07	.02
☐ 159 Houston Star	.15	.07	.02
☐ 160 Ryan Test Free Agency	.15	.07	.02
☐ 161 Awesome Heat	.15	.07	.02
☐ 162 Brotherly Love	.15	.07	.02
☐ 163 Astros Return of The Prodigious Son	.15	.07	.02
☐ 164 Texas Size Decision	.15	.07	.02
☐ 165 Texas Legend	.15	.07	.02
☐ 166 Drawing a Crowd	.15	.07	.02
☐ 167 Great Start	.15	.07	.02
☐ 168 5,000th Strikeout	.15	.07	.02
☐ 169 Texas All-Star	.15	.07	.02
☐ 170 Number Six	.20	.09	.03
☐ 171 300th Win	.20	.09	.03
☐ 172 1990 League Leader	.15	.07	.02
☐ 173 Man of the Year	.25	.11	.03
☐ 174 Spring Training 1991	.15	.07	.02
☐ 175 Fast Ball Grip	.15	.07	.02
☐ 176 Strong Arm	.15	.07	.02
☐ 177 Stanley's Delight	.15	.07	.02
☐ 178 After Nolan's 7th No-Hitter	.20	.09	.03
☐ 179 Stretching Before the Game	.15	.07	.02
☐ 180 The Rangers Sign Nolan For 1992 and 1993	.15	.07	.02
☐ 181 Heading to the Bullpen to Warmup	.15	.07	.02
☐ 182 Nolan Ryan Banker	.15	.07	.02
☐ 183 Time with Fans	.15	.07	.02
☐ 184 Solid 1991 Season	.15	.07	.02
☐ 185 Ranger Team Leader	.15	.07	.02
☐ 186 Nolan Sets More Records	.15	.07	.02
☐ 187 Number Seven	.20	.09	.03
☐ 188 Nolan Passes Niekro	.20	.09	.03
☐ 189 Ryan Trails Sutton	.20	.09	.03
☐ 190 Ranger Strikeout Mark	.15	.07	.02
☐ 191 Consecutive K's	.15	.07	.02
☐ 192 5,500th Strikeout	.15	.07	.02
☐ 193 Twenty-Five First Timers	.15	.07	.02
☐ 194 No-Hitters Ended in the Ninth	.15	.07	.02
☐ 195 Constant Work-Outs	.15	.07	.02
☐ 196 Nolan In Motion	.15	.07	.02
☐ 197 Nolan Pitching in Fenway Park	.15	.07	.02
☐ 198 Goose and Nolan	.20	.09	.03
☐ 199 Talking Over Strategy	.15	.07	.02
☐ 200 Don't Mess With Texas	.15	.07	.02
☐ 201 314-278 Thru 1991	.15	.07	.02
☐ 202 All-Time Leader	.15	.07	.02
☐ 203 High Praise	.15	.07	.02
☐ 204 Manager's Delight	.15	.07	.02
☐ 205 733 Major League Starts	.15	.07	.02
☐ 206 Ryan the Quarterback	.20	.09	.03
☐ 207 Hard Work Pays Off	.15	.07	.02
☐ 208 Passing Along Wisdom	.15	.07	.02
☐ 209 Still Dominant	.15	.07	.02
☐ 210 Nolan's Fast Ball Is Just a Blur	.15	.07	.02
☐ 211 Nolan Ryan Seven No-Hitters	.20	.09	.03
☐ 212 Training for Perfection	.15	.07	.02
☐ 213 Nolans' Edge--Speed	.15	.07	.02
☐ 214 This One was for Them	.15	.07	.02
☐ 215 Another Day's Work	.15	.07	.02
☐ 216 Pick Off at Third	.15	.07	.02
☐ 217 Ready to Pitch	.15	.07	.02
☐ 218 Spring Training 1992	.15	.07	.02
☐ 219 Nolan Receives The Victor Award	.20	.09	.03
☐ 220 1992: Nolan's 26th Season	.20	.09	.03

1992 Pacific Nolan Ryan Gold

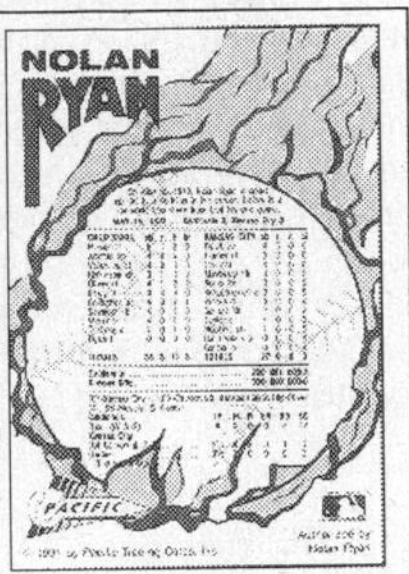

These eight standard size (2 1/2" by 3 1/2") cards were one of two insert subsets randomly packed in 1992 Pacific Nolan Ryan Texas Express II 12-card and 24-card foil packs. Supposedly 10,000 of each card were produced. The cards feature high gloss color action photos of Ryan pitching his seven no-hitters. The pictures are bordered in gold foil and either red/orange (1-4) or purple/red border (5-8) stripes. Inside a flaming baseball design, the backs of cards 1-7 display statistics for that no-hitter while card number 8 summarizes all seven no-hitters. The cards are unnumbered and checklisted below in chronological order of the events.

	MT	EX-MT	VG
COMPLETE SET (8)	175.00	80.00	22.00
COMMON PLAYER (1-8)	25.00	11.50	3.10
☐ 1 Nolan Ryan Number One	25.00	11.50	3.10
☐ 2 Nolan Ryan Number Two	25.00	11.50	3.10
☐ 3 Nolan Ryan Number Three	25.00	11.50	3.10
☐ 4 Nolan Ryan Number Four	25.00	11.50	3.10
☐ 5 Nolan Ryan Number Five	25.00	11.50	3.10
☐ 6 Nolan Ryan Number Six	25.00	11.50	3.10
☐ 7 Nolan Ryan Number Seven	25.00	11.50	3.10
☐ 8 Nolan Ryan Seven No-Hitters	25.00	11.50	3.10

1992 Pacific Nolan Ryan Limited

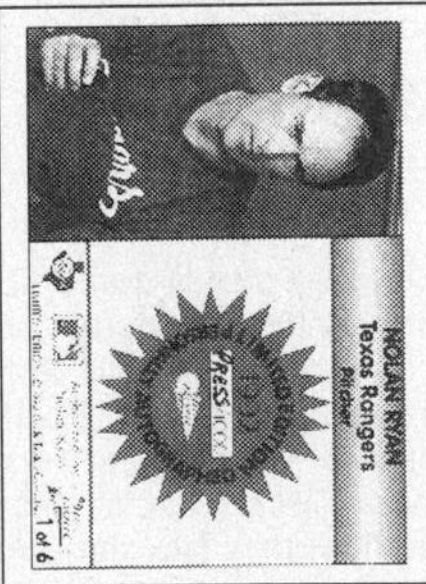

These six standard size (2 1/2" by 3 1/2") cards were one of two insert subsets randomly packed in 1992 Pacific Nolan Ryan Texas Express II 12-card and 24-card foil packs. Only 3,000 of each card were produced and, as an added bonus, 1,000 of card number 1 were autographed by Ryan. A similar-looking pair of two-card strips was inserted (bound)

into all issues of the July 1992 Volume 2, Issue 2 of Trading Cards magazine. However these "magazine cards" lack the words "Limited Edition" on the copyright line on their backs. The six career highlight cards feature high gloss color action photos on their fronts edged by a graded blue stripe on the left side and framed by a white outer border. The Texas Rangers and Pacific logos overlap the picture. The horizontal backs feature a second action color photo. Nolan's name appears in a red, white, and blue bar above a red box containing either career highlights (2, 3, 6), statistics (4) or a poem (5). The cards are numbered on the back.

	MT	EX-MT	VG
COMPLETE SET (6)	175.00	80.00	22.00
COMMON PLAYER (1-6)	35.00	16.00	4.40
☐ 1 Nolan Ryan (Pitching, side view, limited edition on back)	35.00	16.00	4.40
☐ 2 Nolan Ryan (Pitching, front view, gray uniform, limited edition on back)	35.00	16.00	4.40
☐ 3 Nolan Ryan The Texas Express (Limited edition on back)	35.00	16.00	4.40
☐ 4 Nolan Ryan The Seventh No-Hitter (Limited edition on back)	35.00	16.00	4.40
☐ 5 Nolan Ryan A Texas Legacy (Limited edition on back)	35.00	16.00	4.40
☐ 6 Nolan Ryan A Quarter of a Century (Limited edition on back)	35.00	16.00	4.40

1992 Pacific Nolan Ryan Magazine

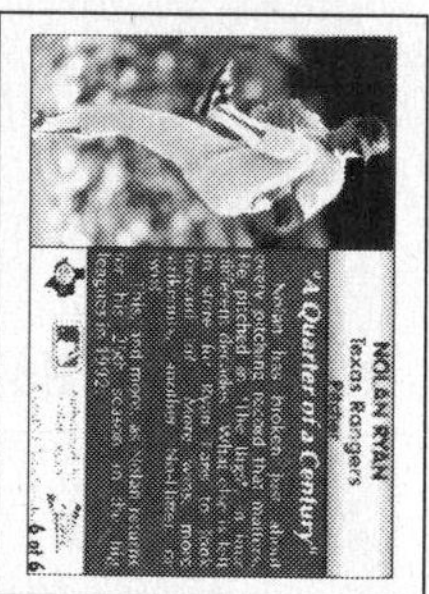

These six standard size (2 1/2" by 3 1/2") cards were inserted (bound) into the July 1992 Volume 2, Issue 2 of Trading Cards magazine as a pair of two-card strips. These are very similar to the hard-to-find inserts that Pacific inserted into the Ryan Texas Express second series foil packs. These "magazine cards" are only differentiable by the fact that they lack the words "Limited Edition" on the copyright line on their backs. The cards are numbered on the back.

	MT	EX-MT	VG
COMPLETE SET (6)	7.50	3.40	.95
COMMON PLAYER (1-6)	1.50	.65	.19
☐ 1 Nolan Ryan (Pitching, side view, does not say Limited edition on back)	1.50	.65	.19
☐ 2 Nolan Ryan (Pitching, front view, gray uniform, does not say Limited edition on back)	1.50	.65	.19
☐ 3 Nolan Ryan The Texas Express (Does not say Limited edition on back)	1.50	.65	.19
☐ 4 Nolan Ryan The Seventh No-Hitter (Does not say Limited edition on back)	1.50	.65	.19
☐ 5 Nolan Ryan A Texas Legacy (Does not say Limited edition on back)	1.50	.65	.19
☐ 6 Nolan Ryan A Quarter of a Century (Does not say Limited edition on back)	1.50	.65	.19

1992 Pacific Tom Seaver

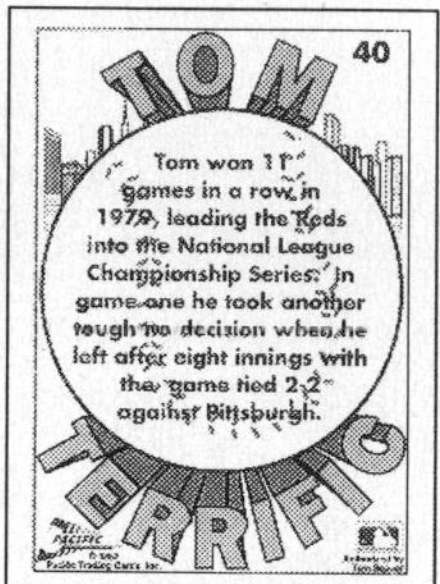

This 110-card set measures the standard size (2 1/2" by 3 1/2") and traces the career of Tom Seaver. The set was sold in 12-card foil packs or as a factory set for 12.95 through a mail-in offer. The fronts feature glossy color player photos with silver, purple, or red borders. Also white border stripes appear on the left and right sides of the pictures. At the lower left corner the nickname "Tom Terrific" in yellow lettering wraps around a white baseball icon. The back design is based on a larger version of this baseball icon, with a second color photo, career summary, or highlights inside the ball. Behind the ball appears a skyline with tall buildings. The cards are numbered on the back.

	MT	EX-MT	VG
COMPLETE SET (110)	9.00	4.00	1.15
COMMON PLAYER (1-110)	.15	.07	.02
☐ 1 Stand-out High School Basketball Player	.25	.11	.03
☐ 2 Pro Ball Player	.15	.07	.02
☐ 3 Destined to be a Met	.15	.07	.02
☐ 4 Brave or Met	.15	.07	.02
☐ 5 Mets Luck of the Draw	.15	.07	.02
☐ 6 Sent to Jacksonville	.15	.07	.02
☐ 7 First Major League Win	.15	.07	.02
☐ 8 1967 Rookie of the Year	.20	.09	.03
☐ 9 Humble Beginnings	.15	.07	.02
☐ 10 Predicting the Future	.15	.07	.02
☐ 11 Rookie All-Star	.15	.07	.02
☐ 12 16 Wins in 1968	.15	.07	.02
☐ 13 1968 National League All-Star	.15	.07	.02
☐ 14 The Amazing Mets	.15	.07	.02
☐ 15 1969 Cy Young Winner	.20	.09	.03
☐ 16 Pitcher of the Year	.20	.09	.03
☐ 17 Strikeout Leader	.15	.07	.02
☐ 18 Seaver Ties Major League Record	.15	.07	.02
☐ 19 Mr. Consistency	.15	.07	.02

	No.	Card			
□	20	Finishing in Style	.15	.07	.02
□	21	Twenty-Game Winner	.15	.07	.02
□	22	Second Cy Young Award	.20	.09	.03
□	23	Batting Star	.15	.07	.02
□	24	At Bat in the World Series	.15	.07	.02
□	25	Championship Series Record	.15	.07	.02
□	26	Injury Plagued Season	.15	.07	.02
□	27	Comeback	.15	.07	.02
□	28	Super September	.15	.07	.02
□	29	Sporting News All-Star	.15	.07	.02
□	30	Strikeout Record	.15	.07	.02
□	31	USC Alumni Star	.15	.07	.02
□	32	Winning Smile	.15	.07	.02
□	33	One-Hitter	.15	.07	.02
□	34	Traded to the Reds	.15	.07	.02
□	35	New York Mets Pitcher	.15	.07	.02
□	36	Winning with the Reds	.15	.07	.02
□	37	Tom's No-Hitter	.15	.07	.02
□	38	National League Leader	.15	.07	.02
□	39	Smooth Swing	.15	.07	.02
□	40	No Decision in the Championship Series	.15	.07	.02
□	41	Injury Shortened Season	.15	.07	.02
□	42	Bouncing Back	.15	.07	.02
□	43	Eighth All-Star Appearance	.15	.07	.02
□	44	Spring Training 1982	.15	.07	.02
□	45	Back to New York	.15	.07	.02
□	46	Cincinnati Reds Pitcher	.15	.07	.02
□	47	Back in the Big Apple	.15	.07	.02
□	48	Opening Day Star	.15	.07	.02
□	49	Not Much Run Support	.15	.07	.02
□	50	A Pair of Shutouts	.15	.07	.02
□	51	4,000 Inning Mark	.15	.07	.02
□	52	One Season in New York	.15	.07	.02
□	53	Chicago Bound	.15	.07	.02
□	54	Chicago White Sox Pitcher	.20	.09	.03
□	55	Win 300	.15	.07	.02
□	56	16 Wins in 1985	.15	.07	.02
□	57	Blast From the Past	.15	.07	.02
□	58	Moving Up in the Record Book	.15	.07	.02
□	59	Cy Young Winners	.20	.09	.03
□	60	Two Legends of the Game	.25	.11	.03
□	61	Singing Praise	.15	.07	.02
□	62	300th Win Tribute	.15	.07	.02
□	63	The Seaver Family	.20	.09	.03
□	64	20th Major League Season	.15	.07	.02
□	65	Traded to the Red Sox	.20	.09	.03
□	66	Chicago White Sox Career Record	.15	.07	.02
□	67	Red Sox Man	.20	.09	.03
□	68	Boston Red Sox Pitcher	.20	.09	.03
□	69	One Last Try	.15	.07	.02
□	70	Major League Records	.15	.07	.02
□	71	Lowest National League Career ERA	.15	.07	.02
□	72	Pitching in Comiskey Park	.15	.07	.02
□	73	273 National League Wins	.15	.07	.02
□	74	300 Win Honors	.15	.07	.02
□	75	311 Major League Wins	.15	.07	.02
□	76	41 Retired	.15	.07	.02
□	77	Championship Series 2.84 ERA	.15	.07	.02
□	78	June 1976 Age 32	.15	.07	.02
□	79	8-Time National League All-Star Pitcher	.15	.07	.02
□	80	Broadcasting Career	.15	.07	.02
□	81	300th Game Win Celebration	.15	.07	.02
□	82	Tom and Nolan	.35	.16	.04
□	83	4th Best ERA All-Time	.15	.07	.02
□	84	15th All-Time in Victories	.15	.07	.02
□	85	300 Win Club	.15	.07	.02
□	86	Hall of Fame	.15	.07	.02
□	87	Pitching in Wrigley Field	.15	.07	.02
□	88	Power Pitching	.15	.07	.02
□	89	Spring Training 1980	.15	.07	.02
□	90	Pitching in Riverfront Stadium 1980	.15	.07	.02
□	91	Tom Terrific	.20	.09	.03
□	92	Super Seaver	.20	.09	.03
□	93	Top 10 All-Time	.15	.07	.02
□	94	16 Opening Day Starting Asignments	.15	.07	.02
□	95	3,272 Major League Strikeouts	.15	.07	.02
□	96	Six Opening Day Wins	.15	.07	.02
□	97	239 Innings Pitched in 1985	.15	.07	.02
□	98	A Day Off	.15	.07	.02
□	99	Concentration (You Can't Let Up)	.15	.07	.02
□	100	Velocity, Movement, and Location	.15	.07	.02
□	101	Strikeout King	.15	.07	.02
□	102	The Most Important Pitch	.15	.07	.02
□	103	Cincinnati Reds Number 41	.15	.07	.02
□	104	George Thomas Seaver	.20	.09	.03
□	105	Dazzling Dean of the Reds' Staff	.15	.07	.02
□	106	Tom Receives the Judge Emil Fuchs Award	.20	.09	.03
□	107	Boston Mound Ace	.15	.07	.02
□	108	Fly Ball to Center	.15	.07	.02
□	109	August 4, 1985 Yankee Stadium	.15	.07	.02
□	110	Breaking Walter Johnson's Strikeout Record	.25	.11	.03

1992 Pacific Tom Seaver Inserts

These six standard-size (2 1/2" by 3 1/2") cards were one of two insert subsets (depicting career highlights of Tom Seaver) randomly packed in 1992 Pacific Tom Seaver 12-card foil packs. The two insert sets are numbered the same, the primary physical difference being a white border or a gold foil border on the card front. Only 3,000 of each non-gold card were produced and, as an added bonus, 1,000 of card number 1 were autographed by Seaver. According to Pacific, 10,000 of each gold card were produced. The six career highlight cards feature high gloss color action player photos on their fronts edged by a color stripe on the left and framed by a white (or gold) outer border. The "Tom Terrific" logo overlays the stripe at the lower left corner. The horizontal backs display a second action color photo. Seaver's name and the card subtitle appear in a graded color bar above a color-coded panel containing career highlights. The backs of the gold foil insert cards are identical to those of the regular inserts and are distinguished only by their non-glossy finish. The cards are numbered on the back. The values for the gold and white versions are the same at this time.

	MT	EX-MT	VG
COMPLETE SET (6)	125.00	57.50	15.50
COMMON PLAYER (1-6)	25.00	11.50	3.10
☐ 1 Tom Seaver Rookie Phenomenon	25.00	11.50	3.10
☐ 2 Tom Seaver Miracle Mets	25.00	11.50	3.10
☐ 3 Tom Seaver Strikeout Record	25.00	11.50	3.10
☐ 4 Tom Seaver No-Hitter	25.00	11.50	3.10
☐ 5 Tom Seaver 300th Win	25.00	11.50	3.10
☐ 6 Tom Seaver Hall of Fame	25.00	11.50	3.10

1958 Packard Bell

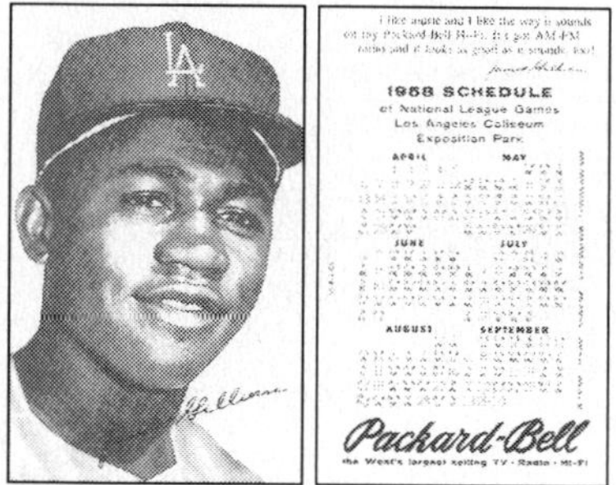

This seven-card set included members of the Los Angeles Dodgers and San Francisco Giants and was issued in both teams' first year on the West Coast. This black and white, unnumbered set features cards measuring approximately 3 3/8" by 5 3/8". The backs are advertisements for Packard Bell (a television and radio manufacturer) along with a schedule for either the Giants or Dodgers. There were four Giants printed and three Dodgers. The catalog designation for this set is H805-5. Since the cards are unnumbered, they are listed below alphabetically.

	NRMT	VG-E	GOOD
COMPLETE SET (7)	450.00	200.00	57.50
COMMON CARD (1-7)	40.00	18.00	5.00
☐ 1 Walt Alston MG Los Angeles Dodgers	75.00	34.00	9.50
☐ 2 Johnny Antonelli San Francisco Giants	40.00	18.00	5.00
☐ 3 Jim Gilliam Los Angeles Dodgers	50.00	23.00	6.25
☐ 4 Gil Hodges Los Angeles Dodgers	100.00	45.00	12.50
☐ 5 Willie Mays San Francisco Giants	225.00	100.00	28.00
☐ 6 Bill Rigney MG San Francisco Giants	40.00	18.00	5.00
☐ 7 Hank Sauer San Francisco Giants	40.00	18.00	5.00

1977 Padres Schedule Cards

This 40-card set was issued in 1977 and featured members of the 1977 San Diego Padres. The cards measure approximately 2 1/4" by 3 3/8" and had brown and white photos on the front of the cards with a schedule of the 1977 Padres special events on the back. A thin line borders the

front photo with the team name and player name appearing below in the same sepia tone. The set is checklisted alphabetically in the list below. The complete set price below refers to the set with all variations listed. The blank-backed cards may have been issued in a different year than the other schedule-back cards.

	NRMT-MT	EXC	G-VG
COMPLETE SET (89)	90.00	40.00	11.50
COMMON PLAYER (1-65)	.40	.18	.05
☐ 1A Bill Almon (Kneeling)	.75	.35	.09
☐ 1B Bill Almon (Shown chest up, bat on shoulder)	.75	.35	.09
☐ 2 Matty Alou	1.25	.55	.16
☐ 3 Joe Amalfitano CO	.40	.18	.05
☐ 4A Steve Arlin (Follow through)	.60	.25	.08
☐ 4B Steve Arlin (Glove to chest)	.60	.25	.08
☐ 5 Bob Barton	.75	.35	.09
☐ 6 Buzzie Bavasi GM	.50	.23	.06
☐ 7 Glenn Beckert	1.25	.55	.16
☐ 8 Vic Bernal	.50	.23	.06
☐ 9 Ollie Brown	1.00	.45	.13
☐ 10A Dave Campbell (Bat on shoulder)	1.00	.45	.13
☐ 10B Dave Campbell (Kneeling, capless)	1.00	.45	.13
☐ 11 Mike Champion	.40	.18	.05
☐ 12 Mike Champion and Bill Almon	.50	.23	.06
☐ 13A Nate Colbert (Shown waist up)	1.25	.55	.16
☐ 13B Nate Colbert (Shown full figure; blank back)	2.00	.90	.25
☐ 14 Nate Colbert and friend (Kneeling next to child with bat)	1.25	.55	.16
☐ 15 Jerry Coleman ANN	1.00	.45	.13
☐ 16 Roger Craig CO	.50	.23	.06
☐ 17 John D'Acquisto	.40	.18	.05
☐ 18 Bob Davis	.40	.18	.05
☐ 19 Willie Davis	1.25	.55	.16
☐ 20 Jim Eakle (Tuba Man)	.75	.35	.09
☐ 21A Rollie Fingers (Shown waist up, both hands in glove, in front of body)	3.00	1.35	.40
☐ 21B Rollie Fingers (Head shot)	3.00	1.35	.40
☐ 22A Dave Freisleben (Washington jersey and cap, blank back)	5.00	2.30	.60
☐ 22B Dave Freisleben (Kneeling)	.50	.23	.06
☐ 23A Clarence Gaston (Bat on shoulder, "adres" on jersey)	1.25	.55	.16
☐ 23B Clarence Gaston (Bat on shoulder, "dre" on jersey)	1.25	.55	.16
☐ 24 Tom Griffin	.40	.18	.05
☐ 25 Johnny Grubb	.50	.23	.06
☐ 26A George Hendrick (Shown chest up, wearing warm-up jacket)	1.00	.45	.13
☐ 26B George Hendrick	1.00	.45	.13

Card			
(Shown waist up, wearing white jersey)			
☐ 27 Enzo Hernandez	.40	.18	.05
☐ 28 Enzo Hernandez and Nate Colbert	.75	.35	.09
☐ 29A Mike Ivie (Batting pose, shown from thighs up)	.75	.35	.09
☐ 29B Mike Ivie (Batting pose, shown from shoulders up, blank back)	.75	.35	.09
☐ 29C Mike Ivie (Bat on shoulder)	.75	.35	.09
☐ 30A Randy Jones (Following Through)	1.00	.45	.13
☐ 30B Randy Jones (Holding Cy Young Award)	1.50	.65	.19
☐ 31 Randy Jones and Bowie Kuhn (Randy holding trophy)	2.00	.90	.25
☐ 32A Fred Kendall (Batting pose)	.75	.35	.09
☐ 32B Fred Kendall (Ball in right hand)	.75	.35	.09
☐ 33 Mike Kilkenny (Blank back)	.75	.35	.09
☐ 34A Clay Kirby (Follow through)	.75	.35	.09
☐ 34B Clay Kirby (Glove near to chest)	.75	.35	.09
☐ 35 Ray Kroc OWN (Blank back)	1.50	.65	.19
☐ 36 Dave Marshall	.75	.35	.09
☐ 37A Willie McCovey With mustache, bat on shoulder)	4.00	1.80	.50
☐ 37B Willie McCovey Without mustache, blank back)	4.00	1.80	.50
☐ 38A John McNamara MG (Looking to his left, blank back)	.75	.35	.09
☐ 38B John McNamara MG (Looking to his right)	.75	.35	.09
☐ 38C John McNamara MG (Looking straight ahead, smiling)	.75	.35	.09
☐ 39 Luis Melendez	.40	.18	.05
☐ 40 Butch Metzger	.40	.18	.05
☐ 41 Bob Miller	.50	.23	.06
☐ 42A Fred Norman (Short hair, kneeling)	.75	.35	.09
☐ 42B Fred Norman (Long hair, arms over head)	.75	.35	.09
☐ 43 Bob Owchinko	.40	.18	.05
☐ 44 Doug Rader	.75	.35	.09
☐ 45 Merv Rettenmund	.50	.23	.06
☐ 46A Gene Richards (Shown chest up, stands in background)	.75	.35	.09
☐ 46B Gene Richards (Shown from thighs up)	.75	.35	.09
☐ 47 Dave Roberts	.40	.18	.05
☐ 48 Rick Sawyer	.40	.18	.05
☐ 49 Bob Shirley	.40	.18	.05
☐ 50 Bob Skinner CO	.50	.23	.06
☐ 51 Ballard Smith GM	1.00	.45	.13
☐ 52 Ed Spiezio	.75	.35	.09
☐ 53 Dan Spillner	.40	.18	.05
☐ 54 Brent Strom	.40	.18	.05
☐ 55 Gary Sutherland	.40	.18	.05
☐ 56 Gene Tenace	1.00	.45	.13
☐ 57A Derrell Thomas (Head shot, wearing glasses)	1.00	.45	.13
☐ 57B Derrell Thomas (Kneeling, not wearing glasses)	1.00	.45	.13
☐ 58A Bobby Tolan (Batting pose)	1.00	.45	.13
☐ 58B Bobby Tolan (Kneeling, holding cleats in hand)	1.00	.45	.13
☐ 59 Dave Tomlin	.40	.18	.05
☐ 60A Jerry Turner (Batting pose, gloveless, wall in background)	.75	.35	.09
☐ 60B Jerry Turner (Batting pose, both hands gloved)	.75	.35	.09
☐ 61 Bobby Valentine	1.25	.55	.16
☐ 62 Dave Wehrmeister	.40	.18	.05
☐ 63 Whitey Wietelmann CO	.40	.18	.05
☐ 64 Don Williams CO	.40	.18	.05
☐ 65A Dave Winfield (Batting pose, waist up, field in background)	6.00	2.70	.75
☐ 65B Dave Winfield (Batting, stands in background, black bat telescoped)	6.00	2.70	.75
☐ 65C Dave Winfield (Two bats on shoulder)	6.00	2.70	.75
☐ 65D Dave Winfield (Full figure, leaning on bat, blank back)	6.00	2.70	.75

1978 Padres Family Fun

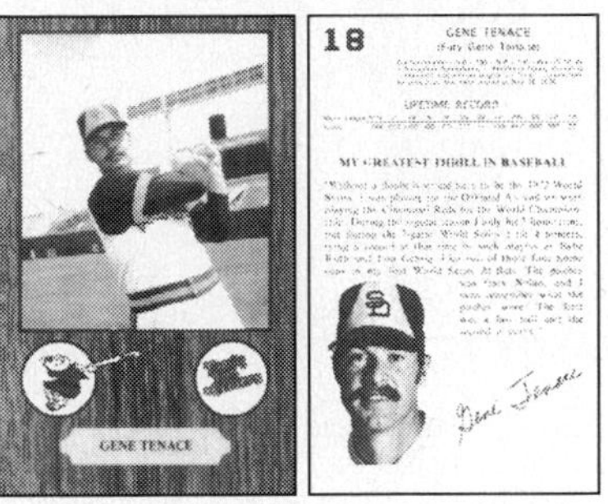

This 39-card set features members of the 1978 San Diego Padres. These large cards measure approximately 3 1/2" by 5 1/2" and are framed in a style similar to the 1962 Topps set with wood-grain borders. The cards have full color photos on the front of the card along with the Padres logo and Family Fun Centers underneath the photo in circles and the name of the player on the bottom of the card. The backs of the card asked each person what their greatest thrill in Baseball was. This set is especially noteworthy for having one of the earliest Ozzie Smith cards printed. The set is checklisted alphabetically in the list below.

	NRMT-MT	EXC	G-VG
COMPLETE SET (39)	30.00	13.50	3.80
COMMON PLAYER (1-39)	.40	.18	.05
☐ 1 Bill Almon	.50	.23	.06
☐ 2 Tucker Ashford	.40	.18	.05
☐ 3 Chuck Baker	.40	.18	.05
☐ 4 Dave Campbell ANN	.40	.18	.05
☐ 5 Mike Champion	.40	.18	.05
☐ 6 Jerry Coleman ANN	.50	.23	.06
☐ 7 Roger Craig MG	.60	.25	.08
☐ 8 John D'Acquisto	.40	.18	.05
☐ 9 Bob Davis	.40	.18	.05
☐ 10 Chuck Estrada CO	.50	.23	.06
☐ 11 Rollie Fingers	2.50	1.15	.30
☐ 12 Dave Freisleben	.40	.18	.05
☐ 13 Oscar Gamble	.60	.25	.08
☐ 14 Fernando Gonzalez	.40	.18	.05
☐ 15 Billy Herman CO	.75	.35	.09
☐ 16 Randy Jones	.60	.25	.08
☐ 17 Ray Kroc (Owner)	1.00	.45	.13
☐ 18 Mark Lee	.40	.18	.05
☐ 19 Mickey Lolich	.75	.35	.09
☐ 20 Bob Owchinko	.40	.18	.05
☐ 21 Broderick Perkins	.40	.18	.05
☐ 22 Gaylord Perry	2.50	1.15	.30
☐ 23 Eric Rasmussen	.40	.18	.05
☐ 24 Don Reynolds	.40	.18	.05
☐ 25 Gene Richards	.40	.18	.05
☐ 26 Dave Roberts	.40	.18	.05
☐ 27 Phil Roof CO	.40	.18	.05
☐ 28 Bob Shirley	.40	.18	.05
☐ 29 Ozzie Smith	20.00	9.00	2.50
☐ 30 Dan Spillner	.40	.18	.05
☐ 31 Rick Sweet	.40	.18	.05
☐ 32 Gene Tenace	.50	.23	.06
☐ 33 Derrel Thomas	.40	.18	.05

☐ 34 Jerry Turner	.40	.18	.05
☐ 35 Dave Wehrmeister	.40	.18	.05
☐ 36 Whitey Wietelmann CO	.40	.18	.05
☐ 37 Don Williams CO	.40	.18	.05
☐ 38 Dave Winfield	5.00	2.30	.60
☐ 39 1978 All-Star Game	.40	.18	.05

1987 Padres Bohemian Hearth Bread

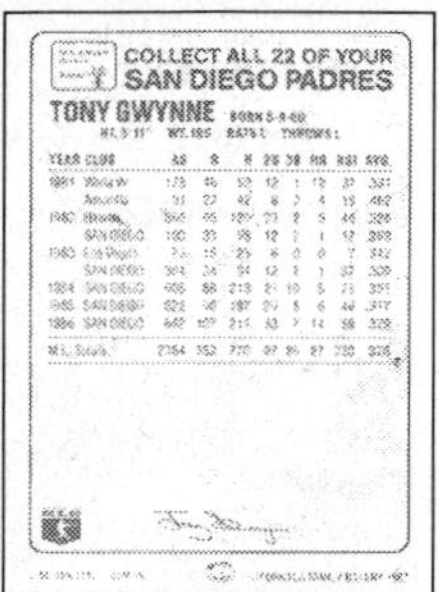

The Bohemian Hearth Bread Company issued this 22-card set of San Diego Padres. The cards measure 2 1/2" by 3 1/2" and feature a distinctive yellow border on the front of the cards. Card backs provide career year-by-year statistics and are numbered.

	MT	EX-MT	VG
COMPLETE SET (22)	50.00	23.00	6.25
COMMON PLAYER	.75	.35	.09
☐ 1 Garry Templeton	1.00	.45	.13
☐ 4 Joey Cora	.75	.35	.09
☐ 5 Randy Ready	1.00	.45	.13
☐ 6 Steve Garvey	6.00	2.70	.75
☐ 7 Kevin Mitchell	7.50	3.40	.95
☐ 8 John Kruk	5.00	2.30	.60
☐ 9 Benito Santiago	6.00	2.70	.75
☐ 10 Larry Bowa MG	1.00	.45	.13
☐ 11 Tim Flannery	.75	.35	.09
☐ 14 Carmelo Martinez	.75	.35	.09
☐ 16 Marvell Wynne	.75	.35	.09
☐ 19 Tony Gwynn	18.00	8.00	2.30
☐ 21 James Steels	.75	.35	.09
☐ 22 Stan Jefferson	.75	.35	.09
☐ 30 Eric Show	.75	.35	.09
☐ 31 Ed Whitson	1.00	.45	.13
☐ 34 Storm Davis	1.00	.45	.13
☐ 37 Craig Lefferts	1.50	.65	.19
☐ 40 Andy Hawkins	.75	.35	.09
☐ 41 Lance McCullers	.75	.35	.09
☐ 43 Dave Dravecky	2.50	1.15	.30
☐ 54 Rich Gossage	2.50	1.15	.30

1988 Padres Coke

These cards were actually issued as two separate promotions. The first eight cards were issued as a perforated sheet (approximately 7 1/2" by 10 1/2") as a Coca Cola Junior Padres Club promotion. The other 12 cards were issued later on specific game days to members of the Junior Padres Club. All the cards are standard size, 2 1/2" by 3 1/2" and are unnumbered. Cards that were on the perforated panel are indicated by PAN in the checklist below. Since the cards are unnumbered, they are listed below by uniform number, which is featured prominently on the card fronts.

	MT	EX-MT	VG
COMPLETE SET (21)	40.00	18.00	5.00
COMMON PANEL PLAYER	.50	.23	.06
COMMON NON-PAN PLAYER	1.25	.55	.16
☐ 1 Garry Templeton PAN	.50	.23	.06
☐ 5 Randy Ready PAN	.50	.23	.06
☐ 7 Keith Moreland	1.25	.55	.16
☐ 8 John Kruk	4.00	1.80	.50
☐ 9 Benito Santiago	5.00	2.30	.60
☐ 10 Larry Bowa MG PAN	.60	.25	.08
☐ 11 Tim Flannery PAN	.50	.23	.06
☐ 14 Carmelo Martinez	1.25	.55	.16
☐ 15 Jack McKeon MG	1.50	.65	.19
☐ 19 Tony Gwynn	15.00	6.75	1.90
☐ 22 Stan Jefferson	1.25	.55	.16
☐ 27 Mark Parent	1.25	.55	.16
☐ 30 Eric Show	1.25	.55	.16
☐ 31 Eddie Whitson	1.50	.65	.19
☐ 35 Chris Brown PAN	.50	.23	.06
☐ 41 Lance McCullers	1.25	.55	.16
☐ 45 Jimmy Jones PAN	.60	.25	.08
☐ 48 Mark Davis PAN	1.50	.65	.19
☐ 51 Greg Booker	1.25	.55	.16
☐ 55 Mark Grant PAN	.50	.23	.06
☐ NNO Padres Logo PAN (Program explanation on reverse)	.50	.23	.06

1989 Padres Coke

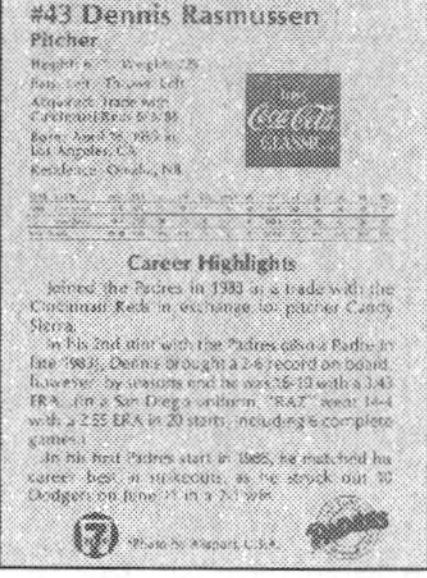

These cards were actually issued as two separate promotions. The first nine cards were issued as a perforated sheet (approximately 7 1/2" by 10 1/2") as a Coca Cola Junior Padres Club promotion. The other 12 cards were issued later on specific game days to members of the Junior Padres Club. All the cards are standard size, 2 1/2" by 3 1/2" and are unnumbered. Cards that were on the perforated panel are indicated by PAN in the checklist below. Since the cards are unnumbered, they are listed below in alphabetical order by subject. Marvell Wynne was planned for the set but was not issued since he was traded before the set was released; Walt Terrell also is tougher to find due to his mid-season trade.

	MT	EX-MT	VG
COMPLETE SET (21)	40.00	18.00	5.00
COMMON PLAYER (1-21)	1.25	.55	.16
COMMON PLAYER PAN	.50	.23	.06
☐ 1 Roberto Alomar PAN	5.00	2.30	.60
☐ 2 Jack Clark	2.00	.90	.25
☐ 3 Mark Davis	2.00	.90	.25
☐ 4 Tim Flannery	1.25	.55	.16
☐ 5 Mark Grant	1.25	.55	.16
☐ 6 Tony Gwynn	12.00	5.50	1.50
☐ 7 Bruce Hurst	2.50	1.15	.30
☐ 8 Chris James	1.50	.65	.19
☐ 9 Carmelo Martinez PAN	.50	.23	.06
☐ 10 Jack McKeon MG PAN	.60	.25	.08
☐ 11 Mark Parent	1.25	.55	.16
☐ 12 Dennis Rasmussen PAN	.50	.23	.06
☐ 13 Randy Ready PAN	.50	.23	.06
☐ 14 Bip Roberts	2.50	1.15	.30
☐ 15 Luis Salazar	1.25	.55	.16
☐ 16 Benito Santiago	3.50	1.55	.45
☐ 17 Eric Show PAN	.60	.25	.08
☐ 18 Garry Templeton PAN	.60	.25	.08
☐ 19 Walt Terrell SP	6.50	2.90	.80
☐ 20 Ed Whitson PAN	.60	.25	.08
☐ NNO Padres Logo PAN	.50	.23	.06

1989 Padres Magazine

PADRES FLASHBACK
Garvey's Dramatic Homer Ties N.L. Playoff Series

These 2 1/2" by 3 1/2" cards came as an insert in issues of "Padres" magazine sold in San Diego. These cards were sponsored by San Diego Sports Collectibles, a major hobby dealer. The cards feature beautiful full-color photos on the front and interesting did-you-know facts on the back along with one line of career statistics. The cards of retired Padres feature an highlight of their career in San Diego. The suggested retail price of each of the six different Padres magazines was 1.50.

	MT	EX-MT	VG
COMPLETE SET (24)	12.50	5.75	1.55
COMMON PLAYER (1-24)	.30	.14	.04
☐ 1 Jack McKeon MG	.30	.14	.04
☐ 2 Sandy Alomar Jr.	1.00	.45	.13
☐ 3 Tony Gwynn	3.50	1.55	.45
☐ 4 Willie McCovey (McCovey hits 16th career grand slam)	1.00	.45	.13
☐ 5 John Kruk	.75	.35	.09
☐ 6 Jack Clark	.50	.23	.06
☐ 7 Eric Show	.30	.14	.04
☐ 8 Rollie Fingers (Fingers wins NL Saves title for second time)	1.00	.45	.13
☐ 9 The Alomars Sandy Alomar Sr. Sandy Alomar Jr. Roberto Alomar	1.25	.55	.16
☐ 10 Carmelo Martinez	.30	.14	.04
☐ 11 Benito Santiago	1.00	.45	.13
☐ 12 Nate Colbert (Colbert 5 HR's, 13 RBI's in Doubleheader)	.30	.14	.04
☐ 13 Mark Davis	.40	.18	.05
☐ 14 Roberto Alomar	3.00	1.35	.40
☐ 15 Tim Flannery	.30	.14	.04
☐ 16 Randy Jones (Jones wins Cy Young Award)	.40	.18	.05
☐ 17 Dennis Rasmussen	.30	.14	.04
☐ 18 Greg W. Harris	.50	.23	.06
☐ 19 Garry Templeton	.40	.18	.05
☐ 20 Steve Garvey (Garvey's HR ties NLCS)	.60	.25	.08
☐ 21 Bruce Hurst	.50	.23	.06
☐ 22 Ed Whitson	.40	.18	.05
☐ 23 Chris James	.40	.18	.05
☐ 24 Gaylord Perry (Perry Wins Cy Young Award in Both Leagues)	1.00	.45	.13

1990 Padres Coke

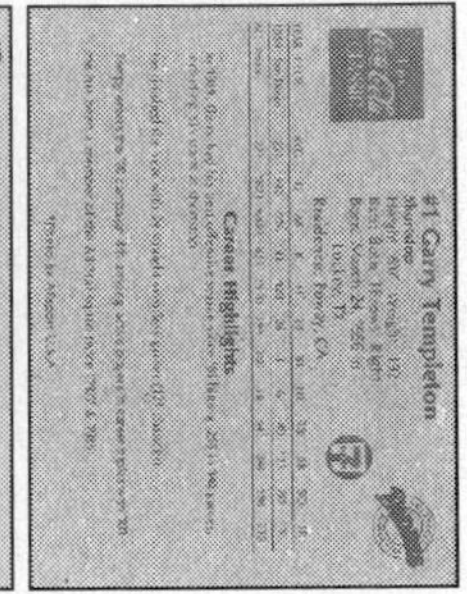

These standard-size cards (2 1/2" by 3 1/2") were issued in two forms: a 7 1/2" by 10 5/8" perforated sheet featuring eight player cards and the Padre logo card (marked by PAN below) as well as 12 individual player cards. The sheet was issued to Coca-Cola Junior Padres Club Members as a starter set, and club members who attended the first six Junior Padres Club games received two additional cards per game. The fronts have color action player photos, with two-toned brown borders on a beige card face. The team logo appears in the upper right corner, and the lower left corner of each picture is cut out to provide space for the player's number and position. In dark brown lettering, the horizontally oriented backs present biography, statistics, and career highlights. The cards are unnumbered and checklisted below in alphabetical order, with the team logo card listed at the end.

	MT	EX-MT	VG
COMPLETE SET (21)	30.00	13.50	3.80
COMMON PLAYER PAN	.40	.18	.05
COMMON PLAYER NON-PAN	1.00	.45	.13
☐ 1 Roberto Alomar	6.00	2.70	.75
☐ 2 Andy Benes PAN	.75	.35	.09
☐ 3 Joe Carter	4.00	1.80	.50
☐ 4 Jack Clark	1.50	.65	.19
☐ 5 Mark Grant PAN	.40	.18	.05
☐ 6 Tony Gwynn	7.50	3.40	.95
☐ 7 Greg W. Harris	1.25	.55	.16
☐ 8 Bruce Hurst	1.50	.65	.19
☐ 9 Craig Lefferts	1.50	.65	.19
☐ 10 Fred Lynn	1.50	.65	.19
☐ 11 Jack McKeon MG PAN	.50	.23	.06
☐ 12 Mike Pagliarulo	1.00	.45	.13
☐ 13 Mark Parent PAN	.40	.18	.05
☐ 14 Dennis Rasmussen PAN	.50	.23	.06
☐ 15 Bip Roberts PAN	.75	.35	.09
☐ 16 Benito Santiago	2.50	1.15	.30
☐ 17 Calvin Schiraldi	1.00	.45	.13
☐ 18 Eric Show PAN	.40	.18	.05
☐ 19 Garry Templeton	1.00	.45	.13
☐ 20 Ed Whitson PAN	.40	.18	.05
☐ NNO Padres Logo PAN	.40	.18	.05

1990 Padres Magazine/Unocal

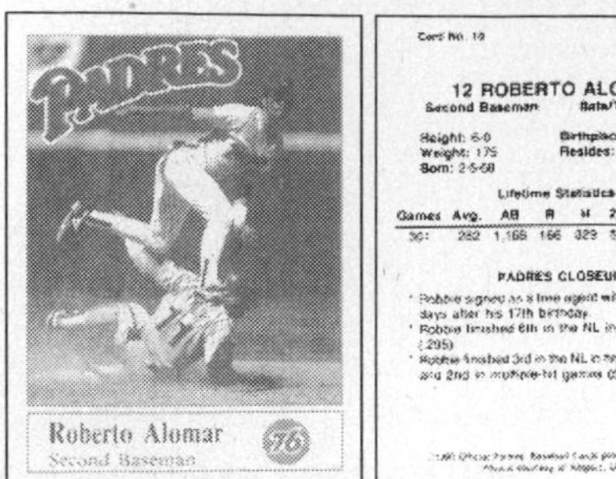

This 24-card set was sponsored by Unocal 76 and was available in the San Diego Padres' game programs for 17.50. The cards were divided into six series, and each series was issued on a 5" by 9" sheet of four cards with a sponsor's coupon. After perforation, the cards measure the standard size (2 1/2" by 3 1/2"). Some players appear in more than one series. The front features a color action player photo with white borders. The player's name is given in a tan stripe below the picture, with the Unocal 76 logo to the right of the name. The backs are printed in black on white and have biography, statistics, and career highlights. The cards are numbered on the back. Coupons from the magazine were to be turned into Unocal for 25 Jack McKeon, 26 Bip Roberts, and 27 Joe Carter.

	MT	EX-MT	VG
COMPLETE SET (27)	16.00	7.25	2.00
COMMON PLAYER (1-24)	.30	.14	.04
COMMON PLAYER (25-27)	.75	.35	.09

	MT	EX-MT	VG
☐ 1 Tony Gwynn	2.50	1.15	.30
☐ 2 Benito Santiago	1.00	.45	.13
☐ 3 Mike Pagliarulo	.40	.18	.05
☐ 4 Dennis Rasmussen	.30	.14	.04
☐ 5 Eric Show	.30	.14	.04
☐ 6 Darrin Jackson	.75	.35	.09
☐ 7 Mark Parent	.30	.14	.04
☐ 8 Padres Announcers Jerry Coleman Rick Monday	.40	.18	.05
☐ 9 Andy Benes	1.00	.45	.13
☐ 10 Roberto Alomar	2.50	1.15	.30
☐ 11 Craig Lefferts	.60	.25	.08
☐ 12 Ed Whitson	.30	.14	.04
☐ 13 Calvin Schiraldi	.30	.14	.04
☐ 14 Garry Templeton	.40	.18	.05
☐ 15 Tony Gwynn	2.50	1.15	.30
☐ 16 Padres Announcers Bob Chandler and Ted Leitner	.30	.14	.04
☐ 17 Fred Lynn	.50	.23	.06
☐ 18 Jack Clark	.50	.23	.06
☐ 19 Mike Dunne	.30	.14	.04
☐ 20 Mark Grant	.30	.14	.04
☐ 21 Benito Santiago	1.00	.45	.13
☐ 22 The Coaches Sandy Alomar Sr. Pat Dobson Amos Otis Greg Riddoch Denny Sommers	.40	.18	.05
☐ 23 Bruce Hurst	.50	.23	.06
☐ 24 Greg W. Harris	.40	.18	.05
☐ 25 Jack McKeon MG	.75	.35	.09
☐ 26 Bip Roberts	1.25	.55	.16
☐ 27 Joe Carter	3.00	1.35	.40

1991 Padres Magazine/Rally's

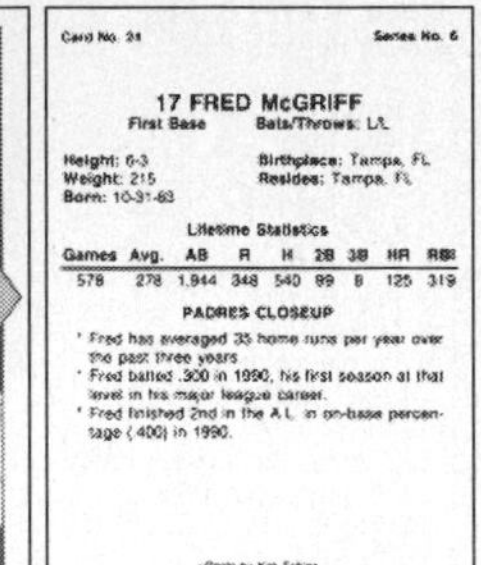

This 24-card set was sponsored by Rally's Hamburgers. The first 24 cards were divided into six series, and each series was issued on a 5" by 9" sheet of four cards with a sponsor's coupon. After perforation, the cards measure the standard size (2 1/2" by 3 1/2"). The front features a color pose shot (from the waist up) of the player, inside a tan baseball diamond framework. Outside the diamond the card background is dark blue, with white borders. The player's name is given in an orange banner at the bottom of the card. Team and sponsor logos in the upper corners round out the front. The backs are printed in black on white and have biography, statistics, and career highlights. The cards are numbered on the back. Some players appear in more than one series. Moreover, there are reportedly variations involving Schiraldi, Gardner, and Presley, who were released during the season. The last three cards were available as part of a promotion whereby fans could tear out a coupon from the Padres Magazine and bring the coupon to one of eight Rally's Hamburgers locations in San Diego County in order to redeem one card.

	MT	EX-MT	VG
COMPLETE SET (27)	12.00	5.50	1.50
COMMON PLAYER (1-24)	.30	.14	.04
COMMON PLAYER (25-27)	.75	.35	.09

	MT	EX-MT	VG
☐ 1 Greg Riddoch MG	.30	.14	.04
☐ 2 Dennis Rasmussen	.40	.18	.05
☐ 3 Thomas Howard	.50	.23	.06
☐ 4 Tom Lampkin	.30	.14	.04
☐ 5 Bruce Hurst	.50	.23	.06
☐ 6 Darrin Jackson	.50	.23	.06
☐ 7 Jerald Clark	.50	.23	.06
☐ 8 Shawn Abner	.30	.14	.04
☐ 9 Bip Roberts	.60	.25	.08
☐ 10 Marty Barrett	.30	.14	.04
☐ 11 Jim Vatcher	.30	.14	.04
☐ 12 Greg Gross CO	.30	.14	.04
☐ 13 Greg W. Harris	.40	.18	.05
☐ 14 Ed Whitson	.30	.14	.04
☐ 15 Jerald Clark	.50	.23	.06
☐ 16 Rich Rodriguez	.30	.14	.04
☐ 17 Larry Andersen	.30	.14	.04
☐ 18 Andy Benes	.75	.35	.09
☐ 19 Bruce Hurst	.50	.23	.06
☐ 20 Paul Faries	.30	.14	.04
☐ 21 Craig Lefferts	.50	.23	.06
☐ 22 Tony Gwynn	2.00	.90	.25
☐ 23 Jim Presley	.30	.14	.04
☐ 24 Fred McGriff	2.00	.90	.25
☐ 25 Gaylord Perry	1.25	.55	.16
☐ 26 Benito Santiago	1.25	.55	.16
☐ 27 Tony Fernandez	.75	.35	.09

1992 Padres Carl's Jr.

This 25-card set was sponsored by Carl's Jr. restaurants and issued in perforated nine-card sheets or in a precut set. The cards are printed on thick card stock and measure slightly larger than standard size (2 9/16" by 3 9/16"). The fronts feature color action player photos bordered in white. The team name appears in tan lettering above the picture while the player's position and name are printed in blue lettering beneath the picture. A unique feature about the player's name is that the first and last letter of his name are oversized. On navy blue lettering on a white background, the horizontally oriented backs present statistics, biography, and career highlights. The sponsor logo in pink rounds out the back. The cards are unnumbered and checklisted below in alphabetical order.

	MT	EX-MT	VG
COMPLETE SET (25)	15.00	6.75	1.90
COMMON PLAYER (1-25)	.35	.16	.04
☐ 1 Larry Andersen	.35	.16	.04
☐ 2 Oscar Azocar	.35	.16	.04
☐ 3 Andy Benes	.90	.40	.11
☐ 4 Dann Bilardello	.35	.16	.04
☐ 5 Jerald Clark	.50	.23	.06
☐ 6 Tony Fernandez	.50	.23	.06
☐ 7 Tony Gwynn	2.50	1.15	.30
☐ 8 Greg W. Harris	.50	.23	.06
☐ 9 Bruce Hurst	.60	.25	.08
☐ 10 Darrin Jackson	.60	.25	.08
☐ 11 Craig Lefferts	.50	.23	.06
☐ 12 Mike Maddux	.35	.16	.04
☐ 13 Fred McGriff	2.50	1.15	.30
☐ 14 Jose Melendez	.50	.23	.06
☐ 15 Randy Myers	.50	.23	.06
☐ 16 Greg Riddoch MG	.35	.16	.04
☐ 17 Rich Rodriguez	.35	.16	.04
☐ 18 Benito Santiago	.75	.35	.09
☐ 19 Gary Sheffield	2.50	1.15	.30
☐ 20 Craig Shipley	.50	.23	.06
☐ 21 Kurt Stillwell	.35	.16	.04
☐ 22 Tim Teufel	.35	.16	.04
☐ 23 Kevin Ward	.35	.16	.04
☐ 24 Ed Whitson	.35	.16	.04
☐ 25 All-Star Game Logo	.35	.16	.04

1989 Pepsi McGwire

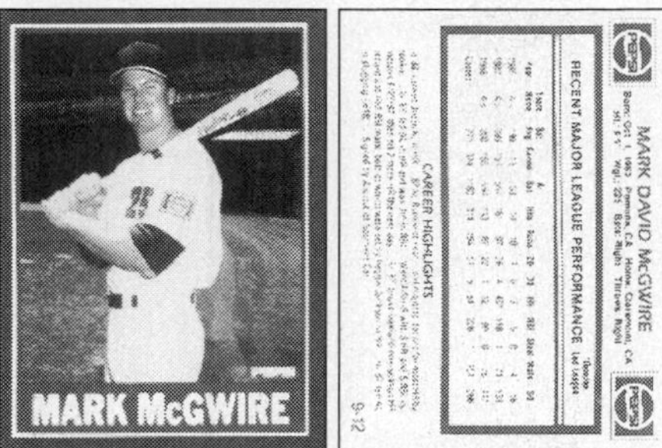

This set includes 12 cards each depicting Mark McGwire. The cards are standard size, 2 1/2" by 3 1/2" and are printed on rather thin card stock. The cards have a distinctive blue outer border. The cards are numbered on the back in the lower right corner. The Pepsi logo is shown on the front and back of each card. All the pictures used in the set are posed showing McGwire in a generic uniform with a Pepsi patch on his upper arm and his number 25 on his chest; in each case his cap or batting helmet is in the Oakland colors but without their logo. The card backs all contain exactly the same statistical and biographical information, only the card number is different. Supposedly cards were distributed inside specially marked 12-packs of Pepsi in the Northern California area.

	MT	EX-MT	VG
COMPLETE SET (12)	20.00	9.00	2.50
COMMON PLAYER (1-12)	2.00	.90	.25
☐ 1 Mark McGwire (Batting stance with left foot lifted)	2.00	.90	.25
☐ 2 Mark McGwire (Fielding position at first base)	2.00	.90	.25
☐ 3 Mark McGwire (Reaching out with glove for ball)	2.00	.90	.25
☐ 4 Mark McGwire (Batting stance in empty stadium)	2.00	.90	.25
☐ 5 Mark McGwire (On one knee with bat)	2.00	.90	.25
☐ 6 Mark McGwire (Stretching for ball at first base)	2.00	.90	.25
☐ 7 Mark McGwire (Smiling with bat on shoulder facing camera)	2.00	.90	.25
☐ 8 Mark McGwire (Holding bat in green windbreaker)	2.00	.90	.25
☐ 9 Mark McGwire (Rawlings bat on left shoulder)	2.00	.90	.25
☐ 10 Mark McGwire (Holding bat parallel to ground in green windbreaker)	2.00	.90	.25
☐ 11 Mark McGwire (Holding bat parallel to ground in uniform, toothy smile)	2.00	.90	.25
☐ 12 Mark McGwire (Serious looking follow through)	2.00	.90	.25

1990 Pepsi Jose Canseco

This ten-card, standard-size set of 2 1/2" by 3 1/2" cards was issued in conjunction with Pepsi-Cola. These blue-bordered cards do not have the team logos. This set is very similar in style to the Pepsi McGwire set issued the year before. All the pictures used in the set are posed showing Canseco in a generic uniform with a Pepsi patch.

	MT	EX-MT	VG
COMPLETE SET (10)	7.50	3.40	.95
COMMON PLAYER (1-10)	1.00	.45	.13
☐ 1 Jose Canseco (Follow Through Waist)	1.00	.45	.13
☐ 2 Jose Canseco	1.00	.45	.13

	MT	EX-MT	VG
(Follow Through Shoulder)			
☐ 3 Jose Canseco (Catching Ball)	1.00	.45	.13
☐ 4 Jose Canseco (Batting Pose)	1.00	.45	.13
☐ 5 Jose Canseco (Glove Over Chest)	1.00	.45	.13
☐ 6 Jose Canseco (Action Follow Through)	1.00	.45	.13
☐ 7 Jose Canseco (Sitting on Dugout Steps)	1.00	.45	.13
☐ 8 Jose Canseco (Waiting for Pitch)	1.00	.45	.13
☐ 9 Jose Canseco (Portrait/Bat at Waist)	1.00	.45	.13
☐ 10 Jose Canseco (Portrait)	1.00	.45	.13

1991 Pepsi Ken Griffey Jr.

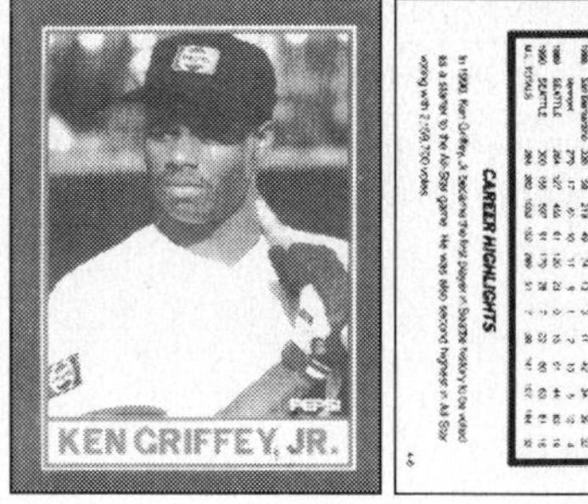

This eight-card set was sponsored by Pepsi-Cola, and the its company logo appears on the front and back of each card. The cards measure the standard size (2 1/2" by 3 1/2"). The color player photos are bordered in red, white, and purple, with Ken Griffey, Jr. in red block lettering below each picture. The backs are either horizontally or vertically oriented and present biographical as well as statistical information in black print on a white background. The cards are numbered on the back.

	MT	EX-MT	VG
COMPLETE SET (8)	10.00	4.50	1.25
COMMON PLAYER (1-6)	2.00	.90	.25
COMMON PLAYER (7-8)	.50	.23	.06
☐ 1 Ken Griffey Jr. (Swinging the bat)	2.00	.90	.25
☐ 2 Ken Griffey Jr. (Throwing from the outfield)	2.00	.90	.25
☐ 3 Ken Griffey Jr. (Catching ball at wall)	2.00	.90	.25
☐ 4 Ken Griffey Jr. (Posing with bat on shoulder)	2.00	.90	.25
☐ 5 Ken Griffey Jr. (Posing with Dad seated)	2.00	.90	.25
☐ 6 Ken Griffey Jr. (Standing beside Dad)	2.00	.90	.25
☐ 7 Ken Griffey Sr. (At bat)	.50	.23	.06
☐ 8 Ken Griffey Sr. (Catching fly ball)	.50	.23	.06

1991 Pepsi Rickey Henderson

These standard-size (2 1/2" by 3 1/2") cards were sponsored by Pepsi and feature Rickey Henderson. The front design has a color player photo, enframed by red borders on blue and white pinstripe background. The white pinstripes become farther and farther apart as one moves toward the right side of the card. An icon of a baseball and baserunner in the lower right corner rounds out the card face. In a horizontal format, the backs have the same career performance statistics but differing career highlights. The cards are numbered on the back.

	MT	EX-MT	VG
COMPLETE SET (10)	10.00	4.50	1.25
COMMON PLAYER (1-10)	1.25	.55	.16
☐ 1 Rickey Henderson (Follow through, left side)	1.25	.55	.16
☐ 2 Rickey Henderson (Running bases)	1.25	.55	.16
☐ 3 Rickey Henderson (Stretching hamstring)	1.25	.55	.16
☐ 4 Rickey Henderson (Ready to run)	1.25	.55	.16
☐ 5 Rickey Henderson (Bat on shoulder)	1.25	.55	.16
☐ 6 Rickey Henderson (Follow through, Right side)	1.25	.55	.16
☐ 7 Rickey Henderson (Squatting with bat)	1.25	.55	.16
☐ 8 Rickey Henderson (After throw)	1.25	.55	.16
☐ 9 Rickey Henderson (Leading off base)	1.25	.55	.16
☐ 10 Rickey Henderson (Warming up with bat)	1.25	.55	.16

1991 Pepsi Superstar

This 17-card set was sponsored by Pepsi-Cola of Florida as part of the "Flavor of Baseball" promotion. The promotion featured a chance to win one of 104 rare, older cards, including one 1952 Mickey Mantle Rookie Card. The Superstar cards were glued inside specially marked 12 packs of Pepsi-Cola products in Orlando, Tampa, and

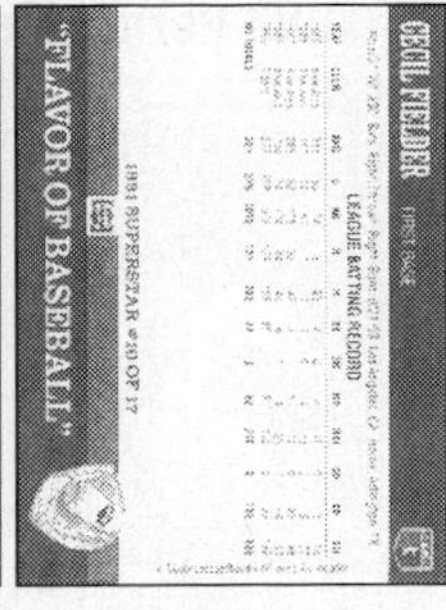

Miami. It is difficult to remove the cards without creasing them; supposedly area supervisors for Pepsi each received a few sets. The cards measure slightly wider than standard size (2 5/8" by 3 1/2"). The fronts have color action player photos, with a baseball glove "catching" a can of Pepsi superimposed at the upper right corner of the picture. The player photo has two top (purple and red/blue) and two bottom (red and purple) color stripes serving as borders but none on its sides. In a horizontal format, the backs have blue and red stripes, and present Major League statistics as well as biography. The cards are numbered on the back.

	MT	EX-MT	VG
COMPLETE SET (17)	75.00	34.00	9.50
COMMON PLAYER (1-17)	1.50	.65	.19
☐ 1 Dwight Gooden	3.50	1.55	.45
☐ 2 Andre Dawson	5.00	2.30	.60
☐ 3 Ryne Sandberg	10.00	4.50	1.25
☐ 4 Dave Stieb	1.50	.65	.19
☐ 5 Jose Rijo	1.50	.65	.19
☐ 6 Roger Clemens	10.00	4.50	1.25
☐ 7 Barry Bonds	6.00	2.70	.75
☐ 8 Cal Ripken	12.00	5.50	1.50
☐ 9 Dave Justice	7.50	3.40	.95
☐ 10 Cecil Fielder	6.00	2.70	.75
☐ 11 Don Mattingly	7.50	3.40	.95
☐ 12 Ozzie Smith	5.00	2.30	.60
☐ 13 Kirby Puckett	9.00	4.00	1.15
☐ 14 Rafael Palmiero	3.50	1.55	.45
☐ 15 Bobby Bonilla	5.00	2.30	.60
☐ 16 Len Dykstra	1.50	.65	.19
☐ 17 Jose Canseco	9.00	4.00	1.15

1992 Pepsi Diet Canada MSA

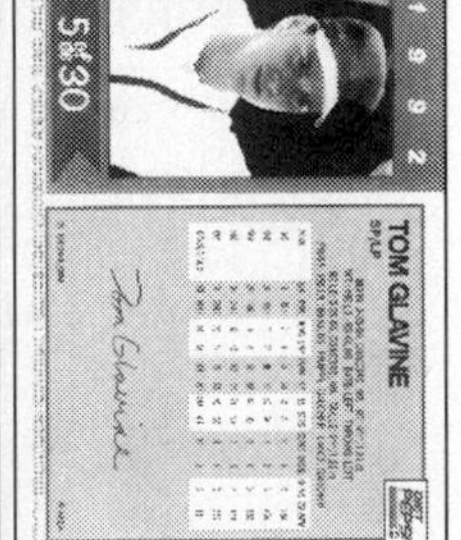

This 30-card standard-size (2 1/2" by 3 1/2") set was issued by MSA (Michael Schechter Associates) for Diet Pepsi in Canada. The glossy color action photos are framed by white borders. The top is edged with a royal blue stripe while a red stripe, with sponsor logos and player's name, edges the bottom. As is typical of MSA sets, the team logos have been airbrushed out. The horizontally oriented backs carry a close-up color photo bordered in red with biography and complete career statistics on a light blue box. A facsimile autograph rounds out the back. The cards are numbered on the back.

	MT	EX-MT	VG
COMPLETE SET (30)	20.00	9.00	2.50
COMMON PLAYER (1-30)	.35	.16	.04
☐ 1 Roger Clemens	1.50	.65	.19
☐ 2 Dwight Gooden	.50	.23	.06
☐ 3 Tom Henke	.35	.16	.04
☐ 4 Dennis Martinez	.35	.16	.04
☐ 5 Tom Glavine	1.00	.45	.13
☐ 6 Jack Morris	.50	.23	.06
☐ 7 Dennis Eckersley	.60	.25	.08
☐ 8 Jeff Reardon	.50	.23	.06
☐ 9 Bryan Harvey	.35	.16	.04
☐ 10 Sandy Alomar Jr.	.35	.16	.04
☐ 11 Carlton Fisk	.60	.25	.08
☐ 12 Gary Carter	.50	.23	.06
☐ 13 Cecil Fielder	.75	.35	.09
☐ 14 Will Clark	1.25	.55	.16
☐ 15 Roberto Alomar	1.50	.65	.19
☐ 16 Ryne Sandberg	2.00	.90	.25
☐ 17 Cal Ripken	2.50	1.15	.30
☐ 18 Barry Larkin	.60	.25	.08
☐ 19 Ozzie Smith	.60	.25	.08
☐ 20 Kelly Gruber	.35	.16	.04
☐ 21 Wade Boggs	.75	.35	.09
☐ 22 Tim Wallach	.35	.16	.04
☐ 23 Howard Johnson	.35	.16	.04
☐ 24 Jose Canseco	1.25	.55	.16
☐ 25 Joe Carter	.75	.35	.09
☐ 26 Ken Griffey Jr.	2.50	1.15	.30
☐ 27 Kirby Puckett	1.50	.65	.19
☐ 28 Rickey Henderson	1.00	.45	.13
☐ 29 Barry Bonds	.75	.35	.09
☐ 30 Dave Winfield	.75	.35	.09

1981 Perma-Graphic All-Stars

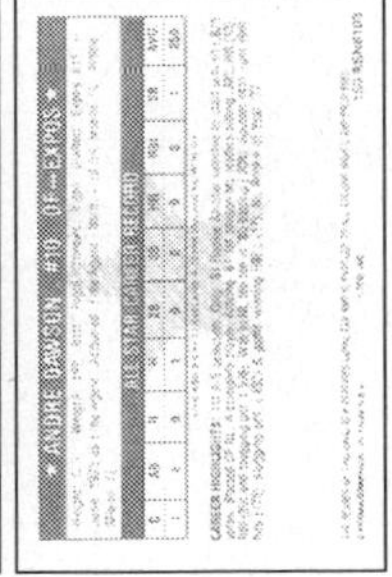

This set commemorates the starters of the 1981 All-Star game. This 18-card set measure 2 1/8" by 3 3/8" and has rounded corners. Because of the players strike of 1981 plenty of time was available to prepare the player's biography with appropriate notes. The set is framed on the front in red for the National League and blue for the American League.

	NRMT-MT	EXC	G-VG
COMPLETE SET (18)	35.00	16.00	4.40
COMMON PLAYER (1-18)	1.25	.55	.16
☐ 1 Gary Carter	2.00	.90	.25
☐ 2 Dave Concepcion	1.50	.65	.19
☐ 3 Andre Dawson	2.50	1.15	.30
☐ 4 George Foster	1.25	.55	.16
☐ 5 Davey Lopes	1.25	.55	.16
☐ 6 Dave Parker	1.50	.65	.19
☐ 7 Pete Rose	4.00	1.80	.50
☐ 8 Mike Schmidt	5.00	2.30	.60
☐ 9 Fernando Valenzuela	1.50	.65	.19
☐ 10 George Brett	4.50	2.00	.55
☐ 11 Rod Carew	2.50	1.15	.30
☐ 12 Bucky Dent	1.25	.55	.16

☐ 13 Carlton Fisk	3.00	1.35	.40
☐ 14 Reggie Jackson	3.50	1.55	.45
☐ 15 Jack Morris	2.00	.90	.25
☐ 16 Willie Randolph	1.25	.55	.16
☐ 17 Ken Singleton	1.25	.55	.16
☐ 18 Dave Winfield	3.50	1.55	.45

1981 Perma-Graphic Credit Cards

Perma-Graphic began their three-year foray into card manufacturing with this 32-card set of "credit cards" each measuring approximately 2 1/8" by 3 3/8". The set featured 32 of the leading players of 1981. This set's design is split on the front between a full-color photo of the player and an identification of said player while the back has one line of career statistics and lines of career highlights. These sets (made of plastic) were issued with the cooperation of Topps Chewing Gum. This first set of Perma-Graphic cards seems to have been produced in greater quantities than the other five Perma-Graphic sets.

	NRMT-MT	EXC	G-VG
COMPLETE SET (32)	35.00	16.00	4.40
COMMON PLAYER (1-32)	1.00	.45	.13
☐ 1 Johnny Bench	3.00	1.35	.40
☐ 2 Mike Schmidt	4.50	2.00	.55
☐ 3 George Brett	3.50	1.55	.45
☐ 4 Carl Yastrzemski	2.00	.90	.25
☐ 5 Pete Rose	3.00	1.35	.40
☐ 6 Bob Horner	1.00	.45	.13
☐ 7 Reggie Jackson	3.00	1.35	.40
☐ 8 Keith Hernandez	1.25	.55	.16
☐ 9 George Foster	1.00	.45	.13
☐ 10 Garry Templeton	1.00	.45	.13
☐ 11 Tom Seaver	3.00	1.35	.40
☐ 12 Steve Garvey	1.50	.65	.19
☐ 13 Dave Parker	1.25	.55	.16
☐ 14 Willie Stargell	1.75	.80	.22
☐ 15 Cecil Cooper	1.00	.45	.13
☐ 16 Steve Carlton	2.00	.90	.25
☐ 17 Ted Simmons	1.25	.55	.16
☐ 18 Dave Kingman	1.25	.55	.16
☐ 19 Rickey Henderson	3.00	1.35	.40
☐ 20 Fred Lynn	1.25	.55	.16
☐ 21 Dave Winfield	3.00	1.35	.40
☐ 22 Rod Carew	2.00	.90	.25
☐ 23 Jim Rice	1.50	.65	.19
☐ 24 Bruce Sutter	1.00	.45	.13
☐ 25 Cesar Cedeno	1.00	.45	.13
☐ 26 Nolan Ryan	6.00	2.70	.75
☐ 27 Dusty Baker	1.25	.55	.16
☐ 28 Jim Palmer	2.00	.90	.25
☐ 29 Gorman Thomas	1.00	.45	.13
☐ 30 Ben Oglivie	1.00	.45	.13
☐ 31 Willie Wilson	1.25	.55	.16
☐ 32 Gary Carter	2.00	.90	.25

1982 Perma-Graphic All-Stars

For the second time Perma-Graphic issued a special set commemorating the starters of the 1982 All-Star game. This 18-card set measures 2 1/8" by 3 3/8" and features a colorful design framing the players photo on the front The back again feature one line of complete All-Star game statistics including the 1982 game and career highlites. Perma-Graphic also issued the set in a limited (reportedly 1200 sets produced) "gold" edition, i.e., with a gold tint to the cards. The gold edition cards are valued at double the prices listed below.

	NRMT-MT	EXC	G-VG
COMPLETE SET (18)	35.00	16.00	4.40
COMMON PLAYER (1-18)	1.25	.55	.16
☐ 1 Dennis Eckersley	2.50	1.15	.30
☐ 2 Cecil Cooper	1.25	.55	.16
☐ 3 Carlton Fisk	2.50	1.15	.30
☐ 4 Robin Yount	3.50	1.55	.45
☐ 5 Bobby Grich	1.25	.55	.16
☐ 6 Rickey Henderson	3.50	1.55	.45
☐ 7 Reggie Jackson	3.00	1.35	.40
☐ 8 Fred Lynn	1.50	.65	.19
☐ 9 George Brett	3.50	1.55	.45
☐ 10 Gary Carter	2.00	.90	.25
☐ 11 Dave Concepcion	1.50	.65	.19
☐ 12 Andre Dawson	2.50	1.15	.30
☐ 13 Tim Raines	1.50	.65	.19
☐ 14 Dale Murphy	2.00	.90	.25
☐ 15 Steve Rogers	1.25	.55	.16
☐ 16 Pete Rose	3.50	1.55	.45
☐ 17 Mike Schmidt	4.00	1.80	.50
☐ 18 Manny Trillo	1.25	.55	.16

1982 Perma-Graphic Credit Cards

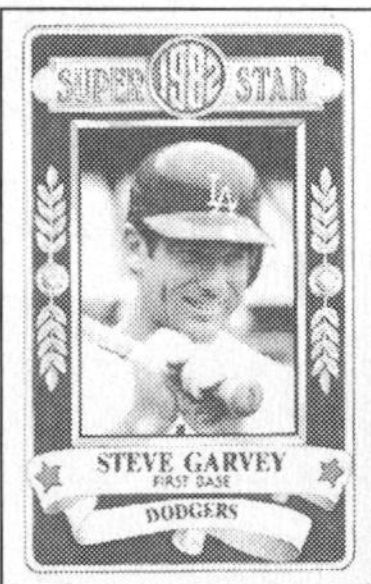

For the second year Perma-Graphic, in association with Topps produced a high-quality set on plastic honoring the leading players in baseball of 1982. The players photo is on the front middle of the card and is framed by a brown border with many innovative designs. This 24-card set features plastic cards each measuring approximately 2 1/8" by 3 3/8". On the card back there is one line of career statistics along with career highlights. Perma-Graphic also issued the set in a limited (reportedly 900 sets produced) "gold" edition, i.e., with a gold tint to the cards. The gold edition cards are valued at double the prices listed below. Again in 1982 Perma-Graphic issued these sets in conjuction and with the approval of Topps Chewing Gum.

	NRMT-MT	EXC	G-VG
COMPLETE SET (24)	45.00	20.00	5.75
COMMON PLAYER (1-24)	1.25	.55	.16
☐ 1 Johnny Bench	3.00	1.35	.40
☐ 2 Tom Seaver	3.00	1.35	.40
☐ 3 Mike Schmidt	4.00	1.80	.50
☐ 4 Gary Carter	2.00	.90	.25
☐ 5 Willie Stargell	2.00	.90	.25
☐ 6 Tim Raines	1.50	.65	.19
☐ 7 Bill Madlock	1.25	.55	.16
☐ 8 Keith Hernandez	1.50	.65	.19
☐ 9 Pete Rose	3.50	1.55	.45
☐ 10 Steve Carlton	2.50	1.15	.30
☐ 11 Steve Garvey	2.00	.90	.25
☐ 12 Fernando Valenzuela	1.50	.65	.19
☐ 13 Carl Yastrzemski	3.00	1.35	.40
☐ 14 Dave Winfield	3.50	1.55	.45
☐ 15 Carney Lansford	1.25	.55	.16
☐ 16 Rollie Fingers	2.50	1.15	.30
☐ 17 Tony Armas	1.25	.55	.16
☐ 18 Cecil Cooper	1.25	.55	.16
☐ 19 George Brett	4.00	1.80	.50
☐ 20 Reggie Jackson	3.50	1.55	.45
☐ 21 Rod Carew	2.50	1.15	.30
☐ 22 Eddie Murray	3.00	1.35	.40
☐ 23 Rickey Henderson	3.50	1.55	.45
☐ 24 Kirk Gibson	1.50	.65	.19

1983 Perma-Graphic All-Stars

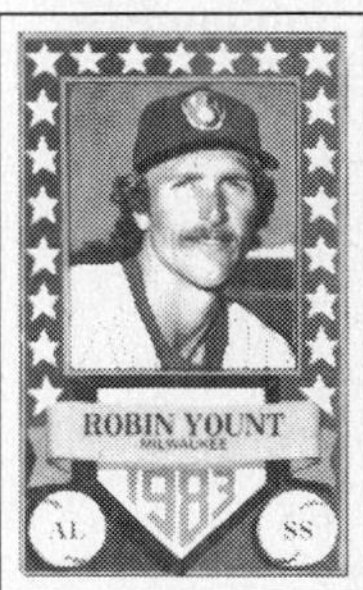

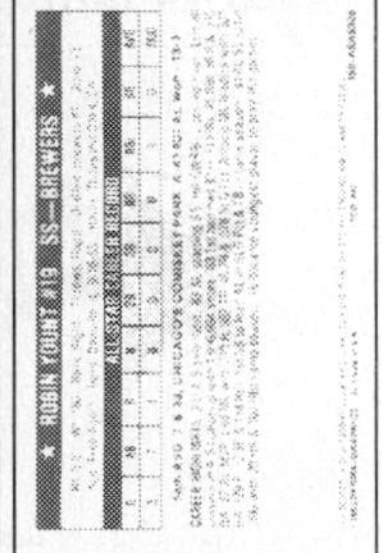

The 1983 All-Star Set was the third set Perma-Graphic issued commemorating the starters of the All-Star game. Again, Perma-Graphic used the Topps photos and issued their sets on plastics. This 18-card set features cards each measuring approximately 2 1/8" by 3 3/8". Perma-Graphic also issued the set in a limited "gold" edition, i.e., with a gold tint to the cards. The gold edition cards are valued at double the prices listed below.

	NRMT-MT	EXC	G-VG
COMPLETE SET (18)	35.00	16.00	4.40
COMMON PLAYER (1-18)	1.25	.55	.16
☐ 1 George Brett	4.00	1.80	.50
☐ 2 Rod Carew	2.50	1.15	.30
☐ 3 Fred Lynn	1.50	.65	.19
☐ 4 Jim Rice	1.50	.65	.19
☐ 5 Ted Simmons	1.50	.65	.19
☐ 6 Dave Stieb	1.25	.55	.16
☐ 7 Dave Winfield	3.00	1.35	.40
☐ 8 Manny Trillo	1.25	.55	.16
☐ 9 Robin Yount	4.00	1.80	.50
☐ 10 Gary Carter	2.00	.90	.25
☐ 11 Andre Dawson	2.50	1.15	.30
☐ 12 Dale Murphy	2.00	.90	.25
☐ 13 Al Oliver	1.25	.55	.16
☐ 14 Tim Raines	1.50	.65	.19
☐ 15 Steve Sax	1.25	.55	.16
☐ 16 Mike Schmidt	4.00	1.80	.50
☐ 17 Ozzie Smith	2.50	1.15	.30
☐ 18 Mario Soto	1.25	.55	.16

1983 Perma-Graphic Credit Cards

This set was the third straight year Perma-Graphic, with approval from Topps issued their high-quality plastic set. This 36-card set which measures 2 1/8" by 3 3/8" have the players photos framed by colorful backgrounds. The backs again feature one line of career statistics and several informative lines of career highlights. Perma-Graphic also issued the set in a limited (reportedly 1000 sets produced) "gold" edition, i.e., with a gold tint to the cards. The gold edition cards are valued at double the prices listed below.

	NRMT-MT	EXC	G-VG
COMPLETE SET (36)	55.00	25.00	7.00
COMMON PLAYER (1-36)	1.25	.55	.16
☐ 1 Bill Buckner	1.50	.65	.19
☐ 2 Steve Carlton	2.50	1.15	.30
☐ 3 Gary Carter	2.00	.90	.25
☐ 4 Andre Dawson	2.50	1.15	.30
☐ 5 Pedro Guerrero	1.50	.65	.19
☐ 6 George Hendrick	1.25	.55	.16
☐ 7 Keith Hernandez	1.50	.65	.19
☐ 8 Bill Madlock	1.25	.55	.16
☐ 9 Dale Murphy	2.00	.90	.25
☐ 10 Al Oliver	1.25	.55	.16
☐ 11 Dave Parker	1.50	.65	.19
☐ 12 Darrell Porter	1.25	.55	.16
☐ 13 Pete Rose	3.50	1.55	.45
☐ 14 Mike Schmidt	4.00	1.80	.50
☐ 15 Lonnie Smith	1.25	.55	.16
☐ 16 Ozzie Smith	2.50	1.15	.30
☐ 17 Bruce Sutter	1.50	.65	.19
☐ 18 Fernando Valenzuela	1.50	.65	.19
☐ 19 George Brett	4.00	1.80	.50
☐ 20 Rod Carew	2.50	1.15	.30
☐ 21 Cecil Cooper	1.25	.55	.16
☐ 22 Doug DeCinces	1.25	.55	.16
☐ 23 Rollie Fingers	2.50	1.15	.30
☐ 24 Damaso Garcia	1.25	.55	.16
☐ 25 Toby Harrah	1.25	.55	.16
☐ 26 Rickey Henderson	3.50	1.55	.45
☐ 27 Reggie Jackson	3.50	1.55	.45
☐ 28 Hal McRae	1.50	.65	.19
☐ 29 Eddie Murray	2.50	1.15	.30
☐ 30 Lance Parrish	1.50	.65	.19
☐ 31 Jim Rice	1.50	.65	.19
☐ 32 Gorman Thomas	1.25	.55	.16
☐ 33 Willie Wilson	1.25	.55	.16
☐ 34 Dave Winfield	3.50	1.55	.45
☐ 35 Carl Yastrzemski	3.00	1.35	.40
☐ 36 Robin Yount	4.00	1.80	.50

1991 Petro-Canada Standups

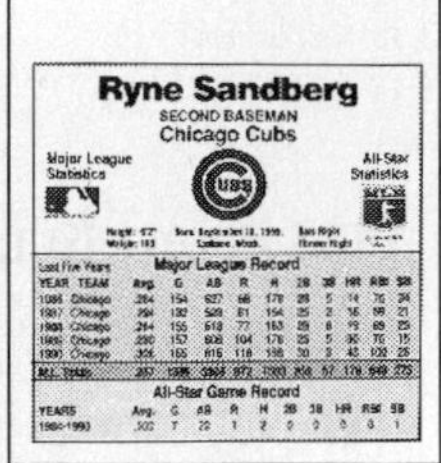

These 3-D action collector cards consist of three cardboard sheets measuring approximately 2 7/8" by 3 13/16" and joined at one end. The front cover has blue and red stripe borders and features either an American or National league logo inside a baseball diamond. The inside cover has a color photo of the crowd at the game. The middle sheet consists of a 3-D standup of the player. The inside of the last sheet has biographical information, career regular season statistics, and All-Star game statistics. The back has career highlights in a sky blue box and "Play the All Star Quiz" questions and answers. The set was first released in Toronto at the All-Star Game in conjunction with the All-Star Fanfest. The cards are numbered on the front.

	MT	EX-MT	VG
COMPLETE SET (26)	30.00	13.50	3.80
COMMON PLAYER (1-26)	.75	.35	.09
☐ 1 Cal Ripken	4.00	1.80	.50
☐ 2 Greg Olson	.75	.35	.09
☐ 3 Roger Clemens	3.00	1.35	.40
☐ 4 Ryne Sandberg	3.50	1.55	.45
☐ 5 Dave Winfield	2.00	.90	.25
☐ 6 Eric Davis	1.25	.55	.16
☐ 7 Carlton Fisk	1.25	.55	.16
☐ 8 Mike Scott	.75	.35	.09
☐ 9 Sandy Alomar Jr.	.75	.35	.09
☐ 10 Tim Wallach	.75	.35	.09
☐ 11 Cecil Fielder	2.00	.90	.25
☐ 12 Dwight Gooden	1.25	.55	.16
☐ 13 George Brett	2.00	.90	.25
☐ 14 Dale Murphy	1.50	.65	.19
☐ 15 Paul Molitor	1.25	.55	.16
☐ 16 Barry Bonds	1.50	.65	.19
☐ 17 Kirby Puckett	2.50	1.15	.30
☐ 18 Ozzie Smith	1.50	.65	.19
☐ 19 Don Mattingly	2.00	.90	.25
☐ 20 Will Clark	2.50	1.15	.30
☐ 21 Rickey Henderson	2.50	1.15	.30
☐ 22 Orel Hershiser	1.00	.45	.13
☐ 23 Ken Griffey Jr.	6.00	2.70	.75
☐ 24 Tony Gwynn	2.50	1.15	.30
☐ 25 Nolan Ryan	6.00	2.70	.75
☐ 26 Kelly Gruber	.90	.40	.11

1964 Phillies Philadelphia Bulletin

This 27-player set was produced by the Philadelphia Bulletin, a newspaper. The catalog designation for this set is M130-5. These large, approximately 8" by 10", photo cards are unnumbered and blank backed.

	NRMT	VG-E	GOOD
COMPLETE SET (27)	150.00	70.00	19.00
COMMON PLAYER (1-27)	5.00	2.30	.60
☐ 1 Richie Allen	20.00	9.00	2.50
☐ 2 Ruben Amaro	6.00	2.70	.75
☐ 3 Jack Baldschun	5.00	2.30	.60
☐ 4 Dennis Bennett	5.00	2.30	.60
☐ 5 John Boozer	5.00	2.30	.60
☐ 6 Johnny Briggs	5.00	2.30	.60
☐ 7 Jim Bunning (2)	12.50	5.75	1.55
☐ 8 Johnny Callison	6.00	2.70	.75
☐ 9 Danny Cater	5.00	2.30	.60
☐ 10 Wes Covington	6.00	2.70	.75
☐ 11 Ray Culp	5.00	2.30	.60
☐ 12 Clay Dalrymple	5.00	2.30	.60
☐ 13 Tony Gonzalez	6.00	2.70	.75
☐ 14 John Herrnstein	5.00	2.30	.60
☐ 15 Alex Johnson	6.00	2.70	.75
☐ 16 Art Mahaffey	5.00	2.30	.60
☐ 17 Gene Mauch MG	7.50	3.40	.95
☐ 18 Vic Power	6.00	2.70	.75
☐ 19 Ed Roebuck	5.00	2.30	.60
☐ 20 Cookie Rojas	6.00	2.70	.75
☐ 21 Bobby Shantz	6.00	2.70	.75
☐ 22 Chris Short	6.00	2.70	.75
☐ 23 Tony Taylor	6.00	2.70	.75
☐ 24 Frank Thomas	6.00	2.70	.75
☐ 25 Gus Triandos	6.00	2.70	.75
☐ 26 Bobby Wine	6.00	2.70	.75
☐ 27 Rick Wise	6.00	2.70	.75

1974 Phillies Johnny Pro

This 12-card set measures approximately 3 3/4" by 7 1/8" and features members of the 1974 Philadelphia Phillies. The most significant player in this series is an early card of Mike Schmidt. The cards are designed to be pushed out and have the players photo against a solid white background. The backs are blank and marked the second straight year that Johnny Pro issued cards of a major league team. The set is checklisted by uniform number. According to informed sources, there were less than 15,000 sets produced.

	NRMT-MT	EXC	G-VG
COMPLETE SET (12)	175.00	80.00	22.00
COMMON PLAYER	4.00	1.80	.50
☐ 8 Bob Boone C	15.00	6.75	1.90
☐ 10 Larry Bowa IF	6.00	2.70	.75
☐ 16 Dave Cash IF	4.00	1.80	.50
☐ 19 Greg Luzinski OF	8.00	3.60	1.00
☐ 20 Mike Schmidt IF	125.00	57.50	15.50
☐ 22 Mike Anderson OF	4.00	1.80	.50
☐ 24 Bill Robinson OF	6.00	2.70	.75
☐ 25 Del Unser OF	6.00	2.70	.75

☐ 27 Willie Montanez IF	4.00	1.80	.50
☐ 32 Steve Carlton P	25.00	11.50	3.10
☐ 37 Ron Schueler P	4.00	1.80	.50
☐ 41 Jim Lonborg P	6.00	2.70	.75

1984 Phillies Tastykake

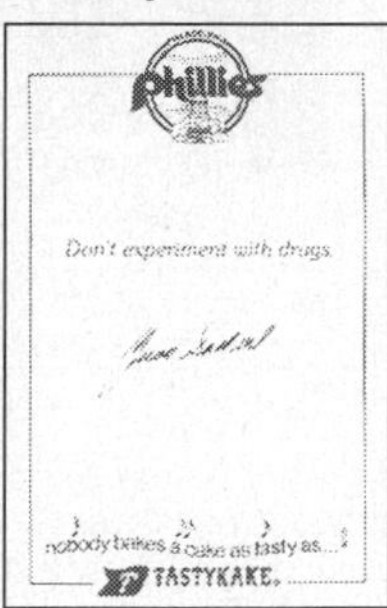

This set features the Philadelphia Phillies and was sponsored by Tastykake. The card fronts feature a colorful picture of the player or subject inside a white border. The cards measure approximately 3 1/2" by 5 1/4". The set was distributed to fans attending a specific game. There were four additional cards which were put out late in the year updating new players (after the first 40 had been out for some time). The update cards are numbered 41-44 after the first group. The card backs contain a brief message (tip) from the player with his facsimile autograph. The cards are unnumbered but the title card gives a numbering system essentially alphabetically within position; that system is used below for the first 40 cards.

	NRMT-MT	EXC	G-VG
COMPLETE SET (44)	12.00	5.50	1.50
COMMON PLAYER (1-40)	.25	.11	.03
COMMON PLAYER (41-44)	.50	.23	.06
☐ 1 Logo Card/Checklist	.35	.16	.04
☐ 2 Team Photo	.35	.16	.04
☐ 3 Phillie Phanatic	.35	.16	.04
☐ 4 Veterans Stadium	.25	.11	.03
☐ 5 Steve Carlton Hall of Fame	1.50	.65	.19
☐ 6 Mike Schmidt Hall of Fame	2.00	.90	.25
☐ 7 Phillies Broadcasters	.25	.11	.03
☐ 8 Paul Owens MG	.25	.11	.03
☐ 9 Dave Bristol CO	.25	.11	.03
☐ 10 John Felske CO	.25	.11	.03
☐ 11 Deron Johnson CO	.25	.11	.03
☐ 12 Claude Osteen CO	.25	.11	.03
☐ 13 Mike Ryan CO	.25	.11	.03
☐ 14 Larry Andersen	.25	.11	.03
☐ 15 Marty Bystrom	.25	.11	.03
☐ 16 Bill Campbell	.25	.11	.03
☐ 17 Steve Carlton	1.50	.65	.19
☐ 18 John Denny	.35	.16	.04
☐ 19 Tony Ghelfi	.25	.11	.03
☐ 20 Kevin Gross	.50	.23	.06
☐ 21 Al Holland	.25	.11	.03
☐ 22 Charles Hudson	.25	.11	.03
☐ 23 Jerry Koosman	.35	.16	.04
☐ 24 Tug McGraw	.50	.23	.06
☐ 25 Bo Diaz	.25	.11	.03
☐ 26 Ozzie Virgil	.25	.11	.03
☐ 27 John Wockenfuss	.25	.11	.03
☐ 28 Luis Aguayo	.25	.11	.03
☐ 29 Ivan DeJesus	.25	.11	.03
☐ 30 Kiko Garcia	.25	.11	.03
☐ 31 Len Matuszek	.25	.11	.03
☐ 32 Juan Samuel	.50	.23	.06
☐ 33 Mike Schmidt	2.00	.90	.25
☐ 34 Tim Corcoran	.25	.11	.03
☐ 35 Greg Gross	.25	.11	.03
☐ 36 Von Hayes	.35	.16	.04
☐ 37 Joe Lefebvre	.25	.11	.03
☐ 38 Sixto Lezcano	.25	.11	.03
☐ 39 Garry Maddox	.35	.16	.04
☐ 40 Glenn Wilson	.25	.11	.03
☐ 41 Don Carman	.50	.23	.06
☐ 42 John Russell	.50	.23	.06
☐ 43 Jeff Stone	.50	.23	.06
☐ 44 Dave Wehrmeister	.50	.23	.06

1985 Phillies CIGNA

This colorful 16-card set (measuring approximately 2 5/8" by 4 1/8") features the Philadelphia Phillies and was also sponsored by CIGNA Corporation. Cards are numbered on the back and contain a safety tip as such the set is frequently categorized and referenced as a safety set. Cards are also numbered by uniform number on the front.

	NRMT-MT	EXC	G-VG
COMPLETE SET (16)	8.00	3.60	1.00
COMMON PLAYER (1-16)	.25	.11	.03
☐ 1 Juan Samuel	.50	.23	.06
☐ 2 Von Hayes	.35	.16	.04
☐ 3 Ozzie Virgil	.25	.11	.03
☐ 4 Mike Schmidt	3.00	1.35	.40
☐ 5 Greg Gross	.25	.11	.03
☐ 6 Tim Corcoran	.25	.11	.03
☐ 7 Jerry Koosman	.50	.23	.06
☐ 8 Jeff Stone	.25	.11	.03
☐ 9 Glenn Wilson	.25	.11	.03
☐ 10 Steve Jeltz	.25	.11	.03
☐ 11 Garry Maddox	.35	.16	.04
☐ 12 Steve Carlton	2.00	.90	.25
☐ 13 John Denny	.35	.16	.04
☐ 14 Kevin Gross	.50	.23	.06
☐ 15 Shane Rawley	.35	.16	.04
☐ 16 Charlie Hudson	.25	.11	.03

1985 Phillies Tastykake

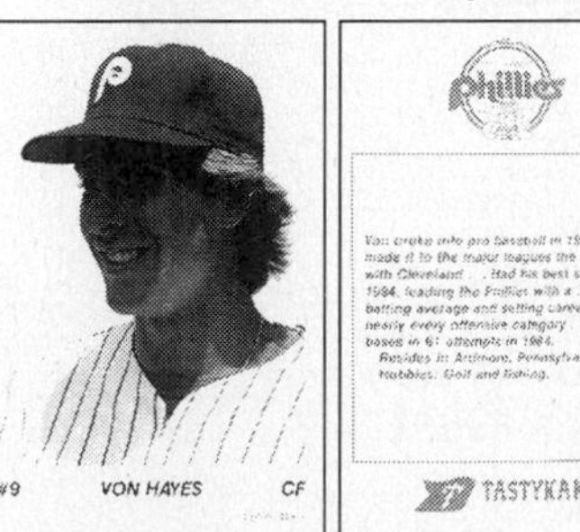

The 1985 Tastykake Philadelphia Phillies set consists of 47 cards, each measuring approximately 3 1/2" by 5 1/4". They feature a color photo of the player framed against white borders. The group shots of the various parts of the teams were posed after the other cards were issued so there are stylistic differences between the group shots and the individual shots. The backs feature brief biographies of the players. The cards are arranged below by position and in alphabetical order within these positions.

	NRMT-MT	EXC	G-VG
COMPLETE SET (47)	11.00	4.90	1.40
COMMON PLAYER (1-47)	.25	.11	.03

	NRMT-MT	EXC	G-VG
☐ 1 Checklist Card	.35	.16	.04
☐ 2 John Felske MG	.25	.11	.03
☐ 3 Dave Bristol CO	.25	.11	.03
☐ 4 Lee Elia CO	.25	.11	.03
☐ 5 Claude Osteen CO	.25	.11	.03
☐ 6 Mike Ryan CO	.25	.11	.03
☐ 7 Del Unser CO	.25	.11	.03
☐ 8 John Felske MG and Del Unser CO Dave Bristol CO Lee Elia CO Mike Ryan CO Hank King CO Claude Osteen CO	.25	.11	.03
☐ 9 Pitching Staff Zachry, Andersen, Hudson, Rawley, Denny, Carlton, Gross, Holland, Koosman, Carman, Bill Campbell	.35	.16	.04
☐ 10 Catchers Darren Daulton, Bo Diaz, Ozzie Virgil	.35	.16	.04
☐ 11 Infielders Schmidt, Jeltz, Ivan DeJesus, Samuel, Aguayo, Russell	.35	.16	.04
☐ 12 Outfielders Corcoran, Gross, Hayes, Lefebvre, Stone, Wilson	.25	.11	.03
☐ 13 Larry Andersen	.25	.11	.03
☐ 14 Steve Carlton	1.50	.65	.19
☐ 15 Don Carman	.25	.11	.03
☐ 16 John Denny	.35	.16	.04
☐ 17 Tony Ghelfi	.25	.11	.03
☐ 18 Kevin Gross	.35	.16	.04
☐ 19 Al Holland	.25	.11	.03
☐ 20 Charles Hudson	.25	.11	.03
☐ 21 Jerry Koosman	.35	.16	.04
☐ 22 Shane Rawley	.25	.11	.03
☐ 23 Pat Zachry	.25	.11	.03
☐ 24 Darren Daulton	1.50	.65	.19
☐ 25 Bo Diaz	.25	.11	.03
☐ 26 Ozzie Virgil	.25	.11	.03
☐ 27 John Wockenfuss	.25	.11	.03
☐ 28 Luis Aguayo	.25	.11	.03
☐ 29 Kiko Garcia	.25	.11	.03
☐ 30 Steve Jeltz	.25	.11	.03
☐ 31 John Russell	.25	.11	.03
☐ 32 Juan Samuel	.35	.16	.04
☐ 33 Mike Schmidt	2.00	.90	.25
☐ 34 Tim Corcoran	.25	.11	.03
☐ 35 Greg Gross	.25	.11	.03
☐ 36 Von Hayes	.35	.16	.04
☐ 37 Joe Lefebvre	.25	.11	.03
☐ 38 Garry Maddox	.35	.16	.04
☐ 39 Jeff Stone	.25	.11	.03
☐ 40 Glenn Wilson	.25	.11	.03
☐ 41 Ramon Caraballo and Mike Diaz	.25	.11	.03
☐ 42 Mike Maddux and Rodger Cole	.25	.11	.03
☐ 43 Rick Schu and Chris James	.35	.16	.04
☐ 44 Francisco Melendez and Ken Jackson	.25	.11	.03
☐ 45 Randy Salava and Rocky Childress	.25	.11	.03
☐ 46 Rich Surhoff and Ralph Citarella	.25	.11	.03
☐ 47 Team Photo	.35	.16	.04

1986 Phillies CIGNA

This 16-card set was sponsored by CIGNA Corp. and was given away by the Philadelphia area Fire Departments. Cards measure approximately 2 3/4" by 4 1/8" and feature full color fronts. The card backs are printed in maroon and black on white card stock. Although the uniform numbers are given on the front of the card, the cards are numbered on the back in the order listed below.

	MT	EX-MT	VG
COMPLETE SET (16)	7.00	3.10	.85
COMMON PLAYER (1-16)	.25	.11	.03

	MT	EX-MT	VG
☐ 1 Juan Samuel	.35	.16	.04
☐ 2 Don Carman	.25	.11	.03
☐ 3 Von Hayes	.35	.16	.04
☐ 4 Kent Tekulve	.35	.16	.04
☐ 5 Greg Gross	.25	.11	.03
☐ 6 Shane Rawley	.35	.16	.04
☐ 7 Darren Daulton	2.00	.90	.25
☐ 8 Kevin Gross	.35	.16	.04
☐ 9 Steve Jeltz	.25	.11	.03
☐ 10 Mike Schmidt	3.00	1.35	.40
☐ 11 Steve Bedrosian	.50	.23	.06
☐ 12 Gary Redus	.35	.16	.04
☐ 13 Charles Hudson	.25	.11	.03
☐ 14 John Russell	.25	.11	.03
☐ 15 Fred Toliver	.25	.11	.03
☐ 16 Glenn Wilson	.25	.11	.03

1986 Phillies Tastykake

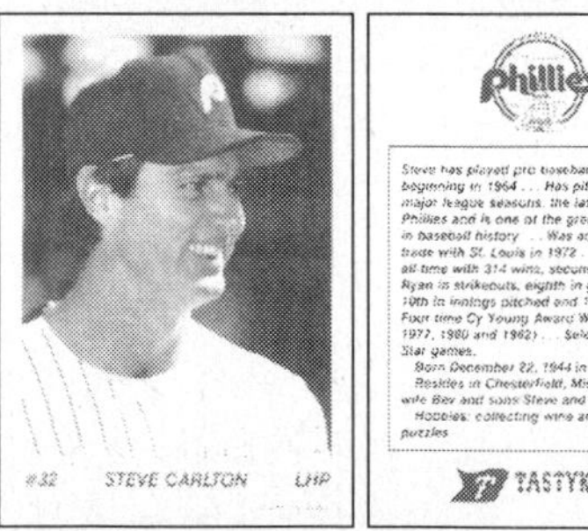

The 1986 Tastykake Philadelphia Phillies set consists of 47 cards, which measure approximately 3 1/2" by 5 1/4". This set features members of the 1986 Philadelphia Phillies. The front of the cards features a full-color photo of the player against white borders while the back has brief biographies. The set has been checklisted for reference below in order by uniform number.

	MT	EX-MT	VG
COMPLETE SET (47)	11.00	4.90	1.40
COMMON PLAYER	.25	.11	.03

☐ 2 Jim Davenport CO	.35	.16	.04
☐ 3 Claude Osteen CO	.25	.11	.03
☐ 4 Lee Elia CO	.25	.11	.03
☐ 5 Mike Ryan CO	.25	.11	.03
☐ 6 John Russell	.25	.11	.03
☐ 7 John Felske MG	.25	.11	.03
☐ 8 Juan Samuel	.35	.16	.04
☐ 9 Von Hayes	.35	.16	.04
☐ 10 Darren Daulton	1.00	.45	.13
☐ 11 Tom Foley	.25	.11	.03
☐ 12 Glenn Wilson	.25	.11	.03
☐ 14 Jeff Stone	.25	.11	.03
☐ 15 Rick Schu	.25	.11	.03
☐ 16 Luis Aguayo	.25	.11	.03
☐ 20 Mike Schmidt	2.00	.90	.25
☐ 21 Greg Gross	.25	.11	.03
☐ 22 Gary Redus	.35	.16	.04
☐ 23 Joe Lefebvre	.25	.11	.03
☐ 24 Milt Thompson	.35	.16	.04
☐ 25 Del Unser CO	.25	.11	.03
☐ 26 Chris James	.35	.16	.04
☐ 27 Kent Tekulve	.35	.16	.04
☐ 28 Shane Rawley	.25	.11	.03
☐ 29 Ronn Reynolds	.25	.11	.03
☐ 30 Steve Jeltz	.25	.11	.03
☐ 31 Garry Maddox	.35	.16	.04
☐ 32 Steve Carlton	1.50	.65	.19
☐ 33 David Shipanoff	.25	.11	.03
☐ 35 Randy Lerch	.25	.11	.03
☐ 36 Robin Roberts	1.00	.45	.13
☐ 39 Dave Rucker	.25	.11	.03
☐ 40 Steve Bedrosian	.35	.16	.04
☐ 41 Tom Hume	.25	.11	.03
☐ 42 Don Carman	.25	.11	.03
☐ 43 Fred Toliver	.25	.11	.03
☐ 46 Kevin Gross	.35	.16	.04
☐ 47 Larry Andersen	.25	.11	.03
☐ 48 Dave Stewart	1.00	.45	.13
☐ 49 Charles Hudson	.25	.11	.03
☐ 50 Rocky Childress	.25	.11	.03
☐ xx Future Phillies Ramon Caraballo Joe Cipolloni	.25	.11	.03
☐ xx Future Phillies Arturo Gonzalez Mike Maddux	.25	.11	.03
☐ xx Future Phillies Francisco Melendez Ricky Jordan	.35	.16	.04
☐ xx Future Phillies Kevin Ward Randy Day	.25	.11	.03
☐ xx Night to Remember 26-7, June 11, 1985	.35	.16	.04
☐ xx Pennant Winning Team 1915 Phillies	.35	.16	.04
☐ xx Pennant Winning Team 1950 Phillies	.35	.16	.04
☐ xx Pennant Winning Team 1980 Phillies	.35	.16	.04
☐ xx Pennant Winning Team 1983 Phillies	.35	.16	.04

1987 Phillies Champion

This four-card set which measured approximately 3" by 4 3/4" (with scratch-off tab) is unusual in that there is no way to determine the player's identity other than knowing and recognizing whose photo it is. The top part of the card has a color photo of the player surrounded in the upper left hand corner with a Champion spark plug logo. The Philadelphia Phillies logo is in the upper right hand part of the card. A Pep Boys ad is in the lower left hand corner of the photo and the WIP Philadelphia Sports Radio promo is in the lower right hand corner of the photo. The set is checklisted alphabetically by subject since the cards are unnumbered.

	MT	EX-MT	VG
COMPLETE SET (4)	18.00	8.00	2.30
COMMON PLAYER (1-4)	1.50	.65	.19
☐ 1 Von Hayes	2.00	.90	.25
☐ 2 Steve Jeltz	1.50	.65	.19
☐ 3 Juan Samuel	2.00	.90	.25
☐ 4 Mike Schmidt	15.00	6.75	1.90

1987 Phillies Tastykake

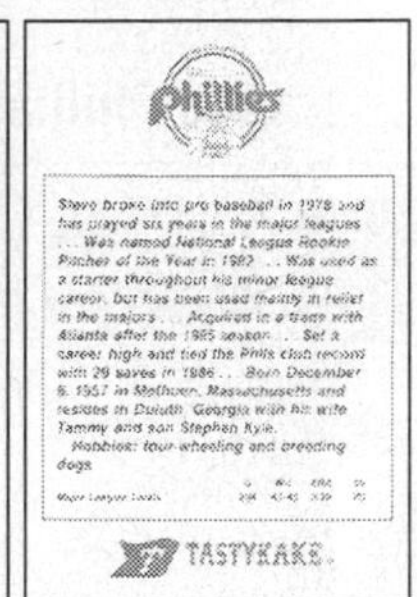

The 1987 Tastykake Philadelphia Phillies set consists of 47 cards which measure approximately 3 1/2" by 5 1/4". The sets again feature full-color photos against a solid white background. There were two number 39s in this set as the Phillies changed personnel during the season, Joe Cowley and Bob Scanlon. For convenience uniform numbers are used below as a basis for numbering and checklisting this set.

	MT	EX-MT	VG
COMPLETE SET (47)	11.00	4.90	1.40
COMMON PLAYER	.25	.11	.03
☐ 6 John Russell	.25	.11	.03
☐ 7 John Felske MG	.25	.11	.03
☐ 8 Juan Samuel	.35	.16	.04
☐ 9 Von Hayes	.35	.16	.04
☐ 10 Darren Daulton	.90	.40	.11
☐ 11 Greg Legg	.25	.11	.03
☐ 12 Glenn Wilson	.25	.11	.03
☐ 13 Lance Parrish	.50	.23	.06
☐ 14 Jeff Stone	.25	.11	.03
☐ 15 Rick Schu	.25	.11	.03
☐ 16 Luis Aguayo	.25	.11	.03
☐ 17 Ron Roenicke	.25	.11	.03
☐ 18 Chris James	.35	.16	.04
☐ 20 Mike Schmidt	2.00	.90	.25
☐ 21 Greg Gross	.25	.11	.03
☐ 23 Joe Cipolloni	.25	.11	.03
☐ 24 Milt Thompson	.35	.16	.04
☐ 27 Kent Tekulve	.35	.16	.04
☐ 28 Shane Rawley	.25	.11	.03
☐ 29 Ronn Reynolds	.25	.11	.03
☐ 30 Steve Jeltz	.25	.11	.03
☐ 33 Mike Jackson	.50	.23	.06
☐ 34 Mike Easler	.25	.11	.03
☐ 35 Dan Schatzeder	.25	.11	.03
☐ 37 Ken Howell	.25	.11	.03
☐ 38 Jim Olander	.25	.11	.03
☐ 39A Joe Cowley	.25	.11	.03
☐ 39B Bob Scanlan	.35	.16	.04
☐ 40 Steve Bedrosian	.35	.16	.04
☐ 41 Tom Hume	.25	.11	.03
☐ 42 Don Carman	.25	.11	.03

☐ 43	Freddie Toliver	.25	.11	.03
☐ 44	Mike Maddux	.25	.11	.03
☐ 45	Greg Jelks	.25	.11	.03
☐ 46	Kevin Gross	.35	.16	.04
☐ 47	Bruce Ruffin	.25	.11	.03
☐ 48	Marvin Freeman	.25	.11	.03
☐ 49	Len Watts	.25	.11	.03
☐ 50	Tom Newell	.35	.16	.04
☐ 51	Ken Jackson	.25	.11	.03
☐ 52	Todd Frohwirth	.25	.11	.03
☐ 58	Doug Bair	.25	.11	.03
☐ xx	Phillie Phanatic (Team mascot)	.35	.16	.04
☐ xx	Team Photo	.35	.16	.04
☐ xx	Shawn Barton and Rick Lundblade	.25	.11	.03
☐ xx	Jeff Kaye and Darren Loy	.25	.11	.03
☐ xx	Coaches Card Claude Osteen CO Del Unser CO Jim Davenport CO Mike Ryan CO Lee Elia CO	.25	.11	.03

1988 Phillies Tastykake

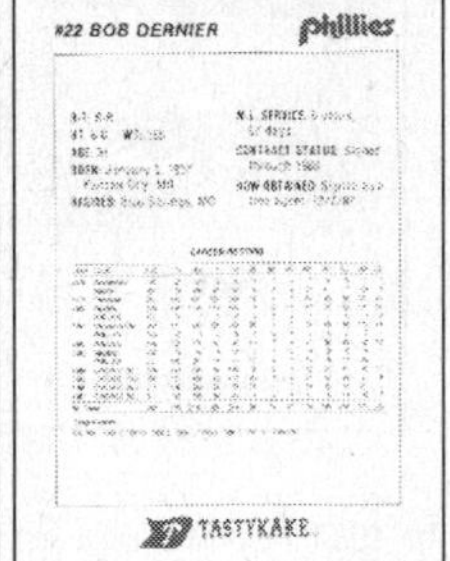

The 1988 Tastykake Philadelphia Phillies set is a 30-card set measuring approximately 4 7/8" by 6 1/4". This set is listed below alphabetically by player. The cards have a full-color photo front and complete player history on the back. There was also a nine-card update set issued later in the year which included a Ricky Jordan card; the update cards are numbered as 31-39 and are blank backed.

		MT	EX-MT	VG
	COMPLETE SET (39)	10.00	4.50	1.25
	COMMON PLAYER (1-30)	.25	.11	.03
	COMMON PLAYER (31-39)	.35	.16	.04
☐ 1	Luis Aguayo	.25	.11	.03
☐ 2	Bill Almon	.25	.11	.03
☐ 3	Steve Bedrosian	.35	.16	.04
☐ 4	Phil Bradley	.35	.16	.04
☐ 5	Jeff Calhoun	.25	.11	.03
☐ 6	Don Carman	.25	.11	.03
☐ 7	Darren Daulton	.75	.35	.09
☐ 8	Bob Dernier	.25	.11	.03
☐ 9A	Lee Elia MG (Vertical format)	.35	.16	.04
☐ 9B	Lee Elia MG (Horizontal format)	.35	.16	.04
☐ 10	Todd Frohwirth	.25	.11	.03
☐ 11	Greg Gross	.25	.11	.03
☐ 12	Kevin Gross	.35	.16	.04
☐ 13	Von Hayes	.35	.16	.04
☐ 14	Chris James	.35	.16	.04
☐ 15	Steve Jeltz	.25	.11	.03
☐ 16	Mike Maddux	.25	.11	.03
☐ 17	Dave Palmer	.35	.16	.04
☐ 18	Lance Parrish	.45	.20	.06
☐ 19	Shane Rawley	.25	.11	.03
☐ 20	Wally Ritchie	.25	.11	.03
☐ 21	Bruce Ruffin	.25	.11	.03
☐ 22	Juan Samuel	.35	.16	.04
☐ 23	Mike Schmidt	1.50	.65	.19
☐ 24	Kent Tekulve	.35	.16	.04
☐ 25	Milt Thompson	.35	.16	.04
☐ 26	Mike Young	.25	.11	.03
☐ 27	Phillies Prospects Tom Barrett Brad Brink Steve DeAngelis Ron Jones Keith Miller Brad Moore Howard Nichols Shane Turner	.35	.16	.04
☐ 28	Team Card	.35	.16	.04
☐ 29	Phillies Coaches Claude Osteen Del Unser John Vuckovich Dave Bristol Tony Taylor Mike Ryan	.25	.11	.03
☐ 30	Phillie Phanatic (Mascot)	.35	.16	.04
☐ 31	Larry Bowa CO	.45	.20	.06
☐ 32	Lee Elia CO	.35	.16	.04
☐ 33	Jackie Gutierrez	.35	.16	.04
☐ 34	Greg A. Harris	.35	.16	.04
☐ 35	Ricky Jordan	.45	.20	.06
☐ 36	Keith Miller	.45	.20	.06
☐ 37	John Russell	.35	.16	.04
☐ 38	John Vuckovich CO	.35	.16	.04
☐ 39	Phillies Announcers Garry Maddox Richie Ashburn Chris Wheeler Harry Kalas Andy Musser	.45	.20	.06

1989 Phillies Tastykake

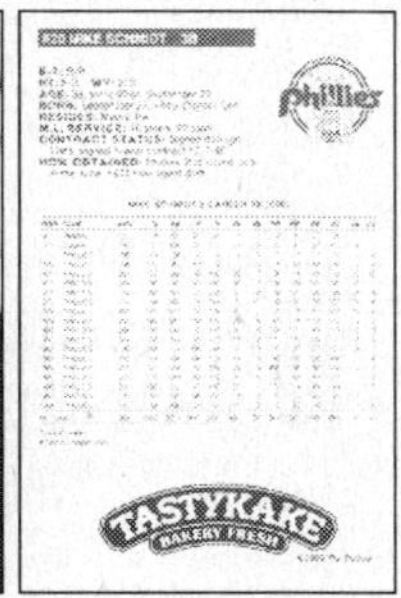

This set was a 36-card set of Philadelphia Phillies measuring approximately 4 1/8" by 6" featuring full-color fronts with complete biographical information and career stats on the back. The set is checklisted alphabetically in the list below. The set was a give away to fans attending the Phillies Tastykake Photocard Night on May 13, 1989 and was later available from a mail-away offer. There was also a nine-player extended set issued later during the 1989 season; the extended players are numbered below in alphabetical order, numbers 37-45. Chris James' card lists him as uniform number 26, but his number is 18 as 26 was Ron Jones' number.

		MT	EX-MT	VG
	COMPLETE SET (45)	12.00	5.50	1.50
	COMMON PLAYER (1-36)	.25	.11	.03
	COMMON PLAYER (37-45)	.35	.16	.04
☐ 1	Steve Bedrosian	.35	.16	.04
☐ 2	Larry Bowa CO	.35	.16	.04
☐ 3	Don Carman	.25	.11	.03
☐ 4	Darren Daulton	.75	.35	.09
☐ 5	Bob Dernier	.25	.11	.03
☐ 6	Curt Ford	.25	.11	.03
☐ 7	Todd Frohwirth	.25	.11	.03
☐ 8	Greg A. Harris	.25	.11	.03
☐ 9	Von Hayes	.35	.16	.04

	MT	EX-MT	VG
☐ 10 Tom Herr	.35	.16	.04
☐ 11 Ken Howell	.35	.16	.04
☐ 12 Chris James UER (Wrong uniform number on card)	.35	.16	.04
☐ 13 Steve Jeltz	.25	.11	.03
☐ 14 Ron Jones	.25	.11	.03
☐ 15 Ricky Jordan	.35	.16	.04
☐ 16 Darold Knowles CO	.25	.11	.03
☐ 17 Steve Lake	.25	.11	.03
☐ 18 Nick Levya MG	.25	.11	.03
☐ 19 Mike Maddux	.25	.11	.03
☐ 20 Alex Madrid	.25	.11	.03
☐ 21 Larry McWilliams	.25	.11	.03
☐ 22 Denis Menke CO	.25	.11	.03
☐ 23 Dwayne Murphy	.25	.11	.03
☐ 24 Tom Nieto	.25	.11	.03
☐ 25 Randy O'Neal	.25	.11	.03
☐ 26 Steve Ontiveros	.25	.11	.03
☐ 27 Jeff Parrett	.50	.23	.06
☐ 28 Bruce Ruffin	.25	.11	.03
☐ 29 Mike Ryal	.25	.11	.03
☐ 30 Mike Ryan CO	.25	.11	.03
☐ 31 Juan Samuel	.35	.16	.04
☐ 32 Mike Schmidt	1.50	.65	.19
☐ 33 Tony Taylor CO	.25	.11	.03
☐ 34 Dickie Thon	.35	.16	.04
☐ 35 John Vuckovich CO	.25	.11	.03
☐ 36 Floyd Youmans	.25	.11	.03
☐ 37 Jim Adduci	.35	.16	.04
☐ 38 Eric Bullock	.35	.16	.04
☐ 39 Dennis Cook	.50	.23	.06
☐ 40 Len Dykstra	.60	.25	.08
☐ 41 Charlie Hayes	.75	.35	.09
☐ 42 John Kruk	.75	.35	.09
☐ 43 Roger McDowell	.50	.23	.06
☐ 44 Terry Mulholland	.75	.35	.09
☐ 45 Randy Ready	.35	.16	.04

1990 Phillies Tastykake

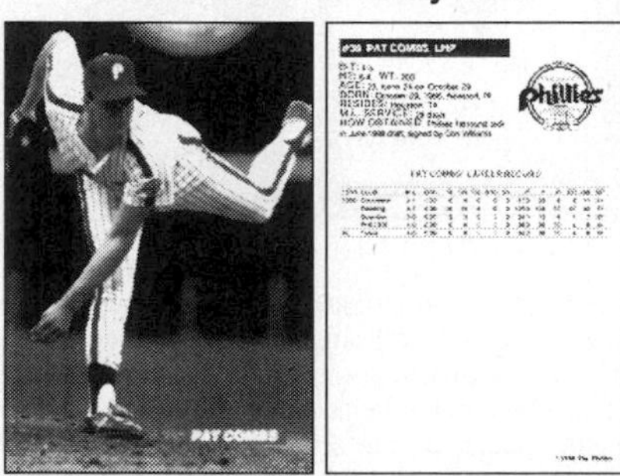

The 1990 Tastykake Philadelphia Phillies set is a 36-card set measuring approximately 4 1/8" by 6" which features players, coaches and manager, four players who have had their uniform numbers retired, broadcasters, and even the Phillies Mascot. The set is checklisted alphabetically, with complete biography and complete stats on the back.

	MT	EX-MT	VG
COMPLETE SET (36)	9.00	4.00	1.15
COMMON PLAYER (1-36)	.25	.11	.03
☐ 1 Darrel Akerfelds	.35	.16	.04
☐ 2 Rod Booker	.25	.11	.03
☐ 3 Sil Campusano	.35	.16	.04
☐ 4 Don Carman	.25	.11	.03
☐ 5 Pat Combs	.50	.23	.06
☐ 6 Dennis Cook	.35	.16	.04
☐ 7 Darren Daulton	.75	.35	.09
☐ 8 Len Dykstra	.60	.25	.08
☐ 9 Curt Ford	.25	.11	.03
☐ 10 Jason Grimsley	.35	.16	.04
☐ 11 Charlie Hayes	.50	.23	.06
☐ 12 Von Hayes	.35	.16	.04
☐ 13 Tommy Herr	.35	.16	.04
☐ 14 Dave Hollins	1.00	.45	.13
☐ 15 Ken Howell	.25	.11	.03
☐ 16 Ron Jones	.25	.11	.03
☐ 17 Ricky Jordan	.35	.16	.04
☐ 18 John Kruk	.60	.25	.08
☐ 19 Steve Lake	.25	.11	.03
☐ 20 Nick Levya MG	.25	.11	.03
☐ 21 Carmelo Martinez	.25	.11	.03
☐ 22 Roger McDowell	.35	.16	.04
☐ 23 Chuck McElroy	.35	.16	.04
☐ 24 Terry Mulholland	.50	.23	.06
☐ 25 Jeff Parrett	.35	.16	.04
☐ 26 Randy Ready	.25	.11	.03
☐ 27 Bruce Ruffin	.25	.11	.03
☐ 28 Dickie Thon	.35	.16	.04
☐ 29 Richie Ashburn	.60	.25	.08
☐ 30 Steve Carlton	1.00	.45	.13
☐ 31 Robin Roberts	.75	.35	.09
☐ 32 Mike Schmidt	1.50	.65	.19
☐ 33 Phillie Phanatic (Mascot)	.35	.16	.04
☐ 34 Phillie Coaches: Denis Menke, Mike Ryan, John Vuckovich, Hal Lanier, Darold Knowles, Larry Bowa	.25	.11	.03
☐ 35 Phillies Broadcasters: Chris Wheeler, Andy Musser, Harry Kalas, Richie Ashburn	.35	.16	.04
☐ 36 Phillies Broadcasters: Mike Schmidt, Jim Barniak, Garry Maddox	.50	.23	.06

1991 Phillies Medford

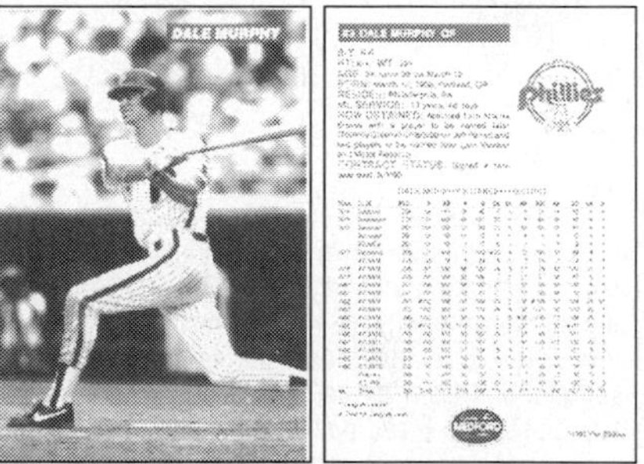

This 35-card set was sponsored by Medford (rather than by Tastykake as in past years), and its company logo is found on the bottom of the reverse. The oversized cards measure approximately 4 1/8" by 6" and feature borderless glossy color action player photos on the obverse. The player's name is given in a red bar at either the top or bottom of the picture. The backs are printed in red and black on white and present biographical as well as statistical information. The cards are unnumbered and checklisted below in alphabetical order.

	MT	EX-MT	VG
COMPLETE SET (35)	9.00	4.00	1.15
COMMON PLAYER (1-35)	.25	.11	.03
☐ 1 Darrel Akerfelds	.25	.11	.03
☐ 2 Andy Ashby	.35	.16	.04
☐ 3 Wally Backman	.25	.11	.03
☐ 4 Joe Boever	.25	.11	.03
☐ 5 Rod Booker	.25	.11	.03
☐ 6 Larry Bowa CO	.35	.16	.04
☐ 7 Sil Campusano	.25	.11	.03
☐ 8 Wes Chamberlain	.75	.35	.09
☐ 9 Pat Combs	.35	.16	.04
☐ 10 Danny Cox	.25	.11	.03
☐ 11 Darren Daulton	.75	.35	.09
☐ 12 Jose DeJesus	.25	.11	.03
☐ 13 Len Dykstra	.50	.23	.06
☐ 14 Darrin Fletcher	.25	.11	.03

		MT	EX-MT	VG
☐ 15	Tommy Greene	.50	.23	.06
☐ 16	Jason Grimsley	.35	.16	.04
☐ 17	Charlie Hayes	.50	.23	.06
☐ 18	Von Hayes	.35	.16	.04
☐ 19	Dave Hollins	.75	.35	.09
☐ 20	Ken Howell	.25	.11	.03
☐ 21	Ricky Jordan	.35	.16	.04
☐ 22	John Kruk	.50	.23	.06
☐ 23	Steve Lake	.25	.11	.03
☐ 24	Hal Lanier CO	.25	.11	.03
☐ 25	Tim Mauser	.35	.16	.04
☐ 26	Roger McDowell	.35	.16	.04
☐ 27	Denis Menke CO	.25	.11	.03
☐ 28	Mickey Morandini	.50	.23	.06
☐ 29	John Morris	.25	.11	.03
☐ 30	Terry Mulholland	.50	.23	.06
☐ 31	Dale Murphy	.75	.35	.09
☐ 32	Johnny Podres CO	.35	.16	.04
☐ 33	Randy Ready	.25	.11	.03
☐ 34	Dickie Thon	.35	.16	.04
☐ 35	John Vukovich CO	.25	.11	.03

1992 Phillies Medford

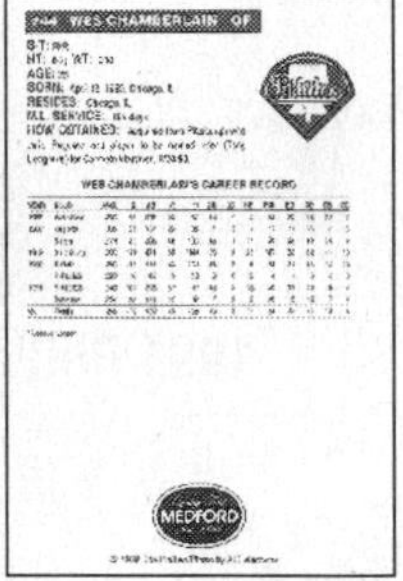

For the second consecutive year, Medford has sponsored a Phillies set, consisting of a first series of 36 cards measuring approximately 4 1/8" by 6" and an extended update series of another ten cards of the same size. The players featured in the update series were mostly mid-season call-ups from the minor leagues. The card fronts feature glossy full-bleed posed color player photos, shot against a studio background. The player's name appears in white lettering in a short red stripe. In black and red print on white, the backs present basic biographical information, career statistics, and the team logo. The sponsor logo at the bottom rounds out the back. The cards are unnumbered and checklisted below alphabetically within series, with the nonplayer cards listed at the end.

	MT	EX-MT	VG
COMPLETE SET (46)	10.00	4.50	1.25
COMMON PLAYER (1-36)	.25	.11	.03
COMMON PLAYER (37-46)	.35	.16	.04

		MT	EX-MT	VG
☐ 1	Kyle Abbott	.35	.16	.04
☐ 2	Ruben Amaro	.35	.16	.04
☐ 3	Andy Ashby	.35	.16	.04
☐ 4	Wally Backman	.25	.11	.03
☐ 5	Kim Batiste	.35	.16	.04
☐ 6	Larry Bowa CO	.35	.16	.04
☐ 7	Cliff Brantley	.35	.16	.04
☐ 8	Wes Chamberlain	.50	.23	.06
☐ 9	Danny Cox	.25	.11	.03
☐ 10	Darren Daulton	.60	.25	.08
☐ 11	Mariano Duncan	.35	.16	.04
☐ 12	Len Dykstra	.50	.23	.06
☐ 13	Jim Fregosi MG	.35	.16	.04
☐ 14	Tommy Greene	.35	.16	.04
☐ 15	Dave Hollins	.60	.25	.08
☐ 16	Barry Jones	.25	.11	.03
☐ 17	John Kruk	.50	.23	.06
☐ 18	Steve Lake	.25	.11	.03
☐ 19	Jim Lindeman	.25	.11	.03
☐ 20	Denis Menke CO	.25	.11	.03
☐ 21	Mickey Morandini	.50	.23	.06
☐ 22	Terry Mulholland	.35	.16	.04
☐ 23	Dale Murphy	.60	.25	.08
☐ 24	Johnny Podres CO	.35	.16	.04
☐ 25	Wally Ritchie	.35	.16	.04
☐ 26	Mel Roberts CO	.25	.11	.03
☐ 27	Mike Ryan CO	.25	.11	.03
☐ 28	Curt Schilling	.50	.23	.06
☐ 29	Steve Searcy	.25	.11	.03
☐ 30	Dale Sveum	.25	.11	.03
☐ 31	John Vukovich Dugout Assistant	.25	.11	.03
☐ 32	Mitch Williams	.35	.16	.04
☐ 33	Phillie Phanatic Mascot	.35	.16	.04
☐ 34	Team Photo	.35	.16	.04
☐ 35	Veterans Stadium	.25	.11	.03
☐ 36	Uniforms Through The Years	.35	.16	.04
☐ 37	Bob Ayrault	.35	.16	.04
☐ 38	Brad Brink	.35	.16	.04
☐ 39	Pat Combs	.50	.23	.06
☐ 40	Jeff Grotewold	.35	.16	.04
☐ 41	Mike Hartley	.35	.16	.04
☐ 42	Ricky Jordan	.50	.23	.06
☐ 43	Tom Marsh	.50	.23	.06
☐ 44	Terry Mulholland	.50	.23	.06
☐ 45	Ben Rivera	.75	.35	.09
☐ 46	Don Robinson	.35	.16	.04

1992 Pinnacle

The 1992 Score Pinnacle baseball set consists of two series each with 310 cards measuring the standard size (2 1/2" by 3 1/2"). Series I count goods pack had 16 cards per pack, while the cello pack featured 27 cards. Two 12-card bonus subsets, displaying the artwork of Chris Greco, were randomly inserted in series I and II count good packs. The fronts feature glossy color player photos, on a black background accented by thin white borders. On a black background, the horizontally oriented backs carry a close-up portrait, statistics (1991 and career), and an in-depth player profile. An anti-counterfeit device appears in the bottom border of each card back. Special subsets featured include '92 Rookie Prospects (52, 55, 168, 247-261, 263-280), Idols (281-286), Sidelines (287-294), Draft Picks (295-304), Shades (305-310), Idols (584-591), Sidelines (592-596), Shades (601-605), Grips (606-612), and Technicians (614-620). The cards are numbered on the back. Key Rookie Cards in the set include Cliff Floyd, Tyler Green, Pat Listach, Manny Ramirez, Al Shirley, and Bob Zupcic.

	MT	EX-MT	VG
COMPLETE SET (620)	60.00	27.00	7.50
COMPLETE SERIES 1 (310)	35.00	16.00	4.40
COMPLETE SERIES 2 (310)	25.00	11.50	3.10
COMMON PLAYER (1-310)	.08	.04	.01
COMMON PLAYER (311-620)	.08	.04	.01

		MT	EX-MT	VG
☐ 1	Frank Thomas	3.00	1.35	.40
☐ 2	Benito Santiago	.12	.05	.02
☐ 3	Carlos Baerga	.50	.23	.06
☐ 4	Cecil Fielder	.30	.14	.04
☐ 5	Barry Larkin	.20	.09	.03

☐ 6 Ozzie Smith	.20	.09	.03
☐ 7 Willie McGee	.10	.04	.01
☐ 8 Paul Molitor	.12	.05	.02
☐ 9 Andy Van Slyke	.12	.05	.02
☐ 10 Ryne Sandberg	.60	.25	.08
☐ 11 Kevin Seitzer	.10	.04	.01
☐ 12 Len Dykstra	.10	.04	.01
☐ 13 Edgar Martinez	.10	.04	.01
☐ 14 Ruben Sierra	.40	.18	.05
☐ 15 Howard Johnson	.10	.04	.01
☐ 16 Dave Henderson	.08	.04	.01
☐ 17 Devon White	.10	.04	.01
☐ 18 Terry Pendleton	.12	.05	.02
☐ 19 Steve Finley	.10	.04	.01
☐ 20 Kirby Puckett	.60	.25	.08
☐ 21 Orel Hershiser	.12	.05	.02
☐ 22 Hal Morris	.10	.04	.01
☐ 23 Don Mattingly	.30	.14	.04
☐ 24 Delino DeShields	.25	.11	.03
☐ 25 Dennis Eckersley	.15	.07	.02
☐ 26 Ellis Burks	.10	.04	.01
☐ 27 Jay Buhner	.10	.04	.01
☐ 28 Matt Williams	.12	.05	.02
☐ 29 Lou Whitaker	.12	.05	.02
☐ 30 Alex Fernandez	.10	.04	.01
☐ 31 Albert Belle	.30	.14	.04
☐ 32 Todd Zeile	.08	.04	.01
☐ 33 Tony Pena	.08	.04	.01
☐ 34 Jay Bell	.08	.04	.01
☐ 35 Rafael Palmeiro	.12	.05	.02
☐ 36 Wes Chamberlain	.12	.05	.02
☐ 37 George Bell	.10	.04	.01
☐ 38 Robin Yount	.25	.11	.03
☐ 39 Vince Coleman	.10	.04	.01
☐ 40 Bruce Hurst	.10	.04	.01
☐ 41 Harold Baines	.10	.04	.01
☐ 42 Chuck Finley	.08	.04	.01
☐ 43 Ken Caminiti	.10	.04	.01
☐ 44 Ben McDonald	.15	.07	.02
☐ 45 Roberto Alomar	.50	.23	.06
☐ 46 Chili Davis	.10	.04	.01
☐ 47 Bill Doran	.08	.04	.01
☐ 48 Jerald Clark	.08	.04	.01
☐ 49 Jose Lind	.08	.04	.01
☐ 50 Nolan Ryan	1.50	.65	.19
☐ 51 Phil Plantier	.30	.14	.04
☐ 52 Gary DiSarcina	.10	.04	.01
☐ 53 Kevin Bass	.08	.04	.01
☐ 54 Pat Kelly	.12	.05	.02
☐ 55 Mark Wohlers	.20	.09	.03
☐ 56 Walt Weiss	.08	.04	.01
☐ 57 Lenny Harris	.08	.04	.01
☐ 58 Ivan Calderon	.08	.04	.01
☐ 59 Harold Reynolds	.08	.04	.01
☐ 60 George Brett	.25	.11	.03
☐ 61 Gregg Olson	.10	.04	.01
☐ 62 Orlando Merced	.12	.05	.02
☐ 63 Steve Decker	.08	.04	.01
☐ 64 John Franco	.10	.04	.01
☐ 65 Greg Maddux	.15	.07	.02
☐ 66 Alex Cole	.08	.04	.01
☐ 67 Dave Hollins	.25	.11	.03
☐ 68 Kent Hrbek	.10	.04	.01
☐ 69 Tom Pagnozzi	.08	.04	.01
☐ 70 Jeff Bagwell	.75	.35	.09
☐ 71 Jim Gantner	.08	.04	.01
☐ 72 Matt Nokes	.08	.04	.01
☐ 73 Brian Harper	.08	.04	.01
☐ 74 Andy Benes	.12	.05	.02
☐ 75 Tom Glavine	.30	.14	.04
☐ 76 Terry Steinbach	.10	.04	.01
☐ 77 Dennis Martinez	.10	.04	.01
☐ 78 John Olerud	.25	.11	.03
☐ 79 Ozzie Guillen	.08	.04	.01
☐ 80 Darryl Strawberry	.30	.14	.04
☐ 81 Gary Gaetti	.08	.04	.01
☐ 82 Dave Righetti	.08	.04	.01
☐ 83 Chris Hoiles	.12	.05	.02
☐ 84 Andujar Cedeno	.12	.05	.02
☐ 85 Jack Clark	.10	.04	.01
☐ 86 David Howard	.08	.04	.01
☐ 87 Bill Gullickson	.08	.04	.01
☐ 88 Bernard Gilkey	.12	.05	.02
☐ 89 Kevin Elster	.08	.04	.01
☐ 90 Kevin Maas	.10	.04	.01
☐ 91 Mark Lewis	.08	.04	.01
☐ 92 Greg Vaughn	.10	.04	.01
☐ 93 Bret Barberie	.12	.05	.02
☐ 94 Dave Smith	.08	.04	.01
☐ 95 Roger Clemens	.60	.25	.08
☐ 96 Doug Drabek	.10	.04	.01
☐ 97 Omar Vizquel	.08	.04	.01
☐ 98 Jose Guzman	.08	.04	.01
☐ 99 Juan Samuel	.08	.04	.01
☐ 100 Dave Justice	.75	.35	.09
☐ 101 Tom Browning	.08	.04	.01
☐ 102 Mark Gubicza	.08	.04	.01
☐ 103 Mickey Morandini	.10	.04	.01
☐ 104 Ed Whitson	.08	.04	.01
☐ 105 Lance Parrish	.10	.04	.01
☐ 106 Scott Erickson	.15	.07	.02
☐ 107 Jack McDowell	.12	.05	.02
☐ 108 Dave Stieb	.08	.04	.01
☐ 109 Mike Moore	.08	.04	.01
☐ 110 Travis Fryman	1.00	.45	.13
☐ 111 Dwight Gooden	.12	.05	.02
☐ 112 Fred McGriff	.30	.14	.04
☐ 113 Alan Trammell	.12	.05	.02
☐ 114 Roberto Kelly	.12	.05	.02
☐ 115 Andre Dawson	.20	.09	.03
☐ 116 Bill Landrum	.08	.04	.01
☐ 117 Brian McRae	.12	.05	.02
☐ 118 B.J. Surhoff	.08	.04	.01
☐ 119 Chuck Knoblauch	.50	.23	.06
☐ 120 Steve Olin	.08	.04	.01
☐ 121 Robin Ventura	.50	.23	.06
☐ 122 Will Clark	.50	.23	.06
☐ 123 Tino Martinez	.12	.05	.02
☐ 124 Dale Murphy	.12	.05	.02
☐ 125 Pete O'Brien	.08	.04	.01
☐ 126 Ray Lankford	.40	.18	.05
☐ 127 Juan Gonzalez	1.25	.55	.16
☐ 128 Ron Gant	.20	.09	.03
☐ 129 Marquis Grissom	.25	.11	.03
☐ 130 Jose Canseco	.50	.23	.06
☐ 131 Mike Greenwell	.12	.05	.02
☐ 132 Mark Langston	.10	.04	.01
☐ 133 Brett Butler	.10	.04	.01
☐ 134 Kelly Gruber	.10	.04	.01
☐ 135 Chris Sabo	.10	.04	.01
☐ 136 Mark Grace	.12	.05	.02
☐ 137 Tony Fernandez	.10	.04	.01
☐ 138 Glenn Davis	.10	.04	.01
☐ 139 Pedro Munoz	.12	.05	.02
☐ 140 Craig Biggio	.10	.04	.01
☐ 141 Pete Schourek	.10	.04	.01
☐ 142 Mike Boddicker	.08	.04	.01
☐ 143 Robby Thompson	.08	.04	.01
☐ 144 Mel Hall	.08	.04	.01
☐ 145 Bryan Harvey	.08	.04	.01
☐ 146 Mike LaValliere	.08	.04	.01
☐ 147 John Kruk	.10	.04	.01
☐ 148 Joe Carter	.30	.14	.04
☐ 149 Greg Olson	.08	.04	.01
☐ 150 Julio Franco	.10	.04	.01
☐ 151 Darryl Hamilton	.10	.04	.01
☐ 152 Felix Fermin	.08	.04	.01
☐ 153 Jose Offerman	.10	.04	.01
☐ 154 Paul O'Neill	.10	.04	.01
☐ 155 Tommy Greene	.08	.04	.01
☐ 156 Ivan Rodriguez	1.00	.45	.13
☐ 157 Dave Stewart	.10	.04	.01
☐ 158 Jeff Reardon	.12	.05	.02
☐ 159 Felix Jose	.10	.04	.01
☐ 160 Doug Dascenzo	.08	.04	.01
☐ 161 Tim Wallach	.10	.04	.01
☐ 162 Dan Plesac	.08	.04	.01
☐ 163 Luis Gonzalez	.12	.05	.02
☐ 164 Mike Henneman	.08	.04	.01
☐ 165 Mike Devereaux	.10	.04	.01
☐ 166 Luis Polonia	.10	.04	.01
☐ 167 Mike Sharperson	.08	.04	.01
☐ 168 Chris Donnels	.08	.04	.01
☐ 169 Greg W. Harris	.08	.04	.01
☐ 170 Deion Sanders	.40	.18	.05
☐ 171 Mike Schooler	.08	.04	.01
☐ 172 Jose DeJesus	.08	.04	.01
☐ 173 Jeff Montgomery	.08	.04	.01
☐ 174 Milt Cuyler	.08	.04	.01
☐ 175 Wade Boggs	.30	.14	.04
☐ 176 Kevin Tapani	.10	.04	.01
☐ 177 Bill Spiers	.08	.04	.01
☐ 178 Tim Raines	.12	.05	.02
☐ 179 Randy Milligan	.08	.04	.01
☐ 180 Rob Dibble	.10	.04	.01
☐ 181 Kirt Manwaring	.08	.04	.01
☐ 182 Pascual Perez	.08	.04	.01
☐ 183 Juan Guzman	1.75	.80	.22
☐ 184 John Smiley	.10	.04	.01
☐ 185 David Segui	.08	.04	.01
☐ 186 Omar Olivares	.08	.04	.01
☐ 187 Joe Slusarski	.08	.04	.01
☐ 188 Erik Hanson	.08	.04	.01
☐ 189 Mark Portugal	.08	.04	.01
☐ 190 Walt Terrell	.08	.04	.01
☐ 191 John Smoltz	.20	.09	.03

☐ 192 Wilson Alvarez .08 .04 .01
☐ 193 Jimmy Key .08 .04 .01
☐ 194 Larry Walker .35 .16 .04
☐ 195 Lee Smith .10 .04 .01
☐ 196 Pete Harnisch .10 .04 .01
☐ 197 Mike Harkey .10 .04 .01
☐ 198 Frank Tanana .08 .04 .01
☐ 199 Terry Mulholland .08 .04 .01
☐ 200 Cal Ripken .75 .35 .09
☐ 201 Dave Magadan .10 .04 .01
☐ 202 Bud Black .08 .04 .01
☐ 203 Terry Shumpert .08 .04 .01
☐ 204 Mike Mussina 1.75 .80 .22
☐ 205 Mo Vaughn .12 .05 .02
☐ 206 Steve Farr .08 .04 .01
☐ 207 Darrin Jackson .10 .04 .01
☐ 208 Jerry Browne .08 .04 .01
☐ 209 Jeff Russell .08 .04 .01
☐ 210 Mike Scioscia .08 .04 .01
☐ 211 Rick Aguilera .10 .04 .01
☐ 212 Jaime Navarro .10 .04 .01
☐ 213 Randy Tomlin .12 .05 .02
☐ 214 Bobby Thigpen .08 .04 .01
☐ 215 Mark Gardner .08 .04 .01
☐ 216 Norm Charlton .10 .04 .01
☐ 217 Mark McGwire .50 .23 .06
☐ 218 Skeeter Barnes .08 .04 .01
☐ 219 Bob Tewksbury .10 .04 .01
☐ 220 Junior Felix .08 .04 .01
☐ 221 Sam Horn .08 .04 .01
☐ 222 Jody Reed .08 .04 .01
☐ 223 Luis Sojo .08 .04 .01
☐ 224 Jerome Walton .08 .04 .01
☐ 225 Darryl Kile .10 .04 .01
☐ 226 Mickey Tettleton .10 .04 .01
☐ 227 Dan Pasqua .08 .04 .01
☐ 228 Jim Gott .08 .04 .01
☐ 229 Bernie Williams .25 .11 .03
☐ 230 Shane Mack .10 .04 .01
☐ 231 Steve Avery .50 .23 .06
☐ 232 Dave Valle .08 .04 .01
☐ 233 Mark Leonard .08 .04 .01
☐ 234 Spike Owen .08 .04 .01
☐ 235 Gary Sheffield .75 .35 .09
☐ 236 Steve Chitren .08 .04 .01
☐ 237 Zane Smith .08 .04 .01
☐ 238 Tom Gordon .08 .04 .01
☐ 239 Jose Oquendo .08 .04 .01
☐ 240 Todd Stottlemyre .10 .04 .01
☐ 241 Darren Daulton .10 .04 .01
☐ 242 Tim Naehring .10 .04 .01
☐ 243 Tony Phillips .08 .04 .01
☐ 244 Shawon Dunston .10 .04 .01
☐ 245 Manuel Lee .08 .04 .01
☐ 246 Mike Pagliarulo .08 .04 .01
☐ 247 Jim Thome .25 .11 .03
☐ 248 Luis Mercedes .25 .11 .03
☐ 249 Cal Eldred 1.00 .45 .13
☐ 250 Derek Bell .30 .14 .04
☐ 251 Arthur Rhodes .40 .18 .05
☐ 252 Scott Cooper .25 .11 .03
☐ 253 Roberto Hernandez .20 .09 .03
☐ 254 Mo Sanford .15 .07 .02
☐ 255 Scott Servais .08 .04 .01
☐ 256 Eric Karros 1.75 .80 .22
☐ 257 Andy Mota .08 .04 .01
☐ 258 Keith Mitchell .15 .07 .02
☐ 259 Joel Johnston .08 .04 .01
☐ 260 John Wehner .12 .05 .02
☐ 261 Gino Minutelli .08 .04 .01
☐ 262 Greg Gagne .08 .04 .01
☐ 263 Stan Royer .15 .07 .02
☐ 264 Carlos Garcia .20 .09 .03
☐ 265 Andy Ashby .08 .04 .01
☐ 266 Kim Batiste .15 .07 .02
☐ 267 Julio Valera .15 .07 .02
☐ 268 Royce Clayton .40 .18 .05
☐ 269 Gary Scott .10 .04 .01
☐ 270 Kirk Dressendorfer .08 .04 .01
☐ 271 Sean Berry .12 .05 .02
☐ 272 Lance Dickson .12 .05 .02
☐ 273 Rob Maurer .20 .09 .03
☐ 274 Scott Brosius .12 .05 .02
☐ 275 Dave Fleming 1.00 .45 .13
☐ 276 Lenny Webster .08 .04 .01
☐ 277 Mike Humphreys .10 .04 .01
☐ 278 Freddie Benavides .08 .04 .01
☐ 279 Harvey Pulliam .12 .05 .02
☐ 280 Jeff Carter .08 .04 .01
☐ 281 Jim Abbott I .40 .18 .05
☐ 282 Wade Boggs I .20 .09 .03
☐ 283 Ken Griffey Jr. I .75 .35 .09
☐ 284 Wally Joyner I .08 .04 .01
☐ 285 Chuck Knoblauch I .25 .11 .03
☐ 286 Robin Ventura I .30 .14 .04
☐ 287 Robin Yount SI .20 .09 .03
☐ 288 Bob Tewksbury SI .08 .04 .01
☐ 289 Kirby Puckett SI .25 .11 .03
☐ 290 Kenny Lofton SI .40 .18 .05
☐ 291 Jack McDowell SI .12 .05 .02
☐ 292 John Burkett SI .08 .04 .01
☐ 293 Dwight Smith SI .08 .04 .01
☐ 294 Nolan Ryan SI .75 .35 .09
☐ 295 Manny Ramirez DP 1.25 .55 .16
☐ 296 Cliff Floyd DP 1.50 .65 .19
☐ 297 Al Shirley DP .40 .18 .05
☐ 298 Brian Barber DP .40 .18 .05
☐ 299 Jon Farrell DP .20 .09 .03
☐ 300 Scott Ruffcorn DP .50 .23 .06
☐ 301 Tyrone Hill DP .75 .35 .09
☐ 302 Benji Gil DP .40 .18 .05
☐ 303 Tyler Green DP .60 .25 .08
☐ 304 Allen Watson DP .50 .23 .06
☐ 305 Jay Buhner SH .08 .04 .01
☐ 306 Roberto Alomar SH .30 .14 .04
☐ 307 Chuck Knoblauch SH .25 .11 .03
☐ 308 Darryl Strawberry SH .20 .09 .03
☐ 309 Danny Tartabull SH .08 .04 .01
☐ 310 Bobby Bonilla SH .10 .04 .01
☐ 311 Mike Felder .08 .04 .01
☐ 312 Storm Davis .08 .04 .01
☐ 313 Tim Teufel .08 .04 .01
☐ 314 Tom Brunansky .10 .04 .01
☐ 315 Rex Hudler .08 .04 .01
☐ 316 Dave Otto .08 .04 .01
☐ 317 Jeff King .08 .04 .01
☐ 318 Dan Gladden .08 .04 .01
☐ 319 Bill Pecota .08 .04 .01
☐ 320 Franklin Stubbs .08 .04 .01
☐ 321 Gary Carter .10 .04 .01
☐ 322 Melido Perez .10 .04 .01
☐ 323 Eric Davis .12 .05 .02
☐ 324 Greg Myers .08 .04 .01
☐ 325 Pete Incaviglia .08 .04 .01
☐ 326 Von Hayes .08 .04 .01
☐ 327 Greg Swindell .10 .04 .01
☐ 328 Steve Sax .10 .04 .01
☐ 329 Chuck McElroy .08 .04 .01
☐ 330 Gregg Jefferies .10 .04 .01
☐ 331 Joe Oliver .08 .04 .01
☐ 332 Paul Faries .08 .04 .01
☐ 333 David West .08 .04 .01
☐ 334 Craig Grebeck .08 .04 .01
☐ 335 Chris Hammond .08 .04 .01
☐ 336 Billy Ripken .08 .04 .01
☐ 337 Scott Sanderson .08 .04 .01
☐ 338 Dick Schofield .08 .04 .01
☐ 339 Bob Milacki .08 .04 .01
☐ 340 Kevin Reimer .10 .04 .01
☐ 341 Jose DeLeon .08 .04 .01
☐ 342 Henry Cotto .08 .04 .01
☐ 343 Daryl Boston .08 .04 .01
☐ 344 Kevin Gross .08 .04 .01
☐ 345 Milt Thompson .08 .04 .01
☐ 346 Luis Rivera .08 .04 .01
☐ 347 Al Osuna .08 .04 .01
☐ 348 Rob Deer .10 .04 .01
☐ 349 Tim Leary .08 .04 .01
☐ 350 Mike Stanton .08 .04 .01
☐ 351 Dean Palmer .12 .05 .02
☐ 352 Trevor Wilson .08 .04 .01
☐ 353 Mark Eichhorn .08 .04 .01
☐ 354 Scott Aldred .08 .04 .01
☐ 355 Mark Whiten .08 .04 .01
☐ 356 Leo Gomez .20 .09 .03
☐ 357 Rafael Belliard .08 .04 .01
☐ 358 Carlos Quintana .08 .04 .01
☐ 359 Mark Davis .08 .04 .01
☐ 360 Chris Nabholz .10 .04 .01
☐ 361 Carlton Fisk .20 .09 .03
☐ 362 Joe Orsulak .08 .04 .01
☐ 363 Eric Anthony .12 .05 .02
☐ 364 Greg Hibbard .08 .04 .01
☐ 365 Scott Leius .08 .04 .01
☐ 366 Hensley Meulens .08 .04 .01
☐ 367 Chris Bosio .08 .04 .01
☐ 368 Brian Downing .08 .04 .01
☐ 369 Sammy Sosa .08 .04 .01
☐ 370 Stan Belinda .08 .04 .01
☐ 371 Joe Grahe .08 .04 .01
☐ 372 Luis Salazar .08 .04 .01
☐ 373 Lance Johnson .08 .04 .01
☐ 374 Kal Daniels .08 .04 .01
☐ 375 Dave Winfield .20 .09 .03
☐ 376 Brook Jacoby .08 .04 .01
☐ 377 Mariano Duncan .08 .04 .01

☐	378	Ron Darling	.10	.04	.01
☐	379	Randy Johnson	.10	.04	.01
☐	380	Chito Martinez	.08	.04	.01
☐	381	Andres Galarraga	.08	.04	.01
☐	382	Willie Randolph	.10	.04	.01
☐	383	Charles Nagy	.25	.11	.03
☐	384	Tim Belcher	.10	.04	.01
☐	385	Duane Ward	.08	.04	.01
☐	386	Vicente Palacios	.08	.04	.01
☐	387	Mike Gallego	.08	.04	.01
☐	388	Rich DeLucia	.08	.04	.01
☐	389	Scott Radinsky	.08	.04	.01
☐	390	Damon Berryhill	.08	.04	.01
☐	391	Kirk McCaskill	.08	.04	.01
☐	392	Pedro Guerrero	.10	.04	.01
☐	393	Kevin Mitchell	.12	.05	.02
☐	394	Dickie Thon	.08	.04	.01
☐	395	Bobby Bonilla	.15	.07	.02
☐	396	Bill Wegman	.08	.04	.01
☐	397	Dave Martinez	.08	.04	.01
☐	398	Rick Sutcliffe	.10	.04	.01
☐	399	Larry Andersen	.08	.04	.01
☐	400	Tony Gwynn	.35	.16	.04
☐	401	Rickey Henderson	.25	.11	.03
☐	402	Greg Cadaret	.08	.04	.01
☐	403	Keith Miller	.08	.04	.01
☐	404	Bip Roberts	.10	.04	.01
☐	405	Kevin Brown	.10	.04	.01
☐	406	Mitch Williams	.08	.04	.01
☐	407	Frank Viola	.10	.04	.01
☐	408	Darren Lewis	.10	.04	.01
☐	409	Bob Welch	.08	.04	.01
☐	410	Bob Walk	.08	.04	.01
☐	411	Todd Frohwirth	.08	.04	.01
☐	412	Brian Hunter	.20	.09	.03
☐	413	Ron Karkovice	.08	.04	.01
☐	414	Mike Morgan	.08	.04	.01
☐	415	Joe Hesketh	.08	.04	.01
☐	416	Don Slaught	.08	.04	.01
☐	417	Tom Henke	.10	.04	.01
☐	418	Kurt Stillwell	.08	.04	.01
☐	419	Hector Villaneuva	.08	.04	.01
☐	420	Glenallen Hill	.08	.04	.01
☐	421	Pat Borders	.08	.04	.01
☐	422	Charlie Hough	.08	.04	.01
☐	423	Charlie Leibrandt	.08	.04	.01
☐	424	Eddie Murray	.20	.09	.03
☐	425	Jesse Barfield	.08	.04	.01
☐	426	Mark Lemke	.08	.04	.01
☐	427	Kevin McReynolds	.10	.04	.01
☐	428	Gilberto Reyes	.08	.04	.01
☐	429	Ramon Martinez	.12	.05	.02
☐	430	Steve Buechele	.08	.04	.01
☐	431	David Wells	.08	.04	.01
☐	432	Kyle Abbott	.15	.07	.02
☐	433	John Habyan	.08	.04	.01
☐	434	Kevin Appier	.10	.04	.01
☐	435	Gene Larkin	.08	.04	.01
☐	436	Sandy Alomar Jr.	.10	.04	.01
☐	437	Mike Jackson	.08	.04	.01
☐	438	Todd Benzinger	.08	.04	.01
☐	439	Teddy Higuera	.08	.04	.01
☐	440	Reggie Sanders	.75	.35	.09
☐	441	Mark Carreon	.08	.04	.01
☐	442	Bret Saberhagen	.10	.04	.01
☐	443	Gene Nelson	.08	.04	.01
☐	444	Jay Howell	.08	.04	.01
☐	445	Roger McDowell	.08	.04	.01
☐	446	Sid Bream	.08	.04	.01
☐	447	Mackey Sasser	.08	.04	.01
☐	448	Bill Swift	.08	.04	.01
☐	449	Hubie Brooks	.08	.04	.01
☐	450	David Cone	.12	.05	.02
☐	451	Bobby Witt	.08	.04	.01
☐	452	Brady Anderson	.10	.04	.01
☐	453	Lee Stevens	.08	.04	.01
☐	454	Luis Aquino	.08	.04	.01
☐	455	Carney Lansford	.10	.04	.01
☐	456	Carlos Hernandez	.08	.04	.01
☐	457	Danny Jackson	.08	.04	.01
☐	458	Gerald Young	.08	.04	.01
☐	459	Tom Candiotti	.08	.04	.01
☐	460	Billy Hatcher	.08	.04	.01
☐	461	John Wetteland	.08	.04	.01
☐	462	Mike Bordick	.15	.07	.02
☐	463	Don Robinson	.08	.04	.01
☐	464	Jeff Johnson	.08	.04	.01
☐	465	Lonnie Smith	.08	.04	.01
☐	466	Paul Assenmacher	.08	.04	.01
☐	467	Alvin Davis	.08	.04	.01
☐	468	Jim Eisenreich	.08	.04	.01
☐	469	Brent Mayne	.08	.04	.01
☐	470	Jeff Brantley	.08	.04	.01
☐	471	Tim Burke	.08	.04	.01
☐	472	Pat Mahomes	.40	.18	.05
☐	473	Ryan Bowen	.15	.07	.02
☐	474	Bryn Smith	.08	.04	.01
☐	475	Mike Flanagan	.08	.04	.01
☐	476	Reggie Jefferson	.12	.05	.02
☐	477	Jeff Blauser	.08	.04	.01
☐	478	Craig Lefferts	.08	.04	.01
☐	479	Todd Worrell	.08	.04	.01
☐	480	Scott Scudder	.08	.04	.01
☐	481	Kirk Gibson	.10	.04	.01
☐	482	Kenny Rogers	.08	.04	.01
☐	483	Jack Morris	.15	.07	.02
☐	484	Russ Swan	.08	.04	.01
☐	485	Mike Huff	.08	.04	.01
☐	486	Ken Hill	.08	.04	.01
☐	487	Geronimo Pena	.12	.05	.02
☐	488	Charlie O'Brien	.08	.04	.01
☐	489	Mike Maddux	.08	.04	.01
☐	490	Scott Livingstone	.20	.09	.03
☐	491	Carl Willis	.08	.04	.01
☐	492	Kelly Downs	.08	.04	.01
☐	493	Dennis Cook	.08	.04	.01
☐	494	Joe Magrane	.08	.04	.01
☐	495	Bob Kipper	.08	.04	.01
☐	496	Jose Mesa	.08	.04	.01
☐	497	Charlie Hayes	.08	.04	.01
☐	498	Joe Girardi	.08	.04	.01
☐	499	Doug Jones	.08	.04	.01
☐	500	Barry Bonds	.50	.23	.06
☐	501	Bill Krueger	.08	.04	.01
☐	502	Glenn Braggs	.08	.04	.01
☐	503	Eric King	.08	.04	.01
☐	504	Frank Castillo	.15	.07	.02
☐	505	Mike Gardiner	.08	.04	.01
☐	506	Cory Snyder	.08	.04	.01
☐	507	Steve Howe	.08	.04	.01
☐	508	Jose Rijo	.10	.04	.01
☐	509	Sid Fernandez	.10	.04	.01
☐	510	Archi Cianfrocco	.25	.11	.03
☐	511	Mark Guthrie	.08	.04	.01
☐	512	Bob Ojeda	.08	.04	.01
☐	513	John Doherty	.08	.04	.01
☐	514	Dante Bichette	.08	.04	.01
☐	515	Juan Berenguer	.08	.04	.01
☐	516	Jeff M. Robinson	.08	.04	.01
☐	517	Mike Macfarlane	.08	.04	.01
☐	518	Matt Young	.08	.04	.01
☐	519	Otis Nixon	.08	.04	.01
☐	520	Brian Holman	.08	.04	.01
☐	521	Chris Haney	.12	.05	.02
☐	522	Jeff Kent	.50	.23	.06
☐	523	Chad Curtis	.50	.23	.06
☐	524	Vince Horsman	.12	.05	.02
☐	525	Rod Nichols	.08	.04	.01
☐	526	Peter Hoy	.12	.05	.02
☐	527	Shawn Boskie	.08	.04	.01
☐	528	Alejandro Pena	.08	.04	.01
☐	529	Dave Burba	.08	.04	.01
☐	530	Ricky Jordan	.08	.04	.01
☐	531	Dave Silvestri	.30	.14	.04
☐	532	John Patterson	.20	.09	.03
☐	533	Jeff Branson	.08	.04	.01
☐	534	Derrick May	.10	.04	.01
☐	535	Esteban Beltre	.15	.07	.02
☐	536	Jose Melendez	.12	.05	.02
☐	537	Wally Joyner	.10	.04	.01
☐	538	Eddie Taubensee	.20	.09	.03
☐	539	Jim Abbott	.20	.09	.03
☐	540	Brian Williams	.50	.23	.06
☐	541	Donovan Osborne	.60	.25	.08
☐	542	Patrick Lennon	.12	.05	.02
☐	543	Mike Groppuso	.15	.07	.02
☐	544	Jarvis Brown	.12	.05	.02
☐	545	Shawn Livsey	.20	.09	.03
☐	546	Jeff Ware	.25	.11	.03
☐	547	Danny Tartabull	.12	.05	.02
☐	548	Bobby Jones	.75	.35	.09
☐	549	Ken Griffey Jr.	2.00	.90	.25
☐	550	Rey Sanchez	.20	.09	.03
☐	551	Pedro Astacio	.75	.35	.09
☐	552	Juan Guerrero	.20	.09	.03
☐	553	Jacob Brumfield	.12	.05	.02
☐	554	Ben Rivera	.15	.07	.02
☐	555	Brian Jordan	.40	.18	.05
☐	556	Denny Neagle	.12	.05	.02
☐	557	Cliff Brantley	.08	.04	.01
☐	558	Anthony Young	.12	.05	.02
☐	559	John Vander Wal	.25	.11	.03
☐	560	Monty Fariss	.15	.07	.02
☐	561	Russ Springer	.30	.14	.04
☐	562	Pat Listach	2.50	1.15	.30
☐	563	Pat Hentgen	.15	.07	.02

		MT	EX-MT	VG
☐ 564	Andy Stankiewicz	.25	.11	.03
☐ 565	Mike Perez	.15	.07	.02
☐ 566	Mike Bielecki	.08	.04	.01
☐ 567	Butch Henry	.20	.09	.03
☐ 568	Dave Nilsson	.40	.18	.05
☐ 569	Scott Hatteberg	.20	.09	.03
☐ 570	Ruben Amaro Jr.	.12	.05	.02
☐ 571	Todd Hundley	.08	.04	.01
☐ 572	Moises Alou	.10	.04	.01
☐ 573	Hector Fajardo	.25	.11	.03
☐ 574	Todd Van Poppel	.40	.18	.05
☐ 575	Willie Banks	.20	.09	.03
☐ 576	Bob Zupcic	.50	.23	.06
☐ 577	J.J. Johnson	.30	.14	.04
☐ 578	John Burkett	.08	.04	.01
☐ 579	Trever Miller	.15	.07	.02
☐ 580	Scott Bankhead	.08	.04	.01
☐ 581	Rich Amaral	.08	.04	.01
☐ 582	Kenny Lofton	1.25	.55	.16
☐ 583	Matt Stairs	.30	.14	.04
☐ 584	Rod Carew Don Mattingly	.20	.09	.03
☐ 585	Jack Morris Steve Avery	.25	.11	.03
☐ 586	Sandy Alomar Roberto Alomar	.25	.11	.03
☐ 587	Catfish Hunter Scott Sanderson	.08	.04	.01
☐ 588	Dave Justice Willie Stargell	.40	.18	.05
☐ 589	Roger Staubach Rex Hudler	.20	.09	.03
☐ 590	Jackie Gleason David Cone	.12	.05	.02
☐ 591	Tony Gwynn Willie Davis	.20	.09	.03
☐ 592	Orel Hershiser	.12	.05	.02
☐ 593	John Wetteland	.08	.04	.01
☐ 594	Tom Glavine	.20	.09	.03
☐ 595	Randy Johnson	.10	.04	.01
☐ 596	Jim Gott	.08	.04	.01
☐ 597	Donald Harris	.08	.04	.01
☐ 598	Shawn Hare	.12	.05	.02
☐ 599	Chris Gardner	.15	.07	.02
☐ 600	Rusty Meacham	.08	.04	.01
☐ 601	Benito Santiago	.12	.05	.02
☐ 602	Eric Davis	.12	.05	.02
☐ 603	Jose Lind	.08	.04	.01
☐ 604	Dave Justice	.40	.18	.05
☐ 605	Tim Raines	.12	.05	.02
☐ 606	Randy Tomlin	.08	.04	.01
☐ 607	Jack McDowell	.12	.05	.02
☐ 608	Greg Maddux	.12	.05	.02
☐ 609	Charles Nagy	.12	.05	.02
☐ 610	Tom Candiotti	.08	.04	.01
☐ 611	David Cone	.12	.05	.02
☐ 612	Steve Avery	.20	.09	.03
☐ 613	Rod Beck	.20	.09	.03
☐ 614	Rickey Henderson	.25	.11	.03
☐ 615	Benito Santiago	.12	.05	.02
☐ 616	Ruben Sierra	.25	.11	.03
☐ 617	Ryne Sandberg	.35	.16	.04
☐ 618	Nolan Ryan	.60	.25	.08
☐ 619	Brett Butler	.10	.04	.01
☐ 620	Dave Justice	.40	.18	.05

1992 Pinnacle Mickey Mantle

This 30-card set commemorates the life and career of Mickey Mantle. Only 3,750 numbered caes were produced, with 48 sets per case. Each set was packaged in a black and blue box that featured a picture of Mantle and a checklist. The cards measure the standard size (2 1/2" by 3 1/2"). The fronts feature a mix of black and white, full-color, and colorized photos in a full-bleed design with gold-foil stamping. At the bottom of each photo appears a purple bar bearing his uniform number (7) and name. The horizontal or vertical backs carry a second player photo and summarize chapters from his life and career on a royal blue panel with navy blue borders. The cards are numbered on the back.

	MT	EX-MT	VG
COMPLETE SET (30)	20.00	9.00	2.50
COMMON PLAYER (1-30)	1.00	.45	.13

		MT	EX-MT	VG
☐ 1	Father and Son	1.50	.65	.19
☐ 2	High School	1.00	.45	.13
☐ 3	Commerce Comet	1.00	.45	.13
☐ 4	Spring Training	1.00	.45	.13
☐ 5	The Beginning	1.00	.45	.13
☐ 6	Number 6	1.00	.45	.13
☐ 7	The Rookie	1.00	.45	.13
☐ 8	Tape-Measure Shots	1.00	.45	.13
☐ 9	Shortstop	1.00	.45	.13
☐ 10	Outfield	1.00	.45	.13
☐ 11	Speed, Speed, Speed	1.00	.45	.13
☐ 12	Contracts	1.00	.45	.13
☐ 13	Three-time MVP	1.00	.45	.13
☐ 14	Triple Crown	1.00	.45	.13
☐ 15	Series Slam	1.00	.45	.13
☐ 16	Series Star	1.00	.45	.13
☐ 17	Switch Hitter	1.00	.45	.13
☐ 18	Fan Favorite	1.00	.45	.13
☐ 19	Milestones	1.00	.45	.13
☐ 20	Enthusiasm	1.00	.45	.13
☐ 21	Hitting	1.00	.45	.13
☐ 22	First Base	1.00	.45	.13
☐ 23	Courage	1.00	.45	.13
☐ 24	Mick and Stan Stan Musial	2.00	.90	.25
☐ 25	Whitey and Yogi Whitey Ford Yogi Berra	1.50	.65	.19
☐ 26	Mick and Billy Billy Martin	1.50	.65	.19
☐ 27	Mick and Casey Casey Stengel	1.50	.65	.19
☐ 28	Awards	1.00	.45	.13
☐ 29	Retirement	1.00	.45	.13
☐ 30	Cooperstown	1.50	.65	.19

1992 Pinnacle Rookie Idols

This 18-card insert set is a spin-off on the Idols subset featured in the regular series. The set features full-bleed color photos of 18 rookies along with their pick of sports figures or other individuals who had the greatest impact on their careers. The standard-size (2 1/2" by 3 1/2") cards were randomly inserted in Series II wax packs. Both sides of the cards are horizontally oriented. The fronts carry a close-up photo of the rookie superimposed on an action game shot of his idol. On a background that shades from white to light blue, the backs feature text comparing the two players flanked by a color photo of each player. The cards are numbered on the back.

	MT	EX-MT	VG
COMPLETE SET (18)	250.00	115.00	31.00
COMMON PAIR (1-18)	12.00	5.50	1.50
☐ 1 Reggie Sanders and Eric Davis	20.00	9.00	2.50
☐ 2 Hector Fajardo and Jim Abbott	15.00	6.75	1.90
☐ 3 Gary Cooper and George Brett	20.00	9.00	2.50
☐ 4 Mark Wohlers and Roger Clemens	30.00	13.50	3.80
☐ 5 Luis Mercedes and Julio Franco	15.00	6.75	1.90
☐ 6 Willie Banks and Doc Gooden	15.00	6.75	1.90
☐ 7 Kenny Lofton and Rickey Henderson	30.00	13.50	3.80
☐ 8 Keith Mitchell and Dave Henderson	12.00	5.50	1.50
☐ 9 Kim Batiste and Barry Larkin	15.00	6.75	1.90
☐ 10 Todd Hundley and Thurman Munson	15.00	6.75	1.90
☐ 11 Eddie Zosky and Cal Ripken	30.00	13.50	3.80
☐ 12 Todd Van Poppel and Nolan Ryan	50.00	23.00	6.25
☐ 13 Jim Thome and Ryne Sandberg	30.00	13.50	3.80
☐ 14 Dave Fleming and Bobby Murcer	20.00	9.00	2.50
☐ 15 Royce Clayton and Ozzie Smith	20.00	9.00	2.50
☐ 16 Donald Harris and Darryl Strawberry	15.00	6.75	1.90
☐ 17 Chad Curtis and Alan Trammell	15.00	6.75	1.90
☐ 18 Derek Bell and Dave Winfield	20.00	9.00	2.50

1992 Pinnacle Rookies

This 30-card boxed set features top rookies of the 1992 season, with at least one player from each team. Each of the 3,000 sequentially numbered cases contained 60 sets. The fronts feature full-bleed color action player photos except at the bottom where a team-color coded bar carries the player's name (in gold foil lettering) and a black bar has the words "1992 Rookie." The team logo appears in a gold foil circle at the lower right corner. The horizontally oriented backs carry a second large color player photo, again edged at the bottom by a team-color coded bar with the player's name and a black bar carrying a player profile. The cards are numbered on the back. The key Rookie Cards in this set are Chad Curtis, Pat Mahomes, and Brian Williams.

	MT	EX-MT	VG
COMPLETE SET (30)	12.00	5.50	1.50
COMMON PLAYER (1-30)	.10	.05	.01
☐ 1 Luis Mercedes	.30	.14	.04
☐ 2 Scott Cooper	.30	.14	.04
☐ 3 Kenny Lofton	1.75	.80	.22
☐ 4 John Doherty	.25	.11	.03
☐ 5 Pat Listach	3.50	1.55	.45
☐ 6 Andy Stankiewicz	.30	.14	.04
☐ 7 Derek Bell	.40	.18	.05
☐ 8 Gary DiSarcina	.10	.05	.01
☐ 9 Roberto Hernandez	.25	.11	.03
☐ 10 Joel Johnston	.10	.05	.01
☐ 11 Pat Mahomes	.60	.25	.08
☐ 12 Todd Van Poppel	.75	.35	.09
☐ 13 Dave Fleming	1.50	.65	.19
☐ 14 Monty Fariss	.20	.09	.03
☐ 15 Gary Scott	.15	.07	.02
☐ 16 Moises Alou	.25	.11	.03
☐ 17 Todd Hundley	.10	.05	.01
☐ 18 Kim Batiste	.20	.09	.03
☐ 19 Denny Neagle	.15	.07	.02
☐ 20 Donovan Osborne	.75	.35	.09
☐ 21 Mark Wohlers	.25	.11	.03
☐ 22 Reggie Sanders	1.00	.45	.13
☐ 23 Brian Williams	.60	.25	.08
☐ 24 Eric Karros	3.00	1.35	.40
☐ 25 Frank Seminara	.50	.23	.06
☐ 26 Royce Clayton	.50	.23	.06
☐ 27 Dave Nilsson	.50	.23	.06
☐ 28 Matt Stairs	.35	.16	.04
☐ 29 Chad Curtis	.60	.25	.08
☐ 30 Carlos Hernandez	.10	.05	.01

1992 Pinnacle Slugfest

This 15-card set measures the standard size (2 1/2" by 3 1/2"). The horizontally oriented fronts feature glossy photos of players at bat. The player's name is printed in gold and the word "Slugfest" is printed in red in a black border across the bottom of the picture. The back design includes a color action player photo on the right half of the card, and statistics and a career summary on the left. The cards are numbered on the back. The cards were issued as an insert with specially marked cello packs.

	MT	EX-MT	VG
COMPLETE SET (15)	40.00	18.00	5.00
COMMON PLAYER (1-15)	1.50	.65	.19
☐ 1 Cecil Fielder	2.00	.90	.25
☐ 2 Mark McGwire	3.50	1.55	.45
☐ 3 Jose Canseco	3.50	1.55	.45
☐ 4 Barry Bonds	3.50	1.55	.45
☐ 5 Dave Justice	3.00	1.35	.40
☐ 6 Bobby Bonilla	1.50	.65	.19
☐ 7 Ken Griffey Jr.	7.00	3.10	.85
☐ 8 Ron Gant	1.50	.65	.19
☐ 9 Ryne Sandberg	3.50	1.55	.45
☐ 10 Ruben Sierra	2.50	1.15	.30
☐ 11 Frank Thomas	10.00	4.50	1.25
☐ 12 Will Clark	3.50	1.55	.45
☐ 13 Kirby Puckett	3.50	1.55	.45
☐ 14 Cal Ripken	5.00	2.30	.60
☐ 15 Jeff Bagwell	3.00	1.35	.40

1992 Pinnacle Team Pinnacle

This 12-card, double-sided subset features the National League and American League All-Star team as selected by Pinnacle. The standard-size (2 1/2" by 3 1/2") were randomly inserted in Series I wax packs. There is one card per position, including two cards for pitchers and two cards for relief pitchers for a total set of twelve. The cards feature illustrations by sports artist Chris Greco of the National League All-Star on one side and the American League All-Star on the other. The words "Team Pinnacle" are printed vertically down the left side of the card in red for American League on one side and blue for National League on the other. The player's name appears in a gold stripe at the bottom. There is no text. The cards are numbered in the black bottom stripe on the side featuring the National League All-Star.

	MT	EX-MT	VG
COMPLETE SET (12)	450.00	200.00	57.50
COMMON PAIR (1-12)	20.00	9.00	2.50
☐ 1 Roger Clemens and Ramon Martinez	50.00	23.00	6.25
☐ 2 Jim Abbott and Steve Avery	40.00	18.00	5.00
☐ 3 Ivan Rodriguez and Benito Santiago	40.00	18.00	5.00
☐ 4 Frank Thomas and Will Clark	100.00	45.00	12.50
☐ 5 Roberto Alomar and Ryne Sandberg	75.00	34.00	9.50
☐ 6 Robin Ventura and Matt Williams	35.00	16.00	4.40
☐ 7 Cal Ripken and Barry Larkin	75.00	34.00	9.50
☐ 8 Danny Tartabull and Barry Bonds	45.00	20.00	5.75
☐ 9 Ken Griffey Jr. and Brett Butler	75.00	34.00	9.50
☐ 10 Ruben Sierra and Dave Justice	45.00	20.00	5.75
☐ 11 Dennis Eckersley and Rob Dibble	30.00	13.50	3.80
☐ 12 Scott Radinsky and John Franco	20.00	9.00	2.50

1992 Pinnacle Team 2000

This 80-card standard-size (2 1/2" by 3 1/2") set focuses on young players who will be still be stars in the year 2000. Cards 1-40 were inserted in Series 1 jumbo packs while cards 41-80 were featured in Series 2 jumbo packs. The fronts features action color player photos. The cards are bordered by a 1/2" black stripe that runs along the left edge and bottom forming a right angle. The two ends of the black stripe are sloped. The words "Team 2000" and the player's name appear in gold foil in the stripe. The team logo is

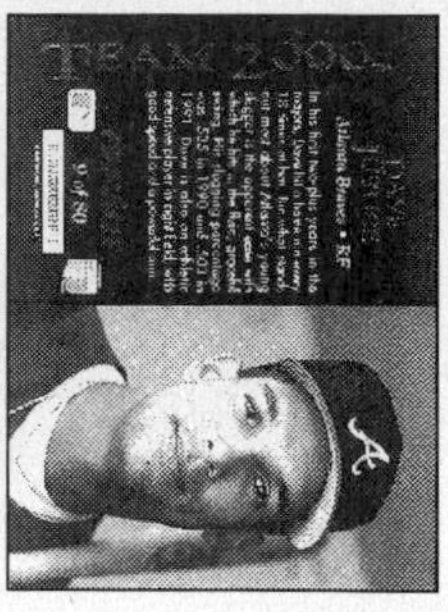

displayed in the lower left corner. The horizontally oriented backs show a close-up color player photo and a career summary on a black background. The cards are numbered on the back.

	MT	EX-MT	VG
COMPLETE SET (80)	50.00	23.00	6.25
COMPLETE SERIES 1 (40)	30.00	13.50	3.80
COMPLETE SERIES 2 (40)	20.00	9.00	2.50
COMMON PLAYER (1-40)	.15	.07	.02
COMMON PLAYER (41-80)	.15	.07	.02
☐ 1 Mike Mussina	3.50	1.55	.45
☐ 2 Phil Plantier	.60	.25	.08
☐ 3 Frank Thomas	6.00	2.70	.75
☐ 4 Travis Fryman	2.00	.90	.25
☐ 5 Kevin Appier	.15	.07	.02
☐ 6 Chuck Knoblauch	1.00	.45	.13
☐ 7 Pat Kelly	.15	.07	.02
☐ 8 Ivan Rodriguez	2.00	.90	.25
☐ 9 Dave Justice	1.50	.65	.19
☐ 10 Jeff Bagwell	1.50	.65	.19
☐ 11 Marquis Grissom	.50	.23	.06
☐ 12 Andy Benes	.15	.07	.02
☐ 13 Gregg Olson	.15	.07	.02
☐ 14 Kevin Morton	.15	.07	.02
☐ 15 Tim Naehring	.15	.07	.02
☐ 16 Dave Hollins	.50	.23	.06
☐ 17 Sandy Alomar Jr.	.15	.07	.02
☐ 18 Albert Belle	.60	.25	.08
☐ 19 Charles Nagy	.50	.23	.06
☐ 20 Brian McRae	.20	.09	.03
☐ 21 Larry Walker	.75	.35	.09
☐ 22 Delino DeShields	.50	.23	.06
☐ 23 Jeff Johnson	.15	.07	.02
☐ 24 Bernie Williams	.50	.23	.06
☐ 25 Jose Offerman	.15	.07	.02
☐ 26 Juan Gonzalez	2.50	1.15	.30
☐ 27A Juan Guzman (Pinnacle logo at top)	3.50	1.55	.45
☐ 27B Juan Guzman (Pinnacle logo at bottom)	3.50	1.55	.45
☐ 28 Eric Anthony	.15	.07	.02
☐ 29 Brian Hunter	.40	.18	.05
☐ 30 John Smoltz	.35	.16	.04
☐ 31 Deion Sanders	.75	.35	.09
☐ 32 Greg Maddux	.30	.14	.04
☐ 33 Andujar Cedeno	.20	.09	.03
☐ 34 Royce Clayton	.75	.35	.09
☐ 35 Kenny Lofton	2.50	1.15	.30
☐ 36 Cal Eldred	2.00	.90	.25
☐ 37 Jim Thome	.40	.18	.05
☐ 38 Gary DiSarcina	.15	.07	.02
☐ 39 Brian Jordan	.75	.35	.09
☐ 40 Chad Curtis	1.00	.45	.13
☐ 41 Ben McDonald	.30	.14	.04
☐ 42 Jim Abbott	.40	.18	.05
☐ 43 Robin Ventura	1.00	.45	.13
☐ 44 Milt Cuyler	.15	.07	.02
☐ 45 Gregg Jefferies	.15	.07	.02
☐ 46 Scott Radinsky	.15	.07	.02
☐ 47 Ken Griffey Jr.	4.00	1.80	.50
☐ 48 Roberto Alomar	1.00	.45	.13
☐ 49 Ramon Martinez	.15	.07	.02
☐ 50 Bret Barberie	.20	.09	.03
☐ 51 Ray Lankford	.75	.35	.09
☐ 52 Leo Gomez	.40	.18	.05
☐ 53 Tommy Greene	.15	.07	.02
☐ 54 Mo Vaughn	.25	.11	.03
☐ 55 Sammy Sosa	.15	.07	.02
☐ 56 Carlos Baerga	.75	.35	.09
☐ 57 Mark Lewis	.15	.07	.02

☐ 58 Tom Gordon	.15	.07	.02
☐ 59 Gary Sheffield	1.50	.65	.19
☐ 60 Scott Erickson	.30	.14	.04
☐ 61 Pedro Munoz	.25	.11	.03
☐ 62 Tino Martinez	.20	.09	.03
☐ 63 Darren Lewis	.15	.07	.02
☐ 64 Dean Palmer	.50	.23	.06
☐ 65 John Olerud	.50	.23	.06
☐ 66 Steve Avery	.90	.40	.11
☐ 67 Pete Harnisch	.15	.07	.02
☐ 68 Luis Gonzalez	.25	.11	.03
☐ 69 Kim Batiste	.30	.14	.04
☐ 70 Reggie Sanders	1.50	.65	.19
☐ 71 Luis Mercedes	.50	.23	.06
☐ 72 Todd Van Poppel	1.00	.45	.13
☐ 73 Gary Scott	.15	.07	.02
☐ 74 Monty Fariss	.30	.14	.04
☐ 75 Kyle Abbott	.15	.07	.02
☐ 76 Eric Karros	3.50	1.55	.45
☐ 77 Mo Sanford	.15	.07	.02
☐ 78 Todd Hundley	.15	.07	.02
☐ 79 Reggie Jefferson	.35	.16	.04
☐ 80 Pat Mahomes	.75	.35	.09

1963 Pirates IDL

This 26-card set measures approximately 4" by 5" and is blank backed. The fronts have black and white photos on the top of the card along with the IDL Drug Store logo in the lower left corner of the card and the players name printed in block letters underneath the picture. The only card which has any designation as to position is the manager card of Danny Murtaugh. These cards are unnumbered and feature members of the Pittsburgh Pirates. The catalog designation for the set is H801-13 although it is infrequently referenced. The Stargell card is one of his few cards from 1963, his rookie year for cards.

	NRMT	VG-E	GOOD
COMPLETE SET (26)	80.00	36.00	10.00
COMMON PLAYER (1-26)	2.00	.90	.25
☐ 1 Bob Bailey	2.00	.90	.25
☐ 2 Smoky Burgess	2.50	1.15	.30
☐ 3 Don Cardwell	2.00	.90	.25
☐ 4 Roberto Clemente	30.00	13.50	3.80
☐ 5 Donn Clendenon	3.00	1.35	.40
☐ 6 Roy Face	3.00	1.35	.40
☐ 7 Earl Francis	2.00	.90	.25
☐ 8 Bob Friend	2.50	1.15	.30
☐ 9 Joe Gibbon	2.00	.90	.25
☐ 10 Julio Gotay	2.00	.90	.25
☐ 11 Harvey Haddix	2.50	1.15	.30
☐ 12 Johnny Logan	2.50	1.15	.30
☐ 13 Bill Mazeroski	6.00	2.70	.75
☐ 14 Al McBean	2.00	.90	.25
☐ 15 Danny Murtaugh MG	2.00	.90	.25
☐ 16 Sam Narron CO	2.00	.90	.25
☐ 17 Ron Northey CO	2.00	.90	.25
☐ 18 Frank Oceak CO	2.00	.90	.25
☐ 19 Jim Pagliaroni	2.00	.90	.25
☐ 20 Ted Savage	2.00	.90	.25
☐ 21 Dick Schofield	2.00	.90	.25
☐ 22 Willie Stargell	30.00	13.50	3.80
☐ 23 Tom Sturdivant	2.00	.90	.25
☐ 24 Virgil Trucks CO	2.00	.90	.25
☐ 25 Bob Veale	3.00	1.35	.40
☐ 26 Bill Virdon	3.00	1.35	.40

1966 Pirates East Hills

The 1966 East Hills Pirates set consists of 25 large (approximately 3 1/4" by 4 1/4"), full color photos of Pittsburgh Pirate ballplayers. These blank-backed cards are numbered in the lower right corner according to the uniform number of the individual depicted. The set was distributed by various stores located in the East Hills Shopping Center. The catalog number for this set is F405.

	NRMT	VG-E	GOOD
COMPLETE SET (25)	35.00	16.00	4.40
COMMON PLAYER	.45	.20	.06
☐ 3 Harry Walker MG	.60	.25	.08
☐ 7 Bob Bailey	.45	.20	.06
☐ 8 Willie Stargell	10.00	4.50	1.25
☐ 9 Bill Mazeroski	2.50	1.15	.30
☐ 10 Jim Pagliaroni	.45	.20	.06
☐ 11 Jose Pagan	.45	.20	.06
☐ 12 Jerry May	.45	.20	.06
☐ 14 Gene Alley	.75	.35	.09
☐ 15 Manny Mota	.75	.35	.09
☐ 16 Andre Rodgers UER (Andy on card)	.45	.20	.06
☐ 17 Donn Clendenon	.75	.35	.09
☐ 18 Matty Alou	1.00	.45	.13
☐ 19 Pete Mikkelsen	.45	.20	.06
☐ 20 Jesse Gonder	.45	.20	.06
☐ 21 Bob Clemente	20.00	9.00	2.50
☐ 22 Woody Fryman	.60	.25	.08
☐ 24 Jerry Lynch	.45	.20	.06
☐ 25 Tommie Sisk	.45	.20	.06
☐ 26 Roy Face	1.25	.55	.16
☐ 28 Steve Blass	.75	.35	.09
☐ 32 Vernon Law	1.00	.45	.13
☐ 34 Al McBean	.45	.20	.06
☐ 39 Bob Veale	.75	.35	.09
☐ 43 Don Cardwell	.45	.20	.06
☐ 45 Gene Michael	.60	.25	.08

1968 Pirates KDKA

This 23-card set measures approximately 2 3/8" by 4" and was issued by radio and television station KDKA to promote the Pittsburgh Pirates, whom they were covering at the time. The fronts have the players' photo on the top 2/3 of the card and a facsimile autograph, the players name and position and uniform number on the lower left hand corner and an ad for KDKA on the lower right corner of the card. The back has an advertisment for both KDKA radio and television. The set is checklisted below by uniform number.

	NRMT-MT	EXC	G-VG
COMPLETE SET (23)	75.00	34.00	9.50
COMMON PLAYER	2.00	.90	.25

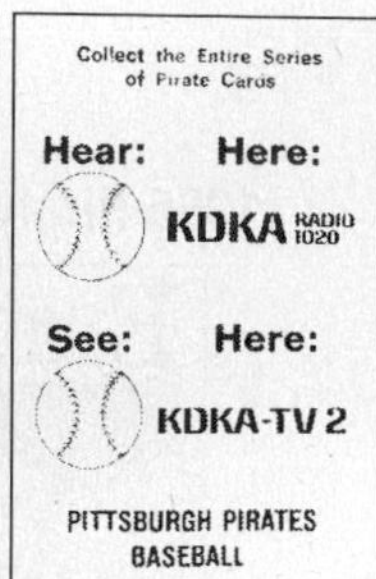

☐ 7 Larry Shepard MG	2.00	.90	.25
☐ 8 Willie Stargell	18.00	8.00	2.30
☐ 9 Bill Mazeroski	6.00	2.70	.75
☐ 10 Gary Kolb	2.00	.90	.25
☐ 11 Jose Pagan	2.00	.90	.25
☐ 12 Jerry May	2.00	.90	.25
☐ 14 Jim Bunning	6.00	2.70	.75
☐ 15 Manny Mota	3.00	1.35	.40
☐ 17 Donn Clendenon	3.00	1.35	.40
☐ 18 Matty Alou	2.50	1.15	.30
☐ 21 Bob Clemente	35.00	16.00	4.40
☐ 22 Gene Alley	2.50	1.15	.30
☐ 25 Tommy Sisk	2.00	.90	.25
☐ 26 Roy Face	3.00	1.35	.40
☐ 27 Ron Kline	2.00	.90	.25
☐ 28 Steve Blass	2.50	1.15	.30
☐ 29 Juan Pizzaro	2.00	.90	.25
☐ 30 Maury Wills	6.00	2.70	.75
☐ 34 Al McBean	2.00	.90	.25
☐ 35 Manny Sanguillen	4.00	1.80	.50
☐ 38 Bob Moose	2.50	1.15	.30
☐ 39 Bob Veale	2.50	1.15	.30
☐ 40 Dave Wickersham	2.00	.90	.25

1989 Pirates Very Fine Juice

The 1989 Very Fine Juice Pittsburgh Pirates set is a 30-card set with cards measuring approximately 2 1/2" by 3 1/2" featuring the members of the 1989 Pittsburgh Pirates. This set was issued on three separate perforated sheets: two panels contain 15 player cards each, while the third panel serves as a cover for the set and displays color action photos of the Pirates. These panels were given away to fans attending the Pirates home game on April 23, 1989. There was a coupon (expiring on 10/31/89) on the back that could be redeemed for a free can of juice. The cards are numbered by uniform number in the list below. The cards are very colorful.

	MT	EX-MT	VG
COMPLETE SET (30)	14.00	6.25	1.75
COMMON PLAYER	.50	.23	.06
☐ 0 Junior Ortiz	.50	.23	.06
☐ 2 Gary Redus	.60	.25	.08
☐ 3 Jay Bell	.90	.40	.11
☐ 5 Sid Bream	.60	.25	.08
☐ 6 Rafael Belliard	.50	.23	.06
☐ 10 Jim Leyland MG	.60	.25	.08
☐ 11 Glenn Wilson	.50	.23	.06
☐ 12 Mike LaValliere	.50	.23	.06
☐ 13 Jose Lind	.60	.25	.08
☐ 14 Ken Oberkfell	.50	.23	.06
☐ 15 Doug Drabek	1.25	.55	.16
☐ 16 Bob Kipper	.50	.23	.06
☐ 17 Bob Walk	.50	.23	.06
☐ 18 Andy Van Slyke	1.50	.65	.19
☐ 23 R.J. Reynolds	.50	.23	.06
☐ 24 Barry Bonds	3.50	1.55	.45
☐ 25 Bobby Bonilla	2.00	.90	.25
☐ 26 Neal Heaton	.50	.23	.06
☐ 30 Benny Distefano	.50	.23	.06
☐ 31 Ray Miller CO and 37 Tommy Sandt CO	.50	.23	.06
☐ 35 Jim Gott	.50	.23	.06
☐ 36 Bruce Kimm CO and 32 Gene Lamont CO	.50	.23	.06
☐ 39 Milt May CO and 45 Rich Donnelly CO	.50	.23	.06
☐ 41 Mike Dunne	.50	.23	.06
☐ 43 Bill Landrum	.60	.25	.08
☐ 44 John Cangelosi	.50	.23	.06
☐ 49 Jeff D. Robinson	.50	.23	.06
☐ 52 Dorn Taylor	.50	.23	.06
☐ 54 Brian Fisher	.50	.23	.06
☐ 57 John Smiley	1.00	.45	.13

1990 Pirates Homers Cookies

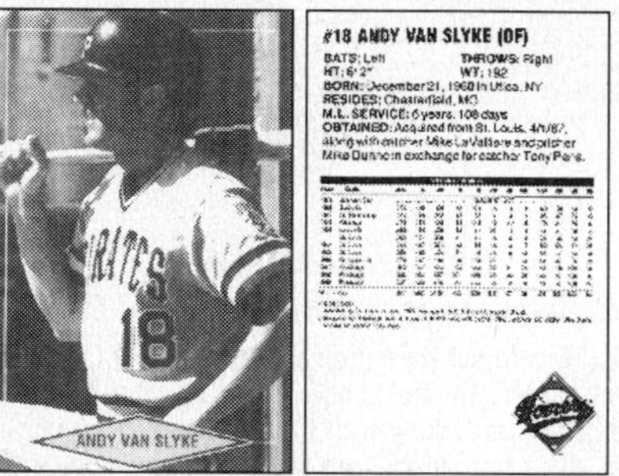

The 1990 Homers Cookies Pittsburgh Pirates set is an attractive 31-card set measuring approximately 4" by 6", used as a giveaway at a Pirates home game. It has been reported that 25,000 of these sets were produced. Four Homers Baseball trivia question cards were also included with the complete set. The fronts are full-color action photos with the backs containing complete statistical information. The set has been checklisted alphabetically below.

	MT	EX-MT	VG
COMPLETE SET (31)	12.50	5.75	1.55
COMMON PLAYER (1-31)	.35	.16	.04
☐ 1 Wally Backman	.35	.16	.04
☐ 2 Doug Bair	.35	.16	.04
☐ 3 Rafael Belliard	.45	.20	.06
☐ 4 Jay Bell	.75	.35	.09
☐ 5 Barry Bonds	2.50	1.15	.30
☐ 6 Bobby Bonilla	1.50	.65	.19
☐ 7 Sid Bream	.45	.20	.06
☐ 8 John Cangelosi	.35	.16	.04
☐ 9 Rich Donnelly CO	.35	.16	.04
☐ 10 Doug Drabek	1.25	.55	.16
☐ 11 Billy Hatcher	.45	.20	.06
☐ 12 Neal Heaton	.35	.16	.04
☐ 13 Jeff King	.60	.25	.08
☐ 14 Bob Kipper	.35	.16	.04
☐ 15 Randy Kramer	.35	.16	.04
☐ 16 Gene Lamont CO	.45	.20	.06
☐ 17 Bill Landrum	.35	.16	.04
☐ 18 Mike LaValliere	.35	.16	.04
☐ 19 Jim Leyland MG	.45	.20	.06
☐ 20 Jose Lind	.45	.20	.06

☐ 21 Milt May	.35	.16	.04
☐ 22 Ray Miller CO	.35	.16	.04
☐ 23 Ted Power	.35	.16	.04
☐ 24 Gary Redus	.35	.16	.04
☐ 25 R.J. Reynolds	.35	.16	.04
☐ 26 Tommy Sandt CO	.35	.16	.04
☐ 27 Don Slaught	.35	.16	.04
☐ 28 Walt Terrell	.35	.16	.04
☐ 29 Andy Van Slyke	1.25	.55	.16
☐ 30 John Smiley	.75	.35	.09
☐ 31 Bob Walk	.35	.16	.04

1992 Pirates Nationwide Insurance

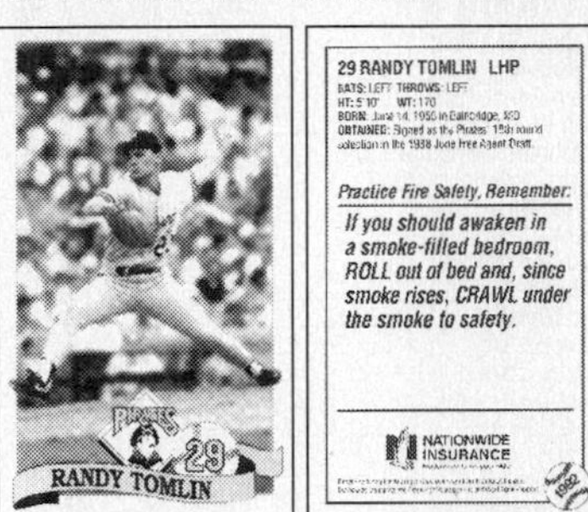

This 25-card set was sponsored by Nationwide Insurance, the Pittsburgh Bureau of Fire, and West Penn Hospital. The cards are oversized and measure 3 1/2" by 5 3/4". The color action player photos on the front are edged by a thin red and a wider white border. Superimposed at the bottom of the picture are the team logo, the player's name in a yellow banner, and his jersey number in a baseball icon. The backs feature statistical information about the player and fire safety tips. The cards are unnumbered and checklisted below in alphabetical order.

	MT	EX-MT	VG
COMPLETE SET (25)	8.00	3.60	1.00
COMMON PLAYER (1-25)	.35	.16	.04
☐ 1 Stan Belinda	.45	.20	.06
☐ 2 Jay Bell	.60	.25	.08
☐ 3 Barry Bonds	1.50	.65	.19
☐ 4 Steve Buechele	.35	.16	.04
☐ 5 Terry Collins CO	.35	.16	.04
☐ 6 Rich Donnelly CO	.35	.16	.04
☐ 7 Doug Drabek	.75	.35	.09
☐ 8 Cecil Espy	.35	.16	.04
☐ 9 Jeff King	.45	.20	.06
☐ 10 Mike LaValliere	.35	.16	.04
☐ 11 Jim Leyland MG	.45	.20	.06
☐ 12 Jose Lind	.35	.16	.04
☐ 13 Roger Mason	.35	.16	.04
☐ 14 Milt May CO	.35	.16	.04
☐ 15 Lloyd McClendon	.35	.16	.04
☐ 16 Orlando Merced	.45	.20	.06
☐ 17 Denny Neagle	.35	.16	.04
☐ 18 Bob Patterson	.35	.16	.04
☐ 19 Gary Redus	.35	.16	.04
☐ 20 Don Slaught	.35	.16	.04
☐ 21 Zane Smith	.45	.20	.06
☐ 22 Randy Tomlin	.45	.20	.06
☐ 23 Andy Van Slyke	.75	.35	.09
☐ 24 Gary Varsho	.35	.16	.04
☐ 25 Bob Walk	.35	.16	.04

1979 Police Giants

The cards in this 30-card set measure approximately 2 5/8" by 4 1/8". The 1979 Police Giants set features cards numbered by the player's uniform number. This full color

set features the player's photo, the Giants' logo, and the player's name, number and position on the front of the cards. A facsimile autograph in an attractive blue ink is also contained on the front. The backs, printed in orange and black, feature Tips from the Giants, the Giants' and sponsoring radio station, KNBR, logos and a line listing the Giants, KNBR, and the San Francisco Police Department as sponsors of the set. The 15 cards which are shown with an asterisk below were available only from the Police. The other 15 cards were given away at the ballpark on June 17, 1979. These cards look very similar to the Giants police set issued in 1980, the following year. Both sets credit Dennis Desprois photographically on each card but this (1979) set seems to have a fuzzier focus on the pictures. The sets can be distinguished on the front since this set's cards have a number sign before the player's uniform number on the front. Also on the card backs the KNBR logo is usually left justified for the cards in the 1979 set whereas the 1980 set has the KNBR logo centered on the card back.

	NRMT-MT	EXC	G-VG
COMPLETE SET (30)	16.00	7.25	2.00
COMMON PLAYER	.50	.23	.06
☐ 1 Dave Bristol MG	.50	.23	.06
☐ 2 Marc Hill	.50	.23	.06
☐ 3 Mike Sadek *	.60	.25	.08
☐ 5 Tom Haller	.50	.23	.06
☐ 6 Joe Altobelli CO *	.60	.25	.08
☐ 8 Larry Shepard CO *	.60	.25	.08
☐ 9 Heity Cruz	.50	.23	.06
☐ 10 Johnnie LeMaster	.50	.23	.06
☐ 12 Jim Davenport CO	.60	.25	.08
☐ 14 Vida Blue	.75	.35	.09
☐ 15 Mike Ivie	.50	.23	.06
☐ 16 Roger Metzger	.50	.23	.06
☐ 17 Randy Moffitt	.50	.23	.06
☐ 18 Bill Madlock	.75	.35	.09
☐ 21 Rob Andrews *	.60	.25	.08
☐ 22 Jack Clark *	2.00	.90	.25
☐ 25 Dave Roberts	.50	.23	.06
☐ 26 John Montefusco	.60	.25	.08
☐ 28 Ed Halicki *	.60	.25	.08
☐ 30 John Tamargo	.50	.23	.06
☐ 31 Larry Herndon	.50	.23	.06
☐ 36 Bill North *	.60	.25	.08
☐ 39 Bob Knepper *	.75	.35	.09
☐ 40 John Curtis *	.60	.25	.08
☐ 41 Darrell Evans *	1.25	.55	.16
☐ 43 Tom Griffin *	.60	.25	.08
☐ 44 Willie McCovey *	3.50	1.55	.45
☐ 45 Terry Whitfield *	.60	.25	.08
☐ 46 Gary Lavelle *	.60	.25	.08
☐ 49 Max Venable *	.60	.25	.08

1980 Police Dodgers

The cards in this 30-card set measure approximately 2 13/16" by 4 1/8". The full color 1980 Police Los Angeles Dodgers set features the player's name, uniform number,

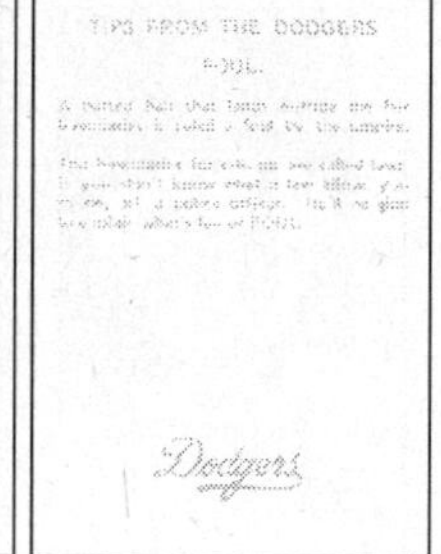

position, and biographical data on the fronts in addition to the photo. The backs feature Tips from the Dodgers, the LAPD logo, and the Dodgers' logo. The cards are listed below according to uniform number.

	NRMT-MT	EXC	G-VG
COMPLETE SET (30)	10.00	4.50	1.25
COMMON PLAYER	.35	.16	.04
☐ 5 Johnny Oates	.60	.25	.08
☐ 6 Steve Garvey	1.00	.45	.13
☐ 7 Steve Yeager	.45	.20	.06
☐ 8 Reggie Smith	.60	.25	.08
☐ 9 Gary Thomasson	.35	.16	.04
☐ 10 Ron Cey	.60	.25	.08
☐ 12 Dusty Baker	.75	.35	.09
☐ 13 Joe Ferguson	.45	.20	.06
☐ 15 Davey Lopes	.60	.25	.08
☐ 16 Rick Monday	.45	.20	.06
☐ 18 Bill Russell	.60	.25	.08
☐ 20 Don Sutton	1.00	.45	.13
☐ 21 Jay Johnstone	.60	.25	.08
☐ 23 Teddy Martinez	.35	.16	.04
☐ 27 Joe Beckwith	.35	.16	.04
☐ 28 Pedro Guerrero	.90	.40	.11
☐ 29 Don Stanhouse	.35	.16	.04
☐ 30 Derrel Thomas	.35	.16	.04
☐ 31 Doug Rau	.35	.16	.04
☐ 34 Ken Brett	.35	.16	.04
☐ 35 Bob Welch	.90	.40	.11
☐ 37 Robert Castillo	.35	.16	.04
☐ 38 Dave Goltz	.35	.16	.04
☐ 41 Jerry Reuss	.45	.20	.06
☐ 43 Rick Sutcliffe	1.00	.45	.13
☐ 44 Mickey Hatcher	.35	.16	.04
☐ 46 Burt Hooton	.35	.16	.04
☐ 49 Charlie Hough	.45	.20	.06
☐ NNO Team Card	.45	.20	.06

1980 Police Giants

The cards in this 31-card set measure approximately 2 5/8" by 4 1/8". The 1980 Police San Francisco Giants set features cards numbered by the player's uniform number. This full color set features the player's photo, the Giants' logo, and the player's name, number and position on the front of the cards. A facsimile autograph in an attractive blue ink is also contained on the front. The backs, printed in orange and black, feature Tips from the Giants, the Giants' and sponsoring radio station, KNBR, logos and a line listing the Giants, KNBR, and the San Francisco Police Department as sponsors of the set. The sets were given away at the ballpark on May 31, 1980.

	NRMT-MT	EXC	G-VG
COMPLETE SET (31)	12.00	5.50	1.50
COMMON PLAYER	.35	.16	.04
☐ 1 Dave Bristol MG	.35	.16	.04
☐ 2 Marc Hill	.35	.16	.04
☐ 3 Mike Sadek	.35	.16	.04
☐ 5 Jim Lefebvre CO	.45	.20	.06
☐ 6 Rennie Stennett	.35	.16	.04
☐ 7 Milt May	.35	.16	.04
☐ 8 Vern Benson CO	.35	.16	.04
☐ 9 Jim Wohlford	.35	.16	.04
☐ 10 Johnnie LeMaster	.35	.16	.04
☐ 12 Jim Davenport CO	.45	.20	.06
☐ 14 Vida Blue	.60	.25	.08
☐ 15 Mike Ivie	.35	.16	.04
☐ 16 Roger Metzger	.35	.16	.04
☐ 17 Randy Moffitt	.35	.16	.04
☐ 19 Al Holland	.35	.16	.04
☐ 20 Joe Strain	.35	.16	.04
☐ 22 Jack Clark	1.50	.65	.19
☐ 26 John Montefusco	.45	.20	.06
☐ 28 Ed Halicki	.35	.16	.04
☐ 31 Larry Herndon	.35	.16	.04
☐ 32 Ed Whitson	.45	.20	.06
☐ 36 Bill North	.35	.16	.04
☐ 38 Greg Minton	.35	.16	.04
☐ 39 Bob Knepper	.45	.20	.06
☐ 41 Darrell Evans	1.00	.45	.13
☐ 42 John Van Ornum	.35	.16	.04
☐ 43 Tom Griffin	.35	.16	.04
☐ 44 Willie McCovey	2.50	1.15	.30
☐ 45 Terry Whitfield	.35	.16	.04
☐ 46 Gary Lavelle	.35	.16	.04
☐ 47 Don McMahon CO	.35	.16	.04

1981 Police Braves

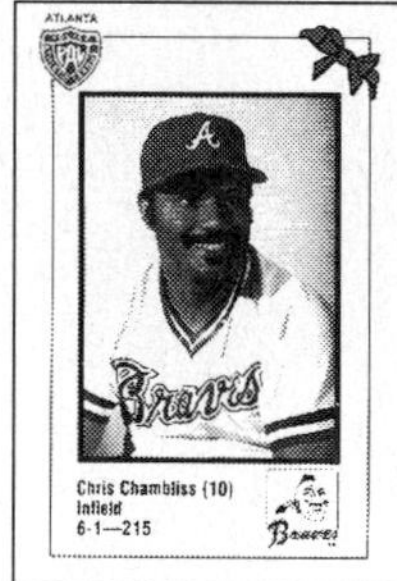

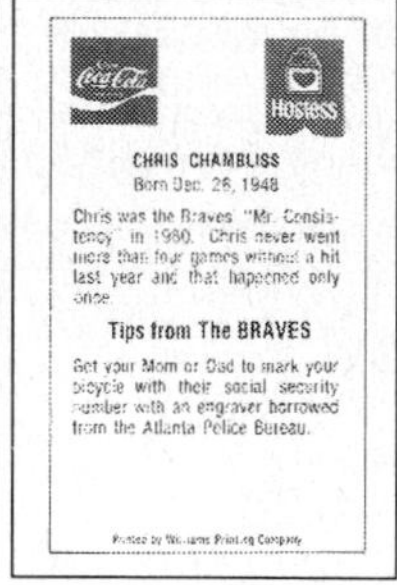

The cards in this 27-card set measure approximately 2 5/8" by 4 1/8". This first Atlanta Police set features full color cards sponsored by the Braves, the Atlanta Police Department, Coca-Cola and Hostess. The cards are numbered by uniform number, which is contained on the front along with an Atlanta Police Athletic League logo, a black and white Braves logo, and a green bow in the upper right corner of the frameline. The backs feature brief player biographies, logos of Coke and Hostess, and Tips from the Braves. It is reported that 33,000 of these sets were printed. The Terry Harper card is supposed to be slightly more difficult to obtain than other cards in the set.

	NRMT-MT	EXC	G-VG
COMPLETE SET (27)	10.00	4.50	1.25
COMMON PLAYER	.35	.16	.04
☐ 1 Jerry Royster	.35	.16	.04
☐ 3 Dale Murphy	2.50	1.15	.30

☐ 4 Biff Pocoroba	.35	.16	.04
☐ 5 Bob Horner	.60	.25	.08
☐ 6 Bobby Cox MG	.60	.25	.08
☐ 9 Luis Gomez	.35	.16	.04
☐ 10 Chris Chambliss	.60	.25	.08
☐ 15 Bill Nahorodny	.35	.16	.04
☐ 16 Rafael Ramirez	.45	.20	.06
☐ 17 Glenn Hubbard	.35	.16	.04
☐ 18 Claudell Washington	.45	.20	.06
☐ 19 Terry Harper SP	.75	.35	.09
☐ 20 Bruce Benedict	.35	.16	.04
☐ 24 John Montefusco	.45	.20	.06
☐ 25 Rufino Linares	.35	.16	.04
☐ 26 Gene Garber	.45	.20	.06
☐ 30 Brian Asselstine	.35	.16	.04
☐ 34 Larry Bradford	.35	.16	.04
☐ 35 Phil Niekro	1.75	.80	.22
☐ 37 Rick Camp	.35	.16	.04
☐ 39 Al Hrabosky	.45	.20	.06
☐ 40 Tommy Boggs	.35	.16	.04
☐ 42 Rick Mahler	.45	.20	.06
☐ 44 Hank Aaron CO	2.50	1.15	.30
☐ 45 Ed Miller	.35	.16	.04
☐ 46 Gaylord Perry	1.75	.80	.22
☐ 49 Preston Hanna	.35	.16	.04

1981 Police Dodgers

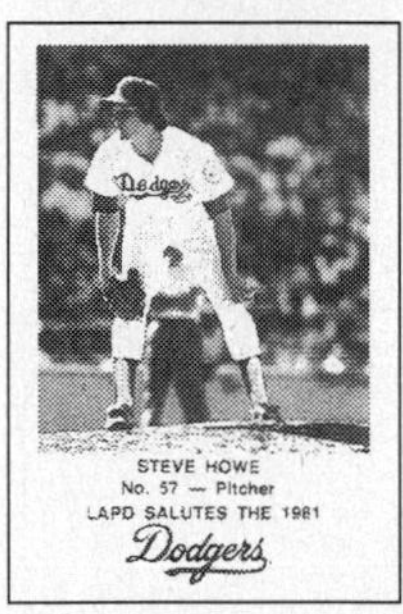

The cards in this 32-card set measure approximately 2 13/16" by 4 1/8". The full color set of 1981 Los Angeles Dodgers features the player's name, number, position and a line stating that the LAPD salutes the 1981 Dodgers, in addition to the player's photo. The backs feature the LAPD logo and short narratives, attributable to the player on the front of the card, revealing police associated tips. The cards of Ken Landreaux and Dave Stewart are reported to be more difficult to obtain than other cards in this set due to the fact that they are replacements for Stanhouse (released 4/17/81) and Hatcher (traded for Landreaux 3/30/81). The complete set price below refers to all 32 cards, i.e., including the variations.

	NRMT-MT	EXC	G-VG
COMPLETE SET (32)	12.00	5.50	1.50
COMMON PLAYER	.35	.16	.04
☐ 2 Tom Lasorda MG	.75	.35	.09
☐ 3 Rudy Law	.35	.16	.04
☐ 6 Steve Garvey	1.00	.45	.13
☐ 7 Steve Yeager	.45	.20	.06
☐ 8 Reggie Smith	.60	.25	.08
☐ 10 Ron Cey	.60	.25	.08
☐ 12 Dusty Baker	.75	.35	.09
☐ 13 Joe Ferguson	.45	.20	.06
☐ 14 Mike Scioscia	.60	.25	.08
☐ 15 Davey Lopes	.60	.25	.08
☐ 16 Rick Monday	.45	.20	.06
☐ 18 Bill Russell	.60	.25	.08
☐ 21 Jay Johnstone	.60	.25	.08
☐ 26 Don Stanhouse	.45	.20	.06
☐ 27 Joe Beckwith	.35	.16	.04
☐ 28 Pedro Guerrero	.75	.35	.09
☐ 30 Derrel Thomas	.35	.16	.04
☐ 34 Fernando Valenzuela	1.50	.65	.19
☐ 35 Bob Welch	.60	.25	.08
☐ 36 Pepe Frias	.35	.16	.04
☐ 37 Robert Castillo	.35	.16	.04
☐ 38 Dave Goltz	.35	.16	.04
☐ 41 Jerry Reuss	.45	.20	.06
☐ 43 Rick Sutcliffe	.60	.25	.08
☐ 44A Mickey Hatcher	.45	.20	.06
☐ 44B Ken Landreaux SP	1.25	.55	.16
☐ 46 Burt Hooton	.35	.16	.04
☐ 48 Dave Stewart SP	2.50	1.15	.30
☐ 51 Terry Forster	.45	.20	.06
☐ 57 Steve Howe	.45	.20	.06
☐ NNO Team Photo/Checklist	.45	.20	.06
☐ NNO Coaching Staff Monty Basgall Tom Lasorda MG Danny Ozark Ron Perranoski Manny Mota Mark Creese	.45	.20	.06

1981 Police Mariners

The cards in this 16-card set measure approximately 2 5/8" by 4 1/8". The full color Seattle Mariners Police set of this year was sponsored by the Washington State Crime Prevention Association, the Kiwanis Club, Coca-Cola and Ernst Home Centers. The fronts feature the player's name, his position, and the Seattle Mariners name in addition to the player's photo. The backs, in red and blue, feature Tips from the Mariners and the logos of the four sponsors of the set. The cards are numbered in the lower left corners of the backs.

	NRMT-MT	EXC	G-VG
COMPLETE SET (16)	7.00	3.10	.85
COMMON PLAYER (1-16)	.45	.20	.06
☐ 1 Jeff Burroughs	.60	.25	.08
☐ 2 Floyd Bannister	.60	.25	.08
☐ 3 Glenn Abbott	.45	.20	.06
☐ 4 Jim Anderson	.45	.20	.06
☐ 5 Danny Meyer	.45	.20	.06
☐ 6 Julio Cruz	.60	.25	.08
☐ 7 Dave Edler	.45	.20	.06
☐ 8 Kenny Clay	.45	.20	.06
☐ 9 Lenny Randle	.45	.20	.06
☐ 10 Mike Parrott	.45	.20	.06
☐ 11 Tom Paciorek	.60	.25	.08
☐ 12 Jerry Narron	.45	.20	.06
☐ 13 Richie Zisk	.60	.25	.08
☐ 14 Maury Wills MG	.75	.35	.09
☐ 15 Joe Simpson	.45	.20	.06
☐ 16 Shane Rawley	.60	.25	.08

1981 Police Royals

The cards in this 10-card set measure approximately 2 1/2" by 4 1/8". The 1981 Police Kansas City Royals set features full color cards of Royals players. The fronts feature the player's name, position, height and weight, and the Royals'

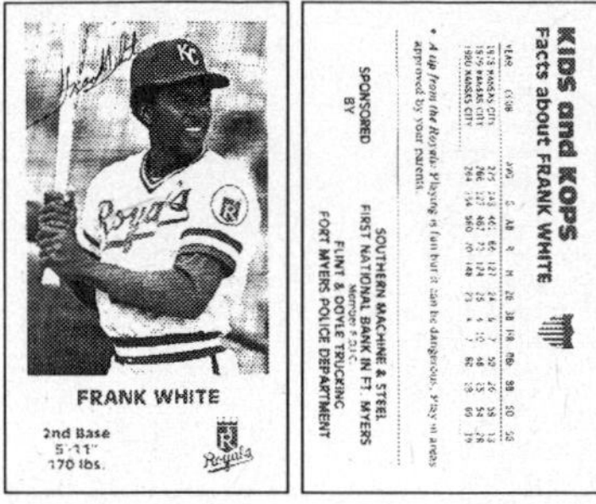

logo in addition to the photo and facsimile autograph of the player. The backs feature player statistics, Tips from the Royals, and identification of the sponsoring organizations. This set can be distinguished from the 1983 Police Royals set by the statistics on the backs of these 1981 cards, whereas the 1983 cards only show a biographical paragraph in tyhe same space.

	NRMT-MT	EXC	G-VG
COMPLETE SET (10)	25.00	11.50	3.10
COMMON PLAYER (1-10)	1.50	.65	.19
☐ 1 Willie Aikens	1.50	.65	.19
☐ 2 George Brett	16.50	7.50	2.10
☐ 3 Rich Gale	1.50	.65	.19
☐ 4 Clint Hurdle	2.00	.90	.25
☐ 5 Dennis Leonard	2.00	.90	.25
☐ 6 Hal McRae	3.00	1.35	.40
☐ 7 Amos Otis	2.00	.90	.25
☐ 8 U.L. Washington	1.50	.65	.19
☐ 9 Frank White	3.00	1.35	.40
☐ 10 Willie Wilson	3.00	1.35	.40

1982 Police Braves

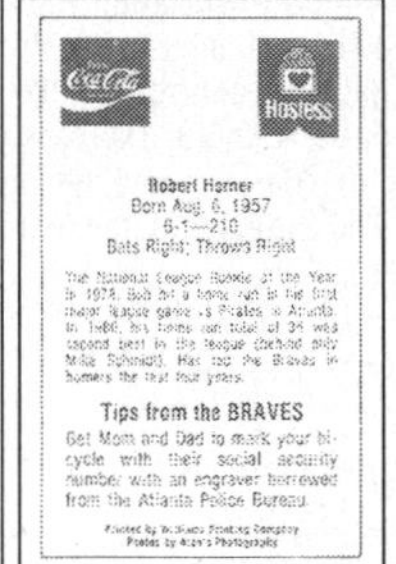

The cards in this 30-card set measure approximately 2 5/8" by 4 1/8". The Atlanta Police Department followed up on their successful 1981 safety set by publishing a new Braves set for 1982. Featured in excellent color photos are manager Joe Torre, 24 players, and 5 coaches. The cards are numbered, by uniform number, on the front only, while the backs contain a short biography of the individual and a Tips from the Braves section. The logos for the Atlanta PAL and the Braves appear on the front; those of Coca-Cola and Hostess are found on the back. A line commemorating Atlanta's record-shattering, season-beginning win streak is located in the upper right corner on every card obverse. The player list on the reverse of the Torre card is a roster list and not a checklist for the set. There were 8,000 sets reportedly printed. The Bob Watson card is supposedly more difficult to obtain than others in this set.

	NRMT-MT	EXC	G-VG
COMPLETE SET (30)	18.00	8.00	2.30
COMMON PLAYER	.50	.23	.06
☐ 1 Jerry Royster	.50	.23	.06
☐ 3 Dale Murphy	4.00	1.80	.50
☐ 4 Biff Pocoroba	.50	.23	.06
☐ 5 Bob Horner	.75	.35	.09
☐ 6 Randy Johnson	.50	.23	.06
☐ 8 Bob Watson SP	1.50	.65	.19
☐ 9 Joe Torre MG	1.00	.45	.13
☐ 10 Chris Chambliss	.75	.35	.09
☐ 15 Claudell Washington	.60	.25	.08
☐ 16 Rafael Ramirez	.50	.23	.06
☐ 17 Glenn Hubbard	.50	.23	.06
☐ 20 Bruce Benedict	.50	.23	.06
☐ 22 Brett Butler	1.50	.65	.19
☐ 23 Tommy Aaron CO	.75	.35	.09
☐ 25 Rufino Linares	.50	.23	.06
☐ 26 Gene Garber	.60	.25	.08
☐ 27 Larry McWilliams	.50	.23	.06
☐ 28 Larry Whisenton	.50	.23	.06
☐ 32 Steve Bedrosian	.90	.40	.11
☐ 35 Phil Niekro	2.50	1.15	.30
☐ 37 Rick Camp	.50	.23	.06
☐ 38 Joe Cowley	.50	.23	.06
☐ 39 Al Hrabosky	.60	.25	.08
☐ 42 Rick Mahler	.50	.23	.06
☐ 43 Bob Walk	.60	.25	.08
☐ 45 Bob Gibson CO	1.50	.65	.19
☐ 49 Preston Hanna	.50	.23	.06
☐ 52 Joe Pignatano CO	.50	.23	.06
☐ 53 Dal Maxvill CO	.50	.23	.06
☐ 54 Rube Walker CO	.50	.23	.06

1982 Police Brewers

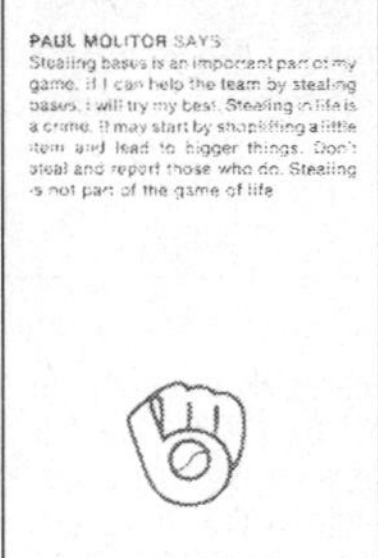

The cards in this 30-card set measure approximately 2 13/16" by 4 1/8". This set of Milwaukee Brewers baseball cards is noted for its excellent color photographs set upon a simple white background. The set was initially distributed at the stadium on May 5th, but was also handed out by several local police departments, and credit lines for the Wisconsin State Fair Park Police (no shield design on reverse), Milwaukee, Brookfield, and Wauwatosa PD's have already been found. The reverses feature advice concerning safety measures, social situations, and crime prevention (Romero card in both Spanish and English). The team card carries a checklist which lists the Brewer's coaches separately although they all appear on a single card; VP/GM Harry Dalton is not mentioned on this list but is included in the set.The prices below are for the basic set without regard to the Police Department listed on the backs. Cards from the more obscure corners and small towns of Wisconsin (where fewer cards were produced) will be valued higher.

	NRMT-MT	EXC	G-VG
COMPLETE SET (30)	15.00	6.75	1.90
COMMON PLAYER	.40	.18	.05
☐ 4 Paul Molitor	2.00	.90	.25
☐ 5 Ned Yost	.40	.18	.05
☐ 7 Don Money	.50	.23	.06

☐ 9 Larry Hisle	.50	.23	.06
☐ 10 Bob McClure	.40	.18	.05
☐ 11 Ed Romero	.40	.18	.05
☐ 13 Roy Howell	.40	.18	.05
☐ 15 Cecil Cooper	.75	.35	.09
☐ 17 Jim Gantner	.75	.35	.09
☐ 19 Robin Yount	4.00	1.80	.50
☐ 20 Gorman Thomas	.60	.25	.08
☐ 22 Charlie Moore	.40	.18	.05
☐ 23 Ted Simmons	1.00	.45	.13
☐ 24 Ben Oglivie	.60	.25	.08
☐ 26 Kevin Bass	.60	.25	.08
☐ 28 Jamie Easterly	.40	.18	.05
☐ 29 Mark Brouhard	.40	.18	.05
☐ 30 Moose Haas	.50	.23	.06
☐ 34 Rollie Fingers	2.00	.90	.25
☐ 35 Randy Lerch	.40	.18	.05
☐ 41 Jim Slaton	.40	.18	.05
☐ 45 Doug Jones	1.00	.45	.13
☐ 46 Jerry Augustine	.40	.18	.05
☐ 47 Dwight Bernard	.40	.18	.05
☐ 48 Mike Caldwell	.50	.23	.06
☐ 50 Pete Vuckovich	.50	.23	.06
☐ NNO Team Card	.60	.25	.08
☐ NNO Harry Dalton GM	.40	.18	.05
☐ NNO Buck Rodgers MG	.50	.23	.06
☐ NNO Brewer Coaches Ron Hansen Bob Rodgers MG Harry Warner Larry Haney Cal McLish	.40	.18	.05

1982 Police Dodgers

The cards in this 30-card set measure approximately 2 13/16" by 4 1/8". The 1982 Los Angeles Dodgers police set depicts the players and events of the 1981 season. There is a World Series trophy card, three cards commemorating the Division, League, and World Series wins, one manager card, and 25 player cards. The obverses have brilliant color photos set on white, and the player cards are numbered according to the uniform number of the individual. The reverses contain biographical material, information about stadium events, and a safety feature emphasizing "the team that wouldn't quit."

	NRMT-MT	EXC	G-VG
COMPLETE SET (30)	9.00	4.00	1.15
COMMON PLAYER	.25	.11	.03
☐ 2 Tom Lasorda MG	.45	.20	.06
☐ 6 Steve Garvey	1.00	.45	.13
☐ 7 Steve Yeager	.35	.16	.04
☐ 8 Mark Belanger	.35	.16	.04
☐ 10 Ron Cey	.45	.20	.06
☐ 12 Dusty Baker	.45	.20	.06
☐ 14 Mike Scioscia	.35	.16	.04
☐ 16 Rick Monday	.35	.16	.04
☐ 18 Bill Russell	.35	.16	.04
☐ 21 Jay Johnstone	.35	.16	.04
☐ 26 Alejandro Pena	.45	.20	.06
☐ 28 Pedro Guerrero	.75	.35	.09
☐ 30 Derrel Thomas	.25	.11	.03
☐ 31 Jorge Orta	.25	.11	.03
☐ 34 Fernando Valenzuela	.90	.40	.11
☐ 35 Bob Welch	.45	.20	.06
☐ 38 Dave Goltz	.25	.11	.03
☐ 40 Ron Roenicke	.25	.11	.03
☐ 41 Jerry Reuss	.35	.16	.04
☐ 44 Ken Landreaux	.25	.11	.03
☐ 46 Burt Hooton	.25	.11	.03
☐ 48 Dave Stewart	.75	.35	.09
☐ 49 Tom Niedenfuer	.25	.11	.03
☐ 51 Terry Forster	.35	.16	.04
☐ 52 Steve Sax	1.00	.45	.13
☐ 57 Steve Howe	.35	.16	.04
☐ NNO World Series Trophy (Checklist back)	.35	.16	.04
☐ NNO World Series Commemorative	.25	.11	.03
☐ NNO NL Champions	.25	.11	.03
☐ NNO Division Champs	.25	.11	.03

1983 Police Braves

The cards in this 30-card set measure approximately 2 5/8" by 4 1/8". For the third year in a row, the Atlanta Braves, in cooperation with the Atlanta Police Department, Coca-Cola, and Hostess, issued a full color safety set. The set features Joe Torre, five coaches, and 24 of the Atlanta Braves. Numbered only by uniform number, the statement that the Braves were the 1982 National League Western Division Champions is included on the fronts along with the Braves and Police Athletic biographies, a short narrative on the player, Tips from the Braves, and the Coke and Hostess logos.

	NRMT-MT	EXC	G-VG
COMPLETE SET (30)	12.00	5.50	1.50
COMMON PLAYER	.35	.16	.04
☐ 1 Jerry Royster	.35	.16	.04
☐ 3 Dale Murphy	3.00	1.35	.40
☐ 4 Biff Pocoroba	.35	.16	.04
☐ 5 Bob Horner	.60	.25	.08
☐ 6 Randy Johnson	.35	.16	.04
☐ 8 Bob Watson	.50	.23	.06
☐ 9 Joe Torre MG	.75	.35	.09
☐ 10 Chris Chambliss	.60	.25	.08
☐ 11 Ken Smith	.35	.16	.04
☐ 15 Claudell Washington	.50	.23	.06
☐ 16 Rafael Ramirez	.35	.16	.04
☐ 17 Glenn Hubbard	.35	.16	.04
☐ 19 Terry Harper	.35	.16	.04
☐ 20 Bruce Benedict	.35	.16	.04
☐ 22 Brett Butler	.90	.40	.11
☐ 24 Larry Owen	.35	.16	.04
☐ 26 Gene Garber	.35	.16	.04
☐ 27 Pascual Perez	.60	.25	.08
☐ 29 Craig McMurtry	.35	.16	.04
☐ 32 Steve Bedrosian	.60	.25	.08
☐ 33 Pete Falcone	.35	.16	.04
☐ 35 Phil Niekro	1.50	.65	.19
☐ 36 Sonny Jackson CO	.35	.16	.04
☐ 37 Rick Camp	.35	.16	.04
☐ 45 Bob Gibson CO	1.50	.65	.19
☐ 49 Rick Behenna	.35	.16	.04
☐ 51 Terry Forster	.50	.23	.06
☐ 52 Joe Pignatano CO	.35	.16	.04
☐ 53 Dal Maxvill CO	.35	.16	.04
☐ 54 Rube Walker CO	.35	.16	.04

1983 Police Brewers

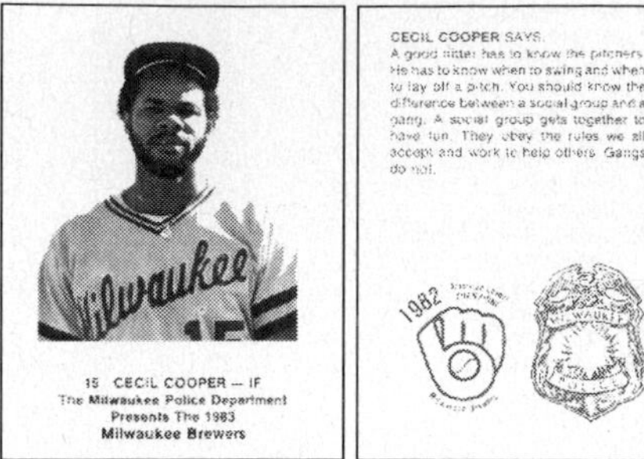

The cards in this 30-card set measure approximately 2 13/16" by 4 1/8". The 1983 Police Milwaukee Brewers set contains full color cards issued by the Milwaukee Police Department in conjunction with the Brewers. The cards are numbered on the fronts by the player uniform number and contain the line, "The Milwaukee Police Department Presents the 1983 Milwaukee Braves." The backs contain a brief narrative attributable to the player on the front, the Milwaukee Police logo, and a Milwaukee Brewers logo stating that they were the 1982 American League Champions. In all, 28 variations of these Police sets have been found to date. Prices below are for the basic set without regard to the Police Department listed on the backs of the cards; cards from the more obscure corners and small towns of Wisconsin (whose cards were produced in lesser quantities) will be valued higher.

	NRMT-MT	EXC	G-VG
COMPLETE SET (30)	9.00	4.00	1.15
COMMON PLAYER	.25	.11	.03
☐ 4 Paul Molitor	1.25	.55	.16
☐ 5 Ned Yost	.25	.11	.03
☐ 7 Don Money	.35	.16	.04
☐ 8 Rob Picciolo	.25	.11	.03
☐ 10 Bob McClure	.25	.11	.03
☐ 11 Ed Romero	.25	.11	.03
☐ 13 Roy Howell	.25	.11	.03
☐ 15 Cecil Cooper	.50	.23	.06
☐ 16 Marshall Edwards	.25	.11	.03
☐ 17 Jim Gantner	.50	.23	.06
☐ 19 Robin Yount	2.50	1.15	.30
☐ 20 Gorman Thomas	.60	.25	.08
☐ 21 Don Sutton	1.00	.45	.13
☐ 22 Charlie Moore	.25	.11	.03
☐ 23 Ted Simmons	.75	.35	.09
☐ 24 Ben Oglivie	.35	.16	.04
☐ 26 Bob Skube	.25	.11	.03
☐ 27 Pete Ladd	.25	.11	.03
☐ 28 Jamie Easterly	.25	.11	.03
☐ 30 Moose Haas	.35	.16	.04
☐ 32 Harvey Kuenn MG	.50	.23	.06
☐ 34 Rollie Fingers	1.25	.55	.16
☐ 40 Bob L. Gibson	.25	.11	.03
☐ 41 Jim Slaton	.25	.11	.03
☐ 42 Tom Tellmann	.25	.11	.03
☐ 46 Jerry Augustine	.25	.11	.03
☐ 48 Mike Caldwell	.35	.16	.04
☐ 50 Pete Vuckovich	.35	.16	.04
☐ NNO Coaches Card Pat Dobson Ron Hansen Larry Haney Dave Garcia	.35	.16	.04
☐ NNO Team Photo (Checklist back)	.35	.16	.04

1983 Police Dodgers

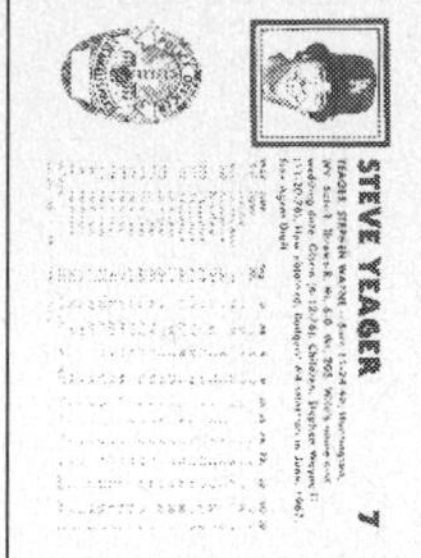

The cards in this 30-card set measure approximately 2 13/16" by 4 1/8". The full color Police Los Angeles Dodgers set of 1983 features the player's name and uniform number on the front along with the Dodger's logo, the year, and the player's photo. The backs feature a small insert portrait picture of the player, player biographies, and career statistics. The logo of the Los Angeles Police Department, the sponsor of the set, is found on the backs of the cards.

	NRMT-MT	EXC	G-VG
COMPLETE SET (30)	8.00	3.60	1.00
COMMON PLAYER	.25	.11	.03
☐ 2 Tom Lasorda MG	.45	.20	.06
☐ 3 Steve Sax	.75	.35	.09
☐ 5 Mike Marshall	.35	.16	.04
☐ 7 Steve Yeager	.35	.16	.04
☐ 12 Dusty Baker	.45	.20	.06
☐ 14 Mike Scioscia	.35	.16	.04
☐ 16 Rick Monday	.35	.16	.04
☐ 17 Greg Brock	.25	.11	.03
☐ 18 Bill Russell	.35	.16	.04
☐ 20 Candy Maldonado	.45	.20	.06
☐ 21 Ricky Wright	.25	.11	.03
☐ 22 Mark Bradley	.25	.11	.03
☐ 23 Dave Sax	.25	.11	.03
☐ 26 Alejandro Pena	.35	.16	.04
☐ 27 Joe Beckwith	.25	.11	.03
☐ 28 Pedro Guerrero	.60	.25	.08
☐ 30 Derrel Thomas	.25	.11	.03
☐ 34 Fernando Valenzuela	.60	.25	.08
☐ 35 Bob Welch	.50	.23	.06
☐ 38 Pat Zachry	.25	.11	.03
☐ 40 Ron Roenicke	.25	.11	.03
☐ 41 Jerry Reuss	.35	.16	.04
☐ 43 Jose Morales	.25	.11	.03
☐ 44 Ken Landreaux	.35	.16	.04
☐ 46 Burt Hooton	.25	.11	.03
☐ 47 Larry White	.25	.11	.03
☐ 48 Dave Stewart	.75	.35	.09
☐ 49 Tom Niedenfuer	.25	.11	.03
☐ 57 Steve Howe	.35	.16	.04
☐ NNO Coaching Staff Ron Perranoski Joe Amalfitano Monty Basgall Mark Cresse Manny Mota	.25	.11	.03

1983 Police Royals

The cards in this ten-card set measure approximately 2 1/2" by 4 1/8". The 1983 Police Kansas City Royals set features full color cards of Royals players. The fronts feature the player's name, height and weight, and the Royals' logo in addition to the player's photo and a facsimile autograph. The backs feature Kids and Cops Facts about the players, Tips from the Royals, and identification of the sponsors of the set. The cards are unnumbered. This set can be

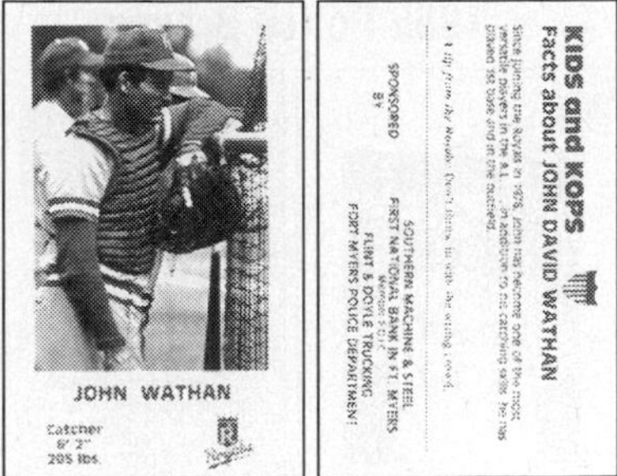

distinguished from the 1981 Police Royals set by the absence of statistics on the backs of these 1983 cards, since these 1983 cards only show a brief biographical paragraph.

	NRMT-MT	EXC	G-VG
COMPLETE SET (10)	25.00	11.50	3.10
COMMON PLAYER (1-10)	1.50	.65	.19
☐ 1 Willie Aikens	1.50	.65	.19
☐ 2 George Brett	16.50	7.50	2.10
☐ 3 Dennis Leonard	2.00	.90	.25
☐ 4 Hal McRae	3.00	1.35	.40
☐ 5 Amos Otis	2.00	.90	.25
☐ 6 Dan Quisenberry	3.00	1.35	.40
☐ 7 U.L. Washington	1.50	.65	.19
☐ 8 John Wathan	2.00	.90	.25
☐ 9 Frank White	3.00	1.35	.40
☐ 10 Willie Wilson	3.00	1.35	.40

1984 Police Braves

The cards in this 30-card set measure approximately 2 5/8" by 4 1/8". For the fourth straight year, the Atlanta Police Department issued a full color set of Atlanta Braves. The cards were given out two per week by Atlanta police officers. In addition to the police department, the set was sponsored by Coke and Hostess. The backs of the cards of Perez and Ramirez are in Spanish. The Joe Torre card contains the checklist.

	NRMT-MT	EXC	G-VG
COMPLETE SET (30)	11.00	4.90	1.40
COMMON PLAYER	.30	.14	.04
☐ 1 Jerry Royster	.30	.14	.04
☐ 3 Dale Murphy	2.00	.90	.25
☐ 5 Bob Horner	.60	.25	.08
☐ 6 Randy Johnson	.30	.14	.04
☐ 8 Bob Watson	.40	.18	.05
☐ 9 Joe Torre MG (Checklist back)	.60	.25	.08
☐ 10 Chris Chambliss	.50	.23	.06
☐ 11 Mike Jorgensen	.30	.14	.04
☐ 15 Claudell Washington	.40	.18	.05
☐ 16 Rafael Ramirez	.30	.14	.04
☐ 17 Glenn Hubbard	.30	.14	.04
☐ 19 Terry Harper	.30	.14	.04
☐ 20 Bruce Benedict	.30	.14	.04
☐ 25 Alex Trevino	.30	.14	.04
☐ 26 Gene Garber	.40	.18	.05
☐ 27 Pascual Perez	.50	.23	.06
☐ 28 Gerald Perry	.40	.18	.05
☐ 29 Craig McMurtry	.30	.14	.04
☐ 31 Donnie Moore	.30	.14	.04
☐ 32 Steve Bedrosian	.50	.23	.06
☐ 33 Pete Falcone	.30	.14	.04
☐ 37 Rick Camp	.30	.14	.04
☐ 39 Len Barker	.40	.18	.05
☐ 42 Rick Mahler	.30	.14	.04
☐ 45 Bob Gibson CO	1.00	.45	.13
☐ 51 Terry Forster	.40	.18	.05
☐ 52 Joe Pignatano CO	.30	.14	.04
☐ 53 Dal Maxvill CO	.30	.14	.04
☐ 54 Rube Walker CO	.30	.14	.04
☐ 55 Luke Appling CO	.60	.25	.08

1984 Police Brewers

14 DION JAMES — OF
Village of Brown Deer Police Dept
Presents The 1984
MILWAUKEE BREWERS

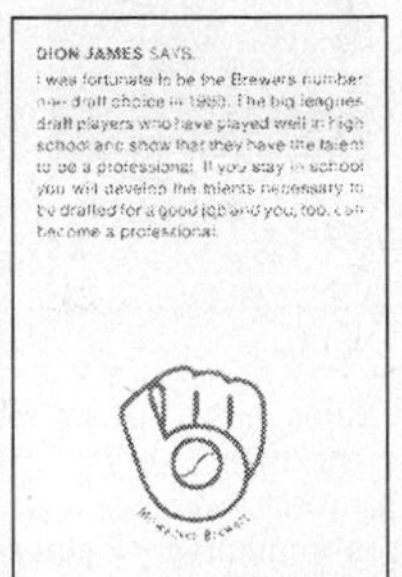

The cards in this 30-card set measure approximately 2 13/16" by 4 1/8". Again this year, the police departments in and around Milwaukee issued sets of the Milwaukee Brewers. Although each set contained the same players and numbers, the individual police departments placed their own name on the fronts of cards to show that they were the particular jurisdiction issuing the set. The backs contain the Brewers logo, a safety tip, and in some cases, a badge of the jurisdiction. To date, 59 variations of this set have been found. Prices below are for the basic set without regard to the Police Department issuing the cards; cards from the more obscure corners and small towns of Wisconsin will be valued higher. Cards are numbered by uniform number.

	NRMT-MT	EXC	G-VG
COMPLETE SET (30)	7.00	3.10	.85
COMMON PLAYER	.25	.11	.03
☐ 2 Randy Ready	.25	.11	.03
☐ 4 Paul Molitor	1.00	.45	.13
☐ 8 Jim Sundberg	.35	.16	.04
☐ 9 Rene Lachemann MG	.35	.16	.04
☐ 10 Bob McClure	.25	.11	.03
☐ 11 Ed Romero	.25	.11	.03
☐ 13 Roy Howell	.25	.11	.03
☐ 14 Dion James	.35	.16	.04
☐ 15 Cecil Cooper	.45	.20	.06
☐ 17 Jim Gantner	.45	.20	.06
☐ 19 Robin Yount	2.00	.90	.25
☐ 20 Don Sutton	.75	.35	.09
☐ 21 Bill Schroeder	.25	.11	.03
☐ 22 Charlie Moore	.25	.11	.03
☐ 23 Ted Simmons	.75	.35	.09
☐ 24 Ben Oglivie	.45	.20	.06
☐ 25 Bob Clark	.25	.11	.03
☐ 27 Pete Ladd	.25	.11	.03
☐ 28 Rick Manning	.25	.11	.03
☐ 29 Mark Brouhard	.25	.11	.03
☐ 30 Moose Haas	.35	.16	.04
☐ 34 Rollie Fingers	1.00	.45	.13
☐ 42 Tom Tellmann	.25	.11	.03
☐ 43 Chuck Porter	.25	.11	.03
☐ 46 Jerry Augustine	.25	.11	.03

☐ 47 Jaime Cocanower	.25	.11	.03
☐ 48 Mike Caldwell	.25	.11	.03
☐ 50 Pete Vuckovich	.35	.16	.04
☐ NNO Coaches Card Dave Garcia Pat Dobson Andy Etchebarren Tom Trebelhorn	.25	.11	.03
☐ NNO Team Photo (Checklist back)	.35	.16	.04

1984 Police Dodgers

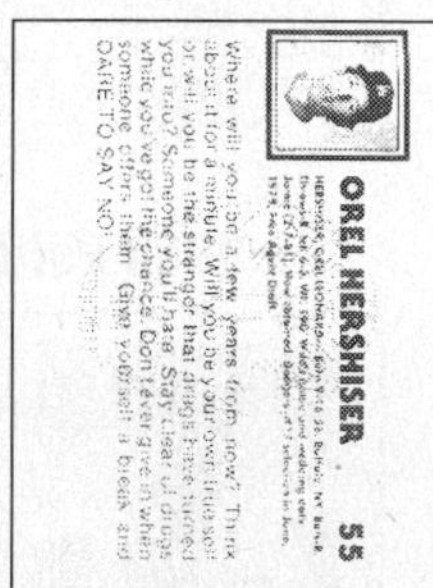

The cards in this 30-card set measure 2 13/16" by 4 1/8". For the fifth straight year, the Los Angeles Police Department sponsored a set of Dodger baseball cards. The set is numbered by player uniform number, which is featured on both the fronts and backs of the cards. The Dodgers' logo appears on the front, and the LAPD logo is superimposed on the backs of the cards. The backs are printed in Dodger blue ink and contain a small photo of the player on the front. Player biographical data and "Dare to Say No" antidrug information are featured on the back. The set features an early card of Orel Hershiser predating his Rookie Cards issued the following year.

	NRMT-MT	EXC	G-VG
COMPLETE SET (30)	8.00	3.60	1.00
COMMON PLAYER	.25	.11	.03
☐ 2 Tom Lasorda MG	.45	.20	.06
☐ 3 Steve Sax	.60	.25	.08
☐ 5 Mike Marshall	.35	.16	.04
☐ 7 Steve Yeager	.35	.16	.04
☐ 9 Greg Brock	.25	.11	.03
☐ 10 Dave Anderson	.25	.11	.03
☐ 14 Mike Scioscia	.35	.16	.04
☐ 16 Rick Monday	.35	.16	.04
☐ 17 Rafael Landestoy	.25	.11	.03
☐ 18 Bill Russell	.35	.16	.04
☐ 20 Candy Maldonado	.35	.16	.04
☐ 21 Bob Bailor	.25	.11	.03
☐ 25 German Rivera	.25	.11	.03
☐ 26 Alejandro Pena	.35	.16	.04
☐ 27 Carlos Diaz	.25	.11	.03
☐ 28 Pedro Guerrero	.60	.25	.08
☐ 31 Jack Fimple	.25	.11	.03
☐ 34 Fernando Valenzuela	.60	.25	.08
☐ 35 Bob Welch	.50	.23	.06
☐ 38 Pat Zachry	.25	.11	.03
☐ 40 Rick Honeycutt	.35	.16	.04
☐ 41 Jerry Reuss	.35	.16	.04
☐ 43 Jose Morales	.25	.11	.03
☐ 44 Ken Landreaux	.35	.16	.04
☐ 45 Terry Whitfield	.25	.11	.03
☐ 46 Burt Hooton	.25	.11	.03
☐ 49 Tom Niedenfuer	.25	.11	.03
☐ 55 Orel Hershiser	2.50	1.15	.30
☐ 56 Richard Rodas	.25	.11	.03
☐ NNO Coaching Staff Monty Basgall Joe Amalfitano Mark Cresse Manny Mota Ron Perranoski	.25	.11	.03

1985 Police Braves

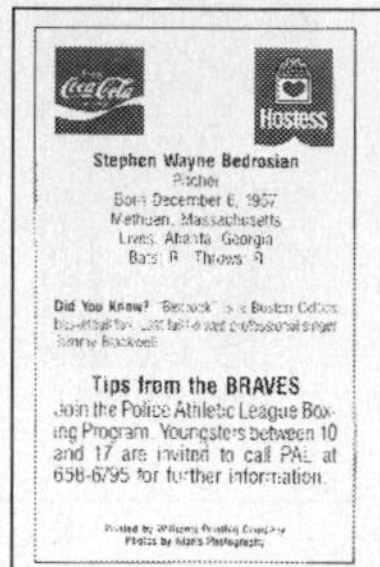

The cards in this 30-card set measure 2 5/8" by 4 1/8". For the fifth straight year, the Atlanta Police Department issued a full color set of Atlanta Braves. The set was also sponsored by Coca Cola and Hostess. In the upper right of the obverse is a logo commemorating the 20th anniversary of the Braves in Atlanta. Cards are numbered by uniform number. Cards feature a safety tip on the back. Each card except for Manager Haas has an interesting "Did You Know" fact about the player.

	NRMT-MT	EXC	G-VG
COMPLETE SET (30)	10.00	4.50	1.25
COMMON PLAYER	.30	.14	.04
☐ 2 Albert Hall	.40	.18	.05
☐ 3 Dale Murphy	2.00	.90	.25
☐ 5 Rick Cerone	.30	.14	.04
☐ 7 Bobby Wine CO	.30	.14	.04
☐ 10 Chris Chambliss	.50	.23	.06
☐ 11 Bob Horner	.60	.25	.08
☐ 12 Paul Runge	.30	.14	.04
☐ 15 Claudell Washington	.40	.18	.05
☐ 16 Rafael Ramirez	.30	.14	.04
☐ 17 Glenn Hubbard	.30	.14	.04
☐ 18 Paul Zuvella	.30	.14	.04
☐ 19 Terry Harper	.30	.14	.04
☐ 20 Bruce Benedict	.30	.14	.04
☐ 22 Eddie Haas MG	.30	.14	.04
☐ 24 Ken Oberkfell	.30	.14	.04
☐ 26 Gene Garber	.40	.18	.05
☐ 27 Pascual Perez	.50	.23	.06
☐ 28 Gerald Perry	.30	.14	.04
☐ 29 Craig McMurtry	.30	.14	.04
☐ 32 Steve Bedrosian	.50	.23	.06
☐ 33 Johnny Sain CO	.60	.25	.08
☐ 34 Zane Smith	.50	.23	.06
☐ 36 Brad Komminsk	.40	.18	.05
☐ 37 Rick Camp	.30	.14	.04
☐ 39 Len Barker	.40	.18	.05
☐ 40 Bruce Sutter	.60	.25	.08
☐ 42 Rick Mahler	.30	.14	.04
☐ 51 Terry Forster	.40	.18	.05
☐ 52 Leo Mazzone CO	.30	.14	.04
☐ 53 Bobby Dews CO	.30	.14	.04

1985 Police Brewers

The cards in this 30-card set measure 2 3/4" by 4 1/8". Again this year, the police departments in and around Milwaukee issued sets of the Milwaukee Brewers. The backs contain the Brewers logo, a safety tip, and in some cases, a badge of the jurisdiction. Prices below are for the basic set without regard to the Police Department issuing the cards; cards from the more obscure corners and small towns of Wisconsin (smaller production) will be valued higher. Cards are numbered by uniform number.

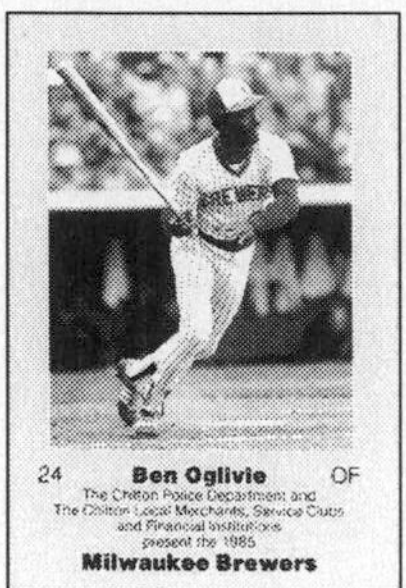

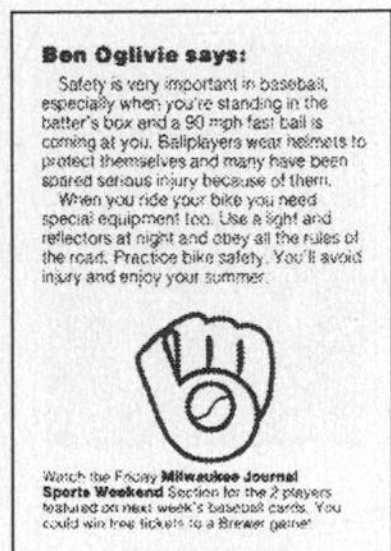

	NRMT-MT	EXC	G-VG
COMPLETE SET (30)	7.00	3.10	.85
COMMON PLAYER	.25	.11	.03
□ 2 Randy Ready	.25	.11	.03
□ 4 Paul Molitor	1.00	.45	.13
□ 5 Doug Loman	.25	.11	.03
□ 7 Paul Householder	.25	.11	.03
□ 10 Bob McClure	.25	.11	.03
□ 11 Ed Romero	.25	.11	.03
□ 14 Dion James	.25	.11	.03
□ 15 Cecil Cooper	.45	.20	.06
□ 17 Jim Gantner	.45	.20	.06
□ 18 Danny Darwin	.25	.11	.03
□ 19 Robin Yount	2.00	.90	.25
□ 21 Bill Schroeder	.25	.11	.03
□ 22 Charlie Moore	.25	.11	.03
□ 23 Ted Simmons	.60	.25	.08
□ 24 Ben Oglivie	.35	.16	.04
□ 26 Brian Giles	.25	.11	.03
□ 27 Pete Ladd	.25	.11	.03
□ 28 Rick Manning	.25	.11	.03
□ 29 Mark Brouhard	.25	.11	.03
□ 30 Moose Haas	.25	.11	.03
□ 31 George Bamberger MG	.25	.11	.03
□ 34 Rollie Fingers	1.00	.45	.13
□ 40 Bob L. Gibson	.25	.11	.03
□ 41 Ray Searage	.25	.11	.03
□ 47 Jaime Cocanower	.25	.11	.03
□ 48 Ray Burris	.25	.11	.03
□ 49 Ted Higuera	.50	.23	.06
□ 50 Pete Vuckovich	.35	.16	.04
□ NNO Team Roster	.35	.16	.04
□ NNO Coaches Card Herm Sterrette Tony Muser Frank Howard Larry Haney Andy Etchebarren	.35	.16	.04
□ NNO Newspaper Carrier	.25	.11	.03

1985 Police Mets/Yankees

This 12-card set was supposedly issued courtesy of the Kiwanis Club, a local law enforcement agency, and the New York Mets and New York Yankees. The cards measure approximately 2 9/16" by 4 1/16". The fronts feature color player photos with white borders. Beneath the photo, player information appears between the team logo and the Kiwanis International logo. The backs have anti-drug messages introduced by the words "New York Mets Say" or "New York Yankees Say." The cards are numbered on the back and are indicated below by a prefix for Mets or Yankees.

	NRMT-MT	EXC	G-VG
COMPLETE SET (12)	8.00	3.60	1.00
COMMON PLAYER (M1-M6)	.50	.23	.06
COMMON PLAYER (Y1-Y6)	.50	.23	.06
□ M1 George Foster and Bill Robinson CO	.75	.35	.09
□ M2 Davey Johnson MG and Gary Carter	.90	.40	.11
□ M3 Dwight Gooden	2.00	.90	.25
□ M4 Mookie Wilson	.50	.23	.06
□ M5 Keith Hernandez	.60	.25	.08
□ M6 Darryl Strawberry	2.00	.90	.25
□ Y1 Willie Randolph	.50	.23	.06
□ Y2 Phil Niekro	1.00	.45	.13
□ Y3 Ron Guidry	.75	.35	.09
□ Y4 Dave Winfield	2.00	.90	.25
□ Y5 Dave Righetti	.60	.25	.08
□ Y6 Billy Martin MG	.75	.35	.09

1986 Police Astros

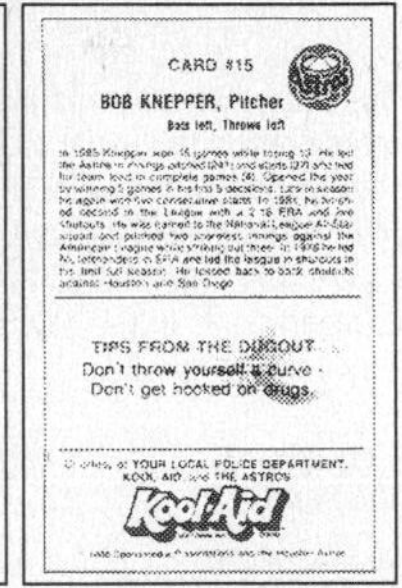

This 26-card safety set was also sponsored by Kool-Aid. The backs contain a biographical paragraph above a "Tip from the Dugout". The front features a full-color photo of the player, his name, and uniform number. The cards are numbered on the back and measure 2 5/8" by 4 1/8". The backs are printed in orange and blue on white card stock. Sets were distributed at the Astrodome on June 14th as well as given away throughout the summer by the Houston Police.

	MT	EX-MT	VG
COMPLETE SET (26)	8.00	3.60	1.00
COMMON PLAYER (1-26)	.25	.11	.03
□ 1 Jim Pankovits	.25	.11	.03
□ 2 Nolan Ryan	4.00	1.80	.50
□ 3 Mike Scott	.50	.23	.06
□ 4 Kevin Bass	.35	.16	.04
□ 5 Bill Doran	.35	.16	.04
□ 6 Hal Lanier MG	.25	.11	.03
□ 7 Denny Walling	.25	.11	.03
□ 8 Alan Ashby	.25	.11	.03
□ 9 Phil Garner	.35	.16	.04
□ 10 Charlie Kerfeld	.25	.11	.03
□ 11 Dave Smith	.35	.16	.04
□ 12 Jose Cruz	.50	.23	.06
□ 13 Craig Reynolds	.25	.11	.03
□ 14 Mark Bailey	.25	.11	.03
□ 15 Bob Knepper	.25	.11	.03
□ 16 Julio Solano	.25	.11	.03
□ 17 Dickie Thon	.35	.16	.04
□ 18 Mike Madden	.25	.11	.03
□ 19 Jeff Calhoun	.25	.11	.03
□ 20 Tony Walker	.25	.11	.03
□ 21 Terry Puhl	.35	.16	.04
□ 22 Glenn Davis	1.25	.55	.16
□ 23 Billy Hatcher	.35	.16	.04

		MT	EX-MT	VG
☐ 24	Jim Deshaies	.25	.11	.03
☐ 25	Frank DiPino	.25	.11	.03
☐ 26	Coaching Staff Gene Tenace Matt Galante Denis Menke Yogi Berra Les Moss	.35	.16	.04

1986 Police Braves

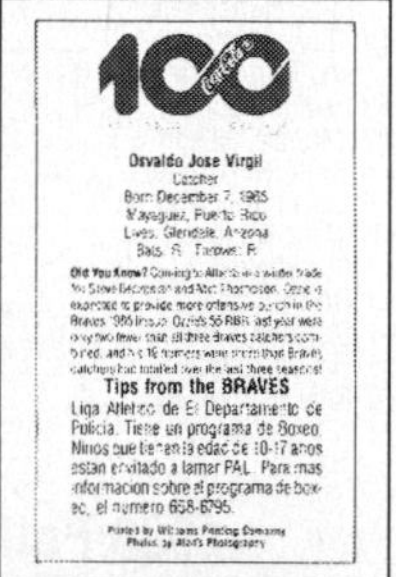

This 30-card safety set was also sponsored by Coca-Cola. The backs contain the usual biographical info and safety tip. The front features a full-color photo of the player, his name, and uniform number. The cards measure 2 5/8" by 4 1/8". Cards were freely distributed throughout the summer by the Police Departments in the Atlanta area. Cards are numbered below by uniform number.

		MT	EX-MT	VG
COMPLETE SET (30)		9.00	4.00	1.15
COMMON PLAYER		.30	.14	.04
☐ 2	Russ Nixon CO	.30	.14	.04
☐ 3	Dale Murphy	2.00	.90	.25
☐ 4	Bob Skinner CO	.40	.18	.05
☐ 5	Billy Sample	.40	.18	.05
☐ 7	Chuck Tanner MG	.40	.18	.05
☐ 8	Willie Stargell CO	1.00	.45	.13
☐ 9	Ozzie Virgil	.30	.14	.04
☐ 10	Chris Chambliss	.50	.23	.06
☐ 11	Bob Horner	.50	.23	.06
☐ 14	Andres Thomas	.30	.14	.04
☐ 15	Claudell Washington	.40	.18	.05
☐ 16	Rafael Ramirez	.30	.14	.04
☐ 17	Glenn Hubbard	.30	.14	.04
☐ 18	Omar Moreno	.30	.14	.04
☐ 19	Terry Harper	.30	.14	.04
☐ 20	Bruce Benedict	.30	.14	.04
☐ 23	Ted Simmons	.60	.25	.08
☐ 24	Ken Oberkfell	.30	.14	.04
☐ 26	Gene Garber	.40	.18	.05
☐ 29	Craig McMurtry	.30	.14	.04
☐ 30	Paul Assenmacher	.30	.14	.04
☐ 33	Johnny Sain CO	.50	.23	.06
☐ 34	Zane Smith	.50	.23	.06
☐ 38	Joe Johnson	.30	.14	.04
☐ 40	Bruce Sutter	.60	.25	.08
☐ 42	Rick Mahler	.40	.18	.05
☐ 46	David Palmer	.40	.18	.05
☐ 48	Duane Ward	.60	.25	.08
☐ 49	Jeff Dedmon	.30	.14	.04
☐ 52	Al Monchak CO	.30	.14	.04

1986 Police Brewers

This 32-card safety set was also sponsored by WTMJ Radio and Kinney Shoes. The backs contain the usual biographical info and safety tip. The front features a full-color photo of the player, his name, position, and uniform number. The cards measure approximately 2 5/8" by 4 1/8". Cards were freely distributed throughout the summer by the Police Departments in the Milwaukee area. Cards are numbered below by uniform number.

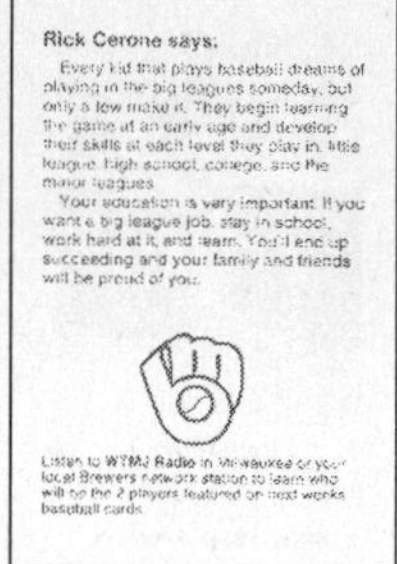

		MT	EX-MT	VG
COMPLETE SET (32)		6.50	2.90	.80
COMMON PLAYER		.25	.11	.03
☐ 1	Ernest Riles	.35	.16	.04
☐ 2	Randy Ready	.25	.11	.03
☐ 3	Juan Castillo	.25	.11	.03
☐ 4	Paul Molitor	.75	.35	.09
☐ 7	Paul Householder	.25	.11	.03
☐ 8	Andy Etchebarren CO	.25	.11	.03
☐ 10	Bob McClure	.25	.11	.03
☐ 11	Rick Cerone	.25	.11	.03
☐ 12	Larry Haney CO	.25	.11	.03
☐ 13	Billy Joe Robidoux	.35	.16	.04
☐ 15	Cecil Cooper	.35	.16	.04
☐ 16	Mike Felder	.35	.16	.04
☐ 17	Jim Gantner	.35	.16	.04
☐ 18	Danny Darwin	.25	.11	.03
☐ 19	Robin Yount	1.50	.65	.19
☐ 20	Juan Nieves	.35	.16	.04
☐ 21	Bill Schroeder	.25	.11	.03
☐ 22	Charlie Moore	.25	.11	.03
☐ 24	Ben Oglivie	.35	.16	.04
☐ 25	Mark Clear	.25	.11	.03
☐ 28	Rick Manning	.25	.11	.03
☐ 31	George Bamberger MG	.25	.11	.03
☐ 33	Frank Howard CO	.35	.16	.04
☐ 35	Tony Muser CO	.25	.11	.03
☐ 37	Dan Plesac	.35	.16	.04
☐ 38	Herm Starrette CO	.25	.11	.03
☐ 39	Tim Leary	.35	.16	.04
☐ 42	Tom Trebelhorn CO	.35	.16	.04
☐ 45	Rob Deer	.60	.25	.08
☐ 46	Bill Wegman	.35	.16	.04
☐ 47	Jaime Cocanower	.25	.11	.03
☐ 49	Teddy Higuera	.45	.20	.06

1986 Police Dodgers

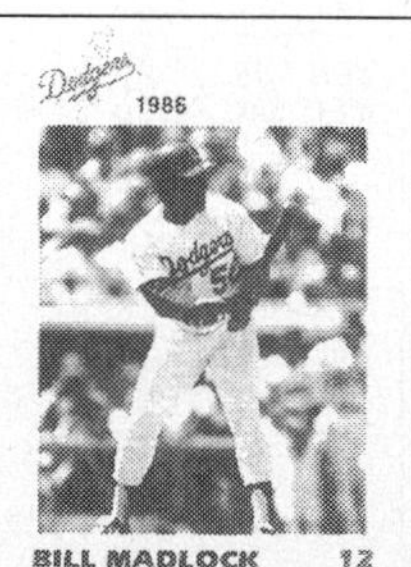

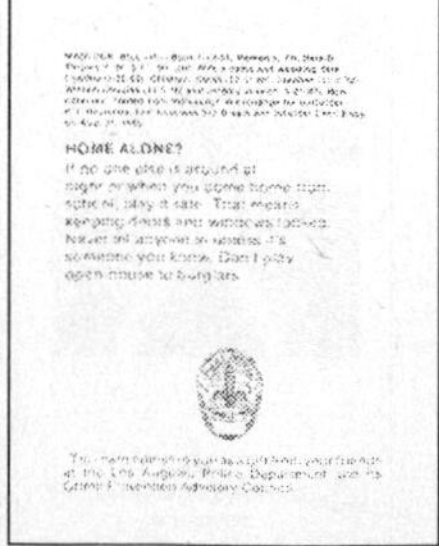

This 30-card set features full-color cards each measuring 2 13/16" by 4 1/8". The cards are unnumbered except for uniform numbers. The backs give a safety tip as well as a short capsule biography. The sets were given away at Dodger Stadium on May 18th.

	MT	EX-MT	VG
COMPLETE SET (30)	6.50	2.90	.80
COMMON PLAYER	.25	.11	.03
☐ 2 Tom Lasorda MG	.45	.20	.06
☐ 3 Steve Sax	.60	.25	.08
☐ 5 Mike Marshall	.35	.16	.04
☐ 9 Greg Brock	.25	.11	.03
☐ 10 Dave Anderson	.25	.11	.03
☐ 12 Bill Madlock	.35	.16	.04
☐ 14 Mike Scioscia	.35	.16	.04
☐ 17 Len Matuszek	.25	.11	.03
☐ 18 Bill Russell	.35	.16	.04
☐ 22 Franklin Stubbs	.35	.16	.04
☐ 23 Enos Cabell	.25	.11	.03
☐ 25 Mariano Duncan	.35	.16	.04
☐ 26 Alejandro Pena	.35	.16	.04
☐ 27 Carlos Diaz	.25	.11	.03
☐ 28 Pedro Guerrero	.60	.25	.08
☐ 29 Alex Trevino	.25	.11	.03
☐ 31 Ed VandeBerg	.25	.11	.03
☐ 34 Fernando Valenzuela	.60	.25	.08
☐ 35 Bob Welch	.45	.20	.06
☐ 40 Rick Honeycutt	.25	.11	.03
☐ 41 Jerry Reuss	.35	.16	.04
☐ 43 Ken Howell	.25	.11	.03
☐ 44 Ken Landreaux	.35	.16	.04
☐ 45 Terry Whitfield	.25	.11	.03
☐ 48 Dennis Powell	.25	.11	.03
☐ 49 Tom Niedenfuer	.25	.11	.03
☐ 51 Reggie Williams	.25	.11	.03
☐ 55 Orel Hershiser	.90	.40	.11
☐ NNO Coaching Staff	.25	.11	.03
Don McMahon			
Mark Cresse			
Ben Hines			
Ron Perranoski			
Monty Basgall			
Manny Mota			
Joe Amalfitano			
☐ NNO Team Photo	.35	.16	.04
(Checklist back)			

1987 Police Astros

This 26-card safety set was sponsored by the Astros, Deer Park Hospital, and Sportsmedia Presentations. The backs contain a biographical paragraph above a "Tip from the Dugout". The front features a full-color photo of the player, his name, position, and uniform number. The cards are numbered on the back and measure 2 5/8" by 4 1/8". The first twelve cards were distributed at the Astrodome on July 14th and the rest were given away later in the summer by the Deer Park Hospital.

	MT	EX-MT	VG
COMPLETE SET (26)	7.00	3.10	.85
COMMON PLAYER (1-26)	.25	.11	.03
☐ 1 Larry Andersen	.25	.11	.03
☐ 2 Mark Bailey	.25	.11	.03
☐ 3 Jose Cruz	.35	.16	.04
☐ 4 Danny Darwin	.25	.11	.03
☐ 5 Bill Doran	.35	.16	.04
☐ 6 Billy Hatcher	.35	.16	.04
☐ 7 Hal Lanier MG	.25	.11	.03
☐ 8 Davey Lopes	.35	.16	.04
☐ 9 Dave Meads	.25	.11	.03
☐ 10 Craig Reynolds	.35	.16	.04
☐ 11 Mike Scott	.60	.25	.08
☐ 12 Denny Walling	.25	.11	.03
☐ 13 Aurelio Lopez	.25	.11	.03
☐ 14 Dickie Thon	.35	.16	.04
☐ 15 Terry Puhl	.35	.16	.04
☐ 16 Nolan Ryan	3.50	1.55	.45
☐ 17 Dave Smith	.35	.16	.04
☐ 18 Julio Solano	.25	.11	.03
☐ 19 Jim Deshaies	.25	.11	.03
☐ 20 Bob Knepper	.25	.11	.03
☐ 21 Alan Ashby	.25	.11	.03
☐ 22 Kevin Bass	.35	.16	.04
☐ 23 Glenn Davis	.60	.25	.08
☐ 24 Phil Garner	.35	.16	.04
☐ 25 Jim Pankovits	.25	.11	.03
☐ 26 Coaching Staff	.35	.16	.04
Gene Tenace			
Matt Galante			
Denis Menke			
Yogi Berra			
Les Moss			

1987 Police Brewers

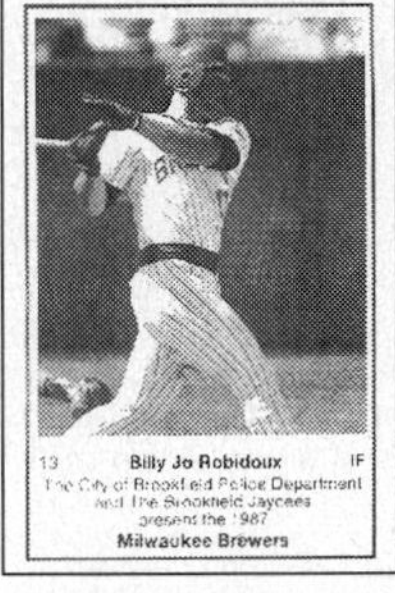

This 30-card safety set was also sponsored by WTMJ Radio and Kinney Shoes. The backs contain the usual biographical info and safety tip. The front features a full-color photo of the player, his name, position, and uniform number. The cards measure 2 5/8" by 4 1/8". Cards were freely distributed throughout the summer by the Police Departments in the Milwaukee area and throughout other parts of Wisconsin. Cards are numbered below by uniform number.

	MT	EX-MT	VG
COMPLETE SET (30)	6.50	2.90	.80
COMMON PLAYER	.25	.11	.03
☐ 1 Ernest Riles	.25	.11	.03
☐ 2 Edgar Diaz	.25	.11	.03
☐ 3 Juan Castillo	.25	.11	.03
☐ 4 Paul Molitor	.75	.35	.09
☐ 5 B.J. Surhoff	.50	.23	.06
☐ 7 Dale Sveum	.25	.11	.03
☐ 9 Greg Brock	.25	.11	.03
☐ 13 Billy Joe Robidoux	.25	.11	.03
☐ 14 Jim Paciorek	.25	.11	.03
☐ 15 Cecil Cooper	.35	.16	.04
☐ 16 Mike Felder	.35	.16	.04
☐ 17 Jim Gantner	.35	.16	.04
☐ 19 Robin Yount	1.50	.65	.19
☐ 20 Juan Nieves	.25	.11	.03
☐ 21 Bill Schroeder	.25	.11	.03
☐ 25 Mark Clear	.25	.11	.03
☐ 26 Glenn Braggs	.35	.16	.04
☐ 28 Rick Manning	.25	.11	.03
☐ 29 Chris Bosio	.75	.35	.09
☐ 32 Chuck Crim	.25	.11	.03
☐ 34 Mark Ciardi	.25	.11	.03
☐ 37 Dan Plesac	.35	.16	.04
☐ 38 John Henry Johnson	.25	.11	.03
☐ 40 Mike Birkbeck	.25	.11	.03
☐ 42 Tom Trebelhorn MG	.35	.16	.04
☐ 45 Rob Deer	.45	.20	.06
☐ 46 Bill Wegman	.35	.16	.04

	MT	EX-MT	VG
☐ 49 Teddy Higuera	.45	.20	.06
☐ NNO Coaching Staff Andy Etchebarren Larry Haney Chuck Hartenstein Dave Hilton Tony Muser	.25	.11	.03
☐ NNO Brewers Team (Checklist on back)	.35	.16	.04

1987 Police Dodgers

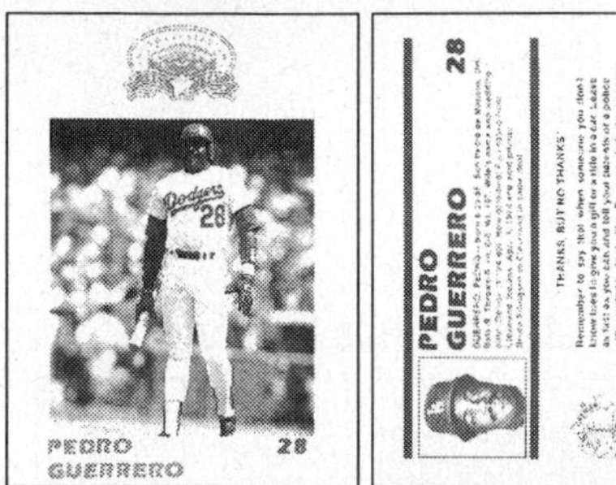

This 30-card set features full-color cards each measuring approximately 2 13/16" by 4 1/8". The cards are unnumbered except for uniform numbers. The backs give a safety tip as well as a short capsule biography. Cards were given away at Dodger Stadium on April 24th and later during the summer by LAPD officers at a rate of two cards per week.

	MT	EX-MT	VG
COMPLETE SET (30)	6.50	2.90	.80
COMMON PLAYER (1-30)	.25	.11	.03
☐ 1 Tom Lasorda MG 2	.45	.20	.06
☐ 2 Steve Sax 3	.60	.25	.08
☐ 3 Mike Marshall 5	.35	.16	.04
☐ 4 Dave Anderson 10	.25	.11	.03
☐ 5 Bill Madlock 12	.35	.16	.04
☐ 6 Mike Scioscia 14	.35	.16	.04
☐ 7 Gilberto Reyes 15	.35	.16	.04
☐ 8 Len Matuszek 17	.25	.11	.03
☐ 9 Reggie Williams 21	.25	.11	.03
☐ 10 Franklin Stubbs 22	.35	.16	.04
☐ 11 Tim Leary 23	.35	.16	.04
☐ 12 Mariano Duncan 25	.35	.16	.04
☐ 13 Alejandro Pena 26	.35	.16	.04
☐ 14 Pedro Guerrero 28	.60	.25	.08
☐ 15 Alex Trevino 29	.25	.11	.03
☐ 16 Jeff Hamilton 33	.35	.16	.04
☐ 17 Fernando Valenzuela 34	.60	.25	.08
☐ 18 Bob Welch 35	.45	.20	.06
☐ 19 Matt Young 36	.35	.16	.04
☐ 20 Rick Honeycutt 40	.25	.11	.03
☐ 21 Jerry Reuss 41	.35	.16	.04
☐ 22 Ken Howell 43	.25	.11	.03
☐ 23 Ken Landreaux 44	.35	.16	.04
☐ 24 Ralph Bryant 46	.25	.11	.03
☐ 25 Jose Gonzalez 47	.25	.11	.03
☐ 26 Tom Niedenfuer 49	.25	.11	.03
☐ 27 Brian Holton 51	.25	.11	.03
☐ 28 Orel Hershiser 55	.75	.35	.09
☐ 29 Coaching Staff Ron Perranoski Tom Lasorda Joe Amalfitano Don McMahon Manny Mota Bill Russell Mark Cresse (Unnumbered)	.25	.11	.03
☐ 30 Dodgers Stadium (25th Anniversary)	.25	.11	.03

1988 Police Astros

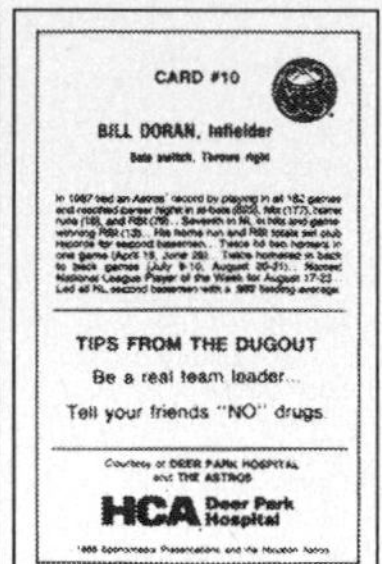

This 26-card safety set was sponsored by the Astros, Deer Park Hospital, and Sportsmedia Presentations. The backs contain a biographical paragraph above "Tips from the Dugout". The front features a full-color photo of the player, his name, position, and uniform number. The cards are numbered on the back and measure 2 5/8" by 4 1/8". The sets were supposedly distributed to the first 15,000 youngsters attending the New York Mets game against the Astros at the Astrodome on July 9th.

	MT	EX-MT	VG
COMPLETE SET (26)	7.00	3.10	.85
COMMON PLAYER (1-26)	.25	.11	.03
☐ 1 Juan Agosto	.25	.11	.03
☐ 2 Larry Andersen	.25	.11	.03
☐ 3 Joaquin Andujar	.35	.16	.04
☐ 4 Alan Ashby	.25	.11	.03
☐ 5 Mark Bailey	.25	.11	.03
☐ 6 Kevin Bass	.35	.16	.04
☐ 7 Danny Darwin	.25	.11	.03
☐ 8 Glenn Davis	.60	.25	.08
☐ 9 Jim Deshaies	.25	.11	.03
☐ 10 Bill Doran	.35	.16	.04
☐ 11 Billy Hatcher	.35	.16	.04
☐ 12 Jeff Heathcock	.25	.11	.03
☐ 13 Steve Henderson	.25	.11	.03
☐ 14 Chuck Jackson	.25	.11	.03
☐ 15 Bob Knepper	.25	.11	.03
☐ 16 Jim Pankovits	.25	.11	.03
☐ 17 Terry Puhl	.35	.16	.04
☐ 18 Rafael Ramirez	.25	.11	.03
☐ 19 Craig Reynolds	.35	.16	.04
☐ 20 Nolan Ryan	3.50	1.55	.45
☐ 21 Mike Scott	.60	.25	.08
☐ 22 Dave Smith	.35	.16	.04
☐ 23 Denny Walling	.25	.11	.03
☐ 24 Gerald Young	.25	.11	.03
☐ 25 Hal Lanier MG	.25	.11	.03
☐ 26 Coaching Staff	.35	.16	.04

1988 Police Brewers

This 30-card safety set was also sponsored by WTMJ Radio and Stadia Athletic Shoes. The backs contain the usual biographical info and safety tip. The front features a full-color photo of the player, his name, position, and uniform number. The cards measure approximately 2 7/8" by 4 1/8". Cards were freely distributed throughout the summer by the Police Departments in the Milwaukee area and throughout other parts of Wisconsin. Cards are numbered below by uniform number.

	MT	EX-MT	VG
COMPLETE SET (30)	6.00	2.70	.75
COMMON PLAYER	.25	.11	.03
☐ 1 Ernest Riles	.25	.11	.03
☐ 3 Juan Castillo	.25	.11	.03

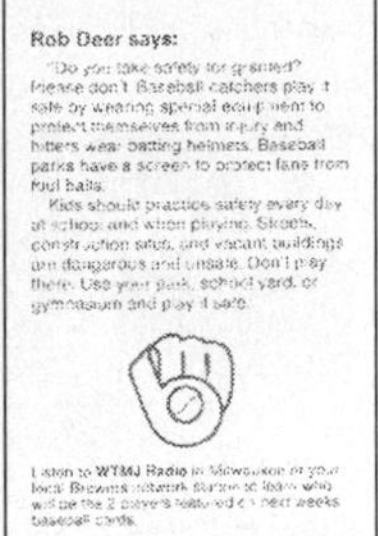

☐ 4 Paul Molitor	.75	.35	.09
☐ 5 B.J. Surhoff	.35	.16	.04
☐ 7 Dale Sveum	.25	.11	.03
☐ 9 Greg Brock	.25	.11	.03
☐ 11 Charlie O'Brien	.25	.11	.03
☐ 14 Jim Adduci	.25	.11	.03
☐ 16 Mike Felder	.25	.11	.03
☐ 17 Jim Gantner	.35	.16	.04
☐ 19 Robin Yount	1.50	.65	.19
☐ 20 Juan Nieves	.25	.11	.03
☐ 21 Bill Schroeder	.25	.11	.03
☐ 23 Joey Meyer	.25	.11	.03
☐ 25 Mark Clear	.25	.11	.03
☐ 26 Glenn Braggs	.25	.11	.03
☐ 28 Odell Jones	.25	.11	.03
☐ 29 Chris Bosio	.50	.23	.06
☐ 30 Steve Kiefer	.25	.11	.03
☐ 32 Chuck Crim	.25	.11	.03
☐ 33 Jay Aldrich	.25	.11	.03
☐ 37 Dan Plesac	.35	.16	.04
☐ 40 Mike Birkbeck	.25	.11	.03
☐ 42 Tom Trebelhorn MG	.35	.16	.04
☐ 43 Dave Stapleton	.25	.11	.03
☐ 45 Rob Deer	.45	.20	.06
☐ 46 Bill Wegman	.35	.16	.04
☐ 49 Ted Higuera	.35	.16	.04
☐ NNO Team Photo HOR	.35	.16	.04
☐ NNO Manager/Coaches HOR Andy Etchebarren Larry Haney Chuck Hartenstein Dave Hilton Tony Muser	.25	.11	.03

1988 Police Dodgers

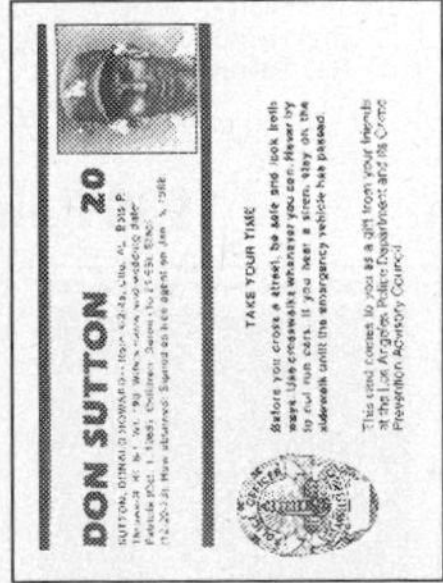

This 30-card set features full-color cards each measuring approximately 2 13/16" by 4 1/8". The cards are unnumbered except for uniform numbers. The backs give a safety tip as well as a short capsule biography. Cards were given during the summer by LAPD officers. The set is very similar to the 1987 set, the 1988 set is distinguished by the fact that it does not have the 25th anniversary (of Dodger Stadium) logo on the card front.

	MT	EX-MT	VG
COMPLETE SET (30)	6.00	2.70	.75
COMMON PLAYER	.25	.11	.03
☐ 2 Tom Lasorda MG	.45	.20	.06
☐ 3 Steve Sax	.45	.20	.06
☐ 5 Mike Marshall	.35	.16	.04
☐ 7 Alfredo Griffin	.25	.11	.03
☐ 9 Mickey Hatcher	.25	.11	.03
☐ 10 Dave Anderson	.25	.11	.03
☐ 12 Danny Heep	.25	.11	.03
☐ 14 Mike Scioscia	.35	.16	.04
☐ 20 Don Sutton	.60	.25	.08
☐ 21 Tito Landrum and 17 Len Matuszak	.25	.11	.03
☐ 22 Franklin Stubbs	.35	.16	.04
☐ 23 Kirk Gibson	.60	.25	.08
☐ 25 Mariano Duncan	.35	.16	.04
☐ 26 Alejandro Pena	.35	.16	.04
☐ 27 Mike Sharperson and 52}Tim Crews	.35	.16	.04
☐ 28 Pedro Guerrero	.45	.20	.06
☐ 29 Alex Trevino	.25	.11	.03
☐ 31 John Shelby	.25	.11	.03
☐ 33 Jeff Hamilton	.25	.11	.03
☐ 34 Fernando Valenzuela	.45	.20	.06
☐ 37 Mike Davis	.25	.11	.03
☐ 41 Brad Havens	.25	.11	.03
☐ 43 Ken Howell	.25	.11	.03
☐ 47 Jesse Orosco	.25	.11	.03
☐ 49 Tim Belcher and 57}Shawn Hillegas	.35	.16	.04
☐ 50 Jay Howell	.35	.16	.04
☐ 51 Brian Holton	.25	.11	.03
☐ 54 Tim Leary	.35	.16	.04
☐ 55 Orel Hershiser	.75	.35	.09
☐ NNO Tom Lasorda MG and Coaches	.35	.16	.04

1988 Police Tigers

This set was sponsored by the Michigan State Police and the Detroit Tigers organization. There are 14 blue-bordered cards in the set; each card measures approximately 2 1/2" by 3 1/2". The cards are completely unnumbered as there is not even any reference to uniform numbers on the cards; the cards are listed below in alphabetical order.

	MT	EX-MT	VG
COMPLETE SET (14)	35.00	16.00	4.40
COMMON PLAYER (1-14)	1.50	.65	.19
☐ 1 Doyle Alexander	2.00	.90	.25
☐ 2 Sparky Anderson MG	3.50	1.55	.45
☐ 3 Dave Bergman	1.50	.65	.19
☐ 4 Tom Brookens	1.50	.65	.19
☐ 5 Darrell Evans	2.50	1.15	.30
☐ 6 Larry Herndon	1.50	.65	.19
☐ 7 Chet Lemon	2.00	.90	.25
☐ 8 Jack Morris	7.50	3.40	.95
☐ 9 Matt Nokes	3.50	1.55	.45
☐ 10 Jeff M. Robinson	2.00	.90	.25
☐ 11 Frank Tanana	2.50	1.15	.30
☐ 12 Walt Terrell	1.50	.65	.19
☐ 13 Alan Trammell	7.50	3.40	.95
☐ 14 Lou Whitaker	7.50	3.40	.95

1989 Police Brewers

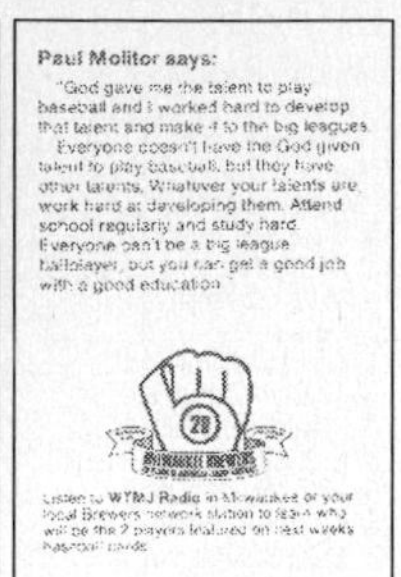

The 1989 Police Milwaukee Brewers set contains 30 cards measuring approximately 2 3/4" by 4 1/4". The fronts have color photos with white borders; the backs feature safety tips. The unnumbered cards were given away by various local Wisconsin police departments. The cards are numbered below by uniform number.

	MT	EX-MT	VG
COMPLETE SET (30)	6.00	2.70	.75
COMMON PLAYER	.25	.11	.03
☐ 1 Gary Sheffield	1.50	.65	.19
☐ 4 Paul Molitor	.75	.35	.09
☐ 5 B.J. Surhoff	.35	.16	.04
☐ 6 Bill Spiers	.35	.16	.04
☐ 7 Dale Sveum	.25	.11	.03
☐ 9 Greg Brock	.25	.11	.03
☐ 14 Gus Polidor	.25	.11	.03
☐ 16 Mike Felder	.25	.11	.03
☐ 17 Jim Gantner	.35	.16	.04
☐ 19 Robin Yount	1.50	.65	.19
☐ 20 Juan Nieves	.25	.11	.03
☐ 22 Charlie O'Brien	.25	.11	.03
☐ 23 Joey Meyer	.25	.11	.03
☐ 25 Dave Engle	.25	.11	.03
☐ 26 Glenn Braggs	.25	.11	.03
☐ 27 Paul Mirabella	.25	.11	.03
☐ 29 Chris Bosio	.50	.23	.06
☐ 30 Terry Francona	.25	.11	.03
☐ 32 Chuck Crim	.25	.11	.03
☐ 37 Dan Plesac	.25	.11	.03
☐ 38 Don August	.25	.11	.03
☐ 40 Mike Birkbeck	.25	.11	.03
☐ 41 Mark Knudson	.25	.11	.03
☐ 42 Tom Trebelhorn MG	.35	.16	.04
☐ 45 Rob Deer	.45	.20	.06
☐ 46 Bill Wegman	.35	.16	.04
☐ 48 Bryan Clutterbuck	.25	.11	.03
☐ 49 Teddy Higuera	.35	.16	.04
☐ NNO Team Card (Checklist on back)	.35	.16	.04
☐ NNO Coaches Card Duffy Dyer Andy Etchebarren Larry Haney Chuck Hartenstein Tony Muser	.25	.11	.03

1989 Police Dodgers

The 1989 Police Los Angeles Dodgers set contains 30 cards measuring approximately 2 5/8" by 4 1/4". The fronts have color photos with white borders; the backs feature safety tips and biographical information. The unnumbered cards were given away by various Los Angeles-area police departments. The cards were also issued as an uncut, perforated sheet to children (age 14 and under) at Dodger Stadium on Baseball Card Night, May 5, 1989.

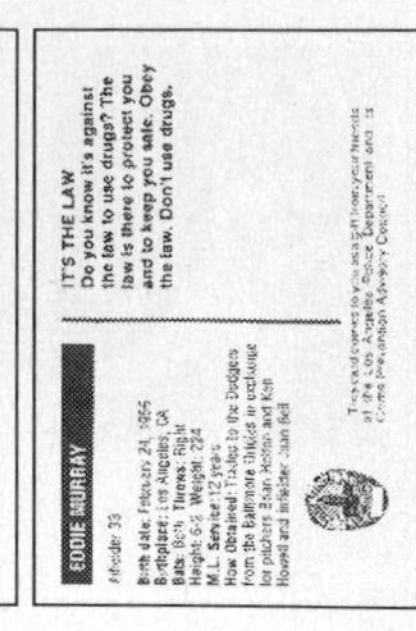

	MT	EX-MT	VG
COMPLETE SET (30)	6.00	2.70	.75
COMMON PLAYER	.25	.11	.03
☐ 1 Dodger Coaches (Unnumbered) Ben Hines Ron Perranoski Tom Lasorda MG Joe Amalfitano Joe Ferguson Mark Cresse Bill Russell Manny Mota	.35	.16	.04
☐ 2 Tom Lasorda MG	.35	.16	.04
☐ 3 Jeff Hamilton	.25	.11	.03
☐ 4 Mike Marshall	.35	.16	.04
☐ 5 Alfredo Griffin	.25	.11	.03
☐ 6 Mickey Hatcher	.25	.11	.03
☐ 7 Dave Anderson	.25	.11	.03
☐ 8 Willie Randolph	.35	.16	.04
☐ 9 Mike Scioscia	.35	.16	.04
☐ 10 Rick Dempsey	.35	.16	.04
☐ 11 Mike Davis	.25	.11	.03
☐ 12 Tracy Woodson	.25	.11	.03
☐ 13 Franklin Stubbs	.25	.11	.03
☐ 14 Kirk Gibson	.45	.20	.06
☐ 15 Mariano Duncan	.35	.16	.04
☐ 16 Alejandro Pena	.35	.16	.04
☐ 17 Mike Sharperson	.25	.11	.03
☐ 18 Ricky Horton	.25	.11	.03
☐ 19 John Tudor	.35	.16	.04
☐ 20 John Shelby	.25	.11	.03
☐ 21 Eddie Murray	.60	.25	.08
☐ 22 Fernando Valenzuela	.45	.20	.06
☐ 23 Mike Morgan	.35	.16	.04
☐ 24 Ramon Martinez	.75	.35	.09
☐ 25 Tim Belcher	.35	.16	.04
☐ 26 Jay Howell	.35	.16	.04
☐ 27 Tim Crews	.25	.11	.03
☐ 28 Tim Leary	.35	.16	.04
☐ 29 Orel Hershiser	.60	.25	.08
☐ 30 Ray Searage	.25	.11	.03

1989 Police Tigers

The 1989 Police Detroit Tigers set contains 14 standard-size (2 1/2" by 3 1/2") cards. The fronts have color photos with blue and orange borders; the backs feature safety tips.

These unnumbered cards were given away by the Michigan state police. The cards are numbered below according to uniform number.

	MT	EX-MT	VG
COMPLETE SET (14)	12.00	5.50	1.50
COMMON PLAYER	.60	.25	.08
☐ 1 Lou Whitaker	2.50	1.15	.30
☐ 3 Alan Trammell	2.50	1.15	.30
☐ 9 Fred Lynn	1.00	.45	.13
☐ 14 Dave Bergman	.60	.25	.08
☐ 15 Pat Sheridan	.60	.25	.08
☐ 19 Doyle Alexander	.75	.35	.09
☐ 21 Willie Hernandez	.75	.35	.09
☐ 26 Frank Tanana	.90	.40	.11
☐ 33 Matt Nokes	1.00	.45	.13
☐ 34 Chet Lemon	.75	.35	.09
☐ 39 Mike Henneman	1.00	.45	.13
☐ 44 Jeff M. Robinson	.60	.25	.08
☐ 47 Jack Morris	2.50	1.15	.30
☐ NNO Sparky Anderson MG	1.25	.55	.16

1990 Police Brewers

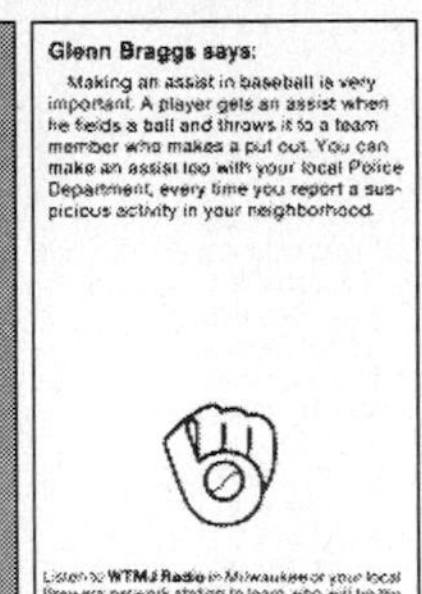

This 30-card police set was issued in conjunction with the Fan Appreciation store of Waukesha, Wisconsin and the Waukesha Police department. This set measures approximately 2 13/16" by 4 1/8" and is checklisted by uniform number. The front of the card is a full-color photo surrounded by a blue border while the back has anti-crime tips.

	MT	EX-MT	VG
COMPLETE SET (30)	6.00	2.70	.75
COMMON PLAYER	.25	.11	.03
☐ 2 Edgar Diaz	.25	.11	.03
☐ 4 Paul Molitor	.60	.25	.08
☐ 7 Dale Sveum	.25	.11	.03
☐ 11 Gary Sheffield	1.00	.45	.13
☐ 14 Gus Polidor	.25	.11	.03
☐ 16 Mike Felder	.25	.11	.03
☐ 17 Jim Gantner	.35	.16	.04
☐ 19 Robin Yount	1.25	.55	.16
☐ 20 Juan Nieves	.25	.11	.03
☐ 22 Charlie O'Brien	.25	.11	.03
☐ 23 Greg Vaughn	.50	.23	.06
☐ 24 Darryl Hamilton	.50	.23	.06
☐ 26 Glenn Braggs	.25	.11	.03
☐ 27 Paul Mirabella	.25	.11	.03
☐ 28 Tom Filer	.25	.11	.03
☐ 29 Chris Bosio	.50	.23	.06
☐ 30 Terry Francona	.25	.11	.03
☐ 31 Jaime Navarro	.50	.23	.06
☐ 32 Chuck Crim	.25	.11	.03
☐ 34 Billy Bates	.25	.11	.03
☐ 36 Tony Fossas	.25	.11	.03
☐ 37 Dan Plesac	.35	.16	.04
☐ 38 Don August	.25	.11	.03
☐ 39 Dave Parker	.50	.23	.06
☐ 40 Mike Birkbeck	.25	.11	.03
☐ 41 Mark Knudson	.25	.11	.03
☐ 42 Tom Trebelhorn MG	.35	.16	.04
☐ 45 Rob Deer	.45	.20	.06
☐ 46 Bill Wegman	.35	.16	.04
☐ 47 Bill Krueger	.35	.16	.04
☐ 49 Teddy Higuera	.35	.16	.04
☐ NNO Coaches	.25	.11	.03

Larry Haney 12
Don Baylor 25
Ray Burris 50
Andy Etchebarren 8
Duffy Dyer 10

1990 Police Dodgers

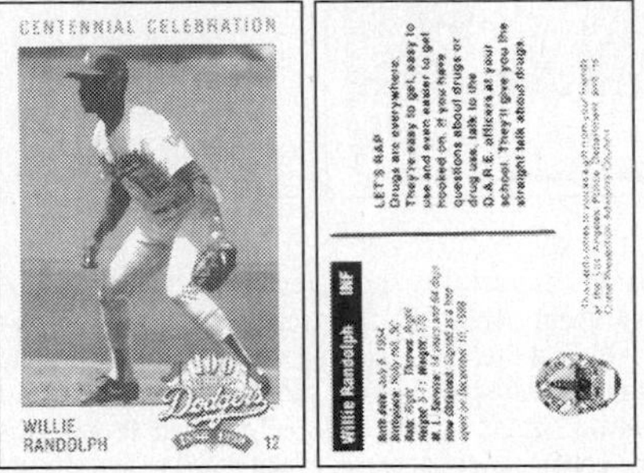

This 26-card set measures approximately 2 13/16" by 4 1/8" and was distributed by both the Los Angeles Police Department and at a pre-season Dodger-Angel exhibition game. This set also commemorated the 100th anniversary of the Dodgers existence. The front has a full-color photo of the player on the front while the back has a brief profile of the player with an anti-crime message. This set is checklisted below by uniform number.

	MT	EX-MT	VG
COMPLETE SET (26)	5.00	2.30	.60
COMMON PLAYER	.25	.11	.03
☐ 1 Tommy Lasorda MG	.35	.16	.04
☐ 3 Jeff Hamilton	.25	.11	.03
☐ 7 Alfredo Griffin	.25	.11	.03
☐ 8 Mickey Hatcher	.25	.11	.03
☐ 10 Juan Samuel	.35	.16	.04
☐ 12 Willie Randolph	.35	.16	.04
☐ 14 Mike Scioscia	.35	.16	.04
☐ 15 Chris Gwynn	.35	.16	.04
☐ 17 Rick Dempsey	.25	.11	.03
☐ 21 Hubie Brooks	.35	.16	.04
☐ 22 Franklin Stubbs	.25	.11	.03
☐ 23 Kirk Gibson	.50	.23	.06
☐ 27 Mike Sharperson	.35	.16	.04
☐ 28 Kal Daniels	.35	.16	.04
☐ 29 Lenny Harris	.35	.16	.04
☐ 31 John Shelby	.25	.11	.03
☐ 33 Eddie Murray	.60	.25	.08
☐ 34 Fernando Valenzuela	.45	.20	.06
☐ 35 Jim Gott	.25	.11	.03
☐ 36 Mike Morgan	.35	.16	.04
☐ 38 Jose Gonzalez	.25	.11	.03
☐ 39 Jim Neidlinger	.35	.16	.04
☐ 46 Mike Hartley	.25	.11	.03
☐ 49 Tim Belcher	.35	.16	.04
☐ 50 Jay Howell	.35	.16	.04
☐ 52 Tim Crews	.25	.11	.03
☐ 55 Orel Hershiser	.45	.20	.06
☐ 57 John Wetteland	.50	.23	.06
☐ 59 Ray Searage	.25	.11	.03
☐ NNO Coaches Card	.25	.11	.03

Ben Hines
Ron Perranowski
Mark Cresse
Manny Mota
Tommy Lasorda MG
Joe Amalfitano
Joe Ferguson
Bill Russell

1991 Police Brewers

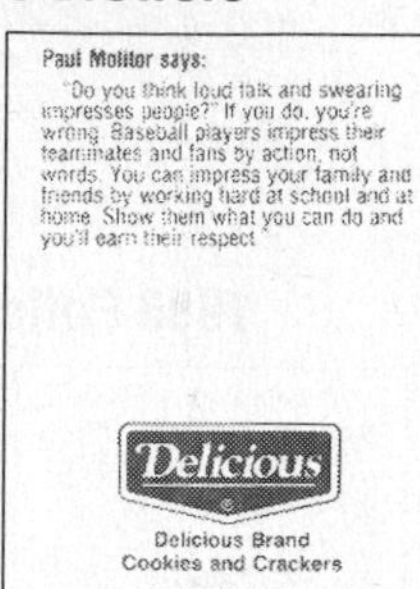

This 30-card set was sponsored by the Waukesha Police Department, Waukesha Sportscards, and Delicious Brand Cookies and Crackers. These sponsors are mentioned at the bottom of both sides of the card. The cards measure the standard size (2 1/2" by 3 1/2"). The fronts feature mostly color action player photos with light gray borders. The team logo is superimposed at the upper right corner. The backs have black print on a white background and feature public service tips by the players. The cards are numbered on the back.

	MT	EX-MT	VG
COMPLETE SET (30)	6.00	2.70	.75
COMMON PLAYER (1-30)	.25	.11	.03
☐ 1 Don August	.25	.11	.03
☐ 2 Dante Bichette	.45	.20	.06
☐ 3 Chris Bosio	.45	.20	.06
☐ 4 Greg Brock	.25	.11	.03
☐ 5 Kevin D. Brown	.25	.11	.03
☐ 6 Chuck Crim	.25	.11	.03
☐ 7 Rick Dempsey	.35	.16	.04
☐ 8 Jim Gantner	.35	.16	.04
☐ 9 Darryl Hamilton	.35	.16	.04
☐ 10 Teddy Higuera	.35	.16	.04
☐ 11 Mark Lee	.25	.11	.03
☐ 12 Mark Knudson	.25	.11	.03
☐ 13 Julio Machado	.35	.16	.04
☐ 14 Candy Maldonado	.35	.16	.04
☐ 15 Paul Molitor	.60	.25	.08
☐ 16 Jaime Navarro	.45	.20	.06
☐ 17 Edwin Nunez	.25	.11	.03
☐ 18 Dan Plesac	.25	.11	.03
☐ 19 Willie Randolph	.35	.16	.04
☐ 20 Ron Robinson	.25	.11	.03
☐ 20 Gary Sheffield	.60	.25	.08
☐ 21 Bill Spiers	.35	.16	.04
☐ 22 Franklin Stubbs	.25	.11	.03
☐ 23 B.J. Surhoff	.35	.16	.04
☐ 24 Dale Sveum	.25	.11	.03
☐ 25 Tom Trebelhorn MG	.25	.11	.03
☐ 26 Greg Vaughn	.45	.20	.06
☐ 27 Bill Wegman	.35	.16	.04
☐ 28 Robin Yount	1.00	.45	.13
☐ NNO Coaches Card Don Baylor Ray Burris Duffy Dyer Andy Etchebarren Larry Haney Fred Stanley	.35	.16	.04

1991 Police Cardinals

This 24-card police set was sponsored by the Kansas City Life Insurance Company and distributed by Greater St. Louis Law Enforcement Agencies. The cards measure 2 5/8" by 4 1/8" and feature on the fronts a mix of posed and action color player photos with white borders. The team name, uniform number, and player's name appear in the white

border below the pictures. In red print on white, the backs have biography, statistics, a safety cartoon with caption, and sponsor's logo. The cards are checklisted below by uniform number.

	MT	EX-MT	VG
COMPLETE SET (24)	12.00	5.50	1.50
COMMON PLAYER	.50	.23	.06
☐ 1 Ozzie Smith	1.25	.55	.16
☐ 7 Geronimo Pena	.75	.35	.09
☐ 9 Joe Torre MG	.75	.35	.09
☐ 10 Rex Hudler	.60	.25	.08
☐ 11 Jose Oquendo	.50	.23	.06
☐ 12 Craig Wilson	.50	.23	.06
☐ 16 Ray Lankford	1.50	.65	.19
☐ 19 Tom Pagnozzi	.75	.35	.09
☐ 21 Gerald Perry	.50	.23	.06
☐ 23 Bernard Gilkey	1.00	.45	.13
☐ 25 Milt Thompson	.60	.25	.08
☐ 27 Todd Zeile	1.00	.45	.13
☐ 28 Pedro Guerrero	.75	.35	.09
☐ 29 Rich Gedman	.50	.23	.06
☐ 34 Felix Jose	1.00	.45	.13
☐ 35 Frank DiPino	.50	.23	.06
☐ 36 Bryn Smith	.60	.25	.08
☐ 37 Scott Terry	.50	.23	.06
☐ 38 Todd Worrell	.75	.35	.09
☐ 39 Bob Tewksbury	.75	.35	.09
☐ 43 Ken Hill	.75	.35	.09
☐ 47 Lee Smith	.75	.35	.09
☐ 48 Jose DeLeon	.50	.23	.06
☐ 49 Juan Agosto	.50	.23	.06

1991 Police Dodgers

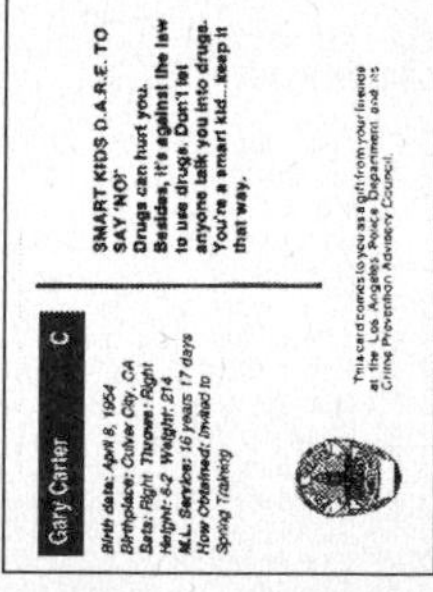

This 30-card set was sponsored by the Los Angeles Police Department and its Crime Prevention Advisory Council. The cards measure approximately 2 13/16" by 4 1/8". The fronts feature color action player photos with the top corners rounded off and white borders on all sides. A black line divides the horizontally oriented back into two halves. While the left half presents biographical information, the right half has an anti-drug or alcohol message. The cards are skip-numbered by uniform number on the fronts.

	MT	EX-MT	VG
COMPLETE SET (30)	5.00	2.30	.60
COMMON PLAYER	.25	.11	.03
☐ 3 Jeff Hamilton	.25	.11	.03
☐ 5 Stan Javier	.25	.11	.03
☐ 7 Alfredo Griffin	.25	.11	.03
☐ 10 Juan Samuel	.35	.16	.04
☐ 12 Gary Carter	.45	.20	.06
☐ 14 Mike Scioscia	.35	.16	.04
☐ 15 Chris Gwynn	.35	.16	.04
☐ 17 Bob Ojeda	.35	.16	.04
☐ 22 Brett Butler	.45	.20	.06
☐ 25 Dennis Cook	.25	.11	.03
☐ 27 Mike Sharperson	.25	.11	.03
☐ 28 Kal Daniels	.35	.16	.04
☐ 29 Lenny Harris	.35	.16	.04
☐ 30 Jose Offerman	.45	.20	.06
☐ 31 Jim Neidlinger	.25	.11	.03
☐ 33 Eddie Murray	.45	.20	.06
☐ 35 Jim Gott	.35	.16	.04
☐ 36 Mike Morgan	.35	.16	.04
☐ 38 Jose Gonzalez	.25	.11	.03
☐ 40 Barry Lyons	.25	.11	.03
☐ 44 Darryl Strawberry	.75	.35	.09
☐ 45 Kevin Gross	.35	.16	.04
☐ 46 Mike Hartley	.25	.11	.03
☐ 48 Ramon Martinez	.45	.20	.06
☐ 49 Tim Belcher	.35	.16	.04
☐ 50 Jay Howell	.35	.16	.04
☐ 52 Tim Crews	.25	.11	.03
☐ 54 John Candelaria	.25	.11	.03
☐ 55 Orel Hershiser	.45	.20	.06
☐ NNO Coaches Card	.25	.11	.03
Ben Hines			
Ron Perranoski			
Mark Cresse			
Manny Mota			
Tommy Lasorda MG			
Joe Amalfitano			
Joe Ferguson			
Bill Russell			

1991 Police Royals

This 27-card set was distributed by the Metropolitan Chiefs and Sheriffs Association. The cards measure approximately 2 5/8" by 4 1/8". The front design has glossy color action photos with white borders. The player's number and name appear below the picture. In blue print, the backs present biography, statistics, and a cartoon with a public service announcement by the player. The cards are unnumbered and checklisted below in alphabetical order, with the coaches' cards listed at the end. Supposedly many of the Bo Jackson cards were burned after Bo was cut from the team.

	MT	EX-MT	VG
COMPLETE SET (27)	15.00	6.75	1.90
COMMON PLAYER (1-27)	.25	.11	.03
☐ 1 Kevin Appier	.60	.25	.08
☐ 2 Luis Aquino	.25	.11	.03
☐ 3 Mike Boddicker	.35	.16	.04
☐ 4 George Brett	1.50	.65	.19
☐ 5 Steve Crawford	.25	.11	.03
☐ 6 Mark Davis	.35	.16	.04
☐ 7 Storm Davis	.35	.16	.04
☐ 8 Jim Eisenreich	.35	.16	.04
☐ 9 Kirk Gibson	.45	.20	.06
☐ 10 Tom Gordon	.45	.20	.06
☐ 11 Mark Gubicza	.35	.16	.04
☐ 12 Bo Jackson SP	7.50	3.40	.95
☐ 13 Mike Macfarlane	.45	.20	.06
☐ 14 Andy McGaffigan	.25	.11	.03
☐ 15 Brian McRae	.60	.25	.08
☐ 16 Jeff Montgomery	.45	.20	.06
☐ 17 Bill Pecota	.25	.11	.03
☐ 18 Bret Saberhagen	.75	.35	.09
☐ 19 Kevin Seitzer	.35	.16	.04
☐ 20 Terry Shumpert	.35	.16	.04
☐ 21 Kurt Stillwell	.35	.16	.04
☐ 22 Danny Tartabull	1.00	.45	.13
☐ 23 Gary Thurman	.25	.11	.03
☐ 24 John Wathan MG	.25	.11	.03
☐ 25 Coaches	.25	.11	.03
Pat Dodson			
Adrian Garrett			
☐ 26 Coaches	.25	.11	.03
Glenn Ezell			
Lynn Jones			
Bob Schaefer			
☐ 27 Checklist Card	.35	.16	.04

1991 Police Tigers

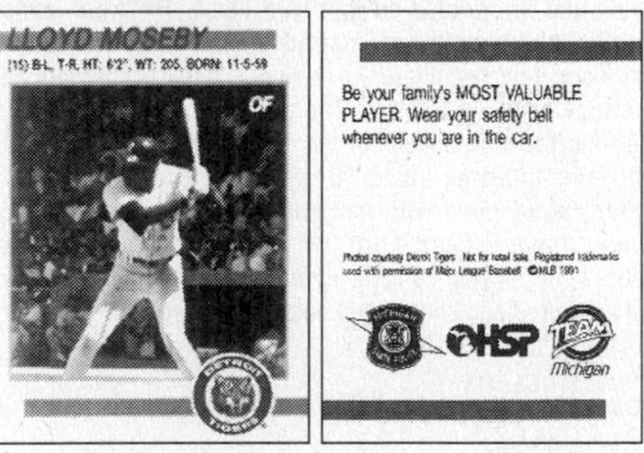

This 14-card set was sponsored by the Michigan State Police, HSP, and Team Michigan, and their sponsor logos appear on the backs. The cards measure the standard size (2 1/2" by 3 1/2") and feature a mix of posed and action color player photos. The player's name appears in blue lettering in an orange stripe above the picture, while a second orange stripe below the picture intersects the team logo at the lower right corner. The backs contain safety tips. The cards are unnumbered and checklisted below in alphabetical order.

	MT	EX-MT	VG
COMPLETE SET (14)	25.00	11.50	3.10
COMMON PLAYER (1-14)	1.25	.55	.16
☐ 1 Sparky Anderson MG	2.50	1.15	.30
☐ 2 Dave Bergman	1.25	.55	.16
☐ 3 Cecil Fielder	7.00	3.10	.85
☐ 4 Travis Fryman	9.00	4.00	1.15
☐ 5 Paul Gibson	1.25	.55	.16
☐ 6 Jerry Don Gleaton	1.25	.55	.16
☐ 7 Lloyd Moseby	1.25	.55	.16
☐ 8 Dan Petry	1.25	.55	.16
☐ 9 Tony Phillips	2.00	.90	.25
☐ 10 Mark Salas	1.25	.55	.16
☐ 11 John Shelby	1.25	.55	.16
☐ 12 Frank Tanana	2.00	.90	.25
☐ 13 Alan Trammell	5.00	2.30	.60
☐ 14 Lou Whitaker	5.00	2.30	.60

1992 Police Angels

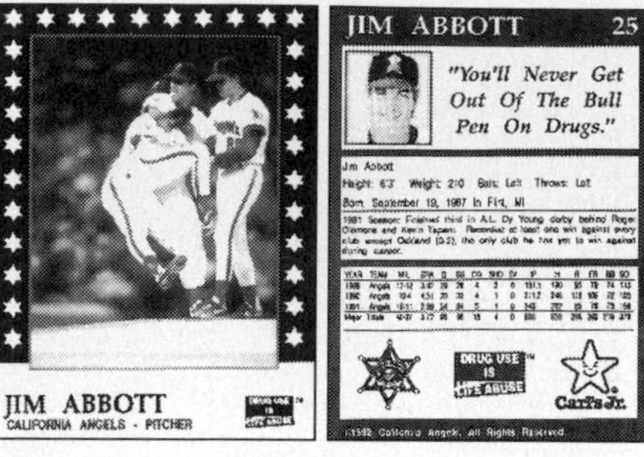

This 18-card set was cosponsored by the Orange County Sheriff's Department and Carl's Jr. Restaurants in Orange County, California. Deputies and police officers distributed the cards to children in grades K through 6, and 15,000 sets were given out at the September 19 Angel home game. The total number of cards produced was 870,000 individual cards. The cards measure the standard size (2 1/2" by 3 1/2") and are printed on thin card stock. The front design has color action player photos inside a red frame and enclosed on three sides by a navy blue outer border studded with six-point white stars. The player's name, team name, and his position appear in the bottom white border along with the anti-drug motto "Drug Use is Life Abuse." On a white background with navy blue print and borders, the backs have a head shot, an anti-drug player quote, biography, statistics, and sponsor logos. The cards are unnumbered and checklisted below in alphabetical order.

	MT	EX-MT	VG
COMPLETE SET (18)	7.50	3.40	.95
COMMON PLAYER (1-18)	.40	.18	.05
☐ 1 Jim Abbott	.75	.35	.09
☐ 2 Gene Autry OWN	.75	.35	.09
☐ 3 Bert Blyleven	.60	.25	.08
☐ 4 Hubie Brooks	.50	.23	.06
☐ 5 Chad Curtis	1.00	.45	.13
☐ 6 Alvin Davis	.50	.23	.06
☐ 7 Gary DiSarcina	.50	.23	.06
☐ 8 Junior Felix	.50	.23	.06
☐ 9 Chuck Finley	.50	.23	.06
☐ 10 Gary Gaetti	.50	.23	.06
☐ 11 Rene Gonzales	.50	.23	.06
☐ 12 Von Hayes	.50	.23	.06
☐ 13 Carl Karcher Founder of Carl's Jr. Restaurants	.40	.18	.05
☐ 14 Mark Langston	.50	.23	.06
☐ 15 Luis Polonia	.50	.23	.06
☐ 16 Bobby Rose	.40	.18	.05
☐ 17 Lee Stevens	.50	.23	.06
☐ 18 Happy Star (Title Card)	.40	.18	.05

1992 Police Brewers

For the second consecutive year, this 30-card set was sponsored by the Waukesha Police Department, Waukesha Sports Cards, and Delicious Brand Cookies and Crackers. The cards measure the standard 2 1/2" by 3 1/2". The obverse features a color action photo on a bright yellow card face. The team name and year appear in the border on the top, while the team logo overlaps the photo and border in the upper right corner. The player's name and position are below the picture. The sponsors are mentioned at the

Pat Listach Says . . .

"Drug dealers are always trying to tempt ballplayers. They like to hang around celebrities and try to get us to join them at parties. We learn to just say no. We tell them to get lost or we'll call the police.

Call it what you want, pot, grass, crack, speed, angel dust, or coke — it's dangerous stuff that can hurt you and even kill. If you're approached, just say no and then call your local police or tell your parents."

Delicious

Delicious Brand Cookies and Crackers

bottom of both sides of the card. The backs have black print on a white background and feature public service tips from the players. The cards are unnumbered and checklisted below in alphabetical order.

	MT	EX-MT	VG
COMPLETE SET (30)	5.00	2.30	.60
COMMON PLAYER (1-30)	.25	.11	.03
☐ 1 Andy Allanson	.25	.11	.03
☐ 2 James Austin	.35	.16	.04
☐ 3 Dante Bichette	.35	.16	.04
☐ 4 Ricky Bones	.35	.16	.04
☐ 5 Chris Bosio	.35	.16	.04
☐ 6 Mike Fetters	.25	.11	.03
☐ 7 Scott Fletcher	.25	.11	.03
☐ 8 Jim Gantner	.35	.16	.04
☐ 9 Phil Garner MG	.35	.16	.04
☐ 10 Darryl Hamilton	.35	.16	.04
☐ 11 Doug Henry	.35	.16	.04
☐ 12 Teddy Higuera	.35	.16	.04
☐ 13 Pat Listach	1.50	.65	.19
☐ 14 Tim McIntosh	.35	.16	.04
☐ 15 Paul Molitor	.50	.23	.06
☐ 16 Jaime Navarro	.35	.16	.04
☐ 17 Edwin Nunez	.25	.11	.03
☐ 18 Jesse Orosco	.35	.16	.04
☐ 19 Dan Plesac	.35	.16	.04
☐ 20 Ron Robinson	.25	.11	.03
☐ 21 Bruce Ruffin	.25	.11	.03
☐ 22 Kevin Seitzer	.35	.16	.04
☐ 23 Bill Spiers	.25	.11	.03
☐ 24 Franklin Stubbs	.25	.11	.03
☐ 25 William Suero	.25	.11	.03
☐ 26 B.J. Surhoff	.35	.16	.04
☐ 27 Greg Vaughn	.35	.16	.04
☐ 28 Bill Wegman	.35	.16	.04
☐ 29 Robin Yount	.90	.40	.11
☐ 30 Coaches Mike Easler Bill Castro Don Rowe Duffy Dyer Tim Foli	.25	.11	.03

1992 Police Cardinals

This 26-card set commemorates the 100th anniversary of the Cardinals. The set was sponsored by the Kansas City

Life Insurance Company and distributed by the Greater St. Louis Law Enforcement Agencies. The cards measure 2 5/8" by 4 1/8" and feature color action player photos with white borders. One corner of the photo is cut off to create space for the the St. Louis Cardinals 100th Anniversary logo. Placement of the logo varies on the cards from the upper right, upper left, or lower right corner. The team name is printed in red on the bottom border, while the player's name and jersey number are in black. The backs are printed in red on a white background and feature biographical and statistical information as well as a cartoon and a corresponding public service player quote. The sponsors are printed at the bottom. The cards are unnumbered and checklisted below in alphabetical order.

	MT	EX-MT	VG
COMPLETE SET (27)	7.00	3.10	.85
COMMON PLAYER (1-27)	.25	.11	.03
☐ 1 Juan Agosto	.25	.11	.03
☐ 2 Cris Carpenter	.25	.11	.03
☐ 3 Jose DeLeon	.25	.11	.03
☐ 4 Andres Galarraga	.35	.16	.04
☐ 5 Rich Gedman	.25	.11	.03
☐ 6 Bernard Gilkey	.50	.23	.06
☐ 7 Pedro Guerrero	.35	.16	.04
☐ 8 Rex Hudler	.35	.16	.04
☐ 9 Felix Jose	.50	.23	.06
☐ 10 Ray Lankford	.75	.35	.09
☐ 11 Joe Magrane	.35	.16	.04
☐ 12 Omar Olivares	.35	.16	.04
☐ 13 Jose Oquendo	.25	.11	.03
☐ 14 Tom Pagnozzi	.35	.16	.04
☐ 15 Geronimo Pena	.35	.16	.04
☐ 16 Gerald Perry	.25	.11	.03
☐ 17 Bryn Smith	.25	.11	.03
☐ 18 Lee Smith	.50	.23	.06
☐ 19 Ozzie Smith	.90	.40	.11
☐ 20 Scott Terry	.25	.11	.03
☐ 21 Bob Tewksbury	.45	.20	.06
☐ 22 Milt Thompson	.35	.16	.04
☐ 23 Joe Torre MG	.35	.16	.04
☐ 24 Craig Wilson	.25	.11	.03
☐ 25 Todd Worrell	.35	.16	.04
☐ 26 Todd Zeile	.50	.23	.06
☐ 27 Checklist	.35	.16	.04

1992 Police Dodgers

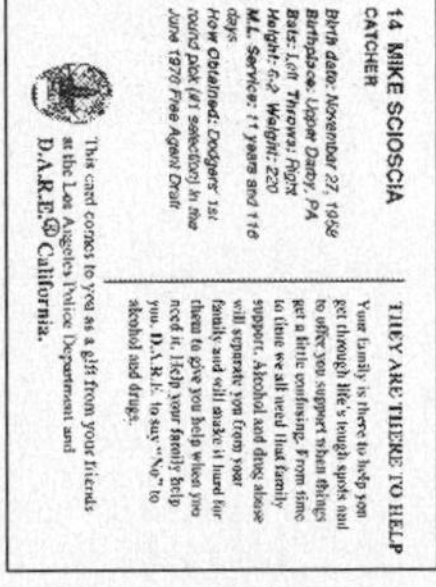

This 30-card standard size (2 1/2" by 3 1/2") set was given out as a promotion at the ball park and was sponsored by the Los Angeles Police Department and D.A.R.E. California. The set, which commemorates the 30th anniversary of Dodger Stadium, features color action photos with rounded corners on a white card face with a navy blue stripe bordering the photos. A commemorative logo is superimposed on the photo at the lower left corner and overlaps onto the white card face. The player's name and uniform number appear at the bottom. The horizontally oriented backs display biographical information and anti-drug or alcohol messages. The cards are skip-numbered by uniform number on the front and back.

	MT	EX-MT	VG
COMPLETE SET (30)	5.00	2.30	.60
COMMON PLAYER	.25	.11	.03
☐ 2 Tommy Lasorda MG	.35	.16	.04
☐ 3 Jeff Hamilton	.25	.11	.03
☐ 5 Stan Javier	.25	.11	.03
☐ 10 Juan Samuel	.35	.16	.04
☐ 14 Mike Scioscia	.35	.16	.04
☐ 15 Dave Hansen	.35	.16	.04
☐ 17 Bob Ojeda	.35	.16	.04
☐ 20 Mitch Webster	.25	.11	.03
☐ 22 Brett Butler	.45	.20	.06
☐ 23 Eric Karros	1.50	.65	.19
☐ 27 Mike Sharperson	.25	.11	.03
☐ 28 Kal Daniels	.35	.16	.04
☐ 29 Lenny Harris	.35	.16	.04
☐ 30 Jose Offerman	.35	.16	.04
☐ 31 Roger McDowell	.25	.11	.03
☐ 33 Eric Davis	.45	.20	.06
☐ 35 Jim Gott	.25	.11	.03
☐ 36 Todd Benzinger	.25	.11	.03
☐ 38 Steve Wilson	.25	.11	.03
☐ 41 Carlos Hernandez	.35	.16	.04
☐ 44 Darryl Strawberry	.60	.25	.08
☐ 46 Kevin Gross	.25	.11	.03
☐ 48 Ramon Martinez	.45	.20	.06
☐ 49 Tom Candiotti	.35	.16	.04
☐ 50 Jay Howell	.35	.16	.04
☐ 52 Tim Crews	.25	.11	.03
☐ 54 John Candelaria	.35	.16	.04
☐ 55 Orel Hershiser	.45	.20	.06
☐ 57 Kip Gross	.25	.11	.03
☐ NNO Coaching Staff Ben Hines Ron Perranoski Tommy Lasorda Joe Amalfitano Ron Roenicke Joe Ferguson Manny Mota Mark Cresse	.25	.11	.03

1992 Police Royals

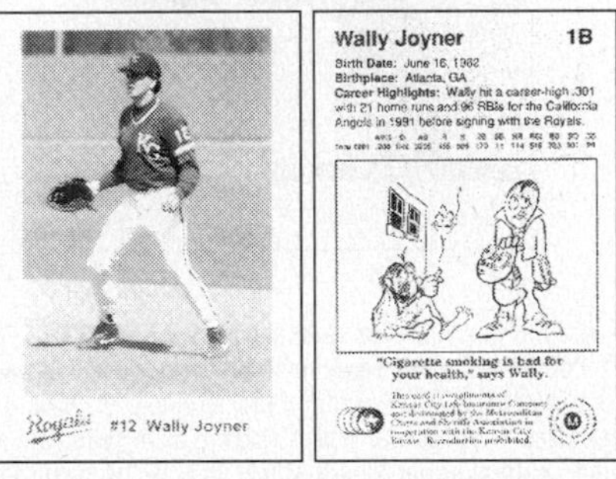

This 27-set, given out as a promotion at the stadium, was sponsored by the Kansas City Life Insurance Company and distributed by the Metropolitan Chiefs and Sheriffs Association. It is rumored that two cards were pulled prior to release (the cards of Kevin Seitzer, who went to Milwaukee, and Kirk Gibson, who went to Pittsburgh). The cards measure 2 5/8" by 4 1/8" and feature action color player photos with white borders. The team name appears in royal blue on the bottom border, while the player's name and jersey number are in black. The backs are printed in blue on a white background and feature biographical and statistical information as well as a cartoon and a corresponding public service player quote. The sponsors are listed at the bottom. The cards are unnumbered and checklisted below in alphabetical order.

	MT	EX-MT	VG
COMPLETE SET (27)	7.00	3.10	.85
COMMON PLAYER (1-27)	.25	.11	.03
☐ 1 Kevin Appier	.45	.20	.06
☐ 2 Luis Aquino	.25	.11	.03
☐ 3 Mike Boddicker	.35	.16	.04
☐ 4 George Brett	1.00	.45	.13
☐ 5 Mark Davis	.35	.16	.04
☐ 6 Jim Eisenreich	.35	.16	.04
☐ 7 Kirk Gibson	.45	.20	.06
☐ 8 Tom Gordon	.35	.16	.04
☐ 9 Mark Gubicza	.35	.16	.04
☐ 10 Chris Gwynn	.35	.16	.04
☐ 11 David Howard	.25	.11	.03
☐ 12 Gregg Jefferies	.60	.25	.08
☐ 13 Joel Johnston	.35	.16	.04
☐ 14 Wally Joyner	.45	.20	.06
☐ 15 Mike Macfarlane	.35	.16	.04
☐ 16 Mike Magnante	.25	.11	.03
☐ 17 Brent Mayne	.35	.16	.04
☐ 18 Brian McRae	.35	.16	.04
☐ 19 Hal McRae MG	.35	.16	.04
☐ 20 Kevin McReynolds	.35	.16	.04
☐ 21 Bob Melvin CO	.25	.11	.03
☐ 22 Keith Miller	.35	.16	.04
☐ 23 Jeff Montgomery	.35	.16	.04
☐ 24 Kevin Seitzer	.35	.16	.04
☐ 25 Terry Shumpert	.25	.11	.03
☐ 26 Gary Thurman	.25	.11	.03
☐ 27 Coaches Glenn Ezell Adrian Garrett Guy Hansen Lynn Jones Bruce Kison Lee May	.25	.11	.03

1961 Post Cereal

The cards in this 200-card set measure 2 1/2" by 3 1/2". The 1961 Post set was this company's first major set. The cards were available on thick cardbox stock, singly or in various panel sizes from cereal boxes (BOX), or in team sheets, printed on thinner cardboard stock, directly from the Post Cereal Company (COM). It is difficult to differentiate the COM cards from the BOX cards; the thickness of the card stock is the best indicator. Many variations exist and are noted in the checklist below. There are many cards which were produced in lesser quantities; the prices below reflect the relative scarcity of the cards. Cards 10, 23, 70, 73, 94, 113, 135, 163, and 183 are examples of cards printed in limited quantities and hence commanding premium prices. The cards are numbered essentially in team groups, i.e., New York Yankees (1-18), Chicago White Sox (19-34), Detroit (35-46), Boston (47-56), Cleveland (57-67), Baltimore (68-80), Kansas City (81-90), Minnesota (91-100), Milwaukee (101-114), Philadelphia (115-124), Pittsburgh (125-140), San Francisco (141-155), Los Angeles Dodgers (156-170), St. Louis (171-180), Cincinnati (181-190), and Chicago Cubs (191-200). The catalog number is F278-33. The complete set price refers to the maximal set with all variations (357). There was also an album produced by Post to hold the cards.

	NRMT	VG-E	GOOD
COMPLETE SET (357)	2800.00	1250.00	350.00
COMMON PLAYER (1-200)	3.00	1.35	.40
☐ 1A Yogi Berra COM	27.00	12.00	3.40
☐ 1B Yogi Berra BOX	27.00	12.00	3.40
☐ 2A Elston Howard COM	4.00	1.80	.50
☐ 2B Elston Howard BOX	4.00	1.80	.50
☐ 3A Bill Skowron COM	3.50	1.55	.45
☐ 3B Bill Skowron BOX	3.50	1.55	.45
☐ 4A Mickey Mantle COM	125.00	57.50	15.50
☐ 4B Mickey Mantle BOX	125.00	57.50	15.50
☐ 5 Bob Turley COM only	20.00	9.00	2.50
☐ 6A Whitey Ford COM	9.00	4.00	1.15
☐ 6B Whitey Ford BOX	9.00	4.00	1.15
☐ 7A Roger Maris COM	30.00	13.50	3.80
☐ 7B Roger Maris BOX	30.00	13.50	3.80
☐ 8A Bobby Richardson COM	3.50	1.55	.45
☐ 8B Bobby Richardson BOX	3.50	1.55	.45
☐ 9A Tony Kubek COM	3.50	1.55	.45
☐ 9B Tony Kubek BOX	3.50	1.55	.45
☐ 10 Gil McDougald BOX only	40.00	18.00	5.00
☐ 11 Cletis Boyer BOX only	3.00	1.35	.40
☐ 12A Hector Lopes COM	3.00	1.35	.40
☐ 12B Hector Lopes BOX	3.00	1.35	.40
☐ 13 Bob Cerv BOX only	3.00	1.35	.40
☐ 14 Ryne Duren BOX only	3.00	1.35	.40
☐ 15 Bobby Shantz BOX only	3.00	1.35	.40
☐ 16 Art Ditmar BOX only	3.00	1.35	.40
☐ 17 Jim Coates BOX only	3.00	1.35	.40
☐ 18 J.Blanchard BOX only	3.00	1.35	.40
☐ 19A Luis Aparicio COM	7.00	3.10	.85
☐ 19B Luis Aparicio BOX	7.00	3.10	.85
☐ 20A Nelson Fox COM	5.00	2.30	.60
☐ 20B Nelson Fox BOX	5.00	2.30	.60
☐ 21A Bill Pierce COM	5.00	2.30	.60
☐ 21B Bill Pierce BOX	5.00	2.30	.60
☐ 22A Early Wynn COM	12.00	5.50	1.50
☐ 22B Early Wynn BOX	12.00	5.50	1.50
☐ 23 Bob Shaw BOX only	100.00	45.00	12.50
☐ 24A Al Smith COM	3.00	1.35	.40
☐ 24B Al Smith BOX	3.00	1.35	.40
☐ 25A Minnie Minoso COM	3.50	1.55	.45
☐ 25B Minnie Minoso BOX	3.50	1.55	.45
☐ 26A Roy Sievers COM	3.00	1.35	.40
☐ 26B Roy Sievers BOX	3.00	1.35	.40
☐ 27A Jim Landis COM	3.00	1.35	.40
☐ 27B Jim Landis BOX	3.00	1.35	.40
☐ 28A Sherm Lollar COM	3.00	1.35	.40
☐ 28B Sherm Lollar BOX	3.00	1.35	.40
☐ 29 Gerry Staley BOX only	3.00	1.35	.40
☐ 30A Gene Freese COM (Reds)	9.00	4.00	1.15
☐ 30B Gene Freese BOX (White Sox)	3.00	1.35	.40
☐ 31 Ted Kluszewski BOX only	4.00	1.80	.50
☐ 32 Turk Lown BOX only	3.00	1.35	.40
☐ 33A Jim Rivera COM	3.00	1.35	.40
☐ 33B Jim Rivera BOX	3.00	1.35	.40
☐ 34 Frank Baumann BOX only	3.00	1.35	.40
☐ 35A Al Kaline COM	18.00	8.00	2.30
☐ 35B Al Kaline BOX	18.00	8.00	2.30
☐ 36A Rocky Colavito COM	6.00	2.70	.75
☐ 36B Rocky Colavito BOX	6.00	2.70	.75
☐ 37A Charlie Maxwell COM	3.00	1.35	.40
☐ 37B Charlie Maxwell BOX	3.00	1.35	.40
☐ 38A Frank Lary COM	3.00	1.35	.40
☐ 38B Frank Lary BOX	3.00	1.35	.40
☐ 39A Jim Bunning COM	4.50	2.00	.55
☐ 39B Jim Bunning BOX	4.50	2.00	.55
☐ 40A Norm Cash COM	3.50	1.55	.45
☐ 40B Norm Cash BOX	3.50	1.55	.45
☐ 41A Frank Bolling COM (Braves, "Charlie Gehringer" in bio)	5.00	2.30	.60
☐ 41B Frank Bolling BOX (Tigers, "Charlie Derringer" in bio)	7.50	3.40	.95
☐ 42A Don Mossi COM	3.00	1.35	.40
☐ 42B Don Mossi BOX	3.00	1.35	.40
☐ 43A Lou Berberet COM	3.00	1.35	.40
☐ 43B Lou Berberet BOX	3.00	1.35	.40
☐ 44 Dave Sisler BOX only	3.00	1.35	.40
☐ 45 Ed Yost BOX only	3.00	1.35	.40
☐ 46 Pete Burnside BOX only	3.00	1.35	.40

Card			
☐ 47A Pete Runnels COM	3.50	1.55	.45
☐ 47B Pete Runnels BOX	3.50	1.55	.45
☐ 48A Frank Malzone COM	3.00	1.35	.40
☐ 48B Frank Malzone BOX	3.00	1.35	.40
☐ 49A Vic Wertz COM	5.00	2.30	.60
☐ 49B Vic Wertz BOX	5.00	2.30	.60
☐ 50A Tom Brewer COM	3.00	1.35	.40
☐ 50B Tom Brewer BOX	3.00	1.35	.40
☐ 51A Willie Tasby COM (Sold to Wash.)	6.00	2.70	.75
☐ 51B Willie Tasby BOX (No sale mention)	3.00	1.35	.40
☐ 52A Russ Nixon COM	3.00	1.35	.40
☐ 52B Russ Nixon BOX	3.00	1.35	.40
☐ 53A Don Buddin COM	3.00	1.35	.40
☐ 53B Don Buddin BOX	3.00	1.35	.40
☐ 54A Bill Monbouquette COM	3.00	1.35	.40
☐ 54B Bill Monbouquette BOX	3.00	1.35	.40
☐ 55A Frank Sullivan COM (Phillies)	9.00	4.00	1.15
☐ 55B Frank Sullivan BOX (Red Sox)	3.00	1.35	.40
☐ 56A Haywood Sullivan COM	3.00	1.35	.40
☐ 56B Haywood Sullivan BOX	3.00	1.35	.40
☐ 57A Harvey Kuenn COM (Giants)	6.00	2.70	.75
☐ 57B Harvey Kuenn BOX (Indians)	4.00	1.80	.50
☐ 58A Gary Bell COM	4.50	2.00	.55
☐ 58B Gary Bell BOX	4.50	2.00	.55
☐ 59A Jim Perry COM	3.00	1.35	.40
☐ 59B Jim Perry BOX	3.00	1.35	.40
☐ 60A Jim Grant COM	3.50	1.55	.45
☐ 60B Jim Grant BOX	3.50	1.55	.45
☐ 61A Johnny Temple COM	3.00	1.35	.40
☐ 61B Johnny Temple BOX	3.00	1.35	.40
☐ 62A Paul Foytack COM	3.00	1.35	.40
☐ 62B Paul Foytack BOX	3.00	1.35	.40
☐ 63A Vic Power COM	3.00	1.35	.40
☐ 63B Vic Power BOX	3.00	1.35	.40
☐ 64A Tito Francona COM	3.00	1.35	.40
☐ 64B Tito Francona BOX	3.00	1.35	.40
☐ 65A Ken Aspromonte COM (Sold to L.A.)	7.50	3.40	.95
☐ 65B Ken Aspromonte BOX (No sale mention)	7.50	3.40	.95
☐ 66 Bob Wilson BOX only	3.00	1.35	.40
☐ 67A John Romano COM	3.00	1.35	.40
☐ 67B John Romano BOX	3.00	1.35	.40
☐ 68A Jim Gentile COM	4.00	1.80	.50
☐ 68B Jim Gentile BOX	4.00	1.80	.50
☐ 69A Gus Triandos COM	3.50	1.55	.45
☐ 69B Gus Triandos BOX	3.50	1.55	.45
☐ 70 Gene Woodling BOX only	35.00	16.00	4.40
☐ 71A Milt Pappas COM	4.00	1.80	.50
☐ 71B Milt Pappas BOX	4.00	1.80	.50
☐ 72A Ron Hansen COM	3.00	1.35	.40
☐ 72B Ron Hansen BOX	3.00	1.35	.40
☐ 73 Chuck Estrada COM only	100.00	45.00	12.50
☐ 74A Steve Barber COM	3.00	1.35	.40
☐ 74B Steve Barber BOX	3.00	1.35	.40
☐ 75A Brooks Robinson COM	25.00	11.50	3.10
☐ 75B Brooks Robinson BOX	25.00	11.50	3.10
☐ 76A Jackie Brandt COM	3.00	1.35	.40
☐ 76B Jackie Brandt BOX	3.00	1.35	.40
☐ 77A Marv Breeding COM	3.00	1.35	.40
☐ 77B Marv Breeding BOX	3.00	1.35	.40
☐ 78 Hal Brown BOX only	3.00	1.35	.40
☐ 79 Billy Klaus BOX only	3.00	1.35	.40
☐ 80A Hoyt Wilhelm COM	7.50	3.40	.95
☐ 80B Hoyt Wilhelm BOX	7.50	3.40	.95
☐ 81A Jerry Lumpe COM	5.00	2.30	.60
☐ 81B Jerry Lumpe BOX	5.00	2.30	.60
☐ 82A Norm Siebern COM	3.00	1.35	.40
☐ 82B Norm Siebern BOX	3.00	1.35	.40
☐ 83A Bud Daley COM	3.50	1.55	.45
☐ 83B Bud Daley BOX	3.50	1.55	.45
☐ 84A Bill Tuttle COM	3.00	1.35	.40
☐ 84B Bill Tuttle BOX	3.00	1.35	.40
☐ 85A Marv Throneberry COM	3.50	1.55	.45
☐ 85B Marv Throneberry BOX	3.50	1.55	.45
☐ 86A Dick Williams COM	3.50	1.55	.45
☐ 86B Dick Williams BOX	3.50	1.55	.45
☐ 87A Ray Herbert COM	3.00	1.35	.40
☐ 87B Ray Herbert BOX	3.00	1.35	.40
☐ 88A Whitey Herzog COM	3.50	1.55	.45
☐ 88B Whitey Herzog BOX	3.50	1.55	.45
☐ 89A Ken Hamlin COM (Sold to L.A.)	18.00	8.00	2.30
☐ 89B Ken Hamlin BOX (No sale mention)	3.00	1.35	.40
☐ 90A Hank Bauer COM	3.50	1.55	.45
☐ 90B Hank Bauer BOX	3.50	1.55	.45
☐ 91A Bob Allison COM (Minnesota)	5.00	2.30	.60
☐ 91B Bob Allison BOX (Minneapolis)	5.00	2.30	.60
☐ 92A Harmon Killebrew (Minnesota) COM	35.00	16.00	4.40
☐ 92B Harmon Killebrew (Minneapolis) BOX	25.00	11.50	3.10
☐ 93A Jim Lemon COM (Minnesota)	20.00	9.00	2.50
☐ 93B Jim Lemon BOX (Minneapolis)	60.00	27.00	7.50
☐ 94A Chuck Stobbs (Minnesota) COM only	175.00	80.00	22.00
☐ 95A Reno Bertoia COM (Minnesota)	5.00	2.30	.60
☐ 95B Reno Bertoia BOX (Minneapolis)	3.00	1.35	.40
☐ 96A Billy Gardner COM (Minnesota)	5.00	2.30	.60
☐ 96B Billy Gardner BOX (Minneapolis)	3.00	1.35	.40
☐ 97A Earl Battey COM (Minnesota)	5.00	2.30	.60
☐ 97B Earl Battey BOX (Minneapolis)	3.00	1.35	.40
☐ 98A Pedro Ramos COM (Minnesota)	5.00	2.30	.60
☐ 98B Pedro Ramos BOX (Minneapolis)	3.00	1.35	.40
☐ 99A Camilo Pascual COM (Minnesota)	5.00	2.30	.60
☐ 99B Camilo Pascual BOX (Minneapolis)	3.00	1.35	.40
☐ 100A Billy Consolo COM (Minnesota)	5.00	2.30	.60
☐ 100B Billy Consolo BOX (Minneapolis)	3.00	1.35	.40
☐ 101A Warren Spahn COM	25.00	11.50	3.10
☐ 101B Warren Spahn BOX	25.00	11.50	3.10
☐ 102A Lew Burdette COM	3.50	1.55	.45
☐ 102B Lew Burdette BOX	3.50	1.55	.45
☐ 103A Bob Buhl COM	3.00	1.35	.40
☐ 103B Bob Buhl BOX	3.00	1.35	.40
☐ 104A Joe Adcock COM	4.00	1.80	.50
☐ 104B Joe Adcock BOX	4.00	1.80	.50
☐ 105A John Logan COM	4.00	1.80	.50
☐ 105B John Logan BOX	4.00	1.80	.50
☐ 106 Ed Mathews COM only	30.00	13.50	3.80
☐ 107A Hank Aaron COM	30.00	13.50	3.80
☐ 107B Hank Aaron BOX	30.00	13.50	3.80
☐ 108A Wes Covington COM	3.00	1.35	.40
☐ 108B Wes Covington BOX	3.00	1.35	.40
☐ 109A Bill Bruton COM (Tigers)	6.00	2.70	.75
☐ 109B Bill Bruton BOX (Braves)	6.00	2.70	.75
☐ 110A Del Crandall COM	4.00	1.80	.50
☐ 110B Del Crandall BOX	4.00	1.80	.50
☐ 111 Red Schoendienst BOX only	4.00	1.80	.50
☐ 112 Juan Pizarro BOX only	3.00	1.35	.40
☐ 113 Chuck Cottier BOX only	15.00	6.75	1.90
☐ 114 Al Spangler BOX only	3.00	1.35	.40
☐ 115A Dick Farrell COM	5.00	2.30	.60
☐ 115B Dick Farrell BOX	5.00	2.30	.60
☐ 116A Jim Owens COM	5.00	2.30	.60
☐ 116B Jim Owens BOX	5.00	2.30	.60
☐ 117A Robin Roberts COM	7.50	3.40	.95
☐ 117B Robin Roberts BOX	7.50	3.40	.95
☐ 118A Tony Taylor COM	3.00	1.35	.40
☐ 118B Tony Taylor BOX	3.00	1.35	.40
☐ 119A Lee Walls COM	3.00	1.35	.40
☐ 119B Lee Walls BOX	3.00	1.35	.40
☐ 120A Tony Curry COM	3.00	1.35	.40
☐ 120B Tony Curry BOX	3.00	1.35	.40
☐ 121A Pancho Herrera COM	3.00	1.35	.40
☐ 121B Pancho Herrera BOX	3.00	1.35	.40
☐ 122A Ken Walters COM	3.00	1.35	.40
☐ 122B Ken Walters BOX	3.00	1.35	.40
☐ 123A John Callison COM	3.00	1.35	.40
☐ 123B John Callison BOX	3.00	1.35	.40
☐ 124A Gene Conley COM (Red Sox)	9.00	4.00	1.15
☐ 124B Gene Conley BOX (Phillies)	3.00	1.35	.40
☐ 125A Bob Friend COM	4.00	1.80	.50
☐ 125B Bob Friend BOX	4.00	1.80	.50
☐ 126A Vernon Law COM	4.00	1.80	.50

☐	126B Vernon Law BOX	4.00	1.80	.50
☐	127A Dick Stuart COM	3.00	1.35	.40
☐	127B Dick Stuart BOX	3.00	1.35	.40
☐	128A Bill Mazeroski COM	3.50	1.55	.45
☐	128B Bill Mazeroski BOX	3.50	1.55	.45
☐	129A Dick Groat COM	3.50	1.55	.45
☐	129B Dick Groat BOX	3.50	1.55	.45
☐	130A Don Hoak COM	3.00	1.35	.40
☐	130B Don Hoak BOX	3.00	1.35	.40
☐	131A Bob Skinner COM	3.00	1.35	.40
☐	131B Bob Skinner BOX	3.00	1.35	.40
☐	132A Bob Clemente COM	35.00	16.00	4.40
☐	132B Bob Clemente BOX	35.00	16.00	4.40
☐	133 Roy Face BOX only	4.00	1.80	.50
☐	134 Harvey Haddix BOX only	3.00	1.35	.40
☐	135 Bill Virdon BOX only	40.00	18.00	5.00
☐	136A Gino Cimoli COM	3.00	1.35	.40
☐	136B Gino Cimoli BOX	3.00	1.35	.40
☐	137 Rocky Nelson BOX only	3.00	1.35	.40
☐	138A Smoky Burgess COM	3.50	1.55	.45
☐	138B Smoky Burgess BOX	3.50	1.55	.45
☐	139 Hal Smith BOX only	3.00	1.35	.40
☐	140 Wilmer Mizell BOX only	3.00	1.35	.40
☐	141A Mike McCormick COM	3.00	1.35	.40
☐	141B Mike McCormick BOX	3.00	1.35	.40
☐	142A John Antonelli COM (Cleveland)	5.00	2.30	.60
☐	142B John Antonelli BOX (San Francisco)	4.00	1.80	.50
☐	143A Sam Jones COM	4.50	2.00	.55
☐	143B Sam Jones BOX	4.50	2.00	.55
☐	144A Orlando Cepeda COM	6.00	2.70	.75
☐	144B Orlando Cepeda BOX	6.00	2.70	.75
☐	145A Willie Mays COM	35.00	16.00	4.40
☐	145B Willie Mays BOX	35.00	16.00	4.40
☐	146A Willie Kirkland (Cleveland) COM	6.00	2.70	.75
☐	146B Willie Kirkland (San Francisco) BOX	4.00	1.80	.50
☐	147A Willie McCovey COM	10.00	4.50	1.25
☐	147B Willie McCovey BOX	10.00	4.50	1.25
☐	148A Don Blasingame COM	3.00	1.35	.40
☐	148B Don Blasingame BOX	3.00	1.35	.40
☐	149A Jim Davenport COM	3.50	1.55	.45
☐	149B Jim Davenport BOX	3.50	1.55	.45
☐	150A Hobie Landrith COM	3.00	1.35	.40
☐	150B Hobie Landrith BOX	3.00	1.35	.40
☐	151 Bob Schmidt BOX only	3.00	1.35	.40
☐	152A Ed Bressoud COM	3.00	1.35	.40
☐	152B Ed Bressoud BOX	3.00	1.35	.40
☐	153A Andre Rodgers (no trade mention) BOX only	20.00	9.00	2.50
☐	153B Andre Rodgers (Traded to Milw.) BOX only	4.00	1.80	.50
☐	154 Jack Sanford BOX only	3.00	1.35	.40
☐	155 Billy O'Dell BOX only	3.00	1.35	.40
☐	156A Norm Larker COM	3.00	1.35	.40
☐	156B Norm Larker BOX	3.00	1.35	.40
☐	157A Charlie Neal COM	3.00	1.35	.40
☐	157B Charlie Neal BOX	3.00	1.35	.40
☐	158A Jim Gilliam COM	4.50	2.00	.55
☐	158B Jim Gilliam BOX	4.50	2.00	.55
☐	159A Wally Moon COM	3.50	1.55	.45
☐	159B Wally Moon BOX	3.50	1.55	.45
☐	160A Don Drysdale COM	10.00	4.50	1.25
☐	160B Don Drysdale BOX	10.00	4.50	1.25
☐	161A Larry Sherry COM	3.50	1.55	.45
☐	161B Larry Sherry BOX	3.50	1.55	.45
☐	162 Stan Williams BOX only	6.00	2.70	.75
☐	163 Mel Roach BOX only	75.00	34.00	9.50
☐	164A Maury Wills COM	7.50	3.40	.95
☐	164B Maury Wills BOX	7.50	3.40	.95
☐	165 Tommy Davis BOX only	3.00	1.35	.40
☐	166A John Roseboro COM	3.00	1.35	.40
☐	166B John Roseboro BOX	3.00	1.35	.40
☐	167A Duke Snider COM	7.50	3.40	.95
☐	167B Duke Snider BOX	7.50	3.40	.95
☐	168A Gil Hodges COM	7.50	3.40	.95
☐	168B Gil Hodges BOX	7.50	3.40	.95
☐	169 John Podres BOX only	3.00	1.35	.40
☐	170 Ed Roebuck BOX only	3.00	1.35	.40
☐	171A Ken Boyer COM	7.50	3.40	.95
☐	171B Ken Boyer BOX	7.50	3.40	.95
☐	172A Joe Cunningham COM	3.00	1.35	.40
☐	172B Joe Cunningham BOX	3.00	1.35	.40
☐	173A Daryl Spencer COM	3.00	1.35	.40
☐	173B Daryl Spencer BOX	3.00	1.35	.40
☐	174A Larry Jackson COM	3.00	1.35	.40
☐	174B Larry Jackson BOX	3.00	1.35	.40
☐	175A Lindy McDaniel COM	3.00	1.35	.40
☐	175B Lindy McDaniel BOX	3.00	1.35	.40
☐	176A Bill White COM	3.50	1.55	.45
☐	176B Bill White BOX	3.50	1.55	.45
☐	177A Alex Grammas COM	3.00	1.35	.40
☐	177B Alex Grammas BOX	3.00	1.35	.40
☐	178A Curt Flood COM	3.50	1.55	.45
☐	178B Curt Flood BOX	3.50	1.55	.45
☐	179A Ernie Broglio COM	3.00	1.35	.40
☐	179B Ernie Broglio BOX	3.00	1.35	.40
☐	180A Hal Smith COM	3.00	1.35	.40
☐	180B Hal Smith BOX	3.00	1.35	.40
☐	181A Vada Pinson COM	3.50	1.55	.45
☐	181B Vada Pinson BOX	3.50	1.55	.45
☐	182A Frank Robinson COM	35.00	16.00	4.40
☐	182B Frank Robinson BOX	35.00	16.00	4.40
☐	183 Roy McMillan BOX only	90.00	40.00	11.50
☐	184A Bob Purkey COM	3.00	1.35	.40
☐	184B Bob Purkey BOX	3.00	1.35	.40
☐	185A Ed Kasko COM	3.00	1.35	.40
☐	185B Ed Kasko BOX	3.00	1.35	.40
☐	186A Gus Bell COM	3.00	1.35	.40
☐	186B Gus Bell BOX	3.00	1.35	.40
☐	187A Jerry Lynch COM	3.00	1.35	.40
☐	187B Jerry Lynch BOX	3.00	1.35	.40
☐	188A Ed Bailey COM	3.00	1.35	.40
☐	188B Ed Bailey BOX	3.00	1.35	.40
☐	189A Jim O'Toole COM	3.00	1.35	.40
☐	189B Jim O'Toole BOX	3.00	1.35	.40
☐	190A Billy Martin COM (Sold to Milwaukee)	9.00	4.00	1.15
☐	190B Billy Martin BOX (No sale mention)	4.00	1.80	.50
☐	191A Ernie Banks COM	25.00	11.50	3.10
☐	191B Ernie Banks BOX	25.00	11.50	3.10
☐	192A Richie Ashburn COM	4.50	2.00	.55
☐	192B Richie Ashburn BOX	4.50	2.00	.55
☐	193A Frank Thomas COM	30.00	13.50	3.80
☐	193B Frank Thomas BOX	30.00	13.50	3.80
☐	194A Don Cardwell COM	3.00	1.35	.40
☐	194B Don Cardwell BOX	3.00	1.35	.40
☐	195A George Altman COM	3.00	1.35	.40
☐	195B George Altman BOX	3.00	1.35	.40
☐	196A Ron Santo COM	5.00	2.30	.60
☐	196B Ron Santo BOX	5.00	2.30	.60
☐	197A Glen Hobbie COM	3.00	1.35	.40
☐	197B Glen Hobbie BOX	3.00	1.35	.40
☐	198A Sam Taylor COM	3.00	1.35	.40
☐	198B Sam Taylor BOX	3.00	1.35	.40
☐	199A Jerry Kindall COM	3.00	1.35	.40
☐	199B Jerry Kindall BOX	3.00	1.35	.40
☐	200A Don Elston COM	3.00	1.35	.40
☐	200B Don Elston BOX	3.00	1.35	.40

1962 Post Cereal

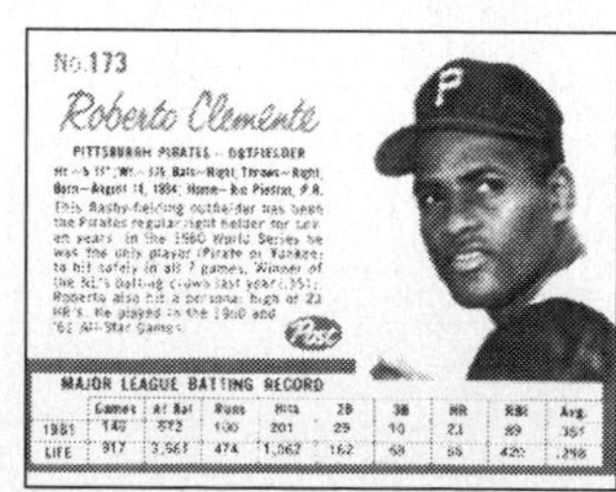

The cards in this 200-player series measure 2 1/2" by 3 1/2" and are oriented horizontally. The 1962 Post set is the easiest of the Post sets to complete. The cards are grouped numerically by team, for example, New York Yankees (1-13), Detroit (14-26), Baltimore (27-36), Cleveland (37-45), Chicago White Sox (46-55), Boston (56-64), Washington (65-73), Los Angeles Angels (74-82), Minnesota (83-91),

Kansas City (92-100), Los Angeles Dodgers (101-115), Cincinnati (116-130), San Francisco (131-144), Milwaukee (145-157), St. Louis (158-168), Pittsburgh (169-181), Chicago Cubs (182-191), and Philadelphia (192-200). Cards 5B and 6B were printed on thin stock in a two-card panel and distributed in a Life magazine promotion. The scarce cards are 55, 69, 83, 92, 101, 103, 113, 116, 122, 125, 127, 131, 140, 144, and 158. The checklist for this set is the same as that of 1962 Jello and 1962 Post Canadian, but those sets are considered separate issues. The catalog number for this set is F278-37.

	NRMT	VG-E	GOOD
COMPLETE SET (210)	2000.00	900.00	250.00
COMMON PLAYER (1-200)	2.50	1.15	.30
☐ 1 Bill Skowron	3.00	1.35	.40
☐ 2 Bobby Richardson	3.00	1.35	.40
☐ 3 Cletis Boyer	2.50	1.15	.30
☐ 4 Tony Kubek	3.00	1.35	.40
☐ 5A Mickey Mantle	100.00	45.00	12.50
☐ 5B Mickey Mantle AD	100.00	45.00	12.50
☐ 6A Roger Maris	25.00	11.50	3.10
☐ 6B Roger Maris AD	25.00	11.50	3.10
☐ 7 Yogi Berra	21.00	9.50	2.60
☐ 8 Elston Howard	3.00	1.35	.40
☐ 9 Whitey Ford	9.00	4.00	1.15
☐ 10 Ralph Terry	2.50	1.15	.30
☐ 11 John Blanchard	2.50	1.15	.30
☐ 12 Luis Arroyo	2.50	1.15	.30
☐ 13 Bill Stafford	2.50	1.15	.30
☐ 14A Norm Cash ERR (Throws: right)	20.00	9.00	2.50
☐ 14B Norm Cash COR (Throws: left)	2.50	1.15	.30
☐ 15 Jake Wood	2.50	1.15	.30
☐ 16 Steve Boros	2.50	1.15	.30
☐ 17 Chico Fernandez	2.50	1.15	.30
☐ 18 Bill Bruton	2.50	1.15	.30
☐ 19 Rocky Colavito	3.50	1.55	.45
☐ 20 Al Kaline	15.00	6.75	1.90
☐ 21 Dick Brown	2.50	1.15	.30
☐ 22 Frank Lary	2.50	1.15	.30
☐ 23 Don Mossi	2.50	1.15	.30
☐ 24 Phil Regan	2.50	1.15	.30
☐ 25 Charley Maxwell	2.50	1.15	.30
☐ 26 Jim Bunning	4.00	1.80	.50
☐ 27A Jim Gentile (Home: Baltimore)	3.00	1.35	.40
☐ 27B Jim Gentile (Home: San Lorenzo)	20.00	9.00	2.50
☐ 28 Marv Breeding	2.50	1.15	.30
☐ 29 Brooks Robinson	15.00	6.75	1.90
☐ 30A Ron Hansen (At-Bats)	3.50	1.55	.45
☐ 30B Ron Hansen (At Bats)	3.50	1.55	.45
☐ 31 Jackie Brandt	2.50	1.15	.30
☐ 32 Dick Williams	2.50	1.15	.30
☐ 33 Gus Triandos	2.50	1.15	.30
☐ 34 Milt Pappas	2.50	1.15	.30
☐ 35 Hoyt Wilhelm	8.00	3.60	1.00
☐ 36 Chuck Estrada	7.00	3.10	.85
☐ 37 Vic Power	2.50	1.15	.30
☐ 38 Johnny Temple	2.50	1.15	.30
☐ 39 Bubba Phillips	2.50	1.15	.30
☐ 40 Tito Francona	2.50	1.15	.30
☐ 41 Willie Kirkland	2.50	1.15	.30
☐ 42 John Romano	2.50	1.15	.30
☐ 43 Jim Perry	2.50	1.15	.30
☐ 44 Woodie Held	2.50	1.15	.30
☐ 45 Chuck Essegian	2.50	1.15	.30
☐ 46 Roy Sievers	2.50	1.15	.30
☐ 47 Nellie Fox	3.50	1.55	.45
☐ 48 Al Smith	2.50	1.15	.30
☐ 49 Luis Aparicio	4.00	1.80	.50
☐ 50 Jim Landis	2.50	1.15	.30
☐ 51 Minnie Minoso	3.00	1.35	.40
☐ 52 Andy Carey	2.50	1.15	.30
☐ 53 Sherman Lollar	2.50	1.15	.30
☐ 54 Bill Pierce	3.00	1.35	.40
☐ 55 Early Wynn	30.00	13.50	3.80
☐ 56 Chuck Schilling	2.50	1.15	.30
☐ 57 Pete Runnels	2.50	1.15	.30
☐ 58 Frank Malzone	2.50	1.15	.30
☐ 59 Don Buddin	2.50	1.15	.30
☐ 60 Gary Geiger	2.50	1.15	.30
☐ 61 Carl Yastrzemski	40.00	18.00	5.00
☐ 62 Jackie Jensen	2.50	1.15	.30
☐ 63 Jim Pagliaroni	2.50	1.15	.30
☐ 64 Don Schwall	2.50	1.15	.30
☐ 65 Dale Long	2.50	1.15	.30
☐ 66 Chuck Cottier	2.50	1.15	.30
☐ 67 Billy Klaus	2.50	1.15	.30
☐ 68 Coot Veal	2.50	1.15	.30
☐ 69 Marty Keough	35.00	16.00	4.40
☐ 70 Willie Tasby	2.50	1.15	.30
☐ 71 Gene Woodling	2.50	1.15	.30
☐ 72 Gene Green	2.50	1.15	.30
☐ 73 Dick Donovan	2.50	1.15	.30
☐ 74 Steve Bilko	2.50	1.15	.30
☐ 75 Rocky Bridges	2.50	1.15	.30
☐ 76 Eddie Yost	2.50	1.15	.30
☐ 77 Leon Wagner	2.50	1.15	.30
☐ 78 Albie Pearson	2.50	1.15	.30
☐ 79 Ken Hunt	2.50	1.15	.30
☐ 80 Earl Averill Jr.	2.50	1.15	.30
☐ 81 Ryne Duren	2.50	1.15	.30
☐ 82 Ted Kluszewski	3.00	1.35	.40
☐ 83 Bob Allison	30.00	13.50	3.80
☐ 84 Billy Martin	3.50	1.55	.45
☐ 85 Harmon Killebrew	10.00	4.50	1.25
☐ 86 Zoilo Versalles	2.50	1.15	.30
☐ 87 Lenny Green	2.50	1.15	.30
☐ 88 Bill Tuttle	2.50	1.15	.30
☐ 89 Jim Lemon	2.50	1.15	.30
☐ 90 Earl Battey	2.50	1.15	.30
☐ 91 Camilo Pascual	2.50	1.15	.30
☐ 92 Norm Siebern	75.00	34.00	9.50
☐ 93 Jerry Lumpe	2.50	1.15	.30
☐ 94 Dick Howser	3.00	1.35	.40
☐ 95A Gene Stephens (Born: Jan. 5)	3.00	1.35	.40
☐ 95B Gene Stephens (Born: Jan. 20)	20.00	9.00	2.50
☐ 96 Leo Posada	2.50	1.15	.30
☐ 97 Joe Pignatano	2.50	1.15	.30
☐ 98 Jim Archer	2.50	1.15	.30
☐ 99 Haywood Sullivan	2.50	1.15	.30
☐ 100 Art Ditmar	2.50	1.15	.30
☐ 101 Gil Hodges	125.00	57.50	15.50
☐ 102 Charlie Neal	2.50	1.15	.30
☐ 103 Daryl Spencer	25.00	11.50	3.10
☐ 104 Maury Wills	5.00	2.30	.60
☐ 105 Tommy Davis	3.00	1.35	.40
☐ 106 Willie Davis	3.00	1.35	.40
☐ 107 John Roseboro	2.50	1.15	.30
☐ 108 John Podres	3.00	1.35	.40
☐ 109A Sandy Koufax	30.00	13.50	3.80
☐ 109B Sandy Koufax (With blue lines)	100.00	45.00	12.50
☐ 110 Don Drysdale	10.00	4.50	1.25
☐ 111 Larry Sherry	3.50	1.55	.45
☐ 112 Jim Gilliam	3.00	1.35	.40
☐ 113 Norm Larker	35.00	16.00	4.40
☐ 114 Duke Snider	8.00	3.60	1.00
☐ 115 Stan Williams	2.50	1.15	.30
☐ 116 Gordy Coleman	100.00	45.00	12.50
☐ 117 Don Blasingame	2.50	1.15	.30
☐ 118 Gene Freese	2.50	1.15	.30
☐ 119 Ed Kasko	2.50	1.15	.30
☐ 120 Gus Bell	2.50	1.15	.30
☐ 121 Vada Pinson	3.00	1.35	.40
☐ 122 Frank Robinson	30.00	13.50	3.80
☐ 123 Bob Purkey	2.50	1.15	.30
☐ 124A Joey Jay	3.00	1.35	.40
☐ 124B Joey Jay (With blue lines)	20.00	9.00	2.50
☐ 125 Jim Brosnan	30.00	13.50	3.80
☐ 126 Jim O'Toole	2.50	1.15	.30
☐ 127 Jerry Lynch	60.00	27.00	7.50
☐ 128 Wally Post	2.50	1.15	.30
☐ 129 Ken Hunt	2.50	1.15	.30
☐ 130 Jerry Zimmerman	2.50	1.15	.30
☐ 131 Willie McCovey	100.00	45.00	12.50
☐ 132 Jose Pagan	2.50	1.15	.30
☐ 133 Felipe Alou UER (Misspelled Filipe in text)	3.00	1.35	.40
☐ 134 Jim Davenport	2.50	1.15	.30
☐ 135 Harvey Kuenn	3.00	1.35	.40
☐ 136 Orlando Cepeda	4.50	2.00	.55
☐ 137 Ed Bailey	2.50	1.15	.30
☐ 138 Sam Jones	2.50	1.15	.30
☐ 139 Mike McCormick	2.50	1.15	.30
☐ 140 Juan Marichal	125.00	57.50	15.50
☐ 141 Jack Sanford	2.50	1.15	.30
☐ 142 Willie Mays	40.00	18.00	5.00
☐ 143 Stu Miller	7.50	3.40	.95
☐ 144 Joe Amalfitano	20.00	9.00	2.50
☐ 145A Joe Adock (sic) ERR	90.00	40.00	11.50
☐ 145B Joe Adcock CORR	3.00	1.35	.40
☐ 146 Frank Bolling	2.50	1.15	.30

☐ 147 Ed Mathews	12.00	5.50	1.50
☐ 148 Roy McMillan	2.50	1.15	.30
☐ 149 Hank Aaron	35.00	16.00	4.40
☐ 150 Gino Cimoli	2.50	1.15	.30
☐ 151 Frank Thomas	2.50	1.15	.30
☐ 152 Joe Torre	3.50	1.55	.45
☐ 153 Lew Burdette	3.00	1.35	.40
☐ 154 Bob Buhl	2.50	1.15	.30
☐ 155 Carlton Willey	2.50	1.15	.30
☐ 156 Lee Maye	2.50	1.15	.30
☐ 157 Al Spangler	2.50	1.15	.30
☐ 158 Bill White	45.00	20.00	5.75
☐ 159 Ken Boyer	3.50	1.55	.45
☐ 160 Joe Cunningham	2.50	1.15	.30
☐ 161 Carl Warwick	2.50	1.15	.30
☐ 162 Carl Sawatski	2.50	1.15	.30
☐ 163 Lindy McDaniel	2.50	1.15	.30
☐ 164 Ernie Broglio	2.50	1.15	.30
☐ 165 Larry Jackson	2.50	1.15	.30
☐ 166 Curt Flood	3.00	1.35	.40
☐ 167 Curt Simmons	2.50	1.15	.30
☐ 168 Alex Grammas	2.50	1.15	.30
☐ 169 Dick Stuart	2.50	1.15	.30
☐ 170 Bill Mazeroski UER (Bio reads 1959, should read 1960)	3.00	1.35	.40
☐ 171 Don Hoak	2.50	1.15	.30
☐ 172 Dick Groat	3.00	1.35	.40
☐ 173A Roberto Clemente	30.00	13.50	3.80
☐ 173B Roberto Clemente (With blue lines)	125.00	57.50	15.50
☐ 174 Bob Skinner	2.50	1.15	.30
☐ 175 Bill Virdon	2.50	1.15	.30
☐ 176 Smoky Burgess	2.50	1.15	.30
☐ 177 Elroy Face	3.00	1.35	.40
☐ 178 Bob Friend	2.50	1.15	.30
☐ 179 Vernon Law	2.50	1.15	.30
☐ 180 Harvey Haddix	2.50	1.15	.30
☐ 181 Hal Smith	2.50	1.15	.30
☐ 182 Ed Bouchee	2.50	1.15	.30
☐ 183 Don Zimmer	2.50	1.15	.30
☐ 184 Ron Santo	3.00	1.35	.40
☐ 185 Andre Rodgers	2.50	1.15	.30
☐ 186 Richie Ashburn	4.00	1.80	.50
☐ 187 George Altman	2.50	1.15	.30
☐ 188 Ernie Banks	15.00	6.75	1.90
☐ 189 Sam Taylor	4.50	2.00	.55
☐ 190 Don Elston	2.50	1.15	.30
☐ 191 Jerry Kindall	2.50	1.15	.30
☐ 192 Pancho Herrera	2.50	1.15	.30
☐ 193 Tony Taylor	2.50	1.15	.30
☐ 194 Ruben Amaro	2.50	1.15	.30
☐ 195 Don Demeter	2.50	1.15	.30
☐ 196 Bobby Gene Smith	2.50	1.15	.30
☐ 197 Clay Dalrymple	2.50	1.15	.30
☐ 198 Robin Roberts	7.50	3.40	.95
☐ 199 Art Mahaffey	2.50	1.15	.30
☐ 200 John Buzhardt	2.50	1.15	.30

1963 Post Cereal

The cards in this 200-card set measure 2 1/2" by 3 1/2". The players are grouped by team with American Leaguers comprising 1-100 and National Leaguers 101-200. The ordering of teams is as follows: Minnesota (1-11), New York Yankees, Los Angeles Angels (24-34), Chicago White Sox (35-45), Detroit (46-56), Baltimore (57-66), Cleveland (67-76), Boston (77-84), Kansas City (85-92), Washington (93-100), San Francisco (101-112), Los Angeles Dodgers (113-124), Cincinnati (125-136), Pittsburgh (137-147), Milwaukee (148-157), St. Louis (158-168), Chicago Cubs (169-176), Philadelphia (177-184), Houston (185-192), and New York Mets (193-200). In contrast to the 1962 issue, the 1963 Post baseball card series is very difficult to complete. There are many card scarcities reflected in the price list below. Cards of the Post set are easily confused with those of the 1963 Jello set, which are 1/4" narrower (a difference which is often eliminated by bad cutting). The catalog designation is F278-38. There was also an album produced by Post to hold the cards.

	NRMT	VG-E	GOOD
COMPLETE SET (206)	4250.00	1900.00	525.00
COMMON PLAYER (1-200)	3.00	1.35	.40
☐ 1 Vic Power	3.00	1.35	.40
☐ 2 Bernie Allen	3.00	1.35	.40
☐ 3 Zoilo Versalles	3.00	1.35	.40
☐ 4 Rich Rollins	3.00	1.35	.40
☐ 5 Harmon Killebrew	18.00	8.00	2.30
☐ 6 Lenny Green	45.00	20.00	5.75
☐ 7 Bob Allison	3.00	1.35	.40
☐ 8 Earl Battey	3.00	1.35	.40
☐ 9 Camilo Pascual	3.00	1.35	.40
☐ 10 Jim Kaat	4.00	1.80	.50
☐ 11 Jack Kralick	3.00	1.35	.40
☐ 12 Bill Skowron	3.50	1.55	.45
☐ 13 Bobby Richardson	4.00	1.80	.50
☐ 14 Cletis Boyer	3.00	1.35	.40
☐ 15 Mickey Mantle	300.00	135.00	38.00
☐ 16 Roger Maris	175.00	80.00	22.00
☐ 17 Yogi Berra	20.00	9.00	2.50
☐ 18 Elston Howard	3.50	1.55	.45
☐ 19 Whitey Ford	12.50	5.75	1.55
☐ 20 Ralph Terry	3.00	1.35	.40
☐ 21 John Blanchard	3.00	1.35	.40
☐ 22 Bill Stafford	3.00	1.35	.40
☐ 23 Tom Tresh	3.00	1.35	.40
☐ 24 Steve Bilko	3.00	1.35	.40
☐ 25 Bill Moran	3.00	1.35	.40
☐ 26A Joe Koppe (BA: .277)	3.00	1.35	.40
☐ 26B Joe Koppe (BA: .227)	20.00	9.00	2.50
☐ 27 Felix Torres	3.00	1.35	.40
☐ 28A Leon Wagner (BA: .278)	3.00	1.35	.40
☐ 28B Leon Wagner (BA: .272)	20.00	9.00	2.50
☐ 29 Albie Pearson	3.00	1.35	.40
☐ 30 Lee Thomas UER (Photo actually George Thomas)	90.00	40.00	11.50
☐ 31 Bob Rodgers	3.00	1.35	.40
☐ 32 Dean Chance	3.00	1.35	.40
☐ 33 Ken McBride	3.00	1.35	.40
☐ 34 George Thomas UER (Photo actually Lee Thomas)	3.00	1.35	.40
☐ 35 Joe Cunningham	3.00	1.35	.40
☐ 36 Nelson Fox	4.00	1.80	.50
☐ 37 Luis Aparicio	6.00	2.70	.75
☐ 38 Al Smith	40.00	18.00	5.00
☐ 39 Floyd Robinson	110.00	50.00	14.00
☐ 40 Jim Landis	3.00	1.35	.40
☐ 41 Charlie Maxwell	3.00	1.35	.40
☐ 42 Sherman Lollar	3.00	1.35	.40
☐ 43 Early Wynn	7.50	3.40	.95
☐ 44 Juan Pizarro	3.00	1.35	.40
☐ 45 Ray Herbert	3.00	1.35	.40
☐ 46 Norm Cash	3.50	1.55	.45
☐ 47 Steve Boros	3.00	1.35	.40
☐ 48 Dick McAuliffe	25.00	11.50	3.10
☐ 49 Bill Bruton	3.50	1.55	.45
☐ 50 Rocky Colavito	5.00	2.30	.60
☐ 51 Al Kaline	21.00	9.50	2.60
☐ 52 Dick Brown	3.00	1.35	.40
☐ 53 Jim Bunning	165.00	75.00	21.00
☐ 54 Hank Aguirre	3.00	1.35	.40
☐ 55 Frank Lary	3.00	1.35	.40
☐ 56 Don Mossi	3.00	1.35	.40
☐ 57 Jim Gentile	3.00	1.35	.40
☐ 58 Jackie Brandt	3.00	1.35	.40
☐ 59 Brooks Robinson	24.00	11.00	3.00
☐ 60 Ron Hansen	3.50	1.55	.45
☐ 61 Jerry Adair	200.00	90.00	25.00

☐ 62 John(Boog) Powell	4.00	1.80	.50
☐ 63 Russ Snyder	3.00	1.35	.40
☐ 64 Steve Barber	3.00	1.35	.40
☐ 65 Milt Pappas	3.00	1.35	.40
☐ 66 Robin Roberts	7.50	3.40	.95
☐ 67 Tito Francona	3.00	1.35	.40
☐ 68 Jerry Kindall	3.00	1.35	.40
☐ 69 Woody Held	3.00	1.35	.40
☐ 70 Bubba Phillips	14.00	6.25	1.75
☐ 71 Chuck Essegian	3.00	1.35	.40
☐ 72 Willie Kirkland	3.00	1.35	.40
☐ 73 Al Luplow	3.00	1.35	.40
☐ 74 Ty Cline	3.00	1.35	.40
☐ 75 Dick Donovan	3.00	1.35	.40
☐ 76 John Romano	3.00	1.35	.40
☐ 77 Pete Runnels	3.00	1.35	.40
☐ 78 Ed Bressoud	3.00	1.35	.40
☐ 79 Frank Malzone	3.00	1.35	.40
☐ 80 Carl Yastrzemski	300.00	135.00	38.00
☐ 81 Gary Geiger	3.00	1.35	.40
☐ 82 Lou Clinton	3.00	1.35	.40
☐ 83 Earl Wilson	3.00	1.35	.40
☐ 84 Bill Monbouquette	3.00	1.35	.40
☐ 85 Norm Siebern	3.00	1.35	.40
☐ 86 Jerry Lumpe	120.00	55.00	15.00
☐ 87 Manny Jimenez	120.00	55.00	15.00
☐ 88 Gino Cimoli	3.00	1.35	.40
☐ 89 Ed Charles	3.00	1.35	.40
☐ 90 Ed Rakow	3.00	1.35	.40
☐ 91 Bob Del Greco	3.00	1.35	.40
☐ 92 Haywood Sullivan	3.00	1.35	.40
☐ 93 Chuck Hinton	3.00	1.35	.40
☐ 94 Ken Retzer	3.00	1.35	.40
☐ 95 Harry Bright	3.00	1.35	.40
☐ 96 Bob Johnson	3.00	1.35	.40
☐ 97 Dave Stenhouse	14.00	6.25	1.75
☐ 98 Chuck Cottier	24.00	11.00	3.00
☐ 99 Tom Cheney	3.00	1.35	.40
☐ 100 Claude Osteen	14.00	6.25	1.75
☐ 101 Orlando Cepeda	5.00	2.30	.60
☐ 102 Chuck Hiller	3.00	1.35	.40
☐ 103 Jose Pagan	3.00	1.35	.40
☐ 104 Jim Davenport	3.00	1.35	.40
☐ 105 Harvey Kuenn	3.50	1.55	.45
☐ 106 Willie Mays	45.00	20.00	5.75
☐ 107 Felipe Alou	3.00	1.35	.40
☐ 108 Tom Haller	120.00	55.00	15.00
☐ 109 Juan Marichal	7.00	3.10	.85
☐ 110 Jack Sanford	3.00	1.35	.40
☐ 111 Bill O'Dell	3.00	1.35	.40
☐ 112 Willie McCovey	9.00	4.00	1.15
☐ 113 Lee Walls	3.00	1.35	.40
☐ 114 Jim Gilliam	3.50	1.55	.45
☐ 115 Maury Wills	4.00	1.80	.50
☐ 116 Ron Fairly	3.00	1.35	.40
☐ 117 Tommy Davis	3.00	1.35	.40
☐ 118 Duke Snider	10.00	4.50	1.25
☐ 119 Willie Davis	200.00	90.00	25.00
☐ 120 John Roseboro	3.00	1.35	.40
☐ 121 Sandy Koufax	35.00	16.00	4.40
☐ 122 Stan Williams	3.00	1.35	.40
☐ 123 Don Drysdale	8.00	3.60	1.00
☐ 124 Daryl Spencer	3.00	1.35	.40
☐ 125 Gordy Coleman	3.00	1.35	.40
☐ 126 Don Blasingame	3.00	1.35	.40
☐ 127 Leo Cardenas	3.00	1.35	.40
☐ 128 Eddie Kasko	200.00	90.00	25.00
☐ 129 Jerry Lynch	15.00	6.75	1.90
☐ 130 Vada Pinson	3.50	1.55	.45
☐ 131A Frank Robinson (No stripes)	20.00	9.00	2.50
☐ 131B Frank Robinson (Stripes on hat)	50.00	23.00	6.25
☐ 132 John Edwards	3.00	1.35	.40
☐ 133 Joey Jay	3.00	1.35	.40
☐ 134 Bob Purkey	3.00	1.35	.40
☐ 135 Marty Keough	30.00	13.50	3.80
☐ 136 Jim O'Toole	3.00	1.35	.40
☐ 137 Dick Stuart	3.00	1.35	.40
☐ 138 Bill Mazeroski	4.00	1.80	.50
☐ 139 Dick Groat	3.50	1.55	.45
☐ 140 Don Hoak	35.00	16.00	4.40
☐ 141 Bob Skinner	18.00	8.00	2.30
☐ 142 Bill Virdon	3.50	1.55	.45
☐ 143 Roberto Clemente	35.00	16.00	4.40
☐ 144 Smoky Burgess	3.00	1.35	.40
☐ 145 Bob Friend	3.00	1.35	.40
☐ 146 Al McBean	3.00	1.35	.40
☐ 147 Elroy Face	3.50	1.55	.45
☐ 148 Joe Adcock	3.50	1.55	.45
☐ 149 Frank Bolling	3.00	1.35	.40
☐ 150 Roy McMillan	3.00	1.35	.40
☐ 151 Eddie Mathews	18.00	8.00	2.30
☐ 152 Hank Aaron	135.00	60.00	17.00
☐ 153 Del Crandall	35.00	16.00	4.40
☐ 154A Bob Shaw COR	3.00	1.35	.40
☐ 154B Bob Shaw ERR (Two "in 1959" in same sentence)	15.00	6.75	1.90
☐ 155 Lew Burdette	3.50	1.55	.45
☐ 156 Joe Torre	4.00	1.80	.50
☐ 157 Tony Cloninger	3.00	1.35	.40
☐ 158A Bill White (Ht. 6'0")	4.00	1.80	.50
☐ 158B Bill White (Ht. 6';)	4.00	1.80	.50
☐ 159 Julian Javier	3.00	1.35	.40
☐ 160 Ken Boyer	4.00	1.80	.50
☐ 161 Julio Gotay	3.00	1.35	.40
☐ 162 Curt Flood	135.00	60.00	17.00
☐ 163 Charlie James	4.00	1.80	.50
☐ 164 Gene Oliver	3.00	1.35	.40
☐ 165 Ernie Broglio	3.00	1.35	.40
☐ 166 Bob Gibson	8.00	3.60	1.00
☐ 167A Lindy McDaniel (No asterisk)	6.00	2.70	.75
☐ 167B Lindy McDaniel (Asterisk traded line)	6.00	2.70	.75
☐ 168 Ray Washburn	3.00	1.35	.40
☐ 169 Ernie Banks	15.00	6.75	1.90
☐ 170 Ron Santo	4.00	1.80	.50
☐ 171 George Altman	3.00	1.35	.40
☐ 172 Billy Williams	165.00	75.00	21.00
☐ 173 Andre Rodgers	15.00	6.75	1.90
☐ 174 Ken Hubbs	30.00	13.50	3.80
☐ 175 Don Landrum	3.00	1.35	.40
☐ 176 Dick Bertell	18.00	8.00	2.30
☐ 177 Roy Sievers	3.00	1.35	.40
☐ 178 Tony Taylor	3.00	1.35	.40
☐ 179 John Callison	3.00	1.35	.40
☐ 180 Don Demeter	3.00	1.35	.40
☐ 181 Tony Gonzalez	14.00	6.25	1.75
☐ 182 Wes Covington	24.00	11.00	3.00
☐ 183 Art Mahaffey	3.00	1.35	.40
☐ 184 Clay Dalrymple	3.00	1.35	.40
☐ 185 Al Spangler	3.50	1.55	.45
☐ 186 Roman Mejias	3.00	1.35	.40
☐ 187 Bob Aspromonte	375.00	170.00	47.50
☐ 188 Norm Larker	35.00	16.00	4.40
☐ 189 Johnny Temple	3.00	1.35	.40
☐ 190 Carl Warwick	3.00	1.35	.40
☐ 191 Bob Lillis	3.00	1.35	.40
☐ 192 Dick Farrell	3.00	1.35	.40
☐ 193 Gil Hodges	8.00	3.60	1.00
☐ 194 Marv Throneberry	3.00	1.35	.40
☐ 195 Charlie Neal	9.00	4.00	1.15
☐ 196 Frank Thomas	200.00	90.00	25.00
☐ 197 Richie Ashburn	25.00	11.50	3.10
☐ 198 Felix Mantilla	3.00	1.35	.40
☐ 199 Rod Kanehl	18.00	8.00	2.30
☐ 200 Roger Craig	3.50	1.55	.45

1990 Post

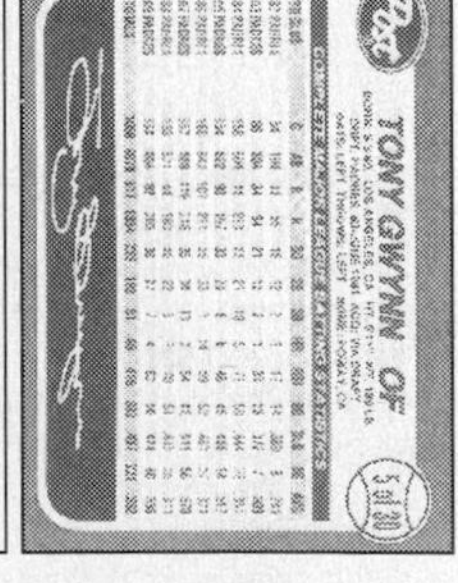

The 1990 Post Cereal set is a 30-card, standard-size (2 1/2" by 3 1/2") set issued with the assistance of Mike Schechter Associates. The sets do not have either team logos or other uniform identification on them. There is also a facsimile autograph on the back of the cards. The cards were inserted randomly as a cello pack (with three cards) inside specially marked boxes of Post cereals. The cards feature red, white, and blue fronts with the words, "First Collector Series". Card backs feature a facsimile autograph. The relatively high cost of the set is due to the fact that the cards were not available as a complete set as a part of any mail-in offer from the company.

	MT	EX-MT	VG
COMPLETE SET (30)	18.00	8.00	2.30
COMMON PLAYER (1-30)	.50	.23	.06
☐ 1 Don Mattingly	1.25	.55	.16
☐ 2 Roger Clemens	1.50	.65	.19
☐ 3 Kirby Puckett	1.25	.55	.16
☐ 4 George Brett	1.25	.55	.16
☐ 5 Tony Gwynn	1.00	.45	.13
☐ 6 Ozzie Smith	1.00	.45	.13
☐ 7 Will Clark	1.25	.55	.16
☐ 8 Orel Hershiser	.50	.23	.06
☐ 9 Ryne Sandberg	1.50	.65	.19
☐ 10 Darryl Strawberry	1.00	.45	.13
☐ 11 Nolan Ryan	2.50	1.15	.30
☐ 12 Mark McGwire	1.25	.55	.16
☐ 13 Jim Abbott	1.00	.45	.13
☐ 14 Bo Jackson	1.50	.65	.19
☐ 15 Kevin Mitchell	.50	.23	.06
☐ 16 Jose Canseco	1.50	.65	.19
☐ 17 Wade Boggs	1.00	.45	.13
☐ 18 Dale Murphy	.60	.25	.08
☐ 19 Mark Grace	.75	.35	.09
☐ 20 Mike Scott	.50	.23	.06
☐ 21 Cal Ripken	2.00	.90	.25
☐ 22 Pedro Guerrero	.50	.23	.06
☐ 23 Ken Griffey Jr.	3.50	1.55	.45
☐ 24 Eric Davis	.60	.25	.08
☐ 25 Rickey Henderson	1.25	.55	.16
☐ 26 Robin Yount	1.25	.55	.16
☐ 27 Von Hayes	.50	.23	.06
☐ 28 Alan Trammell	.60	.25	.08
☐ 29 Dwight Gooden	.75	.35	.09
☐ 30 Joe Carter	1.00	.45	.13

1991 Post

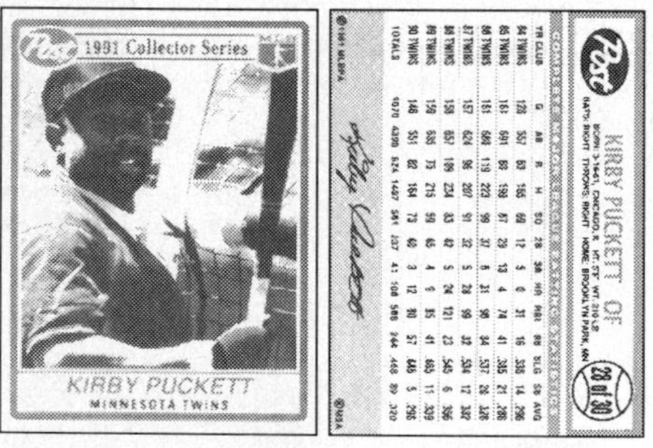

This 30-card set, which measures the standard 2 1/2" by 3 1/2", was released early in 1991 by Post Cereal in conjunction with Michael Schechter Associates (MSA). The players pictured are some of the star players of baseball entering the 1991 season. The design of the set features the Post logo in the upper left hand corner, the MLB logo in the upper right hand corner, and the players name and team underneath the portrait shot of the player pictured on the card. The cards were inserted three-at-a-time in boxes of the following cereals: Post Honeycomb, Super Golden Crisp, Cocoa Pebbles, Fruity Pebbles, Alpha-Bits, and Marshmallow Alpha-Bits. The fronts feature either posed or action color player photos, with blue and yellow borders. The words "1991 Collector Series" appear in a white stripe at the card top. Some cards (numbers 1, 6, 25, and 30) have a banner at the top that reads "Rookie Star". The player's name is given in a white stripe below the picture. The horizontally oriented backs are printed in aqua and dark blue on white and present complete Major League statistical information and a facsimile autograph on the bottom of the card. The cards are numbered on the back.

	MT	EX-MT	VG
COMPLETE SET (30)	10.00	4.50	1.25
COMMON PLAYER (1-30)	.30	.14	.04
☐ 1 Dave Justice	1.00	.45	.13
☐ 2 Mark McGwire	1.00	.45	.13
☐ 3 Will Clark	1.00	.45	.13
☐ 4 Jose Canseco	1.00	.45	.13
☐ 5 Vince Coleman	.30	.14	.04
☐ 6 Sandy Alomar Jr.	.40	.18	.05
☐ 7 Darryl Strawberry	1.00	.45	.13
☐ 8 Len Dykstra	.30	.14	.04
☐ 9 Gregg Jefferies	.50	.23	.06
☐ 10 Tony Gwynn	.75	.35	.09
☐ 11 Ken Griffey Jr.	2.00	.90	.25
☐ 12 Roger Clemens	1.25	.55	.16
☐ 13 Chris Sabo	.30	.14	.04
☐ 14 Bobby Bonilla	.50	.23	.06
☐ 15 Gary Sheffield	1.00	.45	.13
☐ 16 Ryne Sandberg	1.25	.55	.16
☐ 17 Nolan Ryan	2.00	.90	.25
☐ 18 Barry Larkin	.50	.23	.06
☐ 19 Cal Ripken	1.25	.55	.16
☐ 20 Jim Abbott	.60	.25	.08
☐ 21 Barry Bonds	.90	.40	.11
☐ 22 Mark Grace	.60	.25	.08
☐ 23 Cecil Fielder	.75	.35	.09
☐ 24 Kevin Mitchell	.40	.18	.05
☐ 25 Todd Zeile	.30	.14	.04
☐ 26 George Brett	1.00	.45	.13
☐ 27 Rickey Henderson	1.00	.45	.13
☐ 28 Kirby Puckett	1.00	.45	.13
☐ 29 Don Mattingly	1.00	.45	.13
☐ 30 Kevin Maas	.40	.18	.05

1991 Post Canada

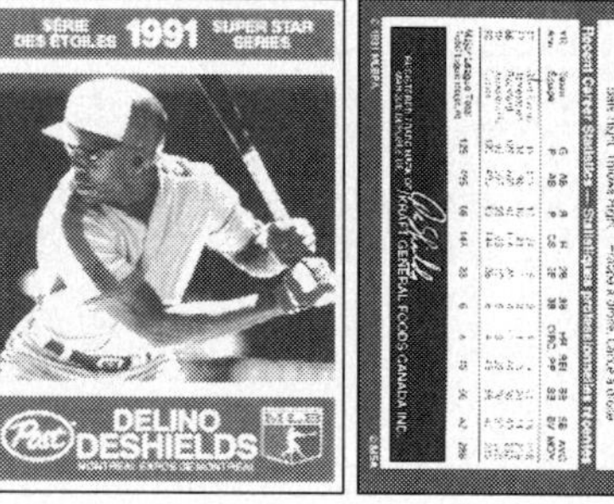

This 30-card Super Stars set was sponsored by Post and features 14 National League and 16 American League players. Two cards were inserted in specially marked boxes of Post Alpha-Bits, Sugar Crisp, and Honeycomb sold in Canada. The cards measure the standard size (2 1/2" by 3 1/2") and are bilingual (French and English) on both sides. While all the cards feature color player photos (action or posed) on the fronts, the NL cards (1-14) are accentuated with red stripes while the AL cards (15-30) have royal blue stripes. In a horizontal format, the backs have biography, recent career statistics, and a facsimile autograph. The cards are numbered on the back. The side panel also included a checklist, an offer for a baseball player poster-album, and an offer to order ten additional cards to complete the set.

	MT	EX-MT	VG
COMPLETE SET (30)	40.00	18.00	5.00
COMMON PLAYER (1-30)	1.00	.45	.13
☐ 1 Delino DeShields	2.50	1.15	.30

☐ 2 Tim Wallach	1.00	.45	.13
☐ 3 Andres Galarraga	1.00	.45	.13
☐ 4 Dave Magadan	1.00	.45	.13
☐ 5 Barry Bonds UER (Career BA .256, should be .265)	3.00	1.35	.40
☐ 6 Len Dykstra	1.00	.45	.13
☐ 7 Andre Dawson	2.50	1.15	.30
☐ 8 Ozzie Smith	2.50	1.15	.30
☐ 9 Will Clark	3.50	1.55	.45
☐ 10 Chris Sabo	1.00	.45	.13
☐ 11 Eddie Murray	2.00	.90	.25
☐ 12 Dave Justice	4.00	1.80	.50
☐ 13 Benito Santiago	1.25	.55	.16
☐ 14 Glenn Davis	1.00	.45	.13
☐ 15 Kelly Gruber	1.00	.45	.13
☐ 16 Dave Stieb	1.00	.45	.13
☐ 17 John Olerud	2.50	1.15	.30
☐ 18 Roger Clemens	4.00	1.80	.50
☐ 19 Cecil Fielder	2.50	1.15	.30
☐ 20 Kevin Maas	1.50	.65	.19
☐ 21 Robin Yount	3.00	1.35	.40
☐ 22 Cal Ripken	4.00	1.80	.50
☐ 23 Sandy Alomar Jr.	1.00	.45	.13
☐ 24 Rickey Henderson	3.00	1.35	.40
☐ 25 Bobby Thigpen	1.00	.45	.13
☐ 26 Ken Griffey Jr.	7.50	3.40	.95
☐ 27 Nolan Ryan	6.00	2.70	.75
☐ 28 Dave Winfield	3.00	1.35	.40
☐ 29 George Brett	3.00	1.35	.40
☐ 30 Kirby Puckett	3.50	1.55	.45

1992 Post

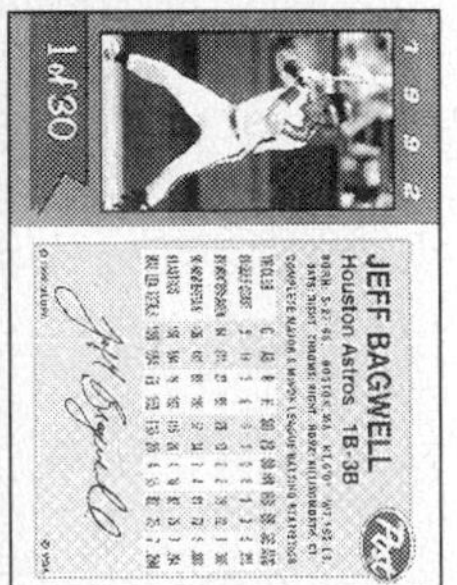

This 30-card set, measuring the standard size (2 1/2" by 3 1/2"), was manufactured by MSA (Michael Schechter Associates) for Post Cereal. Three-card packs were inserted in the following Post cereals: Honeycomb, Super Golden Crisp, Cocoa Pebbles, Fruity Pebbles, Alpha-Bits, Marshmallow Alpha-Bits and, for the first time, Raisin Bran. In the last-mentioned cereal, the cards were protected in cello packs that also had a 50 cent manufacturers coupon good on the next purchase. The other cereals contained tan paper wrapped packs. The complete set could also be obtained via a mail-in offer for 1.00 and five UPC symbols. The fronts feature either posed or action color player photos. A royal blue stripe, which borders the card top, intersects the Post logo at the upper left corner. The player's name and team name appear in a red stripe at the card bottom. The Bagwell and Knoblauch cards display the words "Rookie Star" in a yellow banner at the card top. The horizontally oriented backs show red-bordered posed or action color player photos with biography, statistics and a facsimile autograph on a light-blue box. The cards are numbered on the back.

	MT	EX-MT	VG
COMPLETE SET (30)	8.00	3.60	1.00
COMMON PLAYER (1-30)	.25	.11	.03
☐ 1 Jeff Bagwell	.75	.35	.09
☐ 2 Ryne Sandberg	.75	.35	.09
☐ 3 Don Mattingly	.45	.20	.06
☐ 4 Wally Joyner	.25	.11	.03
☐ 5 Dwight Gooden	.35	.16	.04
☐ 6 Chuck Knoblauch	.45	.20	.06
☐ 7 Kirby Puckett	.75	.35	.09
☐ 8 Ozzie Smith	.45	.20	.06
☐ 9 Cal Ripken	1.00	.45	.13
☐ 10 Darryl Strawberry	.45	.20	.06
☐ 11 George Brett	.45	.20	.06
☐ 12 Joe Carter	.45	.20	.06
☐ 13 Cecil Fielder	.45	.20	.06
☐ 14 Will Clark	.75	.35	.09
☐ 15 Barry Bonds	.45	.20	.06
☐ 16 Roger Clemens	.75	.35	.09
☐ 17 Paul Molitor	.35	.16	.04
☐ 18 Scott Erickson	.35	.16	.04
☐ 19 Wade Boggs	.45	.20	.06
☐ 20 Ken Griffey Jr.	1.25	.55	.16
☐ 21 Bobby Bonilla	.35	.16	.04
☐ 22 Terry Pendleton	.35	.16	.04
☐ 23 Barry Larkin	.35	.16	.04
☐ 24 Frank Thomas	1.50	.65	.19
☐ 25 Jose Canseco	.75	.35	.09
☐ 26 Tony Gwynn	.45	.20	.06
☐ 27 Nolan Ryan	1.25	.55	.16
☐ 28 Howard Johnson	.25	.11	.03
☐ 29 Dave Justice	.45	.20	.06
☐ 30 Danny Tartabull	.35	.16	.04

1992 Post Canada

This 18-card Post Super Star II stand-up set was sponsored by Post and measures the standard size (2 1/2" by 3 1/2"). The set features nine American League and nine National League players and is bilingual (French and English) on both sides. The fronts show posed color player photos with team logos airbrushed out. The NL cards (1-9) are accented with a red stripe at the top and bottom of the photo and the AL cards (10-18) are accented with blue stripes. The Post and MLB logos appear in the bottom stripe along with the player's name and team. The backs feature perforated color action player photos that can be displayed standing. As on the front, the NL photos on the back are bordered in red and the AL in blue. The player's name appears in the bottom border. The cards are numbered on the back.

	MT	EX-MT	VG
COMPLETE SET (18)	20.00	9.00	2.50
COMMON PLAYER (1-18)	.50	.23	.06
☐ 1 Dennis Martinez	.50	.23	.06
☐ 2 Benito Santiago	.50	.23	.06
☐ 3 Will Clark	2.00	.90	.25
☐ 4 Ryne Sandberg	3.00	1.35	.40
☐ 5 Tim Wallach	.50	.23	.06
☐ 6 Ozzie Smith	1.00	.45	.13
☐ 7 Darryl Strawberry	1.25	.55	.16
☐ 8 Brett Butler	.50	.23	.06
☐ 9 Barry Bonds	1.50	.65	.19
☐ 10 Roger Clemens	3.00	1.35	.40
☐ 11 Sandy Alomar Jr.	.50	.23	.06
☐ 12 Cecil Fielder	1.25	.55	.16
☐ 13 Roberto Alomar	3.00	1.35	.40
☐ 14 Kelly Gruber	.50	.23	.06
☐ 15 Cal Ripken	4.00	1.80	.50

☐ 16 Jose Canseco	2.50	1.15	.30
☐ 17 Kirby Puckett	3.00	1.35	.40
☐ 18 Rickey Henderson	1.50	.65	.19

1986 Quaker Granola

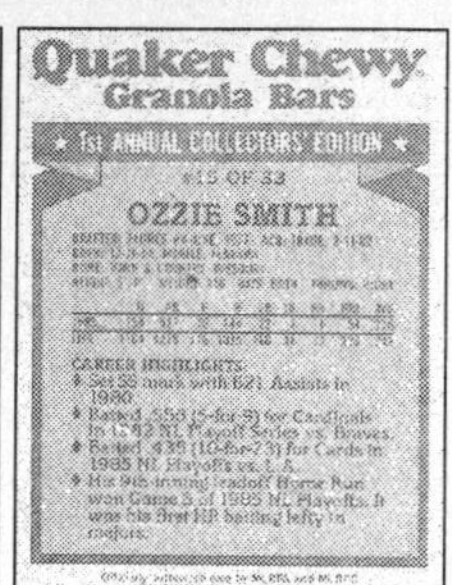

This set of 33 cards was available in packages of Quaker Oats Chewy Granola, three player cards plus a complete set offer card in each package. The set was also available through a mail-in offer where anyone sending in four UPC seals from Chewy Granola (before 12/31/86) would receive a complete set. The cards were produced by Topps for Quaker Oats and are 2 1/2" by 3 1/2". Card backs are printed in red and blue on gray card stock. The cards are numbered on the front and the back. Cards 1-17 feature National League players and cards 18-33 feature American League players. The first three cards in each sequence depict that league's MVP, Cy Young, and Rookie of the Year, respectively. The rest of the cards in each sequence are ordered alphabetically.

	MT	EX-MT	VG
COMPLETE SET (33)	7.00	3.10	.85
COMMON PLAYER (1-33)	.20	.09	.03
☐ 1 Willie McGee	.20	.09	.03
☐ 2 Dwight Gooden	.40	.18	.05
☐ 3 Vince Coleman	.30	.14	.04
☐ 4 Gary Carter	.30	.14	.04
☐ 5 Jack Clark	.20	.09	.03
☐ 6 Steve Garvey	.30	.14	.04
☐ 7 Tony Gwynn	.60	.25	.08
☐ 8 Dale Murphy	.30	.14	.04
☐ 9 Dave Parker	.20	.09	.03
☐ 10 Tim Raines	.20	.09	.03
☐ 11 Pete Rose	.60	.25	.08
☐ 12 Nolan Ryan	1.25	.55	.16
☐ 13 Ryne Sandberg	.75	.35	.09
☐ 14 Mike Schmidt	.75	.35	.09
☐ 15 Ozzie Smith	.40	.18	.05
☐ 16 Darryl Strawberry	.50	.23	.06
☐ 17 Fernando Valenzuela	.20	.09	.03
☐ 18 Don Mattingly	.60	.25	.08
☐ 19 Bret Saberhagen	.30	.14	.04
☐ 20 Ozzie Guillen	.20	.09	.03
☐ 21 Bert Blyleven	.20	.09	.03
☐ 22 Wade Boggs	.60	.25	.08
☐ 23 George Brett	.60	.25	.08
☐ 24 Darrell Evans	.20	.09	.03
☐ 25 Rickey Henderson	.75	.35	.09
☐ 26 Reggie Jackson	.60	.25	.08
☐ 27 Eddie Murray	.40	.18	.05
☐ 28 Phil Niekro	.30	.14	.04
☐ 29 Dan Quisenberry	.20	.09	.03
☐ 30 Jim Rice	.20	.09	.03
☐ 31 Cal Ripken	.75	.35	.09
☐ 32 Tom Seaver	.50	.23	.06
☐ 33 Dave Winfield	.40	.18	.05
☐ NNO Offer Card for the complete set	.10	.05	.01

1984 Ralston Purina

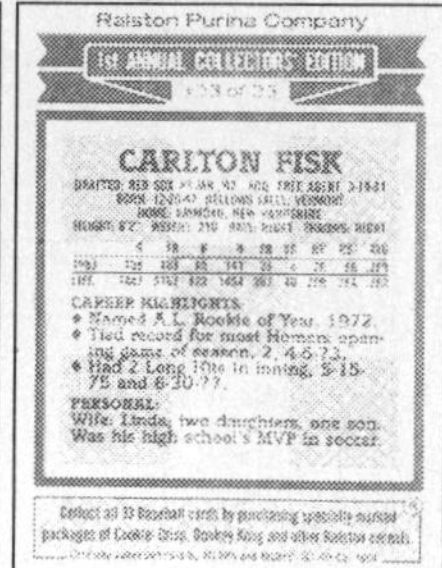

The cards in this 33-card set measure 2 1/2" by 3 1/2". In 1984 the Ralston Purina Company issued what it has entitled "The First Annual Collectors Edition of Baseball Cards." The cards feature portrait photos of the players rather than batting action shots. The Topps logo appears along with the Ralston logo on the front of the card. The backs are completely different from the Topps cards of this year; in fact, they contain neither a Topps logo nor a Topps copyright. Large quantities of these cards were obtained by card dealers for direct distribution into the organized hobby, hence the relatively low price of the set.

	NRMT-MT	EXC	G-VG
COMPLETE SET (33)	4.00	1.80	.50
COMMON PLAYER (1-33)	.10	.05	.01
☐ 1 Eddie Murray	.30	.14	.04
☐ 2 Ozzie Smith	.30	.14	.04
☐ 3 Ted Simmons	.10	.05	.01
☐ 4 Pete Rose	.50	.23	.06
☐ 5 Greg Luzinski	.10	.05	.01
☐ 6 Andre Dawson	.30	.14	.04
☐ 7 Dave Winfield	.35	.16	.04
☐ 8 Tom Seaver	.40	.18	.05
☐ 9 Jim Rice	.10	.05	.01
☐ 10 Fernando Valenzuela	.10	.05	.01
☐ 11 Wade Boggs	.40	.18	.05
☐ 12 Dale Murphy	.25	.11	.03
☐ 13 George Brett	.50	.23	.06
☐ 14 Nolan Ryan	.90	.40	.11
☐ 15 Rickey Henderson	.50	.23	.06
☐ 16 Steve Carlton	.25	.11	.03
☐ 17 Rod Carew	.25	.11	.03
☐ 18 Steve Garvey	.20	.09	.03
☐ 19 Reggie Jackson	.50	.23	.06
☐ 20 Dave Concepcion	.10	.05	.01
☐ 21 Robin Yount	.50	.23	.06
☐ 22 Mike Schmidt	.60	.25	.08
☐ 23 Jim Palmer	.20	.09	.03
☐ 24 Bruce Sutter	.10	.05	.01
☐ 25 Dan Quisenberry	.10	.05	.01
☐ 26 Bill Madlock	.10	.05	.01
☐ 27 Cecil Cooper	.10	.05	.01
☐ 28 Gary Carter	.15	.07	.02
☐ 29 Fred Lynn	.10	.05	.01
☐ 30 Pedro Guerrero	.10	.05	.01
☐ 31 Ron Guidry	.10	.05	.01
☐ 32 Keith Hernandez	.10	.05	.01
☐ 33 Carlton Fisk	.30	.14	.04

1987 Ralston Purina

The Ralston Purina Company issued a set of 15 cards picturing players without their respective team logos. The cards measure approximately 2 1/2" by 3 3/8" and are in full-color on the front. The cards are numbered on the back in the lower right hand corner; the player's uniform number is prominently displayed on the front. The cards were distributed as inserts inside packages of certain flavors of

Ralston Purina's breakfast cereals. Three cards and a contest card were packaged in cellophane and inserted within the cereal box. The set was also available as an uncut sheet through a mail-in offer. Since the uncut sheets are relatively common, the value of the sheet is essentially the same as the value of the sum of the individual cards. In fact there were two uncut sheets issued, one had "Honey Graham Chex" printed at the top and the other had "Cookie Crisp" printed at the top. Also cards were issued with (cards from cereal boxes) and without (cards cut from the uncut sheets) the words "1987 Collectors Edition" printed in blue on the front. The uncut sheet cards Supposedly 100,000 of the uncut sheets were given away free via instant win certificates inserted in with the cereal or collectors could send in two non-winning contest cards plus 1.00 for each uncut sheet.

	MT	EX-MT	VG
COMPLETE SET (15)	12.00	5.50	1.50
COMMON PLAYER (1-15)	.50	.23	.06
☐ 1 Nolan Ryan	3.00	1.35	.40
☐ 2 Steve Garvey	.60	.25	.08
☐ 3 Wade Boggs	1.50	.65	.19
☐ 4 Dave Winfield	1.25	.55	.16
☐ 5 Don Mattingly	1.50	.65	.19
☐ 6 Don Sutton	.60	.25	.08
☐ 7 Dave Parker	.50	.23	.06
☐ 8 Eddie Murray	1.00	.45	.13
☐ 9 Gary Carter	.75	.35	.09
☐ 10 Roger Clemens	2.00	.90	.25
☐ 11 Fernando Valenzuela	.60	.25	.08
☐ 12 Cal Ripken	2.00	.90	.25
☐ 13 Ozzie Smith	1.00	.45	.13
☐ 14 Mike Schmidt	1.50	.65	.19
☐ 15 Ryne Sandberg	1.50	.65	.19

1983 Rangers Affiliated Food

The cards in this 28-card set measure 2 3/8" by 3 1/2". The Affiliated Food Stores chain of Arlington, Texas, produced this set of Texas Rangers late during the 1983 baseball season. Complete sets were given to children 13 and under at the September 3, 1983, Rangers game. The cards are numbered by uniform number and feature the player's name, card number, and the words "1983 Rangers" on the bottom front. The backs contain biographical data, career totals, a small black and white insert picture of the player, and the Affiliated Food Stores' logo. The coaches card is unnumbered.

	NRMT-MT	EXC	G-VG
COMPLETE SET (28)	7.00	3.10	.85
COMMON PLAYER	.25	.11	.03
☐ 1 Bill Stein	.25	.11	.03
☐ 2 Mike Richardt	.25	.11	.03
☐ 3 Wayne Tolleson	.25	.11	.03
☐ 5 Billy Sample	.35	.16	.04
☐ 6 Bobby Jones	.25	.11	.03
☐ 7 Bucky Dent	.45	.20	.06
☐ 8 Bobby Johnson	.25	.11	.03
☐ 9 Pete O'Brien	.60	.25	.08
☐ 10 Jim Sundberg	.45	.20	.06
☐ 11 Doug Rader MG	.35	.16	.04
☐ 12 Dave Hostetler	.35	.16	.04
☐ 14 Larry Biittner	.25	.11	.03
☐ 15 Larry Parrish	.35	.16	.04
☐ 17 Mickey Rivers	.35	.16	.04
☐ 21 Odell Jones	.25	.11	.03
☐ 24 Dave Schmidt	.25	.11	.03
☐ 25 Buddy Bell	.60	.25	.08
☐ 26 George Wright	.25	.11	.03
☐ 28 Frank Tanana	.45	.20	.06
☐ 29 John Butcher	.25	.11	.03
☐ 32 Jon Matlack	.35	.16	.04
☐ 40 Rick Honeycutt	.25	.11	.03
☐ 41 Dave Tobik	.25	.11	.03
☐ 44 Danny Darwin	.35	.16	.04
☐ 46 Jim Anderson	.25	.11	.03
☐ 48 Mike Smithson	.25	.11	.03
☐ 49 Charlie Hough	.35	.16	.04
☐ NNO Rangers Coaches Wayne Terwilliger 42 Merv Rettenmund 22 Dick Such 52 Glenn Ezell 18 Rich Donnelly 37	.25	.11	.03

1984 Rangers Jarvis Press

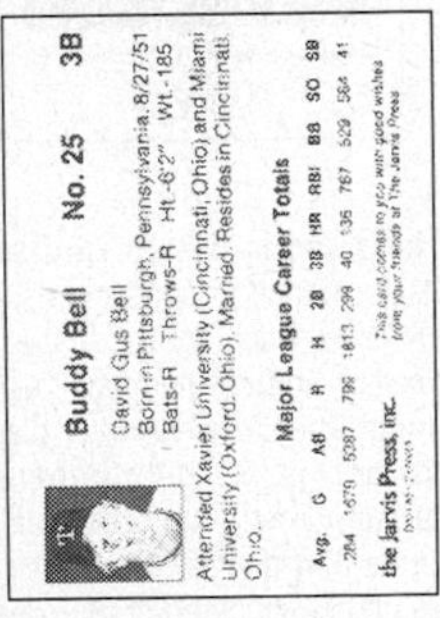

The cards in this 30-card set measure 2 1/2" by 3 1/2". The Jarvis Press of Dallas issued this full-color regional set of Texas Rangers. Cards are numbered on the front by the players uniform number. The cards were issued on an uncut sheet. Twenty-seven player cards, a manager card, a trainer card (unnumbered) and a coaches card (unnumbered) comprise this set. The backs are black and white and contain biographical information, statistics, and an additional photo of the player.

	NRMT-MT	EXC	G-VG
COMPLETE SET (30)	7.00	3.10	.85
COMMON PLAYER	.25	.11	.03
☐ 1 Bill Stein	.25	.11	.03
☐ 2 Alan Bannister	.25	.11	.03

☐ 3 Wayne Tolleson	.25	.11	.03
☐ 5 Billy Sample	.35	.16	.04
☐ 6 Bobby Jones	.25	.11	.03
☐ 7 Ned Yost	.25	.11	.03
☐ 9 Pete O'Brien	.45	.20	.06
☐ 11 Doug Rader MG	.35	.16	.04
☐ 13 Tommy Dunbar	.25	.11	.03
☐ 14 Jim Anderson	.25	.11	.03
☐ 15 Larry Parrish	.35	.16	.04
☐ 16 Mike Mason	.25	.11	.03
☐ 17 Mickey Rivers	.35	.16	.04
☐ 19 Curtis Wilkerson	.25	.11	.03
☐ 20 Jeff Kunkel	.35	.16	.04
☐ 21 Odell Jones	.25	.11	.03
☐ 24 Dave Schmidt	.25	.11	.03
☐ 25 Buddy Bell	.60	.25	.08
☐ 26 George Wright	.25	.11	.03
☐ 28 Frank Tanana	.45	.20	.06
☐ 30 Marv Foley	.25	.11	.03
☐ 31 Dave Stewart	.90	.40	.11
☐ 32 Gary Ward	.25	.11	.03
☐ 36 Dickie Noles	.25	.11	.03
☐ 43 Donnie Scott	.25	.11	.03
☐ 44 Danny Darwin	.35	.16	.04
☐ 49 Charlie Hough	.35	.16	.04
☐ 53 Joey McLaughlin	.25	.11	.03
☐ NNO Bill Ziegler TR	.25	.11	.03
☐ NNO Rangers Coaches Merv Rettenmund 22 Rich Donnelly 37 Glenn Ezell 18 Dick Such 52 Wayne Terwilliger 42	.35	.16	.04

1985 Rangers Performance

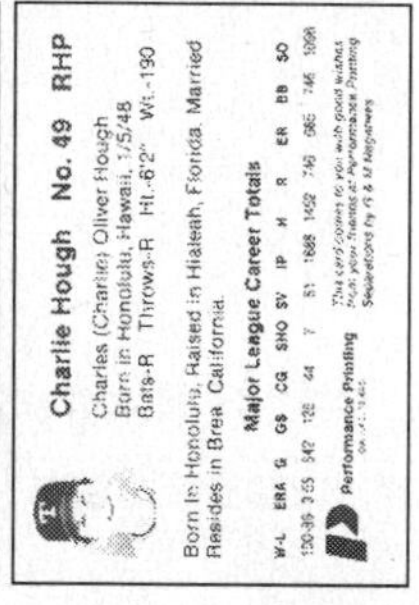

The cards in this 28-card set measure 2 3/8" by 3 1/2". Performance Printing sponsored this full-color regional set of Texas Rangers. Cards are numbered on the back by the players uniform number. The cards were also issued on an uncut sheet. Twenty-five player cards, a manager card, a trainer card (unnumbered) and a coaches card (unnumbered) comprise this set. The backs are black and white and contain biographical information, statistics, and an additional photo of the player.

	NRMT-MT	EXC	G-VG
COMPLETE SET (28)	7.00	3.10	.85
COMMON PLAYER	.25	.11	.03
☐ 0 Oddibe McDowell	.35	.16	.04
☐ 1 Bill Stein	.25	.11	.03
☐ 2 Bobby Valentine MG	.35	.16	.04
☐ 3 Wayne Tolleson	.25	.11	.03
☐ 4 Don Slaught	.35	.16	.04
☐ 5 Alan Bannister	.25	.11	.03
☐ 6 Bobby Jones	.25	.11	.03
☐ 7 Glenn Brummer	.25	.11	.03
☐ 8 Luis Pujols	.25	.11	.03
☐ 9 Pete O'Brien	.45	.20	.06
☐ 11 Toby Harrah	.45	.20	.06
☐ 13 Tommy Dunbar	.25	.11	.03
☐ 15 Larry Parrish	.35	.16	.04
☐ 16 Mike Mason	.25	.11	.03
☐ 19 Curtis Wilkerson	.25	.11	.03
☐ 24 Dave Schmidt	.25	.11	.03
☐ 25 Buddy Bell	.60	.25	.08
☐ 27 Greg A. Harris	.35	.16	.04
☐ 30 Dave Rozema	.25	.11	.03
☐ 32 Gary Ward	.25	.11	.03
☐ 36 Dickie Noles	.25	.11	.03
☐ 41 Chris Welsh	.25	.11	.03
☐ 44 Cliff Johnson	.35	.16	.04
☐ 46 Burt Hooton	.25	.11	.03
☐ 48 Dave Stewart	.75	.35	.09
☐ 49 Charlie Hough	.35	.16	.04
☐ NNO Trainers:Bill Ziegler and Danny Wheat	.25	.11	.03
☐ NNO Rangers Coaches Art Howe 10 Rich Donnelly 37 Glenn Ezell 18 Tom House 35 Wayne Terwilliger 42	.35	.16	.04

1986 Rangers Performance

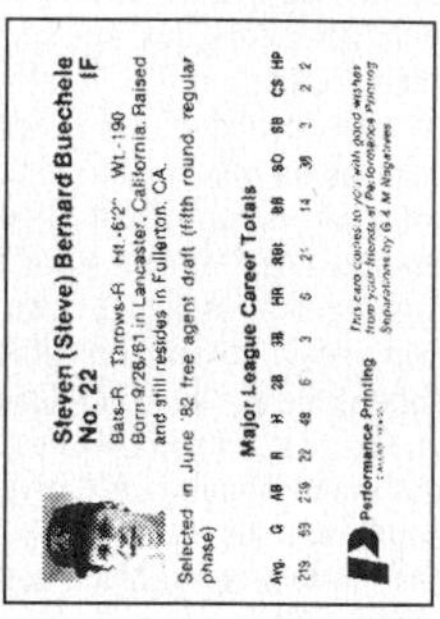

Performance Printing of Dallas produced a 28-card set of Texas Rangers which were given out at the stadium on August 23rd. Cards measure approximately 2 3/8" by 3 1/2" and are in full color. The cards are unnumbered except for uniform number which is given on the card back. Card backs feature black printing on white card stock with a small picture of the player's head in the upper left corner. The set seems to be more desirable than the previous Ranger sets due to the Rangers' 1986 success which was directly related to their outstanding rookie crop.

	MT	EX-MT	VG
COMPLETE SET (28)	10.00	4.50	1.25
COMMON PLAYER	.20	.09	.03
☐ 0 Oddibe McDowell	.30	.14	.04
☐ 1 Scott Fletcher	.30	.14	.04
☐ 2 Bobby Valentine MG	.30	.14	.04
☐ 3 Ruben Sierra	4.00	1.80	.50
☐ 4 Don Slaught	.30	.14	.04
☐ 9 Pete O'Brien	.30	.14	.04
☐ 11 Toby Harrah	.30	.14	.04
☐ 12 Geno Petralli	.20	.09	.03
☐ 15 Larry Parrish	.30	.14	.04
☐ 16 Mike Mason	.20	.09	.03
☐ 17 Darrell Porter	.30	.14	.04
☐ 18 Edwin Correa	.20	.09	.03
☐ 19 Curtis Wilkerson	.20	.09	.03
☐ 22 Steve Buechele	.50	.23	.06
☐ 23 Jose Guzman	.60	.25	.08
☐ 24 Ricky Wright	.20	.09	.03
☐ 27 Greg A. Harris	.20	.09	.03
☐ 28 Mitch Williams	.50	.23	.06
☐ 29 Pete Incaviglia	.60	.25	.08
☐ 32 Gary Ward	.20	.09	.03
☐ 34 Dale Mohorcic	.20	.09	.03
☐ 40 Jeff Russell	.40	.18	.05
☐ 44 Tom Paciorek	.20	.09	.03
☐ 46 Mike Loynd	.20	.09	.03
☐ 48 Bobby Witt	.60	.25	.08
☐ 49 Charlie Hough	.30	.14	.04
☐ NNO Coaching Staff Art Howe 10 Joe Ferguson 13 Tim Foli 14 Tom Robson 31	.20	.09	.03

	NRMT	VG-E	GOOD
Tom House 35 ☐ NNO Trainers:Bill Zeigler and Danny Wheat	.20	.09	.03

1954 Red Heart

The cards in this 33-card set measure approximately 2 5/8" by 3 3/4". The 1954 Red Heart baseball series was marketed by Red Heart dog food, which, incidentally, was a subsidiary of Morrell Meats. The set consists of three series of eleven unnumbered cards each of which could be ordered from the company via an offer (two can labels plus ten cents for each series) on the can label. Each series has a specific color background (red, green or blue) behind the color player photo. Cards with red backgrounds are considered scarcer and are marked with an asterisk in the checklist (which has been alphabetized and numbered for reference). The catalog designation is F156.

	NRMT	VG-E	GOOD
COMPLETE SET (33)	2250.00	1000.00	275.00
COMMON PLAYER (1-33)	30.00	13.50	3.80
COMMON * (RED) PLAYER	35.00	16.00	4.40
☐ 1 Richie Ashburn *	65.00	29.00	8.25
☐ 2 Frank Baumholtz *	35.00	16.00	4.40
☐ 3 Gus Bell	30.00	13.50	3.80
☐ 4 Billy Cox	30.00	13.50	3.80
☐ 5 Alvin Dark	35.00	16.00	4.40
☐ 6 Carl Erskine *	45.00	20.00	5.75
☐ 7 Ferris Fain	30.00	13.50	3.80
☐ 8 Dee Fondy	30.00	13.50	3.80
☐ 9 Nelson Fox	50.00	23.00	6.25
☐ 10 Jim Gilliam	35.00	16.00	4.40
☐ 11 Jim Hegan *	35.00	16.00	4.40
☐ 12 George Kell	60.00	27.00	7.50
☐ 13 Ralph Kiner *	85.00	38.00	10.50
☐ 14 Ted Kluszewski *	65.00	29.00	8.25
☐ 15 Harvey Kuenn	35.00	16.00	4.40
☐ 16 Bob Lemon *	75.00	34.00	9.50
☐ 17 Sherman Lollar	30.00	13.50	3.80
☐ 18 Mickey Mantle	500.00	230.00	65.00
☐ 19 Billy Martin	65.00	29.00	8.25
☐ 20 Gil McDougald *	45.00	20.00	5.75
☐ 21 Roy McMillan	30.00	13.50	3.80
☐ 22 Minnie Minoso	35.00	16.00	4.40
☐ 23 Stan Musial *	350.00	160.00	45.00
☐ 24 Billy Pierce	35.00	16.00	4.40
☐ 25 Al Rosen *	45.00	20.00	5.75
☐ 26 Hank Sauer	30.00	13.50	3.80
☐ 27 Red Schoendienst *	75.00	34.00	9.50
☐ 28 Enos Slaughter	70.00	32.00	8.75
☐ 29 Duke Snider	125.00	57.50	15.50
☐ 30 Warren Spahn	65.00	29.00	8.25
☐ 31 Sammy White	30.00	13.50	3.80
☐ 32 Eddie Yost	30.00	13.50	3.80
☐ 33 Gus Zernial	30.00	13.50	3.80

1952 Red Man

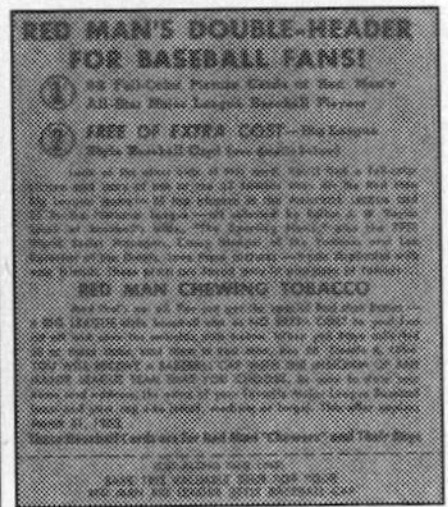

The cards in this 52-card set measure approximately 3 1/2" by 4" (or 3 1/2" by 3 5/8" without the tab). This Red Man issue was the first nationally available tobacco issue since the T cards of the teens early in this century. This 52-card set contains 26 top players from each league. Cards that have the tab (coupon) attached are generally worth two and a half times the price of cards with the tab removed. Card numbers are located on the tabs. The prices listed below refer to cards without tabs. The numbering of the set is alphabetical by player within league with the exception of the managers who are listed first.

	NRMT	VG-E	GOOD
COMPLETE SET (52)	900.00	400.00	115.00
COMMON PLAYER	8.00	3.60	1.00
☐ AL1 Casey Stengel MG	25.00	11.50	3.10
☐ AL2 Roberto Avila	8.00	3.60	1.00
☐ AL3 Yogi Berra	50.00	23.00	6.25
☐ AL4 Gil Coan	8.00	3.60	1.00
☐ AL5 Dom DiMaggio	12.00	5.50	1.50
☐ AL6 Larry Doby	9.00	4.00	1.15
☐ AL7 Ferris Fain	8.00	3.60	1.00
☐ AL8 Bob Feller	33.00	15.00	4.10
☐ AL9 Nelson Fox	14.00	6.25	1.75
☐ AL10 Johnny Groth	8.00	3.60	1.00
☐ AL11 Jim Hegan	8.00	3.60	1.00
☐ AL12 Eddie Joost	8.00	3.60	1.00
☐ AL13 George Kell	18.00	8.00	2.30
☐ AL14 Gil McDougald	12.00	5.50	1.50
☐ AL15 Minnie Minoso	12.00	5.50	1.50
☐ AL16 Billy Pierce	9.00	4.00	1.15
☐ AL17 Bob Porterfield	8.00	3.60	1.00
☐ AL18 Eddie Robinson	8.00	3.60	1.00
☐ AL19 Saul Rogovin	8.00	3.60	1.00
☐ AL20 Bobby Shantz	8.00	3.60	1.00
☐ AL21 Vern Stephens	8.00	3.60	1.00
☐ AL22 Vic Wertz	8.00	3.60	1.00
☐ AL23 Ted Williams	125.00	57.50	15.50
☐ AL24 Early Wynn	18.00	8.00	2.30
☐ AL25 Eddie Yost	8.00	3.60	1.00
☐ AL26 Gus Zernial	8.00	3.60	1.00
☐ NL1 Leo Durocher MG	18.00	8.00	2.30
☐ NL2 Richie Ashburn	16.00	7.25	2.00
☐ NL3 Ewell Blackwell	8.00	3.60	1.00
☐ NL4 Cliff Chambers	8.00	3.60	1.00
☐ NL5 Murry Dickson	8.00	3.60	1.00
☐ NL6 Sid Gordon	8.00	3.60	1.00
☐ NL7 Granny Hamner	8.00	3.60	1.00
☐ NL8 Jim Hearn	8.00	3.60	1.00
☐ NL9 Monte Irvin	16.00	7.25	2.00
☐ NL10 Larry Jansen	8.00	3.60	1.00
☐ NL11 Willie Jones	8.00	3.60	1.00
☐ NL12 Ralph Kiner	24.00	11.00	3.00
☐ NL13 Whitey Lockman	8.00	3.60	1.00
☐ NL14 Sal Maglie	12.00	5.50	1.50
☐ NL15 Willie Mays	100.00	45.00	12.50
☐ NL16 Stan Musial	100.00	45.00	12.50
☐ NL17 Pee Wee Reese	33.00	15.00	4.10
☐ NL18 Robin Roberts	22.00	10.00	2.80
☐ NL19 Al Schoendienst	18.00	8.00	2.30
☐ NL20 Enos Slaughter	22.00	10.00	2.80
☐ NL21 Duke Snider	60.00	27.00	7.50
☐ NL22 Warren Spahn	27.00	12.00	3.40
☐ NL23 Ed Stanky	9.00	4.00	1.15
☐ NL24 Bobby Thomson	10.00	4.50	1.25
☐ NL25 Earl Torgeson	8.00	3.60	1.00
☐ NL26 Wes Westrum	8.00	3.60	1.00

1953 Red Man

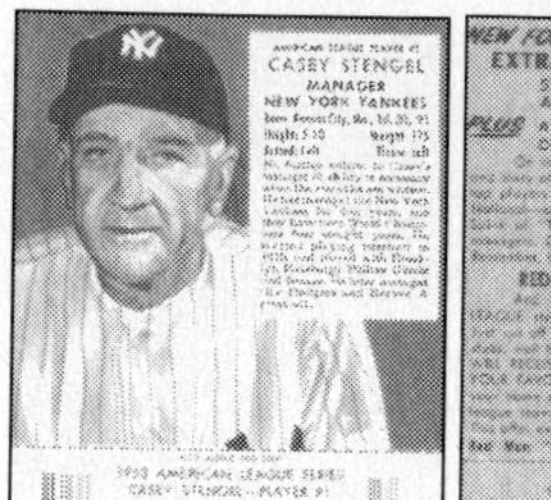

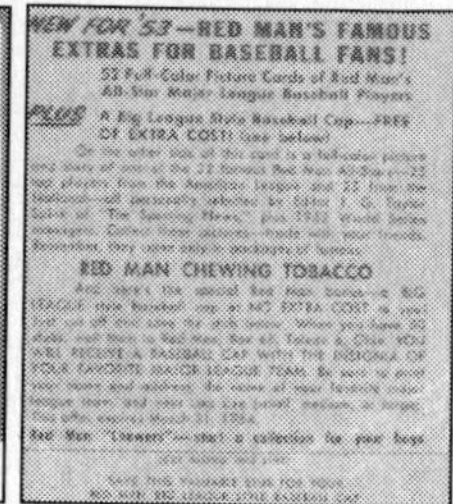

The cards in this 52-card set measure approximately 3 1/2" by 4" (or 3 1/2" by 3 5/8" without the tab). The 1953 Red Man set contains 26 National League stars and 26 American League stars. Card numbers are located both on the write-up of the player and on the tab. Cards that have the tab (coupon) attached are generally worth two and a half times the price of cards with the tab removed. The prices listed below refer to cards without tabs.

	NRMT	VG-E	GOOD
COMPLETE SET (52)	800.00	350.00	100.00
COMMON PLAYER	8.00	3.60	1.00
☐ AL1 Casey Stengel MG	25.00	11.50	3.10
☐ AL2 Hank Bauer	11.00	4.90	1.40
☐ AL3 Yogi Berra	50.00	23.00	6.25
☐ AL4 Walt Dropo	8.00	3.60	1.00
☐ AL5 Nelson Fox	14.00	6.25	1.75
☐ AL6 Jackie Jensen	11.00	4.90	1.40
☐ AL7 Eddie Joost	8.00	3.60	1.00
☐ AL8 George Kell	18.00	8.00	2.30
☐ AL9 Dale Mitchell	8.00	3.60	1.00
☐ AL10 Phil Rizzuto	20.00	9.00	2.50
☐ AL11 Eddie Robinson	8.00	3.60	1.00
☐ AL12 Gene Woodling	9.00	4.00	1.15
☐ AL13 Gus Zernial	8.00	3.60	1.00
☐ AL14 Early Wynn	18.00	8.00	2.30
☐ AL15 Joe Dobson	8.00	3.60	1.00
☐ AL16 Billy Pierce	9.00	4.00	1.15
☐ AL17 Bob Lemon	18.00	8.00	2.30
☐ AL18 Johnny Mize	22.00	10.00	2.80
☐ AL19 Bob Porterfield	8.00	3.60	1.00
☐ AL20 Bobby Shantz	8.00	3.60	1.00
☐ AL21 Mickey Vernon	9.00	4.00	1.15
☐ AL22 Dom DiMaggio	12.00	5.50	1.50
☐ AL23 Gil McDougald	11.00	4.90	1.40
☐ AL24 Al Rosen	11.00	4.90	1.40
☐ AL25 Mel Parnell	8.00	3.60	1.00
☐ AL26 Bobby Avila	8.00	3.60	1.00
☐ NL1 Charlie Dressen MG	8.00	3.60	1.00
☐ NL2 Bobby Adams	8.00	3.60	1.00
☐ NL3 Richie Ashburn	16.00	7.25	2.00
☐ NL4 Joe Black	10.00	4.50	1.25
☐ NL5 Roy Campanella	60.00	27.00	7.50
☐ NL6 Ted Kluszewski	16.00	7.25	2.00
☐ NL7 Whitey Lockman	8.00	3.60	1.00
☐ NL8 Sal Maglie	12.00	5.50	1.50
☐ NL9 Andy Pafko	8.00	3.60	1.00
☐ NL10 Pee Wee Reese	33.00	15.00	4.10
☐ NL11 Robin Roberts	22.00	10.00	2.80
☐ NL12 Al Schoendienst	18.00	8.00	2.30
☐ NL13 Enos Slaughter	22.00	10.00	2.80
☐ NL14 Duke Snider	60.00	27.00	7.50
☐ NL15 Ralph Kiner	24.00	11.00	3.00
☐ NL16 Hank Sauer	8.00	3.60	1.00
☐ NL17 Del Ennis	8.00	3.60	1.00
☐ NL18 Granny Hamner	8.00	3.60	1.00
☐ NL19 Warren Spahn	27.00	12.00	3.40
☐ NL20 Wes Westrum	8.00	3.60	1.00
☐ NL21 Hoyt Wilhelm	20.00	9.00	2.50
☐ NL22 Murry Dickson	8.00	3.60	1.00
☐ NL23 Warren Hacker	8.00	3.60	1.00
☐ NL24 Gerry Staley	8.00	3.60	1.00
☐ NL25 Bobby Thomson	10.00	4.50	1.25
☐ NL26 Stan Musial	100.00	45.00	12.50

1954 Red Man

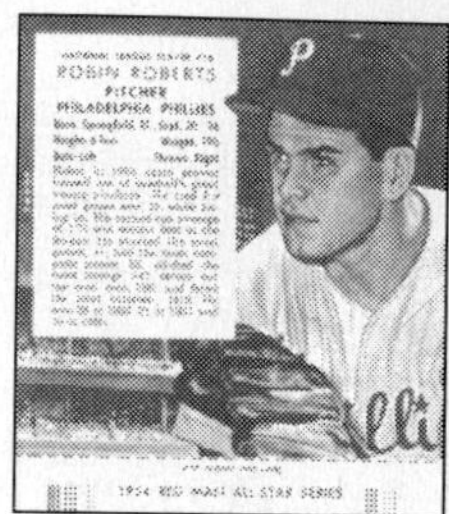

The cards in this 50-card set measure approximately 3 1/2" by 4" (or 3 1/2" by 3 5/8" without the tab). The 1954 Red Man set witnessed a reduction to 25 players from each league. George Kell, Sam Mele, and Dave Philley are known to exist with two different teams. Card number 19 of the National League exists as Enos Slaughter and as Gus Bell. Card numbers are on the write-ups of the players. Cards that have the tab (coupon) attached are generally worth two and a half times the price of cards with the tab removed. The prices listed below refer to cards without tabs. The complete set price below refers to all 54 cards including the four variations.

	NRMT	VG-E	GOOD
COMPLETE SET (54)	1000.00	450.00	125.00
COMMON PLAYERS	8.00	3.60	1.00
☐ AL1 Bobby Avila	8.00	3.60	1.00
☐ AL2 Jim Busby	8.00	3.60	1.00
☐ AL3 Nelson Fox	14.00	6.25	1.75
☐ AL4A George Kell (Boston)	25.00	11.50	3.10
☐ AL4B George Kell (Chicago)	60.00	27.00	7.50
☐ AL5 Sherman Lollar	8.00	3.60	1.00
☐ AL6A Sam Mele (Baltimore)	12.00	5.50	1.50
☐ AL6B Sam Mele (Chicago)	35.00	16.00	4.40
☐ AL7 Minnie Minoso	11.00	4.90	1.40
☐ AL8 Mel Parnell	8.00	3.60	1.00
☐ AL9A Dave Philley (Cleveland)	12.00	5.50	1.50
☐ AL9B Dave Philley (Philadelphia)	35.00	16.00	4.40
☐ AL10 Billy Pierce	9.00	4.00	1.15
☐ AL11 Jim Piersall	11.00	4.90	1.40
☐ AL12 Al Rosen	11.00	4.90	1.40
☐ AL13 Mickey Vernon	9.00	4.00	1.15
☐ AL14 Sammy White	8.00	3.60	1.00
☐ AL15 Gene Woodling	9.00	4.00	1.15
☐ AL16 Whitey Ford	33.00	15.00	4.10
☐ AL17 Phil Rizzuto	20.00	9.00	2.50
☐ AL18 Bob Porterfield	8.00	3.60	1.00
☐ AL19 Chico Carrasquel	8.00	3.60	1.00
☐ AL20 Yogi Berra	50.00	23.00	6.25
☐ AL21 Bob Lemon	18.00	8.00	2.30
☐ AL22 Ferris Fain	8.00	3.60	1.00
☐ AL23 Hank Bauer	11.00	4.90	1.40
☐ AL24 Jim Delsing	8.00	3.60	1.00
☐ AL25 Gil McDougald	11.00	4.90	1.40
☐ NL1 Richie Ashburn	16.00	7.25	2.00
☐ NL2 Billy Cox	8.00	3.60	1.00
☐ NL3 Del Crandall	8.00	3.60	1.00
☐ NL4 Carl Erskine	10.00	4.50	1.25
☐ NL5 Monte Irvin	16.00	7.25	2.00
☐ NL6 Ted Kluszewski	16.00	7.25	2.00
☐ NL7 Don Mueller	8.00	3.60	1.00
☐ NL8 Andy Pafko	8.00	3.60	1.00
☐ NL9 Del Rice	8.00	3.60	1.00
☐ NL10 Al Schoendienst	18.00	8.00	2.30
☐ NL11 Warren Spahn	27.00	12.00	3.40
☐ NL12 Curt Simmons	8.00	3.60	1.00
☐ NL13 Roy Campanella	60.00	27.00	7.50
☐ NL14 Jim Gilliam	11.00	4.90	1.40
☐ NL15 Pee Wee Reese	33.00	15.00	4.10

☐ NL16 Duke Snider	60.00	27.00	7.50
☐ NL17 Rip Repulski	8.00	3.60	1.00
☐ NL18 Robin Roberts	22.00	10.00	2.80
☐ NL19A Enos Slaughter	65.00	29.00	8.25
☐ NL19B Gus Bell	30.00	13.50	3.80
☐ NL20 Johnny Logan	8.00	3.60	1.00
☐ NL21 John Antonelli	8.00	3.60	1.00
☐ NL22 Gil Hodges	24.00	11.00	3.00
☐ NL23 Eddie Mathews	27.00	12.00	3.40
☐ NL24 Lew Burdette	10.00	4.50	1.25
☐ NL25 Willie Mays	100.00	45.00	12.50

1955 Red Man

The cards in this 50-card set measure approximately 3 1/2" by 4" (or 3 1/2" by 3 5/8" without the tab). The 1955 Red Man set contains 25 players from each league. Card numbers are on the write-ups of the players. Cards that have the tab (coupon) attached are generally worth two and a half times the price of cards with the tab removed. The prices listed below refer to cards without tabs.

	NRMT	VG-E	GOOD
COMPLETE SET (50)	700.00	325.00	90.00
COMMON PLAYER	8.00	3.60	1.00
☐ AL1 Ray Boone	8.00	3.60	1.00
☐ AL2 Jim Busby	8.00	3.60	1.00
☐ AL3 Whitey Ford	33.00	15.00	4.10
☐ AL4 Nelson Fox	14.00	6.25	1.75
☐ AL5 Bob Grim	8.00	3.60	1.00
☐ AL6 Jack Harshman	8.00	3.60	1.00
☐ AL7 Jim Hegan	8.00	3.60	1.00
☐ AL8 Bob Lemon	18.00	8.00	2.30
☐ AL9 Irv Noren	8.00	3.60	1.00
☐ AL10 Bob Porterfield	8.00	3.60	1.00
☐ AL11 Al Rosen	11.00	4.90	1.40
☐ AL12 Mickey Vernon	8.00	3.60	1.00
☐ AL13 Vic Wertz	8.00	3.60	1.00
☐ AL14 Early Wynn	18.00	8.00	2.30
☐ AL15 Bobby Avila	8.00	3.60	1.00
☐ AL16 Yogi Berra	50.00	23.00	6.25
☐ AL17 Joe Coleman	8.00	3.60	1.00
☐ AL18 Larry Doby	9.00	4.00	1.15
☐ AL19 Jackie Jensen	8.00	3.60	1.00
☐ AL20 Pete Runnels	8.00	3.60	1.00
☐ AL21 Jim Piersall	11.00	4.90	1.40
☐ AL22 Hank Bauer	11.00	4.90	1.40
☐ AL23 Chico Carrasquel	8.00	3.60	1.00
☐ AL24 Minnie Minoso	11.00	4.90	1.40
☐ AL25 Sandy Consuegra	8.00	3.60	1.00
☐ NL1 Richie Ashburn	16.00	7.25	2.00
☐ NL2 Del Crandall	8.00	3.60	1.00
☐ NL3 Gil Hodges	24.00	11.00	3.00
☐ NL4 Brooks Lawrence	8.00	3.60	1.00
☐ NL5 Johnny Logan	8.00	3.60	1.00
☐ NL6 Sal Maglie	10.00	4.50	1.25
☐ NL7 Willie Mays	100.00	45.00	12.50
☐ NL8 Don Mueller	8.00	3.60	1.00
☐ NL9 Bill Sarni	8.00	3.60	1.00
☐ NL10 Warren Spahn	27.00	12.00	3.40
☐ NL11 Hank Thompson	8.00	3.60	1.00
☐ NL12 Hoyt Wilhelm	18.00	8.00	2.30
☐ NL13 John Antonelli	8.00	3.60	1.00
☐ NL14 Carl Erskine	9.00	4.00	1.15
☐ NL15 Granny Hamner	8.00	3.60	1.00
☐ NL16 Ted Kluszewski	16.00	7.25	2.00
☐ NL17 Pee Wee Reese	33.00	15.00	4.10
☐ NL18 Al Schoendienst	18.00	8.00	2.30
☐ NL19 Duke Snider	60.00	27.00	7.50
☐ NL20 Frank Thomas	8.00	3.60	1.00
☐ NL21 Ray Jablonski	8.00	3.60	1.00
☐ NL22 Dusty Rhodes	8.00	3.60	1.00
☐ NL23 Gus Bell	8.00	3.60	1.00
☐ NL24 Curt Simmons	8.00	3.60	1.00
☐ NL25 Marv Grissom	8.00	3.60	1.00

1982 Red Sox Coke

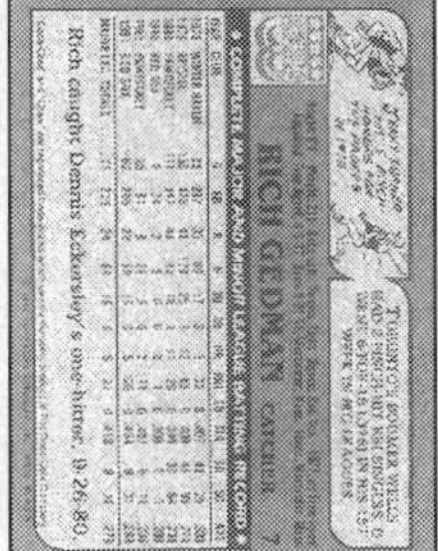

The cards in this 23-card set measure 2 1/2" by 3 1/2". This set of Boston Red Sox ballplayers was issued locally in the Boston area as a joint promotion by Brigham's Ice Cream Stores and Coca-Cola. The pictures are identical to those in the Topps regular 1982 issue, except that the colors are brighter and the Brigham and Coke logos appear inside the frame line. The reverses are done in red, black and gray, in contrast to the Topps set, and the number appears to the right of the position listing. The cards were initally distributed in three-card cello packs with an ice cream or Coca-Cola purchase but later became available as sets within the hobby. The unnumbered title or advertising card carries a premium offer on the reverse. The set numbering is in alphabetical order by player's name.

	NRMT-MT	EXC	G-VG
COMPLETE SET (23)	7.50	3.40	.95
COMMON PLAYER (1-22)	.10	.05	.01
☐ 1 Gary Allenson	.10	.05	.01
☐ 2 Tom Burgmeier	.10	.05	.01
☐ 3 Mark Clear	.10	.05	.01
☐ 4 Steve Crawford	.10	.05	.01
☐ 5 Dennis Eckersley	2.00	.90	.25
☐ 6 Dwight Evans	.75	.35	.09
☐ 7 Rich Gedman	.20	.09	.03
☐ 8 Garry Hancock	.10	.05	.01
☐ 9 Glen Hoffman	.10	.05	.01
☐ 10 Carney Lansford	.50	.23	.06
☐ 11 Rick Miller	.10	.05	.01
☐ 12 Reid Nichols	.10	.05	.01
☐ 13 Bob Ojeda	.50	.23	.06
☐ 14 Tony Perez	1.00	.45	.13
☐ 15 Chuck Rainey	.10	.05	.01
☐ 16 Jerry Remy	.10	.05	.01
☐ 17 Jim Rice	1.00	.45	.13
☐ 18 Bob Stanley	.15	.07	.02
☐ 19 Dave Stapleton	.10	.05	.01
☐ 20 Mike Torrez	.15	.07	.02
☐ 21 John Tudor	.30	.14	.04
☐ 22 Carl Yastrzemski	3.50	1.55	.45
☐ NNO Title Card	.05	.02	.01

1990 Red Sox Pepsi

The 1990 Pepsi Boston Red Sox set is a 20-card standard-size (2 1/2" by 3 1/2") set, which is checklisted alphabetically below. This set was apparently prepared very early in the 1990 season as Bill Buckner and Lee Smith were

still members of the Red Sox in this set. The top of the front of the card have Boston Red Sox printed while the bottom of the card has the players name surrounded by the Pepsi and the Diet Pepsi logo. The backs of the cards have the Score feel to them except the Pepsi and Diet Pepsi logos are again featured prominently on the back of the cards. The cards were supposedly available as a store promotion with one card per specially marked 12-pack of Pepsi. The cards were difficult to remove from the boxes, thus making perfect mint cards worth an extra premium.

	MT	EX-MT	VG
COMPLETE SET (20)	35.00	16.00	4.40
COMMON PLAYER (1-20)	1.25	.55	.16
☐ 1 Marty Barrett	1.25	.55	.16
☐ 2 Mike Boddicker	1.25	.55	.16
☐ 3 Wade Boggs	7.50	3.40	.95
☐ 4 Bill Buckner	1.50	.65	.19
☐ 5 Ellis Burks	2.50	1.15	.30
☐ 6 Roger Clemens	15.00	6.75	1.90
☐ 7 John Dopson	1.25	.55	.16
☐ 8 Dwight Evans	2.50	1.15	.30
☐ 9 Wes Gardner	1.25	.55	.16
☐ 10 Rich Gedman	1.25	.55	.16
☐ 11 Mike Greenwell	3.50	1.55	.45
☐ 12 Dennis Lamp	1.25	.55	.16
☐ 13 Rob Murphy	1.25	.55	.16
☐ 14 Tony Pena	1.50	.65	.19
☐ 15 Carlos Quintana	1.50	.65	.19
☐ 16 Jeff Reardon	2.50	1.15	.30
☐ 17 Jody Reed	1.75	.80	.22
☐ 18 Luis Rivera	1.25	.55	.16
☐ 19 Kevin Romine	1.25	.55	.16
☐ 20 Lee Smith	2.00	.90	.25

1991 Red Sox Pepsi

This 20-card set was sponsored by Pepsi and officially licensed by Mike Schechter Associates on behalf of the MLBPA. The 1991 edition consists of 100,000 sets that were available from July 1 through August 10, 1991 in the New England area, with one card per specially marked pack of Pepsi and Diet Pepsi. The promotion also includes a sweepstakes offering a grand prize trip for four to Red Sox Spring training camp. The standard-size (2 1/2" by 3 1/2") cards have color action player photos with a red, white, and blue front design. Two Pepsi logos adorn the card face below the picture. The backs are bordered in red and have a color head shot, biography, professional batting record, and career summary. The cards are unnumbered and checklisted below in alphabetical order.

	MT	EX-MT	VG
COMPLETE SET (20)	20.00	9.00	2.50
COMMON PLAYER (1-20)	.75	.35	.09
☐ 1 Tom Bolton	.75	.35	.09
☐ 2 Tom Brunansky	.90	.40	.11
☐ 3 Ellis Burks	1.25	.55	.16
☐ 4 Jack Clark	.90	.40	.11
☐ 5 Roger Clemens	7.50	3.40	.95
☐ 6 Danny Darwin	.75	.35	.09
☐ 7 Jeff Gray	.75	.35	.09
☐ 8 Mike Greenwell	1.50	.65	.19
☐ 9 Greg A. Harris	.75	.35	.09
☐ 10 Dana Kiecker	.75	.35	.09
☐ 11 Dennis Lamp	.75	.35	.09
☐ 12 John Marzano	.75	.35	.09
☐ 13 Tim Naehring	.90	.40	.11
☐ 14 Tony Pena	.90	.40	.11
☐ 15 Phil Plantier	3.00	1.35	.40
☐ 16 Carlos Quintana	1.00	.45	.13
☐ 17 Jeff Reardon	1.25	.55	.16
☐ 18 Jody Reed	1.00	.45	.13
☐ 19 Luis Rivera	.75	.35	.09
☐ 20 Matt Young	.75	.35	.09

1992 Red Sox Dunkin' Donuts

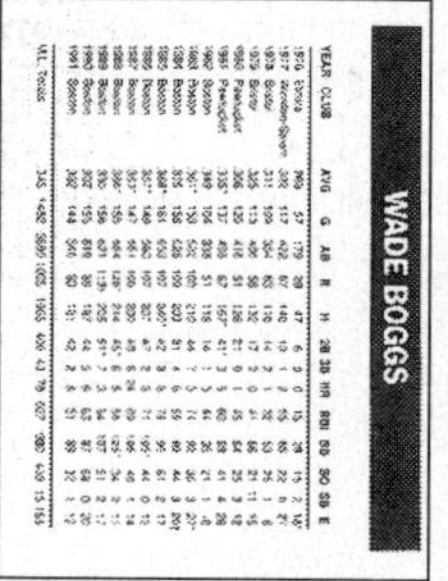

The 1992 Boston Red Sox Player Photo Collection was sponsored by Dunkin' Donuts and WVIT Channel 30 (Connecticut's NBC Station). It consists of three large sheets (each measuring approximately 9 3/8" by 10 3/4") joined together to form one continuous sheet. The first panel displays a color picture of Fenway Park and a WVIT Red Sox Schedule. The second and third panels, which are perforated, feature 15 player cards each. After perforation, the cards measure approximately 2 1/8" by 3 1/8". On a white card face, the fronts have color game shots framed by black border stripes. The player's name, his position, and sponsor logos appear in a bottom white border. On the backs, the player's name appears in a red stripe, and the statistical information is printed in blue on a white background. The cards are unnumbered and checklisted below in alphabetical order.

	MT	EX-MT	VG
COMPLETE SET (30)	10.00	4.50	1.25
COMMON PLAYER (1-30)	.35	.16	.04
☐ 1 Gary Allenson CO	.35	.16	.04
☐ 2 Wade Boggs	.90	.40	.11
☐ 3 Tom Bolton	.35	.16	.04
☐ 4 Tom Brunansky	.45	.20	.06

☐ 5 Al Bumbry CO	.35	.16	.04
☐ 6 Ellis Burks	.60	.25	.08
☐ 7 Rick Burleson CO	.35	.16	.04
☐ 8 Jack Clark	.45	.20	.06
☐ 9 Roger Clemens	1.50	.65	.19
☐ 10 Danny Darwin	.35	.16	.04
☐ 11 Tony Fossas	.35	.16	.04
☐ 12 Rich Gale CO	.35	.16	.04
☐ 13 Mike Gardiner	.35	.16	.04
☐ 14 Mike Greenwell	.60	.25	.08
☐ 15 Greg A. Harris	.35	.16	.04
☐ 16 Joe Hesketh	.35	.16	.04
☐ 17 Butch Hobson MG	.45	.20	.06
☐ 18 John Marzano	.35	.16	.04
☐ 19 Kevin Morton	.35	.16	.04
☐ 20 Tim Naehring	.45	.20	.06
☐ 21 Tony Pena	.45	.20	.06
☐ 22 Phil Plantier	.75	.35	.09
☐ 23 Carlos Quintana	.45	.20	.06
☐ 24 Jeff Reardon	.45	.20	.06
☐ 25 Jody Reed	.45	.20	.06
☐ 26 Luis Rivera	.35	.16	.04
☐ 27 Mo Vaughn	.60	.25	.08
☐ 28 Frank Viola	.60	.25	.08
☐ 29 Matt Young	.35	.16	.04
☐ 30 Don Zimmer CO	.35	.16	.04

1957 Reds Sohio

The 1957 Sohio Cincinnati Reds set consists of 18 perforated photos, approximately 5" by 7", in black and white with facsimile autographs on the front which were designed to be pasted into a special photo album issued by SOHIO (Standard Oil of Ohio). The set features an early Frank Robinson card. These unnumbered cards are listed below in alphabetical order for convenience.

	NRMT	VG-E	GOOD
COMPLETE SET (18)	150.00	70.00	19.00
COMMON PLAYER (1-18)	5.00	2.30	.60
☐ 1 Ed Bailey	5.00	2.30	.60
☐ 2 Gus Bell	6.00	2.70	.75
☐ 3 Rocky Bridges	5.00	2.30	.60
☐ 4 Smoky Burgess	6.00	2.70	.75
☐ 5 Hersh Freeman	5.00	2.30	.60
☐ 6 Alex Grammas	5.00	2.30	.60
☐ 7 Don Gross	5.00	2.30	.60
☐ 8 Warren Hacker	5.00	2.30	.60
☐ 9 Don Hoak	5.00	2.30	.60
☐ 10 Hal Jeffcoat	5.00	2.30	.60
☐ 11 Johnny Klippstein	5.00	2.30	.60
☐ 12 Ted Kluszewski	20.00	9.00	2.50
☐ 13 Brooks Lawrence	5.00	2.30	.60
☐ 14 Roy McMillan	5.00	2.30	.60
☐ 15 Joe Nuxhall	6.00	2.70	.75
☐ 16 Wally Post	6.00	2.70	.75
☐ 17 Frank Robinson	90.00	40.00	11.50
☐ 18 John Temple	6.00	2.70	.75

1982 Reds Coke

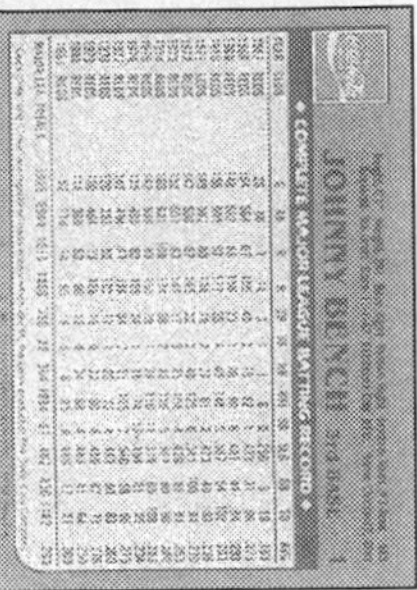

The cards in this 23-card set measure 2 1/2" by 3 1/2". The 1982 Coca-Cola Cincinnati Reds set, issued in conjunction with Topps, contains 22 cards of current Reds players. Although the cards of 15 players feature the exact photo used in the Topps' regular issue, the Coke photos have better coloration and appear sharper than their Topps counterparts. Six players, Cedeno, Harris, Hurdle, Kern, Krenchicki, and Trevino are new to the Redleg uniform via trades, while Paul Householder had formerly appeared on the Reds' 1982 Topps "Future Stars" card. The cards are numbered 1 to 22 on the red and gray reverse, and the Coke logo appears on both sides of the card. There is an unnumbered title card which contains a premium offer on the reverse. The set numbering is in alphabetical order by player's name.

	NRMT-MT	EXC	G-VG
COMPLETE SET (23)	7.50	3.40	.95
COMMON PLAYER (1-22)	.10	.05	.01
☐ 1 Johnny Bench	3.50	1.55	.45
☐ 2 Bruce Berenyi	.10	.05	.01
☐ 3 Larry Biittner	.10	.05	.01
☐ 4 Cesar Cedeno	.20	.09	.03
☐ 5 Dave Concepcion	.40	.18	.05
☐ 6 Dan Driessen	.15	.07	.02
☐ 7 Greg Harris	.35	.16	.04
☐ 8 Paul Householder	.10	.05	.01
☐ 9 Tom Hume	.10	.05	.01
☐ 10 Clint Hurdle	.15	.07	.02
☐ 11 Jim Kern	.10	.05	.01
☐ 12 Wayne Krenchicki	.10	.05	.01
☐ 13 Rafael Landestoy	.10	.05	.01
☐ 14 Charlie Leibrandt	.50	.23	.06
☐ 15 Mike O'Berry	.10	.05	.01
☐ 16 Ron Oester	.15	.07	.02
☐ 17 Frank Pastore	.10	.05	.01
☐ 18 Joe Price	.10	.05	.01
☐ 19 Tom Seaver	3.50	1.55	.45
☐ 20 Mario Soto	.15	.07	.02
☐ 21 Alex Trevino	.10	.05	.01
☐ 22 Mike Vail	.10	.05	.01
☐ NNO Title Card	.05	.02	.01

1986 Reds Texas Gold

Texas Gold Ice Cream is the sponsor of this 28-card set of Cincinnati Reds. The cards are 2 1/2" by 3 1/2" and feature player photos in full color with a red and white border on the front of the card. The set was distributed to fans attending the Reds game at Riverfront Stadium on September 19th. The card backs contain the player's career statistics, uniform number, name, position, and the Texas Gold logo.

	MT	EX-MT	VG
COMPLETE SET (28)	30.00	13.50	3.80
COMMON PLAYER	.60	.25	.08

☐ 6 Bo Diaz	.60	.25	.08
☐ 9 Max Venable	.60	.25	.08
☐ 11 Kurt Stillwell	.75	.35	.09
☐ 12 Nick Esasky	.60	.25	.08
☐ 13 Dave Concepcion	1.25	.55	.16
☐ 14A Pete Rose INF	3.00	1.35	.40
☐ 14B Pete Rose MG	3.00	1.35	.40
☐ 14C Pete Rose (Commemorative)	3.00	1.35	.40
☐ 16 Ron Oester	.60	.25	.08
☐ 20 Eddie Milner	.60	.25	.08
☐ 22 Sal Butera	.60	.25	.08
☐ 24 Tony Perez	2.00	.90	.25
☐ 25 Buddy Bell	.75	.35	.09
☐ 28 Kal Daniels	1.50	.65	.19
☐ 29 Tracy Jones	.60	.25	.08
☐ 31 John Franco	1.00	.45	.13
☐ 32 Tom Browning	1.00	.45	.13
☐ 33 Ron Robinson	.60	.25	.08
☐ 34 Bill Gullickson	.75	.35	.09
☐ 36 Mario Soto	.75	.35	.09
☐ 39 Dave Parker	1.25	.55	.16
☐ 40 John Denny	.75	.35	.09
☐ 44 Eric Davis	5.00	2.30	.60
☐ 45 Chris Welsh	.60	.25	.08
☐ 48 Ted Power	.60	.25	.08
☐ 49 Joe Price	.60	.25	.08
☐ NNO Reds Coaches George Scherger Bruce Kimm Billy DeMars Tommy Helms Scott Breeden Jim Lett	.60	.25	.08
☐ NNO Preferred Customer Card (Discount Coupon)	.60	.25	.08

1991 Reds Pepsi

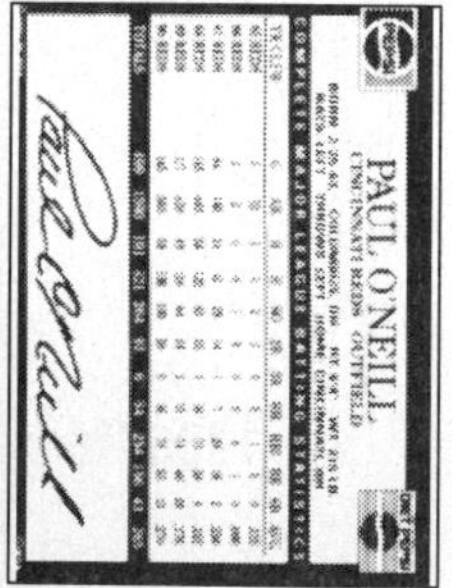

This 20-card set was produced by MSA (Michael Schechter Associates) for Pepsi-Cola of Ohio, and Pepsi logos adorn the upper corners of the card face. The cards measure the standard size (2 1/2" by 3 1/2") and were placed inside of 24-soda packs of Pepsi, Diet Pepsi, Caffeine-Free Pepsi, Caffeine Free Diet-Pepsi, Mountain Dew, and Diet Mountain Dew. The fronts display color player photos bordered in white and red and with the team logos airbrushed away. The horizontally oriented backs are trimmed in navy blue and present biography, statistics, and the player's autograph. The cards are unnumbered and checklisted below in alphabetical order.

	MT	EX-MT	VG
COMPLETE SET (20)	12.50	5.75	1.55
COMMON PLAYER (1-20)	.50	.23	.06
☐ 1 Jack Armstrong	.60	.25	.08
☐ 2 Todd Benzinger	.50	.23	.06
☐ 3 Glenn Braggs	.50	.23	.06
☐ 4 Tom Browning	.75	.35	.09
☐ 5 Norm Charlton	.60	.25	.08
☐ 6 Eric Davis	1.25	.55	.16
☐ 7 Rob Dibble	.75	.35	.09
☐ 8 Bill Doran	.60	.25	.08
☐ 9 Mariano Duncan	.60	.25	.08
☐ 10 Billy Hatcher	.60	.25	.08
☐ 11 Barry Larkin	1.50	.65	.19
☐ 12 Hal Morris	1.25	.55	.16
☐ 13 Randy Myers	.75	.35	.09
☐ 14 Joe Oliver	.60	.25	.08
☐ 15 Paul O'Neill	.75	.35	.09
☐ 16 Lou Piniella MG	.75	.35	.09
☐ 17 Jeff Reed	.50	.23	.06
☐ 18 Jose Rijo	.75	.35	.09
☐ 19 Chris Sabo	1.00	.45	.13
☐ 20 Herm Winningham	.50	.23	.06

1992 Rembrandt Ultra-Pro Promos

The 1992 Rembrandt Ultra-Pro set of 18 cards was issued one-per-package inside specially marked packages of Rembrandt Ultra-Pro sheets. The cards are standard size (2 1/2" by 3 1/2") and are numbered with a P prefix. The cards contain a high-gloss UV coating and feature an exclusive anti-counterfeiting hologram on the back. The set was also available direct from Rembrandt for 35.95 (37.95 or 39.95) plus 4.00 shipping and handling along with three (two or one) UPC's or other proofs of purchase.

	MT	EX-MT	VG
COMPLETE SET (18)	40.00	18.00	5.00
COMMON PLAYER (1-18)	2.00	.90	.25
☐ P1 Bobby Bonilla (Holding both ends of bat across neck)	3.00	1.35	.40
☐ P2 Bobby Bonilla (Front pose, shot from waist up)	3.00	1.35	.40
☐ P3 Bobby Bonilla (Follow-through after golf swing)	3.00	1.35	.40
☐ P4 Jose Canseco (Posed in car)	4.00	1.80	.50
☐ P5 Jose Canseco (Batting stance)	4.00	1.80	.50
☐ P6 Jose Canseco (Front pose, bat resting on shoulder)	4.00	1.80	.50
☐ P7 Hal Morris (Front pose, bat resting on shoulder)	2.00	.90	.25
☐ P8 Hal Morris	2.00	.90	.25

(Posed with tennis racket in hand)			
☐ P9 Hal Morris (Pose, shot from waist up)	2.00	.90	.25
☐ P10 Scott Erickson (Posed with skis on shoulder)	2.00	.90	.25
☐ P11 Scott Erickson (Front pose, shot from waist up	2.00	.90	.25
☐ P12 Scott Erickson (Batting stance)	2.00	.90	.25
☐ P13 Danny Tartabull (Batting stance)	2.00	.90	.25
☐ P14 Danny Tartabull (Front pose, bat resting on shoulder)	2.00	.90	.25
☐ P15 Danny Tartabull (Posed with chrome dumbbell in left hand)	2.00	.90	.25
☐ P16 Danny Tartabull and Bobby Bonilla (Posed in tuxedos, bat on shoulder)	3.00	1.35	.40
☐ P17 Bobby Bonilla (Posed in tuxedo)	3.00	1.35	.40
☐ P18 Danny Tartabull and Bobby Bonilla (Hologram)	5.00	2.30	.60

1955 Rodeo Meats

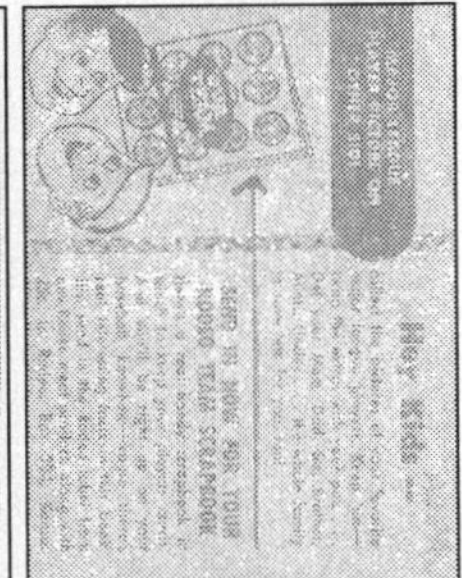

The cards in this 47-card set measure 2 1/2" by 3 1/2". The 1955 Rodeo Meats set contains unnumbered, color cards of the first Kansas City A's team. There are many background color variations noted in the checklist, and the card reverses carry a scrapbook offer. The Grimes and Kryhoski cards listed in the scrapbook album were apparently never issued. The catalog number for this set is F152-1. The cards have been arranged in alphabetical order and assigned numbers for reference.

	NRMT	VG-E	GOOD
COMPLETE SET (47)	5000.00	2300.00	650.00
COMMON PLAYER (1-47)	80.00	36.00	10.00
☐ 1 Joe Astroth	80.00	36.00	10.00
☐ 2 Harold Bevan	100.00	45.00	12.50
☐ 3 Charles Bishop	100.00	45.00	12.50
☐ 4 Don Bollweg	100.00	45.00	12.50
☐ 5 Lou Boudreau MG	250.00	115.00	31.00
☐ 6 Cloyd Boyer (Salmon)	80.00	36.00	10.00
☐ 7 Cloyd Boyer (Light blue)	125.00	57.50	15.50
☐ 8 Ed Burtschy	150.00	70.00	19.00
☐ 9 Art Ceccarelli	100.00	45.00	12.50
☐ 10 Joe DeMaestri (Yellow)	80.00	36.00	10.00
☐ 11 Joe DeMaestri (Green)	80.00	36.00	10.00
☐ 12 Art Ditmar	80.00	36.00	10.00
☐ 13 John Dixon	100.00	45.00	12.50
☐ 14 Jim Finigan	80.00	36.00	10.00
☐ 15 Marion Fricano	100.00	45.00	12.50
☐ 16 Tom Gorman	80.00	36.00	10.00
☐ 17 John Gray	100.00	45.00	12.50
☐ 18 Ray Herbert	80.00	36.00	10.00
☐ 19 Forrest Jacobs	150.00	70.00	19.00
☐ 20 Alex Kellner	80.00	36.00	10.00
☐ 21 Harry Kraft CO (Craft, sic)	80.00	36.00	10.00
☐ 22 Jack Littrell	80.00	36.00	10.00
☐ 23 Hector Lopez	90.00	40.00	11.50
☐ 24 Oscar Melillo CO	80.00	36.00	10.00
☐ 25 Arnold Portocarrero (Purple)	125.00	57.50	15.50
☐ 26 Arnold Portocarrero (Gray)	80.00	36.00	10.00
☐ 27 Vic Power (Yellow)	80.00	36.00	10.00
☐ 28 Vic Power (Pink)	125.00	57.50	15.50
☐ 29 Vic Raschi	125.00	57.50	15.50
☐ 30 Bill Renna (Lavender)	80.00	36.00	10.00
☐ 31 Bill Renna (Dark pink)	125.00	57.50	15.50
☐ 32 Al Robertson	100.00	45.00	12.50
☐ 33 Johnny Sain	175.00	80.00	22.00
☐ 34 Bobby Schantz ERR (Misspelling)	250.00	115.00	31.00
☐ 35 Bobby Shantz COR	150.00	70.00	19.00
☐ 36 Wilmer Shantz (Orange)	80.00	36.00	10.00
☐ 37 Wilmer Shantz (Lavender)	80.00	36.00	10.00
☐ 38 Harry Simpson	80.00	36.00	10.00
☐ 39 Enos Slaughter	300.00	135.00	38.00
☐ 40 Lou Sleater	80.00	36.00	10.00
☐ 41 George Susce CO	100.00	45.00	12.50
☐ 42 Bob Trice	100.00	45.00	12.50
☐ 43 Elmer Valo (Yellow)	125.00	57.50	15.50
☐ 44 Elmer Valo (Green sky)	90.00	40.00	11.50
☐ 45 Bill Wilson (Yellow)	125.00	57.50	15.50
☐ 46 Bill Wilson (Lavender sky)	80.00	36.00	10.00
☐ 47 Gus Zernial	90.00	40.00	11.50

1956 Rodeo Meats

The cards in this 12-card set measure 2 1/2" by 3 1/2". The unnumbered, color cards of the 1956 Rodeo baseball series are easily distinguished from their 1955 counterparts by the absence of the scrapbook offer on the reverse. They were available only in packages of Rodeo All-Meat Wieners. The catalog designation for this set is F152-2, and the cards have been assigned numbers in alphabetical order in the checklist below.

	NRMT	VG-E	GOOD
COMPLETE SET (12)	1350.00	600.00	170.00
COMMON PLAYER (1-12)	80.00	36.00	10.00
☐ 1 Joe Astroth	80.00	36.00	10.00
☐ 2 Lou Boudreau MG	250.00	115.00	31.00
☐ 3 Joe DeMaestri	80.00	36.00	10.00
☐ 4 Art Ditmar	80.00	36.00	10.00
☐ 5 Jim Finigan	80.00	36.00	10.00
☐ 6 Hector Lopez	90.00	40.00	11.50

☐ 7 Vic Power	80.00	36.00	10.00
☐ 8 Bobby Shantz	125.00	57.50	15.50
☐ 9 Harry Simpson	80.00	36.00	10.00
☐ 10 Enos Slaughter	300.00	135.00	38.00
☐ 11 Elmer Valo	90.00	40.00	11.50
☐ 12 Gus Zernial	90.00	40.00	11.50

1986 Royals National Photo

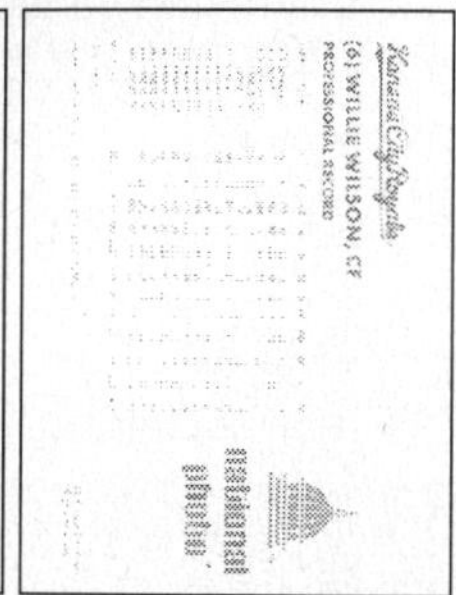

The set contains 24 cards which are numbered only by uniform number except for the checklist card and discount card, which entitles the bearer to a 40 percent discount at National Photo. Cards measure approximately 2 7/8" by 4 1/4". Cards were distributed at the stadium on August 14th. The set was supposedly later available for 3.00 directly from the Royals.

	MT	EX-MT	VG
COMPLETE SET (24)	12.00	5.50	1.50
COMMON PLAYER	.35	.16	.04
☐ 1 Buddy Biancalana	.35	.16	.04
☐ 3 Jorge Orta	.35	.16	.04
☐ 4 Greg Pryor	.35	.16	.04
☐ 5 George Brett	5.00	2.30	.60
☐ 6 Willie Wilson	.75	.35	.09
☐ 8 Jim Sundberg	.45	.20	.06
☐ 10 Dick Howser MG	.60	.25	.08
☐ 11 Hal McRae	.75	.35	.09
☐ 20 Frank White	.60	.25	.08
☐ 21 Lonnie Smith	.75	.35	.09
☐ 22 Dennis Leonard	.60	.25	.08
☐ 23 Mark Gubicza	1.00	.45	.13
☐ 24 Darryl Motley	.35	.16	.04
☐ 25 Danny Jackson	.60	.25	.08
☐ 26 Steve Farr	.60	.25	.08
☐ 29 Dan Quisenberry	.75	.35	.09
☐ 31 Bret Saberhagen	1.25	.55	.16
☐ 35 Lynn Jones	.35	.16	.04
☐ 37 Charlie Leibrandt	.60	.25	.08
☐ 38 Mark Huismann	.35	.16	.04
☐ 40 Bud Black	.45	.20	.06
☐ 45 Steve Balboni	.45	.20	.06
☐ NNO Discount card	.35	.16	.04
☐ NNO Checklist card	.45	.20	.06

1991 S.F. Examiner Athletics

The fifteen 6" by 9" giant-sized cards in this set were issued on yellow cardboard sheets measuring approximately 8 1/2" by 11" and designed for storage in a three-ring binder. The card fronts are green and have color player photos enframed by thin yellow border stripes. The team name appears in a green banner at the top, while the words "Examiner's Finest" appear in a yellow stripe at the bottom of the card. The back has a black and white head shot, biography, career summary, and complete Major League statistics. The cards are unnumbered and checklisted below in alphabetical order.

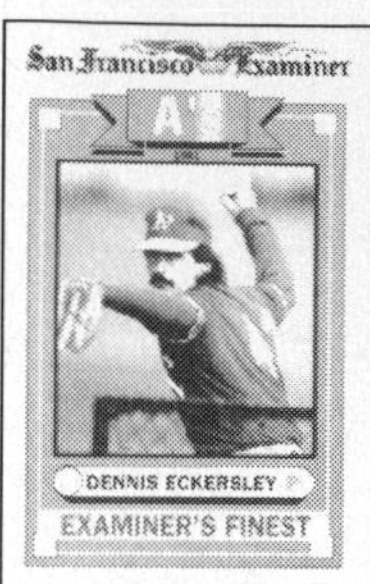

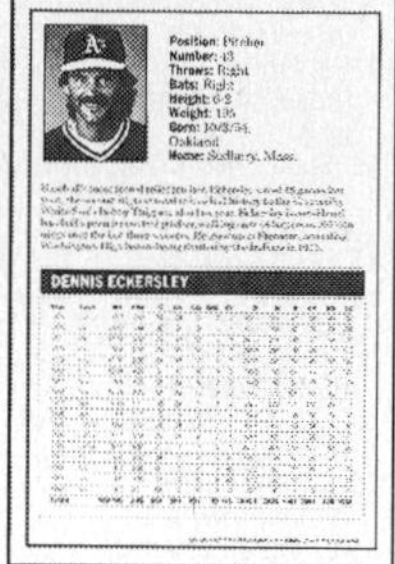

	MT	EX-MT	VG
COMPLETE SET (15)	24.00	11.00	3.00
COMMON PLAYER (1-15)	1.00	.45	.13
☐ 1 Harold Baines	1.50	.65	.19
☐ 2 Jose Canseco	5.00	2.30	.60
☐ 3 Dennis Eckersley	3.00	1.35	.40
☐ 4 Mike Gallego	1.00	.45	.13
☐ 5 Dave Henderson	1.25	.55	.16
☐ 6 Rickey Henderson	3.50	1.55	.45
☐ 7 Rick Honeycutt	1.00	.45	.13
☐ 8 Mark McGwire	3.50	1.55	.45
☐ 9 Mike Moore	1.50	.65	.19
☐ 10 Gene Nelson	1.00	.45	.13
☐ 11 Eric Show	1.00	.45	.13
☐ 12 Terry Steinbach	1.50	.65	.19
☐ 13 Dave Stewart	2.00	.90	.25
☐ 14 Walt Weiss	1.25	.55	.16
☐ 15 Bob Welch	1.25	.55	.16

1991 S.F. Examiner Giants

The sixteen 6" by 9" giant-sized cards in this set were issued on orange cardboard sheets measuring approximately 8 1/2" by 11" and designed for storage in a three-ring binder. The cards fronts are light gray and have color player photos enframed by thin orange border stripes. The team name appears in a black banner at the top, while the words "Examiner's Finest" appear in an orange stripe at the bottom of the card. The back has a black and white head shot, biography, career summary, and complete Major League statistics. The cards are unnumbered and checklisted below in alphabetical order.

	MT	EX-MT	VG
COMPLETE SET (16)	21.00	9.50	2.60
COMMON PLAYER (1-16)	1.00	.45	.13
☐ 1 Kevin Bass	1.00	.45	.13
☐ 2 Mike Benjamin	1.00	.45	.13
☐ 3 Bud Black	1.00	.45	.13
☐ 4 Jeff Brantley	1.25	.55	.16
☐ 5 John Burkett	1.50	.65	.19
☐ 6 Will Clark	5.00	2.30	.60
☐ 7 Steve Decker	2.00	.90	.25

☐ 8 Scott Garrelts	1.00	.45	.13
☐ 9 Mike LaCoss	1.00	.45	.13
☐ 10 Willie McGee	1.50	.65	.19
☐ 11 Kevin Mitchell	2.00	.90	.25
☐ 12 Dave Righetti	1.25	.55	.16
☐ 13 Don Robinson	1.00	.45	.13
☐ 14 Robby Thompson	1.50	.65	.19
☐ 15 Jose Uribe	1.00	.45	.13
☐ 16 Matt Williams	2.50	1.15	.30

1987-88 Score Test Samples

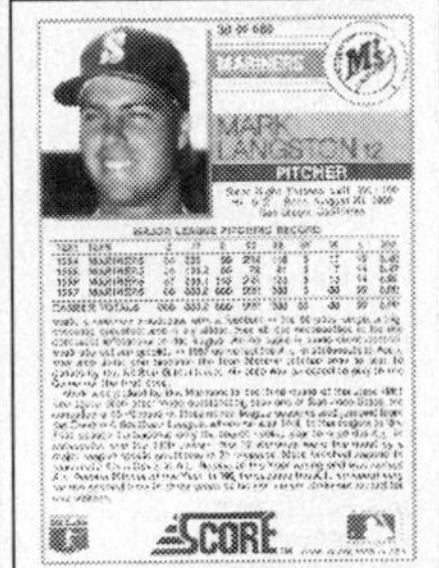

Late in 1987 near the end of the season, Score prepared some samples to show prospective dealers and buyers of the new Score cards what they would look like. These sample cards are distinguished by the fact that there is a row of zeroes for the 1987 season statistics since the season was not over when these sample cards were being printed. The cards are standard size, 2 1/2" by 3 1/2", and are virtually indistinguishable from the regular 1988 Score cards of the same players except for border color variations in a few instances.

	MT	EX-MT	VG
COMPLETE SET (6)	40.00	18.00	5.00
COMMON PLAYER	6.00	2.70	.75
☐ 30 Mark Langston	9.00	4.00	1.15
☐ 48 Tony Pena	7.50	3.40	.95
☐ 71 Keith Moreland	6.00	2.70	.75
☐ 72 Barry Larkin	15.00	6.75	1.90
☐ 121 Dennis Boyd	6.00	2.70	.75
☐ 145 Denny Walling	6.00	2.70	.75

1988 Score

This 660-card set was distributed by Major League Marketing. Cards measure 2 1/2" by 3 1/2" and feature six distinctive border colors on the front. Highlights (652-660) and Rookie Prospects (623-647) are included in the set. Reggie Jackson's career is honored with a five-card subset on cards 500-504. Card number 501, showing Reggie as a member of the Baltimore Orioles, is one of the few opportunities collectors have to visually remember (on a regular card) Reggie's one-year stay with the Orioles. The set is distinguished by the fact that each card back shows a full-color picture of the player. The key Rookie Cards in this set are Ellis Burks, Ron Gant, Tom Glavine, Gregg Jefferies, Roberto Kelly and Matt Williams. The company also produced a very limited "glossy" set, that is valued at eight times the value of the regular (non-glossy) set. Although exact production quantities of this glossy set are not known, it has been speculated, but not confirmed, that 5,000 glossy sets were produced. It is generally accepted that the number of Score glossy sets produced in 1988 was much smaller (estimated only 10 percent to 15 percent as many) than the number of Topps Tiffany or Fleer Tin sets. These Score glossy cards, when bought or sold individually, are valued approximately five to ten times the values listed below.

	MT	EX-MT	VG
COMPLETE SET (660)	20.00	9.00	2.50
COMPLETE FACT.SET (660)	20.00	9.00	2.50
COMMON PLAYER (1-660)	.04	.02	.01
☐ 1 Don Mattingly	.30	.14	.04
☐ 2 Wade Boggs	.30	.14	.04
☐ 3 Tim Raines	.07	.03	.01
☐ 4 Andre Dawson	.20	.09	.03
☐ 5 Mark McGwire	.50	.23	.06
☐ 6 Kevin Seitzer	.07	.03	.01
☐ 7 Wally Joyner	.12	.05	.02
☐ 8 Jesse Barfield	.04	.02	.01
☐ 9 Pedro Guerrero	.07	.03	.01
☐ 10 Eric Davis	.10	.05	.01
☐ 11 George Brett	.25	.11	.03
☐ 12 Ozzie Smith	.20	.09	.03
☐ 13 Rickey Henderson	.30	.14	.04
☐ 14 Jim Rice	.07	.03	.01
☐ 15 Matt Nokes	.20	.09	.03
☐ 16 Mike Schmidt	.40	.18	.05
☐ 17 Dave Parker	.07	.03	.01
☐ 18 Eddie Murray	.20	.09	.03
☐ 19 Andres Galarraga	.04	.02	.01
☐ 20 Tony Fernandez	.07	.03	.01
☐ 21 Kevin McReynolds	.07	.03	.01
☐ 22 B.J. Surhoff	.07	.03	.01
☐ 23 Pat Tabler	.04	.02	.01
☐ 24 Kirby Puckett	.40	.18	.05
☐ 25 Benny Santiago	.10	.05	.01
☐ 26 Ryne Sandberg	.50	.23	.06
☐ 27 Kelly Downs (Will Clark in background, out of focus)	.07	.03	.01
☐ 28 Jose Cruz	.04	.02	.01
☐ 29 Pete O'Brien	.04	.02	.01
☐ 30 Mark Langston	.07	.03	.01
☐ 31 Lee Smith	.15	.07	.02
☐ 32 Juan Samuel	.04	.02	.01
☐ 33 Kevin Bass	.04	.02	.01
☐ 34 R.J. Reynolds	.04	.02	.01
☐ 35 Steve Sax	.07	.03	.01
☐ 36 John Kruk	.15	.07	.02
☐ 37 Alan Trammell	.07	.03	.01
☐ 38 Chris Bosio	.07	.03	.01
☐ 39 Brook Jacoby	.04	.02	.01
☐ 40 Willie McGee UER (Excited misspelled as excitd)	.07	.03	.01
☐ 41 Dave Magadan	.07	.03	.01
☐ 42 Fred Lynn	.07	.03	.01
☐ 43 Kent Hrbek	.07	.03	.01
☐ 44 Brian Downing	.04	.02	.01
☐ 45 Jose Canseco	.60	.25	.08
☐ 46 Jim Presley	.04	.02	.01
☐ 47 Mike Stanley	.04	.02	.01
☐ 48 Tony Pena	.04	.02	.01
☐ 49 David Cone	.50	.23	.06
☐ 50 Rick Sutcliffe	.07	.03	.01
☐ 51 Doug Drabek	.10	.05	.01
☐ 52 Bill Doran	.04	.02	.01
☐ 53 Mike Scioscia	.04	.02	.01
☐ 54 Candy Maldonado	.04	.02	.01
☐ 55 Dave Winfield	.25	.11	.03
☐ 56 Lou Whitaker	.04	.02	.01
☐ 57 Tom Henke	.07	.03	.01
☐ 58 Ken Gerhart	.04	.02	.01
☐ 59 Glenn Braggs	.04	.02	.01

Card			
☐ 60 Julio Franco	.10	.05	.01
☐ 61 Charlie Leibrandt	.04	.02	.01
☐ 62 Gary Gaetti	.04	.02	.01
☐ 63 Bob Boone	.07	.03	.01
☐ 64 Luis Polonia	.25	.11	.03
☐ 65 Dwight Evans	.07	.03	.01
☐ 66 Phil Bradley	.04	.02	.01
☐ 67 Mike Boddicker	.04	.02	.01
☐ 68 Vince Coleman	.07	.03	.01
☐ 69 Howard Johnson	.10	.05	.01
☐ 70 Tim Wallach	.07	.03	.01
☐ 71 Keith Moreland	.04	.02	.01
☐ 72 Barry Larkin	.25	.11	.03
☐ 73 Alan Ashby	.04	.02	.01
☐ 74 Rick Rhoden	.04	.02	.01
☐ 75 Darrell Evans	.07	.03	.01
☐ 76 Dave Stieb	.07	.03	.01
☐ 77 Dan Plesac	.04	.02	.01
☐ 78 Will Clark UER (Born 3/17/64, should be 3/13/64)	.60	.25	.08
☐ 79 Frank White	.04	.02	.01
☐ 80 Joe Carter	.25	.11	.03
☐ 81 Mike Witt	.04	.02	.01
☐ 82 Terry Steinbach	.07	.03	.01
☐ 83 Alvin Davis	.04	.02	.01
☐ 84 Tommy Herr (Will Clark shown sliding into second)	.07	.03	.01
☐ 85 Vance Law	.04	.02	.01
☐ 86 Kal Daniels	.07	.03	.01
☐ 87 Rick Honeycutt UER (Wrong years for stats on back)	.04	.02	.01
☐ 88 Alfredo Griffin	.04	.02	.01
☐ 89 Bret Saberhagen	.10	.05	.01
☐ 90 Bert Blyleven	.07	.03	.01
☐ 91 Jeff Reardon	.12	.05	.02
☐ 92 Cory Snyder	.07	.03	.01
☐ 93A Greg Walker ERR (93 of 66)	3.00	1.35	.40
☐ 93B Greg Walker COR (93 of 660)	.04	.02	.01
☐ 94 Joe Magrane	.10	.05	.01
☐ 95 Rob Deer	.07	.03	.01
☐ 96 Ray Knight	.07	.03	.01
☐ 97 Casey Candaele	.04	.02	.01
☐ 98 John Cerutti	.04	.02	.01
☐ 99 Buddy Bell	.07	.03	.01
☐ 100 Jack Clark	.07	.03	.01
☐ 101 Eric Bell	.04	.02	.01
☐ 102 Willie Wilson	.04	.02	.01
☐ 103 Dave Schmidt	.04	.02	.01
☐ 104 Dennis Eckersley UER (Complete games stats are wrong)	.15	.07	.02
☐ 105 Don Sutton	.10	.05	.01
☐ 106 Danny Tartabull	.15	.07	.02
☐ 107 Fred McGriff	.40	.18	.05
☐ 108 Les Straker	.04	.02	.01
☐ 109 Lloyd Moseby	.04	.02	.01
☐ 110 Roger Clemens	.50	.23	.06
☐ 111 Glenn Hubbard	.04	.02	.01
☐ 112 Ken Williams	.04	.02	.01
☐ 113 Ruben Sierra	.40	.18	.05
☐ 114 Stan Jefferson	.04	.02	.01
☐ 115 Milt Thompson	.04	.02	.01
☐ 116 Bobby Bonilla	.25	.11	.03
☐ 117 Wayne Tolleson	.04	.02	.01
☐ 118 Matt Williams	.90	.40	.11
☐ 119 Chet Lemon	.04	.02	.01
☐ 120 Dale Sveum	.04	.02	.01
☐ 121 Dennis Boyd	.04	.02	.01
☐ 122 Brett Butler	.10	.05	.01
☐ 123 Terry Kennedy	.04	.02	.01
☐ 124 Jack Howell	.04	.02	.01
☐ 125 Curt Young	.04	.02	.01
☐ 126A Dave Valle ERR (Misspelled Dale on card front)	.12	.05	.02
☐ 126B Dave Valle COR	.04	.02	.01
☐ 127 Curt Wilkerson	.04	.02	.01
☐ 128 Tim Teufel	.04	.02	.01
☐ 129 Ozzie Virgil	.04	.02	.01
☐ 130 Brian Fisher	.04	.02	.01
☐ 131 Lance Parrish	.07	.03	.01
☐ 132 Tom Browning	.04	.02	.01
☐ 133A Larry Andersen ERR (Misspelled Anderson on card front)	.12	.05	.02
☐ 133B Larry Andersen COR	.04	.02	.01
☐ 134A Bob Brenly ERR (Misspelled Brenley on card front)	.12	.05	.02
☐ 134B Bob Brenly COR	.04	.02	.01
☐ 135 Mike Marshall	.04	.02	.01
☐ 136 Gerald Perry	.04	.02	.01
☐ 137 Bobby Meacham	.04	.02	.01
☐ 138 Larry Herndon	.04	.02	.01
☐ 139 Fred Manrique	.04	.02	.01
☐ 140 Charlie Hough	.04	.02	.01
☐ 141 Ron Darling	.07	.03	.01
☐ 142 Herm Winningham	.04	.02	.01
☐ 143 Mike Diaz	.04	.02	.01
☐ 144 Mike Jackson	.10	.05	.01
☐ 145 Denny Walling	.04	.02	.01
☐ 146 Robby Thompson	.07	.03	.01
☐ 147 Franklin Stubbs	.04	.02	.01
☐ 148 Albert Hall	.04	.02	.01
☐ 149 Bobby Witt	.07	.03	.01
☐ 150 Lance McCullers	.04	.02	.01
☐ 151 Scott Bradley	.04	.02	.01
☐ 152 Mark McLemore	.04	.02	.01
☐ 153 Tim Laudner	.04	.02	.01
☐ 154 Greg Swindell	.15	.07	.02
☐ 155 Marty Barrett	.04	.02	.01
☐ 156 Mike Heath	.04	.02	.01
☐ 157 Gary Ward	.04	.02	.01
☐ 158A Lee Mazzilli ERR (Misspelled Mazilli on card front)	.12	.05	.02
☐ 158B Lee Mazzilli COR	.04	.02	.01
☐ 159 Tom Foley	.04	.02	.01
☐ 160 Robin Yount	.25	.11	.03
☐ 161 Steve Bedrosian	.04	.02	.01
☐ 162 Bob Walk	.04	.02	.01
☐ 163 Nick Esasky	.04	.02	.01
☐ 164 Ken Caminiti	.30	.14	.04
☐ 165 Jose Uribe	.04	.02	.01
☐ 166 Dave Anderson	.04	.02	.01
☐ 167 Ed Whitson	.04	.02	.01
☐ 168 Ernie Whitt	.04	.02	.01
☐ 169 Cecil Cooper	.07	.03	.01
☐ 170 Mike Pagliarulo	.04	.02	.01
☐ 171 Pat Sheridan	.04	.02	.01
☐ 172 Chris Bando	.04	.02	.01
☐ 173 Lee Lacy	.04	.02	.01
☐ 174 Steve Lombardozzi	.04	.02	.01
☐ 175 Mike Greenwell	.10	.05	.01
☐ 176 Greg Minton	.04	.02	.01
☐ 177 Moose Haas	.04	.02	.01
☐ 178 Mike Kingery	.04	.02	.01
☐ 179 Greg A. Harris	.04	.02	.01
☐ 180 Bo Jackson	.30	.14	.04
☐ 181 Carmelo Martinez	.04	.02	.01
☐ 182 Alex Trevino	.04	.02	.01
☐ 183 Ron Oester	.04	.02	.01
☐ 184 Danny Darwin	.04	.02	.01
☐ 185 Mike Krukow	.04	.02	.01
☐ 186 Rafael Palmeiro	.30	.14	.04
☐ 187 Tim Burke	.04	.02	.01
☐ 188 Roger McDowell	.04	.02	.01
☐ 189 Garry Templeton	.04	.02	.01
☐ 190 Terry Pendleton	.15	.07	.02
☐ 191 Larry Parrish	.04	.02	.01
☐ 192 Rey Quinones	.04	.02	.01
☐ 193 Joaquin Andujar	.04	.02	.01
☐ 194 Tom Brunansky	.07	.03	.01
☐ 195 Donnie Moore	.04	.02	.01
☐ 196 Dan Pasqua	.04	.02	.01
☐ 197 Jim Gantner	.04	.02	.01
☐ 198 Mark Eichhorn	.04	.02	.01
☐ 199 John Grubb	.04	.02	.01
☐ 200 Bill Ripken	.10	.05	.01
☐ 201 Sam Horn	.12	.05	.02
☐ 202 Todd Worrell	.07	.03	.01
☐ 203 Terry Leach	.04	.02	.01
☐ 204 Garth Iorg	.04	.02	.01
☐ 205 Brian Dayett	.04	.02	.01
☐ 206 Bo Diaz	.04	.02	.01
☐ 207 Craig Reynolds	.04	.02	.01
☐ 208 Brian Holton	.04	.02	.01
☐ 209 Marvell Wynne UER (Misspelled Marvelle on card front)	.04	.02	.01
☐ 210 Dave Concepcion	.07	.03	.01
☐ 211 Mike Davis	.04	.02	.01
☐ 212 Devon White	.10	.05	.01
☐ 213 Mickey Brantley	.04	.02	.01
☐ 214 Greg Gagne	.07	.03	.01
☐ 215 Oddibe McDowell	.04	.02	.01
☐ 216 Jimmy Key	.07	.03	.01
☐ 217 Dave Bergman	.04	.02	.01
☐ 218 Calvin Schiraldi	.04	.02	.01
☐ 219 Larry Sheets	.04	.02	.01
☐ 220 Mike Easler	.04	.02	.01
☐ 221 Kurt Stillwell	.04	.02	.01

☐ 222 Chuck Jackson	.04	.02	.01
☐ 223 Dave Martinez	.07	.03	.01
☐ 224 Tim Leary	.04	.02	.01
☐ 225 Steve Garvey	.12	.05	.02
☐ 226 Greg Mathews	.04	.02	.01
☐ 227 Doug Sisk	.04	.02	.01
☐ 228 Dave Henderson	.07	.03	.01
☐ 229 Jimmy Dwyer	.04	.02	.01
☐ 230 Larry Owen	.04	.02	.01
☐ 231 Andre Thornton	.04	.02	.01
☐ 232 Mark Salas	.04	.02	.01
☐ 233 Tom Brookens	.04	.02	.01
☐ 234 Greg Brock	.04	.02	.01
☐ 235 Rance Mulliniks	.04	.02	.01
☐ 236 Bob Brower	.04	.02	.01
☐ 237 Joe Niekro	.07	.03	.01
☐ 238 Scott Bankhead	.04	.02	.01
☐ 239 Doug DeCinces	.04	.02	.01
☐ 240 Tommy John	.07	.03	.01
☐ 241 Rich Gedman	.04	.02	.01
☐ 242 Ted Power	.04	.02	.01
☐ 243 Dave Meads	.04	.02	.01
☐ 244 Jim Sundberg	.04	.02	.01
☐ 245 Ken Oberkfell	.04	.02	.01
☐ 246 Jimmy Jones	.04	.02	.01
☐ 247 Ken Landreaux	.04	.02	.01
☐ 248 Jose Oquendo	.04	.02	.01
☐ 249 John Mitchell	.04	.02	.01
☐ 250 Don Baylor	.07	.03	.01
☐ 251 Scott Fletcher	.04	.02	.01
☐ 252 Al Newman	.04	.02	.01
☐ 253 Carney Lansford	.07	.03	.01
☐ 254 Johnny Ray	.04	.02	.01
☐ 255 Gary Pettis	.04	.02	.01
☐ 256 Ken Phelps	.04	.02	.01
☐ 257 Rick Leach	.04	.02	.01
☐ 258 Tim Stoddard	.04	.02	.01
☐ 259 Ed Romero	.04	.02	.01
☐ 260 Sid Bream	.07	.03	.01
☐ 261A Tom Niedenfuer ERR (Misspelled Neidenfuer on card front)	.12	.05	.02
☐ 261B Tom Niedenfuer COR	.04	.02	.01
☐ 262 Rick Dempsey	.04	.02	.01
☐ 263 Lonnie Smith	.04	.02	.01
☐ 264 Bob Forsch	.04	.02	.01
☐ 265 Barry Bonds	.60	.25	.08
☐ 266 Willie Randolph	.07	.03	.01
☐ 267 Mike Ramsey	.04	.02	.01
☐ 268 Don Slaught	.04	.02	.01
☐ 269 Mickey Tettleton	.12	.05	.02
☐ 270 Jerry Reuss	.04	.02	.01
☐ 271 Marc Sullivan	.04	.02	.01
☐ 272 Jim Morrison	.04	.02	.01
☐ 273 Steve Balboni	.04	.02	.01
☐ 274 Dick Schofield	.04	.02	.01
☐ 275 John Tudor	.04	.02	.01
☐ 276 Gene Larkin	.10	.05	.01
☐ 277 Harold Reynolds	.04	.02	.01
☐ 278 Jerry Browne	.04	.02	.01
☐ 279 Willie Upshaw	.04	.02	.01
☐ 280 Ted Higuera	.04	.02	.01
☐ 281 Terry McGriff	.04	.02	.01
☐ 282 Terry Puhl	.04	.02	.01
☐ 283 Mark Wasinger	.04	.02	.01
☐ 284 Luis Salazar	.04	.02	.01
☐ 285 Ted Simmons	.07	.03	.01
☐ 286 John Shelby	.04	.02	.01
☐ 287 John Smiley	.40	.18	.05
☐ 288 Curt Ford	.04	.02	.01
☐ 289 Steve Crawford	.04	.02	.01
☐ 290 Dan Quisenberry	.07	.03	.01
☐ 291 Alan Wiggins	.04	.02	.01
☐ 292 Randy Bush	.04	.02	.01
☐ 293 John Candelaria	.04	.02	.01
☐ 294 Tony Phillips	.04	.02	.01
☐ 295 Mike Morgan	.07	.03	.01
☐ 296 Bill Wegman	.04	.02	.01
☐ 297A Terry Francona ERR (Misspelled Franconia on card front)	.12	.05	.02
☐ 297B Terry Francona COR	.04	.02	.01
☐ 298 Mickey Hatcher	.04	.02	.01
☐ 299 Andres Thomas	.04	.02	.01
☐ 300 Bob Stanley	.04	.02	.01
☐ 301 Al Pedrique	.04	.02	.01
☐ 302 Jim Lindeman	.04	.02	.01
☐ 303 Wally Backman	.04	.02	.01
☐ 304 Paul O'Neill	.10	.05	.01
☐ 305 Hubie Brooks	.04	.02	.01
☐ 306 Steve Buechele	.04	.02	.01
☐ 307 Bobby Thigpen	.07	.03	.01
☐ 308 George Hendrick	.04	.02	.01
☐ 309 John Moses	.04	.02	.01
☐ 310 Ron Guidry	.07	.03	.01
☐ 311 Bill Schroeder	.04	.02	.01
☐ 312 Jose Nunez	.04	.02	.01
☐ 313 Bud Black	.04	.02	.01
☐ 314 Joe Sambito	.04	.02	.01
☐ 315 Scott McGregor	.04	.02	.01
☐ 316 Rafael Santana	.04	.02	.01
☐ 317 Frank Williams	.04	.02	.01
☐ 318 Mike Fitzgerald	.04	.02	.01
☐ 319 Rick Mahler	.04	.02	.01
☐ 320 Jim Gott	.04	.02	.01
☐ 321 Mariano Duncan	.04	.02	.01
☐ 322 Jose Guzman	.07	.03	.01
☐ 323 Lee Guetterman	.04	.02	.01
☐ 324 Dan Gladden	.04	.02	.01
☐ 325 Gary Carter	.10	.05	.01
☐ 326 Tracy Jones	.04	.02	.01
☐ 327 Floyd Youmans	.04	.02	.01
☐ 328 Bill Dawley	.04	.02	.01
☐ 329 Paul Noce	.04	.02	.01
☐ 330 Angel Salazar	.04	.02	.01
☐ 331 Goose Gossage	.07	.03	.01
☐ 332 George Frazier	.04	.02	.01
☐ 333 Ruppert Jones	.04	.02	.01
☐ 334 Billy Joe Robidoux	.04	.02	.01
☐ 335 Mike Scott	.07	.03	.01
☐ 336 Randy Myers	.07	.03	.01
☐ 337 Bob Sebra	.04	.02	.01
☐ 338 Eric Show	.04	.02	.01
☐ 339 Mitch Williams	.07	.03	.01
☐ 340 Paul Molitor	.12	.05	.02
☐ 341 Gus Polidor	.04	.02	.01
☐ 342 Steve Trout	.04	.02	.01
☐ 343 Jerry Don Gleaton	.04	.02	.01
☐ 344 Bob Knepper	.04	.02	.01
☐ 345 Mitch Webster	.04	.02	.01
☐ 346 John Morris	.04	.02	.01
☐ 347 Andy Hawkins	.04	.02	.01
☐ 348 Dave Leiper	.04	.02	.01
☐ 349 Ernest Riles	.04	.02	.01
☐ 350 Dwight Gooden	.12	.05	.02
☐ 351 Dave Righetti	.04	.02	.01
☐ 352 Pat Dodson	.04	.02	.01
☐ 353 John Habyan	.04	.02	.01
☐ 354 Jim Deshaies	.04	.02	.01
☐ 355 Butch Wynegar	.04	.02	.01
☐ 356 Bryn Smith	.04	.02	.01
☐ 357 Matt Young	.04	.02	.01
☐ 358 Tom Pagnozzi	.25	.11	.03
☐ 359 Floyd Rayford	.04	.02	.01
☐ 360 Darryl Strawberry	.30	.14	.04
☐ 361 Sal Butera	.04	.02	.01
☐ 362 Domingo Ramos	.04	.02	.01
☐ 363 Chris Brown	.04	.02	.01
☐ 364 Jose Gonzalez	.04	.02	.01
☐ 365 Dave Smith	.04	.02	.01
☐ 366 Andy McGaffigan	.04	.02	.01
☐ 367 Stan Javier	.04	.02	.01
☐ 368 Henry Cotto	.04	.02	.01
☐ 369 Mike Birkbeck	.04	.02	.01
☐ 370 Len Dykstra	.07	.03	.01
☐ 371 Dave Collins	.04	.02	.01
☐ 372 Spike Owen	.04	.02	.01
☐ 373 Geno Petralli	.04	.02	.01
☐ 374 Ron Karkovice	.04	.02	.01
☐ 375 Shane Rawley	.04	.02	.01
☐ 376 DeWayne Buice	.04	.02	.01
☐ 377 Bill Pecota	.10	.05	.01
☐ 378 Leon Durham	.04	.02	.01
☐ 379 Ed Olwine	.04	.02	.01
☐ 380 Bruce Hurst	.07	.03	.01
☐ 381 Bob McClure	.04	.02	.01
☐ 382 Mark Thurmond	.04	.02	.01
☐ 383 Buddy Biancalana	.04	.02	.01
☐ 384 Tim Conroy	.04	.02	.01
☐ 385 Tony Gwynn	.30	.14	.04
☐ 386 Greg Gross	.04	.02	.01
☐ 387 Barry Lyons	.04	.02	.01
☐ 388 Mike Felder	.04	.02	.01
☐ 389 Pat Clements	.04	.02	.01
☐ 390 Ken Griffey	.07	.03	.01
☐ 391 Mark Davis	.04	.02	.01
☐ 392 Jose Rijo	.10	.05	.01
☐ 393 Mike Young	.04	.02	.01
☐ 394 Willie Fraser	.04	.02	.01
☐ 395 Dion James	.04	.02	.01
☐ 396 Steve Shields	.04	.02	.01
☐ 397 Randy St.Claire	.04	.02	.01
☐ 398 Danny Jackson	.04	.02	.01
☐ 399 Cecil Fielder	.30	.14	.04
☐ 400 Keith Hernandez	.07	.03	.01
☐ 401 Don Carman	.04	.02	.01

☐ 402	Chuck Crim	.04	.02	.01
☐ 403	Rob Woodward	.04	.02	.01
☐ 404	Junior Ortiz	.04	.02	.01
☐ 405	Glenn Wilson	.04	.02	.01
☐ 406	Ken Howell	.04	.02	.01
☐ 407	Jeff Kunkel	.04	.02	.01
☐ 408	Jeff Reed	.04	.02	.01
☐ 409	Chris James	.04	.02	.01
☐ 410	Zane Smith	.04	.02	.01
☐ 411	Ken Dixon	.04	.02	.01
☐ 412	Ricky Horton	.04	.02	.01
☐ 413	Frank DiPino	.04	.02	.01
☐ 414	Shane Mack	.30	.14	.04
☐ 415	Danny Cox	.04	.02	.01
☐ 416	Andy Van Slyke	.10	.05	.01
☐ 417	Danny Heep	.04	.02	.01
☐ 418	John Cangelosi	.04	.02	.01
☐ 419A	John Christensen ERR (Christiansen on card front)	.12	.05	.02
☐ 419B	John Christensen COR	.04	.02	.01
☐ 420	Joey Cora	.07	.03	.01
☐ 421	Mike LaValliere	.04	.02	.01
☐ 422	Kelly Gruber	.07	.03	.01
☐ 423	Bruce Benedict	.04	.02	.01
☐ 424	Len Matuszek	.04	.02	.01
☐ 425	Kent Tekulve	.04	.02	.01
☐ 426	Rafael Ramirez	.04	.02	.01
☐ 427	Mike Flanagan	.04	.02	.01
☐ 428	Mike Gallego	.04	.02	.01
☐ 429	Juan Castillo	.04	.02	.01
☐ 430	Neal Heaton	.04	.02	.01
☐ 431	Phil Garner	.07	.03	.01
☐ 432	Mike Dunne	.04	.02	.01
☐ 433	Wallace Johnson	.04	.02	.01
☐ 434	Jack O'Connor	.04	.02	.01
☐ 435	Steve Jeltz	.04	.02	.01
☐ 436	Donell Nixon	.04	.02	.01
☐ 437	Jack Lazorko	.04	.02	.01
☐ 438	Keith Comstock	.04	.02	.01
☐ 439	Jeff D. Robinson (Pirates pitcher)	.04	.02	.01
☐ 440	Graig Nettles	.07	.03	.01
☐ 441	Mel Hall	.04	.02	.01
☐ 442	Gerald Young	.04	.02	.01
☐ 443	Gary Redus	.04	.02	.01
☐ 444	Charlie Moore	.04	.02	.01
☐ 445	Bill Madlock	.07	.03	.01
☐ 446	Mark Clear	.04	.02	.01
☐ 447	Greg Booker	.04	.02	.01
☐ 448	Rick Schu	.04	.02	.01
☐ 449	Ron Kittle	.04	.02	.01
☐ 450	Dale Murphy	.10	.05	.01
☐ 451	Bob Dernier	.04	.02	.01
☐ 452	Dale Mohorcic	.04	.02	.01
☐ 453	Rafael Belliard	.04	.02	.01
☐ 454	Charlie Puleo	.04	.02	.01
☐ 455	Dwayne Murphy	.04	.02	.01
☐ 456	Jim Eisenreich	.04	.02	.01
☐ 457	David Palmer	.04	.02	.01
☐ 458	Dave Stewart	.07	.03	.01
☐ 459	Pascual Perez	.04	.02	.01
☐ 460	Glenn Davis	.07	.03	.01
☐ 461	Dan Petry	.04	.02	.01
☐ 462	Jim Winn	.04	.02	.01
☐ 463	Darrell Miller	.04	.02	.01
☐ 464	Mike Moore	.04	.02	.01
☐ 465	Mike LaCoss	.04	.02	.01
☐ 466	Steve Farr	.04	.02	.01
☐ 467	Jerry Mumphrey	.04	.02	.01
☐ 468	Kevin Gross	.04	.02	.01
☐ 469	Bruce Bochy	.04	.02	.01
☐ 470	Orel Hershiser	.07	.03	.01
☐ 471	Eric King	.04	.02	.01
☐ 472	Ellis Burks	.25	.11	.03
☐ 473	Darren Daulton	.07	.03	.01
☐ 474	Mookie Wilson	.07	.03	.01
☐ 475	Frank Viola	.07	.03	.01
☐ 476	Ron Robinson	.04	.02	.01
☐ 477	Bob Melvin	.04	.02	.01
☐ 478	Jeff Musselman	.04	.02	.01
☐ 479	Charlie Kerfeld	.04	.02	.01
☐ 480	Richard Dotson	.04	.02	.01
☐ 481	Kevin Mitchell	.15	.07	.02
☐ 482	Gary Roenicke	.04	.02	.01
☐ 483	Tim Flannery	.04	.02	.01
☐ 484	Rich Yett	.04	.02	.01
☐ 485	Pete Incaviglia	.07	.03	.01
☐ 486	Rick Cerone	.04	.02	.01
☐ 487	Tony Armas	.04	.02	.01
☐ 488	Jerry Reed	.04	.02	.01
☐ 489	Dave Lopes	.07	.03	.01
☐ 490	Frank Tanana	.04	.02	.01

☐ 491	Mike Loynd	.04	.02	.01
☐ 492	Bruce Ruffin	.04	.02	.01
☐ 493	Chris Speier	.04	.02	.01
☐ 494	Tom Hume	.04	.02	.01
☐ 495	Jesse Orosco	.04	.02	.01
☐ 496	Robbie Wine UER (Misspelled Robby on card front)	.04	.02	.01
☐ 497	Jeff Montgomery	.35	.16	.04
☐ 498	Jeff Dedmon	.04	.02	.01
☐ 499	Luis Aguayo	.04	.02	.01
☐ 500	Reggie Jackson (Oakland A's)	.30	.14	.04
☐ 501	Reggie Jackson (Baltimore Orioles)	.30	.14	.04
☐ 502	Reggie Jackson (New York Yankees)	.30	.14	.04
☐ 503	Reggie Jackson (California Angels)	.30	.14	.04
☐ 504	Reggie Jackson (Oakland A's)	.30	.14	.04
☐ 505	Billy Hatcher	.04	.02	.01
☐ 506	Ed Lynch	.04	.02	.01
☐ 507	Willie Hernandez	.04	.02	.01
☐ 508	Jose DeLeon	.04	.02	.01
☐ 509	Joel Youngblood	.04	.02	.01
☐ 510	Bob Welch	.07	.03	.01
☐ 511	Steve Ontiveros	.04	.02	.01
☐ 512	Randy Ready	.04	.02	.01
☐ 513	Juan Nieves	.04	.02	.01
☐ 514	Jeff Russell	.04	.02	.01
☐ 515	Von Hayes	.04	.02	.01
☐ 516	Mark Gubicza	.04	.02	.01
☐ 517	Ken Dayley	.04	.02	.01
☐ 518	Don Aase	.04	.02	.01
☐ 519	Rick Reuschel	.04	.02	.01
☐ 520	Mike Henneman	.15	.07	.02
☐ 521	Rick Aguilera	.07	.03	.01
☐ 522	Jay Howell	.04	.02	.01
☐ 523	Ed Correa	.04	.02	.01
☐ 524	Manny Trillo	.04	.02	.01
☐ 525	Kirk Gibson	.07	.03	.01
☐ 526	Wally Ritchie	.04	.02	.01
☐ 527	Al Nipper	.04	.02	.01
☐ 528	Atlee Hammaker	.04	.02	.01
☐ 529	Shawon Dunston	.07	.03	.01
☐ 530	Jim Clancy	.04	.02	.01
☐ 531	Tom Paciorek	.07	.03	.01
☐ 532	Joel Skinner	.04	.02	.01
☐ 533	Scott Garrelts	.04	.02	.01
☐ 534	Tom O'Malley	.04	.02	.01
☐ 535	John Franco	.07	.03	.01
☐ 536	Paul Kilgus	.04	.02	.01
☐ 537	Darrell Porter	.04	.02	.01
☐ 538	Walt Terrell	.04	.02	.01
☐ 539	Bill Long	.04	.02	.01
☐ 540	George Bell	.10	.05	.01
☐ 541	Jeff Sellers	.04	.02	.01
☐ 542	Joe Boever	.04	.02	.01
☐ 543	Steve Howe	.04	.02	.01
☐ 544	Scott Sanderson	.04	.02	.01
☐ 545	Jack Morris	.12	.05	.02
☐ 546	Todd Benzinger	.10	.05	.01
☐ 547	Steve Henderson	.04	.02	.01
☐ 548	Eddie Milner	.04	.02	.01
☐ 549	Jeff M. Robinson	.04	.02	.01
☐ 550	Cal Ripken	.60	.25	.08
☐ 551	Jody Davis	.04	.02	.01
☐ 552	Kirk McCaskill	.04	.02	.01
☐ 553	Craig Lefferts	.04	.02	.01
☐ 554	Darnell Coles	.04	.02	.01
☐ 555	Phil Niekro	.15	.07	.02
☐ 556	Mike Aldrete	.04	.02	.01
☐ 557	Pat Perry	.04	.02	.01
☐ 558	Juan Agosto	.04	.02	.01
☐ 559	Rob Murphy	.04	.02	.01
☐ 560	Dennis Rasmussen	.04	.02	.01
☐ 561	Manny Lee	.04	.02	.01
☐ 562	Jeff Blauser	.25	.11	.03
☐ 563	Bob Ojeda	.04	.02	.01
☐ 564	Dave Dravecky	.07	.03	.01
☐ 565	Gene Garber	.04	.02	.01
☐ 566	Ron Roenicke	.04	.02	.01
☐ 567	Tommy Hinzo	.04	.02	.01
☐ 568	Eric Nolte	.04	.02	.01
☐ 569	Ed Hearn	.04	.02	.01
☐ 570	Mark Davidson	.04	.02	.01
☐ 571	Jim Walewander	.04	.02	.01
☐ 572	Donnie Hill	.04	.02	.01
☐ 573	Jamie Moyer	.04	.02	.01
☐ 574	Ken Schrom	.04	.02	.01
☐ 575	Nolan Ryan	.75	.35	.09
☐ 576	Jim Acker	.04	.02	.01

☐ 577 Jamie Quirk .04 .02 .01
☐ 578 Jay Aldrich .04 .02 .01
☐ 579 Claudell Washington .04 .02 .01
☐ 580 Jeff Leonard .04 .02 .01
☐ 581 Carmen Castillo .04 .02 .01
☐ 582 Daryl Boston .04 .02 .01
☐ 583 Jeff DeWillis .04 .02 .01
☐ 584 John Marzano .04 .02 .01
☐ 585 Bill Gullickson .04 .02 .01
☐ 586 Andy Allanson .04 .02 .01
☐ 587 Lee Tunnell UER .04 .02 .01
(1987 stat line
reads .4.84 ERA)
☐ 588 Gene Nelson .04 .02 .01
☐ 589 Dave LaPoint .04 .02 .01
☐ 590 Harold Baines .07 .03 .01
☐ 591 Bill Buckner .07 .03 .01
☐ 592 Carlton Fisk .20 .09 .03
☐ 593 Rick Manning .04 .02 .01
☐ 594 Doug Jones .25 .11 .03
☐ 595 Tom Candiotti .04 .02 .01
☐ 596 Steve Lake .04 .02 .01
☐ 597 Jose Lind .15 .07 .02
☐ 598 Ross Jones .04 .02 .01
☐ 599 Gary Matthews .04 .02 .01
☐ 600 Fernando Valenzuela .07 .03 .01
☐ 601 Dennis Martinez .07 .03 .01
☐ 602 Les Lancaster .04 .02 .01
☐ 603 Ozzie Guillen .07 .03 .01
☐ 604 Tony Bernazard .04 .02 .01
☐ 605 Chili Davis .07 .03 .01
☐ 606 Roy Smalley .04 .02 .01
☐ 607 Ivan Calderon .07 .03 .01
☐ 608 Jay Tibbs .04 .02 .01
☐ 609 Guy Hoffman .04 .02 .01
☐ 610 Doyle Alexander .04 .02 .01
☐ 611 Mike Bielecki .04 .02 .01
☐ 612 Shawn Hillegas .04 .02 .01
☐ 613 Keith Atherton .04 .02 .01
☐ 614 Eric Plunk .04 .02 .01
☐ 615 Sid Fernandez .07 .03 .01
☐ 616 Dennis Lamp .04 .02 .01
☐ 617 Dave Engle .04 .02 .01
☐ 618 Harry Spilman .04 .02 .01
☐ 619 Don Robinson .04 .02 .01
☐ 620 John Farrell .04 .02 .01
☐ 621 Nelson Liriano .04 .02 .01
☐ 622 Floyd Bannister .04 .02 .01
☐ 623 Randy Milligan .25 .11 .03
☐ 624 Kevin Elster .05 .02 .01
☐ 625 Jody Reed .25 .11 .03
☐ 626 Shawn Abner .05 .02 .01
☐ 627 Kirt Manwaring .10 .05 .01
☐ 628 Pete Stanicek .05 .02 .01
☐ 629 Rob Ducey .05 .02 .01
☐ 630 Steve Kiefer .05 .02 .01
☐ 631 Gary Thurman .05 .02 .01
☐ 632 Darrel Akerfelds .05 .02 .01
☐ 633 Dave Clark .05 .02 .01
☐ 634 Roberto Kelly .90 .40 .11
☐ 635 Keith Hughes .05 .02 .01
☐ 636 John Davis .05 .02 .01
☐ 637 Mike Devereaux .90 .40 .11
☐ 638 Tom Glavine 2.25 1.00 .30
☐ 639 Keith A. Miller .20 .09 .03
☐ 640 Chris Gwynn UER .12 .05 .02
(Wrong batting and
throwing on back)
☐ 641 Tim Crews .05 .02 .01
☐ 642 Mackey Sasser .10 .05 .01
☐ 643 Vicente Palacios .10 .05 .01
☐ 644 Kevin Romine .05 .02 .01
☐ 645 Gregg Jefferies 1.00 .45 .13
☐ 646 Jeff Treadway .10 .05 .01
☐ 647 Ron Gant 1.50 .65 .19
☐ 648 Mark McGwire and .20 .09 .03
Matt Nokes
(Rookie Sluggers)
☐ 649 Eric Davis and .08 .04 .01
Tim Raines
(Speed and Power)
☐ 650 Don Mattingly and .10 .05 .01
Jack Clark
☐ 651 Tony Fernandez, .20 .09 .03
Alan Trammell, and
Cal Ripken
☐ 652 Vince Coleman HL .05 .02 .01
100 Stolen Bases
☐ 653 Kirby Puckett HL .20 .09 .03
10 Hits in a Row
☐ 654 Benito Santiago HL .05 .02 .01
Hitting Streak
☐ 655 Juan Nieves HL .05 .02 .01
No Hitter
☐ 656 Steve Bedrosian HL .05 .02 .01
Saves Record
☐ 657 Mike Schmidt HL .20 .09 .03
500 Homers
☐ 658 Don Mattingly HL .15 .07 .02
Home Run Streak
☐ 659 Mark McGwire HL .25 .11 .03
Rookie HR Record
☐ 660 Paul Molitor HL .08 .04 .01
Hitting Streak

1988 Score Box Bottoms

There are six different wax box bottom panels each featuring three players and a trivia (related to a particular stadium for a given year) question. The players and trivia question cards are individually numbered. The trivia are numbered below with the prefix T in order to avoid confusion. The trivia cards are very unpopular with collectors since they do not picture any players. When panels of four are cut into individuals, the cards are standard size, 2/1/2" by 3 1/2". The card backs of the players feature the respective League logos most prominently.

	MT	EX-MT	VG
COMPLETE SET (24)	7.50	3.40	.95
COMMON PLAYER (1-18)	.15	.07	.02
COMMON TRIVIA (T1-T6)	.05	.02	.01
☐ 1 Terry Kennedy	.15	.07	.02
☐ 2 Don Mattingly	.75	.35	.09
☐ 3 Willie Randolph	.15	.07	.02
☐ 4 Wade Boggs	.75	.35	.09
☐ 5 Cal Ripken	1.00	.45	.13
☐ 6 George Bell	.25	.11	.03
☐ 7 Rickey Henderson	.75	.35	.09
☐ 8 Dave Winfield	.60	.25	.08
☐ 9 Bret Saberhagen	.25	.11	.03
☐ 10 Gary Carter	.25	.11	.03
☐ 11 Jack Clark	.15	.07	.02
☐ 12 Ryne Sandberg	.90	.40	.11
☐ 13 Mike Schmidt	.75	.35	.09
☐ 14 Ozzie Smith	.40	.18	.05
☐ 15 Eric Davis	.30	.14	.04
☐ 16 Andre Dawson	.40	.18	.05
☐ 17 Darryl Strawberry	.75	.35	.09
☐ 18 Mike Scott	.15	.07	.02
☐ T1 Fenway Park '60 Ted (Williams) Hits To The End	.10	.05	.01
☐ T2 Comiskey Park '83 Grand Slam (Fred Lynn) Breaks Jinx	.05	.02	.01
☐ T3 Anaheim Stadium '87 Old Rookie Record Falls (Mark McGwire)	.15	.07	.02
☐ T4 Wrigley Field '38 Gabby (Hartnett) Gets Pennant Homer	.05	.02	.01
☐ T5 Comiskey Park '50 Red (Schoendienst) Rips Winning HR	.05	.02	.01
☐ T6 County Stadium '87 Rookie (John Farrell) Stops Hit Streak (Paul Molitor)	.05	.02	.01

1988 Score Rookie/Traded

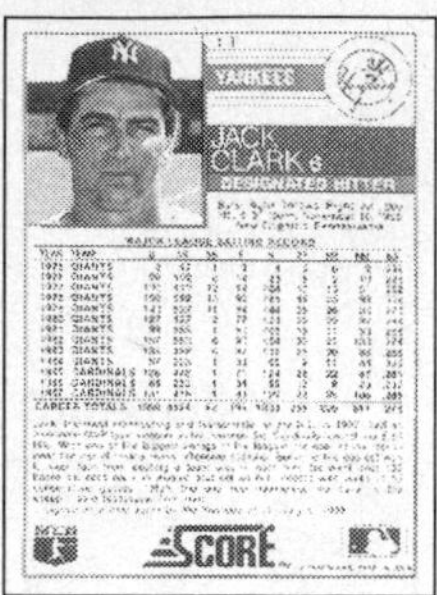

This 110-card set featured traded players (1-65) and rookies (66-110) for the 1988 season. The cards are distinguishable from the regular Score set by the orange borders and by the fact that the numbering on the back has a T suffix. The cards are standard size, 2 1/2" by 3 1/2", and were distributed by Score as a collated set in a special collector box along with some trivia cards. Score also produced a limited "glossy" Rookie and Traded set, that is valued at two to three times the value of the regular (non-glossy) set. It should be noted that the set itself (non-glossy) is now considered somewhat scarce. Apparently Score's first attempt at a Rookie/Traded set was produced very conservatively, resulting in a set which is now recognized as being much tougher to find than the other Rookie/Traded sets from the other major companies of that year. The key (extended) Rookie Cards in this set are Roberto Alomar, Brady Anderson, Craig Biggio, Jay Buhner, Rob Dibble, Mark Grace, Bryan Harvey, Jack McDowell, Melido Perez, Chris Sabo, Todd Stottlemyre, and Walt Weiss.

	MT	EX-MT	VG
COMPLETE SET (110)	90.00	40.00	11.50
COMMON PLAYER (1T-65T)	.15	.07	.02
COMMON PLAYER (66T-110T)	.15	.07	.02
☐ 1T Jack Clark	.25	.11	.03
☐ 2T Danny Jackson	.15	.07	.02
☐ 3T Brett Butler	.40	.18	.05
☐ 4T Kurt Stillwell	.15	.07	.02
☐ 5T Tom Brunansky	.25	.11	.03
☐ 6T Dennis Lamp	.15	.07	.02
☐ 7T Jose DeLeon	.15	.07	.02
☐ 8T Tom Herr	.15	.07	.02
☐ 9T Keith Moreland	.15	.07	.02
☐ 10T Kirk Gibson	.25	.11	.03
☐ 11T Bud Black	.15	.07	.02
☐ 12T Rafael Ramirez	.15	.07	.02
☐ 13T Luis Salazar	.15	.07	.02
☐ 14T Goose Gossage	.25	.11	.03
☐ 15T Bob Welch	.25	.11	.03
☐ 16T Vance Law	.15	.07	.02
☐ 17T Ray Knight	.25	.11	.03
☐ 18T Dan Quisenberry	.25	.11	.03
☐ 19T Don Slaught	.15	.07	.02
☐ 20T Lee Smith	1.00	.45	.13
☐ 21T Rick Cerone	.15	.07	.02
☐ 22T Pat Tabler	.15	.07	.02
☐ 23T Larry McWilliams	.15	.07	.02
☐ 24T Ricky Horton	.15	.07	.02
☐ 25T Graig Nettles	.25	.11	.03
☐ 26T Dan Petry	.15	.07	.02
☐ 27T Jose Rijo	.40	.18	.05
☐ 28T Chili Davis	.25	.11	.03
☐ 29T Dickie Thon	.15	.07	.02
☐ 30T Mackey Sasser	.25	.11	.03
☐ 31T Mickey Tettleton	.40	.18	.05
☐ 32T Rick Dempsey	.15	.07	.02
☐ 33T Ron Hassey	.15	.07	.02
☐ 34T Phil Bradley	.15	.07	.02
☐ 35T Jay Howell	.15	.07	.02
☐ 36T Bill Buckner	.25	.11	.03
☐ 37T Alfredo Griffin	.15	.07	.02
☐ 38T Gary Pettis	.15	.07	.02
☐ 39T Calvin Schiraldi	.15	.07	.02
☐ 40T John Candelaria	.15	.07	.02
☐ 41T Joe Orsulak	.15	.07	.02
☐ 42T Willie Upshaw	.15	.07	.02
☐ 43T Herm Winningham	.15	.07	.02
☐ 44T Ron Kittle	.15	.07	.02
☐ 45T Bob Dernier	.15	.07	.02
☐ 46T Steve Balboni	.15	.07	.02
☐ 47T Steve Shields	.15	.07	.02
☐ 48T Henry Cotto	.15	.07	.02
☐ 49T Dave Henderson	.25	.11	.03
☐ 50T Dave Parker	.25	.11	.03
☐ 51T Mike Young	.15	.07	.02
☐ 52T Mark Salas	.15	.07	.02
☐ 53T Mike Davis	.15	.07	.02
☐ 54T Rafael Santana	.15	.07	.02
☐ 55T Don Baylor	.25	.11	.03
☐ 56T Dan Pasqua	.15	.07	.02
☐ 57T Ernest Riles	.15	.07	.02
☐ 58T Glenn Hubbard	.15	.07	.02
☐ 59T Mike Smithson	.15	.07	.02
☐ 60T Richard Dotson	.15	.07	.02
☐ 61T Jerry Reuss	.15	.07	.02
☐ 62T Mike Jackson	.15	.07	.02
☐ 63T Floyd Bannister	.15	.07	.02
☐ 64T Jesse Orosco	.15	.07	.02
☐ 65T Larry Parrish	.15	.07	.02
☐ 66T Jeff Bittiger	.15	.07	.02
☐ 67T Ray Hayward	.15	.07	.02
☐ 68T Ricky Jordan	.50	.23	.06
☐ 69T Tommy Gregg	.15	.07	.02
☐ 70T Brady Anderson	8.00	3.60	1.00
☐ 71T Jeff Montgomery	.50	.23	.06
☐ 72T Darryl Hamilton	1.50	.65	.19
☐ 73T Cecil Espy	.30	.14	.04
☐ 74T Greg Briley	.30	.14	.04
☐ 75T Joey Meyer	.15	.07	.02
☐ 76T Mike Macfarlane	1.50	.65	.19
☐ 77T Oswald Peraza	.15	.07	.02
☐ 78T Jack Armstrong	.60	.25	.08
☐ 79T Don Heinkel	.15	.07	.02
☐ 80T Mark Grace	15.00	6.75	1.90
☐ 81T Steve Curry	.15	.07	.02
☐ 82T Damon Berryhill	.60	.25	.08
☐ 83T Steve Ellsworth	.15	.07	.02
☐ 84T Pete Smith	2.50	1.15	.30
☐ 85T Jack McDowell	15.00	6.75	1.90
☐ 86T Rob Dibble	2.50	1.15	.30
☐ 87T Bryan Harvey	2.00	.90	.25
☐ 88T John Dopson	.15	.07	.02
☐ 89T Dave Gallagher	.15	.07	.02
☐ 90T Todd Stottlemyre	2.00	.90	.25
☐ 91T Mike Schooler	.50	.23	.06
☐ 92T Don Gordon	.15	.07	.02
☐ 93T Sil Campusano	.15	.07	.02
☐ 94T Jeff Pico	.15	.07	.02
☐ 95T Jay Buhner	3.00	1.35	.40
☐ 96T Nelson Santovenia	.15	.07	.02
☐ 97T Al Leiter	.15	.07	.02
☐ 98T Luis Alicea	.35	.16	.04
☐ 99T Pat Borders	3.00	1.35	.40
☐ 100T Chris Sabo	3.50	1.55	.45
☐ 101T Tim Belcher	.60	.25	.08
☐ 102T Walt Weiss	.60	.25	.08
☐ 103T Craig Biggio	5.50	2.50	.70
☐ 104T Don August	.15	.07	.02
☐ 105T Roberto Alomar	60.00	27.00	7.50
☐ 106T Todd Burns	.15	.07	.02
☐ 107T John Costello	.15	.07	.02
☐ 108T Melido Perez	2.00	.90	.25
☐ 109T Darrin Jackson	2.00	.90	.25
☐ 110T Orestes Destrade	.90	.40	.11

1988 Score Young Superstars I

This attractive high-gloss 40-card set of "Young Superstars" was distributed in a small blue box which had the checklist of the set on a side panel of the box. The cards were also distributed as an insert, one per rak pak. These attractive cards are in full color on the front and also have a full-color small portrait on the card back. The cards are standard size, 2 1/2" by 3 1/2". The cards in this series are distinguishable from the cards in Series II by the fact that this series has a blue and green border on the card front instead of the (Series II) blue and pink border.

	MT	EX-MT	VG
COMPLETE SET (40)	8.00	3.60	1.00
COMMON PLAYER (1-40)	.20	.09	.03
☐ 1 Mark McGwire	.75	.35	.09
☐ 2 Benito Santiago	.40	.18	.05
☐ 3 Sam Horn	.20	.09	.03
☐ 4 Chris Bosio	.30	.14	.04
☐ 5 Matt Nokes	.30	.14	.04
☐ 6 Ken Williams	.20	.09	.03
☐ 7 Dion James	.20	.09	.03
☐ 8 B.J. Surhoff	.30	.14	.04
☐ 9 Joe Magrane	.20	.09	.03
☐ 10 Kevin Seitzer	.30	.14	.04
☐ 11 Stanley Jefferson	.20	.09	.03
☐ 12 Devon White	.30	.14	.04
☐ 13 Nelson Liriano	.20	.09	.03
☐ 14 Chris James	.20	.09	.03
☐ 15 Mike Henneman	.30	.14	.04
☐ 16 Terry Steinbach	.30	.14	.04
☐ 17 John Kruk	.40	.18	.05
☐ 18 Matt Williams	.90	.40	.11
☐ 19 Kelly Downs	.20	.09	.03
☐ 20 Bill Ripken	.20	.09	.03
☐ 21 Ozzie Guillen	.20	.09	.03
☐ 22 Luis Polonia	.30	.14	.04
☐ 23 Dave Magadan	.20	.09	.03
☐ 24 Mike Greenwell	.50	.23	.06
☐ 25 Will Clark	1.00	.45	.13
☐ 26 Mike Dunne	.20	.09	.03
☐ 27 Wally Joyner	.30	.14	.04
☐ 28 Robby Thompson	.20	.09	.03
☐ 29 Ken Caminiti	.40	.18	.05
☐ 30 Jose Canseco	1.00	.45	.13
☐ 31 Todd Benzinger	.20	.09	.03
☐ 32 Pete Incaviglia	.20	.09	.03
☐ 33 John Farrell	.20	.09	.03
☐ 34 Casey Candaele	.20	.09	.03
☐ 35 Mike Aldrete	.20	.09	.03
☐ 36 Ruben Sierra	.75	.35	.09
☐ 37 Ellis Burks	.50	.23	.06
☐ 38 Tracy Jones	.20	.09	.03
☐ 39 Kal Daniels	.20	.09	.03
☐ 40 Cory Snyder	.20	.09	.03

1988 Score Young Superstars II

This attractive high-gloss 40-card set of "Young Superstars" was distributed in a small purple box which had the checklist of the set on a side panel of the box. The cards were not distributed as an insert with rak paks as the first series was, but were only available as a complete set from hobby dealers or through a mail-in offer direct from the company. These attractive cards are in full color on the front and also have a full-color small portrait on the card back. The cards are standard size, 2 1/2" by 3 1/2". The cards in this series are distinguishable from the cards in Series I by the fact that this series has a blue and pink border on the card front instead of the (Series I) blue and green border.

	MT	EX-MT	VG
COMPLETE SET (40)	7.00	3.10	.85
COMMON PLAYER (1-40)	.20	.09	.03
☐ 1 Don Mattingly	.75	.35	.09
☐ 2 Glenn Braggs	.20	.09	.03
☐ 3 Dwight Gooden	.40	.18	.05
☐ 4 Jose Lind	.30	.14	.04
☐ 5 Danny Tartabull	.50	.23	.06
☐ 6 Tony Fernandez	.20	.09	.03
☐ 7 Julio Franco	.30	.14	.04
☐ 8 Andres Galarraga	.20	.09	.03
☐ 9 Bobby Bonilla	.50	.23	.06
☐ 10 Eric Davis	.40	.18	.05
☐ 11 Gerald Young	.20	.09	.03
☐ 12 Barry Bonds	.75	.35	.09
☐ 13 Jerry Browne	.30	.14	.04
☐ 14 Jeff Blauser	.30	.14	.04
☐ 15 Mickey Brantley	.20	.09	.03
☐ 16 Floyd Youmans	.20	.09	.03
☐ 17 Bret Saberhagen	.30	.14	.04
☐ 18 Shawon Dunston	.30	.14	.04
☐ 19 Len Dykstra	.30	.14	.04
☐ 20 Darryl Strawberry	.75	.35	.09
☐ 21 Rick Aguilera	.30	.14	.04
☐ 22 Ivan Calderon	.20	.09	.03
☐ 23 Roger Clemens	1.00	.45	.13
☐ 24 Vince Coleman	.30	.14	.04
☐ 25 Gary Thurman	.20	.09	.03
☐ 26 Jeff Treadway	.20	.09	.03
☐ 27 Oddibe McDowell	.20	.09	.03
☐ 28 Fred McGriff	.60	.25	.08
☐ 29 Mark McLemore	.20	.09	.03
☐ 30 Jeff Musselman	.20	.09	.03
☐ 31 Matt Williams	.75	.35	.09
☐ 32 Dan Plesac	.20	.09	.03
☐ 33 Juan Nieves	.20	.09	.03
☐ 34 Barry Larkin	.50	.23	.06
☐ 35 Greg Mathews	.20	.09	.03
☐ 36 Shane Mack	.40	.18	.05
☐ 37 Scott Bankhead	.30	.14	.04
☐ 38 Eric Bell	.20	.09	.03
☐ 39 Greg Swindell	.30	.14	.04
☐ 40 Kevin Elster	.20	.09	.03

1989 Score

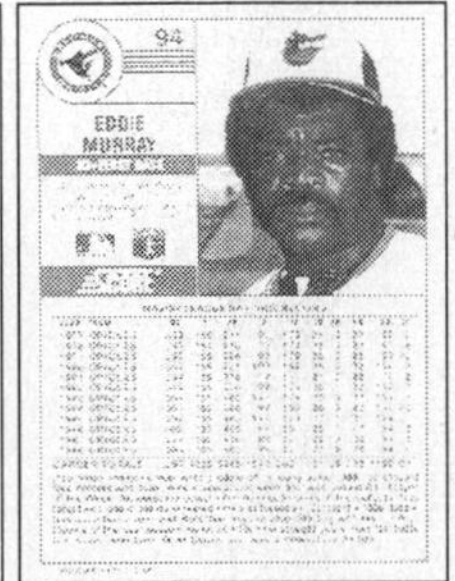

This 660-card set was distributed by Major League Marketing. Cards measure 2 1/2" by 3 1/2" and feature six distinctive inner border (inside a white outer border) colors on the front. Highlights (652-660) and Rookie Prospects (621-651) are included in the set. The set is distinguished by the fact that each card back shows a full-color picture (portrait) of the player. Score "missed" many of the mid-season and later trades; there are numerous examples of inconsistency with regard to the treatment of these players. Study as examples of this inconsistency of handling of late trades, cards numbered 49, 71, 77, 83, 106, 126, 139, 145, 173, 177, 242, 348, 384, 420, 439, 488, 494, and 525. The key Rookie Cards in this set are Sandy Alomar Jr., Felix Jose, Ramon Martinez, Gary Sheffield, and John Smoltz.

	MT	EX-MT	VG
COMPLETE SET (660)	20.00	9.00	2.50
COMPLETE FACT.SET (660)	20.00	9.00	2.50
COMMON PLAYER (1-660)	.04	.02	.01
☐ 1 Jose Canseco	.40	.18	.05
☐ 2 Andre Dawson	.15	.07	.02
☐ 3 Mark McGwire UER	.40	.18	.05
(Bio says 116 RBI's, should be 118)			
☐ 4 Benito Santiago	.07	.03	.01
☐ 5 Rick Reuschel	.04	.02	.01
☐ 6 Fred McGriff	.25	.11	.03
☐ 7 Kal Daniels	.07	.03	.01
☐ 8 Gary Gaetti	.04	.02	.01
☐ 9 Ellis Burks	.07	.03	.01
☐ 10 Darryl Strawberry	.25	.11	.03
☐ 11 Julio Franco	.07	.03	.01
☐ 12 Lloyd Moseby	.04	.02	.01
☐ 13 Jeff Pico	.04	.02	.01
☐ 14 Johnny Ray	.04	.02	.01
☐ 15 Cal Ripken	.50	.23	.06
☐ 16 Dick Schofield	.04	.02	.01
☐ 17 Mel Hall	.04	.02	.01
☐ 18 Bill Ripken	.04	.02	.01
☐ 19 Brook Jacoby	.04	.02	.01
☐ 20 Kirby Puckett	.40	.18	.05
☐ 21 Bill Doran	.04	.02	.01
☐ 22 Pete O'Brien	.04	.02	.01
☐ 23 Matt Nokes	.07	.03	.01
☐ 24 Brian Fisher	.04	.02	.01
☐ 25 Jack Clark	.07	.03	.01
☐ 26 Gary Pettis	.04	.02	.01
☐ 27 Dave Valle	.04	.02	.01
☐ 28 Willie Wilson	.04	.02	.01
☐ 29 Curt Young	.04	.02	.01
☐ 30 Dale Murphy	.10	.05	.01
☐ 31 Barry Larkin	.15	.07	.02
☐ 32 Dave Stewart	.07	.03	.01
☐ 33 Mike LaValliere	.04	.02	.01
☐ 34 Glenn Hubbard	.04	.02	.01
☐ 35 Ryne Sandberg	.40	.18	.05
☐ 36 Tony Pena	.04	.02	.01
☐ 37 Greg Walker	.04	.02	.01
☐ 38 Von Hayes	.04	.02	.01
☐ 39 Kevin Mitchell	.10	.05	.01
☐ 40 Tim Raines	.07	.03	.01
☐ 41 Keith Hernandez	.07	.03	.01
☐ 42 Keith Moreland	.04	.02	.01
☐ 43 Ruben Sierra	.30	.14	.04
☐ 44 Chet Lemon	.04	.02	.01
☐ 45 Willie Randolph	.07	.03	.01
☐ 46 Andy Allanson	.04	.02	.01
☐ 47 Candy Maldonado	.04	.02	.01
☐ 48 Sid Bream	.04	.02	.01
☐ 49 Denny Walling	.04	.02	.01
☐ 50 Dave Winfield	.20	.09	.03
☐ 51 Alvin Davis	.04	.02	.01
☐ 52 Cory Snyder	.04	.02	.01
☐ 53 Hubie Brooks	.04	.02	.01
☐ 54 Chili Davis	.07	.03	.01
☐ 55 Kevin Seitzer	.07	.03	.01
☐ 56 Jose Uribe	.04	.02	.01
☐ 57 Tony Fernandez	.07	.03	.01
☐ 58 Tim Teufel	.04	.02	.01
☐ 59 Oddibe McDowell	.04	.02	.01
☐ 60 Les Lancaster	.04	.02	.01
☐ 61 Billy Hatcher	.04	.02	.01
☐ 62 Dan Gladden	.04	.02	.01
☐ 63 Marty Barrett	.04	.02	.01
☐ 64 Nick Esasky	.04	.02	.01
☐ 65 Wally Joyner	.08	.04	.01
☐ 66 Mike Greenwell	.07	.03	.01
☐ 67 Ken Williams	.04	.02	.01
☐ 68 Bob Horner	.04	.02	.01
☐ 69 Steve Sax	.07	.03	.01
☐ 70 Rickey Henderson	.25	.11	.03
☐ 71 Mitch Webster	.04	.02	.01
☐ 72 Rob Deer	.07	.03	.01
☐ 73 Jim Presley	.04	.02	.01
☐ 74 Albert Hall	.04	.02	.01
☐ 75A George Brett ERR	.75	.35	.09
(At age 33)			
☐ 75B George Brett COR	.20	.09	.03
(At age 35)			
☐ 76 Brian Downing	.04	.02	.01
☐ 77 Dave Martinez	.07	.03	.01
☐ 78 Scott Fletcher	.04	.02	.01
☐ 79 Phil Bradley	.04	.02	.01
☐ 80 Ozzie Smith	.15	.07	.02
☐ 81 Larry Sheets	.04	.02	.01
☐ 82 Mike Aldrete	.04	.02	.01
☐ 83 Darnell Coles	.04	.02	.01
☐ 84 Len Dykstra	.07	.03	.01
☐ 85 Jim Rice	.07	.03	.01
☐ 86 Jeff Treadway	.04	.02	.01
☐ 87 Jose Lind	.04	.02	.01
☐ 88 Willie McGee	.07	.03	.01
☐ 89 Mickey Brantley	.04	.02	.01
☐ 90 Tony Gwynn	.25	.11	.03
☐ 91 R.J. Reynolds	.04	.02	.01
☐ 92 Milt Thompson	.04	.02	.01
☐ 93 Kevin McReynolds	.07	.03	.01
☐ 94 Eddie Murray UER	.15	.07	.02
('86 batting .205, should be .305)			
☐ 95 Lance Parrish	.07	.03	.01
☐ 96 Ron Kittle	.04	.02	.01
☐ 97 Gerald Young	.04	.02	.01
☐ 98 Ernie Whitt	.04	.02	.01
☐ 99 Jeff Reed	.04	.02	.01
☐ 100 Don Mattingly	.25	.11	.03
☐ 101 Gerald Perry	.04	.02	.01
☐ 102 Vance Law	.04	.02	.01
☐ 103 John Shelby	.04	.02	.01
☐ 104 Chris Sabo	.30	.14	.04
☐ 105 Danny Tartabull	.12	.05	.02
☐ 106 Glenn Wilson	.04	.02	.01
☐ 107 Mark Davidson	.04	.02	.01
☐ 108 Dave Parker	.07	.03	.01
☐ 109 Eric Davis	.12	.05	.02
☐ 110 Alan Trammell	.07	.03	.01
☐ 111 Ozzie Virgil	.04	.02	.01
☐ 112 Frank Tanana	.04	.02	.01
☐ 113 Rafael Ramirez	.04	.02	.01
☐ 114 Dennis Martinez	.07	.03	.01
☐ 115 Jose DeLeon	.04	.02	.01
☐ 116 Bob Ojeda	.04	.02	.01
☐ 117 Doug Drabek	.07	.03	.01
☐ 118 Andy Hawkins	.04	.02	.01
☐ 119 Greg Maddux	.30	.14	.04
☐ 120 Cecil Fielder UER	.25	.11	.03
(Photo on back reversed)			
☐ 121 Mike Scioscia	.04	.02	.01
☐ 122 Dan Petry	.04	.02	.01
☐ 123 Terry Kennedy	.04	.02	.01
☐ 124 Kelly Downs	.04	.02	.01
☐ 125 Greg Gross UER	.04	.02	.01
(Gregg on back)			
☐ 126 Fred Lynn	.07	.03	.01
☐ 127 Barry Bonds	.40	.18	.05
☐ 128 Harold Baines	.07	.03	.01
☐ 129 Doyle Alexander	.04	.02	.01
☐ 130 Kevin Elster	.04	.02	.01
☐ 131 Mike Heath	.04	.02	.01
☐ 132 Teddy Higuera	.04	.02	.01
☐ 133 Charlie Leibrandt	.04	.02	.01
☐ 134 Tim Laudner	.04	.02	.01
☐ 135A Ray Knight ERR	.60	.25	.08
(Reverse negative)			
☐ 135B Ray Knight COR	.15	.07	.02
☐ 136 Howard Johnson	.07	.03	.01
☐ 137 Terry Pendleton	.12	.05	.02
☐ 138 Andy McGaffigan	.04	.02	.01
☐ 139 Ken Oberkfell	.04	.02	.01
☐ 140 Butch Wynegar	.04	.02	.01
☐ 141 Rob Murphy	.04	.02	.01
☐ 142 Rich Renteria	.04	.02	.01
☐ 143 Jose Guzman	.07	.03	.01
☐ 144 Andres Galarraga	.04	.02	.01
☐ 145 Ricky Horton	.04	.02	.01
☐ 146 Frank DiPino	.04	.02	.01
☐ 147 Glenn Braggs	.04	.02	.01
☐ 148 John Kruk	.07	.03	.01
☐ 149 Mike Schmidt	.40	.18	.05
☐ 150 Lee Smith	.07	.03	.01
☐ 151 Robin Yount	.20	.09	.03
☐ 152 Mark Eichhorn	.04	.02	.01
☐ 153 DeWayne Buice	.04	.02	.01
☐ 154 B.J. Surhoff	.04	.02	.01
☐ 155 Vince Coleman	.07	.03	.01
☐ 156 Tony Phillips	.04	.02	.01
☐ 157 Willie Fraser	.04	.02	.01
☐ 158 Lance McCullers	.04	.02	.01
☐ 159 Greg Gagne	.04	.02	.01

☐ 160	Jesse Barfield	.04	.02	.01
☐ 161	Mark Langston	.07	.03	.01
☐ 162	Kurt Stillwell	.04	.02	.01
☐ 163	Dion James	.04	.02	.01
☐ 164	Glenn Davis	.07	.03	.01
☐ 165	Walt Weiss	.07	.03	.01
☐ 166	Dave Concepcion	.07	.03	.01
☐ 167	Alfredo Griffin	.04	.02	.01
☐ 168	Don Heinkel	.04	.02	.01
☐ 169	Luis Rivera	.04	.02	.01
☐ 170	Shane Rawley	.04	.02	.01
☐ 171	Darrell Evans	.07	.03	.01
☐ 172	Robby Thompson	.04	.02	.01
☐ 173	Jody Davis	.04	.02	.01
☐ 174	Andy Van Slyke	.10	.05	.01
☐ 175	Wade Boggs UER (Bio says .364, should be .356)	.25	.11	.03
☐ 176	Garry Templeton ('85 stats off-centered)	.04	.02	.01
☐ 177	Gary Redus	.04	.02	.01
☐ 178	Craig Lefferts	.04	.02	.01
☐ 179	Carney Lansford	.07	.03	.01
☐ 180	Ron Darling	.07	.03	.01
☐ 181	Kirk McCaskill	.04	.02	.01
☐ 182	Tony Armas	.04	.02	.01
☐ 183	Steve Farr	.04	.02	.01
☐ 184	Tom Brunansky	.07	.03	.01
☐ 185	Bryan Harvey UER ('87 games 47, should be 3)	.25	.11	.03
☐ 186	Mike Marshall	.04	.02	.01
☐ 187	Bo Diaz	.04	.02	.01
☐ 188	Willie Upshaw	.04	.02	.01
☐ 189	Mike Pagliarulo	.04	.02	.01
☐ 190	Mike Krukow	.04	.02	.01
☐ 191	Tommy Herr	.04	.02	.01
☐ 192	Jim Pankovits	.04	.02	.01
☐ 193	Dwight Evans	.07	.03	.01
☐ 194	Kelly Gruber	.07	.03	.01
☐ 195	Bobby Bonilla	.20	.09	.03
☐ 196	Wallace Johnson	.04	.02	.01
☐ 197	Dave Stieb	.07	.03	.01
☐ 198	Pat Borders	.30	.14	.04
☐ 199	Rafael Palmeiro	.20	.09	.03
☐ 200	Dwight Gooden	.12	.05	.02
☐ 201	Pete Incaviglia	.04	.02	.01
☐ 202	Chris James	.04	.02	.01
☐ 203	Marvell Wynne	.04	.02	.01
☐ 204	Pat Sheridan	.04	.02	.01
☐ 205	Don Baylor	.07	.03	.01
☐ 206	Paul O'Neill	.07	.03	.01
☐ 207	Pete Smith	.07	.03	.01
☐ 208	Mark McLemore	.04	.02	.01
☐ 209	Henry Cotto	.04	.02	.01
☐ 210	Kirk Gibson	.07	.03	.01
☐ 211	Claudell Washington	.04	.02	.01
☐ 212	Randy Bush	.04	.02	.01
☐ 213	Joe Carter	.25	.11	.03
☐ 214	Bill Buckner	.07	.03	.01
☐ 215	Bert Blyleven UER (Wrong birth year)	.07	.03	.01
☐ 216	Brett Butler	.07	.03	.01
☐ 217	Lee Mazzilli	.04	.02	.01
☐ 218	Spike Owen	.04	.02	.01
☐ 219	Bill Swift	.07	.03	.01
☐ 220	Tim Wallach	.07	.03	.01
☐ 221	David Cone	.15	.07	.02
☐ 222	Don Carman	.04	.02	.01
☐ 223	Rich Gossage	.07	.03	.01
☐ 224	Bob Walk	.04	.02	.01
☐ 225	Dave Righetti	.04	.02	.01
☐ 226	Kevin Bass	.04	.02	.01
☐ 227	Kevin Gross	.04	.02	.01
☐ 228	Tim Burke	.04	.02	.01
☐ 229	Rick Mahler	.04	.02	.01
☐ 230	Lou Whitaker UER (252 games in '85, should be 152)	.07	.03	.01
☐ 231	Luis Alicea	.10	.05	.01
☐ 232	Roberto Alomar	.75	.35	.09
☐ 233	Bob Boone	.07	.03	.01
☐ 234	Dickie Thon	.04	.02	.01
☐ 235	Shawon Dunston	.07	.03	.01
☐ 236	Pete Stanicek	.04	.02	.01
☐ 237	Craig Biggio (Inconsistent design, portrait on front)	.40	.18	.05
☐ 238	Dennis Boyd	.04	.02	.01
☐ 239	Tom Candiotti	.04	.02	.01
☐ 240	Gary Carter	.07	.03	.01
☐ 241	Mike Stanley	.04	.02	.01
☐ 242	Ken Phelps	.04	.02	.01
☐ 243	Chris Bosio	.04	.02	.01
☐ 244	Les Straker	.04	.02	.01
☐ 245	Dave Smith	.04	.02	.01
☐ 246	John Candelaria	.04	.02	.01
☐ 247	Joe Orsulak	.04	.02	.01
☐ 248	Storm Davis	.04	.02	.01
☐ 249	Floyd Bannister UER (ML Batting Record)	.04	.02	.01
☐ 250	Jack Morris	.12	.05	.02
☐ 251	Bret Saberhagen	.07	.03	.01
☐ 252	Tom Niedenfuer	.04	.02	.01
☐ 253	Neal Heaton	.04	.02	.01
☐ 254	Eric Show	.04	.02	.01
☐ 255	Juan Samuel	.04	.02	.01
☐ 256	Dale Sveum	.04	.02	.01
☐ 257	Jim Gott	.04	.02	.01
☐ 258	Scott Garrelts	.04	.02	.01
☐ 259	Larry McWilliams	.04	.02	.01
☐ 260	Steve Bedrosian	.04	.02	.01
☐ 261	Jack Howell	.04	.02	.01
☐ 262	Jay Tibbs	.04	.02	.01
☐ 263	Jamie Moyer	.04	.02	.01
☐ 264	Doug Sisk	.04	.02	.01
☐ 265	Todd Worrell	.07	.03	.01
☐ 266	John Farrell	.04	.02	.01
☐ 267	Dave Collins	.04	.02	.01
☐ 268	Sid Fernandez	.07	.03	.01
☐ 269	Tom Brookens	.04	.02	.01
☐ 270	Shane Mack	.07	.03	.01
☐ 271	Paul Kilgus	.04	.02	.01
☐ 272	Chuck Crim	.04	.02	.01
☐ 273	Bob Knepper	.04	.02	.01
☐ 274	Mike Moore	.04	.02	.01
☐ 275	Guillermo Hernandez	.04	.02	.01
☐ 276	Dennis Eckersley	.12	.05	.02
☐ 277	Graig Nettles	.07	.03	.01
☐ 278	Rich Dotson	.04	.02	.01
☐ 279	Larry Herndon	.04	.02	.01
☐ 280	Gene Larkin	.04	.02	.01
☐ 281	Roger McDowell	.04	.02	.01
☐ 282	Greg Swindell	.07	.03	.01
☐ 283	Juan Agosto	.04	.02	.01
☐ 284	Jeff M. Robinson	.04	.02	.01
☐ 285	Mike Dunne	.04	.02	.01
☐ 286	Greg Mathews	.04	.02	.01
☐ 287	Kent Tekulve	.04	.02	.01
☐ 288	Jerry Mumphrey	.04	.02	.01
☐ 289	Jack McDowell	.40	.18	.05
☐ 290	Frank Viola	.07	.03	.01
☐ 291	Mark Gubicza	.04	.02	.01
☐ 292	Dave Schmidt	.04	.02	.01
☐ 293	Mike Henneman	.07	.03	.01
☐ 294	Jimmy Jones	.04	.02	.01
☐ 295	Charlie Hough	.04	.02	.01
☐ 296	Rafael Santana	.04	.02	.01
☐ 297	Chris Speier	.04	.02	.01
☐ 298	Mike Witt	.04	.02	.01
☐ 299	Pascual Perez	.04	.02	.01
☐ 300	Nolan Ryan	.60	.25	.08
☐ 301	Mitch Williams	.07	.03	.01
☐ 302	Mookie Wilson	.07	.03	.01
☐ 303	Mackey Sasser	.04	.02	.01
☐ 304	John Cerutti	.04	.02	.01
☐ 305	Jeff Reardon	.07	.03	.01
☐ 306	Randy Myers UER (6 hits in '87, should be 61)	.07	.03	.01
☐ 307	Greg Brock	.04	.02	.01
☐ 308	Bob Welch	.07	.03	.01
☐ 309	Jeff D. Robinson	.04	.02	.01
☐ 310	Harold Reynolds	.04	.02	.01
☐ 311	Jim Walewander	.04	.02	.01
☐ 312	Dave Magadan	.07	.03	.01
☐ 313	Jim Gantner	.04	.02	.01
☐ 314	Walt Terrell	.04	.02	.01
☐ 315	Wally Backman	.04	.02	.01
☐ 316	Luis Salazar	.04	.02	.01
☐ 317	Rick Rhoden	.04	.02	.01
☐ 318	Tom Henke	.07	.03	.01
☐ 319	Mike Macfarlane	.15	.07	.02
☐ 320	Dan Plesac	.04	.02	.01
☐ 321	Calvin Schiraldi	.04	.02	.01
☐ 322	Stan Javier	.04	.02	.01
☐ 323	Devon White	.07	.03	.01
☐ 324	Scott Bradley	.04	.02	.01
☐ 325	Bruce Hurst	.07	.03	.01
☐ 326	Manny Lee	.04	.02	.01
☐ 327	Rick Aguilera	.07	.03	.01
☐ 328	Bruce Ruffin	.04	.02	.01
☐ 329	Ed Whitson	.04	.02	.01
☐ 330	Bo Jackson	.20	.09	.03
☐ 331	Ivan Calderon	.04	.02	.01

☐ 332 Mickey Hatcher .04 .02 .01
☐ 333 Barry Jones .04 .02 .01
☐ 334 Ron Hassey .04 .02 .01
☐ 335 Bill Wegman .04 .02 .01
☐ 336 Damon Berryhill .04 .02 .01
☐ 337 Steve Ontiveros .04 .02 .01
☐ 338 Dan Pasqua .04 .02 .01
☐ 339 Bill Pecota .04 .02 .01
☐ 340 Greg Cadaret .04 .02 .01
☐ 341 Scott Bankhead .04 .02 .01
☐ 342 Ron Guidry .07 .03 .01
☐ 343 Danny Heep .04 .02 .01
☐ 344 Bob Brower .04 .02 .01
☐ 345 Rich Gedman .04 .02 .01
☐ 346 Nelson Santovenia .04 .02 .01
☐ 347 George Bell .10 .05 .01
☐ 348 Ted Power .04 .02 .01
☐ 349 Mark Grant .04 .02 .01
☐ 350A Roger Clemens ERR 3.50 1.55 .45
(778 career wins)
☐ 350B Roger Clemens COR .40 .18 .05
(78 career wins)
☐ 351 Bill Long .04 .02 .01
☐ 352 Jay Bell .07 .03 .01
☐ 353 Steve Balboni .04 .02 .01
☐ 354 Bob Kipper .04 .02 .01
☐ 355 Steve Jeltz .04 .02 .01
☐ 356 Jesse Orosco .04 .02 .01
☐ 357 Bob Dernier .04 .02 .01
☐ 358 Mickey Tettleton .07 .03 .01
☐ 359 Duane Ward .07 .03 .01
☐ 360 Darrin Jackson .15 .07 .02
☐ 361 Rey Quinones .04 .02 .01
☐ 362 Mark Grace .40 .18 .05
☐ 363 Steve Lake .04 .02 .01
☐ 364 Pat Perry .04 .02 .01
☐ 365 Terry Steinbach .07 .03 .01
☐ 366 Alan Ashby .04 .02 .01
☐ 367 Jeff Montgomery .07 .03 .01
☐ 368 Steve Buechele .04 .02 .01
☐ 369 Chris Brown .04 .02 .01
☐ 370 Orel Hershiser .07 .03 .01
☐ 371 Todd Benzinger .04 .02 .01
☐ 372 Ron Gant .40 .18 .05
☐ 373 Paul Assenmacher .04 .02 .01
☐ 374 Joey Meyer .04 .02 .01
☐ 375 Neil Allen .04 .02 .01
☐ 376 Mike Davis .04 .02 .01
☐ 377 Jeff Parrett .04 .02 .01
☐ 378 Jay Howell .04 .02 .01
☐ 379 Rafael Belliard .04 .02 .01
☐ 380 Luis Polonia UER .07 .03 .01
(2 triples in '87,
should be 10)
☐ 381 Keith Atherton .04 .02 .01
☐ 382 Kent Hrbek .07 .03 .01
☐ 383 Bob Stanley .04 .02 .01
☐ 384 Dave LaPoint .04 .02 .01
☐ 385 Rance Mulliniks .04 .02 .01
☐ 386 Melido Perez .15 .07 .02
☐ 387 Doug Jones .07 .03 .01
☐ 388 Steve Lyons .04 .02 .01
☐ 389 Alejandro Pena .04 .02 .01
☐ 390 Frank White .04 .02 .01
☐ 391 Pat Tabler .04 .02 .01
☐ 392 Eric Plunk .04 .02 .01
☐ 393 Mike Maddux .04 .02 .01
☐ 394 Allan Anderson .04 .02 .01
☐ 395 Bob Brenly .04 .02 .01
☐ 396 Rick Cerone .04 .02 .01
☐ 397 Scott Terry .04 .02 .01
☐ 398 Mike Jackson .04 .02 .01
☐ 399 Bobby Thigpen UER .04 .02 .01
(Bio says 37 saves in
'88, should be 34)
☐ 400 Don Sutton .10 .05 .01
☐ 401 Cecil Espy .04 .02 .01
☐ 402 Junior Ortiz .04 .02 .01
☐ 403 Mike Smithson .04 .02 .01
☐ 404 Bud Black .04 .02 .01
☐ 405 Tom Foley .04 .02 .01
☐ 406 Andres Thomas .04 .02 .01
☐ 407 Rick Sutcliffe .07 .03 .01
☐ 408 Brian Harper .07 .03 .01
☐ 409 John Smiley .07 .03 .01
☐ 410 Juan Nieves .04 .02 .01
☐ 411 Shawn Abner .04 .02 .01
☐ 412 Wes Gardner .04 .02 .01
☐ 413 Darren Daulton .07 .03 .01
☐ 414 Juan Berenguer .04 .02 .01
☐ 415 Charles Hudson .04 .02 .01
☐ 416 Rick Honeycutt .04 .02 .01
☐ 417 Greg Booker .04 .02 .01
☐ 418 Tim Belcher .07 .03 .01
☐ 419 Don August .04 .02 .01
☐ 420 Dale Mohorcic .04 .02 .01
☐ 421 Steve Lombardozzi .04 .02 .01
☐ 422 Atlee Hammaker .04 .02 .01
☐ 423 Jerry Don Gleaton .04 .02 .01
☐ 424 Scott Bailes .04 .02 .01
☐ 425 Bruce Sutter .07 .03 .01
☐ 426 Randy Ready .04 .02 .01
☐ 427 Jerry Reed .04 .02 .01
☐ 428 Bryn Smith .04 .02 .01
☐ 429 Tim Leary .04 .02 .01
☐ 430 Mark Clear .04 .02 .01
☐ 431 Terry Leach .04 .02 .01
☐ 432 John Moses .04 .02 .01
☐ 433 Ozzie Guillen .04 .02 .01
☐ 434 Gene Nelson .04 .02 .01
☐ 435 Gary Ward .04 .02 .01
☐ 436 Luis Aguayo .04 .02 .01
☐ 437 Fernando Valenzuela .07 .03 .01
☐ 438 Jeff Russell UER .04 .02 .01
(Saves total does
not add up correctly)
☐ 439 Cecilio Guante .04 .02 .01
☐ 440 Don Robinson .04 .02 .01
☐ 441 Rick Anderson .04 .02 .01
☐ 442 Tom Glavine .50 .23 .06
☐ 443 Daryl Boston .04 .02 .01
☐ 444 Joe Price .04 .02 .01
☐ 445 Stewart Cliburn .04 .02 .01
☐ 446 Manny Trillo .04 .02 .01
☐ 447 Joel Skinner .04 .02 .01
☐ 448 Charlie Puleo .04 .02 .01
☐ 449 Carlton Fisk .15 .07 .02
☐ 450 Will Clark .40 .18 .05
☐ 451 Otis Nixon .07 .03 .01
☐ 452 Rick Schu .04 .02 .01
☐ 453 Todd Stottlemyre UER .10 .05 .01
(ML Batting Record)
☐ 454 Tim Birtsas .04 .02 .01
☐ 455 Dave Gallagher .04 .02 .01
☐ 456 Barry Lyons .04 .02 .01
☐ 457 Fred Manrique .04 .02 .01
☐ 458 Ernest Riles .04 .02 .01
☐ 459 Doug Jennings .04 .02 .01
☐ 460 Joe Magrane .04 .02 .01
☐ 461 Jamie Quirk .04 .02 .01
☐ 462 Jack Armstrong .12 .05 .02
☐ 463 Bobby Witt .07 .03 .01
☐ 464 Keith A. Miller .04 .02 .01
☐ 465 Todd Burns .04 .02 .01
☐ 466 John Dopson .04 .02 .01
☐ 467 Rich Yett .04 .02 .01
☐ 468 Craig Reynolds .04 .02 .01
☐ 469 Dave Bergman .04 .02 .01
☐ 470 Rex Hudler .04 .02 .01
☐ 471 Eric King .04 .02 .01
☐ 472 Joaquin Andujar .04 .02 .01
☐ 473 Sil Campusano .04 .02 .01
☐ 474 Terry Mulholland .10 .05 .01
☐ 475 Mike Flanagan .04 .02 .01
☐ 476 Greg A. Harris .04 .02 .01
☐ 477 Tommy John .07 .03 .01
☐ 478 Dave Anderson .04 .02 .01
☐ 479 Fred Toliver .04 .02 .01
☐ 480 Jimmy Key .07 .03 .01
☐ 481 Donell Nixon .04 .02 .01
☐ 482 Mark Portugal .04 .02 .01
☐ 483 Tom Pagnozzi .04 .02 .01
☐ 484 Jeff Kunkel .04 .02 .01
☐ 485 Frank Williams .04 .02 .01
☐ 486 Jody Reed .04 .02 .01
☐ 487 Roberto Kelly .15 .07 .02
☐ 488 Shawn Hillegas UER .04 .02 .01
(165 innings in '87,
should be 165.2)
☐ 489 Jerry Reuss .04 .02 .01
☐ 490 Mark Davis .04 .02 .01
☐ 491 Jeff Sellers .04 .02 .01
☐ 492 Zane Smith .04 .02 .01
☐ 493 Al Newman .04 .02 .01
☐ 494 Mike Young .04 .02 .01
☐ 495 Larry Parrish .04 .02 .01
☐ 496 Herm Winningham .04 .02 .01
☐ 497 Carmen Castillo .04 .02 .01
☐ 498 Joe Hesketh .04 .02 .01
☐ 499 Darrell Miller .04 .02 .01
☐ 500 Mike LaCoss .04 .02 .01
☐ 501 Charlie Lea .04 .02 .01
☐ 502 Bruce Benedict .04 .02 .01
☐ 503 Chuck Finley .07 .03 .01
☐ 504 Brad Wellman .04 .02 .01
☐ 505 Tim Crews .04 .02 .01

Card			
☐ 506 Ken Gerhart	.04	.02	.01
☐ 507A Brian Holton ERR	.04	.02	.01
(Born 1/25/65 Denver, should be 11/29/59 in McKeesport)			
☐ 507B Brian Holton COR	3.00	1.35	.40
☐ 508 Dennis Lamp	.04	.02	.01
☐ 509 Bobby Meacham UER	.04	.02	.01
('84 games 099)			
☐ 510 Tracy Jones	.04	.02	.01
☐ 511 Mike R. Fitzgerald	.04	.02	.01
Montreal Expos			
☐ 512 Jeff Bittiger	.04	.02	.01
☐ 513 Tim Flannery	.04	.02	.01
☐ 514 Ray Hayward	.04	.02	.01
☐ 515 Dave Leiper	.04	.02	.01
☐ 516 Rod Scurry	.04	.02	.01
☐ 517 Carmelo Martinez	.04	.02	.01
☐ 518 Curtis Wilkerson	.04	.02	.01
☐ 519 Stan Jefferson	.04	.02	.01
☐ 520 Dan Quisenberry	.07	.03	.01
☐ 521 Lloyd McClendon	.04	.02	.01
☐ 522 Steve Trout	.04	.02	.01
☐ 523 Larry Andersen	.04	.02	.01
☐ 524 Don Aase	.04	.02	.01
☐ 525 Bob Forsch	.04	.02	.01
☐ 526 Geno Petralli	.04	.02	.01
☐ 527 Angel Salazar	.04	.02	.01
☐ 528 Mike Schooler	.10	.05	.01
☐ 529 Jose Oquendo	.04	.02	.01
☐ 530 Jay Buhner	.12	.05	.02
☐ 531 Tom Bolton	.04	.02	.01
☐ 532 Al Nipper	.04	.02	.01
☐ 533 Dave Henderson	.07	.03	.01
☐ 534 John Costello	.04	.02	.01
☐ 535 Donnie Moore	.04	.02	.01
☐ 536 Mike Laga	.04	.02	.01
☐ 537 Mike Gallego	.04	.02	.01
☐ 538 Jim Clancy	.04	.02	.01
☐ 539 Joel Youngblood	.04	.02	.01
☐ 540 Rick Leach	.04	.02	.01
☐ 541 Kevin Romine	.04	.02	.01
☐ 542 Mark Salas	.04	.02	.01
☐ 543 Greg Minton	.04	.02	.01
☐ 544 Dave Palmer	.04	.02	.01
☐ 545 Dwayne Murphy UER	.04	.02	.01
(Game-sinning)			
☐ 546 Jim Deshaies	.04	.02	.01
☐ 547 Don Gordon	.04	.02	.01
☐ 548 Ricky Jordan	.10	.05	.01
☐ 549 Mike Boddicker	.04	.02	.01
☐ 550 Mike Scott	.04	.02	.01
☐ 551 Jeff Ballard	.04	.02	.01
☐ 552A Jose Rijo ERR	.60	.25	.08
(Uniform listed as 27 on back)			
☐ 552B Jose Rijo COR	.15	.07	.02
(Uniform listed as 24 on back)			
☐ 553 Danny Darwin	.04	.02	.01
☐ 554 Tom Browning	.07	.03	.01
☐ 555 Danny Jackson	.04	.02	.01
☐ 556 Rick Dempsey	.04	.02	.01
☐ 557 Jeffrey Leonard	.04	.02	.01
☐ 558 Jeff Musselman	.04	.02	.01
☐ 559 Ron Robinson	.04	.02	.01
☐ 560 John Tudor	.04	.02	.01
☐ 561 Don Slaught UER	.04	.02	.01
(237 games in 1987)			
☐ 562 Dennis Rasmussen	.04	.02	.01
☐ 563 Brady Anderson	.60	.25	.08
☐ 564 Pedro Guerrero	.07	.03	.01
☐ 565 Paul Molitor	.10	.05	.01
☐ 566 Terry Clark	.04	.02	.01
☐ 567 Terry Puhl	.04	.02	.01
☐ 568 Mike Campbell	.04	.02	.01
☐ 569 Paul Mirabella	.04	.02	.01
☐ 570 Jeff Hamilton	.04	.02	.01
☐ 571 Oswald Peraza	.04	.02	.01
☐ 572 Bob McClure	.04	.02	.01
☐ 573 Jose Bautista	.04	.02	.01
☐ 574 Alex Trevino	.04	.02	.01
☐ 575 John Franco	.07	.03	.01
☐ 576 Mark Parent	.04	.02	.01
☐ 577 Nelson Liriano	.04	.02	.01
☐ 578 Steve Shields	.04	.02	.01
☐ 579 Odell Jones	.04	.02	.01
☐ 580 Al Leiter	.04	.02	.01
☐ 581 Dave Stapleton	.04	.02	.01
☐ 582 World Series '88	.07	.03	.01
Orel Hershiser			
Jose Canseco			
Kirk Gibson			
Dave Stewart			
☐ 583 Donnie Hill	.04	.02	.01
☐ 584 Chuck Jackson	.04	.02	.01
☐ 585 Rene Gonzales	.04	.02	.01
☐ 586 Tracy Woodson	.04	.02	.01
☐ 587 Jim Adduci	.04	.02	.01
☐ 588 Mario Soto	.04	.02	.01
☐ 589 Jeff Blauser	.07	.03	.01
☐ 590 Jim Traber	.04	.02	.01
☐ 591 Jon Perlman	.04	.02	.01
☐ 592 Mark Williamson	.04	.02	.01
☐ 593 Dave Meads	.04	.02	.01
☐ 594 Jim Eisenreich	.04	.02	.01
☐ 595A Paul Gibson P1	1.00	.45	.13
☐ 595B Paul Gibson P2	.04	.02	.01
(Airbrushed leg on player in background)			
☐ 596 Mike Birkbeck	.04	.02	.01
☐ 597 Terry Francona	.04	.02	.01
☐ 598 Paul Zuvella	.04	.02	.01
☐ 599 Franklin Stubbs	.04	.02	.01
☐ 600 Gregg Jefferies	.20	.09	.03
☐ 601 John Cangelosi	.04	.02	.01
☐ 602 Mike Sharperson	.04	.02	.01
☐ 603 Mike Diaz	.04	.02	.01
☐ 604 Gary Varsho	.04	.02	.01
☐ 605 Terry Blocker	.04	.02	.01
☐ 606 Charlie O'Brien	.04	.02	.01
☐ 607 Jim Eppard	.04	.02	.01
☐ 608 John Davis	.04	.02	.01
☐ 609 Ken Griffey Sr.	.07	.03	.01
☐ 610 Buddy Bell	.07	.03	.01
☐ 611 Ted Simmons UER	.07	.03	.01
('78 stats Cardinal)			
☐ 612 Matt Williams	.15	.07	.02
☐ 613 Danny Cox	.04	.02	.01
☐ 614 Al Pedrique	.04	.02	.01
☐ 615 Ron Oester	.04	.02	.01
☐ 616 John Smoltz	.60	.25	.08
☐ 617 Bob Melvin	.04	.02	.01
☐ 618 Rob Dibble	.20	.09	.03
☐ 619 Kirt Manwaring	.04	.02	.01
☐ 620 Felix Fermin	.04	.02	.01
☐ 621 Doug Dascenzo	.05	.02	.01
☐ 622 Bill Brennan	.05	.02	.01
☐ 623 Carlos Quintana	.10	.05	.01
☐ 624 Mike Harkey UER	.12	.05	.02
(13 and 31 walks in '88, should be 35 and 33)			
☐ 625 Gary Sheffield	2.00	.90	.25
☐ 626 Tom Prince	.05	.02	.01
☐ 627 Steve Searcy	.05	.02	.01
☐ 628 Charlie Hayes	.25	.11	.03
(Listed as outfielder)			
☐ 629 Felix Jose UER	.75	.35	.09
(Modesto misspelled as Modesta)			
☐ 630 Sandy Alomar Jr.	.25	.11	.03
(Inconsistent design, portrait on front)			
☐ 631 Derek Lilliquist	.10	.05	.01
☐ 632 Geronimo Berroa	.05	.02	.01
☐ 633 Luis Medina	.05	.02	.01
☐ 634 Tom Gordon UER	.10	.05	.01
(Height 6'0")			
☐ 635 Ramon Martinez	.50	.23	.06
☐ 636 Craig Worthington	.05	.02	.01
☐ 637 Edgar Martinez	.40	.18	.05
☐ 638 Chad Kreuter	.05	.02	.01
☐ 639 Ron Jones	.05	.02	.01
☐ 640 Van Snider	.05	.02	.01
☐ 641 Lance Blankenship	.10	.05	.01
☐ 642 Dwight Smith UER	.10	.05	.01
(10 HR's in '87, should be 18)			
☐ 643 Cameron Drew	.05	.02	.01
☐ 644 Jerald Clark	.15	.07	.02
☐ 645 Randy Johnson	.35	.16	.04
☐ 646 Norm Charlton	.20	.09	.03
☐ 647 Todd Frohwirth UER	.05	.02	.01
(Southpaw on back)			
☐ 648 Luis De Los Santos	.05	.02	.01
☐ 649 Tim Jones	.05	.02	.01
☐ 650 Dave West UER	.10	.05	.01
(ML hits 3, should be 6)			
☐ 651 Bob Milacki	.10	.05	.01
☐ 652 Wrigley Field HL	.05	.02	.01
(Let There Be Lights)			
☐ 653 Orel Hershiser HL	.08	.04	.01
(The Streak)			
☐ 654A Wade Boggs HL ERR	3.00	1.35	.40
(Wade Whacks 'Em)			

Card	MT	EX-MT	VG
("seaason" on back)			
☐ 654B Wade Boggs HL COR	.12	.05	.02
(Wade Whacks 'Em)			
☐ 655 Jose Canseco HL	.20	.09	.03
(One of a Kind)			
☐ 656 Doug Jones HL	.05	.02	.01
(Doug Sets Saves)			
☐ 657 Rickey Henderson HL	.12	.05	.02
(Rickey Rocks 'Em)			
☐ 658 Tom Browning HL	.05	.02	.01
(Tom Perfect Pitches)			
☐ 659 Mike Greenwell HL	.08	.04	.01
(Greenwell Gamers)			
☐ 660 Boston Red Sox HL	.05	.02	.01
(Joe Morgan MG, Sox Sock 'Em)			

1989 Score Hottest 100 Rookies

This set was distributed by Publications International in January 1989 through many retail stores and chains; the card set was packaged along with a colorful 48-page book for a suggested retail price of 12.95. Supposedly 225,000 sets were produced. The cards measure the standard 2 1/2" by 3 1/2" and show full color on both sides of the card. The cards were produced by Score as indicated on the card backs. The set is subtitled "Rising Star" on the reverse. The first six cards (1-6) of a 12-card set of Score's trivia cards, subtitled "Rookies to Remember" is included along with each set. The cards are numbered on the back. This set is distinguished by the sharp blue borders and the player's first initial inside a yellow triangle in the lower left corner of the obverse.

	MT	EX-MT	VG
COMPLETE SET (100)	10.00	4.50	1.25
COMMON PLAYER (1-100)	.05	.02	.01
☐ 1 Gregg Jefferies	.75	.35	.09
☐ 2 Vicente Palacios	.05	.02	.01
☐ 3 Cameron Drew	.05	.02	.01
☐ 4 Doug Dascenzo	.05	.02	.01
☐ 5 Luis Medina	.05	.02	.01
☐ 6 Craig Worthington	.05	.02	.01
☐ 7 Rob Ducey	.10	.05	.01
☐ 8 Hal Morris	.60	.25	.08
☐ 9 Bill Brennan	.05	.02	.01
☐ 10 Gary Sheffield	1.25	.55	.16
☐ 11 Mike Devereaux	.20	.09	.03
☐ 12 Hensley Meulens	.20	.09	.03
☐ 13 Carlos Quintana	.15	.07	.02
☐ 14 Todd Frohwirth	.05	.02	.01
☐ 15 Scott Lusader	.05	.02	.01
☐ 16 Mark Carreon	.10	.05	.01
☐ 17 Torey Lovullo	.05	.02	.01
☐ 18 Randy Velarde	.05	.02	.01
☐ 19 Billy Bean	.05	.02	.01
☐ 20 Lance Blankenship	.05	.02	.01
☐ 21 Chris Gwynn	.10	.05	.01
☐ 22 Felix Jose	.40	.18	.05
☐ 23 Derek Lilliquist	.05	.02	.01
☐ 24 Gary Thurman	.05	.02	.01
☐ 25 Ron Jones	.05	.02	.01
☐ 26 Dave Justice	1.25	.55	.16
☐ 27 Johnny Paredes	.05	.02	.01
☐ 28 Tim Jones	.05	.02	.01
☐ 29 Jose Gonzalez	.05	.02	.01
☐ 30 Geronimo Berroa	.10	.05	.01
☐ 31 Trevor Wilson	.10	.05	.01
☐ 32 Morris Madden	.05	.02	.01
☐ 33 Lance Johnson	.10	.05	.01
☐ 34 Marvin Freeman	.05	.02	.01
☐ 35 Jose Cecena	.05	.02	.01
☐ 36 Jim Corsi	.05	.02	.01
☐ 37 Rolando Roomes	.05	.02	.01
☐ 38 Scott Medvin	.05	.02	.01
☐ 39 Charlie Hayes	.15	.07	.02
☐ 40 Edgar Martinez	.50	.23	.06
☐ 41 Van Snider	.05	.02	.01
☐ 42 John Fishel	.05	.02	.01
☐ 43 Bruce Fields	.05	.02	.01
☐ 44 Darryl Hamilton	.15	.07	.02
☐ 45 Tom Prince	.05	.02	.01
☐ 46 Kirt Manwaring	.05	.02	.01
☐ 47 Steve Searcy	.05	.02	.01
☐ 48 Mike Harkey	.25	.11	.03
☐ 49 German Gonzalez	.05	.02	.01
☐ 50 Tony Perezchica	.05	.02	.01
☐ 51 Chad Kreuter	.05	.02	.01
☐ 52 Luis De los Santos	.10	.05	.01
☐ 53 Steve Curry	.05	.02	.01
☐ 54 Greg Briley	.10	.05	.01
☐ 55 Ramon Martinez	.60	.25	.08
☐ 56 Ron Tingley	.05	.02	.01
☐ 57 Randy Kramer	.05	.02	.01
☐ 58 Alex Madrid	.05	.02	.01
☐ 59 Kevin Reimer	.15	.07	.02
☐ 60 Dave Otto	.05	.02	.01
☐ 61 Ken Patterson	.05	.02	.01
☐ 62 Keith Miller	.10	.05	.01
☐ 63 Randy Johnson	.40	.18	.05
☐ 64 Dwight Smith	.15	.07	.02
☐ 65 Eric Yelding	.05	.02	.01
☐ 66 Bob Geren	.05	.02	.01
☐ 67 Shane Turner	.05	.02	.01
☐ 68 Tom Gordon	.20	.09	.03
☐ 69 Jeff Huson	.05	.02	.01
☐ 70 Marty Brown	.05	.02	.01
☐ 71 Nelson Santovenia	.05	.02	.01
☐ 72 Roberto Alomar	1.00	.45	.13
☐ 73 Mike Schooler	.15	.07	.02
☐ 74 Pete Smith	.25	.11	.03
☐ 75 John Costello	.05	.02	.01
☐ 76 Chris Sabo	.40	.18	.05
☐ 77 Damon Berryhill	.15	.07	.02
☐ 78 Mark Grace	.75	.35	.09
☐ 79 Melido Perez	.25	.11	.03
☐ 80 Al Leiter	.05	.02	.01
☐ 81 Todd Stottlemyre	.15	.07	.02
☐ 82 Mackey Sasser	.10	.05	.01
☐ 83 Don August	.05	.02	.01
☐ 84 Jeff Treadway	.05	.02	.01
☐ 85 Jody Reed	.10	.05	.01
☐ 86 Mike Campbell	.05	.02	.01
☐ 87 Ron Gant	.75	.35	.09
☐ 88 Ricky Jordan	.10	.05	.01
☐ 89 Terry Clark	.05	.02	.01
☐ 90 Roberto Kelly	.40	.18	.05
☐ 91 Pat Borders	.25	.11	.03
☐ 92 Bryan Harvey	.25	.11	.03
☐ 93 Joey Meyer	.05	.02	.01
☐ 94 Tim Belcher	.10	.05	.01
☐ 95 Walt Weiss	.20	.09	.03
☐ 96 Dave Gallagher	.05	.02	.01
☐ 97 Mike Macfarlane	.15	.07	.02
☐ 98 Craig Biggio	.40	.18	.05
☐ 99 Jack Armstrong	.15	.07	.02
☐ 100 Todd Burns	.05	.02	.01

1989 Score Hottest 100 Stars

This set was distributed by Publications International in January 1989 through many retail stores and chains; the card set was packaged along with a colorful 48-page book for a suggested retail price of 12.95. Supposedly 225,000 sets were produced. The cards measure the standard 2 1/2" by 3 1/2" and show full color on both sides of the card. The cards were produced by Score as indicated on the card backs. The set is subtitled "Superstar" on the reverse. The last six cards (7-12) of a 12-card set of Score's trivia cards,

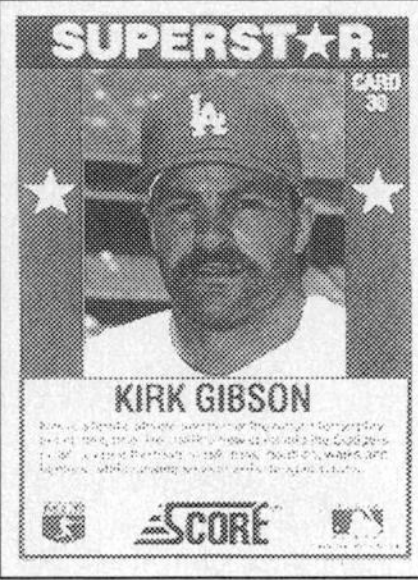

subtitled "Rookies to Remember" is included along with each set. The cards are numbered on the back. This set is distinguished by the sharp red borders and the player's first initial inside a yellow triangle in the upper left corner of the obverse.

	MT	EX-MT	VG
COMPLETE SET (100)	10.00	4.50	1.25
COMMON PLAYER (1-100)	.05	.02	.01
□ 1 Jose Canseco	.75	.35	.09
□ 2 David Cone	.30	.14	.04
□ 3 Dave Winfield	.40	.18	.05
□ 4 George Brett	.45	.20	.06
□ 5 Frank Viola	.10	.05	.01
□ 6 Cory Snyder	.05	.02	.01
□ 7 Alan Trammell	.15	.07	.02
□ 8 Dwight Evans	.10	.05	.01
□ 9 Tim Leary	.05	.02	.01
□ 10 Don Mattingly	.75	.35	.09
□ 11 Kirby Puckett	.75	.35	.09
□ 12 Carney Lansford	.10	.05	.01
□ 13 Dennis Martinez	.10	.05	.01
□ 14 Kent Hrbek	.10	.05	.01
□ 15 Dwight Gooden	.25	.11	.03
□ 16 Dennis Eckersley	.25	.11	.03
□ 17 Kevin Seitzer	.05	.02	.01
□ 18 Lee Smith	.10	.05	.01
□ 19 Danny Tartabull	.20	.09	.03
□ 20 Gerald Perry	.05	.02	.01
□ 21 Gary Gaetti	.05	.02	.01
□ 22 Rick Reuschel	.05	.02	.01
□ 23 Keith Hernandez	.10	.05	.01
□ 24 Jeff Reardon	.10	.05	.01
□ 25 Mark McGwire	.60	.25	.08
□ 26 Juan Samuel	.05	.02	.01
□ 27 Jack Clark	.10	.05	.01
□ 28 Robin Yount	.45	.20	.06
□ 29 Steve Bedrosian	.05	.02	.01
□ 30 Kirk Gibson	.10	.05	.01
□ 31 Barry Bonds	.60	.25	.08
□ 32 Dan Plesac	.05	.02	.01
□ 33 Steve Sax	.10	.05	.01
□ 34 Jeff M. Robinson	.05	.02	.01
□ 35 Orel Hershiser	.10	.05	.01
□ 36 Julio Franco	.15	.07	.02
□ 37 Dave Righetti	.05	.02	.01
□ 38 Bob Knepper	.05	.02	.01
□ 39 Carlton Fisk	.30	.14	.04
□ 40 Tony Gwynn	.60	.25	.08
□ 41 Doug Jones	.05	.02	.01
□ 42 Bobby Bonilla	.45	.20	.06
□ 43 Ellis Burks	.15	.07	.02
□ 44 Pedro Guerrero	.10	.05	.01
□ 45 Rickey Henderson	.60	.25	.08
□ 46 Glenn Davis	.10	.05	.01
□ 47 Benito Santiago	.10	.05	.01
□ 48 Greg Maddux	.25	.11	.03
□ 49 Teddy Higuera	.05	.02	.01
□ 50 Darryl Strawberry	.60	.25	.08
□ 51 Ozzie Guillen	.10	.05	.01
□ 52 Barry Larkin	.25	.11	.03
□ 53 Tony Fernandez	.10	.05	.01
□ 54 Ryne Sandberg	.90	.40	.11
□ 55 Joe Carter	.40	.18	.05
□ 56 Rafael Palmeiro	.30	.14	.04
□ 57 Paul Molitor	.25	.11	.03
□ 58 Eric Davis	.25	.11	.03
□ 59 Mike Henneman	.10	.05	.01
□ 60 Mike Scott	.10	.05	.01
□ 61 Tom Browning	.10	.05	.01
□ 62 Mark Davis	.05	.02	.01
□ 63 Tom Henke	.10	.05	.01
□ 64 Nolan Ryan	1.50	.65	.19
□ 65 Fred McGriff	.60	.25	.08
□ 66 Dale Murphy	.25	.11	.03
□ 67 Mark Langston	.10	.05	.01
□ 68 Bobby Thigpen	.10	.05	.01
□ 69 Mark Gubicza	.05	.02	.01
□ 70 Mike Greenwell	.25	.11	.03
□ 71 Ron Darling	.10	.05	.01
□ 72 Gerald Young	.05	.02	.01
□ 73 Wally Joyner	.10	.05	.01
□ 74 Andres Galarraga	.05	.02	.01
□ 75 Danny Jackson	.05	.02	.01
□ 76 Mike Schmidt	.75	.35	.09
□ 77 Cal Ripken	1.00	.45	.13
□ 78 Alvin Davis	.05	.02	.01
□ 79 Bruce Hurst	.10	.05	.01
□ 80 Andre Dawson	.35	.16	.04
□ 81 Bob Boone	.10	.05	.01
□ 82 Harold Reynolds	.05	.02	.01
□ 83 Eddie Murray	.30	.14	.04
□ 84 Robby Thompson	.05	.02	.01
□ 85 Will Clark	.75	.35	.09
□ 86 Vince Coleman	.15	.07	.02
□ 87 Doug Drabek	.20	.09	.03
□ 88 Ozzie Smith	.35	.16	.04
□ 89 Bob Welch	.10	.05	.01
□ 90 Roger Clemens	1.00	.45	.13
□ 91 George Bell	.15	.07	.02
□ 92 Andy Van Slyke	.20	.09	.03
□ 93 Willie McGee	.10	.05	.01
□ 94 Todd Worrell	.10	.05	.01
□ 95 Tim Raines	.15	.07	.02
□ 96 Kevin McReynolds	.10	.05	.01
□ 97 John Franco	.10	.05	.01
□ 98 Jim Gott	.05	.02	.01
□ 99 Johnny Ray	.05	.02	.01
□ 100 Wade Boggs	.50	.23	.06

1989 Score Rookie/Traded

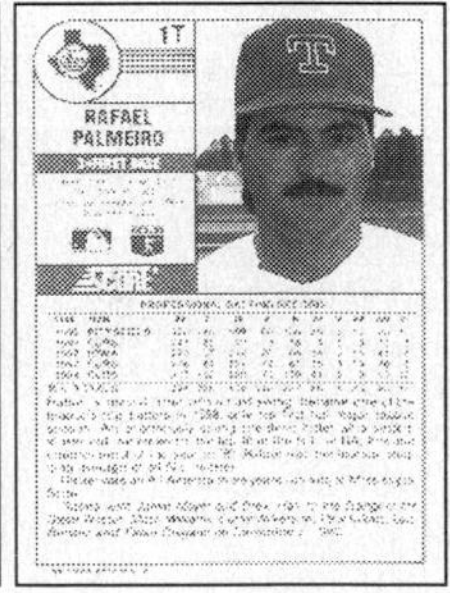

The 1989 Score Rookie and Traded set contains 110 standard-size (2 1/2" by 3 1/2") cards. The fronts have coral green borders with pink diamonds at the bottom. The vertically oriented backs have color facial shots, career stats, and biographical information. Cards 1-80 feature traded players; cards 81-110 feature 1989 rookies. The set was distributed in a blue box with 10 Magic Motion trivia cards. The key Rookie Cards in this set are Jim Abbott, Joey (Albert) Belle, Junior Felix, Ken Griffey Jr., and Jerome Walton.

	MT	EX-MT	VG
COMPLETE SET (110)	10.00	4.50	1.25
COMMON PLAYER (1T-80T)	.05	.02	.01
COMMON PLAYER (81T-110T)	.05	.02	.01
□ 1T Rafael Palmeiro	.20	.09	.03
□ 2T Nolan Ryan	1.50	.65	.19
□ 3T Jack Clark	.08	.04	.01
□ 4T Dave LaPoint	.05	.02	.01
□ 5T Mike Moore	.05	.02	.01
□ 6T Pete O'Brien	.05	.02	.01
□ 7T Jeffrey Leonard	.05	.02	.01
□ 8T Rob Murphy	.05	.02	.01
□ 9T Tom Herr	.05	.02	.01

☐ 10T Claudell Washington	.05	.02	.01
☐ 11T Mike Pagliarulo	.05	.02	.01
☐ 12T Steve Lake	.05	.02	.01
☐ 13T Spike Owen	.05	.02	.01
☐ 14T Andy Hawkins	.05	.02	.01
☐ 15T Todd Benzinger	.05	.02	.01
☐ 16T Mookie Wilson	.08	.04	.01
☐ 17T Bert Blyleven	.08	.04	.01
☐ 18T Jeff Treadway	.08	.04	.01
☐ 19T Bruce Hurst	.08	.04	.01
☐ 20T Steve Sax	.08	.04	.01
☐ 21T Juan Samuel	.05	.02	.01
☐ 22T Jesse Barfield	.05	.02	.01
☐ 23T Carmen Castillo	.05	.02	.01
☐ 24T Terry Leach	.05	.02	.01
☐ 25T Mark Langston	.08	.04	.01
☐ 26T Eric King	.05	.02	.01
☐ 27T Steve Balboni	.05	.02	.01
☐ 28T Len Dykstra	.08	.04	.01
☐ 29T Keith Moreland	.05	.02	.01
☐ 30T Terry Kennedy	.05	.02	.01
☐ 31T Eddie Murray	.15	.07	.02
☐ 32T Mitch Williams	.08	.04	.01
☐ 33T Jeff Parrett	.05	.02	.01
☐ 34T Wally Backman	.05	.02	.01
☐ 35T Julio Franco	.08	.04	.01
☐ 36T Lance Parrish	.08	.04	.01
☐ 37T Nick Esasky	.05	.02	.01
☐ 38T Luis Polonia	.08	.04	.01
☐ 39T Kevin Gross	.05	.02	.01
☐ 40T John Dopson	.05	.02	.01
☐ 41T Willie Randolph	.08	.04	.01
☐ 42T Jim Clancy	.05	.02	.01
☐ 43T Tracy Jones	.05	.02	.01
☐ 44T Phil Bradley	.05	.02	.01
☐ 45T Milt Thompson	.05	.02	.01
☐ 46T Chris James	.05	.02	.01
☐ 47T Scott Fletcher	.05	.02	.01
☐ 48T Kal Daniels	.05	.02	.01
☐ 49T Steve Bedrosian	.05	.02	.01
☐ 50T Rickey Henderson	.25	.11	.03
☐ 51T Dion James	.05	.02	.01
☐ 52T Tim Leary	.05	.02	.01
☐ 53T Roger McDowell	.05	.02	.01
☐ 54T Mel Hall	.05	.02	.01
☐ 55T Dickie Thon	.05	.02	.01
☐ 56T Zane Smith	.05	.02	.01
☐ 57T Danny Heep	.05	.02	.01
☐ 58T Bob McClure	.05	.02	.01
☐ 59T Brian Holton	.05	.02	.01
☐ 60T Randy Ready	.05	.02	.01
☐ 61T Bob Melvin	.05	.02	.01
☐ 62T Harold Baines	.08	.04	.01
☐ 63T Lance McCullers	.05	.02	.01
☐ 64T Jody Davis	.05	.02	.01
☐ 65T Darrell Evans	.08	.04	.01
☐ 66T Joel Youngblood	.05	.02	.01
☐ 67T Frank Viola	.08	.04	.01
☐ 68T Mike Aldrete	.05	.02	.01
☐ 69T Greg Cadaret	.05	.02	.01
☐ 70T John Kruk	.08	.04	.01
☐ 71T Pat Sheridan	.05	.02	.01
☐ 72T Oddibe McDowell	.05	.02	.01
☐ 73T Tom Brookens	.05	.02	.01
☐ 74T Bob Boone	.08	.04	.01
☐ 75T Walt Terrell	.05	.02	.01
☐ 76T Joel Skinner	.05	.02	.01
☐ 77T Randy Johnson	.15	.07	.02
☐ 78T Felix Fermin	.05	.02	.01
☐ 79T Rick Mahler	.05	.02	.01
☐ 80T Richard Dotson	.05	.02	.01
☐ 81T Cris Carpenter	.10	.05	.01
☐ 82T Bill Spiers	.10	.05	.01
☐ 83T Junior Felix	.25	.11	.03
☐ 84T Joe Girardi	.15	.07	.02
☐ 85T Jerome Walton	.10	.05	.01
☐ 86T Greg Litton	.05	.02	.01
☐ 87T Greg W.Harris	.10	.05	.01
☐ 88T Jim Abbott	1.25	.55	.16
☐ 89T Kevin Brown	.30	.14	.04
☐ 90T John Wetteland	.40	.18	.05
☐ 91T Gary Wayne	.05	.02	.01
☐ 92T Rich Monteleone	.05	.02	.01
☐ 93T Bob Geren	.05	.02	.01
☐ 94T Clay Parker	.05	.02	.01
☐ 95T Steve Finley	.40	.18	.05
☐ 96T Gregg Olson	.50	.23	.06
☐ 97T Ken Patterson	.05	.02	.01
☐ 98T Ken Hill	.40	.18	.05
☐ 99T Scott Scudder	.12	.05	.02
☐ 100T Ken Griffey Jr.	5.00	2.30	.60
☐ 101T Jeff Brantley	.10	.05	.01
☐ 102T Donn Pall	.05	.02	.01
☐ 103T Carlos Martinez	.10	.05	.01
☐ 104T Joe Oliver	.20	.09	.03
☐ 105T Omar Vizquel	.15	.07	.02
☐ 106T Joey Belle	2.00	.90	.25
☐ 107T Kenny Rogers	.08	.04	.01
☐ 108T Mark Carreon	.05	.02	.01
☐ 109T Rolando Roomes	.05	.02	.01
☐ 110T Pete Harnisch	.25	.11	.03

1989 Score Scoremasters

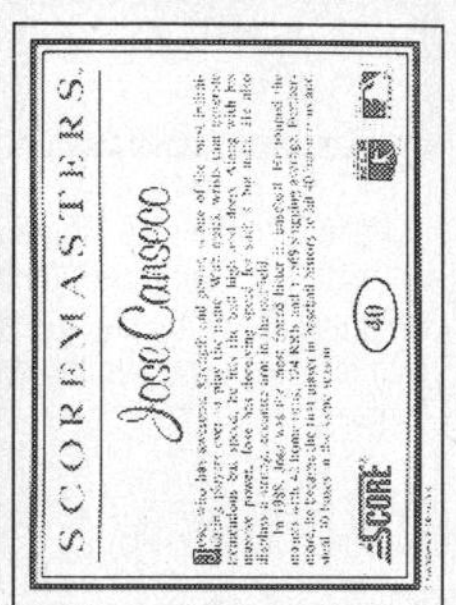

The 1989 Score Scoremasters set contains 42 standard-size (2 1/2" by 3 1/2") cards. The fronts are "pure" with attractively drawn action portraits. The backs feature write-ups of the players' careers. The cards were distributed as a boxed set.

	MT	EX-MT	VG
COMPLETE SET (42)	9.00	4.00	1.15
COMMON PLAYER (1-42)	.20	.09	.03
☐ 1 Bo Jackson	.75	.35	.09
☐ 2 Jerome Walton	.30	.14	.04
☐ 3 Cal Ripken	1.00	.45	.13
☐ 4 Mike Scott	.20	.09	.03
☐ 5 Nolan Ryan	1.50	.65	.19
☐ 6 Don Mattingly	.60	.25	.08
☐ 7 Tom Gordon	.30	.14	.04
☐ 8 Jack Morris	.30	.14	.04
☐ 9 Carlton Fisk	.50	.23	.06
☐ 10 Will Clark	1.00	.45	.13
☐ 11 George Brett	.60	.25	.08
☐ 12 Kevin Mitchell	.30	.14	.04
☐ 13 Mark Langston	.20	.09	.03
☐ 14 Dave Stewart	.20	.09	.03
☐ 15 Dale Murphy	.30	.14	.04
☐ 16 Gary Gaetti	.20	.09	.03
☐ 17 Wade Boggs	.60	.25	.08
☐ 18 Eric Davis	.40	.18	.05
☐ 19 Kirby Puckett	1.00	.45	.13
☐ 20 Roger Clemens	1.00	.45	.13
☐ 21 Orel Hershiser	.30	.14	.04
☐ 22 Mark Grace	.75	.35	.09
☐ 23 Ryne Sandberg	1.00	.45	.13
☐ 24 Barry Larkin	.30	.14	.04
☐ 25 Ellis Burks	.20	.09	.03
☐ 26 Dwight Gooden	.30	.14	.04
☐ 27 Ozzie Smith	.40	.18	.05
☐ 28 Andre Dawson	.40	.18	.05
☐ 29 Julio Franco	.30	.14	.04
☐ 30 Ken Griffey Jr.	2.00	.90	.25
☐ 31 Ruben Sierra	.60	.25	.08
☐ 32 Mark McGwire	.75	.35	.09
☐ 33 Andres Galarraga	.20	.09	.03
☐ 34 Joe Carter	.40	.18	.05
☐ 35 Vince Coleman	.30	.14	.04
☐ 36 Mike Greenwell	.30	.14	.04
☐ 37 Tony Gwynn	.60	.25	.08
☐ 38 Andy Van Slyke	.30	.14	.04
☐ 39 Gregg Jefferies	.60	.25	.08
☐ 40 Jose Canseco	1.00	.45	.13
☐ 41 Dave Winfield	.50	.23	.06
☐ 42 Darryl Strawberry	.60	.25	.08

1989 Score Young Superstars I

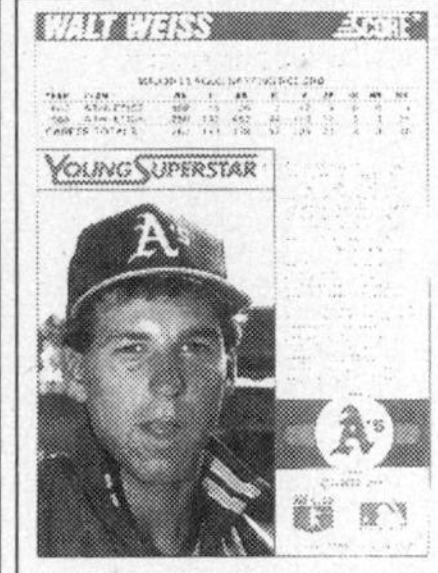

The 1989 Score Young Superstars set I contains 42 standard-size (2 1/2" by 3 1/2") cards. The fronts are pink, white and blue. The vertically oriented backs have color facial shots, 1988 and career stats, and biographical information. One card was included in each 1989 Score rack pack, and the cards were also distributed as a boxed set with five Magic Motion trivia cards.

	MT	EX-MT	VG
COMPLETE SET (42)	7.00	3.10	.85
COMMON PLAYER (1-42)	.15	.07	.02

	MT	EX-MT	VG
☐ 1 Gregg Jefferies	.60	.25	.08
☐ 2 Jody Reed	.15	.07	.02
☐ 3 Mark Grace	.60	.25	.08
☐ 4 Dave Gallagher	.15	.07	.02
☐ 5 Bo Jackson	.75	.35	.09
☐ 6 Jay Buhner	.35	.16	.04
☐ 7 Melido Perez	.25	.11	.03
☐ 8 Bobby Witt	.25	.11	.03
☐ 9 David Cone	.35	.16	.04
☐ 10 Chris Sabo	.35	.16	.04
☐ 11 Pat Borders	.25	.11	.03
☐ 12 Mark Grant	.15	.07	.02
☐ 13 Mike Macfarlane	.25	.11	.03
☐ 14 Mike Jackson	.15	.07	.02
☐ 15 Ricky Jordan	.25	.11	.03
☐ 16 Ron Gant	.75	.35	.09
☐ 17 Al Leiter	.15	.07	.02
☐ 18 Jeff Parrett	.25	.11	.03
☐ 19 Pete Smith	.35	.16	.04
☐ 20 Walt Weiss	.25	.11	.03
☐ 21 Doug Drabek	.25	.11	.03
☐ 22 Kirt Manwaring	.15	.07	.02
☐ 23 Keith Miller	.15	.07	.02
☐ 24 Damon Berryhill	.15	.07	.02
☐ 25 Gary Sheffield	1.25	.55	.16
☐ 26 Brady Anderson	.50	.23	.06
☐ 27 Mitch Williams	.25	.11	.03
☐ 28 Roberto Alomar	.75	.35	.09
☐ 29 Bobby Thigpen	.25	.11	.03
☐ 30 Bryan Harvey UER (47 games in '87)	.25	.11	.03
☐ 31 Jose Rijo	.25	.11	.03
☐ 32 Dave West	.25	.11	.03
☐ 33 Joey Meyer	.15	.07	.02
☐ 34 Allan Anderson	.15	.07	.02
☐ 35 Rafael Palmeiro	.35	.16	.04
☐ 36 Tim Belcher UER (Back reads 1937, should read 1987)	.25	.11	.03
☐ 37 John Smiley	.25	.11	.03
☐ 38 Mackey Sasser	.15	.07	.02
☐ 39 Greg Maddux	.35	.16	.04
☐ 40 Ramon Martinez	.50	.23	.06
☐ 41 Randy Myers	.25	.11	.03
☐ 42 Scott Bankhead	.15	.07	.02

1989 Score Young Superstars II

The 1989 Score Young Superstars II set contains 42 standard-size (2 1/2" by 3 1/2") cards. The fronts are

orange, white and purple. The vertically oriented backs have color facial shots, 1988 and career stats, and biographical information. The cards were distributed as a boxed set with five Magic Motion trivia cards.

	MT	EX-MT	VG
COMPLETE SET (42)	6.00	2.70	.75
COMMON PLAYER (1-42)	.15	.07	.02

	MT	EX-MT	VG
☐ 1 Sandy Alomar Jr.	.50	.23	.06
☐ 2 Tom Gordon	.25	.11	.03
☐ 3 Ron Jones	.15	.07	.02
☐ 4 Todd Burns	.15	.07	.02
☐ 5 Paul O'Neill	.25	.11	.03
☐ 6 Gene Larkin	.15	.07	.02
☐ 7 Eric King	.15	.07	.02
☐ 8 Jeff M. Robinson	.15	.07	.02
☐ 9 Bill Wegman	.25	.11	.03
☐ 10 Cecil Espy	.15	.07	.02
☐ 11 Jose Guzman	.25	.11	.03
☐ 12 Kelly Gruber	.25	.11	.03
☐ 13 Duane Ward	.25	.11	.03
☐ 14 Mark Gubicza	.15	.07	.02
☐ 15 Norm Charlton	.25	.11	.03
☐ 16 Jose Oquendo	.15	.07	.02
☐ 17 Geronimo Berroa	.25	.11	.03
☐ 18 Ken Griffey Jr.	2.50	1.15	.30
☐ 19 Lance McCullers	.15	.07	.02
☐ 20 Todd Stottlemyre	.35	.16	.04
☐ 21 Craig Worthington	.15	.07	.02
☐ 22 Mike Devereaux	.25	.11	.03
☐ 23 Tom Glavine	.75	.35	.09
☐ 24 Dale Sveum	.15	.07	.02
☐ 25 Roberto Kelly	.35	.16	.04
☐ 26 Luis Medina	.15	.07	.02
☐ 27 Steve Searcy	.15	.07	.02
☐ 28 Don August	.15	.07	.02
☐ 29 Shawn Hillegas	.15	.07	.02
☐ 30 Mike Campbell	.15	.07	.02
☐ 31 Mike Harkey	.35	.16	.04
☐ 32 Randy Johnson	.35	.16	.04
☐ 33 Craig Biggio	.50	.23	.06
☐ 34 Mike Schooler	.25	.11	.03
☐ 35 Andres Thomas	.15	.07	.02
☐ 36 Jerome Walton	.25	.11	.03
☐ 37 Cris Carpenter	.25	.11	.03
☐ 38 Kevin Mitchell	.35	.16	.04
☐ 39 Eddie Williams	.15	.07	.02
☐ 40 Chad Kreuter	.15	.07	.02
☐ 41 Danny Jackson	.15	.07	.02
☐ 42 Kurt Stillwell	.25	.11	.03

1990 Score

The 1990 Score set contains 704 standard-size (2 1/2" by 3 1/2") cards. The front borders are red, blue, green or white. The vertically oriented backs are white with borders that match the fronts, and feature color mugshots. Cards numbered 661-682 contain the first round draft picks subset noted as DC for "draft choice" in the checklist below. Cards numbered 683-695 contain the "Dream Team" subset noted by DT in the checklist below. The key Rookie Cards in this set are Delino DeShields, Cal Eldred, Juan Gonzalez, Dave Justice, Chuck Knoblauch, Kevin Maas, Ben McDonald, John

Olerud, Dean Palmer, Frank Thomas, Mo Vaughn, and Larry Walker. A ten-card set of Dream Team Rookies was inserted into each hobby factory set, but was not included in retail factory sets. These cards carry a B prefix on the card number and include a player at each position plus a commemorative card honoring the late Baseball Commissioner A. Bartlett Giamatti.

	MT	EX-MT	VG
COMPLETE SET (704)	20.00	9.00	2.50
COMPLETE FACT.SET (704)	20.00	9.00	2.50
COMPLETE FACT.SET (714)	30.00	13.50	3.80
COMMON PLAYER (1-704)	.04	.02	.01
COMMON PLAYER (B1-B10)	.25	.11	.03

	Card	MT	EX-MT	VG
☐	1 Don Mattingly	.20	.09	.03
☐	2 Cal Ripken	.40	.18	.05
☐	3 Dwight Evans	.07	.03	.01
☐	4 Barry Bonds	.30	.14	.04
☐	5 Kevin McReynolds	.07	.03	.01
☐	6 Ozzie Guillen	.04	.02	.01
☐	7 Terry Kennedy	.04	.02	.01
☐	8 Bryan Harvey	.07	.03	.01
☐	9 Alan Trammell	.07	.03	.01
☐	10 Cory Snyder	.04	.02	.01
☐	11 Jody Reed	.04	.02	.01
☐	12 Roberto Alomar	.40	.18	.05
☐	13 Pedro Guerrero	.07	.03	.01
☐	14 Gary Redus	.04	.02	.01
☐	15 Marty Barrett	.04	.02	.01
☐	16 Ricky Jordan	.04	.02	.01
☐	17 Joe Magrane	.04	.02	.01
☐	18 Sid Fernandez	.07	.03	.01
☐	19 Richard Dotson	.04	.02	.01
☐	20 Jack Clark	.07	.03	.01
☐	21 Bob Walk	.04	.02	.01
☐	22 Ron Karkovice	.04	.02	.01
☐	23 Lenny Harris	.04	.02	.01
☐	24 Phil Bradley	.04	.02	.01
☐	25 Andres Galarraga	.04	.02	.01
☐	26 Brian Downing	.04	.02	.01
☐	27 Dave Martinez	.07	.03	.01
☐	28 Eric King	.04	.02	.01
☐	29 Barry Lyons	.04	.02	.01
☐	30 Dave Schmidt	.04	.02	.01
☐	31 Mike Boddicker	.04	.02	.01
☐	32 Tom Foley	.04	.02	.01
☐	33 Brady Anderson	.12	.05	.02
☐	34 Jim Presley	.04	.02	.01
☐	35 Lance Parrish	.07	.03	.01
☐	36 Von Hayes	.04	.02	.01
☐	37 Lee Smith	.07	.03	.01
☐	38 Herm Winningham	.04	.02	.01
☐	39 Alejandro Pena	.04	.02	.01
☐	40 Mike Scott	.04	.02	.01
☐	41 Joe Orsulak	.04	.02	.01
☐	42 Rafael Ramirez	.04	.02	.01
☐	43 Gerald Young	.04	.02	.01
☐	44 Dick Schofield	.04	.02	.01
☐	45 Dave Smith	.04	.02	.01
☐	46 Dave Magadan	.07	.03	.01
☐	47 Dennis Martinez	.07	.03	.01
☐	48 Greg Minton	.04	.02	.01
☐	49 Milt Thompson	.04	.02	.01
☐	50 Orel Hershiser	.07	.03	.01
☐	51 Bip Roberts	.07	.03	.01
☐	52 Jerry Browne	.04	.02	.01
☐	53 Bob Ojeda	.04	.02	.01
☐	54 Fernando Valenzuela	.07	.03	.01
☐	55 Matt Nokes	.04	.02	.01
☐	56 Brook Jacoby	.04	.02	.01
☐	57 Frank Tanana	.04	.02	.01
☐	58 Scott Fletcher	.04	.02	.01
☐	59 Ron Oester	.04	.02	.01
☐	60 Bob Boone	.07	.03	.01
☐	61 Dan Gladden	.04	.02	.01
☐	62 Darnell Coles	.04	.02	.01
☐	63 Gregg Olson	.10	.05	.01
☐	64 Todd Burns	.04	.02	.01
☐	65 Todd Benzinger	.04	.02	.01
☐	66 Dale Murphy	.10	.05	.01
☐	67 Mike Flanagan	.04	.02	.01
☐	68 Jose Oquendo	.04	.02	.01
☐	69 Cecil Espy	.04	.02	.01
☐	70 Chris Sabo	.07	.03	.01
☐	71 Shane Rawley	.04	.02	.01
☐	72 Tom Brunansky	.07	.03	.01
☐	73 Vance Law	.04	.02	.01
☐	74 B.J. Surhoff	.04	.02	.01
☐	75 Lou Whitaker	.07	.03	.01
☐	76 Ken Caminiti UER (Euclid, Ohio should be Hanford, California)	.07	.03	.01
☐	77 Nelson Liriano	.04	.02	.01
☐	78 Tommy Gregg	.04	.02	.01
☐	79 Don Slaught	.04	.02	.01
☐	80 Eddie Murray	.10	.05	.01
☐	81 Joe Boever	.04	.02	.01
☐	82 Charlie Leibrandt	.04	.02	.01
☐	83 Jose Lind	.04	.02	.01
☐	84 Tony Phillips	.04	.02	.01
☐	85 Mitch Webster	.04	.02	.01
☐	86 Dan Plesac	.04	.02	.01
☐	87 Rick Mahler	.04	.02	.01
☐	88 Steve Lyons	.04	.02	.01
☐	89 Tony Fernandez	.07	.03	.01
☐	90 Ryne Sandberg	.35	.16	.04
☐	91 Nick Esasky	.04	.02	.01
☐	92 Luis Salazar	.04	.02	.01
☐	93 Pete Incaviglia	.04	.02	.01
☐	94 Ivan Calderon	.04	.02	.01
☐	95 Jeff Treadway	.04	.02	.01
☐	96 Kurt Stillwell	.04	.02	.01
☐	97 Gary Sheffield	.50	.23	.06
☐	98 Jeffrey Leonard	.04	.02	.01
☐	99 Andres Thomas	.04	.02	.01
☐	100 Roberto Kelly	.10	.05	.01
☐	101 Alvaro Espinoza	.04	.02	.01
☐	102 Greg Gagne	.04	.02	.01
☐	103 John Farrell	.04	.02	.01
☐	104 Willie Wilson	.04	.02	.01
☐	105 Glenn Braggs	.04	.02	.01
☐	106 Chet Lemon	.04	.02	.01
☐	107A Jamie Moyer ERR (Scintilating)	.04	.02	.01
☐	107B Jamie Moyer COR (Scintillating)	.25	.11	.03
☐	108 Chuck Crim	.04	.02	.01
☐	109 Dave Valle	.04	.02	.01
☐	110 Walt Weiss	.04	.02	.01
☐	111 Larry Sheets	.04	.02	.01
☐	112 Don Robinson	.04	.02	.01
☐	113 Danny Heep	.04	.02	.01
☐	114 Carmelo Martinez	.04	.02	.01
☐	115 Dave Gallagher	.04	.02	.01
☐	116 Mike LaValliere	.04	.02	.01
☐	117 Bob McClure	.04	.02	.01
☐	118 Rene Gonzales	.04	.02	.01
☐	119 Mark Parent	.04	.02	.01
☐	120 Wally Joyner	.07	.03	.01
☐	121 Mark Gubicza	.04	.02	.01
☐	122 Tony Pena	.04	.02	.01
☐	123 Carmen Castillo	.04	.02	.01
☐	124 Howard Johnson	.07	.03	.01
☐	125 Steve Sax	.07	.03	.01
☐	126 Tim Belcher	.07	.03	.01
☐	127 Tim Burke	.04	.02	.01
☐	128 Al Newman	.04	.02	.01
☐	129 Dennis Rasmussen	.04	.02	.01
☐	130 Doug Jones	.07	.03	.01
☐	131 Fred Lynn	.07	.03	.01
☐	132 Jeff Hamilton	.04	.02	.01
☐	133 German Gonzalez	.04	.02	.01
☐	134 John Morris	.04	.02	.01
☐	135 Dave Parker	.07	.03	.01
☐	136 Gary Pettis	.04	.02	.01
☐	137 Dennis Boyd	.04	.02	.01
☐	138 Candy Maldonado	.04	.02	.01
☐	139 Rick Cerone	.04	.02	.01
☐	140 George Brett	.15	.07	.02
☐	141 Dave Clark	.04	.02	.01
☐	142 Dickie Thon	.04	.02	.01
☐	143 Junior Ortiz	.04	.02	.01
☐	144 Don August	.04	.02	.01

☐ 145 Gary Gaetti	.04	.02	.01
☐ 146 Kirt Manwaring	.04	.02	.01
☐ 147 Jeff Reed	.04	.02	.01
☐ 148 Jose Alvarez	.04	.02	.01
☐ 149 Mike Schooler	.04	.02	.01
☐ 150 Mark Grace	.20	.09	.03
☐ 151 Geronimo Berroa	.04	.02	.01
☐ 152 Barry Jones	.04	.02	.01
☐ 153 Geno Petralli	.04	.02	.01
☐ 154 Jim Deshaies	.04	.02	.01
☐ 155 Barry Larkin	.12	.05	.02
☐ 156 Alfredo Griffin	.04	.02	.01
☐ 157 Tom Henke	.07	.03	.01
☐ 158 Mike Jeffcoat	.04	.02	.01
☐ 159 Bob Welch	.07	.03	.01
☐ 160 Julio Franco	.07	.03	.01
☐ 161 Henry Cotto	.04	.02	.01
☐ 162 Terry Steinbach	.07	.03	.01
☐ 163 Damon Berryhill	.04	.02	.01
☐ 164 Tim Crews	.04	.02	.01
☐ 165 Tom Browning	.04	.02	.01
☐ 166 Fred Manrique	.04	.02	.01
☐ 167 Harold Reynolds	.04	.02	.01
☐ 168A Ron Hassey ERR (27 on back)	.04	.02	.01
☐ 168B Ron Hassey COR (24 on back)	1.00	.45	.13
☐ 169 Shawon Dunston	.07	.03	.01
☐ 170 Bobby Bonilla	.12	.05	.02
☐ 171 Tommy Herr	.04	.02	.01
☐ 172 Mike Heath	.04	.02	.01
☐ 173 Rich Gedman	.04	.02	.01
☐ 174 Bill Ripken	.04	.02	.01
☐ 175 Pete O'Brien	.04	.02	.01
☐ 176A Lloyd McClendon ERR (Uniform number on back listed as 1)	.75	.35	.09
☐ 176B Lloyd McClendon COR (Uniform number on back listed as 10)	.04	.02	.01
☐ 177 Brian Holton	.04	.02	.01
☐ 178 Jeff Blauser	.07	.03	.01
☐ 179 Jim Eisenreich	.04	.02	.01
☐ 180 Bert Blyleven	.07	.03	.01
☐ 181 Rob Murphy	.04	.02	.01
☐ 182 Bill Doran	.04	.02	.01
☐ 183 Curt Ford	.04	.02	.01
☐ 184 Mike Henneman	.04	.02	.01
☐ 185 Eric Davis	.10	.05	.01
☐ 186 Lance McCullers	.04	.02	.01
☐ 187 Steve Davis	.04	.02	.01
☐ 188 Bill Wegman	.04	.02	.01
☐ 189 Brian Harper	.07	.03	.01
☐ 190 Mike Moore	.04	.02	.01
☐ 191 Dale Mohorcic	.04	.02	.01
☐ 192 Tim Wallach	.07	.03	.01
☐ 193 Keith Hernandez	.07	.03	.01
☐ 194 Dave Righetti	.04	.02	.01
☐ 195A Bret Saberhagen ERR (Joke)	.08	.04	.01
☐ 195B Bret Saberhagen COR (Joker)	.25	.11	.03
☐ 196 Paul Kilgus	.04	.02	.01
☐ 197 Bud Black	.04	.02	.01
☐ 198 Juan Samuel	.04	.02	.01
☐ 199 Kevin Seitzer	.07	.03	.01
☐ 200 Darryl Strawberry	.20	.09	.03
☐ 201 Dave Stieb	.07	.03	.01
☐ 202 Charlie Hough	.04	.02	.01
☐ 203 Jack Morris	.10	.05	.01
☐ 204 Rance Mulliniks	.04	.02	.01
☐ 205 Alvin Davis	.04	.02	.01
☐ 206 Jack Howell	.04	.02	.01
☐ 207 Ken Patterson	.04	.02	.01
☐ 208 Terry Pendleton	.10	.05	.01
☐ 209 Craig Lefferts	.04	.02	.01
☐ 210 Kevin Brown UER (First mention of '89 Rangers should be '88)	.10	.05	.01
☐ 211 Dan Petry	.04	.02	.01
☐ 212 Dave Leiper	.04	.02	.01
☐ 213 Daryl Boston	.04	.02	.01
☐ 214 Kevin Hickey	.04	.02	.01
☐ 215 Mike Krukow	.04	.02	.01
☐ 216 Terry Francona	.04	.02	.01
☐ 217 Kirk McCaskill	.04	.02	.01
☐ 218 Scott Bailes	.04	.02	.01
☐ 219 Bob Forsch	.04	.02	.01
☐ 220A Mike Aldrete ERR (25 on back)	.04	.02	.01
☐ 220B Mike Aldrete COR (24 on back)	.25	.11	.03
☐ 221 Steve Buechele	.04	.02	.01
☐ 222 Jesse Barfield	.04	.02	.01
☐ 223 Juan Berenguer	.04	.02	.01
☐ 224 Andy McGaffigan	.04	.02	.01
☐ 225 Pete Smith	.07	.03	.01
☐ 226 Mike Witt	.04	.02	.01
☐ 227 Jay Howell	.04	.02	.01
☐ 228 Scott Bradley	.04	.02	.01
☐ 229 Jerome Walton	.07	.03	.01
☐ 230 Greg Swindell	.07	.03	.01
☐ 231 Atlee Hammaker	.04	.02	.01
☐ 232A Mike Devereaux ERR (RF on front)	.08	.04	.01
☐ 232B Mike Devereaux COR (CF on front)	1.00	.45	.13
☐ 233 Ken Hill	.15	.07	.02
☐ 234 Craig Worthington	.04	.02	.01
☐ 235 Scott Terry	.04	.02	.01
☐ 236 Brett Butler	.07	.03	.01
☐ 237 Doyle Alexander	.04	.02	.01
☐ 238 Dave Anderson	.04	.02	.01
☐ 239 Bob Milacki	.04	.02	.01
☐ 240 Dwight Smith	.04	.02	.01
☐ 241 Otis Nixon	.07	.03	.01
☐ 242 Pat Tabler	.04	.02	.01
☐ 243 Derek Lilliquist	.04	.02	.01
☐ 244 Danny Tartabull	.10	.05	.01
☐ 245 Wade Boggs	.20	.09	.03
☐ 246 Scott Garrelts (Should say Relief Pitcher on front)	.04	.02	.01
☐ 247 Spike Owen	.04	.02	.01
☐ 248 Norm Charlton	.07	.03	.01
☐ 249 Gerald Perry	.04	.02	.01
☐ 250 Nolan Ryan	.50	.23	.06
☐ 251 Kevin Gross	.04	.02	.01
☐ 252 Randy Milligan	.04	.02	.01
☐ 253 Mike LaCoss	.04	.02	.01
☐ 254 Dave Bergman	.04	.02	.01
☐ 255 Tony Gwynn	.20	.09	.03
☐ 256 Felix Fermin	.04	.02	.01
☐ 257 Greg W. Harris	.04	.02	.01
☐ 258 Junior Felix	.07	.03	.01
☐ 259 Mark Davis	.04	.02	.01
☐ 260 Vince Coleman	.07	.03	.01
☐ 261 Paul Gibson	.04	.02	.01
☐ 262 Mitch Williams	.07	.03	.01
☐ 263 Jeff Russell	.04	.02	.01
☐ 264 Omar Vizquel	.07	.03	.01
☐ 265 Andre Dawson	.12	.05	.02
☐ 266 Storm Davis	.04	.02	.01
☐ 267 Guillermo Hernandez	.04	.02	.01
☐ 268 Mike Felder	.04	.02	.01
☐ 269 Tom Candiotti	.04	.02	.01
☐ 270 Bruce Hurst	.07	.03	.01
☐ 271 Fred McGriff	.20	.09	.03
☐ 272 Glenn Davis	.07	.03	.01
☐ 273 John Franco	.07	.03	.01
☐ 274 Rich Yett	.04	.02	.01
☐ 275 Craig Biggio	.10	.05	.01
☐ 276 Gene Larkin	.04	.02	.01
☐ 277 Rob Dibble	.07	.03	.01
☐ 278 Randy Bush	.04	.02	.01
☐ 279 Kevin Bass	.04	.02	.01
☐ 280A Bo Jackson ERR (Watham)	.12	.05	.02
☐ 280B Bo Jackson COR (Wathan)	.50	.23	.06
☐ 281 Wally Backman	.04	.02	.01
☐ 282 Larry Andersen	.04	.02	.01
☐ 283 Chris Bosio	.04	.02	.01
☐ 284 Juan Agosto	.04	.02	.01
☐ 285 Ozzie Smith	.12	.05	.02
☐ 286 George Bell	.07	.03	.01
☐ 287 Rex Hudler	.04	.02	.01
☐ 288 Pat Borders	.07	.03	.01
☐ 289 Danny Jackson	.04	.02	.01
☐ 290 Carlton Fisk	.10	.05	.01
☐ 291 Tracy Jones	.04	.02	.01
☐ 292 Allan Anderson	.04	.02	.01
☐ 293 Johnny Ray	.04	.02	.01
☐ 294 Lee Guetterman	.04	.02	.01
☐ 295 Paul O'Neill	.07	.03	.01
☐ 296 Carney Lansford	.07	.03	.01
☐ 297 Tom Brookens	.04	.02	.01
☐ 298 Claudell Washington	.04	.02	.01
☐ 299 Hubie Brooks	.04	.02	.01
☐ 300 Will Clark	.30	.14	.04
☐ 301 Kenny Rogers	.04	.02	.01
☐ 302 Darrell Evans	.07	.03	.01
☐ 303 Greg Briley	.04	.02	.01
☐ 304 Donn Pall	.04	.02	.01
☐ 305 Teddy Higuera	.04	.02	.01
☐ 306 Dan Pasqua	.04	.02	.01

307	Dave Winfield	.15	.07	.02
308	Dennis Powell	.04	.02	.01
309	Jose DeLeon	.04	.02	.01
310	Roger Clemens UER (Dominate, should say dominant)	.35	.16	.04
311	Melido Perez	.07	.03	.01
312	Devon White	.07	.03	.01
313	Dwight Gooden	.10	.05	.01
314	Carlos Martinez	.04	.02	.01
315	Dennis Eckersley	.12	.05	.02
316	Clay Parker UER (Height 6'11")	.04	.02	.01
317	Rick Honeycutt	.04	.02	.01
318	Tim Laudner	.04	.02	.01
319	Joe Carter	.20	.09	.03
320	Robin Yount	.15	.07	.02
321	Felix Jose	.20	.09	.03
322	Mickey Tettleton	.07	.03	.01
323	Mike Gallego	.04	.02	.01
324	Edgar Martinez	.20	.09	.03
325	Dave Henderson	.04	.02	.01
326	Chili Davis	.07	.03	.01
327	Steve Balboni	.04	.02	.01
328	Jody Davis	.04	.02	.01
329	Shawn Hillegas	.04	.02	.01
330	Jim Abbott	.20	.09	.03
331	John Dopson	.04	.02	.01
332	Mark Williamson	.04	.02	.01
333	Jeff D. Robinson	.04	.02	.01
334	John Smiley	.07	.03	.01
335	Bobby Thigpen	.04	.02	.01
336	Garry Templeton	.04	.02	.01
337	Marvell Wynne	.04	.02	.01
338A	Ken Griffey Sr. ERR (Uniform number on back listed as 25)	.08	.04	.01
338B	Ken Griffey Sr. COR (Uniform number on back listed as 30)	1.50	.65	.19
339	Steve Finley	.07	.03	.01
340	Ellis Burks	.07	.03	.01
341	Frank Williams	.04	.02	.01
342	Mike Morgan	.04	.02	.01
343	Kevin Mitchell	.10	.05	.01
344	Joel Youngblood	.04	.02	.01
345	Mike Greenwell	.07	.03	.01
346	Glenn Wilson	.04	.02	.01
347	John Costello	.04	.02	.01
348	Wes Gardner	.04	.02	.01
349	Jeff Ballard	.04	.02	.01
350	Mark Thurmond UER (ERA is 192, should be 1.92)	.04	.02	.01
351	Randy Myers	.07	.03	.01
352	Shawn Abner	.04	.02	.01
353	Jesse Orosco	.04	.02	.01
354	Greg Walker	.04	.02	.01
355	Pete Harnisch	.07	.03	.01
356	Steve Farr	.04	.02	.01
357	Dave LaPoint	.04	.02	.01
358	Willie Fraser	.04	.02	.01
359	Mickey Hatcher	.04	.02	.01
360	Rickey Henderson	.20	.09	.03
361	Mike Fitzgerald	.04	.02	.01
362	Bill Schroeder	.04	.02	.01
363	Mark Carreon	.04	.02	.01
364	Ron Jones	.04	.02	.01
365	Jeff Montgomery	.07	.03	.01
366	Bill Krueger	.04	.02	.01
367	John Cangelosi	.04	.02	.01
368	Jose Gonzalez	.04	.02	.01
369	Greg Hibbard	.20	.09	.03
370	John Smoltz	.25	.11	.03
371	Jeff Brantley	.04	.02	.01
372	Frank White	.04	.02	.01
373	Ed Whitson	.04	.02	.01
374	Willie McGee	.07	.03	.01
375	Jose Canseco	.30	.14	.04
376	Randy Ready	.04	.02	.01
377	Don Aase	.04	.02	.01
378	Tony Armas	.04	.02	.01
379	Steve Bedrosian	.04	.02	.01
380	Chuck Finley	.07	.03	.01
381	Kent Hrbek	.07	.03	.01
382	Jim Gantner	.04	.02	.01
383	Mel Hall	.04	.02	.01
384	Mike Marshall	.04	.02	.01
385	Mark McGwire	.30	.14	.04
386	Wayne Tolleson	.04	.02	.01
387	Brian Holman	.04	.02	.01
388	John Wetteland	.07	.03	.01
389	Darren Daulton	.07	.03	.01

390	Rob Deer	.07	.03	.01
391	John Moses	.04	.02	.01
392	Todd Worrell	.04	.02	.01
393	Chuck Cary	.04	.02	.01
394	Stan Javier	.04	.02	.01
395	Willie Randolph	.07	.03	.01
396	Bill Buckner	.07	.03	.01
397	Robby Thompson	.04	.02	.01
398	Mike Scioscia	.04	.02	.01
399	Lonnie Smith	.04	.02	.01
400	Kirby Puckett	.30	.14	.04
401	Mark Langston	.07	.03	.01
402	Danny Darwin	.04	.02	.01
403	Greg Maddux	.20	.09	.03
404	Lloyd Moseby	.04	.02	.01
405	Rafael Palmeiro	.10	.05	.01
406	Chad Kreuter	.04	.02	.01
407	Jimmy Key	.07	.03	.01
408	Tim Birtsas	.04	.02	.01
409	Tim Raines	.07	.03	.01
410	Dave Stewart	.07	.03	.01
411	Eric Yelding	.04	.02	.01
412	Kent Anderson	.04	.02	.01
413	Les Lancaster	.04	.02	.01
414	Rick Dempsey	.04	.02	.01
415	Randy Johnson	.07	.03	.01
416	Gary Carter	.07	.03	.01
417	Rolando Roomes	.04	.02	.01
418	Dan Schatzeder	.04	.02	.01
419	Bryn Smith	.04	.02	.01
420	Ruben Sierra	.20	.09	.03
421	Steve Jeltz	.04	.02	.01
422	Ken Oberkfell	.04	.02	.01
423	Sid Bream	.04	.02	.01
424	Jim Clancy	.04	.02	.01
425	Kelly Gruber	.07	.03	.01
426	Rick Leach	.04	.02	.01
427	Len Dykstra	.07	.03	.01
428	Jeff Pico	.04	.02	.01
429	John Cerutti	.04	.02	.01
430	David Cone	.12	.05	.02
431	Jeff Kunkel	.04	.02	.01
432	Luis Aquino	.04	.02	.01
433	Ernie Whitt	.04	.02	.01
434	Bo Diaz	.04	.02	.01
435	Steve Lake	.04	.02	.01
436	Pat Perry	.04	.02	.01
437	Mike Davis	.04	.02	.01
438	Cecilio Guante	.04	.02	.01
439	Duane Ward	.04	.02	.01
440	Andy Van Slyke	.10	.05	.01
441	Gene Nelson	.04	.02	.01
442	Luis Polonia	.07	.03	.01
443	Kevin Elster	.04	.02	.01
444	Keith Moreland	.04	.02	.01
445	Roger McDowell	.04	.02	.01
446	Ron Darling	.07	.03	.01
447	Ernest Riles	.04	.02	.01
448	Mookie Wilson	.04	.02	.01
449A	Billy Spiers ERR (No birth year)	.75	.35	.09
449B	Billy Spiers COR (Born in 1966)	.04	.02	.01
450	Rick Sutcliffe	.07	.03	.01
451	Nelson Santovenia	.04	.02	.01
452	Andy Allanson	.04	.02	.01
453	Bob Melvin	.04	.02	.01
454	Benito Santiago	.07	.03	.01
455	Jose Uribe	.04	.02	.01
456	Bill Landrum	.04	.02	.01
457	Bobby Witt	.07	.03	.01
458	Kevin Romine	.04	.02	.01
459	Lee Mazzilli	.04	.02	.01
460	Paul Molitor	.10	.05	.01
461	Ramon Martinez	.15	.07	.02
462	Frank DiPino	.04	.02	.01
463	Walt Terrell	.04	.02	.01
464	Bob Geren	.04	.02	.01
465	Rick Reuschel	.04	.02	.01
466	Mark Grant	.04	.02	.01
467	John Kruk	.07	.03	.01
468	Gregg Jefferies	.12	.05	.02
469	R.J. Reynolds	.04	.02	.01
470	Harold Baines	.07	.03	.01
471	Dennis Lamp	.04	.02	.01
472	Tom Gordon	.07	.03	.01
473	Terry Puhl	.04	.02	.01
474	Curt Wilkerson	.04	.02	.01
475	Dan Quisenberry	.07	.03	.01
476	Oddibe McDowell	.04	.02	.01
477	Zane Smith UER (Career ERA .393)	.04	.02	.01
478	Franklin Stubbs	.04	.02	.01

☐ 479 Wallace Johnson	.04	.02	.01
☐ 480 Jay Tibbs	.04	.02	.01
☐ 481 Tom Glavine	.25	.11	.03
☐ 482 Manny Lee	.04	.02	.01
☐ 483 Joe Hesketh UER (Says Rookiess on back, should say Rookies)	.04	.02	.01
☐ 484 Mike Bielecki	.04	.02	.01
☐ 485 Greg Brock	.04	.02	.01
☐ 486 Pascual Perez	.04	.02	.01
☐ 487 Kirk Gibson	.07	.03	.01
☐ 488 Scott Sanderson	.04	.02	.01
☐ 489 Domingo Ramos	.04	.02	.01
☐ 490 Kal Daniels	.04	.02	.01
☐ 491A David Wells ERR (Reverse negative photo on card back)	1.50	.65	.19
☐ 491B David Wells COR	.07	.03	.01
☐ 492 Jerry Reed	.04	.02	.01
☐ 493 Eric Show	.04	.02	.01
☐ 494 Mike Pagliarulo	.04	.02	.01
☐ 495 Ron Robinson	.04	.02	.01
☐ 496 Brad Komminsk	.04	.02	.01
☐ 497 Greg Litton	.04	.02	.01
☐ 498 Chris James	.04	.02	.01
☐ 499 Luis Quinones	.04	.02	.01
☐ 500 Frank Viola	.04	.02	.01
☐ 501 Tim Teufel UER (Twins '85, the s is lower case, should be upper case)	.04	.02	.01
☐ 502 Terry Leach	.04	.02	.01
☐ 503 Matt Williams	.10	.05	.01
☐ 504 Tim Leary	.04	.02	.01
☐ 505 Doug Drabek	.07	.03	.01
☐ 506 Mariano Duncan	.04	.02	.01
☐ 507 Charlie Hayes	.07	.03	.01
☐ 508 Joey Belle	.50	.23	.06
☐ 509 Pat Sheridan	.04	.02	.01
☐ 510 Mackey Sasser	.04	.02	.01
☐ 511 Jose Rijo	.07	.03	.01
☐ 512 Mike Smithson	.04	.02	.01
☐ 513 Gary Ward	.04	.02	.01
☐ 514 Dion James	.04	.02	.01
☐ 515 Jim Gott	.04	.02	.01
☐ 516 Drew Hall	.04	.02	.01
☐ 517 Doug Bair	.04	.02	.01
☐ 518 Scott Scudder	.04	.02	.01
☐ 519 Rick Aguilera	.07	.03	.01
☐ 520 Rafael Belliard	.04	.02	.01
☐ 521 Jay Buhner	.07	.03	.01
☐ 522 Jeff Reardon	.07	.03	.01
☐ 523 Steve Rosenberg	.04	.02	.01
☐ 524 Randy Velarde	.04	.02	.01
☐ 525 Jeff Musselman	.04	.02	.01
☐ 526 Bill Long	.04	.02	.01
☐ 527 Gary Wayne	.04	.02	.01
☐ 528 Dave Johnson (P)	.04	.02	.01
☐ 529 Ron Kittle	.04	.02	.01
☐ 530 Erik Hanson UER (5th line on back says seson, should say season)	.07	.03	.01
☐ 531 Steve Wilson	.04	.02	.01
☐ 532 Joey Meyer	.04	.02	.01
☐ 533 Curt Young	.04	.02	.01
☐ 534 Kelly Downs	.04	.02	.01
☐ 535 Joe Girardi	.04	.02	.01
☐ 536 Lance Blankenship	.04	.02	.01
☐ 537 Greg Mathews	.04	.02	.01
☐ 538 Donell Nixon	.04	.02	.01
☐ 539 Mark Knudson	.04	.02	.01
☐ 540 Jeff Wetherby	.04	.02	.01
☐ 541 Darrin Jackson	.07	.03	.01
☐ 542 Terry Mulholland	.07	.03	.01
☐ 543 Eric Hetzel	.04	.02	.01
☐ 544 Rick Reed	.04	.02	.01
☐ 545 Dennis Cook	.04	.02	.01
☐ 546 Mike Jackson	.04	.02	.01
☐ 547 Brian Fisher	.04	.02	.01
☐ 548 Gene Harris	.07	.03	.01
☐ 549 Jeff King	.07	.03	.01
☐ 550 Dave Dravecky	.07	.03	.01
☐ 551 Randy Kutcher	.04	.02	.01
☐ 552 Mark Portugal	.04	.02	.01
☐ 553 Jim Corsi	.04	.02	.01
☐ 554 Todd Stottlemyre	.07	.03	.01
☐ 555 Scott Bankhead	.04	.02	.01
☐ 556 Ken Dayley	.04	.02	.01
☐ 557 Rick Wrona	.04	.02	.01
☐ 558 Sammy Sosa	.15	.07	.02
☐ 559 Keith Miller	.04	.02	.01
☐ 560 Ken Griffey Jr.	1.25	.55	.16
☐ 561A Ryne Sandberg HL ERR (Position on front listed as 3B)	10.00	4.50	1.25
☐ 561B Ryne Sandberg HL COR	.20	.09	.03
☐ 562 Billy Hatcher	.04	.02	.01
☐ 563 Jay Bell	.07	.03	.01
☐ 564 Jack Daugherty	.04	.02	.01
☐ 565 Rich Monteleone	.04	.02	.01
☐ 566 Bo Jackson AS-MVP	.12	.05	.02
☐ 567 Tony Fossas	.04	.02	.01
☐ 568 Roy Smith	.04	.02	.01
☐ 569 Jaime Navarro	.20	.09	.03
☐ 570 Lance Johnson	.07	.03	.01
☐ 571 Mike Dyer	.04	.02	.01
☐ 572 Kevin Ritz	.10	.05	.01
☐ 573 Dave West	.04	.02	.01
☐ 574 Gary Mielke	.04	.02	.01
☐ 575 Scott Lusader	.04	.02	.01
☐ 576 Joe Oliver	.04	.02	.01
☐ 577 Sandy Alomar Jr.	.10	.05	.01
☐ 578 Andy Benes UER (Extra comma between day and year)	.20	.09	.03
☐ 579 Tim Jones	.04	.02	.01
☐ 580 Randy McCament	.04	.02	.01
☐ 581 Curt Schilling	.15	.07	.02
☐ 582 John Orton	.10	.05	.01
☐ 583A Milt Cuyler ERR (998 games)	1.00	.45	.13
☐ 583B Milt Cuyler COR (98 games)	.20	.09	.03
☐ 584 Eric Anthony	.30	.14	.04
☐ 585 Greg Vaughn	.15	.07	.02
☐ 586 Deion Sanders	.50	.23	.06
☐ 587 Jose DeJesus	.04	.02	.01
☐ 588 Chip Hale	.04	.02	.01
☐ 589 John Olerud	.60	.25	.08
☐ 590 Steve Olin	.20	.09	.03
☐ 591 Marquis Grissom	.60	.25	.08
☐ 592 Moises Alou	.50	.23	.06
☐ 593 Mark Lemke	.07	.03	.01
☐ 594 Dean Palmer	.60	.25	.08
☐ 595 Robin Ventura	.75	.35	.09
☐ 596 Tino Martinez	.12	.05	.02
☐ 597 Mike Huff	.10	.05	.01
☐ 598 Scott Hemond	.10	.05	.01
☐ 599 Wally Whitehurst	.04	.02	.01
☐ 600 Todd Zeile	.15	.07	.02
☐ 601 Glenallen Hill	.07	.03	.01
☐ 602 Hal Morris	.15	.07	.02
☐ 603 Juan Bell	.04	.02	.01
☐ 604 Bobby Rose	.07	.03	.01
☐ 605 Matt Merullo	.04	.02	.01
☐ 606 Kevin Maas	.25	.11	.03
☐ 607 Randy Nosek	.04	.02	.01
☐ 608A Billy Bates (Text mentions 12 triples in tenth line)	.10	.05	.01
☐ 608B Billy Bates (Text has no mention of triples)	.10	.05	.01
☐ 609 Mike Stanton	.15	.07	.02
☐ 610 Mauro Gozzo	.04	.02	.01
☐ 611 Charles Nagy	.50	.23	.06
☐ 612 Scott Coolbaugh	.04	.02	.01
☐ 613 Jose Vizcaino	.10	.05	.01
☐ 614 Greg Smith	.10	.05	.01
☐ 615 Jeff Huson	.10	.05	.01
☐ 616 Mickey Weston	.04	.02	.01
☐ 617 John Pawlowski	.04	.02	.01
☐ 618A Joe Skalski ERR (27 on back)	.04	.02	.01
☐ 618B Joe Skalski COR (67 on back)	1.00	.45	.13
☐ 619 Bernie Williams	.30	.14	.04
☐ 620 Shawn Holman	.04	.02	.01
☐ 621 Gary Eave	.04	.02	.01
☐ 622 Darrin Fletcher UER (Elmherst, should be Elmhurst)	.10	.05	.01
☐ 623 Pat Combs	.07	.03	.01
☐ 624 Mike Blowers	.04	.02	.01
☐ 625 Kevin Appier	.25	.11	.03
☐ 626 Pat Austin	.04	.02	.01
☐ 627 Kelly Mann	.04	.02	.01
☐ 628 Matt Kinzer	.07	.03	.01
☐ 629 Chris Hammond	.20	.09	.03
☐ 630 Dean Wilkins	.04	.02	.01
☐ 631 Larry Walker UER (Uniform number 55 on front and 33 on back)	.90	.40	.11
☐ 632 Blaine Beatty	.04	.02	.01
☐ 633A Tommy Barrett ERR	.04	.02	.01

(29 on back)			
☐ 633B Tommy Barrett COR (14 on back)	2.00	.90	.25
☐ 634 Stan Belinda	.15	.07	.02
☐ 635 Mike (Tex) Smith	.04	.02	.01
☐ 636 Hensley Meulens	.07	.03	.01
☐ 637 Juan Gonzalez	2.00	.90	.25
☐ 638 Lenny Webster	.10	.05	.01
☐ 639 Mark Gardner	.12	.05	.02
☐ 640 Tommy Greene	.12	.05	.02
☐ 641 Mike Hartley	.04	.02	.01
☐ 642 Phil Stephenson	.04	.02	.01
☐ 643 Kevin Mmahat	.04	.02	.01
☐ 644 Ed Whited	.04	.02	.01
☐ 645 Delino DeShields	.60	.25	.08
☐ 646 Kevin Blankenship	.04	.02	.01
☐ 647 Paul Sorrento	.25	.11	.03
☐ 648 Mike Roesler	.04	.02	.01
☐ 649 Jason Grimsley	.10	.05	.01
☐ 650 Dave Justice	1.25	.55	.16
☐ 651 Scott Cooper	.40	.18	.05
☐ 652 Dave Eiland	.04	.02	.01
☐ 653 Mike Munoz	.04	.02	.01
☐ 654 Jeff Fischer	.04	.02	.01
☐ 655 Terry Jorgensen	.04	.02	.01
☐ 656 George Canale	.04	.02	.01
☐ 657 Brian DuBois UER (Misspelled Dubois on card)	.10	.05	.01
☐ 658 Carlos Quintana	.07	.03	.01
☐ 659 Luis de los Santos	.04	.02	.01
☐ 660 Jerald Clark	.07	.03	.01
☐ 661 Donald Harris DC	.10	.05	.01
☐ 662 Paul Coleman DC	.12	.05	.02
☐ 663 Frank Thomas DC	6.00	2.70	.75
☐ 664 Brent Mayne DC	.15	.07	.02
☐ 665 Eddie Zosky DC	.15	.07	.02
☐ 666 Steve Hosey DC	.60	.25	.08
☐ 667 Scott Bryant DC	.12	.05	.02
☐ 668 Tom Goodwin DC	.15	.07	.02
☐ 669 Cal Eldred DC	1.25	.55	.16
☐ 670 Earl Cunningham DC	.12	.05	.02
☐ 671 Alan Zinter DC	.10	.05	.01
☐ 672 Chuck Knoblauch DC	1.25	.55	.16
☐ 673 Kyle Abbott DC	.20	.09	.03
☐ 674 Roger Salkeld DC	.20	.09	.03
☐ 675 Maurice Vaughn DC	.40	.18	.05
☐ 676 Keith(Kiki) Jones DC	.10	.05	.01
☐ 677 Tyler Houston DC	.10	.05	.01
☐ 678 Jeff Jackson DC	.10	.05	.01
☐ 679 Greg Gohr DC	.15	.07	.02
☐ 680 Ben McDonald DC	.50	.23	.06
☐ 681 Greg Blosser DC	.25	.11	.03
☐ 682 Willie Green DC UER (Name misspelled on card, should be Greene)	.50	.23	.06
☐ 683 Wade Boggs DT UER (Text says 215 hits in '89, should be 205)	.10	.05	.01
☐ 684 Will Clark DT	.15	.07	.02
☐ 685 Tony Gwynn DT UER (Text reads battling instead of batting)	.12	.05	.02
☐ 686 Rickey Henderson DT	.10	.05	.01
☐ 687 Bo Jackson DT	.15	.07	.02
☐ 688 Mark Langston DT	.05	.02	.01
☐ 689 Barry Larkin DT	.10	.05	.01
☐ 690 Kirby Puckett DT	.12	.05	.02
☐ 691 Ryne Sandberg DT	.20	.09	.03
☐ 692 Mike Scott DT	.05	.02	.01
☐ 693A Terry Steinbach DT ERR (cathers)	.05	.02	.01
☐ 693B Terry Steinbach DT COR (catchers)	.25	.11	.03
☐ 694 Bobby Thigpen DT	.05	.02	.01
☐ 695 Mitch Williams DT	.05	.02	.01
☐ 696 Nolan Ryan HL	.30	.14	.04
☐ 697 Bo Jackson FB/BB	1.50	.65	.19
☐ 698 Rickey Henderson ALCS-MVP	.10	.05	.01
☐ 699 Will Clark NLCS-MVP	.12	.05	.02
☐ 700 WS Games 1/2 (Dave Stewart and Mike Moore)	.05	.02	.01
☐ 701 Lights Out: Candlestick 5:04pm (10/17/89)	.08	.04	.01
☐ 702 WS Game 3 Bashers Blast Giants (Carney Lansford, Ricky Henderson, Jose Canseco, Dave Henderson)	.05	.02	.01
☐ 703 WS Game 4/Wrap-up A's Sweep Battle of the Bay (A's Celebrate)	.05	.02	.01
☐ 704 Wade Boggs HL Wade Raps 200	.10	.05	.01
☐ B1 A.Bartlett Giamatti COMM MEM	1.00	.45	.13
☐ B2 Pat Combs	.25	.11	.03
☐ B3 Todd Zeile	.90	.40	.11
☐ B4 Luis de los Santos	.25	.11	.03
☐ B5 Mark Lemke	.40	.18	.05
☐ B6 Robin Ventura	8.00	3.60	1.00
☐ B7 Jeff Huson	.25	.11	.03
☐ B8 Greg Vaughn	1.00	.45	.13
☐ B9 Marquis Grissom	4.00	1.80	.50
☐ B10 Eric Anthony	1.50	.65	.19

1990 Score McDonald's

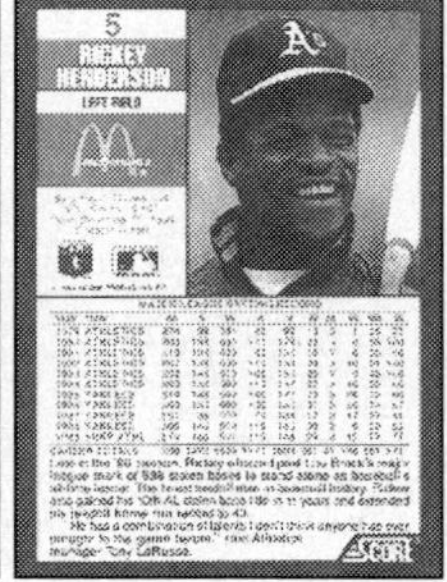

This 25-card set was produced by Score for McDonald's restaurants; included with the set were 15 World Series Trivia cards. The player cards were given away four to a pack and free with the purchase of fries and a drink, at only 11 McDonald's in the United States (in Idaho and Eastern Oregon) during a special promotion which lasted approximately three weeks. The cards measure the standard size (2 1/2" by 3 1/2"). The front has color action player photos, with white and yellow borders on a purple card face that fades as one moves toward the middle of the card. The upper left corner of the picture is cut off to allow space for the McDonald's logo; the player's name and team logo at the bottom round out the card face. The backs have color mugshots, biography, statistics, and career summary. The cards are numbered on the back.

	MT	EX-MT	VG
COMPLETE SET (25)	165.00	75.00	21.00
COMMON PLAYER (1-25)	3.00	1.35	.40
☐ 1 Will Clark	20.00	9.00	2.50
☐ 2 Sandy Alomar Jr.	4.00	1.80	.50
☐ 3 Julio Franco	4.00	1.80	.50
☐ 4 Carlton Fisk	12.00	5.50	1.50
☐ 5 Rickey Henderson	16.00	7.25	2.00
☐ 6 Matt Williams	6.00	2.70	.75
☐ 7 John Franco	3.00	1.35	.40
☐ 8 Ryne Sandberg	24.00	11.00	3.00
☐ 9 Kelly Gruber	4.00	1.80	.50
☐ 10 Andre Dawson	10.00	4.50	1.25
☐ 11 Barry Bonds	14.00	6.25	1.75
☐ 12 Gary Sheffield	16.00	7.25	2.00
☐ 13 Ramon Martinez	6.00	2.70	.75
☐ 14 Len Dykstra	4.00	1.80	.50
☐ 15 Benito Santiago	5.00	2.30	.60
☐ 16 Cecil Fielder	14.00	6.25	1.75
☐ 17 John Olerud	12.00	5.50	1.50
☐ 18 Roger Clemens	22.00	10.00	2.80
☐ 19 George Brett	14.00	6.25	1.75
☐ 20 George Bell	4.00	1.80	.50
☐ 21 Ozzie Guillen	3.00	1.35	.40
☐ 22 Steve Sax	4.00	1.80	.50
☐ 23 Dave Stewart	4.00	1.80	.50

☐ 24 Ozzie Smith	10.00	4.50	1.25
☐ 25 Robin Yount	14.00	6.25	1.75

1990 Score Nolan Ryan Commemorative

This 2 1/2" by 3 1/2" card was issued by Optigraphics (producer of Score and Sportflics) to commemorate the 11th National Sports Card Collectors Convention held in Arlington, Texas in July of 1990. This card featured a Score front similar to the Ryan 1990 Score highlight card except for the 11th National Convention Logo on the bottom right of the card. On the other side a Ryan Sportflics card was printed that stated (reflected) either Sportflics or 1990 National Sports Collectors Convention on the bottom of the card. This issue was limited to a printing of 600 cards with Ryan himself destroying the plates.

	MT	EX-MT	VG
COMPLETE SET (1)	600.00	275.00	75.00
☐ NNO Nolan Ryan (No number on back; card back is actually another front in Sportflics style)	600.00	275.00	75.00

1990 Score 100 Rising Stars

The 1990 Score Rising Stars set contains 100 standard size (2 1/2" by 3 1/2") cards. The fronts are green, blue and white. The vertically oriented backs feature a large color facial shot and career highlights. The cards were distributed as a set in a blister pack, which also included a full color booklet with more information about each player.

	MT	EX-MT	VG
COMPLETE SET (100)	10.00	4.50	1.25
COMMON PLAYER (1-100)	.05	.02	.01

☐ 1 Tom Gordon	.10	.05	.01
☐ 2 Jerome Walton	.10	.05	.01
☐ 3 Ken Griffey Jr.	1.50	.65	.19
☐ 4 Dwight Smith	.10	.05	.01
☐ 5 Jim Abbott	.50	.23	.06
☐ 6 Todd Zeile	.20	.09	.03
☐ 7 Donn Pall	.05	.02	.01
☐ 8 Rick Reed	.05	.02	.01
☐ 9 Joey Belle	.40	.18	.05
☐ 10 Gregg Jefferies	.25	.11	.03
☐ 11 Kevin Ritz	.10	.05	.01
☐ 12 Charlie Hayes	.10	.05	.01
☐ 13 Kevin Appier	.20	.09	.03
☐ 14 Jeff Huson	.05	.02	.01
☐ 15 Gary Wayne	.05	.02	.01
☐ 16 Eric Yelding	.05	.02	.01
☐ 17 Clay Parker	.05	.02	.01
☐ 18 Junior Felix	.10	.05	.01
☐ 19 Derek Lilliquist	.05	.02	.01
☐ 20 Gary Sheffield	.75	.35	.09
☐ 21 Craig Worthington	.05	.02	.01
☐ 22 Jeff Brantley	.05	.02	.01
☐ 23 Eric Hetzel	.05	.02	.01
☐ 24 Greg W.Harris	.10	.05	.01
☐ 25 John Wetteland	.10	.05	.01
☐ 26 Joe Oliver	.05	.02	.01
☐ 27 Kevin Maas	.30	.14	.04
☐ 28 Kevin Brown	.10	.05	.01
☐ 29 Mike Stanton	.10	.05	.01
☐ 30 Greg Vaughn	.25	.11	.03
☐ 31 Ron Jones	.05	.02	.01
☐ 32 Gregg Olson	.20	.09	.03
☐ 33 Joe Girardi	.10	.05	.01
☐ 34 Ken Hill	.15	.07	.02
☐ 35 Sammy Sosa	.20	.09	.03
☐ 36 Geronimo Berroa	.05	.02	.01
☐ 37 Omar Vizquel	.10	.05	.01
☐ 38 Dean Palmer	.40	.18	.05
☐ 39 John Olerud	.75	.35	.09
☐ 40 Deion Sanders	.75	.35	.09
☐ 41 Randy Kramer	.05	.02	.01
☐ 42 Scott Lusader	.05	.02	.01
☐ 43 Dave Johnson (P)	.05	.02	.01
☐ 44 Jeff Wetherby	.05	.02	.01
☐ 45 Eric Anthony	.50	.23	.06
☐ 46 Kenny Rogers	.05	.02	.01
☐ 47 Matt Winters	.05	.02	.01
☐ 48 Mauro Gozzo	.05	.02	.01
☐ 49 Carlos Quintana	.05	.02	.01
☐ 50 Bob Geren	.05	.02	.01
☐ 51 Chad Kreuter	.05	.02	.01
☐ 52 Randy Johnson	.15	.07	.02
☐ 53 Hensley Meulens	.15	.07	.02
☐ 54 Gene Harris	.10	.05	.01
☐ 55 Bill Spiers	.05	.02	.01
☐ 56 Kelly Mann	.05	.02	.01
☐ 57 Tom McCarthy	.05	.02	.01
☐ 58 Steve Finley	.10	.05	.01
☐ 59 Ramon Martinez	.35	.16	.04
☐ 60 Greg Briley	.05	.02	.01
☐ 61 Jack Daugherty	.05	.02	.01
☐ 62 Tim Jones	.05	.02	.01
☐ 63 Doug Strange	.05	.02	.01
☐ 64 John Orton	.05	.02	.01
☐ 65 Scott Scudder	.10	.05	.01
☐ 66 Mark Gardner	.05	.02	.01
☐ 67 Mark Carreon	.05	.02	.01
☐ 68 Bob Milacki	.05	.02	.01
☐ 69 Andy Benes	.35	.16	.04
☐ 70 Carlos Martinez	.10	.05	.01
☐ 71 Jeff King	.10	.05	.01
☐ 72 Brad Arnsberg	.05	.02	.01
☐ 73 Rick Wrona	.05	.02	.01
☐ 74 Cris Carpenter	.10	.05	.01
☐ 75 Dennis Cook	.05	.02	.01
☐ 76 Pete Harnisch	.10	.05	.01
☐ 77 Greg Hibbard	.10	.05	.01
☐ 78 Ed Whited	.05	.02	.01
☐ 79 Scott Coolbaugh	.05	.02	.01
☐ 80 Billy Bates	.05	.02	.01
☐ 81 German Gonzalez	.05	.02	.01
☐ 82 Lance Blankenship	.05	.02	.01
☐ 83 Lenny Harris	.10	.05	.01
☐ 84 Milt Cuyler	.25	.11	.03
☐ 85 Erik Hanson	.10	.05	.01
☐ 86 Kent Anderson	.05	.02	.01
☐ 87 Hal Morris	.35	.16	.04
☐ 88 Mike Brumley	.05	.02	.01
☐ 89 Ken Patterson	.05	.02	.01
☐ 90 Mike Devereaux	.15	.07	.02
☐ 91 Greg Litton	.05	.02	.01
☐ 92 Rolando Roomes	.05	.02	.01
☐ 93 Ben McDonald	.35	.16	.04

		MT	EX-MT	VG
☐ 94	Curt Schilling	.15	.07	.02
☐ 95	Jose DeJesus	.05	.02	.01
☐ 96	Robin Ventura	.75	.35	.09
☐ 97	Steve Searcy	.05	.02	.01
☐ 98	Chip Hale	.05	.02	.01
☐ 99	Marquis Grissom	.60	.25	.08
☐ 100	Luis de los Santos	.05	.02	.01

1990 Score 100 Superstars

The 1990 Score Superstars set contains 100 standard size (2 1/2" by 3 1/2") cards. The fronts are red, white, blue and purple. The vertically oriented backs feature a large color facial shot and career highlights. The cards were distributed as a set in a blister pack, which also included a full color booklet with more information about each player.

		MT	EX-MT	VG
COMPLETE SET (100)		10.00	4.50	1.25
COMMON PLAYER (1-100)		.05	.02	.01
☐ 1	Kirby Puckett	.75	.35	.09
☐ 2	Steve Sax	.10	.05	.01
☐ 3	Tony Gwynn	.50	.23	.06
☐ 4	Willie Randolph	.10	.05	.01
☐ 5	Jose Canseco	.75	.35	.09
☐ 6	Ozzie Smith	.30	.14	.04
☐ 7	Rick Reuschel	.05	.02	.01
☐ 8	Bill Doran	.05	.02	.01
☐ 9	Mickey Tettleton	.15	.07	.02
☐ 10	Don Mattingly	.60	.25	.08
☐ 11	Greg Swindell	.10	.05	.01
☐ 12	Bert Blyleven	.10	.05	.01
☐ 13	Dave Stewart	.10	.05	.01
☐ 14	Andres Galarraga	.05	.02	.01
☐ 15	Darryl Strawberry	.50	.23	.06
☐ 16	Ellis Burks	.20	.09	.03
☐ 17	Paul O'Neill	.10	.05	.01
☐ 18	Bruce Hurst	.10	.05	.01
☐ 19	Dave Smith	.05	.02	.01
☐ 20	Carney Lansford	.10	.05	.01
☐ 21	Robby Thompson	.05	.02	.01
☐ 22	Gary Gaetti	.05	.02	.01
☐ 23	Jeff Russell	.05	.02	.01
☐ 24	Chuck Finley	.05	.02	.01
☐ 25	Mark McGwire	.50	.23	.06
☐ 26	Alvin Davis	.05	.02	.01
☐ 27	George Bell	.15	.07	.02
☐ 28	Cory Snyder	.05	.02	.01
☐ 29	Keith Hernandez	.10	.05	.01
☐ 30	Will Clark	.75	.35	.09
☐ 31	Steve Bedrosian	.05	.02	.01
☐ 32	Ryne Sandberg	.90	.40	.11
☐ 33	Tom Browning	.10	.05	.01
☐ 34	Tim Burke	.05	.02	.01
☐ 35	John Smoltz	.25	.11	.03
☐ 36	Phil Bradley	.05	.02	.01
☐ 37	Bobby Bonilla	.35	.16	.04
☐ 38	Kirk McCaskill	.05	.02	.01
☐ 39	Dave Righetti	.05	.02	.01
☐ 40	Bo Jackson	.75	.35	.09
☐ 41	Alan Trammell	.10	.05	.01
☐ 42	Mike Moore UER (Uniform number is 21, not 23 as on front)	.05	.02	.01
☐ 43	Harold Reynolds	.05	.02	.01
☐ 44	Nolan Ryan	1.25	.55	.16
☐ 45	Fred McGriff	.35	.16	.04
☐ 46	Brian Downing	.05	.02	.01
☐ 47	Brett Butler	.10	.05	.01
☐ 48	Mike Scioscia	.05	.02	.01
☐ 49	John Franco	.05	.02	.01
☐ 50	Kevin Mitchell	.25	.11	.03
☐ 51	Mark Davis	.05	.02	.01
☐ 52	Glenn Davis	.10	.05	.01
☐ 53	Barry Bonds	.50	.23	.06
☐ 54	Dwight Evans	.10	.05	.01
☐ 55	Terry Steinbach	.10	.05	.01
☐ 56	Dave Gallagher	.05	.02	.01
☐ 57	Roberto Kelly	.20	.09	.03
☐ 58	Rafael Palmeiro	.25	.11	.03
☐ 59	Joe Carter	.35	.16	.04
☐ 60	Mark Grace	.50	.23	.06
☐ 61	Pedro Guerrero	.10	.05	.01
☐ 62	Von Hayes	.05	.02	.01
☐ 63	Benito Santiago	.15	.07	.02
☐ 64	Dale Murphy	.25	.11	.03
☐ 65	John Smiley	.10	.05	.01
☐ 66	Cal Ripken	1.00	.45	.13
☐ 67	Mike Greenwell	.20	.09	.03
☐ 68	Devon White	.15	.07	.02
☐ 69	Ed Whitson	.05	.02	.01
☐ 70	Carlton Fisk	.30	.14	.04
☐ 71	Lou Whitaker	.15	.07	.02
☐ 72	Danny Tartabull	.25	.11	.03
☐ 73	Vince Coleman	.15	.07	.02
☐ 74	Andre Dawson	.35	.16	.04
☐ 75	Tim Raines	.15	.07	.02
☐ 76	George Brett	.45	.20	.06
☐ 77	Tom Herr	.05	.02	.01
☐ 78	Andy Van Slyke	.20	.09	.03
☐ 79	Roger Clemens	.90	.40	.11
☐ 80	Wade Boggs	.60	.25	.08
☐ 81	Wally Joyner	.15	.07	.02
☐ 82	Lonnie Smith	.05	.02	.01
☐ 83	Howard Johnson	.15	.07	.02
☐ 84	Julio Franco	.10	.05	.01
☐ 85	Ruben Sierra	.45	.20	.06
☐ 86	Dan Plesac	.05	.02	.01
☐ 87	Bobby Thigpen	.10	.05	.01
☐ 88	Kevin Seitzer	.05	.02	.01
☐ 89	Dave Stieb	.10	.05	.01
☐ 90	Rickey Henderson	.60	.25	.08
☐ 91	Jeffrey Leonard	.05	.02	.01
☐ 92	Robin Yount	.50	.23	.06
☐ 93	Mitch Williams	.10	.05	.01
☐ 94	Orel Hershiser	.15	.07	.02
☐ 95	Eric Davis	.25	.11	.03
☐ 96	Mark Langston	.10	.05	.01
☐ 97	Mike Scott	.10	.05	.01
☐ 98	Paul Molitor	.15	.07	.02
☐ 99	Dwight Gooden	.20	.09	.03
☐ 100	Kevin Bass	.05	.02	.01

1990 Score Rookie/Traded

The 1990 Score Rookie and Traded set marks the third consecutive year Score has issued an end of the year set to mark trades and give rookies early cards. The set consists of 110 cards each measuring the standard size of 2 1/2" by 3 1/2". The first 66 cards are traded players while the last 44 cards are Rookie Cards. Included in the rookie part of the set are cross-athletes Eric Lindros (hockey) and D.J. Dozier (football). The key baseball player Rookie Cards in the set are Carlos Baerga, Derek Bell, and Ray Lankford.

	MT	EX-MT	VG
COMPLETE SET (110)	16.00	7.25	2.00
COMMON PLAYER (1T-66T)	.05	.02	.01
COMMON PLAYER (67T-110T)	.05	.02	.01
☐ 1T Dave Winfield	.15	.07	.02
☐ 2T Kevin Bass	.05	.02	.01
☐ 3T Nick Esasky	.05	.02	.01
☐ 4T Mitch Webster	.05	.02	.01
☐ 5T Pascual Perez	.05	.02	.01
☐ 6T Gary Pettis	.05	.02	.01
☐ 7T Tony Pena	.05	.02	.01
☐ 8T Candy Maldonado	.05	.02	.01
☐ 9T Cecil Fielder	.20	.09	.03
☐ 10T Carmelo Martinez	.05	.02	.01
☐ 11T Mark Langston	.08	.04	.01
☐ 12T Dave Parker	.08	.04	.01
☐ 13T Don Slaught	.05	.02	.01
☐ 14T Tony Phillips	.05	.02	.01
☐ 15T John Franco	.08	.04	.01
☐ 16T Randy Myers	.08	.04	.01
☐ 17T Jeff Reardon	.08	.04	.01
☐ 18T Sandy Alomar Jr.	.10	.05	.01
☐ 19T Joe Carter	.20	.09	.03
☐ 20T Fred Lynn	.08	.04	.01
☐ 21T Storm Davis	.05	.02	.01
☐ 22T Craig Lefferts	.05	.02	.01
☐ 23T Pete O'Brien	.05	.02	.01
☐ 24T Dennis Boyd	.05	.02	.01
☐ 25T Lloyd Moseby	.05	.02	.01
☐ 26T Mark Davis	.05	.02	.01
☐ 27T Tim Leary	.05	.02	.01
☐ 28T Gerald Perry	.05	.02	.01
☐ 29T Don Aase	.05	.02	.01
☐ 30T Ernie Whitt	.05	.02	.01
☐ 31T Dale Murphy	.08	.04	.01
☐ 32T Alejandro Pena	.05	.02	.01
☐ 33T Juan Samuel	.05	.02	.01
☐ 34T Hubie Brooks	.05	.02	.01
☐ 35T Gary Carter	.08	.04	.01
☐ 36T Jim Presley	.05	.02	.01
☐ 37T Wally Backman	.05	.02	.01
☐ 38T Matt Nokes	.05	.02	.01
☐ 39T Dan Petry	.05	.02	.01
☐ 40T Franklin Stubbs	.05	.02	.01
☐ 41T Jeff Huson	.05	.02	.01
☐ 42T Billy Hatcher	.05	.02	.01
☐ 43T Terry Leach	.05	.02	.01
☐ 44T Phil Bradley	.05	.02	.01
☐ 45T Claudell Washington	.05	.02	.01
☐ 46T Luis Polonia	.08	.04	.01
☐ 47T Daryl Boston	.05	.02	.01
☐ 48T Lee Smith	.08	.04	.01
☐ 49T Tom Brunansky	.08	.04	.01
☐ 50T Mike Witt	.05	.02	.01
☐ 51T Willie Randolph	.08	.04	.01
☐ 52T Stan Javier	.05	.02	.01
☐ 53T Brad Komminsk	.05	.02	.01
☐ 54T John Candelaria	.05	.02	.01
☐ 55T Bryn Smith	.05	.02	.01
☐ 56T Glenn Braggs	.05	.02	.01
☐ 57T Keith Hernandez	.08	.04	.01
☐ 58T Ken Oberkfell	.05	.02	.01
☐ 59T Steve Jeltz	.05	.02	.01
☐ 60T Chris James	.05	.02	.01
☐ 61T Scott Sanderson	.05	.02	.01
☐ 62T Bill Long	.05	.02	.01
☐ 63T Rick Cerone	.05	.02	.01
☐ 64T Scott Bailes	.05	.02	.01
☐ 65T Larry Sheets	.05	.02	.01
☐ 66T Junior Ortiz	.05	.02	.01
☐ 67T Francisco Cabrera	.10	.05	.01
☐ 68T Gary DiSarcina	.20	.09	.03
☐ 69T Greg Olson	.10	.05	.01
☐ 70T Beau Allred	.05	.02	.01
☐ 71T Oscar Azocar	.05	.02	.01
☐ 72T Kent Mercker	.12	.05	.02
☐ 73T John Burkett	.10	.05	.01
☐ 74T Carlos Baerga	1.25	.55	.16
☐ 75T Dave Hollins	.60	.25	.08
☐ 76T Todd Hundley	.15	.07	.02
☐ 77T Rick Parker	.05	.02	.01
☐ 78T Steve Cummings	.05	.02	.01
☐ 79T Bill Sampen	.05	.02	.01
☐ 80T Jerry Kutzler	.05	.02	.01
☐ 81T Derek Bell	1.00	.45	.13
☐ 82T Kevin Tapani	.35	.16	.04
☐ 83T Jim Leyritz	.10	.05	.01
☐ 84T Ray Lankford	1.00	.45	.13
☐ 85T Wayne Edwards	.05	.02	.01
☐ 86T Frank Thomas	6.50	2.90	.80
☐ 87T Tim Naehring	.15	.07	.02
☐ 88T Willie Blair	.05	.02	.01
☐ 89T Alan Mills	.12	.05	.02
☐ 90T Scott Radinsky	.15	.07	.02
☐ 91T Howard Farmer	.05	.02	.01
☐ 92T Julio Machado	.08	.04	.01
☐ 93T Rafael Valdez	.10	.05	.01
☐ 94T Shawn Boskie	.10	.05	.01
☐ 95T David Segui	.10	.05	.01
☐ 96T Chris Hoiles	.40	.18	.05
☐ 97T D.J. Dozier	.20	.09	.03
☐ 98T Hector Villanueva	.10	.05	.01
☐ 99T Eric Gunderson	.10	.05	.01
☐ 100T Eric Lindros	7.00	3.10	.85
☐ 101T Dave Otto	.05	.02	.01
☐ 102T Dana Kiecker	.05	.02	.01
☐ 103T Tim Drummond	.05	.02	.01
☐ 104T Mickey Pina	.05	.02	.01
☐ 105T Craig Grebeck	.15	.07	.02
☐ 106T Bernard Gilkey	.40	.18	.05
☐ 107T Tim Layana	.05	.02	.01
☐ 108T Scott Chiamparino	.10	.05	.01
☐ 109T Steve Avery	1.00	.45	.13
☐ 110T Terry Shumpert	.08	.04	.01

1990 Score Young Superstars I

1990 Score Young Superstars I are glossy full color cards featuring 42 of the most popular young players. The first series was issued with Score rak packs while the second series was available only via a mailaway from the Company. The set contains standard-size (2 1/2" by 3 1/2") cards.

	MT	EX-MT	VG
COMPLETE SET (42)	5.00	2.30	.60
COMMON PLAYER (1-42)	.15	.07	.02
☐ 1 Bo Jackson	.75	.35	.09
☐ 2 Dwight Smith	.15	.07	.02
☐ 3 Joey Belle	.50	.23	.06
☐ 4 Gregg Olson	.25	.11	.03
☐ 5 Jim Abbott	.50	.23	.06
☐ 6 Felix Fermin	.15	.07	.02
☐ 7 Brian Holman	.15	.07	.02
☐ 8 Clay Parker	.15	.07	.02
☐ 9 Junior Felix	.25	.11	.03
☐ 10 Joe Oliver	.15	.07	.02
☐ 11 Steve Finley	.25	.11	.03
☐ 12 Greg Briley	.15	.07	.02
☐ 13 Greg Vaughn	.35	.16	.04
☐ 14 Bill Spiers	.15	.07	.02
☐ 15 Eric Yelding	.15	.07	.02
☐ 16 Jose Gonzalez	.15	.07	.02
☐ 17 Mark Carreon	.15	.07	.02
☐ 18 Greg W. Harris	.25	.11	.03
☐ 19 Felix Jose	.35	.16	.04
☐ 20 Bob Milacki	.15	.07	.02
☐ 21 Kenny Rogers	.15	.07	.02
☐ 22 Rolando Roomes	.15	.07	.02
☐ 23 Bip Roberts	.25	.11	.03
☐ 24 Jeff Brantley	.15	.07	.02
☐ 25 Jeff Ballard	.15	.07	.02
☐ 26 John Dopson	.15	.07	.02
☐ 27 Ken Patterson	.15	.07	.02
☐ 28 Omar Vizquel	.25	.11	.03
☐ 29 Kevin Brown	.25	.11	.03
☐ 30 Derek Lilliquist	.15	.07	.02
☐ 31 David Wells	.25	.11	.03
☐ 32 Ken Hill	.25	.11	.03
☐ 33 Greg Litton	.15	.07	.02
☐ 34 Rob Ducey	.15	.07	.02

		MT	EX-MT	VG
☐ 35	Carlos Martinez	.25	.11	.03
☐ 36	John Smoltz	.50	.23	.06
☐ 37	Lenny Harris	.25	.11	.03
☐ 38	Charlie Hayes	.35	.16	.04
☐ 39	Tommy Gregg	.15	.07	.02
☐ 40	John Wetteland	.25	.11	.03
☐ 41	Jeff Huson	.15	.07	.02
☐ 42	Eric Anthony	.35	.16	.04

1990 Score Young Superstars II

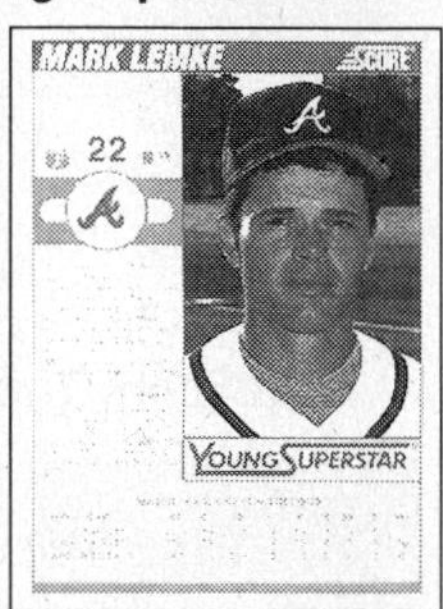

1990 Score Young Superstars II are glossy full color cards featuring 42 of the most popular young players. Whereas the first series was issued with Score rak packs, this second series was available only via a mailaway from the Company. The set contains standard-size (2 1/2" by 3 1/2") cards.

	MT	EX-MT	VG
COMPLETE SET (42)	5.00	2.30	.60
COMMON PLAYER (1-42)	.15	.07	.02

		MT	EX-MT	VG
☐ 1	Todd Zeile	.25	.11	.03
☐ 2	Ben McDonald	.35	.16	.04
☐ 3	Delino DeShields	.50	.23	.06
☐ 4	Pat Combs	.15	.07	.02
☐ 5	John Olerud	.60	.25	.08
☐ 6	Marquis Grissom	.50	.23	.06
☐ 7	Mike Stanton	.25	.11	.03
☐ 8	Robin Ventura	.75	.35	.09
☐ 9	Larry Walker	.60	.25	.08
☐ 10	Dante Bichette	.25	.11	.03
☐ 11	Jack Armstrong	.25	.11	.03
☐ 12	Jay Bell	.25	.11	.03
☐ 13	Andy Benes	.35	.16	.04
☐ 14	Joey Cora	.15	.07	.02
☐ 15	Rob Dibble	.25	.11	.03
☐ 16	Jeff King	.25	.11	.03
☐ 17	Jeff Hamilton	.15	.07	.02
☐ 18	Erik Hanson	.15	.07	.02
☐ 19	Pete Harnisch	.25	.11	.03
☐ 20	Greg Hibbard	.15	.07	.02
☐ 21	Stan Javier	.15	.07	.02
☐ 22	Mark Lemke	.15	.07	.02
☐ 23	Steve Olin	.15	.07	.02
☐ 24	Tommy Greene	.25	.11	.03
☐ 25	Sammy Sosa	.25	.11	.03
☐ 26	Gary Wayne	.15	.07	.02
☐ 27	Deion Sanders	.60	.25	.08
☐ 28	Steve Wilson	.15	.07	.02
☐ 29	Joe Girardi	.15	.07	.02
☐ 30	John Orton	.15	.07	.02
☐ 31	Kevin Tapani	.35	.16	.04
☐ 32	Carlos Baerga	.75	.35	.09
☐ 33	Glenallen Hill	.25	.11	.03
☐ 34	Mike Blowers	.15	.07	.02
☐ 35	Dave Hollins	.50	.23	.06
☐ 36	Lance Blankenship	.15	.07	.02
☐ 37	Hal Morris	.35	.16	.04
☐ 38	Lance Johnson	.25	.11	.03
☐ 39	Chris Gwynn	.15	.07	.02
☐ 40	Doug Dascenzo	.15	.07	.02
☐ 41	Jerald Clark	.15	.07	.02
☐ 42	Carlos Quintana	.15	.07	.02

1991 Score

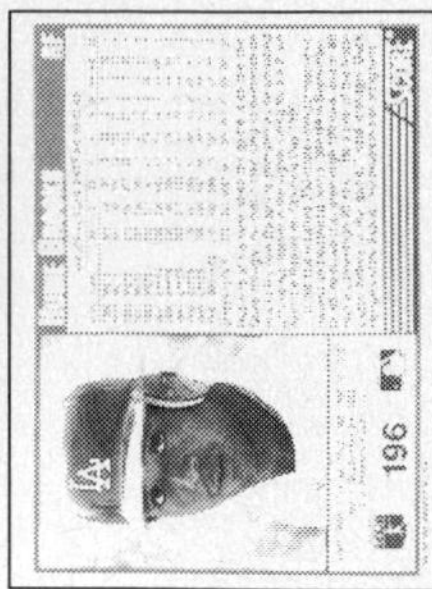

The 1991 Score set contains 893 cards. The cards feature a solid color border framing the full-color photo of the cards. The cards measure the standard card size of 2 1/2" by 3 1/2" and also feature Score trademark full-color photos on the back. The backs also include a brief biography on each player. This set marks the fourth consecutive year that Score has issued a major set but the first time Score issued the set in two series. Score also reused their successful Dream Team concept by using non-baseball photos of Today's stars. Series one contains 441 cards and ends with the Annie Leibowitz photo of Jose Canseco used in American Express ads. This first series also includes 49 Rookie prospects, 12 First Round Draft Picks and five each of the Master Blaster, K-Man, and Rifleman subsets. The All-Star sets in the first series are all American Leaguers (which are all caricatures). The key Rookie Cards in the set are Jeromy Burnitz, Wes Chamberlain, Brian McRae, Mike Mussina, Marc Newfield, Phil Plantier, and Todd Van Poppel. There are a number of pitchers whose card backs show Innings Pitched totals which do not equal the added year-by-year total; the following card numbers were affected, 4, 24, 29, 30, 51, 81, 109, 111, 118, 141, 150, 156, 177, 204, 218, 232, 235, 255, 287, 289, 311, and 328. The second series was issued approximately three months after the release of series one and included many of the special cards Score is noted for, e.g., the continuation of the Dream Team set begun in Series One, All-Star Cartoons featuring National Leaguers, a continuation of the 1990 first round draft picks, and 61 rookie prospects.

	MT	EX-MT	VG
COMPLETE SET (893)	20.00	9.00	2.50
COMPLETE FACT.SET (900)	25.00	11.50	3.10
COMMON PLAYER (1-441)	.04	.02	.01
COMMON PLAYER (442-893)	.04	.02	.01

		MT	EX-MT	VG
☐ 1	Jose Canseco	.20	.09	.03
☐ 2	Ken Griffey Jr.	.50	.23	.06
☐ 3	Ryne Sandberg	.25	.11	.03
☐ 4	Nolan Ryan	.40	.18	.05
☐ 5	Bo Jackson	.12	.05	.02
☐ 6	Bret Saberhagen UER (In bio, missed misspelled as mised)	.07	.03	.01
☐ 7	Will Clark	.20	.09	.03
☐ 8	Ellis Burks	.07	.03	.01
☐ 9	Joe Carter	.12	.05	.02
☐ 10	Rickey Henderson	.12	.05	.02
☐ 11	Ozzie Guillen	.04	.02	.01
☐ 12	Wade Boggs	.12	.05	.02
☐ 13	Jerome Walton	.04	.02	.01
☐ 14	John Franco	.07	.03	.01
☐ 15	Ricky Jordan UER (League misspelled as legue)	.04	.02	.01
☐ 16	Wally Backman	.04	.02	.01
☐ 17	Rob Dibble	.07	.03	.01
☐ 18	Glenn Braggs	.04	.02	.01
☐ 19	Cory Snyder	.04	.02	.01

☐ 20 Kal Daniels .04 .02 .01
☐ 21 Mark Langston .07 .03 .01
☐ 22 Kevin Gross .04 .02 .01
☐ 23 Don Mattingly UER .15 .07 .02
(First line, ' is
missing from Yankee)
☐ 24 Dave Righetti .04 .02 .01
☐ 25 Roberto Alomar .20 .09 .03
☐ 26 Robby Thompson .04 .02 .01
☐ 27 Jack McDowell .10 .05 .01
☐ 28 Bip Roberts UER .07 .03 .01
(Bio reads playd)
☐ 29 Jay Howell .04 .02 .01
☐ 30 Dave Stieb UER .04 .02 .01
(17 wins in bio,
18 in stats)
☐ 31 Johnny Ray .04 .02 .01
☐ 32 Steve Sax .07 .03 .01
☐ 33 Terry Mulholland .04 .02 .01
☐ 34 Lee Guetterman .04 .02 .01
☐ 35 Tim Raines .07 .03 .01
☐ 36 Scott Fletcher .04 .02 .01
☐ 37 Lance Parrish .07 .03 .01
☐ 38 Tony Phillips UER .04 .02 .01
(Born 4/15,
should be 4/25)
☐ 39 Todd Stottlemyre .07 .03 .01
☐ 40 Alan Trammell .07 .03 .01
☐ 41 Todd Burns .04 .02 .01
☐ 42 Mookie Wilson .04 .02 .01
☐ 43 Chris Bosio .04 .02 .01
☐ 44 Jeffrey Leonard .04 .02 .01
☐ 45 Doug Jones .04 .02 .01
☐ 46 Mike Scott UER .04 .02 .01
(In first line,
dominate should
read dominating)
☐ 47 Andy Hawkins .04 .02 .01
☐ 48 Harold Reynolds .04 .02 .01
☐ 49 Paul Molitor .10 .05 .01
☐ 50 John Farrell .04 .02 .01
☐ 51 Danny Darwin .04 .02 .01
☐ 52 Jeff Blauser .04 .02 .01
☐ 53 John Tudor UER .04 .02 .01
(41 wins in '81)
☐ 54 Milt Thompson .04 .02 .01
☐ 55 Dave Justice .30 .14 .04
☐ 56 Greg Olson .04 .02 .01
☐ 57 Willie Blair .04 .02 .01
☐ 58 Rick Parker .04 .02 .01
☐ 59 Shawn Boskie .04 .02 .01
☐ 60 Kevin Tapani .07 .03 .01
☐ 61 Dave Hollins .12 .05 .02
☐ 62 Scott Radinsky .04 .02 .01
☐ 63 Francisco Cabrera .04 .02 .01
☐ 64 Tim Layana .04 .02 .01
☐ 65 Jim Leyritz .04 .02 .01
☐ 66 Wayne Edwards .04 .02 .01
☐ 67 Lee Stevens .04 .02 .01
☐ 68 Bill Sampen UER .04 .02 .01
(Fourth line, long
is spelled along)
☐ 69 Craig Grebeck UER .04 .02 .01
(Born in Cerritos,
not Johnstown)
☐ 70 John Burkett .04 .02 .01
☐ 71 Hector Villanueva .04 .02 .01
☐ 72 Oscar Azocar .04 .02 .01
☐ 73 Alan Mills .04 .02 .01
☐ 74 Carlos Baerga .20 .09 .03
☐ 75 Charles Nagy .25 .11 .03
☐ 76 Tim Drummond .04 .02 .01
☐ 77 Dana Kiecker .04 .02 .01
☐ 78 Tom Edens .10 .05 .01
☐ 79 Kent Mercker .07 .03 .01
☐ 80 Steve Avery .20 .09 .03
☐ 81 Lee Smith .07 .03 .01
☐ 82 Dave Martinez .04 .02 .01
☐ 83 Dave Winfield .10 .05 .01
☐ 84 Bill Spiers .04 .02 .01
☐ 85 Dan Pasqua .04 .02 .01
☐ 86 Randy Milligan .04 .02 .01
☐ 87 Tracy Jones .04 .02 .01
☐ 88 Greg Myers .04 .02 .01
☐ 89 Keith Hernandez .07 .03 .01
☐ 90 Todd Benzinger .04 .02 .01
☐ 91 Mike Jackson .04 .02 .01
☐ 92 Mike Stanley .04 .02 .01
☐ 93 Candy Maldonado .04 .02 .01
☐ 94 John Kruk UER .07 .03 .01
(No decimal point
before 1990 BA)
☐ 95 Cal Ripken UER .30 .14 .04
(Genius spelled genuis)
☐ 96 Willie Fraser .04 .02 .01
☐ 97 Mike Felder .04 .02 .01
☐ 98 Bill Landrum .04 .02 .01
☐ 99 Chuck Crim .04 .02 .01
☐ 100 Chuck Finley .07 .03 .01
☐ 101 Kirt Manwaring .04 .02 .01
☐ 102 Jaime Navarro .07 .03 .01
☐ 103 Dickie Thon .04 .02 .01
☐ 104 Brian Downing .04 .02 .01
☐ 105 Jim Abbott .12 .05 .02
☐ 106 Tom Brookens .04 .02 .01
☐ 107 Darryl Hamilton UER .07 .03 .01
(Bio info is for
Jeff Hamilton)
☐ 108 Bryan Harvey .04 .02 .01
☐ 109 Greg A. Harris UER .04 .02 .01
(Shown pitching lefty,
bio says righty)
☐ 110 Greg Swindell .07 .03 .01
☐ 111 Juan Berenguer .04 .02 .01
☐ 112 Mike Heath .04 .02 .01
☐ 113 Scott Bradley .04 .02 .01
☐ 114 Jack Morris .10 .05 .01
☐ 115 Barry Jones .04 .02 .01
☐ 116 Kevin Romine .04 .02 .01
☐ 117 Garry Templeton .04 .02 .01
☐ 118 Scott Sanderson .04 .02 .01
☐ 119 Roberto Kelly .07 .03 .01
☐ 120 George Brett .10 .05 .01
☐ 121 Oddibe McDowell .04 .02 .01
☐ 122 Jim Acker .04 .02 .01
☐ 123 Bill Swift UER .04 .02 .01
(Born 12/27/61,
should be 10/27)
☐ 124 Eric King .04 .02 .01
☐ 125 Jay Buhner .07 .03 .01
☐ 126 Matt Young .04 .02 .01
☐ 127 Alvaro Espinoza .04 .02 .01
☐ 128 Greg Hibbard .04 .02 .01
☐ 129 Jeff M. Robinson .04 .02 .01
☐ 130 Mike Greenwell .07 .03 .01
☐ 131 Dion James .04 .02 .01
☐ 132 Donn Pall UER .04 .02 .01
(1988 ERA in stats 0.00)
☐ 133 Lloyd Moseby .04 .02 .01
☐ 134 Randy Velarde .04 .02 .01
☐ 135 Allan Anderson .04 .02 .01
☐ 136 Mark Davis .04 .02 .01
☐ 137 Eric Davis .07 .03 .01
☐ 138 Phil Stephenson .04 .02 .01
☐ 139 Felix Fermin .04 .02 .01
☐ 140 Pedro Guerrero .07 .03 .01
☐ 141 Charlie Hough .04 .02 .01
☐ 142 Mike Henneman .04 .02 .01
☐ 143 Jeff Montgomery .04 .02 .01
☐ 144 Lenny Harris .04 .02 .01
☐ 145 Bruce Hurst .07 .03 .01
☐ 146 Eric Anthony .07 .03 .01
☐ 147 Paul Assenmacher .04 .02 .01
☐ 148 Jesse Barfield .04 .02 .01
☐ 149 Carlos Quintana .04 .02 .01
☐ 150 Dave Stewart .07 .03 .01
☐ 151 Roy Smith .04 .02 .01
☐ 152 Paul Gibson .04 .02 .01
☐ 153 Mickey Hatcher .04 .02 .01
☐ 154 Jim Eisenreich .04 .02 .01
☐ 155 Kenny Rogers .04 .02 .01
☐ 156 Dave Schmidt .04 .02 .01
☐ 157 Lance Johnson .04 .02 .01
☐ 158 Dave West .04 .02 .01
☐ 159 Steve Balboni .04 .02 .01
☐ 160 Jeff Brantley .04 .02 .01
☐ 161 Craig Biggio .07 .03 .01
☐ 162 Brook Jacoby .04 .02 .01
☐ 163 Dan Gladden .04 .02 .01
☐ 164 Jeff Reardon UER .07 .03 .01
(Total IP shown as
943.2, should be 943.1)
☐ 165 Mark Carreon .04 .02 .01
☐ 166 Mel Hall .04 .02 .01
☐ 167 Gary Mielke .04 .02 .01
☐ 168 Cecil Fielder .12 .05 .02
☐ 169 Darrin Jackson .07 .03 .01
☐ 170 Rick Aguilera .07 .03 .01
☐ 171 Walt Weiss .04 .02 .01
☐ 172 Steve Farr .04 .02 .01
☐ 173 Jody Reed .04 .02 .01
☐ 174 Mike Jeffcoat .04 .02 .01
☐ 175 Mark Grace .10 .05 .01
☐ 176 Larry Sheets .04 .02 .01
☐ 177 Bill Gullickson .04 .02 .01
☐ 178 Chris Gwynn .04 .02 .01
☐ 179 Melido Perez .07 .03 .01

☐ 180 Sid Fernandez UER............. .07 .03 .01
(779 runs in 1990)
☐ 181 Tim Burke .04 .02 .01
☐ 182 Gary Pettis .04 .02 .01
☐ 183 Rob Murphy .04 .02 .01
☐ 184 Craig Lefferts .04 .02 .01
☐ 185 Howard Johnson .07 .03 .01
☐ 186 Ken Caminiti .07 .03 .01
☐ 187 Tim Belcher .07 .03 .01
☐ 188 Greg Cadaret .04 .02 .01
☐ 189 Matt Williams .07 .03 .01
☐ 190 Dave Magadan .07 .03 .01
☐ 191 Geno Petralli .04 .02 .01
☐ 192 Jeff D. Robinson .04 .02 .01
☐ 193 Jim Deshaies .04 .02 .01
☐ 194 Willie Randolph .07 .03 .01
☐ 195 George Bell .07 .03 .01
☐ 196 Hubie Brooks .04 .02 .01
☐ 197 Tom Gordon .07 .03 .01
☐ 198 Mike Fitzgerald .04 .02 .01
☐ 199 Mike Pagliarulo .04 .02 .01
☐ 200 Kirby Puckett .20 .09 .03
☐ 201 Shawon Dunston .07 .03 .01
☐ 202 Dennis Boyd .04 .02 .01
☐ 203 Junior Felix UER .04 .02 .01
(Text has him in NL)
☐ 204 Alejandro Pena .04 .02 .01
☐ 205 Pete Smith .07 .03 .01
☐ 206 Tom Glavine UER .20 .09 .03
(Lefty spelled leftie)
☐ 207 Luis Salazar .04 .02 .01
☐ 208 John Smoltz .10 .05 .01
☐ 209 Doug Dascenzo .04 .02 .01
☐ 210 Tim Wallach .07 .03 .01
☐ 211 Greg Gagne .04 .02 .01
☐ 212 Mark Gubicza .04 .02 .01
☐ 213 Mark Parent .04 .02 .01
☐ 214 Ken Oberkfell .04 .02 .01
☐ 215 Gary Carter .07 .03 .01
☐ 216 Rafael Palmeiro .10 .05 .01
☐ 217 Tom Niedenfuer .04 .02 .01
☐ 218 Dave LaPoint .04 .02 .01
☐ 219 Jeff Treadway .04 .02 .01
☐ 220 Mitch Williams UER .04 .02 .01
('89 ERA shown as 2.76,
should be 2.64)
☐ 221 Jose DeLeon .04 .02 .01
☐ 222 Mike LaValliere .04 .02 .01
☐ 223 Darrel Akerfelds .04 .02 .01
☐ 224A Kent Anderson ERR .08 .04 .01
(First line, flachy
should read flashy)
☐ 224B Kent Anderson COR .08 .04 .01
(Corrected in
factory sets)
☐ 225 Dwight Evans .07 .03 .01
☐ 226 Gary Redus .04 .02 .01
☐ 227 Paul O'Neill .07 .03 .01
☐ 228 Marty Barrett .04 .02 .01
☐ 229 Tom Browning .04 .02 .01
☐ 230 Terry Pendleton .10 .05 .01
☐ 231 Jack Armstrong .04 .02 .01
☐ 232 Mike Boddicker .04 .02 .01
☐ 233 Neal Heaton .04 .02 .01
☐ 234 Marquis Grissom .15 .07 .02
☐ 235 Bert Blyleven .07 .03 .01
☐ 236 Curt Young .04 .02 .01
☐ 237 Don Carman .04 .02 .01
☐ 238 Charlie Hayes .04 .02 .01
☐ 239 Mark Knudson .04 .02 .01
☐ 240 Todd Zeile .07 .03 .01
☐ 241 Larry Walker UER .20 .09 .03
(Maple River, should
be Maple Ridge)
☐ 242 Jerald Clark .04 .02 .01
☐ 243 Jeff Ballard .04 .02 .01
☐ 244 Jeff King .04 .02 .01
☐ 245 Tom Brunansky .07 .03 .01
☐ 246 Darren Daulton .07 .03 .01
☐ 247 Scott Terry .04 .02 .01
☐ 248 Rob Deer .07 .03 .01
☐ 249 Brady Anderson UER .07 .03 .01
(1990 Hagerstown 1 hit,
should say 13 hits)
☐ 250 Len Dykstra .07 .03 .01
☐ 251 Greg W. Harris .04 .02 .01
☐ 252 Mike Hartley .04 .02 .01
☐ 253 Joey Cora .04 .02 .01
☐ 254 Ivan Calderon .04 .02 .01
☐ 255 Ted Power .04 .02 .01
☐ 256 Sammy Sosa .07 .03 .01
☐ 257 Steve Buechele .04 .02 .01
☐ 258 Mike Devereaux UER .07 .03 .01
(No comma between
city and state)
☐ 259 Brad Komminsk UER .04 .02 .01
(Last text line,
Ba should be BA)
☐ 260 Teddy Higuera .04 .02 .01
☐ 261 Shawn Abner .04 .02 .01
☐ 262 Dave Valle .04 .02 .01
☐ 263 Jeff Huson .04 .02 .01
☐ 264 Edgar Martinez .07 .03 .01
☐ 265 Carlton Fisk .10 .05 .01
☐ 266 Steve Finley .07 .03 .01
☐ 267 John Wetteland .07 .03 .01
☐ 268 Kevin Appier .07 .03 .01
☐ 269 Steve Lyons .04 .02 .01
☐ 270 Mickey Tettleton .07 .03 .01
☐ 271 Luis Rivera .04 .02 .01
☐ 272 Steve Jeltz .04 .02 .01
☐ 273 R.J. Reynolds .04 .02 .01
☐ 274 Carlos Martinez .04 .02 .01
☐ 275 Dan Plesac .04 .02 .01
☐ 276 Mike Morgan UER .04 .02 .01
(Total IP shown as
1149.1, should be 1149)
☐ 277 Jeff Russell .04 .02 .01
☐ 278 Pete Incaviglia .04 .02 .01
☐ 279 Kevin Seitzer UER .07 .03 .01
(Bio has 200 hits twice
and .300 four times,
should be once and
three times)
☐ 280 Bobby Thigpen .04 .02 .01
☐ 281 Stan Javier UER .04 .02 .01
(Born 1/9,
should say 9/1)
☐ 282 Henry Cotto .04 .02 .01
☐ 283 Gary Wayne .04 .02 .01
☐ 284 Shane Mack .07 .03 .01
☐ 285 Brian Holman .04 .02 .01
☐ 286 Gerald Perry .04 .02 .01
☐ 287 Steve Crawford .04 .02 .01
☐ 288 Nelson Liriano .04 .02 .01
☐ 289 Don Aase .04 .02 .01
☐ 290 Randy Johnson .07 .03 .01
☐ 291 Harold Baines .07 .03 .01
☐ 292 Kent Hrbek .07 .03 .01
☐ 293A Les Lancaster ERR .04 .02 .01
(No comma between
Dallas and Texas)
☐ 293B Les Lancaster COR .04 .02 .01
(Corrected in
factory sets)
☐ 294 Jeff Musselman .04 .02 .01
☐ 295 Kurt Stillwell .04 .02 .01
☐ 296 Stan Belinda .04 .02 .01
☐ 297 Lou Whitaker .07 .03 .01
☐ 298 Glenn Wilson .04 .02 .01
☐ 299 Omar Vizquel UER .04 .02 .01
(Born 5/15, should be
4/24, there is a decimal
before GP total for '90)
☐ 300 Ramon Martinez .10 .05 .01
☐ 301 Dwight Smith .04 .02 .01
☐ 302 Tim Crews .04 .02 .01
☐ 303 Lance Blankenship .04 .02 .01
☐ 304 Sid Bream .04 .02 .01
☐ 305 Rafael Ramirez .04 .02 .01
☐ 306 Steve Wilson .04 .02 .01
☐ 307 Mackey Sasser .04 .02 .01
☐ 308 Franklin Stubbs .04 .02 .01
☐ 309 Jack Daugherty UER .04 .02 .01
(Born 6/3/60,
should say July)
☐ 310 Eddie Murray .10 .05 .01
☐ 311 Bob Welch .04 .02 .01
☐ 312 Brian Harper .04 .02 .01
☐ 313 Lance McCullers .04 .02 .01
☐ 314 Dave Smith .04 .02 .01
☐ 315 Bobby Bonilla .10 .05 .01
☐ 316 Jerry Don Gleaton .04 .02 .01
☐ 317 Greg Maddux .10 .05 .01
☐ 318 Keith Miller .04 .02 .01
☐ 319 Mark Portugal .04 .02 .01
☐ 320 Robin Ventura .20 .09 .03
☐ 321 Bob Ojeda .04 .02 .01
☐ 322 Mike Harkey .07 .03 .01
☐ 323 Jay Bell .07 .03 .01
☐ 324 Mark McGwire .20 .09 .03
☐ 325 Gary Gaetti .04 .02 .01
☐ 326 Jeff Pico .04 .02 .01
☐ 327 Kevin McReynolds .07 .03 .01
☐ 328 Frank Tanana .04 .02 .01
☐ 329 Eric Yelding UER .04 .02 .01
(Listed as 6'3",

should be 5'11")			
☐ 330 Barry Bonds	.20	.09	.03
☐ 331 Brian McRae RP UER (No comma between city and state)	.20	.09	.03
☐ 332 Pedro Munoz RP	.25	.11	.03
☐ 333 Daryl Irvine RP	.05	.02	.01
☐ 334 Chris Hoiles RP	.10	.05	.01
☐ 335 Thomas Howard RP	.10	.05	.01
☐ 336 Jeff Schulz RP	.05	.02	.01
☐ 337 Jeff Manto RP	.05	.02	.01
☐ 338 Beau Allred RP	.05	.02	.01
☐ 339 Mike Bordick RP	.35	.16	.04
☐ 340 Todd Hundley RP	.08	.04	.01
☐ 341 Jim Vatcher RP UER (Height 6'9", should be 5'9")	.05	.02	.01
☐ 342 Luis Sojo RP	.08	.04	.01
☐ 343 Jose Offerman RP UER (Born 1969, should say 1968)	.10	.05	.01
☐ 344 Pete Coachman RP	.05	.02	.01
☐ 345 Mike Benjamin RP	.05	.02	.01
☐ 346 Ozzie Canseco RP	.10	.05	.01
☐ 347 Tim McIntosh RP	.05	.02	.01
☐ 348 Phil Plantier RP	.50	.23	.06
☐ 349 Terry Shumpert RP	.05	.02	.01
☐ 350 Darren Lewis RP	.10	.05	.01
☐ 351 David Walsh RP	.10	.05	.01
☐ 352A Scott Chiamparino RP ERR (Bats left, should be right)	.05	.02	.01
☐ 352B Scott Chiamparino RP COR (corrected in factory sets)	.05	.02	.01
☐ 353 Julio Valera RP UER (Progressed mis-spelled as progessed)	.15	.07	.02
☐ 354 Anthony Telford RP	.05	.02	.01
☐ 355 Kevin Wickander RP	.05	.02	.01
☐ 356 Tim Naehring RP	.08	.04	.01
☐ 357 Jim Poole RP	.05	.02	.01
☐ 358 Mark Whiten RP UER (Shown hitting lefty, bio says righty)	.12	.05	.02
☐ 359 Terry Wells RP	.10	.05	.01
☐ 360 Rafael Valdez RP	.05	.02	.01
☐ 361 Mel Stottlemyre Jr. RP	.05	.02	.01
☐ 362 David Segui RP	.05	.02	.01
☐ 363 Paul Abbott RP	.10	.05	.01
☐ 364 Steve Howard RP	.08	.04	.01
☐ 365 Karl Rhodes RP	.05	.02	.01
☐ 366 Rafael Novoa RP	.10	.05	.01
☐ 367 Joe Grahe RP	.15	.07	.02
☐ 368 Darren Reed RP	.05	.02	.01
☐ 369 Jeff McKnight RP	.05	.02	.01
☐ 370 Scott Leius RP	.10	.05	.01
☐ 371 Mark Dewey RP	.10	.05	.01
☐ 372 Mark Lee RP UER (Shown hitting lefty, bio says righty, born in Dakota, should say North Dakota)	.10	.05	.01
☐ 373 Rosario Rodriguez RP (Shown hitting lefty, bio says righty) UER	.10	.05	.01
☐ 374 Chuck McElroy RP	.05	.02	.01
☐ 375 Mike Bell RP	.10	.05	.01
☐ 376 Mickey Morandini RP	.12	.05	.02
☐ 377 Bill Haselman RP	.10	.05	.01
☐ 378 Dave Pavlas RP	.10	.05	.01
☐ 379 Derrick May RP	.10	.05	.01
☐ 380 Jeromy Burnitz FDP	.30	.14	.04
☐ 381 Donald Peters FDP	.10	.05	.01
☐ 382 Alex Fernandez FDP	.15	.07	.02
☐ 383 Mike Mussina FDP	1.50	.65	.19
☐ 384 Dan Smith FDP	.20	.09	.03
☐ 385 Lance Dickson FDP	.10	.05	.01
☐ 386 Carl Everett FDP	.25	.11	.03
☐ 387 Thomas Nevers FDP	.12	.05	.02
☐ 388 Adam Hyzdu FDP	.15	.07	.02
☐ 389 Todd Van Poppel FDP	.50	.23	.06
☐ 390 Rondell White FDP	.50	.23	.06
☐ 391 Marc Newfield FDP	.40	.18	.05
☐ 392 Julio Franco AS	.05	.02	.01
☐ 393 Wade Boggs AS	.10	.05	.01
☐ 394 Ozzie Guillen AS	.05	.02	.01
☐ 395 Cecil Fielder AS	.10	.05	.01
☐ 396 Ken Griffey Jr. AS	.25	.11	.03
☐ 397 Rickey Henderson AS	.10	.05	.01
☐ 398 Jose Canseco AS	.12	.05	.02
☐ 399 Roger Clemens AS	.12	.05	.02
☐ 400 Sandy Alomar Jr. AS	.05	.02	.01
☐ 401 Bobby Thigpen AS	.05	.02	.01
☐ 402 Bobby Bonilla MB	.08	.04	.01
☐ 403 Eric Davis MB	.08	.04	.01
☐ 404 Fred McGriff MB	.10	.05	.01
☐ 405 Glenn Davis MB	.05	.02	.01
☐ 406 Kevin Mitchell MB	.05	.02	.01
☐ 407 Rob Dibble KM	.05	.02	.01
☐ 408 Ramon Martinez KM	.05	.02	.01
☐ 409 David Cone KM	.08	.04	.01
☐ 410 Bobby Witt KM	.05	.02	.01
☐ 411 Mark Langston KM	.05	.02	.01
☐ 412 Bo Jackson RIF	.10	.05	.01
☐ 413 Shawon Dunston RIF UER (In the baseball, should say in baseball)	.05	.02	.01
☐ 414 Jesse Barfield RIF	.05	.02	.01
☐ 415 Ken Caminiti RIF	.05	.02	.01
☐ 416 Benito Santiago RIF	.05	.02	.01
☐ 417 Nolan Ryan HL	.25	.11	.03
☐ 418 Bobby Thigpen HL UER (Back refers to Hal McRae Jr., should say Brian McRae)	.05	.02	.01
☐ 419 Ramon Martinez HL	.05	.02	.01
☐ 420 Bo Jackson HL	.10	.05	.01
☐ 421 Carlton Fisk HL	.10	.05	.01
☐ 422 Jimmy Key	.04	.02	.01
☐ 423 Junior Noboa	.04	.02	.01
☐ 424 Al Newman	.04	.02	.01
☐ 425 Pat Borders	.04	.02	.01
☐ 426 Von Hayes	.04	.02	.01
☐ 427 Tim Teufel	.04	.02	.01
☐ 428 Eric Plunk UER (Text says Eric's had, no apostrophe needed)	.04	.02	.01
☐ 429 John Moses	.04	.02	.01
☐ 430 Mike Witt	.04	.02	.01
☐ 431 Otis Nixon	.07	.03	.01
☐ 432 Tony Fernandez	.07	.03	.01
☐ 433 Rance Mulliniks	.04	.02	.01
☐ 434 Dan Petry	.04	.02	.01
☐ 435 Bob Geren	.04	.02	.01
☐ 436 Steve Frey	.04	.02	.01
☐ 437 Jamie Moyer	.04	.02	.01
☐ 438 Junior Ortiz	.04	.02	.01
☐ 439 Tom O'Malley	.04	.02	.01
☐ 440 Pat Combs	.04	.02	.01
☐ 441 Jose Canseco DT	1.25	.55	.16
☐ 442 Alfredo Griffin	.04	.02	.01
☐ 443 Andres Galarraga	.04	.02	.01
☐ 444 Bryn Smith	.04	.02	.01
☐ 445 Andre Dawson	.10	.05	.01
☐ 446 Juan Samuel	.04	.02	.01
☐ 447 Mike Aldrete	.04	.02	.01
☐ 448 Ron Gant	.12	.05	.02
☐ 449 Fernando Valenzuela	.07	.03	.01
☐ 450 Vince Coleman UER (Should say topped majors in steals four times, not three times)	.07	.03	.01
☐ 451 Kevin Mitchell	.07	.03	.01
☐ 452 Spike Owen	.04	.02	.01
☐ 453 Mike Bielecki	.04	.02	.01
☐ 454 Dennis Martinez	.07	.03	.01
☐ 455 Brett Butler	.07	.03	.01
☐ 456 Ron Darling	.07	.03	.01
☐ 457 Dennis Rasmussen	.04	.02	.01
☐ 458 Ken Howell	.04	.02	.01
☐ 459 Steve Bedrosian	.04	.02	.01
☐ 460 Frank Viola	.07	.03	.01
☐ 461 Jose Lind	.04	.02	.01
☐ 462 Chris Sabo	.07	.03	.01
☐ 463 Dante Bichette	.04	.02	.01
☐ 464 Rick Mahler	.04	.02	.01
☐ 465 John Smiley	.07	.03	.01
☐ 466 Devon White	.07	.03	.01
☐ 467 John Orton	.04	.02	.01
☐ 468 Mike Stanton	.04	.02	.01
☐ 469 Billy Hatcher	.04	.02	.01
☐ 470 Wally Joyner	.07	.03	.01
☐ 471 Gene Larkin	.04	.02	.01
☐ 472 Doug Drabek	.07	.03	.01
☐ 473 Gary Sheffield	.25	.11	.03
☐ 474 David Wells	.04	.02	.01
☐ 475 Andy Van Slyke	.10	.05	.01
☐ 476 Mike Gallego	.04	.02	.01
☐ 477 B.J. Surhoff	.04	.02	.01
☐ 478 Gene Nelson	.04	.02	.01
☐ 479 Mariano Duncan	.04	.02	.01
☐ 480 Fred McGriff	.12	.05	.02
☐ 481 Jerry Browne	.04	.02	.01
☐ 482 Alvin Davis	.04	.02	.01
☐ 483 Bill Wegman	.04	.02	.01
☐ 484 Dave Parker	.07	.03	.01

□ 485 Dennis Eckersley .10 .05 .01
□ 486 Erik Hanson UER .04 .02 .01
(Basketball misspelled as baseketball)
□ 487 Bill Ripken .04 .02 .01
□ 488 Tom Candiotti .04 .02 .01
□ 489 Mike Schooler .04 .02 .01
□ 490 Gregg Olson .07 .03 .01
□ 491 Chris James .04 .02 .01
□ 492 Pete Harnisch .07 .03 .01
□ 493 Julio Franco .07 .03 .01
□ 494 Greg Briley .04 .02 .01
□ 495 Ruben Sierra .15 .07 .02
□ 496 Steve Olin .07 .03 .01
□ 497 Mike Fetters .04 .02 .01
□ 498 Mark Williamson .04 .02 .01
□ 499 Bob Tewksbury .07 .03 .01
□ 500 Tony Gwynn .12 .05 .02
□ 501 Randy Myers .07 .03 .01
□ 502 Keith Comstock .04 .02 .01
□ 503 Craig Worthington UER .04 .02 .01
(DeCinces misspelled DiCinces on back)
□ 504 Mark Eichhorn UER .04 .02 .01
(Stats incomplete, doesn't have '89 Braves stint)
□ 505 Barry Larkin .10 .05 .01
□ 506 Dave Johnson .04 .02 .01
□ 507 Bobby Witt .04 .02 .01
□ 508 Joe Orsulak .04 .02 .01
□ 509 Pete O'Brien .04 .02 .01
□ 510 Brad Arnsberg .04 .02 .01
□ 511 Storm Davis .04 .02 .01
□ 512 Bob Milacki .04 .02 .01
□ 513 Bill Pecota .04 .02 .01
□ 514 Glenallen Hill .04 .02 .01
□ 515 Danny Tartabull .07 .03 .01
□ 516 Mike Moore .04 .02 .01
□ 517 Ron Robinson UER .04 .02 .01
(577 K's in 1990)
□ 518 Mark Gardner .04 .02 .01
□ 519 Rick Wrona .04 .02 .01
□ 520 Mike Scioscia .04 .02 .01
□ 521 Frank Wills .04 .02 .01
□ 522 Greg Brock .04 .02 .01
□ 523 Jack Clark .07 .03 .01
□ 524 Bruce Ruffin .04 .02 .01
□ 525 Robin Yount .10 .05 .01
□ 526 Tom Foley .04 .02 .01
□ 527 Pat Perry .04 .02 .01
□ 528 Greg Vaughn .08 .04 .01
□ 529 Wally Whitehurst .04 .02 .01
□ 530 Norm Charlton .07 .03 .01
□ 531 Marvell Wynne .04 .02 .01
□ 532 Jim Gantner .04 .02 .01
□ 533 Greg Litton .04 .02 .01
□ 534 Manny Lee .04 .02 .01
□ 535 Scott Bailes .04 .02 .01
□ 536 Charlie Leibrandt .04 .02 .01
□ 537 Roger McDowell .04 .02 .01
□ 538 Andy Benes .10 .05 .01
□ 539 Rick Honeycutt .04 .02 .01
□ 540 Dwight Gooden .07 .03 .01
□ 541 Scott Garrelts .04 .02 .01
□ 542 Dave Clark .04 .02 .01
□ 543 Lonnie Smith .04 .02 .01
□ 544 Rick Reuschel .04 .02 .01
□ 545 Delino DeShields UER .15 .07 .02
(Rockford misspelled as Rock Ford in '88)
□ 546 Mike Sharperson .04 .02 .01
□ 547 Mike Kingery .04 .02 .01
□ 548 Terry Kennedy .04 .02 .01
□ 549 David Cone .10 .05 .01
□ 550 Orel Hershiser .07 .03 .01
□ 551 Matt Nokes .04 .02 .01
□ 552 Eddie Williams .04 .02 .01
□ 553 Frank DiPino .04 .02 .01
□ 554 Fred Lynn .07 .03 .01
□ 555 Alex Cole .04 .02 .01
□ 556 Terry Leach .04 .02 .01
□ 557 Chet Lemon .04 .02 .01
□ 558 Paul Mirabella .04 .02 .01
□ 559 Bill Long .04 .02 .01
□ 560 Phil Bradley .04 .02 .01
□ 561 Duane Ward .04 .02 .01
□ 562 Dave Bergman .04 .02 .01
□ 563 Eric Show .04 .02 .01
□ 564 Xavier Hernandez .04 .02 .01
□ 565 Jeff Parrett .04 .02 .01
□ 566 Chuck Cary .04 .02 .01
□ 567 Ken Hill .07 .03 .01
□ 568 Bob Welch Hand .04 .02 .01
(Complement should be compliment) UER
□ 569 John Mitchell .04 .02 .01
□ 570 Travis Fryman .60 .25 .08
□ 571 Derek Lilliquist .04 .02 .01
□ 572 Steve Lake .04 .02 .01
□ 573 John Barfield .04 .02 .01
□ 574 Randy Bush .04 .02 .01
□ 575 Joe Magrane .04 .02 .01
□ 576 Eddie Diaz .04 .02 .01
□ 577 Casey Candaele .04 .02 .01
□ 578 Jesse Orosco .04 .02 .01
□ 579 Tom Henke .07 .03 .01
□ 580 Rick Cerone UER .04 .02 .01
(Actually his third go-round with Yankees)
□ 581 Drew Hall .04 .02 .01
□ 582 Tony Castillo .04 .02 .01
□ 583 Jimmy Jones .04 .02 .01
□ 584 Rick Reed .04 .02 .01
□ 585 Joe Girardi .04 .02 .01
□ 586 Jeff Gray .04 .02 .01
□ 587 Luis Polonia .07 .03 .01
□ 588 Joe Klink .04 .02 .01
□ 589 Rex Hudler .04 .02 .01
□ 590 Kirk McCaskill .04 .02 .01
□ 591 Juan Agosto .04 .02 .01
□ 592 Wes Gardner .04 .02 .01
□ 593 Rich Rodriguez .10 .05 .01
□ 594 Mitch Webster .04 .02 .01
□ 595 Kelly Gruber .07 .03 .01
□ 596 Dale Mohorcic .04 .02 .01
□ 597 Willie McGee .07 .03 .01
□ 598 Bill Krueger .04 .02 .01
□ 599 Bob Walk UER .04 .02 .01
(Cards says he's 33, but actually he's 34)
□ 600 Kevin Maas .08 .04 .01
□ 601 Danny Jackson .04 .02 .01
□ 602 Craig McMurtry UER .04 .02 .01
(Anonymously misspelled anonimously)
□ 603 Curtis Wilkerson .04 .02 .01
□ 604 Adam Peterson .04 .02 .01
□ 605 Sam Horn .04 .02 .01
□ 606 Tommy Gregg .04 .02 .01
□ 607 Ken Dayley .04 .02 .01
□ 608 Carmelo Castillo .04 .02 .01
□ 609 John Shelby .04 .02 .01
□ 610 Don Slaught .04 .02 .01
□ 611 Calvin Schiraldi .04 .02 .01
□ 612 Dennis Lamp .04 .02 .01
□ 613 Andres Thomas .04 .02 .01
□ 614 Jose Gonzalez .04 .02 .01
□ 615 Randy Ready .04 .02 .01
□ 616 Kevin Bass .04 .02 .01
□ 617 Mike Marshall .04 .02 .01
□ 618 Daryl Boston .04 .02 .01
□ 619 Andy McGaffigan .04 .02 .01
□ 620 Joe Oliver .04 .02 .01
□ 621 Jim Gott .04 .02 .01
□ 622 Jose Oquendo .04 .02 .01
□ 623 Jose DeJesus .04 .02 .01
□ 624 Mike Brumley .04 .02 .01
□ 625 John Olerud .15 .07 .02
□ 626 Ernest Riles .04 .02 .01
□ 627 Gene Harris .04 .02 .01
□ 628 Jose Uribe .04 .02 .01
□ 629 Darnell Coles .04 .02 .01
□ 630 Carney Lansford .07 .03 .01
□ 631 Tim Leary .04 .02 .01
□ 632 Tim Hulett .04 .02 .01
□ 633 Kevin Elster .04 .02 .01
□ 634 Tony Fossas .04 .02 .01
□ 635 Francisco Oliveras .04 .02 .01
□ 636 Bob Patterson .04 .02 .01
□ 637 Gary Ward .04 .02 .01
□ 638 Rene Gonzales .04 .02 .01
□ 639 Don Robinson .04 .02 .01
□ 640 Darryl Strawberry .12 .05 .02
□ 641 Dave Anderson .04 .02 .01
□ 642 Scott Scudder .04 .02 .01
□ 643 Reggie Harris UER .10 .05 .01
(Hepatitis misspelled as hepititis)
□ 644 Dave Henderson .04 .02 .01
□ 645 Ben McDonald .10 .05 .01
□ 646 Bob Kipper .04 .02 .01
□ 647 Hal Morris UER .07 .03 .01
(It's should be its)
□ 648 Tim Birtsas .04 .02 .01
□ 649 Steve Searcy .04 .02 .01

☐ 650 Dale Murphy .07 .03 .01
☐ 651 Ron Oester .04 .02 .01
☐ 652 Mike LaCoss .04 .02 .01
☐ 653 Ron Jones .04 .02 .01
☐ 654 Kelly Downs .04 .02 .01
☐ 655 Roger Clemens .25 .11 .03
☐ 656 Herm Winningham .04 .02 .01
☐ 657 Trevor Wilson .04 .02 .01
☐ 658 Jose Rijo .07 .03 .01
☐ 659 Dann Bilardello UER .04 .02 .01
(Bio has 13 games, 1
hit, and 32 AB, stats
show 19, 2, and 37)
☐ 660 Gregg Jefferies .07 .03 .01
☐ 661 Doug Drabek AS UER .05 .02 .01
(Through is mis-
spelled though)
☐ 662 Randy Myers AS .05 .02 .01
☐ 663 Benny Santiago AS .05 .02 .01
☐ 664 Will Clark AS .10 .05 .01
☐ 665 Ryne Sandberg AS .12 .05 .02
☐ 666 Barry Larkin AS UER .08 .04 .01
(Line 13, coolly
misspelled cooly)
☐ 667 Matt Williams AS .05 .02 .01
☐ 668 Barry Bonds AS .10 .05 .01
☐ 669 Eric Davis AS .05 .02 .01
☐ 670 Bobby Bonilla AS .08 .04 .01
☐ 671 Chipper Jones FDP .75 .35 .09
☐ 672 Eric Christopherson .15 .07 .02
FDP
☐ 673 Robbie Beckett FDP .12 .05 .02
☐ 674 Shane Andrews FDP .20 .09 .03
☐ 675 Steve Karsay FDP .25 .11 .03
☐ 676 Aaron Holbert FDP .12 .05 .02
☐ 677 Donovan Osborne FDP .50 .23 .06
☐ 678 Todd Ritchie FDP .10 .05 .01
☐ 679 Ron Walden FDP .10 .05 .01
☐ 680 Tim Costo FDP .20 .09 .03
☐ 681 Dan Wilson FDP .15 .07 .02
☐ 682 Kurt Miller FDP .25 .11 .03
☐ 683 Mike Lieberthal FDP .20 .09 .03
☐ 684 Roger Clemens KM .12 .05 .02
☐ 685 Doc Gooden KM .08 .04 .01
☐ 686 Nolan Ryan KM .25 .11 .03
☐ 687 Frank Viola KM .05 .02 .01
☐ 688 Erik Hanson KM .05 .02 .01
☐ 689 Matt Williams MB .05 .02 .01
☐ 690 Jose Canseco MB UER .12 .05 .02
(Mammoth misspelled
as monmouth)
☐ 691 Darryl Strawberry MB .10 .05 .01
☐ 692 Bo Jackson MB .10 .05 .01
☐ 693 Cecil Fielder MB .10 .05 .01
☐ 694 Sandy Alomar Jr. RF .05 .02 .01
☐ 695 Cory Snyder RF .05 .02 .01
☐ 696 Eric Davis RF .08 .04 .01
☐ 697 Ken Griffey Jr. RF .25 .11 .03
☐ 698 Andy Van Slyke RF UER .05 .02 .01
(Line 2, outfielders
does not need)
☐ 699 Langston/Witt NH .05 .02 .01
Mark Langston
Mike Witt
☐ 700 Randy Johnson NH .05 .02 .01
☐ 701 Nolan Ryan NH .25 .11 .03
☐ 702 Dave Stewart NH .05 .02 .01
☐ 703 Fernando Valenzuela NH .05 .02 .01
☐ 704 Andy Hawkins NH .05 .02 .01
☐ 705 Melido Perez NH .05 .02 .01
☐ 706 Terry Mulholland NH .05 .02 .01
☐ 707 Dave Stieb NH .05 .02 .01
☐ 708 Brian Barnes RP .12 .05 .02
☐ 709 Bernard Gilkey RP .12 .05 .02
☐ 710 Steve Decker RP .15 .07 .02
☐ 711 Paul Faries RP .04 .02 .01
☐ 712 Paul Marak RP .04 .02 .01
☐ 713 Wes Chamberlain RP .20 .09 .03
☐ 714 Kevin Belcher RP .10 .05 .01
☐ 715 Dan Boone RP UER .04 .02 .01
(IP adds up to 101,
but card has 101.2)
☐ 716 Steve Adkins RP .10 .05 .01
☐ 717 Geronimo Pena RP .10 .05 .01
☐ 718 Howard Farmer RP .04 .02 .01
☐ 719 Mark Leonard RP .10 .05 .01
☐ 720 Tom Lampkin RP .04 .02 .01
☐ 721 Mike Gardiner RP .10 .05 .01
☐ 722 Jeff Conine RP .25 .11 .03
☐ 723 Efrain Valdez RP .04 .02 .01
☐ 724 Chuck Malone RP .04 .02 .01
☐ 725 Leo Gomez RP .25 .11 .03
☐ 726 Paul McClellan RP .04 .02 .01
☐ 727 Mark Leiter RP .10 .05 .01
☐ 728 Rich DeLucia RP UER .04 .02 .01
(Line 2, all told
is written alltold)
☐ 729 Mel Rojas RP .10 .05 .01
☐ 730 Hector Wagner RP .04 .02 .01
☐ 731 Ray Lankford RP .30 .14 .04
☐ 732 Turner Ward RP .10 .05 .01
☐ 733 Gerald Alexander RP .10 .05 .01
☐ 734 Scott Anderson RP .10 .05 .01
☐ 735 Tony Perezchica RP .04 .02 .01
☐ 736 Jimmy Kremers RP .04 .02 .01
☐ 737 American Flag .30 .14 .04
(Pray for Peace)
☐ 738 Mike York RP .04 .02 .01
☐ 739 Mike Rochford RP .04 .02 .01
☐ 740 Scott Aldred RP .10 .05 .01
☐ 741 Rico Brogna RP .12 .05 .02
☐ 742 Dave Burba RP .10 .05 .01
☐ 743 Ray Stephens RP .10 .05 .01
☐ 744 Eric Gunderson RP .04 .02 .01
☐ 745 Troy Afenir RP .10 .05 .01
☐ 746 Jeff Shaw RP .04 .02 .01
☐ 747 Orlando Merced RP .20 .09 .03
☐ 748 Omar Olivares RP UER .12 .05 .02
(Line 9, league is
misspelled legaue)
☐ 749 Jerry Kutzler RP .04 .02 .01
☐ 750 Mo Vaughn RP UER .20 .09 .03
(44 SB's in 1990)
☐ 751 Matt Stark RP .10 .05 .01
☐ 752 Randy Hennis RP .10 .05 .01
☐ 753 Andujar Cedeno RP .12 .05 .02
☐ 754 Kelvin Torve RP .04 .02 .01
☐ 755 Joe Kraemer RP .04 .02 .01
☐ 756 Phil Clark RP .15 .07 .02
☐ 757 Ed Vosberg RP .10 .05 .01
☐ 758 Mike Perez RP .15 .07 .02
☐ 759 Scott Lewis RP .10 .05 .01
☐ 760 Steve Chitren RP .10 .05 .01
☐ 761 Ray Young RP .10 .05 .01
☐ 762 Andres Santana RP .10 .05 .01
☐ 763 Rodney McCray RP .04 .02 .01
☐ 764 Sean Berry RP UER .12 .05 .02
(Name misspelled
Barry on card front)
☐ 765 Brent Mayne RP .07 .03 .01
☐ 766 Mike Simms RP .10 .05 .01
☐ 767 Glenn Sutko RP .04 .02 .01
☐ 768 Gary DiSarcina RP .07 .03 .01
☐ 769 George Brett HL .10 .05 .01
☐ 770 Cecil Fielder HL .10 .05 .01
☐ 771 Jim Presley .04 .02 .01
☐ 772 John Dopson .04 .02 .01
☐ 773 Bo Jackson Breaker .15 .07 .02
☐ 774 Brent Knackert UER .07 .03 .01
(Born in 1954, shown
throwing righty, but
bio says lefty)
☐ 775 Bill Doran UER .04 .02 .01
(Reds in NL East)
☐ 776 Dick Schofield .04 .02 .01
☐ 777 Nelson Santovenia .04 .02 .01
☐ 778 Mark Guthrie .04 .02 .01
☐ 779 Mark Lemke .04 .02 .01
☐ 780 Terry Steinbach .07 .03 .01
☐ 781 Tom Bolton .04 .02 .01
☐ 782 Randy Tomlin .20 .09 .03
☐ 783 Jeff Kunkel .04 .02 .01
☐ 784 Felix Jose .07 .03 .01
☐ 785 Rick Sutcliffe .07 .03 .01
☐ 786 John Cerutti .04 .02 .01
☐ 787 Jose Vizcaino UER .04 .02 .01
(Offerman not Opperman)
☐ 788 Curt Schilling .07 .03 .01
☐ 789 Ed Whitson .04 .02 .01
☐ 790 Tony Pena .04 .02 .01
☐ 791 John Candelaria .04 .02 .01
☐ 792 Carmelo Martinez .04 .02 .01
☐ 793 Sandy Alomar Jr. UER .07 .03 .01
(Indian's should
say Indians')
☐ 794 Jim Neidlinger .04 .02 .01
☐ 795 Barry Larkin WS .07 .03 .01
and Chris Sabo
☐ 796 Paul Sorrento .07 .03 .01
☐ 797 Tom Pagnozzi .04 .02 .01
☐ 798 Tino Martinez .08 .04 .01
☐ 799 Scott Ruskin UER .04 .02 .01
(Text says first three
seasons but lists
averages for four)
☐ 800 Kirk Gibson .07 .03 .01

☐ 801 Walt Terrell	.04	.02	.01
☐ 802 John Russell	.04	.02	.01
☐ 803 Chili Davis	.07	.03	.01
☐ 804 Chris Nabholz	.10	.05	.01
☐ 805 Juan Gonzalez	.35	.16	.04
☐ 806 Ron Hassey	.04	.02	.01
☐ 807 Todd Worrell	.04	.02	.01
☐ 808 Tommy Greene	.04	.02	.01
☐ 809 Joel Skinner UER (Joel, not Bob, was drafted in 1979)	.04	.02	.01
☐ 810 Benito Santiago	.07	.03	.01
☐ 811 Pat Tabler UER (Line 3, always misspelled alway)	.04	.02	.01
☐ 812 Scott Erickson UER (Record spelled rcord)	.20	.09	.03
☐ 813 Moises Alou	.15	.07	.02
☐ 814 Dale Sveum	.04	.02	.01
☐ 815 Ryne Sandberg MANYR	.20	.09	.03
☐ 816 Rick Dempsey	.04	.02	.01
☐ 817 Scott Bankhead	.04	.02	.01
☐ 818 Jason Grimsley	.04	.02	.01
☐ 819 Doug Jennings	.04	.02	.01
☐ 820 Tom Herr	.04	.02	.01
☐ 821 Rob Ducey	.04	.02	.01
☐ 822 Luis Quinones	.04	.02	.01
☐ 823 Greg Minton	.04	.02	.01
☐ 824 Mark Grant	.04	.02	.01
☐ 825 Ozzie Smith UER (Shortstop misspelled shortsop)	.10	.05	.01
☐ 826 Dave Eiland	.04	.02	.01
☐ 827 Danny Heep	.04	.02	.01
☐ 828 Hensley Meulens	.07	.03	.01
☐ 829 Charlie O'Brien	.04	.02	.01
☐ 830 Glenn Davis	.07	.03	.01
☐ 831 John Marzano UER (International misspelled Internaional)	.04	.02	.01
☐ 832 Steve Ontiveros	.04	.02	.01
☐ 833 Ron Karkovice	.04	.02	.01
☐ 834 Jerry Goff	.04	.02	.01
☐ 835 Ken Griffey Sr.	.07	.03	.01
☐ 836 Kevin Reimer	.10	.05	.01
☐ 837 Randy Kutcher UER (Infectious misspelled infectous)	.04	.02	.01
☐ 838 Mike Blowers	.04	.02	.01
☐ 839 Mike Macfarlane	.04	.02	.01
☐ 840 Frank Thomas UER (1989 Sarasota stats, 15 games but 188 AB)	1.25	.55	.16
☐ 841 The Griffeys Ken Griffey Jr. Ken Griffey Sr.	.50	.23	.06
☐ 842 Jack Howell	.04	.02	.01
☐ 843 Goose Gozzo	.04	.02	.01
☐ 844 Gerald Young	.04	.02	.01
☐ 845 Zane Smith	.04	.02	.01
☐ 846 Kevin Brown	.07	.03	.01
☐ 847 Sil Campusano	.04	.02	.01
☐ 848 Larry Andersen	.04	.02	.01
☐ 849 Cal Ripken FRAN	.15	.07	.02
☐ 850 Roger Clemens FRAN	.12	.05	.02
☐ 851 Sandy Alomar Jr. FRAN	.05	.02	.01
☐ 852 Alan Trammell FRAN	.08	.04	.01
☐ 853 George Brett FRAN	.10	.05	.01
☐ 854 Robin Yount FRAN	.10	.05	.01
☐ 855 Kirby Puckett FRAN	.12	.05	.02
☐ 856 Don Mattingly FRAN	.10	.05	.01
☐ 857 Rickey Henderson FRAN	.10	.05	.01
☐ 858 Ken Griffey Jr. FRAN	.25	.11	.03
☐ 859 Ruben Sierra FRAN	.10	.05	.01
☐ 860 John Olerud FRAN	.10	.05	.01
☐ 861 Dave Justice FRAN	.15	.07	.02
☐ 862 Ryne Sandberg FRAN	.12	.05	.02
☐ 863 Eric Davis FRAN	.08	.04	.01
☐ 864 Darryl Strawberry FRAN	.10	.05	.01
☐ 865 Tim Wallach FRAN	.05	.02	.01
☐ 866 Doc Gooden FRAN	.08	.04	.01
☐ 867 Len Dykstra FRAN	.05	.02	.01
☐ 868 Barry Bonds FRAN	.10	.05	.01
☐ 869 Todd Zeile FRAN UER (Powerful misspelled as poweful)	.05	.02	.01
☐ 870 Benito Santiago FRAN	.05	.02	.01
☐ 871 Will Clark FRAN	.10	.05	.01
☐ 872 Craig Biggio FRAN	.05	.02	.01
☐ 873 Wally Joyner FRAN	.05	.02	.01
☐ 874 Frank Thomas FRAN	.75	.35	.09
☐ 875 Rickey Henderson MVP	.10	.05	.01
☐ 876 Barry Bonds MVP	.10	.05	.01
☐ 877 Bob Welch CY	.05	.02	.01
☐ 878 Doug Drabek CY	.05	.02	.01
☐ 879 Sandy Alomar Jr ROY	.05	.02	.01
☐ 880 Dave Justice ROY	.15	.07	.02
☐ 881 Damon Berryhill	.04	.02	.01
☐ 882 Frank Viola DT	.10	.05	.01
☐ 883 Dave Stewart DT	.10	.05	.01
☐ 884 Doug Jones DT	.10	.05	.01
☐ 885 Randy Myers DT	.10	.05	.01
☐ 886 Will Clark DT	.40	.18	.05
☐ 887 Roberto Alomar DT	.40	.18	.05
☐ 888 Barry Larkin DT	.10	.05	.01
☐ 889 Wade Boggs DT	.20	.09	.03
☐ 890 Rickey Henderson DT	.30	.14	.04
☐ 891 Kirby Puckett DT	.40	.18	.05
☐ 892 Ken Griffey Jr DT	1.25	.55	.16
☐ 893 Benny Santiago DT	.10	.05	.01

1991 Score All-Star Fanfest

This ten-card set was issued with a 3-D 1946 World Series trivia card. The cards measure the standard size (2 1/2" by 3 1/2") and feature on the fronts color action player photos, with red borders above and below the pictures. The card face is lime green with miniature yellow baseballs and blue player icons, and it can be seen at the top and bottom of the card front. The backs have a similar pattern on a white background and present biographical information as well as career highlights. The cards are numbered on the back.

	MT	EX-MT	VG
COMPLETE SET (10)	15.00	6.75	1.90
COMMON PLAYER (1-10)	1.00	.45	.13
☐ 1 Ray Lankford	4.00	1.80	.50
☐ 2 Steve Decker	1.50	.65	.19
☐ 3 Gary Scott	1.50	.65	.19
☐ 4 Hensley Meulens	1.50	.65	.19
☐ 5 Tim Naehring	1.25	.55	.16
☐ 6 Mark Whiten	1.50	.65	.19
☐ 7 Ed Sprague	1.50	.65	.19
☐ 8 Charles Nagy	2.00	.90	.25
☐ 9 Terry Shumpert	1.00	.45	.13
☐ 10 Chuck Knoblauch	4.00	1.80	.50

1991 Score Cooperstown

This seven-card set measures the standard 2 1/2" by 3 1/2" and was available only as an insert with 1991 Score factory sets. The card design is not like the regular 1991 Score cards. The card front features a portrait of the player in an oval on a white background. The words "Cooperstown Card" are prominently displayed on the card front. The cards are numbered on the back with a B prefix.

	MT	EX-MT	VG
COMPLETE SET (7)	8.00	3.60	1.00
COMMON PLAYER (B1-B7)	.75	.35	.09

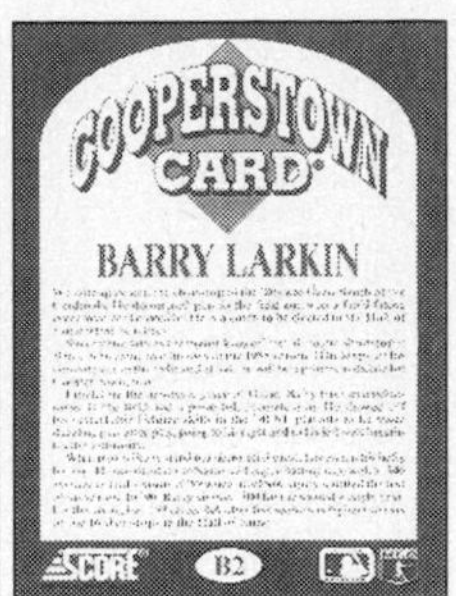

☐ B1 Wade Boggs	1.00	.45	.13
☐ B2 Barry Larkin	.75	.35	.09
☐ B3 Ken Griffey Jr.	3.00	1.35	.40
☐ B4 Rickey Henderson	1.00	.45	.13
☐ B5 George Brett	1.00	.45	.13
☐ B6 Will Clark	1.50	.65	.19
☐ B7 Nolan Ryan	3.00	1.35	.40

1991 Score Hot Rookies

This ten-card set measures the standard size (2 1/2" by 3 1/2"), and one of these cards was inserted in the 1991 Score blister (100-card) packs. The front features a color action player photo, with white borders and the words "Hot Rookie" in yellow above the picture. The card background shades from orange to yellow to orange as one moves down the card face. In a horizontal format, the left half of the back has a color head shot, while the right half has career summary. The cards are numbered on the back.

	MT	EX-MT	VG
COMPLETE SET (10)	18.00	8.00	2.30
COMMON PLAYER (1-10)	.60	.25	.08
☐ 1 Dave Justice	3.00	1.35	.40
☐ 2 Kevin Maas	1.00	.45	.13
☐ 3 Hal Morris	.60	.25	.08
☐ 4 Frank Thomas	8.00	3.60	1.00
☐ 5 Jeff Conine	1.00	.45	.13
☐ 6 Sandy Alomar Jr.	.60	.25	.08
☐ 7 Ray Lankford	2.00	.90	.25
☐ 8 Steve Decker	.60	.25	.08
☐ 9 Juan Gonzalez	5.00	2.30	.60
☐ 10 Jose Offerman	.75	.35	.09

1991 Score Mickey Mantle Promos

This seven-card set measures the standard 2 1/2" by 3 1/2" and features Mickey Mantle at various points in his career. This set was released to dealers and media members on

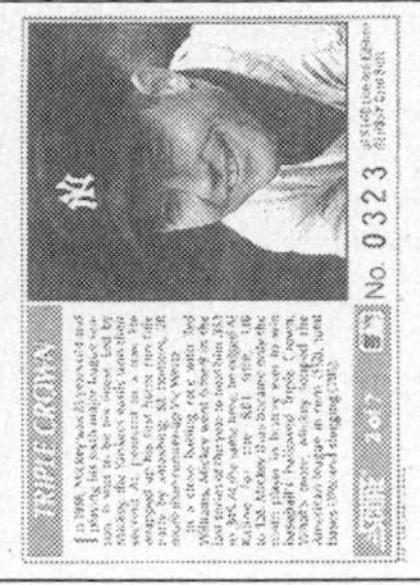

Score's mailing list and was individually numbered on the back. This numbered dealer/media set was limited to 5,000 sets produced. The cards were sent in seven-card packs in the Yankees colors. The fronts are full-color glossy shots of Mantle while the backs are in a horizontal format with a full-color photo and some narrative information. The pictures have red and white borders, with the caption appearing in a blue stripe below the photo. The card number and the set serial number appear on the back. These were essentially the same cards Score used in their second series promotion.

	MT	EX-MT	VG
COMPLETE SET (7)	300.00	135.00	38.00
COMMON MANTLE (1-7)	50.00	23.00	6.25
☐ 1 The Rookie (With Billy Martin)	50.00	23.00	6.25
☐ 2 Triple Crown	50.00	23.00	6.25
☐ 3 World Series	50.00	23.00	6.25
☐ 4 Going, Going, Gone	50.00	23.00	6.25
☐ 5 Speed and Grace	50.00	23.00	6.25
☐ 6 A True Yankee	50.00	23.00	6.25
☐ 7 Twilight	50.00	23.00	6.25
☐ AU0 Mickey Mantle (Autographed with certified signature)	600.00	275.00	75.00

1991 Score Nolan Ryan Life and Times

This four-card standard-size (2 1/2" by 3 1/2") set was manufactured by Score to commemorate four significant milestones in Nolan Ryan's illustrious career beginning with his years growing up in Alvin, Texas, his years with the Mets and Angels, with the Astros and Rangers, and his career statistics. Each card commemorates a career milestone (all occur with the Rangers) and features Ryan's color photo on the front. They are part of "The Life and Times of Nolan Ryan," by Tarrant Printing, a special collector set that consists of four volumes (8 1/2" by 11" booklets) along with the cards packaged in a folder. The color action photos on the fronts are full-bleed, except on the left side, where blue and red border stripes run the length of the card. The horizontally oriented backs feature a different color player photo on the left half. The right half is accented with blue and red stripes and has career highlights on a pale yellow background. The cards are numbered on the back.

	MT	EX-MT	VG
COMPLETE SET (4)	24.00	11.00	3.00
COMMON PLAYER (1-4)	7.50	3.40	.95
☐ 1 Nolan Ryan (5,000th Career Strikeout)	7.50	3.40	.95
☐ 2 Nolan Ryan (6th Career No-Hitter)	7.50	3.40	.95
☐ 3 Nolan Ryan HOR (300th Career Victory)	7.50	3.40	.95
☐ 4 Nolan Ryan HOR (7th Career No-Hitter)	7.50	3.40	.95

1991 Score 100 Rising Stars

The 1991 Score 100 Rising Stars sets were issued by Score with or without special books which goes with the cards. The cards, which feature 100 of the most popular rising stars, are the standard size 2 1/2" by 3 1/2". The fronts of the cards are beautiful full-color photos surrounded by blue and green borders while the backs have a full color photo on the back and give a brief biography of the player. The sets (with the special book with brief biography on the players) are marketed for retail purposes at a suggested price of 12.95.

	MT	EX-MT	VG
COMPLETE SET (100)	10.00	4.50	1.25
COMMON PLAYER (1-100)	.05	.02	.01
☐ 1 Sandy Alomar Jr.	.15	.07	.02
☐ 2 Tom Edens	.05	.02	.01
☐ 3 Terry Shumpert	.05	.02	.01
☐ 4 Shawn Boskie	.05	.02	.01
☐ 5 Steve Avery	.50	.23	.06
☐ 6 Deion Sanders	.50	.23	.06
☐ 7 John Burkett	.10	.05	.01
☐ 8 Stan Belinda	.10	.05	.01
☐ 9 Thomas Howard	.10	.05	.01
☐ 10 Wayne Edwards	.05	.02	.01
☐ 11 Rick Parker	.05	.02	.01
☐ 12 Randy Veres	.05	.02	.01
☐ 13 Alex Cole	.15	.07	.02
☐ 14 Scott Chiamparino	.10	.05	.01
☐ 15 Greg Olson	.05	.02	.01
☐ 16 Jose DeJesus	.05	.02	.01
☐ 17 Mike Blowers	.05	.02	.01
☐ 18 Jeff Huson	.05	.02	.01
☐ 19 Willie Blair	.05	.02	.01
☐ 20 Howard Farmer	.10	.05	.01
☐ 21 Larry Walker	.25	.11	.03
☐ 22 Scott Hemond	.10	.05	.01
☐ 23 Mel Stottlemyre Jr.	.05	.02	.01
☐ 24 Mark Whiten	.15	.07	.02
☐ 25 Jeff Schulz	.05	.02	.01
☐ 26 Gary DiSarcina	.10	.05	.01
☐ 27 George Canale	.05	.02	.01
☐ 28 Dean Palmer	.45	.20	.06
☐ 29 Jim Leyritz	.05	.02	.01
☐ 30 Carlos Baerga	.60	.25	.08
☐ 31 Rafael Valdez	.10	.05	.01
☐ 32 Derek Bell	.45	.20	.06
☐ 33 Francisco Cabrera	.20	.09	.03
☐ 34 Chris Hoiles	.15	.07	.02
☐ 35 Craig Grebeck	.10	.05	.01
☐ 36 Scott Coolbaugh	.05	.02	.01
☐ 37 Kevin Wickander	.05	.02	.01
☐ 38 Marquis Grissom	.40	.18	.05
☐ 39 Chip Hale	.05	.02	.01
☐ 40 Kevin Maas	.25	.11	.03
☐ 41 Juan Gonzalez	1.00	.45	.13
☐ 42 Eric Anthony	.25	.11	.03
☐ 43 Luis Sojo	.10	.05	.01
☐ 44 Paul Sorrento	.10	.05	.01
☐ 45 Dave Justice	.60	.25	.08
☐ 46 Oscar Azocar	.05	.02	.01
☐ 47 Charles Nagy	.25	.11	.03
☐ 48 Robin Ventura	.60	.25	.08
☐ 49 Reggie Harris	.10	.05	.01
☐ 50 Ben McDonald	.25	.11	.03
☐ 51 Hector Villanueva	.10	.05	.01
☐ 52 Kevin Tapani	.15	.07	.02
☐ 53 Brian Bohanon	.10	.05	.01
☐ 54 Tim Layana	.05	.02	.01
☐ 55 Delino DeShields	.40	.18	.05
☐ 56 Beau Allred	.10	.05	.01
☐ 57 Eric Gunderson	.05	.02	.01
☐ 58 Kent Mercker	.10	.05	.01
☐ 59 Juan Bell	.10	.05	.01
☐ 60 Glenallen Hill	.10	.05	.01
☐ 61 David Segui	.10	.05	.01
☐ 62 Alan Mills	.10	.05	.01
☐ 63 Mike Harkey	.15	.07	.02
☐ 64 Bill Sampen	.05	.02	.01
☐ 65 Greg Vaughn	.20	.09	.03
☐ 66 Alex Fernandez	.20	.09	.03
☐ 67 Mike Hartley	.05	.02	.01
☐ 68 Travis Fryman	.75	.35	.09
☐ 69 Dave Rohde	.05	.02	.01
☐ 70 Tom Lampkin	.05	.02	.01
☐ 71 Mark Gardner	.05	.02	.01
☐ 72 Pat Combs	.05	.02	.01
☐ 73 Kevin Appier	.15	.07	.02
☐ 74 Mike Fetters	.10	.05	.01
☐ 75 Greg Myers	.05	.02	.01
☐ 76 Steve Searcy	.05	.02	.01
☐ 77 Tim Naehring	.15	.07	.02
☐ 78 Frank Thomas	1.50	.65	.19
☐ 79 Todd Hundley	.15	.07	.02
☐ 80 Ed Vosberg	.05	.02	.01
☐ 81 Todd Zeile	.15	.07	.02
☐ 82 Lee Stevens	.15	.07	.02
☐ 83 Scott Radinsky	.10	.05	.01
☐ 84 Hensley Meulens	.10	.05	.01
☐ 85 Brian DuBois	.05	.02	.01
☐ 86 Steve Olin	.10	.05	.01
☐ 87 Julio Machado	.05	.02	.01
☐ 88 Jose Vizcaino	.05	.02	.01
☐ 89 Mark Lemke	.10	.05	.01
☐ 90 Felix Jose	.25	.11	.03
☐ 91 Wally Whitehurst	.05	.02	.01
☐ 92 Dana Kiecker	.05	.02	.01
☐ 93 Mike Munoz	.05	.02	.01
☐ 94 Adam Peterson	.05	.02	.01
☐ 95 Tim Drummond	.05	.02	.01
☐ 96 Dave Hollins	.35	.16	.04
☐ 97 Craig Wilson	.10	.05	.01
☐ 98 Hal Morris	.20	.09	.03
☐ 99 Jose Offerman	.15	.07	.02
☐ 100 John Olerud	.40	.18	.05

1991 Score 100 Superstars

The 1991 Score 100 Superstars sets were issued by Score with or without special books which goes with the cards. The cards, which feature 100 of the most popular superstars, are the standard size 2 1/2" by 3 1/2". The fronts of the cards feature beautiful full-color photos surrounded by red, white and blue borders while the backs are surrounded by red and blue borders and feature a full-color photo on the back along with a brief biography. The sets

(with the special book with brief biography on the players) are marketed for retail purposes at a suggested price of 12.95.

	MT	EX-MT	VG
COMPLETE SET (1-100)	10.00	4.50	1.25
COMMON PLAYER (1-100)	.05	.02	.01
☐ 1 Jose Canseco	.60	.25	.08
☐ 2 Bo Jackson	.75	.35	.09
☐ 3 Wade Boggs	.45	.20	.06
☐ 4 Will Clark	.60	.25	.08
☐ 5 Ken Griffey Jr.	1.25	.55	.16
☐ 6 Doug Drabek	.15	.07	.02
☐ 7 Kirby Puckett	.50	.23	.06
☐ 8 Joe Orsulak	.05	.02	.01
☐ 9 Eric Davis	.20	.09	.03
☐ 10 Rickey Henderson	.60	.25	.08
☐ 11 Len Dykstra	.10	.05	.01
☐ 12 Ruben Sierra	.35	.16	.04
☐ 13 Paul Molitor	.15	.07	.02
☐ 14 Ron Gant	.35	.16	.04
☐ 15 Ozzie Guillen	.10	.05	.01
☐ 16 Ramon Martinez	.20	.09	.03
☐ 17 Edgar Martinez	.20	.09	.03
☐ 18 Ozzie Smith	.25	.11	.03
☐ 19 Charlie Hayes	.10	.05	.01
☐ 20 Barry Larkin	.20	.09	.03
☐ 21 Cal Ripken	.75	.35	.09
☐ 22 Andy Van Slyke	.15	.07	.02
☐ 23 Don Mattingly	.60	.25	.08
☐ 24 Dave Stewart	.10	.05	.01
☐ 25 Nolan Ryan	1.00	.45	.13
☐ 26 Barry Bonds	.45	.20	.06
☐ 27 Gregg Olson	.15	.07	.02
☐ 28 Chris Sabo	.15	.07	.02
☐ 29 John Franco	.05	.02	.01
☐ 30 Gary Sheffield	.45	.20	.06
☐ 31 Jeff Treadway	.05	.02	.01
☐ 32 Tom Browning	.05	.02	.01
☐ 33 Jose Lind	.05	.02	.01
☐ 34 Dave Magadan	.05	.02	.01
☐ 35 Dale Murphy	.20	.09	.03
☐ 36 Tom Candiotti	.10	.05	.01
☐ 37 Willie McGee	.10	.05	.01
☐ 38 Robin Yount	.45	.20	.06
☐ 39 Mark McGwire	.45	.20	.06
☐ 40 George Bell	.10	.05	.01
☐ 41 Carlton Fisk	.30	.14	.04
☐ 42 Bobby Bonilla	.30	.14	.04
☐ 43 Randy Milligan	.05	.02	.01
☐ 44 Dave Parker	.10	.05	.01
☐ 45 Shawon Dunston	.10	.05	.01
☐ 46 Brian Harper	.05	.02	.01
☐ 47 John Tudor	.05	.02	.01
☐ 48 Ellis Burks	.15	.07	.02
☐ 49 Bob Welch	.10	.05	.01
☐ 50 Roger Clemens	.75	.35	.09
☐ 51 Mike Henneman	.10	.05	.01
☐ 52 Eddie Murray	.20	.09	.03
☐ 53 Kal Daniels	.05	.02	.01
☐ 54 Doug Jones	.05	.02	.01
☐ 55 Craig Biggio	.15	.07	.02
☐ 56 Rafael Palmeiro	.20	.09	.03
☐ 57 Wally Joyner	.15	.07	.02
☐ 58 Tim Wallach	.05	.02	.01
☐ 59 Bret Saberhagen	.15	.07	.02
☐ 60 Ryne Sandberg	.75	.35	.09
☐ 61 Benito Santiago	.10	.05	.01
☐ 62 Darryl Strawberry	.50	.23	.06
☐ 63 Alan Trammell	.15	.07	.02
☐ 64 Kelly Gruber	.10	.05	.01
☐ 65 Dwight Gooden	.20	.09	.03
☐ 66 Dave Winfield	.35	.16	.04
☐ 67 Rick Aguilera	.05	.02	.01
☐ 68 Dave Righetti	.05	.02	.01
☐ 69 Jim Abbott	.30	.14	.04
☐ 70 Frank Viola	.10	.05	.01
☐ 71 Fred McGriff	.30	.14	.04
☐ 72 Steve Sax	.10	.05	.01
☐ 73 Dennis Eckersley	.20	.09	.03
☐ 74 Cory Snyder	.05	.02	.01
☐ 75 Mackey Sasser	.05	.02	.01
☐ 76 Candy Maldonado	.10	.05	.01
☐ 77 Matt Williams	.20	.09	.03
☐ 78 Kent Hrbek	.10	.05	.01
☐ 79 Randy Myers	.10	.05	.01
☐ 80 Gregg Jefferies	.20	.09	.03
☐ 81 Joe Carter	.30	.14	.04
☐ 82 Mike Greenwell	.20	.09	.03
☐ 83 Jack Armstong	.10	.05	.01
☐ 84 Julio Franco	.15	.07	.02
☐ 85 George Brett	.45	.20	.06
☐ 86 Howard Johnson	.15	.07	.02
☐ 87 Andre Dawson	.25	.11	.03
☐ 88 Cecil Fielder	.45	.20	.06
☐ 89 Tim Raines	.10	.05	.01
☐ 90 Chuck Finley	.05	.02	.01
☐ 91 Mark Grace	.35	.16	.04
☐ 92 Brook Jacoby	.05	.02	.01
☐ 93 Dave Stieb	.10	.05	.01
☐ 94 Tony Gwynn	.40	.18	.05
☐ 95 Bobby Thigpen	.10	.05	.01
☐ 96 Roberto Kelly	.20	.09	.03
☐ 97 Kevin Seitzer	.05	.02	.01
☐ 98 Kevin Mitchell	.20	.09	.03
☐ 99 Dwight Evans	.10	.05	.01
☐ 100 Roberto Alomar	.50	.23	.06

1991 Score Rookies 40

This 40-card set measuring the standard size (2 1/2" by 3 1/2") was distributed with five magic motion trivia cards. The fronts feature high glossy color action player photos, on a blue card face with meandering green lines. The picture has a yellow border on its right side, and red and yellow borders below. The words "1991 Rookie" appear to the left of the picture running the length of the card. The team logo in the lower right corner rounds out the card face. On a yellow background, the backs have a color head shot, biography, and career highlights. The cards are numbered on the back.

	MT	EX-MT	VG
COMPLETE SET (40)	6.00	2.70	.75
COMMON PLAYER (1-40)	.15	.07	.02
☐ 1 Mel Rojas	.25	.11	.03
☐ 2 Ray Lankford	1.00	.45	.13
☐ 3 Scott Aldred	.25	.11	.03
☐ 4 Turner Ward	.15	.07	.02
☐ 5 Omar Olivares	.25	.11	.03
☐ 6 Mo Vaughn	.50	.23	.06
☐ 7 Phil Clark	.25	.11	.03
☐ 8 Brent Mayne	.25	.11	.03
☐ 9 Scott Lewis	.15	.07	.02
☐ 10 Brian Barnes	.25	.11	.03
☐ 11 Bernard Gilkey	.50	.23	.06
☐ 12 Steve Decker	.35	.16	.04

☐ 13 Paul Marak	.15	.07	.02
☐ 14 Wes Chamberlain	.35	.16	.04
☐ 15 Kevin Belcher	.15	.07	.02
☐ 16 Steve Adkins	.15	.07	.02
☐ 17 Geronimo Pena	.25	.11	.03
☐ 18 Mark Leonard	.15	.07	.02
☐ 19 Jeff Conine	.35	.16	.04
☐ 20 Leo Gomez	.50	.23	.06
☐ 21 Chuck Malone	.15	.07	.02
☐ 22 Beau Allred	.25	.11	.03
☐ 23 Todd Hundley	.35	.16	.04
☐ 24 Lance Dickson	.25	.11	.03
☐ 25 Mike Benjamin	.15	.07	.02
☐ 26 Jose Offerman	.25	.11	.03
☐ 27 Terry Shumpert	.15	.07	.02
☐ 28 Darren Lewis	.25	.11	.03
☐ 29 Scott Chiamparino	.25	.11	.03
☐ 30 Tim Naehring	.25	.11	.03
☐ 31 David Segui	.25	.11	.03
☐ 32 Karl Rhodes	.15	.07	.02
☐ 33 Mickey Morandini	.35	.16	.04
☐ 34 Chuck McElroy	.25	.11	.03
☐ 35 Tim McIntosh	.25	.11	.03
☐ 36 Derrick May	.50	.23	.06
☐ 37 Rich DeLucia	.15	.07	.02
☐ 38 Tino Martinez	.35	.16	.04
☐ 39 Hensley Meulens	.25	.11	.03
☐ 40 Andujar Cedeno	.50	.23	.06

1991 Score Rookie/Traded

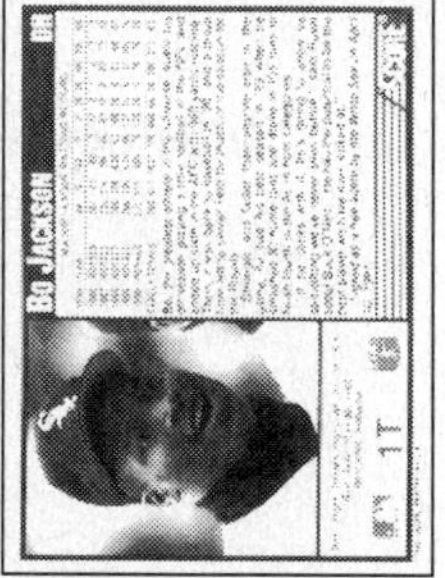

The 1991 Score Rookie and Traded set contains 110 standard-size (2 1/2" by 3 1/2") player cards and 10 "World Series II" magic motion trivia cards. The front design features glossy color action photos, with white and purple borders on a mauve card face. The player's name, team, and position are given above the pictures. In a horizontal format, the left portion of the back has a color head shot and biography, while the right portion has statistics and player profile on a pale yellow background. The cards are numbered on the back. Cards 1-80 feature traded players, while cards 81-110 focus on rookies. The only noteworthy Rookie Cards in the set are Jeff Bagwell and Ivan Rodriguez.

	MT	EX-MT	VG
COMPLETE SET (110)	6.00	2.70	.75
COMMON PLAYER (1T-80T)	.05	.02	.01
COMMON PLAYER (81T-110T)	.05	.02	.01
☐ 1T Bo Jackson	.15	.07	.02
☐ 2T Mike Flanagan	.05	.02	.01
☐ 3T Pete Incaviglia	.05	.02	.01
☐ 4T Jack Clark	.08	.04	.01
☐ 5T Hubie Brooks	.05	.02	.01
☐ 6T Ivan Calderon	.05	.02	.01
☐ 7T Glenn Davis	.08	.04	.01
☐ 8T Wally Backman	.05	.02	.01
☐ 9T Dave Smith	.05	.02	.01
☐ 10T Tim Raines	.08	.04	.01
☐ 11T Joe Carter	.12	.05	.02
☐ 12T Sid Bream	.05	.02	.01
☐ 13T George Bell	.08	.04	.01
☐ 14T Steve Bedrosian	.05	.02	.01
☐ 15T Willie Wilson	.05	.02	.01
☐ 16T Darryl Strawberry	.12	.05	.02
☐ 17T Danny Jackson	.05	.02	.01
☐ 18T Kirk Gibson	.08	.04	.01
☐ 19T Willie McGee	.08	.04	.01
☐ 20T Junior Felix	.05	.02	.01
☐ 21T Steve Farr	.05	.02	.01
☐ 22T Pat Tabler	.05	.02	.01
☐ 23T Brett Butler	.08	.04	.01
☐ 24T Danny Darwin	.05	.02	.01
☐ 25T Mickey Tettleton	.08	.04	.01
☐ 26T Gary Carter	.08	.04	.01
☐ 27T Mitch Williams	.05	.02	.01
☐ 28T Candy Maldonado	.05	.02	.01
☐ 29T Otis Nixon	.08	.04	.01
☐ 30T Brian Downing	.05	.02	.01
☐ 31T Tom Candiotti	.05	.02	.01
☐ 32T John Candelaria	.05	.02	.01
☐ 33T Rob Murphy	.05	.02	.01
☐ 34T Deion Sanders	.20	.09	.03
☐ 35T Willie Randolph	.08	.04	.01
☐ 36T Pete Harnisch	.08	.04	.01
☐ 37T Dante Bichette	.05	.02	.01
☐ 38T Garry Templeton	.05	.02	.01
☐ 39T Gary Gaetti	.05	.02	.01
☐ 40T John Cerutti	.05	.02	.01
☐ 41T Rick Cerone	.05	.02	.01
☐ 42T Mike Pagliarulo	.05	.02	.01
☐ 43T Ron Hassey	.05	.02	.01
☐ 44T Roberto Alomar	.20	.09	.03
☐ 45T Mike Boddicker	.05	.02	.01
☐ 46T Bud Black	.05	.02	.01
☐ 47T Rob Deer	.08	.04	.01
☐ 48T Devon White	.08	.04	.01
☐ 49T Luis Sojo	.05	.02	.01
☐ 50T Terry Pendleton	.10	.05	.01
☐ 51T Kevin Gross	.05	.02	.01
☐ 52T Mike Huff	.05	.02	.01
☐ 53T Dave Righetti	.05	.02	.01
☐ 54T Matt Young	.05	.02	.01
☐ 55T Earnest Riles	.05	.02	.01
☐ 56T Bill Gullickson	.05	.02	.01
☐ 57T Vince Coleman	.08	.04	.01
☐ 58T Fred McGriff	.15	.07	.02
☐ 59T Franklin Stubbs	.05	.02	.01
☐ 60T Eric King	.05	.02	.01
☐ 61T Cory Snyder	.05	.02	.01
☐ 62T Dwight Evans	.08	.04	.01
☐ 63T Gerald Perry	.05	.02	.01
☐ 64T Eric Show	.05	.02	.01
☐ 65T Shawn Hillegas	.05	.02	.01
☐ 66T Tony Fernandez	.08	.04	.01
☐ 67T Tim Teufel	.05	.02	.01
☐ 68T Mitch Webster	.05	.02	.01
☐ 69T Mike Heath	.05	.02	.01
☐ 70T Chili Davis	.08	.04	.01
☐ 71T Larry Andersen	.05	.02	.01
☐ 72T Gary Varsho	.05	.02	.01
☐ 73T Juan Berenguer	.05	.02	.01
☐ 74T Jack Morris	.10	.05	.01
☐ 75T Barry Jones	.05	.02	.01
☐ 76T Rafael Belliard	.05	.02	.01
☐ 77T Steve Buechele	.05	.02	.01
☐ 78T Scott Sanderson	.05	.02	.01
☐ 79T Bob Ojeda	.05	.02	.01
☐ 80T Curt Schilling	.08	.04	.01
☐ 81T Brian Drahman	.10	.05	.01
☐ 82T Ivan Rodriguez	1.25	.55	.16
☐ 83T David Howard	.10	.05	.01
☐ 84T Heathcliff Slocumb	.05	.02	.01
☐ 85T Mike Timlin	.10	.05	.01
☐ 86T Darryl Kile	.10	.05	.01
☐ 87T Pete Schourek	.12	.05	.02
☐ 88T Bruce Walton	.05	.02	.01
☐ 89T Al Osuna	.10	.05	.01
☐ 90T Gary Scott	.15	.07	.02
☐ 91T Doug Simons	.05	.02	.01
☐ 92T Chris Jones	.05	.02	.01
☐ 93T Chuck Knoblauch	.30	.14	.04
☐ 94T Dana Allison	.10	.05	.01
☐ 95T Erik Pappas	.05	.02	.01
☐ 96T Jeff Bagwell	1.25	.55	.16
☐ 97T Kirk Dressendorfer	.10	.05	.01
☐ 98T Freddie Benavides	.05	.02	.01
☐ 99T Luis Gonzalez	.20	.09	.03
☐ 100T Wade Taylor	.05	.02	.01
☐ 101T Ed Sprague	.20	.09	.03
☐ 102T Bob Scanlan	.10	.05	.01
☐ 103T Rick Wilkins	.10	.05	.01
☐ 104T Chris Donnels	.12	.05	.02
☐ 105T Joe Slusarski	.10	.05	.01
☐ 106T Mark Lewis	.12	.05	.02
☐ 107T Pat Kelly	.15	.07	.02
☐ 108T John Briscoe	.10	.05	.01

	MT	EX-MT	VG
☐ 109T Luis Lopez	.10	.05	.01
☐ 110T Jeff Johnson	.10	.05	.01

1992 Score Previews

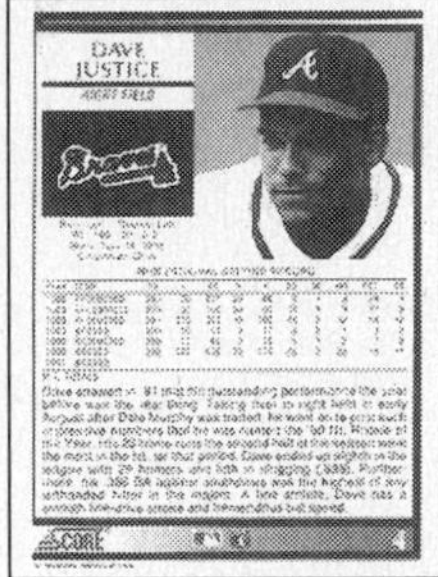

The 1992 Score Preview set contains six cards, each measuring standard size, 2 1/2" by 3 1/2", done in the same style as the 1992 Score baseball cards. Supposedly the Sandberg and Mack cards are tougher as they were only available at the St. Louis card show that Score attended in November 1991.

	MT	EX-MT	VG
COMPLETE SET (6)	35.00	16.00	4.40
COMMON PLAYER (1-6)	4.00	1.80	.50
☐ 1 Ken Griffey Jr.	9.00	4.00	1.15
☐ 2 Dave Justice	6.00	2.70	.75
☐ 3 Robin Ventura	6.00	2.70	.75
☐ 4 Steve Avery	4.00	1.80	.50
☐ 5 Ryne Sandberg	10.00	4.50	1.25
☐ 6 Shane Mack	7.50	3.40	.95

1992 Score

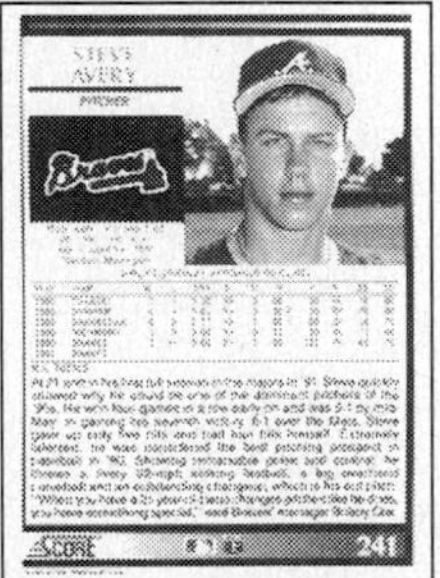

The 1992 Score set marked the second year that Score released their set in two different series. The first series contains 442 cards measuring the standard size (2 1/2" by 3 1/2"). The second series contains 451 more cards sequentially numbered. The glossy color action photos on the fronts are bordered above and below by stripes of the same color, and a thicker, different color stripe runs the length of the card to one side of the picture. The backs have a color close-up shot in the upper right corner, with biography, complete career statistics, and player profile printed on a yellow background. Hall of Famer Joe DiMaggio is remembered in a five-card subset. He autographed 2,500 cards; 2,495 of these were randomly inserted in Series I packs, while the other five were given away through a mail-in sweepstakes. Another 150,000 unsigned DiMaggio cards were inserted in Series I Count Goods packs only. Score later extended its DiMaggio promotion to Series I blister packs; one hundred signed and twelve thousand unsigned cards were randomly inserted in these packs. Also a special "World Series II" trivia card was inserted into each pack. These cards highlight crucial games and heroes from past Octobers. Topical subsets included in the set focus on Rookie Prospects (395-424), No-Hit Club (425-428), Highlights (429-430), AL All-Stars (431-440; with color montages displaying Chris Greco's player caricatures), Dream Team (441-442), Rookie Prospects (736-772, 814-877), NL All-Stars (773-782), Highlights (783, 795-797), No-Hit Club (784-787), Draft Picks (799-810), Memorabilia (878-882), and Dream Team (883-893). All of the Rookie Prospects (736-772) can be found with or without the Rookie Prospect stripe. The cards are numbered on the back. Key Rookie Cards in the set include Cliff Floyd, Brent Gates, Tyler Green, Manny Ramirez, Aaron Sele, and Bob Zupcic. Chuck Knoblauch, 1991 American League Rookie of the Year, autographed 3,000 of his own 1990 Score Draft Pick cards (card number 672) in gold ink, 2,989 were randomly inserted in Series 2 poly packs, while the other 11 were given away in a sweepstakes. The backs of these Knoblauch autograph cards have special holograms to differentiate them.

	MT	EX-MT	VG
COMPLETE SET (893)	20.00	9.00	2.50
COMPLETE FACT.SET (910)	30.00	13.50	3.80
COMPLETE SERIES 1 (442)	10.00	4.50	1.25
COMPLETE SERIES 2 (451)	10.00	4.50	1.25
COMMON PLAYER (1-442)	.04	.02	.01
COMMON PLAYER (443-893)	.04	.02	.01
☐ 1 Ken Griffey Jr.	.50	.23	.06
☐ 2 Nolan Ryan	.40	.18	.05
☐ 3 Will Clark	.20	.09	.03
☐ 4 Dave Justice	.20	.09	.03
☐ 5 Dave Henderson	.04	.02	.01
☐ 6 Bret Saberhagen	.07	.03	.01
☐ 7 Fred McGriff	.12	.05	.02
☐ 8 Erik Hanson	.04	.02	.01
☐ 9 Darryl Strawberry	.12	.05	.02
☐ 10 Dwight Gooden	.07	.03	.01
☐ 11 Juan Gonzalez	.35	.16	.04
☐ 12 Mark Langston	.07	.03	.01
☐ 13 Lonnie Smith	.04	.02	.01
☐ 14 Jeff Montgomery	.04	.02	.01
☐ 15 Roberto Alomar	.20	.09	.03
☐ 16 Delino DeShields	.10	.05	.01
☐ 17 Steve Bedrosian	.04	.02	.01
☐ 18 Terry Pendleton	.10	.05	.01
☐ 19 Mark Carreon	.04	.02	.01
☐ 20 Mark McGwire	.20	.09	.03
☐ 21 Roger Clemens	.25	.11	.03
☐ 22 Chuck Crim	.04	.02	.01
☐ 23 Don Mattingly	.12	.05	.02
☐ 24 Dickie Thon	.04	.02	.01
☐ 25 Ron Gant	.10	.05	.01
☐ 26 Milt Cuyler	.04	.02	.01
☐ 27 Mike Macfarlane	.04	.02	.01
☐ 28 Dan Gladden	.04	.02	.01
☐ 29 Melido Perez	.07	.03	.01
☐ 30 Willie Randolph	.07	.03	.01
☐ 31 Albert Belle	.12	.05	.02
☐ 32 Dave Winfield	.10	.05	.01
☐ 33 Jimmy Jones	.04	.02	.01
☐ 34 Kevin Gross	.04	.02	.01
☐ 35 Andres Galarraga	.04	.02	.01
☐ 36 Mike Devereaux	.07	.03	.01
☐ 37 Chris Bosio	.04	.02	.01
☐ 38 Mike LaValliere	.04	.02	.01
☐ 39 Gary Gaetti	.04	.02	.01
☐ 40 Felix Jose	.07	.03	.01
☐ 41 Alvaro Espinoza	.04	.02	.01
☐ 42 Rick Aguilera	.07	.03	.01
☐ 43 Mike Gallego	.04	.02	.01
☐ 44 Eric Davis	.07	.03	.01
☐ 45 George Bell	.07	.03	.01
☐ 46 Tom Brunansky	.07	.03	.01
☐ 47 Steve Farr	.04	.02	.01
☐ 48 Duane Ward	.04	.02	.01
☐ 49 David Wells	.04	.02	.01

☐ 50 Cecil Fielder	.12	.05	.02
☐ 51 Walt Weiss	.04	.02	.01
☐ 52 Todd Zeile	.04	.02	.01
☐ 53 Doug Jones	.04	.02	.01
☐ 54 Bob Walk	.04	.02	.01
☐ 55 Rafael Palmeiro	.07	.03	.01
☐ 56 Rob Deer	.07	.03	.01
☐ 57 Paul O'Neill	.07	.03	.01
☐ 58 Jeff Reardon	.07	.03	.01
☐ 59 Randy Ready	.04	.02	.01
☐ 60 Scott Erickson	.10	.05	.01
☐ 61 Paul Molitor	.07	.03	.01
☐ 62 Jack McDowell	.07	.03	.01
☐ 63 Jim Acker	.04	.02	.01
☐ 64 Jay Buhner	.07	.03	.01
☐ 65 Travis Fryman	.30	.14	.04
☐ 66 Marquis Grissom	.10	.05	.01
☐ 67 Mike Harkey	.07	.03	.01
☐ 68 Luis Polonia	.07	.03	.01
☐ 69 Ken Caminiti	.07	.03	.01
☐ 70 Chris Sabo	.07	.03	.01
☐ 71 Gregg Olson	.07	.03	.01
☐ 72 Carlton Fisk	.10	.05	.01
☐ 73 Juan Samuel	.04	.02	.01
☐ 74 Todd Stottlemyre	.07	.03	.01
☐ 75 Andre Dawson	.10	.05	.01
☐ 76 Alvin Davis	.04	.02	.01
☐ 77 Bill Doran	.04	.02	.01
☐ 78 B.J. Surhoff	.04	.02	.01
☐ 79 Kirk McCaskill	.04	.02	.01
☐ 80 Dale Murphy	.07	.03	.01
☐ 81 Jose DeLeon	.04	.02	.01
☐ 82 Alex Fernandez	.07	.03	.01
☐ 83 Ivan Calderon	.04	.02	.01
☐ 84 Brent Mayne	.04	.02	.01
☐ 85 Jody Reed	.04	.02	.01
☐ 86 Randy Tomlin	.04	.02	.01
☐ 87 Randy Milligan	.04	.02	.01
☐ 88 Pascual Perez	.04	.02	.01
☐ 89 Hensley Meulens	.04	.02	.01
☐ 90 Joe Carter	.12	.05	.02
☐ 91 Mike Moore	.04	.02	.01
☐ 92 Ozzie Guillen	.04	.02	.01
☐ 93 Shawn Hillegas	.04	.02	.01
☐ 94 Chili Davis	.07	.03	.01
☐ 95 Vince Coleman	.07	.03	.01
☐ 96 Jimmy Key	.04	.02	.01
☐ 97 Billy Ripken	.04	.02	.01
☐ 98 Dave Smith	.04	.02	.01
☐ 99 Tom Bolton	.04	.02	.01
☐ 100 Barry Larkin	.10	.05	.01
☐ 101 Kenny Rogers	.04	.02	.01
☐ 102 Mike Boddicker	.04	.02	.01
☐ 103 Kevin Elster	.04	.02	.01
☐ 104 Ken Hill	.04	.02	.01
☐ 105 Charlie Leibrandt	.04	.02	.01
☐ 106 Pat Combs	.04	.02	.01
☐ 107 Hubie Brooks	.04	.02	.01
☐ 108 Julio Franco	.07	.03	.01
☐ 109 Vicente Palacios	.04	.02	.01
☐ 110 Kal Daniels	.04	.02	.01
☐ 111 Bruce Hurst	.07	.03	.01
☐ 112 Willie McGee	.07	.03	.01
☐ 113 Ted Power	.04	.02	.01
☐ 114 Milt Thompson	.04	.02	.01
☐ 115 Doug Drabek	.07	.03	.01
☐ 116 Rafael Belliard	.04	.02	.01
☐ 117 Scott Garrelts	.04	.02	.01
☐ 118 Terry Mulholland	.04	.02	.01
☐ 119 Jay Howell	.04	.02	.01
☐ 120 Danny Jackson	.04	.02	.01
☐ 121 Scott Ruskin	.04	.02	.01
☐ 122 Robin Ventura	.15	.07	.02
☐ 123 Bip Roberts	.07	.03	.01
☐ 124 Jeff Russell	.04	.02	.01
☐ 125 Hal Morris	.07	.03	.01
☐ 126 Teddy Higuera	.04	.02	.01
☐ 127 Luis Sojo	.04	.02	.01
☐ 128 Carlos Baerga	.15	.07	.02
☐ 129 Jeff Ballard	.04	.02	.01
☐ 130 Tom Gordon	.04	.02	.01
☐ 131 Sid Bream	.04	.02	.01
☐ 132 Rance Mulliniks	.04	.02	.01
☐ 133 Andy Benes	.07	.03	.01
☐ 134 Mickey Tettleton	.07	.03	.01
☐ 135 Rich DeLucia	.04	.02	.01
☐ 136 Tom Pagnozzi	.04	.02	.01
☐ 137 Harold Baines	.07	.03	.01
☐ 138 Danny Darwin	.04	.02	.01
☐ 139 Kevin Bass	.04	.02	.01
☐ 140 Chris Nabholz	.07	.03	.01
☐ 141 Pete O'Brien	.04	.02	.01
☐ 142 Jeff Treadway	.04	.02	.01
☐ 143 Mickey Morandini	.07	.03	.01
☐ 144 Eric King	.04	.02	.01
☐ 145 Danny Tartabull	.07	.03	.01
☐ 146 Lance Johnson	.04	.02	.01
☐ 147 Casey Candaele	.04	.02	.01
☐ 148 Felix Fermin	.04	.02	.01
☐ 149 Rich Rodriguez	.04	.02	.01
☐ 150 Dwight Evans	.07	.03	.01
☐ 151 Joe Klink	.04	.02	.01
☐ 152 Kevin Reimer	.07	.03	.01
☐ 153 Orlando Merced	.07	.03	.01
☐ 154 Mel Hall	.04	.02	.01
☐ 155 Randy Myers	.07	.03	.01
☐ 156 Greg A. Harris	.04	.02	.01
☐ 157 Jeff Brantley	.04	.02	.01
☐ 158 Jim Eisenreich	.04	.02	.01
☐ 159 Luis Rivera	.04	.02	.01
☐ 160 Cris Carpenter	.04	.02	.01
☐ 161 Bruce Ruffin	.04	.02	.01
☐ 162 Omar Vizquel	.04	.02	.01
☐ 163 Gerald Alexander	.04	.02	.01
☐ 164 Mark Guthrie	.04	.02	.01
☐ 165 Scott Lewis	.04	.02	.01
☐ 166 Bill Sampen	.04	.02	.01
☐ 167 Dave Anderson	.04	.02	.01
☐ 168 Kevin McReynolds	.07	.03	.01
☐ 169 Jose Vizcaino	.04	.02	.01
☐ 170 Bob Geren	.04	.02	.01
☐ 171 Mike Morgan	.04	.02	.01
☐ 172 Jim Gott	.04	.02	.01
☐ 173 Mike Pagliarulo	.04	.02	.01
☐ 174 Mike Jeffcoat	.04	.02	.01
☐ 175 Craig Lefferts	.04	.02	.01
☐ 176 Steve Finley	.07	.03	.01
☐ 177 Wally Backman	.04	.02	.01
☐ 178 Kent Mercker	.04	.02	.01
☐ 179 John Cerutti	.04	.02	.01
☐ 180 Jay Bell	.04	.02	.01
☐ 181 Dale Sveum	.04	.02	.01
☐ 182 Greg Gagne	.04	.02	.01
☐ 183 Donnie Hill	.04	.02	.01
☐ 184 Rex Hudler	.04	.02	.01
☐ 185 Pat Kelly	.07	.03	.01
☐ 186 Jeff D. Robinson	.04	.02	.01
☐ 187 Jeff Gray	.04	.02	.01
☐ 188 Jerry Willard	.04	.02	.01
☐ 189 Carlos Quintana	.04	.02	.01
☐ 190 Dennis Eckersley	.10	.05	.01
☐ 191 Kelly Downs	.04	.02	.01
☐ 192 Gregg Jefferies	.07	.03	.01
☐ 193 Darrin Fletcher	.04	.02	.01
☐ 194 Mike Jackson	.04	.02	.01
☐ 195 Eddie Murray	.10	.05	.01
☐ 196 Bill Landrum	.04	.02	.01
☐ 197 Eric Yelding	.04	.02	.01
☐ 198 Devon White	.07	.03	.01
☐ 199 Larry Walker	.15	.07	.02
☐ 200 Ryne Sandberg	.25	.11	.03
☐ 201 Dave Magadan	.07	.03	.01
☐ 202 Steve Chitren	.04	.02	.01
☐ 203 Scott Fletcher	.04	.02	.01
☐ 204 Dwayne Henry	.04	.02	.01
☐ 205 Scott Coolbaugh	.04	.02	.01
☐ 206 Tracy Jones	.04	.02	.01
☐ 207 Von Hayes	.04	.02	.01
☐ 208 Bob Melvin	.04	.02	.01
☐ 209 Scott Scudder	.04	.02	.01
☐ 210 Luis Gonzalez	.07	.03	.01
☐ 211 Scott Sanderson	.04	.02	.01
☐ 212 Chris Donnels	.04	.02	.01
☐ 213 Heathcliff Slocumb	.04	.02	.01
☐ 214 Mike Timlin	.04	.02	.01
☐ 215 Brian Harper	.04	.02	.01
☐ 216 Juan Berenguer UER (Decimal point missing in IP total)	.04	.02	.01
☐ 217 Mike Henneman	.04	.02	.01
☐ 218 Bill Spiers	.04	.02	.01
☐ 219 Scott Terry	.04	.02	.01
☐ 220 Frank Viola	.07	.03	.01
☐ 221 Mark Eichhorn	.04	.02	.01
☐ 222 Ernest Riles	.04	.02	.01
☐ 223 Ray Lankford	.15	.07	.02
☐ 224 Pete Harnisch	.04	.02	.01
☐ 225 Bobby Bonilla	.10	.05	.01
☐ 226 Mike Scioscia	.04	.02	.01
☐ 227 Joel Skinner	.04	.02	.01
☐ 228 Brian Holman	.04	.02	.01
☐ 229 Gilberto Reyes	.04	.02	.01
☐ 230 Matt Williams	.07	.03	.01
☐ 231 Jaime Navarro	.07	.03	.01
☐ 232 Jose Rijo	.07	.03	.01
☐ 233 Atlee Hammaker	.04	.02	.01

☐ 234	Tim Teufel	.04	.02	.01
☐ 235	John Kruk	.07	.03	.01
☐ 236	Kurt Stillwell	.04	.02	.01
☐ 237	Dan Pasqua	.04	.02	.01
☐ 238	Tim Crews	.04	.02	.01
☐ 239	Dave Gallagher	.04	.02	.01
☐ 240	Leo Gomez	.10	.05	.01
☐ 241	Steve Avery	.15	.07	.02
☐ 242	Bill Gullickson	.04	.02	.01
☐ 243	Mark Portugal	.04	.02	.01
☐ 244	Lee Guetterman	.04	.02	.01
☐ 245	Benito Santiago	.07	.03	.01
☐ 246	Jim Gantner	.04	.02	.01
☐ 247	Robby Thompson	.04	.02	.01
☐ 248	Terry Shumpert	.04	.02	.01
☐ 249	Mike Bell	.04	.02	.01
☐ 250	Harold Reynolds	.04	.02	.01
☐ 251	Mike Felder	.04	.02	.01
☐ 252	Bill Pecota	.04	.02	.01
☐ 253	Bill Krueger	.04	.02	.01
☐ 254	Alfredo Griffin	.04	.02	.01
☐ 255	Lou Whitaker	.07	.03	.01
☐ 256	Roy Smith	.04	.02	.01
☐ 257	Jerald Clark	.04	.02	.01
☐ 258	Sammy Sosa	.04	.02	.01
☐ 259	Tim Naehring	.07	.03	.01
☐ 260	Dave Righetti	.04	.02	.01
☐ 261	Paul Gibson	.04	.02	.01
☐ 262	Chris James	.04	.02	.01
☐ 263	Larry Andersen	.04	.02	.01
☐ 264	Storm Davis	.04	.02	.01
☐ 265	Jose Lind	.04	.02	.01
☐ 266	Greg Hibbard	.04	.02	.01
☐ 267	Norm Charlton	.07	.03	.01
☐ 268	Paul Kilgus	.04	.02	.01
☐ 269	Greg Maddux	.07	.03	.01
☐ 270	Ellis Burks	.07	.03	.01
☐ 271	Frank Tanana	.04	.02	.01
☐ 272	Gene Larkin	.04	.02	.01
☐ 273	Ron Hassey	.04	.02	.01
☐ 274	Jeff M. Robinson	.04	.02	.01
☐ 275	Steve Howe	.04	.02	.01
☐ 276	Daryl Boston	.04	.02	.01
☐ 277	Mark Lee	.04	.02	.01
☐ 278	Jose Segura	.10	.05	.01
☐ 279	Lance Blankenship	.04	.02	.01
☐ 280	Don Slaught	.04	.02	.01
☐ 281	Russ Swan	.04	.02	.01
☐ 282	Bob Tewksbury	.07	.03	.01
☐ 283	Geno Petralli	.04	.02	.01
☐ 284	Shane Mack	.07	.03	.01
☐ 285	Bob Scanlan	.04	.02	.01
☐ 286	Tim Leary	.04	.02	.01
☐ 287	John Smoltz	.10	.05	.01
☐ 288	Pat Borders	.04	.02	.01
☐ 289	Mark Davidson	.04	.02	.01
☐ 290	Sam Horn	.04	.02	.01
☐ 291	Lenny Harris	.04	.02	.01
☐ 292	Franklin Stubbs	.04	.02	.01
☐ 293	Thomas Howard	.04	.02	.01
☐ 294	Steve Lyons	.04	.02	.01
☐ 295	Francisco Oliveras	.04	.02	.01
☐ 296	Terry Leach	.04	.02	.01
☐ 297	Barry Jones	.04	.02	.01
☐ 298	Lance Parrish	.07	.03	.01
☐ 299	Wally Whitehurst	.04	.02	.01
☐ 300	Bob Welch	.04	.02	.01
☐ 301	Charlie Hayes	.04	.02	.01
☐ 302	Charlie Hough	.04	.02	.01
☐ 303	Gary Redus	.04	.02	.01
☐ 304	Scott Bradley	.04	.02	.01
☐ 305	Jose Oquendo	.04	.02	.01
☐ 306	Pete Incaviglia	.04	.02	.01
☐ 307	Marvin Freeman	.04	.02	.01
☐ 308	Gary Pettis	.04	.02	.01
☐ 309	Joe Slusarski	.04	.02	.01
☐ 310	Kevin Seitzer	.07	.03	.01
☐ 311	Jeff Reed	.04	.02	.01
☐ 312	Pat Tabler	.04	.02	.01
☐ 313	Mike Maddux	.04	.02	.01
☐ 314	Bob Milacki	.04	.02	.01
☐ 315	Eric Anthony	.07	.03	.01
☐ 316	Dante Bichette	.04	.02	.01
☐ 317	Steve Decker	.07	.03	.01
☐ 318	Jack Clark	.07	.03	.01
☐ 319	Doug Dascenzo	.04	.02	.01
☐ 320	Scott Leius	.04	.02	.01
☐ 321	Jim Lindeman	.04	.02	.01
☐ 322	Bryan Harvey	.04	.02	.01
☐ 323	Spike Owen	.04	.02	.01
☐ 324	Roberto Kelly	.07	.03	.01
☐ 325	Stan Belinda	.04	.02	.01
☐ 326	Joey Cora	.04	.02	.01
☐ 327	Jeff Innis	.04	.02	.01
☐ 328	Willie Wilson	.04	.02	.01
☐ 329	Juan Agosto	.04	.02	.01
☐ 330	Charles Nagy	.10	.05	.01
☐ 331	Scott Bailes	.04	.02	.01
☐ 332	Pete Schourek	.07	.03	.01
☐ 333	Mike Flanagan	.04	.02	.01
☐ 334	Omar Olivares	.04	.02	.01
☐ 335	Dennis Lamp	.04	.02	.01
☐ 336	Tommy Greene	.04	.02	.01
☐ 337	Randy Velarde	.04	.02	.01
☐ 338	Tom Lampkin	.04	.02	.01
☐ 339	John Russell	.04	.02	.01
☐ 340	Bob Kipper	.04	.02	.01
☐ 341	Todd Burns	.04	.02	.01
☐ 342	Ron Jones	.04	.02	.01
☐ 343	Dave Valle	.04	.02	.01
☐ 344	Mike Heath	.04	.02	.01
☐ 345	John Olerud	.10	.05	.01
☐ 346	Gerald Young	.04	.02	.01
☐ 347	Ken Patterson	.04	.02	.01
☐ 348	Les Lancaster	.04	.02	.01
☐ 349	Steve Crawford	.04	.02	.01
☐ 350	John Candelaria	.04	.02	.01
☐ 351	Mike Aldrete	.04	.02	.01
☐ 352	Mariano Duncan	.04	.02	.01
☐ 353	Julio Machado	.04	.02	.01
☐ 354	Ken Williams	.04	.02	.01
☐ 355	Walt Terrell	.04	.02	.01
☐ 356	Mitch Williams	.04	.02	.01
☐ 357	Al Newman	.04	.02	.01
☐ 358	Bud Black	.04	.02	.01
☐ 359	Joe Hesketh	.04	.02	.01
☐ 360	Paul Assenmacher	.04	.02	.01
☐ 361	Bo Jackson	.12	.05	.02
☐ 362	Jeff Blauser	.04	.02	.01
☐ 363	Mike Brumley	.04	.02	.01
☐ 364	Jim Deshaies	.04	.02	.01
☐ 365	Brady Anderson	.07	.03	.01
☐ 366	Chuck McElroy	.04	.02	.01
☐ 367	Matt Merullo	.04	.02	.01
☐ 368	Tim Belcher	.07	.03	.01
☐ 369	Luis Aquino	.04	.02	.01
☐ 370	Joe Oliver	.04	.02	.01
☐ 371	Greg Swindell	.07	.03	.01
☐ 372	Lee Stevens	.04	.02	.01
☐ 373	Mark Knudson	.04	.02	.01
☐ 374	Bill Wegman	.04	.02	.01
☐ 375	Jerry Don Gleaton	.04	.02	.01
☐ 376	Pedro Guerrero	.07	.03	.01
☐ 377	Randy Bush	.04	.02	.01
☐ 378	Greg W. Harris	.04	.02	.01
☐ 379	Eric Plunk	.04	.02	.01
☐ 380	Jose DeJesus	.04	.02	.01
☐ 381	Bobby Witt	.04	.02	.01
☐ 382	Curtis Wilkerson	.04	.02	.01
☐ 383	Gene Nelson	.04	.02	.01
☐ 384	Wes Chamberlain	.07	.03	.01
☐ 385	Tom Henke	.07	.03	.01
☐ 386	Mark Lemke	.04	.02	.01
☐ 387	Greg Briley	.04	.02	.01
☐ 388	Rafael Ramirez	.04	.02	.01
☐ 389	Tony Fossas	.04	.02	.01
☐ 390	Henry Cotto	.04	.02	.01
☐ 391	Tim Hulett	.04	.02	.01
☐ 392	Dean Palmer	.10	.05	.01
☐ 393	Glenn Braggs	.04	.02	.01
☐ 394	Mark Salas	.04	.02	.01
☐ 395	Rusty Meacham	.05	.02	.01
☐ 396	Andy Ashby	.05	.02	.01
☐ 397	Jose Melendez	.05	.02	.01
☐ 398	Warren Newson	.05	.02	.01
☐ 399	Frank Castillo	.08	.04	.01
☐ 400	Chito Martinez	.05	.02	.01
☐ 401	Bernie Williams	.10	.05	.01
☐ 402	Derek Bell	.10	.05	.01
☐ 403	Javier Ortiz	.05	.02	.01
☐ 404	Tim Sherrill	.05	.02	.01
☐ 405	Rob MacDonald	.05	.02	.01
☐ 406	Phil Plantier	.15	.07	.02
☐ 407	Troy Afenir	.05	.02	.01
☐ 408	Gino Minutelli	.05	.02	.01
☐ 409	Reggie Jefferson	.10	.05	.01
☐ 410	Mike Remlinger	.05	.02	.01
☐ 411	Carlos Rodriguez	.05	.02	.01
☐ 412	Joe Redfield	.10	.05	.01
☐ 413	Alonzo Powell	.05	.02	.01
☐ 414	Scott Livingstone UER (Travis Fryman, not Woody, should be referenced on back)	.10	.05	.01
☐ 415	Scott Kamieniecki	.05	.02	.01
☐ 416	Tim Spehr	.05	.02	.01

☐ 417 Brian Hunter .10 .05 .01
☐ 418 Ced Landrum .05 .02 .01
☐ 419 Bret Barberie .05 .02 .01
☐ 420 Kevin Morton .05 .02 .01
☐ 421 Doug Henry .15 .07 .02
☐ 422 Doug Piatt .05 .02 .01
☐ 423 Pat Rice .10 .05 .01
☐ 424 Juan Guzman .75 .35 .09
☐ 425 Nolan Ryan NH .25 .11 .03
☐ 426 Tommy Greene NH .05 .02 .01
☐ 427 Bob Milacki and .05 .02 .01
Mike Flanagan NH
(Mark Williamson
and Gregg Olson)
☐ 428 Wilson Alvarez NH .05 .02 .01
☐ 429 Otis Nixon HL .05 .02 .01
☐ 430 Rickey Henderson HL .10 .05 .01
☐ 431 Cecil Fielder AS .10 .05 .01
☐ 432 Julio Franco AS .05 .02 .01
☐ 433 Cal Ripken AS .15 .07 .02
☐ 434 Wade Boggs AS .10 .05 .01
☐ 435 Joe Carter AS .10 .05 .01
☐ 436 Ken Griffey Jr. AS .25 .11 .03
☐ 437 Ruben Sierra AS .10 .05 .01
☐ 438 Scott Erickson AS .08 .04 .01
☐ 439 Tom Henke AS .05 .02 .01
☐ 440 Terry Steinbach AS .05 .02 .01
☐ 441 Rickey Henderson DT .20 .09 .03
☐ 442 Ryne Sandberg DT .40 .18 .05
☐ 443 Otis Nixon .04 .02 .01
☐ 444 Scott Radinsky .04 .02 .01
☐ 445 Mark Grace .07 .03 .01
☐ 446 Tony Pena .04 .02 .01
☐ 447 Billy Hatcher .04 .02 .01
☐ 448 Glenallen Hill .04 .02 .01
☐ 449 Chris Gwynn .04 .02 .01
☐ 450 Tom Glavine .12 .05 .02
☐ 451 John Habyan .04 .02 .01
☐ 452 Al Osuna .04 .02 .01
☐ 453 Tony Phillips .04 .02 .01
☐ 454 Greg Cadaret .04 .02 .01
☐ 455 Rob Dibble .04 .02 .01
☐ 456 Rick Honeycutt .04 .02 .01
☐ 457 Jerome Walton .04 .02 .01
☐ 458 Mookie Wilson .04 .02 .01
☐ 459 Mark Gubicza .04 .02 .01
☐ 460 Craig Biggio .07 .03 .01
☐ 461 Dave Cochrane .04 .02 .01
☐ 462 Keith Miller .04 .02 .01
☐ 463 Alex Cole .04 .02 .01
☐ 464 Pete Smith .07 .03 .01
☐ 465 Brett Butler .07 .03 .01
☐ 466 Jeff Huson .04 .02 .01
☐ 467 Steve Lake .04 .02 .01
☐ 468 Lloyd Moseby .04 .02 .01
☐ 469 Tim McIntosh .04 .02 .01
☐ 470 Dennis Martinez .07 .03 .01
☐ 471 Greg Myers .04 .02 .01
☐ 472 Mackey Sasser .04 .02 .01
☐ 473 Junior Ortiz .04 .02 .01
☐ 474 Greg Olson .04 .02 .01
☐ 475 Steve Sax .07 .03 .01
☐ 476 Ricky Jordan .04 .02 .01
☐ 477 Max Venable .04 .02 .01
☐ 478 Brian McRae .07 .03 .01
☐ 479 Doug Simons .04 .02 .01
☐ 480 Rickey Henderson .12 .05 .02
☐ 481 Gary Varsho .04 .02 .01
☐ 482 Carl Willis .04 .02 .01
☐ 483 Rick Wilkins .04 .02 .01
☐ 484 Donn Pall .04 .02 .01
☐ 485 Edgar Martinez .07 .03 .01
☐ 486 Tom Foley .04 .02 .01
☐ 487 Mark Williamson .04 .02 .01
☐ 488 Jack Armstrong .04 .02 .01
☐ 489 Gary Carter .07 .03 .01
☐ 490 Ruben Sierra .15 .07 .02
☐ 491 Gerald Perry .04 .02 .01
☐ 492 Rob Murphy .04 .02 .01
☐ 493 Zane Smith .04 .02 .01
☐ 494 Darryl Kile .04 .02 .01
☐ 495 Kelly Gruber .07 .03 .01
☐ 496 Jerry Browne .04 .02 .01
☐ 497 Darryl Hamilton .07 .03 .01
☐ 498 Mike Stanton .04 .02 .01
☐ 499 Mark Leonard .04 .02 .01
☐ 500 Jose Canseco .20 .09 .03
☐ 501 Dave Martinez .04 .02 .01
☐ 502 Jose Guzman .04 .02 .01
☐ 503 Terry Kennedy .04 .02 .01
☐ 504 Ed Sprague .07 .03 .01
☐ 505 Frank Thomas UER .75 .35 .09
(His Gulf Coast League
stats are wrong)
☐ 506 Darren Daulton .07 .03 .01
☐ 507 Kevin Tapani .07 .03 .01
☐ 508 Luis Salazar .04 .02 .01
☐ 509 Paul Faries .04 .02 .01
☐ 510 Sandy Alomar Jr. .07 .03 .01
☐ 511 Jeff King .04 .02 .01
☐ 512 Gary Thurman .04 .02 .01
☐ 513 Chris Hammond .04 .02 .01
☐ 514 Pedro Munoz .07 .03 .01
☐ 515 Alan Trammell .07 .03 .01
☐ 516 Geronimo Pena .04 .02 .01
☐ 517 Rodney McCray UER .04 .02 .01
(Stole 6 bases in
1990, not 5; career
totals are correct at 7)
☐ 518 Manny Lee .04 .02 .01
☐ 519 Junior Felix .04 .02 .01
☐ 520 Kirk Gibson .07 .03 .01
☐ 521 Darrin Jackson .07 .03 .01
☐ 522 John Burkett .04 .02 .01
☐ 523 Jeff Johnson .04 .02 .01
☐ 524 Jim Corsi .04 .02 .01
☐ 525 Robin Yount .10 .05 .01
☐ 526 Jamie Quirk .04 .02 .01
☐ 527 Bob Ojeda .04 .02 .01
☐ 528 Mark Lewis .04 .02 .01
☐ 529 Bryn Smith .04 .02 .01
☐ 530 Kent Hrbek .07 .03 .01
☐ 531 Dennis Boyd .04 .02 .01
☐ 532 Ron Karkovice .04 .02 .01
☐ 533 Don August .04 .02 .01
☐ 534 Todd Frohwirth .04 .02 .01
☐ 535 Wally Joyner .07 .03 .01
☐ 536 Dennis Rasmussen .04 .02 .01
☐ 537 Andy Allanson .04 .02 .01
☐ 538 Goose Gossage .07 .03 .01
☐ 539 John Marzano .04 .02 .01
☐ 540 Cal Ripken .25 .11 .03
☐ 541 Bill Swift UER .04 .02 .01
(Brewers logo on front)
☐ 542 Kevin Appier .07 .03 .01
☐ 543 Dave Bergman .04 .02 .01
☐ 544 Bernard Gilkey .07 .03 .01
☐ 545 Mike Greenwell .07 .03 .01
☐ 546 Jose Uribe .04 .02 .01
☐ 547 Jesse Orosco .04 .02 .01
☐ 548 Bob Patterson .04 .02 .01
☐ 549 Mike Stanley .04 .02 .01
☐ 550 Howard Johnson .07 .03 .01
☐ 551 Joe Orsulak .04 .02 .01
☐ 552 Dick Schofield .04 .02 .01
☐ 553 Dave Hollins .07 .03 .01
☐ 554 David Segui .04 .02 .01
☐ 555 Barry Bonds .15 .07 .02
☐ 556 Mo Vaughn .07 .03 .01
☐ 557 Craig Wilson .04 .02 .01
☐ 558 Bobby Rose .04 .02 .01
☐ 559 Rod Nichols .04 .02 .01
☐ 560 Len Dykstra .07 .03 .01
☐ 561 Craig Grebeck .04 .02 .01
☐ 562 Darren Lewis .07 .03 .01
☐ 563 Todd Benzinger .04 .02 .01
☐ 564 Ed Whitson .04 .02 .01
☐ 565 Jesse Barfield .04 .02 .01
☐ 566 Lloyd McClendon .04 .02 .01
☐ 567 Dan Plesac .04 .02 .01
☐ 568 Danny Cox .04 .02 .01
☐ 569 Skeeter Barnes .04 .02 .01
☐ 570 Bobby Thigpen .04 .02 .01
☐ 571 Deion Sanders .15 .07 .02
☐ 572 Chuck Knoblauch .20 .09 .03
☐ 573 Matt Nokes .04 .02 .01
☐ 574 Herm Winningham .04 .02 .01
☐ 575 Tom Candiotti .04 .02 .01
☐ 576 Jeff Bagwell .25 .11 .03
☐ 577 Brook Jacoby .04 .02 .01
☐ 578 Chico Walker .04 .02 .01
☐ 579 Brian Downing .04 .02 .01
☐ 580 Dave Stewart .07 .03 .01
☐ 581 Francisco Cabrera .04 .02 .01
☐ 582 Rene Gonzales .04 .02 .01
☐ 583 Stan Javier .04 .02 .01
☐ 584 Randy Johnson .07 .03 .01
☐ 585 Chuck Finley .04 .02 .01
☐ 586 Mark Gardner .04 .02 .01
☐ 587 Mark Whiten .04 .02 .01
☐ 588 Garry Templeton .04 .02 .01
☐ 589 Gary Sheffield .20 .09 .03
☐ 590 Ozzie Smith .10 .05 .01
☐ 591 Candy Maldonado .04 .02 .01
☐ 592 Mike Sharperson .04 .02 .01
☐ 593 Carlos Martinez .04 .02 .01
☐ 594 Scott Bankhead .04 .02 .01

☐	595	Tim Wallach	.07	.03	.01
☐	596	Tino Martinez	.07	.03	.01
☐	597	Roger McDowell	.04	.02	.01
☐	598	Cory Snyder	.04	.02	.01
☐	599	Andujar Cedeno	.07	.03	.01
☐	600	Kirby Puckett	.20	.09	.03
☐	601	Rick Parker	.04	.02	.01
☐	602	Todd Hundley	.04	.02	.01
☐	603	Greg Litton	.04	.02	.01
☐	604	Dave Johnson	.04	.02	.01
☐	605	John Franco	.07	.03	.01
☐	606	Mike Fetters	.04	.02	.01
☐	607	Luis Alicea	.04	.02	.01
☐	608	Trevor Wilson	.04	.02	.01
☐	609	Rob Ducey	.04	.02	.01
☐	610	Ramon Martinez	.07	.03	.01
☐	611	Dave Burba	.04	.02	.01
☐	612	Dwight Smith	.04	.02	.01
☐	613	Kevin Maas	.07	.03	.01
☐	614	John Costello	.04	.02	.01
☐	615	Glenn Davis	.07	.03	.01
☐	616	Shawn Abner	.04	.02	.01
☐	617	Scott Hemond	.04	.02	.01
☐	618	Tom Prince	.04	.02	.01
☐	619	Wally Ritchie	.04	.02	.01
☐	620	Jim Abbott	.12	.05	.02
☐	621	Charlie O'Brien	.04	.02	.01
☐	622	Jack Daugherty	.04	.02	.01
☐	623	Tommy Gregg	.04	.02	.01
☐	624	Jeff Shaw	.04	.02	.01
☐	625	Tony Gwynn	.12	.05	.02
☐	626	Mark Leiter	.04	.02	.01
☐	627	Jim Clancy	.04	.02	.01
☐	628	Tim Layana	.04	.02	.01
☐	629	Jeff Schaefer	.04	.02	.01
☐	630	Lee Smith	.07	.03	.01
☐	631	Wade Taylor	.04	.02	.01
☐	632	Mike Simms	.04	.02	.01
☐	633	Terry Steinbach	.07	.03	.01
☐	634	Shawon Dunston	.07	.03	.01
☐	635	Tim Raines	.07	.03	.01
☐	636	Kirt Manwaring	.04	.02	.01
☐	637	Warren Cromartie	.04	.02	.01
☐	638	Luis Quinones	.04	.02	.01
☐	639	Greg Vaughn	.07	.03	.01
☐	640	Kevin Mitchell	.07	.03	.01
☐	641	Chris Hoiles	.07	.03	.01
☐	642	Tom Browning	.04	.02	.01
☐	643	Mitch Webster	.04	.02	.01
☐	644	Steve Olin	.04	.02	.01
☐	645	Tony Fernandez	.07	.03	.01
☐	646	Juan Bell	.04	.02	.01
☐	647	Joe Boever	.04	.02	.01
☐	648	Carney Lansford	.07	.03	.01
☐	649	Mike Benjamin	.04	.02	.01
☐	650	George Brett	.10	.05	.01
☐	651	Tim Burke	.04	.02	.01
☐	652	Jack Morris	.10	.05	.01
☐	653	Orel Hershiser	.07	.03	.01
☐	654	Mike Schooler	.04	.02	.01
☐	655	Andy Van Slyke	.07	.03	.01
☐	656	Dave Stieb	.04	.02	.01
☐	657	Dave Clark	.04	.02	.01
☐	658	Ben McDonald	.10	.05	.01
☐	659	John Smiley	.07	.03	.01
☐	660	Wade Boggs	.12	.05	.02
☐	661	Eric Bullock	.04	.02	.01
☐	662	Eric Show	.04	.02	.01
☐	663	Lenny Webster	.04	.02	.01
☐	664	Mike Huff	.04	.02	.01
☐	665	Rick Sutcliffe	.07	.03	.01
☐	666	Jeff Manto	.04	.02	.01
☐	667	Mike Fitzgerald	.04	.02	.01
☐	668	Matt Young	.04	.02	.01
☐	669	Dave West	.04	.02	.01
☐	670	Mike Hartley	.04	.02	.01
☐	671	Curt Schilling	.07	.03	.01
☐	672	Brian Bohanon	.04	.02	.01
☐	673	Cecil Espy	.04	.02	.01
☐	674	Joe Grahe	.04	.02	.01
☐	675	Sid Fernandez	.07	.03	.01
☐	676	Edwin Nunez	.04	.02	.01
☐	677	Hector Villanueva	.04	.02	.01
☐	678	Sean Berry	.04	.02	.01
☐	679	Dave Eiland	.04	.02	.01
☐	680	Dave Cone	.07	.03	.01
☐	681	Mike Bordick	.08	.04	.01
☐	682	Tony Castillo	.04	.02	.01
☐	683	John Barfield	.04	.02	.01
☐	684	Jeff Hamilton	.04	.02	.01
☐	685	Ken Dayley	.04	.02	.01
☐	686	Carmelo Martinez	.04	.02	.01
☐	687	Mike Capel	.04	.02	.01
☐	688	Scott Chiamparino	.04	.02	.01
☐	689	Rich Gedman	.04	.02	.01
☐	690	Rich Monteleone	.04	.02	.01
☐	691	Alejandro Pena	.04	.02	.01
☐	692	Oscar Azocar	.04	.02	.01
☐	693	Jim Poole	.04	.02	.01
☐	694	Mike Gardiner	.04	.02	.01
☐	695	Steve Buechele	.04	.02	.01
☐	696	Rudy Seanez	.04	.02	.01
☐	697	Paul Abbott	.04	.02	.01
☐	698	Steve Searcy	.04	.02	.01
☐	699	Jose Offerman	.07	.03	.01
☐	700	Ivan Rodriguez	.30	.14	.04
☐	701	Joe Girardi	.04	.02	.01
☐	702	Tony Perezchica	.04	.02	.01
☐	703	Paul McClellan	.04	.02	.01
☐	704	David Howard	.04	.02	.01
☐	705	Dan Petry	.04	.02	.01
☐	706	Jack Howell	.04	.02	.01
☐	707	Jose Mesa	.04	.02	.01
☐	708	Randy St. Claire	.04	.02	.01
☐	709	Kevin Brown	.07	.03	.01
☐	710	Ron Darling	.07	.03	.01
☐	711	Jason Grimsley	.04	.02	.01
☐	712	John Orton	.04	.02	.01
☐	713	Shawn Boskie	.04	.02	.01
☐	714	Pat Clements	.04	.02	.01
☐	715	Brian Barnes	.04	.02	.01
☐	716	Luis Lopez	.04	.02	.01
☐	717	Bob McClure	.04	.02	.01
☐	718	Mark Davis	.04	.02	.01
☐	719	Dann Bilardello	.04	.02	.01
☐	720	Tom Edens	.04	.02	.01
☐	721	Willie Fraser	.04	.02	.01
☐	722	Curt Young	.04	.02	.01
☐	723	Neal Heaton	.04	.02	.01
☐	724	Craig Worthington	.04	.02	.01
☐	725	Mel Rojas	.04	.02	.01
☐	726	Daryl Irvine	.04	.02	.01
☐	727	Roger Mason	.04	.02	.01
☐	728	Kirk Dressendorfer	.04	.02	.01
☐	729	Scott Aldred	.04	.02	.01
☐	730	Willie Blair	.04	.02	.01
☐	731	Allan Anderson	.04	.02	.01
☐	732	Dana Kiecker	.04	.02	.01
☐	733	Jose Gonzalez	.04	.02	.01
☐	734	Brian Drahman	.04	.02	.01
☐	735	Brad Komminsk	.04	.02	.01
☐	736	Arthur Rhodes	.15	.07	.02
☐	737	Terry Mathews	.10	.05	.01
☐	738	Jeff Fassero	.05	.02	.01
☐	739	Mike Magnante	.12	.05	.02
☐	740	Kip Gross	.10	.05	.01
☐	741	Jim Hunter	.10	.05	.01
☐	742	Jose Mota	.05	.02	.01
☐	743	Joe Bitker	.05	.02	.01
☐	744	Tim Mauser	.10	.05	.01
☐	745	Ramon Garcia	.05	.02	.01
☐	746	Rod Beck	.12	.05	.02
☐	747	Jim Austin	.10	.05	.01
☐	748	Keith Mitchell	.08	.04	.01
☐	749	Wayne Rosenthal	.10	.05	.01
☐	750	Bryan Hickerson	.10	.05	.01
☐	751	Bruce Egloff	.05	.02	.01
☐	752	John Wehner	.05	.02	.01
☐	753	Darren Holmes	.05	.02	.01
☐	754	Dave Hansen	.05	.02	.01
☐	755	Mike Mussina	.50	.23	.06
☐	756	Anthony Young	.08	.04	.01
☐	757	Ron Tingley	.05	.02	.01
☐	758	Ricky Bones	.08	.04	.01
☐	759	Mark Wohlers	.10	.05	.01
☐	760	Wilson Alvarez	.05	.02	.01
☐	761	Harvey Pulliam	.08	.04	.01
☐	762	Ryan Bowen	.08	.04	.01
☐	763	Terry Bross	.05	.02	.01
☐	764	Joel Johnston	.05	.02	.01
☐	765	Terry McDaniel	.10	.05	.01
☐	766	Esteban Beltre	.10	.05	.01
☐	767	Rob Maurer	.12	.05	.02
☐	768	Ted Wood	.10	.05	.01
☐	769	Mo Sanford	.05	.02	.01
☐	770	Jeff Carter	.05	.02	.01
☐	771	Gil Heredia	.10	.05	.01
☐	772	Monty Fariss	.08	.04	.01
☐	773	Will Clark AS	.10	.05	.01
☐	774	Ryne Sandberg AS	.12	.05	.02
☐	775	Barry Larkin AS	.08	.04	.01
☐	776	Howard Johnson AS	.05	.02	.01
☐	777	Barry Bonds AS	.10	.05	.01
☐	778	Brett Butler AS	.05	.02	.01
☐	779	Tony Gwynn AS	.10	.05	.01
☐	780	Ramon Martinez AS	.05	.02	.01

☐ 781 Lee Smith AS .05 .02 .01
☐ 782 Mike Scioscia AS .05 .02 .01
☐ 783 Dennis Martinez HL UER .05 .02 .01
(Card has both 13th and 15th perfect game in Major League history)
☐ 784 Dennis Martinez .05 .02 .01
No-Hit Club
☐ 785 Mark Gardner .05 .02 .01
No-Hit Club
☐ 786 Bret Saberhagen .05 .02 .01
No-Hit Club
☐ 787 Kent Mercker .05 .02 .01
Mark Wohlers
Alejandro Pena
No-Hit Club
☐ 788 Cal Ripken MVP .15 .07 .02
☐ 789 Terry Pendleton MVP .08 .04 .01
☐ 790 Roger Clemens CY .12 .05 .02
☐ 791 Tom Glavine CY .10 .05 .01
☐ 792 Chuck Knoblauch ROY .15 .07 .02
☐ 793 Jeff Bagwell ROY .15 .07 .02
☐ 794 Cal Ripken .15 .07 .02
Man of the Year
☐ 795 David Cone HL .08 .04 .01
☐ 796 Kirby Puckett HL .12 .05 .02
☐ 797 Steve Avery HL .10 .05 .01
☐ 798 Jack Morris HL .08 .04 .01
☐ 799 Allen Watson Draft .25 .11 .03
☐ 800 Manny Ramirez Draft .60 .25 .08
☐ 801 Cliff Floyd Draft .75 .35 .09
☐ 802 Al Shirley Draft .25 .11 .03
☐ 803 Brian Barber Draft .20 .09 .03
☐ 804 Jon Farrell Draft .10 .05 .01
☐ 805 Brent Gates Draft .50 .23 .06
☐ 806 Scott Ruffcorn Draft .25 .11 .03
☐ 807 Tyrone Hill Draft .35 .16 .04
☐ 808 Benji Gil Draft .20 .09 .03
☐ 809 Aaron Sele Draft .40 .18 .05
☐ 810 Tyler Green Draft .25 .11 .03
☐ 811 Chris Jones .04 .02 .01
☐ 812 Steve Wilson .04 .02 .01
☐ 813 Freddie Benavides .04 .02 .01
☐ 814 Don Wakamatsu .10 .05 .01
☐ 815 Mike Humphreys .08 .04 .01
☐ 816 Scott Servais .05 .02 .01
☐ 817 Rico Rossy .10 .05 .01
☐ 818 John Ramos .05 .02 .01
☐ 819 Rob Mallicoat .05 .02 .01
☐ 820 Milt Hill .10 .05 .01
☐ 821 Carlos Garcia .10 .05 .01
☐ 822 Stan Royer .05 .02 .01
☐ 823 Jeff Plympton .10 .05 .01
☐ 824 Braulio Castillo .15 .07 .02
☐ 825 David Haas .05 .02 .01
☐ 826 Luis Mercedes .08 .04 .01
☐ 827 Eric Karros .50 .23 .06
☐ 828 Shawn Hare .10 .05 .01
☐ 829 Reggie Sanders .25 .11 .03
☐ 830 Tom Goodwin .05 .02 .01
☐ 831 Dan Gakeler .05 .02 .01
☐ 832 Stacy Jones .10 .05 .01
☐ 833 Kim Batiste .05 .02 .01
☐ 834 Cal Eldred .35 .16 .04
☐ 835 Chris George .05 .02 .01
☐ 836 Wayne Housie .10 .05 .01
☐ 837 Mike Ignasiak .12 .05 .02
☐ 838 Josias Manzanillo .10 .05 .01
☐ 839 Jim Olander .10 .05 .01
☐ 840 Gary Cooper .10 .05 .01
☐ 841 Royce Clayton .15 .07 .02
☐ 842 Hector Fajardo .12 .05 .02
☐ 843 Blaine Beatty .05 .02 .01
☐ 844 Jorge Pedre .10 .05 .01
☐ 845 Kenny Lofton .40 .18 .05
☐ 846 Scott Brosius .10 .05 .01
☐ 847 Chris Cron .10 .05 .01
☐ 848 Denis Boucher .05 .02 .01
☐ 849 Kyle Abbott .08 .04 .01
☐ 850 Robert Zupcic .25 .11 .03
☐ 851 Rheal Cormier .05 .02 .01
☐ 852 Jim Lewis .10 .05 .01
☐ 853 Anthony Telford .05 .02 .01
☐ 854 Cliff Brantley .10 .05 .01
☐ 855 Kevin Campbell .10 .05 .01
☐ 856 Craig Shipley .10 .05 .01
☐ 857 Chuck Carr .08 .04 .01
☐ 858 Tony Eusebio .10 .05 .01
☐ 859 Jim Thome .12 .05 .02
☐ 860 Vinny Castilla .10 .05 .01
☐ 861 Dann Howitt .05 .02 .01
☐ 862 Kevin Ward .10 .05 .01
☐ 863 Steve Wapnick .05 .02 .01
☐ 864 Rod Brewer .15 .07 .02
☐ 865 Todd Van Poppel .20 .09 .03
☐ 866 Jose Hernandez .10 .05 .01
☐ 867 Amalio Carreno .10 .05 .01
☐ 868 Calvin Jones .10 .05 .01
☐ 869 Jeff Gardner .10 .05 .01
☐ 870 Jarvis Brown .10 .05 .01
☐ 871 Eddie Taubensee .12 .05 .02
☐ 872 Andy Mota .05 .02 .01
☐ 873 Chris Haney .05 .02 .01
☐ 874 Roberto Hernandez .12 .05 .02
☐ 875 Laddie Renfroe .10 .05 .01
☐ 876 Scott Cooper .08 .04 .01
☐ 877 Armando Reynoso .10 .05 .01
☐ 878 Ty Cobb .30 .14 .04
(Memorabilia)
☐ 879 Babe Ruth .40 .18 .05
(Memorabilia)
☐ 880 Honus Wagner .20 .09 .03
(Memorabilia)
☐ 881 Lou Gehrig .35 .16 .04
(Memorabilia)
☐ 882 Satchel Paige .20 .09 .03
(Memorabilia)
☐ 883 Will Clark DT .30 .14 .04
☐ 884 Cal Ripken DT .50 .23 .06
☐ 885 Wade Boggs DT .20 .09 .03
☐ 886 Kirby Puckett DT .30 .14 .04
☐ 887 Tony Gwynn DT .20 .09 .03
☐ 888 Craig Biggio DT .10 .05 .01
☐ 889 Scott Erickson DT .12 .05 .02
☐ 890 Tom Glavine DT .20 .09 .03
☐ 891 Rob Dibble DT .10 .05 .01
☐ 892 Mitch Williams DT .10 .05 .01
☐ 893 Frank Thomas DT 1.00 .45 .13
☐ X672 Chuck Knoblauch 125.00 57.50 15.50
(1990 Score card, autographed with special hologram on back)

1992 Score Joe DiMaggio

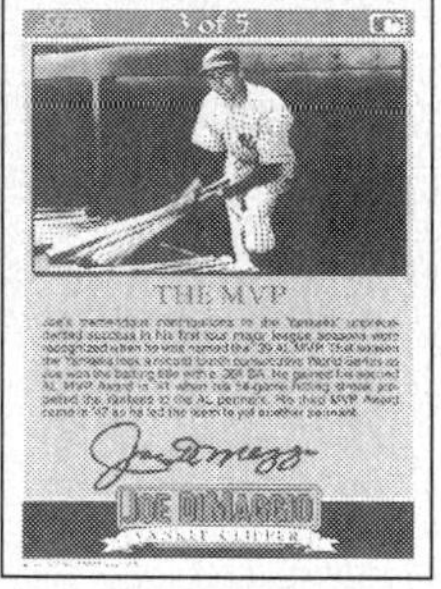

This five-card standard-size (2 1/2" by 3 1/2") set was issued in honor of one of baseball's all-time greats, Joe DiMaggio. Supposedly 30,000 of each card were produced. On a white card face, the fronts have vintage photos that have been colorized and accented by red, white, and blue border stripes. The player's name appears in an orange bar and the card title in a white banner beneath the picture. The backs feature a different colorized player photo and career highlights (on gray), framed between a red top stripe and a navy blue bottom stripe. The cards are numbered on the back.

	MT	EX-MT	VG
COMPLETE SET (5)	150.00	70.00	19.00
COMMON DIMAGGIO (1-5)	30.00	13.50	3.80
☐ 1 Joe DiMaggio The Minors	30.00	13.50	3.80
☐ 2 Joe DiMaggio The Rookie	30.00	13.50	3.80
☐ 3 Joe DiMaggio The MVP	30.00	13.50	3.80
☐ 4 Joe DiMaggio The Streak	30.00	13.50	3.80

	MT	EX-MT	VG
☐ 5 Joe DiMaggio The Legend	30.00	13.50	3.80
☐ AU Joe DiMaggio (Autographed with certified signature)	600.00	275.00	75.00

1992 Score Factory Inserts

This 17-card insert set was included in 1992 Score factory sets and consists of four topical subsets. Cards B1-B7 capture a moment from each game of the 1991 World Series. Cards B8-B11 are Cooperstown cards, honoring future Hall of Famers. Cards B12-B14 form a "Joe D" subset paying tribute to Joe DiMaggio. Cards B15-B17, subtitled "Yaz", conclude the set by commemorating Carl Yastrzemski's heroic feats twenty-five years ago in winning the Triple Crown and lifting the Red Sox to their first American League pennant in 21 years. The cards measure the standard size (2 1/2" by 3 1/2"), and each subset displays a different front design. The World Series cards carry full-bleed color action photos except for a blue stripe at the bottom, while the Cooperstown cards have a color portrait on a white card face. Both the DiMaggio and Yastrzemski subsets have action photos with silver borders; they differ in that the DiMaggio photos are black and white, the Yastrzemski photos color. The DiMaggio and Yastrzemski subsets are numbered on the back within each subset (e.g., "1 of 3") and as a part of the 17-card insert set (e.g., "B1").

	MT	EX-MT	VG
COMPLETE SET (17)	10.00	4.50	1.25
COMMON WS (B1-B7)	.25	.11	.03
COMMON COOPERSTOWN (B8-B11) .16		1.25	.55
COMMON DIMAGGIO (B12-B14)	1.50	.65	.19
COMMON YAZ (B15-B17)	.75	.35	.09
☐ B1 1991 WS Game 1 (Greg) Gagne powers Twins to win	.25	.11	.03
☐ B2 1991 WS Game 2 (Scott) Leius lifts Twins to 2-0 lead	.25	.11	.03
☐ B3 1991 WS Game 3 (Mark) Lemke leaves Twins limp (David Justice)	.25	.11	.03
☐ B4 1991 WS Game 4 Braves gain series tie (Lonnie Smith and Brian Harper)	.25	.11	.03
☐ B5 1991 WS Game 5 Braves bomb Twins (David Justice)	.60	.25	.08
☐ B6 1991 WS Game 6 Kirby (Puckett) keeps the Twins alive	1.50	.65	.19
☐ B7 1991 WS Game 7 A Classic win for the Twins (Gene Larkin)	.25	.11	.03
☐ B8 Carlton Fisk Cooperstown Card	1.25	.55	.16
☐ B9 Ozzie Smith Cooperstown Card	1.25	.55	.16
☐ B10 Dave Winfield Cooperstown Card	1.25	.55	.16
☐ B11 Robin Yount Cooperstown Card	1.50	.65	.19
☐ B12 Joe DiMaggio The Hard Hitter	1.50	.65	.19
☐ B13 Joe DiMaggio The Stylish Fielder	1.50	.65	.19
☐ B14 Joe DiMaggio The Championship Player	1.50	.65	.19
☐ B15 Carl Yastrzemski The Impossible Dream	.75	.35	.09
☐ B16 Carl Yastrzemski The Triple Crown	.75	.35	.09
☐ B17 Carl Yastrzemski The World Series	.75	.35	.09

1992 Score Hot Rookies

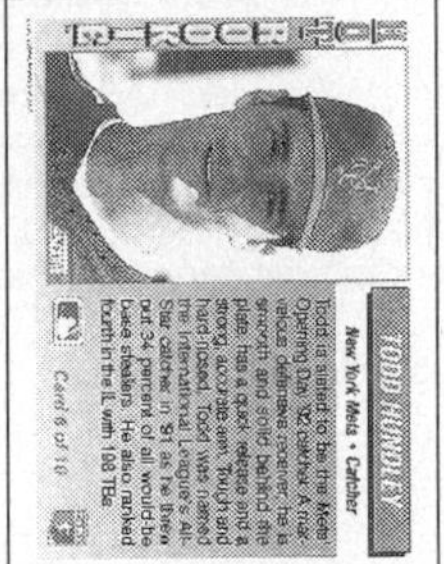

This ten-card set measures the standard size (2 1/2" by 3 1/2"). The front design features color action player photos on a white face. The words "Hot Rookie" appear in orange and yellow vertically along the left edge of the photo, and the team logo is in the lower left corner. The player's name is printed in yellow on a red box accented with a shadow detail. The Score brand mark is superimposed on the lower right corner of the picture. The horizontally oriented backs display color close-up photos. As on the fronts, the words "Hot Rookie" appear along the left photo edge. The player's name is also printed on the back as it is on the front. A career summary is shown in a graded orange background. The cards are numbered on the back.

	MT	EX-MT	VG
COMPLETE SET (10)	10.00	4.50	1.25
COMMON PLAYER (1-10)	.75	.35	.09
☐ 1 Cal Eldred	2.50	1.15	.30
☐ 2 Royce Clayton	1.50	.65	.19
☐ 3 Kenny Lofton	3.00	1.35	.40
☐ 4 Todd Van Poppel	2.00	.90	.25
☐ 5 Scott Cooper	1.25	.55	.16
☐ 6 Todd Hundley	.75	.35	.09
☐ 7 Tino Martinez	1.00	.45	.13
☐ 8 Anthony Telford	.75	.35	.09
☐ 9 Derek Bell	1.25	.55	.16
☐ 10 Reggie Jefferson	1.25	.55	.16

1992 Score Impact Players

The 1992 Score Impact Players insert set was issued in two series each with 45 cards with the respective series of the 1992 regular issue Score cards. Five cards from the 45-card first (second) series were randomly inserted in each 1992 Score I (II) jumbo pack. The cards measure the standard size (2 1/2" by 3 1/2") and the fronts feature full-bleed color

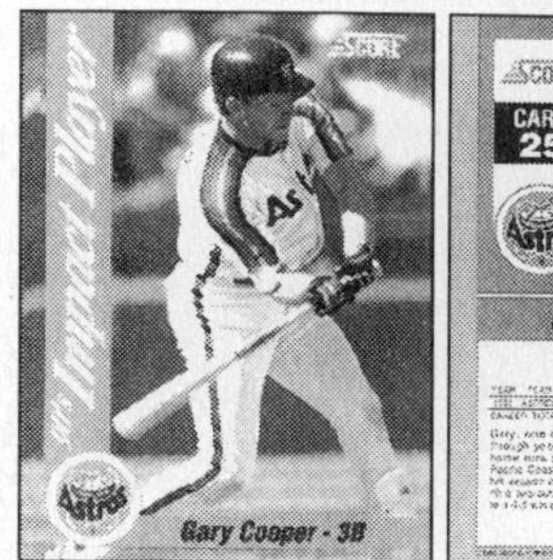

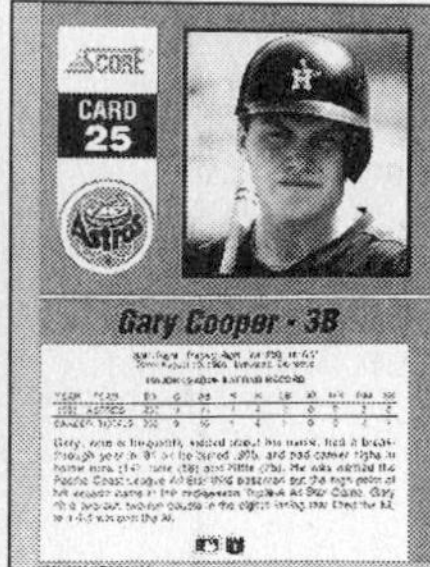

action player photos. The pictures are enhanced by a wide vertical stripe running near the left edge containing the words "90's Impact Player" and a narrower stripe at the bottom printed with the player's name. The stripes are team color-coded and intersect at the team logo in the lower left corner. The backs display close-up color player photos. The picture borders and background colors reflect the team's colors. A white box below the photo contains biographical and statistical information as well as a career summary. The cards are numbered on the back.

	MT	EX-MT	VG
COMPLETE SET (90)	20.00	9.00	2.50
COMPLETE SERIES 1 (45)	13.00	5.75	1.65
COMPLETE SERIES 2 (45)	7.00	3.10	.85
COMMON PLAYER (1-45)	.10	.05	.01
COMMON PLAYER (46-90)	.10	.05	.01

	MT	EX-MT	VG
☐ 1 Chuck Knoblauch	.50	.23	.06
☐ 2 Jeff Bagwell	.75	.35	.09
☐ 3 Juan Guzman	1.75	.80	.22
☐ 4 Milt Cuyler	.10	.05	.01
☐ 5 Ivan Rodriguez	1.00	.45	.13
☐ 6 Rich DeLucia	.10	.05	.01
☐ 7 Orlando Merced	.12	.05	.02
☐ 8 Ray Lankford	.40	.18	.05
☐ 9 Brian Hunter	.20	.09	.03
☐ 10 Roberto Alomar	.50	.23	.06
☐ 11 Wes Chamberlain	.12	.05	.02
☐ 12 Steve Avery	.50	.23	.06
☐ 13 Scott Erickson	.15	.07	.02
☐ 14 Jim Abbott	.20	.09	.03
☐ 15 Mark Whiten	.10	.05	.01
☐ 16 Leo Gomez	.20	.09	.03
☐ 17 Doug Henry	.30	.14	.04
☐ 18 Brent Mayne	.10	.05	.01
☐ 19 Charles Nagy	.12	.05	.02
☐ 20 Phil Plantier	.30	.14	.04
☐ 21 Mo Vaughn	.12	.05	.02
☐ 22 Craig Biggio	.12	.05	.02
☐ 23 Derek Bell	.30	.14	.04
☐ 24 Royce Clayton	.40	.18	.05
☐ 25 Gary Cooper	.15	.07	.02
☐ 26 Scott Cooper	.25	.11	.03
☐ 27 Juan Gonzalez	1.25	.55	.16
☐ 28 Ken Griffey Jr.	2.00	.90	.25
☐ 29 Larry Walker	.40	.18	.05
☐ 30 John Smoltz	.20	.09	.03
☐ 31 Todd Hundley	.10	.05	.01
☐ 32 Kenny Lofton	1.25	.55	.16
☐ 33 Andy Mota	.10	.05	.01
☐ 34 Todd Zeile	.10	.05	.01
☐ 35 Arthur Rhodes	.40	.18	.05
☐ 36 Jim Thome	.25	.11	.03
☐ 37 Todd Van Poppel	.40	.18	.05
☐ 38 Mark Wohlers	.20	.09	.03
☐ 39 Anthony Young	.12	.05	.02
☐ 40 Sandy Alomar Jr.	.12	.05	.02
☐ 41 John Olerud	.25	.11	.03
☐ 42 Robin Ventura	.50	.23	.06
☐ 43 Frank Thomas	3.00	1.35	.40
☐ 44 Dave Justice	.75	.35	.09
☐ 45 Hal Morris	.12	.05	.02
☐ 46 Ruben Sierra	.40	.18	.05
☐ 47 Travis Fryman	1.00	.45	.13
☐ 48 Mike Mussina	1.75	.80	.22
☐ 49 Tom Glavine	.30	.14	.04
☐ 50 Barry Larkin	.20	.09	.03
☐ 51 Will Clark	.50	.23	.06
☐ 52 Jose Canseco	.50	.23	.06
☐ 53 Bo Jackson	.25	.11	.03
☐ 54 Dwight Gooden	.12	.05	.02
☐ 55 Barry Bonds	.50	.23	.06
☐ 56 Fred McGriff	.30	.14	.04
☐ 57 Roger Clemens	.60	.25	.08
☐ 58 Benito Santiago	.12	.05	.02
☐ 59 Darryl Strawberry	.30	.14	.04
☐ 60 Cecil Fielder	.30	.14	.04
☐ 61 John Franco	.10	.05	.01
☐ 62 Matt Williams	.12	.05	.02
☐ 63 Marquis Grissom	.25	.11	.03
☐ 64 Danny Tartabull	.12	.05	.02
☐ 65 Ron Gant	.20	.09	.03
☐ 66 Paul O'Neill	.10	.05	.01
☐ 67 Devon White	.10	.05	.01
☐ 68 Rafael Palmeiro	.12	.05	.02
☐ 69 Tom Gordon	.10	.05	.01
☐ 70 Shawon Dunston	.10	.05	.01
☐ 71 Rob Dibble	.10	.05	.01
☐ 72 Eddie Zosky	.10	.05	.01
☐ 73 Jack McDowell	.12	.05	.02
☐ 74 Len Dykstra	.10	.05	.01
☐ 75 Ramon Martinez	.12	.05	.02
☐ 76 Reggie Sanders	.75	.35	.09
☐ 77 Greg Maddux	.12	.05	.02
☐ 78 Ellis Burks	.10	.05	.01
☐ 79 John Smiley	.10	.05	.01
☐ 80 Roberto Kelly	.10	.05	.01
☐ 81 Ben McDonald	.15	.07	.02
☐ 82 Mark Lewis	.10	.05	.01
☐ 83 Jose Rijo	.10	.05	.01
☐ 84 Ozzie Guillen	.10	.05	.01
☐ 85 Lance Dickson	.10	.05	.01
☐ 86 Kim Batiste	.15	.07	.02
☐ 87 Gregg Olson	.10	.05	.01
☐ 88 Andy Benes	.12	.05	.02
☐ 89 Cal Eldred	1.00	.45	.13
☐ 90 David Cone	.12	.05	.02

1992 Score 100 Rising Stars

The 1992 Score Rising Stars set contains 100 player cards and six "Magic Motion" trivia cards. The cards measure the standard size (2 1/2" by 3 1/2"). The fronts display color action player photos on a card face that shades from green to yellow and back to green. The words "Rising Star" appear above the picture, with the player's name in a blue stripe at the card bottom. The horizontally oriented backs have a color head shot on the left half, with player profile and team logo on the right half. The cards are numbered on the back.

	MT	EX-MT	VG
COMPLETE SET (100)	9.00	4.00	1.15
COMMON PLAYER (1-100)	.05	.02	.01

	MT	EX-MT	VG
☐ 1 Milt Cuyler	.10	.05	.01
☐ 2 David Howard	.05	.02	.01
☐ 3 Brian Hunter	.15	.07	.02
☐ 4 Darryl Kile	.10	.05	.01
☐ 5 Pat Kelly	.10	.05	.01
☐ 6 Luis Gonzalez	.10	.05	.01
☐ 7 Mike Benjamin	.05	.02	.01
☐ 8 Eric Anthony	.15	.07	.02
☐ 9 Moises Alou	.20	.09	.03
☐ 10 Darren Lewis	.10	.05	.01
☐ 11 Chuck Knoblauch	.25	.11	.03
☐ 12 Geronimo Pena	.10	.05	.01

☐ 13 Jeff Plympton	.05	.02	.01
☐ 14 Bret Barberie	.15	.07	.02
☐ 15 Chris Haney	.10	.05	.01
☐ 16 Rick Wilkins	.05	.02	.01
☐ 17 Julio Valera	.05	.02	.01
☐ 18 Joe Slusarski	.10	.05	.01
☐ 19 Jose Melendez	.10	.05	.01
☐ 20 Pete Schourek	.05	.02	.01
☐ 21 Jeff Conine	.25	.11	.03
☐ 22 Paul Faries	.05	.02	.01
☐ 23 Scott Kamieniecki	.05	.02	.01
☐ 24 Bernard Gilkey	.15	.07	.02
☐ 25 Wes Chamberlain	.15	.07	.02
☐ 26 Charles Nagy	.20	.09	.03
☐ 27 Juan Guzman	.40	.18	.05
☐ 28 Heath Slocumb	.05	.02	.01
☐ 29 Eddie Taubensee	.10	.05	.01
☐ 30 Cedric Landrum	.05	.02	.01
☐ 31 Jose Offerman	.10	.05	.01
☐ 32 Andres Santana	.15	.07	.02
☐ 33 David Segui	.05	.02	.01
☐ 34 Bernie Williams	.25	.11	.03
☐ 35 Jeff Bagwell	.60	.25	.08
☐ 36 Kevin Morton	.05	.02	.01
☐ 37 Kirk Dressendorfer	.10	.05	.01
☐ 38 Mike Fetters	.05	.02	.01
☐ 39 Darren Holmes	.10	.05	.01
☐ 40 Jeff Johnson	.10	.05	.01
☐ 41 Scott Aldred	.05	.02	.01
☐ 42 Kevin Ward	.10	.05	.01
☐ 43 Ray Lankford	.30	.14	.04
☐ 44 Terry Shumpert	.05	.02	.01
☐ 45 Wade Taylor	.05	.02	.01
☐ 46 Rob MacDonald	.05	.02	.01
☐ 47 Jose Mota	.10	.05	.01
☐ 48 Reggie Harris	.05	.02	.01
☐ 49 Mike Remlinger	.05	.02	.01
☐ 50 Mark Lewis	.15	.07	.02
☐ 51 Tino Martinez	.15	.07	.02
☐ 52 Ed Sprague	.15	.07	.02
☐ 53 Freddie Benavides	.05	.02	.01
☐ 54 Rich DeLucia	.05	.02	.01
☐ 55 Brian Drahman	.05	.02	.01
☐ 56 Steve Decker	.10	.05	.01
☐ 57 Scott Livingstone	.10	.05	.01
☐ 58 Mike Timlin	.10	.05	.01
☐ 59 Bob Scanlan	.05	.02	.01
☐ 60 Dean Palmer	.25	.11	.03
☐ 61 Frank Castillo	.05	.02	.01
☐ 62 Mark Leonard	.05	.02	.01
☐ 63 Chuck McElroy	.05	.02	.01
☐ 64 Derek Bell	.20	.09	.03
☐ 65 Andujar Cedeno	.20	.09	.03
☐ 66 Leo Gomez	.25	.11	.03
☐ 67 Rusty Meacham	.10	.05	.01
☐ 68 Dann Howitt	.05	.02	.01
☐ 69 Chris Jones	.05	.02	.01
☐ 70 Dave Cochrane	.05	.02	.01
☐ 71 Carlos Martinez	.05	.02	.01
☐ 72 Hensley Meulens	.10	.05	.01
☐ 73 Rich Reed	.05	.02	.01
☐ 74 Pedro Munoz	.15	.07	.02
☐ 75 Orlando Merced	.15	.07	.02
☐ 76 Chito Martinez	.15	.07	.02
☐ 77 Ivan Rodriguez	.60	.25	.08
☐ 78 Brian Barnes	.10	.05	.01
☐ 79 Chris Donnels	.10	.05	.01
☐ 80 Todd Hundley	.10	.05	.01
☐ 81 Gary Scott	.10	.05	.01
☐ 82 John Wehner	.10	.05	.01
☐ 83 Al Osuna	.05	.02	.01
☐ 84 Luis Lopez	.10	.05	.01
☐ 85 Brent Mayne	.10	.05	.01
☐ 86 Phil Plantier	.40	.18	.05
☐ 87 Joe Bitker	.05	.02	.01
☐ 88 Scott Cooper	.15	.07	.02
☐ 89 Chris Hammond	.10	.05	.01
☐ 90 Tim Sherrill	.05	.02	.01
☐ 91 Doug Simons	.05	.02	.01
☐ 92 Kip Gross	.05	.02	.01
☐ 93 Tim McIntosh	.10	.05	.01
☐ 94 Larry Casian	.05	.02	.01
☐ 95 Mike Dalton	.10	.05	.01
☐ 96 Lance Dickson	.15	.07	.02
☐ 97 Joe Grahe	.10	.05	.01
☐ 98 Glenn Sutko	.05	.02	.01
☐ 99 Gerald Alexander	.05	.02	.01
☐ 100 Mo Vaughn	.25	.11	.03

1992 Score 100 Superstars

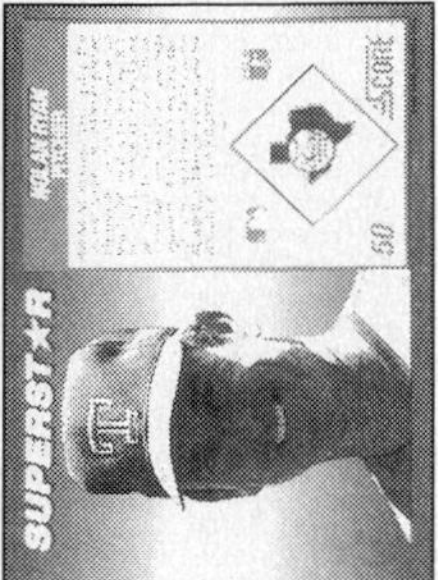

The 1992 Score Superstars set contains 100 player cards and six "Magic Motion" trivia cards. The cards measure the standard size (2 1/2" by 3 1/2"). The fronts display color action player photos on a card face that shades from reddish-orange to yellow and back to reddish-orange again. The words "Superstar" appear above the pictures, with the player's name in a purple stripe at the card bottom. The horizontally oriented backs have a color head shot on the left half, with player profile and team logo on the right half. The cards are numbered on the back.

	MT	EX-MT	VG
COMPLETE SET (100)	9.00	4.00	1.15
COMMON PLAYER (1-100)	.05	.02	.01
☐ 1 Ken Griffey Jr.	.75	.35	.09
☐ 2 Scott Erickson	.15	.07	.02
☐ 3 John Smiley	.05	.02	.01
☐ 4 Rick Aguilera	.05	.02	.01
☐ 5 Jeff Reardon	.10	.05	.01
☐ 6 Chuck Finley	.05	.02	.01
☐ 7 Kirby Puckett	.45	.20	.06
☐ 8 Paul Molitor	.15	.07	.02
☐ 9 Dave Winfield	.35	.16	.04
☐ 10 Mike Greenwell	.15	.07	.02
☐ 11 Bret Saberhagen	.10	.05	.01
☐ 12 Pete Harnisch	.05	.02	.01
☐ 13 Ozzie Guillen	.05	.02	.01
☐ 14 Hal Morris	.10	.05	.01
☐ 15 Tom Glavine	.25	.11	.03
☐ 16 David Cone	.15	.07	.02
☐ 17 Edgar Martinez	.15	.07	.02
☐ 18 Willie McGee	.10	.05	.01
☐ 19 Jim Abbott	.20	.09	.03
☐ 20 Mark Grace	.25	.11	.03
☐ 21 George Brett	.35	.16	.04
☐ 22 Jack McDowell	.15	.07	.02
☐ 23 Don Mattingly	.35	.16	.04
☐ 24 Will Clark	.45	.20	.06
☐ 25 Dwight Gooden	.15	.07	.02
☐ 26 Barry Bonds	.25	.11	.03
☐ 27 Rafael Palmeiro	.15	.07	.02
☐ 28 Lee Smith	.10	.05	.01
☐ 29 Wally Joyner	.10	.05	.01
☐ 30 Wade Boggs	.35	.16	.04
☐ 31 Tom Henke	.10	.05	.01
☐ 32 Mark Langston	.10	.05	.01
☐ 33 Robin Ventura	.30	.14	.04
☐ 34 Steve Avery	.25	.11	.03
☐ 35 Joe Carter	.25	.11	.03
☐ 36 Benito Santiago	.10	.05	.01
☐ 37 Dave Stieb	.05	.02	.01
☐ 38 Julio Franco	.10	.05	.01
☐ 39 Albert Belle	.15	.07	.02
☐ 40 Dale Murphy	.15	.07	.02
☐ 41 Rob Dibble	.10	.05	.01
☐ 42 Dave Justice	.30	.14	.04
☐ 43 Jose Rijo	.10	.05	.01
☐ 44 Eric Davis	.15	.07	.02
☐ 45 Terry Pendleton	.15	.07	.02
☐ 46 Kevin Maas	.10	.05	.01
☐ 47 Ozzie Smith	.20	.09	.03
☐ 48 Andre Dawson	.20	.09	.03
☐ 49 Sandy Alomar Jr.	.10	.05	.01
☐ 50 Nolan Ryan	.75	.35	.09
☐ 51 Frank Thomas	1.00	.45	.13
☐ 52 Craig Biggio	.10	.05	.01

☐ 53 Doug Drabek	.10	.05	.01
☐ 54 Bobby Thigpen	.10	.05	.01
☐ 55 Darryl Strawberry	.35	.16	.04
☐ 56 Dennis Eckersley	.15	.07	.02
☐ 57 John Franco	.05	.02	.01
☐ 58 Paul O'Neill	.05	.02	.01
☐ 59 Scott Sanderson	.05	.02	.01
☐ 60 Dave Stewart	.10	.05	.01
☐ 61 Ivan Calderon	.05	.02	.01
☐ 62 Frank Viola	.10	.05	.01
☐ 63 Mark McGwire	.35	.16	.04
☐ 64 Kelly Gruber	.10	.05	.01
☐ 65 Fred McGriff	.25	.11	.03
☐ 66 Cecil Fielder	.25	.11	.03
☐ 67 Jose Canseco	.45	.20	.06
☐ 68 Howard Johnson	.10	.05	.01
☐ 69 Juan Gonzalez	.45	.20	.06
☐ 70 Tim Wallach	.05	.02	.01
☐ 71 John Olerud	.20	.09	.03
☐ 72 Carlton Fisk	.20	.09	.03
☐ 73 Otis Nixon	.10	.05	.01
☐ 74 Roger Clemens	.45	.20	.06
☐ 75 Ramon Martinez	.15	.07	.02
☐ 76 Ron Gant	.20	.09	.03
☐ 77 Barry Larkin	.20	.09	.03
☐ 78 Eddie Murray	.20	.09	.03
☐ 79 Vince Coleman	.10	.05	.01
☐ 80 Bobby Bonilla	.15	.07	.02
☐ 81 Tony Gwynn	.25	.11	.03
☐ 82 Roberto Alomar	.35	.16	.04
☐ 83 Ellis Burks	.10	.05	.01
☐ 84 Robin Yount	.35	.16	.04
☐ 85 Ryne Sandberg	.45	.20	.06
☐ 86 Len Dykstra	.10	.05	.01
☐ 87 Ruben Sierra	.25	.11	.03
☐ 88 George Bell	.10	.05	.01
☐ 89 Cal Ripken	.50	.23	.06
☐ 90 Danny Tartabull	.15	.07	.02
☐ 91 Gregg Olson	.10	.05	.01
☐ 92 Dave Henderson	.05	.02	.01
☐ 93 Kevin Mitchell	.15	.07	.02
☐ 94 Ben McDonald	.15	.07	.02
☐ 95 Matt Williams	.15	.07	.02
☐ 96 Roberto Kelly	.15	.07	.02
☐ 97 Dennis Martinez	.10	.05	.01
☐ 98 Kent Hrbek	.10	.05	.01
☐ 99 Felix Jose	.15	.07	.02
☐ 100 Rickey Henderson	.35	.16	.04

1992 Score Proctor and Gamble

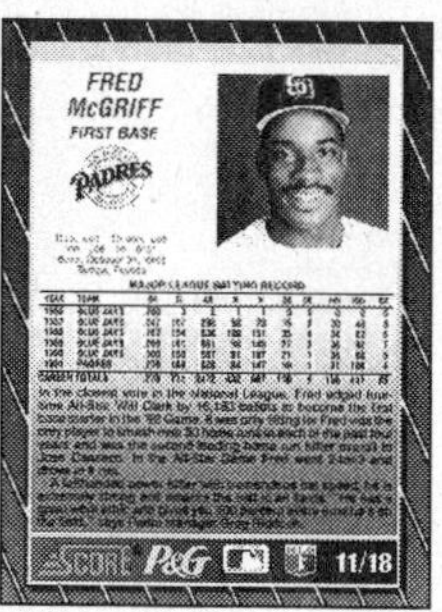

This 18-card standard-size (2 1/2" by 3 1/2") set was produced by Score for Proctor and Gamble as a mail-in premium and contains 18 players from the 1992 All-Star Game line-up. The production run comprised 2,000,000 sets and 25 uncut sheets. A three-card sample set was also produced for sales representatives with a print run of 5,000,000 sets and 25 uncut sheets. The three sample cards, featuring Griffey, Sandberg, and Henderson, are stamped "sample" on the back. Collectors could obtain the set by sending in a required certificate, 99 cents, three UPC symbols from three different Proctor and Gamble products, and 50 cents for postage and handling. The certificate was published in a flyer inserted in Sunday, August 16 newspapers. The card fronts feature color action player cutouts superimposed on a diagonally striped background showing a large star behind the player. Card numbers 1-9 have a blue star on a graded magenta background, while card numbers 10-18 show a red star on blue-green. The backs display a close-up photo, biographical and statistical information, and career summary on a graded yellow-orange background. The cards are numbered "X/18" at the lower right corner.

	MT	EX-MT	VG
COMPLETE SET (18)	9.00	4.00	1.15
COMMON PLAYER (1-18)	.35	.16	.04
☐ 1 Sandy Alomar Jr.	.35	.16	.04
☐ 2 Mark McGwire	.75	.35	.09
☐ 3 Roberto Alomar	.75	.35	.09
☐ 4 Wade Boggs	.50	.23	.06
☐ 5 Cal Ripken	1.00	.45	.13
☐ 6 Kirby Puckett	.75	.35	.09
☐ 7 Ken Griffey Jr.	1.50	.65	.19
☐ 8 Jose Canseco	.75	.35	.09
☐ 9 Kevin Brown	.35	.16	.04
☐ 10 Benito Santiago	.35	.16	.04
☐ 11 Fred McGriff	.50	.23	.06
☐ 12 Ryne Sandberg	1.00	.45	.13
☐ 13 Terry Pendleton	.50	.23	.06
☐ 14 Ozzie Smith	.50	.23	.06
☐ 15 Barry Bonds	.60	.25	.08
☐ 16 Tony Gwynn	.50	.23	.06
☐ 17 Andy Van Slyke	.35	.16	.04
☐ 18 Tom Glavine	.60	.25	.08

1992 Score Rookies

This 40-card boxed set measures the standard size (2 1/2" by 3 1/2") and features glossy color action player photos on a kelly green face with meandering purple stripes. The words "1992 Rookie" are printed in white and red along the left edge of the photo. The player's name appears in white on a red banner at the bottom. The banner and the right edge of the picture are edged in canary yellow. The team logo is superimposed on the photo and the red banner. The back design features close-up player photos with kelly green shadow border on a graded royal blue face. The player's name is printed in red below the picture followed by biography and player profile. The words "1992 Rookie" appear, as on the front, in white and red along the left edge of the card. The cards are numbered on the back.

	MT	EX-MT	VG
COMPLETE SET (40)	6.00	2.70	.75
COMMON PLAYER (1-40)	.15	.07	.02
☐ 1 Todd Van Poppel	.60	.25	.08
☐ 2 Kyle Abbott	.15	.07	.02
☐ 3 Derek Bell	.25	.11	.03
☐ 4 Jim Thome	.25	.11	.03
☐ 5 Mark Wohlers	.25	.11	.03
☐ 6 Todd Hundley	.15	.07	.02
☐ 7 Arthur Lee Rhodes	.35	.16	.04
☐ 8 John Ramos	.15	.07	.02
☐ 9 Chris George	.15	.07	.02

☐ 10 Kenny Lofton	.75	.35	.09
☐ 11 Ted Wood	.25	.11	.03
☐ 12 Royce Clayton	.35	.16	.04
☐ 13 Scott Cooper	.25	.11	.03
☐ 14 Anthony Young	.25	.11	.03
☐ 15 Joel Johnston	.15	.07	.02
☐ 16 Andy Mota	.25	.11	.03
☐ 17 Lenny Webster	.15	.07	.02
☐ 18 Andy Ashby	.15	.07	.02
☐ 19 Jose Mota	.15	.07	.02
☐ 20 Tim McIntosh	.15	.07	.02
☐ 21 Terry Bross	.15	.07	.02
☐ 22 Harvey Pulliam	.25	.11	.03
☐ 23 Hector Fajardo	.25	.11	.03
☐ 24 Esteban Beltre	.25	.11	.03
☐ 25 Gary DiSarcina	.25	.11	.03
☐ 26 Mike Humphreys	.15	.07	.02
☐ 27 Jarvis Brown	.15	.07	.02
☐ 28 Gary Cooper	.15	.07	.02
☐ 29 Chris Donnels	.15	.07	.02
☐ 30 Monty Fariss	.15	.07	.02
☐ 31 Eric Karros	1.00	.45	.13
☐ 32 Braulio Castillo	.25	.11	.03
☐ 33 Cal Eldred	.60	.25	.08
☐ 34 Tom Goodwin	.25	.11	.03
☐ 35 Reggie Sanders	.60	.25	.08
☐ 36 Scott Servais	.15	.07	.02
☐ 37 Kim Batiste	.25	.11	.03
☐ 38 Eric Wedge	.35	.16	.04
☐ 39 Willie Banks	.25	.11	.03
☐ 40 Mo Sanford	.25	.11	.03

1992 Score Rookie/Traded

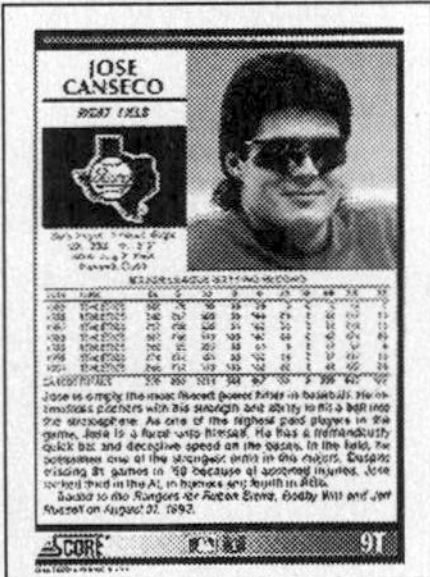

The 1992 Score Rookie and Traded set contains 110 standard-size (2 1/2" by 3 1/2") cards featuring traded veterans and rookies. The fronts display color action player photos edged on one side by an orange stripe that fades to white as one moves down the card face. The player's name appears in a purple bar above the picture, while his position is printed in a purple bar below the picture. The backs carry a color close-up photo, biography, and on a yellow panel, batting or pitching statistics and career summary. The cards are numbered on the back with the "T" suffix. The set is arranged numerically such that cards 1-79 are traded players and cards 80-110 feature rookies.

	MT	EX-MT	VG
COMPLETE SET (110)	14.00	6.25	1.75
COMMON PLAYER (1T-79T)	.05	.02	.01
COMMON PLAYER (80T-110T)	.05	.02	.01

☐ 1T Gary Sheffield	.25	.11	.03
☐ 2T Kevin Seitzer	.08	.04	.01
☐ 3T Danny Tartabull	.08	.04	.01
☐ 4T Steve Sax	.08	.04	.01
☐ 5T Bobby Bonilla	.10	.05	.01
☐ 6T Frank Viola	.08	.04	.01
☐ 7T Dave Winfield	.10	.05	.01
☐ 8T Rick Sutcliffe	.08	.04	.01
☐ 9T Jose Canseco	.25	.11	.03
☐ 10T Greg Swindell	.08	.04	.01
☐ 11T Eddie Murray	.10	.05	.01
☐ 12T Randy Myers	.08	.04	.01
☐ 13T Wally Joyner	.08	.04	.01
☐ 14T Kenny Lofton	.35	.16	.04
☐ 15T Jack Morris	.10	.05	.01
☐ 16T Charlie Hayes	.05	.02	.01
☐ 17T Pete Incaviglia	.05	.02	.01
☐ 18T Kevin Mitchell	.08	.04	.01
☐ 19T Kurt Stillwell	.05	.02	.01
☐ 20T Bret Saberhagen	.08	.04	.01
☐ 21T Steve Buechele	.05	.02	.01
☐ 22T John Smiley	.08	.04	.01
☐ 23T Sammy Sosa	.05	.02	.01
☐ 24T George Bell	.08	.04	.01
☐ 25T Curt Schilling	.08	.04	.01
☐ 26T Dick Schofield	.05	.02	.01
☐ 27T David Cone	.08	.04	.01
☐ 28T Dan Gladden	.05	.02	.01
☐ 29T Kirk McCaskill	.05	.02	.01
☐ 30T Mike Gallego	.05	.02	.01
☐ 31T Kevin McReynolds	.08	.04	.01
☐ 32T Bill Swift	.05	.02	.01
☐ 33T Dave Martinez	.05	.02	.01
☐ 34T Storm Davis	.05	.02	.01
☐ 35T Willie Randolph	.08	.04	.01
☐ 36T Melido Perez	.08	.04	.01
☐ 37T Mark Carreon	.05	.02	.01
☐ 38T Doug Jones	.05	.02	.01
☐ 39T Gregg Jefferies	.08	.04	.01
☐ 40T Mike Jackson	.05	.02	.01
☐ 41T Dickie Thon	.05	.02	.01
☐ 42T Eric King	.05	.02	.01
☐ 43T Herm Winningham	.05	.02	.01
☐ 44T Derek Lilliquist	.05	.02	.01
☐ 45T Dave Anderson	.05	.02	.01
☐ 46T Jeff Reardon	.08	.04	.01
☐ 47T Scott Bankhead	.05	.02	.01
☐ 48T Cory Snyder	.05	.02	.01
☐ 49T Al Newman	.05	.02	.01
☐ 50T Keith Miller	.05	.02	.01
☐ 51T Dave Burba	.05	.02	.01
☐ 52T Bill Pecota	.05	.02	.01
☐ 53T Chuck Crim	.05	.02	.01
☐ 54T Mariano Duncan	.05	.02	.01
☐ 55T Dave Gallagher	.05	.02	.01
☐ 56T Chris Gwynn	.05	.02	.01
☐ 57T Scott Ruskin	.05	.02	.01
☐ 58T Jack Armstrong	.05	.02	.01
☐ 59T Gary Carter	.08	.04	.01
☐ 60T Andres Galarraga	.05	.02	.01
☐ 61T Ken Hill	.08	.04	.01
☐ 62T Eric Davis	.08	.04	.01
☐ 63T Ruben Sierra	.20	.09	.03
☐ 64T Darrin Fletcher	.05	.02	.01
☐ 65T Tim Belcher	.08	.04	.01
☐ 66T Mike Morgan	.05	.02	.01
☐ 67T Scott Scudder	.05	.02	.01
☐ 68T Tom Candiotti	.05	.02	.01
☐ 69T Hubie Brooks	.05	.02	.01
☐ 70T Kal Daniels	.05	.02	.01
☐ 71T Bruce Ruffin	.05	.02	.01
☐ 72T Billy Hatcher	.05	.02	.01
☐ 73T Bob Melvin	.05	.02	.01
☐ 74T Lee Guetterman	.05	.02	.01
☐ 75T Rene Gonzales	.05	.02	.01
☐ 76T Kevin Bass	.05	.02	.01
☐ 77T Tom Bolton	.05	.02	.01
☐ 78T John Wetteland	.05	.02	.01
☐ 79T Bip Roberts	.08	.04	.01
☐ 80T Pat Listach	1.50	.65	.19
☐ 81T John Doherty	.15	.07	.02
☐ 82T Sam Militello	.30	.14	.04
☐ 83T Brian Jordan	.25	.11	.03
☐ 84T Jeff Kent	.25	.11	.03
☐ 85T Dave Fleming	.50	.23	.06
☐ 86T Jeff Tackett	.10	.05	.01
☐ 87T Chad Curtis	.30	.14	.04
☐ 88T Eric Fox	.12	.05	.02
☐ 89T Denny Neagle	.05	.02	.01
☐ 90T Donovan Osborne	.30	.14	.04
☐ 91T Carlos Hernandez	.05	.02	.01
☐ 92T Tim Wakefield	3.00	1.35	.40
☐ 93T Tim Salmon	.50	.23	.06
☐ 94T Dave Nilsson	.15	.07	.02
☐ 95T Mike Perez	.08	.04	.01
☐ 96T Pat Hentgen	.10	.05	.01
☐ 97T Frank Seminara	.20	.09	.03
☐ 98T Ruben Amaro Jr.	.05	.02	.01
☐ 99T Archi Cianfrocco	.15	.07	.02
☐ 100T Andy Stankiewicz	.15	.07	.02
☐ 101T Jim Bullinger	.10	.05	.01
☐ 102T Pat Mahomes	.25	.11	.03
☐ 103T Hipolito Pichardo	.10	.05	.01
☐ 104T Bret Boone	.50	.23	.06
☐ 105T John Vander Wal	.15	.07	.02
☐ 106T Vince Horsman	.10	.05	.01

☐ 107T James Austin	.10	.05	.01
☐ 108T Brian Williams	.25	.11	.03
☐ 109T Dan Walters	.15	.07	.02
☐ 110T Wilfredo Cordero	.15	.07	.02

1992 Score The Franchise

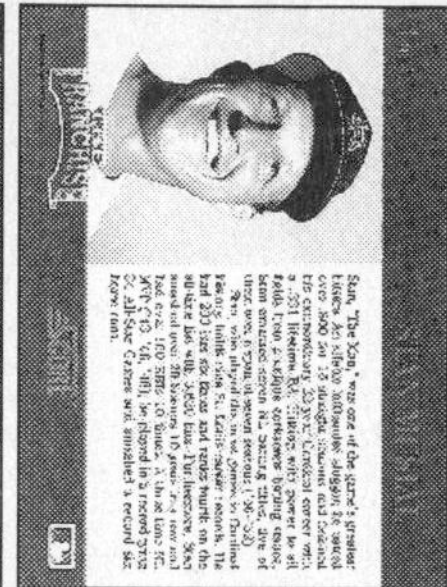

This four-card set features three all-time greats, Stan Musial, Mickey Mantle, and Carl Yastrzemski, and measures the standard size (2 1/2" by 3 1/2"). Each former player autographed 2,000 of his 1992 Score cards, and 500 of the combo cards were signed by all three. In addition to these signed cards, Score produced 600,000 unsigned cards (150,000 of each Franchise card), and both signed and unsigned cards were randomly inserted in 1992 Score Series II poly packs, blister packs, and cello packs. The first three cards feature color action photos of each player. The fourth is horizontally oriented and pictures each player in a batting stance. A forest green stripe borders the top and bottom. The words "The Franchise" and the Score logo appear at the top, and the player's name is printed on the green stripe at the bottom. The backs of the first three cards have a close-up photo and a career summary. The fourth card is a combo card, summarizing the career of all three players. The cards are numbered on the back.

	MT	EX-MT	VG
COMPLETE SET (4)	40.00	18.00	5.00
COMMON PLAYER (1-4)	10.00	4.50	1.25
☐ 1 Stan Musial	10.00	4.50	1.25
☐ 1AU Stan Musial (Autographed with certified signature)	200.00	90.00	25.00
☐ 2 Mickey Mantle	15.00	6.75	1.90
☐ 2AU Mickey Mantle (Autographed with certified signature)	500.00	230.00	65.00
☐ 3 Carl Yastrzemski	10.00	4.50	1.25
☐ 3AU Carl Yastrzemski (Autographed with certified signature)	200.00	90.00	25.00
☐ 4 The Franchise Players Stan Musial Mickey Mantle Carl Yastrzemski	15.00	6.75	1.90
☐ 4AU Franchise Players Stan Musial Mickey Mantle Carl Yastrzemski (Autographed with certified signatures of all three)	1000.00	450.00	125.00

1993 Score Select Promos

These five promo cards were issued to provide dealers with a preview of Score's new Select series cards. The cards

measure the standard size (2 1/2" by 3 1/2") and feature glossy color player photos edged on two sides by a two-toned green border area. The back design is similar to the fronts but with a smaller player photo to create space for player profile and statistics. These promo cards are distinguished from the regular issue by the zeroes in the statistic lines. The cards are numbered on the back.

	MT	EX-MT	VG
COMPLETE SET (5)	20.00	9.00	2.50
COMMON PLAYER (1-5)	2.00	.90	.25
☐ 22 Robin Yount	6.00	2.70	.75
☐ 24 Don Mattingly	6.00	2.70	.75
☐ 26 Sandy Alomar Jr.	2.50	1.15	.30
☐ 41 Gary Sheffield	6.00	2.70	.75
☐ 75 John Smiley	2.00	.90	.25

1993 Score Select

Seeking a niche in the premium, mid-price market, Score has produced a new 405-card baseball set. The set includes regular players, rookies, and draft picks, and was sold in 15-card packs and 28-card super packs. Themed Chase Cards (24 in all) were randomly inserted into the 15-card packs. The cards measure the standard size (2 1/2" by 3 1/2"). The front photos, composed either horizontally or vertically, are ultra-violet coated while the two-toned green borders received a matte finish. The player's name appears in mustard-colored lettering in the bottom border. The backs carry a second color photo as well as 1992 statistics, career totals, and an in-depth player profile, all on a two-toned green background. The cards are numbered on the back. The set includes Draft Pick (291, 297, 303, 310, 352-360) and Rookie (271-290, 292-296, 298-302, 304-309, 311-351, 383, 385, 391, 394, 400-405) subsets.

	MT	EX-MT	VG
COMPLETE SET (405)	30.00	13.50	3.80
COMMON PLAYER (1-405)	.07	.03	.01
☐ 1 Barry Bonds	.30	.14	.04

Card			
☐ 2 Ken Griffey Jr.	.75	.35	.09
☐ 3 Will Clark	.30	.14	.04
☐ 4 Kirby Puckett	.30	.14	.04
☐ 5 Tony Gwynn	.20	.09	.03
☐ 6 Frank Thomas	1.00	.45	.13
☐ 7 Tom Glavine	.20	.09	.03
☐ 8 Roberto Alomar	.35	.16	.04
☐ 9 Andre Dawson	.15	.07	.02
☐ 10 Ron Darling	.10	.05	.01
☐ 11 Bobby Bonilla	.15	.07	.02
☐ 12 Danny Tartabull	.10	.05	.01
☐ 13 Darren Daulton	.10	.05	.01
☐ 14 Roger Clemens	.35	.16	.04
☐ 15 Ozzie Smith	.15	.07	.02
☐ 16 Mark McGwire	.30	.14	.04
☐ 17 Terry Pendleton	.10	.05	.01
☐ 18 Cal Ripken	.40	.18	.05
☐ 19 Fred McGriff	.15	.07	.02
☐ 20 Cecil Fielder	.20	.09	.03
☐ 21 Darryl Strawberry	.20	.09	.03
☐ 22 Robin Yount	.15	.07	.02
☐ 23 Barry Larkin	.15	.07	.02
☐ 24 Don Mattingly	.20	.09	.03
☐ 25 Craig Biggio	.10	.05	.01
☐ 26 Sandy Alomar Jr.	.10	.05	.01
☐ 27 Larry Walker	.20	.09	.03
☐ 28 Junior Felix	.07	.03	.01
☐ 29 Eddie Murray	.15	.07	.02
☐ 30 Robin Ventura	.25	.11	.03
☐ 31 Greg Maddux	.15	.07	.02
☐ 32 Dave Winfield	.15	.07	.02
☐ 33 John Kruk	.10	.05	.01
☐ 34 Wally Joyner	.10	.05	.01
☐ 35 Andy Van Slyke	.10	.05	.01
☐ 36 Chuck Knoblauch	.25	.11	.03
☐ 37 Tom Pagnozzi	.07	.03	.01
☐ 38 Dennis Eckersley	.12	.05	.02
☐ 39 Dave Justice	.30	.14	.04
☐ 40 Juan Gonzalez	.40	.18	.05
☐ 41 Gary Sheffield	.25	.11	.03
☐ 42 Paul Molitor	.10	.05	.01
☐ 43 Delino DeShields	.15	.07	.02
☐ 44 Travis Fryman	.30	.14	.04
☐ 45 Hal Morris	.10	.05	.01
☐ 46 Greg Olson	.10	.05	.01
☐ 47 Ken Caminiti	.07	.03	.01
☐ 48 Wade Boggs	.20	.09	.03
☐ 49 Orel Hershiser	.07	.03	.01
☐ 50 Albert Belle	.20	.09	.03
☐ 51 Bill Swift	.07	.03	.01
☐ 52 Mark Langston	.10	.05	.01
☐ 53 Joe Girardi	.07	.03	.01
☐ 54 Keith Miller	.07	.03	.01
☐ 55 Gary Carter	.10	.05	.01
☐ 56 Brady Anderson	.10	.05	.01
☐ 57 Dwight Gooden	.10	.05	.01
☐ 58 Julio Franco	.10	.05	.01
☐ 59 Lenny Dykstra	.10	.05	.01
☐ 60 Mickey Tettleton	.10	.05	.01
☐ 61 Randy Tomlin	.07	.03	.01
☐ 62 B.J. Surhoff	.07	.03	.01
☐ 63 Todd Zeile	.07	.03	.01
☐ 64 Roberto Kelly	.10	.05	.01
☐ 65 Rob Dibble	.10	.05	.01
☐ 66 Leo Gomez	.10	.05	.01
☐ 67 Doug Jones	.07	.03	.01
☐ 68 Ellis Burks	.10	.05	.01
☐ 69 Mike Scioscia	.07	.03	.01
☐ 70 Charles Nagy	.10	.05	.01
☐ 71 Cory Snyder	.07	.03	.01
☐ 72 Devon White	.10	.05	.01
☐ 73 Mark Grace	.10	.05	.01
☐ 74 Luis Polonia	.07	.03	.01
☐ 75 John Smiley	.10	.05	.01
☐ 76 Carlton Fisk	.15	.07	.02
☐ 77 Luis Sojo	.07	.03	.01
☐ 78 George Brett	.15	.07	.02
☐ 79 Mitch Williams	.07	.03	.01
☐ 80 Kent Hrbek	.10	.05	.01
☐ 81 Jay Bell	.07	.03	.01
☐ 82 Edgar Martinez	.10	.05	.01
☐ 83 Lee Smith	.10	.05	.01
☐ 84 Deion Sanders	.20	.09	.03
☐ 85 Bill Gullickson	.07	.03	.01
☐ 86 Paul O'Neill	.10	.05	.01
☐ 87 Kevin Seitzer	.10	.05	.01
☐ 88 Steve Finley	.07	.03	.01
☐ 89 Mel Hall	.07	.03	.01
☐ 90 Nolan Ryan	.60	.25	.08
☐ 91 Eric Davis	.10	.05	.01
☐ 92 Mike Mussina	.40	.18	.05
☐ 93 Tony Fernandez	.10	.05	.01
☐ 94 Frank Viola	.10	.05	.01
☐ 95 Matt Williams	.10	.05	.01
☐ 96 Joe Carter	.20	.09	.03
☐ 97 Ryne Sandberg	.35	.16	.04
☐ 98 Jim Abbott	.15	.07	.02
☐ 99 Marquis Grissom	.15	.07	.02
☐ 100 George Bell	.10	.05	.01
☐ 101 Howard Johnson	.10	.05	.01
☐ 102 Kevin Appier	.10	.05	.01
☐ 103 Dale Murphy	.10	.05	.01
☐ 104 Shane Mack	.10	.05	.01
☐ 105 Jose Lind	.07	.03	.01
☐ 106 Rickey Henderson	.20	.09	.03
☐ 107 Bob Tewksbury	.07	.03	.01
☐ 108 Kevin Mitchell	.10	.05	.01
☐ 109 Steve Avery	.20	.09	.03
☐ 110 Candy Maldonado	.07	.03	.01
☐ 111 Bip Roberts	.10	.05	.01
☐ 112 Lou Whitaker	.10	.05	.01
☐ 113 Jeff Bagwell	.30	.14	.04
☐ 114 Dante Bichette	.07	.03	.01
☐ 115 Brett Butler	.10	.05	.01
☐ 116 Melido Perez	.07	.03	.01
☐ 117 Andy Benes	.10	.05	.01
☐ 118 Randy Johnson	.10	.05	.01
☐ 119 Willie McGee	.10	.05	.01
☐ 120 Jody Reed	.07	.03	.01
☐ 121 Shawon Dunston	.10	.05	.01
☐ 122 Carlos Baerga	.25	.11	.03
☐ 123 Bret Saberhagen	.07	.03	.01
☐ 124 John Olerud	.15	.07	.02
☐ 125 Ivan Calderon	.07	.03	.01
☐ 126 Bryan Harvey	.07	.03	.01
☐ 127 Terry Mulholland	.07	.03	.01
☐ 128 Ozzie Guillen	.07	.03	.01
☐ 129 Steve Buechele	.07	.03	.01
☐ 130 Kevin Tapani	.10	.05	.01
☐ 131 Felix Jose	.10	.05	.01
☐ 132 Terry Steinbach	.10	.05	.01
☐ 133 Ron Gant	.12	.05	.02
☐ 134 Harold Reynolds	.07	.03	.01
☐ 135 Chris Sabo	.10	.05	.01
☐ 136 Ivan Rodriguez	.30	.14	.04
☐ 137 Eric Anthony	.10	.05	.01
☐ 138 Mike Henneman	.07	.03	.01
☐ 139 Robby Thompson	.07	.03	.01
☐ 140 Scott Fletcher	.07	.03	.01
☐ 141 Bruce Hurst	.10	.05	.01
☐ 142 Kevin Maas	.10	.05	.01
☐ 143 Tom Candiotti	.07	.03	.01
☐ 144 Chris Hoiles	.10	.05	.01
☐ 145 Mike Morgan	.07	.03	.01
☐ 146 Mark Whiten	.07	.03	.01
☐ 147 Dennis Martinez	.10	.05	.01
☐ 148 Tony Pena	.07	.03	.01
☐ 149 Dave Magadan	.07	.03	.01
☐ 150 Mark Lewis	.07	.03	.01
☐ 151 Mariano Duncan	.07	.03	.01
☐ 152 Gregg Jefferies	.10	.05	.01
☐ 153 Doug Drabek	.10	.05	.01
☐ 154 Brian Harper	.07	.03	.01
☐ 155 Ray Lankford	.15	.07	.02
☐ 156 Carney Lansford	.10	.05	.01
☐ 157 Mike Sharperson	.07	.03	.01
☐ 158 Jack Morris	.12	.05	.02
☐ 159 Otis Nixon	.07	.03	.01
☐ 160 Steve Sax	.10	.05	.01
☐ 161 Mark Lemke	.07	.03	.01
☐ 162 Rafael Palmeiro	.10	.05	.01
☐ 163 Jose Rijo	.10	.05	.01
☐ 164 Omar Vizquel	.07	.03	.01
☐ 165 Sammy Sosa	.07	.03	.01
☐ 166 Milt Cuyler	.07	.03	.01
☐ 167 John Franco	.07	.03	.01
☐ 168 Darryl Hamilton	.07	.03	.01
☐ 169 Ken Hill	.07	.03	.01
☐ 170 Mike Devereaux	.10	.05	.01
☐ 171 Don Slaught	.07	.03	.01
☐ 172 Steve Farr	.07	.03	.01
☐ 173 Bernard Gilkey	.10	.05	.01
☐ 174 Mike Fetters	.07	.03	.01
☐ 175 Vince Coleman	.10	.05	.01
☐ 176 Kevin McReynolds	.10	.05	.01
☐ 177 John Smoltz	.12	.05	.02
☐ 178 Greg Gagne	.07	.03	.01
☐ 179 Greg Swindell	.10	.05	.01
☐ 180 Juan Guzman	.40	.18	.05
☐ 181 Kal Daniels	.07	.03	.01
☐ 182 Rick Sutcliffe	.10	.05	.01
☐ 183 Orlando Merced	.07	.03	.01
☐ 184 Bill Wegman	.07	.03	.01
☐ 185 Mark Gardner	.07	.03	.01
☐ 186 Rob Deer	.10	.05	.01
☐ 187 Dave Hollins	.10	.05	.01

☐ 188 Jack Clark	.10	.05	.01
☐ 189 Brian Hunter	.10	.05	.01
☐ 190 Tim Wallach	.07	.03	.01
☐ 191 Tim Belcher	.10	.05	.01
☐ 192 Walt Weiss	.07	.03	.01
☐ 193 Kurt Stillwell	.07	.03	.01
☐ 194 Charlie Hayes	.07	.03	.01
☐ 195 Willie Randolph	.10	.05	.01
☐ 196 Jack McDowell	.10	.05	.01
☐ 197 Jose Offerman	.10	.05	.01
☐ 198 Chuck Finley	.07	.03	.01
☐ 199 Darrin Jackson	.07	.03	.01
☐ 200 Kelly Gruber	.10	.05	.01
☐ 201 John Wetteland	.07	.03	.01
☐ 202 Jay Buhner	.10	.05	.01
☐ 203 Mike LaValliere	.07	.03	.01
☐ 204 Kevin Brown	.10	.05	.01
☐ 205 Luis Gonzalez	.10	.05	.01
☐ 206 Rick Aguilera	.07	.03	.01
☐ 207 Norm Charlton	.10	.05	.01
☐ 208 Mike Bordick	.10	.05	.01
☐ 209 Charlie Leibrandt	.07	.03	.01
☐ 210 Tom Brunansky	.10	.05	.01
☐ 211 Tom Henke	.10	.05	.01
☐ 212 Randy Milligan	.07	.03	.01
☐ 213 Ramon Martinez	.10	.05	.01
☐ 214 Mo Vaughn	.10	.05	.01
☐ 215 Randy Myers	.10	.05	.01
☐ 216 Greg Hibbard	.07	.03	.01
☐ 217 Wes Chamberlain	.07	.03	.01
☐ 218 Tony Phillips	.07	.03	.01
☐ 219 Pete Harnisch	.07	.03	.01
☐ 220 Mike Gallego	.07	.03	.01
☐ 221 Bud Black	.07	.03	.01
☐ 222 Greg Vaughn	.10	.05	.01
☐ 223 Milt Thompson	.07	.03	.01
☐ 224 Ben McDonald	.10	.05	.01
☐ 225 Billy Hatcher	.07	.03	.01
☐ 226 Paul Sorrento	.07	.03	.01
☐ 227 Mark Gubicza	.07	.03	.01
☐ 228 Mike Greenwell	.10	.05	.01
☐ 229 Curt Schilling	.07	.03	.01
☐ 230 Alan Trammell	.10	.05	.01
☐ 231 Zane Smith	.07	.03	.01
☐ 232 Bobby Thigpen	.07	.03	.01
☐ 233 Greg Olson	.07	.03	.01
☐ 234 Joe Orsulak	.07	.03	.01
☐ 235 Joe Oliver	.07	.03	.01
☐ 236 Tim Raines	.10	.05	.01
☐ 237 Juan Samuel	.07	.03	.01
☐ 238 Chili Davis	.10	.05	.01
☐ 239 Spike Owen	.07	.03	.01
☐ 240 Dave Stewart	.10	.05	.01
☐ 241 Jim Eisenreich	.07	.03	.01
☐ 242 Phil Plantier	.10	.05	.01
☐ 243 Sid Fernandez	.10	.05	.01
☐ 244 Dan Gladden	.07	.03	.01
☐ 245 Mickey Morandini	.07	.03	.01
☐ 246 Tino Martinez	.10	.05	.01
☐ 247 Kirt Manwaring	.07	.03	.01
☐ 248 Dean Palmer	.12	.05	.02
☐ 249 Tom Browning	.07	.03	.01
☐ 250 Brian McRae	.07	.03	.01
☐ 251 Scott Leius	.07	.03	.01
☐ 252 Bert Blyleven	.10	.05	.01
☐ 253 Scott Erickson	.10	.05	.01
☐ 254 Bob Welch	.07	.03	.01
☐ 255 Pat Kelly	.10	.05	.01
☐ 256 Felix Fermin	.07	.03	.01
☐ 257 Harold Baines	.10	.05	.01
☐ 258 Duane Ward	.07	.03	.01
☐ 259 Bill Spiers	.07	.03	.01
☐ 260 Jaime Navarro	.10	.05	.01
☐ 261 Scott Sanderson	.07	.03	.01
☐ 262 Gary Gaetti	.07	.03	.01
☐ 263 Bob Ojeda	.07	.03	.01
☐ 264 Jeff Montgomery	.07	.03	.01
☐ 265 Scott Bankhead	.07	.03	.01
☐ 266 Lance Johnson	.07	.03	.01
☐ 267 Rafael Belliard	.07	.03	.01
☐ 268 Kevin Reimer	.07	.03	.01
☐ 269 Benito Santiago	.10	.05	.01
☐ 270 Mike Moore	.07	.03	.01
☐ 271 Dave Fleming	.30	.14	.04
☐ 272 Moises Alou	.10	.05	.01
☐ 273 Pat Listach	.60	.25	.08
☐ 274 Reggie Sanders	.20	.09	.03
☐ 275 Kenny Lofton	.30	.14	.04
☐ 276 Donovan Osborne	.20	.09	.03
☐ 277 Rusty Meacham	.07	.03	.01
☐ 278 Eric Karros	.50	.23	.06
☐ 279 Andy Stankiewicz	.07	.03	.01
☐ 280 Brian Jordan	.15	.07	.02
☐ 281 Gary DiSarcina	.07	.03	.01
☐ 282 Mark Wohlers	.10	.05	.01
☐ 283 Dave Nilsson	.10	.05	.01
☐ 284 Anthony Young	.10	.05	.01
☐ 285 Jim Bullinger	.07	.03	.01
☐ 286 Derek Bell	.10	.05	.01
☐ 287 Brian Williams	.12	.05	.02
☐ 288 Julio Valera	.07	.03	.01
☐ 289 Dan Walters	.10	.05	.01
☐ 290 Chad Curtis	.15	.07	.02
☐ 291 Michael Tucker DP	1.00	.45	.13
☐ 292 Bob Zupcic	.10	.05	.01
☐ 293 Todd Hundley	.07	.03	.01
☐ 294 Jeff Tackett	.07	.03	.01
☐ 295 Greg Colbrunn	.10	.05	.01
☐ 296 Cal Eldred	.30	.14	.04
☐ 297 Chris Roberts DP	.40	.18	.05
☐ 298 John Doherty	.07	.03	.01
☐ 299 Denny Neagle	.07	.03	.01
☐ 300 Arthur Rhodes	.10	.05	.01
☐ 301 Mark Clark	.07	.03	.01
☐ 302 Scott Cooper	.10	.05	.01
☐ 303 Jamie Arnold DP	.30	.14	.04
☐ 304 Jim Thome	.10	.05	.01
☐ 305 Frank Seminara	.07	.03	.01
☐ 306 Kurt Knudsen	.07	.03	.01
☐ 307 Tim Wakefield	.90	.40	.11
☐ 308 John Jaha	.15	.07	.02
☐ 309 Pat Hentgen	.07	.03	.01
☐ 310 B.J. Wallace DP	.60	.25	.08
☐ 311 Roberto Hernandez	.10	.05	.01
☐ 312 Hipolito Pichardo	.07	.03	.01
☐ 313 Eric Fox	.07	.03	.01
☐ 314 Willie Banks	.10	.05	.01
☐ 315 Sam Militello	.25	.11	.03
☐ 316 Vince Horsman	.07	.03	.01
☐ 317 Carlos Hernandez	.07	.03	.01
☐ 318 Jeff Kent	.10	.05	.01
☐ 319 Mike Perez	.07	.03	.01
☐ 320 Scott Livingstone	.07	.03	.01
☐ 321 Jeff Conine	.10	.05	.01
☐ 322 James Austin	.07	.03	.01
☐ 323 John Vander Wal	.07	.03	.01
☐ 324 Pat Mahomes	.12	.05	.02
☐ 325 Pedro Astacio	.25	.11	.03
☐ 326 Bret Boone	.40	.18	.05
☐ 327 Matt Stairs	.07	.03	.01
☐ 328 Damion Easley	.20	.09	.03
☐ 329 Ben Rivera	.10	.05	.01
☐ 330 Reggie Jefferson	.10	.05	.01
☐ 331 Luis Mercedes	.10	.05	.01
☐ 332 Kyle Abbott	.07	.03	.01
☐ 333 Eddie Taubensee	.07	.03	.01
☐ 334 Tim McIntosh	.07	.03	.01
☐ 335 Phil Clark	.07	.03	.01
☐ 336 Wilfredo Cordero	.15	.07	.02
☐ 337 Russ Springer	.15	.07	.02
☐ 338 Craig Colbert	.07	.03	.01
☐ 339 Tim Salmon	.40	.18	.05
☐ 340 Braulio Castillo	.10	.05	.01
☐ 341 Donald Harris	.07	.03	.01
☐ 342 Eric Young	.20	.09	.03
☐ 343 Bob Wickman	.25	.11	.03
☐ 344 John Valentin	.15	.07	.02
☐ 345 Dan Wilson	.07	.03	.01
☐ 346 Steve Hosey	.20	.09	.03
☐ 347 Mike Piazza	.40	.18	.05
☐ 348 Willie Greene	.25	.11	.03
☐ 349 Tom Goodwin	.07	.03	.01
☐ 350 Eric Hillman	.15	.07	.02
☐ 351 Steve Reed	.15	.07	.02
☐ 352 Dan Serafini DP	.40	.18	.05
☐ 353 Todd Steverson DP	.30	.14	.04
☐ 354 Benji Grigsby DP	.30	.14	.04
☐ 355 Shannon Stewart DP	.40	.18	.05
☐ 356 Sean Lowe DP	.35	.16	.04
☐ 357 Derek Wallace DP	.35	.16	.04
☐ 358 Rick Helling DP	.15	.07	.02
☐ 359 Jason Kendall DP	.35	.16	.04
☐ 360 Derek Jeter DP	.50	.23	.06
☐ 361 David Cone	.10	.05	.01
☐ 362 Jeff Reardon	.10	.05	.01
☐ 363 Bobby Witt	.07	.03	.01
☐ 364 Jose Canseco	.35	.16	.04
☐ 365 Jeff Russell	.07	.03	.01
☐ 366 Ruben Sierra	.20	.09	.03
☐ 367 Alan Mills	.07	.03	.01
☐ 368 Matt Nokes	.07	.03	.01
☐ 369 Pat Borders	.07	.03	.01
☐ 370 Pedro Munoz	.10	.05	.01
☐ 371 Danny Jackson	.07	.03	.01
☐ 372 Geronimo Pena	.07	.03	.01
☐ 373 Craig Lefferts	.07	.03	.01

☐ 374 Joe Grahe	.07	.03	.01
☐ 375 Roger McDowell	.07	.03	.01
☐ 376 Jimmy Key	.07	.03	.01
☐ 377 Steve Olin	.07	.03	.01
☐ 378 Glenn Davis	.10	.05	.01
☐ 379 Rene Gonzales	.07	.03	.01
☐ 380 Manuel Lee	.07	.03	.01
☐ 381 Ron Karkovice	.07	.03	.01
☐ 382 Sid Bream	.07	.03	.01
☐ 383 Gerald Williams	.12	.05	.02
☐ 384 Lenny Harris	.07	.03	.01
☐ 385 J.T. Snow	.75	.35	.09
☐ 386 Dave Stieb	.07	.03	.01
☐ 387 Kirk McCaskill	.07	.03	.01
☐ 388 Lance Parrish	.10	.05	.01
☐ 389 Craig Grebeck	.07	.03	.01
☐ 390 Rick Wilkins	.07	.03	.01
☐ 391 Manny Alexander	.15	.07	.02
☐ 392 Mike Schooler	.07	.03	.01
☐ 393 Bernie Williams	.10	.05	.01
☐ 394 Kevin Koslofski	.07	.03	.01
☐ 395 Willie Wilson	.07	.03	.01
☐ 396 Jeff Parrett	.07	.03	.01
☐ 397 Mike Harkey	.10	.05	.01
☐ 398 Frank Tanana	.07	.03	.01
☐ 399 Doug Henry	.07	.03	.01
☐ 400 Royce Clayton	.15	.07	.02
☐ 401 Eric Wedge	.50	.23	.06
☐ 402 Derrick May	.10	.05	.01
☐ 403 Carlos Garcia	.10	.05	.01
☐ 404 Henry Rodriguez	.10	.05	.01
☐ 405 Ryan Klesko	.40	.18	.05

1993 Score Select Aces

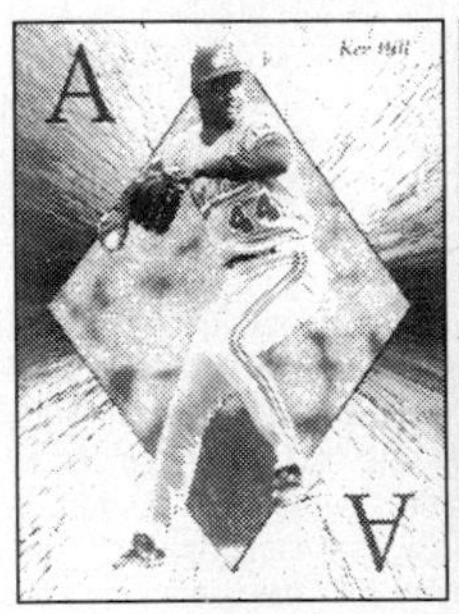

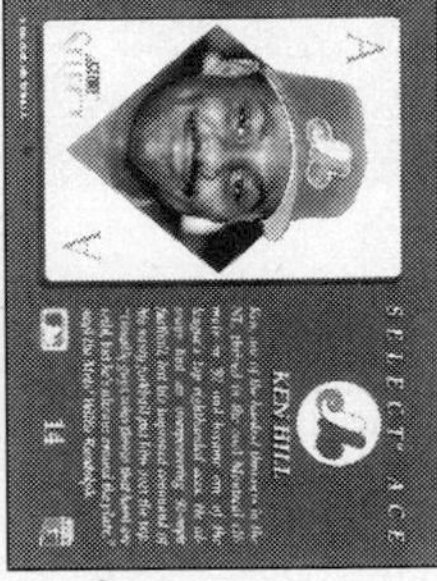

This 24-card set of the top starting pitchers in both leagues was randomly inserted in 1993 Score Select 28-card super packs. According to Score, the chances of finding an Ace card are not less than one in eight packs. The fronts display an action player pose cut out and superimposed on a metallic variegated red and silver diamond design. The diamond itself rests on a background consisting of silver metallic streaks that emanate from the center of the card. In imitation of playing card design, the fronts have a large "A" for Ace in upper left and lower right corners. The player's name in the upper right corner rounds out the card face. On a red background, the horizontal backs have a white "Ace" playing card with a color head shot emanating from a diamond, team logo, and player profile. The cards are numbered on the back.

	MT	EX-MT	VG
COMPLETE SET (24)	80.00	36.00	10.00
COMMON PLAYER (1-24)	3.00	1.35	.40
☐ 1 Roger Clemens	9.00	4.00	1.15
☐ 2 Tom Glavine	5.00	2.30	.60
☐ 3 Jack McDowell	4.00	1.80	.50
☐ 4 Greg Maddux	5.00	2.30	.60
☐ 5 Jack Morris	4.00	1.80	.50
☐ 6 Dennis Martinez	3.00	1.35	.40
☐ 7 Kevin Brown	3.50	1.55	.45
☐ 8 Dwight Gooden	3.50	1.55	.45
☐ 9 Kevin Appier	3.50	1.55	.45
☐ 10 Mike Morgan	3.00	1.35	.40
☐ 11 Juan Guzman	10.00	4.50	1.25
☐ 12 Charles Nagy	4.00	1.80	.50
☐ 13 John Smiley	3.00	1.35	.40
☐ 14 Ken Hill	3.00	1.35	.40
☐ 15 Bob Tewksbury	3.00	1.35	.40
☐ 16 Doug Drabek	3.50	1.55	.45
☐ 17 John Smoltz	4.00	1.80	.50
☐ 18 Greg Swindell	3.50	1.55	.45
☐ 19 Bruce Hurst	3.00	1.35	.40
☐ 20 Mike Mussina	10.00	4.50	1.25
☐ 21 Cal Eldred	7.00	3.10	.85
☐ 22 Melido Perez	3.00	1.35	.40
☐ 23 Dave Fleming	7.00	3.10	.85
☐ 24 Kevin Tapani	3.00	1.35	.40

1993 Score Select Chase Rookies

This 21-card set showcases rookies. The cards were randomly inserted in hobby packs only with at least two cards per box of 36 15-card packs. The fronts exhibit Score's "dufex" printing process, in which a color photo is printed on a metallic base creating an unusual, three-dimensional look. The pictures are tilted slightly to the left and edged on the left and bottom by red metallic borders. On a two-toned red background, the backs present a color headshot in a triangular design and player profile. The cards are numbered on the back at the bottom center.

	MT	EX-MT	VG
COMPLETE SET (21)	90.00	40.00	11.50
COMMON PLAYER (1-21)	3.00	1.35	.40
☐ 1 Pat Listach	10.00	4.50	1.25
☐ 2 Moises Alou	3.50	1.55	.45
☐ 3 Reggie Sanders	7.00	3.10	.85
☐ 4 Kenny Lofton	8.00	3.60	1.00
☐ 5 Eric Karros	10.00	4.50	1.25
☐ 6 Brian Williams	5.00	2.30	.60
☐ 7 Donovan Osborne	6.00	2.70	.75
☐ 8 Sam Militello	6.00	2.70	.75
☐ 9 Chad Curtis	4.00	1.80	.50
☐ 10 Bob Zupcic	4.00	1.80	.50
☐ 11 Tim Salmon	7.00	3.10	.85
☐ 12 Jeff Conine	3.50	1.55	.45
☐ 13 Pedro Astacio	5.00	2.30	.60
☐ 14 Arthur Rhodes	4.00	1.80	.50
☐ 15 Cal Eldred	7.00	3.10	.85
☐ 16 Tim Wakefield	10.00	4.50	1.25
☐ 17 Andy Stankiewicz	3.00	1.35	.40
☐ 18 Wilfredo Cordero	4.00	1.80	.50
☐ 19 Todd Hundley	3.00	1.35	.40
☐ 20 Dave Fleming	7.00	3.10	.85
☐ 21 Bret Boone	7.00	3.10	.85

1993 Score Select Chase Stars

This 24-card set showcases the top players in Major League Baseball. The cards were randomly inserted in retail packs only with at least two cards per box of 36 15-card packs.

The fronts exhibit Score's "dufex" printing process, in which a color photo is printed on a metallic base creating an unusual, three-dimensional look. The pictures are tilted slightly to the left and edged on the left and bottom by green metallic borders. On a two-toned green background, the backs present a color headshot in a triangular design and player profile. The cards are numbered on the back at the bottom center.

	MT	EX-MT	VG
COMPLETE SET (24)	100.00	45.00	12.50
COMMON PLAYER (1-24)	3.00	1.35	.40
☐ 1 Fred McGriff	6.00	2.70	.75
☐ 2 Ryne Sandberg	8.00	3.60	1.00
☐ 3 Ozzie Smith	4.50	2.00	.55
☐ 4 Gary Sheffield	6.00	2.70	.75
☐ 5 Darren Daulton	3.00	1.35	.40
☐ 6 Andy Van Slyke	3.50	1.55	.45
☐ 7 Barry Bonds	7.00	3.10	.85
☐ 8 Tony Gwynn	6.00	2.70	.75
☐ 9 Greg Maddux	5.00	2.30	.60
☐ 10 Tom Glavine	5.00	2.30	.60
☐ 11 John Franco	3.00	1.35	.40
☐ 12 Lee Smith	3.50	1.55	.45
☐ 13 Cecil Fielder	6.00	2.70	.75
☐ 14 Roberto Alomar	8.00	3.60	1.00
☐ 15 Cal Ripken	9.00	4.00	1.15
☐ 16 Edgar Martinez	3.50	1.55	.45
☐ 17 Ivan Rodriguez	8.00	3.60	1.00
☐ 18 Kirby Puckett	7.00	3.10	.85
☐ 19 Ken Griffey Jr.	10.00	4.50	1.25
☐ 20 Joe Carter	6.00	2.70	.75
☐ 21 Roger Clemens	8.00	3.60	1.00
☐ 22 Dave Fleming	7.00	3.10	.85
☐ 23 Paul Molitor	3.50	1.55	.45
☐ 24 Dennis Eckersley	3.50	1.55	.45

1993 Score Select Triple Crown

Honoring Triple Crown winners, this 3-card set was randomly inserted in hobby packs only with at least two cards per box of 36 15-card packs. The fronts exhibit Score's "dufex" printing process, in which a color photo is printed on a metallic base creating an unusual, three-dimensional look. The color player photos on the fronts have a forest green metallic border. The player's name and the year he won the Triple Crown appear above the picture, while the words "Triple Crown" are written in script beneath it. On a forest green background, the backs carry a black and white close-up photo of the player wearing a crown and a summary of the player's award winning performance. The cards are numbered on the back "X of 3" at the lower right corner.

	MT	EX-MT	VG
COMPLETE SET (3)	25.00	11.50	3.10
COMMON PLAYER (1-3)	6.50	2.90	.80
☐ 1 Mickey Mantle	15.00	6.75	1.90
☐ 2 Carl Yastrzemski	6.50	2.90	.80
☐ 3 Frank Robinson	6.50	2.90	.80

1992 Sentry Robin Yount

Robin Yount
First Hit
April 12, 1974

Robin Yount opens his major league career hitless in his first 10 at bats before his first souvenir baseball makes it to the trophy case. Milwaukee opens a 3-game series with the Baltimore Orioles at County Stadium. Dave McNally, who would go on to lead the Birds to the American League East pennant with a 16-10 record, is on the mound when Robin Yount strolls to the plate in the fourth. Yount bounces a single up the middle for his first big league hit. He also scores his first run in the Brewers 5-3 loss.

Sentry FOODS

Sponsored by Sentry Foods, this four-card standard-size (2 1/2" by 3 1/2") captures four moments in the career of Robin Yount, who reached 3,000 career hits during the 1992 season. On a purple marbleized card face, the fronts display color action player photos framed by gold foil borders. A baseball glove icon and the player's name appear in the bottom border. The backs carry text describing Yount's hitting achievement portrayed on the card. The sponsor logo at the bottom rounds out the back. The cards are unnumbered and checklisted below in chronological order.

	MT	EX-MT	VG
COMPLETE SET (4)	20.00	9.00	2.50
COMMON PLAYER (1-4)	6.00	2.70	.75
☐ 1 Robin Yount First Hit (4/12/74)	6.00	2.70	.75
☐ 2 Robin Yount 1,000 (8/16/80)	6.00	2.70	.75
☐ 3 Robin Yount 2,000 (9/6/86)	6.00	2.70	.75
☐ 4 Robin Yount 3,000 (9/9/92)	6.00	2.70	.75

1961 7-Eleven

The 1961 7-Eleven set consists of 29 cards, each measuring 2 7/16" by 3 3/8". The checklist card states that this is the first series, and that a new series was to be released every two weeks (though apparently no other series were issued). The cards are printed on pink cardboard stock and the backs are blank. The fronts have a black and white headshot in the upper left portion and brief biographical information to the right of the picture. The player's name appears across the top of each front. The remainder of the front carries "1960

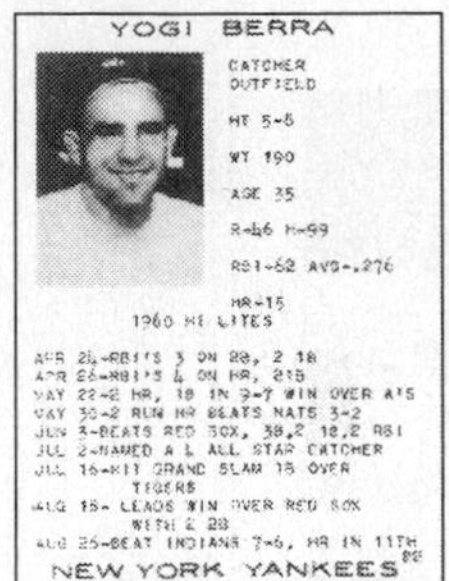

Hi Lites," which consist of a list of dates and the player's achievements on those dates. The team name across the bottom of the card rounds out the front. The cards are numbered on the front in the lower right corner.

	NRMT	VG-E	GOOD
COMPLETE SET (29)	300.00	135.00	38.00
COMMON PLAYER (1-29)	5.00	2.30	.60
☐ 1 Dave Sisler	5.00	2.30	.60
☐ 2 Don Mossi	6.00	2.70	.75
☐ 3 Joey Jay	5.00	2.30	.60
☐ 4 Bob Purkey	5.00	2.30	.60
☐ 5 Jack Fisher	5.00	2.30	.60
☐ 6 John Romano	5.00	2.30	.60
☐ 7 Russ Snyder	5.00	2.30	.60
☐ 8 Johnny Temple	5.00	2.30	.60
☐ 9 Roy Sievers	6.00	2.70	.75
☐ 10 Ron Hansen	5.00	2.30	.60
☐ 11 Pete Runnels	6.00	2.70	.75
☐ 12 Gene Woodling	6.00	2.70	.75
☐ 13 Clint Courtney	5.00	2.30	.60
☐ 14 Whitey Herzog	7.50	3.40	.95
☐ 15 Warren Spahn	25.00	11.50	3.10
☐ 16 Stan Musial	50.00	23.00	6.25
☐ 17 Willie Mays	60.00	27.00	7.50
☐ 18 Ken Boyer	10.00	4.50	1.25
☐ 19 Joe Cunningham	6.00	2.70	.75
☐ 20 Orlando Cepeda	10.00	4.50	1.25
☐ 21 Gil Hodges	15.00	6.75	1.90
☐ 22 Yogi Berra	35.00	16.00	4.40
☐ 23 Ernie Banks	35.00	16.00	4.40
☐ 24 Lou Burdette	7.50	3.40	.95
☐ 25 Roger Maris	45.00	20.00	5.75
☐ 26 Charlie Smith	5.00	2.30	.60
☐ 27 Jimmie Foxx	10.00	4.50	1.25
☐ 28 Mel Ott	10.00	4.50	1.25
☐ 29 Don Nottebart	5.00	2.30	.60

1991 SilverStar Holograms

These hologram cards measure the standard size (2 1/2" by 3 1/2") and were issued to commemorate outstanding achievements of the players. The backs of the hologram cards are brightly colored and have statistics as well as a player profile. Each card also comes with a 2 1/16" by 5 3/8" blank-backed ticket. The tickets have a color player photo, serial number, and a description of the achievement honored. The Henderson hologram honors him as the all-time stolen base leader; the Ryan hologram celebrates his 7th no-hitter; and the Justice hologram commemorates his two-run homer against the Reds on October 1 that led to a 7-6 Braves' victory during the NL West pennant race. The cards are unnumbered and checklisted below chronologically by release dates.

	MT	EX-MT	VG
COMPLETE SET (4)	15.00	6.75	1.90
COMMON PLAYER (1-4)	5.00	2.30	.60
☐ 1 Rickey Henderson (On May 1, 1991, Rickey broke Lou Brock's all-time ...)	4.00	1.80	.50
☐ 2 Nolan Ryan (The Express walked off ... May 1, 1991 with his 7th no-hitter)	5.00	2.30	.60
☐ 3 Dave Justice (On October 1, 1991, ... Justice crushed a two-run homer ...)	4.00	1.80	.50
☐ 4 Cal Ripken (September, 1991: Cal went on a rampage and was named AL POM ...)	5.00	2.30	.60

1984 Smokey Angels

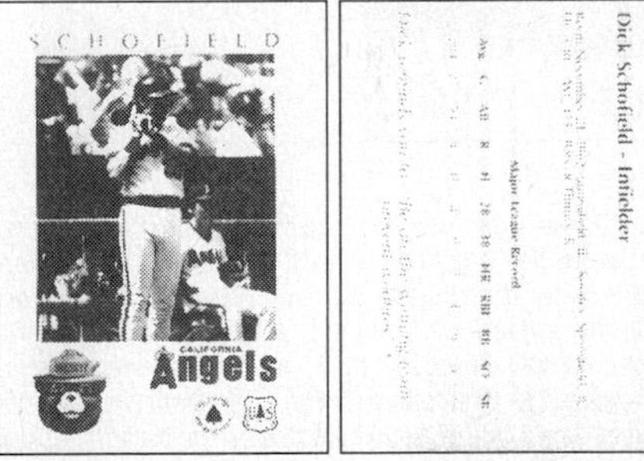

The cards in this 32-card set measure approximately 2 1/2" by 3 3/4" and feature the California Angels in full color. Sets were given out to persons 15 and under attending the June 16th game against the Indians. Unlike the Padres set of this year, Smokey the Bear is not featured on these cards. The player's photo, the Angels' logo, and the Smokey the Bear logo appear on the front, in addition to the California Department of Forestry and the U.S. Forest Service logos. The abbreviated backs contain short biographical data, career statistics, and an anti-wildfire hint from the player on the front. Since the cards are unnumbered, they are ordered and numbered below alphabetically by the player's name.

	NRMT-MT	EXC	G-VG
COMPLETE SET (32)	9.00	4.00	1.15
COMMON PLAYER (1-32)	.25	.11	.03
☐ 1 Don Aase	.25	.11	.03

☐ 2 Juan Beniquez	.25	.11	.03
☐ 3 Bob Boone	.50	.23	.06
☐ 4 Rick Burleson	.35	.16	.04
☐ 5 Rod Carew	1.50	.65	.19
☐ 6 John Curtis	.25	.11	.03
☐ 7 Doug DeCinces	.50	.23	.06
☐ 8 Brian Downing	.35	.16	.04
☐ 9 Ken Forsch	.25	.11	.03
☐ 10 Bobby Grich	.50	.23	.06
☐ 11 Reggie Jackson	2.00	.90	.25
☐ 12 Ron Jackson	.25	.11	.03
☐ 13 Tommy John	.60	.25	.08
☐ 14 Curt Kaufman	.25	.11	.03
☐ 15 Bruce Kison	.25	.11	.03
☐ 16 Frank LaCorte	.25	.11	.03
☐ 17 Logo Card (Forestry Dept.)	.25	.11	.03
☐ 18 Fred Lynn	.35	.16	.04
☐ 19 John McNamara MG	.25	.11	.03
☐ 20 Jerry Narron	.25	.11	.03
☐ 21 Gary Pettis	.50	.23	.06
☐ 22 Rob Picciolo	.25	.11	.03
☐ 23 Ron Romanick	.25	.11	.03
☐ 24 Luis Sanchez	.25	.11	.03
☐ 25 Dick Schofield	.35	.16	.04
☐ 26 Daryl Sconiers	.25	.11	.03
☐ 27 Jim Slaton	.25	.11	.03
☐ 28 Smokey the Bear	.25	.11	.03
☐ 29 Ellis Valentine	.25	.11	.03
☐ 30 Rob Wilfong	.25	.11	.03
☐ 31 Mike Witt	.35	.16	.04
☐ 32 Geoff Zahn	.25	.11	.03

1984 Smokey Dodgers

This four-card set was not widely distributed and has not proven to be very popular with collectors. Cards were supposedly distributed by fire agencies in Southern California at fairs, mall displays, and special events. Cards measure approximately 5" by 7" and feature a color picture of Smokey the Bear with a Dodger. The cards were printed on relatively thin card stock; printing on the back is black on white.

	NRMT-MT	EXC	G-VG
COMPLETE SET (4)	15.00	6.75	1.90
COMMON PLAYER (1-4)	2.50	1.15	.30
☐ 1 Ken Landreaux with Smokey	3.50	1.55	.45
☐ 2 Tom Niedenfuer with Smokey	3.50	1.55	.45
☐ 3 Steve Sax with Smokey	8.50	3.80	1.05
☐ 4 Smokey the Bear (Batting pose)	2.50	1.15	.30

1984 Smokey Padres

The cards in this 29-card set measure 2 1/2" by 3 3/4". This unnumbered, full color set features the Fire Prevention Bear

and a Padres player, coach, manager, or associate on each card. The set was given out at the ballpark at the May 14th game against the Expos. Logos of the California Department of Forestry and the U.S. Forest Service appear in conjunction with a Smokey the Bear logo on the obverse. The set commemorates the 40th birthday of Smokey the Bear. The backs contain short biographical data, statistics and a fire prevention hint from the player pictured on the front.

	NRMT-MT	EXC	G-VG
COMPLETE SET (29)	11.00	4.90	1.40
COMMON PLAYER (1-29)	.30	.14	.04
☐ 1 Kurt Bevacqua	.30	.14	.04
☐ 2 Bobby Brown	.30	.14	.04
☐ 3 Dave Campbell ANN	.30	.14	.04
☐ 4 The Chicken (Mascot)	.75	.35	.09
☐ 5 Jerry Coleman ANN	.40	.18	.05
☐ 6 Luis DeLeon	.30	.14	.04
☐ 7 Dave Dravecky	1.00	.45	.13
☐ 8 Harry Dunlop CO	.30	.14	.04
☐ 9 Tim Flannery	.30	.14	.04
☐ 10 Steve Garvey	1.00	.45	.13
☐ 11 Doug Gwosdz	.30	.14	.04
☐ 12 Tony Gwynn	2.50	1.15	.30
☐ 13 Doug Harvey UMP	.40	.18	.05
☐ 14 Terry Kennedy	.40	.18	.05
☐ 15 Jack Krol CO	.30	.14	.04
☐ 16 Tim Lollar	.30	.14	.04
☐ 17 Jack McKeon (VP for Baseball Operations)	.50	.23	.06
☐ 18 Kevin McReynolds	1.25	.55	.16
☐ 19 Sid Monge	.30	.14	.04
☐ 20 Luis Salazar	.40	.18	.05
☐ 21 Norm Sherry CO	.30	.14	.04
☐ 22 Eric Show	.40	.18	.05
☐ 23 Smokey the Bear	.30	.14	.04
☐ 24 Garry Templeton	.40	.18	.05
☐ 25 Mark Thurmond	.30	.14	.04
☐ 26 Ozzie Virgil CO	.30	.14	.04
☐ 27 Ed Whitson	.40	.18	.05
☐ 28 Alan Wiggins	.30	.14	.04
☐ 29 Dick Williams MG	.40	.18	.05

1985 Smokey Angels

The cards in this 24-card set measure approximately 4 1/4" by 6" and feature the California Angels in full color. The player's photo, the Angels' logo, and the Smokey the Bear logo appear on the front, in addition to the California Department of Forestry and the U.S. Forest Service logos. The abbreviated backs contain short biographical data and an anti-wildfire hint.

	NRMT-MT	EXC	G-VG
COMPLETE SET (24)	7.00	3.10	.85
COMMON PLAYER (1-24)	.25	.11	.03
☐ 1 Mike Witt	.35	.16	.04
☐ 2 Reggie Jackson	1.50	.65	.19
☐ 3 Bob Boone	.60	.25	.08
☐ 4 Mike Brown	.25	.11	.03

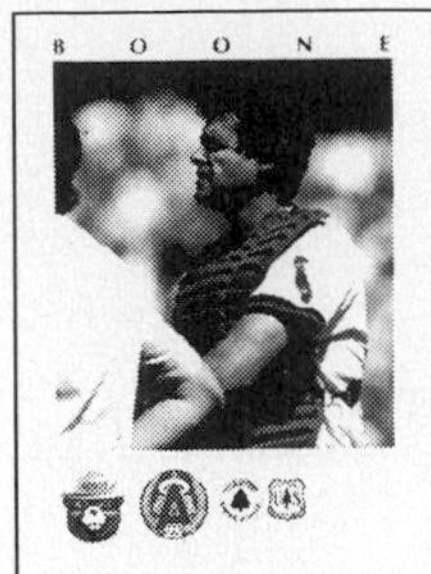

☐ 5 Rod Carew	1.00	.45	.13
☐ 6 Doug DeCinces	.45	.20	.06
☐ 7 Brian Downing	.35	.16	.04
☐ 8 Ken Forsch	.25	.11	.03
☐ 9 Gary Pettis	.35	.16	.04
☐ 10 Jerry Narron	.25	.11	.03
☐ 11 Ron Romanick	.25	.11	.03
☐ 12 Bobby Grich	.45	.20	.06
☐ 13 Dick Schofield	.35	.16	.04
☐ 14 Juan Beniquez	.25	.11	.03
☐ 15 Geoff Zahn	.25	.11	.03
☐ 16 Luis Sanchez	.25	.11	.03
☐ 17 Jim Slaton	.25	.11	.03
☐ 18 Doug Corbett	.25	.11	.03
☐ 19 Ruppert Jones	.25	.11	.03
☐ 20 Rob Wilfong	.25	.11	.03
☐ 21 Donnie Moore	.25	.11	.03
☐ 22 Pat Clements	.25	.11	.03
☐ 23 Tommy John	.60	.25	.08
☐ 24 Gene Mauch MG	.35	.16	.04

1986 Smokey Angels

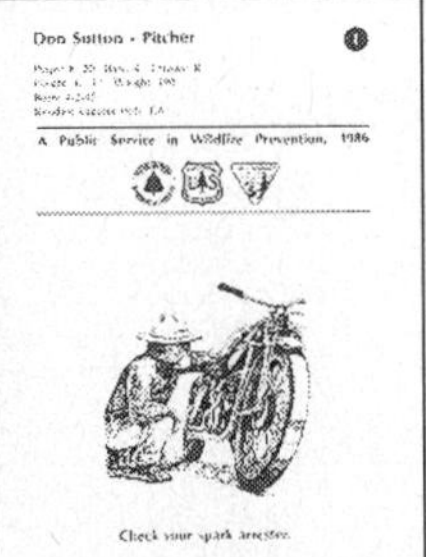

The Forestry Service (in conjunction with the California Angels) produced this large, attractive 24-card set. The cards feature Smokey the Bear pictured in the upper right corner of the card. The card backs give a fire safety tip. The set was given out free at Anaheim Stadium on August 9th. The cards measure approximately 4 1/4" by 6" and are subtitled "Wildfire Prevention" on the front.

	MT	EX-MT	VG
COMPLETE SET (24)	8.00	3.60	1.00
COMMON PLAYER (1-24)	.25	.11	.03
☐ 1 Mike Witt	.35	.16	.04
☐ 2 Reggie Jackson	1.50	.65	.19
☐ 3 Bob Boone	.60	.25	.08
☐ 4 Don Sutton	.75	.35	.09
☐ 5 Kirk McCaskill	.45	.20	.06
☐ 6 Doug DeCinces	.45	.20	.06
☐ 7 Brian Downing	.35	.16	.04
☐ 8 Doug Corbett	.25	.11	.03
☐ 9 Gary Pettis	.35	.16	.04
☐ 10 Jerry Narron	.25	.11	.03
☐ 11 Ron Romanick	.25	.11	.03
☐ 12 Bobby Grich	.45	.20	.06
☐ 13 Dick Schofield	.35	.16	.04
☐ 14 George Hendrick	.35	.16	.04
☐ 15 Rick Burleson	.35	.16	.04
☐ 16 John Candelaria	.35	.16	.04
☐ 17 Jim Slaton	.25	.11	.03
☐ 18 Darrell Miller	.35	.16	.04
☐ 19 Ruppert Jones	.25	.11	.03
☐ 20 Rob Wilfong	.25	.11	.03
☐ 21 Donnie Moore	.25	.11	.03
☐ 22 Wally Joyner	2.00	.90	.25
☐ 23 Terry Forster	.25	.11	.03
☐ 24 Gene Mauch MG	.35	.16	.04

1987 Smokey A's Colorgrams

These cards are actually pages of a booklet featuring members of the Oakland A's and Smokey's fire safety tips. The booklet has 12 pages each containing a black and white photo card (approximately 2 1/2" by 3 3/4") and a black and white player caricature (oversized head) postcard (approximately 3 3/4" by 5 5/8"). The cards are unnumbered but they have biographical information and a fire-prevention cartoon on the back of the card.

	MT	EX-MT	VG
COMPLETE SET (12)	12.00	5.50	1.50
COMMON PLAYER (1-12)	.60	.25	.08
☐ 1 Joaquin Andujar	.75	.35	.09
☐ 2 Jose Canseco	4.50	2.00	.55
☐ 3 Mike Davis	.60	.25	.08
☐ 4 Alfredo Griffin	.60	.25	.08
☐ 5 Moose Haas	.60	.25	.08
☐ 6 Jay Howell	.90	.40	.11
☐ 7 Reggie Jackson	2.00	.90	.25
☐ 8 Carney Lansford	1.00	.45	.13
☐ 9 Dwayne Murphy	.60	.25	.08
☐ 10 Tony Phillips	.90	.40	.11
☐ 11 Dave Stewart	1.25	.55	.16
☐ 12 Curt Young	.60	.25	.08

1987 Smokey American League

The U.S. Forestry Service (in conjunction with Major League Baseball) produced this large, attractive 14-player card set to commemorate the 43rd birthday of Smokey. The cards feature Smokey the Bear pictured on every card with the player. The card backs give a fire safety tip. The cards measure approximately 4" by 6" and are subtitled "National Smokey Bear Day 1987" on the front. The cards were printed on an uncut (but perforated) sheet that measured 18" by 24".

	MT	EX-MT	VG
COMPLETE SET (16)	7.00	3.10	.85
COMMON PLAYER (1-16)	.30	.14	.04
☐ 1 Jose Canseco	2.00	.90	.25
☐ 2 Dennis Oil Can Boyd	.30	.14	.04

☐ 3 John Candelaria	.30	.14	.04
☐ 4 Harold Baines	.40	.18	.05
☐ 5 Joe Carter	1.00	.45	.13
☐ 6 Jack Morris	.60	.25	.08
☐ 7 Buddy Biancalana	.30	.14	.04
☐ 8 Kirby Puckett	2.00	.90	.25
☐ 9 Mike Pagliarulo	.40	.18	.05
☐ 10 Larry Sheets	.30	.14	.04
☐ 11 Mike Moore	.40	.18	.05
☐ 12 Charlie Hough	.40	.18	.05
☐ 13 National Smokey Bear Day 1987	.30	.14	.04
☐ 14 Tom Henke	.40	.18	.05
☐ 15 Jim Gantner	.30	.14	.04
☐ 16 American League Smokey Bear Day 1987	.30	.14	.04

1987 Smokey Angels

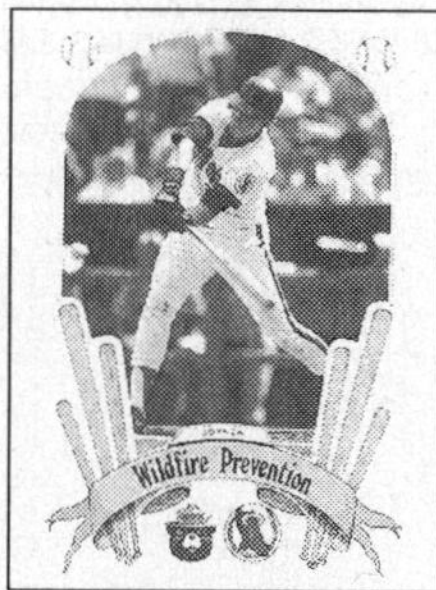

The U.S. Forestry Service (in conjunction with the California Angels) produced this large, attractive 24-card set to commemorate the 43rd birthday of Smokey. The cards feature Smokey the Bear pictured at the bottom of every card. The card backs give a cartoon fire safety tip. The cards measure approximately 4" by 6" and are subtitled "Wildfire Prevention" on the front.

	MT	EX-MT	VG
COMPLETE SET (24)	8.00	3.60	1.00
COMMON PLAYER (1-24)	.30	.14	.04
☐ 1 John Candelaria	.40	.18	.05
☐ 2 Don Sutton	.75	.35	.09
☐ 3 Mike Witt	.40	.18	.05
☐ 4 Gary Lucas	.30	.14	.04
☐ 5 Kirk McCaskill	.40	.18	.05
☐ 6 Chuck Finley	.75	.35	.09
☐ 7 Willie Fraser	.30	.14	.04
☐ 8 Donnie Moore	.30	.14	.04
☐ 9 Urbano Lugo	.30	.14	.04
☐ 10 Butch Wynegar	.30	.14	.04
☐ 11 Darrell Miller	.30	.14	.04
☐ 12 Wally Joyner	1.00	.45	.13
☐ 13 Mark McLemore	.40	.18	.05
☐ 14 Mark Ryal	.30	.14	.04
☐ 15 Dick Schofield	.40	.18	.05
☐ 16 Jack Howell	.40	.18	.05

☐ 17 Doug DeCinces	.50	.23	.06
☐ 18 Gus Polidor	.30	.14	.04
☐ 19 Brian Downing	.40	.18	.05
☐ 20 Gary Pettis	.40	.18	.05
☐ 21 Ruppert Jones	.30	.14	.04
☐ 22 George Hendrick	.40	.18	.05
☐ 23 Devon White	1.00	.45	.13
☐ 24 Checklist Card	.40	.18	.05

1987 Smokey Braves

The U.S. Forestry Service (in conjunction with the Atlanta Braves) produced this large, attractive 27-card set to commemorate the 43rd birthday of Smokey. The cards feature Smokey the Bear pictured in the top right corner of every card. The card backs give a cartoon fire safety tip. The cards measure approximately 4" by 6" and are subtitled "Wildfire Prevention" on the front. Distribution of the cards was gradual at the stadium throughout the summer. These large cards are numbered on the back.

	MT	EX-MT	VG
COMPLETE SET (27)	20.00	9.00	2.50
COMMON PLAYER (1-26)	.65	.30	.08
☐ 1 Zane Smith	.90	.40	.11
☐ 2 Charlie Puleo	.65	.30	.08
☐ 3 Randy O'Neal	.65	.30	.08
☐ 4 David Palmer	.65	.30	.08
☐ 5 Rick Mahler	.65	.30	.08
☐ 6 Ed Olwine	.65	.30	.08
☐ 7 Jeff Dedmon	.65	.30	.08
☐ 8 Paul Assenmacher	.90	.40	.11
☐ 9 Gene Garber	.75	.35	.09
☐ 10 Jim Acker	.65	.30	.08
☐ 11 Bruce Benedict	.65	.30	.08
☐ 12 Ozzie Virgil	.65	.30	.08
☐ 13 Ted Simmons	1.25	.55	.16
☐ 14 Dale Murphy	2.50	1.15	.30
☐ 15 Graig Nettles	1.00	.45	.13
☐ 16 Ken Oberkfell	.65	.30	.08
☐ 17 Gerald Perry	.65	.30	.08
☐ 18 Rafael Ramirez	.65	.30	.08
☐ 19 Ken Griffey	1.00	.45	.13
☐ 20 Andres Thomas	.90	.40	.11
☐ 21 Glenn Hubbard	.65	.30	.08
☐ 22 Damaso Garcia	.65	.30	.08
☐ 23 Gary Roenicke	.65	.30	.08
☐ 24 Dion James	.65	.30	.08
☐ 25 Albert Hall	.65	.30	.08
☐ 26 Chuck Tanner MG	.65	.30	.08
☐ NNO Smokey/Checklist	.90	.40	.11

1987 Smokey Cardinals

The U.S. Forestry Service (in conjunction with the St. Louis Cardinals) produced this large, attractive 25-card set to commemorate the 43rd birthday of Smokey. The cards feature Smokey the Bear pictured in the top right corner of every card. The card backs give a cartoon fire safety tip. The

cards measure approximately 4" by 6" and are subtitled "Wildfire Prevention" on the front. Sets were supposedly available from the Cardinals team for 3.50 postpaid. Also a limited number of 8 1/2" by 12" full-color team photos were available from the team to those who sent in a large SASE. The large team photo is not considered part of the complete set.

	MT	EX-MT	VG
COMPLETE SET (25)	12.00	5.50	1.50
COMMON PLAYER (1-25)	.45	.20	.06
☐ 1 Ray Soff	.45	.20	.06
☐ 2 Todd Worrell	.75	.35	.09
☐ 3 John Tudor	.60	.25	.08
☐ 4 Pat Perry	.45	.20	.06
☐ 5 Rick Horton	.45	.20	.06
☐ 6 Danny Cox	.60	.25	.08
☐ 7 Bob Forsch	.45	.20	.06
☐ 8 Greg Mathews	.45	.20	.06
☐ 9 Bill Dawley	.45	.20	.06
☐ 10 Steve Lake	.45	.20	.06
☐ 11 Tony Pena	.60	.25	.08
☐ 12 Tom Pagnozzi	.60	.25	.08
☐ 13 Jack Clark	.75	.35	.09
☐ 14 Jim Lindeman	.45	.20	.06
☐ 15 Mike Laga	.45	.20	.06
☐ 16 Terry Pendleton	1.25	.55	.16
☐ 17 Ozzie Smith	2.00	.90	.25
☐ 18 Jose Oquendo	.60	.25	.08
☐ 19 Tom Lawless	.45	.20	.06
☐ 20 Tom Herr	.60	.25	.08
☐ 21 Curt Ford	.45	.20	.06
☐ 22 Willie McGee	.90	.40	.11
☐ 23 Tito Landrum	.45	.20	.06
☐ 24 Vince Coleman	1.25	.55	.16
☐ 25 Whitey Herzog MG	.75	.35	.09
☐ NNO Team Photo (large)	2.50	1.15	.30

1987 Smokey Dodger All-Stars

This 40-card set was issued by the U.S. Forestry Service to commemorate the Los Angeles Dodgers selected for the All-Star game over the past 25 years. The cards measure approximately 2 1/2" by 3 3/4" and have full-color fronts. The card fronts are distinguished by their thick silver borders and the bats, balls, and stadium design layout. The 25th anniversary logo for Dodger Stadium is in the lower right corner of each card. The set numbering is alphabetical by subject's name.

	MT	EX-MT	VG
COMPLETE SET (40)	13.50	6.00	1.70
COMMON PLAYER (1-40)	.30	.14	.04
☐ 1 Walt Alston MG	.60	.25	.08
☐ 2 Dusty Baker	.50	.23	.06
☐ 3 Jim Brewer	.30	.14	.04
☐ 4 Ron Cey	.50	.23	.06
☐ 5 Tommy Davis	.40	.18	.05
☐ 6 Willie Davis	.40	.18	.05
☐ 7 Don Drysdale	1.00	.45	.13
☐ 8 Steve Garvey	.90	.40	.11
☐ 9 Bill Grabarkewitz	.30	.14	.04
☐ 10 Pedro Guerrero	.50	.23	.06
☐ 11 Tom Haller	.30	.14	.04
☐ 12 Orel Hershiser	.50	.23	.06
☐ 13 Burt Hooton	.30	.14	.04
☐ 14 Steve Howe	.30	.14	.04
☐ 15 Tommy John	.50	.23	.06
☐ 16 Sandy Koufax	1.50	.65	.19
☐ 17 Tom Lasorda MG	.50	.23	.06
☐ 18 Jim Lefebvre	.30	.14	.04
☐ 19 Davey Lopes	.40	.18	.05
☐ 20 Mike G. Marshall P	.40	.18	.05
☐ 21 Mike A. Marshall OF	.40	.18	.05
☐ 22 Andy Messersmith	.40	.18	.05
☐ 23 Rick Monday	.30	.14	.04
☐ 24 Manny Mota	.40	.18	.05
☐ 25 Claude Osteen	.30	.14	.04
☐ 26 Johnny Podres	.40	.18	.05
☐ 27 Phil Regan	.30	.14	.04
☐ 28 Jerry Reuss	.30	.14	.04
☐ 29 Rick Rhoden	.30	.14	.04
☐ 30 John Roseboro	.40	.18	.05
☐ 31 Bill Russell	.40	.18	.05
☐ 32 Steve Sax	.50	.23	.06
☐ 33 Bill Singer	.30	.14	.04
☐ 34 Reggie Smith	.40	.18	.05
☐ 35 Don Sutton	.90	.40	.11
☐ 36 Fernando Valenzuela	.50	.23	.06
☐ 37 Bob Welch	.40	.18	.05
☐ 38 Maury Wills	.60	.25	.08
☐ 39 Jim Wynn	.40	.18	.05
☐ 40 Checklist Card	.40	.18	.05

1987 Smokey National League

The U.S. Forestry Service (in conjunction with Major League Baseball) produced this large, attractive 14 player card set to commemorate the 43rd birthday of Smokey. The cards feature Smokey the Bear pictured on every card with the player. The card backs give a fire safety tip. The cards measure approximately 4" by 6" and are subtitled "National Smokey Bear Day 1987" on the front. The set price below does not include the more difficult variation cards.

	MT	EX-MT	VG
COMPLETE SET (15)	7.00	3.10	.85
COMMON PLAYER (1-15)	.25	.11	.03
☐ 1 Steve Sax	.50	.23	.06

	MT	EX-MT	VG
☐ 2A Dale Murphy (Holding bat)	2.00	.90	.25
☐ 2B Dale Murphy (No bat, arm around Smokey)	12.50	5.75	1.55
☐ 3A Jody Davis (Kneeling with Smokey)	.50	.23	.06
☐ 3B Jody Davis (Standing, shaking Smokey's hand)	7.50	3.40	.95
☐ 4 Bill Gullickson	.35	.16	.04
☐ 5 Mike Scott	.35	.16	.04
☐ 6 Roger McDowell	.35	.16	.04
☐ 7 Steve Bedrosian	.35	.16	.04
☐ 8 Johnny Ray	.25	.11	.03
☐ 9 Ozzie Smith	1.00	.45	.13
☐ 10 Steve Garvey	.75	.35	.09
☐ 11 National Smokey Bear Day	.35	.16	.04
☐ 12 Mike Krukow	.25	.11	.03
☐ 13 Smokey the Bear	.25	.11	.03
☐ 14 Mike Fitzgerald	.25	.11	.03
☐ 15 National League Logo	.25	.11	.03

1987 Smokey Rangers

The U.S. Forestry Service (in conjunction with the Texas Rangers) produced this large, attractive 32-card set. The cards feature Smokey the Bear pictured in the upper-right corner of every player's card. The card backs give a cartoon fire safety tip. The cards measure approximately 4 1/4" by 6" and are subtitled "Wildfire Prevention" on the front. These large cards are numbered on the back. Cards 4 Mike Mason and 14 Tom Paciorek were withdrawn and were never formally released as part of the set and hence are quite scarce.

	MT	EX-MT	VG
COMPLETE SET (32)	80.00	36.00	10.00
COMMON PLAYER (1-32)	.35	.16	.04
☐ 1 Charlie Hough	.60	.25	.08
☐ 2 Greg A. Harris	.35	.16	.04
☐ 3 Jose Guzman	.75	.35	.09
☐ 4 Mike Mason SP	35.00	16.00	4.40
☐ 5 Dale Mohorcic	.35	.16	.04
☐ 6 Bobby Witt	1.00	.45	.13
☐ 7 Mitch Williams	.75	.35	.09
☐ 8 Geno Petralli	.35	.16	.04
☐ 9 Don Slaught	.50	.23	.06
☐ 10 Darrell Porter	.35	.16	.04
☐ 11 Steve Buechele	.60	.25	.08
☐ 12 Pete O'Brien	.50	.23	.06
☐ 13 Scott Fletcher	.35	.16	.04
☐ 14 Tom Paciorek SP	35.00	16.00	4.40
☐ 15 Pete Incaviglia	.90	.40	.11
☐ 16 Oddibe McDowell	.50	.23	.06
☐ 17 Ruben Sierra	4.00	1.80	.50
☐ 18 Larry Parrish	.50	.23	.06
☐ 19 Bobby Valentine MG	.50	.23	.06
☐ 20 Tom House CO	.35	.16	.04
☐ 21 Tom Robson CO	.35	.16	.04
☐ 22 Edwin Correa	.35	.16	.04
☐ 23 Mike Stanley	.35	.16	.04
☐ 24 Joe Ferguson CO	.35	.16	.04
☐ 25 Art Howe CO	.50	.23	.06
☐ 26 Bob Brower	.35	.16	.04
☐ 27 Mike Loynd	.35	.16	.04
☐ 28 Curtis Wilkerson	.35	.16	.04
☐ 29 Tim Foli CO	.35	.16	.04
☐ 30 Dave Oliver CO	.35	.16	.04
☐ 31 Jerry Browne	.50	.23	.06
☐ 32 Jeff Russell	.60	.25	.08

1988 Smokey Angels

The U.S. Forestry Service (in conjunction with the California Angels) produced this attractive 25-card set. The cards feature Smokey the Bear pictured at the bottom of every card. The card backs give a cartoon fire safety tip. The cards measure approximately 2 1/2" by 3 1/2" and are in full color. The cards are numbered on the back. They were distributed during promotions on August 28, September 4, and September 18.

	MT	EX-MT	VG
COMPLETE SET (25)	10.00	4.50	1.25
COMMON PLAYER (1-24)	.35	.16	.04
☐ 1 Cookie Rojas MG	.35	.16	.04
☐ 2 Johnny Ray	.45	.20	.06
☐ 3 Jack Howell	.35	.16	.04
☐ 4 Mike Witt	.35	.16	.04
☐ 5 Tony Armas	.45	.20	.06
☐ 6 Gus Polidor	.35	.16	.04
☐ 7 DeWayne Buice	.35	.16	.04
☐ 8 Dan Petry	.35	.16	.04
☐ 9 Bob Boone	.75	.35	.09
☐ 10 Chili Davis	.60	.25	.08
☐ 11 Greg Minton	.35	.16	.04
☐ 12 Kirk McCaskill	.35	.16	.04
☐ 13 Devon White	.75	.35	.09
☐ 14 Willie Fraser	.35	.16	.04
☐ 15 Chuck Finley	.45	.20	.06
☐ 16 Dick Schofield	.45	.20	.06
☐ 17 Wally Joyner	.90	.40	.11
☐ 18 Brian Downing	.45	.20	.06
☐ 19 Stewart Cliburn	.35	.16	.04
☐ 20 Donnie Moore	.35	.16	.04
☐ 21 Bryan Harvey	.90	.40	.11
☐ 22 Mark McLemore	.45	.20	.06
☐ 23 Butch Wynegar	.35	.16	.04
☐ 24 George Hendrick	.45	.20	.06
☐ NNO Checklist/Logo Card	.45	.20	.06

1988 Smokey Cardinals

The U.S. Forestry Service (in conjunction with the St. Louis Cardinals) produced this attractive 25-card set. The cards feature Smokey the Bear pictured in the lower right corner of every card. The card backs give a cartoon fire safety tip. The cards measure approximately 3" by 5" and are in full color. The cards are numbered on the backs. The sets were

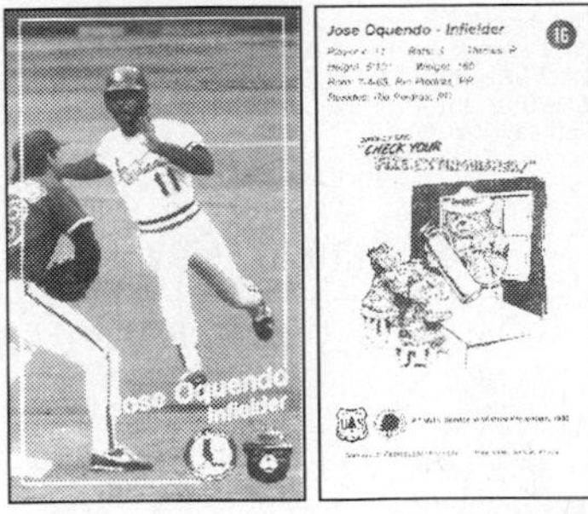

distributed on July 19th during the Cardinals' game against the Los Angeles Dodgers to fans 15 years of age and under.

	MT	EX-MT	VG
COMPLETE SET (25)	12.00	5.50	1.50
COMMON PLAYER (1-25)	.40	.18	.05
☐ 1 Whitey Herzog MG	.60	.25	.08
☐ 2 Danny Cox	.50	.23	.06
☐ 3 Ken Dayley	.40	.18	.05
☐ 4 Jose DeLeon	.40	.18	.05
☐ 5 Bob Forsch	.40	.18	.05
☐ 6 Joe Magrane	.50	.23	.06
☐ 7 Greg Mathews	.40	.18	.05
☐ 8 Scott Terry	.40	.18	.05
☐ 9 John Tudor	.50	.23	.06
☐ 10 Todd Worrell	.60	.25	.08
☐ 11 Steve Lake	.40	.18	.05
☐ 12 Tom Pagnozzi	.60	.25	.08
☐ 13 Tony Pena	.50	.23	.06
☐ 14 Bob Horner	.50	.23	.06
☐ 15 Tom Lawless	.40	.18	.05
☐ 16 Jose Oquendo	.50	.23	.06
☐ 17 Terry Pendleton	1.00	.45	.13
☐ 18 Ozzie Smith	1.25	.55	.16
☐ 19 Vince Coleman	1.00	.45	.13
☐ 20 Curt Ford	.40	.18	.05
☐ 21 Willie McGee	.75	.35	.09
☐ 22 Larry McWilliams	.40	.18	.05
☐ 23 Steve Peters	.40	.18	.05
☐ 24 Luis Alicea	.40	.18	.05
☐ 25 Tom Brunansky	.60	.25	.08

1988 Smokey Dodgers

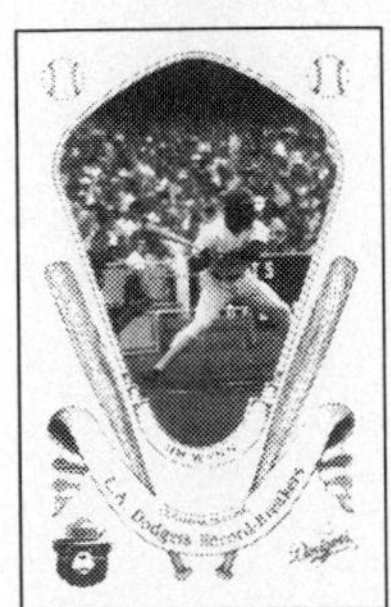

This 32-card set was issued by the U.S. Forestry Service as a perforated sheet that could be separated into individual cards. The set commemorates Los Angeles Dodgers who hold various team and league records, i.e., "L.A. Dodgers Record-Breakers." The cards measure approximately 2 1/2" by 4" and have full-color fronts. The card fronts are distinguished by their thick light blue borders and the bats, balls, and stadium design layout. The sheets of cards were distributed at the Dodgers' Smokey Bear Day game on September 9th.

	MT	EX-MT	VG
COMPLETE SET (32)	12.00	5.50	1.50
COMMON PLAYER (1-32)	.35	.16	.04
☐ 1 Walter Alston MG	.60	.25	.08
☐ 2 John Roseboro	.35	.16	.04
☐ 3 Frank Howard	.45	.20	.06
☐ 4 Sandy Koufax	1.00	.45	.13
☐ 5 Manny Mota	.45	.20	.06
☐ 6 Sandy Koufax, Jerry Reuss, and Bill Singer	.45	.20	.06
☐ 7 Maury Wills	.60	.25	.08
☐ 8 Tommy Davis	.45	.20	.06
☐ 9 Phil Regan	.35	.16	.04
☐ 10 Wes Parker	.45	.20	.06
☐ 11 Don Drysdale	.75	.35	.09
☐ 12 Willie Davis	.45	.20	.06
☐ 13 Bill Russell	.45	.20	.06
☐ 14 Jim Brewer	.35	.16	.04
☐ 15 Steve Garvey, Davey Lopes, Bill Russell, and Ron Cey	.60	.25	.08
☐ 16 Mike Marshall	.45	.20	.06
☐ 17 Steve Garvey	.75	.35	.09
☐ 18 Davey Lopes	.45	.20	.06
☐ 19 Burt Hooton	.35	.16	.04
☐ 20 Jim Wynn	.45	.20	.06
☐ 21 Dusty Baker, Ron Cey, Steve Garvey, and Reggie Smith	.60	.25	.08
☐ 22 Dusty Baker	.60	.25	.08
☐ 23 Tommy Lasorda MG	.60	.25	.08
☐ 24 Fernando Valenzuela	.60	.25	.08
☐ 25 Steve Sax	.60	.25	.08
☐ 26 Dodger Stadium	.35	.16	.04
☐ 27 Ron Cey	.45	.20	.06
☐ 28 Pedro Guerrero	.60	.25	.08
☐ 29 Mike Marshall	.45	.20	.06
☐ 30 Don Sutton	.75	.35	.09
☐ NNO Checklist Card	.45	.20	.06
☐ NNO Smokey Bear	.35	.16	.04

1988 Smokey Padres

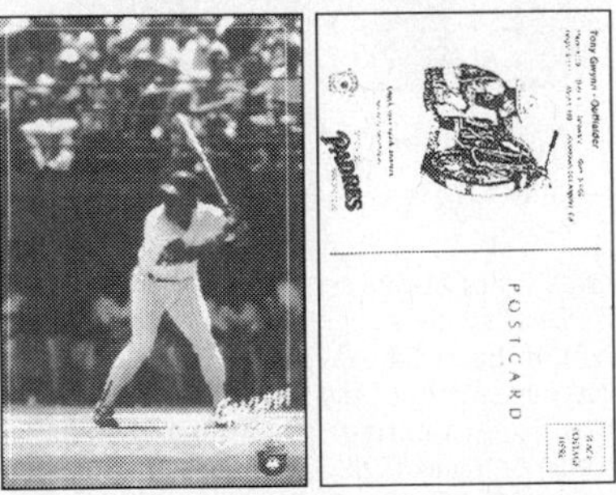

The cards in this 31-card set measure approximately 3 3/4" by 5 3/4". This unnumbered, full color set features the Fire Prevention Bear, Smokey, and a Padres player, coach, manager, or associate on each card. The set was given out at Jack Murphy Stadium to fans under the age of 14 during the Smokey Bear Day game promotion. The logo of the California Department of Forestry appears on the reverse in conjunction with a Smokey the Bear logo on the obverse. The backs contain short biographical data and a fire prevention hint from Smokey. The set is numbered below in alphabetical order. The card backs are actually postcards that can be addressed and mailed. Cards of Larry Bowa and Candy Sierra were printed but were not officially released since they were no longer members of the Padres by the time the cards were to be distributed.

	MT	EX-MT	VG
COMPLETE SET (31)	24.00	11.00	3.00

COMMON PLAYER (1-31)	.60	.25	.08
☐ 1 Shawn Abner	.75	.35	.09
☐ 2 Roberto Alomar	6.00	2.70	.75
☐ 3 Sandy Alomar CO	.75	.35	.09
☐ 4 Greg Booker	.60	.25	.08
☐ 5 Chris Brown	.60	.25	.08
☐ 6 Mark Davis	.90	.40	.11
☐ 7 Pat Dobson CO	.75	.35	.09
☐ 8 Tim Flannery	.60	.25	.08
☐ 9 Mark Grant	.60	.25	.08
☐ 10 Tony Gwynn	4.00	1.80	.50
☐ 11 Andy Hawkins	.60	.25	.08
☐ 12 Stan Jefferson	.60	.25	.08
☐ 13 Jimmy Jones	.60	.25	.08
☐ 14 John Kruk	1.25	.55	.16
☐ 15 Dave Leiper	.60	.25	.08
☐ 16 Shane Mack	1.50	.65	.19
☐ 17 Carmelo Martinez	.60	.25	.08
☐ 18 Lance McCullers	.60	.25	.08
☐ 19 Keith Moreland	.60	.25	.08
☐ 20 Eric Nolte	.60	.25	.08
☐ 21 Amos Otis CO	.75	.35	.09
☐ 22 Mark Parent	.60	.25	.08
☐ 23 Randy Ready	.60	.25	.08
☐ 24 Greg Riddoch CO	.60	.25	.08
☐ 25 Benito Santiago	2.50	1.15	.30
☐ 26 Eric Show	.60	.25	.08
☐ 27 Denny Sommers CO	.60	.25	.08
☐ 28 Garry Templeton	.75	.35	.09
☐ 29 Dickie Thon	.60	.25	.08
☐ 30 Ed Whitson	.60	.25	.08
☐ 31 Marvell Wynne	.60	.25	.08

1988 Smokey Rangers

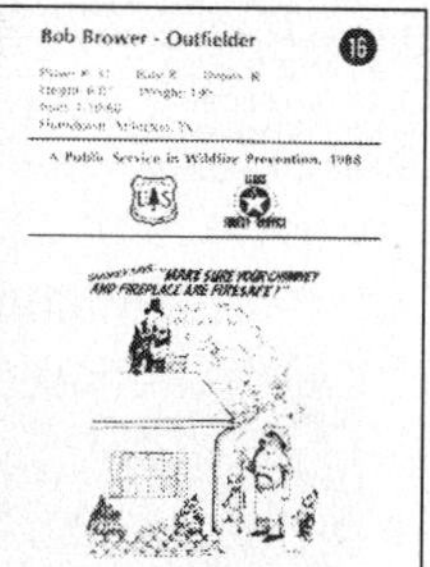

The cards in this 21-card set measure approximately 3 1/2" by 5". This numbered, full color set features the Fire Prevention Bear, Smokey, and a Rangers player (or manager) on each card. The set was given out at Arlington Stadium to fans during the Smokey Bear Day game promotion on August 7th. The logos of the Texas Forest Service and the U.S. Forestry Service appear on the reverse in conjunction with a Smokey the Bear logo on the obverse. The backs contain short biographical data and a fire prevention hint from Smokey.

	MT	EX-MT	VG
COMPLETE SET (21)	12.00	5.50	1.50
COMMON PLAYER (1-21)	.60	.25	.08
☐ 1 Tom O'Malley	.60	.25	.08
☐ 2 Pete O'Brien	.75	.35	.09
☐ 3 Geno Petralli	.60	.25	.08
☐ 4 Pete Incaviglia	.90	.40	.11
☐ 5 Oddibe McDowell	.75	.35	.09
☐ 6 Dale Mohorcic	.60	.25	.08
☐ 7 Bobby Witt	.90	.40	.11
☐ 8 Bobby Valentine MG	.75	.35	.09
☐ 9 Ruben Sierra	2.50	1.15	.30
☐ 10 Scott Fletcher	.60	.25	.08
☐ 11 Mike Stanley	.60	.25	.08
☐ 12 Steve Buechele	.75	.35	.09
☐ 13 Charlie Hough	.75	.35	.09
☐ 14 Larry Parrish	.75	.35	.09
☐ 15 Jerry Browne	.75	.35	.09
☐ 16 Bob Brower	.60	.25	.08
☐ 17 Jeff Russell	.75	.35	.09
☐ 18 Edwin Correa	.60	.25	.08
☐ 19 Mitch Williams	.75	.35	.09
☐ 20 Jose Guzman	.90	.40	.11
☐ 21 Curtis Wilkerson	.60	.25	.08

1988 Smokey Royals

This set of 28 cards features caricatures of the Kansas City Royals players. The cards are nunmbered on the back except for the unnumbered title/checklist card. The card set was distributed as a giveaway item at the stadium on August 14th to kids age 14 and under. The cards are approximately 3" by 5" and are in full color on the card fronts. The Smokey logo is in the upper right corner of every obverse.

	MT	EX-MT	VG
COMPLETE SET (28)	12.00	5.50	1.50
COMMON PLAYER (1-27)	.40	.18	.05
☐ 1 John Wathan MG	.50	.23	.06
☐ 2 Royals Coaches	.40	.18	.05
☐ 3 Willie Wilson	.60	.25	.08
☐ 4 Danny Tartabull	1.25	.55	.16
☐ 5 Bo Jackson	2.00	.90	.25
☐ 6 Gary Thurman	.40	.18	.05
☐ 7 Jerry Don Gleaton	.40	.18	.05
☐ 8 Floyd Bannister	.40	.18	.05
☐ 9 Bud Black	.50	.23	.06
☐ 10 Steve Farr	.75	.35	.09
☐ 11 Gene Garber	.50	.23	.06
☐ 12 Mark Gubicza	.75	.35	.09
☐ 13 Charlie Liebrandt	.60	.25	.08
☐ 14 Ted Power	.40	.18	.05
☐ 15 Dan Quisenberry	.75	.35	.09
☐ 16 Bret Saberhagen	1.00	.45	.13
☐ 17 Mike Macfarlane	.75	.35	.09
☐ 18 Scotti Madison	.40	.18	.05
☐ 19 Jamie Quirk	.40	.18	.05
☐ 20 George Brett	2.00	.90	.25
☐ 21 Kevin Seitzer	.60	.25	.08
☐ 22 Bill Pecota	.50	.23	.06
☐ 23 Kurt Stillwell	.50	.23	.06
☐ 24 Brad Wellman	.40	.18	.05
☐ 25 Frank White	.60	.25	.08
☐ 26 Jim Eisenreich	.50	.23	.06
☐ 27 Smokey Bear	.40	.18	.05
☐ NNO Checklist Card	.50	.23	.06

1988 Smokey Twins Colorgrams

These cards are actually pages of a booklet featuring members of the Minnesota Twins and Smokey's fire safety tips. The booklet has 12 pages each containing a black and white photo card (approximately 2 1/2" by 3 3/4") and a black and white player caricature (oversized head) postcard (approximately 3 3/4" by 5 5/8"). The cards are unnumbered but they have biographical information and a fire-prevention cartoon on the back of the card.

	MT	EX-MT	VG
COMPLETE SET (12)	12.00	5.50	1.50
COMMON PLAYER (1-12)	.60	.25	.08
☐ 1 Frank Viola	1.25	.55	.16
☐ 2 Gary Gaetti	.75	.35	.09
☐ 3 Kent Hrbek	1.25	.55	.16
☐ 4 Jeff Reardon	1.50	.65	.19
☐ 5 Gene Larkin	.75	.35	.09
☐ 6 Bert Blyleven	1.25	.55	.16
☐ 7 Tim Laudner	.60	.25	.08
☐ 8 Greg Gagne	1.00	.45	.13
☐ 9 Randy Bush	.60	.25	.08
☐ 10 Dan Gladden	.60	.25	.08
☐ 11 Al Newman	.60	.25	.08
☐ 12 Kirby Puckett	4.00	1.80	.50

1989 Smokey Angels All-Stars

The 1989 Smokey Angels All-Stars set contains 20 standard-size (2 1/2" by 3 1/2") cards. The fronts have red and white borders. The backs are blue and red and feature career highlights. This set, which depicts current and former Angels who appeared in the All-Star game, was given away at the June 25, 1989 Angels home game. The set numbering is ordered chronologically according to when each subject participated in the respective All-Star Game as an Angel representative.

	MT	EX-MT	VG
COMPLETE SET (20)	7.50	3.40	.95
COMMON PLAYER (1-20)	.25	.11	.03
☐ 1 Bill Rigney MG	.25	.11	.03
☐ 2 Dean Chance	.35	.16	.04
☐ 3 Jim Fregosi	.35	.16	.04
☐ 4 Bobby Knoop	.25	.11	.03
☐ 5 Don Mincher	.25	.11	.03
☐ 6 Clyde Wright	.25	.11	.03
☐ 7 Nolan Ryan	3.00	1.35	.40
☐ 8 Frank Robinson	.75	.35	.09
☐ 9 Frank Tanana	.45	.20	.06
☐ 10 Rod Carew	1.00	.45	.13
☐ 11 Bobby Grich	.35	.16	.04
☐ 12 Brian Downing	.35	.16	.04
☐ 13 Don Baylor	.45	.20	.06
☐ 14 Fred Lynn	.35	.16	.04
☐ 15 Reggie Jackson	1.25	.55	.16
☐ 16 Doug DeCinces	.45	.20	.06
☐ 17 Bob Boone	.45	.20	.06
☐ 18 Wally Joyner	.75	.35	.09
☐ 19 Mike Witt	.25	.11	.03
☐ 20 Johnny Ray	.25	.11	.03

1989 Smokey Cardinals

The 1989 Smokey Cardinals set contains 24 cards measuring approximately 4" by 6". The fronts have color photos with white and red borders. The backs feature biographical information. The cards are unnumbered so they are listed below in alphabetical order for reference.

	MT	EX-MT	VG
COMPLETE SET (24)	10.00	4.50	1.25
COMMON PLAYER (1-24)	.35	.16	.04
☐ 1 Tom Brunansky	.60	.25	.08
☐ 2 Vince Coleman	.90	.40	.11
☐ 3 John Costello	.35	.16	.04
☐ 4 Ken Dayley	.35	.16	.04
☐ 5 Jose DeLeon	.35	.16	.04
☐ 6 Frank DiPino	.35	.16	.04
☐ 7 Pedro Guerrero	.75	.35	.09
☐ 8 Whitey Herzog MG	.60	.25	.08
☐ 9 Ken Hill	.75	.35	.09
☐ 10 Tim Jones	.35	.16	.04
☐ 11 Jim Lindeman	.35	.16	.04
☐ 12 Joe Magrane	.45	.20	.06
☐ 13 Willie McGee	.60	.25	.08
☐ 14 John Morris	.35	.16	.04
☐ 15 Jose Oquendo	.45	.20	.06
☐ 16 Tom Pagnozzi	.60	.25	.08
☐ 17 Tony Pena	.45	.20	.06
☐ 18 Terry Pendleton	1.00	.45	.13
☐ 19 Dan Quisenberry	.60	.25	.08
☐ 20 Ozzie Smith	1.00	.45	.13
☐ 21 Scott Terry	.35	.16	.04
☐ 22 Milt Thompson	.35	.16	.04
☐ 23 Denny Walling	.35	.16	.04
☐ 24 Todd Worrell	.60	.25	.08

1989 Smokey Colt .45s

The 1989 Smokey Houston Colt .45s set contains 29 standard-size (2 1/2" by 3 1/2") cards. The fronts have black and white photos with white and light blue borders. This set depicts old Houston Colt .45s' players from their inaugural 1962 season.

	MT	EX-MT	VG
COMPLETE SET (29)	6.00	2.70	.75
COMMON PLAYER (1-29)	.25	.11	.03
☐ 1 Bob Bruce	.25	.11	.03
☐ 2 Al Cicotte	.25	.11	.03
☐ 3 Dave Giusti	.35	.16	.04
☐ 4 Jim Golden	.25	.11	.03
☐ 5 Ken Johnson	.25	.11	.03

☐ 6 Tom Borland	.25	.11	.03
☐ 7 Bobby Shantz	.35	.16	.04
☐ 8 Dick Farrell	.35	.16	.04
☐ 9 Jim Umbricht	.25	.11	.03
☐ 10 Hal Woodeshick	.25	.11	.03
☐ 11 Merritt Ranew	.25	.11	.03
☐ 12 Hal Smith	.25	.11	.03
☐ 13 Jim Campbell	.25	.11	.03
☐ 14 Norm Larker	.25	.11	.03
☐ 15 Joe Amalfitano	.25	.11	.03
☐ 16 Bob Aspromonte	.25	.11	.03
☐ 17 Bob Lillis	.35	.16	.04
☐ 18 Dick Gernert	.25	.11	.03
☐ 19 Don Buddin	.25	.11	.03
☐ 20 Pidge Browne	.25	.11	.03
☐ 21 Von McDaniel	.25	.11	.03
☐ 22 Don Taussig	.25	.11	.03
☐ 23 Al Spangler	.35	.16	.04
☐ 24 Al Heist	.25	.11	.03
☐ 25 Jim Pendleton	.25	.11	.03
☐ 26 Johnny Weekly	.25	.11	.03
☐ 27 Harry Craft MG	.25	.11	.03
☐ 28 Colt Coaches	.25	.11	.03
☐ 29 1962 Houston Colt 45s	.35	.16	.04

1989 Smokey Dodger Greats

The 1989 Smokey Dodger Greats set contains 104 standard-size (2 1/2" by 3 1/2") cards. The fronts and backs have white and blue borders. The backs are vertically oriented and feature career totals and fire prevention cartoons. The set depicts notable Dodgers of all eras, and was distributed in perforated sheet format. Cards 1-36 are ordered alphabetically and (except for number 31) depict Dodger members of the Hall of Fame. Cards 37-64 (except for number 57) represent Brooklyn Dodgers whereas cards 65-101 represent Los Angeles Dodgers. The last three cards in the set (102-104) are Hall of Famers apparently overlooked in the first group.

	MT	EX-MT	VG
COMPLETE SET (104)	18.00	8.00	2.30
COMMON PLAYER (1-104)	.10	.05	.01
☐ 1 Walter Alston	.40	.18	.05
☐ 2 David Bancroft	.30	.14	.04
☐ 3 Dan Brouthers	.30	.14	.04
☐ 4 Roy Campanella	.75	.35	.09
☐ 5 Max Carey	.30	.14	.04
☐ 6 Hazen(Kiki) Cuyler	.30	.14	.04
☐ 7 Don Drysdale	.40	.18	.05
☐ 8 Burleigh Grimes	.30	.14	.04
☐ 9 Billy Herman	.30	.14	.04
☐ 10 Waite Hoyt	.30	.14	.04
☐ 11 Hughie Jennings	.30	.14	.04
☐ 12 Willie Keeler	.30	.14	.04
☐ 13 Joseph Kelley	.30	.14	.04
☐ 14 George Kelly	.30	.14	.04
☐ 15 Sandy Koufax	.75	.35	.09
☐ 16 Heinie Manush	.30	.14	.04
☐ 17 Juan Marichal	.40	.18	.05
☐ 18 Rabbit Maranville	.30	.14	.04
☐ 19 Rube Marquard	.30	.14	.04
☐ 20 Thomas McCarthy	.30	.14	.04
☐ 21 Joseph McGinnity	.30	.14	.04
☐ 22 Joe Medwick	.30	.14	.04
☐ 23 Pee Wee Reese	.40	.18	.05
☐ 24 Frank Robinson	.40	.18	.05
☐ 25 Jackie Robinson	1.00	.45	.13
☐ 26 George"Babe" Ruth	1.25	.55	.16
☐ 27 Duke Snider	.75	.35	.09
☐ 28 Casey Stengel	.60	.25	.08
☐ 29 Dazzy Vance	.30	.14	.04
☐ 30 Arky Vaughan	.30	.14	.04
☐ 31 Mike Scioscia	.10	.05	.01
☐ 32 Lloyd Waner	.30	.14	.04
☐ 33 John"Monte" Ward	.30	.14	.04
☐ 34 Zack Wheat	.30	.14	.04
☐ 35 Hoyt Wilhelm	.30	.14	.04
☐ 36 Hack Wilson	.30	.14	.04
☐ 37 Tony Cuccinello	.10	.05	.01
☐ 38 Al Lopez	.30	.14	.04
☐ 39 Leo Durocher	.30	.14	.04
☐ 40 Cookie Lavagetto	.10	.05	.01
☐ 41 Babe Phelps	.10	.05	.01
☐ 42 Dolph Camilli	.15	.07	.02
☐ 43 Whitlow Wyatt	.10	.05	.01
☐ 44 Mickey Owen	.10	.05	.01
☐ 45 Van Mungo	.10	.05	.01
☐ 46 Pete Coscarart	.10	.05	.01
☐ 47 Pete Reiser	.15	.07	.02
☐ 48 Augie Galan	.10	.05	.01
☐ 49 Dixie Walker	.10	.05	.01
☐ 50 Kirby Higbe	.10	.05	.01
☐ 51 Ralph Branca	.20	.09	.03
☐ 52 Bruce Edwards	.10	.05	.01
☐ 53 Eddie Stanky	.15	.07	.02
☐ 54 Gil Hodges	.30	.14	.04
☐ 55 Don Newcombe	.20	.09	.03
☐ 56 Preacher Roe	.20	.09	.03
☐ 57 Willie Randolph	.15	.07	.02
☐ 58 Carl Furillo	.20	.09	.03
☐ 59 Charlie Dressen	.10	.05	.01
☐ 60 Carl Erskine	.20	.09	.03
☐ 61 Clem Labine	.15	.07	.02
☐ 62 Gino Cimoli	.10	.05	.01
☐ 63 Johnny Podres	.20	.09	.03
☐ 64 Johnny Roseboro	.15	.07	.02
☐ 65 Wally Moon	.15	.07	.02
☐ 66 Charlie Neal	.15	.07	.02
☐ 67 Norm Larker	.10	.05	.01
☐ 68 Stan Williams	.10	.05	.01
☐ 69 Maury Wills	.25	.11	.03
☐ 70 Tommy Davis	.20	.09	.03
☐ 71 Jim Lefebvre	.15	.07	.02
☐ 72 Phil Regan	.10	.05	.01
☐ 73 Claude Osteen	.10	.05	.01
☐ 74 Tom Haller	.10	.05	.01
☐ 75 Bill Singer	.10	.05	.01
☐ 76 Bill Grabarkewitz	.10	.05	.01
☐ 77 Willie Davis	.15	.07	.02
☐ 78 Don Sutton	.25	.11	.03
☐ 79 Jim Brewer	.10	.05	.01
☐ 80 Manny Mota	.15	.07	.02
☐ 81 Bill Russell	.15	.07	.02
☐ 82 Ron Cey	.15	.07	.02
☐ 83 Steve Garvey	.30	.14	.04
☐ 84 Mike G. Marshall	.15	.07	.02
☐ 85 Andy Messersmith	.15	.07	.02
☐ 86 Jimmy Wynn	.15	.07	.02
☐ 87 Rick Rhoden	.10	.05	.01
☐ 88 Reggie Smith	.15	.07	.02
☐ 89 Jay Howell	.15	.07	.02
☐ 90 Rick Monday	.10	.05	.01
☐ 91 Tommy John	.20	.09	.03
☐ 92 Bob Welch	.15	.07	.02
☐ 93 Dusty Baker	.20	.09	.03
☐ 94 Pedro Guerrero	.20	.09	.03

	MT	EX-MT	VG
☐ 95 Burt Hooton	.10	.05	.01
☐ 96 Davey Lopes	.15	.07	.02
☐ 97 Fernando Valenzuela	.20	.09	.03
☐ 98 Steve Howe	.15	.07	.02
☐ 99 Steve Sax	.20	.09	.03
☐ 100 Orel Hershiser	.25	.11	.03
☐ 101 Mike A. Marshall	.15	.07	.02
☐ 102 Ernie Lombardi	.30	.14	.04
☐ 103 Fred Lindstrom	.30	.14	.04
☐ 104 Wilbert Robinson	.30	.14	.04

1989 Smokey Rangers

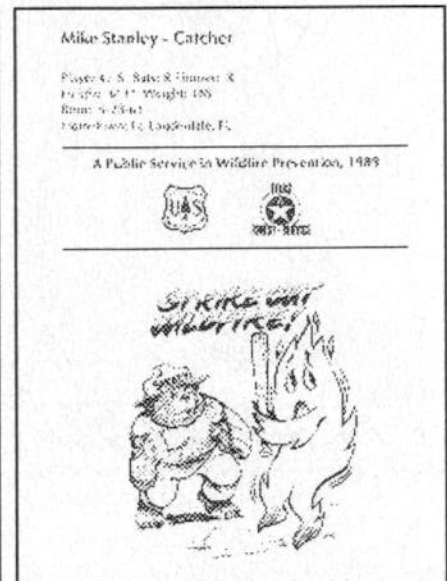

The 1989 Smokey Rangers set features 34 unnumbered cards measuring approximately 4 1/4" by 6". The fronts feature mugshot photos with white borders. The backs feature biographical information and fire prevention tips. The set was given away at a 1989 Rangers' home game.

	MT	EX-MT	VG
COMPLETE SET (34)	18.00	8.00	2.30
COMMON PLAYER (1-34)	.50	.23	.06
☐ 1 Darrel Akerfelds	.50	.23	.06
☐ 2 Brad Arnsberg	.50	.23	.06
☐ 3 Buddy Bell	.75	.35	.09
☐ 4 Kevin Brown	1.00	.45	.13
☐ 5 Steve Buechele	.60	.25	.08
☐ 6 Dick Egan CO	.50	.23	.06
☐ 7 Cecil Espy	.50	.23	.06
☐ 8 Scott Fletcher	.50	.23	.06
☐ 9 Julio Franco	1.00	.45	.13
☐ 10 Cecilio Guante	.50	.23	.06
☐ 11 Jose Guzman	.75	.35	.09
☐ 12 Drew Hall	.50	.23	.06
☐ 13 Toby Harrah CO	.60	.25	.08
☐ 14 Charlie Hough	.60	.25	.08
☐ 15 Tom House CO	.50	.23	.06
☐ 16 Pete Incaviglia	.75	.35	.09
☐ 17 Chad Kreuter	.50	.23	.06
☐ 18 Jeff Kunkel	.50	.23	.06
☐ 19 Rick Leach	.50	.23	.06
☐ 20 Davey Lopes	.60	.25	.08
☐ 21 Craig McMurtry	.50	.23	.06
☐ 22 Jamie Moyer	.50	.23	.06
☐ 23 Dave Oliver CO	.50	.23	.06
☐ 24 Rafael Palmeiro	1.25	.55	.16
☐ 25 Geno Petralli	.50	.23	.06
☐ 26 Tom Robson CO	.50	.23	.06
☐ 27 Kenny Rogers	.60	.25	.08
☐ 28 Jeff Russell	.60	.25	.08
☐ 29 Nolan Ryan	4.00	1.80	.50
☐ 30 Ruben Sierra	3.00	1.35	.40
☐ 31 Mike Stanley	.50	.23	.06
☐ 32 Jim Sundberg	.75	.35	.09
☐ 33 Bobby Valentine MG	.60	.25	.08
☐ 34 Bobby Witt	.75	.35	.09

1990 Smokey Angels

The 1990 Smokey Angels set contains standard-size (2 1/2" by 3 1/2") cards which were produced by the U.S. Forest

Service and Bureau of Land Management in conjunction with the California Department of Forestry. The first 18 cards in the set are alphabetically arranged. Bailes and McClure were apparently added to the checklist later than these 18, after they were acquired by the Angels.

	MT	EX-MT	VG
COMPLETE SET (20)	7.00	3.10	.85
COMMON PLAYER (1-20)	.30	.14	.04
☐ 1 Jim Abbott	1.25	.55	.16
☐ 2 Bert Blyleven	.60	.25	.08
☐ 3 Chili Davis	.40	.18	.05
☐ 4 Brian Downing	.40	.18	.05
☐ 5 Chuck Finley	.30	.14	.04
☐ 6 Willie Fraser	.30	.14	.04
☐ 7 Bryan Harvey	.60	.25	.08
☐ 8 Jack Howell	.30	.14	.04
☐ 9 Wally Joyner	.75	.35	.09
☐ 10 Mark Langston	.50	.23	.06
☐ 11 Kirk McCaskill	.30	.14	.04
☐ 12 Mark McLemore	.30	.14	.04
☐ 13 Lance Parrish	.50	.23	.06
☐ 14 Johnny Ray	.40	.18	.05
☐ 15 Dick Schofield	.40	.18	.05
☐ 16 Mike Witt	.30	.14	.04
☐ 17 Claudell Washington	.40	.18	.05
☐ 18 Devon White	.50	.23	.06
☐ 19 Scott Bailes	.30	.14	.04
☐ 20 Bob McClure	.30	.14	.04

1990 Smokey Cardinals

This 27-card, approximately 3" by 5", set was issued about the 1990 St. Louis Cardinals in conjuction with the US Forest Service which was using the popular character Smokey the Bear. The set has full color action photos of the Cardinals on the front of the card while the back of the card has fire safety tips on the bottom of the card. The set has been checklisted alphabetically for reference. The cards are unnumbered; not even uniform numbers are displayed prominently.

	MT	EX-MT	VG
COMPLETE SET (27)	12.00	5.50	1.50
COMMON PLAYER (1-27)	.45	.20	.06

	MT	EX-MT	VG
☐ 1 Vince Coleman	.90	.40	.11
☐ 2 Dave Collins	.45	.20	.06
☐ 3 Danny Cox	.45	.20	.06
☐ 4 Ken Dayley	.45	.20	.06
☐ 5 Frank DiPino	.45	.20	.06
☐ 6 Jose DeLeon	.45	.20	.06
☐ 7 Pedro Guerrero	.75	.35	.09
☐ 8 Whitey Herzog MG	.60	.25	.08
☐ 9 Rick Horton	.45	.20	.06
☐ 10 Rex Hudler	.60	.25	.08
☐ 11 Tim Jones	.45	.20	.06
☐ 12 Joe Magrane	.60	.25	.08
☐ 13 Greg Mathews	.45	.20	.06
☐ 14 Willie McGee	.75	.35	.09
☐ 15 John Morris	.45	.20	.06
☐ 16 Tom Niedenfuer	.45	.20	.06
☐ 17 Jose Oquendo	.45	.20	.06
☐ 18 Tom Pagnozzi	.60	.25	.08
☐ 19 Terry Pendleton	1.00	.45	.13
☐ 20 Bryn Smith	.60	.25	.08
☐ 21 Lee Smith	.75	.35	.09
☐ 22 Ozzie Smith	1.00	.45	.13
☐ 23 Scott Terry	.45	.20	.06
☐ 24 Milt Thompson	.60	.25	.08
☐ 25 John Tudor	.60	.25	.08
☐ 26 Denny Walling	.45	.20	.06
☐ 27 Todd Zeile	.75	.35	.09

1990 Smokey Southern Cal

This 12-card set was sponsored by the USDA Forest Service in conjunction with other federal agencies. The standard-size cards (2 1/2" by 3 1/2") have on their fronts black and white photos of outstanding players (except for legendary coach Rod Dedeaux) from past USC baseball teams who went on to play in the major Leagues. The team name and player information appear in maroon stripes above and below the picture. A yellow stripe on the bottom and right side of the picture serve as a shadow border. School and Smokey logos superimposed on the picture round out the card face. In black lettering on white, each back has career summary and a fire prevention cartoon starring Smokey. The cards are unnumbered and checklisted below in alphabetical order, with the player's number after the name. The set was also issued as a an uncut sheet, with three rows of four cards each. The card sets were given away to the first 1,000 fans who attended any game during a series between USC and Stanford, February 23-25, at Dedeaux Field.

	MT	EX-MT	VG
COMPLETE SET (12)	9.00	4.00	1.15
COMMON PLAYER (1-12)	.50	.23	.06

	MT	EX-MT	VG
☐ 1 Don Buford	.60	.25	.08
☐ 2 Steve Busby	.60	.25	.08
☐ 3 Rich Dauer	.50	.23	.06
☐ 4 Rod Dedeaux CO	.50	.23	.06
☐ 5 Ron Fairly	.60	.25	.08
☐ 6 Steve Kemp	.50	.23	.06
☐ 7 Dave Kingman	.75	.35	.09
☐ 8 Bill Lee	.60	.25	.08
☐ 9 Fred Lynn	.75	.35	.09
☐ 10 Mark McGwire	3.00	1.35	.40
☐ 11 Tom Seaver	4.00	1.80	.50
☐ 12 Roy Smalley	.50	.23	.06

1991 Smokey Angels

This 20-card set was sponsored by the USDA Forest Service and USDI Bureau of Land Management in cooperation with the California Department of Forestry. The standard size (2 1/2" by 3 1/2") cards have on their fronts color action player photos with gray borders. Also a dark blue stripe borders the picture above and below. The player's name appears in the white stripe at the card bottom, sandwiched between the team logo and Smokey icon. The player's position is given in a red vertical stripe in the lower left corner. The backs are printed in blue and red on white, and present biography as well as a fire prevention cartoon starring Smokey. The cards are numbered in the upper right corner on the back.

	MT	EX-MT	VG
COMPLETE SET (20)	6.00	2.70	.75
COMMON PLAYER (1-20)	.30	.14	.04

	MT	EX-MT	VG
☐ 1 Luis Polonia	.60	.25	.08
☐ 2 Junior Felix	.50	.23	.06
☐ 3 Dave Winfield	1.00	.45	.13
☐ 4 Dave Parker	.60	.25	.08
☐ 5 Lance Parrish	.50	.23	.06
☐ 6 Wally Joyner	.75	.35	.09
☐ 7 Jim Abbott	.75	.35	.09
☐ 8 Mark Langston	.50	.23	.06
☐ 9 Chuck Finley	.30	.14	.04
☐ 10 Kirk McCaskill	.30	.14	.04
☐ 11 Jack Howell	.30	.14	.04
☐ 12 Donnie Hill	.30	.14	.04
☐ 13 Gary Gaetti	.30	.14	.04
☐ 14 Dick Schofield	.40	.18	.05
☐ 15 Luis Sojo	.50	.23	.06
☐ 16 Mark Eichorn	.40	.18	.05
☐ 17 Bryan Harvey	.50	.23	.06
☐ 18 Jeff D. Robinson	.30	.14	.04
☐ 19 Scott Lewis	.30	.14	.04
☐ 20 John Orton	.30	.14	.04

1992 Smokey Padres

This 36-card set was issued in the postcard format and measures approximately 3 13/16" by 5 11/16". The fronts feature full-bleed color action player photos. The Smokey the Bear logo is superimposed in one of the upper corners while the player's name and position are printed in burnt orange lettering in a navy blue stripe edging the bottom of the card. The left portion of the horizontally oriented backs

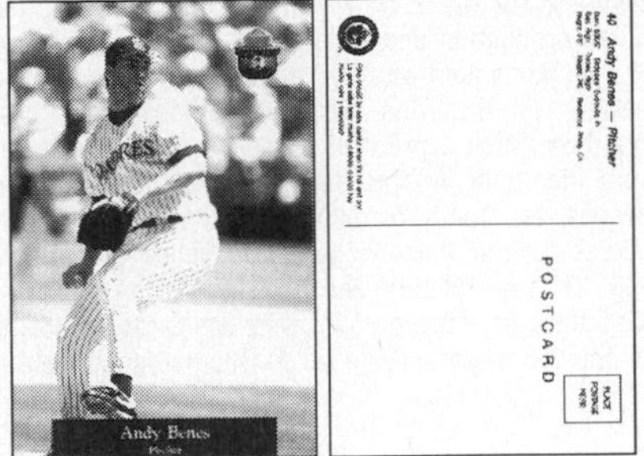

presents brief biographical information and a fire prevention tip in English and Spanish. The cards are unnumbered and checklisted below in alphabetical order.

	MT	EX-MT	VG
COMPLETE SET (36)	20.00	9.00	2.50
COMMON PLAYER (1-36)	.50	.23	.06
☐ 1 Larry Andersen	.50	.23	.06
☐ 2 Oscar Azocar	.50	.23	.06
☐ 3 Andy Benes	1.00	.45	.13
☐ 4 Dann Bilardello	.50	.23	.06
☐ 5 Jerald Clark	.75	.35	.09
☐ 6 Pat Clements	.50	.23	.06
☐ 7 Dave Eiland	.50	.23	.06
☐ 8 Tony Fernandez	.75	.35	.09
☐ 9 Tony Gwynn	2.50	1.15	.30
☐ 10 Gene Harris	.50	.23	.06
☐ 11 Greg W. Harris	.60	.25	.08
☐ 12 Jeremy Hernandez	.60	.25	.08
☐ 13 Bruce Hurst	.60	.25	.08
☐ 14 Darrin Jackson	.75	.35	.09
☐ 15 Tom Lampkin	.50	.23	.06
☐ 16 Bruce Kimm CO	.50	.23	.06
☐ 17 Craig Lefferts	.75	.35	.09
☐ 18 Mike Maddux	.50	.23	.06
☐ 19 Fred McGriff	1.50	.65	.19
☐ 20 Jose Melendez	.75	.35	.09
☐ 21 Randy Myers	.75	.35	.09
☐ 22 Gary Pettis	.60	.25	.08
☐ 23 Rob Picciolo CO	.50	.23	.06
☐ 24 Merv Rettenmund CO	.50	.23	.06
☐ 25 Greg Riddoch MG	.50	.23	.06
☐ 26 Mike Roarke CO	.50	.23	.06
☐ 27 Rich Rodriguez	.50	.23	.06
☐ 28 Benito Santiago	1.00	.45	.13
☐ 29 Frank Seminara	.75	.35	.09
☐ 30 Gary Sheffield	2.00	.90	.25
☐ 31 Craig Shipley	.60	.25	.08
☐ 32 Jim Snyder CO	.50	.23	.06
☐ 33 Dave Staton	.75	.35	.09
☐ 34 Kurt Stillwell	.50	.23	.06
☐ 35 Tim Teufel	.50	.23	.06
☐ 36 Kevin Ward	.60	.25	.08

1989 Socko Orel Hershiser

The 1989 Socko Orel Hershiser set contains seven unnumbered standard-size (2 1/2" by 3 1/2") cards. The fronts are blue, green and yellow, and feature full color photos of Hershiser with the Dodger logos airbrushed out. The backs are white and include "Tips from Orel." The cards were distributed as a promotional set through Socko beverages.

	MT	EX-MT	VG
COMPLETE SET (7)	13.50	6.00	1.70
COMMON PLAYER (1-7)	2.50	1.15	.30
☐ 1 Orel Hershiser The Kick	2.50	1.15	.30
☐ 2 Orel Hershiser The Follow-Through	2.50	1.15	.30
☐ 3 Orel Hershiser The Release	2.50	1.15	.30
☐ 4 Orel Hershiser Backing Up The Catcher	2.50	1.15	.30
☐ 5 Orel Hershiser Barehanding the Ball	2.50	1.15	.30
☐ 6 Orel Hershiser The Grip	2.50	1.15	.30
☐ 7 Orel Hershiser Pitching from the Stretch	2.50	1.15	.30

1985-86 Sportflics Prototypes

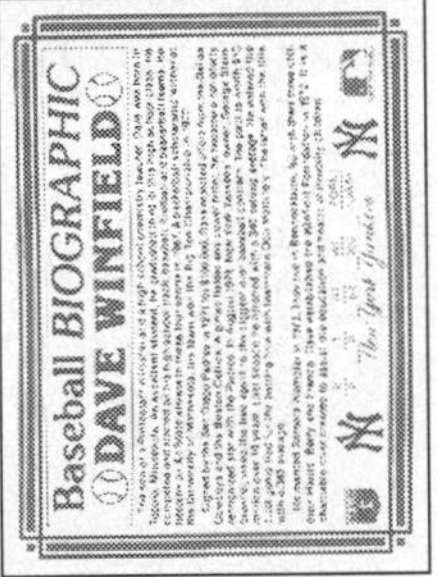

The 1985-86 Sportflics Proof set contains four standard-size (2 1/2" by 3 1/2") unnumbered cards, one mini (1 5/16" by 1 5/16") Joe DiMaggio card, and one trivia card (1 3/4" by 2"). The standard-size cards resemble regular 1986 Sportflics cards, but have different photos and stats only through 1984. One of the Winfield cards has a bio only; unfortunately the biographical statements on the back are incorrect in several instances. The DiMaggio card has black and white photos on the front, and career totals on the back. The trivia card is the same as those distributed with 1986 Sportflics, except it shows the major league baseball logo on the front. These test cards were apparently produced in limited quantity to show Major League Baseball and the Major League Baseball Players Association what Sportflics was proposing in order to be a new licensee for producing cards. These cards are very difficult to find. These cards are considerably rarer than the Sportflics Test cards which were given out after the Sportflics license had been granted.

	NRMT-MT	EXC	G-VG
COMPLETE SET (5)	150.00	70.00	19.00
COMMON PLAYER (1-5)	12.50	5.75	1.55
☐ 1 Joe DiMaggio (Small size)	50.00	23.00	6.25
☐ 2 Mike Schmidt (Stats on back)	50.00	23.00	6.25
☐ 3 Bruce Sutter (Stats on back)	12.50	5.75	1.55
☐ 4 Dave Winfield (Biographical back)	30.00	13.50	3.80
☐ 5 Dave Winfield (Stats on back)	40.00	18.00	5.00

1985-86 Sportflics Test

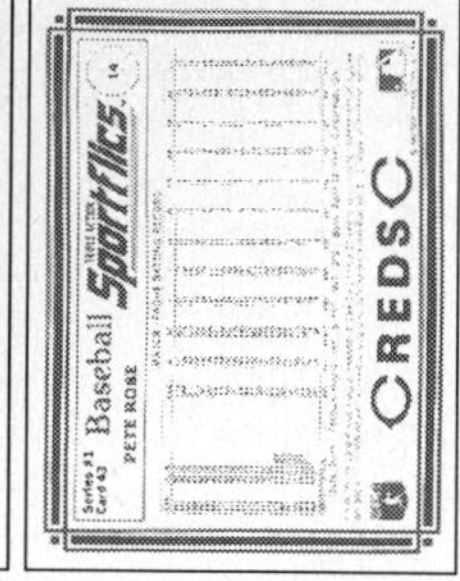

This three-card pack was a test, distributed freely by salesmen to potential buyers to show them what the new Sportflics product would look like. The set is sometimes referred to as the Vendor Sample Kit. Some of these packs even found their way to the retail counters. They are not rare although they are obviously much less common than the regular issue of Sportflics. The cards show statistics only up through 1984. The copyright date on the card backs shows 1986. The cards are standard size, 2 1/2" by 3 1/2".

	NRMT-MT	EXC	G-VG
COMPLETE SET (3)	25.00	11.50	3.10
COMMON PLAYER	6.00	2.70	.75
☐ 1 RBI Sluggers Mike Schmidt Dale Murphy Jim Rice	6.00	2.70	.75
☐ 43 Pete Rose (Pictured with batting helmet; Pete is number 50 in regular 1986 set)	12.50	5.75	1.55
☐ 45 Tom Seaver (Tom is number 25 in regular 1986 set)	12.50	5.75	1.55

1986 Sportflics

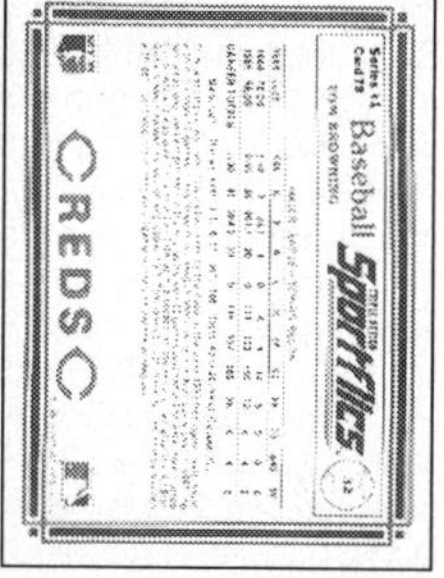

This 200-card set was marketed with 133 small trivia cards. This inaugural set for Sportflics was initially fairly well received by the public. Sportflics was distributed by Major League Marketing; the company also maintained distribution agreements with Wrigley and Amurol. The set features 139 single player "magic motion" cards (which can be tilted to show three different pictures of the same player), 50 "Tri-Stars" (which show three different players), 10 "Big Six" cards (which show six players who share similar achievements), and one World Champs card featuring 12 members of the victorious Kansas City Royals. All cards measure 2 1/2" by 3 1/2". Some of the cards also have (limited production and rarely seen) proof versions with some player selection differences; a proof version of number 178 includes Jim Wilson instead of Mark Funderburk. Also a proof of number 179 with Karl Best, Mark Funderburk, Andres Galarraga, Dwayne Henry, Pete Incaviglia, and Todd Worrell was produced. The following sequences can be found to be in alphabetical order, 26-49, 76-99, 101-124, 151-174, and 187-199. Cards 1-24 seem to be Sportflics' selection of top players and cards 25, 50, 100, 125, and 175 all set milestones or records during the 1985 season.

	MT	EX-MT	VG
COMPLETE SET (200)	40.00	18.00	5.00
COMMON PLAYER (1-200)	.10	.05	.01
☐ 1 George Brett	1.50	.65	.19
☐ 2 Don Mattingly	2.00	.90	.25
☐ 3 Wade Boggs	1.50	.65	.19
☐ 4 Eddie Murray	.90	.40	.11
☐ 5 Dale Murphy	.50	.23	.06
☐ 6 Rickey Henderson	2.00	.90	.25
☐ 7 Harold Baines	.20	.09	.03
☐ 8 Cal Ripken	2.50	1.15	.30
☐ 9 Orel Hershiser	.40	.18	.05
☐ 10 Bret Saberhagen	.40	.18	.05
☐ 11 Tim Raines	.30	.14	.04
☐ 12 Fernando Valenzuela	.20	.09	.03
☐ 13 Tony Gwynn	1.50	.65	.19
☐ 14 Pedro Guerrero	.15	.07	.02
☐ 15 Keith Hernandez	.15	.07	.02
☐ 16 Earnie Riles	.10	.05	.01
☐ 17 Jim Rice	.25	.11	.03
☐ 18 Ron Guidry	.20	.09	.03
☐ 19 Willie McGee	.20	.09	.03
☐ 20 Ryne Sandberg	2.50	1.15	.30
☐ 21 Kirk Gibson	.20	.09	.03
☐ 22 Ozzie Guillen	.30	.14	.04
☐ 23 Dave Parker	.20	.09	.03
☐ 24 Vince Coleman	1.50	.65	.19
☐ 25 Tom Seaver	1.00	.45	.13
☐ 26 Brett Butler	.30	.14	.04
☐ 27 Steve Carlton	.50	.23	.06
☐ 28 Gary Carter	.50	.23	.06
☐ 29 Cecil Cooper	.15	.07	.02
☐ 30 Jose Cruz	.10	.05	.01
☐ 31 Alvin Davis	.10	.05	.01
☐ 32 Dwight Evans	.20	.09	.03
☐ 33 Julio Franco	.30	.14	.04
☐ 34 Damaso Garcia	.10	.05	.01
☐ 35 Steve Garvey	.40	.18	.05
☐ 36 Kent Hrbek	.20	.09	.03
☐ 37 Reggie Jackson	1.25	.55	.16
☐ 38 Fred Lynn	.20	.09	.03
☐ 39 Paul Molitor	.35	.16	.04
☐ 40 Jim Presley	.10	.05	.01
☐ 41 Dave Righetti	.15	.07	.02
☐ 42A Robin Yount ERR New York Yankees	15.00	6.75	1.90
☐ 42B Robin Yount COR Milwaukee Brewers	2.00	.90	.25
☐ 43 Nolan Ryan	4.50	2.00	.55
☐ 44 Mike Schmidt	2.00	.90	.25
☐ 45 Lee Smith	.20	.09	.03
☐ 46 Rick Sutcliffe	.15	.07	.02
☐ 47 Bruce Sutter	.15	.07	.02
☐ 48 Lou Whitaker	.25	.11	.03
☐ 49 Dave Winfield	.75	.35	.09
☐ 50 Pete Rose	1.25	.55	.16
☐ 51 NL MVP's Ryne Sandberg Steve Garvey Pete Rose	.75	.35	.09
☐ 52 Slugging Stars George Brett Harold Baines Jim Rice	.40	.18	.05
☐ 53 No-Hitters Phil Niekro Jerry Reuss Mike Witt	.20	.09	.03
☐ 54 Big Hitters Don Mattingly Cal Ripken Robin Yount	1.25	.55	.16
☐ 55 Bullpen Aces Dan Quisenberry Goose Gossage	.20	.09	.03

	Lee Smith			
☐ 56	Rookies of The Year	.75	.35	.09
	Darryl Strawberry			
	Steve Sax			
	Pete Rose			
☐ 57	AL MVP's	.60	.25	.08
	Cal Ripken			
	Don Baylor			
	Reggie Jackson			
☐ 58	Repeat Batting Champs	.60	.25	.08
	Dave Parker			
	Bill Madlock			
	Pete Rose			
☐ 59	Cy Young Winners	.15	.07	.02
	LaMarr Hoyt			
	Mike Flanagan			
	Ron Guidry			
☐ 60	Double Award Winners	.30	.14	.04
	Fernando Valenzuela			
	Rick Sutcliffe			
	Tom Seaver			
☐ 61	Home Run Champs	.60	.25	.08
	Reggie Jackson			
	Jim Rice			
	Tony Armas			
☐ 62	NL MVP's	.45	.20	.06
	Keith Hernandez			
	Dale Murphy			
	Mike Schmidt			
☐ 63	AL MVP's	.50	.23	.06
	Robin Yount			
	George Brett			
	Fred Lynn			
☐ 64	Comeback Players	.10	.05	.01
	Bert Blyleven			
	Jerry Koosman			
	John Denny			
☐ 65	Cy Young Relievers	.20	.09	.03
	Willie Hernandez			
	Rollie Fingers			
	Bruce Sutter			
☐ 66	Rookies of The Year	.20	.09	.03
	Bob Horner			
	Andre Dawson			
	Gary Matthews			
☐ 67	Rookies of The Year	.45	.20	.06
	Ron Kittle			
	Carlton Fisk			
	Tom Seaver			
☐ 68	Home Run Champs	.30	.14	.04
	Mike Schmidt			
	George Foster			
	Dave Kingman			
☐ 69	Double Award Winners	1.25	.55	.16
	Cal Ripken			
	Rod Carew			
	Pete Rose			
☐ 70	Cy Young Winners	.40	.18	.05
	Rick Sutcliffe			
	Steve Carlton			
	Tom Seaver			
☐ 71	Top Sluggers	.45	.20	.06
	Reggie Jackson			
	Fred Lynn			
	Robin Yount			
☐ 72	Rookies of The Year	.15	.07	.02
	Dave Righetti			
	Fernando Valenzuela			
	Rick Sutcliffe			
☐ 73	Rookies of The Year	.75	.35	.09
	Fred Lynn			
	Eddie Murray			
	Cal Ripken			
☐ 74	Rookies of The Year	.20	.09	.03
	Alvin Davis			
	Lou Whitaker			
	Rod Carew			
☐ 75	Batting Champs	.75	.35	.09
	Don Mattingly			
	Wade Boggs			
	Carney Lansford			
☐ 76	Jesse Barfield	.10	.05	.01
☐ 77	Phil Bradley	.10	.05	.01
☐ 78	Chris Brown	.10	.05	.01
☐ 79	Tom Browning	.15	.07	.02
☐ 80	Tom Brunansky	.20	.09	.03
☐ 81	Bill Buckner	.15	.07	.02
☐ 82	Chili Davis	.15	.07	.02
☐ 83	Mike Davis	.10	.05	.01
☐ 84	Rich Gedman	.10	.05	.01
☐ 85	Willie Hernandez	.10	.05	.01
☐ 86	Ron Kittle	.15	.07	.02
☐ 87	Lee Lacy	.10	.05	.01
☐ 88	Bill Madlock	.15	.07	.02
☐ 89	Mike Marshall	.10	.05	.01
☐ 90	Keith Moreland	.10	.05	.01
☐ 91	Graig Nettles	.20	.09	.03
☐ 92	Lance Parrish	.25	.11	.03
☐ 93	Kirby Puckett	3.00	1.35	.40
☐ 94	Juan Samuel	.15	.07	.02
☐ 95	Steve Sax	.20	.09	.03
☐ 96	Dave Stieb	.15	.07	.02
☐ 97	Darryl Strawberry	1.50	.65	.19
☐ 98	Willie Upshaw	.10	.05	.01
☐ 99	Frank Viola	.30	.14	.04
☐ 100	Dwight Gooden	1.00	.45	.13
☐ 101	Joaquin Andujar	.10	.05	.01
☐ 102	George Bell	.25	.11	.03
☐ 103	Bert Blyleven	.20	.09	.03
☐ 104	Mike Boddicker	.10	.05	.01
☐ 105	Britt Burns	.10	.05	.01
☐ 106	Rod Carew	.75	.35	.09
☐ 107	Jack Clark	.15	.07	.02
☐ 108	Danny Cox	.10	.05	.01
☐ 109	Ron Darling	.30	.14	.04
☐ 110	Andre Dawson	1.00	.45	.13
☐ 111	Leon Durham	.10	.05	.01
☐ 112	Tony Fernandez	.15	.07	.02
☐ 113	Tommy Herr	.10	.05	.01
☐ 114	Teddy Higuera	.15	.07	.02
☐ 115	Bob Horner	.15	.07	.02
☐ 116	Dave Kingman	.20	.09	.03
☐ 117	Jack Morris	.40	.18	.05
☐ 118	Dan Quisenberry	.20	.09	.03
☐ 119	Jeff Reardon	.30	.14	.04
☐ 120	Bryn Smith	.10	.05	.01
☐ 121	Ozzie Smith	1.00	.45	.13
☐ 122	John Tudor	.15	.07	.02
☐ 123	Tim Wallach	.15	.07	.02
☐ 124	Willie Wilson	.15	.07	.02
☐ 125	Carlton Fisk	.90	.40	.11
☐ 126	RBI Sluggers	.15	.07	.02
	Gary Carter			
	Al Oliver			
	George Foster			
☐ 127	Run Scorers	.40	.18	.05
	Tim Raines			
	Ryne Sandberg			
	Keith Hernandez			
☐ 128	Run Scorers	.45	.20	.06
	Paul Molitor			
	Cal Ripken			
	Willie Wilson			
☐ 129	No-Hitters	.15	.07	.02
	John Candelaria			
	Dennis Eckersley			
	Bob Forsch			
☐ 130	World Series MVP's	.50	.23	.06
	Pete Rose			
	Ron Cey			
	Rollie Fingers			
☐ 131	All-Star Game MVP's	.15	.07	.02
	Dave Concepcion			
	George Foster			
	Bill Madlock			
☐ 132	Cy Young Winners	.10	.05	.01
	John Denny			
	Fernando Valenzuela			
	Vida Blue			
☐ 133	Comeback Players	.10	.05	.01
	Rich Dotson			
	Joaquin Andujar			
	Doyle Alexander			
☐ 134	Big Winners	.30	.14	.04
	Rick Sutcliffe			
	Tom Seaver			
	John Denny			
☐ 135	Veteran Pitchers	.60	.25	.08
	Tom Seaver			
	Phil Niekro			
	Don Sutton			
☐ 136	Rookies of The Year	.35	.16	.04
	Dwight Gooden			
	Vince Coleman			
	Alfredo Griffin			
☐ 137	All-Star Game MVP's	.25	.11	.03
	Gary Carter			
	Fred Lynn			
	Steve Garvey			
☐ 138	Veteran Hitters	.50	.23	.06
	Tony Perez			
	Rusty Staub			
	Pete Rose			
☐ 139	Power Hitters	.50	.23	.06
	Mike Schmidt			
	Jim Rice			
	George Foster			

☐ 140 Batting Champs .25 .11 .03
Tony Gwynn
Al Oliver
Bill Buckner
☐ 141 No-Hitters 1.00 .45 .13
Nolan Ryan
Jack Morris
Dave Righetti
☐ 142 No-Hitters .30 .14 .04
Tom Seaver
Bert Blyleven
Vida Blue
☐ 143 Strikeout Kings 1.00 .45 .13
Nolan Ryan
Fernando Valenzuela
Dwight Gooden
☐ 144 Base Stealers .15 .07 .02
Tim Raines
Willie Wilson
Davey Lopes
☐ 145 RBI Sluggers .20 .09 .03
Tony Armas
Cecil Cooper
Eddie Murray
☐ 146 AL MVP's .50 .23 .06
Rod Carew
Jim Rice
Rollie Fingers
☐ 147 World Series MVP's .30 .14 .04
Alan Trammell
Rick Dempsey
Reggie Jackson
☐ 148 World Series MVP's .30 .14 .04
Darrell Porter
Pedro Guerrero
Mike Schmidt
☐ 149 ERA Leaders .10 .05 .01
Mike Boddicker
Rick Sutcliffe
Ron Guidry
☐ 150 Comeback Players .30 .14 .04
Reggie Jackson
Dave Kingman
Fred Lynn
☐ 151 Buddy Bell .15 .07 .02
☐ 152 Dennis Boyd .10 .05 .01
☐ 153 Dave Concepcion .20 .09 .03
☐ 154 Brian Downing .15 .07 .02
☐ 155 Shawon Dunston .30 .14 .04
☐ 156 John Franco .20 .09 .03
☐ 157 Scott Garrelts .15 .07 .02
☐ 158 Bob James .10 .05 .01
☐ 159 Charlie Leibrandt .15 .07 .02
☐ 160 Oddibe McDowell .15 .07 .02
☐ 161 Roger McDowell .15 .07 .02
☐ 162 Mike Moore .20 .09 .03
☐ 163 Phil Niekro .30 .14 .04
☐ 164 Al Oliver .15 .07 .02
☐ 165 Tony Pena .10 .05 .01
☐ 166 Ted Power .10 .05 .01
☐ 167 Mike Scioscia .10 .05 .01
☐ 168 Mario Soto .10 .05 .01
☐ 169 Bob Stanley .10 .05 .01
☐ 170 Garry Templeton .15 .07 .02
☐ 171 Andre Thornton .10 .05 .01
☐ 172 Alan Trammell .35 .16 .04
☐ 173 Doug DeCinces .15 .07 .02
☐ 174 Greg Walker .10 .05 .01
☐ 175 Don Sutton .40 .18 .05
☐ 176 1985 Award Winners .75 .35 .09
Ozzie Guillen
Bret Saberhagen
Don Mattingly
Vince Coleman
Dwight Gooden
Willie McGee
☐ 177 1985 Hot Rookies .20 .09 .03
Stew Cliburn
Brian Fisher UER
(Photo actually
Mike Pagliarulo)
Joe Hesketh
Joe Orsulak
Mark Salas
Larry Sheets
☐ 178 1986 Rookies To Watch 9.00 4.00 1.15
Jose Canseco
Mark Funderburk
Mike Greenwell
Steve Lombardozzi UER
(Photo actually
Mark Salas)
Billy Joe Robidoux
Danny Tartabull
☐ 179 1985 Gold Glovers .60 .25 .08
George Brett
Ron Guidry
Keith Hernandez
Don Mattingly
Willie McGee
Dale Murphy
☐ 180 Active Lifetime .300 .60 .25 .08
Wade Boggs
George Brett
Rod Carew
Cecil Cooper
Don Mattingly
Willie Wilson
☐ 181 Active Lifetime .300 .50 .23 .06
Tony Gwynn
Bill Madlock
Pedro Guerrero
Dave Parker
Pete Rose
Keith Hernandez
☐ 182 1985 Milestones .60 .25 .08
Rod Carew
Phil Niekro
Pete Rose
Nolan Ryan
Tom Seaver
Matt Tallman (fan)
☐ 183 1985 Triple Crown .60 .25 .08
Wade Boggs
Darrell Evans
Don Mattingly
Willie McGee
Dale Murphy
Dave Parker
☐ 184 1985 Highlights .60 .25 .08
Wade Boggs
Dwight Gooden
Rickey Henderson
Don Mattingly
Willie McGee
John Tudor
☐ 185 1985 20 Game Winners .40 .18 .05
Dwight Gooden
Ron Guidry
John Tudor
Joaquin Andujar
Bret Saberhagen
Tom Browning
☐ 186 World Series Champs .25 .11 .03
L.Smith, D.Iorg
W.Wilson, C.Leibrandt
G.Brett, B.Saberhagen
D.Motley, D.Quisenberry
D.Jackson, J.Sundberg
S.Balboni, F.White
☐ 187 Hubie Brooks .10 .05 .01
☐ 188 Glenn Davis .60 .25 .08
☐ 189 Darrell Evans .15 .07 .02
☐ 190 Rich Gossage .20 .09 .03
☐ 191 Andy Hawkins .10 .05 .01
☐ 192 Jay Howell .15 .07 .02
☐ 193 LaMarr Hoyt .10 .05 .01
☐ 194 Davey Lopes .10 .05 .01
☐ 195 Mike Scott .15 .07 .02
☐ 196 Ted Simmons .20 .09 .03
☐ 197 Gary Ward .10 .05 .01
☐ 198 Bob Welch .15 .07 .02
☐ 199 Mike Young .10 .05 .01
☐ 200 Buddy Biancalana .10 .05 .01

1986 Sportflics Decade Greats

This set of 75 three-phase "animated" cards was produced by Sportflics and manufactured by Opti-Graphics of Arlington, Texas. Cards are standard size, 2 1/2" by 3 1/2", and feature both sepia (players of the '30s and '40s) and full color cards. The concept of the set was that the best players at each position for each decade (from the '30s to the '80s) were chosen. The bios were written by Les Woodcock. Also included with the set in the specially designed collector box are 51 trivia cards with historical questions about the six decades of All-Star games. Sample cards of Dwight Gooden

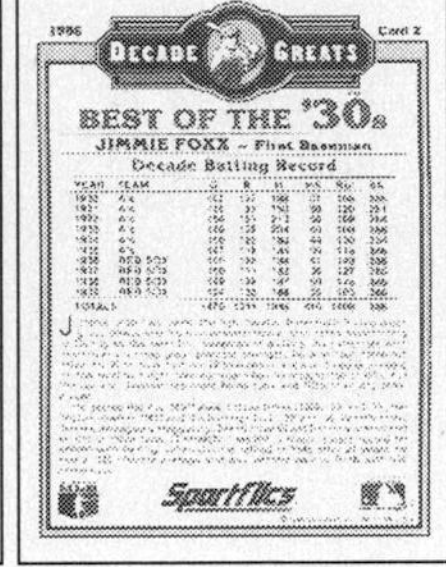

and Mel Ott, which are blank backed except for bing stamped "Sample" on the back, also exist.

	MT	EX-MT	VG
COMPLETE SET (75)	20.00	9.00	2.50
COMMON PLAYER (1-75)	.15	.07	.02

	MT	EX-MT	VG
☐ 1 Babe Ruth	3.50	1.55	.45
☐ 2 Jimmie Foxx	.35	.16	.04
☐ 3 Lefty Grove	.35	.16	.04
☐ 4 Hank Greenberg	.35	.16	.04
☐ 5 Al Simmons	.25	.11	.03
☐ 6 Carl Hubbell	.25	.11	.03
☐ 7 Joe Cronin	.25	.11	.03
☐ 8 Mel Ott	.35	.16	.04
☐ 9 Lefty Gomez	.35	.16	.04
☐ 10 Lou Gehrig (Best '30s Player)	1.50	.65	.19
☐ 11 Pie Traynor	.25	.11	.03
☐ 12 Charlie Gehringer	.25	.11	.03
☐ 13 Best '30s Catchers Bill Dickey Mickey Cochrane Gabby Hartnett	.25	.11	.03
☐ 14 Best '30s Pitchers Dizzy Dean Red Ruffing Paul Derringer	.25	.11	.03
☐ 15 Best '30s Outfielders Paul Waner Joe Medwick Earl Averill	.15	.07	.02
☐ 16 Bob Feller	.75	.35	.09
☐ 17 Lou Boudreau	.25	.11	.03
☐ 18 Enos Slaughter	.35	.16	.04
☐ 19 Hal Newhouser	.25	.11	.03
☐ 20 Joe DiMaggio	2.50	1.15	.30
☐ 21 Pee Wee Reese	.50	.23	.06
☐ 22 Phil Rizzuto	.35	.16	.04
☐ 23 Ernie Lombardi	.15	.07	.02
☐ 24 Best '40s Infielders Johnny Mize Joe Gordon George Kell	.25	.11	.03
☐ 25 Ted Williams (Best '40s Player)	1.50	.65	.19
☐ 26 Mickey Mantle	3.50	1.55	.45
☐ 27 Warren Spahn	.35	.16	.04
☐ 28 Jackie Robinson	1.00	.45	.13
☐ 29 Ernie Banks	.35	.16	.04
☐ 30 Stan Musial (Best '50s Player)	1.00	.45	.13
☐ 31 Yogi Berra	.75	.35	.09
☐ 32 Duke Snider	.75	.35	.09
☐ 33 Roy Campanella	.75	.35	.09
☐ 34 Eddie Mathews	.35	.16	.04
☐ 35 Ralph Kiner	.25	.11	.03
☐ 36 Early Wynn	.25	.11	.03
☐ 37 Double Play Duo Nellie Fox Luis Aparicio	.35	.16	.04
☐ 38 Best '50s First Base Gil Hodges Ted Kluszewski Mickey Vernon	.15	.07	.02
☐ 39 Best '50s Pitchers Bob Lemon Don Newcombe Robin Roberts	.15	.07	.02
☐ 40 Henry Aaron	1.25	.55	.16
☐ 41 Frank Robinson	.35	.16	.04
☐ 42 Bob Gibson	.35	.16	.04
☐ 43 Roberto Clemente	1.00	.45	.13
☐ 44 Whitey Ford	.50	.23	.06
☐ 45 Brooks Robinson	.60	.25	.08
☐ 46 Juan Marichal	.25	.11	.03
☐ 47 Carl Yastrzemski	.75	.35	.09
☐ 48 Best '60s First Base Willie McCovey Harmon Killebrew Orlando Cepeda	.25	.11	.03
☐ 49 Best '60s Catchers Joe Torre Elston Howard Bill Freehan	.15	.07	.02
☐ 50 Willie Mays (Best '50s Player)	1.25	.55	.16
☐ 51 Best '60s Outfielders Al Kaline Tony Oliva Billy Williams	.25	.11	.03
☐ 52 Tom Seaver	1.25	.55	.16
☐ 53 Reggie Jackson	1.00	.45	.13
☐ 54 Steve Carlton	.75	.35	.09
☐ 55 Mike Schmidt	1.25	.55	.16
☐ 56 Joe Morgan	.50	.23	.06
☐ 57 Jim Rice	.25	.11	.03
☐ 58 Jim Palmer	.50	.23	.06
☐ 59 Lou Brock	.35	.16	.04
☐ 60 Pete Rose (Best '70s Player)	1.00	.45	.13
☐ 61 Steve Garvey	.35	.16	.04
☐ 62 Best '70s Catchers Thurman Munson Carlton Fisk Ted Simmons	.50	.23	.06
☐ 63 Best '70s Pitchers Vida Blue Catfish Hunter Nolan Ryan	.50	.23	.06
☐ 64 George Brett	1.25	.55	.16
☐ 65 Don Mattingly	1.25	.55	.16
☐ 66 Fernando Valenzuela	.15	.07	.02
☐ 67 Dale Murphy	.50	.23	.06
☐ 68 Wade Boggs	.75	.35	.09
☐ 69 Rickey Henderson	1.00	.45	.13
☐ 70 Eddie Murray (Best '80s Player)	.60	.25	.08
☐ 71 Ron Guidry	.15	.07	.02
☐ 72 Best '80s Catchers Gary Carter Lance Parrish Tony Pena	.25	.11	.03
☐ 73 Best '80s Infielders Cal Ripken Lou Whitaker Robin Yount	.35	.16	.04
☐ 74 Best '80s Outfielders Pedro Guerrero Tim Raines Dave Winfield	.25	.11	.03
☐ 75 Dwight Gooden	.50	.23	.06

1986 Sportflics Rookies

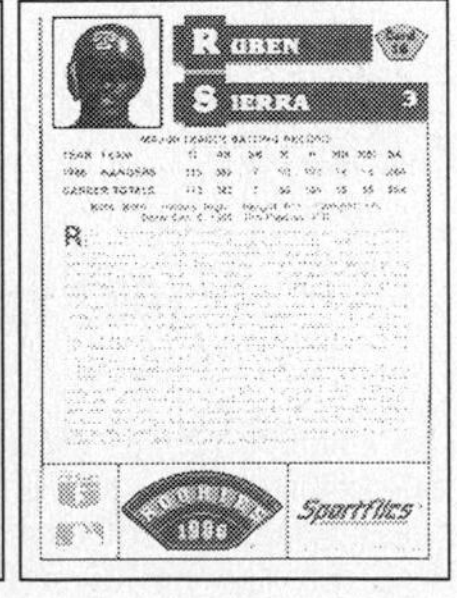

This set of 50 three-phase "animated" cards features top rookies of 1986 as well as a few outstanding rookies from the past. These "Magic Motion" cards are standard size, 2 1/2" by 3 1/2", and feature a distinctive light blue border on the front of the card. Cards were distributed in a light blue box, which also contained 34 trivia cards, each measuring 1 3/4" by 2". There are 47 single player cards along with two Tri-Stars and one Big Six. The statistics on the card backs are inclusive up through the just-completed 1986 season.

	MT	EX-MT	VG
COMPLETE SET (50)	18.00	8.00	2.30
COMMON PLAYER (1-50)	.10	.05	.01
☐ 1 John Kruk	.60	.25	.08
☐ 2 Edwin Correa	.10	.05	.01
☐ 3 Pete Incaviglia	.35	.16	.04
☐ 4 Dale Sveum	.10	.05	.01
☐ 5 Juan Nieves	.10	.05	.01
☐ 6 Will Clark	5.00	2.30	.60
☐ 7 Wally Joyner	1.25	.55	.16
☐ 8 Lance McCullers	.10	.05	.01
☐ 9 Scott Bailes	.10	.05	.01
☐ 10 Dan Plesac	.10	.05	.01
☐ 11 Jose Canseco	5.00	2.30	.60
☐ 12 Bobby Witt	.35	.16	.04
☐ 13 Barry Bonds	4.00	1.80	.50
☐ 14 Andres Thomas	.10	.05	.01
☐ 15 Jim Deshaies	.10	.05	.01
☐ 16 Ruben Sierra	3.50	1.55	.45
☐ 17 Steve Lombardozzi	.10	.05	.01
☐ 18 Cory Snyder	.15	.07	.02
☐ 19 Reggie Williams	.10	.05	.01
☐ 20 Mitch Williams	.15	.07	.02
☐ 21 Glenn Braggs	.10	.05	.01
☐ 22 Danny Tartabull	1.25	.55	.16
☐ 23 Charlie Kerfeld	.10	.05	.01
☐ 24 Paul Assenmacher	.10	.05	.01
☐ 25 Robby Thompson	.20	.09	.03
☐ 26 Bobby Bonilla	2.00	.90	.25
☐ 27 Andres Galarraga	.20	.09	.03
☐ 28 Billy Joe Robidoux	.10	.05	.01
☐ 29 Bruce Ruffin	.10	.05	.01
☐ 30 Greg Swindell	.25	.11	.03
☐ 31 John Cangelosi	.10	.05	.01
☐ 32 Jim Traber	.10	.05	.01
☐ 33 Russ Morman	.10	.05	.01
☐ 34 Barry Larkin	2.00	.90	.25
☐ 35 Todd Worrell	.30	.14	.04
☐ 36 John Cerutti	.10	.05	.01
☐ 37 Mike Kingery	.10	.05	.01
☐ 38 Mark Eichhorn	.10	.05	.01
☐ 39 Scott Bankhead	.15	.07	.02
☐ 40 Bo Jackson	4.00	1.80	.50
☐ 41 Greg Mathews	.10	.05	.01
☐ 42 Eric King	.10	.05	.01
☐ 43 Kal Daniels	.20	.09	.03
☐ 44 Calvin Schiraldi	.10	.05	.01
☐ 45 Mickey Brantley	.10	.05	.01
☐ 46 Tri-Stars Willie Mays Pete Rose Fred Lynn	.40	.18	.05
☐ 47 Tri-Stars Tom Seaver Fern. Valenzuela Dwight Gooden	.40	.18	.05
☐ 48 Big Six Eddie Murray, Lou Whitaker, Dave Righetti, Steve Sax, Cal Ripken, Darryl Strawberry	.30	.14	.04
☐ 49 Kevin Mitchell	1.50	.65	.19
☐ 50 Mike Diaz	.10	.05	.01

1987 Sportflics

This 200-card set was produced by Sportflics and again features three sequence action pictures on each card. Cards measure 2 1/2" by 3 1/2" and are in full color. Also included with the cards were 136 small team logo and trivia cards. There are 165 individual players, 20 Tri-Stars (the top three players in each league at each position), and 15 other miscellaneous multi-player cards. The cards feature a red border on the front. A full-color face shot of the player is printed on the back of the card. Cards are numbered on the back in the upper right corner. The cards in the factory-collated sets are copyrighted 1986, while the cards in the

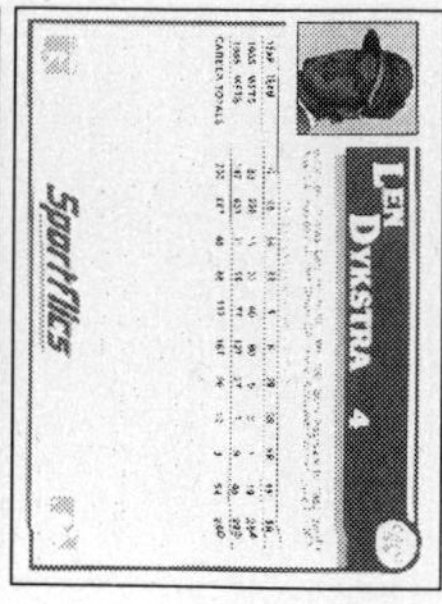

wax packs are copyrighted 1987 or show no copyright year on the back. Cards from wax packs with 1987 copyright are 1-35, 41-75, 81-115, 121-155, and 161-195; the rest of the numbers (when taken from wax packs) are found without a copyright year.

	MT	EX-MT	VG
COMPLETE SET (200)	30.00	13.50	3.80
COMMON PLAYER (1-200)	.10	.05	.01
☐ 1 Don Mattingly	1.25	.55	.16
☐ 2 Wade Boggs	.90	.40	.11
☐ 3 Dale Murphy	.40	.18	.05
☐ 4 Rickey Henderson	1.25	.55	.16
☐ 5 George Brett	.90	.40	.11
☐ 6 Eddie Murray	.75	.35	.09
☐ 7 Kirby Puckett	1.25	.55	.16
☐ 8 Ryne Sandberg	1.50	.65	.19
☐ 9 Cal Ripken	1.50	.65	.19
☐ 10 Roger Clemens	1.50	.65	.19
☐ 11 Ted Higuera	.10	.05	.01
☐ 12 Steve Sax	.15	.07	.02
☐ 13 Chris Brown	.10	.05	.01
☐ 14 Jesse Barfield	.15	.07	.02
☐ 15 Kent Hrbek	.15	.07	.02
☐ 16 Robin Yount	.90	.40	.11
☐ 17 Glenn Davis	.30	.14	.04
☐ 18 Hubie Brooks	.10	.05	.01
☐ 19 Mike Scott	.15	.07	.02
☐ 20 Darryl Strawberry	.90	.40	.11
☐ 21 Alvin Davis	.10	.05	.01
☐ 22 Eric Davis	.35	.16	.04
☐ 23 Danny Tartabull	.50	.23	.06
☐ 24A Cory Snyder ERR '86 (Photo on front is Pat Tabler)	4.00	1.80	.50
☐ 24B Cory Snyder ERR '87 (Photos on front and back are Pat Tabler)	2.00	.90	.25
☐ 24C Cory Snyder COR '86	2.00	.90	.25
☐ 25 Pete Rose	.90	.40	.11
☐ 26 Wally Joyner	.75	.35	.09
☐ 27 Pedro Guerrero	.15	.07	.02
☐ 28 Tom Seaver	.75	.35	.09
☐ 29 Bob Knepper	.10	.05	.01
☐ 30 Mike Schmidt	1.00	.45	.13
☐ 31 Tony Gwynn	.90	.40	.11
☐ 32 Don Slaught	.10	.05	.01
☐ 33 Todd Worrell	.15	.07	.02
☐ 34 Tim Raines	.15	.07	.02
☐ 35 Dave Parker	.15	.07	.02
☐ 36 Bob Ojeda	.10	.05	.01
☐ 37 Pete Incaviglia	.20	.09	.03
☐ 38 Bruce Hurst	.15	.07	.02
☐ 39 Bobby Witt	.25	.11	.03
☐ 40 Steve Garvey	.35	.16	.04
☐ 41 Dave Winfield	.60	.25	.08
☐ 42 Jose Cruz	.10	.05	.01
☐ 43 Orel Hershiser	.20	.09	.03
☐ 44 Reggie Jackson	.75	.35	.09
☐ 45 Chili Davis	.15	.07	.02
☐ 46 Robby Thompson	.15	.07	.02
☐ 47 Dennis Boyd	.10	.05	.01
☐ 48 Kirk Gibson	.20	.09	.03
☐ 49 Fred Lynn	.15	.07	.02
☐ 50 Gary Carter	.35	.16	.04
☐ 51 George Bell	.25	.11	.03
☐ 52 Pete O'Brien	.10	.05	.01
☐ 53 Ron Darling	.20	.09	.03
☐ 54 Paul Molitor	.25	.11	.03
☐ 55 Mike Pagliarulo	.10	.05	.01
☐ 56 Mike Boddicker	.10	.05	.01

☐ 57 Dave Righetti	.15	.07	.02
☐ 58 Len Dykstra	.25	.11	.03
☐ 59 Mike Witt	.10	.05	.01
☐ 60 Tony Bernazard	.10	.05	.01
☐ 61 John Kruk	.25	.11	.03
☐ 62 Mike Krukow	.10	.05	.01
☐ 63 Sid Fernandez	.15	.07	.02
☐ 64 Gary Gaetti	.10	.05	.01
☐ 65 Vince Coleman	.35	.16	.04
☐ 66 Pat Tabler	.10	.05	.01
☐ 67 Mike Scioscia	.10	.05	.01
☐ 68 Scott Garrelts	.10	.05	.01
☐ 69 Brett Butler	.20	.09	.03
☐ 70 Bill Buckner	.15	.07	.02
☐ 71A Dennis Rasmussen	1.00	.45	.13
ERR '86 copyright			
(Photo on back			
is John Montefusco)			
☐ 71B Dennis Rasmussen	.50	.23	.06
COR '87 copyright			
(Photo with mustache)			
☐ 72 Tim Wallach	.15	.07	.02
☐ 73 Bob Horner	.15	.07	.02
☐ 74 Willie McGee	.15	.07	.02
☐ 75 Tri-Stars	.75	.35	.09
Don Mattingly			
Wally Joyner			
Eddie Murray			
☐ 76A Jesse Orosco COR	.35	.16	.04
'86 copyright			
☐ 76B Jesse Orosco ERR	.15	.07	.02
'87 copyright			
(Number on back is 96)			
☐ 77 Tri-Stars	.20	.09	.03
Todd Worrell			
Jeff Reardon			
Dave Smith			
☐ 78 Candy Maldonado	.15	.07	.02
☐ 79 Tri-Stars	.20	.09	.03
Ozzie Smith			
Hubie Brooks			
Shawon Dunston			
☐ 80 Tri-Stars	.60	.25	.08
George Bell			
Jose Canseco			
Jim Rice			
☐ 81 Bert Blyleven	.15	.07	.02
☐ 82 Mike Marshall	.15	.07	.02
☐ 83 Ron Guidry	.15	.07	.02
☐ 84 Julio Franco	.20	.09	.03
☐ 85 Willie Wilson	.15	.07	.02
☐ 86 Lee Lacy	.10	.05	.01
☐ 87 Jack Morris	.30	.14	.04
☐ 88 Ray Knight	.20	.09	.03
☐ 89 Phil Bradley	.10	.05	.01
☐ 90 Jose Canseco	1.50	.65	.19
☐ 91 Gary Ward	.10	.05	.01
☐ 92 Mike Easler	.10	.05	.01
☐ 93 Tony Pena	.10	.05	.01
☐ 94 Dave Smith	.10	.05	.01
☐ 95 Will Clark	1.50	.65	.19
☐ 96 Lloyd Moseby	.10	.05	.01
(See also 76B)			
☐ 97 Jim Rice	.20	.09	.03
☐ 98 Shawon Dunston	.15	.07	.02
☐ 99 Don Sutton	.30	.14	.04
☐ 100 Dwight Gooden	.45	.20	.06
☐ 101 Lance Parrish	.15	.07	.02
☐ 102 Mark Langston	.15	.07	.02
☐ 103 Floyd Youmans	.10	.05	.01
☐ 104 Lee Smith	.20	.09	.03
☐ 105 Willie Hernandez	.10	.05	.01
☐ 106 Doug DeCinces	.15	.07	.02
☐ 107 Ken Schrom	.10	.05	.01
☐ 108 Don Carman	.10	.05	.01
☐ 109 Brook Jacoby	.10	.05	.01
☐ 110 Steve Bedrosian	.10	.05	.01
☐ 111 Tri-Stars	.50	.23	.06
Roger Clemens			
Jack Morris			
Ted Higuera			
☐ 112 Tri-Stars	.10	.05	.01
Marty Barrett			
Tony Bernazard			
Lou Whitaker			
☐ 113 Tri-Stars	.30	.14	.04
Cal Ripken			
Scott Fletcher			
Tony Fernandez			
☐ 114 Tri-Stars	.60	.25	.08
Wade Boggs			
George Brett			
Gary Gaetti			
☐ 115 Tri-Stars	.40	.18	.05
Mike Schmidt			
Chris Brown			
Tim Wallach			
☐ 116 Tri-Stars	.35	.16	.04
Ryne Sandberg			
Johnny Ray			
Bill Doran			
☐ 117 Tri-Stars	.20	.09	.03
Dave Parker			
Tony Gwynn			
Kevin Bass			
☐ 118 Big Six Rookies	.75	.35	.09
Ty Gainey			
Terry Steinbach			
Dave Clark			
Pat Dodson			
Phil Lombardi			
Benito Santiago			
☐ 119 Hi-Lite Tri-Stars	.15	.07	.02
Dave Righetti			
Fernando Valenzuela			
Mike Scott			
☐ 120 Tri-Stars	.25	.11	.03
Fernando Valenzuela			
Mike Scott			
Dwight Gooden			
☐ 121 Johnny Ray	.10	.05	.01
☐ 122 Keith Moreland	.10	.05	.01
☐ 123 Juan Samuel	.15	.07	.02
☐ 124 Wally Backman	.10	.05	.01
☐ 125 Nolan Ryan	2.00	.90	.25
☐ 126 Greg A. Harris	.10	.05	.01
☐ 127 Kirk McCaskill	.10	.05	.01
☐ 128 Dwight Evans	.15	.07	.02
☐ 129 Rick Rhoden	.10	.05	.01
☐ 130 Bill Madlock	.10	.05	.01
☐ 131 Oddibe McDowell	.10	.05	.01
☐ 132 Darrell Evans	.15	.07	.02
☐ 133 Keith Hernandez	.15	.07	.02
☐ 134 Tom Brunansky	.15	.07	.02
☐ 135 Kevin McReynolds	.20	.09	.03
☐ 136 Scott Fletcher	.10	.05	.01
☐ 137 Lou Whitaker	.20	.09	.03
☐ 138 Carney Lansford	.15	.07	.02
☐ 139 Andre Dawson	.60	.25	.08
☐ 140 Carlton Fisk	.60	.25	.08
☐ 141 Buddy Bell	.15	.07	.02
☐ 142 Ozzie Smith	.60	.25	.08
☐ 143 Dan Pasqua	.15	.07	.02
☐ 144 Kevin Mitchell	.50	.23	.06
☐ 145 Bret Saberhagen	.25	.11	.03
☐ 146 Charlie Kerfeld	.10	.05	.01
☐ 147 Phil Niekro	.25	.11	.03
☐ 148 John Candelaria	.10	.05	.01
☐ 149 Rich Gedman	.10	.05	.01
☐ 150 Fernando Valenzuela	.15	.07	.02
☐ 151 Tri-Stars	.15	.07	.02
Gary Carter			
Mike Scioscia			
Tony Pena			
☐ 152 Tri-Stars	.25	.11	.03
Tim Raines			
Jose Cruz			
Vince Coleman			
☐ 153 Tri-Stars	.25	.11	.03
Jesse Barfield			
Harold Baines			
Dave Winfield			
☐ 154 Tri-Stars	.10	.05	.01
Lance Parrish			
Don Slaught			
Rich Gedman			
☐ 155 Tri-Stars	.25	.11	.03
Dale Murphy			
Kevin McReynolds			
Eric Davis			
☐ 156 Hi-Lite Tri-Stars	.40	.18	.05
Don Sutton			
Mike Schmidt			
Jim Deshaies			
☐ 157 Speedburners	.25	.11	.03
Rickey Henderson			
John Cangelosi			
Gary Pettis			
☐ 158 Big Six Rookies	.50	.23	.06
Randy Asadoor			
Casey Candaele			
Kevin Seitzer			
Rafael Palmeiro			
Tim Pyznarski			
Dave Cochrane			
☐ 159 Big Six	.75	.35	.09

	MT	EX-MT	VG
Don Mattingly			
Rickey Henderson			
Roger Clemens			
Dale Murphy			
Eddie Murray			
Dwight Gooden			
☐ 160 Roger McDowell	.10	.05	.01
☐ 161 Brian Downing	.10	.05	.01
☐ 162 Bill Doran	.15	.07	.02
☐ 163 Don Baylor	.15	.07	.02
☐ 164A Alfredo Griffin ERR (No uniform number on card back) '87	.25	.11	.03
☐ 164B Alfredo Griffin COR '86	.25	.11	.03
☐ 165 Don Aase	.10	.05	.01
☐ 166 Glenn Wilson	.10	.05	.01
☐ 167 Dan Quisenberry	.15	.07	.02
☐ 168 Frank White	.10	.05	.01
☐ 169 Cecil Cooper	.15	.07	.02
☐ 170 Jody Davis	.10	.05	.01
☐ 171 Harold Baines	.15	.07	.02
☐ 172 Rob Deer	.20	.09	.03
☐ 173 John Tudor	.10	.05	.01
☐ 174 Larry Parrish	.10	.05	.01
☐ 175 Kevin Bass	.10	.05	.01
☐ 176 Joe Carter	.75	.35	.09
☐ 177 Mitch Webster	.10	.05	.01
☐ 178 Dave Kingman	.15	.07	.02
☐ 179 Jim Presley	.10	.05	.01
☐ 180 Mel Hall	.20	.09	.03
☐ 181 Shane Rawley	.10	.05	.01
☐ 182 Marty Barrett	.10	.05	.01
☐ 183 Damaso Garcia	.10	.05	.01
☐ 184 Bobby Grich	.15	.07	.02
☐ 185 Leon Durham	.10	.05	.01
☐ 186 Ozzie Guillen	.15	.07	.02
☐ 187 Tony Fernandez	.15	.07	.02
☐ 188 Alan Trammell	.25	.11	.03
☐ 189 Jim Clancy	.10	.05	.01
☐ 190 Bo Jackson	1.50	.65	.19
☐ 191 Bob Forsch	.10	.05	.01
☐ 192 John Franco	.10	.05	.01
☐ 193 Von Hayes	.10	.05	.01
☐ 194 Tri-Stars	.10	.05	.01
Don Aase			
Dave Righetti			
Mark Eichhorn			
☐ 195 Tri-Stars	.40	.18	.05
Keith Hernandez			
Will Clark			
Glenn Davis			
☐ 196 Hi-Lite Tri-Stars	.35	.16	.04
Roger Clemens			
Joe Cowley			
Bob Horner			
☐ 197 Big Six	.60	.25	.08
George Brett			
Hubie Brooks			
Tony Gwynn			
Ryne Sandberg			
Tim Raines			
Wade Boggs			
☐ 198 Tri-Stars	.50	.23	.06
Kirby Puckett			
Rickey Henderson			
Fred Lynn			
☐ 199 Speedburners	.25	.11	.03
Tim Raines			
Vince Coleman			
Eric Davis			
☐ 200 Steve Carlton	.35	.16	.04

1987 Sportflics Dealer Panels

These "Magic Motion" card panels of four were issued only to dealers who were ordering other Sportflics product in quantity. If cut into individual cards, the interior white borders will be slightly narrower than the regular issue Sportflics since the panels of four measure a shade under 4 7/8" by 6 7/8". The cards have a 1986 copyright on the back same as the factory collated sets. Other than the slight difference in size, these cards are essentially styled the same as the regular issue of 1987 Sportflics. This set of sixteen top players was accompanied by the inclusion of

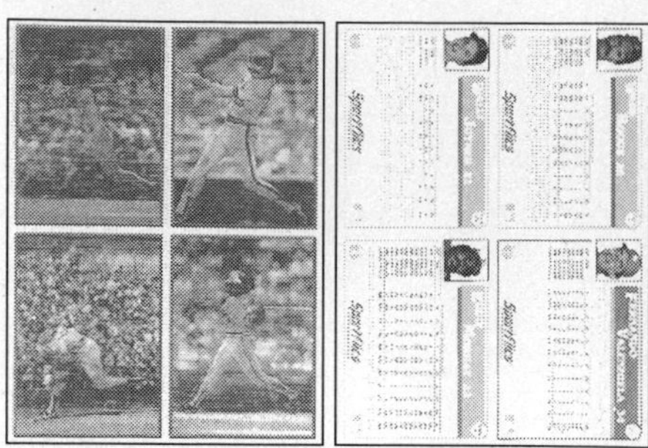

four smaller panels of four team logo/team fact cards. The 16 small team cards correspond directly to the 16 players in the sets. The checklist below prices the panels and gives the card number for each player, which is the same as the player's card number in the Sportflics regular set.

	MT	EX-MT	VG
COMPLETE SET (4)	12.00	5.50	1.50
COMMON PANEL (1-4)	3.00	1.35	.40
☐ 1 Don Mattingly 1	4.50	2.00	.55
Roger Clemens 10			
Mike Schmidt 30			
Tim Raines 34			
☐ 2 Wade Boggs 2	3.50	1.55	.45
Eddie Murray 6			
Wally Joyner 26			
Fern.Valenzuela 150			
☐ 3 Dale Murphy 3	3.00	1.35	.40
Tony Gwynn 31			
Jim Rice 97			
Keith Hernandez 133			
☐ 4 Rickey Henderson 4	4.50	2.00	.55
George Brett 5			
Cal Ripken 9			
Dwight Gooden 100			

1987 Sportflics Rookie Packs

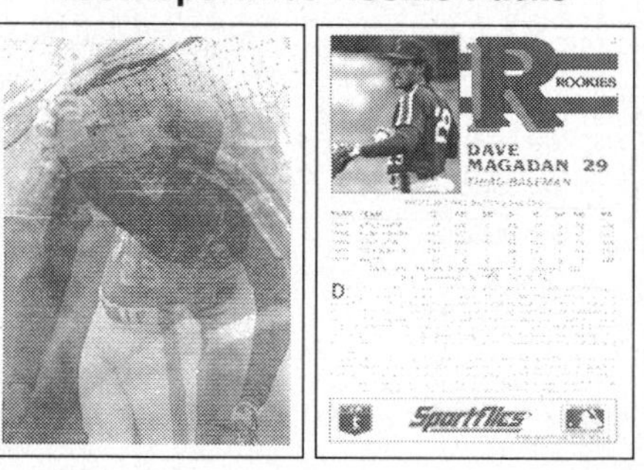

This two pack-set consists of ten "rookie" players and two trivia cards. Each of the two different packs had half the set and the outside of the wrapper told which cards were inside. The cards are all 2 1/2" by 3 1/2". The set includes the first major league baseball cards ever of Alonzo Powell, John Smiley, and Brick Smith. Dealers received one rookie pack with every Team Preview set they ordered. The card backs also feature a full-color small photo of the player.

	MT	EX-MT	VG
COMPLETE SET (10)	6.00	2.70	.75
COMMON PLAYER (1-10)	.40	.18	.05
☐ 1 Terry Steinbach (Pack two)	1.00	.45	.13
☐ 2 Rafael Palmeiro (Pack one)	2.00	.90	.25

	MT	EX-MT	VG
☐ 3 Dave Magadan (Pack two)	.75	.35	.09
☐ 4 Marvin Freeman (Pack two)	.40	.18	.05
☐ 5 Brick Smith (Pack two)	.40	.18	.05
☐ 6 B.J. Surhoff (Pack one)	.75	.35	.09
☐ 7 John Smiley (Pack one)	1.00	.45	.13
☐ 8 Alonzo Powell (Pack two)	.40	.18	.05
☐ 9 Benito Santiago (Pack one)	1.50	.65	.19
☐ 10 Devon White (Pack one)	1.00	.45	.13

1987 Sportflics Rookies I

These "Magic Motion" cards were issued as a series of 25 cards packaged in its own complete set box, along with 17 trivia cards. Cards are 2 1/2" by 3 1/2." The three front photos show the player in two action poses and one portrait pose. The card backs also provide a full-color photo (1 3/8" by 2 1/4") of the player as well as the usual statistics and biographical notes. The front photos are framed by a wide, round-cornered, red border and have the player's name and uniform number at the bottom. The cards in the set are numbered essentially in alphabetical order by player's name.

	MT	EX-MT	VG
COMPLETE SET (25)	7.00	3.10	.85
COMMON PLAYER (1-25)	.10	.05	.01
☐ 1 Eric Bell	.10	.05	.01
☐ 2 Chris Bosio	.30	.14	.04
☐ 3 Bob Brower	.10	.05	.01
☐ 4 Jerry Browne	.20	.09	.03
☐ 5 Ellis Burks	.50	.23	.06
☐ 6 Casey Candaele	.10	.05	.01
☐ 7 Ken Gerhart	.10	.05	.01
☐ 8 Mike Greenwell	.90	.40	.11
☐ 9 Stan Jefferson	.10	.05	.01
☐ 10 Dave Magadan	.20	.09	.03
☐ 11 Joe Magrane	.20	.09	.03
☐ 12 Fred McGriff	1.50	.65	.19
☐ 13 Mark McGwire	2.00	.90	.25
☐ 14 Mark McLemore	.15	.07	.02
☐ 15 Jeff Musselman	.10	.05	.01
☐ 16 Matt Nokes	.30	.14	.04
☐ 17 Paul O'Neill	.30	.14	.04
☐ 18 Luis Polonia	.40	.18	.05
☐ 19 Benito Santiago	.75	.35	.09
☐ 20 Kevin Seitzer	.30	.14	.04
☐ 21 John Smiley	.40	.18	.05
☐ 22 Terry Steinbach	.30	.14	.04
☐ 23 B.J. Surhoff	.20	.09	.03
☐ 24 Devon White	.30	.14	.04
☐ 25 Matt Williams	1.75	.80	.22

1987 Sportflics Rookies II

These "Magic Motion" cards were issued as a series of 25 cards packaged in its own complete set box along with 17 trivia cards. Cards are 2 1/2" by 3 1/2." In this second set the card numbering begins with number 26. The three front photos show the player in two action poses and one portrait pose. The card backs also provide a full-color photo (approximately 1 3/8" by 2 1/4") of the player as well as the usual statistics and biographical notes. The front photos are framed by a wide, round-cornered, red border and have the player's name and uniform number at the bottom.

	MT	EX-MT	VG
COMPLETE SET (25)	4.00	1.80	.50
COMMON PLAYER (26-50)	.10	.05	.01
☐ 26 DeWayne Buice	.10	.05	.01
☐ 27 Willie Fraser	.10	.05	.01
☐ 28 Billy Ripken	.15	.07	.02
☐ 29 Mike Henneman	.20	.09	.03
☐ 30 Shawn Hillegas	.10	.05	.01
☐ 31 Shane Mack	.35	.16	.04
☐ 32 Rafael Palmeiro	1.25	.55	.16
☐ 33 Mike Jackson	.15	.07	.02
☐ 34 Gene Larkin	.20	.09	.03
☐ 35 Jimmy Jones	.10	.05	.01
☐ 36 Gerald Young	.10	.05	.01
☐ 37 Ken Caminiti	.30	.14	.04
☐ 38 Sam Horn	.15	.07	.02
☐ 39 David Cone	1.00	.45	.13
☐ 40 Mike Dunne	.10	.05	.01
☐ 41 Ken Williams	.10	.05	.01
☐ 42 John Morris	.10	.05	.01
☐ 43 Jim Lindeman	.10	.05	.01
☐ 44 Mike Stanley	.10	.05	.01
☐ 45 Les Straker	.10	.05	.01
☐ 46 Jeff M. Robinson	.10	.05	.01
☐ 47 Todd Benzinger	.20	.09	.03
☐ 48 Jeff Blauser	.20	.09	.03
☐ 49 John Marzano	.10	.05	.01
☐ 50 Keith Miller	.25	.11	.03

1987 Sportflics Team Preview

This 26-card set features a card for each Major League team. Each card shows 12 different players on that team via four "Magic Motion" trios. The cards are numbered on the backs. The narrative on the back gives Outlook, Newcomers to Watch, and Summary for each team. The list of players appearing on the front is given at the bottom of the reverse of each card. Cards are standard size, 2 1/2" by 3 1/2". The was distributed as a complete set in its own box along with 26 team logo trivia cards measuring approximately 1 3/4" by 2".

	MT	EX-MT	VG
COMPLETE SET (26)	5.00	2.30	.60
COMMON PLAYER (1-26)	.30	.14	.04

	MT	EX-MT	VG
☐ 1 Texas Rangers	.30	.14	.04
☐ 2 New York Mets	.40	.18	.05
☐ 3 Cleveland Indians	.30	.14	.04
☐ 4 Cincinnati Reds	.40	.18	.05
☐ 5 Toronto Blue Jays	.30	.14	.04
☐ 6 Philadelphia Phillies	.30	.14	.04
☐ 7 New York Yankees	.40	.18	.05
☐ 8 Houston Astros	.30	.14	.04
☐ 9 Boston Red Sox	.40	.18	.05
☐ 10 San Francisco Giants	.30	.14	.04
☐ 11 California Angels	.30	.14	.04
☐ 12 St. Louis Cardinals	.40	.18	.05
☐ 13 Kansas City Royals	.40	.18	.05
☐ 14 Los Angeles Dodgers	.40	.18	.05
☐ 15 Detroit Tigers	.40	.18	.05
☐ 16 San Diego Padres	.30	.14	.04
☐ 17 Minnesota Twins	.40	.18	.05
☐ 18 Pittsburgh Pirates	.30	.14	.04
☐ 19 Milwaukee Brewers	.30	.14	.04
☐ 20 Montreal Expos	.30	.14	.04
☐ 21 Baltimore Orioles	.40	.18	.05
☐ 22 Chicago Cubs	.30	.14	.04
☐ 23 Oakland Athletics	.40	.18	.05
☐ 24 Atlanta Braves	.30	.14	.04
☐ 25 Seattle Mariners	.30	.14	.04
☐ 26 Chicago White Sox	.30	.14	.04

1988 Sportflics

This 225-card set was produced by Sportflics and again features three sequence action pictures on each card. Cards measure 2 1/2" by 3 1/2" and are in full color. There are 219 individual players, three Highlights trios, and three Rookie Prospect trio cards. The cards feature a red border on the front. A full-color action picture of the player is printed on the back of the card. Cards are numbered on the back in the lower right corner.

	MT	EX-MT	VG
COMPLETE SET (225)	35.00	16.00	4.40
COMMON PLAYER (1-225)	.10	.05	.01
☐ 1 Don Mattingly	1.00	.45	.13
☐ 2 Tim Raines	.20	.09	.03
☐ 3 Andre Dawson	.45	.20	.06
☐ 4 George Bell	.20	.09	.03
☐ 5 Joe Carter	.45	.20	.06
☐ 6 Matt Nokes	.20	.09	.03
☐ 7 Dave Winfield	.45	.20	.06
☐ 8 Kirby Puckett	1.00	.45	.13
☐ 9 Will Clark	1.25	.55	.16
☐ 10 Eric Davis	.35	.16	.04
☐ 11 Rickey Henderson	1.00	.45	.13
☐ 12 Ryne Sandberg	1.25	.55	.16
☐ 13 Jesse Barfield UER (Misspelled Jessie on card back)	.15	.07	.02
☐ 14 Ozzie Guillen	.15	.07	.02
☐ 15 Bret Saberhagen	.20	.09	.03
☐ 16 Tony Gwynn	.75	.35	.09
☐ 17 Kevin Seitzer	.20	.09	.03
☐ 18 Jack Clark	.15	.07	.02
☐ 19 Danny Tartabull	.35	.16	.04
☐ 20 Ted Higuera	.10	.05	.01
☐ 21 Charlie Leibrandt UER (Misspelled Liebrandt on card front)	.15	.07	.02
☐ 22 Benito Santiago	.35	.16	.04
☐ 23 Fred Lynn	.15	.07	.02
☐ 24 Robby Thompson	.10	.05	.01
☐ 25 Alan Trammell	.20	.09	.03
☐ 26 Tony Fernandez	.15	.07	.02
☐ 27 Rick Sutcliffe	.10	.05	.01
☐ 28 Gary Carter	.25	.11	.03
☐ 29 Cory Snyder	.15	.07	.02
☐ 30 Lou Whitaker	.20	.09	.03
☐ 31 Keith Hernandez	.15	.07	.02
☐ 32 Mike Witt	.10	.05	.01
☐ 33 Harold Baines	.15	.07	.02
☐ 34 Robin Yount	.75	.35	.09
☐ 35 Mike Schmidt	1.00	.45	.13
☐ 36 Dion James	.10	.05	.01
☐ 37 Tom Candiotti	.15	.07	.02
☐ 38 Tracy Jones	.10	.05	.01
☐ 39 Nolan Ryan	2.50	1.15	.30
☐ 40 Fernando Valenzuela	.15	.07	.02
☐ 41 Vance Law	.10	.05	.01
☐ 42 Roger McDowell	.10	.05	.01
☐ 43 Carlton Fisk	.50	.23	.06
☐ 44 Scott Garrelts	.10	.05	.01
☐ 45 Lee Guetterman	.10	.05	.01
☐ 46 Mark Langston	.15	.07	.02
☐ 47 Willie Randolph	.15	.07	.02
☐ 48 Bill Doran	.10	.05	.01
☐ 49 Larry Parrish	.10	.05	.01
☐ 50 Wade Boggs	.75	.35	.09
☐ 51 Shane Rawley	.10	.05	.01
☐ 52 Alvin Davis	.10	.05	.01
☐ 53 Jeff Reardon	.25	.11	.03
☐ 54 Jim Presley	.10	.05	.01
☐ 55 Kevin Bass	.10	.05	.01
☐ 56 Kevin McReynolds	.20	.09	.03
☐ 57 B.J. Surhoff	.15	.07	.02
☐ 58 Julio Franco	.20	.09	.03
☐ 59 Eddie Murray	.45	.20	.06
☐ 60 Jody Davis	.10	.05	.01
☐ 61 Todd Worrell	.20	.09	.03
☐ 62 Von Hayes	.10	.05	.01
☐ 63 Billy Hatcher	.15	.07	.02
☐ 64 John Kruk	.25	.11	.03
☐ 65 Tom Henke	.15	.07	.02
☐ 66 Mike Scott	.15	.07	.02
☐ 67 Vince Coleman	.20	.09	.03
☐ 68 Ozzie Smith	.45	.20	.06
☐ 69 Ken Williams	.10	.05	.01
☐ 70 Steve Bedrosian	.10	.05	.01
☐ 71 Luis Polonia	.30	.14	.04
☐ 72 Brook Jacoby	.10	.05	.01
☐ 73 Ron Darling	.15	.07	.02
☐ 74 Lloyd Moseby	.10	.05	.01
☐ 75 Wally Joyner	.25	.11	.03
☐ 76 Dan Quisenberry	.15	.07	.02
☐ 77 Scott Fletcher	.10	.05	.01
☐ 78 Kirk McCaskill	.10	.05	.01
☐ 79 Paul Molitor	.30	.14	.04
☐ 80 Mike Aldrete	.10	.05	.01
☐ 81 Neal Heaton	.10	.05	.01
☐ 82 Jeffrey Leonard	.10	.05	.01
☐ 83 Dave Magadan	.15	.07	.02
☐ 84 Danny Cox	.10	.05	.01
☐ 85 Lance McCullers	.10	.05	.01
☐ 86 Jay Howell	.10	.05	.01
☐ 87 Charlie Hough	.15	.07	.02
☐ 88 Gene Garber	.10	.05	.01
☐ 89 Jesse Orosco	.10	.05	.01
☐ 90 Don Robinson	.10	.05	.01
☐ 91 Willie McGee	.15	.07	.02
☐ 92 Bert Blyleven	.15	.07	.02
☐ 93 Phil Bradley	.10	.05	.01

☐ 94 Terry Kennedy	.10	.05	.01
☐ 95 Kent Hrbek	.15	.07	.02
☐ 96 Juan Samuel	.10	.05	.01
☐ 97 Pedro Guerrero	.15	.07	.02
☐ 98 Sid Bream	.10	.05	.01
☐ 99 Devon White	.20	.09	.03
☐ 100 Mark McGwire	1.00	.45	.13
☐ 101 Dave Parker	.20	.09	.03
☐ 102 Glenn Davis	.20	.09	.03
☐ 103 Greg Walker	.10	.05	.01
☐ 104 Rick Rhoden	.10	.05	.01
☐ 105 Mitch Webster	.10	.05	.01
☐ 106 Len Dykstra	.20	.09	.03
☐ 107 Gene Larkin	.15	.07	.02
☐ 108 Floyd Youmans	.10	.05	.01
☐ 109 Andy Van Slyke	.25	.11	.03
☐ 110 Mike Scioscia	.10	.05	.01
☐ 111 Kirk Gibson	.20	.09	.03
☐ 112 Kal Daniels	.15	.07	.02
☐ 113 Ruben Sierra	1.00	.45	.13
☐ 114 Sam Horn	.15	.07	.02
☐ 115 Ray Knight	.15	.07	.02
☐ 116 Jimmy Key	.15	.07	.02
☐ 117 Bo Diaz	.10	.05	.01
☐ 118 Mike Greenwell	.40	.18	.05
☐ 119 Barry Bonds	.90	.40	.11
☐ 120 Reggie Jackson UER	.75	.35	.09
(463 lifetime homers)			
☐ 121 Mike Pagliarulo	.10	.05	.01
☐ 122 Tommy John	.20	.09	.03
☐ 123 Bill Madlock	.10	.05	.01
☐ 124 Ken Caminiti	.25	.11	.03
☐ 125 Gary Ward	.10	.05	.01
☐ 126 Candy Maldonado	.15	.07	.02
☐ 127 Harold Reynolds	.10	.05	.01
☐ 128 Joe Magrane	.15	.07	.02
☐ 129 Mike Henneman	.20	.09	.03
☐ 130 Jim Gantner	.15	.07	.02
☐ 131 Bobby Bonilla	.40	.18	.05
☐ 132 John Farrell	.10	.05	.01
☐ 133 Frank Tanana	.15	.07	.02
☐ 134 Zane Smith	.10	.05	.01
☐ 135 Dave Righetti	.15	.07	.02
☐ 136 Rick Reuschel	.15	.07	.02
☐ 137 Dwight Evans	.15	.07	.02
☐ 138 Howard Johnson	.25	.11	.03
☐ 139 Terry Leach	.10	.05	.01
☐ 140 Casey Candaele	.10	.05	.01
☐ 141 Tom Herr	.10	.05	.01
☐ 142 Tony Pena	.10	.05	.01
☐ 143 Lance Parrish	.15	.07	.02
☐ 144 Ellis Burks	.35	.16	.04
☐ 145 Pete O'Brien	.10	.05	.01
☐ 146 Mike Boddicker	.10	.05	.01
☐ 147 Buddy Bell	.15	.07	.02
☐ 148 Bo Jackson	1.25	.55	.16
☐ 149 Frank White	.15	.07	.02
☐ 150 George Brett	.75	.35	.09
☐ 151 Tim Wallach	.15	.07	.02
☐ 152 Cal Ripken	1.25	.55	.16
☐ 153 Brett Butler	.15	.07	.02
☐ 154 Gary Gaetti	.10	.05	.01
☐ 155 Darryl Strawberry	.75	.35	.09
☐ 156 Alredo Griffin	.10	.05	.01
☐ 157 Marty Barrett	.10	.05	.01
☐ 158 Jim Rice	.20	.09	.03
☐ 159 Terry Pendleton	.35	.16	.04
☐ 160 Orel Hershiser	.20	.09	.03
☐ 161 Larry Sheets	.10	.05	.01
☐ 162 Dave Stewart UER	.25	.11	.03
(Braves logo)			
☐ 163 Shawon Dunston	.20	.09	.03
☐ 164 Keith Moreland	.10	.05	.01
☐ 165 Ken Oberkfell	.10	.05	.01
☐ 166 Ivan Calderon	.20	.09	.03
☐ 167 Bob Welch	.15	.07	.02
☐ 168 Fred McGriff	.75	.35	.09
☐ 169 Pete Incaviglia	.15	.07	.02
☐ 170 Dale Murphy	.25	.11	.03
☐ 171 Mike Dunne	.10	.05	.01
☐ 172 Chili Davis	.15	.07	.02
☐ 173 Milt Thompson	.10	.05	.01
☐ 174 Terry Steinbach	.15	.07	.02
☐ 175 Oddibe McDowell	.10	.05	.01
☐ 176 Jack Morris	.25	.11	.03
☐ 177 Sid Fernandez	.15	.07	.02
☐ 178 Ken Griffey	.20	.09	.03
☐ 179 Lee Smith	.20	.09	.03
☐ 180 Highlights 1987	.45	.20	.06
Kirby Puckett			
Juan Nieves			
Mike Schmidt			
☐ 181 Brian Downing	.10	.05	.01
☐ 182 Andres Galarraga	.15	.07	.02
☐ 183 Rob Deer	.20	.09	.03
☐ 184 Greg Brock	.10	.05	.01
☐ 185 Doug DeCinces	.15	.07	.02
☐ 186 Johnny Ray	.10	.05	.01
☐ 187 Hubie Brooks	.10	.05	.01
☐ 188 Darrell Evans	.15	.07	.02
☐ 189 Mel Hall	.15	.07	.02
☐ 190 Jim Deshaies	.10	.05	.01
☐ 191 Dan Plesac	.10	.05	.01
☐ 192 Willie Wilson	.15	.07	.02
☐ 193 Mike LaValliere	.10	.05	.01
☐ 194 Tom Brunansky	.15	.07	.02
☐ 195 John Franco	.15	.07	.02
☐ 196 Frank Viola	.25	.11	.03
☐ 197 Bruce Hurst	.15	.07	.02
☐ 198 John Tudor	.10	.05	.01
☐ 199 Bob Forsch	.10	.05	.01
☐ 200 Dwight Gooden	.30	.14	.04
☐ 201 Jose Canseco	1.25	.55	.16
☐ 202 Carney Lansford	.15	.07	.02
☐ 203 Kelly Downs	.10	.05	.01
☐ 204 Glenn Wilson	.10	.05	.01
☐ 205 Pat Tabler	.10	.05	.01
☐ 206 Mike Davis	.10	.05	.01
☐ 207 Roger Clemens	1.25	.55	.16
☐ 208 Dave Smith	.10	.05	.01
☐ 209 Curt Young	.10	.05	.01
☐ 210 Mark Eichhorn	.15	.07	.02
☐ 211 Juan Nieves	.10	.05	.01
☐ 212 Bob Boone	.15	.07	.02
☐ 213 Don Sutton	.20	.09	.03
☐ 214 Willie Upshaw	.10	.05	.01
☐ 215 Jim Clancy	.10	.05	.01
☐ 216 Bill Ripken	.15	.07	.02
☐ 217 Ozzie Virgil	.10	.05	.01
☐ 218 Dave Concepcion	.20	.09	.03
☐ 219 Alan Ashby	.10	.05	.01
☐ 220 Mike Marshall	.15	.07	.02
☐ 221 Highlights 1987	.40	.18	.05
Mark McGwire			
Paul Molitor			
Vince Coleman			
☐ 222 Highlights 1987	.40	.18	.05
Benito Santiago			
Steve Bedrosian			
Don Mattingly			
☐ 223 Rookie Prospects	.25	.11	.03
Shawn Abner			
Jay Buhner			
Gary Thurman			
☐ 224 Rookie Prospects	.15	.07	.02
Tim Crews			
Vincente Palacios			
John Davis			
☐ 225 Rookie Prospects	.25	.11	.03
Jody Reed			
Jeff Treadway			
Keith Miller			

1988 Sportflics Gamewinners

This 25-card set of "Gamewinners" was distributed in a green and yellow box along with 17 trivia cards by Weiser Card Company of New Jersey. The 25 players selected for the set show a strong New York preference. The set was ostensibly produced for use as a youth organizational fund raiser. The cards are the standard size, 2 1/2" by 3 1/2" and are done in the typical Sportflics' Magic Motion (three picture) style. The cards are numbered on the back.

	MT	EX-MT	VG
COMPLETE SET (25)	12.00	5.50	1.50
COMMON PLAYER (1-25)	.20	.09	.03
☐ 1 Don Mattingly	1.25	.55	.16
☐ 2 Mark McGwire	1.00	.45	.13
☐ 3 Wade Boggs	1.00	.45	.13
☐ 4 Will Clark	1.25	.55	.16
☐ 5 Eric Davis	.50	.23	.06
☐ 6 Willie Randolph	.20	.09	.03
☐ 7 Dave Winfield	.75	.35	.09
☐ 8 Rickey Henderson	1.00	.45	.13
☐ 9 Dwight Gooden	.50	.23	.06
☐ 10 Benito Santiago	.50	.23	.06
☐ 11 Keith Hernandez	.30	.14	.04
☐ 12 Juan Samuel	.20	.09	.03
☐ 13 Kevin Seitzer	.25	.11	.03
☐ 14 Gary Carter	.50	.23	.06
☐ 15 Darryl Strawberry	1.00	.45	.13
☐ 16 Rick Rhoden	.20	.09	.03
☐ 17 Howard Johnson	.30	.14	.04
☐ 18 Matt Nokes	.30	.14	.04
☐ 19 Dave Righetti	.20	.09	.03
☐ 20 Roger Clemens	1.25	.55	.16
☐ 21 Mike Schmidt	1.00	.45	.13
☐ 22 Kevin McReynolds	.20	.09	.03
☐ 23 Mike Pagliarulo	.20	.09	.03
☐ 24 Kevin Elster	.20	.09	.03
☐ 25 Jack Clark	.20	.09	.03

1989 Sportflics

This 225-card set was produced by Sportflics (distributed by Major League Marketing) and again features three sequence action pictures on each card. Cards measure 2 1/2" by 3 1/2" and are in full color. There are 220 individual players, two Highlights trios, and three Rookie Prospect trio cards. The cards feature a white border on the front with red and blue inner trim colors. A full-color action picture of the player is printed on the back of the card. Cards are numbered on the back in the lower right corner.

	MT	EX-MT	VG
COMPLETE SET (225)	35.00	16.00	4.40
COMMON PLAYER (1-225)	.10	.05	.01
☐ 1 Jose Canseco	1.00	.45	.13
☐ 2 Wally Joyner	.25	.11	.03
☐ 3 Roger Clemens	1.00	.45	.13
☐ 4 Greg Swindell	.20	.09	.03
☐ 5 Jack Morris	.20	.09	.03
☐ 6 Mickey Brantley	.10	.05	.01
☐ 7 Jim Presley	.10	.05	.01
☐ 8 Pete O'Brien	.10	.05	.01
☐ 9 Jesse Barfield	.15	.07	.02
☐ 10 Frank Viola	.15	.07	.02
☐ 11 Kevin Bass	.10	.05	.01
☐ 12 Glenn Wilson	.10	.05	.01
☐ 13 Chris Sabo	.30	.14	.04
☐ 14 Fred McGriff	.50	.23	.06
☐ 15 Mark Grace	.75	.35	.09
☐ 16 Devon White	.15	.07	.02
☐ 17 Juan Samuel	.10	.05	.01
☐ 18 Lou Whitaker UER (Card back says Bats: Right and Throws: Left)	.20	.09	.03
☐ 19 Greg Walker	.10	.05	.01
☐ 20 Roberto Alomar	1.25	.55	.16
☐ 21 Mike Schmidt	.75	.35	.09
☐ 22 Benito Santiago	.25	.11	.03
☐ 23 Dave Stewart	.20	.09	.03
☐ 24 Dave Winfield	.50	.23	.06
☐ 25 George Bell	.20	.09	.03
☐ 26 Jack Clark	.15	.07	.02
☐ 27 Doug Drabek	.25	.11	.03
☐ 28 Ron Gant	.75	.35	.09
☐ 29 Glenn Braggs	.10	.05	.01
☐ 30 Rafael Palmeiro	.25	.11	.03
☐ 31 Brett Butler	.20	.09	.03
☐ 32 Ron Darling	.15	.07	.02
☐ 33 Alvin Davis	.10	.05	.01
☐ 34 Bob Walk	.10	.05	.01
☐ 35 Dave Stieb	.15	.07	.02
☐ 36 Orel Hershiser	.20	.09	.03
☐ 37 John Farrell	.10	.05	.01
☐ 38 Doug Jones	.15	.07	.02
☐ 39 Kelly Downs	.10	.05	.01
☐ 40 Bob Boone	.15	.07	.02
☐ 41 Gary Sheffield UER (7 career triples, should be 0)	2.00	.90	.25
☐ 42 Doug Dascenzo	.10	.05	.01
☐ 43 Chad Kreuter	.10	.05	.01
☐ 44 Ricky Jordan	.15	.07	.02
☐ 45 Dave West	.10	.05	.01
☐ 46 Danny Tartabull	.35	.16	.04
☐ 47 Teddy Higuera	.10	.05	.01
☐ 48 Gary Gaetti	.10	.05	.01
☐ 49 Dave Parker	.15	.07	.02
☐ 50 Don Mattingly	.75	.35	.09
☐ 51 David Cone	.35	.16	.04
☐ 52 Kal Daniels	.15	.07	.02
☐ 53 Carney Lansford	.15	.07	.02
☐ 54 Mike Marshall	.10	.05	.01
☐ 55 Kevin Seitzer	.15	.07	.02
☐ 56 Mike Henneman	.15	.07	.02
☐ 57 Bill Doran	.10	.05	.01
☐ 58 Steve Sax	.15	.07	.02
☐ 59 Lance Parrish	.15	.07	.02
☐ 60 Keith Hernandez	.15	.07	.02
☐ 61 Jose Uribe	.10	.05	.01
☐ 62 Jose Lind	.10	.05	.01
☐ 63 Steve Bedrosian	.10	.05	.01
☐ 64 George Brett UER (Text says .380 in 1980, should be .390)	.50	.23	.06
☐ 65 Kirk Gibson	.20	.09	.03
☐ 66 Cal Ripken	1.00	.45	.13
☐ 67 Mitch Webster	.10	.05	.01
☐ 68 Fred Lynn	.15	.07	.02
☐ 69 Eric Davis	.25	.11	.03
☐ 70 Bo Jackson	.75	.35	.09
☐ 71 Kevin Elster	.10	.05	.01
☐ 72 Rick Reuschel	.10	.05	.01
☐ 73 Tim Burke	.10	.05	.01
☐ 74 Mark Davis	.10	.05	.01
☐ 75 Claudell Washington	.10	.05	.01
☐ 76 Lance McCullers	.10	.05	.01
☐ 77 Mike Moore	.15	.07	.02
☐ 78 Robby Thompson	.15	.07	.02
☐ 79 Roger McDowell	.10	.05	.01
☐ 80 Danny Jackson	.10	.05	.01
☐ 81 Tim Leary	.10	.05	.01
☐ 82 Bobby Witt	.15	.07	.02
☐ 83 Jim Gott	.10	.05	.01
☐ 84 Andy Hawkins	.10	.05	.01
☐ 85 Ozzie Guillen	.15	.07	.02
☐ 86 John Tudor	.10	.05	.01
☐ 87 Todd Burns	.10	.05	.01
☐ 88 Dave Gallagher	.10	.05	.01
☐ 89 Jay Buhner	.25	.11	.03
☐ 90 Gregg Jefferies	.75	.35	.09
☐ 91 Bob Welch	.15	.07	.02
☐ 92 Charlie Hough	.10	.05	.01
☐ 93 Tony Fernandez	.15	.07	.02
☐ 94 Ozzie Virgil	.10	.05	.01
☐ 95 Andre Dawson	.35	.16	.04
☐ 96 Hubie Brooks	.10	.05	.01
☐ 97 Kevin McReynolds	.15	.07	.02
☐ 98 Mike LaValliere	.10	.05	.01
☐ 99 Terry Pendleton	.35	.16	.04
☐ 100 Wade Boggs	.60	.25	.08
☐ 101 Dennis Eckersley	.25	.11	.03
☐ 102 Mark Gubicza	.15	.07	.02
☐ 103 Frank Tanana	.15	.07	.02

☐ 104	Joe Carter	.40	.18	.05
☐ 105	Ozzie Smith	.35	.16	.04
☐ 106	Dennis Martinez	.15	.07	.02
☐ 107	Jeff Treadway	.10	.05	.01
☐ 108	Greg Maddux	.35	.16	.04
☐ 109	Bret Saberhagen	.20	.09	.03
☐ 110	Dale Murphy	.25	.11	.03
☐ 111	Rob Deer	.15	.07	.02
☐ 112	Pete Incaviglia	.15	.07	.02
☐ 113	Vince Coleman	.20	.09	.03
☐ 114	Tim Wallach	.15	.07	.02
☐ 115	Nolan Ryan	2.50	1.15	.30
☐ 116	Walt Weiss	.15	.07	.02
☐ 117	Brian Downing	.10	.05	.01
☐ 118	Melido Perez	.25	.11	.03
☐ 119	Terry Steinbach	.15	.07	.02
☐ 120	Mike Scott	.15	.07	.02
☐ 121	Tim Belcher	.15	.07	.02
☐ 122	Mike Boddicker	.10	.05	.01
☐ 123	Len Dykstra	.15	.07	.02
☐ 124	Fernando Valenzuela	.15	.07	.02
☐ 125	Gerald Young	.10	.05	.01
☐ 126	Tom Henke	.15	.07	.02
☐ 127	Dave Henderson	.10	.05	.01
☐ 128	Dan Plesac	.10	.05	.01
☐ 129	Chili Davis	.15	.07	.02
☐ 130	Bryan Harvey	.25	.11	.03
☐ 131	Don August	.10	.05	.01
☐ 132	Mike Harkey	.25	.11	.03
☐ 133	Luis Polonia	.25	.11	.03
☐ 134	Craig Worthington	.10	.05	.01
☐ 135	Joey Meyer	.10	.05	.01
☐ 136	Barry Larkin	.35	.16	.04
☐ 137	Glenn Davis	.20	.09	.03
☐ 138	Mike Scioscia	.10	.05	.01
☐ 139	Andres Galarraga	.15	.07	.02
☐ 140	Dwight Gooden	.25	.11	.03
☐ 141	Keith Moreland	.10	.05	.01
☐ 142	Kevin Mitchell	.25	.11	.03
☐ 143	Mike Greenwell	.25	.11	.03
☐ 144	Mel Hall	.15	.07	.02
☐ 145	Rickey Henderson	.60	.25	.08
☐ 146	Barry Bonds	.60	.25	.08
☐ 147	Eddie Murray	.30	.14	.04
☐ 148	Lee Smith	.20	.09	.03
☐ 149	Julio Franco	.20	.09	.03
☐ 150	Tim Raines	.15	.07	.02
☐ 151	Mitch Williams	.15	.07	.02
☐ 152	Tim Laudner	.10	.05	.01
☐ 153	Mike Pagliarulo	.10	.05	.01
☐ 154	Floyd Bannister	.10	.05	.01
☐ 155	Gary Carter	.20	.09	.03
☐ 156	Kirby Puckett	.75	.35	.09
☐ 157	Harold Baines	.15	.07	.02
☐ 158	Dave Righetti	.10	.05	.01
☐ 159	Mark Langston	.15	.07	.02
☐ 160	Tony Gwynn	.50	.23	.06
☐ 161	Tom Brunansky	.15	.07	.02
☐ 162	Vance Law	.10	.05	.01
☐ 163	Kelly Gruber	.15	.07	.02
☐ 164	Gerald Perry	.10	.05	.01
☐ 165	Harold Reynolds	.10	.05	.01
☐ 166	Andy Van Slyke	.20	.09	.03
☐ 167	Jimmy Key	.15	.07	.02
☐ 168	Jeff Reardon	.25	.11	.03
☐ 169	Milt Thompson	.10	.05	.01
☐ 170	Will Clark	1.00	.45	.13
☐ 171	Chet Lemon	.10	.05	.01
☐ 172	Pat Tabler	.10	.05	.01
☐ 173	Jim Rice	.20	.09	.03
☐ 174	Billy Hatcher	.10	.05	.01
☐ 175	Bruce Hurst	.15	.07	.02
☐ 176	John Franco	.15	.07	.02
☐ 177	Van Snider	.10	.05	.01
☐ 178	Ron Jones	.10	.05	.01
☐ 179	Jerald Clark	.20	.09	.03
☐ 180	Tom Browning	.15	.07	.02
☐ 181	Von Hayes	.10	.05	.01
☐ 182	Bobby Bonilla	.35	.16	.04
☐ 183	Todd Worrell	.15	.07	.02
☐ 184	John Kruk	.20	.09	.03
☐ 185	Scott Fletcher	.10	.05	.01
☐ 186	Willie Wilson	.15	.07	.02
☐ 187	Jody Davis	.10	.05	.01
☐ 188	Kent Hrbek	.15	.07	.02
☐ 189	Ruben Sierra	.50	.23	.06
☐ 190	Shawon Dunston	.15	.07	.02
☐ 191	Ellis Burks	.25	.11	.03
☐ 192	Brook Jacoby	.10	.05	.01
☐ 193	Jeff M. Robinson	.10	.05	.01
☐ 194	Rich Dotson	.10	.05	.01
☐ 195	Johnny Ray	.10	.05	.01
☐ 196	Cory Snyder	.15	.07	.02
☐ 197	Mike Witt	.10	.05	.01
☐ 198	Marty Barrett	.10	.05	.01
☐ 199	Robin Yount	.50	.23	.06
☐ 200	Mark McGwire	.60	.25	.08
☐ 201	Ryne Sandberg	.75	.35	.09
☐ 202	John Candelaria	.10	.05	.01
☐ 203	Matt Nokes	.15	.07	.02
☐ 204	Dwight Evans	.15	.07	.02
☐ 205	Darryl Strawberry	.60	.25	.08
☐ 206	Willie McGee	.15	.07	.02
☐ 207	Bobby Thigpen	.15	.07	.02
☐ 208	B.J. Surhoff	.15	.07	.02
☐ 209	Paul Molitor	.25	.11	.03
☐ 210	Jody Reed	.15	.07	.02
☐ 211	Doyle Alexander	.10	.05	.01
☐ 212	Dennis Rasmussen	.10	.05	.01
☐ 213	Kevin Gross	.10	.05	.01
☐ 214	Kirk McCaskill	.10	.05	.01
☐ 215	Alan Trammell	.20	.09	.03
☐ 216	Damon Berryhill	.15	.07	.02
☐ 217	Rick Sutcliffe	.10	.05	.01
☐ 218	Don Slaught	.10	.05	.01
☐ 219	Carlton Fisk	.40	.18	.05
☐ 220	Allan Anderson	.10	.05	.01
☐ 221	Jose Canseco Wade Boggs Mike Greenwell	.60	.25	.08
☐ 222	Orel Hershiser Dennis Eckersley Tom Browning	.20	.09	.03
☐ 223	Gary Sheffield Gregg Jefferies Sandy Alomar Jr.	1.50	.65	.19
☐ 224	Bob Milacki Randy Johnson Ramon Martinez	.35	.16	.04
☐ 225	Cameron Drew Geronimo Berroa Ron Jones	.10	.05	.01

1990 Sportflics

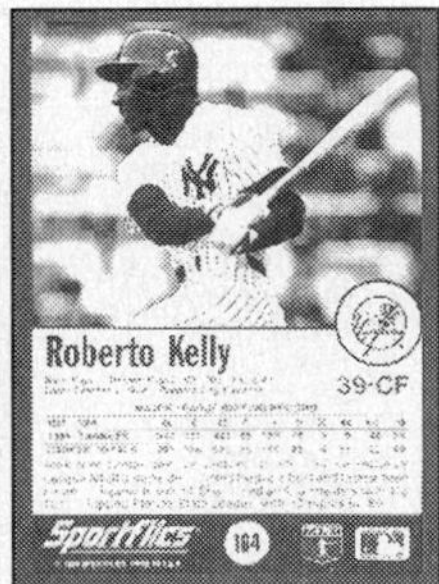

The 1990 Sportflics set contains 225 standard-size (2 1/2" by 3 1/2") cards. On the fronts, the black, white, orange, and yellow borders surround two photos, which can each be seen depending on the angle. The set is considered an improvement over the previous years' versions by many collectors due to the increased clarity of the fronts, caused by having two images rather than three. The backs are dominated by large color photos.

		MT	EX-MT	VG
COMPLETE SET (225)		40.00	18.00	5.00
COMMON PLAYER (1-225)		.10	.05	.01
☐ 1	Kevin Mitchell	.25	.11	.03
☐ 2	Wade Boggs	.50	.23	.06
☐ 3	Cory Snyder	.15	.07	.02
☐ 4	Paul O'Neill	.15	.07	.02
☐ 5	Will Clark	.75	.35	.09
☐ 6	Tony Fernandez	.15	.07	.02
☐ 7	Ken Griffey Jr.	4.50	2.00	.55
☐ 8	Nolan Ryan	2.50	1.15	.30
☐ 9	Rafael Palmeiro	.25	.11	.03
☐ 10	Jesse Barfield	.15	.07	.02
☐ 11	Kirby Puckett	.60	.25	.08
☐ 12	Steve Sax	.15	.07	.02

☐	13	Fred McGriff	.35	.16	.04
☐	14	Gregg Jefferies	.35	.16	.04
☐	15	Mark Grace	.35	.16	.04
☐	16	Ozzie Smith	.30	.14	.04
☐	17	George Bell	.20	.09	.03
☐	18	Robin Yount	.50	.23	.06
☐	19	Glenn Davis	.15	.07	.02
☐	20	Jeffrey Leonard	.10	.05	.01
☐	21	Chili Davis	.15	.07	.02
☐	22	Craig Biggio	.35	.16	.04
☐	23	Jose Canseco	.75	.35	.09
☐	24	Derek Lilliquist	.10	.05	.01
☐	25	Chris Bosio	.20	.09	.03
☐	26	Dave Stieb	.15	.07	.02
☐	27	Bobby Thigpen	.15	.07	.02
☐	28	Jack Clark	.15	.07	.02
☐	29	Kevin Ritz	.10	.05	.01
☐	30	Tom Gordon	.15	.07	.02
☐	31	Bryan Harvey	.20	.09	.03
☐	32	Jim Deshaies	.10	.05	.01
☐	33	Terry Steinbach	.15	.07	.02
☐	34	Tom Glavine	.50	.23	.06
☐	35	Bob Welch	.15	.07	.02
☐	36	Charlie Hayes	.15	.07	.02
☐	37	Jeff Reardon	.20	.09	.03
☐	38	Joe Orsulak	.10	.05	.01
☐	39	Scott Garrelts	.10	.05	.01
☐	40	Bob Boone	.15	.07	.02
☐	41	Scott Bankhead	.10	.05	.01
☐	42	Tom Henke	.15	.07	.02
☐	43	Greg Briley	.10	.05	.01
☐	44	Teddy Higuera	.10	.05	.01
☐	45	Pat Borders	.15	.07	.02
☐	46	Kevin Seitzer	.15	.07	.02
☐	47	Bruce Hurst	.10	.05	.01
☐	48	Ozzie Guillen	.15	.07	.02
☐	49	Wally Joyner	.20	.09	.03
☐	50	Mike Greenwell	.20	.09	.03
☐	51	Gary Gaetti	.10	.05	.01
☐	52	Gary Sheffield UER (Uniform listed as 21, should be 1)	.60	.25	.08
☐	53	Dennis Martinez	.15	.07	.02
☐	54	Ryne Sandberg	.75	.35	.09
☐	55	Mike Scott	.15	.07	.02
☐	56	Todd Benzinger	.10	.05	.01
☐	57	Kelly Gruber	.15	.07	.02
☐	58	Jose Lind	.10	.05	.01
☐	59	Allan Anderson	.10	.05	.01
☐	60	Robby Thompson	.10	.05	.01
☐	61	John Smoltz	.30	.14	.04
☐	62	Mark Davis	.10	.05	.01
☐	63	Tom Herr	.10	.05	.01
☐	64	Randy Johnson	.20	.09	.03
☐	65	Lonnie Smith	.10	.05	.01
☐	66	Pedro Guerrero	.15	.07	.02
☐	67	Jerome Walton	.15	.07	.02
☐	68	Ramon Martinez	.35	.16	.04
☐	69	Tim Raines	.15	.07	.02
☐	70	Matt Williams	.25	.11	.03
☐	71	Joe Oliver	.15	.07	.02
☐	72	Nick Esasky	.10	.05	.01
☐	73	Kevin Brown	.20	.09	.03
☐	74	Walt Weiss	.15	.07	.02
☐	75	Roger McDowell	.10	.05	.01
☐	76	Jose DeLeon	.10	.05	.01
☐	77	Brian Downing	.10	.05	.01
☐	78	Jay Howell	.10	.05	.01
☐	79	Jose Uribe	.10	.05	.01
☐	80	Ellis Burks	.20	.09	.03
☐	81	Sammy Sosa	.30	.14	.04
☐	82	Johnny Ray	.10	.05	.01
☐	83	Danny Darwin	.10	.05	.01
☐	84	Carney Lansford	.15	.07	.02
☐	85	Jose Oquendo	.10	.05	.01
☐	86	John Cerutti	.10	.05	.01
☐	87	Dave Winfield	.35	.16	.04
☐	88	Dave Righetti	.10	.05	.01
☐	89	Danny Jackson	.10	.05	.01
☐	90	Andy Benes	.35	.16	.04
☐	91	Tom Browning	.10	.05	.01
☐	92	Pete O'Brien	.10	.05	.01
☐	93	Roberto Alomar	.60	.25	.08
☐	94	Bret Saberhagen	.20	.09	.03
☐	95	Phil Bradley	.10	.05	.01
☐	96	Doug Jones	.15	.07	.02
☐	97	Eric Davis	.20	.09	.03
☐	98	Tony Gwynn	.45	.20	.06
☐	99	Jim Abbott	.60	.25	.08
☐	100	Cal Ripken	.75	.35	.09
☐	101	Andy Van Slyke	.20	.09	.03
☐	102	Dan Plesac	.10	.05	.01
☐	103	Lou Whitaker	.15	.07	.02
☐	104	Steve Bedrosian	.10	.05	.01
☐	105	Dave Gallagher	.10	.05	.01
☐	106	Keith Hernandez	.15	.07	.02
☐	107	Duane Ward	.15	.07	.02
☐	108	Andre Dawson	.30	.14	.04
☐	109	Howard Johnson	.20	.09	.03
☐	110	Mark Langston	.15	.07	.02
☐	111	Jerry Browne	.10	.05	.01
☐	112	Alvin Davis	.10	.05	.01
☐	113	Sid Fernandez	.15	.07	.02
☐	114	Mike Devereaux	.20	.09	.03
☐	115	Benito Santiago	.20	.09	.03
☐	116	Bip Roberts	.15	.07	.02
☐	117	Craig Worthington	.10	.05	.01
☐	118	Kevin Elster	.10	.05	.01
☐	119	Harold Reynolds	.10	.05	.01
☐	120	Joe Carter	.35	.16	.04
☐	121	Brian Harper	.10	.05	.01
☐	122	Frank Viola	.15	.07	.02
☐	123	Jeff Ballard	.10	.05	.01
☐	124	John Kruk	.20	.09	.03
☐	125	Harold Baines	.15	.07	.02
☐	126	Tom Candiotti	.15	.07	.02
☐	127	Kevin McReynolds	.15	.07	.02
☐	128	Mookie Wilson	.10	.05	.01
☐	129	Danny Tartabull	.25	.11	.03
☐	130	Craig Lefferts	.15	.07	.02
☐	131	Jose DeJesus	.10	.05	.01
☐	132	John Orton	.10	.05	.01
☐	133	Curt Schilling	.15	.07	.02
☐	134	Marquis Grissom	.60	.25	.08
☐	135	Greg Vaughn	.40	.18	.05
☐	136	Brett Butler	.15	.07	.02
☐	137	Rob Deer	.15	.07	.02
☐	138	John Franco	.10	.05	.01
☐	139	Keith Moreland	.10	.05	.01
☐	140	Dave Smith	.10	.05	.01
☐	141	Mark McGwire	.50	.23	.06
☐	142	Vince Coleman	.20	.09	.03
☐	143	Barry Bonds	.45	.20	.06
☐	144	Mike Henneman	.15	.07	.02
☐	145	Dwight Gooden	.25	.11	.03
☐	146	Darryl Strawberry	.45	.20	.06
☐	147	Von Hayes	.10	.05	.01
☐	148	Andres Galarraga	.15	.07	.02
☐	149	Roger Clemens	.75	.35	.09
☐	150	Don Mattingly	.60	.25	.08
☐	151	Joe Magrane	.15	.07	.02
☐	152	Dwight Smith	.10	.05	.01
☐	153	Ricky Jordan	.15	.07	.02
☐	154	Alan Trammell	.20	.09	.03
☐	155	Brook Jacoby	.10	.05	.01
☐	156	Len Dykstra	.15	.07	.02
☐	157	Mike LaValliere	.10	.05	.01
☐	158	Julio Franco	.20	.09	.03
☐	159	Joey Belle	.60	.25	.08
☐	160	Barry Larkin	.25	.11	.03
☐	161	Rick Reuschel	.15	.07	.02
☐	162	Nelson Santovenia	.10	.05	.01
☐	163	Mike Scioscia	.10	.05	.01
☐	164	Damon Berryhill	.10	.05	.01
☐	165	Todd Worrell	.15	.07	.02
☐	166	Jim Eisenreich	.10	.05	.01
☐	167	Ivan Calderon	.15	.07	.02
☐	168	Mauro Gozzo	.10	.05	.01
☐	169	Kirk McCaskill	.10	.05	.01
☐	170	Dennis Eckersley	.25	.11	.03
☐	171	Mickey Tettleton	.20	.09	.03
☐	172	Chuck Finley	.10	.05	.01
☐	173	Dave Magadan	.15	.07	.02
☐	174	Terry Pendleton	.25	.11	.03
☐	175	Willie Randolph	.15	.07	.02
☐	176	Jeff Huson	.10	.05	.01
☐	177	Todd Zeile	.35	.16	.04
☐	178	Steve Olin	.10	.05	.01
☐	179	Eric Anthony	.45	.20	.06
☐	180	Scott Coolbaugh	.10	.05	.01
☐	181	Rick Sutcliffe	.15	.07	.02
☐	182	Tim Wallach	.15	.07	.02
☐	183	Paul Molitor	.25	.11	.03
☐	184	Roberto Kelly	.20	.09	.03
☐	185	Mike Moore	.15	.07	.02
☐	186	Junior Felix	.20	.09	.03
☐	187	Mike Schooler	.10	.05	.01
☐	188	Ruben Sierra	.40	.18	.05
☐	189	Dale Murphy	.25	.11	.03
☐	190	Dan Gladden	.10	.05	.01
☐	191	John Smiley	.15	.07	.02
☐	192	Jeff Russell	.10	.05	.01
☐	193	Bert Blyleven	.15	.07	.02
☐	194	Dave Stewart	.15	.07	.02
☐	195	Bobby Bonilla	.30	.14	.04
☐	196	Mitch Williams	.15	.07	.02

☐ 197 Orel Hershiser	.20	.09	.03
☐ 198 Kevin Bass	.10	.05	.01
☐ 199 Tim Burke	.10	.05	.01
☐ 200 Bo Jackson	.75	.35	.09
☐ 201 David Cone	.25	.11	.03
☐ 202 Gary Pettis	.10	.05	.01
☐ 203 Kent Hrbek	.15	.07	.02
☐ 204 Carlton Fisk	.35	.16	.04
☐ 205 Bob Geren	.10	.05	.01
☐ 206 Bill Spiers	.10	.05	.01
☐ 207 Oddibe McDowell	.10	.05	.01
☐ 208 Rickey Henderson	.60	.25	.08
☐ 209 Ken Caminiti	.15	.07	.02
☐ 210 Devon White	.15	.07	.02
☐ 211 Greg Maddux	.25	.11	.03
☐ 212 Ed Whitson	.10	.05	.01
☐ 213 Carlos Martinez	.10	.05	.01
☐ 214 George Brett	.50	.23	.06
☐ 215 Gregg Olson	.20	.09	.03
☐ 216 Kenny Rogers	.10	.05	.01
☐ 217 Dwight Evans	.15	.07	.02
☐ 218 Pat Tabler	.10	.05	.01
☐ 219 Jeff Treadway	.10	.05	.01
☐ 220 Scott Fletcher	.10	.05	.01
☐ 221 Deion Sanders	.75	.35	.09
☐ 222 Robin Ventura	.75	.35	.09
☐ 223 Chip Hale	.10	.05	.01
☐ 224 Tommy Greene	.20	.09	.03
☐ 225 Dean Palmer	.60	.25	.08

1981 Squirt

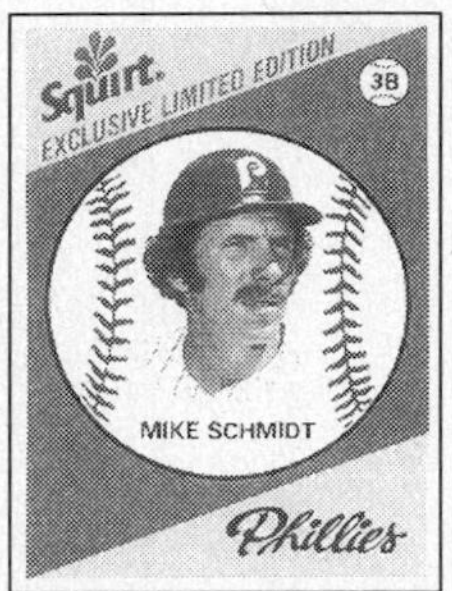

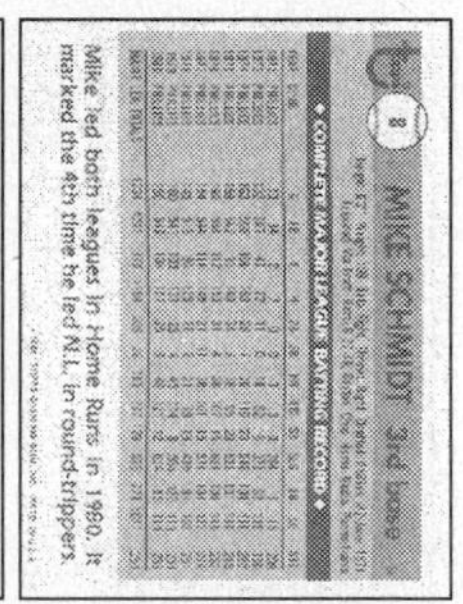

The cards in this 22-panel set consist of 33 different individual cards, each measuring 2 1/2" by 3 1/2". The set was also available as two-card panels measuring approximately 2 1/2" by 10 1/2". Cards numbered 1-11 appear twice, whereas cards 12-33 appear only once in the 22-panel set. The pattern for pairings was 1/12 and 1/23, 2/13 and 2/24, 3/14 and 3/25, and so forth on up to 11/22 and 11/33. Two card panels have a value equal to the sum of the individual cards on the panel. Supposedly panels 4/15, 4/26, 5/27, and 6/28 are more difficult to find than the other panels and are marked as SP in the checklist below.

	NRMT-MT	EXC	G-VG
COMPLETE PANEL SET	20.00	9.00	2.50
COMPLETE IND. SET	12.00	5.50	1.50
COMMON PANEL	.40	.18	.05
COMMON PLAYER (1-11) DP	.25	.11	.03
COMMON PLAYER (12-33)	.25	.11	.03
☐ 1 George Brett DP	.75	.35	.09
☐ 2 George Foster DP	.25	.11	.03
☐ 3 Ben Oglivie DP	.25	.11	.03
☐ 4 Steve Garvey DP	.50	.23	.06
☐ 5 Reggie Jackson DP	.90	.40	.11
☐ 6 Bill Buckner DP	.25	.11	.03
☐ 7 Jim Rice DP	.30	.14	.04
☐ 8 Mike Schmidt DP	.90	.40	.11
☐ 9 Rod Carew DP	.60	.25	.08
☐ 10 Dave Parker DP	.30	.14	.04
☐ 11 Pete Rose DP	.90	.40	.11
☐ 12 Garry Templeton	.25	.11	.03
☐ 13 Rick Burleson	.25	.11	.03
☐ 14 Dave Kingman	.25	.11	.03
☐ 15 Eddie Murray SP	4.00	1.80	.50
☐ 16 Don Sutton	.60	.25	.08
☐ 17 Dusty Baker	.25	.11	.03
☐ 18 Jack Clark	.35	.16	.04
☐ 19 Dave Winfield	1.50	.65	.19
☐ 20 Johnny Bench	1.25	.55	.16
☐ 21 Lee Mazzilli	.25	.11	.03
☐ 22 Al Oliver	.25	.11	.03
☐ 23 Jerry Mumphrey	.25	.11	.03
☐ 24 Tony Armas	.25	.11	.03
☐ 25 Fred Lynn	.30	.14	.04
☐ 26 Ron LeFlore SP	1.00	.45	.13
☐ 27 Steve Kemp SP	1.00	.45	.13
☐ 28 Rickey Henderson SP	8.00	3.60	1.00
☐ 29 John Castino	.25	.11	.03
☐ 30 Cecil Cooper	.25	.11	.03
☐ 31 Bruce Bochte	.25	.11	.03
☐ 32 Joe Charboneau	.25	.11	.03
☐ 33 Chet Lemon	.25	.11	.03

1982 Squirt

The cards in this 22-card set measure 2 1/2" by 3 1/2". Although the 1982 "Exclusive Limited Edition" was prepared for Squirt by Topps, the format and pictures are completely different from the regular Topps cards of this year. Each color picture is obliquely cut and the word Squirt is printed in red in the top left corner. The cards are numbered 1 through 22 and the reverses are yellow and black on white. The cards were issued on four types of panels: (1) yellow attachment card at top with picture card in center and scratch-off game at bottom; (2) yellow attachment card at top with scratch-off game in center and picture card at bottom; (3) white attachment card at top with "Collect all 22" panel in center and picture card at bottom; (4) two card panel with attachment card at top. The two card panels have parallel cards; that is, numbers 1 and 12 together, numbers 2 and 13 together, etc. Two card panels have a value equal to the sum of the individual cards on the panel. The two types (1 and 2) with the scratch-off games are more slightly difficult to obtain than the other two types and hence command prices double those below.

	NRMT-MT	EXC	G-VG
COMPLETE SET (22)	9.00	4.00	1.15
COMMON PLAYER (1-22)	.25	.11	.03
☐ 1 Cecil Cooper	.30	.14	.04
☐ 2 Jerry Remy	.25	.11	.03
☐ 3 George Brett	1.00	.45	.13
☐ 4 Alan Trammell	.50	.23	.06
☐ 5 Reggie Jackson	.90	.40	.11
☐ 6 Kirk Gibson	.40	.18	.05
☐ 7 Dave Winfield	.75	.35	.09
☐ 8 Carlton Fisk	.60	.25	.08
☐ 9 Ron Guidry	.35	.16	.04
☐ 10 Dennis Leonard	.25	.11	.03
☐ 11 Rollie Fingers	.60	.25	.08
☐ 12 Pete Rose	1.00	.45	.13
☐ 13 Phil Garner	.30	.14	.04
☐ 14 Mike Schmidt	1.00	.45	.13
☐ 15 Dave Concepcion	.35	.16	.04
☐ 16 George Hendrick	.25	.11	.03

☐ 17 Andre Dawson	.75	.35	.09
☐ 18 George Foster	.35	.16	.04
☐ 19 Gary Carter	.50	.23	.06
☐ 20 Fernando Valenzuela	.35	.16	.04
☐ 21 Tom Seaver	1.00	.45	.13
☐ 22 Bruce Sutter	.35	.16	.04

1976 SSPC

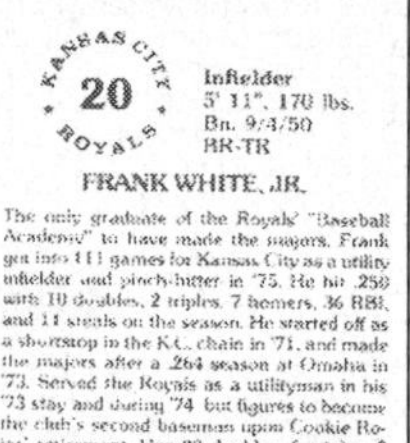

The cards in this 630-card set measure 2 1/2" by 3 1/2". The 1976 "Pure Card" set issued by TCMA derives its name from the lack of borders, logos, signatures, etc., which often clutter up the picture areas of some baseball sets. It differs from other sets produced by this company in that it cannot be re-issued due to an agreement entered into by the manufacturer. Thus, while not technically a legitimate issue, it is significant because it cannot be reprinted, unlike other collector issues. There are no scarcities known. The cards are numbered in team groups, i.e., Atlanta (1-21), Cincinnati (22-46), Houston (47-65), Los Angeles (66-91), San Francisco (92-113), San Diego (114-133), Chicago White Sox (134-158), Kansas City (159-195), California (186-204), Minnesota (205-225), Milwaukee (226-251), Texas (252-273), St. Louis (274-300), Chicago Cubs (301-321), Montreal (322-351), Detroit (352-373), Baltimore (374-401), Boston (402-424), New York Yankees (425-455), Philadelphia (456-477), Oakland (478-503), Cleveland (504-532), New York Mets (533-560), and Pittsburgh (561-586). The rest of the numbers are filled in with checklists (589-595), miscellaneous players, and a heavy dose of coaches. There are a few instances in the set where the team identified on the back is different from the team shown on the front due to trades made after the completion of the 1975 season.

	NRMT-MT	EXC	G-VG
COMPLETE SET (630)	125.00	57.50	15.50
COMMON PLAYER (1-630)	.10	.05	.01
☐ 1 Buzz Capra	.10	.05	.01
☐ 2 Tom House	.15	.07	.02
☐ 3 Max Leon	.10	.05	.01
☐ 4 Carl Morton	.10	.05	.01
☐ 5 Phil Niekro	2.00	.90	.25
☐ 6 Mike Thompson	.10	.05	.01
☐ 7 Elias Sosa	.10	.05	.01
☐ 8 Larvell Blanks	.10	.05	.01
☐ 9 Darrell Evans	.30	.14	.04
☐ 10 Rod Gilbreath	.10	.05	.01
☐ 11 Mike Lum	.10	.05	.01
☐ 12 Craig Robinson	.10	.05	.01
☐ 13 Earl Williams	.10	.05	.01
☐ 14 Vic Correll	.10	.05	.01
☐ 15 Biff Pocoroba	.10	.05	.01
☐ 16 Dusty Baker	.25	.11	.03
☐ 17 Ralph Garr	.15	.07	.02
☐ 18 Cito Gaston	.30	.14	.04
☐ 19 Dave May	.10	.05	.01
☐ 20 Rowland Office	.10	.05	.01
☐ 21 Bob Beall	.10	.05	.01
☐ 22 Sparky Anderson MG	.50	.23	.06
☐ 23 Jack Billingham	.10	.05	.01
☐ 24 Pedro Borbon	.10	.05	.01
☐ 25 Clay Carroll	.10	.05	.01
☐ 26 Pat Darcy	.10	.05	.01
☐ 27 Don Gullett	.15	.07	.02
☐ 28 Clay Kirby	.10	.05	.01
☐ 29 Gary Nolan	.10	.05	.01
☐ 30 Fred Norman	.10	.05	.01
☐ 31 Johnny Bench	7.50	3.40	.95
☐ 32 Bill Plummer	.10	.05	.01
☐ 33 Darrel Chaney	.10	.05	.01
☐ 34 Dave Concepcion	.35	.16	.04
☐ 35 Terry Crowley	.10	.05	.01
☐ 36 Dan Driessen	.20	.09	.03
☐ 37 Doug Flynn	.10	.05	.01
☐ 38 Joe Morgan	4.50	2.00	.55
☐ 39 Tony Perez	1.50	.65	.19
☐ 40 Ken Griffey	1.00	.45	.13
☐ 41 Pete Rose	10.00	4.50	1.25
☐ 42 Ed Armbrister	.10	.05	.01
☐ 43 John Vukovich	.10	.05	.01
☐ 44 George Foster	1.00	.45	.13
☐ 45 Cesar Geronimo	.10	.05	.01
☐ 46 Merv Rettenmund	.10	.05	.01
☐ 47 Jim Crawford	.10	.05	.01
☐ 48 Ken Forsch	.10	.05	.01
☐ 49 Doug Konieczny	.10	.05	.01
☐ 50 Joe Niekro	.25	.11	.03
☐ 51 Cliff Johnson	.10	.05	.01
☐ 52 Skip Jutze	.10	.05	.01
☐ 53 Milt May	.10	.05	.01
☐ 54 Rob Andrews	.10	.05	.01
☐ 55 Ken Boswell	.10	.05	.01
☐ 56 Tommy Helms	.15	.07	.02
☐ 57 Roger Metzger	.10	.05	.01
☐ 58 Larry Milbourne	.10	.05	.01
☐ 59 Doug Rader	.15	.07	.02
☐ 60 Bob Watson	.20	.09	.03
☐ 61 Enos Cabell	.10	.05	.01
☐ 62 Jose Cruz	.25	.11	.03
☐ 63 Cesar Cedeno	.20	.09	.03
☐ 64 Greg Gross	.10	.05	.01
☐ 65 Wilbur Howard	.10	.05	.01
☐ 66 Al Downing	.10	.05	.01
☐ 67 Burt Hooton	.10	.05	.01
☐ 68 Charlie Hough	.20	.09	.03
☐ 69 Tommy John	.75	.35	.09
☐ 70 Andy Messersmith	.15	.07	.02
☐ 71 Doug Rau	.10	.05	.01
☐ 72 Rick Rhoden	.20	.09	.03
☐ 73 Don Sutton	1.50	.65	.19
☐ 74 Rick Auerbach	.10	.05	.01
☐ 75 Ron Cey	.40	.18	.05
☐ 76 Ivan DeJesus	.10	.05	.01
☐ 77 Steve Garvey	2.50	1.15	.30
☐ 78 Lee Lacy	.10	.05	.01
☐ 79 Dave Lopes	.15	.07	.02
☐ 80 Ken McMullen	.10	.05	.01
☐ 81 Joe Ferguson	.10	.05	.01
☐ 82 Paul Powell	.10	.05	.01
☐ 83 Steve Yeager	.10	.05	.01
☐ 84 Willie Crawford	.10	.05	.01
☐ 85 Henry Cruz	.10	.05	.01
☐ 86 Charlie Manuel	.10	.05	.01
☐ 87 Manny Mota	.15	.07	.02
☐ 88 Tom Paciorek	.10	.05	.01
☐ 89 Jim Wynn	.20	.09	.03
☐ 90 Walt Alston MG	.60	.25	.08
☐ 91 Bill Buckner	.35	.16	.04
☐ 92 Jim Barr	.10	.05	.01
☐ 93 Mike Caldwell	.15	.07	.02
☐ 94 John D'Acquisto	.10	.05	.01
☐ 95 Dave Heaverlo	.10	.05	.01
☐ 96 Gary Lavelle	.10	.05	.01
☐ 97 John Montefusco	.15	.07	.02
☐ 98 Charlie Williams	.10	.05	.01
☐ 99 Chris Arnold	.10	.05	.01
☐ 100 Marc Hill	.10	.05	.01
☐ 101 Dave Rader	.10	.05	.01
☐ 102 Bruce Miller	.10	.05	.01
☐ 103 Willie Montanez	.10	.05	.01
☐ 104 Steve Ontiveros	.10	.05	.01
☐ 105 Chris Speier	.10	.05	.01
☐ 106 Derrel Thomas	.10	.05	.01
☐ 107 Gary Thomasson	.10	.05	.01
☐ 108 Glenn Adams	.10	.05	.01
☐ 109 Von Joshua	.10	.05	.01
☐ 110 Gary Matthews	.15	.07	.02
☐ 111 Bobby Murcer	.35	.16	.04
☐ 112 Horace Speed	.10	.05	.01
☐ 113 Wes Westrum MG	.10	.05	.01
☐ 114 Rich Folkers	.10	.05	.01

☐ 115 Alan Foster .10 .05 .01
☐ 116 Dave Freisleben .10 .05 .01
☐ 117 Dan Frisella .10 .05 .01
☐ 118 Randy Jones .20 .09 .03
☐ 119 Dan Spillner .10 .05 .01
☐ 120 Larry Hardy .10 .05 .01
☐ 121 Randy Hundley .10 .05 .01
☐ 122 Fred Kendall .10 .05 .01
☐ 123 John McNamara MG .10 .05 .01
☐ 124 Tito Fuentes .10 .05 .01
☐ 125 Enzo Hernandez .10 .05 .01
☐ 126 Steve Huntz .10 .05 .01
☐ 127 Mike Ivie .10 .05 .01
☐ 128 Hector Torres .10 .05 .01
☐ 129 Ted Kubiak .10 .05 .01
☐ 130 John Grubb .10 .05 .01
☐ 131 John Scott .10 .05 .01
☐ 132 Bob Tolan .15 .07 .02
☐ 133 Dave Winfield 15.00 6.75 1.90
☐ 134 Bill Gogolewski .10 .05 .01
☐ 135 Dan Osborn .10 .05 .01
☐ 136 Jim Kaat .60 .25 .08
☐ 137 Claude Osteen .15 .07 .02
☐ 138 Cecil Upshaw .10 .05 .01
☐ 139 Wilbur Wood .15 .07 .02
☐ 140 Lloyd Allen .10 .05 .01
☐ 141 Brian Downing .25 .11 .03
☐ 142 Jim Essian .20 .09 .03
☐ 143 Bucky Dent .35 .16 .04
☐ 144 Jorge Orta .10 .05 .01
☐ 145 Lee Richard .10 .05 .01
☐ 146 Bill Stein .10 .05 .01
☐ 147 Ken Henderson .10 .05 .01
☐ 148 Carlos May .10 .05 .01
☐ 149 Nyls Nyman .10 .05 .01
☐ 150 Bob Coluccio .10 .05 .01
☐ 151 Chuck Tanner MG .15 .07 .02
☐ 152 Pat Kelly .10 .05 .01
☐ 153 Jerry Hairston .10 .05 .01
☐ 154 Pete Varney .10 .05 .01
☐ 155 Bill Melton .10 .05 .01
☐ 156 Rich Gossage 1.50 .65 .19
☐ 157 Terry Forster .15 .07 .02
☐ 158 Rich Hinton .10 .05 .01
☐ 159 Nelson Briles .10 .05 .01
☐ 160 Al Fitzmorris .10 .05 .01
☐ 161 Steve Mingori .10 .05 .01
☐ 162 Marty Pattin .10 .05 .01
☐ 163 Paul Splittorff .15 .07 .02
☐ 164 Dennis Leonard .15 .07 .02
☐ 165 Buck Martinez .10 .05 .01
☐ 166 Bob Stinson .10 .05 .01
☐ 167 George Brett 25.00 11.50 3.10
☐ 168 Harmon Killebrew 3.50 1.55 .45
☐ 169 John Mayberry .15 .07 .02
☐ 170 Fred Patek .10 .05 .01
☐ 171 Cookie Rojas .15 .07 .02
☐ 172 Rodney Scott .10 .05 .01
☐ 173 Tony Solaita .10 .05 .01
☐ 174 Frank White .30 .14 .04
☐ 175 Al Cowens .20 .09 .03
☐ 176 Hal McRae .35 .16 .04
☐ 177 Amos Otis .20 .09 .03
☐ 178 Vada Pinson .30 .14 .04
☐ 179 Jim Wohlford .10 .05 .01
☐ 180 Doug Bird .10 .05 .01
☐ 181 Mark Littell .10 .05 .01
☐ 182 Bob McClure .15 .07 .02
☐ 183 Steve Busby .15 .07 .02
☐ 184 Fran Healy .10 .05 .01
☐ 185 Whitey Herzog MG .30 .14 .04
☐ 186 Andy Hassler .10 .05 .01
☐ 187 Nolan Ryan 25.00 11.50 3.10
☐ 188 Bill Singer .10 .05 .01
☐ 189 Frank Tanana .25 .11 .03
☐ 190 Ed Figueroa .10 .05 .01
☐ 191 Dave Collins .20 .09 .03
☐ 192 Dick Williams MG .15 .07 .02
☐ 193 Ellie Rodriguez .10 .05 .01
☐ 194 Dave Chalk .10 .05 .01
☐ 195 Winston Llenas .10 .05 .01
☐ 196 Rudy Meoli .10 .05 .01
☐ 197 Orlando Ramirez .10 .05 .01
☐ 198 Jerry Remy .20 .09 .03
☐ 199 Billy Smith .10 .05 .01
☐ 200 Bruce Bochte .10 .05 .01
☐ 201 Joe Lahoud .10 .05 .01
☐ 202 Morris Nettles .10 .05 .01
☐ 203 Mickey Rivers .15 .07 .02
☐ 204 Leroy Stanton .10 .05 .01
☐ 205 Vic Albury .10 .05 .01
☐ 206 Tom Burgmeier .10 .05 .01
☐ 207 Bill Butler .10 .05 .01
☐ 208 Bill Campbell .10 .05 .01
☐ 209 Ray Corbin .10 .05 .01
☐ 210 Joe Decker .10 .05 .01
☐ 211 Jim Hughes .10 .05 .01
☐ 212 Ed Bane UER .10 .05 .01
(Photo actually
Mike Pazik)
☐ 213 Glenn Borgmann .10 .05 .01
☐ 214 Rod Carew 7.00 3.10 .85
☐ 215 Steve Brye .10 .05 .01
☐ 216 Dan Ford .10 .05 .01
☐ 217 Tony Oliva 1.00 .45 .13
☐ 218 Dave Goltz .10 .05 .01
☐ 219 Bert Blyleven 1.00 .45 .13
☐ 220 Larry Hisle .10 .05 .01
☐ 221 Steve Braun .10 .05 .01
☐ 222 Jerry Terrell .10 .05 .01
☐ 223 Eric Soderholm .10 .05 .01
☐ 224 Phil Roof .10 .05 .01
☐ 225 Danny Thompson .10 .05 .01
☐ 226 Jim Colborn .10 .05 .01
☐ 227 Tom Murphy .10 .05 .01
☐ 228 Ed Rodriguez .10 .05 .01
☐ 229 Jim Slaton .10 .05 .01
☐ 230 Ed Sprague .15 .07 .02
☐ 231 Charlie Moore .10 .05 .01
☐ 232 Darrell Porter .15 .07 .02
☐ 233 Kurt Bevacqua .10 .05 .01
☐ 234 Pedro Garcia .10 .05 .01
☐ 235 Mike Hegan .10 .05 .01
☐ 236 Don Money .15 .07 .02
☐ 237 George Scott .20 .09 .03
☐ 238 Robin Yount 25.00 11.50 3.10
☐ 239 Hank Aaron 12.00 5.50 1.50
☐ 240 Rob Ellis .10 .05 .01
☐ 241 Sixto Lezcano .15 .07 .02
☐ 242 Bob Mitchell .10 .05 .01
☐ 243 Gorman Thomas .25 .11 .03
☐ 244 Bill Travers .10 .05 .01
☐ 245 Pete Broberg .10 .05 .01
☐ 246 Bill Sharp .10 .05 .01
☐ 247 Bobby Darwin .10 .05 .01
☐ 248 Rick Austin UER .10 .05 .01
(Photo actually
Larry Anderson)
☐ 249 Larry Anderson UER .10 .05 .01
(Photo actually
Rick Austin)
☐ 250 Tom Bianco .10 .05 .01
☐ 251 Lafayette Currence .10 .05 .01
☐ 252 Steve Foucault .10 .05 .01
☐ 253 Bill Hands .10 .05 .01
☐ 254 Steve Hargan .10 .05 .01
☐ 255 Fergie Jenkins 3.50 1.55 .45
☐ 256 Bob Sheldon .10 .05 .01
☐ 257 Jim Umbarger .10 .05 .01
☐ 258 Clyde Wright .10 .05 .01
☐ 259 Bill Fahey .10 .05 .01
☐ 260 Jim Sundberg .20 .09 .03
☐ 261 Leo Cardenas .10 .05 .01
☐ 262 Jim Fregosi .20 .09 .03
☐ 263 Mike Hargrove .20 .09 .03
☐ 264 Toby Harrah .15 .07 .02
☐ 265 Roy Howell .10 .05 .01
☐ 266 Lenny Randle .10 .05 .01
☐ 267 Roy Smalley .20 .09 .03
☐ 268 Jim Spencer .10 .05 .01
☐ 269 Jeff Burroughs .20 .09 .03
☐ 270 Tom Grieve .20 .09 .03
☐ 271 Joe Lovitto .10 .05 .01
☐ 272 Frank Lucchesi MG .10 .05 .01
☐ 273 Dave Nelson .10 .05 .01
☐ 274 Ted Simmons 1.00 .45 .13
☐ 275 Lou Brock 4.50 2.00 .55
☐ 276 Ron Fairly .10 .05 .01
☐ 277 Bake McBride .10 .05 .01
☐ 278 Reggie Smith .25 .11 .03
☐ 279 Willie Davis .15 .07 .02
☐ 280 Ken Reitz .10 .05 .01
☐ 281 Buddy Bradford .10 .05 .01
☐ 282 Luis Melendez .10 .05 .01
☐ 283 Mike Tyson .10 .05 .01
☐ 284 Ted Sizemore .10 .05 .01
☐ 285 Mario Guerrero .10 .05 .01
☐ 286 Larry Lintz .10 .05 .01
☐ 287 Ken Rudolph .10 .05 .01
☐ 288 Dick Billings .10 .05 .01
☐ 289 Jerry Mumphrey .15 .07 .02
☐ 290 Mike Wallace .10 .05 .01
☐ 291 Al Hrabosky .15 .07 .02
☐ 292 Ken Reynolds .10 .05 .01
☐ 293 Mike Garman .10 .05 .01
☐ 294 Bob Forsch .15 .07 .02

☐	295	John Denny	.15	.07	.02
☐	296	Harry Rasmussen	.10	.05	.01
☐	297	Lynn McGlothen	.10	.05	.01
☐	298	Mike Barlow	.10	.05	.01
☐	299	Greg Terlecky	.10	.05	.01
☐	300	Red Schoendienst MG	.75	.35	.09
☐	301	Rick Reuschel	.35	.16	.04
☐	302	Steve Stone	.15	.07	.02
☐	303	Bill Bonham	.10	.05	.01
☐	304	Oscar Zamora	.10	.05	.01
☐	305	Ken Frailing	.10	.05	.01
☐	306	Milt Wilcox	.10	.05	.01
☐	307	Darold Knowles	.10	.05	.01
☐	308	Jim Marshall MG	.10	.05	.01
☐	309	Bill Madlock	.75	.35	.09
☐	310	Jose Cardenal	.15	.07	.02
☐	311	Rick Monday	.15	.07	.02
☐	312	Jerry Morales	.10	.05	.01
☐	313	Tim Hosley	.10	.05	.01
☐	314	Gene Hiser	.10	.05	.01
☐	315	Don Kessinger	.15	.07	.02
☐	316	Manny Trillo	.15	.07	.02
☐	317	Pete LaCock	.10	.05	.01
☐	318	George Mitterwald	.10	.05	.01
☐	319	Steve Swisher	.10	.05	.01
☐	320	Rob Sperring	.10	.05	.01
☐	321	Vic Harris	.10	.05	.01
☐	322	Ron Dunn	.10	.05	.01
☐	323	Jose Morales	.10	.05	.01
☐	324	Pete Mackanin	.10	.05	.01
☐	325	Jim Cox	.10	.05	.01
☐	326	Larry Parrish	.25	.11	.03
☐	327	Mike Jorgensen	.10	.05	.01
☐	328	Tim Foli	.10	.05	.01
☐	329	Hal Breeden	.10	.05	.01
☐	330	Nate Colbert	.15	.07	.02
☐	331	Pepe Frias	.10	.05	.01
☐	332	Pat Scanlon	.10	.05	.01
☐	333	Bob Bailey	.10	.05	.01
☐	334	Gary Carter	6.00	2.70	.75
☐	335	Pepe Mangual	.10	.05	.01
☐	336	Larry Biittner	.10	.05	.01
☐	337	Jim Lyttle	.10	.05	.01
☐	338	Gary Roenicke	.10	.05	.01
☐	339	Tony Scott	.10	.05	.01
☐	340	Jerry White	.10	.05	.01
☐	341	Jim Dwyer	.10	.05	.01
☐	342	Ellis Valentine	.15	.07	.02
☐	343	Fred Scherman	.10	.05	.01
☐	344	Dennis Blair	.10	.05	.01
☐	345	Woodie Fryman	.10	.05	.01
☐	346	Chuck Taylor	.10	.05	.01
☐	347	Dan Warthen	.10	.05	.01
☐	348	Dan Carrithers	.10	.05	.01
☐	349	Steve Rogers	.20	.09	.03
☐	350	Dale Murray	.10	.05	.01
☐	351	Duke Snider CO	3.00	1.35	.40
☐	352	Ralph Houk MG	.20	.09	.03
☐	353	John Hiller	.20	.09	.03
☐	354	Mickey Lolich	.40	.18	.05
☐	355	Dave Lemancyzk	.10	.05	.01
☐	356	Lerrin LaGrow	.10	.05	.01
☐	357	Fred Arroyo	.10	.05	.01
☐	358	Joe Coleman	.10	.05	.01
☐	359	Ben Oglivie	.20	.09	.03
☐	360	Willie Horton	.20	.09	.03
☐	361	John Knox	.10	.05	.01
☐	362	Leon Roberts	.10	.05	.01
☐	363	Ron LeFlore	.20	.09	.03
☐	364	Gary Sutherland	.10	.05	.01
☐	365	Dan Meyer	.10	.05	.01
☐	366	Aurelio Rodriguez	.10	.05	.01
☐	367	Tom Veryzer	.10	.05	.01
☐	368	Jack Pierce	.10	.05	.01
☐	369	Gene Michael	.15	.07	.02
☐	370	Billy Baldwin	.10	.05	.01
☐	371	Gates Brown	.20	.09	.03
☐	372	Mickey Stanley	.20	.09	.03
☐	373	Terry Humphrey	.10	.05	.01
☐	374	Doyle Alexander	.25	.11	.03
☐	375	Mike Cuellar	.20	.09	.03
☐	376	Wayne Garland	.15	.07	.02
☐	377	Ross Grimsley	.10	.05	.01
☐	378	Grant Jackson	.10	.05	.01
☐	379	Dyar Miller	.10	.05	.01
☐	380	Jim Palmer	5.00	2.30	.60
☐	381	Mike Torrez	.15	.07	.02
☐	382	Mike Willis	.10	.05	.01
☐	383	Dave Duncan	.20	.09	.03
☐	384	Ellie Hendricks	.10	.05	.01
☐	385	Jim Hutto	.10	.05	.01
☐	386	Bob Bailor	.10	.05	.01
☐	387	Doug DeCinces	.30	.14	.04
☐	388	Bob Grich	.25	.11	.03
☐	389	Lee May	.25	.11	.03
☐	390	Tony Muser	.10	.05	.01
☐	391	Tim Nordbrook	.10	.05	.01
☐	392	Brooks Robinson	5.00	2.30	.60
☐	393	Royle Stillman	.10	.05	.01
☐	394	Don Baylor	.50	.23	.06
☐	395	Paul Blair	.15	.07	.02
☐	396	Al Bumbry	.10	.05	.01
☐	397	Larry Harlow	.10	.05	.01
☐	398	Tommy Davis	.20	.09	.03
☐	399	Jim Northrup	.20	.09	.03
☐	400	Ken Singleton	.25	.11	.03
☐	401	Tom Shopay	.10	.05	.01
☐	402	Fred Lynn	1.50	.65	.19
☐	403	Carlton Fisk	4.00	1.80	.50
☐	404	Cecil Cooper	.50	.23	.06
☐	405	Jim Rice	3.00	1.35	.40
☐	406	Juan Beniquez	.15	.07	.02
☐	407	Denny Doyle	.10	.05	.01
☐	408	Dwight Evans	1.00	.45	.13
☐	409	Carl Yastrzemski	7.00	3.10	.85
☐	410	Rick Burleson	.20	.09	.03
☐	411	Bernie Carbo	.10	.05	.01
☐	412	Doug Griffin	.10	.05	.01
☐	413	Rico Petrocelli	.15	.07	.02
☐	414	Bob Montgomery	.10	.05	.01
☐	415	Tim Blackwell	.10	.05	.01
☐	416	Rick Miller	.10	.05	.01
☐	417	Darrell Johnson MG	.10	.05	.01
☐	418	Jim Burton	.10	.05	.01
☐	419	Jim Willoughby	.10	.05	.01
☐	420	Rogelio Moret	.10	.05	.01
☐	421	Bill Lee	.15	.07	.02
☐	422	Dick Drago	.10	.05	.01
☐	423	Diego Segui	.10	.05	.01
☐	424	Luis Tiant	.35	.16	.04
☐	425	Jim Hunter	3.50	1.55	.45
☐	426	Rick Sawyer	.10	.05	.01
☐	427	Rudy May	.10	.05	.01
☐	428	Dick Tidrow	.10	.05	.01
☐	429	Sparky Lyle	.50	.23	.06
☐	430	Doc Medich	.10	.05	.01
☐	431	Pat Dobson	.15	.07	.02
☐	432	Dave Pagan	.10	.05	.01
☐	433	Thurman Munson	5.00	2.30	.60
☐	434	Chris Chambliss	.35	.16	.04
☐	435	Roy White	.20	.09	.03
☐	436	Walt Williams	.10	.05	.01
☐	437	Graig Nettles	.75	.35	.09
☐	438	Rick Dempsey	.20	.09	.03
☐	439	Bobby Bonds	.75	.35	.09
☐	440	Ed Herrmann	.10	.05	.01
☐	441	Sandy Alomar	.15	.07	.02
☐	442	Fred Stanley	.10	.05	.01
☐	443	Terry Whitfield	.10	.05	.01
☐	444	Rich Bladt	.10	.05	.01
☐	445	Lou Piniella	.60	.25	.08
☐	446	Rich Coggins	.10	.05	.01
☐	447	Ed Brinkman	.10	.05	.01
☐	448	Jim Mason	.10	.05	.01
☐	449	Larry Murray	.10	.05	.01
☐	450	Ron Blomberg	.10	.05	.01
☐	451	Elliott Maddox	.10	.05	.01
☐	452	Kerry Dineen	.10	.05	.01
☐	453	Billy Martin MG	1.00	.45	.13
☐	454	Dave Bergman	.10	.05	.01
☐	455	Otto Velez	.10	.05	.01
☐	456	Joe Hoerner	.10	.05	.01
☐	457	Tug McGraw	.40	.18	.05
☐	458	Gene Garber	.15	.07	.02
☐	459	Steve Carlton	5.00	2.30	.60
☐	460	Larry Christenson	.10	.05	.01
☐	461	Tom Underwood	.10	.05	.01
☐	462	Jim Lonborg	.20	.09	.03
☐	463	Jay Johnstone	.20	.09	.03
☐	464	Larry Bowa	.35	.16	.04
☐	465	Dave Cash	.15	.07	.02
☐	466	Ollie Brown	.10	.05	.01
☐	467	Greg Luzinski	.35	.16	.04
☐	468	Johnny Oates	.25	.11	.03
☐	469	Mike Anderson	.10	.05	.01
☐	470	Mike Schmidt	20.00	9.00	2.50
☐	471	Bob Boone	.60	.25	.08
☐	472	Tom Hutton	.10	.05	.01
☐	473	Rich Allen	.50	.23	.06
☐	474	Tony Taylor	.15	.07	.02
☐	475	Jerry Martin	.10	.05	.01
☐	476	Danny Ozark MG	.10	.05	.01
☐	477	Dick Ruthven	.10	.05	.01
☐	478	Jim Todd	.10	.05	.01
☐	479	Paul Lindblad	.10	.05	.01
☐	480	Rollie Fingers	3.50	1.55	.45

☐ 481 Vida Blue .30 .14 .04
☐ 482 Ken Holtzman .15 .07 .02
☐ 483 Dick Bosman .10 .05 .01
☐ 484 Sonny Siebert .10 .05 .01
☐ 485 Glenn Abbott .10 .05 .01
☐ 486 Stan Bahnsen .10 .05 .01
☐ 487 Mike Norris .15 .07 .02
☐ 488 Alvin Dark MG .15 .07 .02
☐ 489 Claudell Washington .20 .09 .03
☐ 490 Joe Rudi .20 .09 .03
☐ 491 Bill North .10 .05 .01
☐ 492 Bert Campaneris .20 .09 .03
☐ 493 Gene Tenace .20 .09 .03
☐ 494 Reggie Jackson 15.00 6.75 1.90
☐ 495 Phil Garner .30 .14 .04
☐ 496 Billy Williams 3.00 1.35 .40
☐ 497 Sal Bando .20 .09 .03
☐ 498 Jim Holt .10 .05 .01
☐ 499 Ted Martinez .10 .05 .01
☐ 500 Ray Fosse .15 .07 .02
☐ 501 Matt Alexander .10 .05 .01
☐ 502 Larry Haney .10 .05 .01
☐ 503 Angel Mangual .10 .05 .01
☐ 504 Fred Beene .10 .05 .01
☐ 505 Tom Buskey .10 .05 .01
☐ 506 Dennis Eckersley 30.00 13.50 3.80
☐ 507 Roric Harrison .10 .05 .01
☐ 508 Don Hood .10 .05 .01
☐ 509 Jim Kern .10 .05 .01
☐ 510 Dave LaRoche .10 .05 .01
☐ 511 Fritz Peterson .10 .05 .01
☐ 512 Jim Strickland .10 .05 .01
☐ 513 Rick Waits .10 .05 .01
☐ 514 Alan Ashby .10 .05 .01
☐ 515 John Ellis .10 .05 .01
☐ 516 Rick Cerone .15 .07 .02
☐ 517 Buddy Bell .35 .16 .04
☐ 518 Jack Brohamer .10 .05 .01
☐ 519 Rico Carty .20 .09 .03
☐ 520 Ed Crosby .10 .05 .01
☐ 521 Frank Duffy .10 .05 .01
☐ 522 Duane Kuiper UER .10 .05 .01
(Photo actually
Rick Manning)
☐ 523 Joe Lis .10 .05 .01
☐ 524 Boog Powell .60 .25 .08
☐ 525 Frank Robinson 4.50 2.00 .55
☐ 526 Oscar Gamble .20 .09 .03
☐ 527 George Hendrick .20 .09 .03
☐ 528 John Lowenstein .10 .05 .01
☐ 529 Rick Manning UER .15 .07 .02
(Photo actually
Duane Kuiper)
☐ 530 Tommy Smith .10 .05 .01
☐ 531 Charlie Spikes .10 .05 .01
☐ 532 Steve Kline .10 .05 .01
☐ 533 Ed Kranepool .20 .09 .03
☐ 534 Mike Vail .10 .05 .01
☐ 535 Del Unser .10 .05 .01
☐ 536 Felix Millan .10 .05 .01
☐ 537 Rusty Staub .40 .18 .05
☐ 538 Jesus Alou .10 .05 .01
☐ 539 Wayne Garrett .10 .05 .01
☐ 540 Mike Phillips .10 .05 .01
☐ 541 Joe Torre .60 .25 .08
☐ 542 Dave Kingman .75 .35 .09
☐ 543 Gene Clines .10 .05 .01
☐ 544 Jack Heidemann .10 .05 .01
☐ 545 Bud Harrelson .20 .09 .03
☐ 546 John Stearns .20 .09 .03
☐ 547 John Milner .10 .05 .01
☐ 548 Bob Apodaca .10 .05 .01
☐ 549 Skip Lockwood .10 .05 .01
☐ 550 Ken Sanders .10 .05 .01
☐ 551 Tom Seaver 9.00 4.00 1.15
☐ 552 Rick Baldwin .10 .05 .01
☐ 553 Hank Webb .10 .05 .01
☐ 554 Jon Matlack .20 .09 .03
☐ 555 Randy Tate .10 .05 .01
☐ 556 Tom Hall .10 .05 .01
☐ 557 George Stone .10 .05 .01
☐ 558 Craig Swan .15 .07 .02
☐ 559 Jerry Cram .10 .05 .01
☐ 560 Roy Staiger .10 .05 .01
☐ 561 Kent Tekulve .25 .11 .03
☐ 562 Jerry Reuss .15 .07 .02
☐ 563 John Candelaria .25 .11 .03
☐ 564 Larry Demery .10 .05 .01
☐ 565 Dave Giusti .15 .07 .02
☐ 566 Jim Rooker .10 .05 .01
☐ 567 Ramon Hernandez .10 .05 .01
☐ 568 Bruce Kison .10 .05 .01
☐ 569 Ken Brett .10 .05 .01
☐ 570 Bob Moose .20 .09 .03
☐ 571 Manny Sanguillen .20 .09 .03
☐ 572 Dave Parker 3.00 1.35 .40
☐ 573 Willie Stargell 4.50 2.00 .55
☐ 574 Richie Zisk .15 .07 .02
☐ 575 Rennie Stennett .10 .05 .01
☐ 576 Al Oliver .75 .35 .09
☐ 577 Bill Robinson .35 .16 .04
☐ 578 Bob Robertson .10 .05 .01
☐ 579 Rich Hebner .10 .05 .01
☐ 580 Ed Kirkpatrick .10 .05 .01
☐ 581 Duffy Dyer .10 .05 .01
☐ 582 Craig Reynolds .10 .05 .01
☐ 583 Frank Taveras .10 .05 .01
☐ 584 Willie Randolph 2.00 .90 .25
☐ 585 Art Howe .25 .11 .03
☐ 586 Danny Murtaugh MG .10 .05 .01
☐ 587 Rick McKinney .10 .05 .01
☐ 588 Ed Goodson .10 .05 .01
☐ 589 Checklist 1 2.00 .90 .25
George Brett
Al Cowens
☐ 590 Checklist 2 1.25 .55 .16
Keith Hernandez
Lou Brock
☐ 591 Checklist 3 1.00 .45 .13
Jerry Koosman
Duke Snider
☐ 592 Checklist 4 .30 .14 .04
Maury Wills
John Knox
☐ 593A Checklist 5 ERR 25.00 11.50 3.10
Jim Hunter
Nolan Ryan
(Noland on front)
☐ 593B Checklist 5 COR 6.00 2.70 .75
Jim Hunter
Nolan Ryan
☐ 594 Checklist 6 .40 .18 .05
Ralph Branca
Carl Erskine
Pee Wee Reese
☐ 595 Checklist 7 1.00 .45 .13
Willie Mays
Herb Score
☐ 596 Larry Cox .10 .05 .01
☐ 597 Gene Mauch MG .15 .07 .02
☐ 598 Whitey Wietelmann CO .10 .05 .01
☐ 599 Wayne Simpson .10 .05 .01
☐ 600 Mel Thomason .10 .05 .01
☐ 601 Ike Hampton .10 .05 .01
☐ 602 Ken Crosby .10 .05 .01
☐ 603 Ralph Rowe .10 .05 .01
☐ 604 Jim Tyrone .10 .05 .01
☐ 605 Mick Kelleher .10 .05 .01
☐ 606 Mario Mendoza .10 .05 .01
☐ 607 Mike Rogodzinski .10 .05 .01
☐ 608 Bob Gallagher .10 .05 .01
☐ 609 Jerry Koosman .25 .11 .03
☐ 610 Joe Frazier MG .10 .05 .01
☐ 611 Karl Kuehl MG .10 .05 .01
☐ 612 Frank LaCorte .10 .05 .01
☐ 613 Ray Bare .10 .05 .01
☐ 614 Billy Muffett CO .10 .05 .01
☐ 615 Bill Laxton .10 .05 .01
☐ 616 Willie Mays CO 8.00 3.60 1.00
☐ 617 Phil Cavarretta CO .20 .09 .03
☐ 618 Ted Kluszewski CO .40 .18 .05
☐ 619 Elston Howard CO .30 .14 .04
☐ 620 Alex Grammas CO .10 .05 .01
☐ 621 Mickey Vernon CO .15 .07 .02
☐ 622 Dick Sisler CO .10 .05 .01
☐ 623 Harvey Haddix CO .15 .07 .02
☐ 624 Bobby Winkles CO .10 .05 .01
☐ 625 John Pesky CO .15 .07 .02
☐ 626 Jim Davenport CO .15 .07 .02
☐ 627 Dave Tomlin .10 .05 .01
☐ 628 Roger Craig CO .25 .11 .03
☐ 629 Joe Amalfitano CO .10 .05 .01
☐ 630 Jim Reese CO .20 .09 .03

1991 Stadium Club

This 600-card standard size (2 1/2" by 3 1/2") set marked Topps first entry into the mass market with a premium quality set. The set features borderless full-color action photos on the front with the name of the player and the

Topps Stadium club logo on the bottom of the card, while the back of the card has the basic biographical information as well as making use of the Fastball BARS system and an inset photo of the player's Topps Rookie Card. The set was issued in two series of 300 cards each. The cards are numbered on the back. The key Rookie Cards in the first series are Greg Colbrunn, Lance Dickson, and Randy Tomlin; however the key cards in the first series are those of Steve Avery, Juan Gonzalez, Ken Griffey Jr., Dave Justice, Nolan Ryan, and Frank Thomas. Series II cards were also available at McDonald's restaurants in the Northeast at three cards per pack. The key Rookie Cards in the second series are Jeff Bagwell, Wes Chamberlain, Pedro Munoz, and Phil Plantier.

	MT	EX-MT	VG
COMPLETE SET (600)	225.00	100.00	28.00
COMPLETE SERIES 1 (300)	135.00	60.00	17.00
COMPLETE SERIES 2 (300)	90.00	40.00	11.50
COMMON PLAYER (1-300)	.25	.11	.03
COMMON PLAYER (301-600)	.25	.11	.03
☐ 1 Dave Stewart (Wearing Tuxedo)	.60	.25	.08
☐ 2 Wally Joyner	.30	.14	.04
☐ 3 Shawon Dunston	.30	.14	.04
☐ 4 Darren Daulton	.35	.16	.04
☐ 5 Will Clark	3.00	1.35	.40
☐ 6 Sammy Sosa	.30	.14	.04
☐ 7 Dan Plesac	.25	.11	.03
☐ 8 Marquis Grissom	2.00	.90	.25
☐ 9 Erik Hanson	.25	.11	.03
☐ 10 Geno Petralli	.25	.11	.03
☐ 11 Jose Rijo	.30	.14	.04
☐ 12 Carlos Quintana	.25	.11	.03
☐ 13 Junior Ortiz	.25	.11	.03
☐ 14 Bob Walk	.25	.11	.03
☐ 15 Mike Macfarlane	.25	.11	.03
☐ 16 Eric Yelding	.25	.11	.03
☐ 17 Bryn Smith	.25	.11	.03
☐ 18 Bip Roberts	.30	.14	.04
☐ 19 Mike Scioscia	.25	.11	.03
☐ 20 Mark Williamson	.25	.11	.03
☐ 21 Don Mattingly	1.50	.65	.19
☐ 22 John Franco	.30	.14	.04
☐ 23 Chet Lemon	.25	.11	.03
☐ 24 Tom Henke	.30	.14	.04
☐ 25 Jerry Browne	.25	.11	.03
☐ 26 Dave Justice	9.00	4.00	1.15
☐ 27 Mark Langston	.30	.14	.04
☐ 28 Damon Berryhill	.25	.11	.03
☐ 29 Kevin Bass	.25	.11	.03
☐ 30 Scott Fletcher	.25	.11	.03
☐ 31 Moises Alou	1.50	.65	.19
☐ 32 Dave Valle	.25	.11	.03
☐ 33 Jody Reed	.25	.11	.03
☐ 34 Dave West	.25	.11	.03
☐ 35 Kevin McReynolds	.30	.14	.04
☐ 36 Pat Combs	.25	.11	.03
☐ 37 Eric Davis	.40	.18	.05
☐ 38 Bret Saberhagen	.30	.14	.04
☐ 39 Stan Javier	.25	.11	.03
☐ 40 Chuck Cary	.25	.11	.03
☐ 41 Tony Phillips	.25	.11	.03
☐ 42 Lee Smith	.40	.18	.05
☐ 43 Tim Teufel	.25	.11	.03
☐ 44 Lance Dickson	.40	.18	.05
☐ 45 Greg Litton	.25	.11	.03
☐ 46 Teddy Higuera	.25	.11	.03
☐ 47 Edgar Martinez	.90	.40	.11
☐ 48 Steve Avery	4.00	1.80	.50
☐ 49 Walt Weiss	.25	.11	.03
☐ 50 David Segui	.25	.11	.03
☐ 51 Andy Benes	1.00	.45	.13
☐ 52 Karl Rhodes	.25	.11	.03
☐ 53 Neal Heaton	.25	.11	.03
☐ 54 Danny Gladden	.25	.11	.03
☐ 55 Luis Rivera	.25	.11	.03
☐ 56 Kevin Brown	.50	.23	.06
☐ 57 Frank Thomas	30.00	13.50	3.80
☐ 58 Terry Mulholland	.25	.11	.03
☐ 59 Dick Schofield	.25	.11	.03
☐ 60 Ron Darling	.30	.14	.04
☐ 61 Sandy Alomar Jr.	.30	.14	.04
☐ 62 Dave Stieb	.25	.11	.03
☐ 63 Alan Trammell	.30	.14	.04
☐ 64 Matt Nokes	.25	.11	.03
☐ 65 Lenny Harris	.25	.11	.03
☐ 66 Milt Thompson	.25	.11	.03
☐ 67 Storm Davis	.25	.11	.03
☐ 68 Joe Oliver	.25	.11	.03
☐ 69 Andres Galarraga	.25	.11	.03
☐ 70 Ozzie Guillen	.25	.11	.03
☐ 71 Ken Howell	.25	.11	.03
☐ 72 Garry Templeton	.25	.11	.03
☐ 73 Derrick May	.30	.14	.04
☐ 74 Xavier Hernandez	.25	.11	.03
☐ 75 Dave Parker	.30	.14	.04
☐ 76 Rick Aguilera	.30	.14	.04
☐ 77 Robby Thompson	.25	.11	.03
☐ 78 Pete Incaviglia	.25	.11	.03
☐ 79 Bob Welch	.25	.11	.03
☐ 80 Randy Milligan	.25	.11	.03
☐ 81 Chuck Finley	.30	.14	.04
☐ 82 Alvin Davis	.25	.11	.03
☐ 83 Tim Naehring	.35	.16	.04
☐ 84 Jay Bell	.30	.14	.04
☐ 85 Joe Magrane	.25	.11	.03
☐ 86 Howard Johnson	.30	.14	.04
☐ 87 Jack McDowell	1.25	.55	.16
☐ 88 Kevin Seitzer	.30	.14	.04
☐ 89 Bruce Ruffin	.25	.11	.03
☐ 90 Fernando Valenzuela	.30	.14	.04
☐ 91 Terry Kennedy	.25	.11	.03
☐ 92 Barry Larkin	1.25	.55	.16
☐ 93 Larry Walker	3.00	1.35	.40
☐ 94 Luis Salazar	.25	.11	.03
☐ 95 Gary Sheffield	5.00	2.30	.60
☐ 96 Bobby Witt	.25	.11	.03
☐ 97 Lonnie Smith	.25	.11	.03
☐ 98 Bryan Harvey	.25	.11	.03
☐ 99 Mookie Wilson	.25	.11	.03
☐ 100 Dwight Gooden	.40	.18	.05
☐ 101 Lou Whitaker	.30	.14	.04
☐ 102 Ron Karkovice	.25	.11	.03
☐ 103 Jesse Barfield	.25	.11	.03
☐ 104 Jose DeJesus	.25	.11	.03
☐ 105 Benito Santiago	.30	.14	.04
☐ 106 Brian Holman	.25	.11	.03
☐ 107 Rafael Ramirez	.25	.11	.03
☐ 108 Ellis Burks	.30	.14	.04
☐ 109 Mike Bielecki	.25	.11	.03
☐ 110 Kirby Puckett	3.00	1.35	.40
☐ 111 Terry Shumpert	.25	.11	.03
☐ 112 Chuck Crim	.25	.11	.03
☐ 113 Todd Benzinger	.25	.11	.03
☐ 114 Brian Barnes	.50	.23	.06
☐ 115 Carlos Baerga	4.00	1.80	.50
☐ 116 Kal Daniels	.25	.11	.03
☐ 117 Dave Johnson	.25	.11	.03
☐ 118 Andy Van Slyke	.40	.18	.05
☐ 119 John Burkett	.25	.11	.03
☐ 120 Rickey Henderson	1.50	.65	.19
☐ 121 Tim Jones	.25	.11	.03
☐ 122 Daryl Irvine	.25	.11	.03
☐ 123 Ruben Sierra	2.00	.90	.25
☐ 124 Jim Abbott	1.50	.65	.19
☐ 125 Daryl Boston	.25	.11	.03
☐ 126 Greg Maddux	1.50	.65	.19
☐ 127 Von Hayes	.25	.11	.03
☐ 128 Mike Fitzgerald	.25	.11	.03
☐ 129 Wayne Edwards	.25	.11	.03
☐ 130 Greg Briley	.25	.11	.03
☐ 131 Rob Dibble	.30	.14	.04
☐ 132 Gene Larkin	.25	.11	.03
☐ 133 David Wells	.25	.11	.03
☐ 134 Steve Balboni	.25	.11	.03
☐ 135 Greg Vaughn	.50	.23	.06
☐ 136 Mark Davis	.25	.11	.03
☐ 137 Dave Rhode	.25	.11	.03
☐ 138 Eric Show	.25	.11	.03

☐ 139 Bobby Bonilla	1.00	.45	.13
☐ 140 Dana Kiecker	.25	.11	.03
☐ 141 Gary Pettis	.25	.11	.03
☐ 142 Dennis Boyd	.25	.11	.03
☐ 143 Mike Benjamin	.25	.11	.03
☐ 144 Luis Polonia	.30	.14	.04
☐ 145 Doug Jones	.25	.11	.03
☐ 146 Al Newman	.25	.11	.03
☐ 147 Alex Fernandez	.75	.35	.09
☐ 148 Bill Doran	.25	.11	.03
☐ 149 Kevin Elster	.25	.11	.03
☐ 150 Len Dykstra	.30	.14	.04
☐ 151 Mike Gallego	.25	.11	.03
☐ 152 Tim Belcher	.30	.14	.04
☐ 153 Jay Buhner	.30	.14	.04
☐ 154 Ozzie Smith UER (Rookie card is 1979, but card back says '78)	.90	.40	.11
☐ 155 Jose Canseco	3.00	1.35	.40
☐ 156 Gregg Olson	.30	.14	.04
☐ 157 Charlie O'Brien	.25	.11	.03
☐ 158 Frank Tanana	.25	.11	.03
☐ 159 George Brett	1.25	.55	.16
☐ 160 Jeff Huson	.25	.11	.03
☐ 161 Kevin Tapani	.75	.35	.09
☐ 162 Jerome Walton	.25	.11	.03
☐ 163 Charlie Hayes	.25	.11	.03
☐ 164 Chris Bosio	.25	.11	.03
☐ 165 Chris Sabo	.30	.14	.04
☐ 166 Lance Parrish	.30	.14	.04
☐ 167 Don Robinson	.25	.11	.03
☐ 168 Manny Lee	.25	.11	.03
☐ 169 Dennis Rasmussen	.25	.11	.03
☐ 170 Wade Boggs	1.50	.65	.19
☐ 171 Bob Geren	.25	.11	.03
☐ 172 Mackey Sasser	.25	.11	.03
☐ 173 Julio Franco	.30	.14	.04
☐ 174 Otis Nixon	.30	.14	.04
☐ 175 Bert Blyleven	.30	.14	.04
☐ 176 Craig Biggio	.50	.23	.06
☐ 177 Eddie Murray	.90	.40	.11
☐ 178 Randy Tomlin	1.25	.55	.16
☐ 179 Tino Martinez	.75	.35	.09
☐ 180 Carlton Fisk	.90	.40	.11
☐ 181 Dwight Smith	.25	.11	.03
☐ 182 Scott Garrelts	.25	.11	.03
☐ 183 Jim Gantner	.25	.11	.03
☐ 184 Dickie Thon	.25	.11	.03
☐ 185 John Farrell	.25	.11	.03
☐ 186 Cecil Fielder	1.50	.65	.19
☐ 187 Glenn Braggs	.25	.11	.03
☐ 188 Allan Anderson	.25	.11	.03
☐ 189 Kurt Stillwell	.25	.11	.03
☐ 190 Jose Oquendo	.25	.11	.03
☐ 191 Joe Orsulak	.25	.11	.03
☐ 192 Ricky Jordan	.25	.11	.03
☐ 193 Kelly Downs	.25	.11	.03
☐ 194 Delino DeShields	2.00	.90	.25
☐ 195 Omar Vizquel	.25	.11	.03
☐ 196 Mark Carreon	.25	.11	.03
☐ 197 Mike Harkey	.30	.14	.04
☐ 198 Jack Howell	.25	.11	.03
☐ 199 Lance Johnson	.25	.11	.03
☐ 200 Nolan Ryan (Wearing Tuxedo)	12.00	5.50	1.50
☐ 201 John Marzano	.25	.11	.03
☐ 202 Doug Drabek	.30	.14	.04
☐ 203 Mark Lemke	.25	.11	.03
☐ 204 Steve Sax	.30	.14	.04
☐ 205 Greg Harris	.25	.11	.03
☐ 206 B.J. Surhoff	.25	.11	.03
☐ 207 Todd Burns	.25	.11	.03
☐ 208 Jose Gonzalez	.25	.11	.03
☐ 209 Mike Scott	.25	.11	.03
☐ 210 Dave Magadan	.30	.14	.04
☐ 211 Dante Bichette	.35	.16	.04
☐ 212 Trevor Wilson	.25	.11	.03
☐ 213 Hector Villanueva	.25	.11	.03
☐ 214 Dan Pasqua	.25	.11	.03
☐ 215 Greg Colbrunn	1.25	.55	.16
☐ 216 Mike Jeffcoat	.25	.11	.03
☐ 217 Harold Reynolds	.25	.11	.03
☐ 218 Paul O'Neill	.30	.14	.04
☐ 219 Mark Guthrie	.25	.11	.03
☐ 220 Barry Bonds	3.00	1.35	.40
☐ 221 Jimmy Key	.25	.11	.03
☐ 222 Billy Ripken	.25	.11	.03
☐ 223 Tom Pagnozzi	.25	.11	.03
☐ 224 Bo Jackson	1.00	.45	.13
☐ 225 Sid Fernandez	.30	.14	.04
☐ 226 Mike Marshall	.25	.11	.03
☐ 227 John Kruk	.35	.16	.04
☐ 228 Mike Fetters	.25	.11	.03
☐ 229 Eric Anthony	.30	.14	.04
☐ 230 Ryne Sandberg	3.50	1.55	.45
☐ 231 Carney Lansford	.30	.14	.04
☐ 232 Melido Perez	.30	.14	.04
☐ 233 Jose Lind	.25	.11	.03
☐ 234 Darryl Hamilton	.30	.14	.04
☐ 235 Tom Browning	.25	.11	.03
☐ 236 Spike Owen	.25	.11	.03
☐ 237 Juan Gonzalez	18.00	8.00	2.30
☐ 238 Felix Fermin	.25	.11	.03
☐ 239 Keith Miller	.25	.11	.03
☐ 240 Mark Gubicza	.25	.11	.03
☐ 241 Kent Anderson	.25	.11	.03
☐ 242 Alvaro Espinoza	.25	.11	.03
☐ 243 Dale Murphy	.40	.18	.05
☐ 244 Orel Hershiser	.30	.14	.04
☐ 245 Paul Molitor	.50	.23	.06
☐ 246 Eddie Whitson	.25	.11	.03
☐ 247 Joe Girardi	.25	.11	.03
☐ 248 Kent Hrbek	.30	.14	.04
☐ 249 Bill Sampen	.25	.11	.03
☐ 250 Kevin Mitchell	.35	.16	.04
☐ 251 Mariano Duncan	.25	.11	.03
☐ 252 Scott Bradley	.25	.11	.03
☐ 253 Mike Greenwell	.30	.14	.04
☐ 254 Tom Gordon	.30	.14	.04
☐ 255 Todd Zeile	.40	.18	.05
☐ 256 Bobby Thigpen	.25	.11	.03
☐ 257 Gregg Jefferies	.60	.25	.08
☐ 258 Kenny Rogers	.25	.11	.03
☐ 259 Shane Mack	.50	.23	.06
☐ 260 Zane Smith	.25	.11	.03
☐ 261 Mitch Williams	.25	.11	.03
☐ 262 Jim Deshaies	.25	.11	.03
☐ 263 Dave Winfield	1.00	.45	.13
☐ 264 Ben McDonald	1.25	.55	.16
☐ 265 Randy Ready	.25	.11	.03
☐ 266 Pat Borders	.25	.11	.03
☐ 267 Jose Uribe	.25	.11	.03
☐ 268 Derek Lilliquist	.25	.11	.03
☐ 269 Greg Brock	.25	.11	.03
☐ 270 Ken Griffey Jr.	12.00	5.50	1.50
☐ 271 Jeff Gray	.25	.11	.03
☐ 272 Danny Tartabull	.50	.23	.06
☐ 273 Denny Martinez	.30	.14	.04
☐ 274 Robin Ventura	4.00	1.80	.50
☐ 275 Randy Myers	.30	.14	.04
☐ 276 Jack Daugherty	.25	.11	.03
☐ 277 Greg Gagne	.25	.11	.03
☐ 278 Jay Howell	.25	.11	.03
☐ 279 Mike LaValliere	.25	.11	.03
☐ 280 Rex Hudler	.25	.11	.03
☐ 281 Mike Simms	.35	.16	.04
☐ 282 Kevin Maas	.50	.23	.06
☐ 283 Jeff Ballard	.25	.11	.03
☐ 284 Dave Henderson	.25	.11	.03
☐ 285 Pete O'Brien	.25	.11	.03
☐ 286 Brook Jacoby	.25	.11	.03
☐ 287 Mike Henneman	.25	.11	.03
☐ 288 Greg Olson	.25	.11	.03
☐ 289 Greg Myers	.25	.11	.03
☐ 290 Mark Grace	1.25	.55	.16
☐ 291 Shawn Abner	.25	.11	.03
☐ 292 Frank Viola	.30	.14	.04
☐ 293 Lee Stevens	.35	.16	.04
☐ 294 Jason Grimsley	.25	.11	.03
☐ 295 Matt Williams	.50	.23	.06
☐ 296 Ron Robinson	.25	.11	.03
☐ 297 Tom Brunansky	.30	.14	.04
☐ 298 Checklist 1-100	.25	.03	.01
☐ 299 Checklist 101-200	.25	.03	.01
☐ 300 Checklist 201-300	.25	.03	.01
☐ 301 Darryl Strawberry	1.50	.65	.19
☐ 302 Bud Black	.25	.11	.03
☐ 303 Harold Baines	.30	.14	.04
☐ 304 Roberto Alomar	5.00	2.30	.60
☐ 305 Norm Charlton	.30	.14	.04
☐ 306 Gary Thurman	.25	.11	.03
☐ 307 Mike Felder	.25	.11	.03
☐ 308 Tony Gwynn	1.50	.65	.19
☐ 309 Roger Clemens	3.50	1.55	.45
☐ 310 Andre Dawson	.90	.40	.11
☐ 311 Scott Radinsky	.25	.11	.03
☐ 312 Bob Melvin	.25	.11	.03
☐ 313 Kirk McCaskill	.25	.11	.03
☐ 314 Pedro Guerrero	.30	.14	.04
☐ 315 Walt Terrell	.25	.11	.03
☐ 316 Sam Horn	.25	.11	.03
☐ 317 Wes Chamberlain	1.25	.55	.16
☐ 318 Pedro Munoz	1.50	.65	.19
☐ 319 Roberto Kelly	.40	.18	.05
☐ 320 Mark Portugal	.25	.11	.03
☐ 321 Tim McIntosh	.25	.11	.03

☐ 322	Jesse Orosco	.25	.11	.03
☐ 323	Gary Green	.25	.11	.03
☐ 324	Greg Harris	.25	.11	.03
☐ 325	Hubie Brooks	.25	.11	.03
☐ 326	Chris Nabholz	.40	.18	.05
☐ 327	Terry Pendleton	.60	.25	.08
☐ 328	Eric King	.25	.11	.03
☐ 329	Chili Davis	.30	.14	.04
☐ 330	Anthony Telford	.25	.11	.03
☐ 331	Kelly Gruber	.30	.14	.04
☐ 332	Dennis Eckersley	.50	.23	.06
☐ 333	Mel Hall	.25	.11	.03
☐ 334	Bob Kipper	.25	.11	.03
☐ 335	Willie McGee	.30	.14	.04
☐ 336	Steve Olin	.25	.11	.03
☐ 337	Steve Buechele	.25	.11	.03
☐ 338	Scott Leius	.40	.18	.05
☐ 339	Hal Morris	.40	.18	.05
☐ 340	Jose Offerman	.40	.18	.05
☐ 341	Kent Mercker	.30	.14	.04
☐ 342	Ken Griffey Sr.	.30	.14	.04
☐ 343	Pete Harnisch	.30	.14	.04
☐ 344	Kirk Gibson	.30	.14	.04
☐ 345	Dave Smith	.25	.11	.03
☐ 346	Dave Martinez	.25	.11	.03
☐ 347	Atlee Hammaker	.25	.11	.03
☐ 348	Brian Downing	.25	.11	.03
☐ 349	Todd Hundley	.35	.16	.04
☐ 350	Candy Maldonado	.25	.11	.03
☐ 351	Dwight Evans	.30	.14	.04
☐ 352	Steve Searcy	.25	.11	.03
☐ 353	Gary Gaetti	.25	.11	.03
☐ 354	Jeff Reardon	.35	.16	.04
☐ 355	Travis Fryman	12.00	5.50	1.50
☐ 356	Dave Righetti	.25	.11	.03
☐ 357	Fred McGriff	1.50	.65	.19
☐ 358	Don Slaught	.25	.11	.03
☐ 359	Gene Nelson	.25	.11	.03
☐ 360	Billy Spiers	.25	.11	.03
☐ 361	Lee Guetterman	.25	.11	.03
☐ 362	Darren Lewis	.40	.18	.05
☐ 363	Duane Ward	.25	.11	.03
☐ 364	Lloyd Moseby	.25	.11	.03
☐ 365	John Smoltz	1.50	.65	.19
☐ 366	Felix Jose	.60	.25	.08
☐ 367	David Cone	.75	.35	.09
☐ 368	Wally Backman	.25	.11	.03
☐ 369	Jeff Montgomery	.25	.11	.03
☐ 370	Rich Garces	.35	.16	.04
☐ 371	Billy Hatcher	.25	.11	.03
☐ 372	Bill Swift	.25	.11	.03
☐ 373	Jim Eisenreich	.25	.11	.03
☐ 374	Rob Ducey	.25	.11	.03
☐ 375	Tim Crews	.25	.11	.03
☐ 376	Steve Finley	.30	.14	.04
☐ 377	Jeff Blauser	.25	.11	.03
☐ 378	Willie Wilson	.25	.11	.03
☐ 379	Gerald Perry	.25	.11	.03
☐ 380	Jose Mesa	.25	.11	.03
☐ 381	Pat Kelly	.60	.25	.08
☐ 382	Matt Merullo	.25	.11	.03
☐ 383	Ivan Calderon	.25	.11	.03
☐ 384	Scott Chiamparino	.30	.14	.04
☐ 385	Lloyd McClendon	.25	.11	.03
☐ 386	Dave Bergman	.25	.11	.03
☐ 387	Ed Sprague	.75	.35	.09
☐ 388	Jeff Bagwell	9.00	4.00	1.15
☐ 389	Brett Butler	.30	.14	.04
☐ 390	Larry Andersen	.25	.11	.03
☐ 391	Glenn Davis	.30	.14	.04
☐ 392	Alex Cole UER (Front photo actually Otis Nixon)	.25	.11	.03
☐ 393	Mike Heath	.25	.11	.03
☐ 394	Danny Darwin	.25	.11	.03
☐ 395	Steve Lake	.25	.11	.03
☐ 396	Tim Layana	.25	.11	.03
☐ 397	Terry Leach	.25	.11	.03
☐ 398	Bill Wegman	.25	.11	.03
☐ 399	Mark McGwire	3.00	1.35	.40
☐ 400	Mike Boddicker	.25	.11	.03
☐ 401	Steve Howe	.25	.11	.03
☐ 402	Bernard Gilkey	.60	.25	.08
☐ 403	Thomas Howard	.35	.16	.04
☐ 404	Rafael Belliard	.25	.11	.03
☐ 405	Tom Candiotti	.25	.11	.03
☐ 406	Rene Gonzales	.25	.11	.03
☐ 407	Chuck McElroy	.25	.11	.03
☐ 408	Paul Sorrento	.50	.23	.06
☐ 409	Randy Johnson	.30	.14	.04
☐ 410	Brady Anderson	.60	.25	.08
☐ 411	Dennis Cook	.25	.11	.03
☐ 412	Mickey Tettleton	.35	.16	.04
☐ 413	Mike Stanton	.25	.11	.03
☐ 414	Ken Oberkfell	.25	.11	.03
☐ 415	Rick Honeycutt	.25	.11	.03
☐ 416	Nelson Santovenia	.25	.11	.03
☐ 417	Bob Tewksbury	.30	.14	.04
☐ 418	Brent Mayne	.35	.16	.04
☐ 419	Steve Farr	.25	.11	.03
☐ 420	Phil Stephenson	.25	.11	.03
☐ 421	Jeff Russell	.25	.11	.03
☐ 422	Chris James	.25	.11	.03
☐ 423	Tim Leary	.25	.11	.03
☐ 424	Gary Carter	.30	.14	.04
☐ 425	Glenallen Hill	.25	.11	.03
☐ 426	Matt Young UER (Card mentions 83T/Tr as RC, but 84T shown)	.25	.11	.03
☐ 427	Sid Bream	.25	.11	.03
☐ 428	Greg Swindell	.35	.16	.04
☐ 429	Scott Aldred	.40	.18	.05
☐ 430	Cal Ripken	4.00	1.80	.50
☐ 431	Bill Landrum	.25	.11	.03
☐ 432	Earnest Riles	.25	.11	.03
☐ 433	Danny Jackson	.25	.11	.03
☐ 434	Casey Candaele	.25	.11	.03
☐ 435	Ken Hill	.30	.14	.04
☐ 436	Jaime Navarro	.75	.35	.09
☐ 437	Lance Blankenship	.25	.11	.03
☐ 438	Randy Velarde	.25	.11	.03
☐ 439	Frank DiPino	.25	.11	.03
☐ 440	Carl Nichols	.25	.11	.03
☐ 441	Jeff M. Robinson	.25	.11	.03
☐ 442	Deion Sanders	2.50	1.15	.30
☐ 443	Vicente Palacios	.25	.11	.03
☐ 444	Devon White	.30	.14	.04
☐ 445	John Cerutti	.25	.11	.03
☐ 446	Tracy Jones	.25	.11	.03
☐ 447	Jack Morris	.60	.25	.08
☐ 448	Mitch Webster	.25	.11	.03
☐ 449	Bob Ojeda	.25	.11	.03
☐ 450	Oscar Azocar	.25	.11	.03
☐ 451	Luis Aquino	.25	.11	.03
☐ 452	Mark Whiten	.50	.23	.06
☐ 453	Stan Belinda	.25	.11	.03
☐ 454	Ron Gant	1.50	.65	.19
☐ 455	Jose DeLeon	.25	.11	.03
☐ 456	Mark Salas UER (Back has 85T photo, but calls it 86T)	.25	.11	.03
☐ 457	Junior Felix	.25	.11	.03
☐ 458	Wally Whitehurst	.25	.11	.03
☐ 459	Phil Plantier	5.00	2.30	.60
☐ 460	Juan Berenguer	.25	.11	.03
☐ 461	Franklin Stubbs	.25	.11	.03
☐ 462	Joe Boever	.25	.11	.03
☐ 463	Tim Wallach	.30	.14	.04
☐ 464	Mike Moore	.25	.11	.03
☐ 465	Albert Belle	2.50	1.15	.30
☐ 466	Mike Witt	.25	.11	.03
☐ 467	Craig Worthington	.25	.11	.03
☐ 468	Jerald Clark	.25	.11	.03
☐ 469	Scott Terry	.25	.11	.03
☐ 470	Milt Cuyler	.35	.16	.04
☐ 471	John Smiley	.30	.14	.04
☐ 472	Charles Nagy	2.50	1.15	.30
☐ 473	Alan Mills	.35	.16	.04
☐ 474	John Russell	.25	.11	.03
☐ 475	Bruce Hurst	.30	.14	.04
☐ 476	Andujar Cedeno	.75	.35	.09
☐ 477	Dave Eiland	.25	.11	.03
☐ 478	Brian McRae	1.25	.55	.16
☐ 479	Mike LaCoss	.25	.11	.03
☐ 480	Chris Gwynn	.25	.11	.03
☐ 481	Jamie Moyer	.25	.11	.03
☐ 482	John Olerud	2.00	.90	.25
☐ 483	Efrain Valdez	.25	.11	.03
☐ 484	Sil Campusano	.25	.11	.03
☐ 485	Pascual Perez	.25	.11	.03
☐ 486	Gary Redus	.25	.11	.03
☐ 487	Andy Hawkins	.25	.11	.03
☐ 488	Cory Snyder	.25	.11	.03
☐ 489	Chris Hoiles	1.00	.45	.13
☐ 490	Ron Hassey	.25	.11	.03
☐ 491	Gary Wayne	.25	.11	.03
☐ 492	Mark Lewis	.75	.35	.09
☐ 493	Scott Coolbaugh	.25	.11	.03
☐ 494	Gerald Young	.25	.11	.03
☐ 495	Juan Samuel	.25	.11	.03
☐ 496	Willie Fraser	.25	.11	.03
☐ 497	Jeff Treadway	.25	.11	.03
☐ 498	Vince Coleman	.30	.14	.04
☐ 499	Cris Carpenter	.25	.11	.03
☐ 500	Jack Clark	.30	.14	.04
☐ 501	Kevin Appier	1.25	.55	.16

☐ 502 Rafael Palmeiro	.75	.35	.09
☐ 503 Hensley Meulens	.30	.14	.04
☐ 504 George Bell	.35	.16	.04
☐ 505 Tony Pena	.25	.11	.03
☐ 506 Roger McDowell	.25	.11	.03
☐ 507 Luis Sojo	.25	.11	.03
☐ 508 Mike Schooler	.25	.11	.03
☐ 509 Robin Yount	1.25	.55	.16
☐ 510 Jack Armstrong	.25	.11	.03
☐ 511 Rick Cerone	.25	.11	.03
☐ 512 Curt Wilkerson	.25	.11	.03
☐ 513 Joe Carter	1.50	.65	.19
☐ 514 Tim Burke	.25	.11	.03
☐ 515 Tony Fernandez	.30	.14	.04
☐ 516 Ramon Martinez	.60	.25	.08
☐ 517 Tim Hulett	.25	.11	.03
☐ 518 Terry Steinbach	.30	.14	.04
☐ 519 Pete Smith	.40	.18	.05
☐ 520 Ken Caminiti	.30	.14	.04
☐ 521 Shawn Boskie	.25	.11	.03
☐ 522 Mike Pagliarulo	.25	.11	.03
☐ 523 Tim Raines	.30	.14	.04
☐ 524 Alfredo Griffin	.25	.11	.03
☐ 525 Henry Cotto	.25	.11	.03
☐ 526 Mike Stanley	.25	.11	.03
☐ 527 Charlie Leibrandt	.25	.11	.03
☐ 528 Jeff King	.25	.11	.03
☐ 529 Eric Plunk	.25	.11	.03
☐ 530 Tom Lampkin	.25	.11	.03
☐ 531 Steve Bedrosian	.25	.11	.03
☐ 532 Tom Herr	.25	.11	.03
☐ 533 Craig Lefferts	.25	.11	.03
☐ 534 Jeff Reed	.25	.11	.03
☐ 535 Mickey Morandini	.50	.23	.06
☐ 536 Greg Cadaret	.25	.11	.03
☐ 537 Ray Lankford	5.00	2.30	.60
☐ 538 John Candelaria	.25	.11	.03
☐ 539 Rob Deer	.30	.14	.04
☐ 540 Brad Arnsberg	.25	.11	.03
☐ 541 Mike Sharperson	.25	.11	.03
☐ 542 Jeff D. Robinson	.25	.11	.03
☐ 543 Mo Vaughn	1.25	.55	.16
☐ 544 Jeff Parrett	.25	.11	.03
☐ 545 Willie Randolph	.30	.14	.04
☐ 546 Herm Winningham	.25	.11	.03
☐ 547 Jeff Innis	.25	.11	.03
☐ 548 Chuck Knoblauch	6.00	2.70	.75
☐ 549 Tommy Greene UER	.25	.11	.03
(Born in North Carolina, not South Carolina)			
☐ 550 Jeff Hamilton	.25	.11	.03
☐ 551 Barry Jones	.25	.11	.03
☐ 552 Ken Dayley	.25	.11	.03
☐ 553 Rick Dempsey	.25	.11	.03
☐ 554 Greg Smith	.25	.11	.03
☐ 555 Mike Devereaux	.50	.23	.06
☐ 556 Keith Comstock	.25	.11	.03
☐ 557 Paul Faries	.25	.11	.03
☐ 558 Tom Glavine	2.50	1.15	.30
☐ 559 Craig Grebeck	.25	.11	.03
☐ 560 Scott Erickson	1.50	.65	.19
☐ 561 Joel Skinner	.25	.11	.03
☐ 562 Mike Morgan	.25	.11	.03
☐ 563 Dave Gallagher	.25	.11	.03
☐ 564 Todd Stottlemyre	.30	.14	.04
☐ 565 Rich Rodriguez	.35	.16	.04
☐ 566 Craig Wilson	.35	.16	.04
☐ 567 Jeff Brantley	.25	.11	.03
☐ 568 Scott Kamieniecki	.35	.16	.04
☐ 569 Steve Decker	.60	.25	.08
☐ 570 Juan Agosto	.25	.11	.03
☐ 571 Tommy Gregg	.25	.11	.03
☐ 572 Kevin Wickander	.25	.11	.03
☐ 573 Jamie Quirk UER	.25	.11	.03
(Rookie card is 1976, but card back is 1990)			
☐ 574 Jerry Don Gleaton	.25	.11	.03
☐ 575 Chris Hammond	.50	.23	.06
☐ 576 Luis Gonzalez	1.25	.55	.16
☐ 577 Russ Swan	.25	.11	.03
☐ 578 Jeff Conine	1.25	.55	.16
☐ 579 Charlie Hough	.25	.11	.03
☐ 580 Jeff Kunkel	.25	.11	.03
☐ 581 Darrel Akerfelds	.25	.11	.03
☐ 582 Jeff Manto	.25	.11	.03
☐ 583 Alejandro Pena	.25	.11	.03
☐ 584 Mark Davidson	.25	.11	.03
☐ 585 Bob MacDonald	.35	.16	.04
☐ 586 Paul Assenmacher	.25	.11	.03
☐ 587 Dan Wilson	.60	.25	.08
☐ 588 Tom Bolton	.25	.11	.03
☐ 589 Brian Harper	.25	.11	.03
☐ 590 John Habyan	.25	.11	.03
☐ 591 John Orton	.25	.11	.03
☐ 592 Mark Gardner	.25	.11	.03
☐ 593 Turner Ward	.35	.16	.04
☐ 594 Bob Patterson	.25	.11	.03
☐ 595 Ed Nunez	.25	.11	.03
☐ 596 Gary Scott UER	.75	.35	.09
(Major League Batting Record should be Minor League)			
☐ 597 Scott Bankhead	.25	.11	.03
☐ 598 Checklist 301-400	.25	.03	.01
☐ 599 Checklist 401-500	.25	.03	.01
☐ 600 Checklist 501-600	.25	.03	.01

1991 Stadium Club Charter Member *

This 50-card multi-sport set was sent to charter members in the Topps Stadium Club. The sports represented in the set are baseball (1-32), football (33-41), and hockey (42-50). The standard-size (2 1/2" and 3 1/2") cards feature on the fronts full-bleed posed and action glossy color player photos. The player's name is shown in the light blue stripe that intersects the Stadium Club logo near the bottom of the picture. The words "Charter Member" are printed in gold foil lettering immediately below the stripe. The back design features a newspaper-like masthead (The Stadium Club Herald) complete with a headline announcing a major event in the player's season with copy below providing more information about the event. The cards are unnumbered and arranged below alphabetically within sports. Also included in the nice black box that held and delivered the Stadium Club cards was a Nolan Ryan bronze metallic card and a key chain.

	MT	EX-MT	VG
COMPLETE SET (50)	30.00	13.50	3.80
COMMON PLAYER (1-32)	.15	.07	.02
COMMON FOOTBALL (33-41)	.15	.07	.02
COMMON HOCKEY (42-50)	.75	.35	.09
☐ 1 Sandy Alomar	.20	.09	.03
☐ 2 George Brett	.75	.35	.09
☐ 3 Barry Bonds	1.00	.45	.13
☐ 4 Ellis Burks	.25	.11	.03
☐ 5 Eric Davis	.25	.11	.03
☐ 6 Delino DeShields	.75	.35	.09
☐ 7 Doug Drabek	.25	.11	.03
☐ 8 Cecil Fielder	.75	.35	.09
☐ 9 Carlton Fisk	.50	.23	.06
☐ 10 Ken Griffey Jr. and Ken Griffey Sr.	4.00	1.80	.50
☐ 11 Billy Hatcher	.15	.07	.02
☐ 12 Andy Hawkins	.15	.07	.02
☐ 13 Rickey Henderson A.L. Recognizes Rickey As MVP	.75	.35	.09
☐ 14 Rickey Henderson Rickey is A.L.'s Leading Thief	.75	.35	.09
☐ 15 Randy Johnson	.25	.11	.03
☐ 16 Dave Justice	1.50	.65	.19

	#	Player	MT	EX-MT	VG
☐	17	Mark Langston and Mike Witt	.15	.07	.02
☐	18	Kevin Maas	.25	.11	.03
☐	19	Ramon Martinez	.25	.11	.03
☐	20	Willie McGee	.15	.07	.02
☐	21	Terry Mulholland	.15	.07	.02
☐	22	Jose Offerman	.25	.11	.03
☐	23	Melido Perez	.25	.11	.03
☐	24	Nolan Ryan A No-Hitter For The Ages	4.00	1.80	.50
☐	25	Nolan Ryan Nolan Ryan Earns 300th Career Win	4.00	1.80	.50
☐	26	Ryne Sandberg	2.00	.90	.25
☐	27	Dave Stewart	.25	.11	.03
☐	28	Dave Stieb	.15	.07	.02
☐	29	Bobby Thigpen	.15	.07	.02
☐	30	Fernando Valenzuela	.15	.07	.02
☐	31	Frank Viola	.25	.11	.03
☐	32	Bob Welch	.15	.07	.02
☐	33	Ottis Anderson Andeson MVP of Super Bowl XXV	.25	.11	.03
☐	34	Ottis Anderson Ottis The Giant Reaches 10,000	.25	.11	.03
☐	35	Randall Cunningham	1.25	.55	.16
☐	36	Warren Moon	1.25	.55	.16
☐	37	Barry Sanders	3.00	1.35	.40
☐	38	Pete Stoyanovich	.15	.07	.02
☐	39	Lawrence Taylor	.50	.23	.06
☐	40	Derrick Thomas	1.00	.45	.13
☐	41	Richmond Webb	.15	.07	.02
☐	42	Ed Belfour Belfour Cops The Vezina	1.50	.65	.19
☐	43	Ed Belfour Belfour Is Top Goalie	1.50	.65	.19
☐	44	Ray Bourque	.75	.35	.09
☐	45	Paul Coffey	.75	.35	.09
☐	46	Wayne Gretzky Gretzky Takes No. 2000	4.00	1.80	.50
☐	47	Wayne Gretzky The 700 Club	4.00	1.80	.50
☐	48	Brett Hull Brett's All Hart	2.50	1.15	.30
☐	49	Brett Hull Hull Joins 50-50 Club	2.50	1.15	.30
☐	50	Mario Lemieux	4.00	1.80	.50

1991 Stadium Club Members Only *

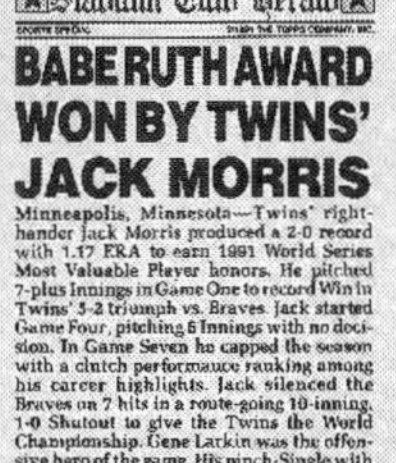

★Stadium Club Herald★

BABE RUTH AWARD WON BY TWINS' JACK MORRIS

Minneapolis, Minnesota—Twins' right-hander Jack Morris produced a 2-0 record with 1.17 ERA to earn 1991 World Series Most Valuable Player honors. He pitched 7-plus Innings in Game One to record Win in Twins' 5-2 triumph vs. Braves. Jack started Game Four, pitching 6 Innings with no decision. In Game Seven he capped the season with a clutch performance ranking among his career highlights. Jack silenced the Braves on 7 hits in a route-going 10-inning, 1-0 Shutout to give the Twins the World Championship. Gene Larkin was the offensive hero of the game. His pinch-Single with the bases loaded won the contest.

This 50-card multi-sport set was sent in three installments to members in the Topps Stadium Club. The first and second installments featured baseball players (card numbers 1-10 and 11-30), while the third spotlighted football (31-37) and hockey (38-50) players. The standard-size (2 1/2" and 3 1/2") feature on the fronts full-bleed posed and action glossy color player photos. The player's name is shown in the light blue stripe that intersects the Stadium Club logo near the bottom of the picture. The words "Members Only" are printed in gold foil lettering immediately below the stripe. The back design features a newspaper-like masthead (The Stadium Club Herald) complete with a headline announcing a major event in the player's season with copy below providing more information about the event. The cards are unnumbered and arranged below alphabetically according to and within installments.

	MT	EX-MT	VG
COMPLETE SET (50)	27.00	12.00	3.40
COMMON PLAYER (1-10)	.15	.07	.02
COMMON PLAYER (11-30)	.15	.07	.02
COMMON FOOTBALL (31-37)	.15	.07	.02
COMMON HOCKEY (38-50)	.25	.11	.03

	#	Player	MT	EX-MT	VG
☐	1	Wilson Alvarez	.25	.11	.03
☐	2	Andy Ashby	.15	.07	.02
☐	3	Tommy Greene	.15	.07	.02
☐	4	Rickey Henderson Rickey Is Top Thief in History	.75	.35	.09
☐	5	Denny Martinez	.15	.07	.02
☐	6	Paul Molitor	.35	.16	.04
☐	7	Nolan Ryan Ryan Extends Record With 7th No-Hitter	3.00	1.35	.40
☐	8	Robby Thompson	.15	.07	.02
☐	9	Dave Winfield	.50	.23	.06
☐	10	Orioles No-Hitter Bob Milacki Mike Flanagan Mark Williamson Gregg Olson Chris Hoiles (C)	.15	.07	.02
☐	11	Jeff Bagwell	1.25	.55	.16
☐	12	Roger Clemens	1.50	.65	.19
☐	13	David Cone	.35	.16	.04
☐	14	Carlton Fisk	.50	.23	.06
☐	15	Julio Franco	.25	.11	.03
☐	16	Tom Glavine	.75	.35	.09
☐	17	Pete Harnisch	.25	.11	.03
☐	18	Rickey Henderson Rickey Leads A.L. In Thefts For 11th Time	.75	.35	.09
☐	19	Howard Johnson	.25	.11	.03
☐	20	Chuck Knoblauch	.75	.35	.09
☐	21	Ray Lankford	.75	.35	.09
☐	22	Jack Morris	.35	.16	.04
☐	23	Terry Pendleton NL's Leading Batsman	.35	.16	.04
☐	24	Terry Pendleton Close MVP Race Favors Terry	.35	.16	.04
☐	25	Jeff Reardon	.25	.11	.03
☐	26	Cal Ripken	2.00	.90	.25
☐	27	Nolan Ryan Ryan's 22nd Straight Year With Over 100 Strikeouts	3.00	1.35	.40
☐	28	Bret Saberhagen	.25	.11	.03
☐	29	AL Home Run Leaders Cecil Fielder Jose Canseco	.75	.35	.09
☐	30	Braves No Hitter Kent Mercker Mark Wohlers Alejandro Pena	.15	.07	.02
☐	31	Art Monk	.60	.25	.08
☐	32	Warren Moon	.90	.40	.11
☐	33	Leonard Russell	.50	.23	.06
☐	34	Mark Rypien	.75	.35	.09
☐	35	Barry Sanders	2.00	.90	.25
☐	36	Emmitt Smith	3.00	1.35	.40
☐	37	Tony Zendejas	.15	.07	.02
☐	38	Pavel Bure	2.50	1.15	.30
☐	39	Guy Carbonneau	.15	.07	.02
☐	40	Paul Coffey	.45	.20	.06
☐	41	Mike Gartner Mike Makes It Two	.35	.16	.04
☐	42	Mike Gartner Mike Makes It 500	.35	.16	.04
☐	43	Michel Goulet	.25	.11	.03
☐	44	Wayne Gretzky	2.50	1.15	.30
☐	45	Brett Hull	1.50	.65	.19
☐	46	Brian Leetch	.75	.35	.09
☐	47	Mario Lemieux Mario Repeats As MVP	2.50	1.15	.30
☐	48	Mario Lemieux Lemieux Takes 3rd Ross Trophy	2.50	1.15	.30
☐	49	Mark Messier	.90	.40	.11
☐	50	Patrick Roy	.90	.40	.11

1992 Stadium Club

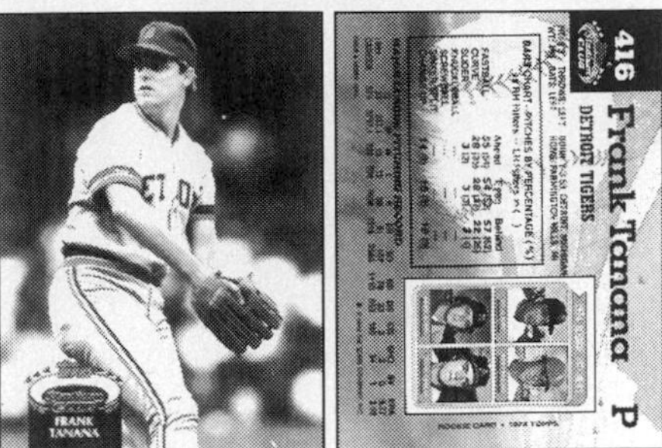

The 1992 Topps Stadium Club baseball card set consists of 900 standard-size (2 1/2" by 3 1/2") cards issued in three series of 300 cards each. The glossy color player photos on the fronts are full-bleed. The "Topps Stadium Club" logo is superimposed at the bottom of the card face, with the player's name appearing immediately below the logo. Some cards in the set have the Stadium Club logo printed upside down. The backs display a mini reprint of the player's Rookie Card and "BARS" (Baseball Analysis and Reporting System) statistics. A card-like application form for membership in Topps Stadium Club was inserted in each wax pack. The cards are numbered on the back. The only noteworthy Rookie Card in the first series is Braulio Castillo. Card numbers 591-600 in the second series form a "Members Choice" subset. The only noteworthy Rookie Card in the second series is Rob Maurer. Card numbers 601-610 in the third series form a "Members Choice" subset. The only noteworthy Rookie Cards in the third series are Pat Listach and Bob Zupcic.

	MT	EX-MT	VG
COMPLETE SET (900)	90.00	40.00	11.50
COMPLETE SERIES 1 (300)	32.00	14.50	4.00
COMPLETE SERIES 2 (300)	32.00	14.50	4.00
COMPLETE SERIES 3 (300)	32.00	14.50	4.00
COMMON PLAYER (1-300)	.15	.07	.02
COMMON PLAYER (301-600)	.15	.07	.02
COMMON PLAYER (601-900)	.15	.07	.02
□ 1 Cal Ripken UER (Misspelled Ripkin on card back)	2.50	1.15	.30
□ 2 Eric Yelding	.15	.07	.02
□ 3 Geno Petralli	.15	.07	.02
□ 4 Wally Backman	.15	.07	.02
□ 5 Milt Cuyler	.15	.07	.02
□ 6 Kevin Bass	.15	.07	.02
□ 7 Dante Bichette	.15	.07	.02
□ 8 Ray Lankford	.75	.35	.09
□ 9 Mel Hall	.15	.07	.02
□ 10 Joe Carter	.60	.25	.08
□ 11 Juan Samuel	.15	.07	.02
□ 12 Jeff Montgomery	.15	.07	.02
□ 13 Glenn Braggs	.15	.07	.02
□ 14 Henry Cotto	.15	.07	.02
□ 15 Deion Sanders	.75	.35	.09
□ 16 Dick Schofield	.15	.07	.02
□ 17 David Cone	.25	.11	.03
□ 18 Chili Davis	.20	.09	.03
□ 19 Tom Foley	.15	.07	.02
□ 20 Ozzie Guillen	.15	.07	.02
□ 21 Luis Salazar	.15	.07	.02
□ 22 Terry Steinbach	.20	.09	.03
□ 23 Chris James	.15	.07	.02
□ 24 Jeff King	.15	.07	.02
□ 25 Carlos Quintana	.15	.07	.02
□ 26 Mike Maddux	.15	.07	.02
□ 27 Tommy Greene	.15	.07	.02
□ 28 Jeff Russell	.15	.07	.02
□ 29 Steve Finley	.20	.09	.03
□ 30 Mike Flanagan	.15	.07	.02
□ 31 Darren Lewis	.20	.09	.03
□ 32 Mark Lee	.15	.07	.02
□ 33 Willie Fraser	.15	.07	.02
□ 34 Mike Henneman	.15	.07	.02
□ 35 Kevin Maas	.20	.09	.03
□ 36 Dave Hansen	.20	.09	.03
□ 37 Erik Hanson	.15	.07	.02
□ 38 Bill Doran	.15	.07	.02
□ 39 Mike Boddicker	.15	.07	.02
□ 40 Vince Coleman	.20	.09	.03
□ 41 Devon White	.20	.09	.03
□ 42 Mark Gardner	.15	.07	.02
□ 43 Scott Lewis	.15	.07	.02
□ 44 Juan Berenguer	.15	.07	.02
□ 45 Carney Lansford	.20	.09	.03
□ 46 Curt Wilkerson	.15	.07	.02
□ 47 Shane Mack	.20	.09	.03
□ 48 Bip Roberts	.20	.09	.03
□ 49 Greg A. Harris	.15	.07	.02
□ 50 Ryne Sandberg	1.25	.55	.16
□ 51 Mark Whiten	.20	.09	.03
□ 52 Jack McDowell	.25	.11	.03
□ 53 Jimmy Jones	.15	.07	.02
□ 54 Steve Lake	.15	.07	.02
□ 55 Bud Black	.15	.07	.02
□ 56 Dave Valle	.15	.07	.02
□ 57 Kevin Reimer	.20	.09	.03
□ 58 Rich Gedman UER (Wrong BARS chart used)	.15	.07	.02
□ 59 Travis Fryman	2.00	.90	.25
□ 60 Steve Avery	.90	.40	.11
□ 61 Francisco de la Rosa	.20	.09	.03
□ 62 Scott Hemond	.15	.07	.02
□ 63 Hal Morris	.20	.09	.03
□ 64 Hensley Meulens	.15	.07	.02
□ 65 Frank Castillo	.30	.14	.04
□ 66 Gene Larkin	.15	.07	.02
□ 67 Jose DeLeon	.15	.07	.02
□ 68 Al Osuna	.15	.07	.02
□ 69 Dave Cochrane	.15	.07	.02
□ 70 Robin Ventura	1.00	.45	.13
□ 71 John Cerutti	.15	.07	.02
□ 72 Kevin Gross	.15	.07	.02
□ 73 Ivan Calderon	.15	.07	.02
□ 74 Mike Macfarlane	.15	.07	.02
□ 75 Stan Belinda	.15	.07	.02
□ 76 Shawn Hillegas	.15	.07	.02
□ 77 Pat Borders	.15	.07	.02
□ 78 Jim Vatcher	.15	.07	.02
□ 79 Bobby Rose	.15	.07	.02
□ 80 Roger Clemens	1.25	.55	.16
□ 81 Craig Worthington	.15	.07	.02
□ 82 Jeff Treadway	.15	.07	.02
□ 83 Jamie Quirk	.15	.07	.02
□ 84 Randy Bush	.15	.07	.02
□ 85 Anthony Young	.30	.14	.04
□ 86 Trevor Wilson	.15	.07	.02
□ 87 Jaime Navarro	.20	.09	.03
□ 88 Les Lancaster	.15	.07	.02
□ 89 Pat Kelly	.20	.09	.03
□ 90 Alvin Davis	.15	.07	.02
□ 91 Larry Andersen	.15	.07	.02
□ 92 Rob Deer	.20	.09	.03
□ 93 Mike Sharperson	.15	.07	.02
□ 94 Lance Parrish	.20	.09	.03
□ 95 Cecil Espy	.15	.07	.02
□ 96 Tim Spehr	.15	.07	.02
□ 97 Dave Stieb	.15	.07	.02
□ 98 Terry Mulholland	.15	.07	.02
□ 99 Dennis Boyd	.15	.07	.02
□ 100 Barry Larkin	.35	.16	.04
□ 101 Ryan Bowen	.30	.14	.04
□ 102 Felix Fermin	.15	.07	.02
□ 103 Luis Alicea	.15	.07	.02
□ 104 Tim Hulett	.15	.07	.02
□ 105 Rafael Belliard	.15	.07	.02
□ 106 Mike Gallego	.15	.07	.02
□ 107 Dave Righetti	.15	.07	.02
□ 108 Jeff Schaefer	.15	.07	.02
□ 109 Ricky Bones	.35	.16	.04
□ 110 Scott Erickson	.25	.11	.03
□ 111 Matt Nokes	.15	.07	.02
□ 112 Bob Scanlan	.15	.07	.02
□ 113 Tom Candiotti	.15	.07	.02
□ 114 Sean Berry	.30	.14	.04
□ 115 Kevin Morton	.15	.07	.02
□ 116 Scott Fletcher	.15	.07	.02
□ 117 B.J. Surhoff	.15	.07	.02
□ 118 Dave Magadan UER (Born Tampa, not Tamps)	.20	.09	.03
□ 119 Bill Gullickson	.15	.07	.02
□ 120 Marquis Grissom	.50	.23	.06
□ 121 Lenny Harris	.15	.07	.02
□ 122 Wally Joyner	.20	.09	.03
□ 123 Kevin Brown	.20	.09	.03

☐ 124 Braulio Castillo	.40	.18	.05
☐ 125 Eric King	.15	.07	.02
☐ 126 Mark Portugal	.15	.07	.02
☐ 127 Calvin Jones	.30	.14	.04
☐ 128 Mike Heath	.15	.07	.02
☐ 129 Todd Van Poppel	.90	.40	.11
☐ 130 Benny Santiago	.25	.11	.03
☐ 131 Gary Thurman	.15	.07	.02
☐ 132 Joe Girardi	.15	.07	.02
☐ 133 Dave Eiland	.15	.07	.02
☐ 134 Orlando Merced	.30	.14	.04
☐ 135 Joe Orsulak	.15	.07	.02
☐ 136 John Burkett	.15	.07	.02
☐ 137 Ken Dayley	.15	.07	.02
☐ 138 Ken Hill	.20	.09	.03
☐ 139 Walt Terrell	.15	.07	.02
☐ 140 Mike Scioscia	.15	.07	.02
☐ 141 Junior Felix	.15	.07	.02
☐ 142 Ken Caminiti	.20	.09	.03
☐ 143 Carlos Baerga	1.00	.45	.13
☐ 144 Tony Fossas	.15	.07	.02
☐ 145 Craig Grebeck	.15	.07	.02
☐ 146 Scott Bradley	.15	.07	.02
☐ 147 Kent Mercker	.15	.07	.02
☐ 148 Derrick May	.20	.09	.03
☐ 149 Jerald Clark	.15	.07	.02
☐ 150 George Brett	.50	.23	.06
☐ 151 Luis Quinones	.15	.07	.02
☐ 152 Mike Pagliarulo	.15	.07	.02
☐ 153 Jose Guzman	.15	.07	.02
☐ 154 Charlie O'Brien	.15	.07	.02
☐ 155 Darren Holmes	.15	.07	.02
☐ 156 Joe Boever	.15	.07	.02
☐ 157 Rich Monteleone	.15	.07	.02
☐ 158 Reggie Harris	.15	.07	.02
☐ 159 Roberto Alomar	1.00	.45	.13
☐ 160 Robby Thompson	.15	.07	.02
☐ 161 Chris Hoiles	.20	.09	.03
☐ 162 Tom Pagnozzi	.15	.07	.02
☐ 163 Omar Vizquel	.15	.07	.02
☐ 164 John Candelaria	.15	.07	.02
☐ 165 Terry Shumpert	.15	.07	.02
☐ 166 Andy Mota	.20	.09	.03
☐ 167 Scott Bailes	.15	.07	.02
☐ 168 Jeff Blauser	.15	.07	.02
☐ 169 Steve Olin	.15	.07	.02
☐ 170 Doug Drabek	.20	.09	.03
☐ 171 Dave Bergman	.15	.07	.02
☐ 172 Eddie Whitson	.15	.07	.02
☐ 173 Gilberto Reyes	.15	.07	.02
☐ 174 Mark Grace	.25	.11	.03
☐ 175 Paul O'Neill	.20	.09	.03
☐ 176 Greg Cadaret	.15	.07	.02
☐ 177 Mark Williamson	.15	.07	.02
☐ 178 Casey Candaele	.15	.07	.02
☐ 179 Candy Maldonado	.15	.07	.02
☐ 180 Lee Smith	.20	.09	.03
☐ 181 Harold Reynolds	.15	.07	.02
☐ 182 David Justice	1.50	.65	.19
☐ 183 Lenny Webster	.15	.07	.02
☐ 184 Donn Pall	.15	.07	.02
☐ 185 Gerald Alexander	.15	.07	.02
☐ 186 Jack Clark	.20	.09	.03
☐ 187 Stan Javier	.15	.07	.02
☐ 188 Ricky Jordan	.15	.07	.02
☐ 189 Franklin Stubbs	.15	.07	.02
☐ 190 Dennis Eckersley	.25	.11	.03
☐ 191 Danny Tartabull	.20	.09	.03
☐ 192 Pete O'Brien	.15	.07	.02
☐ 193 Mark Lewis	.20	.09	.03
☐ 194 Mike Felder	.15	.07	.02
☐ 195 Mickey Tettleton	.20	.09	.03
☐ 196 Dwight Smith	.15	.07	.02
☐ 197 Shawn Abner	.15	.07	.02
☐ 198 Jim Leyritz UER (Career totals less than 1991 totals)	.15	.07	.02
☐ 199 Mike Devereaux	.20	.09	.03
☐ 200 Craig Biggio	.20	.09	.03
☐ 201 Kevin Elster	.15	.07	.02
☐ 202 Rance Mulliniks	.15	.07	.02
☐ 203 Tony Fernandez	.20	.09	.03
☐ 204 Allan Anderson	.15	.07	.02
☐ 205 Herm Winningham	.15	.07	.02
☐ 206 Tim Jones	.15	.07	.02
☐ 207 Ramon Martinez	.25	.11	.03
☐ 208 Teddy Higuera	.15	.07	.02
☐ 209 John Kruk	.20	.09	.03
☐ 210 Jim Abbott	.35	.16	.04
☐ 211 Dean Palmer	1.00	.45	.13
☐ 212 Mark Davis	.15	.07	.02
☐ 213 Jay Buhner	.20	.09	.03
☐ 214 Jesse Barfield	.15	.07	.02
☐ 215 Kevin Mitchell	.25	.11	.03
☐ 216 Mike LaValliere	.15	.07	.02
☐ 217 Mark Wohlers	.40	.18	.05
☐ 218 Dave Henderson	.15	.07	.02
☐ 219 Dave Smith	.15	.07	.02
☐ 220 Albert Belle	.60	.25	.08
☐ 221 Spike Owen	.15	.07	.02
☐ 222 Jeff Gray	.15	.07	.02
☐ 223 Paul Gibson	.15	.07	.02
☐ 224 Bobby Thigpen	.15	.07	.02
☐ 225 Mike Mussina	3.50	1.55	.45
☐ 226 Darrin Jackson	.20	.09	.03
☐ 227 Luis Gonzalez	.25	.11	.03
☐ 228 Greg Briley	.15	.07	.02
☐ 229 Brent Mayne	.15	.07	.02
☐ 230 Paul Molitor	.25	.11	.03
☐ 231 Al Leiter	.15	.07	.02
☐ 232 Andy Van Slyke	.25	.11	.03
☐ 233 Ron Tingley	.15	.07	.02
☐ 234 Bernard Gilkey	.20	.09	.03
☐ 235 Kent Hrbek	.20	.09	.03
☐ 236 Eric Karros	3.50	1.55	.45
☐ 237 Randy Velarde	.15	.07	.02
☐ 238 Andy Allanson	.15	.07	.02
☐ 239 Willie McGee	.20	.09	.03
☐ 240 Juan Gonzalez	2.50	1.15	.30
☐ 241 Karl Rhodes	.15	.07	.02
☐ 242 Luis Mercedes	.50	.23	.06
☐ 243 Billy Swift	.15	.07	.02
☐ 244 Tommy Gregg	.15	.07	.02
☐ 245 David Howard	.15	.07	.02
☐ 246 Dave Hollins	.50	.23	.06
☐ 247 Kip Gross	.20	.09	.03
☐ 248 Walt Weiss	.15	.07	.02
☐ 249 Mackey Sasser	.15	.07	.02
☐ 250 Cecil Fielder	.60	.25	.08
☐ 251 Jerry Browne	.15	.07	.02
☐ 252 Doug Dascenzo	.15	.07	.02
☐ 253 Darryl Hamilton	.20	.09	.03
☐ 254 Dann Bilardello	.15	.07	.02
☐ 255 Luis Rivera	.15	.07	.02
☐ 256 Larry Walker	.75	.35	.09
☐ 257 Ron Karkovice	.15	.07	.02
☐ 258 Bob Tewksbury	.20	.09	.03
☐ 259 Jimmy Key	.15	.07	.02
☐ 260 Bernie Williams	.50	.23	.06
☐ 261 Gary Wayne	.15	.07	.02
☐ 262 Mike Simms UER (Reversed negative)	.15	.07	.02
☐ 263 John Orton	.15	.07	.02
☐ 264 Marvin Freeman	.15	.07	.02
☐ 265 Mike Jeffcoat	.15	.07	.02
☐ 266 Roger Mason	.15	.07	.02
☐ 267 Edgar Martinez	.20	.09	.03
☐ 268 Henry Rodriguez	.40	.18	.05
☐ 269 Sam Horn	.15	.07	.02
☐ 270 Brian McRae	.20	.09	.03
☐ 271 Kirt Manwaring	.15	.07	.02
☐ 272 Mike Bordick	.30	.14	.04
☐ 273 Chris Sabo	.20	.09	.03
☐ 274 Jim Olander	.20	.09	.03
☐ 275 Greg W. Harris	.15	.07	.02
☐ 276 Dan Gakeler	.15	.07	.02
☐ 277 Bill Sampen	.15	.07	.02
☐ 278 Joel Skinner	.15	.07	.02
☐ 279 Curt Schilling	.20	.09	.03
☐ 280 Dale Murphy	.25	.11	.03
☐ 281 Lee Stevens	.15	.07	.02
☐ 282 Lonnie Smith	.15	.07	.02
☐ 283 Manuel Lee	.15	.07	.02
☐ 284 Shawn Boskie	.15	.07	.02
☐ 285 Kevin Seitzer	.20	.09	.03
☐ 286 Stan Royer	.25	.11	.03
☐ 287 John Dopson	.15	.07	.02
☐ 288 Scott Bullett	.30	.14	.04
☐ 289 Ken Patterson	.15	.07	.02
☐ 290 Todd Hundley	.15	.07	.02
☐ 291 Tim Leary	.15	.07	.02
☐ 292 Brett Butler	.20	.09	.03
☐ 293 Gregg Olson	.20	.09	.03
☐ 294 Jeff Brantley	.15	.07	.02
☐ 295 Brian Holman	.15	.07	.02
☐ 296 Brian Harper	.15	.07	.02
☐ 297 Brian Bohanon	.15	.07	.02
☐ 298 Checklist 1-100	.15	.02	.00
☐ 299 Checklist 101-200	.15	.02	.00
☐ 300 Checklist 201-300	.15	.02	.00
☐ 301 Frank Thomas	6.00	2.70	.75
☐ 302 Lloyd McClendon	.15	.07	.02
☐ 303 Brady Anderson	.20	.09	.03
☐ 304 Julio Valera	.30	.14	.04
☐ 305 Mike Aldrete	.15	.07	.02
☐ 306 Joe Oliver	.15	.07	.02

☐ 307	Todd Stottlemyre	.20	.09	.03
☐ 308	Rey Sanchez	.35	.16	.04
☐ 309	Gary Sheffield UER (Listed as 5'1", should be 5'11")	1.50	.65	.19
☐ 310	Andujar Cedeno	.20	.09	.03
☐ 311	Kenny Rogers	.15	.07	.02
☐ 312	Bruce Hurst	.20	.09	.03
☐ 313	Mike Schooler	.15	.07	.02
☐ 314	Mike Benjamin	.15	.07	.02
☐ 315	Chuck Finley	.15	.07	.02
☐ 316	Mark Lemke	.15	.07	.02
☐ 317	Scott Livingstone	.40	.18	.05
☐ 318	Chris Nabholz	.20	.09	.03
☐ 319	Mike Humphreys	.20	.09	.03
☐ 320	Pedro Guerrero	.20	.09	.03
☐ 321	Willie Banks	.50	.23	.06
☐ 322	Tom Goodwin	.30	.14	.04
☐ 323	Hector Wagner	.15	.07	.02
☐ 324	Wally Ritchie	.15	.07	.02
☐ 325	Mo Vaughn	.25	.11	.03
☐ 326	Joe Klink	.15	.07	.02
☐ 327	Cal Eldred	2.00	.90	.25
☐ 328	Daryl Boston	.15	.07	.02
☐ 329	Mike Huff	.15	.07	.02
☐ 330	Jeff Bagwell	1.50	.65	.19
☐ 331	Bob Milacki	.15	.07	.02
☐ 332	Tom Prince	.15	.07	.02
☐ 333	Pat Tabler	.15	.07	.02
☐ 334	Ced Landrum	.15	.07	.02
☐ 335	Reggie Jefferson	.40	.18	.05
☐ 336	Mo Sanford	.30	.14	.04
☐ 337	Kevin Ritz	.15	.07	.02
☐ 338	Gerald Perry	.15	.07	.02
☐ 339	Jeff Hamilton	.15	.07	.02
☐ 340	Tim Wallach	.20	.09	.03
☐ 341	Jeff Huson	.15	.07	.02
☐ 342	Jose Melendez	.15	.07	.02
☐ 343	Willie Wilson	.15	.07	.02
☐ 344	Mike Stanton	.15	.07	.02
☐ 345	Joel Johnston	.15	.07	.02
☐ 346	Lee Guetterman	.15	.07	.02
☐ 347	Francisco Oliveras	.15	.07	.02
☐ 348	Dave Burba	.15	.07	.02
☐ 349	Tim Crews	.15	.07	.02
☐ 350	Scott Leius	.15	.07	.02
☐ 351	Danny Cox	.15	.07	.02
☐ 352	Wayne Housie	.25	.11	.03
☐ 353	Chris Donnels	.15	.07	.02
☐ 354	Chris George	.15	.07	.02
☐ 355	Gerald Young	.15	.07	.02
☐ 356	Roberto Hernandez	.40	.18	.05
☐ 357	Neal Heaton	.15	.07	.02
☐ 358	Todd Frohwirth	.15	.07	.02
☐ 359	Jose Vizcaino	.15	.07	.02
☐ 360	Jim Thome	.50	.23	.06
☐ 361	Craig Wilson	.15	.07	.02
☐ 362	Dave Haas	.15	.07	.02
☐ 363	Billy Hatcher	.15	.07	.02
☐ 364	John Barfield	.15	.07	.02
☐ 365	Luis Aquino	.15	.07	.02
☐ 366	Charlie Leibrandt	.15	.07	.02
☐ 367	Howard Farmer	.15	.07	.02
☐ 368	Bryn Smith	.15	.07	.02
☐ 369	Mickey Morandini	.20	.09	.03
☐ 370	Jose Canseco (See also 597)	1.00	.45	.13
☐ 371	Jose Uribe	.15	.07	.02
☐ 372	Bob MacDonald	.15	.07	.02
☐ 373	Luis Sojo	.15	.07	.02
☐ 374	Craig Shipley	.20	.09	.03
☐ 375	Scott Bankhead	.15	.07	.02
☐ 376	Greg Gagne	.15	.07	.02
☐ 377	Scott Cooper	.50	.23	.06
☐ 378	Jose Offerman	.20	.09	.03
☐ 379	Billy Spiers	.15	.07	.02
☐ 380	John Smiley	.20	.09	.03
☐ 381	Jeff Carter	.15	.07	.02
☐ 382	Heathcliff Slocumb	.15	.07	.02
☐ 383	Jeff Tackett	.25	.11	.03
☐ 384	John Kiely	.20	.09	.03
☐ 385	John Vander Wal	.40	.18	.05
☐ 386	Omar Olivares	.15	.07	.02
☐ 387	Ruben Sierra	.75	.35	.09
☐ 388	Tom Gordon	.15	.07	.02
☐ 389	Charles Nagy	.50	.23	.06
☐ 390	Dave Stewart	.20	.09	.03
☐ 391	Pete Harnisch	.20	.09	.03
☐ 392	Tim Burke	.15	.07	.02
☐ 393	Roberto Kelly	.20	.09	.03
☐ 394	Freddie Benavides	.15	.07	.02
☐ 395	Tom Glavine	.60	.25	.08
☐ 396	Wes Chamberlain	.20	.09	.03
☐ 397	Eric Gunderson	.15	.07	.02
☐ 398	Dave West	.15	.07	.02
☐ 399	Ellis Burks	.20	.09	.03
☐ 400	Ken Griffey Jr.	4.00	1.80	.50
☐ 401	Thomas Howard	.15	.07	.02
☐ 402	Juan Guzman	3.50	1.55	.45
☐ 403	Mitch Webster	.15	.07	.02
☐ 404	Matt Merullo	.15	.07	.02
☐ 405	Steve Buechele	.15	.07	.02
☐ 406	Danny Jackson	.15	.07	.02
☐ 407	Felix Jose	.20	.09	.03
☐ 408	Doug Piatt	.15	.07	.02
☐ 409	Jim Eisenreich	.15	.07	.02
☐ 410	Bryan Harvey	.15	.07	.02
☐ 411	Jim Austin	.20	.09	.03
☐ 412	Jim Poole	.15	.07	.02
☐ 413	Glenallen Hill	.15	.07	.02
☐ 414	Gene Nelson	.15	.07	.02
☐ 415	Ivan Rodriguez	2.00	.90	.25
☐ 416	Frank Tanana	.15	.07	.02
☐ 417	Steve Decker	.15	.07	.02
☐ 418	Jason Grimsley	.15	.07	.02
☐ 419	Tim Layana	.15	.07	.02
☐ 420	Don Mattingly	.60	.25	.08
☐ 421	Jerome Walton	.15	.07	.02
☐ 422	Rob Ducey	.15	.07	.02
☐ 423	Andy Benes	.25	.11	.03
☐ 424	John Marzano	.15	.07	.02
☐ 425	Gene Harris	.15	.07	.02
☐ 426	Tim Raines	.25	.11	.03
☐ 427	Bret Barberie	.20	.09	.03
☐ 428	Harvey Pulliam	.25	.11	.03
☐ 429	Cris Carpenter	.15	.07	.02
☐ 430	Howard Johnson	.20	.09	.03
☐ 431	Orel Hershiser	.25	.11	.03
☐ 432	Brian Hunter	.40	.18	.05
☐ 433	Kevin Tapani	.20	.09	.03
☐ 434	Rick Reed	.15	.07	.02
☐ 435	Ron Witmeyer	.20	.09	.03
☐ 436	Gary Gaetti	.15	.07	.02
☐ 437	Alex Cole	.15	.07	.02
☐ 438	Chito Martinez	.15	.07	.02
☐ 439	Greg Litton	.15	.07	.02
☐ 440	Julio Franco	.20	.09	.03
☐ 441	Mike Munoz	.15	.07	.02
☐ 442	Erik Pappas	.15	.07	.02
☐ 443	Pat Combs	.15	.07	.02
☐ 444	Lance Johnson	.15	.07	.02
☐ 445	Ed Sprague	.20	.09	.03
☐ 446	Mike Greenwell	.25	.11	.03
☐ 447	Milt Thompson	.15	.07	.02
☐ 448	Mike Magnante	.30	.14	.04
☐ 449	Chris Haney	.20	.09	.03
☐ 450	Robin Yount	.50	.23	.06
☐ 451	Rafael Ramirez	.15	.07	.02
☐ 452	Gino Minutelli	.15	.07	.02
☐ 453	Tom Lampkin	.15	.07	.02
☐ 454	Tony Perezchica	.15	.07	.02
☐ 455	Dwight Gooden	.25	.11	.03
☐ 456	Mark Guthrie	.15	.07	.02
☐ 457	Jay Howell	.15	.07	.02
☐ 458	Gary DiSarcina	.15	.07	.02
☐ 459	John Smoltz	.35	.16	.04
☐ 460	Will Clark	1.00	.45	.13
☐ 461	Dave Otto	.15	.07	.02
☐ 462	Rob Maurer	.40	.18	.05
☐ 463	Dwight Evans	.20	.09	.03
☐ 464	Tom Brunansky	.20	.09	.03
☐ 465	Shawn Hare	.25	.11	.03
☐ 466	Geronimo Pena	.25	.11	.03
☐ 467	Alex Fernandez	.20	.09	.03
☐ 468	Greg Myers	.15	.07	.02
☐ 469	Jeff Fassero	.15	.07	.02
☐ 470	Len Dykstra	.20	.09	.03
☐ 471	Jeff Johnson	.15	.07	.02
☐ 472	Russ Swan	.15	.07	.02
☐ 473	Archie Corbin	.30	.14	.04
☐ 474	Chuck McElroy	.15	.07	.02
☐ 475	Mark McGwire	1.00	.45	.13
☐ 476	Wally Whitehurst	.15	.07	.02
☐ 477	Tim McIntosh	.15	.07	.02
☐ 478	Sid Bream	.15	.07	.02
☐ 479	Jeff Juden	.30	.14	.04
☐ 480	Carlton Fisk	.40	.18	.05
☐ 481	Jeff Plympton	.20	.09	.03
☐ 482	Carlos Martinez	.15	.07	.02
☐ 483	Jim Gott	.15	.07	.02
☐ 484	Bob McClure	.15	.07	.02
☐ 485	Tim Teufel	.15	.07	.02
☐ 486	Vicente Palacios	.15	.07	.02
☐ 487	Jeff Reed	.15	.07	.02
☐ 488	Tony Phillips	.15	.07	.02
☐ 489	Mel Rojas	.15	.07	.02

☐ 490	Ben McDonald	.30	.14	.04
☐ 491	Andres Santana	.20	.09	.03
☐ 492	Chris Beasley	.20	.09	.03
☐ 493	Mike Timlin	.15	.07	.02
☐ 494	Brian Downing	.15	.07	.02
☐ 495	Kirk Gibson	.20	.09	.03
☐ 496	Scott Sanderson	.15	.07	.02
☐ 497	Nick Esasky	.15	.07	.02
☐ 498	Johnny Guzman	.50	.23	.06
☐ 499	Mitch Williams	.15	.07	.02
☐ 500	Kirby Puckett	1.00	.45	.13
☐ 501	Mike Harkey	.20	.09	.03
☐ 502	Jim Gantner	.15	.07	.02
☐ 503	Bruce Egloff	.15	.07	.02
☐ 504	Josias Manzanillo	.25	.11	.03
☐ 505	Delino DeShields	.50	.23	.06
☐ 506	Rheal Cormier	.30	.14	.04
☐ 507	Jay Bell	.15	.07	.02
☐ 508	Rich Rowland	.25	.11	.03
☐ 509	Scott Servais	.15	.07	.02
☐ 510	Terry Pendleton	.20	.09	.03
☐ 511	Rich DeLucia	.15	.07	.02
☐ 512	Warren Newson	.15	.07	.02
☐ 513	Paul Faries	.15	.07	.02
☐ 514	Kal Daniels	.15	.07	.02
☐ 515	Jarvis Brown	.20	.09	.03
☐ 516	Rafael Palmeiro	.25	.11	.03
☐ 517	Kelly Downs	.15	.07	.02
☐ 518	Steve Chitren	.15	.07	.02
☐ 519	Moises Alou	.25	.11	.03
☐ 520	Wade Boggs	.60	.25	.08
☐ 521	Pete Schourek	.20	.09	.03
☐ 522	Scott Terry	.15	.07	.02
☐ 523	Kevin Appier	.20	.09	.03
☐ 524	Gary Redus	.15	.07	.02
☐ 525	George Bell	.20	.09	.03
☐ 526	Jeff Kaiser	.15	.07	.02
☐ 527	Alvaro Espinoza	.15	.07	.02
☐ 528	Luis Polonia	.20	.09	.03
☐ 529	Darren Daulton	.20	.09	.03
☐ 530	Norm Charlton	.20	.09	.03
☐ 531	John Olerud	.50	.23	.06
☐ 532	Dan Plesac	.15	.07	.02
☐ 533	Billy Ripken	.15	.07	.02
☐ 534	Rod Nichols	.15	.07	.02
☐ 535	Joey Cora	.15	.07	.02
☐ 536	Harold Baines	.20	.09	.03
☐ 537	Bob Ojeda	.15	.07	.02
☐ 538	Mark Leonard	.15	.07	.02
☐ 539	Danny Darwin	.15	.07	.02
☐ 540	Shawon Dunston	.20	.09	.03
☐ 541	Pedro Munoz	.25	.11	.03
☐ 542	Mark Gubicza	.15	.07	.02
☐ 543	Kevin Baez	.20	.09	.03
☐ 544	Todd Zeile	.15	.07	.02
☐ 545	Don Slaught	.15	.07	.02
☐ 546	Tony Eusebio	.20	.09	.03
☐ 547	Alonzo Powell	.15	.07	.02
☐ 548	Gary Pettis	.15	.07	.02
☐ 549	Brian Barnes	.15	.07	.02
☐ 550	Lou Whitaker	.25	.11	.03
☐ 551	Keith Mitchell	.30	.14	.04
☐ 552	Oscar Azocar	.15	.07	.02
☐ 553	Stu Cole	.25	.11	.03
☐ 554	Steve Wapnick	.15	.07	.02
☐ 555	Derek Bell	.60	.25	.08
☐ 556	Luis Lopez	.20	.09	.03
☐ 557	Anthony Telford	.15	.07	.02
☐ 558	Tim Mauser	.20	.09	.03
☐ 559	Glen Sutko	.15	.07	.02
☐ 560	Darryl Strawberry	.60	.25	.08
☐ 561	Tom Bolton	.15	.07	.02
☐ 562	Cliff Young	.15	.07	.02
☐ 563	Bruce Walton	.15	.07	.02
☐ 564	Chico Walker	.15	.07	.02
☐ 565	John Franco	.20	.09	.03
☐ 566	Paul McClellan	.15	.07	.02
☐ 567	Paul Abbott	.15	.07	.02
☐ 568	Gary Varsho	.15	.07	.02
☐ 569	Carlos Maldonado	.20	.09	.03
☐ 570	Kelly Gruber	.20	.09	.03
☐ 571	Jose Oquendo	.15	.07	.02
☐ 572	Steve Frey	.15	.07	.02
☐ 573	Tino Martinez	.20	.09	.03
☐ 574	Bill Haselman	.15	.07	.02
☐ 575	Eric Anthony	.25	.11	.03
☐ 576	John Habyan	.15	.07	.02
☐ 577	Jeff McNeeley	.40	.18	.05
☐ 578	Chris Bosio	.15	.07	.02
☐ 579	Joe Grahe	.15	.07	.02
☐ 580	Fred McGriff	.60	.25	.08
☐ 581	Rick Honeycutt	.15	.07	.02
☐ 582	Matt Williams	.20	.09	.03
☐ 583	Cliff Brantley	.20	.09	.03
☐ 584	Rob Dibble	.20	.09	.03
☐ 585	Skeeter Barnes	.15	.07	.02
☐ 586	Greg Hibbard	.15	.07	.02
☐ 587	Randy Milligan	.15	.07	.02
☐ 588	Checklist 301-400	.15	.02	.00
☐ 589	Checklist 401-500	.15	.02	.00
☐ 590	Checklist 501-600	.15	.02	.00
☐ 591	Frank Thomas MC	4.00	1.80	.50
☐ 592	David Justice MC	1.00	.45	.13
☐ 593	Roger Clemens MC	1.00	.45	.13
☐ 594	Steve Avery MC	.75	.35	.09
☐ 595	Cal Ripken MC	1.50	.65	.19
☐ 596	Barry Larkin MC UER (Ranked in AL, should be NL)	.20	.09	.03
☐ 597	Jose Canseco MC UER (Mistakenly numbered 370 on card back)	.90	.40	.11
☐ 598	Will Clark MC	.75	.35	.09
☐ 599	Cecil Fielder MC	.50	.23	.06
☐ 600	Ryne Sandberg MC	1.00	.45	.13
☐ 601	Chuck Knoblauch MC	.75	.35	.09
☐ 602	Doc Gooden MC	.20	.09	.03
☐ 603	Ken Griffey Jr. MC	3.00	1.35	.40
☐ 604	Barry Bonds MC	.75	.35	.09
☐ 605	Nolan Ryan MC	2.50	1.15	.30
☐ 606	Jeff Bagwell MC	1.00	.45	.13
☐ 607	Robin Yount MC	.40	.18	.05
☐ 608	Bobby Bonilla MC	.20	.09	.03
☐ 609	George Brett MC	.40	.18	.05
☐ 610	Howard Johnson MC	.20	.09	.03
☐ 611	Esteban Beltre	.30	.14	.04
☐ 612	Mike Christopher	.20	.09	.03
☐ 613	Troy Afenir	.15	.07	.02
☐ 614	Mariano Duncan	.15	.07	.02
☐ 615	Doug Henry	.60	.25	.08
☐ 616	Doug Jones	.15	.07	.02
☐ 617	Alvin Davis	.15	.07	.02
☐ 618	Craig Lefferts	.15	.07	.02
☐ 619	Kevin McReynolds	.20	.09	.03
☐ 620	Barry Bonds	1.00	.45	.13
☐ 621	Turner Ward	.15	.07	.02
☐ 622	Joe Magrane	.15	.07	.02
☐ 623	Mark Parent	.15	.07	.02
☐ 624	Tom Browning	.15	.07	.02
☐ 625	John Smiley	.20	.09	.03
☐ 626	Steve Wilson	.15	.07	.02
☐ 627	Mike Gallego	.15	.07	.02
☐ 628	Sammy Sosa	.15	.07	.02
☐ 629	Rico Rossy	.20	.09	.03
☐ 630	Royce Clayton	.75	.35	.09
☐ 631	Clay Parker	.15	.07	.02
☐ 632	Pete Smith	.20	.09	.03
☐ 633	Jeff McKnight	.15	.07	.02
☐ 634	Jack Daugherty	.15	.07	.02
☐ 635	Steve Sax	.20	.09	.03
☐ 636	Joe Hesketh	.15	.07	.02
☐ 637	Vince Horsman	.20	.09	.03
☐ 638	Eric King	.15	.07	.02
☐ 639	Joe Boever	.15	.07	.02
☐ 640	Jack Morris	.30	.14	.04
☐ 641	Arthur Rhodes	.75	.35	.09
☐ 642	Bob Melvin	.15	.07	.02
☐ 643	Rick Wilkins	.15	.07	.02
☐ 644	Scott Scudder	.15	.07	.02
☐ 645	Bip Roberts	.20	.09	.03
☐ 646	Julio Valera	.30	.14	.04
☐ 647	Kevin Campbell	.20	.09	.03
☐ 648	Steve Searcy	.15	.07	.02
☐ 649	Scott Kamieniecki	.15	.07	.02
☐ 650	Kurt Stillwell	.15	.07	.02
☐ 651	Bob Welch	.15	.07	.02
☐ 652	Andres Galarraga	.15	.07	.02
☐ 653	Mike Jackson	.15	.07	.02
☐ 654	Bo Jackson	.50	.23	.06
☐ 655	Sid Fernandez	.20	.09	.03
☐ 656	Mike Bielecki	.15	.07	.02
☐ 657	Jeff Reardon	.20	.09	.03
☐ 658	Wayne Rosenthal	.20	.09	.03
☐ 659	Eric Bullock	.15	.07	.02
☐ 660	Eric Davis	.25	.11	.03
☐ 661	Randy Tomlin	.20	.09	.03
☐ 662	Tom Edens	.15	.07	.02
☐ 663	Rob Murphy	.15	.07	.02
☐ 664	Leo Gomez	.40	.18	.05
☐ 665	Greg Maddux	.30	.14	.04
☐ 666	Greg Vaughn	.20	.09	.03
☐ 667	Wade Taylor	.15	.07	.02
☐ 668	Brad Arnsberg	.15	.07	.02
☐ 669	Mike Moore	.15	.07	.02
☐ 670	Mark Langston	.20	.09	.03
☐ 671	Barry Jones	.15	.07	.02

☐	672 Bill Landrum	.15	.07	.02
☐	673 Greg Swindell	.20	.09	.03
☐	674 Wayne Edwards	.15	.07	.02
☐	675 Greg Olson	.15	.07	.02
☐	676 Bill Pulsipher	.25	.11	.03
☐	677 Bobby Witt	.15	.07	.02
☐	678 Mark Carreon	.15	.07	.02
☐	679 Patrick Lennon	.25	.11	.03
☐	680 Ozzie Smith	.40	.18	.05
☐	681 John Briscoe	.20	.09	.03
☐	682 Matt Young	.15	.07	.02
☐	683 Jeff Conine	.15	.07	.02
☐	684 Phil Stephenson	.15	.07	.02
☐	685 Ron Darling	.20	.09	.03
☐	686 Bryan Hickerson	.20	.09	.03
☐	687 Dale Sveum	.15	.07	.02
☐	688 Kirk McCaskill	.15	.07	.02
☐	689 Rich Amaral	.20	.09	.03
☐	690 Danny Tartabull	.25	.11	.03
☐	691 Donald Harris	.15	.07	.02
☐	692 Doug Davis	.20	.09	.03
☐	693 John Farrell	.15	.07	.02
☐	694 Paul Gibson	.15	.07	.02
☐	695 Kenny Lofton	2.50	1.15	.30
☐	696 Mike Fetters	.15	.07	.02
☐	697 Rosario Rodriguez	.20	.09	.03
☐	698 Chris Jones	.15	.07	.02
☐	699 Jeff Manto	.15	.07	.02
☐	700 Rick Sutcliffe	.20	.09	.03
☐	701 Scott Bankhead	.15	.07	.02
☐	702 Donnie Hill	.15	.07	.02
☐	703 Todd Worrell	.15	.07	.02
☐	704 Rene Gonzales	.15	.07	.02
☐	705 Rick Cerone	.15	.07	.02
☐	706 Tony Pena	.15	.07	.02
☐	707 Paul Sorrento	.20	.09	.03
☐	708 Gary Scott	.20	.09	.03
☐	709 Junior Noboa	.15	.07	.02
☐	710 Wally Joyner	.20	.09	.03
☐	711 Charlie Hayes	.15	.07	.02
☐	712 Rich Rodriguez	.20	.09	.03
☐	713 Rudy Seanez	.20	.09	.03
☐	714 Jim Bullinger	.30	.14	.04
☐	715 Jeff M. Robinson	.15	.07	.02
☐	716 Jeff Branson	.15	.07	.02
☐	717 Andy Ashby	.25	.11	.03
☐	718 Dave Burba	.15	.07	.02
☐	719 Rich Gossage	.20	.09	.03
☐	720 Randy Johnson	.20	.09	.03
☐	721 David Wells	.15	.07	.02
☐	722 Paul Kilgus	.15	.07	.02
☐	723 Dave Martinez	.15	.07	.02
☐	724 Denny Neagle	.25	.11	.03
☐	725 Andy Stankiewicz	.40	.18	.05
☐	726 Rick Aguilera	.20	.09	.03
☐	727 Junior Ortiz	.15	.07	.02
☐	728 Storm Davis	.15	.07	.02
☐	729 Don Robinson	.15	.07	.02
☐	730 Ron Gant	.35	.16	.04
☐	731 Paul Assenmacher	.15	.07	.02
☐	732 Mike Gardiner	.15	.07	.02
☐	733 Milt Hill	.20	.09	.03
☐	734 Jeremy Hernandez	.25	.11	.03
☐	735 Ken Hill	.20	.09	.03
☐	736 Xavier Hernandez	.15	.07	.02
☐	737 Gregg Jefferies	.20	.09	.03
☐	738 Dick Schofield	.15	.07	.02
☐	739 Ron Robinson	.15	.07	.02
☐	740 Sandy Alomar	.20	.09	.03
☐	741 Mike Stanley	.15	.07	.02
☐	742 Butch Henry	.40	.18	.05
☐	743 Floyd Bannister	.15	.07	.02
☐	744 Brian Drahman	.15	.07	.02
☐	745 Dave Winfield	.40	.18	.05
☐	746 Bob Walk	.15	.07	.02
☐	747 Chris James	.15	.07	.02
☐	748 Don Prybylinski	.20	.09	.03
☐	749 Dennis Rasmussen	.15	.07	.02
☐	750 Rickey Henderson	.50	.23	.06
☐	751 Chris Hammond	.15	.07	.02
☐	752 Bob Kipper	.15	.07	.02
☐	753 Dave Rohde	.15	.07	.02
☐	754 Hubie Brooks	.15	.07	.02
☐	755 Bret Saberhagen	.25	.11	.03
☐	756 Jeff D. Robinson	.15	.07	.02
☐	757 Pat Listach	4.00	1.80	.50
☐	758 Bill Wegman	.15	.07	.02
☐	759 John Wetteland	.15	.07	.02
☐	760 Phil Plantier	.60	.25	.08
☐	761 Wilson Alvarez	.15	.07	.02
☐	762 Scott Aldred	.15	.07	.02
☐	763 Armando Reynoso	.25	.11	.03
☐	764 Todd Benzinger	.15	.07	.02
☐	765 Kevin Mitchell	.25	.11	.03
☐	766 Gary Sheffield	1.50	.65	.19
☐	767 Allan Anderson	.15	.07	.02
☐	768 Rusty Meacham	.15	.07	.02
☐	769 Rick Parker	.15	.07	.02
☐	770 Nolan Ryan	3.00	1.35	.40
☐	771 Jeff Ballard	.15	.07	.02
☐	772 Cory Snyder	.15	.07	.02
☐	773 Denis Boucher	.20	.09	.03
☐	774 Jose Gonzalez	.15	.07	.02
☐	775 Juan Guerrero	.40	.18	.05
☐	776 Ed Nunez	.15	.07	.02
☐	777 Scott Ruskin	.15	.07	.02
☐	778 Terry Leach	.15	.07	.02
☐	779 Carl Willis	.15	.07	.02
☐	780 Bobby Bonilla	.35	.16	.04
☐	781 Duane Ward	.15	.07	.02
☐	782 Joe Slusarski	.15	.07	.02
☐	783 David Segui	.15	.07	.02
☐	784 Kirk Gibson	.20	.09	.03
☐	785 Frank Viola	.20	.09	.03
☐	786 Keith Miller	.15	.07	.02
☐	787 Mike Morgan	.15	.07	.02
☐	788 Kim Batiste	.30	.14	.04
☐	789 Sergio Valdez	.15	.07	.02
☐	790 Eddie Taubensee	.40	.18	.05
☐	791 Jack Armstrong	.15	.07	.02
☐	792 Scott Fletcher	.15	.07	.02
☐	793 Steve Farr	.15	.07	.02
☐	794 Dan Pasqua	.15	.07	.02
☐	795 Eddie Murray	.40	.18	.05
☐	796 John Morris	.15	.07	.02
☐	797 Francisco Cabrera	.15	.07	.02
☐	798 Mike Perez	.30	.14	.04
☐	799 Ted Wood	.30	.14	.04
☐	800 Jose Rijo	.20	.09	.03
☐	801 Danny Gladden	.15	.07	.02
☐	802 Archi Cianfrocco	.50	.23	.06
☐	803 Monty Fariss	.30	.14	.04
☐	804 Roger McDowell	.15	.07	.02
☐	805 Randy Myers	.20	.09	.03
☐	806 Kirk Dressendorfer	.15	.07	.02
☐	807 Zane Smith	.15	.07	.02
☐	808 Glenn Davis	.20	.09	.03
☐	809 Torey Lovullo	.15	.07	.02
☐	810 Andre Dawson	.40	.18	.05
☐	811 Bill Pecota	.15	.07	.02
☐	812 Ted Power	.15	.07	.02
☐	813 Willie Blair	.15	.07	.02
☐	814 Dave Fleming	2.00	.90	.25
☐	815 Chris Gwynn	.15	.07	.02
☐	816 Jody Reed	.15	.07	.02
☐	817 Mark Dewey	.20	.09	.03
☐	818 Kyle Abbott	.30	.14	.04
☐	819 Tom Henke	.20	.09	.03
☐	820 Kevin Seitzer	.20	.09	.03
☐	821 Al Newman	.15	.07	.02
☐	822 Tim Sherrill	.20	.09	.03
☐	823 Chuck Crim	.15	.07	.02
☐	824 Darren Reed	.15	.07	.02
☐	825 Tony Gwynn	.60	.25	.08
☐	826 Steve Foster	.25	.11	.03
☐	827 Steve Howe	.15	.07	.02
☐	828 Brook Jacoby	.15	.07	.02
☐	829 Rodney McCray	.15	.07	.02
☐	830 Chuck Knoblauch	1.00	.45	.13
☐	831 John Wehner	.20	.09	.03
☐	832 Scott Garrelts	.15	.07	.02
☐	833 Alejandro Pena	.15	.07	.02
☐	834 Jeff Parrett	.15	.07	.02
☐	835 Juan Bell	.15	.07	.02
☐	836 Lance Dickson	.20	.09	.03
☐	837 Darryl Kile	.30	.14	.04
☐	838 Efrain Valdez	.15	.07	.02
☐	839 Bob Zupcic	.75	.35	.09
☐	840 George Bell	.20	.09	.03
☐	841 Dave Gallagher	.15	.07	.02
☐	842 Tim Belcher	.20	.09	.03
☐	843 Jeff Shaw	.15	.07	.02
☐	844 Mike Fitzgerald	.15	.07	.02
☐	845 Gary Carter	.20	.09	.03
☐	846 John Russell	.15	.07	.02
☐	847 Eric Hillman	.60	.25	.08
☐	848 Mike Witt	.15	.07	.02
☐	849 Curt Wilkerson	.15	.07	.02
☐	850 Alan Trammell	.25	.11	.03
☐	851 Rex Hudler	.15	.07	.02
☐	852 Mike Walkden	.30	.14	.04
☐	853 Kevin Ward	.20	.09	.03
☐	854 Tim Naehring	.15	.07	.02
☐	855 Bill Swift	.15	.07	.02
☐	856 Damon Berryhill	.15	.07	.02
☐	857 Mark Eichhorn	.15	.07	.02

☐ 858 Hector Villanueva	.15	.07	.02
☐ 859 Jose Lind	.15	.07	.02
☐ 860 Denny Martinez	.20	.09	.03
☐ 861 Bill Krueger	.15	.07	.02
☐ 862 Mike Kingery	.15	.07	.02
☐ 863 Jeff Innis	.15	.07	.02
☐ 864 Derek Lilliquist	.15	.07	.02
☐ 865 Reggie Sanders	1.50	.65	.19
☐ 866 Ramon Garcia	.15	.07	.02
☐ 867 Bruce Ruffin	.15	.07	.02
☐ 868 Dickie Thon	.15	.07	.02
☐ 869 Melido Perez	.20	.09	.03
☐ 870 Ruben Amaro	.20	.09	.03
☐ 871 Alan Mills	.15	.07	.02
☐ 872 Matt Sinatro	.15	.07	.02
☐ 873 Eddie Zosky	.30	.14	.04
☐ 874 Pete Incaviglia	.15	.07	.02
☐ 875 Tom Candiotti	.15	.07	.02
☐ 876 Bob Patterson	.15	.07	.02
☐ 877 Neal Heaton	.15	.07	.02
☐ 878 Terrel Hansen	.40	.18	.05
☐ 879 Dave Eiland	.15	.07	.02
☐ 880 Von Hayes	.15	.07	.02
☐ 881 Tim Scott	.25	.11	.03
☐ 882 Otis Nixon	.20	.09	.03
☐ 883 Herm Winningham	.15	.07	.02
☐ 884 Dion James	.15	.07	.02
☐ 885 Dave Wainhouse	.20	.09	.03
☐ 886 Frank DiPino	.15	.07	.02
☐ 887 Dennis Cook	.15	.07	.02
☐ 888 Jose Mesa	.15	.07	.02
☐ 889 Mark Leiter	.15	.07	.02
☐ 890 Willie Randolph	.20	.09	.03
☐ 891 Craig Colbert	.20	.09	.03
☐ 892 Dwayne Henry	.15	.07	.02
☐ 893 Jim Lindeman	.15	.07	.02
☐ 894 Charlie Hough	.15	.07	.02
☐ 895 Gil Heredia	.20	.09	.03
☐ 896 Scott Chiamparino	.15	.07	.02
☐ 897 Lance Blankenship	.15	.07	.02
☐ 898 Checklist 601-700	.15	.02	.00
☐ 899 Checklist 701-800	.15	.02	.00
☐ 900 Checklist 801-900	.15	.02	.00

1992 Stadium Club Dome

The 1992 Topps Stadium Club Special Stadium set features 100 top draft picks, 56 1991 All-Star Game cards, 25 1991 Team U.S.A. cards, and 19 1991 Championship and World Series cards, all packaged in a set box inside a molded-plastic SkyDome display. Topps actually references this set as a 1991 set and the copyright lines on the card backs say 1991, but the set was released well into 1992. The standard-size (2 1/2" by 3 1/2" cards display full-bleed glossy player photos on the fronts. The player's name appears in an sky-blue stripe that is accented by parallel gold stripes. These stripes intersect the Topps Stadium Club logo. The horizontally oriented backs present biography, statistics, or highlights on a colorful artwork background depicting some aspect of baseball. The cards are numbered on the back. The key Rookie Cards in this set are Cliff Floyd, Tyler Green, Tyrone Hill, Manny Ramirez, Aaron Sele, and Brien Taylor.

	MT	EX-MT	VG
COMPLETE SET (200)	40.00	18.00	5.00
COMMON PLAYER (1-200)	.15	.07	.02
☐ 1 Terry Adams	.20	.09	.03
☐ 2 Tommy Adams	.60	.25	.08
☐ 3 Rick Aguilera	.15	.07	.02
☐ 4 Ron Allen	.25	.11	.03
☐ 5 Roberto Alomar	.50	.23	.06
☐ 6 Sandy Alomar	.15	.07	.02
☐ 7 Greg Anthony	.40	.18	.05
☐ 8 James Austin	.20	.09	.03
☐ 9 Steve Avery	.60	.25	.08
☐ 10 Harold Baines	.15	.07	.02
☐ 11 Brian Barber	.90	.40	.11
☐ 12 Jon Barnes	.20	.09	.03
☐ 13 George Bell	.15	.07	.02
☐ 14 Doug Bennett	.25	.11	.03
☐ 15 Sean Bergman	.25	.11	.03
☐ 16 Craig Biggio	.15	.07	.02
☐ 17 Bill Bliss	.20	.09	.03
☐ 18 Wade Boggs	.35	.16	.04
☐ 19 Bobby Bonilla	.15	.07	.02
☐ 20 Russell Brock	.20	.09	.03
☐ 21 Tarrik Brock	.20	.09	.03
☐ 22 Tom Browning	.15	.07	.02
☐ 23 Brett Butler	.15	.07	.02
☐ 24 Ivan Calderon	.15	.07	.02
☐ 25 Joe Carter	.30	.14	.04
☐ 26 Joe Caruso	.40	.18	.05
☐ 27 Dan Cholowsky	.60	.25	.08
☐ 28 Will Clark	.60	.25	.08
☐ 29 Roger Clemens	.75	.35	.09
☐ 30 Shawn Curran	.20	.09	.03
☐ 31 Chris Curtis	.20	.09	.03
☐ 32 Chili Davis	.15	.07	.02
☐ 33 Andre Dawson	.20	.09	.03
☐ 34 Joe DeBerry	.30	.14	.04
☐ 35 John Dettmer	.40	.18	.05
☐ 36 Rob Dibble	.15	.07	.02
☐ 37 John Donati	.20	.09	.03
☐ 38 Dave Doorneweerd	.40	.18	.05
☐ 39 Darren Dreifort	.75	.35	.09
☐ 40 Mike Durant	.35	.16	.04
☐ 41 Chris Durkin	.30	.14	.04
☐ 42 Dennis Eckersley	.25	.11	.03
☐ 43 Brian Edmondson	.30	.14	.04
☐ 44 Vaughn Eshelman	.20	.09	.03
☐ 45 Shawn Estes	.60	.25	.08
☐ 46 Jorge Fabregas	.35	.16	.04
☐ 47 Jon Farrell	.40	.18	.05
☐ 48 Cecil Fielder	.35	.16	.04
☐ 49 Carlton Fisk	.20	.09	.03
☐ 50 Tim Flannelly	.25	.11	.03
☐ 51 Cliff Floyd	3.00	1.35	.40
☐ 52 Julio Franco	.15	.07	.02
☐ 53 Greg Gagne	.15	.07	.02
☐ 54 Chris Gambs	.20	.09	.03
☐ 55 Ron Gant	.25	.11	.03
☐ 56 Brent Gates	1.50	.65	.19
☐ 57 Dwayne Gerald	.20	.09	.03
☐ 58 Jason Giambi	.90	.40	.11
☐ 59 Benji Gil	.75	.35	.09
☐ 60 Mark Gipner	.20	.09	.03
☐ 61 Danny Gladden	.15	.07	.02
☐ 62 Tom Glavine	.35	.16	.04
☐ 63 Jimmy Gonzalez	.20	.09	.03
☐ 64 Jeff Granger	.60	.25	.08
☐ 65 Dan Grapenthien	.20	.09	.03
☐ 66 Dennis Gray	.25	.11	.03
☐ 67 Shawn Green	1.00	.45	.13
☐ 68 Tyler Green	1.25	.55	.16
☐ 69 Todd Greene	.60	.25	.08
☐ 70 Ken Griffey Jr.	2.00	.90	.25
☐ 71 Kelly Gruber	.15	.07	.02
☐ 72 Ozzie Guillen	.15	.07	.02
☐ 73 Tony Gwynn	.40	.18	.05
☐ 74 Shane Halter	.20	.09	.03
☐ 75 Jeffrey Hammonds	5.00	2.30	.60
☐ 76 Larry Hanlon	.20	.09	.03
☐ 77 Pete Harnisch	.15	.07	.02
☐ 78 Mike Harrison	.25	.11	.03
☐ 79 Bryan Harvey	.15	.07	.02
☐ 80 Scott Hatteberg	.30	.14	.04
☐ 81 Rick Helling	.75	.35	.09
☐ 82 Dave Henderson	.15	.07	.02
☐ 83 Rickey Henderson	.30	.14	.04
☐ 84 Tyrone Hill	1.50	.65	.19
☐ 85 Todd Hollandsworth	.50	.23	.06
☐ 86 Brian Holliday	.20	.09	.03
☐ 87 Terry Horn	.20	.09	.03
☐ 88 Jeff Hostetler	.40	.18	.05
☐ 89 Kent Hrbek	.15	.07	.02
☐ 90 Mark Hubbard	.20	.09	.03

☐ 91 Charles Johnson	4.00	1.80	.50
☐ 92 Howard Johnson	.15	.07	.02
☐ 93 Todd Johnson	.50	.23	.06
☐ 94 Bobby Jones	1.50	.65	.19
☐ 95 Dan Jones	.25	.11	.03
☐ 96 Felix Jose	.15	.07	.02
☐ 97 David Justice	1.00	.45	.13
☐ 98 Jimmy Key	.15	.07	.02
☐ 99 Marc Kroon	.20	.09	.03
☐ 100 John Kruk	.15	.07	.02
☐ 101 Mark Langston	.15	.07	.02
☐ 102 Barry Larkin	.20	.09	.03
☐ 103 Mike LaValliere	.15	.07	.02
☐ 104 Scott Leius	.15	.07	.02
☐ 105 Mark Lemke	.15	.07	.02
☐ 106 Donnie Leshnock	.50	.23	.06
☐ 107 Jimmy Lewis	.40	.18	.05
☐ 108 Shane Livesy	.35	.16	.04
☐ 109 Ryan Long	.35	.16	.04
☐ 110 Trevor Mallory	.20	.09	.03
☐ 111 Denny Martinez	.15	.07	.02
☐ 112 Justin Mashore	.20	.09	.03
☐ 113 Jason McDonald	.40	.18	.05
☐ 114 Jack McDowell	.20	.09	.03
☐ 115 Tom McKinnon	.30	.14	.04
☐ 116 Billy McMillon	.35	.16	.04
☐ 117 Buck McNabb	.30	.14	.04
☐ 118 Jim Mecir	.20	.09	.03
☐ 119 Dan Melendez	.60	.25	.08
☐ 120 Shawn Miller	.20	.09	.03
☐ 121 Trever Miller	.30	.14	.04
☐ 122 Paul Molitor	.20	.09	.03
☐ 123 Vincent Moore	.25	.11	.03
☐ 124 Mike Morgan	.15	.07	.02
☐ 125 Jack Morris WS	.15	.07	.02
☐ 126 Jack Morris AS	.15	.07	.02
☐ 127 Sean Mulligan	.30	.14	.04
☐ 128 Eddie Murray	.25	.11	.03
☐ 129 Mike Neill	1.50	.65	.19
☐ 130 Phil Nevin	6.00	2.70	.75
☐ 131 Mark O'Brien	.25	.11	.03
☐ 132 Alex Ochoa	.35	.16	.04
☐ 133 Chad Ogea	1.25	.55	.16
☐ 134 Greg Olson	.15	.07	.02
☐ 135 Paul O'Neill	.15	.07	.02
☐ 136 Jared Osentowski	.20	.09	.03
☐ 137 Mike Pagliarulo	.15	.07	.02
☐ 138 Rafael Palmeiro	.20	.09	.03
☐ 139 Rodney Pedraza	.30	.14	.04
☐ 140 Tony Phillips (P)	.30	.14	.04
☐ 141 Scott Pisciotta	.50	.23	.06
☐ 142 Christopher Pritchett	.40	.18	.05
☐ 143 Jason Pruitt	.20	.09	.03
☐ 144 Kirby Puckett WS UER (Championship series AB and BA is wrong)	.75	.35	.09
☐ 145 Kirby Puckett AS	.75	.35	.09
☐ 146 Manny Ramirez	2.50	1.15	.30
☐ 147 Eddie Ramos	.30	.14	.04
☐ 148 Mark Ratekin	.20	.09	.03
☐ 149 Jeff Reardon	.20	.09	.03
☐ 150 Sean Rees	.20	.09	.03
☐ 151 Calvin Reese	.60	.25	.08
☐ 152 Desmond Relaford	.20	.09	.03
☐ 153 Eric Richardson	.25	.11	.03
☐ 154 Cal Ripken	1.00	.45	.13
☐ 155 Chris Roberts	1.50	.65	.19
☐ 156 Mike Robertson	.40	.18	.05
☐ 157 Steve Rodriguez	.40	.18	.05
☐ 158 Mike Rossiter	.25	.11	.03
☐ 159 Scott Ruffcorn	1.25	.55	.16
☐ 160 Chris Sabo	.20	.09	.03
☐ 161 Juan Samuel	.15	.07	.02
☐ 162 Ryne Sandberg UER (On 5th line, prior misspelled as prilor)	.75	.35	.09
☐ 163 Scott Sanderson	.15	.07	.02
☐ 164 Benny Santiago	.20	.09	.03
☐ 165 Gene Schall	.25	.11	.03
☐ 166 Chad Schoenvogel	.20	.09	.03
☐ 167 Chris Seelbach	.30	.14	.04
☐ 168 Aaron Sele	1.50	.65	.19
☐ 169 Basil Shabazz	.50	.23	.06
☐ 170 Al Shirley	.75	.35	.09
☐ 171 Paul Shuey	1.00	.45	.13
☐ 172 Ruben Sierra	.35	.16	.04
☐ 173 John Smiley	.15	.07	.02
☐ 174 Lee Smith	.15	.07	.02
☐ 175 Ozzie Smith	.20	.09	.03
☐ 176 Tim Smith	.20	.09	.03
☐ 177 Zane Smith	.15	.07	.02
☐ 178 John Smoltz	.20	.09	.03
☐ 179 Scott Stahoviak	.75	.35	.09
☐ 180 Kennie Steenstra	.40	.18	.05
☐ 181 Kevin Stocker	.25	.11	.03
☐ 182 Chris Stynes	.35	.16	.04
☐ 183 Danny Tartabull	.20	.09	.03
☐ 184 Brien Taylor	10.00	4.50	1.25
☐ 185 Todd Taylor	.40	.18	.05
☐ 186 Larry Thomas	.90	.40	.11
☐ 187 Ozzie Timmons (See also 188)	.60	.25	.08
☐ 188 David Tuttle UER (Mistakenly numbered as 187 on card)	.40	.18	.05
☐ 189 Andy Van Slyke	.20	.09	.03
☐ 190 Frank Viola	.15	.07	.02
☐ 191 Michael Walkden	.30	.14	.04
☐ 192 Jeff Ware	.50	.23	.06
☐ 193 Allen Watson	1.25	.55	.16
☐ 194 Steve Whitaker	.20	.09	.03
☐ 195 Jerry Willard	.15	.07	.02
☐ 196 Craig Wilson	.50	.23	.06
☐ 197 Chris Wimmer	.75	.35	.09
☐ 198 Steve Wojciechowski	.25	.11	.03
☐ 199 Joel Wolfe	.30	.14	.04
☐ 200 Ivan Zweig	.40	.18	.05

1992 Stadium Club First Draft Picks

This three-card subset, featuring Major League Baseball's Number 1 draft pick for 1990, 1991, and 1992, was randomly inserted into 1992 Topps Stadium Club Series III packs. Topps estimated that one of these cards can be found in every 72 packs. One card also was mailed to each member of Topps Stadium Club. The cards measure the standard size (2 1/2" by 3 1/2") and feature on the fronts full-bleed posed color player photos. The player's draft year is printed on an orange circle in the upper right corner and is accented by gold foil stripes of varying lengths that run vertically down the right edge of the card. The player's name appears on the Stadium Club logo at the bottom. The number "1" is gold-foil stamped in a black diamond at the lower left and is followed by a red stripe gold-foil stamped with the words "Draft Pick of the '90s". The back design features color photos on a black and red background with the player's signature gold-foil stamped across the bottom of the photo and gold foil bars running down the right edge of the picture. The team name and biographical information is included in a yellow and white box. The cards are numbered on the back.

	MT	EX-MT	VG
COMPLETE SET (3)	24.00	11.00	3.00
COMMON PLAYER (1-3)	8.00	3.60	1.00
☐ 1 Chipper Jones	8.00	3.60	1.00
☐ 2 Brien Taylor	10.00	4.50	1.25
☐ 3 Phil Nevin	8.00	3.60	1.00

1992 Stadium Club Master Photos

In the first package of materials sent to 1992 Topps Stadium Club members, along with an 11-card boxed set, members received a randomly chosen "Master Photo" printed on (approximately) 5" by 7" white card stock to demonstrate how the photos are cropped to create a borderless design. Each master photo has the Topps Stadium Club logo and the words "Master Photo" above a gold foil picture frame enclosing the color player photo. The backs are blank. The cards are unnumbered and checklisted below alphabetically. Master photos were also available through a special promotion at Walmart as an insert one-per-box in specially marked wax boxes of regular Topps Stadium Club cards.

	MT	EX-MT	VG
COMPLETE SET (15)	75.00	34.00	9.50
COMMON PLAYER (1-15)	2.00	.90	.25
☐ 1 Wade Boggs	5.00	2.30	.60
☐ 2 Barry Bonds	5.00	2.30	.60
☐ 3 Jose Canseco	6.00	2.70	.75
☐ 4 Will Clark	6.00	2.70	.75
☐ 5 Cecil Fielder	5.00	2.30	.60
☐ 6 Dwight Gooden	4.00	1.80	.50
☐ 7 Ken Griffey Jr.	9.00	4.00	1.15
☐ 8 Rickey Henderson	5.00	2.30	.60
☐ 9 Lance Johnson	2.00	.90	.25
☐ 10 Cal Ripken	7.50	3.40	.95
☐ 11 Nolan Ryan	9.00	4.00	1.15
☐ 12 Deion Sanders	6.00	2.70	.75
☐ 13 Darryl Strawberry	5.00	2.30	.60
☐ 14 Danny Tartabull	4.00	1.80	.50
☐ 15 Frank Thomas	12.00	5.50	1.50

1992 Stadium Club Members Only

This ten-card boxed set was the first package of materials sent to 1992 Stadium Club members. The set features ten "Members Only" limited edition Stadium Club cards, one "Top Draft Picks of the '90s" card (as a bonus), and a randomly chosen "Master Photo" printed on 5" by 7" white card stock to demonstrate how the photos are cropped to create a borderless design. The cards measure the standard size (2 1/2" by 3 1/2") and feature full-bleed glossy color player photos. The fronts of the regular cards have the words "Members Only" printed in gold foil at the bottom along with the player's name and the Stadium Club logo. The backs feature a stadium scene with the scoreboard displaying, in yellow neon, a career highlight. The cards are unnumbered and checklisted below alphabetically, with the two-player cards listed at the end.

	MT	EX-MT	VG
COMPLETE SET (10)	5.00	2.30	.60
COMMON PLAYER (1-10)	.15	.07	.02
☐ 1 Wade Boggs	.60	.25	.08
☐ 2 George Brett	.60	.25	.08
☐ 3 Gary Carter	.35	.16	.04
☐ 4 Dave Eiland	.15	.07	.02
☐ 5 Jack Morris	.35	.16	.04
☐ 6 Eddie Murray	.50	.23	.06
☐ 7 Ozzie Smith (2,000th Hit)	.50	.23	.06
☐ 8 Ozzie Smith (7,000th Career Assist)	.50	.23	.06
☐ 9 Roger Clemens and Matt Young	.75	.35	.09
☐ 10 Gary Sheffield and Dwight Gooden	1.25	.55	.16

1953 Stahl Meyer

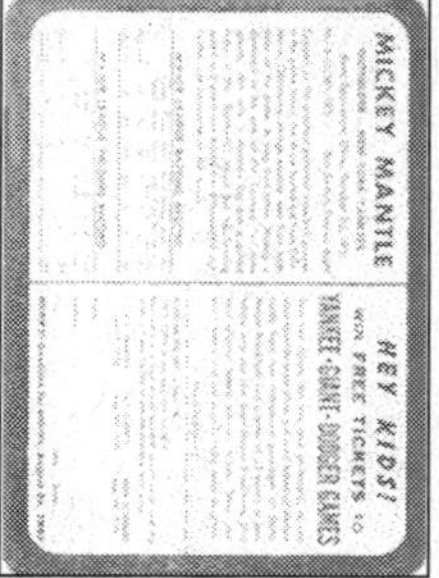

The cards in this nine-card set measure approximately 3 1/4" by 4 1/2". The 1953 Stahl Meyer set of full color, unnumbered cards includes three players from each of the three New York teams. The cards have white borders. The Lockman card is the most plentiful of any card in the set. Some batting and fielding statistics and short biography are included on the back. The cards are ordered in the checklist below by alphabetical order without regard to team affiliation.

	NRMT	VG-E	GOOD
COMPLETE SET	4500.00	2000.00	575.00
COMMON PLAYER (1-9)	125.00	57.50	15.50
☐ 1 Hank Bauer	150.00	70.00	19.00
☐ 2 Roy Campanella	600.00	275.00	75.00
☐ 3 Gil Hodges	300.00	135.00	38.00
☐ 4 Monte Irvin	200.00	90.00	25.00
☐ 5 Whitey Lockman	125.00	57.50	15.50
☐ 6 Mickey Mantle	2250.00	750.00	250.00
☐ 7 Phil Rizzuto	300.00	135.00	38.00
☐ 8 Duke Snider	600.00	275.00	75.00
☐ 9 Bobby Thomson	150.00	70.00	19.00

1954 Stahl Meyer

The cards in this 12-card set measure approximately 3 1/4" by 4 1/2". The 1954 Stahl Meyer set of full color,

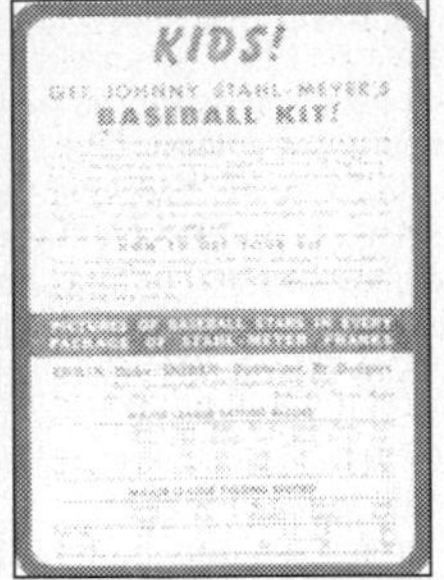

unnumbered cards includes four players from each of the three New York teams. The cards have yellow borders and the backs, oriented horizontally, include an ad for a baseball kit and the player's statistics. No player biography is included on the back. The cards are ordered in the checklist below by alphabetical order without regard to team affiliation.

	NRMT	VG-E	GOOD
COMPLETE SET	7000.00	3200.00	900.00
COMMON PLAYER (1-12)	175.00	80.00	22.00
☐ 1 Hank Bauer	200.00	90.00	25.00
☐ 2 Carl Erskine	200.00	90.00	25.00
☐ 3 Gil Hodges	325.00	145.00	40.00
☐ 4 Monte Irvin	275.00	125.00	34.00
☐ 5 Whitey Lockman	175.00	80.00	22.00
☐ 6 Mickey Mantle	3000.00	1000.00	300.00
☐ 7 Willie Mays	1500.00	500.00	150.00
☐ 8 Gil McDougald	200.00	90.00	25.00
☐ 9 Don Mueller	175.00	80.00	22.00
☐ 10 Don Newcombe	200.00	90.00	25.00
☐ 11 Phil Rizzuto	325.00	145.00	40.00
☐ 12 Duke Snider	650.00	300.00	80.00

1955 Stahl Meyer

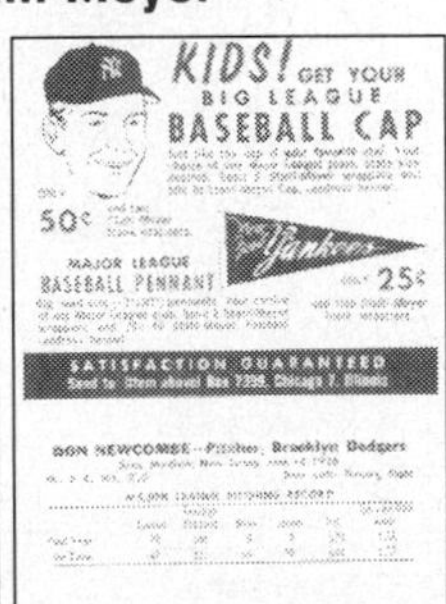

The cards in this 12-card set measure approximately 3 1/4" by 4 1/2". The 1955 Stahl Meyer set of full color, unnumbered cards contains four players each from the three New York teams. As in the 1954 set, the cards have yellow borders; however, the back of the cards contain a sketch of Mickey Mantle with an ad for a baseball cap or a pennant. The cards are ordered in the checklist below by alphabetical order without regard to team affiliation.

	NRMT	VG-E	GOOD
COMPLETE SET	5600.00	2500.00	700.00
COMMON PLAYER (1-12)	175.00	80.00	22.00
☐ 1 Hank Bauer	200.00	90.00	25.00
☐ 2 Carl Erskine	200.00	90.00	25.00
☐ 3 Gil Hodges	325.00	145.00	40.00
☐ 4 Monte Irvin	275.00	125.00	34.00
☐ 5 Whitey Lockman	175.00	80.00	22.00
☐ 6 Mickey Mantle	3000.00	1000.00	300.00
☐ 7 Gil McDougald	200.00	90.00	25.00
☐ 8 Don Mueller	175.00	80.00	22.00
☐ 9 Don Newcombe	200.00	90.00	25.00
☐ 10 Dusty Rhodes	175.00	80.00	22.00
☐ 11 Phil Rizzuto	325.00	145.00	40.00
☐ 12 Duke Snider	650.00	300.00	80.00

1990 Starline Long John Silver

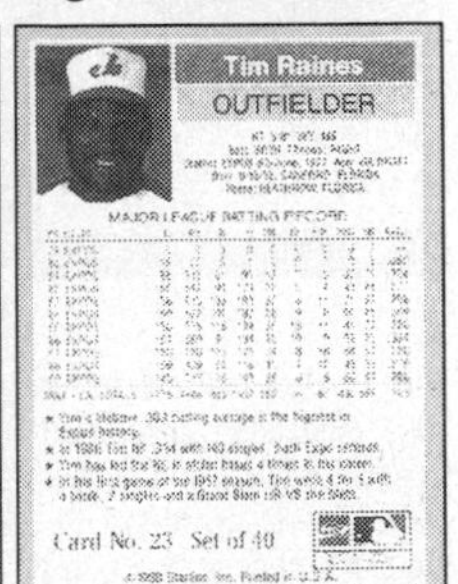

The 1990 Starline Long John Silver set was issued over an eight-week promotion, five cards at a time within a cello pack. The set was initially available only through the Long John Silver seafood fast-food chain with one pack being given to each customer who ordered a meal with a 32-ounce Coke. This 40-card, standard-size (2 1/2" by 3 1/2") set featured the best of today's players. There are several cards for some of the players in the set. After the promotion at Long John Silver had been completed, there were reportedly more than 100,000 sets left over that were released into the organized hobby.

	MT	EX-MT	VG
COMPLETE SET (40)	9.00	4.00	1.15
COMMON PLAYER (1-40)	.20	.09	.03
☐ 1 Don Mattingly	.60	.25	.08
☐ 2 Mark Grace	.50	.23	.06
☐ 3 Eric Davis	.30	.14	.04
☐ 4 Tony Gwynn	.50	.23	.06
☐ 5 Bobby Bonilla	.40	.18	.05
☐ 6 Wade Boggs	.50	.23	.06
☐ 7 Frank Viola	.20	.09	.03
☐ 8 Ruben Sierra	.40	.18	.05
☐ 9 Mark McGwire	.60	.25	.08
☐ 10 Alan Trammell	.30	.14	.04
☐ 11 Mark McGwire	.50	.23	.06
☐ 12 Gregg Jefferies	.40	.18	.05
☐ 13 Nolan Ryan	.75	.35	.09
☐ 14 John Smoltz	.40	.18	.05
☐ 15 Glenn Davis	.20	.09	.03
☐ 16 Mark Grace	.50	.23	.06
☐ 17 Wade Boggs	.50	.23	.06
☐ 18 Frank Viola	.20	.09	.03
☐ 19 Bret Saberhagen	.20	.09	.03
☐ 20 Chris Sabo	.20	.09	.03
☐ 21 Darryl Strawberry	.50	.23	.06
☐ 22 Wade Boggs	.50	.23	.06
☐ 23 Tim Raines	.20	.09	.03
☐ 24 Alan Trammell	.30	.14	.04
☐ 25 Chris Sabo	.20	.09	.03
☐ 26 Nolan Ryan	.75	.35	.09
☐ 27 Mark McGwire	.60	.25	.08
☐ 28 Don Mattingly	.60	.25	.08
☐ 29 Tony Gwynn	.50	.23	.06
☐ 30 Glenn Davis	.20	.09	.03
☐ 31 Bobby Bonilla	.40	.18	.05
☐ 32 Gregg Jefferies	.40	.18	.05
☐ 33 Ruben Sierra	.40	.18	.05
☐ 34 John Smoltz	.40	.18	.05
☐ 35 Don Mattingly	.60	.25	.08
☐ 36 Bret Saberhagen	.20	.09	.03
☐ 37 Darryl Strawberry	.50	.23	.06
☐ 38 Eric Davis	.30	.14	.04
☐ 39 Tim Raines	.20	.09	.03
☐ 40 Mark Grace	.50	.23	.06

1991 Studio Previews

This 18-card preview set was issued (four at a time) within 1991 (specially marked) Donruss retail factory sets in order to show dealers and collectors the look of their new Studio cards. The standard-size (2 1/2" by 3 1/2") cards are exactly the same style as those in the Studio series, with black and white player photos bordered in mauve and player information on the backs. The cards are numbered on the back.

	MT	EX-MT	VG
COMPLETE SET (18)	40.00	18.00	5.00
COMMON PLAYER (1-17)	1.50	.65	.19
☐ 1 Juan Bell	1.50	.65	.19
☐ 2 Roger Clemens	8.00	3.60	1.00
☐ 3 Dave Parker	1.50	.65	.19
☐ 4 Tim Raines	1.50	.65	.19
☐ 5 Kevin Seitzer	1.50	.65	.19
☐ 6 Ted Higuera	1.50	.65	.19
☐ 7 Bernie Williams	3.00	1.35	.40
☐ 8 Harold Baines	1.50	.65	.19
☐ 9 Gary Pettis	1.50	.65	.19
☐ 10 Dave Justice	8.00	3.60	1.00
☐ 11 Eric Davis	2.50	1.15	.30
☐ 12 Andujar Cedeno	2.50	1.15	.30
☐ 13 Tom Foley	1.50	.65	.19
☐ 14 Dwight Gooden	2.50	1.15	.30
☐ 15 Doug Drabek	1.50	.65	.19
☐ 16 Steve Decker	2.50	1.15	.30
☐ 17 Joe Torre MG	1.50	.65	.19
☐ NNO Title card	2.00	.90	.25

1991 Studio

The 1991 Leaf Studio set contains 264 cards and a puzzle of recently inducted Hall of Famer Rod Carew. The Carew puzzle was issued on twenty-one 2 1/2" by 3 1/2" cards, with 3 puzzle pieces per card, for a total of 63 pieces. The player cards measure the standard-size (2 1/2" by 3 1/2"), and the fronts feature posed black and white head-and-shoulders player photos with mauve borders. The team logo, player's name, and position appear along the bottom of the card face. The backs are printed in black and white and have four categories of information: personal, career, hobbies and interests, and heroes. The cards are numbered on the back. The cards are checklisted below alphabetically within and according to teams for each league as follows: Baltimore Orioles (1-10), Boston Red Sox (11-20), California Angels (21-30), Chicago White Sox (31-40), Cleveland Indians (41-50), Detroit Tigers (51-60), Kansas City Royals (61-70), Milwaukee Brewers (71-80), Minnesota Twins (81-90), New York Yankees (91-100), Oakland Athletics (101-110), Seattle Mariners (111-120), Texas Rangers (121-130), Toronto Blue Jays (131-140), Atlanta Braves (141-150), Chicago Cubs (151-160), Cincinnati Reds (161-170), Houston Astros (171-180), Los Angeles Dodgers (181-190), Montreal Expos (191-200), New York Mets (201-210), Philadelphia Phillies (211-220), Pittsburgh Pirates (221-230), St. Louis Cardinals (231-240), San Diego Padres (241-250), and San Francisco Giants (251-260). The key Rookie Cards in the set are Jeff Bagwell, Wes Chamberlain, Phil Plantier, and Todd Van Poppel. Among the other notable cards are Frank Thomas and Dave Justice.

	MT	EX-MT	VG
COMPLETE SET (264)	32.00	14.50	4.00
COMMON PLAYER (1-263)	.08	.04	.01
☐ 1 Glenn Davis	.10	.04	.01
☐ 2 Dwight Evans	.10	.04	.01
☐ 3 Leo Gomez	.75	.35	.09
☐ 4 Chris Hoiles	.30	.14	.04
☐ 5 Sam Horn	.08	.04	.01
☐ 6 Ben McDonald	.25	.11	.03
☐ 7 Randy Milligan	.08	.04	.01
☐ 8 Gregg Olson	.10	.04	.01
☐ 9 Cal Ripken	1.00	.45	.13
☐ 10 David Segui	.08	.04	.01
☐ 11 Wade Boggs	.40	.18	.05
☐ 12 Ellis Burks	.10	.04	.01
☐ 13 Jack Clark	.10	.04	.01
☐ 14 Roger Clemens	.90	.40	.11
☐ 15 Mike Greenwell	.12	.05	.02
☐ 16 Tim Naehring	.15	.07	.02
☐ 17 Tony Pena	.08	.04	.01
☐ 18 Phil Plantier	1.50	.65	.19
☐ 19 Jeff Reardon	.12	.05	.02
☐ 20 Mo Vaughn	.60	.25	.08
☐ 21 Jimmy Reese CO	.10	.04	.01
☐ 22 Jim Abbott UER (Born in 1967, not 1969)	.40	.18	.05
☐ 23 Bert Blyleven	.10	.04	.01
☐ 24 Chuck Finley	.10	.04	.01
☐ 25 Gary Gaetti	.08	.04	.01
☐ 26 Wally Joyner	.10	.04	.01
☐ 27 Mark Langston	.10	.04	.01
☐ 28 Kirk McCaskill	.08	.04	.01
☐ 29 Lance Parrish	.10	.04	.01
☐ 30 Dave Winfield	.25	.11	.03
☐ 31 Alex Fernandez	.30	.14	.04
☐ 32 Carlton Fisk	.30	.14	.04
☐ 33 Scott Fletcher	.08	.04	.01
☐ 34 Greg Hibbard	.08	.04	.01
☐ 35 Charlie Hough	.08	.04	.01
☐ 36 Jack McDowell	.30	.14	.04
☐ 37 Tim Raines	.12	.05	.02
☐ 38 Sammy Sosa	.10	.04	.01
☐ 39 Bobby Thigpen	.08	.04	.01
☐ 40 Frank Thomas	6.00	2.70	.75
☐ 41 Sandy Alomar Jr.	.10	.04	.01
☐ 42 John Farrell	.08	.04	.01
☐ 43 Glenallen Hill	.08	.04	.01
☐ 44 Brook Jacoby	.08	.04	.01
☐ 45 Chris James	.08	.04	.01
☐ 46 Doug Jones	.08	.04	.01
☐ 47 Eric King	.08	.04	.01
☐ 48 Mark Lewis	.25	.11	.03
☐ 49 Greg Swindell UER (Photo actually Turner Ward)	.10	.04	.01
☐ 50 Mark Whiten	.20	.09	.03
☐ 51 Milt Cuyler	.15	.07	.02
☐ 52 Rob Deer	.10	.04	.01
☐ 53 Cecil Fielder	.40	.18	.05
☐ 54 Travis Fryman	3.50	1.55	.45
☐ 55 Bill Gullickson	.08	.04	.01

☐ 56 Lloyd Moseby	.08	.04	.01
☐ 57 Frank Tanana	.08	.04	.01
☐ 58 Mickey Tettleton	.10	.04	.01
☐ 59 Alan Trammell	.12	.05	.02
☐ 60 Lou Whitaker	.12	.05	.02
☐ 61 Mike Boddicker	.08	.04	.01
☐ 62 George Brett	.35	.16	.04
☐ 63 Jeff Conine	.60	.25	.08
☐ 64 Warren Cromartie	.08	.04	.01
☐ 65 Storm Davis	.08	.04	.01
☐ 66 Kirk Gibson	.10	.04	.01
☐ 67 Mark Gubicza	.08	.04	.01
☐ 68 Brian McRae	.60	.25	.08
☐ 69 Bret Saberhagen	.10	.04	.01
☐ 70 Kurt Stillwell	.08	.04	.01
☐ 71 Tim McIntosh	.08	.04	.01
☐ 72 Candy Maldonado	.08	.04	.01
☐ 73 Paul Molitor	.15	.07	.02
☐ 74 Willie Randolph	.10	.04	.01
☐ 75 Ron Robinson	.08	.04	.01
☐ 76 Gary Sheffield	1.25	.55	.16
☐ 77 Franklin Stubbs	.08	.04	.01
☐ 78 B.J. Surhoff	.08	.04	.01
☐ 79 Greg Vaughn	.15	.07	.02
☐ 80 Robin Yount	.35	.16	.04
☐ 81 Rick Aguilera	.10	.04	.01
☐ 82 Steve Bedrosian	.08	.04	.01
☐ 83 Scott Erickson	.60	.25	.08
☐ 84 Greg Gagne	.08	.04	.01
☐ 85 Dan Gladden	.08	.04	.01
☐ 86 Brian Harper	.08	.04	.01
☐ 87 Kent Hrbek	.10	.04	.01
☐ 88 Shane Mack	.10	.04	.01
☐ 89 Jack Morris	.12	.05	.02
☐ 90 Kirby Puckett	.75	.35	.09
☐ 91 Jesse Barfield	.08	.04	.01
☐ 92 Steve Farr	.08	.04	.01
☐ 93 Steve Howe	.08	.04	.01
☐ 94 Roberto Kelly	.12	.05	.02
☐ 95 Tim Leary	.08	.04	.01
☐ 96 Kevin Maas	.15	.07	.02
☐ 97 Don Mattingly	.40	.18	.05
☐ 98 Hensley Meulens	.10	.04	.01
☐ 99 Scott Sanderson	.08	.04	.01
☐ 100 Steve Sax	.10	.04	.01
☐ 101 Jose Canseco	.75	.35	.09
☐ 102 Dennis Eckersley	.15	.07	.02
☐ 103 Dave Henderson	.08	.04	.01
☐ 104 Rickey Henderson	.40	.18	.05
☐ 105 Rick Honeycutt	.08	.04	.01
☐ 106 Mark McGwire	.75	.35	.09
☐ 107 Dave Stewart UER (No-hitter against Toronto, not Texas)	.10	.04	.01
☐ 108 Eric Show	.08	.04	.01
☐ 109 Todd Van Poppel	2.00	.90	.25
☐ 110 Bob Welch	.08	.04	.01
☐ 111 Alvin Davis	.08	.04	.01
☐ 112 Ken Griffey Jr.	2.00	.90	.25
☐ 113 Ken Griffey Sr.	.10	.04	.01
☐ 114 Erik Hanson UER (Misspelled Eric)	.08	.04	.01
☐ 115 Brian Holman	.08	.04	.01
☐ 116 Randy Johnson	.10	.04	.01
☐ 117 Edgar Martinez	.25	.11	.03
☐ 118 Tino Martinez	.25	.11	.03
☐ 119 Harold Reynolds	.08	.04	.01
☐ 120 David Valle	.08	.04	.01
☐ 121 Kevin Belcher	.15	.07	.02
☐ 122 Scott Chiamparino	.10	.04	.01
☐ 123 Julio Franco	.10	.04	.01
☐ 124 Juan Gonzalez	4.00	1.80	.50
☐ 125 Rich Gossage	.10	.04	.01
☐ 126 Jeff Kunkel	.08	.04	.01
☐ 127 Rafael Palmeiro	.20	.09	.03
☐ 128 Nolan Ryan	2.00	.90	.25
☐ 129 Ruben Sierra	.50	.23	.06
☐ 130 Bobby Witt	.08	.04	.01
☐ 131 Roberto Alomar	1.00	.45	.13
☐ 132 Tom Candiotti	.08	.04	.01
☐ 133 Joe Carter	.40	.18	.05
☐ 134 Ken Dayley	.08	.04	.01
☐ 135 Kelly Gruber	.10	.04	.01
☐ 136 John Olerud	.50	.23	.06
☐ 137 Dave Stieb	.08	.04	.01
☐ 138 Turner Ward	.15	.07	.02
☐ 139 Devon White	.10	.04	.01
☐ 140 Mookie Wilson	.08	.04	.01
☐ 141 Steve Avery	.90	.40	.11
☐ 142 Sid Bream	.08	.04	.01
☐ 143 Nick Esasky UER (Homers abbreviated RH)	.08	.04	.01
☐ 144 Ron Gant	.40	.18	.05
☐ 145 Tom Glavine	.75	.35	.09
☐ 146 David Justice	2.00	.90	.25
☐ 147 Kelly Mann	.08	.04	.01
☐ 148 Terry Pendleton	.15	.07	.02
☐ 149 John Smoltz	.40	.18	.05
☐ 150 Jeff Treadway	.08	.04	.01
☐ 151 George Bell	.10	.04	.01
☐ 152 Shawn Boskie	.08	.04	.01
☐ 153 Andre Dawson	.25	.11	.03
☐ 154 Lance Dickson	.20	.09	.03
☐ 155 Shawon Dunston	.10	.04	.01
☐ 156 Joe Girardi	.08	.04	.01
☐ 157 Mark Grace	.30	.14	.04
☐ 158 Ryne Sandberg	.90	.40	.11
☐ 159 Gary Scott	.35	.16	.04
☐ 160 Dave Smith	.08	.04	.01
☐ 161 Tom Browning	.08	.04	.01
☐ 162 Eric Davis	.15	.07	.02
☐ 163 Rob Dibble	.10	.04	.01
☐ 164 Mariano Duncan	.08	.04	.01
☐ 165 Chris Hammond	.15	.07	.02
☐ 166 Billy Hatcher	.08	.04	.01
☐ 167 Barry Larkin	.25	.11	.03
☐ 168 Hal Morris	.10	.04	.01
☐ 169 Paul O'Neill	.10	.04	.01
☐ 170 Chris Sabo	.10	.04	.01
☐ 171 Eric Anthony	.12	.05	.02
☐ 172 Jeff Bagwell	3.00	1.35	.40
☐ 173 Craig Biggio	.15	.07	.02
☐ 174 Ken Caminiti	.10	.04	.01
☐ 175 Jim Deshaies	.08	.04	.01
☐ 176 Steve Finley	.10	.04	.01
☐ 177 Pete Harnisch	.10	.04	.01
☐ 178 Darryl Kile	.30	.14	.04
☐ 179 Curt Schilling	.10	.04	.01
☐ 180 Mike Scott	.08	.04	.01
☐ 181 Brett Butler	.10	.04	.01
☐ 182 Gary Carter	.10	.04	.01
☐ 183 Orel Hershiser	.12	.05	.02
☐ 184 Ramon Martinez	.15	.07	.02
☐ 185 Eddie Murray	.25	.11	.03
☐ 186 Jose Offerman	.15	.07	.02
☐ 187 Bob Ojeda	.08	.04	.01
☐ 188 Juan Samuel	.08	.04	.01
☐ 189 Mike Scioscia	.08	.04	.01
☐ 190 Darryl Strawberry	.40	.18	.05
☐ 191 Moises Alou	.50	.23	.06
☐ 192 Brian Barnes	.25	.11	.03
☐ 193 Oil Can Boyd	.08	.04	.01
☐ 194 Ivan Calderon	.08	.04	.01
☐ 195 Delino DeShields	.50	.23	.06
☐ 196 Mike Fitzgerald	.08	.04	.01
☐ 197 Andres Galarraga	.08	.04	.01
☐ 198 Marquis Grissom	.50	.23	.06
☐ 199 Bill Sampen	.08	.04	.01
☐ 200 Tim Wallach	.10	.04	.01
☐ 201 Daryl Boston	.08	.04	.01
☐ 202 Vince Coleman	.10	.04	.01
☐ 203 John Franco	.10	.04	.01
☐ 204 Dwight Gooden	.15	.07	.02
☐ 205 Tom Herr	.08	.04	.01
☐ 206 Gregg Jefferies	.20	.09	.03
☐ 207 Howard Johnson	.10	.04	.01
☐ 208 Dave Magadan UER (Born 1862, should be 1962)	.10	.04	.01
☐ 209 Kevin McReynolds	.10	.04	.01
☐ 210 Frank Viola	.10	.04	.01
☐ 211 Wes Chamberlain	.60	.25	.08
☐ 212 Darren Daulton	.10	.04	.01
☐ 213 Len Dykstra	.10	.04	.01
☐ 214 Charlie Hayes	.08	.04	.01
☐ 215 Ricky Jordan	.08	.04	.01
☐ 216 Steve Lake (Pictured with parrot on his shoulder)	.08	.04	.01
☐ 217 Roger McDowell	.08	.04	.01
☐ 218 Mickey Morandini	.25	.11	.03
☐ 219 Terry Mulholland	.08	.04	.01
☐ 220 Dale Murphy	.12	.05	.02
☐ 221 Jay Bell	.10	.04	.01
☐ 222 Barry Bonds	.60	.25	.08
☐ 223 Bobby Bonilla	.25	.11	.03
☐ 224 Doug Drabek	.10	.04	.01
☐ 225 Bill Landrum	.08	.04	.01
☐ 226 Mike LaValliere	.08	.04	.01
☐ 227 Jose Lind	.08	.04	.01
☐ 228 Don Slaught	.08	.04	.01
☐ 229 John Smiley	.10	.04	.01
☐ 230 Andy Van Slyke	.20	.09	.03
☐ 231 Bernard Gilkey	.30	.14	.04
☐ 232 Pedro Guerrero	.10	.04	.01
☐ 233 Rex Hudler	.08	.04	.01

☐ 234 Ray Lankford	1.50	.65	.19
☐ 235 Joe Magrane	.08	.04	.01
☐ 236 Jose Oquendo	.08	.04	.01
☐ 237 Lee Smith	.10	.04	.01
☐ 238 Ozzie Smith	.25	.11	.03
☐ 239 Milt Thompson	.08	.04	.01
☐ 240 Todd Zeile	.15	.07	.02
☐ 241 Larry Andersen	.08	.04	.01
☐ 242 Andy Benes	.30	.14	.04
☐ 243 Paul Faries	.08	.04	.01
☐ 244 Tony Fernandez	.10	.04	.01
☐ 245 Tony Gwynn	.40	.18	.05
☐ 246 Atlee Hammaker	.08	.04	.01
☐ 247 Fred McGriff	.40	.18	.05
☐ 248 Bip Roberts	.10	.04	.01
☐ 249 Benito Santiago	.12	.05	.02
☐ 250 Ed Whitson	.08	.04	.01
☐ 251 Dave Anderson	.08	.04	.01
☐ 252 Mike Benjamin	.08	.04	.01
☐ 253 John Burkett UER (Front photo actually Trevor Wilson)	.08	.04	.01
☐ 254 Will Clark	.75	.35	.09
☐ 255 Scott Garrelts	.08	.04	.01
☐ 256 Willie McGee	.10	.04	.01
☐ 257 Kevin Mitchell	.12	.05	.02
☐ 258 Dave Righetti	.08	.04	.01
☐ 259 Matt Williams	.12	.05	.02
☐ 260 Black and Decker Bud Black Steve Decker	.08	.04	.01
☐ 261 Checklist Card 1-88 Sparky Anderson MG	.10	.01	.00
☐ 262 Checklist Card 89-176 Tom Lasorda MG	.10	.01	.00
☐ 263 Checklist Card 177-263 Tony LaRussa MG	.10	.01	.00
☐ NNO Title Card	.10	.05	.01

1992 Studio Previews

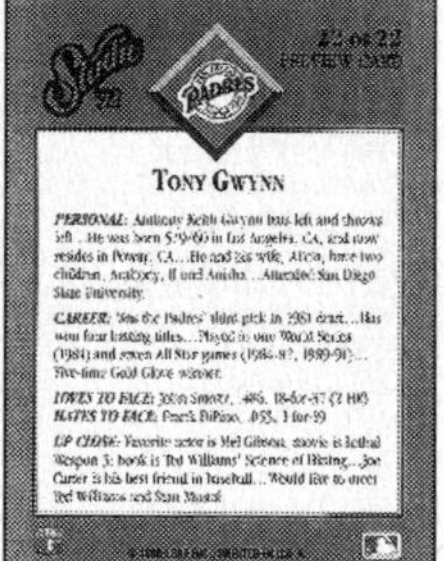

This 22-card set was issued by Leaf to preview the design of the 1992 Leaf Studio series. The cards measure the standard size (2 1/2" by 3 1/2"). A color posed player photo has been cut out and superimposed against the background of a black and white action shot of the player. These pictures are framed in black on a gold card face. The player's name and team name appear in the bottom gold border. On a white panel bordered in gold, the backs feature player information under five headings (Personal, Career, Loves to face, Hates to face, and Up Close). The cards are numbered on the back. Four Studio Preview cards were included as a special insert in each 1992 Donruss retail factory set. It appears that Roberto Alomar and Ozzie Smith may be a little more difficult to find than the other 20 cards; they are designated SP in the checklist below.

	MT	EX-MT	VG
COMPLETE SET (22)	90.00	40.00	11.50
COMMON PLAYER (1-22)	1.50	.65	.19
☐ 1 Ruben Sierra	6.00	2.70	.75
☐ 2 Kirby Puckett	7.00	3.10	.85
☐ 3 Ryne Sandberg	8.00	3.60	1.00
☐ 4 John Kruk	1.50	.65	.19
☐ 5 Cal Ripken	10.00	4.50	1.25
☐ 6 Robin Yount	4.00	1.80	.50
☐ 7 Dwight Gooden	2.50	1.15	.30
☐ 8 David Justice	7.00	3.10	.85
☐ 9 Don Mattingly	4.00	1.80	.50
☐ 10 Wally Joyner	1.50	.65	.19
☐ 11 Will Clark	7.00	3.10	.85
☐ 12 Rob Dibble	1.50	.65	.19
☐ 13 Roberto Alomar SP	12.00	5.50	1.50
☐ 14 Wade Boggs	4.00	1.80	.50
☐ 15 Barry Bonds	7.00	3.10	.85
☐ 16 Jeff Bagwell	6.00	2.70	.75
☐ 17 Mark McGwire	7.00	3.10	.85
☐ 18 Frank Thomas	15.00	6.75	1.90
☐ 19 Brett Butler	1.50	.65	.19
☐ 20 Ozzie Smith SP	10.00	4.50	1.25
☐ 21 Jim Abbott	3.00	1.35	.40
☐ 22 Tony Gwynn	4.50	2.00	.55

1992 Studio

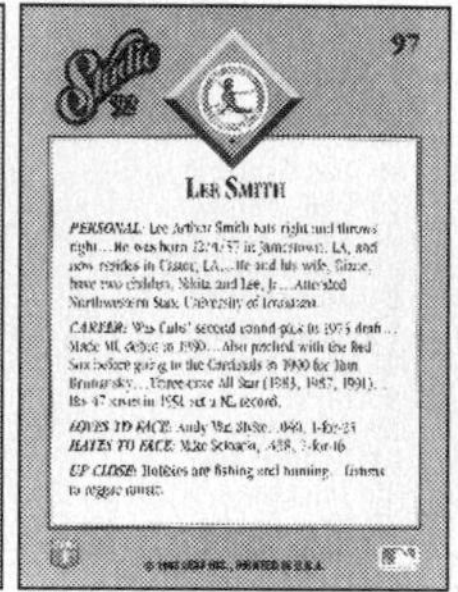

The 1992 Leaf Studio set consists of ten players from each of the 26 major league teams, three checklists, and an introduction card for a total of 264 cards. A Heritage series eight-card subset, featuring today's star players dressed in vintage uniforms, was randomly inserted in 12-card foil packs. The cards measure the standard size (2 1/2" by 3 1/2"). Inside champagne color metallic borders, the fronts carry a color close-up shot superimposed on a black and white action player photo. The backs focus on the personal side of each player by providing an up-close look, and unusual statistics show the batter or pitcher each player "Loves to Face" or "Hates to Face". The cards are numbered on the back. The key Rookie Cards in this set are Chad Curtis and Pat Mahomes.

	MT	EX-MT	VG
COMPLETE SET (264)	25.00	11.50	3.10
COMMON PLAYER (1-264)	.08	.04	.01
☐ 1 Steve Avery	.50	.23	.06
☐ 2 Sid Bream	.08	.04	.01
☐ 3 Ron Gant	.20	.09	.03
☐ 4 Tom Glavine	.30	.14	.04
☐ 5 David Justice	.75	.35	.09
☐ 6 Mark Lemke	.08	.04	.01
☐ 7 Greg Olson	.08	.04	.01
☐ 8 Terry Pendleton	.12	.05	.02
☐ 9 Deion Sanders	.40	.18	.05
☐ 10 John Smoltz	.20	.09	.03
☐ 11 Doug Dascenzo	.08	.04	.01
☐ 12 Andre Dawson	.20	.09	.03
☐ 13 Joe Girardi	.08	.04	.01
☐ 14 Mark Grace	.15	.07	.02
☐ 15 Greg Maddux	.15	.07	.02
☐ 16 Chuck McElroy	.08	.04	.01
☐ 17 Mike Morgan	.08	.04	.01
☐ 18 Ryne Sandberg	.60	.25	.08
☐ 19 Gary Scott	.10	.04	.01
☐ 20 Sammy Sosa	.08	.04	.01
☐ 21 Norm Charlton	.10	.04	.01
☐ 22 Rob Dibble	.10	.04	.01
☐ 23 Barry Larkin	.20	.09	.03
☐ 24 Hal Morris	.10	.04	.01

☐ 25	Paul O'Neill	.10	.04	.01
☐ 26	Jose Rijo	.10	.04	.01
☐ 27	Bip Roberts	.10	.04	.01
☐ 28	Chris Sabo	.10	.04	.01
☐ 29	Reggie Sanders	.75	.35	.09
☐ 30	Greg Swindell	.10	.04	.01
☐ 31	Jeff Bagwell	.75	.35	.09
☐ 32	Craig Biggio	.10	.04	.01
☐ 33	Ken Caminiti	.10	.04	.01
☐ 34	Andujar Cedeno	.10	.05	.01
☐ 35	Steve Finley	.10	.04	.01
☐ 36	Pete Harnisch	.08	.04	.01
☐ 37	Butch Henry	.20	.09	.03
☐ 38	Doug Jones	.10	.04	.01
☐ 39	Darryl Kile	.15	.07	.02
☐ 40	Eddie Taubensee	.20	.09	.03
☐ 41	Brett Butler	.10	.04	.01
☐ 42	Tom Candiotti	.08	.04	.01
☐ 43	Eric Davis	.12	.05	.02
☐ 44	Orel Hershiser	.12	.05	.02
☐ 45	Eric Karros	1.75	.80	.22
☐ 46	Ramon Martinez	.12	.05	.02
☐ 47	Jose Offerman	.10	.04	.01
☐ 48	Mike Scioscia	.08	.04	.01
☐ 49	Mike Sharperson	.08	.04	.01
☐ 50	Darryl Strawberry	.30	.14	.04
☐ 51	Bret Barberie	.12	.05	.02
☐ 52	Ivan Calderon	.08	.04	.01
☐ 53	Gary Carter	.10	.04	.01
☐ 54	Delino DeShields	.25	.11	.03
☐ 55	Marquis Grissom	.25	.11	.03
☐ 56	Ken Hill	.08	.04	.01
☐ 57	Dennis Martinez	.10	.04	.01
☐ 58	Spike Owen	.08	.04	.01
☐ 59	Larry Walker	.35	.16	.04
☐ 60	Tim Wallach	.10	.04	.01
☐ 61	Bobby Bonilla	.15	.07	.02
☐ 62	Tim Burke	.08	.04	.01
☐ 63	Vince Coleman	.10	.04	.01
☐ 64	John Franco	.10	.04	.01
☐ 65	Dwight Gooden	.12	.05	.02
☐ 66	Todd Hundley	.08	.04	.01
☐ 67	Howard Johnson	.10	.04	.01
☐ 68	Eddie Murray	.20	.09	.03
☐ 69	Bret Saberhagen	.12	.05	.02
☐ 70	Anthony Young	.12	.05	.02
☐ 71	Kim Batiste	.15	.07	.02
☐ 72	Wes Chamberlain	.12	.05	.02
☐ 73	Darren Daulton	.10	.04	.01
☐ 74	Mariano Duncan	.08	.04	.01
☐ 75	Len Dykstra	.10	.04	.01
☐ 76	John Kruk	.10	.04	.01
☐ 77	Mickey Morandini	.10	.04	.01
☐ 78	Terry Mulholland	.08	.04	.01
☐ 79	Dale Murphy	.12	.05	.02
☐ 80	Mitch Williams	.08	.04	.01
☐ 81	Jay Bell	.08	.04	.01
☐ 82	Barry Bonds	.50	.23	.06
☐ 83	Steve Buechele	.08	.04	.01
☐ 84	Doug Drabek	.10	.04	.01
☐ 85	Mike LaValliere	.08	.04	.01
☐ 86	Jose Lind	.08	.04	.01
☐ 87	Denny Neagle	.12	.05	.02
☐ 88	Randy Tomlin	.12	.05	.02
☐ 89	Andy Van Slyke	.12	.05	.02
☐ 90	Gary Varsho	.08	.04	.01
☐ 91	Pedro Guerrero	.10	.04	.01
☐ 92	Rex Hudler	.08	.04	.01
☐ 93	Brian Jordan	.40	.18	.05
☐ 94	Felix Jose	.10	.04	.01
☐ 95	Donovan Osborne	.60	.25	.08
☐ 96	Tom Pagnozzi	.08	.04	.01
☐ 97	Lee Smith	.10	.04	.01
☐ 98	Ozzie Smith	.20	.09	.03
☐ 99	Todd Worrell	.08	.04	.01
☐ 100	Todd Zeile	.08	.04	.01
☐ 101	Andy Benes	.12	.05	.02
☐ 102	Jerald Clark	.08	.04	.01
☐ 103	Tony Fernandez	.10	.04	.01
☐ 104	Tony Gwynn	.30	.14	.04
☐ 105	Greg W. Harris	.08	.04	.01
☐ 106	Fred McGriff	.30	.14	.04
☐ 107	Benito Santiago	.12	.05	.02
☐ 108	Gary Sheffield	.75	.35	.09
☐ 109	Kurt Stillwell	.08	.04	.01
☐ 110	Tim Teufel	.08	.04	.01
☐ 111	Kevin Bass	.08	.04	.01
☐ 112	Jeff Brantley	.08	.04	.01
☐ 113	John Burkett	.08	.04	.01
☐ 114	Will Clark	.50	.23	.06
☐ 115	Royce Clayton	.40	.18	.05
☐ 116	Mike Jackson	.08	.04	.01
☐ 117	Darren Lewis	.10	.04	.01
☐ 118	Bill Swift	.08	.04	.01
☐ 119	Robby Thompson	.08	.04	.01
☐ 120	Matt Williams	.10	.05	.01
☐ 121	Brady Anderson	.10	.04	.01
☐ 122	Glenn Davis	.10	.04	.01
☐ 123	Mike Devereaux	.10	.04	.01
☐ 124	Chris Hoiles	.12	.05	.02
☐ 125	Sam Horn	.08	.04	.01
☐ 126	Ben McDonald	.15	.07	.02
☐ 127	Mike Mussina	1.75	.80	.22
☐ 128	Gregg Olson	.10	.04	.01
☐ 129	Cal Ripken Jr.	.75	.35	.09
☐ 130	Rick Sutcliffe	.10	.04	.01
☐ 131	Wade Boggs	.30	.14	.04
☐ 132	Roger Clemens	.60	.25	.08
☐ 133	Greg A. Harris	.08	.04	.01
☐ 134	Tim Naehring	.10	.04	.01
☐ 135	Tony Pena	.08	.04	.01
☐ 136	Phil Plantier	.30	.14	.04
☐ 137	Jeff Reardon	.12	.05	.02
☐ 138	Jody Reed	.08	.04	.01
☐ 139	Mo Vaughn	.12	.05	.02
☐ 140	Frank Viola	.10	.04	.01
☐ 141	Jim Abbott	.20	.09	.03
☐ 142	Hubie Brooks	.08	.04	.01
☐ 143	Chad Curtis	.50	.23	.06
☐ 144	Gary DiSarcina	.08	.04	.01
☐ 145	Chuck Finley	.08	.04	.01
☐ 146	Bryan Harvey	.08	.04	.01
☐ 147	Von Hayes	.08	.04	.01
☐ 148	Mark Langston	.10	.04	.01
☐ 149	Lance Parrish	.10	.04	.01
☐ 150	Lee Stevens	.08	.04	.01
☐ 151	George Bell	.10	.04	.01
☐ 152	Alex Fernandez	.10	.04	.01
☐ 153	Greg Hibbard	.08	.04	.01
☐ 154	Lance Johnson	.08	.04	.01
☐ 155	Kirk McCaskill	.08	.04	.01
☐ 156	Tim Raines	.12	.05	.02
☐ 157	Steve Sax	.10	.04	.01
☐ 158	Bobby Thigpen	.08	.04	.01
☐ 159	Frank Thomas	3.00	1.35	.40
☐ 160	Robin Ventura	.50	.23	.06
☐ 161	Sandy Alomar Jr.	.10	.04	.01
☐ 162	Jack Armstrong	.08	.04	.01
☐ 163	Carlos Baerga	.40	.18	.05
☐ 164	Albert Belle	.30	.14	.04
☐ 165	Alex Cole	.08	.04	.01
☐ 166	Glenallen Hill	.08	.04	.01
☐ 167	Mark Lewis	.10	.04	.01
☐ 168	Kenny Lofton	1.25	.55	.16
☐ 169	Paul Sorrento	.10	.04	.01
☐ 170	Mark Whiten	.08	.04	.01
☐ 171	Milt Cuyler	.08	.04	.01
☐ 172	Rob Deer	.10	.04	.01
☐ 173	Cecil Fielder	.30	.14	.04
☐ 174	Travis Fryman	1.00	.45	.13
☐ 175	Mike Henneman	.08	.04	.01
☐ 176	Tony Phillips	.08	.04	.01
☐ 177	Frank Tanana	.08	.04	.01
☐ 178	Mickey Tettleton	.10	.04	.01
☐ 179	Alan Trammell	.12	.05	.02
☐ 180	Lou Whitaker	.12	.05	.02
☐ 181	George Brett	.25	.11	.03
☐ 182	Tom Gordon	.08	.04	.01
☐ 183	Mark Gubicza	.08	.04	.01
☐ 184	Gregg Jefferies	.10	.04	.01
☐ 185	Wally Joyner	.10	.04	.01
☐ 186	Brent Mayne	.08	.04	.01
☐ 187	Brian McRae	.12	.05	.02
☐ 188	Kevin McReynolds	.10	.04	.01
☐ 189	Keith Miller	.08	.04	.01
☐ 190	Jeff Montgomery	.08	.04	.01
☐ 191	Dante Bichette	.08	.04	.01
☐ 192	Ricky Bones	.15	.07	.02
☐ 193	Scott Fletcher	.08	.04	.01
☐ 194	Paul Molitor	.12	.05	.02
☐ 195	Jaime Navarro	.10	.04	.01
☐ 196	Franklin Stubbs	.08	.04	.01
☐ 197	B.J. Surhoff	.08	.04	.01
☐ 198	Greg Vaughn	.10	.04	.01
☐ 199	Bill Wegman	.08	.04	.01
☐ 200	Robin Yount	.25	.11	.03
☐ 201	Rick Aguilera	.10	.04	.01
☐ 202	Scott Erickson	.15	.07	.02
☐ 203	Greg Gagne	.08	.04	.01
☐ 204	Brian Harper	.08	.04	.01
☐ 205	Kent Hrbek	.10	.04	.01
☐ 206	Scott Leius	.08	.04	.01
☐ 207	Shane Mack	.10	.04	.01
☐ 208	Pat Mahomes	.40	.18	.05
☐ 209	Kirby Puckett	.50	.23	.06
☐ 210	John Smiley	.10	.04	.01

☐ 211 Mike Gallego	.08	.04	.01
☐ 212 Charlie Hayes	.08	.04	.01
☐ 213 Pat Kelly	.10	.05	.01
☐ 214 Roberto Kelly	.10	.05	.01
☐ 215 Kevin Maas	.10	.04	.01
☐ 216 Don Mattingly	.30	.14	.04
☐ 217 Matt Nokes	.08	.04	.01
☐ 218 Melido Perez	.10	.04	.01
☐ 219 Scott Sanderson	.08	.04	.01
☐ 220 Danny Tartabull	.12	.05	.02
☐ 221 Harold Baines	.10	.04	.01
☐ 222 Jose Canseco	.50	.23	.06
☐ 223 Dennis Eckersley	.15	.07	.02
☐ 224 Dave Henderson	.08	.04	.01
☐ 225 Carney Lansford	.10	.04	.01
☐ 226 Mark McGwire	.50	.23	.06
☐ 227 Mike Moore	.08	.04	.01
☐ 228 Randy Ready	.08	.04	.01
☐ 229 Terry Steinbach	.10	.04	.01
☐ 230 Dave Stewart	.10	.04	.01
☐ 231 Jay Buhner	.10	.04	.01
☐ 232 Ken Griffey Jr.	2.00	.90	.25
☐ 233 Erik Hanson	.08	.04	.01
☐ 234 Randy Johnson	.10	.04	.01
☐ 235 Edgar Martinez	.10	.04	.01
☐ 236 Tino Martinez	.10	.05	.01
☐ 237 Kevin Mitchell	.12	.05	.02
☐ 238 Pete O'Brien	.08	.04	.01
☐ 239 Harold Reynolds	.08	.04	.01
☐ 240 David Valle	.08	.04	.01
☐ 241 Julio Franco	.10	.04	.01
☐ 242 Juan Gonzalez	1.25	.55	.16
☐ 243 Jose Guzman	.08	.04	.01
☐ 244 Rafael Palmeiro	.12	.05	.02
☐ 245 Dean Palmer	.50	.23	.06
☐ 246 Ivan Rodriguez	1.00	.45	.13
☐ 247 Jeff Russell	.08	.04	.01
☐ 248 Nolan Ryan	1.50	.65	.19
☐ 249 Ruben Sierra	.40	.18	.05
☐ 250 Dickie Thon	.08	.04	.01
☐ 251 Roberto Alomar	.50	.23	.06
☐ 252 Derek Bell	.30	.14	.04
☐ 253 Pat Borders	.08	.04	.01
☐ 254 Joe Carter	.30	.14	.04
☐ 255 Kelly Gruber	.10	.04	.01
☐ 256 Juan Guzman	1.75	.80	.22
☐ 257 Jack Morris	.15	.07	.02
☐ 258 John Olerud	.25	.11	.03
☐ 259 Devon White	.10	.04	.01
☐ 260 Dave Winfield	.20	.09	.03
☐ 261 Checklist	.10	.01	.00
☐ 262 Checklist	.10	.01	.00
☐ 263 Checklist	.10	.01	.00
☐ 264 History Card	.15	.07	.02

1992 Studio Heritage

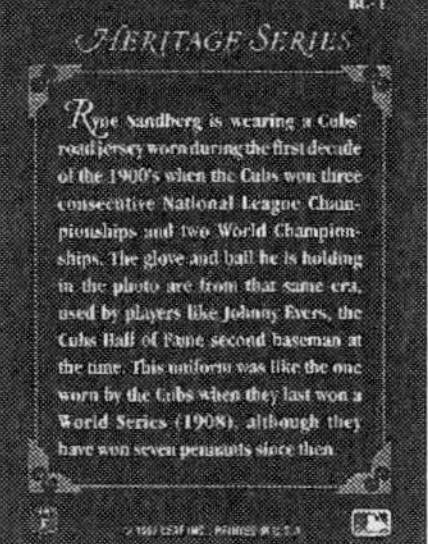

The 1992 Leaf Studio Heritage series subset presents today's star players dressed in vintage uniforms. Cards numbered 1-8 were randomly inserted in 12-card Leaf Studio foil packs while cards numbered 9-14 were featured only in 28-card Leaf Studio jumbo packs. The cards measure the standard size (2 1/2" by 3 1/2"). The fronts display sepia-toned portraits of the players dressed in vintage uniforms of their current teams. The pictures are bordered by dark turquoise and have bronze foil picture holders at each corner. The set title "Heritage Series" also appears in bronze foil lettering above the pictures. Within a bronze picture frame design on dark turquoise, the backs give a brief history of the team with special reference to the year of the vintage uniform. The cards are numbered on the back with a BC prefix.

	MT	EX-MT	VG
COMPLETE SET (14)	35.00	16.00	4.40
COMPLETE FOIL SET (8)	25.00	11.50	3.10
COMPLETE JUMBO SET (6)	10.00	4.50	1.25
COMMON PLAYER (1-8)	2.00	.90	.25
COMMON PLAYER (9-14)	.75	.35	.09
☐ 1 Ryne Sandberg 1908 Cubs	5.00	2.30	.60
☐ 2 Carlton Fisk 1917 White Sox	2.00	.90	.25
☐ 3 Wade Boggs 1918 Red Sox	2.50	1.15	.30
☐ 4 Jose Canseco 1929 Athletics	4.00	1.80	.50
☐ 5 Don Mattingly 1939 Yankees	2.50	1.15	.30
☐ 6 Darryl Strawberry 1944 Dodgers	2.50	1.15	.30
☐ 7 Cal Ripken 1951 Browns	6.00	2.70	.75
☐ 8 Will Clark 1951 Giants	4.00	1.80	.50
☐ 9 Andre Dawson 1944 Cubs	1.75	.80	.22
☐ 10 Andy Van Slyke 1960 Pirates	1.00	.45	.13
☐ 11 Paul Molitor 1969 Pilots	1.00	.45	.13
☐ 12 Jeff Bagwell 1962 Colt 45s	3.00	1.35	.40
☐ 13 Darren Daulton 1945 Phillies	.75	.35	.09
☐ 14 Kirby Puckett 1960 Senators	4.00	1.80	.50

1962 Sugardale

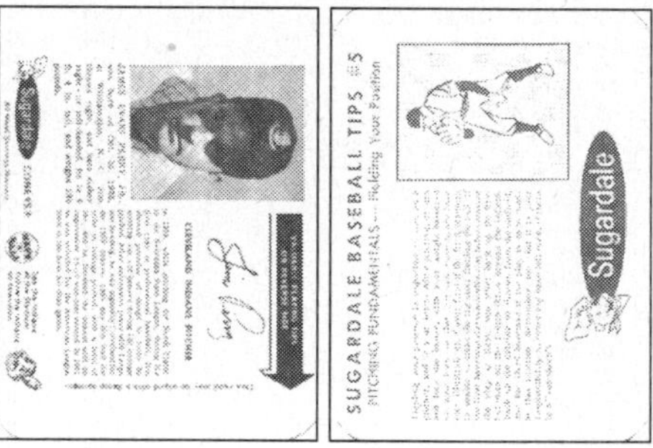

The cards in this 22-card set measure approximately 3 3/4" by 5 1/8". The 1962 Sugardale Meats set of black and white, numbered and lettered cards features the Cleveland Indians and the Pittsburgh Pirates. The Indians are numbered while the Pirates are lettered. The backs, in red print, give player tips. The Bob Nieman card was just recently discovered and is quite scarce. The catalog designation is F174-1.

	NRMT	VG-E	GOOD
COMPLETE SET (22)	2250.00	1000.00	275.00
COMMON PLAYER (1-19)	50.00	23.00	6.25
COMMON PLAYER (A-D)	75.00	34.00	9.50
☐ 1 Barry Latman	50.00	23.00	6.25
☐ 2 Gary Bell	50.00	23.00	6.25
☐ 3 Dick Donovan	50.00	23.00	6.25
☐ 4 Frank Funk	50.00	23.00	6.25
☐ 5 Jim Perry	75.00	34.00	9.50
☐ 6 Not issued	.00	.00	.00
☐ 7 John Romano	50.00	23.00	6.25
☐ 8 Ty Cline	50.00	23.00	6.25

☐ 9 Tito Francona	50.00	23.00	6.25
☐ 10 Bob Nieman SP	250.00	115.00	31.00
☐ 11 Willie Kirkland	50.00	23.00	6.25
☐ 12 Woody Held	50.00	23.00	6.25
☐ 13 Jerry Kindall	50.00	23.00	6.25
☐ 14 Bubba Phillips	50.00	23.00	6.25
☐ 15 Mel Harder CO	60.00	27.00	7.50
☐ 16 Salty Parker CO	50.00	23.00	6.25
☐ 17 Ray Katt CO	50.00	23.00	6.25
☐ 18 Mel McGaha MG	50.00	23.00	6.25
☐ 19 Pedro Ramos	50.00	23.00	6.25
☐ A0 Dick Groat	100.00	45.00	12.50
☐ B0 Roberto Clemente	1000.00	400.00	125.00
☐ C0 Don Hoak	75.00	34.00	9.50
☐ D0 Dick Stuart	100.00	45.00	12.50

1963 Sugardale

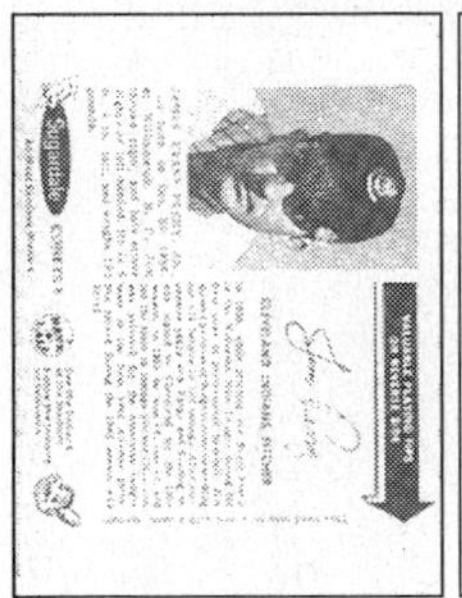

The cards in this 31-card set measure approximately 3 3/4" by 5 1/8". The 1963 Sugardale Meats set of 31 black and white, numbered cards features the Cleveland Indians and Pittsburgh Pirates. The backs are printed in red and give player tips. The 1963 Sugardale set can be distinguished from the 1962 Sugardale set by examining the biographies on the card for mention of the 1962 season. The Perry and Skinner cards were withdrawn after June trades and are difficult to obtain.

	NRMT	VG-E	GOOD
COMPLETE SET (31)	1900.00	850.00	240.00
COMMON PLAYER (1-33)	50.00	23.00	6.25
COMMON PLAYER (34-38)	75.00	34.00	9.50
☐ 1 Barry Latman	50.00	23.00	6.25
☐ 2 Gary Bell	50.00	23.00	6.25
☐ 3 Dick Donovan	50.00	23.00	6.25
☐ 4 Joe Adcock	75.00	34.00	9.50
☐ 5 Jim Perry SP	175.00	80.00	22.00
☐ 6 Not issued	.00	.00	.00
☐ 7 John Romano	50.00	23.00	6.25
☐ 8 Mike de la Hoz	50.00	23.00	6.25
☐ 9 Tito Francona	60.00	27.00	7.50
☐ 10 Gene Green	50.00	23.00	6.25
☐ 11 Willie Kirkland	50.00	23.00	6.25
☐ 12 Woody Held	50.00	23.00	6.25
☐ 13 Jerry Kindall	50.00	23.00	6.25
☐ 14 Max Alvis	50.00	23.00	6.25
☐ 15 Mel Harder CO	60.00	27.00	7.50
☐ 16 George Strickland CO	50.00	23.00	6.25
☐ 17 Elmer Valo CO	50.00	23.00	6.25
☐ 18 Birdie Tebbetts MG	50.00	23.00	6.25
☐ 19 Pedro Ramos	50.00	23.00	6.25
☐ 20 Al Luplow	50.00	23.00	6.25
☐ 21 Not issued	.00	.00	.00
☐ 22 Not issued	.00	.00	.00
☐ 23 Jim Grant	60.00	27.00	7.50
☐ 24 Victor Davalillo	60.00	27.00	7.50
☐ 25 Jerry Walker	60.00	27.00	7.50
☐ 26 Sam McDowell	75.00	34.00	9.50
☐ 27 Fred Whitfield	50.00	23.00	6.25
☐ 28 Jack Kralick	50.00	23.00	6.25
☐ 29 Not issued	.00	.00	.00
☐ 30 Not issued	.00	.00	.00
☐ 31 Not issued	.00	.00	.00
☐ 32 Not issued	.00	.00	.00
☐ 33 Bob Allen	50.00	23.00	6.25
☐ 34 Don Cardwell	75.00	34.00	9.50
☐ 35 Bob Skinner SP	250.00	115.00	31.00
☐ 36 Don Schwall	75.00	34.00	9.50
☐ 37 Jim Pagliaroni	75.00	34.00	9.50
☐ 38 Dick Schofield	75.00	34.00	9.50

1990 Sunflower Seeds

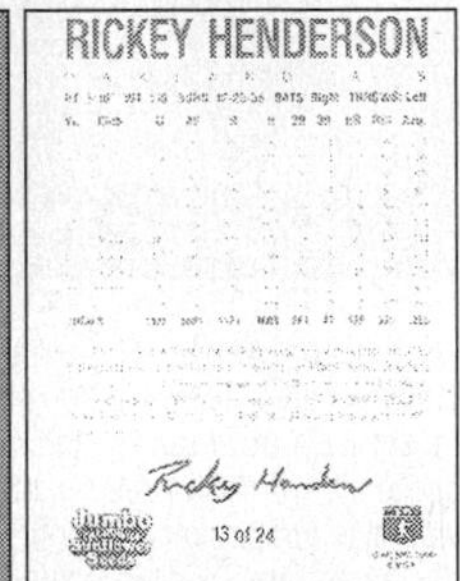

This 24-card, standard-size (2 1/2" by 3 1/2") set is an attractive set which frames the players photo by solid blue borders. In the upper left hand of the card the description, Jumbo California Sunflower Seeds, was placed and underneath the photo is the player's name in red and the team name in very small printing in white. The back of the card features the complete major league record of the player and a short write up as well. This set was issued by Stagi and Scriven Farms Inc. with the cooperation of Michael Schechter Associates (MSA) and features some of the big-name stars in baseball at the time of printing of the set. The set was an attempt by the company to promote sunflower seeds as an alternative to chewing tobacco in the dugout. Three cards were available as an insert in each specially marked bag of Jumbo California Sunflower Seeds.

	MT	EX-MT	VG
COMPLETE SET (24)	18.00	8.00	2.30
COMMON PLAYER (1-24)	.50	.23	.06
☐ 1 Kevin Mitchell	.75	.35	.09
☐ 2 Ken Griffey Jr.	3.00	1.35	.40
☐ 3 Howard Johnson	.60	.25	.08
☐ 4 Bo Jackson	1.25	.55	.16
☐ 5 Kirby Puckett	1.25	.55	.16
☐ 6 Robin Yount	1.00	.45	.13
☐ 7 Dave Stieb	.50	.23	.06
☐ 8 Don Mattingly	1.25	.55	.16
☐ 9 Barry Bonds	1.00	.45	.13
☐ 10 Pedro Guerrero	.50	.23	.06
☐ 11 Tony Gwynn	1.00	.45	.13
☐ 12 Von Hayes	.50	.23	.06
☐ 13 Rickey Henderson	1.25	.55	.16
☐ 14 Tim Raines	.50	.23	.06
☐ 15 Alan Trammell	.60	.25	.08
☐ 16 Dave Stewart	.50	.23	.06
☐ 17 Will Clark	1.25	.55	.16
☐ 18 Roger Clemens	1.50	.65	.19
☐ 19 Wally Joyner	.60	.25	.08
☐ 20 Ryne Sandberg	1.50	.65	.19
☐ 21 Eric Davis	.75	.35	.09
☐ 22 Mike Scott	.50	.23	.06
☐ 23 Cal Ripken	1.50	.65	.19
☐ 24 Eddie Murray	.90	.40	.11

1991 Sunflower Seeds

This 24-card, standard-size (2 1/2" by 3 1/2") set was sponsored by Jumbo California Sunflower Seeds. The posed color player photos are framed by white and yellow borders on a red background. The company logo and the words

"Autograph Series II" appear above the photo, with the player's name, team, and position given below the picture. A facsimile autograph is inscribed across the picture. The backs are printed in red on white and present Major League statistics and career highlights. The cards are numbered on the back. The set was again issued by Stagi and Scriven Farms Inc. with the cooperation of Michael Schechter Associates (MSA). The set was another attempt by the company to promote sunflower seeds as an alternative to chewing tobacco in the dugout. Two cards were available as an insert in each specially marked bag of Jumbo California Sunflower Seeds.

	MT	EX-MT	VG
COMPLETE SET (24)	15.00	6.75	1.90
COMMON PLAYER (1-24)	.40	.18	.05
☐ 1 Ozzie Smith	.75	.35	.09
☐ 2 Wade Boggs	1.00	.45	.13
☐ 3 Bobby Bonilla	.60	.25	.08
☐ 4 George Brett	1.00	.45	.13
☐ 5 Kal Daniels	.40	.18	.05
☐ 6 Glenn Davis	.50	.23	.06
☐ 7 Chuck Finley	.40	.18	.05
☐ 8 Cecil Fielder	1.00	.45	.13
☐ 9 Len Dykstra	.40	.18	.05
☐ 10 Dwight Gooden	.60	.25	.08
☐ 11 Ken Griffey Jr.	2.50	1.15	.30
☐ 12 Kelly Gruber	.40	.18	.05
☐ 13 Kent Hrbek	.40	.18	.05
☐ 14 Andre Dawson	.75	.35	.09
☐ 15 Dave Justice	1.25	.55	.16
☐ 16 Barry Larkin	.60	.25	.08
☐ 17 Ben McDonald	.60	.25	.08
☐ 18 Mark McGwire	1.00	.45	.13
☐ 19 Roberto Alomar	1.25	.55	.16
☐ 20 Nolan Ryan	2.50	1.15	.30
☐ 21 Sandy Alomar Jr.	.40	.18	.05
☐ 22 Bobby Thigpen	.40	.18	.05
☐ 23 Tim Wallach	.40	.18	.05
☐ 24 Matt Williams	.50	.23	.06

1992 Sunflower Seeds

This 24-card, standard-size (2 1/2" by 3 1/2") set was sponsored by Jumbo California Sunflower Seeds and produced by Michael Schechter Associates (MSA). The posed color player photos are framed in white and bright blue on a white background. The company log appears in the upper left corner. The words "Autograph Series III" are printed in red at the top. The player's name, team, and position are given in the blue border below the picture. A facsimile autograph is inscribed across the picture. The backs feature statistical information and career highlights printed in blue on a white background. The cards are numbered on the back.

	MT	EX-MT	VG
COMPLETE SET (24)	12.50	5.75	1.55
COMMON PLAYER (1-24)	.40	.18	.05

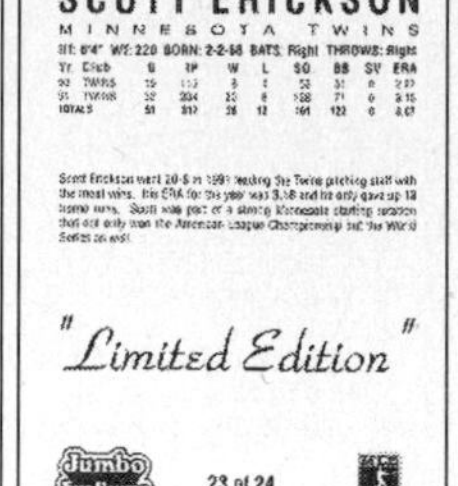

☐ 1 Jeff Reardon	.50	.23	.06
☐ 2 Bill Gullickson	.40	.18	.05
☐ 3 Todd Zeile	.40	.18	.05
☐ 4 Terry Mulholland	.40	.18	.05
☐ 5 Kirby Puckett	1.25	.55	.16
☐ 6 Howard Johnson	.50	.23	.06
☐ 7 Terry Pendleton	.75	.35	.09
☐ 8 Will Clark	1.00	.45	13
☐ 9 Cal Ripken	1.50	.65	.19
☐ 10 Chris Sabo	.40	.18	.05
☐ 11 Jim Abbott	.60	.25	.08
☐ 12 Joe Carter	.75	.35	.09
☐ 13 Paul Molitor	.60	.25	.08
☐ 14 Ken Griffey Jr.	2.00	.90	.25
☐ 15 Randy Johnson	.50	.23	.06
☐ 16 Bobby Bonilla	.60	.25	.08
☐ 17 John Smiley	.50	.23	.06
☐ 18 Jose Canseco	1.00	.45	.13
☐ 19 Tom Glavine	.90	.40	.11
☐ 20 Darryl Strawberry	.75	.35	.09
☐ 21 Brett Butler	.50	.23	.06
☐ 22 Devon White	.50	.23	.06
☐ 23 Scott Erickson	.60	.25	.08
☐ 24 Willie McGee	.40	.18	.05

1948 Swell Sport Thrills

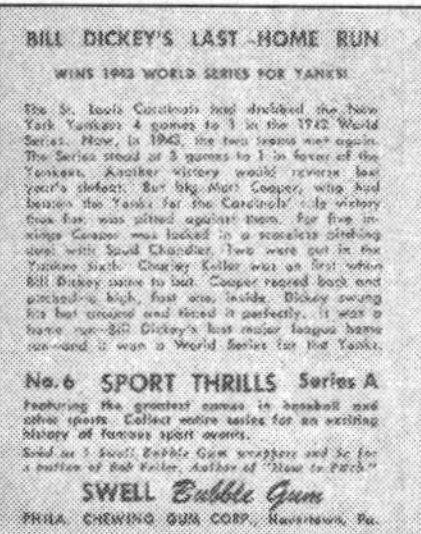

The cards in this 20-card set measure approximately 2 7/16" by 3". The 1948 Swell Gum Sports Thrills set of black and white, numbered cards highlights events from baseball history. The cards have picture framed borders with the title "Sports Thrills Highlights in the World of Sport" on the front. The backs of the cards give the story of the event pictured on the front. Cards numbered 9, 11, 16, and 20 are more difficult to obtain than the other cards in this set. The catalog designation is R448.

	NRMT	VG-E	GOOD
COMPLETE SET (20)	1000.00	450.00	125.00
COMMON PLAYER (1-20)	20.00	9.00	2.50
☐ 1 Greatest Single Inning: Athletics' 10 Run Rally	20.00	9.00	2.50
☐ 2 Amazing Record: Reiser's Debut	20.00	9.00	2.50

With Dodgers			
☐ 3 Dramatic Debut: Jackie Robinson ROY	150.00	70.00	19.00
☐ 4 Greatest Pitcher of Them All: W.Johnson	60.00	27.00	7.50
☐ 5 Three Strikes Not Out: Lost Third Strike Changes Tide of 1941 World Series	20.00	9.00	2.50
☐ 6 Home Run Wins Series: Bill Dickey's Last Home Run	30.00	13.50	3.80
☐ 7 Never Say Die Pitcher: Schumacher Pitching	20.00	9.00	2.50
☐ 8 Five Strikeouts: Nationals Lose All Star Game (Hubbell)	30.00	13.50	3.80
☐ 9 Greatest Catch: Al Gionfriddo's Catch	30.00	13.50	3.80
☐ 10 No Hits No Runs: VanderMeer Comes Back	30.00	13.50	3.80
☐ 11 Bases Loaded: Alexander The Great	45.00	20.00	5.75
☐ 12 Most Dramatic Homer: Babe Ruth Points	175.00	80.00	22.00
☐ 13 Winning Run: Bridges' Pitching and Goslin's Single Wins 1935 World Series	20.00	9.00	2.50
☐ 14 Great Slugging: Lou Gehrig's Four Homers	110.00	50.00	14.00
☐ 15 Four Men To Stop Him: DiMaggio's Bat Streak	50.00	23.00	6.25
☐ 16 Three Run Homer in Ninth: Williams' Homer	165.00	75.00	21.00
☐ 17 Football Block: Lindell's Football Block Paves Way For Yank's Series Victory	20.00	9.00	2.50
☐ 18 Home Run To Fame: Reese's Grand Slam	50.00	23.00	6.25
☐ 19 Strikeout Record: Feller Whiffs Five	50.00	23.00	6.25
☐ 20 Rifle Arm: Furillo	45.00	20.00	5.75

1989 Swell Baseball Greats

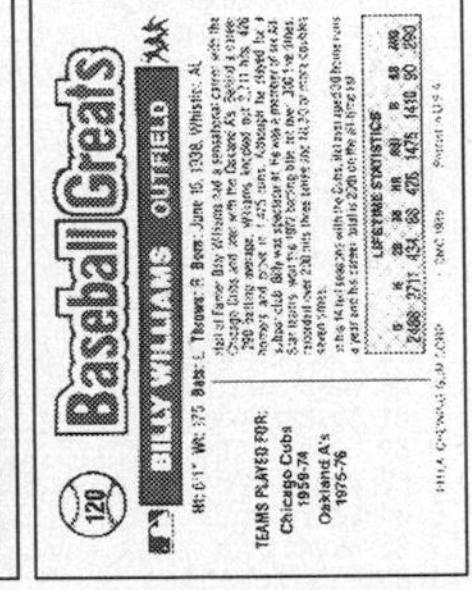

The 1989 Swell Baseball Greats set contains 135 standard-size (2 1/2" by 3 1/2") cards. The fronts have vintage color photos with beige, red and white borders. The horizontally oriented backs are white and scarlet, and feature career highlights and lifetime stats. The set was produced by Philadelphia Chewing Gum Corporation.

	MT	EX-MT	VG
COMPLETE SET (135)	10.00	4.50	1.25
COMMON PLAYER (1-135)	.05	.02	.01
☐ 1 Babe Ruth	1.25	.55	.16
☐ 2 Ty Cobb	.75	.35	.09
☐ 3 Walter Johnson	.35	.16	.04
☐ 4 Honus Wagner	.35	.16	.04
☐ 5 Cy Young	.25	.11	.03
☐ 6 Joe Adcock	.05	.02	.01
☐ 7 Jim Bunning	.10	.05	.01
☐ 8 Orlando Cepeda	.10	.05	.01
☐ 9 Harvey Kuenn	.05	.02	.01
☐ 10 Jim Hunter	.20	.09	.03
☐ 11 Johnny VanderMeer	.10	.05	.01
☐ 12 Tony Oliva	.10	.05	.01
☐ 13 Harvey Haddix UER (Reverse negative)	.10	.05	.01
☐ 14 Dick McAuliffe	.05	.02	.01
☐ 15 Lefty Grove	.20	.09	.03
☐ 16 Bo Belinsky	.05	.02	.01
☐ 17 Claude Osteen	.05	.02	.01
☐ 18 Doc Medich	.05	.02	.01
☐ 19 Del Ennis	.05	.02	.01
☐ 20 Rogers Hornsby	.25	.11	.03
☐ 21 Bob Buhl	.05	.02	.01
☐ 22 Phil Niekro	.20	.09	.03
☐ 23 Don Zimmer	.05	.02	.01
☐ 24 Greg Luzinski	.05	.02	.01
☐ 25 Lou Gehrig	.75	.35	.09
☐ 26 Ken Singleton	.10	.05	.01
☐ 27 Bob Allison	.05	.02	.01
☐ 28 Ed Kranepool	.05	.02	.01
☐ 29 Manny Sanguillen	.05	.02	.01
☐ 30 Luke Appling	.20	.09	.03
☐ 31 Ralph Terry	.05	.02	.01
☐ 32 Smoky Burgess	.05	.02	.01
☐ 33 Gil Hodges	.20	.09	.03
☐ 34 Harry Walker	.05	.02	.01
☐ 35 Edd Roush	.15	.07	.02
☐ 36 Ron Santo	.10	.05	.01
☐ 37 Jim Perry	.05	.02	.01
☐ 38 Jose Morales	.05	.02	.01
☐ 39 Stan Bahnsen	.05	.02	.01
☐ 40 Al Kaline	.35	.16	.04
☐ 41 Mel Harder	.05	.02	.01
☐ 42 Ralph Houk	.05	.02	.01
☐ 43 Jack Billingham	.05	.02	.01
☐ 44 Carl Erskine	.10	.05	.01
☐ 45 Hoyt Wilhelm	.20	.09	.03
☐ 46 Dick Radatz	.05	.02	.01
☐ 47 Roy Sievers	.05	.02	.01
☐ 48 Jim Lonborg	.05	.02	.01
☐ 49 Bobby Richardson	.10	.05	.01
☐ 50 Whitey Ford	.30	.14	.04
☐ 51 Roy Face	.10	.05	.01
☐ 52 Tom Tresh	.05	.02	.01
☐ 53 Joe Nuxhall	.05	.02	.01
☐ 54 Mickey Vernon	.05	.02	.01
☐ 55 Johnny Mize	.20	.09	.03
☐ 56 Scott McGregor	.05	.02	.01
☐ 57 Billy Pierce	.10	.05	.01
☐ 58 Dave Giusti	.05	.02	.01
☐ 59 Minnie Minoso	.10	.05	.01
☐ 60 Early Wynn	.15	.07	.02
☐ 61 Jose Cardenal	.05	.02	.01
☐ 62 Sam Jethroe	.05	.02	.01
☐ 63 Sal Bando	.05	.02	.01
☐ 64 Elrod Hendricks	.05	.02	.01
☐ 65 Enos Slaughter	.20	.09	.03
☐ 66 Jim Bouton	.05	.02	.01
☐ 67 Bill Mazeroski	.10	.05	.01
☐ 68 Tony Kubek	.10	.05	.01
☐ 69 Joe Black	.05	.02	.01
☐ 70 Harmon Killebrew	.25	.11	.03
☐ 71 Sam McDowell	.05	.02	.01
☐ 72 Bucky Dent	.10	.05	.01
☐ 73 Virgil Trucks	.05	.02	.01
☐ 74 Andy Pafko	.05	.02	.01
☐ 75 Bob Feller	.35	.16	.04
☐ 76 Tito Francona	.05	.02	.01
☐ 77 Al Dark	.05	.02	.01
☐ 78 Larry Dierker	.05	.02	.01
☐ 79 Nellie Briles	.05	.02	.01
☐ 80 Lou Boudreau	.20	.09	.03
☐ 81 Wally Moon	.05	.02	.01
☐ 82 Hank Bauer	.05	.02	.01
☐ 83 Jim Piersall	.05	.02	.01
☐ 84 Jim Grant	.05	.02	.01
☐ 85 Richie Ashburn	.15	.07	.02
☐ 86 Bob Friend	.05	.02	.01
☐ 87 Ken Keltner	.05	.02	.01
☐ 88 Jim Kaat	.10	.05	.01
☐ 89 Dean Chance	.05	.02	.01
☐ 90 Al Lopez	.15	.07	.02
☐ 91 Dick Groat	.10	.05	.01
☐ 92 Johnny Blanchard	.05	.02	.01
☐ 93 Chuck Hinton	.05	.02	.01
☐ 94 Clete Boyer	.05	.02	.01
☐ 95 Steve Carlton	.30	.14	.04
☐ 96 Tug McGraw	.10	.05	.01
☐ 97 Mickey Lolich	.10	.05	.01
☐ 98 Earl Weaver MG	.10	.05	.01

☐ 99 Sal Maglie	.10	.05	.01
☐ 100 Ted Williams	.75	.35	.09
☐ 101 Allie Reynolds UER (Photo actually Marius Russo)	.20	.09	.03
☐ 102 Gene Woodling UER (Photo actually Irv Noren)	.20	.09	.03
☐ 103 Moe Drabowsky	.05	.02	.01
☐ 104 Mickey Stanley	.05	.02	.01
☐ 105 Jim Palmer	.30	.14	.04
☐ 106 Bill Freehan	.10	.05	.01
☐ 107 Bob Robertson	.05	.02	.01
☐ 108 Walt Dropo	.05	.02	.01
☐ 109 Jerry Koosman	.10	.05	.01
☐ 110 Bobby Doerr	.20	.09	.03
☐ 111 Phil Rizzuto	.25	.11	.03
☐ 112 Don Kessinger	.10	.05	.01
☐ 113 Milt Pappas	.10	.05	.01
☐ 114 Herb Score	.10	.05	.01
☐ 115 Larry Doby	.10	.05	.01
☐ 116 Glenn Beckert	.05	.02	.01
☐ 117 Andre Thornton	.05	.02	.01
☐ 118 Gary Matthews	.05	.02	.01
☐ 119 Bill Virdon	.10	.05	.01
☐ 120 Billy Williams	.20	.09	.03
☐ 121 Johnny Sain	.10	.05	.01
☐ 122 Don Newcombe	.10	.05	.01
☐ 123 Rico Petrocelli	.05	.02	.01
☐ 124 Dick Bosman	.05	.02	.01
☐ 125 Roberto Clemente	.50	.23	.06
☐ 126 Rocky Colavito	.15	.07	.02
☐ 127 Wilbur Wood	.05	.02	.01
☐ 128 Duke Sims	.05	.02	.01
☐ 129 Ken Holtzman	.05	.02	.01
☐ 130 Casey Stengel	.20	.09	.03
☐ 131 Bobby Shantz	.10	.05	.01
☐ 132 Del Crandall	.10	.05	.01
☐ 133 Bobby Thomson	.10	.05	.01
☐ 134 Brooks Robinson	.35	.16	.04
☐ 135 Checklist Card	.10	.05	.01

1990 Swell Baseball Greats

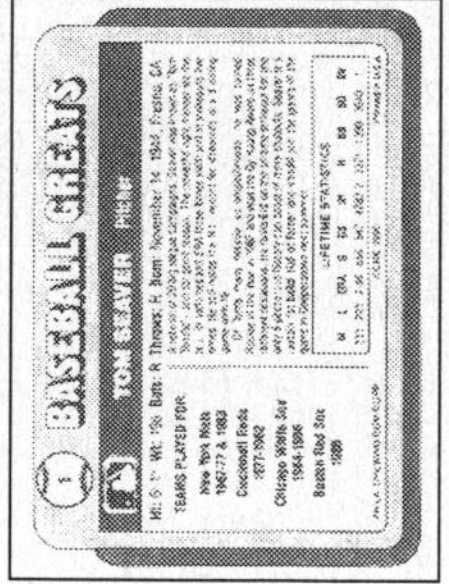

The 1990 Swell Baseball Greats set is a standard-size (2 1/2" by 3 1/2"), 135-card set. The words Baseball Greats is boldly proclaimed on the top of the card. This set was issued by Swell in both complete set form and in 10-card wax packs.

	MT	EX-MT	VG
COMPLETE SET (135)	10.00	4.50	1.25
COMMON PLAYER (1-135)	.05	.02	.01
☐ 1 Tom Seaver	.60	.25	.08
☐ 2 Hank Aaron	.60	.25	.08
☐ 3 Mickey Cochrane	.15	.07	.02
☐ 4 Rod Carew	.45	.20	.06
☐ 5 Carl Yastrzemski	.45	.20	.06
☐ 6 Dizzy Dean	.30	.14	.04
☐ 7 Sal Bando	.05	.02	.01
☐ 8 Whitey Ford	.25	.11	.03
☐ 9 Bill White	.10	.05	.01
☐ 10 Babe Ruth	1.25	.55	.16
☐ 11 Robin Roberts	.20	.09	.03
☐ 12 Warren Spahn	.25	.11	.03
☐ 13 Billy Williams	.20	.09	.03
☐ 14 Joe Garagiola	.20	.09	.03
☐ 15 Ty Cobb	.75	.35	.09
☐ 16 Boog Powell	.10	.05	.01
☐ 17 Tom Tresh	.05	.02	.01
☐ 18 Luke Appling	.20	.09	.03
☐ 19 Tommie Agee	.05	.02	.01
☐ 20 Roberto Clemente	.50	.23	.06
☐ 21 Bobby Thomson	.10	.05	.01
☐ 22 Charlie Keller	.10	.05	.01
☐ 23 George Bamberger	.05	.02	.01
☐ 24 Eddie Lopat	.10	.05	.01
☐ 25 Lou Gehrig	.75	.35	.09
☐ 26 Manny Mota	.05	.02	.01
☐ 27 Steve Stone	.05	.02	.01
☐ 28 Orlando Cepeda	.15	.07	.02
☐ 29 Al Bumbry	.05	.02	.01
☐ 30 Grover Alexander	.20	.09	.03
☐ 31 Lou Boudreau	.15	.07	.02
☐ 32 Herb Score	.10	.05	.01
☐ 33 Harry Walker	.05	.02	.01
☐ 34 Deron Johnson	.05	.02	.01
☐ 35 Edd Roush	.10	.05	.01
☐ 36 Carl Erskine	.10	.05	.01
☐ 37 Ken Forsch	.05	.02	.01
☐ 38 Sal Maglie	.10	.05	.01
☐ 39 Al Rosen	.10	.05	.01
☐ 40 Casey Stengel	.20	.09	.03
☐ 41 Cesar Cedeno	.05	.02	.01
☐ 42 Roy White	.05	.02	.01
☐ 43 Larry Doby	.10	.05	.01
☐ 44 Rod Kanehl	.05	.02	.01
☐ 45 Tris Speaker	.25	.11	.03
☐ 46 Ralph Garr	.05	.02	.01
☐ 47 Andre Thornton	.05	.02	.01
☐ 48 Frankie Crosetti	.10	.05	.01
☐ 49 Dick Groat	.10	.05	.01
☐ 50 Honus Wagner	.35	.16	.04
☐ 51 Rogers Hornsby	.25	.11	.03
☐ 52 Ken Brett	.05	.02	.01
☐ 53 Lenny Randle	.05	.02	.01
☐ 54 Enos Slaughter	.20	.09	.03
☐ 55 Mel Ott	.25	.11	.03
☐ 56 Rico Petrocelli	.05	.02	.01
☐ 57 Walt Dropo	.05	.02	.01
☐ 58 Bob Grich	.05	.02	.01
☐ 59 Billy Herman	.10	.05	.01
☐ 60 Bob Feller	.35	.16	.04
☐ 61 Davey Johnson	.10	.05	.01
☐ 62 Don Drysdale	.25	.11	.03
☐ 63 Lary Sorensen	.05	.02	.01
☐ 64 Ron Santo	.10	.05	.01
☐ 65 Eddie Mathews	.25	.11	.03
☐ 66 Gaylord Perry	.20	.09	.03
☐ 67 Lee May	.05	.02	.01
☐ 68 Johnnie LeMaster	.05	.02	.01
☐ 69 Don Kessinger	.10	.05	.01
☐ 70 Lefty Grove	.25	.11	.03
☐ 71 Lou Brock	.25	.11	.03
☐ 72 Don Cardwell	.05	.02	.01
☐ 73 Harvey Haddix	.05	.02	.01
☐ 74 Frank Torre	.05	.02	.01
☐ 75 Walter Johnson	.35	.16	.04
☐ 76 Don Newcombe	.10	.05	.01
☐ 77 Marv Throneberry	.05	.02	.01
☐ 78 Jim Northrup	.05	.02	.01
☐ 79 Fritz Peterson	.05	.02	.01
☐ 80 Ralph Kiner	.20	.09	.03
☐ 81 Mickey Lolich	.10	.05	.01
☐ 82 Donn Clendenon	.05	.02	.01
☐ 83 Pete Vuckovich	.05	.02	.01
☐ 84 Lefty Gomez	.25	.11	.03
☐ 85 Monte Irvin	.15	.07	.02
☐ 86 Rick Ferrell	.15	.07	.02
☐ 87 Tommy Hutton	.05	.02	.01
☐ 88 Julio Cruz	.05	.02	.01
☐ 89 Vida Blue	.10	.05	.01
☐ 90 Johnny Mize	.20	.09	.03
☐ 91 Rusty Staub	.10	.05	.01
☐ 92 Jimmy Piersall	.10	.05	.01
☐ 93 Bill Mazeroski	.10	.05	.01
☐ 94 Lee Lacy	.05	.02	.01
☐ 95 Ernie Banks	.35	.16	.04
☐ 96 Bobby Doerr	.20	.09	.03
☐ 97 George Foster	.10	.05	.01
☐ 98 Eric Soderholm	.05	.02	.01
☐ 99 Johnny Vander Meer	.10	.05	.01
☐ 100 Cy Young	.30	.14	.04
☐ 101 Jimmie Foxx	.35	.16	.04
☐ 102 Clete Boyer	.10	.05	.01
☐ 103 Steve Garvey	.20	.09	.03
☐ 104 Johnny Podres	.10	.05	.01
☐ 105 Yogi Berra	.40	.18	.05
☐ 106 Bill Monbouquette	.05	.02	.01
☐ 107 Milt Pappas	.05	.02	.01

☐ 108 Dave LaRoche	.05	.02	.01
☐ 109 Elliott Maddox	.05	.02	.01
☐ 110 Steve Carlton	.35	.16	.04
☐ 111 Bud Harrelson	.10	.05	.01
☐ 112 Mark Littell	.05	.02	.01
☐ 113 Frank Thomas	.05	.02	.01
☐ 114 Bill Robinson	.10	.05	.01
☐ 115 Satchel Paige	.35	.16	.04
☐ 116 John Denny	.05	.02	.01
☐ 117 Clyde King	.05	.02	.01
☐ 118 Billy Sample	.05	.02	.01
☐ 119 Rocky Colavito	.15	.07	.02
☐ 120 Bob Gibson	.35	.16	.04
☐ 121 Bert Campaneris	.05	.02	.01
☐ 122 Mark Fidrych	.10	.05	.01
☐ 123 Ed Charles	.05	.02	.01
☐ 124 Jim Lonborg	.10	.05	.01
☐ 125 Ted Williams	.75	.35	.09
☐ 126 Manny Sanguillen	.10	.05	.01
☐ 127 Matt Keough	.05	.02	.01
☐ 128 Vern Ruhle	.05	.02	.01
☐ 129 Bob Skinner	.05	.02	.01
☐ 130 Joe Torre	.15	.07	.02
☐ 131 Ralph Houk	.05	.02	.01
☐ 132 Gil Hodges	.25	.11	.03
☐ 133 Ralph Branca	.10	.05	.01
☐ 134 Christy Mathewson	.35	.16	.04
☐ 135 Checklist Card	.10	.05	.01

1991 Swell Baseball Greats

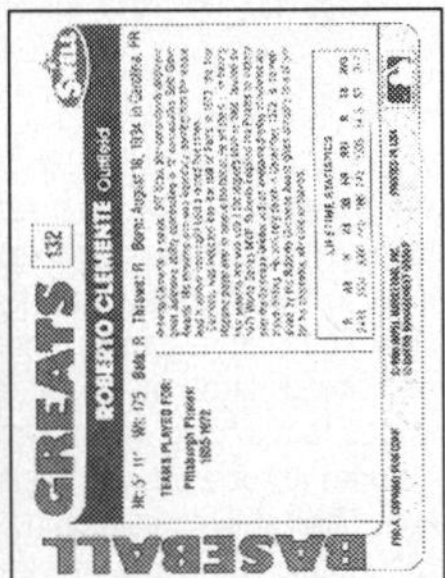

This set marks the third year Philadelphia Chewing Gum (using the Swell trade name) issued a set honoring famous and other important retired players. The front of the cards feature yellow and red borders framing the full-color photo of the player (where full color was available) The cards were issued with cooperation from Impel Marketing. This 150-card set measures the now-standard size of 2 1/2" by 3 1/2" and is sequenced in several alphabetical orders.

	MT	EX-MT	VG
COMPLETE SET (150)	10.00	4.50	1.25
COMMON PLAYER (1-150)	.05	.02	.01
☐ 1 Tommie Agee	.05	.02	.01
☐ 2 Matty Alou	.05	.02	.01
☐ 3 Luke Appling	.20	.09	.03
☐ 4 Richie Ashburn	.15	.07	.02
☐ 5 Ernie Banks	.35	.16	.04
☐ 6 Don Baylor	.10	.05	.01
☐ 7 Buddy Bell	.10	.05	.01
☐ 8 Yogi Berra	.40	.18	.05
☐ 9 Joe Black	.10	.05	.01
☐ 10 Vida Blue	.10	.05	.01
☐ 11 Bobby Bonds	.10	.05	.01
☐ 12 Lou Boudreau	.15	.07	.02
☐ 13 Lou Brock	.25	.11	.03
☐ 14 Ralph Branca	.10	.05	.01
☐ 15 Bobby Brown	.10	.05	.01
☐ 16 Lou Burdette	.10	.05	.01
☐ 17 Steve Carlton	.35	.16	.04
☐ 18 Rico Carty	.10	.05	.01
☐ 19 Jerry Coleman	.10	.05	.01
☐ 20 Frankie Crosetti	.10	.05	.01
☐ 21 Julio Cruz	.05	.02	.01
☐ 22 Alvin Dark	.05	.02	.01
☐ 23 Doug DeCinces	.05	.02	.01
☐ 24 Larry Doby	.10	.05	.01
☐ 25 Bobby Doerr	.20	.09	.03
☐ 26 Don Drysdale	.20	.09	.03
☐ 27 Carl Erskine	.10	.05	.01
☐ 28 Elroy Face	.10	.05	.01
☐ 29 Rick Ferrell	.15	.07	.02
☐ 30 Rollie Fingers	.25	.11	.03
☐ 31 Joe Garagiola	.20	.09	.03
☐ 32 Steve Garvey	.25	.11	.03
☐ 33 Bob Gibson	.30	.14	.04
☐ 34 Mudcat Grant	.05	.02	.01
☐ 35 Dick Groat	.10	.05	.01
☐ 36 Jerry Grote	.05	.02	.01
☐ 37 Toby Harrah	.05	.02	.01
☐ 38 Bud Harrelson	.05	.02	.01
☐ 39 Billy Herman	.15	.07	.02
☐ 40 Ken Holtzman	.05	.02	.01
☐ 41 Willie Horton	.05	.02	.01
☐ 42 Ralph Houk	.05	.02	.01
☐ 43 Al Hrabosky	.05	.02	.01
☐ 44 Monte Irvin	.20	.09	.03
☐ 45 Fergie Jenkins	.25	.11	.03
☐ 46 Davey Johnson	.05	.02	.01
☐ 47 George Kell	.20	.09	.03
☐ 48 Charlie Keller	.10	.05	.01
☐ 49 Harmon Killebrew	.25	.11	.03
☐ 50 Ralph Kiner	.25	.11	.03
☐ 51 Clyde King	.05	.02	.01
☐ 52 Dave Kingman	.10	.05	.01
☐ 53 Al Kaline	.35	.16	.04
☐ 54 Clem Labine	.10	.05	.01
☐ 55 Vern Law	.10	.05	.01
☐ 56 Mickey Lolich	.10	.05	.01
☐ 57 Jim Lonborg	.10	.05	.01
☐ 58 Eddie Lopat	.10	.05	.01
☐ 59 Sal Maglie	.10	.05	.01
☐ 60 Bill Mazeroski	.10	.05	.01
☐ 61 Johnny VanderMeer	.10	.05	.01
☐ 62 Johnny Mize	.20	.09	.03
☐ 63 Manny Mota	.05	.02	.01
☐ 64 Wally Moon	.05	.02	.01
☐ 65 Rick Monday	.05	.02	.01
☐ 66 Tom Tresh	.10	.05	.01
☐ 67 Graig Nettles	.10	.05	.01
☐ 68 Don Newcombe	.10	.05	.01
☐ 69 Milt Pappas	.05	.02	.01
☐ 70 Gaylord Perry	.25	.11	.03
☐ 71 Rico Petrocelli	.05	.02	.01
☐ 72 Jimmy Piersall	.10	.05	.01
☐ 73 Johnny Podres	.10	.05	.01
☐ 74 Boog Powell	.10	.05	.01
☐ 75 Bobby Richardson	.10	.05	.01
☐ 76 Vern Ruhle	.05	.02	.01
☐ 77 Robin Roberts	.20	.09	.03
☐ 78 Al Rosen	.10	.05	.01
☐ 79 Billy Sample	.10	.05	.01
☐ 80 Manny Sanguillen	.10	.05	.01
☐ 81 Ron Santo	.10	.05	.01
☐ 82 Herb Score	.10	.05	.01
☐ 83 Bobby Shantz	.05	.02	.01
☐ 84 Enos Slaughter	.20	.09	.03
☐ 85 Eric Soderholm	.05	.02	.01
☐ 86 Warren Spahn	.25	.11	.03
☐ 87 Rusty Staub	.10	.05	.01
☐ 88 Bobby Thomson	.10	.05	.01
☐ 89 Marv Throneberry	.05	.02	.01
☐ 90 Luis Tiant	.10	.05	.01
☐ 91 Frank Torre	.05	.02	.01
☐ 92 Joe Torre	.15	.07	.02
☐ 93 Bill Virdon	.10	.05	.01
☐ 94 Harry Walker	.05	.02	.01
☐ 95 Earl Weaver	.10	.05	.01
☐ 96 Bill White	.10	.05	.01
☐ 97 Roy White	.05	.02	.01
☐ 98 Billy Williams	.20	.09	.03
☐ 99 Dick Williams	.05	.02	.01
☐ 100 Ted Williams	.75	.35	.09
☐ 101 Gene Woodling	.10	.05	.01
☐ 102 Hank Aaron	.60	.25	.08
☐ 103 Rod Carew	.45	.20	.06
☐ 104 Cesar Cedeno	.10	.05	.01
☐ 105 Orlando Cepeda	.15	.07	.02
☐ 106 Willie Mays	.60	.25	.08
☐ 107 Tom Seaver	.60	.25	.08
☐ 108 Carl Yastrzemski	.45	.20	.06
☐ 109 Clete Boyer	.10	.05	.01
☐ 110 Bert Campaneris	.05	.02	.01
☐ 111 Walt Dropo	.05	.02	.01
☐ 112 George Foster	.10	.05	.01
☐ 113 Phil Garner	.10	.05	.01
☐ 114 Harvey Kuenn	.10	.05	.01
☐ 115 Don Kessinger	.05	.02	.01
☐ 116 Rocky Colavito	.15	.07	.02

☐ 117 Bobby Murcer	.10	.05	.01
☐ 118 Mel Parnell	.05	.02	.01
☐ 119 Ken Reitz	.05	.02	.01
☐ 120 Earl Wilson	.05	.02	.01
☐ 121 Wilbur Wood	.05	.02	.01
☐ 122 Ed Yost	.05	.02	.01
☐ 123 Jim Bouton	.10	.05	.01
☐ 124 Babe Ruth	1.25	.55	.16
☐ 125 Lou Gehrig	.75	.35	.09
☐ 126 Honus Wagner	.35	.16	.04
☐ 127 Ty Cobb	.75	.35	.09
☐ 128 Grover C. Alexander	.25	.11	.03
☐ 129 Lefty Gomez	.25	.11	.03
☐ 130 Walter Johnson	.35	.16	.04
☐ 131 Gil Hodges	.20	.09	.03
☐ 132 Roberto Clemente	.50	.23	.06
☐ 133 Satchel Paige	.35	.16	.04
☐ 134 Edd Roush	.15	.07	.02
☐ 135 Cy Young	.30	.14	.04
☐ 136 Casey Stengel	.25	.11	.03
☐ 137 Rogers Hornsby	.25	.11	.03
☐ 138 Dizzy Dean	.35	.16	.04
☐ 139 Lefty Grove	.25	.11	.03
☐ 140 Tris Speaker	.25	.11	.03
☐ 141 Christy Mathewson	.35	.16	.04
☐ 142 Mickey Cochrane	.15	.07	.02
☐ 143 Jimmie Foxx	.35	.16	.04
☐ 144 Mel Ott	.30	.14	.04
☐ 145 Bob Feller	.35	.16	.04
☐ 146 Brooks Robinson	.25	.11	.03
☐ 147 Eddie Mathews	.25	.11	.03
☐ 148 Pie Traynor	.15	.07	.02
☐ 149 Thurman Munson	.25	.11	.03
☐ 150 Checklist Card	.10	.05	.01

1957 Swifts Franks

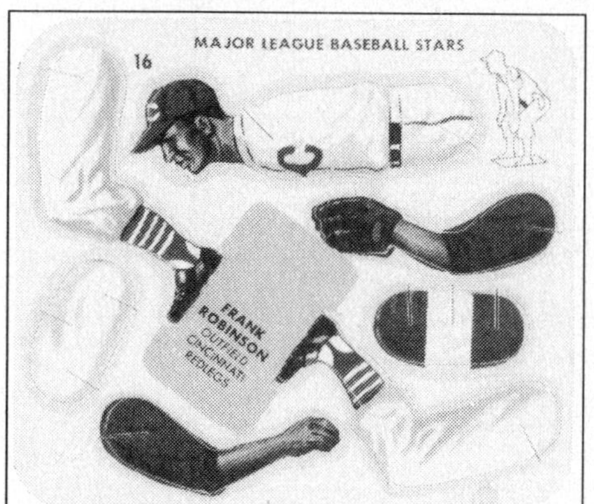

The cards in this 18-card set measure approximately 3 1/2" by 4". These full color, numbered cards issued in 1957 by the Swift Company are die-cut and have rounded corners. Each card consists of several pieces which can be punched out and assembled to form a stand-up model of the player. The cards and a game board were available directly from the company. The company-direct set consisted of three panels each containing six cards; sets found in this "uncut" state carry a value 25 percent higher than the values listed below. The catalog designation for this set is F162.

	NRMT	VG-E	GOOD
COMPLETE SET (18)	2000.00	900.00	250.00
COMMON PLAYER (1-18)	60.00	27.00	7.50
☐ 1 John Podres	70.00	32.00	8.75
☐ 2 Gus Triandos	60.00	27.00	7.50
☐ 3 Dale Long	60.00	27.00	7.50
☐ 4 Billy Pierce	70.00	32.00	8.75
☐ 5 Ed Bailey	60.00	27.00	7.50
☐ 6 Vic Wertz	60.00	27.00	7.50
☐ 7 Nelson Fox	100.00	45.00	12.50
☐ 8 Ken Boyer	90.00	40.00	11.50
☐ 9 Gil McDougald	80.00	36.00	10.00
☐ 10 Junior Gilliam	80.00	36.00	10.00
☐ 11 Eddie Yost	60.00	27.00	7.50
☐ 12 Johnny Logan	60.00	27.00	7.50
☐ 13 Hank Aaron	600.00	275.00	75.00
☐ 14 Bill Tuttle	60.00	27.00	7.50
☐ 15 Jackie Jensen	80.00	36.00	10.00
☐ 16 Frank Robinson	200.00	90.00	25.00
☐ 17 Richie Ashburn	135.00	60.00	17.00
☐ 18 Rocky Colavito	120.00	55.00	15.00

1953 Tigers Glendale

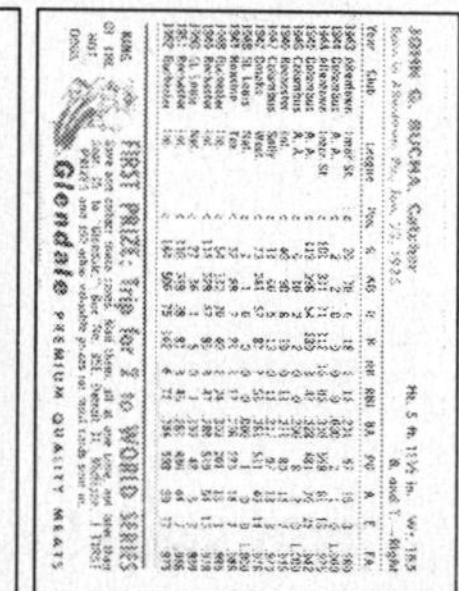

The cards in this 28-card set measure approximately 2 5/8" by 3 3/4". The 1953 Glendale Meats set of full-color, unnumbered cards features Detroit Tiger ballplayers exclusively and was distributed one per package of Glendale Meats in the Detroit area. The back contains the complete major and minor league record through the 1952 season. The scarcer cards of the set command higher prices, with the Houtteman card being the most difficult to find. There is an album associated with the set (which also is quite scarce now). The catalog designation for this scarce regional set is F151. Since the cards are unnumbered, they are ordered below alphabetically.

	NRMT	VG-E	GOOD
COMPLETE SET (28)	6500.00	2900.00	800.00
COMMON PLAYER (1-28)	150.00	70.00	19.00
☐ 1 Matt Batts	150.00	70.00	19.00
☐ 2 Johnny Bucha	150.00	70.00	19.00
☐ 3 Frank Carswell	150.00	70.00	19.00
☐ 4 Jim Delsing	150.00	70.00	19.00
☐ 5 Walt Dropo	175.00	80.00	22.00
☐ 6 Hal Erickson	150.00	70.00	19.00
☐ 7 Paul Foytack	150.00	70.00	19.00
☐ 8 Owen Friend	150.00	70.00	19.00
☐ 9 Ned Garver	150.00	70.00	19.00
☐ 10 Joe Ginsberg SP	375.00	170.00	47.50
☐ 11 Ted Gray	150.00	70.00	19.00
☐ 12 Fred Hatfield	150.00	70.00	19.00
☐ 13 Ray Herbert	150.00	70.00	19.00
☐ 14 Bill Hitchcock	150.00	70.00	19.00
☐ 15 Bill Hoeft SP	250.00	115.00	31.00
☐ 16 Art Houtteman SP	2250.00	900.00	300.00
☐ 17 Milt Jordan	150.00	70.00	19.00
☐ 18 Harvey Kuenn	500.00	230.00	65.00
☐ 19 Don Lund	150.00	70.00	19.00
☐ 20 Dave Madison	150.00	70.00	19.00
☐ 21 Dick Marlowe	150.00	70.00	19.00
☐ 22 Pat Mullin	150.00	70.00	19.00
☐ 23 Bob Nieman	150.00	70.00	19.00
☐ 24 Johnny Pesky	175.00	80.00	22.00
☐ 25 Jerry Priddy	150.00	70.00	19.00
☐ 26 Steve Souchock	150.00	70.00	19.00
☐ 27 Russ Sullivan	150.00	70.00	19.00
☐ 28 Bill Wight	150.00	70.00	19.00

1981 Tigers Detroit News

This 135-card, standard-size, 2 1/2" by 3 1/2" set was issued in 1981 to celebrate the centennial of professional baseball in Detroit. This set features black and white photos surrounded by solid red borders, while the back provides information about either the player or event featured on the front of the card. This set was issued by the Detroit newspaper, the Detroit News and covered players from the nineteenth century right up to players and other personnel active at the time of issue.

	NRMT-MT	EXC	G-VG
COMPLETE SET (135)	18.00	8.00	2.30
COMMON PLAYER (1-135)	.12	.05	.02
☐ 1 Detroit's Boys of Summer 100th Anniversary	.30	.14	.04
☐ 2 Charles W. Bennett	.12	.05	.02
☐ 3 Mickey Cochrane	.40	.18	.05
☐ 4 Harry Heilmann	.35	.16	.04
☐ 5 Walter O. Briggs OWN	.12	.05	.02
☐ 6 Mark Fidrych	.20	.09	.03
☐ 7 1887 Tigers	.15	.07	.02
☐ 8 Tiger Stadium	.12	.05	.02
☐ 9 Rudy York	.12	.05	.02
☐ 10 George Kell	.25	.11	.03
☐ 11 Steve O'Neill MG	.12	.05	.02
☐ 12 John Hiller	.15	.07	.02
☐ 13 1934 Tigers	.15	.07	.02
☐ 14 Charlie Gehringer	.35	.16	.04
☐ 15 Denny McLain	.25	.11	.03
☐ 16 Billy Rogell	.12	.05	.02
☐ 17 Ty Cobb	2.00	.90	.25
☐ 18 Sparky Anderson MG	.25	.11	.03
☐ 19 Davy Jones	.12	.05	.02
☐ 20 Kirk Gibson	.15	.07	.02
☐ 21 Pat Mullin	.12	.05	.02
☐ 22 1972 Tigers	.15	.07	.02
☐ 23 What A Night	.12	.05	.02
☐ 24 Doc Cramer	.12	.05	.02
☐ 25 Mickey Stanley	.12	.05	.02
☐ 26 John Lipon	.12	.05	.02
☐ 27 Jo Jo White	.12	.05	.02
☐ 28 Recreation Park	.12	.05	.02
☐ 29 Wild Bill Donovan	.12	.05	.02
☐ 30 Ray Oyler	.12	.05	.02
☐ 31 Earl Whitehill	.12	.05	.02
☐ 32 Billy Hoeft	.12	.05	.02
☐ 33 Johnny Groth	.12	.05	.02
☐ 34 Hughie Jennings P/MG	.30	.14	.04
☐ 35 Mayo Smith MG	.12	.05	.02
☐ 36 Bennett Park	.12	.05	.02
☐ 37 Tigers Win	.12	.05	.02
☐ 38 Donie Bush P/MG	.12	.05	.02
☐ 39 Harry Coveleski	.12	.05	.02
☐ 40 Paul Richards	.12	.05	.02
☐ 41 Jonathon Stone	.12	.05	.02
☐ 42 Bob Swift	.12	.05	.02
☐ 43 Roy Cullenbine	.12	.05	.02
☐ 44 Hoot Evers	.12	.05	.02
☐ 45 Tigers Win Series	.15	.07	.02
☐ 46 Art Houtteman	.12	.05	.02
☐ 47 Aurelio Rodriguez	.12	.05	.02
☐ 48 Fred Hutchinson P/MG	.15	.07	.02
☐ 49 Don Mossi	.15	.07	.02
☐ 50 Lou Gehrig Streak Ends in Detroit At 2130 Games	.35	.16	.04
☐ 51 Earl Wilson	.12	.05	.02
☐ 52 Jim Northrup	.12	.05	.02
☐ 53 1907 Tigers	.12	.05	.02
☐ 54 Hank Greenberg Hits Two Homers to Draw Even With Ruth	.35	.16	.04
☐ 55 Mickey Lolich	.25	.11	.03
☐ 56 Tommy Bridges	.12	.05	.02
☐ 57 Al Benton	.12	.05	.02
☐ 58 Del Baker MG	.12	.05	.02
☐ 59 Lou Whitaker	.50	.23	.06
☐ 60 Navin Field	.12	.05	.02
☐ 61 1945 Tigers	.15	.07	.02
☐ 62 Ernie Harwell ANN	.25	.11	.03
☐ 63 Tigers League Champs	.15	.07	.02
☐ 64 Bobo Newsom	.15	.07	.02
☐ 65 Don Wert	.12	.05	.02
☐ 66 Ed Summers	.12	.05	.02
☐ 67 Billy Martin MG	.35	.16	.04
☐ 68 Alan Trammell	.50	.23	.06
☐ 69 Dale Alexander	.12	.05	.02
☐ 70 Ed Brinkman	.12	.05	.02
☐ 71 Right Man in Right Place in Right Park Wins Game	.15	.07	.02
☐ 72 Bill Freehan	.25	.11	.03
☐ 73 Norm Cash	.25	.11	.03
☐ 74 George Dauss	.12	.05	.02
☐ 75 Aurelio Lopez	.12	.05	.02
☐ 76 Charlie Maxwell	.15	.07	.02
☐ 77 Ed Barrow MG	.20	.09	.03
☐ 78 Willie Horton	.15	.07	.02
☐ 79 Denny McLain Sets Record 31 Wins	.20	.09	.03
☐ 80 Dan Brouthers	.30	.14	.04
☐ 81 John E. Fetzer OWN	.12	.05	.02
☐ 82 Heinie Manush	.25	.11	.03
☐ 83 1935 Tigers	.15	.07	.02
☐ 84 Ray Boone	.15	.07	.02
☐ 85 Bob Fothergill	.12	.05	.02
☐ 86 Steve Kemp	.15	.07	.02
☐ 87 Ed Killian	.12	.05	.02
☐ 88 Floyd Giebell Is Ineligible for Series But ...	.12	.05	.02
☐ 89 Pinky Higgins	.12	.05	.02
☐ 90 Lance Parrish	.20	.09	.03
☐ 91 Eldon Auker	.12	.05	.02
☐ 92 Birdie Tebbetts	.12	.05	.02
☐ 93 Schoolboy Rowe	.15	.07	.02
☐ 94 Tiger Rally Gives Denny McLain 30	.20	.09	.03
☐ 95 1909 Tigers	.15	.07	.02
☐ 96 Harvey Kuenn	.25	.11	.03
☐ 97 Jim Bunning	.25	.11	.03
☐ 98 1940 Tigers	.15	.07	.02
☐ 99 Rocky Colavito	.30	.14	.04
☐ 100 Al Kaline Enters Hall Of Fame	.50	.23	.06
☐ 101 Billy Bruton	.12	.05	.02
☐ 102 Germany Schaefer	.12	.05	.02
☐ 103 Frank Bolling	.12	.05	.02
☐ 104 Briggs Stadium	.12	.05	.02
☐ 105 Bucky Harris P/MG	.20	.09	.03
☐ 106 Gates Brown	.15	.07	.02
☐ 107 Billy Martin Made the Difference	.25	.11	.03
☐ 108 1908 Tigers	.15	.07	.02
☐ 109 Gee Walker	.12	.05	.02
☐ 110 Pete Fox	.12	.05	.02
☐ 111 Virgil Trucks	.12	.05	.02
☐ 112 1968 Tigers	.25	.11	.03
☐ 113 Dizzy Trout	.12	.05	.02
☐ 114 Barney McCosky	.12	.05	.02
☐ 115 Lu Blue	.12	.05	.02
☐ 116 Hal Newhouser	.35	.16	.04
☐ 117 Tigers Are Home To Prepare For World's Championship Series	.12	.05	.02
☐ 118 Bobby Veach	.12	.05	.02
☐ 119 George Mullin	.12	.05	.02
☐ 120 Reggie Jackson's Super Homer Ignites A.L.	.30	.14	.04
☐ 121 Sam Crawford	.25	.11	.03
☐ 122 Hank Aguirre	.12	.05	.02
☐ 123 Vic Wertz	.15	.07	.02
☐ 124 Goose Goslin	.25	.11	.03
☐ 125 Frank Lary	.15	.07	.02
☐ 126 Joe Coleman	.12	.05	.02
☐ 127 Ed Katalinas Scout	.12	.05	.02
☐ 128 Jack Morris	.45	.20	.06
☐ 129 Tigers Picked As Winners Of Pirate	.12	.05	.02

Battle			
☐ 130 James A. Campbell GM	.15	.07	.02
☐ 131 Ted Gray	.12	.05	.02
☐ 132 Al Kaline	1.00	.45	.13
☐ 133 Hank Greenberg	.40	.18	.05
☐ 134 Dick McAuliffe	.12	.05	.02
☐ 135 Ozzie Virgil	.12	.05	.02

1983 Tigers Al Kaline Story

This 72-card set was issued in 1983 to celebrate Al Kaline's thirtieth year of association with the Detroit Tigers. The set was issued in its own orange box and most of the cards in the series have orange borders. There are some cards which have black borders and those cards are the cards in the set which feature color photos. The set is basically in chronological order and covers events crucial to Kaline's career and the backs of the cards give further details about the picture on the front. The set was produced by Homeplate Sports Cards.

	NRMT-MT	EXC	G-VG
COMPLETE SET (73)	15.00	6.75	1.90
COMMON PLAYER (1-72)	.20	.09	.03
COMMON PLAYER COLOR	.30	.14	.04
☐ 1A Autographed Title Card (Color)	5.00	2.30	.60
☐ 1B I'd play for nothing (Color)	.40	.18	.05
☐ 2 Sandlot Days	.20	.09	.03
☐ 3 Prep MVP	.20	.09	.03
☐ 4 Learning the Ropes	.20	.09	.03
☐ 5 Working for a Living	.20	.09	.03
☐ 6 Pleasing a Young Fan	.20	.09	.03
☐ 7 The Newlyweds Al and Louise Kaline	.30	.14	.04
☐ 8 Al and Pat Mullin	.20	.09	.03
☐ 9 How Al Does It, 1	.20	.09	.03
☐ 10 How Al Does It, 2	.20	.09	.03
☐ 11 Silver Bat 1955	.30	.14	.04
☐ 12 Al and George Stark	.20	.09	.03
☐ 13 Al watching Gordie Howe (Howe taking batting practice)	1.00	.45	.13
☐ 14 Kaline and Mantle	1.50	.65	.19
☐ 15 1958 Group Photo (Jim Hegan, Billy Martin, Ray Boone, Harvey Kuenn, Jim Bunning, Al Kaline)	.50	.23	.06
☐ 16 AL All-Stars Billy Martin, Al Kaline, Harvey Kuenn, Mickey Mantle, Whitey Ford (color)	1.00	.45	.13
☐ 17 Crossing the Plate	.20	.09	.03
☐ 18 1959 All-Star Game (Bill Skowron and Al Kaline)	.30	.14	.04
☐ 19 1960 Tigers Stars (Norm Cash, Rocky Colavito, Al Kaline)	.50	.23	.06
☐ 20 Kaline Slides Under Fox (Al Kaline and Nellie Fox)	.50	.23	.06
☐ 21 1961 Gold Glove	.30	.14	.04
☐ 22 1962 Tigers Al Kaline, Jim Campbell GM, Norm Cash	.40	.18	.05
☐ 23 Costly Catch	.20	.09	.03
☐ 24 Japanese Tour 1962 (Jim Bunning, Al Kaline, Norm Cash, and others)	.40	.18	.05
☐ 25 Perfect Form	.20	.09	.03
☐ 26 Receiving Awards (Ernie Harwell ANN, Al Kaline, George Kell ANN)	.50	.23	.06
☐ 27 Life Isn't Always Easy	.20	.09	.03
☐ 28 Family Game 1964 (Al, Michael, and Mark Kaline)	.20	.09	.03
☐ 29 Al and Charlie Dressen	.20	.09	.03
☐ 30 George Kell and Al	.50	.23	.06
☐ 31 Al and Hal Newhouser	.50	.23	.06
☐ 32 The Kaline Family (Michael, Louise, Al, and Mark Kaline)	.20	.09	.03
☐ 33 Receiving Gold Glove (Al Kaline, Charlie Gehringer, and Bill Freehan)	.50	.23	.06
☐ 34 Rapping a Hit, 1967 (Color)	.40	.18	.05
☐ 35 Veteran Rivals (Mickey Mantle and Al)	1.50	.65	.19
☐ 36 Al Homers vs. Boston	.20	.09	.03
☐ 37 1968 World Series Homer	.20	.09	.03
☐ 38 Premier Fielder	.20	.09	.03
☐ 39 1969 All-Time Tigers (Hank Greenberg, Hal Newhouser, Billy Rogell, Al Kaline, John Fetzer OWN, Dennis McLain, George Kell, Charlie Gehringer)	.50	.23	.06
☐ 40 Part of the Game	.20	.09	.03
☐ 41 Family Portrait (Color)	.40	.18	.05
☐ 42 Spring Training Tribute	.20	.09	.03
☐ 43 Billy Martin and Al	.50	.23	.06
☐ 44 First 100,000 Tiger (With John Fetzer OWN and Jim Campbell GM)	.30	.14	.04
☐ 45 On Deck, 1972 (Color)	.40	.18	.05
☐ 46 A Close Call	.20	.09	.03
☐ 47 On Deck in Baltimore	.20	.09	.03
☐ 48 Hit Number 3,000	.30	.14	.04
☐ 49 April 17, 1955, Three Homers	.20	.09	.03
☐ 50 All-Star Game Record	.20	.09	.03
☐ 51 1968 World Series (Al Kaline and Orlando Cepeda)	.50	.23	.06
☐ 52 1968 World Series Celebration (Al Kaline, John Hiller, Jim Northrup)	.40	.18	.05
☐ 53 Al Kaline Day (Color)	.50	.23	.06
☐ 54 3,000 Hit Day (Al Kaline, Father and Mother, Lee McPhail PRES, Jim Campbell GM)	.30	.14	.04
☐ 55 September 29, 1974, Thank You	.20	.09	.03
☐ 56 Silver Salute	.20	.09	.03
☐ 57 Al and George Kell (Color)	.50	.23	.06
☐ 58 Voices of the Tigers Al and George Kell	.40	.18	.05
☐ 59 Tiger Record Setter (Color)	.30	.14	.04
☐ 60 Al's Last All-Star Team (Color)	.30	.14	.04
☐ 61 Pat Mullin and Al	.20	.09	.03
☐ 62 Al and Mickey Lolich (Color)	.50	.23	.06
☐ 63 Hall of Fame Plaque	.20	.09	.03
☐ 64 Al and Bowie Kuhn (Color)	.40	.18	.05
☐ 65 Al and Parents (Nicholas and Naomi Kaline) (color)	.30	.14	.04
☐ 66 Kaline Family at Hall (color)	.30	.14	.04

☐ 67 The Man and the Boy (Stan Musial and Al)	.75	.35	.09
☐ 68 Two Kids (Ted Williams and Al)	.75	.35	.09
☐ 69 Master Glovemen (Al and Brooks Robinson) (color)	.60	.25	.08
☐ 70 Coach and Pupil (Al and Pat Underwood)	.20	.09	.03
☐ 71 Al at Batting Cage	.20	.09	.03
☐ 72 A Tiger Forever (Color)	.50	.23	.06

1985 Tigers Wendy's/Coke

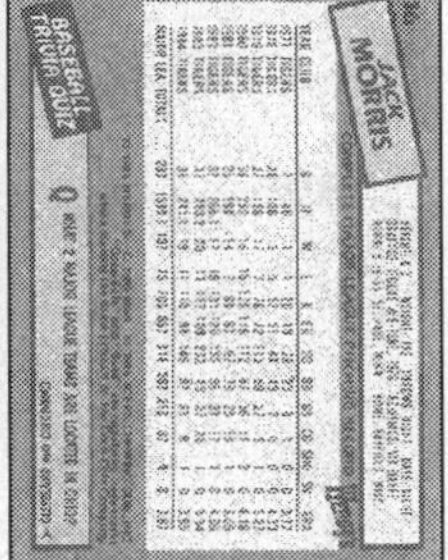

This 22-card set features Detroit Tigers; cards measure 2 1/2" by 3 1/2". The set was co-sponsored by Wendy's and Coca-Cola and was distributed in the Detroit metropolitan area. Coca-Cola purchasers were given a pack which contained three Tiger cards plus a header card. The orange-bordered player photos are different from those used by Topps in their regular set. The cards were produced by Topps as evidenced by the similarity of the card backs with the Topps regular set backs. The set is numbered on the back; the order corresponds to the alphabetical order of the player's names.

	NRMT-MT	EXC	G-VG
COMPLETE SET (22)	9.00	4.00	1.15
COMMON PLAYER (1-22)	.30	.14	.04
☐ 1 Sparky Anderson MG (Checklist back)	.60	.25	.08
☐ 2 Doug Bair	.30	.14	.04
☐ 3 Juan Berenguer	.30	.14	.04
☐ 4 Dave Bergman	.30	.14	.04
☐ 5 Tom Brookens	.30	.14	.04
☐ 6 Marty Castillo	.30	.14	.04
☐ 7 Darrell Evans	.50	.23	.06
☐ 8 Barbaro Garbey	.30	.14	.04
☐ 9 Kirk Gibson	1.00	.45	.13
☐ 10 Johnny Grubb	.30	.14	.04
☐ 11 Willie Hernandez	.40	.18	.05
☐ 12 Larry Herndon	.30	.14	.04
☐ 13 Rusty Kuntz	.30	.14	.04
☐ 14 Chet Lemon	.40	.18	.05
☐ 15 Aurelio Lopez	.30	.14	.04
☐ 16 Jack Morris	2.00	.90	.25
☐ 17 Lance Parrish	1.00	.45	.13
☐ 18 Dan Petry	.40	.18	.05
☐ 19 Bill Scherrer	.30	.14	.04
☐ 20 Alan Trammell	2.00	.90	.25
☐ 21 Lou Whitaker	2.00	.90	.25
☐ 22 Milt Wilcox	.30	.14	.04

1987 Tigers Coke

Coca-Cola, in collaboration with S. Abraham and Sons, issued a set of 18 cards featuring the Detroit Tigers. The cards are numbered on the back. The cards are

NO. 17 OF 18
Tom Brookens

distinguished by the bright yellow border framing the full-color picture of the player on the front. The cards were issued in panels of four: three player cards and a team logo card. The cards measure the standard 2 1/2" by 3 1/2" and were produced by MSA, Mike Schechter Associates.

	MT	EX-MT	VG
COMPLETE SET (18)	7.50	3.40	.95
COMMON PLAYER (1-18)	.35	.16	.04
☐ 1 Kirk Gibson	.75	.35	.09
☐ 2 Larry Herndon	.35	.16	.04
☐ 3 Walt Terrell	.35	.16	.04
☐ 4 Alan Trammell	1.25	.55	.16
☐ 5 Frank Tanana	.60	.25	.08
☐ 6 Pat Sheridan	.35	.16	.04
☐ 7 Jack Morris	1.25	.55	.16
☐ 8 Mike Heath	.35	.16	.04
☐ 9 Dave Bergman	.35	.16	.04
☐ 10 Chet Lemon	.45	.20	.06
☐ 11 Dwight Lowry	.35	.16	.04
☐ 12 Dan Petry	.35	.16	.04
☐ 13 Darrell Evans	.60	.25	.08
☐ 14 Darnell Coles	.50	.23	.06
☐ 15 Willie Hernandez	.45	.20	.06
☐ 16 Lou Whitaker	1.00	.45	.13
☐ 17 Tom Brookens	.35	.16	.04
☐ 18 John Grubb	.35	.16	.04

1988 Tigers Domino's

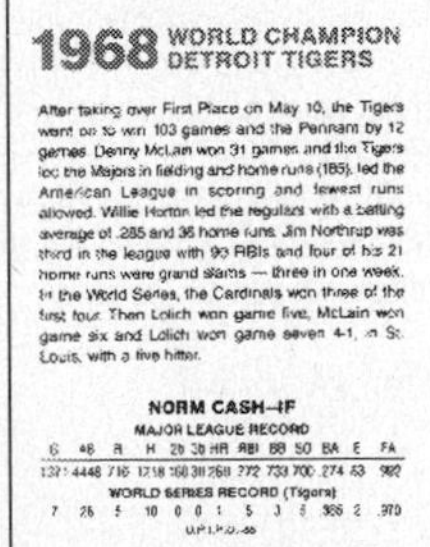
1968 WORLD CHAMPION DETROIT TIGERS

After taking over First Place on May 10, the Tigers went on to win 103 games and the Pennant by 12 games. Denny McLain won 31 games and the Tigers led the Majors in fielding and home runs (185), led the American League in scoring and fewest runs allowed. Willie Horton led the regulars with a batting average of .285 and 36 home runs. Jim Northrup was third in the league with 90 RBIs and four of his 21 home runs were grand slams — three in one week. In the World Series, the Cardinals won three of the first four. Then Lolich won game five, McLain won game six and Lolich won game seven 4-1, in St. Louis, with a five hitter.

NORM CASH—1F

This rather unattractive set commemorates the 20th anniversary of the Detroit Tigers' World Championship season in 1968. The card stock used is rather thin. The cards measure approximately 2 1/2" by 3 1/2". There are a number of errors in the set including biographical errors, misspellings, and photo misidentifications. Players are pictured in black and white inside a red and blue horseshoe. The numerous factual errors in the set detract from the set's collectibility in the eyes of many collectors. The set numbering is in alphabetical order by player's name.

	MT	EX-MT	VG
COMPLETE SET (28)	5.00	2.30	.60
COMMON PLAYER (1-28)	.15	.07	.02

		MT	EX-MT	VG
☐ 1	Gates Brown	.20	.09	.03
☐ 2	Norm Cash	.50	.23	.06
☐ 3	Wayne Comer	.15	.07	.02
☐ 4	Pat Dobson	.20	.09	.03
☐ 5	Bill Freehan	.50	.23	.06
☐ 6	Ernie Harwell ANN	.35	.16	.04
☐ 7	John Hiller	.25	.11	.03
☐ 8	Willie Horton	.25	.11	.03
☐ 9	Al Kaline	1.50	.65	.19
☐ 10	Fred Lasher	.15	.07	.02
☐ 11	Mickey Lolich	.50	.23	.06
☐ 12	Tom Matchick	.15	.07	.02
☐ 13	Ed Mathews	1.00	.45	.13
☐ 14	Dick McAuliffe	.25	.11	.03
☐ 15	Denny McLain	.50	.23	.06
☐ 16	Don McMahon	.20	.09	.03
☐ 17	Jim Northrup	.20	.09	.03
☐ 18	Ray Oyler	.15	.07	.02
☐ 19	Daryl Patterson	.15	.07	.02
☐ 20	Jim Price	.15	.07	.02
☐ 21	Joe Sparma	.15	.07	.02
☐ 22	Mickey Stanley	.25	.11	.03
☐ 23	Dick Tracewski	.15	.07	.02
☐ 24	Jon Warden	.15	.07	.02
☐ 25	Don Wert	.15	.07	.02
☐ 26	Earl Wilson	.20	.09	.03
☐ 27	Pizza Buck Coupon	.15	.07	.02
☐ 28	Title Card Old Timers Game 1988	.15	.07	.02

1988 Tigers Pepsi/Kroger

This set of 25 cards features members of the Detroit Tigers and was sponsored by Pepsi Cola and Kroger. The cards are in full color on the fronts and measure approximately 2 7/8" by 4 1/4". The card backs contain complete Major and Minor League season-by-season statistics. The cards are unnumbered so they are listed below by uniform number, which is given on the card.

		MT	EX-MT	VG
	COMPLETE SET (25)	9.00	4.00	1.15
	COMMON PLAYER	.35	.16	.04
☐ 1	Lou Whitaker	1.00	.45	.13
☐ 2	Alan Trammell	1.00	.45	.13
☐ 8	Mike Heath	.35	.16	.04
☐ 11	Sparky Anderson MG	.45	.20	.06
☐ 12	Luis Salazar	.35	.16	.04
☐ 14	Dave Bergman	.35	.16	.04
☐ 15	Pat Sheridan	.35	.16	.04
☐ 16	Tom Brookens	.35	.16	.04
☐ 19	Doyle Alexander	.45	.20	.06
☐ 21	Willie Hernandez	.45	.20	.06
☐ 22	Ray Knight	.45	.20	.06
☐ 24	Gary Pettis	.35	.16	.04
☐ 25	Eric King	.35	.16	.04
☐ 26	Frank Tanana	.45	.20	.06
☐ 31	Larry Herndon	.35	.16	.04
☐ 32	Jim Walewander	.35	.16	.04
☐ 33	Matt Nokes	.60	.25	.08
☐ 34	Chet Lemon	.45	.20	.06
☐ 35	Walt Terrell	.35	.16	.04
☐ 39	Mike Henneman	.60	.25	.08
☐ 41	Darrell Evans	.60	.25	.08
☐ 44	Jeff M. Robinson	.35	.16	.04
☐ 47	Jack Morris	1.00	.45	.13
☐ 48	Paul Gibson	.35	.16	.04
☐ NNO	Tigers Coaches Billy Consolo Alex Grammas Billy Muffett Vada Pinson Dick Tracewski	.45	.20	.06

1989 Tigers Marathon

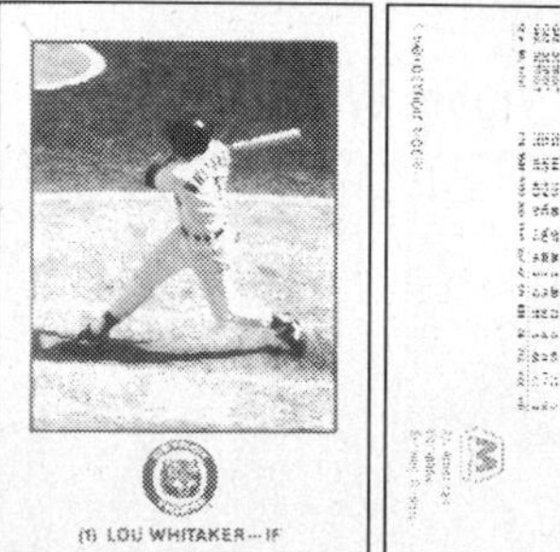

The 1989 Marathon Tigers set features 28 cards measuring approximately 2 3/4" by 4 1/2". The set features color photos surrounded by blue borders and a white background. The Tigers logo is featured prominently under the photo and then the players uniform number name and position is underneath the Tiger logo. The horizontally oriented backs show career stats. The set was given away at the July 15, 1989 Tigers home game against the Seattle Mariners. The cards are numbered by the players' uniform numbers.

		MT	EX-MT	VG
	COMPLETE SET (28)	8.00	3.60	1.00
	COMMON PLAYER	.25	.11	.03
☐ 1	Lou Whitaker	.90	.40	.11
☐ 3	Alan Trammell	.90	.40	.11
☐ 8	Mike Heath	.25	.11	.03
☐ 9	Fred Lynn	.45	.20	.06
☐ 10	Keith Moreland	.25	.11	.03
☐ 11	Sparky Anderson MG	.45	.20	.06
☐ 12	Mike Brumley	.25	.11	.03
☐ 14	Dave Bergman	.25	.11	.03
☐ 15	Pat Sheridan	.25	.11	.03
☐ 17	Al Pedrique	.25	.11	.03
☐ 18	Ramon Pena	.25	.11	.03
☐ 19	Doyle Alexander	.35	.16	.04
☐ 21	Willie Hernandez	.35	.16	.04
☐ 23	Torey Lovullo	.25	.11	.03
☐ 24	Gary Pettis	.25	.11	.03
☐ 25	Ken Williams	.25	.11	.03
☐ 26	Frank Tanana	.45	.20	.06
☐ 27	Charles Hudson	.25	.11	.03
☐ 32	Gary Ward	.25	.11	.03
☐ 33	Matt Nokes	.45	.20	.06
☐ 34	Chet Lemon	.35	.16	.04
☐ 35	Rick Schu	.25	.11	.03
☐ 36	Frank Williams	.25	.11	.03
☐ 39	Mike Henneman	.45	.20	.06
☐ 44	Jeff M. Robinson	.35	.16	.04
☐ 47	Jack Morris	1.00	.45	.13
☐ 48	Paul Gibson	.25	.11	.03
☐ xx	Tiger Coaches Billy Consolo Alex Grammas Billy Muffett Vada Pinson Dick Tracewski	.35	.16	.04

1990 Tigers Coke/Kroger

The 1990 Coke/Kroger Detroit Tigers set contains 28 cards, measuring approximately 2 7/8" by 4 1/4", which was used

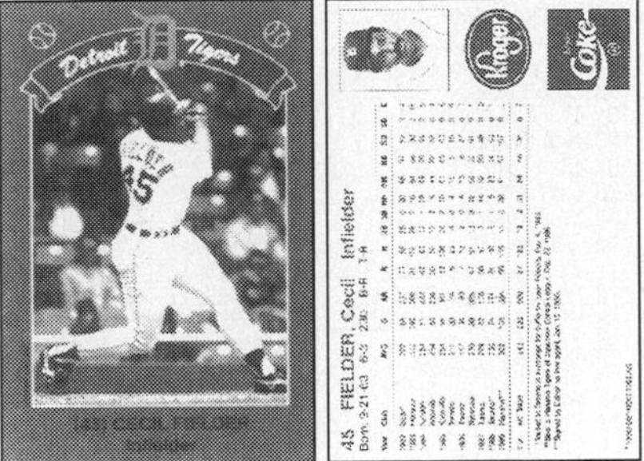

as a giveaway at the July 14th Detroit Tigers home game. The player photo is surrounded by green borders with complete career statistical information printed on the back of each card. This set is checklisted alphabetically in the listings below.

	MT	EX-MT	VG
COMPLETE SET (28)	7.50	3.40	.95
COMMON PLAYER (1-28)	.25	.11	.03
☐ 1 Sparky Anderson MG	.45	.20	.06
☐ 2 Dave Bergman	.25	.11	.03
☐ 3 Brian DuBois	.35	.16	.04
☐ 4 Cecil Fielder	1.25	.55	.16
☐ 5 Paul Gibson	.25	.11	.03
☐ 6 Jerry Don Gleaton	.25	.11	.03
☐ 7 Mike Heath	.25	.11	.03
☐ 8 Mike Henneman	.45	.20	.06
☐ 9 Tracy Jones	.25	.11	.03
☐ 10 Chet Lemon	.35	.16	.04
☐ 11 Urbano Lugo	.25	.11	.03
☐ 12 Jack Morris	1.00	.45	.13
☐ 13 Lloyd Moseby	.35	.16	.04
☐ 14 Matt Nokes	.45	.20	.06
☐ 15 Edwin Nunez	.25	.11	.03
☐ 16 Dan Petry	.35	.16	.04
☐ 17 Tony Phillips	.45	.20	.06
☐ 18 Kevin Ritz	.35	.16	.04
☐ 19 Jeff M. Robinson	.25	.11	.03
☐ 20 Ed Romero	.25	.11	.03
☐ 21 Mark Salas	.25	.11	.03
☐ 22 Larry Sheets	.25	.11	.03
☐ 23 Frank Tanana	.45	.20	.06
☐ 24 Alan Trammell	1.00	.45	.13
☐ 25 Gary Ward	.25	.11	.03
☐ 26 Lou Whitaker	1.00	.45	.13
☐ 27 Ken Williams	.25	.11	.03
☐ 28 Tigers Coaches Billy Consolo Alex Grammas Billy Muffet UER (Sic, Muffett) Vada Pinson Dick Tracewski	.35	.16	.04

1991 Tigers Coke/Kroger

The 1991 Coke/Kroger Tigers set contains 27 cards measuring approximately 2 7/8" by 4 1/4". The fronts feature a mix of action or posed color player photos with white borders. The player's name is written vertically in a purple stripe on the right side of the picture, and the player's number appears in an inverted orange triangle toward the bottom of the stripe. In a horizontal format the back has the sponsors' logos and presents complete statistical information. The set is skip-numbered by uniform number and checklisted below accordingly.

	MT	EX-MT	VG
COMPLETE SET (27)	7.00	3.10	.85
COMMON PLAYER	.25	.11	.03
☐ 1 Lou Whitaker	1.00	.45	.13
☐ 3 Alan Trammell	1.00	.45	.13
☐ 4 Tony Phillips	.60	.25	.08
☐ 10 Andy Allanson	.25	.11	.03
☐ 11 Sparky Anderson MG	.45	.20	.06
☐ 14 Dave Bergman	.25	.11	.03
☐ 15 Lloyd Moseby	.35	.16	.04
☐ 19 Jerry Don Gleaton	.25	.11	.03
☐ 20 Mickey Tettleton	.60	.25	.08
☐ 22 Milt Cuyler	.50	.23	.06
☐ 23 Mark Leiter	.25	.11	.03
☐ 24 Travis Fryman	1.50	.65	.19
☐ 25 John Shelby	.25	.11	.03
☐ 26 Frank Tanana	.45	.20	.06
☐ 27 Mark Salas	.25	.11	.03
☐ 29 Pete Incaviglia	.45	.20	.06
☐ 31 Kevin Ritz	.25	.11	.03
☐ 35 Walt Terrell	.25	.11	.03
☐ 36 Bill Gullickson	.45	.20	.06
☐ 39 Mike Henneman	.45	.20	.06
☐ 44 Rob Deer	.45	.20	.06
☐ 45 Cecil Fielder	1.00	.45	.13
☐ 46 Dan Petry	.35	.16	.04
☐ 48 Paul Gibson	.25	.11	.03
☐ 49 Steve Searcy	.25	.11	.03
☐ 55 John Cerutti	.25	.11	.03
☐ NNO Coaches Card Billy Consolo Jim Davenport Alex Grammas Billy Muffett Vada Pinson Dick Tracewski	.35	.16	.04

1947 Tip Top

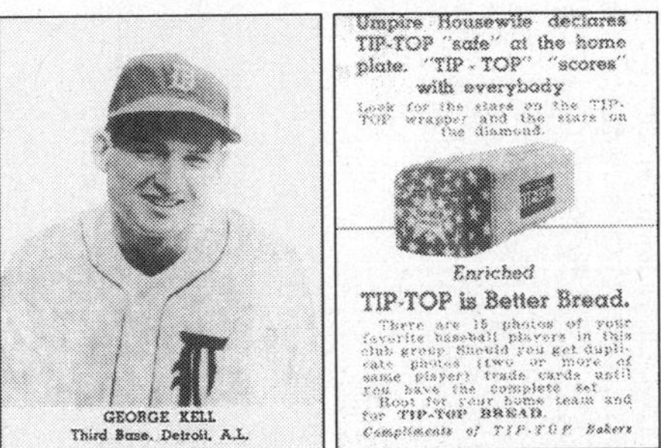

The cards in this 163-card set measure approximately 2 1/4" by 3". The 1947 Tip Top Bread issue contains unnumbered cards with black and white player photos. The set is of interest to baseball historians in that it contains cards of many players not appearing in any other card sets. The cards were issued locally for the eleven following teams: Red Sox (1-15), White Sox (16-30), Tigers (31-45), Yankees (46-60), Browns (61-75), Braves (76-90), Dodgers (91-104), Cubs (105-119), Giants (120-135), Pirates (136-149), and Cardinals (150-164). Players of the Red Sox, Tigers, White Sox, Braves, and the Cubs are scarcer than those of the other teams; players from these tougher teams are marked by SP below to indicate their scarcity. The catalog designation is D323. These unnumbered cards are listed in alphabetical order within teams for convenience.

	NRMT	VG-E	GOOD
COMPLETE SET (163)	10500.	4700.	1300.
COMMON PLAYER (1-164)	25.00	11.50	3.10
COMMON SP PLAYER	85.00	38.00	10.50
☐ 1 Leon Culberson SP	85.00	38.00	10.50
☐ 2 Dom DiMaggio SP	150.00	70.00	19.00
☐ 3 Joe Dobson SP	85.00	38.00	10.50
☐ 4 Bob Doerr SP	250.00	115.00	31.00
☐ 5 Dave(Boo) Ferris SP	85.00	38.00	10.50
☐ 6 Mickey Harris SP	85.00	38.00	10.50
☐ 7 Frank Hayes SP	85.00	38.00	10.50
☐ 8 Cecil Hughson SP	85.00	38.00	10.50
☐ 9 Earl Johnson SP	85.00	38.00	10.50

☐	10	Roy Partee SP	85.00	38.00	10.50
☐	11	Johnny Pesky SP	100.00	45.00	12.50
☐	12	Rip Russell SP	85.00	38.00	10.50
☐	13	Hal Wagner SP	85.00	38.00	10.50
☐	14	Rudy York SP	110.00	50.00	14.00
☐	15	Bill Zuber SP	85.00	38.00	10.50
☐	16	Floyd Baker SP	85.00	38.00	10.50
☐	17	Earl Caldwell SP	85.00	38.00	10.50
☐	18	Lloyd Christopher SP	85.00	38.00	10.50
☐	19	George Dickey SP	85.00	38.00	10.50
☐	20	Ralph Hodgin SP	85.00	38.00	10.50
☐	21	Bob Kennedy SP	85.00	38.00	10.50
☐	22	Joe Kuhel SP	85.00	38.00	10.50
☐	23	Thornton Lee SP	85.00	38.00	10.50
☐	24	Ed Lopat SP	150.00	70.00	19.00
☐	25	Cass Michaels SP	85.00	38.00	10.50
☐	26	John Rigney SP	85.00	38.00	10.50
☐	27	Mike Tresh SP	100.00	45.00	12.50
☐	28	Thurman Tucker SP	85.00	38.00	10.50
☐	29	Jack Wallasca SP	85.00	38.00	10.50
☐	30	Taft Wright SP	85.00	38.00	10.50
☐	31	Walter(Hoot)Evers SP	85.00	38.00	10.50
☐	32	John Gorsica SP	85.00	38.00	10.50
☐	33	Fred Hutchinson SP	110.00	50.00	14.00
☐	34	George Kell SP	400.00	180.00	50.00
☐	35	Eddie Lake SP	85.00	38.00	10.50
☐	36	Ed Mayo SP	85.00	38.00	10.50
☐	37	Arthur Mills SP	85.00	38.00	10.50
☐	38	Pat Mullin SP	85.00	38.00	10.50
☐	39	James Outlaw SP	85.00	38.00	10.50
☐	40	Frank Overmire SP	85.00	38.00	10.50
☐	41	Bob Swift SP	85.00	38.00	10.50
☐	42	Birdie Tebbetts SP	85.00	38.00	10.50
☐	43	Paul(Diz) Trout SP	100.00	45.00	12.50
☐	44	Virgil Trucks SP	100.00	45.00	12.50
☐	45	Dick Wakefield SP	85.00	38.00	10.50
☐	46	Yogi Berra (Listed as Larry on card)	400.00	180.00	50.00
☐	47	Floyd(Bill) Bevans	25.00	11.50	3.10
☐	48	Bobby Brown	45.00	20.00	5.75
☐	49	Thomas Byrne	25.00	11.50	3.10
☐	50	Frank Crosetti	40.00	18.00	5.00
☐	51	Tom Henrich	40.00	18.00	5.00
☐	52	Charlie Keller	35.00	16.00	4.40
☐	53	Johnny Lindell	25.00	11.50	3.10
☐	54	Joe Page	25.00	11.50	3.10
☐	55	Mel Queen	25.00	11.50	3.10
☐	56	Allie Reynolds	45.00	20.00	5.75
☐	57	Phil Rizzuto	135.00	60.00	17.00
☐	58	Aaron Robinson	25.00	11.50	3.10
☐	59	George Stirnweiss	25.00	11.50	3.10
☐	60	Charles Wensloff	25.00	11.50	3.10
☐	61	John Berardino	30.00	13.50	3.80
☐	62	Clifford Fannin	25.00	11.50	3.10
☐	63	Dennis Galehouse	25.00	11.50	3.10
☐	64	Jeff Heath	25.00	11.50	3.10
☐	65	Walter Judnich	25.00	11.50	3.10
☐	66	Jack Kramer	25.00	11.50	3.10
☐	67	Paul Lehner	25.00	11.50	3.10
☐	68	Lester Moss	25.00	11.50	3.10
☐	69	Bob Muncrief	25.00	11.50	3.10
☐	70	Nelson Potter	25.00	11.50	3.10
☐	71	Fred Sanford	25.00	11.50	3.10
☐	72	Joe Schultz	25.00	11.50	3.10
☐	73	Vern Stephens	35.00	16.00	4.40
☐	74	Jerry Witte	25.00	11.50	3.10
☐	75	Al Zarilla	25.00	11.50	3.10
☐	76	Charles Barrett SP	85.00	38.00	10.50
☐	77	Hank Camelli SP	85.00	38.00	10.50
☐	78	Dick Culler SP	85.00	38.00	10.50
☐	79	Nanny Fernandez SP	85.00	38.00	10.50
☐	80	Si Johnson SP	85.00	38.00	10.50
☐	81	Danny Litwhiler SP	85.00	38.00	10.50
☐	82	Phil Masi SP	85.00	38.00	10.50
☐	83	Carvel Rowell SP	85.00	38.00	10.50
☐	84	Connie Ryan SP	85.00	38.00	10.50
☐	85	John Sain SP	150.00	70.00	19.00
☐	86	Ray Sanders SP	85.00	38.00	10.50
☐	87	Sibby Sisti SP	85.00	38.00	10.50
☐	88	Billy Southworth SP	85.00	38.00	10.50
☐	89	Warren Spahn SP	500.00	230.00	65.00
☐	90	Ed Wright SP	85.00	38.00	10.50
☐	91	Bob Bragan	30.00	13.50	3.80
☐	92	Ralph Branca	35.00	16.00	4.40
☐	93	Hugh Casey	25.00	11.50	3.10
☐	94	Bruce Edwards	25.00	11.50	3.10
☐	95	Hal Gregg	25.00	11.50	3.10
☐	96	Joe Hatten	25.00	11.50	3.10
☐	97	Gene Hermanski	25.00	11.50	3.10
☐	98	John Jorgensen	25.00	11.50	3.10
☐	99	Harry Lavagetto	25.00	11.50	3.10
☐	100	Vic Lombardi	25.00	11.50	3.10
☐	101	Frank Melton	25.00	11.50	3.10
☐	102	Ed Miksis	25.00	11.50	3.10
☐	103	Marv Rackley	25.00	11.50	3.10
☐	104	Ed Stevens	25.00	11.50	3.10
☐	105	Phil Cavarretta SP	135.00	60.00	17.00
☐	106	Bob Chipman SP	85.00	38.00	10.50
☐	107	Stan Hack SP	100.00	45.00	12.50
☐	108	Don Johnson SP	85.00	38.00	10.50
☐	109	Emil Kush SP	85.00	38.00	10.50
☐	110	Bill Lee SP	100.00	45.00	12.50
☐	111	Mickey Livingston SP	85.00	38.00	10.50
☐	112	Harry Lowrey SP	85.00	38.00	10.50
☐	113	Clyde McCullough SP	85.00	38.00	10.50
☐	114	Andy Pafko SP	100.00	45.00	12.50
☐	115	Marv Rickert SP	85.00	38.00	10.50
☐	116	John Schmitz SP	85.00	38.00	10.50
☐	117	Bobby Sturgeon SP	85.00	38.00	10.50
☐	118	Ed Waitkus SP	85.00	38.00	10.50
☐	119	Henry Wyse SP	85.00	38.00	10.50
☐	120	Bill Ayers	25.00	11.50	3.10
☐	121	Robert Blattner	25.00	11.50	3.10
☐	122	Mike Budnick	25.00	11.50	3.10
☐	123	Sid Gordon	25.00	11.50	3.10
☐	124	Clint Hartung	25.00	11.50	3.10
☐	125	Monte Kennedy	25.00	11.50	3.10
☐	126	Dave Koslo	25.00	11.50	3.10
☐	127	Whitey Lockman	30.00	13.50	3.80
☐	128	Jack Lohrke	25.00	11.50	3.10
☐	129	Ernie Lombardi	80.00	36.00	10.00
☐	130	Willard Marshall	25.00	11.50	3.10
☐	131	John Mize	100.00	45.00	12.50
☐	132	Eugene Thompson (Does not exist)	.00	.00	.00
☐	133	Ken Trinkle	25.00	11.50	3.10
☐	134	Bill Voiselle	25.00	11.50	3.10
☐	135	Mickey Witek	25.00	11.50	3.10
☐	136	Eddie Basinski	25.00	11.50	3.10
☐	137	Ernie Bonham	25.00	11.50	3.10
☐	138	Billy Cox	30.00	13.50	3.80
☐	139	Elbie Fletcher	25.00	11.50	3.10
☐	140	Frank Gustine	25.00	11.50	3.10
☐	141	Kirby Higbe	25.00	11.50	3.10
☐	142	Leroy Jarvis	25.00	11.50	3.10
☐	143	Ralph Kiner	100.00	45.00	12.50
☐	144	Fred Ostermueller	25.00	11.50	3.10
☐	145	Preacher Roe	45.00	20.00	5.75
☐	146	Jim Russell	25.00	11.50	3.10
☐	147	Rip Sewell	25.00	11.50	3.10
☐	148	Nick Strincevich	25.00	11.50	3.10
☐	149	Honus Wagner CO	125.00	57.50	15.50
☐	150	Alpha Brazle	25.00	11.50	3.10
☐	151	Ken Burkhart	25.00	11.50	3.10
☐	152	Bernard Creger	25.00	11.50	3.10
☐	153	Joffre Cross	25.00	11.50	3.10
☐	154	Charles E. Diering	25.00	11.50	3.10
☐	155	Ervin Dusak	25.00	11.50	3.10
☐	156	Joe Garagiola	100.00	45.00	12.50
☐	157	Tony Kaufmann	25.00	11.50	3.10
☐	158	George Kurowski	25.00	11.50	3.10
☐	159	Marty Marion	50.00	23.00	6.25
☐	160	George Munger	25.00	11.50	3.10
☐	161	Del Rice	25.00	11.50	3.10
☐	162	Dick Sisler	30.00	13.50	3.80
☐	163	Enos Slaughter	100.00	45.00	12.50
☐	164	Ted Wilks	25.00	11.50	3.10

1988 T/M Umpires

This set of 64 cards was distributed as a small boxed set featuring Major League umpires exclusively. The box itself is blank, white, and silver. The set was produced by T and M Sports under licenses from Major League Baseball and the Major League Umpires Association. The cards are in color and are standard size, 2 1/2" by 3 1/2". Card backs are printed in black on light blue. All the cards are black bordered, but the American Leaguers have a red thin inner border, whereas the National Leaguers have a green thin inner border. A short biographical sketch is given on the back for each umpire. The cards are numbered on the back; the number on the front of each card refers to the umpire's uniform number.

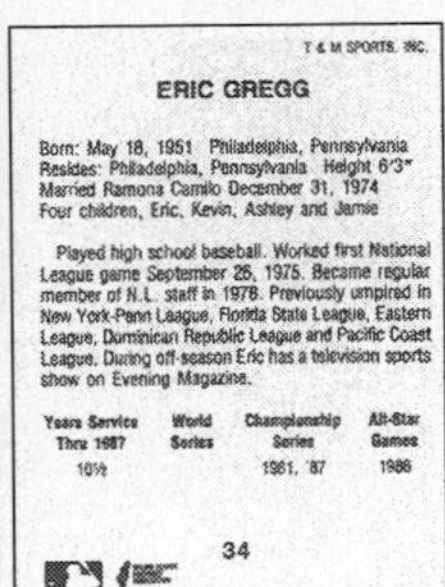

	MT	EX-MT	VG
COMPLETE SET (64)	10.00	4.50	1.25
COMMON PLAYER (1-64)	.25	.11	.03
☐ 1 Doug Harvey	.50	.23	.06
☐ 2 Lee Weyer	.25	.11	.03
☐ 3 Billy Williams	.25	.11	.03
☐ 4 John Kibler	.25	.11	.03
☐ 5 Bob Engel	.50	.23	.06
☐ 6 Harry Wendelstedt	.35	.16	.04
☐ 7 Larry Barnett	.25	.11	.03
☐ 8 Don Denkinger	.35	.16	.04
☐ 9 Dave Phillips	.35	.16	.04
☐ 10 Larry McCoy	.25	.11	.03
☐ 11 Bruce Froemming	.35	.16	.04
☐ 12 John McSherry	.35	.16	.04
☐ 13 Jim Evans	.25	.11	.03
☐ 14 Frank Pulli	.25	.11	.03
☐ 15 Joe Brinkman	.25	.11	.03
☐ 16 Terry Tata	.25	.11	.03
☐ 17 Paul Runge	.25	.11	.03
☐ 18 Dutch Rennert	.25	.11	.03
☐ 19 Nick Bremigan	.25	.11	.03
☐ 20 Jim McKean	.25	.11	.03
☐ 21 Terry Cooney	.25	.11	.03
☐ 22 Rich Garcia	.35	.16	.04
☐ 23 Dale Ford	.25	.11	.03
☐ 24 Al Clark	.25	.11	.03
☐ 25 Greg Kose	.25	.11	.03
☐ 26 Jim Quick	.25	.11	.03
☐ 27 Ed Montague	.25	.11	.03
☐ 28 Jerry Crawford	.25	.11	.03
☐ 29 Steve Palermo	.75	.35	.09
☐ 30 Durwood Merrill	.25	.11	.03
☐ 31 Ken Kaiser	.35	.16	.04
☐ 32 Vic Voltaggio	.25	.11	.03
☐ 33 Mike Reilly	.25	.11	.03
☐ 34 Eric Gregg	.45	.20	.06
☐ 35 Ted Hendry	.25	.11	.03
☐ 36 Joe West	.25	.11	.03
☐ 37 Dave Pallone	.35	.16	.04
☐ 38 Fred Brocklander	.25	.11	.03
☐ 39 John Shulock	.25	.11	.03
☐ 40 Derryl Cousins	.25	.11	.03
☐ 41 Charlie Williams	.25	.11	.03
☐ 42 Rocky Roe	.25	.11	.03
☐ 43 Randy Marsh	.25	.11	.03
☐ 44 Bob Davidson	.25	.11	.03
☐ 45 Drew Coble	.25	.11	.03
☐ 46 Tim McClelland	.25	.11	.03
☐ 47 Dan Morrison	.25	.11	.03
☐ 48 Rick Reed	.25	.11	.03
☐ 49 Steve Rippley	.25	.11	.03
☐ 50 John Hirshbeck	.50	.23	.06
☐ 51 Mark Johnson	.25	.11	.03
☐ 52 Gerry Davis	.25	.11	.03
☐ 53 Dana DeMuth	.25	.11	.03
☐ 54 Larry Young	.25	.11	.03
☐ 55 Tim Welke	.25	.11	.03
☐ 56 Greg Bonin	.25	.11	.03
☐ 57 Tom Hallion	.25	.11	.03
☐ 58 Dale Scott	.25	.11	.03
☐ 59 Tim Tschida	.25	.11	.03
☐ 60 Dick Stello MEM	.25	.11	.03
☐ 61 All-Star Game	.25	.11	.03
☐ 62 World Series	.25	.11	.03
☐ 63 Jocko Conlan HOF	.60	.25	.08
☐ 64 Checklist Card	.35	.16	.04

1989 T/M Umpires

The 1989 Umpires set contains 63 standard-size (2 1/2" by 3 1/2") cards. The fronts have borderless color photos with AL or NL logos. The backs are grey and include biographical information. The cards were distributed as a boxed set along with a custom album.

	MT	EX-MT	VG
COMPLETE SET (63)	9.00	4.00	1.15
COMMON PLAYER (1-63)	.25	.11	.03
☐ 1 Doug Harvey	.50	.23	.06
☐ 2 John Kibler	.25	.11	.03
☐ 3 Bob Engel	.50	.23	.06
☐ 4 Harry Wendelstedt	.35	.16	.04
☐ 5 Larry Barnett	.25	.11	.03
☐ 6 Don Denkinger	.35	.16	.04
☐ 7 Dave Phillips	.35	.16	.04
☐ 8 Larry McCoy	.25	.11	.03
☐ 9 Bruce Froemming	.35	.16	.04
☐ 10 John McSherry	.35	.16	.04
☐ 11 Jim Evans	.25	.11	.03
☐ 12 Frank Pulli	.25	.11	.03
☐ 13 Joe Brinkman	.25	.11	.03
☐ 14 Terry Tata	.25	.11	.03
☐ 15 Nick Bremigan	.25	.11	.03
☐ 16 Jim McKean	.25	.11	.03
☐ 17 Paul Runge	.25	.11	.03
☐ 18 Dutch Rennert	.25	.11	.03
☐ 19 Terry Cooney	.25	.11	.03
☐ 20 Rich Garcia	.35	.16	.04
☐ 21 Dale Ford	.25	.11	.03
☐ 22 Al Clark	.25	.11	.03
☐ 23 Greg Kosc	.25	.11	.03
☐ 24 Jim Quick	.25	.11	.03
☐ 25 Eddie Montague	.25	.11	.03
☐ 26 Jerry Crawford	.25	.11	.03
☐ 27 Steve Palermo	.75	.35	.09
☐ 28 Durwood Merrill	.25	.11	.03
☐ 29 Ken Kaiser	.35	.16	.04
☐ 30 Vic Voltaggio	.25	.11	.03
☐ 31 Mike Reilly	.25	.11	.03
☐ 32 Eric Gregg	.45	.20	.06
☐ 33 Ted Hendry	.25	.11	.03
☐ 34 Joe West	.25	.11	.03
☐ 35 Dave Pallone	.35	.16	.04
☐ 36 Fred Brocklander	.25	.11	.03
☐ 37 John Shulock	.25	.11	.03
☐ 38 Derryl Cousins	.25	.11	.03
☐ 39 Charlie Williams	.25	.11	.03
☐ 40 Rocky Roe	.25	.11	.03
☐ 41 Randy Marsh	.25	.11	.03
☐ 42 Bob Davidson	.25	.11	.03
☐ 43 Drew Coble	.25	.11	.03
☐ 44 Tim McClelland	.25	.11	.03
☐ 45 Dan Morrison	.25	.11	.03
☐ 46 Rick Reed	.25	.11	.03
☐ 47 Steve Rippley	.25	.11	.03
☐ 48 John Hirschbeck	.50	.23	.06
☐ 49 Mark Johnson	.25	.11	.03
☐ 50 Gerry Davis	.25	.11	.03
☐ 51 Dana DeMuth	.25	.11	.03
☐ 52 Larry Young	.25	.11	.03
☐ 53 Tim Welke	.25	.11	.03
☐ 54 Greg Bonin	.25	.11	.03
☐ 55 Tom Hallion	.25	.11	.03
☐ 56 Dale Scott	.25	.11	.03
☐ 57 Tim Tschida	.25	.11	.03
☐ 58 Gary Darling	.25	.11	.03
☐ 59 Mark Hirschbeck	.50	.23	.06

		MT	EX-MT	VG
☐ 60	All Star Randy Marsh Terry Tata Frank Pulli Dan Morrison Dale Ford Larry Barnett	.25	.11	.03
☐ 61	World Series	.25	.11	.03
☐ 62	Lee Weyer	.25	.11	.03
☐ 63	Connolly/Klem	.50	.23	.06

1989-90 T/M Senior League

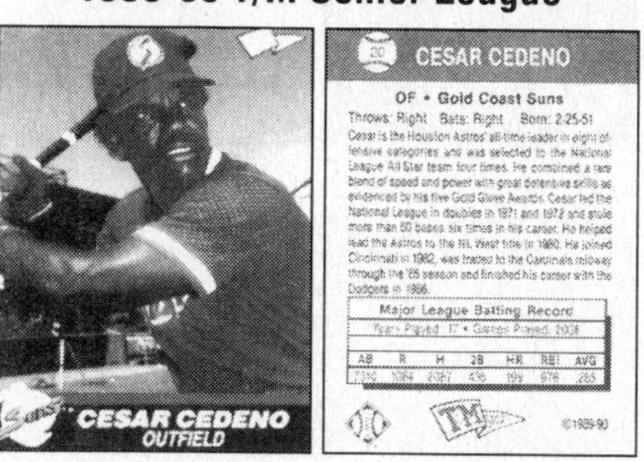

The 1989-90 T/M Senior League set contains 120 standard-size (2 1/2" by 3 1/2") cards depicting members of the new Senior League. The fronts are borderless, with full color photos and black bands at the bottom with player names and positions. The vertically oriented backs are gray and red, and show career major league totals and highlights. The cards were distributed as a boxed set with a checklist card and eight card-sized puzzle pieces. The set ordering is essentially alphabetical according to the player's name.

		MT	EX-MT	VG
COMPLETE SET (121)		9.00	4.00	1.15
COMMON PLAYER (1-120)		.10	.05	.01
☐ 1	Curt Flood COMM	.30	.14	.04
☐ 2	Willie Aikens	.20	.09	.03
☐ 3	Gary Allenson	.10	.05	.01
☐ 4	Stan Bahnsen	.10	.05	.01
☐ 5	Alan Bannister	.10	.05	.01
☐ 6	Juan Beniquez	.15	.07	.02
☐ 7	Jim Bibby	15	.07	.02
☐ 8	Paul Blair	.15	.07	.02
☐ 9	Vida Blue	.20	.09	.03
☐ 10	Bobby Bonds	.35	.16	.04
☐ 11	Pedro Borbon	.10	.05	.01
☐ 12	Clete Boyer	.20	.09	.03
☐ 13	Gates Brown	.20	.09	.03
☐ 14	Al Bumbry	.10	.05	.01
☐ 15	Sal Butera	.10	.05	.01
☐ 16	Bert Campaneris	.20	.09	.03
☐ 17	Bill Campbell	.10	.05	.01
☐ 18	Bernie Carbo	.10	.05	.01
☐ 19	Dave Cash	.10	.05	.01
☐ 20	Cesar Cedeno	.20	.09	.03
☐ 21	Gene Clines	.10	.05	.01
☐ 22	Dave Collins	.20	.09	.03
☐ 23	Cecil Cooper	.20	.09	.03
☐ 24	Doug Corbett	.10	.05	.01
☐ 25	Al Cowens	.20	.09	.03
☐ 26	Jose Cruz	.20	.09	.03
☐ 27	Mike Cuellar	.15	.07	.02
☐ 28	Pat Dobson	.15	.07	.02
☐ 29	Dick Drago	.10	.05	.01
☐ 30	Dan Driessen	.15	.07	.02
☐ 31	Jamie Easterly	.10	.05	.01
☐ 32	Juan Eichelberger	.10	.05	.01
☐ 33	Dock Ellis	.10	.05	.01
☐ 34	Ed Figueroa	.10	.05	.01
☐ 35	Rollie Fingers	1.00	.45	.13
☐ 36	George Foster	.30	.14	.04
☐ 37	Oscar Gamble	.20	.09	.03
☐ 38	Wayne Garland	.10	.05	.01
☐ 39	Wayne Garrett	.10	.05	.01
☐ 40	Ross Grimsley	.10	.05	.01
☐ 41	Jerry Grote	.15	.07	.02
☐ 42	Johnny Grubb	.10	.05	.01
☐ 43	Mario Guerrero	.10	.05	.01
☐ 44	Toby Harrah	.15	.07	.02
☐ 45	Steve Henderson	.10	.05	.01
☐ 46	George Hendrick	.15	.07	.02
☐ 47	Butch Hobson	.20	.09	.03
☐ 48	Roy Howell	.10	.05	.01
☐ 49	Al Hrabosky	.15	.07	.02
☐ 50	Clint Hurdle	.15	.07	.02
☐ 51	Garth Iorg	.10	.05	.01
☐ 52	Tim Ireland	.10	.05	.01
☐ 53	Grant Jackson	.10	.05	.01
☐ 54	Ron Jackson	.10	.05	.01
☐ 55	Ferguson Jenkins	1.00	.45	.13
☐ 56	Odell Jones	.10	.05	.01
☐ 57	Mike Kekich	.10	.05	.01
☐ 58	Steve Kemp	.15	.07	.02
☐ 59	Dave Kingman	.30	.14	.04
☐ 60	Bruce Kison	.10	.05	.01
☐ 61	Lee Lacy	.10	.05	.01
☐ 62	Rafael Landestoy	.10	.05	.01
☐ 63	Ken Landreaux	.15	.07	.02
☐ 64	Tito Landrum	.10	.05	.01
☐ 65	Dave LaRoche	.10	.05	.01
☐ 66	Bill Lee	.15	.07	.02
☐ 67	Ron LeFlore	.15	.07	.02
☐ 68	Dennis Leonard	.15	.07	.02
☐ 69	Bill Madlock	.25	.11	.03
☐ 70	Mickey Mahler	.10	.05	.01
☐ 71	Rich Manning	.10	.05	.01
☐ 72	Tippy Martinez	.10	.05	.01
☐ 73	Jon Matlack	.15	.07	.02
☐ 74	Bake McBride	.15	.07	.02
☐ 75	Steve McCatty	.10	.05	.01
☐ 76	Hal McRae	.25	.11	.03
☐ 77	Dan Meyer	.10	.05	.01
☐ 78	Felix Millan	.10	.05	.01
☐ 79	Paul Mirabella	.10	.05	.01
☐ 80	Omar Moreno	.10	.05	.01
☐ 81	Jim Morrison	.10	.05	.01
☐ 82	Graig Nettles	.30	.14	.04
☐ 83	Al Oliver	.30	.14	.04
☐ 84	Amos Otis	.20	.09	.03
☐ 85	Tom Paciorek	.10	.05	.01
☐ 86	Lowell Palmer	.10	.05	.01
☐ 87	Pat Putnam	.10	.05	.01
☐ 88	Lenny Randle	.10	.05	.01
☐ 89	Ken Reitz	.10	.05	.01
☐ 90	Gene Richards	.10	.05	.01
☐ 91	Mickey Rivers	.15	.07	.02
☐ 92	Leon Roberts	.10	.05	.01
☐ 93	Joe Sambito	.10	.05	.01
☐ 94	Rodney Scott	.10	.05	.01
☐ 95	Bob Shirley	.10	.05	.01
☐ 96	Jim Slaton	.10	.05	.01
☐ 97	Elias Sosa	.10	.05	.01
☐ 98	Fred Stanley	.10	.05	.01
☐ 99	Bill Stein	.10	.05	.01
☐ 100	Rennie Stennett	.10	.05	.01
☐ 101	Sammy Stewart	.10	.05	.01
☐ 102	Tim Stoddard	.10	.05	.01
☐ 103	Champ Summers	.10	.05	.01
☐ 104	Derrel Thomas	.10	.05	.01
☐ 105	Luis Tiant	.30	.14	.04
☐ 106	Bobby Tolan MG	.15	.07	.02
☐ 107	Bill Travers	.10	.05	.01
☐ 108	Tom Underwood	.10	.05	.01
☐ 109	Rick Waits	.10	.05	.01
☐ 110	Ron Washington	.10	.05	.01
☐ 111	U.L. Washington	.10	.05	.01
☐ 112	Earl Weaver MG	.30	.14	.04
☐ 113	Jerry White	.10	.05	.01
☐ 114	Milt Wilcox	.10	.05	.01
☐ 115	Dick Williams MG	.15	.07	.02
☐ 116	Walt Williams	.15	.07	.02
☐ 117	Rick Wise	.15	.07	.02
☐ 118	Favorite Suns Luis Tiant Cesar Cedeno	.20	.09	.03
☐ 119	Home Run Legends George Foster Bobby Bonds	.35	.16	.04
☐ 120	Sunshine Skippers Earl Weaver Dick Williams	.15	.07	.02
☐ NNO	Checklist 1-120	.15	.07	.02

1990 T/M Umpires

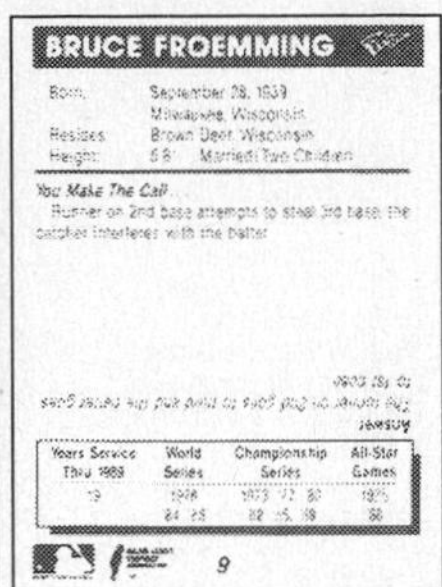

The 1990 T/M Umpires set is a standard-size (2 1/2" by 3 1/2") set which features a picture of each umpire on the front of the card with a baseball rules question on the back of the card. The set was issued as a boxed set as well as in packs.

	MT	EX-MT	VG
COMPLETE SET (70)	9.00	4.00	1.15
COMMON PLAYER (1-70)	.20	.09	.03
☐ 1 Doug Harvey	.40	.18	.05
☐ 2 John Kibler	.20	.09	.03
☐ 3 Bob Engel	.40	.18	.05
☐ 4 Harry Wendelstedt	.30	.14	.04
☐ 5 Larry Barnett	.20	.09	.03
☐ 6 Don Denkinger	.30	.14	.04
☐ 7 Dave Phillips	.30	.14	.04
☐ 8 Larry McCoy	.20	.09	.03
☐ 9 Bruce Froemming	.30	.14	.04
☐ 10 John McSherry	.20	.09	.03
☐ 11 Jim Evans	.20	.09	.03
☐ 12 Frank Pulli	.20	.09	.03
☐ 13 Joe Brinkman	.20	.09	.03
☐ 14 Terry Tata	.20	.09	.03
☐ 15 Jim McKean	.20	.09	.03
☐ 16 Dutch Rennert	.20	.09	.03
☐ 17 Paul Runge	.20	.09	.03
☐ 18 Terry Cooney	.20	.09	.03
☐ 19 Rich Garcia	.30	.14	.04
☐ 20 Dale Ford	.20	.09	.03
☐ 21 Al Clark	.20	.09	.03
☐ 22 Greg Kosc	.20	.09	.03
☐ 23 Jim Quick	.20	.09	.03
☐ 24 Eddie Montague	.20	.09	.03
☐ 25 Jerry Crawford	.20	.09	.03
☐ 26 Steve Palermo	.60	.25	.08
☐ 27 Durwood Merrill	.20	.09	.03
☐ 28 Ken Kaiser	.40	.18	.05
☐ 29 Vic Voltaggio	.20	.09	.03
☐ 30 Mike Reilly	.20	.09	.03
☐ 31 Eric Gregg	.40	.18	.05
☐ 32 Ted Hendry	.20	.09	.03
☐ 33 Joe West	.20	.09	.03
☐ 34 Fred Brocklander	.20	.09	.03
☐ 35 John Shulock	.20	.09	.03
☐ 36 Derryl Cousins	.20	.09	.03
☐ 37 Charlie Williams	.20	.09	.03
☐ 38 Rocky Roe	.20	.09	.03
☐ 39 Randy Marsh	.20	.09	.03
☐ 40 Bob Davidson	.20	.09	.03
☐ 41 Drew Coble	.20	.09	.03
☐ 42 Tim McClelland	.20	.09	.03
☐ 43 Dan Morrison	.20	.09	.03
☐ 44 Rick Reed	.20	.09	.03
☐ 45 Steve Rippley	.20	.09	.03
☐ 46 John Hirschbeck	.40	.18	.05
☐ 47 Mark Johnson	.20	.09	.03
☐ 48 Gerry Davis	.20	.09	.03
☐ 49 Dana DeMuth	.20	.09	.03
☐ 50 Larry Young	.20	.09	.03
☐ 51 Tim Welke	.20	.09	.03
☐ 52 Greg Bonin	.20	.09	.03
☐ 53 Tom Hallion	.20	.09	.03
☐ 54 Dale Scott	.20	.09	.03
☐ 55 Tim Tschida	.20	.09	.03
☐ 56 Gary Darling	.20	.09	.03
☐ 57 Mark Hirschbeck	.40	.18	.05
☐ 58 Jerry Layne	.20	.09	.03
☐ 59 Jim Joyce	.20	.09	.03
☐ 60 Bill Hohn	.20	.09	.03
☐ 61 All-Star Game	.20	.09	.03
☐ 62 World Series	.20	.09	.03
☐ 63 Nick Bremigan	.20	.09	.03
☐ 64 The Runges	.30	.14	.04
☐ 65 Bart Giamatti MEM	.50	.23	.06
☐ 66 Puzzle Piece 1	.20	.09	.03
☐ 67 Puzzle Piece 2	.20	.09	.03
☐ 68 Puzzle Piece 3	.20	.09	.03
☐ 69 Puzzle Piece 4	.20	.09	.03
☐ 70 Checklist Card	.20	.09	.03
☐ 71 Al Barlick HOF	1.00	.45	.13

1951 Topps Blue Backs

The cards in this 52-card set measure 2" by 2 5/8". The 1951 Topps series of blue-backed baseball cards could be used to play a baseball game by shuffling the cards and drawing them from a pile. These cards were marketed with a piece of caramel candy, which often melted or was squashed in such a way as to damage the card and wrapper (despite the fact that a paper shield was inserted between candy and card). Blue Backs are more difficult to obtain than the similarly styled Red Backs. The set is denoted on the cards as "Set B" and the Red Back set is correspondingly Set A. Appropriately leading off the set is Eddie Yost. The only notable Rookie Card in the set is Billy Pierce.

	NRMT	VG-E	GOOD
COMPLETE SET (52)	2100.00	950.00	275.00
COMMON PLAYER (1-52)	35.00	16.00	4.40
☐ 1 Eddie Yost	55.00	25.00	7.00
☐ 2 Hank Majeski	35.00	16.00	4.40
☐ 3 Richie Ashburn	170.00	75.00	21.00
☐ 4 Del Ennis	40.00	18.00	5.00
☐ 5 Johnny Pesky	40.00	18.00	5.00
☐ 6 Red Schoendienst	125.00	57.50	15.50
☐ 7 Gerry Staley	35.00	16.00	4.40
☐ 8 Dick Sisler	35.00	16.00	4.40
☐ 9 Johnny Sain	45.00	20.00	5.75
☐ 10 Joe Page	40.00	18.00	5.00
☐ 11 Johnny Groth	35.00	16.00	4.40
☐ 12 Sam Jethroe	37.50	17.00	4.70
☐ 13 Mickey Vernon	40.00	18.00	5.00
☐ 14 Red Munger	35.00	16.00	4.40
☐ 15 Eddie Joost	35.00	16.00	4.40
☐ 16 Murry Dickson	35.00	16.00	4.40
☐ 17 Roy Smalley	35.00	16.00	4.40
☐ 18 Ned Garver	35.00	16.00	4.40
☐ 19 Phil Masi	35.00	16.00	4.40
☐ 20 Ralph Branca	45.00	20.00	5.75
☐ 21 Billy Johnson	35.00	16.00	4.40
☐ 22 Bob Kuzava	35.00	16.00	4.40
☐ 23 Dizzy Trout	37.50	17.00	4.70
☐ 24 Sherman Lollar	37.50	17.00	4.70
☐ 25 Sam Mele	35.00	16.00	4.40
☐ 26 Chico Carrasquel	40.00	18.00	5.00
☐ 27 Andy Pafko	37.50	17.00	4.70
☐ 28 Harry Brecheen	37.50	17.00	4.70
☐ 29 Granville Hamner	35.00	16.00	4.40
☐ 30 Enos Slaughter	130.00	57.50	16.50
☐ 31 Lou Brissie	35.00	16.00	4.40
☐ 32 Bob Elliott	37.50	17.00	4.70
☐ 33 Don Lenhardt	35.00	16.00	4.40

☐ 34 Earl Torgeson	35.00	16.00	4.40
☐ 35 Tommy Byrne	35.00	16.00	4.40
☐ 36 Cliff Fannin	35.00	16.00	4.40
☐ 37 Bobby Doerr	110.00	50.00	14.00
☐ 38 Irv Noren	37.50	17.00	4.70
☐ 39 Ed Lopat	45.00	20.00	5.75
☐ 40 Vic Wertz	37.50	17.00	4.70
☐ 41 Johnny Schmitz	35.00	16.00	4.40
☐ 42 Bruce Edwards	35.00	16.00	4.40
☐ 43 Willie Jones	35.00	16.00	4.40
☐ 44 Johnny Wyrostek	35.00	16.00	4.40
☐ 45 Billy Pierce	50.00	23.00	6.25
☐ 46 Gerry Priddy	35.00	16.00	4.40
☐ 47 Herman Wehmeier	35.00	16.00	4.40
☐ 48 Billy Cox	40.00	18.00	5.00
☐ 49 Hank Sauer	40.00	18.00	5.00
☐ 50 Johnny Mize	150.00	70.00	19.00
☐ 51 Eddie Waitkus	35.00	16.00	4.40
☐ 52 Sam Chapman	50.00	23.00	6.25

1951 Topps Red Backs

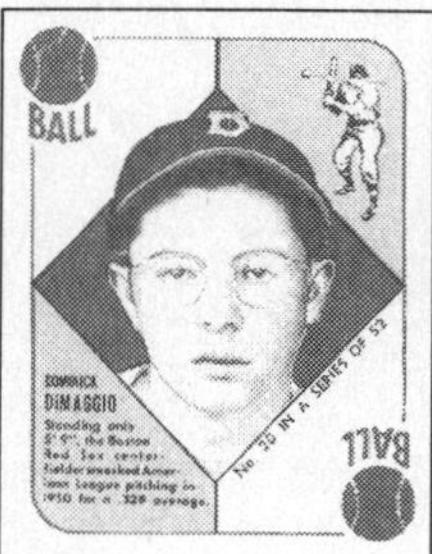

The cards in this 52-card set measure 2" by 2 5/8". The 1951 Topps Red Back set is identical in style to the Blue Back set of the same year. The cards have rounded corners and were designed to be used as a baseball game. Zernial, number 36, is listed with either the White Sox or Athletics, and Holmes, number 52, with either the Braves or Hartford. The set is denoted on the cards as "Set A" and the Blue Back set is correspondingly Set B. The only notable Rookie Card in the set is Monte Irvin.

	NRMT	VG-E	GOOD
COMPLETE SET (54)	750.00	350.00	95.00
COMMON PLAYER (1-52)	7.00	3.10	.85
☐ 1 Yogi Berra	140.00	65.00	17.50
☐ 2 Sid Gordon	7.00	3.10	.85
☐ 3 Ferris Fain	8.00	3.60	1.00
☐ 4 Vern Stephens	8.00	3.60	1.00
☐ 5 Phil Rizzuto	36.00	16.00	4.50
☐ 6 Allie Reynolds	12.00	5.50	1.50
☐ 7 Howie Pollet	7.00	3.10	.85
☐ 8 Early Wynn	21.00	9.50	2.60
☐ 9 Roy Sievers	8.00	3.60	1.00
☐ 10 Mel Parnell	8.00	3.60	1.00
☐ 11 Gene Hermanski	7.00	3.10	.85
☐ 12 Jim Hegan	8.00	3.60	1.00
☐ 13 Dale Mitchell	8.00	3.60	1.00
☐ 14 Wayne Terwilliger	7.00	3.10	.85
☐ 15 Ralph Kiner	30.00	13.50	3.80
☐ 16 Preacher Roe	10.00	4.50	1.25
☐ 17 Gus Bell	10.00	4.50	1.25
☐ 18 Jerry Coleman	10.00	4.50	1.25
☐ 19 Dick Kokos	7.00	3.10	.85
☐ 20 Dom DiMaggio	14.00	6.25	1.75
☐ 21 Larry Jansen	8.00	3.60	1.00
☐ 22 Bob Feller	50.00	23.00	6.25
☐ 23 Ray Boone	12.00	5.50	1.50
☐ 24 Hank Bauer	14.00	6.25	1.75
☐ 25 Cliff Chambers	7.00	3.10	.85
☐ 26 Luke Easter	10.00	4.50	1.25
☐ 27 Wally Westlake	7.00	3.10	.85
☐ 28 Elmer Valo	7.00	3.10	.85
☐ 29 Bob Kennedy	8.00	3.60	1.00
☐ 30 Warren Spahn	50.00	23.00	6.25
☐ 31 Gil Hodges	36.00	16.00	4.50
☐ 32 Henry Thompson	8.00	3.60	1.00
☐ 33 William Werle	7.00	3.10	.85
☐ 34 Grady Hatton	7.00	3.10	.85
☐ 35 Al Rosen	14.00	6.25	1.75
☐ 36A Gus Zernial (Chicago)	36.00	16.00	4.50
☐ 36B Gus Zernial (Philadelphia)	20.00	9.00	2.50
☐ 37 Wes Westrum	8.00	3.60	1.00
☐ 38 Duke Snider	80.00	36.00	10.00
☐ 39 Ted Kluszewski	18.00	8.00	2.30
☐ 40 Mike Garcia	8.00	3.60	1.00
☐ 41 Whitey Lockman	8.00	3.60	1.00
☐ 42 Ray Scarborough	7.00	3.10	.85
☐ 43 Maurice McDermott	7.00	3.10	.85
☐ 44 Sid Hudson	7.00	3.10	.85
☐ 45 Andy Seminick	7.00	3.10	.85
☐ 46 Billy Goodman	8.00	3.60	1.00
☐ 47 Tommy Glaviano	7.00	3.10	.85
☐ 48 Eddie Stanky	8.00	3.60	1.00
☐ 49 Al Zarilla	7.00	3.10	.85
☐ 50 Monte Irvin	45.00	20.00	5.75
☐ 51 Eddie Robinson	7.00	3.10	.85
☐ 52A Tommy Holmes (Boston)	36.00	16.00	4.50
☐ 52B Tommy Holmes (Hartford)	22.00	10.00	2.80

1951 Topps Connie Mack

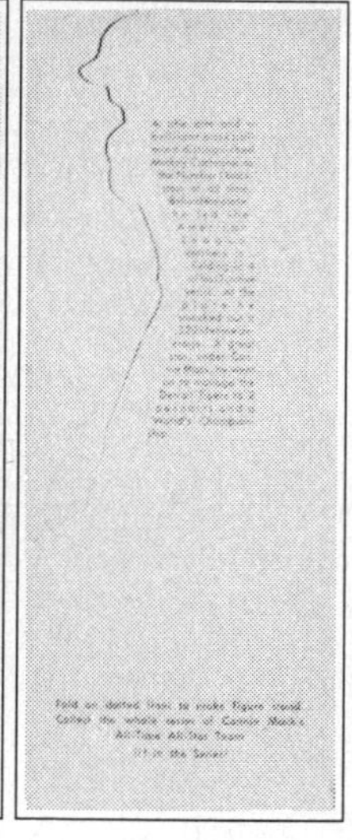

The cards in this 11-card set measure approximately 2 1/16" by 5 1/4". The series of die-cut cards which comprise the set entitled Connie Mack All-Stars was one of Topps' most distinctive and fragile card designs. Printed on thin cardboard, these elegant cards were protected in the wrapper by panels of accompanying Red Backs, but once removed were easily damaged (after all, they were intended to be folded and used as toy figures). Cards without tops have a value less than one-half of that listed below. The cards are unnumbered and are listed below in alphabetical order.

	NRMT	VG-E	GOOD
COMPLETE SET (11)	7000.00	3200.00	900.00
COMMON PLAYER (1-11)	150.00	70.00	19.00
☐ 1 Grover C. Alexander	400.00	180.00	50.00
☐ 2 Mickey Cochrane	300.00	135.00	38.00
☐ 3 Ed Collins	150.00	70.00	19.00
☐ 4 Jimmy Collins	150.00	70.00	19.00
☐ 5 Lou Gehrig	2000.00	800.00	250.00
☐ 6 Walter Johnson	650.00	300.00	80.00

	NRMT	VG-E	GOOD
☐ 7 Connie Mack	350.00	160.00	45.00
☐ 8 Christy Mathewson	350.00	160.00	45.00
☐ 9 Babe Ruth	2500.00	1000.00	300.00
☐ 10 Tris Speaker	150.00	70.00	19.00
☐ 11 Honus Wagner	350.00	160.00	45.00

1951 Topps Current AS

The cards in this 11-card set measure approximately 2 1/16" by 5 1/4". The 1951 Topps Current All-Star series is probably the rarest of all legitimate, nationally issued, post war baseball issues. The set price listed below does not include the prices for the cards of Konstanty, Roberts and Stanky, which likely never were released to the public in gum packs. These three cards (SP in the checklist below) were probably obtained directly from the company and exist in extremely limited numbers. As with the Connie Mack set, cards without the die-cut background are worth half of the value listed below. The cards are unnumbered and are listed below in alphabetical order.

	NRMT	VG-E	GOOD
COMPLETE SET (8)	4500.00	2000.00	575.00
COMMON PLAYER (1-11)	250.00	115.00	31.00
☐ 1 Yogi Berra	1500.00	600.00	200.00
☐ 2 Larry Doby	300.00	135.00	38.00
☐ 3 Walt Dropo	250.00	115.00	31.00
☐ 4 Hoot Evers	250.00	115.00	31.00
☐ 5 George Kell	600.00	275.00	75.00
☐ 6 Ralph Kiner	750.00	350.00	95.00
☐ 7 Jim Konstanty SP	12500.	5500.	1500.
☐ 8 Bob Lemon	600.00	275.00	75.00
☐ 9 Phil Rizzuto	600.00	275.00	75.00
☐ 10 Robin Roberts SP	15000.	6000.	1600.
☐ 11 Eddie Stanky SP	12500.	5500.	1500.

1951 Topps Teams

The cards in this nine-card set measure approximately 2 1/16" by 5 1/4". These unnumbered team cards issued by Topps in 1951 carry black and white photographs framed by a yellow border. These cards were issued in the same five-cent wrapper as the Connie Mack and Current All Stars.

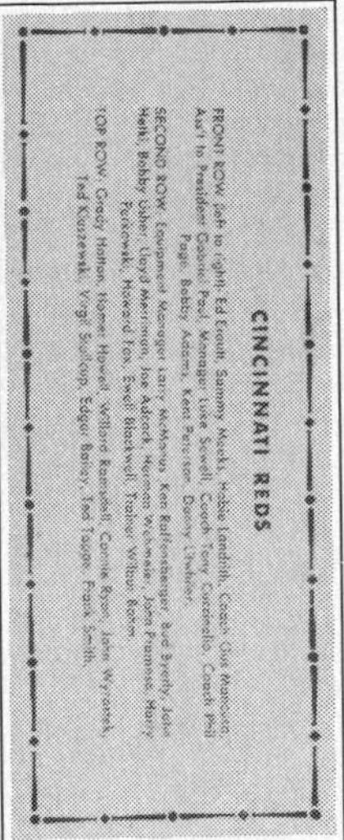

They have been assigned reference numbers in the checklist alphabetically by team city and name. They are found with or without "1950" printed in the name panel before the team name. Although the dated variations are slightly more difficult to find, there is usually no difference in value.

	NRMT	VG-E	GOOD
COMPLETE SET (9)	2000.00	900.00	250.00
COMMON TEAM (1-9)	175.00	80.00	22.00
☐ 1 Boston Red Sox	350.00	160.00	45.00
☐ 2 Brooklyn Dodgers	250.00	115.00	31.00
☐ 3 Chicago White Sox	200.00	90.00	25.00
☐ 4 Cincinnati Reds	175.00	80.00	22.00
☐ 5 New York Giants	200.00	90.00	25.00
☐ 6 Philadelphia Athletics	175.00	80.00	22.00
☐ 7 Philadelphia Phillies	175.00	80.00	22.00
☐ 8 St. Louis Cardinals	325.00	145.00	40.00
☐ 9 Washington Senators	175.00	80.00	22.00

1952 Topps

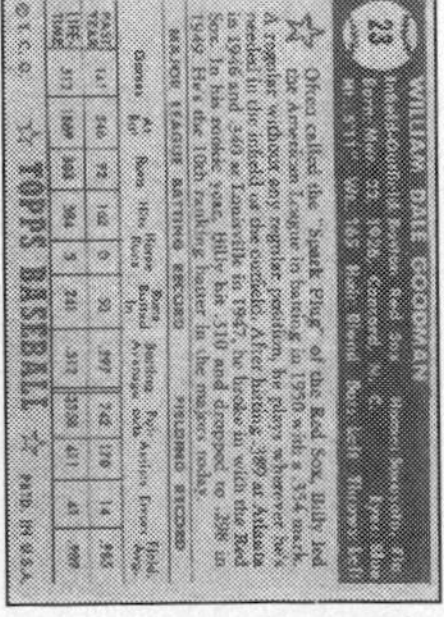

The cards in this 407-card set measure approximately 2 5/8" by 3 3/4". The 1952 Topps set is Topps' first truly major set. Card numbers 1 to 80 were issued with red or black backs, both of which are less plentiful than card numbers 81 to 250. In fact, the first series is considered the most difficult with respect to finding perfect condition cards. Card number

48 (Joe Page) and number 49 (Johnny Sain) can be found with each other's write-up on their back. Card numbers 251 to 310 are somewhat scarce and numbers 311 to 407 are quite scarce. Cards 281-300 were single printed compared to the other cards in the next to last series. Cards 311-313 were double printed on the last high number printing sheet. The key card in the set is obviously Mickey Mantle, number 311, Mickey's first of many Topps cards. Although rarely seen, there exist salesman sample panels of three cards containing the fronts of regular cards with ad information on the back. Two such panels seen are Bob Mahoney/Robin Roberts/Sid Hudson and Wally Westlake/Dizzy Trout/Irv Noren. The key rookies in this set are Billy Martin, Eddie Mathews, and Hoyt Wilhelm.

	NRMT	VG-E	GOOD
COMPLETE SET (407)	66000.	29700.	8300.
COMMON PLAYER (1-80)	60.00	27.00	7.50
COMMON PLAYER (81-250)	30.00	13.50	3.80
COMMON PLAYER (251-280)	50.00	23.00	6.25
COMMON PLAYER (281-300)	60.00	27.00	7.50
COMMON PLAYER (301-310)	50.00	23.00	6.25
COMMON PLAYER (311-407)	190.00	85.00	24.00
1 Andy Pafko	1300.00	130.00	39.00
2 Pete Runnels	70.00	32.00	8.75
3 Hank Thompson	65.00	29.00	8.25
4 Don Lenhardt	60.00	27.00	7.50
5 Larry Jansen	65.00	29.00	8.25
6 Grady Hatton	60.00	27.00	7.50
7 Wayne Terwilliger	60.00	27.00	7.50
8 Fred Marsh	60.00	27.00	7.50
9 Robert Hogue	60.00	27.00	7.50
10 Al Rosen	90.00	40.00	11.50
11 Phil Rizzuto	190.00	85.00	24.00
12 Monty Basgall	60.00	27.00	7.50
13 Johnny Wyrostek	60.00	27.00	7.50
14 Bob Elliott	65.00	29.00	8.25
15 Johnny Pesky	65.00	29.00	8.25
16 Gene Hermanski	60.00	27.00	7.50
17 Jim Hegan	65.00	29.00	8.25
18 Merrill Combs	60.00	27.00	7.50
19 Johnny Bucha	60.00	27.00	7.50
20 Billy Loes	115.00	52.50	14.50
21 Ferris Fain	65.00	29.00	8.25
22 Dom DiMaggio	100.00	45.00	12.50
23 Billy Goodman	65.00	29.00	8.25
24 Luke Easter	65.00	29.00	8.25
25 Johnny Groth	60.00	27.00	7.50
26 Monte Irvin	110.00	50.00	14.00
27 Sam Jethroe	65.00	29.00	8.25
28 Jerry Priddy	60.00	27.00	7.50
29 Ted Kluszewski	100.00	45.00	12.50
30 Mel Parnell	65.00	29.00	8.25
31 Gus Zernial	70.00	32.00	8.75
32 Eddie Robinson	60.00	27.00	7.50
33 Warren Spahn	250.00	115.00	31.00
34 Elmer Valo	60.00	27.00	7.50
35 Hank Sauer	70.00	32.00	8.75
36 Gil Hodges	175.00	80.00	22.00
37 Duke Snider	300.00	135.00	38.00
38 Wally Westlake	60.00	27.00	7.50
39 Dizzy Trout	65.00	29.00	8.25
40 Irv Noren	65.00	29.00	8.25
41 Bob Wellman	60.00	27.00	7.50
42 Lou Kretlow	60.00	27.00	7.50
43 Ray Scarborough	60.00	27.00	7.50
44 Con Dempsey	60.00	27.00	7.50
45 Eddie Joost	60.00	27.00	7.50
46 Gordon Goldsberry	60.00	27.00	7.50
47 Willie Jones	60.00	27.00	7.50
48A Joe Page COR	80.00	36.00	10.00
48B Joe Page ERR (Bio for Sain)	300.00	135.00	38.00
49A Johnny Sain COR	110.00	50.00	14.00
49B Johnny Sain ERR (Bio for Page)	325.00	145.00	40.00
50 Marv Rickert	60.00	27.00	7.50
51 Jim Russell	60.00	27.00	7.50
52 Don Mueller	65.00	29.00	8.25
53 Chris Van Cuyk	60.00	27.00	7.50
54 Leo Kiely	60.00	27.00	7.50
55 Ray Boone	65.00	29.00	8.25
56 Tommy Glaviano	60.00	27.00	7.50
57 Ed Lopat	110.00	50.00	14.00
58 Bob Mahoney	60.00	27.00	7.50
59 Robin Roberts	175.00	80.00	22.00
60 Sid Hudson	60.00	27.00	7.50
61 Tookie Gilbert	60.00	27.00	7.50
62 Chuck Stobbs	60.00	27.00	7.50
63 Howie Pollet	60.00	27.00	7.50
64 Roy Sievers	65.00	29.00	8.25
65 Enos Slaughter	150.00	70.00	19.00
66 Preacher Roe	110.00	50.00	14.00
67 Allie Reynolds	115.00	52.50	14.50
68 Cliff Chambers	60.00	27.00	7.50
69 Virgil Stallcup	60.00	27.00	7.50
70 Al Zarilla	60.00	27.00	7.50
71 Tom Upton	60.00	27.00	7.50
72 Karl Olson	60.00	27.00	7.50
73 Bill Werle	60.00	27.00	7.50
74 Andy Hansen	60.00	27.00	7.50
75 Wes Westrum	65.00	29.00	8.25
76 Eddie Stanky	70.00	32.00	8.75
77 Bob Kennedy	65.00	29.00	8.25
78 Ellis Kinder	60.00	27.00	7.50
79 Gerry Staley	60.00	27.00	7.50
80 Herman Wehmeier	60.00	27.00	7.50
81 Vernon Law	35.00	16.00	4.40
82 Duane Pillette	30.00	13.50	3.80
83 Billy Johnson	30.00	13.50	3.80
84 Vern Stephens	33.00	15.00	4.10
85 Bob Kuzava	33.00	15.00	4.10
86 Ted Gray	30.00	13.50	3.80
87 Dale Coogan	30.00	13.50	3.80
88 Bob Feller	175.00	80.00	22.00
89 Johnny Lipon	30.00	13.50	3.80
90 Mickey Grasso	30.00	13.50	3.80
91 Red Schoendienst	90.00	40.00	11.50
92 Dale Mitchell	33.00	15.00	4.10
93 Al Sima	30.00	13.50	3.80
94 Sam Mele	30.00	13.50	3.80
95 Ken Holcombe	30.00	13.50	3.80
96 Willard Marshall	30.00	13.50	3.80
97 Earl Torgeson	30.00	13.50	3.80
98 Billy Pierce	35.00	16.00	4.40
99 Gene Woodling	60.00	27.00	7.50
100 Del Rice	30.00	13.50	3.80
101 Max Lanier	30.00	13.50	3.80
102 Bill Kennedy	30.00	13.50	3.80
103 Cliff Mapes	30.00	13.50	3.80
104 Don Kolloway	30.00	13.50	3.80
105 Johnny Pramesa	30.00	13.50	3.80
106 Mickey Vernon	35.00	16.00	4.40
107 Connie Ryan	30.00	13.50	3.80
108 Jim Konstanty	35.00	16.00	4.40
109 Ted Wilks	30.00	13.50	3.80
110 Dutch Leonard	30.00	13.50	3.80
111 Peanuts Lowrey	30.00	13.50	3.80
112 Hank Majeski	30.00	13.50	3.80
113 Dick Sisler	33.00	15.00	4.10
114 Willard Ramsdell	30.00	13.50	3.80
115 Red Munger	30.00	13.50	3.80
116 Carl Scheib	30.00	13.50	3.80
117 Sherm Lollar	33.00	15.00	4.10
118 Ken Raffensberger	30.00	13.50	3.80
119 Mickey McDermott	30.00	13.50	3.80
120 Bob Chakales	30.00	13.50	3.80
121 Gus Niarhos	30.00	13.50	3.80
122 Jackie Jensen	75.00	34.00	9.50
123 Eddie Yost	33.00	15.00	4.10
124 Monte Kennedy	30.00	13.50	3.80
125 Bill Rigney	30.00	13.50	3.80
126 Fred Hutchinson	33.00	15.00	4.10
127 Paul Minner	30.00	13.50	3.80
128 Don Bollweg	30.00	13.50	3.80
129 Johnny Mize	90.00	40.00	11.50
130 Sheldon Jones	30.00	13.50	3.80
131 Morrie Martin	30.00	13.50	3.80
132 Clyde Kluttz	30.00	13.50	3.80
133 Al Widmar	30.00	13.50	3.80
134 Joe Tipton	30.00	13.50	3.80
135 Dixie Howell	30.00	13.50	3.80
136 Johnny Schmitz	30.00	13.50	3.80
137 Roy McMillan	35.00	16.00	4.40
138 Bill MacDonald	30.00	13.50	3.80
139 Ken Wood	30.00	13.50	3.80
140 Johnny Antonelli	33.00	15.00	4.10
141 Clint Hartung	30.00	13.50	3.80
142 Harry Perkowski	30.00	13.50	3.80
143 Les Moss	30.00	13.50	3.80
144 Ed Blake	30.00	13.50	3.80
145 Joe Haynes	30.00	13.50	3.80
146 Frank House	30.00	13.50	3.80
147 Bob Young	30.00	13.50	3.80
148 Johnny Klippstein	30.00	13.50	3.80
149 Dick Kryhoski	30.00	13.50	3.80
150 Ted Beard	30.00	13.50	3.80
151 Wally Post	35.00	16.00	4.40
152 Al Evans	30.00	13.50	3.80
153 Bob Rush	30.00	13.50	3.80

☐ 154 Joe Muir	30.00	13.50	3.80
☐ 155 Frank Overmire	30.00	13.50	3.80
☐ 156 Frank Hiller	30.00	13.50	3.80
☐ 157 Bob Usher	30.00	13.50	3.80
☐ 158 Eddie Waitkus	30.00	13.50	3.80
☐ 159 Saul Rogovin	30.00	13.50	3.80
☐ 160 Owen Friend	30.00	13.50	3.80
☐ 161 Bud Byerly	30.00	13.50	3.80
☐ 162 Del Crandall	33.00	15.00	4.10
☐ 163 Stan Rojek	30.00	13.50	3.80
☐ 164 Walt Dubiel	30.00	13.50	3.80
☐ 165 Eddie Kazak	30.00	13.50	3.80
☐ 166 Paul LaPalme	30.00	13.50	3.80
☐ 167 Bill Howerton	30.00	13.50	3.80
☐ 168 Charlie Silvera	35.00	16.00	4.40
☐ 169 Howie Judson	30.00	13.50	3.80
☐ 170 Gus Bell	33.00	15.00	4.10
☐ 171 Ed Erautt	30.00	13.50	3.80
☐ 172 Eddie Miksis	30.00	13.50	3.80
☐ 173 Roy Smalley	30.00	13.50	3.80
☐ 174 Clarence Marshall	30.00	13.50	3.80
☐ 175 Billy Martin	380.00	170.00	47.50
☐ 176 Hank Edwards	30.00	13.50	3.80
☐ 177 Bill Wight	30.00	13.50	3.80
☐ 178 Cass Michaels	30.00	13.50	3.80
☐ 179 Frank Smith	30.00	13.50	3.80
☐ 180 Charlie Maxwell	35.00	16.00	4.40
☐ 181 Bob Swift	30.00	13.50	3.80
☐ 182 Billy Hitchcock	30.00	13.50	3.80
☐ 183 Erv Dusak	30.00	13.50	3.80
☐ 184 Bob Ramazzotti	30.00	13.50	3.80
☐ 185 Bill Nicholson	33.00	15.00	4.10
☐ 186 Walt Masterson	30.00	13.50	3.80
☐ 187 Bob Miller	30.00	13.50	3.80
☐ 188 Clarence Podbielan	30.00	13.50	3.80
☐ 189 Pete Reiser	35.00	16.00	4.40
☐ 190 Don Johnson	30.00	13.50	3.80
☐ 191 Yogi Berra	425.00	190.00	52.50
☐ 192 Myron Ginsberg	30.00	13.50	3.80
☐ 193 Harry Simpson	33.00	15.00	4.10
☐ 194 Joe Hatton	30.00	13.50	3.80
☐ 195 Minnie Minoso	125.00	57.50	15.50
☐ 196 Solly Hemus	35.00	16.00	4.40
☐ 197 George Strickland	30.00	13.50	3.80
☐ 198 Phil Haugstad	30.00	13.50	3.80
☐ 199 George Zuverink	30.00	13.50	3.80
☐ 200 Ralph Houk	65.00	29.00	8.25
☐ 201 Alex Kellner	30.00	13.50	3.80
☐ 202 Joe Collins	40.00	18.00	5.00
☐ 203 Curt Simmons	35.00	16.00	4.40
☐ 204 Ron Northey	30.00	13.50	3.80
☐ 205 Clyde King	30.00	13.50	3.80
☐ 206 Joe Ostrowski	30.00	13.50	3.80
☐ 207 Mickey Harris	30.00	13.50	3.80
☐ 208 Marlin Stuart	30.00	13.50	3.80
☐ 209 Howie Fox	30.00	13.50	3.80
☐ 210 Dick Fowler	30.00	13.50	3.80
☐ 211 Ray Coleman	30.00	13.50	3.80
☐ 212 Ned Garver	30.00	13.50	3.80
☐ 213 Nippy Jones	30.00	13.50	3.80
☐ 214 Johnny Hopp	33.00	15.00	4.10
☐ 215 Hank Bauer	55.00	25.00	7.00
☐ 216 Richie Ashburn	110.00	50.00	14.00
☐ 217 Snuffy Stirnweiss	33.00	15.00	4.10
☐ 218 Clyde McCullough	30.00	13.50	3.80
☐ 219 Bobby Shantz	40.00	18.00	5.00
☐ 220 Joe Presko	30.00	13.50	3.80
☐ 221 Granny Hamner	30.00	13.50	3.80
☐ 222 Hoot Evers	30.00	13.50	3.80
☐ 223 Del Ennis	33.00	15.00	4.10
☐ 224 Bruce Edwards	30.00	13.50	3.80
☐ 225 Frank Baumholtz	30.00	13.50	3.80
☐ 226 Dave Philley	30.00	13.50	3.80
☐ 227 Joe Garagiola	125.00	57.50	15.50
☐ 228 Al Brazle	30.00	13.50	3.80
☐ 229 Gene Bearden UER (Misspelled Beardon)	30.00	13.50	3.80
☐ 230 Matt Batts	30.00	13.50	3.80
☐ 231 Sam Zoldak	30.00	13.50	3.80
☐ 232 Billy Cox	33.00	15.00	4.10
☐ 233 Bob Friend	40.00	18.00	5.00
☐ 234 Steve Souchock	30.00	13.50	3.80
☐ 235 Walt Dropo	33.00	15.00	4.10
☐ 236 Ed Fitzgerald	30.00	13.50	3.80
☐ 237 Jerry Coleman	33.00	15.00	4.10
☐ 238 Art Houtteman	30.00	13.50	3.80
☐ 239 Rocky Bridges	30.00	13.50	3.80
☐ 240 Jack Phillips	30.00	13.50	3.80
☐ 241 Tommy Byrne	30.00	13.50	3.80
☐ 242 Tom Poholsky	30.00	13.50	3.80
☐ 243 Larry Doby	40.00	18.00	5.00
☐ 244 Vic Wertz	33.00	15.00	4.10
☐ 245 Sherry Robertson	30.00	13.50	3.80
☐ 246 George Kell	85.00	38.00	10.50
☐ 247 Randy Gumpert	30.00	13.50	3.80
☐ 248 Frank Shea	30.00	13.50	3.80
☐ 249 Bobby Adams	30.00	13.50	3.80
☐ 250 Carl Erskine	70.00	32.00	8.75
☐ 251 Chico Carrasquel	50.00	23.00	6.25
☐ 252 Vern Bickford	50.00	23.00	6.25
☐ 253 Johnny Berardino	55.00	25.00	7.00
☐ 254 Joe Dobson	50.00	23.00	6.25
☐ 255 Clyde Vollmer	50.00	23.00	6.25
☐ 256 Pete Suder	50.00	23.00	6.25
☐ 257 Bobby Avila	55.00	25.00	7.00
☐ 258 Steve Gromek	50.00	23.00	6.25
☐ 259 Bob Addis	50.00	23.00	6.25
☐ 260 Pete Castiglione	50.00	23.00	6.25
☐ 261 Willie Mays	2600.00	1150.00	325.00
☐ 262 Virgil Trucks	55.00	25.00	7.00
☐ 263 Harry Brecheen	55.00	25.00	7.00
☐ 264 Roy Hartsfield	50.00	23.00	6.25
☐ 265 Chuck Diering	50.00	23.00	6.25
☐ 266 Murry Dickson	50.00	23.00	6.25
☐ 267 Sid Gordon	50.00	23.00	6.25
☐ 268 Bob Lemon	185.00	85.00	23.00
☐ 269 Willard Nixon	50.00	23.00	6.25
☐ 270 Lou Brissie	50.00	23.00	6.25
☐ 271 Jim Delsing	50.00	23.00	6.25
☐ 272 Mike Garcia	55.00	25.00	7.00
☐ 273 Erv Palica	50.00	23.00	6.25
☐ 274 Ralph Branca	85.00	38.00	10.50
☐ 275 Pat Mullin	50.00	23.00	6.25
☐ 276 Jim Wilson	50.00	23.00	6.25
☐ 277 Early Wynn	190.00	85.00	24.00
☐ 278 Allie Clark	50.00	23.00	6.25
☐ 279 Eddie Stewart	50.00	23.00	6.25
☐ 280 Cloyd Boyer	55.00	25.00	7.00
☐ 281 Tommy Brown SP	60.00	27.00	7.50
☐ 282 Birdie Tebbetts SP	65.00	29.00	8.25
☐ 283 Phil Masi SP	60.00	27.00	7.50
☐ 284 Hank Arft SP	60.00	27.00	7.50
☐ 285 Cliff Fannin SP	60.00	27.00	7.50
☐ 286 Joe DeMaestri SP	60.00	27.00	7.50
☐ 287 Steve Bilko SP	60.00	27.00	7.50
☐ 288 Chet Nichols SP	60.00	27.00	7.50
☐ 289 Tommy Holmes SP	65.00	29.00	8.25
☐ 290 Joe Astroth SP	60.00	27.00	7.50
☐ 291 Gil Coan SP	60.00	27.00	7.50
☐ 292 Floyd Baker SP	60.00	27.00	7.50
☐ 293 Sibby Sisti SP	60.00	27.00	7.50
☐ 294 Walker Cooper SP	60.00	27.00	7.50
☐ 295 Phil Cavarretta SP	65.00	29.00	8.25
☐ 296 Red Rolfe SP MG	65.00	29.00	8.25
☐ 297 Andy Seminick SP	60.00	27.00	7.50
☐ 298 Bob Ross SP	60.00	27.00	7.50
☐ 299 Ray Murray SP	60.00	27.00	7.50
☐ 300 Barney McCosky SP	60.00	27.00	7.50
☐ 301 Bob Porterfield	50.00	23.00	6.25
☐ 302 Max Surkont	50.00	23.00	6.25
☐ 303 Harry Dorish	50.00	23.00	6.25
☐ 304 Sam Dente	50.00	23.00	6.25
☐ 305 Paul Richards MG	55.00	25.00	7.00
☐ 306 Lou Sleater	50.00	23.00	6.25
☐ 307 Frank Campos	50.00	23.00	6.25
☐ 308 Luis Aloma	50.00	23.00	6.25
☐ 309 Jim Busby	50.00	23.00	6.25
☐ 310 George Metkovich	60.00	27.00	7.50
☐ 311 Mickey Mantle DP	32000.	9600.	3200.
☐ 312 Jackie Robinson DP	1350.00	600.00	170.00
☐ 313 Bobby Thomson DP	250.00	115.00	31.00
☐ 314 Roy Campanella	2100.00	950.00	275.00
☐ 315 Leo Durocher MG	375.00	170.00	47.50
☐ 316 Dave Williams	225.00	100.00	28.00
☐ 317 Conrado Marrero	200.00	90.00	25.00
☐ 318 Harold Gregg	190.00	85.00	24.00
☐ 319 Al Walker	190.00	85.00	24.00
☐ 320 John Rutherford	200.00	90.00	25.00
☐ 321 Joe Black	250.00	115.00	31.00
☐ 322 Randy Jackson	190.00	85.00	24.00
☐ 323 Bubba Church	190.00	85.00	24.00
☐ 324 Warren Hacker	190.00	85.00	24.00
☐ 325 Bill Serena	190.00	85.00	24.00
☐ 326 George Shuba	250.00	115.00	31.00
☐ 327 Al Wilson	190.00	85.00	24.00
☐ 328 Bob Borkowski	190.00	85.00	24.00
☐ 329 Ike Delock	200.00	90.00	25.00
☐ 330 Turk Lown	190.00	85.00	24.00
☐ 331 Tom Morgan	190.00	85.00	24.00
☐ 332 Anthony Bartirome	190.00	85.00	24.00
☐ 333 Pee Wee Reese	1250.00	575.00	160.00
☐ 334 Wilmer Mizell	210.00	95.00	26.00
☐ 335 Ted Lepcio	190.00	85.00	24.00
☐ 336 Dave Koslo	190.00	85.00	24.00
☐ 337 Jim Hearn	190.00	85.00	24.00
☐ 338 Sal Yvars	190.00	85.00	24.00

☐ 339 Russ Meyer	190.00	85.00	24.00
☐ 340 Bob Hooper	190.00	85.00	24.00
☐ 341 Hal Jeffcoat	190.00	85.00	24.00
☐ 342 Clem Labine	225.00	100.00	28.00
☐ 343 Dick Gernert	190.00	85.00	24.00
☐ 344 Ewell Blackwell	225.00	100.00	28.00
☐ 345 Sammy White	190.00	85.00	24.00
☐ 346 George Spencer	190.00	85.00	24.00
☐ 347 Joe Adcock	225.00	100.00	28.00
☐ 348 Robert Kelly	190.00	85.00	24.00
☐ 349 Bob Cain	190.00	85.00	24.00
☐ 350 Cal Abrams	190.00	85.00	24.00
☐ 351 Alvin Dark	225.00	100.00	28.00
☐ 352 Karl Drews	190.00	85.00	24.00
☐ 353 Bobby Del Greco	190.00	85.00	24.00
☐ 354 Fred Hatfield	190.00	85.00	24.00
☐ 355 Bobby Morgan	190.00	85.00	24.00
☐ 356 Toby Atwell	190.00	85.00	24.00
☐ 357 Smoky Burgess	250.00	115.00	31.00
☐ 358 John Kucab	190.00	85.00	24.00
☐ 359 Dee Fondy	190.00	85.00	24.00
☐ 360 George Crowe	200.00	90.00	25.00
☐ 361 William Posedel CO	190.00	85.00	24.00
☐ 362 Ken Heintzelman	190.00	85.00	24.00
☐ 363 Dick Rozek	190.00	85.00	24.00
☐ 364 Clyde Sukeforth CO	190.00	85.00	24.00
☐ 365 Cookie Lavagetto CO	200.00	90.00	25.00
☐ 366 Dave Madison	190.00	85.00	24.00
☐ 367 Ben Thorpe	190.00	85.00	24.00
☐ 368 Ed Wright	190.00	85.00	24.00
☐ 369 Dick Groat	350.00	160.00	45.00
☐ 370 Billy Hoeft	200.00	90.00	25.00
☐ 371 Bobby Hofman	190.00	85.00	24.00
☐ 372 Gil McDougald	350.00	160.00	45.00
☐ 373 Jim Turner CO	200.00	90.00	25.00
☐ 374 John Benton	190.00	85.00	24.00
☐ 375 John Merson	190.00	85.00	24.00
☐ 376 Faye Throneberry	190.00	85.00	24.00
☐ 377 Chuck Dressen MG	200.00	90.00	25.00
☐ 378 Leroy Fusselman	190.00	85.00	24.00
☐ 379 Joe Rossi	190.00	85.00	24.00
☐ 380 Clem Koshorek	190.00	85.00	24.00
☐ 381 Milton Stock CO	190.00	85.00	24.00
☐ 382 Sam Jones	200.00	90.00	25.00
☐ 383 Del Wilber	190.00	85.00	24.00
☐ 384 Frank Crosetti CO	250.00	115.00	31.00
☐ 385 Herman Franks CO	200.00	90.00	25.00
☐ 386 John Yuhas	190.00	85.00	24.00
☐ 387 Billy Meyer MG	190.00	85.00	24.00
☐ 388 Bob Chipman	190.00	85.00	24.00
☐ 389 Ben Wade	190.00	85.00	24.00
☐ 390 Glenn Nelson	190.00	85.00	24.00
☐ 391 Ben Chapman UER CO (Photo actually Sam Chapman)	190.00	85.00	24.00
☐ 392 Hoyt Wilhelm	725.00	325.00	90.00
☐ 393 Ebba St.Claire	190.00	85.00	24.00
☐ 394 Billy Herman CO	300.00	135.00	38.00
☐ 395 Jake Pitler CO	190.00	85.00	24.00
☐ 396 Dick Williams	250.00	115.00	31.00
☐ 397 Forrest Main	190.00	85.00	24.00
☐ 398 Hal Rice	190.00	85.00	24.00
☐ 399 Jim Fridley	190.00	85.00	24.00
☐ 400 Bill Dickey CO	700.00	325.00	90.00
☐ 401 Bob Schultz	190.00	85.00	24.00
☐ 402 Earl Harrist	190.00	85.00	24.00
☐ 403 Bill Miller	190.00	85.00	24.00
☐ 404 Dick Brodowski	190.00	85.00	24.00
☐ 405 Eddie Pellagrini	190.00	85.00	24.00
☐ 406 Joe Nuxhall	250.00	115.00	31.00
☐ 407 Eddie Mathews	3250.00	800.00	250.00

1953 Topps

The cards in this 274-card set measure 2 5/8" by 3 3/4". Although the last card is numbered 280, there are only 274 cards in the set since numbers 253, 261, 267, 268, 271, and 275 were never issued. The 1953 Topps series contains line drawings of players in full color. The name and team panel at the card base is easily damaged, making it very difficult to complete a mint set. The high number series, 221 to 280, was produced in shorter supply late in the year and hence is more difficult to complete than the lower numbers. The key cards in the set are Mickey Mantle (82) and Willie Mays (244). The key rookies in this set are Roy Face, Jim Gilliam,

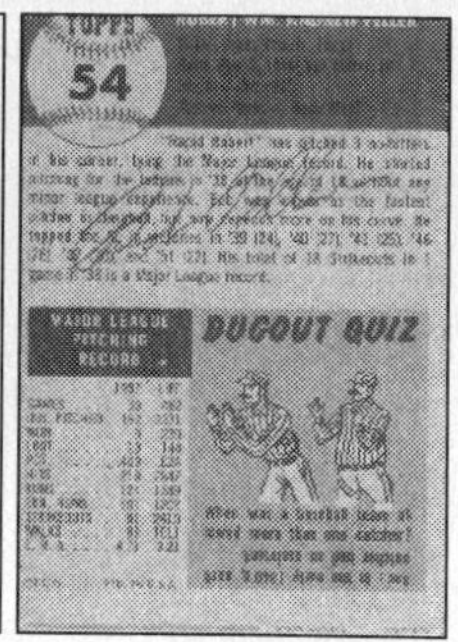

and Johnny Podres, all from the last series. There are a number of double-printed cards (actually not double but 50 percent more of each of these numbers were printed compared to the other cards in the series) indicated by DP in the checklist below. There were five players (10 Smoky Burgess, 44 Ellis Kinder, 61 Early Wynn, 72 Fred Hutchinson, and 81 Joe Black) held out of the first run of 1-85 (but printed in with numbers 86-165), who are each marked by SP in the checklist below. In addition, there are five numbers which were printed in with the more plentiful series 166-220; these cards (94, 107, 131, 145, and 156) are also indicated by DP in the checklist below. There were some three-card advertising panels produced by Topps; the players include Johnny Mize/Clem Koshorek/Toby Atwell and Mickey Mantle/Johnny Wyrostek/Sal Yvars. When cut apart, these advertising cards are distinguished by the non-standard card back, i.e., part of an advertisement for the 1953 Topps set instead of the typical statistics and biographical information about the player pictured.

	NRMT	VG-E	GOOD
COMPLETE SET (274)	14250.	6400.	1800.
COMMON PLAYER (1-165)	28.00	12.50	3.50
COMMON PLAYER (166-220)	22.00	10.00	2.80
COMMON PLAYER (221-280)	100.00	45.00	12.50
☐ 1 Jackie Robinson DP	600.00	275.00	75.00
☐ 2 Luke Easter DP	17.00	7.75	2.10
☐ 3 George Crowe	28.00	12.50	3.50
☐ 4 Ben Wade	28.00	12.50	3.50
☐ 5 Joe Dobson	28.00	12.50	3.50
☐ 6 Sam Jones	30.00	13.50	3.80
☐ 7 Bob Borkowski DP	16.00	7.25	2.00
☐ 8 Clem Koshorek DP	16.00	7.25	2.00
☐ 9 Joe Collins	35.00	16.00	4.40
☐ 10 Smoky Burgess SP	50.00	23.00	6.25
☐ 11 Sal Yvars	28.00	12.50	3.50
☐ 12 Howie Judson DP	16.00	7.25	2.00
☐ 13 Conrado Marrero DP	16.00	7.25	2.00
☐ 14 Clem Labine DP	18.00	8.00	2.30
☐ 15 Bobo Newsom DP	25.00	11.50	3.10
☐ 16 Peanuts Lowrey DP	16.00	7.25	2.00
☐ 17 Billy Hitchcock	28.00	12.50	3.50
☐ 18 Ted Lepcio DP	16.00	7.25	2.00
☐ 19 Mel Parnell DP	17.00	7.75	2.10
☐ 20 Hank Thompson	30.00	13.50	3.80
☐ 21 Billy Johnson	28.00	12.50	3.50
☐ 22 Howie Fox	28.00	12.50	3.50
☐ 23 Toby Atwell DP	16.00	7.25	2.00
☐ 24 Ferris Fain	30.00	13.50	3.80
☐ 25 Ray Boone	30.00	13.50	3.80
☐ 26 Dale Mitchell DP	17.00	7.75	2.10
☐ 27 Roy Campanella DP	210.00	95.00	26.00
☐ 28 Eddie Pellagrini	28.00	12.50	3.50
☐ 29 Hal Jeffcoat	28.00	12.50	3.50
☐ 30 Willard Nixon	28.00	12.50	3.50
☐ 31 Ewell Blackwell	45.00	20.00	5.75
☐ 32 Clyde Vollmer	28.00	12.50	3.50
☐ 33 Bob Kennedy DP	17.00	7.75	2.10
☐ 34 George Shuba	28.00	12.50	3.50
☐ 35 Irv Noren DP	17.00	7.75	2.10
☐ 36 Johnny Groth DP	16.00	7.25	2.00
☐ 37 Eddie Mathews DP	110.00	50.00	14.00
☐ 38 Jim Hearn DP	16.00	7.25	2.00
☐ 39 Eddie Miksis	28.00	12.50	3.50

☐ 40	John Lipon	28.00	12.50	3.50
☐ 41	Enos Slaughter	90.00	40.00	11.50
☐ 42	Gus Zernial DP	18.00	8.00	2.30
☐ 43	Gil McDougald	50.00	23.00	6.25
☐ 44	Ellis Kinder SP	35.00	16.00	4.40
☐ 45	Grady Hatton DP	16.00	7.25	2.00
☐ 46	Johnny Klippstein DP	16.00	7.25	2.00
☐ 47	Bubba Church DP	16.00	7.25	2.00
☐ 48	Bob Del Greco DP	16.00	7.25	2.00
☐ 49	Faye Throneberry DP	16.00	7.25	2.00
☐ 50	Chuck Dressen MG DP	25.00	11.50	3.10
☐ 51	Frank Campos DP	16.00	7.25	2.00
☐ 52	Ted Gray DP	16.00	7.25	2.00
☐ 53	Sherm Lollar DP	17.00	7.75	2.10
☐ 54	Bob Feller DP	110.00	50.00	14.00
☐ 55	Maurice McDermott DP	16.00	7.25	2.00
☐ 56	Gerry Staley DP	16.00	7.25	2.00
☐ 57	Carl Scheib	28.00	12.50	3.50
☐ 58	George Metkovich	28.00	12.50	3.50
☐ 59	Karl Drews DP	16.00	7.25	2.00
☐ 60	Cloyd Boyer DP	16.00	7.25	2.00
☐ 61	Early Wynn SP	100.00	45.00	12.50
☐ 62	Monte Irvin DP	40.00	18.00	5.00
☐ 63	Gus Niarhos DP	16.00	7.25	2.00
☐ 64	Dave Philley	28.00	12.50	3.50
☐ 65	Earl Harrist	28.00	12.50	3.50
☐ 66	Minnie Minoso	45.00	20.00	5.75
☐ 67	Roy Sievers DP	17.00	7.75	2.10
☐ 68	Del Rice	28.00	12.50	3.50
☐ 69	Dick Brodowski	28.00	12.50	3.50
☐ 70	Ed Yuhas	28.00	12.50	3.50
☐ 71	Tony Bartirome	28.00	12.50	3.50
☐ 72	Fred Hutchinson SP MG	40.00	18.00	5.00
☐ 73	Eddie Robinson	28.00	12.50	3.50
☐ 74	Joe Rossi	28.00	12.50	3.50
☐ 75	Mike Garcia	30.00	13.50	3.80
☐ 76	Pee Wee Reese	165.00	75.00	21.00
☐ 77	Johnny Mize DP	60.00	27.00	7.50
☐ 78	Red Schoendienst	65.00	29.00	8.25
☐ 79	Johnny Wyrostek	28.00	12.50	3.50
☐ 80	Jim Hegan	30.00	13.50	3.80
☐ 81	Joe Black SP	65.00	29.00	8.25
☐ 82	Mickey Mantle	3300.00	1500.00	425.00
☐ 83	Howie Pollet	28.00	12.50	3.50
☐ 84	Bob Hooper DP	16.00	7.25	2.00
☐ 85	Bobby Morgan DP	16.00	7.25	2.00
☐ 86	Billy Martin	150.00	70.00	19.00
☐ 87	Ed Lopat	40.00	18.00	5.00
☐ 88	Willie Jones DP	16.00	7.25	2.00
☐ 89	Chuck Stobbs DP	16.00	7.25	2.00
☐ 90	Hank Edwards DP	16.00	7.25	2.00
☐ 91	Ebba St.Claire DP	16.00	7.25	2.00
☐ 92	Paul Minner DP	16.00	7.25	2.00
☐ 93	Hal Rice DP	16.00	7.25	2.00
☐ 94	Bill Kennedy DP	16.00	7.25	2.00
☐ 95	Willard Marshall DP	16.00	7.25	2.00
☐ 96	Virgil Trucks	30.00	13.50	3.80
☐ 97	Don Kolloway DP	16.00	7.25	2.00
☐ 98	Cal Abrams DP	16.00	7.25	2.00
☐ 99	Dave Madison	28.00	12.50	3.50
☐ 100	Bill Miller	28.00	12.50	3.50
☐ 101	Ted Wilks	28.00	12.50	3.50
☐ 102	Connie Ryan DP	16.00	7.25	2.00
☐ 103	Joe Astroth DP	16.00	7.25	2.00
☐ 104	Yogi Berra	275.00	125.00	34.00
☐ 105	Joe Nuxhall DP	17.00	7.75	2.10
☐ 106	Johnny Antonelli	30.00	13.50	3.80
☐ 107	Danny O'Connell DP	16.00	7.25	2.00
☐ 108	Bob Porterfield DP	16.00	7.25	2.00
☐ 109	Alvin Dark	35.00	16.00	4.40
☐ 110	Herman Wehmeier DP	16.00	7.25	2.00
☐ 111	Hank Sauer DP	17.00	7.75	2.10
☐ 112	Ned Garver DP	16.00	7.25	2.00
☐ 113	Jerry Priddy	28.00	12.50	3.50
☐ 114	Phil Rizzuto	125.00	57.50	15.50
☐ 115	George Spencer	28.00	12.50	3.50
☐ 116	Frank Smith DP	16.00	7.25	2.00
☐ 117	Sid Gordon DP	16.00	7.25	2.00
☐ 118	Gus Bell DP	17.00	7.75	2.10
☐ 119	Johnny Sain SP	45.00	20.00	5.75
☐ 120	Davey Williams	30.00	13.50	3.80
☐ 121	Walt Dropo	30.00	13.50	3.80
☐ 122	Elmer Valo	28.00	12.50	3.50
☐ 123	Tommy Byrne DP	16.00	7.25	2.00
☐ 124	Sibby Sisti DP	16.00	7.25	2.00
☐ 125	Dick Williams DP	20.00	9.00	2.50
☐ 126	Bill Connelly DP	16.00	7.25	2.00
☐ 127	Clint Courtney DP	16.00	7.25	2.00
☐ 128	Wilmer Mizell DP (Inconsistent design, logo on front with black birds)	17.00	7.75	2.10
☐ 129	Keith Thomas	28.00	12.50	3.50

☐ 130	Turk Lown DP	16.00	7.25	2.00
☐ 131	Harry Byrd DP	16.00	7.25	2.00
☐ 132	Tom Morgan	28.00	12.50	3.50
☐ 133	Gil Coan	28.00	12.50	3.50
☐ 134	Rube Walker	30.00	13.50	3.80
☐ 135	Al Rosen DP	35.00	16.00	4.40
☐ 136	Ken Heintzelman DP	16.00	7.25	2.00
☐ 137	John Rutherford DP	16.00	7.25	2.00
☐ 138	George Kell	55.00	25.00	7.00
☐ 139	Sammy White	28.00	12.50	3.50
☐ 140	Tommy Glaviano	28.00	12.50	3.50
☐ 141	Allie Reynolds DP	35.00	16.00	4.40
☐ 142	Vic Wertz	30.00	13.50	3.80
☐ 143	Billy Pierce	35.00	16.00	4.40
☐ 144	Bob Schultz DP	16.00	7.25	2.00
☐ 145	Harry Dorish DP	16.00	7.25	2.00
☐ 146	Granny Hamner	28.00	12.50	3.50
☐ 147	Warren Spahn	140.00	65.00	17.50
☐ 148	Mickey Grasso	28.00	12.50	3.50
☐ 149	Dom DiMaggio DP	35.00	16.00	4.40
☐ 150	Harry Simpson DP	16.00	7.25	2.00
☐ 151	Hoyt Wilhelm	70.00	32.00	8.75
☐ 152	Bob Adams DP	16.00	7.25	2.00
☐ 153	Andy Seminick DP	16.00	7.25	2.00
☐ 154	Dick Groat	40.00	18.00	5.00
☐ 155	Dutch Leonard	28.00	12.50	3.50
☐ 156	Jim Rivera DP	17.00	7.75	2.10
☐ 157	Bob Addis DP	16.00	7.25	2.00
☐ 158	Johnny Logan	35.00	16.00	4.40
☐ 159	Wayne Terwilliger DP	16.00	7.25	2.00
☐ 160	Bob Young	28.00	12.50	3.50
☐ 161	Vern Bickford DP	16.00	7.25	2.00
☐ 162	Ted Kluszewski	50.00	23.00	6.25
☐ 163	Fred Hatfield DP	16.00	7.25	2.00
☐ 164	Frank Shea DP	16.00	7.25	2.00
☐ 165	Billy Hoeft	30.00	13.50	3.80
☐ 166	Billy Hunter	22.00	10.00	2.80
☐ 167	Art Schult	22.00	10.00	2.80
☐ 168	Willard Schmidt	22.00	10.00	2.80
☐ 169	Dizzy Trout	24.00	11.00	3.00
☐ 170	Bill Werle	22.00	10.00	2.80
☐ 171	Bill Glynn	22.00	10.00	2.80
☐ 172	Rip Repulski	22.00	10.00	2.80
☐ 173	Preston Ward	22.00	10.00	2.80
☐ 174	Billy Loes	27.00	12.00	3.40
☐ 175	Ron Kline	22.00	10.00	2.80
☐ 176	Don Hoak	30.00	13.50	3.80
☐ 177	Jim Dyck	22.00	10.00	2.80
☐ 178	Jim Waugh	22.00	10.00	2.80
☐ 179	Gene Hermanski	22.00	10.00	2.80
☐ 180	Virgil Stallcup	22.00	10.00	2.80
☐ 181	Al Zarilla	22.00	10.00	2.80
☐ 182	Bobby Hofman	22.00	10.00	2.80
☐ 183	Stu Miller	27.00	12.00	3.40
☐ 184	Hal Brown	22.00	10.00	2.80
☐ 185	Jim Pendleton	22.00	10.00	2.80
☐ 186	Charlie Bishop	22.00	10.00	2.80
☐ 187	Jim Fridley	22.00	10.00	2.80
☐ 188	Andy Carey	35.00	16.00	4.40
☐ 189	Ray Jablonski	22.00	10.00	2.80
☐ 190	Dixie Walker CO	24.00	11.00	3.00
☐ 191	Ralph Kiner	65.00	29.00	8.25
☐ 192	Wally Westlake	22.00	10.00	2.80
☐ 193	Mike Clark	22.00	10.00	2.80
☐ 194	Eddie Kazak	22.00	10.00	2.80
☐ 195	Ed McGhee	22.00	10.00	2.80
☐ 196	Bob Keegan	22.00	10.00	2.80
☐ 197	Del Crandall	24.00	11.00	3.00
☐ 198	Forrest Main	22.00	10.00	2.80
☐ 199	Marion Fricano	22.00	10.00	2.80
☐ 200	Gordon Goldsberry	22.00	10.00	2.80
☐ 201	Paul LaPalme	22.00	10.00	2.80
☐ 202	Carl Sawatski	22.00	10.00	2.80
☐ 203	Cliff Fannin	22.00	10.00	2.80
☐ 204	Dick Bokelman	22.00	10.00	2.80
☐ 205	Vern Benson	22.00	10.00	2.80
☐ 206	Ed Bailey	27.00	12.00	3.40
☐ 207	Whitey Ford	165.00	75.00	21.00
☐ 208	Jim Wilson	22.00	10.00	2.80
☐ 209	Jim Greengrass	22.00	10.00	2.80
☐ 210	Bob Cerv	30.00	13.50	3.80
☐ 211	J.W. Porter	22.00	10.00	2.80
☐ 212	Jack Dittmer	22.00	10.00	2.80
☐ 213	Ray Scarborough	22.00	10.00	2.80
☐ 214	Bill Bruton	27.00	12.00	3.40
☐ 215	Gene Conley	27.00	12.00	3.40
☐ 216	Jim Hughes	22.00	10.00	2.80
☐ 217	Murray Wall	22.00	10.00	2.80
☐ 218	Les Fusselman	22.00	10.00	2.80
☐ 219	Pete Runnels UER (Photo actually Don Johnson)	24.00	11.00	3.00
☐ 220	Satchel Paige UER	475.00	210.00	60.00

(Misspelled Satchell on card front)

☐ 221 Bob Milliken	100.00	45.00	12.50
☐ 222 Vic Janowicz DP	55.00	25.00	7.00
☐ 223 Johnny O'Brien DP	55.00	25.00	7.00
☐ 224 Lou Sleater DP	50.00	23.00	6.25
☐ 225 Bobby Shantz	110.00	50.00	14.00
☐ 226 Ed Erautt	100.00	45.00	12.50
☐ 227 Morrie Martin	100.00	45.00	12.50
☐ 228 Hal Newhouser	150.00	70.00	19.00
☐ 229 Rocky Krsnich	100.00	45.00	12.50
☐ 230 Johnny Lindell DP	50.00	23.00	6.25
☐ 231 Solly Hemus DP	50.00	23.00	6.25
☐ 232 Dick Kokos	100.00	45.00	12.50
☐ 233 Al Aber	100.00	45.00	12.50
☐ 234 Ray Murray DP	50.00	23.00	6.25
☐ 235 John Hetki DP	50.00	23.00	6.25
☐ 236 Harry Perkowski DP	50.00	23.00	6.25
☐ 237 Bud Podbielan DP	50.00	23.00	6.25
☐ 238 Cal Hogue DP	50.00	23.00	6.25
☐ 239 Jim Delsing	100.00	45.00	12.50
☐ 240 Fred Marsh	100.00	45.00	12.50
☐ 241 Al Sima DP	50.00	23.00	6.25
☐ 242 Charlie Silvera	110.00	50.00	14.00
☐ 243 Carlos Bernier DP	50.00	23.00	6.25
☐ 244 Willie Mays	2500.00	750.00	250.00
☐ 245 Bill Norman CO	100.00	45.00	12.50
☐ 246 Roy Face DP	90.00	40.00	11.50
☐ 247 Mike Sandlock DP	50.00	23.00	6.25
☐ 248 Gene Stephens DP	50.00	23.00	6.25
☐ 249 Eddie O'Brien	100.00	45.00	12.50
☐ 250 Bob Wilson	100.00	45.00	12.50
☐ 251 Sid Hudson	100.00	45.00	12.50
☐ 252 Hank Foiles	100.00	45.00	12.50
☐ 253 Does not exist	.00	.00	.00
☐ 254 Preacher Roe DP	90.00	40.00	11.50
☐ 255 Dixie Howell	100.00	45.00	12.50
☐ 256 Les Peden	100.00	45.00	12.50
☐ 257 Bob Boyd	100.00	45.00	12.50
☐ 258 Jim Gilliam	275.00	125.00	34.00
☐ 259 Roy McMillan DP	55.00	25.00	7.00
☐ 260 Sam Calderone	100.00	45.00	12.50
☐ 261 Does not exist	.00	.00	.00
☐ 262 Bob Oldis	100.00	45.00	12.50
☐ 263 Johnny Podres	275.00	125.00	34.00
☐ 264 Gene Woodling DP	65.00	29.00	8.25
☐ 265 Jackie Jensen	115.00	52.50	14.50
☐ 266 Bob Cain	100.00	45.00	12.50
☐ 267 Does not exist	.00	.00	.00
☐ 268 Does not exist	.00	.00	.00
☐ 269 Duane Pillette	100.00	45.00	12.50
☐ 270 Vern Stephens	110.00	50.00	14.00
☐ 271 Does not exist	.00	.00	.00
☐ 272 Bill Antonello	100.00	45.00	12.50
☐ 273 Harvey Haddix	125.00	57.50	15.50
☐ 274 John Riddle CO	100.00	45.00	12.50
☐ 275 Does not exist	.00	.00	.00
☐ 276 Ken Raffensberger	100.00	45.00	12.50
☐ 277 Don Lund	100.00	45.00	12.50
☐ 278 Willie Miranda	100.00	45.00	12.50
☐ 279 Joe Coleman DP	50.00	23.00	6.25
☐ 280 Milt Bolling	325.00	65.00	19.50

1954 Topps

The cards in this 250-card set measure approximately 2 5/8" by 3 3/4". Each of the cards in the 1954 Topps set contains a large "head" shot of the player in color plus a smaller full-length photo in black and white set against a color background. This series contains the Rookie Cards of Hank Aaron, Ernie Banks, and Al Kaline and two separate cards of Ted Williams (number 1 and number 250). Conspicuous by his absence is Mickey Mantle who apparently was the exclusive property of Bowman during 1954 (and 1955). The first two issues of Sports Illustrated magazine contained "card" inserts on regular paper stock which showed actual cards in the set in color and some created cards in black and white, including Mickey Mantle.

	NRMT	VG-E	GOOD
COMPLETE SET (250)	8250.00	3700.00	1050.00
COMMON PLAYER (1-50)	15.00	6.75	1.90
COMMON PLAYER (51-75)	30.00	13.50	3.80
COMMON PLAYER (76-125)	15.00	6.75	1.90
COMMON PLAYER (126-250)	15.00	6.75	1.90
☐ 1 Ted Williams	650.00	200.00	65.00
☐ 2 Gus Zernial	16.00	7.25	2.00
☐ 3 Monte Irvin	35.00	16.00	4.40
☐ 4 Hank Sauer	16.00	7.25	2.00
☐ 5 Ed Lopat	22.50	10.00	2.80
☐ 6 Pete Runnels	16.00	7.25	2.00
☐ 7 Ted Kluszewski	30.00	13.50	3.80
☐ 8 Bob Young	15.00	6.75	1.90
☐ 9 Harvey Haddix	16.00	7.25	2.00
☐ 10 Jackie Robinson	300.00	135.00	38.00
☐ 11 Paul Leslie Smith	15.00	6.75	1.90
☐ 12 Del Crandall	16.00	7.25	2.00
☐ 13 Billy Martin	85.00	38.00	10.50
☐ 14 Preacher Roe	21.00	9.50	2.60
☐ 15 Al Rosen	25.00	11.50	3.10
☐ 16 Vic Janowicz	18.00	8.00	2.30
☐ 17 Phil Rizzuto	75.00	34.00	9.50
☐ 18 Walt Dropo	16.00	7.25	2.00
☐ 19 Johnny Lipon	15.00	6.75	1.90
☐ 20 Warren Spahn	100.00	45.00	12.50
☐ 21 Bobby Shantz	16.00	7.25	2.00
☐ 22 Jim Greengrass	15.00	6.75	1.90
☐ 23 Luke Easter	16.00	7.25	2.00
☐ 24 Granny Hamner	15.00	6.75	1.90
☐ 25 Harvey Kuenn	40.00	18.00	5.00
☐ 26 Ray Jablonski	15.00	6.75	1.90
☐ 27 Ferris Fain	16.00	7.25	2.00
☐ 28 Paul Minner	15.00	6.75	1.90
☐ 29 Jim Hegan	16.00	7.25	2.00
☐ 30 Eddie Mathews	100.00	45.00	12.50
☐ 31 Johnny Klippstein	15.00	6.75	1.90
☐ 32 Duke Snider	150.00	70.00	19.00
☐ 33 Johnny Schmitz	15.00	6.75	1.90
☐ 34 Jim Rivera	15.00	6.75	1.90
☐ 35 Jim Gilliam	30.00	13.50	3.80
☐ 36 Hoyt Wilhelm	50.00	23.00	6.25
☐ 37 Whitey Ford	110.00	50.00	14.00
☐ 38 Eddie Stanky MG	16.00	7.25	2.00
☐ 39 Sherm Lollar	16.00	7.25	2.00
☐ 40 Mel Parnell	16.00	7.25	2.00
☐ 41 Willie Jones	15.00	6.75	1.90
☐ 42 Don Mueller	16.00	7.25	2.00
☐ 43 Dick Groat	20.00	9.00	2.50
☐ 44 Ned Garver	15.00	6.75	1.90
☐ 45 Richie Ashburn	45.00	20.00	5.75
☐ 46 Ken Raffensberger	15.00	6.75	1.90
☐ 47 Ellis Kinder	15.00	6.75	1.90
☐ 48 Billy Hunter	15.00	6.75	1.90
☐ 49 Ray Murray	15.00	6.75	1.90
☐ 50 Yogi Berra	250.00	115.00	31.00
☐ 51 Johnny Lindell	32.50	14.50	4.10
☐ 52 Vic Power	35.00	16.00	4.40
☐ 53 Jack Dittmer	30.00	13.50	3.80
☐ 54 Vern Stephens	32.50	14.50	4.10
☐ 55 Phil Cavarretta MG	35.00	16.00	4.40
☐ 56 Willie Miranda	30.00	13.50	3.80
☐ 57 Luis Aloma	30.00	13.50	3.80
☐ 58 Bob Wilson	30.00	13.50	3.80
☐ 59 Gene Conley	32.50	14.50	4.10
☐ 60 Frank Baumholtz	30.00	13.50	3.80
☐ 61 Bob Cain	30.00	13.50	3.80
☐ 62 Eddie Robinson	30.00	13.50	3.80
☐ 63 Johnny Pesky	35.00	16.00	4.40
☐ 64 Hank Thompson	35.00	16.00	4.40
☐ 65 Bob Swift CO	30.00	13.50	3.80
☐ 66 Ted Lepcio	30.00	13.50	3.80
☐ 67 Jim Willis	30.00	13.50	3.80
☐ 68 Sam Calderone	30.00	13.50	3.80
☐ 69 Bud Podbielan	30.00	13.50	3.80
☐ 70 Larry Doby	70.00	32.00	8.75
☐ 71 Frank Smith	30.00	13.50	3.80
☐ 72 Preston Ward	30.00	13.50	3.80

☐ 73	Wayne Terwilliger	30.00	13.50	3.80
☐ 74	Bill Taylor	30.00	13.50	3.80
☐ 75	Fred Haney MG	30.00	13.50	3.80
☐ 76	Bob Scheffing CO	15.00	6.75	1.90
☐ 77	Ray Boone	16.00	7.25	2.00
☐ 78	Ted Kazanski	15.00	6.75	1.90
☐ 79	Andy Pafko	16.00	7.25	2.00
☐ 80	Jackie Jensen	20.00	9.00	2.50
☐ 81	Dave Hoskins	15.00	6.75	1.90
☐ 82	Milt Bolling	15.00	6.75	1.90
☐ 83	Joe Collins	18.00	8.00	2.30
☐ 84	Dick Cole	15.00	6.75	1.90
☐ 85	Bob Turley	30.00	13.50	3.80
☐ 86	Billy Herman CO	27.00	12.00	3.40
☐ 87	Roy Face	17.50	8.00	2.20
☐ 88	Matt Batts	15.00	6.75	1.90
☐ 89	Howie Pollet	15.00	6.75	1.90
☐ 90	Willie Mays	525.00	240.00	65.00
☐ 91	Bob Oldis	15.00	6.75	1.90
☐ 92	Wally Westlake	15.00	6.75	1.90
☐ 93	Sid Hudson	15.00	6.75	1.90
☐ 94	Ernie Banks	825.00	375.00	105.00
☐ 95	Hal Rice	15.00	6.75	1.90
☐ 96	Charlie Silvera	16.00	7.25	2.00
☐ 97	Jerald Hal Lane	15.00	6.75	1.90
☐ 98	Joe Black	23.00	10.50	2.90
☐ 99	Bobby Hofman	15.00	6.75	1.90
☐ 100	Bob Keegan	15.00	6.75	1.90
☐ 101	Gene Woodling	24.00	11.00	3.00
☐ 102	Gil Hodges	85.00	38.00	10.50
☐ 103	Jim Lemon	20.00	9.00	2.50
☐ 104	Mike Sandlock	15.00	6.75	1.90
☐ 105	Andy Carey	20.00	9.00	2.50
☐ 106	Dick Kokos	15.00	6.75	1.90
☐ 107	Duane Pillette	15.00	6.75	1.90
☐ 108	Thornton Kipper	15.00	6.75	1.90
☐ 109	Bill Bruton	16.00	7.25	2.00
☐ 110	Harry Dorish	15.00	6.75	1.90
☐ 111	Jim Delsing	15.00	6.75	1.90
☐ 112	Bill Renna	15.00	6.75	1.90
☐ 113	Bob Boyd	15.00	6.75	1.90
☐ 114	Dean Stone	15.00	6.75	1.90
☐ 115	Rip Repulski	15.00	6.75	1.90
☐ 116	Steve Bilko	15.00	6.75	1.90
☐ 117	Solly Hemus	15.00	6.75	1.90
☐ 118	Carl Scheib	15.00	6.75	1.90
☐ 119	Johnny Antonelli	16.00	7.25	2.00
☐ 120	Roy McMillan	16.00	7.25	2.00
☐ 121	Clem Labine	20.00	9.00	2.50
☐ 122	Johnny Logan	16.00	7.25	2.00
☐ 123	Bobby Adams	15.00	6.75	1.90
☐ 124	Marion Fricano	15.00	6.75	1.90
☐ 125	Harry Perkowski	15.00	6.75	1.90
☐ 126	Ben Wade	15.00	6.75	1.90
☐ 127	Steve O'Neill MG	15.00	6.75	1.90
☐ 128	Hank Aaron	2100.00	950.00	275.00
☐ 129	Forrest Jacobs	15.00	6.75	1.90
☐ 130	Hank Bauer	35.00	16.00	4.40
☐ 131	Reno Bertoia	15.00	6.75	1.90
☐ 132	Tom Lasorda	165.00	75.00	21.00
☐ 133	Dave Baker CO	15.00	6.75	1.90
☐ 134	Cal Hogue	15.00	6.75	1.90
☐ 135	Joe Presko	15.00	6.75	1.90
☐ 136	Connie Ryan	15.00	6.75	1.90
☐ 137	Wally Moon	30.00	13.50	3.80
☐ 138	Bob Borkowski	15.00	6.75	1.90
☐ 139	The O'Briens Johnny O'Brien Eddie O'Brien	30.00	13.50	3.80
☐ 140	Tom Wright	15.00	6.75	1.90
☐ 141	Joey Jay	20.00	9.00	2.50
☐ 142	Tom Poholsky	15.00	6.75	1.90
☐ 143	Rollie Hemsley CO	15.00	6.75	1.90
☐ 144	Bill Werle	15.00	6.75	1.90
☐ 145	Elmer Valo	15.00	6.75	1.90
☐ 146	Don Johnson	15.00	6.75	1.90
☐ 147	Johnny Riddle CO	15.00	6.75	1.90
☐ 148	Bob Trice	15.00	6.75	1.90
☐ 149	Al Robertson	15.00	6.75	1.90
☐ 150	Dick Kryhoski	15.00	6.75	1.90
☐ 151	Alex Grammas	15.00	6.75	1.90
☐ 152	Michael Blyzka	15.00	6.75	1.90
☐ 153	Al Walker	15.00	6.75	1.90
☐ 154	Mike Fornieles	15.00	6.75	1.90
☐ 155	Bob Kennedy	16.00	7.25	2.00
☐ 156	Joe Coleman	15.00	6.75	1.90
☐ 157	Don Lenhardt	15.00	6.75	1.90
☐ 158	Peanuts Lowrey	15.00	6.75	1.90
☐ 159	Dave Philley	15.00	6.75	1.90
☐ 160	Ralph Kress CO	15.00	6.75	1.90
☐ 161	John Hetki	15.00	6.75	1.90
☐ 162	Herman Wehmeier	15.00	6.75	1.90
☐ 163	Frank House	15.00	6.75	1.90
☐ 164	Stu Miller	16.00	7.25	2.00
☐ 165	Jim Pendleton	15.00	6.75	1.90
☐ 166	Johnny Podres	30.00	13.50	3.80
☐ 167	Don Lund	15.00	6.75	1.90
☐ 168	Morrie Martin	15.00	6.75	1.90
☐ 169	Jim Hughes	15.00	6.75	1.90
☐ 170	James(Dusty) Rhodes	20.00	9.00	2.50
☐ 171	Leo Kiely	15.00	6.75	1.90
☐ 172	Harold Brown	15.00	6.75	1.90
☐ 173	Jack Harshman	15.00	6.75	1.90
☐ 174	Tom Qualters	15.00	6.75	1.90
☐ 175	Frank Leja	22.00	10.00	2.80
☐ 176	Robert Keely CO	15.00	6.75	1.90
☐ 177	Bob Milliken	15.00	6.75	1.90
☐ 178	Bill Glynn	15.00	6.75	1.90
☐ 179	Gair Allie	15.00	6.75	1.90
☐ 180	Wes Westrum	16.00	7.25	2.00
☐ 181	Mel Roach	15.00	6.75	1.90
☐ 182	Chuck Harmon	15.00	6.75	1.90
☐ 183	Earle Combs CO	27.00	12.00	3.40
☐ 184	Ed Bailey	18.00	8.00	2.30
☐ 185	Chuck Stobbs	15.00	6.75	1.90
☐ 186	Karl Olson	15.00	6.75	1.90
☐ 187	Heinie Manush CO	27.00	12.00	3.40
☐ 188	Dave Jolly	15.00	6.75	1.90
☐ 189	Bob Ross	15.00	6.75	1.90
☐ 190	Ray Herbert	15.00	6.75	1.90
☐ 191	John(Dick) Schofield	20.00	9.00	2.50
☐ 192	Ellis Deal CO	15.00	6.75	1.90
☐ 193	Johnny Hopp CO	16.00	7.25	2.00
☐ 194	Bill Sarni	15.00	6.75	1.90
☐ 195	Billy Consolo	18.00	8.00	2.30
☐ 196	Stan Jok	15.00	6.75	1.90
☐ 197	Lynwood Rowe CO ("Schoolboy")	16.00	7.25	2.00
☐ 198	Carl Sawatski	15.00	6.75	1.90
☐ 199	Glenn(Rocky) Nelson	15.00	6.75	1.90
☐ 200	Larry Jansen	16.00	7.25	2.00
☐ 201	Al Kaline	900.00	400.00	115.00
☐ 202	Bob Purkey	20.00	9.00	2.50
☐ 203	Harry Brecheen CO	16.00	7.25	2.00
☐ 204	Angel Scull	15.00	6.75	1.90
☐ 205	Johnny Sain	30.00	13.50	3.80
☐ 206	Ray Crone	15.00	6.75	1.90
☐ 207	Tom Oliver CO	15.00	6.75	1.90
☐ 208	Grady Hatton	15.00	6.75	1.90
☐ 209	Chuck Thompson	15.00	6.75	1.90
☐ 210	Bob Buhl	20.00	9.00	2.50
☐ 211	Don Hoak	18.00	8.00	2.30
☐ 212	Bob Micelotta	15.00	6.75	1.90
☐ 213	Johnny Fitzpatrick CO	15.00	6.75	1.90
☐ 214	Arnie Portocarrero	15.00	6.75	1.90
☐ 215	Ed McGhee	15.00	6.75	1.90
☐ 216	Al Sima	15.00	6.75	1.90
☐ 217	Paul Schreiber CO	15.00	6.75	1.90
☐ 218	Fred Marsh	15.00	6.75	1.90
☐ 219	Chuck Kress	15.00	6.75	1.90
☐ 220	Ruben Gomez	16.00	7.25	2.00
☐ 221	Dick Brodowski	15.00	6.75	1.90
☐ 222	Bill Wilson	15.00	6.75	1.90
☐ 223	Joe Haynes CO	15.00	6.75	1.90
☐ 224	Dick Weik	15.00	6.75	1.90
☐ 225	Don Liddle	15.00	6.75	1.90
☐ 226	Jehosie Heard	15.00	6.75	1.90
☐ 227	Colonel Mills CO	15.00	6.75	1.90
☐ 228	Gene Hermanski	15.00	6.75	1.90
☐ 229	Bob Talbot	15.00	6.75	1.90
☐ 230	Bob Kuzava	16.00	7.25	2.00
☐ 231	Roy Smalley	15.00	6.75	1.90
☐ 232	Lou Limmer	15.00	6.75	1.90
☐ 233	Augie Galan CO	15.00	6.75	1.90
☐ 234	Jerry Lynch	20.00	9.00	2.50
☐ 235	Vernon Law	16.00	7.25	2.00
☐ 236	Paul Penson	15.00	6.75	1.90
☐ 237	Mike Ryba CO	15.00	6.75	1.90
☐ 238	Al Aber	15.00	6.75	1.90
☐ 239	Bill Skowron	85.00	38.00	10.50
☐ 240	Sam Mele	15.00	6.75	1.90
☐ 241	Robert Miller	15.00	6.75	1.90
☐ 242	Curt Roberts	15.00	6.75	1.90
☐ 243	Ray Blades CO	15.00	6.75	1.90
☐ 244	Leroy Wheat	15.00	6.75	1.90
☐ 245	Roy Sievers	18.00	8.00	2.30
☐ 246	Howie Fox	15.00	6.75	1.90
☐ 247	Ed Mayo CO	15.00	6.75	1.90
☐ 248	Al Smith	20.00	9.00	2.50
☐ 249	Wilmer Mizell	16.00	7.25	2.00
☐ 250	Ted Williams	700.00	210.00	70.00

1955 Topps

The cards in this 206-card set measure approximately 2 5/8" by 3 3/4". Both the large "head" shot and the smaller full-length photos used on each card of the 1955 Topps set are in color. The card fronts were designed horizontally for the first time in Topps' history. The first card features Dusty Rhodes, hitting star for the Giants' 1954 World Series sweep over the Indians. A "high" series, 161 to 210, is more difficult to find than cards 1 to 160. Numbers 175, 186, 203, and 209 were never issued. To fill in for the four cards not issued in the high number series, Topps double printed four players, those appearing on cards 170, 172, 184, and 188. Although rarely seen, there exist salesman sample panels of three cards containing the fronts of regular cards with ad information for the 1955 Topps regular and the 1955 Topps Doubleheaders on the back. One such ad panel depicts (from top to bottom) Danny Schell, Jake Thies, and Howie Pollet. The key rookies in this set are Ken Boyer, Roberto Clemente, Harmon Killebrew, and Sandy Koufax.

	NRMT	VG-E	GOOD
COMPLETE SET (206)	7600.00	3400.00	950.00
COMMON PLAYER (1-150)	9.00	4.00	1.15
COMMON PLAYER (151-160)	18.00	8.00	2.30
COMMON PLAYER (161-210)	28.00	12.50	3.50

	NRMT	VG-E	GOOD
☐ 1 Dusty Rhodes	45.00	9.00	2.70
☐ 2 Ted Williams	425.00	190.00	52.50
☐ 3 Art Fowler	10.00	4.50	1.25
☐ 4 Al Kaline	250.00	115.00	31.00
☐ 5 Jim Gilliam	15.00	6.75	1.90
☐ 6 Stan Hack MG	11.00	4.90	1.40
☐ 7 Jim Hegan	10.00	4.50	1.25
☐ 8 Harold Smith	9.00	4.00	1.15
☐ 9 Robert Miller	9.00	4.00	1.15
☐ 10 Bob Keegan	9.00	4.00	1.15
☐ 11 Ferris Fain	10.00	4.50	1.25
☐ 12 Vernon(Jake) Thies	9.00	4.00	1.15
☐ 13 Fred Marsh	9.00	4.00	1.15
☐ 14 Jim Finigan	9.00	4.00	1.15
☐ 15 Jim Pendleton	9.00	4.00	1.15
☐ 16 Roy Sievers	10.00	4.50	1.25
☐ 17 Bobby Hofman	9.00	4.00	1.15
☐ 18 Russ Kemmerer	9.00	4.00	1.15
☐ 19 Billy Herman CO	15.00	6.75	1.90
☐ 20 Andy Carey	12.00	5.50	1.50
☐ 21 Alex Grammas	9.00	4.00	1.15
☐ 22 Bill Skowron	20.00	9.00	2.50
☐ 23 Jack Parks	9.00	4.00	1.15
☐ 24 Hal Newhouser	20.00	9.00	2.50
☐ 25 Johnny Podres	20.00	9.00	2.50
☐ 26 Dick Groat	12.00	5.50	1.50
☐ 27 Billy Gardner	10.00	4.50	1.25
☐ 28 Ernie Banks	225.00	100.00	28.00
☐ 29 Herman Wehmeier	9.00	4.00	1.15
☐ 30 Vic Power	10.00	4.50	1.25
☐ 31 Warren Spahn	85.00	38.00	10.50
☐ 32 Warren McGhee	9.00	4.00	1.15
☐ 33 Tom Qualters	9.00	4.00	1.15
☐ 34 Wayne Terwilliger	9.00	4.00	1.15
☐ 35 Dave Jolly	9.00	4.00	1.15
☐ 36 Leo Kiely	9.00	4.00	1.15
☐ 37 Joe Cunningham	12.50	5.75	1.55
☐ 38 Bob Turley	15.00	6.75	1.90
☐ 39 Bill Glynn	9.00	4.00	1.15
☐ 40 Don Hoak	10.00	4.50	1.25
☐ 41 Chuck Stobbs	9.00	4.00	1.15
☐ 42 John(Windy) McCall	9.00	4.00	1.15
☐ 43 Harvey Haddix	10.00	4.50	1.25
☐ 44 Harold Valentine	9.00	4.00	1.15
☐ 45 Hank Sauer	10.00	4.50	1.25
☐ 46 Ted Kazanski	9.00	4.00	1.15
☐ 47 Hank Aaron UER (Birth incorrectly listed as 2/10)	400.00	180.00	50.00
☐ 48 Bob Kennedy	10.00	4.50	1.25
☐ 49 J.W. Porter	9.00	4.00	1.15
☐ 50 Jackie Robinson	250.00	115.00	31.00
☐ 51 Jim Hughes	9.00	4.00	1.15
☐ 52 Bill Tremel	9.00	4.00	1.15
☐ 53 Bill Taylor	9.00	4.00	1.15
☐ 54 Lou Limmer	9.00	4.00	1.15
☐ 55 Rip Repulski	9.00	4.00	1.15
☐ 56 Ray Jablonski	9.00	4.00	1.15
☐ 57 Billy O'Dell	9.00	4.00	1.15
☐ 58 Jim Rivera	9.00	4.00	1.15
☐ 59 Gair Allie	9.00	4.00	1.15
☐ 60 Dean Stone	9.00	4.00	1.15
☐ 61 Forrest Jacobs	9.00	4.00	1.15
☐ 62 Thornton Kipper	9.00	4.00	1.15
☐ 63 Joe Collins	10.00	4.50	1.25
☐ 64 Gus Triandos	12.50	5.75	1.55
☐ 65 Ray Boone	10.00	4.50	1.25
☐ 66 Ron Jackson	9.00	4.00	1.15
☐ 67 Wally Moon	10.00	4.50	1.25
☐ 68 Jim Davis	9.00	4.00	1.15
☐ 69 Ed Bailey	10.00	4.50	1.25
☐ 70 Al Rosen	14.00	6.25	1.75
☐ 71 Ruben Gomez	9.00	4.00	1.15
☐ 72 Karl Olson	9.00	4.00	1.15
☐ 73 Jack Shepard	9.00	4.00	1.15
☐ 74 Bob Borkowski	9.00	4.00	1.15
☐ 75 Sandy Amoros	25.00	11.50	3.10
☐ 76 Howie Pollet	9.00	4.00	1.15
☐ 77 Arnie Portocarrero	9.00	4.00	1.15
☐ 78 Gordon Jones	9.00	4.00	1.15
☐ 79 Clyde(Danny) Schell	9.00	4.00	1.15
☐ 80 Bob Grim	15.00	6.75	1.90
☐ 81 Gene Conley	10.00	4.50	1.25
☐ 82 Chuck Harmon	9.00	4.00	1.15
☐ 83 Tom Brewer	9.00	4.00	1.15
☐ 84 Camilo Pascual	15.00	6.75	1.90
☐ 85 Don Mossi	15.00	6.75	1.90
☐ 86 Bill Wilson	9.00	4.00	1.15
☐ 87 Frank House	9.00	4.00	1.15
☐ 88 Bob Skinner	15.00	6.75	1.90
☐ 89 Joe Frazier	10.00	4.50	1.25
☐ 90 Karl Spooner	15.00	6.75	1.90
☐ 91 Milt Bolling	9.00	4.00	1.15
☐ 92 Don Zimmer	40.00	18.00	5.00
☐ 93 Steve Bilko	9.00	4.00	1.15
☐ 94 Reno Bertoia	9.00	4.00	1.15
☐ 95 Preston Ward	9.00	4.00	1.15
☐ 96 Chuck Bishop	9.00	4.00	1.15
☐ 97 Carlos Paula	9.00	4.00	1.15
☐ 98 John Riddle CO	9.00	4.00	1.15
☐ 99 Frank Leja	11.00	4.90	1.40
☐ 100 Monte Irvin	30.00	13.50	3.80
☐ 101 Johnny Gray	9.00	4.00	1.15
☐ 102 Wally Westlake	9.00	4.00	1.15
☐ 103 Chuck White	9.00	4.00	1.15
☐ 104 Jack Harshman	9.00	4.00	1.15
☐ 105 Chuck Diering	9.00	4.00	1.15
☐ 106 Frank Sullivan	9.00	4.00	1.15
☐ 107 Curt Roberts	9.00	4.00	1.15
☐ 108 Al Walker	9.00	4.00	1.15
☐ 109 Ed Lopat	15.00	6.75	1.90
☐ 110 Gus Zernial	10.00	4.50	1.25
☐ 111 Bob Milliken	9.00	4.00	1.15
☐ 112 Nelson King	9.00	4.00	1.15
☐ 113 Harry Brecheen CO	10.00	4.50	1.25
☐ 114 Louis Ortiz	9.00	4.00	1.15
☐ 115 Ellis Kinder	9.00	4.00	1.15
☐ 116 Tom Hurd	9.00	4.00	1.15
☐ 117 Mel Roach	9.00	4.00	1.15
☐ 118 Bob Purkey	9.00	4.00	1.15
☐ 119 Bob Lennon	9.00	4.00	1.15
☐ 120 Ted Kluszewski	25.00	11.50	3.10
☐ 121 Bill Renna	9.00	4.00	1.15
☐ 122 Carl Sawatski	9.00	4.00	1.15
☐ 123 Sandy Koufax	1300.00	575.00	160.00
☐ 124 Harmon Killebrew	425.00	190.00	52.50
☐ 125 Ken Boyer	75.00	34.00	9.50
☐ 126 Dick Hall	9.00	4.00	1.15
☐ 127 Dale Long	12.50	5.75	1.55
☐ 128 Ted Lepcio	9.00	4.00	1.15

☐	129 Elvin Tappe	9.00	4.00	1.15
☐	130 Mayo Smith MG	9.00	4.00	1.15
☐	131 Grady Hatton	9.00	4.00	1.15
☐	132 Bob Trice	9.00	4.00	1.15
☐	133 Dave Hoskins	9.00	4.00	1.15
☐	134 Joey Jay	10.00	4.50	1.25
☐	135 Johnny O'Brien	10.00	4.50	1.25
☐	136 Veston(Bunky) Stewart	9.00	4.00	1.15
☐	137 Harry Elliott	9.00	4.00	1.15
☐	138 Ray Herbert	9.00	4.00	1.15
☐	139 Steve Kraly	9.00	4.00	1.15
☐	140 Mel Parnell	10.00	4.50	1.25
☐	141 Tom Wright	9.00	4.00	1.15
☐	142 Jerry Lynch	10.00	4.50	1.25
☐	143 John(Dick) Schofield	10.00	4.50	1.25
☐	144 John(Joe) Amalfitano	12.50	5.75	1.55
☐	145 Elmer Valo	9.00	4.00	1.15
☐	146 Dick Donovan	12.50	5.75	1.55
☐	147 Hugh Pepper	9.00	4.00	1.15
☐	148 Hector Brown	9.00	4.00	1.15
☐	149 Ray Crone	9.00	4.00	1.15
☐	150 Mike Higgins MG	9.00	4.00	1.15
☐	151 Ralph Kress CO	18.00	8.00	2.30
☐	152 Harry Agganis	85.00	38.00	10.50
☐	153 Bud Podbielan	18.00	8.00	2.30
☐	154 Willie Miranda	18.00	8.00	2.30
☐	155 Eddie Mathews	130.00	57.50	16.50
☐	156 Joe Black	35.00	16.00	4.40
☐	157 Robert Miller	18.00	8.00	2.30
☐	158 Tommy Carroll	18.00	8.00	2.30
☐	159 Johnny Schmitz	18.00	8.00	2.30
☐	160 Ray Narleski	25.00	11.50	3.10
☐	161 Chuck Tanner	35.00	16.00	4.40
☐	162 Joe Coleman	28.00	12.50	3.50
☐	163 Faye Throneberry	28.00	12.50	3.50
☐	164 Roberto Clemente	1650.00	750.00	210.00
☐	165 Don Johnson	28.00	12.50	3.50
☐	166 Hank Bauer	55.00	25.00	7.00
☐	167 Thomas Casagrande	28.00	12.50	3.50
☐	168 Duane Pillette	28.00	12.50	3.50
☐	169 Bob Oldis	28.00	12.50	3.50
☐	170 Jim Pearce DP	16.00	7.25	2.00
☐	171 Dick Brodowski	28.00	12.50	3.50
☐	172 Frank Baumholtz DP	16.00	7.25	2.00
☐	173 Bob Kline	28.00	12.50	3.50
☐	174 Rudy Minarcin	28.00	12.50	3.50
☐	175 Does not exist	.00	.00	.00
☐	176 Norm Zauchin	28.00	12.50	3.50
☐	177 Al Robertson	28.00	12.50	3.50
☐	178 Bobby Adams	28.00	12.50	3.50
☐	179 Jim Bolger	28.00	12.50	3.50
☐	180 Clem Labine	35.00	16.00	4.40
☐	181 Roy McMillan	30.00	13.50	3.80
☐	182 Humberto Robinson	28.00	12.50	3.50
☐	183 Anthony Jacobs	28.00	12.50	3.50
☐	184 Harry Perkowski DP	16.00	7.25	2.00
☐	185 Don Ferrarese	28.00	12.50	3.50
☐	186 Does not exist	.00	.00	.00
☐	187 Gil Hodges	165.00	75.00	21.00
☐	188 Charlie Silvera DP	16.00	7.25	2.00
☐	189 Phil Rizzuto	165.00	75.00	21.00
☐	190 Gene Woodling	35.00	16.00	4.40
☐	191 Eddie Stanky MG	35.00	16.00	4.40
☐	192 Jim Delsing	28.00	12.50	3.50
☐	193 Johnny Sain	45.00	20.00	5.75
☐	194 Willie Mays	550.00	250.00	70.00
☐	195 Ed Roebuck	35.00	16.00	4.40
☐	196 Gale Wade	28.00	12.50	3.50
☐	197 Al Smith	30.00	13.50	3.80
☐	198 Yogi Berra	250.00	115.00	31.00
☐	199 Odbert Hamric	28.00	12.50	3.50
☐	200 Jackie Jensen	50.00	23.00	6.25
☐	201 Sherm Lollar	33.00	15.00	4.10
☐	202 Jim Owens	28.00	12.50	3.50
☐	203 Does not exist	.00	.00	.00
☐	204 Frank Smith	28.00	12.50	3.50
☐	205 Gene Freese	35.00	16.00	4.40
☐	206 Pete Daley	28.00	12.50	3.50
☐	207 Billy Consolo	28.00	12.50	3.50
☐	208 Ray Moore	28.00	12.50	3.50
☐	209 Does not exist	.00	.00	.00
☐	210 Duke Snider	550.00	140.00	45.00

1955 Topps Double Header

The cards in ths 66-card set measure approximately 2 1/16" by 4 7/8". Borrowing a design from the T201 Mecca series, Topps issued a 132-player "Double Header" set in a separate wrapper in 1955. Each player is numbered in the biographical section on the reverse. When open, with perforated flap up, one player is revealed; when the flap is lowered, or closed, the player design on top incorporates a portion of the inside player artwork. When the cards are placed side by side, a continuous ballpark background is formed. Some cards have been found without perforations, and all players pictured appear in the low series of the 1955 regular issue.

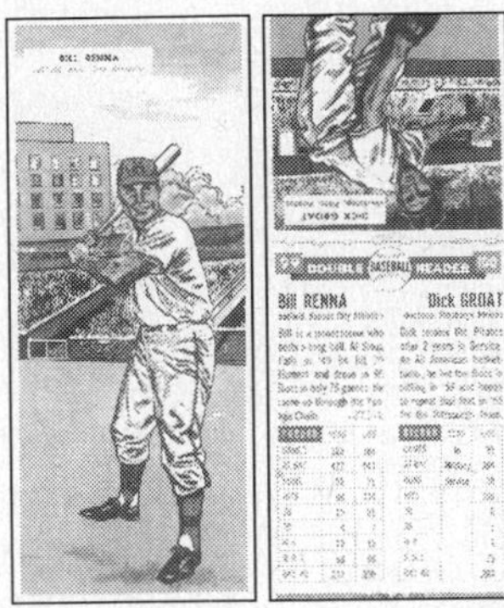

		NRMT	VG-E	GOOD
	COMPLETE SET (66)	4000.00	1800.00	500.00
	COMMON PAIR (1-132)	40.00	18.00	5.00
☐	1 Al Rosen and 2 Chuck Diering	50.00	23.00	6.25
☐	3 Monte Irvin and 4 Russ Kemmerer	60.00	27.00	7.50
☐	5 Ted Kazanski and 6 Gordon Jones	40.00	18.00	5.00
☐	7 Bill Taylor and 8 Billy O'Dell	40.00	18.00	5.00
☐	9 J.W. Porter and 10 Thornton Kipper	40.00	18.00	5.00
☐	11 Curt Roberts and 12 Arnie Portocarrero	40.00	18.00	5.00
☐	13 Wally Westlake and 14 Frank House	40.00	18.00	5.00
☐	15 Rube Walker and 16 Lou Limmer	40.00	18.00	5.00
☐	17 Dean Stone and 18 Charlie White	40.00	18.00	5.00
☐	19 Karl Spooner and 20 Jim Hughes	40.00	18.00	5.00
☐	21 Bill Skowron and 22 Frank Sullivan	50.00	23.00	6.25
☐	23 Jack Shepard and 24 Stan Hack MG	40.00	18.00	5.00
☐	25 Jackie Robinson and 26 Don Hoak	225.00	100.00	28.00
☐	27 Dusty Rhodes and 28 Jim Davis	40.00	18.00	5.00
☐	29 Vic Power and 30 Ed Bailey	40.00	18.00	5.00
☐	31 Howie Pollet and 32 Ernie Banks	225.00	100.00	28.00
☐	33 Jim Pendleton and 34 Gene Conley	40.00	18.00	5.00
☐	35 Karl Olson and 36 Andy Carey	40.00	18.00	5.00
☐	37 Wally Moon and 38 Joe Cunningham	50.00	23.00	6.25
☐	39 Freddie Marsh and 40 Vernon Thies	40.00	18.00	5.00
☐	41 Eddie Lopat and 42 Harvey Haddix	50.00	23.00	6.25
☐	43 Leo Kiely and 44 Chuck Stobbs	40.00	18.00	5.00
☐	45 Al Kaline and 46 Harold Valentine	225.00	100.00	28.00
☐	47 Forrest Jacobs and 48 Johnny Gray	40.00	18.00	5.00
☐	49 Ron Jackson and 50 Jim Finigan	40.00	18.00	5.00
☐	51 Ray Jablonski and 52 Bob Keegan	40.00	18.00	5.00
☐	53 Billy Herman CO and	60.00	27.00	7.50

54 Sandy Amoros			
☐ 55 Chuck Harmon and 56 Bob Skinner	40.00	18.00	5.00
☐ 57 Dick Hall and 58 Bob Grim	40.00	18.00	5.00
☐ 59 Billy Glynn and 60 Bob Miller	40.00	18.00	5.00
☐ 61 Billy Gardner and 62 John Hetki	40.00	18.00	5.00
☐ 63 Bob Borkowski and 64 Bob Turley	50.00	23.00	6.25
☐ 65 Joe Collins and 66 Jack Harshman	40.00	18.00	5.00
☐ 67 Jim Hegan and 68 Jack Parks	40.00	18.00	5.00
☐ 69 Ted Williams and 70 Mayo Smith MG	375.00	170.00	47.50
☐ 71 Gair Allie and 72 Grady Hatton	40.00	18.00	5.00
☐ 73 Jerry Lynch and 74 Harry Brecheen	40.00	18.00	5.00
☐ 75 Tom Wright and 76 Vernon Stewart	40.00	18.00	5.00
☐ 77 Dave Hoskins and 78 Warren McGhee	40.00	18.00	5.00
☐ 79 Roy Sievers and 80 Art Fowler	40.00	18.00	5.00
☐ 81 Danny Schell and 82 Gus Triandos	40.00	18.00	5.00
☐ 83 Joe Frazier and 84 Don Mossi	40.00	18.00	5.00
☐ 85 Elmer Valo and 86 Hector Brown	40.00	18.00	5.00
☐ 87 Bob Kennedy and 88 Windy McCall	40.00	18.00	5.00
☐ 89 Ruben Gomez and 90 Jim Rivera	40.00	18.00	5.00
☐ 91 Louis Ortiz and 92 Milt Bolling	40.00	18.00	5.00
☐ 93 Carl Sawatski and 94 El Tappe	40.00	18.00	5.00
☐ 95 Dave Jolly and 96 Bobby Hofman	40.00	18.00	5.00
☐ 97 Preston Ward and 98 Don Zimmer	50.00	23.00	6.25
☐ 99 Bill Renna and 100 Dick Groat	50.00	23.00	6.25
☐ 101 Bill Wilson and 102 Bill Tremel	40.00	18.00	5.00
☐ 103 Hank Sauer and 104 Camilo Pascual	50.00	23.00	6.25
☐ 105 Hank Aaron and 106 Ray Herbert	500.00	230.00	65.00
☐ 107 Alex Grammas and 108 Tom Qualters	40.00	18.00	5.00
☐ 109 Hal Newhouser and 110 Chuck Bishop	75.00	34.00	9.50
☐ 111 Harmon Killebrew and 112 John Podres	200.00	90.00	25.00
☐ 113 Ray Boone and 114 Bob Purkey	40.00	18.00	5.00
☐ 115 Dale Long and 116 Ferris Fain	40.00	18.00	5.00
☐ 117 Steve Bilko and 118 Bob Milliken	40.00	18.00	5.00
☐ 119 Mel Parnell and 120 Tom Hurd	40.00	18.00	5.00
☐ 121 Ted Kluszewski and 122 Jim Owens	60.00	27.00	7.50
☐ 123 Gus Zernial and 124 Bob Trice	40.00	18.00	5.00
☐ 125 Rip Repulski and 126 Ted Lepcio	40.00	18.00	5.00
☐ 127 Warren Spahn and 128 Tom Brewer	150.00	70.00	19.00
☐ 129 Jim Gilliam and 130 Ellis Kinder	50.00	23.00	6.25
☐ 131 Herm Wehmeier and 132 Wayne Terwilliger	40.00	18.00	5.00

1956 Topps

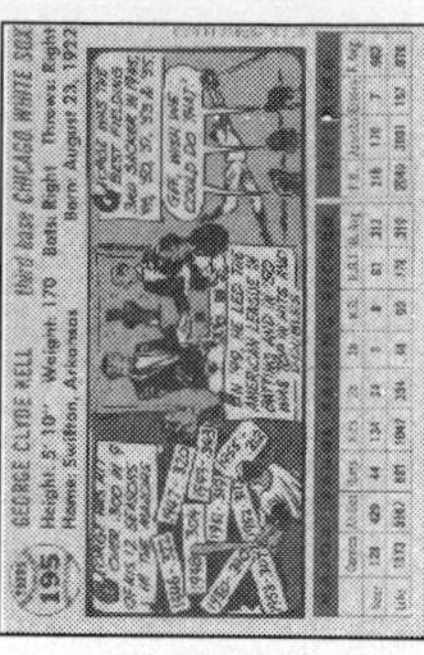

The cards in this 340-card set measure approximately 2 5/8" by 3 3/4". Following up with another horizontally oriented card in 1956, Topps improved the format by layering the color "head" shot onto an actual action sequence involving the player. Cards 1 to 180 come with either white or gray backs: in the 1 to 100 sequence, gray backs are less common (worth about 10 percent more) and in the 101 to 180 sequence, white backs are less common (worth 30 percent more). The team cards, used for the first time in a regular set by Topps, are found dated 1955, or undated, with the team name appearing on either side. The dated team cards in the first series were not printed on the gray stock. The two unnumbered checklist cards are highly prized (must be unmarked to qualify as excellent or mint). The complete set price below does not include the unnumbered checklist cards or any of the variations. The key rookies in this set are Walt Alston, Luis Aparicio, and Roger Craig. There are ten double-printed cards in the first series as evidenced by the discovery of an uncut sheet of 110 cards (10 by 11); these DP's are listed below.

	NRMT	VG-E	GOOD
COMPLETE SET (340)	7700.00	3500.00	950.00
COMMON PLAYER (1-100)	8.50	3.80	1.05
COMMON PLAYER (101-180)	11.50	5.25	1.45
COMMON PLAYER (181-260)	16.00	7.25	2.00
COMMON PLAYER (261-340)	12.50	5.75	1.55
☐ 1 William Harridge (AL President)	125.00	31.00	10.00
☐ 2 Warren Giles (NL President)	20.00	9.00	2.50
☐ 3 Elmer Valo	8.50	3.80	1.05
☐ 4 Carlos Paula	8.50	3.80	1.05
☐ 5 Ted Williams	325.00	145.00	40.00
☐ 6 Ray Boone	10.00	4.50	1.25
☐ 7 Ron Negray	8.50	3.80	1.05
☐ 8 Walter Alston MG	42.00	19.00	5.25
☐ 9 Ruben Gomez DP	8.50	3.80	1.05
☐ 10 Warren Spahn	85.00	38.00	10.50
☐ 11A Chicago Cubs (Centered)	30.00	13.50	3.80
☐ 11B Cubs Team (Dated 1955)	60.00	27.00	7.50
☐ 11C Cubs Team (Name at far left)	30.00	13.50	3.80
☐ 12 Andy Carey	10.00	4.50	1.25
☐ 13 Roy Face	11.00	4.90	1.40
☐ 14 Ken Boyer DP	15.00	6.75	1.90
☐ 15 Ernie Banks DP	100.00	45.00	12.50
☐ 16 Hector Lopez	12.50	5.75	1.55
☐ 17 Gene Conley	10.00	4.50	1.25
☐ 18 Dick Donovan	8.50	3.80	1.05
☐ 19 Chuck Diering	8.50	3.80	1.05
☐ 20 Al Kaline	125.00	57.50	15.50
☐ 21 Joe Collins DP	10.00	4.50	1.25
☐ 22 Jim Finigan	8.50	3.80	1.05
☐ 23 Fred Marsh	8.50	3.80	1.05
☐ 24 Dick Groat	12.50	5.75	1.55
☐ 25 Ted Kluszewski	25.00	11.50	3.10
☐ 26 Grady Hatton	8.50	3.80	1.05
☐ 27 Nelson Burbrink	8.50	3.80	1.05
☐ 28 Bobby Hofman	8.50	3.80	1.05
☐ 29 Jack Harshman	8.50	3.80	1.05
☐ 30 Jackie Robinson DP	165.00	75.00	21.00
☐ 31 Hank Aaron UER (Small photo actually W.Mays)	275.00	125.00	34.00
☐ 32 Frank House	8.50	3.80	1.05
☐ 33 Roberto Clemente	425.00	190.00	52.50
☐ 34 Tom Brewer	8.50	3.80	1.05
☐ 35 Al Rosen	12.50	5.75	1.55

No.	Player			
☐	36 Rudy Minarcin	8.50	3.80	1.05
☐	37 Alex Grammas	8.50	3.80	1.05
☐	38 Bob Kennedy	10.00	4.50	1.25
☐	39 Don Mossi	10.00	4.50	1.25
☐	40 Bob Turley	12.50	5.75	1.55
☐	41 Hank Sauer	10.00	4.50	1.25
☐	42 Sandy Amoros	14.00	6.25	1.75
☐	43 Ray Moore	8.50	3.80	1.05
☐	44 Windy McCall	8.50	3.80	1.05
☐	45 Gus Zernial	10.00	4.50	1.25
☐	46 Gene Freese DP	8.50	3.80	1.05
☐	47 Art Fowler	8.50	3.80	1.05
☐	48 Jim Hegan	10.00	4.50	1.25
☐	49 Pedro Ramos	8.50	3.80	1.05
☐	50 Dusty Rhodes	10.00	4.50	1.25
☐	51 Ernie Oravetz	8.50	3.80	1.05
☐	52 Bob Grim	10.00	4.50	1.25
☐	53 Arnie Portocarrero	8.50	3.80	1.05
☐	54 Bob Keegan	8.50	3.80	1.05
☐	55 Wally Moon	10.00	4.50	1.25
☐	56 Dale Long	10.00	4.50	1.25
☐	57 Duke Maas	8.50	3.80	1.05
☐	58 Ed Roebuck	10.00	4.50	1.25
☐	59 Jose Santiago	8.50	3.80	1.05
☐	60 Mayo Smith MG DP	8.50	3.80	1.05
☐	61 Bill Skowron	18.00	8.00	2.30
☐	62 Hal Smith	8.50	3.80	1.05
☐	63 Roger Craig	30.00	13.50	3.80
☐	64 Luis Arroyo	12.50	5.75	1.55
☐	65 Johnny O'Brien	10.00	4.50	1.25
☐	66 Bob Speake	8.50	3.80	1.05
☐	67 Vic Power	10.00	4.50	1.25
☐	68 Chuck Stobbs	8.50	3.80	1.05
☐	69 Chuck Tanner	12.50	5.75	1.55
☐	70 Jim Rivera	8.50	3.80	1.05
☐	71 Frank Sullivan	8.50	3.80	1.05
☐	72A Phillies Team (Centered)	30.00	13.50	3.80
☐	72B Phillies Team (Dated 1955)	60.00	27.00	7.50
☐	72C Phillies Team (Name at far left)	30.00	13.50	3.80
☐	73 Wayne Terwilliger	8.50	3.80	1.05
☐	74 Jim King	8.50	3.80	1.05
☐	75 Roy Sievers DP	10.00	4.50	1.25
☐	76 Ray Crone	8.50	3.80	1.05
☐	77 Harvey Haddix	10.00	4.50	1.25
☐	78 Herman Wehmeier	8.50	3.80	1.05
☐	79 Sandy Koufax	425.00	190.00	52.50
☐	80 Gus Triandos DP	10.00	4.50	1.25
☐	81 Wally Westlake	8.50	3.80	1.05
☐	82 Bill Renna	8.50	3.80	1.05
☐	83 Karl Spooner	10.00	4.50	1.25
☐	84 Babe Birrer	8.50	3.80	1.05
☐	85A Cleveland Indians (Centered)	30.00	13.50	3.80
☐	85B Indians Team (Dated 1955)	60.00	27.00	7.50
☐	85C Indians Team (Name at far left)	30.00	13.50	3.80
☐	86 Ray Jablonski DP	8.50	3.80	1.05
☐	87 Dean Stone	8.50	3.80	1.05
☐	88 Johnny Kucks	12.50	5.75	1.55
☐	89 Norm Zauchin	8.50	3.80	1.05
☐	90A Cincinnati Redlegs Team (Centered)	30.00	13.50	3.80
☐	90B Reds Team (Dated 1955)	60.00	27.00	7.50
☐	90C Reds Team (Name at far left)	30.00	13.50	3.80
☐	91 Gail Harris	8.50	3.80	1.05
☐	92 Bob(Red) Wilson	8.50	3.80	1.05
☐	93 George Susce	8.50	3.80	1.05
☐	94 Ron Kline	8.50	3.80	1.05
☐	95A Milwaukee Braves Team (Centered)	35.00	16.00	4.40
☐	95B Braves Team (Dated 1955)	70.00	32.00	8.75
☐	95C Braves Team (Name at far left)	35.00	16.00	4.40
☐	96 Bill Tremel	8.50	3.80	1.05
☐	97 Jerry Lynch	10.00	4.50	1.25
☐	98 Camilo Pascual	10.00	4.50	1.25
☐	99 Don Zimmer	18.00	8.00	2.30
☐	100A Baltimore Orioles Team (centered)	35.00	16.00	4.40
☐	100B Orioles Team (Dated 1955)	70.00	32.00	8.75
☐	100C Orioles Team (Name at far left)	35.00	16.00	4.40
☐	101 Roy Campanella	140.00	65.00	17.50
☐	102 Jim Davis	11.50	5.25	1.45
☐	103 Willie Miranda	11.50	5.25	1.45
☐	104 Bob Lennon	11.50	5.25	1.45
☐	105 Al Smith	11.50	5.25	1.45
☐	106 Joe Astroth	11.50	5.25	1.45
☐	107 Eddie Mathews	65.00	29.00	8.25
☐	108 Laurin Pepper	11.50	5.25	1.45
☐	109 Enos Slaughter	35.00	16.00	4.40
☐	110 Yogi Berra	160.00	70.00	20.00
☐	111 Boston Red Sox Team Card	35.00	16.00	4.40
☐	112 Dee Fondy	11.50	5.25	1.45
☐	113 Phil Rizzuto	60.00	27.00	7.50
☐	114 Jim Owens	11.50	5.25	1.45
☐	115 Jackie Jensen	15.00	6.75	1.90
☐	116 Eddie O'Brien	11.50	5.25	1.45
☐	117 Virgil Trucks	13.00	5.75	1.65
☐	118 Nellie Fox	35.00	16.00	4.40
☐	119 Larry Jackson	15.00	6.75	1.90
☐	120 Richie Ashburn	35.00	16.00	4.40
☐	121 Pittsburgh Pirates Team Card	35.00	16.00	4.40
☐	122 Willard Nixon	11.50	5.25	1.45
☐	123 Roy McMillan	13.00	5.75	1.65
☐	124 Don Kaiser	11.50	5.25	1.45
☐	125 Minnie Minoso	25.00	11.50	3.10
☐	126 Jim Brady	11.50	5.25	1.45
☐	127 Willie Jones	11.50	5.25	1.45
☐	128 Eddie Yost	13.00	5.75	1.65
☐	129 Jake Martin	11.50	5.25	1.45
☐	130 Willie Mays	375.00	170.00	47.50
☐	131 Bob Roselli	11.50	5.25	1.45
☐	132 Bobby Avila	11.50	5.25	1.45
☐	133 Ray Narleski	11.50	5.25	1.45
☐	134 St. Louis Cardinals Team Card	35.00	16.00	4.40
☐	135 Mickey Mantle	1150.00	525.00	145.00
☐	136 Johnny Logan	13.00	5.75	1.65
☐	137 Al Silvera	11.50	5.25	1.45
☐	138 Johnny Antonelli	13.00	5.75	1.65
☐	139 Tommy Carroll	11.50	5.25	1.45
☐	140 Herb Score	35.00	16.00	4.40
☐	141 Joe Frazier	11.50	5.25	1.45
☐	142 Gene Baker	11.50	5.25	1.45
☐	143 Jim Piersall	16.00	7.25	2.00
☐	144 Leroy Powell	11.50	5.25	1.45
☐	145 Gil Hodges	55.00	25.00	7.00
☐	146 Washington Nationals Team Card	35.00	16.00	4.40
☐	147 Earl Torgeson	11.50	5.25	1.45
☐	148 Alvin Dark	15.00	6.75	1.90
☐	149 Dixie Howell	11.50	5.25	1.45
☐	150 Duke Snider	150.00	70.00	19.00
☐	151 Spook Jacobs	13.00	5.75	1.65
☐	152 Billy Hoeft	13.00	5.75	1.65
☐	153 Frank Thomas	14.00	6.25	1.75
☐	154 Dave Pope	11.50	5.25	1.45
☐	155 Harvey Kuenn	18.00	8.00	2.30
☐	156 Wes Westrum	13.00	5.75	1.65
☐	157 Dick Brodowski	11.50	5.25	1.45
☐	158 Wally Post	13.00	5.75	1.65
☐	159 Clint Courtney	11.50	5.25	1.45
☐	160 Billy Pierce	15.00	6.75	1.90
☐	161 Joe DeMaestri	11.50	5.25	1.45
☐	162 Dave(Gus) Bell	13.00	5.75	1.65
☐	163 Gene Woodling	15.00	6.75	1.90
☐	164 Harmon Killebrew	175.00	80.00	22.00
☐	165 Red Schoendienst	32.00	14.50	4.00
☐	166 Brooklyn Dodgers Team Card	190.00	85.00	24.00
☐	167 Harry Dorish	11.50	5.25	1.45
☐	168 Sammy White	11.50	5.25	1.45
☐	169 Bob Nelson	11.50	5.25	1.45
☐	170 Bill Virdon	16.00	7.25	2.00
☐	171 Jim Wilson	11.50	5.25	1.45
☐	172 Frank Torre	15.00	6.75	1.90
☐	173 Johnny Podres	18.00	8.00	2.30
☐	174 Glen Gorbous	11.50	5.25	1.45
☐	175 Del Crandall	13.00	5.75	1.65
☐	176 Alex Kellner	11.50	5.25	1.45
☐	177 Hank Bauer	21.00	9.50	2.60
☐	178 Joe Black	16.00	7.25	2.00
☐	179 Harry Chiti	11.50	5.25	1.45
☐	180 Robin Roberts	40.00	18.00	5.00
☐	181 Billy Martin	100.00	45.00	12.50
☐	182 Paul Minner	16.00	7.25	2.00
☐	183 Stan Lopata	16.00	7.25	2.00
☐	184 Don Bessent	16.00	7.25	2.00
☐	185 Bill Bruton	18.00	8.00	2.30
☐	186 Ron Jackson	16.00	7.25	2.00
☐	187 Early Wynn	40.00	18.00	5.00
☐	188 Chicago White Sox Team Card	40.00	18.00	5.00
☐	189 Ned Garver	16.00	7.25	2.00
☐	190 Carl Furillo	30.00	13.50	3.80

☐	191 Frank Lary	20.00	9.00	2.50
☐	192 Smoky Burgess	18.00	8.00	2.30
☐	193 Wilmer Mizell	18.00	8.00	2.30
☐	194 Monte Irvin	35.00	16.00	4.40
☐	195 George Kell	35.00	16.00	4.40
☐	196 Tom Poholsky	16.00	7.25	2.00
☐	197 Granny Hamner	16.00	7.25	2.00
☐	198 Ed Fitzgerald	16.00	7.25	2.00
☐	199 Hank Thompson	18.00	8.00	2.30
☐	200 Bob Feller	150.00	70.00	19.00
☐	201 Rip Repulski	16.00	7.25	2.00
☐	202 Jim Hearn	16.00	7.25	2.00
☐	203 Bill Tuttle	16.00	7.25	2.00
☐	204 Art Swanson	16.00	7.25	2.00
☐	205 Whitey Lockman	18.00	8.00	2.30
☐	206 Erv Palica	16.00	7.25	2.00
☐	207 Jim Small	16.00	7.25	2.00
☐	208 Elston Howard	55.00	25.00	7.00
☐	209 Max Surkont	16.00	7.25	2.00
☐	210 Mike Garcia	18.00	8.00	2.30
☐	211 Murry Dickson	16.00	7.25	2.00
☐	212 Johnny Temple	20.00	9.00	2.50
☐	213 Detroit Tigers Team Card	55.00	25.00	7.00
☐	214 Bob Rush	16.00	7.25	2.00
☐	215 Tommy Byrne	16.00	7.25	2.00
☐	216 Jerry Schoonmaker	16.00	7.25	2.00
☐	217 Billy Klaus	16.00	7.25	2.00
☐	218 Joe Nuxhall UER (Misspelled Nuxall)	18.00	8.00	2.30
☐	219 Lew Burdette	22.00	10.00	2.80
☐	220 Del Ennis	18.00	8.00	2.30
☐	221 Bob Friend	18.00	8.00	2.30
☐	222 Dave Philley	16.00	7.25	2.00
☐	223 Randy Jackson	16.00	7.25	2.00
☐	224 Bud Podbielan	16.00	7.25	2.00
☐	225 Gil McDougald	30.00	13.50	3.80
☐	226 New York Giants Team Card	75.00	34.00	9.50
☐	227 Russ Meyer	16.00	7.25	2.00
☐	228 Mickey Vernon	18.00	8.00	2.30
☐	229 Harry Brecheen CO	18.00	8.00	2.30
☐	230 Chico Carrasquel	16.00	7.25	2.00
☐	231 Bob Hale	16.00	7.25	2.00
☐	232 Toby Atwell	16.00	7.25	2.00
☐	233 Carl Erskine	30.00	13.50	3.80
☐	234 Pete Runnels	18.00	8.00	2.30
☐	235 Don Newcombe	55.00	25.00	7.00
☐	236 Kansas City Athletics Team Card	35.00	16.00	4.40
☐	237 Jose Valdivielso	16.00	7.25	2.00
☐	238 Walt Dropo	18.00	8.00	2.30
☐	239 Harry Simpson	16.00	7.25	2.00
☐	240 Whitey Ford	150.00	70.00	19.00
☐	241 Don Mueller UER (6" tall)	18.00	8.00	2.30
☐	242 Hershell Freeman	16.00	7.25	2.00
☐	243 Sherm Lollar	18.00	8.00	2.30
☐	244 Bob Buhl	18.00	8.00	2.30
☐	245 Billy Goodman	18.00	8.00	2.30
☐	246 Tom Gorman	16.00	7.25	2.00
☐	247 Bill Sarni	16.00	7.25	2.00
☐	248 Bob Porterfield	16.00	7.25	2.00
☐	249 Johnny Klippstein	16.00	7.25	2.00
☐	250 Larry Doby	25.00	11.50	3.10
☐	251 New York Yankees Team Card UER (Don Larsen misspelled as Larson on front)	210.00	95.00	26.00
☐	252 Vern Law	18.00	8.00	2.30
☐	253 Irv Noren	20.00	9.00	2.50
☐	254 George Crowe	16.00	7.25	2.00
☐	255 Bob Lemon	35.00	16.00	4.40
☐	256 Tom Hurd	16.00	7.25	2.00
☐	257 Bobby Thomson	25.00	11.50	3.10
☐	258 Art Ditmar	16.00	7.25	2.00
☐	259 Sam Jones	18.00	8.00	2.30
☐	260 Pee Wee Reese	150.00	70.00	19.00
☐	261 Bobby Shantz	14.00	6.25	1.75
☐	262 Howie Pollet	12.50	5.75	1.55
☐	263 Bob Miller	12.50	5.75	1.55
☐	264 Ray Monzant	12.50	5.75	1.55
☐	265 Sandy Consuegra	12.50	5.75	1.55
☐	266 Don Ferrarese	12.50	5.75	1.55
☐	267 Bob Nieman	12.50	5.75	1.55
☐	268 Dale Mitchell	18.00	8.00	2.30
☐	269 Jack Meyer	12.50	5.75	1.55
☐	270 Billy Loes	14.00	6.25	1.75
☐	271 Foster Castleman	12.50	5.75	1.55
☐	272 Danny O'Connell	12.50	5.75	1.55
☐	273 Walker Cooper	12.50	5.75	1.55
☐	274 Frank Baumholtz	12.50	5.75	1.55
☐	275 Jim Greengrass	12.50	5.75	1.55
☐	276 George Zuverink	12.50	5.75	1.55
☐	277 Daryl Spencer	12.50	5.75	1.55
☐	278 Chet Nichols	12.50	5.75	1.55
☐	279 Johnny Groth	12.50	5.75	1.55
☐	280 Jim Gilliam	21.00	9.50	2.60
☐	281 Art Houtteman	12.50	5.75	1.55
☐	282 Warren Hacker	12.50	5.75	1.55
☐	283 Hal Smith	12.50	5.75	1.55
☐	284 Ike Delock	12.50	5.75	1.55
☐	285 Eddie Miksis	12.50	5.75	1.55
☐	286 Bill Wight	12.50	5.75	1.55
☐	287 Bobby Adams	12.50	5.75	1.55
☐	288 Bob Cerv	30.00	13.50	3.80
☐	289 Hal Jeffcoat	12.50	5.75	1.55
☐	290 Curt Simmons	14.00	6.25	1.75
☐	291 Frank Kellert	12.50	5.75	1.55
☐	292 Luis Aparicio	150.00	70.00	19.00
☐	293 Stu Miller	15.00	6.75	1.90
☐	294 Ernie Johnson	14.00	6.25	1.75
☐	295 Clem Labine	15.00	6.75	1.90
☐	296 Andy Seminick	12.50	5.75	1.55
☐	297 Bob Skinner	14.00	6.25	1.75
☐	298 Johnny Schmitz	12.50	5.75	1.55
☐	299 Charlie Neal	30.00	13.50	3.80
☐	300 Vic Wertz	14.00	6.25	1.75
☐	301 Marv Grissom	12.50	5.75	1.55
☐	302 Eddie Robinson	12.50	5.75	1.55
☐	303 Jim Dyck	12.50	5.75	1.55
☐	304 Frank Malzone	20.00	9.00	2.50
☐	305 Brooks Lawrence	12.50	5.75	1.55
☐	306 Curt Roberts	12.50	5.75	1.55
☐	307 Hoyt Wilhelm	35.00	16.00	4.40
☐	308 Chuck Harmon	12.50	5.75	1.55
☐	309 Don Blasingame	15.00	6.75	1.90
☐	310 Steve Gromek	12.50	5.75	1.55
☐	311 Hal Naragon	12.50	5.75	1.55
☐	312 Andy Pafko	14.00	6.25	1.75
☐	313 Gene Stephens	12.50	5.75	1.55
☐	314 Hobie Landrith	12.50	5.75	1.55
☐	315 Milt Bolling	12.50	5.75	1.55
☐	316 Jerry Coleman	15.00	6.75	1.90
☐	317 Al Aber	12.50	5.75	1.55
☐	318 Fred Hatfield	12.50	5.75	1.55
☐	319 Jack Crimian	12.50	5.75	1.55
☐	320 Joe Adcock	15.00	6.75	1.90
☐	321 Jim Konstanty	15.00	6.75	1.90
☐	322 Karl Olson	12.50	5.75	1.55
☐	323 Willard Schmidt	12.50	5.75	1.55
☐	324 Rocky Bridges	12.50	5.75	1.55
☐	325 Don Liddle	12.50	5.75	1.55
☐	326 Connie Johnson	12.50	5.75	1.55
☐	327 Bob Wiesler	12.50	5.75	1.55
☐	328 Preston Ward	12.50	5.75	1.55
☐	329 Lou Berberet	12.50	5.75	1.55
☐	330 Jim Busby	12.50	5.75	1.55
☐	331 Dick Hall	12.50	5.75	1.55
☐	332 Don Larsen	45.00	20.00	5.75
☐	333 Rube Walker	12.50	5.75	1.55
☐	334 Bob Miller	12.50	5.75	1.55
☐	335 Don Hoak	14.00	6.25	1.75
☐	336 Ellis Kinder	12.50	5.75	1.55
☐	337 Bobby Morgan	12.50	5.75	1.55
☐	338 Jim Delsing	12.50	5.75	1.55
☐	339 Rance Pless	12.50	5.75	1.55
☐	340 Mickey McDermott	50.00	10.00	3.00
☐	NNO Checklist 1/3	300.00	45.00	15.00
☐	NNO Checklist 2/4	300.00	45.00	15.00

1957 Topps

The cards in this 407-card set measure 2 1/2" by 3 1/2". In 1957, Topps returned to the vertical obverse, adopted what we now call the standard card size, and used a large, uncluttered color photo for the first time since 1952. Cards in the series 265 to 352 and the unnumbered checklist cards are scarcer than other cards in the set. However within this scarce series (265-352) there are 22 cards which were printed in double the quantity of the other cards in the series; these 22 double prints are indicated by DP in the checklist below. The first star combination cards, cards 400 and 407, are quite popular with collectors. They feature the big stars of the previous season's World Series teams, the Dodgers (Furillo, Hodges, Campanella, and Snider) and

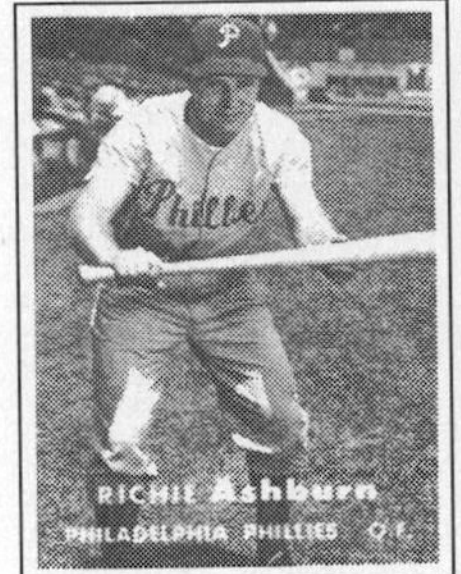

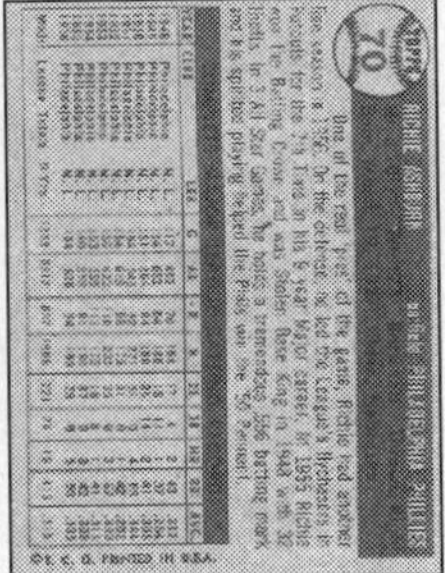

Yankees (Berra and Mantle). The complete set price below does not include the unnumbered checklist cards. The key rookies in this set are Jim Bunning, Rocky Colavito, Don Drysdale, Whitey Herzog, Tony Kubek, Bobby Richardson, Brooks Robinson, and Frank Robinson.

	NRMT	VG-E	GOOD
COMPLETE SET (407)	7700.00	3500.00	950.00
COMMON PLAYER (1-88)	8.50	3.80	1.05
COMMON PLAYER (89-176)	7.50	3.40	.95
COMMON PLAYER (177-264)	6.50	2.90	.80
COMMON PLAYER (265-352)	22.00	10.00	2.80
COMMON PLAYER (353-407)	7.00	3.10	.85
☐ 1 Ted Williams	450.00	135.00	45.00
☐ 2 Yogi Berra	150.00	70.00	19.00
☐ 3 Dale Long	9.50	4.30	1.20
☐ 4 Johnny Logan	10.00	4.50	1.25
☐ 5 Sal Maglie	11.00	4.90	1.40
☐ 6 Hector Lopez	9.50	4.30	1.20
☐ 7 Luis Aparicio	45.00	20.00	5.75
☐ 8 Don Mossi	9.50	4.30	1.20
☐ 9 Johnny Temple	9.50	4.30	1.20
☐ 10 Willie Mays	250.00	115.00	31.00
☐ 11 George Zuverink	8.50	3.80	1.05
☐ 12 Dick Groat	11.00	4.90	1.40
☐ 13 Wally Burnette	8.50	3.80	1.05
☐ 14 Bob Nieman	8.50	3.80	1.05
☐ 15 Robin Roberts	27.00	12.00	3.40
☐ 16 Walt Moryn	8.50	3.80	1.05
☐ 17 Billy Gardner	8.50	3.80	1.05
☐ 18 Don Drysdale	225.00	100.00	28.00
☐ 19 Bob Wilson	8.50	3.80	1.05
☐ 20 Hank Aaron UER (Reverse negative photo on front)	250.00	115.00	31.00
☐ 21 Frank Sullivan	8.50	3.80	1.05
☐ 22 Jerry Snyder UER (Photo actually Ed Fitzgerald)	8.50	3.80	1.05
☐ 23 Sherm Lollar	9.50	4.30	1.20
☐ 24 Bill Mazeroski	70.00	32.00	8.75
☐ 25 Whitey Ford	65.00	29.00	8.25
☐ 26 Bob Boyd	8.50	3.80	1.05
☐ 27 Ted Kazanski	8.50	3.80	1.05
☐ 28 Gene Conley	9.50	4.30	1.20
☐ 29 Whitey Herzog	35.00	16.00	4.40
☐ 30 Pee Wee Reese	70.00	32.00	8.75
☐ 31 Ron Northey	8.50	3.80	1.05
☐ 32 Hershell Freeman	8.50	3.80	1.05
☐ 33 Jim Small	8.50	3.80	1.05
☐ 34 Tom Sturdivant	8.50	3.80	1.05
☐ 35 Frank Robinson	300.00	135.00	38.00
☐ 36 Bob Grim	8.50	3.80	1.05
☐ 37 Frank Torre	9.50	4.30	1.20
☐ 38 Nellie Fox	25.00	11.50	3.10
☐ 39 Al Worthington	8.50	3.80	1.05
☐ 40 Early Wynn	25.00	11.50	3.10
☐ 41 Hal W. Smith	8.50	3.80	1.05
☐ 42 Dee Fondy	8.50	3.80	1.05
☐ 43 Connie Johnson	8.50	3.80	1.05
☐ 44 Joe DeMaestri	8.50	3.80	1.05
☐ 45 Carl Furillo	18.00	8.00	2.30
☐ 46 Robert J. Miller	8.50	3.80	1.05
☐ 47 Don Blasingame	8.50	3.80	1.05
☐ 48 Bill Bruton	10.00	4.50	1.25
☐ 49 Daryl Spencer	8.50	3.80	1.05
☐ 50 Herb Score	18.00	8.00	2.30
☐ 51 Clint Courtney	8.50	3.80	1.05
☐ 52 Lee Walls	8.50	3.80	1.05
☐ 53 Clem Labine	11.00	4.90	1.40
☐ 54 Elmer Valo	8.50	3.80	1.05
☐ 55 Ernie Banks	120.00	55.00	15.00
☐ 56 Dave Sisler	8.50	3.80	1.05
☐ 57 Jim Lemon	9.50	4.30	1.20
☐ 58 Ruben Gomez	8.50	3.80	1.05
☐ 59 Dick Williams	10.50	4.70	1.30
☐ 60 Billy Hoeft	9.50	4.30	1.20
☐ 61 James(Dusty) Rhodes	9.50	4.30	1.20
☐ 62 Billy Martin	50.00	23.00	6.25
☐ 63 Ike Delock	8.50	3.80	1.05
☐ 64 Pete Runnels	9.50	4.30	1.20
☐ 65 Wally Moon	9.50	4.30	1.20
☐ 66 Brooks Lawrence	8.50	3.80	1.05
☐ 67 Chico Carrasquel	8.50	3.80	1.05
☐ 68 Ray Crone	8.50	3.80	1.05
☐ 69 Roy McMillan	9.50	4.30	1.20
☐ 70 Richie Ashburn	25.00	11.50	3.10
☐ 71 Murry Dickson	8.50	3.80	1.05
☐ 72 Bill Tuttle	8.50	3.80	1.05
☐ 73 George Crowe	8.50	3.80	1.05
☐ 74 Vito Valentinetti	8.50	3.80	1.05
☐ 75 Jim Piersall	12.50	5.75	1.55
☐ 76 Roberto Clemente	250.00	115.00	31.00
☐ 77 Paul Foytack	8.50	3.80	1.05
☐ 78 Vic Wertz	9.50	4.30	1.20
☐ 79 Lindy McDaniel	12.50	5.75	1.55
☐ 80 Gil Hodges	50.00	23.00	6.25
☐ 81 Herman Wehmeier	8.50	3.80	1.05
☐ 82 Elston Howard	20.00	9.00	2.50
☐ 83 Lou Skizas	8.50	3.80	1.05
☐ 84 Moe Drabowsky	9.50	4.30	1.20
☐ 85 Larry Doby	11.00	4.90	1.40
☐ 86 Bill Sarni	8.50	3.80	1.05
☐ 87 Tom Gorman	8.50	3.80	1.05
☐ 88 Harvey Kuenn	12.00	5.50	1.50
☐ 89 Roy Sievers	8.50	3.80	1.05
☐ 90 Warren Spahn	75.00	34.00	9.50
☐ 91 Mack Burk	7.50	3.40	.95
☐ 92 Mickey Vernon	8.50	3.80	1.05
☐ 93 Hal Jeffcoat	7.50	3.40	.95
☐ 94 Bobby Del Greco	7.50	3.40	.95
☐ 95 Mickey Mantle	1100.00	325.00	110.00
☐ 96 Hank Aguirre	7.50	3.40	.95
☐ 97 New York Yankees Team Card	60.00	27.00	7.50
☐ 98 Alvin Dark	9.00	4.00	1.15
☐ 99 Bob Keegan	7.50	3.40	.95
☐ 100 League Presidents Warren Giles Will Harridge	12.00	5.50	1.50
☐ 101 Chuck Stobbs	7.50	3.40	.95
☐ 102 Ray Boone	8.50	3.80	1.05
☐ 103 Joe Nuxhall	8.50	3.80	1.05
☐ 104 Hank Foiles	7.50	3.40	.95
☐ 105 Johnny Antonelli	8.50	3.80	1.05
☐ 106 Ray Moore	7.50	3.40	.95
☐ 107 Jim Rivera	7.50	3.40	.95
☐ 108 Tommy Byrne	7.50	3.40	.95
☐ 109 Hank Thompson	8.50	3.80	1.05
☐ 110 Bill Virdon	9.00	4.00	1.15
☐ 111 Hal R. Smith	7.50	3.40	.95
☐ 112 Tom Brewer	7.50	3.40	.95
☐ 113 Wilmer Mizell	8.50	3.80	1.05
☐ 114 Milwaukee Braves Team Card	20.00	9.00	2.50
☐ 115 Jim Gilliam	12.50	5.75	1.55
☐ 116 Mike Fornieles	7.50	3.40	.95
☐ 117 Joe Adcock	9.00	4.00	1.15
☐ 118 Bob Porterfield	7.50	3.40	.95
☐ 119 Stan Lopata	7.50	3.40	.95
☐ 120 Bob Lemon	25.00	11.50	3.10
☐ 121 Clete Boyer	25.00	11.50	3.10
☐ 122 Ken Boyer	15.00	6.75	1.90
☐ 123 Steve Ridzik	7.50	3.40	.95
☐ 124 Dave Philley	7.50	3.40	.95
☐ 125 Al Kaline	110.00	50.00	14.00
☐ 126 Bob Wiesler	7.50	3.40	.95
☐ 127 Bob Buhl	8.50	3.80	1.05
☐ 128 Ed Bailey	8.50	3.80	1.05
☐ 129 Saul Rogovin	7.50	3.40	.95
☐ 130 Don Newcombe	15.00	6.75	1.90
☐ 131 Milt Bolling	7.50	3.40	.95
☐ 132 Art Ditmar	8.50	3.80	1.05
☐ 133 Del Crandall	8.50	3.80	1.05
☐ 134 Don Kaiser	7.50	3.40	.95
☐ 135 Bill Skowron	15.00	6.75	1.90
☐ 136 Jim Hegan	8.50	3.80	1.05
☐ 137 Bob Rush	7.50	3.40	.95
☐ 138 Minnie Minoso	15.00	6.75	1.90
☐ 139 Lou Kretlow	7.50	3.40	.95
☐ 140 Frank Thomas	8.50	3.80	1.05
☐ 141 Al Aber	7.50	3.40	.95
☐ 142 Charley Thompson	7.50	3.40	.95
☐ 143 Andy Pafko	8.50	3.80	1.05

☐ 144 Ray Narleski	7.50	3.40	.95
☐ 145 Al Smith	7.50	3.40	.95
☐ 146 Don Ferrarese	7.50	3.40	.95
☐ 147 Al Walker	7.50	3.40	.95
☐ 148 Don Mueller	8.50	3.80	1.05
☐ 149 Bob Kennedy	8.50	3.80	1.05
☐ 150 Bob Friend	8.50	3.80	1.05
☐ 151 Willie Miranda	7.50	3.40	.95
☐ 152 Jack Harshman	7.50	3.40	.95
☐ 153 Karl Olson	7.50	3.40	.95
☐ 154 Red Schoendienst	25.00	11.50	3.10
☐ 155 Jim Brosnan	8.50	3.80	1.05
☐ 156 Gus Triandos	8.50	3.80	1.05
☐ 157 Wally Post	8.50	3.80	1.05
☐ 158 Curt Simmons	8.50	3.80	1.05
☐ 159 Solly Drake	7.50	3.40	.95
☐ 160 Billy Pierce	10.00	4.50	1.25
☐ 161 Pittsburgh Pirates Team Card	15.00	6.75	1.90
☐ 162 Jack Meyer	7.50	3.40	.95
☐ 163 Sammy White	7.50	3.40	.95
☐ 164 Tommy Carroll	7.50	3.40	.95
☐ 165 Ted Kluszewski	36.00	16.00	4.50
☐ 166 Roy Face	9.50	4.30	1.20
☐ 167 Vic Power	8.50	3.80	1.05
☐ 168 Frank Lary	8.50	3.80	1.05
☐ 169 Herb Plews	7.50	3.40	.95
☐ 170 Duke Snider	110.00	50.00	14.00
☐ 171 Boston Red Sox Team Card	15.00	6.75	1.90
☐ 172 Gene Woodling	8.50	3.80	1.05
☐ 173 Roger Craig	15.00	6.75	1.90
☐ 174 Willie Jones	7.50	3.40	.95
☐ 175 Don Larsen	20.00	9.00	2.50
☐ 176A Gene Baker ERR (Misspelled Bakep on card back)	350.00	160.00	45.00
☐ 176B Gene Baker COR	7.50	3.40	.95
☐ 177 Eddie Yost	7.50	3.40	.95
☐ 178 Don Bessent	6.50	2.90	.80
☐ 179 Ernie Oravetz	6.50	2.90	.80
☐ 180 Gus Bell	7.50	3.40	.95
☐ 181 Dick Donovan	6.50	2.90	.80
☐ 182 Hobie Landrith	6.50	2.90	.80
☐ 183 Chicago Cubs Team Card	15.00	6.75	1.90
☐ 184 Tito Francona	9.00	4.00	1.15
☐ 185 Johnny Kucks	6.50	2.90	.80
☐ 186 Jim King	6.50	2.90	.80
☐ 187 Virgil Trucks	7.50	3.40	.95
☐ 188 Felix Mantilla	8.50	3.80	1.05
☐ 189 Willard Nixon	6.50	2.90	.80
☐ 190 Randy Jackson	6.50	2.90	.80
☐ 191 Joe Margoneri	6.50	2.90	.80
☐ 192 Jerry Coleman	7.50	3.40	.95
☐ 193 Del Rice	6.50	2.90	.80
☐ 194 Hal Brown	6.50	2.90	.80
☐ 195 Bobby Avila	6.50	2.90	.80
☐ 196 Larry Jackson	7.50	3.40	.95
☐ 197 Hank Sauer	7.50	3.40	.95
☐ 198 Detroit Tigers Team Card	15.00	6.75	1.90
☐ 199 Vern Law	7.50	3.40	.95
☐ 200 Gil McDougald	15.00	6.75	1.90
☐ 201 Sandy Amoros	8.50	3.80	1.05
☐ 202 Dick Gernert	6.50	2.90	.80
☐ 203 Hoyt Wilhelm	22.00	10.00	2.80
☐ 204 Kansas City Athletics Team Card	15.00	6.75	1.90
☐ 205 Charlie Maxwell	7.50	3.40	.95
☐ 206 Willard Schmidt	6.50	2.90	.80
☐ 207 Gordon(Billy) Hunter	6.50	2.90	.80
☐ 208 Lou Burdette	10.00	4.50	1.25
☐ 209 Bob Skinner	7.50	3.40	.95
☐ 210 Roy Campanella	110.00	50.00	14.00
☐ 211 Camilo Pascual	7.50	3.40	.95
☐ 212 Rocky Colavito	135.00	60.00	17.00
☐ 213 Les Moss	6.50	2.90	.80
☐ 214 Philadelphia Phillies Team Card	15.00	6.75	1.90
☐ 215 Enos Slaughter	27.00	12.00	3.40
☐ 216 Marv Grissom	6.50	2.90	.80
☐ 217 Gene Stephens	6.50	2.90	.80
☐ 218 Ray Jablonski	6.50	2.90	.80
☐ 219 Tom Acker	6.50	2.90	.80
☐ 220 Jackie Jensen	11.00	4.90	1.40
☐ 221 Dixie Howell	6.50	2.90	.80
☐ 222 Alex Grammas	6.50	2.90	.80
☐ 223 Frank House	6.50	2.90	.80
☐ 224 Marv Blaylock	6.50	2.90	.80
☐ 225 Harry Simpson	6.50	2.90	.80
☐ 226 Preston Ward	6.50	2.90	.80
☐ 227 Gerry Staley	6.50	2.90	.80
☐ 228 Smoky Burgess UER (Misspelled Smokey on card back)	8.50	3.80	1.05
☐ 229 George Susce	6.50	2.90	.80
☐ 230 George Kell	22.00	10.00	2.80
☐ 231 Solly Hemus	6.50	2.90	.80
☐ 232 Whitey Lockman	7.50	3.40	.95
☐ 233 Art Fowler	6.50	2.90	.80
☐ 234 Dick Cole	6.50	2.90	.80
☐ 235 Tom Poholsky	6.50	2.90	.80
☐ 236 Joe Ginsberg	6.50	2.90	.80
☐ 237 Foster Castleman	6.50	2.90	.80
☐ 238 Eddie Robinson	6.50	2.90	.80
☐ 239 Tom Morgan	6.50	2.90	.80
☐ 240 Hank Bauer	15.00	6.75	1.90
☐ 241 Joe Lonnett	6.50	2.90	.80
☐ 242 Charlie Neal	8.50	3.80	1.05
☐ 243 St. Louis Cardinals Team Card	15.00	6.75	1.90
☐ 244 Billy Loes	7.50	3.40	.95
☐ 245 Rip Repulski	6.50	2.90	.80
☐ 246 Jose Valdivielso	6.50	2.90	.80
☐ 247 Turk Lown	6.50	2.90	.80
☐ 248 Jim Finigan	6.50	2.90	.80
☐ 249 Dave Pope	6.50	2.90	.80
☐ 250 Eddie Mathews	45.00	20.00	5.75
☐ 251 Baltimore Orioles Team Card	15.00	6.75	1.90
☐ 252 Carl Erskine	12.50	5.75	1.55
☐ 253 Gus Zernial	7.50	3.40	.95
☐ 254 Ron Negray	6.50	2.90	.80
☐ 255 Charlie Silvera	7.50	3.40	.95
☐ 256 Ron Kline	6.50	2.90	.80
☐ 257 Walt Dropo	6.50	2.90	.80
☐ 258 Steve Gromek	6.50	2.90	.80
☐ 259 Eddie O'Brien	6.50	2.90	.80
☐ 260 Del Ennis	7.50	3.40	.95
☐ 261 Bob Chakales	6.50	2.90	.80
☐ 262 Bobby Thomson	12.00	5.50	1.50
☐ 263 George Strickland	6.50	2.90	.80
☐ 264 Bob Turley	15.00	6.75	1.90
☐ 265 Harvey Haddix DP	15.00	6.75	1.90
☐ 266 Ken Kuhn DP	13.00	5.75	1.65
☐ 267 Danny Kravitz	22.00	10.00	2.80
☐ 268 Jack Collum	22.00	10.00	2.80
☐ 269 Bob Cerv	24.00	11.00	3.00
☐ 270 Washington Senators Team Card	50.00	23.00	6.25
☐ 271 Danny O'Connell DP	13.00	5.75	1.65
☐ 272 Bobby Shantz	30.00	13.50	3.80
☐ 273 Jim Davis	22.00	10.00	2.80
☐ 274 Don Hoak	24.00	11.00	3.00
☐ 275 Cleveland Indians Team Card	50.00	23.00	6.25
☐ 276 Jim Pyburn	22.00	10.00	2.80
☐ 277 Johnny Podres DP	55.00	25.00	7.00
☐ 278 Fred Hatfield DP	13.00	5.75	1.65
☐ 279 Bob Thurman	22.00	10.00	2.80
☐ 280 Alex Kellner	22.00	10.00	2.80
☐ 281 Gail Harris	22.00	10.00	2.80
☐ 282 Jack Dittmer DP	13.00	5.75	1.65
☐ 283 Wes Covington DP	15.00	6.75	1.90
☐ 284 Don Zimmer	30.00	13.50	3.80
☐ 285 Ned Garver	22.00	10.00	2.80
☐ 286 Bobby Richardson	130.00	57.50	16.50
☐ 287 Sam Jones	24.00	11.00	3.00
☐ 288 Ted Lepcio	22.00	10.00	2.80
☐ 289 Jim Bolger DP	13.00	5.75	1.65
☐ 290 Andy Carey DP	15.00	6.75	1.90
☐ 291 Windy McCall	22.00	10.00	2.80
☐ 292 Billy Klaus	22.00	10.00	2.80
☐ 293 Ted Abernathy	22.00	10.00	2.80
☐ 294 Rocky Bridges DP	13.00	5.75	1.65
☐ 295 Joe Collins DP	15.00	6.75	1.90
☐ 296 Johnny Klippstein	22.00	10.00	2.80
☐ 297 Jack Crimian	22.00	10.00	2.80
☐ 298 Irv Noren DP	13.00	5.75	1.65
☐ 299 Chuck Harmon	22.00	10.00	2.80
☐ 300 Mike Garcia	24.00	11.00	3.00
☐ 301 Sammy Esposito DP	13.00	5.75	1.65
☐ 302 Sandy Koufax DP	360.00	160.00	45.00
☐ 303 Billy Goodman	24.00	11.00	3.00
☐ 304 Joe Cunningham	24.00	11.00	3.00
☐ 305 Chico Fernandez	22.00	10.00	2.80
☐ 306 Darrell Johnson DP	15.00	6.75	1.90
☐ 307 Jack D. Phillips DP	13.00	5.75	1.65
☐ 308 Dick Hall	22.00	10.00	2.80
☐ 309 Jim Busby DP	13.00	5.75	1.65
☐ 310 Max Surkont DP	13.00	5.75	1.65
☐ 311 Al Pilarcik DP	13.00	5.75	1.65
☐ 312 Tony Kubek DP	125.00	57.50	15.50
☐ 313 Mel Parnell	24.00	11.00	3.00
☐ 314 Ed Bouchee DP	13.00	5.75	1.65

		NRMT	VG-E	GOOD
☐ 315	Lou Berberet DP	13.00	5.75	1.65
☐ 316	Billy O'Dell	22.00	10.00	2.80
☐ 317	New York Giants Team Card	60.00	27.00	7.50
☐ 318	Mickey McDermott	22.00	10.00	2.80
☐ 319	Gino Cimoli	25.00	11.50	3.10
☐ 320	Neil Chrisley	22.00	10.00	2.80
☐ 321	John(Red) Murff	22.00	10.00	2.80
☐ 322	Cincinnati Reds Team Card	60.00	27.00	7.50
☐ 323	Wes Westrum	24.00	11.00	3.00
☐ 324	Brooklyn Dodgers Team Card	120.00	55.00	15.00
☐ 325	Frank Bolling	22.00	10.00	2.80
☐ 326	Pedro Ramos	22.00	10.00	2.80
☐ 327	Jim Pendleton	22.00	10.00	2.80
☐ 328	Brooks Robinson	425.00	190.00	52.50
☐ 329	Chicago White Sox Team Card	50.00	23.00	6.25
☐ 330	Jim Wilson	22.00	10.00	2.80
☐ 331	Ray Katt	22.00	10.00	2.80
☐ 332	Bob Bowman	22.00	10.00	2.80
☐ 333	Ernie Johnson	24.00	11.00	3.00
☐ 334	Jerry Schoonmaker	22.00	10.00	2.80
☐ 335	Granny Hamner	22.00	10.00	2.80
☐ 336	Haywood Sullivan	25.00	11.50	3.10
☐ 337	Rene Valdes	22.00	10.00	2.80
☐ 338	Jim Bunning	150.00	70.00	19.00
☐ 339	Bob Speake	22.00	10.00	2.80
☐ 340	Bill Wight	22.00	10.00	2.80
☐ 341	Don Gross	22.00	10.00	2.80
☐ 342	Gene Mauch	25.00	11.50	3.10
☐ 343	Taylor Phillips	22.00	10.00	2.80
☐ 344	Paul LaPalme	22.00	10.00	2.80
☐ 345	Paul Smith	22.00	10.00	2.80
☐ 346	Dick Littlefield	22.00	10.00	2.80
☐ 347	Hal Naragon	22.00	10.00	2.80
☐ 348	Jim Hearn	22.00	10.00	2.80
☐ 349	Nellie King	22.00	10.00	2.80
☐ 350	Eddie Miksis	22.00	10.00	2.80
☐ 351	Dave Hillman	22.00	10.00	2.80
☐ 352	Ellis Kinder	22.00	10.00	2.80
☐ 353	Cal Neeman	7.00	3.10	.85
☐ 354	W. (Rip) Coleman	7.00	3.10	.85
☐ 355	Frank Malzone	9.00	4.00	1.15
☐ 356	Faye Throneberry	7.00	3.10	.85
☐ 357	Earl Torgeson	7.00	3.10	.85
☐ 358	Jerry Lynch	8.00	3.60	1.00
☐ 359	Tom Cheney	8.00	3.60	1.00
☐ 360	Johnny Groth	7.00	3.10	.85
☐ 361	Curt Barclay	7.00	3.10	.85
☐ 362	Roman Mejias	8.00	3.60	1.00
☐ 363	Eddie Kasko	7.00	3.10	.85
☐ 364	Cal McLish	8.00	3.60	1.00
☐ 365	Ozzie Virgil	7.00	3.10	.85
☐ 366	Ken Lehman	7.00	3.10	.85
☐ 367	Ed Fitzgerald	7.00	3.10	.85
☐ 368	Bob Purkey	7.00	3.10	.85
☐ 369	Milt Graff	7.00	3.10	.85
☐ 370	Warren Hacker	7.00	3.10	.85
☐ 371	Bob Lennon	7.00	3.10	.85
☐ 372	Norm Zauchin	7.00	3.10	.85
☐ 373	Pete Whisenant	7.00	3.10	.85
☐ 374	Don Cardwell	7.00	3.10	.85
☐ 375	Jim Landis	8.00	3.60	1.00
☐ 376	Don Elston	7.00	3.10	.85
☐ 377	Andre Rodgers	7.00	3.10	.85
☐ 378	Elmer Singleton	7.00	3.10	.85
☐ 379	Don Lee	7.00	3.10	.85
☐ 380	Walker Cooper	7.00	3.10	.85
☐ 381	Dean Stone	7.00	3.10	.85
☐ 382	Jim Brideweser	7.00	3.10	.85
☐ 383	Juan Pizarro	7.00	3.10	.85
☐ 384	Bobby G. Smith	7.00	3.10	.85
☐ 385	Art Houtteman	7.00	3.10	.85
☐ 386	Lyle Luttrell	7.00	3.10	.85
☐ 387	Jack Sanford	9.00	4.00	1.15
☐ 388	Pete Daley	7.00	3.10	.85
☐ 389	Dave Jolly	7.00	3.10	.85
☐ 390	Reno Bertoia	7.00	3.10	.85
☐ 391	Ralph Terry	11.00	4.90	1.40
☐ 392	Chuck Tanner	8.00	3.60	1.00
☐ 393	Raul Sanchez	7.00	3.10	.85
☐ 394	Luis Arroyo	8.00	3.60	1.00
☐ 395	Bubba Phillips	7.00	3.10	.85
☐ 396	Casey Wise	7.00	3.10	.85
☐ 397	Roy Smalley	7.00	3.10	.85
☐ 398	Al Cicotte	8.00	3.60	1.00
☐ 399	Billy Consolo	7.00	3.10	.85
☐ 400	Dodgers' Sluggers Carl Furillo Gil Hodges Roy Campanella Duke Snider	225.00	100.00	28.00
☐ 401	Earl Battey	9.00	4.00	1.15
☐ 402	Jim Pisoni	7.00	3.10	.85
☐ 403	Dick Hyde	7.00	3.10	.85
☐ 404	Harry Anderson	7.00	3.10	.85
☐ 405	Duke Maas	7.00	3.10	.85
☐ 406	Bob Hale	7.00	3.10	.85
☐ 407	Yankee Power Hitters Mickey Mantle Yogi Berra	400.00	180.00	50.00
☐ NNO	Checklist 1/2	250.00	115.00	31.00
☐ NNO	Checklist 2/3	400.00	180.00	50.00
☐ NNO	Checklist 3/4	700.00	325.00	90.00
☐ NNO	Checklist 4/5	900.00	400.00	115.00
☐ NNO	Saturday, May 4th Boston Red Sox vs. Cincinnati Redlegs Cleveland Indians vs. New York Giants	30.00	13.50	3.80
☐ NNO	Saturday, June 22nd Brooklyn Dodgers vs. Chicago White Sox St. Louis Cardinals vs. New York Yankees	30.00	13.50	3.80

1958 Topps

The cards in this 494-card set measure 2 1/2" by 3 1/2". Although the last card is numbered 495, number 145 was not issued, bringing the set total to 494 cards. The 1958 Topps set contains the first Sport Magazine All-Star Selection series (475-495) and expanded use of combination cards. The team cards carried series checklists on back (Milwaukee, Detroit, Baltimore, and Cincinnati are also found with players listed alphabetically). Cards with the scarce yellow name (YL) or team (YT) lettering, as opposed to the common white lettering, are noted in the checklist. In the last series, cards of Stan Musial and Mickey Mantle were triple printed; the cards they replaced (443, 446, 450, and 462) on the printing sheet were hence printed in shorter supply than other cards in the last series and are marked with an SP in the list below. Technically the New York Giants team card (19) is an error as the Giants had already moved to San Francisco. The key rookies in this set are Orlando Cepeda, Curt Flood, Roger Maris, and Vada Pinson.

	NRMT	VG-E	GOOD
COMPLETE SET (494)	5500.00	2500.00	700.00
COMMON PLAYER (1-110)	8.25	3.70	1.05
COMMON PLAYER (111-198)	6.00	2.70	.75
COMMON PLAYER (199-352)	5.00	2.30	.60
COMMON PLAYER (353-440)	4.50	2.00	.55
COMMON PLAYER (441-474)	4.25	1.90	.55
COMMON AS (475-495)	4.50	2.00	.55

☐ 1	Ted Williams	375.00	115.00	38.00
☐ 2A	Bob Lemon	22.00	10.00	2.80
☐ 2B	Bob Lemon YT	45.00	20.00	5.75
☐ 3	Alex Kellner	8.25	3.70	1.05
☐ 4	Hank Foiles	8.25	3.70	1.05
☐ 5	Willie Mays	200.00	90.00	25.00
☐ 6	George Zuverink	8.25	3.70	1.05
☐ 7	Dale Long	9.00	4.00	1.15

☐ 8A Eddie Kasko	8.25	3.70	1.05
☐ 8B Eddie Kasko YL	35.00	16.00	4.40
☐ 9 Hank Bauer	13.00	5.75	1.65
☐ 10 Lou Burdette	10.50	4.70	1.30
☐ 11A Jim Rivera	8.25	3.70	1.05
☐ 11B Jim Rivera YT	30.00	13.50	3.80
☐ 12 George Crowe	8.25	3.70	1.05
☐ 13A Billy Hoeft	8.25	3.70	1.05
☐ 13B Billy Hoeft YL	35.00	16.00	4.40
☐ 14 Rip Repulski	8.25	3.70	1.05
☐ 15 Jim Lemon	9.00	4.00	1.15
☐ 16 Charlie Neal	9.00	4.00	1.15
☐ 17 Felix Mantilla	8.25	3.70	1.05
☐ 18 Frank Sullivan	8.25	3.70	1.05
☐ 19 New York Giants Team Card (Checklist on back)	35.00	16.00	4.40
☐ 20A Gil McDougald	13.00	5.75	1.65
☐ 20B Gil McDougald YL	40.00	18.00	5.00
☐ 21 Curt Barclay	8.25	3.70	1.05
☐ 22 Hal Naragon	8.25	3.70	1.05
☐ 23A Bill Tuttle	8.25	3.70	1.05
☐ 23B Bill Tuttle YL	35.00	16.00	4.40
☐ 24A Hobie Landrith	8.25	3.70	1.05
☐ 24B Hobie Landrith YL	35.00	16.00	4.40
☐ 25 Don Drysdale	80.00	36.00	10.00
☐ 26 Ron Jackson	8.25	3.70	1.05
☐ 27 Bud Freeman	8.25	3.70	1.05
☐ 28 Jim Busby	8.25	3.70	1.05
☐ 29 Ted Lepcio	8.25	3.70	1.05
☐ 30A Hank Aaron	210.00	95.00	26.00
☐ 30B Hank Aaron YL	350.00	160.00	45.00
☐ 31 Tex Clevenger	8.25	3.70	1.05
☐ 32A J.W. Porter	8.25	3.70	1.05
☐ 32B J.W. Porter YL	35.00	16.00	4.40
☐ 33A Cal Neeman	8.25	3.70	1.05
☐ 33B Cal Neeman YT	30.00	13.50	3.80
☐ 34 Bob Thurman	8.25	3.70	1.05
☐ 35A Don Mossi	9.00	4.00	1.15
☐ 35B Don Mossi YT	30.00	13.50	3.80
☐ 36 Ted Kazanski	8.25	3.70	1.05
☐ 37 Mike McCormick UER (Photo actually Ray Monzant)	10.00	4.50	1.25
☐ 38 Dick Gernert	8.25	3.70	1.05
☐ 39 Bob Martyn	8.25	3.70	1.05
☐ 40 George Kell	16.00	7.25	2.00
☐ 41 Dave Hillman	8.25	3.70	1.05
☐ 42 John Roseboro	16.00	7.25	2.00
☐ 43 Sal Maglie	10.00	4.50	1.25
☐ 44 Washington Senators Team Card (Checklist on back)	20.00	9.00	2.50
☐ 45 Dick Groat	10.00	4.50	1.25
☐ 46A Lou Sleater	8.25	3.70	1.05
☐ 46B Lou Sleater YL	35.00	16.00	4.40
☐ 47 Roger Maris	450.00	200.00	57.50
☐ 48 Chuck Harmon	8.25	3.70	1.05
☐ 49 Smoky Burgess	9.00	4.00	1.15
☐ 50A Billy Pierce	10.00	4.50	1.25
☐ 50B Billy Pierce YT	35.00	16.00	4.40
☐ 51 Del Rice	8.25	3.70	1.05
☐ 52A Bob Clemente	200.00	90.00	25.00
☐ 52B Bob Clemente YT	325.00	145.00	40.00
☐ 53A Morrie Martin	8.25	3.70	1.05
☐ 53B Morrie Martin YL	35.00	16.00	4.40
☐ 54 Norm Siebern	10.00	4.50	1.25
☐ 55 Chico Carrasquel	8.25	3.70	1.05
☐ 56 Bill Fischer	8.25	3.70	1.05
☐ 57A Tim Thompson	8.25	3.70	1.05
☐ 57B Tim Thompson YL	35.00	16.00	4.40
☐ 58A Art Schult	8.25	3.70	1.05
☐ 58B Art Schult YT	30.00	13.50	3.80
☐ 59 Dave Sisler	8.25	3.70	1.05
☐ 60A Del Ennis	9.00	4.00	1.15
☐ 60B Del Ennis YL	35.00	16.00	4.40
☐ 61A Darrell Johnson	9.00	4.00	1.15
☐ 61B Darrell Johnson YL	35.00	16.00	4.40
☐ 62 Joe DeMaestri	8.25	3.70	1.05
☐ 63 Joe Nuxhall	9.00	4.00	1.15
☐ 64 Joe Lonnett	8.25	3.70	1.05
☐ 65A Von McDaniel	10.00	4.50	1.25
☐ 65B Von McDaniel YL	36.00	16.00	4.50
☐ 66 Lee Walls	8.25	3.70	1.05
☐ 67 Joe Ginsberg	8.25	3.70	1.05
☐ 68 Daryl Spencer	8.25	3.70	1.05
☐ 69 Wally Burnette	8.25	3.70	1.05
☐ 70A Al Kaline	90.00	40.00	11.50
☐ 70B Al Kaline YL	175.00	80.00	22.00
☐ 71 Dodgers Team (Checklist on back)	45.00	20.00	5.75
☐ 72 Bud Byerly	8.25	3.70	1.05
☐ 73 Pete Daley	8.25	3.70	1.05
☐ 74 Roy Face	9.00	4.00	1.15
☐ 75 Gus Bell	9.00	4.00	1.15
☐ 76A Dick Farrell	9.00	4.00	1.15
☐ 76B Dick Farrell YT	30.00	13.50	3.80
☐ 77A Don Zimmer	12.50	5.75	1.55
☐ 77B Don Zimmer YT	35.00	16.00	4.40
☐ 78A Ernie Johnson	9.00	4.00	1.15
☐ 78B Ernie Johnson YL	35.00	16.00	4.40
☐ 79A Dick Williams	10.00	4.50	1.25
☐ 79B Dick Williams YT	35.00	16.00	4.40
☐ 80 Dick Drott	8.25	3.70	1.05
☐ 81A Steve Boros	10.00	4.50	1.25
☐ 81B Steve Boros YT	35.00	16.00	4.40
☐ 82 Ron Kline	8.25	3.70	1.05
☐ 83 Bob Hazle	10.00	4.50	1.25
☐ 84 Billy O'Dell	8.25	3.70	1.05
☐ 85A Luis Aparicio	26.00	11.50	3.30
☐ 85B Luis Aparicio YT	50.00	23.00	6.25
☐ 86 Valmy Thomas	8.25	3.70	1.05
☐ 87 Johnny Kucks	8.25	3.70	1.05
☐ 88 Duke Snider	75.00	34.00	9.50
☐ 89 Billy Klaus	8.25	3.70	1.05
☐ 90 Robin Roberts	22.00	10.00	2.80
☐ 91 Chuck Tanner	9.00	4.00	1.15
☐ 92A Clint Courtney	8.25	3.70	1.05
☐ 92B Clint Courtney YL	35.00	16.00	4.40
☐ 93 Sandy Amoros	9.00	4.00	1.15
☐ 94 Bob Skinner	9.00	4.00	1.15
☐ 95 Frank Bolling	8.25	3.70	1.05
☐ 96 Joe Durham	8.25	3.70	1.05
☐ 97A Larry Jackson	9.00	4.00	1.15
☐ 97B Larry Jackson YL	35.00	16.00	4.40
☐ 98A Billy Hunter	8.25	3.70	1.05
☐ 98B Billy Hunter YL	35.00	16.00	4.40
☐ 99 Bobby Adams	8.25	3.70	1.05
☐ 100A Early Wynn	22.00	10.00	2.80
☐ 100B Early Wynn YT	50.00	23.00	6.25
☐ 101A Bobby Richardson	21.00	9.50	2.60
☐ 101B Bobby Richardson YL	45.00	20.00	5.75
☐ 102 George Strickland	8.25	3.70	1.05
☐ 103 Jerry Lynch	9.00	4.00	1.15
☐ 104 Jim Pendleton	8.25	3.70	1.05
☐ 105 Billy Gardner	8.25	3.70	1.05
☐ 106 Dick Schofield	9.00	4.00	1.15
☐ 107 Ossie Virgil	8.25	3.70	1.05
☐ 108A Jim Landis	8.25	3.70	1.05
☐ 108B Jim Landis YT	30.00	13.50	3.80
☐ 109 Herb Plews	8.25	3.70	1.05
☐ 110 Johnny Logan	9.00	4.00	1.15
☐ 111 Stu Miller	8.00	3.60	1.00
☐ 112 Gus Zernial	6.50	2.90	.80
☐ 113 Jerry Walker	8.00	3.60	1.00
☐ 114 Irv Noren	6.50	2.90	.80
☐ 115 Jim Bunning	22.00	10.00	2.80
☐ 116 Dave Philley	6.00	2.70	.75
☐ 117 Frank Torre	6.50	2.90	.80
☐ 118 Harvey Haddix	6.50	2.90	.80
☐ 119 Harry Chiti	6.00	2.70	.75
☐ 120 Johnny Podres	10.00	4.50	1.25
☐ 121 Eddie Miksis	6.00	2.70	.75
☐ 122 Walt Moryn	6.00	2.70	.75
☐ 123 Dick Tomanek	6.00	2.70	.75
☐ 124 Bobby Usher	6.00	2.70	.75
☐ 125 Alvin Dark	7.50	3.40	.95
☐ 126 Stan Palys	6.00	2.70	.75
☐ 127 Tom Sturdivant	6.50	2.90	.80
☐ 128 Willie Kirkland	6.50	2.90	.80
☐ 129 Jim Derrington	6.00	2.70	.75
☐ 130 Jackie Jensen	12.00	5.50	1.50
☐ 131 Bob Henrich	6.00	2.70	.75
☐ 132 Vern Law	6.50	2.90	.80
☐ 133 Russ Nixon	7.50	3.40	.95
☐ 134 Philadelphia Phillies Team Card (Checklist on back)	14.00	6.25	1.75
☐ 135 Mike(Moe) Drabowsky	6.50	2.90	.80
☐ 136 Jim Finigan	6.00	2.70	.75
☐ 137 Russ Kemmerer	6.00	2.70	.75
☐ 138 Earl Torgeson	6.00	2.70	.75
☐ 139 George Brunet	6.00	2.70	.75
☐ 140 Wes Covington	6.50	2.90	.80
☐ 141 Ken Lehman	6.00	2.70	.75
☐ 142 Enos Slaughter	25.00	11.50	3.10
☐ 143 Billy Muffett	7.50	3.40	.95
☐ 144 Bobby Morgan	6.00	2.70	.75
☐ 145 Never issued	.00	.00	.00
☐ 146 Dick Gray	6.00	2.70	.75
☐ 147 Don McMahon	9.00	4.00	1.15
☐ 148 Billy Consolo	6.00	2.70	.75
☐ 149 Tom Acker	6.00	2.70	.75
☐ 150 Mickey Mantle	600.00	275.00	75.00
☐ 151 Buddy Pritchard	6.00	2.70	.75
☐ 152 Johnny Antonelli	6.50	2.90	.80

□ 153 Les Moss	6.00	2.70	.75
□ 154 Harry Byrd	6.00	2.70	.75
□ 155 Hector Lopez	6.50	2.90	.80
□ 156 Dick Hyde	6.00	2.70	.75
□ 157 Dee Fondy	6.00	2.70	.75
□ 158 Cleveland Indians Team Card (Checklist on back)	14.00	6.25	1.75
□ 159 Taylor Phillips	6.00	2.70	.75
□ 160 Don Hoak	6.50	2.90	.80
□ 161 Don Larsen	12.50	5.75	1.55
□ 162 Gil Hodges	30.00	13.50	3.80
□ 163 Jim Wilson	6.00	2.70	.75
□ 164 Bob Taylor	6.00	2.70	.75
□ 165 Bob Nieman	6.00	2.70	.75
□ 166 Danny O'Connell	6.00	2.70	.75
□ 167 Frank Baumann	6.00	2.70	.75
□ 168 Joe Cunningham	6.50	2.90	.80
□ 169 Ralph Terry	6.50	2.90	.80
□ 170 Vic Wertz	6.50	2.90	.80
□ 171 Harry Anderson	6.00	2.70	.75
□ 172 Don Gross	6.00	2.70	.75
□ 173 Eddie Yost	6.50	2.90	.80
□ 174 Athletics Team (Checklist on back)	14.00	6.25	1.75
□ 175 Marv Throneberry	12.50	5.75	1.55
□ 176 Bob Buhl	6.50	2.90	.80
□ 177 Al Smith	6.00	2.70	.75
□ 178 Ted Kluszewski	12.50	5.75	1.55
□ 179 Willie Miranda	6.00	2.70	.75
□ 180 Lindy McDaniel	6.50	2.90	.80
□ 181 Willie Jones	6.00	2.70	.75
□ 182 Joe Caffie	6.00	2.70	.75
□ 183 Dave Jolly	6.00	2.70	.75
□ 184 Elvin Tappe	6.00	2.70	.75
□ 185 Ray Boone	6.50	2.90	.80
□ 186 Jack Meyer	6.00	2.70	.75
□ 187 Sandy Koufax	225.00	100.00	28.00
□ 188 Milt Bolling UER (Photo actually Lou Berberet)	6.00	2.70	.75
□ 189 George Susce	6.00	2.70	.75
□ 190 Red Schoendienst	21.00	9.50	2.60
□ 191 Art Ceccarelli	6.00	2.70	.75
□ 192 Milt Graff	6.00	2.70	.75
□ 193 Jerry Lumpe	7.50	3.40	.95
□ 194 Roger Craig	10.00	4.50	1.25
□ 195 Whitey Lockman	6.50	2.90	.80
□ 196 Mike Garcia	6.50	2.90	.80
□ 197 Haywood Sullivan	6.50	2.90	.80
□ 198 Bill Virdon	7.50	3.40	.95
□ 199 Don Blasingame	5.00	2.30	.60
□ 200 Bob Keegan	5.00	2.30	.60
□ 201 Jim Bolger	5.00	2.30	.60
□ 202 Woody Held	6.50	2.90	.80
□ 203 Al Walker	5.00	2.30	.60
□ 204 Leo Kiely	5.00	2.30	.60
□ 205 Johnny Temple	5.50	2.50	.70
□ 206 Bob Shaw	6.50	2.90	.80
□ 207 Solly Hemus	5.00	2.30	.60
□ 208 Cal McLish	5.00	2.30	.60
□ 209 Bob Anderson	5.00	2.30	.60
□ 210 Wally Moon	5.50	2.50	.70
□ 211 Pete Burnside	5.00	2.30	.60
□ 212 Bubba Phillips	5.00	2.30	.60
□ 213 Red Wilson	5.00	2.30	.60
□ 214 Willard Schmidt	5.00	2.30	.60
□ 215 Jim Gilliam	10.50	4.70	1.30
□ 216 St. Louis Cardinals Team Card (Checklist on back)	14.00	6.25	1.75
□ 217 Jack Harshman	5.00	2.30	.60
□ 218 Dick Rand	5.00	2.30	.60
□ 219 Camilo Pascual	5.50	2.50	.70
□ 220 Tom Brewer	5.00	2.30	.60
□ 221 Jerry Kindall	6.50	2.90	.80
□ 222 Bud Daley	5.00	2.30	.60
□ 223 Andy Pafko	5.50	2.50	.70
□ 224 Bob Grim	5.50	2.50	.70
□ 225 Billy Goodman	5.50	2.50	.70
□ 226 Bob Smith	5.00	2.30	.60
□ 227 Gene Stephens	5.00	2.30	.60
□ 228 Duke Maas	5.00	2.30	.60
□ 229 Frank Zupo	5.00	2.30	.60
□ 230 Richie Ashburn	18.00	8.00	2.30
□ 231 Lloyd Merritt	5.00	2.30	.60
□ 232 Reno Bertoia	5.00	2.30	.60
□ 233 Mickey Vernon	5.50	2.50	.70
□ 234 Carl Sawatski	5.00	2.30	.60
□ 235 Tom Gorman	5.00	2.30	.60
□ 236 Ed Fitzgerald	5.00	2.30	.60
□ 237 Bill Wight	5.00	2.30	.60
□ 238 Bill Mazeroski	16.00	7.25	2.00
□ 239 Chuck Stobbs	5.00	2.30	.60
□ 240 Bill Skowron	13.00	5.75	1.65
□ 241 Dick Littlefield	5.00	2.30	.60
□ 242 Johnny Klippstein	5.00	2.30	.60
□ 243 Larry Raines	5.00	2.30	.60
□ 244 Don Demeter	5.00	2.30	.60
□ 245 Frank Lary	5.50	2.50	.70
□ 246 New York Yankees Team Card (Checklist on back)	50.00	23.00	6.25
□ 247 Casey Wise	5.00	2.30	.60
□ 248 Herman Wehmeier	5.00	2.30	.60
□ 249 Ray Moore	5.00	2.30	.60
□ 250 Roy Sievers	5.50	2.50	.70
□ 251 Warren Hacker	5.00	2.30	.60
□ 252 Bob Trowbridge	5.00	2.30	.60
□ 253 Don Mueller	5.50	2.50	.70
□ 254 Alex Grammas	5.00	2.30	.60
□ 255 Bob Turley	10.00	4.50	1.25
□ 256 Chicago White Sox Team Card (Checklist on back)	14.00	6.25	1.75
□ 257 Hal Smith	5.00	2.30	.60
□ 258 Carl Erskine	10.00	4.50	1.25
□ 259 Al Pilarcik	5.00	2.30	.60
□ 260 Frank Malzone	5.50	2.50	.70
□ 261 Turk Lown	5.00	2.30	.60
□ 262 Johnny Groth	5.00	2.30	.60
□ 263 Eddie Bressoud	5.50	2.50	.70
□ 264 Jack Sanford	5.50	2.50	.70
□ 265 Pete Runnels	5.50	2.50	.70
□ 266 Connie Johnson	5.00	2.30	.60
□ 267 Sherm Lollar	5.50	2.50	.70
□ 268 Granny Hamner	5.00	2.30	.60
□ 269 Paul Smith	5.00	2.30	.60
□ 270 Warren Spahn	60.00	27.00	7.50
□ 271 Billy Martin	21.00	9.50	2.60
□ 272 Ray Crone	5.00	2.30	.60
□ 273 Hal Smith	5.00	2.30	.60
□ 274 Rocky Bridges	5.00	2.30	.60
□ 275 Elston Howard	15.00	6.75	1.90
□ 276 Bobby Avila	5.00	2.30	.60
□ 277 Virgil Trucks	5.50	2.50	.70
□ 278 Mack Burk	5.00	2.30	.60
□ 279 Bob Boyd	5.00	2.30	.60
□ 280 Jim Piersall	7.50	3.40	.95
□ 281 Sammy Taylor	5.00	2.30	.60
□ 282 Paul Foytack	5.00	2.30	.60
□ 283 Ray Shearer	5.00	2.30	.60
□ 284 Ray Katt	5.00	2.30	.60
□ 285 Frank Robinson	110.00	50.00	14.00
□ 286 Gino Cimoli	5.00	2.30	.60
□ 287 Sam Jones	5.50	2.50	.70
□ 288 Harmon Killebrew	95.00	42.50	12.00
□ 289 Series Hurling Rivals Lou Burdette Bobby Shantz	6.50	2.90	.80
□ 290 Dick Donovan	5.00	2.30	.60
□ 291 Don Landrum	5.00	2.30	.60
□ 292 Ned Garver	5.00	2.30	.60
□ 293 Gene Freese	5.00	2.30	.60
□ 294 Hal Jeffcoat	5.00	2.30	.60
□ 295 Minnie Minoso	10.00	4.50	1.25
□ 296 Ryne Duren	13.50	6.00	1.70
□ 297 Don Buddin	5.00	2.30	.60
□ 298 Jim Hearn	5.00	2.30	.60
□ 299 Harry Simpson	5.00	2.30	.60
□ 300 League Presidents Will Harridge Warren Giles	8.50	3.80	1.05
□ 301 Randy Jackson	5.00	2.30	.60
□ 302 Mike Baxes	5.00	2.30	.60
□ 303 Neil Chrisley	5.00	2.30	.60
□ 304 Tigers' Big Bats Harvey Kuenn Al Kaline	17.00	7.75	2.10
□ 305 Clem Labine	5.50	2.50	.70
□ 306 Whammy Douglas	5.00	2.30	.60
□ 307 Brooks Robinson	125.00	57.50	15.50
□ 308 Paul Giel	5.50	2.50	.70
□ 309 Gail Harris	5.00	2.30	.60
□ 310 Ernie Banks	100.00	45.00	12.50
□ 311 Bob Purkey	5.00	2.30	.60
□ 312 Boston Red Sox Team Card (Checklist on back)	14.00	6.25	1.75
□ 313 Bob Rush	5.00	2.30	.60
□ 314 Dodgers' Boss and Power: Duke Snider Walt Alston MG	25.00	11.50	3.10
□ 315 Bob Friend	5.50	2.50	.70
□ 316 Tito Francona	5.50	2.50	.70
□ 317 Albie Pearson	5.50	2.50	.70

318	Frank House	5.00	2.30	.60
319	Lou Skizas	5.00	2.30	.60
320	Whitey Ford	50.00	23.00	6.25
321	Sluggers Supreme Ted Kluszewski Ted Williams	45.00	20.00	5.75
322	Harding Peterson	5.50	2.50	.70
323	Elmer Valo	5.00	2.30	.60
324	Hoyt Wilhelm	20.00	9.00	2.50
325	Joe Adcock	7.00	3.10	.85
326	Bob Miller	5.00	2.30	.60
327	Chicago Cubs Team Card (Checklist on back)	14.00	6.25	1.75
328	Ike Delock	5.00	2.30	.60
329	Bob Cerv	5.50	2.50	.70
330	Ed Bailey	5.50	2.50	.70
331	Pedro Ramos	5.00	2.30	.60
332	Jim King	5.00	2.30	.60
333	Andy Carey	5.50	2.50	.70
334	Mound Aces Bob Friend Billy Pierce	5.50	2.50	.70
335	Ruben Gomez	5.00	2.30	.60
336	Bert Hamric	5.00	2.30	.60
337	Hank Aguirre	5.00	2.30	.60
338	Walt Dropo	5.50	2.50	.70
339	Fred Hatfield	5.00	2.30	.60
340	Don Newcombe	10.00	4.50	1.25
341	Pittsburgh Pirates Team Card (Checklist on back)	14.00	6.25	1.75
342	Jim Brosnan	5.50	2.50	.70
343	Orlando Cepeda	80.00	36.00	10.00
344	Bob Porterfield	5.00	2.30	.60
345	Jim Hegan	5.50	2.50	.70
346	Steve Bilko	5.00	2.30	.60
347	Don Rudolph	5.00	2.30	.60
348	Chico Fernandez	5.00	2.30	.60
349	Murry Dickson	5.00	2.30	.60
350	Ken Boyer	13.00	5.75	1.65
351	Braves Fence Busters Del Crandall Eddie Mathews Hank Aaron Joe Adcock	30.00	13.50	3.80
352	Herb Score	8.50	3.80	1.05
353	Stan Lopata	4.50	2.00	.55
354	Art Ditmar	5.00	2.30	.60
355	Bill Bruton	5.00	2.30	.60
356	Bob Malkmus	4.50	2.00	.55
357	Danny McDevitt	4.50	2.00	.55
358	Gene Baker	4.50	2.00	.55
359	Billy Loes	5.00	2.30	.60
360	Roy McMillan	5.00	2.30	.60
361	Mike Fornieles	4.50	2.00	.55
362	Ray Jablonski	4.50	2.00	.55
363	Don Elston	4.50	2.00	.55
364	Earl Battey	4.50	2.00	.55
365	Tom Morgan	4.50	2.00	.55
366	Gene Green	4.50	2.00	.55
367	Jack Urban	4.50	2.00	.55
368	Rocky Colavito	35.00	16.00	4.40
369	Ralph Lumenti	4.50	2.00	.55
370	Yogi Berra	100.00	45.00	12.50
371	Marty Keough	4.50	2.00	.55
372	Don Cardwell	4.50	2.00	.55
373	Joe Pignatano	4.50	2.00	.55
374	Brooks Lawrence	4.50	2.00	.55
375	Pee Wee Reese	55.00	25.00	7.00
376	Charley Rabe	4.50	2.00	.55
377A	Milwaukee Braves Team Card (Alphabetical)	14.00	6.25	1.75
377B	Milwaukee Team numerical checklist	85.00	38.00	10.50
378	Hank Sauer	5.00	2.30	.60
379	Ray Herbert	4.50	2.00	.55
380	Charlie Maxwell	5.00	2.30	.60
381	Hal Brown	4.50	2.00	.55
382	Al Cicotte	4.50	2.00	.55
383	Lou Berberet	4.50	2.00	.55
384	John Goryl	4.50	2.00	.55
385	Wilmer Mizell	5.00	2.30	.60
386	Birdie's Sluggers Ed Bailey Birdie Tebbetts MG Frank Robinson	10.00	4.50	1.25
387	Wally Post	5.00	2.30	.60
388	Billy Moran	4.50	2.00	.55
389	Bill Taylor	4.50	2.00	.55
390	Del Crandall	5.00	2.30	.60
391	Dave Melton	4.50	2.00	.55

392	Bennie Daniels	4.50	2.00	.55
393	Tony Kubek	20.00	9.00	2.50
394	Jim Grant	7.00	3.10	.85
395	Willard Nixon	4.50	2.00	.55
396	Dutch Dotterer	4.50	2.00	.55
397A	Detroit Tigers Team Card (Alphabetical)	14.00	6.25	1.75
397B	Detroit Team numerical checklist	85.00	38.00	10.50
398	Gene Woodling	5.00	2.30	.60
399	Marv Grissom	4.50	2.00	.55
400	Nellie Fox	15.00	6.75	1.90
401	Don Bessent	4.50	2.00	.55
402	Bobby Gene Smith	4.50	2.00	.55
403	Steve Korcheck	4.50	2.00	.55
404	Curt Simmons	5.00	2.30	.60
405	Ken Aspromonte	4.50	2.00	.55
406	Vic Power	5.00	2.30	.60
407	Carlton Willey	5.00	2.30	.60
408A	Baltimore Orioles Team Card (Alphabetical)	14.00	6.25	1.75
408B	Baltimore Team numerical checklist	85.00	38.00	10.50
409	Frank Thomas	5.00	2.30	.60
410	Murray Wall	4.50	2.00	.55
411	Tony Taylor	8.00	3.60	1.00
412	Gerry Staley	4.50	2.00	.55
413	Jim Davenport	7.00	3.10	.85
414	Sammy White	4.50	2.00	.55
415	Bob Bowman	4.50	2.00	.55
416	Foster Castleman	4.50	2.00	.55
417	Carl Furillo	10.00	4.50	1.25
418	World Series Batting Foes: Mickey Mantle Hank Aaron	175.00	80.00	22.00
419	Bobby Shantz	5.00	2.30	.60
420	Vada Pinson	30.00	13.50	3.80
421	Dixie Howell	4.50	2.00	.55
422	Norm Zauchin	4.50	2.00	.55
423	Phil Clark	4.50	2.00	.55
424	Larry Doby	7.00	3.10	.85
425	Sammy Esposito	4.50	2.00	.55
426	Johnny O'Brien	5.00	2.30	.60
427	Al Worthington	4.50	2.00	.55
428A	Cincinnati Reds Team Card (Alphabetical)	14.00	6.25	1.75
428B	Cincinnati Team numerical checklist	85.00	38.00	10.50
429	Gus Triandos	5.00	2.30	.60
430	Bobby Thomson	7.00	3.10	.85
431	Gene Conley	5.00	2.30	.60
432	John Powers	4.50	2.00	.55
433A	Pancho Herrer ERR	500.00	230.00	65.00
433B	Pancho Herrera COR	4.50	2.00	.55
434	Harvey Kuenn	7.00	3.10	.85
435	Ed Roebuck	5.00	2.30	.60
436	Rival Fence Busters Willie Mays Duke Snider	60.00	27.00	7.50
437	Bob Speake	4.50	2.00	.55
438	Whitey Herzog	8.00	3.60	1.00
439	Ray Narleski	4.50	2.00	.55
440	Eddie Mathews	40.00	18.00	5.00
441	Jim Marshall	4.75	2.10	.60
442	Phil Paine	4.25	1.90	.55
443	Billy Harrell SP	15.00	6.75	1.90
444	Danny Kravitz	4.25	1.90	.55
445	Bob Smith	4.25	1.90	.55
446	Carroll Hardy SP	15.00	6.75	1.90
447	Ray Monzant	4.25	1.90	.55
448	Charlie Lau	8.00	3.60	1.00
449	Gene Fodge	4.25	1.90	.55
450	Preston Ward SP	15.00	6.75	1.90
451	Joe Taylor	4.25	1.90	.55
452	Roman Mejias	4.25	1.90	.55
453	Tom Qualters	4.25	1.90	.55
454	Harry Hanebrink	4.25	1.90	.55
455	Hal Griggs	4.25	1.90	.55
456	Dick Brown	4.25	1.90	.55
457	Milt Pappas	7.00	3.10	.85
458	Julio Becquer	4.25	1.90	.55
459	Ron Blackburn	4.25	1.90	.55
460	Chuck Essegian	4.25	1.90	.55
461	Ed Mayer	4.25	1.90	.55
462	Gary Geiger SP	15.00	6.75	1.90
463	Vito Valentinetti	4.25	1.90	.55
464	Curt Flood	26.00	11.50	3.30
465	Arnie Portocarrero	4.25	1.90	.55
466	Pete Whisenant	4.25	1.90	.55
467	Glen Hobbie	4.25	1.90	.55

☐ 468 Bob Schmidt	4.25	1.90	.55
☐ 469 Don Ferrarese	4.25	1.90	.55
☐ 470 R.C. Stevens	4.25	1.90	.55
☐ 471 Lenny Green	4.25	1.90	.55
☐ 472 Joey Jay	4.75	2.10	.60
☐ 473 Bill Renna	4.25	1.90	.55
☐ 474 Roman Semproch	4.25	1.90	.55
☐ 475 Fred Haney AS MG and Casey Stengel AS MG (Checklist back)	20.00	9.00	2.50
☐ 476 Stan Musial AS TP	40.00	18.00	5.00
☐ 477 Bill Skowron AS	7.50	3.40	.95
☐ 478 Johnny Temple AS	4.50	2.00	.55
☐ 479 Nellie Fox AS	8.50	3.80	1.05
☐ 480 Eddie Mathews AS	16.00	7.25	2.00
☐ 481 Frank Malzone AS	4.50	2.00	.55
☐ 482 Ernie Banks AS	25.00	11.50	3.10
☐ 483 Luis Aparicio AS	15.00	6.75	1.90
☐ 484 Frank Robinson AS	25.00	11.50	3.10
☐ 485 Ted Williams AS	75.00	34.00	9.50
☐ 486 Willie Mays AS	50.00	23.00	6.25
☐ 487 Mickey Mantle AS TP	100.00	45.00	12.50
☐ 488 Hank Aaron AS	50.00	23.00	6.25
☐ 489 Jackie Jensen AS	5.00	2.30	.60
☐ 490 Ed Bailey AS	4.50	2.00	.55
☐ 491 Sherm Lollar AS	4.50	2.00	.55
☐ 492 Bob Friend AS	4.50	2.00	.55
☐ 493 Bob Turley AS	5.00	2.30	.60
☐ 494 Warren Spahn AS	17.50	8.00	2.20
☐ 495 Herb Score AS	16.00	3.20	.95
☐ xx Contest Cards !	20.00	9.00	2.50

1959 Topps

The cards in this 572-card set measure 2 1/2" by 3 1/2". The 1959 Topps set contains bust pictures of the players in a colored circle. Card numbers 551 to 572 are Sporting News All-Star Selections. High numbers 507 to 572 have the card number in a black background on the reverse rather than a green background as in the lower numbers. The high numbers are more difficult to obtain. Several cards in the 300s exist with or without an extra traded or option line on the back of the card. Cards 199 to 286 exist with either white or gray backs. Cards 461 to 470 contain "Highlights" while cards 116 to 146 give an alphabetically ordered listing of "Rookie Prospects." These Rookie Prospects (RP) were Topps' first organized inclusion of untested "Rookie" cards. Card 440 features Lew Burdette erroneously posing as a left-handed pitcher. There were some three-card advertising panels produced by Topps; the players included are from the first series. One advertising panel shows Don McMahon, Red Wilson, and Bob Boyd on the front with Ted Kluszewski's reverse on one of the backs. Another panel shows Joe Pignatano, Sam Jones, and Jack Urban on the front with Ted Kluszewski's reverse on one of the backs. Another panel shows Billy Hunter, Chuck Stobbs, and Carl Sawatski on the front with Nellie Fox's reverse on one of the backs. Another panel shows Vito Valentinetti, Ken Lehman, and Ed Bouchee on the front with Nellie Fox's reverse on one of the backs. When cut apart, these advertising cards are distinguished by the non-standard card back, i.e., part of an advertisement for the 1959 Topps set instead of the typical statistics and biographical information about the player pictured. The key rookies in this set are Sparky Anderson, Bob Gibson, and Bill White.

	NRMT	VG-E	GOOD
COMPLETE SET (572)	5400.00	2400.00	700.00
COMMON PLAYER (1-110)	6.50	2.90	.80
COMMON PLAYER (111-198)	4.00	1.80	.50
COMMON PLAYER (199-506)	3.75	1.70	.45
COMMON PLAYER (507-550)	17.00	7.75	2.10
COMMON AS (551-572)	18.00	8.00	2.30
☐ 1 Ford Frick COMM (Commissioner)	80.00	16.00	4.80
☐ 2 Eddie Yost	7.00	3.10	.85
☐ 3 Don McMahon	7.00	3.10	.85
☐ 4 Albie Pearson	7.00	3.10	.85
☐ 5 Dick Donovan	6.50	2.90	.80
☐ 6 Alex Grammas	6.50	2.90	.80
☐ 7 Al Pilarcik	6.50	2.90	.80
☐ 8 Phillies Team (Checklist on back)	40.00	8.00	2.40
☐ 9 Paul Giel	7.00	3.10	.85
☐ 10 Mickey Mantle	475.00	210.00	60.00
☐ 11 Billy Hunter	6.50	2.90	.80
☐ 12 Vern Law	7.00	3.10	.85
☐ 13 Dick Gernert	6.50	2.90	.80
☐ 14 Pete Whisenant	6.50	2.90	.80
☐ 15 Dick Drott	6.50	2.90	.80
☐ 16 Joe Pignatano	6.50	2.90	.80
☐ 17 Danny's Stars Frank Thomas Danny Murtaugh MG Ted Kluszewski	7.00	3.10	.85
☐ 18 Jack Urban	6.50	2.90	.80
☐ 19 Eddie Bressoud	6.50	2.90	.80
☐ 20 Duke Snider	65.00	29.00	8.25
☐ 21 Connie Johnson	6.50	2.90	.80
☐ 22 Al Smith	6.50	2.90	.80
☐ 23 Murry Dickson	7.00	3.10	.85
☐ 24 Red Wilson	6.50	2.90	.80
☐ 25 Don Hoak	7.00	3.10	.85
☐ 26 Chuck Stobbs	6.50	2.90	.80
☐ 27 Andy Pafko	7.00	3.10	.85
☐ 28 Al Worthington	6.50	2.90	.80
☐ 29 Jim Bolger	6.50	2.90	.80
☐ 30 Nellie Fox	15.00	6.75	1.90
☐ 31 Ken Lehman	6.50	2.90	.80
☐ 32 Don Buddin	6.50	2.90	.80
☐ 33 Ed Fitzgerald	6.50	2.90	.80
☐ 34 Pitchers Beware Al Kaline Charley Maxwell	14.00	6.25	1.75
☐ 35 Ted Kluszewski	12.50	5.75	1.55
☐ 36 Hank Aguirre	6.50	2.90	.80
☐ 37 Gene Green	6.50	2.90	.80
☐ 38 Morrie Martin	6.50	2.90	.80
☐ 39 Ed Bouchee	6.50	2.90	.80
☐ 40A Warren Spahn ERR (Born 1931)	90.00	40.00	11.50
☐ 40B Warren Spahn ERR (Born 1931, but three is partially obscured)	125.00	57.50	15.50
☐ 40C Warren Spahn COR (Born 1921)	60.00	27.00	7.50
☐ 41 Bob Martyn	6.50	2.90	.80
☐ 42 Murray Wall	6.50	2.90	.80
☐ 43 Steve Bilko	6.50	2.90	.80
☐ 44 Vito Valentinetti	6.50	2.90	.80
☐ 45 Andy Carey	7.00	3.10	.85
☐ 46 Bill R. Henry	6.50	2.90	.80
☐ 47 Jim Finigan	6.50	2.90	.80
☐ 48 Orioles Team (Checklist on back)	22.00	4.40	1.30
☐ 49 Bill Hall	6.50	2.90	.80
☐ 50 Willie Mays	180.00	80.00	23.00
☐ 51 Rip Coleman	6.50	2.90	.80
☐ 52 Coot Veal	6.50	2.90	.80
☐ 53 Stan Williams	10.00	4.50	1.25
☐ 54 Mel Roach	6.50	2.90	.80
☐ 55 Tom Brewer	6.50	2.90	.80
☐ 56 Carl Sawatski	6.50	2.90	.80
☐ 57 Al Cicotte	6.50	2.90	.80
☐ 58 Eddie Miksis	6.50	2.90	.80
☐ 59 Irv Noren	7.00	3.10	.85
☐ 60 Bob Turley	10.00	4.50	1.25
☐ 61 Dick Brown	6.50	2.90	.80
☐ 62 Tony Taylor	7.00	3.10	.85
☐ 63 Jim Hearn	6.50	2.90	.80
☐ 64 Joe DeMaestri	6.50	2.90	.80

☐ 65 Frank Torre	7.00	3.10	.85
☐ 66 Joe Ginsberg	6.50	2.90	.80
☐ 67 Brooks Lawrence	6.50	2.90	.80
☐ 68 Dick Schofield	7.00	3.10	.85
☐ 69 Giants Team	22.00	4.40	1.30
(Checklist on back)			
☐ 70 Harvey Kuenn	10.00	4.50	1.25
☐ 71 Don Bessent	6.50	2.90	.80
☐ 72 Bill Renna	6.50	2.90	.80
☐ 73 Ron Jackson	6.50	2.90	.80
☐ 74 Directing Power	7.00	3.10	.85
Jim Lemon			
Cookie Lavagetto MG			
Roy Sievers			
☐ 75 Sam Jones	7.00	3.10	.85
☐ 76 Bobby Richardson	18.00	8.00	2.30
☐ 77 John Goryl	6.50	2.90	.80
☐ 78 Pedro Ramos	6.50	2.90	.80
☐ 79 Harry Chiti	6.50	2.90	.80
☐ 80 Minnie Minoso	10.00	4.50	1.25
☐ 81 Hal Jeffcoat	6.50	2.90	.80
☐ 82 Bob Boyd	6.50	2.90	.80
☐ 83 Bob Smith	6.50	2.90	.80
☐ 84 Reno Bertoia	6.50	2.90	.80
☐ 85 Harry Anderson	6.50	2.90	.80
☐ 86 Bob Keegan	6.50	2.90	.80
☐ 87 Danny O'Connell	6.50	2.90	.80
☐ 88 Herb Score	9.00	4.00	1.15
☐ 89 Billy Gardner	6.50	2.90	.80
☐ 90 Bill Skowron	12.50	5.75	1.55
☐ 91 Herb Moford	6.50	2.90	.80
☐ 92 Dave Philley	6.50	2.90	.80
☐ 93 Julio Becquer	6.50	2.90	.80
☐ 94 White Sox Team	22.00	4.40	1.30
(Checklist on back)			
☐ 95 Carl Willey	6.50	2.90	.80
☐ 96 Lou Berberet	6.50	2.90	.80
☐ 97 Jerry Lynch	7.00	3.10	.85
☐ 98 Arnie Portocarrero	6.50	2.90	.80
☐ 99 Ted Kazanski	6.50	2.90	.80
☐ 100 Bob Cerv	7.00	3.10	.85
☐ 101 Alex Kellner	6.50	2.90	.80
☐ 102 Felipe Alou	25.00	11.50	3.10
☐ 103 Billy Goodman	7.00	3.10	.85
☐ 104 Del Rice	6.50	2.90	.80
☐ 105 Lee Walls	6.50	2.90	.80
☐ 106 Hal Woodeshick	6.50	2.90	.80
☐ 107 Norm Larker	7.00	3.10	.85
☐ 108 Zack Monroe	7.00	3.10	.85
☐ 109 Bob Schmidt	6.50	2.90	.80
☐ 110 George Witt	7.00	3.10	.85
☐ 111 Redlegs Team	11.00	2.20	.65
(Checklist on back)			
☐ 112 Billy Consolo	4.00	1.80	.50
☐ 113 Taylor Phillips	4.00	1.80	.50
☐ 114 Earl Battey	4.00	1.80	.50
☐ 115 Mickey Vernon	4.50	2.00	.55
☐ 116 Bob Allison RP	8.00	3.60	1.00
☐ 117 John Blanchard RP	7.50	3.40	.95
☐ 118 John Buzhardt RP	4.50	2.00	.55
☐ 119 John Callison RP	8.00	3.60	1.00
☐ 120 Chuck Coles RP	4.50	2.00	.55
☐ 121 Bob Conley RP	4.50	2.00	.55
☐ 122 Bennie Daniels RP	4.50	2.00	.55
☐ 123 Don Dillard RP	4.50	2.00	.55
☐ 124 Dan Dobbek RP	4.50	2.00	.55
☐ 125 Ron Fairly RP	7.50	3.40	.95
☐ 126 Ed Haas RP	5.00	2.30	.60
☐ 127 Kent Hadley RP	4.50	2.00	.55
☐ 128 Bob Hartman RP	4.50	2.00	.55
☐ 129 Frank Herrera RP	4.50	2.00	.55
☐ 130 Lou Jackson RP	5.00	2.30	.60
☐ 131 Deron Johnson RP	7.00	3.10	.85
☐ 132 Don Lee RP	4.50	2.00	.55
☐ 133 Bob Lillis RP	5.00	2.30	.60
☐ 134 Jim McDaniel RP	4.50	2.00	.55
☐ 135 Gene Oliver RP	4.50	2.00	.55
☐ 136 Jim O'Toole RP	5.00	2.30	.60
☐ 137 Dick Ricketts RP	5.00	2.30	.60
☐ 138 John Romano RP	5.00	2.30	.60
☐ 139 Ed Sadowski RP	4.50	2.00	.55
☐ 140 Charlie Secrest RP	4.50	2.00	.55
☐ 141 Joe Shipley RP	4.50	2.00	.55
☐ 142 Dick Stigman RP	4.50	2.00	.55
☐ 143 Willie Tasby RP	5.00	2.30	.60
☐ 144 Jerry Walker RP	5.00	2.30	.60
☐ 145 Dom Zanni RP	4.50	2.00	.55
☐ 146 Jerry Zimmerman RP	4.50	2.00	.55
☐ 147 Cubs Clubbers	12.50	5.75	1.55
Dale Long			
Ernie Banks			
Walt Moryn			
☐ 148 Mike McCormick	4.50	2.00	.55
☐ 149 Jim Bunning	12.00	5.50	1.50
☐ 150 Stan Musial	175.00	80.00	22.00
☐ 151 Bob Malkmus	4.00	1.80	.50
☐ 152 Johnny Klippstein	4.00	1.80	.50
☐ 153 Jim Marshall	4.00	1.80	.50
☐ 154 Ray Herbert	4.00	1.80	.50
☐ 155 Enos Slaughter	20.00	9.00	2.50
☐ 156 Ace Hurlers	7.00	3.10	.85
Billy Pierce			
Robin Roberts			
☐ 157 Felix Mantilla	4.00	1.80	.50
☐ 158 Walt Dropo	4.00	1.80	.50
☐ 159 Bob Shaw	4.00	1.80	.50
☐ 160 Dick Groat	4.50	2.00	.55
☐ 161 Frank Baumann	4.00	1.80	.50
☐ 162 Bobby G. Smith	4.00	1.80	.50
☐ 163 Sandy Koufax	175.00	80.00	22.00
☐ 164 Johnny Groth	4.00	1.80	.50
☐ 165 Bill Bruton	4.00	1.80	.50
☐ 166 Destruction Crew	7.00	3.10	.85
Minnie Minoso			
Rocky Colavito			
(Misspelled Colovito			
on card back)			
Larry Doby			
☐ 167 Duke Maas	4.00	1.80	.50
☐ 168 Carroll Hardy	4.00	1.80	.50
☐ 169 Ted Abernathy	4.00	1.80	.50
☐ 170 Gene Woodling	4.50	2.00	.55
☐ 171 Willard Schmidt	4.00	1.80	.50
☐ 172 Athletics Team	11.00	2.20	.65
(Checklist on back)			
☐ 173 Bill Monbouquette	4.50	2.00	.55
☐ 174 Jim Pendleton	4.00	1.80	.50
☐ 175 Dick Farrell	4.50	2.00	.55
☐ 176 Preston Ward	4.00	1.80	.50
☐ 177 John Briggs	4.00	1.80	.50
☐ 178 Ruben Amaro	6.00	2.70	.75
☐ 179 Don Rudolph	4.00	1.80	.50
☐ 180 Yogi Berra	90.00	40.00	11.50
☐ 181 Bob Porterfield	4.00	1.80	.50
☐ 182 Milt Graff	4.00	1.80	.50
☐ 183 Stu Miller	4.50	2.00	.55
☐ 184 Harvey Haddix	4.50	2.00	.55
☐ 185 Jim Busby	4.00	1.80	.50
☐ 186 Mudcat Grant	4.50	2.00	.55
☐ 187 Bubba Phillips	4.00	1.80	.50
☐ 188 Juan Pizarro	4.00	1.80	.50
☐ 189 Neil Chrisley	4.00	1.80	.50
☐ 190 Bill Virdon	5.50	2.50	.70
☐ 191 Russ Kemmerer	4.00	1.80	.50
☐ 192 Charlie Beamon	4.00	1.80	.50
☐ 193 Sammy Taylor	4.00	1.80	.50
☐ 194 Jim Brosnan	4.50	2.00	.55
☐ 195 Rip Repulski	4.00	1.80	.50
☐ 196 Billy Moran	4.00	1.80	.50
☐ 197 Ray Semproch	4.00	1.80	.50
☐ 198 Jim Davenport	4.50	2.00	.55
☐ 199 Leo Kiely	3.75	1.70	.45
☐ 200 Warren Giles	6.00	2.70	.75
(NL President)			
☐ 201 Tom Acker	3.75	1.70	.45
☐ 202 Roger Maris	150.00	70.00	19.00
☐ 203 Ossie Virgil	3.75	1.70	.45
☐ 204 Casey Wise	3.75	1.70	.45
☐ 205 Don Larsen	5.50	2.50	.70
☐ 206 Carl Furillo	5.50	2.50	.70
☐ 207 George Strickland	3.75	1.70	.45
☐ 208 Willie Jones	3.75	1.70	.45
☐ 209 Lenny Green	3.75	1.70	.45
☐ 210 Ed Bailey	3.75	1.70	.45
☐ 211 Bob Blaylock	3.75	1.70	.45
☐ 212 Fence Busters	45.00	20.00	5.75
Hank Aaron			
Eddie Mathews			
☐ 213 Jim Rivera	3.75	1.70	.45
☐ 214 Marcelino Solis	3.75	1.70	.45
☐ 215 Jim Lemon	4.25	1.90	.55
☐ 216 Andre Rodgers	3.75	1.70	.45
☐ 217 Carl Erskine	5.50	2.50	.70
☐ 218 Roman Mejias	3.75	1.70	.45
☐ 219 George Zuverink	3.75	1.70	.45
☐ 220 Frank Malzone	4.25	1.90	.55
☐ 221 Bob Bowman	3.75	1.70	.45
☐ 222 Bobby Shantz	5.00	2.30	.60
☐ 223 Cardinals Team	11.00	2.20	.65
(Checklist on back)			
☐ 224 Claude Osteen	6.00	2.70	.75
☐ 225 Johnny Logan	4.25	1.90	.55
☐ 226 Art Ceccarelli	3.75	1.70	.45
☐ 227 Hal W. Smith	3.75	1.70	.45
☐ 228 Don Gross	3.75	1.70	.45
☐ 229 Vic Power	4.25	1.90	.55

☐	230 Bill Fischer	3.75	1.70	.45
☐	231 Ellis Burton	3.75	1.70	.45
☐	232 Eddie Kasko	3.75	1.70	.45
☐	233 Paul Foytack	3.75	1.70	.45
☐	234 Chuck Tanner	4.25	1.90	.55
☐	235 Valmy Thomas	3.75	1.70	.45
☐	236 Ted Bowsfield	3.75	1.70	.45
☐	237 Run Preventers Gil McDougald Bob Turley Bobby Richardson	8.00	3.60	1.00
☐	238 Gene Baker	3.75	1.70	.45
☐	239 Bob Trowbridge	3.75	1.70	.45
☐	240 Hank Bauer	5.50	2.50	.70
☐	241 Billy Muffett	3.75	1.70	.45
☐	242 Ron Samford	3.75	1.70	.45
☐	243 Marv Grissom	3.75	1.70	.45
☐	244 Ted Gray	3.75	1.70	.45
☐	245 Ned Garver	3.75	1.70	.45
☐	246 J.W. Porter	3.75	1.70	.45
☐	247 Don Ferrarese	3.75	1.70	.45
☐	248 Red Sox Team (Checklist on back)	11.00	2.20	.65
☐	249 Bobby Adams	3.75	1.70	.45
☐	250 Billy O'Dell	3.75	1.70	.45
☐	251 Clete Boyer	5.50	2.50	.70
☐	252 Ray Boone	4.25	1.90	.55
☐	253 Seth Morehead	3.75	1.70	.45
☐	254 Zeke Bella	3.75	1.70	.45
☐	255 Del Ennis	4.25	1.90	.55
☐	256 Jerry Davie	3.75	1.70	.45
☐	257 Leon Wagner	5.25	2.40	.65
☐	258 Fred Kipp	3.75	1.70	.45
☐	259 Jim Pisoni	3.75	1.70	.45
☐	260 Early Wynn UER (1957 Cleevland)	15.00	6.75	1.90
☐	261 Gene Stephens	3.75	1.70	.45
☐	262 Hitters' Foes Johnny Podres Clem Labine Don Drysdale	7.50	3.40	.95
☐	263 Bud Daley	3.75	1.70	.45
☐	264 Chico Carrasquel	3.75	1.70	.45
☐	265 Ron Kline	3.75	1.70	.45
☐	266 Woody Held	3.75	1.70	.45
☐	267 John Romonosky	3.75	1.70	.45
☐	268 Tito Francona	4.25	1.90	.55
☐	269 Jack Meyer	3.75	1.70	.45
☐	270 Gil Hodges	21.00	9.50	2.60
☐	271 Orlando Pena	3.75	1.70	.45
☐	272 Jerry Lumpe	3.75	1.70	.45
☐	273 Joey Jay	4.25	1.90	.55
☐	274 Jerry Kindall	4.25	1.90	.55
☐	275 Jack Sanford	4.25	1.90	.55
☐	276 Pete Daley	3.75	1.70	.45
☐	277 Turk Lown	3.75	1.70	.45
☐	278 Chuck Essegian	3.75	1.70	.45
☐	279 Ernie Johnson	4.25	1.90	.55
☐	280 Frank Bolling	3.75	1.70	.45
☐	281 Walt Craddock	3.75	1.70	.45
☐	282 R.C. Stevens	3.75	1.70	.45
☐	283 Russ Heman	3.75	1.70	.45
☐	284 Steve Korcheck	3.75	1.70	.45
☐	285 Joe Cunningham	4.25	1.90	.55
☐	286 Dean Stone	3.75	1.70	.45
☐	287 Don Zimmer	4.25	1.90	.55
☐	288 Dutch Dotterer	3.75	1.70	.45
☐	289 Johnny Kucks	3.75	1.70	.45
☐	290 Wes Covington	4.25	1.90	.55
☐	291 Pitching Partners Pedro Ramos Camilo Pascual	4.25	1.90	.55
☐	292 Dick Williams	4.25	1.90	.55
☐	293 Ray Moore	3.75	1.70	.45
☐	294 Hank Foiles	3.75	1.70	.45
☐	295 Billy Martin	15.00	6.75	1.90
☐	296 Ernie Broglio	5.00	2.30	.60
☐	297 Jackie Brandt	3.75	1.70	.45
☐	298 Tex Clevenger	3.75	1.70	.45
☐	299 Billy Klaus	3.75	1.70	.45
☐	300 Richie Ashburn	12.50	5.75	1.55
☐	301 Earl Averill	3.75	1.70	.45
☐	302 Don Mossi	4.25	1.90	.55
☐	303 Marty Keough	3.75	1.70	.45
☐	304 Cubs Team (Checklist on back)	11.00	2.20	.65
☐	305 Curt Raydon	3.75	1.70	.45
☐	306 Jim Gilliam	6.00	2.70	.75
☐	307 Curt Barclay	3.75	1.70	.45
☐	308 Norm Siebern	3.75	1.70	.45
☐	309 Sal Maglie	5.00	2.30	.60
☐	310 Luis Aparicio	20.00	9.00	2.50
☐	311 Norm Zauchin	3.75	1.70	.45

☐	312 Don Newcombe	5.00	2.30	.60
☐	313 Frank House	3.75	1.70	.45
☐	314 Don Cardwell	3.75	1.70	.45
☐	315 Joe Adcock	4.25	1.90	.55
☐	316A Ralph Lumenti UER (Option) (Photo actually Camilo Pascual)	3.75	1.70	.45
☐	316B Ralph Lumenti UER (No option) (Photo actually Camilo Pascual)	90.00	40.00	11.50
☐	317 Hitting Kings Willie Mays Richie Ashburn	30.00	13.50	3.80
☐	318 Rocky Bridges	3.75	1.70	.45
☐	319 Dave Hillman	3.75	1.70	.45
☐	320 Bob Skinner	4.25	1.90	.55
☐	321A Bob Giallombardo (Option)	3.75	1.70	.45
☐	321B Bob Giallombardo (No option)	90.00	40.00	11.50
☐	322A Harry Hanebrink (Traded)	3.75	1.70	.45
☐	322B Harry Hanebrink (No trade)	90.00	40.00	11.50
☐	323 Frank Sullivan	3.75	1.70	.45
☐	324 Don Demeter	3.75	1.70	.45
☐	325 Ken Boyer	9.00	4.00	1.15
☐	326 Marv Throneberry	5.00	2.30	.60
☐	327 Gary Bell	3.75	1.70	.45
☐	328 Lou Skizas	3.75	1.70	.45
☐	329 Tigers Team (Checklist on back)	11.00	2.20	.65
☐	330 Gus Triandos	4.25	1.90	.55
☐	331 Steve Boros	3.75	1.70	.45
☐	332 Ray Monzant	3.75	1.70	.45
☐	333 Harry Simpson	3.75	1.70	.45
☐	334 Glen Hobbie	3.75	1.70	.45
☐	335 Johnny Temple	4.25	1.90	.55
☐	336A Billy Loes (With traded line)	4.25	1.90	.55
☐	336B Billy Loes (No trade)	90.00	40.00	11.50
☐	337 George Crowe	3.75	1.70	.45
☐	338 Sparky Anderson	45.00	20.00	5.75
☐	339 Roy Face	5.00	2.30	.60
☐	340 Roy Sievers	4.25	1.90	.55
☐	341 Tom Qualters	3.75	1.70	.45
☐	342 Ray Jablonski	3.75	1.70	.45
☐	343 Billy Hoeft	3.75	1.70	.45
☐	344 Russ Nixon	3.75	1.70	.45
☐	345 Gil McDougald	7.50	3.40	.95
☐	346 Batter Bafflers Dave Sisler Tom Brewer	3.75	1.70	.45
☐	347 Bob Buhl	4.25	1.90	.55
☐	348 Ted Lepcio	3.75	1.70	.45
☐	349 Hoyt Wilhelm	18.00	8.00	2.30
☐	350 Ernie Banks	75.00	34.00	9.50
☐	351 Earl Torgeson	3.75	1.70	.45
☐	352 Robin Roberts	18.00	8.00	2.30
☐	353 Curt Flood	5.50	2.50	.70
☐	354 Pete Burnside	3.75	1.70	.45
☐	355 Jim Piersall	5.00	2.30	.60
☐	356 Bob Mabe	3.75	1.70	.45
☐	357 Dick Stuart	6.00	2.70	.75
☐	358 Ralph Terry	4.25	1.90	.55
☐	359 Bill White	30.00	13.50	3.80
☐	360 Al Kaline	70.00	32.00	8.75
☐	361 Willard Nixon	3.75	1.70	.45
☐	362A Dolan Nichols (With option line)	3.75	1.70	.45
☐	362B Dolan Nichols (No option)	90.00	40.00	11.50
☐	363 Bobby Avila	3.75	1.70	.45
☐	364 Danny McDevitt	3.75	1.70	.45
☐	365 Gus Bell	4.25	1.90	.55
☐	366 Humberto Robinson	3.75	1.70	.45
☐	367 Cal Neeman	3.75	1.70	.45
☐	368 Don Mueller	4.25	1.90	.55
☐	369 Dick Tomanek	3.75	1.70	.45
☐	370 Pete Runnels	4.25	1.90	.55
☐	371 Dick Brodowski	3.75	1.70	.45
☐	372 Jim Hegan	4.25	1.90	.55
☐	373 Herb Plews	3.75	1.70	.45
☐	374 Art Ditmar	3.75	1.70	.45
☐	375 Bob Nieman	3.75	1.70	.45
☐	376 Hal Naragon	3.75	1.70	.45
☐	377 John Antonelli	4.25	1.90	.55
☐	378 Gail Harris	3.75	1.70	.45
☐	379 Bob Miller	3.75	1.70	.45
☐	380 Hank Aaron	125.00	57.50	15.50

☐ 381 Mike Baxes	3.75	1.70	.45
☐ 382 Curt Simmons	4.25	1.90	.55
☐ 383 Words of Wisdom	9.00	4.00	1.15
Don Larsen			
Casey Stengel MG			
☐ 384 Dave Sisler	3.75	1.70	.45
☐ 385 Sherm Lollar	4.25	1.90	.55
☐ 386 Jim Delsing	3.75	1.70	.45
☐ 387 Don Drysdale	40.00	18.00	5.00
☐ 388 Bob Will	3.75	1.70	.45
☐ 389 Joe Nuxhall	4.25	1.90	.55
☐ 390 Orlando Cepeda	20.00	9.00	2.50
☐ 391 Milt Pappas	4.25	1.90	.55
☐ 392 Whitey Herzog	6.00	2.70	.75
☐ 393 Frank Lary	4.25	1.90	.55
☐ 394 Randy Jackson	3.75	1.70	.45
☐ 395 Elston Howard	9.00	4.00	1.15
☐ 396 Bob Rush	3.75	1.70	.45
☐ 397 Senators Team	11.00	2.20	.65
(Checklist on back)			
☐ 398 Wally Post	4.25	1.90	.55
☐ 399 Larry Jackson	3.75	1.70	.45
☐ 400 Jackie Jensen	5.00	2.30	.60
☐ 401 Ron Blackburn	3.75	1.70	.45
☐ 402 Hector Lopez	4.25	1.90	.55
☐ 403 Clem Labine	4.25	1.90	.55
☐ 404 Hank Sauer	4.25	1.90	.55
☐ 405 Roy McMillan	4.25	1.90	.55
☐ 406 Solly Drake	3.75	1.70	.45
☐ 407 Moe Drabowsky	4.25	1.90	.55
☐ 408 Keystone Combo	9.00	4.00	1.15
Nellie Fox			
Luis Aparicio			
☐ 409 Gus Zernial	4.25	1.90	.55
☐ 410 Billy Pierce	4.75	2.10	.60
☐ 411 Whitey Lockman	4.25	1.90	.55
☐ 412 Stan Lopata	3.75	1.70	.45
☐ 413 Camilo Pascual UER	4.25	1.90	.55
(Listed as Camillo on front and Pasqual on back)			
☐ 414 Dale Long	4.25	1.90	.55
☐ 415 Bill Mazeroski	8.50	3.80	1.05
☐ 416 Haywood Sullivan	4.25	1.90	.55
☐ 417 Virgil Trucks	4.25	1.90	.55
☐ 418 Gino Cimoli	3.75	1.70	.45
☐ 419 Braves Team	11.00	4.90	1.40
(Checklist on back)			
☐ 420 Rocky Colavito	20.00	9.00	2.50
☐ 421 Herman Wehmeier	3.75	1.70	.45
☐ 422 Hobie Landrith	3.75	1.70	.45
☐ 423 Bob Grim	4.25	1.90	.55
☐ 424 Ken Aspromonte	3.75	1.70	.45
☐ 425 Del Crandall	4.25	1.90	.55
☐ 426 Gerry Staley	3.75	1.70	.45
☐ 427 Charlie Neal	4.25	1.90	.55
☐ 428 Buc Hill Aces	4.25	1.90	.55
Ron Kline			
Bob Friend			
Vernon Law			
Roy Face			
☐ 429 Bobby Thomson	5.00	2.30	.60
☐ 430 Whitey Ford	45.00	20.00	5.75
☐ 431 Whammy Douglas	3.75	1.70	.45
☐ 432 Smoky Burgess	4.25	1.90	.55
☐ 433 Billy Harrell	3.75	1.70	.45
☐ 434 Hal Griggs	3.75	1.70	.45
☐ 435 Frank Robinson	55.00	25.00	7.00
☐ 436 Granny Hamner	3.75	1.70	.45
☐ 437 Ike Delock	3.75	1.70	.45
☐ 438 Sammy Esposito	3.75	1.70	.45
☐ 439 Brooks Robinson	65.00	29.00	8.25
☐ 440 Lou Burdette	7.00	3.10	.85
(Posing as if lefthanded)			
☐ 441 John Roseboro	4.25	1.90	.55
☐ 442 Ray Narleski	3.75	1.70	.45
☐ 443 Daryl Spencer	3.75	1.70	.45
☐ 444 Ron Hansen	5.00	2.30	.60
☐ 445 Cal McLish	3.75	1.70	.45
☐ 446 Rocky Nelson	3.75	1.70	.45
☐ 447 Bob Anderson	3.75	1.70	.45
☐ 448 Vada Pinson UER	7.00	3.10	.85
(Born: 8/8/38, should be 8/11/38)			
☐ 449 Tom Gorman	3.75	1.70	.45
☐ 450 Eddie Mathews	30.00	13.50	3.80
☐ 451 Jimmy Constable	3.75	1.70	.45
☐ 452 Chico Fernandez	3.75	1.70	.45
☐ 453 Les Moss	3.75	1.70	.45
☐ 454 Phil Clark	3.75	1.70	.45
☐ 455 Larry Doby	5.00	2.30	.60
☐ 456 Jerry Casale	3.75	1.70	.45
☐ 457 Dodgers Team	20.00	4.00	1.20
(Checklist on back)			
☐ 458 Gordon Jones	3.75	1.70	.45
☐ 459 Bill Tuttle	3.75	1.70	.45
☐ 460 Bob Friend	4.25	1.90	.55
☐ 461 Mickey Mantle Hits Homer	55.00	25.00	7.00
☐ 462 Rocky Colavito's Catch	10.00	4.50	1.25
☐ 463 Al Kaline Batting Champ	16.00	7.25	2.00
☐ 464 Willie Mays' Series Catch	25.00	11.50	3.10
☐ 465 Roy Sievers Sets Mark	5.00	2.30	.60
☐ 466 Billy Pierce All-Star	5.00	2.30	.60
☐ 467 Hank Aaron Clubs Homer	25.00	11.50	3.10
☐ 468 Duke Snider's Play	17.00	7.75	2.10
☐ 469 Hustler Ernie Banks	17.00	7.75	2.10
☐ 470 Stan Musial's 3000th Hit	21.00	9.50	2.60
☐ 471 Tom Sturdivant	3.75	1.70	.45
☐ 472 Gene Freese	3.75	1.70	.45
☐ 473 Mike Fornieles	3.75	1.70	.45
☐ 474 Moe Thacker	3.75	1.70	.45
☐ 475 Jack Harshman	3.75	1.70	.45
☐ 476 Indians Team	11.00	2.20	.65
(Checklist on back)			
☐ 477 Barry Latman	3.75	1.70	.45
☐ 478 Bob Clemente	125.00	57.50	15.50
☐ 479 Lindy McDaniel	4.25	1.90	.55
☐ 480 Red Schoendienst	15.00	6.75	1.90
☐ 481 Charlie Maxwell	4.25	1.90	.55
☐ 482 Russ Meyer	3.75	1.70	.45
☐ 483 Clint Courtney	3.75	1.70	.45
☐ 484 Willie Kirkland	3.75	1.70	.45
☐ 485 Ryne Duren	6.00	2.70	.75
☐ 486 Sammy White	3.75	1.70	.45
☐ 487 Hal Brown	3.75	1.70	.45
☐ 488 Walt Moryn	3.75	1.70	.45
☐ 489 John Powers	3.75	1.70	.45
☐ 490 Frank Thomas	4.25	1.90	.55
☐ 491 Don Blasingame	3.75	1.70	.45
☐ 492 Gene Conley	4.25	1.90	.55
☐ 493 Jim Landis	3.75	1.70	.45
☐ 494 Don Pavletich	3.75	1.70	.45
☐ 495 Johnny Podres	5.00	2.30	.60
☐ 496 Wayne Terwilliger UER	3.75	1.70	.45
(Athlftics on front)			
☐ 497 Hal R. Smith	3.75	1.70	.45
☐ 498 Dick Hyde	3.75	1.70	.45
☐ 499 Johnny O'Brien	4.25	1.90	.55
☐ 500 Vic Wertz	4.25	1.90	.55
☐ 501 Bob Tiefenauer	3.75	1.70	.45
☐ 502 Alvin Dark	5.00	2.30	.60
☐ 503 Jim Owens	3.75	1.70	.45
☐ 504 Ossie Alvarez	3.75	1.70	.45
☐ 505 Tony Kubek	12.50	5.75	1.55
☐ 506 Bob Purkey	3.75	1.70	.45
☐ 507 Bob Hale	17.00	7.75	2.10
☐ 508 Art Fowler	17.00	7.75	2.10
☐ 509 Norm Cash	70.00	32.00	8.75
☐ 510 Yankees Team	85.00	17.00	5.10
(Checklist on back)			
☐ 511 George Susce	17.00	7.75	2.10
☐ 512 George Altman	17.00	7.75	2.10
☐ 513 Tommy Carroll	17.00	7.75	2.10
☐ 514 Bob Gibson	400.00	180.00	50.00
☐ 515 Harmon Killebrew	150.00	70.00	19.00
☐ 516 Mike Garcia	19.00	8.50	2.40
☐ 517 Joe Koppe	17.00	7.75	2.10
☐ 518 Mike Cueller UER	25.00	11.50	3.10
(Sic, Cuellar)			
☐ 519 Infield Power	19.00	8.50	2.40
Pete Runnels			
Dick Gernert			
Frank Malzone			
☐ 520 Don Elston	17.00	7.75	2.10
☐ 521 Gary Geiger	17.00	7.75	2.10
☐ 522 Gene Snyder	17.00	7.75	2.10
☐ 523 Harry Bright	17.00	7.75	2.10
☐ 524 Larry Osborne	17.00	7.75	2.10
☐ 525 Jim Coates	17.00	7.75	2.10
☐ 526 Bob Speake	17.00	7.75	2.10
☐ 527 Solly Hemus	17.00	7.75	2.10
☐ 528 Pirates Team	50.00	10.00	3.00
(Checklist on back)			
☐ 529 George Bamberger	20.00	9.00	2.50
☐ 530 Wally Moon	19.00	8.50	2.40
☐ 531 Ray Webster	17.00	7.75	2.10
☐ 532 Mark Freeman	17.00	7.75	2.10
☐ 533 Darrell Johnson	19.00	8.50	2.40
☐ 534 Faye Throneberry	17.00	7.75	2.10

☐ 535 Ruben Gomez	17.00	7.75	2.10
☐ 536 Danny Kravitz	17.00	7.75	2.10
☐ 537 Rudolph Arias	17.00	7.75	2.10
☐ 538 Chick King	17.00	7.75	2.10
☐ 539 Gary Blaylock	17.00	7.75	2.10
☐ 540 Willie Miranda	17.00	7.75	2.10
☐ 541 Bob Thurman	17.00	7.75	2.10
☐ 542 Jim Perry	25.00	11.50	3.10
☐ 543 Corsair Trio Bob Skinner Bill Virdon Roberto Clemente	70.00	32.00	8.75
☐ 544 Lee Tate	17.00	7.75	2.10
☐ 545 Tom Morgan	17.00	7.75	2.10
☐ 546 Al Schroll	17.00	7.75	2.10
☐ 547 Jim Baxes	17.00	7.75	2.10
☐ 548 Elmer Singleton	17.00	7.75	2.10
☐ 549 Howie Nunn	17.00	7.75	2.10
☐ 550 Roy Campanella (Symbol of Courage)	175.00	80.00	22.00
☐ 551 Fred Haney MG AS	18.00	8.00	2.30
☐ 552 Casey Stengel MG AS	35.00	16.00	4.40
☐ 553 Orlando Cepeda AS	25.00	11.50	3.10
☐ 554 Bill Skowron AS	25.00	11.50	3.10
☐ 555 Bill Mazeroski AS	25.00	11.50	3.10
☐ 556 Nellie Fox AS	25.00	11.50	3.10
☐ 557 Ken Boyer AS	25.00	11.50	3.10
☐ 558 Frank Malzone AS	18.00	8.00	2.30
☐ 559 Ernie Banks AS	55.00	25.00	7.00
☐ 560 Luis Aparicio AS	35.00	16.00	4.40
☐ 561 Hank Aaron AS	130.00	57.50	16.50
☐ 562 Al Kaline AS	60.00	27.00	7.50
☐ 563 Willie Mays AS	130.00	57.50	16.50
☐ 564 Mickey Mantle AS	300.00	135.00	38.00
☐ 565 Wes Covington AS	18.00	8.00	2.30
☐ 566 Roy Sievers AS	18.00	8.00	2.30
☐ 567 Del Crandall AS	18.00	8.00	2.30
☐ 568 Gus Triandos AS	18.00	8.00	2.30
☐ 569 Bob Friend AS	18.00	8.00	2.30
☐ 570 Bob Turley AS	18.00	8.00	2.30
☐ 571 Warren Spahn AS	40.00	18.00	5.00
☐ 572 Billy Pierce AS	35.00	8.75	2.80

1960 Topps

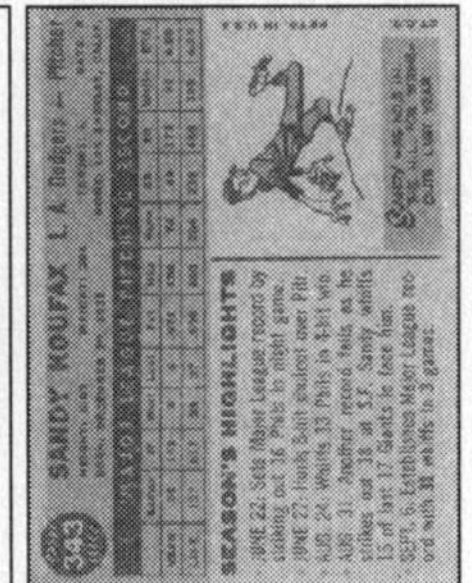

The cards in this 572-card set measure 2 1/2" by 3 1/2". The 1960 Topps set is the only Topps standard size issue to use a horizontally oriented front. World Series cards appeared for the first time (385 to 391), and there is a Rookie Prospect (RP) series (117-148), the most famous of which is Carl Yastrzemski, and a Sport Magazine All-Star Selection (AS) series (553-572). There are 16 manager cards listed alphabetically from 212 through 227. The 1959 Topps All-Rookie team is featured on cards 316-325. The coaching staff of each team was also afforded their own card in a 16-card subset (455-470). Cards 375 to 440 come with either gray or white backs, and the high series (507-572) were printed on a more limited basis than the rest of the set. The team cards have series checklists on the reverse. The key rookies in this set are Willie McCovey and Carl Yastrzemski.

	NRMT	VG-E	GOOD
COMPLETE SET (572)	4000.00	1800.00	500.00
COMMON PLAYER (1-110)	3.75	1.70	.45
COMMON PLAYER (111-198)	3.00	1.35	.40
COMMON PLAYER (199-286)	3.50	1.55	.45
COMMON PLAYER (287-440)	3.75	1.70	.45
COMMON PLAYER (441-506)	5.00	2.30	.60
COMMON PLAYER (507-552)	12.00	5.50	1.50
COMMON AS (553-572)	15.00	6.75	1.90

☐ 1 Early Wynn	40.00	10.00	3.20
☐ 2 Roman Mejias	3.75	1.70	.45
☐ 3 Joe Adcock	4.25	1.90	.55
☐ 4 Bob Purkey	3.75	1.70	.45
☐ 5 Wally Moon	4.25	1.90	.55
☐ 6 Lou Berberet	3.75	1.70	.45
☐ 7 Master and Mentor Willie Mays Bill Rigney MG	20.00	9.00	2.50
☐ 8 Bud Daley	3.75	1.70	.45
☐ 9 Faye Throneberry	3.75	1.70	.45
☐ 10 Ernie Banks	55.00	25.00	7.00
☐ 11 Norm Siebern	3.75	1.70	.45
☐ 12 Milt Pappas	4.25	1.90	.55
☐ 13 Wally Post	4.25	1.90	.55
☐ 14 Jim Grant	4.25	1.90	.55
☐ 15 Pete Runnels	4.25	1.90	.55
☐ 16 Ernie Broglio	4.25	1.90	.55
☐ 17 Johnny Callison	5.00	2.30	.60
☐ 18 Dodgers Team (Checklist on back)	20.00	9.00	2.50
☐ 19 Felix Mantilla	3.75	1.70	.45
☐ 20 Roy Face	5.00	2.30	.60
☐ 21 Dutch Dotterer	3.75	1.70	.45
☐ 22 Rocky Bridges	3.75	1.70	.45
☐ 23 Eddie Fisher	3.75	1.70	.45
☐ 24 Dick Gray	3.75	1.70	.45
☐ 25 Roy Sievers	4.25	1.90	.55
☐ 26 Wayne Terwilliger	3.75	1.70	.45
☐ 27 Dick Drott	3.75	1.70	.45
☐ 28 Brooks Robinson	55.00	25.00	7.00
☐ 29 Clem Labine	4.25	1.90	.55
☐ 30 Tito Francona	3.75	1.70	.45
☐ 31 Sammy Esposito	3.75	1.70	.45
☐ 32 Sophomore Stalwarts Jim O'Toole Vada Pinson	3.75	1.70	.45
☐ 33 Tom Morgan	3.75	1.70	.45
☐ 34 Sparky Anderson	11.00	4.90	1.40
☐ 35 Whitey Ford	45.00	20.00	5.75
☐ 36 Russ Nixon	3.75	1.70	.45
☐ 37 Bill Bruton	3.75	1.70	.45
☐ 38 Jerry Casale	3.75	1.70	.45
☐ 39 Earl Averill	3.75	1.70	.45
☐ 40 Joe Cunningham	4.25	1.90	.55
☐ 41 Barry Latman	3.75	1.70	.45
☐ 42 Hobie Landrith	3.75	1.70	.45
☐ 43 Senators Team (Checklist on back)	9.00	4.00	1.15
☐ 44 Bobby Locke	3.75	1.70	.45
☐ 45 Roy McMillan	4.25	1.90	.55
☐ 46 Jerry Fisher	3.75	1.70	.45
☐ 47 Don Zimmer	4.25	1.90	.55
☐ 48 Hal W. Smith	3.75	1.70	.45
☐ 49 Curt Raydon	3.75	1.70	.45
☐ 50 Al Kaline	55.00	25.00	7.00
☐ 51 Jim Coates	3.75	1.70	.45
☐ 52 Dave Philley	3.75	1.70	.45
☐ 53 Jackie Brandt	3.75	1.70	.45
☐ 54 Mike Fornieles	3.75	1.70	.45
☐ 55 Bill Mazeroski	7.00	3.10	.85
☐ 56 Steve Korcheck	3.75	1.70	.45
☐ 57 Win Savers Turk Lown Gerry Staley	3.75	1.70	.45
☐ 58 Gino Cimoli	3.75	1.70	.45
☐ 59 Juan Pizarro	3.75	1.70	.45
☐ 60 Gus Triandos	4.25	1.90	.55
☐ 61 Eddie Kasko	3.75	1.70	.45
☐ 62 Roger Craig	5.50	2.50	.70
☐ 63 George Strickland	3.75	1.70	.45
☐ 64 Jack Meyer	3.75	1.70	.45
☐ 65 Elston Howard	7.00	3.10	.85
☐ 66 Bob Trowbridge	3.75	1.70	.45
☐ 67 Jose Pagan	3.75	1.70	.45
☐ 68 Dave Hillman	3.75	1.70	.45
☐ 69 Billy Goodman	4.25	1.90	.55
☐ 70 Lew Burdette	6.00	2.70	.75
☐ 71 Marty Keough	3.75	1.70	.45
☐ 72 Tigers Team (Checklist on back)	9.00	4.00	1.15
☐ 73 Bob Gibson	70.00	32.00	8.75
☐ 74 Walt Moryn	3.75	1.70	.45
☐ 75 Vic Power	4.25	1.90	.55
☐ 76 Bill Fischer	3.75	1.70	.45
☐ 77 Hank Foiles	3.75	1.70	.45
☐ 78 Bob Grim	3.75	1.70	.45

☐ 79 Walt Dropo	3.75	1.70	.45
☐ 80 Johnny Antonelli	4.25	1.90	.55
☐ 81 Russ Snyder	3.75	1.70	.45
☐ 82 Ruben Gomez	3.75	1.70	.45
☐ 83 Tony Kubek	7.50	3.40	.95
☐ 84 Hal R. Smith	3.75	1.70	.45
☐ 85 Frank Lary	4.25	1.90	.55
☐ 86 Dick Gernert	3.75	1.70	.45
☐ 87 John Romonosky	3.75	1.70	.45
☐ 88 John Roseboro	4.25	1.90	.55
☐ 89 Hal Brown	3.75	1.70	.45
☐ 90 Bobby Avila	3.75	1.70	.45
☐ 91 Bennie Daniels	3.75	1.70	.45
☐ 92 Whitey Herzog	5.50	2.50	.70
☐ 93 Art Schult	3.75	1.70	.45
☐ 94 Leo Kiely	3.75	1.70	.45
☐ 95 Frank Thomas	4.25	1.90	.55
☐ 96 Ralph Terry	4.25	1.90	.55
☐ 97 Ted Lepcio	3.75	1.70	.45
☐ 98 Gordon Jones	3.75	1.70	.45
☐ 99 Lenny Green	3.75	1.70	.45
☐ 100 Nellie Fox	10.00	4.50	1.25
☐ 101 Bob Miller	3.75	1.70	.45
☐ 102 Kent Hadley	3.75	1.70	.45
☐ 103 Dick Farrell	4.25	1.90	.55
☐ 104 Dick Schofield	4.25	1.90	.55
☐ 105 Larry Sherry	5.50	2.50	.70
☐ 106 Billy Gardner	3.75	1.70	.45
☐ 107 Carlton Willey	3.75	1.70	.45
☐ 108 Pete Daley	3.75	1.70	.45
☐ 109 Clete Boyer	6.50	2.90	.80
☐ 110 Cal McLish	3.75	1.70	.45
☐ 111 Vic Wertz	3.50	1.55	.45
☐ 112 Jack Harshman	3.00	1.35	.40
☐ 113 Bob Skinner	3.50	1.55	.45
☐ 114 Ken Aspromonte	3.00	1.35	.40
☐ 115 Fork and Knuckler Roy Face Hoyt Wilhelm	6.00	2.70	.75
☐ 116 Jim Rivera	3.00	1.35	.40
☐ 117 Tom Borland RP	3.50	1.55	.45
☐ 118 Bob Bruce RP	3.50	1.55	.45
☐ 119 Chico Cardenas RP	4.00	1.80	.50
☐ 120 Duke Carmel RP	3.50	1.55	.45
☐ 121 Camilo Carreon RP	3.50	1.55	.45
☐ 122 Don Dillard RP	3.50	1.55	.45
☐ 123 Dan Dobbek RP	3.50	1.55	.45
☐ 124 Jim Donohue RP	3.50	1.55	.45
☐ 125 Dick Ellsworth RP	5.00	2.30	.60
☐ 126 Chuck Estrada RP	5.00	2.30	.60
☐ 127 Ron Hansen RP	4.00	1.80	.50
☐ 128 Bill Harris RP	3.50	1.55	.45
☐ 129 Bob Hartman RP	3.50	1.55	.45
☐ 130 Frank Herrera RP	3.50	1.55	.45
☐ 131 Ed Hobaugh RP	3.50	1.55	.45
☐ 132 Frank Howard RP	18.00	8.00	2.30
☐ 133 Manuel Javier RP (Sic, Julian)	5.50	2.50	.70
☐ 134 Deron Johnson RP	4.00	1.80	.50
☐ 135 Ken Johnson RP	4.00	1.80	.50
☐ 136 Jim Kaat RP	40.00	18.00	5.00
☐ 137 Lou Klimchock RP	3.50	1.55	.45
☐ 138 Art Mahaffey RP	3.50	1.55	.45
☐ 139 Carl Mathias RP	3.50	1.55	.45
☐ 140 Julio Navarro RP	5.00	2.30	.60
☐ 141 Jim Proctor RP	3.50	1.55	.45
☐ 142 Bill Short RP	3.50	1.55	.45
☐ 143 Al Spangler RP	3.50	1.55	.45
☐ 144 Al Stieglitz RP	3.50	1.55	.45
☐ 145 Jim Umbricht RP	3.50	1.55	.45
☐ 146 Ted Wieand RP	3.50	1.55	.45
☐ 147 Bob Will RP	3.50	1.55	.45
☐ 148 Carl Yastrzemski RP	300.00	135.00	38.00
☐ 149 Bob Nieman	3.00	1.35	.40
☐ 150 Billy Pierce	3.50	1.55	.45
☐ 151 Giants Team (Checklist on back)	8.00	3.60	1.00
☐ 152 Gail Harris	3.00	1.35	.40
☐ 153 Bobby Thomson	3.50	1.55	.45
☐ 154 Jim Davenport	3.50	1.55	.45
☐ 155 Charlie Neal	3.50	1.55	.45
☐ 156 Art Ceccarelli	3.00	1.35	.40
☐ 157 Rocky Nelson	3.00	1.35	.40
☐ 158 Wes Covington	3.50	1.55	.45
☐ 159 Jim Piersall	4.50	2.00	.55
☐ 160 Rival All-Stars Mickey Mantle Ken Boyer	55.00	25.00	7.00
☐ 161 Ray Narleski	3.00	1.35	.40
☐ 162 Sammy Taylor	3.00	1.35	.40
☐ 163 Hector Lopez	3.50	1.55	.45
☐ 164 Reds Team (Checklist on back)	8.00	3.60	1.00
☐ 165 Jack Sanford	3.50	1.55	.45
☐ 166 Chuck Essegian	3.00	1.35	.40
☐ 167 Valmy Thomas	3.00	1.35	.40
☐ 168 Alex Grammas	3.00	1.35	.40
☐ 169 Jake Striker	3.00	1.35	.40
☐ 170 Del Crandall	3.50	1.55	.45
☐ 171 Johnny Groth	3.00	1.35	.40
☐ 172 Willie Kirkland	3.00	1.35	.40
☐ 173 Billy Martin	12.00	5.50	1.50
☐ 174 Indians Team (Checklist on back)	8.00	3.60	1.00
☐ 175 Pedro Ramos	3.00	1.35	.40
☐ 176 Vada Pinson	5.50	2.50	.70
☐ 177 Johnny Kucks	3.00	1.35	.40
☐ 178 Woody Held	3.00	1.35	.40
☐ 179 Rip Coleman	3.00	1.35	.40
☐ 180 Harry Simpson	3.00	1.35	.40
☐ 181 Billy Loes	3.50	1.55	.45
☐ 182 Glen Hobbie	3.00	1.35	.40
☐ 183 Eli Grba	3.00	1.35	.40
☐ 184 Gary Geiger	3.00	1.35	.40
☐ 185 Jim Owens	3.00	1.35	.40
☐ 186 Dave Sisler	3.00	1.35	.40
☐ 187 Jay Hook	3.00	1.35	.40
☐ 188 Dick Williams	3.50	1.55	.45
☐ 189 Don McMahon	3.00	1.35	.40
☐ 190 Gene Woodling	3.50	1.55	.45
☐ 191 Johnny Klippstein	3.00	1.35	.40
☐ 192 Danny O'Connell	3.00	1.35	.40
☐ 193 Dick Hyde	3.00	1.35	.40
☐ 194 Bobby Gene Smith	3.00	1.35	.40
☐ 195 Lindy McDaniel	3.50	1.55	.45
☐ 196 Andy Carey	3.50	1.55	.45
☐ 197 Ron Kline	3.00	1.35	.40
☐ 198 Jerry Lynch	3.50	1.55	.45
☐ 199 Dick Donovan	4.00	1.80	.50
☐ 200 Willie Mays	125.00	57.50	15.50
☐ 201 Larry Osborne	3.50	1.55	.45
☐ 202 Fred Kipp	3.50	1.55	.45
☐ 203 Sammy White	3.50	1.55	.45
☐ 204 Ryne Duren	5.00	2.30	.60
☐ 205 Johnny Logan	4.00	1.80	.50
☐ 206 Claude Osteen	4.00	1.80	.50
☐ 207 Bob Boyd	3.50	1.55	.45
☐ 208 White Sox Team (Checklist on back)	8.00	3.60	1.00
☐ 209 Ron Blackburn	3.50	1.55	.45
☐ 210 Harmon Killebrew	30.00	13.50	3.80
☐ 211 Taylor Phillips	3.50	1.55	.45
☐ 212 Walt Alston MG	12.00	5.50	1.50
☐ 213 Chuck Dressen MG	4.25	1.90	.55
☐ 214 Jimmy Dykes MG	4.25	1.90	.55
☐ 215 Bob Elliott MG	4.25	1.90	.55
☐ 216 Joe Gordon MG	4.25	1.90	.55
☐ 217 Charlie Grimm MG	4.25	1.90	.55
☐ 218 Solly Hemus MG	3.75	1.70	.45
☐ 219 Fred Hutchinson MG	4.25	1.90	.55
☐ 220 Billy Jurges MG	3.75	1.70	.45
☐ 221 Cookie Lavagetto MG	3.75	1.70	.45
☐ 222 Al Lopez MG	6.50	2.90	.80
☐ 223 Danny Murtaugh MG	4.50	2.00	.55
☐ 224 Paul Richards MG	4.25	1.90	.55
☐ 225 Bill Rigney MG	3.75	1.70	.45
☐ 226 Eddie Sawyer MG	3.75	1.70	.45
☐ 227 Casey Stengel MG	20.00	9.00	2.50
☐ 228 Ernie Johnson	4.00	1.80	.50
☐ 229 Joe M. Morgan	4.50	2.00	.55
☐ 230 Mound Magicians Lou Burdette Warren Spahn Bob Buhl	7.00	3.10	.85
☐ 231 Hal Naragon	3.50	1.55	.45
☐ 232 Jim Busby	3.50	1.55	.45
☐ 233 Don Elston	3.50	1.55	.45
☐ 234 Don Demeter	3.50	1.55	.45
☐ 235 Gus Bell	4.00	1.80	.50
☐ 236 Dick Ricketts	3.50	1.55	.45
☐ 237 Elmer Valo	3.50	1.55	.45
☐ 238 Danny Kravitz	3.50	1.55	.45
☐ 239 Joe Shipley	3.50	1.55	.45
☐ 240 Luis Aparicio	15.00	6.75	1.90
☐ 241 Albie Pearson	4.00	1.80	.50
☐ 242 Cardinals Team (Checklist on back)	8.00	3.60	1.00
☐ 243 Bubba Phillips	3.50	1.55	.45
☐ 244 Hal Griggs	3.50	1.55	.45
☐ 245 Eddie Yost	4.00	1.80	.50
☐ 246 Lee Maye	4.00	1.80	.50
☐ 247 Gil McDougald	5.25	2.40	.65
☐ 248 Del Rice	3.50	1.55	.45
☐ 249 Earl Wilson	5.00	2.30	.60
☐ 250 Stan Musial	110.00	50.00	14.00
☐ 251 Bob Malkmus	3.50	1.55	.45

☐ 252 Ray Herbert	3.50	1.55	.45
☐ 253 Eddie Bressoud	3.50	1.55	.45
☐ 254 Arnie Portocarrero	3.50	1.55	.45
☐ 255 Jim Gilliam	5.00	2.30	.60
☐ 256 Dick Brown	3.50	1.55	.45
☐ 257 Gordy Coleman	5.00	2.30	.60
☐ 258 Dick Groat	5.50	2.50	.70
☐ 259 George Altman	3.50	1.55	.45
☐ 260 Power Plus Rocky Colavito Tito Francona	5.25	2.40	.65
☐ 261 Pete Burnside	3.50	1.55	.45
☐ 262 Hank Bauer	4.25	1.90	.55
☐ 263 Darrell Johnson	3.50	1.55	.45
☐ 264 Robin Roberts	14.00	6.25	1.75
☐ 265 Rip Repulski	3.50	1.55	.45
☐ 266 Joey Jay	4.00	1.80	.50
☐ 267 Jim Marshall	3.50	1.55	.45
☐ 268 Al Worthington	3.50	1.55	.45
☐ 269 Gene Green	3.50	1.55	.45
☐ 270 Bob Turley	5.00	2.30	.60
☐ 271 Julio Becquer	3.50	1.55	.45
☐ 272 Fred Green	3.50	1.55	.45
☐ 273 Neil Chrisley	3.50	1.55	.45
☐ 274 Tom Acker	3.50	1.55	.45
☐ 275 Curt Flood	5.00	2.30	.60
☐ 276 Ken McBride	3.50	1.55	.45
☐ 277 Harry Bright	3.50	1.55	.45
☐ 278 Stan Williams	4.00	1.80	.50
☐ 279 Chuck Tanner	4.00	1.80	.50
☐ 280 Frank Sullivan	3.50	1.55	.45
☐ 281 Ray Boone	4.00	1.80	.50
☐ 282 Joe Nuxhall	4.00	1.80	.50
☐ 283 John Blanchard	4.50	2.00	.55
☐ 284 Don Gross	3.50	1.55	.45
☐ 285 Harry Anderson	3.50	1.55	.45
☐ 286 Ray Semproch	3.50	1.55	.45
☐ 287 Felipe Alou	7.00	3.10	.85
☐ 288 Bob Mabe	3.75	1.70	.45
☐ 289 Willie Jones	3.75	1.70	.45
☐ 290 Jerry Lumpe	3.75	1.70	.45
☐ 291 Bob Keegan	3.75	1.70	.45
☐ 292 Dodger Backstops Joe Pignatano John Roseboro	4.25	1.90	.55
☐ 293 Gene Conley	4.25	1.90	.55
☐ 294 Tony Taylor	4.25	1.90	.55
☐ 295 Gil Hodges	20.00	9.00	2.50
☐ 296 Nelson Chittum	3.75	1.70	.45
☐ 297 Reno Bertoia	3.75	1.70	.45
☐ 298 George Witt	3.75	1.70	.45
☐ 299 Earl Torgeson	3.75	1.70	.45
☐ 300 Hank Aaron	125.00	57.50	15.50
☐ 301 Jerry Davie	3.75	1.70	.45
☐ 302 Phillies Team (Checklist on back)	8.00	3.60	1.00
☐ 303 Billy O'Dell	3.75	1.70	.45
☐ 304 Joe Ginsberg	3.75	1.70	.45
☐ 305 Richie Ashburn	10.00	4.50	1.25
☐ 306 Frank Baumann	3.75	1.70	.45
☐ 307 Gene Oliver	3.75	1.70	.45
☐ 308 Dick Hall	3.75	1.70	.45
☐ 309 Bob Hale	3.75	1.70	.45
☐ 310 Frank Malzone	4.25	1.90	.55
☐ 311 Raul Sanchez	3.75	1.70	.45
☐ 312 Charley Lau	4.25	1.90	.55
☐ 313 Turk Lown	3.75	1.70	.45
☐ 314 Chico Fernandez	3.75	1.70	.45
☐ 315 Bobby Shantz	4.25	1.90	.55
☐ 316 Willie McCovey	250.00	115.00	31.00
☐ 317 Pumpsie Green	4.75	2.10	.60
☐ 318 Jim Baxes	4.25	1.90	.55
☐ 319 Joe Koppe	4.25	1.90	.55
☐ 320 Bob Allison	5.00	2.30	.60
☐ 321 Ron Fairly	5.00	2.30	.60
☐ 322 Willie Tasby	4.25	1.90	.55
☐ 323 John Romano	4.25	1.90	.55
☐ 324 Jim Perry	5.00	2.30	.60
☐ 325 Jim O'Toole	4.75	2.10	.60
☐ 326 Bob Clemente	125.00	57.50	15.50
☐ 327 Ray Sadecki	5.00	2.30	.60
☐ 328 Earl Battey	3.75	1.70	.45
☐ 329 Zack Monroe	3.75	1.70	.45
☐ 330 Harvey Kuenn	5.00	2.30	.60
☐ 331 Henry Mason	3.75	1.70	.45
☐ 332 Yankees Team (Checklist on back)	30.00	13.50	3.80
☐ 333 Danny McDevitt	3.75	1.70	.45
☐ 334 Ted Abernathy	3.75	1.70	.45
☐ 335 Red Schoendienst	12.50	5.75	1.55
☐ 336 Ike Delock	3.75	1.70	.45
☐ 337 Cal Neeman	3.75	1.70	.45
☐ 338 Ray Monzant	3.75	1.70	.45
☐ 339 Harry Chiti	3.75	1.70	.45
☐ 340 Harvey Haddix	4.25	1.90	.55
☐ 341 Carroll Hardy	3.75	1.70	.45
☐ 342 Casey Wise	3.75	1.70	.45
☐ 343 Sandy Koufax	150.00	70.00	19.00
☐ 344 Clint Courtney	3.75	1.70	.45
☐ 345 Don Newcombe	5.00	2.30	.60
☐ 346 J.C. Martin UER (Face actually Gary Peters)	4.25	1.90	.55
☐ 347 Ed Bouchee	3.75	1.70	.45
☐ 348 Barry Shetrone	3.75	1.70	.45
☐ 349 Moe Drabowsky	4.25	1.90	.55
☐ 350 Mickey Mantle	400.00	180.00	50.00
☐ 351 Don Nottebart	3.75	1.70	.45
☐ 352 Cincy Clouters Gus Bell Frank Robinson Jerry Lynch	6.50	2.90	.80
☐ 353 Don Larsen	4.50	2.00	.55
☐ 354 Bob Lillis	3.75	1.70	.45
☐ 355 Bill White	7.50	3.40	.95
☐ 356 Joe Amalfitano	3.75	1.70	.45
☐ 357 Al Schroll	3.75	1.70	.45
☐ 358 Joe DeMaestri	3.75	1.70	.45
☐ 359 Buddy Gilbert	3.75	1.70	.45
☐ 360 Herb Score	5.00	2.30	.60
☐ 361 Bob Oldis	3.75	1.70	.45
☐ 362 Russ Kemmerer	3.75	1.70	.45
☐ 363 Gene Stephens	3.75	1.70	.45
☐ 364 Paul Foytack	3.75	1.70	.45
☐ 365 Minnie Minoso	5.50	2.50	.70
☐ 366 Dallas Green	9.00	4.00	1.15
☐ 367 Bill Tuttle	3.75	1.70	.45
☐ 368 Daryl Spencer	3.75	1.70	.45
☐ 369 Billy Hoeft	3.75	1.70	.45
☐ 370 Bill Skowron	8.00	3.60	1.00
☐ 371 Bud Byerly	3.75	1.70	.45
☐ 372 Frank House	3.75	1.70	.45
☐ 373 Don Hoak	4.25	1.90	.55
☐ 374 Bob Buhl	4.25	1.90	.55
☐ 375 Dale Long	4.25	1.90	.55
☐ 376 John Briggs	3.75	1.70	.45
☐ 377 Roger Maris	120.00	55.00	15.00
☐ 378 Stu Miller	4.25	1.90	.55
☐ 379 Red Wilson	3.75	1.70	.45
☐ 380 Bob Shaw	3.75	1.70	.45
☐ 381 Braves Team (Checklist on back)	8.00	3.60	1.00
☐ 382 Ted Bowsfield	3.75	1.70	.45
☐ 383 Leon Wagner	3.75	1.70	.45
☐ 384 Don Cardwell	3.75	1.70	.45
☐ 385 World Series Game 1 Charlie Neal Steals Second	6.00	2.70	.75
☐ 386 World Series Game 2 Charlie Neal Belts Second Homer	6.00	2.70	.75
☐ 387 World Series Game 3 Carl Furillo Breaks Game	6.00	2.70	.75
☐ 388 World Series Game 4 Gil Hodges' Homer	10.00	4.50	1.25
☐ 389 World Series Game 5 Luis Aparicio Swipes Base	10.00	4.50	1.25
☐ 390 World Series Game 6 Scrambling After Ball	6.00	2.70	.75
☐ 391 World Series Summary The Champs Celebrate	6.00	2.70	.75
☐ 392 Tex Clevenger	3.75	1.70	.45
☐ 393 Smoky Burgess	4.25	1.90	.55
☐ 394 Norm Larker	4.25	1.90	.55
☐ 395 Hoyt Wilhelm	12.50	5.75	1.55
☐ 396 Steve Bilko	3.75	1.70	.45
☐ 397 Don Blasingame	3.75	1.70	.45
☐ 398 Mike Cuellar	4.25	1.90	.55
☐ 399 Young Hill Stars Milt Pappas Jack Fisher Jerry Walker	4.25	1.90	.55
☐ 400 Rocky Colavito	12.50	5.75	1.55
☐ 401 Bob Duliba	3.75	1.70	.45
☐ 402 Dick Stuart	4.25	1.90	.55
☐ 403 Ed Sadowski	3.75	1.70	.45
☐ 404 Bob Rush	3.75	1.70	.45
☐ 405 Bobby Richardson	8.50	3.80	1.05
☐ 406 Billy Klaus	3.75	1.70	.45
☐ 407 Gary Peters UER (Face actually J.C. Martin)	5.00	2.30	.60
☐ 408 Carl Furillo	6.00	2.70	.75
☐ 409 Ron Samford	3.75	1.70	.45

☐ 410 Sam Jones	4.25	1.90	.55
☐ 411 Ed Bailey	3.75	1.70	.45
☐ 412 Bob Anderson	3.75	1.70	.45
☐ 413 Athletics Team (Checklist on back)	8.00	3.60	1.00
☐ 414 Don Williams	3.75	1.70	.45
☐ 415 Bob Cerv	3.75	1.70	.45
☐ 416 Humberto Robinson	3.75	1.70	.45
☐ 417 Chuck Cottier	5.00	2.30	.60
☐ 418 Don Mossi	4.25	1.90	.55
☐ 419 George Crowe	3.75	1.70	.45
☐ 420 Eddie Mathews	35.00	16.00	4.40
☐ 421 Duke Maas	3.75	1.70	.45
☐ 422 John Powers	3.75	1.70	.45
☐ 423 Ed Fitzgerald	3.75	1.70	.45
☐ 424 Pete Whisenant	3.75	1.70	.45
☐ 425 Johnny Podres	5.00	2.30	.60
☐ 426 Ron Jackson	3.75	1.70	.45
☐ 427 Al Grunwald	3.75	1.70	.45
☐ 428 Al Smith	3.75	1.70	.45
☐ 429 AL Kings Nellie Fox Harvey Kuenn	6.00	2.70	.75
☐ 430 Art Ditmar	3.75	1.70	.45
☐ 431 Andre Rodgers	3.75	1.70	.45
☐ 432 Chuck Stobbs	3.75	1.70	.45
☐ 433 Irv Noren	3.75	1.70	.45
☐ 434 Brooks Lawrence	3.75	1.70	.45
☐ 435 Gene Freese	3.75	1.70	.45
☐ 436 Marv Throneberry	4.50	2.00	.55
☐ 437 Bob Friend	4.25	1.90	.55
☐ 438 Jim Coker	3.75	1.70	.45
☐ 439 Tom Brewer	3.75	1.70	.45
☐ 440 Jim Lemon	4.25	1.90	.55
☐ 441 Gary Bell	5.00	2.30	.60
☐ 442 Joe Pignatano	5.00	2.30	.60
☐ 443 Charlie Maxwell	5.50	2.50	.70
☐ 444 Jerry Kindall	5.50	2.50	.70
☐ 445 Warren Spahn	55.00	25.00	7.00
☐ 446 Ellis Burton	5.00	2.30	.60
☐ 447 Ray Moore	5.00	2.30	.60
☐ 448 Jim Gentile	12.50	5.75	1.55
☐ 449 Jim Brosnan	5.50	2.50	.70
☐ 450 Orlando Cepeda	20.00	9.00	2.50
☐ 451 Curt Simmons	5.50	2.50	.70
☐ 452 Ray Webster	5.00	2.30	.60
☐ 453 Vern Law	7.00	3.10	.85
☐ 454 Hal Woodeshick	5.00	2.30	.60
☐ 455 Baltimore Coaches Eddie Robinson Harry Brecheen Luman Harris	6.00	2.70	.75
☐ 456 Red Sox Coaches Rudy York Billy Herman Sal Maglie Del Baker	7.50	3.40	.95
☐ 457 Cubs Coaches Charlie Root Lou Klein Elvin Tappe	6.00	2.70	.75
☐ 458 White Sox Coaches Johnny Cooney Don Gutteridge Tony Cuccinello Ray Berres	6.00	2.70	.75
☐ 459 Reds Coaches Reggie Otero Cot Deal Wally Moses	6.00	2.70	.75
☐ 460 Indians Coaches Mel Harder Jo-Jo White Bob Lemon Ralph(Red) Kress	7.50	3.40	.95
☐ 461 Tigers Coaches Tom Ferrick Luke Appling Billy Hitchcock	7.50	3.40	.95
☐ 462 Athletics Coaches Fred Fitzsimmons Don Heffner Walker Cooper	6.00	2.70	.75
☐ 463 Dodgers Coaches Bobby Bragan Pete Reiser Joe Becker Greg Mulleavy	6.50	2.90	.80
☐ 464 Braves Coaches Bob Scheffing Whitlow Wyatt Andy Pafko George Myatt	6.00	2.70	.75
☐ 465 Yankees Coaches Bill Dickey Ralph Houk Frank Crosetti Ed Lopat	15.00	6.75	1.90
☐ 466 Phillies Coaches Ken Silvestri Dick Carter Andy Cohen	6.00	2.70	.75
☐ 467 Pirates Coaches Mickey Vernon Frank Oceak Sam Narron Bill Burwell	6.00	2.70	.75
☐ 468 Cardinals Coaches Johnny Keane Howie Pollet Ray Katt Harry Walker	6.00	2.70	.75
☐ 469 Giants Coaches Wes Westrum Salty Parker Bill Posedel	6.00	2.70	.75
☐ 470 Senators Coaches Bob Swift Ellis Clary Sam Mele	6.00	2.70	.75
☐ 471 Ned Garver	5.00	2.30	.60
☐ 472 Alvin Dark	5.50	2.50	.70
☐ 473 Al Cicotte	5.00	2.30	.60
☐ 474 Haywood Sullivan	5.50	2.50	.70
☐ 475 Don Drysdale	50.00	23.00	6.25
☐ 476 Lou Johnson	5.00	2.30	.60
☐ 477 Don Ferrarese	5.00	2.30	.60
☐ 478 Frank Torre	5.50	2.50	.70
☐ 479 Georges Maranda	5.00	2.30	.60
☐ 480 Yogi Berra	85.00	38.00	10.50
☐ 481 Wes Stock	5.50	2.50	.70
☐ 482 Frank Bolling	5.00	2.30	.60
☐ 483 Camilo Pascual	5.50	2.50	.70
☐ 484 Pirates Team (Checklist on back)	25.00	11.50	3.10
☐ 485 Ken Boyer	12.50	5.75	1.55
☐ 486 Bobby Del Greco	5.00	2.30	.60
☐ 487 Tom Sturdivant	5.00	2.30	.60
☐ 488 Norm Cash	12.50	5.75	1.55
☐ 489 Steve Ridzik	5.00	2.30	.60
☐ 490 Frank Robinson	65.00	29.00	8.25
☐ 491 Mel Roach	5.00	2.30	.60
☐ 492 Larry Jackson	5.00	2.30	.60
☐ 493 Duke Snider	65.00	29.00	8.25
☐ 494 Orioles Team (Checklist on back)	12.50	5.75	1.55
☐ 495 Sherm Lollar	5.50	2.50	.70
☐ 496 Bill Virdon	7.00	3.10	.85
☐ 497 John Tsitouris	5.00	2.30	.60
☐ 498 Al Pilarcik	5.00	2.30	.60
☐ 499 Johnny James	5.00	2.30	.60
☐ 500 Johnny Temple	5.50	2.50	.70
☐ 501 Bob Schmidt	5.00	2.30	.60
☐ 502 Jim Bunning	12.50	5.75	1.55
☐ 503 Don Lee	5.00	2.30	.60
☐ 504 Seth Morehead	5.00	2.30	.60
☐ 505 Ted Kluszewski	12.50	5.75	1.55
☐ 506 Lee Walls	5.00	2.30	.60
☐ 507 Dick Stigman	14.50	6.50	1.80
☐ 508 Billy Consolo	12.00	5.50	1.50
☐ 509 Tommy Davis	30.00	13.50	3.80
☐ 510 Gerry Staley	12.00	5.50	1.50
☐ 511 Ken Walters	12.00	5.50	1.50
☐ 512 Joe Gibbon	12.00	5.50	1.50
☐ 513 Chicago Cubs Team Card (Checklist on back)	36.00	16.00	4.50
☐ 514 Steve Barber	18.00	8.00	2.30
☐ 515 Stan Lopata	12.00	5.50	1.50
☐ 516 Marty Kutyna	12.00	5.50	1.50
☐ 517 Charlie James	12.00	5.50	1.50
☐ 518 Tony Gonzalez	14.50	6.50	1.80
☐ 519 Ed Roebuck	12.00	5.50	1.50
☐ 520 Don Buddin	12.00	5.50	1.50
☐ 521 Mike Lee	12.00	5.50	1.50
☐ 522 Ken Hunt	12.00	5.50	1.50
☐ 523 Clay Dalrymple	12.00	5.50	1.50
☐ 524 Bill Henry	12.00	5.50	1.50
☐ 525 Marv Breeding	12.00	5.50	1.50
☐ 526 Paul Giel	14.50	6.50	1.80
☐ 527 Jose Valdivielso	12.00	5.50	1.50
☐ 528 Ben Johnson	12.00	5.50	1.50
☐ 529 Norm Sherry	18.00	8.00	2.30
☐ 530 Mike McCormick	14.50	6.50	1.80
☐ 531 Sandy Amoros	14.50	6.50	1.80
☐ 532 Mike Garcia	14.50	6.50	1.80

Card			
☐ 533 Lu Clinton	12.00	5.50	1.50
☐ 534 Ken MacKenzie	12.00	5.50	1.50
☐ 535 Whitey Lockman	14.50	6.50	1.80
☐ 536 Wynn Hawkins	12.00	5.50	1.50
☐ 537 Boston Red Sox	36.00	16.00	4.50
Team Card			
(Checklist on back)			
☐ 538 Frank Barnes	12.00	5.50	1.50
☐ 539 Gene Baker	12.00	5.50	1.50
☐ 540 Jerry Walker	12.00	5.50	1.50
☐ 541 Tony Curry	12.00	5.50	1.50
☐ 542 Ken Hamlin	12.00	5.50	1.50
☐ 543 Elio Chacon	12.00	5.50	1.50
☐ 544 Bill Monbouquette	12.00	5.50	1.50
☐ 545 Carl Sawatski	12.00	5.50	1.50
☐ 546 Hank Aguirre	12.00	5.50	1.50
☐ 547 Bob Aspromonte	12.00	5.50	1.50
☐ 548 Don Mincher	14.50	6.50	1.80
☐ 549 John Buzhardt	12.00	5.50	1.50
☐ 550 Jim Landis	12.00	5.50	1.50
☐ 551 Ed Rakow	12.00	5.50	1.50
☐ 552 Walt Bond	12.00	5.50	1.50
☐ 553 Bill Skowron AS	18.00	8.00	2.30
☐ 554 Willie McCovey AS	70.00	32.00	8.75
☐ 555 Nellie Fox AS	20.00	9.00	2.50
☐ 556 Charlie Neal AS	15.00	6.75	1.90
☐ 557 Frank Malzone AS	15.00	6.75	1.90
☐ 558 Eddie Mathews AS	35.00	16.00	4.40
☐ 559 Luis Aparicio AS	25.00	11.50	3.10
☐ 560 Ernie Banks AS	60.00	27.00	7.50
☐ 561 Al Kaline AS	60.00	27.00	7.50
☐ 562 Joe Cunningham AS	15.00	6.75	1.90
☐ 563 Mickey Mantle AS	300.00	135.00	38.00
☐ 564 Willie Mays AS	125.00	57.50	15.50
☐ 565 Roger Maris AS	120.00	55.00	15.00
☐ 566 Hank Aaron AS	125.00	57.50	15.50
☐ 567 Sherm Lollar AS	15.00	6.75	1.90
☐ 568 Del Crandall AS	15.00	6.75	1.90
☐ 569 Camilo Pascual AS	15.00	6.75	1.90
☐ 570 Don Drysdale AS	35.00	16.00	4.40
☐ 571 Billy Pierce AS	15.00	6.75	1.90
☐ 572 Johnny Antonelli AS	25.00	7.50	2.50

1961 Topps

GIL HODGES
First Base-Catcher
Los Angeles Dodgers

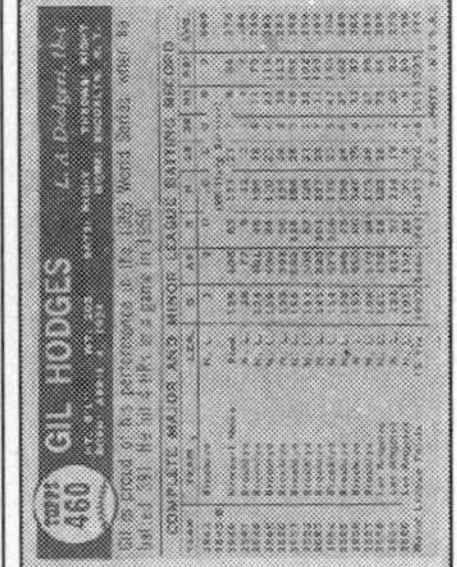

The cards in this 587-card set measure 2 1/2" by 3 1/2". In 1961, Topps returned to the vertical obverse format. Introduced for the first time were "League Leaders" (41 to 50) and separate, numbered checklist cards. Two number 463s exist: the Braves team card carrying that number was meant to be number 426. There are three versions of the second series checklist card number 98; the variations are distinguished by the color of the "CHECKLIST" headline on the front of the card, the color of the printing of the card number on the bottom of the reverse, and the presence of the copyright notice running vertically on the card back. There are two groups of managers (131-139 and 219-226) as well as separate series of World Series cards (306-313), Baseball Thrills (401 to 410), previous MVP's (AL 471-478 and NL 479-486) and Sporting News All-Stars (566 to 589). The usual last series scarcity (523 to 589) exists. The set actually totals 587 cards since numbers 587 and 588 were never issued. The key rookies in this set are ex-Cubs Ron Santo and Billy Williams.

	NRMT	VG-E	GOOD
COMPLETE SET (587)	5850.00	2600.00	750.00
COMMON PLAYER (1-109)	3.00	1.35	.40
COMMON PLAYER (110-370)	3.00	1.35	.40
COMMON PLAYER (371-446)	4.50	2.00	.55
COMMON PLAYER (447-522)	5.50	2.50	.70
COMMON PLAYER (523-565)	34.00	15.50	4.20
COMMON AS (566-589)	36.00	16.00	4.50
☐ 1 Dick Groat	20.00	4.00	1.20
☐ 2 Roger Maris	180.00	80.00	23.00
☐ 3 John Buzhardt	3.00	1.35	.40
☐ 4 Lenny Green	3.00	1.35	.40
☐ 5 John Romano	3.00	1.35	.40
☐ 6 Ed Roebuck	3.00	1.35	.40
☐ 7 White Sox Team	6.50	2.90	.80
☐ 8 Dick Williams	3.50	1.55	.45
☐ 9 Bob Purkey	3.00	1.35	.40
☐ 10 Brooks Robinson	35.00	16.00	4.40
☐ 11 Curt Simmons	3.50	1.55	.45
☐ 12 Moe Thacker	3.00	1.35	.40
☐ 13 Chuck Cottier	3.00	1.35	.40
☐ 14 Don Mossi	3.50	1.55	.45
☐ 15 Willie Kirkland	3.00	1.35	.40
☐ 16 Billy Muffett	3.00	1.35	.40
☐ 17 Checklist 1	10.00	2.00	.60
☐ 18 Jim Grant	3.50	1.55	.45
☐ 19 Clete Boyer	4.50	2.00	.55
☐ 20 Robin Roberts	12.50	5.75	1.55
☐ 21 Zorro Versalles UER	4.50	2.00	.55
(First name should			
be Zoilo)			
☐ 22 Clem Labine	3.50	1.55	.45
☐ 23 Don Demeter	3.00	1.35	.40
☐ 24 Ken Johnson	3.00	1.35	.40
☐ 25 Reds' Heavy Artillery	7.00	3.10	.85
Vada Pinson			
Gus Bell			
Frank Robinson			
☐ 26 Wes Stock	3.00	1.35	.40
☐ 27 Jerry Kindall	3.00	1.35	.40
☐ 28 Hector Lopez	3.00	1.35	.40
☐ 29 Don Nottebart	3.00	1.35	.40
☐ 30 Nellie Fox	7.50	3.40	.95
☐ 31 Bob Schmidt	3.00	1.35	.40
☐ 32 Ray Sadecki	3.00	1.35	.40
☐ 33 Gary Geiger	3.00	1.35	.40
☐ 34 Wynn Hawkins	3.00	1.35	.40
☐ 35 Ron Santo	55.00	25.00	7.00
☐ 36 Jack Kralick	3.00	1.35	.40
☐ 37 Charlie Maxwell	3.50	1.55	.45
☐ 38 Bob Lillis	3.00	1.35	.40
☐ 39 Leo Posada	3.00	1.35	.40
☐ 40 Bob Turley	3.50	1.55	.45
☐ 41 NL Batting Leaders	9.00	4.00	1.15
Dick Groat			
Norm Larker			
Willie Mays			
Roberto Clemente			
☐ 42 AL Batting Leaders	5.00	2.30	.60
Pete Runnels			
Al Smith			
Minnie Minoso			
Bill Skowron			
☐ 43 NL Home Run Leaders	12.00	5.50	1.50
Ernie Banks			
Hank Aaron			
Ed Mathews			
Ken Boyer			
☐ 44 AL Home Run Leaders	35.00	16.00	4.40
Mickey Mantle			
Roger Maris			
Jim Lemon			
Rocky Colavito			
☐ 45 NL ERA Leaders	5.00	2.30	.60
Mike McCormick			
Ernie Broglio			
Don Drysdale			
Bob Friend			
Stan Williams			
☐ 46 AL ERA Leaders	5.00	2.30	.60
Frank Baumann			
Jim Bunning			
Art Ditmar			
Hal Brown			
☐ 47 NL Pitching Leaders	5.00	2.30	.60
Ernie Broglio			
Warren Spahn			
Vern Law			
Lou Burdette			
☐ 48 AL Pitching Leaders	5.00	2.30	.60
Chuck Estrada			

Jim Perry
Bud Daley
Art Ditmar
Frank Lary
Milt Pappas

☐ 49	NL Strikeout Leaders Don Drysdale Sandy Koufax Sam Jones Ernie Broglio	7.00	3.10	.85
☐ 50	AL Strikeout Leaders Jim Bunning Pedro Ramos Early Wynn Frank Lary	5.00	2.30	.60
☐ 51	Detroit Tigers Team Card	6.50	2.90	.80
☐ 52	George Crowe	3.00	1.35	.40
☐ 53	Russ Nixon	3.00	1.35	.40
☐ 54	Earl Francis	3.00	1.35	.40
☐ 55	Jim Davenport	3.50	1.55	.45
☐ 56	Russ Kemmerer	3.00	1.35	.40
☐ 57	Marv Throneberry	4.00	1.80	.50
☐ 58	Joe Schaffernoth	3.00	1.35	.40
☐ 59	Jim Woods	3.00	1.35	.40
☐ 60	Woody Held	3.00	1.35	.40
☐ 61	Ron Piche	3.00	1.35	.40
☐ 62	Al Pilarcik	3.00	1.35	.40
☐ 63	Jim Kaat	8.50	3.80	1.05
☐ 64	Alex Grammas	3.00	1.35	.40
☐ 65	Ted Kluszewski	6.00	2.70	.75
☐ 66	Bill Henry	3.00	1.35	.40
☐ 67	Ossie Virgil	3.00	1.35	.40
☐ 68	Deron Johnson	3.50	1.55	.45
☐ 69	Earl Wilson	3.50	1.55	.45
☐ 70	Bill Virdon	3.50	1.55	.45
☐ 71	Jerry Adair	3.00	1.35	.40
☐ 72	Stu Miller	3.50	1.55	.45
☐ 73	Al Spangler	3.00	1.35	.40
☐ 74	Joe Pignatano	3.00	1.35	.40
☐ 75	Lindy Shows Larry Lindy McDaniel Larry Jackson	3.50	1.55	.45
☐ 76	Harry Anderson	3.00	1.35	.40
☐ 77	Dick Stigman	3.00	1.35	.40
☐ 78	Lee Walls	3.00	1.35	.40
☐ 79	Joe Ginsberg	3.00	1.35	.40
☐ 80	Harmon Killebrew	25.00	11.50	3.10
☐ 81	Tracy Stallard	3.00	1.35	.40
☐ 82	Joe Christopher	3.00	1.35	.40
☐ 83	Bob Bruce	3.00	1.35	.40
☐ 84	Lee Maye	3.00	1.35	.40
☐ 85	Jerry Walker	3.00	1.35	.40
☐ 86	Los Angeles Dodgers Team Card	6.50	2.90	.80
☐ 87	Joe Amalfitano	3.00	1.35	.40
☐ 88	Richie Ashburn	8.00	3.60	1.00
☐ 89	Billy Martin	8.50	3.80	1.05
☐ 90	Gerry Staley	3.00	1.35	.40
☐ 91	Walt Moryn	3.00	1.35	.40
☐ 92	Hal Naragon	3.00	1.35	.40
☐ 93	Tony Gonzalez	3.00	1.35	.40
☐ 94	Johnny Kucks	3.00	1.35	.40
☐ 95	Norm Cash	6.50	2.90	.80
☐ 96	Billy O'Dell	3.00	1.35	.40
☐ 97	Jerry Lynch	3.50	1.55	.45
☐ 98A	Checklist 2 (Red "Checklist", 98 black on white)	10.00	2.00	.60
☐ 98B	Checklist 2 (Yellow "Checklist", 98 black on white)	10.00	2.00	.60
☐ 98C	Checklist 2 (Yellow "Checklist", 98 white on black, no copyright)	10.00	2.00	.60
☐ 99	Don Buddin UER (66 HR's)	3.00	1.35	.40
☐ 100	Harvey Haddix	3.50	1.55	.45
☐ 101	Bubba Phillips	3.00	1.35	.40
☐ 102	Gene Stephens	3.00	1.35	.40
☐ 103	Ruben Amaro	3.00	1.35	.40
☐ 104	John Blanchard	3.50	1.55	.45
☐ 105	Carl Willey	3.00	1.35	.40
☐ 106	Whitey Herzog	5.00	2.30	.60
☐ 107	Seth Morehead	3.00	1.35	.40
☐ 108	Dan Dobbek	3.00	1.35	.40
☐ 109	Johnny Podres	3.50	1.55	.45
☐ 110	Vada Pinson	4.50	2.00	.55
☐ 111	Jack Meyer	3.00	1.35	.40
☐ 112	Chico Fernandez	3.00	1.35	.40
☐ 113	Mike Fornieles	3.00	1.35	.40
☐ 114	Hobie Landrith	3.00	1.35	.40
☐ 115	Johnny Antonelli	3.50	1.55	.45
☐ 116	Joe DeMaestri	3.00	1.35	.40
☐ 117	Dale Long	3.50	1.55	.45
☐ 118	Chris Cannizzaro	3.00	1.35	.40
☐ 119	A's Big Armor Norm Siebern Hank Bauer Jerry Lumpe	3.50	1.55	.45
☐ 120	Eddie Mathews	30.00	13.50	3.80
☐ 121	Eli Grba	3.00	1.35	.40
☐ 122	Chicago Cubs Team Card	6.50	2.90	.80
☐ 123	Billy Gardner	3.00	1.35	.40
☐ 124	J.C. Martin	3.00	1.35	.40
☐ 125	Steve Barber	3.00	1.35	.40
☐ 126	Dick Stuart	3.50	1.55	.45
☐ 127	Ron Kline	3.00	1.35	.40
☐ 128	Rip Repulski	3.00	1.35	.40
☐ 129	Ed Hobaugh	3.00	1.35	.40
☐ 130	Norm Larker	3.00	1.35	.40
☐ 131	Paul Richards MG	4.00	1.80	.50
☐ 132	Al Lopez MG	4.50	2.00	.55
☐ 133	Ralph Houk MG	5.00	2.30	.60
☐ 134	Mickey Vernon MG	4.00	1.80	.50
☐ 135	Fred Hutchinson MG	4.00	1.80	.50
☐ 136	Walt Alston MG	6.00	2.70	.75
☐ 137	Chuck Dressen MG	4.00	1.80	.50
☐ 138	Danny Murtaugh MG	4.50	2.00	.55
☐ 139	Solly Hemus MG	3.50	1.55	.45
☐ 140	Gus Triandos	3.50	1.55	.45
☐ 141	Billy Williams	110.00	50.00	14.00
☐ 142	Luis Arroyo	3.50	1.55	.45
☐ 143	Russ Snyder	3.00	1.35	.40
☐ 144	Jim Coker	3.00	1.35	.40
☐ 145	Bob Buhl	3.50	1.55	.45
☐ 146	Marty Keough	3.00	1.35	.40
☐ 147	Ed Rakow	3.00	1.35	.40
☐ 148	Julian Javier	3.50	1.55	.45
☐ 149	Bob Oldis	3.00	1.35	.40
☐ 150	Willie Mays	125.00	57.50	15.50
☐ 151	Jim Donohue	3.00	1.35	.40
☐ 152	Earl Torgeson	3.00	1.35	.40
☐ 153	Don Lee	3.00	1.35	.40
☐ 154	Bobby Del Greco	3.00	1.35	.40
☐ 155	Johnny Temple	3.50	1.55	.45
☐ 156	Ken Hunt	3.00	1.35	.40
☐ 157	Cal McLish	3.00	1.35	.40
☐ 158	Pete Daley	3.00	1.35	.40
☐ 159	Orioles Team	6.50	2.90	.80
☐ 160	Whitey Ford UER (Incorrectly listed as 5'0" tall)	40.00	18.00	5.00
☐ 161	Sherman Jones UER (Photo actually Eddie Fisher)	3.00	1.35	.40
☐ 162	Jay Hook	3.00	1.35	.40
☐ 163	Ed Sadowski	3.00	1.35	.40
☐ 164	Felix Mantilla	3.00	1.35	.40
☐ 165	Gino Cimoli	3.00	1.35	.40
☐ 166	Danny Kravitz	3.00	1.35	.40
☐ 167	San Francisco Giants Team Card	6.50	2.90	.80
☐ 168	Tommy Davis	6.00	2.70	.75
☐ 169	Don Elston	3.00	1.35	.40
☐ 170	Al Smith	3.00	1.35	.40
☐ 171	Paul Foytack	3.00	1.35	.40
☐ 172	Don Dillard	3.00	1.35	.40
☐ 173	Beantown Bombers Frank Malzone Vic Wertz Jackie Jensen	3.50	1.55	.45
☐ 174	Ray Semproch	3.00	1.35	.40
☐ 175	Gene Freese	3.00	1.35	.40
☐ 176	Ken Aspromonte	3.00	1.35	.40
☐ 177	Don Larsen	4.50	2.00	.55
☐ 178	Bob Nieman	3.00	1.35	.40
☐ 179	Joe Koppe	3.00	1.35	.40
☐ 180	Bobby Richardson	8.00	3.60	1.00
☐ 181	Fred Green	3.00	1.35	.40
☐ 182	Dave Nicholson	3.00	1.35	.40
☐ 183	Andre Rodgers	3.00	1.35	.40
☐ 184	Steve Bilko	3.00	1.35	.40
☐ 185	Herb Score	4.50	2.00	.55
☐ 186	Elmer Valo	3.00	1.35	.40
☐ 187	Billy Klaus	3.00	1.35	.40
☐ 188	Jim Marshall	3.00	1.35	.40
☐ 189A	Checklist 3 (Copyright symbol almost adjacent to 263 Ken Hamlin)	10.00	2.00	.60
☐ 189B	Checklist 3 (Copyright symbol adjacent to 264 Glen Hobbie)	10.00	2.00	.60

☐	190	Stan Williams	3.50	1.55	.45
☐	191	Mike DeLaHoz	3.00	1.35	.40
☐	192	Dick Brown	3.00	1.35	.40
☐	193	Gene Conley	3.50	1.55	.45
☐	194	Gordy Coleman	3.50	1.55	.45
☐	195	Jerry Casale	3.00	1.35	.40
☐	196	Ed Bouchee	3.00	1.35	.40
☐	197	Dick Hall	3.00	1.35	.40
☐	198	Carl Sawatski	3.00	1.35	.40
☐	199	Bob Boyd	3.00	1.35	.40
☐	200	Warren Spahn	35.00	16.00	4.40
☐	201	Pete Whisenant	3.00	1.35	.40
☐	202	Al Neiger	3.00	1.35	.40
☐	203	Eddie Bressoud	3.00	1.35	.40
☐	204	Bob Skinner	3.50	1.55	.45
☐	205	Billy Pierce	3.50	1.55	.45
☐	206	Gene Green	3.00	1.35	.40
☐	207	Dodger Southpaws Sandy Koufax Johnny Podres	21.00	9.50	2.60
☐	208	Larry Osborne	3.00	1.35	.40
☐	209	Ken McBride	3.00	1.35	.40
☐	210	Pete Runnels	3.50	1.55	.45
☐	211	Bob Gibson	40.00	18.00	5.00
☐	212	Haywood Sullivan	3.50	1.55	.45
☐	213	Bill Stafford	3.00	1.35	.40
☐	214	Danny Murphy	3.00	1.35	.40
☐	215	Gus Bell	3.50	1.55	.45
☐	216	Ted Bowsfield	3.00	1.35	.40
☐	217	Mel Roach	3.00	1.35	.40
☐	218	Hal Brown	3.00	1.35	.40
☐	219	Gene Mauch MG	4.00	1.80	.50
☐	220	Alvin Dark MG	4.00	1.80	.50
☐	221	Mike Higgins MG	3.50	1.55	.45
☐	222	Jimmy Dykes MG	4.50	2.00	.55
☐	223	Bob Scheffing MG	3.50	1.55	.45
☐	224	Joe Gordon MG	4.50	2.00	.55
☐	225	Bill Rigney MG	3.50	1.55	.45
☐	226	Cookie Lavagetto MG	3.50	1.55	.45
☐	227	Juan Pizarro	3.00	1.35	.40
☐	228	New York Yankees Team Card	30.00	13.50	3.80
☐	229	Rudy Hernandez	3.00	1.35	.40
☐	230	Don Hoak	3.50	1.55	.45
☐	231	Dick Drott	3.00	1.35	.40
☐	232	Bill White	6.00	2.70	.75
☐	233	Joey Jay	3.50	1.55	.45
☐	234	Ted Lepcio	3.00	1.35	.40
☐	235	Camilo Pascual	3.50	1.55	.45
☐	236	Don Gile	3.00	1.35	.40
☐	237	Billy Loes	3.50	1.55	.45
☐	238	Jim Gilliam	4.50	2.00	.55
☐	239	Dave Sisler	3.00	1.35	.40
☐	240	Ron Hansen	3.00	1.35	.40
☐	241	Al Cicotte	3.00	1.35	.40
☐	242	Hal Smith	3.00	1.35	.40
☐	243	Frank Lary	3.50	1.55	.45
☐	244	Chico Cardenas	3.50	1.55	.45
☐	245	Joe Adcock	3.50	1.55	.45
☐	246	Bob Davis	3.00	1.35	.40
☐	247	Billy Goodman	3.50	1.55	.45
☐	248	Ed Keegan	3.00	1.35	.40
☐	249	Cincinnati Reds Team Card	6.50	2.90	.80
☐	250	Buc Hill Aces Vern Law Roy Face	3.50	1.55	.45
☐	251	Bill Bruton	3.00	1.35	.40
☐	252	Bill Short	3.00	1.35	.40
☐	253	Sammy Taylor	3.00	1.35	.40
☐	254	Ted Sadowski	3.00	1.35	.40
☐	255	Vic Power	3.50	1.55	.45
☐	256	Billy Hoeft	3.00	1.35	.40
☐	257	Carroll Hardy	3.00	1.35	.40
☐	258	Jack Sanford	3.50	1.55	.45
☐	259	John Schaive	3.00	1.35	.40
☐	260	Don Drysdale	30.00	13.50	3.80
☐	261	Charlie Lau	3.50	1.55	.45
☐	262	Tony Curry	3.00	1.35	.40
☐	263	Ken Hamlin	3.00	1.35	.40
☐	264	Glen Hobbie	3.00	1.35	.40
☐	265	Tony Kubek	9.00	4.00	1.15
☐	266	Lindy McDaniel	3.50	1.55	.45
☐	267	Norm Siebern	3.00	1.35	.40
☐	268	Ike Delock	3.00	1.35	.40
☐	269	Harry Chiti	3.00	1.35	.40
☐	270	Bob Friend	3.50	1.55	.45
☐	271	Jim Landis	3.00	1.35	.40
☐	272	Tom Morgan	3.00	1.35	.40
☐	273A	Checklist 4 (Copyright symbol adjacent to 336 Don Mincher)	15.00	3.00	.90
☐	273B	Checklist 4 (Copyright symbol adjacent to 339 Gene Baker)	10.00	2.00	.60
☐	274	Gary Bell	3.00	1.35	.40
☐	275	Gene Woodling	3.50	1.55	.45
☐	276	Ray Rippelmeyer	3.00	1.35	.40
☐	277	Hank Foiles	3.00	1.35	.40
☐	278	Don McMahon	3.00	1.35	.40
☐	279	Jose Pagan	3.00	1.35	.40
☐	280	Frank Howard	5.50	2.50	.70
☐	281	Frank Sullivan	3.00	1.35	.40
☐	282	Faye Throneberry	3.00	1.35	.40
☐	283	Bob Anderson	3.00	1.35	.40
☐	284	Dick Gernert	3.00	1.35	.40
☐	285	Sherm Lollar	3.50	1.55	.45
☐	286	George Witt	3.00	1.35	.40
☐	287	Carl Yastrzemski	150.00	70.00	19.00
☐	288	Albie Pearson	3.50	1.55	.45
☐	289	Ray Moore	3.00	1.35	.40
☐	290	Stan Musial	110.00	50.00	14.00
☐	291	Tex Clevenger	3.00	1.35	.40
☐	292	Jim Baumer	3.00	1.35	.40
☐	293	Tom Sturdivant	3.00	1.35	.40
☐	294	Don Blasingame	3.00	1.35	.40
☐	295	Milt Pappas	3.50	1.55	.45
☐	296	Wes Covington	3.50	1.55	.45
☐	297	Athletics Team	6.50	2.90	.80
☐	298	Jim Golden	3.00	1.35	.40
☐	299	Clay Dalrymple	3.00	1.35	.40
☐	300	Mickey Mantle	425.00	190.00	52.50
☐	301	Chet Nichols	3.00	1.35	.40
☐	302	Al Heist	3.00	1.35	.40
☐	303	Gary Peters	3.50	1.55	.45
☐	304	Rocky Nelson	3.00	1.35	.40
☐	305	Mike McCormick	3.50	1.55	.45
☐	306	World Series Game 1 Bill Virdon Saves Game	7.25	3.30	.90
☐	307	World Series Game 2 Mickey Mantle Two Homers	40.00	18.00	5.00
☐	308	World Series Game 3 Bobby Richardson Is Hero	7.25	3.30	.90
☐	309	World Series Game 4 Gino Cimoli Safe	7.25	3.30	.90
☐	310	World Series Game 5 Roy Face Saves Day	7.25	3.30	.90
☐	311	World Series Game 6 Whitey Ford Second Shutout	11.00	4.90	1.40
☐	312	World Series Game 7 Bill Mazeroski's Homer	12.50	5.75	1.55
☐	313	World Series Summary Pirates Celebrate	9.00	4.00	1.15
☐	314	Bob Miller	3.00	1.35	.40
☐	315	Earl Battey	3.00	1.35	.40
☐	316	Bobby Gene Smith	3.00	1.35	.40
☐	317	Jim Brewer	3.00	1.35	.40
☐	318	Danny O'Connell	3.00	1.35	.40
☐	319	Valmy Thomas	3.00	1.35	.40
☐	320	Lou Burdette	3.50	1.55	.45
☐	321	Marv Breeding	3.00	1.35	.40
☐	322	Bill Kunkel	3.50	1.55	.45
☐	323	Sammy Esposito	3.00	1.35	.40
☐	324	Hank Aguirre	3.00	1.35	.40
☐	325	Wally Moon	3.50	1.55	.45
☐	326	Dave Hillman	3.00	1.35	.40
☐	327	Matty Alou	7.00	3.10	.85
☐	328	Jim O'Toole	3.50	1.55	.45
☐	329	Julio Becquer	3.00	1.35	.40
☐	330	Rocky Colavito	12.00	5.50	1.50
☐	331	Ned Garver	3.00	1.35	.40
☐	332	Dutch Dotterer UER (Photo actually Tommy Dotterer, Dutch's brother)	3.00	1.35	.40
☐	333	Fritz Brickell	3.00	1.35	.40
☐	334	Walt Bond	3.00	1.35	.40
☐	335	Frank Bolling	3.00	1.35	.40
☐	336	Don Mincher	3.50	1.55	.45
☐	337	Al's Aces Early Wynn Al Lopez Herb Score	5.00	2.30	.60
☐	338	Don Landrum	3.00	1.35	.40
☐	339	Gene Baker	3.00	1.35	.40
☐	340	Vic Wertz	3.50	1.55	.45
☐	341	Jim Owens	3.00	1.35	.40
☐	342	Clint Courtney	3.00	1.35	.40
☐	343	Earl Robinson	3.00	1.35	.40
☐	344	Sandy Koufax	110.00	50.00	14.00
☐	345	Jim Piersall	4.00	1.80	.50

☐ 346 Howie Nunn 3.00 1.35 .40
☐ 347 St. Louis Cardinals 6.50 2.90 .80
Team Card
☐ 348 Steve Boros 3.00 1.35 .40
☐ 349 Danny McDevitt 3.00 1.35 .40
☐ 350 Ernie Banks 40.00 18.00 5.00
☐ 351 Jim King 3.00 1.35 .40
☐ 352 Bob Shaw 3.00 1.35 .40
☐ 353 Howie Bedell 3.00 1.35 .40
☐ 354 Billy Harrell 3.00 1.35 .40
☐ 355 Bob Allison 3.50 1.55 .45
☐ 356 Ryne Duren 4.00 1.80 .50
☐ 357 Daryl Spencer 3.00 1.35 .40
☐ 358 Earl Averill 3.00 1.35 .40
☐ 359 Dallas Green 4.00 1.80 .50
☐ 360 Frank Robinson 45.00 20.00 5.75
☐ 361A Checklist 5 10.00 2.00 .60
(No ad on back)
☐ 361B Checklist 5 15.00 3.00 .90
(Special Feature
ad on back)
☐ 362 Frank Funk 3.00 1.35 .40
☐ 363 John Roseboro 3.50 1.55 .45
☐ 364 Moe Drabowsky 3.50 1.55 .45
☐ 365 Jerry Lumpe 3.00 1.35 .40
☐ 366 Eddie Fisher 3.00 1.35 .40
☐ 367 Jim Rivera 3.00 1.35 .40
☐ 368 Bennie Daniels 3.00 1.35 .40
☐ 369 Dave Philley 3.00 1.35 .40
☐ 370 Roy Face 4.00 1.80 .50
☐ 371 Bill Skowron SP 40.00 18.00 5.00
☐ 372 Bob Hendley 4.50 2.00 .55
☐ 373 Boston Red Sox 9.00 4.00 1.15
Team Card
☐ 374 Paul Giel 5.00 2.30 .60
☐ 375 Ken Boyer 8.00 3.60 1.00
☐ 376 Mike Roarke 5.00 2.30 .60
☐ 377 Ruben Gomez 4.50 2.00 .55
☐ 378 Wally Post 5.00 2.30 .60
☐ 379 Bobby Shantz 5.00 2.30 .60
☐ 380 Minnie Minoso 5.00 2.30 .60
☐ 381 Dave Wickersham 4.50 2.00 .55
☐ 382 Frank Thomas 5.50 2.50 .70
☐ 383 Frisco First Liners 5.00 2.30 .60
Mike McCormick
Jack Sanford
Billy O'Dell
☐ 384 Chuck Essegian 4.50 2.00 .55
☐ 385 Jim Perry 5.00 2.30 .60
☐ 386 Joe Hicks 4.50 2.00 .55
☐ 387 Duke Maas 4.50 2.00 .55
☐ 388 Bob Clemente 110.00 50.00 14.00
☐ 389 Ralph Terry 5.50 2.50 .70
☐ 390 Del Crandall 5.50 2.50 .70
☐ 391 Winston Brown 4.50 2.00 .55
☐ 392 Reno Bertoia 4.50 2.00 .55
☐ 393 Batter Bafflers 4.50 2.00 .55
Don Cardwell
Glen Hobbie
☐ 394 Ken Walters 4.50 2.00 .55
☐ 395 Chuck Estrada 5.00 2.30 .60
☐ 396 Bob Aspromonte 4.50 2.00 .55
☐ 397 Hal Woodeshick 4.50 2.00 .55
☐ 398 Hank Bauer 5.00 2.30 .60
☐ 399 Cliff Cook 4.50 2.00 .55
☐ 400 Vern Law 5.50 2.50 .70
☐ 401 Babe Ruth 60th Homer 30.00 13.50 3.80
☐ 402 Perfect Game 20.00 9.00 2.50
(Don Larsen)
☐ 403 26 Inning Tie 6.00 2.70 .75
☐ 404 Rogers Hornsby .424 10.00 4.50 1.25
Average
☐ 405 Lou Gehrig's Streak 25.00 11.50 3.10
☐ 406 Mickey Mantle 565 55.00 25.00 7.00
Foot Homer
☐ 407 Jack Chesbro Wins 41 6.00 2.70 .75
☐ 408 Christy Mathewson 10.00 4.50 1.25
Fans 267
☐ 409 Walter Johnson 10.00 4.50 1.25
Shutouts
☐ 410 Harvey Haddix 12 7.00 3.10 .85
Perfect Innings
☐ 411 Tony Taylor 5.00 2.30 .60
☐ 412 Larry Sherry 5.00 2.30 .60
☐ 413 Eddie Yost 5.00 2.30 .60
☐ 414 Dick Donovan 4.50 2.00 .55
☐ 415 Hank Aaron 135.00 60.00 17.00
☐ 416 Dick Howser 9.00 4.00 1.15
☐ 417 Juan Marichal 150.00 70.00 19.00
☐ 418 Ed Bailey 5.00 2.30 .60
☐ 419 Tom Borland 4.50 2.00 .55
☐ 420 Ernie Broglio 5.00 2.30 .60
☐ 421 Ty Cline 4.50 2.00 .55
☐ 422 Bud Daley 4.50 2.00 .55
☐ 423 Charlie Neal SP 10.00 4.50 1.25
☐ 424 Turk Lown 4.50 2.00 .55
☐ 425 Yogi Berra 75.00 34.00 9.50
☐ 426 Milwaukee Braves 9.00 4.00 1.15
Team Card
(Back numbered 463)
☐ 427 Dick Ellsworth 5.00 2.30 .60
☐ 428 Ray Barker SP 10.00 4.50 1.25
☐ 429 Al Kaline 45.00 20.00 5.75
☐ 430 Bill Mazeroski SP 40.00 18.00 5.00
☐ 431 Chuck Stobbs 4.50 2.00 .55
☐ 432 Coot Veal 4.50 2.00 .55
☐ 433 Art Mahaffey 4.50 2.00 .55
☐ 434 Tom Brewer 4.50 2.00 .55
☐ 435 Orlando Cepeda UER 11.00 4.90 1.40
(San Francis on
card front)
☐ 436 Jim Maloney 10.00 4.50 1.25
☐ 437A Checklist 6 15.00 3.00 .90
440 Louis Aparicio
☐ 437B Checklist 6 15.00 3.00 .90
440 Luis Aparicio
☐ 438 Curt Flood 5.50 2.50 .70
☐ 439 Phil Regan 5.00 2.30 .60
☐ 440 Luis Aparicio 15.00 6.75 1.90
☐ 441 Dick Bertell 4.50 2.00 .55
☐ 442 Gordon Jones 4.50 2.00 .55
☐ 443 Duke Snider 45.00 20.00 5.75
☐ 444 Joe Nuxhall 5.50 2.50 .70
☐ 445 Frank Malzone 5.00 2.30 .60
☐ 446 Bob Taylor 4.50 2.00 .55
☐ 447 Harry Bright 5.50 2.50 .70
☐ 448 Del Rice 5.50 2.50 .70
☐ 449 Bob Bolin 5.50 2.50 .70
☐ 450 Jim Lemon 6.00 2.70 .75
☐ 451 Power for Ernie 6.50 2.90 .80
Daryl Spencer
Bill White
Ernie Broglio
☐ 452 Bob Allen 5.50 2.50 .70
☐ 453 Dick Schofield 6.00 2.70 .75
☐ 454 Pumpsie Green 6.00 2.70 .75
☐ 455 Early Wynn 14.00 6.25 1.75
☐ 456 Hal Bevan 5.50 2.50 .70
☐ 457 Johnny James 5.50 2.50 .70
(Listed as Angel,
but wearing Yankee
uniform and cap)
☐ 458 Willie Tasby 5.50 2.50 .70
☐ 459 Terry Fox 5.50 2.50 .70
☐ 460 Gil Hodges 16.00 7.25 2.00
☐ 461 Smoky Burgess 6.50 2.90 .80
☐ 462 Lou Klimchock 5.50 2.50 .70
☐ 463 Jack Fisher 6.00 2.70 .75
(See also 426)
☐ 464 Lee Thomas 7.00 3.10 .85
(Pictured with Yankee
cap but listed as
Los Angeles Angel)
☐ 465 Roy McMillan 6.00 2.70 .75
☐ 466 Ron Moeller 5.50 2.50 .70
☐ 467 Cleveland Indians 9.00 4.00 1.15
Team Card
☐ 468 John Callison 6.50 2.90 .80
☐ 469 Ralph Lumenti 5.50 2.50 .70
☐ 470 Roy Sievers 6.00 2.70 .75
☐ 471 Phil Rizzuto MVP 15.00 6.75 1.90
☐ 472 Yogi Berra MVP 55.00 25.00 7.00
☐ 473 Bob Shantz MVP 6.50 2.90 .80
☐ 474 Al Rosen MVP 6.50 2.90 .80
☐ 475 Mickey Mantle MVP 125.00 57.50 15.50
☐ 476 Jackie Jensen MVP 6.50 2.90 .80
☐ 477 Nellie Fox MVP 8.50 3.80 1.05
☐ 478 Roger Maris MVP 45.00 20.00 5.75
☐ 479 Jim Konstanty MVP 6.50 2.90 .80
☐ 480 Roy Campanella MVP 35.00 16.00 4.40
☐ 481 Hank Sauer MVP 6.50 2.90 .80
☐ 482 Willie Mays MVP 45.00 20.00 5.75
☐ 483 Don Newcombe MVP 6.50 2.90 .80
☐ 484 Hank Aaron MVP 45.00 20.00 5.75
☐ 485 Ernie Banks MVP 30.00 13.50 3.80
☐ 486 Dick Groat MVP 6.50 2.90 .80
☐ 487 Gene Oliver 5.50 2.50 .70
☐ 488 Joe McClain 5.50 2.50 .70
☐ 489 Walt Dropo 5.50 2.50 .70
☐ 490 Jim Bunning 10.00 4.50 1.25
☐ 491 Philadelphia Phillies 9.00 4.00 1.15
Team Card
☐ 492 Ron Fairly 6.00 2.70 .75
☐ 493 Don Zimmer UER 7.00 3.10 .85
(Brooklyn A.L.)
☐ 494 Tom Cheney 5.50 2.50 .70

☐ 495 Elston Howard	9.50	4.30	1.20
☐ 496 Ken MacKenzie	5.50	2.50	.70
☐ 497 Willie Jones	5.50	2.50	.70
☐ 498 Ray Herbert	5.50	2.50	.70
☐ 499 Chuck Schilling	5.50	2.50	.70
☐ 500 Harvey Kuenn	7.00	3.10	.85
☐ 501 John DeMerit	5.50	2.50	.70
☐ 502 Clarence Coleman	7.00	3.10	.85
☐ 503 Tito Francona	5.50	2.50	.70
☐ 504 Billy Consolo	5.50	2.50	.70
☐ 505 Red Schoendienst	15.00	6.75	1.90
☐ 506 Willie Davis	18.00	8.00	2.30
☐ 507 Pete Burnside	5.50	2.50	.70
☐ 508 Rocky Bridges	5.50	2.50	.70
☐ 509 Camilo Carreon	5.50	2.50	.70
☐ 510 Art Ditmar	5.50	2.50	.70
☐ 511 Joe M. Morgan	6.00	2.70	.75
☐ 512 Bob Will	5.50	2.50	.70
☐ 513 Jim Brosnan	6.50	2.90	.80
☐ 514 Jake Wood	5.50	2.50	.70
☐ 515 Jackie Brandt	5.50	2.50	.70
☐ 516 Checklist 7	15.00	3.00	.90
☐ 517 Willie McCovey	65.00	29.00	8.25
☐ 518 Andy Carey	6.00	2.70	.75
☐ 519 Jim Pagliaroni	6.00	2.70	.75
☐ 520 Joe Cunningham	6.00	2.70	.75
☐ 521 Brother Battery Norm Sherry Larry Sherry	6.00	2.70	.75
☐ 522 Dick Farrell UER (Phillies cap, but listed on Dodgers)	6.00	2.70	.75
☐ 523 Joe Gibbon	34.00	15.50	4.20
☐ 524 Johnny Logan	40.00	18.00	5.00
☐ 525 Ron Perranoski	40.00	18.00	5.00
☐ 526 R.C. Stevens	34.00	15.50	4.20
☐ 527 Gene Leek	34.00	15.50	4.20
☐ 528 Pedro Ramos	34.00	15.50	4.20
☐ 529 Bob Roselli	34.00	15.50	4.20
☐ 530 Bob Malkmus	34.00	15.50	4.20
☐ 531 Jim Coates	34.00	15.50	4.20
☐ 532 Bob Hale	34.00	15.50	4.20
☐ 533 Jack Curtis	34.00	15.50	4.20
☐ 534 Eddie Kasko	34.00	15.50	4.20
☐ 535 Larry Jackson	34.00	15.50	4.20
☐ 536 Bill Tuttle	34.00	15.50	4.20
☐ 537 Bobby Locke	34.00	15.50	4.20
☐ 538 Chuck Hiller	34.00	15.50	4.20
☐ 539 Johnny Klippstein	34.00	15.50	4.20
☐ 540 Jackie Jensen	40.00	18.00	5.00
☐ 541 Roland Sheldon	40.00	18.00	5.00
☐ 542 Minnesota Twins Team Card	70.00	32.00	8.75
☐ 543 Roger Craig	40.00	18.00	5.00
☐ 544 George Thomas	34.00	15.50	4.20
☐ 545 Hoyt Wilhelm	65.00	29.00	8.25
☐ 546 Marty Kutyna	34.00	15.50	4.20
☐ 547 Leon Wagner	34.00	15.50	4.20
☐ 548 Ted Wills	34.00	15.50	4.20
☐ 549 Hal R. Smith	34.00	15.50	4.20
☐ 550 Frank Baumann	34.00	15.50	4.20
☐ 551 George Altman	34.00	15.50	4.20
☐ 552 Jim Archer	34.00	15.50	4.20
☐ 553 Bill Fischer	34.00	15.50	4.20
☐ 554 Pittsburgh Pirates Team Card	70.00	32.00	8.75
☐ 555 Sam Jones	37.50	17.00	4.70
☐ 556 Ken R. Hunt	34.00	15.50	4.20
☐ 557 Jose Valdivielso	34.00	15.50	4.20
☐ 558 Don Ferrarese	34.00	15.50	4.20
☐ 559 Jim Gentile	37.50	17.00	4.70
☐ 560 Barry Latman	34.00	15.50	4.20
☐ 561 Charley James	34.00	15.50	4.20
☐ 562 Bill Monbouquette	34.00	15.50	4.20
☐ 563 Bob Cerv	40.00	18.00	5.00
☐ 564 Don Cardwell	34.00	15.50	4.20
☐ 565 Felipe Alou	45.00	20.00	5.75
☐ 566 Paul Richards MG AS	36.00	16.00	4.50
☐ 567 Danny Murtaugh MG AS	36.00	16.00	4.50
☐ 568 Bill Skowron AS	40.00	18.00	5.00
☐ 569 Frank Herrera AS	36.00	16.00	4.50
☐ 570 Nellie Fox AS	45.00	20.00	5.75
☐ 571 Bill Mazeroski AS	40.00	18.00	5.00
☐ 572 Brooks Robinson AS	100.00	45.00	12.50
☐ 573 Ken Boyer AS	40.00	18.00	5.00
☐ 574 Luis Aparicio AS	50.00	23.00	6.25
☐ 575 Ernie Banks AS	100.00	45.00	12.50
☐ 576 Roger Maris AS	165.00	75.00	21.00
☐ 577 Hank Aaron AS	175.00	80.00	22.00
☐ 578 Mickey Mantle AS	400.00	180.00	50.00
☐ 579 Willie Mays AS	175.00	80.00	22.00
☐ 580 Al Kaline AS	100.00	45.00	12.50
☐ 581 Frank Robinson AS	100.00	45.00	12.50
☐ 582 Earl Battey AS	36.00	16.00	4.50
☐ 583 Del Crandall AS	36.00	16.00	4.50
☐ 584 Jim Perry AS	36.00	16.00	4.50
☐ 585 Bob Friend AS	36.00	16.00	4.50
☐ 586 Whitey Ford AS	100.00	45.00	12.50
☐ 587 Does not exist	.00	.00	.00
☐ 588 Does not exist	.00	.00	.00
☐ 589 Warren Spahn AS	160.00	70.00	20.00

1962 Topps

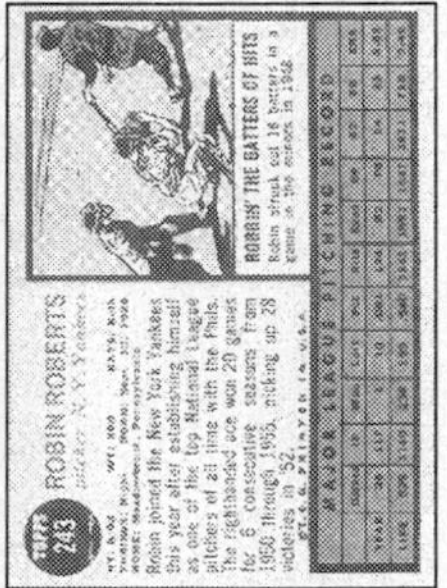

The cards in this 598-card set measure 2 1/2" by 3 1/2". The 1962 Topps set contains a mini-series spotlighting Babe Ruth (135-144). Other subsets in the set include League Leaders (51-60), World Series cards (232-237), In Action cards (311-319), NL All Stars (390-399), AL All Stars (466-475), and Rookie Prospects (591-598). The All-Star selections were again provided by Sport Magazine, as in 1958 and 1960. The second series had two distinct printings which are distinguishable by numerous color and pose variations. Those cards with a distinctive "green tint" are valued at a slight premuim as they are basically the result of a flawed printing process occurring early in the second series run. Card number 139 exists as A: Babe Ruth Special card, B: Hal Reniff with arms over head, or C: Hal Reniff in the same pose as card number 159. In addition, two poses exist for players depicted on card numbers 129, 132, 134, 147, 174, 176, and 190. The high number series, 523 to 598, is somewhat more difficult to obtain than other cards in the set. Within the last series (523-598) there are 43 cards which were printed in lesser quantities; these are marked SP in the checklist below. The set price listed does not include the pose variations (see checklist below for individual values). The key rookies in this set are Lou Brock, Tim McCarver, Gaylord Perry, and Bob Uecker.

	NRMT	VG-E	GOOD
COMPLETE SET (598)	5400.00	2400.00	700.00
COMMON PLAYER (1-109)	2.50	1.15	.30
COMMON PLAYER (110-196)	2.50	1.15	.30
COMMON PLAYER (197-283)	3.00	1.35	.40
COMMON PLAYER (284-370)	3.50	1.55	.45
COMMON PLAYER (371-446)	5.50	2.50	.70
COMMON PLAYER (447-522)	7.00	3.10	.85
COMMON PLAYER (523-590)	15.00	6.75	1.90
COMMON ROOKIES (591-598)	33.00	15.00	4.10
☐ 1 Roger Maris	250.00	115.00	31.00
☐ 2 Jim Brosnan	2.50	1.15	.30
☐ 3 Pete Runnels	3.00	1.35	.40
☐ 4 John DeMerit	2.50	1.15	.30
☐ 5 Sandy Koufax UER (Struck ou 18)	125.00	57.50	15.50
☐ 6 Marv Breeding	2.50	1.15	.30
☐ 7 Frank Thomas	3.50	1.55	.45
☐ 8 Ray Herbert	2.50	1.15	.30
☐ 9 Jim Davenport	3.00	1.35	.40
☐ 10 Bob Clemente	115.00	52.50	14.50
☐ 11 Tom Morgan	2.50	1.15	.30
☐ 12 Harry Craft MG	2.50	1.15	.30
☐ 13 Dick Howser	3.00	1.35	.40

☐ 14 Bill White	4.50	2.00	.55
☐ 15 Dick Donovan	2.50	1.15	.30
☐ 16 Darrell Johnson	2.50	1.15	.30
☐ 17 John Callison	3.00	1.35	.40
☐ 18 Managers' Dream	125.00	57.50	15.50
Mickey Mantle			
Willie Mays			
☐ 19 Ray Washburn	2.50	1.15	.30
☐ 20 Rocky Colavito	10.00	4.50	1.25
☐ 21 Jim Kaat	6.00	2.70	.75
☐ 22A Checklist 1 ERR	10.00	1.50	.50
(121-176 on back)			
☐ 22B Checklist 1 COR	10.00	1.50	.50
☐ 23 Norm Larker	2.50	1.15	.30
☐ 24 Tigers Team	6.00	2.70	.75
☐ 25 Ernie Banks	45.00	20.00	5.75
☐ 26 Chris Cannizzaro	2.50	1.15	.30
☐ 27 Chuck Cottier	2.50	1.15	.30
☐ 28 Minnie Minoso	4.50	2.00	.55
☐ 29 Casey Stengel MG	20.00	9.00	2.50
☐ 30 Eddie Mathews	20.00	9.00	2.50
☐ 31 Tom Tresh	18.00	8.00	2.30
☐ 32 John Roseboro	3.00	1.35	.40
☐ 33 Don Larsen	3.00	1.35	.40
☐ 34 Johnny Temple	3.00	1.35	.40
☐ 35 Don Schwall	3.00	1.35	.40
☐ 36 Don Leppert	2.50	1.15	.30
☐ 37 Tribe Hill Trio	3.00	1.35	.40
Barry Latman			
Dick Stigman			
Jim Perry			
☐ 38 Gene Stephens	2.50	1.15	.30
☐ 39 Joe Koppe	2.50	1.15	.30
☐ 40 Orlando Cepeda	9.00	4.00	1.15
☐ 41 Cliff Cook	2.50	1.15	.30
☐ 42 Jim King	2.50	1.15	.30
☐ 43 Los Angeles Dodgers	6.00	2.70	.75
Team Card			
☐ 44 Don Taussig	2.50	1.15	.30
☐ 45 Brooks Robinson	40.00	18.00	5.00
☐ 46 Jack Baldschun	2.50	1.15	.30
☐ 47 Bob Will	2.50	1.15	.30
☐ 48 Ralph Terry	3.00	1.35	.40
☐ 49 Hal Jones	2.50	1.15	.30
☐ 50 Stan Musial	110.00	50.00	14.00
☐ 51 AL Batting Leaders	5.00	2.30	.60
Norm Cash			
Jim Piersall			
Al Kaline			
Elston Howard			
☐ 52 NL Batting Leaders	6.50	2.90	.80
Bob Clemente			
Vada Pinson			
Ken Boyer			
Wally Moon			
☐ 53 AL Home Run Leaders	50.00	23.00	6.25
Roger Maris			
Mickey Mantle			
Jim Gentile			
Harmon Killebrew			
☐ 54 NL Home Run Leaders	7.00	3.10	.85
Orlando Cepeda			
Willie Mays			
Frank Robinson			
☐ 55 AL ERA Leaders	4.50	2.00	.55
Dick Donovan			
Bill Stafford			
Don Mossi			
Milt Pappas			
☐ 56 NL ERA Leaders	5.00	2.30	.60
Warren Spahn			
Jim O'Toole			
Curt Simmons			
Mike McCormick			
☐ 57 AL Wins Leaders	5.00	2.30	.60
Whitey Ford			
Frank Lary			
Steve Barber			
Jim Bunning			
☐ 58 NL Wins Leaders	5.00	2.30	.60
Warren Spahn			
Joe Jay			
Jim O'Toole			
☐ 59 AL Strikeout Leaders	4.50	2.00	.55
Camilo Pascual			
Whitey Ford			
Jim Bunning			
Juan Pizzaro			
☐ 60 NL Strikeout Leaders	8.00	3.60	1.00
Sandy Koufax			
Stan Williams			
Don Drysdale			
Jim O'Toole			
☐ 61 Cardinals Team	6.00	2.70	.75
☐ 62 Steve Boros	2.50	1.15	.30
☐ 63 Tony Cloninger	3.50	1.55	.45
☐ 64 Russ Snyder	2.50	1.15	.30
☐ 65 Bobby Richardson	6.50	2.90	.80
☐ 66 Cuno Barragan	2.50	1.15	.30
☐ 67 Harvey Haddix	3.00	1.35	.40
☐ 68 Ken Hunt	2.50	1.15	.30
☐ 69 Phil Ortega	2.50	1.15	.30
☐ 70 Harmon Killebrew	20.00	9.00	2.50
☐ 71 Dick LeMay	2.50	1.15	.30
☐ 72 Bob's Pupils	2.50	1.15	.30
Steve Boros			
Bob Scheffing MG			
Jake Wood			
☐ 73 Nellie Fox	7.00	3.10	.85
☐ 74 Bob Lillis	2.50	1.15	.30
☐ 75 Milt Pappas	3.00	1.35	.40
☐ 76 Howie Bedell	2.50	1.15	.30
☐ 77 Tony Taylor	3.00	1.35	.40
☐ 78 Gene Green	2.50	1.15	.30
☐ 79 Ed Hobaugh	2.50	1.15	.30
☐ 80 Vada Pinson	4.50	2.00	.55
☐ 81 Jim Pagliaroni	2.50	1.15	.30
☐ 82 Deron Johnson	3.00	1.35	.40
☐ 83 Larry Jackson	2.50	1.15	.30
☐ 84 Lenny Green	2.50	1.15	.30
☐ 85 Gil Hodges	16.00	7.25	2.00
☐ 86 Donn Clendenon	4.00	1.80	.50
☐ 87 Mike Roarke	2.50	1.15	.30
☐ 88 Ralph Houk MG	3.50	1.55	.45
(Berra in background)			
☐ 89 Barney Schultz	2.50	1.15	.30
☐ 90 Jim Piersall	3.00	1.35	.40
☐ 91 J.C. Martin	2.50	1.15	.30
☐ 92 Sam Jones	2.50	1.15	.30
☐ 93 John Blanchard	3.00	1.35	.40
☐ 94 Jay Hook	2.50	1.15	.30
☐ 95 Don Hoak	3.00	1.35	.40
☐ 96 Eli Grba	2.50	1.15	.30
☐ 97 Tito Francona	2.50	1.15	.30
☐ 98 Checklist 2	10.00	1.50	.50
☐ 99 John (Boog) Powell	21.00	9.50	2.60
☐ 100 Warren Spahn	32.00	14.50	4.00
☐ 101 Carroll Hardy	2.50	1.15	.30
☐ 102 Al Schroll	2.50	1.15	.30
☐ 103 Don Blasingame	2.50	1.15	.30
☐ 104 Ted Savage	2.50	1.15	.30
☐ 105 Don Mossi	3.00	1.35	.40
☐ 106 Carl Sawatski	2.50	1.15	.30
☐ 107 Mike McCormick	3.00	1.35	.40
☐ 108 Willie Davis	4.00	1.80	.50
☐ 109 Bob Shaw	2.50	1.15	.30
☐ 110 Bill Skowron	5.00	2.30	.60
☐ 111 Dallas Green	3.00	1.35	.40
☐ 112 Hank Foiles	2.50	1.15	.30
☐ 113 Chicago White Sox	6.00	2.70	.75
Team Card			
☐ 114 Howie Koplitz	2.50	1.15	.30
☐ 115 Bob Skinner	3.00	1.35	.40
☐ 116 Herb Score	4.00	1.80	.50
☐ 117 Gary Geiger	2.50	1.15	.30
☐ 118 Julian Javier	3.00	1.35	.40
☐ 119 Danny Murphy	2.50	1.15	.30
☐ 120 Bob Purkey	2.50	1.15	.30
☐ 121 Billy Hitchcock MG	2.50	1.15	.30
☐ 122 Norm Bass	2.50	1.15	.30
☐ 123 Mike De La Hoz	2.50	1.15	.30
☐ 124 Bill Pleis	2.50	1.15	.30
☐ 125 Gene Woodling	3.00	1.35	.40
☐ 126 Al Cicotte	2.50	1.15	.30
☐ 127 Pride of A's	3.00	1.35	.40
Norm Siebern			
Hank Bauer MG			
Jerry Lumpe			
☐ 128 Art Fowler	2.50	1.15	.30
☐ 129A Lee Walls	2.50	1.15	.30
(Facing right)			
☐ 129B Lee Walls	26.00	11.50	3.30
(Facing left)			
☐ 130 Frank Bolling	2.50	1.15	.30
☐ 131 Pete Richert	2.50	1.15	.30
☐ 132A Angels Team	6.00	2.70	.75
(Without photo)			
☐ 132B Angels Team	26.00	11.50	3.30
(With photo)			
☐ 133 Felipe Alou	5.00	2.30	.60
☐ 134A Billy Hoeft	2.50	1.15	.30
(Facing right)			
☐ 134B Billy Hoeft	26.00	11.50	3.30
(Facing straight)			
☐ 135 Babe Ruth Special 1	18.00	8.00	2.30
Babe as a Boy			

☐ 136 Babe Ruth Special 2	18.00	8.00	2.30
Babe Joins Yanks			
☐ 137 Babe Ruth Special 3	18.00	8.00	2.30
Babe with Huggins			
☐ 138 Babe Ruth Special 4	18.00	8.00	2.30
Famous Slugger			
☐ 139A Babe Ruth Special 5	25.00	11.50	3.10
Babe Hits 60			
☐ 139B Hal Reniff PORT	13.00	5.75	1.65
☐ 139C Hal Reniff	55.00	25.00	7.00
(Pitching)			
☐ 140 Babe Ruth Special 6	25.00	11.50	3.10
Gehrig and Ruth			
☐ 141 Babe Ruth Special 7	18.00	8.00	2.30
Twilight Years			
☐ 142 Babe Ruth Special 8	18.00	8.00	2.30
Coaching Dodgers			
☐ 143 Babe Ruth Special 9	18.00	8.00	2.30
Greatest Sports Hero			
☐ 144 Babe Ruth Special 10	18.00	8.00	2.30
Farewell Speech			
☐ 145 Barry Latman	2.50	1.15	.30
☐ 146 Don Demeter	2.50	1.15	.30
☐ 147A Bill Kunkel PORT	2.50	1.15	.30
☐ 147B Bill Kunkel	26.00	11.50	3.30
(Pitching pose)			
☐ 148 Wally Post	3.00	1.35	.40
☐ 149 Bob Duliba	2.50	1.15	.30
☐ 150 Al Kaline	35.00	16.00	4.40
☐ 151 Johnny Klippstein	2.50	1.15	.30
☐ 152 Mickey Vernon MG	3.00	1.35	.40
☐ 153 Pumpsie Green	3.00	1.35	.40
☐ 154 Lee Thomas	3.00	1.35	.40
☐ 155 Stu Miller	3.00	1.35	.40
☐ 156 Merritt Ranew	2.50	1.15	.30
☐ 157 Wes Covington	3.00	1.35	.40
☐ 158 Braves Team	6.00	2.70	.75
☐ 159 Hal Reniff	4.00	1.80	.50
☐ 160 Dick Stuart	3.00	1.35	.40
☐ 161 Frank Baumann	2.50	1.15	.30
☐ 162 Sammy Drake	2.50	1.15	.30
☐ 163 Hot Corner Guard	3.00	1.35	.40
Billy Gardner			
Cletis Boyer			
☐ 164 Hal Naragon	2.50	1.15	.30
☐ 165 Jackie Brandt	2.50	1.15	.30
☐ 166 Don Lee	2.50	1.15	.30
☐ 167 Tim McCarver	35.00	16.00	4.40
☐ 168 Leo Posada	2.50	1.15	.30
☐ 169 Bob Cerv	3.00	1.35	.40
☐ 170 Ron Santo	12.00	5.50	1.50
☐ 171 Dave Sisler	2.50	1.15	.30
☐ 172 Fred Hutchinson MG	3.00	1.35	.40
☐ 173 Chico Fernandez	2.50	1.15	.30
☐ 174A Carl Willey	2.50	1.15	.30
(Capless)			
☐ 174B Carl Willey	26.00	11.50	3.30
(With cap)			
☐ 175 Frank Howard	5.00	2.30	.60
☐ 176A Eddie Yost PORT	3.00	1.35	.40
☐ 176B Eddie Yost BATTING	26.00	11.50	3.30
☐ 177 Bobby Shantz	3.00	1.35	.40
☐ 178 Camilo Carreon	2.50	1.15	.30
☐ 179 Tom Sturdivant	2.50	1.15	.30
☐ 180 Bob Allison	3.00	1.35	.40
☐ 181 Paul Brown	2.50	1.15	.30
☐ 182 Bob Nieman	2.50	1.15	.30
☐ 183 Roger Craig	4.00	1.80	.50
☐ 184 Haywood Sullivan	3.00	1.35	.40
☐ 185 Roland Sheldon	2.50	1.15	.30
☐ 186 Mack Jones	2.50	1.15	.30
☐ 187 Gene Conley	3.00	1.35	.40
☐ 188 Chuck Hiller	2.50	1.15	.30
☐ 189 Dick Hall	2.50	1.15	.30
☐ 190A Wally Moon PORT	3.00	1.35	.40
☐ 190B Wally Moon BATTING	26.00	11.50	3.30
☐ 191 Jim Brewer	2.50	1.15	.30
☐ 192A Checklist 3	10.00	1.50	.50
(Without comma)			
☐ 192B Checklist 3	10.00	1.50	.50
(Comma after			
Checklist)			
☐ 193 Eddie Kasko	2.50	1.15	.30
☐ 194 Dean Chance	4.00	1.80	.50
☐ 195 Joe Cunningham	3.00	1.35	.40
☐ 196 Terry Fox	2.50	1.15	.30
☐ 197 Daryl Spencer	3.00	1.35	.40
☐ 198 Johnny Keane MG	3.50	1.55	.45
☐ 199 Gaylord Perry	180.00	80.00	23.00
☐ 200 Mickey Mantle	500.00	230.00	65.00
☐ 201 Ike Delock	3.00	1.35	.40
☐ 202 Carl Warwick	3.00	1.35	.40
☐ 203 Jack Fisher	3.00	1.35	.40
☐ 204 Johnny Weekly	3.00	1.35	.40
☐ 205 Gene Freese	3.00	1.35	.40
☐ 206 Senators Team	6.00	2.70	.75
☐ 207 Pete Burnside	3.00	1.35	.40
☐ 208 Billy Martin	8.00	3.60	1.00
☐ 209 Jim Fregosi	9.50	4.30	1.20
☐ 210 Roy Face	4.00	1.80	.50
☐ 211 Midway Masters	3.50	1.55	.45
Frank Bolling			
Roy McMillan			
☐ 212 Jim Owens	3.00	1.35	.40
☐ 213 Richie Ashburn	10.00	4.50	1.25
☐ 214 Dom Zanni	3.00	1.35	.40
☐ 215 Woody Held	3.00	1.35	.40
☐ 216 Ron Kline	3.00	1.35	.40
☐ 217 Walt Alston MG	5.00	2.30	.60
☐ 218 Joe Torre	25.00	11.50	3.10
☐ 219 Al Downing	5.00	2.30	.60
☐ 220 Roy Sievers	3.50	1.55	.45
☐ 221 Bill Short	3.00	1.35	.40
☐ 222 Jerry Zimmerman	3.00	1.35	.40
☐ 223 Alex Grammas	3.00	1.35	.40
☐ 224 Don Rudolph	3.00	1.35	.40
☐ 225 Frank Malzone	3.50	1.55	.45
☐ 226 San Francisco Giants	6.00	2.70	.75
Team Card			
☐ 227 Bob Tiefenauer	3.00	1.35	.40
☐ 228 Dale Long	3.50	1.55	.45
☐ 229 Jesus McFarlane	3.00	1.35	.40
☐ 230 Camilo Pascual	3.50	1.55	.45
☐ 231 Ernie Bowman	3.00	1.35	.40
☐ 232 World Series Game 1	5.50	2.50	.70
Yanks win opener			
☐ 233 World Series Game 2	5.50	2.50	.70
Joey Jay ties it up			
☐ 234 World Series Game 3	20.00	9.00	2.50
Roger Maris wins			
in 9th			
☐ 235 World Series Game 4	8.50	3.80	1.05
Whitey Ford sets			
new mark			
☐ 236 World Series Game 5	5.50	2.50	.70
Yanks crush Reds			
☐ 237 World Series Summary	5.50	2.50	.70
Yanks celebrate			
☐ 238 Norm Sherry	3.50	1.55	.45
☐ 239 Cecil Butler	3.00	1.35	.40
☐ 240 George Altman	3.00	1.35	.40
☐ 241 Johnny Kucks	3.00	1.35	.40
☐ 242 Mel McGaha MG	3.00	1.35	.40
☐ 243 Robin Roberts	12.50	5.75	1.55
☐ 244 Don Gile	3.00	1.35	.40
☐ 245 Ron Hansen	3.00	1.35	.40
☐ 246 Art Ditmar	3.00	1.35	.40
☐ 247 Joe Pignatano	3.00	1.35	.40
☐ 248 Bob Aspromonte	3.00	1.35	.40
☐ 249 Ed Keegan	3.00	1.35	.40
☐ 250 Norm Cash	7.00	3.10	.85
☐ 251 New York Yankees	24.00	11.00	3.00
Team Card			
☐ 252 Earl Francis	3.00	1.35	.40
☐ 253 Harry Chiti MG	3.00	1.35	.40
☐ 254 Gordon Windhorn	3.00	1.35	.40
☐ 255 Juan Pizarro	3.00	1.35	.40
☐ 256 Elio Chacon	3.00	1.35	.40
☐ 257 Jack Spring	3.00	1.35	.40
☐ 258 Marty Keough	3.00	1.35	.40
☐ 259 Lou Klimchock	3.00	1.35	.40
☐ 260 Billy Pierce	3.50	1.55	.45
☐ 261 George Alusik	3.00	1.35	.40
☐ 262 Bob Schmidt	3.00	1.35	.40
☐ 263 The Right Pitch	3.50	1.55	.45
Bob Purkey			
Jim Turner CO			
Joe Jay			
☐ 264 Dick Ellsworth	3.50	1.55	.45
☐ 265 Joe Adcock	3.50	1.55	.45
☐ 266 John Anderson	3.00	1.35	.40
☐ 267 Dan Dobbek	3.00	1.35	.40
☐ 268 Ken McBride	3.00	1.35	.40
☐ 269 Bob Oldis	3.00	1.35	.40
☐ 270 Dick Groat	4.00	1.80	.50
☐ 271 Ray Rippelmeyer	3.00	1.35	.40
☐ 272 Earl Robinson	3.00	1.35	.40
☐ 273 Gary Bell	3.00	1.35	.40
☐ 274 Sammy Taylor	3.00	1.35	.40
☐ 275 Norm Siebern	3.00	1.35	.40
☐ 276 Hal Kolstad	3.00	1.35	.40
☐ 277 Checklist 4	10.00	1.50	.50
☐ 278 Ken Johnson	3.00	1.35	.40
☐ 279 Hobie Landrith UER	3.00	1.35	.40
(Wrong birthdate)			
☐ 280 Johnny Podres	3.50	1.55	.45

☐ 281 Jake Gibbs 3.50 1.55 .45
☐ 282 Dave Hillman 3.00 1.35 .40
☐ 283 Charlie Smith 3.00 1.35 .40
☐ 284 Ruben Amaro 3.50 1.55 .45
☐ 285 Curt Simmons 4.00 1.80 .50
☐ 286 Al Lopez MG 5.00 2.30 .60
☐ 287 George Witt 3.50 1.55 .45
☐ 288 Billy Williams 45.00 20.00 5.75
☐ 289 Mike Krsnich 3.50 1.55 .45
☐ 290 Jim Gentile 5.50 2.50 .70
☐ 291 Hal Stowe 3.50 1.55 .45
☐ 292 Jerry Kindall 3.50 1.55 .45
☐ 293 Bob Miller 3.50 1.55 .45
☐ 294 Phillies Team 7.00 3.10 .85
☐ 295 Vern Law 4.00 1.80 .50
☐ 296 Ken Hamlin 3.50 1.55 .45
☐ 297 Ron Perranoski 4.00 1.80 .50
☐ 298 Bill Tuttle 3.50 1.55 .45
☐ 299 Don Wert 3.50 1.55 .45
☐ 300 Willie Mays 150.00 70.00 19.00
☐ 301 Galen Cisco 5.00 2.30 .60
☐ 302 Johnny Edwards 3.50 1.55 .45
☐ 303 Frank Torre 4.00 1.80 .50
☐ 304 Dick Farrell 3.50 1.55 .45
☐ 305 Jerry Lumpe 3.50 1.55 .45
☐ 306 Redbird Rippers 4.00 1.80 .50
Lindy McDaniel
Larry Jackson
☐ 307 Jim Grant 4.00 1.80 .50
☐ 308 Neil Chrisley 3.50 1.55 .45
☐ 309 Moe Morhardt 3.50 1.55 .45
☐ 310 Whitey Ford 40.00 18.00 5.00
☐ 311 Tony Kubek IA 6.50 2.90 .80
☐ 312 Warren Spahn IA 10.00 4.50 1.25
☐ 313 Roger Maris IA 24.00 11.00 3.00
☐ 314 Rocky Colavito IA 6.00 2.70 .75
☐ 315 Whitey Ford IA 10.00 4.50 1.25
☐ 316 Harmon Killebrew IA 10.00 4.50 1.25
☐ 317 Stan Musial IA 20.00 9.00 2.50
☐ 318 Mickey Mantle IA 65.00 29.00 8.25
☐ 319 Mike McCormick IA 4.00 1.80 .50
☐ 320 Hank Aaron 150.00 70.00 19.00
☐ 321 Lee Stange 3.50 1.55 .45
☐ 322 Alvin Dark MG 4.00 1.80 .50
☐ 323 Don Landrum 3.50 1.55 .45
☐ 324 Joe McClain 3.50 1.55 .45
☐ 325 Luis Aparicio 15.00 6.75 1.90
☐ 326 Tom Parsons 3.50 1.55 .45
☐ 327 Ozzie Virgil 3.50 1.55 .45
☐ 328 Ken Walters 3.50 1.55 .45
☐ 329 Bob Bolin 3.50 1.55 .45
☐ 330 John Romano 3.50 1.55 .45
☐ 331 Moe Drabowsky 4.00 1.80 .50
☐ 332 Don Buddin 3.50 1.55 .45
☐ 333 Frank Cipriani 3.50 1.55 .45
☐ 334 Boston Red Sox 7.00 3.10 .85
Team Card
☐ 335 Bill Bruton 3.50 1.55 .45
☐ 336 Billy Muffett 3.50 1.55 .45
☐ 337 Jim Marshall 3.50 1.55 .45
☐ 338 Billy Gardner 3.50 1.55 .45
☐ 339 Jose Valdivielso 3.50 1.55 .45
☐ 340 Don Drysdale 40.00 18.00 5.00
☐ 341 Mike Hershberger 3.50 1.55 .45
☐ 342 Ed Rakow 3.50 1.55 .45
☐ 343 Albie Pearson 4.00 1.80 .50
☐ 344 Ed Bauta 3.50 1.55 .45
☐ 345 Chuck Schilling 3.50 1.55 .45
☐ 346 Jack Kralick 3.50 1.55 .45
☐ 347 Chuck Hinton 3.50 1.55 .45
☐ 348 Larry Burright 3.50 1.55 .45
☐ 349 Paul Foytack 3.50 1.55 .45
☐ 350 Frank Robinson 50.00 23.00 6.25
☐ 351 Braves' Backstops 6.00 2.70 .75
Joe Torre
Del Crandall
☐ 352 Frank Sullivan 3.50 1.55 .45
☐ 353 Bill Mazeroski 7.50 3.40 .95
☐ 354 Roman Mejias 3.50 1.55 .45
☐ 355 Steve Barber 3.50 1.55 .45
☐ 356 Tom Haller 5.00 2.30 .60
☐ 357 Jerry Walker 3.50 1.55 .45
☐ 358 Tommy Davis 6.50 2.90 .80
☐ 359 Bobby Locke 3.50 1.55 .45
☐ 360 Yogi Berra 80.00 36.00 10.00
☐ 361 Bob Hendley 3.50 1.55 .45
☐ 362 Ty Cline 3.50 1.55 .45
☐ 363 Bob Roselli 3.50 1.55 .45
☐ 364 Ken Hunt 3.50 1.55 .45
☐ 365 Charlie Neal 5.00 2.30 .60
☐ 366 Phil Regan 4.00 1.80 .50
☐ 367 Checklist 5 10.00 1.50 .50
☐ 368 Bob Tillman 3.50 1.55 .45
☐ 369 Ted Bowsfield 3.50 1.55 .45
☐ 370 Ken Boyer 7.00 3.10 .85
☐ 371 Earl Battey 5.50 2.50 .70
☐ 372 Jack Curtis 5.50 2.50 .70
☐ 373 Al Heist 5.50 2.50 .70
☐ 374 Gene Mauch MG 6.00 2.70 .75
☐ 375 Ron Fairly 6.00 2.70 .75
☐ 376 Bud Daley 5.50 2.50 .70
☐ 377 John Orsino 5.50 2.50 .70
☐ 378 Bennie Daniels 5.50 2.50 .70
☐ 379 Chuck Essegian 5.50 2.50 .70
☐ 380 Lou Burdette 6.50 2.90 .80
☐ 381 Chico Cardenas 6.00 2.70 .75
☐ 382 Dick Williams 6.00 2.70 .75
☐ 383 Ray Sadecki 5.50 2.50 .70
☐ 384 K.C. Athletics 10.00 4.50 1.25
Team Card
☐ 385 Early Wynn 20.00 9.00 2.50
☐ 386 Don Mincher 6.00 2.70 .75
☐ 387 Lou Brock 250.00 115.00 31.00
☐ 388 Ryne Duren 7.00 3.10 .85
☐ 389 Smoky Burgess 6.00 2.70 .75
☐ 390 Orlando Cepeda AS 8.00 3.60 1.00
☐ 391 Bill Mazeroski AS 8.00 3.60 1.00
☐ 392 Ken Boyer AS 8.00 3.60 1.00
☐ 393 Roy McMillan AS 6.00 2.70 .75
☐ 394 Hank Aaron AS 45.00 20.00 5.75
☐ 395 Willie Mays AS 45.00 20.00 5.75
☐ 396 Frank Robinson AS 15.00 6.75 1.90
☐ 397 John Roseboro AS 6.00 2.70 .75
☐ 398 Don Drysdale AS 15.00 6.75 1.90
☐ 399 Warren Spahn AS 15.00 6.75 1.90
☐ 400 Elston Howard 10.00 4.50 1.25
☐ 401 AL/NL Homer Kings 40.00 18.00 5.00
Roger Maris
Orlando Cepeda
☐ 402 Gino Cimoli 5.50 2.50 .70
☐ 403 Chet Nichols 5.50 2.50 .70
☐ 404 Tim Harkness 5.50 2.50 .70
☐ 405 Jim Perry 7.00 3.10 .85
☐ 406 Bob Taylor 5.50 2.50 .70
☐ 407 Hank Aguirre 5.50 2.50 .70
☐ 408 Gus Bell 6.00 2.70 .75
☐ 409 Pittsburgh Pirates 10.00 4.50 1.25
Team Card
☐ 410 Al Smith 5.50 2.50 .70
☐ 411 Danny O'Connell 5.50 2.50 .70
☐ 412 Charlie James 5.50 2.50 .70
☐ 413 Matty Alou 6.50 2.90 .80
☐ 414 Joe Gaines 5.50 2.50 .70
☐ 415 Bill Virdon 6.00 2.70 .75
☐ 416 Bob Scheffing MG 5.50 2.50 .70
☐ 417 Joe Azcue 5.50 2.50 .70
☐ 418 Andy Carey 5.50 2.50 .70
☐ 419 Bob Bruce 5.50 2.50 .70
☐ 420 Gus Triandos 6.00 2.70 .75
☐ 421 Ken MacKenzie 5.50 2.50 .70
☐ 422 Steve Bilko 5.50 2.50 .70
☐ 423 Rival League 7.00 3.10 .85
Relief Aces:
Roy Face
Hoyt Wilhelm
☐ 424 Al McBean 6.00 2.70 .75
☐ 425 Carl Yastrzemski 225.00 100.00 28.00
☐ 426 Bob Farley 5.50 2.50 .70
☐ 427 Jake Wood 5.50 2.50 .70
☐ 428 Joe Hicks 5.50 2.50 .70
☐ 429 Billy O'Dell 5.50 2.50 .70
☐ 430 Tony Kubek 10.00 4.50 1.25
☐ 431 Bob Rodgers 8.00 3.60 1.00
☐ 432 Jim Pendleton 5.50 2.50 .70
☐ 433 Jim Archer 5.50 2.50 .70
☐ 434 Clay Dalrymple 5.50 2.50 .70
☐ 435 Larry Sherry 6.00 2.70 .75
☐ 436 Felix Mantilla 5.50 2.50 .70
☐ 437 Ray Moore 5.50 2.50 .70
☐ 438 Dick Brown 5.50 2.50 .70
☐ 439 Jerry Buchek 5.50 2.50 .70
☐ 440 Joey Jay 5.50 2.50 .70
☐ 441 Checklist 6 15.00 2.30 .75
☐ 442 Wes Stock 5.50 2.50 .70
☐ 443 Del Crandall 6.00 2.70 .75
☐ 444 Ted Wills 5.50 2.50 .70
☐ 445 Vic Power 6.00 2.70 .75
☐ 446 Don Elston 5.50 2.50 .70
☐ 447 Willie Kirkland 7.00 3.10 .85
☐ 448 Joe Gibbon 7.00 3.10 .85
☐ 449 Jerry Adair 7.00 3.10 .85
☐ 450 Jim O'Toole 8.00 3.60 1.00
☐ 451 Jose Tartabull 8.50 3.80 1.05
☐ 452 Earl Averill Jr. 7.00 3.10 .85
☐ 453 Cal McLish 7.00 3.10 .85
☐ 454 Floyd Robinson 7.00 3.10 .85

☐ 455 Luis Arroyo 8.00 3.60 1.00
☐ 456 Joe Amalfitano 7.00 3.10 .85
☐ 457 Lou Clinton 7.00 3.10 .85
☐ 458A Bob Buhl 8.00 3.60 1.00
(Braves emblem
on cap)
☐ 458B Bob Buhl 50.00 23.00 6.25
(No emblem on cap)
☐ 459 Ed Bailey 7.00 3.10 .85
☐ 460 Jim Bunning 11.00 4.90 1.40
☐ 461 Ken Hubbs 25.00 11.50 3.10
☐ 462A Willie Tasby 7.00 3.10 .85
(Senators emblem
on cap)
☐ 462B Willie Tasby 50.00 23.00 6.25
(No emblem on cap)
☐ 463 Hank Bauer MG 8.00 3.60 1.00
☐ 464 Al Jackson 9.00 4.00 1.15
☐ 465 Reds Team 14.00 6.25 1.75
☐ 466 Norm Cash AS 9.00 4.00 1.15
☐ 467 Chuck Schilling AS 7.50 3.40 .95
☐ 468 Brooks Robinson AS 18.00 8.00 2.30
☐ 469 Luis Aparicio AS 11.00 4.90 1.40
☐ 470 Al Kaline AS 20.00 9.00 2.50
☐ 471 Mickey Mantle AS 150.00 70.00 19.00
☐ 472 Rocky Colavito AS 10.00 4.50 1.25
☐ 473 Elston Howard AS 9.00 4.00 1.15
☐ 474 Frank Lary AS 7.50 3.40 .95
☐ 475 Whitey Ford AS 15.00 6.75 1.90
☐ 476 Orioles Team 14.00 6.25 1.75
☐ 477 Andre Rodgers 7.00 3.10 .85
☐ 478 Don Zimmer 8.50 3.80 1.05
(Shown with Mets cap,
but listed as with
Cincinnati)
☐ 479 Joel Horlen 9.00 4.00 1.15
☐ 480 Harvey Kuenn 8.50 3.80 1.05
☐ 481 Vic Wertz 8.00 3.60 1.00
☐ 482 Sam Mele MG 7.00 3.10 .85
☐ 483 Don McMahon 7.00 3.10 .85
☐ 484 Dick Schofield 7.00 3.10 .85
☐ 485 Pedro Ramos 7.00 3.10 .85
☐ 486 Jim Gilliam 9.00 4.00 1.15
☐ 487 Jerry Lynch 7.00 3.10 .85
☐ 488 Hal Brown 7.00 3.10 .85
☐ 489 Julio Gotay 7.00 3.10 .85
☐ 490 Clete Boyer 9.00 4.00 1.15
☐ 491 Leon Wagner 7.00 3.10 .85
☐ 492 Hal W. Smith 7.00 3.10 .85
☐ 493 Danny McDevitt 7.00 3.10 .85
☐ 494 Sammy White 7.00 3.10 .85
☐ 495 Don Cardwell 7.00 3.10 .85
☐ 496 Wayne Causey 7.00 3.10 .85
☐ 497 Ed Bouchee 7.00 3.10 .85
☐ 498 Jim Donohue 7.00 3.10 .85
☐ 499 Zoilo Versalles 7.50 3.40 .95
☐ 500 Duke Snider 55.00 25.00 7.00
☐ 501 Claude Osteen 7.50 3.40 .95
☐ 502 Hector Lopez 7.50 3.40 .95
☐ 503 Danny Murtaugh MG 7.50 3.40 .95
☐ 504 Eddie Bressoud 7.00 3.10 .85
☐ 505 Juan Marichal 45.00 20.00 5.75
☐ 506 Charlie Maxwell 7.50 3.40 .95
☐ 507 Ernie Broglio 7.50 3.40 .95
☐ 508 Gordy Coleman 7.50 3.40 .95
☐ 509 Dave Giusti 9.00 4.00 1.15
☐ 510 Jim Lemon 7.00 3.10 .85
☐ 511 Bubba Phillips 7.00 3.10 .85
☐ 512 Mike Fornieles 7.00 3.10 .85
☐ 513 Whitey Herzog 8.50 3.80 1.05
☐ 514 Sherm Lollar 7.50 3.40 .95
☐ 515 Stan Williams 7.50 3.40 .95
☐ 516 Checklist 7 15.00 2.30 .75
☐ 517 Dave Wickersham 7.00 3.10 .85
☐ 518 Lee Maye 7.00 3.10 .85
☐ 519 Bob Johnson 7.00 3.10 .85
☐ 520 Bob Friend 8.00 3.60 1.00
☐ 521 Jacke Davis UER 7.00 3.10 .85
(Listed as OF on
front and P on back)
☐ 522 Lindy McDaniel 8.00 3.60 1.00
☐ 523 Russ Nixon SP 26.00 11.50 3.30
☐ 524 Howie Nunn SP 26.00 11.50 3.30
☐ 525 George Thomas 15.00 6.75 1.90
☐ 526 Hal Woodeshick SP 26.00 11.50 3.30
☐ 527 Dick McAuliffe 20.00 9.00 2.50
☐ 528 Turk Lown 15.00 6.75 1.90
☐ 529 John Schaive SP 26.00 11.50 3.30
☐ 530 Bob Gibson SP 175.00 80.00 22.00
☐ 531 Bobby G. Smith 15.00 6.75 1.90
☐ 532 Dick Stigman 15.00 6.75 1.90
☐ 533 Charley Lau SP 27.00 12.00 3.40
☐ 534 Tony Gonzalez SP 26.00 11.50 3.30
☐ 535 Ed Roebuck 15.00 6.75 1.90
☐ 536 Dick Gernert 15.00 6.75 1.90
☐ 537 Cleveland Indians 42.50 19.00 5.25
Team Card
☐ 538 Jack Sanford 16.00 7.25 2.00
☐ 539 Billy Moran 15.00 6.75 1.90
☐ 540 Jim Landis SP 26.00 11.50 3.30
☐ 541 Don Nottebart SP 26.00 11.50 3.30
☐ 542 Dave Philley 15.00 6.75 1.90
☐ 543 Bob Allen SP 26.00 11.50 3.30
☐ 544 Willie McCovey SP 175.00 80.00 22.00
☐ 545 Hoyt Wilhelm SP 55.00 25.00 7.00
☐ 546 Moe Thacker SP 26.00 11.50 3.30
☐ 547 Don Ferrarese 15.00 6.75 1.90
☐ 548 Bobby Del Greco 15.00 6.75 1.90
☐ 549 Bill Rigney MG SP 26.00 11.50 3.30
☐ 550 Art Mahaffey SP 26.00 11.50 3.30
☐ 551 Harry Bright 15.00 6.75 1.90
☐ 552 Chicago Cubs SP 50.00 23.00 6.25
Team Card
☐ 553 Jim Coates 15.00 6.75 1.90
☐ 554 Bubba Morton SP 26.00 11.50 3.30
☐ 555 John Buzhardt SP 26.00 11.50 3.30
☐ 556 Al Spangler 15.00 6.75 1.90
☐ 557 Bob Anderson SP 26.00 11.50 3.30
☐ 558 John Goryl 15.00 6.75 1.90
☐ 559 Mike Higgins MG 15.00 6.75 1.90
☐ 560 Chuck Estrada SP 26.00 11.50 3.30
☐ 561 Gene Oliver SP 26.00 11.50 3.30
☐ 562 Bill Henry 15.00 6.75 1.90
☐ 563 Ken Aspromonte 15.00 6.75 1.90
☐ 564 Bob Grim 15.00 6.75 1.90
☐ 565 Jose Pagan 15.00 6.75 1.90
☐ 566 Marty Kutyna SP 26.00 11.50 3.30
☐ 567 Tracy Stallard SP 26.00 11.50 3.30
☐ 568 Jim Golden 15.00 6.75 1.90
☐ 569 Ed Sadowski SP 26.00 11.50 3.30
☐ 570 Bill Stafford SP 30.00 13.50 3.80
☐ 571 Billy Klaus SP 26.00 11.50 3.30
☐ 572 Bob G. Miller SP 30.00 13.50 3.80
☐ 573 Johnny Logan 16.00 7.25 2.00
☐ 574 Dean Stone 15.00 6.75 1.90
☐ 575 Red Schoendienst SP 50.00 23.00 6.25
☐ 576 Russ Kemmerer SP 26.00 11.50 3.30
☐ 577 Dave Nicholson SP 26.00 11.50 3.30
☐ 578 Jim Duffalo 15.00 6.75 1.90
☐ 579 Jim Schaffer SP 26.00 11.50 3.30
☐ 580 Bill Monbouquette 15.00 6.75 1.90
☐ 581 Mel Roach 15.00 6.75 1.90
☐ 582 Ron Piche 15.00 6.75 1.90
☐ 583 Larry Osborne 15.00 6.75 1.90
☐ 584 Minnesota Twins SP 50.00 23.00 6.25
Team Card
☐ 585 Glen Hobbie SP 26.00 11.50 3.30
☐ 586 Sammy Esposito SP 26.00 11.50 3.30
☐ 587 Frank Funk SP 26.00 11.50 3.30
☐ 588 Birdie Tebbetts MG 17.50 8.00 2.20
☐ 589 Bob Turley 16.00 7.25 2.00
☐ 590 Curt Flood 20.00 9.00 2.50
☐ 591 Rookie Pitchers SP 60.00 27.00 7.50
Sam McDowell
Ron Taylor
Ron Nischwitz
Art Quirk
Dick Radatz
☐ 592 Rookie Pitchers SP 75.00 34.00 9.50
Dan Pfister
Bo Belinsky
Dave Stenhouse
Jim Bouton
Joe Bonikowski
☐ 593 Rookie Pitchers SP 33.00 15.00 4.10
Jack Lamabe
Craig Anderson
Jack Hamilton
Bob Moorhead
Bob Veale
☐ 594 Rookie Catchers SP 100.00 45.00 12.50
Doc Edwards
Ken Retzer
Bob Uecker
Doug Camilli
Don Pavletich
☐ 595 Rookie Infielders SP 33.00 15.00 4.10
Bob Sadowski
Felix Torres
Marlan Coughtry
Ed Charles
☐ 596 Rookie Infielders SP 65.00 29.00 8.25
Bernie Allen
Joe Pepitone
Phil Linz
Rich Rollins

☐ 597 Rookie Infielders SP........... 40.00 18.00 5.00
Jim McKnight
Rod Kanehl
Amado Samuel
Denis Menke
☐ 598 Rookie Outfielders SP........ 75.00 34.00 9.50
Al Luplow
Manny Jimenez
Howie Goss
Jim Hickman
Ed Olivares

1963 Topps

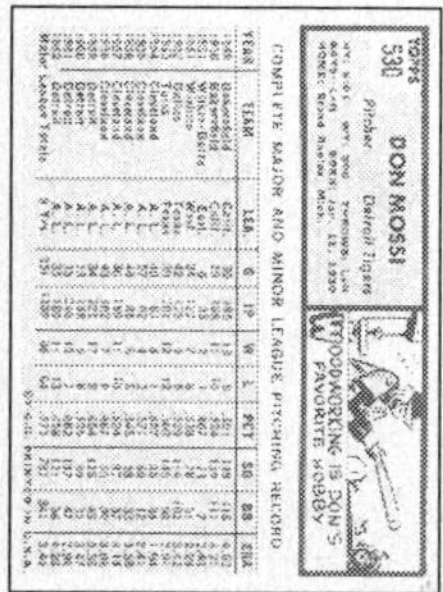

The cards in this 576-card set measure 2 1/2" by 3 1/2". The sharp color photographs of the 1963 set are a vivid contrast to the drab pictures of 1962. In addition to the "League Leaders" series (1-10) and World Series cards (142-148), the seventh and last series of cards (523-576) contains seven Rookie Cards (each depicting four players). There were some three-card advertising panels produced by Topps; the players included are from the first series; one panel shows Hoyt Wilhelm, Don Lock, and Bob Duliba on the front with a Stan Musial ad/endorsement on one of the backs. This set has gained special prominence in recent years since it contains the Rookie Card of Pete Rose (537). Other key rookies in this set are Tony Oliva, Willie Stargell, and Rusty Staub.

	NRMT	VG-E	GOOD
COMPLETE SET (576)........................	5300.00	2400.00	650.00
COMMON PLAYER (1-109)..............	2.00	.90	.25
COMMON PLAYER (110-196)..........	2.25	1.00	.30
COMMON PLAYER (197-283)..........	3.00	1.35	.40
COMMON PLAYER (284-370)..........	4.00	1.80	.50
COMMON PLAYER (371-446)..........	4.50	2.00	.55
COMMON PLAYER (447-522)..........	14.00	6.25	1.75
COMMON PLAYER (523-576)..........	10.00	4.50	1.25

☐ 1 NL Batting Leaders................. 36.00 7.25 2.20
Tommy Davis
Frank Robinson
Stan Musial
Hank Aaron
Bill White
☐ 2 AL Batting Leaders................. 20.00 9.00 2.50
Pete Runnels
Mickey Mantle
Floyd Robinson
Norm Siebern
Chuck Hinton
☐ 3 NL Home Run Leaders........... 20.00 9.00 2.50
Willie Mays
Hank Aaron
Frank Robinson
Orlando Cepeda
Ernie Banks
☐ 4 AL Home Run Leaders........... 7.50 3.40 .95
Harmon Killebrew
Norm Cash
Rocky Colavito
Roger Maris
Jim Gentile
Leon Wagner
☐ 5 NL ERA Leaders...................... 8.00 3.60 1.00
Sandy Koufax
Bob Shaw
Bob Purkey
Bob Gibson
Don Drysdale
☐ 6 AL ERA Leaders...................... 5.00 2.30 .60
Hank Aguirre
Robin Roberts
Whitey Ford
Eddie Fisher
Dean Chance
☐ 7 NL Pitching Leaders............... 5.00 2.30 .60
Don Drysdale
Jack Sanford
Bob Purkey
Billy O'Dell
Art Mahaffey
Joe Jay
☐ 8 AL Pitching Leaders............... 4.50 2.00 .55
Ralph Terry
Dick Donovan
Ray Herbert
Jim Bunning
Camilo Pascual
☐ 9 NL Strikeout Leaders............. 8.00 3.60 1.00
Don Drysdale
Sandy Koufax
Bob Gibson
Billy O'Dell
Dick Farrell
☐ 10 AL Strikeout Leaders............ 4.50 2.00 .55
Camilo Pascual
Jim Bunning
Ralph Terry
Juan Pizarro
Jim Kaat
☐ 11 Lee Walls............................. 2.00 .90 .25
☐ 12 Steve Barber......................... 2.00 .90 .25
☐ 13 Philadelphia Phillies............. 4.50 2.00 .55
Team Card
☐ 14 Pedro Ramos......................... 2.00 .90 .25
☐ 15 Ken Hubbs UER..................... 3.50 1.55 .45
(No position listed
on front of card)
☐ 16 Al Smith................................ 2.00 .90 .25
☐ 17 Ryne Duren........................... 2.50 1.15 .30
☐ 18 Buc Blasters.......................... 15.00 6.75 1.90
Smoky Burgess
Dick Stuart
Bob Clemente
Bob Skinner
☐ 19 Pete Burnside........................ 2.00 .90 .25
☐ 20 Tony Kubek........................... 4.50 2.00 .55
☐ 21 Marty Keough........................ 2.00 .90 .25
☐ 22 Curt Simmons........................ 2.50 1.15 .30
☐ 23 Ed Lopat MG.......................... 2.50 1.15 .30
☐ 24 Bob Bruce.............................. 2.00 .90 .25
☐ 25 Al Kaline................................ 35.00 16.00 4.40
☐ 26 Ray Moore............................. 2.00 .90 .25
☐ 27 Choo Choo Coleman.............. 2.00 .90 .25
☐ 28 Mike Fornieles....................... 2.00 .90 .25
☐ 29A 1962 Rookie Stars.............. 5.50 2.50 .70
Sammy Ellis
Ray Culp
John Boozer
Jesse Gonder
☐ 29B 1963 Rookie Stars.............. 3.25 1.45 .40
Sammy Ellis
Ray Culp
John Boozer
Jesse Gonder
☐ 30 Harvey Kuenn........................ 2.50 1.15 .30
☐ 31 Cal Koonce............................ 2.00 .90 .25
☐ 32 Tony Gonzalez....................... 2.00 .90 .25
☐ 33 Bo Belinsky........................... 2.50 1.15 .30
☐ 34 Dick Schofield....................... 2.00 .90 .25
☐ 35 John Buzhardt........................ 2.00 .90 .25
☐ 36 Jerry Kindall.......................... 2.00 .90 .25
☐ 37 Jerry Lynch............................ 2.00 .90 .25
☐ 38 Bud Daley.............................. 2.00 .90 .25
☐ 39 Angels Team......................... 4.50 2.00 .55
☐ 40 Vic Power.............................. 2.50 1.15 .30
☐ 41 Charley Lau........................... 2.50 1.15 .30
☐ 42 Stan Williams......................... 2.50 1.15 .30
(Listed as Yankee on
card but LA cap)
☐ 43 Veteran Masters..................... 4.00 1.80 .50
Casey Stengel MG
Gene Woodling
☐ 44 Terry Fox............................... 2.00 .90 .25
☐ 45 Bob Aspromonte..................... 2.00 .90 .25
☐ 46 Tommie Aaron....................... 3.25 1.45 .40
☐ 47 Don Lock................................ 2.00 .90 .25
☐ 48 Birdie Tebbetts MG................ 2.50 1.15 .30

☐ 49 Dal Maxvill	3.25	1.45	.40
☐ 50 Billy Pierce	2.50	1.15	.30
☐ 51 George Alusik	2.00	.90	.25
☐ 52 Chuck Schilling	2.00	.90	.25
☐ 53 Joe Moeller	2.00	.90	.25
☐ 54A 1962 Rookie Stars	14.00	6.25	1.75
Nelson Mathews			
Harry Fanok			
Jack Cullen			
Dave DeBusschere			
☐ 54B 1963 Rookie Stars	6.00	2.70	.75
Nelson Mathews			
Harry Fanok			
Jack Cullen			
Dave DeBusschere			
☐ 55 Bill Virdon	2.50	1.15	.30
☐ 56 Dennis Bennett	2.00	.90	.25
☐ 57 Billy Moran	2.00	.90	.25
☐ 58 Bob Will	2.00	.90	.25
☐ 59 Craig Anderson	2.00	.90	.25
☐ 60 Elston Howard	6.00	2.70	.75
☐ 61 Ernie Bowman	2.00	.90	.25
☐ 62 Bob Hendley	2.00	.90	.25
☐ 63 Reds Team	4.50	2.00	.55
☐ 64 Dick McAuliffe	2.50	1.15	.30
☐ 65 Jackie Brandt	2.00	.90	.25
☐ 66 Mike Joyce	2.00	.90	.25
☐ 67 Ed Charles	2.00	.90	.25
☐ 68 Friendly Foes	11.00	4.90	1.40
Duke Snider			
Gil Hodges			
☐ 69 Bud Zipfel	2.00	.90	.25
☐ 70 Jim O'Toole	2.50	1.15	.30
☐ 71 Bobby Wine	2.50	1.15	.30
☐ 72 Johnny Romano	2.00	.90	.25
☐ 73 Bobby Bragan MG	3.00	1.35	.40
☐ 74 Denny Lemaster	2.00	.90	.25
☐ 75 Bob Allison	2.50	1.15	.30
☐ 76 Earl Wilson	2.50	1.15	.30
☐ 77 Al Spangler	2.00	.90	.25
☐ 78 Marv Throneberry	3.00	1.35	.40
☐ 79 Checklist 1	10.00	1.50	.50
☐ 80 Jim Gilliam	3.50	1.55	.45
☐ 81 Jim Schaffer	2.00	.90	.25
☐ 82 Ed Rakow	2.00	.90	.25
☐ 83 Charley James	2.00	.90	.25
☐ 84 Ron Kline	2.00	.90	.25
☐ 85 Tom Haller	2.50	1.15	.30
☐ 86 Charley Maxwell	2.50	1.15	.30
☐ 87 Bob Veale	2.50	1.15	.30
☐ 88 Ron Hansen	2.00	.90	.25
☐ 89 Dick Stigman	2.00	.90	.25
☐ 90 Gordy Coleman	2.50	1.15	.30
☐ 91 Dallas Green	2.50	1.15	.30
☐ 92 Hector Lopez	2.50	1.15	.30
☐ 93 Galen Cisco	2.00	.90	.25
☐ 94 Bob Schmidt	2.00	.90	.25
☐ 95 Larry Jackson	2.00	.90	.25
☐ 96 Lou Clinton	2.00	.90	.25
☐ 97 Bob Duliba	2.00	.90	.25
☐ 98 George Thomas	2.00	.90	.25
☐ 99 Jim Umbricht	2.00	.90	.25
☐ 100 Joe Cunningham	2.00	.90	.25
☐ 101 Joe Gibbon	2.00	.90	.25
☐ 102A Checklist 2	10.00	1.50	.50
(Red on yellow)			
☐ 102B Checklist 2	10.00	1.50	.50
(White on red)			
☐ 103 Chuck Essegian	2.00	.90	.25
☐ 104 Lew Krausse	2.00	.90	.25
☐ 105 Ron Fairly	2.50	1.15	.30
☐ 106 Bobby Bolin	2.00	.90	.25
☐ 107 Jim Hickman	2.50	1.15	.30
☐ 108 Hoyt Wilhelm	10.50	4.70	1.30
☐ 109 Lee Maye	2.00	.90	.25
☐ 110 Rich Rollins	2.75	1.25	.35
☐ 111 Al Jackson	2.25	1.00	.30
☐ 112 Dick Brown	2.25	1.00	.30
☐ 113 Don Landrum UER	2.25	1.00	.30
(Photo actually			
Ron Santo)			
☐ 114 Dan Osinski	2.25	1.00	.30
☐ 115 Carl Yastrzemski	65.00	29.00	8.25
☐ 116 Jim Brosnan	2.75	1.25	.35
☐ 117 Jacke Davis	2.25	1.00	.30
☐ 118 Sherm Lollar	2.25	1.00	.30
☐ 119 Bob Lillis	2.25	1.00	.30
☐ 120 Roger Maris	65.00	29.00	8.25
☐ 121 Jim Hannan	2.25	1.00	.30
☐ 122 Julio Gotay	2.25	1.00	.30
☐ 123 Frank Howard	3.50	1.55	.45
☐ 124 Dick Howser	2.75	1.25	.35
☐ 125 Robin Roberts	11.00	4.90	1.40

☐ 126 Bob Uecker	25.00	11.50	3.10
☐ 127 Bill Tuttle	2.25	1.00	.30
☐ 128 Matty Alou	2.75	1.25	.35
☐ 129 Gary Bell	2.25	1.00	.30
☐ 130 Dick Groat	3.25	1.45	.40
☐ 131 Washington Senators	4.50	2.00	.55
Team Card			
☐ 132 Jack Hamilton	2.25	1.00	.30
☐ 133 Gene Freese	2.25	1.00	.30
☐ 134 Bob Scheffing MG	2.25	1.00	.30
☐ 135 Richie Ashburn	9.50	4.30	1.20
☐ 136 Ike Delock	2.25	1.00	.30
☐ 137 Mack Jones	2.25	1.00	.30
☐ 138 Pride of NL	36.00	16.00	4.50
Willie Mays			
Stan Musial			
☐ 139 Earl Averill	2.25	1.00	.30
☐ 140 Frank Lary	2.75	1.25	.35
☐ 141 Manny Mota	6.50	2.90	.80
☐ 142 World Series Game 1	7.00	3.10	.85
Whitey Ford wins			
series opener			
☐ 143 World Series Game 2	5.00	2.30	.60
Jack Sanford flashes			
shutout magic			
☐ 144 World Series Game 3	11.00	4.90	1.40
Roger Maris sparks			
Yankee rally			
☐ 145 World Series Game 4	5.00	2.30	.60
Chuck Hiller blasts			
grand slammer			
☐ 146 World Series Game 5	5.00	2.30	.60
Tom Tresh's homer			
defeats Giants			
☐ 147 World Series Game 6	5.00	2.30	.60
Billy Pierce stars in			
3 hit victory			
☐ 148 World Series Game 7	5.00	2.30	.60
Yanks celebrate			
as Ralph Terry wins			
☐ 149 Marv Breeding	2.25	1.00	.30
☐ 150 Johnny Podres	2.75	1.25	.35
☐ 151 Pirates Team	4.50	2.00	.55
☐ 152 Ron Nischwitz	2.25	1.00	.30
☐ 153 Hal Smith	2.25	1.00	.30
☐ 154 Walt Alston MG	4.50	2.00	.55
☐ 155 Bill Stafford	2.25	1.00	.30
☐ 156 Roy McMillan	2.75	1.25	.35
☐ 157 Diego Segui	2.25	1.00	.30
☐ 158 Rookie Stars	4.00	1.80	.50
Rogelio Alvares			
Dave Roberts			
Tommy Harper			
Bob Saverine			
☐ 159 Jim Pagliaroni	2.25	1.00	.30
☐ 160 Juan Pizarro	2.25	1.00	.30
☐ 161 Frank Torre	2.75	1.25	.35
☐ 162 Twins Team	4.50	2.00	.55
☐ 163 Don Larsen	2.75	1.25	.35
☐ 164 Bubba Morton	2.25	1.00	.30
☐ 165 Jim Kaat	5.25	2.40	.65
☐ 166 Johnny Keane MG	2.25	1.00	.30
☐ 167 Jim Fregosi	4.00	1.80	.50
☐ 168 Russ Nixon	2.25	1.00	.30
☐ 169 Rookie Stars	35.00	16.00	4.40
Dick Egan			
Julio Navarro			
Tommie Sisk			
Gaylord Perry			
☐ 170 Joe Adcock	3.50	1.55	.45
☐ 171 Steve Hamilton	2.25	1.00	.30
☐ 172 Gene Oliver	2.25	1.00	.30
☐ 173 Bombers' Best	80.00	36.00	10.00
Tom Tresh			
Mickey Mantle			
Bobby Richardson			
☐ 174 Larry Burright	2.25	1.00	.30
☐ 175 Bob Buhl	2.75	1.25	.35
☐ 176 Jim King	2.25	1.00	.30
☐ 177 Bubba Phillips	2.25	1.00	.30
☐ 178 Johnny Edwards	2.25	1.00	.30
☐ 179 Ron Piche	2.25	1.00	.30
☐ 180 Bill Skowron	4.00	1.80	.50
☐ 181 Sammy Esposito	2.25	1.00	.30
☐ 182 Albie Pearson	2.75	1.25	.35
☐ 183 Joe Pepitone	4.00	1.80	.50
☐ 184 Vern Law	2.75	1.25	.35
☐ 185 Chuck Hiller	2.25	1.00	.30
☐ 186 Jerry Zimmerman	2.25	1.00	.30
☐ 187 Willie Kirkland	2.25	1.00	.30
☐ 188 Eddie Bressoud	2.25	1.00	.30
☐ 189 Dave Giusti	2.75	1.25	.35
☐ 190 Minnie Minoso	4.00	1.80	.50

☐ 191 Checklist 3 .... 10.00 1.50 .50
☐ 192 Clay Dalrymple .... 2.25 1.00 .30
☐ 193 Andre Rodgers .... 2.25 1.00 .30
☐ 194 Joe Nuxhall .... 2.75 1.25 .35
☐ 195 Manny Jimenez .... 2.25 1.00 .30
☐ 196 Doug Camilli .... 2.25 1.00 .30
☐ 197 Roger Craig .... 4.00 1.80 .50
☐ 198 Lenny Green .... 3.00 1.35 .40
☐ 199 Joe Amalfitano .... 3.00 1.35 .40
☐ 200 Mickey Mantle 450.00 200.00 57.50
☐ 201 Cecil Butler .... 3.00 1.35 .40
☐ 202 Boston Red Sox .... 6.00 2.70 .75
Team Card
☐ 203 Chico Cardenas .... 3.50 1.55 .45
☐ 204 Don Nottebart .... 3.00 1.35 .40
☐ 205 Luis Aparicio 15.00 6.75 1.90
☐ 206 Ray Washburn .... 3.00 1.35 .40
☐ 207 Ken Hunt .... 3.00 1.35 .40
☐ 208 Rookie Stars .... 3.00 1.35 .40
Ron Herbel
John Miller
Wally Wolf
Ron Taylor
☐ 209 Hobie Landrith .... 3.00 1.35 .40
☐ 210 Sandy Koufax 175.00 80.00 22.00
☐ 211 Fred Whitfield .... 3.00 1.35 .40
☐ 212 Glen Hobbie .... 3.00 1.35 .40
☐ 213 Billy Hitchcock MG .... 3.00 1.35 .40
☐ 214 Orlando Pena .... 3.00 1.35 .40
☐ 215 Bob Skinner .... 3.50 1.55 .45
☐ 216 Gene Conley .... 3.50 1.55 .45
☐ 217 Joe Christopher .... 3.00 1.35 .40
☐ 218 Tiger Twirlers .... 3.50 1.55 .45
Frank Lary
Don Mossi
Jim Bunning
☐ 219 Chuck Cottier .... 3.00 1.35 .40
☐ 220 Camilo Pascual .... 3.50 1.55 .45
☐ 221 Cookie Rojas .... 4.50 2.00 .55
☐ 222 Cubs Team .... 6.00 2.70 .75
☐ 223 Eddie Fisher .... 3.00 1.35 .40
☐ 224 Mike Roarke .... 3.00 1.35 .40
☐ 225 Joey Jay .... 3.00 1.35 .40
☐ 226 Julian Javier .... 3.50 1.55 .45
☐ 227 Jim Grant .... 3.50 1.55 .45
☐ 228 Rookie Stars 55.00 25.00 7.00
Max Alvis
Bob Bailey
Tony Oliva
(Listed as Pedro)
Ed Kranepool
☐ 229 Willie Davis .... 3.50 1.55 .45
☐ 230 Pete Runnels .... 3.50 1.55 .45
☐ 231 Eli Grba UER .... 3.00 1.35 .40
(Large photo is
Ryne Duren)
☐ 232 Frank Malzone .... 3.50 1.55 .45
☐ 233 Casey Stengel MG 17.00 7.75 2.10
☐ 234 Dave Nicholson .... 3.00 1.35 .40
☐ 235 Billy O'Dell .... 3.00 1.35 .40
☐ 236 Bill Bryan .... 3.00 1.35 .40
☐ 237 Jim Coates .... 3.00 1.35 .40
☐ 238 Lou Johnson .... 3.50 1.55 .45
☐ 239 Harvey Haddix .... 3.50 1.55 .45
☐ 240 Rocky Colavito 10.00 4.50 1.25
☐ 241 Bob Smith .... 3.00 1.35 .40
☐ 242 Power Plus 35.00 16.00 4.40
Ernie Banks
Hank Aaron
☐ 243 Don Leppert .... 3.00 1.35 .40
☐ 244 John Tsitouris .... 3.00 1.35 .40
☐ 245 Gil Hodges 20.00 9.00 2.50
☐ 246 Lee Stange .... 3.00 1.35 .40
☐ 247 Yankees Team 20.00 9.00 2.50
☐ 248 Tito Francona .... 3.00 1.35 .40
☐ 249 Leo Burke .... 3.00 1.35 .40
☐ 250 Stan Musial 125.00 57.50 15.50
☐ 251 Jack Lamabe .... 3.00 1.35 .40
☐ 252 Ron Santo .... 7.50 3.40 .95
☐ 253 Rookie Stars .... 3.50 1.55 .45
Len Gabrielson
Pete Jernigan
John Wojcik
Deacon Jones
☐ 254 Mike Hershberger .... 3.00 1.35 .40
☐ 255 Bob Shaw .... 3.00 1.35 .40
☐ 256 Jerry Lumpe .... 3.00 1.35 .40
☐ 257 Hank Aguirre .... 3.00 1.35 .40
☐ 258 Alvin Dark MG .... 3.50 1.55 .45
☐ 259 Johnny Logan .... 3.50 1.55 .45
☐ 260 Jim Gentile .... 3.50 1.55 .45
☐ 261 Bob Miller .... 3.00 1.35 .40
☐ 262 Ellis Burton .... 3.00 1.35 .40
☐ 263 Dave Stenhouse .... 3.00 1.35 .40
☐ 264 Phil Linz .... 3.50 1.55 .45
☐ 265 Vada Pinson .... 5.00 2.30 .60
☐ 266 Bob Allen .... 3.00 1.35 .40
☐ 267 Carl Sawatski .... 3.00 1.35 .40
☐ 268 Don Demeter .... 3.00 1.35 .40
☐ 269 Don Mincher .... 3.00 1.35 .40
☐ 270 Felipe Alou .... 5.00 2.30 .60
☐ 271 Dean Stone .... 3.00 1.35 .40
☐ 272 Danny Murphy .... 3.00 1.35 .40
☐ 273 Sammy Taylor .... 3.00 1.35 .40
☐ 274 Checklist 4 .... 10.00 1.50 .50
☐ 275 Eddie Mathews 20.00 9.00 2.50
☐ 276 Barry Shetrone .... 3.00 1.35 .40
☐ 277 Dick Farrell .... 3.00 1.35 .40
☐ 278 Chico Fernandez .... 3.00 1.35 .40
☐ 279 Wally Moon .... 3.50 1.55 .45
☐ 280 Bob Rodgers .... 5.00 2.30 .60
☐ 281 Tom Sturdivant .... 3.00 1.35 .40
☐ 282 Bobby Del Greco .... 3.00 1.35 .40
☐ 283 Roy Sievers .... 3.50 1.55 .45
☐ 284 Dave Sisler .... 4.00 1.80 .50
☐ 285 Dick Stuart .... 4.50 2.00 .55
☐ 286 Stu Miller .... 4.50 2.00 .55
☐ 287 Dick Bertell .... 4.00 1.80 .50
☐ 288 Chicago White Sox 9.00 4.00 1.15
Team Card
☐ 289 Hal Brown .... 4.00 1.80 .50
☐ 290 Bill White .... 6.50 2.90 .80
☐ 291 Don Rudolph .... 4.00 1.80 .50
☐ 292 Pumpsie Green .... 4.50 2.00 .55
☐ 293 Bill Pleis .... 4.00 1.80 .50
☐ 294 Bill Rigney MG .... 4.00 1.80 .50
☐ 295 Ed Roebuck .... 4.00 1.80 .50
☐ 296 Doc Edwards .... 4.00 1.80 .50
☐ 297 Jim Golden .... 4.00 1.80 .50
☐ 298 Don Dillard .... 4.00 1.80 .50
☐ 299 Rookie Stars .... 4.50 2.00 .55
Dave Morehead
Bob Dustal
Tom Butters
Dan Schneider
☐ 300 Willie Mays 180.00 80.00 23.00
☐ 301 Bill Fischer .... 4.00 1.80 .50
☐ 302 Whitey Herzog .... 6.50 2.90 .80
☐ 303 Earl Francis .... 4.00 1.80 .50
☐ 304 Harry Bright .... 4.00 1.80 .50
☐ 305 Don Hoak .... 4.50 2.00 .55
☐ 306 Star Receivers .... 5.00 2.30 .60
Earl Battey
Elston Howard
☐ 307 Chet Nichols .... 4.00 1.80 .50
☐ 308 Camilo Carreon .... 4.00 1.80 .50
☐ 309 Jim Brewer .... 4.00 1.80 .50
☐ 310 Tommy Davis .... 6.00 2.70 .75
☐ 311 Joe McClain .... 4.00 1.80 .50
☐ 312 Houston Colts 15.00 6.75 1.90
Team Card
☐ 313 Ernie Broglio .... 4.50 2.00 .55
☐ 314 John Goryl .... 4.00 1.80 .50
☐ 315 Ralph Terry .... 4.50 2.00 .55
☐ 316 Norm Sherry .... 4.50 2.00 .55
☐ 317 Sam McDowell .... 5.00 2.30 .60
☐ 318 Gene Mauch MG .... 4.50 2.00 .55
☐ 319 Joe Gaines .... 4.00 1.80 .50
☐ 320 Warren Spahn 40.00 18.00 5.00
☐ 321 Gino Cimoli .... 4.00 1.80 .50
☐ 322 Bob Turley .... 4.50 2.00 .55
☐ 323 Bill Mazeroski .... 6.50 2.90 .80
☐ 324 Rookie Stars .... 5.00 2.30 .60
George Williams
Pete Ward
Phil Roof
Vic Davalillo
☐ 325 Jack Sanford .... 4.00 1.80 .50
☐ 326 Hank Foiles .... 4.00 1.80 .50
☐ 327 Paul Foytack .... 4.00 1.80 .50
☐ 328 Dick Williams .... 4.50 2.00 .55
☐ 329 Lindy McDaniel .... 4.50 2.00 .55
☐ 330 Chuck Hinton .... 4.00 1.80 .50
☐ 331 Series Foes .... 4.50 2.00 .55
Bill Stafford
Bill Pierce
☐ 332 Joel Horlen .... 4.50 2.00 .55
☐ 333 Carl Warwick .... 4.00 1.80 .50
☐ 334 Wynn Hawkins .... 4.00 1.80 .50
☐ 335 Leon Wagner .... 4.00 1.80 .50
☐ 336 Ed Bauta .... 4.00 1.80 .50
☐ 337 Dodgers Team 12.50 5.75 1.55
☐ 338 Russ Kemmerer .... 4.00 1.80 .50
☐ 339 Ted Bowsfield .... 4.00 1.80 .50
☐ 340 Yogi Berra 75.00 34.00 9.50
(Player/coach)

☐ 341 Jack Baldschun 4.00 1.80 .50
☐ 342 Gene Woodling 4.50 2.00 .55
☐ 343 Johnny Pesky MG 4.50 2.00 .55
☐ 344 Don Schwall 4.50 2.00 .55
☐ 345 Brooks Robinson 55.00 25.00 7.00
☐ 346 Billy Hoeft 4.00 1.80 .50
☐ 347 Joe Torre 8.50 3.80 1.05
☐ 348 Vic Wertz 4.50 2.00 .55
☐ 349 Zoilo Versalles 4.50 2.00 .55
☐ 350 Bob Purkey 4.00 1.80 .50
☐ 351 Al Luplow 4.00 1.80 .50
☐ 352 Ken Johnson 4.00 1.80 .50
☐ 353 Billy Williams 25.00 11.50 3.10
☐ 354 Dom Zanni 4.00 1.80 .50
☐ 355 Dean Chance 5.00 2.30 .60
☐ 356 John Schaive 4.00 1.80 .50
☐ 357 George Altman 4.00 1.80 .50
☐ 358 Milt Pappas 4.50 2.00 .55
☐ 359 Haywood Sullivan 4.50 2.00 .55
☐ 360 Don Drysdale 40.00 18.00 5.00
☐ 361 Clete Boyer 6.50 2.90 .80
☐ 362 Checklist 5 10.00 1.50 .50
☐ 363 Dick Radatz 5.00 2.30 .60
☐ 364 Howie Goss 4.00 1.80 .50
☐ 365 Jim Bunning 10.00 4.50 1.25
☐ 366 Tony Taylor 4.50 2.00 .55
☐ 367 Tony Cloninger 4.00 1.80 .50
☐ 368 Ed Bailey 4.00 1.80 .50
☐ 369 Jim Lemon 4.00 1.80 .50
☐ 370 Dick Donovan 4.00 1.80 .50
☐ 371 Rod Kanehl 4.50 2.00 .55
☐ 372 Don Lee 4.50 2.00 .55
☐ 373 Jim Campbell 4.50 2.00 .55
☐ 374 Claude Osteen 5.00 2.30 .60
☐ 375 Ken Boyer 9.00 4.00 1.15
☐ 376 John Wyatt 4.50 2.00 .55
☐ 377 Baltimore Orioles 9.00 4.00 1.15
Team Card
☐ 378 Bill Henry 4.50 2.00 .55
☐ 379 Bob Anderson 4.50 2.00 .55
☐ 380 Ernie Banks 70.00 32.00 8.75
☐ 381 Frank Baumann 4.50 2.00 .55
☐ 382 Ralph Houk MG 6.50 2.90 .80
☐ 383 Pete Richert 4.50 2.00 .55
☐ 384 Bob Tillman 4.50 2.00 .55
☐ 385 Art Mahaffey 4.50 2.00 .55
☐ 386 Rookie Stars 5.00 2.30 .60
Ed Kirkpatrick
John Bateman
Larry Bearnarth
Garry Roggenburk
☐ 387 Al McBean 4.50 2.00 .55
☐ 388 Jim Davenport 5.00 2.30 .60
☐ 389 Frank Sullivan 4.50 2.00 .55
☐ 390 Hank Aaron 150.00 70.00 19.00
☐ 391 Bill Dailey 4.50 2.00 .55
☐ 392 Tribe Thumpers 4.50 2.00 .55
Johnny Romano
Tito Francona
☐ 393 Ken MacKenzie 4.50 2.00 .55
☐ 394 Tim McCarver 15.00 6.75 1.90
☐ 395 Don McMahon 4.50 2.00 .55
☐ 396 Joe Koppe 4.50 2.00 .55
☐ 397 Kansas City Athletics 9.00 4.00 1.15
Team Card
☐ 398 Boog Powell 25.00 11.50 3.10
☐ 399 Dick Ellsworth 5.00 2.30 .60
☐ 400 Frank Robinson 50.00 23.00 6.25
☐ 401 Jim Bouton 9.50 4.30 1.20
☐ 402 Mickey Vernon MG 5.00 2.30 .60
☐ 403 Ron Perranoski 5.00 2.30 .60
☐ 404 Bob Oldis 4.50 2.00 .55
☐ 405 Floyd Robinson 4.50 2.00 .55
☐ 406 Howie Koplitz 4.50 2.00 .55
☐ 407 Rookie Stars 4.50 2.00 .55
Frank Kostro
Chico Ruiz
Larry Elliot
Dick Simpson
☐ 408 Billy Gardner 4.50 2.00 .55
☐ 409 Roy Face 5.50 2.50 .70
☐ 410 Earl Battey 4.50 2.00 .55
☐ 411 Jim Constable 4.50 2.00 .55
☐ 412 Dodger Big Three 35.00 16.00 4.40
Johnny Podres
Don Drysdale
Sandy Koufax
☐ 413 Jerry Walker 4.50 2.00 .55
☐ 414 Ty Cline 4.50 2.00 .55
☐ 415 Bob Gibson 50.00 23.00 6.25
☐ 416 Alex Grammas 4.50 2.00 .55
☐ 417 Giants Team 9.00 4.00 1.15
☐ 418 John Orsino 4.50 2.00 .55

☐ 419 Tracy Stallard 4.50 2.00 .55
☐ 420 Bobby Richardson 11.00 4.90 1.40
☐ 421 Tom Morgan 4.50 2.00 .55
☐ 422 Fred Hutchinson MG 5.00 2.30 .60
☐ 423 Ed Hobaugh 4.50 2.00 .55
☐ 424 Charlie Smith 4.50 2.00 .55
☐ 425 Smoky Burgess 5.00 2.30 .60
☐ 426 Barry Latman 4.50 2.00 .55
☐ 427 Bernie Allen 4.50 2.00 .55
☐ 428 Carl Boles 4.50 2.00 .55
☐ 429 Lou Burdette 6.00 2.70 .75
☐ 430 Norm Siebern 4.50 2.00 .55
☐ 431A Checklist 6 10.00 1.50 .50
(White on red)
☐ 431B Checklist 6 22.00 3.30 1.10
(Black on orange)
☐ 432 Roman Mejias 4.50 2.00 .55
☐ 433 Denis Menke 4.50 2.00 .55
☐ 434 John Callison 5.00 2.30 .60
☐ 435 Woody Held 4.50 2.00 .55
☐ 436 Tim Harkness 4.50 2.00 .55
☐ 437 Bill Bruton 4.50 2.00 .55
☐ 438 Wes Stock 4.50 2.00 .55
☐ 439 Don Zimmer 6.50 2.90 .80
☐ 440 Juan Marichal 30.00 13.50 3.80
☐ 441 Lee Thomas 5.00 2.30 .60
☐ 442 J.C. Hartman 4.50 2.00 .55
☐ 443 Jim Piersall 5.50 2.50 .70
☐ 444 Jim Maloney 6.50 2.90 .80
☐ 445 Norm Cash 6.50 2.90 .80
☐ 446 Whitey Ford 40.00 18.00 5.00
☐ 447 Felix Mantilla 14.00 6.25 1.75
☐ 448 Jack Kralick 14.00 6.25 1.75
☐ 449 Jose Tartabull 14.00 6.25 1.75
☐ 450 Bob Friend 16.00 7.25 2.00
☐ 451 Indians Team 35.00 16.00 4.40
☐ 452 Barney Schultz 14.00 6.25 1.75
☐ 453 Jake Wood 14.00 6.25 1.75
☐ 454A Art Fowler 14.00 6.25 1.75
(Card number on
white background)
☐ 454B Art Fowler 28.00 12.50 3.50
(Card number on
orange background)
☐ 455 Ruben Amaro 14.00 6.25 1.75
☐ 456 Jim Coker 14.00 6.25 1.75
☐ 457 Tex Clevenger 14.00 6.25 1.75
☐ 458 Al Lopez MG 20.00 9.00 2.50
☐ 459 Dick LeMay 14.00 6.25 1.75
☐ 460 Del Crandall 16.00 7.25 2.00
☐ 461 Norm Bass 14.00 6.25 1.75
☐ 462 Wally Post 16.00 7.25 2.00
☐ 463 Joe Schaffernoth 14.00 6.25 1.75
☐ 464 Ken Aspromonte 14.00 6.25 1.75
☐ 465 Chuck Estrada 14.00 6.25 1.75
☐ 466 Rookie Stars SP 55.00 25.00 7.00
Nate Oliver
Tony Martinez
Bill Freehan
Jerry Robinson
☐ 467 Phil Ortega 14.00 6.25 1.75
☐ 468 Carroll Hardy 14.00 6.25 1.75
☐ 469 Jay Hook 14.00 6.25 1.75
☐ 470 Tom Tresh SP 50.00 23.00 6.25
☐ 471 Ken Retzer 14.00 6.25 1.75
☐ 472 Lou Brock 150.00 70.00 19.00
☐ 473 New York Mets 120.00 55.00 15.00
Team Card
☐ 474 Jack Fisher 14.00 6.25 1.75
☐ 475 Gus Triandos 16.00 7.25 2.00
☐ 476 Frank Funk 14.00 6.25 1.75
☐ 477 Donn Clendenon 16.00 7.25 2.00
☐ 478 Paul Brown 14.00 6.25 1.75
☐ 479 Ed Brinkman 14.00 6.25 1.75
☐ 480 Bill Monbouquette 14.00 6.25 1.75
☐ 481 Bob Taylor 14.00 6.25 1.75
☐ 482 Felix Torres 14.00 6.25 1.75
☐ 483 Jim Owens 14.00 6.25 1.75
☐ 484 Dale Long SP 22.00 10.00 2.80
☐ 485 Jim Landis 14.00 6.25 1.75
☐ 486 Ray Sadecki 14.00 6.25 1.75
☐ 487 John Roseboro 16.00 7.25 2.00
☐ 488 Jerry Adair 14.00 6.25 1.75
☐ 489 Paul Toth 14.00 6.25 1.75
☐ 490 Willie McCovey 150.00 70.00 19.00
☐ 491 Harry Craft MG 14.00 6.25 1.75
☐ 492 Dave Wickersham 14.00 6.25 1.75
☐ 493 Walt Bond 14.00 6.25 1.75
☐ 494 Phil Regan 16.00 7.25 2.00
☐ 495 Frank Thomas SP 25.00 11.50 3.10
☐ 496 Rookie Stars 14.00 6.25 1.75
Steve Dalkowski
Fred Newman

Card	NRMT	VG-E	GOOD
Jack Smith			
Carl Bouldin			
☐ 497 Bennie Daniels	14.00	6.25	1.75
☐ 498 Eddie Kasko	14.00	6.25	1.75
☐ 499 J.C. Martin	14.00	6.25	1.75
☐ 500 Harmon Killebrew SP	150.00	70.00	19.00
☐ 501 Joe Azcue	14.00	6.25	1.75
☐ 502 Daryl Spencer	14.00	6.25	1.75
☐ 503 Braves Team	35.00	16.00	4.40
☐ 504 Bob Johnson	14.00	6.25	1.75
☐ 505 Curt Flood	20.00	9.00	2.50
☐ 506 Gene Green	14.00	6.25	1.75
☐ 507 Roland Sheldon	14.00	6.25	1.75
☐ 508 Ted Savage	14.00	6.25	1.75
☐ 509A Checklist 7	22.00	3.30	1.10
(Copyright centered)			
☐ 509B Checklist 7	22.00	3.30	1.10
(Copyright to right)			
☐ 510 Ken McBride	14.00	6.25	1.75
☐ 511 Charlie Neal	16.00	7.25	2.00
☐ 512 Cal McLish	14.00	6.25	1.75
☐ 513 Gary Geiger	14.00	6.25	1.75
☐ 514 Larry Osborne	14.00	6.25	1.75
☐ 515 Don Elston	14.00	6.25	1.75
☐ 516 Purnell Goldy	14.00	6.25	1.75
☐ 517 Hal Woodeshick	14.00	6.25	1.75
☐ 518 Don Blasingame	14.00	6.25	1.75
☐ 519 Claude Raymond	18.00	8.00	2.30
☐ 520 Orlando Cepeda	25.00	11.50	3.10
☐ 521 Dan Pfister	14.00	6.25	1.75
☐ 522 Rookie Stars	16.00	7.25	2.00
Mel Nelson			
Gary Peters			
Jim Roland			
Art Quirk			
☐ 523 Bill Kunkel	10.00	4.50	1.25
☐ 524 Cardinals Team	25.00	11.50	3.10
☐ 525 Nellie Fox	20.00	9.00	2.50
☐ 526 Dick Hall	10.00	4.50	1.25
☐ 527 Ed Sadowski	10.00	4.50	1.25
☐ 528 Carl Willey	10.00	4.50	1.25
☐ 529 Wes Covington	11.00	4.90	1.40
☐ 530 Don Mossi	11.00	4.90	1.40
☐ 531 Sam Mele MG	10.00	4.50	1.25
☐ 532 Steve Boros	10.00	4.50	1.25
☐ 533 Bobby Shantz	12.50	5.75	1.55
☐ 534 Ken Walters	10.00	4.50	1.25
☐ 535 Jim Perry	12.50	5.75	1.55
☐ 536 Norm Larker	10.00	4.50	1.25
☐ 537 Rookie Stars	925.00	425.00	115.00
Pedro Gonzalez			
Ken McMullen			
Al Weis			
Pete Rose			
☐ 538 George Brunet	10.00	4.50	1.25
☐ 539 Wayne Causey	10.00	4.50	1.25
☐ 540 Bob Clemente	225.00	100.00	28.00
☐ 541 Ron Moeller	10.00	4.50	1.25
☐ 542 Lou Klimchock	10.00	4.50	1.25
☐ 543 Russ Snyder	10.00	4.50	1.25
☐ 544 Rookie Stars	42.00	19.00	5.25
Duke Carmel			
Bill Haas			
Rusty Staub			
Dick Phillips			
☐ 545 Jose Pagan	10.00	4.50	1.25
☐ 546 Hal Reniff	10.00	4.50	1.25
☐ 547 Gus Bell	11.00	4.90	1.40
☐ 548 Tom Satriano	10.00	4.50	1.25
☐ 549 Rookie Stars	10.00	4.50	1.25
Marcelino Lopez			
Pete Lovrich			
Paul Ratliff			
Elmo Plaskett			
☐ 550 Duke Snider	85.00	38.00	10.50
☐ 551 Billy Klaus	10.00	4.50	1.25
☐ 552 Detroit Tigers	32.00	14.50	4.00
Team Card			
☐ 553 Rookie Stars	275.00	125.00	34.00
Brock Davis			
Jim Gosger			
Willie Stargell			
John Herrnstein			
☐ 554 Hank Fischer	10.00	4.50	1.25
☐ 555 John Blanchard	11.00	4.90	1.40
☐ 556 Al Worthington	10.00	4.50	1.25
☐ 557 Cuno Barragan	10.00	4.50	1.25
☐ 558 Rookie Stars	15.00	6.75	1.90
Bill Faul			
Ron Hunt			
Al Moran			
Bob Lipski			
☐ 559 Danny Murtaugh MG	11.00	4.90	1.40
☐ 560 Ray Herbert	10.00	4.50	1.25
☐ 561 Mike De La Hoz	10.00	4.50	1.25
☐ 562 Rookie Stars	20.00	9.00	2.50
Randy Cardinal			
Dave McNally			
Ken Rowe			
Don Rowe			
☐ 563 Mike McCormick	11.00	4.90	1.40
☐ 564 George Banks	10.00	4.50	1.25
☐ 565 Larry Sherry	11.00	4.90	1.40
☐ 566 Cliff Cook	10.00	4.50	1.25
☐ 567 Jim Duffalo	10.00	4.50	1.25
☐ 568 Bob Sadowski	10.00	4.50	1.25
☐ 569 Luis Arroyo	11.00	4.90	1.40
☐ 570 Frank Bolling	10.00	4.50	1.25
☐ 571 Johnny Klippstein	10.00	4.50	1.25
☐ 572 Jack Spring	10.00	4.50	1.25
☐ 573 Coot Veal	10.00	4.50	1.25
☐ 574 Hal Kolstad	10.00	4.50	1.25
☐ 575 Don Cardwell	10.00	4.50	1.25
☐ 576 Johnny Temple	15.00	6.75	1.90

1964 Topps

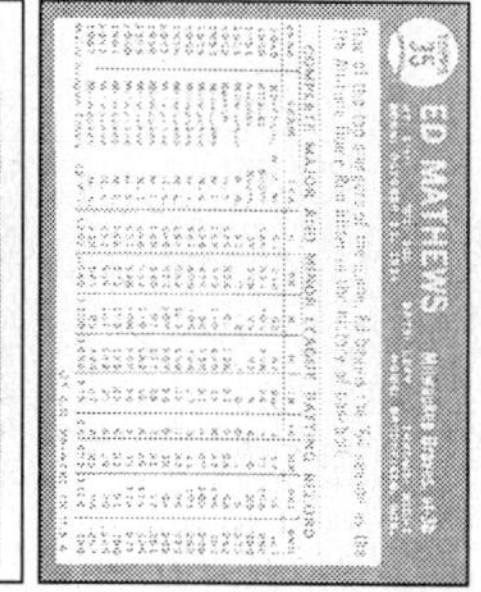

The cards in this 587-card set measure 2 1/2" by 3 1/2". Players in the 1964 Topps baseball series were easy to sort by team due to the giant block lettering found at the top of each card. The name and position of the player are found underneath the picture, and the card is numbered in a ball design on the orange-colored back. The usual last series scarcity holds for this set (523 to 587). Subsets within this set include League Leaders (1-12) and World Series cards (136-140). There were some three-card advertising panels produced by Topps: the players included are from the first series; one panel shows Walt Alston, Bill Henry, and Vada Pinson on the front with a Mickey Mantle card back on one of the backs. Another panel shows Carl Willey, White Sox Rookies, and Bob Friend on the front with a Mickey Mantle card back on one of the backs. The key Rookie Cards in this set are Richie Allen, Tommy John, Tony LaRussa, Lou Piniella, and Phil Niekro.

	NRMT	VG-E	GOOD
COMPLETE SET (587)	3400.00	1500.00	425.00
COMMON PLAYER (1-196)	2.00	.90	.25
COMMON PLAYER (197-370)	3.00	1.35	.40
COMMON PLAYER (371-522)	5.00	2.30	.60
COMMON PLAYER (523-587)	10.00	4.50	1.25
☐ 1 NL ERA Leaders	20.00	5.00	1.60
Sandy Koufax			
Dick Ellsworth			
Bob Friend			
☐ 2 AL ERA Leaders	3.50	1.55	.45
Gary Peters			
Juan Pizarro			
Camilo Pascual			
☐ 3 NL Pitching Leaders	11.00	4.90	1.40
Sandy Koufax			
Juan Marichal			
Warren Spahn			
Jim Maloney			
☐ 4 AL Pitching Leaders	4.00	1.80	.50
Whitey Ford			

	Camilo Pascual			
	Jim Bouton			
☐ 5	NL Strikeout Leaders	9.00	4.00	1.15
	Sandy Koufax			
	Jim Maloney			
	Don Drysdale			
☐ 6	AL Strikeout Leaders	3.50	1.55	.45
	Camilo Pascual			
	Jim Bunning			
	Dick Stigman			
☐ 7	NL Batting Leaders	8.00	3.60	1.00
	Tommy Davis			
	Bob Clemente			
	Dick Groat			
	Hank Aaron			
☐ 8	AL Batting Leaders	8.00	3.60	1.00
	Carl Yastrzemski			
	Al Kaline			
	Rich Rollins			
☐ 9	NL Home Run Leaders	15.00	6.75	1.90
	Hank Aaron			
	Willie McCovey			
	Willie Mays			
	Orlando Cepeda			
☐ 10	AL Home Run Leaders	4.50	2.00	.55
	Harmon Killebrew			
	Dick Stuart			
	Bob Allison			
☐ 11	NL RBI Leaders	8.00	3.60	1.00
	Hank Aaron			
	Ken Boyer			
	Bill White			
☐ 12	AL RBI Leaders	6.00	2.70	.75
	Dick Stuart			
	Al Kaline			
	Harmon Killebrew			
☐ 13	Hoyt Wilhelm	9.00	4.00	1.15
☐ 14	Dodgers Rookies	2.00	.90	.25
	Dick Nen			
	Nick Willhite			
☐ 15	Zoilo Versalles	2.50	1.15	.30
☐ 16	John Boozer	2.00	.90	.25
☐ 17	Willie Kirkland	2.00	.90	.25
☐ 18	Billy O'Dell	2.00	.90	.25
☐ 19	Don Wert	2.00	.90	.25
☐ 20	Bob Friend	2.50	1.15	.30
☐ 21	Yogi Berra MG	40.00	18.00	5.00
☐ 22	Jerry Adair	2.00	.90	.25
☐ 23	Chris Zachary	2.00	.90	.25
☐ 24	Carl Sawatski	2.00	.90	.25
☐ 25	Bill Monbouquette	2.00	.90	.25
☐ 26	Gino Cimoli	2.00	.90	.25
☐ 27	New York Mets	7.00	3.10	.85
	Team Card			
☐ 28	Claude Osteen	2.50	1.15	.30
☐ 29	Lou Brock	40.00	18.00	5.00
☐ 30	Ron Perranoski	2.50	1.15	.30
☐ 31	Dave Nicholson	2.00	.90	.25
☐ 32	Dean Chance	3.00	1.35	.40
☐ 33	Reds Rookies	2.50	1.15	.30
	Sammy Ellis			
	Mel Queen			
☐ 34	Jim Perry	2.50	1.15	.30
☐ 35	Eddie Mathews	20.00	9.00	2.50
☐ 36	Hal Reniff	2.00	.90	.25
☐ 37	Smoky Burgess	2.50	1.15	.30
☐ 38	Jim Wynn	6.50	2.90	.80
☐ 39	Hank Aguirre	2.00	.90	.25
☐ 40	Dick Groat	2.50	1.15	.30
☐ 41	Friendly Foes	5.00	2.30	.60
	Willie McCovey			
	Leon Wagner			
☐ 42	Moe Drabowsky	2.50	1.15	.30
☐ 43	Roy Sievers	2.50	1.15	.30
☐ 44	Duke Carmel	2.00	.90	.25
☐ 45	Milt Pappas	2.50	1.15	.30
☐ 46	Ed Brinkman	2.00	.90	.25
☐ 47	Giants Rookies	3.50	1.55	.45
	Jesus Alou			
	Ron Herbel			
☐ 48	Bob Perry	2.00	.90	.25
☐ 49	Bill Henry	2.00	.90	.25
☐ 50	Mickey Mantle	250.00	115.00	31.00
☐ 51	Pete Richert	2.00	.90	.25
☐ 52	Chuck Hinton	2.00	.90	.25
☐ 53	Denis Menke	2.00	.90	.25
☐ 54	Sam Mele MG	2.00	.90	.25
☐ 55	Ernie Banks	30.00	13.50	3.80
☐ 56	Hal Brown	2.00	.90	.25
☐ 57	Tim Harkness	2.00	.90	.25
☐ 58	Don Demeter	2.00	.90	.25
☐ 59	Ernie Broglio	2.00	.90	.25
☐ 60	Frank Malzone	2.50	1.15	.30
☐ 61	Angel Backstops	2.50	1.15	.30

	Bob Rodgers			
	Ed Sadowski			
☐ 62	Ted Savage	2.00	.90	.25
☐ 63	John Orsino	2.00	.90	.25
☐ 64	Ted Abernathy	2.00	.90	.25
☐ 65	Felipe Alou	3.50	1.55	.45
☐ 66	Eddie Fisher	2.00	.90	.25
☐ 67	Tigers Team	4.00	1.80	.50
☐ 68	Willie Davis	2.50	1.15	.30
☐ 69	Clete Boyer	3.00	1.35	.40
☐ 70	Joe Torre	4.50	2.00	.55
☐ 71	Jack Spring	2.00	.90	.25
☐ 72	Chico Cardenas	2.50	1.15	.30
☐ 73	Jimmie Hall	2.50	1.15	.30
☐ 74	Pirates Rookies	2.00	.90	.25
	Bob Priddy			
	Tom Butters			
☐ 75	Wayne Causey	2.00	.90	.25
☐ 76	Checklist 1	9.00	1.35	.45
☐ 77	Jerry Walker	2.00	.90	.25
☐ 78	Merritt Ranew	2.00	.90	.25
☐ 79	Bob Heffner	2.00	.90	.25
☐ 80	Vada Pinson	3.50	1.55	.45
☐ 81	All-Star Vets	7.00	3.10	.85
	Nellie Fox			
	Harmon Killebrew			
☐ 82	Jim Davenport	2.50	1.15	.30
☐ 83	Gus Triandos	2.50	1.15	.30
☐ 84	Carl Willey	2.00	.90	.25
☐ 85	Pete Ward	2.00	.90	.25
☐ 86	Al Downing	3.00	1.35	.40
☐ 87	St. Louis Cardinals	5.00	2.30	.60
	Team Card			
☐ 88	John Roseboro	2.50	1.15	.30
☐ 89	Boog Powell	5.00	2.30	.60
☐ 90	Earl Battey	2.00	.90	.25
☐ 91	Bob Bailey	2.50	1.15	.30
☐ 92	Steve Ridzik	2.00	.90	.25
☐ 93	Gary Geiger	2.00	.90	.25
☐ 94	Braves Rookies	2.00	.90	.25
	Jim Britton			
	Larry Maxie			
☐ 95	George Altman	2.00	.90	.25
☐ 96	Bob Buhl	2.50	1.15	.30
☐ 97	Jim Fregosi	2.50	1.15	.30
☐ 98	Bill Bruton	2.00	.90	.25
☐ 99	Al Stanek	2.00	.90	.25
☐ 100	Elston Howard	5.00	2.30	.60
☐ 101	Walt Alston MG	4.00	1.80	.50
☐ 102	Checklist 2	9.00	1.35	.45
☐ 103	Curt Flood	3.00	1.35	.40
☐ 104	Art Mahaffey	2.00	.90	.25
☐ 105	Woody Held	2.00	.90	.25
☐ 106	Joe Nuxhall	2.50	1.15	.30
☐ 107	White Sox Rookies	2.00	.90	.25
	Bruce Howard			
	Frank Kreutzer			
☐ 108	John Wyatt	2.00	.90	.25
☐ 109	Rusty Staub	7.50	3.40	.95
☐ 110	Albie Pearson	2.50	1.15	.30
☐ 111	Don Elston	2.00	.90	.25
☐ 112	Bob Tillman	2.00	.90	.25
☐ 113	Grover Powell	2.00	.90	.25
☐ 114	Don Lock	2.00	.90	.25
☐ 115	Frank Bolling	2.00	.90	.25
☐ 116	Twins Rookies	15.00	6.75	1.90
	Jay Ward			
	Tony Oliva			
☐ 117	Earl Francis	2.00	.90	.25
☐ 118	John Blanchard	2.50	1.15	.30
☐ 119	Gary Kolb	2.00	.90	.25
☐ 120	Don Drysdale	20.00	9.00	2.50
☐ 121	Pete Runnels	2.50	1.15	.30
☐ 122	Don McMahon	2.00	.90	.25
☐ 123	Jose Pagan	2.00	.90	.25
☐ 124	Orlando Pena	2.00	.90	.25
☐ 125	Pete Rose	175.00	80.00	22.00
☐ 126	Russ Snyder	2.00	.90	.25
☐ 127	Angels Rookies	2.00	.90	.25
	Aubrey Gatewood			
	Dick Simpson			
☐ 128	Mickey Lolich	18.00	8.00	2.30
☐ 129	Amado Samuel	2.00	.90	.25
☐ 130	Gary Peters	2.50	1.15	.30
☐ 131	Steve Boros	2.00	.90	.25
☐ 132	Braves Team	4.00	1.80	.50
☐ 133	Jim Grant	2.50	1.15	.30
☐ 134	Don Zimmer	2.50	1.15	.30
☐ 135	Johnny Callison	2.50	1.15	.30
☐ 136	World Series Game 1	14.00	6.25	1.75
	Sandy Koufax			
	strikes out 15			
☐ 137	World Series Game 2	4.00	1.80	.50
	Tommy Davis			

	Card			
	sparks rally			
☐	138 World Series Game 3	4.00	1.80	.50
	LA Three Straight (Ron Fairly)			
☐	139 World Series Game 4	4.00	1.80	.50
	Sealing Yanks doom (Frank Howard)			
☐	140 World Series Summary	4.00	1.80	.50
	Dodgers celebrate			
☐	141 Danny Murtaugh MG	2.50	1.15	.30
☐	142 John Bateman	2.00	.90	.25
☐	143 Bubba Phillips	2.00	.90	.25
☐	144 Al Worthington	2.00	.90	.25
☐	145 Norm Siebern	2.00	.90	.25
☐	146 Indians Rookies	70.00	32.00	8.75
	Tommy John			
	Bob Chance			
☐	147 Ray Sadecki	2.00	.90	.25
☐	148 J.C. Martin	2.00	.90	.25
☐	149 Paul Foytack	2.00	.90	.25
☐	150 Willie Mays	110.00	50.00	14.00
☐	151 Athletics Team	4.00	1.80	.50
☐	152 Denny Lemaster	2.00	.90	.25
☐	153 Dick Williams	2.50	1.15	.30
☐	154 Dick Tracewski	3.00	1.35	.40
☐	155 Duke Snider	33.00	15.00	4.10
☐	156 Bill Dailey	2.00	.90	.25
☐	157 Gene Mauch MG	2.50	1.15	.30
☐	158 Ken Johnson	2.00	.90	.25
☐	159 Charlie Dees	2.00	.90	.25
☐	160 Ken Boyer	5.50	2.50	.70
☐	161 Dave McNally	3.50	1.55	.45
☐	162 Hitting Area	2.50	1.15	.30
	Dick Sisler CO			
	Vada Pinson			
☐	163 Donn Clendenon	2.50	1.15	.30
☐	164 Bud Daley	2.00	.90	.25
☐	165 Jerry Lumpe	2.00	.90	.25
☐	166 Marty Keough	2.00	.90	.25
☐	167 Senators Rookies	32.00	14.50	4.00
	Mike Brumley			
	Lou Piniella			
☐	168 Al Weis	2.00	.90	.25
☐	169 Del Crandall	2.50	1.15	.30
☐	170 Dick Radatz	2.50	1.15	.30
☐	171 Ty Cline	2.00	.90	.25
☐	172 Indians Team	4.00	1.80	.50
☐	173 Ryne Duren	2.50	1.15	.30
☐	174 Doc Edwards	2.00	.90	.25
☐	175 Billy Williams	20.00	9.00	2.50
☐	176 Tracy Stallard	2.00	.90	.25
☐	177 Harmon Killebrew	20.00	9.00	2.50
☐	178 Hank Bauer MG	2.50	1.15	.30
☐	179 Carl Warwick	2.00	.90	.25
☐	180 Tommy Davis	3.50	1.55	.45
☐	181 Dave Wickersham	2.00	.90	.25
☐	182 Sox Sockers	12.50	5.75	1.55
	Carl Yastrzemski			
	Chuck Schilling			
☐	183 Ron Taylor	2.00	.90	.25
☐	184 Al Luplow	2.00	.90	.25
☐	185 Jim O'Toole	2.50	1.15	.30
☐	186 Roman Mejias	2.00	.90	.25
☐	187 Ed Roebuck	2.00	.90	.25
☐	188 Checklist 3	9.00	1.35	.45
☐	189 Bob Hendley	2.00	.90	.25
☐	190 Bobby Richardson	6.50	2.90	.80
☐	191 Clay Dalrymple	2.00	.90	.25
☐	192 Cubs Rookies	2.00	.90	.25
	John Boccabella			
	Billy Cowan			
☐	193 Jerry Lynch	2.00	.90	.25
☐	194 John Goryl	2.00	.90	.25
☐	195 Floyd Robinson	2.00	.90	.25
☐	196 Jim Gentile	3.50	1.55	.45
☐	197 Frank Lary	3.50	1.55	.45
☐	198 Len Gabrielson	3.00	1.35	.40
☐	199 Joe Azcue	3.00	1.35	.40
☐	200 Sandy Koufax	110.00	50.00	14.00
☐	201 Orioles Rookies	3.50	1.55	.45
	Sam Bowens			
	Wally Bunker			
☐	202 Galen Cisco	3.50	1.55	.45
☐	203 John Kennedy	3.50	1.55	.45
☐	204 Matty Alou	4.00	1.80	.50
☐	205 Nellie Fox	6.00	2.70	.75
☐	206 Steve Hamilton	3.00	1.35	.40
☐	207 Fred Hutchinson MG	3.50	1.55	.45
☐	208 Wes Covington	3.50	1.55	.45
☐	209 Bob Allen	3.00	1.35	.40
☐	210 Carl Yastrzemski	65.00	29.00	8.25
☐	211 Jim Coker	3.00	1.35	.40
☐	212 Pete Lovrich	3.00	1.35	.40
☐	213 Angels Team	6.00	2.70	.75
☐	214 Ken McMullen	3.50	1.55	.45
☐	215 Ray Herbert	3.00	1.35	.40
☐	216 Mike DeLaHoz	3.00	1.35	.40
☐	217 Jim King	3.00	1.35	.40
☐	218 Hank Fischer	3.00	1.35	.40
☐	219 Young Aces	4.50	2.00	.55
	Al Downing			
	Jim Bouton			
☐	220 Dick Ellsworth	3.50	1.55	.45
☐	221 Bob Saverine	3.00	1.35	.40
☐	222 Billy Pierce	3.50	1.55	.45
☐	223 George Banks	3.00	1.35	.40
☐	224 Tommie Sisk	3.00	1.35	.40
☐	225 Roger Maris	65.00	29.00	8.25
☐	226 Colts Rookies	5.00	2.30	.60
	Jerry Grote			
	Larry Yellen			
☐	227 Barry Latman	3.00	1.35	.40
☐	228 Felix Mantilla	3.00	1.35	.40
☐	229 Charley Lau	3.50	1.55	.45
☐	230 Brooks Robinson	35.00	16.00	4.40
☐	231 Dick Calmus	3.00	1.35	.40
☐	232 Al Lopez MG	5.00	2.30	.60
☐	233 Hal Smith	3.00	1.35	.40
☐	234 Gary Bell	3.00	1.35	.40
☐	235 Ron Hunt	3.00	1.35	.40
☐	236 Bill Faul	3.00	1.35	.40
☐	237 Cubs Team	6.00	2.70	.75
☐	238 Roy McMillan	3.50	1.55	.45
☐	239 Herm Starrette	3.00	1.35	.40
☐	240 Bill White	4.50	2.00	.55
☐	241 Jim Owens	3.00	1.35	.40
☐	242 Harvey Kuenn	3.50	1.55	.45
☐	243 Phillies Rookies	25.00	11.50	3.10
	Richie Allen			
	John Herrnstein			
☐	244 Tony LaRussa	25.00	11.50	3.10
☐	245 Dick Stigman	3.00	1.35	.40
☐	246 Manny Mota	4.00	1.80	.50
☐	247 Dave DeBusschere	4.00	1.80	.50
☐	248 Johnny Pesky MG	3.50	1.55	.45
☐	249 Doug Camilli	3.00	1.35	.40
☐	250 Al Kaline	35.00	16.00	4.40
☐	251 Choo Choo Coleman	3.00	1.35	.40
☐	252 Ken Aspromonte	3.00	1.35	.40
☐	253 Wally Post	3.50	1.55	.45
☐	254 Don Hoak	3.50	1.55	.45
☐	255 Lee Thomas	3.50	1.55	.45
☐	256 Johnny Weekly	3.00	1.35	.40
☐	257 San Francisco Giants	6.00	2.70	.75
	Team Card			
☐	258 Garry Roggenburk	3.00	1.35	.40
☐	259 Harry Bright	3.00	1.35	.40
☐	260 Frank Robinson	27.00	12.00	3.40
☐	261 Jim Hannan	3.00	1.35	.40
☐	262 Cards Rookies	6.00	2.70	.75
	Mike Shannon			
	Harry Fanok			
☐	263 Chuck Estrada	3.00	1.35	.40
☐	264 Jim Landis	3.00	1.35	.40
☐	265 Jim Bunning	6.00	2.70	.75
☐	266 Gene Freese	3.00	1.35	.40
☐	267 Wilbur Wood	6.00	2.70	.75
☐	268 Bill's Got It	3.50	1.55	.45
	Danny Murtaugh MG			
	Bill Virdon			
☐	269 Ellis Burton	3.00	1.35	.40
☐	270 Rich Rollins	3.50	1.55	.45
☐	271 Bob Sadowski	3.00	1.35	.40
☐	272 Jake Wood	3.00	1.35	.40
☐	273 Mel Nelson	3.00	1.35	.40
☐	274 Checklist 4	9.00	1.35	.45
☐	275 John Tsitouris	3.00	1.35	.40
☐	276 Jose Tartabull	3.50	1.55	.45
☐	277 Ken Retzer	3.00	1.35	.40
☐	278 Bobby Shantz	3.50	1.55	.45
☐	279 Joe Koppe UER	3.50	1.55	.45
	(Glove on wrong hand)			
☐	280 Juan Marichal	12.50	5.75	1.55
☐	281 Yankees Rookies	3.50	1.55	.45
	Jake Gibbs			
	Tom Metcalf			
☐	282 Bob Bruce	3.00	1.35	.40
☐	283 Tom McCraw	4.00	1.80	.50
☐	284 Dick Schofield	3.00	1.35	.40
☐	285 Robin Roberts	10.00	4.50	1.25
☐	286 Don Landrum	3.00	1.35	.40
☐	287 Red Sox Rookies	35.00	16.00	4.40
	Tony Conigliaro			
	Bill Spanswick			
☐	288 Al Moran	3.00	1.35	.40
☐	289 Frank Funk	3.00	1.35	.40
☐	290 Bob Allison	3.50	1.55	.45

☐ 291	Phil Ortega	3.00	1.35	.40
☐ 292	Mike Roarke	3.00	1.35	.40
☐ 293	Phillies Team	6.00	2.70	.75
☐ 294	Ken L. Hunt	3.00	1.35	.40
☐ 295	Roger Craig	3.50	1.55	.45
☐ 296	Ed Kirkpatrick	3.00	1.35	.40
☐ 297	Ken MacKenzie	3.00	1.35	.40
☐ 298	Harry Craft MG	3.00	1.35	.40
☐ 299	Bill Stafford	3.00	1.35	.40
☐ 300	Hank Aaron	125.00	57.50	15.50
☐ 301	Larry Brown	3.00	1.35	.40
☐ 302	Dan Pfister	3.00	1.35	.40
☐ 303	Jim Campbell	3.00	1.35	.40
☐ 304	Bob Johnson	3.00	1.35	.40
☐ 305	Jack Lamabe	3.00	1.35	.40
☐ 306	Giant Gunners	25.00	11.50	3.10
	Willie Mays			
	Orlando Cepeda			
☐ 307	Joe Gibbon	3.00	1.35	.40
☐ 308	Gene Stephens	3.00	1.35	.40
☐ 309	Paul Toth	3.00	1.35	.40
☐ 310	Jim Gilliam	4.50	2.00	.55
☐ 311	Tom Brown	3.00	1.35	.40
☐ 312	Tigers Rookies	3.00	1.35	.40
	Fritz Fisher			
	Fred Gladding			
☐ 313	Chuck Hiller	3.00	1.35	.40
☐ 314	Jerry Buchek	3.00	1.35	.40
☐ 315	Bo Belinsky	3.50	1.55	.45
☐ 316	Gene Oliver	3.00	1.35	.40
☐ 317	Al Smith	3.00	1.35	.40
☐ 318	Minnesota Twins	6.00	2.70	.75
	Team Card			
☐ 319	Paul Brown	3.00	1.35	.40
☐ 320	Rocky Colavito	8.00	3.60	1.00
☐ 321	Bob Lillis	3.00	1.35	.40
☐ 322	George Brunet	3.00	1.35	.40
☐ 323	John Buzhardt	3.00	1.35	.40
☐ 324	Casey Stengel MG	17.00	7.75	2.10
☐ 325	Hector Lopez	3.50	1.55	.45
☐ 326	Ron Brand	3.00	1.35	.40
☐ 327	Don Blasingame	3.00	1.35	.40
☐ 328	Bob Shaw	3.00	1.35	.40
☐ 329	Russ Nixon	3.00	1.35	.40
☐ 330	Tommy Harper	3.50	1.55	.45
☐ 331	AL Bombers	125.00	57.50	15.50
	Roger Maris			
	Norm Cash			
	Mickey Mantle			
	Al Kaline			
☐ 332	Ray Washburn	3.00	1.35	.40
☐ 333	Billy Moran	3.00	1.35	.40
☐ 334	Lew Krausse	3.00	1.35	.40
☐ 335	Don Mossi	3.50	1.55	.45
☐ 336	Andre Rodgers	3.00	1.35	.40
☐ 337	Dodgers Rookies	8.50	3.80	1.05
	Al Ferrara			
	Jeff Torborg			
☐ 338	Jack Kralick	3.00	1.35	.40
☐ 339	Walt Bond	3.00	1.35	.40
☐ 340	Joe Cunningham	3.00	1.35	.40
☐ 341	Jim Roland	3.00	1.35	.40
☐ 342	Willie Stargell	45.00	20.00	5.75
☐ 343	Senators Team	6.00	2.70	.75
☐ 344	Phil Linz	3.50	1.55	.45
☐ 345	Frank Thomas	3.50	1.55	.45
☐ 346	Joey Jay	3.00	1.35	.40
☐ 347	Bobby Wine	3.00	1.35	.40
☐ 348	Ed Lopat MG	3.50	1.55	.45
☐ 349	Art Fowler	3.00	1.35	.40
☐ 350	Willie McCovey	30.00	13.50	3.80
☐ 351	Dan Schneider	3.00	1.35	.40
☐ 352	Eddie Bressoud	3.00	1.35	.40
☐ 353	Wally Moon	3.50	1.55	.45
☐ 354	Dave Giusti	3.00	1.35	.40
☐ 355	Vic Power	3.50	1.55	.45
☐ 356	Reds Rookies	3.50	1.55	.45
	Bill McCool			
	Chico Ruiz			
☐ 357	Charley James	3.00	1.35	.40
☐ 358	Ron Kline	3.00	1.35	.40
☐ 359	Jim Schaffer	3.00	1.35	.40
☐ 360	Joe Pepitone	4.50	2.00	.55
☐ 361	Jay Hook	3.00	1.35	.40
☐ 362	Checklist 5	9.00	1.35	.45
☐ 363	Dick McAuliffe	3.50	1.55	.45
☐ 364	Joe Gaines	3.00	1.35	.40
☐ 365	Cal McLish	3.00	1.35	.40
☐ 366	Nelson Mathews	3.00	1.35	.40
☐ 367	Fred Whitfield	3.00	1.35	.40
☐ 368	White Sox Rookies	3.50	1.55	.45
	Fritz Ackley			
	Don Buford			
☐ 369	Jerry Zimmerman	3.00	1.35	.40
☐ 370	Hal Woodeshick	3.00	1.35	.40
☐ 371	Frank Howard	6.50	2.90	.80
☐ 372	Howie Koplitz	5.00	2.30	.60
☐ 373	Pirates Team	10.00	4.50	1.25
☐ 374	Bobby Bolin	5.00	2.30	.60
☐ 375	Ron Santo	7.00	3.10	.85
☐ 376	Dave Morehead	5.00	2.30	.60
☐ 377	Bob Skinner	5.50	2.50	.70
☐ 378	Braves Rookies	6.00	2.70	.75
	Woody Woodward			
	Jack Smith			
☐ 379	Tony Gonzalez	5.00	2.30	.60
☐ 380	Whitey Ford	30.00	13.50	3.80
☐ 381	Bob Taylor	5.00	2.30	.60
☐ 382	Wes Stock	5.00	2.30	.60
☐ 383	Bill Rigney MG	5.00	2.30	.60
☐ 384	Ron Hansen	5.00	2.30	.60
☐ 385	Curt Simmons	5.50	2.50	.70
☐ 386	Lenny Green	5.00	2.30	.60
☐ 387	Terry Fox	5.00	2.30	.60
☐ 388	A's Rookies	5.50	2.50	.70
	John O'Donoghue			
	George Williams			
☐ 389	Jim Umbricht	5.50	2.50	.70
	(Card back mentions			
	his death)			
☐ 390	Orlando Cepeda	8.50	3.80	1.05
☐ 391	Sam McDowell	5.50	2.50	.70
☐ 392	Jim Pagliaroni	5.00	2.30	.60
☐ 393	Casey Teaches	6.50	2.90	.80
	Casey Stengel MG			
	Ed Kranepool			
☐ 394	Bob Miller	5.00	2.30	.60
☐ 395	Tom Tresh	7.00	3.10	.85
☐ 396	Dennis Bennett	5.00	2.30	.60
☐ 397	Chuck Cottier	5.00	2.30	.60
☐ 398	Mets Rookies	5.00	2.30	.60
	Bill Haas			
	Dick Smith			
☐ 399	Jackie Brandt	5.00	2.30	.60
☐ 400	Warren Spahn	36.00	16.00	4.50
☐ 401	Charlie Maxwell	5.50	2.50	.70
☐ 402	Tom Sturdivant	5.00	2.30	.60
☐ 403	Reds Team	10.00	4.50	1.25
☐ 404	Tony Martinez	5.00	2.30	.60
☐ 405	Ken McBride	5.00	2.30	.60
☐ 406	Al Spangler	5.00	2.30	.60
☐ 407	Bill Freehan	6.50	2.90	.80
☐ 408	Cubs Rookies	5.00	2.30	.60
	Jim Stewart			
	Fred Burdette			
☐ 409	Bill Fischer	5.00	2.30	.60
☐ 410	Dick Stuart	5.50	2.50	.70
☐ 411	Lee Walls	5.00	2.30	.60
☐ 412	Ray Culp	5.00	2.30	.60
☐ 413	Johnny Keane MG	5.00	2.30	.60
☐ 414	Jack Sanford	5.00	2.30	.60
☐ 415	Tony Kubek	8.00	3.60	1.00
☐ 416	Lee Maye	5.00	2.30	.60
☐ 417	Don Cardwell	5.00	2.30	.60
☐ 418	Orioles Rookies	5.50	2.50	.70
	Darold Knowles			
	Les Narum			
☐ 419	Ken Harrelson	8.50	3.80	1.05
☐ 420	Jim Maloney	5.50	2.50	.70
☐ 421	Camilo Carreon	5.00	2.30	.60
☐ 422	Jack Fisher	5.00	2.30	.60
☐ 423	Tops in NL	110.00	50.00	14.00
	Hank Aaron			
	Willie Mays			
☐ 424	Dick Bertell	5.00	2.30	.60
☐ 425	Norm Cash	6.50	2.90	.80
☐ 426	Bob Rodgers	5.50	2.50	.70
☐ 427	Don Rudolph	5.00	2.30	.60
☐ 428	Red Sox Rookies	5.00	2.30	.60
	Archie Skeen			
	Pete Smith			
	(Back states Archie			
	has retired)			
☐ 429	Tim McCarver	9.00	4.00	1.15
☐ 430	Juan Pizarro	5.00	2.30	.60
☐ 431	George Alusik	5.00	2.30	.60
☐ 432	Ruben Amaro	5.00	2.30	.60
☐ 433	Yankees Team	15.00	6.75	1.90
☐ 434	Don Nottebart	5.00	2.30	.60
☐ 435	Vic Davalillo	5.00	2.30	.60
☐ 436	Charlie Neal	5.50	2.50	.70
☐ 437	Ed Bailey	5.00	2.30	.60
☐ 438	Checklist 6	15.00	2.30	.75
☐ 439	Harvey Haddix	5.50	2.50	.70
☐ 440	Bob Clemente UER	150.00	70.00	19.00
	(1960 Pittsburfh)			

☐ 441 Bob Duliba 5.00 2.30 .60
☐ 442 Pumpsie Green 5.50 2.50 .70
☐ 443 Chuck Dressen MG 5.50 2.50 .70
☐ 444 Larry Jackson 5.00 2.30 .60
☐ 445 Bill Skowron 6.00 2.70 .75
☐ 446 Julian Javier 5.50 2.50 .70
☐ 447 Ted Bowsfield 5.00 2.30 .60
☐ 448 Cookie Rojas 5.50 2.50 .70
☐ 449 Deron Johnson 5.50 2.50 .70
☐ 450 Steve Barber 5.00 2.30 .60
☐ 451 Joe Amalfitano 5.00 2.30 .60
☐ 452 Giants Rookies 7.00 3.10 .85
Gil Garrido
Jim Ray Hart
☐ 453 Frank Baumann 5.00 2.30 .60
☐ 454 Tommie Aaron 5.50 2.50 .70
☐ 455 Bernie Allen 5.00 2.30 .60
☐ 456 Dodgers Rookies 7.50 3.40 .95
Wes Parker
John Werhas
☐ 457 Jesse Gonder 5.00 2.30 .60
☐ 458 Ralph Terry 5.50 2.50 .70
☐ 459 Red Sox Rookies 5.00 2.30 .60
Pete Charton
Dalton Jones
☐ 460 Bob Gibson 40.00 18.00 5.00
☐ 461 George Thomas 5.00 2.30 .60
☐ 462 Birdie Tebbetts MG 5.50 2.50 .70
☐ 463 Don Leppert 5.00 2.30 .60
☐ 464 Dallas Green 5.50 2.50 .70
☐ 465 Mike Hershberger 5.00 2.30 .60
☐ 466 A's Rookies 5.50 2.50 .70
Dick Green
Aurelio Monteagudo
☐ 467 Bob Aspromonte 5.00 2.30 .60
☐ 468 Gaylord Perry 45.00 20.00 5.75
☐ 469 Cubs Rookies 5.50 2.50 .70
Fred Norman
Sterling Slaughter
☐ 470 Jim Bouton 7.00 3.10 .85
☐ 471 Gates Brown 8.00 3.60 1.00
☐ 472 Vern Law 5.50 2.50 .70
☐ 473 Baltimore Orioles 10.00 4.50 1.25
Team Card
☐ 474 Larry Sherry 5.50 2.50 .70
☐ 475 Ed Charles 5.00 2.30 .60
☐ 476 Braves Rookies 10.00 4.50 1.25
Rico Carty
Dick Kelley
☐ 477 Mike Joyce 5.00 2.30 .60
☐ 478 Dick Howser 5.50 2.50 .70
☐ 479 Cardinals Rookies 5.00 2.30 .60
Dave Bakenhaster
Johnny Lewis
☐ 480 Bob Purkey 5.00 2.30 .60
☐ 481 Chuck Schilling 5.00 2.30 .60
☐ 482 Phillies Rookies 5.50 2.50 .70
John Briggs
Danny Cater
☐ 483 Fred Valentine 5.00 2.30 .60
☐ 484 Bill Pleis 5.00 2.30 .60
☐ 485 Tom Haller 5.50 2.50 .70
☐ 486 Bob Kennedy MG 5.50 2.50 .70
☐ 487 Mike McCormick 5.50 2.50 .70
☐ 488 Yankees Rookies 5.50 2.50 .70
Pete Mikkelsen
Bob Meyer
☐ 489 Julio Navarro 5.00 2.30 .60
☐ 490 Ron Fairly 5.50 2.50 .70
☐ 491 Ed Rakow 5.00 2.30 .60
☐ 492 Colts Rookies 6.00 2.70 .75
Jim Beauchamp
Mike White
☐ 493 Don Lee 5.00 2.30 .60
☐ 494 Al Jackson 5.00 2.30 .60
☐ 495 Bill Virdon 5.50 2.50 .70
☐ 496 White Sox Team 10.00 4.50 1.25
☐ 497 Jeoff Long 5.00 2.30 .60
☐ 498 Dave Stenhouse 5.00 2.30 .60
☐ 499 Indians Rookies 5.50 2.50 .70
Chico Salmon
Gordon Seyfried
☐ 500 Camilo Pascual 5.50 2.50 .70
☐ 501 Bob Veale 5.50 2.50 .70
☐ 502 Angels Rookies 6.00 2.70 .75
Bobby Knoop
Bob Lee
☐ 503 Earl Wilson 5.50 2.50 .70
☐ 504 Claude Raymond 5.50 2.50 .70
☐ 505 Stan Williams 5.50 2.50 .70
☐ 506 Bobby Bragan MG 5.00 2.30 .60
☐ 507 Johnny Edwards 5.00 2.30 .60
☐ 508 Diego Segui 5.00 2.30 .60
☐ 509 Pirates Rookies 10.00 4.50 1.25
Gene Alley
Orlando McFarlane
☐ 510 Lindy McDaniel 5.50 2.50 .70
☐ 511 Lou Jackson 5.50 2.50 .70
☐ 512 Tigers Rookies 14.00 6.25 1.75
Willie Horton
Joe Sparma
☐ 513 Don Larsen 6.50 2.90 .80
☐ 514 Jim Hickman 5.50 2.50 .70
☐ 515 Johnny Romano 5.00 2.30 .60
☐ 516 Twins Rookies 5.00 2.30 .60
Jerry Arrigo
Dwight Siebler
☐ 517A Checklist 7 ERR 25.00 3.80 1.25
(Incorrect numbering
sequence on back)
☐ 517B Checklist 7 COR 15.00 2.30 .75
(Correct numbering
on back)
☐ 518 Carl Bouldin 5.00 2.30 .60
☐ 519 Charlie Smith 5.00 2.30 .60
☐ 520 Jack Baldschun 5.00 2.30 .60
☐ 521 Tom Satriano 5.00 2.30 .60
☐ 522 Bob Tiefenauer 5.00 2.30 .60
☐ 523 Lou Burdette UER 10.00 4.50 1.25
(Pitching lefty)
☐ 524 Reds Rookies 10.00 4.50 1.25
Jim Dickson
Bobby Klaus
☐ 525 Al McBean 10.00 4.50 1.25
☐ 526 Lou Clinton 10.00 4.50 1.25
☐ 527 Larry Bearnarth 10.00 4.50 1.25
☐ 528 A's Rookies 15.00 6.75 1.90
Dave Duncan
Tommie Reynolds
☐ 529 Alvin Dark MG 12.00 5.50 1.50
☐ 530 Leon Wagner 10.00 4.50 1.25
☐ 531 Los Angeles Dodgers 24.00 11.00 3.00
Team Card
☐ 532 Twins Rookies 12.00 5.50 1.50
Bud Bloomfield
(Bloomfield photo
actually Jay Ward)
Joe Nossek
☐ 533 Johnny Klippstein 10.00 4.50 1.25
☐ 534 Gus Bell 12.00 5.50 1.50
☐ 535 Phil Regan 12.00 5.50 1.50
☐ 536 Mets Rookies 10.00 4.50 1.25
Larry Elliot
John Stephenson
☐ 537 Dan Osinski 10.00 4.50 1.25
☐ 538 Minnie Minoso 12.50 5.75 1.55
☐ 539 Roy Face 12.00 5.50 1.50
☐ 540 Luis Aparicio 21.00 9.50 2.60
☐ 541 Braves Rookies 210.00 95.00 26.00
Phil Roof
Phil Niekro
☐ 542 Don Mincher 10.00 4.50 1.25
☐ 543 Bob Uecker 50.00 23.00 6.25
☐ 544 Colts Rookies 12.00 5.50 1.50
Steve Hertz
Joe Hoerner
☐ 545 Max Alvis 10.00 4.50 1.25
☐ 546 Joe Christopher 10.00 4.50 1.25
☐ 547 Gil Hodges MG 15.00 6.75 1.90
☐ 548 NL Rookies 10.00 4.50 1.25
Wayne Schurr
Paul Speckenbach
☐ 549 Joe Moeller 10.00 4.50 1.25
☐ 550 Ken Hubbs MEM 25.00 11.50 3.10
(In memoriam)
☐ 551 Billy Hoeft 10.00 4.50 1.25
☐ 552 Indians Rookies 12.00 5.50 1.50
Tom Kelley
Sonny Siebert
☐ 553 Jim Brewer 10.00 4.50 1.25
☐ 554 Hank Foiles 10.00 4.50 1.25
☐ 555 Lee Stange 10.00 4.50 1.25
☐ 556 Mets Rookies 10.00 4.50 1.25
Steve Dillon
Ron Locke
☐ 557 Leo Burke 10.00 4.50 1.25
☐ 558 Don Schwall 10.00 4.50 1.25
☐ 559 Dick Phillips 10.00 4.50 1.25
☐ 560 Dick Farrell 10.00 4.50 1.25
☐ 561 Phillies Rookies UER 12.50 5.75 1.55
Dave Bennett
(19 ... is 18)
Rick Wise
☐ 562 Pedro Ramos 10.00 4.50 1.25
☐ 563 Dal Maxvill 12.00 5.50 1.50
☐ 564 AL Rookies 10.00 4.50 1.25

Joe McCabe			
Jerry McNertney			
□ 565 Stu Miller	12.00	5.50	1.50
□ 566 Ed Kranepool	14.00	6.25	1.75
□ 567 Jim Kaat	15.00	6.75	1.90
□ 568 NL Rookies	10.00	4.50	1.25
Phil Gagliano			
Cap Peterson			
□ 569 Fred Newman	10.00	4.50	1.25
□ 570 Bill Mazeroski	15.00	6.75	1.90
□ 571 Gene Conley	12.00	5.50	1.50
□ 572 AL Rookies	10.00	4.50	1.25
Dave Gray			
Dick Egan			
□ 573 Jim Duffalo	10.00	4.50	1.25
□ 574 Manny Jimenez	10.00	4.50	1.25
□ 575 Tony Cloninger	10.00	4.50	1.25
□ 576 Mets Rookies	10.00	4.50	1.25
Jerry Hinsley			
Bill Wakefield			
□ 577 Gordy Coleman	12.00	5.50	1.50
□ 578 Glen Hobbie	10.00	4.50	1.25
□ 579 Red Sox Team	20.00	9.00	2.50
□ 580 Johnny Podres	12.00	5.50	1.50
□ 581 Yankees Rookies	10.00	4.50	1.25
Pedro Gonzalez			
Archie Moore			
□ 582 Rod Kanehl	10.00	4.50	1.25
□ 583 Tito Francona	10.00	4.50	1.25
□ 584 Joel Horlen	12.00	5.50	1.50
□ 585 Tony Taylor	12.00	5.50	1.50
□ 586 Jim Piersall	12.50	5.75	1.55
□ 587 Bennie Daniels	14.00	6.25	1.75

1964 Topps Giants

The cards in this 60-card set measure approximately 3 1/8" by 5 1/4". The 1964 Topps Giants are postcard size cards containing color player photographs. They are numbered on the backs, which also contain biographical information presented in a newspaper format. These "giant size" cards were distributed in both cellophane and waxed gum packs apart from the Topps regular issue of 1964. Cards 3, 28, 42, 45, 47, 51 and 60 are more difficult to find and are indicated by SP in the checklist below.

	NRMT	VG-E	GOOD
COMPLETE SET (60)	150.00	70.00	19.00
COMMON PLAYER (1-60)	.35	.16	.04
□ 1 Gary Peters	.35	.16	.04
□ 2 Ken Johnson	.35	.16	.04
□ 3 Sandy Koufax SP	30.00	13.50	3.80
□ 4 Bob Bailey	.35	.16	.04
□ 5 Milt Pappas	.35	.16	.04
□ 6 Ron Hunt	.35	.16	.04
□ 7 Whitey Ford	3.50	1.55	.45
□ 8 Roy McMillan	.35	.16	.04
□ 9 Rocky Colavito	.75	.35	.09
□ 10 Jim Bunning	.75	.35	.09
□ 11 Bob Clemente	7.50	3.40	.95
□ 12 Al Kaline	5.00	2.30	.60
□ 13 Nellie Fox	.75	.35	.09
□ 14 Tony Gonzalez	.35	.16	.04
□ 15 Jim Gentile	.35	.16	.04
□ 16 Dean Chance	.35	.16	.04
□ 17 Dick Ellsworth	.35	.16	.04
□ 18 Jim Fregosi	.50	.23	.06
□ 19 Dick Groat	.50	.23	.06
□ 20 Chuck Hinton	.35	.16	.04
□ 21 Elston Howard	.50	.23	.06
□ 22 Dick Farrell	.35	.16	.04
□ 23 Albie Pearson	.35	.16	.04
□ 24 Frank Howard	.50	.23	.06
□ 25 Mickey Mantle	20.00	9.00	2.50
□ 26 Joe Torre	.50	.23	.06
□ 27 Eddie Brinkman	.35	.16	.04
□ 28 Bob Friend SP	7.50	3.40	.95
□ 29 Frank Robinson	3.50	1.55	.45
□ 30 Bill Freehan	.60	.25	.08
□ 31 Warren Spahn	3.50	1.55	.45
□ 32 Camilo Pascual	.35	.16	.04
□ 33 Pete Ward	.35	.16	.04
□ 34 Jim Maloney	.35	.16	.04
□ 35 Dave Wickersham	.35	.16	.04
□ 36 Johnny Callison	.50	.23	.06
□ 37 Juan Marichal	2.50	1.15	.30
□ 38 Harmon Killebrew	2.50	1.15	.30
□ 39 Luis Aparicio	2.00	.90	.25
□ 40 Dick Radatz	.35	.16	.04
□ 41 Bob Gibson	3.50	1.55	.45
□ 42 Dick Stuart SP	7.50	3.40	.95
□ 43 Tommy Davis	.35	.16	.04
□ 44 Tony Oliva	.75	.35	.09
□ 45 Wayne Causey SP	7.50	3.40	.95
□ 46 Max Alvis	.35	.16	.04
□ 47 Galen Cisco SP	7.50	3.40	.95
□ 48 Carl Yastrzemski	5.00	2.30	.60
□ 49 Hank Aaron	7.50	3.40	.95
□ 50 Brooks Robinson	4.50	2.00	.55
□ 51 Willie Mays SP	30.00	13.50	3.80
□ 52 Billy Williams	2.50	1.15	.30
□ 53 Juan Pizarro	.35	.16	.04
□ 54 Leon Wagner	.35	.16	.04
□ 55 Orlando Cepeda	.75	.35	.09
□ 56 Vada Pinson	.50	.23	.06
□ 57 Ken Boyer	.60	.25	.08
□ 58 Ron Santo	.75	.35	.09
□ 59 John Romano	.35	.16	.04
□ 60 Bill Skowron SP	10.00	4.50	1.25

1964 Topps Stand Ups

In 1964 Topps produced a die-cut "Stand-Up" card design for the first time since their Connie Mack and Current All Stars of 1951. The cards have full-length, color player photos set against a green and yellow background. Of the 77 cards in the set, 22 were single printed and these are marked in the checklist below with an SP. These unnumbered cards are standard-size (2 1/2" by 3 1/2"), blank backed, and have been numbered here for reference in alphabetical order of players.

	NRMT	VG-E	GOOD
COMPLETE SET (77)	2500.00	1150.00	325.00
COMMON PLAYER (1-77)	6.00	2.70	.75
COMMON PLAYER SP	24.00	11.00	3.00
□ 1 Hank Aaron	125.00	57.50	15.50
□ 2 Hank Aguirre	6.00	2.70	.75
□ 3 George Altman	6.00	2.70	.75
□ 4 Max Alvis	6.00	2.70	.75
□ 5 Bob Aspromonte	6.00	2.70	.75
□ 6 Jack Baldschun SP	24.00	11.00	3.00

☐ 7 Ernie Banks	50.00	23.00	6.25
☐ 8 Steve Barber	6.00	2.70	.75
☐ 9 Earl Battey	6.00	2.70	.75
☐ 10 Ken Boyer	8.00	3.60	1.00
☐ 11 Ernie Broglio	6.00	2.70	.75
☐ 12 John Callison	7.00	3.10	.85
☐ 13 Norm Cash SP	30.00	13.50	3.80
☐ 14 Wayne Causey	6.00	2.70	.75
☐ 15 Orlando Cepeda	10.00	4.50	1.25
☐ 16 Ed Charles	6.00	2.70	.75
☐ 17 Bob Clemente	100.00	45.00	12.50
☐ 18 Donn Clendenon SP	24.00	11.00	3.00
☐ 19 Rocky Colavito	10.00	4.50	1.25
☐ 20 Ray Culp SP	24.00	11.00	3.00
☐ 21 Tommy Davis	8.00	3.60	1.00
☐ 22 Don Drysdale SP	90.00	40.00	11.50
☐ 23 Dick Ellsworth	6.00	2.70	.75
☐ 24 Dick Farrell	6.00	2.70	.75
☐ 25 Jim Fregosi	7.00	3.10	.85
☐ 26 Bob Friend	6.00	2.70	.75
☐ 27 Jim Gentile	6.00	2.70	.75
☐ 28 Jesse Gonder SP	24.00	11.00	3.00
☐ 29 Tony Gonzalez SP	24.00	11.00	3.00
☐ 30 Dick Groat	8.00	3.60	1.00
☐ 31 Woody Held	6.00	2.70	.75
☐ 32 Chuck Hinton	6.00	2.70	.75
☐ 33 Elston Howard	8.00	3.60	1.00
☐ 34 Frank Howard SP	30.00	13.50	3.80
☐ 35 Ron Hunt	6.00	2.70	.75
☐ 36 Al Jackson	6.00	2.70	.75
☐ 37 Ken Johnson	6.00	2.70	.75
☐ 38 Al Kaline	60.00	27.00	7.50
☐ 39 Harmon Killebrew	40.00	18.00	5.00
☐ 40 Sandy Koufax	100.00	45.00	12.50
☐ 41 Don Lock SP	24.00	11.00	3.00
☐ 42 Jerry Lumpe SP	24.00	11.00	3.00
☐ 43 Jim Maloney	7.00	3.10	.85
☐ 44 Frank Malzone	6.00	2.70	.75
☐ 45 Mickey Mantle	500.00	230.00	65.00
☐ 46 Juan Marichal SP	90.00	40.00	11.50
☐ 47 Eddie Mathews SP	100.00	45.00	12.50
☐ 48 Willie Mays	125.00	57.50	15.50
☐ 49 Bill Mazeroski	8.00	3.60	1.00
☐ 50 Ken McBride	6.00	2.70	.75
☐ 51 Willie McCovey SP	100.00	45.00	12.50
☐ 52 Claude Osteen	6.00	2.70	.75
☐ 53 Jim O'Toole	6.00	2.70	.75
☐ 54 Camilo Pascual	6.00	2.70	.75
☐ 55 Albie Pearson SP	24.00	11.00	3.00
☐ 56 Gary Peters	6.00	2.70	.75
☐ 57 Vada Pinson	8.00	3.60	1.00
☐ 58 Juan Pizarro	6.00	2.70	.75
☐ 59 Boog Powell	10.00	4.50	1.25
☐ 60 Bobby Richardson	10.00	4.50	1.25
☐ 61 Brooks Robinson	50.00	23.00	6.25
☐ 62 Floyd Robinson	6.00	2.70	.75
☐ 63 Frank Robinson	45.00	20.00	5.75
☐ 64 Ed Roebuck SP	24.00	11.00	3.00
☐ 65 Rich Rollins	6.00	2.70	.75
☐ 66 John Romano	6.00	2.70	.75
☐ 67 Ron Santo SP	30.00	13.50	3.80
☐ 68 Norm Siebern	6.00	2.70	.75
☐ 69 Warren Spahn SP	100.00	45.00	12.50
☐ 70 Dick Stuart SP	24.00	11.00	3.00
☐ 71 Lee Thomas	6.00	2.70	.75
☐ 72 Joe Torre	10.00	4.50	1.25
☐ 73 Pete Ward	6.00	2.70	.75
☐ 74 Bill White SP	30.00	13.50	3.80
☐ 75 Billy Williams SP	90.00	40.00	11.50
☐ 76 Hal Woodeshick SP	24.00	11.00	3.00
☐ 77 Carl Yastrzemski SP	400.00	180.00	50.00

1965 Topps

The cards in this 598-card set measure 2 1/2" by 3 1/2". The cards comprising the 1965 Topps set have team names located within a distinctive pennant design below the picture. The cards have blue borders on the reverse and were issued by series. Cards 523 to 598 are more difficult to obtain than all other series. Within this last series there are 44 cards that were printed in lesser quantities than the other cards in that series; these shorter-printed cards are marked by SP in the checklist below. In addition, the sixth series (447-522) is more difficult to obtain than series one through five. Featured subsets within this set include League Leaders

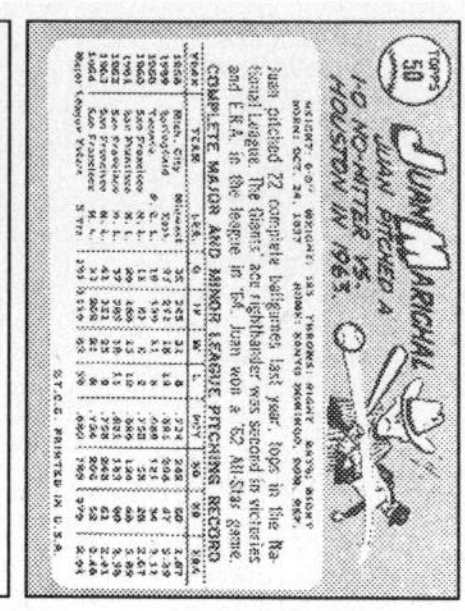

(1-12) and World Series cards (132-139). Key cards in this set include Steve Carlton's rookie, Mickey Mantle, and Pete Rose. Other key rookies in this set are Jim Hunter, Joe Morgan, and Tony Perez.

	NRMT	VG-E	GOOD
COMPLETE SET (598)	3750.00	1700.00	475.00
COMMON PLAYER (1-196)	1.50	.65	.19
COMMON PLAYER (197-283)	2.00	.90	.25
COMMON PLAYER (284-370)	3.50	1.55	.45
COMMON PLAYER (371-446)	5.00	2.30	.60
COMMON PLAYER (447-522)	6.00	2.70	.75
COMMON PLAYER (523-598)	6.00	2.70	.75
☐ 1 AL Batting Leaders	15.00	4.50	1.50
Tony Oliva			
Elston Howard			
Brooks Robinson			
☐ 2 NL Batting Leaders	9.00	4.00	1.15
Bob Clemente			
Hank Aaron			
Rico Carty			
☐ 3 AL Home Run Leaders	20.00	9.00	2.50
Harmon Killebrew			
Mickey Mantle			
Boog Powell			
☐ 4 NL Home Run Leaders	7.50	3.40	.95
Willie Mays			
Billy Williams			
Jim Ray Hart			
Orlando Cepeda			
Johnny Callison			
☐ 5 AL RBI Leaders	20.00	9.00	2.50
Brooks Robinson			
Harmon Killebrew			
Mickey Mantle			
Dick Stuart			
☐ 6 NL RBI Leaders	5.00	2.30	.60
Ken Boyer			
Willie Mays			
Ron Santo			
☐ 7 AL ERA Leaders	3.00	1.35	.40
Dean Chance			
Joel Horlen			
☐ 8 NL ERA Leaders	9.50	4.30	1.20
Sandy Koufax			
Don Drysdale			
☐ 9 AL Pitching Leaders	3.00	1.35	.40
Dean Chance			
Gary Peters			
Dave Wickersham			
Juan Pizarro			
Wally Bunker			
☐ 10 NL Pitching Leaders	3.00	1.35	.40
Larry Jackson			
Ray Sadecki			
Juan Marichal			
☐ 11 AL Strikeout Leaders	3.00	1.35	.40
Al Downing			
Dean Chance			
Camilo Pascual			
☐ 12 NL Strikeout Leaders	4.50	2.00	.55
Bob Veale			
Don Drysdale			
Bob Gibson			
☐ 13 Pedro Ramos	1.50	.65	.19
☐ 14 Len Gabrielson	1.50	.65	.19
☐ 15 Robin Roberts	8.00	3.60	1.00
☐ 16 Houston Rookies	175.00	80.00	22.00
Joe Morgan			
Sonny Jackson			
☐ 17 Johnny Romano	1.50	.65	.19

☐ 18 Bill McCool 1.50 .65 .19
☐ 19 Gates Brown 2.00 .90 .25
☐ 20 Jim Bunning 4.50 2.00 .55
☐ 21 Don Blasingame 1.50 .65 .19
☐ 22 Charlie Smith 1.50 .65 .19
☐ 23 Bob Tiefenauer 1.50 .65 .19
☐ 24 Minnesota Twins 3.00 1.35 .40
Team Card
☐ 25 Al McBean 1.50 .65 .19
☐ 26 Bobby Knoop 1.50 .65 .19
☐ 27 Dick Bertell 1.50 .65 .19
☐ 28 Barney Schultz 1.50 .65 .19
☐ 29 Felix Mantilla 1.50 .65 .19
☐ 30 Jim Bouton 3.00 1.35 .40
☐ 31 Mike White 1.50 .65 .19
☐ 32 Herman Franks MG 1.50 .65 .19
☐ 33 Jackie Brandt 1.50 .65 .19
☐ 34 Cal Koonce 1.50 .65 .19
☐ 35 Ed Charles 1.50 .65 .19
☐ 36 Bobby Wine 1.50 .65 .19
☐ 37 Fred Gladding 1.50 .65 .19
☐ 38 Jim King 1.50 .65 .19
☐ 39 Gerry Arrigo 1.50 .65 .19
☐ 40 Frank Howard 3.00 1.35 .40
☐ 41 White Sox Rookies 1.50 .65 .19
Bruce Howard
Marv Staehle
☐ 42 Earl Wilson 2.00 .90 .25
☐ 43 Mike Shannon 2.00 .90 .25
(Name in red, other
Cardinals in yellow)
☐ 44 Wade Blasingame 1.50 .65 .19
☐ 45 Roy McMillan 2.00 .90 .25
☐ 46 Bob Lee 1.50 .65 .19
☐ 47 Tommy Harper 2.00 .90 .25
☐ 48 Claude Raymond 2.00 .90 .25
☐ 49 Orioles Rookies 2.50 1.15 .30
Curt Blefary
John Miller
☐ 50 Juan Marichal 11.00 4.90 1.40
☐ 51 Bill Bryan 1.50 .65 .19
☐ 52 Ed Roebuck 1.50 .65 .19
☐ 53 Dick McAuliffe 2.00 .90 .25
☐ 54 Joe Gibbon 1.50 .65 .19
☐ 55 Tony Conigliaro 9.00 4.00 1.15
☐ 56 Ron Kline 1.50 .65 .19
☐ 57 Cardinals Team 3.00 1.35 .40
☐ 58 Fred Talbot 1.50 .65 .19
☐ 59 Nate Oliver 1.50 .65 .19
☐ 60 Jim O'Toole 2.00 .90 .25
☐ 61 Chris Cannizzaro 1.50 .65 .19
☐ 62 Jim Katt UER 4.50 2.00 .55
(Sic, Kaat)
☐ 63 Ty Cline 1.50 .65 .19
☐ 64 Lou Burdette 2.00 .90 .25
☐ 65 Tony Kubek 4.00 1.80 .50
☐ 66 Bill Rigney MG 1.50 .65 .19
☐ 67 Harvey Haddix 2.00 .90 .25
☐ 68 Del Crandall 2.00 .90 .25
☐ 69 Bill Virdon 2.00 .90 .25
☐ 70 Bill Skowron 2.00 .90 .25
☐ 71 John O'Donoghue 1.50 .65 .19
☐ 72 Tony Gonzalez 1.50 .65 .19
☐ 73 Dennis Ribant 1.50 .65 .19
☐ 74 Red Sox Rookies 7.00 3.10 .85
Rico Petrocelli
Jerry Stephenson
☐ 75 Deron Johnson 2.00 .90 .25
☐ 76 Sam McDowell 2.00 .90 .25
☐ 77 Doug Camilli 1.50 .65 .19
☐ 78 Dal Maxvill 1.50 .65 .19
☐ 79A Checklist 1 9.00 1.35 .45
(61 Cannizzaro)
☐ 79B Checklist 1 9.00 1.35 .45
(61 C.Cannizzaro)
☐ 80 Turk Farrell 1.50 .65 .19
☐ 81 Don Buford 2.00 .90 .25
☐ 82 Braves Rookies 4.00 1.80 .50
Santos Alomar
John Braun
☐ 83 George Thomas 1.50 .65 .19
☐ 84 Ron Herbel 1.50 .65 .19
☐ 85 Willie Smith 1.50 .65 .19
☐ 86 Les Narum 1.50 .65 .19
☐ 87 Nelson Mathews 1.50 .65 .19
☐ 88 Jack Lamabe 1.50 .65 .19
☐ 89 Mike Hershberger 1.50 .65 .19
☐ 90 Rich Rollins 2.00 .90 .25
☐ 91 Cubs Team 3.00 1.35 .40
☐ 92 Dick Howser 2.00 .90 .25
☐ 93 Jack Fisher 1.50 .65 .19
☐ 94 Charlie Lau 2.00 .90 .25
☐ 95 Bill Mazeroski 3.50 1.55 .45
☐ 96 Sonny Siebert 2.00 .90 .25
☐ 97 Pedro Gonzalez 1.50 .65 .19
☐ 98 Bob Miller 1.50 .65 .19
☐ 99 Gil Hodges MG 6.00 2.70 .75
☐ 100 Ken Boyer 3.50 1.55 .45
☐ 101 Fred Newman 1.50 .65 .19
☐ 102 Steve Boros 1.50 .65 .19
☐ 103 Harvey Kuenn 2.00 .90 .25
☐ 104 Checklist 2 9.00 1.35 .45
☐ 105 Chico Salmon 1.50 .65 .19
☐ 106 Gene Oliver 1.50 .65 .19
☐ 107 Phillies Rookies 2.50 1.15 .30
Pat Corrales
Costen Shockley
☐ 108 Don Mincher 1.50 .65 .19
☐ 109 Walt Bond 1.50 .65 .19
☐ 110 Ron Santo 4.00 1.80 .50
☐ 111 Lee Thomas 2.00 .90 .25
☐ 112 Derrell Griffith 1.50 .65 .19
☐ 113 Steve Barber 1.50 .65 .19
☐ 114 Jim Hickman 2.00 .90 .25
☐ 115 Bobby Richardson 4.00 1.80 .50
☐ 116 Cardinals Rookies 2.50 1.15 .30
Dave Dowling
Bob Tolan
☐ 117 Wes Stock 1.50 .65 .19
☐ 118 Hal Lanier 2.50 1.15 .30
☐ 119 John Kennedy 1.50 .65 .19
☐ 120 Frank Robinson 30.00 13.50 3.80
☐ 121 Gene Alley 2.00 .90 .25
☐ 122 Bill Pleis 1.50 .65 .19
☐ 123 Frank Thomas 2.00 .90 .25
☐ 124 Tom Satriano 1.50 .65 .19
☐ 125 Juan Pizarro 1.50 .65 .19
☐ 126 Dodgers Team 4.00 1.80 .50
☐ 127 Frank Lary 1.50 .65 .19
☐ 128 Vic Davalillo 1.50 .65 .19
☐ 129 Bennie Daniels 1.50 .65 .19
☐ 130 Al Kaline 30.00 13.50 3.80
☐ 131 Johnny Keane MG 1.50 .65 .19
☐ 132 World Series Game 1 4.00 1.80 .50
Cards take opener
(Mike Shannon)
☐ 133 World Series Game 2 4.00 1.80 .50
Mel Stottlemyre wins
☐ 134 World Series Game 3 45.00 20.00 5.75
Mickey Mantle's homer
☐ 135 World Series Game 4 4.00 1.80 .50
Ken Boyer's grand-slam
☐ 136 World Series Game 5 4.00 1.80 .50
10th inning triumph
(Tim McCarver being
greeted at home)
☐ 137 World Series Game 6 4.00 1.80 .50
Jim Bouton wins again
☐ 138 World Series Game 7 10.00 4.50 1.25
Bob Gibson wins finale
☐ 139 World Series Summary 4.00 1.80 .50
Cards celebrate
☐ 140 Dean Chance 2.00 .90 .25
☐ 141 Charlie James 1.50 .65 .19
☐ 142 Bill Monbouquette 1.50 .65 .19
☐ 143 Pirates Rookies 1.50 .65 .19
John Gelnar
Jerry May
☐ 144 Ed Kranepool 2.00 .90 .25
☐ 145 Luis Tiant 15.00 6.75 1.90
☐ 146 Ron Hansen 1.50 .65 .19
☐ 147 Dennis Bennett 1.50 .65 .19
☐ 148 Willie Kirkland 1.50 .65 .19
☐ 149 Wayne Schurr 1.50 .65 .19
☐ 150 Brooks Robinson 30.00 13.50 3.80
☐ 151 Athletics Team 3.00 1.35 .40
☐ 152 Phil Ortega 1.50 .65 .19
☐ 153 Norm Cash 4.00 1.80 .50
☐ 154 Bob Humphreys 1.50 .65 .19
☐ 155 Roger Maris 65.00 29.00 8.25
☐ 156 Bob Sadowski 1.50 .65 .19
☐ 157 Zoilo Versalles 2.50 1.15 .30
☐ 158 Dick Sisler 1.50 .65 .19
☐ 159 Jim Duffalo 1.50 .65 .19
☐ 160 Bob Clemente UER 80.00 36.00 10.00
(1960 Pittsburfh)
☐ 161 Frank Baumann 1.50 .65 .19
☐ 162 Russ Nixon 1.50 .65 .19
☐ 163 Johnny Briggs 1.50 .65 .19
☐ 164 Al Spangler 1.50 .65 .19
☐ 165 Dick Ellsworth 1.50 .65 .19
☐ 166 Indians Rookies 3.50 1.55 .45
George Culver
Tommie Agee
☐ 167 Bill Wakefield 1.50 .65 .19
☐ 168 Dick Green 1.50 .65 .19

169 Dave Vineyard 1.50 .65 .19
170 Hank Aaron 100.00 45.00 12.50
171 Jim Roland 1.50 .65 .19
172 Jim Piersall 2.00 .90 .25
173 Detroit Tigers 3.00 1.35 .40
Team Card
174 Joey Jay 1.50 .65 .19
175 Bob Aspromonte 1.50 .65 .19
176 Willie McCovey 20.00 9.00 2.50
177 Pete Mikkelsen 1.50 .65 .19
178 Dalton Jones 1.50 .65 .19
179 Hal Woodeshick 1.50 .65 .19
180 Bob Allison 2.00 .90 .25
181 Senators Rookies 1.50 .65 .19
Don Loun
Joe McCabe
182 Mike DeLaHoz 1.50 .65 .19
183 Dave Nicholson 1.50 .65 .19
184 John Boozer 1.50 .65 .19
185 Max Alvis 1.50 .65 .19
186 Billy Cowan 1.50 .65 .19
187 Casey Stengel MG 15.00 6.75 1.90
188 Sam Bowens 1.50 .65 .19
189 Checklist 3 9.00 1.35 .45
190 Bill White 3.50 1.55 .45
191 Phil Regan 2.00 .90 .25
192 Jim Coker 1.50 .65 .19
193 Gaylord Perry 20.00 9.00 2.50
194 Rookie Stars 1.50 .65 .19
Bill Kelso
Rick Reichardt
195 Bob Veale 2.00 .90 .25
196 Ron Fairly 1.50 .65 .19
197 Diego Segui 2.00 .90 .25
198 Smoky Burgess 2.50 1.15 .30
199 Bob Heffner 2.00 .90 .25
200 Joe Torre 4.50 2.00 .55
201 Twins Rookies 3.00 1.35 .40
Sandy Valdespino
Cesar Tovar
202 Leo Burke 2.00 .90 .25
203 Dallas Green 2.50 1.15 .30
204 Russ Snyder 2.00 .90 .25
205 Warren Spahn 27.00 12.00 3.40
206 Willie Horton 3.50 1.55 .45
207 Pete Rose 175.00 80.00 22.00
208 Tommy John 15.00 6.75 1.90
209 Pirates Team 4.00 1.80 .50
210 Jim Fregosi 2.50 1.15 .30
211 Steve Ridzik 2.00 .90 .25
212 Ron Brand 2.00 .90 .25
213 Jim Davenport 2.00 .90 .25
214 Bob Purkey 2.00 .90 .25
215 Pete Ward 2.00 .90 .25
216 Al Worthington 2.00 .90 .25
217 Walt Alston MG 4.00 1.80 .50
218 Dick Schofield 2.00 .90 .25
219 Bob Meyer 2.00 .90 .25
220 Billy Williams 15.00 6.75 1.90
221 John Tsitouris 2.00 .90 .25
222 Bob Tillman 2.00 .90 .25
223 Dan Osinski 2.00 .90 .25
224 Bob Chance 2.00 .90 .25
225 Bo Belinsky 2.50 1.15 .30
226 Yankees Rookies 2.00 .90 .25
Elvio Jimenez
Jake Gibbs
227 Bobby Klaus 2.00 .90 .25
228 Jack Sanford 2.00 .90 .25
229 Lou Clinton 2.00 .90 .25
230 Ray Sadecki 2.00 .90 .25
231 Jerry Adair 2.00 .90 .25
232 Steve Blass 3.50 1.55 .45
233 Don Zimmer 2.50 1.15 .30
234 White Sox Team 4.00 1.80 .50
235 Chuck Hinton 2.00 .90 .25
236 Denny McLain 25.00 11.50 3.10
237 Bernie Allen 2.00 .90 .25
238 Joe Moeller 2.00 .90 .25
239 Doc Edwards 2.00 .90 .25
240 Bob Bruce 2.00 .90 .25
241 Mack Jones 2.00 .90 .25
242 George Brunet 2.00 .90 .25
243 Reds Rookies 3.00 1.35 .40
Ted Davidson
Tommy Helms
244 Lindy McDaniel 2.50 1.15 .30
245 Joe Pepitone 2.50 1.15 .30
246 Tom Butters 2.00 .90 .25
247 Wally Moon 2.50 1.15 .30
248 Gus Triandos 2.50 1.15 .30
249 Dave McNally 3.00 1.35 .40
250 Willie Mays 100.00 45.00 12.50
251 Billy Herman MG 2.50 1.15 .30
252 Pete Richert 2.00 .90 .25
253 Danny Cater 2.00 .90 .25
254 Roland Sheldon 2.00 .90 .25
255 Camilo Pascual 2.50 1.15 .30
256 Tito Francona 2.00 .90 .25
257 Jim Wynn 3.00 1.35 .40
258 Larry Bearnarth 2.00 .90 .25
259 Tigers Rookies 4.50 2.00 .55
Jim Northrup
Ray Oyler
260 Don Drysdale 20.00 9.00 2.50
261 Duke Carmel 2.00 .90 .25
262 Bud Daley 2.00 .90 .25
263 Marty Keough 2.00 .90 .25
264 Bob Buhl 2.50 1.15 .30
265 Jim Pagliaroni 2.00 .90 .25
266 Bert Campaneris 8.00 3.60 1.00
267 Senators Team 4.00 1.80 .50
268 Ken McBride 2.00 .90 .25
269 Frank Bolling 2.00 .90 .25
270 Milt Pappas 2.50 1.15 .30
271 Don Wert 2.00 .90 .25
272 Chuck Schilling 2.00 .90 .25
273 Checklist 4 9.00 1.35 .45
274 Lum Harris MG 2.00 .90 .25
275 Dick Groat 3.00 1.35 .40
276 Hoyt Wilhelm 8.00 3.60 1.00
277 Johnny Lewis 2.00 .90 .25
278 Ken Retzer 2.00 .90 .25
279 Dick Tracewski 2.00 .90 .25
280 Dick Stuart 2.50 1.15 .30
281 Bill Stafford 2.00 .90 .25
282 Giants Rookies 5.00 2.30 .60
Dick Estelle
Masanori Murakami
283 Fred Whitfield 2.00 .90 .25
284 Nick Willhite 3.50 1.55 .45
285 Ron Hunt 3.50 1.55 .45
286 Athletics Rookies 3.50 1.55 .45
Jim Dickson
Aurelio Monteagudo
287 Gary Kolb 3.50 1.55 .45
288 Jack Hamilton 3.50 1.55 .45
289 Gordy Coleman 4.00 1.80 .50
290 Wally Bunker 4.00 1.80 .50
291 Jerry Lynch 3.50 1.55 .45
292 Larry Yellen 3.50 1.55 .45
293 Angels Team 6.50 2.90 .80
294 Tim McCarver 6.00 2.70 .75
295 Dick Radatz 4.00 1.80 .50
296 Tony Taylor 3.50 1.55 .45
297 Dave DeBusschere 4.00 1.80 .50
298 Jim Stewart 3.50 1.55 .45
299 Jerry Zimmerman 3.50 1.55 .45
300 Sandy Koufax 125.00 57.50 15.50
301 Birdie Tebbetts MG 4.00 1.80 .50
302 Al Stanek 3.50 1.55 .45
303 John Orsino 3.50 1.55 .45
304 Dave Stenhouse 3.50 1.55 .45
305 Rico Carty 4.50 2.00 .55
306 Bubba Phillips 3.50 1.55 .45
307 Barry Latman 3.50 1.55 .45
308 Mets Rookies 7.50 3.40 .95
Cleon Jones
Tom Parsons
309 Steve Hamilton 3.50 1.55 .45
310 Johnny Callison 4.00 1.80 .50
311 Orlando Pena 3.50 1.55 .45
312 Joe Nuxhall 4.00 1.80 .50
313 Jim Schaffer 3.50 1.55 .45
314 Sterling Slaughter 3.50 1.55 .45
315 Frank Malzone 4.00 1.80 .50
316 Reds Team 6.50 2.90 .80
317 Don McMahon 3.50 1.55 .45
318 Matty Alou 4.00 1.80 .50
319 Ken McMullen 3.50 1.55 .45
320 Bob Gibson 35.00 16.00 4.40
321 Rusty Staub 6.00 2.70 .75
322 Rick Wise 4.00 1.80 .50
323 Hank Bauer MG 4.00 1.80 .50
324 Bobby Locke 3.50 1.55 .45
325 Donn Clendenon 4.00 1.80 .50
326 Dwight Siebler 3.50 1.55 .45
327 Denis Menke 3.50 1.55 .45
328 Eddie Fisher 3.50 1.55 .45
329 Hawk Taylor 3.50 1.55 .45
330 Whitey Ford 35.00 16.00 4.40
331 Dodgers Rookies 4.00 1.80 .50
Al Ferrara
John Purdin
332 Ted Abernathy 3.50 1.55 .45
333 Tom Reynolds 3.50 1.55 .45

☐ 334 Vic Roznovsky 3.50 1.55 .45
☐ 335 Mickey Lolich 6.00 2.70 .75
☐ 336 Woody Held 3.50 1.55 .45
☐ 337 Mike Cuellar 4.00 1.80 .50
☐ 338 Philadelphia Phillies 6.50 2.90 .80
Team Card
☐ 339 Ryne Duren 4.00 1.80 .50
☐ 340 Tony Oliva 12.50 5.75 1.55
☐ 341 Bob Bolin 3.50 1.55 .45
☐ 342 Bob Rodgers 4.00 1.80 .50
☐ 343 Mike McCormick 4.00 1.80 .50
☐ 344 Wes Parker 4.00 1.80 .50
☐ 345 Floyd Robinson 3.50 1.55 .45
☐ 346 Bobby Bragan MG 3.50 1.55 .45
☐ 347 Roy Face 4.50 2.00 .55
☐ 348 George Banks 3.50 1.55 .45
☐ 349 Larry Miller 3.50 1.55 .45
☐ 350 Mickey Mantle 500.00 230.00 65.00
☐ 351 Jim Perry 4.00 1.80 .50
☐ 352 Alex Johnson 4.50 2.00 .55
☐ 353 Jerry Lumpe 3.50 1.55 .45
☐ 354 Cubs Rookies 3.50 1.55 .45
Billy Ott
Jack Warner
☐ 355 Vada Pinson 4.00 1.80 .50
☐ 356 Bill Spanswick 3.50 1.55 .45
☐ 357 Carl Warwick 3.50 1.55 .45
☐ 358 Albie Pearson 4.00 1.80 .50
☐ 359 Ken Johnson 3.50 1.55 .45
☐ 360 Orlando Cepeda 8.00 3.60 1.00
☐ 361 Checklist 5 3.50 .55 .18
☐ 362 Don Schwall 3.50 1.55 .45
☐ 363 Bob Johnson 3.50 1.55 .45
☐ 364 Galen Cisco 3.50 1.55 .45
☐ 365 Jim Gentile 4.00 1.80 .50
☐ 366 Dan Schneider 3.50 1.55 .45
☐ 367 Leon Wagner 3.50 1.55 .45
☐ 368 White Sox Rookies 4.00 1.80 .50
Ken Berry
Joel Gibson
☐ 369 Phil Linz 4.00 1.80 .50
☐ 370 Tommy Davis 4.00 1.80 .50
☐ 371 Frank Kreutzer 5.00 2.30 .60
☐ 372 Clay Dalrymple 5.00 2.30 .60
☐ 373 Curt Simmons 5.50 2.50 .70
☐ 374 Angels Rookies 7.00 3.10 .85
Jose Cardenal
Dick Simpson
☐ 375 Dave Wickersham 5.00 2.30 .60
☐ 376 Jim Landis 5.00 2.30 .60
☐ 377 Willie Stargell 32.00 14.50 4.00
☐ 378 Chuck Estrada 5.00 2.30 .60
☐ 379 Giants Team 9.00 4.00 1.15
☐ 380 Rocky Colavito 9.00 4.00 1.15
☐ 381 Al Jackson 5.00 2.30 .60
☐ 382 J.C. Martin 5.00 2.30 .60
☐ 383 Felipe Alou 6.50 2.90 .80
☐ 384 Johnny Klippstein 5.00 2.30 .60
☐ 385 Carl Yastrzemski 85.00 38.00 10.50
☐ 386 Cubs Rookies 5.00 2.30 .60
Paul Jaeckel
Fred Norman
☐ 387 Johnny Podres 5.50 2.50 .70
☐ 388 John Blanchard 5.00 2.30 .60
☐ 389 Don Larsen 5.50 2.50 .70
☐ 390 Bill Freehan 6.50 2.90 .80
☐ 391 Mel McGaha MG 5.00 2.30 .60
☐ 392 Bob Friend 5.50 2.50 .70
☐ 393 Ed Kirkpatrick 5.00 2.30 .60
☐ 394 Jim Hannan 5.00 2.30 .60
☐ 395 Jim Ray Hart 5.50 2.50 .70
☐ 396 Frank Bertaina 5.00 2.30 .60
☐ 397 Jerry Buchek 5.00 2.30 .60
☐ 398 Reds Rookies 5.50 2.50 .70
Dan Neville
Art Shamsky
☐ 399 Ray Herbert 5.00 2.30 .60
☐ 400 Harmon Killebrew 35.00 16.00 4.40
☐ 401 Carl Willey 5.00 2.30 .60
☐ 402 Joe Amalfitano 5.00 2.30 .60
☐ 403 Boston Red Sox 9.00 4.00 1.15
Team Card
☐ 404 Stan Williams 5.50 2.50 .70
(Listed as Indian
but Yankee cap)
☐ 405 John Roseboro 5.50 2.50 .70
☐ 406 Ralph Terry 5.50 2.50 .70
☐ 407 Lee Maye 5.00 2.30 .60
☐ 408 Larry Sherry 5.50 2.50 .70
☐ 409 Astros Rookies 6.50 2.90 .80
Jim Beauchamp
Larry Dierker
☐ 410 Luis Aparicio 10.00 4.50 1.25
☐ 411 Roger Craig 5.50 2.50 .70
☐ 412 Bob Bailey 5.50 2.50 .70
☐ 413 Hal Reniff 5.00 2.30 .60
☐ 414 Al Lopez MG 6.50 2.90 .80
☐ 415 Curt Flood 7.50 3.40 .95
☐ 416 Jim Brewer 5.00 2.30 .60
☐ 417 Ed Brinkman 5.00 2.30 .60
☐ 418 Johnny Edwards 5.00 2.30 .60
☐ 419 Ruben Amaro 5.00 2.30 .60
☐ 420 Larry Jackson 5.00 2.30 .60
☐ 421 Twins Rookies 5.00 2.30 .60
Gary Dotter
Jay Ward
☐ 422 Aubrey Gatewood 5.00 2.30 .60
☐ 423 Jesse Gonder 5.00 2.30 .60
☐ 424 Gary Bell 5.00 2.30 .60
☐ 425 Wayne Causey 5.00 2.30 .60
☐ 426 Braves Team 9.00 4.00 1.15
☐ 427 Bob Saverine 5.00 2.30 .60
☐ 428 Bob Shaw 5.00 2.30 .60
☐ 429 Don Demeter 5.00 2.30 .60
☐ 430 Gary Peters 5.00 2.30 .60
☐ 431 Cards Rookies 6.50 2.90 .80
Nelson Briles
Wayne Spiezio
☐ 432 Jim Grant 5.50 2.50 .70
☐ 433 John Bateman 5.00 2.30 .60
☐ 434 Dave Morehead 5.00 2.30 .60
☐ 435 Willie Davis 5.50 2.50 .70
☐ 436 Don Elston 5.00 2.30 .60
☐ 437 Chico Cardenas 5.50 2.50 .70
☐ 438 Harry Walker MG 5.00 2.30 .60
☐ 439 Moe Drabowsky 5.50 2.50 .70
☐ 440 Tom Tresh 6.00 2.70 .75
☐ 441 Denny Lemaster 5.00 2.30 .60
☐ 442 Vic Power 5.50 2.50 .70
☐ 443 Checklist 6 12.00 1.80 .60
☐ 444 Bob Hendley 5.00 2.30 .60
☐ 445 Don Lock 5.00 2.30 .60
☐ 446 Art Mahaffey 5.00 2.30 .60
☐ 447 Julian Javier 6.50 2.90 .80
☐ 448 Lee Stange 6.00 2.70 .75
☐ 449 Mets Rookies 6.00 2.70 .75
Jerry Hinsley
Gary Kroll
☐ 450 Elston Howard 8.00 3.60 1.00
☐ 451 Jim Owens 6.00 2.70 .75
☐ 452 Gary Geiger 6.00 2.70 .75
☐ 453 Dodgers Rookies 6.50 2.90 .80
Willie Crawford
John Werhas
☐ 454 Ed Rakow 6.00 2.70 .75
☐ 455 Norm Siebern 6.00 2.70 .75
☐ 456 Bill Henry 6.00 2.70 .75
☐ 457 Bob Kennedy MG 6.50 2.90 .80
☐ 458 John Buzhardt 6.00 2.70 .75
☐ 459 Frank Kostro 6.00 2.70 .75
☐ 460 Richie Allen 27.00 12.00 3.40
☐ 461 Braves Rookies 60.00 27.00 7.50
Clay Carroll
Phil Niekro
☐ 462 Lew Krausse UER 6.50 2.90 .80
(Photo actually
Pete Lovrich)
☐ 463 Manny Mota 7.00 3.10 .85
☐ 464 Ron Piche 6.00 2.70 .75
☐ 465 Tom Haller 7.00 3.10 .85
☐ 466 Senators Rookies 6.00 2.70 .75
Pete Craig
Dick Nen
☐ 467 Ray Washburn 6.00 2.70 .75
☐ 468 Larry Brown 6.00 2.70 .75
☐ 469 Don Nottebart 6.00 2.70 .75
☐ 470 Yogi Berra P/CO 60.00 27.00 7.50
☐ 471 Billy Hoeft 6.00 2.70 .75
☐ 472 Don Pavletich 6.00 2.70 .75
☐ 473 Orioles Rookies 12.50 5.75 1.55
Paul Blair
Dave Johnson
☐ 474 Cookie Rojas 7.00 3.10 .85
☐ 475 Clete Boyer 7.50 3.40 .95
☐ 476 Billy O'Dell 6.00 2.70 .75
☐ 477 Cards Rookies 575.00 250.00 70.00
Fritz Ackley
Steve Carlton
☐ 478 Wilbur Wood 7.00 3.10 .85
☐ 479 Ken Harrelson 7.50 3.40 .95
☐ 480 Joel Horlen 6.00 2.70 .75
☐ 481 Cleveland Indians 12.00 5.50 1.50
Team Card
☐ 482 Bob Priddy 6.00 2.70 .75
☐ 483 George Smith 6.00 2.70 .75
☐ 484 Ron Perranoski 7.00 3.10 .85

☐ 485 Nellie Fox P/CO 12.00 5.50 1.50
☐ 486 Angels Rookies 6.00 2.70 .75
Tom Egan
Pat Rogan
☐ 487 Woody Woodward 6.50 2.90 .80
☐ 488 Ted Wills 6.00 2.70 .75
☐ 489 Gene Mauch MG 6.50 2.90 .80
☐ 490 Earl Battey 6.00 2.70 .75
☐ 491 Tracy Stallard 6.00 2.70 .75
☐ 492 Gene Freese 6.00 2.70 .75
☐ 493 Tigers Rookies 6.00 2.70 .75
Bill Roman
Bruce Brubaker
☐ 494 Jay Ritchie 6.00 2.70 .75
☐ 495 Joe Christopher 6.00 2.70 .75
☐ 496 Joe Cunningham 6.00 2.70 .75
☐ 497 Giants Rookies 6.50 2.90 .80
Ken Henderson
Jack Hiatt
☐ 498 Gene Stephens 6.00 2.70 .75
☐ 499 Stu Miller 6.50 2.90 .80
☐ 500 Eddie Mathews 36.00 16.00 4.50
☐ 501 Indians Rookies 6.00 2.70 .75
Ralph Gagliano
Jim Rittwage
☐ 502 Don Cardwell 6.00 2.70 .75
☐ 503 Phil Gagliano 6.00 2.70 .75
☐ 504 Jerry Grote 6.00 2.70 .75
☐ 505 Ray Culp 6.00 2.70 .75
☐ 506 Sam Mele MG 6.00 2.70 .75
☐ 507 Sammy Ellis 6.00 2.70 .75
☐ 508 Checklist 7 12.00 1.80 .60
☐ 509 Red Sox Rookies 6.00 2.70 .75
Bob Guindon
Gerry Vezendy
☐ 510 Ernie Banks 80.00 36.00 10.00
☐ 511 Ron Locke 6.00 2.70 .75
☐ 512 Cap Peterson 6.00 2.70 .75
☐ 513 New York Yankees 16.00 7.25 2.00
Team Card
☐ 514 Joe Azcue 6.00 2.70 .75
☐ 515 Vern Law 7.00 3.10 .85
☐ 516 Al Weis 6.00 2.70 .75
☐ 517 Angels Rookies 6.50 2.90 .80
Paul Schaal
Jack Warner
☐ 518 Ken Rowe 6.00 2.70 .75
☐ 519 Bob Uecker UER 35.00 16.00 4.40
(Posing as a left-handed batter)
☐ 520 Tony Cloninger 6.00 2.70 .75
☐ 521 Phillies Rookies 6.00 2.70 .75
Dave Bennett
Morrie Stevens
☐ 522 Hank Aguirre 6.00 2.70 .75
☐ 523 Mike Brumley SP 11.00 4.90 1.40
☐ 524 Dave Giusti SP 11.00 4.90 1.40
☐ 525 Eddie Bressoud 6.00 2.70 .75
☐ 526 Athletics Rookies SP 150.00 70.00 19.00
Rene Lachemann
Johnny Odom
Jim Hunter ERR
("Tim" on back)
Skip Lockwood
☐ 527 Jeff Torborg SP 15.00 6.75 1.90
☐ 528 George Altman 6.00 2.70 .75
☐ 529 Jerry Fosnow SP 11.00 4.90 1.40
☐ 530 Jim Maloney 7.00 3.10 .85
☐ 531 Chuck Hiller 6.00 2.70 .75
☐ 532 Hector Lopez 6.50 2.90 .80
☐ 533 Mets Rookies SP 32.00 14.50 4.00
Dan Napoleon
Ron Swoboda
Tug McGraw
Jim Bethke
☐ 534 John Herrnstein 6.00 2.70 .75
☐ 535 Jack Kralick SP 11.00 4.90 1.40
☐ 536 Andre Rodgers SP 11.00 4.90 1.40
☐ 537 Angels Rookies 7.50 3.40 .95
Marcelino Lopez
Phil Roof
Rudy May
☐ 538 Chuck Dressen MG SP 12.00 5.50 1.50
☐ 539 Herm Starrette 6.00 2.70 .75
☐ 540 Lou Brock SP 50.00 23.00 6.25
☐ 541 White Sox Rookies 6.00 2.70 .75
Greg Bollo
Bob Locker
☐ 542 Lou Klimchock 6.00 2.70 .75
☐ 543 Ed Connolly SP 11.00 4.90 1.40
☐ 544 Howie Reed 6.00 2.70 .75
☐ 545 Jesus Alou SP 11.00 4.90 1.40
☐ 546 Indians Rookies 6.00 2.70 .75
Bill Davis
Mike Hedlund
Ray Barker
Floyd Weaver
☐ 547 Jake Wood SP 11.00 4.90 1.40
☐ 548 Dick Stigman 6.00 2.70 .75
☐ 549 Cubs Rookies SP 17.00 7.75 2.10
Roberto Pena
Glenn Beckert
☐ 550 Mel Stottlemyre SP 35.00 16.00 4.40
☐ 551 New York Mets SP 35.00 16.00 4.40
Team Card
☐ 552 Julio Gotay 6.00 2.70 .75
☐ 553 Astros Rookies 6.00 2.70 .75
Dan Coombs
Gene Ratliff
Jack McClure
☐ 554 Chico Ruiz SP 11.00 4.90 1.40
☐ 555 Jack Baldschun SP 11.00 4.90 1.40
☐ 556 Red Schoendienst MG SP 20.00 9.00 2.50
☐ 557 Jose Santiago 6.00 2.70 .75
☐ 558 Tommie Sisk 6.00 2.70 .75
☐ 559 Ed Bailey SP 11.00 4.90 1.40
☐ 560 Boog Powell SP 20.00 9.00 2.50
☐ 561 Dodgers Rookies 12.50 5.75 1.55
Dennis Daboll
Mike Kekich
Hector Valle
Jim Lefebvre
☐ 562 Billy Moran 6.00 2.70 .75
☐ 563 Julio Navarro 6.00 2.70 .75
☐ 564 Mel Nelson 6.00 2.70 .75
☐ 565 Ernie Broglio SP 11.00 4.90 1.40
☐ 566 Yankees Rookies SP 11.00 4.90 1.40
Gil Blanco
Ross Moschitto
Art Lopez
☐ 567 Tommie Aaron 7.00 3.10 .85
☐ 568 Ron Taylor SP 11.00 4.90 1.40
☐ 569 Gino Cimoli SP 11.00 4.90 1.40
☐ 570 Claude Osteen SP 11.00 4.90 1.40
☐ 571 Ossie Virgil SP 11.00 4.90 1.40
☐ 572 Baltimore Orioles SP 30.00 13.50 3.80
Team Card
☐ 573 Red Sox Rookies SP 25.00 11.50 3.10
Jim Lonborg
Gerry Moses
Bill Schlesinger
Mike Ryan
☐ 574 Roy Sievers 7.00 3.10 .85
☐ 575 Jose Pagan 6.00 2.70 .75
☐ 576 Terry Fox SP 11.00 4.90 1.40
☐ 577 AL Rookie Stars SP 12.00 5.50 1.50
Darold Knowles
Don Buschhorn
Richie Scheinblum
☐ 578 Camilo Carreon SP 11.00 4.90 1.40
☐ 579 Dick Smith SP 11.00 4.90 1.40
☐ 580 Jimmie Hall SP 11.00 4.90 1.40
☐ 581 NL Rookie Stars SP 165.00 75.00 21.00
Tony Perez
Dave Ricketts
Kevin Collins
☐ 582 Bob Schmidt SP 11.00 4.90 1.40
☐ 583 Wes Covington SP 11.00 4.90 1.40
☐ 584 Harry Bright 6.00 2.70 .75
☐ 585 Hank Fischer 6.00 2.70 .75
☐ 586 Tom McCraw SP 11.00 4.90 1.40
☐ 587 Joe Sparma 6.00 2.70 .75
☐ 588 Lenny Green 6.00 2.70 .75
☐ 589 Giants Rookies SP 11.00 4.90 1.40
Frank Linzy
Bob Schroder
☐ 590 John Wyatt 6.00 2.70 .75
☐ 591 Bob Skinner SP 12.00 5.50 1.50
☐ 592 Frank Bork SP 11.00 4.90 1.40
☐ 593 Tigers Rookies SP 15.00 6.75 1.90
Jackie Moore
John Sullivan
☐ 594 Joe Gaines 6.00 2.70 .75
☐ 595 Don Lee 6.00 2.70 .75
☐ 596 Don Landrum SP 11.00 4.90 1.40
☐ 597 Twins Rookies 6.00 2.70 .75
Joe Nossek
John Sevcik
Dick Reese
☐ 598 Al Downing SP 20.00 9.00 2.50

1966 Topps

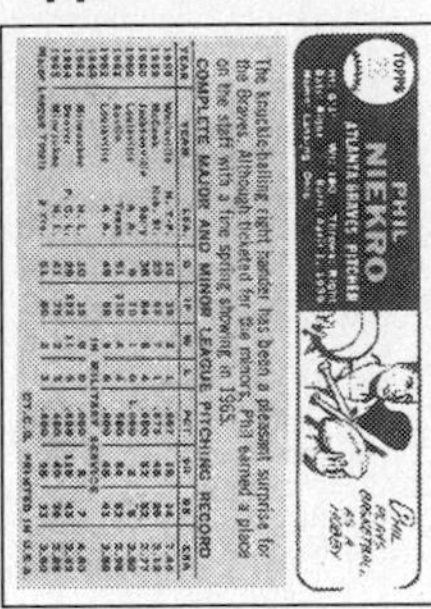

The cards in this 598-card set measure 2 1/2" by 3 1/2". There are the same number of cards as in the 1965 set. Once again, the seventh series cards (523 to 598) are considered more difficult to obtain than the cards of any other series in the set. Within this last series there are 43 cards that were printed in lesser quantities than the other cards in that series; these shorter-printed cards are marked by SP in the checklist below. The only featured subset within this set is League Leaders (215-226). Noteworthy Rookie Cards in the set include Jim Palmer (126), Ferguson Jenkins (254), and Don Sutton (288). Palmer is described in the bio (on his card back) as a left-hander.

	NRMT	VG-E	GOOD
COMPLETE SET (598)	4400.00	2000.00	550.00
COMMON PLAYER (1-109)	1.50	.65	.19
COMMON PLAYER (110-196)	2.00	.90	.25
COMMON PLAYER (197-283)	2.50	1.15	.30
COMMON PLAYER (284-370)	3.00	1.35	.40
COMMON PLAYER (371-446)	4.50	2.00	.55
COMMON PLAYER (447-522)	7.50	3.40	.95
COMMON PLAYER (523-598)	15.00	6.75	1.90
☐ 1 Willie Mays	150.00	45.00	15.00
☐ 2 Ted Abernathy	1.50	.65	.19
☐ 3 Sam Mele MG	1.50	.65	.19
☐ 4 Ray Culp	1.50	.65	.19
☐ 5 Jim Fregosi	2.00	.90	.25
☐ 6 Chuck Schilling	1.50	.65	.19
☐ 7 Tracy Stallard	1.50	.65	.19
☐ 8 Floyd Robinson	1.50	.65	.19
☐ 9 Clete Boyer	2.00	.90	.25
☐ 10 Tony Cloninger	1.50	.65	.19
☐ 11 Senators Rookies	1.50	.65	.19
Brant Alyea			
Pete Craig			
☐ 12 John Tsitouris	1.50	.65	.19
☐ 13 Lou Johnson	2.00	.90	.25
☐ 14 Norm Siebern	1.50	.65	.19
☐ 15 Vern Law	2.00	.90	.25
☐ 16 Larry Brown	1.50	.65	.19
☐ 17 John Stephenson	1.50	.65	.19
☐ 18 Roland Sheldon	1.50	.65	.19
☐ 19 San Francisco Giants	3.00	1.35	.40
Team Card			
☐ 20 Willie Horton	2.00	.90	.25
☐ 21 Don Nottebart	1.50	.65	.19
☐ 22 Joe Nossek	1.50	.65	.19
☐ 23 Jack Sanford	1.50	.65	.19
☐ 24 Don Kessinger	4.00	1.80	.50
☐ 25 Pete Ward	1.50	.65	.19
☐ 26 Ray Sadecki	1.50	.65	.19
☐ 27 Orioles Rookies	1.50	.65	.19
Darold Knowles			
Andy Etchebarren			
☐ 28 Phil Niekro	20.00	9.00	2.50
☐ 29 Mike Brumley	1.50	.65	.19
☐ 30 Pete Rose DP	50.00	23.00	6.25
☐ 31 Jack Cullen	1.50	.65	.19
☐ 32 Adolfo Phillips	1.50	.65	.19
☐ 33 Jim Pagliaroni	1.50	.65	.19
☐ 34 Checklist 1	8.00	1.20	.40
☐ 35 Ron Swoboda	2.50	1.15	.30
☐ 36 Jim Hunter UER	30.00	13.50	3.80
(Stats say 1963 and			
1964, should be			
1963 and 1964)			
☐ 37 Billy Herman MG	2.00	.90	.25
☐ 38 Ron Nischwitz	1.50	.65	.19
☐ 39 Ken Henderson	1.50	.65	.19
☐ 40 Jim Grant	1.50	.65	.19
☐ 41 Don LeJohn	1.50	.65	.19
☐ 42 Aubrey Gatewood	1.50	.65	.19
☐ 43A Don Landrum	2.00	.90	.25
(Dark button on pants			
showing)			
☐ 43B Don Landrum	2.00	.90	.25
(Button on pants			
partially airbrushed)			
☐ 43C Don Landrum	2.00	.90	.25
(Button on pants			
not showing)			
☐ 44 Indians Rookies	1.50	.65	.19
Bill Davis			
Tom Kelley			
☐ 45 Jim Gentile	2.00	.90	.25
☐ 46 Howie Koplitz	1.50	.65	.19
☐ 47 J.C. Martin	1.50	.65	.19
☐ 48 Paul Blair	2.00	.90	.25
☐ 49 Woody Woodward	2.00	.90	.25
☐ 50 Mickey Mantle DP	200.00	90.00	25.00
☐ 51 Gordon Richardson	1.50	.65	.19
☐ 52 Power Plus	2.00	.90	.25
Wes Covington			
Johnny Callison			
☐ 53 Bob Duliba	1.50	.65	.19
☐ 54 Jose Pagan	1.50	.65	.19
☐ 55 Ken Harrelson	2.00	.90	.25
☐ 56 Sandy Valdespino	1.50	.65	.19
☐ 57 Jim Lefebvre	2.00	.90	.25
☐ 58 Dave Wickersham	1.50	.65	.19
☐ 59 Reds Team	3.00	1.35	.40
☐ 60 Curt Flood	2.00	.90	.25
☐ 61 Bob Bolin	1.50	.65	.19
☐ 62A Merritt Ranew	1.50	.65	.19
(With sold line)			
☐ 62B Merritt Ranew	32.00	14.50	4.00
(Without sold line)			
☐ 63 Jim Stewart	1.50	.65	.19
☐ 64 Bob Bruce	1.50	.65	.19
☐ 65 Leon Wagner	1.50	.65	.19
☐ 66 Al Weis	1.50	.65	.19
☐ 67 Mets Rookies	2.00	.90	.25
Cleon Jones			
Dick Selma			
☐ 68 Hal Reniff	1.50	.65	.19
☐ 69 Ken Hamlin	1.50	.65	.19
☐ 70 Carl Yastrzemski	40.00	18.00	5.00
☐ 71 Frank Carpin	1.50	.65	.19
☐ 72 Tony Perez	35.00	16.00	4.40
☐ 73 Jerry Zimmerman	1.50	.65	.19
☐ 74 Don Mossi	2.00	.90	.25
☐ 75 Tommy Davis	2.00	.90	.25
☐ 76 Red Schoendienst MG	4.00	1.80	.50
☐ 77 John Orsino	1.50	.65	.19
☐ 78 Frank Linzy	1.50	.65	.19
☐ 79 Joe Pepitone	2.00	.90	.25
☐ 80 Richie Allen	4.50	2.00	.55
☐ 81 Ray Oyler	1.50	.65	.19
☐ 82 Bob Hendley	1.50	.65	.19
☐ 83 Albie Pearson	2.00	.90	.25
☐ 84 Braves Rookies	1.50	.65	.19
Jim Beauchamp			
Dick Kelley			
☐ 85 Eddie Fisher	1.50	.65	.19
☐ 86 John Bateman	1.50	.65	.19
☐ 87 Dan Napoleon	1.50	.65	.19
☐ 88 Fred Whitfield	1.50	.65	.19
☐ 89 Ted Davidson	1.50	.65	.19
☐ 90 Luis Aparicio	7.00	3.10	.85
☐ 91A Bob Uecker TR	16.00	7.25	2.00
☐ 91B Bob Uecker NTR	55.00	25.00	7.00
☐ 92 Yankees Team	4.00	1.80	.50
☐ 93 Jim Lonborg	3.00	1.35	.40
☐ 94 Matty Alou	2.00	.90	.25
☐ 95 Pete Richert	1.50	.65	.19
☐ 96 Felipe Alou	2.00	.90	.25
☐ 97 Jim Merritt	1.50	.65	.19
☐ 98 Don Demeter	1.50	.65	.19
☐ 99 Buc Belters	4.00	1.80	.50
Willie Stargell			
Donn Clendenon			
☐ 100 Sandy Koufax	110.00	50.00	14.00
☐ 101A Checklist 2	16.00	2.40	.80
(115 W. Spahn) ERR			
☐ 101B Checklist 2	10.00	1.50	.50
(115 Bill Henry) COR			
☐ 102 Ed Kirkpatrick	1.50	.65	.19
☐ 103A Dick Groat TR	2.00	.90	.25
☐ 103B Dick Groat NTR	32.00	14.50	4.00

☐ 104A Alex Johnson TR	2.00	.90	.25
☐ 104B Alex Johnson NTR	32.00	14.50	4.00
☐ 105 Milt Pappas	2.00	.90	.25
☐ 106 Rusty Staub	3.50	1.55	.45
☐ 107 A's Rookies Larry Stahl Ron Tompkins	1.50	.65	.19
☐ 108 Bobby Klaus	1.50	.65	.19
☐ 109 Ralph Terry	2.00	.90	.25
☐ 110 Ernie Banks	25.00	11.50	3.10
☐ 111 Gary Peters	2.00	.90	.25
☐ 112 Manny Mota	2.50	1.15	.30
☐ 113 Hank Aguirre	2.00	.90	.25
☐ 114 Jim Gosger	2.00	.90	.25
☐ 115 Bill Henry	2.00	.90	.25
☐ 116 Walt Alston MG	4.00	1.80	.50
☐ 117 Jake Gibbs	2.50	1.15	.30
☐ 118 Mike McCormick	2.50	1.15	.30
☐ 119 Art Shamsky	2.00	.90	.25
☐ 120 Harmon Killebrew	20.00	9.00	2.50
☐ 121 Ray Herbert	2.00	.90	.25
☐ 122 Joe Gaines	2.00	.90	.25
☐ 123 Pirates Rookies Frank Bork Jerry May	2.00	.90	.25
☐ 124 Tug McGraw	5.00	2.30	.60
☐ 125 Lou Brock	25.00	11.50	3.10
☐ 126 Jim Palmer UER (Described as a lefthander on card back)	225.00	100.00	28.00
☐ 127 Ken Berry	2.00	.90	.25
☐ 128 Jim Landis	2.00	.90	.25
☐ 129 Jack Kralick	2.00	.90	.25
☐ 130 Joe Torre	4.00	1.80	.50
☐ 131 Angels Team	4.00	1.80	.50
☐ 132 Orlando Cepeda	6.00	2.70	.75
☐ 133 Don McMahon	2.00	.90	.25
☐ 134 Wes Parker	2.50	1.15	.30
☐ 135 Dave Morehead	2.00	.90	.25
☐ 136 Woody Held	2.00	.90	.25
☐ 137 Pat Corrales	2.50	1.15	.30
☐ 138 Roger Repoz	2.00	.90	.25
☐ 139 Cubs Rookies Byron Browne Don Young	2.00	.90	.25
☐ 140 Jim Maloney	2.50	1.15	.30
☐ 141 Tom McCraw	2.00	.90	.25
☐ 142 Don Dennis	2.00	.90	.25
☐ 143 Jose Tartabull	2.50	1.15	.30
☐ 144 Don Schwall	2.00	.90	.25
☐ 145 Bill Freehan	3.00	1.35	.40
☐ 146 George Altman	2.00	.90	.25
☐ 147 Lum Harris MG	2.00	.90	.25
☐ 148 Bob Johnson	2.00	.90	.25
☐ 149 Dick Nen	2.00	.90	.25
☐ 150 Rocky Colavito	5.00	2.30	.60
☐ 151 Gary Wagner	2.00	.90	.25
☐ 152 Frank Malzone	2.50	1.15	.30
☐ 153 Rico Carty	2.50	1.15	.30
☐ 154 Chuck Hiller	2.00	.90	.25
☐ 155 Marcelino Lopez	2.00	.90	.25
☐ 156 Double Play Combo Dick Schofield Hal Lanier	2.00	.90	.25
☐ 157 Rene Lachemann	2.50	1.15	.30
☐ 158 Jim Brewer	2.00	.90	.25
☐ 159 Chico Ruiz	2.00	.90	.25
☐ 160 Whitey Ford	25.00	11.50	3.10
☐ 161 Jerry Lumpe	2.00	.90	.25
☐ 162 Lee Maye	2.00	.90	.25
☐ 163 Tito Francona	2.00	.90	.25
☐ 164 White Sox Rookies Tommie Agee Marv Staehle	2.50	1.15	.30
☐ 165 Don Lock	2.00	.90	.25
☐ 166 Chris Krug	2.00	.90	.25
☐ 167 Boog Powell	4.50	2.00	.55
☐ 168 Dan Osinski	2.00	.90	.25
☐ 169 Duke Sims	2.00	.90	.25
☐ 170 Cookie Rojas	2.50	1.15	.30
☐ 171 Nick Willhite	2.00	.90	.25
☐ 172 Mets Team	4.00	1.80	.50
☐ 173 Al Spangler	2.00	.90	.25
☐ 174 Ron Taylor	2.00	.90	.25
☐ 175 Bert Campaneris	2.50	1.15	.30
☐ 176 Jim Davenport	2.00	.90	.25
☐ 177 Hector Lopez	2.00	.90	.25
☐ 178 Bob Tillman	2.00	.90	.25
☐ 179 Cards Rookies Dennis Aust Bob Tolan	2.50	1.15	.30
☐ 180 Vada Pinson	2.50	1.15	.30
☐ 181 Al Worthington	2.00	.90	.25
☐ 182 Jerry Lynch	2.00	.90	.25
☐ 183A Checklist 3 (Large print on front)	8.00	1.20	.40
☐ 183B Checklist 3 (Small print on front)	8.00	1.20	.40
☐ 184 Denis Menke	2.00	.90	.25
☐ 185 Bob Buhl	2.50	1.15	.30
☐ 186 Ruben Amaro	2.00	.90	.25
☐ 187 Chuck Dressen MG	2.50	1.15	.30
☐ 188 Al Luplow	2.00	.90	.25
☐ 189 John Roseboro	2.50	1.15	.30
☐ 190 Jimmie Hall	2.00	.90	.25
☐ 191 Darrell Sutherland	2.00	.90	.25
☐ 192 Vic Power	2.50	1.15	.30
☐ 193 Dave McNally	2.50	1.15	.30
☐ 194 Senators Team	4.00	1.80	.50
☐ 195 Joe Morgan	45.00	20.00	5.75
☐ 196 Don Pavletich	2.00	.90	.25
☐ 197 Sonny Siebert	2.50	1.15	.30
☐ 198 Mickey Stanley	3.50	1.55	.45
☐ 199 Chisox Clubbers Bill Skowron Johnny Romano Floyd Robinson	3.00	1.35	.40
☐ 200 Eddie Mathews	12.50	5.75	1.55
☐ 201 Jim Dickson	2.50	1.15	.30
☐ 202 Clay Dalrymple	2.50	1.15	.30
☐ 203 Jose Santiago	2.50	1.15	.30
☐ 204 Cubs Team	4.50	2.00	.55
☐ 205 Tom Tresh	3.00	1.35	.40
☐ 206 Al Jackson	2.50	1.15	.30
☐ 207 Frank Quilici	2.50	1.15	.30
☐ 208 Bob Miller	2.50	1.15	.30
☐ 209 Tigers Rookies Fritz Fisher John Hiller	3.50	1.55	.45
☐ 210 Bill Mazeroski	3.75	1.70	.45
☐ 211 Frank Kreutzer	2.50	1.15	.30
☐ 212 Ed Kranepool	3.00	1.35	.40
☐ 213 Fred Newman	2.50	1.15	.30
☐ 214 Tommy Harper	3.00	1.35	.40
☐ 215 NL Batting Leaders Bob Clemente Hank Aaron Willie Mays	25.00	11.50	3.10
☐ 216 AL Batting Leaders Tony Oliva Carl Yastrzemski Vic Davalillo	5.50	2.50	.70
☐ 217 NL Home Run Leaders Willie Mays Willie McCovey Billy Williams	15.00	6.75	1.90
☐ 218 AL Home Run Leaders Tony Conigliaro Norm Cash Willie Horton	3.75	1.70	.45
☐ 219 NL RBI Leaders Deron Johnson Frank Robinson Willie Mays	7.00	3.10	.85
☐ 220 AL RBI Leaders Rocky Colavito Willie Horton Tony Oliva	3.75	1.70	.45
☐ 221 NL ERA Leaders Sandy Koufax Juan Marichal Vern Law	7.00	3.10	.85
☐ 222 AL ERA Leaders Sam McDowell Eddie Fisher Sonny Siebert	3.75	1.70	.45
☐ 223 NL Pitching Leaders Sandy Koufax Tony Cloninger Don Drysdale	7.00	3.10	.85
☐ 224 AL Pitching Leaders Jim Grant Mel Stottlemyre Jim Kaat	3.75	1.70	.45
☐ 225 NL Strikeout Leaders Sandy Koufax Bob Veale Bob Gibson	7.00	3.10	.85
☐ 226 AL Strikeout Leaders Sam McDowell Mickey Lolich Dennis McLain Sonny Siebert	3.75	1.70	.45

☐ 227 Russ Nixon	2.50	1.15	.30
☐ 228 Larry Dierker	2.50	1.15	.30
☐ 229 Hank Bauer MG	3.00	1.35	.40
☐ 230 Johnny Callison	3.00	1.35	.40
☐ 231 Floyd Weaver	2.50	1.15	.30
☐ 232 Glenn Beckert	3.00	1.35	.40
☐ 233 Dom Zanni	2.50	1.15	.30
☐ 234 Yankees Rookies Rich Beck Roy White	7.00	3.10	.85
☐ 235 Don Cardwell	2.50	1.15	.30
☐ 236 Mike Hershberger	2.50	1.15	.30
☐ 237 Billy O'Dell	2.50	1.15	.30
☐ 238 Dodgers Team	4.50	2.00	.55
☐ 239 Orlando Pena	2.50	1.15	.30
☐ 240 Earl Battey	2.50	1.15	.30
☐ 241 Dennis Ribant	2.50	1.15	.30
☐ 242 Jesus Alou	2.50	1.15	.30
☐ 243 Nelson Briles	3.00	1.35	.40
☐ 244 Astros Rookies Chuck Harrison Sonny Jackson	2.50	1.15	.30
☐ 245 John Buzhardt	2.50	1.15	.30
☐ 246 Ed Bailey	2.50	1.15	.30
☐ 247 Carl Warwick	2.50	1.15	.30
☐ 248 Pete Mikkelsen	2.50	1.15	.30
☐ 249 Bill Rigney MG	2.50	1.15	.30
☐ 250 Sammy Ellis	2.50	1.15	.30
☐ 251 Ed Brinkman	2.50	1.15	.30
☐ 252 Denny Lemaster	2.50	1.15	.30
☐ 253 Don Wert	2.50	1.15	.30
☐ 254 Phillies Rookies Ferguson Jenkins Bill Sorrell	135.00	60.00	17.00
☐ 255 Willie Stargell	20.00	9.00	2.50
☐ 256 Lew Krausse	2.50	1.15	.30
☐ 257 Jeff Torborg	3.00	1.35	.40
☐ 258 Dave Giusti	2.50	1.15	.30
☐ 259 Boston Red Sox Team Card	4.50	2.00	.55
☐ 260 Bob Shaw	2.50	1.15	.30
☐ 261 Ron Hansen	2.50	1.15	.30
☐ 262 Jack Hamilton	2.50	1.15	.30
☐ 263 Tom Egan	2.50	1.15	.30
☐ 264 Twins Rookies Andy Kosco Ted Uhlaender	2.50	1.15	.30
☐ 265 Stu Miller	3.00	1.35	.40
☐ 266 Pedro Gonzalez UER (Misspelled Gonzales on card back)	2.50	1.15	.30
☐ 267 Joe Sparma	2.50	1.15	.30
☐ 268 John Blanchard	2.50	1.15	.30
☐ 269 Don Heffner MG	2.50	1.15	.30
☐ 270 Claude Osteen	3.00	1.35	.40
☐ 271 Hal Lanier	2.50	1.15	.30
☐ 272 Jack Baldschun	2.50	1.15	.30
☐ 273 Astro Aces Bob Aspromonte Rusty Staub	3.00	1.35	.40
☐ 274 Buster Narum	2.50	1.15	.30
☐ 275 Tim McCarver	5.00	2.30	.60
☐ 276 Jim Bouton	3.50	1.55	.45
☐ 277 George Thomas	2.50	1.15	.30
☐ 278 Cal Koonce	2.50	1.15	.30
☐ 279 Checklist 4	8.00	1.20	.40
☐ 280 Bobby Knoop	2.50	1.15	.30
☐ 281 Bruce Howard	2.50	1.15	.30
☐ 282 Johnny Lewis	2.50	1.15	.30
☐ 283 Jim Perry	3.00	1.35	.40
☐ 284 Bobby Wine	3.50	1.55	.45
☐ 285 Luis Tiant	4.50	2.00	.55
☐ 286 Gary Geiger	3.00	1.35	.40
☐ 287 Jack Aker	3.00	1.35	.40
☐ 288 Dodgers Rookies Bill Singer Don Sutton	150.00	70.00	19.00
☐ 289 Larry Sherry	3.50	1.55	.45
☐ 290 Ron Santo	4.50	2.00	.55
☐ 291 Moe Drabowsky	3.50	1.55	.45
☐ 292 Jim Coker	3.00	1.35	.40
☐ 293 Mike Shannon	3.50	1.55	.45
☐ 294 Steve Ridzik	3.00	1.35	.40
☐ 295 Jim Ray Hart	3.50	1.55	.45
☐ 296 Johnny Keane MG	3.00	1.35	.40
☐ 297 Jim Owens	3.00	1.35	.40
☐ 298 Rico Petrocelli	4.00	1.80	.50
☐ 299 Lou Burdette	3.50	1.55	.45
☐ 300 Bob Clemente	100.00	45.00	12.50
☐ 301 Greg Bollo	3.00	1.35	.40
☐ 302 Ernie Bowman	3.00	1.35	.40
☐ 303 Cleveland Indians Team Card	5.00	2.30	.60
☐ 304 John Herrnstein	3.00	1.35	.40
☐ 305 Camilo Pascual	3.50	1.55	.45
☐ 306 Ty Cline	3.00	1.35	.40
☐ 307 Clay Carroll	3.50	1.55	.45
☐ 308 Tom Haller	3.50	1.55	.45
☐ 309 Diego Segui	3.00	1.35	.40
☐ 310 Frank Robinson	40.00	18.00	5.00
☐ 311 Reds Rookies Tommy Helms Dick Simpson	3.50	1.55	.45
☐ 312 Bob Saverine	3.00	1.35	.40
☐ 313 Chris Zachary	3.00	1.35	.40
☐ 314 Hector Valle	3.00	1.35	.40
☐ 315 Norm Cash	4.00	1.80	.50
☐ 316 Jack Fisher	3.00	1.35	.40
☐ 317 Dalton Jones	3.00	1.35	.40
☐ 318 Harry Walker MG	3.00	1.35	.40
☐ 319 Gene Freese	3.00	1.35	.40
☐ 320 Bob Gibson	30.00	13.50	3.80
☐ 321 Rick Reichardt	3.00	1.35	.40
☐ 322 Bill Faul	3.00	1.35	.40
☐ 323 Ray Barker	3.00	1.35	.40
☐ 324 John Boozer	3.00	1.35	.40
☐ 325 Vic Davalillo	3.00	1.35	.40
☐ 326 Braves Team	5.00	2.30	.60
☐ 327 Bernie Allen	3.00	1.35	.40
☐ 328 Jerry Grote	3.00	1.35	.40
☐ 329 Pete Charton	3.00	1.35	.40
☐ 330 Ron Fairly	3.50	1.55	.45
☐ 331 Ron Herbel	3.00	1.35	.40
☐ 332 Bill Bryan	3.00	1.35	.40
☐ 333 Senators Rookies Joe Coleman Jim French	3.50	1.55	.45
☐ 334 Marty Keough	3.00	1.35	.40
☐ 335 Juan Pizarro	3.00	1.35	.40
☐ 336 Gene Alley	3.50	1.55	.45
☐ 337 Fred Gladding	3.00	1.35	.40
☐ 338 Dal Maxvill	3.00	1.35	.40
☐ 339 Del Crandall	3.50	1.55	.45
☐ 340 Dean Chance	3.50	1.55	.45
☐ 341 Wes Westrum MG	3.50	1.55	.45
☐ 342 Bob Humphreys	3.00	1.35	.40
☐ 343 Joe Christopher	3.00	1.35	.40
☐ 344 Steve Blass	3.50	1.55	.45
☐ 345 Bob Allison	3.50	1.55	.45
☐ 346 Mike DeLaHoz	3.00	1.35	.40
☐ 347 Phil Regan	3.50	1.55	.45
☐ 348 Orioles Team	5.00	2.30	.60
☐ 349 Cap Peterson	3.00	1.35	.40
☐ 350 Mel Stottlemyre	4.50	2.00	.55
☐ 351 Fred Valentine	3.00	1.35	.40
☐ 352 Bob Aspromonte	3.00	1.35	.40
☐ 353 Al McBean	3.00	1.35	.40
☐ 354 Smoky Burgess	3.50	1.55	.45
☐ 355 Wade Blasingame	3.00	1.35	.40
☐ 356 Red Sox Rookies Owen Johnson Ken Sanders	3.00	1.35	.40
☐ 357 Gerry Arrigo	3.00	1.35	.40
☐ 358 Charlie Smith	3.00	1.35	.40
☐ 359 Johnny Briggs	3.00	1.35	.40
☐ 360 Ron Hunt	3.00	1.35	.40
☐ 361 Tom Satriano	3.00	1.35	.40
☐ 362 Gates Brown	3.50	1.55	.45
☐ 363 Checklist 5	10.00	1.50	.50
☐ 364 Nate Oliver	3.00	1.35	.40
☐ 365 Roger Maris	60.00	27.00	7.50
☐ 366 Wayne Causey	3.00	1.35	.40
☐ 367 Mel Nelson	3.00	1.35	.40
☐ 368 Charlie Lau	3.50	1.55	.45
☐ 369 Jim King	3.00	1.35	.40
☐ 370 Chico Cardenas	3.00	1.35	.40
☐ 371 Lee Stange	4.50	2.00	.55
☐ 372 Harvey Kuenn	5.00	2.30	.60
☐ 373 Giants Rookies Jack Hiatt Dick Estelle	5.00	2.30	.60
☐ 374 Bob Locker	4.50	2.00	.55
☐ 375 Donn Clendenon	5.00	2.30	.60
☐ 376 Paul Schaal	4.50	2.00	.55
☐ 377 Turk Farrell	4.50	2.00	.55
☐ 378 Dick Tracewski	4.50	2.00	.55
☐ 379 Cardinal Team	8.00	3.60	1.00
☐ 380 Tony Conigliaro	8.50	3.80	1.05
☐ 381 Hank Fischer	4.50	2.00	.55
☐ 382 Phil Roof	4.50	2.00	.55
☐ 383 Jackie Brandt	4.50	2.00	.55
☐ 384 Al Downing	5.00	2.30	.60
☐ 385 Ken Boyer	5.50	2.50	.70
☐ 386 Gil Hodges MG	7.00	3.10	.85
☐ 387 Howie Reed	4.50	2.00	.55
☐ 388 Don Mincher	4.50	2.00	.55

☐ 389 Jim O'Toole	5.00	2.30	.60
☐ 390 Brooks Robinson	35.00	16.00	4.40
☐ 391 Chuck Hinton	4.50	2.00	.55
☐ 392 Cubs Rookies Bill Hands Randy Hundley	5.00	2.30	.60
☐ 393 George Brunet	4.50	2.00	.55
☐ 394 Ron Brand	4.50	2.00	.55
☐ 395 Len Gabrielson	4.50	2.00	.55
☐ 396 Jerry Stephenson	4.50	2.00	.55
☐ 397 Bill White	5.50	2.50	.70
☐ 398 Danny Cater	4.50	2.00	.55
☐ 399 Ray Washburn	4.50	2.00	.55
☐ 400 Zoilo Versalles	4.50	2.00	.55
☐ 401 Ken McMullen	4.50	2.00	.55
☐ 402 Jim Hickman	4.50	2.00	.55
☐ 403 Fred Talbot	4.50	2.00	.55
☐ 404 Pittsburgh Pirates Team Card	8.00	3.60	1.00
☐ 405 Elston Howard	6.00	2.70	.75
☐ 406 Joey Jay	4.50	2.00	.55
☐ 407 John Kennedy	4.50	2.00	.55
☐ 408 Lee Thomas	5.00	2.30	.60
☐ 409 Billy Hoeft	4.50	2.00	.55
☐ 410 Al Kaline	33.00	15.00	4.10
☐ 411 Gene Mauch MG	5.00	2.30	.60
☐ 412 Sam Bowens	4.50	2.00	.55
☐ 413 Johnny Romano	4.50	2.00	.55
☐ 414 Dan Coombs	4.50	2.00	.55
☐ 415 Max Alvis	4.50	2.00	.55
☐ 416 Phil Ortega	4.50	2.00	.55
☐ 417 Angels Rookies Jim McGlothlin Ed Sukla	5.00	2.30	.60
☐ 418 Phil Gagliano	4.50	2.00	.55
☐ 419 Mike Ryan	4.50	2.00	.55
☐ 420 Juan Marichal	12.50	5.75	1.55
☐ 421 Roy McMillan	5.00	2.30	.60
☐ 422 Ed Charles	4.50	2.00	.55
☐ 423 Ernie Broglio	4.50	2.00	.55
☐ 424 Reds Rookies Lee May Darrell Osteen	7.50	3.40	.95
☐ 425 Bob Veale	5.00	2.30	.60
☐ 426 White Sox Team	8.00	3.60	1.00
☐ 427 John Miller	4.50	2.00	.55
☐ 428 Sandy Alomar	5.00	2.30	.60
☐ 429 Bill Monbouquette	4.50	2.00	.55
☐ 430 Don Drysdale	20.00	9.00	2.50
☐ 431 Walt Bond	4.50	2.00	.55
☐ 432 Bob Heffner	4.50	2.00	.55
☐ 433 Alvin Dark MG	5.00	2.30	.60
☐ 434 Willie Kirkland	4.50	2.00	.55
☐ 435 Jim Bunning	7.50	3.40	.95
☐ 436 Julian Javier	5.00	2.30	.60
☐ 437 Al Stanek	4.50	2.00	.55
☐ 438 Willie Smith	4.50	2.00	.55
☐ 439 Pedro Ramos	4.50	2.00	.55
☐ 440 Deron Johnson	5.00	2.30	.60
☐ 441 Tommie Sisk	4.50	2.00	.55
☐ 442 Orioles Rookies Ed Barnowski Eddie Watt	4.50	2.00	.55
☐ 443 Bill Wakefield	4.50	2.00	.55
☐ 444 Checklist 6	10.00	1.50	.50
☐ 445 Jim Kaat	7.50	3.40	.95
☐ 446 Mack Jones	4.50	2.00	.55
☐ 447 Dick Ellsworth UER (Photo actually Ken Hubbs)	9.00	4.00	1.15
☐ 448 Eddie Stanky MG	8.50	3.80	1.05
☐ 449 Joe Moeller	7.50	3.40	.95
☐ 450 Tony Oliva	11.00	4.90	1.40
☐ 451 Barry Latman	7.50	3.40	.95
☐ 452 Joe Azcue	7.50	3.40	.95
☐ 453 Ron Kline	7.50	3.40	.95
☐ 454 Jerry Buchek	7.50	3.40	.95
☐ 455 Mickey Lolich	10.00	4.50	1.25
☐ 456 Red Sox Rookies Darrell Brandon Joe Foy	7.50	3.40	.95
☐ 457 Joe Gibbon	7.50	3.40	.95
☐ 458 Manny Jiminez	7.50	3.40	.95
☐ 459 Bill McCool	7.50	3.40	.95
☐ 460 Curt Blefary	7.50	3.40	.95
☐ 461 Roy Face	8.50	3.80	1.05
☐ 462 Bob Rodgers	8.50	3.80	1.05
☐ 463 Philadelphia Phillies Team Card	12.00	5.50	1.50
☐ 464 Larry Bearnarth	7.50	3.40	.95
☐ 465 Don Buford	8.50	3.80	1.05
☐ 466 Ken Johnson	7.50	3.40	.95
☐ 467 Vic Roznovsky	7.50	3.40	.95
☐ 468 Johnny Podres	8.50	3.80	1.05
☐ 469 Yankees Rookies Bobby Murcer Dooley Womack	27.00	12.00	3.40
☐ 470 Sam McDowell	8.50	3.80	1.05
☐ 471 Bob Skinner	8.50	3.80	1.05
☐ 472 Terry Fox	7.50	3.40	.95
☐ 473 Rich Rollins	7.50	3.40	.95
☐ 474 Dick Schofield	7.50	3.40	.95
☐ 475 Dick Radatz	8.50	3.80	1.05
☐ 476 Bobby Bragan MG	7.50	3.40	.95
☐ 477 Steve Barber	7.50	3.40	.95
☐ 478 Tony Gonzalez	7.50	3.40	.95
☐ 479 Jim Hannan	7.50	3.40	.95
☐ 480 Dick Stuart	8.50	3.80	1.05
☐ 481 Bob Lee	7.50	3.40	.95
☐ 482 Cubs Rookies John Boccabella Dave Dowling	7.50	3.40	.95
☐ 483 Joe Nuxhall	8.50	3.80	1.05
☐ 484 Wes Covington	7.50	3.40	.95
☐ 485 Bob Bailey	8.00	3.60	1.00
☐ 486 Tommy John	15.00	6.75	1.90
☐ 487 Al Ferrara	7.50	3.40	.95
☐ 488 George Banks	7.50	3.40	.95
☐ 489 Curt Simmons	8.50	3.80	1.05
☐ 490 Bobby Richardson	12.50	5.75	1.55
☐ 491 Dennis Bennett	7.50	3.40	.95
☐ 492 Athletics Team	12.00	5.50	1.50
☐ 493 Johnny Klippstein	7.50	3.40	.95
☐ 494 Gordy Coleman	8.50	3.80	1.05
☐ 495 Dick McAuliffe	8.50	3.80	1.05
☐ 496 Lindy McDaniel	8.50	3.80	1.05
☐ 497 Chris Cannizzaro	7.50	3.40	.95
☐ 498 Pirates Rookies Luke Walker Woody Fryman	8.50	3.80	1.05
☐ 499 Wally Bunker	7.50	3.40	.95
☐ 500 Hank Aaron	125.00	57.50	15.50
☐ 501 John O'Donoghue	7.50	3.40	.95
☐ 502 Lenny Green UER (Born: aJn. 6, 1933)	7.50	3.40	.95
☐ 503 Steve Hamilton	7.50	3.40	.95
☐ 504 Grady Hatton MG	7.50	3.40	.95
☐ 505 Jose Cardenal	8.50	3.80	1.05
☐ 506 Bo Belinsky	8.50	3.80	1.05
☐ 507 Johnny Edwards	7.50	3.40	.95
☐ 508 Steve Hargan	9.00	4.00	1.15
☐ 509 Jake Wood	7.50	3.40	.95
☐ 510 Hoyt Wilhelm	14.00	6.25	1.75
☐ 511 Giants Rookies Bob Barton Tito Fuentes	9.00	4.00	1.15
☐ 512 Dick Stigman	7.50	3.40	.95
☐ 513 Camilo Carreon	7.50	3.40	.95
☐ 514 Hal Woodeshick	7.50	3.40	.95
☐ 515 Frank Howard	10.00	4.50	1.25
☐ 516 Eddie Bressoud	7.50	3.40	.95
☐ 517A Checklist 7 529 White Sox Rookies 544 Cardinals Rookies	16.00	2.40	.80
☐ 517B Checklist 7 529 W. Sox Rookies 544 Cards Rookies	16.00	2.40	.80
☐ 518 Braves Rookies Herb Hippauf Arnie Umbach	7.50	3.40	.95
☐ 519 Bob Friend	9.00	4.00	1.15
☐ 520 Jim Wynn	8.50	3.80	1.05
☐ 521 John Wyatt	7.50	3.40	.95
☐ 522 Phil Linz	8.50	3.80	1.05
☐ 523 Bob Sadowski	17.50	8.00	2.20
☐ 524 Giants Rookies SP Ollie Brown Don Mason	30.00	13.50	3.80
☐ 525 Gary Bell SP	30.00	13.50	3.80
☐ 526 Twins Team SP	75.00	34.00	9.50
☐ 527 Julio Navarro	15.00	6.75	1.90
☐ 528 Jesse Gonder SP	30.00	13.50	3.80
☐ 529 White Sox Rookies Lee Elia Dennis Higgins Bill Voss	17.50	8.00	2.20
☐ 530 Robin Roberts	50.00	23.00	6.25
☐ 531 Joe Cunningham	15.00	6.75	1.90
☐ 532 Aurelio Monteagudo SP	30.00	13.50	3.80
☐ 533 Jerry Adair SP	30.00	13.50	3.80
☐ 534 Mets Rookies Dave Eilers Rob Gardner	15.00	6.75	1.90
☐ 535 Willie Davis SP	50.00	23.00	6.25
☐ 536 Dick Egan	15.00	6.75	1.90
☐ 537 Herman Franks MG	15.00	6.75	1.90

Card	NRMT	VG-E	GOOD
☐ 538 Bob Allen SP	30.00	13.50	3.80
☐ 539 Astros Rookies	15.00	6.75	1.90
Bill Heath			
Carroll Sembera			
☐ 540 Denny McLain SP	75.00	34.00	9.50
☐ 541 Gene Oliver SP	30.00	13.50	3.80
☐ 542 George Smith	15.00	6.75	1.90
☐ 543 Roger Craig SP	40.00	18.00	5.00
☐ 544 Cardinals Rookies SP	35.00	16.00	4.40
Joe Hoerner			
George Kernek			
Jimy Williams UER			
(Misspelled Jimmy			
on card)			
☐ 545 Dick Green SP	30.00	13.50	3.80
☐ 546 Dwight Siebler	15.00	6.75	1.90
☐ 547 Horace Clarke SP	50.00	23.00	6.25
☐ 548 Gary Kroll SP	30.00	13.50	3.80
☐ 549 Senators Rookies	15.00	6.75	1.90
Al Closter			
Casey Cox			
☐ 550 Willie McCovey SP	125.00	57.50	15.50
☐ 551 Bob Purkey SP	30.00	13.50	3.80
☐ 552 Birdie Tebbetts	30.00	13.50	3.80
MG SP			
☐ 553 Rookie Stars	15.00	6.75	1.90
Pat Garrett			
Jackie Warner			
☐ 554 Jim Northrup SP	30.00	13.50	3.80
☐ 555 Ron Perranoski SP	30.00	13.50	3.80
☐ 556 Mel Queen SP	30.00	13.50	3.80
☐ 557 Felix Mantilla SP	30.00	13.50	3.80
☐ 558 Red Sox Rookies	27.00	12.00	3.40
Guido Grilli			
Pete Magrini			
George Scott			
☐ 559 Roberto Pena SP	30.00	13.50	3.80
☐ 560 Joel Horlen	15.00	6.75	1.90
☐ 561 ChooChoo Coleman SP	50.00	23.00	6.25
☐ 562 Russ Snyder	15.00	6.75	1.90
☐ 563 Twins Rookies	15.00	6.75	1.90
Pete Cimino			
Cesar Tovar			
☐ 564 Bob Chance SP	30.00	13.50	3.80
☐ 565 Jim Piersall SP	40.00	18.00	5.00
☐ 566 Mike Cuellar SP	35.00	16.00	4.40
☐ 567 Dick Howser SP	35.00	16.00	4.40
☐ 568 Athletics Rookies	17.50	8.00	2.20
Paul Lindblad			
Ron Stone			
☐ 569 Orlando McFarlane SP	30.00	13.50	3.80
☐ 570 Art Mahaffey SP	30.00	13.50	3.80
☐ 571 Dave Roberts SP	30.00	13.50	3.80
☐ 572 Bob Priddy	15.00	6.75	1.90
☐ 573 Derrell Griffith	15.00	6.75	1.90
☐ 574 Mets Rookies	15.00	6.75	1.90
Bill Hepler			
Bill Murphy			
☐ 575 Earl Wilson	17.50	8.00	2.20
☐ 576 Dave Nicholson SP	30.00	13.50	3.80
☐ 577 Jack Lamabe SP	30.00	13.50	3.80
☐ 578 Chi Chi Olivo SP	30.00	13.50	3.80
☐ 579 Orioles Rookies	18.00	8.00	2.30
Frank Bertaina			
Gene Brabender			
Dave Johnson			
☐ 580 Billy Williams SP	100.00	45.00	12.50
☐ 581 Tony Martinez	15.00	6.75	1.90
☐ 582 Garry Roggenburk	15.00	6.75	1.90
☐ 583 Tigers Team SP	140.00	65.00	17.50
☐ 584 Yankees Rookies	15.00	6.75	1.90
Frank Fernandez			
Fritz Peterson			
☐ 585 Tony Taylor	15.00	6.75	1.90
☐ 586 Claude Raymond SP	30.00	13.50	3.80
☐ 587 Dick Bertell	15.00	6.75	1.90
☐ 588 Athletics Rookies	15.00	6.75	1.90
Chuck Dobson			
Ken Suarez			
☐ 589 Lou Klimchock SP	35.00	16.00	4.40
☐ 590 Bill Skowron SP	45.00	20.00	5.75
☐ 591 NL Rookies SP	50.00	23.00	6.25
Bart Shirley			
Grant Jackson			
☐ 592 Andre Rodgers	15.00	6.75	1.90
☐ 593 Doug Camilli SP	30.00	13.50	3.80
☐ 594 Chico Salmon	15.00	6.75	1.90
☐ 595 Larry Jackson	15.00	6.75	1.90
☐ 596 Astros Rookies SP	18.00	8.00	2.30
Nate Colbert			
Greg Sims			
☐ 597 John Sullivan	15.00	6.75	1.90
☐ 598 Gaylord Perry SP	300.00	135.00	38.00

1967 Topps

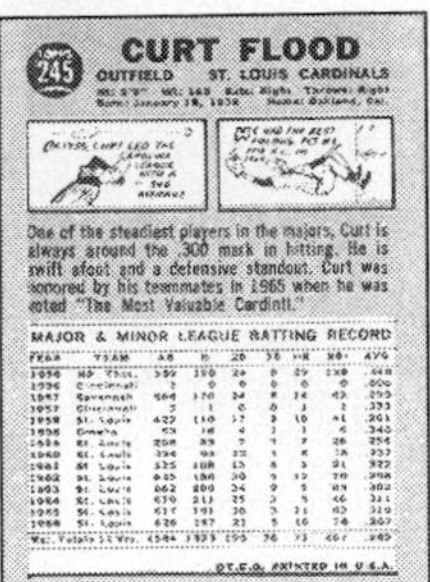

The cards in this 609-card set measure 2 1/2" by 3 1/2". The 1967 Topps series is considered by some collectors to be one of the company's finest accomplishments in baseball card production. Excellent color photographs are combined with easy-to-read backs. Cards 458 to 533 are slightly harder to find than numbers 1 to 457, and the inevitable (difficult to find) high series (534 to 609) exists. Each checklist card features a small circular picture of a popular player included in that series. Printing discrepancies resulted in some high series cards being in shorter supply. The checklist below identifies (by DP) 22 double-printed high numbers; of the 76 cards in the last series, 54 cards were short printed and the other 22 cards are much more plentiful. Featured subsets within this set include World Series cards (151-155) and League Leaders (233-244). Although there are several relatively expensive cards in this popular set, the key cards in the set are undoubtedly the Tom Seaver Rookie Card (581) and the Rod Carew Rookie Card (569). Although rarely seen, there exists a salesman's sample panel of three cards, that pictures Earl Battey, Manny Mota, and Gene Brabender with ad information on the back about the "new" Topps cards.

	NRMT	VG-E	GOOD
COMPLETE SET (609)	5250.00	2400.00	650.00
COMMON PLAYER (1-109)	1.50	.65	.19
COMMON PLAYER (110-196)	2.00	.90	.25
COMMON PLAYER (197-283)	2.50	1.15	.30
COMMON PLAYER (284-370)	3.00	1.35	.40
COMMON PLAYER (371-457)	4.00	1.80	.50
COMMON PLAYER (458-533)	7.00	3.10	.85
COMMON PLAYER (534-609)	18.00	8.00	2.30
☐ 1 The Champs DP	18.00	5.50	1.80
Frank Robinson			
Hank Bauer MG			
Brooks Robinson			
☐ 2 Jack Hamilton	1.50	.65	.19
☐ 3 Duke Sims	1.50	.65	.19
☐ 4 Hal Lanier	1.50	.65	.19
☐ 5 Whitey Ford UER	20.00	9.00	2.50
(1953 listed as			
1933 in stats on back)			
☐ 6 Dick Simpson	1.50	.65	.19
☐ 7 Don McMahon	1.50	.65	.19
☐ 8 Chuck Harrison	1.50	.65	.19
☐ 9 Ron Hansen	1.50	.65	.19
☐ 10 Matty Alou	2.00	.90	.25
☐ 11 Barry Moore	1.50	.65	.19
☐ 12 Dodgers Rookies	2.00	.90	.25
Jim Campanis			
Bill Singer			
☐ 13 Joe Sparma	1.50	.65	.19
☐ 14 Phil Linz	2.00	.90	.25
☐ 15 Earl Battey	1.50	.65	.19
☐ 16 Bill Hands	1.50	.65	.19
☐ 17 Jim Gosger	1.50	.65	.19
☐ 18 Gene Oliver	1.50	.65	.19
☐ 19 Jim McGlothlin	1.50	.65	.19
☐ 20 Orlando Cepeda	7.50	3.40	.95
☐ 21 Dave Bristol MG	1.50	.65	.19
☐ 22 Gene Brabender	1.50	.65	.19

☐ 23 Larry Elliot	1.50	.65	.19
☐ 24 Bob Allen	1.50	.65	.19
☐ 25 Elston Howard	4.00	1.80	.50
☐ 26A Bob Priddy NTR	30.00	13.50	3.80
☐ 26B Bob Priddy TR	1.50	.65	.19
☐ 27 Bob Saverine	1.50	.65	.19
☐ 28 Barry Latman	1.50	.65	.19
☐ 29 Tom McCraw	1.50	.65	.19
☐ 30 Al Kaline DP	16.00	7.25	2.00
☐ 31 Jim Brewer	1.50	.65	.19
☐ 32 Bob Bailey	2.00	.90	.25
☐ 33 Athletic Rookies Sal Bando Randy Schwartz	4.50	2.00	.55
☐ 34 Pete Cimino	1.50	.65	.19
☐ 35 Rico Carty	2.00	.90	.25
☐ 36 Bob Tillman	1.50	.65	.19
☐ 37 Rick Wise	2.00	.90	.25
☐ 38 Bob Johnson	1.50	.65	.19
☐ 39 Curt Simmons	2.00	.90	.25
☐ 40 Rick Reichardt	1.50	.65	.19
☐ 41 Joe Hoerner	1.50	.65	.19
☐ 42 Mets Team	3.00	1.35	.40
☐ 43 Chico Salmon	1.50	.65	.19
☐ 44 Joe Nuxhall	2.00	.90	.25
☐ 45 Roger Maris	50.00	23.00	6.25
☐ 46 Lindy McDaniel	2.00	.90	.25
☐ 47 Ken McMullen	1.50	.65	.19
☐ 48 Bill Freehan	2.00	.90	.25
☐ 49 Roy Face	2.00	.90	.25
☐ 50 Tony Oliva	5.00	2.30	.60
☐ 51 Astros Rookies Dave Adlesh Wes Bales	1.50	.65	.19
☐ 52 Dennis Higgins	1.50	.65	.19
☐ 53 Clay Dalrymple	1.50	.65	.19
☐ 54 Dick Green	1.50	.65	.19
☐ 55 Don Drysdale	15.00	6.75	1.90
☐ 56 Jose Tartabull	2.00	.90	.25
☐ 57 Pat Jarvis	1.50	.65	.19
☐ 58 Paul Schaal	1.50	.65	.19
☐ 59 Ralph Terry	2.00	.90	.25
☐ 60 Luis Aparicio	6.50	2.90	.80
☐ 61 Gordy Coleman	2.00	.90	.25
☐ 62 Checklist 1 Frank Robinson	6.50	1.95	.65
☐ 63 Cards' Clubbers Lou Brock Curt Flood	7.50	3.40	.95
☐ 64 Fred Valentine	1.50	.65	.19
☐ 65 Tom Haller	2.00	.90	.25
☐ 66 Manny Mota	2.00	.90	.25
☐ 67 Ken Berry	1.50	.65	.19
☐ 68 Bob Buhl	2.00	.90	.25
☐ 69 Vic Davalillo	1.50	.65	.19
☐ 70 Ron Santo	3.50	1.55	.45
☐ 71 Camilo Pascual	2.00	.90	.25
☐ 72 Tigers Rookies George Korince (Photo actually James Murray Brown) John (Tom) Matchick	1.50	.65	.19
☐ 73 Rusty Staub	3.50	1.55	.45
☐ 74 Wes Stock	1.50	.65	.19
☐ 75 George Scott	2.50	1.15	.30
☐ 76 Jim Barbieri	1.50	.65	.19
☐ 77 Dooley Womack	1.50	.65	.19
☐ 78 Pat Corrales	2.00	.90	.25
☐ 79 Bubba Morton	1.50	.65	.19
☐ 80 Jim Maloney	2.00	.90	.25
☐ 81 Eddie Stanky MG	2.00	.90	.25
☐ 82 Steve Barber	1.50	.65	.19
☐ 83 Ollie Brown	1.50	.65	.19
☐ 84 Tommie Sisk	1.50	.65	.19
☐ 85 Johnny Callison	2.00	.90	.25
☐ 86A Mike McCormick NTR (Senators on front and Senators on back)	30.00	13.50	3.80
☐ 86B Mike McCormick TR (Traded line at end of bio; Senators on front, but Giants on back)	2.00	.90	.25
☐ 87 George Altman	1.50	.65	.19
☐ 88 Mickey Lolich	4.00	1.80	.50
☐ 89 Felix Millan	2.00	.90	.25
☐ 90 Jim Nash	1.50	.65	.19
☐ 91 Johnny Lewis	1.50	.65	.19
☐ 92 Ray Washburn	1.50	.65	.19
☐ 93 Yankees Rookies Stan Bahnsen Bobby Murcer	3.50	1.55	.45
☐ 94 Ron Fairly	2.00	.90	.25
☐ 95 Sonny Siebert	1.50	.65	.19
☐ 96 Art Shamsky	1.50	.65	.19
☐ 97 Mike Cuellar	2.00	.90	.25
☐ 98 Rich Rollins	1.50	.65	.19
☐ 99 Lee Stange	1.50	.65	.19
☐ 100 Frank Robinson DP	18.00	8.00	2.30
☐ 101 Ken Johnson	1.50	.65	.19
☐ 102 Philadelphia Phillies Team Card	3.00	1.35	.40
☐ 103 Checklist 2 Mickey Mantle	9.00	2.70	.90
☐ 104 Minnie Rojas	1.50	.65	.19
☐ 105 Ken Boyer	3.00	1.35	.40
☐ 106 Randy Hundley	2.00	.90	.25
☐ 107 Joel Horlen	1.50	.65	.19
☐ 108 Alex Johnson	2.00	.90	.25
☐ 109 Tribe Thumpers Rocky Colavito Leon Wagner	2.50	1.15	.30
☐ 110 Jack Aker	2.50	1.15	.30
☐ 111 John Kennedy	2.00	.90	.25
☐ 112 Dave Wickersham	2.00	.90	.25
☐ 113 Dave Nicholson	2.00	.90	.25
☐ 114 Jack Baldschun	2.00	.90	.25
☐ 115 Paul Casanova	2.00	.90	.25
☐ 116 Herman Franks MG	2.00	.90	.25
☐ 117 Darrell Brandon	2.00	.90	.25
☐ 118 Bernie Allen	2.00	.90	.25
☐ 119 Wade Blasingame	2.00	.90	.25
☐ 120 Floyd Robinson	2.00	.90	.25
☐ 121 Eddie Bressoud	2.00	.90	.25
☐ 122 George Brunet	2.00	.90	.25
☐ 123 Pirates Rookies Jim Price Luke Walker	2.00	.90	.25
☐ 124 Jim Stewart	2.00	.90	.25
☐ 125 Moe Drabowsky	2.50	1.15	.30
☐ 126 Tony Taylor	2.00	.90	.25
☐ 127 John O'Donoghue	2.00	.90	.25
☐ 128 Ed Spiezio	2.00	.90	.25
☐ 129 Phil Roof	2.00	.90	.25
☐ 130 Phil Regan	2.50	1.15	.30
☐ 131 Yankees Team	5.00	2.30	.60
☐ 132 Ozzie Virgil	2.00	.90	.25
☐ 133 Ron Kline	2.00	.90	.25
☐ 134 Gates Brown	2.50	1.15	.30
☐ 135 Deron Johnson	2.50	1.15	.30
☐ 136 Carroll Sembera	2.00	.90	.25
☐ 137 Twins Rookies Ron Clark Jim Ollum	2.50	1.15	.30
☐ 138 Dick Kelley	2.00	.90	.25
☐ 139 Dalton Jones	2.00	.90	.25
☐ 140 Willie Stargell	20.00	9.00	2.50
☐ 141 John Miller	2.00	.90	.25
☐ 142 Jackie Brandt	2.00	.90	.25
☐ 143 Sox Sockers Pete Ward Don Buford	2.00	.90	.25
☐ 144 Bill Hepler	2.00	.90	.25
☐ 145 Larry Brown	2.00	.90	.25
☐ 146 Steve Carlton	125.00	57.50	15.50
☐ 147 Tom Egan	2.00	.90	.25
☐ 148 Adolfo Phillips	2.00	.90	.25
☐ 149 Joe Moeller	2.00	.90	.25
☐ 150 Mickey Mantle	250.00	115.00	31.00
☐ 151 World Series Game 1 Moe mows down 11 (Moe Drabowsky)	3.75	1.70	.45
☐ 152 World Series Game 2 Jim Palmer blanks Dodgers	7.00	3.10	.85
☐ 153 World Series Game 3 Paul Blair's homer defeats L.A.	3.75	1.70	.45
☐ 154 World Series Game 4 Orioles 4 straight (Brooks Robinson and Dave McNally)	3.75	1.70	.45
☐ 155 World Series Summary Winners celebrate	3.75	1.70	.45
☐ 156 Ron Herbel	2.00	.90	.25
☐ 157 Danny Cater	2.00	.90	.25
☐ 158 Jimmie Coker	2.00	.90	.25
☐ 159 Bruce Howard	2.00	.90	.25
☐ 160 Willie Davis	2.50	1.15	.30
☐ 161 Dick Williams MG	2.50	1.15	.30
☐ 162 Billy O'Dell	2.00	.90	.25
☐ 163 Vic Roznovsky	2.00	.90	.25
☐ 164 Dwight Siebler UER (Last line of stats shows 1960 Minnesota)	2.00	.90	.25
☐ 165 Cleon Jones	2.50	1.15	.30

☐ 166 Eddie Mathews	13.00	5.75	1.65
☐ 167 Senators Rookies	2.00	.90	.25
Joe Coleman			
Tim Cullen			
☐ 168 Ray Culp	2.00	.90	.25
☐ 169 Horace Clarke	2.00	.90	.25
☐ 170 Dick McAuliffe	2.50	1.15	.30
☐ 171 Cal Koonce	2.00	.90	.25
☐ 172 Bill Heath	2.00	.90	.25
☐ 173 St. Louis Cardinals	4.00	1.80	.50
Team Card			
☐ 174 Dick Radatz	2.50	1.15	.30
☐ 175 Bobby Knoop	2.00	.90	.25
☐ 176 Sammy Ellis	2.00	.90	.25
☐ 177 Tito Fuentes	2.00	.90	.25
☐ 178 John Buzhardt	2.00	.90	.25
☐ 179 Braves Rookies	2.00	.90	.25
Charles Vaughan			
Cecil Upshaw			
☐ 180 Curt Blefary	2.00	.90	.25
☐ 181 Terry Fox	2.00	.90	.25
☐ 182 Ed Charles	2.00	.90	.25
☐ 183 Jim Pagliaroni	2.00	.90	.25
☐ 184 George Thomas	2.00	.90	.25
☐ 185 Ken Holtzman	4.50	2.00	.55
☐ 186 Mets Maulers	2.50	1.15	.30
Ed Kranepool			
Ron Swoboda			
☐ 187 Pedro Ramos	2.00	.90	.25
☐ 188 Ken Harrelson	2.50	1.15	.30
☐ 189 Chuck Hinton	2.00	.90	.25
☐ 190 Turk Farrell	2.00	.90	.25
☐ 191A Checklist 3	7.50	2.30	.75
(214 Tom Kelley)			
(Willie Mays)			
☐ 191B Checklist 3	12.50	3.80	1.25
(214 Dick Kelley)			
(Willie Mays)			
☐ 192 Fred Gladding	2.00	.90	.25
☐ 193 Jose Cardenal	2.50	1.15	.30
☐ 194 Bob Allison	2.50	1.15	.30
☐ 195 Al Jackson	2.00	.90	.25
☐ 196 Johnny Romano	2.00	.90	.25
☐ 197 Ron Perranoski	3.00	1.35	.40
☐ 198 Chuck Hiller	2.50	1.15	.30
☐ 199 Billy Hitchcock MG	2.50	1.15	.30
☐ 200 Willie Mays UER	100.00	45.00	12.50
('63 Sna Francisco			
on card back stats)			
☐ 201 Hal Reniff	2.50	1.15	.30
☐ 202 Johnny Edwards	2.50	1.15	.30
☐ 203 Al McBean	2.50	1.15	.30
☐ 204 Orioles Rookies	3.00	1.35	.40
Mike Epstein			
Tom Phoebus			
☐ 205 Dick Groat	3.00	1.35	.40
☐ 206 Dennis Bennett	2.50	1.15	.30
☐ 207 John Orsino	2.50	1.15	.30
☐ 208 Jack Lamabe	2.50	1.15	.30
☐ 209 Joe Nossek	2.50	1.15	.30
☐ 210 Bob Gibson	20.00	9.00	2.50
☐ 211 Twins Team	4.00	1.80	.50
☐ 212 Chris Zachary	2.50	1.15	.30
☐ 213 Jay Johnstone	3.50	1.55	.45
☐ 214 Dick Kelley	2.50	1.15	.30
☐ 215 Ernie Banks	20.00	9.00	2.50
☐ 216 Bengal Belters	8.50	3.80	1.05
Norm Cash			
Al Kaline			
☐ 217 Rob Gardner	2.50	1.15	.30
☐ 218 Wes Parker	3.00	1.35	.40
☐ 219 Clay Carroll	3.00	1.35	.40
☐ 220 Jim Ray Hart	3.00	1.35	.40
☐ 221 Woody Fryman	3.00	1.35	.40
☐ 222 Reds Rookies	3.00	1.35	.40
Darrell Osteen			
Lee May			
☐ 223 Mike Ryan	2.50	1.15	.30
☐ 224 Walt Bond	2.50	1.15	.30
☐ 225 Mel Stottlemyre	3.50	1.55	.45
☐ 226 Julian Javier	3.00	1.35	.40
☐ 227 Paul Lindblad	2.50	1.15	.30
☐ 228 Gil Hodges MG	5.00	2.30	.60
☐ 229 Larry Jackson	2.50	1.15	.30
☐ 230 Boog Powell	4.00	1.80	.50
☐ 231 John Bateman	2.50	1.15	.30
☐ 232 Don Buford	2.50	1.15	.30
☐ 233 AL ERA Leaders	3.50	1.55	.45
Gary Peters			
Joel Horlen			
Steve Hargan			
☐ 234 NL ERA Leaders	8.00	3.60	1.00
Sandy Koufax			
Mike Cuellar			
Juan Marichal			
☐ 235 AL Pitching Leaders	3.50	1.55	.45
Jim Kaat			
Denny McLain			
Earl Wilson			
☐ 236 NL Pitching Leaders	15.00	6.75	1.90
Sandy Koufax			
Juan Marichal			
Bob Gibson			
Gaylord Perry			
☐ 237 AL Strikeout Leaders	3.50	1.55	.45
Sam McDowell			
Jim Kaat			
Earl Wilson			
☐ 238 NL Strikeout Leaders	6.50	2.90	.80
Sandy Koufax			
Jim Bunning			
Bob Veale			
☐ 239 AL Batting Leaders	6.00	2.70	.75
Frank Robinson			
Tony Oliva			
Al Kaline			
☐ 240 NL Batting Leaders	3.50	1.55	.45
Matty Alou			
Felipe Alou			
Rico Carty			
☐ 241 AL RBI Leaders	6.00	2.70	.75
Frank Robinson			
Harmon Killebrew			
Boog Powell			
☐ 242 NL RBI Leaders	10.00	4.50	1.25
Hank Aaron			
Bob Clemente			
Richie Allen			
☐ 243 AL Home Run Leaders	6.00	2.70	.75
Frank Robinson			
Harmon Killebrew			
Boog Powell			
☐ 244 NL Home Run Leaders	10.00	4.50	1.25
Hank Aaron			
Richie Allen			
Willie Mays			
☐ 245 Curt Flood	3.50	1.55	.45
☐ 246 Jim Perry	3.00	1.35	.40
☐ 247 Jerry Lumpe	2.50	1.15	.30
☐ 248 Gene Mauch MG	3.00	1.35	.40
☐ 249 Nick Willhite	2.50	1.15	.30
☐ 250 Hank Aaron UER	100.00	45.00	12.50
(Second 1961 in stats			
should be 1962)			
☐ 251 Woody Held	2.50	1.15	.30
☐ 252 Bob Bolin	2.50	1.15	.30
☐ 253 Indians Rookies	2.50	1.15	.30
Bill Davis			
Gus Gil			
☐ 254 Milt Pappas	3.00	1.35	.40
(No facsimile auto-			
graph on card front)			
☐ 255 Frank Howard	3.50	1.55	.45
☐ 256 Bob Hendley	2.50	1.15	.30
☐ 257 Charlie Smith	2.50	1.15	.30
☐ 258 Lee Maye	2.50	1.15	.30
☐ 259 Don Dennis	2.50	1.15	.30
☐ 260 Jim Lefebvre	3.00	1.35	.40
☐ 261 John Wyatt	2.50	1.15	.30
☐ 262 Athletics Team	4.00	1.80	.50
☐ 263 Hank Aguirre	2.50	1.15	.30
☐ 264 Ron Swoboda	3.00	1.35	.40
☐ 265 Lou Burdette	3.00	1.35	.40
☐ 266 Pitt Power	4.00	1.80	.50
Willie Stargell			
Donn Clendenon			
☐ 267 Don Schwall	2.50	1.15	.30
☐ 268 Johnny Briggs	2.50	1.15	.30
☐ 269 Don Nottebart	2.50	1.15	.30
☐ 270 Zoilo Versalles	2.50	1.15	.30
☐ 271 Eddie Watt	2.50	1.15	.30
☐ 272 Cubs Rookies	3.50	1.55	.45
Bill Connors			
Dave Dowling			
☐ 273 Dick Lines	2.50	1.15	.30
☐ 274 Bob Aspromonte	2.50	1.15	.30
☐ 275 Fred Whitfield	2.50	1.15	.30
☐ 276 Bruce Brubaker	2.50	1.15	.30
☐ 277 Steve Whitaker	2.50	1.15	.30
☐ 278 Checklist 4	6.50	1.95	.65
Jim Kaat			
☐ 279 Frank Linzy	2.50	1.15	.30
☐ 280 Tony Conigliaro	7.50	3.40	.95
☐ 281 Bob Rodgers	3.00	1.35	.40
☐ 282 John Odom	2.50	1.15	.30
☐ 283 Gene Alley	3.00	1.35	.40
☐ 284 Johnny Podres	3.50	1.55	.45

☐ 285 Lou Brock 25.00 11.50 3.10
☐ 286 Wayne Causey 3.00 1.35 .40
☐ 287 Mets Rookies 3.00 1.35 .40
Greg Goossen
Bart Shirley
☐ 288 Denny Lemaster 3.00 1.35 .40
☐ 289 Tom Tresh 4.00 1.80 .50
☐ 290 Bill White 4.00 1.80 .50
☐ 291 Jim Hannan 3.00 1.35 .40
☐ 292 Don Pavletich 3.00 1.35 .40
☐ 293 Ed Kirkpatrick 3.00 1.35 .40
☐ 294 Walt Alston MG 4.00 1.80 .50
☐ 295 Sam McDowell 3.50 1.55 .45
☐ 296 Glenn Beckert 3.50 1.55 .45
☐ 297 Dave Morehead 3.00 1.35 .40
☐ 298 Ron Davis 3.00 1.35 .40
☐ 299 Norm Siebern 3.00 1.35 .40
☐ 300 Jim Kaat 4.50 2.00 .55
☐ 301 Jesse Gonder 3.00 1.35 .40
☐ 302 Orioles Team 6.00 2.70 .75
☐ 303 Gil Blanco 3.00 1.35 .40
☐ 304 Phil Gagliano 3.00 1.35 .40
☐ 305 Earl Wilson 3.50 1.55 .45
☐ 306 Bud Harrelson 4.50 2.00 .55
☐ 307 Jim Beauchamp 3.00 1.35 .40
☐ 308 Al Downing 3.50 1.55 .45
☐ 309 Hurlers Beware 3.50 1.55 .45
Johnny Callison
Richie Allen
☐ 310 Gary Peters 3.00 1.35 .40
☐ 311 Ed Brinkman 3.00 1.35 .40
☐ 312 Don Mincher 3.00 1.35 .40
☐ 313 Bob Lee 3.00 1.35 .40
☐ 314 Red Sox Rookies 8.00 3.60 1.00
Mike Andrews
Reggie Smith
☐ 315 Billy Williams 12.50 5.75 1.55
☐ 316 Jack Kralick 3.00 1.35 .40
☐ 317 Cesar Tovar 3.50 1.55 .45
☐ 318 Dave Giusti 3.00 1.35 .40
☐ 319 Paul Blair 3.50 1.55 .45
☐ 320 Gaylord Perry 15.00 6.75 1.90
☐ 321 Mayo Smith MG 3.00 1.35 .40
☐ 322 Jose Pagan 3.00 1.35 .40
☐ 323 Mike Hershberger 3.00 1.35 .40
☐ 324 Hal Woodeshick 3.00 1.35 .40
☐ 325 Chico Cardenas 3.50 1.55 .45
☐ 326 Bob Uecker 20.00 9.00 2.50
☐ 327 California Angels 6.00 2.70 .75
Team Card
☐ 328 Clete Boyer UER 3.50 1.55 .45
(Stats only go up
through 1965)
☐ 329 Charlie Lau 3.50 1.55 .45
☐ 330 Claude Osteen 3.50 1.55 .45
☐ 331 Joe Foy 3.00 1.35 .40
☐ 332 Jesus Alou 3.00 1.35 .40
☐ 333 Fergie Jenkins 35.00 16.00 4.40
☐ 334 Twin Terrors 4.50 2.00 .55
Bob Allison
Harmon Killebrew
☐ 335 Bob Veale 3.50 1.55 .45
☐ 336 Joe Azcue 3.00 1.35 .40
☐ 337 Joe Morgan 25.00 11.50 3.10
☐ 338 Bob Locker 3.00 1.35 .40
☐ 339 Chico Ruiz 3.00 1.35 .40
☐ 340 Joe Pepitone 3.50 1.55 .45
☐ 341 Giants Rookies 3.00 1.35 .40
Dick Dietz
Bill Sorrell
☐ 342 Hank Fischer 3.00 1.35 .40
☐ 343 Tom Satriano 3.00 1.35 .40
☐ 344 Ossie Chavarria 3.00 1.35 .40
☐ 345 Stu Miller 3.50 1.55 .45
☐ 346 Jim Hickman 3.00 1.35 .40
☐ 347 Grady Hatton MG 3.00 1.35 .40
☐ 348 Tug McGraw 4.50 2.00 .55
☐ 349 Bob Chance 3.00 1.35 .40
☐ 350 Joe Torre 4.50 2.00 .55
☐ 351 Vern Law 3.50 1.55 .45
☐ 352 Ray Oyler 3.00 1.35 .40
☐ 353 Bill McCool 3.00 1.35 .40
☐ 354 Cubs Team 6.00 2.70 .75
☐ 355 Carl Yastrzemski 80.00 36.00 10.00
☐ 356 Larry Jaster 3.00 1.35 .40
☐ 357 Bill Skowron 3.50 1.55 .45
☐ 358 Ruben Amaro 3.00 1.35 .40
☐ 359 Dick Ellsworth 3.00 1.35 .40
☐ 360 Leon Wagner 3.00 1.35 .40
☐ 361 Checklist 5 7.50 2.30 .75
Roberto Clemente
☐ 362 Darold Knowles 3.00 1.35 .40
☐ 363 Dave Johnson 3.50 1.55 .45
☐ 364 Claude Raymond 3.00 1.35 .40
☐ 365 John Roseboro 3.50 1.55 .45
☐ 366 Andy Kosco 3.00 1.35 .40
☐ 367 Angels Rookies 3.00 1.35 .40
Bill Kelso
Don Wallace
☐ 368 Jack Hiatt 3.00 1.35 .40
☐ 369 Jim Hunter 20.00 9.00 2.50
☐ 370 Tommy Davis 3.50 1.55 .45
☐ 371 Jim Lonborg 5.00 2.30 .60
☐ 372 Mike DeLaHoz 4.00 1.80 .50
☐ 373 White Sox Rookies DP 4.00 1.80 .50
Duane Josephson
Fred Klages
☐ 374A Mel Queen ERR DP 4.00 1.80 .50
(Incomplete stat
line on back)
☐ 374B Mel Queen COR DP 4.00 1.80 .50
(Complete stat
line on back)
☐ 375 Jake Gibbs 4.00 1.80 .50
☐ 376 Don Lock DP 4.00 1.80 .50
☐ 377 Luis Tiant 5.00 2.30 .60
☐ 378 Detroit Tigers 8.00 3.60 1.00
Team Card UER
(Willie Horton with
262 RBI's in 1966)
☐ 379 Jerry May DP 4.00 1.80 .50
☐ 380 Dean Chance DP 4.00 1.80 .50
☐ 381 Dick Schofield DP 4.00 1.80 .50
☐ 382 Dave McNally 4.50 2.00 .55
☐ 383 Ken Henderson DP 4.00 1.80 .50
☐ 384 Cardinals Rookies 4.00 1.80 .50
Jim Cosman
Dick Hughes
☐ 385 Jim Fregosi 4.50 2.00 .55
(Batting wrong)
☐ 386 Dick Selma DP 4.00 1.80 .50
☐ 387 Cap Peterson DP 4.00 1.80 .50
☐ 388 Arnold Earley DP 4.00 1.80 .50
☐ 389 Alvin Dark MG DP 4.50 2.00 .55
☐ 390 Jim Wynn DP 4.50 2.00 .55
☐ 391 Wilbur Wood DP 4.50 2.00 .55
☐ 392 Tommy Harper DP 4.50 2.00 .55
☐ 393 Jim Bouton DP 4.50 2.00 .55
☐ 394 Jake Wood DP 4.00 1.80 .50
☐ 395 Chris Short 4.50 2.00 .55
☐ 396 Atlanta Aces 4.00 1.80 .50
Denis Menke
Tony Cloninger
☐ 397 Willie Smith DP 4.00 1.80 .50
☐ 398 Jeff Torborg 4.50 2.00 .55
☐ 399 Al Worthington DP 4.00 1.80 .50
☐ 400 Bob Clemente DP 75.00 34.00 9.50
☐ 401 Jim Coates 4.00 1.80 .50
☐ 402 Phillies Rookies DP 4.50 2.00 .55
Grant Jackson
Billy Wilson
☐ 403 Dick Nen 4.00 1.80 .50
☐ 404 Nelson Briles 4.50 2.00 .55
☐ 405 Russ Snyder 4.00 1.80 .50
☐ 406 Lee Elia DP 4.00 1.80 .50
☐ 407 Reds Team 8.00 3.60 1.00
☐ 408 Jim Northrup DP 4.50 2.00 .55
☐ 409 Ray Sadecki 4.00 1.80 .50
☐ 410 Lou Johnson DP 4.00 1.80 .50
☐ 411 Dick Howser DP 4.50 2.00 .55
☐ 412 Astros Rookies 4.50 2.00 .55
Norm Miller
Doug Rader
☐ 413 Jerry Grote 4.00 1.80 .50
☐ 414 Casey Cox 4.00 1.80 .50
☐ 415 Sonny Jackson 4.00 1.80 .50
☐ 416 Roger Repoz 4.00 1.80 .50
☐ 417A Bob Bruce ERR DP 30.00 13.50 3.80
(RBAVES on back)
☐ 417B Bob Bruce COR DP 4.00 1.80 .50
☐ 418 Sam Mele MG 4.00 1.80 .50
☐ 419 Don Kessinger DP 4.50 2.00 .55
☐ 420 Denny McLain 7.50 3.40 .95
☐ 421 Dal Maxvill DP 4.00 1.80 .50
☐ 422 Hoyt Wilhelm 9.00 4.00 1.15
☐ 423 Fence Busters DP 25.00 11.50 3.10
Willie Mays
Willie McCovey
☐ 424 Pedro Gonzalez 4.00 1.80 .50
☐ 425 Pete Mikkelsen 4.00 1.80 .50
☐ 426 Lou Clinton 4.00 1.80 .50
☐ 427A Ruben Gomez ERR DP 4.00 1.80 .50
(Incomplete stat
line on back)
☐ 427B Ruben Gomez COR DP 4.00 1.80 .50
(Complete stat

line on back)
□ 428 Dodgers Rookies DP 4.50 2.00 .55
Tom Hutton
Gene Michael
□ 429 Garry Roggenburk DP 4.00 1.80 .50
□ 430 Pete Rose 80.00 36.00 10.00
□ 431 Ted Uhlaender 4.00 1.80 .50
□ 432 Jimmie Hall DP 4.00 1.80 .50
□ 433 Al Luplow DP 4.00 1.80 .50
□ 434 Eddie Fisher DP 4.00 1.80 .50
□ 435 Mack Jones DP 4.00 1.80 .50
□ 436 Pete Ward 4.00 1.80 .50
□ 437 Senators Team 8.00 3.60 1.00
□ 438 Chuck Dobson 4.00 1.80 .50
□ 439 Byron Browne 4.00 1.80 .50
□ 440 Steve Hargan 4.00 1.80 .50
□ 441 Jim Davenport 4.00 1.80 .50
□ 442 Yankees Rookies DP 4.50 2.00 .55
Bill Robinson
Joe Verbanic
□ 443 Tito Francona DP 4.00 1.80 .50
□ 444 George Smith 4.00 1.80 .50
□ 445 Don Sutton 36.00 16.00 4.50
□ 446 Russ Nixon DP 4.00 1.80 .50
□ 447A Bo Belinsky ERR DP 4.50 2.00 .55
(Incomplete stat
line on back)
□ 447B Bo Belinsky COR DP 4.50 2.00 .55
(Complete stat
line on back)
□ 448 Harry Walker MG DP 4.00 1.80 .50
□ 449 Orlando Pena 4.00 1.80 .50
□ 450 Richie Allen 7.50 3.40 .95
□ 451 Fred Newman DP 4.00 1.80 .50
□ 452 Ed Kranepool 4.50 2.00 .55
□ 453 Aurelio Monteagudo DP 4.00 1.80 .50
□ 454A Checklist 6 DP 7.50 2.30 .75
Juan Marichal
(Missing left ear)
□ 454B Checklist 6 DP 7.50 2.30 .75
Juan Marichal
(left ear showing)
□ 455 Tommie Agee 4.50 2.00 .55
□ 456 Phil Niekro 18.00 8.00 2.30
□ 457 Andy Etchebarren DP 4.50 2.00 .55
□ 458 Lee Thomas 8.00 3.60 1.00
□ 459 Senators Rookies 8.00 3.60 1.00
Dick Bosman
Pete Craig
□ 460 Harmon Killebrew 55.00 25.00 7.00
□ 461 Bob Miller 7.00 3.10 .85
□ 462 Bob Barton 7.00 3.10 .85
□ 463 Hill Aces 8.00 3.60 1.00
Sam McDowell
Sonny Siebert
□ 464 Dan Coombs 7.00 3.10 .85
□ 465 Willie Horton 8.00 3.60 1.00
□ 466 Bobby Wine 7.00 3.10 .85
□ 467 Jim O'Toole 8.00 3.60 1.00
□ 468 Ralph Houk MG 8.00 3.60 1.00
□ 469 Len Gabrielson 7.00 3.10 .85
□ 470 Bob Shaw 7.00 3.10 .85
□ 471 Rene Lachemann 8.00 3.60 1.00
□ 472 Rookies Pirates 7.00 3.10 .85
John Gelnar
George Spriggs
□ 473 Jose Santiago 7.00 3.10 .85
□ 474 Bob Tolan 8.00 3.60 1.00
□ 475 Jim Palmer 110.00 50.00 14.00
□ 476 Tony Perez SP 100.00 45.00 12.50
□ 477 Braves Team 14.00 6.25 1.75
□ 478 Bob Humphreys 7.00 3.10 .85
□ 479 Gary Bell 7.00 3.10 .85
□ 480 Willie McCovey 40.00 18.00 5.00
□ 481 Leo Durocher MG 13.00 5.75 1.65
□ 482 Bill Monbouquette 7.00 3.10 .85
□ 483 Jim Landis 7.00 3.10 .85
□ 484 Jerry Adair 7.00 3.10 .85
□ 485 Tim McCarver 25.00 11.50 3.10
□ 486 Twins Rookies 7.00 3.10 .85
Rich Reese
Bill Whitby
□ 487 Tommie Reynolds 7.00 3.10 .85
□ 488 Gerry Arrigo 7.00 3.10 .85
□ 489 Doug Clemens 7.00 3.10 .85
□ 490 Tony Cloninger 7.00 3.10 .85
□ 491 Sam Bowens 7.00 3.10 .85
□ 492 Pittsburgh Pirates 14.00 6.25 1.75
Team Card
□ 493 Phil Ortega 7.00 3.10 .85
□ 494 Bill Rigney MG 7.00 3.10 .85
□ 495 Fritz Peterson 7.00 3.10 .85
□ 496 Orlando McFarlane 7.00 3.10 .85
□ 497 Ron Campbell 7.00 3.10 .85
□ 498 Larry Dierker 7.00 3.10 .85
□ 499 Indians Rookies 7.00 3.10 .85
George Culver
Jose Vidal
□ 500 Juan Marichal 25.00 11.50 3.10
□ 501 Jerry Zimmerman 7.00 3.10 .85
□ 502 Derrell Griffith 7.00 3.10 .85
□ 503 Los Angeles Dodgers 14.00 6.25 1.75
Team Card
□ 504 Orlando Martinez 7.00 3.10 .85
□ 505 Tommy Helms 8.00 3.60 1.00
□ 506 Smoky Burgess 8.00 3.60 1.00
□ 507 Orioles Rookies 7.00 3.10 .85
Ed Barnowski
Larry Haney
□ 508 Dick Hall 7.00 3.10 .85
□ 509 Jim King 7.00 3.10 .85
□ 510 Bill Mazeroski 12.50 5.75 1.55
□ 511 Don Wert 7.00 3.10 .85
□ 512 Red Schoendienst MG 12.50 5.75 1.55
□ 513 Marcelino Lopez 7.00 3.10 .85
□ 514 John Werhas 7.00 3.10 .85
□ 515 Bert Campaneris 8.00 3.60 1.00
□ 516 Giants Team 14.00 6.25 1.75
□ 517 Fred Talbot 7.00 3.10 .85
□ 518 Denis Menke 7.00 3.10 .85
□ 519 Ted Davidson 7.00 3.10 .85
□ 520 Max Alvis 7.00 3.10 .85
□ 521 Bird Bombers 8.00 3.60 1.00
Boog Powell
Curt Blefary
□ 522 John Stephenson 7.00 3.10 .85
□ 523 Jim Merritt 7.00 3.10 .85
□ 524 Felix Mantilla 7.00 3.10 .85
□ 525 Ron Hunt 7.00 3.10 .85
□ 526 Tigers Rookies 9.00 4.00 1.15
Pat Dobson
George Korince
(See 67T-72)
□ 527 Dennis Ribant 7.00 3.10 .85
□ 528 Rico Petrocelli 11.00 4.90 1.40
□ 529 Gary Wagner 7.00 3.10 .85
□ 530 Felipe Alou 11.00 4.90 1.40
□ 531 Checklist 7 12.50 3.80 1.25
Brooks Robinson
□ 532 Jim Hicks 7.00 3.10 .85
□ 533 Jack Fisher 7.00 3.10 .85
□ 534 Hank Bauer MG DP 10.00 4.50 1.25
□ 535 Donn Clendenon 20.50 9.25 2.60
□ 536 Cubs Rookies 40.00 18.00 5.00
Joe Niekro
Paul Popovich
□ 537 Chuck Estrada DP 10.00 4.50 1.25
□ 538 J.C. Martin 18.00 8.00 2.30
□ 539 Dick Egan DP 10.00 4.50 1.25
□ 540 Norm Cash 50.00 23.00 6.25
□ 541 Joe Gibbon 18.00 8.00 2.30
□ 542 Athletics Rookies DP 12.50 5.75 1.55
Rick Monday
Tony Pierce
□ 543 Dan Schneider 18.00 8.00 2.30
□ 544 Cleveland Indians 30.00 13.50 3.80
Team Card
□ 545 Jim Grant 18.00 8.00 2.30
□ 546 Woody Woodward 20.50 9.25 2.60
□ 547 Red Sox Rookies DP 10.00 4.50 1.25
Russ Gibson
Bill Rohr
□ 548 Tony Gonzalez DP 10.00 4.50 1.25
□ 549 Jack Sanford 18.00 8.00 2.30
□ 550 Vada Pinson DP 12.50 5.75 1.55
□ 551 Doug Camilli DP 10.00 4.50 1.25
□ 552 Ted Savage 18.00 8.00 2.30
□ 553 Yankees Rookies 35.00 16.00 4.40
Mike Hegan
Thad Tillotson
□ 554 Andre Rodgers DP 10.00 4.50 1.25
□ 555 Don Cardwell 18.00 8.00 2.30
□ 556 Al Weis DP 10.00 4.50 1.25
□ 557 Al Ferrara 18.00 8.00 2.30
□ 558 Orioles Rookies 60.00 27.00 7.50
Mark Belanger
Bill Dillman
□ 559 Dick Tracewski DP 10.00 4.50 1.25
□ 560 Jim Bunning 60.00 27.00 7.50
□ 561 Sandy Alomar 20.50 9.25 2.60
□ 562 Steve Blass DP 11.00 4.90 1.40
□ 563 Joe Adcock 25.00 11.50 3.10
□ 564 Astros Rookies DP 11.00 4.90 1.40
Alonzo Harris
Aaron Pointer
□ 565 Lew Krausse 18.00 8.00 2.30
□ 566 Gary Geiger DP 10.00 4.50 1.25

☐ 567 Steve Hamilton	18.00	8.00	2.30
☐ 568 John Sullivan	18.00	8.00	2.30
☐ 569 AL Rookies DP	550.00	250.00	70.00
Rod Carew			
Hank Allen			
☐ 570 Maury Wills	100.00	45.00	12.50
☐ 571 Larry Sherry	18.00	8.00	2.30
☐ 572 Don Demeter	25.00	11.50	3.10
☐ 573 Chicago White Sox	30.00	13.50	3.80
Team Card UER			
(Indians team			
stats on back)			
☐ 574 Jerry Buchek	18.00	8.00	2.30
☐ 575 Dave Boswell	18.00	8.00	2.30
☐ 576 NL Rookies	25.00	11.50	3.10
Ramon Hernandez			
Norm Gigon			
☐ 577 Bill Short	18.00	8.00	2.30
☐ 578 John Boccabella	18.00	8.00	2.30
☐ 579 Bill Henry	18.00	8.00	2.30
☐ 580 Rocky Colavito	80.00	36.00	10.00
☐ 581 Mets Rookies	1400.00	650.00	180.00
Bill Denehy			
Tom Seaver			
☐ 582 Jim Owens DP	10.00	4.50	1.25
☐ 583 Ray Barker	18.00	8.00	2.30
☐ 584 Jim Piersall	30.00	13.50	3.80
☐ 585 Wally Bunker	18.00	8.00	2.30
☐ 586 Manny Jimenez	18.00	8.00	2.30
☐ 587 NL Rookies	30.00	13.50	3.80
Don Shaw			
Gary Sutherland			
☐ 588 Johnny Klippstein DP	10.00	4.50	1.25
☐ 589 Dave Ricketts DP	10.00	4.50	1.25
☐ 590 Pete Richert	18.00	8.00	2.30
☐ 591 Ty Cline	18.00	8.00	2.30
☐ 592 NL Rookies	25.00	11.50	3.10
Jim Shellenback			
Ron Willis			
☐ 593 Wes Westrum MG	20.50	9.25	2.60
☐ 594 Dan Osinski	25.00	11.50	3.10
☐ 595 Cookie Rojas	20.50	9.25	2.60
☐ 596 Galen Cisco DP	10.00	4.50	1.25
☐ 597 Ted Abernathy	18.00	8.00	2.30
☐ 598 White Sox Rookies	20.50	9.25	2.60
Walt Williams			
Ed Stroud			
☐ 599 Bob Duliba DP	10.00	4.50	1.25
☐ 600 Brooks Robinson	250.00	115.00	31.00
☐ 601 Bill Bryan DP	10.00	4.50	1.25
☐ 602 Juan Pizarro	18.00	8.00	2.30
☐ 603 Athletics Rookies	18.00	8.00	2.30
Tim Talton			
Ramon Webster			
☐ 604 Red Sox Team	125.00	57.50	15.50
☐ 605 Mike Shannon	50.00	23.00	6.25
☐ 606 Ron Taylor	18.00	8.00	2.30
☐ 607 Mickey Stanley	40.00	18.00	5.00
☐ 608 Cubs Rookies DP	10.00	4.50	1.25
Rich Nye			
John Upham			
☐ 609 Tommy John	125.00	31.00	10.00

1968 Topps

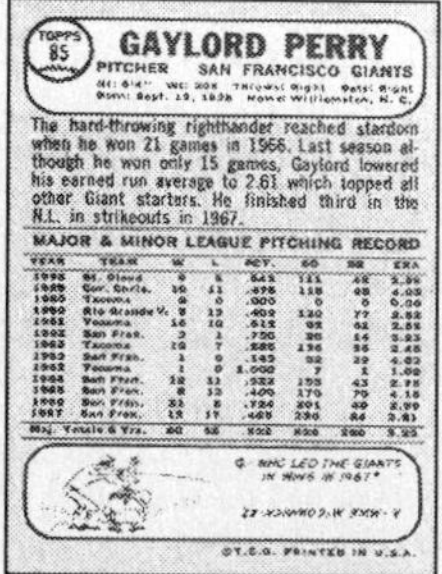

The cards in this 598-card set measure 2 1/2" by 3 1/2". The 1968 Topps set includes Sporting News All-Star Selections as card numbers 361 to 380. Other subsets in the set include League Leaders (1-12) and World Series cards (151-158). The front of each checklist card features a picture of a popular player inside a circle. High numbers 534 to 598 are slightly more difficult to obtain. The first series looks different from the other series, as it has a lighter, wider mesh background on the card front. The later series all had a much darker, finer mesh pattern. Key cards in the set are the Rookie Cards of Johnny Bench (247) and Nolan Ryan (177).

	NRMT-MT	EXC	G-VG
COMPLETE SET (598)	3300.00	1500.00	425.00
COMMON PLAYER (1-109)	1.50	.65	.19
COMMON PLAYER (110-196)	1.50	.65	.19
COMMON PLAYER (197-283)	1.50	.65	.19
COMMON PLAYER (284-370)	1.50	.65	.19
COMMON PLAYER (371-457)	1.50	.65	.19
COMMON PLAYER (458-533)	3.00	1.35	.40
COMMON PLAYER (534-598)	3.75	1.70	.45
☐ 1 NL Batting Leaders	16.00	4.80	1.60
Bob Clemente			
Tony Gonzalez			
Matty Alou			
☐ 2 AL Batting Leaders	10.00	4.50	1.25
Carl Yastrzemski			
Frank Robinson			
Al Kaline			
☐ 3 NL RBI Leaders	7.00	3.10	.85
Orlando Cepeda			
Bob Clemente			
Hank Aaron			
☐ 4 AL RBI Leaders	10.00	4.50	1.25
Carl Yastrzemski			
Harmon Killebrew			
Frank Robinson			
☐ 5 NL Home Run Leaders	6.00	2.70	.75
Hank Aaron			
Jim Wynn			
Ron Santo			
Willie McCovey			
☐ 6 AL Home Run Leaders	7.50	3.40	.95
Carl Yastrzemski			
Harmon Killebrew			
Frank Howard			
☐ 7 NL ERA Leaders	3.00	1.35	.40
Phil Niekro			
Jim Bunning			
Chris Short			
☐ 8 AL ERA Leaders	3.00	1.35	.40
Joel Horlen			
Gary Peters			
Sonny Siebert			
☐ 9 NL Pitching Leaders	3.50	1.55	.45
Mike McCormick			
Ferguson Jenkins			
Jim Bunning			
Claude Osteen			
☐ 10A AL Pitching Leaders	3.50	1.55	.45
Jim Lonborg ERR			
(Misspelled Lonberg			
on card back)			
Earl Wilson			
Dean Chance			
☐ 10B AL Pitching Leaders	3.50	1.55	.45
Jim Lonborg COR			
Earl Wilson			
Dean Chance			
☐ 11 NL Strikeout Leaders	4.00	1.80	.50
Jim Bunning			
Ferguson Jenkins			
Gaylord Perry			
☐ 12 AL Strikeout Leaders	3.00	1.35	.40
Jim Lonborg UER			
(Misspelled Longberg			
on card back)			
Sam McDowell			
Dean Chance			
☐ 13 Chuck Hartenstein	1.50	.65	.19
☐ 14 Jerry McNertney	1.50	.65	.19
☐ 15 Ron Hunt	1.50	.65	.19
☐ 16 Indians Rookies	4.50	2.00	.55
Lou Piniella			
Richie Scheinblum			
☐ 17 Dick Hall	1.50	.65	.19
☐ 18 Mike Hershberger	1.50	.65	.19
☐ 19 Juan Pizarro	1.50	.65	.19
☐ 20 Brooks Robinson	25.00	11.50	3.10
☐ 21 Ron Davis	1.50	.65	.19
☐ 22 Pat Dobson	2.00	.90	.25
☐ 23 Chico Cardenas	2.00	.90	.25
☐ 24 Bobby Locke	1.50	.65	.19

Card			
☐ 25 Julian Javier	2.00	.90	.25
☐ 26 Darrell Brandon	1.50	.65	.19
☐ 27 Gil Hodges MG	7.50	3.40	.95
☐ 28 Ted Uhlaender	1.50	.65	.19
☐ 29 Joe Verbanic	1.50	.65	.19
☐ 30 Joe Torre	3.00	1.35	.40
☐ 31 Ed Stroud	1.50	.65	.19
☐ 32 Joe Gibbon	1.50	.65	.19
☐ 33 Pete Ward	1.50	.65	.19
☐ 34 Al Ferrara	1.50	.65	.19
☐ 35 Steve Hargan	1.50	.65	.19
☐ 36 Pirates Rookies Bob Moose Bob Robertson	2.00	.90	.25
☐ 37 Billy Williams	10.00	4.50	1.25
☐ 38 Tony Pierce	1.50	.65	.19
☐ 39 Cookie Rojas	2.00	.90	.25
☐ 40 Denny McLain	12.50	5.75	1.55
☐ 41 Julio Gotay	1.50	.65	.19
☐ 42 Larry Haney	1.50	.65	.19
☐ 43 Gary Bell	1.50	.65	.19
☐ 44 Frank Kostro	1.50	.65	.19
☐ 45 Tom Seaver	250.00	115.00	31.00
☐ 46 Dave Ricketts	1.50	.65	.19
☐ 47 Ralph Houk MG	2.00	.90	.25
☐ 48 Ted Davidson	1.50	.65	.19
☐ 49A Eddie Brinkman (White team name)	1.50	.65	.19
☐ 49B Eddie Brinkman (Yellow team name)	40.00	18.00	5.00
☐ 50 Willie Mays	70.00	32.00	8.75
☐ 51 Bob Locker	1.50	.65	.19
☐ 52 Hawk Taylor	1.50	.65	.19
☐ 53 Gene Alley	2.00	.90	.25
☐ 54 Stan Williams	2.00	.90	.25
☐ 55 Felipe Alou	2.00	.90	.25
☐ 56 Orioles Rookies Dave Leonhard Dave May	1.50	.65	.19
☐ 57 Dan Schneider	1.50	.65	.19
☐ 58 Eddie Mathews	12.50	5.75	1.55
☐ 59 Don Lock	1.50	.65	.19
☐ 60 Ken Holtzman	2.00	.90	.25
☐ 61 Reggie Smith	2.50	1.15	.30
☐ 62 Chuck Dobson	1.50	.65	.19
☐ 63 Dick Kenworthy	1.50	.65	.19
☐ 64 Jim Merritt	1.50	.65	.19
☐ 65 John Roseboro	2.00	.90	.25
☐ 66A Casey Cox (White team name)	1.50	.65	.19
☐ 66B Casey Cox (Yellow team name)	100.00	45.00	12.50
☐ 67 Checklist 1 Jim Kaat	6.00	1.50	.50
☐ 68 Ron Willis	1.50	.65	.19
☐ 69 Tom Tresh	2.00	.90	.25
☐ 70 Bob Veale	2.00	.90	.25
☐ 71 Vern Fuller	1.50	.65	.19
☐ 72 Tommy John	5.00	2.30	.60
☐ 73 Jim Ray Hart	2.00	.90	.25
☐ 74 Milt Pappas	2.00	.90	.25
☐ 75 Don Mincher	1.50	.65	.19
☐ 76 Braves Rookies Jim Britton Ron Reed	2.00	.90	.25
☐ 77 Don Wilson	2.00	.90	.25
☐ 78 Jim Northrup	2.00	.90	.25
☐ 79 Ted Kubiak	1.50	.65	.19
☐ 80 Rod Carew	150.00	70.00	19.00
☐ 81 Larry Jackson	1.50	.65	.19
☐ 82 Sam Bowens	1.50	.65	.19
☐ 83 John Stephenson	1.50	.65	.19
☐ 84 Bob Tolan	2.00	.90	.25
☐ 85 Gaylord Perry	11.00	4.90	1.40
☐ 86 Willie Stargell	12.50	5.75	1.55
☐ 87 Dick Williams MG	2.00	.90	.25
☐ 88 Phil Regan	2.00	.90	.25
☐ 89 Jake Gibbs	1.50	.65	.19
☐ 90 Vada Pinson	2.50	1.15	.30
☐ 91 Jim Ollom	1.50	.65	.19
☐ 92 Ed Kranepool	2.00	.90	.25
☐ 93 Tony Cloninger	1.50	.65	.19
☐ 94 Lee Maye	1.50	.65	.19
☐ 95 Bob Aspromonte	1.50	.65	.19
☐ 96 Senator Rookies Frank Coggins Dick Nold	1.50	.65	.19
☐ 97 Tom Phoebus	1.50	.65	.19
☐ 98 Gary Sutherland	1.50	.65	.19
☐ 99 Rocky Colavito	4.00	1.80	.50
☐ 100 Bob Gibson	25.00	11.50	3.10
☐ 101 Glenn Beckert	2.00	.90	.25
☐ 102 Jose Cardenal	2.00	.90	.25
☐ 103 Don Sutton	12.50	5.75	1.55
☐ 104 Dick Dietz	1.50	.65	.19
☐ 105 Al Downing	2.00	.90	.25
☐ 106 Dalton Jones	1.50	.65	.19
☐ 107A Checklist 2 Juan Marichal (Tan wide mesh)	6.00	1.50	.50
☐ 107B Checklist 2 Juan Marichal (Brown fine mesh)	6.00	1.50	.50
☐ 108 Don Pavletich	1.50	.65	.19
☐ 109 Bert Campaneris	2.00	.90	.25
☐ 110 Hank Aaron	75.00	34.00	9.50
☐ 111 Rich Reese	1.50	.65	.19
☐ 112 Woody Fryman	1.50	.65	.19
☐ 113 Tigers Rookies Tom Matchick Daryl Patterson	1.50	.65	.19
☐ 114 Ron Swoboda	2.00	.90	.25
☐ 115 Sam McDowell	2.00	.90	.25
☐ 116 Ken McMullen	1.50	.65	.19
☐ 117 Larry Jaster	1.50	.65	.19
☐ 118 Mark Belanger	2.00	.90	.25
☐ 119 Ted Savage	1.50	.65	.19
☐ 120 Mel Stottlemyre	2.50	1.15	.30
☐ 121 Jimmie Hall	1.50	.65	.19
☐ 122 Gene Mauch MG	2.00	.90	.25
☐ 123 Jose Santiago	1.50	.65	.19
☐ 124 Nate Oliver	1.50	.65	.19
☐ 125 Joel Horlen	1.50	.65	.19
☐ 126 Bobby Etheridge	1.50	.65	.19
☐ 127 Paul Lindblad	1.50	.65	.19
☐ 128 Astros Rookies Tom Dukes Alonzo Harris	1.50	.65	.19
☐ 129 Mickey Stanley	2.50	1.15	.30
☐ 130 Tony Perez	15.00	6.75	1.90
☐ 131 Frank Bertaina	1.50	.65	.19
☐ 132 Bud Harrelson	2.00	.90	.25
☐ 133 Fred Whitfield	1.50	.65	.19
☐ 134 Pat Jarvis	1.50	.65	.19
☐ 135 Paul Blair	2.00	.90	.25
☐ 136 Randy Hundley	2.00	.90	.25
☐ 137 Twins Team	3.00	1.35	.40
☐ 138 Ruben Amaro	1.50	.65	.19
☐ 139 Chris Short	1.50	.65	.19
☐ 140 Tony Conigliaro	5.00	2.30	.60
☐ 141 Dal Maxvill	1.50	.65	.19
☐ 142 White Sox Rookies Buddy Bradford Bill Voss	1.50	.65	.19
☐ 143 Pete Cimino	1.50	.65	.19
☐ 144 Joe Morgan	20.00	9.00	2.50
☐ 145 Don Drysdale	11.00	4.90	1.40
☐ 146 Sal Bando	2.00	.90	.25
☐ 147 Frank Linzy	1.50	.65	.19
☐ 148 Dave Bristol MG	1.50	.65	.19
☐ 149 Bob Saverine	1.50	.65	.19
☐ 150 Bob Clemente	55.00	25.00	7.00
☐ 151 World Series Game 1 Lou Brock socks 4 hits in opener	8.00	3.60	1.00
☐ 152 World Series Game 2 Carl Yastrzemski smashes 2 homers	10.00	4.50	1.25
☐ 153 World Series Game 3 Nellie Briles cools Boston	4.00	1.80	.50
☐ 154 World Series Game 4 Bob Gibson hurls shutout	8.00	3.60	1.00
☐ 155 World Series Game 5 Jim Lonborg wins again	4.00	1.80	.50
☐ 156 World Series Game 6 Rico Petrocelli two homers	4.00	1.80	.50
☐ 157 World Series Game 7 St. Louis wins it	4.00	1.80	.50
☐ 158 World Series Summary Cardinals celebrate	4.00	1.80	.50
☐ 159 Don Kessinger	2.00	.90	.25
☐ 160 Earl Wilson	2.00	.90	.25
☐ 161 Norm Miller	1.50	.65	.19
☐ 162 Cards Rookies Hal Gilson Mike Torrez	2.00	.90	.25
☐ 163 Gene Brabender	1.50	.65	.19
☐ 164 Ramon Webster	1.50	.65	.19
☐ 165 Tony Oliva	4.00	1.80	.50
☐ 166 Claude Raymond	1.50	.65	.19
☐ 167 Elston Howard	3.00	1.35	.40
☐ 168 Dodgers Team	3.00	1.35	.40

☐ 169 Bob Bolin 1.50 .65 .19
☐ 170 Jim Fregosi 2.00 .90 .25
☐ 171 Don Nottebart 1.50 .65 .19
☐ 172 Walt Williams 1.50 .65 .19
☐ 173 John Boozer 1.50 .65 .19
☐ 174 Bob Tillman 1.50 .65 .19
☐ 175 Maury Wills 4.50 2.00 .55
☐ 176 Bob Allen 1.50 .65 .19
☐ 177 Mets Rookies 1650.00 750.00 210.00
Jerry Koosman
Nolan Ryan
☐ 178 Don Wert 1.50 .65 .19
☐ 179 Bill Stoneman 1.50 .65 .19
☐ 180 Curt Flood 2.00 .90 .25
☐ 181 Jerry Zimmerman 1.50 .65 .19
☐ 182 Dave Giusti 1.50 .65 .19
☐ 183 Bob Kennedy MG 2.00 .90 .25
☐ 184 Lou Johnson 2.00 .90 .25
☐ 185 Tom Haller 1.50 .65 .19
☐ 186 Eddie Watt 1.50 .65 .19
☐ 187 Sonny Jackson 1.50 .65 .19
☐ 188 Cap Peterson 1.50 .65 .19
☐ 189 Bill Landis 1.50 .65 .19
☐ 190 Bill White 2.50 1.15 .30
☐ 191 Dan Frisella 1.50 .65 .19
☐ 192A Checklist 3 7.50 1.90 .60
Carl Yastrzemski
(Special Baseball
Playing Card)
☐ 192B Checklist 3 7.50 1.90 .60
Carl Yastrzemski
(Special Baseball
Playing Card Game)
☐ 193 Jack Hamilton 1.50 .65 .19
☐ 194 Don Buford 1.50 .65 .19
☐ 195 Joe Pepitone 2.00 .90 .25
☐ 196 Gary Nolan 2.00 .90 .25
☐ 197 Larry Brown 1.50 .65 .19
☐ 198 Roy Face 2.00 .90 .25
☐ 199 A's Rookies 1.50 .65 .19
Roberto Rodriquez
Darrell Osteen
☐ 200 Orlando Cepeda 5.00 2.30 .60
☐ 201 Mike Marshall 3.00 1.35 .40
☐ 202 Adolfo Phillips 1.50 .65 .19
☐ 203 Dick Kelley 1.50 .65 .19
☐ 204 Andy Etchebarren 1.50 .65 .19
☐ 205 Juan Marichal 10.00 4.50 1.25
☐ 206 Cal Ermer MG 1.50 .65 .19
☐ 207 Carroll Sembera 1.50 .65 .19
☐ 208 Willie Davis 2.00 .90 .25
☐ 209 Tim Cullen 1.50 .65 .19
☐ 210 Gary Peters 1.50 .65 .19
☐ 211 J.C. Martin 1.50 .65 .19
☐ 212 Dave Morehead 1.50 .65 .19
☐ 213 Chico Ruiz 1.50 .65 .19
☐ 214 Yankees Rookies 2.00 .90 .25
Stan Bahnsen
Frank Fernandez
☐ 215 Jim Bunning 4.50 2.00 .55
☐ 216 Bubba Morton 1.50 .65 .19
☐ 217 Dick Farrell 1.50 .65 .19
☐ 218 Ken Suarez 1.50 .65 .19
☐ 219 Rob Gardner 1.50 .65 .19
☐ 220 Harmon Killebrew 15.00 6.75 1.90
☐ 221 Braves Team 3.00 1.35 .40
☐ 222 Jim Hardin 1.50 .65 .19
☐ 223 Ollie Brown 1.50 .65 .19
☐ 224 Jack Aker 1.50 .65 .19
☐ 225 Richie Allen 4.50 2.00 .55
☐ 226 Jimmie Price 1.50 .65 .19
☐ 227 Joe Hoerner 1.50 .65 .19
☐ 228 Dodgers Rookies 2.00 .90 .25
Jack Billingham
Jim Fairey
☐ 229 Fred Klages 1.50 .65 .19
☐ 230 Pete Rose 40.00 18.00 5.00
☐ 231 Dave Baldwin 1.50 .65 .19
☐ 232 Denis Menke 1.50 .65 .19
☐ 233 George Scott 2.00 .90 .25
☐ 234 Bill Monbouquette 1.50 .65 .19
☐ 235 Ron Santo 4.00 1.80 .50
☐ 236 Tug McGraw 3.00 1.35 .40
☐ 237 Alvin Dark MG 2.00 .90 .25
☐ 238 Tom Satriano 1.50 .65 .19
☐ 239 Bill Henry 1.50 .65 .19
☐ 240 Al Kaline 25.00 11.50 3.10
☐ 241 Felix Millan 1.50 .65 .19
☐ 242 Moe Drabowsky 2.00 .90 .25
☐ 243 Rich Rollins 1.50 .65 .19
☐ 244 John Donaldson 1.50 .65 .19
☐ 245 Tony Gonzalez 1.50 .65 .19
☐ 246 Fritz Peterson 1.50 .65 .19
☐ 247 Reds Rookies 275.00 125.00 34.00
Johnny Bench
Ron Tompkins
☐ 248 Fred Valentine 1.50 .65 .19
☐ 249 Bill Singer 1.50 .65 .19
☐ 250 Carl Yastrzemski 40.00 18.00 5.00
☐ 251 Manny Sanguillen 5.00 2.30 .60
☐ 252 Angels Team 3.00 1.35 .40
☐ 253 Dick Hughes 1.50 .65 .19
☐ 254 Cleon Jones 2.00 .90 .25
☐ 255 Dean Chance 2.00 .90 .25
☐ 256 Norm Cash 6.00 2.70 .75
☐ 257 Phil Niekro 8.00 3.60 1.00
☐ 258 Cubs Rookies 1.50 .65 .19
Jose Arcia
Bill Schlesinger
☐ 259 Ken Boyer 2.50 1.15 .30
☐ 260 Jim Wynn 2.00 .90 .25
☐ 261 Dave Duncan 2.00 .90 .25
☐ 262 Rick Wise 2.00 .90 .25
☐ 263 Horace Clarke 1.50 .65 .19
☐ 264 Ted Abernathy 1.50 .65 .19
☐ 265 Tommy Davis 2.00 .90 .25
☐ 266 Paul Popovich 1.50 .65 .19
☐ 267 Herman Franks MG 1.50 .65 .19
☐ 268 Bob Humphreys 1.50 .65 .19
☐ 269 Bob Tiefenauer 1.50 .65 .19
☐ 270 Matty Alou 2.00 .90 .25
☐ 271 Bobby Knoop 1.50 .65 .19
☐ 272 Ray Culp 1.50 .65 .19
☐ 273 Dave Johnson 2.00 .90 .25
☐ 274 Mike Cuellar 2.00 .90 .25
☐ 275 Tim McCarver 4.00 1.80 .50
☐ 276 Jim Roland 1.50 .65 .19
☐ 277 Jerry Buchek 1.50 .65 .19
☐ 278 Checklist 4 6.00 1.50 .50
Orlando Cepeda
☐ 279 Bill Hands 1.50 .65 .19
☐ 280 Mickey Mantle 240.00 110.00 30.00
☐ 281 Jim Campanis 1.50 .65 .19
☐ 282 Rick Monday 2.00 .90 .25
☐ 283 Mel Queen 1.50 .65 .19
☐ 284 Johnny Briggs 1.50 .65 .19
☐ 285 Dick McAuliffe 2.00 .90 .25
☐ 286 Cecil Upshaw 1.50 .65 .19
☐ 287 White Sox Rookies 1.50 .65 .19
Mickey Abarbanel
Cisco Carlos
☐ 288 Dave Wickersham 1.50 .65 .19
☐ 289 Woody Held 1.50 .65 .19
☐ 290 Willie McCovey 12.50 5.75 1.55
☐ 291 Dick Lines 1.50 .65 .19
☐ 292 Art Shamsky 1.50 .65 .19
☐ 293 Bruce Howard 1.50 .65 .19
☐ 294 Red Schoendienst MG 4.00 1.80 .50
☐ 295 Sonny Siebert 1.50 .65 .19
☐ 296 Byron Browne 1.50 .65 .19
☐ 297 Russ Gibson 1.50 .65 .19
☐ 298 Jim Brewer 1.50 .65 .19
☐ 299 Gene Michael 2.00 .90 .25
☐ 300 Rusty Staub 3.50 1.55 .45
☐ 301 Twins Rookies 1.50 .65 .19
George Mitterwald
Rick Renick
☐ 302 Gerry Arrigo 1.50 .65 .19
☐ 303 Dick Green 1.50 .65 .19
☐ 304 Sandy Valdespino 1.50 .65 .19
☐ 305 Minnie Rojas 1.50 .65 .19
☐ 306 Mike Ryan 1.50 .65 .19
☐ 307 John Hiller 2.00 .90 .25
☐ 308 Pirates Team 3.00 1.35 .40
☐ 309 Ken Henderson 1.50 .65 .19
☐ 310 Luis Aparicio 6.00 2.70 .75
☐ 311 Jack Lamabe 1.50 .65 .19
☐ 312 Curt Blefary 1.50 .65 .19
☐ 313 Al Weis 1.50 .65 .19
☐ 314 Red Sox Rookies 1.50 .65 .19
Bill Rohr
George Spriggs
☐ 315 Zoilo Versalles 1.50 .65 .19
☐ 316 Steve Barber 1.50 .65 .19
☐ 317 Ron Brand 1.50 .65 .19
☐ 318 Chico Salmon 1.50 .65 .19
☐ 319 George Culver 1.50 .65 .19
☐ 320 Frank Howard 3.00 1.35 .40
☐ 321 Leo Durocher MG 3.00 1.35 .40
☐ 322 Dave Boswell 1.50 .65 .19
☐ 323 Deron Johnson 2.00 .90 .25
☐ 324 Jim Nash 1.50 .65 .19
☐ 325 Manny Mota 2.00 .90 .25
☐ 326 Dennis Ribant 1.50 .65 .19
☐ 327 Tony Taylor 1.50 .65 .19
☐ 328 Angels Rookies 1.50 .65 .19

Card			
Chuck Vinson			
Jim Weaver			
☐ 329 Duane Josephson	1.50	.65	.19
☐ 330 Roger Maris	40.00	18.00	5.00
☐ 331 Dan Osinski	1.50	.65	.19
☐ 332 Doug Rader	2.00	.90	.25
☐ 333 Ron Herbel	1.50	.65	.19
☐ 334 Orioles Team	3.00	1.35	.40
☐ 335 Bob Allison	2.00	.90	.25
☐ 336 John Purdin	1.50	.65	.19
☐ 337 Bill Robinson	2.00	.90	.25
☐ 338 Bob Johnson	1.50	.65	.19
☐ 339 Rich Nye	1.50	.65	.19
☐ 340 Max Alvis	1.50	.65	.19
☐ 341 Jim Lemon MG	1.50	.65	.19
☐ 342 Ken Johnson	1.50	.65	.19
☐ 343 Jim Gosger	1.50	.65	.19
☐ 344 Donn Clendenon	2.00	.90	.25
☐ 345 Bob Hendley	1.50	.65	.19
☐ 346 Jerry Adair	1.50	.65	.19
☐ 347 George Brunet	1.50	.65	.19
☐ 348 Phillies Rookies	1.50	.65	.19
Larry Colton			
Dick Thoenen			
☐ 349 Ed Spiezio	1.50	.65	.19
☐ 350 Hoyt Wilhelm	7.00	3.10	.85
☐ 351 Bob Barton	1.50	.65	.19
☐ 352 Jackie Hernandez	1.50	.65	.19
☐ 353 Mack Jones	1.50	.65	.19
☐ 354 Pete Richert	1.50	.65	.19
☐ 355 Ernie Banks	25.00	11.50	3.10
☐ 356A Checklist 5	6.00	1.50	.50
Ken Holtzman			
(Head centered			
within circle)			
☐ 356B Checklist 5	6.00	1.50	.50
Ken Holtzman			
(Head shifted right			
within circle)			
☐ 357 Len Gabrielson	1.50	.65	.19
☐ 358 Mike Epstein	1.50	.65	.19
☐ 359 Joe Moeller	1.50	.65	.19
☐ 360 Willie Horton	2.50	1.15	.30
☐ 361 Harmon Killebrew AS	8.00	3.60	1.00
☐ 362 Orlando Cepeda AS	3.00	1.35	.40
☐ 363 Rod Carew AS	14.00	6.25	1.75
☐ 364 Joe Morgan AS	10.00	4.50	1.25
☐ 365 Brooks Robinson AS	10.00	4.50	1.25
☐ 366 Ron Santo AS	3.00	1.35	.40
☐ 367 Jim Fregosi AS	2.25	1.00	.30
☐ 368 Gene Alley AS	2.25	1.00	.30
☐ 369 Carl Yastrzemski AS	12.50	5.75	1.55
☐ 370 Hank Aaron AS	15.00	6.75	1.90
☐ 371 Tony Oliva AS	3.00	1.35	.40
☐ 372 Lou Brock AS	10.00	4.50	1.25
☐ 373 Frank Robinson AS	10.00	4.50	1.25
☐ 374 Bob Clemente AS	15.00	6.75	1.90
☐ 375 Bill Freehan AS	2.25	1.00	.30
☐ 376 Tim McCarver AS	3.00	1.35	.40
☐ 377 Joel Horlen AS	2.25	1.00	.30
☐ 378 Bob Gibson AS	10.00	4.50	1.25
☐ 379 Gary Peters AS	2.25	1.00	.30
☐ 380 Ken Holtzman AS	2.25	1.00	.30
☐ 381 Boog Powell	3.00	1.35	.40
☐ 382 Ramon Hernandez	1.50	.65	.19
☐ 383 Steve Whitaker	1.50	.65	.19
☐ 384 Reds Rookies	12.50	5.75	1.55
Bill Henry			
Hal McRae			
☐ 385 Jim Hunter	15.00	6.75	1.90
☐ 386 Greg Goossen	1.50	.65	.19
☐ 387 Joe Foy	1.50	.65	.19
☐ 388 Ray Washburn	1.50	.65	.19
☐ 389 Jay Johnstone	2.00	.90	.25
☐ 390 Bill Mazeroski	3.50	1.55	.45
☐ 391 Bob Priddy	1.50	.65	.19
☐ 392 Grady Hatton MG	1.50	.65	.19
☐ 393 Jim Perry	2.00	.90	.25
☐ 394 Tommie Aaron	2.00	.90	.25
☐ 395 Camilo Pascual	2.00	.90	.25
☐ 396 Bobby Wine	1.50	.65	.19
☐ 397 Vic Davalillo	1.50	.65	.19
☐ 398 Jim Grant	1.50	.65	.19
☐ 399 Ray Oyler	1.50	.65	.19
☐ 400A Mike McCormick	2.00	.90	.25
(Yellow letters)			
☐ 400B Mike McCormick	100.00	45.00	12.50
(Team name in			
white letters)			
☐ 401 Mets Team	3.00	1.35	.40
☐ 402 Mike Hegan	1.50	.65	.19
☐ 403 John Buzhardt	1.50	.65	.19
☐ 404 Floyd Robinson	1.50	.65	.19
☐ 405 Tommy Helms	2.00	.90	.25
☐ 406 Dick Ellsworth	1.50	.65	.19
☐ 407 Gary Kolb	1.50	.65	.19
☐ 408 Steve Carlton	60.00	27.00	7.50
☐ 409 Orioles Rookies	1.50	.65	.19
Frank Peters			
Ron Stone			
☐ 410 Fergie Jenkins	20.00	9.00	2.50
☐ 411 Ron Hansen	1.50	.65	.19
☐ 412 Clay Carroll	2.00	.90	.25
☐ 413 Tom McCraw	1.50	.65	.19
☐ 414 Mickey Lolich	5.00	2.30	.60
☐ 415 Johnny Callison	2.00	.90	.25
☐ 416 Bill Rigney MG	1.50	.65	.19
☐ 417 Willie Crawford	1.50	.65	.19
☐ 418 Eddie Fisher	1.50	.65	.19
☐ 419 Jack Hiatt	1.50	.65	.19
☐ 420 Cesar Tovar	1.50	.65	.19
☐ 421 Ron Taylor	1.50	.65	.19
☐ 422 Rene Lachemann	2.00	.90	.25
☐ 423 Fred Gladding	1.50	.65	.19
☐ 424 Chicago White Sox	3.00	1.35	.40
Team Card			
☐ 425 Jim Maloney	2.00	.90	.25
☐ 426 Hank Allen	1.50	.65	.19
☐ 427 Dick Calmus	1.50	.65	.19
☐ 428 Vic Roznovsky	1.50	.65	.19
☐ 429 Tommie Sisk	1.50	.65	.19
☐ 430 Rico Petrocelli	2.00	.90	.25
☐ 431 Dooley Womack	1.50	.65	.19
☐ 432 Indians Rookies	1.50	.65	.19
Bill Davis			
Jose Vidal			
☐ 433 Bob Rodgers	2.00	.90	.25
☐ 434 Ricardo Joseph	1.50	.65	.19
☐ 435 Ron Perranoski	2.00	.90	.25
☐ 436 Hal Lanier	1.50	.65	.19
☐ 437 Don Cardwell	1.50	.65	.19
☐ 438 Lee Thomas	2.00	.90	.25
☐ 439 Lum Harris MG	1.50	.65	.19
☐ 440 Claude Osteen	2.00	.90	.25
☐ 441 Alex Johnson	2.00	.90	.25
☐ 442 Dick Bosman	1.50	.65	.19
☐ 443 Joe Azcue	1.50	.65	.19
☐ 444 Jack Fisher	1.50	.65	.19
☐ 445 Mike Shannon	2.00	.90	.25
☐ 446 Ron Kline	1.50	.65	.19
☐ 447 Tigers Rookies	1.50	.65	.19
George Korince			
Fred Lasher			
☐ 448 Gary Wagner	1.50	.65	.19
☐ 449 Gene Oliver	1.50	.65	.19
☐ 450 Jim Kaat	4.50	2.00	.55
☐ 451 Al Spangler	1.50	.65	.19
☐ 452 Jesus Alou	1.50	.65	.19
☐ 453 Sammy Ellis	1.50	.65	.19
☐ 454A Checklist 6	7.50	1.90	.60
Frank Robinson			
(Cap complete			
within circle)			
☐ 454B Checklist 6	7.50	1.90	.60
Frank Robinson			
(Cap partially			
within circle)			
☐ 455 Rico Carty	2.00	.90	.25
☐ 456 John O'Donoghue	1.50	.65	.19
☐ 457 Jim Lefebvre	2.00	.90	.25
☐ 458 Lew Krausse	3.50	1.55	.45
☐ 459 Dick Simpson	3.00	1.35	.40
☐ 460 Jim Lonborg	5.00	2.30	.60
☐ 461 Chuck Hiller	3.00	1.35	.40
☐ 462 Barry Moore	3.00	1.35	.40
☐ 463 Jim Schaffer	3.00	1.35	.40
☐ 464 Don McMahon	3.00	1.35	.40
☐ 465 Tommie Agee	3.50	1.55	.45
☐ 466 Bill Dillman	3.00	1.35	.40
☐ 467 Dick Howser	3.50	1.55	.45
☐ 468 Larry Sherry	3.00	1.35	.40
☐ 469 Ty Cline	3.00	1.35	.40
☐ 470 Bill Freehan	5.00	2.30	.60
☐ 471 Orlando Pena	3.00	1.35	.40
☐ 472 Walt Alston MG	4.50	2.00	.55
☐ 473 Al Worthington	3.00	1.35	.40
☐ 474 Paul Schaal	3.00	1.35	.40
☐ 475 Joe Niekro	4.50	2.00	.55
☐ 476 Woody Woodward	3.50	1.55	.45
☐ 477 Philadelphia Phillies	6.00	2.70	.75
Team Card			
☐ 478 Dave McNally	3.50	1.55	.45
☐ 479 Phil Gagliano	3.00	1.35	.40
☐ 480 Manager's Dream	35.00	16.00	4.40
Tony Oliva			
Chico Cardenas			
Bob Clemente			

☐ 481 John Wyatt	3.00	1.35	.40
☐ 482 Jose Pagan	3.00	1.35	.40
☐ 483 Darold Knowles	3.00	1.35	.40
☐ 484 Phil Roof	3.00	1.35	.40
☐ 485 Ken Berry	3.00	1.35	.40
☐ 486 Cal Koonce	3.00	1.35	.40
☐ 487 Lee May	5.00	2.30	.60
☐ 488 Dick Tracewski	3.00	1.35	.40
☐ 489 Wally Bunker	3.00	1.35	.40
☐ 490 Super Stars Harmon Killebrew Willie Mays Mickey Mantle	125.00	57.50	15.50
☐ 491 Denny Lemaster	3.00	1.35	.40
☐ 492 Jeff Torborg	3.50	1.55	.45
☐ 493 Jim McGlothlin	3.00	1.35	.40
☐ 494 Ray Sadecki	3.00	1.35	.40
☐ 495 Leon Wagner	3.00	1.35	.40
☐ 496 Steve Hamilton	3.00	1.35	.40
☐ 497 Cardinals Team	6.00	2.70	.75
☐ 498 Bill Bryan	3.00	1.35	.40
☐ 499 Steve Blass	3.50	1.55	.45
☐ 500 Frank Robinson	30.00	13.50	3.80
☐ 501 John Odom	3.00	1.35	.40
☐ 502 Mike Andrews	3.00	1.35	.40
☐ 503 Al Jackson	3.00	1.35	.40
☐ 504 Russ Snyder	3.00	1.35	.40
☐ 505 Joe Sparma	6.00	2.70	.75
☐ 506 Clarence Jones	5.00	2.30	.60
☐ 507 Wade Blasingame	3.00	1.35	.40
☐ 508 Duke Sims	3.00	1.35	.40
☐ 509 Dennis Higgins	3.00	1.35	.40
☐ 510 Ron Fairly	3.50	1.55	.45
☐ 511 Bill Kelso	3.00	1.35	.40
☐ 512 Grant Jackson	3.00	1.35	.40
☐ 513 Hank Bauer MG	3.50	1.55	.45
☐ 514 Al McBean	3.00	1.35	.40
☐ 515 Russ Nixon	3.00	1.35	.40
☐ 516 Pete Mikkelsen	3.00	1.35	.40
☐ 517 Diego Segui	3.00	1.35	.40
☐ 518A Checklist 7 ERR (539 AL Rookies) (Clete Boyer)	8.00	2.00	.65
☐ 518B Checklist 7 COR (539 ML Rookies) (Clete Boyer)	12.00	3.00	.95
☐ 519 Jerry Stephenson	3.00	1.35	.40
☐ 520 Lou Brock	25.00	11.50	3.10
☐ 521 Don Shaw	3.00	1.35	.40
☐ 522 Wayne Causey	3.00	1.35	.40
☐ 523 John Tsitouris	3.00	1.35	.40
☐ 524 Andy Kosco	3.00	1.35	.40
☐ 525 Jim Davenport	3.00	1.35	.40
☐ 526 Bill Denehy	3.00	1.35	.40
☐ 527 Tito Francona	3.00	1.35	.40
☐ 528 Tigers Team	70.00	32.00	8.75
☐ 529 Bruce Von Hoff	3.00	1.35	.40
☐ 530 Bird Belters Brooks Robinson Frank Robinson	15.00	6.75	1.90
☐ 531 Chuck Hinton	3.00	1.35	.40
☐ 532 Luis Tiant	5.00	2.30	.60
☐ 533 Wes Parker	3.50	1.55	.45
☐ 534 Bob Miller	3.75	1.70	.45
☐ 535 Danny Cater	3.75	1.70	.45
☐ 536 Bill Short	3.75	1.70	.45
☐ 537 Norm Siebern	3.75	1.70	.45
☐ 538 Manny Jimenez	3.75	1.70	.45
☐ 539 Major League Rookies Jim Ray Mike Ferraro	3.75	1.70	.45
☐ 540 Nelson Briles	4.50	2.00	.55
☐ 541 Sandy Alomar	4.50	2.00	.55
☐ 542 John Boccabella	3.75	1.70	.45
☐ 543 Bob Lee	3.75	1.70	.45
☐ 544 Mayo Smith MG	5.00	2.30	.60
☐ 545 Lindy McDaniel	4.50	2.00	.55
☐ 546 Roy White	4.50	2.00	.55
☐ 547 Dan Coombs	3.75	1.70	.45
☐ 548 Bernie Allen	3.75	1.70	.45
☐ 549 Orioles Rookies Curt Motton Roger Nelson	3.75	1.70	.45
☐ 550 Clete Boyer	4.50	2.00	.55
☐ 551 Darrell Sutherland	3.75	1.70	.45
☐ 552 Ed Kirkpatrick	3.75	1.70	.45
☐ 553 Hank Aguirre	3.75	1.70	.45
☐ 554 A's Team	7.50	3.40	.95
☐ 555 Jose Tartabull	4.50	2.00	.55
☐ 556 Dick Selma	3.75	1.70	.45
☐ 557 Frank Quilici	3.75	1.70	.45
☐ 558 Johnny Edwards	3.75	1.70	.45
☐ 559 Pirates Rookies Carl Taylor Luke Walker	3.75	1.70	.45
☐ 560 Paul Casanova	3.75	1.70	.45
☐ 561 Lee Elia	4.25	1.90	.55
☐ 562 Jim Bouton	6.00	2.70	.75
☐ 563 Ed Charles	3.75	1.70	.45
☐ 564 Eddie Stanky MG	4.50	2.00	.55
☐ 565 Larry Dierker	4.25	1.90	.55
☐ 566 Ken Harrelson	4.50	2.00	.55
☐ 567 Clay Dalrymple	3.75	1.70	.45
☐ 568 Willie Smith	3.75	1.70	.45
☐ 569 NL Rookies Ivan Murrell Les Rohr	3.75	1.70	.45
☐ 570 Rick Reichardt	3.75	1.70	.45
☐ 571 Tony LaRussa	8.00	3.60	1.00
☐ 572 Don Bosch	3.75	1.70	.45
☐ 573 Joe Coleman	3.75	1.70	.45
☐ 574 Cincinnati Reds Team Card	7.50	3.40	.95
☐ 575 Jim Palmer	65.00	29.00	8.25
☐ 576 Dave Adlesh	3.75	1.70	.45
☐ 577 Fred Talbot	3.75	1.70	.45
☐ 578 Orlando Martinez	3.75	1.70	.45
☐ 579 NL Rookies Larry Hisle Mike Lum	5.50	2.50	.70
☐ 580 Bob Bailey	3.75	1.70	.45
☐ 581 Garry Roggenburk	3.75	1.70	.45
☐ 582 Jerry Grote	3.75	1.70	.45
☐ 583 Gates Brown	6.00	2.70	.75
☐ 584 Larry Shepard MG	3.75	1.70	.45
☐ 585 Wilbur Wood	4.50	2.00	.55
☐ 586 Jim Pagliaroni	3.75	1.70	.45
☐ 587 Roger Repoz	3.75	1.70	.45
☐ 588 Dick Schofield	3.75	1.70	.45
☐ 589 Twins Rookies Ron Clark Moe Ogier	3.75	1.70	.45
☐ 590 Tommy Harper	4.50	2.00	.55
☐ 591 Dick Nen	3.75	1.70	.45
☐ 592 John Bateman	3.75	1.70	.45
☐ 593 Lee Stange	3.75	1.70	.45
☐ 594 Phil Linz	4.50	2.00	.55
☐ 595 Phil Ortega	3.75	1.70	.45
☐ 596 Charlie Smith	3.75	1.70	.45
☐ 597 Bill McCool	3.75	1.70	.45
☐ 598 Jerry May	5.00	2.30	.60

1968 Topps Game

The cards in this 33-card set measure approximately 2 1/4" by 3 1/4". This "Game" card set of players, issued as inserts with the regular 1968 Topps baseball series, was patterned directly after the Red Back and Blue Back sets of 1951. Each card has a color player photo set upon a pure white background, with a facsimile autograph underneath the picture. The cards have blue backs, and were also sold in boxed sets on a limited basis.

	NRMT-MT	EXC	G-VG
COMPLETE SET (33)	80.00	36.00	10.00
COMMON PLAYER (1-33)	.50	.23	.06
☐ 1 Matty Alou	.50	.23	.06
☐ 2 Mickey Mantle	20.00	9.00	2.50
☐ 3 Carl Yastrzemski	9.00	4.00	1.15

□ 4 Hank Aaron	9.00	4.00	1.15
□ 5 Harmon Killebrew	3.00	1.35	.40
□ 6 Roberto Clemente	8.00	3.60	1.00
□ 7 Frank Robinson	4.00	1.80	.50
□ 8 Willie Mays	9.00	4.00	1.15
□ 9 Brooks Robinson	4.00	1.80	.50
□ 10 Tommy Davis	.50	.23	.06
□ 11 Bill Freehan	.60	.25	.08
□ 12 Claude Osteen	.50	.23	.06
□ 13 Gary Peters	.50	.23	.06
□ 14 Jim Lonborg	.50	.23	.06
□ 15 Steve Hargan	.50	.23	.06
□ 16 Dean Chance	.50	.23	.06
□ 17 Mike McCormick	.50	.23	.06
□ 18 Tim McCarver	.75	.35	.09
□ 19 Ron Santo	.75	.35	.09
□ 20 Tony Gonzalez	.50	.23	.06
□ 21 Frank Howard	.60	.25	.08
□ 22 George Scott	.50	.23	.06
□ 23 Rich Allen	.75	.35	.09
□ 24 Jim Wynn	.50	.23	.06
□ 25 Gene Alley	.50	.23	.06
□ 26 Rick Monday	.50	.23	.06
□ 27 Al Kaline	4.50	2.00	.55
□ 28 Rusty Staub	.75	.35	.09
□ 29 Rod Carew	7.00	3.10	.85
□ 30 Pete Rose	9.00	4.00	1.15
□ 31 Joe Torre	.75	.35	.09
□ 32 Orlando Cepeda	.75	.35	.09
□ 33 Jim Fregosi	.60	.25	.08

1969 Topps

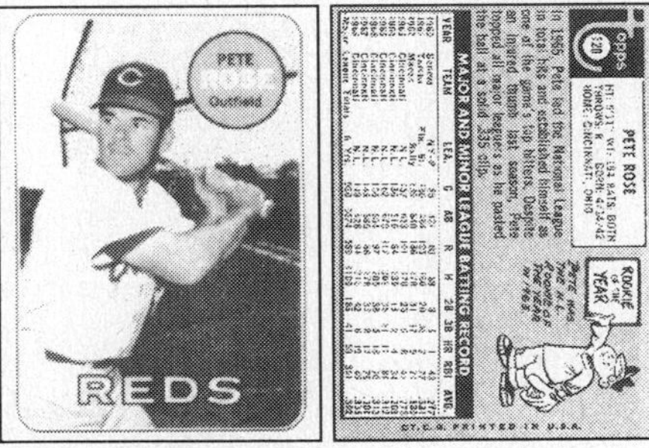

The cards in this 664-card set measure 2 1/2" by 3 1/2". The 1969 Topps set includes Sporting News All-Star Selections as card numbers 416 to 435. Other popular subsets within this set include League Leaders (1-12) and World Series cards (162-169). The fifth series contains several variations; the more difficult variety consists of cards with the player's first name, last name, and/or position in white letters instead of lettering in some other color. These are designated in the checklist below by WL (white letters). Each checklist card features a different popular player's picture inside a circle on the front of the checklist card. Two different poses of Clay Dalrymple and Donn Clendenon exist, as indicated in the checklist. The key Rookie Cards in this set are Rollie Fingers, Reggie Jackson, and Graig Nettles. This was the last year that Topps issued multi-player special star cards, ending a 13-year tradition, which they had begun in 1957. There were cropping differences in checklist cards 57, 214, and 412, due to their each being printed with two different series. The differences are difficult to explain and have not been greatly sought by collectors; hence they are not listed explicitly in the list below. The All-Star cards 426-435, when turned over and placed together, form a puzzle back of Pete Rose.

	NRMT-MT	EXC	G-VG
COMPLETE SET (664)	2650.00	1200.00	325.00
COMMON PLAYER (1-109)	1.50	.65	.19
COMMON PLAYER (110-218)	1.50	.65	.19
COMMON PLAYER (219-327)	2.50	1.15	.30
COMMON PLAYER (328-425)	1.50	.65	.19
COMMON PLAYER (426-512)	1.50	.65	.19
COMMON PLAYER (513-588)	2.00	.90	.25
COMMON PLAYER (589-664)	2.25	1.00	.30

□ 1 AL Batting Leaders Carl Yastrzemski Danny Cater Tony Oliva	12.00	3.60	1.20
□ 2 NL Batting Leaders Pete Rose Matty Alou Felipe Alou	5.50	2.50	.70
□ 3 AL RBI Leaders Ken Harrelson Frank Howard Jim Northrup	3.00	1.35	.40
□ 4 NL RBI Leaders Willie McCovey Ron Santo Billy Williams	4.50	2.00	.55
□ 5 AL Home Run Leaders Frank Howard Willie Horton Ken Harrelson	3.00	1.35	.40
□ 6 NL Home Run Leaders Willie McCovey Richie Allen Ernie Banks	4.50	2.00	.55
□ 7 AL ERA Leaders Luis Tiant Sam McDowell Dave McNally	3.00	1.35	.40
□ 8 NL ERA Leaders Bob Gibson Bobby Bolin Bob Veale	3.00	1.35	.40
□ 9 AL Pitching Leaders Denny McLain Dave McNally Luis Tiant Mel Stottlemyre	3.00	1.35	.40
□ 10 NL Pitching Leaders Juan Marichal Bob Gibson Fergie Jenkins	5.00	2.30	.60
□ 11 AL Strikeout Leaders Sam McDowell Denny McLain Luis Tiant	3.00	1.35	.40
□ 12 NL Strikeout Leaders Bob Gibson Fergie Jenkins Bill Singer	3.50	1.55	.45
□ 13 Mickey Stanley	2.00	.90	.25
□ 14 Al McBean	1.50	.65	.19
□ 15 Boog Powell	3.00	1.35	.40
□ 16 Giants Rookies Cesar Gutierrez Rich Robertson	1.50	.65	.19
□ 17 Mike Marshall	2.00	.90	.25
□ 18 Dick Schofield	1.50	.65	.19
□ 19 Ken Suarez	1.50	.65	.19
□ 20 Ernie Banks	20.00	9.00	2.50
□ 21 Jose Santiago	1.50	.65	.19
□ 22 Jesus Alou	1.50	.65	.19
□ 23 Lew Krausse	1.50	.65	.19
□ 24 Walt Alston MG	2.50	1.15	.30
□ 25 Roy White	2.00	.90	.25
□ 26 Clay Carroll	2.00	.90	.25
□ 27 Bernie Allen	1.50	.65	.19
□ 28 Mike Ryan	1.50	.65	.19
□ 29 Dave Morehead	1.50	.65	.19
□ 30 Bob Allison	2.00	.90	.25
□ 31 Mets Rookies Gary Gentry Amos Otis	3.00	1.35	.40
□ 32 Sammy Ellis	1.50	.65	.19
□ 33 Wayne Causey	1.50	.65	.19
□ 34 Gary Peters	1.50	.65	.19
□ 35 Joe Morgan	12.50	5.75	1.55
□ 36 Luke Walker	1.50	.65	.19
□ 37 Curt Motton	1.50	.65	.19
□ 38 Zoilo Versalles	1.50	.65	.19
□ 39 Dick Hughes	1.50	.65	.19
□ 40 Mayo Smith MG	1.50	.65	.19
□ 41 Bob Barton	1.50	.65	.19
□ 42 Tommy Harper	2.00	.90	.25
□ 43 Joe Niekro	2.00	.90	.25
□ 44 Danny Cater	1.50	.65	.19
□ 45 Maury Wills	3.00	1.35	.40
□ 46 Fritz Peterson	1.50	.65	.19
□ 47A Paul Popovich	1.50	.65	.19

(No helmet emblem)
□ 47B Paul Popovich 25.00 11.50 3.10
(C emblem on helmet)
□ 48 Brant Alyea 1.50 .65 .19
□ 49A Royals Rookies ERR 1.50 .65 .19
Steve Jones
E. Rodriquez "q"
□ 49B Royals Rookies COR 25.00 11.50 3.10
Steve Jones
E. Rodriguez "g"
□ 50 Bob Clemente UER 50.00 23.00 6.25
(Bats Right
listed twice)
□ 51 Woody Fryman 1.50 .65 .19
□ 52 Mike Andrews 1.50 .65 .19
□ 53 Sonny Jackson 1.50 .65 .19
□ 54 Cisco Carlos 1.50 .65 .19
□ 55 Jerry Grote 1.50 .65 .19
□ 56 Rich Reese 1.50 .65 .19
□ 57 Checklist 1 5.50 1.40 .45
Denny McLain
□ 58 Fred Gladding 1.50 .65 .19
□ 59 Jay Johnstone 2.00 .90 .25
□ 60 Nelson Briles 2.00 .90 .25
□ 61 Jimmie Hall 1.50 .65 .19
□ 62 Chico Salmon 1.50 .65 .19
□ 63 Jim Hickman 2.00 .90 .25
□ 64 Bill Monbouquette 1.50 .65 .19
□ 65 Willie Davis 2.00 .90 .25
□ 66 Orioles Rookies 2.00 .90 .25
Mike Adamson
Merv Rettenmund
□ 67 Bill Stoneman 1.50 .65 .19
□ 68 Dave Duncan 2.00 .90 .25
□ 69 Steve Hamilton 1.50 .65 .19
□ 70 Tommy Helms 2.00 .90 .25
□ 71 Steve Whitaker 1.50 .65 .19
□ 72 Ron Taylor 1.50 .65 .19
□ 73 Johnny Briggs 1.50 .65 .19
□ 74 Preston Gomez MG 1.50 .65 .19
□ 75 Luis Aparicio 5.50 2.50 .70
□ 76 Norm Miller 1.50 .65 .19
□ 77A Ron Perranoski 2.00 .90 .25
(No emblem on cap)
□ 77B Ron Perranoski 25.00 11.50 3.10
(LA on cap)
□ 78 Tom Satriano 1.50 .65 .19
□ 79 Milt Pappas 2.00 .90 .25
□ 80 Norm Cash 3.00 1.35 .40
□ 81 Mel Queen 1.50 .65 .19
□ 82 Pirates Rookies 11.00 4.90 1.40
Rich Hebner
Al Oliver
□ 83 Mike Ferraro 2.00 .90 .25
□ 84 Bob Humphreys 1.50 .65 .19
□ 85 Lou Brock 25.00 11.50 3.10
□ 86 Pete Richert 1.50 .65 .19
□ 87 Horace Clarke 1.50 .65 .19
□ 88 Rich Nye 1.50 .65 .19
□ 89 Russ Gibson 1.50 .65 .19
□ 90 Jerry Koosman 6.00 2.70 .75
□ 91 Alvin Dark MG 2.00 .90 .25
□ 92 Jack Billingham 1.50 .65 .19
□ 93 Joe Foy 1.50 .65 .19
□ 94 Hank Aguirre 1.50 .65 .19
□ 95 Johnny Bench 140.00 65.00 17.50
□ 96 Denny Lemaster 1.50 .65 .19
□ 97 Buddy Bradford 1.50 .65 .19
□ 98 Dave Giusti 1.50 .65 .19
□ 99A Twins Rookies 20.00 9.00 2.50
Danny Morris
Graig Nettles
(No loop)
□ 99B Twins Rookies 24.00 11.00 3.00
Danny Morris
Graig Nettles
(Errant loop in
upper left corner
of obverse)
□ 100 Hank Aaron 60.00 27.00 7.50
□ 101 Daryl Patterson 1.50 .65 .19
□ 102 Jim Davenport 1.50 .65 .19
□ 103 Roger Repoz 1.50 .65 .19
□ 104 Steve Blass 2.00 .90 .25
□ 105 Rick Monday 2.00 .90 .25
□ 106 Jim Hannan 1.50 .65 .19
□ 107A Checklist 2 ERR 5.50 1.40 .45
(161 Jim Purdin)
(Bob Gibson)
□ 107B Checklist 2 COR 7.50 1.90 .60
(161 John Purdin)
(Bob Gibson)
□ 108 Tony Taylor 1.50 .65 .19
□ 109 Jim Lonborg 2.00 .90 .25
□ 110 Mike Shannon 2.00 .90 .25
□ 111 Johnny Morris 1.50 .65 .19
□ 112 J.C. Martin 1.50 .65 .19
□ 113 Dave May 1.50 .65 .19
□ 114 Yankees Rookies 1.50 .65 .19
Alan Closter
John Cumberland
□ 115 Bill Hands 1.50 .65 .19
□ 116 Chuck Harrison 1.50 .65 .19
□ 117 Jim Fairey 1.50 .65 .19
□ 118 Stan Williams 1.50 .65 .19
□ 119 Doug Rader 2.00 .90 .25
□ 120 Pete Rose 35.00 16.00 4.40
□ 121 Joe Grzenda 1.50 .65 .19
□ 122 Ron Fairly 2.00 .90 .25
□ 123 Wilbur Wood 2.00 .90 .25
□ 124 Hank Bauer MG 2.00 .90 .25
□ 125 Ray Sadecki 1.50 .65 .19
□ 126 Dick Tracewski 1.50 .65 .19
□ 127 Kevin Collins 2.00 .90 .25
□ 128 Tommie Aaron 2.00 .90 .25
□ 129 Bill McCool 1.50 .65 .19
□ 130 Carl Yastrzemski 30.00 13.50 3.80
□ 131 Chris Cannizzaro 1.50 .65 .19
□ 132 Dave Baldwin 1.50 .65 .19
□ 133 Johnny Callison 2.00 .90 .25
□ 134 Jim Weaver 1.50 .65 .19
□ 135 Tommy Davis 2.00 .90 .25
□ 136 Cards Rookies 1.50 .65 .19
Steve Huntz
Mike Torrez
□ 137 Wally Bunker 1.50 .65 .19
□ 138 John Bateman 1.50 .65 .19
□ 139 Andy Kosco 1.50 .65 .19
□ 140 Jim Lefebvre 2.00 .90 .25
□ 141 Bill Dillman 1.50 .65 .19
□ 142 Woody Woodward 2.00 .90 .25
□ 143 Joe Nossek 1.50 .65 .19
□ 144 Bob Hendley 1.50 .65 .19
□ 145 Max Alvis 1.50 .65 .19
□ 146 Jim Perry 2.00 .90 .25
□ 147 Leo Durocher MG 3.00 1.35 .40
□ 148 Lee Stange 1.50 .65 .19
□ 149 Ollie Brown 1.50 .65 .19
□ 150 Denny McLain 5.00 2.30 .60
□ 151A Clay Dalrymple 1.50 .65 .19
(Portrait, Orioles)
□ 151B Clay Dalrymple 15.00 6.75 1.90
(Catching, Phillies)
□ 152 Tommie Sisk 1.50 .65 .19
□ 153 Ed Brinkman 1.50 .65 .19
□ 154 Jim Britton 1.50 .65 .19
□ 155 Pete Ward 1.50 .65 .19
□ 156 Houston Rookies 1.50 .65 .19
Hal Gilson
Leon McFadden
□ 157 Bob Rodgers 2.00 .90 .25
□ 158 Joe Gibbon 1.50 .65 .19
□ 159 Jerry Adair 1.50 .65 .19
□ 160 Vada Pinson 2.00 .90 .25
□ 161 John Purdin 1.50 .65 .19
□ 162 World Series Game 1 6.00 2.70 .75
Bob Gibson fans 17
□ 163 World Series Game 2 3.50 1.55 .45
Tiger homers
deck the Cards
(Willie Horton)
□ 164 World Series Game 3 6.00 2.70 .75
Tim McCarver's homer
□ 165 World Series Game 4 6.00 2.70 .75
Lou Brock lead-off
homer
□ 166 World Series Game 5 7.50 3.40 .95
Al Kaline's key hit
□ 167 World Series Game 6 3.50 1.55 .45
Jim Northrup grandslam
□ 168 World Series Game 7 6.00 2.70 .75
Mickey Lolich outduels
Bob Gibson
□ 169 World Series Summary 3.50 1.55 .45
Tigers celebrate
(Dick McAuliffe,
Denny McLain, and
Willie Horton)
□ 170 Frank Howard 2.50 1.15 .30
□ 171 Glenn Beckert 2.00 .90 .25
□ 172 Jerry Stephenson 1.50 .65 .19
□ 173 White Sox Rookies 1.50 .65 .19
Bob Christian
Gerry Nyman
□ 174 Grant Jackson 1.50 .65 .19
□ 175 Jim Bunning 3.50 1.55 .45
□ 176 Joe Azcue 1.50 .65 .19

☐ 177 Ron Reed	1.50	.65	.19
☐ 178 Ray Oyler	1.50	.65	.19
☐ 179 Don Pavletich	1.50	.65	.19
☐ 180 Willie Horton	2.00	.90	.25
☐ 181 Mel Nelson	1.50	.65	.19
☐ 182 Bill Rigney MG	1.50	.65	.19
☐ 183 Don Shaw	1.50	.65	.19
☐ 184 Roberto Pena	1.50	.65	.19
☐ 185 Tom Phoebus	1.50	.65	.19
☐ 186 Johnny Edwards	1.50	.65	.19
☐ 187 Leon Wagner	1.50	.65	.19
☐ 188 Rick Wise	2.00	.90	.25
☐ 189 Red Sox Rookies	1.50	.65	.19
Joe Lahoud			
John Thibodeau			
☐ 190 Willie Mays	65.00	29.00	8.25
☐ 191 Lindy McDaniel	2.00	.90	.25
☐ 192 Jose Pagan	1.50	.65	.19
☐ 193 Don Cardwell	1.50	.65	.19
☐ 194 Ted Uhlaender	1.50	.65	.19
☐ 195 John Odom	1.50	.65	.19
☐ 196 Lum Harris MG	1.50	.65	.19
☐ 197 Dick Selma	1.50	.65	.19
☐ 198 Willie Smith	1.50	.65	.19
☐ 199 Jim French	1.50	.65	.19
☐ 200 Bob Gibson	15.00	6.75	1.90
☐ 201 Russ Snyder	1.50	.65	.19
☐ 202 Don Wilson	2.00	.90	.25
☐ 203 Dave Johnson	2.00	.90	.25
☐ 204 Jack Hiatt	1.50	.65	.19
☐ 205 Rick Reichardt	1.50	.65	.19
☐ 206 Phillies Rookies	2.00	.90	.25
Larry Hisle			
Barry Lersch			
☐ 207 Roy Face	2.00	.90	.25
☐ 208A Donn Clendenon (Houston)	2.00	.90	.25
☐ 208B Donn Clendenon (Expos)	15.00	6.75	1.90
☐ 209 Larry Haney UER (Reverse negative)	1.50	.65	.19
☐ 210 Felix Millan	1.50	.65	.19
☐ 211 Galen Cisco	1.50	.65	.19
☐ 212 Tom Tresh	2.00	.90	.25
☐ 213 Gerry Arrigo	1.50	.65	.19
☐ 214 Checklist 3	5.50	1.40	.45
With 69T deckle CL on back (no player)			
☐ 215 Rico Petrocelli	2.00	.90	.25
☐ 216 Don Sutton	9.00	4.00	1.15
☐ 217 John Donaldson	1.50	.65	.19
☐ 218 John Roseboro	2.00	.90	.25
☐ 219 Freddie Patek	4.00	1.80	.50
☐ 220 Sam McDowell	3.00	1.35	.40
☐ 221 Art Shamsky	2.50	1.15	.30
☐ 222 Duane Josephson	2.50	1.15	.30
☐ 223 Tom Dukes	2.50	1.15	.30
☐ 224 Angels Rookies	2.50	1.15	.30
Bill Harrelson			
Steve Kealey			
☐ 225 Don Kessinger	3.00	1.35	.40
☐ 226 Bruce Howard	2.50	1.15	.30
☐ 227 Frank Johnson	2.50	1.15	.30
☐ 228 Dave Leonhard	2.50	1.15	.30
☐ 229 Don Lock	2.50	1.15	.30
☐ 230 Rusty Staub	4.00	1.80	.50
☐ 231 Pat Dobson	3.00	1.35	.40
☐ 232 Dave Ricketts	2.50	1.15	.30
☐ 233 Steve Barber	2.50	1.15	.30
☐ 234 Dave Bristol MG	2.50	1.15	.30
☐ 235 Jim Hunter	15.00	6.75	1.90
☐ 236 Manny Mota	3.00	1.35	.40
☐ 237 Bobby Cox	5.00	2.30	.60
☐ 238 Ken Johnson	2.50	1.15	.30
☐ 239 Bob Taylor	2.50	1.15	.30
☐ 240 Ken Harrelson	3.00	1.35	.40
☐ 241 Jim Brewer	2.50	1.15	.30
☐ 242 Frank Kostro	2.50	1.15	.30
☐ 243 Ron Kline	2.50	1.15	.30
☐ 244 Indians Rookies	3.50	1.55	.45
Ray Fosse			
George Woodson			
☐ 245 Ed Charles	2.50	1.15	.30
☐ 246 Joe Coleman	2.50	1.15	.30
☐ 247 Gene Oliver	2.50	1.15	.30
☐ 248 Bob Priddy	2.50	1.15	.30
☐ 249 Ed Spiezio	2.50	1.15	.30
☐ 250 Frank Robinson	30.00	13.50	3.80
☐ 251 Ron Herbel	2.50	1.15	.30
☐ 252 Chuck Cottier	2.50	1.15	.30
☐ 253 Jerry Johnson	2.50	1.15	.30
☐ 254 Joe Schultz MG	2.50	1.15	.30
☐ 255 Steve Carlton	55.00	25.00	7.00
☐ 256 Gates Brown	3.00	1.35	.40
☐ 257 Jim Ray	2.50	1.15	.30
☐ 258 Jackie Hernandez	2.50	1.15	.30
☐ 259 Bill Short	2.50	1.15	.30
☐ 260 Reggie Jackson	725.00	325.00	90.00
☐ 261 Bob Johnson	2.50	1.15	.30
☐ 262 Mike Kekich	2.50	1.15	.30
☐ 263 Jerry May	2.50	1.15	.30
☐ 264 Bill Landis	2.50	1.15	.30
☐ 265 Chico Cardenas	3.00	1.35	.40
☐ 266 Dodger Rookies	2.50	1.15	.30
Tom Hutton			
Alan Foster			
☐ 267 Vicente Romo	2.50	1.15	.30
☐ 268 Al Spangler	2.50	1.15	.30
☐ 269 Al Weis	2.50	1.15	.30
☐ 270 Mickey Lolich	4.50	2.00	.55
☐ 271 Larry Stahl	2.50	1.15	.30
☐ 272 Ed Stroud	2.50	1.15	.30
☐ 273 Ron Willis	2.50	1.15	.30
☐ 274 Clyde King MG	2.50	1.15	.30
☐ 275 Vic Davalillo	2.50	1.15	.30
☐ 276 Gary Wagner	2.50	1.15	.30
☐ 277 Elrod Hendricks	4.00	1.80	.50
☐ 278 Gary Geiger UER (Batting wrong)	2.50	1.15	.30
☐ 279 Roger Nelson	2.50	1.15	.30
☐ 280 Alex Johnson	3.00	1.35	.40
☐ 281 Ted Kubiak	2.50	1.15	.30
☐ 282 Pat Jarvis	2.50	1.15	.30
☐ 283 Sandy Alomar	3.00	1.35	.40
☐ 284 Expos Rookies	2.50	1.15	.30
Jerry Robertson			
Mike Wegener			
☐ 285 Don Mincher	2.50	1.15	.30
☐ 286 Dock Ellis	3.00	1.35	.40
☐ 287 Jose Tartabull	3.00	1.35	.40
☐ 288 Ken Holtzman	3.00	1.35	.40
☐ 289 Bart Shirley	2.50	1.15	.30
☐ 290 Jim Kaat	4.50	2.00	.55
☐ 291 Vern Fuller	2.50	1.15	.30
☐ 292 Al Downing	3.00	1.35	.40
☐ 293 Dick Dietz	2.50	1.15	.30
☐ 294 Jim Lemon MG	2.50	1.15	.30
☐ 295 Tony Perez	15.00	6.75	1.90
☐ 296 Andy Messersmith	4.00	1.80	.50
☐ 297 Deron Johnson	2.50	1.15	.30
☐ 298 Dave Nicholson	2.50	1.15	.30
☐ 299 Mark Belanger	3.00	1.35	.40
☐ 300 Felipe Alou	4.00	1.80	.50
☐ 301 Darrell Brandon	2.50	1.15	.30
☐ 302 Jim Pagliaroni	2.50	1.15	.30
☐ 303 Cal Koonce	2.50	1.15	.30
☐ 304 Padres Rookies	7.50	3.40	.95
Bill Davis			
Clarence Gaston			
☐ 305 Dick McAuliffe	3.00	1.35	.40
☐ 306 Jim Grant	2.50	1.15	.30
☐ 307 Gary Kolb	2.50	1.15	.30
☐ 308 Wade Blasingame	2.50	1.15	.30
☐ 309 Walt Williams	2.50	1.15	.30
☐ 310 Tom Haller	2.50	1.15	.30
☐ 311 Sparky Lyle	15.00	6.75	1.90
☐ 312 Lee Elia	3.00	1.35	.40
☐ 313 Bill Robinson	3.00	1.35	.40
☐ 314 Checklist 4	5.50	1.40	.45
Don Drysdale			
☐ 315 Eddie Fisher	2.50	1.15	.30
☐ 316 Hal Lanier	2.50	1.15	.30
☐ 317 Bruce Look	2.50	1.15	.30
☐ 318 Jack Fisher	2.50	1.15	.30
☐ 319 Ken McMullen UER	2.50	1.15	.30
(Headings on back are for a pitcher)			
☐ 320 Dal Maxvill	2.50	1.15	.30
☐ 321 Jim McAndrew	2.50	1.15	.30
☐ 322 Jose Vidal	2.50	1.15	.30
☐ 323 Larry Miller	2.50	1.15	.30
☐ 324 Tiger Rookies	2.50	1.15	.30
Les Cain			
Dave Campbell			
☐ 325 Jose Cardenal	3.00	1.35	.40
☐ 326 Gary Sutherland	2.50	1.15	.30
☐ 327 Willie Crawford	2.50	1.15	.30
☐ 328 Joel Horlen	1.50	.65	.19
☐ 329 Rick Joseph	1.50	.65	.19
☐ 330 Tony Conigliaro	4.00	1.80	.50
☐ 331 Braves Rookies	2.50	1.15	.30
Gil Garrido			
Tom House			
☐ 332 Fred Talbot	1.50	.65	.19
☐ 333 Ivan Murrell	1.50	.65	.19
☐ 334 Phil Roof	1.50	.65	.19

☐ 335	Bill Mazeroski	3.00	1.35	.40
☐ 336	Jim Roland	1.50	.65	.19
☐ 337	Marty Martinez	1.50	.65	.19
☐ 338	Del Unser	1.50	.65	.19
☐ 339	Reds Rookies	1.50	.65	.19
	Steve Mingori			
	Jose Pena			
☐ 340	Dave McNally	2.00	.90	.25
☐ 341	Dave Adlesh	1.50	.65	.19
☐ 342	Bubba Morton	1.50	.65	.19
☐ 343	Dan Frisella	1.50	.65	.19
☐ 344	Tom Matchick	1.50	.65	.19
☐ 345	Frank Linzy	1.50	.65	.19
☐ 346	Wayne Comer	1.50	.65	.19
☐ 347	Randy Hundley	1.50	.65	.19
☐ 348	Steve Hargan	1.50	.65	.19
☐ 349	Dick Williams MG	2.00	.90	.25
☐ 350	Richie Allen	4.00	1.80	.50
☐ 351	Carroll Sembera	1.50	.65	.19
☐ 352	Paul Schaal	1.50	.65	.19
☐ 353	Jeff Torborg	2.00	.90	.25
☐ 354	Nate Oliver	1.50	.65	.19
☐ 355	Phil Niekro	6.50	2.90	.80
☐ 356	Frank Quilici	1.50	.65	.19
☐ 357	Carl Taylor	1.50	.65	.19
☐ 358	Athletics Rookies	1.50	.65	.19
	George Lauzerique			
	Roberto Rodriquez			
☐ 359	Dick Kelley	1.50	.65	.19
☐ 360	Jim Wynn	2.00	.90	.25
☐ 361	Gary Holman	1.50	.65	.19
☐ 362	Jim Maloney	2.00	.90	.25
☐ 363	Russ Nixon	1.50	.65	.19
☐ 364	Tommie Agee	2.00	.90	.25
☐ 365	Jim Fregosi	2.00	.90	.25
☐ 366	Bo Belinsky	2.00	.90	.25
☐ 367	Lou Johnson	2.00	.90	.25
☐ 368	Vic Roznovsky	1.50	.65	.19
☐ 369	Bob Skinner	2.00	.90	.25
☐ 370	Juan Marichal	7.50	3.40	.95
☐ 371	Sal Bando	2.00	.90	.25
☐ 372	Adolfo Phillips	1.50	.65	.19
☐ 373	Fred Lasher	1.50	.65	.19
☐ 374	Bob Tillman	1.50	.65	.19
☐ 375	Harmon Killebrew	20.00	9.00	2.50
☐ 376	Royals Rookies	2.50	1.15	.30
	Mike Fiore			
	Jim Rooker			
☐ 377	Gary Bell	1.50	.65	.19
☐ 378	Jose Herrera	1.50	.65	.19
☐ 379	Ken Boyer	2.50	1.15	.30
☐ 380	Stan Bahnsen	1.50	.65	.19
☐ 381	Ed Kranepool	2.00	.90	.25
☐ 382	Pat Corrales	2.00	.90	.25
☐ 383	Casey Cox	1.50	.65	.19
☐ 384	Larry Shepard MG	1.50	.65	.19
☐ 385	Orlando Cepeda	3.50	1.55	.45
☐ 386	Jim McGlothlin	1.50	.65	.19
☐ 387	Bobby Klaus	1.50	.65	.19
☐ 388	Tom McCraw	1.50	.65	.19
☐ 389	Dan Coombs	1.50	.65	.19
☐ 390	Bill Freehan	2.50	1.15	.30
☐ 391	Ray Culp	1.50	.65	.19
☐ 392	Bob Burda	1.50	.65	.19
☐ 393	Gene Brabender	1.50	.65	.19
☐ 394	Pilots Rookies	4.50	2.00	.55
	Lou Piniella			
	Marv Staehle			
☐ 395	Chris Short	1.50	.65	.19
☐ 396	Jim Campanis	1.50	.65	.19
☐ 397	Chuck Dobson	1.50	.65	.19
☐ 398	Tito Francona	1.50	.65	.19
☐ 399	Bob Bailey	1.50	.65	.19
☐ 400	Don Drysdale	11.00	4.90	1.40
☐ 401	Jake Gibbs	1.50	.65	.19
☐ 402	Ken Boswell	1.50	.65	.19
☐ 403	Bob Miller	1.50	.65	.19
☐ 404	Cubs Rookies	1.50	.65	.19
	Vic LaRose			
	Gary Ross			
☐ 405	Lee May	2.00	.90	.25
☐ 406	Phil Ortega	1.50	.65	.19
☐ 407	Tom Egan	1.50	.65	.19
☐ 408	Nate Colbert	1.50	.65	.19
☐ 409	Bob Moose	1.50	.65	.19
☐ 410	Al Kaline	20.00	9.00	2.50
☐ 411	Larry Dierker	1.50	.65	.19
☐ 412	Checklist 5 DP	8.00	2.00	.65
	Mickey Mantle			
☐ 413	Roland Sheldon	1.50	.65	.19
☐ 414	Duke Sims	1.50	.65	.19
☐ 415	Ray Washburn	1.50	.65	.19
☐ 416	Willie McCovey AS	6.50	2.90	.80
☐ 417	Ken Harrelson AS	2.25	1.00	.30
☐ 418	Tommy Helms AS	2.25	1.00	.30
☐ 419	Rod Carew AS	10.00	4.50	1.25
☐ 420	Ron Santo AS	2.50	1.15	.30
☐ 421	Brooks Robinson AS	7.50	3.40	.95
☐ 422	Don Kessinger AS	2.25	1.00	.30
☐ 423	Bert Campaneris AS	2.25	1.00	.30
☐ 424	Pete Rose AS	12.50	5.75	1.55
☐ 425	Carl Yastrzemski AS	12.00	5.50	1.50
☐ 426	Curt Flood AS	2.25	1.00	.30
☐ 427	Tony Oliva AS	2.50	1.15	.30
☐ 428	Lou Brock AS	6.00	2.70	.75
☐ 429	Willie Horton AS	2.25	1.00	.30
☐ 430	Johnny Bench AS	15.00	6.75	1.90
☐ 431	Bill Freehan AS	2.25	1.00	.30
☐ 432	Bob Gibson AS	5.00	2.30	.60
☐ 433	Denny McLain AS	2.25	1.00	.30
☐ 434	Jerry Koosman AS	2.25	1.00	.30
☐ 435	Sam McDowell AS	2.25	1.00	.30
☐ 436	Gene Alley	2.00	.90	.25
☐ 437	Luis Alcaraz	1.50	.65	.19
☐ 438	Gary Waslewski	1.50	.65	.19
☐ 439	White Sox Rookies	1.50	.65	.19
	Ed Herrmann			
	Dan Lazar			
☐ 440A	Willie McCovey	15.00	6.75	1.90
☐ 440B	Willie McCovey WL	100.00	45.00	12.50
	(McCovey white)			
☐ 441A	Dennis Higgins	1.50	.65	.19
☐ 441B	Dennis Higgins WL	21.00	9.50	2.60
	(Higgins white)			
☐ 442	Ty Cline	1.50	.65	.19
☐ 443	Don Wert	1.50	.65	.19
☐ 444A	Joe Moeller	1.50	.65	.19
☐ 444B	Joe Moeller WL	21.00	9.50	2.60
	(Moeller white)			
☐ 445	Bobby Knoop	1.50	.65	.19
☐ 446	Claude Raymond	1.50	.65	.19
☐ 447A	Ralph Houk MG	2.00	.90	.25
☐ 447B	Ralph Houk WL	21.00	9.50	2.60
	MG (Houk white)			
☐ 448	Bob Tolan	2.00	.90	.25
☐ 449	Paul Lindblad	1.50	.65	.19
☐ 450	Billy Williams	6.50	2.90	.80
☐ 451A	Rich Rollins	1.50	.65	.19
☐ 451B	Rich Rollins WL	21.00	9.50	2.60
	(Rich and 3B white)			
☐ 452A	Al Ferrara	1.50	.65	.19
☐ 452B	Al Ferrara WL	21.00	9.50	2.60
	(Al and OF white)			
☐ 453	Mike Cuellar	2.50	1.15	.30
☐ 454A	Phillies Rookies	2.00	.90	.25
	Larry Colton			
	Don Money			
☐ 454B	Phillies Rookies WL	21.00	9.50	2.60
	Larry Colton			
	Don Money			
	(Names in white)			
☐ 455	Sonny Siebert	1.50	.65	.19
☐ 456	Bud Harrelson	2.00	.90	.25
☐ 457	Dalton Jones	1.50	.65	.19
☐ 458	Curt Blefary	1.50	.65	.19
☐ 459	Dave Boswell	1.50	.65	.19
☐ 460	Joe Torre	3.00	1.35	.40
☐ 461A	Mike Epstein	1.50	.65	.19
☐ 461B	Mike Epstein WL	21.00	9.50	2.60
	(Epstein white)			
☐ 462	Red Schoendienst MG	2.50	1.15	.30
☐ 463	Dennis Ribant	1.50	.65	.19
☐ 464A	Dave Marshall	1.50	.65	.19
☐ 464B	Dave Marshall WL	21.00	9.50	2.60
	(Marshall white)			
☐ 465	Tommy John	4.00	1.80	.50
☐ 466	John Boccabella	1.50	.65	.19
☐ 467	Tommie Reynolds	1.50	.65	.19
☐ 468A	Pirates Rookies	1.50	.65	.19
	Bruce Dal Canton			
	Bob Robertson			
☐ 468B	Pirates Rookies WL	21.00	9.50	2.60
	Bruce Dal Canton			
	Bob Robertson			
	(Names in white)			
☐ 469	Chico Ruiz	1.50	.65	.19
☐ 470A	Mel Stottlemyre	2.50	1.15	.30
☐ 470B	Mel Stottlemyre WL	25.00	11.50	3.10
	(Stottlemyre white)			
☐ 471A	Ted Savage	1.50	.65	.19
☐ 471B	Ted Savage WL	21.00	9.50	2.60
	(Savage white)			
☐ 472	Jim Price	1.50	.65	.19
☐ 473A	Jose Arcia	1.50	.65	.19
☐ 473B	Jose Arcia WL	21.00	9.50	2.60

(Jose and 2B white)			
☐ 474 Tom Murphy	1.50	.65	.19
☐ 475 Tim McCarver	3.00	1.35	.40
☐ 476A Boston Rookies	2.50	1.15	.30
Ken Brett			
Gerry Moses			
☐ 476B Boston Rookies WL	22.50	10.00	2.80
Ken Brett			
Gerry Moses			
(Names in white)			
☐ 477 Jeff James	1.50	.65	.19
☐ 478 Don Buford	1.50	.65	.19
☐ 479 Richie Scheinblum	1.50	.65	.19
☐ 480 Tom Seaver	135.00	60.00	17.00
☐ 481 Bill Melton	2.00	.90	.25
☐ 482A Jim Gosger	1.50	.65	.19
☐ 482B Jim Gosger WL	21.00	9.50	2.60
(Jim and OF white)			
☐ 483 Ted Abernathy	1.50	.65	.19
☐ 484 Joe Gordon MG	2.00	.90	.25
☐ 485A Gaylord Perry	10.00	4.50	1.25
☐ 485B Gaylord Perry WL	75.00	34.00	9.50
(Perry white)			
☐ 486A Paul Casanova	1.50	.65	.19
☐ 486B Paul Casanova WL	21.00	9.50	2.60
(Casanova white)			
☐ 487 Denis Menke	1.50	.65	.19
☐ 488 Joe Sparma	1.50	.65	.19
☐ 489 Clete Boyer	2.00	.90	.25
☐ 490 Matty Alou	2.00	.90	.25
☐ 491A Twins Rookies	1.50	.65	.19
Jerry Crider			
George Mitterwald			
☐ 491B Twins Rookies WL	21.00	9.50	2.60
Jerry Crider			
George Mitterwald			
(Names in white)			
☐ 492 Tony Cloninger	1.50	.65	.19
☐ 493A Wes Parker	2.00	.90	.25
☐ 493B Wes Parker WL	21.00	9.50	2.60
(Parker white)			
☐ 494 Ken Berry	1.50	.65	.19
☐ 495 Bert Campaneris	2.00	.90	.25
☐ 496 Larry Jaster	1.50	.65	.19
☐ 497 Julian Javier	2.00	.90	.25
☐ 498 Juan Pizarro	2.00	.90	.25
☐ 499 Astro Rookies	1.50	.65	.19
Don Bryant			
Steve Shea			
☐ 500A Mickey Mantle UER	250.00	115.00	31.00
(No Topps copy-			
right on card back)			
☐ 500B Mickey Mantle WL	650.00	300.00	80.00
(Mantle in white;			
no Topps copyright			
on card back) UER			
☐ 501A Tony Gonzalez	1.50	.65	.19
☐ 501B Tony Gonzalez WL	21.00	9.50	2.60
(Tony and OF white)			
☐ 502 Minnie Rojas	1.50	.65	.19
☐ 503 Larry Brown	1.50	.65	.19
☐ 504 Checklist 6	7.00	1.75	.55
Brooks Robinson			
☐ 505A Bobby Bolin	1.50	.65	.19
☐ 505B Bobby Bolin WL	21.00	9.50	2.60
(Bolin white)			
☐ 506 Paul Blair	2.00	.90	.25
☐ 507 Cookie Rojas	2.00	.90	.25
☐ 508 Moe Drabowsky	1.50	.65	.19
☐ 509 Manny Sanguillen	2.00	.90	.25
☐ 510 Rod Carew	80.00	36.00	10.00
☐ 511A Diego Segui	1.50	.65	.19
☐ 511B Diego Segui WL	21.00	9.50	2.60
(Diego and P white)			
☐ 512 Cleon Jones	2.00	.90	.25
☐ 513 Camilo Pascual	2.50	1.15	.30
☐ 514 Mike Lum	2.00	.90	.25
☐ 515 Dick Green	2.00	.90	.25
☐ 516 Earl Weaver MG	12.50	5.75	1.55
☐ 517 Mike McCormick	2.50	1.15	.30
☐ 518 Fred Whitfield	2.00	.90	.25
☐ 519 Yankees Rookies	2.00	.90	.25
Jerry Kenney			
Len Boehmer			
☐ 520 Bob Veale	2.50	1.15	.30
☐ 521 George Thomas	2.00	.90	.25
☐ 522 Joe Hoerner	2.00	.90	.25
☐ 523 Bob Chance	2.00	.90	.25
☐ 524 Expos Rookies	2.00	.90	.25
Jose Laboy			
Floyd Wicker			
☐ 525 Earl Wilson	2.50	1.15	.30
☐ 526 Hector Torres	2.00	.90	.25
☐ 527 Al Lopez MG	3.00	1.35	.40
☐ 528 Claude Osteen	2.50	1.15	.30
☐ 529 Ed Kirkpatrick	2.00	.90	.25
☐ 530 Cesar Tovar	2.00	.90	.25
☐ 531 Dick Farrell	2.00	.90	.25
☐ 532 Bird Hill Aces	2.50	1.15	.30
Tom Phoebus			
Jim Hardin			
Dave McNally			
Mike Cuellar			
☐ 533 Nolan Ryan	550.00	250.00	70.00
☐ 534 Jerry McNertney	2.00	.90	.25
☐ 535 Phil Regan	2.50	1.15	.30
☐ 536 Padres Rookies	2.00	.90	.25
Danny Breeden			
Dave Roberts			
☐ 537 Mike Paul	2.00	.90	.25
☐ 538 Charlie Smith	2.00	.90	.25
☐ 539 Ted Shows How	7.00	3.10	.85
Mike Epstein			
Ted Williams MG			
☐ 540 Curt Flood	3.00	1.35	.40
☐ 541 Joe Verbanic	2.00	.90	.25
☐ 542 Bob Aspromonte	2.00	.90	.25
☐ 543 Fred Newman	2.00	.90	.25
☐ 544 Tigers Rookies	2.00	.90	.25
Mike Kilkenny			
Ron Woods			
☐ 545 Willie Stargell	16.00	7.25	2.00
☐ 546 Jim Nash	2.00	.90	.25
☐ 547 Billy Martin MG	6.00	2.70	.75
☐ 548 Bob Locker	2.00	.90	.25
☐ 549 Ron Brand	2.00	.90	.25
☐ 550 Brooks Robinson	25.00	11.50	3.10
☐ 551 Wayne Granger	2.00	.90	.25
☐ 552 Dodgers Rookies	3.00	1.35	.40
Ted Sizemore			
Bill Sudakis			
☐ 553 Ron Davis	2.00	.90	.25
☐ 554 Frank Bertaina	2.00	.90	.25
☐ 555 Jim Ray Hart	2.50	1.15	.30
☐ 556 A's Stars	2.50	1.15	.30
Sal Bando			
Bert Campaneris			
Danny Cater			
☐ 557 Frank Fernandez	2.00	.90	.25
☐ 558 Tom Burgmeier	2.50	1.15	.30
☐ 559 Cardinals Rookies	2.00	.90	.25
Joe Hague			
Jim Hicks			
☐ 560 Luis Tiant	3.00	1.35	.40
☐ 561 Ron Clark	2.00	.90	.25
☐ 562 Bob Watson	4.00	1.80	.50
☐ 563 Marty Pattin	2.00	.90	.25
☐ 564 Gil Hodges MG	10.00	4.50	1.25
☐ 565 Hoyt Wilhelm	7.00	3.10	.85
☐ 566 Ron Hansen	2.00	.90	.25
☐ 567 Pirates Rookies	2.00	.90	.25
Elvio Jimenez			
Jim Shellenback			
☐ 568 Cecil Upshaw	2.00	.90	.25
☐ 569 Billy Harris	2.00	.90	.25
☐ 570 Ron Santo	5.50	2.50	.70
☐ 571 Cap Peterson	2.00	.90	.25
☐ 572 Giants Heroes	12.50	5.75	1.55
Willie McCovey			
Juan Marichal			
☐ 573 Jim Palmer	45.00	20.00	5.75
☐ 574 George Scott	2.50	1.15	.30
☐ 575 Bill Singer	2.50	1.15	.30
☐ 576 Phillies Rookies	2.00	.90	.25
Ron Stone			
Bill Wilson			
☐ 577 Mike Hegan	2.00	.90	.25
☐ 578 Don Bosch	2.00	.90	.25
☐ 579 Dave Nelson	2.50	1.15	.30
☐ 580 Jim Northrup	2.50	1.15	.30
☐ 581 Gary Nolan	2.50	1.15	.30
☐ 582A Checklist 7	5.50	1.40	.45
(White circle on back)			
(Tony Oliva)			
☐ 582B Checklist 7	7.50	1.90	.60
(Red circle on back)			
(Tony Oliva)			
☐ 583 Clyde Wright	2.00	.90	.25
☐ 584 Don Mason	2.00	.90	.25
☐ 585 Ron Swoboda	2.50	1.15	.30
☐ 586 Tim Cullen	2.00	.90	.25
☐ 587 Joe Rudi	5.00	2.30	.60
☐ 588 Bill White	3.00	1.35	.40
☐ 589 Joe Pepitone	2.75	1.25	.35
☐ 590 Rico Carty	2.75	1.25	.35
☐ 591 Mike Hedlund	2.25	1.00	.30
☐ 592 Padres Rookies	2.25	1.00	.30

Rafael Robles
Al Santorini
☐ 593 Don Nottebart 2.25 1.00 .30
☐ 594 Dooley Womack 2.25 1.00 .30
☐ 595 Lee Maye 2.25 1.00 .30
☐ 596 Chuck Hartenstein 2.25 1.00 .30
☐ 597 A.L. Rookies 150.00 70.00 19.00
Bob Floyd
Larry Burchart
Rollie Fingers
☐ 598 Ruben Amaro 2.25 1.00 .30
☐ 599 John Boozer 2.25 1.00 .30
☐ 600 Tony Oliva 6.50 2.90 .80
☐ 601 Tug McGraw 4.50 2.00 .55
☐ 602 Cubs Rookies 2.25 1.00 .30
Alec Distaso
Don Young
Jim Qualls
☐ 603 Joe Keough 2.25 1.00 .30
☐ 604 Bobby Etheridge 2.25 1.00 .30
☐ 605 Dick Ellsworth 2.25 1.00 .30
☐ 606 Gene Mauch MG 2.75 1.25 .35
☐ 607 Dick Bosman 2.25 1.00 .30
☐ 608 Dick Simpson 2.25 1.00 .30
☐ 609 Phil Gagliano 2.25 1.00 .30
☐ 610 Jim Hardin 2.25 1.00 .30
☐ 611 Braves Rookies 3.50 1.55 .45
Bob Didier
Walt Hriniak
Gary Neibauer
☐ 612 Jack Aker 2.25 1.00 .30
☐ 613 Jim Beauchamp 2.25 1.00 .30
☐ 614 Houston Rookies 2.25 1.00 .30
Tom Griffin
Skip Guinn
☐ 615 Len Gabrielson 2.25 1.00 .30
☐ 616 Don McMahon 2.25 1.00 .30
☐ 617 Jesse Gonder 2.25 1.00 .30
☐ 618 Ramon Webster 2.25 1.00 .30
☐ 619 Royals Rookies 2.25 1.00 .30
Bill Butler
Pat Kelly
Juan Rios
☐ 620 Dean Chance 2.75 1.25 .35
☐ 621 Bill Voss 2.25 1.00 .30
☐ 622 Dan Osinski 2.25 1.00 .30
☐ 623 Hank Allen 2.25 1.00 .30
☐ 624 NL Rookies 3.50 1.55 .45
Darrel Chaney
Duffy Dyer
Terry Harmon
☐ 625 Mack Jones UER 2.25 1.00 .30
(Batting wrong)
☐ 626 Gene Michael 2.75 1.25 .35
☐ 627 George Stone 2.25 1.00 .30
☐ 628 Red Sox Rookies 4.00 1.80 .50
Bill Conigliaro
Syd O'Brien
Fred Wenz
☐ 629 Jack Hamilton 2.25 1.00 .30
☐ 630 Bobby Bonds 40.00 18.00 5.00
☐ 631 John Kennedy 2.25 1.00 .30
☐ 632 Jon Warden 2.25 1.00 .30
☐ 633 Harry Walker MG 2.25 1.00 .30
☐ 634 Andy Etchebarren 2.25 1.00 .30
☐ 635 George Culver 2.25 1.00 .30
☐ 636 Woody Held 2.25 1.00 .30
☐ 637 Padres Rookies 2.25 1.00 .30
Jerry DaVanon
Frank Reberger
Clay Kirby
☐ 638 Ed Sprague 2.25 1.00 .30
☐ 639 Barry Moore 2.25 1.00 .30
☐ 640 Fergie Jenkins 22.00 10.00 2.80
☐ 641 NL Rookies 2.25 1.00 .30
Bobby Darwin
John Miller
Tommy Dean
☐ 642 John Hiller 2.25 1.00 .30
☐ 643 Billy Cowan 2.25 1.00 .30
☐ 644 Chuck Hinton 2.25 1.00 .30
☐ 645 George Brunet 2.25 1.00 .30
☐ 646 Expos Rookies 2.75 1.25 .35
Dan McGinn
Carl Morton
☐ 647 Dave Wickersham 2.25 1.00 .30
☐ 648 Bobby Wine 2.25 1.00 .30
☐ 649 Al Jackson 2.25 1.00 .30
☐ 650 Ted Williams MG 12.50 5.75 1.55
☐ 651 Gus Gil 2.25 1.00 .30
☐ 652 Eddie Watt 2.25 1.00 .30
☐ 653 Aurelio Rodriguez UER 3.00 1.35 .40
(Photo actually
Angels' batboy)
☐ 654 White Sox Rookies 4.00 1.80 .50
Carlos May
Don Secrist
Rich Morales
☐ 655 Mike Hershberger 2.25 1.00 .30
☐ 656 Dan Schneider 2.25 1.00 .30
☐ 657 Bobby Murcer 5.00 2.30 .60
☐ 658 AL Rookies 2.75 1.25 .35
Tom Hall
Bill Burbach
Jim Miles
☐ 659 Johnny Podres 3.00 1.35 .40
☐ 660 Reggie Smith 4.50 2.00 .55
☐ 661 Jim Merritt 2.25 1.00 .30
☐ 662 Royals Rookies 2.75 1.25 .35
Dick Drago
George Spriggs
Bob Oliver
☐ 663 Dick Radatz 2.75 1.25 .35
☐ 664 Ron Hunt 4.00 1.80 .50

1969 Topps Deckle

The cards in this 33-card set measure approximately 2 1/4" by 3 1/4". This unusual black and white insert set derives its name from the serrated border, or edge, of the cards. The cards were included as inserts in the regularly issued Topps baseball series of 1969. Card number 11 is found with either Hoyt Wilhelm or Jim Wynn, and number 22 with either Rusty Staub or Joe Foy. The set price below does include all variations. The set numbering is arranged in team order by league except for cards 11 and 22.

	NRMT-MT	EXC	G-VG
COMPLETE SET (35)	75.00	34.00	9.50
COMMON PLAYER (1-33)	.50	.23	.06
☐ 1 Brooks Robinson	4.50	2.00	.55
☐ 2 Boog Powell	.75	.35	.09
☐ 3 Ken Harrelson	.60	.25	.08
☐ 4 Carl Yastrzemski	6.00	2.70	.75
☐ 5 Jim Fregosi	.60	.25	.08
☐ 6 Luis Aparicio	1.50	.65	.19
☐ 7 Luis Tiant	.60	.25	.08
☐ 8 Denny McLain	.75	.35	.09
☐ 9 Willie Horton	.60	.25	.08
☐ 10 Bill Freehan	.60	.25	.08
☐ 11A Hoyt Wilhelm	6.00	2.70	.75
☐ 11B Jim Wynn	10.00	4.50	1.25
☐ 12 Rod Carew	5.00	2.30	.60
☐ 13 Mel Stottlemyre	.60	.25	.08
☐ 14 Rick Monday	.50	.23	.06
☐ 15 Tommy Davis	.60	.25	.08
☐ 16 Frank Howard	.60	.25	.08
☐ 17 Felipe Alou	.75	.35	.09
☐ 18 Don Kessinger	.50	.23	.06
☐ 19 Ron Santo	.75	.35	.09
☐ 20 Tommy Helms	.50	.23	.06
☐ 21 Pete Rose	8.00	3.60	1.00
☐ 22A Rusty Staub	3.00	1.35	.40
☐ 22B Joe Foy	10.00	4.50	1.25
☐ 23 Tom Haller	.50	.23	.06
☐ 24 Maury Wills	.75	.35	.09
☐ 25 Jerry Koosman	.75	.35	.09
☐ 26 Richie Allen	.75	.35	.09
☐ 27 Bob Clemente	8.00	3.60	1.00
☐ 28 Curt Flood	.75	.35	.09

□ 29 Bob Gibson	3.50	1.55	.45
□ 30 Al Ferrara	.50	.23	.06
□ 31 Willie McCovey	4.00	1.80	.50
□ 32 Juan Marichal	3.00	1.35	.40
□ 33 Willie Mays	9.00	4.00	1.15

1969 Topps Super

The cards in this 66-card set measure approximately 2 1/4" by 3 1/4". This beautiful Topps set was released independently of the regular baseball series of 1969. It is referred to as "Super Baseball" on the back of the card, a title which was also used for the postcard-size cards issued in 1970 and 1971. Complete sheets, and cards with square corners cut from these sheets, are sometimes encountered. The set numbering is in alphabetical order by teams within league.

	NRMT-MT	EXC	G-VG
COMPLETE SET (66)	5500.00	2500.00	700.00
COMMON PLAYER (1-66)	11.00	4.90	1.40
□ 1 Dave McNally	12.00	5.50	1.50
□ 2 Frank Robinson	175.00	80.00	22.00
□ 3 Brooks Robinson	225.00	100.00	28.00
□ 4 Ken Harrelson	13.50	6.00	1.70
□ 5 Carl Yastrzemski	375.00	170.00	47.50
□ 6 Ray Culp	11.00	4.90	1.40
□ 7 Jim Fregosi	12.00	5.50	1.50
□ 8 Rick Reichardt	11.00	4.90	1.40
□ 9 Vic Davalillo	11.00	4.90	1.40
□ 10 Luis Aparicio	90.00	40.00	11.50
□ 11 Pete Ward	11.00	4.90	1.40
□ 12 Joel Horlen	11.00	4.90	1.40
□ 13 Luis Tiant	13.50	6.00	1.70
□ 14 Sam McDowell	11.00	4.90	1.40
□ 15 Jose Cardenal	11.00	4.90	1.40
□ 16 Willie Horton	12.00	5.50	1.50
□ 17 Denny McLain	15.00	6.75	1.90
□ 18 Bill Freehan	12.00	5.50	1.50
□ 19 Harmon Killebrew	150.00	70.00	19.00
□ 20 Tony Oliva	18.00	8.00	2.30
□ 21 Dean Chance	11.00	4.90	1.40
□ 22 Joe Foy	11.00	4.90	1.40
□ 23 Roger Nelson	11.00	4.90	1.40
□ 24 Mickey Mantle	900.00	400.00	115.00
□ 25 Mel Stottlemyre	13.50	6.00	1.70
□ 26 Roy White	13.50	6.00	1.70
□ 27 Rick Monday	11.00	4.90	1.40
□ 28 Reggie Jackson	650.00	300.00	80.00
□ 29 Bert Campaneris	12.00	5.50	1.50
□ 30 Frank Howard	13.50	6.00	1.70
□ 31 Camilo Pascual	11.00	4.90	1.40
□ 32 Tommy Davis	13.50	6.00	1.70
□ 33 Don Mincher	11.00	4.90	1.40
□ 34 Hank Aaron	450.00	200.00	57.50
□ 35 Felipe Alou	15.00	6.75	1.90
□ 36 Joe Torre	18.00	8.00	2.30
□ 37 Fergie Jenkins	100.00	45.00	12.50
□ 38 Ron Santo	18.00	8.00	2.30
□ 39 Billy Williams	90.00	40.00	11.50
□ 40 Tommy Helms	11.00	4.90	1.40
□ 41 Pete Rose	500.00	230.00	65.00
□ 42 Joe Morgan	135.00	60.00	17.00
□ 43 Jim Wynn	12.00	5.50	1.50
□ 44 Curt Blefary	11.00	4.90	1.40
□ 45 Willie Davis	11.00	4.90	1.40
□ 46 Don Drysdale	100.00	45.00	12.50
□ 47 Tom Haller	11.00	4.90	1.40
□ 48 Rusty Staub	15.00	6.75	1.90
□ 49 Maury Wills	18.00	8.00	2.30
□ 50 Cleon Jones	12.00	5.50	1.50
□ 51 Jerry Koosman	15.00	6.75	1.90
□ 52 Tom Seaver	425.00	190.00	52.50
□ 53 Richie Allen	15.00	6.75	1.90
□ 54 Chris Short	11.00	4.90	1.40
□ 55 Cookie Rojas	11.00	4.90	1.40
□ 56 Matty Alou	11.00	4.90	1.40
□ 57 Steve Blass	11.00	4.90	1.40
□ 58 Bob Clemente	300.00	135.00	38.00
□ 59 Curt Flood	15.00	6.75	1.90
□ 60 Bob Gibson	150.00	70.00	19.00
□ 61 Tim McCarver	18.00	8.00	2.30
□ 62 Dick Selma	11.00	4.90	1.40
□ 63 Ollie Brown	11.00	4.90	1.40
□ 64 Juan Marichal	125.00	57.50	15.50
□ 65 Willie Mays	450.00	200.00	57.50
□ 66 Willie McCovey	175.00	80.00	22.00

1970 Topps

The cards in this 720-card set measure 2 1/2" by 3 1/2". The Topps set for 1970 has color photos surrounded by white frame lines and gray borders. The backs have a blue biographical section and a yellow record section. All-Star selections are featured on cards 450 to 469. Other topical subsets within this set include League Leaders (61-72), Playoffs cards (195-202), and World Series cards (305-310). There are graduations of scarcity, terminating in the high series (634-720), which are outlined in the value summary. The key Rookie Card in this set is Thurman Munson.

	NRMT-MT	EXC	G-VG
COMPLETE SET (720)	2250.00	1000.00	275.00
COMMON PLAYER (1-132)	.70	.30	.09
COMMON PLAYER (133-263)	.80	.35	.10
COMMON PLAYER (264-372)	1.00	.45	.13
COMMON PLAYER (373-459)	1.25	.55	.16
COMMON PLAYER (460-546)	1.50	.65	.19
COMMON PLAYER (547-633)	3.00	1.35	.40
COMMON PLAYER (634-720)	6.00	2.70	.75
□ 1 New York Mets Team Card	12.50	2.50	.75
□ 2 Diego Segui	.70	.30	.09
□ 3 Darrel Chaney	.70	.30	.09
□ 4 Tom Egan	.70	.30	.09
□ 5 Wes Parker	1.00	.45	.13
□ 6 Grant Jackson	.70	.30	.09
□ 7 Indians Rookies Gary Boyd Russ Nagelson	.70	.30	.09
□ 8 Jose Martinez	1.00	.45	.13
□ 9 Checklist 1	5.00	.50	.15
□ 10 Carl Yastrzemski	25.00	11.50	3.10
□ 11 Nate Colbert	.70	.30	.09
□ 12 John Hiller	1.00	.45	.13
□ 13 Jack Hiatt	.70	.30	.09
□ 14 Hank Allen	.70	.30	.09

☐ 15 Larry Dierker .70 .30 .09
☐ 16 Charlie Metro MG .70 .30 .09
☐ 17 Hoyt Wilhelm 4.00 1.80 .50
☐ 18 Carlos May 1.00 .45 .13
☐ 19 John Boccabella .70 .30 .09
☐ 20 Dave McNally 1.00 .45 .13
☐ 21 A's Rookies 7.00 3.10 .85
Vida Blue
Gene Tenace
☐ 22 Ray Washburn .70 .30 .09
☐ 23 Bill Robinson 1.00 .45 .13
☐ 24 Dick Selma .70 .30 .09
☐ 25 Cesar Tovar .70 .30 .09
☐ 26 Tug McGraw 1.50 .65 .19
☐ 27 Chuck Hinton .70 .30 .09
☐ 28 Billy Wilson .70 .30 .09
☐ 29 Sandy Alomar 1.00 .45 .13
☐ 30 Matty Alou 1.00 .45 .13
☐ 31 Marty Pattin .70 .30 .09
☐ 32 Harry Walker MG .70 .30 .09
☐ 33 Don Wert .70 .30 .09
☐ 34 Willie Crawford .70 .30 .09
☐ 35 Joel Horlen .70 .30 .09
☐ 36 Red Rookies 1.00 .45 .13
Danny Breeden
Bernie Carbo
☐ 37 Dick Drago .70 .30 .09
☐ 38 Mack Jones .70 .30 .09
☐ 39 Mike Nagy .70 .30 .09
☐ 40 Rich Allen 2.00 .90 .25
☐ 41 George Lauzerique .70 .30 .09
☐ 42 Tito Fuentes .70 .30 .09
☐ 43 Jack Aker .70 .30 .09
☐ 44 Roberto Pena .70 .30 .09
☐ 45 Dave Johnson 1.00 .45 .13
☐ 46 Ken Rudolph .70 .30 .09
☐ 47 Bob Miller .70 .30 .09
☐ 48 Gil Garrido .70 .30 .09
☐ 49 Tim Cullen .70 .30 .09
☐ 50 Tommie Agee 1.00 .45 .13
☐ 51 Bob Christian .70 .30 .09
☐ 52 Bruce Dal Canton .70 .30 .09
☐ 53 John Kennedy .70 .30 .09
☐ 54 Jeff Torborg 1.00 .45 .13
☐ 55 John Odom .70 .30 .09
☐ 56 Phillies Rookies .70 .30 .09
Joe Lis
Scott Reid
☐ 57 Pat Kelly .70 .30 .09
☐ 58 Dave Marshall .70 .30 .09
☐ 59 Dick Ellsworth .70 .30 .09
☐ 60 Jim Wynn 1.00 .45 .13
☐ 61 NL Batting Leaders 5.00 2.30 .60
Pete Rose
Bob Clemente
Cleon Jones
☐ 62 AL Batting Leaders 3.00 1.35 .40
Rod Carew
Reggie Smith
Tony Oliva
☐ 63 NL RBI Leaders 3.00 1.35 .40
Willie McCovey
Ron Santo
Tony Perez
☐ 64 AL RBI Leaders 4.50 2.00 .55
Harmon Killebrew
Boog Powell
Reggie Jackson
☐ 65 NL Home Run Leaders 4.00 1.80 .50
Willie McCovey
Hank Aaron
Lee May
☐ 66 AL Home Run Leaders 4.50 2.00 .55
Harmon Killebrew
Frank Howard
Reggie Jackson
☐ 67 NL ERA Leaders 5.00 2.30 .60
Juan Marichal
Steve Carlton
Bob Gibson
☐ 68 AL ERA Leaders 2.00 .90 .25
Dick Bosman
Jim Palmer
Mike Cuellar
☐ 69 NL Pitching Leaders 5.00 2.30 .60
Tom Seaver
Phil Niekro
Fergie Jenkins
Juan Marichal
☐ 70 AL Pitching Leaders 2.00 .90 .25
Dennis McLain
Mike Cuellar
Dave Boswell
Dave McNally
Jim Perry
Mel Stottlemyre
☐ 71 NL Strikeout Leaders 3.00 1.35 .40
Fergie Jenkins
Bob Gibson
Bill Singer
☐ 72 AL Strikeout Leaders 2.00 .90 .25
Sam McDowell
Mickey Lolich
Andy Messersmith
☐ 73 Wayne Granger .70 .30 .09
☐ 74 Angels Rookies .70 .30 .09
Greg Washburn
Wally Wolf
☐ 75 Jim Kaat 2.00 .90 .25
☐ 76 Carl Taylor .70 .30 .09
☐ 77 Frank Linzy .70 .30 .09
☐ 78 Joe Lahoud .70 .30 .09
☐ 79 Clay Kirby .70 .30 .09
☐ 80 Don Kessinger 1.00 .45 .13
☐ 81 Dave May .70 .30 .09
☐ 82 Frank Fernandez .70 .30 .09
☐ 83 Don Cardwell .70 .30 .09
☐ 84 Paul Casanova .70 .30 .09
☐ 85 Max Alvis .70 .30 .09
☐ 86 Lum Harris MG .70 .30 .09
☐ 87 Steve Renko .70 .30 .09
☐ 88 Pilots Rookies .70 .30 .09
Miguel Fuentes
Dick Baney
☐ 89 Juan Rios .70 .30 .09
☐ 90 Tim McCarver 1.50 .65 .19
☐ 91 Rich Morales .70 .30 .09
☐ 92 George Culver .70 .30 .09
☐ 93 Rick Renick .70 .30 .09
☐ 94 Freddie Patek 1.00 .45 .13
☐ 95 Earl Wilson 1.00 .45 .13
☐ 96 Cardinals Rookies 3.00 1.35 .40
Leron Lee
Jerry Reuss
☐ 97 Joe Moeller .70 .30 .09
☐ 98 Gates Brown 1.00 .45 .13
☐ 99 Bobby Pfeil .70 .30 .09
☐ 100 Mel Stottlemyre 1.50 .65 .19
☐ 101 Bobby Floyd .70 .30 .09
☐ 102 Joe Rudi 1.00 .45 .13
☐ 103 Frank Reberger .70 .30 .09
☐ 104 Gerry Moses .70 .30 .09
☐ 105 Tony Gonzalez .70 .30 .09
☐ 106 Darold Knowles .70 .30 .09
☐ 107 Bobby Etheridge .70 .30 .09
☐ 108 Tom Burgmeier .70 .30 .09
☐ 109 Expos Rookies .70 .30 .09
Garry Jestadt
Carl Morton
☐ 110 Bob Moose .70 .30 .09
☐ 111 Mike Hegan .70 .30 .09
☐ 112 Dave Nelson .70 .30 .09
☐ 113 Jim Ray .70 .30 .09
☐ 114 Gene Michael 1.00 .45 .13
☐ 115 Alex Johnson 1.00 .45 .13
☐ 116 Sparky Lyle 1.50 .65 .19
☐ 117 Don Young .70 .30 .09
☐ 118 George Mitterwald .70 .30 .09
☐ 119 Chuck Taylor .70 .30 .09
☐ 120 Sal Bando 1.00 .45 .13
☐ 121 Orioles Rookies 1.00 .45 .13
Fred Beene
Terry Crowley
☐ 122 George Stone .70 .30 .09
☐ 123 Don Gutteridge MG .70 .30 .09
☐ 124 Larry Jaster .70 .30 .09
☐ 125 Deron Johnson .70 .30 .09
☐ 126 Marty Martinez .70 .30 .09
☐ 127 Joe Coleman .70 .30 .09
☐ 128A Checklist 2 ERR 5.00 .50 .15
(226 R Perranoski)
☐ 128B Checklist 2 COR 5.00 .50 .15
(226 R. Perranoski)
☐ 129 Jimmie Price .70 .30 .09
☐ 130 Ollie Brown .70 .30 .09
☐ 131 Dodgers Rookies .70 .30 .09
Ray Lamb
Bob Stinson
☐ 132 Jim McGlothlin .70 .30 .09
☐ 133 Clay Carroll .80 .35 .10
☐ 134 Danny Walton .80 .35 .10
☐ 135 Dick Dietz .80 .35 .10
☐ 136 Steve Hargan .80 .35 .10
☐ 137 Art Shamsky .80 .35 .10
☐ 138 Joe Foy .80 .35 .10
☐ 139 Rich Nye .80 .35 .10
☐ 140 Reggie Jackson 200.00 90.00 25.00

☐ 141 Pirates Rookies Dave Cash Johnny Jeter	1.00	.45	.13
☐ 142 Fritz Peterson	.80	.35	.10
☐ 143 Phil Gagliano	.80	.35	.10
☐ 144 Ray Culp	.80	.35	.10
☐ 145 Rico Carty	1.00	.45	.13
☐ 146 Danny Murphy	.80	.35	.10
☐ 147 Angel Hermoso	.80	.35	.10
☐ 148 Earl Weaver MG	2.50	1.15	.30
☐ 149 Billy Champion	.80	.35	.10
☐ 150 Harmon Killebrew	8.50	3.80	1.05
☐ 151 Dave Roberts	.80	.35	.10
☐ 152 Ike Brown	.80	.35	.10
☐ 153 Gary Gentry	.80	.35	.10
☐ 154 Senators Rookies Jim Miles Jan Dukes	.80	.35	.10
☐ 155 Denis Menke	.80	.35	.10
☐ 156 Eddie Fisher	.80	.35	.10
☐ 157 Manny Mota	1.00	.45	.13
☐ 158 Jerry McNertney	.80	.35	.10
☐ 159 Tommy Helms	1.00	.45	.13
☐ 160 Phil Niekro	5.00	2.30	.60
☐ 161 Richie Scheinblum	.80	.35	.10
☐ 162 Jerry Johnson	.80	.35	.10
☐ 163 Syd O'Brien	.80	.35	.10
☐ 164 Ty Cline	.80	.35	.10
☐ 165 Ed Kirkpatrick	.80	.35	.10
☐ 166 Al Oliver	2.50	1.15	.30
☐ 167 Bill Burbach	.80	.35	.10
☐ 168 Dave Watkins	.80	.35	.10
☐ 169 Tom Hall	.80	.35	.10
☐ 170 Billy Williams	7.50	3.40	.95
☐ 171 Jim Nash	.80	.35	.10
☐ 172 Braves Rookies Garry Hill Ralph Garr	2.50	1.15	.30
☐ 173 Jim Hicks	.80	.35	.10
☐ 174 Ted Sizemore	1.00	.45	.13
☐ 175 Dick Bosman	.80	.35	.10
☐ 176 Jim Ray Hart	1.00	.45	.13
☐ 177 Jim Northrup	1.00	.45	.13
☐ 178 Denny Lemaster	.80	.35	.10
☐ 179 Ivan Murrell	.80	.35	.10
☐ 180 Tommy John	3.00	1.35	.40
☐ 181 Sparky Anderson MG	2.50	1.15	.30
☐ 182 Dick Hall	.80	.35	.10
☐ 183 Jerry Grote	.80	.35	.10
☐ 184 Ray Fosse	.80	.35	.10
☐ 185 Don Mincher	.80	.35	.10
☐ 186 Rick Joseph	.80	.35	.10
☐ 187 Mike Hedlund	.80	.35	.10
☐ 188 Manny Sanguillen	1.00	.45	.13
☐ 189 Yankees Rookies Thurman Munson Dave McDonald	100.00	45.00	12.50
☐ 190 Joe Torre	2.50	1.15	.30
☐ 191 Vicente Romo	.80	.35	.10
☐ 192 Jim Qualls	.80	.35	.10
☐ 193 Mike Wegener	.80	.35	.10
☐ 194 Chuck Manuel	.80	.35	.10
☐ 195 NL Playoff Game 1 Tom Seaver wins opener	12.00	5.50	1.50
☐ 196 NL Playoff Game 2 Mets show muscle (Ken Boswell)	2.25	1.00	.30
☐ 197 NL Playoff Game 3 Nolan Ryan saves the day	20.00	9.00	2.50
☐ 198 NL Playoff Summary Mets celebrate (Nolan Ryan)	8.00	3.60	1.00
☐ 199 AL Playoff Game 1 Orioles win squeaker (Mike Cuellar)	2.25	1.00	.30
☐ 200 AL Playoff Game 2 Boog Powell scores winning run	2.25	1.00	.30
☐ 201 AL Playoff Game 3 Birds wrap it up (Boog Powell and Andy Etchebarren)	2.25	1.00	.30
☐ 202 AL Playoff Summary Orioles celebrate	2.25	1.00	.30
☐ 203 Rudy May	.80	.35	.10
☐ 204 Len Gabrielson	.80	.35	.10
☐ 205 Bert Campaneris	1.00	.45	.13
☐ 206 Clete Boyer	1.00	.45	.13
☐ 207 Tigers Rookies Norman McRae Bob Reed	.80	.35	.10
☐ 208 Fred Gladding	.80	.35	.10
☐ 209 Ken Suarez	.80	.35	.10
☐ 210 Juan Marichal	6.00	2.70	.75
☐ 211 Ted Williams MG	9.00	4.00	1.15
☐ 212 Al Santorini	.80	.35	.10
☐ 213 Andy Etchebarren	.80	.35	.10
☐ 214 Ken Boswell	.80	.35	.10
☐ 215 Reggie Smith	2.00	.90	.25
☐ 216 Chuck Hartenstein	.80	.35	.10
☐ 217 Ron Hansen	.80	.35	.10
☐ 218 Ron Stone	.80	.35	.10
☐ 219 Jerry Kenney	.80	.35	.10
☐ 220 Steve Carlton	35.00	16.00	4.40
☐ 221 Ron Brand	.80	.35	.10
☐ 222 Jim Rooker	1.00	.45	.13
☐ 223 Nate Oliver	.80	.35	.10
☐ 224 Steve Barber	.80	.35	.10
☐ 225 Lee May	1.00	.45	.13
☐ 226 Ron Perranoski	1.00	.45	.13
☐ 227 Astros Rookies John Mayberry Bob Watkins	1.50	.65	.19
☐ 228 Aurelio Rodriguez	1.00	.45	.13
☐ 229 Rich Robertson	.80	.35	.10
☐ 230 Brooks Robinson	12.50	5.75	1.55
☐ 231 Luis Tiant	2.00	.90	.25
☐ 232 Bob Didier	.80	.35	.10
☐ 233 Lew Krausse	.80	.35	.10
☐ 234 Tommy Dean	.80	.35	.10
☐ 235 Mike Epstein	.80	.35	.10
☐ 236 Bob Veale	1.00	.45	.13
☐ 237 Russ Gibson	.80	.35	.10
☐ 238 Jose Laboy	.80	.35	.10
☐ 239 Ken Berry	.80	.35	.10
☐ 240 Fergie Jenkins	10.00	4.50	1.25
☐ 241 Royals Rookies Al Fitzmorris Scott Northey	.80	.35	.10
☐ 242 Walter Alston MG	2.00	.90	.25
☐ 243 Joe Sparma	.80	.35	.10
☐ 244A Checklist 3 (Red bat on front)	5.00	.50	.15
☐ 244B Checklist 3 (Brown bat on front)	5.00	.50	.15
☐ 245 Leo Cardenas	.80	.35	.10
☐ 246 Jim McAndrew	.80	.35	.10
☐ 247 Lou Klimchock	.80	.35	.10
☐ 248 Jesus Alou	.80	.35	.10
☐ 249 Bob Locker	.80	.35	.10
☐ 250 Willie McCovey UER (1963 San Francisci)	10.00	4.50	1.25
☐ 251 Dick Schofield	.80	.35	.10
☐ 252 Lowell Palmer	.80	.35	.10
☐ 253 Ron Woods	.80	.35	.10
☐ 254 Camilo Pascual	1.00	.45	.13
☐ 255 Jim Spencer	.80	.35	.10
☐ 256 Vic Davalillo	.80	.35	.10
☐ 257 Dennis Higgins	.80	.35	.10
☐ 258 Paul Popovich	.80	.35	.10
☐ 259 Tommie Reynolds	.80	.35	.10
☐ 260 Claude Osteen	1.00	.45	.13
☐ 261 Curt Motton	.80	.35	.10
☐ 262 Padres Rookies Jerry Morales Jim Williams	.80	.35	.10
☐ 263 Duane Josephson	1.00	.45	.13
☐ 264 Rich Hebner	1.25	.55	.16
☐ 265 Randy Hundley	1.00	.45	.13
☐ 266 Wally Bunker	1.00	.45	.13
☐ 267 Twins Rookies Herman Hill Paul Ratliff	1.00	.45	.13
☐ 268 Claude Raymond	1.00	.45	.13
☐ 269 Cesar Gutierrez	1.00	.45	.13
☐ 270 Chris Short	1.00	.45	.13
☐ 271 Greg Goossen	1.00	.45	.13
☐ 272 Hector Torres	1.00	.45	.13
☐ 273 Ralph Houk MG	1.25	.55	.16
☐ 274 Gerry Arrigo	1.00	.45	.13
☐ 275 Duke Sims	1.00	.45	.13
☐ 276 Ron Hunt	1.00	.45	.13
☐ 277 Paul Doyle	1.00	.45	.13
☐ 278 Tommie Aaron	1.25	.55	.16
☐ 279 Bill Lee	2.00	.90	.25
☐ 280 Donn Clendenon	1.25	.55	.16
☐ 281 Casey Cox	1.00	.45	.13
☐ 282 Steve Huntz	1.00	.45	.13
☐ 283 Angel Bravo	1.00	.45	.13
☐ 284 Jack Baldschun	1.00	.45	.13
☐ 285 Paul Blair	1.25	.55	.16
☐ 286 Dodgers Rookies Jack Jenkins Bill Buckner	9.00	4.00	1.15
☐ 287 Fred Talbot	1.00	.45	.13

☐ 288 Larry Hisle 1.25 .55 .16
☐ 289 Gene Brabender 1.00 .45 .13
☐ 290 Rod Carew 50.00 23.00 6.25
☐ 291 Leo Durocher MG 2.00 .90 .25
☐ 292 Eddie Leon 1.00 .45 .13
☐ 293 Bob Bailey 1.00 .45 .13
☐ 294 Jose Azcue 1.00 .45 .13
☐ 295 Cecil Upshaw 1.00 .45 .13
☐ 296 Woody Woodward 1.25 .55 .16
☐ 297 Curt Blefary 1.00 .45 .13
☐ 298 Ken Henderson 1.00 .45 .13
☐ 299 Buddy Bradford 1.00 .45 .13
☐ 300 Tom Seaver 110.00 50.00 14.00
☐ 301 Chico Salmon 1.00 .45 .13
☐ 302 Jeff James 1.00 .45 .13
☐ 303 Brant Alyea 1.00 .45 .13
☐ 304 Bill Russell 3.50 1.55 .45
☐ 305 World Series Game 1 2.50 1.15 .30
Don Buford leadoff
homer
☐ 306 World Series Game 2 2.50 1.15 .30
Donn Clendenon's
homer breaks ice
☐ 307 World Series Game 3 2.50 1.15 .30
Tommie Agee's catch
saves the day
☐ 308 World Series Game 4 2.50 1.15 .30
J.C. Martin's bunt
ends deadlock
☐ 309 World Series Game 5 2.50 1.15 .30
Jerry Koosman
shuts door
☐ 310 World Series Summary 4.00 1.80 .50
Mets whoop it up
☐ 311 Dick Green 1.00 .45 .13
☐ 312 Mike Torrez 1.25 .55 .16
☐ 313 Mayo Smith MG 1.00 .45 .13
☐ 314 Bill McCool 1.00 .45 .13
☐ 315 Luis Aparicio 4.50 2.00 .55
☐ 316 Skip Guinn 1.00 .45 .13
☐ 317 Red Sox Rookies 1.25 .55 .16
Billy Conigliaro
Luis Alvarado
☐ 318 Willie Smith 1.00 .45 .13
☐ 319 Clay Dalrymple 1.00 .45 .13
☐ 320 Jim Maloney 1.25 .55 .16
☐ 321 Lou Piniella 2.50 1.15 .30
☐ 322 Luke Walker 1.00 .45 .13
☐ 323 Wayne Comer 1.00 .45 .13
☐ 324 Tony Taylor 1.00 .45 .13
☐ 325 Dave Boswell 1.00 .45 .13
☐ 326 Bill Voss 1.00 .45 .13
☐ 327 Hal King 1.00 .45 .13
☐ 328 George Brunet 1.00 .45 .13
☐ 329 Chris Cannizzaro 1.00 .45 .13
☐ 330 Lou Brock 10.00 4.50 1.25
☐ 331 Chuck Dobson 1.00 .45 .13
☐ 332 Bobby Wine 1.00 .45 .13
☐ 333 Bobby Murcer 2.00 .90 .25
☐ 334 Phil Regan 1.25 .55 .16
☐ 335 Bill Freehan 1.25 .55 .16
☐ 336 Del Unser 1.00 .45 .13
☐ 337 Mike McCormick 1.25 .55 .16
☐ 338 Paul Schaal 1.00 .45 .13
☐ 339 Johnny Edwards 1.00 .45 .13
☐ 340 Tony Conigliaro 2.00 .90 .25
☐ 341 Bill Sudakis 1.00 .45 .13
☐ 342 Wilbur Wood 1.25 .55 .16
☐ 343A Checklist 4 5.00 .50 .15
(Red bat on front)
☐ 343B Checklist 4 5.00 .50 .15
(Brown bat on front)
☐ 344 Marcelino Lopez 1.00 .45 .13
☐ 345 Al Ferrara 1.00 .45 .13
☐ 346 Red Schoendienst MG 2.00 .90 .25
☐ 347 Russ Snyder 1.00 .45 .13
☐ 348 Mets Rookies 1.25 .55 .16
Mike Jorgensen
Jesse Hudson
☐ 349 Steve Hamilton 1.00 .45 .13
☐ 350 Roberto Clemente 50.00 23.00 6.25
☐ 351 Tom Murphy 1.00 .45 .13
☐ 352 Bob Barton 1.00 .45 .13
☐ 353 Stan Williams 1.00 .45 .13
☐ 354 Amos Otis 1.25 .55 .16
☐ 355 Doug Rader 1.25 .55 .16
☐ 356 Fred Lasher 1.00 .45 .13
☐ 357 Bob Burda 1.00 .45 .13
☐ 358 Pedro Borbon 1.00 .45 .13
☐ 359 Phil Roof 1.00 .45 .13
☐ 360 Curt Flood 1.75 .80 .22
☐ 361 Ray Jarvis 1.00 .45 .13
☐ 362 Joe Hague 1.00 .45 .13
☐ 363 Tom Shopay 1.00 .45 .13
☐ 364 Dan McGinn 1.00 .45 .13
☐ 365 Zoilo Versalles 1.00 .45 .13
☐ 366 Barry Moore 1.00 .45 .13
☐ 367 Mike Lum 1.00 .45 .13
☐ 368 Ed Herrmann 1.00 .45 .13
☐ 369 Alan Foster 1.00 .45 .13
☐ 370 Tommy Harper 1.25 .55 .16
☐ 371 Rod Gaspar 1.00 .45 .13
☐ 372 Dave Giusti 1.25 .55 .16
☐ 373 Roy White 1.50 .65 .19
☐ 374 Tommie Sisk 1.25 .55 .16
☐ 375 Johnny Callison 1.50 .65 .19
☐ 376 Lefty Phillips MG 1.25 .55 .16
☐ 377 Bill Butler 1.25 .55 .16
☐ 378 Jim Davenport 1.25 .55 .16
☐ 379 Tom Tischinski 1.25 .55 .16
☐ 380 Tony Perez 9.00 4.00 1.15
☐ 381 Athletics Rookies 1.25 .55 .16
Bobby Brooks
Mike Olivo
☐ 382 Jack DiLauro 1.25 .55 .16
☐ 383 Mickey Stanley 1.50 .65 .19
☐ 384 Gary Neibauer 1.25 .55 .16
☐ 385 George Scott 1.50 .65 .19
☐ 386 Bill Dillman 1.25 .55 .16
☐ 387 Baltimore Orioles 2.50 1.15 .30
Team Card
☐ 388 Byron Browne 1.25 .55 .16
☐ 389 Jim Shellenback 1.25 .55 .16
☐ 390 Willie Davis 1.50 .65 .19
☐ 391 Larry Brown 1.25 .55 .16
☐ 392 Walt Hriniak 1.25 .55 .16
☐ 393 John Gelnar 1.25 .55 .16
☐ 394 Gil Hodges MG 4.50 2.00 .55
☐ 395 Walt Williams 1.25 .55 .16
☐ 396 Steve Blass 1.50 .65 .19
☐ 397 Roger Repoz 1.25 .55 .16
☐ 398 Bill Stoneman 1.25 .55 .16
☐ 399 New York Yankees 2.50 1.15 .30
Team Card
☐ 400 Denny McLain 2.00 .90 .25
☐ 401 Giants Rookies 1.25 .55 .16
John Harrell
Bernie Williams
☐ 402 Ellie Rodriguez 1.25 .55 .16
☐ 403 Jim Bunning 3.00 1.35 .40
☐ 404 Rich Reese 1.25 .55 .16
☐ 405 Bill Hands 1.25 .55 .16
☐ 406 Mike Andrews 1.25 .55 .16
☐ 407 Bob Watson 1.50 .65 .19
☐ 408 Paul Lindblad 1.25 .55 .16
☐ 409 Bob Tolan 1.50 .65 .19
☐ 410 Boog Powell 3.50 1.55 .45
☐ 411 Los Angeles Dodgers 2.50 1.15 .30
Team Card
☐ 412 Larry Burchart 1.25 .55 .16
☐ 413 Sonny Jackson 1.25 .55 .16
☐ 414 Paul Edmondson 1.25 .55 .16
☐ 415 Julian Javier 1.50 .65 .19
☐ 416 Joe Verbanic 1.25 .55 .16
☐ 417 John Bateman 1.25 .55 .16
☐ 418 John Donaldson 1.25 .55 .16
☐ 419 Ron Taylor 1.25 .55 .16
☐ 420 Ken McMullen 1.50 .65 .19
☐ 421 Pat Dobson 1.50 .65 .19
☐ 422 Royals Team 2.50 1.15 .30
☐ 423 Jerry May 1.25 .55 .16
☐ 424 Mike Kilkenny 1.25 .55 .16
(Inconsistent design,
card number in
white circle)
☐ 425 Bobby Bonds 7.50 3.40 .95
☐ 426 Bill Rigney MG 1.25 .55 .16
☐ 427 Fred Norman 1.25 .55 .16
☐ 428 Don Buford 1.25 .55 .16
☐ 429 Cubs Rookies 1.25 .55 .16
Randy Bobb
Jim Cosman
☐ 430 Andy Messersmith 1.50 .65 .19
☐ 431 Ron Swoboda 1.50 .65 .19
☐ 432A Checklist 5 5.00 .50 .15
("Baseball" in
yellow letters)
☐ 432B Checklist 5 5.00 .50 .15
("Baseball" in
white letters)
☐ 433 Ron Bryant 1.25 .55 .16
☐ 434 Felipe Alou 1.75 .80 .22
☐ 435 Nelson Briles 1.50 .65 .19
☐ 436 Philadelphia Phillies 2.50 1.15 .30
Team Card
☐ 437 Danny Cater 1.25 .55 .16

Card			
☐ 438 Pat Jarvis	1.25	.55	.16
☐ 439 Lee Maye	1.25	.55	.16
☐ 440 Bill Mazeroski	2.50	1.15	.30
☐ 441 John O'Donoghue	1.25	.55	.16
☐ 442 Gene Mauch MG	1.50	.65	.19
☐ 443 Al Jackson	1.25	.55	.16
☐ 444 White Sox Rookies	1.25	.55	.16
Billy Farmer			
John Matias			
☐ 445 Vada Pinson	2.00	.90	.25
☐ 446 Billy Grabarkewitz	1.25	.55	.16
☐ 447 Lee Stange	1.25	.55	.16
☐ 448 Houston Astros	2.50	1.15	.30
Team Card			
☐ 449 Jim Palmer	25.00	11.50	3.10
☐ 450 Willie McCovey AS	5.50	2.50	.70
☐ 451 Boog Powell AS	1.50	.65	.19
☐ 452 Felix Millan AS	1.50	.65	.19
☐ 453 Rod Carew AS	7.50	3.40	.95
☐ 454 Ron Santo AS	2.50	1.15	.30
☐ 455 Brooks Robinson AS	5.50	2.50	.70
☐ 456 Don Kessinger AS	1.50	.65	.19
☐ 457 Rico Petrocelli AS	1.50	.65	.19
☐ 458 Pete Rose AS	14.00	6.25	1.75
☐ 459 Reggie Jackson AS	27.00	12.00	3.40
☐ 460 Matty Alou AS	2.25	1.00	.30
☐ 461 Carl Yastrzemski AS	12.00	5.50	1.50
☐ 462 Hank Aaron AS	15.00	6.75	1.90
☐ 463 Frank Robinson AS	7.50	3.40	.95
☐ 464 Johnny Bench AS	15.00	6.75	1.90
☐ 465 Bill Freehan AS	2.25	1.00	.30
☐ 466 Juan Marichal AS	4.50	2.00	.55
☐ 467 Denny McLain AS	2.25	1.00	.30
☐ 468 Jerry Koosman AS	2.25	1.00	.30
☐ 469 Sam McDowell AS	2.25	1.00	.30
☐ 470 Willie Stargell	11.00	4.90	1.40
☐ 471 Chris Zachary	1.50	.65	.19
☐ 472 Braves Team	3.00	1.35	.40
☐ 473 Don Bryant	1.50	.65	.19
☐ 474 Dick Kelley	1.50	.65	.19
☐ 475 Dick McAuliffe	2.00	.90	.25
☐ 476 Don Shaw	1.50	.65	.19
☐ 477 Orioles Rookies	1.50	.65	.19
Al Severinsen			
Roger Freed			
☐ 478 Bobby Heise	1.50	.65	.19
☐ 479 Dick Woodson	1.50	.65	.19
☐ 480 Glenn Beckert	2.00	.90	.25
☐ 481 Jose Tartabull	2.00	.90	.25
☐ 482 Tom Hilgendorf	1.50	.65	.19
☐ 483 Gail Hopkins	1.50	.65	.19
☐ 484 Gary Nolan	2.00	.90	.25
☐ 485 Jay Johnstone	2.00	.90	.25
☐ 486 Terry Harmon	1.50	.65	.19
☐ 487 Cisco Carlos	1.50	.65	.19
☐ 488 J.C. Martin	1.50	.65	.19
☐ 489 Eddie Kasko MG	1.50	.65	.19
☐ 490 Bill Singer	2.00	.90	.25
☐ 491 Graig Nettles	6.00	2.70	.75
☐ 492 Astros Rookies	1.50	.65	.19
Keith Lampard			
Scipio Spinks			
☐ 493 Lindy McDaniel	2.00	.90	.25
☐ 494 Larry Stahl	1.50	.65	.19
☐ 495 Dave Morehead	1.50	.65	.19
☐ 496 Steve Whitaker	1.50	.65	.19
☐ 497 Eddie Watt	1.50	.65	.19
☐ 498 Al Weis	1.50	.65	.19
☐ 499 Skip Lockwood	1.50	.65	.19
☐ 500 Hank Aaron	60.00	27.00	7.50
☐ 501 Chicago White Sox	3.00	1.35	.40
Team Card			
☐ 502 Rollie Fingers	40.00	18.00	5.00
☐ 503 Dal Maxvill	1.50	.65	.19
☐ 504 Don Pavletich	1.50	.65	.19
☐ 505 Ken Holtzman	2.00	.90	.25
☐ 506 Ed Stroud	1.50	.65	.19
☐ 507 Pat Corrales	2.00	.90	.25
☐ 508 Joe Niekro	2.00	.90	.25
☐ 509 Montreal Expos	3.00	1.35	.40
Team Card			
☐ 510 Tony Oliva	3.00	1.35	.40
☐ 511 Joe Hoerner	1.50	.65	.19
☐ 512 Billy Harris	1.50	.65	.19
☐ 513 Preston Gomez MG	1.50	.65	.19
☐ 514 Steve Hovley	1.50	.65	.19
☐ 515 Don Wilson	2.00	.90	.25
☐ 516 Yankees Rookies	1.50	.65	.19
John Ellis			
Jim Lyttle			
☐ 517 Joe Gibbon	1.50	.65	.19
☐ 518 Bill Melton	1.50	.65	.19
☐ 519 Don McMahon	1.50	.65	.19
☐ 520 Willie Horton	2.00	.90	.25
☐ 521 Cal Koonce	1.50	.65	.19
☐ 522 Angels Team	3.00	1.35	.40
☐ 523 Jose Pena	1.50	.65	.19
☐ 524 Alvin Dark MG	2.00	.90	.25
☐ 525 Jerry Adair	1.50	.65	.19
☐ 526 Ron Herbel	1.50	.65	.19
☐ 527 Don Bosch	1.50	.65	.19
☐ 528 Elrod Hendricks	1.50	.65	.19
☐ 529 Bob Aspromonte	1.50	.65	.19
☐ 530 Bob Gibson	15.00	6.75	1.90
☐ 531 Ron Clark	1.50	.65	.19
☐ 532 Danny Murtaugh MG	2.00	.90	.25
☐ 533 Buzz Stephen	1.50	.65	.19
☐ 534 Minnesota Twins	3.00	1.35	.40
Team Card			
☐ 535 Andy Kosco	1.50	.65	.19
☐ 536 Mike Kekich	1.50	.65	.19
☐ 537 Joe Morgan	15.00	6.75	1.90
☐ 538 Bob Humphreys	1.50	.65	.19
☐ 539 Phillies Rookies	5.00	2.30	.60
Denny Doyle			
Larry Bowa			
☐ 540 Gary Peters	1.50	.65	.19
☐ 541 Bill Heath	1.50	.65	.19
☐ 542 Checklist 6	5.00	.50	.15
☐ 543 Clyde Wright	1.50	.65	.19
☐ 544 Cincinnati Reds	3.00	1.35	.40
Team Card			
☐ 545 Ken Harrelson	2.00	.90	.25
☐ 546 Ron Reed	1.50	.65	.19
☐ 547 Rick Monday	3.50	1.55	.45
☐ 548 Howie Reed	3.00	1.35	.40
☐ 549 St. Louis Cardinals	6.00	2.70	.75
Team Card			
☐ 550 Frank Howard	5.00	2.30	.60
☐ 551 Dock Ellis	3.50	1.55	.45
☐ 552 Royals Rookies	3.00	1.35	.40
Don O'Riley			
Dennis Paepke			
Fred Rico			
☐ 553 Jim Lefebvre	3.50	1.55	.45
☐ 554 Tom Timmermann	3.00	1.35	.40
☐ 555 Orlando Cepeda	5.50	2.50	.70
☐ 556 Dave Bristol MG	3.00	1.35	.40
☐ 557 Ed Kranepool	3.50	1.55	.45
☐ 558 Vern Fuller	3.00	1.35	.40
☐ 559 Tommy Davis	3.50	1.55	.45
☐ 560 Gaylord Perry	15.00	6.75	1.90
☐ 561 Tom McCraw	3.00	1.35	.40
☐ 562 Ted Abernathy	3.00	1.35	.40
☐ 563 Boston Red Sox	6.00	2.70	.75
Team Card			
☐ 564 Johnny Briggs	3.00	1.35	.40
☐ 565 Jim Hunter	15.00	6.75	1.90
☐ 566 Gene Alley	3.50	1.55	.45
☐ 567 Bob Oliver	3.00	1.35	.40
☐ 568 Stan Bahnsen	3.50	1.55	.45
☐ 569 Cookie Rojas	3.50	1.55	.45
☐ 570 Jim Fregosi	3.50	1.55	.45
☐ 571 Jim Brewer	3.00	1.35	.40
☐ 572 Frank Quilici MG	3.00	1.35	.40
☐ 573 Padres Rookies	3.00	1.35	.40
Mike Corkins			
Rafael Robles			
Ron Slocum			
☐ 574 Bobby Bolin	3.00	1.35	.40
☐ 575 Cleon Jones	3.50	1.55	.45
☐ 576 Milt Pappas	3.50	1.55	.45
☐ 577 Bernie Allen	3.00	1.35	.40
☐ 578 Tom Griffin	3.00	1.35	.40
☐ 579 Detroit Tigers	6.00	2.70	.75
Team Card			
☐ 580 Pete Rose	65.00	29.00	8.25
☐ 581 Tom Satriano	3.00	1.35	.40
☐ 582 Mike Paul	3.00	1.35	.40
☐ 583 Hal Lanier	3.00	1.35	.40
☐ 584 Al Downing	3.50	1.55	.45
☐ 585 Rusty Staub	5.00	2.30	.60
☐ 586 Rickey Clark	3.00	1.35	.40
☐ 587 Jose Arcia	3.00	1.35	.40
☐ 588A Checklist 7 ERR	8.00	.80	.24
(666 Adolfo)			
☐ 588B Checklist 7 COR	5.00	.50	.15
(666 Adolpho)			
☐ 589 Joe Keough	3.00	1.35	.40
☐ 590 Mike Cuellar	3.50	1.55	.45
☐ 591 Mike Ryan UER	3.00	1.35	.40
(Pitching Record			
header on card back)			
☐ 592 Daryl Patterson	3.00	1.35	.40
☐ 593 Chicago Cubs	6.00	2.70	.75
Team Card			

594 Jake Gibbs	3.00	1.35	.40
595 Maury Wills	4.50	2.00	.55
596 Mike Hershberger	3.00	1.35	.40
597 Sonny Siebert	3.00	1.35	.40
598 Joe Pepitone	3.50	1.55	.45
599 Senators Rookies	3.50	1.55	.45
Dick Stelmaszek			
Gene Martin			
Dick Such			
600 Willie Mays	85.00	38.00	10.50
601 Pete Richert	3.00	1.35	.40
602 Ted Savage	3.00	1.35	.40
603 Ray Oyler	3.00	1.35	.40
604 Clarence Gaston	4.00	1.80	.50
605 Rick Wise	3.50	1.55	.45
606 Chico Ruiz	3.00	1.35	.40
607 Gary Waslewski	3.00	1.35	.40
608 Pittsburgh Pirates	6.00	2.70	.75
Team Card			
609 Buck Martinez	4.00	1.80	.50
(Inconsistent design,			
card number in			
white circle)			
610 Jerry Koosman	5.00	2.30	.60
611 Norm Cash	5.00	2.30	.60
612 Jim Hickman	3.50	1.55	.45
613 Dave Baldwin	3.00	1.35	.40
614 Mike Shannon	3.50	1.55	.45
615 Mark Belanger	3.50	1.55	.45
616 Jim Merritt	3.00	1.35	.40
617 Jim French	3.00	1.35	.40
618 Billy Wynne	3.00	1.35	.40
619 Norm Miller	3.00	1.35	.40
620 Jim Perry	5.00	2.30	.60
621 Braves Rookies	30.00	13.50	3.80
Mike McQueen			
Darrell Evans			
Rick Kester			
622 Don Sutton	15.00	6.75	1.90
623 Horace Clarke	3.00	1.35	.40
624 Clyde King MG	3.00	1.35	.40
625 Dean Chance	3.00	1.35	.40
626 Dave Ricketts	3.00	1.35	.40
627 Gary Wagner	3.00	1.35	.40
628 Wayne Garrett	3.00	1.35	.40
629 Merv Rettenmund	3.00	1.35	.40
630 Ernie Banks	40.00	18.00	5.00
631 Oakland Athletics	6.00	2.70	.75
Team Card			
632 Gary Sutherland	3.00	1.35	.40
633 Roger Nelson	3.00	1.35	.40
634 Bud Harrelson	6.50	2.90	.80
635 Bob Allison	6.50	2.90	.80
636 Jim Stewart	6.00	2.70	.75
637 Cleveland Indians	12.00	5.50	1.50
Team Card			
638 Frank Bertaina	6.00	2.70	.75
639 Dave Campbell	6.00	2.70	.75
640 Al Kaline	50.00	23.00	6.25
641 Al McBean	6.00	2.70	.75
642 Angels Rookies	6.00	2.70	.75
Greg Garrett			
Gordon Lund			
Jarvis Tatum			
643 Jose Pagan	6.00	2.70	.75
644 Gerry Nyman	6.00	2.70	.75
645 Don Money	7.00	3.10	.85
646 Jim Britton	6.00	2.70	.75
647 Tom Matchick	6.00	2.70	.75
648 Larry Haney	6.00	2.70	.75
649 Jimmie Hall	6.00	2.70	.75
650 Sam McDowell	7.00	3.10	.85
651 Jim Gosger	6.00	2.70	.75
652 Rich Rollins	6.00	2.70	.75
653 Moe Drabowsky	6.00	2.70	.75
654 NL Rookies	7.00	3.10	.85
Oscar Gamble			
Boots Day			
Angel Mangual			
655 John Roseboro	7.00	3.10	.85
656 Jim Hardin	6.00	2.70	.75
657 San Diego Padres	12.00	5.50	1.50
Team Card			
658 Ken Tatum	6.00	2.70	.75
659 Pete Ward	6.00	2.70	.75
660 Johnny Bench	180.00	80.00	23.00
661 Jerry Robertson	6.00	2.70	.75
662 Frank Lucchesi MG	6.00	2.70	.75
663 Tito Francona	6.00	2.70	.75
664 Bob Robertson	6.00	2.70	.75
665 Jim Lonborg	7.00	3.10	.85
666 Adolpho Phillips	6.00	2.70	.75
667 Bob Meyer	6.00	2.70	.75
668 Bob Tillman	6.00	2.70	.75
669 White Sox Rookies	6.50	2.90	.80
Bart Johnson			
Dan Lazar			
Mickey Scott			
670 Ron Santo	8.50	3.80	1.05
671 Jim Campanis	6.00	2.70	.75
672 Leon McFadden	6.00	2.70	.75
673 Ted Uhlaender	6.00	2.70	.75
674 Dave Leonhard	6.00	2.70	.75
675 Jose Cardenal	7.00	3.10	.85
676 Washington Senators	12.00	5.50	1.50
Team Card			
677 Woodie Fryman	6.00	2.70	.75
678 Dave Duncan	6.50	2.90	.80
679 Ray Sadecki	6.00	2.70	.75
680 Rico Petrocelli	7.00	3.10	.85
681 Bob Garibaldi	6.00	2.70	.75
682 Dalton Jones	6.00	2.70	.75
683 Reds Rookies	8.50	3.80	1.05
Vern Geishert			
Hal McRae			
Wayne Simpson			
684 Jack Fisher	6.00	2.70	.75
685 Tom Haller	6.00	2.70	.75
686 Jackie Hernandez	6.00	2.70	.75
687 Bob Priddy	6.00	2.70	.75
688 Ted Kubiak	6.00	2.70	.75
689 Frank Tepedino	6.00	2.70	.75
690 Ron Fairly	7.00	3.10	.85
691 Joe Grzenda	6.00	2.70	.75
692 Duffy Dyer	6.00	2.70	.75
693 Bob Johnson	6.00	2.70	.75
694 Gary Ross	6.00	2.70	.75
695 Bobby Knoop	6.00	2.70	.75
696 San Francisco Giants	12.00	5.50	1.50
Team Card			
697 Jim Hannan	6.00	2.70	.75
698 Tom Tresh	8.00	3.60	1.00
699 Hank Aguirre	6.00	2.70	.75
700 Frank Robinson	45.00	20.00	5.75
701 Jack Billingham	6.00	2.70	.75
702 AL Rookies	6.00	2.70	.75
Bob Johnson			
Ron Klimkowski			
Bill Zepp			
703 Lou Marone	6.00	2.70	.75
704 Frank Baker	6.00	2.70	.75
705 Tony Cloninger UER	6.00	2.70	.75
(Batter headings			
on card back)			
706 John McNamara MG	6.00	2.70	.75
707 Kevin Collins	7.00	3.10	.85
708 Jose Santiago	6.00	2.70	.75
709 Mike Fiore	6.00	2.70	.75
710 Felix Millan	6.00	2.70	.75
711 Ed Brinkman	6.00	2.70	.75
712 Nolan Ryan	550.00	250.00	70.00
713 Seattle Pilots	25.00	11.50	3.10
Team Card			
714 Al Spangler	6.00	2.70	.75
715 Mickey Lolich	7.50	3.40	.95
716 Cardinals Rookies	7.00	3.10	.85
Sal Campisi			
Reggie Cleveland			
Santiago Guzman			
717 Tom Phoebus	6.00	2.70	.75
718 Ed Spiezio	6.00	2.70	.75
719 Jim Roland	6.00	2.70	.75
720 Rick Reichardt	7.50	3.40	.95

1971 Topps

The cards in this 752-card set measure 2 1/2" by 3 1/2". The 1971 Topps set is a challenge to complete in strict mint condition because the black obverse border is easily scratched and damaged. An unusual feature of this set is that the player is also pictured in black and white on the back of the card. Featured subsets within this set include League Leaders (61-72), Playoffs cards (195-202), and World Series cards (327-332). Cards 524-643 and the last series (644-752) are somewhat scarce. The last series was printed in two sheets of 132. On the printing sheets 44 cards were printed in 50 percent greater quantity than the

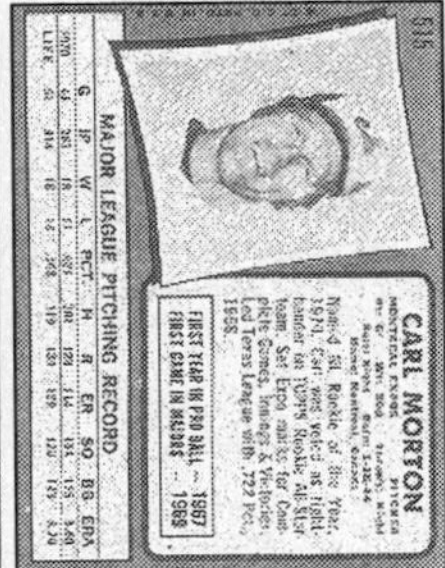

other 66 cards. These 66 (slightly) shorter-printed numbers are identified in the checklist below by SP. The key Rookie Cards in this set are the multi-player Rookie Card of Dusty Baker and Don Baylor and the individual cards of Bert Blyleven, Dave Concepcion, Steve Garvey, and Ted Simmons.

	NRMT-MT	EXC	G-VG
COMPLETE SET (752)	2200.00	1000.00	275.00
COMMON PLAYER (1-132)	.90	.40	.11
COMMON PLAYER (133-263)	1.00	.45	.13
COMMON PLAYER (264-393)	1.25	.55	.16
COMMON PLAYER (394-523)	2.00	.90	.25
COMMON PLAYER (524-643)	4.00	1.80	.50
COMMON PLAYER (644-752)	5.00	2.30	.60

	NRMT-MT	EXC	G-VG
☐ 1 Baltimore Orioles	12.50	2.50	.75
Team Card			
☐ 2 Dock Ellis	1.00	.45	.13
☐ 3 Dick McAuliffe	1.00	.45	.13
☐ 4 Vic Davalillo	.90	.40	.11
☐ 5 Thurman Munson	40.00	18.00	5.00
☐ 6 Ed Spiezio	.90	.40	.11
☐ 7 Jim Holt	.90	.40	.11
☐ 8 Mike McQueen	.90	.40	.11
☐ 9 George Scott	1.00	.45	.13
☐ 10 Claude Osteen	1.00	.45	.13
☐ 11 Elliott Maddox	1.00	.45	.13
☐ 12 Johnny Callison	1.00	.45	.13
☐ 13 White Sox Rookies	.90	.40	.11
Charlie Brinkman			
Dick Moloney			
☐ 14 Dave Concepcion	24.00	11.00	3.00
☐ 15 Andy Messersmith	1.00	.45	.13
☐ 16 Ken Singleton	3.50	1.55	.45
☐ 17 Billy Sorrell	.90	.40	.11
☐ 18 Norm Miller	.90	.40	.11
☐ 19 Skip Pitlock	.90	.40	.11
☐ 20 Reggie Jackson	135.00	60.00	17.00
☐ 21 Dan McGinn	.90	.40	.11
☐ 22 Phil Roof	.90	.40	.11
☐ 23 Oscar Gamble	1.00	.45	.13
☐ 24 Rich Hand	.90	.40	.11
☐ 25 Clarence Gaston	2.00	.90	.25
☐ 26 Bert Blyleven	65.00	29.00	8.25
☐ 27 Pirates Rookies	1.25	.55	.16
Fred Cambria			
Gene Clines			
☐ 28 Ron Klimkowski	.90	.40	.11
☐ 29 Don Buford	.90	.40	.11
☐ 30 Phil Niekro	5.00	2.30	.60
☐ 31 Eddie Kasko MG	.90	.40	.11
☐ 32 Jerry DaVanon	.90	.40	.11
☐ 33 Del Unser	.90	.40	.11
☐ 34 Sandy Vance	.90	.40	.11
☐ 35 Lou Piniella	2.00	.90	.25
☐ 36 Dean Chance	.90	.40	.11
☐ 37 Rich McKinney	.90	.40	.11
☐ 38 Jim Colborn	.90	.40	.11
☐ 39 Tiger Rookies	1.50	.65	.19
Lerrin LaGrow			
Gene Lamont			
☐ 40 Lee May	1.00	.45	.13
☐ 41 Rick Austin	.90	.40	.11
☐ 42 Boots Day	.90	.40	.11
☐ 43 Steve Kealey	.90	.40	.11
☐ 44 Johnny Edwards	.90	.40	.11
☐ 45 Jim Hunter	7.00	3.10	.85
☐ 46 Dave Campbell	.90	.40	.11
☐ 47 Johnny Jeter	.90	.40	.11
☐ 48 Dave Baldwin	.90	.40	.11
☐ 49 Don Money	.90	.40	.11
☐ 50 Willie McCovey	10.00	4.50	1.25
☐ 51 Steve Kline	.90	.40	.11
☐ 52 Braves Rookies	1.25	.55	.16
Oscar Brown			
Earl Williams			
☐ 53 Paul Blair	1.00	.45	.13
☐ 54 Checklist 1	5.00	2.30	.60
☐ 55 Steve Carlton	33.00	15.00	4.10
☐ 56 Duane Josephson	.90	.40	.11
☐ 57 Von Joshua	.90	.40	.11
☐ 58 Bill Lee	1.00	.45	.13
☐ 59 Gene Mauch MG	1.00	.45	.13
☐ 60 Dick Bosman	.90	.40	.11
☐ 61 AL Batting Leaders	3.50	1.55	.45
Alex Johnson			
Carl Yastrzemski			
Tony Oliva			
☐ 62 NL Batting Leaders	2.50	1.15	.30
Rico Carty			
Joe Torre			
Manny Sanguillen			
☐ 63 AL RBI Leaders	2.50	1.15	.30
Frank Howard			
Tony Conigliaro			
Boog Powell			
☐ 64 NL RBI Leaders	4.00	1.80	.50
Johnny Bench			
Tony Perez			
Billy Williams			
☐ 65 AL HR Leaders	3.50	1.55	.45
Frank Howard			
Harmon Killebrew			
Carl Yastrzemski			
☐ 66 NL HR Leaders	4.25	1.90	.55
Johnny Bench			
Billy Williams			
Tony Perez			
☐ 67 AL ERA Leaders	3.00	1.35	.40
Diego Segui			
Jim Palmer			
Clyde Wright			
☐ 68 NL ERA Leaders	3.00	1.35	.40
Tom Seaver			
Wayne Simpson			
Luke Walker			
☐ 69 AL Pitching Leaders	2.50	1.15	.30
Mike Cuellar			
Dave McNally			
Jim Perry			
☐ 70 NL Pitching Leaders	4.25	1.90	.55
Bob Gibson			
Gaylord Perry			
Fergie Jenkins			
☐ 71 AL Strikeout Leaders	2.50	1.15	.30
Sam McDowell			
Mickey Lolich			
Bob Johnson			
☐ 72 NL Strikeout Leaders	5.00	2.30	.60
Tom Seaver			
Bob Gibson			
Fergie Jenkins			
☐ 73 George Brunet	.90	.40	.11
☐ 74 Twins Rookies	.90	.40	.11
Pete Hamm			
Jim Nettles			
☐ 75 Gary Nolan	1.00	.45	.13
☐ 76 Ted Savage	.90	.40	.11
☐ 77 Mike Compton	.90	.40	.11
☐ 78 Jim Spencer	.90	.40	.11
☐ 79 Wade Blasingame	.90	.40	.11
☐ 80 Bill Melton	.90	.40	.11
☐ 81 Felix Millan	.90	.40	.11
☐ 82 Casey Cox	.90	.40	.11
☐ 83 Met Rookies	1.25	.55	.16
Tim Foli			
Randy Bobb			
☐ 84 Marcel Lachemann	1.50	.65	.19
☐ 85 Billy Grabarkewitz	.90	.40	.11
☐ 86 Mike Kilkenny	.90	.40	.11
☐ 87 Jack Heidemann	.90	.40	.11
☐ 88 Hal King	.90	.40	.11
☐ 89 Ken Brett	.90	.40	.11
☐ 90 Joe Pepitone	1.00	.45	.13
☐ 91 Bob Lemon MG	1.75	.80	.22
☐ 92 Fred Wenz	.90	.40	.11
☐ 93 Senators Rookies	.90	.40	.11
Norm McRae			
Denny Riddleberger			
☐ 94 Don Hahn	.90	.40	.11
☐ 95 Luis Tiant	2.00	.90	.25
☐ 96 Joe Hague	.90	.40	.11
☐ 97 Floyd Wicker	.90	.40	.11
☐ 98 Joe Decker	.90	.40	.11

☐ 99 Mark Belanger	1.00	.45	.13
☐ 100 Pete Rose	45.00	20.00	5.75
☐ 101 Les Cain	.90	.40	.11
☐ 102 Astros Rookies Ken Forsch Larry Howard	1.00	.45	.13
☐ 103 Rich Severson	.90	.40	.11
☐ 104 Dan Frisella	.90	.40	.11
☐ 105 Tony Conigliaro	1.75	.80	.22
☐ 106 Tom Dukes	.90	.40	.11
☐ 107 Roy Foster	.90	.40	.11
☐ 108 John Cumberland	.90	.40	.11
☐ 109 Steve Hovley	.90	.40	.11
☐ 110 Bill Mazeroski	2.00	.90	.25
☐ 111 Yankee Rookies Loyd Colson Bobby Mitchell	.90	.40	.11
☐ 112 Manny Mota	1.00	.45	.13
☐ 113 Jerry Crider	.90	.40	.11
☐ 114 Billy Conigliaro	1.00	.45	.13
☐ 115 Donn Clendenon	1.00	.45	.13
☐ 116 Ken Sanders	.90	.40	.11
☐ 117 Ted Simmons	24.00	11.00	3.00
☐ 118 Cookie Rojas	1.00	.45	.13
☐ 119 Frank Lucchesi MG	.90	.40	.11
☐ 120 Willie Horton	1.00	.45	.13
☐ 121 Cubs Rookies Jim Dunegan Roe Skidmore	.90	.40	.11
☐ 122 Eddie Watt	.90	.40	.11
☐ 123A Checklist 2 (Card number at bottom right)	5.00	2.30	.60
☐ 123B Checklist 2 (Card number centered)	5.00	2.30	.60
☐ 124 Don Gullett	1.50	.65	.19
☐ 125 Ray Fosse	1.00	.45	.13
☐ 126 Danny Coombs	.90	.40	.11
☐ 127 Danny Thompson	1.00	.45	.13
☐ 128 Frank Johnson	.90	.40	.11
☐ 129 Aurelio Monteagudo	.90	.40	.11
☐ 130 Denis Menke	.90	.40	.11
☐ 131 Curt Blefary	.90	.40	.11
☐ 132 Jose Laboy	.90	.40	.11
☐ 133 Mickey Lolich	2.00	.90	.25
☐ 134 Jose Arcia	1.00	.45	.13
☐ 135 Rick Monday	1.25	.55	.16
☐ 136 Duffy Dyer	1.00	.45	.13
☐ 137 Marcelino Lopez	1.00	.45	.13
☐ 138 Phillies Rookies Joe Lis Willie Montanez	1.25	.55	.16
☐ 139 Paul Casanova	1.00	.45	.13
☐ 140 Gaylord Perry	8.50	3.80	1.05
☐ 141 Frank Quilici	1.00	.45	.13
☐ 142 Mack Jones	1.00	.45	.13
☐ 143 Steve Blass	1.25	.55	.16
☐ 144 Jackie Hernandez	1.00	.45	.13
☐ 145 Bill Singer	1.25	.55	.16
☐ 146 Ralph Houk MG	1.25	.55	.16
☐ 147 Bob Priddy	1.00	.45	.13
☐ 148 John Mayberry	1.25	.55	.16
☐ 149 Mike Hershberger	1.00	.45	.13
☐ 150 Sam McDowell	1.25	.55	.16
☐ 151 Tommy Davis	1.25	.55	.16
☐ 152 Angels Rookies Lloyd Allen Winston Llenas	1.00	.45	.13
☐ 153 Gary Ross	1.00	.45	.13
☐ 154 Cesar Gutierrez	1.00	.45	.13
☐ 155 Ken Henderson	1.00	.45	.13
☐ 156 Bart Johnson	1.00	.45	.13
☐ 157 Bob Bailey	1.00	.45	.13
☐ 158 Jerry Reuss	2.00	.90	.25
☐ 159 Jarvis Tatum	1.00	.45	.13
☐ 160 Tom Seaver	65.00	29.00	8.25
☐ 161 Coin Checklist	5.00	2.30	.60
☐ 162 Jack Billingham	1.00	.45	.13
☐ 163 Buck Martinez	1.00	.45	.13
☐ 164 Reds Rookies Frank Duffy Milt Wilcox	1.25	.55	.16
☐ 165 Cesar Tovar	1.00	.45	.13
☐ 166 Joe Hoerner	1.00	.45	.13
☐ 167 Tom Grieve	2.00	.90	.25
☐ 168 Bruce Dal Canton	1.00	.45	.13
☐ 169 Ed Herrmann	1.00	.45	.13
☐ 170 Mike Cuellar	1.25	.55	.16
☐ 171 Bobby Wine	1.00	.45	.13
☐ 172 Duke Sims	1.00	.45	.13
☐ 173 Gil Garrido	1.00	.45	.13
☐ 174 Dave LaRoche	1.50	.65	.19
☐ 175 Jim Hickman	1.00	.45	.13
☐ 176 Red Sox Rookies Bob Montgomery Doug Griffin	1.50	.65	.19
☐ 177 Hal McRae	2.50	1.15	.30
☐ 178 Dave Duncan	1.00	.45	.13
☐ 179 Mike Corkins	1.00	.45	.13
☐ 180 Al Kaline UER (Home instead of Birth)	20.00	9.00	2.50
☐ 181 Hal Lanier	1.00	.45	.13
☐ 182 Al Downing	1.25	.55	.16
☐ 183 Gil Hodges MG	5.00	2.30	.60
☐ 184 Stan Bahnsen	1.00	.45	.13
☐ 185 Julian Javier	1.25	.55	.16
☐ 186 Bob Spence	1.00	.45	.13
☐ 187 Ted Abernathy	1.00	.45	.13
☐ 188 Dodgers Rookies Bob Valentine Mike Strahler	4.00	1.80	.50
☐ 189 George Mitterwald	1.00	.45	.13
☐ 190 Bob Tolan	1.25	.55	.16
☐ 191 Mike Andrews	1.00	.45	.13
☐ 192 Billy Wilson	1.00	.45	.13
☐ 193 Bob Grich	5.00	2.30	.60
☐ 194 Mike Lum	1.00	.45	.13
☐ 195 AL Playoff Game 1 Boog Powell muscles Twins	2.50	1.15	.30
☐ 196 AL Playoff Game 2 Dave McNally makes it two straight	2.50	1.15	.30
☐ 197 AL Playoff Game 3 Jim Palmer mows'em down	4.00	1.80	.50
☐ 198 AL Playoff Summary Orioles celebrate	2.50	1.15	.30
☐ 199 NL Playoff Game 1 Ty Cline pinch-triple decides it	2.50	1.15	.30
☐ 200 NL Playoff Game 2 Bobby Tolan scores for third time	2.50	1.15	.30
☐ 201 NL Playoff Game 3 Ty Cline scores winning run	2.50	1.15	.30
☐ 202 NL Playoff Summary Reds celebrate	2.50	1.15	.30
☐ 203 Larry Gura	1.50	.65	.19
☐ 204 Brewers Rookies Bernie Smith George Kopacz	1.00	.45	.13
☐ 205 Gerry Moses	1.00	.45	.13
☐ 206 Checklist 3	5.00	2.30	.60
☐ 207 Alan Foster	1.00	.45	.13
☐ 208 Billy Martin MG	3.50	1.55	.45
☐ 209 Steve Renko	1.00	.45	.13
☐ 210 Rod Carew	48.00	22.00	6.00
☐ 211 Phil Hennigan	1.00	.45	.13
☐ 212 Rich Hebner	1.25	.55	.16
☐ 213 Frank Baker	1.00	.45	.13
☐ 214 Al Ferrara	1.00	.45	.13
☐ 215 Diego Segui	1.00	.45	.13
☐ 216 Cards Rookies Reggie Cleveland Luis Melendez	1.00	.45	.13
☐ 217 Ed Stroud	1.00	.45	.13
☐ 218 Tony Cloninger	1.00	.45	.13
☐ 219 Elrod Hendricks	1.00	.45	.13
☐ 220 Ron Santo	2.50	1.15	.30
☐ 221 Dave Morehead	1.00	.45	.13
☐ 222 Bob Watson	1.25	.55	.16
☐ 223 Cecil Upshaw	1.00	.45	.13
☐ 224 Alan Gallagher	1.00	.45	.13
☐ 225 Gary Peters	1.00	.45	.13
☐ 226 Bill Russell	2.00	.90	.25
☐ 227 Floyd Weaver	1.00	.45	.13
☐ 228 Wayne Garrett	1.00	.45	.13
☐ 229 Jim Hannan	1.00	.45	.13
☐ 230 Willie Stargell	10.00	4.50	1.25
☐ 231 Indians Rookies Vince Colbert John Lowenstein	1.50	.65	.19
☐ 232 John Strohmayer	1.00	.45	.13
☐ 233 Larry Bowa	2.00	.90	.25
☐ 234 Jim Lyttle	1.00	.45	.13
☐ 235 Nate Colbert	1.00	.45	.13
☐ 236 Bob Humphreys	1.00	.45	.13
☐ 237 Cesar Cedeno	3.50	1.55	.45
☐ 238 Chuck Dobson	1.00	.45	.13
☐ 239 Red Schoendienst MG	2.00	.90	.25
☐ 240 Clyde Wright	1.00	.45	.13
☐ 241 Dave Nelson	1.00	.45	.13
☐ 242 Jim Ray	1.00	.45	.13

	No.	Card			
☐	243	Carlos May	1.25	.55	.16
☐	244	Bob Tillman	1.00	.45	.13
☐	245	Jim Kaat	3.00	1.35	.40
☐	246	Tony Taylor	1.00	.45	.13
☐	247	Royals Rookies	1.75	.80	.22
		Jerry Cram			
		Paul Splittorff			
☐	248	Hoyt Wilhelm	4.25	1.90	.55
☐	249	Chico Salmon	1.00	.45	.13
☐	250	Johnny Bench	55.00	25.00	7.00
☐	251	Frank Reberger	1.00	.45	.13
☐	252	Eddie Leon	1.00	.45	.13
☐	253	Bill Sudakis	1.00	.45	.13
☐	254	Cal Koonce	1.00	.45	.13
☐	255	Bob Robertson	1.25	.55	.16
☐	256	Tony Gonzalez	1.00	.45	.13
☐	257	Nelson Briles	1.00	.45	.13
☐	258	Dick Green	1.00	.45	.13
☐	259	Dave Marshall	1.00	.45	.13
☐	260	Tommy Harper	1.25	.55	.16
☐	261	Darold Knowles	1.00	.45	.13
☐	262	Padres Rookies	1.00	.45	.13
		Jim Williams			
		Dave Robinson			
☐	263	John Ellis	1.25	.55	.16
☐	264	Joe Morgan	10.00	4.50	1.25
☐	265	Jim Northrup	1.50	.65	.19
☐	266	Bill Stoneman	1.25	.55	.16
☐	267	Rich Morales	1.25	.55	.16
☐	268	Philadelphia Phillies	2.50	1.15	.30
		Team Card			
☐	269	Gail Hopkins	1.25	.55	.16
☐	270	Rico Carty	1.50	.65	.19
☐	271	Bill Zepp	1.25	.55	.16
☐	272	Tommy Helms	1.50	.65	.19
☐	273	Pete Richert	1.25	.55	.16
☐	274	Ron Slocum	1.25	.55	.16
☐	275	Vada Pinson	2.00	.90	.25
☐	276	Giants Rookies	9.00	4.00	1.15
		Mike Davison			
		George Foster			
☐	277	Gary Waslewski	1.25	.55	.16
☐	278	Jerry Grote	1.25	.55	.16
☐	279	Lefty Phillips MG	1.25	.55	.16
☐	280	Fergie Jenkins	12.00	5.50	1.50
☐	281	Danny Walton	1.25	.55	.16
☐	282	Jose Pagan	1.25	.55	.16
☐	283	Dick Such	1.25	.55	.16
☐	284	Jim Gosger	1.25	.55	.16
☐	285	Sal Bando	1.50	.65	.19
☐	286	Jerry McNertney	1.25	.55	.16
☐	287	Mike Fiore	1.25	.55	.16
☐	288	Joe Moeller	1.25	.55	.16
☐	289	Chicago White Sox	2.50	1.15	.30
		Team Card			
☐	290	Tony Oliva	3.50	1.55	.45
☐	291	George Culver	1.25	.55	.16
☐	292	Jay Johnstone	1.50	.65	.19
☐	293	Pat Corrales	1.50	.65	.19
☐	294	Steve Dunning	1.25	.55	.16
☐	295	Bobby Bonds	4.50	2.00	.55
☐	296	Tom Timmermann	1.25	.55	.16
☐	297	Johnny Briggs	1.25	.55	.16
☐	298	Jim Nelson	1.25	.55	.16
☐	299	Ed Kirkpatrick	1.25	.55	.16
☐	300	Brooks Robinson	20.00	9.00	2.50
☐	301	Earl Wilson	1.35	.60	.17
☐	302	Phil Gagliano	1.25	.55	.16
☐	303	Lindy McDaniel	1.50	.65	.19
☐	304	Ron Brand	1.25	.55	.16
☐	305	Reggie Smith	2.00	.90	.25
☐	306	Jim Nash	1.25	.55	.16
☐	307	Don Wert	1.25	.55	.16
☐	308	St. Louis Cardinals	2.50	1.15	.30
		Team Card			
☐	309	Dick Ellsworth	1.25	.55	.16
☐	310	Tommie Agee	1.50	.65	.19
☐	311	Lee Stange	1.25	.55	.16
☐	312	Harry Walker MG	1.25	.55	.16
☐	313	Tom Hall	1.25	.55	.16
☐	314	Jeff Torborg	1.50	.65	.19
☐	315	Ron Fairly	1.50	.65	.19
☐	316	Fred Scherman	1.25	.55	.16
☐	317	Athletic Rookies	1.25	.55	.16
		Jim Driscoll			
		Angel Mangual			
☐	318	Rudy May	1.25	.55	.16
☐	319	Ty Cline	1.25	.55	.16
☐	320	Dave McNally	1.50	.65	.19
☐	321	Tom Matchick	1.25	.55	.16
☐	322	Jim Beauchamp	1.25	.55	.16
☐	323	Billy Champion	1.25	.55	.16
☐	324	Graig Nettles	3.50	1.55	.45
☐	325	Juan Marichal	6.00	2.70	.75
☐	326	Richie Scheinblum	1.25	.55	.16
☐	327	World Series Game 1	2.50	1.15	.30
		Boog Powell homers			
		to opposite field			
☐	328	World Series Game 2	2.50	1.15	.30
		(Don Buford)			
☐	329	World Series Game 3	4.00	1.80	.50
		Frank Robinson			
		shows muscle			
☐	330	World Series Game 4	2.50	1.15	.30
		Reds stay alive			
☐	331	World Series Game 5	4.50	2.00	.55
		Brooks Robinson			
		commits robbery			
☐	332	World Series Summary	2.50	1.15	.30
		Orioles celebrate			
☐	333	Clay Kirby	1.25	.55	.16
☐	334	Roberto Pena	1.25	.55	.16
☐	335	Jerry Koosman	2.50	1.15	.30
☐	336	Detroit Tigers	2.50	1.15	.30
		Team Card			
☐	337	Jesus Alou	1.25	.55	.16
☐	338	Gene Tenace	2.00	.90	.25
☐	339	Wayne Simpson	1.25	.55	.16
☐	340	Rico Petrocelli	1.50	.65	.19
☐	341	Steve Garvey	70.00	32.00	8.75
☐	342	Frank Tepedino	1.25	.55	.16
☐	343	Pirates Rookies	1.75	.80	.22
		Ed Acosta			
		Milt May			
☐	344	Ellie Rodriguez	1.25	.55	.16
☐	345	Joel Horlen	1.25	.55	.16
☐	346	Lum Harris MG	1.25	.55	.16
☐	347	Ted Uhlaender	1.25	.55	.16
☐	348	Fred Norman	1.25	.55	.16
☐	349	Rich Reese	1.25	.55	.16
☐	350	Billy Williams	6.50	2.90	.80
☐	351	Jim Shellenback	1.25	.55	.16
☐	352	Denny Doyle	1.25	.55	.16
☐	353	Carl Taylor	1.25	.55	.16
☐	354	Don McMahon	1.25	.55	.16
☐	355	Bud Harrelson	1.50	.65	.19
☐	356	Bob Locker	1.25	.55	.16
☐	357	Cincinnati Reds	2.50	1.15	.30
		Team Card			
☐	358	Danny Cater	1.25	.55	.16
☐	359	Ron Reed	1.25	.55	.16
☐	360	Jim Fregosi	1.50	.65	.19
☐	361	Don Sutton	8.00	3.60	1.00
☐	362	Orioles Rookies	1.25	.55	.16
		Mike Adamson			
		Roger Freed			
☐	363	Mike Nagy	1.25	.55	.16
☐	364	Tommy Dean	1.25	.55	.16
☐	365	Bob Johnson	1.25	.55	.16
☐	366	Ron Stone	1.25	.55	.16
☐	367	Dalton Jones	1.25	.55	.16
☐	368	Bob Veale	1.50	.65	.19
☐	369	Checklist 4	5.00	.50	.15
☐	370	Joe Torre	3.50	1.55	.45
☐	371	Jack Hiatt	1.25	.55	.16
☐	372	Lew Krausse	1.25	.55	.16
☐	373	Tom McCraw	1.25	.55	.16
☐	374	Clete Boyer	1.50	.65	.19
☐	375	Steve Hargan	1.25	.55	.16
☐	376	Expos Rookies	1.25	.55	.16
		Clyde Mashore			
		Ernie McAnally			
☐	377	Greg Garrett	1.25	.55	.16
☐	378	Tito Fuentes	1.25	.55	.16
☐	379	Wayne Granger	1.25	.55	.16
☐	380	Ted Williams MG	8.00	3.60	1.00
☐	381	Fred Gladding	1.25	.55	.16
☐	382	Jake Gibbs	1.25	.55	.16
☐	383	Rod Gaspar	1.25	.55	.16
☐	384	Rollie Fingers	17.50	8.00	2.20
☐	385	Maury Wills	2.50	1.15	.30
☐	386	Boston Red Sox	2.50	1.15	.30
		Team Card			
☐	387	Ron Herbel	1.25	.55	.16
☐	388	Al Oliver	3.00	1.35	.40
☐	389	Ed Brinkman	1.25	.55	.16
☐	390	Glenn Beckert	1.50	.65	.19
☐	391	Twins Rookies	1.25	.55	.16
		Steve Brye			
		Cotton Nash			
☐	392	Grant Jackson	1.25	.55	.16
☐	393	Merv Rettenmund	1.50	.65	.19
☐	394	Clay Carroll	2.50	1.15	.30
☐	395	Roy White	2.50	1.15	.30
☐	396	Dick Schofield	2.00	.90	.25
☐	397	Alvin Dark MG	2.50	1.15	.30

☐ 398	Howie Reed	2.00	.90	.25
☐ 399	Jim French	2.00	.90	.25
☐ 400	Hank Aaron	60.00	27.00	7.50
☐ 401	Tom Murphy	2.00	.90	.25
☐ 402	Los Angeles Dodgers Team Card	4.00	1.80	.50
☐ 403	Joe Coleman	2.00	.90	.25
☐ 404	Astros Rookies Buddy Harris Roger Metzger	2.00	.90	.25
☐ 405	Leo Cardenas	2.00	.90	.25
☐ 406	Ray Sadecki	2.00	.90	.25
☐ 407	Joe Rudi	2.50	1.15	.30
☐ 408	Rafael Robles	2.00	.90	.25
☐ 409	Don Pavletich	2.00	.90	.25
☐ 410	Ken Holtzman	2.50	1.15	.30
☐ 411	George Spriggs	2.00	.90	.25
☐ 412	Jerry Johnson	2.00	.90	.25
☐ 413	Pat Kelly	2.50	1.15	.30
☐ 414	Woodie Fryman	2.50	1.15	.30
☐ 415	Mike Hegan	2.00	.90	.25
☐ 416	Gene Alley	2.00	.90	.25
☐ 417	Dick Hall	2.00	.90	.25
☐ 418	Adolfo Phillips	2.00	.90	.25
☐ 419	Ron Hansen	2.00	.90	.25
☐ 420	Jim Merritt	2.00	.90	.25
☐ 421	John Stephenson	2.00	.90	.25
☐ 422	Frank Bertaina	2.00	.90	.25
☐ 423	Tigers Rookies Dennis Saunders Tim Marting	2.00	.90	.25
☐ 424	Roberto Rodriquez	2.00	.90	.25
☐ 425	Doug Rader	2.50	1.15	.30
☐ 426	Chris Cannizzaro	2.00	.90	.25
☐ 427	Bernie Allen	2.00	.90	.25
☐ 428	Jim McAndrew	2.00	.90	.25
☐ 429	Chuck Hinton	2.00	.90	.25
☐ 430	Wes Parker	2.50	1.15	.30
☐ 431	Tom Burgmeier	2.00	.90	.25
☐ 432	Bob Didier	2.00	.90	.25
☐ 433	Skip Lockwood	2.00	.90	.25
☐ 434	Gary Sutherland	2.00	.90	.25
☐ 435	Jose Cardenal	2.50	1.15	.30
☐ 436	Wilbur Wood	2.50	1.15	.30
☐ 437	Danny Murtaugh MG	2.50	1.15	.30
☐ 438	Mike McCormick	2.50	1.15	.30
☐ 439	Phillies Rookies Greg Luzinski Scott Reid	5.00	2.30	.60
☐ 440	Bert Campaneris	2.50	1.15	.30
☐ 441	Milt Pappas	2.50	1.15	.30
☐ 442	California Angels Team Card	4.00	1.80	.50
☐ 443	Rich Robertson	2.00	.90	.25
☐ 444	Jimmie Price	2.00	.90	.25
☐ 445	Art Shamsky	2.00	.90	.25
☐ 446	Bobby Bolin	2.00	.90	.25
☐ 447	Cesar Geronimo	2.50	1.15	.30
☐ 448	Dave Roberts	2.00	.90	.25
☐ 449	Brant Alyea	2.00	.90	.25
☐ 450	Bob Gibson	16.00	7.25	2.00
☐ 451	Joe Keough	2.00	.90	.25
☐ 452	John Boccabella	2.00	.90	.25
☐ 453	Terry Crowley	2.00	.90	.25
☐ 454	Mike Paul	2.00	.90	.25
☐ 455	Don Kessinger	2.50	1.15	.30
☐ 456	Bob Meyer	2.00	.90	.25
☐ 457	Willie Smith	2.00	.90	.25
☐ 458	White Sox Rookies Ron Lolich Dave Lemonds	2.00	.90	.25
☐ 459	Jim Lefebvre	2.00	.90	.25
☐ 460	Fritz Peterson	2.00	.90	.25
☐ 461	Jim Ray Hart	2.50	1.15	.30
☐ 462	Washington Senators Team Card	4.00	1.80	.50
☐ 463	Tom Kelley	2.00	.90	.25
☐ 464	Aurelio Rodriguez	2.00	.90	.25
☐ 465	Tim McCarver	2.50	1.15	.30
☐ 466	Ken Berry	2.00	.90	.25
☐ 467	Al Santorini	2.00	.90	.25
☐ 468	Frank Fernandez	2.00	.90	.25
☐ 469	Bob Aspromonte	2.00	.90	.25
☐ 470	Bob Oliver	2.00	.90	.25
☐ 471	Tom Griffin	2.00	.90	.25
☐ 472	Ken Rudolph	2.00	.90	.25
☐ 473	Gary Wagner	2.00	.90	.25
☐ 474	Jim Fairey	2.00	.90	.25
☐ 475	Ron Perranoski	2.50	1.15	.30
☐ 476	Dal Maxvill	2.00	.90	.25
☐ 477	Earl Weaver MG	3.50	1.55	.45
☐ 478	Bernie Carbo	2.00	.90	.25
☐ 479	Dennis Higgins	2.00	.90	.25
☐ 480	Manny Sanguillen	2.50	1.15	.30
☐ 481	Daryl Patterson	2.00	.90	.25
☐ 482	San Diego Padres Team Card	4.00	1.80	.50
☐ 483	Gene Michael	2.50	1.15	.30
☐ 484	Don Wilson	2.50	1.15	.30
☐ 485	Ken McMullen	2.00	.90	.25
☐ 486	Steve Huntz	2.00	.90	.25
☐ 487	Paul Schaal	2.00	.90	.25
☐ 488	Jerry Stephenson	2.00	.90	.25
☐ 489	Luis Alvarado	2.00	.90	.25
☐ 490	Deron Johnson	2.00	.90	.25
☐ 491	Jim Hardin	2.00	.90	.25
☐ 492	Ken Boswell	2.00	.90	.25
☐ 493	Dave May	2.00	.90	.25
☐ 494	Braves Rookies Ralph Garr Rick Kester	2.50	1.15	.30
☐ 495	Felipe Alou	3.00	1.35	.40
☐ 496	Woody Woodward	2.50	1.15	.30
☐ 497	Horacio Pina	2.00	.90	.25
☐ 498	John Kennedy	2.00	.90	.25
☐ 499	Checklist 5	5.00	.50	.15
☐ 500	Jim Perry	2.50	1.15	.30
☐ 501	Andy Etchebarren	2.00	.90	.25
☐ 502	Chicago Cubs Team Card	4.00	1.80	.50
☐ 503	Gates Brown	2.50	1.15	.30
☐ 504	Ken Wright	2.00	.90	.25
☐ 505	Ollie Brown	2.00	.90	.25
☐ 506	Bobby Knoop	2.00	.90	.25
☐ 507	George Stone	2.00	.90	.25
☐ 508	Roger Repoz	2.00	.90	.25
☐ 509	Jim Grant	2.00	.90	.25
☐ 510	Ken Harrelson	2.50	1.15	.30
☐ 511	Chris Short	2.00	.90	.25
☐ 512	Red Sox Rookies Dick Mills Mike Garman	2.00	.90	.25
☐ 513	Nolan Ryan	250.00	115.00	31.00
☐ 514	Ron Woods	2.00	.90	.25
☐ 515	Carl Morton	2.00	.90	.25
☐ 516	Ted Kubiak	2.00	.90	.25
☐ 517	Charlie Fox MG	2.00	.90	.25
☐ 518	Joe Grzenda	2.00	.90	.25
☐ 519	Willie Crawford	2.00	.90	.25
☐ 520	Tommy John	5.00	2.30	.60
☐ 521	Leron Lee	2.00	.90	.25
☐ 522	Minnesota Twins Team Card	4.00	1.80	.50
☐ 523	John Odom	2.00	.90	.25
☐ 524	Mickey Stanley	4.50	2.00	.55
☐ 525	Ernie Banks	45.00	20.00	5.75
☐ 526	Ray Jarvis	4.00	1.80	.50
☐ 527	Cleon Jones	4.50	2.00	.55
☐ 528	Wally Bunker	4.00	1.80	.50
☐ 529	NL Rookie Infielders Enzo Hernandez Bill Buckner Marty Perez	6.00	2.70	.75
☐ 530	Carl Yastrzemski	40.00	18.00	5.00
☐ 531	Mike Torrez	4.50	2.00	.55
☐ 532	Bill Rigney MG	4.00	1.80	.50
☐ 533	Mike Ryan	4.00	1.80	.50
☐ 534	Luke Walker	4.00	1.80	.50
☐ 535	Curt Flood	5.00	2.30	.60
☐ 536	Claude Raymond	4.00	1.80	.50
☐ 537	Tom Egan	4.00	1.80	.50
☐ 538	Angel Bravo	4.00	1.80	.50
☐ 539	Larry Brown	4.00	1.80	.50
☐ 540	Larry Dierker	4.00	1.80	.50
☐ 541	Bob Burda	4.00	1.80	.50
☐ 542	Bob Miller	4.00	1.80	.50
☐ 543	New York Yankees Team Card	8.00	3.60	1.00
☐ 544	Vida Blue	6.00	2.70	.75
☐ 545	Dick Dietz	4.00	1.80	.50
☐ 546	John Matias	4.00	1.80	.50
☐ 547	Pat Dobson	4.50	2.00	.55
☐ 548	Don Mason	4.00	1.80	.50
☐ 549	Jim Brewer	4.00	1.80	.50
☐ 550	Harmon Killebrew	25.00	11.50	3.10
☐ 551	Frank Linzy	4.00	1.80	.50
☐ 552	Buddy Bradford	4.00	1.80	.50
☐ 553	Kevin Collins	4.50	2.00	.55
☐ 554	Lowell Palmer	4.00	1.80	.50
☐ 555	Walt Williams	4.00	1.80	.50
☐ 556	Jim McGlothlin	4.00	1.80	.50
☐ 557	Tom Satriano	4.00	1.80	.50
☐ 558	Hector Torres	4.00	1.80	.50
☐ 559	AL Rookie Pitchers Terry Cox Bill Gogolewski	4.00	1.80	.50

Gary Jones			
☐ 560 Rusty Staub	5.00	2.30	.60
☐ 561 Syd O'Brien	4.00	1.80	.50
☐ 562 Dave Giusti	4.00	1.80	.50
☐ 563 San Francisco Giants	8.00	3.60	1.00
Team Card			
☐ 564 Al Fitzmorris	4.00	1.80	.50
☐ 565 Jim Wynn	4.50	2.00	.55
☐ 566 Tim Cullen	4.00	1.80	.50
☐ 567 Walt Alston MG	5.00	2.30	.60
☐ 568 Sal Campisi	4.00	1.80	.50
☐ 569 Ivan Murrell	4.00	1.80	.50
☐ 570 Jim Palmer	40.00	18.00	5.00
☐ 571 Ted Sizemore	4.00	1.80	.50
☐ 572 Jerry Kenney	4.00	1.80	.50
☐ 573 Ed Kranepool	4.50	2.00	.55
☐ 574 Jim Bunning	6.00	2.70	.75
☐ 575 Bill Freehan	4.50	2.00	.55
☐ 576 Cubs Rookies	4.00	1.80	.50
Adrian Garrett			
Brock Davis			
Garry Jestadt			
☐ 577 Jim Lonborg	4.50	2.00	.55
☐ 578 Ron Hunt	4.00	1.80	.50
☐ 579 Marty Pattin	4.00	1.80	.50
☐ 580 Tony Perez	13.00	5.75	1.65
☐ 581 Roger Nelson	4.00	1.80	.50
☐ 582 Dave Cash	5.00	2.30	.60
☐ 583 Ron Cook	4.00	1.80	.50
☐ 584 Cleveland Indians	8.00	3.60	1.00
Team Card			
☐ 585 Willie Davis	4.50	2.00	.55
☐ 586 Dick Woodson	4.00	1.80	.50
☐ 587 Sonny Jackson	4.00	1.80	.50
☐ 588 Tom Bradley	4.00	1.80	.50
☐ 589 Bob Barton	4.00	1.80	.50
☐ 590 Alex Johnson	4.50	2.00	.55
☐ 591 Jackie Brown	4.50	2.00	.55
☐ 592 Randy Hundley	4.00	1.80	.50
☐ 593 Jack Aker	4.00	1.80	.50
☐ 594 Cards Rookies	6.00	2.70	.75
Bob Chlupsa			
Bob Stinson			
Al Hrabosky			
☐ 595 Dave Johnson	4.50	2.00	.55
☐ 596 Mike Jorgensen	4.00	1.80	.50
☐ 597 Ken Suarez	4.00	1.80	.50
☐ 598 Rick Wise	4.50	2.00	.55
☐ 599 Norm Cash	6.00	2.70	.75
☐ 600 Willie Mays	90.00	40.00	11.50
☐ 601 Ken Tatum	4.00	1.80	.50
☐ 602 Marty Martinez	4.00	1.80	.50
☐ 603 Pittsburgh Pirates	8.00	3.60	1.00
Team Card			
☐ 604 John Gelnar	4.00	1.80	.50
☐ 605 Orlando Cepeda	6.00	2.70	.75
☐ 606 Chuck Taylor	4.00	1.80	.50
☐ 607 Paul Ratliff	4.00	1.80	.50
☐ 608 Mike Wegener	4.00	1.80	.50
☐ 609 Leo Durocher MG	6.00	2.70	.75
☐ 610 Amos Otis	4.50	2.00	.55
☐ 611 Tom Phoebus	4.00	1.80	.50
☐ 612 Indians Rookies	4.00	1.80	.50
Lou Camilli			
Ted Ford			
Steve Mingori			
☐ 613 Pedro Borbon	4.00	1.80	.50
☐ 614 Billy Cowan	4.00	1.80	.50
☐ 615 Mel Stottlemyre	6.00	2.70	.75
☐ 616 Larry Hisle	4.50	2.00	.55
☐ 617 Clay Dalrymple	4.00	1.80	.50
☐ 618 Tug McGraw	5.50	2.50	.70
☐ 619A Checklist 6 ERR	5.00	.50	.15
(No copyright)			
☐ 619B Checklist 6 COR	10.00	1.00	.30
(Copyright on back)			
☐ 620 Frank Howard	5.50	2.50	.70
☐ 621 Ron Bryant	4.00	1.80	.50
☐ 622 Joe Lahoud	4.00	1.80	.50
☐ 623 Pat Jarvis	4.00	1.80	.50
☐ 624 Oakland Athletics	8.00	3.60	1.00
Team Card			
☐ 625 Lou Brock	30.00	13.50	3.80
☐ 626 Freddie Patek	4.50	2.00	.55
☐ 627 Steve Hamilton	4.00	1.80	.50
☐ 628 John Bateman	4.00	1.80	.50
☐ 629 John Hiller	4.50	2.00	.55
☐ 630 Roberto Clemente	65.00	29.00	8.25
☐ 631 Eddie Fisher	4.00	1.80	.50
☐ 632 Darrel Chaney	4.00	1.80	.50
☐ 633 AL Rookie Outfielders	4.00	1.80	.50
Bobby Brooks			
Pete Koegel			
Scott Northey			

☐ 634 Phil Regan	4.50	2.00	.55
☐ 635 Bobby Murcer	7.00	3.10	.85
☐ 636 Denny Lemaster	4.00	1.80	.50
☐ 637 Dave Bristol MG	4.00	1.80	.50
☐ 638 Stan Williams	4.00	1.80	.50
☐ 639 Tom Haller	4.00	1.80	.50
☐ 640 Frank Robinson	40.00	18.00	5.00
☐ 641 New York Mets	10.00	4.50	1.25
Team Card			
☐ 642 Jim Roland	4.00	1.80	.50
☐ 643 Rick Reichardt	5.00	2.30	.60
☐ 644 Jim Stewart SP	9.00	4.00	1.15
☐ 645 Jim Maloney SP	10.00	4.50	1.25
☐ 646 Bobby Floyd SP	9.00	4.00	1.15
☐ 647 Juan Pizarro	5.00	2.30	.60
☐ 648 Mets Rookies SP	15.00	6.75	1.90
Rich Folkers			
Ted Martinez			
Jon Matlack			
☐ 649 Sparky Lyle SP	15.00	6.75	1.90
☐ 650 Rich Allen SP	27.00	12.00	3.40
☐ 651 Jerry Robertson SP	9.00	4.00	1.15
☐ 652 Atlanta Braves	12.00	5.50	1.50
Team Card			
☐ 653 Russ Snyder SP	9.00	4.00	1.15
☐ 654 Don Shaw SP	9.00	4.00	1.15
☐ 655 Mike Epstein SP	9.00	4.00	1.15
☐ 656 Gerry Nyman SP	9.00	4.00	1.15
☐ 657 Jose Azcue	5.00	2.30	.60
☐ 658 Paul Lindblad SP	9.00	4.00	1.15
☐ 659 Byron Browne SP	9.00	4.00	1.15
☐ 660 Ray Culp	5.00	2.30	.60
☐ 661 Chuck Tanner MG SP	9.00	4.00	1.15
☐ 662 Mike Hedlund SP	9.00	4.00	1.15
☐ 663 Marv Staehle	5.00	2.30	.60
☐ 664 Rookie Pitchers SP	9.00	4.00	1.15
Archie Reynolds			
Bob Reynolds			
Ken Reynolds			
☐ 665 Ron Swoboda SP	12.00	5.50	1.50
☐ 666 Gene Brabender SP	9.00	4.00	1.15
☐ 667 Pete Ward	5.00	2.30	.60
☐ 668 Gary Neibauer	5.00	2.30	.60
☐ 669 Ike Brown SP	9.00	4.00	1.15
☐ 670 Bill Hands	5.00	2.30	.60
☐ 671 Bill Voss SP	9.00	4.00	1.15
☐ 672 Ed Crosby SP	9.00	4.00	1.15
☐ 673 Gerry Janeski SP	9.00	4.00	1.15
☐ 674 Montreal Expos	12.00	5.50	1.50
Team Card			
☐ 675 Dave Boswell	5.00	2.30	.60
☐ 676 Tommie Reynolds	5.00	2.30	.60
☐ 677 Jack DiLauro SP	9.00	4.00	1.15
☐ 678 George Thomas	5.00	2.30	.60
☐ 679 Don O'Riley	5.00	2.30	.60
☐ 680 Don Mincher SP	9.00	4.00	1.15
☐ 681 Bill Butler	5.00	2.30	.60
☐ 682 Terry Harmon	5.00	2.30	.60
☐ 683 Bill Burbach SP	9.00	4.00	1.15
☐ 684 Curt Motton	5.00	2.30	.60
☐ 685 Moe Drabowsky	5.00	2.30	.60
☐ 686 Chico Ruiz SP	9.00	4.00	1.15
☐ 687 Ron Taylor SP	9.00	4.00	1.15
☐ 688 Sparky Anderson MG SP	21.00	9.50	2.60
☐ 689 Frank Baker	5.00	2.30	.60
☐ 690 Bob Moose	5.00	2.30	.60
☐ 691 Bobby Heise	5.00	2.30	.60
☐ 692 AL Rookie Pitchers SP	9.00	4.00	1.15
Hal Haydel			
Rogelio Moret			
Wayne Twitchell			
☐ 693 Jose Pena SP	9.00	4.00	1.15
☐ 694 Rick Renick SP	9.00	4.00	1.15
☐ 695 Joe Niekro	5.50	2.50	.70
☐ 696 Jerry Morales	5.00	2.30	.60
☐ 697 Rickey Clark SP	9.00	4.00	1.15
☐ 698 Milwaukee Brewers SP	18.00	8.00	2.30
Team Card			
☐ 699 Jim Britton	5.00	2.30	.60
☐ 700 Boog Powell SP	20.00	9.00	2.50
☐ 701 Bob Garibaldi	5.00	2.30	.60
☐ 702 Milt Ramirez	5.00	2.30	.60
☐ 703 Mike Kekich	5.00	2.30	.60
☐ 704 J.C. Martin SP	9.00	4.00	1.15
☐ 705 Dick Selma SP	9.00	4.00	1.15
☐ 706 Joe Foy SP	9.00	4.00	1.15
☐ 707 Fred Lasher	5.00	2.30	.60
☐ 708 Russ Nagelson SP	9.00	4.00	1.15
☐ 709 Rookie Outfielders SP	60.00	27.00	7.50
Dusty Baker			
Don Baylor			
Tom Paciorek			
☐ 710 Sonny Siebert	5.00	2.30	.60

☐ 711 Larry Stahl SP	9.00	4.00	1.15
☐ 712 Jose Martinez	5.00	2.30	.60
☐ 713 Mike Marshall SP	9.00	4.00	1.15
☐ 714 Dick Williams MG SP	9.00	4.00	1.15
☐ 715 Horace Clarke SP	9.00	4.00	1.15
☐ 716 Dave Leonhard	5.00	2.30	.60
☐ 717 Tommie Aaron SP	9.00	4.00	1.15
☐ 718 Billy Wynne	5.00	2.30	.60
☐ 719 Jerry May SP	9.00	4.00	1.15
☐ 720 Matty Alou	5.50	2.50	.70
☐ 721 John Morris	5.00	2.30	.60
☐ 722 Houston Astros SP Team Card	18.00	8.00	2.30
☐ 723 Vicente Romo SP	9.00	4.00	1.15
☐ 724 Tom Tischinski SP	9.00	4.00	1.15
☐ 725 Gary Gentry SP	9.00	4.00	1.15
☐ 726 Paul Popovich	5.00	2.30	.60
☐ 727 Ray Lamb SP	9.00	4.00	1.15
☐ 728 NL Rookie Outfielders Wayne Redmond Keith Lampard Bernie Williams	5.00	2.30	.60
☐ 729 Dick Billings	5.00	2.30	.60
☐ 730 Jim Rooker	5.00	2.30	.60
☐ 731 Jim Qualls SP	9.00	4.00	1.15
☐ 732 Bob Reed	5.00	2.30	.60
☐ 733 Lee Maye SP	9.00	4.00	1.15
☐ 734 Rob Gardner SP	9.00	4.00	1.15
☐ 735 Mike Shannon SP	9.00	4.00	1.15
☐ 736 Mel Queen SP	9.00	4.00	1.15
☐ 737 Preston Gomez MG SP	9.00	4.00	1.15
☐ 738 Russ Gibson SP	9.00	4.00	1.15
☐ 739 Barry Lersch SP	9.00	4.00	1.15
☐ 740 Luis Aparicio SP UER (Led AL in steals from 1965 to 1964, should be 1956 to 1964)	21.00	9.50	2.60
☐ 741 Skip Guinn	5.00	2.30	.60
☐ 742 Kansas City Royals Team Card	12.00	5.50	1.50
☐ 743 John O'Donoghue SP	9.00	4.00	1.15
☐ 744 Chuck Manuel SP	9.00	4.00	1.15
☐ 745 Sandy Alomar SP	9.00	4.00	1.15
☐ 746 Andy Kosco	5.00	2.30	.60
☐ 747 NL Rookie Pitchers Al Severinsen Scipio Spinks Balor Moore	5.00	2.30	.60
☐ 748 John Purdin SP	9.00	4.00	1.15
☐ 749 Ken Szotkiewicz	5.00	2.30	.60
☐ 750 Denny McLain SP	18.00	8.00	2.30
☐ 751 Al Weis SP	15.00	6.75	1.90
☐ 752 Dick Drago	9.00	4.00	1.15

1972 Topps

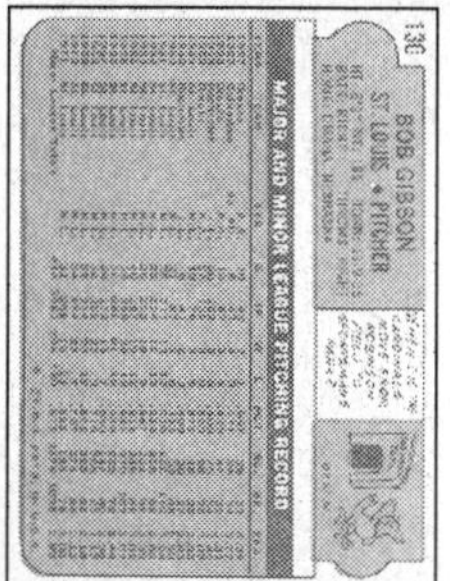

The cards in this 787-card set measure 2 1/2" by 3 1/2". The 1972 Topps set contained the most cards ever for a Topps set to that point in time. Features appearing for the first time were "Boyhood Photos" (KP: 341-348 and 491-498), Awards and Trophy cards (621-626), "In Action" (distributed throughout the set), and "Traded Cards" (TR: 751-757). Other subsets included League Leaders (85-96), Playoffs cards (221-222), and World Series cards (223-230). The curved lines of the color picture are a departure from the rectangular designs of other years. There is a series of intermediate scarcity (526-656) and the usual high numbers (657-787). The key Rookie Card in this set is Carlton Fisk.

	NRMT-MT	EXC	G-VG
COMPLETE SET (787)	2000.00	900.00	250.00
COMMON PLAYER (1-132)	.60	.25	.08
COMMON PLAYER (133-263)	.75	.35	.09
COMMON PLAYER (264-394)	1.00	.45	.13
COMMON PLAYER (395-525)	1.50	.65	.19
COMMON PLAYER (526-656)	3.00	1.35	.40
COMMON PLAYER (657-787)	6.50	2.90	.80
☐ 1 Pittsburgh Pirates Team Card	7.00	1.40	.40
☐ 2 Ray Culp	.60	.25	.08
☐ 3 Bob Tolan	.60	.25	.08
☐ 4 Checklist 1	4.00	.40	.12
☐ 5 John Bateman	.60	.25	.08
☐ 6 Fred Scherman	.60	.25	.08
☐ 7 Enzo Hernandez	.60	.25	.08
☐ 8 Ron Swoboda	.85	.40	.11
☐ 9 Stan Williams	.60	.25	.08
☐ 10 Amos Otis	.85	.40	.11
☐ 11 Bobby Valentine	1.00	.45	.13
☐ 12 Jose Cardenal	.60	.25	.08
☐ 13 Joe Grzenda	.60	.25	.08
☐ 14 Phillies Rookies Pete Koegel Mike Anderson Wayne Twitchell	.60	.25	.08
☐ 15 Walt Williams	.60	.25	.08
☐ 16 Mike Jorgensen	.60	.25	.08
☐ 17 Dave Duncan	.60	.25	.08
☐ 18A Juan Pizarro (Yellow underline C and S of Cubs)	.60	.25	.08
☐ 18B Juan Pizarro (Green underline C and S of Cubs)	5.00	2.30	.60
☐ 19 Billy Cowan	.60	.25	.08
☐ 20 Don Wilson	.60	.25	.08
☐ 21 Atlanta Braves Team Card	1.50	.65	.19
☐ 22 Rob Gardner	.60	.25	.08
☐ 23 Ted Kubiak	.60	.25	.08
☐ 24 Ted Ford	.60	.25	.08
☐ 25 Bill Singer	.60	.25	.08
☐ 26 Andy Etchebarren	.60	.25	.08
☐ 27 Bob Johnson	.60	.25	.08
☐ 28 Twins Rookies Bob Gebhard Steve Brye Hal Haydel	.60	.25	.08
☐ 29A Bill Bonham (Yellow underline C and S of Cubs)	.60	.25	.08
☐ 29B Bill Bonham (Green underline C and S of Cubs)	5.00	2.30	.60
☐ 30 Rico Petrocelli	.85	.40	.11
☐ 31 Cleon Jones	.85	.40	.11
☐ 32 Jones In Action	.60	.25	.08
☐ 33 Billy Martin MG	3.50	1.55	.45
☐ 34 Martin In Action	1.75	.80	.22
☐ 35 Jerry Johnson	.60	.25	.08
☐ 36 Johnson In Action	.60	.25	.08
☐ 37 Carl Yastrzemski	15.00	6.75	1.90
☐ 38 Yastrzemski In Action	7.50	3.40	.95
☐ 39 Bob Barton	.60	.25	.08
☐ 40 Barton In Action	.60	.25	.08
☐ 41 Tommy Davis	.85	.40	.11
☐ 42 Davis In Action	.60	.25	.08
☐ 43 Rick Wise	.85	.40	.11
☐ 44 Wise In Action	.60	.25	.08
☐ 45A Glenn Beckert (Yellow underline C and S of Cubs)	.85	.40	.11
☐ 45B Glenn Beckert (Green underline C and S of Cubs)	5.00	2.30	.60
☐ 46 Beckert In Action	.60	.25	.08
☐ 47 John Ellis	.60	.25	.08
☐ 48 Ellis In Action	.60	.25	.08
☐ 49 Willie Mays	27.00	12.00	3.40
☐ 50 Mays In Action	13.50	6.00	1.70
☐ 51 Harmon Killebrew	6.00	2.70	.75
☐ 52 Killebrew In Action	3.00	1.35	.40
☐ 53 Bud Harrelson	.85	.40	.11
☐ 54 Harrelson In Action	.60	.25	.08
☐ 55 Clyde Wright	.60	.25	.08
☐ 56 Rich Chiles	.60	.25	.08
☐ 57 Bob Oliver	.60	.25	.08

☐ 58	Ernie McAnally	.60	.25	.08
☐ 59	Fred Stanley	.60	.25	.08
☐ 60	Manny Sanguillen	.85	.40	.11
☐ 61	Cubs Rookies Burt Hooton Gene Hiser Earl Stephenson	1.50	.65	.19
☐ 62	Angel Mangual	.60	.25	.08
☐ 63	Duke Sims	.60	.25	.08
☐ 64	Pete Broberg	.60	.25	.08
☐ 65	Cesar Cedeno	1.25	.55	.16
☐ 66	Ray Corbin	.60	.25	.08
☐ 67	Red Schoendienst MG	1.25	.55	.16
☐ 68	Jim York	.60	.25	.08
☐ 69	Roger Freed	.60	.25	.08
☐ 70	Mike Cuellar	.85	.40	.11
☐ 71	California Angels Team Card	1.50	.65	.19
☐ 72	Bruce Kison	1.00	.45	.13
☐ 73	Steve Huntz	.60	.25	.08
☐ 74	Cecil Upshaw	.60	.25	.08
☐ 75	Bert Campaneris	.85	.40	.11
☐ 76	Don Carrithers	.60	.25	.08
☐ 77	Ron Theobald	.60	.25	.08
☐ 78	Steve Arlin	.60	.25	.08
☐ 79	Red Sox Rookies Mike Garman Cecil Cooper Carlton Fisk	120.00	55.00	15.00
☐ 80	Tony Perez	4.50	2.00	.55
☐ 81	Mike Hedlund	.60	.25	.08
☐ 82	Ron Woods	.60	.25	.08
☐ 83	Dalton Jones	.60	.25	.08
☐ 84	Vince Colbert	.60	.25	.08
☐ 85	NL Batting Leaders Joe Torre Ralph Garr Glenn Beckert	1.50	.65	.19
☐ 86	AL Batting Leaders Tony Oliva Bobby Murcer Merv Rettenmund	1.50	.65	.19
☐ 87	NL RBI Leaders Joe Torre Willie Stargell Hank Aaron	3.00	1.35	.40
☐ 88	AL RBI Leaders Harmon Killebrew Frank Robinson Reggie Smith	3.00	1.35	.40
☐ 89	NL Home Run Leaders Willie Stargell Hank Aaron Lee May	2.50	1.15	.30
☐ 90	AL Home Run Leaders Bill Melton Norm Cash Reggie Jackson	1.50	.65	.19
☐ 91	NL ERA Leaders Tom Seaver Dave Roberts UER (Photo actually Danny Coombs) Don Wilson	2.00	.90	.25
☐ 92	AL ERA Leaders Vida Blue Wilbur Wood Jim Palmer	1.50	.65	.19
☐ 93	NL Pitching Leaders Fergie Jenkins Steve Carlton Al Downing Tom Seaver	3.00	1.35	.40
☐ 94	AL Pitching Leaders Mickey Lolich Vida Blue Wilbur Wood	1.50	.65	.19
☐ 95	NL Strikeout Leaders Tom Seaver Fergie Jenkins Bill Stoneman	3.00	1.35	.40
☐ 96	AL Strikeout Leaders Mickey Lolich Vida Blue Joe Coleman	1.50	.65	.19
☐ 97	Tom Kelley	.60	.25	.08
☐ 98	Chuck Tanner MG	.85	.40	.11
☐ 99	Ross Grimsley	.60	.25	.08
☐ 100	Frank Robinson	6.00	2.70	.75
☐ 101	Astros Rookies Bill Greif J.R. Richard Ray Busse	2.00	.90	.25
☐ 102	Lloyd Allen	.60	.25	.08
☐ 103	Checklist 2	4.00	.40	.12
☐ 104	Toby Harrah	2.00	.90	.25
☐ 105	Gary Gentry	.60	.25	.08
☐ 106	Milwaukee Brewers Team Card	1.50	.65	.19
☐ 107	Jose Cruz	2.50	1.15	.30
☐ 108	Gary Waslewski	.60	.25	.08
☐ 109	Jerry May	.60	.25	.08
☐ 110	Ron Hunt	.60	.25	.08
☐ 111	Jim Grant	.60	.25	.08
☐ 112	Greg Luzinski	1.50	.65	.19
☐ 113	Rogelio Moret	.60	.25	.08
☐ 114	Bill Buckner	2.00	.90	.25
☐ 115	Jim Fregosi	.85	.40	.11
☐ 116	Ed Farmer	1.00	.45	.13
☐ 117A	Cleo James (Yellow underline C and S of Cubs)	.60	.25	.08
☐ 117B	Cleo James (Green underline C and S of Cubs)	5.00	2.30	.60
☐ 118	Skip Lockwood	.60	.25	.08
☐ 119	Marty Perez	.60	.25	.08
☐ 120	Bill Freehan	.85	.40	.11
☐ 121	Ed Sprague	.60	.25	.08
☐ 122	Larry Biittner	.60	.25	.08
☐ 123	Ed Acosta	.60	.25	.08
☐ 124	Yankees Rookies Alan Closter Rusty Torres Roger Hambright	.60	.25	.08
☐ 125	Dave Cash	.85	.40	.11
☐ 126	Bart Johnson	.60	.25	.08
☐ 127	Duffy Dyer	.60	.25	.08
☐ 128	Eddie Watt	.60	.25	.08
☐ 129	Charlie Fox MG	.60	.25	.08
☐ 130	Bob Gibson	6.50	2.90	.80
☐ 131	Jim Nettles	.60	.25	.08
☐ 132	Joe Morgan	6.00	2.70	.75
☐ 133	Joe Keough	.75	.35	.09
☐ 134	Carl Morton	.75	.35	.09
☐ 135	Vada Pinson	1.25	.55	.16
☐ 136	Darrel Chaney	.75	.35	.09
☐ 137	Dick Williams MG	1.00	.45	.13
☐ 138	Mike Kekich	.75	.35	.09
☐ 139	Tim McCarver	1.25	.55	.16
☐ 140	Pat Dobson	1.00	.45	.13
☐ 141	Mets Rookies Buzz Capra Lee Stanton Jon Matlack	1.00	.45	.13
☐ 142	Chris Chambliss	3.50	1.55	.45
☐ 143	Garry Jestadt	.75	.35	.09
☐ 144	Marty Pattin	.75	.35	.09
☐ 145	Don Kessinger	1.00	.45	.13
☐ 146	Steve Kealey	.75	.35	.09
☐ 147	Dave Kingman	7.00	3.10	.85
☐ 148	Dick Billings	.75	.35	.09
☐ 149	Gary Neibauer	.75	.35	.09
☐ 150	Norm Cash	1.00	.45	.13
☐ 151	Jim Brewer	.75	.35	.09
☐ 152	Gene Clines	.75	.35	.09
☐ 153	Rick Auerbach	.75	.35	.09
☐ 154	Ted Simmons	3.50	1.55	.45
☐ 155	Larry Dierker	.75	.35	.09
☐ 156	Minnesota Twins Team Card	1.50	.65	.19
☐ 157	Don Gullett	1.00	.45	.13
☐ 158	Jerry Kenney	.75	.35	.09
☐ 159	John Boccabella	.75	.35	.09
☐ 160	Andy Messersmith	1.00	.45	.13
☐ 161	Brock Davis	.75	.35	.09
☐ 162	Brewers Rookies UER Jerry Bell Darrell Porter Bob Reynolds (Porter and Bell photos switched)	1.00	.45	.13
☐ 163	Tug McGraw	1.50	.65	.19
☐ 164	McGraw In Action	1.00	.45	.13
☐ 165	Chris Speier	1.25	.55	.16
☐ 166	Speier In Action	1.00	.45	.13
☐ 167	Deron Johnson	.75	.35	.09
☐ 168	Johnson In Action	.75	.35	.09
☐ 169	Vida Blue	1.50	.65	.19
☐ 170	Blue In Action	1.00	.45	.13
☐ 171	Darrell Evans	2.00	.90	.25
☐ 172	Evans In Action	1.00	.45	.13
☐ 173	Clay Kirby	.75	.35	.09
☐ 174	Kirby In Action	.75	.35	.09
☐ 175	Tom Haller	.75	.35	.09
☐ 176	Haller In Action	.75	.35	.09

☐ 177 Paul Schaal	.75	.35	.09
☐ 178 Schaal In Action	.75	.35	.09
☐ 179 Dock Ellis	.75	.35	.09
☐ 180 Ellis In Action	.75	.35	.09
☐ 181 Ed Kranepool	.75	.35	.09
☐ 182 Kranepool In Action	.75	.35	.09
☐ 183 Bill Melton	.75	.35	.09
☐ 184 Melton In Action	.75	.35	.09
☐ 185 Ron Bryant	.75	.35	.09
☐ 186 Bryant In Action	.75	.35	.09
☐ 187 Gates Brown	1.00	.45	.13
☐ 188 Frank Lucchesi MG	.75	.35	.09
☐ 189 Gene Tenace	1.00	.45	.13
☐ 190 Dave Giusti	.75	.35	.09
☐ 191 Jeff Burroughs	1.25	.55	.16
☐ 192 Chicago Cubs Team Card	1.50	.65	.19
☐ 193 Kurt Bevacqua	.75	.35	.09
☐ 194 Fred Norman	.75	.35	.09
☐ 195 Orlando Cepeda	3.00	1.35	.40
☐ 196 Mel Queen	.75	.35	.09
☐ 197 Johnny Briggs	.75	.35	.09
☐ 198 Dodgers Rookies Charlie Hough Bob O'Brien Mike Strahler	5.00	2.30	.60
☐ 199 Mike Fiore	.75	.35	.09
☐ 200 Lou Brock	6.50	2.90	.80
☐ 201 Phil Roof	.75	.35	.09
☐ 202 Scipio Spinks	.75	.35	.09
☐ 203 Ron Blomberg	.75	.35	.09
☐ 204 Tommy Helms	.75	.35	.09
☐ 205 Dick Drago	.75	.35	.09
☐ 206 Dal Maxvill	.75	.35	.09
☐ 207 Tom Egan	.75	.35	.09
☐ 208 Milt Pappas	1.00	.45	.13
☐ 209 Joe Rudi	1.00	.45	.13
☐ 210 Denny McLain	1.50	.65	.19
☐ 211 Gary Sutherland	.75	.35	.09
☐ 212 Grant Jackson	.75	.35	.09
☐ 213 Angels Rookies Billy Parker Art Kusnyer Tom Silverio	1.00	.45	.13
☐ 214 Mike McQueen	.75	.35	.09
☐ 215 Alex Johnson	1.00	.45	.13
☐ 216 Joe Niekro	1.00	.45	.13
☐ 217 Roger Metzger	.75	.35	.09
☐ 218 Eddie Kasko MG	.75	.35	.09
☐ 219 Rennie Stennett	1.00	.45	.13
☐ 220 Jim Perry	1.00	.45	.13
☐ 221 NL Playoffs Bucs champs	1.50	.65	.19
☐ 222 AL Playoffs Orioles champs (Brooks Robinson)	2.00	.90	.25
☐ 223 World Series Game 1 (Dave McNally pitching)	1.50	.65	.19
☐ 224 World Series Game 2 (Dave Johnson and Mark Belanger)	1.50	.65	.19
☐ 225 World Series Game 3 (Manny Sanguillen scoring)	1.50	.65	.19
☐ 226 World Series Game 4 (Roberto Clemente on second)	3.50	1.55	.45
☐ 227 World Series Game 5 (Nellie Briles pitching)	1.50	.65	.19
☐ 228 World Series Game 6 (Frank Robinson and Manny Sanguillen)	1.50	.65	.19
☐ 229 World Series Game 7 (Steve Blass pitching)	1.50	.65	.19
☐ 230 World Series Summary (Pirates celebrate)	1.50	.65	.19
☐ 231 Casey Cox	.75	.35	.09
☐ 232 Giants Rookies Chris Arnold Jim Barr Dave Rader	.75	.35	.09
☐ 233 Jay Johnstone	1.00	.45	.13
☐ 234 Ron Taylor	.75	.35	.09
☐ 235 Merv Rettenmund	.75	.35	.09
☐ 236 Jim McGlothlin	.75	.35	.09
☐ 237 New York Yankees Team Card	1.50	.65	.19
☐ 238 Leron Lee	.75	.35	.09
☐ 239 Tom Timmermann	.75	.35	.09
☐ 240 Rich Allen	3.00	1.35	.40
☐ 241 Rollie Fingers	8.00	3.60	1.00
☐ 242 Don Mincher	.75	.35	.09
☐ 243 Frank Linzy	.75	.35	.09
☐ 244 Steve Braun	.75	.35	.09
☐ 245 Tommie Agee	1.00	.45	.13
☐ 246 Tom Burgmeier	.75	.35	.09
☐ 247 Milt May	.75	.35	.09
☐ 248 Tom Bradley	.75	.35	.09
☐ 249 Harry Walker MG	.75	.35	.09
☐ 250 Boog Powell	1.50	.65	.19
☐ 251 Checklist 3	4.00	.40	.12
☐ 252 Ken Reynolds	.75	.35	.09
☐ 253 Sandy Alomar	1.00	.45	.13
☐ 254 Boots Day	.75	.35	.09
☐ 255 Jim Lonborg	1.00	.45	.13
☐ 256 George Foster	2.25	1.00	.30
☐ 257 Tigers Rookies Jim Foor Tim Hosley Paul Jata	.75	.35	.09
☐ 258 Randy Hundley	.75	.35	.09
☐ 259 Sparky Lyle	1.25	.55	.16
☐ 260 Ralph Garr	1.00	.45	.13
☐ 261 Steve Mingori	.75	.35	.09
☐ 262 San Diego Padres Team Card	1.50	.65	.19
☐ 263 Felipe Alou	1.25	.55	.16
☐ 264 Tommy John	2.50	1.15	.30
☐ 265 Wes Parker	1.25	.55	.16
☐ 266 Bobby Bolin	1.00	.45	.13
☐ 267 Dave Concepcion	3.50	1.55	.45
☐ 268 A's Rookies Dwain Anderson Chris Floethe	1.00	.45	.13
☐ 269 Don Hahn	1.00	.45	.13
☐ 270 Jim Palmer	15.00	6.75	1.90
☐ 271 Ken Rudolph	1.00	.45	.13
☐ 272 Mickey Rivers	1.50	.65	.19
☐ 273 Bobby Floyd	1.00	.45	.13
☐ 274 Al Severinsen	1.00	.45	.13
☐ 275 Cesar Tovar	1.00	.45	.13
☐ 276 Gene Mauch MG	1.25	.55	.16
☐ 277 Elliott Maddox	1.00	.45	.13
☐ 278 Dennis Higgins	1.00	.45	.13
☐ 279 Larry Brown	1.00	.45	.13
☐ 280 Willie McCovey	6.50	2.90	.80
☐ 281 Bill Parsons	1.00	.45	.13
☐ 282 Houston Astros Team Card	2.00	.90	.25
☐ 283 Darrell Brandon	1.00	.45	.13
☐ 284 Ike Brown	1.00	.45	.13
☐ 285 Gaylord Perry	7.00	3.10	.85
☐ 286 Gene Alley	1.25	.55	.16
☐ 287 Jim Hardin	1.00	.45	.13
☐ 288 Johnny Jeter	1.00	.45	.13
☐ 289 Syd O'Brien	1.00	.45	.13
☐ 290 Sonny Siebert	1.00	.45	.13
☐ 291 Hal McRae	2.00	.90	.25
☐ 292 McRae In Action	1.25	.55	.16
☐ 293 Dan Frisella	1.00	.45	.13
☐ 294 Frisella In Action	1.00	.45	.13
☐ 295 Dick Dietz	1.00	.45	.13
☐ 296 Dietz In Action	1.00	.45	.13
☐ 297 Claude Osteen	1.25	.55	.16
☐ 298 Osteen In Action	1.00	.45	.13
☐ 299 Hank Aaron	35.00	16.00	4.40
☐ 300 Aaron in Action	17.50	8.00	2.20
☐ 301 George Mitterwald	1.00	.45	.13
☐ 302 Mitterwald In Action	1.00	.45	.13
☐ 303 Joe Pepitone	1.25	.55	.16
☐ 304 Pepitone In Action	1.00	.45	.13
☐ 305 Ken Boswell	1.00	.45	.13
☐ 306 Boswell In Action	1.00	.45	.13
☐ 307 Steve Renko	1.00	.45	.13
☐ 308 Renko In Action	1.00	.45	.13
☐ 309 Roberto Clemente	35.00	16.00	4.40
☐ 310 Clemente In Action	17.50	8.00	2.20
☐ 311 Clay Carroll	1.00	.45	.13
☐ 312 Carroll In Action	1.00	.45	.13
☐ 313 Luis Aparicio	3.00	1.35	.40
☐ 314 Aparicio In Action	1.50	.65	.19
☐ 315 Paul Splittorff	1.00	.45	.13
☐ 316 Cardinals Rookies Jim Bibby Jorge Roque Santiago Guzman	1.25	.55	.16
☐ 317 Rich Hand	1.00	.45	.13
☐ 318 Sonny Jackson	1.00	.45	.13
☐ 319 Aurelio Rodriguez	1.00	.45	.13
☐ 320 Steve Blass	1.25	.55	.16
☐ 321 Joe Lahoud	1.00	.45	.13
☐ 322 Jose Pena	1.00	.45	.13
☐ 323 Earl Weaver MG	2.00	.90	.25
☐ 324 Mike Ryan	1.00	.45	.13
☐ 325 Mel Stottlemyre	1.25	.55	.16

☐ 326 Pat Kelly 1.00 .45 .13
☐ 327 Steve Stone 1.75 .80 .22
☐ 328 Boston Red Sox 2.00 .90 .25
Team Card
☐ 329 Roy Foster 1.00 .45 .13
☐ 330 Jim Hunter 5.00 2.30 .60
☐ 331 Stan Swanson 1.00 .45 .13
☐ 332 Buck Martinez 1.00 .45 .13
☐ 333 Steve Barber 1.00 .45 .13
☐ 334 Rangers Rookies 1.00 .45 .13
Bill Fahey
Jim Mason
Tom Ragland
☐ 335 Bill Hands 1.00 .45 .13
☐ 336 Marty Martinez 1.00 .45 .13
☐ 337 Mike Kilkenny 1.00 .45 .13
☐ 338 Bob Grich 1.50 .65 .19
☐ 339 Ron Cook 1.00 .45 .13
☐ 340 Roy White 1.25 .55 .16
☐ 341 KP: Joe Torre 1.25 .55 .16
☐ 342 KP: Wilbur Wood 1.25 .55 .16
☐ 343 KP: Willie Stargell 1.50 .65 .19
☐ 344 KP: Dave McNally 1.25 .55 .16
☐ 345 KP: Rick Wise 1.25 .55 .16
☐ 346 KP: Jim Fregosi 1.25 .55 .16
☐ 347 KP: Tom Seaver 4.00 1.80 .50
☐ 348 KP: Sal Bando 1.25 .55 .16
☐ 349 Al Fitzmorris 1.00 .45 .13
☐ 350 Frank Howard 1.50 .65 .19
☐ 351 Braves Rookies 1.25 .55 .16
Tom House
Rick Kester
Jimmy Britton
☐ 352 Dave LaRoche 1.00 .45 .13
☐ 353 Art Shamsky 1.00 .45 .13
☐ 354 Tom Murphy 1.00 .45 .13
☐ 355 Bob Watson 1.25 .55 .16
☐ 356 Gerry Moses 1.00 .45 .13
☐ 357 Woody Fryman 1.00 .45 .13
☐ 358 Sparky Anderson MG 2.00 .90 .25
☐ 359 Don Pavletich 1.00 .45 .13
☐ 360 Dave Roberts 1.00 .45 .13
☐ 361 Mike Andrews 1.00 .45 .13
☐ 362 New York Mets 2.00 .90 .25
Team Card
☐ 363 Ron Klimkowski 1.00 .45 .13
☐ 364 Johnny Callison 1.25 .55 .16
☐ 365 Dick Bosman 1.00 .45 .13
☐ 366 Jimmy Rosario 1.00 .45 .13
☐ 367 Ron Perranoski 1.25 .55 .16
☐ 368 Danny Thompson 1.00 .45 .13
☐ 369 Jim Lefebvre 1.25 .55 .16
☐ 370 Don Buford 1.00 .45 .13
☐ 371 Denny Lemaster 1.00 .45 .13
☐ 372 Royals Rookies 1.00 .45 .13
Lance Clemons
Monty Montgomery
☐ 373 John Mayberry 1.25 .55 .16
☐ 374 Jack Heidemann 1.00 .45 .13
☐ 375 Reggie Cleveland 1.00 .45 .13
☐ 376 Andy Kosco 1.00 .45 .13
☐ 377 Terry Harmon 1.00 .45 .13
☐ 378 Checklist 4 4.00 .40 .12
☐ 379 Ken Berry 1.00 .45 .13
☐ 380 Earl Williams 1.00 .45 .13
☐ 381 Chicago White Sox 2.00 .90 .25
Team Card
☐ 382 Joe Gibbon 1.00 .45 .13
☐ 383 Brant Alyea 1.00 .45 .13
☐ 384 Dave Campbell 1.00 .45 .13
☐ 385 Mickey Stanley 1.25 .55 .16
☐ 386 Jim Colborn 1.00 .45 .13
☐ 387 Horace Clarke 1.00 .45 .13
☐ 388 Charlie Williams 1.00 .45 .13
☐ 389 Bill Rigney MG 1.00 .45 .13
☐ 390 Willie Davis 1.25 .55 .16
☐ 391 Ken Sanders 1.00 .45 .13
☐ 392 Pirates Rookies 1.50 .65 .19
Fred Cambria
Richie Zisk
☐ 393 Curt Motton 1.00 .45 .13
☐ 394 Ken Forsch 1.25 .55 .16
☐ 395 Matty Alou 1.75 .80 .22
☐ 396 Paul Lindblad 1.50 .65 .19
☐ 397 Philadelphia Phillies 3.00 1.35 .40
Team Card
☐ 398 Larry Hisle 1.75 .80 .22
☐ 399 Milt Wilcox 1.50 .65 .19
☐ 400 Tony Oliva 2.50 1.15 .30
☐ 401 Jim Nash 1.50 .65 .19
☐ 402 Bobby Heise 1.50 .65 .19
☐ 403 John Cumberland 1.50 .65 .19
☐ 404 Jeff Torborg 1.75 .80 .22
☐ 405 Ron Fairly 1.75 .80 .22
☐ 406 George Hendrick 2.00 .90 .25
☐ 407 Chuck Taylor 1.50 .65 .19
☐ 408 Jim Northrup 1.75 .80 .22
☐ 409 Frank Baker 1.50 .65 .19
☐ 410 Fergie Jenkins 7.50 3.40 .95
☐ 411 Bob Montgomery 1.50 .65 .19
☐ 412 Dick Kelley 1.50 .65 .19
☐ 413 White Sox Rookies 1.50 .65 .19
Don Eddy
Dave Lemonds
☐ 414 Bob Miller 1.50 .65 .19
☐ 415 Cookie Rojas 1.75 .80 .22
☐ 416 Johnny Edwards 1.50 .65 .19
☐ 417 Tom Hall 1.50 .65 .19
☐ 418 Tom Shopay 1.50 .65 .19
☐ 419 Jim Spencer 1.50 .65 .19
☐ 420 Steve Carlton 25.00 11.50 3.10
☐ 421 Ellie Rodriguez 1.50 .65 .19
☐ 422 Ray Lamb 1.50 .65 .19
☐ 423 Oscar Gamble 1.75 .80 .22
☐ 424 Bill Gogolewski 1.50 .65 .19
☐ 425 Ken Singleton 2.50 1.15 .30
☐ 426 Singleton In Action 1.75 .80 .22
☐ 427 Tito Fuentes 1.50 .65 .19
☐ 428 Fuentes In Action 1.50 .65 .19
☐ 429 Bob Robertson 1.50 .65 .19
☐ 430 Robertson In Action 1.50 .65 .19
☐ 431 Clarence Gaston 2.50 1.15 .30
☐ 432 Gaston In Action 1.75 .80 .22
☐ 433 Johnny Bench 45.00 20.00 5.75
☐ 434 Bench In Action 22.50 10.00 2.80
☐ 435 Reggie Jackson 55.00 25.00 7.00
☐ 436 Jackson In Action 27.50 12.50 3.40
☐ 437 Maury Wills 2.50 1.15 .30
☐ 438 Wills In Action 2.00 .90 .25
☐ 439 Billy Williams 5.00 2.30 .60
☐ 440 Williams In Action 2.50 1.15 .30
☐ 441 Thurman Munson 20.00 9.00 2.50
☐ 442 Munson In Action 10.00 4.50 1.25
☐ 443 Ken Henderson 1.50 .65 .19
☐ 444 Henderson In Action 1.50 .65 .19
☐ 445 Tom Seaver 40.00 18.00 5.00
☐ 446 Seaver In Action 20.00 9.00 2.50
☐ 447 Willie Stargell 6.00 2.70 .75
☐ 448 Stargell In Action 3.00 1.35 .40
☐ 449 Bob Lemon MG 1.75 .80 .22
☐ 450 Mickey Lolich 2.50 1.15 .30
☐ 451 Tony LaRussa 3.00 1.35 .40
☐ 452 Ed Herrmann 1.50 .65 .19
☐ 453 Barry Lersch 1.50 .65 .19
☐ 454 Oakland A's 3.00 1.35 .40
Team Card
☐ 455 Tommy Harper 1.75 .80 .22
☐ 456 Mark Belanger 1.75 .80 .22
☐ 457 Padres Rookies 1.50 .65 .19
Darcy Fast
Derrel Thomas
Mike Ivie
☐ 458 Aurelio Monteagudo 1.50 .65 .19
☐ 459 Rick Renick 1.50 .65 .19
☐ 460 Al Downing 1.50 .65 .19
☐ 461 Tim Cullen 1.50 .65 .19
☐ 462 Rickey Clark 1.50 .65 .19
☐ 463 Bernie Carbo 1.50 .65 .19
☐ 464 Jim Roland 1.50 .65 .19
☐ 465 Gil Hodges MG 4.50 2.00 .55
☐ 466 Norm Miller 1.50 .65 .19
☐ 467 Steve Kline 1.50 .65 .19
☐ 468 Richie Scheinblum 1.50 .65 .19
☐ 469 Ron Herbel 1.50 .65 .19
☐ 470 Ray Fosse 1.50 .65 .19
☐ 471 Luke Walker 1.50 .65 .19
☐ 472 Phil Gagliano 1.50 .65 .19
☐ 473 Dan McGinn 1.50 .65 .19
☐ 474 Orioles Rookies 7.00 3.10 .85
Don Baylor
Roric Harrison
Johnny Oates
☐ 475 Gary Nolan 1.75 .80 .22
☐ 476 Lee Richard 1.50 .65 .19
☐ 477 Tom Phoebus 1.50 .65 .19
☐ 478 Checklist 5 4.00 .40 .12
☐ 479 Don Shaw 1.50 .65 .19
☐ 480 Lee May 1.75 .80 .22
☐ 481 Billy Conigliaro 1.75 .80 .22
☐ 482 Joe Hoerner 1.50 .65 .19
☐ 483 Ken Suarez 1.50 .65 .19
☐ 484 Lum Harris MG 1.50 .65 .19
☐ 485 Phil Regan 1.75 .80 .22
☐ 486 John Lowenstein 1.50 .65 .19
☐ 487 Detroit Tigers 3.00 1.35 .40
Team Card

☐ 488	Mike Nagy	1.50	.65	.19
☐ 489	Expos Rookies Terry Humphrey Keith Lampard	1.50	.65	.19
☐ 490	Dave McNally	1.75	.80	.22
☐ 491	KP: Lou Piniella	2.00	.90	.25
☐ 492	KP: Mel Stottlemyre	1.75	.80	.22
☐ 493	KP: Bob Bailey	1.75	.80	.22
☐ 494	KP: Willie Horton	1.75	.80	.22
☐ 495	KP: Bill Melton	1.75	.80	.22
☐ 496	KP: Bud Harrelson	1.75	.80	.22
☐ 497	KP: Jim Perry	1.75	.80	.22
☐ 498	KP: Brooks Robinson	2.50	1.15	.30
☐ 499	Vicente Romo	1.50	.65	.19
☐ 500	Joe Torre	2.50	1.15	.30
☐ 501	Pete Hamm	1.50	.65	.19
☐ 502	Jackie Hernandez	1.50	.65	.19
☐ 503	Gary Peters	1.50	.65	.19
☐ 504	Ed Spiezio	1.50	.65	.19
☐ 505	Mike Marshall	1.75	.80	.22
☐ 506	Indians Rookies Terry Ley Jim Moyer Dick Tidrow	1.50	.65	.19
☐ 507	Fred Gladding	1.50	.65	.19
☐ 508	Elrod Hendricks	1.50	.65	.19
☐ 509	Don McMahon	1.50	.65	.19
☐ 510	Ted Williams MG	7.50	3.40	.95
☐ 511	Tony Taylor	1.50	.65	.19
☐ 512	Paul Popovich	1.50	.65	.19
☐ 513	Lindy McDaniel	1.75	.80	.22
☐ 514	Ted Sizemore	1.50	.65	.19
☐ 515	Bert Blyleven	12.50	5.75	1.55
☐ 516	Oscar Brown	1.50	.65	.19
☐ 517	Ken Brett	1.50	.65	.19
☐ 518	Wayne Garrett	1.50	.65	.19
☐ 519	Ted Abernathy	1.50	.65	.19
☐ 520	Larry Bowa	2.00	.90	.25
☐ 521	Alan Foster	1.50	.65	.19
☐ 522	Los Angeles Dodgers Team Card	3.00	1.35	.40
☐ 523	Chuck Dobson	1.50	.65	.19
☐ 524	Reds Rookies Ed Armbrister Mel Behney	1.50	.65	.19
☐ 525	Carlos May	1.75	.80	.22
☐ 526	Bob Bailey	3.50	1.55	.45
☐ 527	Dave Leonhard	3.00	1.35	.40
☐ 528	Ron Stone	3.00	1.35	.40
☐ 529	Dave Nelson	3.00	1.35	.40
☐ 530	Don Sutton	6.50	2.90	.80
☐ 531	Freddie Patek	3.50	1.55	.45
☐ 532	Fred Kendall	3.00	1.35	.40
☐ 533	Ralph Houk MG	3.50	1.55	.45
☐ 534	Jim Hickman	3.50	1.55	.45
☐ 535	Ed Brinkman	3.00	1.35	.40
☐ 536	Doug Rader	3.50	1.55	.45
☐ 537	Bob Locker	3.00	1.35	.40
☐ 538	Charlie Sands	3.00	1.35	.40
☐ 539	Terry Forster	4.00	1.80	.50
☐ 540	Felix Millan	3.00	1.35	.40
☐ 541	Roger Repoz	3.00	1.35	.40
☐ 542	Jack Billingham	3.00	1.35	.40
☐ 543	Duane Josephson	3.00	1.35	.40
☐ 544	Ted Martinez	3.00	1.35	.40
☐ 545	Wayne Granger	3.00	1.35	.40
☐ 546	Joe Hague	3.00	1.35	.40
☐ 547	Cleveland Indians Team Card	6.00	2.70	.75
☐ 548	Frank Reberger	3.00	1.35	.40
☐ 549	Dave May	3.00	1.35	.40
☐ 550	Brooks Robinson	25.00	11.50	3.10
☐ 551	Ollie Brown	3.00	1.35	.40
☐ 552	Brown In Action	3.00	1.35	.40
☐ 553	Wilbur Wood	3.50	1.55	.45
☐ 554	Wood In Action	3.00	1.35	.40
☐ 555	Ron Santo	4.50	2.00	.55
☐ 556	Santo In Action	4.00	1.80	.50
☐ 557	John Odom	3.00	1.35	.40
☐ 558	Odom In Action	3.00	1.35	.40
☐ 559	Pete Rose	50.00	23.00	6.25
☐ 560	Rose In Action	25.00	11.50	3.10
☐ 561	Leo Cardenas	3.00	1.35	.40
☐ 562	Cardenas In Action	3.00	1.35	.40
☐ 563	Ray Sadecki	3.00	1.35	.40
☐ 564	Sadecki In Action	3.00	1.35	.40
☐ 565	Reggie Smith	3.50	1.55	.45
☐ 566	Smith In Action	3.00	1.35	.40
☐ 567	Juan Marichal	7.00	3.10	[illegible]
☐ 568	Marichal In Action	3.50	1.55	.45
☐ 569	Ed Kirkpatrick	3.00	1.35	.40
☐ 570	Kirkpatrick In Action	3.00	1.35	.40
☐ 571	Nate Colbert	3.00	1.35	.40
☐ 572	Colbert In Action	3.00	1.35	.40
☐ 573	Fritz Peterson	3.00	1.35	.40
☐ 574	Peterson In Action	3.00	1.35	.40
☐ 575	Al Oliver	4.00	1.80	.50
☐ 576	Leo Durocher MG	4.00	1.80	.50
☐ 577	Mike Paul	3.00	1.35	.40
☐ 578	Billy Grabarkewitz	3.00	1.35	.40
☐ 579	Doyle Alexander	3.50	1.55	.45
☐ 580	Lou Piniella	5.00	2.30	.60
☐ 581	Wade Blasingame	3.00	1.35	.40
☐ 582	Montreal Expos Team Card	6.00	2.70	.75
☐ 583	Darold Knowles	3.00	1.35	.40
☐ 584	Jerry McNertney	3.00	1.35	.40
☐ 585	George Scott	3.50	1.55	.45
☐ 586	Denis Menke	3.00	1.35	.40
☐ 587	Billy Wilson	3.00	1.35	.40
☐ 588	Jim Holt	3.00	1.35	.40
☐ 589	Hal Lanier	3.00	1.35	.40
☐ 590	Graig Nettles	5.00	2.30	.60
☐ 591	Paul Casanova	3.00	1.35	.40
☐ 592	Lew Krausse	3.00	1.35	.40
☐ 593	Rich Morales	3.00	1.35	.40
☐ 594	Jim Beauchamp	3.00	1.35	.40
☐ 595	Nolan Ryan	260.00	115.00	33.00
☐ 596	Manny Mota	3.50	1.55	.45
☐ 597	Jim Magnuson	3.00	1.35	.40
☐ 598	Hal King	3.00	1.35	.40
☐ 599	Billy Champion	3.00	1.35	.40
☐ 600	Al Kaline	25.00	11.50	3.10
☐ 601	George Stone	3.00	1.35	.40
☐ 602	Dave Bristol MG	3.00	1.35	.40
☐ 603	Jim Ray	3.00	1.35	.40
☐ 604A	Checklist 6 (Copyright on back bottom right)	9.00	.90	.27
☐ 604B	Checklist 6 (Copyright on back bottom left)	9.00	.90	.27
☐ 605	Nelson Briles	3.50	1.55	.45
☐ 606	Luis Melendez	3.00	1.35	.40
☐ 607	Frank Duffy	3.00	1.35	.40
☐ 608	Mike Corkins	3.00	1.35	.40
☐ 609	Tom Grieve	3.50	1.55	.45
☐ 610	Bill Stoneman	3.00	1.35	.40
☐ 611	Rich Reese	3.00	1.35	.40
☐ 612	Joe Decker	3.00	1.35	.40
☐ 613	Mike Ferraro	3.00	1.35	.40
☐ 614	Ted Uhlaender	3.00	1.35	.40
☐ 615	Steve Hargan	3.00	1.35	.40
☐ 616	Joe Ferguson	3.50	1.55	.45
☐ 617	Kansas City Royals Team Card	6.00	2.70	.75
☐ 618	Rich Robertson	3.00	1.35	.40
☐ 619	Rich McKinney	3.00	1.35	.40
☐ 620	Phil Niekro	7.00	3.10	.85
☐ 621	Commissioners Award	4.00	1.80	.50
☐ 622	MVP Award	4.00	1.80	.50
☐ 623	Cy Young Award	4.00	1.80	.50
☐ 624	Minor League Player	4.00	1.80	.50
☐ 625	Rookie of the Year	4.00	1.80	.50
☐ 626	Babe Ruth Award	4.00	1.80	.50
☐ 627	Moe Drabowsky	3.00	1.35	.40
☐ 628	Terry Crowley	3.00	1.35	.40
☐ 629	Paul Doyle	3.00	1.35	.40
☐ 630	Rich Hebner	3.50	1.55	.45
☐ 631	John Strohmayer	3.00	1.35	.40
☐ 632	Mike Hegan	3.00	1.35	.40
☐ 633	Jack Hiatt	3.00	1.35	.40
☐ 634	Dick Woodson	3.00	1.35	.40
☐ 635	Don Money	3.50	1.55	.45
☐ 636	Bill Lee	3.50	1.55	.45
☐ 637	Preston Gomez MG	3.00	1.35	.40
☐ 638	Ken Wright	3.00	1.35	.40
☐ 639	J.C. Martin	3.00	1.35	.40
☐ 640	Joe Coleman	3.00	1.35	.40
☐ 641	Mike Lum	3.00	1.35	.40
☐ 642	Dennis Riddleberger	3.00	1.35	.40
☐ 643	Russ Gibson	3.00	1.35	.40
☐ 644	Bernie Allen	3.00	1.35	.40
☐ 645	Jim Maloney	3.50	1.55	.45
☐ 646	Chico Salmon	3.00	1.35	.40
☐ 647	Bob Moose	3.00	1.35	.40
☐ 648	Jim Lyttle	3.00	1.35	.40
☐ 649	Pete Richert	3.00	1.35	.40
☐ 650	Sal Bando	3.50	1.55	.45
☐ 651	Cincinnati Reds Team Card	6.00	2.70	.75
☐ 652	Marcelino Lopez	3.00	1.35	.40
☐ 653	Jim Fairey	3.00	1.35	.40
☐ 654	Horacio Pina	3.00	1.35	.40
☐ 655	Jerry Grote	3.00	1.35	.40
☐ 656	Rudy May	3.00	1.35	.40

☐ 657 Bobby Wine 6.50 2.90 .80
☐ 658 Steve Dunning 6.50 2.90 .80
☐ 659 Bob Aspromonte 6.50 2.90 .80
☐ 660 Paul Blair 7.50 3.40 .95
☐ 661 Bill Virdon MG 7.50 3.40 .95
☐ 662 Stan Bahnsen 6.50 2.90 .80
☐ 663 Fran Healy 7.50 3.40 .95
☐ 664 Bobby Knoop 6.50 2.90 .80
☐ 665 Chris Short 6.50 2.90 .80
☐ 666 Hector Torres 6.50 2.90 .80
☐ 667 Ray Newman 6.50 2.90 .80
☐ 668 Texas Rangers 15.00 6.75 1.90
Team Card
☐ 669 Willie Crawford 6.50 2.90 .80
☐ 670 Ken Holtzman 7.50 3.40 .95
☐ 671 Donn Clendenon 7.50 3.40 .95
☐ 672 Archie Reynolds 6.50 2.90 .80
☐ 673 Dave Marshall 6.50 2.90 .80
☐ 674 John Kennedy 6.50 2.90 .80
☐ 675 Pat Jarvis 6.50 2.90 .80
☐ 676 Danny Cater 6.50 2.90 .80
☐ 677 Ivan Murrell 6.50 2.90 .80
☐ 678 Steve Luebber 6.50 2.90 .80
☐ 679 Astros Rookies 6.50 2.90 .80
Bob Fenwick
Bob Stinson
☐ 680 Dave Johnson 7.50 3.40 .95
☐ 681 Bobby Pfeil 6.50 2.90 .80
☐ 682 Mike McCormick 7.50 3.40 .95
☐ 683 Steve Hovley 6.50 2.90 .80
☐ 684 Hal Breeden 7.50 3.40 .95
☐ 685 Joel Horlen 6.50 2.90 .80
☐ 686 Steve Garvey 70.00 32.00 8.75
☐ 687 Del Unser 6.50 2.90 .80
☐ 688 St. Louis Cardinals 12.00 5.50 1.50
Team Card
☐ 689 Eddie Fisher 6.50 2.90 .80
☐ 690 Willie Montanez 7.50 3.40 .95
☐ 691 Curt Blefary 6.50 2.90 .80
☐ 692 Blefary In Action 6.50 2.90 .80
☐ 693 Alan Gallagher 6.50 2.90 .80
☐ 694 Gallagher In Action 6.50 2.90 .80
☐ 695 Rod Carew 90.00 40.00 11.50
☐ 696 Carew In Action 45.00 20.00 5.75
☐ 697 Jerry Koosman 15.00 6.75 1.90
☐ 698 Koosman In Action 10.00 4.50 1.25
☐ 699 Bobby Murcer 15.00 6.75 1.90
☐ 700 Murcer In Action 10.00 4.50 1.25
☐ 701 Jose Pagan 6.50 2.90 .80
☐ 702 Pagan In Action 6.50 2.90 .80
☐ 703 Doug Griffin 6.50 2.90 .80
☐ 704 Griffin In Action 6.50 2.90 .80
☐ 705 Pat Corrales 7.50 3.40 .95
☐ 706 Corrales In Action 6.50 2.90 .80
☐ 707 Tim Foli 6.50 2.90 .80
☐ 708 Foli In Action 6.50 2.90 .80
☐ 709 Jim Kaat 15.00 6.75 1.90
☐ 710 Kaat In Action 10.00 4.50 1.25
☐ 711 Bobby Bonds 18.00 8.00 2.30
☐ 712 Bonds In Action 11.50 5.25 1.45
☐ 713 Gene Michael 7.50 3.40 .95
☐ 714 Michael In Action 7.50 3.40 .95
☐ 715 Mike Epstein 6.50 2.90 .80
☐ 716 Jesus Alou 6.50 2.90 .80
☐ 717 Bruce Dal Canton 6.50 2.90 .80
☐ 718 Del Rice MG 6.50 2.90 .80
☐ 719 Cesar Geronimo 6.50 2.90 .80
☐ 720 Sam McDowell 7.50 3.40 .95
☐ 721 Eddie Leon 6.50 2.90 .80
☐ 722 Bill Sudakis 6.50 2.90 .80
☐ 723 Al Santorini 6.50 2.90 .80
☐ 724 AL Rookie Pitchers 6.50 2.90 .80
John Curtis
Rich Hinton
Mickey Scott
☐ 725 Dick McAuliffe 7.50 3.40 .95
☐ 726 Dick Selma 6.50 2.90 .80
☐ 727 Jose Laboy 6.50 2.90 .80
☐ 728 Gail Hopkins 6.50 2.90 .80
☐ 729 Bob Veale 7.50 3.40 .95
☐ 730 Rick Monday 7.50 3.40 .95
☐ 731 Baltimore Orioles 12.00 5.50 1.50
Team Card
☐ 732 George Culver 6.50 2.90 .80
☐ 733 Jim Ray Hart 7.50 3.40 .95
☐ 734 Bob Burda 6.50 2.90 .80
☐ 735 Diego Segui 6.50 2.90 .80
☐ 736 Bill Russell 8.50 3.80 1.05
☐ 737 Len Randle 6.50 2.90 .80
☐ 738 Jim Merritt 6.50 2.90 .80
☐ 739 Don Mason 6.50 2.90 .80
☐ 740 Rico Carty 7.50 3.40 .95
☐ 741 Rookie First Basemen 10.00 4.50 1.25
Tom Hutton
John Milner
Rick Miller
☐ 742 Jim Rooker 6.50 2.90 .80
☐ 743 Cesar Gutierrez 6.50 2.90 .80
☐ 744 Jim Slaton 6.50 2.90 .80
☐ 745 Julian Javier 7.50 3.40 .95
☐ 746 Lowell Palmer 6.50 2.90 .80
☐ 747 Jim Stewart 6.50 2.90 .80
☐ 748 Phil Hennigan 6.50 2.90 .80
☐ 749 Walter Alston MG 10.00 4.50 1.25
☐ 750 Willie Horton 7.50 3.40 .95
☐ 751 Steve Carlton TR 60.00 27.00 7.50
☐ 752 Joe Morgan TR 45.00 20.00 5.75
☐ 753 Denny McLain TR 13.00 5.75 1.65
☐ 754 Frank Robinson TR 35.00 16.00 4.40
☐ 755 Jim Fregosi TR 7.00 3.10 .85
☐ 756 Rick Wise TR 7.00 3.10 .85
☐ 757 Jose Cardenal TR 7.00 3.10 .85
☐ 758 Gil Garrido 6.50 2.90 .80
☐ 759 Chris Cannizzaro 6.50 2.90 .80
☐ 760 Bill Mazeroski 9.00 4.00 1.15
☐ 761 Rookie Outfielders 28.00 12.50 3.50
Ben Oglivie
Ron Cey
Bernie Williams
☐ 762 Wayne Simpson 6.50 2.90 .80
☐ 763 Ron Hansen 6.50 2.90 .80
☐ 764 Dusty Baker 12.00 5.50 1.50
☐ 765 Ken McMullen 6.50 2.90 .80
☐ 766 Steve Hamilton 6.50 2.90 .80
☐ 767 Tom McCraw 6.50 2.90 .80
☐ 768 Denny Doyle 6.50 2.90 .80
☐ 769 Jack Aker 6.50 2.90 .80
☐ 770 Jim Wynn 7.50 3.40 .95
☐ 771 San Francisco Giants 12.00 5.50 1.50
Team Card
☐ 772 Ken Tatum 6.50 2.90 .80
☐ 773 Ron Brand 6.50 2.90 .80
☐ 774 Luis Alvarado 6.50 2.90 .80
☐ 775 Jerry Reuss 7.50 3.40 .95
☐ 776 Bill Voss 6.50 2.90 .80
☐ 777 Hoyt Wilhelm 20.00 9.00 2.50
☐ 778 Twins Rookies 15.00 6.75 1.90
Vic Albury
Rick Dempsey
Jim Strickland
☐ 779 Tony Cloninger 6.50 2.90 .80
☐ 780 Dick Green 6.50 2.90 .80
☐ 781 Jim McAndrew 6.50 2.90 .80
☐ 782 Larry Stahl 6.50 2.90 .80
☐ 783 Les Cain 6.50 2.90 .80
☐ 784 Ken Aspromonte 6.50 2.90 .80
☐ 785 Vic Davalillo 6.50 2.90 .80
☐ 786 Chuck Brinkman 6.50 2.90 .80
☐ 787 Ron Reed 8.00 3.60 1.00

1973 Topps

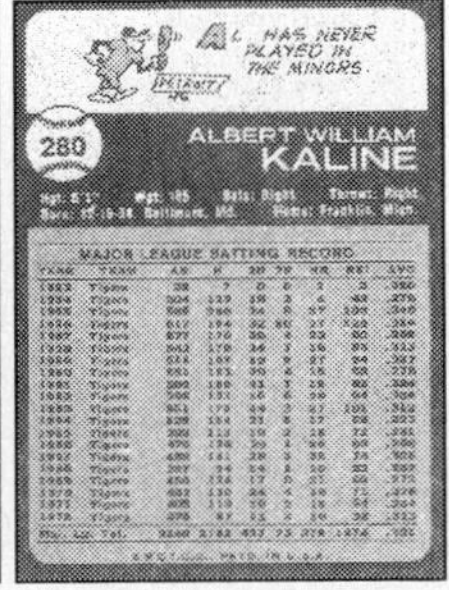

The cards in this 660-card set measure 2 1/2" by 3 1/2". The 1973 Topps set marked the last year in which Topps marketed baseball cards in consecutive series. The last series (529-660) is more difficult to obtain. Beginning in 1974, all Topps cards were printed at the same time, thus eliminating the "high number" factor. The set features team leader cards with small individual pictures of the coaching staff members and a larger picture of the manager. The "background" variations below with respect to these leader cards are subtle and are best understood after a side-by-side comparison of the two varieties. An "All-Time Leaders" series (471-478) appeared for the first time in this set. Kid Pictures appeared again for the second year in a row (341-346). Other topical subsets within the set included League Leaders (61-68), Playoffs cards (201-202), World Series cards (203-210), and Rookie Prospects (601-616). The key Rookie Cards in this set are all in the Rookie Prospect series: Bob Boone, Dwight Evans, and Mike Schmidt.

	NRMT-MT	EXC	G-VG
COMPLETE SET (660)	1200.00	550.00	150.00
COMMON PLAYER (1-132)	.50	.23	.06
COMMON PLAYER (133-264)	.50	.23	.06
COMMON PLAYER (265-396)	.65	.30	.08
COMMON PLAYER (397-528)	1.25	.55	.16
COMMON PLAYER (529-660)	3.00	1.35	.40

Card	NRMT-MT	EXC	G-VG
☐ 1 All-Time HR Leaders	30.00	7.50	2.40
Babe Ruth 714			
Hank Aaron 673			
Willie Mays 654			
☐ 2 Rich Hebner	.75	.35	.09
☐ 3 Jim Lonborg	.75	.35	.09
☐ 4 John Milner	.50	.23	.06
☐ 5 Ed Brinkman	.50	.23	.06
☐ 6 Mac Scarce	.50	.23	.06
☐ 7 Texas Rangers	1.00	.45	.13
Team Card			
☐ 8 Tom Hall	.50	.23	.06
☐ 9 Johnny Oates	.80	.35	.10
☐ 10 Don Sutton	3.50	1.55	.45
☐ 11 Chris Chambliss	1.00	.45	.13
☐ 12A Padres Leaders	.80	.35	.10
Don Zimmer MG			
Dave Garcia CO			
Johnny Podres CO			
Bob Skinner CO			
Whitey Wietelmann CO			
(Podres no right ear)			
☐ 12B Padres Leaders	1.50	.65	.19
(Podres has right ear)			
☐ 13 George Hendrick	.75	.35	.09
☐ 14 Sonny Siebert	.50	.23	.06
☐ 15 Ralph Garr	.75	.35	.09
☐ 16 Steve Braun	.50	.23	.06
☐ 17 Fred Gladding	.50	.23	.06
☐ 18 Leroy Stanton	.50	.23	.06
☐ 19 Tim Foli	.50	.23	.06
☐ 20 Stan Bahnsen	.50	.23	.06
☐ 21 Randy Hundley	.50	.23	.06
☐ 22 Ted Abernathy	.50	.23	.06
☐ 23 Dave Kingman	1.50	.65	.19
☐ 24 Al Santorini	.50	.23	.06
☐ 25 Roy White	.75	.35	.09
☐ 26 Pittsburgh Pirates	1.00	.45	.13
Team Card			
☐ 27 Bill Gogolewski	.50	.23	.06
☐ 28 Hal McRae	1.25	.55	.16
☐ 29 Tony Taylor	.50	.23	.06
☐ 30 Tug McGraw	1.00	.45	.13
☐ 31 Buddy Bell	3.50	1.55	.45
☐ 32 Fred Norman	.50	.23	.06
☐ 33 Jim Breazeale	.50	.23	.06
☐ 34 Pat Dobson	.50	.23	.06
☐ 35 Willie Davis	.75	.35	.09
☐ 36 Steve Barber	.50	.23	.06
☐ 37 Bill Robinson	.75	.35	.09
☐ 38 Mike Epstein	.50	.23	.06
☐ 39 Dave Roberts	.50	.23	.06
☐ 40 Reggie Smith	.90	.40	.11
☐ 41 Tom Walker	.50	.23	.06
☐ 42 Mike Andrews	.50	.23	.06
☐ 43 Randy Moffitt	.50	.23	.06
☐ 44 Rick Monday	.75	.35	.09
☐ 45 Ellie Rodriguez UER	.50	.23	.06
(Photo actually			
John Felske)			
☐ 46 Lindy McDaniel	.75	.35	.09
☐ 47 Luis Melendez	.50	.23	.06
☐ 48 Paul Splittorff	.50	.23	.06
☐ 49A Twins Leaders	.80	.35	.10
Frank Quilici MG			
Vern Morgan CO			
Bob Rodgers CO			
Ralph Rowe CO			
Al Worthington CO			
(Solid backgrounds)			
☐ 49B Twins Leaders	1.50	.65	.19
(Natural backgrounds)			
☐ 50 Roberto Clemente	35.00	16.00	4.40
☐ 51 Chuck Seelbach	.50	.23	.06
☐ 52 Denis Menke	.50	.23	.06
☐ 53 Steve Dunning	.50	.23	.06
☐ 54 Checklist 1	3.00	.30	.09
☐ 55 Jon Matlack	.75	.35	.09
☐ 56 Merv Rettenmund	.50	.23	.06
☐ 57 Derrel Thomas	.50	.23	.06
☐ 58 Mike Paul	.50	.23	.06
☐ 59 Steve Yeager	1.00	.45	.13
☐ 60 Ken Holtzman	.75	.35	.09
☐ 61 Batting Leaders	2.50	1.15	.30
Billy Williams			
Rod Carew			
☐ 62 Home Run Leaders	2.50	1.15	.30
Johnny Bench			
Dick Allen			
☐ 63 RBI Leaders	2.50	1.15	.30
Johnny Bench			
Dick Allen			
☐ 64 Stolen Base Leaders	1.75	.80	.22
Lou Brock			
Bert Campaneris			
☐ 65 ERA Leaders	1.75	.80	.22
Steve Carlton			
Luis Tiant			
☐ 66 Victory Leaders	1.75	.80	.22
Steve Carlton			
Gaylord Perry			
Wilbur Wood			
☐ 67 Strikeout Leaders	10.00	4.50	1.25
Steve Carlton			
Nolan Ryan			
☐ 68 Leading Firemen	1.00	.45	.13
Clay Carroll			
Sparky Lyle			
☐ 69 Phil Gagliano	.50	.23	.06
☐ 70 Milt Pappas	.75	.35	.09
☐ 71 Johnny Briggs	.50	.23	.06
☐ 72 Ron Reed	.50	.23	.06
☐ 73 Ed Herrmann	.50	.23	.06
☐ 74 Billy Champion	.50	.23	.06
☐ 75 Vada Pinson	1.00	.45	.13
☐ 76 Doug Rader	.50	.23	.06
☐ 77 Mike Torrez	.75	.35	.09
☐ 78 Richie Scheinblum	.50	.23	.06
☐ 79 Jim Willoughby	.50	.23	.06
☐ 80 Tony Oliva UER	1.50	.65	.19
(Minnseota on front)			
☐ 81A Cubs Leaders	1.00	.45	.13
Whitey Lockman MG			
Hank Aguirre CO			
Ernie Banks CO			
Larry Jansen CO			
Pete Reiser CO			
(Solid backgrounds)			
☐ 81B Cubs Leaders	2.00	.90	.25
(Natural backgrounds)			
☐ 82 Fritz Peterson	.50	.23	.06
☐ 83 Leron Lee	.50	.23	.06
☐ 84 Rollie Fingers	7.00	3.10	.85
☐ 85 Ted Simmons	2.50	1.15	.30
☐ 86 Tom McCraw	.50	.23	.06
☐ 87 Ken Boswell	.50	.23	.06
☐ 88 Mickey Stanley	.75	.35	.09
☐ 89 Jack Billingham	.50	.23	.06
☐ 90 Brooks Robinson	7.00	3.10	.85
☐ 91 Los Angeles Dodgers	1.00	.45	.13
Team Card			
☐ 92 Jerry Bell	.50	.23	.06
☐ 93 Jesus Alou	.50	.23	.06
☐ 94 Dick Billings	.50	.23	.06
☐ 95 Steve Blass	.75	.35	.09
☐ 96 Doug Griffin	.50	.23	.06
☐ 97 Willie Montanez	.75	.35	.09
☐ 98 Dick Woodson	.50	.23	.06
☐ 99 Carl Taylor	.50	.23	.06
☐ 100 Hank Aaron	25.00	11.50	3.10
☐ 101 Ken Henderson	.50	.23	.06
☐ 102 Rudy May	.50	.23	.06
☐ 103 Celerino Sanchez	.50	.23	.06
☐ 104 Reggie Cleveland	.50	.23	.06
☐ 105 Carlos May	.50	.23	.06
☐ 106 Terry Humphrey	.50	.23	.06
☐ 107 Phil Hennigan	.50	.23	.06
☐ 108 Bill Russell	.75	.35	.09
☐ 109 Doyle Alexander	.75	.35	.09
☐ 110 Bob Watson	.75	.35	.09
☐ 111 Dave Nelson	.50	.23	.06
☐ 112 Gary Ross	.50	.23	.06
☐ 113 Jerry Grote	.50	.23	.06
☐ 114 Lynn McGlothen	.50	.23	.06
☐ 115 Ron Santo	1.00	.45	.13

☐ 116A Yankees Leaders .80 .35 .10
Ralph Houk MG
Jim Hegan CO
Elston Howard CO
Dick Howser CO
Jim Turner CO
(Solid backgrounds)
☐ 116B Yankees Leaders 1.50 .65 .19
(Natural backgrounds)
☐ 117 Ramon Hernandez .50 .23 .06
☐ 118 John Mayberry .75 .35 .09
☐ 119 Larry Bowa 1.00 .45 .13
☐ 120 Joe Coleman .50 .23 .06
☐ 121 Dave Rader .50 .23 .06
☐ 122 Jim Strickland .50 .23 .06
☐ 123 Sandy Alomar .75 .35 .09
☐ 124 Jim Hardin .50 .23 .06
☐ 125 Ron Fairly .50 .23 .06
☐ 126 Jim Brewer .50 .23 .06
☐ 127 Milwaukee Brewers 1.00 .45 .13
Team Card
☐ 128 Ted Sizemore .50 .23 .06
☐ 129 Terry Forster .75 .35 .09
☐ 130 Pete Rose 18.00 8.00 2.30
☐ 131A Red Sox Leaders .80 .35 .10
Eddie Kasko MG
Doug Camilli CO
Don Lenhardt CO
Eddie Popowski CO
(No right ear)
Lee Stange CO
☐ 131B Red Sox Leaders 1.50 .65 .19
(Popowski has right
ear showing)
☐ 132 Matty Alou .75 .35 .09
☐ 133 Dave Roberts .50 .23 .06
☐ 134 Milt Wilcox .50 .23 .06
☐ 135 Lee May UER .75 .35 .09
(Career average .000)
☐ 136A Orioles Leaders 1.00 .45 .13
Earl Weaver MG
George Bamberger CO
Jim Frey CO
Billy Hunter CO
George Staller CO
(Orange backgrounds)
☐ 136B Orioles Leaders 2.00 .90 .25
(Dark pale
backgrounds)
☐ 137 Jim Beauchamp .50 .23 .06
☐ 138 Horacio Pina .50 .23 .06
☐ 139 Carmen Fanzone .50 .23 .06
☐ 140 Lou Piniella 1.00 .45 .13
☐ 141 Bruce Kison .50 .23 .06
☐ 142 Thurman Munson 10.00 4.50 1.25
☐ 143 John Curtis .50 .23 .06
☐ 144 Marty Perez .50 .23 .06
☐ 145 Bobby Bonds 2.00 .90 .25
☐ 146 Woodie Fryman .50 .23 .06
☐ 147 Mike Anderson .50 .23 .06
☐ 148 Dave Goltz .50 .23 .06
☐ 149 Ron Hunt .50 .23 .06
☐ 150 Wilbur Wood .75 .35 .09
☐ 151 Wes Parker .75 .35 .09
☐ 152 Dave May .50 .23 .06
☐ 153 Al Hrabosky .75 .35 .09
☐ 154 Jeff Torborg .75 .35 .09
☐ 155 Sal Bando .75 .35 .09
☐ 156 Cesar Geronimo .50 .23 .06
☐ 157 Denny Riddleberger .50 .23 .06
☐ 158 Houston Astros 1.00 .45 .13
Team Card
☐ 159 Clarence Gaston 1.00 .45 .13
☐ 160 Jim Palmer 12.50 5.75 1.55
☐ 161 Ted Martinez .50 .23 .06
☐ 162 Pete Broberg .50 .23 .06
☐ 163 Vic Davalillo .50 .23 .06
☐ 164 Monty Montgomery .50 .23 .06
☐ 165 Luis Aparicio 2.75 1.25 .35
☐ 166 Terry Harmon .50 .23 .06
☐ 167 Steve Stone .75 .35 .09
☐ 168 Jim Northrup .75 .35 .09
☐ 169 Ron Schueler .75 .35 .09
☐ 170 Harmon Killebrew 5.00 2.30 .60
☐ 171 Bernie Carbo .50 .23 .06
☐ 172 Steve Kline .50 .23 .06
☐ 173 Hal Breeden .50 .23 .06
☐ 174 Rich Gossage 20.00 9.00 2.50
☐ 175 Frank Robinson 6.00 2.70 .75
☐ 176 Chuck Taylor .50 .23 .06
☐ 177 Bill Plummer .50 .23 .06
☐ 178 Don Rose .50 .23 .06
☐ 179A A's Leaders .80 .35 .10
Dick Williams MG
Jerry Adair CO
Vern Hoscheit CO
Irv Noren CO
Wes Stock CO
(Hoscheit left ear
showing)
☐ 179B A's Leaders 1.50 .65 .19
(Hoscheit left ear
not showing)
☐ 180 Fergie Jenkins 5.00 2.30 .60
☐ 181 Jack Brohamer .50 .23 .06
☐ 182 Mike Caldwell .50 .23 .06
☐ 183 Don Buford .50 .23 .06
☐ 184 Jerry Koosman .75 .35 .09
☐ 185 Jim Wynn .75 .35 .09
☐ 186 Bill Fahey .50 .23 .06
☐ 187 Luke Walker .50 .23 .06
☐ 188 Cookie Rojas .75 .35 .09
☐ 189 Greg Luzinski 1.00 .45 .13
☐ 190 Bob Gibson 6.00 2.70 .75
☐ 191 Detroit Tigers 1.00 .45 .13
Team Card
☐ 192 Pat Jarvis .50 .23 .06
☐ 193 Carlton Fisk 45.00 20.00 5.75
☐ 194 Jorge Orta .50 .23 .06
☐ 195 Clay Carroll .50 .23 .06
☐ 196 Ken McMullen .50 .23 .06
☐ 197 Ed Goodson .50 .23 .06
☐ 198 Horace Clarke .50 .23 .06
☐ 199 Bert Blyleven 5.00 2.30 .60
☐ 200 Billy Williams 4.00 1.80 .50
☐ 201 A.L. Playoffs 1.00 .45 .13
A's over Tigers;
George Hendrick
scores winning run
☐ 202 N.L. Playoffs 1.00 .45 .13
Reds over Pirates
George Foster's
run decides
☐ 203 World Series Game 1 1.00 .45 .13
Gene Tenace the Menace
☐ 204 World Series Game 2 1.00 .45 .13
A's two straight
☐ 205 World Series Game 3 1.00 .45 .13
Reds win squeeker
(Tony Perez)
☐ 206 World Series Game 4 1.00 .45 .13
Gene Tenace singles
in ninth
☐ 207 World Series Game 5 1.00 .45 .13
Blue Moon Odom out
at plate
☐ 208 World Series Game 6 1.00 .45 .13
Reds' slugging
ties series
(Johnny Bench)
☐ 209 World Series Game 7 1.00 .45 .13
Bert Campaneris starts
winning rally
☐ 210 World Series Summary 1.00 .45 .13
World champions:
A's Win
☐ 211 Balor Moore .50 .23 .06
☐ 212 Joe Lahoud .50 .23 .06
☐ 213 Steve Garvey 12.50 5.75 1.55
☐ 214 Steve Hamilton .50 .23 .06
☐ 215 Dusty Baker 1.00 .45 .13
☐ 216 Toby Harrah .80 .35 .10
☐ 217 Don Wilson .50 .23 .06
☐ 218 Aurelio Rodriguez .50 .23 .06
☐ 219 St. Louis Cardinals 1.00 .45 .13
Team Card
☐ 220 Nolan Ryan 90.00 40.00 11.50
☐ 221 Fred Kendall .50 .23 .06
☐ 222 Rob Gardner .50 .23 .06
☐ 223 Bud Harrelson .75 .35 .09
☐ 224 Bill Lee .75 .35 .09
☐ 225 Al Oliver 1.25 .55 .16
☐ 226 Ray Fosse .50 .23 .06
☐ 227 Wayne Twitchell .50 .23 .06
☐ 228 Bobby Darwin .50 .23 .06
☐ 229 Roric Harrison .50 .23 .06
☐ 230 Joe Morgan 6.50 2.90 .80
☐ 231 Bill Parsons .50 .23 .06
☐ 232 Ken Singleton .75 .35 .09
☐ 233 Ed Kirkpatrick .50 .23 .06
☐ 234 Bill North .50 .23 .06
☐ 235 Jim Hunter 4.00 1.80 .50
☐ 236 Tito Fuentes .50 .23 .06
☐ 237A Braves Leaders 1.50 .65 .19
Eddie Mathews MG
Lew Burdette CO
Jim Busby CO

Roy Hartsfield CO
Ken Silvestri CO
(Burdette right ear showing)
☐ 237B Braves Leaders .... 3.00 1.35 .40
(Burdette right ear not showing)
☐ 238 Tony Muser .... .50 .23 .06
☐ 239 Pete Richert .... .50 .23 .06
☐ 240 Bobby Murcer .... .80 .35 .10
☐ 241 Dwain Anderson .... .50 .23 .06
☐ 242 George Culver .... .50 .23 .06
☐ 243 California Angels .... 1.00 .45 .13
Team Card
☐ 244 Ed Acosta .... .50 .23 .06
☐ 245 Carl Yastrzemski 15.00 6.75 1.90
☐ 246 Ken Sanders .... .50 .23 .06
☐ 247 Del Unser .... .50 .23 .06
☐ 248 Jerry Johnson .... .50 .23 .06
☐ 249 Larry Biittner .... .50 .23 .06
☐ 250 Manny Sanguillen .... .75 .35 .09
☐ 251 Roger Nelson .... .50 .23 .06
☐ 252A Giants Leaders .... .80 .35 .10
Charlie Fox MG
Joe Amalfitano CO
Andy Gilbert CO
Don McMahon CO
John McNamara CO
(Orange backgrounds)
☐ 252B Giants Leaders .... 1.50 .65 .19
(Dark pale backgrounds)
☐ 253 Mark Belanger .... .75 .35 .09
☐ 254 Bill Stoneman .... .50 .23 .06
☐ 255 Reggie Jackson 33.00 15.00 4.10
☐ 256 Chris Zachary .... .50 .23 .06
☐ 257A Mets Leaders .... 2.50 1.15 .30
Yogi Berra MG
Roy McMillan CO
Joe Pignatano CO
Rube Walker CO
Eddie Yost CO
(Orange backgrounds)
☐ 257B Mets Leaders .... 5.00 2.30 .60
(Dark pale backgrounds)
☐ 258 Tommy John .... 1.75 .80 .22
☐ 259 Jim Holt .... .50 .23 .06
☐ 260 Gary Nolan .... .75 .35 .09
☐ 261 Pat Kelly .... .50 .23 .06
☐ 262 Jack Aker .... .50 .23 .06
☐ 263 George Scott .... .75 .35 .09
☐ 264 Checklist 2 .... 3.00 .30 .09
☐ 265 Gene Michael .... .90 .40 .11
☐ 266 Mike Lum .... .65 .30 .08
☐ 267 Lloyd Allen .... .65 .30 .08
☐ 268 Jerry Morales .... .65 .30 .08
☐ 269 Tim McCarver .... 1.00 .45 .13
☐ 270 Luis Tiant .... .90 .40 .11
☐ 271 Tom Hutton .... .65 .30 .08
☐ 272 Ed Farmer .... .65 .30 .08
☐ 273 Chris Speier .... .65 .30 .08
☐ 274 Darold Knowles .... .65 .30 .08
☐ 275 Tony Perez .... 4.00 1.80 .50
☐ 276 Joe Lovitto .... .65 .30 .08
☐ 277 Bob Miller .... .65 .30 .08
☐ 278 Baltimore Orioles .... 1.25 .55 .16
Team Card
☐ 279 Mike Strahler .... .65 .30 .08
☐ 280 Al Kaline .... 6.00 2.70 .75
☐ 281 Mike Jorgensen .... .65 .30 .08
☐ 282 Steve Hovley .... .65 .30 .08
☐ 283 Ray Sadecki .... .65 .30 .08
☐ 284 Glenn Borgmann .... .65 .30 .08
☐ 285 Don Kessinger .... .90 .40 .11
☐ 286 Frank Linzy .... .65 .30 .08
☐ 287 Eddie Leon .... .65 .30 .08
☐ 288 Gary Gentry .... .65 .30 .08
☐ 289 Bob Oliver .... .65 .30 .08
☐ 290 Cesar Cedeno .... .90 .40 .11
☐ 291 Rogelio Moret .... .65 .30 .08
☐ 292 Jose Cruz .... 1.25 .55 .16
☐ 293 Bernie Allen .... .65 .30 .08
☐ 294 Steve Arlin .... .65 .30 .08
☐ 295 Bert Campaneris .... .90 .40 .11
☐ 296 Reds Leaders .... 1.50 .65 .19
Sparky Anderson MG
Alex Grammas CO
Ted Kluszewski CO
George Scherger CO
Larry Shepard CO
☐ 297 Walt Williams .... .65 .30 .08
☐ 298 Ron Bryant .... .65 .30 .08
☐ 299 Ted Ford .... .65 .30 .08
☐ 300 Steve Carlton 15.00 6.75 1.90
☐ 301 Billy Grabarkewitz .... .65 .30 .08
☐ 302 Terry Crowley .... .65 .30 .08
☐ 303 Nelson Briles .... .90 .40 .11
☐ 304 Duke Sims .... .65 .30 .08
☐ 305 Willie Mays 40.00 18.00 5.00
☐ 306 Tom Burgmeier .... .65 .30 .08
☐ 307 Boots Day .... .65 .30 .08
☐ 308 Skip Lockwood .... .65 .30 .08
☐ 309 Paul Popovich .... .65 .30 .08
☐ 310 Dick Allen .... 1.75 .80 .22
☐ 311 Joe Decker .... .65 .30 .08
☐ 312 Oscar Brown .... .65 .30 .08
☐ 313 Jim Ray .... .65 .30 .08
☐ 314 Ron Swoboda .... .90 .40 .11
☐ 315 John Odom .... .65 .30 .08
☐ 316 San Diego Padres .... 1.25 .55 .16
Team Card
☐ 317 Danny Cater .... .65 .30 .08
☐ 318 Jim McGlothlin .... .65 .30 .08
☐ 319 Jim Spencer .... .65 .30 .08
☐ 320 Lou Brock .... 6.50 2.90 .80
☐ 321 Rich Hinton .... .65 .30 .08
☐ 322 Garry Maddox .... 1.50 .65 .19
☐ 323 Tigers Leaders .... 1.00 .45 .13
Billy Martin MG
Art Fowler CO
Charlie Silvera CO
Dick Tracewski CO
☐ 324 Al Downing .... .65 .30 .08
☐ 325 Boog Powell .... 1.00 .45 .13
☐ 326 Darrell Brandon .... .65 .30 .08
☐ 327 John Lowenstein .... .65 .30 .08
☐ 328 Bill Bonham .... .65 .30 .08
☐ 329 Ed Kranepool .... .65 .30 .08
☐ 330 Rod Carew 18.00 8.00 2.30
☐ 331 Carl Morton .... .65 .30 .08
☐ 332 John Felske .... .65 .30 .08
☐ 333 Gene Clines .... .65 .30 .08
☐ 334 Freddie Patek .... .90 .40 .11
☐ 335 Bob Tolan .... .65 .30 .08
☐ 336 Tom Bradley .... .65 .30 .08
☐ 337 Dave Duncan .... .65 .30 .08
☐ 338 Checklist 3 .... 3.00 .30 .09
☐ 339 Dick Tidrow .... .65 .30 .08
☐ 340 Nate Colbert .... .65 .30 .08
☐ 341 KP: Jim Palmer .... 1.75 .80 .22
☐ 342 KP: Sam McDowell .... .80 .35 .10
☐ 343 KP: Bobby Murcer .... .80 .35 .10
☐ 344 KP: Jim Hunter .... 1.50 .65 .19
☐ 345 KP: Chris Speier .... .80 .35 .10
☐ 346 KP: Gaylord Perry .... 1.50 .65 .19
☐ 347 Kansas City Royals .... 1.25 .55 .16
Team Card
☐ 348 Rennie Stennett .... .65 .30 .08
☐ 349 Dick McAuliffe .... .90 .40 .11
☐ 350 Tom Seaver 30.00 13.50 3.80
☐ 351 Jimmy Stewart .... .65 .30 .08
☐ 352 Don Stanhouse .... .65 .30 .08
☐ 353 Steve Brye .... .65 .30 .08
☐ 354 Billy Parker .... .65 .30 .08
☐ 355 Mike Marshall .... .90 .40 .11
☐ 356 White Sox Leaders .... .80 .35 .10
Chuck Tanner MG
Joe Lonnett CO
Jim Mahoney CO
Al Monchak CO
Johnny Sain CO
☐ 357 Ross Grimsley .... .65 .30 .08
☐ 358 Jim Nettles .... .65 .30 .08
☐ 359 Cecil Upshaw .... .65 .30 .08
☐ 360 Joe Rudi UER .... .90 .40 .11
(Photo actually Gene Tenace)
☐ 361 Fran Healy .... .65 .30 .08
☐ 362 Eddie Watt .... .65 .30 .08
☐ 363 Jackie Hernandez .... .65 .30 .08
☐ 364 Rick Wise .... .65 .30 .08
☐ 365 Rico Petrocelli .... .90 .40 .11
☐ 366 Brock Davis .... .65 .30 .08
☐ 367 Burt Hooton .... .90 .40 .11
☐ 368 Bill Buckner .... 1.00 .45 .13
☐ 369 Lerrin LaGrow .... .65 .30 .08
☐ 370 Willie Stargell .... 5.00 2.30 .60
☐ 371 Mike Kekich .... .65 .30 .08
☐ 372 Oscar Gamble .... .90 .40 .11
☐ 373 Clyde Wright .... .65 .30 .08
☐ 374 Darrell Evans .... 1.00 .45 .13
☐ 375 Larry Dierker .... .65 .30 .08
☐ 376 Frank Duffy .... .65 .30 .08
☐ 377 Expos Leaders .... .80 .35 .10
Gene Mauch MG
Dave Bristol CO

Larry Doby CO
Cal McLish CO
Jerry Zimmerman CO
☐ 378 Len Randle .65 .30 .08
☐ 379 Cy Acosta .65 .30 .08
☐ 380 Johnny Bench 25.00 11.50 3.10
☐ 381 Vicente Romo .65 .30 .08
☐ 382 Mike Hegan .65 .30 .08
☐ 383 Diego Segui .65 .30 .08
☐ 384 Don Baylor 3.00 1.35 .40
☐ 385 Jim Perry .90 .40 .11
☐ 386 Don Money .90 .40 .11
☐ 387 Jim Barr .65 .30 .08
☐ 388 Ben Oglivie .90 .40 .11
☐ 389 New York Mets 3.00 1.35 .40
Team Card
☐ 390 Mickey Lolich .90 .40 .11
☐ 391 Lee Lacy 1.00 .45 .13
☐ 392 Dick Drago .65 .30 .08
☐ 393 Jose Cardenal .65 .30 .08
☐ 394 Sparky Lyle 1.00 .45 .13
☐ 395 Roger Metzger .65 .30 .08
☐ 396 Grant Jackson .90 .40 .11
☐ 397 Dave Cash 1.50 .65 .19
☐ 398 Rich Hand 1.25 .55 .16
☐ 399 George Foster 2.00 .90 .25
☐ 400 Gaylord Perry 5.00 2.30 .60
☐ 401 Clyde Mashore 1.25 .55 .16
☐ 402 Jack Hiatt 1.25 .55 .16
☐ 403 Sonny Jackson 1.25 .55 .16
☐ 404 Chuck Brinkman 1.25 .55 .16
☐ 405 Cesar Tovar 1.25 .55 .16
☐ 406 Paul Lindblad 1.25 .55 .16
☐ 407 Felix Millan 1.25 .55 .16
☐ 408 Jim Colborn 1.25 .55 .16
☐ 409 Ivan Murrell 1.25 .55 .16
☐ 410 Willie McCovey 6.00 2.70 .75
(Bench behind plate)
☐ 411 Ray Corbin 1.25 .55 .16
☐ 412 Manny Mota 1.75 .80 .22
☐ 413 Tom Timmermann 1.25 .55 .16
☐ 414 Ken Rudolph 1.25 .55 .16
☐ 415 Marty Pattin 1.25 .55 .16
☐ 416 Paul Schaal 1.25 .55 .16
☐ 417 Scipio Spinks 1.25 .55 .16
☐ 418 Bob Grich 1.75 .80 .22
☐ 419 Casey Cox 1.25 .55 .16
☐ 420 Tommie Agee 1.50 .65 .19
☐ 421A Angels Leaders 1.50 .65 .19
Bobby Winkles MG
Tom Morgan CO
Salty Parker CO
Jimmie Reese CO
John Roseboro CO
(Orange backgrounds)
☐ 421B Angels Leaders 3.00 1.35 .40
(Dark pale
backgrounds)
☐ 422 Bob Robertson 1.25 .55 .16
☐ 423 Johnny Jeter 1.25 .55 .16
☐ 424 Denny Doyle 1.25 .55 .16
☐ 425 Alex Johnson 1.50 .65 .19
☐ 426 Dave LaRoche 1.25 .55 .16
☐ 427 Rick Auerbach 1.25 .55 .16
☐ 428 Wayne Simpson 1.25 .55 .16
☐ 429 Jim Fairey 1.25 .55 .16
☐ 430 Vida Blue 1.75 .80 .22
☐ 431 Gerry Moses 1.25 .55 .16
☐ 432 Dan Frisella 1.25 .55 .16
☐ 433 Willie Horton 1.75 .80 .22
☐ 434 San Francisco Giants 2.50 1.15 .30
Team Card
☐ 435 Rico Carty 1.75 .80 .22
☐ 436 Jim McAndrew 1.25 .55 .16
☐ 437 John Kennedy 1.25 .55 .16
☐ 438 Enzo Hernandez 1.25 .55 .16
☐ 439 Eddie Fisher 1.25 .55 .16
☐ 440 Glenn Beckert 1.50 .65 .19
☐ 441 Gail Hopkins 1.25 .55 .16
☐ 442 Dick Dietz 1.25 .55 .16
☐ 443 Danny Thompson 1.25 .55 .16
☐ 444 Ken Brett 1.25 .55 .16
☐ 445 Ken Berry 1.25 .55 .16
☐ 446 Jerry Reuss 1.50 .65 .19
☐ 447 Joe Hague 1.25 .55 .16
☐ 448 John Hiller 1.50 .65 .19
☐ 449A Indians Leaders 2.00 .90 .25
Ken Aspromonte MG
Rocky Colavito CO
Joe Lutz CO
Warren Spahn CO
(Spahn's right
ear pointed)
☐ 449B Indians Leaders 4.00 1.80 .50
(Spahn's right
ear round)
☐ 450 Joe Torre 2.00 .90 .25
☐ 451 John Vukovich 1.50 .65 .19
☐ 452 Paul Casanova 1.25 .55 .16
☐ 453 Checklist 4 3.00 .30 .09
☐ 454 Tom Haller 1.25 .55 .16
☐ 455 Bill Melton 1.25 .55 .16
☐ 456 Dick Green 1.25 .55 .16
☐ 457 John Strohmayer 1.25 .55 .16
☐ 458 Jim Mason 1.25 .55 .16
☐ 459 Jimmy Howarth 1.25 .55 .16
☐ 460 Bill Freehan 1.75 .80 .22
☐ 461 Mike Corkins 1.25 .55 .16
☐ 462 Ron Blomberg 1.25 .55 .16
☐ 463 Ken Tatum 1.25 .55 .16
☐ 464 Chicago Cubs 2.50 1.15 .30
Team Card
☐ 465 Dave Giusti 1.25 .55 .16
☐ 466 Jose Arcia 1.25 .55 .16
☐ 467 Mike Ryan 1.25 .55 .16
☐ 468 Tom Griffin 1.25 .55 .16
☐ 469 Dan Monzon 1.25 .55 .16
☐ 470 Mike Cuellar 1.50 .65 .19
☐ 471 Hits Leaders 5.00 2.30 .60
Ty Cobb 4191
☐ 472 Grand Slam Leaders 6.00 2.70 .75
Lou Gehrig 23
☐ 473 Total Bases Leaders 5.00 2.30 .60
Hank Aaron 6172
☐ 474 RBI Leaders 10.00 4.50 1.25
Babe Ruth 2209
☐ 475 Batting Leaders 5.00 2.30 .60
Ty Cobb .367
☐ 476 Shutout Leaders 2.25 1.00 .30
Walter Johnson 113
☐ 477 Victory Leaders 2.25 1.00 .30
Cy Young 511
☐ 478 Strikeout Leaders 2.25 1.00 .30
Walter Johnson 3508
☐ 479 Hal Lanier 1.25 .55 .16
☐ 480 Juan Marichal 5.00 2.30 .60
☐ 481 Chicago White Sox 2.50 1.15 .30
Team Card
☐ 482 Rick Reuschel 4.00 1.80 .50
☐ 483 Dal Maxvill 1.25 .55 .16
☐ 484 Ernie McAnally 1.25 .55 .16
☐ 485 Norm Cash 1.75 .80 .22
☐ 486A Phillies Leaders 1.50 .65 .19
Danny Ozark MG
Carroll Beringer CO
Billy DeMars CO
Ray Rippelmeyer CO
Bobby Wine CO
(Orange backgrounds)
☐ 486B Phillies Leaders 3.00 1.35 .40
(Dark pale
backgrounds)
☐ 487 Bruce Dal Canton 1.25 .55 .16
☐ 488 Dave Campbell 1.25 .55 .16
☐ 489 Jeff Burroughs 1.50 .65 .19
☐ 490 Claude Osteen 1.50 .65 .19
☐ 491 Bob Montgomery 1.25 .55 .16
☐ 492 Pedro Borbon 1.25 .55 .16
☐ 493 Duffy Dyer 1.25 .55 .16
☐ 494 Rich Morales 1.25 .55 .16
☐ 495 Tommy Helms 1.25 .55 .16
☐ 496 Ray Lamb 1.25 .55 .16
☐ 497A Cardinals Leaders 2.00 .90 .25
Red Schoendienst MG
Vern Benson CO
George Kissell CO
Barney Schultz CO
(Orange backgrounds)
☐ 497B Cardinals Leaders 4.00 1.80 .50
(Dark pale
backgrounds)
☐ 498 Graig Nettles 3.00 1.35 .40
☐ 499 Bob Moose 1.25 .55 .16
☐ 500 Oakland A's 2.50 1.15 .30
Team Card
☐ 501 Larry Gura 1.50 .65 .19
☐ 502 Bobby Valentine 1.50 .65 .19
☐ 503 Phil Niekro 5.00 2.30 .60
☐ 504 Earl Williams 1.25 .55 .16
☐ 505 Bob Bailey 1.25 .55 .16
☐ 506 Bart Johnson 1.25 .55 .16
☐ 507 Darrel Chaney 1.25 .55 .16
☐ 508 Gates Brown 1.25 .55 .16
☐ 509 Jim Nash 1.25 .55 .16
☐ 510 Amos Otis 1.75 .80 .22
☐ 511 Sam McDowell 1.50 .65 .19
☐ 512 Dalton Jones 1.25 .55 .16
☐ 513 Dave Marshall 1.25 .55 .16

☐ 514 Jerry Kenney	1.25	.55	.16
☐ 515 Andy Messersmith	1.50	.65	.19
☐ 516 Danny Walton	1.25	.55	.16
☐ 517A Pirates Leaders	1.50	.65	.19
Bill Virdon MG			
Don Leppert CO			
Bill Mazeroski CO			
Dave Ricketts CO			
Mel Wright CO			
(Mazeroski has no right ear)			
☐ 517B Pirates Leaders	3.00	1.35	.40
(Mazeroski has right ear)			
☐ 518 Bob Veale	1.50	.65	.19
☐ 519 Johnny Edwards	1.25	.55	.16
☐ 520 Mel Stottlemyre	1.75	.80	.22
☐ 521 Atlanta Braves	2.50	1.15	.30
Team Card			
☐ 522 Leo Cardenas	1.25	.55	.16
☐ 523 Wayne Granger	1.25	.55	.16
☐ 524 Gene Tenace	1.50	.65	.19
☐ 525 Jim Fregosi	1.75	.80	.22
☐ 526 Ollie Brown	1.25	.55	.16
☐ 527 Dan McGinn	1.25	.55	.16
☐ 528 Paul Blair	1.50	.65	.19
☐ 529 Milt May	3.50	1.55	.45
☐ 530 Jim Kaat	5.00	2.30	.60
☐ 531 Ron Woods	3.00	1.35	.40
☐ 532 Steve Mingori	3.00	1.35	.40
☐ 533 Larry Stahl	3.00	1.35	.40
☐ 534 Dave Lemonds	3.00	1.35	.40
☐ 535 Johnny Callison	3.50	1.55	.45
☐ 536 Philadelphia Phillies	6.00	2.70	.75
Team Card			
☐ 537 Bill Slayback	3.00	1.35	.40
☐ 538 Jim Ray Hart	3.50	1.55	.45
☐ 539 Tom Murphy	3.00	1.35	.40
☐ 540 Cleon Jones	3.50	1.55	.45
☐ 541 Bob Bolin	3.00	1.35	.40
☐ 542 Pat Corrales	3.50	1.55	.45
☐ 543 Alan Foster	3.00	1.35	.40
☐ 544 Von Joshua	3.00	1.35	.40
☐ 545 Orlando Cepeda	4.50	2.00	.55
☐ 546 Jim York	3.00	1.35	.40
☐ 547 Bobby Heise	3.00	1.35	.40
☐ 548 Don Durham	3.00	1.35	.40
☐ 549 Rangers Leaders	5.00	2.30	.60
Whitey Herzog MG			
Chuck Estrada CO			
Chuck Hiller CO			
Jackie Moore CO			
☐ 550 Dave Johnson	3.50	1.55	.45
☐ 551 Mike Kilkenny	3.00	1.35	.40
☐ 552 J.C. Martin	3.00	1.35	.40
☐ 553 Mickey Scott	3.00	1.35	.40
☐ 554 Dave Concepcion	5.00	2.30	.60
☐ 555 Bill Hands	3.00	1.35	.40
☐ 556 New York Yankees	7.50	3.40	.95
Team Card			
☐ 557 Bernie Williams	3.00	1.35	.40
☐ 558 Jerry May	3.00	1.35	.40
☐ 559 Barry Lersch	3.00	1.35	.40
☐ 560 Frank Howard	4.50	2.00	.55
☐ 561 Jim Geddes	3.00	1.35	.40
☐ 562 Wayne Garrett	3.00	1.35	.40
☐ 563 Larry Haney	3.00	1.35	.40
☐ 564 Mike Thompson	3.00	1.35	.40
☐ 565 Jim Hickman	3.00	1.35	.40
☐ 566 Lew Krausse	3.00	1.35	.40
☐ 567 Bob Fenwick	3.00	1.35	.40
☐ 568 Ray Newman	3.00	1.35	.40
☐ 569 Dodgers Leaders	4.50	2.00	.55
Walt Alston MG			
Red Adams CO			
Monty Basgall CO			
Jim Gilliam CO			
Tom Lasorda CO			
☐ 570 Bill Singer	3.50	1.55	.45
☐ 571 Rusty Torres	3.00	1.35	.40
☐ 572 Gary Sutherland	3.00	1.35	.40
☐ 573 Fred Beene	3.00	1.35	.40
☐ 574 Bob Didier	3.00	1.35	.40
☐ 575 Dock Ellis	3.00	1.35	.40
☐ 576 Montreal Expos	6.00	2.70	.75
Team Card			
☐ 577 Eric Soderholm	3.00	1.35	.40
☐ 578 Ken Wright	3.00	1.35	.40
☐ 579 Tom Grieve	3.50	1.55	.45
☐ 580 Joe Pepitone	3.50	1.55	.45
☐ 581 Steve Kealey	3.00	1.35	.40
☐ 582 Darrell Porter	3.50	1.55	.45
☐ 583 Bill Grief	3.00	1.35	.40
☐ 584 Chris Arnold	3.00	1.35	.40
☐ 585 Joe Niekro	3.50	1.55	.45
☐ 586 Bill Sudakis	3.00	1.35	.40
☐ 587 Rich McKinney	3.00	1.35	.40
☐ 588 Checklist 5	20.00	2.00	.60
☐ 589 Ken Forsch	3.00	1.35	.40
☐ 590 Deron Johnson	3.00	1.35	.40
☐ 591 Mike Hedlund	3.00	1.35	.40
☐ 592 John Boccabella	3.00	1.35	.40
☐ 593 Royals Leaders	3.50	1.55	.45
Jack McKeon MG			
Galen Cisco CO			
Harry Dunlop CO			
Charlie Lau CO			
☐ 594 Vic Harris	3.00	1.35	.40
☐ 595 Don Gullett	3.50	1.55	.45
☐ 596 Boston Red Sox	6.00	2.70	.75
Team Card			
☐ 597 Mickey Rivers	3.50	1.55	.45
☐ 598 Phil Roof	3.00	1.35	.40
☐ 599 Ed Crosby	3.00	1.35	.40
☐ 600 Dave McNally	3.50	1.55	.45
☐ 601 Rookie Catchers	3.25	1.45	.40
Sergio Robles			
George Pena			
Rick Stelmaszek			
☐ 602 Rookie Pitchers	3.25	1.45	.40
Mel Behney			
Ralph Garcia			
Doug Rau			
☐ 603 Rookie 3rd Basemen	3.25	1.45	.40
Terry Hughes			
Bill McNulty			
Ken Reitz			
☐ 604 Rookie Pitchers	3.25	1.45	.40
Jesse Jefferson			
Dennis O'Toole			
Bob Strampe			
☐ 605 Rookie 1st Basemen	4.00	1.80	.50
Enos Cabell			
Pat Bourque			
Gonzalo Marquez			
☐ 606 Rookie Outfielders	5.00	2.30	.60
Gary Matthews			
Tom Paciorek			
Jorge Roque			
☐ 607 Rookie Shortstops	3.25	1.45	.40
Pepe Frias			
Ray Busse			
Mario Guerrero			
☐ 608 Rookie Pitchers	4.00	1.80	.50
Steve Busby			
Dick Colpaert			
George Medich			
☐ 609 Rookie 2nd Basemen	5.00	2.30	.60
Larvell Blanks			
Pedro Garcia			
Dave Lopes			
☐ 610 Rookie Pitchers	5.00	2.30	.60
Jimmy Freeman			
Charlie Hough			
Hank Webb			
☐ 611 Rookie Outfielders	3.25	1.45	.40
Rich Coggins			
Jim Wohlford			
Richie Zisk			
☐ 612 Rookie Pitchers	3.25	1.45	.40
Steve Lawson			
Bob Reynolds			
Brent Strom			
☐ 613 Rookie Catchers	50.00	23.00	6.25
Bob Boone			
Skip Jutze			
Mike Ivie			
☐ 614 Rookie Outfielders	60.00	27.00	7.50
Al Bumbry			
Dwight Evans			
Charlie Spikes			
☐ 615 Rookie 3rd Basemen	500.00	230.00	65.00
Ron Cey			
John Hilton			
Mike Schmidt			
☐ 616 Rookie Pitchers	3.25	1.45	.40
Norm Angelini			
Steve Blateric			
Mike Garman			
☐ 617 Rich Chiles	3.00	1.35	.40
☐ 618 Andy Etchebarren	3.00	1.35	.40
☐ 619 Billy Wilson	3.00	1.35	.40
☐ 620 Tommy Harper	3.50	1.55	.45
☐ 621 Joe Ferguson	3.50	1.55	.45
☐ 622 Larry Hisle	3.50	1.55	.45
☐ 623 Steve Renko	3.00	1.35	.40

☐ 624 Astros Leaders	4.50	2.00	.55
Leo Durocher MG			
Preston Gomez CO			
Grady Hatton CO			
Hub Kittle CO			
Jim Owens CO			
☐ 625 Angel Mangual	3.00	1.35	.40
☐ 626 Bob Barton	3.00	1.35	.40
☐ 627 Luis Alvarado	3.00	1.35	.40
☐ 628 Jim Slaton	3.00	1.35	.40
☐ 629 Cleveland Indians	6.00	2.70	.75
Team Card			
☐ 630 Denny McLain	4.50	2.00	.55
☐ 631 Tom Matchick	3.00	1.35	.40
☐ 632 Dick Selma	3.00	1.35	.40
☐ 633 Ike Brown	3.00	1.35	.40
☐ 634 Alan Closter	3.00	1.35	.40
☐ 635 Gene Alley	3.50	1.55	.45
☐ 636 Rickey Clark	3.00	1.35	.40
☐ 637 Norm Miller	3.00	1.35	.40
☐ 638 Ken Reynolds	3.00	1.35	.40
☐ 639 Willie Crawford	3.00	1.35	.40
☐ 640 Dick Bosman	3.00	1.35	.40
☐ 641 Cincinnati Reds	6.00	2.70	.75
Team Card			
☐ 642 Jose Laboy	3.00	1.35	.40
☐ 643 Al Fitzmorris	3.00	1.35	.40
☐ 644 Jack Heidemann	3.00	1.35	.40
☐ 645 Bob Locker	3.00	1.35	.40
☐ 646 Brewers Leaders	3.50	1.55	.45
Del Crandall MG			
Harvey Kuenn CO			
Joe Nossek CO			
Bob Shaw CO			
Jim Walton CO			
☐ 647 George Stone	3.00	1.35	.40
☐ 648 Tom Egan	3.00	1.35	.40
☐ 649 Rich Folkers	3.00	1.35	.40
☐ 650 Felipe Alou	3.50	1.55	.45
☐ 651 Don Carrithers	3.00	1.35	.40
☐ 652 Ted Kubiak	3.00	1.35	.40
☐ 653 Joe Hoerner	3.00	1.35	.40
☐ 654 Minnesota Twins	6.00	2.70	.75
Team Card			
☐ 655 Clay Kirby	3.00	1.35	.40
☐ 656 John Ellis	3.00	1.35	.40
☐ 657 Bob Johnson	3.00	1.35	.40
☐ 658 Elliott Maddox	3.00	1.35	.40
☐ 659 Jose Pagan	3.00	1.35	.40
☐ 660 Fred Scherman	4.00	1.80	.50

1974 Topps

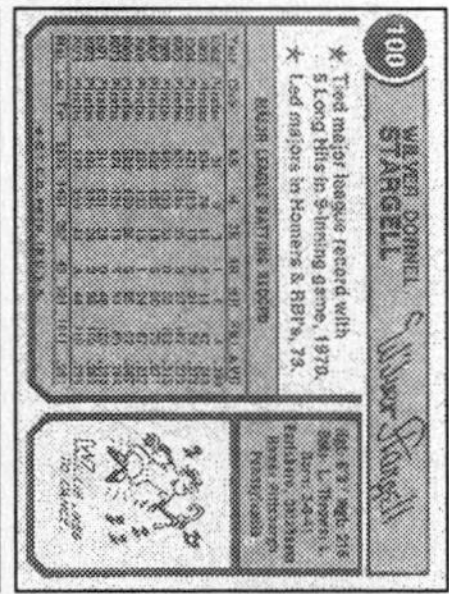

The cards in this 660-card set measure 2 1/2" by 3 1/2". This year marked the first time Topps issued all the cards of its baseball set at the same time rather than in series. Some interesting variations were created by the rumored move of the San Diego Padres to Washington. Fifteen cards (13 players, the team card, and the Rookie Card (599) of the Padres were printed either as "San Diego" (SD) or "Washington." The latter are the scarcer variety and are denoted in the checklist below by WAS. Each team's manager and his coaches again have a combined card with small pictures of each coach below the larger photo of the team's manager. The first six cards in the set (1-6) feature Hank Aaron and his illustrious career. Other topical subsets included in the set are League Leaders (201-208), All-Star selections (331-339), Playoffs cards (470-471), World Series cards (472-479), and Rookie Prospects (596-608). The card backs for the All-Stars (331-339) have no statistics, but form a picture puzzle of Bobby Bonds, the 1973 All-Star Game MVP. The key rookies in this set are Ken Griffey Sr., Dave Parker, and Dave Winfield.

	NRMT-MT	EXC	G-VG
COMPLETE SET (660)	650.00	300.00	80.00
COMMON PLAYER (1-660)	.50	.23	.06
☐ 1 Hank Aaron	30.00	7.50	2.40
All-Time Home Run King			
(Complete ML record)			
☐ 2 Aaron Special 54-57	6.00	2.70	.75
(Records on back)			
☐ 3 Aaron Special 58-61	6.00	2.70	.75
(Memorable homers)			
☐ 4 Aaron Special 62-65	6.00	2.70	.75
(Life in ML's 1954-63)			
☐ 5 Aaron Special 66-69	6.00	2.70	.75
(Life in ML's 1964-73)			
☐ 6 Aaron Special 70-73	6.00	2.70	.75
(Milestone homers)			
☐ 7 Jim Hunter	5.00	2.30	.60
☐ 8 George Theodore	.50	.23	.06
☐ 9 Mickey Lolich	.75	.35	.09
☐ 10 Johnny Bench	17.00	7.75	2.10
☐ 11 Jim Bibby	.50	.23	.06
☐ 12 Dave May	.50	.23	.06
☐ 13 Tom Hilgendorf	.50	.23	.06
☐ 14 Paul Popovich	.50	.23	.06
☐ 15 Joe Torre	1.00	.45	.13
☐ 16 Baltimore Orioles	1.00	.45	.13
Team Card			
☐ 17 Doug Bird	.50	.23	.06
☐ 18 Gary Thomasson	.50	.23	.06
☐ 19 Gerry Moses	.50	.23	.06
☐ 20 Nolan Ryan	75.00	34.00	9.50
☐ 21 Bob Gallagher	.50	.23	.06
☐ 22 Cy Acosta	.50	.23	.06
☐ 23 Craig Robinson	.50	.23	.06
☐ 24 John Hiller	.60	.25	.08
☐ 25 Ken Singleton	.60	.25	.08
☐ 26 Bill Campbell	.50	.23	.06
☐ 27 George Scott	.60	.25	.08
☐ 28 Manny Sanguillen	.60	.25	.08
☐ 29 Phil Niekro	4.00	1.80	.50
☐ 30 Bobby Bonds	1.75	.80	.22
☐ 31 Astros Leaders	.60	.25	.08
Preston Gomez MG			
Roger Craig CO			
Hub Kittle CO			
Grady Hatton CO			
Bob Lillis CO			
☐ 32A Johnny Grubb SD	.50	.23	.06
☐ 32B Johnny Grubb WAS	6.00	2.70	.75
☐ 33 Don Newhauser	.50	.23	.06
☐ 34 Andy Kosco	.50	.23	.06
☐ 35 Gaylord Perry	4.00	1.80	.50
☐ 36 St. Louis Cardinals	1.00	.45	.13
Team Card			
☐ 37 Dave Sells	.50	.23	.06
☐ 38 Don Kessinger	.60	.25	.08
☐ 39 Ken Suarez	.50	.23	.06
☐ 40 Jim Palmer	10.00	4.50	1.25
☐ 41 Bobby Floyd	.50	.23	.06
☐ 42 Claude Osteen	.60	.25	.08
☐ 43 Jim Wynn	.60	.25	.08
☐ 44 Mel Stottlemyre	.60	.25	.08
☐ 45 Dave Johnson	.60	.25	.08
☐ 46 Pat Kelly	.50	.23	.06
☐ 47 Dick Ruthven	.50	.23	.06
☐ 48 Dick Sharon	.50	.23	.06
☐ 49 Steve Renko	.50	.23	.06
☐ 50 Rod Carew	12.50	5.75	1.55
☐ 51 Bobby Heise	.50	.23	.06
☐ 52 Al Oliver	1.00	.45	.13
☐ 53A Fred Kendall SD	.50	.23	.06
☐ 53B Fred Kendall WAS	6.00	2.70	.75
☐ 54 Elias Sosa	.50	.23	.06
☐ 55 Frank Robinson	6.00	2.70	.75
☐ 56 New York Mets	1.00	.45	.13
Team Card			
☐ 57 Darold Knowles	.50	.23	.06
☐ 58 Charlie Spikes	.50	.23	.06
☐ 59 Ross Grimsley	.50	.23	.06
☐ 60 Lou Brock	6.00	2.70	.75
☐ 61 Luis Aparicio	2.50	1.15	.30

☐ 62 Bob Locker .50 .23 .06
☐ 63 Bill Sudakis .50 .23 .06
☐ 64 Doug Rau .50 .23 .06
☐ 65 Amos Otis .60 .25 .08
☐ 66 Sparky Lyle .75 .35 .09
☐ 67 Tommy Helms .50 .23 .06
☐ 68 Grant Jackson .50 .23 .06
☐ 69 Del Unser .50 .23 .06
☐ 70 Dick Allen 1.00 .45 .13
☐ 71 Dan Frisella .50 .23 .06
☐ 72 Aurelio Rodriguez .50 .23 .06
☐ 73 Mike Marshall .60 .25 .08
☐ 74 Minnesota Twins 1.00 .45 .13
Team Card
☐ 75 Jim Colborn .50 .23 .06
☐ 76 Mickey Rivers .60 .25 .08
☐ 77A Rich Troedson SD .50 .23 .06
☐ 77B Rich Troedson WAS 6.00 2.70 .75
☐ 78 Giants Leaders .60 .25 .08
Charlie Fox MG
John McNamara CO
Joe Amalfitano CO
Andy Gilbert CO
Don McMahon CO
☐ 79 Gene Tenace .60 .25 .08
☐ 80 Tom Seaver 21.00 9.50 2.60
☐ 81 Frank Duffy .50 .23 .06
☐ 82 Dave Giusti .50 .23 .06
☐ 83 Orlando Cepeda 1.50 .65 .19
☐ 84 Rick Wise .50 .23 .06
☐ 85 Joe Morgan 6.00 2.70 .75
☐ 86 Joe Ferguson .60 .25 .08
☐ 87 Fergie Jenkins 4.50 2.00 .55
☐ 88 Freddie Patek .60 .25 .08
☐ 89 Jackie Brown .50 .23 .06
☐ 90 Bobby Murcer .75 .35 .09
☐ 91 Ken Forsch .50 .23 .06
☐ 92 Paul Blair .60 .25 .08
☐ 93 Rod Gilbreath .50 .23 .06
☐ 94 Detroit Tigers 1.00 .45 .13
Team Card
☐ 95 Steve Carlton 12.50 5.75 1.55
☐ 96 Jerry Hairston .50 .23 .06
☐ 97 Bob Bailey .50 .23 .06
☐ 98 Bert Blyleven 4.00 1.80 .50
☐ 99 Brewers Leaders .60 .25 .08
Del Crandall MG
Harvey Kuenn CO
Joe Nossek CO
Jim Walton CO
Al Widmar CO
☐ 100 Willie Stargell 4.50 2.00 .55
☐ 101 Bobby Valentine .60 .25 .08
☐ 102A Bill Greif SD .50 .23 .06
☐ 102B Bill Greif WAS 6.00 2.70 .75
☐ 103 Sal Bando .60 .25 .08
☐ 104 Ron Bryant .50 .23 .06
☐ 105 Carlton Fisk 25.00 11.50 3.10
☐ 106 Harry Parker .50 .23 .06
☐ 107 Alex Johnson .50 .23 .06
☐ 108 Al Hrabosky .60 .25 .08
☐ 109 Bob Grich .75 .35 .09
☐ 110 Billy Williams 4.00 1.80 .50
☐ 111 Clay Carroll .50 .23 .06
☐ 112 Dave Lopes 1.00 .45 .13
☐ 113 Dick Drago .50 .23 .06
☐ 114 Angels Team 1.00 .45 .13
☐ 115 Willie Horton .60 .25 .08
☐ 116 Jerry Reuss .60 .25 .08
☐ 117 Ron Blomberg .50 .23 .06
☐ 118 Bill Lee .60 .25 .08
☐ 119 Phillies Leaders .60 .25 .08
Danny Ozark MG
Ray Ripplemeyer CO
Bobby Wine CO
Carroll Beringer CO
Billy DeMars CO
☐ 120 Wilbur Wood .50 .23 .06
☐ 121 Larry Lintz .50 .23 .06
☐ 122 Jim Holt .50 .23 .06
☐ 123 Nelson Briles .60 .25 .08
☐ 124 Bobby Coluccio .50 .23 .06
☐ 125A Nate Colbert SD .60 .25 .08
☐ 125B Nate Colbert WAS 6.00 2.70 .75
☐ 126 Checklist 1 2.50 .25 .07
☐ 127 Tom Paciorek .60 .25 .08
☐ 128 John Ellis .50 .23 .06
☐ 129 Chris Speier .50 .23 .06
☐ 130 Reggie Jackson 33.00 15.00 4.10
☐ 131 Bob Boone 5.00 2.30 .60
☐ 132 Felix Millan .50 .23 .06
☐ 133 David Clyde .60 .25 .08
☐ 134 Denis Menke .50 .23 .06
☐ 135 Roy White .60 .25 .08
☐ 136 Rick Reuschel .75 .35 .09
☐ 137 Al Bumbry .50 .23 .06
☐ 138 Eddie Brinkman .50 .23 .06
☐ 139 Aurelio Monteagudo .50 .23 .06
☐ 140 Darrell Evans .75 .35 .09
☐ 141 Pat Bourque .50 .23 .06
☐ 142 Pedro Garcia .50 .23 .06
☐ 143 Dick Woodson .50 .23 .06
☐ 144 Dodgers Leaders 1.50 .65 .19
Walter Alston MG
Tom Lasorda CO
Jim Gilliam CO
Red Adams CO
Monty Basgall CO
☐ 145 Dock Ellis .50 .23 .06
☐ 146 Ron Fairly .50 .23 .06
☐ 147 Bart Johnson .50 .23 .06
☐ 148A Dave Hilton SD .50 .23 .06
☐ 148B Dave Hilton WAS 6.00 2.70 .75
☐ 149 Mac Scarce .50 .23 .06
☐ 150 John Mayberry .60 .25 .08
☐ 151 Diego Segui .50 .23 .06
☐ 152 Oscar Gamble .60 .25 .08
☐ 153 Jon Matlack .60 .25 .08
☐ 154 Houston Astros 1.00 .45 .13
Team Card
☐ 155 Bert Campaneris .60 .25 .08
☐ 156 Randy Moffitt .50 .23 .06
☐ 157 Vic Harris .50 .23 .06
☐ 158 Jack Billingham .50 .23 .06
☐ 159 Jim Ray Hart .60 .25 .08
☐ 160 Brooks Robinson 6.00 2.70 .75
☐ 161 Ray Burris UER .60 .25 .08
(Card number is
printed sideways)
☐ 162 Bill Freehan .60 .25 .08
☐ 163 Ken Berry .50 .23 .06
☐ 164 Tom House .50 .23 .06
☐ 165 Willie Davis .60 .25 .08
☐ 166 Royals Leaders .60 .25 .08
Jack McKeon MG
Charlie Lau CO
Harry Dunlop CO
Galen Cisco CO
☐ 167 Luis Tiant .75 .35 .09
☐ 168 Danny Thompson .50 .23 .06
☐ 169 Steve Rogers .60 .25 .08
☐ 170 Bill Melton .50 .23 .06
☐ 171 Eduardo Rodriguez .50 .23 .06
☐ 172 Gene Clines .50 .23 .06
☐ 173A Randy Jones SD .80 .35 .10
☐ 173B Randy Jones WAS 8.00 3.60 1.00
☐ 174 Bill Robinson .60 .25 .08
☐ 175 Reggie Cleveland .50 .23 .06
☐ 176 John Lowenstein .50 .23 .06
☐ 177 Dave Roberts .50 .23 .06
☐ 178 Garry Maddox .60 .25 .08
☐ 179 Mets Leaders 2.00 .90 .25
Yogi Berra MG
Rube Walker CO
Eddie Yost CO
Roy McMillan CO
Joe Pignatano CO
☐ 180 Ken Holtzman .60 .25 .08
☐ 181 Cesar Geronimo .50 .23 .06
☐ 182 Lindy McDaniel .60 .25 .08
☐ 183 Johnny Oates .60 .25 .08
☐ 184 Texas Rangers 1.00 .45 .13
Team Card
☐ 185 Jose Cardenal .50 .23 .06
☐ 186 Fred Scherman .50 .23 .06
☐ 187 Don Baylor 2.75 1.25 .35
☐ 188 Rudy Meoli .50 .23 .06
☐ 189 Jim Brewer .50 .23 .06
☐ 190 Tony Oliva 1.50 .65 .19
☐ 191 Al Fitzmorris .50 .23 .06
☐ 192 Mario Guerrero .50 .23 .06
☐ 193 Tom Walker .50 .23 .06
☐ 194 Darrell Porter .60 .25 .08
☐ 195 Carlos May .50 .23 .06
☐ 196 Jim Fregosi .60 .25 .08
☐ 197A Vicente Romo SD .50 .23 .06
☐ 197B Vicente Romo WAS 6.00 2.70 .75
☐ 198 Dave Cash .50 .23 .06
☐ 199 Mike Kekich .50 .23 .06
☐ 200 Cesar Cedeno .60 .25 .08
☐ 201 Batting Leaders 5.00 2.30 .60
Rod Carew
Pete Rose
☐ 202 Home Run Leaders 4.50 2.00 .55
Reggie Jackson
Willie Stargell

☐ 203 RBI Leaders .... 4.50 2.00 .55
Reggie Jackson
Willie Stargell
☐ 204 Stolen Base Leaders .... 1.25 .55 .16
Tommy Harper
Lou Brock
☐ 205 Victory Leaders .... 1.00 .45 .13
Wilbur Wood
Ron Bryant
☐ 206 ERA Leaders .... 5.00 2.30 .60
Jim Palmer
Tom Seaver
☐ 207 Strikeout Leaders 12.00 5.50 1.50
Nolan Ryan
Tom Seaver
☐ 208 Leading Firemen .... 1.00 .45 .13
John Hiller
Mike Marshall
☐ 209 Ted Sizemore .... .50 .23 .06
☐ 210 Bill Singer .... .50 .23 .06
☐ 211 Chicago Cubs Team .... 1.00 .45 .13
☐ 212 Rollie Fingers .... 6.00 2.70 .75
☐ 213 Dave Rader .... .50 .23 .06
☐ 214 Billy Grabarkewitz .... .50 .23 .06
☐ 215 Al Kaline UER .... 6.00 2.70 .75
(No copyright on back)
☐ 216 Ray Sadecki .... .50 .23 .06
☐ 217 Tim Foli .... .50 .23 .06
☐ 218 Johnny Briggs .... .50 .23 .06
☐ 219 Doug Griffin .... .50 .23 .06
☐ 220 Don Sutton .... 4.00 1.80 .50
☐ 221 White Sox Leaders .... .60 .25 .08
Chuck Tanner MG
Jim Mahoney CO
Alex Monchak CO
Johnny Sain CO
Joe Lonnett CO
☐ 222 Ramon Hernandez .... .50 .23 .06
☐ 223 Jeff Burroughs .... .75 .35 .09
☐ 224 Roger Metzger .... .50 .23 .06
☐ 225 Paul Splittorff .... .50 .23 .06
☐ 226A Padres Team SD .... 1.00 .45 .13
☐ 226B Padres Team WAS 8.00 3.60 1.00
☐ 227 Mike Lum .... .50 .23 .06
☐ 228 Ted Kubiak .... .50 .23 .06
☐ 229 Fritz Peterson .... .50 .23 .06
☐ 230 Tony Perez .... 4.00 1.80 .50
☐ 231 Dick Tidrow .... .50 .23 .06
☐ 232 Steve Brye .... .50 .23 .06
☐ 233 Jim Barr .... .50 .23 .06
☐ 234 John Milner .... .50 .23 .06
☐ 235 Dave McNally .... .60 .25 .08
☐ 236 Cardinals Leaders .... .80 .35 .10
Red Schoendienst MG
Barney Schultz CO
George Kissell CO
Johnny Lewis CO
Vern Benson CO
☐ 237 Ken Brett .... .50 .23 .06
☐ 238 Fran Healy HOR .... .60 .25 .08
(Munson sliding
in background)
☐ 239 Bill Russell .... .60 .25 .08
☐ 240 Joe Coleman .... .50 .23 .06
☐ 241A Glenn Beckert SD .... .60 .25 .08
☐ 241B Glenn Beckert WAS .... 6.00 2.70 .75
☐ 242 Bill Gogolewski .... .50 .23 .06
☐ 243 Bob Oliver .... .50 .23 .06
☐ 244 Carl Morton .... .50 .23 .06
☐ 245 Cleon Jones .... .60 .25 .08
☐ 246 Oakland Athletics .... 1.00 .45 .13
Team Card
☐ 247 Rick Miller .... .50 .23 .06
☐ 248 Tom Hall .... .50 .23 .06
☐ 249 George Mitterwald .... .50 .23 .06
☐ 250A Willie McCovey SD .... 6.00 2.70 .75
☐ 250B Willie McCovey WAS 30.00 13.50 3.80
☐ 251 Graig Nettles .... 2.00 .90 .25
☐ 252 Dave Parker 30.00 13.50 3.80
☐ 253 John Boccabella .... .50 .23 .06
☐ 254 Stan Bahnsen .... .50 .23 .06
☐ 255 Larry Bowa .... .75 .35 .09
☐ 256 Tom Griffin .... .50 .23 .06
☐ 257 Buddy Bell .... .90 .40 .11
☐ 258 Jerry Morales .... .50 .23 .06
☐ 259 Bob Reynolds .... .50 .23 .06
☐ 260 Ted Simmons .... 2.50 1.15 .30
☐ 261 Jerry Bell .... .50 .23 .06
☐ 262 Ed Kirkpatrick .... .50 .23 .06
☐ 263 Checklist 2 .... 2.50 .25 .07
☐ 264 Joe Rudi .... .60 .25 .08
☐ 265 Tug McGraw .... 1.00 .45 .13
☐ 266 Jim Northrup .... .60 .25 .08
☐ 267 Andy Messersmith .... .60 .25 .08
☐ 268 Tom Grieve .... .60 .25 .08
☐ 269 Bob Johnson .... .50 .23 .06
☐ 270 Ron Santo .... 1.00 .45 .13
☐ 271 Bill Hands .... .50 .23 .06
☐ 272 Paul Casanova .... .50 .23 .06
☐ 273 Checklist 3 .... 2.50 .25 .07
☐ 274 Fred Beene .... .50 .23 .06
☐ 275 Ron Hunt .... .50 .23 .06
☐ 276 Angels Leaders .... .60 .25 .08
Bobby Winkles MG
John Roseboro CO
Tom Morgan CO
Jimmie Reese CO
Salty Parker CO
☐ 277 Gary Nolan .... .60 .25 .08
☐ 278 Cookie Rojas .... .60 .25 .08
☐ 279 Jim Crawford .... .50 .23 .06
☐ 280 Carl Yastrzemski 12.50 5.75 1.55
☐ 281 San Francisco Giants .... 1.00 .45 .13
Team Card
☐ 282 Doyle Alexander .... .60 .25 .08
☐ 283 Mike Schmidt 100.00 45.00 12.50
☐ 284 Dave Duncan .... .50 .23 .06
☐ 285 Reggie Smith .... .60 .25 .08
☐ 286 Tony Muser .... .50 .23 .06
☐ 287 Clay Kirby .... .50 .23 .06
☐ 288 Gorman Thomas .... 1.75 .80 .22
☐ 289 Rick Auerbach .... .50 .23 .06
☐ 290 Vida Blue .... .75 .35 .09
☐ 291 Don Hahn .... .50 .23 .06
☐ 292 Chuck Seelbach .... .50 .23 .06
☐ 293 Milt May .... .50 .23 .06
☐ 294 Steve Foucault .... .50 .23 .06
☐ 295 Rick Monday .... .60 .25 .08
☐ 296 Ray Corbin .... .50 .23 .06
☐ 297 Hal Breeden .... .50 .23 .06
☐ 298 Roric Harrison .... .50 .23 .06
☐ 299 Gene Michael .... .60 .25 .08
☐ 300 Pete Rose 12.50 5.75 1.55
☐ 301 Bob Montgomery .... .50 .23 .06
☐ 302 Rudy May .... .50 .23 .06
☐ 303 George Hendrick .... .60 .25 .08
☐ 304 Don Wilson .... .50 .23 .06
☐ 305 Tito Fuentes .... .50 .23 .06
☐ 306 Orioles Leaders .... 1.00 .45 .13
Earl Weaver MG
Jim Frey CO
George Bamberger CO
Billy Hunter CO
George Staller CO
☐ 307 Luis Melendez .... .50 .23 .06
☐ 308 Bruce Dal Canton .... .50 .23 .06
☐ 309A Dave Roberts SD .... .50 .23 .06
☐ 309B Dave Roberts WAS 8.00 3.60 1.00
☐ 310 Terry Forster .... .60 .25 .08
☐ 311 Jerry Grote .... .50 .23 .06
☐ 312 Deron Johnson .... .50 .23 .06
☐ 313 Barry Lersch .... .50 .23 .06
☐ 314 Milwaukee Brewers .... 1.00 .45 .13
Team Card
☐ 315 Ron Cey .... 1.00 .45 .13
☐ 316 Jim Perry .... .60 .25 .08
☐ 317 Richie Zisk .... .60 .25 .08
☐ 318 Jim Merritt .... .50 .23 .06
☐ 319 Randy Hundley .... .50 .23 .06
☐ 320 Dusty Baker .... .80 .35 .10
☐ 321 Steve Braun .... .50 .23 .06
☐ 322 Ernie McAnally .... .50 .23 .06
☐ 323 Richie Scheinblum .... .50 .23 .06
☐ 324 Steve Kline .... .50 .23 .06
☐ 325 Tommy Harper .... .60 .25 .08
☐ 326 Reds Leaders .... .80 .35 .10
Sparky Anderson MG
Larry Shepard CO
George Scherger CO
Alex Grammas CO
Ted Kluszewski CO
☐ 327 Tom Timmermann .... .50 .23 .06
☐ 328 Skip Jutze .... .50 .23 .06
☐ 329 Mark Belanger .... .60 .25 .08
☐ 330 Juan Marichal .... 3.00 1.35 .40
☐ 331 All-Star Catchers .... 6.50 2.90 .80
Carlton Fisk
Johnny Bench
☐ 332 All-Star 1B .... 3.50 1.55 .45
Dick Allen
Hank Aaron
☐ 333 All-Star 2B .... 3.00 1.35 .40
Rod Carew
Joe Morgan
☐ 334 All-Star 3B .... 2.00 .90 .25
Brooks Robinson

Ron Santo
☐ 335 All-Star SS .75 .35 .09
Bert Campaneris
Chris Speier
☐ 336 All-Star LF 3.00 1.35 .40
Bobby Murcer
Pete Rose
☐ 337 All-Star CF .75 .35 .09
Amos Otis
Cesar Cedeno
☐ 338 All-Star RF 4.50 2.00 .55
Reggie Jackson
Billy Williams
☐ 339 All-Star Pitchers 1.25 .55 .16
Jim Hunter
Rick Wise
☐ 340 Thurman Munson 10.00 4.50 1.25
☐ 341 Dan Driessen .80 .35 .10
☐ 342 Jim Lonborg .60 .25 .08
☐ 343 Royals Team 1.00 .45 .13
☐ 344 Mike Caldwell .50 .23 .06
☐ 345 Bill North .50 .23 .06
☐ 346 Ron Reed .50 .23 .06
☐ 347 Sandy Alomar .60 .25 .08
☐ 348 Pete Richert .50 .23 .06
☐ 349 John Vukovich .50 .23 .06
☐ 350 Bob Gibson 6.00 2.70 .75
☐ 351 Dwight Evans 12.50 5.75 1.55
☐ 352 Bill Stoneman .50 .23 .06
☐ 353 Rich Coggins .50 .23 .06
☐ 354 Cubs Leaders .60 .25 .08
Whitey Lockman MG
J.C. Martin CO
Hank Aguirre CO
Al Spangler CO
Jim Marshall CO
☐ 355 Dave Nelson .50 .23 .06
☐ 356 Jerry Koosman .75 .35 .09
☐ 357 Buddy Bradford .50 .23 .06
☐ 358 Dal Maxvill .50 .23 .06
☐ 359 Brent Strom .50 .23 .06
☐ 360 Greg Luzinski .75 .35 .09
☐ 361 Don Carrithers .50 .23 .06
☐ 362 Hal King .50 .23 .06
☐ 363 New York Yankees 1.00 .45 .13
Team Card
☐ 364A Cito Gaston SD .75 .35 .09
☐ 364B Cito Gaston WAS 10.00 4.50 1.25
☐ 365 Steve Busby .60 .25 .08
☐ 366 Larry Hisle .60 .25 .08
☐ 367 Norm Cash .75 .35 .09
☐ 368 Manny Mota .60 .25 .08
☐ 369 Paul Lindblad .50 .23 .06
☐ 370 Bob Watson .60 .25 .08
☐ 371 Jim Slaton .50 .23 .06
☐ 372 Ken Reitz .50 .23 .06
☐ 373 John Curtis .50 .23 .06
☐ 374 Marty Perez .50 .23 .06
☐ 375 Earl Williams .50 .23 .06
☐ 376 Jorge Orta .50 .23 .06
☐ 377 Ron Woods .50 .23 .06
☐ 378 Burt Hooton .60 .25 .08
☐ 379 Rangers Leaders 1.00 .45 .13
Billy Martin MG
Frank Lucchesi CO
Art Fowler CO
Charlie Silvera CO
Jackie Moore CO
☐ 380 Bud Harrelson .60 .25 .08
☐ 381 Charlie Sands .50 .23 .06
☐ 382 Bob Moose .50 .23 .06
☐ 383 Philadelphia Phillies 1.00 .45 .13
Team Card
☐ 384 Chris Chambliss .60 .25 .08
☐ 385 Don Gullett .60 .25 .08
☐ 386 Gary Matthews .60 .25 .08
☐ 387A Rich Morales SD .50 .23 .06
☐ 387B Rich Morales WAS 8.00 3.60 1.00
☐ 388 Phil Roof .50 .23 .06
☐ 389 Gates Brown .50 .23 .06
☐ 390 Lou Piniella 1.00 .45 .13
☐ 391 Billy Champion .50 .23 .06
☐ 392 Dick Green .50 .23 .06
☐ 393 Orlando Pena .50 .23 .06
☐ 394 Ken Henderson .50 .23 .06
☐ 395 Doug Rader .50 .23 .06
☐ 396 Tommy Davis .60 .25 .08
☐ 397 George Stone .50 .23 .06
☐ 398 Duke Sims .50 .23 .06
☐ 399 Mike Paul .50 .23 .06
☐ 400 Harmon Killebrew 5.00 2.30 .60
☐ 401 Elliott Maddox .50 .23 .06
☐ 402 Jim Rooker .50 .23 .06
☐ 403 Red Sox Leaders .60 .25 .08
Darrell Johnson MG
Eddie Popowski CO
Lee Stange CO
Don Zimmer CO
Don Bryant CO
☐ 404 Jim Howarth .50 .23 .06
☐ 405 Ellie Rodriguez .50 .23 .06
☐ 406 Steve Arlin .50 .23 .06
☐ 407 Jim Wohlford .50 .23 .06
☐ 408 Charlie Hough .60 .25 .08
☐ 409 Ike Brown .50 .23 .06
☐ 410 Pedro Borbon .50 .23 .06
☐ 411 Frank Baker .50 .23 .06
☐ 412 Chuck Taylor .50 .23 .06
☐ 413 Don Money .60 .25 .08
☐ 414 Checklist 4 2.50 .25 .07
☐ 415 Gary Gentry .50 .23 .06
☐ 416 Chicago White Sox 1.00 .45 .13
Team Card
☐ 417 Rich Folkers .50 .23 .06
☐ 418 Walt Williams .50 .23 .06
☐ 419 Wayne Twitchell .50 .23 .06
☐ 420 Ray Fosse .50 .23 .06
☐ 421 Dan Fife .50 .23 .06
☐ 422 Gonzalo Marquez .50 .23 .06
☐ 423 Fred Stanley .50 .23 .06
☐ 424 Jim Beauchamp .50 .23 .06
☐ 425 Pete Broberg .50 .23 .06
☐ 426 Rennie Stennett .50 .23 .06
☐ 427 Bobby Bolin .50 .23 .06
☐ 428 Gary Sutherland .50 .23 .06
☐ 429 Dick Lange .50 .23 .06
☐ 430 Matty Alou .60 .25 .08
☐ 431 Gene Garber .75 .35 .09
☐ 432 Chris Arnold .50 .23 .06
☐ 433 Lerrin LaGrow .50 .23 .06
☐ 434 Ken McMullen .50 .23 .06
☐ 435 Dave Concepcion 2.50 1.15 .30
☐ 436 Don Hood .50 .23 .06
☐ 437 Jim Lyttle .50 .23 .06
☐ 438 Ed Herrmann .50 .23 .06
☐ 439 Norm Miller .50 .23 .06
☐ 440 Jim Kaat 1.50 .65 .19
☐ 441 Tom Ragland .50 .23 .06
☐ 442 Alan Foster .50 .23 .06
☐ 443 Tom Hutton .50 .23 .06
☐ 444 Vic Davalillo .50 .23 .06
☐ 445 George Medich .50 .23 .06
☐ 446 Len Randle .50 .23 .06
☐ 447 Twins Leaders .60 .25 .08
Frank Quilici MG
Ralph Rowe CO
Bob Rodgers CO
Vern Morgan CO
☐ 448 Ron Hodges .50 .23 .06
☐ 449 Tom McCraw .50 .23 .06
☐ 450 Rich Hebner .60 .25 .08
☐ 451 Tommy John 2.00 .90 .25
☐ 452 Gene Hiser .50 .23 .06
☐ 453 Balor Moore .50 .23 .06
☐ 454 Kurt Bevacqua .50 .23 .06
☐ 455 Tom Bradley .50 .23 .06
☐ 456 Dave Winfield 160.00 70.00 20.00
☐ 457 Chuck Goggin .50 .23 .06
☐ 458 Jim Ray .50 .23 .06
☐ 459 Cincinnati Reds 1.00 .45 .13
Team Card
☐ 460 Boog Powell 1.00 .45 .13
☐ 461 John Odom .50 .23 .06
☐ 462 Luis Alvarado .50 .23 .06
☐ 463 Pat Dobson .50 .23 .06
☐ 464 Jose Cruz .60 .25 .08
☐ 465 Dick Bosman .50 .23 .06
☐ 466 Dick Billings .50 .23 .06
☐ 467 Winston Llenas .50 .23 .06
☐ 468 Pepe Frias .50 .23 .06
☐ 469 Joe Decker .50 .23 .06
☐ 470 AL Playoffs 6.00 2.70 .75
A's over Orioles
(Reggie Jackson)
☐ 471 NL Playoffs 1.00 .45 .13
Mets over Reds
(Jon Matlack pitching)
☐ 472 World Series Game 1 1.00 .45 .13
(Darold Knowles
pitching)
☐ 473 World Series Game 2 5.00 2.30 .60
(Willie Mays batting)
☐ 474 World Series Game 3 1.00 .45 .13
(Bert Campaneris
stealing)
☐ 475 World Series Game 4 1.00 .45 .13
(Rusty Staub batting)
☐ 476 World Series Game 5 1.00 .45 .13

	(Cleon Jones scoring)			
☐ 477	World Series Game 6	6.00	2.70	.75
	(Reggie Jackson)			
☐ 478	World Series Game 7	1.00	.45	.13
	(Bert Campaneris batting)			
☐ 479	World Series Summary	1.00	.45	.13
	A's celebrate; win 2nd consecutive championship			
☐ 480	Willie Crawford	.50	.23	.06
☐ 481	Jerry Terrell	.50	.23	.06
☐ 482	Bob Didier	.50	.23	.06
☐ 483	Atlanta Braves	1.00	.45	.13
	Team Card			
☐ 484	Carmen Fanzone	.50	.23	.06
☐ 485	Felipe Alou	.80	.35	.10
☐ 486	Steve Stone	.60	.25	.08
☐ 487	Ted Martinez	.50	.23	.06
☐ 488	Andy Etchebarren	.50	.23	.06
☐ 489	Pirates Leaders	.60	.25	.08
	Danny Murtaugh MG			
	Don Osborn CO			
	Don Leppert CO			
	Bill Mazeroski CO			
	Bob Skinner CO			
☐ 490	Vada Pinson	.80	.35	.10
☐ 491	Roger Nelson	.50	.23	.06
☐ 492	Mike Rogodzinski	.50	.23	.06
☐ 493	Joe Hoerner	.50	.23	.06
☐ 494	Ed Goodson	.50	.23	.06
☐ 495	Dick McAuliffe	.60	.25	.08
☐ 496	Tom Murphy	.50	.23	.06
☐ 497	Bobby Mitchell	.50	.23	.06
☐ 498	Pat Corrales	.60	.25	.08
☐ 499	Rusty Torres	.50	.23	.06
☐ 500	Lee May	.60	.25	.08
☐ 501	Eddie Leon	.50	.23	.06
☐ 502	Dave LaRoche	.50	.23	.06
☐ 503	Eric Soderholm	.50	.23	.06
☐ 504	Joe Niekro	.60	.25	.08
☐ 505	Bill Buckner	1.00	.45	.13
☐ 506	Ed Farmer	.50	.23	.06
☐ 507	Larry Stahl	.50	.23	.06
☐ 508	Montreal Expos	1.00	.45	.13
	Team Card			
☐ 509	Jesse Jefferson	.50	.23	.06
☐ 510	Wayne Garrett	.50	.23	.06
☐ 511	Toby Harrah	.60	.25	.08
☐ 512	Joe Lahoud	.50	.23	.06
☐ 513	Jim Campanis	.50	.23	.06
☐ 514	Paul Schaal	.50	.23	.06
☐ 515	Willie Montanez	.50	.23	.06
☐ 516	Horacio Pina	.50	.23	.06
☐ 517	Mike Hegan	.50	.23	.06
☐ 518	Derrel Thomas	.50	.23	.06
☐ 519	Bill Sharp	.50	.23	.06
☐ 520	Tim McCarver	.80	.35	.10
☐ 521	Indians Leaders	.60	.25	.08
	Ken Aspromonte MG			
	Clay Bryant CO			
	Tony Pacheco CO			
☐ 522	J.R. Richard	.60	.25	.08
☐ 523	Cecil Cooper	1.75	.80	.22
☐ 524	Bill Plummer	.50	.23	.06
☐ 525	Clyde Wright	.50	.23	.06
☐ 526	Frank Tepedino	.50	.23	.06
☐ 527	Bobby Darwin	.50	.23	.06
☐ 528	Bill Bonham	.50	.23	.06
☐ 529	Horace Clarke	.50	.23	.06
☐ 530	Mickey Stanley	.60	.25	.08
☐ 531	Expos Leaders	.60	.25	.08
	Gene Mauch MG			
	Dave Bristol CO			
	Cal McLish CO			
	Larry Doby CO			
	Jerry Zimmerman CO			
☐ 532	Skip Lockwood	.50	.23	.06
☐ 533	Mike Phillips	.50	.23	.06
☐ 534	Eddie Watt	.50	.23	.06
☐ 535	Bob Tolan	.50	.23	.06
☐ 536	Duffy Dyer	.50	.23	.06
☐ 537	Steve Mingori	.50	.23	.06
☐ 538	Cesar Tovar	.50	.23	.06
☐ 539	Lloyd Allen	.50	.23	.06
☐ 540	Bob Robertson	.50	.23	.06
☐ 541	Cleveland Indians	1.00	.45	.13
	Team Card			
☐ 542	Rich Gossage	5.00	2.30	.60
☐ 543	Danny Cater	.50	.23	.06
☐ 544	Ron Schueler	.50	.23	.06
☐ 545	Billy Conigliaro	.60	.25	.08
☐ 546	Mike Corkins	.50	.23	.06
☐ 547	Glenn Borgmann	.50	.23	.06
☐ 548	Sonny Siebert	.50	.23	.06
☐ 549	Mike Jorgensen	.50	.23	.06
☐ 550	Sam McDowell	.60	.25	.08
☐ 551	Von Joshua	.50	.23	.06
☐ 552	Denny Doyle	.50	.23	.06
☐ 553	Jim Willoughby	.50	.23	.06
☐ 554	Tim Johnson	.50	.23	.06
☐ 555	Woodie Fryman	.50	.23	.06
☐ 556	Dave Campbell	.50	.23	.06
☐ 557	Jim McGlothlin	.50	.23	.06
☐ 558	Bill Fahey	.50	.23	.06
☐ 559	Darrel Chaney	.50	.23	.06
☐ 560	Mike Cuellar	.60	.25	.08
☐ 561	Ed Kranepool	.50	.23	.06
☐ 562	Jack Aker	.50	.23	.06
☐ 563	Hal McRae	1.00	.45	.13
☐ 564	Mike Ryan	.50	.23	.06
☐ 565	Milt Wilcox	.50	.23	.06
☐ 566	Jackie Hernandez	.50	.23	.06
☐ 567	Boston Red Sox	1.00	.45	.13
	Team Card			
☐ 568	Mike Torrez	.60	.25	.08
☐ 569	Rick Dempsey	.75	.35	.09
☐ 570	Ralph Garr	.60	.25	.08
☐ 571	Rich Hand	.50	.23	.06
☐ 572	Enzo Hernandez	.50	.23	.06
☐ 573	Mike Adams	.50	.23	.06
☐ 574	Bill Parsons	.50	.23	.06
☐ 575	Steve Garvey	10.00	4.50	1.25
☐ 576	Scipio Spinks	.50	.23	.06
☐ 577	Mike Sadek	.50	.23	.06
☐ 578	Ralph Houk MG	.60	.25	.08
☐ 579	Cecil Upshaw	.50	.23	.06
☐ 580	Jim Spencer	.50	.23	.06
☐ 581	Fred Norman	.50	.23	.06
☐ 582	Bucky Dent	2.00	.90	.25
☐ 583	Marty Pattin	.50	.23	.06
☐ 584	Ken Rudolph	.50	.23	.06
☐ 585	Merv Rettenmund	.50	.23	.06
☐ 586	Jack Brohamer	.50	.23	.06
☐ 587	Larry Christenson	.50	.23	.06
☐ 588	Hal Lanier	.50	.23	.06
☐ 589	Boots Day	.50	.23	.06
☐ 590	Roger Moret	.50	.23	.06
☐ 591	Sonny Jackson	.50	.23	.06
☐ 592	Ed Bane	.50	.23	.06
☐ 593	Steve Yeager	.60	.25	.08
☐ 594	Leroy Stanton	.50	.23	.06
☐ 595	Steve Blass	.60	.25	.08
☐ 596	Rookie Pitchers	.60	.25	.08
	Wayne Garland			
	Fred Holdsworth			
	Mark Littell			
	Dick Pole			
☐ 597	Rookie Shortstops	.75	.35	.09
	Dave Chalk			
	John Gamble			
	Pete MacKanin			
	Manny Trillo			
☐ 598	Rookie Outfielders	25.00	11.50	3.10
	Dave Augustine			
	Ken Griffey			
	Steve Ontiveros			
	Jim Tyrone			
☐ 599A	Rookie Pitchers WAS	1.00	.45	.13
	Ron Diorio			
	Dave Freisleben			
	Frank Riccelli			
	Greg Shanahan			
☐ 599B	Rookie Pitchers SD	4.00	1.80	.50
	(SD in large print)			
☐ 599C	Rookie Pitchers SD	7.50	3.40	.95
	(SD in small print)			
☐ 600	Rookie Infielders	5.00	2.30	.60
	Ron Cash			
	Jim Cox			
	Bill Madlock			
	Reggie Sanders			
☐ 601	Rookie Outfielders	6.00	2.70	.75
	Ed Armbrister			
	Rich Bladt			
	Brian Downing			
	Bake McBride			
☐ 602	Rookie Pitchers	.70	.30	.09
	Glen Abbott			
	Rick Henninger			
	Craig Swan			
	Dan Vossler			
☐ 603	Rookie Catchers	.60	.25	.08
	Barry Foote			
	Tom Lundstedt			
	Charlie Moore			
	Sergio Robles			

☐ 604 Rookie Infielders Terry Hughes John Knox Andre Thornton Frank White	5.00	2.30	.60
☐ 605 Rookie Pitchers Vic Albury Ken Frailing Kevin Kobel Frank Tanana	5.00	2.30	.60
☐ 606 Rookie Outfielders Jim Fuller Wilbur Howard Tommy Smith Otto Velez	.60	.25	.08
☐ 607 Rookie Shortstops Leo Foster Tom Heintzelman Dave Rosello Frank Taveras	.60	.25	.08
☐ 608A Rookie Pitchers: ERR Bob Apodaco (sic) Dick Baney John D'Acquisto Mike Wallace	2.00	.90	.25
☐ 608B Rookie Pitchers: COR Bob Apodaca Dick Baney John D'Acquisto Mike Wallace	.75	.35	.09
☐ 609 Rico Petrocelli	.60	.25	.08
☐ 610 Dave Kingman	1.25	.55	.16
☐ 611 Rich Stelmaszek	.50	.23	.06
☐ 612 Luke Walker	.50	.23	.06
☐ 613 Dan Monzon	.50	.23	.06
☐ 614 Adrian Devine	.50	.23	.06
☐ 615 Johnny Jeter UER (Misspelled Johnnie on card back)	.50	.23	.06
☐ 616 Larry Gura	.50	.23	.06
☐ 617 Ted Ford	.50	.23	.06
☐ 618 Jim Mason	.50	.23	.06
☐ 619 Mike Anderson	.50	.23	.06
☐ 620 Al Downing	.50	.23	.06
☐ 621 Bernie Carbo	.50	.23	.06
☐ 622 Phil Gagliano	.50	.23	.06
☐ 623 Celerino Sanchez	.50	.23	.06
☐ 624 Bob Miller	.50	.23	.06
☐ 625 Ollie Brown	.50	.23	.06
☐ 626 Pittsburgh Pirates Team Card	1.00	.45	.13
☐ 627 Carl Taylor	.50	.23	.06
☐ 628 Ivan Murrell	.50	.23	.06
☐ 629 Rusty Staub	1.00	.45	.13
☐ 630 Tommie Agee	.60	.25	.08
☐ 631 Steve Barber	.50	.23	.06
☐ 632 George Culver	.50	.23	.06
☐ 633 Dave Hamilton	.50	.23	.06
☐ 634 Braves Leaders Eddie Mathews MG Herm Starrette CO Connie Ryan CO Jim Busby CO Ken Silvestri CO	1.25	.55	.16
☐ 635 Johnny Edwards	.50	.23	.06
☐ 636 Dave Goltz	.50	.23	.06
☐ 637 Checklist 5	2.50	.25	.07
☐ 638 Ken Sanders	.50	.23	.06
☐ 639 Joe Lovitto	.50	.23	.06
☐ 640 Milt Pappas	.60	.25	.08
☐ 641 Chuck Brinkman	.50	.23	.06
☐ 642 Terry Harmon	.50	.23	.06
☐ 643 Dodgers Team	1.00	.45	.13
☐ 644 Wayne Granger	.50	.23	.06
☐ 645 Ken Boswell	.50	.23	.06
☐ 646 George Foster	2.00	.90	.25
☐ 647 Juan Beniquez	.60	.25	.08
☐ 648 Terry Crowley	.50	.23	.06
☐ 649 Fernando Gonzalez	.50	.23	.06
☐ 650 Mike Epstein	.50	.23	.06
☐ 651 Leron Lee	.50	.23	.06
☐ 652 Gail Hopkins	.50	.23	.06
☐ 653 Bob Stinson	.50	.23	.06
☐ 654A Jesus Alou ERR (No position)	.60	.25	.08
☐ 654B Jesus Alou COR (Outfield)	7.00	3.10	.85
☐ 655 Mike Tyson	.50	.23	.06
☐ 656 Adrian Garrett	.50	.23	.06
☐ 657 Jim Shellenback	.50	.23	.06
☐ 658 Lee Lacy	.50	.23	.06
☐ 659 Joe Lis	.50	.23	.06
☐ 660 Larry Dierker	.75	.35	.09

1974 Topps Traded

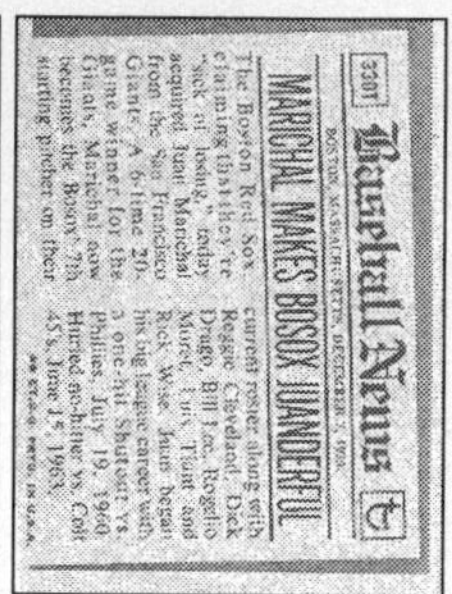

The cards in this 44-card set measure 2 1/2" by 3 1/2". The 1974 Topps Traded set contains 43 player cards and one unnumbered checklist card. The obverses have the word "traded" in block letters and the backs are designed in newspaper style. Card numbers are the same as in the regular set except they are followed by a "T." No known scarcities exist for this set. The cards were issued heavily mixed in with regular wax packs of the 1974 Topps cards toward the end of the distribution cycle; they were produced in large enough quantity that they are no scarcer than the regular Topps cards.

	NRMT-MT	EXC	G-VG
COMPLETE SET (44)	13.00	5.75	1.65
COMMON PLAYER	.35	.16	.04
☐ 23T Craig Robinson	.35	.16	.04
☐ 42T Claude Osteen	.45	.20	.06
☐ 43T Jim Wynn	.45	.20	.06
☐ 51T Bobby Heise	.35	.16	.04
☐ 59T Ross Grimsley	.35	.16	.04
☐ 62T Bob Locker	.35	.16	.04
☐ 63T Bill Sudakis	.35	.16	.04
☐ 73T Mike Marshall	.65	.30	.08
☐ 123T Nelson Briles	.45	.20	.06
☐ 139T Aurelio Monteagudo	.35	.16	.04
☐ 151T Diego Segui	.35	.16	.04
☐ 165T Willie Davis	.45	.20	.06
☐ 175T Reggie Cleveland	.35	.16	.04
☐ 182T Lindy McDaniel	.45	.20	.06
☐ 186T Fred Scherman	.35	.16	.04
☐ 249T George Mitterwald	.35	.16	.04
☐ 262T Ed Kirkpatrick	.35	.16	.04
☐ 269T Bob Johnson	.35	.16	.04
☐ 270T Ron Santo	.65	.30	.08
☐ 313T Barry Lersch	.35	.16	.04
☐ 319T Randy Hundley	.35	.16	.04
☐ 330T Juan Marichal	2.50	1.15	.30
☐ 348T Pete Richert	.35	.16	.04
☐ 373T John Curtis	.35	.16	.04
☐ 390T Lou Piniella	.65	.30	.08
☐ 428T Gary Sutherland	.35	.16	.04
☐ 454T Kurt Bevacqua	.35	.16	.04
☐ 458T Jim Ray	.35	.16	.04
☐ 485T Felipe Alou	.65	.30	.08
☐ 486T Steve Stone	.65	.30	.08
☐ 496T Tom Murphy	.35	.16	.04
☐ 516T Horacio Pina	.35	.16	.04
☐ 534T Eddie Watt	.35	.16	.04
☐ 538T Cesar Tovar	.35	.16	.04
☐ 544T Ron Schueler	.35	.16	.04
☐ 579T Cecil Upshaw	.35	.16	.04
☐ 585T Merv Rettenmund	.35	.16	.04
☐ 612T Luke Walker	.35	.16	.04
☐ 616T Larry Gura	.45	.20	.06
☐ 618T Jim Mason	.35	.16	.04
☐ 630T Tommie Agee	.45	.20	.06
☐ 648T Terry Crowley	.35	.16	.04
☐ 649T Fernando Gonzalez	.35	.16	.04
☐ NNO Traded Checklist	1.00	.10	.03

1975 Topps

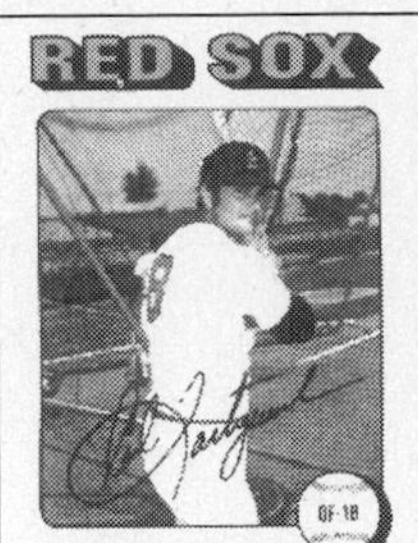

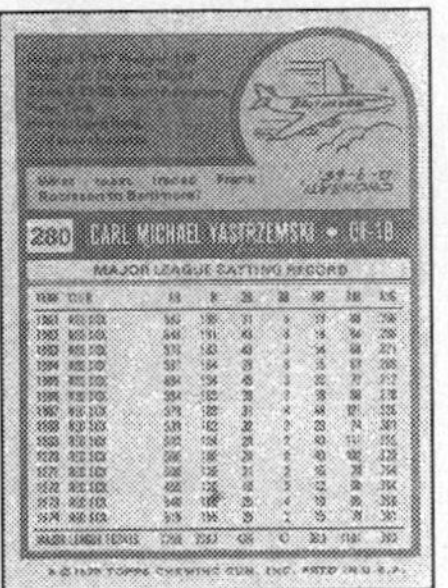

The cards in the 1975 Topps set were issued in two different sizes: a regular standard size (2 1/2" by 3 1/2") and a mini size (2 1/2" by 3 1/8") which was issued as a test in certain areas of the country. The 660-card Topps baseball set for 1975 was radically different in appearance from sets of the preceding years. The most prominent change was the use of a two-color frame surrounding the picture area rather than a single, subdued color. A facsimile autograph appears on the picture, and the backs are printed in red and green on gray. Cards 189-212 depict the MVP's of both leagues from 1951 through 1974. The first seven cards (1-7) feature players (listed in alphabetical order) breaking records or achieving milestones during the previous season. Cards 306-313 picture league leaders in various statistical categories. Cards 459-466 depict the results of post-season action. Team cards feature a checklist back for players on that team and show a small inset photo of the manager on the front. The Phillies Team card number 46 erroneously lists Terry Harmon as number 339 instead of number 399. The following players' regular issue cards are explicitly denoted as All-Stars, 1, 50, 80, 140, 170, 180, 260, 320, 350, 390, 400, 420, 440, 470, 530, 570, and 600. This set is quite popular with collectors, at least in part due to the fact that the Rookie Cards of Robin Yount, George Brett, Gary Carter, Jim Rice, Fred Lynn, and Keith Hernandez are all in the set. Topps minis have the same checklist and are valued from approximately 1.25 times to double the prices listed below.

	NRMT-MT	EXC	G-VG
COMPLETE SET (660)	900.00	400.00	115.00
COMMON PLAYER (1-132)	.50	.23	.06
COMMON PLAYER (133-264)	.50	.23	.06
COMMON PLAYER (265-660)	.50	.23	.06
☐ 1 RB: Hank Aaron Sets Homer Mark	30.00	7.50	2.40
☐ 2 RB: Lou Brock 118 Stolen Bases	3.50	1.55	.45
☐ 3 RB: Bob Gibson 3000th Strikeout	3.50	1.55	.45
☐ 4 RB: Al Kaline 3000 Hit Club	4.00	1.80	.50
☐ 5 RB: Nolan Ryan Fans 300 for 3rd Year in a Row	20.00	9.00	2.50
☐ 6 RB: Mike Marshall Hurls 106 Games	.75	.35	.09
☐ 7 No Hitters Steve Busby Dick Bosman Nolan Ryan	5.00	2.30	.60
☐ 8 Rogelio Moret	.50	.23	.06
☐ 9 Frank Tepedino	.50	.23	.06
☐ 10 Willie Davis	.60	.25	.08
☐ 11 Bill Melton	.50	.23	.06
☐ 12 David Clyde	.50	.23	.06
☐ 13 Gene Locklear	.50	.23	.06
☐ 14 Milt Wilcox	.50	.23	.06
☐ 15 Jose Cardenal	.50	.23	.06
☐ 16 Frank Tanana	2.00	.90	.25
☐ 17 Dave Concepcion	2.50	1.15	.30
☐ 18 Tigers: Team/Mgr. Ralph Houk (Checklist back)	1.50	.65	.19
☐ 19 Jerry Koosman	.75	.35	.09
☐ 20 Thurman Munson	9.00	4.00	1.15
☐ 21 Rollie Fingers	5.00	2.30	.60
☐ 22 Dave Cash	.50	.23	.06
☐ 23 Bill Russell	.60	.25	.08
☐ 24 Al Fitzmorris	.50	.23	.06
☐ 25 Lee May	.60	.25	.08
☐ 26 Dave McNally	.60	.25	.08
☐ 27 Ken Reitz	.50	.23	.06
☐ 28 Tom Murphy	.50	.23	.06
☐ 29 Dave Parker	8.00	3.60	1.00
☐ 30 Bert Blyleven	3.00	1.35	.40
☐ 31 Dave Rader	.50	.23	.06
☐ 32 Reggie Cleveland	.50	.23	.06
☐ 33 Dusty Baker	.75	.35	.09
☐ 34 Steve Renko	.50	.23	.06
☐ 35 Ron Santo	1.00	.45	.13
☐ 36 Joe Lovitto	.50	.23	.06
☐ 37 Dave Freisleben	.50	.23	.06
☐ 38 Buddy Bell	.75	.35	.09
☐ 39 Andre Thornton	.60	.25	.08
☐ 40 Bill Singer	.50	.23	.06
☐ 41 Cesar Geronimo	.50	.23	.06
☐ 42 Joe Coleman	.50	.23	.06
☐ 43 Cleon Jones	.60	.25	.08
☐ 44 Pat Dobson	.50	.23	.06
☐ 45 Joe Rudi	.60	.25	.08
☐ 46 Phillies: Team/Mgr. Danny Ozark UER (Checklist back)	1.50	.65	.19
☐ 47 Tommy John	2.00	.90	.25
☐ 48 Freddie Patek	.60	.25	.08
☐ 49 Larry Dierker	.50	.23	.06
☐ 50 Brooks Robinson	6.00	2.70	.75
☐ 51 Bob Forsch	.90	.40	.11
☐ 52 Darrell Porter	.60	.25	.08
☐ 53 Dave Giusti	.50	.23	.06
☐ 54 Eric Soderholm	.50	.23	.06
☐ 55 Bobby Bonds	1.50	.65	.19
☐ 56 Rick Wise	.60	.25	.08
☐ 57 Dave Johnson	.60	.25	.08
☐ 58 Chuck Taylor	.50	.23	.06
☐ 59 Ken Henderson	.50	.23	.06
☐ 60 Fergie Jenkins	4.50	2.00	.55
☐ 61 Dave Winfield	55.00	25.00	7.00
☐ 62 Fritz Peterson	.50	.23	.06
☐ 63 Steve Swisher	.50	.23	.06
☐ 64 Dave Chalk	.50	.23	.06
☐ 65 Don Gullett	.60	.25	.08
☐ 66 Willie Horton	.60	.25	.08
☐ 67 Tug McGraw	1.00	.45	.13
☐ 68 Ron Blomberg	.50	.23	.06
☐ 69 John Odom	.50	.23	.06
☐ 70 Mike Schmidt	65.00	29.00	8.25
☐ 71 Charlie Hough	.60	.25	.08
☐ 72 Royals: Team/Mgr. Jack McKeon (Checklist back)	1.50	.65	.19
☐ 73 J.R. Richard	.60	.25	.08
☐ 74 Mark Belanger	.60	.25	.08
☐ 75 Ted Simmons	2.00	.90	.25
☐ 76 Ed Sprague	.50	.23	.06
☐ 77 Richie Zisk	.60	.25	.08
☐ 78 Ray Corbin	.50	.23	.06
☐ 79 Gary Matthews	.60	.25	.08
☐ 80 Carlton Fisk	24.00	11.00	3.00
☐ 81 Ron Reed	.50	.23	.06
☐ 82 Pat Kelly	.50	.23	.06
☐ 83 Jim Merritt	.50	.23	.06
☐ 84 Enzo Hernandez	.50	.23	.06
☐ 85 Bill Bonham	.50	.23	.06
☐ 86 Joe Lis	.50	.23	.06
☐ 87 George Foster	2.00	.90	.25
☐ 88 Tom Egan	.50	.23	.06
☐ 89 Jim Ray	.50	.23	.06
☐ 90 Rusty Staub	1.00	.45	.13
☐ 91 Dick Green	.50	.23	.06
☐ 92 Cecil Upshaw	.50	.23	.06
☐ 93 Dave Lopes	1.00	.45	.13
☐ 94 Jim Lonborg	.60	.25	.08
☐ 95 John Mayberry	.60	.25	.08
☐ 96 Mike Cosgrove	.50	.23	.06
☐ 97 Earl Williams	.50	.23	.06
☐ 98 Rich Folkers	.50	.23	.06
☐ 99 Mike Hegan	.50	.23	.06
☐ 100 Willie Stargell	4.00	1.80	.50
☐ 101 Expos: Team/Mgr. Gene Mauch (Checklist back)	1.50	.65	.19

Card			
☐ 102 Joe Decker	.50	.23	.06
☐ 103 Rick Miller	.50	.23	.06
☐ 104 Bill Madlock	1.25	.55	.16
☐ 105 Buzz Capra	.50	.23	.06
☐ 106 Mike Hargrove	.80	.35	.10
☐ 107 Jim Barr	.50	.23	.06
☐ 108 Tom Hall	.50	.23	.06
☐ 109 George Hendrick	.60	.25	.08
☐ 110 Wilbur Wood	.50	.23	.06
☐ 111 Wayne Garrett	.50	.23	.06
☐ 112 Larry Hardy	.50	.23	.06
☐ 113 Elliott Maddox	.50	.23	.06
☐ 114 Dick Lange	.50	.23	.06
☐ 115 Joe Ferguson	.50	.23	.06
☐ 116 Lerrin LaGrow	.50	.23	.06
☐ 117 Orioles: Team/Mgr. Earl Weaver (Checklist back)	1.50	.65	.19
☐ 118 Mike Anderson	.50	.23	.06
☐ 119 Tommy Helms	.50	.23	.06
☐ 120 Steve Busby UER (Photo actually Fran Healy)	.60	.25	.08
☐ 121 Bill North	.50	.23	.06
☐ 122 Al Hrabosky	.60	.25	.08
☐ 123 Johnny Briggs	.50	.23	.06
☐ 124 Jerry Reuss	.60	.25	.08
☐ 125 Ken Singleton	.60	.25	.08
☐ 126 Checklist 1-132	2.00	.20	.06
☐ 127 Glenn Borgmann	.50	.23	.06
☐ 128 Bill Lee	.60	.25	.08
☐ 129 Rick Monday	.60	.25	.08
☐ 130 Phil Niekro	4.00	1.80	.50
☐ 131 Toby Harrah	.60	.25	.08
☐ 132 Randy Moffitt	.50	.23	.06
☐ 133 Dan Driessen	.60	.25	.08
☐ 134 Ron Hodges	.50	.23	.06
☐ 135 Charlie Spikes	.50	.23	.06
☐ 136 Jim Mason	.50	.23	.06
☐ 137 Terry Forster	.60	.25	.08
☐ 138 Del Unser	.50	.23	.06
☐ 139 Horacio Pina	.50	.23	.06
☐ 140 Steve Garvey	7.00	3.10	.85
☐ 141 Mickey Stanley	.60	.25	.08
☐ 142 Bob Reynolds	.50	.23	.06
☐ 143 Cliff Johnson	.60	.25	.08
☐ 144 Jim Wohlford	.50	.23	.06
☐ 145 Ken Holtzman	.60	.25	.08
☐ 146 Padres: Team/Mgr. John McNamara (Checklist back)	1.50	.65	.19
☐ 147 Pedro Garcia	.50	.23	.06
☐ 148 Jim Rooker	.50	.23	.06
☐ 149 Tim Foli	.50	.23	.06
☐ 150 Bob Gibson	6.00	2.70	.75
☐ 151 Steve Brye	.50	.23	.06
☐ 152 Mario Guerrero	.50	.23	.06
☐ 153 Rick Reuschel	.60	.25	.08
☐ 154 Mike Lum	.50	.23	.06
☐ 155 Jim Bibby	.50	.23	.06
☐ 156 Dave Kingman	1.00	.45	.13
☐ 157 Pedro Borbon	.50	.23	.06
☐ 158 Jerry Grote	.50	.23	.06
☐ 159 Steve Arlin	.50	.23	.06
☐ 160 Graig Nettles	1.50	.65	.19
☐ 161 Stan Bahnsen	.50	.23	.06
☐ 162 Willie Montanez	.50	.23	.06
☐ 163 Jim Brewer	.50	.23	.06
☐ 164 Mickey Rivers	.60	.25	.08
☐ 165 Doug Rader	.60	.25	.08
☐ 166 Woodie Fryman	.50	.23	.06
☐ 167 Rich Coggins	.50	.23	.06
☐ 168 Bill Greif	.50	.23	.06
☐ 169 Cookie Rojas	.60	.25	.08
☐ 170 Bert Campaneris	.60	.25	.08
☐ 171 Ed Kirkpatrick	.50	.23	.06
☐ 172 Red Sox: Team/Mgr. Darrell Johnson (Checklist back)	1.50	.65	.19
☐ 173 Steve Rogers	.60	.25	.08
☐ 174 Bake McBride	.60	.25	.08
☐ 175 Don Money	.60	.25	.08
☐ 176 Burt Hooton	.60	.25	.08
☐ 177 Vic Correll	.50	.23	.06
☐ 178 Cesar Tovar	.50	.23	.06
☐ 179 Tom Bradley	.50	.23	.06
☐ 180 Joe Morgan	7.50	3.40	.95
☐ 181 Fred Beene	.50	.23	.06
☐ 182 Don Hahn	.50	.23	.06
☐ 183 Mel Stottlemyre	.60	.25	.08
☐ 184 Jorge Orta	.50	.23	.06
☐ 185 Steve Carlton	10.00	4.50	1.25
☐ 186 Willie Crawford	.50	.23	.06
☐ 187 Denny Doyle	.50	.23	.06
☐ 188 Tom Griffin	.50	.23	.06
☐ 189 1951 MVP's Larry (Yogi) Berra Roy Campanella (Campy never issued)	2.50	1.15	.30
☐ 190 1952 MVP's Bobby Shantz Hank Sauer	1.00	.45	.13
☐ 191 1953 MVP's Al Rosen Roy Campanella	1.25	.55	.16
☐ 192 1954 MVP's Yogi Berra Willie Mays	2.50	1.15	.30
☐ 193 1955 MVP's Yogi Berra Roy Campanella (Campy card never issued, pictured with LA cap, sic)	2.50	1.15	.30
☐ 194 1956 MVP's Mickey Mantle Don Newcombe	7.00	3.10	.85
☐ 195 1957 MVP's Mickey Mantle Hank Aaron	11.00	4.90	1.40
☐ 196 1958 MVP's Jackie Jensen Ernie Banks	1.00	.45	.13
☐ 197 1959 MVP's Nellie Fox Ernie Banks	1.25	.55	.16
☐ 198 1960 MVP's Roger Maris Dick Groat	1.00	.45	.13
☐ 199 1961 MVP's Roger Maris Frank Robinson	2.50	1.15	.30
☐ 200 1962 MVP's Mickey Mantle Maury Wills (Wills never issued)	7.00	3.10	.85
☐ 201 1963 MVP's Elston Howard Sandy Koufax	1.25	.55	.16
☐ 202 1964 MVP's Brooks Robinson Ken Boyer	1.25	.55	.16
☐ 203 1965 MVP's Zoilo Versalles Willie Mays	1.25	.55	.16
☐ 204 1966 MVP's Frank Robinson Bob Clemente	2.50	1.15	.30
☐ 205 1967 MVP's Carl Yastrzemski Orlando Cepeda	1.50	.65	.19
☐ 206 1968 MVP's Denny McLain Bob Gibson	1.50	.65	.19
☐ 207 1969 MVP's Harmon Killebrew Willie McCovey	1.50	.65	.19
☐ 208 1970 MVP's Boog Powell Johnny Bench	1.25	.55	.16
☐ 209 1971 MVP's Vida Blue Joe Torre	1.00	.45	.13
☐ 210 1972 MVP's Rich Allen Johnny Bench	1.25	.55	.16
☐ 211 1973 MVP's Reggie Jackson Pete Rose	6.00	2.70	.75
☐ 212 1974 MVP's Jeff Burroughs Steve Garvey	1.00	.45	.13
☐ 213 Oscar Gamble	.60	.25	.08
☐ 214 Harry Parker	.50	.23	.06
☐ 215 Bobby Valentine	.60	.25	.08
☐ 216 Giants: Team/Mgr. Wes Westrum (Checklist back)	1.50	.65	.19
☐ 217 Lou Piniella	1.00	.45	.13
☐ 218 Jerry Johnson	.50	.23	.06
☐ 219 Ed Herrmann	.50	.23	.06
☐ 220 Don Sutton	4.00	1.80	.50
☐ 221 Aurelio Rodriguez	.50	.23	.06
☐ 222 Dan Spillner	.50	.23	.06
☐ 223 Robin Yount	225.00	100.00	28.00
☐ 224 Ramon Hernandez	.50	.23	.06

☐ 225 Bob Grich .75 .35 .09
☐ 226 Bill Campbell .50 .23 .06
☐ 227 Bob Watson .60 .25 .08
☐ 228 George Brett 225.00 100.00 28.00
☐ 229 Barry Foote .50 .23 .06
☐ 230 Jim Hunter 4.00 1.80 .50
☐ 231 Mike Tyson .50 .23 .06
☐ 232 Diego Segui .50 .23 .06
☐ 233 Billy Grabarkewitz .50 .23 .06
☐ 234 Tom Grieve .60 .25 .08
☐ 235 Jack Billingham .50 .23 .06
☐ 236 Angels: Team/Mgr. 1.50 .65 .19
Dick Williams
(Checklist back)
☐ 237 Carl Morton .50 .23 .06
☐ 238 Dave Duncan .50 .23 .06
☐ 239 George Stone .50 .23 .06
☐ 240 Garry Maddox .60 .25 .08
☐ 241 Dick Tidrow .50 .23 .06
☐ 242 Jay Johnstone .60 .25 .08
☐ 243 Jim Kaat 1.25 .55 .16
☐ 244 Bill Buckner 1.00 .45 .13
☐ 245 Mickey Lolich .75 .35 .09
☐ 246 Cardinals: Team/Mgr. 1.50 .65 .19
Red Schoendienst
(Checklist back)
☐ 247 Enos Cabell .50 .23 .06
☐ 248 Randy Jones .60 .25 .08
☐ 249 Danny Thompson .50 .23 .06
☐ 250 Ken Brett .50 .23 .06
☐ 251 Fran Healy .50 .23 .06
☐ 252 Fred Scherman .50 .23 .06
☐ 253 Jesus Alou .50 .23 .06
☐ 254 Mike Torrez .60 .25 .08
☐ 255 Dwight Evans 6.50 2.90 .80
☐ 256 Billy Champion .50 .23 .06
☐ 257 Checklist: 133-264 2.00 .20 .06
☐ 258 Dave LaRoche .50 .23 .06
☐ 259 Len Randle .50 .23 .06
☐ 260 Johnny Bench 15.00 6.75 1.90
☐ 261 Andy Hassler .50 .23 .06
☐ 262 Rowland Office .50 .23 .06
☐ 263 Jim Perry .60 .25 .08
☐ 264 John Milner .50 .23 .06
☐ 265 Ron Bryant .50 .23 .06
☐ 266 Sandy Alomar .60 .25 .08
☐ 267 Dick Ruthven .50 .23 .06
☐ 268 Hal McRae .75 .35 .09
☐ 269 Doug Rau .50 .23 .06
☐ 270 Ron Fairly .50 .23 .06
☐ 271 Gerry Moses .50 .23 .06
☐ 272 Lynn McGlothen .50 .23 .06
☐ 273 Steve Braun .50 .23 .06
☐ 274 Vicente Romo .50 .23 .06
☐ 275 Paul Blair .60 .25 .08
☐ 276 White Sox Team/Mgr. 1.50 .65 .19
Chuck Tanner
(Checklist back)
☐ 277 Frank Taveras .50 .23 .06
☐ 278 Paul Lindblad .50 .23 .06
☐ 279 Milt May .50 .23 .06
☐ 280 Carl Yastrzemski 10.00 4.50 1.25
☐ 281 Jim Slaton .50 .23 .06
☐ 282 Jerry Morales .50 .23 .06
☐ 283 Steve Foucault .50 .23 .06
☐ 284 Ken Griffey 4.00 1.80 .50
☐ 285 Ellie Rodriguez .50 .23 .06
☐ 286 Mike Jorgensen .50 .23 .06
☐ 287 Roric Harrison .50 .23 .06
☐ 288 Bruce Ellingsen .50 .23 .06
☐ 289 Ken Rudolph .50 .23 .06
☐ 290 Jon Matlack .50 .23 .06
☐ 291 Bill Sudakis .50 .23 .06
☐ 292 Ron Schueler .50 .23 .06
☐ 293 Dick Sharon .50 .23 .06
☐ 294 Geoff Zahn .50 .23 .06
☐ 295 Vada Pinson .75 .35 .09
☐ 296 Alan Foster .50 .23 .06
☐ 297 Craig Kusick .50 .23 .06
☐ 298 Johnny Grubb .50 .23 .06
☐ 299 Bucky Dent .75 .35 .09
☐ 300 Reggie Jackson 28.00 12.50 3.50
☐ 301 Dave Roberts .50 .23 .06
☐ 302 Rick Burleson .75 .35 .09
☐ 303 Grant Jackson .50 .23 .06
☐ 304 Pirates: Team/Mgr. 1.50 .65 .19
Danny Murtaugh
(Checklist back)
☐ 305 Jim Colborn .50 .23 .06
☐ 306 Batting Leaders 1.25 .55 .16
Rod Carew
Ralph Garr
☐ 307 Home Run Leaders 3.00 1.35 .40
Dick Allen
Mike Schmidt
☐ 308 RBI Leaders 1.50 .65 .19
Jeff Burroughs
Johnny Bench
☐ 309 Stolen Base Leaders 1.50 .65 .19
Bill North
Lou Brock
☐ 310 Victory Leaders 1.25 .55 .16
Jim Hunter
Fergie Jenkins
Andy Messersmith
Phil Niekro
☐ 311 ERA Leaders 1.25 .55 .16
Jim Hunter
Buzz Capra
☐ 312 Strikeout Leaders 12.00 5.50 1.50
Nolan Ryan
Steve Carlton
☐ 313 Leading Firemen 1.00 .45 .13
Terry Forster
Mike Marshall
☐ 314 Buck Martinez .50 .23 .06
☐ 315 Don Kessinger .60 .25 .08
☐ 316 Jackie Brown .50 .23 .06
☐ 317 Joe Lahoud .50 .23 .06
☐ 318 Ernie McAnally .50 .23 .06
☐ 319 Johnny Oates .60 .25 .08
☐ 320 Pete Rose 15.00 6.75 1.90
☐ 321 Rudy May .50 .23 .06
☐ 322 Ed Goodson .50 .23 .06
☐ 323 Fred Holdsworth .50 .23 .06
☐ 324 Ed Kranepool .50 .23 .06
☐ 325 Tony Oliva 1.25 .55 .16
☐ 326 Wayne Twitchell .50 .23 .06
☐ 327 Jerry Hairston .50 .23 .06
☐ 328 Sonny Siebert .50 .23 .06
☐ 329 Ted Kubiak .50 .23 .06
☐ 330 Mike Marshall .60 .25 .08
☐ 331 Indians: Team/Mgr. 1.50 .65 .19
Frank Robinson
(Checklist back)
☐ 332 Fred Kendall .50 .23 .06
☐ 333 Dick Drago .50 .23 .06
☐ 334 Greg Gross .50 .23 .06
☐ 335 Jim Palmer 10.00 4.50 1.25
☐ 336 Rennie Stennett .50 .23 .06
☐ 337 Kevin Kobel .50 .23 .06
☐ 338 Rich Stelmaszek .50 .23 .06
☐ 339 Jim Fregosi .60 .25 .08
☐ 340 Paul Splittorff .50 .23 .06
☐ 341 Hal Breeden .50 .23 .06
☐ 342 Leroy Stanton .50 .23 .06
☐ 343 Danny Frisella .50 .23 .06
☐ 344 Ben Oglivie .60 .25 .08
☐ 345 Clay Carroll .50 .23 .06
☐ 346 Bobby Darwin .50 .23 .06
☐ 347 Mike Caldwell .50 .23 .06
☐ 348 Tony Muser .50 .23 .06
☐ 349 Ray Sadecki .50 .23 .06
☐ 350 Bobby Murcer .75 .35 .09
☐ 351 Bob Boone 1.50 .65 .19
☐ 352 Darold Knowles .50 .23 .06
☐ 353 Luis Melendez .50 .23 .06
☐ 354 Dick Bosman .50 .23 .06
☐ 355 Chris Cannizzaro .50 .23 .06
☐ 356 Rico Petrocelli .60 .25 .08
☐ 357 Ken Forsch .50 .23 .06
☐ 358 Al Bumbry .50 .23 .06
☐ 359 Paul Popovich .50 .23 .06
☐ 360 George Scott .60 .25 .08
☐ 361 Dodgers: Team/Mgr. 1.50 .65 .19
Walter Alston
(Checklist back)
☐ 362 Steve Hargan .50 .23 .06
☐ 363 Carmen Fanzone .50 .23 .06
☐ 364 Doug Bird .50 .23 .06
☐ 365 Bob Bailey .50 .23 .06
☐ 366 Ken Sanders .50 .23 .06
☐ 367 Craig Robinson .50 .23 .06
☐ 368 Vic Albury .50 .23 .06
☐ 369 Merv Rettenmund .50 .23 .06
☐ 370 Tom Seaver 20.00 9.00 2.50
☐ 371 Gates Brown .50 .23 .06
☐ 372 John D'Acquisto .50 .23 .06
☐ 373 Bill Sharp .50 .23 .06
☐ 374 Eddie Watt .50 .23 .06
☐ 375 Roy White .60 .25 .08
☐ 376 Steve Yeager .60 .25 .08
☐ 377 Tom Hilgendorf .50 .23 .06
☐ 378 Derrel Thomas .50 .23 .06
☐ 379 Bernie Carbo .50 .23 .06
☐ 380 Sal Bando .60 .25 .08
☐ 381 John Curtis .50 .23 .06

Card			
☐ 382 Don Baylor	2.00	.90	.25
☐ 383 Jim York	.50	.23	.06
☐ 384 Brewers: Team/Mgr.	1.50	.65	.19
Del Crandall			
(Checklist back)			
☐ 385 Dock Ellis	.50	.23	.06
☐ 386 Checklist: 265-396	2.00	.20	.06
☐ 387 Jim Spencer	.50	.23	.06
☐ 388 Steve Stone	.60	.25	.08
☐ 389 Tony Solaita	.50	.23	.06
☐ 390 Ron Cey	1.00	.45	.13
☐ 391 Don DeMola	.50	.23	.06
☐ 392 Bruce Bochte	.50	.23	.06
☐ 393 Gary Gentry	.50	.23	.06
☐ 394 Larvell Blanks	.50	.23	.06
☐ 395 Bud Harrelson	.60	.25	.08
☐ 396 Fred Norman	.50	.23	.06
☐ 397 Bill Freehan	.60	.25	.08
☐ 398 Elias Sosa	.50	.23	.06
☐ 399 Terry Harmon	.50	.23	.06
☐ 400 Dick Allen	1.00	.45	.13
☐ 401 Mike Wallace	.50	.23	.06
☐ 402 Bob Tolan	.50	.23	.06
☐ 403 Tom Buskey	.50	.23	.06
☐ 404 Ted Sizemore	.50	.23	.06
☐ 405 John Montague	.50	.23	.06
☐ 406 Bob Gallagher	.50	.23	.06
☐ 407 Herb Washington	.50	.23	.06
☐ 408 Clyde Wright	.50	.23	.06
☐ 409 Bob Robertson	.50	.23	.06
☐ 410 Mike Cueller UER	.60	.25	.08
(Sic, Cuellar)			
☐ 411 George Mitterwald	.50	.23	.06
☐ 412 Bill Hands	.50	.23	.06
☐ 413 Marty Pattin	.50	.23	.06
☐ 414 Manny Mota	.60	.25	.08
☐ 415 John Hiller	.60	.25	.08
☐ 416 Larry Lintz	.50	.23	.06
☐ 417 Skip Lockwood	.50	.23	.06
☐ 418 Leo Foster	.50	.23	.06
☐ 419 Dave Goltz	.50	.23	.06
☐ 420 Larry Bowa	.75	.35	.09
☐ 421 Mets: Team/Mgr.	1.50	.65	.19
Yogi Berra			
(Checklist back)			
☐ 422 Brian Downing	1.50	.65	.19
☐ 423 Clay Kirby	.50	.23	.06
☐ 424 John Lowenstein	.50	.23	.06
☐ 425 Tito Fuentes	.50	.23	.06
☐ 426 George Medich	.50	.23	.06
☐ 427 Clarence Gaston	.60	.25	.08
☐ 428 Dave Hamilton	.50	.23	.06
☐ 429 Jim Dwyer	.50	.23	.06
☐ 430 Luis Tiant	.75	.35	.09
☐ 431 Rod Gilbreath	.50	.23	.06
☐ 432 Ken Berry	.50	.23	.06
☐ 433 Larry Demery	.50	.23	.06
☐ 434 Bob Locker	.50	.23	.06
☐ 435 Dave Nelson	.50	.23	.06
☐ 436 Ken Frailing	.50	.23	.06
☐ 437 Al Cowens	.60	.25	.08
☐ 438 Don Carrithers	.50	.23	.06
☐ 439 Ed Brinkman	.50	.23	.06
☐ 440 Andy Messersmith	.60	.25	.08
☐ 441 Bobby Heise	.50	.23	.06
☐ 442 Maximino Leon	.50	.23	.06
☐ 443 Twins: Team/Mgr.	1.50	.65	.19
Frank Quilici			
(Checklist back)			
☐ 444 Gene Garber	.60	.25	.08
☐ 445 Felix Millan	.50	.23	.06
☐ 446 Bart Johnson	.50	.23	.06
☐ 447 Terry Crowley	.50	.23	.06
☐ 448 Frank Duffy	.50	.23	.06
☐ 449 Charlie Williams	.50	.23	.06
☐ 450 Willie McCovey	5.00	2.30	.60
☐ 451 Rick Dempsey	.75	.35	.09
☐ 452 Angel Mangual	.50	.23	.06
☐ 453 Claude Osteen	.60	.25	.08
☐ 454 Doug Griffin	.50	.23	.06
☐ 455 Don Wilson	.50	.23	.06
☐ 456 Bob Coluccio	.50	.23	.06
☐ 457 Mario Mendoza	.50	.23	.06
☐ 458 Ross Grimsley	.50	.23	.06
☐ 459 1974 AL Champs	1.00	.45	.13
A's over Orioles			
(Second base action			
pictured)			
☐ 460 1974 NL Champs	1.25	.55	.16
Dodgers over Pirates			
(Frank Taveras and			
Steve Garvey at second)			
☐ 461 World Series Game 1	3.50	1.55	.45
(Reggie Jackson)			
☐ 462 World Series Game 2	1.00	.45	.13
(Dodger dugout)			
☐ 463 World Series Game 3	1.25	.55	.16
(Rollie Fingers			
pitching)			
☐ 464 World Series Game 4	1.00	.45	.13
(A's batter)			
☐ 465 World Series Game 5	1.00	.45	.13
(Joe Rudi rounding			
third)			
☐ 466 World Series Summary	1.25	.55	.16
A's do it again;			
win third straight			
(A's group picture)			
☐ 467 Ed Halicki	.50	.23	.06
☐ 468 Bobby Mitchell	.50	.23	.06
☐ 469 Tom Dettore	.50	.23	.06
☐ 470 Jeff Burroughs	.60	.25	.08
☐ 471 Bob Stinson	.50	.23	.06
☐ 472 Bruce Dal Canton	.50	.23	.06
☐ 473 Ken McMullen	.50	.23	.06
☐ 474 Luke Walker	.50	.23	.06
☐ 475 Darrell Evans	.75	.35	.09
☐ 476 Ed Figueroa	.50	.23	.06
☐ 477 Tom Hutton	.50	.23	.06
☐ 478 Tom Burgmeier	.50	.23	.06
☐ 479 Ken Boswell	.50	.23	.06
☐ 480 Carlos May	.50	.23	.06
☐ 481 Will McEnaney	.50	.23	.06
☐ 482 Tom McCraw	.50	.23	.06
☐ 483 Steve Ontiveros	.50	.23	.06
☐ 484 Glenn Beckert	.60	.25	.08
☐ 485 Sparky Lyle	.75	.35	.09
☐ 486 Ray Fosse	.50	.23	.06
☐ 487 Astros: Team/Mgr.	1.50	.65	.19
Preston Gomez			
(Checklist back)			
☐ 488 Bill Travers	.50	.23	.06
☐ 489 Cecil Cooper	1.25	.55	.16
☐ 490 Reggie Smith	.75	.35	.09
☐ 491 Doyle Alexander	.60	.25	.08
☐ 492 Rich Hebner	.60	.25	.08
☐ 493 Don Stanhouse	.50	.23	.06
☐ 494 Pete LaCock	.50	.23	.06
☐ 495 Nelson Briles	.60	.25	.08
☐ 496 Pepe Frias	.50	.23	.06
☐ 497 Jim Nettles	.50	.23	.06
☐ 498 Al Downing	.50	.23	.06
☐ 499 Marty Perez	.50	.23	.06
☐ 500 Nolan Ryan	75.00	34.00	9.50
☐ 501 Bill Robinson	.60	.25	.08
☐ 502 Pat Bourque	.50	.23	.06
☐ 503 Fred Stanley	.50	.23	.06
☐ 504 Buddy Bradford	.50	.23	.06
☐ 505 Chris Speier	.50	.23	.06
☐ 506 Leron Lee	.50	.23	.06
☐ 507 Tom Carroll	.50	.23	.06
☐ 508 Bob Hansen	.50	.23	.06
☐ 509 Dave Hilton	.50	.23	.06
☐ 510 Vida Blue	.75	.35	.09
☐ 511 Rangers: Team/Mgr.	1.50	.65	.19
Billy Martin			
(Checklist back)			
☐ 512 Larry Milbourne	.50	.23	.06
☐ 513 Dick Pole	.50	.23	.06
☐ 514 Jose Cruz	.75	.35	.09
☐ 515 Manny Sanguillen	.60	.25	.08
☐ 516 Don Hood	.50	.23	.06
☐ 517 Checklist: 397-528	2.00	.20	.06
☐ 518 Leo Cardenas	.50	.23	.06
☐ 519 Jim Todd	.50	.23	.06
☐ 520 Amos Otis	.60	.25	.08
☐ 521 Dennis Blair	.50	.23	.06
☐ 522 Gary Sutherland	.50	.23	.06
☐ 523 Tom Paciorek	.60	.25	.08
☐ 524 John Doherty	.50	.23	.06
☐ 525 Tom House	.50	.23	.06
☐ 526 Larry Hisle	.60	.25	.08
☐ 527 Mac Scarce	.50	.23	.06
☐ 528 Eddie Leon	.50	.23	.06
☐ 529 Gary Thomasson	.50	.23	.06
☐ 530 Gaylord Perry	4.00	1.80	.50
☐ 531 Reds: Team/Mgr.	2.50	1.15	.30
Sparky Anderson			
(Checklist back)			
☐ 532 Gorman Thomas	.75	.35	.09
☐ 533 Rudy Meoli	.50	.23	.06
☐ 534 Alex Johnson	.50	.23	.06
☐ 535 Gene Tenace	.60	.25	.08
☐ 536 Bob Moose	.50	.23	.06
☐ 537 Tommy Harper	.60	.25	.08
☐ 538 Duffy Dyer	.50	.23	.06
☐ 539 Jesse Jefferson	.50	.23	.06

☐ 540 Lou Brock 5.00 2.30 .60
☐ 541 Roger Metzger .50 .23 .06
☐ 542 Pete Broberg .50 .23 .06
☐ 543 Larry Biittner .50 .23 .06
☐ 544 Steve Mingori .50 .23 .06
☐ 545 Billy Williams 4.00 1.80 .50
☐ 546 John Knox .50 .23 .06
☐ 547 Von Joshua .50 .23 .06
☐ 548 Charlie Sands .50 .23 .06
☐ 549 Bill Butler .50 .23 .06
☐ 550 Ralph Garr .60 .25 .08
☐ 551 Larry Christenson .50 .23 .06
☐ 552 Jack Brohamer .50 .23 .06
☐ 553 John Boccabella .50 .23 .06
☐ 554 Rich Gossage 3.00 1.35 .40
☐ 555 Al Oliver 1.00 .45 .13
☐ 556 Tim Johnson .50 .23 .06
☐ 557 Larry Gura .50 .23 .06
☐ 558 Dave Roberts .50 .23 .06
☐ 559 Bob Montgomery .50 .23 .06
☐ 560 Tony Perez 4.00 1.80 .50
☐ 561 A's: Team/Mgr. 1.50 .65 .19
Alvin Dark
(Checklist back)
☐ 562 Gary Nolan .60 .25 .08
☐ 563 Wilbur Howard .50 .23 .06
☐ 564 Tommy Davis .60 .25 .08
☐ 565 Joe Torre 1.00 .45 .13
☐ 566 Ray Burris .50 .23 .06
☐ 567 Jim Sundberg 1.00 .45 .13
☐ 568 Dale Murray .50 .23 .06
☐ 569 Frank White 1.00 .45 .13
☐ 570 Jim Wynn .60 .25 .08
☐ 571 Dave Lemanczyk .50 .23 .06
☐ 572 Roger Nelson .50 .23 .06
☐ 573 Orlando Pena .50 .23 .06
☐ 574 Tony Taylor .50 .23 .06
☐ 575 Gene Clines .50 .23 .06
☐ 576 Phil Roof .50 .23 .06
☐ 577 John Morris .50 .23 .06
☐ 578 Dave Tomlin .50 .23 .06
☐ 579 Skip Pitlock .50 .23 .06
☐ 580 Frank Robinson 5.00 2.30 .60
☐ 581 Darrel Chaney .50 .23 .06
☐ 582 Eduardo Rodriguez .50 .23 .06
☐ 583 Andy Etchebarren .50 .23 .06
☐ 584 Mike Garman .50 .23 .06
☐ 585 Chris Chambliss .60 .25 .08
☐ 586 Tim McCarver .80 .35 .10
☐ 587 Chris Ward .50 .23 .06
☐ 588 Rick Auerbach .50 .23 .06
☐ 589 Braves: Team/Mgr. 1.50 .65 .19
Clyde King
(Checklist back)
☐ 590 Cesar Cedeno .60 .25 .08
☐ 591 Glenn Abbott .50 .23 .06
☐ 592 Balor Moore .50 .23 .06
☐ 593 Gene Lamont .50 .23 .06
☐ 594 Jim Fuller .50 .23 .06
☐ 595 Joe Niekro .60 .25 .08
☐ 596 Ollie Brown .50 .23 .06
☐ 597 Winston Llenas .50 .23 .06
☐ 598 Bruce Kison .50 .23 .06
☐ 599 Nate Colbert .50 .23 .06
☐ 600 Rod Carew 12.00 5.50 1.50
☐ 601 Juan Beniquez .50 .23 .06
☐ 602 John Vukovich .50 .23 .06
☐ 603 Lew Krausse .50 .23 .06
☐ 604 Oscar Zamora .50 .23 .06
☐ 605 John Ellis .50 .23 .06
☐ 606 Bruce Miller .50 .23 .06
☐ 607 Jim Holt .50 .23 .06
☐ 608 Gene Michael .60 .25 .08
☐ 609 Elrod Hendricks .50 .23 .06
☐ 610 Ron Hunt .50 .23 .06
☐ 611 Yankees: Team/Mgr. 1.50 .65 .19
Bill Virdon
(Checklist back)
☐ 612 Terry Hughes .50 .23 .06
☐ 613 Bill Parsons .50 .23 .06
☐ 614 Rookie Pitchers .65 .30 .08
Jack Kucek
Dyar Miller
Vern Ruhle
Paul Siebert
☐ 615 Rookie Pitchers 1.00 .45 .13
Pat Darcy
Dennis Leonard
Tom Underwood
Hank Webb
☐ 616 Rookie Outfielders 24.00 11.00 3.00
Dave Augustine
Pepe Mangual
Jim Rice
John Scott
☐ 617 Rookie Infielders 2.50 1.15 .30
Mike Cubbage
Doug DeCinces
Reggie Sanders
Manny Trillo
☐ 618 Rookie Pitchers 1.25 .55 .16
Jamie Easterly
Tom Johnson
Scott McGregor
Rick Rhoden
☐ 619 Rookie Outfielders .65 .30 .08
Benny Ayala
Nyls Nyman
Tommy Smith
Jerry Turner
☐ 620 Rookie Catcher/OF 50.00 23.00 6.25
Gary Carter
Marc Hill
Danny Meyer
Leon Roberts
☐ 621 Rookie Pitchers 1.00 .45 .13
John Denny
Rawly Eastwick
Jim Kern
Juan Veintidos
☐ 622 Rookie Outfielders 12.00 5.50 1.50
Ed Armbrister
Fred Lynn
Tom Poquette
Terry Whitfield UER
(Listed as Ney York)
☐ 623 Rookie Infielders 20.00 9.00 2.50
Phil Garner
Keith Hernandez UER
(Sic, bats right)
Bob Sheldon
Tom Veryzer
☐ 624 Rookie Pitchers .65 .30 .08
Doug Konieczny
Gary Lavelle
Jim Otten
Eddie Solomon
☐ 625 Boog Powell 1.00 .45 .13
☐ 626 Larry Haney UER .50 .23 .06
(Photo actually
Dave Duncan)
☐ 627 Tom Walker .50 .23 .06
☐ 628 Ron LeFlore .75 .35 .09
☐ 629 Joe Hoerner .50 .23 .06
☐ 630 Greg Luzinski .75 .35 .09
☐ 631 Lee Lacy .50 .23 .06
☐ 632 Morris Nettles .50 .23 .06
☐ 633 Paul Casanova .50 .23 .06
☐ 634 Cy Acosta .50 .23 .06
☐ 635 Chuck Dobson .50 .23 .06
☐ 636 Charlie Moore .50 .23 .06
☐ 637 Ted Martinez .50 .23 .06
☐ 638 Cubs: Team/Mgr. 1.50 .65 .19
Jim Marshall
(Checklist back)
☐ 639 Steve Kline .50 .23 .06
☐ 640 Harmon Killebrew 5.00 2.30 .60
☐ 641 Jim Northrup .50 .23 .06
☐ 642 Mike Phillips .50 .23 .06
☐ 643 Brent Strom .50 .23 .06
☐ 644 Bill Fahey .50 .23 .06
☐ 645 Danny Cater .50 .23 .06
☐ 646 Checklist: 529-660 2.00 .20 .06
☐ 647 Claudell Washington .90 .40 .11
☐ 648 Dave Pagan .50 .23 .06
☐ 649 Jack Heidemann .50 .23 .06
☐ 650 Dave May .50 .23 .06
☐ 651 John Morlan .50 .23 .06
☐ 652 Lindy McDaniel .60 .25 .08
☐ 653 Lee Richard UER .50 .23 .06
(Listed as Richards
on card front)
☐ 654 Jerry Terrell .50 .23 .06
☐ 655 Rico Carty .60 .25 .08
☐ 656 Bill Plummer .50 .23 .06
☐ 657 Bob Oliver .50 .23 .06
☐ 658 Vic Harris .50 .23 .06
☐ 659 Bob Apodaca .50 .23 .06
☐ 660 Hank Aaron 30.00 7.50 2.40

1976 Topps

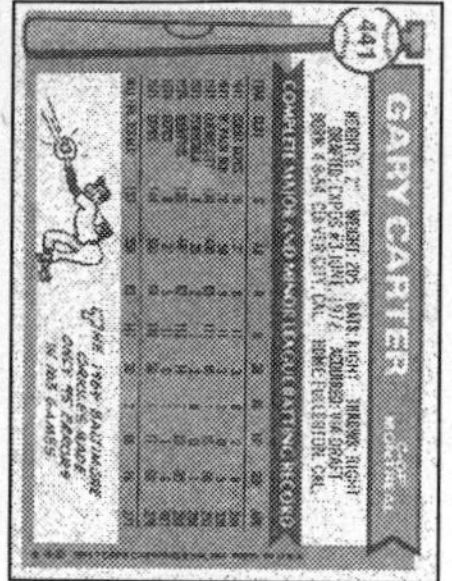

The 1976 Topps set of 660 cards (measuring 2 1/2" by 3 1/2") is known for its sharp color photographs and interesting presentation of subjects. Team cards feature a checklist back for players on that team and show a small inset photo of the manager on the front. A "Father and Son" series (66-70) spotlights five Major Leaguers whose fathers also made the "Big Show." Other subseries include "All Time All Stars" (341-350), "Record Breakers" from the previous season (1-6), League Leaders (191-205), Post-season cards (461-462), and Rookie Prospects (589-599). The following players' regular issue cards are explicitly denoted as All-Stars, 10, 48, 60, 140, 150, 165, 169, 240, 300, 370, 380, 395, 400, 420, 475, 500, 580, and 650. The key rookies in this set are Dennis Eckersley, Ron Guidry, and Willie Randolph.

	NRMT-MT	EXC	G-VG
COMPLETE SET (660)	475.00	210.00	60.00
COMMON PLAYER (1-660)	.30	.14	.04
☐ 1 RB: Hank Aaron Most RBI's, 2262	15.00	6.75	1.90
☐ 2 RB: Bobby Bonds Most leadoff HR's 32; plus three seasons 30 homers/30 steals	.75	.35	.09
☐ 3 RB: Mickey Lolich Lefthander, Most Strikeouts, 2679	.50	.23	.06
☐ 4 RB: Dave Lopes Most Consecutive SB attempts, 38	.50	.23	.06
☐ 5 RB: Tom Seaver Most Cons. seasons with 200 SO's, 8	3.50	1.55	.45
☐ 6 RB: Rennie Stennett Most Hits in a 9 inning game, 7	.50	.23	.06
☐ 7 Jim Umbarger	.30	.14	.04
☐ 8 Tito Fuentes	.30	.14	.04
☐ 9 Paul Lindblad	.30	.14	.04
☐ 10 Lou Brock	5.00	2.30	.60
☐ 11 Jim Hughes	.30	.14	.04
☐ 12 Richie Zisk	.40	.18	.05
☐ 13 John Wockenfuss	.30	.14	.04
☐ 14 Gene Garber	.30	.14	.04
☐ 15 George Scott	.40	.18	.05
☐ 16 Bob Apodaca	.30	.14	.04
☐ 17 New York Yankees Team Card; Billy Martin MG (Checklist back)	1.25	.55	.16
☐ 18 Dale Murray	.30	.14	.04
☐ 19 George Brett	60.00	27.00	7.50
☐ 20 Bob Watson	.40	.18	.05
☐ 21 Dave LaRoche	.30	.14	.04
☐ 22 Bill Russell	.40	.18	.05
☐ 23 Brian Downing	1.00	.45	.13
☐ 24 Cesar Geronimo	.30	.14	.04
☐ 25 Mike Torrez	.40	.18	.05
☐ 26 Andre Thornton	.40	.18	.05
☐ 27 Ed Figueroa	.30	.14	.04
☐ 28 Dusty Baker	.60	.25	.08
☐ 29 Rick Burleson	.40	.18	.05
☐ 30 John Montefusco	.40	.18	.05
☐ 31 Len Randle	.30	.14	.04
☐ 32 Danny Frisella	.30	.14	.04
☐ 33 Bill North	.30	.14	.04
☐ 34 Mike Garman	.30	.14	.04
☐ 35 Tony Oliva	1.00	.45	.13
☐ 36 Frank Taveras	.30	.14	.04
☐ 37 John Hiller	.40	.18	.05
☐ 38 Garry Maddox	.40	.18	.05
☐ 39 Pete Broberg	.30	.14	.04
☐ 40 Dave Kingman	1.00	.45	.13
☐ 41 Tippy Martinez	.40	.18	.05
☐ 42 Barry Foote	.30	.14	.04
☐ 43 Paul Splittorff	.30	.14	.04
☐ 44 Doug Rader	.40	.18	.05
☐ 45 Boog Powell	.75	.35	.09
☐ 46 Los Angeles Dodgers Team Card; Walter Alston MG (Checklist back)	1.25	.55	.16
☐ 47 Jesse Jefferson	.30	.14	.04
☐ 48 Dave Concepcion	1.50	.65	.19
☐ 49 Dave Duncan	.30	.14	.04
☐ 50 Fred Lynn	1.50	.65	.19
☐ 51 Ray Burris	.30	.14	.04
☐ 52 Dave Chalk	.30	.14	.04
☐ 53 Mike Beard	.30	.14	.04
☐ 54 Dave Rader	.30	.14	.04
☐ 55 Gaylord Perry	3.50	1.55	.45
☐ 56 Bob Tolan	.30	.14	.04
☐ 57 Phil Garner	1.00	.45	.13
☐ 58 Ron Reed	.30	.14	.04
☐ 59 Larry Hisle	.40	.18	.05
☐ 60 Jerry Reuss	.40	.18	.05
☐ 61 Ron LeFlore	.40	.18	.05
☐ 62 Johnny Oates	.40	.18	.05
☐ 63 Bobby Darwin	.30	.14	.04
☐ 64 Jerry Koosman	.50	.23	.06
☐ 65 Chris Chambliss	.40	.18	.05
☐ 66 Father and Son Gus Bell Buddy Bell	.50	.23	.06
☐ 67 Father and Son Ray Boone Bob Boone	.75	.35	.09
☐ 68 Father and Son Joe Coleman Joe Coleman Jr.	.50	.23	.06
☐ 69 Father and Son Jim Hegan Mike Hegan	.50	.23	.06
☐ 70 Father and Son Roy Smalley Roy Smalley Jr.	.50	.23	.06
☐ 71 Steve Rogers	.40	.18	.05
☐ 72 Hal McRae	.75	.35	.09
☐ 73 Baltimore Orioles Team Card; Earl Weaver MG (Checklist back)	1.25	.55	.16
☐ 74 Oscar Gamble	.40	.18	.05
☐ 75 Larry Dierker	.30	.14	.04
☐ 76 Willie Crawford	.30	.14	.04
☐ 77 Pedro Borbon	.30	.14	.04
☐ 78 Cecil Cooper	.75	.35	.09
☐ 79 Jerry Morales	.30	.14	.04
☐ 80 Jim Kaat	1.25	.55	.16
☐ 81 Darrell Evans	.50	.23	.06
☐ 82 Von Joshua	.30	.14	.04
☐ 83 Jim Spencer	.30	.14	.04
☐ 84 Brent Strom	.30	.14	.04
☐ 85 Mickey Rivers	.40	.18	.05
☐ 86 Mike Tyson	.30	.14	.04
☐ 87 Tom Burgmeier	.30	.14	.04
☐ 88 Duffy Dyer	.30	.14	.04
☐ 89 Vern Ruhle	.30	.14	.04
☐ 90 Sal Bando	.40	.18	.05
☐ 91 Tom Hutton	.30	.14	.04
☐ 92 Eduardo Rodriguez	.30	.14	.04
☐ 93 Mike Phillips	.30	.14	.04
☐ 94 Jim Dwyer	.30	.14	.04
☐ 95 Brooks Robinson	6.00	2.70	.75
☐ 96 Doug Bird	.30	.14	.04
☐ 97 Wilbur Howard	.30	.14	.04
☐ 98 Dennis Eckersley	65.00	29.00	8.25
☐ 99 Lee Lacy	.30	.14	.04
☐ 100 Jim Hunter	3.50	1.55	.45
☐ 101 Pete LaCock	.30	.14	.04
☐ 102 Jim Willoughby	.30	.14	.04
☐ 103 Biff Pocoroba	.30	.14	.04
☐ 104 Cincinnati Reds Team Card; Sparky Anderson MG (Checklist back)	2.00	.90	.25

☐ 105 Gary Lavelle	.30	.14	.04
☐ 106 Tom Grieve	.40	.18	.05
☐ 107 Dave Roberts	.30	.14	.04
☐ 108 Don Kirkwood	.30	.14	.04
☐ 109 Larry Lintz	.30	.14	.04
☐ 110 Carlos May	.30	.14	.04
☐ 111 Danny Thompson	.30	.14	.04
☐ 112 Kent Tekulve	1.50	.65	.19
☐ 113 Gary Sutherland	.30	.14	.04
☐ 114 Jay Johnstone	.40	.18	.05
☐ 115 Ken Holtzman	.40	.18	.05
☐ 116 Charlie Moore	.30	.14	.04
☐ 117 Mike Jorgensen	.30	.14	.04
☐ 118 Boston Red Sox Team Card; Darrell Johnson MG (Checklist back)	1.25	.55	.16
☐ 119 Checklist 1-132	1.50	.15	.05
☐ 120 Rusty Staub	.75	.35	.09
☐ 121 Tony Solaita	.30	.14	.04
☐ 122 Mike Cosgrove	.30	.14	.04
☐ 123 Walt Williams	.30	.14	.04
☐ 124 Doug Rau	.30	.14	.04
☐ 125 Don Baylor	1.50	.65	.19
☐ 126 Tom Dettore	.30	.14	.04
☐ 127 Larvell Blanks	.30	.14	.04
☐ 128 Ken Griffey	2.50	1.15	.30
☐ 129 Andy Etchebarren	.30	.14	.04
☐ 130 Luis Tiant	.50	.23	.06
☐ 131 Bill Stein	.30	.14	.04
☐ 132 Don Hood	.30	.14	.04
☐ 133 Gary Matthews	.40	.18	.05
☐ 134 Mike Ivie	.30	.14	.04
☐ 135 Bake McBride	.40	.18	.05
☐ 136 Dave Goltz	.30	.14	.04
☐ 137 Bill Robinson	.40	.18	.05
☐ 138 Lerrin LaGrow	.30	.14	.04
☐ 139 Gorman Thomas	.50	.23	.06
☐ 140 Vida Blue	.50	.23	.06
☐ 141 Larry Parrish	1.25	.55	.16
☐ 142 Dick Drago	.30	.14	.04
☐ 143 Jerry Grote	.30	.14	.04
☐ 144 Al Fitzmorris	.30	.14	.04
☐ 145 Larry Bowa	.75	.35	.09
☐ 146 George Medich	.30	.14	.04
☐ 147 Houston Astros Team Card; Bill Virdon MG (Checklist back)	1.25	.55	.16
☐ 148 Stan Thomas	.30	.14	.04
☐ 149 Tommy Davis	.40	.18	.05
☐ 150 Steve Garvey	5.00	2.30	.60
☐ 151 Bill Bonham	.30	.14	.04
☐ 152 Leroy Stanton	.30	.14	.04
☐ 153 Buzz Capra	.30	.14	.04
☐ 154 Bucky Dent	.75	.35	.09
☐ 155 Jack Billingham	.30	.14	.04
☐ 156 Rico Carty	.40	.18	.05
☐ 157 Mike Caldwell	.30	.14	.04
☐ 158 Ken Reitz	.30	.14	.04
☐ 159 Jerry Terrell	.30	.14	.04
☐ 160 Dave Winfield	27.00	12.00	3.40
☐ 161 Bruce Kison	.30	.14	.04
☐ 162 Jack Pierce	.30	.14	.04
☐ 163 Jim Slaton	.30	.14	.04
☐ 164 Pepe Mangual	.30	.14	.04
☐ 165 Gene Tenace	.40	.18	.05
☐ 166 Skip Lockwood	.30	.14	.04
☐ 167 Freddie Patek	.40	.18	.05
☐ 168 Tom Hilgendorf	.30	.14	.04
☐ 169 Graig Nettles	1.50	.65	.19
☐ 170 Rick Wise	.30	.14	.04
☐ 171 Greg Gross	.30	.14	.04
☐ 172 Texas Rangers Team Card; Frank Lucchesi MG (Checklist back)	1.25	.55	.16
☐ 173 Steve Swisher	.30	.14	.04
☐ 174 Charlie Hough	.40	.18	.05
☐ 175 Ken Singleton	.40	.18	.05
☐ 176 Dick Lange	.30	.14	.04
☐ 177 Marty Perez	.30	.14	.04
☐ 178 Tom Buskey	.30	.14	.04
☐ 179 George Foster	1.00	.45	.13
☐ 180 Rich Gossage	2.50	1.15	.30
☐ 181 Willie Montanez	.30	.14	.04
☐ 182 Harry Rasmussen	.30	.14	.04
☐ 183 Steve Braun	.30	.14	.04
☐ 184 Bill Greif	.30	.14	.04
☐ 185 Dave Parker	4.00	1.80	.50
☐ 186 Tom Walker	.30	.14	.04
☐ 187 Pedro Garcia	.30	.14	.04
☐ 188 Fred Scherman	.30	.14	.04
☐ 189 Claudell Washington	.40	.18	.05
☐ 190 Jon Matlack	.30	.14	.04
☐ 191 NL Batting Leaders Bill Madlock Ted Simmons Manny Sanguillen	.75	.35	.09
☐ 192 AL Batting Leaders Rod Carew Fred Lynn Thurman Munson	2.50	1.15	.30
☐ 193 NL Home Run Leaders Mike Schmidt Dave Kingman Greg Luzinski	2.25	1.00	.30
☐ 194 AL Home Run Leaders Reggie Jackson George Scott John Mayberry	2.50	1.15	.30
☐ 195 NL RBI Leaders Greg Luzinski Johnny Bench Tony Perez	1.50	.65	.19
☐ 196 AL RBI Leaders George Scott John Mayberry Fred Lynn	.75	.35	.09
☐ 197 NL Steals Leaders Dave Lopes Joe Morgan Lou Brock	1.50	.65	.19
☐ 198 AL Steals Leaders Mickey Rivers Claudell Washington Amos Otis	.75	.35	.09
☐ 199 NL Victory Leaders Tom Seaver Randy Jones Andy Messersmith	1.25	.55	.16
☐ 200 AL Victory Leaders Jim Hunter Jim Palmer Vida Blue	1.50	.65	.19
☐ 201 NL ERA Leaders Randy Jones Andy Messersmith Tom Seaver	1.25	.55	.16
☐ 202 AL ERA Leaders Jim Palmer Jim Hunter Dennis Eckersley	4.00	1.80	.50
☐ 203 NL Strikeout Leaders Tom Seaver John Montefusco Andy Messersmith	1.25	.55	.16
☐ 204 AL Strikeout Leaders Frank Tanana Bert Blyleven Gaylord Perry	1.00	.45	.13
☐ 205 Leading Firemen Al Hrabosky Rich Gossage	.75	.35	.09
☐ 206 Manny Trillo	.30	.14	.04
☐ 207 Andy Hassler	.30	.14	.04
☐ 208 Mike Lum	.30	.14	.04
☐ 209 Alan Ashby	.40	.18	.05
☐ 210 Lee May	.40	.18	.05
☐ 211 Clay Carroll	.30	.14	.04
☐ 212 Pat Kelly	.30	.14	.04
☐ 213 Dave Heaverlo	.30	.14	.04
☐ 214 Eric Soderholm	.30	.14	.04
☐ 215 Reggie Smith	.50	.23	.06
☐ 216 Montreal Expos Team Card; Karl Kuehl MG (Checklist back)	1.25	.55	.16
☐ 217 Dave Freisleben	.30	.14	.04
☐ 218 John Knox	.30	.14	.04
☐ 219 Tom Murphy	.30	.14	.04
☐ 220 Manny Sanguillen	.40	.18	.05
☐ 221 Jim Todd	.30	.14	.04
☐ 222 Wayne Garrett	.30	.14	.04
☐ 223 Ollie Brown	.30	.14	.04
☐ 224 Jim York	.30	.14	.04
☐ 225 Roy White	.40	.18	.05
☐ 226 Jim Sundberg	.40	.18	.05
☐ 227 Oscar Zamora	.30	.14	.04
☐ 228 John Hale	.30	.14	.04
☐ 229 Jerry Remy	.60	.25	.08
☐ 230 Carl Yastrzemski	8.00	3.60	1.00
☐ 231 Tom House	.30	.14	.04
☐ 232 Frank Duffy	.30	.14	.04
☐ 233 Grant Jackson	.30	.14	.04
☐ 234 Mike Sadek	.30	.14	.04

☐ 235 Bert Blyleven	2.50	1.15	.30
☐ 236 Kansas City Royals Team Card; Whitey Herzog MG (Checklist back)	1.25	.55	.16
☐ 237 Dave Hamilton	.30	.14	.04
☐ 238 Larry Biittner	.30	.14	.04
☐ 239 John Curtis	.30	.14	.04
☐ 240 Pete Rose	12.50	5.75	1.55
☐ 241 Hector Torres	.30	.14	.04
☐ 242 Dan Meyer	.30	.14	.04
☐ 243 Jim Rooker	.30	.14	.04
☐ 244 Bill Sharp	.30	.14	.04
☐ 245 Felix Millan	.30	.14	.04
☐ 246 Cesar Tovar	.30	.14	.04
☐ 247 Terry Harmon	.30	.14	.04
☐ 248 Dick Tidrow	.30	.14	.04
☐ 249 Cliff Johnson	.40	.18	.05
☐ 250 Fergie Jenkins	3.50	1.55	.45
☐ 251 Rick Monday	.40	.18	.05
☐ 252 Tim Nordbrook	.30	.14	.04
☐ 253 Bill Buckner	.75	.35	.09
☐ 254 Rudy Meoli	.30	.14	.04
☐ 255 Fritz Peterson	.30	.14	.04
☐ 256 Rowland Office	.30	.14	.04
☐ 257 Ross Grimsley	.30	.14	.04
☐ 258 Nyls Nyman	.30	.14	.04
☐ 259 Darrel Chaney	.30	.14	.04
☐ 260 Steve Busby	.30	.14	.04
☐ 261 Gary Thomasson	.30	.14	.04
☐ 262 Checklist 133-264	1.50	.15	.05
☐ 263 Lyman Bostock	.50	.23	.06
☐ 264 Steve Renko	.30	.14	.04
☐ 265 Willie Davis	.40	.18	.05
☐ 266 Alan Foster	.30	.14	.04
☐ 267 Aurelio Rodriguez	.30	.14	.04
☐ 268 Del Unser	.30	.14	.04
☐ 269 Rick Austin	.30	.14	.04
☐ 270 Willie Stargell	3.50	1.55	.45
☐ 271 Jim Lonborg	.40	.18	.05
☐ 272 Rick Dempsey	.40	.18	.05
☐ 273 Joe Niekro	.40	.18	.05
☐ 274 Tommy Harper	.40	.18	.05
☐ 275 Rick Manning	.60	.25	.08
☐ 276 Mickey Scott	.30	.14	.04
☐ 277 Chicago Cubs Team Card; Jim Marshall MG (Checklist back)	1.25	.55	.16
☐ 278 Bernie Carbo	.30	.14	.04
☐ 279 Roy Howell	.30	.14	.04
☐ 280 Burt Hooton	.40	.18	.05
☐ 281 Dave May	.30	.14	.04
☐ 282 Dan Osborn	.30	.14	.04
☐ 283 Merv Rettenmund	.30	.14	.04
☐ 284 Steve Ontiveros	.30	.14	.04
☐ 285 Mike Cuellar	.40	.18	.05
☐ 286 Jim Wohlford	.30	.14	.04
☐ 287 Pete Mackanin	.30	.14	.04
☐ 288 Bill Campbell	.30	.14	.04
☐ 289 Enzo Hernandez	.30	.14	.04
☐ 290 Ted Simmons	1.50	.65	.19
☐ 291 Ken Sanders	.30	.14	.04
☐ 292 Leon Roberts	.30	.14	.04
☐ 293 Bill Castro	.50	.23	.06
☐ 294 Ed Kirkpatrick	.30	.14	.04
☐ 295 Dave Cash	.30	.14	.04
☐ 296 Pat Dobson	.30	.14	.04
☐ 297 Roger Metzger	.30	.14	.04
☐ 298 Dick Bosman	.30	.14	.04
☐ 299 Champ Summers	.30	.14	.04
☐ 300 Johnny Bench	12.50	5.75	1.55
☐ 301 Jackie Brown	.30	.14	.04
☐ 302 Rick Miller	.30	.14	.04
☐ 303 Steve Foucault	.30	.14	.04
☐ 304 California Angels Team Card; Dick Williams MG (Checklist back)	1.25	.55	.16
☐ 305 Andy Messersmith	.40	.18	.05
☐ 306 Rod Gilbreath	.30	.14	.04
☐ 307 Al Bumbry	.30	.14	.04
☐ 308 Jim Barr	.30	.14	.04
☐ 309 Bill Melton	.30	.14	.04
☐ 310 Randy Jones	.50	.23	.06
☐ 311 Cookie Rojas	.40	.18	.05
☐ 312 Don Carrithers	.30	.14	.04
☐ 313 Dan Ford	.30	.14	.04
☐ 314 Ed Kranepool	.30	.14	.04
☐ 315 Al Hrabosky	.40	.18	.05
☐ 316 Robin Yount	60.00	27.00	7.50
☐ 317 John Candelaria	3.50	1.55	.45
☐ 318 Bob Boone	1.00	.45	.13
☐ 319 Larry Gura	.30	.14	.04
☐ 320 Willie Horton	.40	.18	.05
☐ 321 Jose Cruz	.50	.23	.06
☐ 322 Glenn Abbott	.30	.14	.04
☐ 323 Rob Sperring	.30	.14	.04
☐ 324 Jim Bibby	.30	.14	.04
☐ 325 Tony Perez	2.50	1.15	.30
☐ 326 Dick Pole	.30	.14	.04
☐ 327 Dave Moates	.30	.14	.04
☐ 328 Carl Morton	.30	.14	.04
☐ 329 Joe Ferguson	.30	.14	.04
☐ 330 Nolan Ryan	60.00	27.00	7.50
☐ 331 San Diego Padres Team Card; John McNamara MG (Checklist back)	1.25	.55	.16
☐ 332 Charlie Williams	.30	.14	.04
☐ 333 Bob Coluccio	.30	.14	.04
☐ 334 Dennis Leonard	.40	.18	.05
☐ 335 Bob Grich	.50	.23	.06
☐ 336 Vic Albury	.30	.14	.04
☐ 337 Bud Harrelson	.40	.18	.05
☐ 338 Bob Bailey	.30	.14	.04
☐ 339 John Denny	.40	.18	.05
☐ 340 Jim Rice	6.50	2.90	.80
☐ 341 All-Time 1B Lou Gehrig	6.50	2.90	.80
☐ 342 All-Time 2B Rogers Hornsby	3.00	1.35	.40
☐ 343 All-Time 3B Pie Traynor	1.00	.45	.13
☐ 344 All-Time SS Honus Wagner	3.50	1.55	.45
☐ 345 All-Time OF Babe Ruth	10.00	4.50	1.25
☐ 346 All-Time OF Ty Cobb	6.50	2.90	.80
☐ 347 All-Time OF Ted Williams	6.50	2.90	.80
☐ 348 All-Time C Mickey Cochrane	1.00	.45	.13
☐ 349 All-Time RHP Walter Johnson	2.50	1.15	.30
☐ 350 All-Time LHP Lefty Grove	1.00	.45	.13
☐ 351 Randy Hundley	.30	.14	.04
☐ 352 Dave Giusti	.30	.14	.04
☐ 353 Sixto Lezcano	.40	.18	.05
☐ 354 Ron Blomberg	.30	.14	.04
☐ 355 Steve Carlton	8.50	3.80	1.05
☐ 356 Ted Martinez	.30	.14	.04
☐ 357 Ken Forsch	.30	.14	.04
☐ 358 Buddy Bell	.50	.23	.06
☐ 359 Rick Reuschel	.40	.18	.05
☐ 360 Jeff Burroughs	.40	.18	.05
☐ 361 Detroit Tigers Team Card; Ralph Houk MG (Checklist back)	1.25	.55	.16
☐ 362 Will McEnaney	.30	.14	.04
☐ 363 Dave Collins	.75	.35	.09
☐ 364 Elias Sosa	.30	.14	.04
☐ 365 Carlton Fisk	11.00	4.90	1.40
☐ 366 Bobby Valentine	.40	.18	.05
☐ 367 Bruce Miller	.30	.14	.04
☐ 368 Wilbur Wood	.30	.14	.04
☐ 369 Frank White	.50	.23	.06
☐ 370 Ron Cey	1.00	.45	.13
☐ 371 Elrod Hendricks	.30	.14	.04
☐ 372 Rick Baldwin	.30	.14	.04
☐ 373 Johnny Briggs	.30	.14	.04
☐ 374 Dan Warthen	.50	.23	.06
☐ 375 Ron Fairly	.30	.14	.04
☐ 376 Rich Hebner	.40	.18	.05
☐ 377 Mike Hegan	.30	.14	.04
☐ 378 Steve Stone	.40	.18	.05
☐ 379 Ken Boswell	.30	.14	.04
☐ 380 Bobby Bonds	1.25	.55	.16
☐ 381 Denny Doyle	.30	.14	.04
☐ 382 Matt Alexander	.30	.14	.04
☐ 383 John Ellis	.30	.14	.04
☐ 384 Philadelphia Phillies Team Card; Danny Ozark MG (Checklist back)	1.25	.55	.16
☐ 385 Mickey Lolich	.50	.23	.06
☐ 386 Ed Goodson	.30	.14	.04
☐ 387 Mike Miley	.30	.14	.04
☐ 388 Stan Perzanowski	.30	.14	.04
☐ 389 Glenn Adams	.30	.14	.04
☐ 390 Don Gullett	.40	.18	.05
☐ 391 Jerry Hairston	.30	.14	.04
☐ 392 Checklist 265-396	1.50	.15	.05

☐ 393 Paul Mitchell	.30	.14	.04
☐ 394 Fran Healy	.30	.14	.04
☐ 395 Jim Wynn	.40	.18	.05
☐ 396 Bill Lee	.30	.14	.04
☐ 397 Tim Foli	.30	.14	.04
☐ 398 Dave Tomlin	.30	.14	.04
☐ 399 Luis Melendez	.30	.14	.04
☐ 400 Rod Carew	9.00	4.00	1.15
☐ 401 Ken Brett	.30	.14	.04
☐ 402 Don Money	.40	.18	.05
☐ 403 Geoff Zahn	.30	.14	.04
☐ 404 Enos Cabell	.30	.14	.04
☐ 405 Rollie Fingers	4.00	1.80	.50
☐ 406 Ed Herrmann	.30	.14	.04
☐ 407 Tom Underwood	.30	.14	.04
☐ 408 Charlie Spikes	.30	.14	.04
☐ 409 Dave Lemanczyk	.30	.14	.04
☐ 410 Ralph Garr	.40	.18	.05
☐ 411 Bill Singer	.30	.14	.04
☐ 412 Toby Harrah	.40	.18	.05
☐ 413 Pete Varney	.30	.14	.04
☐ 414 Wayne Garland	.30	.14	.04
☐ 415 Vada Pinson	.50	.23	.06
☐ 416 Tommy John	1.50	.65	.19
☐ 417 Gene Clines	.30	.14	.04
☐ 418 Jose Morales	.50	.23	.06
☐ 419 Reggie Cleveland	.30	.14	.04
☐ 420 Joe Morgan	6.50	2.90	.80
☐ 421 Oakland A's Team Card; (No MG on front; checklist back)	1.25	.55	.16
☐ 422 Johnny Grubb	.30	.14	.04
☐ 423 Ed Halicki	.30	.14	.04
☐ 424 Phil Roof	.30	.14	.04
☐ 425 Rennie Stennett	.30	.14	.04
☐ 426 Bob Forsch	.30	.14	.04
☐ 427 Kurt Bevacqua	.30	.14	.04
☐ 428 Jim Crawford	.30	.14	.04
☐ 429 Fred Stanley	.30	.14	.04
☐ 430 Jose Cardenal	.30	.14	.04
☐ 431 Dick Ruthven	.30	.14	.04
☐ 432 Tom Veryzer	.30	.14	.04
☐ 433 Rick Waits	.30	.14	.04
☐ 434 Morris Nettles	.30	.14	.04
☐ 435 Phil Niekro	2.50	1.15	.30
☐ 436 Bill Fahey	.30	.14	.04
☐ 437 Terry Forster	.30	.14	.04
☐ 438 Doug DeCinces	.60	.25	.08
☐ 439 Rick Rhoden	.40	.18	.05
☐ 440 John Mayberry	.40	.18	.05
☐ 441 Gary Carter	12.50	5.75	1.55
☐ 442 Hank Webb	.30	.14	.04
☐ 443 San Francisco Giants Team Card; (No MG on front; checklist back)	1.25	.55	.16
☐ 444 Gary Nolan	.30	.14	.04
☐ 445 Rico Petrocelli	.40	.18	.05
☐ 446 Larry Haney	.30	.14	.04
☐ 447 Gene Locklear	.30	.14	.04
☐ 448 Tom Johnson	.30	.14	.04
☐ 449 Bob Robertson	.30	.14	.04
☐ 450 Jim Palmer	8.00	3.60	1.00
☐ 451 Buddy Bradford	.30	.14	.04
☐ 452 Tom Hausman	.30	.14	.04
☐ 453 Lou Piniella	.75	.35	.09
☐ 454 Tom Griffin	.30	.14	.04
☐ 455 Dick Allen	.80	.35	.10
☐ 456 Joe Coleman	.30	.14	.04
☐ 457 Ed Crosby	.30	.14	.04
☐ 458 Earl Williams	.30	.14	.04
☐ 459 Jim Brewer	.30	.14	.04
☐ 460 Cesar Cedeno	.40	.18	.05
☐ 461 NL and AL Champs Reds sweep Bucs, Bosox surprise A's	.60	.25	.08
☐ 462 '75 World Series Reds Champs	.60	.25	.08
☐ 463 Steve Hargan	.30	.14	.04
☐ 464 Ken Henderson	.30	.14	.04
☐ 465 Mike Marshall	.40	.18	.05
☐ 466 Bob Stinson	.30	.14	.04
☐ 467 Woodie Fryman	.30	.14	.04
☐ 468 Jesus Alou	.30	.14	.04
☐ 469 Rawly Eastwick	.30	.14	.04
☐ 470 Bobby Murcer	.75	.35	.09
☐ 471 Jim Burton	.30	.14	.04
☐ 472 Bob Davis	.30	.14	.04
☐ 473 Paul Blair	.40	.18	.05
☐ 474 Ray Corbin	.30	.14	.04
☐ 475 Joe Rudi	.40	.18	.05
☐ 476 Bob Moose	.30	.14	.04
☐ 477 Cleveland Indians Team Card; Frank Robinson MG (Checklist back)	1.25	.55	.16
☐ 478 Lynn McGlothen	.30	.14	.04
☐ 479 Bobby Mitchell	.30	.14	.04
☐ 480 Mike Schmidt	35.00	16.00	4.40
☐ 481 Rudy May	.30	.14	.04
☐ 482 Tim Hosley	.30	.14	.04
☐ 483 Mickey Stanley	.30	.14	.04
☐ 484 Eric Raich	.30	.14	.04
☐ 485 Mike Hargrove	.40	.18	.05
☐ 486 Bruce Dal Canton	.30	.14	.04
☐ 487 Leron Lee	.30	.14	.04
☐ 488 Claude Osteen	.40	.18	.05
☐ 489 Skip Jutze	.30	.14	.04
☐ 490 Frank Tanana	1.00	.45	.13
☐ 491 Terry Crowley	.30	.14	.04
☐ 492 Marty Pattin	.30	.14	.04
☐ 493 Derrel Thomas	.30	.14	.04
☐ 494 Craig Swan	.40	.18	.05
☐ 495 Nate Colbert	.30	.14	.04
☐ 496 Juan Beniquez	.30	.14	.04
☐ 497 Joe McIntosh	.30	.14	.04
☐ 498 Glenn Borgmann	.30	.14	.04
☐ 499 Mario Guerrero	.30	.14	.04
☐ 500 Reggie Jackson	21.00	9.50	2.60
☐ 501 Billy Champion	.30	.14	.04
☐ 502 Tim McCarver	.75	.35	.09
☐ 503 Elliott Maddox	.30	.14	.04
☐ 504 Pittsburgh Pirates Team Card; Danny Murtaugh MG (Checklist back)	1.25	.55	.16
☐ 505 Mark Belanger	.40	.18	.05
☐ 506 George Mitterwald	.30	.14	.04
☐ 507 Ray Bare	.30	.14	.04
☐ 508 Duane Kuiper	.50	.23	.06
☐ 509 Bill Hands	.30	.14	.04
☐ 510 Amos Otis	.40	.18	.05
☐ 511 Jamie Easterley	.30	.14	.04
☐ 512 Ellie Rodriguez	.30	.14	.04
☐ 513 Bart Johnson	.30	.14	.04
☐ 514 Dan Driessen	.40	.18	.05
☐ 515 Steve Yeager	.40	.18	.05
☐ 516 Wayne Granger	.30	.14	.04
☐ 517 John Milner	.30	.14	.04
☐ 518 Doug Flynn	.30	.14	.04
☐ 519 Steve Brye	.30	.14	.04
☐ 520 Willie McCovey	4.00	1.80	.50
☐ 521 Jim Colborn	.30	.14	.04
☐ 522 Ted Sizemore	.30	.14	.04
☐ 523 Bob Montgomery	.30	.14	.04
☐ 524 Pete Falcone	.30	.14	.04
☐ 525 Billy Williams	3.50	1.55	.45
☐ 526 Checklist 397-528	1.50	.15	.05
☐ 527 Mike Anderson	.30	.14	.04
☐ 528 Dock Ellis	.30	.14	.04
☐ 529 Deron Johnson	.30	.14	.04
☐ 530 Don Sutton	3.00	1.35	.40
☐ 531 New York Mets Team Card; Joe Frazier MG (Checklist back)	1.25	.55	.16
☐ 532 Milt May	.30	.14	.04
☐ 533 Lee Richard	.30	.14	.04
☐ 534 Stan Bahnsen	.30	.14	.04
☐ 535 Dave Nelson	.30	.14	.04
☐ 536 Mike Thompson	.30	.14	.04
☐ 537 Tony Muser	.30	.14	.04
☐ 538 Pat Darcy	.30	.14	.04
☐ 539 John Balaz	.30	.14	.04
☐ 540 Bill Freehan	.40	.18	.05
☐ 541 Steve Mingori	.30	.14	.04
☐ 542 Keith Hernandez	4.00	1.80	.50
☐ 543 Wayne Twitchell	.30	.14	.04
☐ 544 Pepe Frias	.30	.14	.04
☐ 545 Sparky Lyle	.60	.25	.08
☐ 546 Dave Rosello	.30	.14	.04
☐ 547 Roric Harrison	.30	.14	.04
☐ 548 Manny Mota	.40	.18	.05
☐ 549 Randy Tate	.30	.14	.04
☐ 550 Hank Aaron	25.00	11.50	3.10
☐ 551 Jerry DaVanon	.30	.14	.04
☐ 552 Terry Humphrey	.30	.14	.04
☐ 553 Randy Moffitt	.30	.14	.04
☐ 554 Ray Fosse	.30	.14	.04
☐ 555 Dyar Miller	.30	.14	.04
☐ 556 Minnesota Twins Team Card; Gene Mauch MG (Checklist back)	1.25	.55	.16
☐ 557 Dan Spillner	.30	.14	.04

☐ 558 Clarence Gaston	.40	.18	.05
☐ 559 Clyde Wright	.30	.14	.04
☐ 560 Jorge Orta	.30	.14	.04
☐ 561 Tom Carroll	.30	.14	.04
☐ 562 Adrian Garrett	.30	.14	.04
☐ 563 Larry Demery	.30	.14	.04
☐ 564 Bubble Gum Champ Kurt Bevacqua	.50	.23	.06
☐ 565 Tug McGraw	.50	.23	.06
☐ 566 Ken McMullen	.30	.14	.04
☐ 567 George Stone	.30	.14	.04
☐ 568 Rob Andrews	.30	.14	.04
☐ 569 Nelson Briles	.40	.18	.05
☐ 570 George Hendrick	.40	.18	.05
☐ 571 Don DeMola	.30	.14	.04
☐ 572 Rich Coggins	.30	.14	.04
☐ 573 Bill Travers	.30	.14	.04
☐ 574 Don Kessinger	.40	.18	.05
☐ 575 Dwight Evans	3.00	1.35	.40
☐ 576 Maximino Leon	.30	.14	.04
☐ 577 Marc Hill	.30	.14	.04
☐ 578 Ted Kubiak	.30	.14	.04
☐ 579 Clay Kirby	.30	.14	.04
☐ 580 Bert Campaneris	.40	.18	.05
☐ 581 St. Louis Cardinals Team Card; Red Schoendienst MG (Checklist back)	1.25	.55	.16
☐ 582 Mike Kekich	.30	.14	.04
☐ 583 Tommy Helms	.30	.14	.04
☐ 584 Stan Wall	.30	.14	.04
☐ 585 Joe Torre	.60	.25	.08
☐ 586 Ron Schueler	.30	.14	.04
☐ 587 Leo Cardenas	.30	.14	.04
☐ 588 Kevin Kobel	.30	.14	.04
☐ 589 Rookie Pitchers Santo Alcala Mike Flanagan Joe Pactwa Pablo Torrealba	2.00	.90	.25
☐ 590 Rookie Outfielders Henry Cruz Chet Lemon Ellis Valentine Terry Whitfield	.75	.35	.09
☐ 591 Rookie Pitchers Steve Grilli Craig Mitchell Jose Sosa George Throop	.50	.23	.06
☐ 592 Rookie Infielders Willie Randolph Dave McKay Jerry Royster Roy Staiger	9.00	4.00	1.15
☐ 593 Rookie Pitchers Larry Anderson Ken Crosby Mark Littell Butch Metzger	.50	.23	.06
☐ 594 Rookie Catchers/OF Andy Merchant Ed Ott Royle Stillman Jerry White	.50	.23	.06
☐ 595 Rookie Pitchers Art DeFillipis Randy Lerch Sid Monge Steve Barr	.50	.23	.06
☐ 596 Rookie Infielders Craig Reynolds Lamar Johnson Johnnie LeMaster Jerry Manuel	.50	.23	.06
☐ 597 Rookie Pitchers Don Aase Jack Kucek Frank LaCorte Mike Pazik	.50	.23	.06
☐ 598 Rookie Outfielders Hector Cruz Jamie Quirk Jerry Turner Joe Wallis	.50	.23	.06
☐ 599 Rookie Pitchers Rob Dressler Ron Guidry Bob McClure Pat Zachry	8.00	3.60	1.00
☐ 600 Tom Seaver	15.00	6.75	1.90
☐ 601 Ken Rudolph	.30	.14	.04
☐ 602 Doug Konieczny	.30	.14	.04
☐ 603 Jim Holt	.30	.14	.04
☐ 604 Joe Lovitto	.30	.14	.04
☐ 605 Al Downing	.30	.14	.04
☐ 606 Milwaukee Brewers Team Card; Alex Grammas MG (Checklist back)	1.25	.55	.16
☐ 607 Rich Hinton	.30	.14	.04
☐ 608 Vic Correll	.30	.14	.04
☐ 609 Fred Norman	.30	.14	.04
☐ 610 Greg Luzinski	.50	.23	.06
☐ 611 Rich Folkers	.30	.14	.04
☐ 612 Joe Lahoud	.30	.14	.04
☐ 613 Tim Johnson	.30	.14	.04
☐ 614 Fernando Arroyo	.30	.14	.04
☐ 615 Mike Cubbage	.30	.14	.04
☐ 616 Buck Martinez	.30	.14	.04
☐ 617 Darold Knowles	.30	.14	.04
☐ 618 Jack Brohamer	.30	.14	.04
☐ 619 Bill Butler	.30	.14	.04
☐ 620 Al Oliver	.75	.35	.09
☐ 621 Tom Hall	.30	.14	.04
☐ 622 Rick Auerbach	.30	.14	.04
☐ 623 Bob Allietta	.30	.14	.04
☐ 624 Tony Taylor	.30	.14	.04
☐ 625 J.R. Richard	.40	.18	.05
☐ 626 Bob Sheldon	.30	.14	.04
☐ 627 Bill Plummer	.30	.14	.04
☐ 628 John D'Acquisto	.30	.14	.04
☐ 629 Sandy Alomar	.40	.18	.05
☐ 630 Chris Speier	.30	.14	.04
☐ 631 Atlanta Braves Team Card; Dave Bristol MG (Checklist back)	1.25	.55	.16
☐ 632 Rogelio Moret	.30	.14	.04
☐ 633 John Stearns	.50	.23	.06
☐ 634 Larry Christenson	.30	.14	.04
☐ 635 Jim Fregosi	.40	.18	.05
☐ 636 Joe Decker	.30	.14	.04
☐ 637 Bruce Bochte	.30	.14	.04
☐ 638 Doyle Alexander	.40	.18	.05
☐ 639 Fred Kendall	.30	.14	.04
☐ 640 Bill Madlock	1.00	.45	.13
☐ 641 Tom Paciorek	.40	.18	.05
☐ 642 Dennis Blair	.30	.14	.04
☐ 643 Checklist 529-660	1.50	.15	.05
☐ 644 Tom Bradley	.30	.14	.04
☐ 645 Darrell Porter	.40	.18	.05
☐ 646 John Lowenstein	.30	.14	.04
☐ 647 Ramon Hernandez	.30	.14	.04
☐ 648 Al Cowens	.30	.14	.04
☐ 649 Dave Roberts	.30	.14	.04
☐ 650 Thurman Munson	8.00	3.60	1.00
☐ 651 John Odom	.30	.14	.04
☐ 652 Ed Armbrister	.30	.14	.04
☐ 653 Mike Norris	.30	.14	.04
☐ 654 Doug Griffin	.30	.14	.04
☐ 655 Mike Vail	.30	.14	.04
☐ 656 Chicago White Sox Team Card; Chuck Tanner MG (Checklist back)	1.25	.55	.16
☐ 657 Roy Smalley	.50	.23	.06
☐ 658 Jerry Johnson	.30	.14	.04
☐ 659 Ben Oglivie	.40	.18	.05
☐ 660 Dave Lopes	1.00	.45	.13

1976 Topps Traded

The cards in this 44-card set measure 2 1/2" by 3 1/2". The 1976 Topps Traded set contains 43 players and one unnumbered checklist card. The individuals pictured were traded after the Topps regular set was printed. A "Sports Extra" heading design is found on each picture and is also used to introduce the biographical section of the reverse. Each card is numbered according to the player's regular 1976 card with the addition of "T" to indicate his new status.

	NRMT-MT	EXC	G-VG
COMPLETE SET (44)	12.00	5.50	1.50
COMMON PLAYER	.30	.14	.04
☐ 27T Ed Figueroa	.30	.14	.04
☐ 28T Dusty Baker	.50	.23	.06
☐ 44T Doug Rader	.40	.18	.05

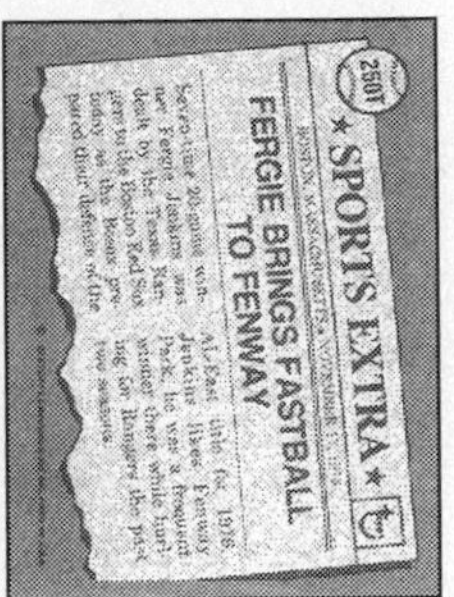

☐ 58T	Ron Reed	.30	.14	.04
☐ 74T	Oscar Gamble	.50	.23	.06
☐ 80T	Jim Kaat	1.00	.45	.13
☐ 83T	Jim Spencer	.30	.14	.04
☐ 85T	Mickey Rivers	.40	.18	.05
☐ 99T	Lee Lacy	.30	.14	.04
☐ 120T	Rusty Staub	.50	.23	.06
☐ 127T	Larvell Blanks	.30	.14	.04
☐ 146T	George Medich	.30	.14	.04
☐ 158T	Ken Reitz	.30	.14	.04
☐ 208T	Mike Lum	.30	.14	.04
☐ 211T	Clay Carroll	.30	.14	.04
☐ 231T	Tom House	.30	.14	.04
☐ 250T	Fergie Jenkins	2.50	1.15	.30
☐ 259T	Darrel Chaney	.30	.14	.04
☐ 292T	Leon Roberts	.30	.14	.04
☐ 296T	Pat Dobson	.30	.14	.04
☐ 309T	Bill Melton	.30	.14	.04
☐ 338T	Bob Bailey	.30	.14	.04
☐ 380T	Bobby Bonds	.75	.35	.09
☐ 383T	John Ellis	.30	.14	.04
☐ 385T	Mickey Lolich	.50	.23	.06
☐ 401T	Ken Brett	.30	.14	.04
☐ 410T	Ralph Garr	.40	.18	.05
☐ 411T	Bill Singer	.30	.14	.04
☐ 428T	Jim Crawford	.30	.14	.04
☐ 434T	Morris Nettles	.30	.14	.04
☐ 464T	Ken Henderson	.30	.14	.04
☐ 497T	Joe McIntosh	.30	.14	.04
☐ 524T	Pete Falcone	.30	.14	.04
☐ 527T	Mike Anderson	.30	.14	.04
☐ 528T	Dock Ellis	.30	.14	.04
☐ 532T	Milt May	.30	.14	.04
☐ 554T	Ray Fosse	.30	.14	.04
☐ 579T	Clay Kirby	.30	.14	.04
☐ 583T	Tommy Helms	.30	.14	.04
☐ 592T	Willie Randolph	4.50	2.00	.55
☐ 618T	Jack Brohamer	.30	.14	.04
☐ 632T	Rogelio Moret	.30	.14	.04
☐ 649T	Dave Roberts	.30	.14	.04
☐ NNO	Traded Checklist	1.00	.10	.03

1977 Topps

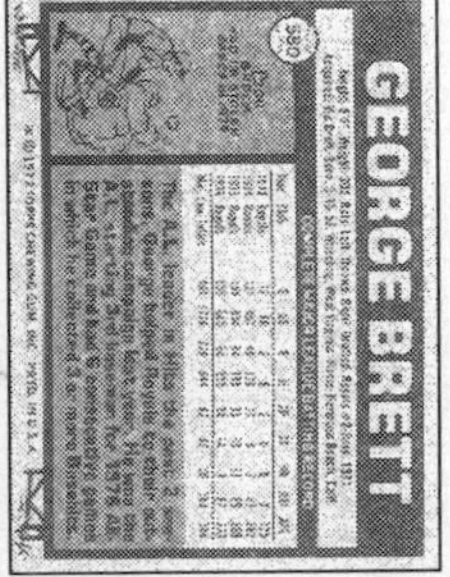

The cards in this 660-card set measure 2 1/2" by 3 1/2". In 1977 for the fifth consecutive year, Topps produced a 660-card baseball set. The player's name, team affiliation, and his position are compactly arranged over the picture area and a facsimile autograph appears on the photo. Team cards feature a checklist of that team's players in the set and a small picture of the manager on the front of the card. Appearing for the first time are the series "Brothers" (631-634) and "Turn Back the Clock" (433-437). Other subseries in the set are League Leaders (1-8), Record Breakers (231-234), Playoffs cards (276-277), World Series cards (411-413), and Rookie Prospects (472-479 and 487-494). The following players' regular issue cards are explicitly denoted as All-Stars, 30, 70, 100, 120, 170, 210, 240, 265, 301, 347, 400, 420, 450, 500, 521, 550, 560, and 580. The key cards in the set are the Rookie Cards of Dale Murphy (476) and Andre Dawson (473). Other notable Rookie Cards in the set include Jack Clark, Dennis Martinez, and Bruce Sutter. Cards numbered 23 or lower, that feature Yankees and do not follow the numbering checklisted below, are not necessarily error cards. They are undoubtedly Burger King cards, a separate set with its own pricing and mass distribution. Burger King cards are indistinguishable from the corresponding Topps cards except for the card numbering difference and the fact that Burger King cards do not have a printing sheet designation (such as A through F like the regular Topps) anywhere on the card back in very small print. There was an aluminum version of the Dale Murphy Rookie Card number 476 produced (legally) in the early '80s; proceeds from the sales (originally priced at 10.00) of this "card" went to the Huntington's Disease Foundation.

	NRMT-MT	EXC	G-VG
COMPLETE SET (660)	440.00	200.00	55.00
COMMON PLAYER (1-660)	.25	.11	.03
☐ 1 Batting Leaders George Brett Bill Madlock	5.00	1.25	.40
☐ 2 Home Run Leaders Graig Nettles Mike Schmidt	1.50	.65	.19
☐ 3 RBI Leaders Lee May George Foster	.50	.23	.06
☐ 4 Stolen Base Leaders Bill North Dave Lopes	.50	.23	.06
☐ 5 Victory Leaders Jim Palmer Randy Jones	.75	.35	.09
☐ 6 Strikeout Leaders Nolan Ryan Tom Seaver	10.00	4.50	1.25
☐ 7 ERA Leaders Mark Fidrych John Denny	.50	.23	.06
☐ 8 Leading Firemen Bill Campbell Rawly Eastwick	.50	.23	.06
☐ 9 Doug Rader	.25	.11	.03
☐ 10 Reggie Jackson	16.00	7.25	2.00
☐ 11 Rob Dressler	.25	.11	.03
☐ 12 Larry Haney	.25	.11	.03
☐ 13 Luis Gomez	.25	.11	.03
☐ 14 Tommy Smith	.25	.11	.03
☐ 15 Don Gullett	.35	.16	.04
☐ 16 Bob Jones	.25	.11	.03
☐ 17 Steve Stone	.35	.16	.04
☐ 18 Indians Team/Mgr. Frank Robinson (Checklist back)	1.00	.45	.13
☐ 19 John D'Acquisto	.25	.11	.03
☐ 20 Graig Nettles	1.00	.45	.13
☐ 21 Ken Forsch	.25	.11	.03
☐ 22 Bill Freehan	.35	.16	.04
☐ 23 Dan Driessen	.25	.11	.03
☐ 24 Carl Morton	.25	.11	.03
☐ 25 Dwight Evans	3.00	1.35	.40
☐ 26 Ray Sadecki	.25	.11	.03
☐ 27 Bill Buckner	.50	.23	.06
☐ 28 Woodie Fryman	.25	.11	.03
☐ 29 Bucky Dent	.60	.25	.08
☐ 30 Greg Luzinski	.45	.20	.06
☐ 31 Jim Todd	.25	.11	.03
☐ 32 Checklist 1	1.25	.13	.04
☐ 33 Wayne Garland	.25	.11	.03

☐ 34 Angels Team/Mgr. Norm Sherry (Checklist back)	1.00	.45	.13
☐ 35 Rennie Stennett	.25	.11	.03
☐ 36 John Ellis	.25	.11	.03
☐ 37 Steve Hargan	.25	.11	.03
☐ 38 Craig Kusick	.25	.11	.03
☐ 39 Tom Griffin	.25	.11	.03
☐ 40 Bobby Murcer	.50	.23	.06
☐ 41 Jim Kern	.25	.11	.03
☐ 42 Jose Cruz	.35	.16	.04
☐ 43 Ray Bare	.25	.11	.03
☐ 44 Bud Harrelson	.35	.16	.04
☐ 45 Rawly Eastwick	.25	.11	.03
☐ 46 Buck Martinez	.25	.11	.03
☐ 47 Lynn McGlothen	.25	.11	.03
☐ 48 Tom Paciorek	.35	.16	.04
☐ 49 Grant Jackson	.25	.11	.03
☐ 50 Ron Cey	.50	.23	.06
☐ 51 Brewers Team/Mgr. Alex Grammas (Checklist back)	1.00	.45	.13
☐ 52 Ellis Valentine	.25	.11	.03
☐ 53 Paul Mitchell	.25	.11	.03
☐ 54 Sandy Alomar	.35	.16	.04
☐ 55 Jeff Burroughs	.35	.16	.04
☐ 56 Rudy May	.25	.11	.03
☐ 57 Marc Hill	.25	.11	.03
☐ 58 Chet Lemon	.35	.16	.04
☐ 59 Larry Christenson	.25	.11	.03
☐ 60 Jim Rice	4.00	1.80	.50
☐ 61 Manny Sanguillen	.35	.16	.04
☐ 62 Eric Raich	.25	.11	.03
☐ 63 Tito Fuentes	.25	.11	.03
☐ 64 Larry Biittner	.25	.11	.03
☐ 65 Skip Lockwood	.25	.11	.03
☐ 66 Roy Smalley	.35	.16	.04
☐ 67 Joaquin Andujar	.60	.25	.08
☐ 68 Bruce Bochte	.25	.11	.03
☐ 69 Jim Crawford	.25	.11	.03
☐ 70 Johnny Bench	10.00	4.50	1.25
☐ 71 Dock Ellis	.25	.11	.03
☐ 72 Mike Anderson	.25	.11	.03
☐ 73 Charlie Williams	.25	.11	.03
☐ 74 A's Team/Mgr. Jack McKeon (Checklist back)	1.00	.45	.13
☐ 75 Dennis Leonard	.35	.16	.04
☐ 76 Tim Foli	.25	.11	.03
☐ 77 Dyar Miller	.25	.11	.03
☐ 78 Bob Davis	.25	.11	.03
☐ 79 Don Money	.35	.16	.04
☐ 80 Andy Messersmith	.35	.16	.04
☐ 81 Juan Beniquez	.25	.11	.03
☐ 82 Jim Rooker	.25	.11	.03
☐ 83 Kevin Bell	.25	.11	.03
☐ 84 Ollie Brown	.25	.11	.03
☐ 85 Duane Kuiper	.25	.11	.03
☐ 86 Pat Zachry	.25	.11	.03
☐ 87 Glenn Borgmann	.25	.11	.03
☐ 88 Stan Wall	.25	.11	.03
☐ 89 Butch Hobson	.80	.35	.10
☐ 90 Cesar Cedeno	.35	.16	.04
☐ 91 John Verhoeven	.25	.11	.03
☐ 92 Dave Rosello	.25	.11	.03
☐ 93 Tom Poquette	.25	.11	.03
☐ 94 Craig Swan	.25	.11	.03
☐ 95 Keith Hernandez	2.00	.90	.25
☐ 96 Lou Piniella	.50	.23	.06
☐ 97 Dave Heaverlo	.25	.11	.03
☐ 98 Milt May	.25	.11	.03
☐ 99 Tom Hausman	.25	.11	.03
☐ 100 Joe Morgan	5.00	2.30	.60
☐ 101 Dick Bosman	.25	.11	.03
☐ 102 Jose Morales	.25	.11	.03
☐ 103 Mike Bacsik	.25	.11	.03
☐ 104 Omar Moreno	.35	.16	.04
☐ 105 Steve Yeager	.35	.16	.04
☐ 106 Mike Flanagan	.50	.23	.06
☐ 107 Bill Melton	.25	.11	.03
☐ 108 Alan Foster	.25	.11	.03
☐ 109 Jorge Orta	.25	.11	.03
☐ 110 Steve Carlton	8.00	3.60	1.00
☐ 111 Rico Petrocelli	.35	.16	.04
☐ 112 Bill Greif	.25	.11	.03
☐ 113 Blue Jays Leaders Roy Hartsfield MG Don Leppert CO Bob Miller CO Jackie Moore CO Harry Warner CO (Checklist back)	1.00	.45	.13
☐ 114 Bruce Dal Canton	.25	.11	.03
☐ 115 Rick Manning	.25	.11	.03
☐ 116 Joe Niekro	.35	.16	.04
☐ 117 Frank White	.35	.16	.04
☐ 118 Rick Jones	.25	.11	.03
☐ 119 John Stearns	.25	.11	.03
☐ 120 Rod Carew	8.00	3.60	1.00
☐ 121 Gary Nolan	.25	.11	.03
☐ 122 Ben Oglivie	.35	.16	.04
☐ 123 Fred Stanley	.25	.11	.03
☐ 124 George Mitterwald	.25	.11	.03
☐ 125 Bill Travers	.25	.11	.03
☐ 126 Rod Gilbreath	.25	.11	.03
☐ 127 Ron Fairly	.25	.11	.03
☐ 128 Tommy John	1.00	.45	.13
☐ 129 Mike Sadek	.25	.11	.03
☐ 130 Al Oliver	.60	.25	.08
☐ 131 Orlando Ramirez	.25	.11	.03
☐ 132 Chip Lang	.25	.11	.03
☐ 133 Ralph Garr	.35	.16	.04
☐ 134 Padres Team/Mgr. John McNamara (Checklist back)	1.00	.45	.13
☐ 135 Mark Belanger	.35	.16	.04
☐ 136 Jerry Mumphrey	.25	.11	.03
☐ 137 Jeff Terpko	.25	.11	.03
☐ 138 Bob Stinson	.25	.11	.03
☐ 139 Fred Norman	.25	.11	.03
☐ 140 Mike Schmidt	25.00	11.50	3.10
☐ 141 Mark Littell	.25	.11	.03
☐ 142 Steve Dillard	.25	.11	.03
☐ 143 Ed Herrmann	.25	.11	.03
☐ 144 Bruce Sutter	5.00	2.30	.60
☐ 145 Tom Veryzer	.25	.11	.03
☐ 146 Dusty Baker	.45	.20	.06
☐ 147 Jackie Brown	.25	.11	.03
☐ 148 Fran Healy	.25	.11	.03
☐ 149 Mike Cubbage	.25	.11	.03
☐ 150 Tom Seaver	12.50	5.75	1.55
☐ 151 Johnny LeMaster	.25	.11	.03
☐ 152 Gaylord Perry	2.50	1.15	.30
☐ 153 Ron Jackson	.25	.11	.03
☐ 154 Dave Giusti	.25	.11	.03
☐ 155 Joe Rudi	.35	.16	.04
☐ 156 Pete Mackanin	.25	.11	.03
☐ 157 Ken Brett	.25	.11	.03
☐ 158 Ted Kubiak	.25	.11	.03
☐ 159 Bernie Carbo	.25	.11	.03
☐ 160 Will McEnaney	.25	.11	.03
☐ 161 Garry Templeton	1.25	.55	.16
☐ 162 Mike Cuellar	.35	.16	.04
☐ 163 Dave Hilton	.25	.11	.03
☐ 164 Tug McGraw	.45	.20	.06
☐ 165 Jim Wynn	.35	.16	.04
☐ 166 Bill Campbell	.25	.11	.03
☐ 167 Rich Hebner	.35	.16	.04
☐ 168 Charlie Spikes	.25	.11	.03
☐ 169 Darold Knowles	.25	.11	.03
☐ 170 Thurman Munson	6.00	2.70	.75
☐ 171 Ken Sanders	.25	.11	.03
☐ 172 John Milner	.25	.11	.03
☐ 173 Chuck Scrivener	.25	.11	.03
☐ 174 Nelson Briles	.35	.16	.04
☐ 175 Butch Wynegar	.25	.11	.03
☐ 176 Bob Robertson	.25	.11	.03
☐ 177 Bart Johnson	.25	.11	.03
☐ 178 Bombo Rivera	.25	.11	.03
☐ 179 Paul Hartzell	.25	.11	.03
☐ 180 Dave Lopes	.45	.20	.06
☐ 181 Ken McMullen	.25	.11	.03
☐ 182 Dan Spillner	.25	.11	.03
☐ 183 Cardinals Team/Mgr. Vern Rapp (Checklist back)	1.00	.45	.13
☐ 184 Bo McLaughlin	.25	.11	.03
☐ 185 Sixto Lezcano	.25	.11	.03
☐ 186 Doug Flynn	.25	.11	.03
☐ 187 Dick Pole	.25	.11	.03
☐ 188 Bob Tolan	.25	.11	.03
☐ 189 Rick Dempsey	.35	.16	.04
☐ 190 Ray Burris	.25	.11	.03
☐ 191 Doug Griffin	.25	.11	.03
☐ 192 Clarence Gaston	.35	.16	.04
☐ 193 Larry Gura	.25	.11	.03
☐ 194 Gary Matthews	.35	.16	.04
☐ 195 Ed Figueroa	.25	.11	.03
☐ 196 Len Randle	.25	.11	.03
☐ 197 Ed Ott	.25	.11	.03
☐ 198 Wilbur Wood	.25	.11	.03
☐ 199 Pepe Frias	.25	.11	.03
☐ 200 Frank Tanana	.75	.35	.09
☐ 201 Ed Kranepool	.25	.11	.03
☐ 202 Tom Johnson	.25	.11	.03
☐ 203 Ed Armbrister	.25	.11	.03

☐	204 Jeff Newman	.40	.18	.05
☐	205 Pete Falcone	.25	.11	.03
☐	206 Boog Powell	.60	.25	.08
☐	207 Glenn Abbott	.25	.11	.03
☐	208 Checklist 2	1.25	.13	.04
☐	209 Rob Andrews	.25	.11	.03
☐	210 Fred Lynn	1.00	.45	.13
☐	211 Giants Team/Mgr. Joe Altobelli (Checklist back)	1.00	.45	.13
☐	212 Jim Mason	.25	.11	.03
☐	213 Maximino Leon	.25	.11	.03
☐	214 Darrell Porter	.35	.16	.04
☐	215 Butch Metzger	.25	.11	.03
☐	216 Doug DeCinces	.35	.16	.04
☐	217 Tom Underwood	.25	.11	.03
☐	218 John Wathan	.75	.35	.09
☐	219 Joe Coleman	.25	.11	.03
☐	220 Chris Chambliss	.35	.16	.04
☐	221 Bob Bailey	.25	.11	.03
☐	222 Francisco Barrios	.25	.11	.03
☐	223 Earl Williams	.25	.11	.03
☐	224 Rusty Torres	.25	.11	.03
☐	225 Bob Apodaca	.25	.11	.03
☐	226 Leroy Stanton	.25	.11	.03
☐	227 Joe Sambito	.25	.11	.03
☐	228 Twins Team/Mgr. Gene Mauch (Checklist back)	1.00	.45	.13
☐	229 Don Kessinger	.35	.16	.04
☐	230 Vida Blue	.45	.20	.06
☐	231 RB: George Brett Most cons. games with 3 or more hits	9.00	4.00	1.15
☐	232 RB: Minnie Minoso Oldest to hit safely	.60	.25	.08
☐	233 RB: Jose Morales, Most pinch-hits, season	.35	.16	.04
☐	234 RB: Nolan Ryan Most seasons, 300 or more strikeouts	13.50	6.00	1.70
☐	235 Cecil Cooper	.60	.25	.08
☐	236 Tom Buskey	.25	.11	.03
☐	237 Gene Clines	.25	.11	.03
☐	238 Tippy Martinez	.35	.16	.04
☐	239 Bill Plummer	.25	.11	.03
☐	240 Ron LeFlore	.35	.16	.04
☐	241 Dave Tomlin	.25	.11	.03
☐	242 Ken Henderson	.25	.11	.03
☐	243 Ron Reed	.25	.11	.03
☐	244 John Mayberry (Cartoon mentions T206 Wagner)	.45	.20	.06
☐	245 Rick Rhoden	.35	.16	.04
☐	246 Mike Vail	.25	.11	.03
☐	247 Chris Knapp	.25	.11	.03
☐	248 Wilbur Howard	.25	.11	.03
☐	249 Pete Redfern	.25	.11	.03
☐	250 Bill Madlock	.60	.25	.08
☐	251 Tony Muser	.25	.11	.03
☐	252 Dale Murray	.25	.11	.03
☐	253 John Hale	.25	.11	.03
☐	254 Doyle Alexander	.25	.11	.03
☐	255 George Scott	.35	.16	.04
☐	256 Joe Hoerner	.25	.11	.03
☐	257 Mike Miley	.25	.11	.03
☐	258 Luis Tiant	.45	.20	.06
☐	259 Mets Team/Mgr. Joe Frazier (Checklist back)	1.00	.45	.13
☐	260 J.R. Richard	.35	.16	.04
☐	261 Phil Garner	.45	.20	.06
☐	262 Al Cowens	.25	.11	.03
☐	263 Mike Marshall	.35	.16	.04
☐	264 Tom Hutton	.25	.11	.03
☐	265 Mark Fidrych	1.75	.80	.22
☐	266 Derrel Thomas	.25	.11	.03
☐	267 Ray Fosse	.25	.11	.03
☐	268 Rick Sawyer	.25	.11	.03
☐	269 Joe Lis	.25	.11	.03
☐	270 Dave Parker	3.00	1.35	.40
☐	271 Terry Forster	.25	.11	.03
☐	272 Lee Lacy	.25	.11	.03
☐	273 Eric Soderholm	.25	.11	.03
☐	274 Don Stanhouse	.25	.11	.03
☐	275 Mike Hargrove	.35	.16	.04
☐	276 AL Champs Chris Chambliss' homer decides it	.50	.23	.06
☐	277 NL Champs Reds sweep Phillies	1.25	.55	.16
☐	278 Danny Frisella	.25	.11	.03
☐	279 Joe Wallis	.25	.11	.03
☐	280 Jim Hunter	2.50	1.15	.30
☐	281 Roy Staiger	.25	.11	.03
☐	282 Sid Monge	.25	.11	.03
☐	283 Jerry DaVanon	.25	.11	.03
☐	284 Mike Norris	.25	.11	.03
☐	285 Brooks Robinson	4.50	2.00	.55
☐	286 Johnny Grubb	.25	.11	.03
☐	287 Reds Team/Mgr. Sparky Anderson (Checklist back)	1.00	.45	.13
☐	288 Bob Montgomery	.25	.11	.03
☐	289 Gene Garber	.25	.11	.03
☐	290 Amos Otis	.35	.16	.04
☐	291 Jason Thompson	.45	.20	.06
☐	292 Rogelio Moret	.25	.11	.03
☐	293 Jack Brohamer	.25	.11	.03
☐	294 George Medich	.25	.11	.03
☐	295 Gary Carter	7.50	3.40	.95
☐	296 Don Hood	.25	.11	.03
☐	297 Ken Reitz	.25	.11	.03
☐	298 Charlie Hough	.35	.16	.04
☐	299 Otto Velez	.25	.11	.03
☐	300 Jerry Koosman	.45	.20	.06
☐	301 Toby Harrah	.35	.16	.04
☐	302 Mike Garman	.25	.11	.03
☐	303 Gene Tenace	.35	.16	.04
☐	304 Jim Hughes	.25	.11	.03
☐	305 Mickey Rivers	.35	.16	.04
☐	306 Rick Waits	.25	.11	.03
☐	307 Gary Sutherland	.25	.11	.03
☐	308 Gene Pentz	.25	.11	.03
☐	309 Red Sox Team/Mgr. Don Zimmer (Checklist back)	1.00	.45	.13
☐	310 Larry Bowa	.45	.20	.06
☐	311 Vern Ruhle	.25	.11	.03
☐	312 Rob Belloir	.25	.11	.03
☐	313 Paul Blair	.35	.16	.04
☐	314 Steve Mingori	.25	.11	.03
☐	315 Dave Chalk	.25	.11	.03
☐	316 Steve Rogers	.25	.11	.03
☐	317 Kurt Bevacqua	.25	.11	.03
☐	318 Duffy Dyer	.25	.11	.03
☐	319 Rich Gossage	1.25	.55	.16
☐	320 Ken Griffey	1.50	.65	.19
☐	321 Dave Goltz	.25	.11	.03
☐	322 Bill Russell	.35	.16	.04
☐	323 Larry Lintz	.25	.11	.03
☐	324 John Curtis	.25	.11	.03
☐	325 Mike Ivie	.25	.11	.03
☐	326 Jesse Jefferson	.25	.11	.03
☐	327 Astros Team/Mgr. Bill Virdon (Checklist back)	1.00	.45	.13
☐	328 Tommy Boggs	.25	.11	.03
☐	329 Ron Hodges	.25	.11	.03
☐	330 George Hendrick	.35	.16	.04
☐	331 Jim Colborn	.25	.11	.03
☐	332 Elliott Maddox	.25	.11	.03
☐	333 Paul Reuschel	.25	.11	.03
☐	334 Bill Stein	.25	.11	.03
☐	335 Bill Robinson	.35	.16	.04
☐	336 Denny Doyle	.25	.11	.03
☐	337 Ron Schueler	.25	.11	.03
☐	338 Dave Duncan	.25	.11	.03
☐	339 Adrian Devine	.25	.11	.03
☐	340 Hal McRae	.45	.20	.06
☐	341 Joe Kerrigan	.40	.18	.05
☐	342 Jerry Remy	.25	.11	.03
☐	343 Ed Halicki	.25	.11	.03
☐	344 Brian Downing	.60	.25	.08
☐	345 Reggie Smith	.45	.20	.06
☐	346 Bill Singer	.25	.11	.03
☐	347 George Foster	1.25	.55	.16
☐	348 Brent Strom	.25	.11	.03
☐	349 Jim Holt	.25	.11	.03
☐	350 Larry Dierker	.25	.11	.03
☐	351 Jim Sundberg	.35	.16	.04
☐	352 Mike Phillips	.25	.11	.03
☐	353 Stan Thomas	.25	.11	.03
☐	354 Pirates Team/Mgr. Chuck Tanner (Checklist back)	1.00	.45	.13
☐	355 Lou Brock	4.00	1.80	.50
☐	356 Checklist 3	1.25	.13	.04
☐	357 Tim McCarver	.50	.23	.06
☐	358 Tom House	.25	.11	.03
☐	359 Willie Randolph	2.50	1.15	.30
☐	360 Rick Monday	.35	.16	.04
☐	361 Eduardo Rodriguez	.25	.11	.03
☐	362 Tommy Davis	.35	.16	.04
☐	363 Dave Roberts	.25	.11	.03
☐	364 Vic Correll	.25	.11	.03

Card			
☐ 365 Mike Torrez	.35	.16	.04
☐ 366 Ted Sizemore	.25	.11	.03
☐ 367 Dave Hamilton	.25	.11	.03
☐ 368 Mike Jorgensen	.25	.11	.03
☐ 369 Terry Humphrey	.25	.11	.03
☐ 370 John Montefusco	.35	.16	.04
☐ 371 Royals Team/Mgr. Whitey Herzog (Checklist back)	1.00	.45	.13
☐ 372 Rich Folkers	.25	.11	.03
☐ 373 Bert Campaneris	.35	.16	.04
☐ 374 Kent Tekulve	.45	.20	.06
☐ 375 Larry Hisle	.35	.16	.04
☐ 376 Nino Espinosa	.25	.11	.03
☐ 377 Dave McKay	.25	.11	.03
☐ 378 Jim Umbarger	.25	.11	.03
☐ 379 Larry Cox	.25	.11	.03
☐ 380 Lee May	.35	.16	.04
☐ 381 Bob Forsch	.25	.11	.03
☐ 382 Charlie Moore	.25	.11	.03
☐ 383 Stan Bahnsen	.25	.11	.03
☐ 384 Darrel Chaney	.25	.11	.03
☐ 385 Dave LaRoche	.25	.11	.03
☐ 386 Manny Mota	.35	.16	.04
☐ 387 Yankees Team (Checklist back)	1.50	.65	.19
☐ 388 Terry Harmon	.25	.11	.03
☐ 389 Ken Kravec	.25	.11	.03
☐ 390 Dave Winfield	20.00	9.00	2.50
☐ 391 Dan Warthen	.25	.11	.03
☐ 392 Phil Roof	.25	.11	.03
☐ 393 John Lowenstein	.25	.11	.03
☐ 394 Bill Laxton	.25	.11	.03
☐ 395 Manny Trillo	.25	.11	.03
☐ 396 Tom Murphy	.25	.11	.03
☐ 397 Larry Herndon	.50	.23	.06
☐ 398 Tom Burgmeier	.25	.11	.03
☐ 399 Bruce Boisclair	.25	.11	.03
☐ 400 Steve Garvey	4.00	1.80	.50
☐ 401 Mickey Scott	.25	.11	.03
☐ 402 Tommy Helms	.25	.11	.03
☐ 403 Tom Grieve	.35	.16	.04
☐ 404 Eric Rasmussen	.25	.11	.03
☐ 405 Claudell Washington	.35	.16	.04
☐ 406 Tim Johnson	.25	.11	.03
☐ 407 Dave Freisleben	.25	.11	.03
☐ 408 Cesar Tovar	.25	.11	.03
☐ 409 Pete Broberg	.25	.11	.03
☐ 410 Willie Montanez	.25	.11	.03
☐ 411 W.S. Games 1 and 2 Joe Morgan homers in opener; Johnny Bench stars as Reds take 2nd game	1.50	.65	.19
☐ 412 W.S. Games 3 and 4 Reds stop Yankees; Johnny Bench's two homers wrap it up	1.25	.55	.16
☐ 413 World Series Summary Cincy wins 2nd straight series	.60	.25	.08
☐ 414 Tommy Harper	.35	.16	.04
☐ 415 Jay Johnstone	.35	.16	.04
☐ 416 Chuck Hartenstein	.25	.11	.03
☐ 417 Wayne Garrett	.25	.11	.03
☐ 418 White Sox Team/Mgr. Bob Lemon (Checklist back)	1.00	.45	.13
☐ 419 Steve Swisher	.25	.11	.03
☐ 420 Rusty Staub	.45	.20	.06
☐ 421 Doug Rau	.25	.11	.03
☐ 422 Freddie Patek	.35	.16	.04
☐ 423 Gary Lavelle	.25	.11	.03
☐ 424 Steve Brye	.25	.11	.03
☐ 425 Joe Torre	.50	.23	.06
☐ 426 Dick Drago	.25	.11	.03
☐ 427 Dave Rader	.25	.11	.03
☐ 428 Rangers Team/Mgr. Frank Lucchesi (Checklist back)	1.00	.45	.13
☐ 429 Ken Boswell	.25	.11	.03
☐ 430 Fergie Jenkins	3.00	1.35	.40
☐ 431 Dave Collins UER (Photo actually Bobby Jones)	.35	.16	.04
☐ 432 Buzz Capra	.25	.11	.03
☐ 433 Turn back clock 1972 Nate Colbert	.35	.16	.04
☐ 434 Turn back clock 1967 Carl Yastrzemski Triple Crown	1.50	.65	.19
☐ 435 Turn back clock 1962 Maury Wills 104 steals	.35	.16	.04
☐ 436 Turn back clock 1957 Bob Keegan hurls Majors' only no-hitter	.35	.16	.04
☐ 437 Turn back clock 1952 Ralph Kiner leads NL in HR's 7th straight year	.50	.23	.06
☐ 438 Marty Perez	.25	.11	.03
☐ 439 Gorman Thomas	.35	.16	.04
☐ 440 Jon Matlack	.25	.11	.03
☐ 441 Larvell Blanks	.25	.11	.03
☐ 442 Braves Team/Mgr. Dave Bristol (Checklist back)	1.00	.45	.13
☐ 443 Lamar Johnson	.25	.11	.03
☐ 444 Wayne Twitchell	.25	.11	.03
☐ 445 Ken Singleton	.35	.16	.04
☐ 446 Bill Bonham	.25	.11	.03
☐ 447 Jerry Turner	.25	.11	.03
☐ 448 Ellie Rodriguez	.25	.11	.03
☐ 449 Al Fitzmorris	.25	.11	.03
☐ 450 Pete Rose	9.00	4.00	1.15
☐ 451 Checklist 4	1.25	.13	.04
☐ 452 Mike Caldwell	.25	.11	.03
☐ 453 Pedro Garcia	.25	.11	.03
☐ 454 Andy Etchebarren	.25	.11	.03
☐ 455 Rick Wise	.25	.11	.03
☐ 456 Leon Roberts	.25	.11	.03
☐ 457 Steve Luebber	.25	.11	.03
☐ 458 Leo Foster	.25	.11	.03
☐ 459 Steve Foucault	.25	.11	.03
☐ 460 Willie Stargell	3.00	1.35	.40
☐ 461 Dick Tidrow	.25	.11	.03
☐ 462 Don Baylor	1.25	.55	.16
☐ 463 Jamie Quirk	.25	.11	.03
☐ 464 Randy Moffitt	.25	.11	.03
☐ 465 Rico Carty	.35	.16	.04
☐ 466 Fred Holdsworth	.25	.11	.03
☐ 467 Phillies Team/Mgr. Danny Ozark (Checklist back)	1.00	.45	.13
☐ 468 Ramon Hernandez	.25	.11	.03
☐ 469 Pat Kelly	.25	.11	.03
☐ 470 Ted Simmons	1.00	.45	.13
☐ 471 Del Unser	.25	.11	.03
☐ 472 Rookie Pitchers Don Aase Bob McClure Gil Patterson Dave Wehrmeister	.35	.16	.04
☐ 473 Rookie Outfielders Andre Dawson Gene Richards John Scott Denny Walling	75.00	34.00	9.50
☐ 474 Rookie Shortstops Bob Bailor Kiko Garcia Craig Reynolds Alex Taveras	.50	.23	.06
☐ 475 Rookie Pitchers Chris Batton Rick Camp Scott McGregor Manny Sarmiento	.50	.23	.06
☐ 476 Rookie Catchers Gary Alexander Rick Cerone Dale Murphy Kevin Pasley	30.00	13.50	3.80
☐ 477 Rookie Infielders Doug Ault Rich Dauer Orlando Gonzalez Phil Mankowski	.35	.16	.04
☐ 478 Rookie Pitchers Jim Gideon Leon Hooten Dave Johnson Mark Lemongello	.35	.16	.04
☐ 479 Rookie Outfielders Brian Asselstine Wayne Gross Sam Mejias Alvis Woods	.35	.16	.04
☐ 480 Carl Yastrzemski	6.00	2.70	.75
☐ 481 Roger Metzger	.25	.11	.03
☐ 482 Tony Solaita	.25	.11	.03
☐ 483 Richie Zisk	.25	.11	.03
☐ 484 Burt Hooton	.35	.16	.04
☐ 485 Roy White	.35	.16	.04
☐ 486 Ed Bane	.25	.11	.03
☐ 487 Rookie Pitchers Larry Anderson	.35	.16	.04

	Ed Glynn			
	Joe Henderson			
	Greg Terlecky			
☐ 488	Rookie Outfielders	10.00	4.50	1.25
	Jack Clark			
	Ruppert Jones			
	Lee Mazzilli			
	Dan Thomas			
☐ 489	Rookie Pitchers	.35	.16	.04
	Len Barker			
	Randy Lerch			
	Greg Minton			
	Mike Overy			
☐ 490	Rookie Shortstops	.35	.16	.04
	Billy Almon			
	Mickey Klutts			
	Tommy McMillan			
	Mark Wagner			
☐ 491	Rookie Pitchers	8.00	3.60	1.00
	Mike Dupree			
	Dennis Martinez			
	Craig Mitchell			
	Bob Sykes			
☐ 492	Rookie Outfielders	.75	.35	.09
	Tony Armas			
	Steve Kemp			
	Carlos Lopez			
	Gary Woods			
☐ 493	Rookie Pitchers	.40	.18	.05
	Mike Krukow			
	Jim Otten			
	Gary Wheelock			
	Mike Willis			
☐ 494	Rookie Infielders	2.00	.90	.25
	Juan Bernhardt			
	Mike Champion			
	Jim Gantner			
	Bump Wills			
☐ 495	Al Hrabosky	.25	.11	.03
☐ 496	Gary Thomasson	.25	.11	.03
☐ 497	Clay Carroll	.25	.11	.03
☐ 498	Sal Bando	.35	.16	.04
☐ 499	Pablo Torrealba	.25	.11	.03
☐ 500	Dave Kingman	.60	.25	.08
☐ 501	Jim Bibby	.25	.11	.03
☐ 502	Randy Hundley	.25	.11	.03
☐ 503	Bill Lee	.25	.11	.03
☐ 504	Dodgers Team/Mgr.	1.00	.45	.13
	Tom Lasorda			
	(Checklist back)			
☐ 505	Oscar Gamble	.35	.16	.04
☐ 506	Steve Grilli	.25	.11	.03
☐ 507	Mike Hegan	.25	.11	.03
☐ 508	Dave Pagan	.25	.11	.03
☐ 509	Cookie Rojas	.35	.16	.04
☐ 510	John Candelaria	.65	.30	.08
☐ 511	Bill Fahey	.25	.11	.03
☐ 512	Jack Billingham	.25	.11	.03
☐ 513	Jerry Terrell	.25	.11	.03
☐ 514	Cliff Johnson	.25	.11	.03
☐ 515	Chris Speier	.25	.11	.03
☐ 516	Bake McBride	.35	.16	.04
☐ 517	Pete Vuckovich	.40	.18	.05
☐ 518	Cubs Team/Mgr.	1.00	.45	.13
	Herman Franks			
	(Checklist back)			
☐ 519	Don Kirkwood	.25	.11	.03
☐ 520	Garry Maddox	.25	.11	.03
☐ 521	Bob Grich	.45	.20	.06
☐ 522	Enzo Hernandez	.25	.11	.03
☐ 523	Rollie Fingers	4.00	1.80	.50
☐ 524	Rowland Office	.25	.11	.03
☐ 525	Dennis Eckersley	20.00	9.00	2.50
☐ 526	Larry Parrish	.35	.16	.04
☐ 527	Dan Meyer	.25	.11	.03
☐ 528	Bill Castro	.25	.11	.03
☐ 529	Jim Essian	.50	.23	.06
☐ 530	Rick Reuschel	.35	.16	.04
☐ 531	Lyman Bostock	.35	.16	.04
☐ 532	Jim Willoughby	.25	.11	.03
☐ 533	Mickey Stanley	.25	.11	.03
☐ 534	Paul Splittorff	.25	.11	.03
☐ 535	Cesar Geronimo	.25	.11	.03
☐ 536	Vic Albury	.25	.11	.03
☐ 537	Dave Roberts	.25	.11	.03
☐ 538	Frank Taveras	.25	.11	.03
☐ 539	Mike Wallace	.25	.11	.03
☐ 540	Bob Watson	.35	.16	.04
☐ 541	John Denny	.35	.16	.04
☐ 542	Frank Duffy	.25	.11	.03
☐ 543	Ron Blomberg	.25	.11	.03
☐ 544	Gary Ross	.25	.11	.03
☐ 545	Bob Boone	.75	.35	.09
☐ 546	Orioles Team/Mgr.	1.00	.45	.13
	Earl Weaver			
	(Checklist back)			
☐ 547	Willie McCovey	4.00	1.80	.50
☐ 548	Joel Youngblood	.25	.11	.03
☐ 549	Jerry Royster	.25	.11	.03
☐ 550	Randy Jones	.35	.16	.04
☐ 551	Bill North	.25	.11	.03
☐ 552	Pepe Mangual	.25	.11	.03
☐ 553	Jack Heidemann	.25	.11	.03
☐ 554	Bruce Kimm	.25	.11	.03
☐ 555	Dan Ford	.25	.11	.03
☐ 556	Doug Bird	.25	.11	.03
☐ 557	Jerry White	.25	.11	.03
☐ 558	Elias Sosa	.25	.11	.03
☐ 559	Alan Bannister	.25	.11	.03
☐ 560	Dave Concepcion	1.00	.45	.13
☐ 561	Pete LaCock	.25	.11	.03
☐ 562	Checklist 5	1.25	.13	.04
☐ 563	Bruce Kison	.25	.11	.03
☐ 564	Alan Ashby	.25	.11	.03
☐ 565	Mickey Lolich	.45	.20	.06
☐ 566	Rick Miller	.25	.11	.03
☐ 567	Enos Cabell	.25	.11	.03
☐ 568	Carlos May	.25	.11	.03
☐ 569	Jim Lonborg	.35	.16	.04
☐ 570	Bobby Bonds	.75	.35	.09
☐ 571	Darrell Evans	.35	.16	.04
☐ 572	Ross Grimsley	.25	.11	.03
☐ 573	Joe Ferguson	.25	.11	.03
☐ 574	Aurelio Rodriguez	.25	.11	.03
☐ 575	Dick Ruthven	.25	.11	.03
☐ 576	Fred Kendall	.25	.11	.03
☐ 577	Jerry Augustine	.25	.11	.03
☐ 578	Bob Randall	.25	.11	.03
☐ 579	Don Carrithers	.25	.11	.03
☐ 580	George Brett	35.00	16.00	4.40
☐ 581	Pedro Borbon	.25	.11	.03
☐ 582	Ed Kirkpatrick	.25	.11	.03
☐ 583	Paul Lindblad	.25	.11	.03
☐ 584	Ed Goodson	.25	.11	.03
☐ 585	Rick Burleson	.35	.16	.04
☐ 586	Steve Renko	.25	.11	.03
☐ 587	Rick Baldwin	.25	.11	.03
☐ 588	Dave Moates	.25	.11	.03
☐ 589	Mike Cosgrove	.25	.11	.03
☐ 590	Buddy Bell	.40	.18	.05
☐ 591	Chris Arnold	.25	.11	.03
☐ 592	Dan Briggs	.25	.11	.03
☐ 593	Dennis Blair	.25	.11	.03
☐ 594	Biff Pocoroba	.25	.11	.03
☐ 595	John Hiller	.25	.11	.03
☐ 596	Jerry Martin	.25	.11	.03
☐ 597	Mariners Leaders	1.00	.45	.13
	Darrell Johnson MG			
	Don Bryant CO			
	Jim Busby CO			
	Vada Pinson CO			
	Wes Stock CO			
	(Checklist back)			
☐ 598	Sparky Lyle	.60	.25	.08
☐ 599	Mike Tyson	.25	.11	.03
☐ 600	Jim Palmer	7.50	3.40	.95
☐ 601	Mike Lum	.25	.11	.03
☐ 602	Andy Hassler	.25	.11	.03
☐ 603	Willie Davis	.35	.16	.04
☐ 604	Jim Slaton	.25	.11	.03
☐ 605	Felix Millan	.25	.11	.03
☐ 606	Steve Braun	.25	.11	.03
☐ 607	Larry Demery	.25	.11	.03
☐ 608	Roy Howell	.25	.11	.03
☐ 609	Jim Barr	.25	.11	.03
☐ 610	Jose Cardenal	.25	.11	.03
☐ 611	Dave Lemanczyk	.25	.11	.03
☐ 612	Barry Foote	.25	.11	.03
☐ 613	Reggie Cleveland	.25	.11	.03
☐ 614	Greg Gross	.25	.11	.03
☐ 615	Phil Niekro	2.50	1.15	.30
☐ 616	Tommy Sandt	.40	.18	.05
☐ 617	Bobby Darwin	.25	.11	.03
☐ 618	Pat Dobson	.25	.11	.03
☐ 619	Johnny Oates	.25	.11	.03
☐ 620	Don Sutton	2.50	1.15	.30
☐ 621	Tigers Team/Mgr.	1.00	.45	.13
	Ralph Houk			
	(Checklist back)			
☐ 622	Jim Wohlford	.25	.11	.03
☐ 623	Jack Kucek	.25	.11	.03
☐ 624	Hector Cruz	.25	.11	.03
☐ 625	Ken Holtzman	.35	.16	.04
☐ 626	Al Bumbry	.25	.11	.03
☐ 627	Bob Myrick	.25	.11	.03
☐ 628	Mario Guerrero	.25	.11	.03
☐ 629	Bobby Valentine	.35	.16	.04
☐ 630	Bert Blyleven	2.00	.90	.25

☐ 631 Big League Brothers George Brett Ken Brett	5.00	2.30	.60
☐ 632 Big League Brothers Bob Forsch Ken Forsch	.35	.16	.04
☐ 633 Big League Brothers Lee May Carlos May	.35	.16	.04
☐ 634 Big League Brothers Paul Reuschel Rick Reuschel UER (Photos switched)	.35	.16	.04
☐ 635 Robin Yount	35.00	16.00	4.40
☐ 636 Santo Alcala	.25	.11	.03
☐ 637 Alex Johnson	.25	.11	.03
☐ 638 Jim Kaat	1.00	.45	.13
☐ 639 Jerry Morales	.25	.11	.03
☐ 640 Carlton Fisk	10.00	4.50	1.25
☐ 641 Dan Larson	.25	.11	.03
☐ 642 Willie Crawford	.25	.11	.03
☐ 643 Mike Pazik	.25	.11	.03
☐ 644 Matt Alexander	.25	.11	.03
☐ 645 Jerry Reuss	.35	.16	.04
☐ 646 Andres Mora	.25	.11	.03
☐ 647 Expos Team/Mgr. Dick Williams (Checklist back)	1.00	.45	.13
☐ 648 Jim Spencer	.25	.11	.03
☐ 649 Dave Cash	.25	.11	.03
☐ 650 Nolan Ryan	40.00	18.00	5.00
☐ 651 Von Joshua	.25	.11	.03
☐ 652 Tom Walker	.25	.11	.03
☐ 653 Diego Segui	.25	.11	.03
☐ 654 Ron Pruitt	.25	.11	.03
☐ 655 Tony Perez	2.00	.90	.25
☐ 656 Ron Guidry	2.00	.90	.25
☐ 657 Mick Kelleher	.25	.11	.03
☐ 658 Marty Pattin	.25	.11	.03
☐ 659 Merv Rettenmund	.25	.11	.03
☐ 660 Willie Horton	.50	.23	.06

1978 Topps

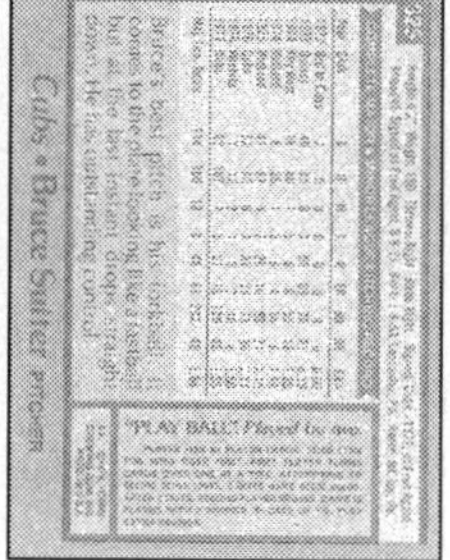

The cards in this 726-card set measure 2 1/2" by 3 1/2". The 1978 Topps set experienced an increase in number of cards from the previous five regular issue sets of 660. Card numbers 1 through 7 feature Record Breakers (RB) of the 1977 season. Other subsets within this set include League Leaders (201-208), Post-season cards (411-413), and Rookie Prospects (701-711). The key Rookie Cards in this set are the multi-player Rookie Card of Paul Molitor and Alan Trammell, Jack Morris, Eddie Murray, Lance Parrish, and Lou Whitaker. The manager cards in the set feature a "then and now" format on the card front showing the manager as he looked many years before, e.g., during his playing days. While no scarcities exist, 66 of the cards are more abundant in supply, as they were "double printed." These 66 double-printed cards are noted in the checklist by DP. Team cards again feature a checklist of that team's players in the set on the back. Cards numbered 23 or lower, that feature Astros, Rangers, Tigers, or Yankees and do not follow the numbering checklisted below, are not necessarily error cards. They are undoubtedly Burger King cards, a separate set with its own pricing and mass distribution. Burger King cards are indistinguishable from the corresponding Topps cards except for the card numbering difference and the fact that Burger King cards do not have a printing sheet designation (such as A through F like the regular Topps) anywhere on the card back in very small print.

	NRMT-MT	EXC	G-VG
COMPLETE SET (726)	325.00	145.00	40.00
COMMON PLAYER (1-726)	.20	.09	.03
COMMON PLAYER DP	.10	.05	.01
☐ 1 RB: Lou Brock Most steals, lifetime	3.00	.75	.24
☐ 2 RB: Sparky Lyle Most games, pure relief, lifetime	.35	.16	.04
☐ 3 RB: Willie McCovey Most times, 2 HR's in inning, lifetime	1.25	.55	.16
☐ 4 RB: Brooks Robinson Most consecutive seasons with one club	1.50	.65	.19
☐ 5 RB: Pete Rose Most hits, switch hitter, lifetime	3.00	1.35	.40
☐ 6 RB: Nolan Ryan Most games with 10 or more strikeouts, lifetime	8.00	3.60	1.00
☐ 7 RB: Reggie Jackson Most homers, one World Series	4.00	1.80	.50
☐ 8 Mike Sadek	.10	.05	.01
☐ 9 Doug DeCinces	.20	.09	.03
☐ 10 Phil Niekro	2.00	.90	.25
☐ 11 Rick Manning	.10	.05	.01
☐ 12 Don Aase	.10	.05	.01
☐ 13 Art Howe	.75	.35	.09
☐ 14 Lerrin LaGrow	.10	.05	.01
☐ 15 Tony Perez DP	.75	.35	.09
☐ 16 Roy White	.20	.09	.03
☐ 17 Mike Krukow	.10	.05	.01
☐ 18 Bob Grich	.30	.14	.04
☐ 19 Darrell Porter	.20	.09	.03
☐ 20 Pete Rose DP	4.00	1.80	.50
☐ 21 Steve Kemp	.10	.05	.01
☐ 22 Charlie Hough	.20	.09	.03
☐ 23 Bump Wills	.10	.05	.01
☐ 24 Don Money DP	.10	.05	.01
☐ 25 Jon Matlack	.10	.05	.01
☐ 26 Rich Hebner	.10	.05	.01
☐ 27 Geoff Zahn	.10	.05	.01
☐ 28 Ed Ott	.10	.05	.01
☐ 29 Bob Lacey	.10	.05	.01
☐ 30 George Hendrick	.20	.09	.03
☐ 31 Glenn Abbott	.10	.05	.01
☐ 32 Garry Templeton	.30	.14	.04
☐ 33 Dave Lemanczyk	.10	.05	.01
☐ 34 Willie McCovey	3.00	1.35	.40
☐ 35 Sparky Lyle	.30	.14	.04
☐ 36 Eddie Murray	75.00	34.00	9.50
☐ 37 Rick Waits	.10	.05	.01
☐ 38 Willie Montanez	.10	.05	.01
☐ 39 Floyd Bannister	.60	.25	.08
☐ 40 Carl Yastrzemski	4.50	2.00	.55
☐ 41 Burt Hooton	.20	.09	.03
☐ 42 Jorge Orta	.10	.05	.01
☐ 43 Bill Atkinson	.10	.05	.01
☐ 44 Toby Harrah	.20	.09	.03
☐ 45 Mark Fidrych	.50	.23	.06
☐ 46 Al Cowens	.10	.05	.01
☐ 47 Jack Billingham	.10	.05	.01
☐ 48 Don Baylor	1.00	.45	.13
☐ 49 Ed Kranepool	.10	.05	.01
☐ 50 Rick Reuschel	.20	.09	.03
☐ 51 Charlie Moore DP	.10	.05	.01
☐ 52 Jim Lonborg	.10	.05	.01
☐ 53 Phil Garner DP	.10	.05	.01
☐ 54 Tom Johnson	.10	.05	.01
☐ 55 Mitchell Page	.10	.05	.01
☐ 56 Randy Jones	.10	.05	.01
☐ 57 Dan Meyer	.10	.05	.01
☐ 58 Bob Forsch	.10	.05	.01
☐ 59 Otto Velez	.10	.05	.01
☐ 60 Thurman Munson	5.00	2.30	.60
☐ 61 Larvell Blanks	.10	.05	.01
☐ 62 Jim Barr	.10	.05	.01
☐ 63 Don Zimmer MG	.20	.09	.03

☐ 64 Gene Pentz	.10	.05	.01
☐ 65 Ken Singleton	.20	.09	.03
☐ 66 Chicago White Sox Team Card (Checklist back)	.75	.35	.09
☐ 67 Claudell Washington	.20	.09	.03
☐ 68 Steve Foucault DP	.10	.05	.01
☐ 69 Mike Vail	.10	.05	.01
☐ 70 Rich Gossage	1.00	.45	.13
☐ 71 Terry Humphrey	.10	.05	.01
☐ 72 Andre Dawson	25.00	11.50	3.10
☐ 73 Andy Hassler	.10	.05	.01
☐ 74 Checklist 1	1.00	.45	.13
☐ 75 Dick Ruthven	.10	.05	.01
☐ 76 Steve Ontiveros	.10	.05	.01
☐ 77 Ed Kirkpatrick	.10	.05	.01
☐ 78 Pablo Torrealba	.10	.05	.01
☐ 79 Darrell Johnson DP MG	.10	.05	.01
☐ 80 Ken Griffey	1.00	.45	.13
☐ 81 Pete Redfern	.10	.05	.01
☐ 82 San Francisco Giants Team Card (Checklist back)	.75	.35	.09
☐ 83 Bob Montgomery	.10	.05	.01
☐ 84 Kent Tekulve	.20	.09	.03
☐ 85 Ron Fairly	.10	.05	.01
☐ 86 Dave Tomlin	.10	.05	.01
☐ 87 John Lowenstein	.10	.05	.01
☐ 88 Mike Phillips	.10	.05	.01
☐ 89 Ken Clay	.10	.05	.01
☐ 90 Larry Bowa	.30	.14	.04
☐ 91 Oscar Zamora	.10	.05	.01
☐ 92 Adrian Devine	.10	.05	.01
☐ 93 Bobby Cox DP	.10	.05	.01
☐ 94 Chuck Scrivener	.10	.05	.01
☐ 95 Jamie Quirk	.10	.05	.01
☐ 96 Baltimore Orioles Team Card (Checklist back)	.75	.35	.09
☐ 97 Stan Bahnsen	.10	.05	.01
☐ 98 Jim Essian	.20	.09	.03
☐ 99 Willie Hernandez	.60	.25	.08
☐ 100 George Brett	25.00	11.50	3.10
☐ 101 Sid Monge	.10	.05	.01
☐ 102 Matt Alexander	.10	.05	.01
☐ 103 Tom Murphy	.10	.05	.01
☐ 104 Lee Lacy	.10	.05	.01
☐ 105 Reggie Cleveland	.10	.05	.01
☐ 106 Bill Plummer	.10	.05	.01
☐ 107 Ed Halicki	.10	.05	.01
☐ 108 Von Joshua	.10	.05	.01
☐ 109 Joe Torre MG	.50	.23	.06
☐ 110 Richie Zisk	.10	.05	.01
☐ 111 Mike Tyson	.10	.05	.01
☐ 112 Houston Astros Team Card (Checklist back)	.75	.35	.09
☐ 113 Don Carrithers	.10	.05	.01
☐ 114 Paul Blair	.20	.09	.03
☐ 115 Gary Nolan	.10	.05	.01
☐ 116 Tucker Ashford	.10	.05	.01
☐ 117 John Montague	.10	.05	.01
☐ 118 Terry Harmon	.10	.05	.01
☐ 119 Dennis Martinez	2.50	1.15	.30
☐ 120 Gary Carter	4.50	2.00	.55
☐ 121 Alvis Woods	.10	.05	.01
☐ 122 Dennis Eckersley	9.00	4.00	1.15
☐ 123 Manny Trillo	.10	.05	.01
☐ 124 Dave Rozema	.10	.05	.01
☐ 125 George Scott	.20	.09	.03
☐ 126 Paul Moskau	.10	.05	.01
☐ 127 Chet Lemon	.20	.09	.03
☐ 128 Bill Russell	.20	.09	.03
☐ 129 Jim Colborn	.10	.05	.01
☐ 130 Jeff Burroughs	.20	.09	.03
☐ 131 Bert Blyleven	1.00	.45	.13
☐ 132 Enos Cabell	.10	.05	.01
☐ 133 Jerry Augustine	.10	.05	.01
☐ 134 Steve Henderson	.10	.05	.01
☐ 135 Ron Guidry DP	.75	.35	.09
☐ 136 Ted Sizemore	.10	.05	.01
☐ 137 Craig Kusick	.10	.05	.01
☐ 138 Larry Demery	.10	.05	.01
☐ 139 Wayne Gross	.10	.05	.01
☐ 140 Rollie Fingers	3.50	1.55	.45
☐ 141 Ruppert Jones	.10	.05	.01
☐ 142 John Montefusco	.20	.09	.03
☐ 143 Keith Hernandez	1.75	.80	.22
☐ 144 Jesse Jefferson	.10	.05	.01
☐ 145 Rick Monday	.20	.09	.03
☐ 146 Doyle Alexander	.10	.05	.01
☐ 147 Lee Mazzilli	.10	.05	.01
☐ 148 Andre Thornton	.20	.09	.03
☐ 149 Dale Murray	.10	.05	.01
☐ 150 Bobby Bonds	.40	.18	.05
☐ 151 Milt Wilcox	.10	.05	.01
☐ 152 Ivan DeJesus	.10	.05	.01
☐ 153 Steve Stone	.20	.09	.03
☐ 154 Cecil Cooper DP	.25	.11	.03
☐ 155 Butch Hobson	.30	.14	.04
☐ 156 Andy Messersmith	.20	.09	.03
☐ 157 Pete LaCock DP	.10	.05	.01
☐ 158 Joaquin Andujar	.20	.09	.03
☐ 159 Lou Piniella	.40	.18	.05
☐ 160 Jim Palmer	5.00	2.30	.60
☐ 161 Bob Boone	.75	.35	.09
☐ 162 Paul Thormodsgard	.10	.05	.01
☐ 163 Bill North	.10	.05	.01
☐ 164 Bob Owchinko	.10	.05	.01
☐ 165 Rennie Stennett	.10	.05	.01
☐ 166 Carlos Lopez	.10	.05	.01
☐ 167 Tim Foli	.10	.05	.01
☐ 168 Reggie Smith	.20	.09	.03
☐ 169 Jerry Johnson	.10	.05	.01
☐ 170 Lou Brock	3.50	1.55	.45
☐ 171 Pat Zachry	.10	.05	.01
☐ 172 Mike Hargrove	.20	.09	.03
☐ 173 Robin Yount UER (Played for Newark in 1973, not 1971)	25.00	11.50	3.10
☐ 174 Wayne Garland	.10	.05	.01
☐ 175 Jerry Morales	.10	.05	.01
☐ 176 Milt May	.10	.05	.01
☐ 177 Gene Garber DP	.10	.05	.01
☐ 178 Dave Chalk	.10	.05	.01
☐ 179 Dick Tidrow	.10	.05	.01
☐ 180 Dave Concepcion	1.00	.45	.13
☐ 181 Ken Forsch	.10	.05	.01
☐ 182 Jim Spencer	.10	.05	.01
☐ 183 Doug Bird	.10	.05	.01
☐ 184 Checklist 2	1.00	.45	.13
☐ 185 Ellis Valentine	.10	.05	.01
☐ 186 Bob Stanley DP	.10	.05	.01
☐ 187 Jerry Royster DP	.10	.05	.01
☐ 188 Al Bumbry	.10	.05	.01
☐ 189 Tom Lasorda MG	.30	.14	.04
☐ 190 John Candelaria	.20	.09	.03
☐ 191 Rodney Scott	.10	.05	.01
☐ 192 San Diego Padres Team Card (Checklist back)	.75	.35	.09
☐ 193 Rich Chiles	.10	.05	.01
☐ 194 Derrel Thomas	.10	.05	.01
☐ 195 Larry Dierker	.10	.05	.01
☐ 196 Bob Bailor	.10	.05	.01
☐ 197 Nino Espinosa	.10	.05	.01
☐ 198 Ron Pruitt	.10	.05	.01
☐ 199 Craig Reynolds	.10	.05	.01
☐ 200 Reggie Jackson	14.00	6.25	1.75
☐ 201 Batting Leaders Dave Parker Rod Carew	1.25	.55	.16
☐ 202 Home Run Leaders DP George Foster Jim Rice	.20	.09	.03
☐ 203 RBI Leaders George Foster Larry Hisle	.40	.18	.05
☐ 204 Steals Leaders DP Frank Taveras Freddie Patek	.20	.09	.03
☐ 205 Victory Leaders Steve Carlton Dave Goltz Dennis Leonard Jim Palmer	1.50	.65	.19
☐ 206 Strikeout Leaders DP Phil Niekro Nolan Ryan	2.00	.90	.25
☐ 207 ERA Leaders DP John Candelaria Frank Tanana	.20	.09	.03
☐ 208 Top Firemen Rollie Fingers Bill Campbell	.75	.35	.09
☐ 209 Dock Ellis	.10	.05	.01
☐ 210 Jose Cardenal	.10	.05	.01
☐ 211 Earl Weaver MG DP	.25	.11	.03
☐ 212 Mike Caldwell	.10	.05	.01
☐ 213 Alan Bannister	.10	.05	.01
☐ 214 California Angels Team Card (Checklist back)	.75	.35	.09
☐ 215 Darrell Evans	.30	.14	.04
☐ 216 Mike Paxton	.10	.05	.01
☐ 217 Rod Gilbreath	.10	.05	.01

☐ 218	Marty Pattin	.10	.05	.01
☐ 219	Mike Cubbage	.10	.05	.01
☐ 220	Pedro Borbon	.10	.05	.01
☐ 221	Chris Speier	.10	.05	.01
☐ 222	Jerry Martin	.10	.05	.01
☐ 223	Bruce Kison	.10	.05	.01
☐ 224	Jerry Tabb	.10	.05	.01
☐ 225	Don Gullett DP	.10	.05	.01
☐ 226	Joe Ferguson	.10	.05	.01
☐ 227	Al Fitzmorris	.10	.05	.01
☐ 228	Manny Mota DP	.10	.05	.01
☐ 229	Leo Foster	.10	.05	.01
☐ 230	Al Hrabosky	.10	.05	.01
☐ 231	Wayne Nordhagen	.10	.05	.01
☐ 232	Mickey Stanley	.10	.05	.01
☐ 233	Dick Pole	.10	.05	.01
☐ 234	Herman Franks MG	.10	.05	.01
☐ 235	Tim McCarver	.20	.09	.03
☐ 236	Terry Whitfield	.10	.05	.01
☐ 237	Rich Dauer	.10	.05	.01
☐ 238	Juan Beniquez	.10	.05	.01
☐ 239	Dyar Miller	.10	.05	.01
☐ 240	Gene Tenace	.20	.09	.03
☐ 241	Pete Vuckovich	.20	.09	.03
☐ 242	Barry Bonnell DP	.10	.05	.01
☐ 243	Bob McClure	.10	.05	.01
☐ 244	Montreal Expos Team Card DP (Checklist back)	.40	.18	.05
☐ 245	Rick Burleson	.20	.09	.03
☐ 246	Dan Driessen	.10	.05	.01
☐ 247	Larry Christenson	.10	.05	.01
☐ 248	Frank White DP	.10	.05	.01
☐ 249	Dave Goltz DP	.10	.05	.01
☐ 250	Graig Nettles DP	.30	.14	.04
☐ 251	Don Kirkwood	.10	.05	.01
☐ 252	Steve Swisher DP	.10	.05	.01
☐ 253	Jim Kern	.10	.05	.01
☐ 254	Dave Collins	.20	.09	.03
☐ 255	Jerry Reuss	.20	.09	.03
☐ 256	Joe Altobelli MG	.10	.05	.01
☐ 257	Hector Cruz	.10	.05	.01
☐ 258	John Hiller	.10	.05	.01
☐ 259	Los Angeles Dodgers Team Card (Checklist back)	.75	.35	.09
☐ 260	Bert Campaneris	.20	.09	.03
☐ 261	Tim Hosley	.10	.05	.01
☐ 262	Rudy May	.10	.05	.01
☐ 263	Danny Walton	.10	.05	.01
☐ 264	Jamie Easterly	.10	.05	.01
☐ 265	Sal Bando DP	.10	.05	.01
☐ 266	Bob Shirley	.10	.05	.01
☐ 267	Doug Ault	.10	.05	.01
☐ 268	Gil Flores	.10	.05	.01
☐ 269	Wayne Twitchell	.10	.05	.01
☐ 270	Carlton Fisk	7.50	3.40	.95
☐ 271	Randy Lerch DP	.10	.05	.01
☐ 272	Royle Stillman	.10	.05	.01
☐ 273	Fred Norman	.10	.05	.01
☐ 274	Freddie Patek	.20	.09	.03
☐ 275	Dan Ford	.10	.05	.01
☐ 276	Bill Bonham DP	.10	.05	.01
☐ 277	Bruce Boisclair	.10	.05	.01
☐ 278	Enrique Romo	.10	.05	.01
☐ 279	Bill Virdon MG	.10	.05	.01
☐ 280	Buddy Bell	.20	.09	.03
☐ 281	Eric Rasmussen DP	.10	.05	.01
☐ 282	New York Yankees Team Card (Checklist back)	1.25	.55	.16
☐ 283	Omar Moreno	.10	.05	.01
☐ 284	Randy Moffitt	.10	.05	.01
☐ 285	Steve Yeager DP	.10	.05	.01
☐ 286	Ben Oglivie	.20	.09	.03
☐ 287	Kiko Garcia	.10	.05	.01
☐ 288	Dave Hamilton	.10	.05	.01
☐ 289	Checklist 3	1.00	.45	.13
☐ 290	Willie Horton	.20	.09	.03
☐ 291	Gary Ross	.10	.05	.01
☐ 292	Gene Richards	.10	.05	.01
☐ 293	Mike Willis	.10	.05	.01
☐ 294	Larry Parrish	.20	.09	.03
☐ 295	Bill Lee	.10	.05	.01
☐ 296	Biff Pocoroba	.10	.05	.01
☐ 297	Warren Brusstar DP	.10	.05	.01
☐ 298	Tony Armas	.20	.09	.03
☐ 299	Whitey Herzog MG	.20	.09	.03
☐ 300	Joe Morgan	3.50	1.55	45
☐ 301	Buddy Schultz	.10	.05	.01
☐ 302	Chicago Cubs Team Card (Checklist back)	.75	.35	.09
☐ 303	Sam Hinds	.10	.05	.01
☐ 304	John Milner	.10	.05	.01
☐ 305	Rico Carty	.20	.09	.03
☐ 306	Joe Niekro	.20	.09	.03
☐ 307	Glenn Borgmann	.10	.05	.01
☐ 308	Jim Rooker	.10	.05	.01
☐ 309	Cliff Johnson	.10	.05	.01
☐ 310	Don Sutton	2.50	1.15	.30
☐ 311	Jose Baez DP	.10	.05	.01
☐ 312	Greg Minton	.10	.05	.01
☐ 313	Andy Etchebarren	.10	.05	.01
☐ 314	Paul Lindblad	.10	.05	.01
☐ 315	Mark Belanger	.20	.09	.03
☐ 316	Henry Cruz DP	.10	.05	.01
☐ 317	Dave Johnson	.10	.05	.01
☐ 318	Tom Griffin	.10	.05	.01
☐ 319	Alan Ashby	.10	.05	.01
☐ 320	Fred Lynn	1.00	.45	.13
☐ 321	Santo Alcala	.10	.05	.01
☐ 322	Tom Paciorek	.20	.09	.03
☐ 323	Jim Fregosi DP	.10	.05	.01
☐ 324	Vern Rapp MG	.10	.05	.01
☐ 325	Bruce Sutter	1.25	.55	.16
☐ 326	Mike Lum DP	.10	.05	.01
☐ 327	Rick Langford DP	.10	.05	.01
☐ 328	Milwaukee Brewers Team Card (Checklist back)	.75	.35	.09
☐ 329	John Verhoeven	.10	.05	.01
☐ 330	Bob Watson	.20	.09	.03
☐ 331	Mark Littell	.10	.05	.01
☐ 332	Duane Kuiper	.10	.05	.01
☐ 333	Jim Todd	.10	.05	.01
☐ 334	John Stearns	.10	.05	.01
☐ 335	Bucky Dent	.60	.25	.08
☐ 336	Steve Busby	.10	.05	.01
☐ 337	Tom Grieve	.20	.09	.03
☐ 338	Dave Heaverlo	.10	.05	.01
☐ 339	Mario Guerrero	.10	.05	.01
☐ 340	Bake McBride	.20	.09	.03
☐ 341	Mike Flanagan	.40	.18	.05
☐ 342	Aurelio Rodriguez	.10	.05	.01
☐ 343	John Wathan DP	.10	.05	.01
☐ 344	Sam Ewing	.10	.05	.01
☐ 345	Luis Tiant	.30	.14	.04
☐ 346	Larry Biittner	.10	.05	.01
☐ 347	Terry Forster	.10	.05	.01
☐ 348	Del Unser	.10	.05	.01
☐ 349	Rick Camp DP	.10	.05	.01
☐ 350	Steve Garvey	3.00	1.35	.40
☐ 351	Jeff Torborg	.20	.09	.03
☐ 352	Tony Scott	.10	.05	.01
☐ 353	Doug Bair	.10	.05	.01
☐ 354	Cesar Geronimo	.10	.05	.01
☐ 355	Bill Travers	.10	.05	.01
☐ 356	New York Mets Team Card (Checklist back)	.75	.35	.09
☐ 357	Tom Poquette	.10	.05	.01
☐ 358	Mark Lemongello	.10	.05	.01
☐ 359	Marc Hill	.10	.05	.01
☐ 360	Mike Schmidt	18.00	8.00	2.30
☐ 361	Chris Knapp	.10	.05	.01
☐ 362	Dave May	.10	.05	.01
☐ 363	Bob Randall	.10	.05	.01
☐ 364	Jerry Turner	.10	.05	.01
☐ 365	Ed Figueroa	.10	.05	.01
☐ 366	Larry Milbourne DP	.10	.05	.01
☐ 367	Rick Dempsey	.20	.09	.03
☐ 368	Balor Moore	.10	.05	.01
☐ 369	Tim Nordbrook	.10	.05	.01
☐ 370	Rusty Staub	.30	.14	.04
☐ 371	Ray Burris	.10	.05	.01
☐ 372	Brian Asselstine	.10	.05	.01
☐ 373	Jim Willoughby	.10	.05	.01
☐ 374	Jose Morales	.10	.05	.01
☐ 375	Tommy John	1.00	.45	.13
☐ 376	Jim Wohlford	.10	.05	.01
☐ 377	Manny Sarmiento	.10	.05	.01
☐ 378	Bobby Winkles MG	.10	.05	.01
☐ 379	Skip Lockwood	.10	.05	.01
☐ 380	Ted Simmons	1.00	.45	.13
☐ 381	Philadelphia Phillies Team Card (Checklist back)	.75	.35	.09
☐ 382	Joe Lahoud	.10	.05	.01
☐ 383	Mario Mendoza	.10	.05	.01
☐ 384	Jack Clark	2.00	.90	.25
☐ 385	Tito Fuentes	.10	.05	.01
☐ 386	Bob Gorinski	.10	.05	.01
☐ 387	Ken Holtzman	.10	.05	.01
☐ 388	Bill Fahey DP	.10	.05	.01
☐ 389	Julio Gonzalez	.10	.05	.01

☐ 390	Oscar Gamble	.20	.09	.03
☐ 391	Larry Haney	.10	.05	.01
☐ 392	Billy Almon	.10	.05	.01
☐ 393	Tippy Martinez	.20	.09	.03
☐ 394	Roy Howell DP	.10	.05	.01
☐ 395	Jim Hughes	.10	.05	.01
☐ 396	Bob Stinson DP	.10	.05	.01
☐ 397	Greg Gross	.10	.05	.01
☐ 398	Don Hood	.10	.05	.01
☐ 399	Pete Mackanin	.10	.05	.01
☐ 400	Nolan Ryan	30.00	13.50	3.80
☐ 401	Sparky Anderson MG	.20	.09	.03
☐ 402	Dave Campbell	.10	.05	.01
☐ 403	Bud Harrelson	.10	.05	.01
☐ 404	Detroit Tigers Team Card (Checklist back)	.75	.35	.09
☐ 405	Rawly Eastwick	.10	.05	.01
☐ 406	Mike Jorgensen	.10	.05	.01
☐ 407	Odell Jones	.10	.05	.01
☐ 408	Joe Zdeb	.10	.05	.01
☐ 409	Ron Schueler	.10	.05	.01
☐ 410	Bill Madlock	.50	.23	.06
☐ 411	AL Champs Yankees rally to defeat Royals	.50	.23	.06
☐ 412	NL Champs Dodgers overpower Phillies in four	.50	.23	.06
☐ 413	World Series Reggie and Yankees reign supreme	4.00	1.80	.50
☐ 414	Darold Knowles DP	.10	.05	.01
☐ 415	Ray Fosse	.10	.05	.01
☐ 416	Jack Brohamer	.10	.05	.01
☐ 417	Mike Garman DP	.10	.05	.01
☐ 418	Tony Muser	.10	.05	.01
☐ 419	Jerry Garvin	.10	.05	.01
☐ 420	Greg Luzinski	.30	.14	.04
☐ 421	Junior Moore	.10	.05	.01
☐ 422	Steve Braun	.10	.05	.01
☐ 423	Dave Rosello	.10	.05	.01
☐ 424	Boston Red Sox Team Card (Checklist back)	.75	.35	.09
☐ 425	Steve Rogers DP	.10	.05	.01
☐ 426	Fred Kendall	.10	.05	.01
☐ 427	Mario Soto	.40	.18	.05
☐ 428	Joel Youngblood	.10	.05	.01
☐ 429	Mike Barlow	.10	.05	.01
☐ 430	Al Oliver	.50	.23	.06
☐ 431	Butch Metzger	.10	.05	.01
☐ 432	Terry Bulling	.10	.05	.01
☐ 433	Fernando Gonzalez	.10	.05	.01
☐ 434	Mike Norris	.10	.05	.01
☐ 435	Checklist 4	1.00	.45	.13
☐ 436	Vic Harris DP	.10	.05	.01
☐ 437	Bo McLaughlin	.10	.05	.01
☐ 438	John Ellis	.10	.05	.01
☐ 439	Ken Kravec	.10	.05	.01
☐ 440	Dave Lopes	.30	.14	.04
☐ 441	Larry Gura	.10	.05	.01
☐ 442	Elliott Maddox	.10	.05	.01
☐ 443	Darrel Chaney	.10	.05	.01
☐ 444	Roy Hartsfield MG	.10	.05	.01
☐ 445	Mike Ivie	.10	.05	.01
☐ 446	Tug McGraw	.30	.14	.04
☐ 447	Leroy Stanton	.10	.05	.01
☐ 448	Bill Castro	.10	.05	.01
☐ 449	Tim Blackwell DP	.10	.05	.01
☐ 450	Tom Seaver	8.00	3.60	1.00
☐ 451	Minnesota Twins Team Card (Checklist back)	.75	.35	.09
☐ 452	Jerry Mumphrey	.10	.05	.01
☐ 453	Doug Flynn	.10	.05	.01
☐ 454	Dave LaRoche	.10	.05	.01
☐ 455	Bill Robinson	.20	.09	.03
☐ 456	Vern Ruhle	.10	.05	.01
☐ 457	Bob Bailey	.10	.05	.01
☐ 458	Jeff Newman	.10	.05	.01
☐ 459	Charlie Spikes	.10	.05	.01
☐ 460	Jim Hunter	2.50	1.15	.30
☐ 461	Rob Andrews DP	.10	.05	.01
☐ 462	Rogelio Moret	.10	.05	.01
☐ 463	Kevin Bell	.10	.05	.01
☐ 464	Jerry Grote	.10	.05	.01
☐ 465	Hal McRae	.30	.14	.04
☐ 466	Dennis Blair	.10	.05	.01
☐ 467	Alvin Dark MG	.20	.09	.03
☐ 468	Warren Cromartie	.40	.18	.05
☐ 469	Rick Cerone	.20	.09	.03
☐ 470	J.R. Richard	.20	.09	.03
☐ 471	Roy Smalley	.20	.09	.03
☐ 472	Ron Reed	.10	.05	.01
☐ 473	Bill Buckner	.40	.18	.05
☐ 474	Jim Slaton	.10	.05	.01
☐ 475	Gary Matthews	.20	.09	.03
☐ 476	Bill Stein	.10	.05	.01
☐ 477	Doug Capilla	.10	.05	.01
☐ 478	Jerry Remy	.10	.05	.01
☐ 479	St. Louis Cardinals Team Card (Checklist back)	.75	.35	.09
☐ 480	Ron LeFlore	.20	.09	.03
☐ 481	Jackson Todd	.10	.05	.01
☐ 482	Rick Miller	.10	.05	.01
☐ 483	Ken Macha	.10	.05	.01
☐ 484	Jim Norris	.10	.05	.01
☐ 485	Chris Chambliss	.20	.09	.03
☐ 486	John Curtis	.10	.05	.01
☐ 487	Jim Tyrone	.10	.05	.01
☐ 488	Dan Spillner	.10	.05	.01
☐ 489	Rudy Meoli	.10	.05	.01
☐ 490	Amos Otis	.20	.09	.03
☐ 491	Scott McGregor	.20	.09	.03
☐ 492	Jim Sundberg	.20	.09	.03
☐ 493	Steve Renko	.10	.05	.01
☐ 494	Chuck Tanner MG	.20	.09	.03
☐ 495	Dave Cash	.10	.05	.01
☐ 496	Jim Clancy DP	.20	.09	.03
☐ 497	Glenn Adams	.10	.05	.01
☐ 498	Joe Sambito	.10	.05	.01
☐ 499	Seattle Mariners Team Card (Checklist back)	.75	.35	.09
☐ 500	George Foster	.90	.40	.11
☐ 501	Dave Roberts	.10	.05	.01
☐ 502	Pat Rockett	.10	.05	.01
☐ 503	Ike Hampton	.10	.05	.01
☐ 504	Roger Freed	.10	.05	.01
☐ 505	Felix Millan	.10	.05	.01
☐ 506	Ron Blomberg	.10	.05	.01
☐ 507	Willie Crawford	.10	.05	.01
☐ 508	Johnny Oates	.10	.05	.01
☐ 509	Brent Strom	.10	.05	.01
☐ 510	Willie Stargell	3.00	1.35	.40
☐ 511	Frank Duffy	.10	.05	.01
☐ 512	Larry Herndon	.10	.05	.01
☐ 513	Barry Foote	.10	.05	.01
☐ 514	Rob Sperring	.10	.05	.01
☐ 515	Tim Corcoran	.10	.05	.01
☐ 516	Gary Beare	.10	.05	.01
☐ 517	Andres Mora	.10	.05	.01
☐ 518	Tommy Boggs DP	.10	.05	.01
☐ 519	Brian Downing	.60	.25	.08
☐ 520	Larry Hisle	.10	.05	.01
☐ 521	Steve Staggs	.10	.05	.01
☐ 522	Dick Williams MG	.20	.09	.03
☐ 523	Donnie Moore	.10	.05	.01
☐ 524	Bernie Carbo	.10	.05	.01
☐ 525	Jerry Terrell	.10	.05	.01
☐ 526	Cincinnati Reds Team Card (Checklist back)	.75	.35	.09
☐ 527	Vic Correll	.10	.05	.01
☐ 528	Rob Picciolo	.10	.05	.01
☐ 529	Paul Hartzell	.10	.05	.01
☐ 530	Dave Winfield	14.00	6.25	1.75
☐ 531	Tom Underwood	.10	.05	.01
☐ 532	Skip Jutze	.10	.05	.01
☐ 533	Sandy Alomar	.20	.09	.03
☐ 534	Wilbur Howard	.10	.05	.01
☐ 535	Checklist 5	1.00	.45	.13
☐ 536	Roric Harrison	.10	.05	.01
☐ 537	Bruce Bochte	.10	.05	.01
☐ 538	Johnny LeMaster	.10	.05	.01
☐ 539	Vic Davalillo DP	.10	.05	.01
☐ 540	Steve Carlton	6.00	2.70	.75
☐ 541	Larry Cox	.10	.05	.01
☐ 542	Tim Johnson	.10	.05	.01
☐ 543	Larry Harlow DP	.10	.05	.01
☐ 544	Len Randle DP	.10	.05	.01
☐ 545	Bill Campbell	.10	.05	.01
☐ 546	Ted Martinez	.10	.05	.01
☐ 547	John Scott	.10	.05	.01
☐ 548	Billy Hunter MG DP	.10	.05	.01
☐ 549	Joe Kerrigan	.10	.05	.01
☐ 550	John Mayberry	.20	.09	.03
☐ 551	Atlanta Braves Team Card (Checklist back)	.75	.35	.09
☐ 552	Francisco Barrios	.10	.05	.01
☐ 553	Terry Puhl	.40	.18	.05
☐ 554	Joe Coleman	.10	.05	.01
☐ 555	Butch Wynegar	.10	.05	.01

☐ 556 Ed Armbrister .10 .05 .01
☐ 557 Tony Solaita .10 .05 .01
☐ 558 Paul Mitchell .10 .05 .01
☐ 559 Phil Mankowski .10 .05 .01
☐ 560 Dave Parker 3.00 1.35 .40
☐ 561 Charlie Williams .10 .05 .01
☐ 562 Glenn Burke .10 .05 .01
☐ 563 Dave Rader .10 .05 .01
☐ 564 Mick Kelleher .10 .05 .01
☐ 565 Jerry Koosman .30 .14 .04
☐ 566 Merv Rettenmund .10 .05 .01
☐ 567 Dick Drago .10 .05 .01
☐ 568 Tom Hutton .10 .05 .01
☐ 569 Lary Sorensen .10 .05 .01
☐ 570 Dave Kingman .50 .23 .06
☐ 571 Buck Martinez .10 .05 .01
☐ 572 Rick Wise .10 .05 .01
☐ 573 Luis Gomez .10 .05 .01
☐ 574 Bob Lemon MG .40 .18 .05
☐ 575 Pat Dobson .10 .05 .01
☐ 576 Sam Mejias .10 .05 .01
☐ 577 Oakland A's .75 .35 .09
Team Card
(Checklist back)
☐ 578 Buzz Capra .10 .05 .01
☐ 579 Rance Mulliniks .10 .05 .01
☐ 580 Rod Carew 6.00 2.70 .75
☐ 581 Lynn McGlothen .10 .05 .01
☐ 582 Fran Healy .10 .05 .01
☐ 583 George Medich .10 .05 .01
☐ 584 John Hale .10 .05 .01
☐ 585 Woodie Fryman DP .10 .05 .01
☐ 586 Ed Goodson .10 .05 .01
☐ 587 John Urrea .10 .05 .01
☐ 588 Jim Mason .10 .05 .01
☐ 589 Bob Knepper .50 .23 .06
☐ 590 Bobby Murcer .30 .14 .04
☐ 591 George Zeber .10 .05 .01
☐ 592 Bob Apodaca .10 .05 .01
☐ 593 Dave Skaggs .10 .05 .01
☐ 594 Dave Freisleben .10 .05 .01
☐ 595 Sixto Lezcano .10 .05 .01
☐ 596 Gary Wheelock .10 .05 .01
☐ 597 Steve Dillard .10 .05 .01
☐ 598 Eddie Solomon .10 .05 .01
☐ 599 Gary Woods .10 .05 .01
☐ 600 Frank Tanana .40 .18 .05
☐ 601 Gene Mauch MG .20 .09 .03
☐ 602 Eric Soderholm .10 .05 .01
☐ 603 Will McEnaney .10 .05 .01
☐ 604 Earl Williams .10 .05 .01
☐ 605 Rick Rhoden .20 .09 .03
☐ 606 Pittsburgh Pirates .75 .35 .09
Team Card
(Checklist back)
☐ 607 Fernando Arroyo .10 .05 .01
☐ 608 Johnny Grubb .10 .05 .01
☐ 609 John Denny .10 .05 .01
☐ 610 Garry Maddox .20 .09 .03
☐ 611 Pat Scanlon .10 .05 .01
☐ 612 Ken Henderson .10 .05 .01
☐ 613 Marty Perez .10 .05 .01
☐ 614 Joe Wallis .10 .05 .01
☐ 615 Clay Carroll .10 .05 .01
☐ 616 Pat Kelly .10 .05 .01
☐ 617 Joe Nolan .10 .05 .01
☐ 618 Tommy Helms .10 .05 .01
☐ 619 Thad Bosley DP .10 .05 .01
☐ 620 Willie Randolph 1.00 .45 .13
☐ 621 Craig Swan DP .10 .05 .01
☐ 622 Champ Summers .10 .05 .01
☐ 623 Eduardo Rodriguez .10 .05 .01
☐ 624 Gary Alexander DP .10 .05 .01
☐ 625 Jose Cruz .20 .09 .03
☐ 626 Toronto Blue Jays .40 .18 .05
Team Card DP
(Checklist back)
☐ 627 David Johnson .10 .05 .01
☐ 628 Ralph Garr .10 .05 .01
☐ 629 Don Stanhouse .10 .05 .01
☐ 630 Ron Cey .40 .18 .05
☐ 631 Danny Ozark MG .10 .05 .01
☐ 632 Rowland Office .10 .05 .01
☐ 633 Tom Veryzer .10 .05 .01
☐ 634 Len Barker .10 .05 .01
☐ 635 Joe Rudi .20 .09 .03
☐ 636 Jim Bibby .10 .05 .01
☐ 637 Duffy Dyer .10 .05 .01
☐ 638 Paul Splittorff .10 .05 .01
☐ 639 Gene Clines .10 .05 .01
☐ 640 Lee May DP .10 .05 .01
☐ 641 Doug Rau .10 .05 .01
☐ 642 Denny Doyle .10 .05 .01
☐ 643 Tom House .10 .05 .01
☐ 644 Jim Dwyer .10 .05 .01
☐ 645 Mike Torrez .20 .09 .03
☐ 646 Rick Auerbach DP .10 .05 .01
☐ 647 Steve Dunning .10 .05 .01
☐ 648 Gary Thomasson .10 .05 .01
☐ 649 Moose Haas .10 .05 .01
☐ 650 Cesar Cedeno .20 .09 .03
☐ 651 Doug Rader .10 .05 .01
☐ 652 Checklist 6 1.00 .45 .13
☐ 653 Ron Hodges DP .10 .05 .01
☐ 654 Pepe Frias .10 .05 .01
☐ 655 Lyman Bostock .20 .09 .03
☐ 656 Dave Garcia MG .10 .05 .01
☐ 657 Bombo Rivera .10 .05 .01
☐ 658 Manny Sanguillen .20 .09 .03
☐ 659 Texas Rangers .75 .35 .09
Team Card
(Checklist back)
☐ 660 Jason Thompson .20 .09 .03
☐ 661 Grant Jackson .10 .05 .01
☐ 662 Paul Dade .10 .05 .01
☐ 663 Paul Reuschel .10 .05 .01
☐ 664 Fred Stanley .10 .05 .01
☐ 665 Dennis Leonard .20 .09 .03
☐ 666 Billy Smith .10 .05 .01
☐ 667 Jeff Byrd .10 .05 .01
☐ 668 Dusty Baker .30 .14 .04
☐ 669 Pete Falcone .10 .05 .01
☐ 670 Jim Rice 3.00 1.35 .40
☐ 671 Gary Lavelle .10 .05 .01
☐ 672 Don Kessinger .20 .09 .03
☐ 673 Steve Brye .10 .05 .01
☐ 674 Ray Knight 2.00 .90 .25
☐ 675 Jay Johnstone .30 .14 .04
☐ 676 Bob Myrick .10 .05 .01
☐ 677 Ed Herrmann .10 .05 .01
☐ 678 Tom Burgmeier .10 .05 .01
☐ 679 Wayne Garrett .10 .05 .01
☐ 680 Vida Blue .30 .14 .04
☐ 681 Rob Belloir .10 .05 .01
☐ 682 Ken Brett .10 .05 .01
☐ 683 Mike Champion .10 .05 .01
☐ 684 Ralph Houk MG .20 .09 .03
☐ 685 Frank Taveras .10 .05 .01
☐ 686 Gaylord Perry 2.50 1.15 .30
☐ 687 Julio Cruz .10 .05 .01
☐ 688 George Mitterwald .10 .05 .01
☐ 689 Cleveland Indians .75 .35 .09
Team Card
(Checklist back)
☐ 690 Mickey Rivers .20 .09 .03
☐ 691 Ross Grimsley .10 .05 .01
☐ 692 Ken Reitz .10 .05 .01
☐ 693 Lamar Johnson .10 .05 .01
☐ 694 Elias Sosa .10 .05 .01
☐ 695 Dwight Evans 2.00 .90 .25
☐ 696 Steve Mingori .10 .05 .01
☐ 697 Roger Metzger .10 .05 .01
☐ 698 Juan Bernhardt .10 .05 .01
☐ 699 Jackie Brown .10 .05 .01
☐ 700 Johnny Bench 5.00 2.30 .60
☐ 701 Rookie Pitchers .30 .14 .04
Tom Hume
Larry Landreth
Steve McCatty
Bruce Taylor
☐ 702 Rookie Catchers .30 .14 .04
Bill Nahorodny
Kevin Pasley
Rick Sweet
Don Werner
☐ 703 Rookie Pitchers DP 18.00 8.00 2.30
Larry Andersen
Tim Jones
Mickey Mahler
Jack Morris
☐ 704 Rookie 2nd Basemen 20.00 9.00 2.50
Garth Iorg
Dave Oliver
Sam Perlozzo
Lou Whitaker
☐ 705 Rookie Outfielders .50 .23 .06
Dave Bergman
Miguel Dilone
Clint Hurdle
Willie Norwood
☐ 706 Rookie 1st Basemen .30 .14 .04
Wayne Cage
Ted Cox
Pat Putnam
Dave Revering
☐ 707 Rookie Shortstops 50.00 23.00 6.25

Mickey Klutts Paul Molitor Alan Trammell U.L. Washington			
☐ 708 Rookie Catchers	16.00	7.25	2.00
Bo Diaz Dale Murphy Lance Parrish Ernie Whitt			
☐ 709 Rookie Pitchers	.30	.14	.04
Steve Burke Matt Keough Lance Rautzhan Dan Schatzeder			
☐ 710 Rookie Outfielders	.60	.25	.08
Dell Alston Rick Bosetti Mike Easler Keith Smith			
☐ 711 Rookie Pitchers DP	.30	.14	.04
Cardell Camper Dennis Lamp Craig Mitchell Roy Thomas			
☐ 712 Bobby Valentine	.20	.09	.03
☐ 713 Bob Davis	.10	.05	.01
☐ 714 Mike Anderson	.10	.05	.01
☐ 715 Jim Kaat	.75	.35	.09
☐ 716 Clarence Gaston	.20	.09	.03
☐ 717 Nelson Briles	.10	.05	.01
☐ 718 Ron Jackson	.10	.05	.01
☐ 719 Randy Elliott	.10	.05	.01
☐ 720 Fergie Jenkins	2.50	1.15	.30
☐ 721 Billy Martin MG	.60	.25	.08
☐ 722 Pete Broberg	.10	.05	.01
☐ 723 John Wockenfuss	.10	.05	.01
☐ 724 Kansas City Royals	.75	.35	.09
Team Card (Checklist back)			
☐ 725 Kurt Bevacqua	.10	.05	.01
☐ 726 Wilbur Wood	.30	.14	.04

1979 Topps

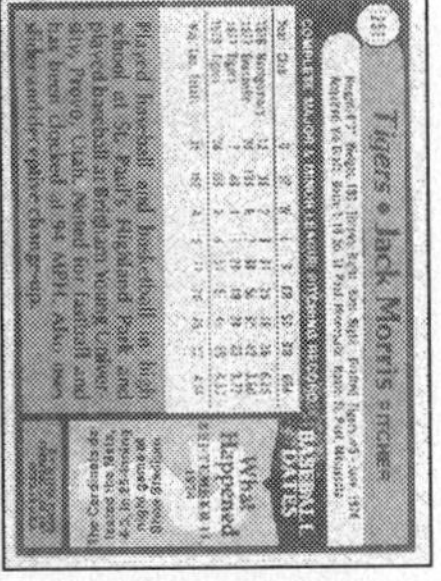

The cards in this 726-card set measure 2 1/2" by 3 1/2". Topps continued with the same number of cards as in 1978. Various series spotlight League Leaders (1-8), "Season and Career Record Holders" (411-418), "Record Breakers of 1978" (201-206), and one "Prospects" card for each team (701-726). Team cards feature a checklist on back of that team's players in the set and a small picture of the manager on the front of the card. There are 66 cards that were double printed and these are noted in the checklist by the abbreviation DP. Bump Wills (369) was initially depicted in a Ranger uniform but with a Blue Jays affiliation; later printings correctly labeled him with Texas. The set price listed does not include the scarcer Wills (Rangers) card. The key Rookie Cards in this set are Pedro Guerrero, Carney Lansford, Ozzie Smith, and Bob Welch. Cards numbered 23 or lower, which feature Phillies or Yankees and do not follow the numbering checklisted below, are not necessarily error cards. They are undoubtedly Burger King cards, separate sets for each team each with its own pricing and mass distribution. Burger King cards are indistinguishable from the corresponding Topps cards except for the card numbering difference and the fact that Burger King cards do not have a printing sheet designation (such as A through F like the regular Topps) anywhere on the card back in very small print.

	NRMT-MT	EXC	G-VG
COMPLETE SET (726)	250.00	115.00	31.00
COMMON PLAYER (1-726)	.15	.07	.02
COMMON PLAYER DP	.08	.04	.01
☐ 1 Batting Leaders	3.00	.60	.18
Rod Carew Dave Parker			
☐ 2 Home Run Leaders	.35	.16	.04
Jim Rice George Foster			
☐ 3 RBI Leaders	.35	.16	.04
Jim Rice George Foster			
☐ 4 Stolen Base Leaders	.35	.16	.04
Ron LeFlore Omar Moreno			
☐ 5 Victory Leaders	.35	.16	.04
Ron Guidry Gaylord Perry			
☐ 6 Strikeout Leaders	4.00	1.80	.50
Nolan Ryan J.R. Richard			
☐ 7 ERA Leaders	.35	.16	.04
Ron Guidry Craig Swan			
☐ 8 Leading Firemen	.50	.23	.06
Rich Gossage Rollie Fingers			
☐ 9 Dave Campbell	.08	.04	.01
☐ 10 Lee May	.18	.08	.02
☐ 11 Marc Hill	.08	.04	.01
☐ 12 Dick Drago	.08	.04	.01
☐ 13 Paul Dade	.08	.04	.01
☐ 14 Rafael Landestoy	.08	.04	.01
☐ 15 Ross Grimsley	.08	.04	.01
☐ 16 Fred Stanley	.08	.04	.01
☐ 17 Donnie Moore	.08	.04	.01
☐ 18 Tony Solaita	.08	.04	.01
☐ 19 Larry Gura DP	.08	.04	.01
☐ 20 Joe Morgan DP	1.25	.55	.16
☐ 21 Kevin Kobel	.08	.04	.01
☐ 22 Mike Jorgensen	.08	.04	.01
☐ 23 Terry Forster	.08	.04	.01
☐ 24 Paul Molitor	14.00	6.25	1.75
☐ 25 Steve Carlton	4.00	1.80	.50
☐ 26 Jamie Quirk	.08	.04	.01
☐ 27 Dave Goltz	.08	.04	.01
☐ 28 Steve Brye	.08	.04	.01
☐ 29 Rick Langford	.08	.04	.01
☐ 30 Dave Winfield	10.00	4.50	1.25
☐ 31 Tom House DP	.08	.04	.01
☐ 32 Jerry Mumphrey	.08	.04	.01
☐ 33 Dave Rozema	.08	.04	.01
☐ 34 Rob Andrews	.08	.04	.01
☐ 35 Ed Figueroa	.08	.04	.01
☐ 36 Alan Ashby	.08	.04	.01
☐ 37 Joe Kerrigan DP	.08	.04	.01
☐ 38 Bernie Carbo	.08	.04	.01
☐ 39 Dale Murphy	7.50	3.40	.95
☐ 40 Dennis Eckersley	7.50	3.40	.95
☐ 41 Twins Team/Mgr.	.60	.25	.08
Gene Mauch (Checklist back)			
☐ 42 Ron Blomberg	.08	.04	.01
☐ 43 Wayne Twitchell	.08	.04	.01
☐ 44 Kurt Bevacqua	.08	.04	.01
☐ 45 Al Hrabosky	.08	.04	.01
☐ 46 Ron Hodges	.08	.04	.01
☐ 47 Fred Norman	.08	.04	.01
☐ 48 Merv Rettenmund	.08	.04	.01
☐ 49 Vern Ruhle	.08	.04	.01
☐ 50 Steve Garvey DP	1.50	.65	.19
☐ 51 Ray Fosse DP	.08	.04	.01
☐ 52 Randy Lerch	.08	.04	.01
☐ 53 Mick Kelleher	.08	.04	.01
☐ 54 Dell Alston DP	.08	.04	.01
☐ 55 Willie Stargell	2.50	1.15	.30
☐ 56 John Hale	.08	.04	.01
☐ 57 Eric Rasmussen	.08	.04	.01
☐ 58 Bob Randall DP	.08	.04	.01
☐ 59 John Denny DP	.08	.04	.01
☐ 60 Mickey Rivers	.18	.08	.02
☐ 61 Bo Diaz	.08	.04	.01
☐ 62 Randy Moffitt	.08	.04	.01

☐ 63 Jack Brohamer .08 .04 .01
☐ 64 Tom Underwood .08 .04 .01
☐ 65 Mark Belanger .18 .08 .02
☐ 66 Tigers Team/Mgr. .60 .25 .08
Les Moss
(Checklist back)
☐ 67 Jim Mason DP .08 .04 .01
☐ 68 Joe Niekro DP .08 .04 .01
☐ 69 Elliott Maddox .08 .04 .01
☐ 70 John Candelaria .18 .08 .02
☐ 71 Brian Downing .50 .23 .06
☐ 72 Steve Mingori .08 .04 .01
☐ 73 Ken Henderson .08 .04 .01
☐ 74 Shane Rawley .35 .16 .04
☐ 75 Steve Yeager .18 .08 .02
☐ 76 Warren Cromartie .18 .08 .02
☐ 77 Dan Briggs DP .08 .04 .01
☐ 78 Elias Sosa .08 .04 .01
☐ 79 Ted Cox .08 .04 .01
☐ 80 Jason Thompson .18 .08 .02
☐ 81 Roger Erickson .08 .04 .01
☐ 82 Mets Team/Mgr. .60 .25 .08
Joe Torre
(Checklist back)
☐ 83 Fred Kendall .08 .04 .01
☐ 84 Greg Minton .08 .04 .01
☐ 85 Gary Matthews .18 .08 .02
☐ 86 Rodney Scott .08 .04 .01
☐ 87 Pete Falcone .08 .04 .01
☐ 88 Bob Molinaro .08 .04 .01
☐ 89 Dick Tidrow .08 .04 .01
☐ 90 Bob Boone .50 .23 .06
☐ 91 Terry Crowley .08 .04 .01
☐ 92 Jim Bibby .08 .04 .01
☐ 93 Phil Mankowski .08 .04 .01
☐ 94 Len Barker .08 .04 .01
☐ 95 Robin Yount 15.00 6.75 1.90
☐ 96 Indians Team/Mgr. .60 .25 .08
Jeff Torborg
(Checklist back)
☐ 97 Sam Mejias .08 .04 .01
☐ 98 Ray Burris .08 .04 .01
☐ 99 John Wathan .18 .08 .02
☐ 100 Tom Seaver DP 3.75 1.70 .45
☐ 101 Roy Howell .08 .04 .01
☐ 102 Mike Anderson .08 .04 .01
☐ 103 Jim Todd .08 .04 .01
☐ 104 Johnny Oates DP .08 .04 .01
☐ 105 Rick Camp DP .08 .04 .01
☐ 106 Frank Duffy .08 .04 .01
☐ 107 Jesus Alou DP .08 .04 .01
☐ 108 Eduardo Rodriguez .08 .04 .01
☐ 109 Joel Youngblood .08 .04 .01
☐ 110 Vida Blue .18 .08 .02
☐ 111 Roger Freed .08 .04 .01
☐ 112 Phillies Team/Mgr. .60 .25 .08
Danny Ozark
(Checklist back)
☐ 113 Pete Redfern .08 .04 .01
☐ 114 Cliff Johnson .08 .04 .01
☐ 115 Nolan Ryan 27.00 12.00 3.40
☐ 116 Ozzie Smith 75.00 34.00 9.50
☐ 117 Grant Jackson .08 .04 .01
☐ 118 Bud Harrelson .08 .04 .01
☐ 119 Don Stanhouse .08 .04 .01
☐ 120 Jim Sundberg .18 .08 .02
☐ 121 Checklist 1 DP .30 .03 .01
☐ 122 Mike Paxton .08 .04 .01
☐ 123 Lou Whitaker 8.00 3.60 1.00
☐ 124 Dan Schatzeder .08 .04 .01
☐ 125 Rick Burleson .08 .04 .01
☐ 126 Doug Bair .08 .04 .01
☐ 127 Thad Bosley .08 .04 .01
☐ 128 Ted Martinez .08 .04 .01
☐ 129 Marty Pattin DP .08 .04 .01
☐ 130 Bob Watson DP .08 .04 .01
☐ 131 Jim Clancy .08 .04 .01
☐ 132 Rowland Office .08 .04 .01
☐ 133 Bill Castro .08 .04 .01
☐ 134 Alan Bannister .08 .04 .01
☐ 135 Bobby Murcer .18 .08 .02
☐ 136 Jim Kaat .75 .35 .09
☐ 137 Larry Wolfe DP .08 .04 .01
☐ 138 Mark Lee .08 .04 .01
☐ 139 Luis Pujols .08 .04 .01
☐ 140 Don Gullett .18 .08 .02
☐ 141 Tom Paciorek .18 .08 .02
☐ 142 Charlie Williams .08 .04 .01
☐ 143 Tony Scott .08 .04 .01
☐ 144 Sandy Alomar .18 .08 .02
☐ 145 Rick Rhoden .08 .04 .01
☐ 146 Duane Kuiper .08 .04 .01
☐ 147 Dave Hamilton .08 .04 .01
☐ 148 Bruce Boisclair .08 .04 .01
☐ 149 Manny Sarmiento .08 .04 .01
☐ 150 Wayne Cage .08 .04 .01
☐ 151 John Hiller .08 .04 .01
☐ 152 Rick Cerone .08 .04 .01
☐ 153 Dennis Lamp .08 .04 .01
☐ 154 Jim Gantner DP .30 .14 .04
☐ 155 Dwight Evans 1.50 .65 .19
☐ 156 Buddy Solomon .08 .04 .01
☐ 157 U.L. Washington UER .08 .04 .01
(Sic, bats left,
should be right)
☐ 158 Joe Sambito .08 .04 .01
☐ 159 Roy White .18 .08 .02
☐ 160 Mike Flanagan .30 .14 .04
☐ 161 Barry Foote .08 .04 .01
☐ 162 Tom Johnson .08 .04 .01
☐ 163 Glenn Burke .08 .04 .01
☐ 164 Mickey Lolich .18 .08 .02
☐ 165 Frank Taveras .08 .04 .01
☐ 166 Leon Roberts .08 .04 .01
☐ 167 Roger Metzger DP .08 .04 .01
☐ 168 Dave Freisleben .08 .04 .01
☐ 169 Bill Nahorodny .08 .04 .01
☐ 170 Don Sutton 1.50 .65 .19
☐ 171 Gene Clines .08 .04 .01
☐ 172 Mike Bruhert .08 .04 .01
☐ 173 John Lowenstein .08 .04 .01
☐ 174 Rick Auerbach .08 .04 .01
☐ 175 George Hendrick .18 .08 .02
☐ 176 Aurelio Rodriguez .08 .04 .01
☐ 177 Ron Reed .08 .04 .01
☐ 178 Alvis Woods .08 .04 .01
☐ 179 Jim Beattie DP .08 .04 .01
☐ 180 Larry Hisle .08 .04 .01
☐ 181 Mike Garman .08 .04 .01
☐ 182 Tim Johnson .08 .04 .01
☐ 183 Paul Splittorff .08 .04 .01
☐ 184 Darrel Chaney .08 .04 .01
☐ 185 Mike Torrez .18 .08 .02
☐ 186 Eric Soderholm .08 .04 .01
☐ 187 Mark Lemongello .08 .04 .01
☐ 188 Pat Kelly .08 .04 .01
☐ 189 Eddie Whitson .75 .35 .09
☐ 190 Ron Cey .40 .18 .05
☐ 191 Mike Norris .08 .04 .01
☐ 192 Cardinals Team/Mgr. .60 .25 .08
Ken Boyer
(Checklist back)
☐ 193 Glenn Adams .08 .04 .01
☐ 194 Randy Jones .08 .04 .01
☐ 195 Bill Madlock .40 .18 .05
☐ 196 Steve Kemp DP .08 .04 .01
☐ 197 Bob Apodaca .08 .04 .01
☐ 198 Johnny Grubb .08 .04 .01
☐ 199 Larry Milbourne .08 .04 .01
☐ 200 Johnny Bench DP 3.00 1.35 .40
☐ 201 RB: Mike Edwards .20 .09 .03
Most unassisted DP's,
second basemen
☐ 202 RB: Ron Guidry, Most .30 .14 .04
strikeouts, lefthander,
nine inning game
☐ 203 RB: J.R. Richard .20 .09 .03
Most strikeouts,
season, righthander
☐ 204 RB: Pete Rose 1.75 .80 .22
Most consecutive
games batting safely
☐ 205 RB: John Stearns .20 .09 .03
Most SB's by
catcher, season
☐ 206 RB: Sammy Stewart .20 .09 .03
7 straight SO's,
first ML game
☐ 207 Dave Lemanczyk .08 .04 .01
☐ 208 Clarence Gaston .18 .08 .02
☐ 209 Reggie Cleveland .08 .04 .01
☐ 210 Larry Bowa .18 .08 .02
☐ 211 Denny Martinez 1.50 .65 .19
☐ 212 Carney Lansford 5.00 2.30 .60
☐ 213 Bill Travers .08 .04 .01
☐ 214 Red Sox Team/Mgr. .60 .25 .08
Don Zimmer
(Checklist back)
☐ 215 Willie McCovey 2.50 1.15 .30
☐ 216 Wilbur Wood .08 .04 .01
☐ 217 Steve Dillard .08 .04 .01
☐ 218 Dennis Leonard .18 .08 .02
☐ 219 Roy Smalley .18 .08 .02
☐ 220 Cesar Geronimo .08 .04 .01
☐ 221 Jesse Jefferson .08 .04 .01
☐ 222 Bob Beall .08 .04 .01

☐ 223 Kent Tekulve .... .18 .08 .02
☐ 224 Dave Revering .... .08 .04 .01
☐ 225 Rich Gossage .... 1.00 .45 .13
☐ 226 Ron Pruitt .... .08 .04 .01
☐ 227 Steve Stone .... .18 .08 .02
☐ 228 Vic Davalillo .... .08 .04 .01
☐ 229 Doug Flynn .... .08 .04 .01
☐ 230 Bob Forsch .... .08 .04 .01
☐ 231 John Wockenfuss .... .08 .04 .01
☐ 232 Jimmy Sexton .... .08 .04 .01
☐ 233 Paul Mitchell .... .08 .04 .01
☐ 234 Toby Harrah .... .18 .08 .02
☐ 235 Steve Rogers .... .08 .04 .01
☐ 236 Jim Dwyer .... .08 .04 .01
☐ 237 Billy Smith .... .08 .04 .01
☐ 238 Balor Moore .... .08 .04 .01
☐ 239 Willie Horton .... .18 .08 .02
☐ 240 Rick Reuschel .... .18 .08 .02
☐ 241 Checklist 2 DP .... .30 .03 .01
☐ 242 Pablo Torrealba .... .08 .04 .01
☐ 243 Buck Martinez DP .... .08 .04 .01
☐ 244 Pirates Team/Mgr. .... .60 .25 .08
Chuck Tanner
(Checklist back)
☐ 245 Jeff Burroughs .... .08 .04 .01
☐ 246 Darrell Jackson .... .08 .04 .01
☐ 247 Tucker Ashford DP .... .08 .04 .01
☐ 248 Pete LaCock .... .08 .04 .01
☐ 249 Paul Thormodsgard .... .08 .04 .01
☐ 250 Willie Randolph .... .75 .35 .09
☐ 251 Jack Morris 8.00 3.60 1.00
☐ 252 Bob Stinson .... .08 .04 .01
☐ 253 Rick Wise .... .08 .04 .01
☐ 254 Luis Gomez .... .08 .04 .01
☐ 255 Tommy John .... 1.00 .45 .13
☐ 256 Mike Sadek .... .08 .04 .01
☐ 257 Adrian Devine .... .08 .04 .01
☐ 258 Mike Phillips .... .08 .04 .01
☐ 259 Reds Team/Mgr. .... .60 .25 .08
Sparky Anderson
(Checklist back)
☐ 260 Richie Zisk .... .08 .04 .01
☐ 261 Mario Guerrero .... .08 .04 .01
☐ 262 Nelson Briles .... .08 .04 .01
☐ 263 Oscar Gamble .... .18 .08 .02
☐ 264 Don Robinson .... .60 .25 .08
☐ 265 Don Money .... .08 .04 .01
☐ 266 Jim Willoughby .... .08 .04 .01
☐ 267 Joe Rudi .... .18 .08 .02
☐ 268 Julio Gonzalez .... .08 .04 .01
☐ 269 Woodie Fryman .... .08 .04 .01
☐ 270 Butch Hobson .... .18 .08 .02
☐ 271 Rawly Eastwick .... .08 .04 .01
☐ 272 Tim Corcoran .... .08 .04 .01
☐ 273 Jerry Terrell .... .08 .04 .01
☐ 274 Willie Norwood .... .08 .04 .01
☐ 275 Junior Moore .... .08 .04 .01
☐ 276 Jim Colborn .... .08 .04 .01
☐ 277 Tom Grieve .... .18 .08 .02
☐ 278 Andy Messersmith .... .18 .08 .02
☐ 279 Jerry Grote DP .... .08 .04 .01
☐ 280 Andre Thornton .... .18 .08 .02
☐ 281 Vic Correll DP .... .08 .04 .01
☐ 282 Blue Jays Team/Mgr. .... .60 .25 .08
Roy Hartsfield
(Checklist back)
☐ 283 Ken Kravec .... .08 .04 .01
☐ 284 Johnnie LeMaster .... .08 .04 .01
☐ 285 Bobby Bonds .... .40 .18 .05
☐ 286 Duffy Dyer .... .08 .04 .01
☐ 287 Andres Mora .... .08 .04 .01
☐ 288 Milt Wilcox .... .08 .04 .01
☐ 289 Jose Cruz .... .18 .08 .02
☐ 290 Dave Lopes .... .18 .08 .02
☐ 291 Tom Griffin .... .08 .04 .01
☐ 292 Don Reynolds .... .08 .04 .01
☐ 293 Jerry Garvin .... .08 .04 .01
☐ 294 Pepe Frias .... .08 .04 .01
☐ 295 Mitchell Page .... .08 .04 .01
☐ 296 Preston Hanna .... .08 .04 .01
☐ 297 Ted Sizemore .... .08 .04 .01
☐ 298 Rich Gale .... .08 .04 .01
☐ 299 Steve Ontiveros .... .08 .04 .01
☐ 300 Rod Carew .... 4.00 1.80 .50
☐ 301 Tom Hume .... .08 .04 .01
☐ 302 Braves Team/Mgr. .... .60 .25 .08
Bobby Cox
(Checklist back)
☐ 303 Lary Sorensen DP .... .08 .04 .01
☐ 304 Steve Swisher .... .08 .04 .01
☐ 305 Willie Montanez .... .08 .04 .01
☐ 306 Floyd Bannister .... .08 .04 .01
☐ 307 Larvell Blanks .... .08 .04 .01
☐ 308 Bert Blyleven .... 1.00 .45 .13
☐ 309 Ralph Garr .... .08 .04 .01
☐ 310 Thurman Munson .... 3.50 1.55 .45
☐ 311 Gary Lavelle .... .08 .04 .01
☐ 312 Bob Robertson .... .08 .04 .01
☐ 313 Dyar Miller .... .08 .04 .01
☐ 314 Larry Harlow .... .08 .04 .01
☐ 315 Jon Matlack .... .08 .04 .01
☐ 316 Milt May .... .08 .04 .01
☐ 317 Jose Cardenal .... .08 .04 .01
☐ 318 Bob Welch .... 6.00 2.70 .75
☐ 319 Wayne Garrett .... .08 .04 .01
☐ 320 Carl Yastrzemski .... 3.50 1.55 .45
☐ 321 Gaylord Perry .... 2.50 1.15 .30
☐ 322 Danny Goodwin .... .08 .04 .01
☐ 323 Lynn McGlothen .... .08 .04 .01
☐ 324 Mike Tyson .... .08 .04 .01
☐ 325 Cecil Cooper .... .35 .16 .04
☐ 326 Pedro Borbon .... .08 .04 .01
☐ 327 Art Howe DP .... .08 .04 .01
☐ 328 Oakland A's Team/Mgr. .... .60 .25 .08
Jack McKeon
(Checklist back)
☐ 329 Joe Coleman .... .08 .04 .01
☐ 330 George Brett 15.00 6.75 1.90
☐ 331 Mickey Mahler .... .08 .04 .01
☐ 332 Gary Alexander .... .08 .04 .01
☐ 333 Chet Lemon .... .18 .08 .02
☐ 334 Craig Swan .... .08 .04 .01
☐ 335 Chris Chambliss .... .18 .08 .02
☐ 336 Bobby Thompson .... .08 .04 .01
☐ 337 John Montague .... .08 .04 .01
☐ 338 Vic Harris .... .08 .04 .01
☐ 339 Ron Jackson .... .08 .04 .01
☐ 340 Jim Palmer .... 3.50 1.55 .45
☐ 341 Willie Upshaw .... .18 .08 .02
☐ 342 Dave Roberts .... .08 .04 .01
☐ 343 Ed Glynn .... .08 .04 .01
☐ 344 Jerry Royster .... .08 .04 .01
☐ 345 Tug McGraw .... .28 .13 .04
☐ 346 Bill Buckner .... .28 .13 .04
☐ 347 Doug Rau .... .08 .04 .01
☐ 348 Andre Dawson 15.00 6.75 1.90
☐ 349 Jim Wright .... .08 .04 .01
☐ 350 Garry Templeton .... .18 .08 .02
☐ 351 Wayne Nordhagen DP .... .08 .04 .01
☐ 352 Steve Renko .... .08 .04 .01
☐ 353 Checklist 3 .... .75 .08 .02
☐ 354 Bill Bonham .... .08 .04 .01
☐ 355 Lee Mazzilli .... .08 .04 .01
☐ 356 Giants Team/Mgr. .... .60 .25 .08
Joe Altobelli
(Checklist back)
☐ 357 Jerry Augustine .... .08 .04 .01
☐ 358 Alan Trammell 9.00 4.00 1.15
☐ 359 Dan Spillner DP .... .08 .04 .01
☐ 360 Amos Otis .... .18 .08 .02
☐ 361 Tom Dixon .... .08 .04 .01
☐ 362 Mike Cubbage .... .08 .04 .01
☐ 363 Craig Skok .... .08 .04 .01
☐ 364 Gene Richards .... .08 .04 .01
☐ 365 Sparky Lyle .... .28 .13 .04
☐ 366 Juan Bernhardt .... .08 .04 .01
☐ 367 Dave Skaggs .... .08 .04 .01
☐ 368 Don Aase .... .08 .04 .01
☐ 369A Bump Wills ERR .... 3.00 1.35 .40
(Blue Jays)
☐ 369B Bump Wills COR .... 3.00 1.35 .40
(Rangers)
☐ 370 Dave Kingman .... .40 .18 .05
☐ 371 Jeff Holly .... .08 .04 .01
☐ 372 Lamar Johnson .... .08 .04 .01
☐ 373 Lance Rautzhan .... .08 .04 .01
☐ 374 Ed Herrmann .... .08 .04 .01
☐ 375 Bill Campbell .... .08 .04 .01
☐ 376 Gorman Thomas .... .18 .08 .02
☐ 377 Paul Moskau .... .08 .04 .01
☐ 378 Rob Picciolo DP .... .08 .04 .01
☐ 379 Dale Murray .... .08 .04 .01
☐ 380 John Mayberry .... .18 .08 .02
☐ 381 Astros Team/Mgr. .... .60 .25 .08
Bill Virdon
(Checklist back)
☐ 382 Jerry Martin .... .08 .04 .01
☐ 383 Phil Garner .... .18 .08 .02
☐ 384 Tommy Boggs .... .08 .04 .01
☐ 385 Dan Ford .... .08 .04 .01
☐ 386 Francisco Barrios .... .08 .04 .01
☐ 387 Gary Thomasson .... .08 .04 .01
☐ 388 Jack Billingham .... .08 .04 .01
☐ 389 Joe Zdeb .... .08 .04 .01
☐ 390 Rollie Fingers .... 2.00 .90 .25
☐ 391 Al Oliver .... .35 .16 .04

No.	Card			
392	Doug Ault	.08	.04	.01
393	Scott McGregor	.18	.08	.02
394	Randy Stein	.08	.04	.01
395	Dave Cash	.08	.04	.01
396	Bill Plummer	.08	.04	.01
397	Sergio Ferrer	.08	.04	.01
398	Ivan DeJesus	.08	.04	.01
399	David Clyde	.08	.04	.01
400	Jim Rice	2.00	.90	.25
401	Ray Knight	.50	.23	.06
402	Paul Hartzell	.08	.04	.01
403	Tim Foli	.08	.04	.01
404	White Sox Team/Mgr Don Kessinger (Checklist back)	.60	.25	.08
405	Butch Wynegar DP	.08	.04	.01
406	Joe Wallis DP	.08	.04	.01
407	Pete Vuckovich	.18	.08	.02
408	Charlie Moore DP	.08	.04	.01
409	Willie Wilson	2.75	1.25	.35
410	Darrell Evans	.28	.13	.04
411	Hits Record Season: George Sisler Career: Ty Cobb	.50	.23	.06
412	RBI Record Season: Hack Wilson Career: Hank Aaron	.50	.23	.06
413	Home Run Record Season: Roger Maris Career: Hank Aaron	1.00	.45	.13
414	Batting Record Season: Rogers Hornsby Career: Ty Cobb	.50	.23	.06
415	Steals Record Season: Lou Brock Career: Lou Brock	.50	.23	.06
416	Wins Record Season: Jack Chesbro Career: Cy Young	.25	.11	.03
417	Strikeout Record DP Season: Nolan Ryan Career: Walter Johnson	1.50	.65	.19
418	ERA Record DP Season: Dutch Leonard Career: Walter Johnson	.12	.05	.02
419	Dick Ruthven	.08	.04	.01
420	Ken Griffey	1.00	.45	.13
421	Doug DeCinces	.18	.08	.02
422	Ruppert Jones	.08	.04	.01
423	Bob Montgomery	.08	.04	.01
424	Angels Team/Mgr. Jim Fregosi (Checklist back)	.60	.25	.08
425	Rick Manning	.08	.04	.01
426	Chris Speier	.08	.04	.01
427	Andy Replogle	.08	.04	.01
428	Bobby Valentine	.18	.08	.02
429	John Urrea DP	.08	.04	.01
430	Dave Parker	2.00	.90	.25
431	Glenn Borgmann	.08	.04	.01
432	Dave Heaverlo	.08	.04	.01
433	Larry Biittner	.08	.04	.01
434	Ken Clay	.08	.04	.01
435	Gene Tenace	.18	.08	.02
436	Hector Cruz	.08	.04	.01
437	Rick Williams	.08	.04	.01
438	Horace Speed	.08	.04	.01
439	Frank White	.18	.08	.02
440	Rusty Staub	.28	.13	.04
441	Lee Lacy	.08	.04	.01
442	Doyle Alexander	.08	.04	.01
443	Bruce Bochte	.08	.04	.01
444	Aurelio Lopez	.08	.04	.01
445	Steve Henderson	.08	.04	.01
446	Jim Lonborg	.08	.04	.01
447	Manny Sanguillen	.18	.08	.02
448	Moose Haas	.08	.04	.01
449	Bombo Rivera	.08	.04	.01
450	Dave Concepcion	.75	.35	.09
451	Royals Team/Mgr. Whitey Herzog (Checklist back)	.60	.25	.08
452	Jerry Morales	.08	.04	.01
453	Chris Knapp	.08	.04	.01
454	Len Randle	.08	.04	.01
455	Bill Lee DP	.08	.04	.01
456	Chuck Baker	.08	.04	.01
457	Bruce Sutter	1.25	.55	.16
458	Jim Essian	.08	.04	.01
459	Sid Monge	.08	.04	.01
460	Graig Nettles	.50	.23	.06
461	Jim Barr DP	.08	.04	.01
462	Otto Velez	.08	.04	.01
463	Steve Comer	.08	.04	.01
464	Joe Nolan	.08	.04	.01
465	Reggie Smith	.18	.08	.02
466	Mark Littell	.08	.04	.01
467	Don Kessinger DP	.08	.04	.01
468	Stan Bahnsen DP	.08	.04	.01
469	Lance Parrish	2.50	1.15	.30
470	Garry Maddox DP	.08	.04	.01
471	Joaquin Andujar	.18	.08	.02
472	Craig Kusick	.08	.04	.01
473	Dave Roberts	.08	.04	.01
474	Dick Davis	.08	.04	.01
475	Dan Driessen	.08	.04	.01
476	Tom Poquette	.08	.04	.01
477	Bob Grich	.18	.08	.02
478	Juan Beniquez	.08	.04	.01
479	Padres Team/Mgr. Roger Craig (Checklist back)	.60	.25	.08
480	Fred Lynn	.75	.35	.09
481	Skip Lockwood	.08	.04	.01
482	Craig Reynolds	.08	.04	.01
483	Checklist 4 DP	.30	.03	.01
484	Rick Waits	.08	.04	.01
485	Bucky Dent	.18	.08	.02
486	Bob Knepper	.08	.04	.01
487	Miguel Dilone	.08	.04	.01
488	Bob Owchinko	.08	.04	.01
489	Larry Cox UER (Photo actually Dave Rader)	.08	.04	.01
490	Al Cowens	.08	.04	.01
491	Tippy Martinez	.18	.08	.02
492	Bob Bailor	.08	.04	.01
493	Larry Christenson	.08	.04	.01
494	Jerry White	.08	.04	.01
495	Tony Perez	1.00	.45	.13
496	Barry Bonnell DP	.08	.04	.01
497	Glenn Abbott	.08	.04	.01
498	Rich Chiles	.08	.04	.01
499	Rangers Team/Mgr. Pat Corrales (Checklist back)	.60	.25	.08
500	Ron Guidry	.75	.35	.09
501	Junior Kennedy	.08	.04	.01
502	Steve Braun	.08	.04	.01
503	Terry Humphrey	.08	.04	.01
504	Larry McWilliams	.08	.04	.01
505	Ed Kranepool	.08	.04	.01
506	John D'Acquisto	.08	.04	.01
507	Tony Armas	.08	.04	.01
508	Charlie Hough	.18	.08	.02
509	Mario Mendoza UER (Career BA .278, should say .204)	.08	.04	.01
510	Ted Simmons	.75	.35	.09
511	Paul Reuschel DP	.08	.04	.01
512	Jack Clark	1.25	.55	.16
513	Dave Johnson	.08	.04	.01
514	Mike Proly	.08	.04	.01
515	Enos Cabell	.08	.04	.01
516	Champ Summers DP	.08	.04	.01
517	Al Bumbry	.08	.04	.01
518	Jim Umbarger	.08	.04	.01
519	Ben Oglivie	.18	.08	.02
520	Gary Carter	4.00	1.80	.50
521	Sam Ewing	.08	.04	.01
522	Ken Holtzman	.08	.04	.01
523	John Milner	.08	.04	.01
524	Tom Burgmeier	.08	.04	.01
525	Freddie Patek	.08	.04	.01
526	Dodgers Team/Mgr. Tom Lasorda (Checklist back)	.60	.25	.08
527	Lerrin LaGrow	.08	.04	.01
528	Wayne Gross DP	.08	.04	.01
529	Brian Asselstine	.08	.04	.01
530	Frank Tanana	.40	.18	.05
531	Fernando Gonzalez	.08	.04	.01
532	Buddy Schultz	.08	.04	.01
533	Leroy Stanton	.08	.04	.01
534	Ken Forsch	.08	.04	.01
535	Ellis Valentine	.08	.04	.01
536	Jerry Reuss	.18	.08	.02
537	Tom Veryzer	.08	.04	.01
538	Mike Ivie DP	.08	.04	.01
539	John Ellis	.08	.04	.01
540	Greg Luzinski	.28	.13	.04
541	Jim Slaton	.08	.04	.01
542	Rick Bosetti	.08	.04	.01
543	Kiko Garcia	.08	.04	.01
544	Fergie Jenkins	1.50	.65	.19
545	John Stearns	.08	.04	.01

☐ 546 Bill Russell	.18	.08	.02
☐ 547 Clint Hurdle	.08	.04	.01
☐ 548 Enrique Romo	.08	.04	.01
☐ 549 Bob Bailey	.08	.04	.01
☐ 550 Sal Bando	.18	.08	.02
☐ 551 Cubs Team/Mgr. Herman Franks (Checklist back)	.60	.25	.08
☐ 552 Jose Morales	.08	.04	.01
☐ 553 Denny Walling	.08	.04	.01
☐ 554 Matt Keough	.08	.04	.01
☐ 555 Biff Pocoroba	.08	.04	.01
☐ 556 Mike Lum	.08	.04	.01
☐ 557 Ken Brett	.08	.04	.01
☐ 558 Jay Johnstone	.18	.08	.02
☐ 559 Greg Pryor	.08	.04	.01
☐ 560 John Montefusco	.08	.04	.01
☐ 561 Ed Ott	.08	.04	.01
☐ 562 Dusty Baker	.28	.13	.04
☐ 563 Roy Thomas	.08	.04	.01
☐ 564 Jerry Turner	.08	.04	.01
☐ 565 Rico Carty	.18	.08	.02
☐ 566 Nino Espinosa	.08	.04	.01
☐ 567 Richie Hebner	.08	.04	.01
☐ 568 Carlos Lopez	.08	.04	.01
☐ 569 Bob Sykes	.08	.04	.01
☐ 570 Cesar Cedeno	.18	.08	.02
☐ 571 Darrell Porter	.08	.04	.01
☐ 572 Rod Gilbreath	.08	.04	.01
☐ 573 Jim Kern	.08	.04	.01
☐ 574 Claudell Washington	.18	.08	.02
☐ 575 Luis Tiant	.18	.08	.02
☐ 576 Mike Parrott	.08	.04	.01
☐ 577 Brewers Team/Mgr. George Bamberger (Checklist back)	.60	.25	.08
☐ 578 Pete Broberg	.08	.04	.01
☐ 579 Greg Gross	.08	.04	.01
☐ 580 Ron Fairly	.08	.04	.01
☐ 581 Darold Knowles	.08	.04	.01
☐ 582 Paul Blair	.18	.08	.02
☐ 583 Julio Cruz	.08	.04	.01
☐ 584 Jim Rooker	.08	.04	.01
☐ 585 Hal McRae	.18	.08	.02
☐ 586 Bob Horner	1.00	.45	.13
☐ 587 Ken Reitz	.08	.04	.01
☐ 588 Tom Murphy	.08	.04	.01
☐ 589 Terry Whitfield	.08	.04	.01
☐ 590 J.R. Richard	.18	.08	.02
☐ 591 Mike Hargrove	.18	.08	.02
☐ 592 Mike Krukow	.08	.04	.01
☐ 593 Rick Dempsey	.18	.08	.02
☐ 594 Bob Shirley	.08	.04	.01
☐ 595 Phil Niekro	1.50	.65	.19
☐ 596 Jim Wohlford	.08	.04	.01
☐ 597 Bob Stanley	.08	.04	.01
☐ 598 Mark Wagner	.08	.04	.01
☐ 599 Jim Spencer	.08	.04	.01
☐ 600 George Foster	.60	.25	.08
☐ 601 Dave LaRoche	.08	.04	.01
☐ 602 Checklist 5	.75	.08	.02
☐ 603 Rudy May	.08	.04	.01
☐ 604 Jeff Newman	.08	.04	.01
☐ 605 Rick Monday DP	.08	.04	.01
☐ 606 Expos Team/Mgr. Dick Williams (Checklist back)	.60	.25	.08
☐ 607 Omar Moreno	.18	.08	.02
☐ 608 Dave McKay	.08	.04	.01
☐ 609 Silvio Martinez	.08	.04	.01
☐ 610 Mike Schmidt	10.00	4.50	1.25
☐ 611 Jim Norris	.08	.04	.01
☐ 612 Rick Honeycutt	.60	.25	.08
☐ 613 Mike Edwards	.08	.04	.01
☐ 614 Willie Hernandez	.18	.08	.02
☐ 615 Ken Singleton	.18	.08	.02
☐ 616 Billy Almon	.08	.04	.01
☐ 617 Terry Puhl	.18	.08	.02
☐ 618 Jerry Remy	.08	.04	.01
☐ 619 Ken Landreaux	.18	.08	.02
☐ 620 Bert Campaneris	.18	.08	.02
☐ 621 Pat Zachry	.08	.04	.01
☐ 622 Dave Collins	.18	.08	.02
☐ 623 Bob McClure	.08	.04	.01
☐ 624 Larry Herndon	.08	.04	.01
☐ 625 Mark Fidrych	.30	.14	.04
☐ 626 Yankees Team/Mgr. Bob Lemon (Checklist back)	.60	.25	.08
☐ 627 Gary Serum	.08	.04	.01
☐ 628 Del Unser	.08	.04	.01
☐ 629 Gene Garber	.08	.04	.01
☐ 630 Bake McBride	.18	.08	.02
☐ 631 Jorge Orta	.08	.04	.01
☐ 632 Don Kirkwood	.08	.04	.01
☐ 633 Rob Wilfong DP	.08	.04	.01
☐ 634 Paul Lindblad	.08	.04	.01
☐ 635 Don Baylor	1.00	.45	.13
☐ 636 Wayne Garland	.08	.04	.01
☐ 637 Bill Robinson	.18	.08	.02
☐ 638 Al Fitzmorris	.08	.04	.01
☐ 639 Manny Trillo	.08	.04	.01
☐ 640 Eddie Murray	25.00	11.50	3.10
☐ 641 Bobby Castillo	.08	.04	.01
☐ 642 Wilbur Howard DP	.08	.04	.01
☐ 643 Tom Hausman	.08	.04	.01
☐ 644 Manny Mota	.18	.08	.02
☐ 645 George Scott DP	.08	.04	.01
☐ 646 Rick Sweet	.08	.04	.01
☐ 647 Bob Lacey	.08	.04	.01
☐ 648 Lou Piniella	.35	.16	.04
☐ 649 John Curtis	.08	.04	.01
☐ 650 Pete Rose	5.00	2.30	.60
☐ 651 Mike Caldwell	.08	.04	.01
☐ 652 Stan Papi	.08	.04	.01
☐ 653 Warren Brusstar DP	.08	.04	.01
☐ 654 Rick Miller	.08	.04	.01
☐ 655 Jerry Koosman	.18	.08	.02
☐ 656 Hosken Powell	.08	.04	.01
☐ 657 George Medich	.08	.04	.01
☐ 658 Taylor Duncan	.08	.04	.01
☐ 659 Mariners Team/Mgr. Darrell Johnson (Checklist back)	.60	.25	.08
☐ 660 Ron LeFlore DP	.08	.04	.01
☐ 661 Bruce Kison	.08	.04	.01
☐ 662 Kevin Bell	.08	.04	.01
☐ 663 Mike Vail	.08	.04	.01
☐ 664 Doug Bird	.08	.04	.01
☐ 665 Lou Brock	3.00	1.35	.40
☐ 666 Rich Dauer	.08	.04	.01
☐ 667 Don Hood	.08	.04	.01
☐ 668 Bill North	.08	.04	.01
☐ 669 Checklist 6	.75	.08	.02
☐ 670 Jim Hunter DP	.75	.35	.09
☐ 671 Joe Ferguson DP	.08	.04	.01
☐ 672 Ed Halicki	.08	.04	.01
☐ 673 Tom Hutton	.08	.04	.01
☐ 674 Dave Tomlin	.08	.04	.01
☐ 675 Tim McCarver	.35	.16	.04
☐ 676 Johnny Sutton	.08	.04	.01
☐ 677 Larry Parrish	.18	.08	.02
☐ 678 Geoff Zahn	.08	.04	.01
☐ 679 Derrel Thomas	.08	.04	.01
☐ 680 Carlton Fisk	6.00	2.70	.75
☐ 681 John Henry Johnson	.08	.04	.01
☐ 682 Dave Chalk	.08	.04	.01
☐ 683 Dan Meyer DP	.08	.04	.01
☐ 684 Jamie Easterly DP	.08	.04	.01
☐ 685 Sixto Lezcano	.08	.04	.01
☐ 686 Ron Schueler DP	.08	.04	.01
☐ 687 Rennie Stennett	.08	.04	.01
☐ 688 Mike Willis	.08	.04	.01
☐ 689 Orioles Team/Mgr. Earl Weaver (Checklist back)	.60	.25	.08
☐ 690 Buddy Bell DP	.08	.04	.01
☐ 691 Dock Ellis DP	.08	.04	.01
☐ 692 Mickey Stanley	.08	.04	.01
☐ 693 Dave Rader	.08	.04	.01
☐ 694 Burt Hooton	.18	.08	.02
☐ 695 Keith Hernandez	1.50	.65	.19
☐ 696 Andy Hassler	.08	.04	.01
☐ 697 Dave Bergman	.08	.04	.01
☐ 698 Bill Stein	.08	.04	.01
☐ 699 Hal Dues	.08	.04	.01
☐ 700 Reggie Jackson DP	3.75	1.70	.45
☐ 701 Orioles Prospects Mark Corey John Flinn Sammy Stewart	.20	.09	.03
☐ 702 Red Sox Prospects Joel Finch Garry Hancock Allen Ripley	.20	.09	.03
☐ 703 Angels Prospects Jim Anderson Dave Frost Bob Slater	.20	.09	.03
☐ 704 White Sox Prospects Ross Baumgarten Mike Colbern Mike Squires	.20	.09	.03
☐ 705 Indians Prospects Alfredo Griffin Tim Norrid	.60	.25	.08

Dave Oliver			
☐ 706 Tigers Prospects	.20	.09	.03
Dave Stegman			
Dave Tobik			
Kip Young			
☐ 707 Royals Prospects	.20	.09	.03
Randy Bass			
Jim Gaudet			
Randy McGilberry			
☐ 708 Brewers Prospects	1.00	.45	.13
Kevin Bass			
Eddie Romero			
Ned Yost			
☐ 709 Twins Prospects	.20	.09	.03
Sam Perlozzo			
Rick Sofield			
Kevin Stanfield			
☐ 710 Yankees Prospects	.30	.14	.04
Brian Doyle			
Mike Heath			
Dave Rajsich			
☐ 711 A's Prospects	.30	.14	.04
Dwayne Murphy			
Bruce Robinson			
Alan Wirth			
☐ 712 Mariners Prospects	.20	.09	.03
Bud Anderson			
Greg Biercevicz			
Byron McLaughlin			
☐ 713 Rangers Prospects	.60	.25	.08
Danny Darwin			
Pat Putnam			
Billy Sample			
☐ 714 Blue Jays Prospects	.20	.09	.03
Victor Cruz			
Pat Kelly			
Ernie Whitt			
☐ 715 Braves Prospects	.20	.09	.03
Bruce Benedict			
Glenn Hubbard			
Larry Whisenton			
☐ 716 Cubs Prospects	.20	.09	.03
Dave Geisel			
Karl Pagel			
Scot Thompson			
☐ 717 Reds Prospects	.35	.16	.04
Mike LaCoss			
Ron Oester			
Harry Spilman			
☐ 718 Astros Prospects	.20	.09	.03
Bruce Bochy			
Mike Fischlin			
Don Pisker			
☐ 719 Dodgers Prospects	6.00	2.70	.75
Pedro Guerrero			
Rudy Law			
Joe Simpson			
☐ 720 Expos Prospects	1.50	.65	.19
Jerry Fry			
Jerry Pirtle			
Scott Sanderson			
☐ 721 Mets Prospects	.30	.14	.04
Juan Berenguer			
Dwight Bernard			
Dan Norman			
☐ 722 Phillies Prospects	1.25	.55	.16
Jim Morrison			
Lonnie Smith			
Jim Wright			
☐ 723 Pirates Prospects	.20	.09	.03
Dale Berra			
Eugenio Cotes			
Ben Wiltbank			
☐ 724 Cardinals Prospects	.60	.25	.08
Tom Bruno			
George Frazier			
Terry Kennedy			
☐ 725 Padres Prospects	.20	.09	.03
Jim Beswick			
Steve Mura			
Broderick Perkins			
☐ 726 Giants Prospects	.30	.14	.04
Greg Johnston			
Joe Strain			
John Tamargo			

1980 Topps

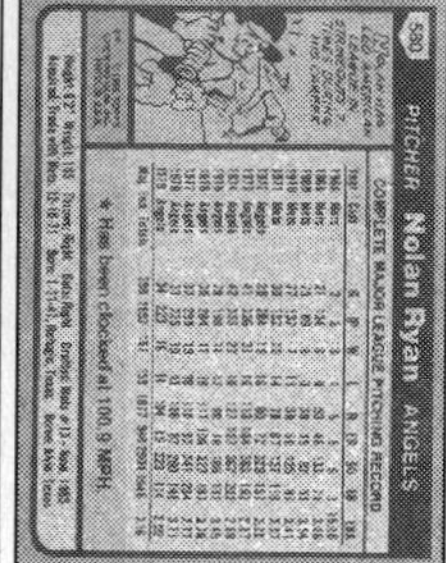

The cards in this 726-card set measure 2 1/2" by 3 1/2". In 1980 Topps released another set of the same size and number of cards as the previous two years. As with those sets, Topps again has produced 66 double-printed cards in the set; they are noted by DP in the checklist below. The player's name appears over the picture and his position and team are found in pennant design. Every card carries a facsimile autograph. Team cards feature a team checklist of players in the set on the back and the manager's name on the front. Cards 1-6 show Highlights (HL) of the 1979 season, cards 201-207 are League Leaders, and cards 661-686 feature American and National League rookie "Future Stars," one card for each team showing three young prospects. The key Rookie Card in this set is Rickey Henderson; other noteworthy rookies included are Dave Stieb and Rick Sutcliffe.

	NRMT-MT	EXC	G-VG
COMPLETE SET (726)	275.00	125.00	34.00
COMMON PLAYER (1-726)	.15	.07	.02
COMMON PLAYER DP	.08	.04	.01
☐ 1 HL: Lou Brock and Carl Yastrzemski Enter 3000 hit circle	2.50	.50	.15
☐ 2 HL: Willie McCovey, 512th homer sets new mark for NL lefties	1.00	.45	.13
☐ 3 HL: Manny Mota, All-time pinch-hits, 145	.25	.11	.03
☐ 4 HL: Pete Rose, Career Record 10th season with 200 or more hits	2.00	.90	.25
☐ 5 HL: Garry Templeton, First with 100 hits from each side of plate	.25	.11	.03
☐ 6 HL: Del Unser, 3rd cons. pinch homer sets new ML standard	.25	.11	.03
☐ 7 Mike Lum	.08	.04	.01
☐ 8 Craig Swan	.08	.04	.01
☐ 9 Steve Braun	.08	.04	.01
☐ 10 Dennis Martinez	.75	.35	.09
☐ 11 Jimmy Sexton	.08	.04	.01
☐ 12 John Curtis DP	.08	.04	.01
☐ 13 Ron Pruitt	.08	.04	.01
☐ 14 Dave Cash	.08	.04	.01
☐ 15 Bill Campbell	.08	.04	.01
☐ 16 Jerry Narron	.08	.04	.01
☐ 17 Bruce Sutter	.75	.35	.09
☐ 18 Ron Jackson	.08	.04	.01
☐ 19 Balor Moore	.08	.04	.01
☐ 20 Dan Ford	.08	.04	.01
☐ 21 Manny Sarmiento	.08	.04	.01
☐ 22 Pat Putnam	.08	.04	.01
☐ 23 Derrel Thomas	.08	.04	.01
☐ 24 Jim Slaton	.08	.04	.01
☐ 25 Lee Mazzilli	.08	.04	.01
☐ 26 Marty Pattin	.08	.04	.01
☐ 27 Del Unser	.08	.04	.01
☐ 28 Bruce Kison	.08	.04	.01
☐ 29 Mark Wagner	.08	.04	.01
☐ 30 Vida Blue	.18	.08	.02
☐ 31 Jay Johnstone	.18	.08	.02

☐ 32 Julio Cruz DP .08 .04 .01
☐ 33 Tony Scott .08 .04 .01
☐ 34 Jeff Newman DP .08 .04 .01
☐ 35 Luis Tiant .18 .08 .02
☐ 36 Rusty Torres .08 .04 .01
☐ 37 Kiko Garcia .08 .04 .01
☐ 38 Dan Spillner DP .08 .04 .01
☐ 39 Rowland Office .08 .04 .01
☐ 40 Carlton Fisk 5.00 2.30 .60
☐ 41 Rangers Team/Mgr. .50 .23 .06
Pat Corrales
(Checklist back)
☐ 42 David Palmer .18 .08 .02
☐ 43 Bombo Rivera .08 .04 .01
☐ 44 Bill Fahey .08 .04 .01
☐ 45 Frank White .18 .08 .02
☐ 46 Rico Carty .18 .08 .02
☐ 47 Bill Bonham DP .08 .04 .01
☐ 48 Rick Miller .08 .04 .01
☐ 49 Mario Guerrero .08 .04 .01
☐ 50 J.R. Richard .18 .08 .02
☐ 51 Joe Ferguson DP .08 .04 .01
☐ 52 Warren Brusstar .08 .04 .01
☐ 53 Ben Oglivie .18 .08 .02
☐ 54 Dennis Lamp .08 .04 .01
☐ 55 Bill Madlock .40 .18 .05
☐ 56 Bobby Valentine .18 .08 .02
☐ 57 Pete Vuckovich .18 .08 .02
☐ 58 Doug Flynn .08 .04 .01
☐ 59 Eddy Putman .08 .04 .01
☐ 60 Bucky Dent .18 .08 .02
☐ 61 Gary Serum .08 .04 .01
☐ 62 Mike Ivie .08 .04 .01
☐ 63 Bob Stanley .08 .04 .01
☐ 64 Joe Nolan .08 .04 .01
☐ 65 Al Bumbry .08 .04 .01
☐ 66 Royals Team/Mgr. .50 .23 .06
Jim Frey
(Checklist back)
☐ 67 Doyle Alexander .08 .04 .01
☐ 68 Larry Harlow .08 .04 .01
☐ 69 Rick Williams .08 .04 .01
☐ 70 Gary Carter 3.00 1.35 .40
☐ 71 John Milner DP .08 .04 .01
☐ 72 Fred Howard DP .08 .04 .01
☐ 73 Dave Collins .08 .04 .01
☐ 74 Sid Monge .08 .04 .01
☐ 75 Bill Russell .18 .08 .02
☐ 76 John Stearns .08 .04 .01
☐ 77 Dave Stieb 3.50 1.55 .45
☐ 78 Ruppert Jones .08 .04 .01
☐ 79 Bob Owchinko .08 .04 .01
☐ 80 Ron LeFlore .18 .08 .02
☐ 81 Ted Sizemore .08 .04 .01
☐ 82 Astros Team/Mgr. .50 .23 .06
Bill Virdon
(Checklist back)
☐ 83 Steve Trout .08 .04 .01
☐ 84 Gary Lavelle .08 .04 .01
☐ 85 Ted Simmons .60 .25 .08
☐ 86 Dave Hamilton .08 .04 .01
☐ 87 Pepe Frias .08 .04 .01
☐ 88 Ken Landreaux .08 .04 .01
☐ 89 Don Hood .08 .04 .01
☐ 90 Manny Trillo .08 .04 .01
☐ 91 Rick Dempsey .18 .08 .02
☐ 92 Rick Rhoden .08 .04 .01
☐ 93 Dave Roberts DP .08 .04 .01
☐ 94 Neil Allen .20 .09 .03
☐ 95 Cecil Cooper .20 .09 .03
☐ 96 A's Team/Mgr. .50 .23 .06
Jim Marshall
(Checklist back)
☐ 97 Bill Lee .08 .04 .01
☐ 98 Jerry Terrell .08 .04 .01
☐ 99 Victor Cruz .08 .04 .01
☐ 100 Johnny Bench 4.50 2.00 .55
☐ 101 Aurelio Lopez .08 .04 .01
☐ 102 Rich Dauer .08 .04 .01
☐ 103 Bill Caudill .08 .04 .01
☐ 104 Manny Mota .18 .08 .02
☐ 105 Frank Tanana .25 .11 .03
☐ 106 Jeff Leonard .40 .18 .05
☐ 107 Francisco Barrios .08 .04 .01
☐ 108 Bob Horner .18 .08 .02
☐ 109 Bill Travers .08 .04 .01
☐ 110 Fred Lynn DP .25 .11 .03
☐ 111 Bob Knepper .08 .04 .01
☐ 112 White Sox Team/Mgr. .50 .23 .06
Tony LaRussa
(Checklist back)
☐ 113 Geoff Zahn .08 .04 .01
☐ 114 Juan Beniquez .08 .04 .01
☐ 115 Sparky Lyle .18 .08 .02
☐ 116 Larry Cox .08 .04 .01
☐ 117 Dock Ellis .08 .04 .01
☐ 118 Phil Garner .18 .08 .02
☐ 119 Sammy Stewart .08 .04 .01
☐ 120 Greg Luzinski .28 .13 .04
☐ 121 Checklist 1 .60 .25 .08
☐ 122 Dave Rosello DP .08 .04 .01
☐ 123 Lynn Jones .08 .04 .01
☐ 124 Dave Lemanczyk .08 .04 .01
☐ 125 Tony Perez 1.00 .45 .13
☐ 126 Dave Tomlin .08 .04 .01
☐ 127 Gary Thomasson .08 .04 .01
☐ 128 Tom Burgmeier .08 .04 .01
☐ 129 Craig Reynolds .08 .04 .01
☐ 130 Amos Otis .18 .08 .02
☐ 131 Paul Mitchell .08 .04 .01
☐ 132 Biff Pocoroba .08 .04 .01
☐ 133 Jerry Turner .08 .04 .01
☐ 134 Matt Keough .08 .04 .01
☐ 135 Bill Buckner .18 .08 .02
☐ 136 Dick Ruthven .08 .04 .01
☐ 137 John Castino .08 .04 .01
☐ 138 Ross Baumgarten .08 .04 .01
☐ 139 Dane Iorg .08 .04 .01
☐ 140 Rich Gossage .75 .35 .09
☐ 141 Gary Alexander .08 .04 .01
☐ 142 Phil Huffman .08 .04 .01
☐ 143 Bruce Bochte DP .08 .04 .01
☐ 144 Steve Comer .08 .04 .01
☐ 145 Darrell Evans .18 .08 .02
☐ 146 Bob Welch .75 .35 .09
☐ 147 Terry Puhl .08 .04 .01
☐ 148 Manny Sanguillen .18 .08 .02
☐ 149 Tom Hume .08 .04 .01
☐ 150 Jason Thompson .18 .08 .02
☐ 151 Tom Hausman DP .08 .04 .01
☐ 152 John Fulgham .08 .04 .01
☐ 153 Tim Blackwell .08 .04 .01
☐ 154 Lary Sorensen .08 .04 .01
☐ 155 Jerry Remy .08 .04 .01
☐ 156 Tony Brizzolara .08 .04 .01
☐ 157 Willie Wilson DP .35 .16 .04
☐ 158 Rob Picciolo DP .08 .04 .01
☐ 159 Ken Clay .08 .04 .01
☐ 160 Eddie Murray 12.50 5.75 1.55
☐ 161 Larry Christenson .08 .04 .01
☐ 162 Bob Randall .08 .04 .01
☐ 163 Steve Swisher .08 .04 .01
☐ 164 Greg Pryor .08 .04 .01
☐ 165 Omar Moreno .08 .04 .01
☐ 166 Glenn Abbott .08 .04 .01
☐ 167 Jack Clark 1.00 .45 .13
☐ 168 Rick Waits .08 .04 .01
☐ 169 Luis Gomez .08 .04 .01
☐ 170 Burt Hooton .18 .08 .02
☐ 171 Fernando Gonzalez .08 .04 .01
☐ 172 Ron Hodges .08 .04 .01
☐ 173 John Henry Johnson .08 .04 .01
☐ 174 Ray Knight .18 .08 .02
☐ 175 Rick Reuschel .18 .08 .02
☐ 176 Champ Summers .08 .04 .01
☐ 177 Dave Heaverlo .08 .04 .01
☐ 178 Tim McCarver .30 .14 .04
☐ 179 Ron Davis .08 .04 .01
☐ 180 Warren Cromartie .08 .04 .01
☐ 181 Moose Haas .08 .04 .01
☐ 182 Ken Reitz .08 .04 .01
☐ 183 Jim Anderson DP .08 .04 .01
☐ 184 Steve Renko DP .08 .04 .01
☐ 185 Hal McRae .18 .08 .02
☐ 186 Junior Moore .08 .04 .01
☐ 187 Alan Ashby .08 .04 .01
☐ 188 Terry Crowley .08 .04 .01
☐ 189 Kevin Kobel .08 .04 .01
☐ 190 Buddy Bell .18 .08 .02
☐ 191 Ted Martinez .08 .04 .01
☐ 192 Braves Team/Mgr. .50 .23 .06
Bobby Cox
(Checklist back)
☐ 193 Dave Goltz .08 .04 .01
☐ 194 Mike Easler .08 .04 .01
☐ 195 John Montefusco .08 .04 .01
☐ 196 Lance Parrish .90 .40 .11
☐ 197 Byron McLaughlin .08 .04 .01
☐ 198 Dell Alston DP .08 .04 .01
☐ 199 Mike LaCoss .08 .04 .01
☐ 200 Jim Rice 1.00 .45 .13
☐ 201 Batting Leaders .30 .14 .04
Keith Hernandez
Fred Lynn
☐ 202 Home Run Leaders .30 .14 .04
Dave Kingman

	Gorman Thomas			
☐ 203	RBI Leaders	1.00	.45	.13
	Dave Winfield			
	Don Baylor			
☐ 204	Stolen Base Leaders	.30	.14	.04
	Omar Moreno			
	Willie Wilson			
☐ 205	Victory Leaders	.30	.14	.04
	Joe Niekro			
	Phil Niekro			
	Mike Flanagan			
☐ 206	Strikeout Leaders	3.00	1.35	.40
	J.R. Richard			
	Nolan Ryan			
☐ 207	ERA Leaders	.30	.14	.04
	J.R. Richard			
	Ron Guidry			
☐ 208	Wayne Cage	.08	.04	.01
☐ 209	Von Joshua	.08	.04	.01
☐ 210	Steve Carlton	4.25	1.90	.55
☐ 211	Dave Skaggs DP	.08	.04	.01
☐ 212	Dave Roberts	.08	.04	.01
☐ 213	Mike Jorgensen DP	.08	.04	.01
☐ 214	Angels Team/Mgr.	.50	.23	.06
	Jim Fregosi			
	(Checklist back)			
☐ 215	Sixto Lezcano	.08	.04	.01
☐ 216	Phil Mankowski	.08	.04	.01
☐ 217	Ed Halicki	.08	.04	.01
☐ 218	Jose Morales	.08	.04	.01
☐ 219	Steve Mingori	.08	.04	.01
☐ 220	Dave Concepcion	.60	.25	.08
☐ 221	Joe Cannon	.08	.04	.01
☐ 222	Ron Hassey	.40	.18	.05
☐ 223	Bob Sykes	.08	.04	.01
☐ 224	Willie Montanez	.08	.04	.01
☐ 225	Lou Piniella	.25	.11	.03
☐ 226	Bill Stein	.08	.04	.01
☐ 227	Len Barker	.08	.04	.01
☐ 228	Johnny Oates	.08	.04	.01
☐ 229	Jim Bibby	.08	.04	.01
☐ 230	Dave Winfield	7.50	3.40	.95
☐ 231	Steve McCatty	.08	.04	.01
☐ 232	Alan Trammell	4.00	1.80	.50
☐ 233	LaRue Washington	.08	.04	.01
☐ 234	Vern Ruhle	.08	.04	.01
☐ 235	Andre Dawson	10.00	4.50	1.25
☐ 236	Marc Hill	.08	.04	.01
☐ 237	Scott McGregor	.18	.08	.02
☐ 238	Rob Wilfong	.08	.04	.01
☐ 239	Don Aase	.08	.04	.01
☐ 240	Dave Kingman	.35	.16	.04
☐ 241	Checklist 2	.60	.25	.08
☐ 242	Lamar Johnson	.08	.04	.01
☐ 243	Jerry Augustine	.08	.04	.01
☐ 244	Cardinals Team/Mgr.	.50	.23	.06
	Ken Boyer			
	(Checklist back)			
☐ 245	Phil Niekro	1.50	.65	.19
☐ 246	Tim Foli DP	.08	.04	.01
☐ 247	Frank Riccelli	.08	.04	.01
☐ 248	Jamie Quirk	.08	.04	.01
☐ 249	Jim Clancy	.08	.04	.01
☐ 250	Jim Kaat	.40	.18	.05
☐ 251	Kip Young	.08	.04	.01
☐ 252	Ted Cox	.08	.04	.01
☐ 253	John Montague	.08	.04	.01
☐ 254	Paul Dade DP	.08	.04	.01
☐ 255	Dusty Baker DP	.08	.04	.01
☐ 256	Roger Erickson	.08	.04	.01
☐ 257	Larry Herndon	.08	.04	.01
☐ 258	Paul Moskau	.08	.04	.01
☐ 259	Mets Team/Mgr.	.50	.23	.06
	Joe Torre			
	(Checklist back)			
☐ 260	Al Oliver	.35	.16	.04
☐ 261	Dave Chalk	.08	.04	.01
☐ 262	Benny Ayala	.08	.04	.01
☐ 263	Dave LaRoche DP	.08	.04	.01
☐ 264	Bill Robinson	.18	.08	.02
☐ 265	Robin Yount	12.50	5.75	1.55
☐ 266	Bernie Carbo	.08	.04	.01
☐ 267	Dan Schatzeder	.08	.04	.01
☐ 268	Rafael Landestoy	.08	.04	.01
☐ 269	Dave Tobik	.08	.04	.01
☐ 270	Mike Schmidt DP	4.50	2.00	.55
☐ 271	Dick Drago DP	.08	.04	.01
☐ 272	Ralph Garr	.08	.04	.01
☐ 273	Eduardo Rodriguez	.08	.04	.01
☐ 274	Dale Murphy	4.00	1.80	.50
☐ 275	Jerry Koosman	.18	.08	.02
☐ 276	Tom Veryzer	.08	.04	.01
☐ 277	Rick Bosetti	.08	.04	.01
☐ 278	Jim Spencer	.08	.04	.01
☐ 279	Rob Andrews	.08	.04	.01
☐ 280	Gaylord Perry	1.50	.65	.19
☐ 281	Paul Blair	.18	.08	.02
☐ 282	Mariners Team/Mgr.	.50	.23	.06
	Darrell Johnson			
	(Checklist back)			
☐ 283	John Ellis	.08	.04	.01
☐ 284	Larry Murray DP	.08	.04	.01
☐ 285	Don Baylor	.60	.25	.08
☐ 286	Darold Knowles DP	.08	.04	.01
☐ 287	John Lowenstein	.08	.04	.01
☐ 288	Dave Rozema	.08	.04	.01
☐ 289	Bruce Bochy	.08	.04	.01
☐ 290	Steve Garvey	1.50	.65	.19
☐ 291	Randy Scarberry	.08	.04	.01
☐ 292	Dale Berra	.08	.04	.01
☐ 293	Elias Sosa	.08	.04	.01
☐ 294	Charlie Spikes	.08	.04	.01
☐ 295	Larry Gura	.08	.04	.01
☐ 296	Dave Rader	.08	.04	.01
☐ 297	Tim Johnson	.08	.04	.01
☐ 298	Ken Holtzman	.08	.04	.01
☐ 299	Steve Henderson	.08	.04	.01
☐ 300	Ron Guidry	.60	.25	.08
☐ 301	Mike Edwards	.08	.04	.01
☐ 302	Dodgers Team/Mgr.	.50	.23	.06
	Tom Lasorda			
	(Checklist back)			
☐ 303	Bill Castro	.08	.04	.01
☐ 304	Butch Wynegar	.08	.04	.01
☐ 305	Randy Jones	.08	.04	.01
☐ 306	Denny Walling	.08	.04	.01
☐ 307	Rick Honeycutt	.18	.08	.02
☐ 308	Mike Hargrove	.18	.08	.02
☐ 309	Larry McWilliams	.08	.04	.01
☐ 310	Dave Parker	1.50	.65	.19
☐ 311	Roger Metzger	.08	.04	.01
☐ 312	Mike Barlow	.08	.04	.01
☐ 313	Johnny Grubb	.08	.04	.01
☐ 314	Tim Stoddard	.08	.04	.01
☐ 315	Steve Kemp	.08	.04	.01
☐ 316	Bob Lacey	.08	.04	.01
☐ 317	Mike Anderson DP	.08	.04	.01
☐ 318	Jerry Reuss	.18	.08	.02
☐ 319	Chris Speier	.08	.04	.01
☐ 320	Dennis Eckersley	4.00	1.80	.50
☐ 321	Keith Hernandez	1.00	.45	.13
☐ 322	Claudell Washington	.18	.08	.02
☐ 323	Mick Kelleher	.08	.04	.01
☐ 324	Tom Underwood	.08	.04	.01
☐ 325	Dan Driessen	.08	.04	.01
☐ 326	Bo McLaughlin	.08	.04	.01
☐ 327	Ray Fosse DP	.08	.04	.01
☐ 328	Twins Team/Mgr.	.50	.23	.06
	Gene Mauch			
	(Checklist back)			
☐ 329	Bert Roberge	.08	.04	.01
☐ 330	Al Cowens	.08	.04	.01
☐ 331	Richie Hebner	.08	.04	.01
☐ 332	Enrique Romo	.08	.04	.01
☐ 333	Jim Norris DP	.08	.04	.01
☐ 334	Jim Beattie	.08	.04	.01
☐ 335	Willie McCovey	2.00	.90	.25
☐ 336	George Medich	.08	.04	.01
☐ 337	Carney Lansford	1.00	.45	.13
☐ 338	John Wockenfuss	.08	.04	.01
☐ 339	John D'Acquisto	.08	.04	.01
☐ 340	Ken Singleton	.18	.08	.02
☐ 341	Jim Essian	.08	.04	.01
☐ 342	Odell Jones	.08	.04	.01
☐ 343	Mike Vail	.08	.04	.01
☐ 344	Randy Lerch	.08	.04	.01
☐ 345	Larry Parrish	.18	.08	.02
☐ 346	Buddy Solomon	.08	.04	.01
☐ 347	Harry Chappas	.08	.04	.01
☐ 348	Checklist 3	.60	.25	.08
☐ 349	Jack Brohamer	.08	.04	.01
☐ 350	George Hendrick	.18	.08	.02
☐ 351	Bob Davis	.08	.04	.01
☐ 352	Dan Briggs	.08	.04	.01
☐ 353	Andy Hassler	.08	.04	.01
☐ 354	Rick Auerbach	.08	.04	.01
☐ 355	Gary Matthews	.18	.08	.02
☐ 356	Padres Team/Mgr.	.50	.23	.06
	Jerry Coleman			
	(Checklist back)			
☐ 357	Bob McClure	.08	.04	.01
☐ 358	Lou Whitaker	4.00	1.80	.50
☐ 359	Randy Moffitt	.08	.04	.01
☐ 360	Darrell Porter DP	.08	.04	.01
☐ 361	Wayne Garland	.08	.04	.01
☐ 362	Danny Goodwin	.08	.04	.01
☐ 363	Wayne Gross	.08	.04	.01

	No.	Player			
☐	364	Ray Burris	.08	.04	.01
☐	365	Bobby Murcer	.18	.08	.02
☐	366	Rob Dressler	.08	.04	.01
☐	367	Billy Smith	.08	.04	.01
☐	368	Willie Aikens	.18	.08	.02
☐	369	Jim Kern	.08	.04	.01
☐	370	Cesar Cedeno	.18	.08	.02
☐	371	Jack Morris	5.00	2.30	.60
☐	372	Joel Youngblood	.08	.04	.01
☐	373	Dan Petry DP	.25	.11	.03
☐	374	Jim Gantner	.18	.08	.02
☐	375	Ross Grimsley	.08	.04	.01
☐	376	Gary Allenson	.25	.11	.03
☐	377	Junior Kennedy	.08	.04	.01
☐	378	Jerry Mumphrey	.08	.04	.01
☐	379	Kevin Bell	.08	.04	.01
☐	380	Garry Maddox	.08	.04	.01
☐	381	Cubs Team/Mgr.	.50	.23	.06
		Preston Gomez			
		(Checklist back)			
☐	382	Dave Freisleben	.08	.04	.01
☐	383	Ed Ott	.08	.04	.01
☐	384	Joey McLaughlin	.08	.04	.01
☐	385	Enos Cabell	.08	.04	.01
☐	386	Darrell Jackson	.08	.04	.01
☐	387A	Fred Stanley	1.00	.45	.13
		(Yellow name on front)			
☐	387B	Fred Stanley	.08	.04	.01
		(Red name on front)			
☐	388	Mike Paxton	.08	.04	.01
☐	389	Pete LaCock	.08	.04	.01
☐	390	Fergie Jenkins	1.50	.65	.19
☐	391	Tony Armas DP	.08	.04	.01
☐	392	Milt Wilcox	.08	.04	.01
☐	393	Ozzie Smith	18.00	8.00	2.30
☐	394	Reggie Cleveland	.08	.04	.01
☐	395	Ellis Valentine	.08	.04	.01
☐	396	Dan Meyer	.08	.04	.01
☐	397	Roy Thomas DP	.08	.04	.01
☐	398	Barry Foote	.08	.04	.01
☐	399	Mike Proly DP	.08	.04	.01
☐	400	George Foster	.50	.23	.06
☐	401	Pete Falcone	.08	.04	.01
☐	402	Merv Rettenmund	.08	.04	.01
☐	403	Pete Redfern DP	.08	.04	.01
☐	404	Orioles Team/Mgr.	.50	.23	.06
		Earl Weaver			
		(Checklist back)			
☐	405	Dwight Evans	1.25	.55	.16
☐	406	Paul Molitor	6.50	2.90	.80
☐	407	Tony Solaita	.08	.04	.01
☐	408	Bill North	.08	.04	.01
☐	409	Paul Splittorff	.08	.04	.01
☐	410	Bobby Bonds	.28	.13	.04
☐	411	Frank LaCorte	.08	.04	.01
☐	412	Thad Bosley	.08	.04	.01
☐	413	Allen Ripley	.08	.04	.01
☐	414	George Scott	.18	.08	.02
☐	415	Bill Atkinson	.08	.04	.01
☐	416	Tom Brookens	.08	.04	.01
☐	417	Craig Chamberlain DP	.08	.04	.01
☐	418	Roger Freed DP	.08	.04	.01
☐	419	Vic Correll	.08	.04	.01
☐	420	Butch Hobson	.18	.08	.02
☐	421	Doug Bird	.08	.04	.01
☐	422	Larry Milbourne	.08	.04	.01
☐	423	Dave Frost	.08	.04	.01
☐	424	Yankees Team/Mgr.	.50	.23	.06
		Dick Howser			
		(Checklist back)			
☐	425	Mark Belanger	.18	.08	.02
☐	426	Grant Jackson	.08	.04	.01
☐	427	Tom Hutton DP	.08	.04	.01
☐	428	Pat Zachry	.08	.04	.01
☐	429	Duane Kuiper	.08	.04	.01
☐	430	Larry Hisle DP	.08	.04	.01
☐	431	Mike Krukow	.08	.04	.01
☐	432	Willie Norwood	.08	.04	.01
☐	433	Rich Gale	.08	.04	.01
☐	434	Johnnie LeMaster	.08	.04	.01
☐	435	Don Gullett	.18	.08	.02
☐	436	Billy Almon	.08	.04	.01
☐	437	Joe Niekro	.18	.08	.02
☐	438	Dave Revering	.08	.04	.01
☐	439	Mike Phillips	.08	.04	.01
☐	440	Don Sutton	1.50	.65	.19
☐	441	Eric Soderholm	.08	.04	.01
☐	442	Jorge Orta	.08	.04	.01
☐	443	Mike Parrott	.08	.04	.01
☐	444	Alvis Woods	.08	.04	.01
☐	445	Mark Fidrych	.18	.08	.02
☐	446	Duffy Dyer	.08	.04	.01
☐	447	Nino Espinosa	.08	.04	.01
☐	448	Jim Wohlford	.08	.04	.01
☐	449	Doug Bair	.08	.04	.01
☐	450	George Brett	12.50	5.75	1.55
☐	451	Indians Team/Mgr.	.50	.23	.06
		Dave Garcia			
		(Checklist back)			
☐	452	Steve Dillard	.08	.04	.01
☐	453	Mike Bacsik	.08	.04	.01
☐	454	Tom Donohue	.08	.04	.01
☐	455	Mike Torrez	.08	.04	.01
☐	456	Frank Taveras	.08	.04	.01
☐	457	Bert Blyleven	.75	.35	.09
☐	458	Billy Sample	.08	.04	.01
☐	459	Mickey Lolich DP	.08	.04	.01
☐	460	Willie Randolph	.75	.35	.09
☐	461	Dwayne Murphy	.08	.04	.01
☐	462	Mike Sadek DP	.08	.04	.01
☐	463	Jerry Royster	.08	.04	.01
☐	464	John Denny	.08	.04	.01
☐	465	Rick Monday	.18	.08	.02
☐	466	Mike Squires	.08	.04	.01
☐	467	Jesse Jefferson	.08	.04	.01
☐	468	Aurelio Rodriguez	.08	.04	.01
☐	469	Randy Niemann DP	.08	.04	.01
☐	470	Bob Boone	.50	.23	.06
☐	471	Hosken Powell DP	.08	.04	.01
☐	472	Willie Hernandez	.18	.08	.02
☐	473	Bump Wills	.08	.04	.01
☐	474	Steve Busby	.08	.04	.01
☐	475	Cesar Geronimo	.08	.04	.01
☐	476	Bob Shirley	.08	.04	.01
☐	477	Buck Martinez	.08	.04	.01
☐	478	Gil Flores	.08	.04	.01
☐	479	Expos Team/Mgr.	.50	.23	.06
		Dick Williams			
		(Checklist back)			
☐	480	Bob Watson	.18	.08	.02
☐	481	Tom Paciorek	.18	.08	.02
☐	482	Rickey Henderson UER	120.00	55.00	15.00
		(7 steals at Modesto,			
		should be at Fresno)			
☐	483	Bo Diaz	.08	.04	.01
☐	484	Checklist 4	.60	.25	.08
☐	485	Mickey Rivers	.18	.08	.02
☐	486	Mike Tyson DP	.08	.04	.01
☐	487	Wayne Nordhagen	.08	.04	.01
☐	488	Roy Howell	.08	.04	.01
☐	489	Preston Hanna DP	.08	.04	.01
☐	490	Lee May	.18	.08	.02
☐	491	Steve Mura DP	.08	.04	.01
☐	492	Todd Cruz	.08	.04	.01
☐	493	Jerry Martin	.08	.04	.01
☐	494	Craig Minetto	.08	.04	.01
☐	495	Bake McBride	.18	.08	.02
☐	496	Silvio Martinez	.08	.04	.01
☐	497	Jim Mason	.08	.04	.01
☐	498	Danny Darwin	.08	.04	.01
☐	499	Giants Team/Mgr.	.50	.23	.06
		Dave Bristol			
		(Checklist back)			
☐	500	Tom Seaver	4.50	2.00	.55
☐	501	Rennie Stennett	.08	.04	.01
☐	502	Rich Wortham DP	.08	.04	.01
☐	503	Mike Cubbage	.08	.04	.01
☐	504	Gene Garber	.08	.04	.01
☐	505	Bert Campaneris	.18	.08	.02
☐	506	Tom Buskey	.08	.04	.01
☐	507	Leon Roberts	.08	.04	.01
☐	508	U.L. Washington	.08	.04	.01
☐	509	Ed Glynn	.08	.04	.01
☐	510	Ron Cey	.35	.16	.04
☐	511	Eric Wilkins	.08	.04	.01
☐	512	Jose Cardenal	.08	.04	.01
☐	513	Tom Dixon DP	.08	.04	.01
☐	514	Steve Ontiveros	.08	.04	.01
☐	515	Mike Caldwell	.08	.04	.01
☐	516	Hector Cruz	.08	.04	.01
☐	517	Don Stanhouse	.08	.04	.01
☐	518	Nelson Norman	.08	.04	.01
☐	519	Steve Nicosia	.08	.04	.01
☐	520	Steve Rogers	.08	.04	.01
☐	521	Ken Brett	.08	.04	.01
☐	522	Jim Morrison	.08	.04	.01
☐	523	Ken Henderson	.08	.04	.01
☐	524	Jim Wright DP	.08	.04	.01
☐	525	Clint Hurdle	.08	.04	.01
☐	526	Phillies Team/Mgr.	.50	.23	.06
		Dallas Green			
		(Checklist back)			
☐	527	Doug Rau DP	.08	.04	.01
☐	528	Adrian Devine	.08	.04	.01
☐	529	Jim Barr	.08	.04	.01
☐	530	Jim Sundberg DP	.08	.04	.01

☐ 531	Eric Rasmussen	.08	.04	.01
☐ 532	Willie Horton	.18	.08	.02
☐ 533	Checklist 5	.60	.25	.08
☐ 534	Andre Thornton	.18	.08	.02
☐ 535	Bob Forsch	.08	.04	.01
☐ 536	Lee Lacy	.08	.04	.01
☐ 537	Alex Trevino	.08	.04	.01
☐ 538	Joe Strain	.08	.04	.01
☐ 539	Rudy May	.08	.04	.01
☐ 540	Pete Rose	4.50	2.00	.55
☐ 541	Miguel Dilone	.08	.04	.01
☐ 542	Joe Coleman	.08	.04	.01
☐ 543	Pat Kelly	.08	.04	.01
☐ 544	Rick Sutcliffe	4.00	1.80	.50
☐ 545	Jeff Burroughs	.08	.04	.01
☐ 546	Rick Langford	.08	.04	.01
☐ 547	John Wathan	.08	.04	.01
☐ 548	Dave Rajsich	.08	.04	.01
☐ 549	Larry Wolfe	.08	.04	.01
☐ 550	Ken Griffey	.60	.25	.08
☐ 551	Pirates Team/Mgr.	.50	.23	.06
	Chuck Tanner			
	(Checklist back)			
☐ 552	Bill Nahorodny	.08	.04	.01
☐ 553	Dick Davis	.08	.04	.01
☐ 554	Art Howe	.18	.08	.02
☐ 555	Ed Figueroa	.08	.04	.01
☐ 556	Joe Rudi	.18	.08	.02
☐ 557	Mark Lee	.08	.04	.01
☐ 558	Alfredo Griffin	.08	.04	.01
☐ 559	Dale Murray	.08	.04	.01
☐ 560	Dave Lopes	.18	.08	.02
☐ 561	Eddie Whitson	.18	.08	.02
☐ 562	Joe Wallis	.08	.04	.01
☐ 563	Will McEnaney	.08	.04	.01
☐ 564	Rick Manning	.08	.04	.01
☐ 565	Dennis Leonard	.18	.08	.02
☐ 566	Bud Harrelson	.08	.04	.01
☐ 567	Skip Lockwood	.08	.04	.01
☐ 568	Gary Roenicke	.18	.08	.02
☐ 569	Terry Kennedy	.18	.08	.02
☐ 570	Roy Smalley	.18	.08	.02
☐ 571	Joe Sambito	.08	.04	.01
☐ 572	Jerry Morales DP	.08	.04	.01
☐ 573	Kent Tekulve	.18	.08	.02
☐ 574	Scot Thompson	.08	.04	.01
☐ 575	Ken Kravec	.08	.04	.01
☐ 576	Jim Dwyer	.08	.04	.01
☐ 577	Blue Jays Team/Mgr.	.50	.23	.06
	Bobby Mattick			
	(Checklist back)			
☐ 578	Scott Sanderson	.40	.18	.05
☐ 579	Charlie Moore	.08	.04	.01
☐ 580	Nolan Ryan	21.00	9.50	2.60
☐ 581	Bob Bailor	.08	.04	.01
☐ 582	Brian Doyle	.08	.04	.01
☐ 583	Bob Stinson	.08	.04	.01
☐ 584	Kurt Bevacqua	.08	.04	.01
☐ 585	Al Hrabosky	.08	.04	.01
☐ 586	Mitchell Page	.08	.04	.01
☐ 587	Garry Templeton	.18	.08	.02
☐ 588	Greg Minton	.08	.04	.01
☐ 589	Chet Lemon	.18	.08	.02
☐ 590	Jim Palmer	3.50	1.55	.45
☐ 591	Rick Cerone	.08	.04	.01
☐ 592	Jon Matlack	.08	.04	.01
☐ 593	Jesus Alou	.08	.04	.01
☐ 594	Dick Tidrow	.08	.04	.01
☐ 595	Don Money	.08	.04	.01
☐ 596	Rick Matula	.08	.04	.01
☐ 597	Tom Poquette	.08	.04	.01
☐ 598	Fred Kendall DP	.08	.04	.01
☐ 599	Mike Norris	.08	.04	.01
☐ 600	Reggie Jackson	8.50	3.80	1.05
☐ 601	Buddy Schultz	.08	.04	.01
☐ 602	Brian Downing	.25	.11	.03
☐ 603	Jack Billingham DP	.08	.04	.01
☐ 604	Glenn Adams	.08	.04	.01
☐ 605	Terry Forster	.08	.04	.01
☐ 606	Reds Team/Mgr.	.50	.23	.06
	John McNamara			
	(Checklist back)			
☐ 607	Woodie Fryman	.08	.04	.01
☐ 608	Alan Bannister	.08	.04	.01
☐ 609	Ron Reed	.08	.04	.01
☐ 610	Willie Stargell	2.00	.90	.25
☐ 611	Jerry Garvin DP	.08	.04	.01
☐ 612	Cliff Johnson	.08	.04	.01
☐ 613	Randy Stein	.08	.04	.01
☐ 614	John Hiller	.08	.04	.01
☐ 615	Doug DeCinces	.18	.08	.02
☐ 616	Gene Richards	.08	.04	.01
☐ 617	Joaquin Andujar	.18	.08	.02
☐ 618	Bob Montgomery DP	.08	.04	.01
☐ 619	Sergio Ferrer	.08	.04	.01
☐ 620	Richie Zisk	.08	.04	.01
☐ 621	Bob Grich	.18	.08	.02
☐ 622	Mario Soto	.08	.04	.01
☐ 623	Gorman Thomas	.18	.08	.02
☐ 624	Lerrin LaGrow	.08	.04	.01
☐ 625	Chris Chambliss	.18	.08	.02
☐ 626	Tigers Team/Mgr.	.50	.23	.06
	Sparky Anderson			
	(Checklist back)			
☐ 627	Pedro Borbon	.08	.04	.01
☐ 628	Doug Capilla	.08	.04	.01
☐ 629	Jim Todd	.08	.04	.01
☐ 630	Larry Bowa	.18	.08	.02
☐ 631	Mark Littell	.08	.04	.01
☐ 632	Barry Bonnell	.08	.04	.01
☐ 633	Bob Apodaca	.08	.04	.01
☐ 634	Glenn Borgmann DP	.08	.04	.01
☐ 635	John Candelaria	.18	.08	.02
☐ 636	Toby Harrah	.18	.08	.02
☐ 637	Joe Simpson	.08	.04	.01
☐ 638	Mark Clear	.08	.04	.01
☐ 639	Larry Biittner	.08	.04	.01
☐ 640	Mike Flanagan	.18	.08	.02
☐ 641	Ed Kranepool	.08	.04	.01
☐ 642	Ken Forsch DP	.08	.04	.01
☐ 643	John Mayberry	.08	.04	.01
☐ 644	Charlie Hough	.18	.08	.02
☐ 645	Rick Burleson	.08	.04	.01
☐ 646	Checklist 6	.60	.25	.08
☐ 647	Milt May	.08	.04	.01
☐ 648	Roy White	.18	.08	.02
☐ 649	Tom Griffin	.08	.04	.01
☐ 650	Joe Morgan	2.00	.90	.25
☐ 651	Rollie Fingers	2.00	.90	.25
☐ 652	Mario Mendoza	.08	.04	.01
☐ 653	Stan Bahnsen	.08	.04	.01
☐ 654	Bruce Boisclair DP	.08	.04	.01
☐ 655	Tug McGraw	.18	.08	.02
☐ 656	Larvell Blanks	.08	.04	.01
☐ 657	Dave Edwards	.08	.04	.01
☐ 658	Chris Knapp	.08	.04	.01
☐ 659	Brewers Team/Mgr.	.50	.23	.06
	George Bamberger			
	(Checklist back)			
☐ 660	Rusty Staub	.18	.08	.02
☐ 661	Orioles Rookies	.20	.09	.03
	Mark Corey			
	Dave Ford			
	Wayne Krenchicki			
☐ 662	Red Sox Rookies	.20	.09	.03
	Joel Finch			
	Mike O'Berry			
	Chuck Rainey			
☐ 663	Angels Rookies	1.00	.45	.13
	Ralph Botting			
	Bob Clark			
	Dickie Thon			
☐ 664	White Sox Rookies	.20	.09	.03
	Mike Colbern			
	Guy Hoffman			
	Dewey Robinson			
☐ 665	Indians Rookies	.30	.14	.04
	Larry Andersen			
	Bobby Cuellar			
	Sandy Wihtol			
☐ 666	Tigers Rookies	.20	.09	.03
	Mike Chris			
	Al Greene			
	Bruce Robbins			
☐ 667	Royals Rookies	2.50	1.15	.30
	Renie Martin			
	Bill Paschall			
	Dan Quisenberry			
☐ 668	Brewers Rookies	.20	.09	.03
	Danny Boitano			
	Willie Mueller			
	Lenn Sakata			
☐ 669	Twins Rookies	.20	.09	.03
	Dan Graham			
	Rick Sofield			
	Gary Ward			
☐ 670	Yankees Rookies	.20	.09	.03
	Bobby Brown			
	Brad Gulden			
	Darryl Jones			
☐ 671	A's Rookies	2.50	1.15	.30
	Derek Bryant			
	Brian Kingman			
	Mike Morgan			
☐ 672	Mariners Rookies	.20	.09	.03
	Charlie Beamon			

Rodney Craig			
Rafael Vasquez			
☐ 673 Rangers Rookies	.20	.09	.03
Brian Allard			
Jerry Don Gleaton			
Greg Mahlberg			
☐ 674 Blue Jays Rookies	.20	.09	.03
Butch Edge			
Pat Kelly			
Ted Wilborn			
☐ 675 Braves Rookies	.20	.09	.03
Bruce Benedict			
Larry Bradford			
Eddie Miller			
☐ 676 Cubs Rookies	.20	.09	.03
Dave Geisel			
Steve Macko			
Karl Pagel			
☐ 677 Reds Rookies	.20	.09	.03
Art DeFreites			
Frank Pastore			
Harry Spilman			
☐ 678 Astros Rookies	.20	.09	.03
Reggie Baldwin			
Alan Knicely			
Pete Ladd			
☐ 679 Dodgers Rookies	.30	.14	.04
Joe Beckwith			
Mickey Hatcher			
Dave Patterson			
☐ 680 Expos Rookies	.30	.14	.04
Tony Bernazard			
Randy Miller			
John Tamargo			
☐ 681 Mets Rookies	3.00	1.35	.40
Dan Norman			
Jesse Orosco			
Mike Scott			
☐ 682 Phillies Rookies	.20	.09	.03
Ramon Aviles			
Dickie Noles			
Kevin Saucier			
☐ 683 Pirates Rookies	.20	.09	.03
Dorian Boyland			
Alberto Lois			
Harry Saferight			
☐ 684 Cardinals Rookies	.60	.25	.08
George Frazier			
Tom Herr			
Dan O'Brien			
☐ 685 Padres Rookies	.20	.09	.03
Tim Flannery			
Brian Greer			
Jim Wilhelm			
☐ 686 Giants Rookies	.20	.09	.03
Greg Johnston			
Dennis Littlejohn			
Phil Nastu			
☐ 687 Mike Heath DP	.08	.04	.01
☐ 688 Steve Stone	.25	.11	.03
☐ 689 Red Sox Team/Mgr.	.50	.23	.06
Don Zimmer			
(Checklist back)			
☐ 690 Tommy John	.50	.23	.06
☐ 691 Ivan DeJesus	.08	.04	.01
☐ 692 Rawly Eastwick DP	.08	.04	.01
☐ 693 Craig Kusick	.08	.04	.01
☐ 694 Jim Rooker	.08	.04	.01
☐ 695 Reggie Smith	.18	.08	.02
☐ 696 Julio Gonzalez	.08	.04	.01
☐ 697 David Clyde	.08	.04	.01
☐ 698 Oscar Gamble	.18	.08	.02
☐ 699 Floyd Bannister	.08	.04	.01
☐ 700 Rod Carew DP	1.75	.80	.22
☐ 701 Ken Oberkfell	.35	.16	.04
☐ 702 Ed Farmer	.08	.04	.01
☐ 703 Otto Velez	.08	.04	.01
☐ 704 Gene Tenace	.18	.08	.02
☐ 705 Freddie Patek	.08	.04	.01
☐ 706 Tippy Martinez	.18	.08	.02
☐ 707 Elliott Maddox	.08	.04	.01
☐ 708 Bob Tolan	.08	.04	.01
☐ 709 Pat Underwood	.08	.04	.01
☐ 710 Graig Nettles	.30	.14	.04
☐ 711 Bob Galasso	.08	.04	.01
☐ 712 Rodney Scott	.08	.04	.01
☐ 713 Terry Whitfield	.08	.04	.01
☐ 714 Fred Norman	.08	.04	.01
☐ 715 Sal Bando	.18	.08	.02
☐ 716 Lynn McGlothen	.08	.04	.01
☐ 717 Mickey Klutts DP	.08	.04	.01
☐ 718 Greg Gross	.08	.04	.01
☐ 719 Don Robinson	.18	.08	.02
☐ 720 Carl Yastrzemski DP	1.75	.80	.22
☐ 721 Paul Hartzell	.08	.04	.01
☐ 722 Jose Cruz	.18	.08	.02
☐ 723 Shane Rawley	.08	.04	.01
☐ 724 Jerry White	.08	.04	.01
☐ 725 Rick Wise	.08	.04	.01
☐ 726 Steve Yeager	.25	.11	.03

1981 Topps

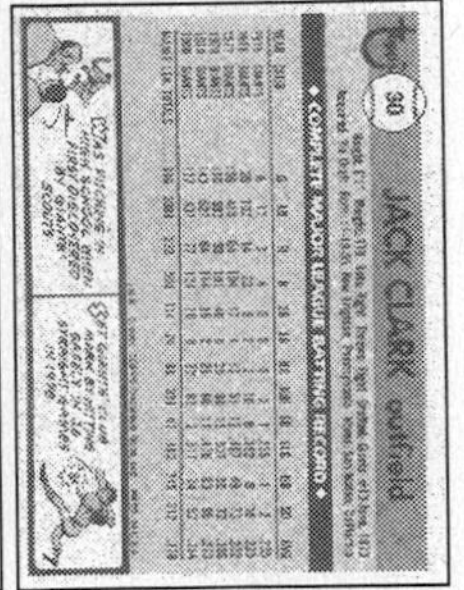

The cards in this 726-card set measure 2 1/2" by 3 1/2". League Leaders (1-8), Record Breakers (201-208), and Post-season cards (401-404) are topical subsets found in this set marketed by Topps in 1981. The team cards are all grouped together (661-686) and feature team checklist backs and a very small photo of the team's manager in the upper right corner of the obverse. The obverses carry the player's position and team in a baseball cap design, and the company name is printed in a small baseball. The backs are red and gray. The 66 double-printed cards are noted in the checklist by DP. The key Rookie Cards in the set include Harold Baines, Kirk Gibson, Bruce Hurst, Tim Raines, Jeff Reardon, and Fernando Valenzuela. Other Rookie Cards in the set are Mike Boddicker, Hubie Brooks, Bill Gullickson, Charlie Leibrandt, Lloyd Moseby, Tony Pena, and John Tudor.

	NRMT-MT	EXC	G-VG
COMPLETE SET (726)	90.00	40.00	11.50
COMMON PLAYER (1-726)	.10	.05	.01
COMMON PLAYER DP	.05	.02	.01
☐ 1 Batting Leaders	2.50	.50	.15
George Brett			
Bill Buckner			
☐ 2 Home Run Leaders	.60	.25	.08
Reggie Jackson			
Ben Oglivie			
Mike Schmidt			
☐ 3 RBI Leaders	.50	.23	.06
Cecil Cooper			
Mike Schmidt			
☐ 4 Stolen Base Leaders	1.75	.80	.22
Rickey Henderson			
Ron LeFlore			
☐ 5 Victory Leaders	.30	.14	.04
Steve Stone			
Steve Carlton			
☐ 6 Strikeout Leaders	.30	.14	.04
Len Barker			
Steve Carlton			
☐ 7 ERA Leaders	.20	.09	.03
Rudy May			
Don Sutton			
☐ 8 Leading Firemen	.35	.16	.04
Dan Quisenberry			
Rollie Fingers			
Tom Hume			
☐ 9 Pete LaCock DP	.05	.02	.01
☐ 10 Mike Flanagan	.10	.05	.01
☐ 11 Jim Wohlford DP	.05	.02	.01
☐ 12 Mark Clear	.05	.02	.01
☐ 13 Joe Charboneau	.10	.05	.01
☐ 14 John Tudor	.50	.23	.06
☐ 15 Larry Parrish	.05	.02	.01

☐ 16 Ron Davis	.05	.02	.01
☐ 17 Cliff Johnson	.05	.02	.01
☐ 18 Glenn Adams	.05	.02	.01
☐ 19 Jim Clancy	.05	.02	.01
☐ 20 Jeff Burroughs	.05	.02	.01
☐ 21 Ron Oester	.05	.02	.01
☐ 22 Danny Darwin	.05	.02	.01
☐ 23 Alex Trevino	.05	.02	.01
☐ 24 Don Stanhouse	.05	.02	.01
☐ 25 Sixto Lezcano	.05	.02	.01
☐ 26 U.L. Washington	.05	.02	.01
☐ 27 Champ Summers DP	.05	.02	.01
☐ 28 Enrique Romo	.05	.02	.01
☐ 29 Gene Tenace	.05	.02	.01
☐ 30 Jack Clark	.40	.18	.05
☐ 31 Checklist 1-121 DP	.15	.02	.01
☐ 32 Ken Oberkfell	.05	.02	.01
☐ 33 Rick Honeycutt	.05	.02	.01
☐ 34 Aurelio Rodriguez	.05	.02	.01
☐ 35 Mitchell Page	.05	.02	.01
☐ 36 Ed Farmer	.05	.02	.01
☐ 37 Gary Roenicke	.05	.02	.01
☐ 38 Win Remmerswaal	.05	.02	.01
☐ 39 Tom Veryzer	.05	.02	.01
☐ 40 Tug McGraw	.10	.05	.01
☐ 41 Ranger Rookies	.12	.05	.02
Bob Babcock			
John Butcher			
Jerry Don Gleaton			
☐ 42 Jerry White DP	.05	.02	.01
☐ 43 Jose Morales	.05	.02	.01
☐ 44 Larry McWilliams	.05	.02	.01
☐ 45 Enos Cabell	.05	.02	.01
☐ 46 Rick Bosetti	.05	.02	.01
☐ 47 Ken Brett	.05	.02	.01
☐ 48 Dave Skaggs	.05	.02	.01
☐ 49 Bob Shirley	.05	.02	.01
☐ 50 Dave Lopes	.10	.05	.01
☐ 51 Bill Robinson DP	.05	.02	.01
☐ 52 Hector Cruz	.05	.02	.01
☐ 53 Kevin Saucier	.05	.02	.01
☐ 54 Ivan DeJesus	.05	.02	.01
☐ 55 Mike Norris	.05	.02	.01
☐ 56 Buck Martinez	.05	.02	.01
☐ 57 Dave Roberts	.05	.02	.01
☐ 58 Joel Youngblood	.05	.02	.01
☐ 59 Dan Petry	.10	.05	.01
☐ 60 Willie Randolph	.10	.05	.01
☐ 61 Butch Wynegar	.05	.02	.01
☐ 62 Joe Pettini	.05	.02	.01
☐ 63 Steve Renko DP	.05	.02	.01
☐ 64 Brian Asselstine	.05	.02	.01
☐ 65 Scott McGregor	.05	.02	.01
☐ 66 Royals Rookies	.12	.05	.02
Manny Castillo			
Tim Ireland			
Mike Jones			
☐ 67 Ken Kravec	.05	.02	.01
☐ 68 Matt Alexander DP	.05	.02	.01
☐ 69 Ed Halicki	.05	.02	.01
☐ 70 Al Oliver DP	.05	.02	.01
☐ 71 Hal Dues	.05	.02	.01
☐ 72 Barry Evans DP	.05	.02	.01
☐ 73 Doug Bair	.05	.02	.01
☐ 74 Mike Hargrove	.10	.05	.01
☐ 75 Reggie Smith	.10	.05	.01
☐ 76 Mario Mendoza	.05	.02	.01
☐ 77 Mike Barlow	.05	.02	.01
☐ 78 Steve Dillard	.05	.02	.01
☐ 79 Bruce Robbins	.05	.02	.01
☐ 80 Rusty Staub	.10	.05	.01
☐ 81 Dave Stapleton	.05	.02	.01
☐ 82 Astros Rookies DP	.12	.05	.02
Danny Heep			
Alan Knicely			
Bobby Sprowl			
☐ 83 Mike Proly	.05	.02	.01
☐ 84 Johnnie LeMaster	.05	.02	.01
☐ 85 Mike Caldwell	.05	.02	.01
☐ 86 Wayne Gross	.05	.02	.01
☐ 87 Rick Camp	.05	.02	.01
☐ 88 Joe Lefebvre	.05	.02	.01
☐ 89 Darrell Jackson	.05	.02	.01
☐ 90 Bake McBride	.05	.02	.01
☐ 91 Tim Stoddard DP	.05	.02	.01
☐ 92 Mike Easler	.05	.02	.01
☐ 93 Ed Glynn DP	.05	.02	.01
☐ 94 Harry Spilman DP	.05	.02	.01
☐ 95 Jim Sundberg	.10	.05	.01
☐ 96 A's Rookies	.12	.05	.02
Dave Beard			
Ernie Camacho			
Pat Dempsey			

☐ 97 Chris Speier	.05	.02	.01
☐ 98 Clint Hurdle	.05	.02	.01
☐ 99 Eric Wilkins	.05	.02	.01
☐ 100 Rod Carew	3.00	1.35	.40
☐ 101 Benny Ayala	.05	.02	.01
☐ 102 Dave Tobik	.05	.02	.01
☐ 103 Jerry Martin	.05	.02	.01
☐ 104 Terry Forster	.05	.02	.01
☐ 105 Jose Cruz	.10	.05	.01
☐ 106 Don Money	.05	.02	.01
☐ 107 Rich Wortham	.05	.02	.01
☐ 108 Bruce Benedict	.05	.02	.01
☐ 109 Mike Scott	.35	.16	.04
☐ 110 Carl Yastrzemski	3.00	1.35	.40
☐ 111 Greg Minton	.05	.02	.01
☐ 112 White Sox Rookies	.12	.05	.02
Rusty Kuntz			
Fran Mullin			
Leo Sutherland			
☐ 113 Mike Phillips	.05	.02	.01
☐ 114 Tom Underwood	.05	.02	.01
☐ 115 Roy Smalley	.05	.02	.01
☐ 116 Joe Simpson	.05	.02	.01
☐ 117 Pete Falcone	.05	.02	.01
☐ 118 Kurt Bevacqua	.05	.02	.01
☐ 119 Tippy Martinez	.10	.05	.01
☐ 120 Larry Bowa	.10	.05	.01
☐ 121 Larry Harlow	.05	.02	.01
☐ 122 John Denny	.05	.02	.01
☐ 123 Al Cowens	.05	.02	.01
☐ 124 Jerry Garvin	.05	.02	.01
☐ 125 Andre Dawson	3.50	1.55	.45
☐ 126 Charlie Leibrandt	1.25	.55	.16
☐ 127 Rudy Law	.05	.02	.01
☐ 128 Gary Allenson DP	.05	.02	.01
☐ 129 Art Howe	.10	.05	.01
☐ 130 Larry Gura	.05	.02	.01
☐ 131 Keith Moreland	.10	.05	.01
☐ 132 Tommy Boggs	.05	.02	.01
☐ 133 Jeff Cox	.05	.02	.01
☐ 134 Steve Mura	.05	.02	.01
☐ 135 Gorman Thomas	.10	.05	.01
☐ 136 Doug Capilla	.05	.02	.01
☐ 137 Hosken Powell	.05	.02	.01
☐ 138 Rich Dotson DP	.05	.02	.01
☐ 139 Oscar Gamble	.05	.02	.01
☐ 140 Bob Forsch	.05	.02	.01
☐ 141 Miguel Dilone	.05	.02	.01
☐ 142 Jackson Todd	.05	.02	.01
☐ 143 Dan Meyer	.05	.02	.01
☐ 144 Allen Ripley	.05	.02	.01
☐ 145 Mickey Rivers	.10	.05	.01
☐ 146 Bobby Castillo	.05	.02	.01
☐ 147 Dale Berra	.05	.02	.01
☐ 148 Randy Niemann	.05	.02	.01
☐ 149 Joe Nolan	.05	.02	.01
☐ 150 Mark Fidrych	.10	.05	.01
☐ 151 Claudell Washington	.05	.02	.01
☐ 152 John Urrea	.05	.02	.01
☐ 153 Tom Poquette	.05	.02	.01
☐ 154 Rick Langford	.05	.02	.01
☐ 155 Chris Chambliss	.10	.05	.01
☐ 156 Bob McClure	.05	.02	.01
☐ 157 John Wathan	.05	.02	.01
☐ 158 Fergie Jenkins	1.00	.45	.13
☐ 159 Brian Doyle	.05	.02	.01
☐ 160 Garry Maddox	.05	.02	.01
☐ 161 Dan Graham	.05	.02	.01
☐ 162 Doug Corbett	.05	.02	.01
☐ 163 Bill Almon	.05	.02	.01
☐ 164 LaMarr Hoyt	.10	.05	.01
☐ 165 Tony Scott	.05	.02	.01
☐ 166 Floyd Bannister	.05	.02	.01
☐ 167 Terry Whitfield	.05	.02	.01
☐ 168 Don Robinson DP	.05	.02	.01
☐ 169 John Mayberry	.05	.02	.01
☐ 170 Ross Grimsley	.05	.02	.01
☐ 171 Gene Richards	.05	.02	.01
☐ 172 Gary Woods	.05	.02	.01
☐ 173 Bump Wills	.05	.02	.01
☐ 174 Doug Rau	.05	.02	.01
☐ 175 Dave Collins	.05	.02	.01
☐ 176 Mike Krukow	.05	.02	.01
☐ 177 Rick Peters	.05	.02	.01
☐ 178 Jim Essian DP	.05	.02	.01
☐ 179 Rudy May	.05	.02	.01
☐ 180 Pete Rose	3.50	1.55	.45
☐ 181 Elias Sosa	.05	.02	.01
☐ 182 Bob Grich	.10	.05	.01
☐ 183 Dick Davis DP	.05	.02	.01
☐ 184 Jim Dwyer	.05	.02	.01
☐ 185 Dennis Leonard	.05	.02	.01
☐ 186 Wayne Nordhagen	.05	.02	.01

☐ 187 Mike Parrott .05 .02 .01
☐ 188 Doug DeCinces .10 .05 .01
☐ 189 Craig Swan .05 .02 .01
☐ 190 Cesar Cedeno .10 .05 .01
☐ 191 Rick Sutcliffe .50 .23 .06
☐ 192 Braves Rookies .25 .11 .03
Terry Harper
Ed Miller
Rafael Ramirez
☐ 193 Pete Vuckovich .10 .05 .01
☐ 194 Rod Scurry .05 .02 .01
☐ 195 Rich Murray .05 .02 .01
☐ 196 Duffy Dyer .05 .02 .01
☐ 197 Jim Kern .05 .02 .01
☐ 198 Jerry Dybzinski .05 .02 .01
☐ 199 Chuck Rainey .05 .02 .01
☐ 200 George Foster .25 .11 .03
☐ 201 RB: Johnny Bench .75 .35 .09
Most homers,
lifetime, catcher
☐ 202 RB: Steve Carlton .75 .35 .09
Most strikeouts,
lefthander, lifetime
☐ 203 RB: Bill Gullickson .35 .16 .04
Most strikeouts,
game, rookie
☐ 204 RB: Ron LeFlore and .20 .09 .03
Rodney Scott
Most stolen bases,
teammates, season
☐ 205 RB: Pete Rose .90 .40 .11
Most cons. seasons
600 or more at-bats
☐ 206 RB: Mike Schmidt 1.25 .55 .16
Most homers, third
baseman, season
☐ 207 RB: Ozzie Smith 1.25 .55 .16
Most assists,
season, shortstop
☐ 208 RB: Willie Wilson .20 .09 .03
Most at-bats, season
☐ 209 Dickie Thon DP .05 .02 .01
☐ 210 Jim Palmer 2.50 1.15 .30
☐ 211 Derrel Thomas .05 .02 .01
☐ 212 Steve Nicosia .05 .02 .01
☐ 213 Al Holland .05 .02 .01
☐ 214 Angels Rookies .12 .05 .02
Ralph Botting
Jim Dorsey
John Harris
☐ 215 Larry Hisle .05 .02 .01
☐ 216 John Henry Johnson .05 .02 .01
☐ 217 Rich Hebner .05 .02 .01
☐ 218 Paul Splittorff .05 .02 .01
☐ 219 Ken Landreaux .05 .02 .01
☐ 220 Tom Seaver 3.00 1.35 .40
☐ 221 Bob Davis .05 .02 .01
☐ 222 Jorge Orta .05 .02 .01
☐ 223 Roy Lee Jackson .05 .02 .01
☐ 224 Pat Zachry .05 .02 .01
☐ 225 Ruppert Jones .05 .02 .01
☐ 226 Manny Sanguillen DP .05 .02 .01
☐ 227 Fred Martinez .05 .02 .01
☐ 228 Tom Paciorek .10 .05 .01
☐ 229 Rollie Fingers 2.00 .90 .25
☐ 230 George Hendrick .10 .05 .01
☐ 231 Joe Beckwith .05 .02 .01
☐ 232 Mickey Klutts .05 .02 .01
☐ 233 Skip Lockwood .05 .02 .01
☐ 234 Lou Whitaker 1.25 .55 .16
☐ 235 Scott Sanderson .10 .05 .01
☐ 236 Mike Ivie .05 .02 .01
☐ 237 Charlie Moore .05 .02 .01
☐ 238 Willie Hernandez .10 .05 .01
☐ 239 Rick Miller DP .05 .02 .01
☐ 240 Nolan Ryan 12.00 5.50 1.50
☐ 241 Checklist 122-242 DP .15 .02 .00
☐ 242 Chet Lemon .05 .02 .01
☐ 243 Sal Butera .05 .02 .01
☐ 244 Cardinals Rookies .05 .02 .01
Tito Landrum
Al Olmsted
Andy Rincon
☐ 245 Ed Figueroa .05 .02 .01
☐ 246 Ed Ott DP .05 .02 .01
☐ 247 Glenn Hubbard DP .05 .02 .01
☐ 248 Joey McLaughlin .05 .02 .01
☐ 249 Larry Cox .05 .02 .01
☐ 250 Ron Guidry .40 .18 .05
☐ 251 Tom Brookens .05 .02 .01
☐ 252 Victor Cruz .05 .02 .01
☐ 253 Dave Bergman .05 .02 .01
☐ 254 Ozzie Smith 5.00 2.30 .60
☐ 255 Mark Littell .05 .02 .01
☐ 256 Bombo Rivera .05 .02 .01
☐ 257 Rennie Stennett .05 .02 .01
☐ 258 Joe Price .05 .02 .01
☐ 259 Mets Rookies 1.50 .65 .19
Juan Berenguer
Hubie Brooks
Mookie Wilson
☐ 260 Ron Cey .10 .05 .01
☐ 261 Rickey Henderson 16.00 7.25 2.00
☐ 262 Sammy Stewart .05 .02 .01
☐ 263 Brian Downing .10 .05 .01
☐ 264 Jim Norris .05 .02 .01
☐ 265 John Candelaria .10 .05 .01
☐ 266 Tom Herr .10 .05 .01
☐ 267 Stan Bahnsen .05 .02 .01
☐ 268 Jerry Royster .05 .02 .01
☐ 269 Ken Forsch .05 .02 .01
☐ 270 Greg Luzinski .10 .05 .01
☐ 271 Bill Castro .05 .02 .01
☐ 272 Bruce Kimm .05 .02 .01
☐ 273 Stan Papi .05 .02 .01
☐ 274 Craig Chamberlain .05 .02 .01
☐ 275 Dwight Evans .50 .23 .06
☐ 276 Dan Spillner .05 .02 .01
☐ 277 Alfredo Griffin .05 .02 .01
☐ 278 Rick Sofield .05 .02 .01
☐ 279 Bob Knepper .05 .02 .01
☐ 280 Ken Griffey .50 .23 .06
☐ 281 Fred Stanley .05 .02 .01
☐ 282 Mariners Rookies .12 .05 .02
Rick Anderson
Greg Biercevicz
Rodney Craig
☐ 283 Billy Sample .05 .02 .01
☐ 284 Brian Kingman .05 .02 .01
☐ 285 Jerry Turner .05 .02 .01
☐ 286 Dave Frost .05 .02 .01
☐ 287 Lenn Sakata .05 .02 .01
☐ 288 Bob Clark .05 .02 .01
☐ 289 Mickey Hatcher .05 .02 .01
☐ 290 Bob Boone DP .05 .02 .01
☐ 291 Aurelio Lopez .05 .02 .01
☐ 292 Mike Squires .05 .02 .01
☐ 293 Charlie Lea .05 .02 .01
☐ 294 Mike Tyson DP .05 .02 .01
☐ 295 Hal McRae .10 .05 .01
☐ 296 Bill Nahorodny DP .05 .02 .01
☐ 297 Bob Bailor .05 .02 .01
☐ 298 Buddy Solomon .05 .02 .01
☐ 299 Elliott Maddox .05 .02 .01
☐ 300 Paul Molitor 2.00 .90 .25
☐ 301 Matt Keough .05 .02 .01
☐ 302 Dodgers Rookies 3.00 1.35 .40
Jack Perconte
Mike Scioscia
Fernando Valenzuela
☐ 303 Johnny Oates .05 .02 .01
☐ 304 John Castino .05 .02 .01
☐ 305 Ken Clay .05 .02 .01
☐ 306 Juan Beniquez DP .05 .02 .01
☐ 307 Gene Garber .05 .02 .01
☐ 308 Rick Manning .05 .02 .01
☐ 309 Luis Salazar .25 .11 .03
☐ 310 Vida Blue DP .05 .02 .01
☐ 311 Freddie Patek .05 .02 .01
☐ 312 Rick Rhoden .05 .02 .01
☐ 313 Luis Pujols .05 .02 .01
☐ 314 Rich Dauer .05 .02 .01
☐ 315 Kirk Gibson 3.00 1.35 .40
☐ 316 Craig Minetto .05 .02 .01
☐ 317 Lonnie Smith .25 .11 .03
☐ 318 Steve Yeager .05 .02 .01
☐ 319 Rowland Office .05 .02 .01
☐ 320 Tom Burgmeier .05 .02 .01
☐ 321 Leon Durham .10 .05 .01
☐ 322 Neil Allen .05 .02 .01
☐ 323 Jim Morrison DP .05 .02 .01
☐ 324 Mike Willis .05 .02 .01
☐ 325 Ray Knight .10 .05 .01
☐ 326 Biff Pocoroba .05 .02 .01
☐ 327 Moose Haas .05 .02 .01
☐ 328 Twins Rookies .12 .05 .02
Dave Engle
Greg Johnston
Gary Ward
☐ 329 Joaquin Andujar .10 .05 .01
☐ 330 Frank White .10 .05 .01
☐ 331 Dennis Lamp .05 .02 .01
☐ 332 Lee Lacy DP .05 .02 .01
☐ 333 Sid Monge .05 .02 .01
☐ 334 Dane Iorg .05 .02 .01
☐ 335 Rick Cerone .05 .02 .01

☐ 336	Eddie Whitson	.05	.02	.01
☐ 337	Lynn Jones	.05	.02	.01
☐ 338	Checklist 243-363	.30	.03	.01
☐ 339	John Ellis	.05	.02	.01
☐ 340	Bruce Kison	.05	.02	.01
☐ 341	Dwayne Murphy	.05	.02	.01
☐ 342	Eric Rasmussen DP	.05	.02	.01
☐ 343	Frank Taveras	.05	.02	.01
☐ 344	Byron McLaughlin	.05	.02	.01
☐ 345	Warren Cromartie	.05	.02	.01
☐ 346	Larry Christenson DP	.05	.02	.01
☐ 347	Harold Baines	4.00	1.80	.50
☐ 348	Bob Sykes	.05	.02	.01
☐ 349	Glenn Hoffman	.05	.02	.01
☐ 350	J.R. Richard	.10	.05	.01
☐ 351	Otto Velez	.05	.02	.01
☐ 352	Dick Tidrow DP	.05	.02	.01
☐ 353	Terry Kennedy	.10	.05	.01
☐ 354	Mario Soto	.05	.02	.01
☐ 355	Bob Horner	.10	.05	.01
☐ 356	Padres Rookies George Stablein Craig Stimac Tom Tellmann	.12	.05	.02
☐ 357	Jim Slaton	.05	.02	.01
☐ 358	Mark Wagner	.05	.02	.01
☐ 359	Tom Hausman	.05	.02	.01
☐ 360	Willie Wilson	.30	.14	.04
☐ 361	Joe Strain	.05	.02	.01
☐ 362	Bo Diaz	.05	.02	.01
☐ 363	Geoff Zahn	.05	.02	.01
☐ 364	Mike Davis	.10	.05	.01
☐ 365	Graig Nettles DP	.05	.02	.01
☐ 366	Mike Ramsey	.05	.02	.01
☐ 367	Dennis Martinez	.50	.23	.06
☐ 368	Leon Roberts	.05	.02	.01
☐ 369	Frank Tanana	.10	.05	.01
☐ 370	Dave Winfield	4.50	2.00	.55
☐ 371	Charlie Hough	.10	.05	.01
☐ 372	Jay Johnstone	.10	.05	.01
☐ 373	Pat Underwood	.05	.02	.01
☐ 374	Tommy Hutton	.05	.02	.01
☐ 375	Dave Concepcion	.25	.11	.03
☐ 376	Ron Reed	.05	.02	.01
☐ 377	Jerry Morales	.05	.02	.01
☐ 378	Dave Rader	.05	.02	.01
☐ 379	Lary Sorensen	.05	.02	.01
☐ 380	Willie Stargell	1.50	.65	.19
☐ 381	Cubs Rookies Carlos Lezcano Steve Macko Randy Martz	.12	.05	.02
☐ 382	Paul Mirabella	.05	.02	.01
☐ 383	Eric Soderholm DP	.05	.02	.01
☐ 384	Mike Sadek	.05	.02	.01
☐ 385	Joe Sambito	.05	.02	.01
☐ 386	Dave Edwards	.05	.02	.01
☐ 387	Phil Niekro	1.00	.45	.13
☐ 388	Andre Thornton	.10	.05	.01
☐ 389	Marty Pattin	.05	.02	.01
☐ 390	Cesar Geronimo	.05	.02	.01
☐ 391	Dave Lemanczyk DP	.05	.02	.01
☐ 392	Lance Parrish	.40	.18	.05
☐ 393	Broderick Perkins	.05	.02	.01
☐ 394	Woodie Fryman	.05	.02	.01
☐ 395	Scot Thompson	.05	.02	.01
☐ 396	Bill Campbell	.05	.02	.01
☐ 397	Julio Cruz	.05	.02	.01
☐ 398	Ross Baumgarten	.05	.02	.01
☐ 399	Orioles Rookies Mike Boddicker Mark Corey Floyd Rayford	.75	.35	.09
☐ 400	Reggie Jackson	4.00	1.80	.50
☐ 401	AL Champs Royals sweep Yanks (George Brett swinging)	1.25	.55	.16
☐ 402	NL Champs Phillies squeak past Astros	.20	.09	.03
☐ 403	1980 World Series Phillies beat Royals in six	.20	.09	.03
☐ 404	1980 World Series Phillies win first World Series	.20	.09	.03
☐ 405	Nino Espinosa	.05	.02	.01
☐ 406	Dickie Noles	.05	.02	.01
☐ 407	Ernie Whitt	.05	.02	.01
☐ 408	Fernando Arroyo	.05	.02	.01
☐ 409	Larry Herndon	.05	.02	.01
☐ 410	Bert Campaneris	.10	.05	.01
☐ 411	Terry Puhl	.05	.02	.01

☐ 412	Britt Burns	.10	.05	.01
☐ 413	Tony Bernazard	.05	.02	.01
☐ 414	John Pacella DP	.05	.02	.01
☐ 415	Ben Oglivie	.10	.05	.01
☐ 416	Gary Alexander	.05	.02	.01
☐ 417	Dan Schatzeder	.05	.02	.01
☐ 418	Bobby Brown	.05	.02	.01
☐ 419	Tom Hume	.05	.02	.01
☐ 420	Keith Hernandez	.50	.23	.06
☐ 421	Bob Stanley	.05	.02	.01
☐ 422	Dan Ford	.05	.02	.01
☐ 423	Shane Rawley	.05	.02	.01
☐ 424	Yankees Rookies Tim Lollar Bruce Robinson Dennis Werth	.12	.05	.02
☐ 425	Al Bumbry	.05	.02	.01
☐ 426	Warren Brusstar	.05	.02	.01
☐ 427	John D'Acquisto	.05	.02	.01
☐ 428	John Stearns	.05	.02	.01
☐ 429	Mick Kelleher	.05	.02	.01
☐ 430	Jim Bibby	.05	.02	.01
☐ 431	Dave Roberts	.05	.02	.01
☐ 432	Len Barker	.05	.02	.01
☐ 433	Rance Mulliniks	.05	.02	.01
☐ 434	Roger Erickson	.05	.02	.01
☐ 435	Jim Spencer	.05	.02	.01
☐ 436	Gary Lucas	.05	.02	.01
☐ 437	Mike Heath DP	.05	.02	.01
☐ 438	John Montefusco	.05	.02	.01
☐ 439	Denny Walling	.05	.02	.01
☐ 440	Jerry Reuss	.10	.05	.01
☐ 441	Ken Reitz	.05	.02	.01
☐ 442	Ron Pruitt	.05	.02	.01
☐ 443	Jim Beattie DP	.05	.02	.01
☐ 444	Garth Iorg	.05	.02	.01
☐ 445	Ellis Valentine	.05	.02	.01
☐ 446	Checklist 364-484	.30	.03	.01
☐ 447	Junior Kennedy DP	.05	.02	.01
☐ 448	Tim Corcoran	.05	.02	.01
☐ 449	Paul Mitchell	.05	.02	.01
☐ 450	Dave Kingman DP	.05	.02	.01
☐ 451	Indians Rookies Chris Bando Tom Brennan Sandy Wihtol	.12	.05	.02
☐ 452	Renie Martin	.05	.02	.01
☐ 453	Rob Wilfong DP	.05	.02	.01
☐ 454	Andy Hassler	.05	.02	.01
☐ 455	Rick Burleson	.05	.02	.01
☐ 456	Jeff Reardon	10.00	4.50	1.25
☐ 457	Mike Lum	.05	.02	.01
☐ 458	Randy Jones	.05	.02	.01
☐ 459	Greg Gross	.05	.02	.01
☐ 460	Rich Gossage	.30	.14	.04
☐ 461	Dave McKay	.05	.02	.01
☐ 462	Jack Brohamer	.05	.02	.01
☐ 463	Milt May	.05	.02	.01
☐ 464	Adrian Devine	.05	.02	.01
☐ 465	Bill Russell	.10	.05	.01
☐ 466	Bob Molinaro	.05	.02	.01
☐ 467	Dave Stieb	.50	.23	.06
☐ 468	John Wockenfuss	.05	.02	.01
☐ 469	Jeff Leonard	.10	.05	.01
☐ 470	Manny Trillo	.05	.02	.01
☐ 471	Mike Vail	.05	.02	.01
☐ 472	Dyar Miller DP	.05	.02	.01
☐ 473	Jose Cardenal	.05	.02	.01
☐ 474	Mike LaCoss	.05	.02	.01
☐ 475	Buddy Bell	.10	.05	.01
☐ 476	Jerry Koosman	.10	.05	.01
☐ 477	Luis Gomez	.05	.02	.01
☐ 478	Juan Eichelberger	.05	.02	.01
☐ 479	Expos Rookies Tim Raines Roberto Ramos Bobby Pate	7.50	3.40	.95
☐ 480	Carlton Fisk	3.00	1.35	.40
☐ 481	Bob Lacey DP	.05	.02	.01
☐ 482	Jim Gantner	.10	.05	.01
☐ 483	Mike Griffin	.05	.02	.01
☐ 484	Max Venable DP	.05	.02	.01
☐ 485	Garry Templeton	.10	.05	.01
☐ 486	Marc Hill	.05	.02	.01
☐ 487	Dewey Robinson	.05	.02	.01
☐ 488	Damaso Garcia	.10	.05	.01
☐ 489	John Littlefield	.05	.02	.01
☐ 490	Eddie Murray	4.00	1.80	.50
☐ 491	Gordy Pladson	.05	.02	.01
☐ 492	Barry Foote	.05	.02	.01
☐ 493	Dan Quisenberry	.40	.18	.05
☐ 494	Bob Walk	.50	.23	.06
☐ 495	Dusty Baker	.10	.05	.01

☐ 496 Paul Dade .05 .02 .01
☐ 497 Fred Norman .05 .02 .01
☐ 498 Pat Putnam .05 .02 .01
☐ 499 Frank Pastore .05 .02 .01
☐ 500 Jim Rice .50 .23 .06
☐ 501 Tim Foli DP .05 .02 .01
☐ 502 Giants Rookies .12 .05 .02
Chris Bourjos
Al Hargesheimer
Mike Rowland
☐ 503 Steve McCatty .05 .02 .01
☐ 504 Dale Murphy 1.50 .65 .19
☐ 505 Jason Thompson .05 .02 .01
☐ 506 Phil Huffman .05 .02 .01
☐ 507 Jamie Quirk .05 .02 .01
☐ 508 Rob Dressler .05 .02 .01
☐ 509 Pete Mackanin .05 .02 .01
☐ 510 Lee Mazzilli .05 .02 .01
☐ 511 Wayne Garland .05 .02 .01
☐ 512 Gary Thomasson .05 .02 .01
☐ 513 Frank LaCorte .05 .02 .01
☐ 514 George Riley .05 .02 .01
☐ 515 Robin Yount 6.00 2.70 .75
☐ 516 Doug Bird .05 .02 .01
☐ 517 Richie Zisk .05 .02 .01
☐ 518 Grant Jackson .05 .02 .01
☐ 519 John Tamargo DP .05 .02 .01
☐ 520 Steve Stone .10 .05 .01
☐ 521 Sam Mejias .05 .02 .01
☐ 522 Mike Colbern .05 .02 .01
☐ 523 John Fulgham .05 .02 .01
☐ 524 Willie Aikens .05 .02 .01
☐ 525 Mike Torrez .05 .02 .01
☐ 526 Phillies Rookies .12 .05 .02
Marty Bystrom
Jay Loviglio
Jim Wright
☐ 527 Danny Goodwin .05 .02 .01
☐ 528 Gary Matthews .10 .05 .01
☐ 529 Dave LaRoche .05 .02 .01
☐ 530 Steve Garvey 1.00 .45 .13
☐ 531 John Curtis .05 .02 .01
☐ 532 Bill Stein .05 .02 .01
☐ 533 Jesus Figueroa .05 .02 .01
☐ 534 Dave Smith .35 .16 .04
☐ 535 Omar Moreno .05 .02 .01
☐ 536 Bob Owchinko DP .05 .02 .01
☐ 537 Ron Hodges .05 .02 .01
☐ 538 Tom Griffin .05 .02 .01
☐ 539 Rodney Scott .05 .02 .01
☐ 540 Mike Schmidt DP 3.00 1.35 .40
☐ 541 Steve Swisher .05 .02 .01
☐ 542 Larry Bradford DP .05 .02 .01
☐ 543 Terry Crowley .05 .02 .01
☐ 544 Rich Gale .05 .02 .01
☐ 545 Johnny Grubb .05 .02 .01
☐ 546 Paul Moskau .05 .02 .01
☐ 547 Mario Guerrero .05 .02 .01
☐ 548 Dave Goltz .05 .02 .01
☐ 549 Jerry Remy .05 .02 .01
☐ 550 Tommy John .30 .14 .04
☐ 551 Pirates Rookies 1.00 .45 .13
Vance Law
Tony Pena
Pascual Perez
☐ 552 Steve Trout .05 .02 .01
☐ 553 Tim Blackwell .05 .02 .01
☐ 554 Bert Blyleven UER .75 .35 .09
(1 is missing from
1980 on card back)
☐ 555 Cecil Cooper .10 .05 .01
☐ 556 Jerry Mumphrey .05 .02 .01
☐ 557 Chris Knapp .05 .02 .01
☐ 558 Barry Bonnell .05 .02 .01
☐ 559 Willie Montanez .05 .02 .01
☐ 560 Joe Morgan 1.25 .55 .16
☐ 561 Dennis Littlejohn .05 .02 .01
☐ 562 Checklist 485-605 .30 .03 .01
☐ 563 Jim Kaat .30 .14 .04
☐ 564 Ron Hassey DP .05 .02 .01
☐ 565 Burt Hooton .05 .02 .01
☐ 566 Del Unser .05 .02 .01
☐ 567 Mark Bomback .05 .02 .01
☐ 568 Dave Revering .05 .02 .01
☐ 569 Al Williams DP .05 .02 .01
☐ 570 Ken Singleton .10 .05 .01
☐ 571 Todd Cruz .05 .02 .01
☐ 572 Jack Morris 3.00 1.35 .40
☐ 573 Phil Garner .10 .05 .01
☐ 574 Bill Caudill .05 .02 .01
☐ 575 Tony Perez .60 .25 .08
☐ 576 Reggie Cleveland .05 .02 .01
☐ 577 Blue Jays Rookies .12 .05 .02
Luis Leal
Brian Milner
Ken Schrom
☐ 578 Bill Gullickson 1.50 .65 .19
☐ 579 Tim Flannery .05 .02 .01
☐ 580 Don Baylor .10 .05 .01
☐ 581 Roy Howell .05 .02 .01
☐ 582 Gaylord Perry 1.00 .45 .13
☐ 583 Larry Milbourne .05 .02 .01
☐ 584 Randy Lerch .05 .02 .01
☐ 585 Amos Otis .10 .05 .01
☐ 586 Silvio Martinez .05 .02 .01
☐ 587 Jeff Newman .05 .02 .01
☐ 588 Gary Lavelle .05 .02 .01
☐ 589 Lamar Johnson .05 .02 .01
☐ 590 Bruce Sutter .30 .14 .04
☐ 591 John Lowenstein .05 .02 .01
☐ 592 Steve Comer .05 .02 .01
☐ 593 Steve Kemp .05 .02 .01
☐ 594 Preston Hanna DP .05 .02 .01
☐ 595 Butch Hobson .10 .05 .01
☐ 596 Jerry Augustine .05 .02 .01
☐ 597 Rafael Landestoy .05 .02 .01
☐ 598 George Vukovich DP .05 .02 .01
☐ 599 Dennis Kinney .05 .02 .01
☐ 600 Johnny Bench 3.00 1.35 .40
☐ 601 Don Aase .05 .02 .01
☐ 602 Bobby Murcer .10 .05 .01
☐ 603 John Verhoeven .05 .02 .01
☐ 604 Rob Picciolo .05 .02 .01
☐ 605 Don Sutton 1.00 .45 .13
☐ 606 Reds Rookies DP .12 .05 .02
Bruce Berenyi
Geoff Combe
Paul Householder
☐ 607 David Palmer .05 .02 .01
☐ 608 Greg Pryor .05 .02 .01
☐ 609 Lynn McGlothen .05 .02 .01
☐ 610 Darrell Porter .05 .02 .01
☐ 611 Rick Matula DP .05 .02 .01
☐ 612 Duane Kuiper .05 .02 .01
☐ 613 Jim Anderson .05 .02 .01
☐ 614 Dave Rozema .05 .02 .01
☐ 615 Rick Dempsey .10 .05 .01
☐ 616 Rick Wise .05 .02 .01
☐ 617 Craig Reynolds .05 .02 .01
☐ 618 John Milner .05 .02 .01
☐ 619 Steve Henderson .05 .02 .01
☐ 620 Dennis Eckersley 2.50 1.15 .30
☐ 621 Tom Donohue .05 .02 .01
☐ 622 Randy Moffitt .05 .02 .01
☐ 623 Sal Bando .10 .05 .01
☐ 624 Bob Welch .50 .23 .06
☐ 625 Bill Buckner .10 .05 .01
☐ 626 Tigers Rookies .12 .05 .02
Dave Steffen
Jerry Ujdur
Roger Weaver
☐ 627 Luis Tiant .10 .05 .01
☐ 628 Vic Correll .05 .02 .01
☐ 629 Tony Armas .10 .05 .01
☐ 630 Steve Carlton 3.00 1.35 .40
☐ 631 Ron Jackson .05 .02 .01
☐ 632 Alan Bannister .05 .02 .01
☐ 633 Bill Lee .05 .02 .01
☐ 634 Doug Flynn .05 .02 .01
☐ 635 Bobby Bonds .10 .05 .01
☐ 636 Al Hrabosky .05 .02 .01
☐ 637 Jerry Narron .05 .02 .01
☐ 638 Checklist 606-726 .30 .03 .01
☐ 639 Carney Lansford .40 .18 .05
☐ 640 Dave Parker .60 .25 .08
☐ 641 Mark Belanger .10 .05 .01
☐ 642 Vern Ruhle .05 .02 .01
☐ 643 Lloyd Moseby .25 .11 .03
☐ 644 Ramon Aviles DP .05 .02 .01
☐ 645 Rick Reuschel .10 .05 .01
☐ 646 Marvis Foley .05 .02 .01
☐ 647 Dick Drago .05 .02 .01
☐ 648 Darrell Evans .10 .05 .01
☐ 649 Manny Sarmiento .05 .02 .01
☐ 650 Bucky Dent .10 .05 .01
☐ 651 Pedro Guerrero .60 .25 .08
☐ 652 John Montague .05 .02 .01
☐ 653 Bill Fahey .05 .02 .01
☐ 654 Ray Burris .05 .02 .01
☐ 655 Dan Driessen .05 .02 .01
☐ 656 Jon Matlack .05 .02 .01
☐ 657 Mike Cubbage DP .05 .02 .01
☐ 658 Milt Wilcox .05 .02 .01
☐ 659 Brewers Rookies .12 .05 .02
John Flinn
Ed Romero
Ned Yost

□ 660 Gary Carter	1.50	.65	.19
□ 661 Orioles Team/Mgr. Earl Weaver (Checklist back)	.25	.11	.03
□ 662 Red Sox Team/Mgr. Ralph Houk (Checklist back)	.25	.11	.03
□ 663 Angels Team/Mgr. Jim Fregosi (Checklist back)	.25	.11	.03
□ 664 White Sox Team/Mgr. Tony LaRussa (Checklist back)	.25	.11	.03
□ 665 Indians Team/Mgr. Dave Garcia (Checklist back)	.25	.11	.03
□ 666 Tigers Team/Mgr. Sparky Anderson (Checklist back)	.25	.11	.03
□ 667 Royals Team/Mgr. Jim Frey (Checklist back)	.25	.11	.03
□ 668 Brewers Team/Mgr. Bob Rodgers (Checklist back)	.25	.11	.03
□ 669 Twins Team/Mgr. John Goryl (Checklist back)	.25	.11	.03
□ 670 Yankees Team/Mgr. Gene Michael (Checklist back)	.25	.11	.03
□ 671 A's Team/Mgr. Billy Martin (Checklist back)	.25	.11	.03
□ 672 Mariners Team/Mgr. Maury Wills (Checklist back)	.25	.11	.03
□ 673 Rangers Team/Mgr. Don Zimmer (Checklist back)	.25	.11	.03
□ 674 Blue Jays Team/Mgr. Bobby Mattick (Checklist back)	.25	.11	.03
□ 675 Braves Team/Mgr. Bobby Cox (Checklist back)	.25	.11	.03
□ 676 Cubs Team/Mgr. Joe Amalfitano (Checklist back)	.25	.11	.03
□ 677 Reds Team/Mgr. John McNamara (Checklist back)	.25	.11	.03
□ 678 Astros Team/Mgr. Bill Virdon (Checklist back)	.25	.11	.03
□ 679 Dodgers Team/Mgr. Tom Lasorda (Checklist back)	.25	.11	.03
□ 680 Expos Team/Mgr. Dick Williams (Checklist back)	.25	.11	.03
□ 681 Mets Team/Mgr. Joe Torre (Checklist back)	.25	.11	.03
□ 682 Phillies Team/Mgr. Dallas Green (Checklist back)	.25	.11	.03
□ 683 Pirates Team/Mgr. Chuck Tanner (Checklist back)	.25	.11	.03
□ 684 Cardinals Team/Mgr. Whitey Herzog (Checklist back)	.25	.11	.03
□ 685 Padres Team/Mgr. Frank Howard (Checklist back)	.25	.11	.03
□ 686 Giants Team/Mgr. Dave Bristol (Checklist back)	.25	.11	.03
□ 687 Jeff Jones	.05	.02	.01
□ 688 Kiko Garcia	.05	.02	.01
□ 689 Red Sox Rookies Bruce Hurst Keith MacWhorter Reid Nichols	2.00	.90	.25
□ 690 Bob Watson	.10	.05	.01
□ 691 Dick Ruthven	.05	.02	.01
□ 692 Lenny Randle	.05	.02	.01
□ 693 Steve Howe	.10	.05	.01
□ 694 Bud Harrelson DP	.05	.02	.01
□ 695 Kent Tekulve	.10	.05	.01
□ 696 Alan Ashby	.05	.02	.01
□ 697 Rick Waits	.05	.02	.01
□ 698 Mike Jorgensen	.05	.02	.01
□ 699 Glenn Abbott	.05	.02	.01
□ 700 George Brett	6.00	2.70	.75
□ 701 Joe Rudi	.10	.05	.01
□ 702 George Medich	.05	.02	.01
□ 703 Alvis Woods	.05	.02	.01
□ 704 Bill Travers DP	.05	.02	.01
□ 705 Ted Simmons	.30	.14	.04
□ 706 Dave Ford	.05	.02	.01
□ 707 Dave Cash	.05	.02	.01
□ 708 Doyle Alexander	.05	.02	.01
□ 709 Alan Trammell DP	1.00	.45	.13
□ 710 Ron LeFlore DP	.05	.02	.01
□ 711 Joe Ferguson	.05	.02	.01
□ 712 Bill Bonham	.05	.02	.01
□ 713 Bill North	.05	.02	.01
□ 714 Pete Redfern	.05	.02	.01
□ 715 Bill Madlock	.10	.05	.01
□ 716 Glenn Borgmann	.05	.02	.01
□ 717 Jim Barr DP	.05	.02	.01
□ 718 Larry Biittner	.05	.02	.01
□ 719 Sparky Lyle	.10	.05	.01
□ 720 Fred Lynn	.10	.05	.01
□ 721 Toby Harrah	.10	.05	.01
□ 722 Joe Niekro	.10	.05	.01
□ 723 Bruce Bochte	.05	.02	.01
□ 724 Lou Piniella	.10	.05	.01
□ 725 Steve Rogers	.05	.02	.01
□ 726 Rick Monday	.25	.11	.03

1981 Topps Traded

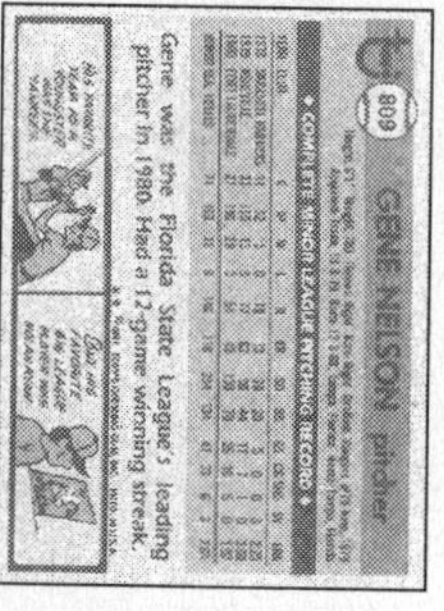

The cards in this 132-card set measure 2 1/2" by 3 1/2". For the first time since 1976, Topps issued a "traded" set in 1981. Unlike the small traded sets of 1974 and 1976, this set contains a larger number of cards and was sequentially numbered, alphabetically, from 727 to 858. Thus, this set gives the impression it is a continuation of their regular issue of this year. The sets were issued only through hobby card dealers and were boxed in complete sets of 132 cards. There are no key Rookie Cards in this set although Tim Raines, Jeff Reardon, and Fernando Valenzuela are depicted in their rookie year for cards.

	NRMT-MT	EXC	G-VG
COMPLETE SET (132)	50.00	23.00	6.25
COMMON PLAYER (727-858)	.15	.07	.02
□ 727 Danny Ainge	4.50	2.00	.55
□ 728 Doyle Alexander	.15	.07	.02
□ 729 Gary Alexander	.15	.07	.02
□ 730 Bill Almon	.15	.07	.02
□ 731 Joaquin Andujar	.25	.11	.03
□ 732 Bob Bailor	.15	.07	.02
□ 733 Juan Beniquez	.15	.07	.02
□ 734 Dave Bergman	.15	.07	.02
□ 735 Tony Bernazard	.15	.07	.02
□ 736 Larry Biittner	.15	.07	.02
□ 737 Doug Bird	.15	.07	.02
□ 738 Bert Blyleven	1.50	.65	.19
□ 739 Mark Bomback	.15	.07	.02
□ 740 Bobby Bonds	.25	.11	.03
□ 741 Rick Bosetti	.15	.07	.02
□ 742 Hubie Brooks	.90	.40	.11
□ 743 Rick Burleson	.15	.07	.02
□ 744 Ray Burris	.15	.07	.02

	Player	NRMT-MT	EXC	G-VG
☐ 745	Jeff Burroughs	.15	.07	.02
☐ 746	Enos Cabell	.15	.07	.02
☐ 747	Ken Clay	.15	.07	.02
☐ 748	Mark Clear	.15	.07	.02
☐ 749	Larry Cox	.15	.07	.02
☐ 750	Hector Cruz	.15	.07	.02
☐ 751	Victor Cruz	.15	.07	.02
☐ 752	Mike Cubbage	.25	.11	.03
☐ 753	Dick Davis	.15	.07	.02
☐ 754	Brian Doyle	.15	.07	.02
☐ 755	Dick Drago	.15	.07	.02
☐ 756	Leon Durham	.25	.11	.03
☐ 757	Jim Dwyer	.15	.07	.02
☐ 758	Dave Edwards	.15	.07	.02
☐ 759	Jim Essian	.15	.07	.02
☐ 760	Bill Fahey	.15	.07	.02
☐ 761	Rollie Fingers	3.50	1.55	.45
☐ 762	Carlton Fisk	7.00	3.10	.85
☐ 763	Barry Foote	.15	.07	.02
☐ 764	Ken Forsch	.15	.07	.02
☐ 765	Kiko Garcia	.15	.07	.02
☐ 766	Cesar Geronimo	.15	.07	.02
☐ 767	Gary Gray	.15	.07	.02
☐ 768	Mickey Hatcher	.15	.07	.02
☐ 769	Steve Henderson	.15	.07	.02
☐ 770	Marc Hill	.15	.07	.02
☐ 771	Butch Hobson	.25	.11	.03
☐ 772	Rick Honeycutt	.15	.07	.02
☐ 773	Roy Howell	.15	.07	.02
☐ 774	Mike Ivie	.15	.07	.02
☐ 775	Roy Lee Jackson	.15	.07	.02
☐ 776	Cliff Johnson	.15	.07	.02
☐ 777	Randy Jones	.15	.07	.02
☐ 778	Ruppert Jones	.15	.07	.02
☐ 779	Mick Kelleher	.15	.07	.02
☐ 780	Terry Kennedy	.25	.11	.03
☐ 781	Dave Kingman	.25	.11	.03
☐ 782	Bob Knepper	.15	.07	.02
☐ 783	Ken Kravec	.15	.07	.02
☐ 784	Bob Lacey	.15	.07	.02
☐ 785	Dennis Lamp	.15	.07	.02
☐ 786	Rafael Landestoy	.15	.07	.02
☐ 787	Ken Landreaux	.15	.07	.02
☐ 788	Carney Lansford	.75	.35	.09
☐ 789	Dave LaRoche	.15	.07	.02
☐ 790	Joe Lefebvre	.15	.07	.02
☐ 791	Ron LeFlore	.25	.11	.03
☐ 792	Randy Lerch	.15	.07	.02
☐ 793	Sixto Lezcano	.15	.07	.02
☐ 794	John Littlefield	.15	.07	.02
☐ 795	Mike Lum	.15	.07	.02
☐ 796	Greg Luzinski	.25	.11	.03
☐ 797	Fred Lynn	.25	.11	.03
☐ 798	Jerry Martin	.15	.07	.02
☐ 799	Buck Martinez	.15	.07	.02
☐ 800	Gary Matthews	.25	.11	.03
☐ 801	Mario Mendoza	.15	.07	.02
☐ 802	Larry Milbourne	.15	.07	.02
☐ 803	Rick Miller	.15	.07	.02
☐ 804	John Montefusco	.15	.07	.02
☐ 805	Jerry Morales	.15	.07	.02
☐ 806	Jose Morales	.15	.07	.02
☐ 807	Joe Morgan	3.00	1.35	.40
☐ 808	Jerry Mumphrey	.15	.07	.02
☐ 809	Gene Nelson	.25	.11	.03
☐ 810	Ed Ott	.15	.07	.02
☐ 811	Bob Owchinko	.15	.07	.02
☐ 812	Gaylord Perry	2.50	1.15	.30
☐ 813	Mike Phillips	.15	.07	.02
☐ 814	Darrell Porter	.15	.07	.02
☐ 815	Mike Proly	.15	.07	.02
☐ 816	Tim Raines	12.00	5.50	1.50
☐ 817	Lenny Randle	.15	.07	.02
☐ 818	Doug Rau	.15	.07	.02
☐ 819	Jeff Reardon	18.00	8.00	2.30
☐ 820	Ken Reitz	.15	.07	.02
☐ 821	Steve Renko	.15	.07	.02
☐ 822	Rick Reuschel	.25	.11	.03
☐ 823	Dave Revering	.15	.07	.02
☐ 824	Dave Roberts	.15	.07	.02
☐ 825	Leon Roberts	.15	.07	.02
☐ 826	Joe Rudi	.25	.11	.03
☐ 827	Kevin Saucier	.15	.07	.02
☐ 828	Tony Scott	.15	.07	.02
☐ 829	Bob Shirley	.15	.07	.02
☐ 830	Ted Simmons	.50	.23	.06
☐ 831	Lary Sorensen	.15	.07	.02
☐ 832	Jim Spencer	.15	.07	.02
☐ 833	Harry Spilman	.15	.07	.02
☐ 834	Fred Stanley	.15	.07	.02
☐ 835	Rusty Staub	.25	.11	.03
☐ 836	Bill Stein	.15	.07	.02
☐ 837	Joe Strain	.15	.07	.02
☐ 838	Bruce Sutter	.50	.23	.06
☐ 839	Don Sutton	2.50	1.15	.30
☐ 840	Steve Swisher	.15	.07	.02
☐ 841	Frank Tanana	.25	.11	.03
☐ 842	Gene Tenace	.15	.07	.02
☐ 843	Jason Thompson	.15	.07	.02
☐ 844	Dickie Thon	.25	.11	.03
☐ 845	Bill Travers	.15	.07	.02
☐ 846	Tom Underwood	.15	.07	.02
☐ 847	John Urrea	.15	.07	.02
☐ 848	Mike Vail	.15	.07	.02
☐ 849	Ellis Valentine	.15	.07	.02
☐ 850	Fernando Valenzuela	2.50	1.15	.30
☐ 851	Pete Vuckovich	.25	.11	.03
☐ 852	Mark Wagner	.15	.07	.02
☐ 853	Bob Walk	.60	.25	.08
☐ 854	Claudell Washington	.15	.07	.02
☐ 855	Dave Winfield	10.00	4.50	1.25
☐ 856	Geoff Zahn	.15	.07	.02
☐ 857	Richie Zisk	.15	.07	.02
☐ 858	Checklist 727-858	.15	.02	.00

1982 Topps

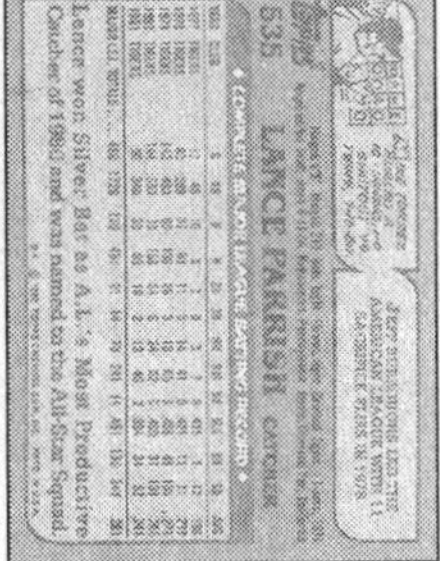

The cards in this 792-card set measure 2 1/2" by 3 1/2". The 1982 baseball series was the first of the largest sets Topps issued at one printing. The 66-card increase from the previous year's total eliminated the "double print" practice, that had occurred in every regular issue since 1978. Cards 1-6 depict Highlights (HL) of the 1981 season, cards 161-168 picture League Leaders, and there are mini-series of AL (547-557) and NL (337-347) All-Stars (AS). The abbreviation "SA" in the checklist is given for the 40 "Super Action" cards introduced in this set. The team cards are actually Team Leader (TL) cards picturing the batting (BA: batting average) and pitching leader for that team with a checklist back. The key Rookie Cards in this set are George Bell, Cal Ripken, Steve Sax, Lee Smith, and Dave Stewart.

	NRMT-MT	EXC	G-VG
COMPLETE SET (792)	150.00	70.00	19.00
COMMON PLAYER (1-792)	.10	.05	.01
☐ 1 HL: Steve Carlton Sets new NL strikeout record	.75	.19	.06
☐ 2 HL: Ron Davis Fans 8 straight in relief	.15	.07	.02
☐ 3 HL: Tim Raines Swipes 71 bases as rookie	.35	.16	.04
☐ 4 HL: Pete Rose Sets NL career hits mark	.75	.35	.09
☐ 5 HL: Nolan Ryan Pitches fifth career no-hitter	3.00	1.35	.40
☐ 6 HL: Fern. Valenzuela 8 shutouts as rookie	.15	.07	.02
☐ 7 Scott Sanderson	.15	.07	.02
☐ 8 Rich Dauer	.10	.05	.01
☐ 9 Ron Guidry	.30	.14	.04
☐ 10 SA: Ron Guidry	.15	.07	.02
☐ 11 Gary Alexander	.10	.05	.01

No.	Card			
☐ 12	Moose Haas	.10	.05	.01
☐ 13	Lamar Johnson	.10	.05	.01
☐ 14	Steve Howe	.10	.05	.01
☐ 15	Ellis Valentine	.10	.05	.01
☐ 16	Steve Comer	.10	.05	.01
☐ 17	Darrell Evans	.15	.07	.02
☐ 18	Fernando Arroyo	.10	.05	.01
☐ 19	Ernie Whitt	.10	.05	.01
☐ 20	Garry Maddox	.10	.05	.01
☐ 21	Orioles Rookies Bob Bonner Cal Ripken Jeff Schneider	75.00	34.00	9.50
☐ 22	Jim Beattie	.10	.05	.01
☐ 23	Willie Hernandez	.15	.07	.02
☐ 24	Dave Frost	.10	.05	.01
☐ 25	Jerry Remy	.10	.05	.01
☐ 26	Jorge Orta	.10	.05	.01
☐ 27	Tom Herr	.15	.07	.02
☐ 28	John Urrea	.10	.05	.01
☐ 29	Dwayne Murphy	.10	.05	.01
☐ 30	Tom Seaver	2.00	.90	.25
☐ 31	SA: Tom Seaver	1.00	.45	.13
☐ 32	Gene Garber	.10	.05	.01
☐ 33	Jerry Morales	.10	.05	.01
☐ 34	Joe Sambito	.10	.05	.01
☐ 35	Willie Aikens	.10	.05	.01
☐ 36	Rangers TL BA: Al Oliver Pitching: Doc Medich	.20	.09	.03
☐ 37	Dan Graham	.10	.05	.01
☐ 38	Charlie Lea	.10	.05	.01
☐ 39	Lou Whitaker	.75	.35	.09
☐ 40	Dave Parker	.50	.23	.06
☐ 41	SA: Dave Parker	.25	.11	.03
☐ 42	Rick Sofield	.10	.05	.01
☐ 43	Mike Cubbage	.10	.05	.01
☐ 44	Britt Burns	.10	.05	.01
☐ 45	Rick Cerone	.10	.05	.01
☐ 46	Jerry Augustine	.10	.05	.01
☐ 47	Jeff Leonard	.10	.05	.01
☐ 48	Bobby Castillo	.10	.05	.01
☐ 49	Alvis Woods	.10	.05	.01
☐ 50	Buddy Bell	.15	.07	.02
☐ 51	Cubs Rookies Jay Howell Carlos Lezcano Ty Waller	.40	.18	.05
☐ 52	Larry Andersen	.10	.05	.01
☐ 53	Greg Gross	.10	.05	.01
☐ 54	Ron Hassey	.10	.05	.01
☐ 55	Rick Burleson	.10	.05	.01
☐ 56	Mark Littell	.10	.05	.01
☐ 57	Craig Reynolds	.10	.05	.01
☐ 58	John D'Acquisto	.10	.05	.01
☐ 59	Rich Gedman	.20	.09	.03
☐ 60	Tony Armas	.10	.05	.01
☐ 61	Tommy Boggs	.10	.05	.01
☐ 62	Mike Tyson	.10	.05	.01
☐ 63	Mario Soto	.10	.05	.01
☐ 64	Lynn Jones	.10	.05	.01
☐ 65	Terry Kennedy	.10	.05	.01
☐ 66	Astros TL BA: Art Howe Pitching: Nolan Ryan	1.00	.45	.13
☐ 67	Rich Gale	.10	.05	.01
☐ 68	Roy Howell	.10	.05	.01
☐ 69	Al Williams	.10	.05	.01
☐ 70	Tim Raines	1.75	.80	.22
☐ 71	Roy Lee Jackson	.10	.05	.01
☐ 72	Rick Auerbach	.10	.05	.01
☐ 73	Buddy Solomon	.10	.05	.01
☐ 74	Bob Clark	.10	.05	.01
☐ 75	Tommy John	.30	.14	.04
☐ 76	Greg Pryor	.10	.05	.01
☐ 77	Miguel Dilone	.10	.05	.01
☐ 78	George Medich	.10	.05	.01
☐ 79	Bob Bailor	.10	.05	.01
☐ 80	Jim Palmer	1.75	.80	.22
☐ 81	SA: Jim Palmer	.75	.35	.09
☐ 82	Bob Welch	.40	.18	.05
☐ 83	Yankees Rookies Steve Balboni Andy McGaffigan Andre Robertson	.15	.07	.02
☐ 84	Rennie Stennett	.10	.05	.01
☐ 85	Lynn McGlothen	.10	.05	.01
☐ 86	Dane Iorg	.10	.05	.01
☐ 87	Matt Keough	.10	.05	.01
☐ 88	Biff Pocoroba	.10	.05	.01
☐ 89	Steve Henderson	.10	.05	.01
☐ 90	Nolan Ryan	11.00	4.90	1.40
☐ 91	Carney Lansford	.15	.07	.02
☐ 92	Brad Havens	.10	.05	.01
☐ 93	Larry Hisle	.10	.05	.01
☐ 94	Andy Hassler	.10	.05	.01
☐ 95	Ozzie Smith	3.00	1.35	.40
☐ 96	Royals TL BA: George Brett Pitching: Larry Gura	.50	.23	.06
☐ 97	Paul Moskau	.10	.05	.01
☐ 98	Terry Bulling	.10	.05	.01
☐ 99	Barry Bonnell	.10	.05	.01
☐ 100	Mike Schmidt	3.50	1.55	.45
☐ 101	SA: Mike Schmidt	1.50	.65	.19
☐ 102	Dan Briggs	.10	.05	.01
☐ 103	Bob Lacey	.10	.05	.01
☐ 104	Rance Mulliniks	.10	.05	.01
☐ 105	Kirk Gibson	.75	.35	.09
☐ 106	Enrique Romo	.10	.05	.01
☐ 107	Wayne Krenchicki	.10	.05	.01
☐ 108	Bob Sykes	.10	.05	.01
☐ 109	Dave Revering	.10	.05	.01
☐ 110	Carlton Fisk	2.00	.90	.25
☐ 111	SA: Carlton Fisk	1.00	.45	.13
☐ 112	Billy Sample	.10	.05	.01
☐ 113	Steve McCatty	.10	.05	.01
☐ 114	Ken Landreaux	.10	.05	.01
☐ 115	Gaylord Perry	.75	.35	.09
☐ 116	Jim Wohlford	.10	.05	.01
☐ 117	Rawly Eastwick	.10	.05	.01
☐ 118	Expos Rookies Terry Francona Brad Mills Bryn Smith	.35	.16	.04
☐ 119	Joe Pittman	.10	.05	.01
☐ 120	Gary Lucas	.10	.05	.01
☐ 121	Ed Lynch	.10	.05	.01
☐ 122	Jamie Easterly UER (Photo actually Reggie Cleveland)	.10	.05	.01
☐ 123	Danny Goodwin	.10	.05	.01
☐ 124	Reid Nichols	.10	.05	.01
☐ 125	Danny Ainge	1.25	.55	.16
☐ 126	Braves TL BA: Claudell Washington Pitching: Rick Mahler	.20	.09	.03
☐ 127	Lonnie Smith	.15	.07	.02
☐ 128	Frank Pastore	.10	.05	.01
☐ 129	Checklist 1-132	.15	.01	.00
☐ 130	Julio Cruz	.10	.05	.01
☐ 131	Stan Bahnsen	.10	.05	.01
☐ 132	Lee May	.10	.05	.01
☐ 133	Pat Underwood	.10	.05	.01
☐ 134	Dan Ford	.10	.05	.01
☐ 135	Andy Rincon	.10	.05	.01
☐ 136	Lenn Sakata	.10	.05	.01
☐ 137	George Cappuzzello	.10	.05	.01
☐ 138	Tony Pena	.25	.11	.03
☐ 139	Jeff Jones	.10	.05	.01
☐ 140	Ron LeFlore	.15	.07	.02
☐ 141	Indians Rookies Chris Bando Tom Brennan Von Hayes	.40	.18	.05
☐ 142	Dave LaRoche	.10	.05	.01
☐ 143	Mookie Wilson	.15	.07	.02
☐ 144	Fred Breining	.10	.05	.01
☐ 145	Bob Horner	.15	.07	.02
☐ 146	Mike Griffin	.10	.05	.01
☐ 147	Denny Walling	.10	.05	.01
☐ 148	Mickey Klutts	.10	.05	.01
☐ 149	Pat Putnam	.10	.05	.01
☐ 150	Ted Simmons	.15	.07	.02
☐ 151	Dave Edwards	.10	.05	.01
☐ 152	Ramon Aviles	.10	.05	.01
☐ 153	Roger Erickson	.10	.05	.01
☐ 154	Dennis Werth	.10	.05	.01
☐ 155	Otto Velez	.10	.05	.01
☐ 156	Oakland A's TL BA: Rickey Henderson Pitching: Steve McCatty	.75	.35	.09
☐ 157	Steve Crawford	.10	.05	.01
☐ 158	Brian Downing	.15	.07	.02
☐ 159	Larry Biittner	.10	.05	.01
☐ 160	Luis Tiant	.15	.07	.02
☐ 161	Batting Leaders Bill Madlock Carney Lansford	.20	.09	.03
☐ 162	Home Run Leaders Mike Schmidt Tony Armas Dwight Evans Bobby Grich Eddie Murray	.50	.23	.06
☐ 163	RBI Leaders	.75	.35	.09

Mike Schmidt			
Eddie Murray			
☐ 164 Stolen Base Leaders	1.50	.65	.19
Tim Raines			
Rickey Henderson			
☐ 165 Victory Leaders	.20	.09	.03
Tom Seaver			
Denny Martinez			
Steve McCatty			
Jack Morris			
Pete Vuckovich			
☐ 166 Strikeout Leaders	.20	.09	.03
Fernando Valenzuela			
Len Barker			
☐ 167 ERA Leaders	1.50	.65	.19
Nolan Ryan			
Steve McCatty			
☐ 168 Leading Firemen	.25	.11	.03
Bruce Sutter			
Rollie Fingers			
☐ 169 Charlie Leibrandt	.15	.07	.02
☐ 170 Jim Bibby	.10	.05	.01
☐ 171 Giants Rookies	1.50	.65	.19
Bob Brenly			
Chili Davis			
Bob Tufts			
☐ 172 Bill Gullickson	.35	.16	.04
☐ 173 Jamie Quirk	.10	.05	.01
☐ 174 Dave Ford	.10	.05	.01
☐ 175 Jerry Mumphrey	.10	.05	.01
☐ 176 Dewey Robinson	.10	.05	.01
☐ 177 John Ellis	.10	.05	.01
☐ 178 Dyar Miller	.10	.05	.01
☐ 179 Steve Garvey	.75	.35	.09
☐ 180 SA: Steve Garvey	.35	.16	.04
☐ 181 Silvio Martinez	.10	.05	.01
☐ 182 Larry Herndon	.10	.05	.01
☐ 183 Mike Proly	.10	.05	.01
☐ 184 Mick Kelleher	.10	.05	.01
☐ 185 Phil Niekro	.75	.35	.09
☐ 186 Cardinals TL	.20	.09	.03
BA: Keith Hernandez			
Pitching: Bob Forsch			
☐ 187 Jeff Newman	.10	.05	.01
☐ 188 Randy Martz	.10	.05	.01
☐ 189 Glenn Hoffman	.10	.05	.01
☐ 190 J.R. Richard	.15	.07	.02
☐ 191 Tim Wallach	1.50	.65	.19
☐ 192 Broderick Perkins	.10	.05	.01
☐ 193 Darrell Jackson	.10	.05	.01
☐ 194 Mike Vail	.10	.05	.01
☐ 195 Paul Molitor	1.50	.65	.19
☐ 196 Willie Upshaw	.10	.05	.01
☐ 197 Shane Rawley	.10	.05	.01
☐ 198 Chris Speier	.10	.05	.01
☐ 199 Don Aase	.10	.05	.01
☐ 200 George Brett	4.00	1.80	.50
☐ 201 SA: George Brett	2.00	.90	.25
☐ 202 Rick Manning	.10	.05	.01
☐ 203 Blue Jays Rookies	.90	.40	.11
Jesse Barfield			
Brian Milner			
Boomer Wells			
☐ 204 Gary Roenicke	.10	.05	.01
☐ 205 Neil Allen	.10	.05	.01
☐ 206 Tony Bernazard	.10	.05	.01
☐ 207 Rod Scurry	.10	.05	.01
☐ 208 Bobby Murcer	.15	.07	.02
☐ 209 Gary Lavelle	.10	.05	.01
☐ 210 Keith Hernandez	.35	.16	.04
☐ 211 Dan Petry	.10	.05	.01
☐ 212 Mario Mendoza	.10	.05	.01
☐ 213 Dave Stewart	4.50	2.00	.55
☐ 214 Brian Asselstine	.10	.05	.01
☐ 215 Mike Krukow	.10	.05	.01
☐ 216 White Sox TL	.20	.09	.03
BA: Chet Lemon			
Pitching: Dennis Lamp			
☐ 217 Bo McLaughlin	.10	.05	.01
☐ 218 Dave Roberts	.10	.05	.01
☐ 219 John Curtis	.10	.05	.01
☐ 220 Manny Trillo	.10	.05	.01
☐ 221 Jim Slaton	.10	.05	.01
☐ 222 Butch Wynegar	.10	.05	.01
☐ 223 Lloyd Moseby	.10	.05	.01
☐ 224 Bruce Bochte	.10	.05	.01
☐ 225 Mike Torrez	.10	.05	.01
☐ 226 Checklist 133-264	.15	.01	.00
☐ 227 Ray Burris	.10	.05	.01
☐ 228 Sam Mejias	.10	.05	.01
☐ 229 Geoff Zahn	.10	.05	.01
☐ 230 Willie Wilson	.15	.07	.02
☐ 231 Phillies Rookies	.30	.14	.04
Mark Davis			
Bob Dernier			
Ozzie Virgil			
☐ 232 Terry Crowley	.10	.05	.01
☐ 233 Duane Kuiper	.10	.05	.01
☐ 234 Ron Hodges	.10	.05	.01
☐ 235 Mike Easler	.10	.05	.01
☐ 236 John Martin	.10	.05	.01
☐ 237 Rusty Kuntz	.10	.05	.01
☐ 238 Kevin Saucier	.10	.05	.01
☐ 239 Jon Matlack	.10	.05	.01
☐ 240 Bucky Dent	.15	.07	.02
☐ 241 SA: Bucky Dent	.10	.05	.01
☐ 242 Milt May	.10	.05	.01
☐ 243 Bob Owchinko	.10	.05	.01
☐ 244 Rufino Linares	.10	.05	.01
☐ 245 Ken Reitz	.10	.05	.01
☐ 246 New York Mets TL	.20	.09	.03
BA: Hubie Brooks			
Pitching: Mike Scott			
☐ 247 Pedro Guerrero	.40	.18	.05
☐ 248 Frank LaCorte	.10	.05	.01
☐ 249 Tim Flannery	.10	.05	.01
☐ 250 Tug McGraw	.15	.07	.02
☐ 251 Fred Lynn	.15	.07	.02
☐ 252 SA: Fred Lynn	.10	.05	.01
☐ 253 Chuck Baker	.10	.05	.01
☐ 254 Jorge Bell	8.00	3.60	1.00
☐ 255 Tony Perez	.50	.23	.06
☐ 256 SA: Tony Perez	.25	.11	.03
☐ 257 Larry Harlow	.10	.05	.01
☐ 258 Bo Diaz	.10	.05	.01
☐ 259 Rodney Scott	.10	.05	.01
☐ 260 Bruce Sutter	.25	.11	.03
☐ 261 Tigers Rookies UER	.12	.05	.02
Howard Bailey			
Marty Castillo			
Dave Rucker			
(Rucker photo act-			
ally Roger Weaver)			
☐ 262 Doug Bair	.10	.05	.01
☐ 263 Victor Cruz	.10	.05	.01
☐ 264 Dan Quisenberry	.15	.07	.02
☐ 265 Al Bumbry	.10	.05	.01
☐ 266 Rick Leach	.10	.05	.01
☐ 267 Kurt Bevacqua	.10	.05	.01
☐ 268 Rickey Keeton	.10	.05	.01
☐ 269 Jim Essian	.10	.05	.01
☐ 270 Rusty Staub	.15	.07	.02
☐ 271 Larry Bradford	.10	.05	.01
☐ 272 Bump Wills	.10	.05	.01
☐ 273 Doug Bird	.10	.05	.01
☐ 274 Bob Ojeda	.60	.25	.08
☐ 275 Bob Watson	.15	.07	.02
☐ 276 Angels TL	.25	.11	.03
BA: Rod Carew			
Pitching: Ken Forsch			
☐ 277 Terry Puhl	.10	.05	.01
☐ 278 John Littlefield	.10	.05	.01
☐ 279 Bill Russell	.15	.07	.02
☐ 280 Ben Oglivie	.15	.07	.02
☐ 281 John Verhoeven	.10	.05	.01
☐ 282 Ken Macha	.10	.05	.01
☐ 283 Brian Allard	.10	.05	.01
☐ 284 Bob Grich	.15	.07	.02
☐ 285 Sparky Lyle	.15	.07	.02
☐ 286 Bill Fahey	.10	.05	.01
☐ 287 Alan Bannister	.10	.05	.01
☐ 288 Garry Templeton	.15	.07	.02
☐ 289 Bob Stanley	.10	.05	.01
☐ 290 Ken Singleton	.15	.07	.02
☐ 291 Pirates Rookies	.20	.09	.03
Vance Law			
Bob Long			
Johnny Ray			
☐ 292 David Palmer	.10	.05	.01
☐ 293 Rob Picciolo	.10	.05	.01
☐ 294 Mike LaCoss	.10	.05	.01
☐ 295 Jason Thompson	.10	.05	.01
☐ 296 Bob Walk	.10	.05	.01
☐ 297 Clint Hurdle	.10	.05	.01
☐ 298 Danny Darwin	.10	.05	.01
☐ 299 Steve Trout	.10	.05	.01
☐ 300 Reggie Jackson	3.00	1.35	.40
☐ 301 SA: Reggie Jackson	1.50	.65	.19
☐ 302 Doug Flynn	.10	.05	.01
☐ 303 Bill Caudill	.10	.05	.01
☐ 304 Johnnie LeMaster	.10	.05	.01
☐ 305 Don Sutton	.75	.35	.09
☐ 306 SA: Don Sutton	.35	.16	.04
☐ 307 Randy Bass	.10	.05	.01
☐ 308 Charlie Moore	.10	.05	.01
☐ 309 Pete Redfern	.10	.05	.01
☐ 310 Mike Hargrove	.15	.07	.02
☐ 311 Dodgers TL	.20	.09	.03

BA: Dusty Baker
Pitching: Burt Hooton

Card			
□ 312 Lenny Randle	.10	.05	.01
□ 313 John Harris	.10	.05	.01
□ 314 Buck Martinez	.10	.05	.01
□ 315 Burt Hooton	.10	.05	.01
□ 316 Steve Braun	.10	.05	.01
□ 317 Dick Ruthven	.10	.05	.01
□ 318 Mike Heath	.10	.05	.01
□ 319 Dave Rozema	.10	.05	.01
□ 320 Chris Chambliss	.15	.07	.02
□ 321 SA: Chris Chambliss	.10	.05	.01
□ 322 Garry Hancock	.10	.05	.01
□ 323 Bill Lee	.10	.05	.01
□ 324 Steve Dillard	.10	.05	.01
□ 325 Jose Cruz	.15	.07	.02
□ 326 Pete Falcone	.10	.05	.01
□ 327 Joe Nolan	.10	.05	.01
□ 328 Ed Farmer	.10	.05	.01
□ 329 U.L. Washington	.10	.05	.01
□ 330 Rick Wise	.10	.05	.01
□ 331 Benny Ayala	.10	.05	.01
□ 332 Don Robinson	.10	.05	.01
□ 333 Brewers Rookies Frank DiPino Marshall Edwards Chuck Porter	.12	.05	.02
□ 334 Aurelio Rodriguez	.10	.05	.01
□ 335 Jim Sundberg	.15	.07	.02
□ 336 Mariners TL BA: Tom Paciorek Pitching: Glenn Abbott	.20	.09	.03
□ 337 Pete Rose AS	.90	.40	.11
□ 338 Dave Lopes AS	.15	.07	.02
□ 339 Mike Schmidt AS	1.25	.55	.16
□ 340 Dave Concepcion AS	.15	.07	.02
□ 341 Andre Dawson AS	1.00	.45	.13
□ 342A George Foster AS (With autograph)	.15	.07	.02
□ 342B George Foster AS (W/o autograph)	1.00	.45	.13
□ 343 Dave Parker AS	.20	.09	.03
□ 344 Gary Carter AS	.50	.23	.06
□ 345 Fernando Valenzuela AS	.15	.07	.02
□ 346A Tom Seaver AS ERR ("t ed")	1.25	.55	.16
□ 346B Tom Seaver AS COR ("tied")	.75	.35	.09
□ 347 Bruce Sutter AS	.15	.07	.02
□ 348 Derrel Thomas	.10	.05	.01
□ 349 George Frazier	.10	.05	.01
□ 350 Thad Bosley	.10	.05	.01
□ 351 Reds Rookies Scott Brown Geoff Combe Paul Householder	.12	.05	.02
□ 352 Dick Davis	.10	.05	.01
□ 353 Jack O'Connor	.10	.05	.01
□ 354 Roberto Ramos	.10	.05	.01
□ 355 Dwight Evans	.35	.16	.04
□ 356 Denny Lewallyn	.10	.05	.01
□ 357 Butch Hobson	.15	.07	.02
□ 358 Mike Parrott	.10	.05	.01
□ 359 Jim Dwyer	.10	.05	.01
□ 360 Len Barker	.10	.05	.01
□ 361 Rafael Landestoy	.10	.05	.01
□ 362 Jim Wright UER (Wrong Jim Wright pictured)	.10	.05	.01
□ 363 Bob Molinaro	.10	.05	.01
□ 364 Doyle Alexander	.10	.05	.01
□ 365 Bill Madlock	.15	.07	.02
□ 366 Padres TL BA: Luis Salazar Pitching: Juan Eichelberger	.20	.09	.03
□ 367 Jim Kaat	.20	.09	.03
□ 368 Alex Trevino	.10	.05	.01
□ 369 Champ Summers	.10	.05	.01
□ 370 Mike Norris	.10	.05	.01
□ 371 Jerry Don Gleaton	.10	.05	.01
□ 372 Luis Gomez	.10	.05	.01
□ 373 Gene Nelson	.10	.05	.01
□ 374 Tim Blackwell	.10	.05	.01
□ 375 Dusty Baker	.15	.07	.02
□ 376 Chris Welsh	.10	.05	.01
□ 377 Kiko Garcia	.10	.05	.01
□ 378 Mike Caldwell	.10	.05	.01
□ 379 Rob Wilfong	.10	.05	.01
□ 380 Dave Stieb	.30	.14	.04
□ 381 Red Sox Rookies Bruce Hurst Dave Schmidt Julio Valdez	.50	.23	.06
□ 382 Joe Simpson	.10	.05	.01
□ 383A Pascual Perez ERR (No position on front)	20.00	9.00	2.50
□ 383B Pascual Perez COR	.15	.07	.02
□ 384 Keith Moreland	.10	.05	.01
□ 385 Ken Forsch	.10	.05	.01
□ 386 Jerry White	.10	.05	.01
□ 387 Tom Veryzer	.10	.05	.01
□ 388 Joe Rudi	.10	.05	.01
□ 389 George Vukovich	.10	.05	.01
□ 390 Eddie Murray	3.00	1.35	.40
□ 391 Dave Tobik	.10	.05	.01
□ 392 Rick Bosetti	.10	.05	.01
□ 393 Al Hrabosky	.10	.05	.01
□ 394 Checklist 265-396	.15	.01	.00
□ 395 Omar Moreno	.10	.05	.01
□ 396 Twins TL BA: John Castino Pitching: Fernando Arroyo	.20	.09	.03
□ 397 Ken Brett	.10	.05	.01
□ 398 Mike Squires	.10	.05	.01
□ 399 Pat Zachry	.10	.05	.01
□ 400 Johnny Bench	2.00	.90	.25
□ 401 SA: Johnny Bench	1.00	.45	.13
□ 402 Bill Stein	.10	.05	.01
□ 403 Jim Tracy	.10	.05	.01
□ 404 Dickie Thon	.10	.05	.01
□ 405 Rick Reuschel	.15	.07	.02
□ 406 Al Holland	.10	.05	.01
□ 407 Danny Boone	.10	.05	.01
□ 408 Ed Romero	.10	.05	.01
□ 409 Don Cooper	.10	.05	.01
□ 410 Ron Cey	.15	.07	.02
□ 411 SA: Ron Cey	.10	.05	.01
□ 412 Luis Leal	.10	.05	.01
□ 413 Dan Meyer	.10	.05	.01
□ 414 Elias Sosa	.10	.05	.01
□ 415 Don Baylor	.15	.07	.02
□ 416 Marty Bystrom	.10	.05	.01
□ 417 Pat Kelly	.10	.05	.01
□ 418 Rangers Rookies John Butcher Bobby Johnson Dave Schmidt	.12	.05	.02
□ 419 Steve Stone	.15	.07	.02
□ 420 George Hendrick	.15	.07	.02
□ 421 Mark Clear	.10	.05	.01
□ 422 Cliff Johnson	.10	.05	.01
□ 423 Stan Papi	.10	.05	.01
□ 424 Bruce Benedict	.10	.05	.01
□ 425 John Candelaria	.10	.05	.01
□ 426 Orioles TL BA: Eddie Murray Pitching: Sammy Stewart	.35	.16	.04
□ 427 Ron Oester	.10	.05	.01
□ 428 LaMarr Hoyt	.10	.05	.01
□ 429 John Wathan	.10	.05	.01
□ 430 Vida Blue	.15	.07	.02
□ 431 SA: Vida Blue	.10	.05	.01
□ 432 Mike Scott	.15	.07	.02
□ 433 Alan Ashby	.10	.05	.01
□ 434 Joe Lefebvre	.10	.05	.01
□ 435 Robin Yount	4.00	1.80	.50
□ 436 Joe Strain	.10	.05	.01
□ 437 Juan Berenguer	.10	.05	.01
□ 438 Pete Mackanin	.10	.05	.01
□ 439 Dave Righetti	.75	.35	.09
□ 440 Jeff Burroughs	.10	.05	.01
□ 441 Astros Rookies Danny Heep Billy Smith Bobby Sprowl	.12	.05	.02
□ 442 Bruce Kison	.10	.05	.01
□ 443 Mark Wagner	.10	.05	.01
□ 444 Terry Forster	.10	.05	.01
□ 445 Larry Parrish	.10	.05	.01
□ 446 Wayne Garland	.10	.05	.01
□ 447 Darrell Porter	.10	.05	.01
□ 448 SA: Darrell Porter	.10	.05	.01
□ 449 Luis Aguayo	.10	.05	.01
□ 450 Jack Morris	2.50	1.15	.30
□ 451 Ed Miller	.10	.05	.01
□ 452 Lee Smith	10.00	4.50	1.25
□ 453 Art Howe	.10	.05	.01
□ 454 Rick Langford	.10	.05	.01
□ 455 Tom Burgmeier	.10	.05	.01
□ 456 Chicago Cubs TL BA: Bill Buckner Pitching: Randy Martz	.20	.09	.03
□ 457 Tim Stoddard	.10	.05	.01
□ 458 Willie Montanez	.10	.05	.01

☐ 459 Bruce Berenyi	.10	.05	.01
☐ 460 Jack Clark	.30	.14	.04
☐ 461 Rich Dotson	.10	.05	.01
☐ 462 Dave Chalk	.10	.05	.01
☐ 463 Jim Kern	.10	.05	.01
☐ 464 Juan Bonilla	.10	.05	.01
☐ 465 Lee Mazzilli	.10	.05	.01
☐ 466 Randy Lerch	.10	.05	.01
☐ 467 Mickey Hatcher	.10	.05	.01
☐ 468 Floyd Bannister	.10	.05	.01
☐ 469 Ed Ott	.10	.05	.01
☐ 470 John Mayberry	.10	.05	.01
☐ 471 Royals Rookies	.12	.05	.02
Atlee Hammaker			
Mike Jones			
Darryl Motley			
☐ 472 Oscar Gamble	.10	.05	.01
☐ 473 Mike Stanton	.10	.05	.01
☐ 474 Ken Oberkfell	.10	.05	.01
☐ 475 Alan Trammell	.90	.40	.11
☐ 476 Brian Kingman	.10	.05	.01
☐ 477 Steve Yeager	.10	.05	.01
☐ 478 Ray Searage	.10	.05	.01
☐ 479 Rowland Office	.10	.05	.01
☐ 480 Steve Carlton	2.00	.90	.25
☐ 481 SA: Steve Carlton	1.00	.45	.13
☐ 482 Glenn Hubbard	.10	.05	.01
☐ 483 Gary Woods	.10	.05	.01
☐ 484 Ivan DeJesus	.10	.05	.01
☐ 485 Kent Tekulve	.15	.07	.02
☐ 486 Yankees TL	.20	.09	.03
BA: Jerry Mumphrey			
Pitching: Tommy John			
☐ 487 Bob McClure	.10	.05	.01
☐ 488 Ron Jackson	.10	.05	.01
☐ 489 Rick Dempsey	.15	.07	.02
☐ 490 Dennis Eckersley	2.50	1.15	.30
☐ 491 Checklist 397-528	.15	.01	.00
☐ 492 Joe Price	.10	.05	.01
☐ 493 Chet Lemon	.10	.05	.01
☐ 494 Hubie Brooks	.35	.16	.04
☐ 495 Dennis Leonard	.10	.05	.01
☐ 496 Johnny Grubb	.10	.05	.01
☐ 497 Jim Anderson	.10	.05	.01
☐ 498 Dave Bergman	.10	.05	.01
☐ 499 Paul Mirabella	.10	.05	.01
☐ 500 Rod Carew	2.00	.90	.25
☐ 501 SA: Rod Carew	1.00	.45	.13
☐ 502 Braves Rookies	3.00	1.35	.40
Steve Bedrosian UER			
(Photo actually			
Larry Owen)			
Brett Butler			
Larry Owen			
☐ 503 Julio Gonzalez	.10	.05	.01
☐ 504 Rick Peters	.10	.05	.01
☐ 505 Graig Nettles	.15	.07	.02
☐ 506 SA: Graig Nettles	.10	.05	.01
☐ 507 Terry Harper	.10	.05	.01
☐ 508 Jody Davis	.15	.07	.02
☐ 509 Harry Spilman	.10	.05	.01
☐ 510 Fernando Valenzuela	.35	.16	.04
☐ 511 Ruppert Jones	.10	.05	.01
☐ 512 Jerry Dybzinski	.10	.05	.01
☐ 513 Rick Rhoden	.10	.05	.01
☐ 514 Joe Ferguson	.10	.05	.01
☐ 515 Larry Bowa	.15	.07	.02
☐ 516 SA: Larry Bowa	.10	.05	.01
☐ 517 Mark Brouhard	.10	.05	.01
☐ 518 Garth Iorg	.10	.05	.01
☐ 519 Glenn Adams	.10	.05	.01
☐ 520 Mike Flanagan	.15	.07	.02
☐ 521 Bill Almon	.10	.05	.01
☐ 522 Chuck Rainey	.10	.05	.01
☐ 523 Gary Gray	.10	.05	.01
☐ 524 Tom Hausman	.10	.05	.01
☐ 525 Ray Knight	.15	.07	.02
☐ 526 Expos TL	.20	.09	.03
BA: Warren Cromartie			
Pitching: Bill Gullickson			
☐ 527 John Henry Johnson	.10	.05	.01
☐ 528 Matt Alexander	.10	.05	.01
☐ 529 Allen Ripley	.10	.05	.01
☐ 530 Dickie Noles	.10	.05	.01
☐ 531 A's Rookies	.12	.05	.02
Rich Bordi			
Mark Budaska			
Kelvin Moore			
☐ 532 Toby Harrah	.15	.07	.02
☐ 533 Joaquin Andujar	.15	.07	.02
☐ 534 Dave McKay	.10	.05	.01
☐ 535 Lance Parrish	.35	.16	.04
☐ 536 Rafael Ramirez	.10	.05	.01

☐ 537 Doug Capilla	.10	.05	.01
☐ 538 Lou Piniella	.15	.07	.02
☐ 539 Vern Ruhle	.10	.05	.01
☐ 540 Andre Dawson	3.00	1.35	.40
☐ 541 Barry Evans	.10	.05	.01
☐ 542 Ned Yost	.10	.05	.01
☐ 543 Bill Robinson	.15	.07	.02
☐ 544 Larry Christenson	.10	.05	.01
☐ 545 Reggie Smith	.15	.07	.02
☐ 546 SA: Reggie Smith	.10	.05	.01
☐ 547 Rod Carew AS	.90	.40	.11
☐ 548 Willie Randolph AS	.15	.07	.02
☐ 549 George Brett AS	1.75	.80	.22
☐ 550 Bucky Dent AS	.15	.07	.02
☐ 551 Reggie Jackson AS	1.50	.65	.19
☐ 552 Ken Singleton AS	.15	.07	.02
☐ 553 Dave Winfield AS	1.50	.65	.19
☐ 554 Carlton Fisk AS	.75	.35	.09
☐ 555 Scott McGregor AS	.15	.07	.02
☐ 556 Jack Morris AS	.60	.25	.08
☐ 557 Rich Gossage AS	.15	.07	.02
☐ 558 John Tudor	.15	.07	.02
☐ 559 Indians TL	.20	.09	.03
BA: Mike Hargrove			
Pitching: Bert Blyleven			
☐ 560 Doug Corbett	.10	.05	.01
☐ 561 Cardinals Rookies	.12	.05	.02
Glenn Brummer			
Luis DeLeon			
Gene Roof			
☐ 562 Mike O'Berry	.10	.05	.01
☐ 563 Ross Baumgarten	.10	.05	.01
☐ 564 Doug DeCinces	.15	.07	.02
☐ 565 Jackson Todd	.10	.05	.01
☐ 566 Mike Jorgensen	.10	.05	.01
☐ 567 Bob Babcock	.10	.05	.01
☐ 568 Joe Pettini	.10	.05	.01
☐ 569 Willie Randolph	.15	.07	.02
☐ 570 SA: Willie Randolph	.10	.05	.01
☐ 571 Glenn Abbott	.10	.05	.01
☐ 572 Juan Beniquez	.10	.05	.01
☐ 573 Rick Waits	.10	.05	.01
☐ 574 Mike Ramsey	.10	.05	.01
☐ 575 Al Cowens	.10	.05	.01
☐ 576 Giants TL	.20	.09	.03
BA: Milt May			
Pitching: Vida Blue			
☐ 577 Rick Monday	.10	.05	.01
☐ 578 Shooty Babitt	.10	.05	.01
☐ 579 Rick Mahler	.10	.05	.01
☐ 580 Bobby Bonds	.15	.07	.02
☐ 581 Ron Reed	.15	.07	.02
☐ 582 Luis Pujols	.10	.05	.01
☐ 583 Tippy Martinez	.10	.05	.01
☐ 584 Hosken Powell	.10	.05	.01
☐ 585 Rollie Fingers	1.00	.45	.13
☐ 586 SA: Rollie Fingers	.50	.23	.06
☐ 587 Tim Lollar	.10	.05	.01
☐ 588 Dale Berra	.10	.05	.01
☐ 589 Dave Stapleton	.10	.05	.01
☐ 590 Al Oliver	.15	.07	.02
☐ 591 SA: Al Oliver	.10	.05	.01
☐ 592 Craig Swan	.10	.05	.01
☐ 593 Billy Smith	.10	.05	.01
☐ 594 Renie Martin	.10	.05	.01
☐ 595 Dave Collins	.10	.05	.01
☐ 596 Damaso Garcia	.10	.05	.01
☐ 597 Wayne Nordhagen	.10	.05	.01
☐ 598 Bob Galasso	.10	.05	.01
☐ 599 White Sox Rookies	.12	.05	.02
Jay Loviglio			
Reggie Patterson			
Leo Sutherland			
☐ 600 Dave Winfield	4.00	1.80	.50
☐ 601 Sid Monge	.10	.05	.01
☐ 602 Freddie Patek	.10	.05	.01
☐ 603 Rich Hebner	.10	.05	.01
☐ 604 Orlando Sanchez	.10	.05	.01
☐ 605 Steve Rogers	.10	.05	.01
☐ 606 Blue Jays TL	.20	.09	.03
BA: John Mayberry			
Pitching: Dave Stieb			
☐ 607 Leon Durham	.10	.05	.01
☐ 608 Jerry Royster	.10	.05	.01
☐ 609 Rick Sutcliffe	.40	.18	.05
☐ 610 Rickey Henderson	7.00	3.10	.85
☐ 611 Joe Niekro	.15	.07	.02
☐ 612 Gary Ward	.10	.05	.01
☐ 613 Jim Gantner	.15	.07	.02
☐ 614 Juan Eichelberger	.10	.05	.01
☐ 615 Bob Boone	.15	.07	.02
☐ 616 SA: Bob Boone	.10	.05	.01
☐ 617 Scott McGregor	.10	.05	.01

Card			
☐ 618 Tim Foli	.10	.05	.01
☐ 619 Bill Campbell	.10	.05	.01
☐ 620 Ken Griffey	.40	.18	.05
☐ 621 SA: Ken Griffey	.20	.09	.03
☐ 622 Dennis Lamp	.10	.05	.01
☐ 623 Mets Rookies	.35	.16	.04
Ron Gardenhire			
Terry Leach			
Tim Leary			
☐ 624 Fergie Jenkins	.75	.35	.09
☐ 625 Hal McRae	.15	.07	.02
☐ 626 Randy Jones	.10	.05	.01
☐ 627 Enos Cabell	.10	.05	.01
☐ 628 Bill Travers	.10	.05	.01
☐ 629 John Wockenfuss	.10	.05	.01
☐ 630 Joe Charboneau	.10	.05	.01
☐ 631 Gene Tenace	.10	.05	.01
☐ 632 Bryan Clark	.10	.05	.01
☐ 633 Mitchell Page	.10	.05	.01
☐ 634 Checklist 529-660	.15	.01	.00
☐ 635 Ron Davis	.10	.05	.01
☐ 636 Phillies TL	.40	.18	.05
BA: Pete Rose			
Pitching: Steve Carlton			
☐ 637 Rick Camp	.10	.05	.01
☐ 638 John Milner	.10	.05	.01
☐ 639 Ken Kravec	.10	.05	.01
☐ 640 Cesar Cedeno	.15	.07	.02
☐ 641 Steve Mura	.10	.05	.01
☐ 642 Mike Scioscia	.25	.11	.03
☐ 643 Pete Vuckovich	.15	.07	.02
☐ 644 John Castino	.10	.05	.01
☐ 645 Frank White	.15	.07	.02
☐ 646 SA: Frank White	.10	.05	.01
☐ 647 Warren Brusstar	.10	.05	.01
☐ 648 Jose Morales	.10	.05	.01
☐ 649 Ken Clay	.10	.05	.01
☐ 650 Carl Yastrzemski	2.00	.90	.25
☐ 651 SA: Carl Yastrzemski	1.00	.45	.13
☐ 652 Steve Nicosia	.10	.05	.01
☐ 653 Angels Rookies	1.25	.55	.16
Tom Brunansky			
Luis Sanchez			
Daryl Sconiers			
☐ 654 Jim Morrison	.10	.05	.01
☐ 655 Joel Youngblood	.10	.05	.01
☐ 656 Eddie Whitson	.10	.05	.01
☐ 657 Tom Poquette	.10	.05	.01
☐ 658 Tito Landrum	.10	.05	.01
☐ 659 Fred Martinez	.10	.05	.01
☐ 660 Dave Concepcion	.15	.07	.02
☐ 661 SA: Dave Concepcion	.10	.05	.01
☐ 662 Luis Salazar	.10	.05	.01
☐ 663 Hector Cruz	.10	.05	.01
☐ 664 Dan Spillner	.10	.05	.01
☐ 665 Jim Clancy	.10	.05	.01
☐ 666 Tigers TL	.20	.09	.03
BA: Steve Kemp			
Pitching: Dan Petry			
☐ 667 Jeff Reardon	3.00	1.35	.40
☐ 668 Dale Murphy	1.50	.65	.19
☐ 669 Larry Milbourne	.10	.05	.01
☐ 670 Steve Kemp	.10	.05	.01
☐ 671 Mike Davis	.10	.05	.01
☐ 672 Bob Knepper	.10	.05	.01
☐ 673 Keith Drumwright	.10	.05	.01
☐ 674 Dave Goltz	.10	.05	.01
☐ 675 Cecil Cooper	.15	.07	.02
☐ 676 Sal Butera	.10	.05	.01
☐ 677 Alfredo Griffin	.10	.05	.01
☐ 678 Tom Paciorek	.15	.07	.02
☐ 679 Sammy Stewart	.10	.05	.01
☐ 680 Gary Matthews	.15	.07	.02
☐ 681 Dodgers Rookies	5.00	2.30	.60
Mike Marshall			
Ron Roenicke			
Steve Sax			
☐ 682 Jesse Jefferson	.10	.05	.01
☐ 683 Phil Garner	.15	.07	.02
☐ 684 Harold Baines	1.25	.55	.16
☐ 685 Bert Blyleven	.50	.23	.06
☐ 686 Gary Allenson	.10	.05	.01
☐ 687 Greg Minton	.10	.05	.01
☐ 688 Leon Roberts	.10	.05	.01
☐ 689 Lary Sorensen	.10	.05	.01
☐ 690 Dave Kingman	.15	.07	.02
☐ 691 Dan Schatzeder	.10	.05	.01
☐ 692 Wayne Gross	.10	.05	.01
☐ 693 Cesar Geronimo	.10	.05	.01
☐ 694 Dave Wehrmeister	.10	.05	.01
☐ 695 Warren Cromartie	.10	.05	.01
☐ 696 Pirates TL	.20	.09	.03
BA: Bill Madlock			
Pitching: Eddie Solomon			
☐ 697 John Montefusco	.10	.05	.01
☐ 698 Tony Scott	.10	.05	.01
☐ 699 Dick Tidrow	.10	.05	.01
☐ 700 George Foster	.15	.07	.02
☐ 701 SA: George Foster	.10	.05	.01
☐ 702 Steve Renko	.10	.05	.01
☐ 703 Brewers TL	.20	.09	.03
BA: Cecil Cooper			
Pitching: Pete Vuckovich			
☐ 704 Mickey Rivers	.10	.05	.01
☐ 705 SA: Mickey Rivers	.10	.05	.01
☐ 706 Barry Foote	.10	.05	.01
☐ 707 Mark Bomback	.10	.05	.01
☐ 708 Gene Richards	.10	.05	.01
☐ 709 Don Money	.10	.05	.01
☐ 710 Jerry Reuss	.10	.05	.01
☐ 711 Mariners Rookies	1.50	.65	.19
Dave Edler			
Dave Henderson			
Reggie Walton			
☐ 712 Dennis Martinez	.40	.18	.05
☐ 713 Del Unser	.10	.05	.01
☐ 714 Jerry Koosman	.15	.07	.02
☐ 715 Willie Stargell	1.00	.45	.13
☐ 716 SA: Willie Stargell	.50	.23	.06
☐ 717 Rick Miller	.10	.05	.01
☐ 718 Charlie Hough	.15	.07	.02
☐ 719 Jerry Narron	.10	.05	.01
☐ 720 Greg Luzinski	.15	.07	.02
☐ 721 SA: Greg Luzinski	.10	.05	.01
☐ 722 Jerry Martin	.10	.05	.01
☐ 723 Junior Kennedy	.10	.05	.01
☐ 724 Dave Rosello	.10	.05	.01
☐ 725 Amos Otis	.15	.07	.02
☐ 726 SA: Amos Otis	.10	.05	.01
☐ 727 Sixto Lezcano	.10	.05	.01
☐ 728 Aurelio Lopez	.10	.05	.01
☐ 729 Jim Spencer	.10	.05	.01
☐ 730 Gary Carter	1.25	.55	.16
☐ 731 Padres Rookies	.12	.05	.02
Mike Armstrong			
Doug Gwosdz			
Fred Kuhaulua			
☐ 732 Mike Lum	.10	.05	.01
☐ 733 Larry McWilliams	.10	.05	.01
☐ 734 Mike Ivie	.10	.05	.01
☐ 735 Rudy May	.10	.05	.01
☐ 736 Jerry Turner	.10	.05	.01
☐ 737 Reggie Cleveland	.10	.05	.01
☐ 738 Dave Engle	.10	.05	.01
☐ 739 Joey McLaughlin	.10	.05	.01
☐ 740 Dave Lopes	.15	.07	.02
☐ 741 SA: Dave Lopes	.10	.05	.01
☐ 742 Dick Drago	.10	.05	.01
☐ 743 John Stearns	.10	.05	.01
☐ 744 Mike Witt	.20	.09	.03
☐ 745 Bake McBride	.10	.05	.01
☐ 746 Andre Thornton	.15	.07	.02
☐ 747 John Lowenstein	.10	.05	.01
☐ 748 Marc Hill	.10	.05	.01
☐ 749 Bob Shirley	.10	.05	.01
☐ 750 Jim Rice	.40	.18	.05
☐ 751 Rick Honeycutt	.10	.05	.01
☐ 752 Lee Lacy	.10	.05	.01
☐ 753 Tom Brookens	.10	.05	.01
☐ 754 Joe Morgan	1.00	.45	.13
☐ 755 SA: Joe Morgan	.50	.23	.06
☐ 756 Reds TL	.35	.16	.04
BA: Ken Griffey			
Pitching: Tom Seaver			
☐ 757 Tom Underwood	.10	.05	.01
☐ 758 Claudell Washington	.10	.05	.01
☐ 759 Paul Splittorff	.10	.05	.01
☐ 760 Bill Buckner	.15	.07	.02
☐ 761 Dave Smith	.10	.05	.01
☐ 762 Mike Phillips	.10	.05	.01
☐ 763 Tom Hume	.10	.05	.01
☐ 764 Steve Swisher	.10	.05	.01
☐ 765 Gorman Thomas	.15	.07	.02
☐ 766 Twins Rookies	3.00	1.35	.40
Lenny Faedo			
Kent Hrbek			
Tim Laudner			
☐ 767 Roy Smalley	.10	.05	.01
☐ 768 Jerry Garvin	.10	.05	.01
☐ 769 Richie Zisk	.10	.05	.01
☐ 770 Rich Gossage	.30	.14	.04
☐ 771 SA: Rich Gossage	.15	.07	.02
☐ 772 Bert Campaneris	.15	.07	.02
☐ 773 John Denny	.10	.05	.01
☐ 774 Jay Johnstone	.15	.07	.02
☐ 775 Bob Forsch	.10	.05	.01
☐ 776 Mark Belanger	.15	.07	.02

☐ 777 Tom Griffin	.10	.05	.01
☐ 778 Kevin Hickey	.10	.05	.01
☐ 779 Grant Jackson	.10	.05	.01
☐ 780 Pete Rose	2.00	.90	.25
☐ 781 SA: Pete Rose	1.00	.45	.13
☐ 782 Frank Taveras	.10	.05	.01
☐ 783 Greg Harris	.30	.14	.04
☐ 784 Milt Wilcox	.10	.05	.01
☐ 785 Dan Driessen	.10	.05	.01
☐ 786 Red Sox TL BA: Carney Lansford Pitching: Mike Torrez	.20	.09	.03
☐ 787 Fred Stanley	.10	.05	.01
☐ 788 Woodie Fryman	.10	.05	.01
☐ 789 Checklist 661-792	.15	.01	.00
☐ 790 Larry Gura	.10	.05	.01
☐ 791 Bobby Brown	.10	.05	.01
☐ 792 Frank Tanana	.20	.09	.03

1982 Topps Traded

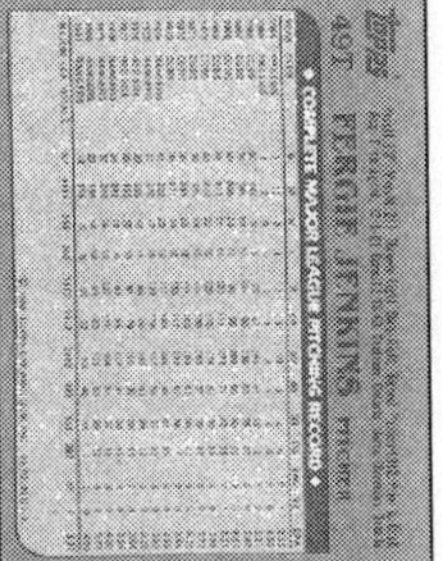

The cards in this 132-card set measure 2 1/2" by 3 1/2". The 1982 Topps Traded or extended series is distinguished by a "T" printed after the number (located on the reverse). This was the first time Topps began a tradition of newly numbering (and alphabetizing) their traded series from 1T to 132T. Of the total cards, 70 players represent the American League and 61 represent the National League, with the remaining card a numbered checklist (132T). The Cubs lead the pack with 12 changes, while the Red Sox are the only team in either league to have no new additions. All 131 player photos used in the set are completely new. Of this total, 112 individuals are seen in the uniform of their new team, 11 others have been elevated to single card status from "Future Stars" cards, and eight more are entirely new to the 1982 Topps lineup. The backs are almost completely red in color with black print. There are no key Rookie Cards in this set. Although the Cal Ripken card is this set's most valuable card, it is not his Rookie Card since he had already been included in the 1982 regular set, albeit on a multi-player card.

	NRMT-MT	EXC	G-VG
COMPLETE SET (132)	300.00	135.00	38.00
COMMON PLAYER (1T-132T)	.40	.18	.05
☐ 1T Doyle Alexander	.40	.18	.05
☐ 2T Jesse Barfield	1.00	.45	.13
☐ 3T Ross Baumgarten	.40	.18	.05
☐ 4T Steve Bedrosian	.50	.23	.06
☐ 5T Mark Belanger	.50	.23	.06
☐ 6T Kurt Bevacqua	.40	.18	.05
☐ 7T Tim Blackwell	.40	.18	.05
☐ 8T Vida Blue	.50	.23	.06
☐ 9T Bob Boone	.50	.23	.06
☐ 10T Larry Bowa	.50	.23	.06
☐ 11T Dan Briggs	.40	.18	.05
☐ 12T Bobby Brown	.40	.18	.05
☐ 13T Tom Brunansky	2.00	.90	.25
☐ 14T Jeff Burroughs	.40	.18	.05
☐ 15T Enos Cabell	.40	.18	.05
☐ 16T Bill Campbell	.40	.18	.05
☐ 17T Bobby Castillo	.40	.18	.05
☐ 18T Bill Caudill	.40	.18	.05
☐ 19T Cesar Cedeno	.50	.23	.06
☐ 20T Dave Collins	.40	.18	.05
☐ 21T Doug Corbett	.40	.18	.05
☐ 22T Al Cowens	.40	.18	.05
☐ 23T Chili Davis	2.00	.90	.25
☐ 24T Dick Davis	.40	.18	.05
☐ 25T Ron Davis	.40	.18	.05
☐ 26T Doug DeCinces	.50	.23	.06
☐ 27T Ivan DeJesus	.40	.18	.05
☐ 28T Bob Dernier	.40	.18	.05
☐ 29T Bo Diaz	.40	.18	.05
☐ 30T Roger Erickson	.40	.18	.05
☐ 31T Jim Essian	.40	.18	.05
☐ 32T Ed Farmer	.40	.18	.05
☐ 33T Doug Flynn	.40	.18	.05
☐ 34T Tim Foli	.40	.18	.05
☐ 35T Dan Ford	.40	.18	.05
☐ 36T George Foster	.50	.23	.06
☐ 37T Dave Frost	.40	.18	.05
☐ 38T Rich Gale	.40	.18	.05
☐ 39T Ron Gardenhire	.40	.18	.05
☐ 40T Ken Griffey	.75	.35	.09
☐ 41T Greg Harris	.50	.23	.06
☐ 42T Von Hayes	.60	.25	.08
☐ 43T Larry Herndon	.40	.18	.05
☐ 44T Kent Hrbek	6.00	2.70	.75
☐ 45T Mike Ivie	.40	.18	.05
☐ 46T Grant Jackson	.40	.18	.05
☐ 47T Reggie Jackson	10.00	4.50	1.25
☐ 48T Ron Jackson	.40	.18	.05
☐ 49T Fergie Jenkins	2.50	1.15	.30
☐ 50T Lamar Johnson	.40	.18	.05
☐ 51T Randy Johnson	.40	.18	.05
☐ 52T Jay Johnstone	.50	.23	.06
☐ 53T Mick Kelleher	.40	.18	.05
☐ 54T Steve Kemp	.40	.18	.05
☐ 55T Junior Kennedy	.40	.18	.05
☐ 56T Jim Kern	.40	.18	.05
☐ 57T Ray Knight	.50	.23	.06
☐ 58T Wayne Krenchicki	.40	.18	.05
☐ 59T Mike Krukow	.40	.18	.05
☐ 60T Duane Kuiper	.40	.18	.05
☐ 61T Mike LaCoss	.40	.18	.05
☐ 62T Chet Lemon	.40	.18	.05
☐ 63T Sixto Lezcano	.40	.18	.05
☐ 64T Dave Lopes	.50	.23	.06
☐ 65T Jerry Martin	.40	.18	.05
☐ 66T Renie Martin	.40	.18	.05
☐ 67T John Mayberry	.40	.18	.05
☐ 68T Lee Mazzilli	.40	.18	.05
☐ 69T Bake McBride	.40	.18	.05
☐ 70T Dan Meyer	.40	.18	.05
☐ 71T Larry Milbourne	.40	.18	.05
☐ 72T Eddie Milner	.40	.18	.05
☐ 73T Sid Monge	.40	.18	.05
☐ 74T John Montefusco	.40	.18	.05
☐ 75T Jose Morales	.40	.18	.05
☐ 76T Keith Moreland	.40	.18	.05
☐ 77T Jim Morrison	.40	.18	.05
☐ 78T Rance Mulliniks	.40	.18	.05
☐ 79T Steve Mura	.40	.18	.05
☐ 80T Gene Nelson	.40	.18	.05
☐ 81T Joe Nolan	.40	.18	.05
☐ 82T Dickie Noles	.40	.18	.05
☐ 83T Al Oliver	.50	.23	.06
☐ 84T Jorge Orta	.40	.18	.05
☐ 85T Tom Paciorek	.50	.23	.06
☐ 86T Larry Parrish	.40	.18	.05
☐ 87T Jack Perconte	.40	.18	.05
☐ 88T Gaylord Perry	2.50	1.15	.30
☐ 89T Rob Picciolo	.40	.18	.05
☐ 90T Joe Pittman	.40	.18	.05
☐ 91T Hosken Powell	.40	.18	.05
☐ 92T Mike Proly	.40	.18	.05
☐ 93T Greg Pryor	.40	.18	.05
☐ 94T Charlie Puleo	.40	.18	.05
☐ 95T Shane Rawley	.40	.18	.05
☐ 96T Johnny Ray	.50	.23	.06
☐ 97T Dave Revering	.40	.18	.05
☐ 98T Cal Ripken	275.00	125.00	34.00
☐ 99T Allen Ripley	.40	.18	.05
☐ 100T Bill Robinson	.50	.23	.06
☐ 101T Aurelio Rodriguez	.40	.18	.05
☐ 102T Joe Rudi	.40	.18	.05
☐ 103T Steve Sax	8.00	3.60	1.00
☐ 104T Dan Schatzeder	.40	.18	.05
☐ 105T Bob Shirley	.40	.18	.05
☐ 106T Eric Show	.50	.23	.06
☐ 107T Roy Smalley	.50	.23	.06
☐ 108T Lonnie Smith	.50	.23	.06
☐ 109T Ozzie Smith	20.00	9.00	2.50

☐ 110T	Reggie Smith	.50	.23	.06
☐ 111T	Lary Sorensen	.40	.18	.05
☐ 112T	Elias Sosa	.40	.18	.05
☐ 113T	Mike Stanton	.40	.18	.05
☐ 114T	Steve Stroughter	.40	.18	.05
☐ 115T	Champ Summers	.40	.18	.05
☐ 116T	Rick Sutcliffe	1.00	.45	.13
☐ 117T	Frank Tanana	.50	.23	.06
☐ 118T	Frank Taveras	.40	.18	.05
☐ 119T	Garry Templeton	.50	.23	.06
☐ 120T	Alex Trevino	.40	.18	.05
☐ 121T	Jerry Turner	.40	.18	.05
☐ 122T	Ed VandeBerg	.40	.18	.05
☐ 123T	Tom Veryzer	.40	.18	.05
☐ 124T	Ron Washington	.40	.18	.05
☐ 125T	Bob Watson	.50	.23	.06
☐ 126T	Dennis Werth	.40	.18	.05
☐ 127T	Eddie Whitson	.40	.18	.05
☐ 128T	Rob Wilfong	.40	.18	.05
☐ 129T	Bump Wills	.40	.18	.05
☐ 130T	Gary Woods	.40	.18	.05
☐ 131T	Butch Wynegar	.40	.18	.05
☐ 132T	Checklist: 1-132	.40	.04	.01

1983 Topps

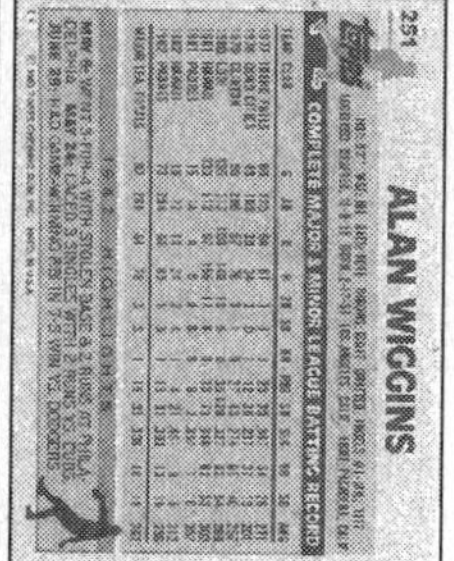

The cards in this 792-card set measure 2 1/2" by 3 1/2". Each regular card of the Topps set for 1983 features a large action shot of a player with a small cameo portrait at bottom right. There are special series for AL and NL All Stars (386-407), League Leaders (701-708), and Record Breakers (1-6). In addition, there are 34 "Super Veteran" (SV) cards and six numbered checklist cards. The Super Veteran cards are oriented horizontally and show two pictures of the featured player, a recent picture and a picture showing the player as a rookie when he broke in. The cards are numbered on the reverse at the upper left corner. The team cards are actually Team Leader (TL) cards picturing the batting (BA: batting average) and pitching leader for that team with a checklist back. The key Rookie Cards in this set are Wade Boggs, Tony Gwynn, Willie McGee, Ryne Sandberg, and Frank Viola.

	NRMT-MT	EXC	G-VG
COMPLETE SET (792)	180.00	80.00	23.00
COMMON PLAYER (1-792)	.10	.05	.01

☐ 1	RB: Tony Armas 11 putouts by rightfielder	.20	.09	.03
☐ 2	RB: Rickey Henderson Sets modern record for steals, season	1.75	.80	.22
☐ 3	RB: Greg Minton 269 1/3 homerless innings streak	.15	.07	.02
☐ 4	RB: Lance Parrish Threw out three baserunners in All-Star game	.15	.07	.02
☐ 5	RB: Manny Trillo 479 consecutive errorless chances, second baseman	.15	.07	.02
☐ 6	RB: John Wathan ML steals record for catchers, 31	.15	.07	.02
☐ 7	Gene Richards	.10	.05	.01
☐ 8	Steve Balboni	.10	.05	.01
☐ 9	Joey McLaughlin	.10	.05	.01
☐ 10	Gorman Thomas	.10	.05	.01
☐ 11	Billy Gardner MG	.10	.05	.01
☐ 12	Paul Mirabella	.10	.05	.01
☐ 13	Larry Herndon	.10	.05	.01
☐ 14	Frank LaCorte	.10	.05	.01
☐ 15	Ron Cey	.15	.07	.02
☐ 16	George Vukovich	.10	.05	.01
☐ 17	Kent Tekulve	.15	.07	.02
☐ 18	SV: Kent Tekulve	.10	.05	.01
☐ 19	Oscar Gamble	.10	.05	.01
☐ 20	Carlton Fisk	2.00	.90	.25
☐ 21	Baltimore Orioles TL BA: Eddie Murray ERA: Jim Palmer	.40	.18	.05
☐ 22	Randy Martz	.10	.05	.01
☐ 23	Mike Heath	.10	.05	.01
☐ 24	Steve Mura	.10	.05	.01
☐ 25	Hal McRae	.15	.07	.02
☐ 26	Jerry Royster	.10	.05	.01
☐ 27	Doug Corbett	.10	.05	.01
☐ 28	Bruce Bochte	.10	.05	.01
☐ 29	Randy Jones	.10	.05	.01
☐ 30	Jim Rice	.30	.14	.04
☐ 31	Bill Gullickson	.25	.11	.03
☐ 32	Dave Bergman	.10	.05	.01
☐ 33	Jack O'Connor	.10	.05	.01
☐ 34	Paul Householder	.10	.05	.01
☐ 35	Rollie Fingers	1.00	.45	.13
☐ 36	SV: Rollie Fingers	.40	.18	.05
☐ 37	Darrell Johnson MG	.10	.05	.01
☐ 38	Tim Flannery	.10	.05	.01
☐ 39	Terry Puhl	.10	.05	.01
☐ 40	Fernando Valenzuela	.25	.11	.03
☐ 41	Jerry Turner	.10	.05	.01
☐ 42	Dale Murray	.10	.05	.01
☐ 43	Bob Dernier	.10	.05	.01
☐ 44	Don Robinson	.10	.05	.01
☐ 45	John Mayberry	.10	.05	.01
☐ 46	Richard Dotson	.10	.05	.01
☐ 47	Dave McKay	.10	.05	.01
☐ 48	Lary Sorensen	.10	.05	.01
☐ 49	Willie McGee	4.00	1.80	.50
☐ 50	Bob Horner UER ('82 RBI total 7)	.15	.07	.02
☐ 51	Chicago Cubs TL BA: Leon Durham ERA: Fergie Jenkins	.20	.09	.03
☐ 52	Onix Concepcion	.10	.05	.01
☐ 53	Mike Witt	.10	.05	.01
☐ 54	Jim Maler	.10	.05	.01
☐ 55	Mookie Wilson	.15	.07	.02
☐ 56	Chuck Rainey	.10	.05	.01
☐ 57	Tim Blackwell	.10	.05	.01
☐ 58	Al Holland	.10	.05	.01
☐ 59	Benny Ayala	.10	.05	.01
☐ 60	Johnny Bench	2.00	.90	.25
☐ 61	SV: Johnny Bench	1.00	.45	.13
☐ 62	Bob McClure	.10	.05	.01
☐ 63	Rick Monday	.10	.05	.01
☐ 64	Bill Stein	.10	.05	.01
☐ 65	Jack Morris	1.75	.80	.22
☐ 66	Bob Lillis MG	.10	.05	.01
☐ 67	Sal Butera	.10	.05	.01
☐ 68	Eric Show	.10	.05	.01
☐ 69	Lee Lacy	.10	.05	.01
☐ 70	Steve Carlton	2.00	.90	.25
☐ 71	SV: Steve Carlton	1.00	.45	.13
☐ 72	Tom Paciorek	.15	.07	.02
☐ 73	Allen Ripley	.10	.05	.01
☐ 74	Julio Gonzalez	.10	.05	.01
☐ 75	Amos Otis	.10	.05	.01
☐ 76	Rick Mahler	.10	.05	.01
☐ 77	Hosken Powell	.10	.05	.01
☐ 78	Bill Caudill	.10	.05	.01
☐ 79	Mick Kelleher	.10	.05	.01
☐ 80	George Foster	.15	.07	.02
☐ 81	Yankees TL BA: Jerry Mumphrey ERA: Dave Righetti	.15	.07	.02
☐ 82	Bruce Hurst	.15	.07	.02
☐ 83	Ryne Sandberg	60.00	27.00	7.50
☐ 84	Milt May	.10	.05	.01
☐ 85	Ken Singleton	.15	.07	.02
☐ 86	Tom Hume	.10	.05	.01
☐ 87	Joe Rudi	.10	.05	.01
☐ 88	Jim Gantner	.15	.07	.02
☐ 89	Leon Roberts	.10	.05	.01

Card			
☐ 90 Jerry Reuss	.10	.05	.01
☐ 91 Larry Milbourne	.10	.05	.01
☐ 92 Mike LaCoss	.10	.05	.01
☐ 93 John Castino	.10	.05	.01
☐ 94 Dave Edwards	.10	.05	.01
☐ 95 Alan Trammell	.90	.40	.11
☐ 96 Dick Howser MG	.10	.05	.01
☐ 97 Ross Baumgarten	.10	.05	.01
☐ 98 Vance Law	.10	.05	.01
☐ 99 Dickie Noles	.10	.05	.01
☐ 100 Pete Rose	2.00	.90	.25
☐ 101 SV: Pete Rose	1.00	.45	.13
☐ 102 Dave Beard	.10	.05	.01
☐ 103 Darrell Porter	.10	.05	.01
☐ 104 Bob Walk	.10	.05	.01
☐ 105 Don Baylor	.15	.07	.02
☐ 106 Gene Nelson	.10	.05	.01
☐ 107 Mike Jorgensen	.10	.05	.01
☐ 108 Glenn Hoffman	.10	.05	.01
☐ 109 Luis Leal	.10	.05	.01
☐ 110 Ken Griffey	.35	.16	.04
☐ 111 Montreal Expos TL	.15	.07	.02
BA: Al Oliver			
ERA: Steve Rogers			
☐ 112 Bob Shirley	.10	.05	.01
☐ 113 Ron Roenicke	.10	.05	.01
☐ 114 Jim Slaton	.10	.05	.01
☐ 115 Chili Davis	.50	.23	.06
☐ 116 Dave Schmidt	.10	.05	.01
☐ 117 Alan Knicely	.10	.05	.01
☐ 118 Chris Welsh	.10	.05	.01
☐ 119 Tom Brookens	.10	.05	.01
☐ 120 Len Barker	.10	.05	.01
☐ 121 Mickey Hatcher	.10	.05	.01
☐ 122 Jimmy Smith	.10	.05	.01
☐ 123 George Frazier	.10	.05	.01
☐ 124 Marc Hill	.10	.05	.01
☐ 125 Leon Durham	.10	.05	.01
☐ 126 Joe Torre MG	.15	.07	.02
☐ 127 Preston Hanna	.10	.05	.01
☐ 128 Mike Ramsey	.10	.05	.01
☐ 129 Checklist: 1-132	.15	.02	.00
☐ 130 Dave Stieb	.25	.11	.03
☐ 131 Ed Ott	.10	.05	.01
☐ 132 Todd Cruz	.10	.05	.01
☐ 133 Jim Barr	.10	.05	.01
☐ 134 Hubie Brooks	.20	.09	.03
☐ 135 Dwight Evans	.35	.16	.04
☐ 136 Willie Aikens	.10	.05	.01
☐ 137 Woodie Fryman	.10	.05	.01
☐ 138 Rick Dempsey	.15	.07	.02
☐ 139 Bruce Berenyi	.10	.05	.01
☐ 140 Willie Randolph	.15	.07	.02
☐ 141 Indians TL	.15	.07	.02
BA: Toby Harrah			
ERA: Rick Sutcliffe			
☐ 142 Mike Caldwell	.10	.05	.01
☐ 143 Joe Pettini	.10	.05	.01
☐ 144 Mark Wagner	.10	.05	.01
☐ 145 Don Sutton	.50	.23	.06
☐ 146 SV: Don Sutton	.25	.11	.03
☐ 147 Rick Leach	.10	.05	.01
☐ 148 Dave Roberts	.10	.05	.01
☐ 149 Johnny Ray	.10	.05	.01
☐ 150 Bruce Sutter	.25	.11	.03
☐ 151 SV: Bruce Sutter	.10	.05	.01
☐ 152 Jay Johnstone	.15	.07	.02
☐ 153 Jerry Koosman	.15	.07	.02
☐ 154 Johnnie LeMaster	.10	.05	.01
☐ 155 Dan Quisenberry	.15	.07	.02
☐ 156 Billy Martin MG	.20	.09	.03
☐ 157 Steve Bedrosian	.10	.05	.01
☐ 158 Rob Wilfong	.10	.05	.01
☐ 159 Mike Stanton	.10	.05	.01
☐ 160 Dave Kingman	.15	.07	.02
☐ 161 SV: Dave Kingman	.10	.05	.01
☐ 162 Mark Clear	.10	.05	.01
☐ 163 Cal Ripken	25.00	11.50	3.10
☐ 164 David Palmer	.10	.05	.01
☐ 165 Dan Driessen	.10	.05	.01
☐ 166 John Pacella	.10	.05	.01
☐ 167 Mark Brouhard	.10	.05	.01
☐ 168 Juan Eichelberger	.10	.05	.01
☐ 169 Doug Flynn	.10	.05	.01
☐ 170 Steve Howe	.10	.05	.01
☐ 171 Giants TL	.20	.09	.03
BA: Joe Morgan			
ERA: Bill Laskey			
☐ 172 Vern Ruhle	.10	.05	.01
☐ 173 Jim Morrison	.10	.05	.01
☐ 174 Jerry Ujdur	.10	.05	.01
☐ 175 Bo Diaz	.10	.05	.01
☐ 176 Dave Righetti	.20	.09	.03
☐ 177 Harold Baines	.75	.35	.09
☐ 178 Luis Tiant	.15	.07	.02
☐ 179 SV: Luis Tiant	.10	.05	.01
☐ 180 Rickey Henderson	5.50	2.50	.70
☐ 181 Terry Felton	.10	.05	.01
☐ 182 Mike Fischlin	.10	.05	.01
☐ 183 Ed VandeBerg	.10	.05	.01
☐ 184 Bob Clark	.10	.05	.01
☐ 185 Tim Lollar	.10	.05	.01
☐ 186 Whitey Herzog MG	.10	.05	.01
☐ 187 Terry Leach	.15	.07	.02
☐ 188 Rick Miller	.10	.05	.01
☐ 189 Dan Schatzeder	.10	.05	.01
☐ 190 Cecil Cooper	.15	.07	.02
☐ 191 Joe Price	.10	.05	.01
☐ 192 Floyd Rayford	.10	.05	.01
☐ 193 Harry Spilman	.10	.05	.01
☐ 194 Cesar Geronimo	.10	.05	.01
☐ 195 Bob Stoddard	.10	.05	.01
☐ 196 Bill Fahey	.10	.05	.01
☐ 197 Jim Eisenreich	.40	.18	.05
☐ 198 Kiko Garcia	.10	.05	.01
☐ 199 Marty Bystrom	.10	.05	.01
☐ 200 Rod Carew	2.00	.90	.25
☐ 201 SV: Rod Carew	1.00	.45	.13
☐ 202 Blue Jays TL	.15	.07	.02
BA: Damaso Garcia			
ERA: Dave Stieb			
☐ 203 Mike Morgan	.50	.23	.06
☐ 204 Junior Kennedy	.10	.05	.01
☐ 205 Dave Parker	.50	.23	.06
☐ 206 Ken Oberkfell	.10	.05	.01
☐ 207 Rick Camp	.10	.05	.01
☐ 208 Dan Meyer	.10	.05	.01
☐ 209 Mike Moore	1.75	.80	.22
☐ 210 Jack Clark	.20	.09	.03
☐ 211 John Denny	.10	.05	.01
☐ 212 John Stearns	.10	.05	.01
☐ 213 Tom Burgmeier	.10	.05	.01
☐ 214 Jerry White	.10	.05	.01
☐ 215 Mario Soto	.10	.05	.01
☐ 216 Tony LaRussa MG	.15	.07	.02
☐ 217 Tim Stoddard	.10	.05	.01
☐ 218 Roy Howell	.10	.05	.01
☐ 219 Mike Armstrong	.10	.05	.01
☐ 220 Dusty Baker	.15	.07	.02
☐ 221 Joe Niekro	.15	.07	.02
☐ 222 Damaso Garcia	.10	.05	.01
☐ 223 John Montefusco	.10	.05	.01
☐ 224 Mickey Rivers	.10	.05	.01
☐ 225 Enos Cabell	.10	.05	.01
☐ 226 Enrique Romo	.10	.05	.01
☐ 227 Chris Bando	.10	.05	.01
☐ 228 Joaquin Andujar	.10	.05	.01
☐ 229 Phillies TL	.20	.09	.03
BA: Bo Diaz			
ERA: Steve Carlton			
☐ 230 Fergie Jenkins	.50	.23	.06
☐ 231 SV: Fergie Jenkins	.25	.11	.03
☐ 232 Tom Brunansky	.30	.14	.04
☐ 233 Wayne Gross	.10	.05	.01
☐ 234 Larry Andersen	.10	.05	.01
☐ 235 Claudell Washington	.10	.05	.01
☐ 236 Steve Renko	.10	.05	.01
☐ 237 Dan Norman	.10	.05	.01
☐ 238 Bud Black	.50	.23	.06
☐ 239 Dave Stapleton	.10	.05	.01
☐ 240 Rich Gossage	.25	.11	.03
☐ 241 SV: Rich Gossage	.10	.05	.01
☐ 242 Joe Nolan	.10	.05	.01
☐ 243 Duane Walker	.10	.05	.01
☐ 244 Dwight Bernard	.10	.05	.01
☐ 245 Steve Sax	1.00	.45	.13
☐ 246 George Bamberger MG	.10	.05	.01
☐ 247 Dave Smith	.10	.05	.01
☐ 248 Bake McBride	.10	.05	.01
☐ 249 Checklist: 133-264	.15	.02	.00
☐ 250 Bill Buckner	.15	.07	.02
☐ 251 Alan Wiggins	.10	.05	.01
☐ 252 Luis Aguayo	.10	.05	.01
☐ 253 Larry McWilliams	.10	.05	.01
☐ 254 Rick Cerone	.10	.05	.01
☐ 255 Gene Garber	.10	.05	.01
☐ 256 SV: Gene Garber	.10	.05	.01
☐ 257 Jesse Barfield	.20	.09	.03
☐ 258 Manny Castillo	.10	.05	.01
☐ 259 Jeff Jones	.10	.05	.01
☐ 260 Steve Kemp	.10	.05	.01
☐ 261 Tigers TL	.15	.07	.02
BA: Larry Herndon			
ERA: Dan Petry			
☐ 262 Ron Jackson	.10	.05	.01
☐ 263 Renie Martin	.10	.05	.01

☐ 264	Jamie Quirk	.10	.05	.01
☐ 265	Joel Youngblood	.10	.05	.01
☐ 266	Paul Boris	.10	.05	.01
☐ 267	Terry Francona	.10	.05	.01
☐ 268	Storm Davis	.25	.11	.03
☐ 269	Ron Oester	.10	.05	.01
☐ 270	Dennis Eckersley	1.75	.80	.22
☐ 271	Ed Romero	.10	.05	.01
☐ 272	Frank Tanana	.15	.07	.02
☐ 273	Mark Belanger	.10	.05	.01
☐ 274	Terry Kennedy	.10	.05	.01
☐ 275	Ray Knight	.15	.07	.02
☐ 276	Gene Mauch MG	.10	.05	.01
☐ 277	Rance Mulliniks	.10	.05	.01
☐ 278	Kevin Hickey	.10	.05	.01
☐ 279	Greg Gross	.10	.05	.01
☐ 280	Bert Blyleven	.40	.18	.05
☐ 281	Andre Robertson	.10	.05	.01
☐ 282	Reggie Smith (Ryne Sandberg ducking back)	.50	.23	.06
☐ 283	SV: Reggie Smith	.10	.05	.01
☐ 284	Jeff Lahti	.10	.05	.01
☐ 285	Lance Parrish	.20	.09	.03
☐ 286	Rick Langford	.10	.05	.01
☐ 287	Bobby Brown	.10	.05	.01
☐ 288	Joe Cowley	.10	.05	.01
☐ 289	Jerry Dybzinski	.10	.05	.01
☐ 290	Jeff Reardon	2.00	.90	.25
☐ 291	Pirates TL BA: Bill Madlock ERA: John Candelaria	.15	.07	.02
☐ 292	Craig Swan	.10	.05	.01
☐ 293	Glenn Gulliver	.10	.05	.01
☐ 294	Dave Engle	.10	.05	.01
☐ 295	Jerry Remy	.10	.05	.01
☐ 296	Greg Harris	.10	.05	.01
☐ 297	Ned Yost	.10	.05	.01
☐ 298	Floyd Chiffer	.10	.05	.01
☐ 299	George Wright	.10	.05	.01
☐ 300	Mike Schmidt	3.00	1.35	.40
☐ 301	SV: Mike Schmidt	1.50	.65	.19
☐ 302	Ernie Whitt	.10	.05	.01
☐ 303	Miguel Dilone	.10	.05	.01
☐ 304	Dave Rucker	.10	.05	.01
☐ 305	Larry Bowa	.15	.07	.02
☐ 306	Tom Lasorda MG	.15	.07	.02
☐ 307	Lou Piniella	.15	.07	.02
☐ 308	Jesus Vega	.10	.05	.01
☐ 309	Jeff Leonard	.10	.05	.01
☐ 310	Greg Luzinski	.15	.07	.02
☐ 311	Glenn Brummer	.10	.05	.01
☐ 312	Brian Kingman	.10	.05	.01
☐ 313	Gary Gray	.10	.05	.01
☐ 314	Ken Dayley	.10	.05	.01
☐ 315	Rick Burleson	.10	.05	.01
☐ 316	Paul Splittorff	.10	.05	.01
☐ 317	Gary Rajsich	.10	.05	.01
☐ 318	John Tudor	.15	.07	.02
☐ 319	Lenn Sakata	.10	.05	.01
☐ 320	Steve Rogers	.10	.05	.01
☐ 321	Brewers TL BA: Robin Yount ERA: Pete Vuckovich	.35	.16	.04
☐ 322	Dave Van Gorder	.10	.05	.01
☐ 323	Luis DeLeon	.10	.05	.01
☐ 324	Mike Marshall	.15	.07	.02
☐ 325	Von Hayes	.15	.07	.02
☐ 326	Garth Iorg	.10	.05	.01
☐ 327	Bobby Castillo	.10	.05	.01
☐ 328	Craig Reynolds	.10	.05	.01
☐ 329	Randy Niemann	.10	.05	.01
☐ 330	Buddy Bell	.15	.07	.02
☐ 331	Mike Krukow	.10	.05	.01
☐ 332	Glenn Wilson	.15	.07	.02
☐ 333	Dave LaRoche	.10	.05	.01
☐ 334	SV: Dave LaRoche	.10	.05	.01
☐ 335	Steve Henderson	.10	.05	.01
☐ 336	Rene Lachemann MG	.10	.05	.01
☐ 337	Tito Landrum	.10	.05	.01
☐ 338	Bob Owchinko	.10	.05	.01
☐ 339	Terry Harper	.10	.05	.01
☐ 340	Larry Gura	.10	.05	.01
☐ 341	Doug DeCinces	.15	.07	.02
☐ 342	Atlee Hammaker	.10	.05	.01
☐ 343	Bob Bailor	.10	.05	.01
☐ 344	Roger LaFrancois	.10	.05	.01
☐ 345	Jim Clancy	.10	.05	.01
☐ 346	Joe Pittman	.10	.05	.01
☐ 347	Sammy Stewart	.10	.05	.01
☐ 348	Alan Bannister	.10	.05	.01
☐ 349	Checklist: 265-396	.15	.02	.00
☐ 350	Robin Yount	3.50	1.55	.45
☐ 351	Reds TL BA: Cesar Cedeno ERA: Mario Soto	.15	.07	.02
☐ 352	Mike Scioscia	.15	.07	.02
☐ 353	Steve Comer	.10	.05	.01
☐ 354	Randy Johnson	.10	.05	.01
☐ 355	Jim Bibby	.10	.05	.01
☐ 356	Gary Woods	.10	.05	.01
☐ 357	Len Matuszek	.10	.05	.01
☐ 358	Jerry Garvin	.10	.05	.01
☐ 359	Dave Collins	.10	.05	.01
☐ 360	Nolan Ryan	9.00	4.00	1.15
☐ 361	SV: Nolan Ryan	4.50	2.00	.55
☐ 362	Bill Almon	.10	.05	.01
☐ 363	John Stuper	.10	.05	.01
☐ 364	Brett Butler	.75	.35	.09
☐ 365	Dave Lopes	.15	.07	.02
☐ 366	Dick Williams MG	.10	.05	.01
☐ 367	Bud Anderson	.10	.05	.01
☐ 368	Richie Zisk	.10	.05	.01
☐ 369	Jesse Orosco	.10	.05	.01
☐ 370	Gary Carter	1.00	.45	.13
☐ 371	Mike Richardt	.10	.05	.01
☐ 372	Terry Crowley	.10	.05	.01
☐ 373	Kevin Saucier	.10	.05	.01
☐ 374	Wayne Krenchicki	.10	.05	.01
☐ 375	Pete Vuckovich	.10	.05	.01
☐ 376	Ken Landreaux	.10	.05	.01
☐ 377	Lee May	.10	.05	.01
☐ 378	SV: Lee May	.10	.05	.01
☐ 379	Guy Sularz	.10	.05	.01
☐ 380	Ron Davis	.10	.05	.01
☐ 381	Red Sox TL BA: Jim Rice ERA: Bob Stanley	.15	.07	.02
☐ 382	Bob Knepper	.10	.05	.01
☐ 383	Ozzie Virgil	.10	.05	.01
☐ 384	Dave Dravecky	.75	.35	.09
☐ 385	Mike Easler	.10	.05	.01
☐ 386	Rod Carew AS	.75	.35	.09
☐ 387	Bob Grich AS	.12	.05	.02
☐ 388	George Brett AS	1.25	.55	.16
☐ 389	Robin Yount AS	1.25	.55	.16
☐ 390	Reggie Jackson AS	.90	.40	.11
☐ 391	Rickey Henderson AS	2.00	.90	.25
☐ 392	Fred Lynn AS	.12	.05	.02
☐ 393	Carlton Fisk AS	.75	.35	.09
☐ 394	Pete Vuckovich AS	.12	.05	.02
☐ 395	Larry Gura AS	.12	.05	.02
☐ 396	Dan Quisenberry AS	.12	.05	.02
☐ 397	Pete Rose AS	.75	.35	.09
☐ 398	Manny Trillo AS	.12	.05	.02
☐ 399	Mike Schmidt AS	1.25	.55	.16
☐ 400	Dave Concepcion AS	.12	.05	.02
☐ 401	Dale Murphy AS	.40	.18	.05
☐ 402	Andre Dawson AS	.90	.40	.11
☐ 403	Tim Raines AS	.35	.16	.04
☐ 404	Gary Carter AS	.40	.18	.05
☐ 405	Steve Rogers AS	.12	.05	.02
☐ 406	Steve Carlton AS	.75	.35	.09
☐ 407	Bruce Sutter AS	.12	.05	.02
☐ 408	Rudy May	.10	.05	.01
☐ 409	Marvis Foley	.10	.05	.01
☐ 410	Phil Niekro	.60	.25	.08
☐ 411	SV: Phil Niekro	.30	.14	.04
☐ 412	Rangers TL BA: Buddy Bell ERA: Charlie Hough	.15	.07	.02
☐ 413	Matt Keough	.10	.05	.01
☐ 414	Julio Cruz	.10	.05	.01
☐ 415	Bob Forsch	.10	.05	.01
☐ 416	Joe Ferguson	.10	.05	.01
☐ 417	Tom Hausman	.10	.05	.01
☐ 418	Greg Pryor	.10	.05	.01
☐ 419	Steve Crawford	.10	.05	.01
☐ 420	Al Oliver	.15	.07	.02
☐ 421	SV: Al Oliver	.10	.05	.01
☐ 422	George Cappuzzello	.10	.05	.01
☐ 423	Tom Lawless	.10	.05	.01
☐ 424	Jerry Augustine	.10	.05	.01
☐ 425	Pedro Guerrero	.35	.16	.04
☐ 426	Earl Weaver MG	.15	.07	.02
☐ 427	Roy Lee Jackson	.10	.05	.01
☐ 428	Champ Summers	.10	.05	.01
☐ 429	Eddie Whitson	.10	.05	.01
☐ 430	Kirk Gibson	.60	.25	.08
☐ 431	Gary Gaetti	.60	.25	.08
☐ 432	Porfirio Altamirano	.10	.05	.01
☐ 433	Dale Berra	.10	.05	.01
☐ 434	Dennis Lamp	.10	.05	.01
☐ 435	Tony Armas	.10	.05	.01
☐ 436	Bill Campbell	.10	.05	.01
☐ 437	Rick Sweet	.10	.05	.01

□ 438 Dave LaPoint	.15	.07	.02
□ 439 Rafael Ramirez	.10	.05	.01
□ 440 Ron Guidry	.25	.11	.03
□ 441 Astros TL	.15	.07	.02
BA: Ray Knight			
ERA: Joe Niekro			
□ 442 Brian Downing	.15	.07	.02
□ 443 Don Hood	.10	.05	.01
□ 444 Wally Backman	.15	.07	.02
□ 445 Mike Flanagan	.15	.07	.02
□ 446 Reid Nichols	.10	.05	.01
□ 447 Bryn Smith	.15	.07	.02
□ 448 Darrell Evans	.15	.07	.02
□ 449 Eddie Milner	.10	.05	.01
□ 450 Ted Simmons	.15	.07	.02
□ 451 SV: Ted Simmons	.10	.05	.01
□ 452 Lloyd Moseby	.10	.05	.01
□ 453 Lamar Johnson	.10	.05	.01
□ 454 Bob Welch	.35	.16	.04
□ 455 Sixto Lezcano	.10	.05	.01
□ 456 Lee Elia MG	.10	.05	.01
□ 457 Milt Wilcox	.10	.05	.01
□ 458 Ron Washington	.10	.05	.01
□ 459 Ed Farmer	.10	.05	.01
□ 460 Roy Smalley	.10	.05	.01
□ 461 Steve Trout	.10	.05	.01
□ 462 Steve Nicosia	.10	.05	.01
□ 463 Gaylord Perry	.60	.25	.08
□ 464 SV: Gaylord Perry	.30	.14	.04
□ 465 Lonnie Smith	.15	.07	.02
□ 466 Tom Underwood	.10	.05	.01
□ 467 Rufino Linares	.10	.05	.01
□ 468 Dave Goltz	.10	.05	.01
□ 469 Ron Gardenhire	.10	.05	.01
□ 470 Greg Minton	.10	.05	.01
□ 471 K.C. Royals TL	.15	.07	.02
BA: Willie Wilson			
ERA: Vida Blue			
□ 472 Gary Allenson	.10	.05	.01
□ 473 John Lowenstein	.10	.05	.01
□ 474 Ray Burris	.10	.05	.01
□ 475 Cesar Cedeno	.15	.07	.02
□ 476 Rob Picciolo	.10	.05	.01
□ 477 Tom Niedenfuer	.10	.05	.01
□ 478 Phil Garner	.15	.07	.02
□ 479 Charlie Hough	.15	.07	.02
□ 480 Toby Harrah	.10	.05	.01
□ 481 Scot Thompson	.10	.05	.01
□ 482 Tony Gwynn UER	40.00	18.00	5.00
(No Topps logo under card number on back)			
□ 483 Lynn Jones	.10	.05	.01
□ 484 Dick Ruthven	.10	.05	.01
□ 485 Omar Moreno	.10	.05	.01
□ 486 Clyde King MG	.10	.05	.01
□ 487 Jerry Hairston	.10	.05	.01
□ 488 Alfredo Griffin	.10	.05	.01
□ 489 Tom Herr	.15	.07	.02
□ 490 Jim Palmer	1.50	.65	.19
□ 491 SV: Jim Palmer	.75	.35	.09
□ 492 Paul Serna	.10	.05	.01
□ 493 Steve McCatty	.10	.05	.01
□ 494 Bob Brenly	.10	.05	.01
□ 495 Warren Cromartie	.10	.05	.01
□ 496 Tom Veryzer	.10	.05	.01
□ 497 Rick Sutcliffe	.30	.14	.04
□ 498 Wade Boggs	35.00	16.00	4.40
□ 499 Jeff Little	.10	.05	.01
□ 500 Reggie Jackson	2.00	.90	.25
□ 501 SV: Reggie Jackson	1.00	.45	.13
□ 502 Atlanta Braves TL	.25	.11	.03
BA: Dale Murphy			
ERA: Phil Niekro			
□ 503 Moose Haas	.10	.05	.01
□ 504 Don Werner	.10	.05	.01
□ 505 Garry Templeton	.15	.07	.02
□ 506 Jim Gott	.20	.09	.03
□ 507 Tony Scott	.10	.05	.01
□ 508 Tom Filer	.10	.05	.01
□ 509 Lou Whitaker	.75	.35	.09
□ 510 Tug McGraw	.15	.07	.02
□ 511 SV: Tug McGraw	.10	.05	.01
□ 512 Doyle Alexander	.10	.05	.01
□ 513 Fred Stanley	.10	.05	.01
□ 514 Rudy Law	.10	.05	.01
□ 515 Gene Tenace	.10	.05	.01
□ 516 Bill Virdon MG	.10	.05	.01
□ 517 Gary Ward	.10	.05	.01
□ 518 Bill Laskey	.10	.05	.01
□ 519 Terry Bulling	.10	.05	.01
□ 520 Fred Lynn	.15	.07	.02
□ 521 Bruce Benedict	.10	.05	.01
□ 522 Pat Zachry	.10	.05	.01
□ 523 Carney Lansford	.15	.07	.02
□ 524 Tom Brennan	.10	.05	.01
□ 525 Frank White	.15	.07	.02
□ 526 Checklist: 397-528	.15	.02	.00
□ 527 Larry Biittner	.10	.05	.01
□ 528 Jamie Easterly	.10	.05	.01
□ 529 Tim Laudner	.10	.05	.01
□ 530 Eddie Murray	2.50	1.15	.30
□ 531 Oakland A's TL	.50	.23	.06
BA: Rickey Henderson			
ERA: Rick Langford			
□ 532 Dave Stewart	1.00	.45	.13
□ 533 Luis Salazar	.10	.05	.01
□ 534 John Butcher	.10	.05	.01
□ 535 Manny Trillo	.10	.05	.01
□ 536 John Wockenfuss	.10	.05	.01
□ 537 Rod Scurry	.10	.05	.01
□ 538 Danny Heep	.10	.05	.01
□ 539 Roger Erickson	.10	.05	.01
□ 540 Ozzie Smith	2.50	1.15	.30
□ 541 Britt Burns	.10	.05	.01
□ 542 Jody Davis	.10	.05	.01
□ 543 Alan Fowlkes	.10	.05	.01
□ 544 Larry Whisenton	.10	.05	.01
□ 545 Floyd Bannister	.10	.05	.01
□ 546 Dave Garcia MG	.10	.05	.01
□ 547 Geoff Zahn	.10	.05	.01
□ 548 Brian Giles	.10	.05	.01
□ 549 Charlie Puleo	.10	.05	.01
□ 550 Carl Yastrzemski	2.00	.90	.25
□ 551 SV: Carl Yastrzemski	1.00	.45	.13
□ 552 Tim Wallach	.30	.14	.04
□ 553 Dennis Martinez	.15	.07	.02
□ 554 Mike Vail	.10	.05	.01
□ 555 Steve Yeager	.10	.05	.01
□ 556 Willie Upshaw	.10	.05	.01
□ 557 Rick Honeycutt	.10	.05	.01
□ 558 Dickie Thon	.10	.05	.01
□ 559 Pete Redfern	.10	.05	.01
□ 560 Ron LeFlore	.15	.07	.02
□ 561 Cardinals TL	.15	.07	.02
BA: Lonnie Smith			
ERA: Joaquin Andujar			
□ 562 Dave Rozema	.10	.05	.01
□ 563 Juan Bonilla	.10	.05	.01
□ 564 Sid Monge	.10	.05	.01
□ 565 Bucky Dent	.15	.07	.02
□ 566 Manny Sarmiento	.10	.05	.01
□ 567 Joe Simpson	.10	.05	.01
□ 568 Willie Hernandez	.15	.07	.02
□ 569 Jack Perconte	.10	.05	.01
□ 570 Vida Blue	.15	.07	.02
□ 571 Mickey Klutts	.10	.05	.01
□ 572 Bob Watson	.15	.07	.02
□ 573 Andy Hassler	.10	.05	.01
□ 574 Glenn Adams	.10	.05	.01
□ 575 Neil Allen	.10	.05	.01
□ 576 Frank Robinson MG	.35	.16	.04
□ 577 Luis Aponte	.10	.05	.01
□ 578 David Green	.10	.05	.01
□ 579 Rich Dauer	.10	.05	.01
□ 580 Tom Seaver	2.00	.90	.25
□ 581 SV: Tom Seaver	1.00	.45	.13
□ 582 Marshall Edwards	.10	.05	.01
□ 583 Terry Forster	.10	.05	.01
□ 584 Dave Hostetler	.10	.05	.01
□ 585 Jose Cruz	.15	.07	.02
□ 586 Frank Viola	5.00	2.30	.60
□ 587 Ivan DeJesus	.10	.05	.01
□ 588 Pat Underwood	.10	.05	.01
□ 589 Alvis Woods	.10	.05	.01
□ 590 Tony Pena	.15	.07	.02
□ 591 White Sox TL	.15	.07	.02
BA: Greg Luzinski			
ERA: LaMarr Hoyt			
□ 592 Shane Rawley	.10	.05	.01
□ 593 Broderick Perkins	.10	.05	.01
□ 594 Eric Rasmussen	.10	.05	.01
□ 595 Tim Raines	1.00	.45	.13
□ 596 Randy Johnson	.10	.05	.01
□ 597 Mike Proly	.10	.05	.01
□ 598 Dwayne Murphy	.10	.05	.01
□ 599 Don Aase	.10	.05	.01
□ 600 George Brett	3.50	1.55	.45
□ 601 Ed Lynch	.10	.05	.01
□ 602 Rich Gedman	.10	.05	.01
□ 603 Joe Morgan	1.00	.45	.13
□ 604 SV: Joe Morgan	.50	.23	.06
□ 605 Gary Roenicke	.10	.05	.01
□ 606 Bobby Cox MG	.10	.05	.01
□ 607 Charlie Leibrandt	.15	.07	.02
□ 608 Don Money	.10	.05	.01
□ 609 Danny Darwin	.10	.05	.01

☐ 610	Steve Garvey	.60	.25	.08
☐ 611	Bert Roberge	.10	.05	.01
☐ 612	Steve Swisher	.10	.05	.01
☐ 613	Mike Ivie	.10	.05	.01
☐ 614	Ed Glynn	.10	.05	.01
☐ 615	Garry Maddox	.10	.05	.01
☐ 616	Bill Nahorodny	.10	.05	.01
☐ 617	Butch Wynegar	.10	.05	.01
☐ 618	LaMarr Hoyt	.10	.05	.01
☐ 619	Keith Moreland	.10	.05	.01
☐ 620	Mike Norris	.10	.05	.01
☐ 621	New York Mets TL	.15	.07	.02
	BA: Mookie Wilson			
	ERA: Craig Swan			
☐ 622	Dave Edler	.10	.05	.01
☐ 623	Luis Sanchez	.10	.05	.01
☐ 624	Glenn Hubbard	.10	.05	.01
☐ 625	Ken Forsch	.10	.05	.01
☐ 626	Jerry Martin	.10	.05	.01
☐ 627	Doug Bair	.10	.05	.01
☐ 628	Julio Valdez	.10	.05	.01
☐ 629	Charlie Lea	.10	.05	.01
☐ 630	Paul Molitor	1.25	.55	.16
☐ 631	Tippy Martinez	.10	.05	.01
☐ 632	Alex Trevino	.10	.05	.01
☐ 633	Vicente Romo	.10	.05	.01
☐ 634	Max Venable	.10	.05	.01
☐ 635	Graig Nettles	.15	.07	.02
☐ 636	SV: Graig Nettles	.10	.05	.01
☐ 637	Pat Corrales MG	.10	.05	.01
☐ 638	Dan Petry	.10	.05	.01
☐ 639	Art Howe	.10	.05	.01
☐ 640	Andre Thornton	.10	.05	.01
☐ 641	Billy Sample	.10	.05	.01
☐ 642	Checklist: 529-660	.15	.02	.00
☐ 643	Bump Wills	.10	.05	.01
☐ 644	Joe Lefebvre	.10	.05	.01
☐ 645	Bill Madlock	.15	.07	.02
☐ 646	Jim Essian	.10	.05	.01
☐ 647	Bobby Mitchell	.10	.05	.01
☐ 648	Jeff Burroughs	.10	.05	.01
☐ 649	Tommy Boggs	.10	.05	.01
☐ 650	George Hendrick	.10	.05	.01
☐ 651	Angels TL	.20	.09	.03
	BA: Rod Carew			
	ERA: Mike Witt			
☐ 652	Butch Hobson	.15	.07	.02
☐ 653	Ellis Valentine	.10	.05	.01
☐ 654	Bob Ojeda	.15	.07	.02
☐ 655	Al Bumbry	.10	.05	.01
☐ 656	Dave Frost	.10	.05	.01
☐ 657	Mike Gates	.10	.05	.01
☐ 658	Frank Pastore	.10	.05	.01
☐ 659	Charlie Moore	.10	.05	.01
☐ 660	Mike Hargrove	.15	.07	.02
☐ 661	Bill Russell	.15	.07	.02
☐ 662	Joe Sambito	.10	.05	.01
☐ 663	Tom O'Malley	.10	.05	.01
☐ 664	Bob Molinaro	.10	.05	.01
☐ 665	Jim Sundberg	.15	.07	.02
☐ 666	Sparky Anderson MG	.15	.07	.02
☐ 667	Dick Davis	.10	.05	.01
☐ 668	Larry Christenson	.10	.05	.01
☐ 669	Mike Squires	.10	.05	.01
☐ 670	Jerry Mumphrey	.10	.05	.01
☐ 671	Lenny Faedo	.10	.05	.01
☐ 672	Jim Kaat	.20	.09	.03
☐ 673	SV: Jim Kaat	.10	.05	.01
☐ 674	Kurt Bevacqua	.10	.05	.01
☐ 675	Jim Beattie	.10	.05	.01
☐ 676	Biff Pocoroba	.10	.05	.01
☐ 677	Dave Revering	.10	.05	.01
☐ 678	Juan Beniquez	.10	.05	.01
☐ 679	Mike Scott	.15	.07	.02
☐ 680	Andre Dawson	2.50	1.15	.30
☐ 681	Dodgers Leaders	.15	.07	.02
	BA: Pedro Guerrero			
	ERA: Fernando Valenzuela			
☐ 682	Bob Stanley	.10	.05	.01
☐ 683	Dan Ford	.10	.05	.01
☐ 684	Rafael Landestoy	.10	.05	.01
☐ 685	Lee Mazzilli	.10	.05	.01
☐ 686	Randy Lerch	.10	.05	.01
☐ 687	U.L. Washington	.10	.05	.01
☐ 688	Jim Wohlford	.10	.05	.01
☐ 689	Ron Hassey	.10	.05	.01
☐ 690	Kent Hrbek	.75	.35	.09
☐ 691	Dave Tobik	.10	.05	.01
☐ 692	Denny Walling	.10	.05	.01
☐ 693	Sparky Lyle	.15	.07	.02
☐ 694	SV: Sparky Lyle	.10	.05	.01
☐ 695	Ruppert Jones	.10	.05	.01
☐ 696	Chuck Tanner MG	.10	.05	.01
☐ 697	Barry Foote	.10	.05	.01
☐ 698	Tony Bernazard	.10	.05	.01
☐ 699	Lee Smith	3.00	1.35	.40
☐ 700	Keith Hernandez	.30	.14	.04
☐ 701	Batting Leaders	.20	.09	.03
	AL: Willie Wilson			
	NL: Al Oliver			
☐ 702	Home Run Leaders	.30	.14	.04
	AL: Reggie Jackson			
	AL: Gorman Thomas			
	NL: Dave Kingman			
☐ 703	RBI Leaders	.20	.09	.03
	AL: Hal McRae			
	NL: Dale Murphy			
	NL: Al Oliver			
☐ 704	SB Leaders	1.00	.45	.13
	AL: Rickey Henderson			
	NL: Tim Raines			
☐ 705	Victory Leaders	.25	.11	.03
	AL: LaMarr Hoyt			
	NL: Steve Carlton			
☐ 706	Strikeout Leaders	.20	.09	.03
	AL: Floyd Bannister			
	NL: Steve Carlton			
☐ 707	ERA Leaders	.20	.09	.03
	AL: Rick Sutcliffe			
	NL: Steve Rogers			
☐ 708	Leading Firemen	.20	.09	.03
	AL: Dan Quisenberry			
	NL: Bruce Sutter			
☐ 709	Jimmy Sexton	.10	.05	.01
☐ 710	Willie Wilson	.15	.07	.02
☐ 711	Mariners TL	.15	.07	.02
	BA: Bruce Bochte			
	ERA: Jim Beattie			
☐ 712	Bruce Kison	.10	.05	.01
☐ 713	Ron Hodges	.10	.05	.01
☐ 714	Wayne Nordhagen	.10	.05	.01
☐ 715	Tony Perez	.40	.18	.05
☐ 716	SV: Tony Perez	.20	.09	.03
☐ 717	Scott Sanderson	.10	.05	.01
☐ 718	Jim Dwyer	.10	.05	.01
☐ 719	Rich Gale	.10	.05	.01
☐ 720	Dave Concepcion	.15	.07	.02
☐ 721	John Martin	.10	.05	.01
☐ 722	Jorge Orta	.10	.05	.01
☐ 723	Randy Moffitt	.10	.05	.01
☐ 724	Johnny Grubb	.10	.05	.01
☐ 725	Dan Spillner	.10	.05	.01
☐ 726	Harvey Kuenn MG	.15	.07	.02
☐ 727	Chet Lemon	.10	.05	.01
☐ 728	Ron Reed	.10	.05	.01
☐ 729	Jerry Morales	.10	.05	.01
☐ 730	Jason Thompson	.10	.05	.01
☐ 731	Al Williams	.10	.05	.01
☐ 732	Dave Henderson	.40	.18	.05
☐ 733	Buck Martinez	.10	.05	.01
☐ 734	Steve Braun	.10	.05	.01
☐ 735	Tommy John	.20	.09	.03
☐ 736	SV: Tommy John	.15	.07	.02
☐ 737	Mitchell Page	.10	.05	.01
☐ 738	Tim Foli	.10	.05	.01
☐ 739	Rick Ownbey	.10	.05	.01
☐ 740	Rusty Staub	.15	.07	.02
☐ 741	SV: Rusty Staub	.10	.05	.01
☐ 742	Padres TL	.15	.07	.02
	BA: Terry Kennedy			
	ERA: Tim Lollar			
☐ 743	Mike Torrez	.10	.05	.01
☐ 744	Brad Mills	.10	.05	.01
☐ 745	Scott McGregor	.10	.05	.01
☐ 746	John Wathan	.10	.05	.01
☐ 747	Fred Breining	.10	.05	.01
☐ 748	Derrel Thomas	.10	.05	.01
☐ 749	Jon Matlack	.10	.05	.01
☐ 750	Ben Oglivie	.10	.05	.01
☐ 751	Brad Havens	.10	.05	.01
☐ 752	Luis Pujols	.10	.05	.01
☐ 753	Elias Sosa	.10	.05	.01
☐ 754	Bill Robinson	.15	.07	.02
☐ 755	John Candelaria	.10	.05	.01
☐ 756	Russ Nixon MG	.10	.05	.01
☐ 757	Rick Manning	.10	.05	.01
☐ 758	Aurelio Rodriguez	.10	.05	.01
☐ 759	Doug Bird	.10	.05	.01
☐ 760	Dale Murphy	1.25	.55	.16
☐ 761	Gary Lucas	.10	.05	.01
☐ 762	Cliff Johnson	.10	.05	.01
☐ 763	Al Cowens	.10	.05	.01
☐ 764	Pete Falcone	.10	.05	.01
☐ 765	Bob Boone	.15	.07	.02
☐ 766	Barry Bonnell	.10	.05	.01
☐ 767	Duane Kuiper	.10	.05	.01

☐ 768 Chris Speier	.10	.05	.01
☐ 769 Checklist: 661-792	.15	.02	.00
☐ 770 Dave Winfield	3.00	1.35	.40
☐ 771 Twins TL BA: Kent Hrbek ERA: Bobby Castillo	.15	.07	.02
☐ 772 Jim Kern	.10	.05	.01
☐ 773 Larry Hisle	.10	.05	.01
☐ 774 Alan Ashby	.10	.05	.01
☐ 775 Burt Hooton	.10	.05	.01
☐ 776 Larry Parrish	.10	.05	.01
☐ 777 John Curtis	.10	.05	.01
☐ 778 Rich Hebner	.10	.05	.01
☐ 779 Rick Waits	.10	.05	.01
☐ 780 Gary Matthews	.15	.07	.02
☐ 781 Rick Rhoden	.10	.05	.01
☐ 782 Bobby Murcer	.15	.07	.02
☐ 783 SV: Bobby Murcer	.10	.05	.01
☐ 784 Jeff Newman	.10	.05	.01
☐ 785 Dennis Leonard	.10	.05	.01
☐ 786 Ralph Houk MG	.10	.05	.01
☐ 787 Dick Tidrow	.10	.05	.01
☐ 788 Dane Iorg	.10	.05	.01
☐ 789 Bryan Clark	.10	.05	.01
☐ 790 Bob Grich	.15	.07	.02
☐ 791 Gary Lavelle	.10	.05	.01
☐ 792 Chris Chambliss	.20	.09	.03

1983 Topps Gaylord Perry

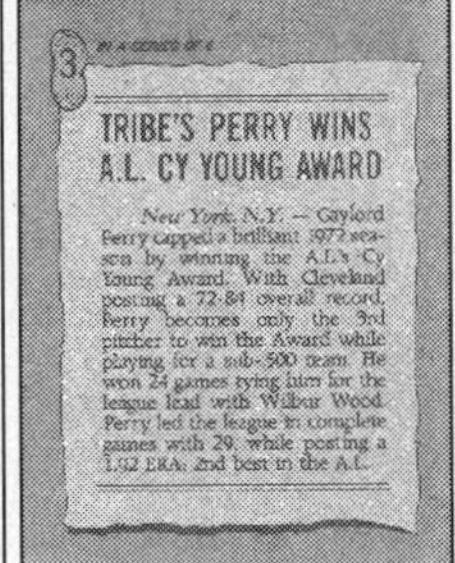

This six-card, standard-size, 2 1/2" by 3 1/2" set depicts Gaylord Perry during various parts of his career. These cards have the looks of Topps cards and were produced by Topps but have no Topps logo on either the front or the back of the card.

	NRMT-MT	EXC	G-VG
COMPLETE SET (6)	15.00	6.75	1.90
COMMON PLAYER (1-6)	3.00	1.35	.40
☐ 1 Gaylord Perry San Francisco Giants (Perry wins first game in 1962)	3.00	1.35	.40
☐ 2 Gaylord Perry San Francisco Giants (Perry pitches no-hitter in 1968)	3.00	1.35	.40
☐ 3 Gaylord Perry Cleveland Indians (Perry wins Cy Young Award in 1972)	3.00	1.35	.40
☐ 4 Gaylord Perry Texas Rangers (Perry strikes out 2,500th in 1975)	3.00	1.35	.40
☐ 5 Gaylord Perry San Diego Padres (Perry wins second Cy Young and strikes out 3,000th in 1978)	3.00	1.35	.40
☐ 6 Gaylord Perry Seattle Mariners (Perry wins 300th game in 1982)	3.00	1.35	.40

1983 Topps Glossy 40

The cards in this 40-card set measure 2 1/2" by 3 1/2". The 1983 Topps "Collector's Edition" or "All-Star Set" (popularly known as "Glossies") consists of color ballplayer picture cards with shiny, glazed surfaces. The player's name appears in small print outside the frame line at bottom left. The backs contain no biography or record and list only the set titles, the player's name, team, position, and the card number.

	NRMT-MT	EXC	G-VG
COMPLETE SET (40)	12.50	5.75	1.55
COMMON PLAYER (1-40)	.20	.09	.03
☐ 1 Carl Yastrzemski	1.00	.45	.13
☐ 2 Mookie Wilson	.25	.11	.03
☐ 3 Andre Thornton	.20	.09	.03
☐ 4 Keith Hernandez	.30	.14	.04
☐ 5 Robin Yount	1.25	.55	.16
☐ 6 Terry Kennedy	.20	.09	.03
☐ 7 Dave Winfield	.75	.35	.09
☐ 8 Mike Schmidt	1.50	.65	.19
☐ 9 Buddy Bell	.20	.09	.03
☐ 10 Fernando Valenzuela	.30	.14	.04
☐ 11 Rich Gossage	.30	.14	.04
☐ 12 Bob Horner	.20	.09	.03
☐ 13 Toby Harrah	.20	.09	.03
☐ 14 Pete Rose	1.25	.55	.16
☐ 15 Cecil Cooper	.25	.11	.03
☐ 16 Dale Murphy	.75	.35	.09
☐ 17 Carlton Fisk	.75	.35	.09
☐ 18 Ray Knight	.25	.11	.03
☐ 19 Jim Palmer	.75	.35	.09
☐ 20 Gary Carter	.50	.23	.06
☐ 21 Richie Zisk	.20	.09	.03
☐ 22 Dusty Baker	[illegible]	.14	.04
☐ 23 Willie Wilson	.30	.14	.04
☐ 24 Bill Buckner	.25	.11	.03
☐ 25 Dave Stieb	.25	.11	.03
☐ 26 Bill Madlock	.25	.11	.03
☐ 27 Lance Parrish	.30	.14	.04
☐ 28 Nolan Ryan	3.00	1.35	.40
☐ 29 Rod Carew	1.00	.45	.13
☐ 30 Al Oliver	.25	.11	.03
☐ 31 George Brett	1.25	.55	.16
☐ 32 Jack Clark	.30	.14	.04
☐ 33 Rickey Henderson	1.25	.55	.16
☐ 34 Dave Concepcion	.30	.14	.04
☐ 35 Kent Hrbek	.40	.18	.05
☐ 36 Steve Carlton	.75	.35	.09
☐ 37 Eddie Murray	1.00	.45	.13
☐ 38 Ruppert Jones	.20	.09	.03
☐ 39 Reggie Jackson	1.00	.45	.13
☐ 40 Bruce Sutter	.30	.14	.04

1983 Topps Traded

The cards in this 132-card set measure 2 1/2" by 3 1/2". For the third year in a row, Topps issued a 132-card Traded (or extended) set featuring some of the year's top rookies and players who had changed teams during the year, but were featured with their old team in the Topps regular issue of

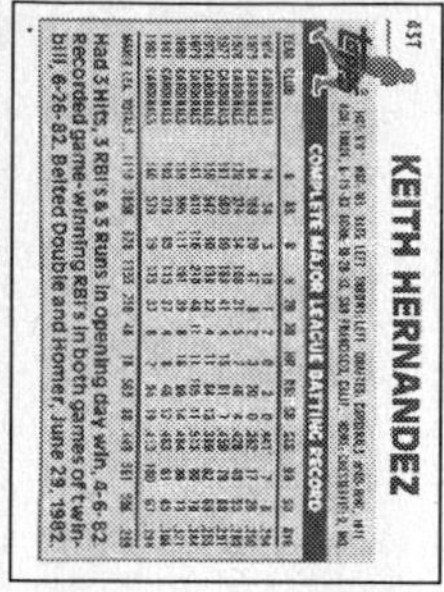

1983. The cards were available through hobby dealers only and were printed in Ireland by the Topps affiliate in that country. The set is numbered alphabetically by the last name of the player of the card. The Darryl Strawberry card number 108 can be found with either one or two asterisks (in the lower left corner of the reverse). The key (extended) Rookie Card in this set is obviously Darryl Strawberry. Also noteworthy is Julio Franco's first Topps (extended) card.

	NRMT-MT	EXC	G-VG
COMPLETE SET (132)	110.00	50.00	14.00
COMMON PLAYER (1T-132T)	.15	.07	.02

Card	NRMT-MT	EXC	G-VG
☐ 1T Neil Allen	.15	.07	.02
☐ 2T Bill Almon	.15	.07	.02
☐ 3T Joe Altobelli MG	.15	.07	.02
☐ 4T Tony Armas	.15	.07	.02
☐ 5T Doug Bair	.15	.07	.02
☐ 6T Steve Baker	.15	.07	.02
☐ 7T Floyd Bannister	.15	.07	.02
☐ 8T Don Baylor	.25	.11	.03
☐ 9T Tony Bernazard	.15	.07	.02
☐ 10T Larry Biittner	.15	.07	.02
☐ 11T Dann Bilardello	.15	.07	.02
☐ 12T Doug Bird	.15	.07	.02
☐ 13T Steve Boros MG	.15	.07	.02
☐ 14T Greg Brock	.25	.11	.03
☐ 15T Mike C. Brown (Red Sox pitcher)	.15	.07	.02
☐ 16T Tom Burgmeier	.15	.07	.02
☐ 17T Randy Bush	.25	.11	.03
☐ 18T Bert Campaneris	.25	.11	.03
☐ 19T Ron Cey	.25	.11	.03
☐ 20T Chris Codiroli	.15	.07	.02
☐ 21T Dave Collins	.15	.07	.02
☐ 22T Terry Crowley	.15	.07	.02
☐ 23T Julio Cruz	.15	.07	.02
☐ 24T Mike Davis	.15	.07	.02
☐ 25T Frank DiPino	.15	.07	.02
☐ 26T Bill Doran	.90	.40	.11
☐ 27T Jerry Dybzinski	.15	.07	.02
☐ 28T Jamie Easterly	.15	.07	.02
☐ 29T Juan Eichelberger	.15	.07	.02
☐ 30T Jim Essian	.15	.07	.02
☐ 31T Pete Falcone	.15	.07	.02
☐ 32T Mike Ferraro MG	.15	.07	.02
☐ 33T Terry Forster	.15	.07	.02
☐ 34T Julio Franco	9.00	4.00	1.15
☐ 35T Rich Gale	.15	.07	.02
☐ 36T Kiko Garcia	.15	.07	.02
☐ 37T Steve Garvey	1.50	.65	.19
☐ 38T Johnny Grubb	.15	.07	.02
☐ 39T Mel Hall	3.00	1.35	.40
☐ 40T Von Hayes	.25	.11	.03
☐ 41T Danny Heep	.15	.07	.02
☐ 42T Steve Henderson	.15	.07	.02
☐ 43T Keith Hernandez	.50	.23	.06
☐ 44T Leo Hernandez	.15	.07	.02
☐ 45T Willie Hernandez	.25	.11	.03
☐ 46T Al Holland	.15	.07	.02
☐ 47T Frank Howard MG	.25	.11	.03
☐ 48T Bobby Johnson	.15	.07	.02
☐ 49T Cliff Johnson	.15	.07	.02
☐ 50T Odell Jones	.15	.07	.02
☐ 51T Mike Jorgensen	.15	.07	.02
☐ 52T Bob Kearney	.15	.07	.02
☐ 53T Steve Kemp	.15	.07	.02
☐ 54T Matt Keough	.15	.07	.02
☐ 55T Ron Kittle	.25	.11	.03
☐ 56T Mickey Klutts	.15	.07	.02
☐ 57T Alan Knicely	.15	.07	.02
☐ 58T Mike Krukow	.15	.07	.02
☐ 59T Rafael Landestoy	.15	.07	.02
☐ 60T Carney Lansford	.25	.11	.03
☐ 61T Joe Lefebvre	.15	.07	.02
☐ 62T Bryan Little	.15	.07	.02
☐ 63T Aurelio Lopez	.15	.07	.02
☐ 64T Mike Madden	.15	.07	.02
☐ 65T Rick Manning	.15	.07	.02
☐ 66T Billy Martin MG	.25	.11	.03
☐ 67T Lee Mazzilli	.15	.07	.02
☐ 68T Andy McGaffigan	.15	.07	.02
☐ 69T Craig McMurtry	.15	.07	.02
☐ 70T John McNamara MG	.15	.07	.02
☐ 71T Orlando Mercado	.15	.07	.02
☐ 72T Larry Milbourne	.15	.07	.02
☐ 73T Randy Moffitt	.15	.07	.02
☐ 74T Sid Monge	.15	.07	.02
☐ 75T Jose Morales	.15	.07	.02
☐ 76T Omar Moreno	.15	.07	.02
☐ 77T Joe Morgan	2.50	1.15	.30
☐ 78T Mike Morgan	.75	.35	.09
☐ 79T Dale Murray	.15	.07	.02
☐ 80T Jeff Newman	.15	.07	.02
☐ 81T Pete O'Brien	.90	.40	.11
☐ 82T Jorge Orta	.15	.07	.02
☐ 83T Alejandro Pena	.75	.35	.09
☐ 84T Pascual Perez	.15	.07	.02
☐ 85T Tony Perez	1.50	.65	.19
☐ 86T Broderick Perkins	.15	.07	.02
☐ 87T Tony Phillips	3.00	1.35	.40
☐ 88T Charlie Puleo	.15	.07	.02
☐ 89T Pat Putnam	.15	.07	.02
☐ 90T Jamie Quirk	.15	.07	.02
☐ 91T Doug Rader MG	.15	.07	.02
☐ 92T Chuck Rainey	.15	.07	.02
☐ 93T Bobby Ramos	.15	.07	.02
☐ 94T Gary Redus	.60	.25	.08
☐ 95T Steve Renko	.15	.07	.02
☐ 96T Leon Roberts	.15	.07	.02
☐ 97T Aurelio Rodriguez	.15	.07	.02
☐ 98T Dick Ruthven	.15	.07	.02
☐ 99T Daryl Sconiers	.15	.07	.02
☐ 100T Mike Scott	.25	.11	.03
☐ 101T Tom Seaver	9.00	4.00	1.15
☐ 102T John Shelby	.25	.11	.03
☐ 103T Bob Shirley	.15	.07	.02
☐ 104T Joe Simpson	.15	.07	.02
☐ 105T Doug Sisk	.15	.07	.02
☐ 106T Mike Smithson	.25	.11	.03
☐ 107T Elias Sosa	.15	.07	.02
☐ 108T Darryl Strawberry	75.00	34.00	9.50
☐ 109T Tom Tellmann	.15	.07	.02
☐ 110T Gene Tenace	.15	.07	.02
☐ 111T Gorman Thomas	.25	.11	.03
☐ 112T Dick Tidrow	.15	.07	.02
☐ 113T Dave Tobik	.15	.07	.02
☐ 114T Wayne Tolleson	.15	.07	.02
☐ 115T Mike Torrez	.15	.07	.02
☐ 116T Manny Trillo	.15	.07	.02
☐ 117T Steve Trout	.15	.07	.02
☐ 118T Lee Tunnell	.15	.07	.02
☐ 119T Mike Vail	.15	.07	.02
☐ 120T Ellis Valentine	.15	.07	.02
☐ 121T Tom Veryzer	.15	.07	.02
☐ 122T George Vukovich	.15	.07	.02
☐ 123T Rick Waits	.15	.07	.02
☐ 124T Greg Walker	.25	.11	.03
☐ 125T Chris Welsh	.15	.07	.02
☐ 126T Len Whitehouse	.15	.07	.02
☐ 127T Eddie Whitson	.15	.07	.02
☐ 128T Jim Wohlford	.15	.07	.02
☐ 129T Matt Young	.25	.11	.03
☐ 130T Joel Youngblood	.15	.07	.02
☐ 131T Pat Zachry	.15	.07	.02
☐ 132T Checklist 1T-132T	.25	.03	.01

1984 Topps

The cards in this 792-card set measure 2 1/2" by 3 1/2". For the second year in a row, Topps utilized a dual picture on the front of the card. A portrait is shown in a square insert and an action shot is featured in the main photo. Card numbers 1-6 feature 1983 Highlights (HL), cards 131-138 depict League Leaders, card numbers 386-407 feature All-Stars, and card numbers 701-718 feature active Major League career leaders in various statistical categories. Each

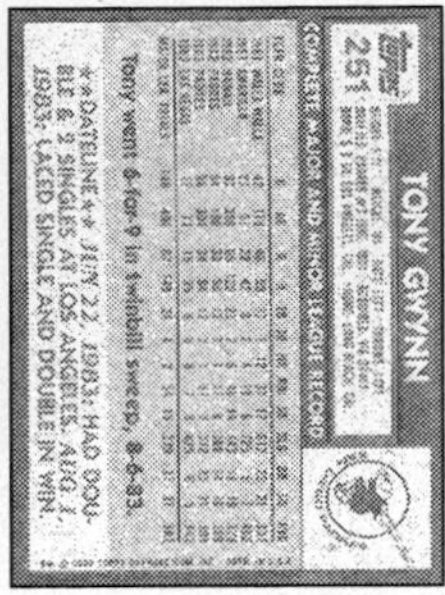

team leader (TL) card features the team's leading hitter and pitcher pictured on the front with a team checklist back. There are six numerical checklist cards in the set. The player cards feature team logos in the upper right corner of the reverse. The key Rookie Cards in this set are Don Mattingly, Darryl Strawberry, and Andy Van Slyke. Topps also produced a specially boxed "glossy" edition, frequently referred to as the Topps Tiffany set. There were supposedly only 10,000 sets of the Tiffany cards produced; they were marketed to hobby dealers. The checklist of cards (792 regular and 132 Traded) is identical to that of the normal non-glossy cards. There are two primary distinguishing features of the Tiffany cards, white card stock reverses and high gloss obverses. These Tiffany cards are valued approximately from five to ten times the values listed below. Topps tested a special send-in offer in Michigan and a few other states whereby collectors could obtain direct from Topps ten cards of their choice. Needless to say most people ordered the key (most valuable) players necessitating the printing of a special sheet to keep up with the demand. The special sheet had five cards of Darryl Strawberry, three cards of Don Mattingly, etc. The test was apparently a failure in Topps' eyes as they have never tried it again.

	NRMT-MT	EXC	G-VG
COMPLETE SET (792)	85.00	38.00	10.50
COMMON PLAYER (1-792)	.08	.04	.01
☐ 1 HL: Steve Carlton	.50	.10	.03
300th win and			
all-time SO king			
☐ 2 HL: Rickey Henderson	1.00	.16	.12
100 stolen bases,			
three times			
☐ 3 HL: Dan Quisenberry	.12	.05	.02
Sets save record			
☐ 4 HL: Nolan Ryan,	.60	.25	.08
Steve Carlton, and			
Gaylord Perry			
(All surpass Johnson)			
☐ 5 HL: Dave Righetti,	.12	.05	.02
Bob Forsch,			
and Mike Warren			
(All pitch no-hitters)			
☐ 6 HL: Johnny Bench,	.40	.18	.05
Gaylord Perry, and			
Carl Yastrzemski			
(Superstars retire)			
☐ 7 Gary Lucas	.08	.04	.01
☐ 8 Don Mattingly	12.00	5.50	1.50
☐ 9 Jim Gott	.08	.04	.01
☐ 10 Robin Yount	2.00	.90	.25
☐ 11 Minnesota Twins TL	.12	.05	.02
Kent Hrbek			
Ken Schrom			
☐ 12 Billy Sample	.08	.04	.01
☐ 13 Scott Holman	.08	.04	.01
☐ 14 Tom Brookens	.08	.04	.01
☐ 15 Burt Hooton	.08	.04	.01
☐ 16 Omar Moreno	.08	.04	.01
☐ 17 John Denny	.08	.04	.01
☐ 18 Dale Berra	.08	.04	.01
☐ 19 Ray Fontenot	.08	.04	.01
☐ 20 Greg Luzinski	.12	.05	.02
☐ 21 Joe Altobelli MG	.08	.04	.01
☐ 22 Bryan Clark	.08	.04	.01
☐ 23 Keith Moreland	.08	.04	.01
☐ 24 John Martin	.08	.04	.01
☐ 25 Glenn Hubbard	.08	.04	.01
☐ 26 Bud Black	.08	.04	.01
☐ 27 Daryl Sconiers	.08	.04	.01
☐ 28 Frank Viola	.50	.23	.06
☐ 29 Danny Heep	.08	.04	.01
☐ 30 Wade Boggs	4.00	1.80	.50
☐ 31 Andy McGaffigan	.08	.04	.01
☐ 32 Bobby Ramos	.08	.04	.01
☐ 33 Tom Burgmeier	.08	.04	.01
☐ 34 Eddie Milner	.08	.04	.01
☐ 35 Don Sutton	.35	.16	.04
☐ 36 Denny Walling	.08	.04	.01
☐ 37 Texas Rangers TL	.12	.05	.02
Buddy Bell			
Rick Honeycutt			
☐ 38 Luis DeLeon	.08	.04	.01
☐ 39 Garth Iorg	.08	.04	.01
☐ 40 Dusty Baker	.12	.05	.02
☐ 41 Tony Bernazard	.08	.04	.01
☐ 42 Johnny Grubb	.08	.04	.01
☐ 43 Ron Reed	.08	.04	.01
☐ 44 Jim Morrison	.08	.04	.01
☐ 45 Jerry Mumphrey	.08	.04	.01
☐ 46 Ray Smith	.08	.04	.01
☐ 47 Rudy Law	.08	.04	.01
☐ 48 Julio Franco	1.00	.45	.13
☐ 49 John Stuper	.08	.04	.01
☐ 50 Chris Chambliss	.12	.05	.02
☐ 51 Jim Frey MG	.08	.04	.01
☐ 52 Paul Splittorff	.08	.04	.01
☐ 53 Juan Beniquez	.08	.04	.01
☐ 54 Jesse Orosco	.08	.04	.01
☐ 55 Dave Concepcion	.12	.05	.02
☐ 56 Gary Allenson	.08	.04	.01
☐ 57 Dan Schatzeder	.08	.04	.01
☐ 58 Max Venable	.08	.04	.01
☐ 59 Sammy Stewart	.08	.04	.01
☐ 60 Paul Molitor UER	.60	.25	.08
('83 stats .272, 613,			
167; should be .270,			
608, 164)			
☐ 61 Chris Codiroli	.08	.04	.01
☐ 62 Dave Hostetler	.08	.04	.01
☐ 63 Ed VandeBerg	.08	.04	.01
☐ 64 Mike Scioscia	.12	.05	.02
☐ 65 Kirk Gibson	.25	.11	.03
☐ 66 Houston Astros TL	.40	.18	.05
Jose Cruz			
Nolan Ryan			
☐ 67 Gary Ward	.08	.04	.01
☐ 68 Luis Salazar	.08	.04	.01
☐ 69 Rod Scurry	.08	.04	.01
☐ 70 Gary Matthews	.12	.05	.02
☐ 71 Leo Hernandez	.08	.04	.01
☐ 72 Mike Squires	.08	.04	.01
☐ 73 Jody Davis	.08	.04	.01
☐ 74 Jerry Martin	.08	.04	.01
☐ 75 Bob Forsch	.08	.04	.01
☐ 76 Alfredo Griffin	.08	.04	.01
☐ 77 Brett Butler	.25	.11	.03
☐ 78 Mike Torrez	.08	.04	.01
☐ 79 Rob Wilfong	.08	.04	.01
☐ 80 Steve Rogers	.08	.04	.01
☐ 81 Billy Martin MG	.15	.07	.02
☐ 82 Doug Bird	.08	.04	.01
☐ 83 Richie Zisk	.08	.04	.01
☐ 84 Lenny Faedo	.08	.04	.01
☐ 85 Atlee Hammaker	.08	.04	.01
☐ 86 John Shelby	.08	.04	.01
☐ 87 Frank Pastore	.08	.04	.01
☐ 88 Rob Picciolo	.08	.04	.01
☐ 89 Mike Smithson	.08	.04	.01
☐ 90 Pedro Guerrero	.12	.05	.02
☐ 91 Dan Spillner	.08	.04	.01
☐ 92 Lloyd Moseby	.08	.04	.01
☐ 93 Bob Knepper	.08	.04	.01
☐ 94 Mario Ramirez	.08	.04	.01
☐ 95 Aurelio Lopez	.08	.04	.01
☐ 96 K.C. Royals TL	.12	.05	.02
Hal McRae			
Larry Gura			
☐ 97 LaMarr Hoyt	.08	.04	.01
☐ 98 Steve Nicosia	.08	.04	.01
☐ 99 Craig Lefferts	.25	.11	.03
☐ 100 Reggie Jackson	1.25	.55	.16
☐ 101 Porfirio Altamirano	.08	.04	.01
☐ 102 Ken Oberkfell	.08	.04	.01
☐ 103 Dwayne Murphy	.08	.04	.01
☐ 104 Ken Dayley	.08	.04	.01
☐ 105 Tony Armas	.08	.04	.01

☐	106 Tim Stoddard	.08	.04	.01
☐	107 Ned Yost	.08	.04	.01
☐	108 Randy Moffitt	.08	.04	.01
☐	109 Brad Wellman	.08	.04	.01
☐	110 Ron Guidry	.12	.05	.02
☐	111 Bill Virdon MG	.08	.04	.01
☐	112 Tom Niedenfuer	.08	.04	.01
☐	113 Kelly Paris	.08	.04	.01
☐	114 Checklist 1-132	.12	.01	.00
☐	115 Andre Thornton	.08	.04	.01
☐	116 George Bjorkman	.08	.04	.01
☐	117 Tom Veryzer	.08	.04	.01
☐	118 Charlie Hough	.12	.05	.02
☐	119 John Wockenfuss	.08	.04	.01
☐	120 Keith Hernandez	.12	.05	.02
☐	121 Pat Sheridan	.08	.04	.01
☐	122 Cecilio Guante	.08	.04	.01
☐	123 Butch Wynegar	.08	.04	.01
☐	124 Damaso Garcia	.08	.04	.01
☐	125 Britt Burns	.08	.04	.01
☐	126 Atlanta Braves TL	.15	.07	.02
	Dale Murphy			
	Craig McMurtry			
☐	127 Mike Madden	.08	.04	.01
☐	128 Rick Manning	.08	.04	.01
☐	129 Bill Laskey	.08	.04	.01
☐	130 Ozzie Smith	1.25	.55	.16
☐	131 Batting Leaders	.60	.25	.08
	Bill Madlock			
	Wade Boggs			
☐	132 Home Run Leaders	.30	.14	.04
	Mike Schmidt			
	Jim Rice			
☐	133 RBI Leaders	.20	.09	.03
	Dale Murphy			
	Cecil Cooper			
	Jim Rice			
☐	134 Stolen Base Leaders	.75	.35	.09
	Tim Raines			
	Rickey Henderson			
☐	135 Victory Leaders	.12	.05	.02
	John Denny			
	LaMarr Hoyt			
☐	136 Strikeout Leaders	.30	.14	.04
	Steve Carlton			
	Jack Morris			
☐	137 ERA Leaders	.12	.05	.02
	Atlee Hammaker			
	Rick Honeycutt			
☐	138 Leading Firemen	.12	.05	.02
	Al Holland			
	Dan Quisenberry			
☐	139 Bert Campaneris	.12	.05	.02
☐	140 Storm Davis	.08	.04	.01
☐	141 Pat Corrales MG	.08	.04	.01
☐	142 Rich Gale	.08	.04	.01
☐	143 Jose Morales	.08	.04	.01
☐	144 Brian Harper	.75	.35	.09
☐	145 Gary Lavelle	.08	.04	.01
☐	146 Ed Romero	.08	.04	.01
☐	147 Dan Petry	.08	.04	.01
☐	148 Joe Lefebvre	.08	.04	.01
☐	149 Jon Matlack	.08	.04	.01
☐	150 Dale Murphy	.75	.35	.09
☐	151 Steve Trout	.08	.04	.01
☐	152 Glenn Brummer	.08	.04	.01
☐	153 Dick Tidrow	.08	.04	.01
☐	154 Dave Henderson	.12	.05	.02
☐	155 Frank White	.12	.05	.02
☐	156 Oakland A's TL	.25	.11	.03
	Rickey Henderson			
	Tim Conroy			
☐	157 Gary Gaetti	.12	.05	.02
☐	158 John Curtis	.08	.04	.01
☐	159 Darryl Cias	.08	.04	.01
☐	160 Mario Soto	.08	.04	.01
☐	161 Junior Ortiz	.08	.04	.01
☐	162 Bob Ojeda	.08	.04	.01
☐	163 Lorenzo Gray	.08	.04	.01
☐	164 Scott Sanderson	.08	.04	.01
☐	165 Ken Singleton	.12	.05	.02
☐	166 Jamie Nelson	.08	.04	.01
☐	167 Marshall Edwards	.08	.04	.01
☐	168 Juan Bonilla	.08	.04	.01
☐	169 Larry Parrish	.08	.04	.01
☐	170 Jerry Reuss	.08	.04	.01
☐	171 Frank Robinson MG	.15	.07	.02
☐	172 Frank DiPino	.08	.04	.01
☐	173 Marvell Wynne	.08	.04	.01
☐	174 Juan Berenguer	.08	.04	.01
☐	175 Graig Nettles	.12	.05	.02
☐	176 Lee Smith	.75	.35	.09
☐	177 Jerry Hairston	.08	.04	.01
☐	178 Bill Krueger	.15	.07	.02
☐	179 Buck Martinez	.08	.04	.01
☐	180 Manny Trillo	.08	.04	.01
☐	181 Roy Thomas	.08	.04	.01
☐	182 Darryl Strawberry	12.00	5.50	1.50
☐	183 Al Williams	.08	.04	.01
☐	184 Mike O'Berry	.08	.04	.01
☐	185 Sixto Lezcano	.08	.04	.01
☐	186 Cardinal TL	.12	.05	.02
	Lonnie Smith			
	John Stuper			
☐	187 Luis Aponte	.08	.04	.01
☐	188 Bryan Little	.08	.04	.01
☐	189 Tim Conroy	.08	.04	.01
☐	190 Ben Oglivie	.08	.04	.01
☐	191 Mike Boddicker	.08	.04	.01
☐	192 Nick Esasky	.12	.05	.02
☐	193 Darrell Brown	.08	.04	.01
☐	194 Domingo Ramos	.08	.04	.01
☐	195 Jack Morris	1.00	.45	.13
☐	196 Don Slaught	.15	.07	.02
☐	197 Garry Hancock	.08	.04	.01
☐	198 Bill Doran	.20	.09	.03
☐	199 Willie Hernandez	.12	.05	.02
☐	200 Andre Dawson	1.25	.55	.16
☐	201 Bruce Kison	.08	.04	.01
☐	202 Bobby Cox MG	.08	.04	.01
☐	203 Matt Keough	.08	.04	.01
☐	204 Bobby Meacham	.08	.04	.01
☐	205 Greg Minton	.08	.04	.01
☐	206 Andy Van Slyke	3.00	1.35	.40
☐	207 Donnie Moore	.08	.04	.01
☐	208 Jose Oquendo	.15	.07	.02
☐	209 Manny Sarmiento	.08	.04	.01
☐	210 Joe Morgan	.40	.18	.05
☐	211 Rick Sweet	.08	.04	.01
☐	212 Broderick Perkins	.08	.04	.01
☐	213 Bruce Hurst	.12	.05	.02
☐	214 Paul Householder	.08	.04	.01
☐	215 Tippy Martinez	.08	.04	.01
☐	216 White Sox TL	.15	.07	.02
	Carlton Fisk			
	Richard Dotson			
☐	217 Alan Ashby	.08	.04	.01
☐	218 Rick Waits	.08	.04	.01
☐	219 Joe Simpson	.08	.04	.01
☐	220 Fernando Valenzuela	.12	.05	.02
☐	221 Cliff Johnson	.08	.04	.01
☐	222 Rick Honeycutt	.08	.04	.01
☐	223 Wayne Krenchicki	.08	.04	.01
☐	224 Sid Monge	.08	.04	.01
☐	225 Lee Mazzilli	.08	.04	.01
☐	226 Juan Eichelberger	.08	.04	.01
☐	227 Steve Braun	.08	.04	.01
☐	228 John Rabb	.08	.04	.01
☐	229 Paul Owens MG	.08	.04	.01
☐	230 Rickey Henderson	4.00	1.80	.50
☐	231 Gary Woods	.08	.04	.01
☐	232 Tim Wallach	.12	.05	.02
☐	233 Checklist 133-264	.12	.01	.00
☐	234 Rafael Ramirez	.08	.04	.01
☐	235 Matt Young	.08	.04	.01
☐	236 Ellis Valentine	.08	.04	.01
☐	237 John Castino	.08	.04	.01
☐	238 Reid Nichols	.08	.04	.01
☐	239 Jay Howell	.12	.05	.02
☐	240 Eddie Murray	1.50	.65	.19
☐	241 Bill Almon	.08	.04	.01
☐	242 Alex Trevino	.08	.04	.01
☐	243 Pete Ladd	.08	.04	.01
☐	244 Candy Maldonado	.25	.11	.03
☐	245 Rick Sutcliffe	.12	.05	.02
☐	246 New York Mets TL	.20	.09	.03
	Mookie Wilson			
	Tom Seaver			
☐	247 Onix Concepcion	.08	.04	.01
☐	248 Bill Dawley	.08	.04	.01
☐	249 Jay Johnstone	.12	.05	.02
☐	250 Bill Madlock	.12	.05	.02
☐	251 Tony Gwynn	5.00	2.30	.60
☐	252 Larry Christenson	.08	.04	.01
☐	253 Jim Wohlford	.08	.04	.01
☐	254 Shane Rawley	.08	.04	.01
☐	255 Bruce Benedict	.08	.04	.01
☐	256 Dave Geisel	.08	.04	.01
☐	257 Julio Cruz	.08	.04	.01
☐	258 Luis Sanchez	.08	.04	.01
☐	259 Sparky Anderson MG	.12	.05	.02
☐	260 Scott McGregor	.08	.04	.01
☐	261 Bobby Brown	.08	.04	.01
☐	262 Tom Candiotti	.50	.23	.06
☐	263 Jack Fimple	.08	.04	.01
☐	264 Doug Frobel	.08	.04	.01

265	Donnie Hill	.08	.04	.01
266	Steve Lubratich	.08	.04	.01
267	Carmelo Martinez	.12	.05	.02
268	Jack O'Connor	.08	.04	.01
269	Aurelio Rodriguez	.08	.04	.01
270	Jeff Russell	.30	.14	.04
271	Moose Haas	.08	.04	.01
272	Rick Dempsey	.12	.05	.02
273	Charlie Puleo	.08	.04	.01
274	Rick Monday	.08	.04	.01
275	Len Matuszek	.08	.04	.01
276	Angels TL Rod Carew Geoff Zahn	.15	.07	.02
277	Eddie Whitson	.08	.04	.01
278	Jorge Bell	.75	.35	.09
279	Ivan DeJesus	.08	.04	.01
280	Floyd Bannister	.08	.04	.01
281	Larry Milbourne	.08	.04	.01
282	Jim Barr	.08	.04	.01
283	Larry Biittner	.08	.04	.01
284	Howard Bailey	.08	.04	.01
285	Darrell Porter	.08	.04	.01
286	Lary Sorensen	.08	.04	.01
287	Warren Cromartie	.08	.04	.01
288	Jim Beattie	.08	.04	.01
289	Randy Johnson	.08	.04	.01
290	Dave Dravecky	.08	.01	.00
291	Chuck Tanner MG	.08	.04	.01
292	Tony Scott	.08	.04	.01
293	Ed Lynch	.08	.04	.01
294	U.L. Washington	.08	.04	.01
295	Mike Flanagan	.08	.04	.01
296	Jeff Newman	.08	.04	.01
297	Bruce Berenyi	.08	.04	.01
298	Jim Gantner	.12	.05	.02
299	John Butcher	.08	.04	.01
300	Pete Rose	1.25	.55	.16
301	Frank LaCorte	.08	.04	.01
302	Barry Bonnell	.08	.04	.01
303	Marty Castillo	.08	.04	.01
304	Warren Brusstar	.08	.04	.01
305	Roy Smalley	.08	.04	.01
306	Dodgers TL Pedro Guerrero Bob Welch	.12	.05	.02
307	Bobby Mitchell	.08	.04	.01
308	Ron Hassey	.08	.04	.01
309	Tony Phillips	.60	.25	.08
310	Willie McGee	.30	.14	.04
311	Jerry Koosman	.12	.05	.02
312	Jorge Orta	.08	.04	.01
313	Mike Jorgensen	.08	.04	.01
314	Orlando Mercado	.08	.04	.01
315	Bob Grich	.12	.05	.02
316	Mark Bradley	.08	.04	.01
317	Greg Pryor	.08	.04	.01
318	Bill Gullickson	.12	.05	.02
319	Al Bumbry	.08	.04	.01
320	Bob Stanley	.08	.04	.01
321	Harvey Kuenn MG	.08	.01	.00
322	Ken Schrom	.08	.04	.01
323	Alan Knicely	.08	.04	.01
324	Alejandro Pena	.20	.09	.03
325	Darrell Evans	.12	.05	.02
326	Bob Kearney	.08	.04	.01
327	Ruppert Jones	.08	.04	.01
328	Vern Ruhle	.08	.04	.01
329	Pat Tabler	.08	.04	.01
330	John Candelaria	.08	.04	.01
331	Bucky Dent	.12	.05	.02
332	Kevin Gross	.15	.07	.02
333	Larry Herndon	.08	.04	.01
334	Chuck Rainey	.08	.04	.01
335	Don Baylor	.12	.05	.02
336	Seattle Mariners TL Pat Putnam Matt Young	.12	.05	.02
337	Kevin Hagen	.08	.04	.01
338	Mike Warren	.08	.04	.01
339	Roy Lee Jackson	.08	.04	.01
340	Hal McRae	.12	.05	.02
341	Dave Tobik	.08	.04	.01
342	Tim Foli	.08	.04	.01
343	Mark Davis	.12	.05	.02
344	Rick Miller	.08	.04	.01
345	Kent Hrbek	.30	.14	.04
346	Kurt Bevacqua	.08	.04	.01
347	Allan Ramirez	.08	.04	.01
348	Toby Harrah	.08	.04	.01
349	Bob L. Gibson (Brewers Pitcher)	.08	.04	.01
350	George Foster	.12	.05	.02
351	Russ Nixon MG	.08	.04	.01
352	Dave Stewart	.30	.14	.04
353	Jim Anderson	.08	.04	.01
354	Jeff Burroughs	.08	.04	.01
355	Jason Thompson	.08	.04	.01
356	Glenn Abbott	.08	.04	.01
357	Ron Cey	.12	.05	.02
358	Bob Dernier	.08	.04	.01
359	Jim Acker	.08	.04	.01
360	Willie Randolph	.12	.05	.02
361	Dave Smith	.08	.04	.01
362	David Green	.08	.04	.01
363	Tim Laudner	.08	.04	.01
364	Scott Fletcher	.08	.04	.01
365	Steve Bedrosian	.12	.05	.02
366	Padres TL Terry Kennedy Dave Dravecky	.12	.05	.02
367	Jamie Easterly	.08	.04	.01
368	Hubie Brooks	.12	.05	.02
369	Steve McCatty	.08	.04	.01
370	Tim Raines	.40	.18	.05
371	Dave Gumpert	.08	.04	.01
372	Gary Roenicke	.08	.04	.01
373	Bill Scherrer	.08	.04	.01
374	Don Money	.08	.04	.01
375	Dennis Leonard	.08	.04	.01
376	Dave Anderson	.12	.05	.02
377	Danny Darwin	.08	.04	.01
378	Bob Brenly	.08	.04	.01
379	Checklist 265-396	.12	.01	.00
380	Steve Garvey	.40	.18	.05
381	Ralph Houk MG	.12	.05	.02
382	Chris Nyman	.08	.04	.01
383	Terry Puhl	.08	.04	.01
384	Lee Tunnell	.08	.04	.01
385	Tony Perez	.25	.11	.03
386	George Hendrick AS	.12	.05	.02
387	Johnny Ray AS	.12	.05	.02
388	Mike Schmidt AS	.75	.35	.09
389	Ozzie Smith AS	.40	.18	.05
390	Tim Raines AS	.15	.07	.02
391	Dale Murphy AS	.25	.11	.03
392	Andre Dawson AS	.40	.18	.05
393	Gary Carter AS	.20	.09	.03
394	Steve Rogers AS	.12	.05	.02
395	Steve Carlton AS	.35	.16	.04
396	Jesse Orosco AS	.12	.05	.02
397	Eddie Murray AS	.40	.18	.05
398	Lou Whitaker AS	.15	.07	.02
399	George Brett AS	.65	.30	.08
400	Cal Ripken AS	2.00	.90	.25
401	Jim Rice AS	.12	.05	.02
402	Dave Winfield AS	.60	.25	.08
403	Lloyd Moseby AS	.12	.05	.02
404	Ted Simmons AS	.12	.05	.02
405	LaMarr Hoyt AS	.12	.05	.02
406	Ron Guidry AS	.12	.05	.02
407	Dan Quisenberry AS	.12	.05	.02
408	Lou Piniella	.12	.05	.02
409	Juan Agosto	.08	.04	.01
410	Claudell Washington	.08	.04	.01
411	Houston Jimenez	.08	.04	.01
412	Doug Rader MG	.08	.04	.01
413	Spike Owen	.15	.07	.02
414	Mitchell Page	.08	.04	.01
415	Tommy John	.12	.05	.02
416	Dane Iorg	.08	.04	.01
417	Mike Armstrong	.08	.04	.01
418	Ron Hodges	.08	.04	.01
419	John Henry Johnson	.08	.04	.01
420	Cecil Cooper	.12	.05	.02
421	Charlie Lea	.08	.04	.01
422	Jose Cruz	.12	.05	.02
423	Mike Morgan	.12	.05	.02
424	Dann Bilardello	.08	.04	.01
425	Steve Howe	.08	.04	.01
426	Orioles TL Cal Ripken Mike Boddicker	1.00	.45	.13
427	Rick Leach	.08	.04	.01
428	Fred Breining	.08	.04	.01
429	Randy Bush	.12	.05	.02
430	Rusty Staub	.12	.05	.02
431	Chris Bando	.08	.04	.01
432	Charles Hudson	.08	.04	.01
433	Rich Hebner	.08	.04	.01
434	Harold Baines	.25	.11	.03
435	Neil Allen	.08	.04	.01
436	Rick Peters	.08	.04	.01
437	Mike Proly	.08	.04	.01
438	Biff Pocoroba	.08	.04	.01
439	Bob Stoddard	.08	.04	.01

☐ 440 Steve Kemp	.08	.04	.01
☐ 441 Bob Lillis MG	.08	.04	.01
☐ 442 Byron McLaughlin	.08	.04	.01
☐ 443 Benny Ayala	.08	.04	.01
☐ 444 Steve Renko	.08	.04	.01
☐ 445 Jerry Remy	.08	.04	.01
☐ 446 Luis Pujols	.08	.04	.01
☐ 447 Tom Brunansky	.12	.05	.02
☐ 448 Ben Hayes	.08	.04	.01
☐ 449 Joe Pettini	.08	.04	.01
☐ 450 Gary Carter	.60	.25	.08
☐ 451 Bob Jones	.08	.04	.01
☐ 452 Chuck Porter	.08	.04	.01
☐ 453 Willie Upshaw	.08	.04	.01
☐ 454 Joe Beckwith	.08	.04	.01
☐ 455 Terry Kennedy	.08	.04	.01
☐ 456 Chicago Cubs TL Keith Moreland Fergie Jenkins	.12	.05	.02
☐ 457 Dave Rozema	.08	.04	.01
☐ 458 Kiko Garcia	.08	.04	.01
☐ 459 Kevin Hickey	.08	.04	.01
☐ 460 Dave Winfield	1.75	.80	.22
☐ 461 Jim Maler	.08	.04	.01
☐ 462 Lee Lacy	.08	.04	.01
☐ 463 Dave Engle	.08	.04	.01
☐ 464 Jeff A. Jones (A's Pitcher)	.08	.04	.01
☐ 465 Mookie Wilson	.12	.05	.02
☐ 466 Gene Garber	.08	.04	.01
☐ 467 Mike Ramsey	.08	.04	.01
☐ 468 Geoff Zahn	.08	.04	.01
☐ 469 Tom O'Malley	.08	.04	.01
☐ 470 Nolan Ryan	6.00	2.70	.75
☐ 471 Dick Howser MG	.08	.04	.01
☐ 472 Mike G. Brown (Red Sox Pitcher)	.08	.04	.01
☐ 473 Jim Dwyer	.08	.04	.01
☐ 474 Greg Bargar	.08	.04	.01
☐ 475 Gary Redus	.15	.07	.02
☐ 476 Tom Tellmann	.08	.04	.01
☐ 477 Rafael Landestoy	.08	.04	.01
☐ 478 Alan Bannister	.08	.04	.01
☐ 479 Frank Tanana	.12	.05	.02
☐ 480 Ron Kittle	.12	.05	.02
☐ 481 Mark Thurmond	.08	.04	.01
☐ 482 Enos Cabell	.08	.04	.01
☐ 483 Fergie Jenkins	.35	.16	.04
☐ 484 Ozzie Virgil	.08	.04	.01
☐ 485 Rick Rhoden	.08	.04	.01
☐ 486 N.Y. Yankees TL Don Baylor Ron Guidry	.12	.05	.02
☐ 487 Ricky Adams	.08	.04	.01
☐ 488 Jesse Barfield	.12	.05	.02
☐ 489 Dave Von Ohlen	.08	.04	.01
☐ 490 Cal Ripken	8.00	3.60	1.00
☐ 491 Bobby Castillo	.08	.04	.01
☐ 492 Tucker Ashford	.08	.04	.01
☐ 493 Mike Norris	.08	.04	.01
☐ 494 Chili Davis	.12	.05	.02
☐ 495 Rollie Fingers	.40	.18	.05
☐ 496 Terry Francona	.08	.04	.01
☐ 497 Bud Anderson	.08	.04	.01
☐ 498 Rich Gedman	.08	.04	.01
☐ 499 Mike Witt	.08	.04	.01
☐ 500 George Brett	2.00	.90	.25
☐ 501 Steve Henderson	.08	.04	.01
☐ 502 Joe Torre MG	.12	.05	.02
☐ 503 Elias Sosa	.08	.04	.01
☐ 504 Mickey Rivers	.08	.04	.01
☐ 505 Pete Vuckovich	.08	.04	.01
☐ 506 Ernie Whitt	.08	.04	.01
☐ 507 Mike LaCoss	.08	.04	.01
☐ 508 Mel Hall	.40	.18	.05
☐ 509 Brad Havens	.08	.04	.01
☐ 510 Alan Trammell	.40	.18	.05
☐ 511 Marty Bystrom	.08	.04	.01
☐ 512 Oscar Gamble	.08	.04	.01
☐ 513 Dave Beard	.08	.04	.01
☐ 514 Floyd Rayford	.08	.04	.01
☐ 515 Gorman Thomas	.08	.04	.01
☐ 516 Montreal Expos TL Al Oliver Charlie Lea	.12	.05	.02
☐ 517 John Moses	.08	.04	.01
☐ 518 Greg Walker	.12	.05	.02
☐ 519 Ron Davis	.08	.04	.01
☐ 520 Bob Boone	.12	.05	.02
☐ 521 Pete Falcone	.08	.04	.01
☐ 522 Dave Bergman	.08	.04	.01
☐ 523 Glenn Hoffman	.08	.04	.01
☐ 524 Carlos Diaz	.08	.04	.01
☐ 525 Willie Wilson	.12	.05	.02
☐ 526 Ron Oester	.08	.04	.01
☐ 527 Checklist 397-528	.12	.01	.00
☐ 528 Mark Brouhard	.08	.04	.01
☐ 529 Keith Atherton	.08	.04	.01
☐ 530 Dan Ford	.08	.04	.01
☐ 531 Steve Boros MG	.08	.04	.01
☐ 532 Eric Show	.08	.04	.01
☐ 533 Ken Landreaux	.08	.04	.01
☐ 534 Pete O'Brien	.20	.09	.03
☐ 535 Bo Diaz	.08	.04	.01
☐ 536 Doug Bair	.08	.04	.01
☐ 537 Johnny Ray	.08	.04	.01
☐ 538 Kevin Bass	.08	.04	.01
☐ 539 George Frazier	.08	.04	.01
☐ 540 George Hendrick	.08	.04	.01
☐ 541 Dennis Lamp	.08	.04	.01
☐ 542 Duane Kuiper	.08	.04	.01
☐ 543 Craig McMurtry	.08	.04	.01
☐ 544 Cesar Geronimo	.08	.04	.01
☐ 545 Bill Buckner	.12	.05	.02
☐ 546 Indians TL Mike Hargrove Lary Sorensen	.12	.05	.02
☐ 547 Mike Moore	.15	.07	.02
☐ 548 Ron Jackson	.08	.04	.01
☐ 549 Walt Terrell	.12	.05	.02
☐ 550 Jim Rice	.15	.07	.02
☐ 551 Scott Ullger	.08	.04	.01
☐ 552 Ray Burris	.08	.04	.01
☐ 553 Joe Nolan	.08	.04	.01
☐ 554 Ted Power	.08	.04	.01
☐ 555 Greg Brock	.08	.04	.01
☐ 556 Joey McLaughlin	.08	.04	.01
☐ 557 Wayne Tolleson	.08	.04	.01
☐ 558 Mike Davis	.08	.04	.01
☐ 559 Mike Scott	.12	.05	.02
☐ 560 Carlton Fisk	1.25	.55	.16
☐ 561 Whitey Herzog MG	.08	.04	.01
☐ 562 Manny Castillo	.08	.04	.01
☐ 563 Glenn Wilson	.08	.04	.01
☐ 564 Al Holland	.08	.04	.01
☐ 565 Leon Durham	.08	.04	.01
☐ 566 Jim Bibby	.08	.04	.01
☐ 567 Mike Heath	.08	.04	.01
☐ 568 Pete Filson	.08	.04	.01
☐ 569 Bake McBride	.08	.04	.01
☐ 570 Dan Quisenberry	.12	.05	.02
☐ 571 Bruce Bochy	.08	.04	.01
☐ 572 Jerry Royster	.08	.04	.01
☐ 573 Dave Kingman	.12	.05	.02
☐ 574 Brian Downing	.12	.05	.02
☐ 575 Jim Clancy	.08	.04	.01
☐ 576 Giants TL Jeff Leonard Atlee Hammaker	.12	.05	.02
☐ 577 Mark Clear	.08	.04	.01
☐ 578 Lenn Sakata	.08	.04	.01
☐ 579 Bob James	.08	.04	.01
☐ 580 Lonnie Smith	.12	.05	.02
☐ 581 Jose DeLeon	.12	.05	.02
☐ 582 Bob McClure	.08	.04	.01
☐ 583 Derrel Thomas	.08	.04	.01
☐ 584 Dave Schmidt	.08	.04	.01
☐ 585 Dan Driessen	.08	.04	.01
☐ 586 Joe Niekro	.12	.05	.02
☐ 587 Von Hayes	.12	.05	.02
☐ 588 Milt Wilcox	.08	.04	.01
☐ 589 Mike Easler	.08	.04	.01
☐ 590 Dave Stieb	.12	.05	.02
☐ 591 Tony LaRussa MG	.12	.05	.02
☐ 592 Andre Robertson	.08	.04	.01
☐ 593 Jeff Lahti	.08	.04	.01
☐ 594 Gene Richards	.08	.04	.01
☐ 595 Jeff Reardon	.75	.35	.09
☐ 596 Ryne Sandberg	8.00	3.60	1.00
☐ 597 Rick Camp	.08	.04	.01
☐ 598 Rusty Kuntz	.08	.04	.01
☐ 599 Doug Sisk	.08	.04	.01
☐ 600 Rod Carew	1.25	.55	.16
☐ 601 John Tudor	.12	.05	.02
☐ 602 John Wathan	.08	.04	.01
☐ 603 Renie Martin	.08	.04	.01
☐ 604 John Lowenstein	.08	.04	.01
☐ 605 Mike Caldwell	.08	.04	.01
☐ 606 Blue Jays TL Lloyd Moseby Dave Stieb	.12	.05	.02
☐ 607 Tom Hume	.08	.04	.01
☐ 608 Bobby Johnson	.08	.04	.01
☐ 609 Dan Meyer	.08	.04	.01
☐ 610 Steve Sax	.30	.14	.04
☐ 611 Chet Lemon	.08	.04	.01

☐	612	Harry Spilman	.08	.04	.01
☐	613	Greg Gross	.08	.04	.01
☐	614	Len Barker	.08	.04	.01
☐	615	Garry Templeton	.12	.05	.02
☐	616	Don Robinson	.08	.04	.01
☐	617	Rick Cerone	.08	.04	.01
☐	618	Dickie Noles	.08	.04	.01
☐	619	Jerry Dybzinski	.08	.04	.01
☐	620	Al Oliver	.12	.05	.02
☐	621	Frank Howard MG	.08	.04	.01
☐	622	Al Cowens	.08	.04	.01
☐	623	Ron Washington	.08	.04	.01
☐	624	Terry Harper	.08	.04	.01
☐	625	Larry Gura	.08	.04	.01
☐	626	Bob Clark	.08	.04	.01
☐	627	Dave LaPoint	.12	.05	.02
☐	628	Ed Jurak	.08	.04	.01
☐	629	Rick Langford	.08	.04	.01
☐	630	Ted Simmons	.12	.05	.02
☐	631	Dennis Martinez	.12	.05	.02
☐	632	Tom Foley	.08	.04	.01
☐	633	Mike Krukow	.08	.04	.01
☐	634	Mike Marshall	.12	.05	.02
☐	635	Dave Righetti	.12	.05	.02
☐	636	Pat Putnam	.08	.04	.01
☐	637	Phillies TL Gary Matthews John Denny	.12	.05	.02
☐	638	George Vukovich	.08	.04	.01
☐	639	Rick Lysander	.08	.04	.01
☐	640	Lance Parrish	.15	.07	.02
☐	641	Mike Richardt	.08	.04	.01
☐	642	Tom Underwood	.08	.04	.01
☐	643	Mike C. Brown (Angels OF)	.08	.04	.01
☐	644	Tim Lollar	.08	.04	.01
☐	645	Tony Pena	.12	.05	.02
☐	646	Checklist 529-660	.12	.01	.00
☐	647	Ron Roenicke	.08	.04	.01
☐	648	Len Whitehouse	.08	.04	.01
☐	649	Tom Herr	.12	.05	.02
☐	650	Phil Niekro	.35	.16	.04
☐	651	John McNamara MG	.08	.04	.01
☐	652	Rudy May	.08	.04	.01
☐	653	Dave Stapleton	.08	.04	.01
☐	654	Bob Bailor	.08	.04	.01
☐	655	Amos Otis	.08	.04	.01
☐	656	Bryn Smith	.08	.04	.01
☐	657	Thad Bosley	.08	.04	.01
☐	658	Jerry Augustine	.08	.04	.01
☐	659	Duane Walker	.08	.04	.01
☐	660	Ray Knight	.12	.05	.02
☐	661	Steve Yeager	.08	.04	.01
☐	662	Tom Brennan	.08	.04	.01
☐	663	Johnnie LeMaster	.08	.04	.01
☐	664	Dave Stegman	.08	.04	.01
☐	665	Buddy Bell	.12	.05	.02
☐	666	Detroit Tigers TL Lou Whitaker Jack Morris	.20	.09	.03
☐	667	Vance Law	.08	.04	.01
☐	668	Larry McWilliams	.08	.04	.01
☐	669	Dave Lopes	.12	.05	.02
☐	670	Rich Gossage	.15	.07	.02
☐	671	Jamie Quirk	.08	.04	.01
☐	672	Ricky Nelson	.08	.04	.01
☐	673	Mike Walters	.08	.04	.01
☐	674	Tim Flannery	.08	.04	.01
☐	675	Pascual Perez	.08	.04	.01
☐	676	Brian Giles	.08	.04	.01
☐	677	Doyle Alexander	.08	.04	.01
☐	678	Chris Speier	.08	.04	.01
☐	679	Art Howe	.08	.04	.01
☐	680	Fred Lynn	.12	.05	.02
☐	681	Tom Lasorda MG	.12	.05	.02
☐	682	Dan Morogiello	.08	.04	.01
☐	683	Marty Barrett	.12	.05	.02
☐	684	Bob Shirley	.08	.04	.01
☐	685	Willie Aikens	.08	.04	.01
☐	686	Joe Price	.08	.04	.01
☐	687	Roy Howell	.08	.04	.01
☐	688	George Wright	.08	.04	.01
☐	689	Mike Fischlin	.08	.04	.01
☐	690	Jack Clark	.12	.05	.02
☐	691	Steve Lake	.08	.04	.01
☐	692	Dickie Thon	.08	.04	.01
☐	693	Alan Wiggins	.08	.04	.01
☐	694	Mike Stanton	.08	.04	.01
☐	695	Lou Whitaker	.40	.18	.05
☐	696	Pirates TL Bill Madlock Rick Rhoden	.12	.05	.02
☐	697	Dale Murray	.08	.04	.01
☐	698	Marc Hill	.08	.04	.01
☐	699	Dave Rucker	.08	.04	.01
☐	700	Mike Schmidt	2.50	1.15	.30
☐	701	NL Active Batting Bill Madlock Pete Rose Dave Parker	.15	.07	.02
☐	702	NL Active Hits Pete Rose Rusty Staub Tony Perez	.15	.07	.02
☐	703	NL Active Home Run Mike Schmidt Tony Perez Dave Kingman	.15	.07	.02
☐	704	NL Active RBI Tony Perez Rusty Staub Al Oliver	.12	.05	.02
☐	705	NL Active Steals Joe Morgan Cesar Cedeno Larry Bowa	.12	.05	.02
☐	706	NL Active Victory Steve Carlton Fergie Jenkins Tom Seaver	.25	.11	.03
☐	707	NL Active Strikeout Steve Carlton Nolan Ryan Tom Seaver	.75	.35	.09
☐	708	NL Active ERA Tom Seaver Steve Carlton Steve Rogers	.20	.09	.03
☐	709	NL Active Save Bruce Sutter Tug McGraw Gene Garber	.12	.05	.02
☐	710	AL Active Batting Rod Carew George Brett Cecil Cooper	.20	.09	.03
☐	711	AL Active Hits Rod Carew Bert Campaneris Reggie Jackson	.20	.09	.03
☐	712	AL Active Home Run Reggie Jackson Graig Nettles Greg Luzinski	.20	.09	.03
☐	713	AL Active RBI Reggie Jackson Ted Simmons Graig Nettles	.20	.09	.03
☐	714	AL Active Steals Bert Campaneris Dave Lopes Omar Moreno	.12	.05	.02
☐	715	AL Active Victory Jim Palmer Don Sutton Tommy John	.15	.07	.02
☐	716	AL Active Strikeout Don Sutton Bert Blyleven Jerry Koosman	.12	.05	.02
☐	717	AL Active ERA Jim Palmer Rollie Fingers Ron Guidry	.15	.07	.02
☐	718	AL Active Save Rollie Fingers Rich Gossage Dan Quisenberry	.15	.07	.02
☐	719	Andy Hassler	.08	.04	.01
☐	720	Dwight Evans	.20	.09	.03
☐	721	Del Crandall MG	.08	.04	.01
☐	722	Bob Welch	.15	.07	.02
☐	723	Rich Dauer	.08	.04	.01
☐	724	Eric Rasmussen	.08	.04	.01
☐	725	Cesar Cedeno	.12	.05	.02
☐	726	Brewers TL Ted Simmons Moose Haas	.12	.05	.02
☐	727	Joel Youngblood	.08	.04	.01
☐	728	Tug McGraw	.12	.05	.02
☐	729	Gene Tenace	.08	.04	.01
☐	730	Bruce Sutter	.12	.05	.02
☐	731	Lynn Jones	.08	.04	.01
☐	732	Terry Crowley	.08	.04	.01
☐	733	Dave Collins	.08	.04	.01
☐	734	Odell Jones	.08	.04	.01

☐ 735 Rick Burleson	.08	.04	.01
☐ 736 Dick Ruthven	.08	.04	.01
☐ 737 Jim Essian	.08	.04	.01
☐ 738 Bill Schroeder	.08	.04	.01
☐ 739 Bob Watson	.12	.05	.02
☐ 740 Tom Seaver	1.25	.55	.16
☐ 741 Wayne Gross	.08	.04	.01
☐ 742 Dick Williams MG	.08	.04	.01
☐ 743 Don Hood	.08	.04	.01
☐ 744 Jamie Allen	.08	.04	.01
☐ 745 Dennis Eckersley	1.00	.45	.13
☐ 746 Mickey Hatcher	.08	.04	.01
☐ 747 Pat Zachry	.08	.04	.01
☐ 748 Jeff Leonard	.08	.04	.01
☐ 749 Doug Flynn	.08	.04	.01
☐ 750 Jim Palmer	1.25	.55	.16
☐ 751 Charlie Moore	.08	.04	.01
☐ 752 Phil Garner	.12	.05	.02
☐ 753 Doug Gwosdz	.08	.04	.01
☐ 754 Kent Tekulve	.12	.05	.02
☐ 755 Garry Maddox	.08	.04	.01
☐ 756 Reds TL	.12	.05	.02
Ron Oester			
Mario Soto			
☐ 757 Larry Bowa	.12	.05	.02
☐ 758 Bill Stein	.08	.04	.01
☐ 759 Richard Dotson	.08	.04	.01
☐ 760 Bob Horner	.12	.05	.02
☐ 761 John Montefusco	.08	.04	.01
☐ 762 Rance Mulliniks	.08	.04	.01
☐ 763 Craig Swan	.08	.04	.01
☐ 764 Mike Hargrove	.12	.05	.02
☐ 765 Ken Forsch	.08	.04	.01
☐ 766 Mike Vail	.08	.04	.01
☐ 767 Carney Lansford	.12	.05	.02
☐ 768 Champ Summers	.08	.04	.01
☐ 769 Bill Caudill	.08	.04	.01
☐ 770 Ken Griffey	.12	.05	.02
☐ 771 Billy Gardner MG	.08	.04	.01
☐ 772 Jim Slaton	.08	.04	.01
☐ 773 Todd Cruz	.08	.04	.01
☐ 774 Tom Gorman	.08	.04	.01
☐ 775 Dave Parker	.25	.11	.03
☐ 776 Craig Reynolds	.08	.04	.01
☐ 777 Tom Paciorek	.12	.05	.02
☐ 778 Andy Hawkins	.12	.05	.02
☐ 779 Jim Sundberg	.12	.05	.02
☐ 780 Steve Carlton	1.25	.55	.16
☐ 781 Checklist 661-792	.12	.01	.00
☐ 782 Steve Balboni	.08	.04	.01
☐ 783 Luis Leal	.08	.04	.01
☐ 784 Leon Roberts	.08	.04	.01
☐ 785 Joaquin Andujar	.08	.04	.01
☐ 786 Red Sox TL	.50	.23	.06
Wade Boggs			
Bob Ojeda			
☐ 787 Bill Campbell	.08	.04	.01
☐ 788 Milt May	.08	.04	.01
☐ 789 Bert Blyleven	.20	.09	.03
☐ 790 Doug DeCinces	.08	.04	.01
☐ 791 Terry Forster	.08	.04	.01
☐ 792 Bill Russell	.12	.05	.02

1984 Topps All-Star Glossy 22

The cards in this 22-card set measure 2 1/2" by 3 1/2". Unlike the 1983 Topps Glossy set which was not distributed with its regular baseball cards, the 1984 Topps Glossy set was distributed as inserts in Topps Rak-Paks. The set features the nine American and National League All-Stars who started in the 1983 All Star game in Chicago. The managers and team captains (Yastrzemski and Bench) complete the set. The cards are numbered on the back and are ordered by position within league (AL: 1-11 and NL: 12-22).

	NRMT-MT	EXC	G-VG
COMPLETE SET (22)	4.00	1.80	.50
COMMON PLAYER (1-22)	.10	.05	.01
☐ 1 Harvey Kuenn MG	.10	.05	.01
☐ 2 Rod Carew	.50	.23	.06
☐ 3 Manny Trillo	.10	.05	.01
☐ 4 George Brett	.75	.35	.09
☐ 5 Robin Yount	.75	.35	.09
☐ 6 Jim Rice	.20	.09	.03
☐ 7 Fred Lynn	.15	.07	.02
☐ 8 Dave Winfield	.50	.23	.06
☐ 9 Ted Simmons	.15	.07	.02
☐ 10 Dave Stieb	.15	.07	.02
☐ 11 Carl Yastrzemski CAPT	.40	.18	.05
☐ 12 Whitey Herzog MG	.10	.05	.01
☐ 13 Al Oliver	.15	.07	.02
☐ 14 Steve Sax	.20	.09	.03
☐ 15 Mike Schmidt	.75	.35	.09
☐ 16 Ozzie Smith	.50	.23	.06
☐ 17 Tim Raines	.25	.11	.03
☐ 18 Andre Dawson	.50	.23	.06
☐ 19 Dale Murphy	.50	.23	.06
☐ 20 Gary Carter	.35	.16	.04
☐ 21 Mario Soto	.10	.05	.01
☐ 22 Johnny Bench CAPT	.35	.16	.04

1984 Topps Cereal

The cards in this 33 card-set measure 2 1/2" by 3 1/2". The cards are numbered both on the front and the back. The 1984 Topps Cereal Series is exactly the same as the Ralston-Purina issue of this year except for a Topps logo and the words "Cereal Series" on the tops of the fronts of the cards in place of the Ralston checkerboard background. The checkerboard background is absent from the reverse, and a Topps logo is on the reverse of the cereal cards. These cards were distributed in unmarked boxes of Ralston-Purina cereal with a pack of four cards (three players and a checklist) being inside random cereal boxes. The back of the checklist details an offer to obtain any twelve cards direct from the issuer for only 1.50.

	NRMT-MT	EXC	G-VG
COMPLETE SET (34)	15.00	6.75	1.90
COMMON PLAYER (1-33)	.35	.16	.04
☐ 1 Eddie Murray	1.00	.45	.13
☐ 2 Ozzie Smith	.60	.25	.08
☐ 3 Ted Simmons	.45	.20	.06
☐ 4 Pete Rose	1.25	.55	.16
☐ 5 Greg Luzinski	.35	.16	.04
☐ 6 Andre Dawson	.60	.25	.08
☐ 7 Dave Winfield	.90	.40	.11
☐ 8 Tom Seaver	1.00	.45	.13
☐ 9 Jim Rice	.45	.20	.06

Card	NRMT-MT	EXC	G-VG
☐ 10 Fernando Valenzuela	.45	.20	.06
☐ 11 Wade Boggs	1.25	.55	.16
☐ 12 Dale Murphy	.75	.35	.09
☐ 13 George Brett	1.25	.55	.16
☐ 14 Nolan Ryan	2.50	1.15	.30
☐ 15 Rickey Henderson	1.25	.55	.16
☐ 16 Steve Carlton	.75	.35	.09
☐ 17 Rod Carew	1.00	.45	.13
☐ 18 Steve Garvey	.60	.25	.08
☐ 19 Reggie Jackson	1.00	.45	.13
☐ 20 Dave Concepcion	.45	.20	.06
☐ 21 Robin Yount	1.25	.55	.16
☐ 22 Mike Schmidt	1.50	.65	.19
☐ 23 Jim Palmer	.75	.35	.09
☐ 24 Bruce Sutter	.45	.20	.06
☐ 25 Dan Quisenberry	.45	.20	.06
☐ 26 Bill Madlock	.35	.16	.04
☐ 27 Cecil Cooper	.35	.16	.04
☐ 28 Gary Carter	.60	.25	.08
☐ 29 Fred Lynn	.45	.20	.06
☐ 30 Pedro Guerrero	.45	.20	.06
☐ 31 Ron Guidry	.45	.20	.06
☐ 32 Keith Hernandez	.45	.20	.06
☐ 33 Carlton Fisk	.75	.35	.09
☐ 34 Checklist card (Unnumbered)	.35	.16	.04

1984 Topps Glossy 40

The cards in this 40-card set measure 2 1/2" by 3 1/2". Similar to last year's glossy set, this set was issued as a bonus prize to Topps All-Star Baseball Game cards found in wax packs. Twenty-five bonus runs from the game cards were necessary to obtain a five card subset of the series. There were eight different subsets of five cards. The cards are numbered and the set contains 20 stars from each league.

	NRMT-MT	EXC	G-VG
COMPLETE SET (40)	12.50	5.75	1.55
COMMON PLAYER (1-40)	.20	.09	.03
☐ 1 Pete Rose	1.25	.55	.16
☐ 2 Lance Parrish	.30	.14	.04
☐ 3 Steve Rogers	.20	.09	.03
☐ 4 Eddie Murray	1.00	.45	.13
☐ 5 Johnny Ray	.20	.09	.03
☐ 6 Rickey Henderson	1.25	.55	.16
☐ 7 Atlee Hammaker	.20	.09	.03
☐ 8 Wade Boggs	1.25	.55	.16
☐ 9 Gary Carter	.50	.23	.06
☐ 10 Jack Morris	.40	.18	.05
☐ 11 Darrell Evans	.20	.09	.03
☐ 12 George Brett	1.25	.55	.16
☐ 13 Bob Horner	.20	.09	.03
☐ 14 Ron Guidry	.30	.14	.04
☐ 15 Nolan Ryan	2.50	1.15	.30
☐ 16 Dave Winfield	.75	.35	.09
☐ 17 Ozzie Smith	.50	.23	.06
☐ 18 Ted Simmons	.30	.14	.04
☐ 19 Bill Madlock	.20	.09	.03
☐ 20 Tony Armas	.20	.09	.03
☐ 21 Al Oliver	.30	.14	.04
☐ 22 Jim Rice	.40	.18	.05
☐ 23 George Hendrick	.20	.09	.03
☐ 24 Dave Stieb	.20	.09	.03
☐ 25 Pedro Guerrero	.30	.14	.04
☐ 26 Rod Carew	1.00	.45	.13
☐ 27 Steve Carlton	.75	.35	.09
☐ 28 Dave Righetti	.20	.09	.03
☐ 29 Darryl Strawberry	1.25	.55	.16
☐ 30 Lou Whitaker	.30	.14	.04
☐ 31 Dale Murphy	.75	.35	.09
☐ 32 LaMarr Hoyt	.20	.09	.03
☐ 33 Jesse Orosco	.20	.09	.03
☐ 34 Cecil Cooper	.30	.14	.04
☐ 35 Andre Dawson	.50	.23	.06
☐ 36 Robin Yount	1.25	.55	.16
☐ 37 Tim Raines	.30	.14	.04
☐ 38 Dan Quisenberry	.30	.14	.04
☐ 39 Mike Schmidt	1.50	.65	.19
☐ 40 Carlton Fisk	.75	.35	.09

1984 Topps Traded

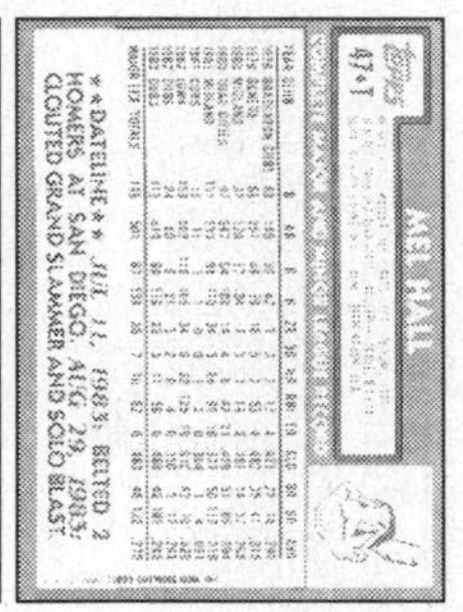

The cards in this 132-card set measure 2 1/2" by 3 1/2". In its now standard procedure, Topps issued its Traded (or extended) set for the fourth year in a row. Because all photos and statistics of its regular set for the year were developed during the fall and winter months of the preceding year, players who changed teams during the fall, winter, and spring months are portrayed with the teams they were with in 1983. The Traded set updates the shortcomings of the regular set by presenting the players with their proper teams for the current year. Several of 1984's top rookies not contained in the regular set are pictured in the Traded set. The key (extended) Rookie Cards in this set are Alvin Davis, Dwight Gooden, Mark Langston, Jose Rijo, and Bret Saberhagen. Again this year, the Topps affiliate in Ireland printed the cards, and the cards were available through hobby channels only. Topps also produced a specially boxed "glossy" edition, frequently referred to as the Topps Traded Tiffany set. There were supposedly only 10,000 sets of the Tiffany cards produced; they were marketed to hobby dealers. The checklist of cards is identical to that of the normal non-glossy cards. There are two primary distinguishing features of the Tiffany cards, white card stock reverses and high gloss obverses. These Tiffany cards are valued approximately from five to ten times the values listed below. The set numbering is in alphabetical order by player's name.

	NRMT-MT	EXC	G-VG
COMPLETE SET (132)	90.00	40.00	11.50
COMMON PLAYER (1T-132T)	.20	.09	.03
☐ 1T Willie Aikens	.20	.09	.03
☐ 2T Luis Aponte	.20	.09	.03
☐ 3T Mike Armstrong	.20	.09	.03
☐ 4T Bob Bailor	.20	.09	.03
☐ 5T Dusty Baker	.30	.14	.04
☐ 6T Steve Balboni	.20	.09	.03
☐ 7T Alan Bannister	.20	.09	.03
☐ 8T Dave Beard	.20	.09	.03
☐ 9T Joe Beckwith	.20	.09	.03
☐ 10T Bruce Berenyi	.20	.09	.03
☐ 11T Dave Bergman	.20	.09	.03

☐ 12T	Tony Bernazard	.20	.09	.03
☐ 13T	Yogi Berra MG	1.00	.45	.13
☐ 14T	Barry Bonnell	.20	.09	.03
☐ 15T	Phil Bradley	.30	.14	.04
☐ 16T	Fred Breining	.20	.09	.03
☐ 17T	Bill Buckner	.30	.14	.04
☐ 18T	Ray Burris	.20	.09	.03
☐ 19T	John Butcher	.20	.09	.03
☐ 20T	Brett Butler	1.00	.45	.13
☐ 21T	Enos Cabell	.20	.09	.03
☐ 22T	Bill Campbell	.20	.09	.03
☐ 23T	Bill Caudill	.20	.09	.03
☐ 24T	Bob Clark	.20	.09	.03
☐ 25T	Bryan Clark	.20	.09	.03
☐ 26T	Jaime Cocanower	.20	.09	.03
☐ 27T	Ron Darling	3.50	1.55	.45
☐ 28T	Alvin Davis	.75	.35	.09
☐ 29T	Ken Dayley	.20	.09	.03
☐ 30T	Jeff Dedmon	.20	.09	.03
☐ 31T	Bob Dernier	.20	.09	.03
☐ 32T	Carlos Diaz	.20	.09	.03
☐ 33T	Mike Easler	.20	.09	.03
☐ 34T	Dennis Eckersley	7.00	3.10	.85
☐ 35T	Jim Essian	.20	.09	.03
☐ 36T	Darrell Evans	.30	.14	.04
☐ 37T	Mike Fitzgerald	.20	.09	.03
☐ 38T	Tim Foli	.20	.09	.03
☐ 39T	George Frazier	.20	.09	.03
☐ 40T	Rich Gale	.20	.09	.03
☐ 41T	Barbaro Garbey	.20	.09	.03
☐ 42T	Dwight Gooden	27.00	12.00	3.40
☐ 43T	Rich Gossage	.50	.23	.06
☐ 44T	Wayne Gross	.20	.09	.03
☐ 45T	Mark Gubicza	1.75	.80	.22
☐ 46T	Jackie Gutierrez	.20	.09	.03
☐ 47T	Mel Hall	.75	.35	.09
☐ 48T	Toby Harrah	.20	.09	.03
☐ 49T	Ron Hassey	.20	.09	.03
☐ 50T	Rich Hebner	.20	.09	.03
☐ 51T	Willie Hernandez	.30	.14	.04
☐ 52T	Ricky Horton	.20	.09	.03
☐ 53T	Art Howe	.20	.09	.03
☐ 54T	Dane Iorg	.20	.09	.03
☐ 55T	Brook Jacoby	.50	.23	.06
☐ 56T	Mike Jeffcoat	.20	.09	.03
☐ 57T	Dave Johnson MG	.30	.14	.04
☐ 58T	Lynn Jones	.20	.09	.03
☐ 59T	Ruppert Jones	.20	.09	.03
☐ 60T	Mike Jorgensen	.20	.09	.03
☐ 61T	Bob Kearney	.20	.09	.03
☐ 62T	Jimmy Key	5.00	2.30	.60
☐ 63T	Dave Kingman	.30	.14	.04
☐ 64T	Jerry Koosman	.30	.14	.04
☐ 65T	Wayne Krenchicki	.20	.09	.03
☐ 66T	Rusty Kuntz	.20	.09	.03
☐ 67T	Rene Lachemann MG	.20	.09	.03
☐ 68T	Frank LaCorte	.20	.09	.03
☐ 69T	Dennis Lamp	.20	.09	.03
☐ 70T	Mark Langston	9.00	4.00	1.15
☐ 71T	Rick Leach	.20	.09	.03
☐ 72T	Craig Lefferts	.50	.23	.06
☐ 73T	Gary Lucas	.20	.09	.03
☐ 74T	Jerry Martin	.20	.09	.03
☐ 75T	Carmelo Martinez	.30	.14	.04
☐ 76T	Mike Mason	.20	.09	.03
☐ 77T	Gary Matthews	.30	.14	.04
☐ 78T	Andy McGaffigan	.20	.09	.03
☐ 79T	Larry Milbourne	.20	.09	.03
☐ 80T	Sid Monge	.20	.09	.03
☐ 81T	Jackie Moore MG	.20	.09	.03
☐ 82T	Joe Morgan	3.50	1.55	.45
☐ 83T	Graig Nettles	.30	.14	.04
☐ 84T	Phil Niekro	3.00	1.35	.40
☐ 85T	Ken Oberkfell	.20	.09	.03
☐ 86T	Mike O'Berry	.20	.09	.03
☐ 87T	Al Oliver	.30	.14	.04
☐ 88T	Jorge Orta	.20	.09	.03
☐ 89T	Amos Otis	.30	.14	.04
☐ 90T	Dave Parker	1.75	.80	.22
☐ 91T	Tony Perez	3.00	1.35	.40
☐ 92T	Gerald Perry	.30	.14	.04
☐ 93T	Gary Pettis	.30	.14	.04
☐ 94T	Rob Picciolo	.20	.09	.03
☐ 95T	Vern Rapp MG	.20	.09	.03
☐ 96T	Floyd Rayford	.20	.09	.03
☐ 97T	Randy Ready	.30	.14	.04
☐ 98T	Ron Reed	.20	.09	.03
☐ 99T	Gene Richards	.20	.09	.03
☐ 100T	Jose Rijo	10.00	4.50	1.25
☐ 101T	Jeff D. Robinson (Giants pitcher)	.30	.14	.04
☐ 102T	Ron Romanick	.20	.09	.03
☐ 103T	Pete Rose	9.00	4.00	1.15
☐ 104T	Bret Saberhagen	14.00	6.25	1.75
☐ 105T	Juan Samuel	1.00	.45	.13
☐ 106T	Scott Sanderson	.20	.09	.03
☐ 107T	Dick Schofield	.50	.23	.06
☐ 108T	Tom Seaver	9.00	4.00	1.15
☐ 109T	Jim Slaton	.20	.09	.03
☐ 110T	Mike Smithson	.20	.09	.03
☐ 111T	Lary Sorensen	.20	.09	.03
☐ 112T	Tim Stoddard	.20	.09	.03
☐ 113T	Champ Summers	.20	.09	.03
☐ 114T	Jim Sundberg	.30	.14	.04
☐ 115T	Rick Sutcliffe	.50	.23	.06
☐ 116T	Craig Swan	.20	.09	.03
☐ 117T	Tim Teufel	.50	.23	.06
☐ 118T	Derrel Thomas	.20	.09	.03
☐ 119T	Gorman Thomas	.20	.09	.03
☐ 120T	Alex Trevino	.20	.09	.03
☐ 121T	Manny Trillo	.20	.09	.03
☐ 122T	John Tudor	.30	.14	.04
☐ 123T	Tom Underwood	.20	.09	.03
☐ 124T	Mike Vail	.20	.09	.03
☐ 125T	Tom Waddell	.20	.09	.03
☐ 126T	Gary Ward	.20	.09	.03
☐ 127T	Curt Wilkerson	.20	.09	.03
☐ 128T	Frank Williams	.20	.09	.03
☐ 129T	Glenn Wilson	.20	.09	.03
☐ 130T	John Wockenfuss	.20	.09	.03
☐ 131T	Ned Yost	.20	.09	.03
☐ 132T	Checklist 1-132	.30	.03	.01

1985 Topps

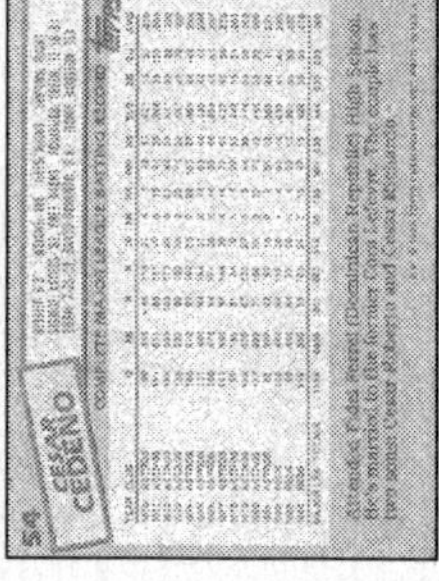

The cards in this 792-card set measure 2 1/2" by 3 1/2". The 1985 Topps set contains full color cards. The fronts feature both the Topps and team logos along with the team name, player's name, and his position. The backs feature player statistics with ink colors of light green and maroon on a gray stock. A trivia quiz is included on the lower portion of the backs. The first ten cards (1-10) are Record Breakers (RB), cards 131-143 are Father and Son (FS) cards, and cards 701 to 722 portray All-Star selections (AS). Cards 271 to 282 represent "First Draft Picks" still active in professional baseball and cards 389-404 feature the coach and eligible (not returning to college) players on the 1984 U.S. Olympic Baseball Team. The manager cards in the set are important in that they contain the checklist of that team's players on the back. The key Rookie Cards in this set are Roger Clemens, Eric Davis, Shawon Dunston, Dwight Gooden, Orel Hershiser, Mark Langston, Shane Mack, Mark McGwire, Terry Pendleton, Kirby Puckett, Jose Rijo, and Bret Saberhagen. Topps also produced a specially boxed "glossy" edition, frequently referred to as the Topps Tiffany set. There were supposedly only 8,000 sets of the Tiffany cards produced; they were marketed to hobby dealers. The checklist of cards (792 regular and 132 Traded) is identical to that of the normal non-glossy cards. There are two primary distinguishing features of the Tiffany cards, white card stock reverses and high gloss obverses. These Tiffany cards are valued approximately from five to ten times the values listed below.

	NRMT-MT	EXC	G-VG
COMPLETE SET (792)	100.00	45.00	12.50
COMMON PLAYER (1-792)	.07	.03	.01
☐ 1 Carlton Fisk RB Longest game by catcher	.40	.10	.03
☐ 2 Steve Garvey RB Consecutive error-less games, 1B	.15	.07	.02
☐ 3 Dwight Gooden RB Most strikeouts, rookie, season	.90	.40	.11
☐ 4 Cliff Johnson RB Most pinch homers, lifetime	.12	.05	.02
☐ 5 Joe Morgan RB Most homers, 2B, lifetime	.15	.07	.02
☐ 6 Pete Rose RB Most singles, lifetime	.40	.18	.05
☐ 7 Nolan Ryan RB Most strikeouts, lifetime	1.25	.55	.16
☐ 8 Juan Samuel RB Most stolen bases, rookie, season	.12	.05	.02
☐ 9 Bruce Sutter RB Most saves, season, NL	.12	.05	.02
☐ 10 Don Sutton RB Most seasons, 100 or more K's	.15	.07	.02
☐ 11 Ralph Houk MG (Checklist back)	.10	.05	.01
☐ 12 Dave Lopes (Now with Cubs on card front)	.10	.05	.01
☐ 13 Tim Lollar	.07	.03	.01
☐ 14 Chris Bando	.07	.03	.01
☐ 15 Jerry Koosman	.10	.05	.01
☐ 16 Bobby Meacham	.07	.03	.01
☐ 17 Mike Scott	.10	.05	.01
☐ 18 Mickey Hatcher	.07	.03	.01
☐ 19 George Frazier	.07	.03	.01
☐ 20 Chet Lemon	.07	.03	.01
☐ 21 Lee Tunnell	.07	.03	.01
☐ 22 Duane Kuiper	.07	.03	.01
☐ 23 Bret Saberhagen	2.00	.90	.25
☐ 24 Jesse Barfield	.10	.05	.01
☐ 25 Steve Bedrosian	.10	.05	.01
☐ 26 Roy Smalley	.07	.03	.01
☐ 27 Bruce Berenyi	.07	.03	.01
☐ 28 Dann Bilardello	.07	.03	.01
☐ 29 Odell Jones	.07	.03	.01
☐ 30 Cal Ripken	4.00	1.80	.50
☐ 31 Terry Whitfield	.07	.03	.01
☐ 32 Chuck Porter	.07	.03	.01
☐ 33 Tito Landrum	.07	.03	.01
☐ 34 Ed Nunez	.07	.03	.01
☐ 35 Graig Nettles	.10	.05	.01
☐ 36 Fred Breining	.07	.03	.01
☐ 37 Reid Nichols	.07	.03	.01
☐ 38 Jackie Moore MG (Checklist back)	.10	.05	.01
☐ 39 John Wockenfuss	.07	.03	.01
☐ 40 Phil Niekro	.20	.09	.03
☐ 41 Mike Fischlin	.07	.03	.01
☐ 42 Luis Sanchez	.07	.03	.01
☐ 43 Andre David	.07	.03	.01
☐ 44 Dickie Thon	.07	.03	.01
☐ 45 Greg Minton	.07	.03	.01
☐ 46 Gary Woods	.07	.03	.01
☐ 47 Dave Rozema	.07	.03	.01
☐ 48 Tony Fernandez	.50	.23	.06
☐ 49 Butch Davis	.07	.03	.01
☐ 50 John Candelaria	.07	.03	.01
☐ 51 Bob Watson	.10	.05	.01
☐ 52 Jerry Dybzinski	.07	.03	.01
☐ 53 Tom Gorman	.07	.03	.01
☐ 54 Cesar Cedeno	.10	.05	.01
☐ 55 Frank Tanana	.10	.05	.01
☐ 56 Jim Dwyer	.07	.03	.01
☐ 57 Pat Zachry	.07	.03	.01
☐ 58 Orlando Mercado	.07	.03	.01
☐ 59 Rick Waits	.07	.03	.01
☐ 60 George Hendrick	.07	.03	.01
☐ 61 Curt Kaufman	.07	.03	.01
☐ 62 Mike Ramsey	.07	.03	.01
☐ 63 Steve McCatty	.07	.03	.01
☐ 64 Mark Bailey	.07	.03	.01
☐ 65 Bill Buckner	.10	.05	.01
☐ 66 Dick Williams MG (Checklist back)	.10	.05	.01
☐ 67 Rafael Santana	.07	.03	.01
☐ 68 Von Hayes	.07	.03	.01
☐ 69 Jim Winn	.07	.03	.01
☐ 70 Don Baylor	.10	.05	.01
☐ 71 Tim Laudner	.07	.03	.01
☐ 72 Rick Sutcliffe	.10	.05	.01
☐ 73 Rusty Kuntz	.07	.03	.01
☐ 74 Mike Krukow	.07	.03	.01
☐ 75 Willie Upshaw	.07	.03	.01
☐ 76 Alan Bannister	.07	.03	.01
☐ 77 Joe Beckwith	.07	.03	.01
☐ 78 Scott Fletcher	.07	.03	.01
☐ 79 Rick Mahler	.07	.03	.01
☐ 80 Keith Hernandez	.10	.05	.01
☐ 81 Lenn Sakata	.07	.03	.01
☐ 82 Joe Price	.07	.03	.01
☐ 83 Charlie Moore	.07	.03	.01
☐ 84 Spike Owen	.07	.03	.01
☐ 85 Mike Marshall	.07	.03	.01
☐ 86 Don Aase	.07	.03	.01
☐ 87 David Green	.07	.03	.01
☐ 88 Bryn Smith	.07	.03	.01
☐ 89 Jackie Gutierrez	.07	.03	.01
☐ 90 Rich Gossage	.10	.05	.01
☐ 91 Jeff Burroughs	.07	.03	.01
☐ 92 Paul Owens MG (Checklist back)	.10	.05	.01
☐ 93 Don Schulze	.07	.03	.01
☐ 94 Toby Harrah	.07	.03	.01
☐ 95 Jose Cruz	.10	.05	.01
☐ 96 Johnny Ray	.07	.03	.01
☐ 97 Pete Filson	.07	.03	.01
☐ 98 Steve Lake	.07	.03	.01
☐ 99 Milt Wilcox	.07	.03	.01
☐ 100 George Brett	1.25	.55	.16
☐ 101 Jim Acker	.07	.03	.01
☐ 102 Tommy Dunbar	.07	.03	.01
☐ 103 Randy Lerch	.07	.03	.01
☐ 104 Mike Fitzgerald	.07	.03	.01
☐ 105 Ron Kittle	.10	.05	.01
☐ 106 Pascual Perez	.07	.03	.01
☐ 107 Tom Foley	.07	.03	.01
☐ 108 Darnell Coles	.10	.05	.01
☐ 109 Gary Roenicke	.07	.03	.01
☐ 110 Alejandro Pena	.07	.03	.01
☐ 111 Doug DeCinces	.07	.03	.01
☐ 112 Tom Tellmann	.07	.03	.01
☐ 113 Tom Herr	.10	.05	.01
☐ 114 Bob James	.07	.03	.01
☐ 115 Rickey Henderson	2.00	.90	.25
☐ 116 Dennis Boyd	.07	.03	.01
☐ 117 Greg Gross	.07	.03	.01
☐ 118 Eric Show	.07	.03	.01
☐ 119 Pat Corrales MG (Checklist back)	.10	.05	.01
☐ 120 Steve Kemp	.07	.03	.01
☐ 121 Checklist: 1-132	.12	.01	.00
☐ 122 Tom Brunansky	.10	.05	.01
☐ 123 Dave Smith	.07	.03	.01
☐ 124 Rich Hebner	.07	.03	.01
☐ 125 Kent Tekulve	.07	.03	.01
☐ 126 Ruppert Jones	.07	.03	.01
☐ 127 Mark Gubicza	.35	.16	.04
☐ 128 Ernie Whitt	.07	.03	.01
☐ 129 Gene Garber	.07	.03	.01
☐ 130 Al Oliver	.10	.05	.01
☐ 131 Buddy/Gus Bell FS	.10	.05	.01
☐ 132 Dale/Yogi Berra FS	.15	.07	.02
☐ 133 Bob/Ray Boone FS	.10	.05	.01
☐ 134 Terry/Tito Francona FS	.10	.05	.01
☐ 135 Terry/Bob Kennedy FS	.10	.05	.01
☐ 136 Jeff/Bill Kunkel FS	.10	.05	.01
☐ 137 Vance/Vern Law FS	.10	.05	.01
☐ 138 Dick/Dick Schofield FS	.10	.05	.01
☐ 139 Joel/Bob Skinner FS	.10	.05	.01
☐ 140 Roy/Roy Smalley FS	.10	.05	.01
☐ 141 Mike/Dave Stenhouse FS	.10	.05	.01
☐ 142 Steve/Dizzy Trout FS	.10	.05	.01
☐ 143 Ozzie/Ossie Virgil FS	.10	.05	.01
☐ 144 Ron Gardenhire	.07	.03	.01
☐ 145 Alvin Davis	.12	.05	.02
☐ 146 Gary Redus	.07	.03	.01
☐ 147 Bill Swaggerty	.07	.03	.01
☐ 148 Steve Yeager	.07	.03	.01
☐ 149 Dickie Noles	.07	.03	.01
☐ 150 Jim Rice	.10	.05	.01
☐ 151 Moose Haas	.07	.03	.01
☐ 152 Steve Braun	.07	.03	.01

☐ 153	Frank LaCorte	.07	.03	.01
☐ 154	Argenis Salazar	.07	.03	.01
☐ 155	Yogi Berra MG (Checklist back)	.20	.09	.03
☐ 156	Craig Reynolds	.07	.03	.01
☐ 157	Tug McGraw	.10	.05	.01
☐ 158	Pat Tabler	.07	.03	.01
☐ 159	Carlos Diaz	.07	.03	.01
☐ 160	Lance Parrish	.10	.05	.01
☐ 161	Ken Schrom	.07	.03	.01
☐ 162	Benny Distefano	.07	.03	.01
☐ 163	Dennis Eckersley	.50	.23	.06
☐ 164	Jorge Orta	.07	.03	.01
☐ 165	Dusty Baker	.10	.05	.01
☐ 166	Keith Atherton	.07	.03	.01
☐ 167	Rufino Linares	.07	.03	.01
☐ 168	Garth Iorg	.07	.03	.01
☐ 169	Dan Spillner	.07	.03	.01
☐ 170	George Foster	.10	.05	.01
☐ 171	Bill Stein	.07	.03	.01
☐ 172	Jack Perconte	.07	.03	.01
☐ 173	Mike Young	.07	.03	.01
☐ 174	Rick Honeycutt	.07	.03	.01
☐ 175	Dave Parker	.20	.09	.03
☐ 176	Bill Schroeder	.07	.03	.01
☐ 177	Dave Von Ohlen	.07	.03	.01
☐ 178	Miguel Dilone	.07	.03	.01
☐ 179	Tommy John	.10	.05	.01
☐ 180	Dave Winfield	1.25	.55	.16
☐ 181	Roger Clemens	25.00	11.50	3.10
☐ 182	Tim Flannery	.07	.03	.01
☐ 183	Larry McWilliams	.07	.03	.01
☐ 184	Carmen Castillo	.07	.03	.01
☐ 185	Al Holland	.07	.03	.01
☐ 186	Bob Lillis MG (Checklist back)	.10	.05	.01
☐ 187	Mike Walters	.07	.03	.01
☐ 188	Greg Pryor	.07	.03	.01
☐ 189	Warren Brusstar	.07	.03	.01
☐ 190	Rusty Staub	.10	.05	.01
☐ 191	Steve Nicosia	.07	.03	.01
☐ 192	Howard Johnson	1.50	.65	.19
☐ 193	Jimmy Key	.75	.35	.09
☐ 194	Dave Stegman	.07	.03	.01
☐ 195	Glenn Hubbard	.07	.03	.01
☐ 196	Pete O'Brien	.10	.05	.01
☐ 197	Mike Warren	.07	.03	.01
☐ 198	Eddie Milner	.07	.03	.01
☐ 199	Dennis Martinez	.10	.05	.01
☐ 200	Reggie Jackson	.75	.35	.09
☐ 201	Burt Hooton	.07	.03	.01
☐ 202	Gorman Thomas	.07	.03	.01
☐ 203	Bob McClure	.07	.03	.01
☐ 204	Art Howe	.07	.03	.01
☐ 205	Steve Rogers	.07	.03	.01
☐ 206	Phil Garner	.10	.05	.01
☐ 207	Mark Clear	.07	.03	.01
☐ 208	Champ Summers	.07	.03	.01
☐ 209	Bill Campbell	.07	.03	.01
☐ 210	Gary Matthews	.07	.03	.01
☐ 211	Clay Christiansen	.07	.03	.01
☐ 212	George Vukovich	.07	.03	.01
☐ 213	Billy Gardner MG (Checklist back)	.10	.05	.01
☐ 214	John Tudor	.10	.05	.01
☐ 215	Bob Brenly	.07	.03	.01
☐ 216	Jerry Don Gleaton	.07	.03	.01
☐ 217	Leon Roberts	.07	.03	.01
☐ 218	Doyle Alexander	.07	.03	.01
☐ 219	Gerald Perry	.07	.03	.01
☐ 220	Fred Lynn	.10	.05	.01
☐ 221	Ron Reed	.07	.03	.01
☐ 222	Hubie Brooks	.10	.05	.01
☐ 223	Tom Hume	.07	.03	.01
☐ 224	Al Cowens	.07	.03	.01
☐ 225	Mike Boddicker	.07	.03	.01
☐ 226	Juan Beniquez	.07	.03	.01
☐ 227	Danny Darwin	.07	.03	.01
☐ 228	Dion James	.07	.03	.01
☐ 229	Dave LaPoint	.07	.03	.01
☐ 230	Gary Carter	.35	.16	.04
☐ 231	Dwayne Murphy	.07	.03	.01
☐ 232	Dave Beard	.07	.03	.01
☐ 233	Ed Jurak	.07	.03	.01
☐ 234	Jerry Narron	.07	.03	.01
☐ 235	Garry Maddox	.07	.03	.01
☐ 236	Mark Thurmond	.07	.03	.01
☐ 237	Julio Franco	.35	.16	.04
☐ 238	Jose Rijo	1.50	.65	.19
☐ 239	Tim Teufel	.12	.05	.02
☐ 240	Dave Stieb	.10	.05	.01
☐ 241	Jim Frey MG (Checklist back)	.10	.05	.01
☐ 242	Greg Harris	.07	.03	.01
☐ 243	Barbaro Garbey	.07	.03	.01
☐ 244	Mike Jones	.07	.03	.01
☐ 245	Chili Davis	.10	.05	.01
☐ 246	Mike Norris	.07	.03	.01
☐ 247	Wayne Tolleson	.07	.03	.01
☐ 248	Terry Forster	.07	.03	.01
☐ 249	Harold Baines	.20	.09	.03
☐ 250	Jesse Orosco	.07	.03	.01
☐ 251	Brad Gulden	.07	.03	.01
☐ 252	Dan Ford	.07	.03	.01
☐ 253	Sid Bream	.40	.18	.05
☐ 254	Pete Vuckovich	.07	.03	.01
☐ 255	Lonnie Smith	.07	.03	.01
☐ 256	Mike Stanton	.07	.03	.01
☐ 257	Bryan Little	.07	.03	.01
☐ 258	Mike C. Brown (Angels Outfielder)	.07	.03	.01
☐ 259	Gary Allenson	.07	.03	.01
☐ 260	Dave Righetti	.10	.05	.01
☐ 261	Checklist: 133-264	.12	.01	.00
☐ 262	Greg Booker	.07	.03	.01
☐ 263	Mel Hall	.12	.05	.02
☐ 264	Joe Sambito	.07	.03	.01
☐ 265	Juan Samuel	.12	.05	.02
☐ 266	Frank Viola	.20	.09	.03
☐ 267	Henry Cotto	.07	.03	.01
☐ 268	Chuck Tanner MG (Checklist back)	.10	.05	.01
☐ 269	Doug Baker	.07	.03	.01
☐ 270	Dan Quisenberry	.10	.05	.01
☐ 271	Tim Foli FDP68	.10	.05	.01
☐ 272	Jeff Burroughs FDP69	.10	.05	.01
☐ 273	Bill Almon FDP74	.10	.05	.01
☐ 274	Floyd Bannister FDP76	.10	.05	.01
☐ 275	Harold Baines FDP77	.15	.07	.02
☐ 276	Bob Horner FDP78	.10	.05	.01
☐ 277	Al Chambers FDP79	.10	.05	.01
☐ 278	Darryl Strawberry FDP80	1.50	.65	.19
☐ 279	Mike Moore FDP81	.12	.05	.02
☐ 280	Shawon Dunston FDP82	.90	.40	.11
☐ 281	Tim Belcher FDP83	1.00	.45	.13
☐ 282	Shawn Abner FDP84	.15	.07	.02
☐ 283	Fran Mullins	.07	.03	.01
☐ 284	Marty Bystrom	.07	.03	.01
☐ 285	Dan Driessen	.07	.03	.01
☐ 286	Rudy Law	.07	.03	.01
☐ 287	Walt Terrell	.07	.03	.01
☐ 288	Jeff Kunkel	.07	.03	.01
☐ 289	Tom Underwood	.07	.03	.01
☐ 290	Cecil Cooper	.10	.05	.01
☐ 291	Bob Welch	.12	.05	.02
☐ 292	Brad Komminsk	.07	.03	.01
☐ 293	Curt Young	.07	.03	.01
☐ 294	Tom Nieto	.07	.03	.01
☐ 295	Joe Niekro	.10	.05	.01
☐ 296	Ricky Nelson	.07	.03	.01
☐ 297	Gary Lucas	.07	.03	.01
☐ 298	Marty Barrett	.07	.03	.01
☐ 299	Andy Hawkins	.07	.03	.01
☐ 300	Rod Carew	.60	.25	.08
☐ 301	John Montefusco	.07	.03	.01
☐ 302	Tim Corcoran	.07	.03	.01
☐ 303	Mike Jeffcoat	.07	.03	.01
☐ 304	Gary Gaetti	.10	.05	.01
☐ 305	Dale Berra	.07	.03	.01
☐ 306	Rick Reuschel	.10	.05	.01
☐ 307	Sparky Anderson MG (Checklist back)	.10	.05	.01
☐ 308	John Wathan	.07	.03	.01
☐ 309	Mike Witt	.07	.03	.01
☐ 310	Manny Trillo	.07	.03	.01
☐ 311	Jim Gott	.07	.03	.01
☐ 312	Marc Hill	.07	.03	.01
☐ 313	Dave Schmidt	.07	.03	.01
☐ 314	Ron Oester	.07	.03	.01
☐ 315	Doug Sisk	.07	.03	.01
☐ 316	John Lowenstein	.07	.03	.01
☐ 317	Jack Lazorko	.07	.03	.01
☐ 318	Ted Simmons	.10	.05	.01
☐ 319	Jeff Jones	.07	.03	.01
☐ 320	Dale Murphy	.40	.18	.05
☐ 321	Ricky Horton	.07	.03	.01
☐ 322	Dave Stapleton	.07	.03	.01
☐ 323	Andy McGaffigan	.07	.03	.01
☐ 324	Bruce Bochy	.07	.03	.01
☐ 325	John Denny	.07	.03	.01
☐ 326	Kevin Bass	.07	.03	.01
☐ 327	Brook Jacoby	.12	.05	.02
☐ 328	Bob Shirley	.07	.03	.01
☐ 329	Ron Washington	.07	.03	.01
☐ 330	Leon Durham	.07	.03	.01

☐ 331	Bill Laskey	.07	.03	.01
☐ 332	Brian Harper	.20	.09	.03
☐ 333	Willie Hernandez	.07	.03	.01
☐ 334	Dick Howser MG (Checklist back)	.10	.05	.01
☐ 335	Bruce Benedict	.07	.03	.01
☐ 336	Rance Mulliniks	.07	.03	.01
☐ 337	Billy Sample	.07	.03	.01
☐ 338	Britt Burns	.07	.03	.01
☐ 339	Danny Heep	.07	.03	.01
☐ 340	Robin Yount	1.25	.55	.16
☐ 341	Floyd Rayford	.07	.03	.01
☐ 342	Ted Power	.07	.03	.01
☐ 343	Bill Russell	.10	.05	.01
☐ 344	Dave Henderson	.10	.05	.01
☐ 345	Charlie Lea	.07	.03	.01
☐ 346	Terry Pendleton	4.00	1.80	.50
☐ 347	Rick Langford	.07	.03	.01
☐ 348	Bob Boone	.10	.05	.01
☐ 349	Domingo Ramos	.07	.03	.01
☐ 350	Wade Boggs	2.00	.90	.25
☐ 351	Juan Agosto	.07	.03	.01
☐ 352	Joe Morgan	.25	.11	.03
☐ 353	Julio Solano	.07	.03	.01
☐ 354	Andre Robertson	.07	.03	.01
☐ 355	Bert Blyleven	.15	.07	.02
☐ 356	Dave Meier	.07	.03	.01
☐ 357	Rich Bordi	.07	.03	.01
☐ 358	Tony Pena	.10	.05	.01
☐ 359	Pat Sheridan	.07	.03	.01
☐ 360	Steve Carlton	.50	.23	.06
☐ 361	Alfredo Griffin	.07	.03	.01
☐ 362	Craig McMurtry	.07	.03	.01
☐ 363	Ron Hodges	.07	.03	.01
☐ 364	Richard Dotson	.07	.03	.01
☐ 365	Danny Ozark MG (Checklist back)	.10	.05	.01
☐ 366	Todd Cruz	.07	.03	.01
☐ 367	Keefe Cato	.07	.03	.01
☐ 368	Dave Bergman	.07	.03	.01
☐ 369	R.J. Reynolds	.07	.03	.01
☐ 370	Bruce Sutter	.10	.05	.01
☐ 371	Mickey Rivers	.07	.03	.01
☐ 372	Roy Howell	.07	.03	.01
☐ 373	Mike Moore	.12	.05	.02
☐ 374	Brian Downing	.10	.05	.01
☐ 375	Jeff Reardon	.40	.18	.05
☐ 376	Jeff Newman	.07	.03	.01
☐ 377	Checklist: 265-396	.12	.01	.00
☐ 378	Alan Wiggins	.07	.03	.01
☐ 379	Charles Hudson	.07	.03	.01
☐ 380	Ken Griffey	.10	.05	.01
☐ 381	Roy Smith	.07	.03	.01
☐ 382	Denny Walling	.07	.03	.01
☐ 383	Rick Lysander	.07	.03	.01
☐ 384	Jody Davis	.07	.03	.01
☐ 385	Jose DeLeon	.07	.03	.01
☐ 386	Dan Gladden	.20	.09	.03
☐ 387	Buddy Biancalana	.07	.03	.01
☐ 388	Bert Roberge	.07	.03	.01
☐ 389	Rod Dedeaux OLY CO	.12	.05	.02
☐ 390	Sid Akins OLY	.12	.05	.02
☐ 391	Flavio Alfaro OLY	.12	.05	.02
☐ 392	Don August OLY	.15	.07	.02
☐ 393	Scott Bankhead OLY	.40	.18	.05
☐ 394	Bob Caffrey OLY	.12	.05	.02
☐ 395	Mike Dunne OLY	.12	.05	.02
☐ 396	Gary Green OLY	.12	.05	.02
☐ 397	John Hoover OLY	.12	.05	.02
☐ 398	Shane Mack OLY	3.00	1.35	.40
☐ 399	John Marzano OLY	.12	.05	.02
☐ 400	Oddibe McDowell OLY	.15	.07	.02
☐ 401	Mark McGwire OLY	30.00	13.50	3.80
☐ 402	Pat Pacillo OLY	.12	.05	.02
☐ 403	Cory Snyder OLY	1.25	.55	.16
☐ 404	Billy Swift OLY	1.00	.45	.13
☐ 405	Tom Veryzer	.07	.03	.01
☐ 406	Len Whitehouse	.07	.03	.01
☐ 407	Bobby Ramos	.07	.03	.01
☐ 408	Sid Monge	.07	.03	.01
☐ 409	Brad Wellman	.07	.03	.01
☐ 410	Bob Horner	.10	.05	.01
☐ 411	Bobby Cox MG (Checklist back)	.10	.05	.01
☐ 412	Bud Black	.07	.03	.01
☐ 413	Vance Law	.07	.03	.01
☐ 414	Gary Ward	.07	.03	.01
☐ 415	Ron Darling UER (No trivia answer)	.20	.09	.03
☐ 416	Wayne Gross	.07	.03	.01
☐ 417	John Franco	.50	.23	.06
☐ 418	Ken Landreaux	.07	.03	.01
☐ 419	Mike Caldwell	.07	.03	.01
☐ 420	Andre Dawson	.75	.35	.09
☐ 421	Dave Rucker	.07	.03	.01
☐ 422	Carney Lansford	.10	.05	.01
☐ 423	Barry Bonnell	.07	.03	.01
☐ 424	Al Nipper	.07	.03	.01
☐ 425	Mike Hargrove	.10	.05	.01
☐ 426	Vern Ruhle	.07	.03	.01
☐ 427	Mario Ramirez	.07	.03	.01
☐ 428	Larry Andersen	.07	.03	.01
☐ 429	Rick Cerone	.07	.03	.01
☐ 430	Ron Davis	.07	.03	.01
☐ 431	U.L. Washington	.07	.03	.01
☐ 432	Thad Bosley	.07	.03	.01
☐ 433	Jim Morrison	.07	.03	.01
☐ 434	Gene Richards	.07	.03	.01
☐ 435	Dan Petry	.07	.03	.01
☐ 436	Willie Aikens	.07	.03	.01
☐ 437	Al Jones	.07	.03	.01
☐ 438	Joe Torre MG (Checklist back)	.10	.05	.01
☐ 439	Junior Ortiz	.07	.03	.01
☐ 440	Fernando Valenzuela	.10	.05	.01
☐ 441	Duane Walker	.07	.03	.01
☐ 442	Ken Forsch	.07	.03	.01
☐ 443	George Wright	.07	.03	.01
☐ 444	Tony Phillips	.10	.05	.01
☐ 445	Tippy Martinez	.07	.03	.01
☐ 446	Jim Sundberg	.10	.05	.01
☐ 447	Jeff Lahti	.07	.03	.01
☐ 448	Derrel Thomas	.07	.03	.01
☐ 449	Phil Bradley	.10	.05	.01
☐ 450	Steve Garvey	.25	.11	.03
☐ 451	Bruce Hurst	.10	.05	.01
☐ 452	John Castino	.07	.03	.01
☐ 453	Tom Waddell	.07	.03	.01
☐ 454	Glenn Wilson	.07	.03	.01
☐ 455	Bob Knepper	.07	.03	.01
☐ 456	Tim Foli	.07	.03	.01
☐ 457	Cecilio Guante	.07	.03	.01
☐ 458	Randy Johnson	.07	.03	.01
☐ 459	Charlie Leibrandt	.10	.05	.01
☐ 460	Ryne Sandberg	4.00	1.80	.50
☐ 461	Marty Castillo	.07	.03	.01
☐ 462	Gary Lavelle	.07	.03	.01
☐ 463	Dave Collins	.07	.03	.01
☐ 464	Mike Mason	.07	.03	.01
☐ 465	Bob Grich	.10	.05	.01
☐ 466	Tony LaRussa MG (Checklist back)	.10	.05	.01
☐ 467	Ed Lynch	.07	.03	.01
☐ 468	Wayne Krenchicki	.07	.03	.01
☐ 469	Sammy Stewart	.07	.03	.01
☐ 470	Steve Sax	.20	.09	.03
☐ 471	Pete Ladd	.07	.03	.01
☐ 472	Jim Essian	.07	.03	.01
☐ 473	Tim Wallach	.10	.05	.01
☐ 474	Kurt Kepshire	.07	.03	.01
☐ 475	Andre Thornton	.07	.03	.01
☐ 476	Jeff Stone	.07	.03	.01
☐ 477	Bob Ojeda	.07	.03	.01
☐ 478	Kurt Bevacqua	.07	.03	.01
☐ 479	Mike Madden	.07	.03	.01
☐ 480	Lou Whitaker	.25	.11	.03
☐ 481	Dale Murray	.07	.03	.01
☐ 482	Harry Spilman	.07	.03	.01
☐ 483	Mike Smithson	.07	.03	.01
☐ 484	Larry Bowa	.10	.05	.01
☐ 485	Matt Young	.07	.03	.01
☐ 486	Steve Balboni	.07	.03	.01
☐ 487	Frank Williams	.07	.03	.01
☐ 488	Joel Skinner	.07	.03	.01
☐ 489	Bryan Clark	.07	.03	.01
☐ 490	Jason Thompson	.07	.03	.01
☐ 491	Rick Camp	.07	.03	.01
☐ 492	Dave Johnson MG (Checklist back)	.10	.05	.01
☐ 493	Orel Hershiser	1.50	.65	.19
☐ 494	Rich Dauer	.07	.03	.01
☐ 495	Mario Soto	.07	.03	.01
☐ 496	Donnie Scott	.07	.03	.01
☐ 497	Gary Pettis UER (Photo actually Gary's little brother, Lynn)	.10	.05	.01
☐ 498	Ed Romero	.07	.03	.01
☐ 499	Danny Cox	.07	.03	.01
☐ 500	Mike Schmidt	2.00	.90	.25
☐ 501	Dan Schatzeder	.07	.03	.01
☐ 502	Rick Miller	.07	.03	.01
☐ 503	Tim Conroy	.07	.03	.01
☐ 504	Jerry Willard	.07	.03	.01
☐ 505	Jim Beattie	.07	.03	.01
☐ 506	Franklin Stubbs	.10	.05	.01

□ 507 Ray Fontenot	.07	.03	.01
□ 508 John Shelby	.07	.03	.01
□ 509 Milt May	.07	.03	.01
□ 510 Kent Hrbek	.20	.09	.03
□ 511 Lee Smith	.40	.18	.05
□ 512 Tom Brookens	.07	.03	.01
□ 513 Lynn Jones	.07	.03	.01
□ 514 Jeff Cornell	.07	.03	.01
□ 515 Dave Concepcion	.10	.05	.01
□ 516 Roy Lee Jackson	.07	.03	.01
□ 517 Jerry Martin	.07	.03	.01
□ 518 Chris Chambliss	.10	.05	.01
□ 519 Doug Rader MG (Checklist back)	.10	.05	.01
□ 520 LaMarr Hoyt	.07	.03	.01
□ 521 Rick Dempsey	.07	.03	.01
□ 522 Paul Molitor	.35	.16	.04
□ 523 Candy Maldonado	.10	.05	.01
□ 524 Rob Wilfong	.07	.03	.01
□ 525 Darrell Porter	.07	.03	.01
□ 526 David Palmer	.07	.03	.01
□ 527 Checklist: 397-528	.12	.01	.00
□ 528 Bill Krueger	.10	.05	.01
□ 529 Rich Gedman	.07	.03	.01
□ 530 Dave Dravecky	.10	.05	.01
□ 531 Joe Lefebvre	.07	.03	.01
□ 532 Frank DiPino	.07	.03	.01
□ 533 Tony Bernazard	.07	.03	.01
□ 534 Brian Dayett	.07	.03	.01
□ 535 Pat Putnam	.07	.03	.01
□ 536 Kirby Puckett	22.00	10.00	2.80
□ 537 Don Robinson	.07	.03	.01
□ 538 Keith Moreland	.07	.03	.01
□ 539 Aurelio Lopez	.07	.03	.01
□ 540 Claudell Washington	.07	.03	.01
□ 541 Mark Davis	.10	.05	.01
□ 542 Don Slaught	.07	.03	.01
□ 543 Mike Squires	.07	.03	.01
□ 544 Bruce Kison	.07	.03	.01
□ 545 Lloyd Moseby	.07	.03	.01
□ 546 Brent Gaff	.07	.03	.01
□ 547 Pete Rose MG (Checklist back)	.40	.18	.05
□ 548 Larry Parrish	.07	.03	.01
□ 549 Mike Scioscia	.10	.05	.01
□ 550 Scott McGregor	.07	.03	.01
□ 551 Andy Van Slyke	.75	.35	.09
□ 552 Chris Codiroli	.07	.03	.01
□ 553 Bob Clark	.07	.03	.01
□ 554 Doug Flynn	.07	.03	.01
□ 555 Bob Stanley	.07	.03	.01
□ 556 Sixto Lezcano	.07	.03	.01
□ 557 Len Barker	.07	.03	.01
□ 558 Carmelo Martinez	.07	.03	.01
□ 559 Jay Howell	.10	.05	.01
□ 560 Bill Madlock	.10	.05	.01
□ 561 Darryl Motley	.07	.03	.01
□ 562 Houston Jimenez	.07	.03	.01
□ 563 Dick Ruthven	.07	.03	.01
□ 564 Alan Ashby	.07	.03	.01
□ 565 Kirk Gibson	.15	.07	.02
□ 566 Ed VandeBerg	.07	.03	.01
□ 567 Joel Youngblood	.07	.03	.01
□ 568 Cliff Johnson	.07	.03	.01
□ 569 Ken Oberkfell	.07	.03	.01
□ 570 Darryl Strawberry	3.00	1.35	.40
□ 571 Charlie Hough	.10	.05	.01
□ 572 Tom Paciorek	.10	.05	.01
□ 573 Jay Tibbs	.07	.03	.01
□ 574 Joe Altobelli MG (Checklist back)	.10	.05	.01
□ 575 Pedro Guerrero	.10	.05	.01
□ 576 Jaime Cocanower	.07	.03	.01
□ 577 Chris Speier	.07	.03	.01
□ 578 Terry Francona	.07	.03	.01
□ 579 Ron Romanick	.07	.03	.01
□ 580 Dwight Evans	.12	.05	.02
□ 581 Mark Wagner	.07	.03	.01
□ 582 Ken Phelps	.07	.03	.01
□ 583 Bobby Brown	.07	.03	.01
□ 584 Kevin Gross	.07	.03	.01
□ 585 Butch Wynegar	.07	.03	.01
□ 586 Bill Scherrer	.07	.03	.01
□ 587 Doug Frobel	.07	.03	.01
□ 588 Bobby Castillo	.07	.03	.01
□ 589 Bob Dernier	.07	.03	.01
□ 590 Ray Knight	.10	.05	.01
□ 591 Larry Herndon	.07	.03	.01
□ 592 Jeff D. Robinson (Giants pitcher)	.10	.05	.01
□ 593 Rick Leach	.07	.03	.01
□ 594 Curt Wilkerson	.07	.03	.01
□ 595 Larry Gura	.07	.03	.01
□ 596 Jerry Hairston	.07	.03	.01
□ 597 Brad Lesley	.07	.03	.01
□ 598 Jose Oquendo	.10	.05	.01
□ 599 Storm Davis	.07	.03	.01
□ 600 Pete Rose	.60	.25	.08
□ 601 Tom Lasorda MG (Checklist back)	.10	.05	.01
□ 602 Jeff Dedmon	.07	.03	.01
□ 603 Rick Manning	.07	.03	.01
□ 604 Daryl Sconiers	.07	.03	.01
□ 605 Ozzie Smith	.90	.40	.11
□ 606 Rich Gale	.07	.03	.01
□ 607 Bill Almon	.07	.03	.01
□ 608 Craig Lefferts	.10	.05	.01
□ 609 Broderick Perkins	.07	.03	.01
□ 610 Jack Morris	.50	.23	.06
□ 611 Ozzie Virgil	.07	.03	.01
□ 612 Mike Armstrong	.07	.03	.01
□ 613 Terry Puhl	.07	.03	.01
□ 614 Al Williams	.07	.03	.01
□ 615 Marvell Wynne	.07	.03	.01
□ 616 Scott Sanderson	.07	.03	.01
□ 617 Willie Wilson	.10	.05	.01
□ 618 Pete Falcone	.07	.03	.01
□ 619 Jeff Leonard	.07	.03	.01
□ 620 Dwight Gooden	3.50	1.55	.45
□ 621 Marvis Foley	.07	.03	.01
□ 622 Luis Leal	.07	.03	.01
□ 623 Greg Walker	.07	.03	.01
□ 624 Benny Ayala	.07	.03	.01
□ 625 Mark Langston	1.25	.55	.16
□ 626 German Rivera	.07	.03	.01
□ 627 Eric Davis	3.50	1.55	.45
□ 628 Rene Lachemann MG (Checklist back)	.10	.05	.01
□ 629 Dick Schofield	.07	.03	.01
□ 630 Tim Raines	.20	.09	.03
□ 631 Bob Forsch	.07	.03	.01
□ 632 Bruce Bochte	.07	.03	.01
□ 633 Glenn Hoffman	.07	.03	.01
□ 634 Bill Dawley	.07	.03	.01
□ 635 Terry Kennedy	.07	.03	.01
□ 636 Shane Rawley	.07	.03	.01
□ 637 Brett Butler	.20	.09	.03
□ 638 Mike Pagliarulo	.10	.05	.01
□ 639 Ed Hodge	.07	.03	.01
□ 640 Steve Henderson	.07	.03	.01
□ 641 Rod Scurry	.07	.03	.01
□ 642 Dave Owen	.07	.03	.01
□ 643 Johnny Grubb	.07	.03	.01
□ 644 Mark Huismann	.07	.03	.01
□ 645 Damaso Garcia	.07	.03	.01
□ 646 Scot Thompson	.07	.03	.01
□ 647 Rafael Ramirez	.07	.03	.01
□ 648 Bob Jones	.07	.03	.01
□ 649 Sid Fernandez	.35	.16	.04
□ 650 Greg Luzinski	.10	.05	.01
□ 651 Jeff Russell	.12	.05	.02
□ 652 Joe Nolan	.07	.03	.01
□ 653 Mark Brouhard	.07	.03	.01
□ 654 Dave Anderson	.07	.03	.01
□ 655 Joaquin Andujar	.07	.03	.01
□ 656 Chuck Cottier MG (Checklist back)	.10	.05	.01
□ 657 Jim Slaton	.07	.03	.01
□ 658 Mike Stenhouse	.07	.03	.01
□ 659 Checklist: 529-660	.12	.01	.00
□ 660 Tony Gwynn	2.50	1.15	.30
□ 661 Steve Crawford	.07	.03	.01
□ 662 Mike Heath	.07	.03	.01
□ 663 Luis Aguayo	.07	.03	.01
□ 664 Steve Farr	.30	.14	.04
□ 665 Don Mattingly	3.00	1.35	.40
□ 666 Mike LaCoss	.07	.03	.01
□ 667 Dave Engle	.07	.03	.01
□ 668 Steve Trout	.07	.03	.01
□ 669 Lee Lacy	.07	.03	.01
□ 670 Tom Seaver	.60	.25	.08
□ 671 Dane Iorg	.07	.03	.01
□ 672 Juan Berenguer	.07	.03	.01
□ 673 Buck Martinez	.07	.03	.01
□ 674 Atlee Hammaker	.07	.03	.01
□ 675 Tony Perez	.15	.07	.02
□ 676 Albert Hall	.07	.03	.01
□ 677 Wally Backman	.07	.03	.01
□ 678 Joey McLaughlin	.07	.03	.01
□ 679 Bob Kearney	.07	.03	.01
□ 680 Jerry Reuss	.07	.03	.01
□ 681 Ben Oglivie	.07	.03	.01
□ 682 Doug Corbett	.07	.03	.01
□ 683 Whitey Herzog MG (Checklist back)	.10	.05	.01
□ 684 Bill Doran	.10	.05	.01

☐ 685	Bill Caudill	.07	.03	.01
☐ 686	Mike Easler	.07	.03	.01
☐ 687	Bill Gullickson	.10	.05	.01
☐ 688	Len Matuszek	.07	.03	.01
☐ 689	Luis DeLeon	.07	.03	.01
☐ 690	Alan Trammell	.25	.11	.03
☐ 691	Dennis Rasmussen	.07	.03	.01
☐ 692	Randy Bush	.07	.03	.01
☐ 693	Tim Stoddard	.07	.03	.01
☐ 694	Joe Carter	4.00	1.80	.50
☐ 695	Rick Rhoden	.07	.03	.01
☐ 696	John Rabb	.07	.03	.01
☐ 697	Onix Concepcion	.07	.03	.01
☐ 698	Jorge Bell	.40	.18	.05
☐ 699	Donnie Moore	.07	.03	.01
☐ 700	Eddie Murray	.90	.40	.11
☐ 701	Eddie Murray AS	.35	.16	.04
☐ 702	Damaso Garcia AS	.10	.05	.01
☐ 703	George Brett AS	.60	.25	.08
☐ 704	Cal Ripken AS	1.25	.55	.16
☐ 705	Dave Winfield AS	.50	.23	.06
☐ 706	Rickey Henderson AS	.60	.25	.08
☐ 707	Tony Armas AS	.10	.05	.01
☐ 708	Lance Parrish AS	.10	.05	.01
☐ 709	Mike Boddicker AS	.10	.05	.01
☐ 710	Frank Viola AS	.15	.07	.02
☐ 711	Dan Quisenberry AS	.10	.05	.01
☐ 712	Keith Hernandez AS	.10	.05	.01
☐ 713	Ryne Sandberg AS	1.50	.65	.19
☐ 714	Mike Schmidt AS	.65	.30	.08
☐ 715	Ozzie Smith AS	.35	.16	.04
☐ 716	Dale Murphy AS	.20	.09	.03
☐ 717	Tony Gwynn AS	.75	.35	.09
☐ 718	Jeff Leonard AS	.10	.05	.01
☐ 719	Gary Carter AS	.15	.07	.02
☐ 720	Rick Sutcliffe AS	.10	.05	.01
☐ 721	Bob Knepper AS	.10	.05	.01
☐ 722	Bruce Sutter AS	.10	.05	.01
☐ 723	Dave Stewart	.20	.09	.03
☐ 724	Oscar Gamble	.07	.03	.01
☐ 725	Floyd Bannister	.07	.03	.01
☐ 726	Al Bumbry	.07	.03	.01
☐ 727	Frank Pastore	.07	.03	.01
☐ 728	Bob Bailor	.07	.03	.01
☐ 729	Don Sutton	.20	.09	.03
☐ 730	Dave Kingman	.10	.05	.01
☐ 731	Neil Allen	.07	.03	.01
☐ 732	John McNamara MG (Checklist back)	.10	.05	.01
☐ 733	Tony Scott	.07	.03	.01
☐ 734	John Henry Johnson	.07	.03	.01
☐ 735	Garry Templeton	.07	.03	.01
☐ 736	Jerry Mumphrey	.07	.03	.01
☐ 737	Bo Diaz	.07	.03	.01
☐ 738	Omar Moreno	.07	.03	.01
☐ 739	Ernie Camacho	.07	.03	.01
☐ 740	Jack Clark	.10	.05	.01
☐ 741	John Butcher	.07	.03	.01
☐ 742	Ron Hassey	.07	.03	.01
☐ 743	Frank White	.10	.05	.01
☐ 744	Doug Bair	.07	.03	.01
☐ 745	Buddy Bell	.10	.05	.01
☐ 746	Jim Clancy	.07	.03	.01
☐ 747	Alex Trevino	.07	.03	.01
☐ 748	Lee Mazzilli	.07	.03	.01
☐ 749	Julio Cruz	.07	.03	.01
☐ 750	Rollie Fingers	.20	.09	.03
☐ 751	Kelvin Chapman	.07	.03	.01
☐ 752	Bob Owchinko	.07	.03	.01
☐ 753	Greg Brock	.07	.03	.01
☐ 754	Larry Milbourne	.07	.03	.01
☐ 755	Ken Singleton	.10	.05	.01
☐ 756	Rob Picciolo	.07	.03	.01
☐ 757	Willie McGee	.20	.09	.03
☐ 758	Ray Burris	.07	.03	.01
☐ 759	Jim Fanning MG (Checklist back)	.10	.05	.01
☐ 760	Nolan Ryan	4.50	2.00	.55
☐ 761	Jerry Remy	.07	.03	.01
☐ 762	Eddie Whitson	.07	.03	.01
☐ 763	Kiko Garcia	.07	.03	.01
☐ 764	Jamie Easterly	.07	.03	.01
☐ 765	Willie Randolph	.10	.05	.01
☐ 766	Paul Mirabella	.07	.03	.01
☐ 767	Darrell Brown	.07	.03	.01
☐ 768	Ron Cey	.10	.05	.01
☐ 769	Joe Cowley	.07	.03	.01
☐ 770	Carlton Fisk	.75	.35	.09
☐ 771	Geoff Zahn	.07	.03	.01
☐ 772	Johnnie LeMaster	.07	.03	.01
☐ 773	Hal McRae	.10	.05	.01
☐ 774	Dennis Lamp	.07	.03	.01
☐ 775	Mookie Wilson	.10	.05	.01
☐ 776	Jerry Royster	.07	.03	.01
☐ 777	Ned Yost	.07	.03	.01
☐ 778	Mike Davis	.07	.03	.01
☐ 779	Nick Esasky	.07	.03	.01
☐ 780	Mike Flanagan	.07	.03	.01
☐ 781	Jim Gantner	.10	.05	.01
☐ 782	Tom Niedenfuer	.07	.03	.01
☐ 783	Mike Jorgensen	.07	.03	.01
☐ 784	Checklist: 661-792	.12	.01	.00
☐ 785	Tony Armas	.07	.03	.01
☐ 786	Enos Cabell	.07	.03	.01
☐ 787	Jim Wohlford	.07	.03	.01
☐ 788	Steve Comer	.07	.03	.01
☐ 789	Luis Salazar	.07	.03	.01
☐ 790	Ron Guidry	.10	.05	.01
☐ 791	Ivan DeJesus	.07	.03	.01
☐ 792	Darrell Evans	.12	.05	.02

1985 Topps All-Star Glossy 22

The cards in this 22-card set measure 2 1/2" by 3 1/2". Similar in design, both front and back, to last year's Glossy set, this edition features the managers, starting nine players and honorary captains of the National and American League teams in the 1984 All-Star game. The set is numbered on the reverse with players essentially ordered by position within league, NL: 1-11 and AL: 12-22.

	NRMT-MT	EXC	G-VG
COMPLETE SET (22)	4.00	1.80	.50
COMMON PLAYER (1-22)	.10	.05	.01

☐ 1	Paul Owens MG	.10	.05	.01
☐ 2	Steve Garvey	.30	.14	.04
☐ 3	Ryne Sandberg	.90	.40	.11
☐ 4	Mike Schmidt	.75	.35	.09
☐ 5	Ozzie Smith	.40	.18	.05
☐ 6	Tony Gwynn	.50	.23	.06
☐ 7	Dale Murphy	.30	.14	.04
☐ 8	Darryl Strawberry	.60	.25	.08
☐ 9	Gary Carter	.30	.14	.04
☐ 10	Charlie Lea	.10	.05	.01
☐ 11	Willie McCovey CAPT	.20	.09	.03
☐ 12	Joe Altobelli MG	.10	.05	.01
☐ 13	Rod Carew	.40	.18	.05
☐ 14	Lou Whitaker	.15	.07	.02
☐ 15	George Brett	.75	.35	.09
☐ 16	Cal Ripken	.90	.40	.11
☐ 17	Dave Winfield	.50	.23	.06
☐ 18	Chet Lemon	.10	.05	.01
☐ 19	Reggie Jackson	.60	.25	.08
☐ 20	Lance Parrish	.20	.09	.03
☐ 21	Dave Stieb	.10	.05	.01
☐ 22	Hank Greenberg CAPT	.20	.09	.03

1985 Topps Glossy 40

The cards in this 40-card set measure 2 1/2" by 3 1/2". Similar to last year's glossy set, this set was issued as a bonus prize to Topps All-Star Baseball Game cards found in wax packs. The set could be obtained by sending in the

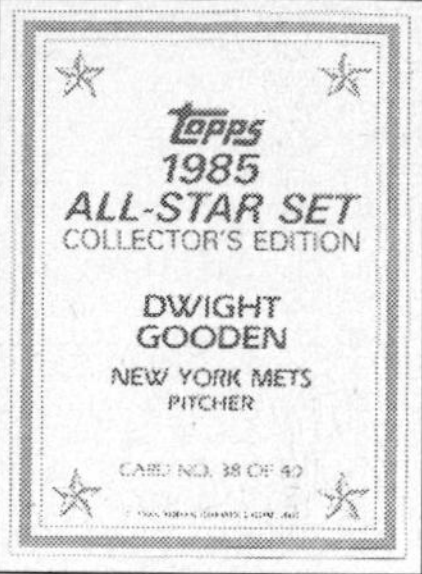

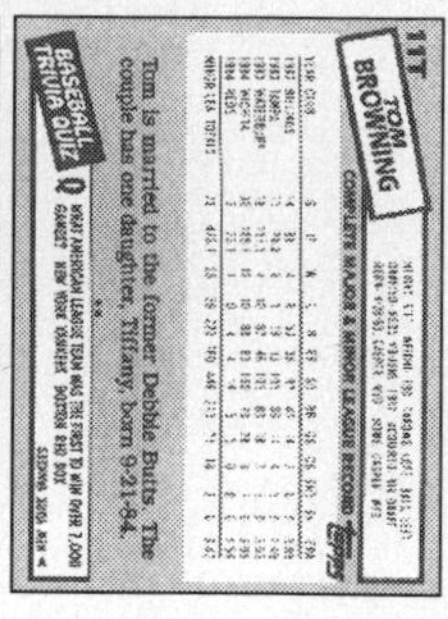

"Bonus Runs" from the "Winning Pitch" game insert cards. For 25 runs and 75 cents, a collector could send in for one of the eight different five card series plus automatically be entered in the Grand Prize Sweepstakes for a chance at a free trip to the All-Star game. The cards are numbered and contain 20 stars from each league.

	NRMT-MT	EXC	G-VG
COMPLETE SET (40)	12.50	5.75	1.55
COMMON PLAYER (1-40)	.20	.09	.03
☐ 1 Dale Murphy	.60	.25	.08
☐ 2 Jesse Orosco	.20	.09	.03
☐ 3 Bob Brenly	.20	.09	.03
☐ 4 Mike Boddicker	.20	.09	.03
☐ 5 Dave Kingman	.30	.14	.04
☐ 6 Jim Rice	.30	.14	.04
☐ 7 Frank Viola	.30	.14	.04
☐ 8 Alvin Davis	.30	.14	.04
☐ 9 Rick Sutcliffe	.20	.09	.03
☐ 10 Pete Rose	1.00	.45	.13
☐ 11 Leon Durham	.20	.09	.03
☐ 12 Joaquin Andujar	.20	.09	.03
☐ 13 Keith Hernandez	.30	.14	.04
☐ 14 Dave Winfield	.75	.35	.09
☐ 15 Reggie Jackson	1.00	.45	.13
☐ 16 Alan Trammell	.40	.18	.05
☐ 17 Bert Blyleven	.30	.14	.04
☐ 18 Tony Armas	.20	.09	.03
☐ 19 Rich Gossage	.30	.14	.04
☐ 20 Jose Cruz	.20	.09	.03
☐ 21 Ryne Sandberg	1.50	.65	.19
☐ 22 Bruce Sutter	.30	.14	.04
☐ 23 Mike Schmidt	1.25	.55	.16
☐ 24 Cal Ripken	1.50	.65	.19
☐ 25 Dan Petry	.20	.09	.03
☐ 26 Jack Morris	.40	.18	.05
☐ 27 Don Mattingly	1.25	.55	.16
☐ 28 Eddie Murray	.75	.35	.09
☐ 29 Tony Gwynn	.90	.40	.11
☐ 30 Charlie Lea	.20	.09	.03
☐ 31 Juan Samuel	.20	.09	.03
☐ 32 Phil Niekro	.40	.18	.05
☐ 33 Alejandro Pena	.20	.09	.03
☐ 34 Harold Baines	.30	.14	.04
☐ 35 Dan Quisenberry	.30	.14	.04
☐ 36 Gary Carter	.50	.23	.06
☐ 37 Mario Soto	.20	.09	.03
☐ 38 Dwight Gooden	.60	.25	.08
☐ 39 Tom Brunansky	.30	.14	.04
☐ 40 Dave Stieb	.20	.09	.03

1985 Topps Traded

The cards in this 132-card set measure 2 1/2" by 3 1/2". In its now standard procedure, Topps issued its Traded (or extended) set for the fifth year in a row. Topps did however test on a limited basis the issuance of these Traded cards in wax packs. Because all photos and statistics of its regular set for the year were developed during the fall and winter months of the preceding year, players who changed teams during the fall, winter, and spring months are portrayed in the 1985 regular issue set with the teams they were with in 1984. The Traded set updates the shortcomings of the regular set by presenting the players with their proper teams for the current year. Most of 1985's top rookies not contained in the regular set are picked up in the Traded set. The key (extended) Rookie Cards in this set are Vince Coleman, Ozzie Guillen, and Mickey Tettleton. Again this year, the Topps affiliate in Ireland printed the cards, and the cards were available through hobby channels only. Topps also produced a specially boxed "glossy" edition, frequently referred to as the Topps Traded Tiffany set. There were supposedly only 8,000 sets of the Tiffany cards produced; they were marketed to hobby dealers. The checklist of cards is identical to that of the normal non-glossy cards. There are two primary distinguishing features of the Tiffany cards, white card stock reverses and high gloss obverses. These Tiffany cards are valued from approximately five to ten times the values listed below. The set numbering is in alphabetical order by player's name.

	NRMT-MT	EXC	G-VG
COMPLETE SET (132)	30.00	13.50	3.80
COMMON PLAYER (1T-132T)	.15	.07	.02
☐ 1T Don Aase	.15	.07	.02
☐ 2T Bill Almon	.15	.07	.02
☐ 3T Benny Ayala	.15	.07	.02
☐ 4T Dusty Baker	.20	.09	.03
☐ 5T Geo.Bamberger MG	.15	.07	.02
☐ 6T Dale Berra	.15	.07	.02
☐ 7T Rich Bordi	.15	.07	.02
☐ 8T Daryl Boston	.25	.11	.03
☐ 9T Hubie Brooks	.20	.09	.03
☐ 10T Chris Brown	.15	.07	.02
☐ 11T Tom Browning	1.00	.45	.13
☐ 12T Al Bumbry	.15	.07	.02
☐ 13T Ray Burris	.15	.07	.02
☐ 14T Jeff Burroughs	.15	.07	.02
☐ 15T Bill Campbell	.15	.07	.02
☐ 16T Don Carman	.15	.07	.02
☐ 17T Gary Carter	1.00	.45	.13
☐ 18T Bobby Castillo	.15	.07	.02
☐ 19T Bill Caudill	.15	.07	.02
☐ 20T Rick Cerone	.15	.07	.02
☐ 21T Bryan Clark	.15	.07	.02
☐ 22T Jack Clark	.20	.09	.03
☐ 23T Pat Clements	.15	.07	.02
☐ 24T Vince Coleman	4.00	1.80	.50
☐ 25T Dave Collins	.15	.07	.02
☐ 26T Danny Darwin	.15	.07	.02
☐ 27T Jim Davenport MG	.15	.07	.02
☐ 28T Jerry Davis	.15	.07	.02
☐ 29T Brian Dayett	.15	.07	.02
☐ 30T Ivan DeJesus	.15	.07	.02
☐ 31T Ken Dixon	.15	.07	.02
☐ 32T Mariano Duncan	1.25	.55	.16
☐ 33T John Felske MG	.15	.07	.02
☐ 34T Mike Fitzgerald	.15	.07	.02
☐ 35T Ray Fontenot	.15	.07	.02
☐ 36T Greg Gagne	.40	.18	.05
☐ 37T Oscar Gamble	.15	.07	.02
☐ 38T Scott Garrelts	.15	.07	.02
☐ 39T Bob L. Gibson	.15	.07	.02
☐ 40T Jim Gott	.15	.07	.02
☐ 41T David Green	.15	.07	.02
☐ 42T Alfredo Griffin	.15	.07	.02
☐ 43T Ozzie Guillen	1.25	.55	.16
☐ 44T Eddie Haas MG	.15	.07	.02

☐ 45T Terry Harper	.15	.07	.02
☐ 46T Toby Harrah	.15	.07	.02
☐ 47T Greg Harris	.15	.07	.02
☐ 48T Ron Hassey	.15	.07	.02
☐ 49T Rickey Henderson	5.00	2.30	.60
☐ 50T Steve Henderson	.15	.07	.02
☐ 51T George Hendrick	.15	.07	.02
☐ 52T Joe Hesketh	.25	.11	.03
☐ 53T Teddy Higuera	.25	.11	.03
☐ 54T Donnie Hill	.15	.07	.02
☐ 55T Al Holland	.15	.07	.02
☐ 56T Burt Hooton	.15	.07	.02
☐ 57T Jay Howell	.20	.09	.03
☐ 58T Ken Howell	.15	.07	.02
☐ 59T LaMarr Hoyt	.15	.07	.02
☐ 60T Tim Hulett	.15	.07	.02
☐ 61T Bob James	.15	.07	.02
☐ 62T Steve Jeltz	.15	.07	.02
☐ 63T Cliff Johnson	.15	.07	.02
☐ 64T Howard Johnson	2.00	.90	.25
☐ 65T Ruppert Jones	.15	.07	.02
☐ 66T Steve Kemp	.15	.07	.02
☐ 67T Bruce Kison	.15	.07	.02
☐ 68T Alan Knicely	.15	.07	.02
☐ 69T Mike LaCoss	.15	.07	.02
☐ 70T Lee Lacy	.15	.07	.02
☐ 71T Dave LaPoint	.15	.07	.02
☐ 72T Gary Lavelle	.15	.07	.02
☐ 73T Vance Law	.15	.07	.02
☐ 74T Johnnie LeMaster	.15	.07	.02
☐ 75T Sixto Lezcano	.15	.07	.02
☐ 76T Tim Lollar	.15	.07	.02
☐ 77T Fred Lynn	.20	.09	.03
☐ 78T Billy Martin MG	.25	.11	.03
☐ 79T Ron Mathis	.15	.07	.02
☐ 80T Len Matuszek	.15	.07	.02
☐ 81T Gene Mauch MG	.15	.07	.02
☐ 82T Oddibe McDowell	.20	.09	.03
☐ 83T Roger McDowell	.40	.18	.05
☐ 84T John McNamara MG	.15	.07	.02
☐ 85T Donnie Moore	.15	.07	.02
☐ 86T Gene Nelson	.15	.07	.02
☐ 87T Steve Nicosia	.15	.07	.02
☐ 88T Al Oliver	.20	.09	.03
☐ 89T Joe Orsulak	.60	.25	.08
☐ 90T Rob Picciolo	.15	.07	.02
☐ 91T Chris Pittaro	.15	.07	.02
☐ 92T Jim Presley	.15	.07	.02
☐ 93T Rick Reuschel	.20	.09	.03
☐ 94T Bert Roberge	.15	.07	.02
☐ 95T Bob Rodgers MG	.15	.07	.02
☐ 96T Jerry Royster	.15	.07	.02
☐ 97T Dave Rozema	.15	.07	.02
☐ 98T Dave Rucker	.15	.07	.02
☐ 99T Vern Ruhle	.15	.07	.02
☐ 100T Paul Runge	.15	.07	.02
☐ 101T Mark Salas	.15	.07	.02
☐ 102T Luis Salazar	.15	.07	.02
☐ 103T Joe Sambito	.15	.07	.02
☐ 104T Rick Schu	.15	.07	.02
☐ 105T Donnie Scott	.15	.07	.02
☐ 106T Larry Sheets	.15	.07	.02
☐ 107T Don Slaught	.15	.07	.02
☐ 108T Roy Smalley	.15	.07	.02
☐ 109T Lonnie Smith	.20	.09	.03
☐ 110T Nate Snell UER (Headings on back for a batter)	.15	.07	.02
☐ 111T Chris Speier	.15	.07	.02
☐ 112T Mike Stenhouse	.15	.07	.02
☐ 113T Tim Stoddard	.15	.07	.02
☐ 114T Jim Sundberg	.20	.09	.03
☐ 115T Bruce Sutter	.20	.09	.03
☐ 116T Don Sutton	.75	.35	.09
☐ 117T Kent Tekulve	.15	.07	.02
☐ 118T Tom Tellmann	.15	.07	.02
☐ 119T Walt Terrell	.15	.07	.02
☐ 120T Mickey Tettleton	5.00	2.30	.60
☐ 121T Derrel Thomas	.15	.07	.02
☐ 122T Rich Thompson	.15	.07	.02
☐ 123T Alex Trevino	.15	.07	.02
☐ 124T John Tudor	.20	.09	.03
☐ 125T Jose Uribe	.25	.11	.03
☐ 126T Bobby Valentine MG	.20	.09	.03
☐ 127T Dave Von Ohlen	.15	.07	.02
☐ 128T U.L. Washington	.15	.07	.02
☐ 129T Earl Weaver MG	.20	.09	.03
☐ 130T Eddie Whitson	.15	.07	.02
☐ 131T Herm Winningham	.30	.14	.04
☐ 132T Checklist 1-132	.20	.02	.01

1986 Topps

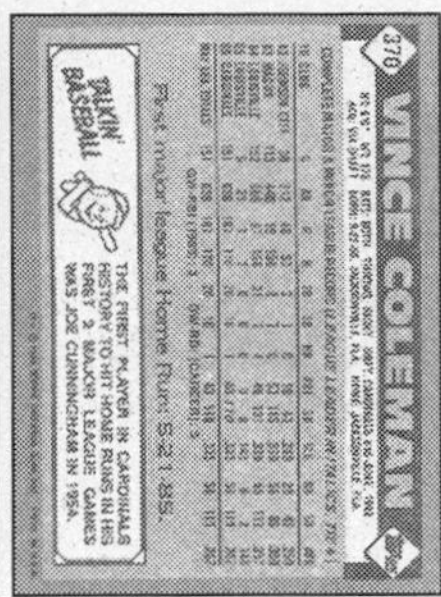

The cards in this 792-card set are standard-size (2 1/2" by 3 1/2"). The first seven cards are a tribute to Pete Rose and his career. Card numbers 2-7 show small photos of Pete's Topps cards of the given years on the front with biographical information pertaining to those years on the back. The team leader cards were done differently with a simple player action shot on a white background; the player pictured is dubbed the "Dean" of that team, i.e., the player with the longest continuous service with that team. Topps again features a "Turn Back the Clock" series (401-405). Record breakers of the previous year are acknowledged on card numbers 201 to 207. Card numbers 701-722 feature All-Star selections from each league. Manager cards feature the team checklist on the reverse. Ryne Sandberg (690) is the only player card in the set without a Topps logo on the front of the card; this omission was never corrected by Topps. There are two other uncorrected errors involving misnumbered cards; see card numbers 51, 57, 141, and 171 in the checklist below. The backs of all the cards have a distinctive red background. The key Rookie Cards in this set are Vince Coleman, Len Dykstra, Cecil Fielder, and Mickey Tettleton. Topps also produced a specially boxed "glossy" edition, frequently referred to as the Topps Tiffany set. There were supposedly only 5,000 sets of the Tiffany cards produced; they were marketed to hobby dealers. The checklist of cards (792 regular and 132 Traded) is identical to that of the normal non-glossy cards. There are two primary distinguishing features of the Tiffany cards, white card stock reverses and high gloss obverses. These Tiffany cards are valued approximately from five to ten times the values listed below.

	MT	EX-MT	VG
COMPLETE SET (792)	40.00	18.00	5.00
COMPLETE FACT.SET (792)	40.00	18.00	5.00
COMMON PLAYER (1-792)	.05	.02	.01
☐ 1 Pete Rose	1.00	.25	.08
☐ 2 Rose Special: '63-'66	.30	.14	.04
☐ 3 Rose Special: '67-'70	.30	.14	.04
☐ 4 Rose Special: '71-'74	.30	.14	.04
☐ 5 Rose Special: '75-'78	.30	.14	.04
☐ 6 Rose Special: '79-'82	.30	.14	.04
☐ 7 Rose Special: '83-'85	.30	.14	.04
☐ 8 Dwayne Murphy	.05	.02	.01
☐ 9 Roy Smith	.05	.02	.01
☐ 10 Tony Gwynn	1.25	.55	.16
☐ 11 Bob Ojeda	.05	.02	.01
☐ 12 Jose Uribe	.10	.05	.01
☐ 13 Bob Kearney	.05	.02	.01
☐ 14 Julio Cruz	.05	.02	.01
☐ 15 Eddie Whitson	.05	.02	.01
☐ 16 Rick Schu	.05	.02	.01
☐ 17 Mike Stenhouse	.05	.02	.01
☐ 18 Brent Gaff	.05	.02	.01
☐ 19 Rich Hebner	.05	.02	.01
☐ 20 Lou Whitaker	.12	.05	.02
☐ 21 George Bamberger MG	.08	.04	.01

	(Checklist back)			
22	Duane Walker	.05	.02	.01
23	Manny Lee	.25	.11	.03
24	Len Barker	.05	.02	.01
25	Willie Wilson	.05	.02	.01
26	Frank DiPino	.05	.02	.01
27	Ray Knight	.08	.04	.01
28	Eric Davis	.50	.23	.06
29	Tony Phillips	.08	.04	.01
30	Eddie Murray	.45	.20	.06
31	Jamie Easterly	.05	.02	.01
32	Steve Yeager	.05	.02	.01
33	Jeff Lahti	.05	.02	.01
34	Ken Phelps	.05	.02	.01
35	Jeff Reardon	.25	.11	.03
36	Tigers Leaders	.08	.04	.01
	Lance Parrish			
37	Mark Thurmond	.05	.02	.01
38	Glenn Hoffman	.05	.02	.01
39	Dave Rucker	.05	.02	.01
40	Ken Griffey	.08	.04	.01
41	Brad Wellman	.05	.02	.01
42	Geoff Zahn	.05	.02	.01
43	Dave Engle	.05	.02	.01
44	Lance McCullers	.05	.02	.01
45	Damaso Garcia	.05	.02	.01
46	Billy Hatcher	.08	.04	.01
47	Juan Berenguer	.05	.02	.01
48	Bill Almon	.05	.02	.01
49	Rick Manning	.05	.02	.01
50	Dan Quisenberry	.08	.04	.01
51	Bobby Wine MG ERR	.08	.04	.01
	(Checklist back)			
	(Number of card on			
	back is actually 57)			
52	Chris Welsh	.05	.02	.01
53	Len Dykstra	.75	.35	.09
54	John Franco	.10	.05	.01
55	Fred Lynn	.08	.04	.01
56	Tom Niedenfuer	.05	.02	.01
57	Bill Doran	.05	.02	.01
	(See also 51)			
58	Bill Krueger	.05	.02	.01
59	Andre Thornton	.05	.02	.01
60	Dwight Evans	.10	.05	.01
61	Karl Best	.05	.02	.01
62	Bob Boone	.08	.04	.01
63	Ron Roenicke	.05	.02	.01
64	Floyd Bannister	.05	.02	.01
65	Dan Driessen	.05	.02	.01
66	Cardinals Leaders	.08	.04	.01
	Bob Forsch			
67	Carmelo Martinez	.05	.02	.01
68	Ed Lynch	.05	.02	.01
69	Luis Aguayo	.05	.02	.01
70	Dave Winfield	.60	.25	.08
71	Ken Schrom	.05	.02	.01
72	Shawon Dunston	.12	.05	.02
73	Randy O'Neal	.05	.02	.01
74	Rance Mulliniks	.05	.02	.01
75	Jose DeLeon	.05	.02	.01
76	Dion James	.05	.02	.01
77	Charlie Leibrandt	.08	.04	.01
78	Bruce Benedict	.05	.02	.01
79	Dave Schmidt	.05	.02	.01
80	Darryl Strawberry	1.00	.45	.13
81	Gene Mauch MG	.08	.04	.01
	(Checklist back)			
82	Tippy Martinez	.05	.02	.01
83	Phil Garner	.08	.04	.01
84	Curt Young	.05	.02	.01
85	Tony Perez	.12	.05	.02
	(Eric Davis also			
	shown on card)			
86	Tom Waddell	.05	.02	.01
87	Candy Maldonado	.08	.04	.01
88	Tom Nieto	.05	.02	.01
89	Randy St.Claire	.05	.02	.01
90	Garry Templeton	.05	.02	.01
91	Steve Crawford	.05	.02	.01
92	Al Cowens	.05	.02	.01
93	Scot Thompson	.05	.02	.01
94	Rich Bordi	.05	.02	.01
95	Ozzie Virgil	.05	.02	.01
96	Blue Jays Leaders	.08	.04	.01
	Jim Clancy			
97	Gary Gaetti	.08	.04	.01
98	Dick Ruthven	.05	.02	.01
99	Buddy Biancalana	.05	.02	.01
100	Nolan Ryan	3.00	1.35	.40
101	Dave Bergman	.05	.02	.01
102	Joe Orsulak	.15	.07	.02
103	Luis Salazar	.05	.02	.01
104	Sid Fernandez	.12	.05	.02
105	Gary Ward	.05	.02	.01
106	Ray Burris	.05	.02	.01
107	Rafael Ramirez	.05	.02	.01
108	Ted Power	.05	.02	.01
109	Len Matuszek	.05	.02	.01
110	Scott McGregor	.05	.02	.01
111	Roger Craig MG	.08	.04	.01
	(Checklist back)			
112	Bill Campbell	.05	.02	.01
113	U.L. Washington	.05	.02	.01
114	Mike C. Brown	.05	.02	.01
	(Pirates Outfielder)			
115	Jay Howell	.08	.04	.01
116	Brook Jacoby	.05	.02	.01
117	Bruce Kison	.05	.02	.01
118	Jerry Royster	.05	.02	.01
119	Barry Bonnell	.05	.02	.01
120	Steve Carlton	.40	.18	.05
121	Nelson Simmons	.05	.02	.01
122	Pete Filson	.05	.02	.01
123	Greg Walker	.05	.02	.01
124	Luis Sanchez	.05	.02	.01
125	Dave Lopes	.08	.04	.01
126	Mets Leaders	.08	.04	.01
	Mookie Wilson			
127	Jack Howell	.05	.02	.01
128	John Wathan	.05	.02	.01
129	Jeff Dedmon	.05	.02	.01
130	Alan Trammell	.15	.07	.02
131	Checklist: 1-132	.10	.01	.00
132	Razor Shines	.05	.02	.01
133	Andy McGaffigan	.05	.02	.01
134	Carney Lansford	.08	.04	.01
135	Joe Niekro	.08	.04	.01
136	Mike Hargrove	.08	.04	.01
137	Charlie Moore	.05	.02	.01
138	Mark Davis	.08	.04	.01
139	Daryl Boston	.05	.02	.01
140	John Candelaria	.05	.02	.01
141	Chuck Cottier MG	.08	.04	.01
	(Checklist back)			
	(See also 171)			
142	Bob Jones	.05	.02	.01
143	Dave Van Gorder	.05	.02	.01
144	Doug Sisk	.05	.02	.01
145	Pedro Guerrero	.10	.05	.01
146	Jack Perconte	.05	.02	.01
147	Larry Sheets	.05	.02	.01
148	Mike Heath	.05	.02	.01
149	Brett Butler	.10	.05	.01
150	Joaquin Andujar	.05	.02	.01
151	Dave Stapleton	.05	.02	.01
152	Mike Morgan	.08	.04	.01
153	Ricky Adams	.05	.02	.01
154	Bert Roberge	.05	.02	.01
155	Bob Grich	.08	.04	.01
156	White Sox Leaders	.08	.04	.01
	Richard Dotson			
157	Ron Hassey	.05	.02	.01
158	Derrel Thomas	.05	.02	.01
159	Orel Hershiser UER	.25	.11	.03
	(82 Alburquerque)			
160	Chet Lemon	.05	.02	.01
161	Lee Tunnell	.05	.02	.01
162	Greg Gagne	.08	.04	.01
163	Pete Ladd	.05	.02	.01
164	Steve Balboni	.05	.02	.01
165	Mike Davis	.05	.02	.01
166	Dickie Thon	.05	.02	.01
167	Zane Smith	.15	.07	.02
168	Jeff Burroughs	.05	.02	.01
169	George Wright	.05	.02	.01
170	Gary Carter	.20	.09	.03
171	Bob Rodgers MG ERR	.08	.04	.01
	(Checklist back)			
	(Number of card on			
	back actually 141)			
172	Jerry Reed	.05	.02	.01
173	Wayne Gross	.05	.02	.01
174	Brian Snyder	.05	.02	.01
175	Steve Sax	.10	.05	.01
176	Jay Tibbs	.05	.02	.01
177	Joel Youngblood	.05	.02	.01
178	Ivan DeJesus	.05	.02	.01
179	Stu Cliburn	.05	.02	.01
180	Don Mattingly	1.00	.45	.13
181	Al Nipper	.05	.02	.01
182	Bobby Brown	.05	.02	.01
183	Larry Andersen	.05	.02	.01
184	Tim Laudner	.05	.02	.01
185	Rollie Fingers	.15	.07	.02
186	Astros Leaders	.08	.04	.01
	Jose Cruz			

☐ 187	Scott Fletcher	.05	.02	.01
☐ 188	Bob Dernier	.05	.02	.01
☐ 189	Mike Mason	.05	.02	.01
☐ 190	George Hendrick	.05	.02	.01
☐ 191	Wally Backman	.05	.02	.01
☐ 192	Milt Wilcox	.05	.02	.01
☐ 193	Daryl Sconiers	.05	.02	.01
☐ 194	Craig McMurtry	.05	.02	.01
☐ 195	Dave Concepcion	.08	.04	.01
☐ 196	Doyle Alexander	.05	.02	.01
☐ 197	Enos Cabell	.05	.02	.01
☐ 198	Ken Dixon	.05	.02	.01
☐ 199	Dick Howser MG (Checklist back)	.08	.04	.01
☐ 200	Mike Schmidt	1.00	.45	.13
☐ 201	RB: Vince Coleman Most stolen bases, season, rookie	.20	.09	.03
☐ 202	RB: Dwight Gooden Youngest 20 game winner	.20	.09	.03
☐ 203	RB: Keith Hernandez Most game-winning RBI's	.10	.05	.01
☐ 204	RB: Phil Niekro Oldest shutout pitcher	.10	.05	.01
☐ 205	RB: Tony Perez Oldest grand slammer	.10	.05	.01
☐ 206	RB: Pete Rose Most hits, lifetime	.30	.14	.04
☐ 207	RB:Fernando Valenzuela Most cons. innings, start of season, no earned runs	.10	.05	.01
☐ 208	Ramon Romero	.05	.02	.01
☐ 209	Randy Ready	.05	.02	.01
☐ 210	Calvin Schiraldi	.05	.02	.01
☐ 211	Ed Wojna	.05	.02	.01
☐ 212	Chris Speier	.05	.02	.01
☐ 213	Bob Shirley	.05	.02	.01
☐ 214	Randy Bush	.05	.02	.01
☐ 215	Frank White	.08	.04	.01
☐ 216	A's Leaders Dwayne Murphy	.08	.04	.01
☐ 217	Bill Scherrer	.05	.02	.01
☐ 218	Randy Hunt	.05	.02	.01
☐ 219	Dennis Lamp	.05	.02	.01
☐ 220	Bob Horner	.08	.04	.01
☐ 221	Dave Henderson	.10	.05	.01
☐ 222	Craig Gerber	.05	.02	.01
☐ 223	Atlee Hammaker	.05	.02	.01
☐ 224	Cesar Cedeno	.08	.04	.01
☐ 225	Ron Darling	.10	.05	.01
☐ 226	Lee Lacy	.05	.02	.01
☐ 227	Al Jones	.05	.02	.01
☐ 228	Tom Lawless	.05	.02	.01
☐ 229	Bill Gullickson	.08	.04	.01
☐ 230	Terry Kennedy	.05	.02	.01
☐ 231	Jim Frey MG (Checklist back)	.08	.04	.01
☐ 232	Rick Rhoden	.05	.02	.01
☐ 233	Steve Lyons	.05	.02	.01
☐ 234	Doug Corbett	.05	.02	.01
☐ 235	Butch Wynegar	.05	.02	.01
☐ 236	Frank Eufemia	.05	.02	.01
☐ 237	Ted Simmons	.08	.04	.01
☐ 238	Larry Parrish	.05	.02	.01
☐ 239	Joel Skinner	.05	.02	.01
☐ 240	Tommy John	.10	.05	.01
☐ 241	Tony Fernandez	.12	.05	.02
☐ 242	Rich Thompson	.05	.02	.01
☐ 243	Johnny Grubb	.05	.02	.01
☐ 244	Craig Lefferts	.08	.04	.01
☐ 245	Jim Sundberg	.08	.04	.01
☐ 246	Phillies Leaders Steve Carlton	.15	.07	.02
☐ 247	Terry Harper	.05	.02	.01
☐ 248	Spike Owen	.05	.02	.01
☐ 249	Rob Deer	.30	.14	.04
☐ 250	Dwight Gooden	.50	.23	.06
☐ 251	Rich Dauer	.05	.02	.01
☐ 252	Bobby Castillo	.05	.02	.01
☐ 253	Dann Bilardello	.05	.02	.01
☐ 254	Ozzie Guillen	.25	.11	.03
☐ 255	Tony Armas	.05	.02	.01
☐ 256	Kurt Kepshire	.05	.02	.01
☐ 257	Doug DeCinces	.05	.02	.01
☐ 258	Tim Burke	.10	.05	.01
☐ 259	Dan Pasqua	.08	.04	.01
☐ 260	Tony Pena	.08	.04	.01
☐ 261	Bobby Valentine MG (Checklist back)	.08	.04	.01
☐ 262	Mario Ramirez	.05	.02	.01
☐ 263	Checklist: 133-264	.10	.01	.00
☐ 264	Darren Daulton	1.00	.45	.13
☐ 265	Ron Davis	.05	.02	.01
☐ 266	Keith Moreland	.05	.02	.01
☐ 267	Paul Molitor	.20	.09	.03
☐ 268	Mike Scott	.08	.04	.01
☐ 269	Dane Iorg	.05	.02	.01
☐ 270	Jack Morris	.35	.16	.04
☐ 271	Dave Collins	.05	.02	.01
☐ 272	Tim Tolman	.05	.02	.01
☐ 273	Jerry Willard	.05	.02	.01
☐ 274	Ron Gardenhire	.05	.02	.01
☐ 275	Charlie Hough	.05	.02	.01
☐ 276	Yankees Leaders Willie Randolph	.08	.04	.01
☐ 277	Jaime Cocanower	.05	.02	.01
☐ 278	Sixto Lezcano	.05	.02	.01
☐ 279	Al Pardo	.05	.02	.01
☐ 280	Tim Raines	.15	.07	.02
☐ 281	Steve Mura	.05	.02	.01
☐ 282	Jerry Mumphrey	.05	.02	.01
☐ 283	Mike Fischlin	.05	.02	.01
☐ 284	Brian Dayett	.05	.02	.01
☐ 285	Buddy Bell	.08	.04	.01
☐ 286	Luis DeLeon	.05	.02	.01
☐ 287	John Christensen	.05	.02	.01
☐ 288	Don Aase	.05	.02	.01
☐ 289	Johnnie LeMaster	.05	.02	.01
☐ 290	Carlton Fisk	.40	.18	.05
☐ 291	Tom Lasorda MG (Checklist back)	.08	.04	.01
☐ 292	Chuck Porter	.05	.02	.01
☐ 293	Chris Chambliss	.08	.04	.01
☐ 294	Danny Cox	.05	.02	.01
☐ 295	Kirk Gibson	.10	.05	.01
☐ 296	Geno Petralli	.05	.02	.01
☐ 297	Tim Lollar	.05	.02	.01
☐ 298	Craig Reynolds	.05	.02	.01
☐ 299	Bryn Smith	.05	.02	.01
☐ 300	George Brett	.75	.35	.09
☐ 301	Dennis Rasmussen	.05	.02	.01
☐ 302	Greg Gross	.05	.02	.01
☐ 303	Curt Wardle	.05	.02	.01
☐ 304	Mike Gallego	.10	.05	.01
☐ 305	Phil Bradley	.05	.02	.01
☐ 306	Padres Leaders Terry Kennedy	.08	.04	.01
☐ 307	Dave Sax	.05	.02	.01
☐ 308	Ray Fontenot	.05	.02	.01
☐ 309	John Shelby	.05	.02	.01
☐ 310	Greg Minton	.05	.02	.01
☐ 311	Dick Schofield	.05	.02	.01
☐ 312	Tom Filer	.05	.02	.01
☐ 313	Joe DeSa	.05	.02	.01
☐ 314	Frank Pastore	.05	.02	.01
☐ 315	Mookie Wilson	.08	.04	.01
☐ 316	Sammy Khalifa	.05	.02	.01
☐ 317	Ed Romero	.05	.02	.01
☐ 318	Terry Whitfield	.05	.02	.01
☐ 319	Rick Camp	.05	.02	.01
☐ 320	Jim Rice	.10	.05	.01
☐ 321	Earl Weaver MG (Checklist back)	.08	.04	.01
☐ 322	Bob Forsch	.05	.02	.01
☐ 323	Jerry Davis	.05	.02	.01
☐ 324	Dan Schatzeder	.05	.02	.01
☐ 325	Juan Beniquez	.05	.02	.01
☐ 326	Kent Tekulve	.05	.02	.01
☐ 327	Mike Pagliarulo	.05	.02	.01
☐ 328	Pete O'Brien	.05	.02	.01
☐ 329	Kirby Puckett	4.00	1.80	.50
☐ 330	Rick Sutcliffe	.08	.04	.01
☐ 331	Alan Ashby	.05	.02	.01
☐ 332	Darryl Motley	.05	.02	.01
☐ 333	Tom Henke	.35	.16	.04
☐ 334	Ken Oberkfell	.05	.02	.01
☐ 335	Don Sutton	.12	.05	.02
☐ 336	Indians Leaders Andre Thornton	.08	.04	.01
☐ 337	Darnell Coles	.08	.04	.01
☐ 338	Jorge Bell	.25	.11	.03
☐ 339	Bruce Berenyi	.05	.02	.01
☐ 340	Cal Ripken	2.50	1.15	.30
☐ 341	Frank Williams	.05	.02	.01
☐ 342	Gary Redus	.05	.02	.01
☐ 343	Carlos Diaz	.05	.02	.01
☐ 344	Jim Wohlford	.05	.02	.01
☐ 345	Donnie Moore	.05	.02	.01
☐ 346	Bryan Little	.05	.02	.01
☐ 347	Teddy Higuera	.10	.05	.01
☐ 348	Cliff Johnson	.05	.02	.01
☐ 349	Mark Clear	.05	.02	.01

☐ 350 Jack Clark	.08	.04	.01
☐ 351 Chuck Tanner MG (Checklist back)	.08	.04	.01
☐ 352 Harry Spilman	.05	.02	.01
☐ 353 Keith Atherton	.05	.02	.01
☐ 354 Tony Bernazard	.05	.02	.01
☐ 355 Lee Smith	.25	.11	.03
☐ 356 Mickey Hatcher	.05	.02	.01
☐ 357 Ed VandeBerg	.05	.02	.01
☐ 358 Rick Dempsey	.05	.02	.01
☐ 359 Mike LaCoss	.05	.02	.01
☐ 360 Lloyd Moseby	.05	.02	.01
☐ 361 Shane Rawley	.05	.02	.01
☐ 362 Tom Paciorek	.08	.04	.01
☐ 363 Terry Forster	.05	.02	.01
☐ 364 Reid Nichols	.05	.02	.01
☐ 365 Mike Flanagan	.05	.02	.01
☐ 366 Reds Leaders Dave Concepcion	.08	.04	.01
☐ 367 Aurelio Lopez	.05	.02	.01
☐ 368 Greg Brock	.05	.02	.01
☐ 369 Al Holland	.05	.02	.01
☐ 370 Vince Coleman	.90	.40	.11
☐ 371 Bill Stein	.05	.02	.01
☐ 372 Ben Oglivie	.05	.02	.01
☐ 373 Urbano Lugo	.05	.02	.01
☐ 374 Terry Francona	.05	.02	.01
☐ 375 Rich Gedman	.05	.02	.01
☐ 376 Bill Dawley	.05	.02	.01
☐ 377 Joe Carter	1.00	.45	.13
☐ 378 Bruce Bochte	.05	.02	.01
☐ 379 Bobby Meacham	.05	.02	.01
☐ 380 LaMarr Hoyt	.05	.02	.01
☐ 381 Ray Miller MG (Checklist back)	.08	.04	.01
☐ 382 Ivan Calderon	.50	.23	.06
☐ 383 Chris Brown	.05	.02	.01
☐ 384 Steve Trout	.05	.02	.01
☐ 385 Cecil Cooper	.08	.04	.01
☐ 386 Cecil Fielder	6.50	2.90	.80
☐ 387 Steve Kemp	.05	.02	.01
☐ 388 Dickie Noles	.05	.02	.01
☐ 389 Glenn Davis	.40	.18	.05
☐ 390 Tom Seaver	.40	.18	.05
☐ 391 Julio Franco	.15	.07	.02
☐ 392 John Russell	.05	.02	.01
☐ 393 Chris Pittaro	.05	.02	.01
☐ 394 Checklist: 265-396	.10	.01	.00
☐ 395 Scott Garrelts	.05	.02	.01
☐ 396 Red Sox Leaders Dwight Evans	.08	.04	.01
☐ 397 Steve Buechele	.40	.18	.05
☐ 398 Earnie Riles	.05	.02	.01
☐ 399 Bill Swift	.15	.07	.02
☐ 400 Rod Carew	.45	.20	.06
☐ 401 Turn Back 5 Years Fernando Valenzuela '81	.10	.05	.01
☐ 402 Turn Back 10 Years Tom Seaver '76	.20	.09	.03
☐ 403 Turn Back 15 Years Willie Mays '71	.15	.07	.02
☐ 404 Turn Back 20 Years Frank Robinson '66	.12	.05	.02
☐ 405 Turn Back 25 Years Roger Maris '61	.15	.07	.02
☐ 406 Scott Sanderson	.05	.02	.01
☐ 407 Sal Butera	.05	.02	.01
☐ 408 Dave Smith	.05	.02	.01
☐ 409 Paul Runge	.05	.02	.01
☐ 410 Dave Kingman	.08	.04	.01
☐ 411 Sparky Anderson MG (Checklist back)	.08	.04	.01
☐ 412 Jim Clancy	.05	.02	.01
☐ 413 Tim Flannery	.05	.02	.01
☐ 414 Tom Gorman	.05	.02	.01
☐ 415 Hal McRae	.08	.04	.01
☐ 416 Dennis Martinez	.08	.04	.01
☐ 417 R.J. Reynolds	.05	.02	.01
☐ 418 Alan Knicely	.05	.02	.01
☐ 419 Frank Wills	.05	.02	.01
☐ 420 Von Hayes	.05	.02	.01
☐ 421 David Palmer	.05	.02	.01
☐ 422 Mike Jorgensen	.05	.02	.01
☐ 423 Dan Spillner	.05	.02	.01
☐ 424 Rick Miller	.05	.02	.01
☐ 425 Larry McWilliams	.05	.02	.01
☐ 426 Brewers Leaders Charlie Moore	.08	.04	.01
☐ 427 Joe Cowley	.05	.02	.01
☐ 428 Max Venable	.05	.02	.01
☐ 429 Greg Booker	.05	.02	.01
☐ 430 Kent Hrbek	.12	.05	.02
☐ 431 George Frazier	.05	.02	.01
☐ 432 Mark Bailey	.05	.02	.01
☐ 433 Chris Codiroli	.05	.02	.01
☐ 434 Curt Wilkerson	.05	.02	.01
☐ 435 Bill Caudill	.05	.02	.01
☐ 436 Doug Flynn	.05	.02	.01
☐ 437 Rick Mahler	.05	.02	.01
☐ 438 Clint Hurdle	.05	.02	.01
☐ 439 Rick Honeycutt	.05	.02	.01
☐ 440 Alvin Davis	.05	.02	.01
☐ 441 Whitey Herzog MG (Checklist back)	.08	.04	.01
☐ 442 Ron Robinson	.05	.02	.01
☐ 443 Bill Buckner	.08	.04	.01
☐ 444 Alex Trevino	.05	.02	.01
☐ 445 Bert Blyleven	.10	.05	.01
☐ 446 Lenn Sakata	.05	.02	.01
☐ 447 Jerry Don Gleaton	.05	.02	.01
☐ 448 Herm Winningham	.10	.05	.01
☐ 449 Rod Scurry	.05	.02	.01
☐ 450 Graig Nettles	.08	.04	.01
☐ 451 Mark Brown	.05	.02	.01
☐ 452 Bob Clark	.05	.02	.01
☐ 453 Steve Jeltz	.05	.02	.01
☐ 454 Burt Hooton	.05	.02	.01
☐ 455 Willie Randolph	.08	.04	.01
☐ 456 Braves Leaders Dale Murphy	.10	.05	.01
☐ 457 Mickey Tettleton	1.00	.45	.13
☐ 458 Kevin Bass	.05	.02	.01
☐ 459 Luis Leal	.05	.02	.01
☐ 460 Leon Durham	.05	.02	.01
☐ 461 Walt Terrell	.05	.02	.01
☐ 462 Domingo Ramos	.05	.02	.01
☐ 463 Jim Gott	.05	.02	.01
☐ 464 Ruppert Jones	.05	.02	.01
☐ 465 Jesse Orosco	.05	.02	.01
☐ 466 Tom Foley	.05	.02	.01
☐ 467 Bob James	.05	.02	.01
☐ 468 Mike Scioscia	.05	.02	.01
☐ 469 Storm Davis	.05	.02	.01
☐ 470 Bill Madlock	.08	.04	.01
☐ 471 Bobby Cox MG (Checklist back)	.08	.04	.01
☐ 472 Joe Hesketh	.08	.04	.01
☐ 473 Mark Brouhard	.05	.02	.01
☐ 474 John Tudor	.08	.04	.01
☐ 475 Juan Samuel	.08	.04	.01
☐ 476 Ron Mathis	.05	.02	.01
☐ 477 Mike Easler	.05	.02	.01
☐ 478 Andy Hawkins	.05	.02	.01
☐ 479 Bob Melvin	.05	.02	.01
☐ 480 Oddibe McDowell	.05	.02	.01
☐ 481 Scott Bradley	.05	.02	.01
☐ 482 Rick Lysander	.05	.02	.01
☐ 483 George Vukovich	.05	.02	.01
☐ 484 Donnie Hill	.05	.02	.01
☐ 485 Gary Matthews	.05	.02	.01
☐ 486 Angels Leaders Bobby Grich	.05	.02	.01
☐ 487 Bret Saberhagen	.40	.18	.05
☐ 488 Lou Thornton	.05	.02	.01
☐ 489 Jim Winn	.05	.02	.01
☐ 490 Jeff Leonard	.05	.02	.01
☐ 491 Pascual Perez	.05	.02	.01
☐ 492 Kelvin Chapman	.05	.02	.01
☐ 493 Gene Nelson	.05	.02	.01
☐ 494 Gary Roenicke	.05	.02	.01
☐ 495 Mark Langston	.20	.09	.03
☐ 496 Jay Johnstone	.08	.04	.01
☐ 497 John Stuper	.05	.02	.01
☐ 498 Tito Landrum	.05	.02	.01
☐ 499 Bob L. Gibson	.05	.02	.01
☐ 500 Rickey Henderson	1.00	.45	.13
☐ 501 Dave Johnson MG (Checklist back)	.08	.04	.01
☐ 502 Glen Cook	.05	.02	.01
☐ 503 Mike Fitzgerald	.05	.02	.01
☐ 504 Denny Walling	.05	.02	.01
☐ 505 Jerry Koosman	.08	.04	.01
☐ 506 Bill Russell	.08	.04	.01
☐ 507 Steve Ontiveros	.05	.02	.01
☐ 508 Alan Wiggins	.05	.02	.01
☐ 509 Ernie Camacho	.05	.02	.01
☐ 510 Wade Boggs	1.00	.45	.13
☐ 511 Ed Nunez	.05	.02	.01
☐ 512 Thad Bosley	.05	.02	.01
☐ 513 Ron Washington	.05	.02	.01
☐ 514 Mike Jones	.05	.02	.01
☐ 515 Darrell Evans	.08	.04	.01
☐ 516 Giants Leaders Greg Minton	.08	.04	.01
☐ 517 Milt Thompson	.10	.05	.01
☐ 518 Buck Martinez	.05	.02	.01

Card			
☐ 519 Danny Darwin	.05	.02	.01
☐ 520 Keith Hernandez	.10	.05	.01
☐ 521 Nate Snell	.05	.02	.01
☐ 522 Bob Bailor	.05	.02	.01
☐ 523 Joe Price	.05	.02	.01
☐ 524 Darrell Miller	.05	.02	.01
☐ 525 Marvell Wynne	.05	.02	.01
☐ 526 Charlie Lea	.05	.02	.01
☐ 527 Checklist: 397-528	.10	.01	.00
☐ 528 Terry Pendleton	.60	.25	.08
☐ 529 Marc Sullivan	.05	.02	.01
☐ 530 Rich Gossage	.10	.05	.01
☐ 531 Tony LaRussa MG (Checklist back)	.08	.04	.01
☐ 532 Don Carman	.05	.02	.01
☐ 533 Billy Sample	.05	.02	.01
☐ 534 Jeff Calhoun	.05	.02	.01
☐ 535 Toby Harrah	.05	.02	.01
☐ 536 Jose Rijo	.25	.11	.03
☐ 537 Mark Salas	.05	.02	.01
☐ 538 Dennis Eckersley	.30	.14	.04
☐ 539 Glenn Hubbard	.05	.02	.01
☐ 540 Dan Petry	.05	.02	.01
☐ 541 Jorge Orta	.05	.02	.01
☐ 542 Don Schulze	.05	.02	.01
☐ 543 Jerry Narron	.05	.02	.01
☐ 544 Eddie Milner	.05	.02	.01
☐ 545 Jimmy Key	.20	.09	.03
☐ 546 Mariners Leaders Dave Henderson	.08	.04	.01
☐ 547 Roger McDowell	.12	.05	.02
☐ 548 Mike Young	.05	.02	.01
☐ 549 Bob Welch	.10	.05	.01
☐ 550 Tom Herr	.05	.02	.01
☐ 551 Dave LaPoint	.05	.02	.01
☐ 552 Marc Hill	.05	.02	.01
☐ 553 Jim Morrison	.05	.02	.01
☐ 554 Paul Householder	.05	.02	.01
☐ 555 Hubie Brooks	.05	.02	.01
☐ 556 John Denny	.05	.02	.01
☐ 557 Gerald Perry	.05	.02	.01
☐ 558 Tim Stoddard	.05	.02	.01
☐ 559 Tommy Dunbar	.05	.02	.01
☐ 560 Dave Righetti	.08	.04	.01
☐ 561 Bob Lillis MG (Checklist back)	.08	.04	.01
☐ 562 Joe Beckwith	.05	.02	.01
☐ 563 Alejandro Sanchez	.05	.02	.01
☐ 564 Warren Brusstar	.05	.02	.01
☐ 565 Tom Brunansky	.08	.04	.01
☐ 566 Alfredo Griffin	.05	.02	.01
☐ 567 Jeff Barkley	.05	.02	.01
☐ 568 Donnie Scott	.05	.02	.01
☐ 569 Jim Acker	.05	.02	.01
☐ 570 Rusty Staub	.08	.04	.01
☐ 571 Mike Jeffcoat	.05	.02	.01
☐ 572 Paul Zuvella	.05	.02	.01
☐ 573 Tom Hume	.05	.02	.01
☐ 574 Ron Kittle	.05	.02	.01
☐ 575 Mike Boddicker	.05	.02	.01
☐ 576 Expos Leaders Andre Dawson	.15	.07	.02
☐ 577 Jerry Reuss	.05	.02	.01
☐ 578 Lee Mazzilli	.05	.02	.01
☐ 579 Jim Slaton	.05	.02	.01
☐ 580 Willie McGee	.10	.05	.01
☐ 581 Bruce Hurst	.08	.04	.01
☐ 582 Jim Gantner	.05	.02	.01
☐ 583 Al Bumbry	.05	.02	.01
☐ 584 Brian Fisher	.05	.02	.01
☐ 585 Garry Maddox	.05	.02	.01
☐ 586 Greg Harris	.05	.02	.01
☐ 587 Rafael Santana	.05	.02	.01
☐ 588 Steve Lake	.05	.02	.01
☐ 589 Sid Bream	.08	.04	.01
☐ 590 Bob Knepper	.05	.02	.01
☐ 591 Jackie Moore MG (Checklist back)	.08	.04	.01
☐ 592 Frank Tanana	.08	.04	.01
☐ 593 Jesse Barfield	.08	.04	.01
☐ 594 Chris Bando	.05	.02	.01
☐ 595 Dave Parker	.12	.05	.02
☐ 596 Onix Concepcion	.05	.02	.01
☐ 597 Sammy Stewart	.05	.02	.01
☐ 598 Jim Presley	.05	.02	.01
☐ 599 Rick Aguilera	.75	.35	.09
☐ 600 Dale Murphy	.25	.11	.03
☐ 601 Gary Lucas	.05	.02	.01
☐ 602 Mariano Duncan	.25	.11	.03
☐ 603 Bill Laskey	.05	.02	.01
☐ 604 Gary Pettis	.05	.02	.01
☐ 605 Dennis Boyd	.05	.02	.01
☐ 606 Royals Leaders Hal McRae	.08	.04	.01
☐ 607 Ken Dayley	.05	.02	.01
☐ 608 Bruce Bochy	.05	.02	.01
☐ 609 Barbaro Garbey	.05	.02	.01
☐ 610 Ron Guidry	.08	.04	.01
☐ 611 Gary Woods	.05	.02	.01
☐ 612 Richard Dotson	.05	.02	.01
☐ 613 Roy Smalley	.05	.02	.01
☐ 614 Rick Waits	.05	.02	.01
☐ 615 Johnny Ray	.05	.02	.01
☐ 616 Glenn Brummer	.05	.02	.01
☐ 617 Lonnie Smith	.05	.02	.01
☐ 618 Jim Pankovits	.05	.02	.01
☐ 619 Danny Heep	.05	.02	.01
☐ 620 Bruce Sutter	.08	.04	.01
☐ 621 John Felske MG (Checklist back)	.08	.04	.01
☐ 622 Gary Lavelle	.05	.02	.01
☐ 623 Floyd Rayford	.05	.02	.01
☐ 624 Steve McCatty	.05	.02	.01
☐ 625 Bob Brenly	.05	.02	.01
☐ 626 Roy Thomas	.05	.02	.01
☐ 627 Ron Oester	.05	.02	.01
☐ 628 Kirk McCaskill	.15	.07	.02
☐ 629 Mitch Webster	.05	.02	.01
☐ 630 Fernando Valenzuela	.08	.04	.01
☐ 631 Steve Braun	.05	.02	.01
☐ 632 Dave Von Ohlen	.05	.02	.01
☐ 633 Jackie Gutierrez	.05	.02	.01
☐ 634 Roy Lee Jackson	.05	.02	.01
☐ 635 Jason Thompson	.05	.02	.01
☐ 636 Cubs Leaders Lee Smith	.15	.07	.02
☐ 637 Rudy Law	.05	.02	.01
☐ 638 John Butcher	.05	.02	.01
☐ 639 Bo Diaz	.05	.02	.01
☐ 640 Jose Cruz	.05	.02	.01
☐ 641 Wayne Tolleson	.05	.02	.01
☐ 642 Ray Searage	.05	.02	.01
☐ 643 Tom Brookens	.05	.02	.01
☐ 644 Mark Gubicza	.08	.04	.01
☐ 645 Dusty Baker	.08	.04	.01
☐ 646 Mike Moore	.10	.05	.01
☐ 647 Mel Hall	.10	.05	.01
☐ 648 Steve Bedrosian	.05	.02	.01
☐ 649 Ronn Reynolds	.05	.02	.01
☐ 650 Dave Stieb	.08	.04	.01
☐ 651 Billy Martin MG (Checklist back)	.10	.05	.01
☐ 652 Tom Browning	.12	.05	.02
☐ 653 Jim Dwyer	.05	.02	.01
☐ 654 Ken Howell	.05	.02	.01
☐ 655 Manny Trillo	.05	.02	.01
☐ 656 Brian Harper	.12	.05	.02
☐ 657 Juan Agosto	.05	.02	.01
☐ 658 Rob Wilfong	.05	.02	.01
☐ 659 Checklist: 529-660	.10	.01	.00
☐ 660 Steve Garvey	.15	.07	.02
☐ 661 Roger Clemens	4.50	2.00	.55
☐ 662 Bill Schroeder	.05	.02	.01
☐ 663 Neil Allen	.05	.02	.01
☐ 664 Tim Corcoran	.05	.02	.01
☐ 665 Alejandro Pena	.05	.02	.01
☐ 666 Rangers Leaders Charlie Hough	.08	.04	.01
☐ 667 Tim Teufel	.05	.02	.01
☐ 668 Cecilio Guante	.05	.02	.01
☐ 669 Ron Cey	.08	.04	.01
☐ 670 Willie Hernandez	.05	.02	.01
☐ 671 Lynn Jones	.05	.02	.01
☐ 672 Rob Picciolo	.05	.02	.01
☐ 673 Ernie Whitt	.05	.02	.01
☐ 674 Pat Tabler	.05	.02	.01
☐ 675 Claudell Washington	.05	.02	.01
☐ 676 Matt Young	.05	.02	.01
☐ 677 Nick Esasky	.05	.02	.01
☐ 678 Dan Gladden	.05	.02	.01
☐ 679 Britt Burns	.05	.02	.01
☐ 680 George Foster	.05	.02	.01
☐ 681 Dick Williams MG (Checklist back)	.08	.04	.01
☐ 682 Junior Ortiz	.05	.02	.01
☐ 683 Andy Van Slyke	.30	.14	.04
☐ 684 Bob McClure	.05	.02	.01
☐ 685 Tim Wallach	.08	.04	.01
☐ 686 Jeff Stone	.05	.02	.01
☐ 687 Mike Trujillo	.05	.02	.01
☐ 688 Larry Herndon	.05	.02	.01
☐ 689 Dave Stewart	.12	.05	.02
☐ 690 Ryne Sandberg UER (No Topps logo on front)	2.00	.90	.25
☐ 691 Mike Madden	.05	.02	.01
☐ 692 Dale Berra	.05	.02	.01

☐ 693 Tom Tellmann .05 .02 .01
☐ 694 Garth Iorg .05 .02 .01
☐ 695 Mike Smithson .05 .02 .01
☐ 696 Dodgers Leaders .08 .04 .01
Bill Russell
☐ 697 Bud Black .05 .02 .01
☐ 698 Brad Komminsk .05 .02 .01
☐ 699 Pat Corrales MG .08 .04 .01
(Checklist back)
☐ 700 Reggie Jackson .40 .18 .05
☐ 701 Keith Hernandez AS .08 .04 .01
☐ 702 Tom Herr AS .08 .04 .01
☐ 703 Tim Wallach AS .08 .04 .01
☐ 704 Ozzie Smith AS .20 .09 .03
☐ 705 Dale Murphy AS .12 .05 .02
☐ 706 Pedro Guerrero AS .08 .04 .01
☐ 707 Willie McGee AS .08 .04 .01
☐ 708 Gary Carter AS .10 .05 .01
☐ 709 Dwight Gooden AS .20 .09 .03
☐ 710 John Tudor AS .08 .04 .01
☐ 711 Jeff Reardon AS .15 .07 .02
☐ 712 Don Mattingly AS .40 .18 .05
☐ 713 Damaso Garcia AS .08 .04 .01
☐ 714 George Brett AS .35 .16 .04
☐ 715 Cal Ripken AS 1.00 .45 .13
☐ 716 Rickey Henderson AS .40 .18 .05
☐ 717 Dave Winfield AS .30 .14 .04
☐ 718 George Bell AS .15 .07 .02
☐ 719 Carlton Fisk AS .20 .09 .03
☐ 720 Bret Saberhagen AS .15 .07 .02
☐ 721 Ron Guidry AS .08 .04 .01
☐ 722 Dan Quisenberry AS .08 .04 .01
☐ 723 Marty Bystrom .05 .02 .01
☐ 724 Tim Hulett .05 .02 .01
☐ 725 Mario Soto .05 .02 .01
☐ 726 Orioles Leaders .08 .04 .01
Rick Dempsey
☐ 727 David Green .05 .02 .01
☐ 728 Mike Marshall .05 .02 .01
☐ 729 Jim Beattie .05 .02 .01
☐ 730 Ozzie Smith .45 .20 .06
☐ 731 Don Robinson .05 .02 .01
☐ 732 Floyd Youmans .05 .02 .01
☐ 733 Ron Romanick .05 .02 .01
☐ 734 Marty Barrett .05 .02 .01
☐ 735 Dave Dravecky .08 .04 .01
☐ 736 Glenn Wilson .05 .02 .01
☐ 737 Pete Vuckovich .05 .02 .01
☐ 738 Andre Robertson .05 .02 .01
☐ 739 Dave Rozema .05 .02 .01
☐ 740 Lance Parrish .08 .04 .01
☐ 741 Pete Rose MG .40 .18 .05
(Checklist back)
☐ 742 Frank Viola .15 .07 .02
☐ 743 Pat Sheridan .05 .02 .01
☐ 744 Lary Sorensen .05 .02 .01
☐ 745 Willie Upshaw .05 .02 .01
☐ 746 Denny Gonzalez .05 .02 .01
☐ 747 Rick Cerone .05 .02 .01
☐ 748 Steve Henderson .05 .02 .01
☐ 749 Ed Jurak .05 .02 .01
☐ 750 Gorman Thomas .05 .02 .01
☐ 751 Howard Johnson .35 .16 .04
☐ 752 Mike Krukow .05 .02 .01
☐ 753 Dan Ford .05 .02 .01
☐ 754 Pat Clements .05 .02 .01
☐ 755 Harold Baines .12 .05 .02
☐ 756 Pirates Leaders .08 .04 .01
Rick Rhoden
☐ 757 Darrell Porter .05 .02 .01
☐ 758 Dave Anderson .05 .02 .01
☐ 759 Moose Haas .05 .02 .01
☐ 760 Andre Dawson .50 .23 .06
☐ 761 Don Slaught .05 .02 .01
☐ 762 Eric Show .05 .02 .01
☐ 763 Terry Puhl .05 .02 .01
☐ 764 Kevin Gross .05 .02 .01
☐ 765 Don Baylor .08 .04 .01
☐ 766 Rick Langford .05 .02 .01
☐ 767 Jody Davis .05 .02 .01
☐ 768 Vern Ruhle .05 .02 .01
☐ 769 Harold Reynolds .25 .11 .03
☐ 770 Vida Blue .08 .04 .01
☐ 771 John McNamara MG .08 .04 .01
(Checklist back)
☐ 772 Brian Downing .08 .04 .01
☐ 773 Greg Pryor .05 .02 .01
☐ 774 Terry Leach .05 .02 .01
☐ 775 Al Oliver .08 .04 .01
☐ 776 Gene Garber .05 .02 .01
☐ 777 Wayne Krenchicki .05 .02 .01
☐ 778 Jerry Hairston .05 .02 .01
☐ 779 Rick Reuschel .08 .04 .01
☐ 780 Robin Yount .75 .35 .09
☐ 781 Joe Nolan .05 .02 .01
☐ 782 Ken Landreaux .05 .02 .01
☐ 783 Ricky Horton .05 .02 .01
☐ 784 Alan Bannister .05 .02 .01
☐ 785 Bob Stanley .05 .02 .01
☐ 786 Twins Leaders .08 .04 .01
Mickey Hatcher
☐ 787 Vance Law .05 .02 .01
☐ 788 Marty Castillo .05 .02 .01
☐ 789 Kurt Bevacqua .05 .02 .01
☐ 790 Phil Niekro .12 .05 .02
☐ 791 Checklist: 661-792 .10 .01 .00
☐ 792 Charles Hudson .08 .02 .01

1986 Topps All-Star Glossy 22

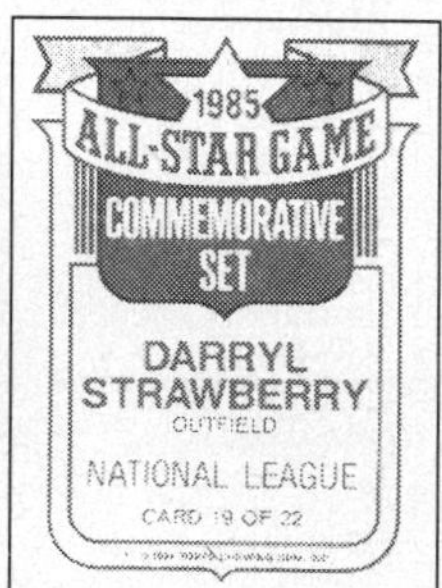

This 22-card set was distributed as an insert, one card per rak pack. The players featured are the starting lineups of the 1985 All-Star Game played in Minnesota. Cards are very colorful with a high gloss finish and are standard-size, 2 1/2" by 3 1/2". Cards are numbered on the back.

	MT	EX-MT	VG
COMPLETE SET (22)	3.50	1.55	.45
COMMON PLAYER (1-22)	.10	.05	.01
☐ 1 Sparky Anderson MG	.10	.05	.01
☐ 2 Eddie Murray	.40	.18	.05
☐ 3 Lou Whitaker	.20	.09	.03
☐ 4 George Brett	.50	.23	.06
☐ 5 Cal Ripken	.75	.35	.09
☐ 6 Jim Rice	.30	.14	.04
☐ 7 Rickey Henderson	.60	.25	.08
☐ 8 Dave Winfield	.50	.23	.06
☐ 9 Carlton Fisk	.50	.23	.06
☐ 10 Jack Morris	.30	.14	.04
☐ 11 AL Team Photo	.10	.05	.01
☐ 12 Dick Williams MG	.10	.05	.01
☐ 13 Steve Garvey	.25	.11	.03
☐ 14 Tom Herr	.10	.05	.01
☐ 15 Graig Nettles	.20	.09	.03
☐ 16 Ozzie Smith	.40	.18	.05
☐ 17 Tony Gwynn	.50	.23	.06
☐ 18 Dale Murphy	.40	.18	.05
☐ 19 Darryl Strawberry	.50	.23	.06
☐ 20 Terry Kennedy	.10	.05	.01
☐ 21 LaMarr Hoyt	.10	.05	.01
☐ 22 NL Team Photo	.10	.05	.01

1986 Topps Glossy Send-In 60

This 60-card glossy set was produced by Topps and distributed ten cards at a time based on the offer found on the wax packs. Cards measure the standard 2 1/2" by 3 1/2". Each series of ten cards was available by sending in 1.00 plus six "special offer" cards inserted one per wax pack. The card backs are printed in red and blue on white card stock. The card fronts feature a white border and a green frame surrounding a full-color photo of the player.

	MT	EX-MT	VG
COMPLETE SET (60)	12.50	5.75	1.55
COMMON PLAYER (1-60)	.20	.09	.03
☐ 1 Oddibe McDowell	.20	.09	.03
☐ 2 Reggie Jackson	.75	.35	.09
☐ 3 Fernando Valenzuela	.25	.11	.03
☐ 4 Jack Clark	.25	.11	.03
☐ 5 Rickey Henderson	.75	.35	.09
☐ 6 Steve Balboni	.20	.09	.03
☐ 7 Keith Hernandez	.30	.14	.04
☐ 8 Lance Parrish	.25	.11	.03
☐ 9 Willie McGee	.30	.14	.04
☐ 10 Chris Brown	.20	.09	.03
☐ 11 Darryl Strawberry	.60	.25	.08
☐ 12 Ron Guidry	.25	.11	.03
☐ 13 Dave Parker	.30	.14	.04
☐ 14 Cal Ripken	1.00	.45	.13
☐ 15 Tim Raines	.40	.18	.05
☐ 16 Rod Carew	.50	.23	.06
☐ 17 Mike Schmidt	1.00	.45	.13
☐ 18 George Brett	.75	.35	.09
☐ 19 Joe Hesketh	.20	.09	.03
☐ 20 Dan Pasqua	.20	.09	.03
☐ 21 Vince Coleman	.40	.18	.05
☐ 22 Tom Seaver	.50	.23	.06
☐ 23 Gary Carter	.40	.18	.05
☐ 24 Orel Hershiser	.35	.16	.04
☐ 25 Pedro Guerrero	.30	.14	.04
☐ 26 Wade Boggs	.75	.35	.09
☐ 27 Bret Saberhagen	.35	.16	.04
☐ 28 Carlton Fisk	.50	.23	.06
☐ 29 Kirk Gibson	.25	.11	.03
☐ 30 Brian Fisher	.20	.09	.03
☐ 31 Don Mattingly	1.00	.45	.13
☐ 32 Tom Herr	.20	.09	.03
☐ 33 Eddie Murray	.50	.23	.06
☐ 34 Ryne Sandberg	1.00	.45	.13
☐ 35 Dan Quisenberry	.30	.14	.04
☐ 36 Jim Rice	.30	.14	.04
☐ 37 Dale Murphy	.40	.18	.05
☐ 38 Steve Garvey	.30	.14	.04
☐ 39 Roger McDowell	.25	.11	.03
☐ 40 Earnie Riles	.20	.09	.03
☐ 41 Dwight Gooden	.40	.18	.05
☐ 42 Dave Winfield	.50	.23	.06
☐ 43 Dave Stieb	.20	.09	.03
☐ 44 Bob Horner	.20	.09	.03
☐ 45 Nolan Ryan	1.50	.65	.19
☐ 46 Ozzie Smith	.50	.23	.06
☐ 47 George Bell	.30	.14	.04
☐ 48 Gorman Thomas	.20	.09	.03
☐ 49 Tom Browning	.30	.14	.04
☐ 50 Larry Sheets	.20	.09	.03
☐ 51 Pete Rose	.75	.35	.09
☐ 52 Brett Butler	.30	.14	.04
☐ 53 John Tudor	.20	.09	.03
☐ 54 Phil Bradley	.20	.09	.03
☐ 55 Jeff Reardon	.40	.18	.05
☐ 56 Rich Gossage	.30	.14	.04
☐ 57 Tony Gwynn	.60	.25	.08
☐ 58 Ozzie Guillen	.35	.16	.04
☐ 59 Glenn Davis	.35	.16	.04
☐ 60 Darrell Evans	.20	.09	.03

1986 Topps Mini Leaders

The 1986 Topps Mini set of Major League Leaders features 66 cards of leaders of the various statistical categories for the 1985 season. The cards are numbered on the back and measure approximately 2 1/8" by 2 15/16". They are very similar in design to the Team Leader "Dean" cards in the 1986 Topps regular issue. The order of the set numbering is alphabetical by player's name as well as alphabetical by team city name within league.

	MT	EX-MT	VG
COMPLETE SET (66)	7.00	3.10	.85
COMMON PLAYER (1-66)	.05	.02	.01
☐ 1 Eddie Murray	.35	.16	.04
☐ 2 Cal Ripken	.75	.35	.09
☐ 3 Wade Boggs	.50	.23	.06
☐ 4 Dennis Boyd	.05	.02	.01
☐ 5 Dwight Evans	.10	.05	.01
☐ 6 Bruce Hurst	.05	.02	.01
☐ 7 Gary Pettis	.05	.02	.01
☐ 8 Harold Baines	.10	.05	.01
☐ 9 Floyd Bannister	.05	.02	.01
☐ 10 Britt Burns	.05	.02	.01
☐ 11 Carlton Fisk	.35	.16	.04
☐ 12 Brett Butler	.10	.05	.01
☐ 13 Darrell Evans	.05	.02	.01
☐ 14 Jack Morris	.15	.07	.02
☐ 15 Lance Parrish	.10	.05	.01
☐ 16 Walt Terrell	.05	.02	.01
☐ 17 Steve Balboni	.05	.02	.01
☐ 18 George Brett	.50	.23	.06
☐ 19 Charlie Leibrandt	.10	.05	.01
☐ 20 Bret Saberhagen	.20	.09	.03
☐ 21 Lonnie Smith	.05	.02	.01
☐ 22 Willie Wilson	.10	.05	.01
☐ 23 Bert Blyleven	.10	.05	.01
☐ 24 Mike Smithson	.05	.02	.01
☐ 25 Frank Viola	.15	.07	.02
☐ 26 Ron Guidry	.10	.05	.01
☐ 27 Rickey Henderson	.50	.23	.06
☐ 28 Don Mattingly	.60	.25	.08
☐ 29 Dave Winfield	.40	.18	.05
☐ 30 Mike Moore	.10	.05	.01
☐ 31 Gorman Thomas	.05	.02	.01
☐ 32 Toby Harrah	.05	.02	.01
☐ 33 Charlie Hough	.05	.02	.01
☐ 34 Doyle Alexander	.05	.02	.01
☐ 35 Jimmy Key	.10	.05	.01
☐ 36 Dave Stieb	.10	.05	.01
☐ 37 Dale Murphy	.20	.09	.03
☐ 38 Keith Moreland	.05	.02	.01
☐ 39 Ryne Sandberg	.75	.35	.09
☐ 40 Tom Browning	.05	.02	.01
☐ 41 Dave Parker	.10	.05	.01
☐ 42 Mario Soto	.05	.02	.01
☐ 43 Nolan Ryan	1.00	.45	.13
☐ 44 Pedro Guerrero	.10	.05	.01
☐ 45 Orel Hershiser	.15	.07	.02
☐ 46 Mike Scioscia	.05	.02	.01
☐ 47 Fernando Valenzuela	.10	.05	.01
☐ 48 Bob Welch	.10	.05	.01
☐ 49 Tim Raines	.15	.07	.02
☐ 50 Gary Carter	.25	.11	.03
☐ 51 Sid Fernandez	.10	.05	.01
☐ 52 Dwight Gooden	.25	.11	.03
☐ 53 Keith Hernandez	.10	.05	.01
☐ 54 Juan Samuel	.05	.02	.01

☐ 55 Mike Schmidt	.75	.35	.09
☐ 56 Glenn Wilson	.05	.02	.01
☐ 57 Rick Reuschel	.05	.02	.01
☐ 58 Joaquin Andujar	.05	.02	.01
☐ 59 Jack Clark	.10	.05	.01
☐ 60 Vince Coleman	.25	.11	.03
☐ 61 Danny Cox	.05	.02	.01
☐ 62 Tom Herr	.05	.02	.01
☐ 63 Willie McGee	.10	.05	.01
☐ 64 John Tudor	.05	.02	.01
☐ 65 Tony Gwynn	.45	.20	.06
☐ 66 Checklist Card	.10	.05	.01

1986 Topps Traded

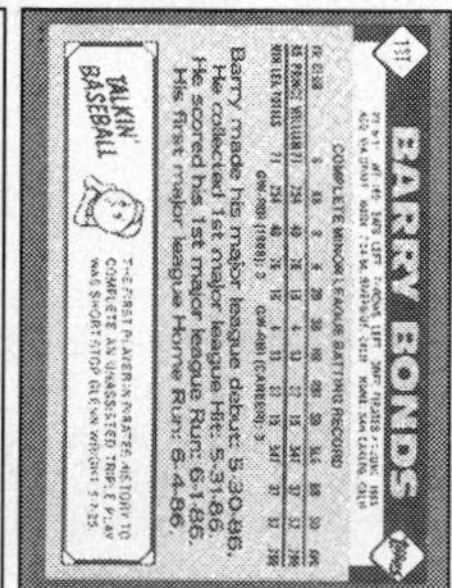

This 132-card Traded or extended set was distributed by Topps to dealers in a special red and white box as a complete set. The card fronts are identical in style to the Topps regular issue and are also 2 1/2" by 3 1/2". The backs are printed in red and black on white card stock. Cards are numbered (with a T suffix) alphabetically according to the name of the player. The key (extended) Rookie Cards in this set are Barry Bonds, Bobby Bonilla, Jose Canseco, Will Clark, Bo Jackson, and Kevin Mitchell. Topps also produced a specially boxed "glossy" edition frequently referred to as the Topps Traded Tiffany set. There were supposedly only 5,000 sets of the Tiffany cards produced; they were marketed to hobby dealers. The checklist of cards is identical to that of the normal non-glossy cards. There are two primary distinguishing features of the Tiffany cards, white card stock reverses and high gloss obverses. These Tiffany cards are valued approximately from five to ten times the values listed below.

	MT	EX-MT	VG
COMPLETE SET (132)	24.00	11.00	3.00
COMMON PLAYER (1T-132T)	.06	.03	.01
☐ 1T Andy Allanson	.06	.03	.01
☐ 2T Neil Allen	.06	.03	.01
☐ 3T Joaquin Andujar	.06	.03	.01
☐ 4T Paul Assenmacher	.06	.03	.01
☐ 5T Scott Bailes	.06	.03	.01
☐ 6T Don Baylor	.10	.04	.01
☐ 7T Steve Bedrosian	.06	.03	.01
☐ 8T Juan Beniquez	.06	.03	.01
☐ 9T Juan Berenguer	.06	.03	.01
☐ 10T Mike Bielecki	.15	.07	.02
☐ 11T Barry Bonds	6.00	2.70	.75
☐ 12T Bobby Bonilla	2.50	1.15	.30
☐ 13T Juan Bonilla	.06	.03	.01
☐ 14T Rich Bordi	.06	.03	.01
☐ 15T Steve Boros MG	.06	.03	.01
☐ 16T Rick Burleson	.06	.03	.01
☐ 17T Bill Campbell	.06	.03	.01
☐ 18T Tom Candiotti	.15	.07	.02
☐ 19T John Cangelosi	.06	.03	.01
☐ 20T Jose Canseco	6.00	2.70	.75
☐ 21T Carmen Castillo	.06	.03	.01
☐ 22T Rick Cerone	.06	.03	.01
☐ 23T John Cerutti	.06	.03	.01
☐ 24T Will Clark	6.00	2.70	.75
☐ 25T Mark Clear	.06	.03	.01
☐ 26T Darnell Coles	.06	.03	.01
☐ 27T Dave Collins	.06	.03	.01
☐ 28T Tim Conroy	.06	.03	.01
☐ 29T Joe Cowley	.06	.03	.01
☐ 30T Joel Davis	.06	.03	.01
☐ 31T Rob Deer	.20	.09	.03
☐ 32T John Denny	.06	.03	.01
☐ 33T Mike Easler	.06	.03	.01
☐ 34T Mark Eichhorn	.10	.04	.01
☐ 35T Steve Farr	.10	.04	.01
☐ 36T Scott Fletcher	.06	.03	.01
☐ 37T Terry Forster	.06	.03	.01
☐ 38T Terry Francona	.06	.03	.01
☐ 39T Jim Fregosi MG	.06	.03	.01
☐ 40T Andres Galarraga	.25	.11	.03
☐ 41T Ken Griffey	.10	.04	.01
☐ 42T Bill Gullickson	.10	.04	.01
☐ 43T Jose Guzman	.30	.14	.04
☐ 44T Moose Haas	.06	.03	.01
☐ 45T Billy Hatcher	.10	.04	.01
☐ 46T Mike Heath	.06	.03	.01
☐ 47T Tom Hume	.06	.03	.01
☐ 48T Pete Incaviglia	.25	.11	.03
☐ 49T Dane Iorg	.06	.03	.01
☐ 50T Bo Jackson	2.50	1.15	.30
☐ 51T Wally Joyner	1.00	.45	.13
☐ 52T Charlie Kerfeld	.10	.04	.01
☐ 53T Eric King	.06	.03	.01
☐ 54T Bob Kipper	.06	.03	.01
☐ 55T Wayne Krenchicki	.06	.03	.01
☐ 56T John Kruk	.90	.40	.11
☐ 57T Mike LaCoss	.06	.03	.01
☐ 58T Pete Ladd	.06	.03	.01
☐ 59T Mike Laga	.06	.03	.01
☐ 60T Hal Lanier MG	.06	.03	.01
☐ 61T Dave LaPoint	.06	.03	.01
☐ 62T Rudy Law	.06	.03	.01
☐ 63T Rick Leach	.06	.03	.01
☐ 64T Tim Leary	.06	.03	.01
☐ 65T Dennis Leonard	.06	.03	.01
☐ 66T Jim Leyland MG	.25	.11	.03
☐ 67T Steve Lyons	.06	.03	.01
☐ 68T Mickey Mahler	.06	.03	.01
☐ 69T Candy Maldonado	.10	.04	.01
☐ 70T Roger Mason	.10	.05	.01
☐ 71T Bob McClure	.06	.03	.01
☐ 72T Andy McGaffigan	.06	.03	.01
☐ 73T Gene Michael MG	.06	.03	.01
☐ 74T Kevin Mitchell	1.25	.55	.16
☐ 75T Omar Moreno	.06	.03	.01
☐ 76T Jerry Mumphrey	.06	.03	.01
☐ 77T Phil Niekro	.25	.11	.03
☐ 78T Randy Niemann	.06	.03	.01
☐ 79T Juan Nieves	.06	.03	.01
☐ 80T Otis Nixon	.60	.25	.08
☐ 81T Bob Ojeda	.06	.03	.01
☐ 82T Jose Oquendo	.06	.03	.01
☐ 83T Tom Paciorek	.10	.04	.01
☐ 84T David Palmer	.06	.03	.01
☐ 85T Frank Pastore	.06	.03	.01
☐ 86T Lou Piniella MG	.10	.04	.01
☐ 87T Dan Plesac	.15	.07	.02
☐ 88T Darrell Porter	.06	.03	.01
☐ 89T Rey Quinones	.06	.03	.01
☐ 90T Gary Redus	.06	.03	.01
☐ 91T Bip Roberts	.60	.25	.08
☐ 92T Billy Joe Robidoux	.06	.03	.01
☐ 93T Jeff D. Robinson	.10	.04	.01
☐ 94T Gary Roenicke	.06	.03	.01
☐ 95T Ed Romero	.06	.03	.01
☐ 96T Argenis Salazar	.06	.03	.01
☐ 97T Joe Sambito	.06	.03	.01
☐ 98T Billy Sample	.06	.03	.01
☐ 99T Dave Schmidt	.06	.03	.01
☐ 100T Ken Schrom	.06	.03	.01
☐ 101T Tom Seaver	.50	.23	.06
☐ 102T Ted Simmons	.10	.04	.01
☐ 103T Sammy Stewart	.06	.03	.01
☐ 104T Kurt Stillwell	.15	.07	.02
☐ 105T Franklin Stubbs	.06	.03	.01
☐ 106T Dale Sveum	.06	.03	.01
☐ 107T Chuck Tanner MG	.06	.03	.01
☐ 108T Danny Tartabull	.90	.40	.11
☐ 109T Tim Teufel	.06	.03	.01
☐ 110T Bob Tewksbury	.40	.18	.05
☐ 111T Andres Thomas	.06	.03	.01
☐ 112T Milt Thompson	.10	.04	.01
☐ 113T Robby Thompson	.25	.11	.03
☐ 114T Jay Tibbs	.06	.03	.01
☐ 115T Wayne Tolleson	.06	.03	.01
☐ 116T Alex Trevino	.06	.03	.01
☐ 117T Manny Trillo	.06	.03	.01
☐ 118T Ed VandeBerg	.06	.03	.01

		MT	EX-MT	VG
☐ 119T	Ozzie Virgil	.06	.03	.01
☐ 120T	Bob Walk	.06	.03	.01
☐ 121T	Gene Walter	.06	.03	.01
☐ 122T	Claudell Washington	.06	.03	.01
☐ 123T	Bill Wegman	.25	.11	.03
☐ 124T	Dick Williams MG	.06	.03	.01
☐ 125T	Mitch Williams	.20	.09	.03
☐ 126T	Bobby Witt	.25	.11	.03
☐ 127T	Todd Worrell	.20	.09	.03
☐ 128T	George Wright	.06	.03	.01
☐ 129T	Ricky Wright	.06	.03	.01
☐ 130T	Steve Yeager	.06	.03	.01
☐ 131T	Paul Zuvella	.06	.03	.01
☐ 132T	Checklist 1-132	.10	.01	.00

1986 Topps Wax Box Cards

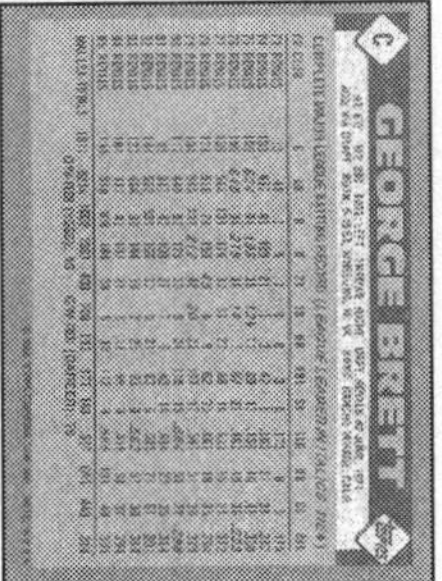

Topps printed cards (each measuring the standard 2 1/2" by 3 1/2") on the bottoms of their wax pack boxes for their regular issue cards; there are four different boxes, each with four cards. These sixteen cards ("numbered" A through P) are listed below; they are not considered an integral part of the regular set but are considered a separate set. The order of the set is alphabetical by player's name. These wax box cards are styled almost exactly like the 1986 Topps regular issue cards. Complete boxes would be worth an additional 25 percent premium over the prices below. The card lettering is sequenced in alphabetical order.

	MT	EX-MT	VG
COMPLETE SET (16)	8.00	3.60	1.00
COMMON PLAYER (A-P)	.15	.07	.02

		MT	EX-MT	VG
☐ A0	George Bell	.25	.11	.03
☐ B0	Wade Boggs	1.00	.45	.13
☐ C0	George Brett	1.00	.45	.13
☐ D0	Vince Coleman	1.00	.45	.13
☐ E0	Carlton Fisk	.75	.35	.09
☐ F0	Dwight Gooden	.75	.35	.09
☐ G0	Pedro Guerrero	.25	.11	.03
☐ H0	Ron Guidry	.25	.11	.03
☐ I0	Reggie Jackson	1.00	.45	.13
☐ J0	Don Mattingly	1.25	.55	.16
☐ K0	Oddibe McDowell	.15	.07	.02
☐ L0	Willie McGee	.25	.11	.03
☐ M0	Dale Murphy	.60	.25	.08
☐ N0	Pete Rose	1.25	.55	.16
☐ O0	Bret Saberhagen	.35	.16	.04
☐ P0	Fernando Valenzuela	.25	.11	.03

1987 Topps

This 792-card set is reminiscent of the 1962 Topps baseball cards with their simulated wood grain borders. The backs are printed in yellow and blue on gray card stock. The manager cards contain a checklist of the respective team's players on the back. Subsets in the set include Record Breakers (1-7), Turn Back the Clock (311-315), and All-Star selections (595-616). The Team Leader cards typically show

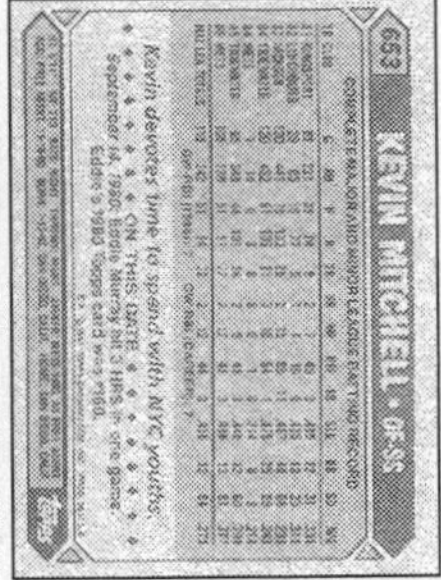

players conferring on the mound inside a white cloud. The wax pack wrapper gives details of "Spring Fever Baseball" where a lucky collector can win a trip for four to Spring Training. The key Rookie Cards in this set are Barry Bonds, Bobby Bonilla, Will Clark, Mike Greenwell, Bo Jackson, Barry Larkin, Dave Magadan, Kevin Mitchell, Rafael Palmiero, and Ruben Sierra. Topps also produced a specially boxed "glossy" edition, frequently referred to as the Topps Tiffany set. This year Topps did not disclose the number of sets they produced or sold. It is apparent from the availability that there were many more sets produced this year compared to the 1984-86 Tiffany sets, perhaps 30,000 sets, more than three times as many. The checklist of cards (792 regular and 132 Traded) is identical to that of the normal non-glossy cards. There are two primary distinguishing features of the Tiffany cards, white card stock reverses and high gloss obverses. These Tiffany cards are valued approximately from three to five times the values listed below.

	MT	EX-MT	VG
COMPLETE SET (792)	25.00	11.50	3.10
COMPLETE FACT.SET (792)	30.00	13.50	3.80
COMMON PLAYER (1-792)	.04	.02	.01

		MT	EX-MT	VG
☐ 1	RB: Roger Clemens Most strikeouts, nine inning game	.40	.10	.03
☐ 2	RB: Jim Deshaies Most cons. K's, start of game	.05	.02	.01
☐ 3	RB: Dwight Evans Earliest home run, season	.05	.02	.01
☐ 4	RB: Davey Lopes Most steals, season, 40-year-old	.05	.02	.01
☐ 5	RB: Dave Righetti Most saves, season	.05	.02	.01
☐ 6	RB: Ruben Sierra Youngest player to switch hit homers in game	.35	.16	.04
☐ 7	RB: Todd Worrell Most saves, season, rookie	.05	.02	.01
☐ 8	Terry Pendleton	.25	.11	.03
☐ 9	Jay Tibbs	.04	.02	.01
☐ 10	Cecil Cooper	.07	.03	.01
☐ 11	Indians Team (Mound conference)	.04	.02	.01
☐ 12	Jeff Sellers	.04	.02	.01
☐ 13	Nick Esasky	.04	.02	.01
☐ 14	Dave Stewart	.10	.05	.01
☐ 15	Claudell Washington	.04	.02	.01
☐ 16	Pat Clements	.04	.02	.01
☐ 17	Pete O'Brien	.04	.02	.01
☐ 18	Dick Howser MG (Checklist back)	.06	.03	.01
☐ 19	Matt Young	.04	.02	.01
☐ 20	Gary Carter	.12	.05	.02
☐ 21	Mark Davis	.04	.02	.01
☐ 22	Doug DeCinces	.04	.02	.01
☐ 23	Lee Smith	.15	.07	.02
☐ 24	Tony Walker	.04	.02	.01
☐ 25	Bert Blyleven	.10	.05	.01

26 Greg Brock	.04	.02	.01
27 Joe Cowley	.04	.02	.01
28 Rick Dempsey	.04	.02	.01
29 Jimmy Key	.07	.03	.01
30 Tim Raines	.10	.05	.01
31 Braves Team	.05	.02	.01
(Glenn Hubbard and			
Rafael Ramirez)			
32 Tim Leary	.04	.02	.01
33 Andy Van Slyke	.20	.09	.03
34 Jose Rijo	.12	.05	.02
35 Sid Bream	.07	.03	.01
36 Eric King	.04	.02	.01
37 Marvell Wynne	.04	.02	.01
38 Dennis Leonard	.04	.02	.01
39 Marty Barrett	.04	.02	.01
40 Dave Righetti	.07	.03	.01
41 Bo Diaz	.04	.02	.01
42 Gary Redus	.04	.02	.01
43 Gene Michael MG	.06	.03	.01
(Checklist back)			
44 Greg Harris	.04	.02	.01
45 Jim Presley	.04	.02	.01
46 Dan Gladden	.04	.02	.01
47 Dennis Powell	.04	.02	.01
48 Wally Backman	.04	.02	.01
49 Terry Harper	.04	.02	.01
50 Dave Smith	.04	.02	.01
51 Mel Hall	.07	.03	.01
52 Keith Atherton	.04	.02	.01
53 Ruppert Jones	.04	.02	.01
54 Bill Dawley	.04	.02	.01
55 Tim Wallach	.07	.03	.01
56 Brewers Team	.05	.02	.01
(Mound conference)			
57 Scott Nielsen	.04	.02	.01
58 Thad Bosley	.04	.02	.01
59 Ken Dayley	.04	.02	.01
60 Tony Pena	.04	.02	.01
61 Bobby Thigpen	.25	.11	.03
62 Bobby Meacham	.04	.02	.01
63 Fred Toliver	.04	.02	.01
64 Harry Spilman	.04	.02	.01
65 Tom Browning	.07	.03	.01
66 Marc Sullivan	.04	.02	.01
67 Bill Swift	.10	.05	.01
68 Tony LaRussa MG	.06	.03	.01
(Checklist back)			
69 Lonnie Smith	.04	.02	.01
70 Charlie Hough	.04	.02	.01
71 Mike Aldrete	.04	.02	.01
72 Walt Terrell	.04	.02	.01
73 Dave Anderson	.04	.02	.01
74 Dan Pasqua	.07	.03	.01
75 Ron Darling	.07	.03	.01
76 Rafael Ramirez	.04	.02	.01
77 Bryan Oelkers	.04	.02	.01
78 Tom Foley	.04	.02	.01
79 Juan Nieves	.04	.02	.01
80 Wally Joyner	.50	.23	.06
81 Padres Team	.05	.02	.01
(Andy Hawkins and			
Terry Kennedy)			
82 Rob Murphy	.04	.02	.01
83 Mike Davis	.04	.02	.01
84 Steve Lake	.04	.02	.01
85 Kevin Bass	.04	.02	.01
86 Nate Snell	.04	.02	.01
87 Mark Salas	.04	.02	.01
88 Ed Wojna	.04	.02	.01
89 Ozzie Guillen	.07	.03	.01
90 Dave Stieb	.07	.03	.01
91 Harold Reynolds	.04	.02	.01
92A Urbano Lugo	.30	.14	.04
ERR (no trademark)			
92B Urbano Lugo COR	.04	.02	.01
93 Jim Leyland MG	.12	.05	.02
(Checklist back)			
94 Calvin Schiraldi	.04	.02	.01
95 Oddibe McDowell	.04	.02	.01
96 Frank Williams	.04	.02	.01
97 Glenn Wilson	.04	.02	.01
98 Bill Scherrer	.04	.02	.01
99 Darryl Motley	.04	.02	.01
(Now with Braves			
on card front)			
100 Steve Garvey	.12	.05	.02
101 Carl Willis	.10	.05	.01
102 Paul Zuvella	.04	.02	.01
103 Rick Aguilera	.12	.05	.02
104 Billy Sample	.04	.02	.01
105 Floyd Youmans	.04	.02	.01
106 Blue Jays Team	.04	.02	.01
(George Bell and			
Jesse Barfield)			
107 John Butcher	.04	.02	.01
108 Jim Gantner UER	.04	.02	.01
(Brewers logo			
reversed)			
109 R.J. Reynolds	.04	.02	.01
110 John Tudor	.07	.03	.01
111 Alfredo Griffin	.04	.02	.01
112 Alan Ashby	.04	.02	.01
113 Neil Allen	.04	.02	.01
114 Billy Beane	.04	.02	.01
115 Donnie Moore	.04	.02	.01
116 Bill Russell	.07	.03	.01
117 Jim Beattie	.04	.02	.01
118 Bobby Valentine MG	.06	.03	.01
(Checklist back)			
119 Ron Robinson	.04	.02	.01
120 Eddie Murray	.25	.11	.03
121 Kevin Romine	.04	.02	.01
122 Jim Clancy	.04	.02	.01
123 John Kruk	.60	.25	.08
124 Ray Fontenot	.04	.02	.01
125 Bob Brenly	.04	.02	.01
126 Mike Loynd	.04	.02	.01
127 Vance Law	.04	.02	.01
128 Checklist 1-132	.06	.01	.00
129 Rick Cerone	.04	.02	.01
130 Dwight Gooden	.20	.09	.03
131 Pirates Team	.05	.02	.01
(Sid Bream and			
Tony Pena)			
132 Paul Assenmacher	.04	.02	.01
133 Jose Oquendo	.04	.02	.01
134 Rich Yett	.04	.02	.01
135 Mike Easler	.04	.02	.01
136 Ron Romanick	.04	.02	.01
137 Jerry Willard	.04	.02	.01
138 Roy Lee Jackson	.04	.02	.01
139 Devon White	.40	.18	.05
140 Bret Saberhagen	.15	.07	.02
141 Herm Winningham	.04	.02	.01
142 Rick Sutcliffe	.07	.03	.01
143 Steve Boros MG	.06	.03	.01
(Checklist back)			
144 Mike Scioscia	.04	.02	.01
145 Charlie Kerfeld	.04	.02	.01
146 Tracy Jones	.04	.02	.01
147 Randy Niemann	.04	.02	.01
148 Dave Collins	.04	.02	.01
149 Ray Searage	.04	.02	.01
150 Wade Boggs	.40	.18	.05
151 Mike LaCoss	.04	.02	.01
152 Toby Harrah	.04	.02	.01
153 Duane Ward	.30	.14	.04
154 Tom O'Malley	.04	.02	.01
155 Eddie Whitson	.04	.02	.01
156 Mariners Team	.05	.02	.01
(Mound conference)			
157 Danny Darwin	.04	.02	.01
158 Tim Teufel	.04	.02	.01
159 Ed Olwine	.04	.02	.01
160 Julio Franco	.15	.07	.02
161 Steve Ontiveros	.04	.02	.01
162 Mike LaValliere	.15	.07	.02
163 Kevin Gross	.04	.02	.01
164 Sammy Khalifa	.04	.02	.01
165 Jeff Reardon	.15	.07	.02
166 Bob Boone	.07	.03	.01
167 Jim Deshaies	.10	.05	.01
168 Lou Piniella MG	.06	.03	.01
(Checklist back)			
169 Ron Washington	.04	.02	.01
170 Bo Jackson	.90	.40	.11
171 Chuck Cary	.04	.02	.01
172 Ron Oester	.04	.02	.01
173 Alex Trevino	.04	.02	.01
174 Henry Cotto	.04	.02	.01
175 Bob Stanley	.04	.02	.01
176 Steve Buechele	.07	.03	.01
177 Keith Moreland	.04	.02	.01
178 Cecil Fielder	.90	.40	.11
179 Bill Wegman	.04	.02	.01
180 Chris Brown	.04	.02	.01
181 Cardinals Team	.05	.02	.01
(Mound conference)			
182 Lee Lacy	.04	.02	.01
183 Andy Hawkins	.04	.02	.01
184 Bobby Bonilla	.90	.40	.11
185 Roger McDowell	.04	.02	.01
186 Bruce Benedict	.04	.02	.01
187 Mark Huismann	.04	.02	.01
188 Tony Phillips	.07	.03	.01
189 Joe Hesketh	.04	.02	.01

Card			
☐ 190 Jim Sundberg	.04	.02	.01
☐ 191 Charles Hudson	.04	.02	.01
☐ 192 Cory Snyder	.10	.05	.01
☐ 193 Roger Craig MG	.06	.03	.01
(Checklist back)			
☐ 194 Kirk McCaskill	.04	.02	.01
☐ 195 Mike Pagliarulo	.04	.02	.01
☐ 196 Randy O'Neal UER	.04	.02	.01
(Wrong ML career W-L totals)			
☐ 197 Mark Bailey	.04	.02	.01
☐ 198 Lee Mazzilli	.04	.02	.01
☐ 199 Mariano Duncan	.04	.02	.01
☐ 200 Pete Rose	.30	.14	.04
☐ 201 John Cangelosi	.04	.02	.01
☐ 202 Ricky Wright	.04	.02	.01
☐ 203 Mike Kingery	.04	.02	.01
☐ 204 Sammy Stewart	.04	.02	.01
☐ 205 Graig Nettles	.07	.03	.01
☐ 206 Twins Team	.05	.02	.01
(Frank Viola and Tim Laudner)			
☐ 207 George Frazier	.04	.02	.01
☐ 208 John Shelby	.04	.02	.01
☐ 209 Rick Schu	.04	.02	.01
☐ 210 Lloyd Moseby	.04	.02	.01
☐ 211 John Morris	.04	.02	.01
☐ 212 Mike Fitzgerald	.04	.02	.01
☐ 213 Randy Myers	.15	.07	.02
☐ 214 Omar Moreno	.04	.02	.01
☐ 215 Mark Langston	.12	.05	.02
☐ 216 B.J. Surhoff	.12	.05	.02
☐ 217 Chris Codiroli	.04	.02	.01
☐ 218 Sparky Anderson MG	.06	.03	.01
(Checklist back)			
☐ 219 Cecilio Guante	.04	.02	.01
☐ 220 Joe Carter	.40	.18	.05
☐ 221 Vern Ruhle	.04	.02	.01
☐ 222 Denny Walling	.04	.02	.01
☐ 223 Charlie Leibrandt	.07	.03	.01
☐ 224 Wayne Tolleson	.04	.02	.01
☐ 225 Mike Smithson	.04	.02	.01
☐ 226 Max Venable	.04	.02	.01
☐ 227 Jamie Moyer	.04	.02	.01
☐ 228 Curt Wilkerson	.04	.02	.01
☐ 229 Mike Birkbeck	.04	.02	.01
☐ 230 Don Baylor	.07	.03	.01
☐ 231 Giants Team	.05	.02	.01
(Bob Brenly and Jim Gott)			
☐ 232 Reggie Williams	.04	.02	.01
☐ 233 Russ Morman	.04	.02	.01
☐ 234 Pat Sheridan	.04	.02	.01
☐ 235 Alvin Davis	.04	.02	.01
☐ 236 Tommy John	.07	.03	.01
☐ 237 Jim Morrison	.04	.02	.01
☐ 238 Bill Krueger	.04	.02	.01
☐ 239 Juan Espino	.04	.02	.01
☐ 240 Steve Balboni	.04	.02	.01
☐ 241 Danny Heep	.04	.02	.01
☐ 242 Rick Mahler	.04	.02	.01
☐ 243 Whitey Herzog MG	.06	.03	.01
(Checklist back)			
☐ 244 Dickie Noles	.04	.02	.01
☐ 245 Willie Upshaw	.04	.02	.01
☐ 246 Jim Dwyer	.04	.02	.01
☐ 247 Jeff Reed	.04	.02	.01
☐ 248 Gene Walter	.04	.02	.01
☐ 249 Jim Pankovits	.04	.02	.01
☐ 250 Teddy Higuera	.04	.02	.01
☐ 251 Rob Wilfong	.04	.02	.01
☐ 252 Dennis Martinez	.07	.03	.01
☐ 253 Eddie Milner	.04	.02	.01
☐ 254 Bob Tewksbury	.25	.11	.03
☐ 255 Juan Samuel	.04	.02	.01
☐ 256 Royals Team	.10	.05	.01
(George Brett and Frank White)			
☐ 257 Bob Forsch	.04	.02	.01
☐ 258 Steve Yeager	.04	.02	.01
☐ 259 Mike Greenwell	.40	.18	.05
☐ 260 Vida Blue	.07	.03	.01
☐ 261 Ruben Sierra	1.75	.80	.22
☐ 262 Jim Winn	.04	.02	.01
☐ 263 Stan Javier	.04	.02	.01
☐ 264 Checklist 133-264	.06	.01	.00
☐ 265 Darrell Evans	.07	.03	.01
☐ 266 Jeff Hamilton	.04	.02	.01
☐ 267 Howard Johnson	.20	.09	.03
☐ 268 Pat Corrales MG	.06	.03	.01
(Checklist back)			
☐ 269 Cliff Speck	.04	.02	.01
☐ 270 Jody Davis	.04	.02	.01
☐ 271 Mike G. Brown	.04	.02	.01
(Mariners pitcher)			
☐ 272 Andres Galarraga	.12	.05	.02
☐ 273 Gene Nelson	.04	.02	.01
☐ 274 Jeff Hearron UER	.04	.02	.01
(Duplicate 1986 stat line on back)			
☐ 275 LaMarr Hoyt	.04	.02	.01
☐ 276 Jackie Gutierrez	.04	.02	.01
☐ 277 Juan Agosto	.04	.02	.01
☐ 278 Gary Pettis	.04	.02	.01
☐ 279 Dan Plesac	.10	.05	.01
☐ 280 Jeff Leonard	.04	.02	.01
☐ 281 Reds Team	.10	.05	.01
(Pete Rose, Bo Diaz, and Bill Gullickson)			
☐ 282 Jeff Calhoun	.04	.02	.01
☐ 283 Doug Drabek	.60	.25	.08
☐ 284 John Moses	.04	.02	.01
☐ 285 Dennis Boyd	.04	.02	.01
☐ 286 Mike Woodard	.04	.02	.01
☐ 287 Dave Von Ohlen	.04	.02	.01
☐ 288 Tito Landrum	.04	.02	.01
☐ 289 Bob Kipper	.04	.02	.01
☐ 290 Leon Durham	.04	.02	.01
☐ 291 Mitch Williams	.15	.07	.02
☐ 292 Franklin Stubbs	.04	.02	.01
☐ 293 Bob Rodgers MG	.06	.03	.01
(Checklist back, inconsistent design on card back)			
☐ 294 Steve Jeltz	.04	.02	.01
☐ 295 Len Dykstra	.12	.05	.02
☐ 296 Andres Thomas	.04	.02	.01
☐ 297 Don Schulze	.04	.02	.01
☐ 298 Larry Herndon	.04	.02	.01
☐ 299 Joel Davis	.04	.02	.01
☐ 300 Reggie Jackson	.30	.14	.04
☐ 301 Luis Aquino UER	.04	.02	.01
(No trademark, never corrected)			
☐ 302 Bill Schroeder	.04	.02	.01
☐ 303 Juan Berenguer	.04	.02	.01
☐ 304 Phil Garner	.07	.03	.01
☐ 305 John Franco	.10	.05	.01
☐ 306 Red Sox Team	.10	.05	.01
(Tom Seaver, John McNamara MG, and Rich Gedman)			
☐ 307 Lee Guetterman	.04	.02	.01
☐ 308 Don Slaught	.04	.02	.01
☐ 309 Mike Young	.04	.02	.01
☐ 310 Frank Viola	.12	.05	.02
☐ 311 Turn Back 1982	.20	.09	.03
Rickey Henderson			
☐ 312 Turn Back 1977	.10	.05	.01
Reggie Jackson			
☐ 313 Turn Back 1972	.10	.05	.01
Roberto Clemente			
☐ 314 Turn Back 1967 UER	.10	.05	.01
Carl Yastrzemski (Sic, 112 RBI's on back)			
☐ 315 Turn Back 1962	.05	.02	.01
Maury Wills			
☐ 316 Brian Fisher	.04	.02	.01
☐ 317 Clint Hurdle	.04	.02	.01
☐ 318 Jim Fregosi MG	.06	.03	.01
(Checklist back)			
☐ 319 Greg Swindell	.60	.25	.08
☐ 320 Barry Bonds	2.25	1.00	.30
☐ 321 Mike Laga	.04	.02	.01
☐ 322 Chris Bando	.04	.02	.01
☐ 323 Al Newman	.04	.02	.01
☐ 324 David Palmer	.04	.02	.01
☐ 325 Garry Templeton	.04	.02	.01
☐ 326 Mark Gubicza	.04	.02	.01
☐ 327 Dale Sveum	.04	.02	.01
☐ 328 Bob Welch	.07	.03	.01
☐ 329 Ron Roenicke	.04	.02	.01
☐ 330 Mike Scott	.07	.03	.01
☐ 331 Mets Team	.15	.07	.02
(Gary Carter and Darryl Strawberry)			
☐ 332 Joe Price	.04	.02	.01
☐ 333 Ken Phelps	.04	.02	.01
☐ 334 Ed Correa	.04	.02	.01
☐ 335 Candy Maldonado	.07	.03	.01
☐ 336 Allan Anderson	.04	.02	.01
☐ 337 Darrell Miller	.04	.02	.01
☐ 338 Tim Conroy	.04	.02	.01
☐ 339 Donnie Hill	.04	.02	.01
☐ 340 Roger Clemens	1.25	.55	.16

☐ 341 Mike C. Brown .04 .02 .01
(Pirates Outfielder)
☐ 342 Bob James .04 .02 .01
☐ 343 Hal Lanier MG .06 .03 .01
(Checklist back)
☐ 344A Joe Niekro .07 .03 .01
(Copyright inside righthand border)
☐ 344B Joe Niekro .30 .14 .04
(Copyright outside righthand border)
☐ 345 Andre Dawson .25 .11 .03
☐ 346 Shawon Dunston .07 .03 .01
☐ 347 Mickey Brantley .04 .02 .01
☐ 348 Carmelo Martinez .04 .02 .01
☐ 349 Storm Davis .04 .02 .01
☐ 350 Keith Hernandez .07 .03 .01
☐ 351 Gene Garber .04 .02 .01
☐ 352 Mike Felder .04 .02 .01
☐ 353 Ernie Camacho .04 .02 .01
☐ 354 Jamie Quirk .04 .02 .01
☐ 355 Don Carman .04 .02 .01
☐ 356 White Sox Team .05 .02 .01
(Mound conference)
☐ 357 Steve Fireovid .04 .02 .01
☐ 358 Sal Butera .04 .02 .01
☐ 359 Doug Corbett .04 .02 .01
☐ 360 Pedro Guerrero .07 .03 .01
☐ 361 Mark Thurmond .04 .02 .01
☐ 362 Luis Quinones .04 .02 .01
☐ 363 Jose Guzman .07 .03 .01
☐ 364 Randy Bush .04 .02 .01
☐ 365 Rick Rhoden .04 .02 .01
☐ 366 Mark McGwire 2.00 .90 .25
☐ 367 Jeff Lahti .04 .02 .01
☐ 368 John McNamara MG .06 .03 .01
(Checklist back)
☐ 369 Brian Dayett .04 .02 .01
☐ 370 Fred Lynn .07 .03 .01
☐ 371 Mark Eichhorn .07 .03 .01
☐ 372 Jerry Mumphrey .04 .02 .01
☐ 373 Jeff Dedmon .04 .02 .01
☐ 374 Glenn Hoffman .04 .02 .01
☐ 375 Ron Guidry .07 .03 .01
☐ 376 Scott Bradley .04 .02 .01
☐ 377 John Henry Johnson .04 .02 .01
☐ 378 Rafael Santana .04 .02 .01
☐ 379 John Russell .04 .02 .01
☐ 380 Rich Gossage .08 .04 .01
☐ 381 Expos Team .05 .02 .01
(Mound conference)
☐ 382 Rudy Law .04 .02 .01
☐ 383 Ron Davis .04 .02 .01
☐ 384 Johnny Grubb .04 .02 .01
☐ 385 Orel Hershiser .12 .05 .02
☐ 386 Dickie Thon .04 .02 .01
☐ 387 T.R. Bryden .04 .02 .01
☐ 388 Geno Petralli .04 .02 .01
☐ 389 Jeff D. Robinson .04 .02 .01
☐ 390 Gary Matthews .07 .03 .01
☐ 391 Jay Howell .07 .03 .01
☐ 392 Checklist 265-396 .06 .01 .00
☐ 393 Pete Rose MG .20 .09 .03
(Checklist back)
☐ 394 Mike Bielecki .04 .02 .01
☐ 395 Damaso Garcia .04 .02 .01
☐ 396 Tim Lollar .04 .02 .01
☐ 397 Greg Walker .04 .02 .01
☐ 398 Brad Havens .04 .02 .01
☐ 399 Curt Ford .04 .02 .01
☐ 400 George Brett .35 .16 .04
☐ 401 Billy Joe Robidoux .04 .02 .01
☐ 402 Mike Trujillo .04 .02 .01
☐ 403 Jerry Royster .04 .02 .01
☐ 404 Doug Sisk .04 .02 .01
☐ 405 Brook Jacoby .04 .02 .01
☐ 406 Yankees Team .20 .09 .03
(Rickey Henderson and Don Mattingly)
☐ 407 Jim Acker .04 .02 .01
☐ 408 John Mizerock .04 .02 .01
☐ 409 Milt Thompson .07 .03 .01
☐ 410 Fernando Valenzuela .07 .03 .01
☐ 411 Darnell Coles .04 .02 .01
☐ 412 Eric Davis .20 .09 .03
☐ 413 Moose Haas .04 .02 .01
☐ 414 Joe Orsulak .04 .02 .01
☐ 415 Bobby Witt .15 .07 .02
☐ 416 Tom Nieto .04 .02 .01
☐ 417 Pat Perry .04 .02 .01
☐ 418 Dick Williams MG .06 .03 .01
(Checklist back)
☐ 419 Mark Portugal .12 .05 .02
☐ 420 Will Clark 2.25 1.00 .30
☐ 421 Jose DeLeon .04 .02 .01
☐ 422 Jack Howell .04 .02 .01
☐ 423 Jaime Cocanower .04 .02 .01
☐ 424 Chris Speier .04 .02 .01
☐ 425 Tom Seaver .25 .11 .03
☐ 426 Floyd Rayford .04 .02 .01
☐ 427 Edwin Nunez .04 .02 .01
☐ 428 Bruce Bochy .04 .02 .01
☐ 429 Tim Pyznarski .04 .02 .01
☐ 430 Mike Schmidt .50 .23 .06
☐ 431 Dodgers Team .05 .02 .01
(Mound conference)
☐ 432 Jim Slaton .04 .02 .01
☐ 433 Ed Hearn .04 .02 .01
☐ 434 Mike Fischlin .04 .02 .01
☐ 435 Bruce Sutter .07 .03 .01
☐ 436 Andy Allanson .04 .02 .01
☐ 437 Ted Power .04 .02 .01
☐ 438 Kelly Downs .10 .05 .01
☐ 439 Karl Best .04 .02 .01
☐ 440 Willie McGee .07 .03 .01
☐ 441 Dave Leiper .04 .02 .01
☐ 442 Mitch Webster .04 .02 .01
☐ 443 John Felske MG .06 .03 .01
(Checklist back)
☐ 444 Jeff Russell .07 .03 .01
☐ 445 Dave Lopes .07 .03 .01
☐ 446 Chuck Finley .20 .09 .03
☐ 447 Bill Almon .04 .02 .01
☐ 448 Chris Bosio .20 .09 .03
☐ 449 Pat Dodson .04 .02 .01
☐ 450 Kirby Puckett 1.00 .45 .13
☐ 451 Joe Sambito .04 .02 .01
☐ 452 Dave Henderson .07 .03 .01
☐ 453 Scott Terry .04 .02 .01
☐ 454 Luis Salazar .04 .02 .01
☐ 455 Mike Boddicker .04 .02 .01
☐ 456 A's Team .05 .02 .01
(Mound conference)
☐ 457 Len Matuszek .04 .02 .01
☐ 458 Kelly Gruber .25 .11 .03
☐ 459 Dennis Eckersley .20 .09 .03
☐ 460 Darryl Strawberry .40 .18 .05
☐ 461 Craig McMurtry .04 .02 .01
☐ 462 Scott Fletcher .04 .02 .01
☐ 463 Tom Candiotti .07 .03 .01
☐ 464 Butch Wynegar .04 .02 .01
☐ 465 Todd Worrell .07 .03 .01
☐ 466 Kal Daniels .10 .05 .01
☐ 467 Randy St.Claire .04 .02 .01
☐ 468 George Bamberger MG .06 .03 .01
(Checklist back)
☐ 469 Mike Diaz .04 .02 .01
☐ 470 Dave Dravecky .07 .03 .01
☐ 471 Ronn Reynolds .04 .02 .01
☐ 472 Bill Doran .04 .02 .01
☐ 473 Steve Farr .07 .03 .01
☐ 474 Jerry Narron .04 .02 .01
☐ 475 Scott Garrelts .04 .02 .01
☐ 476 Danny Tartabull .40 .18 .05
☐ 477 Ken Howell .04 .02 .01
☐ 478 Tim Laudner .04 .02 .01
☐ 479 Bob Sebra .04 .02 .01
☐ 480 Jim Rice .10 .05 .01
☐ 481 Phillies Team .05 .02 .01
(Glenn Wilson, Juan Samuel, and Von Hayes)
☐ 482 Daryl Boston .04 .02 .01
☐ 483 Dwight Lowry .04 .02 .01
☐ 484 Jim Traber .04 .02 .01
☐ 485 Tony Fernandez .10 .05 .01
☐ 486 Otis Nixon .25 .11 .03
☐ 487 Dave Gumpert .04 .02 .01
☐ 488 Ray Knight .07 .03 .01
☐ 489 Bill Gullickson .07 .03 .01
☐ 490 Dale Murphy .15 .07 .02
☐ 491 Ron Karkovice .07 .03 .01
☐ 492 Mike Heath .04 .02 .01
☐ 493 Tom Lasorda MG .06 .03 .01
(Checklist back)
☐ 494 Barry Jones .04 .02 .01
☐ 495 Gorman Thomas .04 .02 .01
☐ 496 Bruce Bochte .04 .02 .01
☐ 497 Dale Mohorcic .04 .02 .01
☐ 498 Bob Kearney .04 .02 .01
☐ 499 Bruce Ruffin .04 .02 .01
☐ 500 Don Mattingly .40 .18 .05
☐ 501 Craig Lefferts .07 .03 .01
☐ 502 Dick Schofield .04 .02 .01
☐ 503 Larry Andersen .04 .02 .01
☐ 504 Mickey Hatcher .04 .02 .01

☐ 505 Bryn Smith	.04	.02	.01
☐ 506 Orioles Team (Mound conference)	.05	.02	.01
☐ 507 Dave L. Stapleton (Infielder)	.04	.02	.01
☐ 508 Scott Bankhead	.04	.02	.01
☐ 509 Enos Cabell	.04	.02	.01
☐ 510 Tom Henke	.07	.03	.01
☐ 511 Steve Lyons	.04	.02	.01
☐ 512 Dave Magadan	.15	.07	.02
☐ 513 Carmen Castillo	.04	.02	.01
☐ 514 Orlando Mercado	.04	.02	.01
☐ 515 Willie Hernandez	.04	.02	.01
☐ 516 Ted Simmons	.07	.03	.01
☐ 517 Mario Soto	.04	.02	.01
☐ 518 Gene Mauch MG (Checklist back)	.06	.03	.01
☐ 519 Curt Young	.04	.02	.01
☐ 520 Jack Clark	.07	.03	.01
☐ 521 Rick Reuschel	.04	.02	.01
☐ 522 Checklist 397-528	.06	.01	.00
☐ 523 Earnie Riles	.04	.02	.01
☐ 524 Bob Shirley	.04	.02	.01
☐ 525 Phil Bradley	.04	.02	.01
☐ 526 Roger Mason	.07	.03	.01
☐ 527 Jim Wohlford	.04	.02	.01
☐ 528 Ken Dixon	.04	.02	.01
☐ 529 Alvaro Espinoza	.10	.05	.01
☐ 530 Tony Gwynn	.50	.23	.06
☐ 531 Astros Team (Yogi Berra conference)	.10	.05	.01
☐ 532 Jeff Stone	.04	.02	.01
☐ 533 Argenis Salazar	.04	.02	.01
☐ 534 Scott Sanderson	.04	.02	.01
☐ 535 Tony Armas	.04	.02	.01
☐ 536 Terry Mulholland	.30	.14	.04
☐ 537 Rance Mulliniks	.04	.02	.01
☐ 538 Tom Niedenfuer	.04	.02	.01
☐ 539 Reid Nichols	.04	.02	.01
☐ 540 Terry Kennedy	.04	.02	.01
☐ 541 Rafael Belliard	.12	.05	.02
☐ 542 Ricky Horton	.04	.02	.01
☐ 543 Dave Johnson MG (Checklist back)	.06	.03	.01
☐ 544 Zane Smith	.04	.02	.01
☐ 545 Buddy Bell	.07	.03	.01
☐ 546 Mike Morgan	.07	.03	.01
☐ 547 Rob Deer	.12	.05	.02
☐ 548 Bill Mooneyham	.04	.02	.01
☐ 549 Bob Melvin	.04	.02	.01
☐ 550 Pete Incaviglia	.15	.07	.02
☐ 551 Frank Wills	.04	.02	.01
☐ 552 Larry Sheets	.04	.02	.01
☐ 553 Mike Maddux	.04	.02	.01
☐ 554 Buddy Biancalana	.04	.02	.01
☐ 555 Dennis Rasmussen	.04	.02	.01
☐ 556 Angels Team (Rene Lachemann CO, Mike Witt, and Bob Boone)	.05	.02	.01
☐ 557 John Cerutti	.04	.02	.01
☐ 558 Greg Gagne	.07	.03	.01
☐ 559 Lance McCullers	.04	.02	.01
☐ 560 Glenn Davis	.12	.05	.02
☐ 561 Rey Quinones	.04	.02	.01
☐ 562 Bryan Clutterbuck	.04	.02	.01
☐ 563 John Stefero	.04	.02	.01
☐ 564 Larry McWilliams	.04	.02	.01
☐ 565 Dusty Baker	.07	.03	.01
☐ 566 Tim Hulett	.04	.02	.01
☐ 567 Greg Mathews	.04	.02	.01
☐ 568 Earl Weaver MG (Checklist back)	.06	.03	.01
☐ 569 Wade Rowdon	.04	.02	.01
☐ 570 Sid Fernandez	.07	.03	.01
☐ 571 Ozzie Virgil	.04	.02	.01
☐ 572 Pete Ladd	.04	.02	.01
☐ 573 Hal McRae	.07	.03	.01
☐ 574 Manny Lee	.07	.03	.01
☐ 575 Pat Tabler	.04	.02	.01
☐ 576 Frank Pastore	.04	.02	.01
☐ 577 Dann Bilardello	.04	.02	.01
☐ 578 Billy Hatcher	.07	.03	.01
☐ 579 Rick Burleson	.04	.02	.01
☐ 580 Mike Krukow	.04	.02	.01
☐ 581 Cubs Team (Ron Cey and Steve Trout)	.05	.02	.01
☐ 582 Bruce Berenyi	.04	.02	.01
☐ 583 Junior Ortiz	.04	.02	.01
☐ 584 Ron Kittle	.04	.02	.01
☐ 585 Scott Bailes	.04	.02	.01
☐ 586 Ben Oglivie	.04	.02	.01
☐ 587 Eric Plunk	.04	.02	.01
☐ 588 Wallace Johnson	.04	.02	.01
☐ 589 Steve Crawford	.04	.02	.01
☐ 590 Vince Coleman	.12	.05	.02
☐ 591 Spike Owen	.04	.02	.01
☐ 592 Chris Welsh	.04	.02	.01
☐ 593 Chuck Tanner MG (Checklist back)	.06	.03	.01
☐ 594 Rick Anderson	.04	.02	.01
☐ 595 Keith Hernandez AS	.05	.02	.01
☐ 596 Steve Sax AS	.05	.02	.01
☐ 597 Mike Schmidt AS	.25	.11	.03
☐ 598 Ozzie Smith AS	.12	.05	.02
☐ 599 Tony Gwynn AS	.25	.11	.03
☐ 600 Dave Parker AS	.05	.02	.01
☐ 601 Darryl Strawberry AS	.25	.11	.03
☐ 602 Gary Carter AS	.08	.04	.01
☐ 603A Dwight Gooden AS ERR (no trademark)	.40	.18	.05
☐ 603B Dwight Gooden AS COR	.12	.05	.02
☐ 604 Fernando Valenzuela AS	.05	.02	.01
☐ 605 Todd Worrell AS	.05	.02	.01
☐ 606A Don Mattingly AS ERR (no trademark)	.75	.35	.09
☐ 606B Don Mattingly AS COR	.25	.11	.03
☐ 607 Tony Bernazard AS	.05	.02	.01
☐ 608 Wade Boggs AS	.20	.09	.03
☐ 609 Cal Ripken AS	.50	.23	.06
☐ 610 Jim Rice AS	.05	.02	.01
☐ 611 Kirby Puckett AS	.50	.23	.06
☐ 612 George Bell AS	.05	.02	.01
☐ 613 Lance Parrish AS UER (Pitcher heading on back)	.05	.02	.01
☐ 614 Roger Clemens AS	.50	.23	.06
☐ 615 Teddy Higuera AS	.05	.02	.01
☐ 616 Dave Righetti AS	.05	.02	.01
☐ 617 Al Nipper	.04	.02	.01
☐ 618 Tom Kelly MG (Checklist back)	.06	.03	.01
☐ 619 Jerry Reed	.04	.02	.01
☐ 620 Jose Canseco	2.00	.90	.25
☐ 621 Danny Cox	.04	.02	.01
☐ 622 Glenn Braggs	.10	.05	.01
☐ 623 Kurt Stillwell	.10	.05	.01
☐ 624 Tim Burke	.04	.02	.01
☐ 625 Mookie Wilson	.07	.03	.01
☐ 626 Joel Skinner	.04	.02	.01
☐ 627 Ken Oberkfell	.04	.02	.01
☐ 628 Bob Walk	.04	.02	.01
☐ 629 Larry Parrish	.04	.02	.01
☐ 630 John Candelaria	.04	.02	.01
☐ 631 Tigers Team (Mound conference)	.05	.02	.01
☐ 632 Rob Woodward	.04	.02	.01
☐ 633 Jose Uribe	.04	.02	.01
☐ 634 Rafael Palmeiro	1.25	.55	.16
☐ 635 Ken Schrom	.04	.02	.01
☐ 636 Darren Daulton	.15	.07	.02
☐ 637 Bip Roberts	.35	.16	.04
☐ 638 Rich Bordi	.04	.02	.01
☐ 639 Gerald Perry	.04	.02	.01
☐ 640 Mark Clear	.04	.02	.01
☐ 641 Domingo Ramos	.04	.02	.01
☐ 642 Al Pulido	.04	.02	.01
☐ 643 Ron Shepherd	.04	.02	.01
☐ 644 John Denny	.04	.02	.01
☐ 645 Dwight Evans	.08	.04	.01
☐ 646 Mike Mason	.04	.02	.01
☐ 647 Tom Lawless	.04	.02	.01
☐ 648 Barry Larkin	1.00	.45	.13
☐ 649 Mickey Tettleton	.15	.07	.02
☐ 650 Hubie Brooks	.04	.02	.01
☐ 651 Benny Distefano	.04	.02	.01
☐ 652 Terry Forster	.04	.02	.01
☐ 653 Kevin Mitchell	.75	.35	.09
☐ 654 Checklist 529-660	.06	.01	.00
☐ 655 Jesse Barfield	.07	.03	.01
☐ 656 Rangers Team (Bobby Valentine MG and Ricky Wright)	.05	.02	.01
☐ 657 Tom Waddell	.04	.02	.01
☐ 658 Robby Thompson	.15	.07	.02
☐ 659 Aurelio Lopez	.04	.02	.01
☐ 660 Bob Horner	.07	.03	.01
☐ 661 Lou Whitaker	.10	.05	.01
☐ 662 Frank DiPino	.04	.02	.01
☐ 663 Cliff Johnson	.04	.02	.01
☐ 664 Mike Marshall	.04	.02	.01
☐ 665 Rod Scurry	.04	.02	.01
☐ 666 Von Hayes	.04	.02	.01
☐ 667 Ron Hassey	.04	.02	.01
☐ 668 Juan Bonilla	.04	.02	.01

Card	MT	EX-MT	VG
☐ 669 Bud Black	.04	.02	.01
☐ 670 Jose Cruz	.04	.02	.01
☐ 671A Ray Soff ERR (No D* before copyright line)	.04	.02	.01
☐ 671B Ray Soff COR (D* before copyright line)	.04	.02	.01
☐ 672 Chili Davis	.07	.03	.01
☐ 673 Don Sutton	.10	.05	.01
☐ 674 Bill Campbell	.04	.02	.01
☐ 675 Ed Romero	.04	.02	.01
☐ 676 Charlie Moore	.04	.02	.01
☐ 677 Bob Grich	.07	.03	.01
☐ 678 Carney Lansford	.07	.03	.01
☐ 679 Kent Hrbek	.10	.05	.01
☐ 680 Ryne Sandberg	.75	.35	.09
☐ 681 George Bell	.15	.07	.02
☐ 682 Jerry Reuss	.04	.02	.01
☐ 683 Gary Roenicke	.04	.02	.01
☐ 684 Kent Tekulve	.04	.02	.01
☐ 685 Jerry Hairston	.04	.02	.01
☐ 686 Doyle Alexander	.04	.02	.01
☐ 687 Alan Trammell	.12	.05	.02
☐ 688 Juan Beniquez	.04	.02	.01
☐ 689 Darrell Porter	.04	.02	.01
☐ 690 Dane Iorg	.04	.02	.01
☐ 691 Dave Parker	.10	.05	.01
☐ 692 Frank White	.04	.02	.01
☐ 693 Terry Puhl	.04	.02	.01
☐ 694 Phil Niekro	.10	.05	.01
☐ 695 Chico Walker	.07	.03	.01
☐ 696 Gary Lucas	.04	.02	.01
☐ 697 Ed Lynch	.04	.02	.01
☐ 698 Ernie Whitt	.04	.02	.01
☐ 699 Ken Landreaux	.04	.02	.01
☐ 700 Dave Bergman	.04	.02	.01
☐ 701 Willie Randolph	.07	.03	.01
☐ 702 Greg Gross	.04	.02	.01
☐ 703 Dave Schmidt	.04	.02	.01
☐ 704 Jesse Orosco	.04	.02	.01
☐ 705 Bruce Hurst	.07	.03	.01
☐ 706 Rick Manning	.04	.02	.01
☐ 707 Bob McClure	.04	.02	.01
☐ 708 Scott McGregor	.04	.02	.01
☐ 709 Dave Kingman	.07	.03	.01
☐ 710 Gary Gaetti	.04	.02	.01
☐ 711 Ken Griffey	.07	.03	.01
☐ 712 Don Robinson	.04	.02	.01
☐ 713 Tom Brookens	.04	.02	.01
☐ 714 Dan Quisenberry	.07	.03	.01
☐ 715 Bob Dernier	.04	.02	.01
☐ 716 Rick Leach	.04	.02	.01
☐ 717 Ed VandeBerg	.04	.02	.01
☐ 718 Steve Carlton	.25	.11	.03
☐ 719 Tom Hume	.04	.02	.01
☐ 720 Richard Dotson	.04	.02	.01
☐ 721 Tom Herr	.04	.02	.01
☐ 722 Bob Knepper	.04	.02	.01
☐ 723 Brett Butler	.10	.05	.01
☐ 724 Greg Minton	.04	.02	.01
☐ 725 George Hendrick	.04	.02	.01
☐ 726 Frank Tanana	.04	.02	.01
☐ 727 Mike Moore	.04	.02	.01
☐ 728 Tippy Martinez	.04	.02	.01
☐ 729 Tom Paciorek	.07	.03	.01
☐ 730 Eric Show	.04	.02	.01
☐ 731 Dave Concepcion	.07	.03	.01
☐ 732 Manny Trillo	.04	.02	.01
☐ 733 Bill Caudill	.04	.02	.01
☐ 734 Bill Madlock	.07	.03	.01
☐ 735 Rickey Henderson	.40	.18	.05
☐ 736 Steve Bedrosian	.04	.02	.01
☐ 737 Floyd Bannister	.04	.02	.01
☐ 738 Jorge Orta	.04	.02	.01
☐ 739 Chet Lemon	.04	.02	.01
☐ 740 Rich Gedman	.04	.02	.01
☐ 741 Paul Molitor	.15	.07	.02
☐ 742 Andy McGaffigan	.04	.02	.01
☐ 743 Dwayne Murphy	.04	.02	.01
☐ 744 Roy Smalley	.04	.02	.01
☐ 745 Glenn Hubbard	.04	.02	.01
☐ 746 Bob Ojeda	.04	.02	.01
☐ 747 Johnny Ray	.04	.02	.01
☐ 748 Mike Flanagan	.04	.02	.01
☐ 749 Ozzie Smith	.25	.11	.03
☐ 750 Steve Trout	.04	.02	.01
☐ 751 Garth Iorg	.04	.02	.01
☐ 752 Dan Petry	.04	.02	.01
☐ 753 Rick Honeycutt	.04	.02	.01
☐ 754 Dave LaPoint	.04	.02	.01
☐ 755 Luis Aguayo	.04	.02	.01
☐ 756 Carlton Fisk	.25	.11	.03
☐ 757 Nolan Ryan	1.00	.45	.13
☐ 758 Tony Bernazard	.04	.02	.01
☐ 759 Joel Youngblood	.04	.02	.01
☐ 760 Mike Witt	.04	.02	.01
☐ 761 Greg Pryor	.04	.02	.01
☐ 762 Gary Ward	.04	.02	.01
☐ 763 Tim Flannery	.04	.02	.01
☐ 764 Bill Buckner	.07	.03	.01
☐ 765 Kirk Gibson	.08	.04	.01
☐ 766 Don Aase	.04	.02	.01
☐ 767 Ron Cey	.07	.03	.01
☐ 768 Dennis Lamp	.04	.02	.01
☐ 769 Steve Sax	.10	.05	.01
☐ 770 Dave Winfield	.30	.14	.04
☐ 771 Shane Rawley	.04	.02	.01
☐ 772 Harold Baines	.10	.05	.01
☐ 773 Robin Yount	.35	.16	.04
☐ 774 Wayne Krenchicki	.04	.02	.01
☐ 775 Joaquin Andujar	.04	.02	.01
☐ 776 Tom Brunansky	.07	.03	.01
☐ 777 Chris Chambliss	.07	.03	.01
☐ 778 Jack Morris	.20	.09	.03
☐ 779 Craig Reynolds	.04	.02	.01
☐ 780 Andre Thornton	.04	.02	.01
☐ 781 Atlee Hammaker	.04	.02	.01
☐ 782 Brian Downing	.04	.02	.01
☐ 783 Willie Wilson	.04	.02	.01
☐ 784 Cal Ripken	1.00	.45	.13
☐ 785 Terry Francona	.04	.02	.01
☐ 786 Jimy Williams MG (Checklist back)	.06	.03	.01
☐ 787 Alejandro Pena	.04	.02	.01
☐ 788 Tim Stoddard	.04	.02	.01
☐ 789 Dan Schatzeder	.04	.02	.01
☐ 790 Julio Cruz	.04	.02	.01
☐ 791 Lance Parrish UER (No trademark, never corrected)	.07	.03	.01
☐ 792 Checklist 661-792	.06	.01	.00

1987 Topps All-Star Glossy 22

This set of 22 glossy cards was inserted one per rack pack. Players selected for the set are the starting players (plus manager and two pitchers) in the 1986 All-Star Game in Houston. Cards measure standard size, 2 1/2" by 3 1/2" and the backs feature red and blue printing on a white card stock.

	MT	EX-MT	VG
COMPLETE SET (22)	3.50	1.55	.45
COMMON PLAYER (1-22)	.10	.05	.01
☐ 1 Whitey Herzog MG	.10	.05	.01
☐ 2 Keith Hernandez	.15	.07	.02
☐ 3 Ryne Sandberg	.60	.25	.08
☐ 4 Mike Schmidt	.50	.23	.06
☐ 5 Ozzie Smith	.35	.16	.04
☐ 6 Tony Gwynn	.35	.16	.04
☐ 7 Dale Murphy	.25	.11	.03
☐ 8 Darryl Strawberry	.35	.16	.04
☐ 9 Gary Carter	.25	.11	.03
☐ 10 Dwight Gooden	.20	.09	.03
☐ 11 Fernando Valenzuela	.15	.07	.02
☐ 12 Dick Howser MG	.10	.05	.01
☐ 13 Wally Joyner	.25	.11	.03
☐ 14 Lou Whitaker	.20	.09	.03
☐ 15 Wade Boggs	.45	.20	.06

	MT	EX-MT	VG
☐ 16 Cal Ripken	.60	.25	.08
☐ 17 Dave Winfield	.40	.18	.05
☐ 18 Rickey Henderson	.50	.23	.06
☐ 19 Kirby Puckett	.50	.23	.06
☐ 20 Lance Parrish	.15	.07	.02
☐ 21 Roger Clemens	.60	.25	.08
☐ 22 Teddy Higuera	.10	.05	.01

1987 Topps Glossy Send-In 60

Topps issued this set through a mail-in offer explained and advertised on the wax packs. This 60-card set features glossy fronts with each card measuring 2 1/2" by 3 1/2". The offer provided your choice of any one of the six 10-card subsets (1-10, 11-20, etc.) for 1.00 plus six of the Special Offer ("Spring Fever Baseball") insert cards, which were found one per wax pack. The last two players (numerically) in each ten-card subset are actually "Hot Prospects."

	MT	EX-MT	VG
COMPLETE SET (60)	12.00	5.50	1.50
COMMON PLAYER (1-60)	.20	.09	.03
☐ 1 Don Mattingly	.75	.35	.09
☐ 2 Tony Gwynn	.60	.25	.08
☐ 3 Gary Gaetti	.20	.09	.03
☐ 4 Glenn Davis	.30	.14	.04
☐ 5 Roger Clemens	1.00	.45	.13
☐ 6 Dale Murphy	.40	.18	.05
☐ 7 Lou Whitaker	.30	.14	.04
☐ 8 Roger McDowell	.20	.09	.03
☐ 9 Cory Snyder	.30	.14	.04
☐ 10 Todd Worrell	.25	.11	.03
☐ 11 Gary Carter	.40	.18	.05
☐ 12 Eddie Murray	.50	.23	.06
☐ 13 Bob Knepper	.20	.09	.03
☐ 14 Harold Baines	.30	.14	.04
☐ 15 Jeff Reardon	.30	.14	.04
☐ 16 Joe Carter	.60	.25	.08
☐ 17 Dave Parker	.30	.14	.04
☐ 18 Wade Boggs	.60	.25	.08
☐ 19 Danny Tartabull	.50	.23	.06
☐ 20 Jim Deshaies	.20	.09	.03
☐ 21 Rickey Henderson	.75	.35	.09
☐ 22 Rob Deer	.30	.14	.04
☐ 23 Ozzie Smith	.40	.18	.05
☐ 24 Dave Righetti	.20	.09	.03
☐ 25 Kent Hrbek	.20	.09	.03
☐ 26 Keith Hernandez	.30	.14	.04
☐ 27 Don Baylor	.30	.14	.04
☐ 28 Mike Schmidt	.75	.35	.09
☐ 29 Pete Incaviglia	.30	.14	.04
☐ 30 Barry Bonds	1.00	.45	.13
☐ 31 George Brett	.75	.35	.09
☐ 32 Darryl Strawberry	.60	.25	.08
☐ 33 Mike Witt	.20	.09	.03
☐ 34 Kevin Bass	.20	.09	.03
☐ 35 Jesse Barfield	.20	.09	.03
☐ 36 Bob Ojeda	.20	.09	.03
☐ 37 Cal Ripken	1.00	.45	.13
☐ 38 Vince Coleman	.30	.14	.04
☐ 39 Wally Joyner	.40	.18	.05
☐ 40 Robby Thompson	.20	.09	.03
☐ 41 Pete Rose	.75	.35	.09
☐ 42 Jim Rice	.30	.14	.04
☐ 43 Tony Bernazard	.20	.09	.03
☐ 44 Eric Davis	.40	.18	.05
☐ 45 George Bell	.30	.14	.04
☐ 46 Hubie Brooks	.20	.09	.03
☐ 47 Jack Morris	.40	.18	.05
☐ 48 Tim Raines	.30	.14	.04
☐ 49 Mark Eichhorn	.20	.09	.03
☐ 50 Kevin Mitchell	.40	.18	.05
☐ 51 Dwight Gooden	.40	.18	.05
☐ 52 Doug DeCinces	.20	.09	.03
☐ 53 Fernando Valenzuela	.30	.14	.04
☐ 54 Reggie Jackson	.50	.23	.06
☐ 55 Johnny Ray	.20	.09	.03
☐ 56 Mike Pagliarulo	.20	.09	.03
☐ 57 Kirby Puckett	.75	.35	.09
☐ 58 Lance Parrish	.30	.14	.04
☐ 59 Jose Canseco	1.00	.45	.13
☐ 60 Greg Mathews	.20	.09	.03

1987 Topps Jumbo Rookies

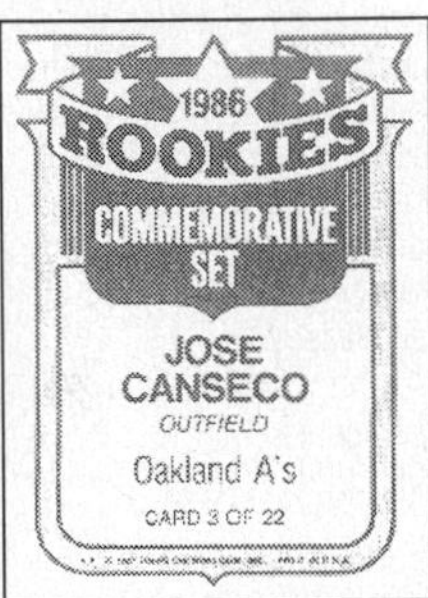

Inserted in each supermarket jumbo pack is a card from this series of 22 of 1986's best rookies as determined by Topps. Jumbo packs consisted of 100 (regular issue 1987 Topps baseball) cards with a stick of gum plus the insert "Rookie" card. The card fronts are in full color and measure 2 1/2" by 3 1/2". The card backs are printed in red and blue on white card stock and are numbered at the bottom essentially by alphabetical order.

	MT	EX-MT	VG
COMPLETE SET (22)	12.00	5.50	1.50
COMMON PLAYER (1-22)	.20	.09	.03
☐ 1 Andy Allanson	.20	.09	.03
☐ 2 John Cangelosi	.20	.09	.03
☐ 3 Jose Canseco	3.00	1.35	.40
☐ 4 Will Clark	3.00	1.35	.40
☐ 5 Mark Eichhorn	.30	.14	.04
☐ 6 Pete Incaviglia	.40	.18	.05
☐ 7 Wally Joyner	.75	.35	.09
☐ 8 Eric King	.20	.09	.03
☐ 9 Dave Magadan	.30	.14	.04
☐ 10 John Morris	.20	.09	.03
☐ 11 Juan Nieves	.20	.09	.03
☐ 12 Rafael Palmeiro	1.00	.45	.13
☐ 13 Billy Joe Robidoux	.20	.09	.03
☐ 14 Bruce Ruffin	.20	.09	.03
☐ 15 Ruben Sierra	2.00	.90	.25
☐ 16 Cory Snyder	.30	.14	.04
☐ 17 Kurt Stillwell	.30	.14	.04
☐ 18 Dale Sveum	.20	.09	.03
☐ 19 Danny Tartabull	.90	.40	.11
☐ 20 Andres Thomas	.20	.09	.03
☐ 21 Robby Thompson	.30	.14	.04
☐ 22 Todd Worrell	.30	.14	.04

1987 Topps Mini Leaders

The 1987 Topps Mini set of Major League Leaders features 77 cards of leaders of the various statistical categories for the 1986 season. The cards are numbered on the back and measure approximately 2 5/32" by 3". The card backs are

printed in orange and brown on white card stock. They are very similar in design to the Team Leader cards in the 1987 Topps regular issue. The cards were distributed as a separate issue in wax packs of seven for 30 cents. Eleven of the cards were double printed and are hence more plentiful; they are marked DP in the checklist below. The order of the set is alphabetical by player's name within team; the teams themselves are ordered alphabetically by city name within each league.

	MT	EX-MT	VG
COMPLETE SET (77)	7.00	3.10	.85
COMMON PLAYER (1-77)	.06	.03	.01
COMMON PLAYER DP	.04	.02	.01
☐ 1 Bob Horner DP	.06	.03	.01
☐ 2 Dale Murphy	.20	.09	.03
☐ 3 Lee Smith	.10	.05	.01
☐ 4 Eric Davis	.30	.14	.04
☐ 5 John Franco	.06	.03	.01
☐ 6 Dave Parker	.10	.05	.01
☐ 7 Kevin Bass	.06	.03	.01
☐ 8 Glenn Davis DP	.10	.05	.01
☐ 9 Bill Doran DP	.06	.03	.01
☐ 10 Bob Knepper DP	.04	.02	.01
☐ 11 Mike Scott	.10	.05	.01
☐ 12 Dave Smith	.06	.03	.01
☐ 13 Mariano Duncan	.06	.03	.01
☐ 14 Orel Hershiser	.15	.07	.02
☐ 15 Steve Sax DP	.10	.05	.01
☐ 16 Fernando Valenzuela	.10	.05	.01
☐ 17 Tim Raines	.15	.07	.02
☐ 18 Jeff Reardon	.15	.07	.02
☐ 19 Floyd Youmans	.06	.03	.01
☐ 20 Gary Carter DP	.12	.05	.02
☐ 21 Ron Darling	.10	.05	.01
☐ 22 Sid Fernandez	.10	.05	.01
☐ 23 Dwight Gooden	.25	.11	.03
☐ 24 Keith Hernandez	.10	.05	.01
☐ 25 Bob Ojeda	.06	.03	.01
☐ 26 Darryl Strawberry	.50	.23	.06
☐ 27 Steve Bedrosian	.06	.03	.01
☐ 28 Von Hayes DP	.04	.02	.01
☐ 29 Juan Samuel	.10	.05	.01
☐ 30 Mike Schmidt	.60	.25	.08
☐ 31 Rick Rhoden	.06	.03	.01
☐ 32 Vince Coleman	.15	.07	.02
☐ 33 Danny Cox	.06	.03	.01
☐ 34 Todd Worrell	.15	.07	.02
☐ 35 Tony Gwynn	.50	.23	.06
☐ 36 Mike Krukow	.06	.03	.01
☐ 37 Candy Maldonado	.10	.05	.01
☐ 38 Don Aase	.06	.03	.01
☐ 39 Eddie Murray	.35	.16	.04
☐ 40 Cal Ripken	.75	.35	.09
☐ 41 Wade Boggs	.50	.23	.06
☐ 42 Roger Clemens	.75	.35	.09
☐ 43 Bruce Hurst	.10	.05	.01
☐ 44 Jim Rice	.15	.07	.02
☐ 45 Wally Joyner	.20	.09	.03
☐ 46 Donnie Moore	.06	.03	.01
☐ 47 Gary Pettis	.06	.03	.01
☐ 48 Mike Witt	.06	.03	.01
☐ 49 John Cangelosi	.06	.03	.01
☐ 50 Tom Candiotti	.10	.05	.01
☐ 51 Joe Carter	.35	.16	.04
☐ 52 Pat Tabler	.06	.03	.01
☐ 53 Kirk Gibson DP	.10	.05	.01
☐ 54 Willie Hernandez	.06	.03	.01
☐ 55 Jack Morris	.15	.07	.02
☐ 56 Alan Trammell DP	.10	.05	.01
☐ 57 George Brett	.50	.23	.06
☐ 58 Willie Wilson	.10	.05	.01
☐ 59 Rob Deer	.10	.05	.01
☐ 60 Teddy Higuera	.06	.03	.01
☐ 61 Bert Blyleven DP	.06	.03	.01
☐ 62 Gary Gaetti DP	.04	.02	.01
☐ 63 Kirby Puckett	.60	.25	.08
☐ 64 Rickey Henderson	.50	.23	.06
☐ 65 Don Mattingly	.60	.25	.08
☐ 66 Dennis Rasmussen	.06	.03	.01
☐ 67 Dave Righetti	.06	.03	.01
☐ 68 Jose Canseco	.75	.35	.09
☐ 69 Dave Kingman	.10	.05	.01
☐ 70 Phil Bradley	.06	.03	.01
☐ 71 Mark Langston	.10	.05	.01
☐ 72 Pete O'Brien	.06	.03	.01
☐ 73 Jesse Barfield	.06	.03	.01
☐ 74 George Bell	.15	.07	.02
☐ 75 Tony Fernandez	.10	.05	.01
☐ 76 Tom Henke	.10	.05	.01
☐ 77 Checklist Card	.10	.05	.01

1987 Topps Traded

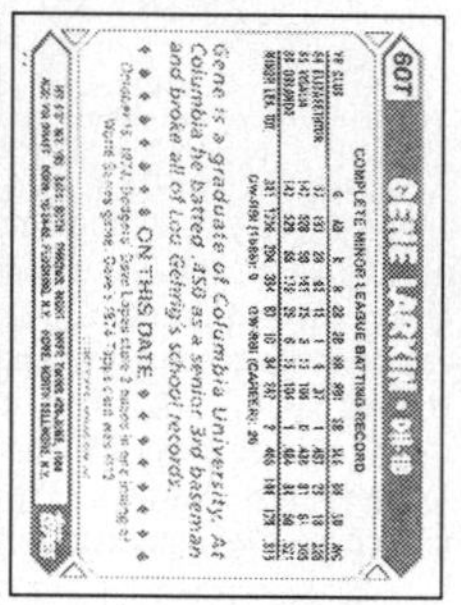

This 132-card Traded or extended set was distributed by Topps to dealers in a special green and white box as a complete set. The card fronts are identical in style to the Topps regular issue and are also 2 1/2" by 3 1/2". The backs are printed in yellow and blue on white card stock. Cards are numbered (with a T suffix) alphabetically according to the name of the player. The key (extended) rookies in this set (without any prior cards) are Ellis Burks and Matt Williams. Extended rookies in this set (with prior cards but not from Topps) are David Cone, Greg Maddux, and Fred McGriff. Topps also produced a specially boxed "glossy" edition, frequently referred to as the Topps Traded Tiffany set. This year Topps did not disclose the number of sets they produced or sold. It is apparent from the availability that there were many more sets produced this year compared to the 1984-86 Tiffany sets, perhaps 30,000 sets, more than three times as many. The checklist of cards is identical to that of the normal non-glossy cards. There are two primary distinguishing features of the Tiffany cards, white card stock reverses and high gloss obverses. These Tiffany cards are valued approximately from three to five times the values listed below.

	MT	EX-MT	VG
COMPLETE SET (132)	10.00	4.50	1.25
COMMON PLAYER (1T-132T)	.05	.02	.01
☐ 1T Bill Almon	.05	.02	.01
☐ 2T Scott Bankhead	.05	.02	.01
☐ 3T Eric Bell	.05	.02	.01
☐ 4T Juan Beniquez	.05	.02	.01
☐ 5T Juan Berenguer	.05	.02	.01
☐ 6T Greg Booker	.05	.02	.01
☐ 7T Thad Bosley	.05	.02	.01
☐ 8T Larry Bowa MG	.08	.04	.01
☐ 9T Greg Brock	.05	.02	.01

☐ 10T Bob Brower .05 .02 .01
☐ 11T Jerry Browne .08 .04 .01
☐ 12T Ralph Bryant .08 .04 .01
☐ 13T DeWayne Buice .05 .02 .01
☐ 14T Ellis Burks .50 .23 .06
☐ 15T Ivan Calderon .12 .05 .02
☐ 16T Jeff Calhoun .05 .02 .01
☐ 17T Casey Candaele .05 .02 .01
☐ 18T John Cangelosi .05 .02 .01
☐ 19T Steve Carlton .25 .11 .03
☐ 20T Juan Castillo .05 .02 .01
☐ 21T Rick Cerone .05 .02 .01
☐ 22T Ron Cey .08 .04 .01
☐ 23T John Christensen .05 .02 .01
☐ 24T David Cone 2.00 .90 .25
☐ 25T Chuck Crim .05 .02 .01
☐ 26T Storm Davis .05 .02 .01
☐ 27T Andre Dawson .30 .14 .04
☐ 28T Rick Dempsey .05 .02 .01
☐ 29T Doug Drabek .40 .18 .05
☐ 30T Mike Dunne .05 .02 .01
☐ 31T Dennis Eckersley .35 .16 .04
☐ 32T Lee Elia MG .05 .02 .01
☐ 33T Brian Fisher .05 .02 .01
☐ 34T Terry Francona .05 .02 .01
☐ 35T Willie Fraser .05 .02 .01
☐ 36T Billy Gardner MG .05 .02 .01
☐ 37T Ken Gerhart .05 .02 .01
☐ 38T Dan Gladden .05 .02 .01
☐ 39T Jim Gott .05 .02 .01
☐ 40T Cecilio Guante .05 .02 .01
☐ 41T Albert Hall .05 .02 .01
☐ 42T Terry Harper .05 .02 .01
☐ 43T Mickey Hatcher .05 .02 .01
☐ 44T Brad Havens .05 .02 .01
☐ 45T Neal Heaton .05 .02 .01
☐ 46T Mike Henneman .25 .11 .03
☐ 47T Donnie Hill .05 .02 .01
☐ 48T Guy Hoffman .05 .02 .01
☐ 49T Brian Holton .05 .02 .01
☐ 50T Charles Hudson .05 .02 .01
☐ 51T Danny Jackson .05 .02 .01
☐ 52T Reggie Jackson .35 .16 .04
☐ 53T Chris James .10 .05 .01
☐ 54T Dion James .05 .02 .01
☐ 55T Stan Jefferson .05 .02 .01
☐ 56T Joe Johnson .05 .02 .01
☐ 57T Terry Kennedy .05 .02 .01
☐ 58T Mike Kingery .05 .02 .01
☐ 59T Ray Knight .08 .04 .01
☐ 60T Gene Larkin .15 .07 .02
☐ 61T Mike LaValliere .08 .04 .01
☐ 62T Jack Lazorko .05 .02 .01
☐ 63T Terry Leach .05 .02 .01
☐ 64T Tim Leary .05 .02 .01
☐ 65T Jim Lindeman .05 .02 .01
☐ 66T Steve Lombardozzi .05 .02 .01
☐ 67T Bill Long .05 .02 .01
☐ 68T Barry Lyons .05 .02 .01
☐ 69T Shane Mack .60 .25 .08
☐ 70T Greg Maddux 3.00 1.35 .40
☐ 71T Bill Madlock .08 .04 .01
☐ 72T Joe Magrane .10 .05 .01
☐ 73T Dave Martinez .15 .07 .02
☐ 74T Fred McGriff 2.25 1.00 .30
☐ 75T Mark McLemore .12 .05 .02
☐ 76T Kevin McReynolds .08 .04 .01
☐ 77T Dave Meads .05 .02 .01
☐ 78T Eddie Milner .05 .02 .01
☐ 79T Greg Minton .05 .02 .01
☐ 80T John Mitchell .05 .02 .01
☐ 81T Kevin Mitchell .50 .23 .06
☐ 82T Charlie Moore .05 .02 .01
☐ 83T Jeff Musselman .05 .02 .01
☐ 84T Gene Nelson .05 .02 .01
☐ 85T Graig Nettles .08 .04 .01
☐ 86T Al Newman .05 .02 .01
☐ 87T Reid Nichols .05 .02 .01
☐ 88T Tom Niedenfuer .05 .02 .01
☐ 89T Joe Niekro .08 .04 .01
☐ 90T Tom Nieto .05 .02 .01
☐ 91T Matt Nokes .25 .11 .03
☐ 92T Dickie Noles .05 .02 .01
☐ 93T Pat Pacillo .05 .02 .01
☐ 94T Lance Parrish .08 .04 .01
☐ 95T Tony Pena .05 .02 .01
☐ 96T Luis Polonia .40 .18 .05
☐ 97T Randy Ready .05 .02 .01
☐ 98T Jeff Reardon .20 .09 .03
☐ 99T Gary Redus .05 .02 .01
☐ 100T Jeff Reed .05 .02 .01
☐ 101T Rick Rhoden .05 .02 .01
☐ 102T Cal Ripken Sr. MG .08 .04 .01
☐ 103T Wally Ritchie .05 .02 .01
☐ 104T Jeff M. Robinson .08 .04 .01
☐ 105T Gary Roenicke .05 .02 .01
☐ 106T Jerry Royster .05 .02 .01
☐ 107T Mark Salas .05 .02 .01
☐ 108T Luis Salazar .05 .02 .01
☐ 109T Benny Santiago .35 .16 .04
☐ 110T Dave Schmidt .05 .02 .01
☐ 111T Kevin Seitzer .25 .11 .03
☐ 112T John Shelby .05 .02 .01
☐ 113T Steve Shields .05 .02 .01
☐ 114T John Smiley .75 .35 .09
☐ 115T Chris Speier .05 .02 .01
☐ 116T Mike Stanley .05 .02 .01
☐ 117T Terry Steinbach .30 .14 .04
☐ 118T Les Straker .05 .02 .01
☐ 119T Jim Sundberg .05 .02 .01
☐ 120T Danny Tartabull .25 .11 .03
☐ 121T Tom Trebelhorn MG .05 .02 .01
☐ 122T Dave Valle .05 .02 .01
☐ 123T Ed VandeBerg .05 .02 .01
☐ 124T Andy Van Slyke .20 .09 .03
☐ 125T Gary Ward .05 .02 .01
☐ 126T Alan Wiggins .05 .02 .01
☐ 127T Bill Wilkinson .05 .02 .01
☐ 128T Frank Williams .05 .02 .01
☐ 129T Matt Williams 1.50 .65 .19
☐ 130T Jim Winn .05 .02 .01
☐ 131T Matt Young .05 .02 .01
☐ 132T Checklist 1T-132T .05 .01 .00

1987 Topps Wax Box Cards

This set of eight cards is really four different sets of two smaller (approximately 2 1/8" by 3") cards which were printed on the side of the wax pack box; these eight cards are lettered A through H and are very similar in design to the Topps regular issue cards. The order of the set is alphabetical by player's name. Complete boxes would be worth an additional 25 percent premium over the prices below. The card backs are done in a newspaper headline style describing something about that player that happened the previous season. The card backs feature blue and yellow ink on gray card stock.

	MT	EX-MT	VG
COMPLETE SET (8)	3.50	1.55	.45
COMMON PLAYER (A-H)	.15	.07	.02

☐ A Don Baylor .25 .11 .03
☐ B Steve Carlton .60 .25 .08
☐ C Ron Cey .15 .07 .02
☐ D Cecil Cooper .15 .07 .02
☐ E Rickey Henderson 1.50 .65 .19
☐ F Jim Rice .25 .11 .03
☐ G Don Sutton .35 .16 .04
☐ H Dave Winfield 1.00 .45 .13

1988 Topps

This 792-card set features backs that are printed in orange and black on light gray card stock. The manager cards contain a checklist of the respective team's players on the back. Subsets in the set include Record Breakers (1-7), Turn Back the Clock (661-665), and All-Star selections (386-407). The Team Leader cards typically show two players together inside a white cloud. The key Rookie Cards in this set are Ellis Burks, Tom Glavine, and Matt Williams. Topps also produced a specially boxed "glossy" edition, frequently referred to as the Topps Tiffany set. This year, again, Topps did not disclose the number of Tiffany sets they produced or sold. It is apparent from the availability that there were many more sets produced this year compared to the 1984-86 Tiffany sets, perhaps 25,000 sets. The checklist of cards (792 regular and 132 Traded) is identical to that of the normal non-glossy cards. There are two primary distinguishing features of the Tiffany cards, white card stock reverses and high gloss obverses. These Tiffany cards are valued approximately from three to five times the values listed below.

	MT	EX-MT	VG
COMPLETE SET (792)	20.00	9.00	2.50
COMPLETE FACT.SET (792)	20.00	9.00	2.50
COMMON PLAYER (1-792)	.04	.02	.01
☐ 1 Vince Coleman RB 100 Steals for Third Cons. Season	.10	.03	.01
☐ 2 Don Mattingly RB Six Grand Slams	.12	.05	.02
☐ 3A Mark McGwire RB Rookie Homer Record (White spot behind left foot)	.40	.18	.05
☐ 3B Mark McGwire RB Rookie Homer Record (No white spot)	.25	.11	.03
☐ 4A Eddie Murray RB Switch Home Runs, Two Straight Games (Caption in box on card front)	.40	.18	.05
☐ 4B Eddie Murray RB Switch Home Runs, Two Straight Games (No caption on front)	.10	.05	.01
☐ 5 Phil/Joe Niekro RB Brothers Win Record	.05	.02	.01
☐ 6 Nolan Ryan RB 11th Season with 200 Strikeouts	.40	.18	.05
☐ 7 Benito Santiago RB 34-Game Hitting Streak, Rookie Record	.05	.02	.01
☐ 8 Kevin Elster	.04	.02	.01
☐ 9 Andy Hawkins	.04	.02	.01
☐ 10 Ryne Sandberg	.50	.23	.06
☐ 11 Mike Young	.04	.02	.01
☐ 12 Bill Schroeder	.04	.02	.01
☐ 13 Andres Thomas	.04	.02	.01
☐ 14 Sparky Anderson MG (Checklist back)	.06	.03	.01
☐ 15 Chili Davis	.07	.03	.01
☐ 16 Kirk McCaskill	.04	.02	.01
☐ 17 Ron Oester	.04	.02	.01
☐ 18A Al Leiter ERR (Photo actually Steve George, right ear visible)	.15	.07	.02
☐ 18B Al Leiter COR (Left ear visible)	.04	.02	.01
☐ 19 Mark Davidson	.04	.02	.01
☐ 20 Kevin Gross	.04	.02	.01
☐ 21 Red Sox TL Wade Boggs and Spike Owen	.08	.04	.01
☐ 22 Greg Swindell	.15	.07	.02
☐ 23 Ken Landreaux	.04	.02	.01
☐ 24 Jim Deshaies	.04	.02	.01
☐ 25 Andres Galarraga	.04	.02	.01
☐ 26 Mitch Williams	.07	.03	.01
☐ 27 R.J. Reynolds	.04	.02	.01
☐ 28 Jose Nunez	.04	.02	.01
☐ 29 Argenis Salazar	.04	.02	.01
☐ 30 Sid Fernandez	.07	.03	.01
☐ 31 Bruce Bochy	.04	.02	.01
☐ 32 Mike Morgan	.07	.03	.01
☐ 33 Rob Deer	.07	.03	.01
☐ 34 Ricky Horton	.04	.02	.01
☐ 35 Harold Baines	.07	.03	.01
☐ 36 Jamie Moyer	.04	.02	.01
☐ 37 Ed Romero	.04	.02	.01
☐ 38 Jeff Calhoun	.04	.02	.01
☐ 39 Gerald Perry	.04	.02	.01
☐ 40 Orel Hershiser	.07	.03	.01
☐ 41 Bob Melvin	.04	.02	.01
☐ 42 Bill Landrum	.07	.03	.01
☐ 43 Dick Schofield	.04	.02	.01
☐ 44 Lou Piniella MG (Checklist back)	.06	.03	.01
☐ 45 Kent Hrbek	.07	.03	.01
☐ 46 Darnell Coles	.04	.02	.01
☐ 47 Joaquin Andujar	.04	.02	.01
☐ 48 Alan Ashby	.04	.02	.01
☐ 49 Dave Clark	.04	.02	.01
☐ 50 Hubie Brooks	.04	.02	.01
☐ 51 Orioles TL Eddie Murray and Cal Ripken	.25	.11	.03
☐ 52 Don Robinson	.04	.02	.01
☐ 53 Curt Wilkerson	.04	.02	.01
☐ 54 Jim Clancy	.04	.02	.01
☐ 55 Phil Bradley	.04	.02	.01
☐ 56 Ed Hearn	.04	.02	.01
☐ 57 Tim Crews	.04	.02	.01
☐ 58 Dave Magadan	.07	.03	.01
☐ 59 Danny Cox	.04	.02	.01
☐ 60 Rickey Henderson	.30	.14	.04
☐ 61 Mark Knudson	.04	.02	.01
☐ 62 Jeff Hamilton	.04	.02	.01
☐ 63 Jimmy Jones	.04	.02	.01
☐ 64 Ken Caminiti	.30	.14	.04
☐ 65 Leon Durham	.04	.02	.01
☐ 66 Shane Rawley	.04	.02	.01
☐ 67 Ken Oberkfell	.04	.02	.01
☐ 68 Dave Dravecky	.07	.03	.01
☐ 69 Mike Hart	.04	.02	.01
☐ 70 Roger Clemens	.50	.23	.06
☐ 71 Gary Pettis	.04	.02	.01
☐ 72 Dennis Eckersley	.15	.07	.02
☐ 73 Randy Bush	.04	.02	.01
☐ 74 Tom Lasorda MG (Checklist back)	.06	.03	.01
☐ 75 Joe Carter	.25	.11	.03
☐ 76 Dennis Martinez	.07	.03	.01
☐ 77 Tom O'Malley	.04	.02	.01
☐ 78 Dan Petry	.04	.02	.01
☐ 79 Ernie Whitt	.04	.02	.01
☐ 80 Mark Langston	.07	.03	.01
☐ 81 Reds TL Ron Robinson and John Franco	.05	.02	.01
☐ 82 Darrel Akerfelds	.04	.02	.01
☐ 83 Jose Oquendo	.04	.02	.01
☐ 84 Cecilio Guante	.04	.02	.01
☐ 85 Howard Johnson	.10	.05	.01
☐ 86 Ron Karkovice	.04	.02	.01
☐ 87 Mike Mason	.04	.02	.01
☐ 88 Earnie Riles	.04	.02	.01
☐ 89 Gary Thurman	.04	.02	.01
☐ 90 Dale Murphy	.10	.05	.01
☐ 91 Joey Cora	.07	.03	.01
☐ 92 Len Matuszek	.04	.02	.01
☐ 93 Bob Sebra	.04	.02	.01
☐ 94 Chuck Jackson	.04	.02	.01

☐ 95 Lance Parrish .07 .03 .01
☐ 96 Todd Benzinger .10 .05 .01
☐ 97 Scott Garrelts .04 .02 .01
☐ 98 Rene Gonzales .12 .05 .02
☐ 99 Chuck Finley .07 .03 .01
☐ 100 Jack Clark .07 .03 .01
☐ 101 Allan Anderson .04 .02 .01
☐ 102 Barry Larkin .25 .11 .03
☐ 103 Curt Young .04 .02 .01
☐ 104 Dick Williams MG .06 .03 .01
(Checklist back)
☐ 105 Jesse Orosco .04 .02 .01
☐ 106 Jim Walewander .04 .02 .01
☐ 107 Scott Bailes .04 .02 .01
☐ 108 Steve Lyons .04 .02 .01
☐ 109 Joel Skinner .04 .02 .01
☐ 110 Teddy Higuera .04 .02 .01
☐ 111 Expos TL .05 .02 .01
Hubie Brooks and
Vance Law
☐ 112 Les Lancaster .04 .02 .01
☐ 113 Kelly Gruber .07 .03 .01
☐ 114 Jeff Russell .04 .02 .01
☐ 115 Johnny Ray .04 .02 .01
☐ 116 Jerry Don Gleaton .04 .02 .01
☐ 117 James Steels .04 .02 .01
☐ 118 Bob Welch .07 .03 .01
☐ 119 Robbie Wine .04 .02 .01
☐ 120 Kirby Puckett .40 .18 .05
☐ 121 Checklist 1-132 .06 .01 .00
☐ 12[illegible] [illegible]ny Bernazard .04 .02 .01
☐ 12[illegible] [illegible]n Candiotti .04 .02 .01
☐ 12[illegible] [illegible]y Knight .07 .03 .01
☐ 12[illegible] [illegible]uce Hurst .07 .03 .01
☐ 126 [illegible]eve Jeltz .04 .02 .01
☐ 127 [illegible]im Gott .04 .02 .01
☐ 128 Johnny Grubb .04 .02 .01
☐ 129 Greg Minton .04 .02 .01
☐ 130 Buddy Bell .07 .03 .01
☐ 131 Don Schulze .04 .02 .01
☐ 132 Donnie Hill .04 .02 .01
☐ 133 Greg Mathews .04 .02 .01
☐ 134 Chuck Tanner MG .06 .03 .01
(Checklist back)
☐ 135 Dennis Rasmussen .04 .02 .01
☐ 136 Brian Dayett .04 .02 .01
☐ 137 Chris Bosio .07 .03 .01
☐ 138 Mitch Webster .04 .02 .01
☐ 139 Jerry Browne .04 .02 .01
☐ 140 Jesse Barfield .04 .02 .01
☐ 141 Royals TL .10 .05 .01
George Brett and
Bret Saberhagen
☐ 142 Andy Van Slyke .10 .05 .01
☐ 143 Mickey Tettleton .12 .05 .02
☐ 144 Don Gordon .04 .02 .01
☐ 145 Bill Madlock .07 .03 .01
☐ 146 Donell Nixon .04 .02 .01
☐ 147 Bill Buckner .07 .03 .01
☐ 148 Carmelo Martinez .04 .02 .01
☐ 149 Ken Howell .04 .02 .01
☐ 150 Eric Davis .10 .05 .01
☐ 151 Bob Knepper .04 .02 .01
☐ 152 Jody Reed .25 .11 .03
☐ 153 John Habyan .04 .02 .01
☐ 154 Jeff Stone .04 .02 .01
☐ 155 Bruce Sutter .07 .03 .01
☐ 156 Gary Matthews .04 .02 .01
☐ 157 Atlee Hammaker .04 .02 .01
☐ 158 Tim Hulett .04 .02 .01
☐ 159 Brad Arnsberg .04 .02 .01
☐ 160 Willie McGee .07 .03 .01
☐ 161 Bryn Smith .04 .02 .01
☐ 162 Mark McLemore .04 .02 .01
☐ 163 Dale Mohorcic .04 .02 .01
☐ 164 Dave Johnson MG .06 .03 .01
(Checklist back)
☐ 165 Robin Yount .25 .11 .03
☐ 166 Rick Rodriquez .04 .02 .01
☐ 167 Rance Mulliniks .04 .02 .01
☐ 168 Barry Jones .04 .02 .01
☐ 169 Ross Jones .04 .02 .01
☐ 170 Rich Gossage .07 .03 .01
☐ 171 Cubs TL .05 .02 .01
Shawon Dunston
and Manny Trillo
☐ 172 Lloyd McClendon .04 .02 .01
☐ 173 Eric Plunk .04 .02 .01
☐ 174 Phil Garner .07 .03 .01
☐ 175 Kevin Bass .04 .02 .01
☐ 176 Jeff Reed .04 .02 .01
☐ 177 Frank Tanana .04 .02 .01
☐ 178 Dwayne Henry .04 .02 .01
☐ 179 Charlie Puleo .04 .02 .01
☐ 180 Terry Kennedy .04 .02 .01
☐ 181 David Cone .50 .23 .06
☐ 182 Ken Phelps .04 .02 .01
☐ 183 Tom Lawless .04 .02 .01
☐ 184 Ivan Calderon .07 .03 .01
☐ 185 Rick Rhoden .04 .02 .01
☐ 186 Rafael Palmeiro .30 .14 .04
☐ 187 Steve Kiefer .04 .02 .01
☐ 188 John Russell .04 .02 .01
☐ 189 Wes Gardner .04 .02 .01
☐ 190 Candy Maldonado .04 .02 .01
☐ 191 John Cerutti .04 .02 .01
☐ 192 Devon White .10 .05 .01
☐ 193 Brian Fisher .04 .02 .01
☐ 194 Tom Kelly MG .06 .03 .01
(Checklist back)
☐ 195 Dan Quisenberry .07 .03 .01
☐ 196 Dave Engle .04 .02 .01
☐ 197 Lance McCullers .04 .02 .01
☐ 198 Franklin Stubbs .04 .02 .01
☐ 199 Dave Meads .04 .02 .01
☐ 200 Wade Boggs .30 .14 .04
☐ 201 Rangers TL .05 .02 .01
Bobby Valentine MG,
Pete O'Brien,
Pete Incaviglia, and
Steve Buechele
☐ 202 Glenn Hoffman .04 .02 .01
☐ 203 Fred Toliver .04 .02 .01
☐ 204 Paul O'Neill .12 .05 .02
☐ 205 Nelson Liriano .04 .02 .01
☐ 206 Domingo Ramos .04 .02 .01
☐ 207 John Mitchell .04 .02 .01
☐ 208 Steve Lake .04 .02 .01
☐ 209 Richard Dotson .04 .02 .01
☐ 210 Willie Randolph .07 .03 .01
☐ 211 Frank DiPino .04 .02 .01
☐ 212 Greg Brock .04 .02 .01
☐ 213 Albert Hall .04 .02 .01
☐ 214 Dave Schmidt .04 .02 .01
☐ 215 Von Hayes .04 .02 .01
☐ 216 Jerry Reuss .04 .02 .01
☐ 217 Harry Spilman .04 .02 .01
☐ 218 Dan Schatzeder .04 .02 .01
☐ 219 Mike Stanley .04 .02 .01
☐ 220 Tom Henke .07 .03 .01
☐ 221 Rafael Belliard .04 .02 .01
☐ 222 Steve Farr .04 .02 .01
☐ 223 Stan Jefferson .04 .02 .01
☐ 224 Tom Trebelhorn MG .06 .03 .01
(Checklist back)
☐ 225 Mike Scioscia .04 .02 .01
☐ 226 Dave Lopes .07 .03 .01
☐ 227 Ed Correa .04 .02 .01
☐ 228 Wallace Johnson .04 .02 .01
☐ 229 Jeff Musselman .04 .02 .01
☐ 230 Pat Tabler .04 .02 .01
☐ 231 Pirates TL .12 .05 .02
Barry Bonds and
Bobby Bonilla
☐ 232 Bob James .04 .02 .01
☐ 233 Rafael Santana .04 .02 .01
☐ 234 Ken Dayley .04 .02 .01
☐ 235 Gary Ward .04 .02 .01
☐ 236 Ted Power .04 .02 .01
☐ 237 Mike Heath .04 .02 .01
☐ 238 Luis Polonia .25 .11 .03
☐ 239 Roy Smalley .04 .02 .01
☐ 240 Lee Smith .15 .07 .02
☐ 241 Damaso Garcia .04 .02 .01
☐ 242 Tom Niedenfuer .04 .02 .01
☐ 243 Mark Ryal .04 .02 .01
☐ 244 Jeff D. Robinson .04 .02 .01
☐ 245 Rich Gedman .04 .02 .01
☐ 246 Mike Campbell .04 .02 .01
☐ 247 Thad Bosley .04 .02 .01
☐ 248 Storm Davis .04 .02 .01
☐ 249 Mike Marshall .04 .02 .01
☐ 250 Nolan Ryan .75 .35 .09
☐ 251 Tom Foley .04 .02 .01
☐ 252 Bob Brower .04 .02 .01
☐ 253 Checklist 133-264 .06 .01 .00
☐ 254 Lee Elia MG .06 .03 .01
(Checklist back)
☐ 255 Mookie Wilson .07 .03 .01
☐ 256 Ken Schrom .04 .02 .01
☐ 257 Jerry Royster .04 .02 .01
☐ 258 Ed Nunez .04 .02 .01
☐ 259 Ron Kittle .04 .02 .01
☐ 260 Vince Coleman .07 .03 .01
☐ 261 Giants TL .05 .02 .01
(Five players)

☐ 262	Drew Hall	.04	.02	.01
☐ 263	Glenn Braggs	.04	.02	.01
☐ 264	Les Straker	.04	.02	.01
☐ 265	Bo Diaz	.04	.02	.01
☐ 266	Paul Assenmacher	.04	.02	.01
☐ 267	Billy Bean	.04	.02	.01
☐ 268	Bruce Ruffin	.04	.02	.01
☐ 269	Ellis Burks	.25	.11	.03
☐ 270	Mike Witt	.04	.02	.01
☐ 271	Ken Gerhart	.04	.02	.01
☐ 272	Steve Ontiveros	.04	.02	.01
☐ 273	Garth Iorg	.04	.02	.01
☐ 274	Junior Ortiz	.04	.02	.01
☐ 275	Kevin Seitzer	.07	.03	.01
☐ 276	Luis Salazar	.04	.02	.01
☐ 277	Alejandro Pena	.04	.02	.01
☐ 278	Jose Cruz	.04	.02	.01
☐ 279	Randy St.Claire	.04	.02	.01
☐ 280	Pete Incaviglia	.07	.03	.01
☐ 281	Jerry Hairston	.04	.02	.01
☐ 282	Pat Perry	.04	.02	.01
☐ 283	Phil Lombardi	.04	.02	.01
☐ 284	Larry Bowa MG (Checklist back)	.06	.03	.01
☐ 285	Jim Presley	.04	.02	.01
☐ 286	Chuck Crim	.04	.02	.01
☐ 287	Manny Trillo	.04	.02	.01
☐ 288	Pat Pacillo (Chris Sabo in background of photo)	.04	.02	.01
☐ 289	Dave Bergman	.04	.02	.01
☐ 290	Tony Fernandez	.07	.03	.01
☐ 291	Astros TL Billy Hatcher and Kevin Bass	.05	.02	.01
☐ 292	Carney Lansford	.07	.03	.01
☐ 293	Doug Jones	.25	.11	.03
☐ 294	Al Pedrique	.04	.02	.01
☐ 295	Bert Blyleven	.07	.03	.01
☐ 296	Floyd Rayford	.04	.02	.01
☐ 297	Zane Smith	.04	.02	.01
☐ 298	Milt Thompson	.04	.02	.01
☐ 299	Steve Crawford	.04	.02	.01
☐ 300	Don Mattingly	.30	.14	.04
☐ 301	Bud Black	.04	.02	.01
☐ 302	Jose Uribe	.04	.02	.01
☐ 303	Eric Show	.04	.02	.01
☐ 304	George Hendrick	.04	.02	.01
☐ 305	Steve Sax	.07	.03	.01
☐ 306	Billy Hatcher	.04	.02	.01
☐ 307	Mike Trujillo	.04	.02	.01
☐ 308	Lee Mazzilli	.04	.02	.01
☐ 309	Bill Long	.04	.02	.01
☐ 310	Tom Herr	.04	.02	.01
☐ 311	Scott Sanderson	.04	.02	.01
☐ 312	Joey Meyer	.04	.02	.01
☐ 313	Bob McClure	.04	.02	.01
☐ 314	Jimy Williams MG (Checklist back)	.06	.03	.01
☐ 315	Dave Parker	.07	.03	.01
☐ 316	Jose Rijo	.10	.05	.01
☐ 317	Tom Nieto	.04	.02	.01
☐ 318	Mel Hall	.04	.02	.01
☐ 319	Mike Loynd	.04	.02	.01
☐ 320	Alan Trammell	.07	.03	.01
☐ 321	White Sox TL Harold Baines and Carlton Fisk	.05	.02	.01
☐ 322	Vicente Palacios	.10	.05	.01
☐ 323	Rick Leach	.04	.02	.01
☐ 324	Danny Jackson	.04	.02	.01
☐ 325	Glenn Hubbard	.04	.02	.01
☐ 326	Al Nipper	.04	.02	.01
☐ 327	Larry Sheets	.04	.02	.01
☐ 328	Greg Cadaret	.04	.02	.01
☐ 329	Chris Speier	.04	.02	.01
☐ 330	Eddie Whitson	.04	.02	.01
☐ 331	Brian Downing	.04	.02	.01
☐ 332	Jerry Reed	.04	.02	.01
☐ 333	Wally Backman	.04	.02	.01
☐ 334	Dave LaPoint	.04	.02	.01
☐ 335	Claudell Washington	.04	.02	.01
☐ 336	Ed Lynch	.04	.02	.01
☐ 337	Jim Gantner	.04	.02	.01
☐ 338	Brian Holton UER (1987 ERA .389, should be 3.89)	.04	.02	.01
☐ 339	Kurt Stillwell	.04	.02	.01
☐ 340	Jack Morris	.12	.05	.02
☐ 341	Carmen Castillo	.04	.02	.01
☐ 342	Larry Andersen	.04	.02	.01
☐ 343	Greg Gagne	.04	.02	.01
☐ 344	Tony LaRussa MG (Checklist back)	.06	.03	.01
☐ 345	Scott Fletcher	.04	.02	.01
☐ 346	Vance Law	.04	.02	.01
☐ 347	Joe Johnson	.04	.02	.01
☐ 348	Jim Eisenreich	.04	.02	.01
☐ 349	Bob Walk	.04	.02	.01
☐ 350	Will Clark	.60	.25	.08
☐ 351	Cardinals TL Red Schoendienst CO and Tony Pena	.05	.02	.01
☐ 352	Billy Ripken	.10	.05	.01
☐ 353	Ed Olwine	.04	.02	.01
☐ 354	Marc Sullivan	.04	.02	.01
☐ 355	Roger McDowell	.04	.02	.01
☐ 356	Luis Aguayo	.04	.02	.01
☐ 357	Floyd Bannister	.04	.02	.01
☐ 358	Rey Quinones	.04	.02	.01
☐ 359	Tim Stoddard	.04	.02	.01
☐ 360	Tony Gwynn	.30	.14	.04
☐ 361	Greg Maddux	.75	.35	.09
☐ 362	Juan Castillo	.04	.02	.01
☐ 363	Willie Fraser	.04	.02	.01
☐ 364	Nick Esasky	.04	.02	.01
☐ 365	Floyd Youmans	.04	.02	.01
☐ 366	Chet Lemon	.04	.02	.01
☐ 367	Tim Leary	.04	.02	.01
☐ 368	Gerald Young	.04	.02	.01
☐ 369	Greg Harris	.04	.02	.01
☐ 370	Jose Canseco	.60	.25	.08
☐ 371	Joe Hesketh	.04	.02	.01
☐ 372	Matt Williams	.90	.40	.11
☐ 373	Checklist 265-396	.06	.01	.00
☐ 374	Doc Edwards MG (Checklist back)	.06	.03	.01
☐ 375	Tom Brunansky	.07	.03	.01
☐ 376	Bill Wilkinson	.04	.02	.01
☐ 377	Sam Horn	.12	.05	.02
☐ 378	Todd Frohwirth	.04	.02	.01
☐ 379	Rafael Ramirez	.04	.02	.01
☐ 380	Joe Magrane	.10	.05	.01
☐ 381	Angels TL Wally Joyner and Jack Howell	.05	.02	.01
☐ 382	Keith A. Miller (New York Mets)	.20	.09	.03
☐ 383	Eric Bell	.04	.02	.01
☐ 384	Neil Allen	.04	.02	.01
☐ 385	Carlton Fisk	.20	.09	.03
☐ 386	Don Mattingly AS	.15	.07	.02
☐ 387	Willie Randolph AS	.05	.02	.01
☐ 388	Wade Boggs AS	.15	.07	.02
☐ 389	Alan Trammell AS	.05	.02	.01
☐ 390	George Bell AS	.05	.02	.01
☐ 391	Kirby Puckett AS	.20	.09	.03
☐ 392	Dave Winfield AS	.15	.07	.02
☐ 393	Matt Nokes AS	.05	.02	.01
☐ 394	Roger Clemens AS	.25	.11	.03
☐ 395	Jimmy Key AS	.05	.02	.01
☐ 396	Tom Henke AS	.05	.02	.01
☐ 397	Jack Clark AS	.05	.02	.01
☐ 398	Juan Samuel AS	.05	.02	.01
☐ 399	Tim Wallach AS	.05	.02	.01
☐ 400	Ozzie Smith AS	.12	.05	.02
☐ 401	Andre Dawson AS	.12	.05	.02
☐ 402	Tony Gwynn AS	.15	.07	.02
☐ 403	Tim Raines AS	.05	.02	.01
☐ 404	Benny Santiago AS	.05	.02	.01
☐ 405	Dwight Gooden AS	.10	.05	.01
☐ 406	Shane Rawley AS	.05	.02	.01
☐ 407	Steve Bedrosian AS	.05	.02	.01
☐ 408	Dion James	.04	.02	.01
☐ 409	Joel McKeon	.04	.02	.01
☐ 410	Tony Pena	.04	.02	.01
☐ 411	Wayne Tolleson	.04	.02	.01
☐ 412	Randy Myers	.07	.03	.01
☐ 413	John Christensen	.04	.02	.01
☐ 414	John McNamara MG (Checklist back)	.06	.03	.01
☐ 415	Don Carman	.04	.02	.01
☐ 416	Keith Moreland	.04	.02	.01
☐ 417	Mark Ciardi	.04	.02	.01
☐ 418	Joel Youngblood	.04	.02	.01
☐ 419	Scott McGregor	.04	.02	.01
☐ 420	Wally Joyner	.12	.05	.02
☐ 421	Ed VandeBerg	.04	.02	.01
☐ 422	Dave Concepcion	.07	.03	.01
☐ 423	John Smiley	.40	.18	.05
☐ 424	Dwayne Murphy	.04	.02	.01
☐ 425	Jeff Reardon	.12	.05	.02
☐ 426	Randy Ready	.04	.02	.01
☐ 427	Paul Kilgus	.04	.02	.01
☐ 428	John Shelby	.04	.02	.01
☐ 429	Tigers TL Alan Trammell and	.05	.02	.01

	Kirk Gibson			
☐ 430	Glenn Davis	.07	.03	.01
☐ 431	Casey Candaele	.04	.02	.01
☐ 432	Mike Moore	.04	.02	.01
☐ 433	Bill Pecota	.10	.05	.01
☐ 434	Rick Aguilera	.07	.03	.01
☐ 435	Mike Pagliarulo	.04	.02	.01
☐ 436	Mike Bielecki	.04	.02	.01
☐ 437	Fred Manrique	.04	.02	.01
☐ 438	Rob Ducey	.04	.02	.01
☐ 439	Dave Martinez	.08	.04	.01
☐ 440	Steve Bedrosian	.04	.02	.01
☐ 441	Rick Manning	.04	.02	.01
☐ 442	Tom Bolton	.04	.02	.01
☐ 443	Ken Griffey	.07	.03	.01
☐ 444	Cal Ripken, Sr. MG (Checklist back) UER (two copyrights)	.06	.03	.01
☐ 445	Mike Krukow	.04	.02	.01
☐ 446	Doug DeCinces (Now with Cardinals on card front)	.04	.02	.01
☐ 447	Jeff Montgomery	.35	.16	.04
☐ 448	Mike Davis	.04	.02	.01
☐ 449	Jeff M. Robinson	.07	.03	.01
☐ 450	Barry Bonds	.60	.25	.08
☐ 451	Keith Atherton	.04	.02	.01
☐ 452	Willie Wilson	.04	.02	.01
☐ 453	Dennis Powell	.04	.02	.01
☐ 454	Marvell Wynne	.04	.02	.01
☐ 455	Shawn Hillegas	.04	.02	.01
☐ 456	Dave Anderson	.04	.02	.01
☐ 457	Terry Leach	.04	.02	.01
☐ 458	Ron Hassey	.04	.02	.01
☐ 459	Yankees TL Dave Winfield and Willie Randolph	.05	.02	.01
☐ 460	Ozzie Smith	.20	.09	.03
☐ 461	Danny Darwin	.04	.02	.01
☐ 462	Don Slaught	.04	.02	.01
☐ 463	Fred McGriff	.75	.35	.09
☐ 464	Jay Tibbs	.04	.02	.01
☐ 465	Paul Molitor	.12	.05	.02
☐ 466	Jerry Mumphrey	.04	.02	.01
☐ 467	Don Aase	.04	.02	.01
☐ 468	Darren Daulton	.07	.03	.01
☐ 469	Jeff Dedmon	.04	.02	.01
☐ 470	Dwight Evans	.07	.03	.01
☐ 471	Donnie Moore	.04	.02	.01
☐ 472	Robby Thompson	.07	.03	.01
☐ 473	Joe Niekro	.07	.03	.01
☐ 474	Tom Brookens	.04	.02	.01
☐ 475	Pete Rose MG (Checklist back)	.20	.09	.03
☐ 476	Dave Stewart	.07	.03	.01
☐ 477	Jamie Quirk	.04	.02	.01
☐ 478	Sid Bream	.07	.03	.01
☐ 479	Brett Butler	.10	.05	.01
☐ 480	Dwight Gooden	.12	.05	.02
☐ 481	Mariano Duncan	.04	.02	.01
☐ 482	Mark Davis	.04	.02	.01
☐ 483	Rod Booker	.04	.02	.01
☐ 484	Pat Clements	.04	.02	.01
☐ 485	Harold Reynolds	.04	.02	.01
☐ 486	Pat Keedy	.04	.02	.01
☐ 487	Jim Pankovits	.04	.02	.01
☐ 488	Andy McGaffigan	.04	.02	.01
☐ 489	Dodgers TL Pedro Guerrero and Fernando Valenzuela	.05	.02	.01
☐ 490	Larry Parrish	.04	.02	.01
☐ 491	B.J. Surhoff	.07	.03	.01
☐ 492	Doyle Alexander	.04	.02	.01
☐ 493	Mike Greenwell	.10	.05	.01
☐ 494	Wally Ritchie	.04	.02	.01
☐ 495	Eddie Murray	.20	.09	.03
☐ 496	Guy Hoffman	.04	.02	.01
☐ 497	Kevin Mitchell	.15	.07	.02
☐ 498	Bob Boone	.07	.03	.01
☐ 499	Eric King	.04	.02	.01
☐ 500	Andre Dawson	.20	.09	.03
☐ 501	Tim Birtsas	.04	.02	.01
☐ 502	Dan Gladden	.04	.02	.01
☐ 503	Junior Noboa	.04	.02	.01
☐ 504	Bob Rodgers MG (Checklist back)	.06	.03	.01
☐ 505	Willie Upshaw	.04	.02	.01
☐ 506	John Cangelosi	.04	.02	.01
☐ 507	Mark Gubicza	.04	.02	.01
☐ 508	Tim Teufel	.04	.02	.01
☐ 509	Bill Dawley	.04	.02	.01
☐ 510	Dave Winfield	.20	.09	.03
☐ 511	Joel Davis	.04	.02	.01
☐ 512	Alex Trevino	.04	.02	.01
☐ 513	Tim Flannery	.04	.02	.01
☐ 514	Pat Sheridan	.04	.02	.01
☐ 515	Juan Nieves	.04	.02	.01
☐ 516	Jim Sundberg	.04	.02	.01
☐ 517	Ron Robinson	.04	.02	.01
☐ 518	Greg Gross	.04	.02	.01
☐ 519	Mariners TL Harold Reynolds and Phil Bradley	.05	.02	.01
☐ 520	Dave Smith	.04	.02	.01
☐ 521	Jim Dwyer	.04	.02	.01
☐ 522	Bob Patterson	.04	.02	.01
☐ 523	Gary Roenicke	.04	.02	.01
☐ 524	Gary Lucas	.04	.02	.01
☐ 525	Marty Barrett	.04	.02	.01
☐ 526	Juan Berenguer	.04	.02	.01
☐ 527	Steve Henderson	.04	.02	.01
☐ 528A	Checklist 397-528 ERR (455 S. Carlton)	.30	.03	.01
☐ 528B	Checklist 397-528 COR (455 S. Hillegas)	.06	.01	.00
☐ 529	Tim Burke	.04	.02	.01
☐ 530	Gary Carter	.10	.05	.01
☐ 531	Rich Yett	.04	.02	.01
☐ 532	Mike Kingery	.04	.02	.01
☐ 533	John Farrell	.04	.02	.01
☐ 534	John Wathan MG (Checklist back)	.06	.03	.01
☐ 535	Ron Guidry	.07	.03	.01
☐ 536	John Morris	.04	.02	.01
☐ 537	Steve Buechele	.04	.02	.01
☐ 538	Bill Wegman	.04	.02	.01
☐ 539	Mike LaValliere	.04	.02	.01
☐ 540	Bret Saberhagen	.10	.05	.01
☐ 541	Juan Beniquez	.04	.02	.01
☐ 542	Paul Noce	.04	.02	.01
☐ 543	Kent Tekulve	.04	.02	.01
☐ 544	Jim Traber	.04	.02	.01
☐ 545	Don Baylor	.07	.03	.01
☐ 546	John Candelaria	.04	.02	.01
☐ 547	Felix Fermin	.04	.02	.01
☐ 548	Shane Mack	.25	.11	.03
☐ 549	Braves TL Albert Hall, Dale Murphy, Ken Griffey, and Dion James	.05	.02	.01
☐ 550	Pedro Guerrero	.07	.03	.01
☐ 551	Terry Steinbach	.07	.03	.01
☐ 552	Mark Thurmond	.04	.02	.01
☐ 553	Tracy Jones	.04	.02	.01
☐ 554	Mike Smithson	.04	.02	.01
☐ 555	Brook Jacoby	.04	.02	.01
☐ 556	Stan Clarke	.04	.02	.01
☐ 557	Craig Reynolds	.04	.02	.01
☐ 558	Bob Ojeda	.04	.02	.01
☐ 559	Ken Williams	.04	.02	.01
☐ 560	Tim Wallach	.07	.03	.01
☐ 561	Rick Cerone	.04	.02	.01
☐ 562	Jim Lindeman	.04	.02	.01
☐ 563	Jose Guzman	.07	.03	.01
☐ 564	Frank Lucchesi MG (Checklist back)	.06	.03	.01
☐ 565	Lloyd Moseby	.04	.02	.01
☐ 566	Charlie O'Brien	.04	.02	.01
☐ 567	Mike Diaz	.04	.02	.01
☐ 568	Chris Brown	.04	.02	.01
☐ 569	Charlie Leibrandt	.04	.02	.01
☐ 570	Jeffrey Leonard	.04	.02	.01
☐ 571	Mark Williamson	.04	.02	.01
☐ 572	Chris James	.04	.02	.01
☐ 573	Bob Stanley	.04	.02	.01
☐ 574	Graig Nettles	.07	.03	.01
☐ 575	Don Sutton	.10	.05	.01
☐ 576	Tommy Hinzo	.04	.02	.01
☐ 577	Tom Browning	.04	.02	.01
☐ 578	Gary Gaetti	.04	.02	.01
☐ 579	Mets TL Gary Carter and Kevin McReynolds	.05	.02	.01
☐ 580	Mark McGwire	.50	.23	.06
☐ 581	Tito Landrum	.04	.02	.01
☐ 582	Mike Henneman	.15	.07	.02
☐ 583	Dave Valle	.04	.02	.01
☐ 584	Steve Trout	.04	.02	.01
☐ 585	Ozzie Guillen	.07	.03	.01
☐ 586	Bob Forsch	.04	.02	.01
☐ 587	Terry Puhl	.04	.02	.01
☐ 588	Jeff Parrett	.04	.02	.01
☐ 589	Geno Petralli	.04	.02	.01
☐ 590	George Bell	.10	.05	.01
☐ 591	Doug Drabek	.10	.05	.01
☐ 592	Dale Sveum	.04	.02	.01

Card			
☐ 593 Bob Tewksbury	.07	.03	.01
☐ 594 Bobby Valentine MG (Checklist back)	.06	.03	.01
☐ 595 Frank White	.04	.02	.01
☐ 596 John Kruk	.15	.07	.02
☐ 597 Gene Garber	.04	.02	.01
☐ 598 Lee Lacy	.04	.02	.01
☐ 599 Calvin Schiraldi	.04	.02	.01
☐ 600 Mike Schmidt	.40	.18	.05
☐ 601 Jack Lazorko	.04	.02	.01
☐ 602 Mike Aldrete	.04	.02	.01
☐ 603 Rob Murphy	.04	.02	.01
☐ 604 Chris Bando	.04	.02	.01
☐ 605 Kirk Gibson	.07	.03	.01
☐ 606 Moose Haas	.04	.02	.01
☐ 607 Mickey Hatcher	.04	.02	.01
☐ 608 Charlie Kerfeld	.04	.02	.01
☐ 609 Twins TL Gary Gaetti and Kent Hrbek	.05	.02	.01
☐ 610 Keith Hernandez	.07	.03	.01
☐ 611 Tommy John	.07	.03	.01
☐ 612 Curt Ford	.04	.02	.01
☐ 613 Bobby Thigpen	.07	.03	.01
☐ 614 Herm Winningham	.04	.02	.01
☐ 615 Jody Davis	.04	.02	.01
☐ 616 Jay Aldrich	.04	.02	.01
☐ 617 Oddibe McDowell	.04	.02	.01
☐ 618 Cecil Fielder	.30	.14	.04
☐ 619 Mike Dunne UER (Inconsistent design, black name on front)	.04	.02	.01
☐ 620 Cory Snyder	.07	.03	.01
☐ 621 Gene Nelson	.04	.02	.01
☐ 622 Kal Daniels	.07	.03	.01
☐ 623 Mike Flanagan	.04	.02	.01
☐ 624 Jim Leyland MG (Checklist back)	.06	.03	.01
☐ 625 Frank Viola	.07	.03	.01
☐ 626 Glenn Wilson	.04	.02	.01
☐ 627 Joe Boever	.04	.02	.01
☐ 628 Dave Henderson	.07	.03	.01
☐ 629 Kelly Downs	.04	.02	.01
☐ 630 Darrell Evans	.07	.03	.01
☐ 631 Jack Howell	.04	.02	.01
☐ 632 Steve Shields	.04	.02	.01
☐ 633 Barry Lyons	.04	.02	.01
☐ 634 Jose DeLeon	.04	.02	.01
☐ 635 Terry Pendleton	.15	.07	.02
☐ 636 Charles Hudson	.04	.02	.01
☐ 637 Jay Bell	.30	.14	.04
☐ 638 Steve Balboni	.04	.02	.01
☐ 639 Brewers TL Glenn Braggs and Tony Muser CO	.05	.02	.01
☐ 640 Garry Templeton UER (Inconsistent design, green border)	.04	.02	.01
☐ 641 Rick Honeycutt	.04	.02	.01
☐ 642 Bob Dernier	.04	.02	.01
☐ 643 Rocky Childress	.04	.02	.01
☐ 644 Terry McGriff	.04	.02	.01
☐ 645 Matt Nokes	.20	.09	.03
☐ 646 Checklist 529-660	.06	.01	.00
☐ 647 Pascual Perez	.04	.02	.01
☐ 648 Al Newman	.04	.02	.01
☐ 649 DeWayne Buice	.04	.02	.01
☐ 650 Cal Ripken	.60	.25	.08
☐ 651 Mike Jackson	.10	.05	.01
☐ 652 Bruce Benedict	.04	.02	.01
☐ 653 Jeff Sellers	.04	.02	.01
☐ 654 Roger Craig MG (Checklist back)	.06	.03	.01
☐ 655 Len Dykstra	.07	.03	.01
☐ 656 Lee Guetterman	.04	.02	.01
☐ 657 Gary Redus	.04	.02	.01
☐ 658 Tim Conroy UER (Inconsistent design, name in white)	.04	.02	.01
☐ 659 Bobby Meacham	.04	.02	.01
☐ 660 Rick Reuschel	.04	.02	.01
☐ 661 Turn Back Clock 1983 Nolan Ryan	.35	.16	.04
☐ 662 Turn Back Clock 1978 Jim Rice	.05	.02	.01
☐ 663 Turn Back Clock 1973 Ron Blomberg	.05	.02	.01
☐ 664 Turn Back Clock 1968 Bob Gibson	.10	.05	.01
☐ 665 Turn Back Clock 1963 Stan Musial	.10	.05	.01
☐ 666 Mario Soto	.04	.02	.01
☐ 667 Luis Quinones	.04	.02	.01
☐ 668 Walt Terrell	.04	.02	.01
☐ 669 Phillies TL Lance Parrish and Mike Ryan CO	.05	.02	.01
☐ 670 Dan Plesac	.04	.02	.01
☐ 671 Tim Laudner	.04	.02	.01
☐ 672 John Davis	.04	.02	.01
☐ 673 Tony Phillips	.04	.02	.01
☐ 674 Mike Fitzgerald	.04	.02	.01
☐ 675 Jim Rice	.07	.03	.01
☐ 676 Ken Dixon	.04	.02	.01
☐ 677 Eddie Milner	.04	.02	.01
☐ 678 Jim Acker	.04	.02	.01
☐ 679 Darrell Miller	.04	.02	.01
☐ 680 Charlie Hough	.04	.02	.01
☐ 681 Bobby Bonilla	.25	.11	.03
☐ 682 Jimmy Key	.07	.03	.01
☐ 683 Julio Franco	.10	.05	.01
☐ 684 Hal Lanier MG (Checklist back)	.06	.03	.01
☐ 685 Ron Darling	.07	.03	.01
☐ 686 Terry Francona	.04	.02	.01
☐ 687 Mickey Brantley	.04	.02	.01
☐ 688 Jim Winn	.04	.02	.01
☐ 689 Tom Pagnozzi	.25	.11	.03
☐ 690 Jay Howell	.04	.02	.01
☐ 691 Dan Pasqua	.04	.02	.01
☐ 692 Mike Birkbeck	.04	.02	.01
☐ 693 Benito Santiago	.10	.05	.01
☐ 694 Eric Nolte	.04	.02	.01
☐ 695 Shawon Dunston	.07	.03	.01
☐ 696 Duane Ward	.07	.03	.01
☐ 697 Steve Lombardozzi	.04	.02	.01
☐ 698 Brad Havens	.04	.02	.01
☐ 699 Padres TL Benito Santiago and Tony Gwynn	.10	.05	.01
☐ 700 George Brett	.25	.11	.03
☐ 701 Sammy Stewart	.04	.02	.01
☐ 702 Mike Gallego	.04	.02	.01
☐ 703 Bob Brenly	.04	.02	.01
☐ 704 Dennis Boyd	.04	.02	.01
☐ 705 Juan Samuel	.04	.02	.01
☐ 706 Rick Mahler	.04	.02	.01
☐ 707 Fred Lynn	.07	.03	.01
☐ 708 Gus Polidor	.04	.02	.01
☐ 709 George Frazier	.04	.02	.01
☐ 710 Darryl Strawberry	.30	.14	.04
☐ 711 Bill Gullickson	.04	.02	.01
☐ 712 John Moses	.04	.02	.01
☐ 713 Willie Hernandez	.04	.02	.01
☐ 714 Jim Fregosi MG (Checklist back)	.06	.03	.01
☐ 715 Todd Worrell	.07	.03	.01
☐ 716 Lenn Sakata	.04	.02	.01
☐ 717 Jay Baller	.04	.02	.01
☐ 718 Mike Felder	.04	.02	.01
☐ 719 Denny Walling	.04	.02	.01
☐ 720 Tim Raines	.07	.03	.01
☐ 721 Pete O'Brien	.04	.02	.01
☐ 722 Manny Lee	.04	.02	.01
☐ 723 Bob Kipper	.04	.02	.01
☐ 724 Danny Tartabull	.15	.07	.02
☐ 725 Mike Boddicker	.04	.02	.01
☐ 726 Alfredo Griffin	.04	.02	.01
☐ 727 Greg Booker	.04	.02	.01
☐ 728 Andy Allanson	.04	.02	.01
☐ 729 Blue Jays TL George Bell and Fred McGriff	.05	.02	.01
☐ 730 John Franco	.07	.03	.01
☐ 731 Rick Schu	.04	.02	.01
☐ 732 David Palmer	.04	.02	.01
☐ 733 Spike Owen	.04	.02	.01
☐ 734 Craig Lefferts	.04	.02	.01
☐ 735 Kevin McReynolds	.07	.03	.01
☐ 736 Matt Young	.04	.02	.01
☐ 737 Butch Wynegar	.04	.02	.01
☐ 738 Scott Bankhead	.04	.02	.01
☐ 739 Daryl Boston	.04	.02	.01
☐ 740 Rick Sutcliffe	.07	.03	.01
☐ 741 Mike Easler	.04	.02	.01
☐ 742 Mark Clear	.04	.02	.01
☐ 743 Larry Herndon	.04	.02	.01
☐ 744 Whitey Herzog MG (Checklist back)	.06	.03	.01
☐ 745 Bill Doran	.04	.02	.01
☐ 746 Gene Larkin	.10	.05	.01
☐ 747 Bobby Witt	.07	.03	.01
☐ 748 Reid Nichols	.04	.02	.01
☐ 749 Mark Eichhorn	.04	.02	.01
☐ 750 Bo Jackson	.30	.14	.04
☐ 751 Jim Morrison	.04	.02	.01

☐ 752 Mark Grant	.04	.02	.01
☐ 753 Danny Heep	.04	.02	.01
☐ 754 Mike LaCoss	.04	.02	.01
☐ 755 Ozzie Virgil	.04	.02	.01
☐ 756 Mike Maddux	.04	.02	.01
☐ 757 John Marzano	.04	.02	.01
☐ 758 Eddie Williams	.04	.02	.01
☐ 759 A's TL UER Mark McGwire and Jose Canseco (two copyrights)	.25	.11	.03
☐ 760 Mike Scott	.07	.03	.01
☐ 761 Tony Armas	.04	.02	.01
☐ 762 Scott Bradley	.04	.02	.01
☐ 763 Doug Sisk	.04	.02	.01
☐ 764 Greg Walker	.04	.02	.01
☐ 765 Neal Heaton	.04	.02	.01
☐ 766 Henry Cotto	.04	.02	.01
☐ 767 Jose Lind	.15	.07	.02
☐ 768 Dickie Noles (Now with Tigers on card front)	.04	.02	.01
☐ 769 Cecil Cooper	.07	.03	.01
☐ 770 Lou Whitaker	.07	.03	.01
☐ 771 Ruben Sierra	.40	.18	.05
☐ 772 Sal Butera	.04	.02	.01
☐ 773 Frank Williams	.04	.02	.01
☐ 774 Gene Mauch MG (Checklist back)	.06	.03	.01
☐ 775 Dave Stieb	.07	.03	.01
☐ 776 Checklist 661-792	.06	.01	.00
☐ 777 Lonnie Smith	.04	.02	.01
☐ 778A Keith Comstock ERR (White "Padres")	2.50	1.15	.30
☐ 778B Keith Comstock COR (Blue "Padres")	.04	.02	.01
☐ 779 Tom Glavine	2.25	1.00	.30
☐ 780 Fernando Valenzuela	.07	.03	.01
☐ 781 Keith Hughes	.04	.02	.01
☐ 782 Jeff Ballard	.04	.02	.01
☐ 783 Ron Roenicke	.04	.02	.01
☐ 784 Joe Sambito	.04	.02	.01
☐ 785 Alvin Davis	.04	.02	.01
☐ 786 Joe Price UER (Inconsistent design, orange team name)	.04	.02	.01
☐ 787 Bill Almon	.04	.02	.01
☐ 788 Ray Searage	.04	.02	.01
☐ 789 Indians' TL Joe Carter and Cory Snyder	.10	.05	.01
☐ 790 Dave Righetti	.04	.02	.01
☐ 791 Ted Simmons	.07	.03	.01
☐ 792 John Tudor	.04	.02	.01

1988 Topps All-Star Glossy 22

This set of 22 glossy cards was inserted one per rack pack. Players selected for the set are the starting players (plus manager and honorary captain) in the 1987 All-Star Game in Oakland. Cards measure standard size, 2 1/2" by 3 1/2" and the backs feature red and blue printing on a white card stock.

	MT	EX-MT	VG
COMPLETE SET (22)	3.50	1.55	.45
COMMON PLAYER (1-22)	.10	.05	.01

☐ 1 John McNamara MG	.10	.05	.01
☐ 2 Don Mattingly	.50	.23	.06
☐ 3 Willie Randolph	.10	.05	.01
☐ 4 Wade Boggs	.40	.18	.05
☐ 5 Cal Ripken	.60	.25	.08
☐ 6 George Bell	.20	.09	.03
☐ 7 Rickey Henderson	.50	.23	.06
☐ 8 Dave Winfield	.35	.16	.04
☐ 9 Terry Kennedy	.10	.05	.01
☐ 10 Bret Saberhagen	.20	.09	.03
☐ 11 Jim Hunter CAPT	.15	.07	.02
☐ 12 Dave Johnson MG	.10	.05	.01
☐ 13 Jack Clark	.15	.07	.02
☐ 14 Ryne Sandberg	.60	.25	.08
☐ 15 Mike Schmidt	.50	.23	.06
☐ 16 Ozzie Smith	.35	.16	.04
☐ 17 Eric Davis	.25	.11	.03
☐ 18 Andre Dawson	.35	.16	.04
☐ 19 Darryl Strawberry	.40	.18	.05
☐ 20 Gary Carter	.25	.11	.03
☐ 21 Mike Scott	.10	.05	.01
☐ 22 Billy Williams CAPT	.15	.07	.02

1988 Topps Big

This set of 264 cards was issued as three separately distributed series of 88 cards each. Cards were distributed in wax packs with seven cards for a suggested retail of 40 cents. These cards are very reminiscent in style of the 1956 Topps card set. The cards measure approximately 2 5/8" by 3 3/4" and are oriented horizontally.

	MT	EX-MT	VG
COMPLETE SET (264)	24.00	11.00	3.00
COMMON PLAYER (1-88)	.05	.02	.01
COMMON PLAYER (89-176)	.05	.02	.01
COMMON PLAYER (177-264)	.05	.02	.01

☐ 1 Paul Molitor	.15	.07	.02
☐ 2 Milt Thompson	.05	.02	.01
☐ 3 Billy Hatcher	.05	.02	.01
☐ 4 Mike Witt	.05	.02	.01
☐ 5 Vince Coleman	.15	.07	.02
☐ 6 Dwight Evans	.10	.05	.01
☐ 7 Tim Wallach	.08	.04	.01
☐ 8 Alan Trammell	.15	.07	.02
☐ 9 Will Clark	1.00	.45	.13
☐ 10 Jeff Reardon	.15	.07	.02
☐ 11 Dwight Gooden	.30	.14	.04
☐ 12 Benito Santiago	.15	.07	.02
☐ 13 Jose Canseco	1.00	.45	.13
☐ 14 Dale Murphy	.30	.14	.04
☐ 15 George Bell	.15	.07	.02
☐ 16 Ryne Sandberg	1.25	.55	.16
☐ 17 Brook Jacoby	.05	.02	.01
☐ 18 Fernando Valenzuela	.08	.04	.01
☐ 19 Scott Fletcher	.05	.02	.01
☐ 20 Eric Davis	.25	.11	.03
☐ 21 Willie Wilson	.08	.04	.01
☐ 22 B.J. Surhoff	.05	.02	.01
☐ 23 Steve Bedrosian	.05	.02	.01
☐ 24 Dave Winfield	.35	.16	.04
☐ 25 Bobby Bonilla	.40	.18	.05
☐ 26 Larry Sheets	.05	.02	.01
☐ 27 Ozzie Guillen	.08	.04	.01
☐ 28 Checklist 1-88	.08	.00	.00
☐ 29 Nolan Ryan	1.75	.80	.22
☐ 30 Bob Boone	.10	.05	.01

☐	31 Tom Herr	.05	.02	.01
☐	32 Wade Boggs	.75	.35	.09
☐	33 Neal Heaton	.05	.02	.01
☐	34 Doyle Alexander	.05	.02	.01
☐	35 Candy Maldonado	.08	.04	.01
☐	36 Kirby Puckett	.75	.35	.09
☐	37 Gary Carter	.25	.11	.03
☐	38 Lance McCullers	.05	.02	.01
☐	39A Terry Steinbach (Topps logo in black)	.15	.07	.02
☐	39B Terry Steinbach (Topps logo in white)	.15	.07	.02
☐	40 Gerald Perry	.05	.02	.01
☐	41 Tom Henke	.08	.04	.01
☐	42 Leon Durham	.05	.02	.01
☐	43 Cory Snyder	.08	.04	.01
☐	44 Dale Sveum	.05	.02	.01
☐	45 Lance Parrish	.08	.04	.01
☐	46 Steve Sax	.10	.05	.01
☐	47 Charlie Hough	.05	.02	.01
☐	48 Kal Daniels	.10	.05	.01
☐	49 Bo Jackson	.75	.35	.09
☐	50 Ron Guidry	.08	.04	.01
☐	51 Bill Doran	.05	.02	.01
☐	52 Wally Joyner	.20	.09	.03
☐	53 Terry Pendleton	.15	.07	.02
☐	54 Marty Barrett	.05	.02	.01
☐	55 Andres Galarraga	.10	.05	.01
☐	56 Larry Herndon	.05	.02	.01
☐	57 Kevin Mitchell	.25	.11	.03
☐	58 Greg Gagne	.05	.02	.01
☐	59 Keith Hernandez	.10	.05	.01
☐	60 John Kruk	.12	.05	.02
☐	61 Mike LaValliere	.05	.02	.01
☐	62 Cal Ripken	1.25	.55	.16
☐	63 Ivan Calderon	.08	.04	.01
☐	64 Alvin Davis	.05	.02	.01
☐	65 Luis Polonia	.15	.07	.02
☐	66 Robin Yount	.75	.35	.09
☐	67 Juan Samuel	.05	.02	.01
☐	68 Andres Thomas	.05	.02	.01
☐	69 Jeff Musselman	.05	.02	.01
☐	70 Jerry Mumphrey	.05	.02	.01
☐	71 Joe Carter	.35	.16	.04
☐	72 Mike Scioscia	.05	.02	.01
☐	73 Pete Incaviglia	.08	.04	.01
☐	74 Barry Larkin	.25	.11	.03
☐	75 Frank White	.08	.04	.01
☐	76 Willie Randolph	.08	.04	.01
☐	77 Kevin Bass	.05	.02	.01
☐	78 Brian Downing	.05	.02	.01
☐	79 Willie McGee	.10	.05	.01
☐	80 Ellis Burks	.25	.11	.03
☐	81 Hubie Brooks	.05	.02	.01
☐	82 Darrell Evans	.08	.04	.01
☐	83 Robby Thompson	.05	.02	.01
☐	84 Kent Hrbek	.08	.04	.01
☐	85 Ron Darling	.10	.05	.01
☐	86 Stan Jefferson	.05	.02	.01
☐	87 Teddy Higuera	.05	.02	.01
☐	88 Mike Schmidt	.75	.35	.09
☐	89 Barry Bonds	.75	.35	.09
☐	90 Jim Presley	.05	.02	.01
☐	91 Orel Hershiser	.15	.07	.02
☐	92 Jesse Barfield	.08	.04	.01
☐	93 Tom Candiotti	.08	.04	.01
☐	94 Bret Saberhagen	.15	.07	.02
☐	95 Jose Uribe	.05	.02	.01
☐	96 Tom Browning	.08	.04	.01
☐	97 Johnny Ray	.05	.02	.01
☐	98 Mike Morgan	.08	.04	.01
☐	99 Lou Whitaker	.12	.05	.02
☐	100 Jim Sundberg	.05	.02	.01
☐	101 Roger McDowell	.05	.02	.01
☐	102 Randy Ready	.05	.02	.01
☐	103 Mike Gallego	.05	.02	.01
☐	104 Steve Buechele	.05	.02	.01
☐	105 Greg Walker	.05	.02	.01
☐	106 Jose Lind	.10	.05	.01
☐	107 Steve Trout	.05	.02	.01
☐	108 Rick Rhoden	.05	.02	.01
☐	109 Jim Pankovits	.05	.02	.01
☐	110 Ken Griffey Sr.	.15	.07	.02
☐	111 Danny Cox	.05	.02	.01
☐	112 Franklin Stubbs	.05	.02	.01
☐	113 Lloyd Moseby	.05	.02	.01
☐	114 Mel Hall	.10	.05	.01
☐	115 Kevin Seitzer	.10	.05	.01
☐	116 Tim Raines	.15	.07	.02
☐	117 Juan Castillo	.05	.02	.01
☐	118 Roger Clemens	1.25	.55	.16
☐	119 Mike Aldrete	.05	.02	.01
☐	120 Mario Soto	.05	.02	.01
☐	121 Jack Howell	.05	.02	.01
☐	122 Rick Schu	.05	.02	.01
☐	123 Jeff Robinson	.05	.02	.01
☐	124 Doug Drabek	.15	.07	.02
☐	125 Henry Cotto	.05	.02	.01
☐	126 Checklist 89-176	.08	.00	.00
☐	127 Gary Gaetti	.05	.02	.01
☐	128 Rick Sutcliffe	.08	.04	.01
☐	129 Howard Johnson	.12	.05	.02
☐	130 Chris Brown	.05	.02	.01
☐	131 Dave Henderson	.08	.04	.01
☐	132 Curt Wilkerson	.05	.02	.01
☐	133 Mike Marshall	.05	.02	.01
☐	134 Kelly Gruber	.12	.05	.02
☐	135 Julio Franco	.15	.07	.02
☐	136 Kurt Stillwell	.05	.02	.01
☐	137 Donnie Hill	.05	.02	.01
☐	138 Mike Pagliarulo	.05	.02	.01
☐	139 Von Hayes	.05	.02	.01
☐	140 Mike Scott	.08	.04	.01
☐	141 Bob Kipper	.05	.02	.01
☐	142 Harold Reynolds	.05	.02	.01
☐	143 Bob Brenly	.05	.02	.01
☐	144 Dave Concepcion	.10	.05	.01
☐	145 Devon White	.10	.05	.01
☐	146 Jeff Stone	.05	.02	.01
☐	147 Chet Lemon	.05	.02	.01
☐	148 Ozzie Virgil	.05	.02	.01
☐	149 Todd Worrell	.10	.05	.01
☐	150 Mitch Webster	.05	.02	.01
☐	151 Rob Deer	.08	.04	.01
☐	152 Rich Gedman	.05	.02	.01
☐	153 Andre Dawson	.35	.16	.04
☐	154 Mike Davis	.05	.02	.01
☐	155 Nelson Liriano	.05	.02	.01
☐	156 Greg Swindell	.15	.07	.02
☐	157 George Brett	.75	.35	.09
☐	158 Kevin McReynolds	.15	.07	.02
☐	159 Brian Fisher	.05	.02	.01
☐	160 Mike Kingery	.05	.02	.01
☐	161 Tony Gwynn	.75	.35	.09
☐	162 Don Baylor	.10	.05	.01
☐	163 Jerry Browne	.05	.02	.01
☐	164 Dan Pasqua	.05	.02	.01
☐	165 Rickey Henderson	1.00	.45	.13
☐	166 Brett Butler	.10	.05	.01
☐	167 Nick Esasky	.05	.02	.01
☐	168 Kirk McCaskill	.05	.02	.01
☐	169 Fred Lynn	.10	.05	.01
☐	170 Jack Morris	.15	.07	.02
☐	171 Pedro Guerrero	.10	.05	.01
☐	172 Dave Stieb	.08	.04	.01
☐	173 Pat Tabler	.05	.02	.01
☐	174 Floyd Bannister	.05	.02	.01
☐	175 Rafael Belliard	.05	.02	.01
☐	176 Mark Langston	.08	.04	.01
☐	177 Greg Mathews	.05	.02	.01
☐	178 Claudell Washington	.05	.02	.01
☐	179 Mark McGwire	1.00	.45	.13
☐	180 Bert Blyleven	.12	.05	.02
☐	181 Jim Rice	.12	.05	.02
☐	182 Mookie Wilson	.05	.02	.01
☐	183 Willie Fraser	.05	.02	.01
☐	184 Andy Van Slyke	.15	.07	.02
☐	185 Matt Nokes	.12	.05	.02
☐	186 Eddie Whitson	.05	.02	.01
☐	187 Tony Fernandez	.08	.04	.01
☐	188 Rick Reuschel	.05	.02	.01
☐	189 Ken Phelps	.05	.02	.01
☐	190 Juan Nieves	.05	.02	.01
☐	191 Kirk Gibson	.15	.07	.02
☐	192 Glenn Davis	.15	.07	.02
☐	193 Zane Smith	.05	.02	.01
☐	194 Jose DeLeon	.05	.02	.01
☐	195 Gary Ward	.05	.02	.01
☐	196 Pascual Perez	.05	.02	.01
☐	197 Carlton Fisk	.35	.16	.04
☐	198 Oddibe McDowell	.05	.02	.01
☐	199 Mark Gubicza	.08	.04	.01
☐	200 Glenn Hubbard	.05	.02	.01
☐	201 Frank Viola	.10	.05	.01
☐	202 Jody Reed	.15	.07	.02
☐	203 Len Dykstra	.10	.05	.01
☐	204 Dick Schofield	.05	.02	.01
☐	205 Sid Bream	.08	.04	.01
☐	206 Willie Hernandez	.05	.02	.01
☐	207 Keith Moreland	.05	.02	.01
☐	208 Mark Eichhorn	.05	.02	.01
☐	209 Rene Gonzales	.05	.02	.01
☐	210 Dave Valle	.05	.02	.01
☐	211 Tom Brunansky	.08	.04	.01
☐	212 Charles Hudson	.05	.02	.01
☐	213 John Farrell	.05	.02	.01

☐	214 Jeff Treadway	.05	.02	.01
☐	215 Eddie Murray	.35	.16	.04
☐	216 Checklist 177-264	.08	.00	.00
☐	217 Greg Brock	.05	.02	.01
☐	218 John Shelby	.05	.02	.01
☐	219 Craig Reynolds	.05	.02	.01
☐	220 Dion James	.05	.02	.01
☐	221 Carney Lansford	.08	.04	.01
☐	222 Juan Berenguer	.05	.02	.01
☐	223 Luis Rivera	.05	.02	.01
☐	224 Harold Baines	.10	.05	.01
☐	225 Shawon Dunston	.10	.05	.01
☐	226 Luis Aguayo	.05	.02	.01
☐	227 Pete O'Brien	.05	.02	.01
☐	228 Ozzie Smith	.30	.14	.04
☐	229 Don Mattingly	1.00	.45	.13
☐	230 Danny Tartabull	.25	.11	.03
☐	231 Andy Allanson	.05	.02	.01
☐	232 John Franco	.05	.02	.01
☐	233 Mike Greenwell	.25	.11	.03
☐	234 Bob Ojeda	.05	.02	.01
☐	235 Chili Davis	.08	.04	.01
☐	236 Mike Dunne	.05	.02	.01
☐	237 Jim Morrison	.05	.02	.01
☐	238 Carmelo Martinez	.05	.02	.01
☐	239 Ernie Whitt	.05	.02	.01
☐	240 Scott Garrelts	.05	.02	.01
☐	241 Mike Moore	.08	.04	.01
☐	242 Dave Parker	.10	.05	.01
☐	243 Tim Laudner	.05	.02	.01
☐	244 Bill Wegman	.08	.04	.01
☐	245 Bob Horner	.08	.04	.01
☐	246 Rafael Santana	.05	.02	.01
☐	247 Alfredo Griffin	.05	.02	.01
☐	248 Mark Bailey	.05	.02	.01
☐	249 Ron Gant	1.00	.45	.13
☐	250 Bryn Smith	.05	.02	.01
☐	251 Lance Johnson	.15	.07	.02
☐	252 Sam Horn	.05	.02	.01
☐	253 Darryl Strawberry	.75	.35	.09
☐	254 Chuck Finley	.08	.04	.01
☐	255 Darnell Coles	.05	.02	.01
☐	256 Mike Henneman	.15	.07	.02
☐	257 Andy Hawkins	.05	.02	.01
☐	258 Jim Clancy	.05	.02	.01
☐	259 Atlee Hammaker	.05	.02	.01
☐	260 Glenn Wilson	.05	.02	.01
☐	261 Larry McWilliams	.05	.02	.01
☐	262 Jack Clark	.08	.04	.01
☐	263 Walt Weiss	.15	.07	.02
☐	264 Gene Larkin	.08	.04	.01

1988 Topps Glossy Send-In 60

Topps issued this set through a mail-in offer explained and advertised on the wax packs. This 60-card set features glossy fronts with each card measuring 2 1/2" by 3 1/2". The offer provided your choice of any one of the six 10-card subsets (1-10, 11-20, etc.) for 1.25 plus six of the Special Offer ("Spring Fever Baseball") insert cards, which were found one per wax pack. One complete set was obtainable by sending 7.50 plus 18 special offer cards. The last two players (numerically) in each ten-card subset are actually "Hot Prospects."

		MT	EX-MT	VG
	COMPLETE SET (60)	11.00	4.90	1.40
	COMMON PLAYER (1-60)	.20	.09	.03
☐	1 Andre Dawson	.40	.18	.05
☐	2 Jesse Barfield	.20	.09	.03
☐	3 Mike Schmidt	.75	.35	.09
☐	4 Ruben Sierra	.60	.25	.08
☐	5 Mike Scott	.20	.09	.03
☐	6 Cal Ripken	1.00	.45	.13
☐	7 Gary Carter	.40	.18	.05
☐	8 Kent Hrbek	.30	.14	.04
☐	9 Kevin Seitzer	.20	.09	.03
☐	10 Mike Henneman	.30	.14	.04
☐	11 Don Mattingly	.60	.25	.08
☐	12 Tim Raines	.30	.14	.04
☐	13 Roger Clemens	1.00	.45	.13
☐	14 Ryne Sandberg	1.00	.45	.13
☐	15 Tony Fernandez	.30	.14	.04
☐	16 Eric Davis	.40	.18	.05
☐	17 Jack Morris	.30	.14	.04
☐	18 Tim Wallach	.20	.09	.03
☐	19 Mike Dunne	.20	.09	.03
☐	20 Mike Greenwell	.40	.18	.05
☐	21 Dwight Evans	.30	.14	.04
☐	22 Darryl Strawberry	.60	.25	.08
☐	23 Cory Snyder	.25	.11	.03
☐	24 Pedro Guerrero	.25	.11	.03
☐	25 Rickey Henderson	.60	.25	.08
☐	26 Dale Murphy	.40	.18	.05
☐	27 Kirby Puckett	.75	.35	.09
☐	28 Steve Bedrosian	.20	.09	.03
☐	29 Devon White	.30	.14	.04
☐	30 Benito Santiago	.40	.18	.05
☐	31 George Bell	.30	.14	.04
☐	32 Keith Hernandez	.30	.14	.04
☐	33 Dave Stewart	.30	.14	.04
☐	34 Dave Parker	.30	.14	.04
☐	35 Tom Henke	.30	.14	.04
☐	36 Willie McGee	.30	.14	.04
☐	37 Alan Trammell	.30	.14	.04
☐	38 Tony Gwynn	.50	.23	.06
☐	39 Mark McGwire	.60	.25	.08
☐	40 Joe Magrane	.20	.09	.03
☐	41 Jack Clark	.30	.14	.04
☐	42 Willie Randolph	.20	.09	.03
☐	43 Juan Samuel	.20	.09	.03
☐	44 Joe Carter	.50	.23	.06
☐	45 Shane Rawley	.20	.09	.03
☐	46 Dave Winfield	.50	.23	.06
☐	47 Ozzie Smith	.40	.18	.05
☐	48 Wally Joyner	.30	.14	.04
☐	49 B.J. Surhoff	.20	.09	.03
☐	50 Ellis Burks	.40	.18	.05
☐	51 Wade Boggs	.50	.23	.06
☐	52 Howard Johnson	.30	.14	.04
☐	53 George Brett	.60	.25	.08
☐	54 Dwight Gooden	.30	14	.04
☐	55 Jose Canseco	.75	.35	.09
☐	56 Lee Smith	.30	.14	.04
☐	57 Paul Molitor	.30	.14	.04
☐	58 Andres Galarraga	.25	.11	.03
☐	59 Matt Nokes	.25	.11	.03
☐	60 Casey Candaele	.20	.09	.03

1988 Topps Jumbo Rookies

Inserted in each supermarket jumbo pack is a card from this series of 22 of 1987's best rookies as determined by Topps.

Jumbo packs consisted of 100 (regular issue 1988 Topps baseball) cards with a stick of gum plus the insert "Rookie" card. The card fronts are in full color and measure 2 1/2" by 3 1/2". The card backs are printed in red and blue on white card stock and are numbered at the bottom.

	MT	EX-MT	VG
COMPLETE SET (22)	7.00	3.10	.85
COMMON PLAYER (1-22)	.20	.09	.03
☐ 1 Billy Ripken	.20	.09	.03
☐ 2 Ellis Burks	.60	.25	.08
☐ 3 Mike Greenwell	.75	.35	.09
☐ 4 DeWayne Buice	.20	.09	.03
☐ 5 Devon White	.40	.18	.05
☐ 6 Fred Manrique	.20	.09	.03
☐ 7 Mike Henneman	.30	.14	.04
☐ 8 Matt Nokes	.50	.23	.06
☐ 9 Kevin Seitzer	.30	.14	.04
☐ 10 B.J. Surhoff	.30	.14	.04
☐ 11 Casey Candaele	.20	.09	.03
☐ 12 Randy Myers	.40	.18	.05
☐ 13 Mark McGwire	1.50	.65	.19
☐ 14 Luis Polonia	.50	.23	.06
☐ 15 Terry Steinbach	.30	.14	.04
☐ 16 Mike Dunne	.20	.09	.03
☐ 17 Al Pedrique	.20	.09	.03
☐ 18 Benito Santiago	.60	.25	.08
☐ 19 Kelly Downs	.20	.09	.03
☐ 20 Joe Magrane	.30	.14	.04
☐ 21 Jerry Browne	.20	.09	.03
☐ 22 Jeff Musselman	.20	.09	.03

1988 Topps Mini Leaders

The 1988 Topps Mini set of Major League Leaders features 77 cards of leaders of the various statistical categories for the 1987 season. The cards are numbered on the back and measure approximately 2 1/8" by 3". The set numbering is alphabetical by player within team and the teams themselves are in alphabetical order as well. The card backs are printed in blue, red, and yellow on white card stock. The cards were distributed as a separate issue in wax packs.

	MT	EX-MT	VG
COMPLETE SET (77)	7.50	3.40	.95
COMMON PLAYER (1-77)	.05	.02	.01
☐ 1 Wade Boggs	.45	.20	.06
☐ 2 Roger Clemens	.75	.35	.09
☐ 3 Dwight Evans	.10	.05	.01
☐ 4 DeWayne Buice	.05	.02	.01
☐ 5 Brian Downing	.05	.02	.01
☐ 6 Wally Joyner	.15	.07	.02
☐ 7 Ivan Calderon	.10	.05	.01
☐ 8 Carlton Fisk	.35	.16	.04
☐ 9 Gary Redus	.05	.02	.01
☐ 10 Darrell Evans	.10	.05	.01
☐ 11 Jack Morris	.20	.09	.03
☐ 12 Alan Trammell	.15	.07	.02
☐ 13 Lou Whitaker	.15	.07	.02
☐ 14 Bret Saberhagen	.15	.07	.02
☐ 15 Kevin Seitzer	.10	.05	.01
☐ 16 Danny Tartabull	.20	.09	.03
☐ 17 Willie Wilson	.10	.05	.01
☐ 18 Teddy Higuera	.05	.02	.01
☐ 19 Paul Molitor	.15	.07	.02
☐ 20 Dan Plesac	.05	.02	.01
☐ 21 Robin Yount	.50	.23	.06
☐ 22 Kent Hrbek	.10	.05	.01
☐ 23 Kirby Puckett	.60	.25	.08
☐ 24 Jeff Reardon	.15	.07	.02
☐ 25 Frank Viola	.10	.05	.01
☐ 26 Rickey Henderson	.60	.25	.08
☐ 27 Don Mattingly	.60	.25	.08
☐ 28 Willie Randolph	.05	.02	.01
☐ 29 Dave Righetti	.05	.02	.01
☐ 30 Jose Canseco	.75	.35	.09
☐ 31 Mark McGwire	.60	.25	.08
☐ 32 Dave Stewart	.10	.05	.01
☐ 33 Phil Bradley	.05	.02	.01
☐ 34 Mark Langston	.08	.04	.01
☐ 35 Harold Reynolds	.05	.02	.01
☐ 36 Charlie Hough	.08	.04	.01
☐ 37 George Bell	.10	.05	.01
☐ 38 Tom Henke	.08	.04	.01
☐ 39 Jimmy Key	.08	.04	.01
☐ 40 Dion James	.05	.02	.01
☐ 41 Dale Murphy	.20	.09	.03
☐ 42 Zane Smith	.05	.02	.01
☐ 43 Andre Dawson	.30	.14	.04
☐ 44 Lee Smith	.10	.05	.01
☐ 45 Rick Sutcliffe	.08	.04	.01
☐ 46 Eric Davis	.20	.09	.03
☐ 47 John Franco	.05	.02	.01
☐ 48 Dave Parker	.10	.05	.01
☐ 49 Billy Hatcher	.05	.02	.01
☐ 50 Nolan Ryan	1.25	.55	.16
☐ 51 Mike Scott	.05	.02	.01
☐ 52 Pedro Guerrero	.08	.04	.01
☐ 53 Orel Hershiser	.12	.05	.02
☐ 54 Fernando Valenzuela	.08	.04	.01
☐ 55 Bob Welch	.08	.04	.01
☐ 56 Andres Galarraga	.08	.04	.01
☐ 57 Tim Raines	.10	.05	.01
☐ 58 Tim Wallach	.05	.02	.01
☐ 59 Len Dykstra	.10	.05	.01
☐ 60 Dwight Gooden	.20	.09	.03
☐ 61 Howard Johnson	.12	.05	.02
☐ 62 Roger McDowell	.05	.02	.01
☐ 63 Darryl Strawberry	.45	.20	.06
☐ 64 Steve Bedrosian	.05	.02	.01
☐ 65 Shane Rawley	.05	.02	.01
☐ 66 Juan Samuel	.05	.02	.01
☐ 67 Mike Schmidt	.75	.35	.09
☐ 68 Mike Dunne	.05	.02	.01
☐ 69 Jack Clark	.08	.04	.01
☐ 70 Vince Coleman	.12	.05	.02
☐ 71 Willie McGee	.08	.04	.01
☐ 72 Ozzie Smith	.30	.14	.04
☐ 73 Todd Worrell	.08	.04	.01
☐ 74 Tony Gwynn	.45	.20	.06
☐ 75 John Kruk	.12	.05	.02
☐ 76 Rick Reuschel	.05	.02	.01
☐ 77 Checklist Card	.08	.04	.01

1988 Topps Revco League Leaders

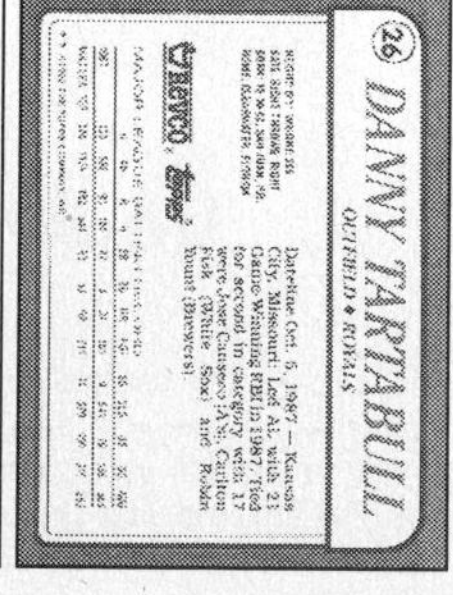

Topps produced this 33-card boxed set for Revco stores subtitled "League Leaders". The cards measure 2 1/2" by 3 1/2" and feature a high-gloss, full-color photo of the player inside a white border. The card backs are printed in red and black on white card stock. The cards are numbered on the back. The statistics provided on the card backs cover only two lines, last season and Major League totals.

	MT	EX-MT	VG
COMPLETE SET (33)	4.00	1.80	.50
COMMON PLAYER (1-33)	.10	.05	.01
☐ 1 Tony Gwynn	.45	.20	.06
☐ 2 Andre Dawson	.35	.16	.04
☐ 3 Vince Coleman	.25	.11	.03
☐ 4 Jack Clark	.15	.07	.02
☐ 5 Tim Raines	.15	.07	.02
☐ 6 Tim Wallach	.15	.07	.02
☐ 7 Juan Samuel	.10	.05	.01
☐ 8 Nolan Ryan	1.25	.55	.16
☐ 9 Rick Sutcliffe	.10	.05	.01
☐ 10 Kent Tekulve	.10	.05	.01
☐ 11 Steve Bedrosian	.10	.05	.01
☐ 12 Orel Hershiser	.15	.07	.02
☐ 13 Rick Reuschel	.10	.05	.01
☐ 14 Fernando Valenzuela	.15	.07	.02
☐ 15 Bob Welch	.10	.05	.01
☐ 16 Wade Boggs	.50	.23	.06
☐ 17 Mark McGwire	.50	.23	.06
☐ 18 George Bell	.20	.09	.03
☐ 19 Harold Reynolds	.10	.05	.01
☐ 20 Paul Molitor	.25	.11	.03
☐ 21 Kirby Puckett	.60	.25	.08
☐ 22 Kevin Seitzer	.15	.07	.02
☐ 23 Brian Downing	.10	.05	.01
☐ 24 Dwight Evans	.15	.07	.02
☐ 25 Willie Wilson	.15	.07	.02
☐ 26 Danny Tartabull	.25	.11	.03
☐ 27 Jimmy Key	.15	.07	.02
☐ 28 Roger Clemens	.60	.25	.08
☐ 29 Dave Stewart	.20	.09	.03
☐ 30 Mark Eichhorn	.10	.05	.01
☐ 31 Tom Henke	.15	.07	.02
☐ 32 Charlie Hough	.15	.07	.02
☐ 33 Mark Langston	.15	.07	.02

1988 Topps Rite-Aid Team MVP's

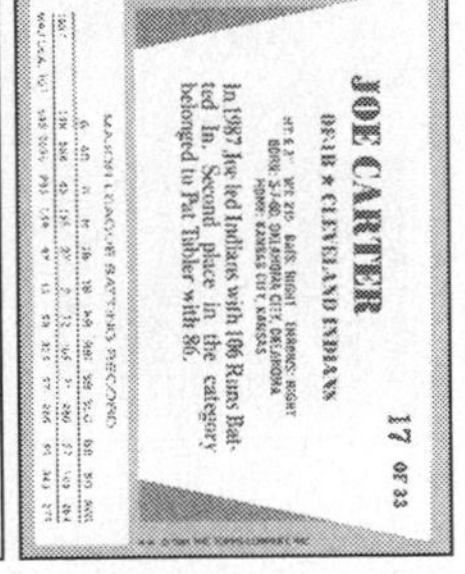

Topps produced this 33-card boxed set for Rite Aid Drug and Discount Stores subtitled "Team MVP's". The Rite Aid logo is at the top of every obverse. The cards measure 2 1/2" by 3 1/2" and feature a high-gloss, full-color photo of the player inside a red, white, and blue border. The card backs are printed in blue and black on white card stock. The cards are numbered on the back and the checklist for the set is found on the back panel of the small collector box. The statistics provided on the card backs cover only two lines, last season and Major League totals.

	MT	EX-MT	VG
COMPLETE SET (33)	4.00	1.80	.50
COMMON PLAYER (1-33)	.10	.05	.01
☐ 1 Dale Murphy	.25	.11	.03
☐ 2 Andre Dawson	.35	.16	.04
☐ 3 Eric Davis	.25	.11	.03
☐ 4 Mike Scott	.15	.07	.02
☐ 5 Pedro Guerrero	.15	.07	.02
☐ 6 Tim Raines	.15	.07	.02
☐ 7 Darryl Strawberry	.45	.20	.06
☐ 8 Mike Schmidt	.60	.25	.08
☐ 9 Mike Dunne	.10	.05	.01
☐ 10 Jack Clark	.15	.07	.02
☐ 11 Tony Gwynn	.45	.20	.06
☐ 12 Will Clark	.60	.25	.08
☐ 13 Cal Ripken	.75	.35	.09
☐ 14 Wade Boggs	.45	.20	.06
☐ 15 Wally Joyner	.20	.09	.03
☐ 16 Harold Baines	.15	.07	.02
☐ 17 Joe Carter	.35	.16	.04
☐ 18 Alan Trammell	.20	.09	.03
☐ 19 Kevin Seitzer	.15	.07	.02
☐ 20 Paul Molitor	.25	.11	.03
☐ 21 Kirby Puckett	.60	.25	.08
☐ 22 Don Mattingly	.50	.23	.06
☐ 23 Mark McGwire	.50	.23	.06
☐ 24 Alvin Davis	.10	.05	.01
☐ 25 Ruben Sierra	.60	.25	.08
☐ 26 George Bell	.15	.07	.02
☐ 27 Jack Morris	.25	.11	.03
☐ 28 Jeff Reardon	.20	.09	.03
☐ 29 John Tudor	.10	.05	.01
☐ 30 Rick Reuschel	.10	.05	.01
☐ 31 Gary Gaetti	.10	.05	.01
☐ 32 Jeffrey Leonard	.10	.05	.01
☐ 33 Frank Viola	.15	.07	.02

1988 Topps Traded

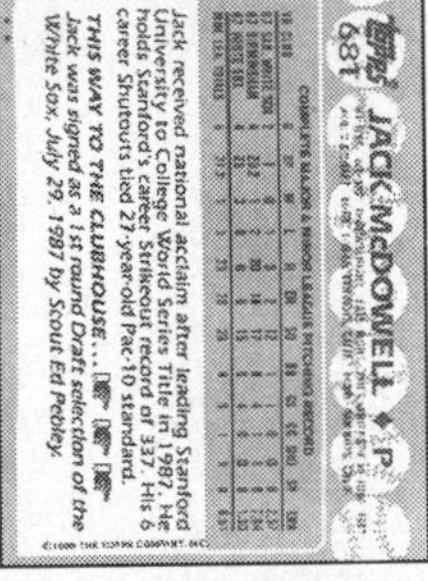

This 132-card Traded or extended set was distributed by Topps to dealers in a special blue and white box as a complete set. The card fronts are identical in style to the Topps regular issue and are also 2 1/2" by 3 1/2". The backs are printed in orange and black on white card stock. Cards are numbered (with a T suffix) alphabetically according to the name of the player. This set has generated additional interest due to the inclusion of the 1988 U.S. Olympic baseball team members. These Olympians are indicated in the checklist below by OLY. The key (extended) Rookie Cards in this set are Jim Abbott, Roberto Alomar, Brady Anderson, Andy Benes, Ron Gant, Mark Grace, Roberto Kelly, Tino Martinez, Jack McDowell, Charles Nagy, Chris Sabo, Robin Ventura, and Walt Weiss. Topps also produced a specially boxed "glossy" edition, frequently referred to as the Topps Traded Tiffany set. This year, again, Topps did not disclose the number of Tiffany sets they produced or sold. It is apparent from the availability that there were many more sets produced this year compared to the 1984-86 Tiffany sets, perhaps 25,000 sets. The checklist of cards is identical to that of the normal non-glossy cards. There are two primary distinguishing features of the Tiffany cards, white card stock reverses and high gloss obverses. These Tiffany cards are valued approximately from three to five times the values listed below.

	MT	EX-MT	VG
COMPLETE SET (132)	30.00	13.50	3.80
COMMON PLAYER (1T-132T)	.05	.02	.01
☐ 1T Jim Abbott OLY	6.50	2.90	.80

☐ 2T Juan Agosto	.05	.02	.01
☐ 3T Luis Alicea	.15	.07	.02
☐ 4T Roberto Alomar	9.00	4.00	1.15
☐ 5T Brady Anderson	1.50	.65	.19
☐ 6T Jack Armstrong	.20	.09	.03
☐ 7T Don August	.05	.02	.01
☐ 8T Floyd Bannister	.05	.02	.01
☐ 9T Bret Barberie OLY	.50	.23	.06
☐ 10T Jose Bautista	.05	.02	.01
☐ 11T Don Baylor	.08	.04	.01
☐ 12T Tim Belcher	.15	.07	.02
☐ 13T Buddy Bell	.08	.04	.01
☐ 14T Andy Benes OLY	3.00	1.35	.40
☐ 15T Damon Berryhill	.20	.09	.03
☐ 16T Bud Black	.05	.02	.01
☐ 17T Pat Borders	.60	.25	.08
☐ 18T Phil Bradley	.05	.02	.01
☐ 19T Jeff Branson OLY	.30	.14	.04
☐ 20T Tom Brunansky	.08	.04	.01
☐ 21T Jay Buhner	.60	.25	.08
☐ 22T Brett Butler	.12	.05	.02
☐ 23T Jim Campanis OLY	.20	.09	.03
☐ 24T Sil Campusano	.05	.02	.01
☐ 25T John Candelaria	.05	.02	.01
☐ 26T Jose Cecena	.05	.02	.01
☐ 27T Rick Cerone	.05	.02	.01
☐ 28T Jack Clark	.08	.04	.01
☐ 29T Kevin Coffman	.05	.02	.01
☐ 30T Pat Combs OLY	.15	.07	.02
☐ 31T Henry Cotto	.05	.02	.01
☐ 32T Chili Davis	.08	.04	.01
☐ 33T Mike Davis	.05	.02	.01
☐ 34T Jose DeLeon	.05	.02	.01
☐ 35T Richard Dotson	.05	.02	.01
☐ 36T Cecil Espy	.10	.05	.01
☐ 37T Tom Filer	.05	.02	.01
☐ 38T Mike Fiore OLY	.05	.02	.01
☐ 39T Ron Gant	2.25	1.00	.30
☐ 40T Kirk Gibson	.08	.04	.01
☐ 41T Rich Gossage	.08	.04	.01
☐ 42T Mark Grace	2.25	1.00	.30
☐ 43T Alfredo Griffin	.05	.02	.01
☐ 44T Ty Griffin OLY	.12	.05	.02
☐ 45T Bryan Harvey	.60	.25	.08
☐ 46T Ron Hassey	.05	.02	.01
☐ 47T Ray Hayward	.05	.02	.01
☐ 48T Dave Henderson	.08	.04	.01
☐ 49T Tom Herr	.05	.02	.01
☐ 50T Bob Horner	.08	.04	.01
☐ 51T Ricky Horton	.05	.02	.01
☐ 52T Jay Howell	.05	.02	.01
☐ 53T Glenn Hubbard	.05	.02	.01
☐ 54T Jeff Innis	.05	.02	.01
☐ 55T Danny Jackson	.05	.02	.01
☐ 56T Darrin Jackson	.50	.23	.06
☐ 57T Roberto Kelly	1.00	.45	.13
☐ 58T Ron Kittle	.05	.02	.01
☐ 59T Ray Knight	.08	.04	.01
☐ 60T Vance Law	.05	.02	.01
☐ 61T Jeffrey Leonard	.05	.02	.01
☐ 62T Mike Macfarlane	.40	.18	.05
☐ 63T Scotti Madison	.05	.02	.01
☐ 64T Kirt Manwaring	.05	.02	.01
☐ 65T Mark Marquess OLY CO	.05	.02	.01
☐ 66T Tino Martinez OLY	1.25	.55	.16
☐ 67T Billy Masse OLY	.12	.05	.02
☐ 68T Jack McDowell	2.25	1.00	.30
☐ 69T Jack McKeon MG	.05	.02	.01
☐ 70T Larry McWilliams	.05	.02	.01
☐ 71T Mickey Morandini OLY	.75	.35	.09
☐ 72T Keith Moreland	.05	.02	.01
☐ 73T Mike Morgan	.05	.02	.01
☐ 74T Charles Nagy OLY	3.00	1.35	.40
☐ 75T Al Nipper	.05	.02	.01
☐ 76T Russ Nixon MG	.05	.02	.01
☐ 77T Jesse Orosco	.05	.02	.01
☐ 78T Joe Orsulak	.05	.02	.01
☐ 79T Dave Palmer	.05	.02	.01
☐ 80T Mark Parent	.05	.02	.01
☐ 81T Dave Parker	.08	.04	.01
☐ 82T Dan Pasqua	.05	.02	.01
☐ 83T Melido Perez	.60	.25	.08
☐ 84T Steve Peters	.05	.02	.01
☐ 85T Dan Petry	.05	.02	.01
☐ 86T Gary Pettis	.05	.02	.01
☐ 87T Jeff Pico	.05	.02	.01
☐ 88T Jim Poole OLY	.12	.05	.02
☐ 89T Ted Power	.05	.02	.01
☐ 90T Rafael Ramirez	.05	.02	.01
☐ 91T Dennis Rasmussen	.05	.02	.01
☐ 92T Jose Rijo	.15	.07	.02
☐ 93T Ernie Riles	.05	.02	.01
☐ 94T Luis Rivera	.05	.02	.01
☐ 95T Doug Robbins OLY	.15	.07	.02
☐ 96T Frank Robinson MG	.15	.07	.02
☐ 97T Cookie Rojas MG	.05	.02	.01
☐ 98T Chris Sabo	.75	.35	.09
☐ 99T Mark Salas	.05	.02	.01
☐ 100T Luis Salazar	.05	.02	.01
☐ 101T Rafael Santana	.05	.02	.01
☐ 102T Nelson Santovenia	.05	.02	.01
☐ 103T Mackey Sasser	.10	.05	.01
☐ 104T Calvin Schiraldi	.05	.02	.01
☐ 105T Mike Schooler	.15	.07	.02
☐ 106T Scott Servais OLY	.20	.09	.03
☐ 107T Dave Silvestri OLY	.40	.18	.05
☐ 108T Don Slaught	.05	.02	.01
☐ 109T Joe Slusarski OLY	.30	.14	.04
☐ 110T Lee Smith	.20	.09	.03
☐ 111T Pete Smith	.50	.23	.06
☐ 112T Jim Snyder MG	.05	.02	.01
☐ 113T Ed Sprague OLY	1.00	.45	.13
☐ 114T Pete Stanicek	.05	.02	.01
☐ 115T Kurt Stillwell	.05	.02	.01
☐ 116T Todd Stottlemyre	.50	.23	.06
☐ 117T Bill Swift	.12	.05	.02
☐ 118T Pat Tabler	.05	.02	.01
☐ 119T Scott Terry	.05	.02	.01
☐ 120T Mickey Tettleton	.20	.09	.03
☐ 121T Dickie Thon	.05	.02	.01
☐ 122T Jeff Treadway	.12	.05	.02
☐ 123T Willie Upshaw	.05	.02	.01
☐ 124T Robin Ventura OLY	10.00	4.50	1.25
☐ 125T Ron Washington	.05	.02	.01
☐ 126T Walt Weiss	.25	.11	.03
☐ 127T Bob Welch	.08	.04	.01
☐ 128T David Wells	.20	.09	.03
☐ 129T Glenn Wilson	.05	.02	.01
☐ 130T Ted Wood OLY	.25	.11	.03
☐ 131T Don Zimmer MG	.08	.04	.01
☐ 132T Checklist 1T-132T	.08	.01	.00

1988 Topps UK Minis

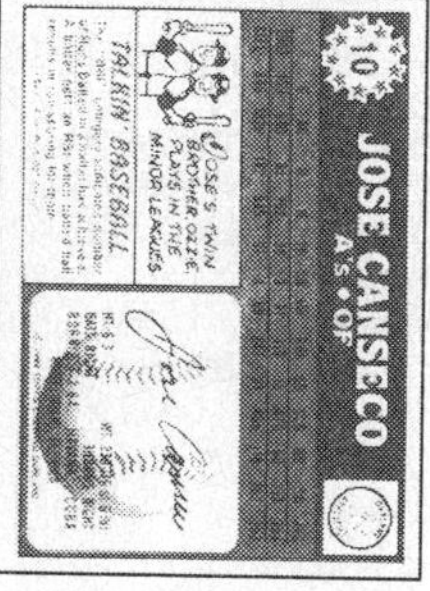

The 1988 Topps UK (United Kingdom) Mini set of "American Baseball" features 88 cards. The cards are numbered on the back and measure approximately 2 1/8" by 3". The card backs are printed in blue, red, and yellow on white card stock. The cards were distributed as a separate issue in packs. A custom black and yellow small set box was also available for holding a complete set; the box has a complete checklist on the back panel. The set player numbering is according to alphabetical order. Topps also produced a specially boxed "glossy" edition frequently referred to as the Topps UK Tiffany set. Topps did not disclose the number of UK Tiffany sets they produced or sold. The checklist of Tiffany cards is identical to that of the normal UK non-glossy cards. These Tiffany cards are valued at approximately two to three times the values listed below.

	MT	EX-MT	VG
COMPLETE SET (88)	8.00	3.60	1.00
COMMON PLAYER (1-88)	.05	.02	.01
☐ 1 Harold Baines	.10	.05	.01
☐ 2 Steve Bedrosian	.05	.02	.01
☐ 3 George Bell	.10	.05	.01

☐ 4 Wade Boggs	.45	.20	.06
☐ 5 Barry Bonds	.60	.25	.08
☐ 6 Bob Boone	.10	.05	.01
☐ 7 George Brett	.45	.20	.06
☐ 8 Hubie Brooks	.05	.02	.01
☐ 9 Ivan Calderon	.05	.02	.01
☐ 10 Jose Canseco	.75	.35	.09
☐ 11 Gary Carter	.20	.09	.03
☐ 12 Joe Carter	.35	.16	.04
☐ 13 Jack Clark	.10	.05	.01
☐ 14 Will Clark	.75	.35	.09
☐ 15 Roger Clemens	1.00	.45	.13
☐ 16 Vince Coleman	.15	.07	.02
☐ 17 Alvin Davis	.05	.02	.01
☐ 18 Eric Davis	.25	.11	.03
☐ 19 Glenn Davis	.15	.07	.02
☐ 20 Andre Dawson	.35	.16	.04
☐ 21 Mike Dunne	.05	.02	.01
☐ 22 Dwight Evans	.10	.05	.01
☐ 23 Tony Fernandez	.10	.05	.01
☐ 24 John Franco	.05	.02	.01
☐ 25 Gary Gaetti	.05	.02	.01
☐ 26 Kirk Gibson	.10	.05	.01
☐ 27 Dwight Gooden	.20	.09	.03
☐ 28 Pedro Guerrero	.10	.05	.01
☐ 29 Tony Gwynn	.50	.23	.06
☐ 30 Billy Hatcher	.05	.02	.01
☐ 31 Rickey Henderson	.60	.25	.08
☐ 32 Tom Henke	.10	.05	.01
☐ 33 Keith Hernandez	.10	.05	.01
☐ 34 Orel Hershiser	.15	.07	.02
☐ 35 Teddy Higuera	.05	.02	.01
☐ 36 Charlie Hough	.05	.02	.01
☐ 37 Kent Hrbek	.10	.05	.01
☐ 38 Brook Jacoby	.05	.02	.01
☐ 39 Dion James	.05	.02	.01
☐ 40 Wally Joyner	.15	.07	.02
☐ 41 John Kruk	.15	.07	.02
☐ 42 Mark Langston	.10	.05	.01
☐ 43 Jeffrey Leonard	.05	.02	.01
☐ 44 Candy Maldonado	.10	.05	.01
☐ 45 Don Mattingly	.60	.25	.08
☐ 46 Willie McGee	.10	.05	.01
☐ 47 Mark McGwire	.60	.25	.08
☐ 48 Kevin Mitchell	.25	.11	.03
☐ 49 Paul Molitor	.20	.09	.03
☐ 50 Jack Morris	.20	.09	.03
☐ 51 Lloyd Moseby	.05	.02	.01
☐ 52 Dale Murphy	.20	.09	.03
☐ 53 Eddie Murray	.40	.18	.05
☐ 54 Matt Nokes	.10	.05	.01
☐ 55 Dave Parker	.10	.05	.01
☐ 56 Larry Parrish	.05	.02	.01
☐ 57 Kirby Puckett	.50	.23	.06
☐ 58 Tim Raines	.10	.05	.01
☐ 59 Willie Randolph	.10	.05	.01
☐ 60 Harold Reynolds	.05	.02	.01
☐ 61 Cal Ripken	.75	.35	.09
☐ 62 Nolan Ryan	1.25	.55	.16
☐ 63 Bret Saberhagen	.15	.07	.02
☐ 64 Juan Samuel	.05	.02	.01
☐ 65 Ryne Sandberg	.75	.35	.09
☐ 66 Benito Santiago	.25	.11	.03
☐ 67 Mike Schmidt	.75	.35	.09
☐ 68 Mike Scott	.10	.05	.01
☐ 69 Kevin Seitzer	.05	.02	.01
☐ 70 Larry Sheets	.05	.02	.01
☐ 71 Ruben Sierra	.50	.23	.06
☐ 72 Ozzie Smith	.35	.16	.04
☐ 73 Zane Smith	.05	.02	.01
☐ 74 Cory Snyder	.10	.05	.01
☐ 75 Dave Stewart	.15	.07	.02
☐ 76 Darryl Strawberry	.50	.23	.06
☐ 77 Rick Sutcliffe	.05	.02	.01
☐ 78 Danny Tartabull	.25	.11	.03
☐ 79 Alan Trammell	.15	.07	.02
☐ 80 Fernando Valenzuela	.10	.05	.01
☐ 81 Andy Van Slyke	.15	.07	.02
☐ 82 Frank Viola	.10	.05	.01
☐ 83 Greg Walker	.05	.02	.01
☐ 84 Tim Wallach	.05	.02	.01
☐ 85 Dave Winfield	.40	.18	.05
☐ 86 Mike Witt	.05	.02	.01
☐ 87 Robin Yount	.50	.23	.06
☐ 88 Checklist Card	.10	.05	.01

1988 Topps Wax Box Cards

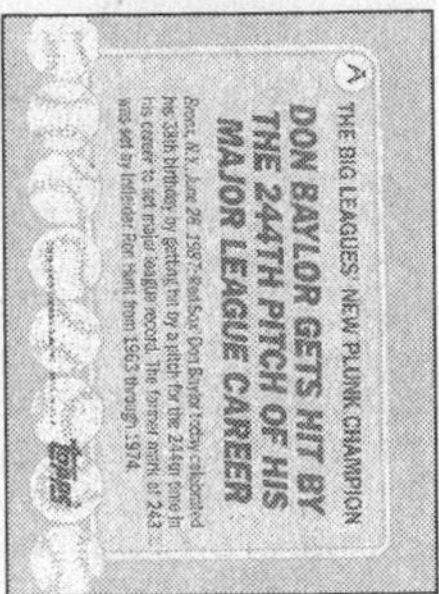

The cards in this 16-card set measure the standard, 2 1/2" by 3 1/2". Cards have essentially the same design as the 1988 Topps regular issue set. The cards were printed on the bottoms of the regular issue wax pack boxes. These 16 cards, "lettered" A through P, are considered a separate set in their own right and are not typically included in a complete set of the regular issue 1988 Topps cards. The value of the panels uncut is slightly greater, perhaps by 25 percent greater, than the value of the individual cards cut up carefully. The card lettering is sequenced alphabetically by player's name.

	MT	EX-MT	VG
COMPLETE SET (16)	7.00	3.10	.85
COMMON PLAYER (A-P)	.15	.07	.02
☐ A Don Baylor	.25	.11	.03
☐ B Steve Bedrosian	.15	.07	.02
☐ C Juan Beniquez	.15	.07	.02
☐ D Bob Boone	.25	.11	.03
☐ E Darrell Evans	.15	.07	.02
☐ F Tony Gwynn	.90	.40	.11
☐ G John Kruk	.35	.16	.04
☐ H Marvell Wynne	.15	.07	.02
☐ I Joe Carter	.75	.35	.09
☐ J Eric Davis	.50	.23	.06
☐ K Howard Johnson	.35	.16	.04
☐ L Darryl Strawberry	.90	.40	.11
☐ M Rickey Henderson	1.00	.45	.13
☐ N Nolan Ryan	1.50	.65	.19
☐ O Mike Schmidt	1.00	.45	.13
☐ P Kent Tekulve	.15	.07	.02

1989 Topps

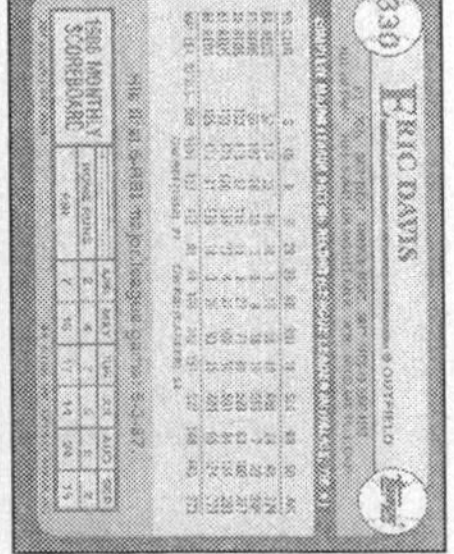

This 792-card set features backs that are printed in pink and black on gray card stock. The manager cards contain a checklist of the respective team's players on the back. Subsets in the set include Record Breakers (1-7), Turn Back the Clock (661-665), and All-Star selections (386-407). The bonus cards distributed throughout the set, which are indicated on the Topps checklist cards, are actually Team Leader (TL) cards. Also sprinkled throughout the set are Future Stars (FS) and First Draft Picks (FDP). There are subtle variations found in the Future Stars cards with respect to the placement of photo and type on the card; in fact, each card has at least two varieties but they are difficult to detect (requiring precise measurement) as well as difficult to explain. The key rookies in this set are Jim Abbott, Sandy Alomar Jr., Brady Anderson, Steve Avery, Andy Benes, Ramon Martinez, Gary Sheffield, John Smoltz, and Robin Ventura. Topps also produced a specially boxed "glossy" edition, frequently referred to as the Topps Tiffany set. This year, again, Topps did not disclose the number of Tiffany sets they produced or sold but it seems that production quantities were roughly similar (or slightly smaller, approximately 15,000 sets) to the previous two years. The checklist of cards (792 regular and 132 Traded) is identical to that of the normal non-glossy cards. There are two primary distinguishing features of the Tiffany cards, white card stock reverses and high gloss obverses. These Tiffany cards are valued approximately from three to five times the values listed below.

	MT	EX-MT	VG
COMPLETE SET (792)	20.00	9.00	2.50
COMPLETE FACT.SET (792)	20.00	9.00	2.50
COMMON PLAYER (1-792)	.04	.02	.01
☐ 1 George Bell RB Slams 3 HR on Opening Day	.10	.05	.01
☐ 2 Wade Boggs RB Gets 200 Hits 6th Straight Season	.12	.05	.02
☐ 3 Gary Carter RB Sets Record for Career Putouts	.05	.02	.01
☐ 4 Andre Dawson RB Logs Double Figures in HR and SB	.08	.04	.01
☐ 5 Orel Hershiser RB Pitches 59 Scoreless Innings	.05	.02	.01
☐ 6 Doug Jones RB UER Earns His 15th Straight Save (Photo actually Chris Codiroli)	.05	.02	.01
☐ 7 Kevin McReynolds RB Steals 21 Without Being Caught	.05	.02	.01
☐ 8 Dave Eiland	.04	.02	.01
☐ 9 Tim Teufel	.04	.02	.01
☐ 10 Andre Dawson	.15	.07	.02
☐ 11 Bruce Sutter	.07	.03	.01
☐ 12 Dale Sveum	.04	.02	.01
☐ 13 Doug Sisk	.04	.02	.01
☐ 14 Tom Kelly MG (Team checklist back)	.06	.03	.01
☐ 15 Robby Thompson	.04	.02	.01
☐ 16 Ron Robinson	.04	.02	.01
☐ 17 Brian Downing	.04	.02	.01
☐ 18 Rick Rhoden	.04	.02	.01
☐ 19 Greg Gagne	.04	.02	.01
☐ 20 Steve Bedrosian	.04	.02	.01
☐ 21 Chicago White Sox TL Greg Walker	.05	.02	.01
☐ 22 Tim Crews	.04	.02	.01
☐ 23 Mike R. Fitzgerald Montreal Expos	.04	.02	.01
☐ 24 Larry Andersen	.04	.02	.01
☐ 25 Frank White	.04	.02	.01
☐ 26 Dale Mohorcic	.04	.02	.01
☐ 27A Orestes Destrade (F* next to copyright)	.20	.09	.03
☐ 27B Orestes Destrade (E*F* next to copyright)	.20	.09	.03
☐ 28 Mike Moore	.04	.02	.01
☐ 29 Kelly Gruber	.07	.03	.01
☐ 30 Dwight Gooden	.12	.05	.02
☐ 31 Terry Francona	.04	.02	.01
☐ 32 Dennis Rasmussen	.04	.02	.01
☐ 33 B.J. Surhoff	.04	.02	.01
☐ 34 Ken Williams	.04	.02	.01
☐ 35 John Tudor UER ('84 Pirates record, should be Red Sox)	.04	.02	.01
☐ 36 Mitch Webster	.04	.02	.01
☐ 37 Bob Stanley	.04	.02	.01
☐ 38 Paul Runge	.04	.02	.01
☐ 39 Mike Maddux	.04	.02	.01
☐ 40 Steve Sax	.07	.03	.01
☐ 41 Terry Mulholland	.07	.03	.01
☐ 42 Jim Eppard	.04	.02	.01
☐ 43 Guillermo Hernandez	.04	.02	.01
☐ 44 Jim Snyder MG (Team checklist back)	.06	.03	.01
☐ 45 Kal Daniels	.07	.03	.01
☐ 46 Mark Portugal	.04	.02	.01
☐ 47 Carney Lansford	.07	.03	.01
☐ 48 Tim Burke	.04	.02	.01
☐ 49 Craig Biggio	.40	.18	.05
☐ 50 George Bell	.10	.05	.01
☐ 51 California Angels TL Mark McLemore	.05	.02	.01
☐ 52 Bob Brenly	.04	.02	.01
☐ 53 Ruben Sierra	.30	.14	.04
☐ 54 Steve Trout	.04	.02	.01
☐ 55 Julio Franco	.07	.03	.01
☐ 56 Pat Tabler	.04	.02	.01
☐ 57 Alejandro Pena	.04	.02	.01
☐ 58 Lee Mazzilli	.04	.02	.01
☐ 59 Mark Davis	.04	.02	.01
☐ 60 Tom Brunansky	.07	.03	.01
☐ 61 Neil Allen	.04	.02	.01
☐ 62 Alfredo Griffin	.04	.02	.01
☐ 63 Mark Clear	.04	.02	.01
☐ 64 Alex Trevino	.04	.02	.01
☐ 65 Rick Reuschel	.04	.02	.01
☐ 66 Manny Trillo	.04	.02	.01
☐ 67 Dave Palmer	.04	.02	.01
☐ 68 Darrell Miller	.04	.02	.01
☐ 69 Jeff Ballard	.04	.02	.01
☐ 70 Mark McGwire	.40	.18	.05
☐ 71 Mike Boddicker	.04	.02	.01
☐ 72 John Moses	.04	.02	.01
☐ 73 Pascual Perez	.04	.02	.01
☐ 74 Nick Leyva MG (Team checklist back)	.06	.03	.01
☐ 75 Tom Henke	.07	.03	.01
☐ 76 Terry Blocker	.04	.02	.01
☐ 77 Doyle Alexander	.04	.02	.01
☐ 78 Jim Sundberg	.04	.02	.01
☐ 79 Scott Bankhead	.04	.02	.01
☐ 80 Cory Snyder	.04	.02	.01
☐ 81 Montreal Expos TL Tim Raines	.05	.02	.01
☐ 82 Dave Leiper	.04	.02	.01
☐ 83 Jeff Blauser	.07	.03	.01
☐ 84 Bill Bene FDP	.04	.02	.01
☐ 85 Kevin McReynolds	.07	.03	.01
☐ 86 Al Nipper	.04	.02	.01
☐ 87 Larry Owen	.04	.02	.01
☐ 88 Darryl Hamilton	.20	.09	.03
☐ 89 Dave LaPoint	.04	.02	.01
☐ 90 Vince Coleman UER (Wrong birth year)	.07	.03	.01
☐ 91 Floyd Youmans	.04	.02	.01
☐ 92 Jeff Kunkel	.04	.02	.01
☐ 93 Ken Howell	.04	.02	.01
☐ 94 Chris Speier	.04	.02	.01
☐ 95 Gerald Young	.04	.02	.01
☐ 96 Rick Cerone (Ellis Burks in background of photo)	.04	.02	.01
☐ 97 Greg Mathews	.04	.02	.01
☐ 98 Larry Sheets	.04	.02	.01
☐ 99 Sherman Corbett	.04	.02	.01
☐ 100 Mike Schmidt	.40	.18	.05
☐ 101 Les Straker	.04	.02	.01
☐ 102 Mike Gallego	.04	.02	.01
☐ 103 Tim Birtsas	.04	.02	.01
☐ 104 Dallas Green MG (Team checklist back)	.06	.03	.01
☐ 105 Ron Darling	.07	.03	.01
☐ 106 Willie Upshaw	.04	.02	.01
☐ 107 Jose DeLeon	.04	.02	.01
☐ 108 Fred Manrique	.04	.02	.01
☐ 109 Hipolito Pena	.04	.02	.01
☐ 110 Paul Molitor	.10	.05	.01
☐ 111 Cincinnati Reds TL Eric Davis (Swinging bat)	.05	.02	.01
☐ 112 Jim Presley	.04	.02	.01
☐ 113 Lloyd Moseby	.04	.02	.01
☐ 114 Bob Kipper	.04	.02	.01
☐ 115 Jody Davis	.04	.02	.01

□ 116 Jeff Montgomery	.07	.03	.01
□ 117 Dave Anderson	.04	.02	.01
□ 118 Checklist 1-132	.05	.01	.00
□ 119 Terry Puhl	.04	.02	.01
□ 120 Frank Viola	.07	.03	.01
□ 121 Garry Templeton	.04	.02	.01
□ 122 Lance Johnson	.07	.03	.01
□ 123 Spike Owen	.04	.02	.01
□ 124 Jim Traber	.04	.02	.01
□ 125 Mike Krukow	.04	.02	.01
□ 126 Sid Bream	.04	.02	.01
□ 127 Walt Terrell	.04	.02	.01
□ 128 Milt Thompson	.04	.02	.01
□ 129 Terry Clark	.04	.02	.01
□ 130 Gerald Perry	.04	.02	.01
□ 131 Dave Otto	.04	.02	.01
□ 132 Curt Ford	.04	.02	.01
□ 133 Bill Long	.04	.02	.01
□ 134 Don Zimmer MG	.06	.03	.01
(Team checklist back)			
□ 135 Jose Rijo	.07	.03	.01
□ 136 Joey Meyer	.04	.02	.01
□ 137 Geno Petralli	.04	.02	.01
□ 138 Wallace Johnson	.04	.02	.01
□ 139 Mike Flanagan	.04	.02	.01
□ 140 Shawon Dunston	.07	.03	.01
□ 141 Cleveland Indians TL	.05	.02	.01
Brook Jacoby			
□ 142 Mike Diaz	.04	.02	.01
□ 143 Mike Campbell	.04	.02	.01
□ 144 Jay Bell	.07	.03	.01
□ 145 Dave Stewart	.07	.03	.01
□ 146 Gary Pettis	.04	.02	.01
□ 147 DeWayne Buice	.04	.02	.01
□ 148 Bill Pecota	.04	.02	.01
□ 149 Doug Dascenzo	.04	.02	.01
□ 150 Fernando Valenzuela	.07	.03	.01
□ 151 Terry McGriff	.04	.02	.01
□ 152 Mark Thurmond	.04	.02	.01
□ 153 Jim Pankovits	.04	.02	.01
□ 154 Don Carman	.04	.02	.01
□ 155 Marty Barrett	.04	.02	.01
□ 156 Dave Gallagher	.04	.02	.01
□ 157 Tom Glavine	.50	.23	.06
□ 158 Mike Aldrete	.04	.02	.01
□ 159 Pat Clements	.04	.02	.01
□ 160 Jeffrey Leonard	.04	.02	.01
□ 161 Gregg Olson FDP UER	.40	.18	.05
(Born Scribner, NE,			
should be Omaha, NE)			
□ 162 John Davis	.04	.02	.01
□ 163 Bob Forsch	.04	.02	.01
□ 164 Hal Lanier MG	.06	.03	.01
(Team checklist back)			
□ 165 Mike Dunne	.04	.02	.01
□ 166 Doug Jennings	.04	.02	.01
□ 167 Steve Searcy FS	.04	.02	.01
□ 168 Willie Wilson	.04	.02	.01
□ 169 Mike Jackson	.04	.02	.01
□ 170 Tony Fernandez	.07	.03	.01
□ 171 Atlanta Braves TL	.05	.02	.01
Andres Thomas			
□ 172 Frank Williams	.04	.02	.01
□ 173 Mel Hall	.04	.02	.01
□ 174 Todd Burns	.04	.02	.01
□ 175 John Shelby	.04	.02	.01
□ 176 Jeff Parrett	.04	.02	.01
□ 177 Monty Fariss FDP	.30	.14	.04
□ 178 Mark Grant	.04	.02	.01
□ 179 Ozzie Virgil	.04	.02	.01
□ 180 Mike Scott	.04	.02	.01
□ 181 Craig Worthington	.04	.02	.01
□ 182 Bob McClure	.04	.02	.01
□ 183 Oddibe McDowell	.04	.02	.01
□ 184 John Costello	.04	.02	.01
□ 185 Claudell Washington	.04	.02	.01
□ 186 Pat Perry	.04	.02	.01
□ 187 Darren Daulton	.07	.03	.01
□ 188 Dennis Lamp	.04	.02	.01
□ 189 Kevin Mitchell	.10	.05	.01
□ 190 Mike Witt	.04	.02	.01
□ 191 Sil Campusano	.04	.02	.01
□ 192 Paul Mirabella	.04	.02	.01
□ 193 Sparky Anderson MG	.06	.03	.01
(Team checklist back)			
UER (553 Salazer)			
□ 194 Greg W. Harris	.10	.05	.01
San Diego Padres			
□ 195 Ozzie Guillen	.04	.02	.01
□ 196 Denny Walling	.04	.02	.01
□ 197 Neal Heaton	.04	.02	.01
□ 198 Danny Heep	.04	.02	.01
□ 199 Mike Schooler	.10	.05	.01
□ 200 George Brett	.20	.09	.03
□ 201 Blue Jays TL	.05	.02	.01
Kelly Gruber			
□ 202 Brad Moore	.04	.02	.01
□ 203 Rob Ducey	.04	.02	.01
□ 204 Brad Havens	.04	.02	.01
□ 205 Dwight Evans	.07	.03	.01
□ 206 Roberto Alomar	.75	.35	.09
□ 207 Terry Leach	.04	.02	.01
□ 208 Tom Pagnozzi	.04	.02	.01
□ 209 Jeff Bittiger	.04	.02	.01
□ 210 Dale Murphy	.10	.05	.01
□ 211 Mike Pagliarulo	.04	.02	.01
□ 212 Scott Sanderson	.04	.02	.01
□ 213 Rene Gonzales	.04	.02	.01
□ 214 Charlie O'Brien	.04	.02	.01
□ 215 Kevin Gross	.04	.02	.01
□ 216 Jack Howell	.04	.02	.01
□ 217 Joe Price	.04	.02	.01
□ 218 Mike LaValliere	.04	.02	.01
□ 219 Jim Clancy	.04	.02	.01
□ 220 Gary Gaetti	.04	.02	.01
□ 221 Cecil Espy	.04	.02	.01
□ 222 Mark Lewis FDP	.30	.14	.04
□ 223 Jay Buhner	.12	.05	.02
□ 224 Tony LaRussa MG	.06	.03	.01
(Team checklist back)			
□ 225 Ramon Martinez	.50	.23	.06
□ 226 Bill Doran	.04	.02	.01
□ 227 John Farrell	.04	.02	.01
□ 228 Nelson Santovenia	.04	.02	.01
□ 229 Jimmy Key	.07	.03	.01
□ 230 Ozzie Smith	.15	.07	.02
□ 231 San Diego Padres TL	.12	.05	.02
Roberto Alomar			
(Gary Carter at plate)			
□ 232 Ricky Horton	.04	.02	.01
□ 233 Gregg Jefferies FS	.25	.11	.03
□ 234 Tom Browning	.04	.02	.01
□ 235 John Kruk	.07	.03	.01
□ 236 Charles Hudson	.04	.02	.01
□ 237 Glenn Hubbard	.04	.02	.01
□ 238 Eric King	.04	.02	.01
□ 239 Tim Laudner	.04	.02	.01
□ 240 Greg Maddux	.30	.14	.04
□ 241 Brett Butler	.07	.03	.01
□ 242 Ed VandeBerg	.04	.02	.01
□ 243 Bob Boone	.07	.03	.01
□ 244 Jim Acker	.04	.02	.01
□ 245 Jim Rice	.07	.03	.01
□ 246 Rey Quinones	.04	.02	.01
□ 247 Shawn Hillegas	.04	.02	.01
□ 248 Tony Phillips	.04	.02	.01
□ 249 Tim Leary	.04	.02	.01
□ 250 Cal Ripken	.50	.23	.06
□ 251 John Dopson	.04	.02	.01
□ 252 Billy Hatcher	.04	.02	.01
□ 253 Jose Alvarez	.04	.02	.01
□ 254 Tom Lasorda MG	.06	.03	.01
(Team checklist back)			
□ 255 Ron Guidry	.07	.03	.01
□ 256 Benny Santiago	.07	.03	.01
□ 257 Rick Aguilera	.07	.03	.01
□ 258 Checklist 133-264	.05	.01	.00
□ 259 Larry McWilliams	.04	.02	.01
□ 260 Dave Winfield	.20	.09	.03
□ 261 St.Louis Cardinals TL	.05	.02	.01
Tom Brunansky			
(With Luis Alicea)			
□ 262 Jeff Pico	.04	.02	.01
□ 263 Mike Felder	.04	.02	.01
□ 264 Rob Dibble	.20	.09	.03
□ 265 Kent Hrbek	.07	.03	.01
□ 266 Luis Aquino	.04	.02	.01
□ 267 Jeff M. Robinson	.04	.02	.01
Detroit Tigers			
□ 268 N. Keith Miller	.04	.02	.01
Philadelphia Phillies			
□ 269 Tom Bolton	.04	.02	.01
□ 270 Wally Joyner	.08	.04	.01
□ 271 Jay Tibbs	.04	.02	.01
□ 272 Ron Hassey	.04	.02	.01
□ 273 Jose Lind	.04	.02	.01
□ 274 Mark Eichhorn	.04	.02	.01
□ 275 Danny Tartabull UER	.12	.05	.02
(Born San Juan, PR			
should be Miami, FL)			
□ 276 Paul Kilgus	.04	.02	.01
□ 277 Mike Davis	.04	.02	.01
□ 278 Andy McGaffigan	.04	.02	.01
□ 279 Scott Bradley	.04	.02	.01
□ 280 Bob Knepper	.04	.02	.01
□ 281 Gary Redus	.04	.02	.01

☐ 282 Cris Carpenter .10 .05 .01
☐ 283 Andy Allanson .04 .02 .01
☐ 284 Jim Leyland MG .06 .03 .01
(Team checklist back)
☐ 285 John Candelaria .04 .02 .01
☐ 286 Darrin Jackson .15 .07 .02
☐ 287 Juan Nieves .04 .02 .01
☐ 288 Pat Sheridan .04 .02 .01
☐ 289 Ernie Whitt .04 .02 .01
☐ 290 John Franco .07 .03 .01
☐ 291 New York Mets TL .08 .04 .01
Darryl Strawberry
(With Keith Hernandez
and Kevin McReynolds)
☐ 292 Jim Corsi .10 .05 .01
☐ 293 Glenn Wilson .04 .02 .01
☐ 294 Juan Berenguer .04 .02 .01
☐ 295 Scott Fletcher .04 .02 .01
☐ 296 Ron Gant .50 .23 .06
☐ 297 Oswald Peraza .04 .02 .01
☐ 298 Chris James .04 .02 .01
☐ 299 Steve Ellsworth .04 .02 .01
☐ 300 Darryl Strawberry .25 .11 .03
☐ 301 Charlie Leibrandt .04 .02 .01
☐ 302 Gary Ward .04 .02 .01
☐ 303 Felix Fermin .04 .02 .01
☐ 304 Joel Youngblood .04 .02 .01
☐ 305 Dave Smith .04 .02 .01
☐ 306 Tracy Woodson .04 .02 .01
☐ 307 Lance McCullers .04 .02 .01
☐ 308 Ron Karkovice .04 .02 .01
☐ 309 Mario Diaz .04 .02 .01
☐ 310 Rafael Palmeiro .20 .09 .03
☐ 311 Chris Bosio .04 .02 .01
☐ 312 Tom Lawless .04 .02 .01
☐ 313 Dennis Martinez .07 .03 .01
☐ 314 Bobby Valentine MG .06 .03 .01
(Team checklist back)
☐ 315 Greg Swindell .07 .03 .01
☐ 316 Walt Weiss .07 .03 .01
☐ 317 Jack Armstrong .12 .05 .02
☐ 318 Gene Larkin .04 .02 .01
☐ 319 Greg Booker .04 .02 .01
☐ 320 Lou Whitaker .07 .03 .01
☐ 321 Boston Red Sox TL .05 .02 .01
Jody Reed
☐ 322 John Smiley .07 .03 .01
☐ 323 Gary Thurman .04 .02 .01
☐ 324 Bob Milacki .10 .05 .01
☐ 325 Jesse Barfield .04 .02 .01
☐ 326 Dennis Boyd .04 .02 .01
☐ 327 Mark Lemke .15 .07 .02
☐ 328 Rick Honeycutt .04 .02 .01
☐ 329 Bob Melvin .04 .02 .01
☐ 330 Eric Davis .12 .05 .02
☐ 331 Curt Wilkerson .04 .02 .01
☐ 332 Tony Armas .04 .02 .01
☐ 333 Bob Ojeda .04 .02 .01
☐ 334 Steve Lyons .04 .02 .01
☐ 335 Dave Righetti .04 .02 .01
☐ 336 Steve Balboni .04 .02 .01
☐ 337 Calvin Schiraldi .04 .02 .01
☐ 338 Jim Adduci .04 .02 .01
☐ 339 Scott Bailes .04 .02 .01
☐ 340 Kirk Gibson .07 .03 .01
☐ 341 Jim Deshaies .04 .02 .01
☐ 342 Tom Brookens .04 .02 .01
☐ 343 Gary Sheffield FS 2.00 .90 .25
☐ 344 Tom Trebelhorn MG .06 .03 .01
(Team checklist back)
☐ 345 Charlie Hough .04 .02 .01
☐ 346 Rex Hudler .04 .02 .01
☐ 347 John Cerutti .04 .02 .01
☐ 348 Ed Hearn .04 .02 .01
☐ 349 Ron Jones .04 .02 .01
☐ 350 Andy Van Slyke .10 .05 .01
☐ 351 San Fran. Giants TL .05 .02 .01
Bob Melvin
(With Bill Fahey CO)
☐ 352 Rick Schu .04 .02 .01
☐ 353 Marvell Wynne .04 .02 .01
☐ 354 Larry Parrish .04 .02 .01
☐ 355 Mark Langston .07 .03 .01
☐ 356 Kevin Elster .04 .02 .01
☐ 357 Jerry Reuss .04 .02 .01
☐ 358 Ricky Jordan .10 .05 .01
☐ 359 Tommy John .07 .03 .01
☐ 360 Ryne Sandberg .40 .18 .05
☐ 361 Kelly Downs .04 .02 .01
☐ 362 Jack Lazorko .04 .02 .01
☐ 363 Rich Yett .04 .02 .01
☐ 364 Rob Deer .07 .03 .01
☐ 365 Mike Henneman .07 .03 .01
☐ 366 Herm Winningham .04 .02 .01
☐ 367 Johnny Paredes .04 .02 .01
☐ 368 Brian Holton .04 .02 .01
☐ 369 Ken Caminiti .07 .03 .01
☐ 370 Dennis Eckersley .12 .05 .02
☐ 371 Manny Lee .04 .02 .01
☐ 372 Craig Lefferts .04 .02 .01
☐ 373 Tracy Jones .04 .02 .01
☐ 374 John Wathan MG .06 .03 .01
(Team checklist back)
☐ 375 Terry Pendleton .12 .05 .02
☐ 376 Steve Lombardozzi .04 .02 .01
☐ 377 Mike Smithson .04 .02 .01
☐ 378 Checklist 265-396 .05 .01 .00
☐ 379 Tim Flannery .04 .02 .01
☐ 380 Rickey Henderson .25 .11 .03
☐ 381 Baltimore Orioles TL .05 .02 .01
Larry Sheets
☐ 382 John Smoltz .60 .25 .08
☐ 383 Howard Johnson .07 .03 .01
☐ 384 Mark Salas .04 .02 .01
☐ 385 Von Hayes .04 .02 .01
☐ 386 Andres Galarraga AS .05 .02 .01
☐ 387 Ryne Sandberg AS .20 .09 .03
☐ 388 Bobby Bonilla AS .10 .05 .01
☐ 389 Ozzie Smith AS .10 .05 .01
☐ 390 Darryl Strawberry AS .12 .05 .02
☐ 391 Andre Dawson AS .10 .05 .01
☐ 392 Andy Van Slyke AS .08 .04 .01
☐ 393 Gary Carter AS .05 .02 .01
☐ 394 Orel Hershiser AS .05 .02 .01
☐ 395 Danny Jackson AS .05 .02 .01
☐ 396 Kirk Gibson AS .05 .02 .01
☐ 397 Don Mattingly AS .12 .05 .02
☐ 398 Julio Franco AS .05 .02 .01
☐ 399 Wade Boggs AS .12 .05 .02
☐ 400 Alan Trammell AS .08 .04 .01
☐ 401 Jose Canseco AS .20 .09 .03
☐ 402 Mike Greenwell AS .08 .04 .01
☐ 403 Kirby Puckett AS .20 .09 .03
☐ 404 Bob Boone AS .05 .02 .01
☐ 405 Roger Clemens AS .20 .09 .03
☐ 406 Frank Viola AS .05 .02 .01
☐ 407 Dave Winfield AS .10 .05 .01
☐ 408 Greg Walker .04 .02 .01
☐ 409 Ken Dayley .04 .02 .01
☐ 410 Jack Clark .07 .03 .01
☐ 411 Mitch Williams .07 .03 .01
☐ 412 Barry Lyons .04 .02 .01
☐ 413 Mike Kingery .04 .02 .01
☐ 414 Jim Fregosi MG .06 .03 .01
(Team checklist back)
☐ 415 Rich Gossage .07 .03 .01
☐ 416 Fred Lynn .07 .03 .01
☐ 417 Mike LaCoss .04 .02 .01
☐ 418 Bob Dernier .04 .02 .01
☐ 419 Tom Filer .04 .02 .01
☐ 420 Joe Carter .25 .11 .03
☐ 421 Kirk McCaskill .04 .02 .01
☐ 422 Bo Diaz .04 .02 .01
☐ 423 Brian Fisher .04 .02 .01
☐ 424 Luis Polonia UER .07 .03 .01
(Wrong birthdate)
☐ 425 Jay Howell .04 .02 .01
☐ 426 Dan Gladden .04 .02 .01
☐ 427 Eric Show .04 .02 .01
☐ 428 Craig Reynolds .04 .02 .01
☐ 429 Minnesota Twins TL .05 .02 .01
Greg Gagne
(Taking throw at 2nd)
☐ 430 Mark Gubicza .04 .02 .01
☐ 431 Luis Rivera .04 .02 .01
☐ 432 Chad Kreuter .04 .02 .01
☐ 433 Albert Hall .04 .02 .01
☐ 434 Ken Patterson .04 .02 .01
☐ 435 Len Dykstra .07 .03 .01
☐ 436 Bobby Meacham .04 .02 .01
☐ 437 Andy Benes FDP .60 .25 .08
☐ 438 Greg Gross .04 .02 .01
☐ 439 Frank DiPino .04 .02 .01
☐ 440 Bobby Bonilla .20 .09 .03
☐ 441 Jerry Reed .04 .02 .01
☐ 442 Jose Oquendo .04 .02 .01
☐ 443 Rod Nichols .04 .02 .01
☐ 444 Moose Stubing MG .06 .03 .01
(Team checklist back)
☐ 445 Matt Nokes .07 .03 .01
☐ 446 Rob Murphy .04 .02 .01
☐ 447 Donell Nixon .04 .02 .01
☐ 448 Eric Plunk .04 .02 .01
☐ 449 Carmelo Martinez .04 .02 .01
☐ 450 Roger Clemens .40 .18 .05
☐ 451 Mark Davidson .04 .02 .01

	Card			
☐	452 Israel Sanchez	.04	.02	.01
☐	453 Tom Prince	.04	.02	.01
☐	454 Paul Assenmacher	.04	.02	.01
☐	455 Johnny Ray	.04	.02	.01
☐	456 Tim Belcher	.07	.03	.01
☐	457 Mackey Sasser	.04	.02	.01
☐	458 Donn Pall	.04	.02	.01
☐	459 Seattle Mariners TL Dave Valle	.05	.02	.01
☐	460 Dave Stieb	.07	.03	.01
☐	461 Buddy Bell	.07	.03	.01
☐	462 Jose Guzman	.07	.03	.01
☐	463 Steve Lake	.04	.02	.01
☐	464 Bryn Smith	.04	.02	.01
☐	465 Mark Grace	.40	.18	.05
☐	466 Chuck Crim	.04	.02	.01
☐	467 Jim Walewander	.04	.02	.01
☐	468 Henry Cotto	.04	.02	.01
☐	469 Jose Bautista	.04	.02	.01
☐	470 Lance Parrish	.07	.03	.01
☐	471 Steve Curry	.04	.02	.01
☐	472 Brian Harper	.07	.03	.01
☐	473 Don Robinson	.04	.02	.01
☐	474 Bob Rodgers MG (Team checklist back)	.06	.03	.01
☐	475 Dave Parker	.07	.03	.01
☐	476 Jon Perlman	.04	.02	.01
☐	477 Dick Schofield	.04	.02	.01
☐	478 Doug Drabek	.07	.03	.01
☐	479 Mike Macfarlane	.15	.07	.02
☐	480 Keith Hernandez	.07	.03	.01
☐	481 Chris Brown	.04	.02	.01
☐	482 Steve Peters	.04	.02	.01
☐	483 Mickey Hatcher	.04	.02	.01
☐	484 Steve Shields	.04	.02	.01
☐	485 Hubie Brooks	.04	.02	.01
☐	486 Jack McDowell	.40	.18	.05
☐	487 Scott Lusader	.04	.02	.01
☐	488 Kevin Coffman ("Now with Cubs")	.04	.02	.01
☐	489 Phila. Phillies TL Mike Schmidt	.10	.05	.01
☐	490 Chris Sabo	.25	.11	.03
☐	491 Mike Birkbeck	.04	.02	.01
☐	492 Alan Ashby	.04	.02	.01
☐	493 Todd Benzinger	.04	.02	.01
☐	494 Shane Rawley	.04	.02	.01
☐	495 Candy Maldonado	.04	.02	.01
☐	496 Dwayne Henry	.04	.02	.01
☐	497 Pete Stanicek	.04	.02	.01
☐	498 Dave Valle	.04	.02	.01
☐	499 Don Heinkel	.04	.02	.01
☐	500 Jose Canseco	.40	.18	.05
☐	501 Vance Law	.04	.02	.01
☐	502 Duane Ward	.07	.03	.01
☐	503 Al Newman	.04	.02	.01
☐	504 Bob Walk	.04	.02	.01
☐	505 Pete Rose MG (Team checklist back)	.15	.07	.02
☐	506 Kirt Manwaring	.04	.02	.01
☐	507 Steve Farr	.04	.02	.01
☐	508 Wally Backman	.04	.02	.01
☐	509 Bud Black	.04	.02	.01
☐	510 Bob Horner	.04	.02	.01
☐	511 Richard Dotson	.04	.02	.01
☐	512 Donnie Hill	.04	.02	.01
☐	513 Jesse Orosco	.04	.02	.01
☐	514 Chet Lemon	.04	.02	.01
☐	515 Barry Larkin	.15	.07	.02
☐	516 Eddie Whitson	.04	.02	.01
☐	517 Greg Brock	.04	.02	.01
☐	518 Bruce Ruffin	.04	.02	.01
☐	519 New York Yankees TL Willie Randolph	.05	.02	.01
☐	520 Rick Sutcliffe	.07	.03	.01
☐	521 Mickey Tettleton	.07	.03	.01
☐	522 Randy Kramer	.04	.02	.01
☐	523 Andres Thomas	.04	.02	.01
☐	524 Checklist 397-528	.05	.01	.00
☐	525 Chili Davis	.07	.03	.01
☐	526 Wes Gardner	.04	.02	.01
☐	527 Dave Henderson	.07	.03	.01
☐	528 Luis Medina (Lower left front has white triangle)	.04	.02	.01
☐	529 Tom Foley	.04	.02	.01
☐	530 Nolan Ryan	.60	.25	.08
☐	531 Dave Hengel	.04	.02	.01
☐	532 Jerry Browne	.04	.02	.01
☐	533 Andy Hawkins	.04	.02	.01
☐	534 Doc Edwards MG (Team checklist back)	.06	.03	.01
☐	535 Todd Worrell UER (4 wins in '88, should be 5)	.07	.03	.01
☐	536 Joel Skinner	.04	.02	.01
☐	537 Pete Smith	.07	.03	.01
☐	538 Juan Castillo	.04	.02	.01
☐	539 Barry Jones	.04	.02	.01
☐	540 Bo Jackson	.20	.09	.03
☐	541 Cecil Fielder	.25	.11	.03
☐	542 Todd Frohwirth	.04	.02	.01
☐	543 Damon Berryhill	.04	.02	.01
☐	544 Jeff Sellers	.04	.02	.01
☐	545 Mookie Wilson	.07	.03	.01
☐	546 Mark Williamson	.04	.02	.01
☐	547 Mark McLemore	.04	.02	.01
☐	548 Bobby Witt	.07	.03	.01
☐	549 Chicago Cubs TL Jamie Moyer (Pitching)	.05	.02	.01
☐	550 Orel Hershiser	.07	.03	.01
☐	551 Randy Ready	.04	.02	.01
☐	552 Greg Cadaret	.04	.02	.01
☐	553 Luis Salazar	.04	.02	.01
☐	554 Nick Esasky	.04	.02	.01
☐	555 Bert Blyleven	.07	.03	.01
☐	556 Bruce Fields	.04	.02	.01
☐	557 Keith A. Miller New York Mets	.04	.02	.01
☐	558 Dan Pasqua	.04	.02	.01
☐	559 Juan Agosto	.04	.02	.01
☐	560 Tim Raines	.07	.03	.01
☐	561 Luis Aguayo	.04	.02	.01
☐	562 Danny Cox	.04	.02	.01
☐	563 Bill Schroeder	.04	.02	.01
☐	564 Russ Nixon MG (Team checklist back)	.06	.03	.01
☐	565 Jeff Russell	.04	.02	.01
☐	566 Al Pedrique	.04	.02	.01
☐	567 David Wells UER (Complete Pitching Recor)	.10	.05	.01
☐	568 Mickey Brantley	.04	.02	.01
☐	569 German Jimenez	.04	.02	.01
☐	570 Tony Gwynn UER ('88 average should be italicized as league leader)	.25	.11	.03
☐	571 Billy Ripken	.04	.02	.01
☐	572 Atlee Hammaker	.04	.02	.01
☐	573 Jim Abbott FDP	1.00	.45	.13
☐	574 Dave Clark	.04	.02	.01
☐	575 Juan Samuel	.04	.02	.01
☐	576 Greg Minton	.04	.02	.01
☐	577 Randy Bush	.04	.02	.01
☐	578 John Morris	.04	.02	.01
☐	579 Houston Astros TL Glenn Davis (Batting stance)	.05	.02	.01
☐	580 Harold Reynolds	.04	.02	.01
☐	581 Gene Nelson	.04	.02	.01
☐	582 Mike Marshall	.04	.02	.01
☐	583 Paul Gibson	.04	.02	.01
☐	584 Randy Velarde UER (Signed 1935, should be 1985)	.04	.02	.01
☐	585 Harold Baines	.07	.03	.01
☐	586 Joe Boever	.04	.02	.01
☐	587 Mike Stanley	.04	.02	.01
☐	588 Luis Alicea	.10	.05	.01
☐	589 Dave Meads	.04	.02	.01
☐	590 Andres Galarraga	.04	.02	.01
☐	591 Jeff Musselman	.04	.02	.01
☐	592 John Cangelosi	.04	.02	.01
☐	593 Drew Hall	.04	.02	.01
☐	594 Jimy Williams MG (Team checklist back)	.06	.03	.01
☐	595 Teddy Higuera	.04	.02	.01
☐	596 Kurt Stillwell	.04	.02	.01
☐	597 Terry Taylor	.04	.02	.01
☐	598 Ken Gerhart	.04	.02	.01
☐	599 Tom Candiotti	.04	.02	.01
☐	600 Wade Boggs	.25	.11	.03
☐	601 Dave Dravecky	.07	.03	.01
☐	602 Devon White	.07	.03	.01
☐	603 Frank Tanana	.04	.02	.01
☐	604 Paul O'Neill	.07	.03	.01
☐	605A Bob Welch ERR (Missing line on back, "Complete M.L. Pitching Record")	2.25	1.00	.30
☐	605B Bob Welch COR	.07	.03	.01
☐	606 Rick Dempsey	.04	.02	.01
☐	607 Willie Ansley FDP	.12	.05	.02
☐	608 Phil Bradley	.04	.02	.01
☐	609 Detroit Tigers TL	.05	.02	.01

Frank Tanana
(With Alan Trammell
and Mike Heath)
☐ 610 Randy Myers .07 .03 .01
☐ 611 Don Slaught .04 .02 .01
☐ 612 Dan Quisenberry .07 .03 .01
☐ 613 Gary Varsho .04 .02 .01
☐ 614 Joe Hesketh .04 .02 .01
☐ 615 Robin Yount .20 .09 .03
☐ 616 Steve Rosenberg .04 .02 .01
☐ 617 Mark Parent .04 .02 .01
☐ 618 Rance Mulliniks .04 .02 .01
☐ 619 Checklist 529-660 .05 .01 .00
☐ 620 Barry Bonds .40 .18 .05
☐ 621 Rick Mahler .04 .02 .01
☐ 622 Stan Javier .04 .02 .01
☐ 623 Fred Toliver .04 .02 .01
☐ 624 Jack McKeon MG .06 .03 .01
(Team checklist back)
☐ 625 Eddie Murray .15 .07 .02
☐ 626 Jeff Reed .04 .02 .01
☐ 627 Greg A. Harris .04 .02 .01
Philadelphia Phillies
☐ 628 Matt Williams .15 .07 .02
☐ 629 Pete O'Brien .04 .02 .01
☐ 630 Mike Greenwell .07 .03 .01
☐ 631 Dave Bergman .04 .02 .01
☐ 632 Bryan Harvey .25 .11 .03
☐ 633 Daryl Boston .04 .02 .01
☐ 634 Marvin Freeman .04 .02 .01
☐ 635 Willie Randolph .07 .03 .01
☐ 636 Bill Wilkinson .04 .02 .01
☐ 637 Carmen Castillo .04 .02 .01
☐ 638 Floyd Bannister .04 .02 .01
☐ 639 Oakland A's TL .05 .02 .01
Walt Weiss
☐ 640 Willie McGee .07 .03 .01
☐ 641 Curt Young .04 .02 .01
☐ 642 Argenis Salazar .04 .02 .01
☐ 643 Louie Meadows .04 .02 .01
☐ 644 Lloyd McClendon .04 .02 .01
☐ 645 Jack Morris .12 .05 .02
☐ 646 Kevin Bass .04 .02 .01
☐ 647 Randy Johnson .35 .16 .04
☐ 648 Sandy Alomar FS .25 .11 .03
☐ 649 Stewart Cliburn .04 .02 .01
☐ 650 Kirby Puckett .40 .18 .05
☐ 651 Tom Niedenfuer .04 .02 .01
☐ 652 Rich Gedman .04 .02 .01
☐ 653 Tommy Barrett .04 .02 .01
☐ 654 Whitey Herzog MG .06 .03 .01
(Team checklist back)
☐ 655 Dave Magadan .07 .03 .01
☐ 656 Ivan Calderon .04 .02 .01
☐ 657 Joe Magrane .04 .02 .01
☐ 658 R.J. Reynolds .04 .02 .01
☐ 659 Al Leiter .04 .02 .01
☐ 660 Will Clark .40 .18 .05
☐ 661 Dwight Gooden TBC84 .10 .05 .01
☐ 662 Lou Brock TBC79 .08 .04 .01
☐ 663 Hank Aaron TBC74 .10 .05 .01
☐ 664 Gil Hodges TBC69 .05 .02 .01
☐ 665A Tony Oliva TBC64 2.00 .90 .25
ERR (fabricated card
is enlarged version
of Oliva's 64T card;
Topps copyright
missing)
☐ 665B Tony Oliva TBC64 .05 .02 .01
COR (fabricated
card)
☐ 666 Randy St.Claire .04 .02 .01
☐ 667 Dwayne Murphy .04 .02 .01
☐ 668 Mike Bielecki .04 .02 .01
☐ 669 L.A. Dodgers TL .05 .02 .01
Orel Hershiser
(Mound conference
with Mike Scioscia)
☐ 670 Kevin Seitzer .07 .03 .01
☐ 671 Jim Gantner .04 .02 .01
☐ 672 Allan Anderson .04 .02 .01
☐ 673 Don Baylor .07 .03 .01
☐ 674 Otis Nixon .07 .03 .01
☐ 675 Bruce Hurst .07 .03 .01
☐ 676 Ernie Riles .04 .02 .01
☐ 677 Dave Schmidt .04 .02 .01
☐ 678 Dion James .04 .02 .01
☐ 679 Willie Fraser .04 .02 .01
☐ 680 Gary Carter .07 .03 .01
☐ 681 Jeff D. Robinson .04 .02 .01
Pittsburgh Pirates
☐ 682 Rick Leach .04 .02 .01
☐ 683 Jose Cecena .04 .02 .01
☐ 684 Dave Johnson MG .06 .03 .01
(Team checklist back)
☐ 685 Jeff Treadway .04 .02 .01
☐ 686 Scott Terry .04 .02 .01
☐ 687 Alvin Davis .04 .02 .01
☐ 688 Zane Smith .04 .02 .01
☐ 689A Stan Jefferson .04 .02 .01
(Pink triangle on
front bottom left)
☐ 689B Stan Jefferson .04 .02 .01
(Violet triangle on
front bottom left)
☐ 690 Doug Jones .07 .03 .01
☐ 691 Roberto Kelly UER .20 .09 .03
(83 Oneonita)
☐ 692 Steve Ontiveros .04 .02 .01
☐ 693 Pat Borders .30 .14 .04
☐ 694 Les Lancaster .04 .02 .01
☐ 695 Carlton Fisk .15 .07 .02
☐ 696 Don August .04 .02 .01
☐ 697A Franklin Stubbs .04 .02 .01
(Team name on front
in white)
☐ 697B Franklin Stubbs .04 .02 .01
(Team name on front
in gray)
☐ 698 Keith Atherton .04 .02 .01
☐ 699 Pittsburgh Pirates TL .05 .02 .01
Al Pedrique
(Tony Gwynn sliding)
☐ 700 Don Mattingly .25 .11 .03
☐ 701 Storm Davis .04 .02 .01
☐ 702 Jamie Quirk .04 .02 .01
☐ 703 Scott Garrelts .04 .02 .01
☐ 704 Carlos Quintana .10 .05 .01
☐ 705 Terry Kennedy .04 .02 .01
☐ 706 Pete Incaviglia .04 .02 .01
☐ 707 Steve Jeltz .04 .02 .01
☐ 708 Chuck Finley .07 .03 .01
☐ 709 Tom Herr .04 .02 .01
☐ 710 David Cone .15 .07 .02
☐ 711 Candy Sierra .04 .02 .01
☐ 712 Bill Swift .07 .03 .01
☐ 713 Ty Griffin FDP .08 .04 .01
☐ 714 Joe Morgan MG .06 .03 .01
(Team checklist back)
☐ 715 Tony Pena .04 .02 .01
☐ 716 Wayne Tolleson .04 .02 .01
☐ 717 Jamie Moyer .04 .02 .01
☐ 718 Glenn Braggs .04 .02 .01
☐ 719 Danny Darwin .04 .02 .01
☐ 720 Tim Wallach .07 .03 .01
☐ 721 Ron Tingley .04 .02 .01
☐ 722 Todd Stottlemyre .10 .05 .01
☐ 723 Rafael Belliard .04 .02 .01
☐ 724 Jerry Don Gleaton .04 .02 .01
☐ 725 Terry Steinbach .07 .03 .01
☐ 726 Dickie Thon .04 .02 .01
☐ 727 Joe Orsulak .04 .02 .01
☐ 728 Charlie Puleo .04 .02 .01
☐ 729 Texas Rangers TL UER .05 .02 .01
Steve Buechele
(Inconsistent design,
team name on front
surrounded by black,
should be white)
☐ 730 Danny Jackson .04 .02 .01
☐ 731 Mike Young .04 .02 .01
☐ 732 Steve Buechele .04 .02 .01
☐ 733 Randy Bockus .04 .02 .01
☐ 734 Jody Reed .04 .02 .01
☐ 735 Roger McDowell .04 .02 .01
☐ 736 Jeff Hamilton .04 .02 .01
☐ 737 Norm Charlton .20 .09 .03
☐ 738 Darnell Coles .04 .02 .01
☐ 739 Brook Jacoby .04 .02 .01
☐ 740 Dan Plesac .04 .02 .01
☐ 741 Ken Phelps .04 .02 .01
☐ 742 Mike Harkey FS .12 .05 .02
☐ 743 Mike Heath .04 .02 .01
☐ 744 Roger Craig MG .06 .03 .01
(Team checklist back)
☐ 745 Fred McGriff .25 .11 .03
☐ 746 German Gonzalez UER .04 .02 .01
(Wrong birthdate)
☐ 747 Wil Tejada .04 .02 .01
☐ 748 Jimmy Jones .04 .02 .01
☐ 749 Rafael Ramirez .04 .02 .01
☐ 750 Bret Saberhagen .07 .03 .01
☐ 751 Ken Oberkfell .04 .02 .01
☐ 752 Jim Gott .04 .02 .01
☐ 753 Jose Uribe .04 .02 .01
☐ 754 Bob Brower .04 .02 .01
☐ 755 Mike Scioscia .04 .02 .01
☐ 756 Scott Medvin .04 .02 .01

☐ 757 Brady Anderson	.60	.25	.08
☐ 758 Gene Walter	.04	.02	.01
☐ 759 Milwaukee Brewers TL Rob Deer	.05	.02	.01
☐ 760 Lee Smith	.07	.03	.01
☐ 761 Dante Bichette	.25	.11	.03
☐ 762 Bobby Thigpen	.04	.02	.01
☐ 763 Dave Martinez	.07	.03	.01
☐ 764 Robin Ventura FDP	1.25	.55	.16
☐ 765 Glenn Davis	.07	.03	.01
☐ 766 Cecilio Guante	.04	.02	.01
☐ 767 Mike Capel	.04	.02	.01
☐ 768 Bill Wegman	.04	.02	.01
☐ 769 Junior Ortiz	.04	.02	.01
☐ 770 Alan Trammell	.07	.03	.01
☐ 771 Ron Kittle	.04	.02	.01
☐ 772 Ron Oester	.04	.02	.01
☐ 773 Keith Moreland	.04	.02	.01
☐ 774 Frank Robinson MG (Team checklist back)	.10	.05	.01
☐ 775 Jeff Reardon	.07	.03	.01
☐ 776 Nelson Liriano	.04	.02	.01
☐ 777 Ted Power	.04	.02	.01
☐ 778 Bruce Benedict	.04	.02	.01
☐ 779 Craig McMurtry	.04	.02	.01
☐ 780 Pedro Guerrero	.07	.03	.01
☐ 781 Greg Briley	.10	.05	.01
☐ 782 Checklist 661-792	.05	.01	.00
☐ 783 Trevor Wilson	.12	.05	.02
☐ 784 Steve Avery FDP	1.25	1.25	1.25
☐ 785 Ellis Burks	.07	.03	.01
☐ 786 Melido Perez	.15	.07	.02
☐ 787 Dave West	.10	.05	.01
☐ 788 Mike Morgan	.07	.03	.01
☐ 789 Kansas City Royals TL Bo Jackson (Throwing)	.10	.05	.01
☐ 790 Sid Fernandez	.07	.03	.01
☐ 791 Jim Lindeman	.04	.02	.01
☐ 792 Rafael Santana	.04	.02	.01

1989 Topps All-Star Glossy 22

These glossy cards were inserted with Topps rack packs and honor the starting line-ups, managers, and honorary captains of the 1988 National and American League All-Star teams. The cards are standard size, 2 1/2" by 3 1/2" and very similar to the design Topps has used since 1984. The backs are printed in red and blue on white card stock.

	MT	EX-MT	VG
COMPLETE SET (22)	3.50	1.55	.45
COMMON PLAYER (1-22)	.10	.05	.01
☐ 1 Tom Kelly MG	.10	.05	.01
☐ 2 Mark McGwire	.40	.18	.05
☐ 3 Paul Molitor	.20	.09	.03
☐ 4 Wade Boggs	.40	.18	.05
☐ 5 Cal Ripken	.60	.25	.08
☐ 6 Jose Canseco	.50	.23	.06
☐ 7 Rickey Henderson	.50	.23	.06
☐ 8 Dave Winfield	.35	.16	.04
☐ 9 Terry Steinbach	.15	.07	.02
☐ 10 Frank Viola	.15	.07	.02
☐ 11 Bobby Doerr CAPT	.15	.07	.02
☐ 12 Whitey Herzog MG	.10	.05	.01
☐ 13 Will Clark	.50	.23	.06
☐ 14 Ryne Sandberg	.60	.25	.08
☐ 15 Bobby Bonilla	.35	.16	.04
☐ 16 Ozzie Smith	.30	.14	.04
☐ 17 Vince Coleman	.20	.09	.03
☐ 18 Andre Dawson	.30	.14	.04
☐ 19 Darryl Strawberry	.40	.18	.05
☐ 20 Gary Carter	.20	.09	.03
☐ 21 Dwight Gooden	.20	.09	.03
☐ 22 Willie Stargell CAPT	.20	.09	.03

1989 Topps Ames 20/20 Club

The 1989 (Topps) Ames 20/20 Club set contains 33 standard-size (2 1/2" by 3 1/2") glossy cards. The fronts resemble plaques with gold and silver trim. The vertically oriented backs show career stats. The cards were distributed at Ames department stores as a boxed set. The set was produced by Topps for Ames; the Topps logo is also on the front of each card. The set includes active major leaguers who have had seasons of at least 20 home runs and 20 stolen bases. The backs include lifetime batting records with home run and stolen base totals for their 20/20 years highlighted. The subject list for the set is printed on the back panel of the set's custom box. These numbered cards are ordered alphabetically by player's name.

	MT	EX-MT	VG
COMPLETE SET (33)	4.00	1.80	.50
COMMON PLAYER (1-33)	.10	.05	.01
☐ 1 Jesse Barfield	.10	.05	.01
☐ 2 Kevin Bass	.10	.05	.01
☐ 3 Don Baylor	.15	.07	.02
☐ 4 George Bell	.20	.09	.03
☐ 5 Barry Bonds	.50	.23	.06
☐ 6 Phil Bradley	.10	.05	.01
☐ 7 Ellis Burks	.20	.09	.03
☐ 8 Jose Canseco	.60	.25	.08
☐ 9 Joe Carter	.35	.16	.04
☐ 10 Kal Daniels	.10	.05	.01
☐ 11 Eric Davis	.20	.09	.03
☐ 12 Mike Davis	.10	.05	.01
☐ 13 Andre Dawson	.30	.14	.04
☐ 14 Kirk Gibson	.15	.07	.02
☐ 15 Pedro Guerrero	.10	.05	.01
☐ 16 Rickey Henderson	.60	.25	.08
☐ 17 Bo Jackson	.60	.25	.08
☐ 18 Howard Johnson	.15	.07	.02
☐ 19 Jeffrey Leonard	.10	.05	.01
☐ 20 Kevin McReynolds	.10	.05	.01
☐ 21 Dale Murphy	.20	.09	.03
☐ 22 Dwayne Murphy	.10	.05	.01
☐ 23 Dave Parker	.15	.07	.02
☐ 24 Kirby Puckett	.50	.23	.06
☐ 25 Juan Samuel	.10	.05	.01
☐ 26 Ryne Sandberg	.60	.25	.08
☐ 27 Mike Schmidt	.50	.23	.06
☐ 28 Darryl Strawberry	.50	.23	.06
☐ 29 Alan Trammell	.20	.09	.03
☐ 30 Andy Van Slyke	.20	.09	.03
☐ 31 Devon White	.15	.07	.02
☐ 32 Dave Winfield	.35	.16	.04
☐ 33 Robin Yount	.50	.23	.06

1989 Topps Big

The 1989 Topps Big Baseball set contains 330 glossy cards measuring approximately 2 1/2" by 3 3/4". The fronts feature mug shots superimposed on action photos. The horizontally oriented backs have color cartoons and statistics for the player's previous season and total career. Team members for the United States Olympic team were also included in this set. The set was released in three series of 110 cards. The cards were distributed in seven-card cello packs marked with the series number.

	MT	EX-MT	VG
COMPLETE SET (330)	30.00	13.50	3.80
COMMON PLAYER (1-110)	.05	.02	.01
COMMON PLAYER (111-220)	.05	.02	.01
COMMON PLAYER (221-330)	.06	.03	.01

		MT	EX-MT	VG
☐ 1	Orel Hershiser	.20	.09	.03
☐ 2	Harold Reynolds	.05	.02	.01
☐ 3	Jody Davis	.05	.02	.01
☐ 4	Greg Walker	.05	.02	.01
☐ 5	Barry Bonds	.50	.23	.06
☐ 6	Bret Saberhagen	.12	.05	.02
☐ 7	Johnny Ray	.05	.02	.01
☐ 8	Mike Fiore	.05	.02	.01
☐ 9	Juan Castillo	.05	.02	.01
☐ 10	Todd Burns	.05	.02	.01
☐ 11	Carmelo Martinez	.05	.02	.01
☐ 12	Geno Petralli	.05	.02	.01
☐ 13	Mel Hall	.08	.04	.01
☐ 14	Tom Browning	.08	.04	.01
☐ 15	Fred McGriff	.40	.18	.05
☐ 16	Kevin Elster	.05	.02	.01
☐ 17	Tim Leary	.05	.02	.01
☐ 18	Jim Rice	.12	.05	.02
☐ 19	Bret Barberie	.20	.09	.03
☐ 20	Jay Buhner	.12	.05	.02
☐ 21	Atlee Hammaker	.05	.02	.01
☐ 22	Lou Whitaker	.12	.05	.02
☐ 23	Paul Runge	.05	.02	.01
☐ 24	Carlton Fisk	.35	.16	.04
☐ 25	Jose Lind	.05	.02	.01
☐ 26	Mark Gubicza	.05	.02	.01
☐ 27	Billy Ripken	.05	.02	.01
☐ 28	Mike Pagliarulo	.05	.02	.01
☐ 29	Jim Deshaies	.05	.02	.01
☐ 30	Mark McLemore	.05	.02	.01
☐ 31	Scott Terry	.05	.02	.01
☐ 32	Franklin Stubbs	.05	.02	.01
☐ 33	Don August	.05	.02	.01
☐ 34	Mark McGwire	.60	.25	.08
☐ 35	Eric Show	.05	.02	.01
☐ 36	Cecil Espy	.05	.02	.01
☐ 37	Ron Tingley	.05	.02	.01
☐ 38	Mickey Brantley	.05	.02	.01
☐ 39	Paul O'Neill	.08	.04	.01
☐ 40	Ed Sprague	.15	.07	.02
☐ 41	Len Dykstra	.10	.05	.01
☐ 42	Roger Clemens	1.00	.45	.13
☐ 43	Ron Gant	.60	.25	.08
☐ 44	Dan Pasqua	.05	.02	.01
☐ 45	Jeff D. Robinson	.05	.02	.01
☐ 46	George Brett	.50	.23	.06
☐ 47	Bryn Smith	.05	.02	.01
☐ 48	Mike Marshall	.05	.02	.01
☐ 49	Doug Robbins	.05	.02	.01
☐ 50	Don Mattingly	.60	.25	.08
☐ 51	Mike Scott	.08	.04	.01
☐ 52	Steve Jeltz	.05	.02	.01
☐ 53	Dick Schofield	.05	.02	.01
☐ 54	Tom Brunansky	.08	.04	.01
☐ 55	Gary Sheffield	1.25	.55	.16
☐ 56	Dave Valle	.05	.02	.01
☐ 57	Carney Lansford	.08	.04	.01
☐ 58	Tony Gwynn	.50	.23	.06
☐ 59	Checklist 1-110	.08	.00	.00
☐ 60	Damon Berryhill	.05	.02	.01
☐ 61	Jack Morris	.15	.07	.02
☐ 62	Brett Butler	.10	.05	.01
☐ 63	Mickey Hatcher	.05	.02	.01
☐ 64	Bruce Sutter	.08	.04	.01
☐ 65	Robin Ventura	1.25	.55	.16
☐ 66	Junior Ortiz	.05	.02	.01
☐ 67	Pat Tabler	.05	.02	.01
☐ 68	Greg Swindell	.08	.04	.01
☐ 69	Jeff Branson	.15	.07	.02
☐ 70	Manny Lee	.08	.04	.01
☐ 71	Dave Magadan	.08	.04	.01
☐ 72	Rich Gedman	.05	.02	.01
☐ 73	Tim Raines	.10	.05	.01
☐ 74	Mike Maddux	.05	.02	.01
☐ 75	Jim Presley	.05	.02	.01
☐ 76	Chuck Finley	.08	.04	.01
☐ 77	Jose Oquendo	.05	.02	.01
☐ 78	Rob Deer	.08	.04	.01
☐ 79	Jay Howell	.08	.04	.01
☐ 80	Terry Steinbach	.08	.04	.01
☐ 81	Ed Whitson	.08	.04	.01
☐ 82	Ruben Sierra	.60	.25	.08
☐ 83	Bruce Benedict	.05	.02	.01
☐ 84	Fred Manrique	.05	.02	.01
☐ 85	John Smiley	.08	.04	.01
☐ 86	Mike Macfarlane	.12	.05	.02
☐ 87	Rene Gonzales	.05	.02	.01
☐ 88	Charles Hudson	.05	.02	.01
☐ 89	Glenn Davis	.12	.05	.02
☐ 90	Les Straker	.05	.02	.01
☐ 91	Carmen Castillo	.05	.02	.01
☐ 92	Tracy Woodson	.05	.02	.01
☐ 93	Tino Martinez	.35	.16	.04
☐ 94	Herm Winningham	.05	.02	.01
☐ 95	Kelly Gruber	.08	.04	.01
☐ 96	Terry Leach	.05	.02	.01
☐ 97	Jody Reed	.08	.04	.01
☐ 98	Nelson Santovenia	.05	.02	.01
☐ 99	Tony Armas	.05	.02	.01
☐ 100	Greg Brock	.05	.02	.01
☐ 101	Dave Stewart	.10	.05	.01
☐ 102	Roberto Alomar	1.00	.45	.13
☐ 103	Jim Sundberg	.05	.02	.01
☐ 104	Albert Hall	.05	.02	.01
☐ 105	Steve Lyons	.05	.02	.01
☐ 106	Sid Bream	.05	.02	.01
☐ 107	Danny Tartabull	.20	.09	.03
☐ 108	Rick Dempsey	.08	.04	.01
☐ 109	Rich Renteria	.05	.02	.01
☐ 110	Ozzie Smith	.30	.14	.04
☐ 111	Steve Sax	.10	.05	.01
☐ 112	Kelly Downs	.05	.02	.01
☐ 113	Larry Sheets	.05	.02	.01
☐ 114	Andy Benes	.50	.23	.06
☐ 115	Pete O'Brien	.05	.02	.01
☐ 116	Kevin McReynolds	.08	.04	.01
☐ 117	Juan Berenguer	.05	.02	.01
☐ 118	Billy Hatcher	.05	.02	.01
☐ 119	Rick Cerone	.05	.02	.01
☐ 120	Andre Dawson	.30	.14	.04
☐ 121	Storm Davis	.05	.02	.01
☐ 122	Devon White	.08	.04	.01
☐ 123	Alan Trammell	.15	.07	.02
☐ 124	Vince Coleman	.15	.07	.02
☐ 125	Al Leiter	.05	.02	.01
☐ 126	Dale Sveum	.05	.02	.01
☐ 127	Pete Incaviglia	.08	.04	.01
☐ 128	Dave Stieb	.08	.04	.01
☐ 129	Kevin Mitchell	.30	.14	.04
☐ 130	Dave Schmidt	.05	.02	.01
☐ 131	Gary Redus	.05	.02	.01
☐ 132	Ron Robinson	.05	.02	.01
☐ 133	Darnell Coles	.05	.02	.01
☐ 134	Benito Santiago	.15	.07	.02
☐ 135	John Farrell	.05	.02	.01
☐ 136	Willie Wilson	.08	.04	.01
☐ 137	Steve Bedrosian	.05	.02	.01
☐ 138	Don Slaught	.05	.02	.01
☐ 139	Darryl Strawberry	.50	.23	.06
☐ 140	Frank Viola	.10	.05	.01
☐ 141	Dave Silvestri	.15	.07	.02
☐ 142	Carlos Quintana	.10	.05	.01
☐ 143	Vance Law	.05	.02	.01
☐ 144	Dave Parker	.10	.05	.01

☐ 145 Tim Belcher	.10	.05	.01
☐ 146 Will Clark	.60	.25	.08
☐ 147 Mark Williamson	.05	.02	.01
☐ 148 Ozzie Guillen	.08	.04	.01
☐ 149 Kirk McCaskill	.05	.02	.01
☐ 150 Pat Sheridan	.05	.02	.01
☐ 151 Terry Pendleton	.15	.07	.02
☐ 152 Roberto Kelly	.20	.09	.03
☐ 153 Joey Meyer	.05	.02	.01
☐ 154 Mark Grant	.05	.02	.01
☐ 155 Joe Carter	.35	.16	.04
☐ 156 Steve Buechele	.05	.02	.01
☐ 157 Tony Fernandez	.08	.04	.01
☐ 158 Jeff Reed	.05	.02	.01
☐ 159 Bobby Bonilla	.25	.11	.03
☐ 160 Henry Cotto	.05	.02	.01
☐ 161 Kurt Stillwell	.05	.02	.01
☐ 162 Mickey Morandini	.20	.09	.03
☐ 163 Robby Thompson	.05	.02	.01
☐ 164 Rick Schu	.05	.02	.01
☐ 165 Stan Jefferson	.05	.02	.01
☐ 166 Ron Darling	.08	.04	.01
☐ 167 Kirby Puckett	.60	.25	.08
☐ 168 Bill Doran	.05	.02	.01
☐ 169 Dennis Lamp	.05	.02	.01
☐ 170 Ty Griffin	.10	.05	.01
☐ 171 Ron Hassey	.05	.02	.01
☐ 172 Dale Murphy	.20	.09	.03
☐ 173 Andres Galarraga	.08	.04	.01
☐ 174 Tim Flannery	.05	.02	.01
☐ 175 Cory Snyder	.08	.04	.01
☐ 176 Checklist 111-220	.08	.00	.00
☐ 177 Tommy Barrett	.05	.02	.01
☐ 178 Dan Petry	.05	.02	.01
☐ 179 Billy Masse	.10	.05	.01
☐ 180 Terry Kennedy	.05	.02	.01
☐ 181 Joe Orsulak	.05	.02	.01
☐ 182 Doyle Alexander	.05	.02	.01
☐ 183 Willie McGee	.08	.04	.01
☐ 184 Jim Gantner	.05	.02	.01
☐ 185 Keith Hernandez	.08	.04	.01
☐ 186 Greg Gagne	.05	.02	.01
☐ 187 Kevin Bass	.05	.02	.01
☐ 188 Mark Eichhorn	.05	.02	.01
☐ 189 Mark Grace	.60	.25	.08
☐ 190 Jose Canseco	.75	.35	.09
☐ 191 Bobby Witt	.08	.04	.01
☐ 192 Rafael Santana	.05	.02	.01
☐ 193 Dwight Evans	.08	.04	.01
☐ 194 Greg Booker	.05	.02	.01
☐ 195 Brook Jacoby	.05	.02	.01
☐ 196 Rafael Belliard	.05	.02	.01
☐ 197 Candy Maldonado	.08	.04	.01
☐ 198 Mickey Tettleton	.12	.05	.02
☐ 199 Barry Larkin	.20	.09	.03
☐ 200 Frank White	.08	.04	.01
☐ 201 Wally Joyner	.12	.05	.02
☐ 202 Chet Lemon	.05	.02	.01
☐ 203 Joe Magrane	.08	.04	.01
☐ 204 Glenn Braggs	.05	.02	.01
☐ 205 Scott Fletcher	.05	.02	.01
☐ 206 Gary Ward	.05	.02	.01
☐ 207 Nelson Liriano	.05	.02	.01
☐ 208 Howard Johnson	.12	.05	.02
☐ 209 Kent Hrbek	.08	.04	.01
☐ 210 Ken Caminiti	.10	.05	.01
☐ 211 Mike Greenwell	.20	.09	.03
☐ 212 Ryne Sandberg	1.00	.45	.13
☐ 213 Joe Slusarski	.10	.05	.01
☐ 214 Donell Nixon	.05	.02	.01
☐ 215 Tim Wallach	.05	.02	.01
☐ 216 John Kruk	.10	.05	.01
☐ 217 Charles Nagy	.35	.16	.04
☐ 218 Alvin Davis	.05	.02	.01
☐ 219 Oswald Peraza	.05	.02	.01
☐ 220 Mike Schmidt	1.00	.45	.13
☐ 221 Spike Owen	.06	.03	.01
☐ 222 Mike Smithson	.06	.03	.01
☐ 223 Dion James	.06	.03	.01
☐ 224 Ernie Whitt	.06	.03	.01
☐ 225 Mike Davis	.06	.03	.01
☐ 226 Gene Larkin	.06	.03	.01
☐ 227 Pat Combs	.10	.05	.01
☐ 228 Jack Howell	.06	.03	.01
☐ 229 Ron Oester	.06	.03	.01
☐ 230 Paul Gibson	.06	.03	.01
☐ 231 Mookie Wilson	.10	.05	.01
☐ 232 Glenn Hubbard	.06	.03	.01
☐ 233 Shawon Dunston	.10	.05	.01
☐ 234 Otis Nixon	.15	.07	.02
☐ 235 Melido Perez	.15	.07	.02
☐ 236 Jerry Browne	.10	.05	.01
☐ 237 Rick Rhoden	.06	.03	.01
☐ 238 Bo Jackson	.75	.35	.09
☐ 239 Randy Velarde	.06	.03	.01
☐ 240 Jack Clark	.10	.05	.01
☐ 241 Wade Boggs	.60	.25	.08
☐ 242 Lonnie Smith	.06	.03	.01
☐ 243 Mike Flanagan	.10	.05	.01
☐ 244 Willie Randolph	.10	.05	.01
☐ 245 Oddibe McDowell	.06	.03	.01
☐ 246 Ricky Jordan	.10	.05	.01
☐ 247 Greg Briley	.10	.05	.01
☐ 248 Rex Hudler	.06	.03	.01
☐ 249 Robin Yount	.60	.25	.08
☐ 250 Lance Parrish	.10	.05	.01
☐ 251 Chris Sabo	.35	.16	.04
☐ 252 Mike Henneman	.10	.05	.01
☐ 253 Gregg Jefferies	.60	.25	.08
☐ 254 Curt Young	.06	.03	.01
☐ 255 Andy Van Slyke	.15	.07	.02
☐ 256 Rod Booker	.06	.03	.01
☐ 257 Rafael Palmeiro	.20	.09	.03
☐ 258 Jose Uribe	.06	.03	.01
☐ 259 Ellis Burks	.20	.09	.03
☐ 260 John Smoltz	.50	.23	.06
☐ 261 Tom Foley	.06	.03	.01
☐ 262 Lloyd Moseby	.06	.03	.01
☐ 263 Jim Poole	.10	.05	.01
☐ 264 Gary Gaetti	.06	.03	.01
☐ 265 Bob Dernier	.06	.03	.01
☐ 266 Harold Baines	.10	.05	.01
☐ 267 Tom Candiotti	.10	.05	.01
☐ 268 Rafael Ramirez	.06	.03	.01
☐ 269 Bob Boone	.10	.05	.01
☐ 270 Buddy Bell	.10	.05	.01
☐ 271 Rickey Henderson	.60	.25	.08
☐ 272 Willie Fraser	.06	.03	.01
☐ 273 Eric Davis	.25	.11	.03
☐ 274 Jeff M. Robinson	.06	.03	.01
☐ 275 Damaso Garcia	.06	.03	.01
☐ 276 Sid Fernandez	.10	.05	.01
☐ 277 Stan Javier	.06	.03	.01
☐ 278 Marty Barrett	.06	.03	.01
☐ 279 Gerald Perry	.06	.03	.01
☐ 280 Rob Ducey	.10	.05	.01
☐ 281 Mike Scioscia	.06	.03	.01
☐ 282 Randy Bush	.06	.03	.01
☐ 283 Tom Herr	.06	.03	.01
☐ 284 Glenn Wilson	.06	.03	.01
☐ 285 Pedro Guerrero	.10	.05	.01
☐ 286 Cal Ripken	1.00	.45	.13
☐ 287 Randy Johnson	.20	.09	.03
☐ 288 Julio Franco	.15	.07	.02
☐ 289 Ivan Calderon	.10	.05	.01
☐ 290 Rich Yett	.06	.03	.01
☐ 291 Scott Servais	.10	.05	.01
☐ 292 Bill Pecota	.06	.03	.01
☐ 293 Ken Phelps	.06	.03	.01
☐ 294 Chili Davis	.10	.05	.01
☐ 295 Manny Trillo	.06	.03	.01
☐ 296 Mike Boddicker	.06	.03	.01
☐ 297 Geronimo Berroa	.10	.05	.01
☐ 298 Todd Stottlemyre	.10	.05	.01
☐ 299 Kirk Gibson	.10	.05	.01
☐ 300 Wally Backman	.06	.03	.01
☐ 301 Hubie Brooks	.06	.03	.01
☐ 302 Von Hayes	.06	.03	.01
☐ 303 Matt Nokes	.10	.05	.01
☐ 304 Dwight Gooden	.20	.09	.03
☐ 305 Walt Weiss	.10	.05	.01
☐ 306 Mike LaValliere	.06	.03	.01
☐ 307 Cris Carpenter	.06	.03	.01
☐ 308 Ted Wood	.25	.11	.03
☐ 309 Jeff Russell	.06	.03	.01
☐ 310 Dave Gallagher	.06	.03	.01
☐ 311 Andy Allanson	.06	.03	.01
☐ 312 Craig Reynolds	.06	.03	.01
☐ 313 Kevin Seitzer	.10	.05	.01
☐ 314 Dave Winfield	.35	.16	.04
☐ 315 Andy McGaffigan	.06	.03	.01
☐ 316 Nick Esasky	.06	.03	.01
☐ 317 Jeff Blauser	.10	.05	.01
☐ 318 George Bell	.15	.07	.02
☐ 319 Eddie Murray	.30	.14	.04
☐ 320 Mark Davidson	.06	.03	.01
☐ 321 Juan Samuel	.06	.03	.01
☐ 322 Jim Abbott	.90	.40	.11
☐ 323 Kal Daniels	.10	.05	.01
☐ 324 Mike Brumley	.06	.03	.01
☐ 325 Gary Carter	.15	.07	.02
☐ 326 Dave Henderson	.10	.05	.01
☐ 327 Checklist 221-330	.10	.01	.00
☐ 328 Garry Templeton	.10	.05	.01
☐ 329 Pat Perry	.06	.03	.01
☐ 330 Paul Molitor	.15	.07	.02

1989 Topps Cap'n Crunch

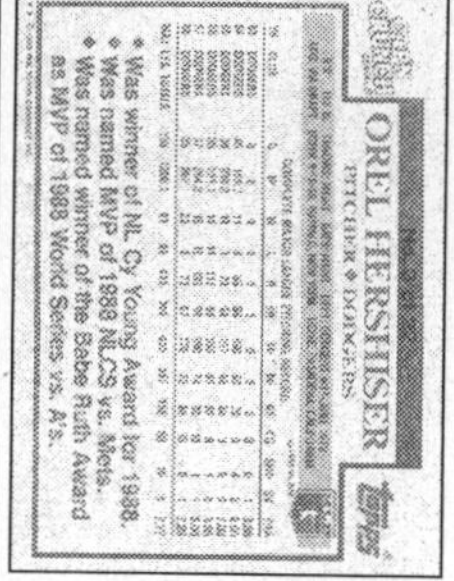

The 1989 Topps Cap'n Crunch set contains 22 standard-size (2 1/2" by 3 1/2") cards. The fronts have red, white and blue borders surrounding "mugshot" photos. The backs are horizontally oriented and show lifetime stats. The set was produced by Topps, but has team logos airbrushed out. Two cards were included (in a cellophane wrapper with a piece of gum) in each specially marked Cap'n Crunch cereal box. The set was not available as a complete set as part of any mail-in offer. The set was produced by Topps.

	MT	EX-MT	VG
COMPLETE SET (22)	12.00	5.50	1.50
COMMON PLAYER (1-22)	.60	.25	.08
☐ 1 Jose Canseco	1.25	.55	.16
☐ 2 Kirk Gibson	.60	.25	.08
☐ 3 Orel Hershiser	.75	.35	.09
☐ 4 Frank Viola	.60	.25	.08
☐ 5 Tony Gwynn	1.00	.45	.13
☐ 6 Cal Ripken	1.50	.65	.19
☐ 7 Darryl Strawberry	1.00	.45	.13
☐ 8 Don Mattingly	1.25	.55	.16
☐ 9 George Brett	1.25	.55	.16
☐ 10 Andre Dawson	1.00	.45	.13
☐ 11 Dale Murphy	.75	.35	.09
☐ 12 Alan Trammell	.60	.25	.08
☐ 13 Eric Davis	.75	.35	.09
☐ 14 Jack Clark	.60	.25	.08
☐ 15 Eddie Murray	.90	.40	.11
☐ 16 Mike Schmidt	1.25	.55	.16
☐ 17 Dwight Gooden	.75	.35	.09
☐ 18 Roger Clemens	1.50	.65	.19
☐ 19 Will Clark	1.25	.55	.16
☐ 20 Kirby Puckett	1.25	.55	.16
☐ 21 Robin Yount	1.25	.55	.16
☐ 22 Mark McGwire	1.00	.45	.13

1989 Topps Glossy Send-In 60

The 1989 Topps Glossy Send-In set contains 60 standard-size (2 1/2" by 3 1/2") cards. The fronts have color photos with white borders; the backs are light blue. The cards were distributed through the mail by Topps in six groups of ten cards. The last two cards out of each group of ten are young players or prospects.

	MT	EX-MT	VG
COMPLETE SET (60)	10.00	4.50	1.25
COMMON PLAYER (1-60)	.15	.07	.02
☐ 1 Kirby Puckett	.60	.25	.08
☐ 2 Eric Davis	.25	.11	.03
☐ 3 Joe Carter	.35	.16	.04
☐ 4 Andy Van Slyke	.25	.11	.03
☐ 5 Wade Boggs	.45	.20	.06
☐ 6 David Cone	.35	.16	.04
☐ 7 Kent Hrbek	.25	.11	.03
☐ 8 Darryl Strawberry	.45	.20	.06
☐ 9 Jay Buhner	.25	.11	.03
☐ 10 Ron Gant	.45	.20	.06
☐ 11 Will Clark	.60	.25	.08
☐ 12 Jose Canseco	.60	.25	.08
☐ 13 Juan Samuel	.15	.07	.02
☐ 14 George Brett	.45	.20	.06
☐ 15 Benito Santiago	.35	.16	.04
☐ 16 Dennis Eckersley	.25	.11	.03
☐ 17 Gary Carter	.25	.11	.03
☐ 18 Frank Viola	.15	.07	.02
☐ 19 Roberto Alomar	.75	.35	.09
☐ 20 Paul Gibson	.15	.07	.02
☐ 21 Dave Winfield	.35	.16	.04
☐ 22 Howard Johnson	.25	.11	.03
☐ 23 Roger Clemens	.75	.35	.09
☐ 24 Bobby Bonilla	.35	.16	.04
☐ 25 Alan Trammell	.25	.11	.03
☐ 26 Kevin McReynolds	.25	.11	.03
☐ 27 George Bell	.25	.11	.03
☐ 28 Bruce Hurst	.15	.07	.02
☐ 29 Mark Grace	.60	.25	.08
☐ 30 Tim Belcher	.25	.11	.03
☐ 31 Mike Greenwell	.25	.11	.03
☐ 32 Glenn Davis	.25	.11	.03
☐ 33 Gary Gaetti	.15	.07	.02
☐ 34 Ryne Sandberg	.75	.35	.09
☐ 35 Rickey Henderson	.60	.25	.08
☐ 36 Dwight Evans	.25	.11	.03
☐ 37 Dwight Gooden	.25	.11	.03
☐ 38 Robin Yount	.45	.20	.06
☐ 39 Damon Berryhill	.20	.09	.03
☐ 40 Chris Sabo	.35	.16	.04
☐ 41 Mark McGwire	.60	.25	.08
☐ 42 Ozzie Smith	.35	.16	.04
☐ 43 Paul Molitor	.25	.11	.03
☐ 44 Andres Galarraga	.20	.09	.03
☐ 45 Dave Stewart	.25	.11	.03
☐ 46 Tom Browning	.15	.07	.02
☐ 47 Cal Ripken	.75	.35	.09
☐ 48 Orel Hershiser	.25	.11	.03
☐ 49 Dave Gallagher	.15	.07	.02
☐ 50 Walt Weiss	.25	.11	.03
☐ 51 Don Mattingly	.60	.25	.08
☐ 52 Tony Fernandez	.25	.11	.03
☐ 53 Tim Raines	.25	.11	.03
☐ 54 Jeff Reardon	.25	.11	.03
☐ 55 Kirk Gibson	.25	.11	.03
☐ 56 Jack Clark	.25	.11	.03
☐ 57 Danny Jackson	.15	.07	.02
☐ 58 Tony Gwynn	.45	.20	.06
☐ 59 Cecil Espy	.15	.07	.02
☐ 60 Jody Reed	.15	.07	.02

1989 Topps Hills Team MVP's

The 1989 Topps Hills Team MVP's set contains 33 glossy standard-size (2 1/2" by 3 1/2") cards. The fronts and backs are yellow, red, white and navy. The horizontally oriented backs are green. The cards were distributed through Hills stores as a boxed set. The set was produced by Topps although it was printed in Ireland. These numbered cards are ordered alphabetically by player's name.

	MT	EX-MT	VG
COMPLETE SET (33)	4.00	1.80	.50
COMMON PLAYER (1-33)	.10	.05	.01
☐ 1 Harold Baines	.15	.07	.02
☐ 2 Wade Boggs	.50	.23	.06

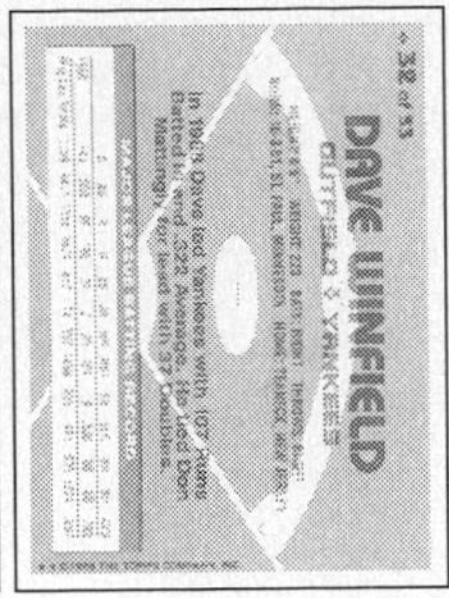

Player	MT	EX-MT	VG
□ 3 George Brett	.50	.23	.06
□ 4 Tom Brunansky	.15	.07	.02
□ 5 Jose Canseco	.60	.25	.08
□ 6 Joe Carter	.35	.16	.04
□ 7 Will Clark	.60	.25	.08
□ 8 Roger Clemens	.75	.35	.09
□ 9 David Cone	.20	.09	.03
□ 10 Glenn Davis	.15	.07	.02
□ 11 Andre Dawson	.30	.14	.04
□ 12 Dennis Eckersley	.20	.09	.03
□ 13 Andres Galarraga	.10	.05	.01
□ 14 Kirk Gibson	.10	.05	.01
□ 15 Mike Greenwell	.20	.09	.03
□ 16 Tony Gwynn	.50	.23	.06
□ 17 Orel Hershiser	.15	.07	.02
□ 18 Danny Jackson	.10	.05	.01
□ 19 Mark Langston	.10	.05	.01
□ 20 Fred McGriff	.25	.11	.03
□ 21 Dale Murphy	.25	.11	.03
□ 22 Eddie Murray	.35	.16	.04
□ 23 Kirby Puckett	.60	.25	.08
□ 24 Johnny Ray	.10	.05	.01
□ 25 Juan Samuel	.10	.05	.01
□ 26 Ruben Sierra	.50	.23	.06
□ 27 Dave Stewart	.20	.09	.03
□ 28 Darryl Strawberry	.50	.23	.06
□ 29 Alan Trammell	.15	.07	.02
□ 30 Andy Van Slyke	.20	.09	.03
□ 31 Frank Viola	.15	.07	.02
□ 32 Dave Winfield	.35	.16	.04
□ 33 Robin Yount	.50	.23	.06

1989 Topps Jumbo Rookies

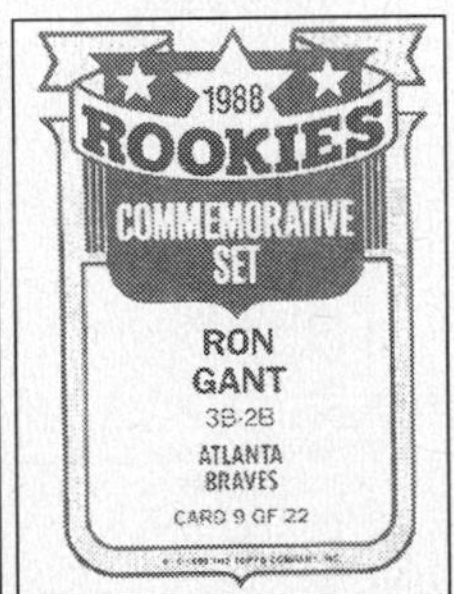

Inserted in each supermarket jumbo pack is a card from this series of 22 of 1988's best rookies as determined by Topps. Jumbo packs consisted of 100 (regular issue 1989 Topps baseball) cards with a stick of gum plus the insert "Rookie" card. The card fronts are in full color and measure 2 1/2" by 3 1/2". The card backs are printed in red and blue on white card stock and are numbered at the bottom. The order of the set is alphabetical by player's name.

	MT	EX-MT	VG
COMPLETE SET (22)	7.50	3.40	.95
COMMON PLAYER (1-22)	.20	.09	.03
□ 1 Roberto Alomar	1.50	.65	.19
□ 2 Brady Anderson	.50	.23	.06
□ 3 Tim Belcher	.30	.14	.04
□ 4 Damon Berryhill	.25	.11	.03
□ 5 Jay Buhner	.40	.18	.05
□ 6 Kevin Elster	.20	.09	.03
□ 7 Cecil Espy	.20	.09	.03
□ 8 Dave Gallagher	.20	.09	.03
□ 9 Ron Gant	.75	.35	.09
□ 10 Paul Gibson	.20	.09	.03
□ 11 Mark Grace	.75	.35	.09
□ 12 Darrin Jackson	.40	.18	.05
□ 13 Gregg Jefferies	.75	.35	.09
□ 14 Ricky Jordan	.30	.14	.04
□ 15 Al Leiter	.20	.09	.03
□ 16 Melido Perez	.35	.16	.04
□ 17 Chris Sabo	.50	.23	.06
□ 18 Nelson Santovenia	.20	.09	.03
□ 19 Mackey Sasser	.20	.09	.03
□ 20 Gary Sheffield	1.50	.65	.19
□ 21 Walt Weiss	.30	.14	.04
□ 22 David Wells	.25	.11	.03

1989 Topps Mini Leaders

The 1989 Topps Mini League Leaders set contains 77 cards measuring approximately 2 1/8" by 3". The fronts have color photos with large white borders. The backs are yellow and feature 1988 and career stats. The cards were distributed in seven-card cello packs. These numbered cards are ordered alphabetically by player within team and the teams themselves are ordered alphabetically.

	MT	EX-MT	VG
COMPLETE SET (77)	7.50	3.40	.95
COMMON PLAYER (1-77)	.05	.02	.01
□ 1 Dale Murphy	.20	.09	.03
□ 2 Gerald Perry	.05	.02	.01
□ 3 Andre Dawson	.25	.11	.03
□ 4 Greg Maddux	.25	.11	.03
□ 5 Rafael Palmeiro	.20	.09	.03
□ 6 Tom Browning	.08	.04	.01
□ 7 Kal Daniels	.08	.04	.01
□ 8 Eric Davis	.20	.09	.03
□ 9 John Franco	.08	.04	.01
□ 10 Danny Jackson	.05	.02	.01
□ 11 Barry Larkin	.20	.09	.03
□ 12 Jose Rijo	.10	.05	.01
□ 13 Chris Sabo	.20	.09	.03
□ 14 Nolan Ryan	1.00	.45	.13
□ 15 Mike Scott	.08	.04	.01
□ 16 Gerald Young	.05	.02	.01
□ 17 Kirk Gibson	.08	.04	.01
□ 18 Orel Hershiser	.12	.05	.02
□ 19 Steve Sax	.10	.05	.01
□ 20 John Tudor	.05	.02	.01
□ 21 Hubie Brooks	.05	.02	.01
□ 22 Andres Galarraga	.08	.04	.01
□ 23 Otis Nixon	.10	.05	.01
□ 24 David Cone	.15	.07	.02
□ 25 Sid Fernandez	.08	.04	.01
□ 26 Dwight Gooden	.20	.09	.03
□ 27 Kevin McReynolds	.08	.04	.01
□ 28 Darryl Strawberry	.50	.23	.06
□ 29 Juan Samuel	.05	.02	.01
□ 30 Bobby Bonilla	.25	.11	.03

☐ 31 Sid Bream	.08	.04	.01
☐ 32 Jim Gott	.05	.02	.01
☐ 33 Andy Van Slyke	.15	.07	.02
☐ 34 Vince Coleman	.12	.05	.02
☐ 35 Jose DeLeon	.05	.02	.01
☐ 36 Joe Magrane	.05	.02	.01
☐ 37 Ozzie Smith	.25	.11	.03
☐ 38 Todd Worrell	.10	.05	.01
☐ 39 Tony Gwynn	.35	.16	.04
☐ 40 Brett Butler	.10	.05	.01
☐ 41 Will Clark	.50	.23	.06
☐ 42 Rick Reuschel	.05	.02	.01
☐ 43 Checklist Card	.08	.04	.01
☐ 44 Eddie Murray	.20	.09	.03
☐ 45 Wade Boggs	.35	.16	.04
☐ 46 Roger Clemens	.50	.23	.06
☐ 47 Dwight Evans	.08	.04	.01
☐ 48 Mike Greenwell	.20	.09	.03
☐ 49 Bruce Hurst	.08	.04	.01
☐ 50 Johnny Ray	.05	.02	.01
☐ 51 Doug Jones	.05	.02	.01
☐ 52 Greg Swindell	.08	.04	.01
☐ 53 Gary Pettis	.05	.02	.01
☐ 54 George Brett	.45	.20	.06
☐ 55 Mark Gubicza	.08	.04	.01
☐ 56 Willie Wilson	.08	.04	.01
☐ 57 Teddy Higuera	.05	.02	.01
☐ 58 Paul Molitor	.15	.07	.02
☐ 59 Robin Yount	.45	.20	.06
☐ 60 Allan Anderson	.05	.02	.01
☐ 61 Gary Gaetti	.05	.02	.01
☐ 62 Kirby Puckett	.45	.20	.06
☐ 63 Jeff Reardon	.10	.05	.01
☐ 64 Frank Viola	.10	.05	.01
☐ 65 Jack Clark	.08	.04	.01
☐ 66 Rickey Henderson	.50	.23	.06
☐ 67 Dave Winfield	.30	.14	.04
☐ 68 Jose Canseco	.60	.25	.08
☐ 69 Dennis Eckersley	.15	.07	.02
☐ 70 Mark McGwire	.50	.23	.06
☐ 71 Dave Stewart	.10	.05	.01
☐ 72 Alvin Davis	.05	.02	.01
☐ 73 Mark Langston	.08	.04	.01
☐ 74 Harold Reynolds	.05	.02	.01
☐ 75 George Bell	.10	.05	.01
☐ 76 Tony Fernandez	.08	.04	.01
☐ 77 Fred McGriff	.25	.11	.03

1989 Topps Traded

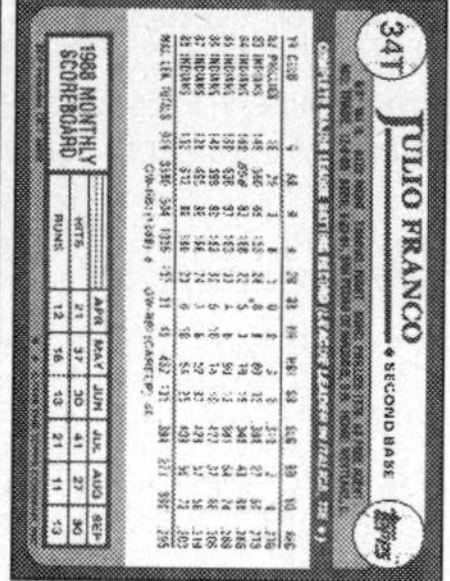

The 1989 Topps Traded set contains 132 standard-size (2 1/2" by 3 1/2") cards. The fronts have white borders; the horizontally oriented backs are red and pink. From the front the cards' style is indistinguishable from the 1989 Topps regular issue. The cards were distributed as a boxed set. The key rookies in this set are Ken Griffey Jr., Deion Sanders, and Jerome Walton. Topps also produced a specially boxed "glossy" edition frequently referred to as the Topps Traded Tiffany set. This year, again, Topps did not disclose the number of Tiffany sets they produced or sold but it seems that production quantities were roughly similar (or slightly smaller, 15,000 sets) to the previous two years. The checklist of cards is identical to that of the normal non-glossy cards. There are two primary distinguishing features of the Tiffany cards, white card stock reverses and high gloss obverses. These Tiffany cards are valued approximately from three to five times the values listed below.

	MT	EX-MT	VG
COMPLETE SET (132)	7.50	3.40	.95
COMMON PLAYER (1T-132T)	.05	.02	.01
☐ 1T Don Aase	.05	.02	.01
☐ 2T Jim Abbott	1.00	.45	.13
☐ 3T Kent Anderson	.05	.02	.01
☐ 4T Keith Atherton	.05	.02	.01
☐ 5T Wally Backman	.05	.02	.01
☐ 6T Steve Balboni	.05	.02	.01
☐ 7T Jesse Barfield	.05	.02	.01
☐ 8T Steve Bedrosian	.05	.02	.01
☐ 9T Todd Benzinger	.05	.02	.01
☐ 10T Geronimo Berroa	.05	.02	.01
☐ 11T Bert Blyleven	.08	.04	.01
☐ 12T Bob Boone	.08	.04	.01
☐ 13T Phil Bradley	.05	.02	.01
☐ 14T Jeff Brantley	.10	.05	.01
☐ 15T Kevin Brown	.30	.14	.04
☐ 16T Jerry Browne	.05	.02	.01
☐ 17T Chuck Cary	.05	.02	.01
☐ 18T Carmen Castillo	.05	.02	.01
☐ 19T Jim Clancy	.05	.02	.01
☐ 20T Jack Clark	.08	.04	.01
☐ 21T Bryan Clutterbuck	.05	.02	.01
☐ 22T Jody Davis	.05	.02	.01
☐ 23T Mike Devereaux	.35	.16	.04
☐ 24T Frank DiPino	.05	.02	.01
☐ 25T Benny Distefano	.05	.02	.01
☐ 26T John Dopson	.05	.02	.01
☐ 27T Len Dykstra	.08	.04	.01
☐ 28T Jim Eisenreich	.05	.02	.01
☐ 29T Nick Esasky	.05	.02	.01
☐ 30T Alvaro Espinoza	.05	.02	.01
☐ 31T Darrell Evans UER (Stat headings on back are for a pitcher)	.08	.04	.01
☐ 32T Junior Felix	.25	.11	.03
☐ 33T Felix Fermin	.05	.02	.01
☐ 34T Julio Franco	.08	.04	.01
☐ 35T Terry Francona	.05	.02	.01
☐ 36T Cito Gaston MG	.08	.04	.01
☐ 37T Bob Geren UER (Photo actually Mike Fennell)	.05	.02	.01
☐ 38T Tom Gordon	.10	.05	.01
☐ 39T Tommy Gregg	.05	.02	.01
☐ 40T Ken Griffey Sr.	.08	.04	.01
☐ 41T Ken Griffey Jr.	4.00	1.80	.50
☐ 42T Kevin Gross	.05	.02	.01
☐ 43T Lee Guetterman	.05	.02	.01
☐ 44T Mel Hall	.05	.02	.01
☐ 45T Erik Hanson	.20	.09	.03
☐ 46T Gene Harris	.10	.05	.01
☐ 47T Andy Hawkins	.05	.02	.01
☐ 48T Rickey Henderson	.25	.11	.03
☐ 49T Tom Herr	.05	.02	.01
☐ 50T Ken Hill	.40	.18	.05
☐ 51T Brian Holman	.10	.05	.01
☐ 52T Brian Holton	.05	.02	.01
☐ 53T Art Howe MG	.05	.02	.01
☐ 54T Ken Howell	.05	.02	.01
☐ 55T Bruce Hurst	.08	.04	.01
☐ 56T Chris James	.05	.02	.01
☐ 57T Randy Johnson	.15	.07	.02
☐ 58T Jimmy Jones	.05	.02	.01
☐ 59T Terry Kennedy	.05	.02	.01
☐ 60T Paul Kilgus	.05	.02	.01
☐ 61T Eric King	.05	.02	.01
☐ 62T Ron Kittle	.05	.02	.01
☐ 63T John Kruk	.08	.04	.01
☐ 64T Randy Kutcher	.05	.02	.01
☐ 65T Steve Lake	.05	.02	.01
☐ 66T Mark Langston	.08	.04	.01
☐ 67T Dave LaPoint	.05	.02	.01
☐ 68T Rick Leach	.05	.02	.01
☐ 69T Terry Leach	.05	.02	.01
☐ 70T Jim Lefebvre MG	.05	.02	.01
☐ 71T Al Leiter	.05	.02	.01
☐ 72T Jeffrey Leonard	.05	.02	.01
☐ 73T Derek Lilliquist	.10	.05	.01
☐ 74T Rick Mahler	.05	.02	.01
☐ 75T Tom McCarthy	.05	.02	.01
☐ 76T Lloyd McClendon	.05	.02	.01
☐ 77T Lance McCullers	.05	.02	.01
☐ 78T Oddibe McDowell	.05	.02	.01
☐ 79T Roger McDowell	.05	.02	.01

☐ 80T Larry McWilliams	.05	.02	.01
☐ 81T Randy Milligan	.05	.02	.01
☐ 82T Mike Moore	.05	.02	.01
☐ 83T Keith Moreland	.05	.02	.01
☐ 84T Mike Morgan	.08	.04	.01
☐ 85T Jamie Moyer	.05	.02	.01
☐ 86T Rob Murphy	.05	.02	.01
☐ 87T Eddie Murray	.15	.07	.02
☐ 88T Pete O'Brien	.05	.02	.01
☐ 89T Gregg Olson	.40	.18	.05
☐ 90T Steve Ontiveros	.05	.02	.01
☐ 91T Jesse Orosco	.05	.02	.01
☐ 92T Spike Owen	.05	.02	.01
☐ 93T Rafael Palmeiro	.20	.09	.03
☐ 94T Clay Parker	.05	.02	.01
☐ 95T Jeff Parrett	.05	.02	.01
☐ 96T Lance Parrish	.08	.04	.01
☐ 97T Dennis Powell	.05	.02	.01
☐ 98T Rey Quinones	.05	.02	.01
☐ 99T Doug Rader MG	.05	.02	.01
☐ 100T Willie Randolph	.08	.04	.01
☐ 101T Shane Rawley	.05	.02	.01
☐ 102T Randy Ready	.05	.02	.01
☐ 103T Bip Roberts	.08	.04	.01
☐ 104T Kenny Rogers	.08	.04	.01
☐ 105T Ed Romero	.05	.02	.01
☐ 106T Nolan Ryan	1.25	.55	.16
☐ 107T Luis Salazar	.05	.02	.01
☐ 108T Juan Samuel	.05	.02	.01
☐ 109T Alex Sanchez	.05	.02	.01
☐ 110T Deion Sanders	2.00	.90	.25
☐ 111T Steve Sax	.08	.04	.01
☐ 112T Rick Schu	.05	.02	.01
☐ 113T Dwight Smith	.10	.05	.01
☐ 114T Lonnie Smith	.05	.02	.01
☐ 115T Billy Spiers	.10	.05	.01
☐ 116T Kent Tekulve	.05	.02	.01
☐ 117T Walt Terrell	.05	.02	.01
☐ 118T Milt Thompson	.05	.02	.01
☐ 119T Dickie Thon	.05	.02	.01
☐ 120T Jeff Torborg MG	.05	.02	.01
☐ 121T Jeff Treadway	.08	.04	.01
☐ 122T Omar Vizquel	.15	.07	.02
☐ 123T Jerome Walton	.10	.05	.01
☐ 124T Gary Ward	.05	.02	.01
☐ 125T Claudell Washington	.05	.02	.01
☐ 126T Curt Wilkerson	.05	.02	.01
☐ 127T Eddie Williams	.05	.02	.01
☐ 128T Frank Williams	.05	.02	.01
☐ 129T Ken Williams	.05	.02	.01
☐ 130T Mitch Williams	.08	.04	.01
☐ 131T Steve Wilson	.05	.02	.01
☐ 132T Checklist 1T-132T	.08	.01	.00

1989 Topps UK Minis

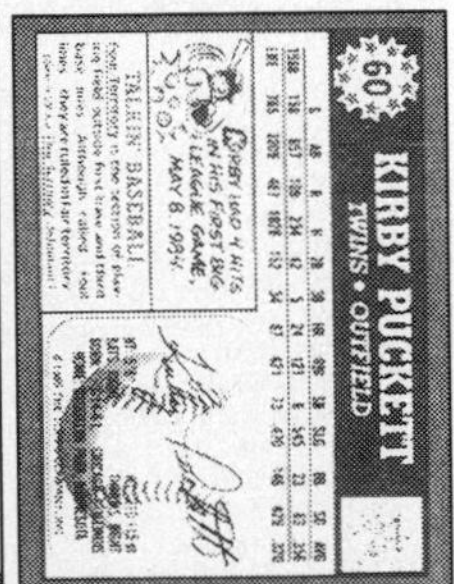

The 1989 Topps UK Minis baseball set contains 88 cards measuring approximately 2 1/8" by 3". The fronts are red, white and blue. The backs are yellow and red, and feature 1988 and career stats. The cards were distributed in five-card poly packs. The card set numbering is in alphabetical order by player's name.

	MT	EX-MT	VG
COMPLETE SET (88)	10.00	4.50	1.25
COMMON PLAYER (1-88)	.05	.02	.01
☐ 1 Brady Anderson	.25	.11	.03
☐ 2 Harold Baines	.08	.04	.01
☐ 3 George Bell	.10	.05	.01
☐ 4 Wade Boggs	.50	.23	.06
☐ 5 Barry Bonds	.60	.25	.08
☐ 6 Bobby Bonilla	.35	.16	.04
☐ 7 George Brett	.50	.23	.06
☐ 8 Hubie Brooks	.05	.02	.01
☐ 9 Tom Brunansky	.08	.04	.01
☐ 10 Jay Buhner	.15	.07	.02
☐ 11 Brett Butler	.10	.05	.01
☐ 12 Jose Canseco	.60	.25	.08
☐ 13 Joe Carter	.35	.16	.04
☐ 14 Jack Clark	.08	.04	.01
☐ 15 Will Clark	.60	.25	.08
☐ 16 Roger Clemens	.75	.35	.09
☐ 17 David Cone	.20	.09	.03
☐ 18 Alvin Davis	.05	.02	.01
☐ 19 Eric Davis	.20	.09	.03
☐ 20 Glenn Davis	.10	.05	.01
☐ 21 Andre Dawson	.30	.14	.04
☐ 22 Bill Doran	.05	.02	.01
☐ 23 Dennis Eckersley	.15	.07	.02
☐ 24 Dwight Evans	.08	.04	.01
☐ 25 Tony Fernandez	.08	.04	.01
☐ 26 Carlton Fisk	.35	.16	.04
☐ 27 John Franco	.08	.04	.01
☐ 28 Andres Galarraga	.05	.02	.01
☐ 29 Ron Gant	.35	.16	.04
☐ 30 Kirk Gibson	.10	.05	.01
☐ 31 Dwight Gooden	.20	.09	.03
☐ 32 Mike Greenwell	.20	.09	.03
☐ 33 Mark Gubicza	.08	.04	.01
☐ 34 Pedro Guerrero	.08	.04	.01
☐ 35 Ozzie Guillen	.08	.04	.01
☐ 36 Tony Gwynn	.45	.20	.06
☐ 37 Rickey Henderson	.60	.25	.08
☐ 38 Orel Hershiser	.12	.05	.02
☐ 39 Teddy Higuera	.05	.02	.01
☐ 40 Charlie Hough	.05	.02	.01
☐ 41 Kent Hrbek	.08	.04	.01
☐ 42 Bruce Hurst	.08	.04	.01
☐ 43 Bo Jackson	.60	.25	.08
☐ 44 Gregg Jefferies	.50	.23	.06
☐ 45 Ricky Jordan	.10	.05	.01
☐ 46 Wally Joyner	.12	.05	.02
☐ 47 Mark Langston	.08	.04	.01
☐ 48 Mike Marshall	.05	.02	.01
☐ 49 Don Mattingly	.50	.23	.06
☐ 50 Fred McGriff	.25	.11	.03
☐ 51 Mark McGwire	.50	.23	.06
☐ 52 Kevin McReynolds	.08	.04	.01
☐ 53 Paul Molitor	.15	.07	.02
☐ 54 Jack Morris	.15	.07	.02
☐ 55 Dale Murphy	.20	.09	.03
☐ 56 Eddie Murray	.25	.11	.03
☐ 57 Pete O'Brien	.05	.02	.01
☐ 58 Rafael Palmeiro	.15	.07	.02
☐ 59 Gerald Perry	.05	.02	.01
☐ 60 Kirby Puckett	.50	.23	.06
☐ 61 Tim Raines	.10	.05	.01
☐ 62 Johnny Ray	.05	.02	.01
☐ 63 Rick Reuschel	.05	.02	.01
☐ 64 Cal Ripken	.75	.35	.09
☐ 65 Chris Sabo	.25	.11	.03
☐ 66 Juan Samuel	.05	.02	.01
☐ 67 Ryne Sandberg	.75	.35	.09
☐ 68 Benito Santiago	.15	.07	.02
☐ 69 Steve Sax	.10	.05	.01
☐ 70 Mike Schmidt	.75	.35	.09
☐ 71 Ruben Sierra	.50	.23	.06
☐ 72 Ozzie Smith	.30	.14	.04
☐ 73 Cory Snyder	.08	.04	.01
☐ 74 Dave Stewart	.10	.05	.01
☐ 75 Darryl Strawberry	.50	.23	.06
☐ 76 Greg Swindell	.08	.04	.01
☐ 77 Alan Trammell	.15	.07	.02
☐ 78 Fernando Valenzuela	.05	.02	.01
☐ 79 Andy Van Slyke	.15	.07	.02
☐ 80 Frank Viola	.10	.05	.01
☐ 81 Claudell Washington	.05	.02	.01
☐ 82 Walt Weiss	.10	.05	.01
☐ 83 Lou Whitaker	.15	.07	.02
☐ 84 Dave Winfield	.35	.16	.04
☐ 85 Mike Witt	.05	.02	.01
☐ 86 Gerald Young	.05	.02	.01
☐ 87 Robin Yount	.45	.20	.06
☐ 88 Checklist Card	.08	.04	.01

1989 Topps Wax Box Cards

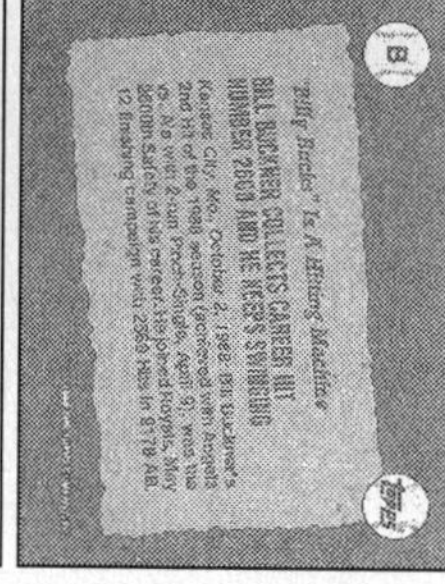

The cards in this 16-card set measure the standard 2 1/2" by 3 1/2". Cards have essentially the same design as the 1989 Topps regular issue set. The cards were printed on the bottoms of the regular issue wax pack boxes. These 16 cards, "lettered" A through P, are considered a separate set in their own right and are not typically included in a complete set of the regular issue 1989 Topps cards. The order of the set is alphabetical by player's name. The value of the panels uncut is slightly greater, perhaps by 25 percent greater, than the value of the individual cards cut up carefully. The sixteen cards in this set honor players (and one manager) who reached career milestones during the 1988 season.

	MT	EX-MT	VG
COMPLETE SET (16)	7.00	3.10	.85
COMMON PLAYER (A-P)	.15	.07	.02
☐ A George Brett 475th Double	1.00	.45	.13
☐ B Bill Buckner 2600th Hit	.25	.11	.03
☐ C Darrell Evans 400th Home Run	.15	.07	.02
☐ D Rich Gossage 300th Save	.25	.11	.03
☐ E Greg Gross 125th Pinch Hit	.15	.07	.02
☐ F Rickey Henderson 775th Stolen Base	1.00	.45	.13
☐ G Keith Hernandez 125th Game- Winning RBI	.25	.11	.03
☐ H Tom Lasorda MG 1000th Managerial Win	.25	.11	.03
☐ I Jim Rice 1400th Run Batted In	.25	.11	.03
☐ J Cal Ripken 1000th Cons. Game	1.25	.55	.16
☐ K Nolan Ryan 4700th Strikeout	1.50	.65	.19
☐ L Mike Schmidt 1000th Long Hit	1.00	.45	.13
☐ M Bruce Sutter 300th Save	.25	.11	.03
☐ N Don Sutton 750th Game Started	.35	.16	.04
☐ O Kent Tekulve 1000th Appearance	.15	.07	.02
☐ P Dave Winfield 1400th Run Batted In	.75	.35	.09

1989-90 Topps Senior League

The 1989-90 Topps Senior League baseball set was issued second among the three sets commemorating the first Senior league season. This set was issued in set form in its own box containing all 132 cards, each standard sized (2 1/2" by 3 1/2").

	MT	EX-MT	VG
COMPLETE SET (132)	7.00	3.10	.85
COMMON PLAYER (1-132)	.06	.03	.01
☐ 1 George Foster	.20	.09	.03
☐ 2 Dwight Lowry	.06	.03	.01
☐ 3 Bob Jones	.06	.03	.01
☐ 4 Clete Boyer MG	.12	.05	.02
☐ 5 Rafael Landestoy	.06	.03	.01
☐ 6 Bob Shirley	.06	.03	.01
☐ 7 Ivan Murrell	.06	.03	.01
☐ 8 Jerry White	.06	.03	.01
☐ 9 Steve Henderson	.06	.03	.01
☐ 10 Marty Castillo	.06	.03	.01
☐ 11 Bruce Kison	.10	.05	.01
☐ 12 George Hendrick	.12	.05	.02
☐ 13 Bernie Carbo	.10	.05	.01
☐ 14 Jerry Martin	.06	.03	.01
☐ 15 Al Hrabosky	.12	.05	.02
☐ 16 Luis Gomez	.06	.03	.01
☐ 17 Dick Drago	.06	.03	.01
☐ 18 Bobby Ramos	.06	.03	.01
☐ 19 Joe Pittman	.06	.03	.01
☐ 20 Ike Blessitt	.10	.05	.01
☐ 21 Bill Travers	.06	.03	.01
☐ 22 Dick Williams MG	.10	.05	.01
☐ 23 Randy Lerch	.06	.03	.01
☐ 24 Tom Spencer	.06	.03	.01
☐ 25 Graig Nettles	.20	.09	.03
☐ 26 Jim Gideon	.06	.03	.01
☐ 27 Al Bumbry	.10	.05	.01
☐ 28 Tom Murphy	.06	.03	.01
☐ 29 Rodney Scott	.06	.03	.01
☐ 30 Alan Bannister	.06	.03	.01
☐ 31 John D'Acquisto	.06	.03	.01
☐ 32 Bert Campaneris	.12	.05	.02
☐ 33 Bill Lee	.12	.05	.02
☐ 34 Jerry Grote	.10	.05	.01
☐ 35 Ken Reitz	.06	.03	.01
☐ 36 Al Oliver	.20	.09	.03
☐ 37 Tim Stoddard	.06	.03	.01
☐ 38 Lenny Randle	.06	.03	.01
☐ 39 Rick Manning	.06	.03	.01
☐ 40 Bobby Bonds	.30	.14	.04
☐ 41 Rick Wise	.12	.05	.02
☐ 42 Sal Butera	.06	.03	.01
☐ 43 Ed Figueroa	.06	.03	.01
☐ 44 Ron Washington	.06	.03	.01
☐ 45 Elias Sosa	.06	.03	.01
☐ 46 Dan Driessen	.10	.05	.01
☐ 47 Wayne Nordhagen	.06	.03	.01
☐ 48 Vida Blue	.15	.07	.02
☐ 49 Butch Hobson	.15	.07	.02
☐ 50 Randy Bass	.10	.05	.01
☐ 51 Paul Mirabella	.06	.03	.01
☐ 52 Steve Kemp	.10	.05	.01
☐ 53 Kim Allen	.06	.03	.01
☐ 54 Stan Cliburn	.06	.03	.01
☐ 55 Derrel Thomas	.06	.03	.01
☐ 56 Pete Falcone	.06	.03	.01
☐ 57 Willie Aikens	.10	.05	.01
☐ 58 Toby Harrah	.10	.05	.01
☐ 59 Bob Tolan	.10	.05	.01
☐ 60 Rick Waits	.06	.03	.01
☐ 61 Jim Morrison	.06	.03	.01
☐ 62 Stan Bahnsen	.06	.03	.01
☐ 63 Gene Richards	.06	.03	.01
☐ 64 Dave Cash	.10	.05	.01
☐ 65 Rollie Fingers	.75	.35	.09
☐ 66 Butch Benton	.06	.03	.01
☐ 67 Tim Ireland	.06	.03	.01
☐ 68 Rick Lysander	.06	.03	.01
☐ 69 Cesar Cedeno	.10	.05	.01

☐ 70 Jim Willoughby	.06	.03	.01
☐ 71 Bill Madlock	.15	.07	.02
☐ 72 Lee Lacy	.06	.03	.01
☐ 73 Milt Wilcox	.06	.03	.01
☐ 74 Ron Pruitt	.06	.03	.01
☐ 75 Wayne Krenchicki	.06	.03	.01
☐ 76 Earl Weaver MG	.15	.07	.02
☐ 77 Pedro Borbon	.06	.03	.01
☐ 78 Jose Cruz	.12	.05	.02
☐ 79 Steve Ontiveros	.06	.03	.01
☐ 80 Mike Easler	.10	.05	.01
☐ 81 Amos Otis	.15	.07	.02
☐ 82 Mickey Mahler	.06	.03	.01
☐ 83 Orlando Gonzalez	.06	.03	.01
☐ 84 Doug Simunic	.06	.03	.01
☐ 85 Felix Millan	.10	.05	.01
☐ 86 Garth Iorg	.06	.03	.01
☐ 87 Pete Broberg	.06	.03	.01
☐ 88 Roy Howell	.06	.03	.01
☐ 89 Dave LaRoche	.06	.03	.01
☐ 90 Jerry Manuel	.06	.03	.01
☐ 91 Tony Scott	.06	.03	.01
☐ 92 Larvell Blanks	.06	.03	.01
☐ 93 Joaquin Andujar	.12	.05	.02
☐ 94 Tito Landrum	.10	.05	.01
☐ 95 Joe Sambito	.10	.05	.01
☐ 96 Pat Dobson	.10	.05	.01
☐ 97 Dan Meyer	.06	.03	.01
☐ 98 Clint Hurdle	.12	.05	.02
☐ 99 Pete LaCock	.10	.05	.01
☐ 100 Bob Galasso	.06	.03	.01
☐ 101 Dave Kingman	.20	.09	.03
☐ 102 Jon Matlack	.12	.05	.02
☐ 103 Larry Harlow	.06	.03	.01
☐ 104 Rick Peterson	.06	.03	.01
☐ 105 Joe Hicks	.06	.03	.01
☐ 106 Bill Campbell	.06	.03	.01
☐ 107 Tom Paciorek	.10	.05	.01
☐ 108 Ray Burris	.10	.05	.01
☐ 109 Ken Landreaux	.10	.05	.01
☐ 110 Steve McCatty	.06	.03	.01
☐ 111 Ron LeFlore	.10	.05	.01
☐ 112 Joe Decker	.06	.03	.01
☐ 113 Leon Roberts	.06	.03	.01
☐ 114 Doug Corbett	.06	.03	.01
☐ 115 Mickey Rivers	.10	.05	.01
☐ 116 Dock Ellis	.06	.03	.01
☐ 117 Ron Jackson	.06	.03	.01
☐ 118 Bob Molinaro	.06	.03	.01
☐ 119 Fergie Jenkins	.90	.40	.11
☐ 120 U.L. Washington	.06	.03	.01
☐ 121 Roy Thomas	.06	.03	.01
☐ 122 Hal McRae	.15	.07	.02
☐ 123 Juan Eichelberger	.06	.03	.01
☐ 124 Gary Rajsich	.06	.03	.01
☐ 125 Dennis Leonard	.10	.05	.01
☐ 126 Walt Williams	.10	.05	.01
☐ 127 Rennie Stennett	.06	.03	.01
☐ 128 Jim Bibby	.10	.05	.01
☐ 129 Dyar Miller	.06	.03	.01
☐ 130 Luis Pujols	.06	.03	.01
☐ 131 Juan Beniquez	.10	.05	.01
☐ 132 Checklist Card	.10	.05	.01

1990 Topps

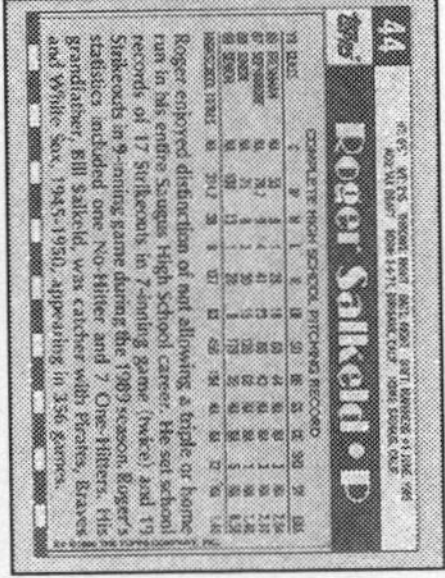

The 1990 Topps set contains 792 standard-size (2 1/2" by 3 1/2") cards. The front borders are various colors. The horizontally oriented backs are yellowish green. Cards 385-407 contain the All-Stars. Cards 661-665 contain the Turn Back the Clock cards. The manager cards this year contain information that had been on the backs of the Team Leader cards in the past few years; the Team Leader cards were discontinued, apparently in order to allow better individual player card selection. Topps really concentrated on individual player cards in this set with 725, the most ever in a baseball card set. The checklist cards are oriented alphabetically by team name and player name. The key Rookie Cards in this set are Delino DeShields, Juan Gonzalez, Marquis Grissom, Ben McDonald, Frank Thomas, and Larry Walker. There exists a printing variation on the Jeff King (454) card where the card number, Topps logo, name, and personal information block on the card back is erroneously shaded in yellow as the rest of the back. Topps also produced a specially boxed "glossy" edition frequently referred to as the Topps Tiffany set. This year, again, Topps did not disclose the number of Tiffany sets they produced or sold but it seems that production quantities were roughly similar (approximately 15,000 sets) to the previous year. The checklist of cards is identical to that of the normal non-glossy cards. There are two primary distinguishing features of the Tiffany cards, white card stock reverses and high gloss obverses. These Tiffany cards are valued approximately from three to five times the values listed below.

	MT	EX-MT	VG
COMPLETE SET (792)	20.00	9.00	2.50
COMPLETE FACT.SET (792)	25.00	11.50	3.10
COMMON PLAYER (1-792)	.04	.02	.01
☐ 1 Nolan Ryan	.60	.25	.08
☐ 2 Nolan Ryan Salute New York Mets	.25	.11	.03
☐ 3 Nolan Ryan Salute California Angels	.25	.11	.03
☐ 4 Nolan Ryan Salute Houston Astros	.25	.11	.03
☐ 5 Nolan Ryan Salute Texas Rangers UER (Says Texas Stadium rather than Arlington Stadium)	.25	.11	.03
☐ 6 Vince Coleman RB (50 consecutive stolen bases)	.05	.02	.01
☐ 7 Rickey Henderson RB (40 career leadoff home runs)	.10	.05	.01
☐ 8 Cal Ripken RB (20 or more homers for 8 consecutive years, record for shortstops)	.20	.09	.03
☐ 9 Eric Plunk	.04	.02	.01
☐ 10 Barry Larkin	.12	.05	.02
☐ 11 Paul Gibson	.04	.02	.01
☐ 12 Joe Girardi	.04	.02	.01
☐ 13 Mark Williamson	.04	.02	.01
☐ 14 Mike Fetters	.10	.05	.01
☐ 15 Teddy Higuera	.04	.02	.01
☐ 16 Kent Anderson	.04	.02	.01
☐ 17 Kelly Downs	.04	.02	.01
☐ 18 Carlos Quintana	.07	.03	.01
☐ 19 Al Newman	.04	.02	.01
☐ 20 Mark Gubicza	.04	.02	.01
☐ 21 Jeff Torborg MG	.04	.02	.01
☐ 22 Bruce Ruffin	.04	.02	.01
☐ 23 Randy Velarde	.04	.02	.01
☐ 24 Joe Hesketh	.04	.02	.01
☐ 25 Willie Randolph	.07	.03	.01
☐ 26 Don Slaught	.04	.02	.01
☐ 27 Rick Leach	.04	.02	.01
☐ 28 Duane Ward	.04	.02	.01
☐ 29 John Cangelosi	.04	.02	.01
☐ 30 David Cone	.12	.05	.02
☐ 31 Henry Cotto	.04	.02	.01
☐ 32 John Farrell	.04	.02	.01
☐ 33 Greg Walker	.04	.02	.01
☐ 34 Tony Fossas	.04	.02	.01
☐ 35 Benito Santiago	.07	.03	.01
☐ 36 John Costello	.04	.02	.01
☐ 37 Domingo Ramos	.04	.02	.01
☐ 38 Wes Gardner	.04	.02	.01

☐ 39 Curt Ford	.04	.02	.01
☐ 40 Jay Howell	.04	.02	.01
☐ 41 Matt Williams	.10	.05	.01
☐ 42 Jeff M. Robinson	.04	.02	.01
☐ 43 Dante Bichette	.07	.03	.01
☐ 44 Roger Salkeld FDP	.25	.11	.03
☐ 45 Dave Parker UER (Born in Jackson, not Calhoun)	.07	.03	.01
☐ 46 Rob Dibble	.07	.03	.01
☐ 47 Brian Harper	.07	.03	.01
☐ 48 Zane Smith	.04	.02	.01
☐ 49 Tom Lawless	.04	.02	.01
☐ 50 Glenn Davis	.07	.03	.01
☐ 51 Doug Rader MG	.04	.02	.01
☐ 52 Jack Daugherty	.04	.02	.01
☐ 53 Mike LaCoss	.04	.02	.01
☐ 54 Joel Skinner	.04	.02	.01
☐ 55 Darrell Evans UER (HR total should be 414, not 424)	.07	.03	.01
☐ 56 Franklin Stubbs	.04	.02	.01
☐ 57 Greg Vaughn	.15	.07	.02
☐ 58 Keith Miller	.04	.02	.01
☐ 59 Ted Power	.04	.02	.01
☐ 60 George Brett	.15	.07	.02
☐ 61 Deion Sanders	.40	.18	.05
☐ 62 Ramon Martinez	.15	.07	.02
☐ 63 Mike Pagliarulo	.04	.02	.01
☐ 64 Danny Darwin	.04	.02	.01
☐ 65 Devon White	.07	.03	.01
☐ 66 Greg Litton	.04	.02	.01
☐ 67 Scott Sanderson	.04	.02	.01
☐ 68 Dave Henderson	.04	.02	.01
☐ 69 Todd Frohwirth	.04	.02	.01
☐ 70 Mike Greenwell	.07	.03	.01
☐ 71 Allan Anderson	.04	.02	.01
☐ 72 Jeff Huson	.10	.05	.01
☐ 73 Bob Milacki	.04	.02	.01
☐ 74 Jeff Jackson FDP	.10	.05	.01
☐ 75 Doug Jones	.07	.03	.01
☐ 76 Dave Valle	.04	.02	.01
☐ 77 Dave Bergman	.04	.02	.01
☐ 78 Mike Flanagan	.04	.02	.01
☐ 79 Ron Kittle	.04	.02	.01
☐ 80 Jeff Russell	.04	.02	.01
☐ 81 Bob Rodgers MG	.04	.02	.01
☐ 82 Scott Terry	.04	.02	.01
☐ 83 Hensley Meulens	.07	.03	.01
☐ 84 Ray Searage	.04	.02	.01
☐ 85 Juan Samuel	.04	.02	.01
☐ 86 Paul Kilgus	.04	.02	.01
☐ 87 Rick Luecken	.04	.02	.01
☐ 88 Glenn Braggs	.04	.02	.01
☐ 89 Clint Zavaras	.04	.02	.01
☐ 90 Jack Clark	.07	.03	.01
☐ 91 Steve Frey	.10	.05	.01
☐ 92 Mike Stanley	.04	.02	.01
☐ 93 Shawn Hillegas	.04	.02	.01
☐ 94 Herm Winningham	.04	.02	.01
☐ 95 Todd Worrell	.04	.02	.01
☐ 96 Jody Reed	.04	.02	.01
☐ 97 Curt Schilling	.15	.07	.02
☐ 98 Jose Gonzalez	.04	.02	.01
☐ 99 Rich Monteleone	.04	.02	.01
☐ 100 Will Clark	.30	.14	.04
☐ 101 Shane Rawley	.04	.02	.01
☐ 102 Stan Javier	.04	.02	.01
☐ 103 Marvin Freeman	.04	.02	.01
☐ 104 Bob Knepper	.04	.02	.01
☐ 105 Randy Myers	.07	.03	.01
☐ 106 Charlie O'Brien	.04	.02	.01
☐ 107 Fred Lynn	.07	.03	.01
☐ 108 Rod Nichols	.04	.02	.01
☐ 109 Roberto Kelly	.10	.05	.01
☐ 110 Tommy Helms MG	.04	.02	.01
☐ 111 Ed Whited	.04	.02	.01
☐ 112 Glenn Wilson	.04	.02	.01
☐ 113 Manny Lee	.04	.02	.01
☐ 114 Mike Bielecki	.04	.02	.01
☐ 115 Tony Pena	.04	.02	.01
☐ 116 Floyd Bannister	.04	.02	.01
☐ 117 Mike Sharperson	.04	.02	.01
☐ 118 Erik Hanson	.07	.03	.01
☐ 119 Billy Hatcher	.04	.02	.01
☐ 120 John Franco	.07	.03	.01
☐ 121 Robin Ventura	.60	.25	.08
☐ 122 Shawn Abner	.04	.02	.01
☐ 123 Rich Gedman	.04	.02	.01
☐ 124 Dave Dravecky	.07	.03	.01
☐ 125 Kent Hrbek	.07	.03	.01
☐ 126 Randy Kramer	.04	.02	.01
☐ 127 Mike Devereaux	.07	.03	.01
☐ 128 Checklist 1	.05	.01	.00
☐ 129 Ron Jones	.04	.02	.01
☐ 130 Bert Blyleven	.07	.03	.01
☐ 131 Matt Nokes	.04	.02	.01
☐ 132 Lance Blankenship	.04	.02	.01
☐ 133 Ricky Horton	.04	.02	.01
☐ 134 Earl Cunningham FDP	.12	.05	.02
☐ 135 Dave Magadan	.07	.03	.01
☐ 136 Kevin Brown	.10	.05	.01
☐ 137 Marty Pevey	.04	.02	.01
☐ 138 Al Leiter	.04	.02	.01
☐ 139 Greg Brock	.04	.02	.01
☐ 140 Andre Dawson	.12	.05	.02
☐ 141 John Hart MG	.04	.02	.01
☐ 142 Jeff Wetherby	.04	.02	.01
☐ 143 Rafael Belliard	.04	.02	.01
☐ 144 Bud Black	.04	.02	.01
☐ 145 Terry Steinbach	.07	.03	.01
☐ 146 Rob Richie	.04	.02	.01
☐ 147 Chuck Finley	.07	.03	.01
☐ 148 Edgar Martinez	.25	.11	.03
☐ 149 Steve Farr	.04	.02	.01
☐ 150 Kirk Gibson	.07	.03	.01
☐ 151 Rick Mahler	.04	.02	.01
☐ 152 Lonnie Smith	.04	.02	.01
☐ 153 Randy Milligan	.04	.02	.01
☐ 154 Mike Maddux	.04	.02	.01
☐ 155 Ellis Burks	.07	.03	.01
☐ 156 Ken Patterson	.04	.02	.01
☐ 157 Craig Biggio	.10	.05	.01
☐ 158 Craig Lefferts	.04	.02	.01
☐ 159 Mike Felder	.04	.02	.01
☐ 160 Dave Righetti	.04	.02	.01
☐ 161 Harold Reynolds	.04	.02	.01
☐ 162 Todd Zeile	.15	.07	.02
☐ 163 Phil Bradley	.04	.02	.01
☐ 164 Jeff Juden FDP	.20	.09	.03
☐ 165 Walt Weiss	.04	.02	.01
☐ 166 Bobby Witt	.07	.03	.01
☐ 167 Kevin Appier	.25	.11	.03
☐ 168 Jose Lind	.04	.02	.01
☐ 169 Richard Dotson	.04	.02	.01
☐ 170 George Bell	.07	.03	.01
☐ 171 Russ Nixon MG	.04	.02	.01
☐ 172 Tom Lampkin	.04	.02	.01
☐ 173 Tim Belcher	.07	.03	.01
☐ 174 Jeff Kunkel	.04	.02	.01
☐ 175 Mike Moore	.04	.02	.01
☐ 176 Luis Quinones	.04	.02	.01
☐ 177 Mike Henneman	.04	.02	.01
☐ 178 Chris James	.04	.02	.01
☐ 179 Brian Holton	.04	.02	.01
☐ 180 Tim Raines	.07	.03	.01
☐ 181 Juan Agosto	.04	.02	.01
☐ 182 Mookie Wilson	.04	.02	.01
☐ 183 Steve Lake	.04	.02	.01
☐ 184 Danny Cox	.04	.02	.01
☐ 185 Ruben Sierra	.20	.09	.03
☐ 186 Dave LaPoint	.04	.02	.01
☐ 187 Rick Wrona	.04	.02	.01
☐ 188 Mike Smithson	.04	.02	.01
☐ 189 Dick Schofield	.04	.02	.01
☐ 190 Rick Reuschel	.04	.02	.01
☐ 191 Pat Borders	.07	.03	.01
☐ 192 Don August	.04	.02	.01
☐ 193 Andy Benes	.15	.07	.02
☐ 194 Glenallen Hill	.07	.03	.01
☐ 195 Tim Burke	.04	.02	.01
☐ 196 Gerald Young	.04	.02	.01
☐ 197 Doug Drabek	.07	.03	.01
☐ 198 Mike Marshall	.04	.02	.01
☐ 199 Sergio Valdez	.04	.02	.01
☐ 200 Don Mattingly	.20	.09	.03
☐ 201 Cito Gaston MG	.07	.03	.01
☐ 202 Mike Macfarlane	.04	.02	.01
☐ 203 Mike Roesler	.04	.02	.01
☐ 204 Bob Dernier	.04	.02	.01
☐ 205 Mark Davis	.04	.02	.01
☐ 206 Nick Esasky	.04	.02	.01
☐ 207 Bob Ojeda	.04	.02	.01
☐ 208 Brook Jacoby	.04	.02	.01
☐ 209 Greg Mathews	.04	.02	.01
☐ 210 Ryne Sandberg	.35	.16	.04
☐ 211 John Cerutti	.04	.02	.01
☐ 212 Joe Orsulak	.04	.02	.01
☐ 213 Scott Bankhead	.04	.02	.01
☐ 214 Terry Francona	.04	.02	.01
☐ 215 Kirk McCaskill	.04	.02	.01
☐ 216 Ricky Jordan	.04	.02	.01
☐ 217 Don Robinson	.04	.02	.01
☐ 218 Wally Backman	.04	.02	.01
☐ 219 Donn Pall	.04	.02	.01
☐ 220 Barry Bonds	.30	.14	.04

☐ 221	Gary Mielke	.04	.02	.01
☐ 222	Kurt Stillwell UER (Graduate misspelled as gradute)	.04	.02	.01
☐ 223	Tommy Gregg	.04	.02	.01
☐ 224	Delino DeShields	.60	.25	.08
☐ 225	Jim Deshaies	.04	.02	.01
☐ 226	Mickey Hatcher	.04	.02	.01
☐ 227	Kevin Tapani	.35	.16	.04
☐ 228	Dave Martinez	.07	.03	.01
☐ 229	David Wells	.07	.03	.01
☐ 230	Keith Hernandez	.07	.03	.01
☐ 231	Jack McKeon MG	.04	.02	.01
☐ 232	Darnell Coles	.04	.02	.01
☐ 233	Ken Hill	.15	.07	.02
☐ 234	Mariano Duncan	.04	.02	.01
☐ 235	Jeff Reardon	.07	.03	.01
☐ 236	Hal Morris	.15	.07	.02
☐ 237	Kevin Ritz	.10	.05	.01
☐ 238	Felix Jose	.20	.09	.03
☐ 239	Eric Show	.04	.02	.01
☐ 240	Mark Grace	.20	.09	.03
☐ 241	Mike Krukow	.04	.02	.01
☐ 242	Fred Manrique	.04	.02	.01
☐ 243	Barry Jones	.04	.02	.01
☐ 244	Bill Schroeder	.04	.02	.01
☐ 245	Roger Clemens	.35	.16	.04
☐ 246	Jim Eisenreich	.04	.02	.01
☐ 247	Jerry Reed	.04	.02	.01
☐ 248	Dave Anderson	.04	.02	.01
☐ 249	Mike(Texas) Smith	.04	.02	.01
☐ 250	Jose Canseco	.30	.14	.04
☐ 251	Jeff Blauser	.07	.03	.01
☐ 252	Otis Nixon	.07	.03	.01
☐ 253	Mark Portugal	.04	.02	.01
☐ 254	Francisco Cabrera	.10	.05	.01
☐ 255	Bobby Thigpen	.04	.02	.01
☐ 256	Marvell Wynne	.04	.02	.01
☐ 257	Jose DeLeon	.04	.02	.01
☐ 258	Barry Lyons	.04	.02	.01
☐ 259	Lance McCullers	.04	.02	.01
☐ 260	Eric Davis	.10	.05	.01
☐ 261	Whitey Herzog MG	.07	.03	.01
☐ 262	Checklist 2	.05	.01	.00
☐ 263	Mel Stottlemyre Jr.	.04	.02	.01
☐ 264	Bryan Clutterbuck	.04	.02	.01
☐ 265	Pete O'Brien	.04	.02	.01
☐ 266	German Gonzalez	.04	.02	.01
☐ 267	Mark Davidson	.04	.02	.01
☐ 268	Rob Murphy	.04	.02	.01
☐ 269	Dickie Thon	.04	.02	.01
☐ 270	Dave Stewart	.07	.03	.01
☐ 271	Chet Lemon	.04	.02	.01
☐ 272	Bryan Harvey	.07	.03	.01
☐ 273	Bobby Bonilla	.12	.05	.02
☐ 274	Mauro Gozzo	.04	.02	.01
☐ 275	Mickey Tettleton	.07	.03	.01
☐ 276	Gary Thurman	.04	.02	.01
☐ 277	Lenny Harris	.04	.02	.01
☐ 278	Pascual Perez	.04	.02	.01
☐ 279	Steve Buechele	.04	.02	.01
☐ 280	Lou Whitaker	.07	.03	.01
☐ 281	Kevin Bass	.04	.02	.01
☐ 282	Derek Lilliquist	.04	.02	.01
☐ 283	Joey Belle	.50	.23	.06
☐ 284	Mark Gardner	.12	.05	.02
☐ 285	Willie McGee	.07	.03	.01
☐ 286	Lee Guetterman	.04	.02	.01
☐ 287	Vance Law	.04	.02	.01
☐ 288	Greg Briley	.04	.02	.01
☐ 289	Norm Charlton	.07	.03	.01
☐ 290	Robin Yount	.15	.07	.02
☐ 291	Dave Johnson MG	.07	.03	.01
☐ 292	Jim Gott	.04	.02	.01
☐ 293	Mike Gallego	.04	.02	.01
☐ 294	Craig McMurtry	.04	.02	.01
☐ 295	Fred McGriff	.20	.09	.03
☐ 296	Jeff Ballard	.04	.02	.01
☐ 297	Tommy Herr	.04	.02	.01
☐ 298	Dan Gladden	.04	.02	.01
☐ 299	Adam Peterson	.04	.02	.01
☐ 300	Bo Jackson	.15	.07	.02
☐ 301	Don Aase	.04	.02	.01
☐ 302	Marcus Lawton	.04	.02	.01
☐ 303	Rick Cerone	.04	.02	.01
☐ 304	Marty Clary	.04	.02	.01
☐ 305	Eddie Murray	.10	.05	.01
☐ 306	Tom Niedenfuer	.04	.02	.01
☐ 307	Bip Roberts	.07	.03	.01
☐ 308	Jose Guzman	.04	.02	.01
☐ 309	Eric Yelding	.04	.02	.01
☐ 310	Steve Bedrosian	.04	.02	.01
☐ 311	Dwight Smith	.04	.02	.01
☐ 312	Dan Quisenberry	.07	.03	.01
☐ 313	Gus Polidor	.04	.02	.01
☐ 314	Donald Harris FDP	.10	.05	.01
☐ 315	Bruce Hurst	.07	.03	.01
☐ 316	Carney Lansford	.07	.03	.01
☐ 317	Mark Guthrie	.04	.02	.01
☐ 318	Wallace Johnson	.04	.02	.01
☐ 319	Dion James	.04	.02	.01
☐ 320	Dave Stieb	.07	.03	.01
☐ 321	Joe Morgan MG	.04	.02	.01
☐ 322	Junior Ortiz	.04	.02	.01
☐ 323	Willie Wilson	.04	.02	.01
☐ 324	Pete Harnisch	.10	.05	.01
☐ 325	Robby Thompson	.04	.02	.01
☐ 326	Tom McCarthy	.04	.02	.01
☐ 327	Ken Williams	.04	.02	.01
☐ 328	Curt Young	.04	.02	.01
☐ 329	Oddibe McDowell	.04	.02	.01
☐ 330	Ron Darling	.07	.03	.01
☐ 331	Juan Gonzalez	2.00	.90	.25
☐ 332	Paul O'Neill	.07	.03	.01
☐ 333	Bill Wegman	.04	.02	.01
☐ 334	Johnny Ray	.04	.02	.01
☐ 335	Andy Hawkins	.04	.02	.01
☐ 336	Ken Griffey Jr.	1.25	.55	.16
☐ 337	Lloyd McClendon	.04	.02	.01
☐ 338	Dennis Lamp	.04	.02	.01
☐ 339	Dave Clark	.04	.02	.01
☐ 340	Fernando Valenzuela	.07	.03	.01
☐ 341	Tom Foley	.04	.02	.01
☐ 342	Alex Trevino	.04	.02	.01
☐ 343	Frank Tanana	.04	.02	.01
☐ 344	George Canale	.04	.02	.01
☐ 345	Harold Baines	.07	.03	.01
☐ 346	Jim Presley	.04	.02	.01
☐ 347	Junior Felix	.07	.03	.01
☐ 348	Gary Wayne	.04	.02	.01
☐ 349	Steve Finley	.10	.05	.01
☐ 350	Bret Saberhagen	.07	.03	.01
☐ 351	Roger Craig MG	.04	.02	.01
☐ 352	Bryn Smith	.04	.02	.01
☐ 353	Sandy Alomar Jr.UER (Not listed as Jr. on card front)	.10	.05	.01
☐ 354	Stan Belinda	.15	.07	.02
☐ 355	Marty Barrett	.04	.02	.01
☐ 356	Randy Ready	.04	.02	.01
☐ 357	Dave West	.04	.02	.01
☐ 358	Andres Thomas	.04	.02	.01
☐ 359	Jimmy Jones	.04	.02	.01
☐ 360	Paul Molitor	.10	.05	.01
☐ 361	Randy McCament	.04	.02	.01
☐ 362	Damon Berryhill	.04	.02	.01
☐ 363	Dan Petry	.04	.02	.01
☐ 364	Rolando Roomes	.04	.02	.01
☐ 365	Ozzie Guillen	.04	.02	.01
☐ 366	Mike Heath	.04	.02	.01
☐ 367	Mike Morgan	.04	.02	.01
☐ 368	Bill Doran	.04	.02	.01
☐ 369	Todd Burns	.04	.02	.01
☐ 370	Tim Wallach	.07	.03	.01
☐ 371	Jimmy Key	.07	.03	.01
☐ 372	Terry Kennedy	.04	.02	.01
☐ 373	Alvin Davis	.04	.02	.01
☐ 374	Steve Cummings	.04	.02	.01
☐ 375	Dwight Evans	.07	.03	.01
☐ 376	Checklist 3 UER (Higuera misalphabet-ized in Brewer list)	.05	.01	.00
☐ 377	Mickey Weston	.04	.02	.01
☐ 378	Luis Salazar	.04	.02	.01
☐ 379	Steve Rosenberg	.04	.02	.01
☐ 380	Dave Winfield	.15	.07	.02
☐ 381	Frank Robinson MG	.07	.03	.01
☐ 382	Jeff Musselman	.04	.02	.01
☐ 383	John Morris	.04	.02	.01
☐ 384	Pat Combs	.07	.03	.01
☐ 385	Fred McGriff AS	.10	.05	.01
☐ 386	Julio Franco AS	.05	.02	.01
☐ 387	Wade Boggs AS	.10	.05	.01
☐ 388	Cal Ripken AS	.20	.09	.03
☐ 389	Robin Yount AS	.10	.05	.01
☐ 390	Ruben Sierra AS	.12	.05	.02
☐ 391	Kirby Puckett AS	.12	.05	.02
☐ 392	Carlton Fisk AS	.08	.04	.01
☐ 393	Bret Saberhagen AS	.05	.02	.01
☐ 394	Jeff Ballard AS	.05	.02	.01
☐ 395	Jeff Russell AS	.05	.02	.01
☐ 396	A.Bartlett Giamatti COMM MEM	.20	.09	.03
☐ 397	Will Clark AS	.15	.07	.02
☐ 398	Ryne Sandberg AS	.20	.09	.03
☐ 399	Howard Johnson AS	.05	.02	.01

Card			
□ 400 Ozzie Smith AS	.08	.04	.01
□ 401 Kevin Mitchell AS	.05	.02	.01
□ 402 Eric Davis AS	.08	.04	.01
□ 403 Tony Gwynn AS	.12	.05	.02
□ 404 Craig Biggio AS	.05	.02	.01
□ 405 Mike Scott AS	.05	.02	.01
□ 406 Joe Magrane AS	.05	.02	.01
□ 407 Mark Davis AS	.05	.02	.01
□ 408 Trevor Wilson	.04	.02	.01
□ 409 Tom Brunansky	.07	.03	.01
□ 410 Joe Boever	.04	.02	.01
□ 411 Ken Phelps	.04	.02	.01
□ 412 Jamie Moyer	.04	.02	.01
□ 413 Brian DuBois	.04	.02	.01
□ 414A Frank Thomas FDP ERR (Name missing on card front)	6.00	2.70	.75
□ 414B Frank Thomas FDP COR	4.00	1.80	.50
□ 415 Shawon Dunston	.07	.03	.01
□ 416 Dave Johnson (P)	.04	.02	.01
□ 417 Jim Gantner	.04	.02	.01
□ 418 Tom Browning	.04	.02	.01
□ 419 Beau Allred	.04	.02	.01
□ 420 Carlton Fisk	.10	.05	.01
□ 421 Greg Minton	.04	.02	.01
□ 422 Pat Sheridan	.04	.02	.01
□ 423 Fred Toliver	.04	.02	.01
□ 424 Jerry Reuss	.04	.02	.01
□ 425 Bill Landrum	.04	.02	.01
□ 426 Jeff Hamilton	.04	.02	.01
□ 427 Carmen Castillo	.04	.02	.01
□ 428 Steve Davis	.04	.02	.01
□ 429 Tom Kelly MG	.04	.02	.01
□ 430 Pete Incaviglia	.04	.02	.01
□ 431 Randy Johnson	.07	.03	.01
□ 432 Damaso Garcia	.04	.02	.01
□ 433 Steve Olin	.20	.09	.03
□ 434 Mark Carreon	.04	.02	.01
□ 435 Kevin Seitzer	.07	.03	.01
□ 436 Mel Hall	.04	.02	.01
□ 437 Les Lancaster	.04	.02	.01
□ 438 Greg Myers	.04	.02	.01
□ 439 Jeff Parrett	.04	.02	.01
□ 440 Alan Trammell	.07	.03	.01
□ 441 Bob Kipper	.04	.02	.01
□ 442 Jerry Browne	.04	.02	.01
□ 443 Cris Carpenter	.04	.02	.01
□ 444 Kyle Abbott FDP	.20	.09	.03
□ 445 Danny Jackson	.04	.02	.01
□ 446 Dan Pasqua	.04	.02	.01
□ 447 Atlee Hammaker	.04	.02	.01
□ 448 Greg Gagne	.04	.02	.01
□ 449 Dennis Rasmussen	.04	.02	.01
□ 450 Rickey Henderson	.20	.09	.03
□ 451 Mark Lemke	.07	.03	.01
□ 452 Luis De Los Santos	.04	.02	.01
□ 453 Jody Davis	.04	.02	.01
□ 454 Jeff King	.07	.03	.01
□ 455 Jeffrey Leonard	.04	.02	.01
□ 456 Chris Gwynn	.04	.02	.01
□ 457 Gregg Jefferies	.12	.05	.02
□ 458 Bob McClure	.04	.02	.01
□ 459 Jim Lefebvre MG	.04	.02	.01
□ 460 Mike Scott	.04	.02	.01
□ 461 Carlos Martinez	.04	.02	.01
□ 462 Denny Walling	.04	.02	.01
□ 463 Drew Hall	.04	.02	.01
□ 464 Jerome Walton	.07	.03	.01
□ 465 Kevin Gross	.04	.02	.01
□ 466 Rance Mulliniks	.04	.02	.01
□ 467 Juan Nieves	.04	.02	.01
□ 468 Bill Ripken	.04	.02	.01
□ 469 John Kruk	.07	.03	.01
□ 470 Frank Viola	.07	.03	.01
□ 471 Mike Brumley	.04	.02	.01
□ 472 Jose Uribe	.04	.02	.01
□ 473 Joe Price	.04	.02	.01
□ 474 Rich Thompson	.04	.02	.01
□ 475 Bob Welch	.07	.03	.01
□ 476 Brad Komminsk	.04	.02	.01
□ 477 Willie Fraser	.04	.02	.01
□ 478 Mike LaValliere	.04	.02	.01
□ 479 Frank White	.04	.02	.01
□ 480 Sid Fernandez	.07	.03	.01
□ 481 Garry Templeton	.04	.02	.01
□ 482 Steve Carter	.04	.02	.01
□ 483 Alejandro Pena	.04	.02	.01
□ 484 Mike Fitzgerald	.04	.02	.01
□ 485 John Candelaria	.04	.02	.01
□ 486 Jeff Treadway	.04	.02	.01
□ 487 Steve Searcy	.04	.02	.01
□ 488 Ken Oberkfell	.04	.02	.01
□ 489 Nick Leyva MG	.04	.02	.01
□ 490 Dan Plesac	.04	.02	.01
□ 491 Dave Cochrane	.10	.05	.01
□ 492 Ron Oester	.04	.02	.01
□ 493 Jason Grimsley	.10	.05	.01
□ 494 Terry Puhl	.04	.02	.01
□ 495 Lee Smith	.07	.03	.01
□ 496 Cecil Espy UER ('88 stats have 3 SB's, should be 33)	.04	.02	.01
□ 497 Dave Schmidt	.04	.02	.01
□ 498 Rick Schu	.04	.02	.01
□ 499 Bill Long	.04	.02	.01
□ 500 Kevin Mitchell	.10	.05	.01
□ 501 Matt Young	.04	.02	.01
□ 502 Mitch Webster	.04	.02	.01
□ 503 Randy St.Claire	.04	.02	.01
□ 504 Tom O'Malley	.04	.02	.01
□ 505 Kelly Gruber	.07	.03	.01
□ 506 Tom Glavine	.25	.11	.03
□ 507 Gary Redus	.04	.02	.01
□ 508 Terry Leach	.04	.02	.01
□ 509 Tom Pagnozzi	.04	.02	.01
□ 510 Dwight Gooden	.10	.05	.01
□ 511 Clay Parker	.04	.02	.01
□ 512 Gary Pettis	.04	.02	.01
□ 513 Mark Eichhorn	.04	.02	.01
□ 514 Andy Allanson	.04	.02	.01
□ 515 Len Dykstra	.07	.03	.01
□ 516 Tim Leary	.04	.02	.01
□ 517 Roberto Alomar	.40	.18	.05
□ 518 Bill Krueger	.04	.02	.01
□ 519 Bucky Dent MG	.04	.02	.01
□ 520 Mitch Williams	.07	.03	.01
□ 521 Craig Worthington	.04	.02	.01
□ 522 Mike Dunne	.04	.02	.01
□ 523 Jay Bell	.07	.03	.01
□ 524 Daryl Boston	.04	.02	.01
□ 525 Wally Joyner	.07	.03	.01
□ 526 Checklist 4	.05	.01	.00
□ 527 Ron Hassey	.04	.02	.01
□ 528 Kevin Wickander	.04	.02	.01
□ 529 Greg Harris	.04	.02	.01
□ 530 Mark Langston	.07	.03	.01
□ 531 Ken Caminiti	.07	.03	.01
□ 532 Cecilio Guante	.04	.02	.01
□ 533 Tim Jones	.04	.02	.01
□ 534 Louie Meadows	.04	.02	.01
□ 535 John Smoltz	.25	.11	.03
□ 536 Bob Geren	.04	.02	.01
□ 537 Mark Grant	.04	.02	.01
□ 538 Bill Spiers UER (Photo actually George Canale)	.04	.02	.01
□ 539 Neal Heaton	.04	.02	.01
□ 540 Danny Tartabull	.10	.05	.01
□ 541 Pat Perry	.04	.02	.01
□ 542 Darren Daulton	.07	.03	.01
□ 543 Nelson Liriano	.04	.02	.01
□ 544 Dennis Boyd	.04	.02	.01
□ 545 Kevin McReynolds	.07	.03	.01
□ 546 Kevin Hickey	.04	.02	.01
□ 547 Jack Howell	.04	.02	.01
□ 548 Pat Clements	.04	.02	.01
□ 549 Don Zimmer MG	.04	.02	.01
□ 550 Julio Franco	.07	.03	.01
□ 551 Tim Crews	.04	.02	.01
□ 552 Mike(Miss.) Smith	.04	.02	.01
□ 553 Scott Scudder UER (Cedar Rap1ds)	.04	.02	.01
□ 554 Jay Buhner	.07	.03	.01
□ 555 Jack Morris	.10	.05	.01
□ 556 Gene Larkin	.04	.02	.01
□ 557 Jeff Innis	.04	.02	.01
□ 558 Rafael Ramirez	.04	.02	.01
□ 559 Andy McGaffigan	.04	.02	.01
□ 560 Steve Sax	.07	.03	.01
□ 561 Ken Dayley	.04	.02	.01
□ 562 Chad Kreuter	.04	.02	.01
□ 563 Alex Sanchez	.04	.02	.01
□ 564 Tyler Houston FDP	.10	.05	.01
□ 565 Scott Fletcher	.04	.02	.01
□ 566 Mark Knudson	.04	.02	.01
□ 567 Ron Gant	.25	.11	.03
□ 568 John Smiley	.07	.03	.01
□ 569 Ivan Calderon	.04	.02	.01
□ 570 Cal Ripken	.40	.18	.05
□ 571 Brett Butler	.07	.03	.01
□ 572 Greg A. Harris	.04	.02	.01
□ 573 Danny Heep	.04	.02	.01
□ 574 Bill Swift	.07	.03	.01
□ 575 Lance Parrish	.07	.03	.01
□ 576 Mike Dyer	.04	.02	.01
□ 577 Charlie Hayes	.12	.05	.02

☐ 578 Joe Magrane	.04	.02	.01
☐ 579 Art Howe MG	.04	.02	.01
☐ 580 Joe Carter	.20	.09	.03
☐ 581 Ken Griffey Sr.	.07	.03	.01
☐ 582 Rick Honeycutt	.04	.02	.01
☐ 583 Bruce Benedict	.04	.02	.01
☐ 584 Phil Stephenson	.04	.02	.01
☐ 585 Kal Daniels	.04	.02	.01
☐ 586 Edwin Nunez	.04	.02	.01
☐ 587 Lance Johnson	.07	.03	.01
☐ 588 Rick Rhoden	.04	.02	.01
☐ 589 Mike Aldrete	.04	.02	.01
☐ 590 Ozzie Smith	.12	.05	.02
☐ 591 Todd Stottlemyre	.04	.02	.01
☐ 592 R.J. Reynolds	.04	.02	.01
☐ 593 Scott Bradley	.04	.02	.01
☐ 594 Luis Sojo	.15	.07	.02
☐ 595 Greg Swindell	.07	.03	.01
☐ 596 Jose DeJesus	.04	.02	.01
☐ 597 Chris Bosio	.04	.02	.01
☐ 598 Brady Anderson	.12	.05	.02
☐ 599 Frank Williams	.04	.02	.01
☐ 600 Darryl Strawberry	.20	.09	.03
☐ 601 Luis Rivera	.04	.02	.01
☐ 602 Scott Garrelts	.04	.02	.01
☐ 603 Tony Armas	.04	.02	.01
☐ 604 Ron Robinson	.04	.02	.01
☐ 605 Mike Scioscia	.04	.02	.01
☐ 606 Storm Davis	.04	.02	.01
☐ 607 Steve Jeltz	.04	.02	.01
☐ 608 Eric Anthony	.30	.14	.04
☐ 609 Sparky Anderson MG	.04	.02	.01
☐ 610 Pedro Guerrero	.07	.03	.01
☐ 611 Walt Terrell	.04	.02	.01
☐ 612 Dave Gallagher	.04	.02	.01
☐ 613 Jeff Pico	.04	.02	.01
☐ 614 Nelson Santovenia	.04	.02	.01
☐ 615 Rob Deer	.07	.03	.01
☐ 616 Brian Holman	.04	.02	.01
☐ 617 Geronimo Berroa	.04	.02	.01
☐ 618 Ed Whitson	.04	.02	.01
☐ 619 Rob Ducey	.04	.02	.01
☐ 620 Tony Castillo	.04	.02	.01
☐ 621 Melido Perez	.07	.03	.01
☐ 622 Sid Bream	.04	.02	.01
☐ 623 Jim Corsi	.04	.02	.01
☐ 624 Darrin Jackson	.07	.03	.01
☐ 625 Roger McDowell	.04	.02	.01
☐ 626 Bob Melvin	.04	.02	.01
☐ 627 Jose Rijo	.07	.03	.01
☐ 628 Candy Maldonado	.04	.02	.01
☐ 629 Eric Hetzel	.04	.02	.01
☐ 630 Gary Gaetti	.04	.02	.01
☐ 631 John Wetteland	.15	.07	.02
☐ 632 Scott Lusader	.04	.02	.01
☐ 633 Dennis Cook	.04	.02	.01
☐ 634 Luis Polonia	.07	.03	.01
☐ 635 Brian Downing	.04	.02	.01
☐ 636 Jesse Orosco	.04	.02	.01
☐ 637 Craig Reynolds	.04	.02	.01
☐ 638 Jeff Montgomery	.07	.03	.01
☐ 639 Tony LaRussa MG	.04	.02	.01
☐ 640 Rick Sutcliffe	.07	.03	.01
☐ 641 Doug Strange	.10	.05	.01
☐ 642 Jack Armstrong	.07	.03	.01
☐ 643 Alfredo Griffin	.04	.02	.01
☐ 644 Paul Assenmacher	.04	.02	.01
☐ 645 Jose Oquendo	.04	.02	.01
☐ 646 Checklist 5	.05	.01	.00
☐ 647 Rex Hudler	.04	.02	.01
☐ 648 Jim Clancy	.04	.02	.01
☐ 649 Dan Murphy	.10	.05	.01
☐ 650 Mike Witt	.04	.02	.01
☐ 651 Rafael Santana	.04	.02	.01
☐ 652 Mike Boddicker	.04	.02	.01
☐ 653 John Moses	.04	.02	.01
☐ 654 Paul Coleman FDP	.12	.05	.02
☐ 655 Gregg Olson	.10	.05	.01
☐ 656 Mackey Sasser	.04	.02	.01
☐ 657 Terry Mulholland	.07	.03	.01
☐ 658 Donell Nixon	.04	.02	.01
☐ 659 Greg Cadaret	.04	.02	.01
☐ 660 Vince Coleman	.07	.03	.01
☐ 661 Dick Howser TBC'85 UER (Seaver's 300th on 7/11/85, should be 8/4/85)	.05	.02	.01
☐ 662 Mike Schmidt TBC'80	.10	.05	.01
☐ 663 Fred Lynn TBC'75	.05	.02	.01
☐ 664 Johnny Bench TBC'70	.08	.04	.01
☐ 665 Sandy Koufax TBC'65	.08	.04	.01
☐ 666 Brian Fisher	.04	.02	.01
☐ 667 Curt Wilkerson	.04	.02	.01
☐ 668 Joe Oliver	.10	.05	.01
☐ 669 Tom Lasorda MG	.07	.03	.01
☐ 670 Dennis Eckersley	.12	.05	.02
☐ 671 Bob Boone	.07	.03	.01
☐ 672 Roy Smith	.04	.02	.01
☐ 673 Joey Meyer	.04	.02	.01
☐ 674 Spike Owen	.04	.02	.01
☐ 675 Jim Abbott	.20	.09	.03
☐ 676 Randy Kutcher	.04	.02	.01
☐ 677 Jay Tibbs	.04	.02	.01
☐ 678 Kirt Manwaring UER ('88 Phoenix stats repeated)	.04	.02	.01
☐ 679 Gary Ward	.04	.02	.01
☐ 680 Howard Johnson	.07	.03	.01
☐ 681 Mike Schooler	.04	.02	.01
☐ 682 Dann Bilardello	.04	.02	.01
☐ 683 Kenny Rogers	.04	.02	.01
☐ 684 Julio Machado	.04	.02	.01
☐ 685 Tony Fernandez	.07	.03	.01
☐ 686 Carmelo Martinez	.04	.02	.01
☐ 687 Tim Birtsas	.04	.02	.01
☐ 688 Milt Thompson	.04	.02	.01
☐ 689 Rich Yett	.04	.02	.01
☐ 690 Mark McGwire	.30	.14	.04
☐ 691 Chuck Cary	.04	.02	.01
☐ 692 Sammy Sosa	.15	.07	.02
☐ 693 Calvin Schiraldi	.04	.02	.01
☐ 694 Mike Stanton	.15	.07	.02
☐ 695 Tom Henke	.07	.03	.01
☐ 696 B.J. Surhoff	.04	.02	.01
☐ 697 Mike Davis	.04	.02	.01
☐ 698 Omar Vizquel	.07	.03	.01
☐ 699 Jim Leyland MG	.04	.02	.01
☐ 700 Kirby Puckett	.30	.14	.04
☐ 701 Bernie Williams	.30	.14	.04
☐ 702 Tony Phillips	.04	.02	.01
☐ 703 Jeff Brantley	.04	.02	.01
☐ 704 Chip Hale	.04	.02	.01
☐ 705 Claudell Washington	.04	.02	.01
☐ 706 Geno Petralli	.04	.02	.01
☐ 707 Luis Aquino	.04	.02	.01
☐ 708 Larry Sheets	.04	.02	.01
☐ 709 Juan Berenguer	.04	.02	.01
☐ 710 Von Hayes	.04	.02	.01
☐ 711 Rick Aguilera	.07	.03	.01
☐ 712 Todd Benzinger	.04	.02	.01
☐ 713 Tim Drummond	.04	.02	.01
☐ 714 Marquis Grissom	.60	.25	.08
☐ 715 Greg Maddux	.20	.09	.03
☐ 716 Steve Balboni	.04	.02	.01
☐ 717 Ron Karkovice	.04	.02	.01
☐ 718 Gary Sheffield	.50	.23	.06
☐ 719 Wally Whitehurst	.04	.02	.01
☐ 720 Andres Galarraga	.04	.02	.01
☐ 721 Lee Mazzilli	.04	.02	.01
☐ 722 Felix Fermin	.04	.02	.01
☐ 723 Jeff D. Robinson	.04	.02	.01
☐ 724 Juan Bell	.04	.02	.01
☐ 725 Terry Pendleton	.10	.05	.01
☐ 726 Gene Nelson	.04	.02	.01
☐ 727 Pat Tabler	.04	.02	.01
☐ 728 Jim Acker	.04	.02	.01
☐ 729 Bobby Valentine MG	.04	.02	.01
☐ 730 Tony Gwynn	.20	.09	.03
☐ 731 Don Carman	.04	.02	.01
☐ 732 Ernest Riles	.04	.02	.01
☐ 733 John Dopson	.04	.02	.01
☐ 734 Kevin Elster	.04	.02	.01
☐ 735 Charlie Hough	.04	.02	.01
☐ 736 Rick Dempsey	.04	.02	.01
☐ 737 Chris Sabo	.07	.03	.01
☐ 738 Gene Harris	.04	.02	.01
☐ 739 Dale Sveum	.04	.02	.01
☐ 740 Jesse Barfield	.04	.02	.01
☐ 741 Steve Wilson	.04	.02	.01
☐ 742 Ernie Whitt	.04	.02	.01
☐ 743 Tom Candiotti	.04	.02	.01
☐ 744 Kelly Mann	.04	.02	.01
☐ 745 Hubie Brooks	.04	.02	.01
☐ 746 Dave Smith	.04	.02	.01
☐ 747 Randy Bush	.04	.02	.01
☐ 748 Doyle Alexander	.04	.02	.01
☐ 749 Mark Parent UER ('87 BA .80, should be .080)	.04	.02	.01
☐ 750 Dale Murphy	.10	.05	.01
☐ 751 Steve Lyons	.04	.02	.01
☐ 752 Tom Gordon	.07	.03	.01
☐ 753 Chris Speier	.04	.02	.01
☐ 754 Bob Walk	.04	.02	.01
☐ 755 Rafael Palmeiro	.10	.05	.01
☐ 756 Ken Howell	.04	.02	.01

☐ 757 Larry Walker	.90	.40	.11
☐ 758 Mark Thurmond	.04	.02	.01
☐ 759 Tom Trebelhorn MG	.04	.02	.01
☐ 760 Wade Boggs	.20	.09	.03
☐ 761 Mike Jackson	.04	.02	.01
☐ 762 Doug Dascenzo	.04	.02	.01
☐ 763 Dennis Martinez	.07	.03	.01
☐ 764 Tim Teufel	.04	.02	.01
☐ 765 Chili Davis	.07	.03	.01
☐ 766 Brian Meyer	.04	.02	.01
☐ 767 Tracy Jones	.04	.02	.01
☐ 768 Chuck Crim	.04	.02	.01
☐ 769 Greg Hibbard	.20	.09	.03
☐ 770 Cory Snyder	.04	.02	.01
☐ 771 Pete Smith	.07	.03	.01
☐ 772 Jeff Reed	.04	.02	.01
☐ 773 Dave Leiper	.04	.02	.01
☐ 774 Ben McDonald	.50	.23	.06
☐ 775 Andy Van Slyke	.10	.05	.01
☐ 776 Charlie Leibrandt	.04	.02	.01
☐ 777 Tim Laudner	.04	.02	.01
☐ 778 Mike Jeffcoat	.04	.02	.01
☐ 779 Lloyd Moseby	.04	.02	.01
☐ 780 Orel Hershiser	.07	.03	.01
☐ 781 Mario Diaz	.04	.02	.01
☐ 782 Jose Alvarez	.04	.02	.01
☐ 783 Checklist 6	.05	.01	.00
☐ 784 Scott Bailes	.04	.02	.01
☐ 785 Jim Rice	.07	.03	.01
☐ 786 Eric King	.04	.02	.01
☐ 787 Rene Gonzales	.04	.02	.01
☐ 788 Frank DiPino	.04	.02	.01
☐ 789 John Wathan MG	.04	.02	.01
☐ 790 Gary Carter	.07	.03	.01
☐ 791 Alvaro Espinoza	.04	.02	.01
☐ 792 Gerald Perry	.04	.02	.01

1990 Topps All-Star Glossy 22

The 1990 Topps Glossy All-Star set contains 22 standard-size (2 1/2" by 3 1/2") glossy cards. The front and back borders are white, and other design elements are red, blue and yellow. This set is almost identical to previous year sets of the same name. One card was included in each 1990 Topps rack pack. The players selected for the set were the starters, managers, and honorary captains in the previous year's All-Star Game.

	MT	EX-MT	VG
COMPLETE SET (22)	3.00	1.35	.40
COMMON PLAYER (1-22)	.10	.05	.01
☐ 1 Tom Lasorda MG	.10	.05	.01
☐ 2 Will Clark	.50	.23	.06
☐ 3 Ryne Sandberg	.60	.25	.08
☐ 4 Howard Johnson	.20	.09	.03
☐ 5 Ozzie Smith	.25	.11	.03
☐ 6 Kevin Mitchell	.25	.11	.03
☐ 7 Eric Davis	.20	.09	.03
☐ 8 Tony Gwynn	.35	.16	.04
☐ 9 Benito Santiago	.15	.07	.02
☐ 10 Rick Reuschel	.10	.05	.01
☐ 11 Don Drysdale CAPT	.15	.07	.02
☐ 12 Tony LaRussa MG	.10	.05	.01
☐ 13 Mark McGwire	.35	.16	.04
☐ 14 Julio Franco	.15	.07	.02
☐ 15 Wade Boggs	.35	.16	.04
☐ 16 Cal Ripken	.60	.25	.08
☐ 17 Bo Jackson	.40	.18	.05
☐ 18 Kirby Puckett	.50	.23	.06
☐ 19 Ruben Sierra	.35	.16	.04
☐ 20 Terry Steinbach	.10	.05	.01
☐ 21 Dave Stewart	.10	.05	.01
☐ 22 Carl Yastrzemski CAPT	.20	.09	.03

1990 Topps Ames All-Stars

The 1990 Topps Ames All-Stars set was issued by Topps for the Ames department stores for the second straight year. This standard-size (2 1/2" by 3 1/2") set featured 33 of the leading hitters active in major league baseball. This set includes an early card of Keith Hernandez as a Cleveland Indian.

	MT	EX-MT	VG
COMPLETE SET (33)	4.00	1.80	.50
COMMON PLAYER (1-33)	.10	.05	.01
☐ 1 Dave Winfield	.30	.14	.04
☐ 2 George Brett	.40	.18	.05
☐ 3 Jim Rice	.15	.07	.02
☐ 4 Dwight Evans	.15	.07	.02
☐ 5 Robin Yount	.40	.18	.05
☐ 6 Dave Parker	.15	.07	.02
☐ 7 Eddie Murray	.30	.14	.04
☐ 8 Keith Hernandez	.15	.07	.02
☐ 9 Andre Dawson	.30	.14	.04
☐ 10 Fred Lynn	.15	.07	.02
☐ 11 Dale Murphy	.25	.11	.03
☐ 12 Jack Clark	.15	.07	.02
☐ 13 Rickey Henderson	.50	.23	.06
☐ 14 Paul Molitor	.15	.07	.02
☐ 15 Cal Ripken	.60	.25	.08
☐ 16 Wade Boggs	.40	.18	.05
☐ 17 Tim Raines	.15	.07	.02
☐ 18 Don Mattingly	.50	.23	.06
☐ 19 Kent Hrbek	.15	.07	.02
☐ 20 Kirk Gibson	.15	.07	.02
☐ 21 Julio Franco	.15	.07	.02
☐ 22 George Bell	.15	.07	.02
☐ 23 Darryl Strawberry	.40	.18	.05
☐ 24 Kirby Puckett	.50	.23	.06
☐ 25 Juan Samuel	.10	.05	.01
☐ 26 Alvin Davis	.10	.05	.01
☐ 27 Joe Carter	.30	.14	.04
☐ 28 Eric Davis	.20	.09	.03
☐ 29 Jose Canseco	.50	.23	.06
☐ 30 Wally Joyner	.20	.09	.03
☐ 31 Will Clark	.50	.23	.06
☐ 32 Ruben Sierra	.40	.18	.05
☐ 33 Danny Tartabull	.20	.09	.03

1990 Topps Big

The 1990 Topps Big set contains 330 cards each measuring an slightly over-sized 2 5/8" by 3 3/4". In 1989 Topps had issued two oversize sets (Bigs and Bowmans), but in 1990

only the Topps Big were issued by Topps as an oversize set. The set was issued in three series of 110 cards.

	MT	EX-MT	VG
COMPLETE SET (330)	30.00	13.50	3.80
COMMON PLAYER (1-110)	.05	.02	.01
COMMON PLAYER (111-220)	.05	.02	.01
COMMON PLAYER (221-330)	.06	.03	.01

	Player	MT	EX-MT	VG
☐ 1	Dwight Evans	.10	.05	.01
☐ 2	Kirby Puckett	.50	.23	.06
☐ 3	Kevin Gross	.05	.02	.01
☐ 4	Ron Hassey	.05	.02	.01
☐ 5	Lloyd McClendon	.05	.02	.01
☐ 6	Bo Jackson	.60	.25	.08
☐ 7	Lonnie Smith	.05	.02	.01
☐ 8	Alvaro Espinoza	.05	.02	.01
☐ 9	Roberto Alomar	.60	.25	.08
☐ 10	Glenn Braggs	.05	.02	.01
☐ 11	David Cone	.20	.09	.03
☐ 12	Claudell Washington	.05	.02	.01
☐ 13	Pedro Guerrero	.08	.04	.01
☐ 14	Todd Benzinger	.05	.02	.01
☐ 15	Jeff Russell	.05	.02	.01
☐ 16	Terry Kennedy	.05	.02	.01
☐ 17	Kelly Gruber	.10	.05	.01
☐ 18	Alfredo Griffin	.05	.02	.01
☐ 19	Mark Grace	.35	.16	.04
☐ 20	Dave Winfield	.30	.14	.04
☐ 21	Bret Saberhagen	.12	.05	.02
☐ 22	Roger Clemens	.75	.35	.09
☐ 23	Bob Walk	.05	.02	.01
☐ 24	Dave Magadan	.08	.04	.01
☐ 25	Spike Owen	.05	.02	.01
☐ 26	Jody Davis	.05	.02	.01
☐ 27	Kent Hrbek	.08	.04	.01
☐ 28	Mark McGwire	.45	.20	.06
☐ 29	Eddie Murray	.30	.14	.04
☐ 30	Paul O'Neill	.08	.04	.01
☐ 31	Jose DeLeon	.05	.02	.01
☐ 32	Steve Lyons	.05	.02	.01
☐ 33	Dan Plesac	.05	.02	.01
☐ 34	Jack Howell	.05	.02	.01
☐ 35	Greg Briley	.05	.02	.01
☐ 36	Andy Hawkins	.05	.02	.01
☐ 37	Cecil Espy	.05	.02	.01
☐ 38	Rick Sutcliffe	.08	.04	.01
☐ 39	Jack Clark	.08	.04	.01
☐ 40	Dale Murphy	.20	.09	.03
☐ 41	Mike Henneman	.08	.04	.01
☐ 42	Rick Honeycutt	.05	.02	.01
☐ 43	Willie Randolph	.08	.04	.01
☐ 44	Marty Barrett	.05	.02	.01
☐ 45	Willie Wilson	.08	.04	.01
☐ 46	Wallace Johnson	.05	.02	.01
☐ 47	Greg Brock	.05	.02	.01
☐ 48	Tom Browning	.08	.04	.01
☐ 49	Gerald Young	.05	.02	.01
☐ 50	Dennis Eckersley	.15	.07	.02
☐ 51	Scott Garrelts	.05	.02	.01
☐ 52	Gary Redus	.05	.02	.01
☐ 53	Al Newman	.05	.02	.01
☐ 54	Daryl Boston	.05	.02	.01
☐ 55	Ron Oester	.05	.02	.01
☐ 56	Danny Tartabull	.20	.09	.03
☐ 57	Gregg Jefferies	.25	.11	.03
☐ 58	Tom Foley	.05	.02	.01
☐ 59	Robin Yount	.40	.18	.05
☐ 60	Pat Borders	.12	.05	.02
☐ 61	Mike Greenwell	.20	.09	.03
☐ 62	Shawon Dunston	.08	.04	.01
☐ 63	Steve Buechele	.05	.02	.01
☐ 64	Dave Stewart	.10	.05	.01
☐ 65	Jose Oquendo	.05	.02	.01
☐ 66	Ron Gant	.30	.14	.04
☐ 67	Mike Scioscia	.05	.02	.01
☐ 68	Randy Velarde	.05	.02	.01
☐ 69	Von Hayes	.05	.02	.01
☐ 70	Tim Wallach	.05	.02	.01
☐ 71	Eric Show	.05	.02	.01
☐ 72	Eric Davis	.20	.09	.03
☐ 73	Mike Gallego	.05	.02	.01
☐ 74	Rob Deer	.08	.04	.01
☐ 75	Ryne Sandberg	.75	.35	.09
☐ 76	Kevin Seitzer	.08	.04	.01
☐ 77	Wade Boggs	.45	.20	.06
☐ 78	Greg Gagne	.05	.02	.01
☐ 79	John Smiley	.08	.04	.01
☐ 80	Ivan Calderon	.08	.04	.01
☐ 81	Pete Incaviglia	.08	.04	.01
☐ 82	Orel Hershiser	.12	.05	.02
☐ 83	Carney Lansford	.08	.04	.01
☐ 84	Mike Fitzgerald	.05	.02	.01
☐ 85	Don Mattingly	.60	.25	.08
☐ 86	Chet Lemon	.05	.02	.01
☐ 87	Rolando Roomes	.05	.02	.01
☐ 88	Billy Spiers	.05	.02	.01
☐ 89	Pat Tabler	.05	.02	.01
☐ 90	Danny Heep	.05	.02	.01
☐ 91	Andre Dawson	.30	.14	.04
☐ 92	Randy Bush	.05	.02	.01
☐ 93	Tony Gwynn	.40	.18	.05
☐ 94	Tom Brunansky	.08	.04	.01
☐ 95	Johnny Ray	.05	.02	.01
☐ 96	Matt Williams	.25	.11	.03
☐ 97	Barry Lyons	.05	.02	.01
☐ 98	Jeff Hamilton	.05	.02	.01
☐ 99	Tom Glavine	.35	.16	.04
☐ 100	Ken Griffey Sr.	.10	.05	.01
☐ 101	Tom Henke	.08	.04	.01
☐ 102	Dave Righetti	.08	.04	.01
☐ 103	Paul Molitor	.15	.07	.02
☐ 104	Mike LaValliere	.05	.02	.01
☐ 105	Frank White	.08	.04	.01
☐ 106	Bob Welch	.10	.05	.01
☐ 107	Ellis Burks	.15	.07	.02
☐ 108	Andres Galarraga	.08	.04	.01
☐ 109	Mitch Williams	.05	.02	.01
☐ 110	Checklist 1-110	.08	.00	.00
☐ 111	Craig Biggio	.15	.07	.02
☐ 112	Dave Stieb	.08	.04	.01
☐ 113	Ron Darling	.08	.04	.01
☐ 114	Bert Blyleven	.10	.05	.01
☐ 115	Dickie Thon	.05	.02	.01
☐ 116	Carlos Martinez	.05	.02	.01
☐ 117	Jeff King	.08	.04	.01
☐ 118	Terry Steinbach	.08	.04	.01
☐ 119	Frank Tanana	.08	.04	.01
☐ 120	Mark Lemke	.05	.02	.01
☐ 121	Chris Sabo	.20	.09	.03
☐ 122	Glenn Davis	.15	.07	.02
☐ 123	Mel Hall	.08	.04	.01
☐ 124	Jim Gantner	.08	.04	.01
☐ 125	Benito Santiago	.20	.09	.03
☐ 126	Milt Thompson	.08	.04	.01
☐ 127	Rafael Palmeiro	.20	.09	.03
☐ 128	Barry Bonds	.50	.23	.06
☐ 129	Mike Bielecki	.05	.02	.01
☐ 130	Lou Whitaker	.12	.05	.02
☐ 131	Bob Ojeda	.05	.02	.01
☐ 132	Dion James	.05	.02	.01
☐ 133	Dennis Martinez	.08	.04	.01
☐ 134	Fred McGriff	.25	.11	.03
☐ 135	Terry Pendleton	.15	.07	.02
☐ 136	Pat Combs	.10	.05	.01
☐ 137	Kevin Mitchell	.20	.09	.03
☐ 138	Marquis Grissom	.50	.23	.06
☐ 139	Chris Bosio	.10	.05	.01
☐ 140	Omar Vizquel	.10	.05	.01
☐ 141	Steve Sax	.10	.05	.01
☐ 142	Nelson Liriano	.05	.02	.01
☐ 143	Kevin Elster	.05	.02	.01
☐ 144	Dan Pasqua	.05	.02	.01
☐ 145	Dave Smith	.05	.02	.01
☐ 146	Craig Worthington	.05	.02	.01
☐ 147	Dan Gladden	.05	.02	.01
☐ 148	Oddibe McDowell	.05	.02	.01
☐ 149	Bip Roberts	.10	.05	.01
☐ 150	Randy Ready	.05	.02	.01
☐ 151	Dwight Smith	.08	.04	.01
☐ 152	Eddie Whitson	.05	.02	.01
☐ 153	George Bell	.15	.07	.02
☐ 154	Tim Raines	.12	.05	.02
☐ 155	Sid Fernandez	.08	.04	.01
☐ 156	Henry Cotto	.05	.02	.01
☐ 157	Harold Baines	.08	.04	.01

□ 158 Willie McGee	.10	.05	.01
□ 159 Bill Doran	.05	.02	.01
□ 160 Steve Balboni	.05	.02	.01
□ 161 Pete Smith	.20	.09	.03
□ 162 Frank Viola	.10	.05	.01
□ 163 Gary Sheffield	.50	.23	.06
□ 164 Bill Landrum	.05	.02	.01
□ 165 Tony Fernandez	.08	.04	.01
□ 166 Mike Heath	.05	.02	.01
□ 167 Jody Reed	.08	.04	.01
□ 168 Wally Joyner	.12	.05	.02
□ 169 Robby Thompson	.05	.02	.01
□ 170 Ken Caminiti	.10	.05	.01
□ 171 Nolan Ryan	1.50	.65	.19
□ 172 Ricky Jordan	.10	.05	.01
□ 173 Lance Blankenship	.05	.02	.01
□ 174 Dwight Gooden	.20	.09	.03
□ 175 Ruben Sierra	.40	.18	.05
□ 176 Carlton Fisk	.30	.14	.04
□ 177 Garry Templeton	.05	.02	.01
□ 178 Mike Devereaux	.10	.05	.01
□ 179 Mookie Wilson	.08	.04	.01
□ 180 Jeff Blauser	.10	.05	.01
□ 181 Scott Bradley	.05	.02	.01
□ 182 Luis Salazar	.05	.02	.01
□ 183 Rafael Ramirez	.05	.02	.01
□ 184 Vince Coleman	.12	.05	.02
□ 185 Doug Drabek	.12	.05	.02
□ 186 Darryl Strawberry	.40	.18	.05
□ 187 Tim Burke	.05	.02	.01
□ 188 Jesse Barfield	.08	.04	.01
□ 189 Barry Larkin	.15	.07	.02
□ 190 Alan Trammell	.15	.07	.02
□ 191 Steve Lake	.05	.02	.01
□ 192 Derek Lilliquist	.05	.02	.01
□ 193 Don Robinson	.05	.02	.01
□ 194 Kevin McReynolds	.08	.04	.01
□ 195 Melido Perez	.10	.05	.01
□ 196 Jose Lind	.05	.02	.01
□ 197 Eric Anthony	.20	.09	.03
□ 198 B.J. Surhoff	.08	.04	.01
□ 199 John Olerud	.60	.25	.08
□ 200 Mike Moore	.08	.04	.01
□ 201 Mark Gubicza	.08	.04	.01
□ 202 Phil Bradley	.05	.02	.01
□ 203 Ozzie Smith	.25	.11	.03
□ 204 Greg Maddux	.15	.07	.02
□ 205 Julio Franco	.10	.05	.01
□ 206 Tom Herr	.05	.02	.01
□ 207 Scott Fletcher	.05	.02	.01
□ 208 Bobby Bonilla	.25	.11	.03
□ 209 Bob Geren	.05	.02	.01
□ 210 Junior Felix	.10	.05	.01
□ 211 Dick Schofield	.05	.02	.01
□ 212 Jim Deshaies	.05	.02	.01
□ 213 Jose Uribe	.05	.02	.01
□ 214 John Kruk	.12	.05	.02
□ 215 Ozzie Guillen	.08	.04	.01
□ 216 Howard Johnson	.12	.05	.02
□ 217 Andy Van Slyke	.15	.07	.02
□ 218 Tim Laudner	.05	.02	.01
□ 219 Manny Lee	.05	.02	.01
□ 220 Checklist 111-220	.08	.00	.00
□ 221 Cory Snyder	.10	.05	.01
□ 222 Billy Hatcher	.06	.03	.01
□ 223 Bud Black	.06	.03	.01
□ 224 Will Clark	.75	.35	.09
□ 225 Kevin Tapani	.15	.07	.02
□ 226 Mike Pagliarulo	.06	.03	.01
□ 227 Dave Parker	.12	.05	.02
□ 228 Ben McDonald	.50	.23	.06
□ 229 Carlos Baerga	.75	.35	.09
□ 230 Roger McDowell	.06	.03	.01
□ 231 Delino DeShields	.60	.25	.08
□ 232 Mark Langston	.10	.05	.01
□ 233 Wally Backman	.06	.03	.01
□ 234 Jim Eisenreich	.06	.03	.01
□ 235 Mike Schooler	.06	.03	.01
□ 236 Kevin Bass	.06	.03	.01
□ 237 John Farrell	.06	.03	.01
□ 238 Kal Daniels	.10	.05	.01
□ 239 Tony Phillips	.10	.05	.01
□ 240 Todd Stottlemyre	.10	.05	.01
□ 241 Greg Olson	.10	.05	.01
□ 242 Charlie Hough	.06	.03	.01
□ 243 Mariano Duncan	.06	.03	.01
□ 244 Bill Ripken	.06	.03	.01
□ 245 Joe Carter	.35	.16	.04
□ 246 Tim Belcher	.15	.07	.02
□ 247 Roberto Kelly	.25	.11	.03
□ 248 Candy Maldonado	.10	.05	.01
□ 249 Mike Scott	.10	.05	.01
□ 250 Ken Griffey Jr.	3.00	1.35	.40
□ 251 Nick Esasky	.06	.03	.01
□ 252 Tom Gordon	.10	.05	.01
□ 253 John Tudor	.06	.03	.01
□ 254 Gary Gaetti	.06	.03	.01
□ 255 Neal Heaton	.06	.03	.01
□ 256 Jerry Browne	.06	.03	.01
□ 257 Jose Rijo	.12	.05	.02
□ 258 Mike Boddicker	.06	.03	.01
□ 259 Brett Butler	.10	.05	.01
□ 260 Andy Benes	.20	.09	.03
□ 261 Kevin Brown	.10	.05	.01
□ 262 Hubie Brooks	.06	.03	.01
□ 263 Randy Milligan	.06	.03	.01
□ 264 John Franco	.10	.05	.01
□ 265 Sandy Alomar Jr.	.15	.07	.02
□ 266 Dave Valle	.06	.03	.01
□ 267 Jerome Walton	.10	.05	.01
□ 268 Bob Boone	.10	.05	.01
□ 269 Ken Howell	.06	.03	.01
□ 270 Jose Canseco	.75	.35	.09
□ 271 Joe Magrane	.06	.03	.01
□ 272 Brian DuBois	.06	.03	.01
□ 273 Carlos Quintana	.10	.05	.01
□ 274 Lance Johnson	.10	.05	.01
□ 275 Steve Bedrosian	.06	.03	.01
□ 276 Brook Jacoby	.06	.03	.01
□ 277 Fred Lynn UER (Pirates logo on card front)	.12	.05	.02
□ 278 Jeff Ballard	.06	.03	.01
□ 279 Otis Nixon	.12	.05	.02
□ 280 Chili Davis	.10	.05	.01
□ 281 Joe Oliver	.10	.05	.01
□ 282 Brian Holman	.06	.03	.01
□ 283 Juan Samuel	.06	.03	.01
□ 284 Rick Aguilera	.10	.05	.01
□ 285 Jeff Reardon	.12	.05	.02
□ 286 Sammy Sosa	.25	.11	.03
□ 287 Carmelo Martinez	.10	.05	.01
□ 288 Greg Swindell	.10	.05	.01
□ 289 Erik Hanson	.10	.05	.01
□ 290 Tony Pena	.06	.03	.01
□ 291 Pascual Perez	.06	.03	.01
□ 292 Rickey Henderson	.60	.25	.08
□ 293 Kurt Stillwell	.06	.03	.01
□ 294 Todd Zeile	.20	.09	.03
□ 295 Bobby Thigpen	.10	.05	.01
□ 296 Larry Walker	.75	.35	.09
□ 297 Rob Murphy	.06	.03	.01
□ 298 Mitch Webster	.06	.03	.01
□ 299 Devon White	.10	.05	.01
□ 300 Len Dykstra	.12	.05	.02
□ 301 Keith Hernandez	.12	.05	.02
□ 302 Gene Larkin	.06	.03	.01
□ 303 Jeffrey Leonard	.06	.03	.01
□ 304 Jim Presley	.06	.03	.01
□ 305 Lloyd Moseby	.06	.03	.01
□ 306 John Smoltz	.20	.09	.03
□ 307 Sam Horn	.06	.03	.01
□ 308 Greg Litton	.06	.03	.01
□ 309 Dave Henderson	.10	.05	.01
□ 310 Mark McLemore	.06	.03	.01
□ 311 Gary Pettis	.06	.03	.01
□ 312 Mark Davis	.06	.03	.01
□ 313 Cecil Fielder	.50	.23	.06
□ 314 Jack Armstrong	.12	.05	.02
□ 315 Alvin Davis	.06	.03	.01
□ 316 Doug Jones	.06	.03	.01
□ 317 Eric Yelding	.06	.03	.01
□ 318 Joe Orsulak	.06	.03	.01
□ 319 Chuck Finley	.06	.03	.01
□ 320 Glenn Wilson	.06	.03	.01
□ 321 Harold Reynolds	.06	.03	.01
□ 322 Teddy Higuera	.06	.03	.01
□ 323 Lance Parrish	.10	.05	.01
□ 324 Bruce Hurst	.10	.05	.01
□ 325 Dave West	.06	.03	.01
□ 326 Kirk Gibson	.12	.05	.02
□ 327 Cal Ripken	.75	.35	.09
□ 328 Rick Reuschel	.06	.03	.01
□ 329 Jim Abbott	.50	.23	.06
□ 330 Checklist 221-330	.10	.01	.00

1990 Topps Debut '89

The 1990 Topps Major League Debut Set is a 152-card, standard-size (2 1/2" by 3 1/2") set arranged in alphabetical order by player's name. Each card front features the date of

the player's first major league appearance. Strangely enough, even though the set commemorates the 1989 Major League debuts, the set was not issued until the 1990 season had almost begun.

	MT	EX-MT	VG
COMPLETE SET (152)	15.00	6.75	1.90
COMMON PLAYER (1-152)	.05	.02	.01
☐ 1 Jim Abbott	.75	.35	.09
☐ 2 Beau Allred	.10	.05	.01
☐ 3 Wilson Alvarez	.10	.05	.01
☐ 4 Kent Anderson	.05	.02	.01
☐ 5 Eric Anthony	.30	.14	.04
☐ 6 Kevin Appier	.15	.07	.02
☐ 7 Larry Arndt	.05	.02	.01
☐ 8 John Barfield	.05	.02	.01
☐ 9 Billy Bates	.05	.02	.01
☐ 10 Kevin Batiste	.10	.05	.01
☐ 11 Blaine Beatty	.05	.02	.01
☐ 12 Stan Belinda	.10	.05	.01
☐ 13 Juan Bell	.10	.05	.01
☐ 14 Joey Belle (Now known as Albert)	.75	.35	.09
☐ 15 Andy Benes	.40	.18	.05
☐ 16 Mike Benjamin	.05	.02	.01
☐ 17 Geronimo Berroa	.10	.05	.01
☐ 18 Mike Blowers	.05	.02	.01
☐ 19 Brian Brady	.10	.05	.01
☐ 20 Francisco Cabrera	.15	.07	.02
☐ 21 George Canale	.05	.02	.01
☐ 22 Jose Cano	.05	.02	.01
☐ 23 Steve Carter	.05	.02	.01
☐ 24 Pat Combs	.10	.05	.01
☐ 25 Scott Coolbaugh	.05	.02	.01
☐ 26 Steve Cummings	.05	.02	.01
☐ 27 Pete Dalena	.05	.02	.01
☐ 28 Jeff Datz	.05	.02	.01
☐ 29 Bobby Davidson	.05	.02	.01
☐ 30 Drew Denson	.05	.02	.01
☐ 31 Gary DiSarcina	.10	.05	.01
☐ 32 Brian DuBois	.05	.02	.01
☐ 33 Mike Dyer	.05	.02	.01
☐ 34 Wayne Edwards	.05	.02	.01
☐ 35 Junior Felix	.15	.07	.02
☐ 36 Mike Fetters	.10	.05	.01
☐ 37 Steve Finley	.20	.09	.03
☐ 38 Darrin Fletcher	.10	.05	.01
☐ 39 LaVel Freeman	.10	.05	.01
☐ 40 Steve Frey	.05	.02	.01
☐ 41 Mark Gardner	.05	.02	.01
☐ 42 Joe Girardi	.10	.05	.01
☐ 43 Juan Gonzalez	2.50	1.15	.30
☐ 44 Goose Gozzo	.05	.02	.01
☐ 45 Tommy Greene	.20	.09	.03
☐ 46 Ken Griffey Jr.	4.00	1.80	.50
☐ 47 Jason Grimsley	.10	.05	.01
☐ 48 Marquis Grissom	.60	.25	.08
☐ 49 Mark Guthrie	.05	.02	.01
☐ 50 Chip Hale	.05	.02	.01
☐ 51 Jack Hardy	.05	.02	.01
☐ 52 Gene Harris	.05	.02	.01
☐ 53 Mike Hartley	.05	.02	.01
☐ 54 Scott Hemond	.05	.02	.01
☐ 55 Xavier Hernandez	.05	.02	.01
☐ 56 Eric Hetzel	.05	.02	.01
☐ 57 Greg Hibbard	.10	.05	.01
☐ 58 Mark Higgins	.05	.02	.01
☐ 59 Glenallen Hill	.10	.05	.01
☐ 60 Chris Hoiles	.25	.11	.03
☐ 61 Shawn Holman	.05	.02	.01
☐ 62 Dann Howitt	.10	.05	.01
☐ 63 Mike Huff	.10	.05	.01
☐ 64 Terry Jorgensen	.15	.07	.02
☐ 65 Dave Justice	2.00	.90	.25
☐ 66 Jeff King	.15	.07	.02
☐ 67 Matt Kinzer	.05	.02	.01
☐ 68 Joe Kraemer	.05	.02	.01
☐ 69 Marcus Lawton	.05	.02	.01
☐ 70 Derek Lilliquist	.05	.02	.01
☐ 71 Scott Little	.05	.02	.01
☐ 72 Greg Litton	.05	.02	.01
☐ 73 Rick Luecken	.05	.02	.01
☐ 74 Julio Machado	.10	.05	.01
☐ 75 Tom Magrann	.05	.02	.01
☐ 76 Kelly Mann	.05	.02	.01
☐ 77 Randy McCament	.05	.02	.01
☐ 78 Ben McDonald	.50	.23	.06
☐ 79 Chuck McElroy	.10	.05	.01
☐ 80 Jeff McKnight	.05	.02	.01
☐ 81 Kent Mercker	.20	.09	.03
☐ 82 Matt Merullo	.05	.02	.01
☐ 83 Hensley Meulens	.15	.07	.02
☐ 84 Kevin Mmahat	.10	.05	.01
☐ 85 Mike Munoz	.05	.02	.01
☐ 86 Dan Murphy	.05	.02	.01
☐ 87 Jaime Navarro	.15	.07	.02
☐ 88 Randy Nosek	.05	.02	.01
☐ 89 John Olerud	.75	.35	.09
☐ 90 Steve Olin	.20	.09	.03
☐ 91 Joe Oliver	.10	.05	.01
☐ 92 Francisco Oliveras	.05	.02	.01
☐ 93 Gregg Olson	.25	.11	.03
☐ 94 John Orton	.10	.05	.01
☐ 95 Dean Palmer	.60	.25	.08
☐ 96 Ramon Pena	.05	.02	.01
☐ 97 Jeff Peterek	.05	.02	.01
☐ 98 Marty Pevey	.05	.02	.01
☐ 99 Rusty Richards	.05	.02	.01
☐ 100 Jeff Richardson	.05	.02	.01
☐ 101 Rob Richie	.05	.02	.01
☐ 102 Kevin Ritz	.05	.02	.01
☐ 103 Rosario Rodriguez	.05	.02	.01
☐ 104 Mike Roesler	.05	.02	.01
☐ 105 Kenny Rogers	.05	.02	.01
☐ 106 Bobby Rose	.05	.02	.01
☐ 107 Alex Sanchez	.05	.02	.01
☐ 108 Deion Sanders	.75	.35	.09
☐ 109 Jeff Schaefer	.05	.02	.01
☐ 110 Jeff Schulz	.05	.02	.01
☐ 111 Mike Schwabe	.05	.02	.01
☐ 112 Dick Scott	.05	.02	.01
☐ 113 Scott Scudder	.15	.07	.02
☐ 114 Rudy Seanez	.15	.07	.02
☐ 115 Joe Skalski	.05	.02	.01
☐ 116 Dwight Smith	.10	.05	.01
☐ 117 Greg Smith	.05	.02	.01
☐ 118 Mike Smith	.05	.02	.01
☐ 119 Paul Sorrento	.15	.07	.02
☐ 120 Sammy Sosa	.25	.11	.03
☐ 121 Billy Spiers	.10	.05	.01
☐ 122 Mike Stanton	.10	.05	.01
☐ 123 Phil Stephenson	.05	.02	.01
☐ 124 Doug Strange	.10	.05	.01
☐ 125 Russ Swan	.10	.05	.01
☐ 126 Kevin Tapani	.25	.11	.03
☐ 127 Stu Tate	.10	.05	.01
☐ 128 Greg Vaughn	.35	.16	.04
☐ 129 Robin Ventura	1.50	.65	.19
☐ 130 Randy Veres	.05	.02	.01
☐ 131 Jose Vizcaino	.15	.07	.02
☐ 132 Omar Vizquel	.20	.09	.03
☐ 133 Larry Walker	.75	.35	.09
☐ 134 Jerome Walton	.15	.07	.02
☐ 135 Gary Wayne	.05	.02	.01
☐ 136 Lenny Webster	.10	.05	.01
☐ 137 Mickey Weston	.05	.02	.01
☐ 138 Jeff Wetherby	.05	.02	.01
☐ 139 John Wetteland	.20	.09	.03
☐ 140 Ed Whited	.05	.02	.01
☐ 141 Wally Whitehurst	.10	.05	.01
☐ 142 Kevin Wickander	.05	.02	.01
☐ 143 Dean Wilkins	.05	.02	.01
☐ 144 Dana Williams	.05	.02	.01
☐ 145 Paul Wilmet	.05	.02	.01
☐ 146 Craig Wilson	.10	.05	.01
☐ 147 Matt Winters	.10	.05	.01
☐ 148 Eric Yelding	.05	.02	.01
☐ 149 Clint Zavaras	.10	.05	.01
☐ 150 Todd Zeile	.35	.16	.04
☐ 151 Checklist Card	.08	.00	.00
☐ 152 Checklist Card	.10	.01	.00

1990 Topps Glossy Send-In 60

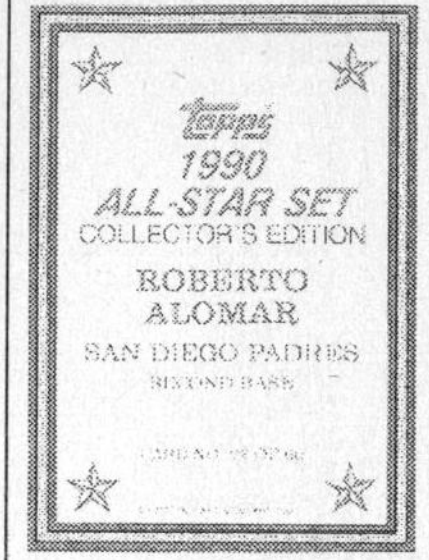

The 1990 Topps Glossy 60 set was issued as a mailaway by Topps for the eighth straight year. This standard-size (2 1/2" by 3 1/2"), 60-card set features two young players among every ten players as Topps again broke down these cards into six series of ten cards each.

	MT	EX-MT	VG
COMPLETE SET (60)	10.00	4.50	1.25
COMMON PLAYER (1-60)	.15	.07	.02
☐ 1 Ryne Sandberg	.75	.35	.09
☐ 2 Nolan Ryan	1.25	.55	.16
☐ 3 Glenn Davis	.25	.11	.03
☐ 4 Dave Stewart	.20	.09	.03
☐ 5 Barry Larkin	.25	.11	.03
☐ 6 Carney Lansford	.15	.07	.02
☐ 7 Darryl Strawberry	.45	.20	.06
☐ 8 Steve Sax	.20	.09	.03
☐ 9 Carlos Martinez	.15	.07	.02
☐ 10 Gary Sheffield	.60	.25	.08
☐ 11 Don Mattingly	.50	.23	.06
☐ 12 Mark Grace	.50	.23	.06
☐ 13 Bret Saberhagen	.25	.11	.03
☐ 14 Mike Scott	.15	.07	.02
☐ 15 Robin Yount	.50	.23	.06
☐ 16 Ozzie Smith	.35	.16	.04
☐ 17 Jeff Ballard	.15	.07	.02
☐ 18 Rick Reuschel	.15	.07	.02
☐ 19 Greg Briley	.15	.07	.02
☐ 20 Ken Griffey Jr.	1.25	.55	.16
☐ 21 Kevin Mitchell	.35	.16	.04
☐ 22 Wade Boggs	.50	.23	.06
☐ 23 Dwight Gooden	.30	.14	.04
☐ 24 George Bell	.25	.11	.03
☐ 25 Eric Davis	.30	.14	.04
☐ 26 Ruben Sierra	.40	.18	.05
☐ 27 Roberto Alomar	.75	.35	.09
☐ 28 Gary Gaetti	.15	.07	.02
☐ 29 Gregg Olson	.25	.11	.03
☐ 30 Tom Gordon	.15	.07	.02
☐ 31 Jose Canseco	.75	.35	.09
☐ 32 Pedro Guerrero	.25	.11	.03
☐ 33 Joe Carter	.35	.16	.04
☐ 34 Mike Scioscia	.15	.07	.02
☐ 35 Julio Franco	.25	.11	.03
☐ 36 Joe Magrane	.15	.07	.02
☐ 37 Rickey Henderson	.60	.25	.08
☐ 38 Tim Raines	.25	.11	.03
☐ 39 Jerome Walton	.20	.09	.03
☐ 40 Bob Geren	.15	.07	.02
☐ 41 Andre Dawson	.35	.16	.04
☐ 42 Mark McGwire	.50	.23	.06
☐ 43 Howard Johnson	.25	.11	.03
☐ 44 Bo Jackson	.75	.35	.09
☐ 45 Shawon Dunston	.15	.07	.02
☐ 46 Carlton Fisk	.35	.16	.04
☐ 47 Mitch Williams	.15	.07	.02
☐ 48 Kirby Puckett	.50	.23	.06
☐ 49 Craig Worthington	.15	.07	.02
☐ 50 Jim Abbott	.35	.16	.04
☐ 51 Cal Ripken	1.00	.45	.13
☐ 52 Will Clark	.75	.35	.09
☐ 53 Dennis Eckersley	.25	.11	.03
☐ 54 Craig Biggio	.25	.11	.03
☐ 55 Fred McGriff	.35	.16	.04
☐ 56 Tony Gwynn	.50	.23	.06
☐ 57 Mickey Tettleton	.25	.11	.03
☐ 58 Mark Davis	.15	.07	.02
☐ 59 Omar Vizquel	.20	.09	.03
☐ 60 Gregg Jefferies	.35	.16	.04

1990 Topps Hills Hit Men

The 1990 Topps Hit Men set is a standard-size (2 1/2" by 3 1/2") 33-card set arranged in order of slugging percentage. The set was produced by Topps for Hills Department stores. Each card in the set has a glossy-coated front.

	MT	EX-MT	VG
COMPLETE SET (33)	4.00	1.80	.50
COMMON PLAYER (1-33)	.10	.05	.01
☐ 1 Eric Davis	.20	.09	.03
☐ 2 Will Clark	.50	.23	.06
☐ 3 Don Mattingly	.50	.23	.06
☐ 4 Darryl Strawberry	.40	.18	.05
☐ 5 Kevin Mitchell	.25	.11	.03
☐ 6 Pedro Guerrero	.15	.07	.02
☐ 7 Jose Canseco	.50	.23	.06
☐ 8 Jim Rice	.15	.07	.02
☐ 9 Danny Tartabull	.20	.09	.03
☐ 10 George Brett	.40	.18	.05
☐ 11 Kent Hrbek	.15	.07	.02
☐ 12 George Bell	.15	.07	.02
☐ 13 Eddie Murray	.30	.14	.04
☐ 14 Fred Lynn	.15	.07	.02
☐ 15 Andre Dawson	.30	.14	.04
☐ 16 Dale Murphy	.25	.11	.03
☐ 17 Dave Winfield	.30	.14	.04
☐ 18 Jack Clark	.15	.07	.02
☐ 19 Wade Boggs	.40	.18	.05
☐ 20 Ruben Sierra	.35	.16	.04
☐ 21 Dave Parker	.15	.07	.02
☐ 22 Glenn Davis	.15	.07	.02
☐ 23 Dwight Evans	.15	.07	.02
☐ 24 Jesse Barfield	.10	.05	.01
☐ 25 Kirk Gibson	.15	.07	.02
☐ 26 Alvin Davis	.10	.05	.01
☐ 27 Kirby Puckett	.45	.20	.06
☐ 28 Joe Carter	.30	.14	.04
☐ 29 Carlton Fisk	.30	.14	.04
☐ 30 Harold Baines	.10	.05	.01
☐ 31 Andres Galarraga	.10	.05	.01
☐ 32 Cal Ripken	.60	.25	.08
☐ 33 Howard Johnson	.20	.09	.03

1990 Topps Jumbo Rookies

The 1990 Topps Jumbo Rookies set contains 33 standard-size (2 1/2" by 3 1/2") glossy cards. The front and back borders are white, and other design elements are red, blue and yellow. This set is almost identical to previous year sets of the same name except that it contains 33 cards rather than only 22. One card was included in each 1990 Topps "jumbo" pack. The cards are numbered in alphabetical order.

	MT	EX-MT	VG
COMPLETE SET (33)	10.00	4.50	1.25
COMMON PLAYER (1-33)	.20	.09	.03
☐ 1 Jim Abbott	.60	.25	.08
☐ 2 Joey Belle	.60	.25	.08
☐ 3 Andy Benes	.50	.23	.06
☐ 4 Greg Briley	.20	.09	.03
☐ 5 Kevin Brown	.30	.14	.04
☐ 6 Mark Carreon	.20	.09	.03
☐ 7 Mike Devereaux	.30	.14	.04
☐ 8 Junior Felix	.30	.14	.04
☐ 9 Bob Geren	.20	.09	.03
☐ 10 Tom Gordon	.30	.14	.04
☐ 11 Ken Griffey Jr.	2.50	1.15	.30
☐ 12 Pete Harnisch	.30	.14	.04
☐ 13 Greg W. Harris	.20	.09	.03
☐ 14 Greg Hibbard	.20	.09	.03
☐ 15 Ken Hill	.30	.14	.04
☐ 16 Gregg Jefferies	.50	.23	.06
☐ 17 Jeff King	.20	.09	.03
☐ 18 Derek Lilliquist	.20	.09	.03
☐ 19 Carlos Martinez	.25	.11	.03
☐ 20 Ramon Martinez	.35	.16	.04
☐ 21 Bob Milacki	.20	.09	.03
☐ 22 Gregg Olson	.40	.18	.05
☐ 23 Donn Pall	.20	.09	.03
☐ 24 Kenny Rogers	.20	.09	.03
☐ 25 Gary Sheffield	1.00	.45	.13
☐ 26 Dwight Smith	.30	.14	.04
☐ 27 Billy Spiers	.20	.09	.03
☐ 28 Omar Vizquel	.30	.14	.04
☐ 29 Jerome Walton	.25	.11	.03
☐ 30 Dave West	.20	.09	.03
☐ 31 John Wetteland	.35	.16	.04
☐ 32 Steve Wilson	.20	.09	.03
☐ 33 Craig Worthington	.20	.09	.03

1990 Topps Mini Leaders

The 1990 Topps League Leader Minis is a 88-card set with cards measuring approximately 2 1/8" by 3". The set features players who finished 1989 in the top five in any major hitting or pitching category. This set marked the fifth year that Topps issued their Mini set. The card numbering is alphabetical by player within team and the teams themselves are ordered alphabetically.

	MT	EX-MT	VG
COMPLETE SET (88)	8.00	3.60	1.00
COMMON PLAYER (1-88)	.06	.03	.01
☐ 1 Jeff Ballard	.06	.03	.01
☐ 2 Phil Bradley	.06	.03	.01
☐ 3 Wade Boggs	.50	.23	.06
☐ 4 Roger Clemens	.75	.35	.09
☐ 5 Nick Esasky	.06	.03	.01
☐ 6 Jody Reed	.10	.05	.01
☐ 7 Bert Blyleven	.10	.05	.01
☐ 8 Chuck Finley	.06	.03	.01
☐ 9 Kirk McCaskill	.06	.03	.01
☐ 10 Devon White	.10	.05	.01
☐ 11 Ivan Calderon	.10	.05	.01
☐ 12 Bobby Thigpen	.10	.05	.01
☐ 13 Joe Carter	.25	.11	.03
☐ 14 Gary Pettis	.06	.03	.01
☐ 15 Tom Gordon	.10	.05	.01
☐ 16 Bo Jackson	.60	.25	.08
☐ 17 Bret Saberhagen	.12	.05	.02
☐ 18 Kevin Seitzer	.10	.05	.01
☐ 19 Chris Bosio	.12	.05	.02
☐ 20 Paul Molitor	.15	.07	.02
☐ 21 Dan Plesac	.06	.03	.01
☐ 22 Robin Yount	.50	.23	.06
☐ 23 Kirby Puckett	.60	.25	.08
☐ 24 Don Mattingly	.60	.25	.08
☐ 25 Steve Sax	.10	.05	.01
☐ 26 Storm Davis	.06	.03	.01
☐ 27 Dennis Eckersley	.15	.07	.02
☐ 28 Rickey Henderson	.50	.23	.06
☐ 29 Carney Lansford	.10	.05	.01
☐ 30 Mark McGwire	.50	.23	.06
☐ 31 Mike Moore	.10	.05	.01
☐ 32 Dave Stewart	.12	.05	.02
☐ 33 Alvin Davis	.06	.03	.01
☐ 34 Harold Reynolds	.06	.03	.01
☐ 35 Mike Schooler	.06	.03	.01
☐ 36 Cecil Espy	.06	.03	.01
☐ 37 Julio Franco	.12	.05	.02
☐ 38 Jeff Russell	.06	.03	.01
☐ 39 Nolan Ryan	1.00	.45	.13
☐ 40 Ruben Sierra	.40	.18	.05
☐ 41 George Bell	.12	.05	.02
☐ 42 Tony Fernandez	.10	.05	.01
☐ 43 Fred McGriff	.20	.09	.03
☐ 44 Dave Stieb	.10	.05	.01
☐ 45 Checklist Card	.10	.05	.01
☐ 46 Lonnie Smith	.06	.03	.01
☐ 47 John Smoltz	.20	.09	.03
☐ 48 Mike Bielecki	.06	.03	.01
☐ 49 Mark Grace	.35	.16	.04
☐ 50 Greg Maddux	.15	.07	.02
☐ 51 Ryne Sandberg	.75	.35	.09
☐ 52 Mitch Williams	.10	.05	.01
☐ 53 Eric Davis	.20	.09	.03
☐ 54 John Franco	.06	.03	.01
☐ 55 Glenn Davis	.12	.05	.02
☐ 56 Mike Scott	.06	.03	.01
☐ 57 Tim Belcher	.10	.05	.01
☐ 58 Orel Hershiser	.12	.05	.02
☐ 59 Jay Howell	.06	.03	.01
☐ 60 Eddie Murray	.20	.09	.03
☐ 61 Tim Burke	.06	.03	.01
☐ 62 Mark Langston	.10	.05	.01
☐ 63 Tim Raines	.12	.05	.02
☐ 64 Tim Wallach	.06	.03	.01
☐ 65 David Cone	.15	.07	.02
☐ 66 Sid Fernandez	.10	.05	.01
☐ 67 Howard Johnson	.12	.05	.02
☐ 68 Juan Samuel	.06	.03	.01
☐ 69 Von Hayes	.06	.03	.01
☐ 70 Barry Bonds	.50	.23	.06
☐ 71 Bobby Bonilla	.25	.11	.03
☐ 72 Andy Van Slyke	.15	.07	.02
☐ 73 Vince Coleman	.15	.07	.02
☐ 74 Jose DeLeon	.06	.03	.01
☐ 75 Pedro Guerrero	.10	.05	.01
☐ 76 Joe Magrane	.06	.03	.01
☐ 77 Roberto Alomar	.50	.23	.06
☐ 78 Jack Clark	.10	.05	.01
☐ 79 Mark Davis	.06	.03	.01
☐ 80 Tony Gwynn	.40	.18	.05
☐ 81 Bruce Hurst	.10	.05	.01
☐ 82 Eddie Whitson	.06	.03	.01
☐ 83 Brett Butler	.10	.05	.01
☐ 84 Will Clark	.60	.25	.08
☐ 85 Scott Garrelts	.06	.03	.01
☐ 86 Kevin Mitchell	.20	.09	.03
☐ 87 Rick Reuschel	.06	.03	.01
☐ 88 Robby Thompson	.10	.05	.01

1990 Topps Traded

The 1990 Topps Traded Set was the tenth consecutive year Topps issued a set at the end of the year. This 132-card standard size (2 1/2" by 3 1/2") set was arranged alphabetically by player and includes a mix of traded players and rookies for whom Topps did not include a card in the regular set. The key Rookie Cards in this set are Carlos Baerga, Scott Erickson, Travis Fryman, Dave Hollins, Dave Justice, Kevin Maas, and John Olerud. Also for the first time, Topps not only issued the set in a special collector boxes (made in Ireland) but distributed (on a significant basis) the set via their own wax packs. The wax pack cards were produced Topps' Duryea, Pennsylvania plant. There were seven cards in the packs and the wrapper highlighted the set as containing promising rookies, players who changed teams, and new managers. The cards differ in that the Irish-made cards have the whiter-type backs typical of the cards made in Ireland while the American cards have the typical Topps gray-type card stock on the back. Topps also produced a specially boxed "glossy" edition frequently referred to as the Topps Traded Tiffany set. This year, again, Topps did not disclose the number of Tiffany sets they produced or sold but it seems that production quantities were roughly similar (approximately 15,000 sets) to the previous year. The checklist of cards is identical to that of the normal non-glossy cards. There are two primary distinguishing features of the Tiffany cards, white card stock reverses and high gloss obverses. These Tiffany cards are valued approximately from three to five times the values listed below.

	MT	EX-MT	VG
COMPLETE SET (132)	6.00	2.70	.75
COMMON PLAYER (1T-132T)	.05	.02	.01
☐ 1T Darrel Akerfelds	.05	.02	.01
☐ 2T Sandy Alomar Jr.	.10	.05	.01
☐ 3T Brad Arnsberg	.05	.02	.01
☐ 4T Steve Avery	.60	.25	.08
☐ 5T Wally Backman	.05	.02	.01
☐ 6T Carlos Baerga	1.25	.55	.16
☐ 7T Kevin Bass	.05	.02	.01
☐ 8T Willie Blair	.10	.05	.01
☐ 9T Mike Blowers	.05	.02	.01
☐ 10T Shawn Boskie	.10	.05	.01
☐ 11T Daryl Boston	.05	.02	.01
☐ 12T Dennis Boyd	.05	.02	.01
☐ 13T Glenn Braggs	.05	.02	.01
☐ 14T Hubie Brooks	.05	.02	.01
☐ 15T Tom Brunansky	.08	.04	.01
☐ 16T John Burkett	.10	.05	.01
☐ 17T Casey Candaele	.05	.02	.01
☐ 18T John Candelaria	.05	.02	.01
☐ 19T Gary Carter	.08	.04	.01
☐ 20T Joe Carter	.20	.09	.03
☐ 21T Rick Cerone	.05	.02	.01
☐ 22T Scott Coolbaugh	.05	.02	.01
☐ 23T Bobby Cox MG	.05	.02	.01
☐ 24T Mark Davis	.05	.02	.01
☐ 25T Storm Davis	.05	.02	.01
☐ 26T Edgar Diaz	.05	.02	.01
☐ 27T Wayne Edwards	.05	.02	.01
☐ 28T Mark Eichhorn	.05	.02	.01
☐ 29T Scott Erickson	.75	.35	.09
☐ 30T Nick Esasky	.05	.02	.01
☐ 31T Cecil Fielder	.20	.09	.03
☐ 32T John Franco	.08	.04	.01
☐ 33T Travis Fryman	1.50	.65	.19
☐ 34T Bill Gullickson	.05	.02	.01
☐ 35T Darryl Hamilton	.08	.04	.01
☐ 36T Mike Harkey	.08	.04	.01
☐ 37T Bud Harrelson MG	.05	.02	.01
☐ 38T Billy Hatcher	.05	.02	.01
☐ 39T Keith Hernandez	.08	.04	.01
☐ 40T Joe Hesketh	.05	.02	.01
☐ 41T Dave Hollins	.60	.25	.08
☐ 42T Sam Horn	.05	.02	.01
☐ 43T Steve Howard	.08	.04	.01
☐ 44T Todd Hundley	.15	.07	.02
☐ 45T Jeff Huson	.05	.02	.01
☐ 46T Chris James	.05	.02	.01
☐ 47T Stan Javier	.05	.02	.01
☐ 48T Dave Justice	1.25	.55	.16
☐ 49T Jeff Kaiser	.05	.02	.01
☐ 50T Dana Kiecker	.05	.02	.01
☐ 51T Joe Klink	.05	.02	.01
☐ 52T Brent Knackert	.10	.05	.01
☐ 53T Brad Komminsk	.05	.02	.01
☐ 54T Mark Langston	.08	.04	.01
☐ 55T Tim Layana	.05	.02	.01
☐ 56T Rick Leach	.05	.02	.01
☐ 57T Terry Leach	.05	.02	.01
☐ 58T Tim Leary	.05	.02	.01
☐ 59T Craig Lefferts	.05	.02	.01
☐ 60T Charlie Leibrandt	.05	.02	.01
☐ 61T Jim Leyritz	.10	.05	.01
☐ 62T Fred Lynn	.08	.04	.01
☐ 63T Kevin Maas	.25	.11	.03
☐ 64T Shane Mack	.08	.04	.01
☐ 65T Candy Maldonado	.05	.02	.01
☐ 66T Fred Manrique	.05	.02	.01
☐ 67T Mike Marshall	.05	.02	.01
☐ 68T Carmelo Martinez	.05	.02	.01
☐ 69T John Marzano	.05	.02	.01
☐ 70T Ben McDonald	.50	.23	.06
☐ 71T Jack McDowell	.20	.09	.03
☐ 72T John McNamara MG	.05	.02	.01
☐ 73T Orlando Mercado	.05	.02	.01
☐ 74T Stump Merrill MG	.05	.02	.01
☐ 75T Alan Mills	.12	.05	.02
☐ 76T Hal Morris	.15	.07	.02
☐ 77T Lloyd Moseby	.05	.02	.01
☐ 78T Randy Myers	.08	.04	.01
☐ 79T Tim Naehring	.15	.07	.02
☐ 80T Junior Noboa	.05	.02	.01
☐ 81T Matt Nokes	.05	.02	.01
☐ 82T Pete O'Brien	.05	.02	.01
☐ 83T John Olerud	.60	.25	.08
☐ 84T Greg Olson	.10	.05	.01
☐ 85T Junior Ortiz	.05	.02	.01
☐ 86T Dave Parker	.08	.04	.01
☐ 87T Rick Parker	.05	.02	.01
☐ 88T Bob Patterson	.05	.02	.01
☐ 89T Alejandro Pena	.05	.02	.01
☐ 90T Tony Pena	.05	.02	.01
☐ 91T Pascual Perez	.05	.02	.01
☐ 92T Gerald Perry	.05	.02	.01
☐ 93T Dan Petry	.05	.02	.01
☐ 94T Gary Pettis	.05	.02	.01
☐ 95T Tony Phillips	.05	.02	.01
☐ 96T Lou Piniella MG	.08	.04	.01
☐ 97T Luis Polonia	.08	.04	.01
☐ 98T Jim Presley	.05	.02	.01
☐ 99T Scott Radinsky	.15	.07	.02
☐ 100T Willie Randolph	.08	.04	.01
☐ 101T Jeff Reardon	.08	.04	.01
☐ 102T Greg Riddoch MG	.05	.02	.01
☐ 103T Jeff Robinson	.05	.02	.01
☐ 104T Ron Robinson	.05	.02	.01
☐ 105T Kevin Romine	.05	.02	.01
☐ 106T Scott Ruskin	.05	.02	.01
☐ 107T John Russell	.05	.02	.01
☐ 108T Bill Sampen	.05	.02	.01
☐ 109T Juan Samuel	.05	.02	.01
☐ 110T Scott Sanderson	.05	.02	.01
☐ 111T Jack Savage	.05	.02	.01
☐ 112T Dave Schmidt	.05	.02	.01
☐ 113T Red Schoendienst MG	.08	.04	.01
☐ 114T Terry Shumpert	.05	.02	.01
☐ 115T Matt Sinatro	.05	.02	.01
☐ 116T Don Slaught	.05	.02	.01
☐ 117T Bryn Smith	.05	.02	.01
☐ 118T Lee Smith	.08	.04	.01

☐ 119T Paul Sorrento	.25	.11	.03
☐ 120T Franklin Stubbs UER ('84 says '99 and has the same stats as '89, '83 stats are missing)	.05	.02	.01
☐ 121T Russ Swan	.10	.05	.01
☐ 122T Bob Tewksbury	.08	.04	.01
☐ 123T Wayne Tolleson	.05	.02	.01
☐ 124T John Tudor	.05	.02	.01
☐ 125T Randy Veres	.05	.02	.01
☐ 126T Hector Villanueva	.10	.05	.01
☐ 127T Mitch Webster	.05	.02	.01
☐ 128T Ernie Whitt	.05	.02	.01
☐ 129T Frank Wills	.05	.02	.01
☐ 130T Dave Winfield	.15	.07	.02
☐ 131T Matt Young	.05	.02	.01
☐ 132T Checklist Card	.08	.01	.00

1990 Topps TV All-Stars

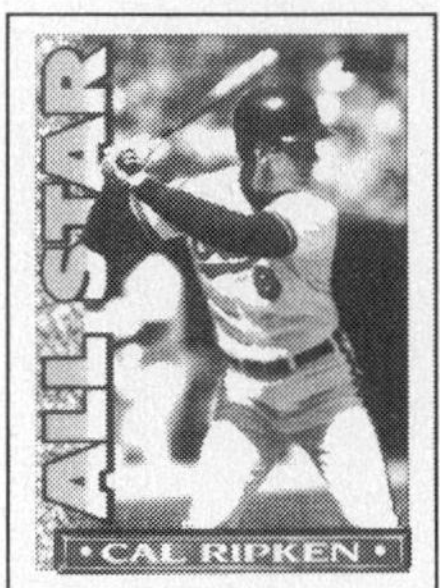

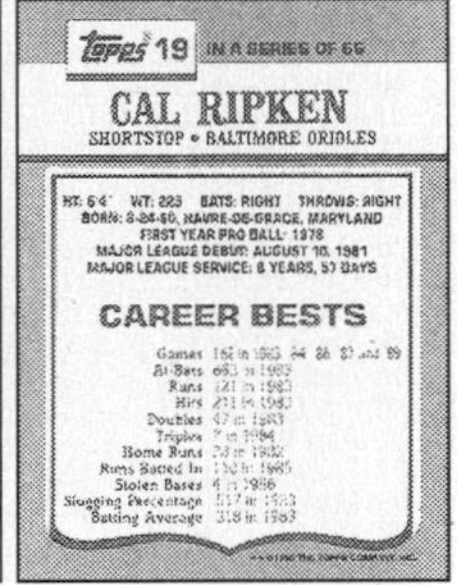

This All-Star team set contains 66 cards measuring the standard size (2 1/2" by 3 1/2"). The fronts feature posed or action color player photos with a high gloss. In block lettering, the words "All-Star" are printed vertically in blue on the left side of the card. The player's name appears in a red plaque below the picture, and white borders round out the card face. The backs are printed in black lettering and have a red and white background. Inside a decal design, biographical information and career bests are superimposed on a blue, pink, and white background. The cards are numbered on the back. These cards were offered only on television as a complete set for sale through an 800 number.

	MT	EX-MT	VG
COMPLETE SET (66)	60.00	27.00	7.50
COMMON PLAYER (1-66)	.60	.25	.08
☐ 1 Mark McGwire	2.00	.90	.25
☐ 2 Julio Franco	.90	.40	.11
☐ 3 Ozzie Guillen	.75	.35	.09
☐ 4 Carney Lansford	.75	.35	.09
☐ 5 Bo Jackson	3.00	1.35	.40
☐ 6 Kirby Puckett	3.50	1.55	.45
☐ 7 Ruben Sierra	2.00	.90	.25
☐ 8 Carlton Fisk	1.50	.65	.19
☐ 9 Nolan Ryan	6.50	2.90	.80
☐ 10 Rickey Henderson	3.00	1.35	.40
☐ 11 Jose Canseco	3.50	1.55	.45
☐ 12 Mark Davis	.60	.25	.08
☐ 13 Dennis Eckersley	.90	.40	.11
☐ 14 Chuck Finley	.60	.25	.08
☐ 15 Bret Saberhagen	.75	.35	.09
☐ 16 Dave Stewart	.75	.35	.09
☐ 17 Don Mattingly	3.00	1.35	.40
☐ 18 Steve Sax	.75	.35	.09
☐ 19 Cal Ripken	4.50	2.00	.55
☐ 20 Wade Boggs	2.00	.90	.25
☐ 21 George Bell	.90	.40	.11
☐ 22 Mike Greenwell	1.00	.45	.13
☐ 23 Robin Yount	2.00	.90	.25
☐ 24 Mickey Tettleton	.75	.35	.09
☐ 25 Roger Clemens	4.50	2.00	.55
☐ 26 Fred McGriff	1.50	.65	.19
☐ 27 Jeff Ballard	.60	.25	.08
☐ 28 Dwight Evans	.75	.35	.09
☐ 29 Paul Molitor	1.25	.55	.16
☐ 30 Gregg Olson	.90	.40	.11
☐ 31 Dan Plesac	.60	.25	.08
☐ 32 Greg Swindell	.75	.35	.09
☐ 33 Tony LaRussa MG and Cito Gaston MG	.60	.25	.08
☐ 34 Will Clark	3.50	1.55	.45
☐ 35 Roberto Alomar	3.00	1.35	.40
☐ 36 Barry Larkin	1.25	.55	.16
☐ 37 Ken Caminiti	.75	.35	.09
☐ 38 Eric Davis	1.25	.55	.16
☐ 39 Tony Gwynn	2.00	.90	.25
☐ 40 Kevin Mitchell	1.25	.55	.16
☐ 41 Craig Biggio	1.00	.45	.13
☐ 42 Mike Scott	.75	.35	.09
☐ 43 Joe Carter	1.50	.65	.19
☐ 44 Jack Clark	.75	.35	.09
☐ 45 Glenn Davis	.75	.35	.09
☐ 46 Orel Hershiser	.75	.35	.09
☐ 47 Jay Howell	.60	.25	.08
☐ 48 Bruce Hurst	.60	.25	.08
☐ 49 Dave Smith	.60	.25	.08
☐ 50 Pedro Guerrero	.60	.25	.08
☐ 51 Ryne Sandberg	4.50	2.00	.55
☐ 52 Ozzie Smith	1.50	.65	.19
☐ 53 Howard Johnson	1.00	.45	.13
☐ 54 Von Hayes	.60	.25	.08
☐ 55 Tim Raines	.90	.40	.11
☐ 56 Darryl Strawberry	2.50	1.15	.30
☐ 57 Mike LaValliere	.60	.25	.08
☐ 58 Dwight Gooden	1.25	.55	.16
☐ 59 Bobby Bonilla	1.25	.55	.16
☐ 60 Tim Burke	.60	.25	.08
☐ 61 Sid Fernandez	.60	.25	.08
☐ 62 Andres Galarraga	.75	.35	.09
☐ 63 Mark Grace	1.25	.55	.16
☐ 64 Joe Magrane	.60	.25	.08
☐ 65 Mitch Williams	.60	.25	.08
☐ 66 Roger Craig MG and Don Zimmer MG	.60	.25	.08

1990 Topps TV Cardinals

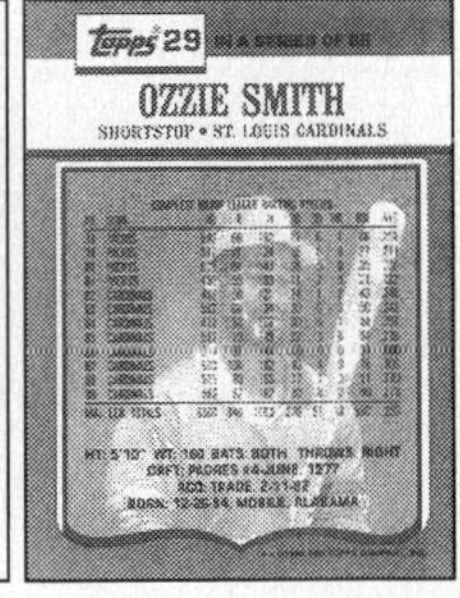

This Cardinals team set contains 66 cards measuring the standard size (2 1/2" by 3 1/2"). The fronts feature posed or action color player photos with a high gloss. In block lettering, the team name is printed vertically in red and pink on the left side of the card. The player's name appears in a blue plaque below the picture, and white borders round out the card face. The backs are printed in black lettering and have a red and white background. Inside a decal design, player information and statistics are superimposed on an indistinct version of the same picture as on the front. The cards are numbered on the back. Cards numbered 1-36 were with the parent club, while cards 37-66 were in the farm system.

	MT	EX-MT	VG
COMPLETE SET (66)	50.00	23.00	6.25
COMMON PLAYER (1-66)	.60	.25	.08
☐ 1 Whitey Herzog MG	1.00	.45	.13
☐ 2 Steve Braun CO	.60	.25	.08
☐ 3 Rich Hacker CO	.60	.25	.08
☐ 4 Dave Ricketts CO	.60	.25	.08

	MT	EX-MT	VG
☐ 5 Jim Riggleman CO	.60	.25	.08
☐ 6 Mike Roarke CO	.60	.25	.08
☐ 7 Cris Carpenter	.60	.25	.08
☐ 8 John Costello	.60	.25	.08
☐ 9 Danny Cox	.75	.35	.09
☐ 10 Ken Dayley	.60	.25	.08
☐ 11 Jose DeLeon	.75	.35	.09
☐ 12 Frank DiPino	.60	.25	.08
☐ 13 Ken Hill	1.25	.55	.16
☐ 14 Howard Hilton	.60	.25	.08
☐ 15 Ricky Horton	.60	.25	.08
☐ 16 Joe Magrane	.75	.35	.09
☐ 17 Greg Mathews	.60	.25	.08
☐ 18 Bryn Smith	.60	.25	.08
☐ 19 Scott Terry	.60	.25	.08
☐ 20 Bob Tewksbury	1.25	.55	.16
☐ 21 John Tudor	.90	.40	.11
☐ 22 Todd Worrell	.90	.40	.11
☐ 23 Tom Pagnozzi	.90	.40	.11
☐ 24 Todd Zeile	2.50	1.15	.30
☐ 25 Pedro Guerrero	1.00	.45	.13
☐ 26 Tim Jones	.60	.25	.08
☐ 27 Jose Oquendo	.75	.35	.09
☐ 28 Terry Pendleton	3.00	1.35	.40
☐ 29 Ozzie Smith	4.50	2.00	.55
☐ 30 Denny Walling	.60	.25	.08
☐ 31 Tom Brunansky	1.00	.45	.13
☐ 32 Vince Coleman	1.50	.65	.19
☐ 33 Dave Collins	.60	.25	.08
☐ 34 Willie McGee	1.50	.65	.19
☐ 35 John Morris	.60	.25	.08
☐ 36 Milt Thompson	.75	.35	.09
☐ 37 Gibson Alba	.60	.25	.08
☐ 38 Scott Arnold	.60	.25	.08
☐ 39 Rod Brewer	1.25	.55	.16
☐ 40 Greg Carmona	.75	.35	.09
☐ 41 Mark Clark	.75	.35	.09
☐ 42 Stan Clarke	.60	.25	.08
☐ 43 Paul Coleman	1.00	.45	.13
☐ 44 Todd Crosby	.60	.25	.08
☐ 45 Brad DuVall	.90	.40	.11
☐ 46 John Ericks	.60	.25	.08
☐ 47 Bien Figueroa	.60	.25	.08
☐ 48 Terry Francona	.60	.25	.08
☐ 49 Ed Fulton	.60	.25	.08
☐ 50 Bernard Gilkey	3.00	1.35	.40
☐ 51 Ernie Camacho	.60	.25	.08
☐ 52 Mike Hinkle	.60	.25	.08
☐ 53 Ray Lankford	6.00	2.70	.75
☐ 54 Julian Martinez	.75	.35	.09
☐ 55 Jesus Mendez	.75	.35	.09
☐ 56 Mike Milchin	1.00	.45	.13
☐ 57 Mauricio Nunez	.75	.35	.09
☐ 58 Omar Olivares	.90	.40	.11
☐ 59 Geronimo Pena	1.25	.55	.16
☐ 60 Mike Perez	1.25	.55	.16
☐ 61 Gaylen Pitts MG	.60	.25	.08
☐ 62 Mark Riggins CO	.60	.25	.08
☐ 63 Tim Sherrill	.60	.25	.08
☐ 64 Roy Silver	.60	.25	.08
☐ 65 Ray Stephens	1.00	.45	.13
☐ 66 Craig Wilson	1.00	.45	.13

1990 Topps TV Cubs

This Cubs team set contains 66 cards measuring the standard size (2 1/2" by 3 1/2"). The fronts feature posed or action color player photos with a high gloss. In block lettering, the team name is printed vertically in blue on the left side of the card. The player's name appears in a gold plaque below the picture, and white borders round out the card face. The backs are printed in black and have a red and white background. Inside a decal design, player information and statistics are superimposed on an indistinct version of the same picture as on the front. The cards are numbered on the back. Cards numbered 1-35 were with the parent club, while cards 36-66 were in the farm system.

	MT	EX-MT	VG
COMPLETE SET (66)	50.00	23.00	6.25
COMMON PLAYER (1-66)	.60	.25	.08
☐ 1 Don Zimmer MG	.75	.35	.09
☐ 2 Joe Altobelli CO	.60	.25	.08
☐ 3 Chuck Cottier CO	.60	.25	.08
☐ 4 Jose Martinez CO	.60	.25	.08
☐ 5 Dick Pole CO	.60	.25	.08
☐ 6 Phil Roof CO	.60	.25	.08
☐ 7 Paul Assenmacher	.60	.25	.08
☐ 8 Mike Bielecki	.60	.25	.08
☐ 9 Mike Harkey	1.50	.65	.19
☐ 10 Joe Kraemer	.60	.25	.08
☐ 11 Les Lancaster	.60	.25	.08
☐ 12 Greg Maddux	2.50	1.15	.30
☐ 13 Jose Nunez	.60	.25	.08
☐ 14 Jeff Pico	.60	.25	.08
☐ 15 Rick Sutcliffe	1.00	.45	.13
☐ 16 Dean Wilkins	1.00	.45	.13
☐ 17 Mitch Williams	.90	.40	.11
☐ 18 Steve Wilson	.75	.35	.09
☐ 19 Damon Berryhill	.75	.35	.09
☐ 20 Joe Girardi	.75	.35	.09
☐ 21 Rick Wrona	.75	.35	.09
☐ 22 Shawon Dunston	1.25	.55	.16
☐ 23 Mark Grace	3.00	1.35	.40
☐ 24 Domingo Ramos	.60	.25	.08
☐ 25 Luis Salazar	.75	.35	.09
☐ 26 Ryne Sandberg	9.00	4.00	1.15
☐ 27 Greg Smith	.60	.25	.08
☐ 28 Curtis Wilkerson	.60	.25	.08
☐ 29 Dave Clark	.60	.25	.08
☐ 30 Doug Dascenzo	.75	.35	.09
☐ 31 Andre Dawson	3.50	1.55	.45
☐ 32 Lloyd McClendon	.60	.25	.08
☐ 33 Dwight Smith	.75	.35	.09
☐ 34 Jerome Walton	.90	.40	.11
☐ 35 Marvell Wynne	.60	.25	.08
☐ 36 Alex Arias	.90	.40	.11
☐ 37 Bob Bafia	.60	.25	.08
☐ 38 Brad Bierley	.60	.25	.08
☐ 39 Shawn Boskie	.75	.35	.09
☐ 40 Danny Clay	.60	.25	.08
☐ 41 Rusty Crockett	.60	.25	.08
☐ 42 Earl Cunningham	1.00	.45	.13
☐ 43 Len Damian	.60	.25	.08
☐ 44 Darrin Duffy	.60	.25	.08
☐ 45 Ty Griffin	.75	.35	.09
☐ 46 Brian Guinn	.60	.25	.08
☐ 47 Phil Hannon	.60	.25	.08
☐ 48 Phil Harrison	.60	.25	.08
☐ 49 Jeff Hearron	.60	.25	.08
☐ 50 Greg Kallevig	.60	.25	.08
☐ 51 Cedric Landrum	.60	.25	.08
☐ 52 Bill Long	.60	.25	.08
☐ 53 Derrick May	2.00	.90	.25
☐ 54 Ray Mullino	.60	.25	.08
☐ 55 Erik Pappas	.90	.40	.11
☐ 56 Steve Parker	.60	.25	.08
☐ 57 Dave Pavlas	.75	.35	.09
☐ 58 Laddie Renfroe	.60	.25	.08
☐ 59 Jeff Small	.60	.25	.08
☐ 60 Doug Strange	.75	.35	.09
☐ 61 Gary Varsho	.60	.25	.08
☐ 62 Hector Villanueva	.75	.35	.09
☐ 63 Rick Wilkins	.90	.40	.11
☐ 64 Dana Williams	.75	.35	.09
☐ 65 Bill Wrona	.75	.35	.09
☐ 66 Fernando Zarranz	.60	.25	.08

1990 Topps TV Mets

This Mets team set contains 66 cards measuring the standard size (2 1/2" by 3 1/2"). The fronts feature posed or action color player photos with a high gloss. In block

lettering, the words "All Star" are printed vertically in orange and yellow on the left side of the card. The player's name appears in a red plaque below the picture, and white borders round out the card face. The backs are printed in black lettering and have a red and white background. Inside a decal design, player information and statistics are superimposed on an indistinct version of the same picture as on the front. The cards are numbered on the back. Cards numbered 1-34 were with the parent club, while cards 35-66 were in the farm system.

	MT	EX-MT	VG
COMPLETE SET (66)	50.00	23.00	6.25
COMMON PLAYER (1-66)	.60	.25	.08
☐ 1 Dave Johnson MG	.75	.35	.09
☐ 2 Mike Cubbage CO	.60	.25	.08
☐ 3 Doc Edwards CO	.60	.25	.08
☐ 4 Bud Harrelson CO	.75	.35	.09
☐ 5 Greg Pavlick CO	.60	.25	.08
☐ 6 Mel Stottlemyre CO	.75	.35	.09
☐ 7 Blaine Beatty	.75	.35	.09
☐ 8 David Cone	2.50	1.15	.30
☐ 9 Ron Darling	1.25	.55	.16
☐ 10 Sid Fernandez	1.00	.45	.13
☐ 11 John Franco	1.00	.45	.13
☐ 12 Dwight Gooden	4.00	1.80	.50
☐ 13 Jeff Innis	.75	.35	.09
☐ 14 Julio Machado	.75	.35	.09
☐ 15 Jeff Musselman	.60	.25	.08
☐ 16 Bob Ojeda	.75	.35	.09
☐ 17 Alejandro Pena	1.00	.45	.13
☐ 18 Frank Viola	1.25	.55	.16
☐ 19 Wally Whitehurst	.75	.35	.09
☐ 20 Barry Lyons	.60	.25	.08
☐ 21 Orlando Mercado	.60	.25	.08
☐ 22 Mackey Sasser	.75	.35	.09
☐ 23 Kevin Elster	.60	.25	.08
☐ 24 Gregg Jefferies	3.00	1.35	.40
☐ 25 Howard Johnson	2.00	.90	.25
☐ 26 Dave Magadan	1.00	.45	.13
☐ 27 Mike Marshall	.75	.35	.09
☐ 28 Tom O'Malley	.60	.25	.08
☐ 29 Tim Teufel	.75	.35	.09
☐ 30 Mark Carreon	.60	.25	.08
☐ 31 Kevin McReynolds	1.00	.45	.13
☐ 32 Keith Miller	.90	.40	.11
☐ 33 Darryl Strawberry	6.00	2.70	.75
☐ 34 Lou Thornton	.60	.25	.08
☐ 35 Shawn Barton	.60	.25	.08
☐ 36 Tim Bogar	.60	.25	.08
☐ 37 Terry Bross	.75	.35	.09
☐ 38 Kevin Brown	.75	.35	.09
☐ 39 Mike DeButch	.60	.25	.08
☐ 40 Alex Diaz	.60	.25	.08
☐ 41 Chris Donnels	1.00	.45	.13
☐ 42 Jeff Gardner	.90	.40	.11
☐ 43 Denny Gonzalez	.60	.25	.08
☐ 44 Kenny Graves	.60	.25	.08
☐ 45 Manny Hernandez	.75	.35	.09
☐ 46 Keith Hughes	.75	.35	.09
☐ 47 Todd Hundley	1.25	.55	.16
☐ 48 Chris Jelic	.75	.35	.09
☐ 49 Dave Liddell	.60	.25	.08
☐ 50 Terry McDaniel	.75	.35	.09
☐ 51 Cesar Mejia	.60	.25	.08
☐ 52 Scott Nielsen	.60	.25	.08
☐ 53 Dale Plummer	.60	.25	.08
☐ 54 Darren Reed	.75	.35	.09
☐ 55 Gil Roca	.60	.25	.08
☐ 56 Jaime Roseboro	.75	.35	.09
☐ 57 Roger Samuels	.60	.25	.08
☐ 58 Zoilo Sanchez	.60	.25	.08
☐ 59 Pete Schourek	.75	.35	.09
☐ 60 Craig Shipley	.75	.35	.09
☐ 61 Ray Soff	.60	.25	.08
☐ 62 Steve Swisher MG	.60	.25	.08
☐ 63 Kelvin Torve	.60	.25	.08
☐ 64 Dave Trautwein	.60	.25	.08
☐ 65 Julio Valera	1.25	.55	.16
☐ 66 Alan Zinter	.90	.40	.11

1990 Topps TV Red Sox

This Red Sox team set contains 66 cards measuring the standard size (2 1/2" by 3 1/2"). The fronts feature posed or action color player photos with a high gloss. In block lettering, the team name is printed vertically in red and yellow on the left side of the card. The player's name appears in a blue plaque below the picture, and white borders round out the card face. The backs are printed in black and have a red and white background. Inside a decal design, player information and statistics are superimposed over an indistinct version of the same picture as on the front. The cards are numbered on the back. Cards numbered 1-33 were with the parent club, while cards 34-66 were in the farm system.

	MT	EX-MT	VG
COMPLETE SET (66)	50.00	23.00	6.25
COMMON PLAYER (1-66)	.60	.25	.08
☐ 1 Joe Morgan MG	.75	.35	.09
☐ 2 Dick Berardino CO	.60	.25	.08
☐ 3 Al Bumbry CO	.60	.25	.08
☐ 4 Bill Fischer CO	.60	.25	.08
☐ 5 Richie Hebner CO	.75	.35	.09
☐ 6 Rac Slider CO	.60	.25	.08
☐ 7 Mike Boddicker	.75	.35	.09
☐ 8 Roger Clemens	7.50	3.40	.95
☐ 9 John Dopson	.60	.25	.08
☐ 10 Wes Gardner	.60	.25	.08
☐ 11 Greg A. Harris	.60	.25	.08
☐ 12 Dana Kiecker	.60	.25	.08
☐ 13 Dennis Lamp	.60	.25	.08
☐ 14 Rob Murphy	.60	.25	.08
☐ 15 Jeff Reardon	1.50	.65	.19
☐ 16 Mike Rochford	.60	.25	.08
☐ 17 Lee Smith	1.50	.65	.19
☐ 18 Rich Gedman	.60	.25	.08
☐ 19 John Marzano	.60	.25	.08
☐ 20 Tony Pena	.75	.35	.09
☐ 21 Marty Barrett	.60	.25	.08
☐ 22 Wade Boggs	4.50	2.00	.55
☐ 23 Bill Buckner	.75	.35	.09
☐ 24 Danny Heep	.60	.25	.08
☐ 25 Jody Reed	.75	.35	.09
☐ 26 Luis Rivera	.60	.25	.08
☐ 27 Billy Joe Robidoux	.60	.25	.08
☐ 28 Ellis Burks	1.50	.65	.19
☐ 29 Dwight Evans	1.25	.55	.16
☐ 30 Mike Greenwell	1.50	.65	.19
☐ 31 Randy Kutcher	.60	.25	.08
☐ 32 Carlos Quintana	1.00	.45	.13
☐ 33 Kevin Romine	.60	.25	.08

☐ 34 Ed Nottle MG	.60	.25	.08
☐ 35 Mark Meleski CO	.60	.25	.08
☐ 36 Steve Bast	.60	.25	.08
☐ 37 Greg Blosser	2.00	.90	.25
☐ 38 Tom Bolton	.75	.35	.09
☐ 39 Scott Cooper	2.00	.90	.25
☐ 40 Zach Crouch	.60	.25	.08
☐ 41 Steve Curry	.75	.35	.09
☐ 42 Mike Dalton	.60	.25	.08
☐ 43 John Flaherty	.60	.25	.08
☐ 44 Angel Gonzalez	.60	.25	.08
☐ 45 Eric Hetzel	.60	.25	.08
☐ 46 Daryl Irvine	.75	.35	.09
☐ 47 Joe Johnson	.60	.25	.08
☐ 48 Rick Lancellotti	.90	.40	.11
☐ 49 John Leister	.90	.40	.11
☐ 50 Derek Livernois	.60	.25	.08
☐ 51 Josias Manzanillo	.60	.25	.08
☐ 52 Kevin Morton	.90	.40	.11
☐ 53 Julius McDougal	1.00	.45	.13
☐ 54 Tim Naehring	1.25	.55	.16
☐ 55 Jim Pankovits	.60	.25	.08
☐ 56 Mickey Pina	.75	.35	.09
☐ 57 Phil Plantier	4.50	2.00	.55
☐ 58 Jerry Reed	.60	.25	.08
☐ 59 Larry Shikles	.60	.25	.08
☐ 60 Tito Stewart	.60	.25	.08
☐ 61 Jeff Stone	.60	.25	.08
☐ 62 John Trautwein	.60	.25	.08
☐ 63 Gary Tremblay	.60	.25	.08
☐ 64 Mo Vaughn	2.00	.90	.25
☐ 65 Scott Wade	.60	.25	.08
☐ 66 Eric Wedge	1.50	.65	.19

1990 Topps TV Yankees

This Yankees team set contains 66 cards measuring the standard size (2 1/2" by 3 1/2"). The fronts feature posed or action color player photos with a high gloss. In block lettering, the team name is printed vertically in light gray on the left side of the card. The player's name appears in a gold plaque below the picture, and white borders round out the card face. The backs are printed in black lettering and have a red and white background. Inside a decal design, player information and statistics are superimposed on an indistinct version of the same picture as on the front. The cards are numbered on the back. Cards numbered 1-34 were with the parent club, while cards 35-66 were in the farm system.

	MT	EX-MT	VG
COMPLETE SET (66)	50.00	23.00	6.25
COMMON PLAYER (1-66)	.60	.25	.08
☐ 1 Bucky Dent MG	.75	.35	.09
☐ 2 Mark Connor CO	.60	.25	.08
☐ 3 Billy Connors CO	.60	.25	.08
☐ 4 Mike Ferraro CO	.60	.25	.08
☐ 5 Joe Sparks CO	.60	.25	.08
☐ 6 Champ Summers CO	.60	.25	.08
☐ 7 Greg Cadaret	.60	.25	.08
☐ 8 Chuck Cary	.60	.25	.08
☐ 9 Lee Guetterman	.60	.25	.08
☐ 10 Andy Hawkins	.60	.25	.08
☐ 11 Dave LaPoint	.60	.25	.08
☐ 12 Tim Leary	.75	.35	.09
☐ 13 Lance McCullers	.60	.25	.08
☐ 14 Alan Mills	1.00	.45	.13
☐ 15 Clay Parker	.60	.25	.08
☐ 16 Pascual Perez	.75	.35	.09
☐ 17 Eric Plunk	.60	.25	.08
☐ 18 Dave Righetti	1.25	.55	.16
☐ 19 Jeff D. Robinson	.60	.25	.08
☐ 20 Rick Cerone	.60	.25	.08
☐ 21 Bob Geren	.60	.25	.08
☐ 22 Steve Balboni	.60	.25	.08
☐ 23 Mike Blowers	.60	.25	.08
☐ 24 Alvaro Espinoza	.60	.25	.08
☐ 25 Don Mattingly	7.50	3.40	.95
☐ 26 Steve Sax	1.00	.45	.13
☐ 27 Wayne Tolleson	.60	.25	.08
☐ 28 Randy Velarde	.60	.25	.08
☐ 29 Jesse Barfield	.75	.35	.09
☐ 30 Mel Hall	1.00	.45	.13
☐ 31 Roberto Kelly	2.50	1.15	.30
☐ 32 Luis Polonia	1.50	.65	.19
☐ 33 Deion Sanders	3.50	1.55	.45
☐ 34 Dave Winfield	3.00	1.35	.40
☐ 35 Steve Adkins	.75	.35	.09
☐ 36 Oscar Azocar	.60	.25	.08
☐ 37 Bob Brower	.60	.25	.08
☐ 38 Britt Burns	.60	.25	.08
☐ 39 Bob Davidson	.60	.25	.08
☐ 40 Brian Dorsett	.90	.40	.11
☐ 41 Dave Eiland	.75	.35	.09
☐ 42 John Fishel	.60	.25	.08
☐ 43 Andy Fox	.60	.25	.08
☐ 44 John Habyan	.60	.25	.08
☐ 45 Cullen Hartzog	.60	.25	.08
☐ 46 Sterling Hitchcock	1.25	.55	.16
☐ 47 Brian Johnson	.60	.25	.08
☐ 48 Jimmy Jones	.60	.25	.08
☐ 49 Scott Kamieniecki	.75	.35	.09
☐ 50 Jim Leyritz	.75	.35	.09
☐ 51 Mark Leiter	.75	.35	.09
☐ 52 Jason Maas	.75	.35	.09
☐ 53 Kevin Maas	2.00	.90	.25
☐ 54 Hensley Meulens	1.00	.45	.13
☐ 55 Kevin Mmahat	.75	.35	.09
☐ 56 Rich Monteleone	.60	.25	.08
☐ 57 Vince Phillips	.75	.35	.09
☐ 58 Carlos Rodriguez	.75	.35	.09
☐ 59 Dave Sax	.60	.25	.08
☐ 60 Willie Smith	.75	.35	.09
☐ 61 Van Snider	.60	.25	.08
☐ 62 Andy Stankiewicz	1.25	.55	.16
☐ 63 Wade Taylor	.75	.35	.09
☐ 64 Ricky Torres	.60	.25	.08
☐ 65 Jim Walewander	.75	.35	.09
☐ 66 Bernie Williams	3.00	1.35	.40

1990 Topps Wax Box Cards

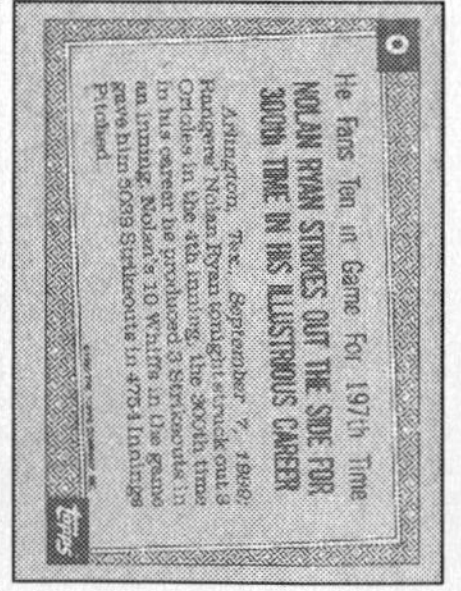

The 1990 Topps wax box cards comprise four different box bottoms with four cards each, for a total of 16 standard-size (2 1/2" by 3 1/2") cards. The front borders are green. The vertically oriented backs are yellowish green. These cards depict various career milestones achieved during the 1989 season. The card numbers are actually the letters A through P. The card ordering is alphabetical by player's name.

	MT	EX-MT	VG
COMPLETE SET (16)	7.50	3.40	.95
COMMON PLAYER (A-P)	.15	.07	.02
☐ A Wade Boggs	.75	.35	.09
☐ B George Brett	.75	.35	.09
☐ C Andre Dawson	.60	.25	.08
☐ D Darrell Evans	.15	.07	.02
☐ E Dwight Gooden	.35	.16	.04
☐ F Rickey Henderson	.75	.35	.09
☐ G Tom Lasorda MG	.25	.11	.03
☐ H Fred Lynn	.15	.07	.02
☐ I Mark McGwire	.75	.35	.09
☐ J Dave Parker	.25	.11	.03
☐ K Jeff Reardon	.25	.11	.03
☐ L Rick Reuschel	.15	.07	.02
☐ M Jim Rice	.25	.11	.03
☐ N Cal Ripken	1.00	.45	.13
☐ O Nolan Ryan	1.25	.55	.16
☐ P Ryne Sandberg	1.00	.45	.13

1991 Topps

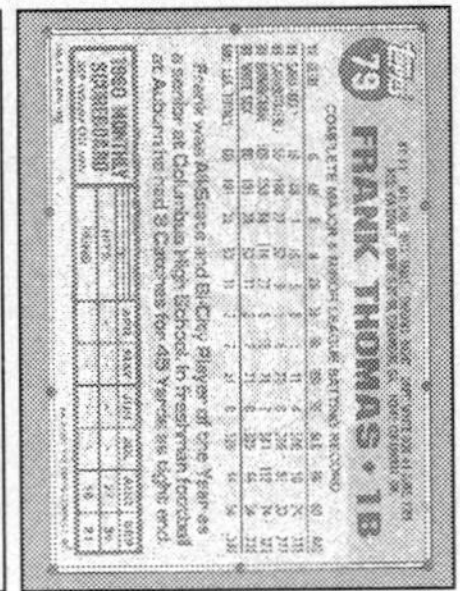

The 1991 Topps Set consists of 792 cards in the now standard size of 2 1/2" by 3 1/2". This set marks Topps tenth consecutive year of issuing a 792-card set. Topps also commemorated their fortieth anniversary by including a "Topps 40" logo on the front and back of each card. Virtually all of the cards have been discovered without the 40th logo on the back. As a special promotion Topps inserted (randomly) into their wax packs one of every previous card they ever issued. Topps again issued their checklists in team order (and alphabetically within team) and included a special 22-card All-Star set (386-407). There are five players listed as Future Stars, 114 Lance Dickson, 211 Brian Barnes, 561 Tim McIntosh, 587 Jose Offerman, and 594 Rich Garces. There are nine players listed as First Draft Picks, 74 Shane Andrews, 103 Tim Costo, 113 Carl Everett, 278 Alex Fernandez, 471 Mike Lieberthal, 491 Kurt Miller, 529 Marc Newfield, 596 Ronnie Walden, and 767 Dan Wilson. The key Rookie Cards in this set are Wes Chamberlain, Brian McRae, Marc Newfield, and Phil Plantier. The complete 1991 Topps set was also issued as a factory set of micro baseball cards with cards measuring approximately one-fourth the size of the regular size cards but identical in other respects. The micro set and its cards are valued at approximately half the values listed below for the regular size cards. The set was also issued with a gold "Operation Desert Shield" emblem stamped on the cards. It has been reported that Topps sent wax cases (equivalent to 6,313 sets) as gifts to U.S. troops stationed in the Persian Gulf. These Desert Shield cards are quite valuable in comparison to the regular issue of Topps; but one must be careful as counterfeits of these cards are known. These counterfeit Desert Shield cards can typically be detected by the shape of the gold shield stamped on the card. The bottom of the shield on the original is rounded, almost flat; the known forgeries come to a point. Due to the scarcity of these Desert Shield cards, they are usually sold at one hundred times the value of the corresponding regular card. Topps also produced a specially boxed "glossy" edition frequently referred to as the Topps Tiffany set. This year, again, Topps did not disclose the number of Tiffany sets they produced or sold. The checklist of cards is identical to that of the normal non-glossy cards. There are two primary distinguishing features of the Tiffany cards, white card stock reverses and high gloss obverses. These Tiffany cards are valued approximately from three to five times the values listed below.

	MT	EX-MT	VG
COMPLETE SET (792)	20.00	9.00	2.50
COMPLETE FACT.SET (792)	25.00	11.50	3.10
COMMON PLAYER (1-792)	.04	.02	.01
☐ 1 Nolan Ryan	.50	.23	.06
☐ 2 George Brett RB	.10	.05	.01
☐ 3 Carlton Fisk RB	.10	.05	.01
☐ 4 Kevin Maas RB	.05	.02	.01
☐ 5 Cal Ripken RB	.15	.07	.02
☐ 6 Nolan Ryan RB	.25	.11	.03
☐ 7 Ryne Sandberg RB	.12	.05	.02
☐ 8 Bobby Thigpen RB	.05	.02	.01
☐ 9 Darrin Fletcher	.04	.02	.01
☐ 10 Gregg Olson	.07	.03	.01
☐ 11 Roberto Kelly	.07	.03	.01
☐ 12 Paul Assenmacher	.04	.02	.01
☐ 13 Mariano Duncan	.04	.02	.01
☐ 14 Dennis Lamp	.04	.02	.01
☐ 15 Von Hayes	.04	.02	.01
☐ 16 Mike Heath	.04	.02	.01
☐ 17 Jeff Brantley	.04	.02	.01
☐ 18 Nelson Liriano	.04	.02	.01
☐ 19 Jeff Robinson New York Yankees	.04	.02	.01
☐ 20 Pedro Guerrero	.07	.03	.01
☐ 21 Joe Morgan MG	.04	.02	.01
☐ 22 Storm Davis	.04	.02	.01
☐ 23 Jim Gantner	.04	.02	.01
☐ 24 Dave Martinez	.04	.02	.01
☐ 25 Tim Belcher	.07	.03	.01
☐ 26 Luis Sojo UER (Born in Barquisimento, not Carquis)	.04	.02	.01
☐ 27 Bobby Witt	.04	.02	.01
☐ 28 Alvaro Espinoza	.04	.02	.01
☐ 29 Bob Walk	.04	.02	.01
☐ 30 Gregg Jefferies	.07	.03	.01
☐ 31 Colby Ward	.04	.02	.01
☐ 32 Mike Simms	.10	.05	.01
☐ 33 Barry Jones	.04	.02	.01
☐ 34 Atlee Hammaker	.04	.02	.01
☐ 35 Greg Maddux	.10	.05	.01
☐ 36 Donnie Hill	.04	.02	.01
☐ 37 Tom Bolton	.04	.02	.01
☐ 38 Scott Bradley	.04	.02	.01
☐ 39 Jim Neidlinger	.04	.02	.01
☐ 40 Kevin Mitchell	.07	.03	.01
☐ 41 Ken Dayley	.04	.02	.01
☐ 42 Chris Hoiles	.15	.07	.02
☐ 43 Roger McDowell	.04	.02	.01
☐ 44 Mike Felder	.04	.02	.01
☐ 45 Chris Sabo	.07	.03	.01
☐ 46 Tim Drummond	.04	.02	.01
☐ 47 Brook Jacoby	.04	.02	.01
☐ 48 Dennis Boyd	.04	.02	.01
☐ 49A Pat Borders ERR (40 steals at Kinston in '86)	.25	.11	.03
☐ 49B Pat Borders COR (0 steals at Kinston in '86)	.04	.02	.01
☐ 50 Bob Welch	.04	.02	.01
☐ 51 Art Howe MG	.04	.02	.01
☐ 52 Francisco Oliveras	.04	.02	.01
☐ 53 Mike Sharperson UER (Born in 1961, not 1960)	.04	.02	.01
☐ 54 Gary Mielke	.04	.02	.01
☐ 55 Jeffrey Leonard	.04	.02	.01
☐ 56 Jeff Parrett	.04	.02	.01
☐ 57 Jack Howell	.04	.02	.01
☐ 58 Mel Stottlemyre Jr.	.04	.02	.01
☐ 59 Eric Yelding	.04	.02	.01
☐ 60 Frank Viola	.07	.03	.01
☐ 61 Stan Javier	.04	.02	.01

☐ 62 Lee Guetterman	.04	.02	.01
☐ 63 Milt Thompson	.04	.02	.01
☐ 64 Tom Herr	.04	.02	.01
☐ 65 Bruce Hurst	.07	.03	.01
☐ 66 Terry Kennedy	.04	.02	.01
☐ 67 Rick Honeycutt	.04	.02	.01
☐ 68 Gary Sheffield	.25	.11	.03
☐ 69 Steve Wilson	.04	.02	.01
☐ 70 Ellis Burks	.07	.03	.01
☐ 71 Jim Acker	.04	.02	.01
☐ 72 Junior Ortiz	.04	.02	.01
☐ 73 Craig Worthington	.04	.02	.01
☐ 74 Shane Andrews	.20	.09	.03
☐ 75 Jack Morris	.10	.05	.01
☐ 76 Jerry Browne	.04	.02	.01
☐ 77 Drew Hall	.04	.02	.01
☐ 78 Geno Petralli	.04	.02	.01
☐ 79 Frank Thomas	1.25	.55	.16
☐ 80A Fernando Valenzuela ERR (104 earned runs in '90 tied for league lead)	.25	.11	.03
☐ 80B Fernando Valenzuela COR (104 earned runs in '90 led league, 20 CG's in 1986 now italicized)	.07	.03	.01
☐ 81 Cito Gaston MG	.04	.02	.01
☐ 82 Tom Glavine	.20	.09	.03
☐ 83 Daryl Boston	.04	.02	.01
☐ 84 Bob McClure	.04	.02	.01
☐ 85 Jesse Barfield	.04	.02	.01
☐ 86 Les Lancaster	.04	.02	.01
☐ 87 Tracy Jones	.04	.02	.01
☐ 88 Bob Tewksbury	.07	.03	.01
☐ 89 Darren Daulton	.07	.03	.01
☐ 90 Danny Tartabull	.07	.03	.01
☐ 91 Greg Colbrunn	.25	.11	.03
☐ 92 Danny Jackson	.04	.02	.01
☐ 93 Ivan Calderon	.04	.02	.01
☐ 94 John Dopson	.04	.02	.01
☐ 95 Paul Molitor	.10	.05	.01
☐ 96 Trevor Wilson	.04	.02	.01
☐ 97A Brady Anderson ERR (September, 2 RBI and 3 hits, should be 3 RBI and 14 hits	.25	.11	.03
☐ 97B Brady Anderson COR	.07	.03	.01
☐ 98 Sergio Valdez	.04	.02	.01
☐ 99 Chris Gwynn	.04	.02	.01
☐ 100A Don Mattingly ERR (10 hits in 1990)	.50	.23	.06
☐ 100B Don Mattingly COR (101 hits in 1990)	.15	.07	.02
☐ 101 Rob Ducey	.04	.02	.01
☐ 102 Gene Larkin	.04	.02	.01
☐ 103 Tim Costo	.20	.09	.03
☐ 104 Don Robinson	.04	.02	.01
☐ 105 Kevin McReynolds	.07	.03	.01
☐ 106 Ed Nunez	.04	.02	.01
☐ 107 Luis Polonia	.07	.03	.01
☐ 108 Matt Young	.04	.02	.01
☐ 109 Greg Riddoch MG	.04	.02	.01
☐ 110 Tom Henke	.07	.03	.01
☐ 111 Andres Thomas	.04	.02	.01
☐ 112 Frank DiPino	.04	.02	.01
☐ 113 Carl Everett	.25	.11	.03
☐ 114 Lance Dickson	.10	.05	.01
☐ 115 Hubie Brooks	.04	.02	.01
☐ 116 Mark Davis	.04	.02	.01
☐ 117 Dion James	.04	.02	.01
☐ 118 Tom Edens	.10	.05	.01
☐ 119 Carl Nichols	.04	.02	.01
☐ 120 Joe Carter	.12	.05	.02
☐ 121 Eric King	.04	.02	.01
☐ 122 Paul O'Neill	.07	.03	.01
☐ 123 Greg A. Harris	.04	.02	.01
☐ 124 Randy Bush	.04	.02	.01
☐ 125 Steve Bedrosian	.04	.02	.01
☐ 126 Bernard Gilkey	.15	.07	.02
☐ 127 Joe Price	.04	.02	.01
☐ 128 Travis Fryman UER (Front has SS, back has SS-3B)	.40	.18	.05
☐ 129 Mark Eichhorn	.04	.02	.01
☐ 130 Ozzie Smith	.10	.05	.01
☐ 131A Checklist 1 ERR 727 Phil Bradley	.15	.02	.00
☐ 131B Checklist 1 COR 717 Phil Bradley	.06	.01	.00
☐ 132 Jamie Quirk	.04	.02	.01
☐ 133 Greg Briley	.04	.02	.01
☐ 134 Kevin Elster	.04	.02	.01
☐ 135 Jerome Walton	.04	.02	.01
☐ 136 Dave Schmidt	.04	.02	.01
☐ 137 Randy Ready	.04	.02	.01
☐ 138 Jamie Moyer	.04	.02	.01
☐ 139 Jeff Treadway	.04	.02	.01
☐ 140 Fred McGriff	.12	.05	.02
☐ 141 Nick Leyva MG	.04	.02	.01
☐ 142 Curt Wilkerson	.04	.02	.01
☐ 143 John Smiley	.07	.03	.01
☐ 144 Dave Henderson	.04	.02	.01
☐ 145 Lou Whitaker	.07	.03	.01
☐ 146 Dan Plesac	.04	.02	.01
☐ 147 Carlos Baerga	.20	.09	.03
☐ 148 Rey Palacios	.04	.02	.01
☐ 149 Al Osuna UER (Shown throwing right, but bio says lefty)	.10	.05	.01
☐ 150 Cal Ripken	.30	.14	.04
☐ 151 Tom Browning	.04	.02	.01
☐ 152 Mickey Hatcher	.04	.02	.01
☐ 153 Bryan Harvey	.04	.02	.01
☐ 154 Jay Buhner	.07	.03	.01
☐ 155A Dwight Evans ERR (Led league with 162 games in '82)	.25	.11	.03
☐ 155B Dwight Evans COR (Tied for lead with 162 games in '82)	.07	.03	.01
☐ 156 Carlos Martinez	.04	.02	.01
☐ 157 John Smoltz	.10	.05	.01
☐ 158 Jose Uribe	.04	.02	.01
☐ 159 Joe Boever	.04	.02	.01
☐ 160 Vince Coleman UER (Wrong birth year, born 9/22/60)	.07	.03	.01
☐ 161 Tim Leary	.04	.02	.01
☐ 162 Ozzie Canseco	.08	.04	.01
☐ 163 Dave Johnson	.04	.02	.01
☐ 164 Edgar Diaz	.04	.02	.01
☐ 165 Sandy Alomar Jr.	.07	.03	.01
☐ 166 Harold Baines	.07	.03	.01
☐ 167A Randy Tomlin ERR (Harriburg)	.50	.23	.06
☐ 167B Randy Tomlin COR (Harrisburg)	.20	.09	.03
☐ 168 John Olerud	.15	.07	.02
☐ 169 Luis Aquino	.04	.02	.01
☐ 170 Carlton Fisk	.10	.05	.01
☐ 171 Tony LaRussa MG	.04	.02	.01
☐ 172 Pete Incaviglia	.04	.02	.01
☐ 173 Jason Grimsley	.04	.02	.01
☐ 174 Ken Caminiti	.07	.03	.01
☐ 175 Jack Armstrong	.04	.02	.01
☐ 176 John Orton	.04	.02	.01
☐ 177 Reggie Harris	.10	.05	.01
☐ 178 Dave Valle	.04	.02	.01
☐ 179 Pete Harnisch	.07	.03	.01
☐ 180 Tony Gwynn	.12	.05	.02
☐ 181 Duane Ward	.04	.02	.01
☐ 182 Junior Noboa	.04	.02	.01
☐ 183 Clay Parker	.04	.02	.01
☐ 184 Gary Green	.04	.02	.01
☐ 185 Joe Magrane	.04	.02	.01
☐ 186 Rod Booker	.04	.02	.01
☐ 187 Greg Cadaret	.04	.02	.01
☐ 188 Damon Berryhill	.04	.02	.01
☐ 189 Daryl Irvine	.04	.02	.01
☐ 190 Matt Williams	.07	.03	.01
☐ 191 Willie Blair	.04	.02	.01
☐ 192 Rob Deer	.07	.03	.01
☐ 193 Felix Fermin	.04	.02	.01
☐ 194 Xavier Hernandez	.04	.02	.01
☐ 195 Wally Joyner	.07	.03	.01
☐ 196 Jim Vatcher	.04	.02	.01
☐ 197 Chris Nabholz	.10	.05	.01
☐ 198 R.J. Reynolds	.04	.02	.01
☐ 199 Mike Hartley	.04	.02	.01
☐ 200 Darryl Strawberry	.12	.05	.02
☐ 201 Tom Kelly MG	.04	.02	.01
☐ 202 Jim Leyritz	.04	.02	.01
☐ 203 Gene Harris	.04	.02	.01
☐ 204 Herm Winningham	.04	.02	.01
☐ 205 Mike Perez	.15	.07	.02
☐ 206 Carlos Quintana	.04	.02	.01
☐ 207 Gary Wayne	.04	.02	.01
☐ 208 Willie Wilson	.04	.02	.01
☐ 209 Ken Howell	.04	.02	.01
☐ 210 Lance Parrish	.07	.03	.01
☐ 211 Brian Barnes	.12	.05	.02
☐ 212 Steve Finley	.07	.03	.01
☐ 213 Frank Wills	.04	.02	.01
☐ 214 Joe Girardi	.04	.02	.01
☐ 215 Dave Smith	.04	.02	.01

☐ 216 Greg Gagne	.04	.02	.01
☐ 217 Chris Bosio	.04	.02	.01
☐ 218 Rick Parker	.04	.02	.01
☐ 219 Jack McDowell	.10	.05	.01
☐ 220 Tim Wallach	.07	.03	.01
☐ 221 Don Slaught	.04	.02	.01
☐ 222 Brian McRae	.20	.09	.03
☐ 223 Allan Anderson	.04	.02	.01
☐ 224 Juan Gonzalez	.35	.16	.04
☐ 225 Randy Johnson	.07	.03	.01
☐ 226 Alfredo Griffin	.04	.02	.01
☐ 227 Steve Avery UER (Pitched 13 games for Durham in 1989, not 2)	.20	.09	.03
☐ 228 Rex Hudler	.04	.02	.01
☐ 229 Rance Mulliniks	.04	.02	.01
☐ 230 Sid Fernandez	.07	.03	.01
☐ 231 Doug Rader MG	.04	.02	.01
☐ 232 Jose DeJesus	.04	.02	.01
☐ 233 Al Leiter	.04	.02	.01
☐ 234 Scott Erickson	.15	.07	.02
☐ 235 Dave Parker	.07	.03	.01
☐ 236A Frank Tanana ERR (Tied for lead with 269 K's in '75)	.25	.11	.03
☐ 236B Frank Tanana COR (Led league with 269 K's in '75)	.04	.02	.01
☐ 237 Rick Cerone	.04	.02	.01
☐ 238 Mike Dunne	.04	.02	.01
☐ 239 Darren Lewis	.10	.05	.01
☐ 240 Mike Scott	.04	.02	.01
☐ 241 Dave Clark UER (Career totals 19 HR and 5 3B, should be 22 and 3)	.04	.02	.01
☐ 242 Mike LaCoss	.04	.02	.01
☐ 243 Lance Johnson	.04	.02	.01
☐ 244 Mike Jeffcoat	.04	.02	.01
☐ 245 Kal Daniels	.04	.02	.01
☐ 246 Kevin Wickander	.04	.02	.01
☐ 247 Jody Reed	.04	.02	.01
☐ 248 Tom Gordon	.07	.03	.01
☐ 249 Bob Melvin	.04	.02	.01
☐ 250 Dennis Eckersley	.10	.05	.01
☐ 251 Mark Lemke	.04	.02	.01
☐ 252 Mel Rojas	.10	.05	.01
☐ 253 Garry Templeton	.04	.02	.01
☐ 254 Shawn Boskie	.04	.02	.01
☐ 255 Brian Downing	.04	.02	.01
☐ 256 Greg Hibbard	.04	.02	.01
☐ 257 Tom O'Malley	.04	.02	.01
☐ 258 Chris Hammond	.10	.05	.01
☐ 259 Hensley Meulens	.07	.03	.01
☐ 260 Harold Reynolds	.04	.02	.01
☐ 261 Bud Harrelson MG	.04	.02	.01
☐ 262 Tim Jones	.04	.02	.01
☐ 263 Checklist 2	.06	.01	.00
☐ 264 Dave Hollins	.12	.05	.02
☐ 265 Mark Gubicza	.04	.02	.01
☐ 266 Carmelo Castillo	.04	.02	.01
☐ 267 Mark Knudson	.04	.02	.01
☐ 268 Tom Brookens	.04	.02	.01
☐ 269 Joe Hesketh	.04	.02	.01
☐ 270A Mark McGwire ERR (1987 Slugging Pctg. listed as 618)	.20	.09	.03
☐ 270B Mark McGwire COR (1987 Slugging Pctg. listed as .618)	.20	.09	.03
☐ 271 Omar Olivares	.12	.05	.02
☐ 272 Jeff King	.04	.02	.01
☐ 273 Johnny Ray	.04	.02	.01
☐ 274 Ken Williams	.04	.02	.01
☐ 275 Alan Trammell	.07	.03	.01
☐ 276 Bill Swift	.04	.02	.01
☐ 277 Scott Coolbaugh	.04	.02	.01
☐ 278 Alex Fernandez UER (No '90 White Sox stats)	.15	.07	.02
☐ 279A Jose Gonzalez ERR (Photo actually Billy Bean)	.25	.11	.03
☐ 279B Jose Gonzalez COR	.04	.02	.01
☐ 280 Bret Saberhagen	.07	.03	.01
☐ 281 Larry Sheets	.04	.02	.01
☐ 282 Don Carman	.04	.02	.01
☐ 283 Marquis Grissom	.15	.07	.02
☐ 284 Billy Spiers	.04	.02	.01
☐ 285 Jim Abbott	.12	.05	.02
☐ 286 Ken Oberkfell	.04	.02	.01
☐ 287 Mark Grant	.04	.02	.01
☐ 288 Derrick May	.07	.03	.01
☐ 289 Tim Birtsas	.04	.02	.01
☐ 290 Steve Sax	.07	.03	.01
☐ 291 John Wathan MG	.04	.02	.01
☐ 292 Bud Black	.04	.02	.01
☐ 293 Jay Bell	.07	.03	.01
☐ 294 Mike Moore	.04	.02	.01
☐ 295 Rafael Palmeiro	.10	.05	.01
☐ 296 Mark Williamson	.04	.02	.01
☐ 297 Manny Lee	.04	.02	.01
☐ 298 Omar Vizquel	.04	.02	.01
☐ 299 Scott Radinsky	.04	.02	.01
☐ 300 Kirby Puckett	.20	.09	.03
☐ 301 Steve Farr	.04	.02	.01
☐ 302 Tim Teufel	.04	.02	.01
☐ 303 Mike Boddicker	.04	.02	.01
☐ 304 Kevin Reimer	.10	.05	.01
☐ 305 Mike Scioscia	.04	.02	.01
☐ 306A Lonnie Smith ERR (136 games in '90)	.25	.11	.03
☐ 306B Lonnie Smith COR (135 games in '90)	.07	.03	.01
☐ 307 Andy Benes	.10	.05	.01
☐ 308 Tom Pagnozzi	.04	.02	.01
☐ 309 Norm Charlton	.07	.03	.01
☐ 310 Gary Carter	.07	.03	.01
☐ 311 Jeff Pico	.04	.02	.01
☐ 312 Charlie Hayes	.04	.02	.01
☐ 313 Ron Robinson	.04	.02	.01
☐ 314 Gary Pettis	.04	.02	.01
☐ 315 Roberto Alomar	.20	.09	.03
☐ 316 Gene Nelson	.04	.02	.01
☐ 317 Mike Fitzgerald	.04	.02	.01
☐ 318 Rick Aguilera	.07	.03	.01
☐ 319 Jeff McKnight	.04	.02	.01
☐ 320 Tony Fernandez	.07	.03	.01
☐ 321 Bob Rodgers MG	.04	.02	.01
☐ 322 Terry Shumpert	.04	.02	.01
☐ 323 Cory Snyder	.04	.02	.01
☐ 324A Ron Kittle ERR (Set another standard ...)	.25	.11	.03
☐ 324B Ron Kittle COR (Tied another standard ...)	.04	.02	.01
☐ 325 Brett Butler	.07	.03	.01
☐ 326 Ken Patterson	.04	.02	.01
☐ 327 Ron Hassey	.04	.02	.01
☐ 328 Walt Terrell	.04	.02	.01
☐ 329 Dave Justice UER (Drafted third round on card, should say fourth pick)	.30	.14	.04
☐ 330 Dwight Gooden	.07	.03	.01
☐ 331 Eric Anthony	.07	.03	.01
☐ 332 Kenny Rogers	.04	.02	.01
☐ 333 Chipper Jones FDP	.75	.35	.09
☐ 334 Todd Benzinger	.04	.02	.01
☐ 335 Mitch Williams	.04	.02	.01
☐ 336 Matt Nokes	.04	.02	.01
☐ 337A Keith Comstock ERR (Cubs logo on front)	.25	.11	.03
☐ 337B Keith Comstock COR (Mariners logo on front)	.04	.02	.01
☐ 338 Luis Rivera	.04	.02	.01
☐ 339 Larry Walker	.20	.09	.03
☐ 340 Ramon Martinez	.08	.04	.01
☐ 341 John Moses	.04	.02	.01
☐ 342 Mickey Morandini	.12	.05	.02
☐ 343 Jose Oquendo	.04	.02	.01
☐ 344 Jeff Russell	.04	.02	.01
☐ 345 Len Dykstra	.07	.03	.01
☐ 346 Jesse Orosco	.04	.02	.01
☐ 347 Greg Vaughn	.08	.04	.01
☐ 348 Todd Stottlemyre	.07	.03	.01
☐ 349 Dave Gallagher	.04	.02	.01
☐ 350 Glenn Davis	.07	.03	.01
☐ 351 Joe Torre MG	.07	.03	.01
☐ 352 Frank White	.04	.02	.01
☐ 353 Tony Castillo	.04	.02	.01
☐ 354 Sid Bream	.04	.02	.01
☐ 355 Chili Davis	.07	.03	.01
☐ 356 Mike Marshall	.04	.02	.01
☐ 357 Jack Savage	.04	.02	.01
☐ 358 Mark Parent	.04	.02	.01
☐ 359 Chuck Cary	.04	.02	.01
☐ 360 Tim Raines	.07	.03	.01
☐ 361 Scott Garrelts	.04	.02	.01
☐ 362 Hector Villenueva	.04	.02	.01
☐ 363 Rick Mahler	.04	.02	.01
☐ 364 Dan Pasqua	.04	.02	.01
☐ 365 Mike Schooler	.04	.02	.01
☐ 366A Checklist 3 ERR 19 Carl Nichols	.15	.02	.00
☐ 366B Checklist 3 COR	.06	.01	.00

119 Carl Nichols
☐ 367 Dave Walsh .10 .05 .01
☐ 368 Felix Jose .07 .03 .01
☐ 369 Steve Searcy .04 .02 .01
☐ 370 Kelly Gruber .07 .03 .01
☐ 371 Jeff Montgomery .04 .02 .01
☐ 372 Spike Owen .04 .02 .01
☐ 373 Darrin Jackson .07 .03 .01
☐ 374 Larry Casian .04 .02 .01
☐ 375 Tony Pena .04 .02 .01
☐ 376 Mike Harkey .07 .03 .01
☐ 377 Rene Gonzales .04 .02 .01
☐ 378A Wilson Alvarez ERR .40 .18 .05
('89 Port Charlotte
and '90 Birmingham
stat lines omitted)
☐ 378B Wilson Alvarez COR .10 .05 .01
(Text still says 143
K's in 1988, whereas
stats say 134)
☐ 379 Randy Velarde .04 .02 .01
☐ 380 Willie McGee .07 .03 .01
☐ 381 Jim Leyland MG .04 .02 .01
☐ 382 Mackey Sasser .04 .02 .01
☐ 383 Pete Smith .07 .03 .01
☐ 384 Gerald Perry .04 .02 .01
☐ 385 Mickey Tettleton .07 .03 .01
☐ 386 Cecil Fielder AS .10 .05 .01
☐ 387 Julio Franco AS .05 .02 .01
☐ 388 Kelly Gruber AS .05 .02 .01
☐ 389 Alan Trammell AS .05 .02 .01
☐ 390 Jose Canseco AS .12 .05 .02
☐ 391 Rickey Henderson AS .10 .05 .01
☐ 392 Ken Griffey Jr. AS .25 .11 .03
☐ 393 Carlton Fisk AS .10 .05 .01
☐ 394 Bob Welch AS .05 .02 .01
☐ 395 Chuck Finley AS .05 .02 .01
☐ 396 Bobby Thigpen AS .05 .02 .01
☐ 397 Eddie Murray AS .10 .05 .01
☐ 398 Ryne Sandberg AS .12 .05 .02
☐ 399 Matt Williams AS .05 .02 .01
☐ 400 Barry Larkin AS .08 .04 .01
☐ 401 Barry Bonds AS .10 .05 .01
☐ 402 Darryl Strawbery AS .10 .05 .01
☐ 403 Bobby Bonilla AS .08 .04 .01
☐ 404 Mike Scioscia AS .05 .02 .01
☐ 405 Doug Drabek AS .05 .02 .01
☐ 406 Frank Viola AS .05 .02 .01
☐ 407 John Franco AS .05 .02 .01
☐ 408 Earnie Riles .04 .02 .01
☐ 409 Mike Stanley .04 .02 .01
☐ 410 Dave Righetti .04 .02 .01
☐ 411 Lance Blankenship .04 .02 .01
☐ 412 Dave Bergman .04 .02 .01
☐ 413 Terry Mulholland .04 .02 .01
☐ 414 Sammy Sosa .07 .03 .01
☐ 415 Rick Sutcliffe .07 .03 .01
☐ 416 Randy Milligan .04 .02 .01
☐ 417 Bill Krueger .04 .02 .01
☐ 418 Nick Esasky .04 .02 .01
☐ 419 Jeff Reed .04 .02 .01
☐ 420 Bobby Thigpen .04 .02 .01
☐ 421 Alex Cole .04 .02 .01
☐ 422 Rick Reuschel .04 .02 .01
☐ 423 Rafael Ramirez UER .04 .02 .01
(Born 1959, not 1958)
☐ 424 Calvin Schiraldi .04 .02 .01
☐ 425 Andy Van Slyke .10 .05 .01
☐ 426 Joe Grahe .15 .07 .02
☐ 427 Rick Dempsey .04 .02 .01
☐ 428 John Barfield .04 .02 .01
☐ 429 Stump Merrill MG .04 .02 .01
☐ 430 Gary Gaetti .04 .02 .01
☐ 431 Paul Gibson .04 .02 .01
☐ 432 Delino DeShields .15 .07 .02
☐ 433 Pat Tabler .04 .02 .01
☐ 434 Julio Machado .04 .02 .01
☐ 435 Kevin Maas .08 .04 .01
☐ 436 Scott Bankhead .04 .02 .01
☐ 437 Doug Dascenzo .04 .02 .01
☐ 438 Vicente Palacios .04 .02 .01
☐ 439 Dickie Thon .04 .02 .01
☐ 440 George Bell .07 .03 .01
☐ 441 Zane Smith .04 .02 .01
☐ 442 Charlie O'Brien .04 .02 .01
☐ 443 Jeff Innis .04 .02 .01
☐ 444 Glenn Braggs .04 .02 .01
☐ 445 Greg Swindell .07 .03 .01
☐ 446 Craig Grebeck .04 .02 .01
☐ 447 John Burkett .04 .02 .01
☐ 448 Craig Lefferts .04 .02 .01
☐ 449 Juan Berenguer .04 .02 .01
☐ 450 Wade Boggs .12 .05 .02
☐ 451 Neal Heaton .04 .02 .01
☐ 452 Bill Schroeder .04 .02 .01
☐ 453 Lenny Harris .04 .02 .01
☐ 454A Kevin Appier ERR .25 .11 .03
('90 Omaha stat
line omitted)
☐ 454B Kevin Appier COR .07 .03 .01
☐ 455 Walt Weiss .04 .02 .01
☐ 456 Charlie Leibrandt .04 .02 .01
☐ 457 Todd Hundley .04 .02 .01
☐ 458 Brian Holman .04 .02 .01
☐ 459 Tom Trebelhorn MG UER .04 .02 .01
(Pitching and batting
columns switched)
☐ 460 Dave Stieb .04 .02 .01
☐ 461 Robin Ventura .20 .09 .03
☐ 462 Steve Frey .04 .02 .01
☐ 463 Dwight Smith .04 .02 .01
☐ 464 Steve Buechele .04 .02 .01
☐ 465 Ken Griffey Sr. .07 .03 .01
☐ 466 Charles Nagy .40 .18 .05
☐ 467 Dennis Cook .04 .02 .01
☐ 468 Tim Hulett .04 .02 .01
☐ 469 Chet Lemon .04 .02 .01
☐ 470 Howard Johnson .07 .03 .01
☐ 471 Mike Lieberthal .20 .09 .03
☐ 472 Kirt Manwaring .04 .02 .01
☐ 473 Curt Young .04 .02 .01
☐ 474 Phil Plantier .50 .23 .06
☐ 475 Teddy Higuera .04 .02 .01
☐ 476 Glenn Wilson .04 .02 .01
☐ 477 Mike Fetters .04 .02 .01
☐ 478 Kurt Stillwell .04 .02 .01
☐ 479 Bob Patterson UER .04 .02 .01
(Has a decimal point
between 7 and 9)
☐ 480 Dave Magadan .07 .03 .01
☐ 481 Eddie Whitson .04 .02 .01
☐ 482 Tino Martinez .10 .05 .01
☐ 483 Mike Aldrete .04 .02 .01
☐ 484 Dave LaPoint .04 .02 .01
☐ 485 Terry Pendleton .10 .05 .01
☐ 486 Tommy Greene .04 .02 .01
☐ 487 Rafael Belliard .04 .02 .01
☐ 488 Jeff Manto .04 .02 .01
☐ 489 Bobby Valentine MG .04 .02 .01
☐ 490 Kirk Gibson .07 .03 .01
☐ 491 Kurt Miller .25 .11 .03
☐ 492 Ernie Whitt .04 .02 .01
☐ 493 Jose Rijo .07 .03 .01
☐ 494 Chris James .04 .02 .01
☐ 495 Charlie Hough .04 .02 .01
☐ 496 Marty Barrett .04 .02 .01
☐ 497 Ben McDonald .10 .05 .01
☐ 498 Mark Salas .04 .02 .01
☐ 499 Melido Perez .07 .03 .01
☐ 500 Will Clark .20 .09 .03
☐ 501 Mike Bielecki .04 .02 .01
☐ 502 Carney Lansford .07 .03 .01
☐ 503 Roy Smith .04 .02 .01
☐ 504 Julio Valera .15 .07 .02
☐ 505 Chuck Finley .07 .03 .01
☐ 506 Darnell Coles .04 .02 .01
☐ 507 Steve Jeltz .04 .02 .01
☐ 508 Mike York .04 .02 .01
☐ 509 Glenallen Hill .04 .02 .01
☐ 510 John Franco .07 .03 .01
☐ 511 Steve Balboni .04 .02 .01
☐ 512 Jose Mesa .04 .02 .01
☐ 513 Jerald Clark .04 .02 .01
☐ 514 Mike Stanton .04 .02 .01
☐ 515 Alvin Davis .04 .02 .01
☐ 516 Karl Rhodes .04 .02 .01
☐ 517 Joe Oliver .04 .02 .01
☐ 518 Cris Carpenter .04 .02 .01
☐ 519 Sparky Anderson MG .04 .02 .01
☐ 520 Mark Grace .10 .05 .01
☐ 521 Joe Orsulak .04 .02 .01
☐ 522 Stan Belinda .04 .02 .01
☐ 523 Rodney McCray .04 .02 .01
☐ 524 Darrel Akerfelds .04 .02 .01
☐ 525 Willie Randolph .07 .03 .01
☐ 526A Moises Alou ERR .50 .23 .06
(37 runs in 2 games
for '90 Pirates)
☐ 526B Moises Alou COR .25 .11 .03
(0 runs in 2 games
for '90 Pirates)
☐ 527A Checklist 4 ERR .15 .02 .00
105 Keith Miller
719 Kevin McReynolds
☐ 527B Checklist 4 COR .06 .01 .00
105 Kevin McReynolds
719 Keith Miller

☐ 528 Denny Martinez .07 .03 .01
☐ 529 Marc Newfield .40 .18 .05
☐ 530 Roger Clemens .25 .11 .03
☐ 531 Dave Rohde .04 .02 .01
☐ 532 Kirk McCaskill .04 .02 .01
☐ 533 Oddibe McDowell .04 .02 .01
☐ 534 Mike Jackson .04 .02 .01
☐ 535 Ruben Sierra UER .15 .07 .02
(Back reads 100 Runs
amd 100 RBI's)
☐ 536 Mike Witt .04 .02 .01
☐ 537 Jose Lind .04 .02 .01
☐ 538 Bip Roberts .07 .03 .01
☐ 539 Scott Terry .04 .02 .01
☐ 540 George Brett .10 .05 .01
☐ 541 Domingo Ramos .04 .02 .01
☐ 542 Rob Murphy .04 .02 .01
☐ 543 Junior Felix .04 .02 .01
☐ 544 Alejandro Pena .04 .02 .01
☐ 545 Dale Murphy .07 .03 .01
☐ 546 Jeff Ballard .04 .02 .01
☐ 547 Mike Pagliarulo .04 .02 .01
☐ 548 Jaime Navarro .07 .03 .01
☐ 549 John McNamara MG .04 .02 .01
☐ 550 Eric Davis .07 .03 .01
☐ 551 Bob Kipper .04 .02 .01
☐ 552 Jeff Hamilton .04 .02 .01
☐ 553 Joe Klink .04 .02 .01
☐ 554 Brian Harper .04 .02 .01
☐ 555 Turner Ward .10 .05 .01
☐ 556 Gary Ward .04 .02 .01
☐ 557 Wally Whitehurst .04 .02 .01
☐ 558 Otis Nixon .07 .03 .01
☐ 559 Adam Peterson .04 .02 .01
☐ 560 Greg Smith .04 .02 .01
☐ 561 Tim McIntosh .04 .02 .01
☐ 562 Jeff Kunkel .04 .02 .01
☐ 563 Brent Knackert .04 .02 .01
☐ 564 Dante Bichette .04 .02 .01
☐ 565 Craig Biggio .07 .03 .01
☐ 566 Craig Wilson .10 .05 .01
☐ 567 Dwayne Henry .04 .02 .01
☐ 568 Ron Karkovice .04 .02 .01
☐ 569 Curt Schilling .07 .03 .01
☐ 570 Barry Bonds .20 .09 .03
☐ 571 Pat Combs .04 .02 .01
☐ 572 Dave Anderson .04 .02 .01
☐ 573 Rich Rodriguez UER .10 .05 .01
(Stats say drafted 4th,
but bio says 9th round)
☐ 574 John Marzano .04 .02 .01
☐ 575 Robin Yount .10 .05 .01
☐ 576 Jeff Kaiser .04 .02 .01
☐ 577 Bill Doran .04 .02 .01
☐ 578 Dave West .04 .02 .01
☐ 579 Roger Craig MG .04 .02 .01
☐ 580 Dave Stewart .07 .03 .01
☐ 581 Luis Quinones .04 .02 .01
☐ 582 Marty Clary .04 .02 .01
☐ 583 Tony Phillips .04 .02 .01
☐ 584 Kevin Brown .07 .03 .01
☐ 585 Pete O'Brien .04 .02 .01
☐ 586 Fred Lynn .07 .03 .01
☐ 587 Jose Offerman UER .10 .05 .01
(Text says he signed
7/24/86, but bio
says 1988)
☐ 588 Mark Whiten .12 .05 .02
☐ 589 Scott Ruskin .04 .02 .01
☐ 590 Eddie Murray .10 .05 .01
☐ 591 Ken Hill .07 .03 .01
☐ 592 B.J. Surhoff .04 .02 .01
☐ 593A Mike Walker ERR .25 .11 .03
('90 Canton-Akron
stat line omitted)
☐ 593B Mike Walker COR .04 .02 .01
☐ 594 Rich Garces .10 .05 .01
☐ 595 Bill Landrum .04 .02 .01
☐ 596 Ronnie Walden .10 .05 .01
☐ 597 Jerry Don Gleaton .04 .02 .01
☐ 598 Sam Horn .04 .02 .01
☐ 599A Greg Myers ERR .25 .11 .03
('90 Syracuse
stat line omitted)
☐ 599B Greg Myers COR .04 .02 .01
☐ 600 Bo Jackson .12 .05 .02
☐ 601 Bob Ojeda .04 .02 .01
☐ 602 Casey Candaele .04 .02 .01
☐ 603A Wes Chamberlain ERR .60 .25 .08
(Photo actually
Louie Meadows)
☐ 603B Wes Chamberlain COR .20 .09 .03
☐ 604 Billy Hatcher .04 .02 .01
☐ 605 Jeff Reardon .07 .03 .01
☐ 606 Jim Gott .04 .02 .01
☐ 607 Edgar Martinez .07 .03 .01
☐ 608 Todd Burns .04 .02 .01
☐ 609 Jeff Torborg MG .04 .02 .01
☐ 610 Andres Galarraga .04 .02 .01
☐ 611 Dave Eiland .04 .02 .01
☐ 612 Steve Lyons .04 .02 .01
☐ 613 Eric Show .04 .02 .01
☐ 614 Luis Salazar .04 .02 .01
☐ 615 Bert Blyleven .07 .03 .01
☐ 616 Todd Zeile .07 .03 .01
☐ 617 Bill Wegman .04 .02 .01
☐ 618 Sil Campusano .04 .02 .01
☐ 619 David Wells .04 .02 .01
☐ 620 Ozzie Guillen .04 .02 .01
☐ 621 Ted Power .04 .02 .01
☐ 622 Jack Daugherty .04 .02 .01
☐ 623 Jeff Blauser .04 .02 .01
☐ 624 Tom Candiotti .04 .02 .01
☐ 625 Terry Steinbach .07 .03 .01
☐ 626 Gerald Young .04 .02 .01
☐ 627 Tim Layana .04 .02 .01
☐ 628 Greg Litton .04 .02 .01
☐ 629 Wes Gardner .04 .02 .01
☐ 630 Dave Winfield .10 .05 .01
☐ 631 Mike Morgan .04 .02 .01
☐ 632 Lloyd Moseby .04 .02 .01
☐ 633 Kevin Tapani .07 .03 .01
☐ 634 Henry Cotto .04 .02 .01
☐ 635 Andy Hawkins .04 .02 .01
☐ 636 Geronimo Pena .10 .05 .01
☐ 637 Bruce Ruffin .04 .02 .01
☐ 638 Mike Macfarlane .04 .02 .01
☐ 639 Frank Robinson MG .10 .05 .01
☐ 640 Andre Dawson .10 .05 .01
☐ 641 Mike Henneman .04 .02 .01
☐ 642 Hal Morris .07 .03 .01
☐ 643 Jim Presley .04 .02 .01
☐ 644 Chuck Crim .04 .02 .01
☐ 645 Juan Samuel .04 .02 .01
☐ 646 Andujar Cedeno .12 .05 .02
☐ 647 Mark Portugal .04 .02 .01
☐ 648 Lee Stevens .04 .02 .01
☐ 649 Bill Sampen .04 .02 .01
☐ 650 Jack Clark .07 .03 .01
☐ 651 Alan Mills .04 .02 .01
☐ 652 Kevin Romine .04 .02 .01
☐ 653 Anthony Telford .04 .02 .01
☐ 654 Paul Sorrento .07 .03 .01
☐ 655 Erik Hanson .04 .02 .01
☐ 656A Checklist 5 ERR .15 .02 .00
348 Vicente Palacios
381 Jose Lind
537 Mike LaValliere
665 Jim Leyland
☐ 656B Checklist 5 ERR .15 .02 .00
433 Vicente Palacios
(Palacios should be 438)
537 Jose Lind
665 Mike LaValliere
381 Jim Leyland
☐ 656C Checklist 5 COR .15 .02 .00
438 Vicente Palacios
537 Jose Lind
665 Mike LaValliere
381 Jim Leyland
☐ 657 Mike Kingery .04 .02 .01
☐ 658 Scott Aldred .10 .05 .01
☐ 659 Oscar Azocar .04 .02 .01
☐ 660 Lee Smith .07 .03 .01
☐ 661 Steve Lake .04 .02 .01
☐ 662 Ron Dibble .07 .03 .01
☐ 663 Greg Brock .04 .02 .01
☐ 664 John Farrell .04 .02 .01
☐ 665 Mike LaValliere .04 .02 .01
☐ 666 Danny Darwin .04 .02 .01
☐ 667 Kent Anderson .04 .02 .01
☐ 668 Bill Long .04 .02 .01
☐ 669 Lou Piniella MG .04 .02 .01
☐ 670 Rickey Henderson .12 .05 .02
☐ 671 Andy McGaffigan .04 .02 .01
☐ 672 Shane Mack .07 .03 .01
☐ 673 Greg Olson UER .04 .02 .01
(6 RBI in '88 at Tide-
water and 2 RBI in '87,
should be 48 and 15)
☐ 674A Kevin Gross ERR .25 .11 .03
(89 BB with Phillies
in '88 tied for
league lead)
☐ 674B Kevin Gross COR .04 .02 .01
(89 BB with Phillies

in '88 led league)
☐ 675 Tom Brunansky .07 .03 .01
☐ 676 Scott Chiamparino .07 .03 .01
☐ 677 Billy Ripken .04 .02 .01
☐ 678 Mark Davidson .04 .02 .01
☐ 679 Bill Bathe .04 .02 .01
☐ 680 David Cone .10 .05 .01
☐ 681 Jeff Schaefer .04 .02 .01
☐ 682 Ray Lankford .40 .18 .05
☐ 683 Derek Lilliquist .04 .02 .01
☐ 684 Milt Cuyler .10 .05 .01
☐ 685 Doug Drabek .07 .03 .01
☐ 686 Mike Gallego .04 .02 .01
☐ 687A John Cerutti ERR .25 .11 .03
(4.46 ERA in '90)
☐ 687B John Cerutti COR .04 .02 .01
(4.76 ERA in '90)
☐ 688 Rosario Rodriguez .10 .05 .01
☐ 689 John Kruk .07 .03 .01
☐ 690 Orel Hershiser .07 .03 .01
☐ 691 Mike Blowers .04 .02 .01
☐ 692A Efrain Valdez ERR .25 .11 .03
(Born 6/11/66)
☐ 692B Efrain Valdez COR .04 .02 .01
(Born 7/11/66 and two
lines of text added)
☐ 693 Francisco Cabrera .04 .02 .01
☐ 694 Randy Veres .04 .02 .01
☐ 695 Kevin Seitzer .07 .03 .01
☐ 696 Steve Olin .07 .03 .01
☐ 697 Shawn Abner .04 .02 .01
☐ 698 Mark Guthrie .04 .02 .01
☐ 699 Jim Lefebvre MG .04 .02 .01
☐ 700 Jose Canseco .20 .09 .03
☐ 701 Pascual Perez .04 .02 .01
☐ 702 Tim Naehring .07 .03 .01
☐ 703 Juan Agosto .04 .02 .01
☐ 704 Devon White .07 .03 .01
☐ 705 Robby Thompson .04 .02 .01
☐ 706A Brad Arnsberg ERR .25 .11 .03
(68.2 IP in '90)
☐ 706B Brad Arnsberg COR .04 .02 .01
(62.2 IP in '90)
☐ 707 Jim Eisenreich .04 .02 .01
☐ 708 John Mitchell .04 .02 .01
☐ 709 Matt Sinatro .04 .02 .01
☐ 710 Kent Hrbek .07 .03 .01
☐ 711 Jose DeLeon .04 .02 .01
☐ 712 Ricky Jordan .04 .02 .01
☐ 713 Scott Scudder .04 .02 .01
☐ 714 Marvell Wynne .04 .02 .01
☐ 715 Tim Burke .04 .02 .01
☐ 716 Bob Geren .04 .02 .01
☐ 717 Phil Bradley .04 .02 .01
☐ 718 Steve Crawford .04 .02 .01
☐ 719 Keith Miller .04 .02 .01
☐ 720 Cecil Fielder .12 .05 .02
☐ 721 Mark Lee .10 .05 .01
☐ 722 Wally Backman .04 .02 .01
☐ 723 Candy Maldonado .04 .02 .01
☐ 724 David Segui .04 .02 .01
☐ 725 Ron Gant .12 .05 .02
☐ 726 Phil Stephenson .04 .02 .01
☐ 727 Mookie Wilson .04 .02 .01
☐ 728 Scott Sanderson .04 .02 .01
☐ 729 Don Zimmer MG .04 .02 .01
☐ 730 Barry Larkin .10 .05 .01
☐ 731 Jeff Gray .04 .02 .01
☐ 732 Franklin Stubbs .04 .02 .01
☐ 733 Kelly Downs .04 .02 .01
☐ 734 John Russell .04 .02 .01
☐ 735 Ron Darling .07 .03 .01
☐ 736 Dick Schofield .04 .02 .01
☐ 737 Tim Crews .04 .02 .01
☐ 738 Mel Hall .04 .02 .01
☐ 739 Russ Swan .04 .02 .01
☐ 740 Ryne Sandberg .25 .11 .03
☐ 741 Jimmy Key .04 .02 .01
☐ 742 Tommy Gregg .04 .02 .01
☐ 743 Bryn Smith .04 .02 .01
☐ 744 Nelson Santovenia .04 .02 .01
☐ 745 Doug Jones .04 .02 .01
☐ 746 John Shelby .04 .02 .01
☐ 747 Tony Fossas .04 .02 .01
☐ 748 Al Newman .04 .02 .01
☐ 749 Greg W. Harris .04 .02 .01
☐ 750 Bobby Bonilla .10 .05 .01
☐ 751 Wayne Edwards .04 .02 .01
☐ 752 Kevin Bass .04 .02 .01
☐ 753 Paul Marak UER .04 .02 .01
(Stats say drafted in
Jan., but bio says May)
☐ 754 Bill Pecota .04 .02 .01
☐ 755 Mark Langston .07 .03 .01
☐ 756 Jeff Huson .04 .02 .01
☐ 757 Mark Gardner .04 .02 .01
☐ 758 Mike Devereaux .07 .03 .01
☐ 759 Bobby Cox MG .04 .02 .01
☐ 760 Benny Santiago .07 .03 .01
☐ 761 Larry Andersen .04 .02 .01
☐ 762 Mitch Webster .04 .02 .01
☐ 763 Dana Kiecker .04 .02 .01
☐ 764 Mark Carreon .04 .02 .01
☐ 765 Shawon Dunston .07 .03 .01
☐ 766 Jeff Robinson .04 .02 .01
☐ 767 Dan Wilson .15 .07 .02
☐ 768 Don Pall .04 .02 .01
☐ 769 Tim Sherrill .10 .05 .01
☐ 770 Jay Howell .04 .02 .01
☐ 771 Gary Redus UER .04 .02 .01
(Born in Tanner,
should say Athens)
☐ 772 Kent Mercker UER .07 .03 .01
(Born in Indianapolis,
should say Dublin, Ohio)
☐ 773 Tom Foley .04 .02 .01
☐ 774 Dennis Rasmussen .04 .02 .01
☐ 775 Julio Franco .07 .03 .01
☐ 776 Brent Mayne .04 .02 .01
☐ 777 John Candelaria .04 .02 .01
☐ 778 Dan Gladden .04 .02 .01
☐ 779 Carmelo Martinez .04 .02 .01
☐ 780A Randy Myers ERR .25 .11 .03
(15 career losses)
☐ 780B Randy Myers COR .07 .03 .01
(19 career losses)
☐ 781 Darryl Hamilton .07 .03 .01
☐ 782 Jim Deshaies .04 .02 .01
☐ 783 Joel Skinner .04 .02 .01
☐ 784 Willie Fraser .04 .02 .01
☐ 785 Scott Fletcher .04 .02 .01
☐ 786 Eric Plunk .04 .02 .01
☐ 787 Checklist 6 .06 .01 .00
☐ 788 Bob Milacki .04 .02 .01
☐ 789 Tom Lasorda MG .04 .02 .01
☐ 790 Ken Griffey Jr. .50 .23 .06
☐ 791 Mike Benjamin .04 .02 .01
☐ 792 Mike Greenwell .07 .03 .01

1991 Topps Archive 1953

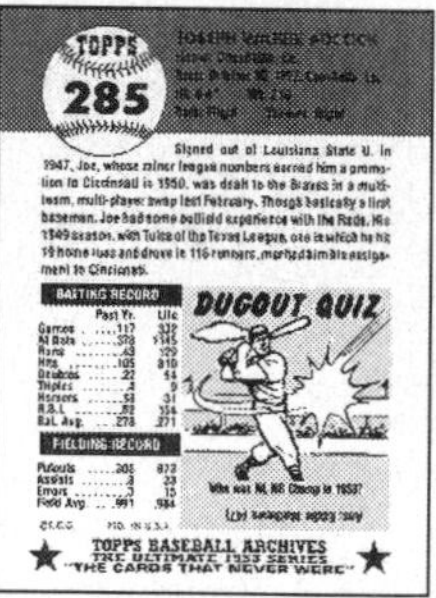

The 1953 Topps Archive set is a reprint of the original 274-card 1953 Topps set. The only card missing from the reprint set is that of Billy Loes (174), who did not give Topps permission to reprint his card. Moreover, the set has been extended by 57 cards, with cards honoring Mrs. Eleanor Engle, Hoyt Wilhelm (who had already been included in the set as card number 151), 1953 HOF inductees Dizzy Dean and Al Simmons, and "prospect" Hank Aaron. Although the original cards measured 2 5/8" by 3 3/4", the reprint cards measure the modern standard, 2 1/2" by 3 1/2". Production quantities were supposedly limited to not more than 18,000 cases.

	MT	EX-MT	VG
COMPLETE SET (330)	70.00	32.00	8.75
COMMON PLAYER (1-220)	.12	.05	.02
COMMON PLAYER (221-280)	.15	.07	.02
COMMON PLAYER (281-337)	.20	.09	.03

☐ 1	Jackie Robinson	3.00	1.35	.40
☐ 2	Luke Easter	.12	.05	.02
☐ 3	George Crowe	.12	.05	.02
☐ 4	Ben Wade	.12	.05	.02
☐ 5	Joe Dobson	.12	.05	.02
☐ 6	Sam Jones	.12	.05	.02
☐ 7	Bob Borkowski	.12	.05	.02
☐ 8	Clem Koshorek	.12	.05	.02
☐ 9	Joe Collins	.15	.07	.02
☐ 10	Smoky Burgess	.15	.07	.02
☐ 11	Sal Yvars	.12	.05	.02
☐ 12	Howie Judson	.12	.05	.02
☐ 13	Conrado Marrero	.12	.05	.02
☐ 14	Clem Labine	.15	.07	.02
☐ 15	Bobo Newsom	.15	.07	.02
☐ 16	Peanuts Lowrey	.12	.05	.02
☐ 17	Billy Hitchcock	.12	.05	.02
☐ 18	Ted Lepcio	.12	.05	.02
☐ 19	Mel Parnell	.15	.07	.02
☐ 20	Hank Thompson	.15	.07	.02
☐ 21	Billy Johnson	.12	.05	.02
☐ 22	Howie Fox	.12	.05	.02
☐ 23	Toby Atwell	.12	.05	.02
☐ 24	Ferris Fain	.15	.07	.02
☐ 25	Ray Boone	.15	.07	.02
☐ 26	Dale Mitchell	.15	.07	.02
☐ 27	Roy Campanella	2.00	.90	.25
☐ 28	Eddie Pellagrini	.12	.05	.02
☐ 29	Hal Jeffcoat	.12	.05	.02
☐ 30	Willard Nixon	.12	.05	.02
☐ 31	Ewell Blackwell	.20	.09	.03
☐ 32	Clyde Vollmer	.12	.05	.02
☐ 33	Bob Kennedy	.12	.05	.02
☐ 34	George Shuba	.15	.07	.02
☐ 35	Irv Noren	.12	.05	.02
☐ 36	Johnny Groth	.12	.05	.02
☐ 37	Eddie Mathews	1.50	.65	.19
☐ 38	Jim Hearn	.12	.05	.02
☐ 39	Eddie Miksis	.12	.05	.02
☐ 40	John Lipon	.12	.05	.02
☐ 41	Enos Slaughter	.75	.35	.09
☐ 42	Gus Zernial	.12	.05	.02
☐ 43	Gil McDougald	.35	.16	.04
☐ 44	Ellis Kinder	.12	.05	.02
☐ 45	Grady Hatton	.12	.05	.02
☐ 46	Johnny Klippstein	.12	.05	.02
☐ 47	Bubba Church	.12	.05	.02
☐ 48	Bob Del Greco	.12	.05	.02
☐ 49	Faye Throneberry	.12	.05	.02
☐ 50	Chuck Dressen MG	.15	.07	.02
☐ 51	Frank Campos	.12	.05	.02
☐ 52	Ted Gray	.12	.05	.02
☐ 53	Sherm Lollar	.15	.07	.02
☐ 54	Bob Feller	1.25	.55	.16
☐ 55	Maurice McDermott	.12	.05	.02
☐ 56	Gerry Staley	.12	.05	.02
☐ 57	Carl Scheib	.12	.05	.02
☐ 58	George Metkovich	.12	.05	.02
☐ 59	Karl Drews	.12	.05	.02
☐ 60	Cloyd Boyer	.12	.05	.02
☐ 61	Early Wynn	.75	.35	.09
☐ 62	Monte Irvin	.50	.23	.06
☐ 63	Gus Niarhos	.12	.05	.02
☐ 64	Dave Philley	.12	.05	.02
☐ 65	Earl Harrist	.12	.05	.02
☐ 66	Minnie Minoso	.40	.18	.05
☐ 67	Roy Sievers	.15	.07	.02
☐ 68	Del Rice	.12	.05	.02
☐ 69	Dick Brodowski	.12	.05	.02
☐ 70	Ed Yuhas	.12	.05	.02
☐ 71	Tony Bartirome	.12	.05	.02
☐ 72	Fred Hutchinson	.15	.07	.02
☐ 73	Eddie Robinson	.12	.05	.02
☐ 74	Joe Rossi	.12	.05	.02
☐ 75	Mike Garcia	.15	.07	.02
☐ 76	Pee Wee Reese	1.25	.55	.16
☐ 77	Johnny Mize	.75	.35	.09
☐ 78	Red Schoendienst	.75	.35	.09
☐ 79	Johnny Wyrostek	.12	.05	.02
☐ 80	Jim Hegan	.15	.07	.02
☐ 81	Joe Black	.25	.11	.03
☐ 82	Mickey Mantle	20.00	9.00	2.50
☐ 83	Howie Pollet	.12	.05	.02
☐ 84	Bob Hooper	.12	.05	.02
☐ 85	Bobby Morgan	.12	.05	.02
☐ 86	Billy Martin	1.25	.55	.16
☐ 87	Ed Lopat	.40	.18	.05
☐ 88	Willie Jones	.12	.05	.02
☐ 89	Chuck Stobbs	.12	.05	.02
☐ 90	Hank Edwards	.12	.05	.02
☐ 91	Ebba St.Claire	.12	.05	.02
☐ 92	Paul Minner	.12	.05	.02
☐ 93	Hal Rice	.12	.05	.02
☐ 94	Bill Kennedy	.12	.05	.02
☐ 95	Willard Marshall	.12	.05	.02
☐ 96	Virgil Trucks	.12	.05	.02
☐ 97	Don Kolloway	.12	.05	.02
☐ 98	Cal Abrams	.12	.05	.02
☐ 99	Dave Madison	.12	.05	.02
☐ 100	Bill Miller	.12	.05	.02
☐ 101	Ted Wilks	.12	.05	.02
☐ 102	Connie Ryan	.12	.05	.02
☐ 103	Joe Astroth	.12	.05	.02
☐ 104	Yogi Berra	2.25	1.00	.30
☐ 105	Joe Nuxhall	.15	.07	.02
☐ 106	Johnny Antonelli	.15	.07	.02
☐ 107	Danny O'Connell	.12	.05	.02
☐ 108	Bob Porterfield	.12	.05	.02
☐ 109	Alvin Dark	.20	.09	.03
☐ 110	Herman Wehmeier	.12	.05	.02
☐ 111	Hank Sauer	.15	.07	.02
☐ 112	Ned Garver	.12	.05	.02
☐ 113	Jerry Priddy	.12	.05	.02
☐ 114	Phil Rizzuto	1.00	.45	.13
☐ 115	George Spencer	.12	.05	.02
☐ 116	Frank Smith	.12	.05	.02
☐ 117	Sid Gordon	.12	.05	.02
☐ 118	Gus Bell	.15	.07	.02
☐ 119	Johnny Sain	.40	.18	.05
☐ 120	Davey Williams	.15	.07	.02
☐ 121	Walt Dropo	.15	.07	.02
☐ 122	Elmer Valo	.12	.05	.02
☐ 123	Tommy Byrne	.12	.05	.02
☐ 124	Sibby Sisti	.12	.05	.02
☐ 125	Dick Williams	.15	.07	.02
☐ 126	Bill Connelly	.12	.05	.02
☐ 127	Clint Courtney	.12	.05	.02
☐ 128	Wilmer Mizell	.12	.05	.02
☐ 129	Keith Thomas	.12	.05	.02
☐ 130	Turk Lown	.12	.05	.02
☐ 131	Harry Byrd	.12	.05	.02
☐ 132	Tom Morgan	.12	.05	.02
☐ 133	Gil Coan	.12	.05	.02
☐ 134	Rube Walker	.15	.07	.02
☐ 135	Al Rosen	.35	.16	.04
☐ 136	Ken Heintzelman	.12	.05	.02
☐ 137	John Rutherford	.12	.05	.02
☐ 138	George Kell	.60	.25	.08
☐ 139	Sammy White	.12	.05	.02
☐ 140	Tommy Glaviano	.12	.05	.02
☐ 141	Allie Reynolds	.35	.16	.04
☐ 142	Vic Wertz	.15	.07	.02
☐ 143	Billy Pierce	.20	.09	.03
☐ 144	Bob Schultz	.12	.05	.02
☐ 145	Harry Dorish	.12	.05	.02
☐ 146	Granny Hamner	.12	.05	.02
☐ 147	Warren Spahn	1.50	.65	.19
☐ 148	Mickey Grasso	.12	.05	.02
☐ 149	Dom DiMaggio	.30	.14	.04
☐ 150	Harry Simpson	.12	.05	.02
☐ 151	Hoyt Wilhelm	.75	.35	.09
☐ 152	Bob Adams	.12	.05	.02
☐ 153	Andy Seminick	.12	.05	.02
☐ 154	Dick Groat	.30	.14	.04
☐ 155	Dutch Leonard	.15	.07	.02
☐ 156	Jim Rivera	.12	.05	.02
☐ 157	Bob Addis	.12	.05	.02
☐ 158	Johnny Logan	.15	.07	.02
☐ 159	Wayne Terwilliger	.12	.05	.02
☐ 160	Bob Young	.12	.05	.02
☐ 161	Vern Bickford	.12	.05	.02
☐ 162	Ted Kluszewski	.40	.18	.05
☐ 163	Fred Hatfield	.12	.05	.02
☐ 164	Frank Shea	.12	.05	.02
☐ 165	Billy Hoeft	.12	.05	.02
☐ 166	Billy Hunter	.12	.05	.02
☐ 167	Art Schult	.12	.05	.02
☐ 168	Willard Schmidt	.12	.05	.02
☐ 169	Dizzy Trout	.12	.05	.02
☐ 170	Bill Werle	.12	.05	.02
☐ 171	Bill Glynn	.12	.05	.02
☐ 172	Rip Repulski	.12	.05	.02
☐ 173	Preston Ward	.12	.05	.02
☐ 174	Billy Loes (Not printed)	.00	.00	.00
☐ 175	Ron Kline	.12	.05	.02
☐ 176	Don Hoak	.20	.09	.03
☐ 177	Jim Dyck	.12	.05	.02
☐ 178	Jim Waugh	.12	.05	.02
☐ 179	Gene Hermanski	.12	.05	.02
☐ 180	Virgil Stallcup	.12	.05	.02
☐ 181	Al Zarilla	.12	.05	.02
☐ 182	Bobby Hofman	.12	.05	.02
☐ 183	Stu Miller	.15	.07	.02
☐ 184	Hal Brown	.12	.05	.02
☐ 185	Jim Pendleton	.12	.05	.02

Card	MT	EX-MT	VG
□ 186 Charlie Bishop	.12	.05	.02
□ 187 Jim Fridley	.12	.05	.02
□ 188 Andy Carey	.20	.09	.03
□ 189 Ray Jablonski	.12	.05	.02
□ 190 Dixie Walker CO	.12	.05	.02
□ 191 Ralph Kiner	.75	.35	.09
□ 192 Wally Westlake	.12	.05	.02
□ 193 Mike Clark	.12	.05	.02
□ 194 Eddie Kazak	.12	.05	.02
□ 195 Ed McGhee	.12	.05	.02
□ 196 Bob Keegan	.12	.05	.02
□ 197 Del Crandall	.15	.07	.02
□ 198 Forrest Main	.12	.05	.02
□ 199 Marion Fricano	.12	.05	.02
□ 200 Gordon Goldsberry	.12	.05	.02
□ 201 Paul LaPalme	.12	.05	.02
□ 202 Carl Sawatski	.12	.05	.02
□ 203 Cliff Fannin	.12	.05	.02
□ 204 Dick Bokelman	.12	.05	.02
□ 205 Vern Benson	.12	.05	.02
□ 206 Ed Bailey	.20	.09	.03
□ 207 Whitey Ford	1.50	.65	.19
□ 208 Jim Wilson	.12	.05	.02
□ 209 Jim Greengrass	.12	.05	.02
□ 210 Bob Cerv	.15	.07	.02
□ 211 J.W. Porter	.12	.05	.02
□ 212 Jack Dittmer	.12	.05	.02
□ 213 Ray Scarborough	.12	.05	.02
□ 214 Bill Bruton	.15	.07	.02
□ 215 Gene Conley	.15	.07	.02
□ 216 Jim Hughes	.12	.05	.02
□ 217 Murray Wall	.12	.05	.02
□ 218 Les Fusselman	.12	.05	.02
□ 219 Pete Runnels UER (Photo actually Don Johnson)	.15	.07	.02
□ 220 Satchel Paige UER (Misspelled Satchell on card front)	4.00	1.80	.50
□ 221 Bob Milliken	.15	.07	.02
□ 222 Vic Janowicz	.25	.11	.03
□ 223 Johnny O'Brien	.25	.11	.03
□ 224 Lou Sleater	.15	.07	.02
□ 225 Bobby Shantz	.25	.11	.03
□ 226 Ed Erautt	.15	.07	.02
□ 227 Morrie Martin	.15	.07	.02
□ 228 Hal Newhouser	1.00	.45	.13
□ 229 Rocky Krsnich	.15	.07	.02
□ 230 Johnny Lindell	.15	.07	.02
□ 231 Solly Hemus	.15	.07	.02
□ 232 Dick Kokos	.15	.07	.02
□ 233 Al Aber	.15	.07	.02
□ 234 Ray Murray	.15	.07	.02
□ 235 John Hetki	.15	.07	.02
□ 236 Harry Perkowski	.15	.07	.02
□ 237 Bud Podbielan	.15	.07	.02
□ 238 Cal Hogue	.15	.07	.02
□ 239 Jim Delsing	.15	.07	.02
□ 240 Fred Marsh	.15	.07	.02
□ 241 Al Sima	.15	.07	.02
□ 242 Charlie Silvera	.20	.09	.03
□ 243 Carlos Bernier	.15	.07	.02
□ 244 Willie Mays	12.00	5.50	1.50
□ 245 Bill Norman CO	.15	.07	.02
□ 246 Roy Face	.35	.16	.04
□ 247 Mike Sandlock	.15	.07	.02
□ 248 Gene Stephens	.15	.07	.02
□ 249 Eddie O'Brien	.25	.11	.03
□ 250 Bob Wilson	.15	.07	.02
□ 251 Sid Hudson	.15	.07	.02
□ 252 Hank Foiles	.15	.07	.02
□ 253 Does not exist	.00	.00	.00
□ 254 Preacher Roe	.35	.16	.04
□ 255 Dixie Howell	.15	.07	.02
□ 256 Les Peden	.15	.07	.02
□ 257 Bob Boyd	.15	.07	.02
□ 258 Jim Gilliam	.50	.23	.06
□ 259 Roy McMillan	.20	.09	.03
□ 260 Sam Calderone	.15	.07	.02
□ 261 Does not exist	.00	.00	.00
□ 262 Bob Oldis	.15	.07	.02
□ 263 Johnny Podres	.50	.23	.06
□ 264 Gene Woodling	.30	.14	.04
□ 265 Jackie Jensen	.40	.18	.05
□ 266 Bob Cain	.15	.07	.02
□ 267 Does not exist	.00	.00	.00
□ 268 Does not exist	.00	.00	.00
□ 269 Duane Pillette	.15	.07	.02
□ 270 Vern Stephens	.20	.09	.03
□ 271 Does not exist	.00	.00	.00
□ 272 Bill Antonello	.15	.07	.02
□ 273 Harvey Haddix	.30	.14	.04
□ 274 John Riddle	.15	.07	.02
□ 275 Does not exist	.00	.00	.00
□ 276 Ken Raffensberger	.15	.07	.02
□ 277 Don Lund	.15	.07	.02
□ 278 Willie Miranda	.15	.07	.02
□ 279 Joe Coleman	.15	.07	.02
□ 280 Milt Bolling	.35	.16	.04
□ 281 Jimmie Dykes MG	.25	.11	.03
□ 282 Ralph Houk	.25	.11	.03
□ 283 Frank Thomas	.25	.11	.03
□ 284 Bob Lemon	.60	.25	.08
□ 285 Joe Adcock	.30	.14	.04
□ 286 Jimmy Piersall	.35	.16	.04
□ 287 Mickey Vernon	.30	.14	.04
□ 288 Robin Roberts	.75	.35	.09
□ 289 Rogers Hornsby MG	.75	.35	.09
□ 290 Hank Bauer	.30	.14	.04
□ 291 Hoot Evers	.20	.09	.03
□ 292 Whitey Lockman	.20	.09	.03
□ 293 Ralph Branca	.30	.14	.04
□ 294 Wally Post	.20	.09	.03
□ 295 Phil Cavarretta MG	.25	.11	.03
□ 296 Gil Hodges	.60	.25	.08
□ 297 Roy Smalley	.20	.09	.03
□ 298 Bob Friend	.25	.11	.03
□ 299 Dusty Rhodes	.25	.11	.03
□ 300 Eddie Stanky	.25	.11	.03
□ 301 Harvey Kuenn	.50	.23	.06
□ 302 Marty Marion	.35	.16	.04
□ 303 Sal Maglie	.35	.16	.04
□ 304 Lou Boudreau MG	.50	.23	.06
□ 305 Carl Furillo	.35	.16	.04
□ 306 Bobo Holloman	.25	.11	.03
□ 307 Steve O'Neill MG	.20	.09	.03
□ 308 Carl Erskine	.35	.16	.04
□ 309 Leo Durocher MG	.50	.23	.06
□ 310 Lew Burdette	.35	.16	.04
□ 311 Richie Ashburn	.60	.25	.08
□ 312 Hoyt Wilhelm	.90	.40	.11
□ 313 Bucky Harris MG	.40	.18	.05
□ 314 Joe Garagiola	.50	.23	.06
□ 315 Johnny Pesky	.25	.11	.03
□ 316 Fred Haney MG	.20	.09	.03
□ 317 Hank Aaron	9.00	4.00	1.15
□ 318 Curt Simmons	.25	.11	.03
□ 319 Ted Williams	9.00	4.00	1.15
□ 320 Don Newcombe	.40	.18	.05
□ 321 Charlie Grimm MG	.25	.11	.03
□ 322 Paul Richards MG	.20	.09	.03
□ 323 Wes Westrum	.20	.09	.03
□ 324 Vern Law	.30	.14	.04
□ 325 Casey Stengel MG	.60	.25	.08
□ 326 Dizzy Dean and Al Simmons (1953 HOF Inductees)	.50	.23	.06
□ 327 Duke Snider	2.25	1.00	.30
□ 328 Bill Rigney	.20	.09	.03
□ 329 Al Lopez MG	.40	.18	.05
□ 330 Bobby Thomson	.30	.14	.04
□ 331 Nellie Fox	.45	.20	.06
□ 332 Eleanor Engle	1.25	.55	.16
□ 333 Larry Doby	.30	.14	.04
□ 334 Billy Goodman	.20	.09	.03
□ 335 Checklist 1-140	.20	.09	.03
□ 336 Checklist 141-280	.20	.09	.03
□ 337 Checklist 281-337	.20	.09	.03

1991 Topps Babe Ruth

This 11-card set was produced by Topps to commemorate the NBC made-for-television movie about Ruth that aired Sunday, October 6, 1991. The standard-size (2 1/2" by 3 1/2") cards have various color shots from the movie on the fronts, with aqua and red borders on a white card face. The name "Babe Ruth" is written in cursive lettering in the lower right corner of each card, and a caption for each card appears below the picture in the red border. The horizontally oriented backs are printed in dark blue and pink on gray and feature an extended caption to the picture on the front. The cards are numbered on the back.

	MT	EX-MT	VG
COMPLETE SET (11)	25.00	11.50	3.10
COMMON PLAYER (1-11)	1.50	.65	.19

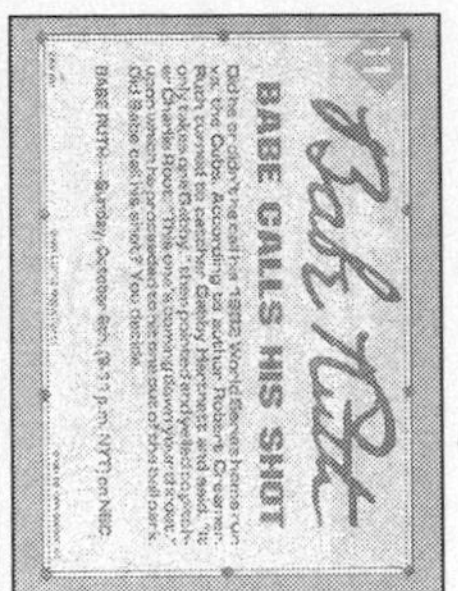

☐ 1 Babe Ruth-Sunday October 6th NBC	2.00	.90	.25
☐ 2 Babe Ruth Stephen Lang as Babe Ruth	2.00	.90	.25
☐ 3 Babe Ruth Bruce Weitz as Miller Huggins	1.50	.65	.19
☐ 4 Babe Ruth Lisa Zane as Claire Ruth	1.50	.65	.19
☐ 5 Babe Ruth Donald Moffat as Jacob Ruppert	1.50	.65	.19
☐ 6 Babe Ruth Neil McDonough as Lou Gehrig	2.00	.90	.25
☐ 7 Babe Ruth Pete Rose as Ty Cobb	10.00	4.50	1.25
☐ 8 Babe Ruth Rod Carew Baseball Consultant	6.00	2.70	.75
☐ 9 Babe Ruth Ruth and Mgr. Huggins	2.50	1.15	.30
☐ 10 Babe Ruth Ruth in Action	2.50	1.15	.30
☐ 11 Babe Ruth Babe Calls His Shot	2.50	1.15	.30

1991 Topps Debut '90

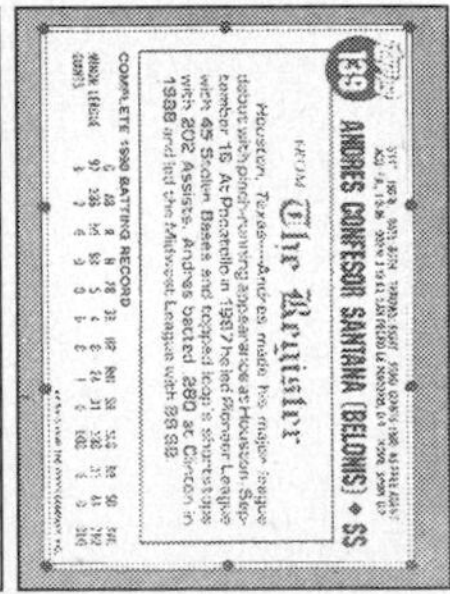

The 1991 Topps Major League Debut Set contains 171 cards measuring the standard size (2 1/2" by 3 1/2"). Although the checklist card is arranged chronologically in order of first major league appearance in 1990, the player cards are arranged alphabetically by the player's last name. The front design features mostly posed color player photos, with two different color stripes on the top and sides of the picture. The card face is white, and the player's name is given in the color stripe below the picture. The horizontally oriented backs have player information and statistics in blue lettering on a pink and white background. The cards are numbered on the back.

	MT	EX-MT	VG
COMPLETE SET (171)	28.00	12.50	3.50
COMMON PLAYER (1-171)	.05	.02	.01
☐ 1 Paul Abbott	.10	.05	.01
☐ 2 Steve Adkins	.05	.02	.01
☐ 3 Scott Aldred	.10	.05	.01
☐ 4 Gerald Alexander	.10	.05	.01
☐ 5 Moises Alou	.25	.11	.03
☐ 6 Steve Avery	2.50	1.15	.30
☐ 7 Oscar Azocar	.10	.05	.01
☐ 8 Carlos Baerga	.60	.25	.08
☐ 9 Kevin Baez	.10	.05	.01
☐ 10 Jeff Baldwin	.10	.05	.01
☐ 11 Brian Barnes	.15	.07	.02
☐ 12 Kevin Bearse	.10	.05	.01
☐ 13 Kevin Belcher	.10	.05	.01
☐ 14 Mike Bell	.15	.07	.02
☐ 15 Sean Berry	.10	.05	.01
☐ 16 Joe Bitker	.10	.05	.01
☐ 17 Willie Blair	.05	.02	.01
☐ 18 Brian Bohanon	.10	.05	.01
☐ 19 Mike Bordick	.20	.09	.03
☐ 20 Shawn Boskie	.10	.05	.01
☐ 21 Rod Brewer	.20	.09	.03
☐ 22 Kevin Brown	.10	.05	.01
☐ 23 Dave Burba	.10	.05	.01
☐ 24 Jim Campbell	.05	.02	.01
☐ 25 Ozzie Canseco	.20	.09	.03
☐ 26 Chuck Carr	.20	.09	.03
☐ 27 Larry Casian	.10	.05	.01
☐ 28 Andujar Cedeno	.35	.16	.04
☐ 29 Wes Chamberlain	.50	.23	.06
☐ 30 Scott Chiamparino	.10	.05	.01
☐ 31 Steve Chitren	.10	.05	.01
☐ 32 Pete Coachman	.05	.02	.01
☐ 33 Alex Cole	.20	.09	.03
☐ 34 Jeff Conine	.30	.14	.04
☐ 35 Scott Cooper	.50	.23	.06
☐ 36 Milt Cuyler	.25	.11	.03
☐ 37 Steve Decker	.25	.11	.03
☐ 38 Rich DeLucia	.05	.02	.01
☐ 39 Delino DeShields	.60	.25	.08
☐ 40 Mark Dewey	.10	.05	.01
☐ 41 Carlos Diaz	.10	.05	.01
☐ 42 Lance Dickson	.15	.07	.02
☐ 43 Narciso Elvira	.10	.05	.01
☐ 44 Luis Encarnacion	.05	.02	.01
☐ 45 Scott Erickson	.50	.23	.06
☐ 46 Paul Faries	.10	.05	.01
☐ 47 Howard Farmer	.10	.05	.01
☐ 48 Alex Fernandez	.30	.14	.04
☐ 49 Travis Fryman	5.00	2.30	.60
☐ 50 Rich Garces	.10	.05	.01
☐ 51 Carlos Garcia	.30	.14	.04
☐ 52 Mike Gardiner	.05	.02	.01
☐ 53 Bernard Gilkey	.50	.23	.06
☐ 54 Tom Gilles	.10	.05	.01
☐ 55 Jerry Goff	.05	.02	.01
☐ 56 Leo Gomez	.50	.23	.06
☐ 57 Luis Gonzalez	.25	.11	.03
☐ 58 Joe Grahe	.15	.07	.02
☐ 59 Craig Grebeck	.15	.07	.02
☐ 60 Kip Gross	.05	.02	.01
☐ 61 Eric Gunderson	.05	.02	.01
☐ 62 Chris Hammond	.15	.07	.02
☐ 63 Dave Hansen	.10	.05	.01
☐ 64 Reggie Harris	.10	.05	.01
☐ 65 Bill Haselman	.10	.05	.01
☐ 66 Randy Hennis	.10	.05	.01
☐ 67 Carlos Hernandez	.15	.07	.02
☐ 68 Howard Hilton	.05	.02	.01
☐ 69 Dave Hollins	.40	.18	.05
☐ 70 Darren Holmes	.15	.07	.02
☐ 71 John Hoover	.05	.02	.01
☐ 72 Steve Howard	.10	.05	.01
☐ 73 Thomas Howard	.10	.05	.01
☐ 74 Todd Hundley	.25	.11	.03
☐ 75 Daryl Irvine	.10	.05	.01
☐ 76 Chris Jelic	.15	.07	.02
☐ 77 Dana Kiecker	.05	.02	.01
☐ 78 Brent Knackert	.15	.07	.02
☐ 79 Jimmy Kremers	.10	.05	.01
☐ 80 Jerry Kutzler	.10	.05	.01
☐ 81 Ray Lankford	1.00	.45	.13
☐ 82 Tim Layana	.10	.05	.01
☐ 83 Terry Lee	.05	.02	.01
☐ 84 Mark Leiter	.10	.05	.01
☐ 85 Scott Leius	.15	.07	.02
☐ 86 Mark Leonard	.10	.05	.01
☐ 87 Darren Lewis	.25	.11	.03
☐ 88 Scott Lewis	.10	.05	.01
☐ 89 Jim Leyritz	.10	.05	.01
☐ 90 Dave Liddell	.10	.05	.01

☐ 91 Luis Lopez	.30	.14	.04
☐ 92 Kevin Maas	.40	.18	.05
☐ 93 Bob MacDonald	.10	.05	.01
☐ 94 Carlos Maldonado	.10	.05	.01
☐ 95 Chuck Malone	.10	.05	.01
☐ 96 Ramon Manon	.15	.07	.02
☐ 97 Jeff Manto	.10	.05	.01
☐ 98 Paul Marak	.05	.02	.01
☐ 99 Tino Martinez	.35	.16	.04
☐ 100 Derrick May	.35	.16	.04
☐ 101 Brent Mayne	.15	.07	.02
☐ 102 Paul McClellan	.15	.07	.02
☐ 103 Rodney McCray	.10	.05	.01
☐ 104 Tim McIntosh	.10	.05	.01
☐ 105 Brian McRae	.30	.14	.04
☐ 106 Jose Melendez	.15	.07	.02
☐ 107 Orlando Merced	.30	.14	.04
☐ 108 Alan Mills	.15	.07	.02
☐ 109 Gino Minutelli	.25	.11	.03
☐ 110 Mickey Morandini	.25	.11	.03
☐ 111 Pedro Munoz	.40	.18	.05
☐ 112 Chris Nabholz	.20	.09	.03
☐ 113 Tim Naehring	.25	.11	.03
☐ 114 Charles Nagy	.30	.14	.04
☐ 115 Jim Neidlinger	.10	.05	.01
☐ 116 Rafael Novoa	.10	.05	.01
☐ 117 Jose Offerman	.25	.11	.03
☐ 118 Omar Olivares	.20	.09	.03
☐ 119 Javier Ortiz	.40	.18	.05
☐ 120 Al Osuna	.10	.05	.01
☐ 121 Rick Parker	.10	.05	.01
☐ 122 Dave Pavlas	.10	.05	.01
☐ 123 Geronimo Pena	.20	.09	.03
☐ 124 Mike Perez	.15	.07	.02
☐ 125 Phil Plantier	.75	.35	.09
☐ 126 Jim Poole	.10	.05	.01
☐ 127 Tom Quinlan	.10	.05	.01
☐ 128 Scott Radinsky	.20	.09	.03
☐ 129 Darren Reed	.10	.05	.01
☐ 130 Karl Rhodes	.05	.02	.01
☐ 131 Jeff Richardson	.05	.02	.01
☐ 132 Rich Rodriguez	.05	.02	.01
☐ 133 Dave Rohde	.05	.02	.01
☐ 134 Mel Rojas	.15	.07	.02
☐ 135 Vic Rosario	.10	.05	.01
☐ 136 Rich Rowland	.15	.07	.02
☐ 137 Scott Ruskin	.10	.05	.01
☐ 138 Bill Sampen	.05	.02	.01
☐ 139 Andres Santana	.25	.11	.03
☐ 140 David Segui	.10	.05	.01
☐ 141 Jeff Shaw	.10	.05	.01
☐ 142 Tim Sherrill	.10	.05	.01
☐ 143 Terry Shumpert	.10	.05	.01
☐ 144 Mike Simms	.15	.07	.02
☐ 145 Daryl Smith	.10	.05	.01
☐ 146 Luis Sojo	.15	.07	.02
☐ 147 Steve Springer	.10	.05	.01
☐ 148 Ray Stephens	.10	.05	.01
☐ 149 Lee Stevens	.25	.11	.03
☐ 150 Mel Stottlemyre Jr.	.05	.02	.01
☐ 151 Glenn Sutko	.10	.05	.01
☐ 152 Anthony Telford	.10	.05	.01
☐ 153 Frank Thomas	7.50	3.40	.95
☐ 154 Randy Tomlin	.30	.14	.04
☐ 155 Brian Traxler	.10	.05	.01
☐ 156 Efrain Valdez	.10	.05	.01
☐ 157 Rafael Valdez	.15	.07	.02
☐ 158 Julio Valera	.20	.09	.03
☐ 159 Jim Vatcher	.10	.05	.01
☐ 160 Hector Villanueva	.10	.05	.01
☐ 161 Hector Wagner	.10	.05	.01
☐ 162 Dave Walsh	.10	.05	.01
☐ 163 Steve Wapnick	.10	.05	.01
☐ 164 Colby Ward	.10	.05	.01
☐ 165 Turner Ward	.15	.07	.02
☐ 166 Terry Wells	.10	.05	.01
☐ 167 Mark Whiten	.15	.07	.02
☐ 168 Mike York	.10	.05	.01
☐ 169 Cliff Young	.10	.05	.01
☐ 170 Checklist Card	.08	.04	.01
☐ 171 Checklist Card	.08	.04	.01

1991 Topps Traded

The 1991 Topps Traded set contains 132 cards measuring the standard size (2 1/2 by 3 1/2"). The set includes a Team U.S.A. subset, featuring 25 of America's top collegiate

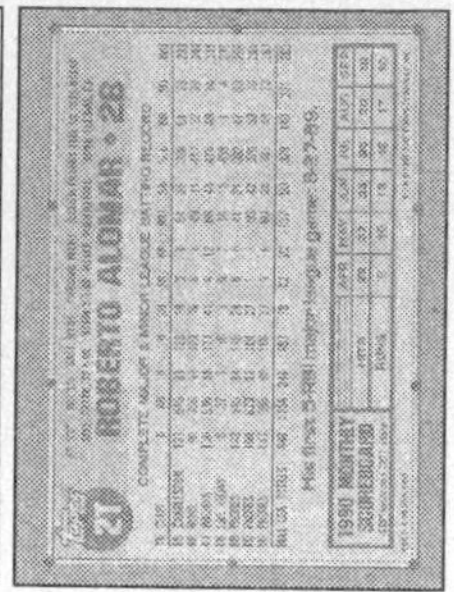

players; these players are indicated in the checklist below by USA. The cards were sold in wax packs as well as factory sets. The cards in the wax packs (gray backs) and collated factory sets (white backs) are from different card stock. The fronts have color action player photos, with two different color borders on a white card face. The player's position and name are given in the thicker border below the picture. In blue print on a pink and gray background, the horizontally oriented backs have biographical information and statistics. The cards are numbered on the back in the upper left corner; the set numbering corresponds to alphabetical order. The key Rookie Cards in this set are Jeff Bagwell, Jeffrey Hammonds, Charles Johnson, Phil Nevin, and Ivan Rodriguez.

	MT	EX-MT	VG
COMPLETE SET (132)	12.00	5.50	1.50
COMMON PLAYER (1T-132T)	.05	.02	.01
☐ 1T Juan Agosto	.05	.02	.01
☐ 2T Roberto Alomar	.20	.09	.03
☐ 3T Wally Backman	.05	.02	.01
☐ 4T Jeff Bagwell	1.25	.55	.16
☐ 5T Skeeter Barnes	.05	.02	.01
☐ 6T Steve Bedrosian	.05	.02	.01
☐ 7T Derek Bell	.30	.14	.04
☐ 8T George Bell	.08	.04	.01
☐ 9T Rafael Belliard	.05	.02	.01
☐ 10T Dante Bichette	.05	.02	.01
☐ 11T Bud Black	.05	.02	.01
☐ 12T Mike Boddicker	.05	.02	.01
☐ 13T Sid Bream	.05	.02	.01
☐ 14T Hubie Brooks	.05	.02	.01
☐ 15T Brett Butler	.08	.04	.01
☐ 16T Ivan Calderon	.05	.02	.01
☐ 17T John Candelaria	.05	.02	.01
☐ 18T Tom Candiotti	.05	.02	.01
☐ 19T Gary Carter	.08	.04	.01
☐ 20T Joe Carter	.12	.05	.02
☐ 21T Rick Cerone	.05	.02	.01
☐ 22T Jack Clark	.08	.04	.01
☐ 23T Vince Coleman	.08	.04	.01
☐ 24T Scott Coolbaugh	.05	.02	.01
☐ 25T Danny Cox	.05	.02	.01
☐ 26T Danny Darwin	.05	.02	.01
☐ 27T Chili Davis	.08	.04	.01
☐ 28T Glenn Davis	.08	.04	.01
☐ 29T Steve Decker	.15	.07	.02
☐ 30T Rob Deer	.08	.04	.01
☐ 31T Rich DeLucia	.05	.02	.01
☐ 32T John Dettmer USA	.20	.09	.03
☐ 33T Brian Downing	.05	.02	.01
☐ 34T Darren Dreifort USA	.35	.16	.04
☐ 35T Kirk Dressendorfer	.10	.05	.01
☐ 36T Jim Essian MG	.05	.02	.01
☐ 37T Dwight Evans	.08	.04	.01
☐ 38T Steve Farr	.05	.02	.01
☐ 39T Jeff Fassero	.10	.05	.01
☐ 40T Junior Felix	.05	.02	.01
☐ 41T Tony Fernandez	.08	.04	.01
☐ 42T Steve Finley	.08	.04	.01
☐ 43T Jim Fregosi MG	.05	.02	.01
☐ 44T Gary Gaetti	.05	.02	.01
☐ 45T Jason Giambi USA	.40	.18	.05
☐ 46T Kirk Gibson	.08	.04	.01
☐ 47T Leo Gomez	.25	.11	.03
☐ 48T Luis Gonzalez	.20	.09	.03
☐ 49T Jeff Granger USA	.30	.14	.04

☐ 50T Todd Greene USA	.25	.11	.03
☐ 51T Jeffrey Hammonds USA	1.50	.65	.19
☐ 52T Mike Hargrove MG	.05	.02	.01
☐ 53T Pete Harnisch	.08	.04	.01
☐ 54T Rick Helling USA UER (Misspelled Hellings on card back)	.40	.18	.05
☐ 55T Glenallen Hill	.05	.02	.01
☐ 56T Charlie Hough	.05	.02	.01
☐ 57T Pete Incaviglia	.05	.02	.01
☐ 58T Bo Jackson	.12	.05	.02
☐ 59T Danny Jackson	.05	.02	.01
☐ 60T Reggie Jefferson	.15	.07	.02
☐ 61T Charles Johnson USA	1.25	.55	.16
☐ 62T Jeff Johnson	.10	.05	.01
☐ 63T Todd Johnson USA	.25	.11	.03
☐ 64T Barry Jones	.05	.02	.01
☐ 65T Chris Jones	.05	.02	.01
☐ 66T Scott Kamieniecki	.10	.05	.01
☐ 67T Pat Kelly	.15	.07	.02
☐ 68T Darryl Kile	.10	.05	.01
☐ 69T Chuck Knoblauch	.40	.18	.05
☐ 70T Bill Krueger	.05	.02	.01
☐ 71T Scott Leius	.10	.05	.01
☐ 72T Donnie Leshnock USA	.25	.11	.03
☐ 73T Mark Lewis	.10	.05	.01
☐ 74T Candy Maldonado	.05	.02	.01
☐ 75T Jason McDonald USA	.20	.09	.03
☐ 76T Willie McGee	.08	.04	.01
☐ 77T Fred McGriff	.12	.05	.02
☐ 78T Billy McMillon USA	.20	.09	.03
☐ 79T Hal McRae MG	.05	.02	.01
☐ 80T Dan Melendez USA	.25	.11	.03
☐ 81T Orlando Merced	.20	.09	.03
☐ 82T Jack Morris	.10	.05	.01
☐ 83T Phil Nevin USA	2.00	.90	.25
☐ 84T Otis Nixon	.08	.04	.01
☐ 85T Johnny Oates MG	.05	.02	.01
☐ 86T Bob Ojeda	.05	.02	.01
☐ 87T Mike Pagliarulo	.05	.02	.01
☐ 88T Dean Palmer	.20	.09	.03
☐ 89T Dave Parker	.08	.04	.01
☐ 90T Terry Pendleton	.10	.05	.01
☐ 91T Tony Phillips (P) USA	.15	.07	.02
☐ 92T Doug Piatt	.10	.05	.01
☐ 93T Ron Polk USA CO	.05	.02	.01
☐ 94T Tim Raines	.08	.04	.01
☐ 95T Willie Randolph	.08	.04	.01
☐ 96T Dave Righetti	.05	.02	.01
☐ 97T Ernie Riles	.05	.02	.01
☐ 98T Chris Roberts USA	.60	.25	.08
☐ 99T Jeff D. Robinson	.05	.02	.01
☐ 100T Jeff M. Robinson	.05	.02	.01
☐ 101T Ivan Rodriguez	1.25	.55	.16
☐ 102T Steve Rodriguez USA	.20	.09	.03
☐ 103T Tom Runnells MG	.05	.02	.01
☐ 104T Scott Sanderson	.05	.02	.01
☐ 105T Bob Scanlan	.10	.05	.01
☐ 106T Pete Schourek	.12	.05	.02
☐ 107T Gary Scott	.15	.07	.02
☐ 108T Paul Shuey USA	.50	.23	.06
☐ 109T Doug Simons	.05	.02	.01
☐ 110T Dave Smith	.05	.02	.01
☐ 111T Cory Snyder	.05	.02	.01
☐ 112T Luis Sojo	.05	.02	.01
☐ 113T Kennie Steenstra USA	.20	.09	.03
☐ 114T Darryl Strawberry	.12	.05	.02
☐ 115T Franklin Stubbs	.05	.02	.01
☐ 116T Todd Taylor USA	.20	.09	.03
☐ 117T Wade Taylor	.05	.02	.01
☐ 118T Garry Templeton	.05	.02	.01
☐ 119T Mickey Tettleton	.08	.04	.01
☐ 120T Tim Teufel	.05	.02	.01
☐ 121T Mike Timlin	.10	.05	.01
☐ 122T David Tuttle USA	.20	.09	.03
☐ 123T Mo Vaughn	.20	.09	.03
☐ 124T Jeff Ware USA	.25	.11	.03
☐ 125T Devon White	.08	.04	.01
☐ 126T Mark Whiten	.10	.05	.01
☐ 127T Mitch Williams	.05	.02	.01
☐ 128T Craig Wilson USA	.20	.09	.03
☐ 129T Willie Wilson	.05	.02	.01
☐ 130T Chris Wimmer	.30	.14	.04
☐ 131T Ivan Zweig USA	.20	.09	.03
☐ 132T Checklist Card	.08	.01	.00

1991 Topps Wax Box Cards

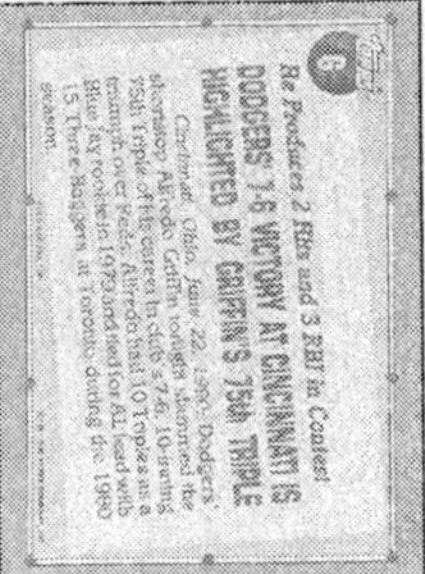

Topps again in 1991 issued cards on the bottom of their wax pack boxes. There are four different boxes, each with four cards and a checklist on the side. These standard-size cards (2 1/2" by 3 1/2") have yellow borders rather than the white borders of the regular issue cards, and they have different photos of the players. The backs are printed in pink and blue on gray cardboard stock and feature outstanding achievements of the players. The cards are numbered by letter on the back. The cards have the typical Topps 1991 design on the front of the card. The set was ordered in alphabetical order, but is "lettered" rather than numbered.

	MT	EX-MT	VG
COMPLETE SET (16)	5.00	2.30	.60
COMMON PLAYER (A-P)	.15	.07	.02
☐ A Bert Blyleven	.25	.11	.03
☐ B George Brett	.60	.25	.08
☐ C Brett Butler	.25	.11	.03
☐ D Andre Dawson	.50	.23	.06
☐ E Dwight Evans	.25	.11	.03
☐ F Carlton Fisk	.35	.16	.04
☐ G Alfredo Griffin	.15	.07	.02
☐ H Rickey Henderson	.75	.35	.09
☐ I Willie McGee	.25	.11	.03
☐ J Dale Murphy	.35	.16	.04
☐ K Eddie Murray	.35	.16	.04
☐ L Dave Parker	.25	.11	.03
☐ M Jeff Reardon	.25	.11	.03
☐ N Nolan Ryan	1.00	.45	.13
☐ O Juan Samuel	.15	.07	.02
☐ P Robin Yount	.60	.25	.08

1992 Topps Promo Sheet

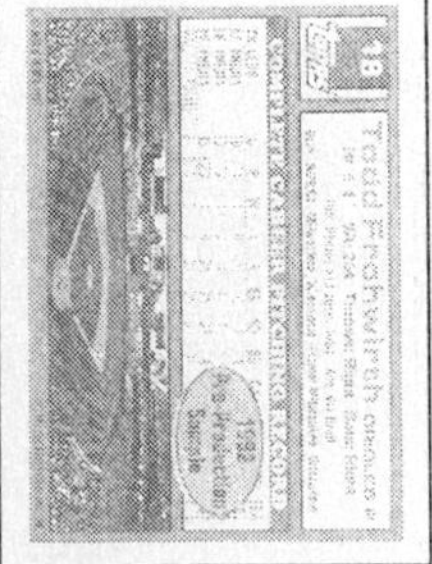

This 1992 Topps pre-production sample sheet measures approximately 7 3/4" by 10 3/4" and features nine player cards. The sheet is unperforated and if cut, the cards would measure the standard size (2 1/2" by 3 1/2"). The fronts have glossy color action photos on a white card face, with different color borders overlaying the picture. In a horizontal format, the backs have biography and complete Major League statistics. Moreover, some of the backs display pictures of baseball stadiums, if the player's career length permits. The cards are numbered on the back and also show an oval-shaped "1992 Pre-Production Sample" over some of the statistics.

	MT	EX-MT	VG
COMPLETE SET (9)	12.00	5.50	1.50
COMMON PLAYER	2.00	.90	.25
☐ 3 Shawon Dunston	2.25	1.00	.30
☐ 16 Mike Heath	2.00	.90	.25
☐ 18 Todd Frohwirth	2.00	.90	.25
☐ 20 Bip Roberts	2.25	1.00	.30
☐ 131 Rob Dibble	2.50	1.15	.30
☐ 174 Otis Nixon	2.25	1.00	.30
☐ 273 Denny Martinez	2.25	1.00	.30
☐ 325 Brett Butler	2.50	1.15	.30
☐ 798 Tom Lasorda MG	2.50	1.15	.30

1992 Topps Gold Promo Sheet

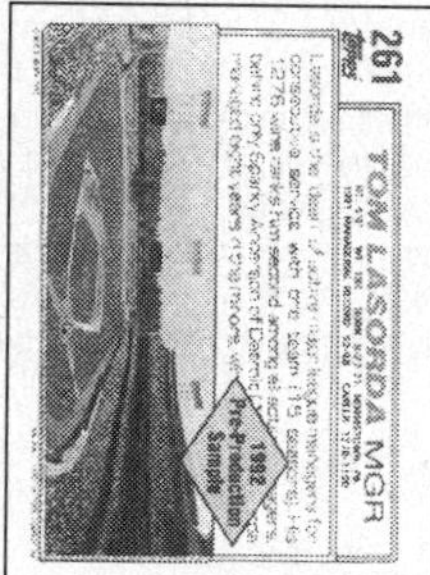

This 1992 Topps Gold pre-production sample sheet measures approximately 7 3/4" by 10 3/4" and features nine player cards. The sheet is unperforated and if cut, the cards would measure the standard size (2 1/2" by 3 1/2"). The fronts have glossy color action photos on a white card face, with different color borders overlaying the picture. In a horizontal format, the backs have biography and complete Major League statistics. Moreover, some of the backs display pictures of baseball stadiums, if the player's career length permits. The cards are numbered on the back and also show a diamond-shaped "1992 Pre-Production Sample" over some of the statistics.

	MT	EX-MT	VG
COMPLETE SET (9)	20.00	9.00	2.50
COMMON PLAYER	2.00	.90	.25
☐ 1 Nolan Ryan	9.00	4.00	1.15
☐ 15 Denny Martinez	2.25	1.00	.30
☐ 20 Bip Roberts	2.25	1.00	.30
☐ 40 Cal Ripken	7.50	3.40	.95
☐ 261 Tom Lasorda MG	2.50	1.15	.30
☐ 370 Shawon Dunston	2.25	1.00	.30
☐ 512 Mike Heath	2.00	.90	.25
☐ 655 Brett Butler	2.50	1.15	.30
☐ 757 Rob Dibble	2.50	1.15	.30

1992 Topps

The 1992 Topps set contains 792 cards measuring the standard size (2 1/2" by 3 1/2"). The fronts have either posed or action color player photos on a white card face. Different color stripes frame the pictures, and the player's name and team name appear in two short color stripes

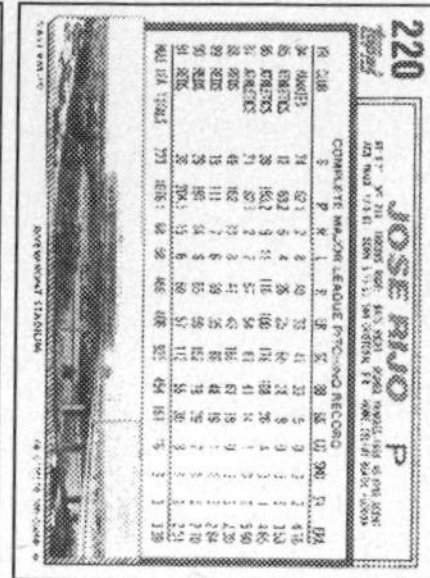

respectively at the bottom. In a horizontal format, the backs have biography and complete career batting or pitching record. In addition, some of the cards have a picture of a baseball field and stadium on the back. Special subsets included are Record Breakers (2-5), Prospects (58, 126, 179, 473, 551, 591, 618, 656, 676), and All-Stars (386-407). The cards are numbered on the back. These cards were not issued with bubble gum and feature white card stock. The key Rookie Cards in this set are Cliff Floyd, Tyler Green, Manny Ramirez, and Brien Taylor.

	MT	EX-MT	VG
COMPLETE SET (792)	20.00	9.00	2.50
COMPLETE FACT.SET (802)	30.00	13.50	3.80
COMPLETE HOLIDAY SET (811)	33.00	15.00	4.10
COMMON PLAYER (1-792)	.04	.02	.01
☐ 1 Nolan Ryan	.40	.18	.05
☐ 2 Ricky Henderson RB (Some cards have print marks that show 1.991 on the front)	.10	.05	.01
☐ 3 Jeff Reardon RB	.04	.02	.01
☐ 4 Nolan Ryan RB	.25	.11	.03
☐ 5 Dave Winfield RB	.10	.05	.01
☐ 6 Brien Taylor	2.50	1.15	.30
☐ 7 Jim Olander	.10	.05	.01
☐ 8 Bryan Hickerson	.10	.05	.01
☐ 9 Jon Farrell	.10	.05	.01
☐ 10 Wade Boggs	.12	.05	.02
☐ 11 Jack McDowell	.07	.03	.01
☐ 12 Luis Gonzalez	.07	.03	.01
☐ 13 Mike Scioscia	.04	.02	.01
☐ 14 Wes Chamberlain	.07	.03	.01
☐ 15 Dennis Martinez	.07	.03	.01
☐ 16 Jeff Montgomery	.04	.02	.01
☐ 17 Randy Milligan	.04	.02	.01
☐ 18 Greg Cadaret	.04	.02	.01
☐ 19 Jamie Quirk	.04	.02	.01
☐ 20 Bip Roberts	.07	.03	.01
☐ 21 Buck Rogers MG	.04	.02	.01
☐ 22 Bill Wegman	.04	.02	.01
☐ 23 Chuck Knoblauch	.20	.09	.03
☐ 24 Randy Myers	.07	.03	.01
☐ 25 Ron Gant	.10	.05	.01
☐ 26 Mike Bielecki	.04	.02	.01
☐ 27 Juan Gonzalez	.35	.16	.04
☐ 28 Mike Schooler	.04	.02	.01
☐ 29 Mickey Tettleton	.07	.03	.01
☐ 30 John Kruk	.07	.03	.01
☐ 31 Bryn Smith	.04	.02	.01
☐ 32 Chris Nabholz	.07	.03	.01
☐ 33 Carlos Baerga	.15	.07	.02
☐ 34 Jeff Juden	.08	.04	.01
☐ 35 Dave Righetti	.04	.02	.01
☐ 36 Scott Ruffcorn	.25	.11	.03
☐ 37 Luis Polonia	.07	.03	.01
☐ 38 Tom Candiotti	.04	.02	.01
☐ 39 Greg Olson	.04	.02	.01
☐ 40 Cal Ripken	.25	.11	.03
☐ 41 Craig Lefferts	.04	.02	.01
☐ 42 Mike Macfarlane	.04	.02	.01
☐ 43 Jose Lind	.04	.02	.01
☐ 44 Rick Aguilera	.07	.03	.01
☐ 45 Gary Carter	.07	.03	.01
☐ 46 Steve Farr	.04	.02	.01
☐ 47 Rex Hudler	.04	.02	.01
☐ 48 Scott Scudder	.04	.02	.01
☐ 49 Damon Berryhill	.04	.02	.01
☐ 50 Ken Griffey Jr.	.50	.23	.06

☐ 51 Tom Runnells MG	.04	.02	.01
☐ 52 Juan Bell	.04	.02	.01
☐ 53 Tommy Gregg	.04	.02	.01
☐ 54 David Wells	.04	.02	.01
☐ 55 Rafael Palmeiro	.07	.03	.01
☐ 56 Charlie O'Brien	.04	.02	.01
☐ 57 Donn Pall	.04	.02	.01
☐ 58 1992 Prospects C	.35	.16	.04
Brad Ausmus			
Jim Campanis Jr.			
Dave Nilsson			
Doug Robbins			
☐ 59 Mo Vaughn	.07	.03	.01
☐ 60 Tony Fernandez	.07	.03	.01
☐ 61 Paul O'Neill	.07	.03	.01
☐ 62 Gene Nelson	.04	.02	.01
☐ 63 Randy Ready	.04	.02	.01
☐ 64 Bob Kipper	.04	.02	.01
☐ 65 Willie McGee	.07	.03	.01
☐ 66 Scott Stahoviak	.20	.09	.03
☐ 67 Luis Salazar	.04	.02	.01
☐ 68 Marvin Freeman	.04	.02	.01
☐ 69 Kenny Lofton	.40	.18	.05
☐ 70 Gary Gaetti	.04	.02	.01
☐ 71 Erik Hanson	.04	.02	.01
☐ 72 Eddie Zosky	.07	.03	.01
☐ 73 Brian Barnes	.04	.02	.01
☐ 74 Scott Leius	.04	.02	.01
☐ 75 Bret Saberhagen	.07	.03	.01
☐ 76 Mike Gallego	.04	.02	.01
☐ 77 Jack Armstrong	.04	.02	.01
☐ 78 Ivan Rodriguez	.30	.14	.04
☐ 79 Jesse Orosco	.04	.02	.01
☐ 80 David Justice	.20	.09	.03
☐ 81 Ced Landrum	.04	.02	.01
☐ 82 Doug Simons	.04	.02	.01
☐ 83 Tommy Greene	.04	.02	.01
☐ 84 Leo Gomez	.10	.05	.01
☐ 85 Jose DeLeon	.04	.02	.01
☐ 86 Steve Finley	.07	.03	.01
☐ 87 Bob MacDonald	.04	.02	.01
☐ 88 Darrin Jackson	.07	.03	.01
☐ 89 Neal Heaton	.04	.02	.01
☐ 90 Robin Yount	.10	.05	.01
☐ 91 Jeff Reed	.04	.02	.01
☐ 92 Lenny Harris	.04	.02	.01
☐ 93 Reggie Jefferson	.07	.03	.01
☐ 94 Sammy Sosa	.04	.02	.01
☐ 95 Scott Bailes	.04	.02	.01
☐ 96 Tom McKinnon	.10	.05	.01
☐ 97 Luis Rivera	.04	.02	.01
☐ 98 Mike Harkey	.07	.03	.01
☐ 99 Jeff Treadway	.04	.02	.01
☐ 100 Jose Canseco	.20	.09	.03
☐ 101 Omar Vizquel	.04	.02	.01
☐ 102 Scott Kamieniecki	.04	.02	.01
☐ 103 Ricky Jordan	.04	.02	.01
☐ 104 Jeff Ballard	.04	.02	.01
☐ 105 Felix Jose	.07	.03	.01
☐ 106 Mike Boddicker	.04	.02	.01
☐ 107 Dan Pasqua	.04	.02	.01
☐ 108 Mike Timlin	.04	.02	.01
☐ 109 Roger Craig MG	.04	.02	.01
☐ 110 Ryne Sandberg	.25	.11	.03
☐ 111 Mark Carreon	.04	.02	.01
☐ 112 Oscar Azocar	.04	.02	.01
☐ 113 Mike Greenwell	.07	.03	.01
☐ 114 Mark Portugal	.04	.02	.01
☐ 115 Terry Pendleton	.10	.05	.01
☐ 116 Willie Randolph	.07	.03	.01
☐ 117 Scott Terry	.04	.02	.01
☐ 118 Chili Davis	.07	.03	.01
☐ 119 Mark Gardner	.04	.02	.01
☐ 120 Alan Trammell	.07	.03	.01
☐ 121 Derek Bell	.10	.05	.01
☐ 122 Gary Varsho	.04	.02	.01
☐ 123 Bob Ojeda	.04	.02	.01
☐ 124 Shawn Livsey	.10	.05	.01
☐ 125 Chris Hoiles	.07	.03	.01
☐ 126 1992 Prospects 1B	.90	.40	.11
Ryan Klesko			
John Jaha			
Rico Brogna			
Dave Staton			
☐ 127 Carlos Quintana	.04	.02	.01
☐ 128 Kurt Stillwell	.04	.02	.01
☐ 129 Melido Perez	.07	.03	.01
☐ 130 Alvin Davis	.04	.02	.01
☐ 131 Checklist 1-132	.05	.01	.00
☐ 132 Eric Show	.04	.02	.01
☐ 133 Rance Mulliniks	.04	.02	.01
☐ 134 Darryl Kile	.04	.02	.01
☐ 135 Von Hayes	.04	.02	.01
☐ 136 Bill Doran	.04	.02	.01
☐ 137 Jeff Robinson	.04	.02	.01
☐ 138 Monty Fariss	.04	.02	.01
☐ 139 Jeff Innis	.04	.02	.01
☐ 140 Mark Grace UER	.07	.03	.01
(Home Calie., should			
be Calif.)			
☐ 141 Jim Leyland MG UER	.04	.02	.01
(No closed parenthesis			
after East in 1991)			
☐ 142 Todd Van Poppel	.20	.09	.03
☐ 143 Paul Gibson	.04	.02	.01
☐ 144 Bill Swift	.04	.02	.01
☐ 145 Danny Tartabull	.07	.03	.01
☐ 146 Al Newman	.04	.02	.01
☐ 147 Cris Carpenter	.04	.02	.01
☐ 148 Anthony Young	.07	.03	.01
☐ 149 Brian Bohanon	.04	.02	.01
☐ 150 Roger Clemens UER	.25	.11	.03
(League leading ERA in			
1990 not italicized)			
☐ 151 Jeff Hamilton	.04	.02	.01
☐ 152 Charlie Leibrandt	.04	.02	.01
☐ 153 Ron Karkovice	.04	.02	.01
☐ 154 Hensley Meulens	.04	.02	.01
☐ 155 Scott Bankhead	.04	.02	.01
☐ 156 Manny Ramirez	.60	.25	.08
☐ 157 Keith Miller	.04	.02	.01
☐ 158 Todd Frohwirth	.04	.02	.01
☐ 159 Darrin Fletcher	.04	.02	.01
☐ 160 Bobby Bonilla	.10	.05	.01
☐ 161 Casey Candaele	.04	.02	.01
☐ 162 Paul Faries	.04	.02	.01
☐ 163 Dana Kiecker	.04	.02	.01
☐ 164 Shane Mack	.07	.03	.01
☐ 165 Mark Langston	.07	.03	.01
☐ 166 Geronimo Pena	.04	.02	.01
☐ 167 Andy Allanson	.04	.02	.01
☐ 168 Dwight Smith	.04	.02	.01
☐ 169 Chuck Crim	.04	.02	.01
☐ 170 Alex Cole	.04	.02	.01
☐ 171 Bill Plummer MG	.04	.02	.01
☐ 172 Juan Berenguer	.04	.02	.01
☐ 173 Brian Downing	.04	.02	.01
☐ 174 Steve Frey	.04	.02	.01
☐ 175 Orel Hershiser	.07	.03	.01
☐ 176 Ramon Garcia	.04	.02	.01
☐ 177 Dan Gladden	.04	.02	.01
☐ 178 Jim Acker	.04	.02	.01
☐ 179 1992 Prospects 2B	.25	.11	.03
Bobby DeJardin			
Cesar Bernhardt			
Armando Moreno			
Andy Stankiewicz			
☐ 180 Kevin Mitchell	.07	.03	.01
☐ 181 Hector Villanueva	.04	.02	.01
☐ 182 Jeff Reardon	.07	.03	.01
☐ 183 Brent Mayne	.04	.02	.01
☐ 184 Jimmy Jones	.04	.02	.01
☐ 185 Benito Santiago	.07	.03	.01
☐ 186 Cliff Floyd	.75	.35	.09
☐ 187 Ernie Riles	.04	.02	.01
☐ 188 Jose Guzman	.04	.02	.01
☐ 189 Junior Felix	.04	.02	.01
☐ 190 Glenn Davis	.07	.03	.01
☐ 191 Charlie Hough	.04	.02	.01
☐ 192 Dave Fleming	.50	.23	.06
☐ 193 Omar Olivares	.04	.02	.01
☐ 194 Eric Karros	.50	.23	.06
☐ 195 David Cone	.07	.03	.01
☐ 196 Frank Castillo	.08	.04	.01
☐ 197 Glenn Braggs	.04	.02	.01
☐ 198 Scott Aldred	.04	.02	.01
☐ 199 Jeff Blauser	.04	.02	.01
☐ 200 Len Dykstra	.07	.03	.01
☐ 201 Buck Showalter MG	.10	.05	.01
☐ 202 Rick Honeycutt	.04	.02	.01
☐ 203 Greg Myers	.04	.02	.01
☐ 204 Trevor Wilson	.04	.02	.01
☐ 205 Jay Howell	.04	.02	.01
☐ 206 Luis Sojo	.04	.02	.01
☐ 207 Jack Clark	.07	.03	.01
☐ 208 Julio Machado	.04	.02	.01
☐ 209 Lloyd McClendon	.04	.02	.01
☐ 210 Ozzie Guillen	.04	.02	.01
☐ 211 Jeremy Hernandez	.10	.05	.01
☐ 212 Randy Velarde	.04	.02	.01
☐ 213 Les Lancaster	.04	.02	.01
☐ 214 Andy Mota	.04	.02	.01
☐ 215 Rich Gossage	.07	.03	.01
☐ 216 Brent Gates	.50	.23	.06
☐ 217 Brian Harper	.04	.02	.01
☐ 218 Mike Flanagan	.04	.02	.01

☐	219	Jerry Browne	.04	.02	.01
☐	220	Jose Rijo	.07	.03	.01
☐	221	Skeeter Barnes	.04	.02	.01
☐	222	Jaime Navarro	.07	.03	.01
☐	223	Mel Hall	.04	.02	.01
☐	224	Bret Barberie	.04	.02	.01
☐	225	Roberto Alomar	.20	.09	.03
☐	226	Pete Smith	.07	.03	.01
☐	227	Daryl Boston	.04	.02	.01
☐	228	Eddie Whitson	.04	.02	.01
☐	229	Shawn Boskie	.04	.02	.01
☐	230	Dick Schofield	.04	.02	.01
☐	231	Brian Drahman	.04	.02	.01
☐	232	John Smiley	.07	.03	.01
☐	233	Mitch Webster	.04	.02	.01
☐	234	Terry Steinbach	.07	.03	.01
☐	235	Jack Morris	.10	.05	.01
☐	236	Bill Pecota	.04	.02	.01
☐	237	Jose Hernandez	.10	.05	.01
☐	238	Greg Litton	.04	.02	.01
☐	239	Brian Holman	.04	.02	.01
☐	240	Andres Galarraga	.04	.02	.01
☐	241	Gerald Young	.04	.02	.01
☐	242	Mike Mussina	.50	.23	.06
☐	243	Alvaro Espinoza	.04	.02	.01
☐	244	Darren Daulton	.07	.03	.01
☐	245	John Smoltz	.10	.05	.01
☐	246	Jason Pruitt	.10	.05	.01
☐	247	Chuck Finley	.04	.02	.01
☐	248	Jim Gantner	.04	.02	.01
☐	249	Tony Fossas	.04	.02	.01
☐	250	Ken Griffey Sr.	.07	.03	.01
☐	251	Kevin Elster	.04	.02	.01
☐	252	Dennis Rasmussen	.04	.02	.01
☐	253	Terry Kennedy	.04	.02	.01
☐	254	Ryan Bowen	.07	.03	.01
☐	255	Robin Ventura	.15	.07	.02
☐	256	Mike Aldrete	.04	.02	.01
☐	257	Jeff Russell	.04	.02	.01
☐	258	Jim Lindeman	.04	.02	.01
☐	259	Ron Darling	.07	.03	.01
☐	260	Devon White	.07	.03	.01
☐	261	Tom Lasorda MG	.04	.02	.01
☐	262	Terry Lee	.04	.02	.01
☐	263	Bob Patterson	.04	.02	.01
☐	264	Checklist 133-264	.05	.01	.00
☐	265	Teddy Higuera	.04	.02	.01
☐	266	Roberto Kelly	.07	.03	.01
☐	267	Steve Bedrosian	.04	.02	.01
☐	268	Brady Anderson	.07	.03	.01
☐	269	Ruben Amaro Jr.	.04	.02	.01
☐	270	Tony Gwynn	.12	.05	.02
☐	271	Tracy Jones	.04	.02	.01
☐	272	Jerry Don Gleaton	.04	.02	.01
☐	273	Craig Grebeck	.04	.02	.01
☐	274	Bob Scanlan	.04	.02	.01
☐	275	Todd Zeile	.04	.02	.01
☐	276	Shawn Green	.25	.11	.03
☐	277	Scott Chiamparino	.04	.02	.01
☐	278	Darryl Hamilton	.07	.03	.01
☐	279	Jim Clancy	.04	.02	.01
☐	280	Carlos Martinez	.04	.02	.01
☐	281	Kevin Appier	.07	.03	.01
☐	282	John Wehner	.04	.02	.01
☐	283	Reggie Sanders	.25	.11	.03
☐	284	Gene Larkin	.04	.02	.01
☐	285	Bob Welch	.04	.02	.01
☐	286	Gilberto Reyes	.04	.02	.01
☐	287	Pete Schourek	.07	.03	.01
☐	288	Andujar Cedeno	.07	.03	.01
☐	289	Mike Morgan	.04	.02	.01
☐	290	Bo Jackson	.12	.05	.02
☐	291	Phil Garner MG	.04	.02	.01
☐	292	Ray Lankford	.15	.07	.02
☐	293	Mike Henneman	.04	.02	.01
☐	294	Dave Valle	.04	.02	.01
☐	295	Alonzo Powell	.04	.02	.01
☐	296	Tom Brunansky	.07	.03	.01
☐	297	Kevin Brown	.07	.03	.01
☐	298	Kelly Gruber	.07	.03	.01
☐	299	Charles Nagy	.10	.05	.01
☐	300	Don Mattingly	.12	.05	.02
☐	301	Kirk McCaskill	.04	.02	.01
☐	302	Joey Cora	.04	.02	.01
☐	303	Dan Plesac	.04	.02	.01
☐	304	Joe Oliver	.04	.02	.01
☐	305	Tom Glavine	.12	.05	.02
☐	306	Al Shirley	.20	.09	03
☐	307	Bruce Ruffin	.04	.02	.01
☐	308	Craig Shipley	.10	.05	.01
☐	309	Dave Martinez	.04	.02	.01
☐	310	Jose Mesa	.04	.02	.01
☐	311	Henry Cotto	.04	.02	.01
☐	312	Mike LaValliere	.04	.02	.01
☐	313	Kevin Tapani	.07	.03	.01
☐	314	Jeff Huson (Shows Jose Canseco sliding into second)	.04	.02	.01
☐	315	Juan Samuel	.04	.02	.01
☐	316	Curt Schilling	.07	.03	.01
☐	317	Mike Bordick	.08	.04	.01
☐	318	Steve Howe	.04	.02	.01
☐	319	Tony Phillips	.04	.02	.01
☐	320	George Bell	.07	.03	.01
☐	321	Lou Piniella MG	.04	.02	.01
☐	322	Tim Burke	.04	.02	.01
☐	323	Milt Thompson	.04	.02	.01
☐	324	Danny Darwin	.04	.02	.01
☐	325	Joe Orsulak	.04	.02	.01
☐	326	Eric King	.04	.02	.01
☐	327	Jay Buhner	.07	.03	.01
☐	328	Joel Johnston	.04	.02	.01
☐	329	Franklin Stubbs	.04	.02	.01
☐	330	Will Clark	.20	.09	.03
☐	331	Steve Lake	.04	.02	.01
☐	332	Chris Jones	.04	.02	.01
☐	333	Pat Tabler	.04	.02	.01
☐	334	Kevin Gross	.04	.02	.01
☐	335	Dave Henderson	.04	.02	.01
☐	336	Greg Anthony	.15	.07	.02
☐	337	Alejandro Pena	.04	.02	.01
☐	338	Shawn Abner	.04	.02	.01
☐	339	Tom Browning	.04	.02	.01
☐	340	Otis Nixon	.07	.03	.01
☐	341	Bob Geren	.04	.02	.01
☐	342	Tim Spehr	.04	.02	.01
☐	343	John Vander Wal	.15	.07	.02
☐	344	Jack Daugherty	.04	.02	.01
☐	345	Zane Smith	.04	.02	.01
☐	346	Rheal Cormier	.04	.02	.01
☐	347	Kent Hrbek	.07	.03	.01
☐	348	Rick Wilkins	.04	.02	.01
☐	349	Steve Lyons	.04	.02	.01
☐	350	Gregg Olson	.07	.03	.01
☐	351	Greg Riddoch MG	.04	.02	.01
☐	352	Ed Nunez	.04	.02	.01
☐	353	Braulio Castillo	.15	.07	.02
☐	354	Dave Bergman	.04	.02	.01
☐	355	Warren Newson	.04	.02	.01
☐	356	Luis Quinones	.04	.02	.01
☐	357	Mike Witt	.04	.02	.01
☐	358	Ted Wood	.10	.05	.01
☐	359	Mike Moore	.04	.02	.01
☐	360	Lance Parrish	.07	.03	.01
☐	361	Barry Jones	.04	.02	.01
☐	362	Javier Ortiz	.04	.02	.01
☐	363	John Candelaria	.04	.02	.01
☐	364	Glenallen Hill	.04	.02	.01
☐	365	Duane Ward	.04	.02	.01
☐	366	Checklist 265-396	.05	.01	.00
☐	367	Rafael Belliard	.04	.02	.01
☐	368	Bill Krueger	.04	.02	.01
☐	369	Steve Whitaker	.10	.05	.01
☐	370	Shawon Dunston	.07	.03	.01
☐	371	Dante Bichette	.04	.02	.01
☐	372	Kip Gross	.10	.05	.01
☐	373	Don Robinson	.04	.02	.01
☐	374	Bernie Williams	.08	.04	.01
☐	375	Bert Blyleven	.07	.03	.01
☐	376	Chris Donnels	.04	.02	.01
☐	377	Bob Zupcic	.25	.11	.03
☐	378	Joel Skinner	.04	.02	.01
☐	379	Steve Chitren	.04	.02	.01
☐	380	Barry Bonds	.15	.07	.02
☐	381	Sparky Anderson MG	.04	.02	.01
☐	382	Sid Fernandez	.07	.03	.01
☐	383	Dave Hollins	.07	.03	.01
☐	384	Mark Lee	.04	.02	.01
☐	385	Tim Wallach	.07	.03	.01
☐	386	Will Clark AS	.10	.05	.01
☐	387	Ryne Sandberg AS	.10	.05	.01
☐	388	Howard Johnson AS	.05	.02	.01
☐	389	Barry Larkin AS	.08	.04	.01
☐	390	Barry Bonds AS	.10	.05	.01
☐	391	Ron Gant AS	.10	.05	.01
☐	392	Bobby Bonilla AS	.08	.04	.01
☐	393	Craig Biggio AS	.05	.02	.01
☐	394	Dennis Martinez AS	.05	.02	.01
☐	395	Tom Glavine AS	.10	.05	.01
☐	396	Lee Smith AS	.05	.02	.01
☐	397	Cecil Fielder AS	.10	.05	.01
☐	398	Julio Franco AS	.05	.02	.01
☐	399	Wade Boggs AS	.10	.05	.01
☐	400	Cal Ripken AS	.15	.07	.02
☐	401	Jose Canseco AS	.10	.05	.01
☐	402	Joe Carter AS	.10	.05	.01

☐ 403	Ruben Sierra AS	.10	.05	.01
☐ 404	Matt Nokes AS	.05	.02	.01
☐ 405	Roger Clemens AS	.12	.05	.02
☐ 406	Jim Abbott AS	.10	.05	.01
☐ 407	Bryan Harvey AS	.05	.02	.01
☐ 408	Bob Milacki	.04	.02	.01
☐ 409	Geno Petralli	.04	.02	.01
☐ 410	Dave Stewart	.07	.03	.01
☐ 411	Mike Jackson	.04	.02	.01
☐ 412	Luis Aquino	.04	.02	.01
☐ 413	Tim Teufel	.04	.02	.01
☐ 414	Jeff Ware	.12	.05	.02
☐ 415	Jim Deshaies	.04	.02	.01
☐ 416	Ellis Burks	.07	.03	.01
☐ 417	Allan Anderson	.04	.02	.01
☐ 418	Alfredo Griffin	.04	.02	.01
☐ 419	Wally Whitehurst	.04	.02	.01
☐ 420	Sandy Alomar Jr.	.07	.03	.01
☐ 421	Juan Agosto	.04	.02	.01
☐ 422	Sam Horn	.04	.02	.01
☐ 423	Jeff Fassero	.04	.02	.01
☐ 424	Paul McClellan	.04	.02	.01
☐ 425	Cecil Fielder	.12	.05	.02
☐ 426	Tim Raines	.07	.03	.01
☐ 427	Eddie Taubensee	.12	.05	.02
☐ 428	Dennis Boyd	.04	.02	.01
☐ 429	Tony LaRussa MG	.04	.02	.01
☐ 430	Steve Sax	.07	.03	.01
☐ 431	Tom Gordon	.04	.02	.01
☐ 432	Billy Hatcher	.04	.02	.01
☐ 433	Cal Eldred	.35	.16	.04
☐ 434	Wally Backman	.04	.02	.01
☐ 435	Mark Eichhorn	.04	.02	.01
☐ 436	Mookie Wilson	.04	.02	.01
☐ 437	Scott Servais	.04	.02	.01
☐ 438	Mike Maddux	.04	.02	.01
☐ 439	Chico Walker	.04	.02	.01
☐ 440	Doug Drabek	.07	.03	.01
☐ 441	Rob Deer	.07	.03	.01
☐ 442	Dave West	.04	.02	.01
☐ 443	Spike Owen	.04	.02	.01
☐ 444	Tyrone Hill	.35	.16	.04
☐ 445	Matt Williams	.07	.03	.01
☐ 446	Mark Lewis	.07	.03	.01
☐ 447	David Segui	.04	.02	.01
☐ 448	Tom Pagnozzi	.04	.02	.01
☐ 449	Jeff Johnson	.04	.02	.01
☐ 450	Mark McGwire	.20	.09	.03
☐ 451	Tom Henke	.07	.03	.01
☐ 452	Wilson Alvarez	.04	.02	.01
☐ 453	Gary Redus	.04	.02	.01
☐ 454	Darren Holmes	.04	.02	.01
☐ 455	Pete O'Brien	.04	.02	.01
☐ 456	Pat Combs	.04	.02	.01
☐ 457	Hubie Brooks	.04	.02	.01
☐ 458	Frank Tanana	.04	.02	.01
☐ 459	Tom Kelly MG	.04	.02	.01
☐ 460	Andre Dawson	.10	.05	.01
☐ 461	Doug Jones	.04	.02	.01
☐ 462	Rich Rodriguez	.04	.02	.01
☐ 463	Mike Simms	.04	.02	.01
☐ 464	Mike Jeffcoat	.04	.02	.01
☐ 465	Barry Larkin	.10	.05	.01
☐ 466	Stan Belinda	.04	.02	.01
☐ 467	Lonnie Smith	.04	.02	.01
☐ 468	Greg Harris	.04	.02	.01
☐ 469	Jim Eisenreich	.04	.02	.01
☐ 470	Pedro Guerrero	.07	.03	.01
☐ 471	Jose DeJesus	.04	.02	.01
☐ 472	Rich Rowland	.12	.05	.02
☐ 473	1992 Prospects 3B UER Frank Bolick Craig Paquette Tom Redington Paul Russo (Line around top border)	.25	.11	.03
☐ 474	Mike Rossiter	.10	.05	.01
☐ 475	Robby Thompson	.04	.02	.01
☐ 476	Randy Bush	.04	.02	.01
☐ 477	Greg Hibbard	.04	.02	.01
☐ 478	Dale Sveum	.04	.02	.01
☐ 479	Chito Martinez	.04	.02	.01
☐ 480	Scott Sanderson	.04	.02	.01
☐ 481	Tino Martinez	.07	.03	.01
☐ 482	Jimmy Key	.04	.02	.01
☐ 483	Terry Shumpert	.04	.02	.01
☐ 484	Mike Hartley	.04	.02	.01
☐ 485	Chris Sabo	.07	.03	.01
☐ 486	Bob Walk	.04	.02	.01
☐ 487	John Cerutti	.04	.02	.01
☐ 488	Scott Cooper	.07	.03	.01
☐ 489	Bobby Cox MG	.04	.02	.01
☐ 490	Julio Franco	.07	.03	.01
☐ 491	Jeff Brantley	.04	.02	.01
☐ 492	Mike Devereaux	.07	.03	.01
☐ 493	Jose Offerman	.07	.03	.01
☐ 494	Gary Thurman	.04	.02	.01
☐ 495	Carney Lansford	.07	.03	.01
☐ 496	Joe Grahe	.04	.02	.01
☐ 497	Andy Ashby	.04	.02	.01
☐ 498	Gerald Perry	.04	.02	.01
☐ 499	Dave Otto	.04	.02	.01
☐ 500	Vince Coleman	.07	.03	.01
☐ 501	Rob Mallicoat	.04	.02	.01
☐ 502	Greg Briley	.04	.02	.01
☐ 503	Pascual Perez	.04	.02	.01
☐ 504	Aaron Sele	.40	.18	.05
☐ 505	Bobby Thigpen	.04	.02	.01
☐ 506	Todd Benzinger	.04	.02	.01
☐ 507	Candy Maldonado	.04	.02	.01
☐ 508	Bill Gullickson	.04	.02	.01
☐ 509	Doug Dascenzo	.04	.02	.01
☐ 510	Frank Viola	.07	.03	.01
☐ 511	Kenny Rogers	.04	.02	.01
☐ 512	Mike Heath	.04	.02	.01
☐ 513	Kevin Bass	.04	.02	.01
☐ 514	Kim Batiste	.04	.02	.01
☐ 515	Delino DeShields	.10	.05	.01
☐ 516	Ed Sprague Jr.	.07	.03	.01
☐ 517	Jim Gott	.04	.02	.01
☐ 518	Jose Melendez	.04	.02	.01
☐ 519	Hal McRae MG	.04	.02	.01
☐ 520	Jeff Bagwell	.25	.11	.03
☐ 521	Joe Hesketh	.04	.02	.01
☐ 522	Milt Cuyler	.04	.02	.01
☐ 523	Shawn Hillegas	.04	.02	.01
☐ 524	Don Slaught	.04	.02	.01
☐ 525	Randy Johnson	.07	.03	.01
☐ 526	Doug Piatt	.04	.02	.01
☐ 527	Checklist 397-528	.05	.01	.00
☐ 528	Steve Foster	.10	.05	.01
☐ 529	Joe Girardi	.04	.02	.01
☐ 530	Jim Abbott	.12	.05	.02
☐ 531	Larry Walker	.15	.07	.02
☐ 532	Mike Huff	.04	.02	.01
☐ 533	Mackey Sasser	.04	.02	.01
☐ 534	Benji Gil	.20	.09	.03
☐ 535	Dave Stieb	.04	.02	.01
☐ 536	Willie Wilson	.04	.02	.01
☐ 537	Mark Leiter	.04	.02	.01
☐ 538	Jose Uribe	.04	.02	.01
☐ 539	Thomas Howard	.04	.02	.01
☐ 540	Ben McDonald	.10	.05	.01
☐ 541	Jose Tolentino	.10	.05	.01
☐ 542	Keith Mitchell	.07	.03	.01
☐ 543	Jerome Walton	.04	.02	.01
☐ 544	Cliff Brantley	.10	.05	.01
☐ 545	Andy Van Slyke	.07	.03	.01
☐ 546	Paul Sorrento	.07	.03	.01
☐ 547	Herm Winningham	.04	.02	.01
☐ 548	Mark Guthrie	.04	.02	.01
☐ 549	Joe Torre MG	.04	.02	.01
☐ 550	Darryl Strawberry	.12	.05	.02
☐ 551	1992 Prospects SS UER Wilfredo Cordero Chipper Jones Manny Alexander Alex Arias (No line around top border)	.60	.25	.08
☐ 552	Dave Gallagher	.04	.02	.01
☐ 553	Edgar Martinez	.07	.03	.01
☐ 554	Donald Harris	.04	.02	.01
☐ 555	Frank Thomas	.75	.35	.09
☐ 556	Storm Davis	.04	.02	.01
☐ 557	Dickie Thon	.04	.02	.01
☐ 558	Scott Garrelts	.04	.02	.01
☐ 559	Steve Olin	.04	.02	.01
☐ 560	Rickey Henderson	.12	.05	.02
☐ 561	Jose Vizcaino	.04	.02	.01
☐ 562	Wade Taylor	.04	.02	.01
☐ 563	Pat Borders	.04	.02	.01
☐ 564	Jimmy Gonzalez	.10	.05	.01
☐ 565	Lee Smith	.07	.03	.01
☐ 566	Bill Sampen	.04	.02	.01
☐ 567	Dean Palmer	.10	.05	.01
☐ 568	Bryan Harvey	.04	.02	.01
☐ 569	Tony Pena	.04	.02	.01
☐ 570	Lou Whitaker	.07	.03	.01
☐ 571	Randy Tomlin	.04	.02	.01
☐ 572	Greg Vaughn	.07	.03	.01
☐ 573	Kelly Downs	.04	.02	.01
☐ 574	Steve Avery UER (Should be 13 games for Durham in 1989)	.15	.07	.02
☐ 575	Kirby Puckett	.20	.09	.03

☐ 576 Heathcliff Slocumb .04 .02 .01
☐ 577 Kevin Seitzer .07 .03 .01
☐ 578 Lee Guetterman .04 .02 .01
☐ 579 Johnny Oates MG .04 .02 .01
☐ 580 Greg Maddux .07 .03 .01
☐ 581 Stan Javier .04 .02 .01
☐ 582 Vicente Palacios .04 .02 .01
☐ 583 Mel Rojas .04 .02 .01
☐ 584 Wayne Rosenthal .10 .05 .01
☐ 585 Lenny Webster .04 .02 .01
☐ 586 Rod Nichols .04 .02 .01
☐ 587 Mickey Morandini .07 .03 .01
☐ 588 Russ Swan .04 .02 .01
☐ 589 Mariano Duncan .04 .02 .01
☐ 590 Howard Johnson .07 .03 .01
☐ 591 1992 Prospects OF .35 .16 .04
Jeromy Burnitz
Jacob Brumfield
Alan Cockrell
D.J. Dozier
☐ 592 Denny Neagle .04 .02 .01
☐ 593 Steve Decker .04 .02 .01
☐ 594 Brian Barber .20 .09 .03
☐ 595 Bruce Hurst .07 .03 .01
☐ 596 Kent Mercker .04 .02 .01
☐ 597 Mike Magnante .12 .05 .02
☐ 598 Jody Reed .04 .02 .01
☐ 599 Steve Searcy .04 .02 .01
☐ 600 Paul Molitor .07 .03 .01
☐ 601 Dave Smith .04 .02 .01
☐ 602 Mike Fetters .04 .02 .01
☐ 603 Luis Mercedes .07 .03 .01
☐ 604 Chris Gwynn .04 .02 .01
☐ 605 Scott Erickson .08 .04 .01
☐ 606 Brook Jacoby .04 .02 .01
☐ 607 Todd Stottlemyre .07 .03 .01
☐ 608 Scott Bradley .04 .02 .01
☐ 609 Mike Hargrove MG .04 .02 .01
☐ 610 Eric Davis .07 .03 .01
☐ 611 Brian Hunter .10 .05 .01
☐ 612 Pat Kelly .07 .03 .01
☐ 613 Pedro Munoz .07 .03 .01
☐ 614 Al Osuna .04 .02 .01
☐ 615 Matt Merullo .04 .02 .01
☐ 616 Larry Andersen .04 .02 .01
☐ 617 Junior Ortiz .04 .02 .01
☐ 618 1992 Prospects OF .40 .18 .05
Cesar Hernandez
Steve Hosey
Jeff McNeely
Dan Peltier
☐ 619 Danny Jackson .04 .02 .01
☐ 620 George Brett .10 .05 .01
☐ 621 Dan Gakeler .04 .02 .01
☐ 622 Steve Buechele .04 .02 .01
☐ 623 Bob Tewksbury .07 .03 .01
☐ 624 Shawn Estes .15 .07 .02
☐ 625 Kevin McReynolds .07 .03 .01
☐ 626 Chris Haney .04 .02 .01
☐ 627 Mike Sharperson .04 .02 .01
☐ 628 Mark Williamson .04 .02 .01
☐ 629 Wally Joyner .07 .03 .01
☐ 630 Carlton Fisk .10 .05 .01
☐ 631 Armando Reynoso .10 .05 .01
☐ 632 Felix Fermin .04 .02 .01
☐ 633 Mitch Williams .04 .02 .01
☐ 634 Manuel Lee .04 .02 .01
☐ 635 Harold Baines .07 .03 .01
☐ 636 Greg Harris .04 .02 .01
☐ 637 Orlando Merced .07 .03 .01
☐ 638 Chris Bosio .04 .02 .01
☐ 639 Wayne Housie .10 .05 .01
☐ 640 Xavier Hernandez .04 .02 .01
☐ 641 David Howard .04 .02 .01
☐ 642 Tim Crews .04 .02 .01
☐ 643 Rick Cerone .04 .02 .01
☐ 644 Terry Leach .04 .02 .01
☐ 645 Deion Sanders .15 .07 .02
☐ 646 Craig Wilson .04 .02 .01
☐ 647 Marquis Grissom .10 .05 .01
☐ 648 Scott Fletcher .04 .02 .01
☐ 649 Norm Charlton .07 .03 .01
☐ 650 Jesse Barfield .04 .02 .01
☐ 651 Joe Slusarski .04 .02 .01
☐ 652 Bobby Rose .04 .02 .01
☐ 653 Dennis Lamp .04 .02 .01
☐ 654 Allen Watson .25 .11 .03
☐ 655 Brett Butler .07 .03 .01
☐ 656 1992 Prospects OF .35 .16 .04
Rudy Pemberton
Henry Rodriguez
Lee Tinsley
Gerald Williams
☐ 657 Dave Johnson .04 .02 .01
☐ 658 Checklist 529-660 .05 .01 .00
☐ 659 Brian McRae .07 .03 .01
☐ 660 Fred McGriff .12 .05 .02
☐ 661 Bill Landrum .04 .02 .01
☐ 662 Juan Guzman .75 .35 .09
☐ 663 Greg Gagne .04 .02 .01
☐ 664 Ken Hill .04 .02 .01
☐ 665 Dave Haas .04 .02 .01
☐ 666 Tom Foley .04 .02 .01
☐ 667 Roberto Hernandez .12 .05 .02
☐ 668 Dwayne Henry .04 .02 .01
☐ 669 Jim Fregosi MG .04 .02 .01
☐ 670 Harold Reynolds .04 .02 .01
☐ 671 Mark Whiten .04 .02 .01
☐ 672 Eric Plunk .04 .02 .01
☐ 673 Todd Hundley .04 .02 .01
☐ 674 Mo Sanford .04 .02 .01
☐ 675 Bobby Witt .04 .02 .01
☐ 676 1992 Prospects P .60 .25 .08
Sam Militello
Pat Mahomes
Turk Wendell
Roger Salkeld
☐ 677 John Marzano .04 .02 .01
☐ 678 Joe Klink .04 .02 .01
☐ 679 Pete Incaviglia .04 .02 .01
☐ 680 Dale Murphy .07 .03 .01
☐ 681 Rene Gonzales .04 .02 .01
☐ 682 Andy Benes .07 .03 .01
☐ 683 Jim Poole .04 .02 .01
☐ 684 Trever Miller .10 .05 .01
☐ 685 Scott Livingstone .10 .05 .01
☐ 686 Rich DeLucia .04 .02 .01
☐ 687 Harvey Pulliam .08 .04 .01
☐ 688 Tim Belcher .07 .03 .01
☐ 689 Mark Lemke .04 .02 .01
☐ 690 John Franco .07 .03 .01
☐ 691 Walt Weiss .04 .02 .01
☐ 692 Scott Ruskin .04 .02 .01
☐ 693 Jeff King .04 .02 .01
☐ 694 Mike Gardiner .04 .02 .01
☐ 695 Gary Sheffield .20 .09 .03
☐ 696 Joe Boever .04 .02 .01
☐ 697 Mike Felder .04 .02 .01
☐ 698 John Habyan .04 .02 .01
☐ 699 Cito Gaston MG .04 .02 .01
☐ 700 Ruben Sierra .15 .07 .02
☐ 701 Scott Radinsky .04 .02 .01
☐ 702 Lee Stevens .04 .02 .01
☐ 703 Mark Wohlers .08 .04 .01
☐ 704 Curt Young .04 .02 .01
☐ 705 Dwight Evans .07 .03 .01
☐ 706 Rob Murphy .04 .02 .01
☐ 707 Gregg Jefferies .07 .03 .01
☐ 708 Tom Bolton .04 .02 .01
☐ 709 Chris James .04 .02 .01
☐ 710 Kevin Maas .07 .03 .01
☐ 711 Ricky Bones .08 .04 .01
☐ 712 Curt Wilkerson .04 .02 .01
☐ 713 Roger McDowell .04 .02 .01
☐ 714 Calvin Reese .15 .07 .02
☐ 715 Craig Biggio .07 .03 .01
☐ 716 Kirk Dressendorfer .04 .02 .01
☐ 717 Ken Dayley .04 .02 .01
☐ 718 B.J. Surhoff .04 .02 .01
☐ 719 Terry Mulholland .04 .02 .01
☐ 720 Kirk Gibson .07 .03 .01
☐ 721 Mike Pagliarulo .04 .02 .01
☐ 722 Walt Terrell .04 .02 .01
☐ 723 Jose Oquendo .04 .02 .01
☐ 724 Kevin Morton .04 .02 .01
☐ 725 Dwight Gooden .07 .03 .01
☐ 726 Kirt Manwaring .04 .02 .01
☐ 727 Chuck McElroy .04 .02 .01
☐ 728 Dave Burba .04 .02 .01
☐ 729 Art Howe MG .04 .02 .01
☐ 730 Ramon Martinez .07 .03 .01
☐ 731 Donnie Hill .04 .02 .01
☐ 732 Nelson Santovenia .04 .02 .01
☐ 733 Bob Melvin .04 .02 .01
☐ 734 Scott Hatteberg .10 .05 .01
☐ 735 Greg Swindell .07 .03 .01
☐ 736 Lance Johnson .04 .02 .01
☐ 737 Kevin Reimer .04 .02 .01
☐ 738 Dennis Eckersley .10 .05 .01
☐ 739 Rob Ducey .04 .02 .01
☐ 740 Ken Caminiti .07 .03 .01
☐ 741 Mark Gubicza .04 .02 .01
☐ 742 Billy Spiers .04 .02 .01
☐ 743 Darren Lewis .07 .03 .01
☐ 744 Chris Hammond .04 .02 .01
☐ 745 Dave Magadan .07 .03 .01

☐ 746	Bernard Gilkey	.07	.03	.01
☐ 747	Willie Banks	.04	.02	.01
☐ 748	Matt Nokes	.04	.02	.01
☐ 749	Jerald Clark	.04	.02	.01
☐ 750	Travis Fryman	.30	.14	.04
☐ 751	Steve Wilson	.04	.02	.01
☐ 752	Billy Ripken	.04	.02	.01
☐ 753	Paul Assenmacher	.04	.02	.01
☐ 754	Charlie Hayes	.04	.02	.01
☐ 755	Alex Fernandez	.07	.03	.01
☐ 756	Gary Pettis	.04	.02	.01
☐ 757	Rob Dibble	.07	.03	.01
☐ 758	Tim Naehring	.07	.03	.01
☐ 759	Jeff Torborg MG	.04	.02	.01
☐ 760	Ozzie Smith	.10	.05	.01
☐ 761	Mike Fitzgerald	.04	.02	.01
☐ 762	John Burkett	.04	.02	.01
☐ 763	Kyle Abbott	.07	.03	.01
☐ 764	Tyler Green	.25	.11	.03
☐ 765	Pete Harnisch	.04	.02	.01
☐ 766	Mark Davis	.04	.02	.01
☐ 767	Kal Daniels	.04	.02	.01
☐ 768	Jim Thome	.12	.05	.02
☐ 769	Jack Howell	.04	.02	.01
☐ 770	Sid Bream	.04	.02	.01
☐ 771	Arthur Rhodes	.15	.07	.02
☐ 772	Garry Templeton	.04	.02	.01
☐ 773	Hal Morris	.07	.03	.01
☐ 774	Bud Black	.04	.02	.01
☐ 775	Ivan Calderon	.04	.02	.01
☐ 776	Doug Henry	.15	.07	.02
☐ 777	John Olerud	.10	.05	.01
☐ 778	Tim Leary	.04	.02	.01
☐ 779	Jay Bell	.04	.02	.01
☐ 780	Eddie Murray	.10	.05	.01
☐ 781	Paul Abbott	.04	.02	.01
☐ 782	Phil Plantier	.15	.07	.02
☐ 783	Joe Magrane	.04	.02	.01
☐ 784	Ken Patterson	.04	.02	.01
☐ 785	Albert Belle	.12	.05	.02
☐ 786	Royce Clayton	.15	.07	.02
☐ 787	Checklist 661-792	.05	.01	.00
☐ 788	Mike Stanton	.04	.02	.01
☐ 789	Bobby Valentine MG	.04	.02	.01
☐ 790	Joe Carter	.12	.05	.02
☐ 791	Danny Cox	.04	.02	.01
☐ 792	Dave Winfield	.10	.05	.01

1992 Topps Debut '91

The 1991 Topps Debut '91 set contains 194 standard-size (2 1/2" by 3 1/2") cards. The fronts feature a mix of either posed or action glossy color player photos, framed with two color border stripes on a white card face. The date of the player's first major league appearance is given in a color bar in the lower right corner. In addition to biography and 1991 batting record, the horizontally oriented backs present player profiles in the form of a newspaper article from The Register. The cards are numbered on the back.

		MT	EX-MT	VG
	COMPLETE SET (194)	18.00	8.00	2.30
	COMMON PLAYER (1-194)	.05	.02	.01
☐ 1	Kyle Abbott	.10	.05	.01
☐ 2	Dana Allison	.10	.05	.01
☐ 3	Rich Amaral	.10	.05	.01
☐ 4	Ruben Amaro Jr.	.15	.07	.02
☐ 5	Andy Ashby	.10	.05	.01
☐ 6	Jim Austin	.10	.05	.01
☐ 7	Jeff Bagwell	1.25	.55	.16
☐ 8	Jeff Banister	.05	.02	.01
☐ 9	Willie Banks	.20	.09	.03
☐ 10	Bret Barberie	.20	.09	.03
☐ 11	Kim Batiste	.10	.05	.01
☐ 12	Chris Beasley	.10	.05	.01
☐ 13	Rod Beck	.20	.09	.03
☐ 14	Derek Bell	.25	.11	.03
☐ 15	Esteban Beltre	.10	.05	.01
☐ 16	Freddie Benavides	.05	.02	.01
☐ 17	Ricky Bones	.15	.07	.02
☐ 18	Denis Boucher	.10	.05	.01
☐ 19	Ryan Bowen	.15	.07	.02
☐ 20	Cliff Brantley	.15	.07	.02
☐ 21	John Briscoe	.10	.05	.01
☐ 22	Scott Brosius	.10	.05	.01
☐ 23	Terry Bross	.05	.02	.01
☐ 24	Jarvis Brown	.10	.05	.01
☐ 25	Scott Bullett	.20	.09	.03
☐ 26	Kevin Campbell	.10	.05	.01
☐ 27	Amalio Carreno	.10	.05	.01
☐ 28	Matias Carrillo	.10	.05	.01
☐ 29	Jeff Carter	.05	.02	.01
☐ 30	Vinny Castilla	.05	.02	.01
☐ 31	Braulio Castillo	.25	.11	.03
☐ 32	Frank Castillo	.10	.05	.01
☐ 33	Darrin Chapin	.15	.07	.02
☐ 34	Mike Christopher	.15	.07	.02
☐ 35	Mark Clark	.10	.05	.01
☐ 36	Royce Clayton	.35	.16	.04
☐ 37	Stu Cole	.10	.05	.01
☐ 38	Gary Cooper	.05	.02	.01
☐ 39	Archie Corbin	.15	.07	.02
☐ 40	Rheal Cormier	.20	.09	.03
☐ 41	Chris Cron	.15	.07	.02
☐ 42	Mike Dalton	.10	.05	.01
☐ 43	Mark Davis	.10	.05	.01
☐ 44	Francisco DeLaRosa	.10	.05	.01
☐ 45	Chris Donnels	.15	.07	.02
☐ 46	Brian Drahman	.10	.05	.01
☐ 47	Tom Drees	.05	.02	.01
☐ 48	Kirk Dressendorfer	.15	.07	.02
☐ 49	Bruce Egloff	.10	.05	.01
☐ 50	Cal Eldred	1.00	.45	.13
☐ 51	Jose Escobar	.10	.05	.01
☐ 52	Tony Eusebio	.10	.05	.01
☐ 53	Hector Fajardo	.15	.07	.02
☐ 54	Monty Fariss	.15	.07	.02
☐ 55	Jeff Fassero	.10	.05	.01
☐ 56	Dave Fleming	.75	.35	.09
☐ 57	Kevin Flora	.10	.05	.01
☐ 58	Steve Foster	.15	.07	.02
☐ 59	Dan Gakeler	.10	.05	.01
☐ 60	Ramon Garcia	.10	.05	.01
☐ 61	Chris Gardner	.10	.05	.01
☐ 62	Jeff Gardner	.10	.05	.01
☐ 63	Chris George	.10	.05	.01
☐ 64	Ray Giannelli	.10	.05	.01
☐ 65	Tom Goodwin	.20	.09	.03
☐ 66	Mark Grater	.10	.05	.01
☐ 67	Johnny Guzman	.30	.14	.04
☐ 68	Juan Guzman	1.25	.55	.16
☐ 69	Dave Haas	.10	.05	.01
☐ 70	Chris Haney	.15	.07	.02
☐ 71	Shawn Hare	.20	.09	.03
☐ 72	Donald Harris	.15	.07	.02
☐ 73	Doug Henry	.10	.05	.01
☐ 74	Pat Hentgen	.20	.09	.03
☐ 75	Gil Heredia	.10	.05	.01
☐ 76	Jeremy Hernandez	.20	.09	.03
☐ 77	Jose Hernandez	.10	.05	.01
☐ 78	Roberto Hernandez	.20	.09	.03
☐ 79	Bryan Hickerson	.10	.05	.01
☐ 80	Milt Hill	.10	.05	.01
☐ 81	Vince Horsman	.10	.05	.01
☐ 82	Wayne Housie	.15	.07	.02
☐ 83	Chris Howard	.10	.05	.01
☐ 84	David Howard	.10	.05	.01
☐ 85	Mike Humphreys	.15	.07	.02
☐ 86	Brian Hunter	.25	.11	.03
☐ 87	Jim Hunter	.15	.07	.02
☐ 88	Mike Ignasiak	.10	.05	.01
☐ 89	Reggie Jefferson	.40	.18	.05
☐ 90	Jeff Johnson	.10	.05	.01
☐ 91	Joel Johnston	.15	.07	.02
☐ 92	Calvin Jones	.15	.07	.02
☐ 93	Chris Jones	.10	.05	.01
☐ 94	Stacy Jones	.10	.05	.01
☐ 95	Jeff Juden	.30	.14	.04
☐ 96	Scott Kamieniecki	.10	.05	.01

☐ 97 Eric Karros	1.25	.55	.16
☐ 98 Pat Kelly	.25	.11	.03
☐ 99 John Kiely	.10	.05	.01
☐ 100 Darryl Kile	.20	.09	.03
☐ 101 Wayne Kirby	.15	.07	.02
☐ 102 Garland Kiser	.10	.05	.01
☐ 103 Chuck Knoblauch	.60	.25	.08
☐ 104 Randy Knorr	.15	.07	.02
☐ 105 Tom Kramer	.10	.05	.01
☐ 106 Ced Landrum	.10	.05	.01
☐ 107 Patrick Lennon	.20	.09	.03
☐ 108 Jim Lewis	.15	.07	.02
☐ 109 Mark Lewis	.25	.11	.03
☐ 110 Doug Lindsey	.10	.05	.01
☐ 111 Scott Livingstone	.20	.09	.03
☐ 112 Kenny Lofton	.50	.23	.06
☐ 113 Ever Magallanes	.10	.05	.01
☐ 114 Mike Magnante	.15	.07	.02
☐ 115 Barry Manuel	.15	.07	.02
☐ 116 Josias Manzanillo	.10	.05	.01
☐ 117 Chito Martinez	.35	.16	.04
☐ 118 Terry Mathews	.10	.05	.01
☐ 119 Rob Maurer	.20	.09	.03
☐ 120 Tim Mauser	.15	.07	.02
☐ 121 Terry McDaniel	.15	.07	.02
☐ 122 Rusty Meacham	.20	.09	.03
☐ 123 Luis Mercedes	.30	.14	.04
☐ 124 Paul Miller	.10	.05	.01
☐ 125 Keith Mitchell	.25	.11	.03
☐ 126 Bobby Moore	.20	.09	.03
☐ 127 Kevin Morton	.10	.05	.01
☐ 128 Andy Mota	.10	.05	.01
☐ 129 Jose Mota	.10	.05	.01
☐ 130 Mike Mussina	1.25	.55	.16
☐ 131 Jeff Mutis	.10	.05	.01
☐ 132 Denny Neagle	.25	.11	.03
☐ 133 Warren Newson	.15	.07	.02
☐ 134 Jim Olander	.10	.05	.01
☐ 135 Erik Pappas	.15	.07	.02
☐ 136 Jorge Pedre	.10	.05	.01
☐ 137 Yorkis Perez	.20	.09	.03
☐ 138 Mark Petkovsek	.10	.05	.01
☐ 139 Doug Piatt	.10	.05	.01
☐ 140 Jeff Plympton	.05	.02	.01
☐ 141 Harvey Pulliam	.15	.07	.02
☐ 142 John Ramos	.25	.11	.03
☐ 143 Mike Remlinger	.05	.02	.01
☐ 144 Laddie Renfroe	.15	.07	.02
☐ 145 Armando Reynoso	.10	.05	.01
☐ 146 Arthur Rhodes	.35	.16	.04
☐ 147 Pat Rice	.15	.07	.02
☐ 148 Nikco Riesgo	.30	.14	.04
☐ 149 Carlos Rodriguez	.20	.09	.03
☐ 150 Ivan Rodriguez	1.25	.55	.16
☐ 151 Wayne Rosenthal	.10	.05	.01
☐ 152 Rico Rossy	.10	.05	.01
☐ 153 Stan Royer	.10	.05	.01
☐ 154 Rey Sanchez	.15	.07	.02
☐ 155 Reggie Sanders	.50	.23	.06
☐ 156 Mo Sanford	.20	.09	.03
☐ 157 Bob Scanlan	.10	.05	.01
☐ 158 Pete Schourek	.10	.05	.01
☐ 159 Gary Scott	.20	.09	.03
☐ 160 Tim Scott	.20	.09	.03
☐ 161 Tony Scruggs	.05	.02	.01
☐ 162 Scott Servais	.10	.05	.01
☐ 163 Doug Simons	.10	.05	.01
☐ 164 Heathcliff Slocumb	.05	.02	.01
☐ 165 Joe Slusarski	.10	.05	.01
☐ 166 Tim Spehr	.20	.09	.03
☐ 167 Ed Sprague	.25	.11	.03
☐ 168 Jeff Tackett	.10	.05	.01
☐ 169 Eddie Taubensee	.15	.07	.02
☐ 170 Wade Taylor	.10	.05	.01
☐ 171 Jim Thome	.35	.16	.04
☐ 172 Mike Timlin	.10	.05	.01
☐ 173 Jose Tolentino	.05	.02	.01
☐ 174 John Vander Wal	.15	.07	.02
☐ 175 Todd Van Poppel	.75	.35	.09
☐ 176 Mo Vaughn	.35	.16	.04
☐ 177 Dave Wainhouse	.10	.05	.01
☐ 178 Don Wakamatsu	.05	.02	.01
☐ 179 Bruce Walton	.10	.05	.01
☐ 180 Kevin Ward	.10	.05	.01
☐ 181 Dave Weathers	.20	.09	.03
☐ 182 Eric Wedge	.30	.14	.04
☐ 183 John Wehner	.20	.09	.03
☐ 184 Rick Wilkins	.15	.07	.02
☐ 185 Bernie Williams	.40	.18	.05
☐ 186 Brian Williams	.20	.09	.03
☐ 187 Ron Witmeyer	.10	.05	.01
☐ 188 Mark Wohlers	.20	.09	.03
☐ 189 Ted Wood	.15	.07	.02
☐ 190 Anthony Young	.20	.09	.03
☐ 191 Eddie Zosky	.15	.07	.02
☐ 192 Bob Zupcic	.35	.16	.04
☐ 193 Checklist 1	.08	.04	.01
☐ 194 Checklist 2	.08	.04	.01

1992 Topps Dairy Queen

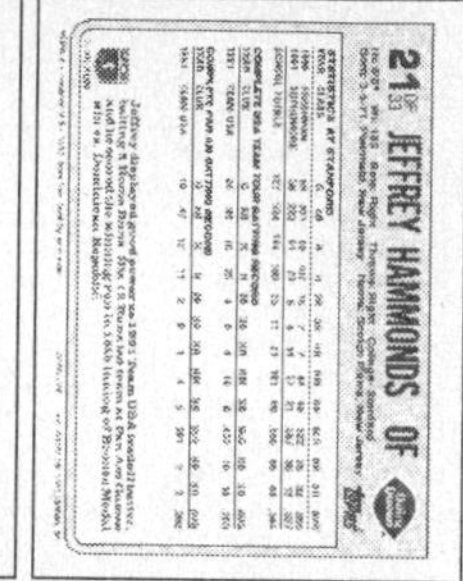

This 33-card standard size (2 1/2" by 3 1/2") set was produced by Topps for Dairy Queen. The set was available in four-card packs with the purchase of a regular-sized sundae in a Team USA helmet during June and July 1992. The set features 16 Team USA players from the 1984 and 1988 teams who are now major league stars as well as 15 1992 Team USA prospects. Completing the set is a 1988 Gold Medal team celebration card and the 1992 Head Coach Ron Fraser. The front design features posed color player photos bordered in blue and red on a white background. The Team USA logo is printed in red and blue at the top. The Dairy Queen logo and the player's name overlay the bottom of the picture. The horizontally oriented backs feature Major League, Team USA tour, and Olympic statistics printed in red and blue on a light blue box. The cards are numbered on the back.

	MT	EX-MT	VG
COMPLETE SET (33)	15.00	6.75	1.90
COMMON PLAYER (1-33)	.15	.07	.02
☐ 1 Mark McGwire	1.00	.45	.13
☐ 2 Will Clark	1.50	.65	.19
☐ 3 John Marzano	.15	.07	.02
☐ 4 Barry Larkin	.60	.25	.08
☐ 5 Bobby Witt	.35	.16	.04
☐ 6 Scott Bankhead	.25	.11	.03
☐ 7 B.J. Surhoff	.35	.16	.04
☐ 8 Shane Mack	.50	.23	.06
☐ 9 Jim Abbott	.75	.35	.09
☐ 10 Ben McDonald	.75	.35	.09
☐ 11 Robin Ventura	1.50	.65	.19
☐ 12 Charles Nagy	.50	.23	.06
☐ 13 Andy Benes	.50	.23	.06
☐ 14 Joe Slusarski	.15	.07	.02
☐ 15 Ed Sprague	.35	.16	.04
☐ 16 Bret Barberie	.15	.07	.02
☐ 17 Team USA Strikes Gold	.50	.23	.06
☐ 18 Jeff Granger	.35	.16	.04
☐ 19 John Dettmer	.25	.11	.03
☐ 20 Todd Greene	.35	.16	.04
☐ 21 Jeffrey Hammonds	2.00	.90	.25
☐ 22 Dan Melendez	.35	.16	.04
☐ 23 Kennie Steenstra	.35	.16	.04
☐ 24 Todd Johnson	.25	.11	.03
☐ 25 Chris Roberts	.75	.35	.09
☐ 26 Steve Rodriguez	.25	.11	.03
☐ 27 Charles Johnson	2.00	.90	.25
☐ 28 Chris Wimmer	.35	.16	.04
☐ 29 Tony Phillips (P)	.25	.11	.03
☐ 30 Craig Wilson	.35	.16	.04
☐ 31 Jason Giambi	.50	.23	.06
☐ 32 Paul Shuey	.75	.35	.09
☐ 33 Ron Fraser CO	.15	.07	.02

1992 Topps Gold

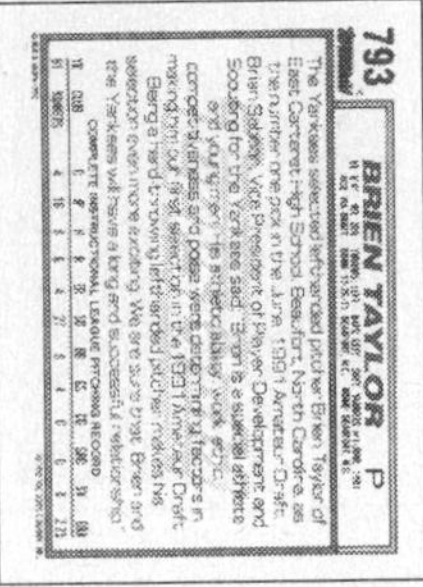

Topps produced a 792-card Topps Gold factory set packaged in a foil display box. Only this set contained an additional card of Brien Taylor, numbered 793 and hand signed by him. The production run was 12,000 sets. The Topps Gold cards were also available in regular series packs. According to Topps, on average collectors would find one Topps Gold card in every 36 wax packs, one in every 18 cello packs, one in every 12 rak packs, five per Vending box, one in every six jumbo packs, and ten per regular set. The packs also featured "Match-the-Stats" game cards in which the consumer could save "Runs". For 2.00 and every 100 Runs saved in this game, the consumer could receive through a mail-in offer ten Topps Gold cards. These particular Topps Gold cards carry the word "Winner" in gold foil on the card front. The checklist cards in the regular set were replaced with six individual Rookie player cards (131, 264, 366, 527, 658, 787) in the gold set. There were a number of uncorrected errors in the Gold set. Chuck Finley (86) has gold band indicating he is Mark Davidson of the Astros. Andujar Cedeno (288) is listed as a member of the New York Yankees. Mike Huff (532) is listed as a member of the Boston Red Sox. Barry Larkin (465) is listed as a member of the Houston Astros but is correctly listed as a member of the Cincinnati Reds on his Gold Winners cards. Typically the individual cards are sold at a multiple of the player's respective value in the regular set.

	MT	EX-MT	VG
COMPLETE SET (792)	400.00	180.00	50.00
COMPLETE FACT.SET (793)	500.00	230.00	65.00
COMMON GOLD CARDS (1G-792G)	.75	.35	.09
COMPLETE WINNERS SET (792)	125.00	57.50	15.50
COMMON WINNERS (1GW-792GW)	.25	.11	.03
☐ 86G Chuck Finley UER (Gold band has Mark Davidson, Astros)	1.50	.65	.19
☐ 131G Terry Mathews (Replaces Checklist 1)	1.50	.65	.19
☐ 131GW Terry Mathews (Replaces Checklist 1)	.50	.23	.06
☐ 264G Rod Beck (Replaces Checklist 2)	3.00	1.35	.40
☐ 264GW Rod Beck (Replaces Checklist 2)	1.00	.45	.13
☐ 288G Andujar Cedeno UER (Listed on Yankees)	1.50	.65	.19
☐ 366G Tony Perezchica (Replaces Checklist 3)	1.50	.65	.19
☐ 366GW Tony Perezchica (Replaces Checklist 3)	.50	.23	.06
☐ 465G Barry Larkin UER (Listed on Astros)	4.50	2.00	.55
☐ 465GWA Barry Larkin ERR (Listed on Astros)	3.00	1.35	.40
☐ 465GWB Barry Larkin COR (Listed on Reds)	3.00	1.35	.40
☐ 527G Terry McDaniel (Replaces Checklist 4)	1.50	.65	.19
☐ 527GW Terry McDaniel (Replaces Checklist 4)	.50	.23	.06
☐ 532G Mike Huff UER (Listed on Red Sox)	1.50	.65	.19
☐ 658G John Ramos (Replaces Checklist 5)	1.50	.65	.19
☐ 658GW John Ramos (Replaces Checklist 5)	.50	.23	.06
☐ 787G Brian Williams (Replaces Checklist 6)	7.50	3.40	.95
☐ 787GW Brian Williams (Replaces Checklist 6)	2.50	1.15	.30
☐ 793G Brien Taylor SP AUTO	135.00	60.00	17.00

1992 Topps Highland Mint Mint-Cards

These cards, from the Highland Mint, measure the standard size (2 1/2" by 3 1/2") and are exact reproductions of 1992 Topps Major League baseball cards. Produced in limited numbers, only 1,000 silver and 5,00 bronze were issued. Each mint-card bears a serial number on its bottom edge. These cards were available only in hobby stores, and were packaged in a lucite display case within an album. Each card comes with a sequentially numbered Certificate of Authenticity. The cards feature future heroes, current, and past stars. The cards are numbered corresponding to their actual original 1992 Topps card number and checklisted below in that manner. The prices below refer to the bronze versions; the silver versions would be valued at approximately four times the values listed below.

	MT	EX-MT	VG
COMPLETE SET (6)	250.00	115.00	31.00
COMMON PLAYER	45.00	20.00	5.75
☐ 1 Nolan Ryan	50.00	23.00	6.25
☐ 40 Cal Ripken	45.00	20.00	5.75
☐ 50 Ken Griffey Jr.	50.00	23.00	6.25
☐ 110 Ryne Sandberg	45.00	20.00	5.75
☐ 150 Roger Clemens	45.00	20.00	5.75
☐ 330 Will Clark	45.00	20.00	5.75

1992 Topps McDonald's Best

This 44-card standard-size (2 1/2" by 3 1/2") set was produced by Topps for McDonald's and distributed in the New York, New Jersey, and Connecticut areas. The set was subtitled "McDonald's Baseball's Best". For 99 cents with the purchase of an Extra Value Meal or 1.79 with any other food purchase, the collector received a 5-card cello pack. The top card of each pack was always one of eleven different rookies (34-44) randomly packed with four other non-Rookie Cards. On the fronts, the color player photos are edged with canary yellow and black borders. The player's name and sponsor logo are gold foil stamped at the bottom.

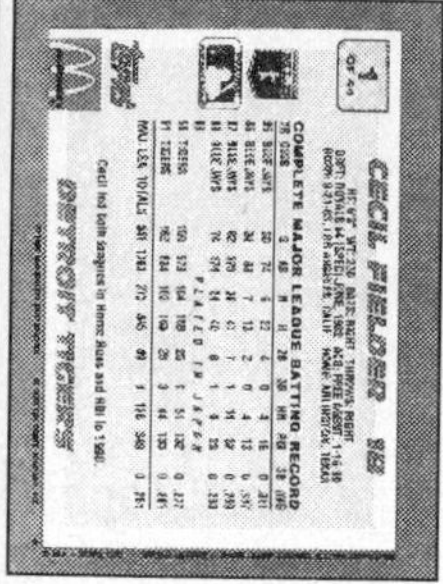

The backs are bordered in red and white and display biographical and statistical information on a orange-yellow background. The cards are numbered on the back.

	MT	EX-MT	VG
COMPLETE SET (44)	30.00	13.50	3.80
COMMON PLAYER (1-44)	.35	.16	.04

	Player	MT	EX-MT	VG
☐ 1	Cecil Fielder	.75	.35	.09
☐ 2	Benny Santiago	.45	.20	.06
☐ 3	Rickey Henderson	1.00	.45	.13
☐ 4	Roberto Alomar	1.50	.65	.19
☐ 5	Ryne Sandberg	2.00	.90	.25
☐ 6	George Brett	.75	.35	.09
☐ 7	Terry Pendleton	.60	.25	.08
☐ 8	Ken Griffey Jr.	4.00	1.80	.50
☐ 9	Bobby Bonilla	.60	.25	.08
☐ 10	Roger Clemens	2.00	.90	.25
☐ 11	Ozzie Smith	.60	.25	.08
☐ 12	Barry Bonds	1.00	.45	.13
☐ 13	Cal Ripken	2.00	.90	.25
☐ 14	Ron Gant	.60	.25	.08
☐ 15	Carlton Fisk	.60	.25	.08
☐ 16	Steve Avery	1.00	.45	.13
☐ 17	Robin Yount	.75	.35	.09
☐ 18	Will Clark	1.50	.65	.19
☐ 19	Kirby Puckett	1.50	.65	.19
☐ 20	Jim Abbott	.60	.25	.08
☐ 21	Barry Larkin	.60	.25	.08
☐ 22	Jose Canseco	1.50	.65	.19
☐ 23	Howard Johnson	.45	.20	.06
☐ 24	Nolan Ryan	3.00	1.35	.40
☐ 25	Frank Thomas	6.00	2.70	.75
☐ 26	Danny Tartabull	.60	.25	.08
☐ 27	Julio Franco	.35	.16	.04
☐ 28	David Justice	1.50	.65	.19
☐ 29	Joe Carter	.75	.35	.09
☐ 30	Dale Murphy	.45	.20	.06
☐ 31	Andre Dawson	.60	.25	.08
☐ 32	Dwight Gooden	.45	.20	.06
☐ 33	Bo Jackson	1.00	.45	.13
☐ 34	Jeff Bagwell	1.25	.55	.16
☐ 35	Chuck Knoblauch	1.00	.45	.13
☐ 36	Derek Bell	.60	.25	.08
☐ 37	Jim Thome	.45	.20	.06
☐ 38	Royce Clayton	.60	.25	.08
☐ 39	Ryan Klesko	1.25	.55	.16
☐ 40	Chito Martinez	.35	.16	.04
☐ 41	Ivan Rodriguez	1.25	.55	.16
☐ 42	Todd Hundley	.35	.16	.04
☐ 43	Eric Karros	1.50	.65	.19
☐ 44	Todd Van Poppel	1.00	.45	.13

1992 Topps Micro Gold Insert

The 12 cards in this set were included as a special insert in the 1992 Topps Micro Baseball set. These micro cards measure approximately 40 percent of the original size (approximately 1" by 1 3/8"). The fronts feature a color cut-out player photo on a gold-foil panel. The panel is bordered in red and blue on a white face. Player information appears at the bottom. The horizontally oriented backs have biographical and statistical information divided into separated blue-bordered and red-bordered boxes. A picture

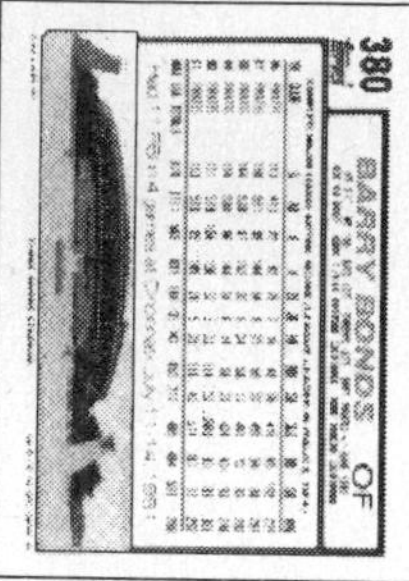

of player's home stadium is at the bottom. The cards are numbered just as in the regular series and are checklisted below accordingly.

	MT	EX-MT	VG
COMPLETE SET (12)	3.50	1.55	.45
COMMON PLAYER	.15	.07	.02

	Player	MT	EX-MT	VG
☐ 1	Nolan Ryan	1.00	.45	.13
☐ 2	Rickey Henderson	.35	.16	.04
☐ 10	Wade Boggs	.30	.14	.04
☐ 50	Ken Griffey Jr.	1.00	.45	.13
☐ 100	Jose Canseco	.50	.23	.06
☐ 270	Tony Gwynn	.30	.14	.04
☐ 300	Don Mattingly	.35	.16	.04
☐ 390	Barry Bonds	.30	.14	.04
☐ 397	Cecil Fielder	.30	.14	.04
☐ 403	Ruben Sierra	.30	.14	.04
☐ 460	Andre Dawson	.25	.11	.03
☐ 725	Dwight Gooden	.15	.07	.02

1992 Topps Kids

This 132-card standard size (2 1/2" by 3 1/2") set was packaged in seven-card wax packs with a stick of bubble gum. The front features action and posed player pictures that are part-photo and part-cartoon on a brightly colored background. The player's name is printed at the bottom in a variety of colors and styles. The backs carry a cartoon with a trivia fact and a "Fun Box" including trivia questions, puzzles, quotable quotes, tips from the pros, or a "Did You Know" feature. Statistical information is shown in a multi-colored grid at the bottom. The cards are numbered on the back. The set numbering is arranged by teams in alphabetical order within division.

	MT	EX-MT	VG
COMPLETE SET (132)	10.00	4.50	1.25
COMMON PLAYER (1-132)	.05	.02	.01

	Player	MT	EX-MT	VG
☐ 1	Ryne Sandberg	.50	.23	.06
☐ 2	Andre Dawson	.20	.09	.03
☐ 3	George Bell	.10	.05	.01
☐ 4	Mark Grace	.15	.07	.02
☐ 5	Shawon Dunston	.05	.02	.01

☐ 6 Tim Wallach	.05	.02	.01
☐ 7 Ivan Calderon	.05	.02	.01
☐ 8 Marquis Grissom	.15	.07	.02
☐ 9 Delino DeShields	.15	.07	.02
☐ 10 Dennis Martinez	.08	.04	.01
☐ 11 Dwight Gooden	.12	.05	.02
☐ 12 Howard Johnson	.08	.04	.01
☐ 13 John Franco	.05	.02	.01
☐ 14 Gregg Jefferies	.12	.05	.02
☐ 15 Kevin McReynolds	.05	.02	.01
☐ 16 David Cone	.12	.05	.02
☐ 17 Len Dykstra	.08	.04	.01
☐ 18 John Kruk	.08	.04	.01
☐ 19 Von Hayes	.05	.02	.01
☐ 20 Mitch Williams	.05	.02	.01
☐ 21 Barry Bonds	.25	.11	.03
☐ 22 Bobby Bonilla	.15	.07	.02
☐ 23 Andy Van Slyke	.12	.05	.02
☐ 24 Doug Drabek	.08	.04	.01
☐ 25 Ozzie Smith	.20	.09	.03
☐ 26 Pedro Guerrero	.08	.04	.01
☐ 27 Todd Zeile	.08	.04	.01
☐ 28 Lee Smith	.10	.05	.01
☐ 29 Felix Jose	.08	.04	.01
☐ 30 Jose DeLeon	.05	.02	.01
☐ 31 David Justice	.25	.11	.03
☐ 32 Ron Gant	.12	.05	.02
☐ 33 Terry Pendleton	.10	.05	.01
☐ 34 Tom Glavine	.20	.09	.03
☐ 35 Otis Nixon	.08	.04	.01
☐ 36 Steve Avery	.20	.09	.03
☐ 37 Barry Larkin	.15	.07	.02
☐ 38 Eric Davis	.12	.05	.02
☐ 39 Chris Sabo	.08	.04	.01
☐ 40 Rob Dibble	.05	.02	.01
☐ 41 Paul O'Neill	.05	.02	.01
☐ 42 Jose Rijo	.05	.02	.01
☐ 43 Craig Biggio	.08	.04	.01
☐ 44 Jeff Bagwell	.25	.11	.03
☐ 45 Ken Caminiti	.08	.04	.01
☐ 46 Steve Finley	.05	.02	.01
☐ 47 Darryl Strawberry	.25	.11	.03
☐ 48 Ramon Martinez	.12	.05	.02
☐ 49 Brett Butler	.08	.04	.01
☐ 50 Eddie Murray	.12	.05	.02
☐ 51 Kal Daniels	.05	.02	.01
☐ 52 Orel Hershiser	.08	.04	.01
☐ 53 Tony Gwynn	.20	.09	.03
☐ 54 Benito Santiago	.10	.05	.01
☐ 55 Fred McGriff	.20	.09	.03
☐ 56 Bip Roberts	.08	.04	.01
☐ 57 Tony Fernandez	.08	.04	.01
☐ 58 Will Clark	.30	.14	.04
☐ 59 Kevin Mitchell	.10	.05	.01
☐ 60 Matt Williams	.10	.05	.01
☐ 61 Willie McGee	.08	.04	.01
☐ 62 Dave Righetti	.05	.02	.01
☐ 63 Cal Ripken	.50	.23	.06
☐ 64 Ben McDonald	.10	.05	.01
☐ 65 Glenn Davis	.08	.04	.01
☐ 66 Gregg Olson	.08	.04	.01
☐ 67 Roger Clemens	.40	.18	.05
☐ 68 Wade Boggs	.25	.11	.03
☐ 69 Mike Greenwell	.08	.04	.01
☐ 70 Ellis Burks	.08	.04	.01
☐ 71 Sandy Alomar Jr.	.08	.04	.01
☐ 72 Greg Swindell	.08	.04	.01
☐ 73 Albert Belle	.15	.07	.02
☐ 74 Mark Whiten	.08	.04	.01
☐ 75 Alan Trammell	.10	.05	.01
☐ 76 Cecil Fielder	.20	.09	.03
☐ 77 Lou Whitaker	.10	.05	.01
☐ 78 Travis Fryman	.40	.18	.05
☐ 79 Tony Phillips	.08	.04	.01
☐ 80 Robin Yount	.20	.09	.03
☐ 81 Paul Molitor	.12	.05	.02
☐ 82 B.J. Surhoff	.05	.02	.01
☐ 83 Greg Vaughn	.08	.04	.01
☐ 84 Don Mattingly	.25	.11	.03
☐ 85 Steve Sax	.08	.04	.01
☐ 86 Kevin Maas	.10	.05	.01
☐ 87 Mel Hall	.08	.04	.01
☐ 88 Roberto Kelly	.10	.05	.01
☐ 89 Joe Carter	.20	.09	.03
☐ 90 Roberto Alomar	.35	.16	.04
☐ 91 Dave Stieb	.05	.02	.01
☐ 92 Kelly Gruber	.08	.04	.01
☐ 93 Tom Henke	.08	.04	.01
☐ 94 Chuck Finley	.05	.02	.01
☐ 95 Wally Joyner	.08	.04	.01
☐ 96 Dave Winfield	.20	.09	.03
☐ 97 Jim Abbott	.15	.07	.02
☐ 98 Mark Langston	.08	.04	.01
☐ 99 Frank Thomas	1.00	.45	.13
☐ 100 Ozzie Guillen	.05	.02	.01
☐ 101 Bobby Thigpen	.05	.02	.01
☐ 102 Robin Ventura	.20	.09	.03
☐ 103 Bo Jackson	.15	.07	.02
☐ 104 Tim Raines	.08	.04	.01
☐ 105 George Brett	.20	.09	.03
☐ 106 Danny Tartabull	.10	.05	.01
☐ 107 Bret Saberhagen	.08	.04	.01
☐ 108 Brian McRae	.10	.05	.01
☐ 109 Kirby Puckett	.40	.18	.05
☐ 110 Scott Erickson	.10	.05	.01
☐ 111 Kent Hrbek	.08	.04	.01
☐ 112 Chuck Knoblauch	.25	.11	.03
☐ 113 Chili Davis	.05	.02	.01
☐ 114 Rick Aguilera	.08	.04	.01
☐ 115 Jose Canseco	.40	.18	.05
☐ 116 Dave Henderson	.05	.02	.01
☐ 117 Dave Stewart	.08	.04	.01
☐ 118 Rickey Henderson	.25	.11	.03
☐ 119 Dennis Eckersley	.12	.05	.02
☐ 120 Harold Baines	.08	.04	.01
☐ 121 Mark McGwire	.35	.16	.04
☐ 122 Ken Griffey Jr.	.75	.35	.09
☐ 123 Harold Reynolds	.05	.02	.01
☐ 124 Erik Hanson	.05	.02	.01
☐ 125 Edgar Martinez	.10	.05	.01
☐ 126 Randy Johnson	.08	.04	.01
☐ 127 Nolan Ryan	.75	.35	.09
☐ 128 Ruben Sierra	.25	.11	.03
☐ 129 Julio Franco	.08	.04	.01
☐ 130 Rafael Palmeiro	.10	.05	.01
☐ 131 Juan Gonzalez	.40	.18	.05
☐ 132 Checklist	.08	.04	.01

1992 Topps Traded

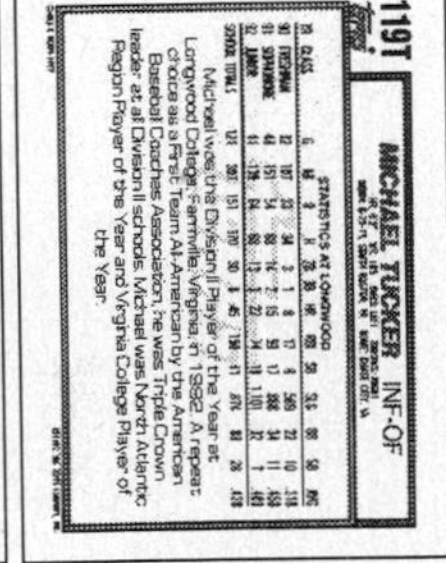

The 1992 Topps Traded set comprises 132 cards, each measuring the standard size (2 1/2" by 3 1/2"). As in past editions, the set focuses on promising rookies, new managers, and players who changed teams. The set also includes a Team U.S.A. subset, featuring 25 of America's top college players and the Team U.S.A. coach. Inside a white outer border, the fronts display color action photos that have two-color (white and another color) picture frames. The player's name appears in a short color bar at the lower left corner while the team name is given in a different color bar at the lower right corner. In a horizontal format, the backs carry biography, statistics, player summary, or a small color picture of the team's stadium . The cards are arranged in alphabetical order by player's last name and numbered on the back. The key Rookie Cards in this set are Pat Listach, Calvin Murray, Michael Tucker, and B.J. Wallace.

	MT	EX-MT	VG
COMPLETE SET (132)	14.00	6.25	1.75
COMMON PLAYER (1T-132T)	.05	.02	.01
☐ 1T Willie Adams USA	.20	.09	.03
☐ 2T Jeff Alkire USA	.30	.14	.04
☐ 3T Felipe Alou MG	.05	.02	.01
☐ 4T Moises Alou	.10	.05	.01

☐ 5T Ruben Amaro	.05	.02	.01
☐ 6T Jack Armstrong	.05	.02	.01
☐ 7T Scott Bankhead	.05	.02	.01
☐ 8T Tim Belcher	.08	.04	.01
☐ 9T George Bell	.08	.04	.01
☐ 10T Freddie Benavides	.05	.02	.01
☐ 11T Todd Benzinger	.05	.02	.01
☐ 12T Joe Boever	.05	.02	.01
☐ 13T Ricky Bones	.08	.04	.01
☐ 14T Bobby Bonilla	.10	.05	.01
☐ 15T Hubie Brooks	.05	.02	.01
☐ 16T Jerry Browne	.05	.02	.01
☐ 17T Jim Bullinger	.10	.05	.01
☐ 18T Dave Burba	.05	.02	.01
☐ 19T Kevin Campbell	.10	.05	.01
☐ 20T Tom Candiotti	.05	.02	.01
☐ 21T Mark Carreon	.05	.02	.01
☐ 22T Gary Carter	.08	.04	.01
☐ 23T Archi Cianfrocco	.15	.07	.02
☐ 24T Phil Clark	.05	.02	.01
☐ 25T Chad Curtis	.25	.11	.03
☐ 26T Eric Davis	.08	.04	.01
☐ 27T Tim Davis USA	.20	.09	.03
☐ 28T Gary DiSarcina	.05	.02	.01
☐ 29T Darren Dreifort USA	.15	.07	.02
☐ 30T Mariano Duncan	.05	.02	.01
☐ 31T Mike Fitzgerald	.05	.02	.01
☐ 32T John Flaherty	.10	.05	.01
☐ 33T Darrin Fletcher	.05	.02	.01
☐ 34T Scott Fletcher	.05	.02	.01
☐ 35T Ron Fraser CO USA	.12	.05	.02
☐ 36T Andres Galarraga	.05	.02	.01
☐ 37T Dave Gallagher	.05	.02	.01
☐ 38T Mike Gallego	.05	.02	.01
☐ 39T Nomar Garciaparra USA	.30	.14	.04
☐ 40T Jason Giambi USA	.15	.07	.02
☐ 41T Danny Gladden	.05	.02	.01
☐ 42T Rene Gonzales	.05	.02	.01
☐ 43T Jeff Granger USA	.12	.05	.02
☐ 44T Rick Greene USA	.25	.11	.03
☐ 45T Jeffrey Hammonds USA	.75	.35	.09
☐ 46T Charlie Hayes	.05	.02	.01
☐ 47T Von Hayes	.05	.02	.01
☐ 48T Rick Helling USA	.15	.07	.02
☐ 49T Butch Henry	.12	.05	.02
☐ 50T Carlos Hernandez	.05	.02	.01
☐ 51T Ken Hill	.08	.04	.01
☐ 52T Butch Hobson	.05	.02	.01
☐ 53T Vince Horsman	.10	.05	.01
☐ 54T Pete Incaviglia	.05	.02	.01
☐ 55T Gregg Johnson	.10	.05	.01
☐ 56T Charles Johnson USA	.50	.23	.06
☐ 57T Doug Jones	.05	.02	.01
☐ 58T Brian Jordan	.25	.11	.03
☐ 59T Wally Joyner	.08	.04	.01
☐ 60T Daron Kirkreit USA	.35	.16	.04
☐ 61T Bill Krueger	.05	.02	.01
☐ 62T Gene Lamont MG	.05	.02	.01
☐ 63T Jim Lefebvre MG	.05	.02	.01
☐ 64T Danny Leon	.10	.05	.01
☐ 65T Pat Listach	1.50	.65	.19
☐ 66T Kenny Lofton	.40	.18	.05
☐ 67T Dave Martinez	.05	.02	.01
☐ 68T Derrick May	.08	.04	.01
☐ 69T Kirk McCaskill	.05	.02	.01
☐ 70T Chad McConnell USA	.30	.14	.04
☐ 71T Kevin McReynolds	.08	.04	.01
☐ 72T Rusty Meacham	.05	.02	.01
☐ 73T Keith Miller	.05	.02	.01
☐ 74T Kevin Mitchell	.08	.04	.01
☐ 75T Jason Moler USA	.20	.09	.03
☐ 76T Mike Morgan	.05	.02	.01
☐ 77T Jack Morris	.10	.05	.01
☐ 78T Calvin Murray USA	.75	.35	.09
☐ 79T Eddie Murray	.10	.05	.01
☐ 80T Randy Myers	.08	.04	.01
☐ 81T Denny Neagle	.05	.02	.01
☐ 82T Phil Nevin USA	1.00	.45	.13
☐ 83T Dave Nilsson	.15	.07	.02
☐ 84T Junior Ortiz	.05	.02	.01
☐ 85T Donovan Osborne	.30	.14	.04
☐ 86T Bill Pecota	.05	.02	.01
☐ 87T Melido Perez	.08	.04	.01
☐ 88T Mike Perez	.05	.02	.01
☐ 89T Hipolito Pichardo	.10	.05	.01
☐ 90T Willie Randolph	.08	.04	.01
☐ 91T Darren Reed	.05	.02	.01
☐ 92T Bip Roberts	.08	.04	.01
☐ 93T Chris Roberts USA	.25	.11	.03
☐ 94T Steve Rodriguez USA	.10	.05	.01
☐ 95T Bruce Ruffin	.05	.02	.01
☐ 96T Scott Ruskin	.05	.02	.01
☐ 97T Bret Saberhagen	.08	.04	.01
☐ 98T Rey Sanchez	.12	.05	.02
☐ 99T Steve Sax	.08	.04	.01
☐ 100T Curt Schilling	.08	.04	.01
☐ 101T Dick Schofield	.05	.02	.01
☐ 102T Gary Scott	.08	.04	.01
☐ 103T Kevin Seitzer	.08	.04	.01
☐ 104T Frank Seminara	.20	.09	.03
☐ 105T Gary Sheffield	.25	.11	.03
☐ 106T John Smiley	.08	.04	.01
☐ 107T Cory Snyder	.05	.02	.01
☐ 108T Paul Sorrento	.08	.04	.01
☐ 109T Sammy Sosa	.05	.02	.01
☐ 110T Matt Stairs	.15	.07	.02
☐ 111T Andy Stankiewicz	.15	.07	.02
☐ 112T Kurt Stillwell	.05	.02	.01
☐ 113T Rick Sutcliffe	.08	.04	.01
☐ 114T Bill Swift	.05	.02	.01
☐ 115T Jeff Tackett	.08	.04	.01
☐ 116T Danny Tartabull	.08	.04	.01
☐ 117T Eddie Taubensee	.10	.05	.01
☐ 118T Dickie Thon	.05	.02	.01
☐ 119T Michael Tucker USA	1.25	.55	.16
☐ 120T Scooter Tucker	.10	.05	.01
☐ 121T Marc Valdes USA	.20	.09	.03
☐ 122T Julio Valera	.08	.04	.01
☐ 123T Jason Varitek USA	.30	.14	.04
☐ 124T Ron Villone USA	.25	.11	.03
☐ 125T Frank Viola	.08	.04	.01
☐ 126T B.J. Wallace USA	1.00	.45	.13
☐ 127T Dan Walters	.15	.07	.02
☐ 128T Craig Wilson USA	.12	.05	.02
☐ 129T Chris Wimmer USA	.10	.05	.01
☐ 130T Dave Winfield	.12	.05	.02
☐ 131T Herm Winningham	.05	.02	.01
☐ 132T Checklist Card	.08	.01	.00

1993 Topps Pre-Production Sheet

The 1993 Topps Pre-Production sheet was sent out to give collectors a preview of the design of Topps' 1993 regular issue cards. The sheet measures 8" by 11" and features nine standard-size (2 1/2" by 3 1/2") cards. The fronts feature color action player photos with white borders. The player's name appears in a stripe at the bottom of the picture, and this stripe and two short diagonal stripes at the bottom corners of the picture are team color-coded. The backs are colorful and carry a color head shot, biography, complete statistical information, with a career highlight if space permits. A gray circle with the message "1993 Pre-Production Sample: For General Look Only" is superimposed over the statistical section. The cards are all numbered "000" and are therefore checklisted below in alphabetical order.

	MT	EX-MT	VG
COMPLETE SET (9)	10.00	4.50	1.25
COMMON PLAYER (1-9)	.75	.35	.09
☐ 1 Roberto Alomar	2.50	1.15	.30
☐ 2 Bobby Bonilla	1.50	.65	.19
☐ 3 Gary Carter	1.25	.55	.16
☐ 4 Andre Dawson	1.50	.65	.19
☐ 5 Dave Fleming	1.50	.65	.19
☐ 6 Ken Griffey Jr.	3.50	1.55	.45

☐ 7 Pete Incaviglia	.75	.35	.09
☐ 8 Spike Owen	.75	.35	.09
☐ 9 Larry Walker	1.50	.65	.19

1993 Topps Holiday Previews

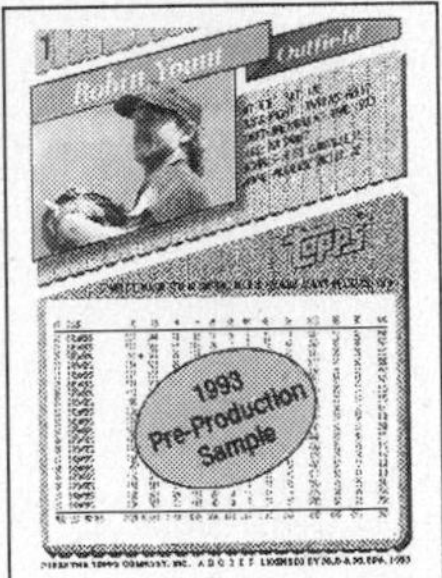

These nine pre-production cards were included in the 1992 Topps Holiday set as a special insert set. The cards are standard size, 2 1/2" by 3 1/2" and were done in the style of the 1993 Topps baseball cards. The fronts feature color action player photos bordered in white. A team color-coded horizontal bar and two short diagonal bars accent the pictures at the bottom. The backs carry a color close-up photo, biography, statistics, and (where space allows) a summary of the player's outstanding performance during a game. The cards say "1993 Pre-Production Sample" inside an oval in the middle of the card back. The cards are numbered on the back.

	MT	EX-MT	VG
COMPLETE SET (9)	7.50	3.40	.95
COMMON PLAYER	.35	.16	.04
☐ 1 Robin Yount	1.00	.45	.13
☐ 2 Barry Bonds	1.00	.45	.13
☐ 11 Eric Karros	.75	.35	.09
☐ 32 Don Mattingly	1.25	.55	.16
☐ 100 Mark McGwire	1.25	.55	.16
☐ 150 Frank Thomas	2.50	1.15	.30
☐ 179 Ken Griffey Jr.	2.50	1.15	.30
☐ 230 Carlton Fisk	.75	.35	.09
☐ 250 Chuck Knoblauch	.35	.16	.04

1993 Topps

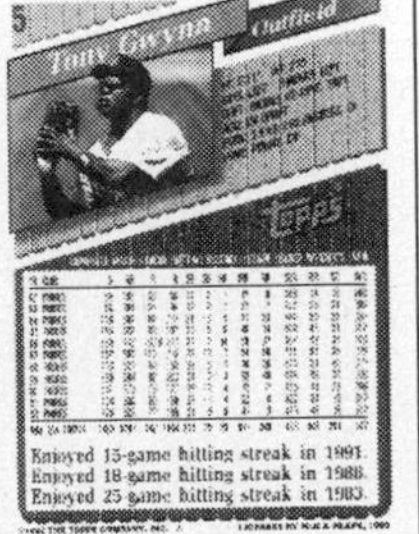

The 1993 Topps baseball set (first series) consists of 396 cards measuring the standard size (2 1/2" by 3 1/2"). A Topps Gold card was inserted in every 15-card pack, and Topps Black Gold cards were randomly inserted throughout the packs. The fronts feature color action player photos with white borders. The player's name appears in a stripe at the bottom of the picture, and this stripe and two short diagonal stripes at the bottom corners of the picture are team color-coded. The backs are colorful and carry a color head shot, biography, complete statistical information, with a career highlight if space permitted. The cards are numbered on the back.

	MT	EX-MT	VG
COMPLETE SET (396)	15.00	6.75	1.90
COMMON PLAYER (1-396)	.04	.02	.01
GOLD COMPLETE SET (396)	150.00	70.00	19.00
GOLD COMMON (1-396)	.25	.11	.03
☐ 1 Robin Yount	.10	.05	.01
☐ 2 Barry Bonds	.15	.07	.02
☐ 3 Ryne Sandberg	.20	.09	.03
☐ 4 Roger Clemens	.25	.11	.03
☐ 5 Tony Gwynn	.12	.05	.02
☐ 6 Jeff Tackett	.25	.11	.03
☐ 7 Pete Incaviglia	.25	.11	.03
☐ 8 Mark Wohlers	.28	.13	.04
☐ 9 Kent Hrbek	.28	.13	.04
☐ 10 Will Clark	.15	.07	.02
☐ 11 Eric Karros	.35	.16	.04
☐ 12 Lee Smith	.25	.11	.03
☐ 13 Esteban Beltre	.25	.11	.03
☐ 14 Greg Briley	.25	.11	.03
☐ 15 Marquis Grissom	.10	.05	.01
☐ 16 Dan Plesac	.25	.11	.03
☐ 17 Dave Hollins	.28	.13	.04
☐ 18 Terry Steinbach	.28	.13	.04
☐ 19 Ed Nunez	.25	.11	.03
☐ 20 Tim Salmon	.25	.11	.03
☐ 21 Luis Salazar	.25	.11	.03
☐ 22 Jim Eisenreich	.25	.11	.03
☐ 23 Todd Stottlemyre	.25	.11	.03
☐ 24 Tim Naehring	.25	.11	.03
☐ 25 John Franco	.25	.11	.03
☐ 26 Skeeter Barnes	.25	.11	.03
☐ 27 Carlos Garcia	.25	.11	.03
☐ 28 Joe Orsulak	.25	.11	.03
☐ 29 Dwayne Henry	.25	.11	.03
☐ 30 Fred McGriff	.12	.05	.02
☐ 31 Derek Lilliquist	.25	.11	.03
☐ 32 Don Mattingly	.12	.05	.02
☐ 33 B.J. Wallace	.40	.18	.05
☐ 34 Juan Gonzalez	.30	.14	.04
☐ 35 John Smoltz	.10	.05	.01
☐ 36 Scott Servais	.25	.11	.03
☐ 37 Lenny Webster	.25	.11	.03
☐ 38 Chris James	.25	.11	.03
☐ 39 Roger McDowell	.25	.11	.03
☐ 40 Ozzie Smith	.10	.05	.01
☐ 41 Alex Fernandez	.28	.13	.04
☐ 42 Spike Owen	.25	.11	.03
☐ 43 Ruben Amaro	.25	.11	.03
☐ 44 Kevin Seitzer	.28	.13	.04
☐ 45 Dave Fleming	.20	.09	.03
☐ 46 Eric Fox	.25	.11	.03
☐ 47 Bob Scanlan	.25	.11	.03
☐ 48 Bert Blyleven	.28	.13	.04
☐ 49 Brian McRae	.25	.11	.03
☐ 50 Roberto Alomar	.20	.09	.03
☐ 51 Mo Vaughn	.28	.13	.04
☐ 52 Bobby Bonilla	.10	.05	.01
☐ 53 Frank Tanana	.25	.11	.03
☐ 54 Mike LaValliere	.25	.11	.03
☐ 55 Mark McLemore	.25	.11	.03
☐ 56 Chad Mottola	.75	.35	.09
☐ 57 Norm Charlton	.28	.13	.04
☐ 58 Jose Melendez	.25	.11	.03
☐ 59 Carlos Martinez	.25	.11	.03
☐ 60 Roberto Kelly	.28	.13	.04
☐ 61 Gene Larkin	.25	.11	.03
☐ 62 Rafael Belliard	.25	.11	.03
☐ 63 Al Osuna	.25	.11	.03
☐ 64 Scott Chiamparino	.25	.11	.03
☐ 65 Brett Butler	.28	.13	.04
☐ 66 John Burkett	.25	.11	.03
☐ 67 Felix Jose	.28	.13	.04
☐ 68 Omar Vizquel	.25	.11	.03
☐ 69 John Vander Wal	.25	.11	.03
☐ 70 Roberto Hernandez	.25	.11	.03
☐ 71 Ricky Bones	.25	.11	.03
☐ 72 Jeff Grotewold	.25	.11	.03
☐ 73 Mike Moore	.25	.11	.03
☐ 74 Steve Buechele	.25	.11	.03
☐ 75 Juan Guzman	.30	.14	.04
☐ 76 Kevin Appier	.28	.13	.04
☐ 77 Junior Felix	.25	.11	.03

☐ 78 Greg W. Harris .25 .11 .03
☐ 79 Dick Schofield .25 .11 .03
☐ 80 Cecil Fielder .12 .05 .02
☐ 81 Lloyd McClendon .25 .11 .03
☐ 82 David Segui .25 .11 .03
☐ 83 Reggie Sanders .12 .05 .02
☐ 84 Kurt Stillwell .25 .11 .03
☐ 85 Sandy Alomar .28 .13 .04
☐ 86 John Habyan .25 .11 .03
☐ 87 Kevin Reimer .25 .11 .03
☐ 88 Mike Stanton .25 .11 .03
☐ 89 Eric Anthony .28 .13 .04
☐ 90 Scott Erickson .28 .13 .04
☐ 91 Craig Colbert .25 .11 .03
☐ 92 Tom Pagnozzi .25 .11 .03
☐ 93 Pedro Astacio .20 .09 .03
☐ 94 Lance Johnson .25 .11 .03
☐ 95 Larry Walker .12 .05 .02
☐ 96 Russ Swan .25 .11 .03
☐ 97 Scott Fletcher .25 .11 .03
☐ 98 Derek Jeter .30 .14 .04
☐ 99 Mike Williams .10 .05 .01
☐ 100 Mark McGwire .15 .07 .02
☐ 101 Jim Bullinger .25 .11 .03
☐ 102 Brian Hunter .28 .13 .04
☐ 103 Jody Reed .25 .11 .03
☐ 104 Mike Butcher .25 .11 .03
☐ 105 Gregg Jefferies .28 .13 .04
☐ 106 Howard Johnson .28 .13 .04
☐ 107 John Kiely .25 .11 .03
☐ 108 Jose Lind .25 .11 .03
☐ 109 Sam Horn .25 .11 .03
☐ 110 Barry Larkin .10 .05 .01
☐ 111 Bruce Hurst .28 .13 .04
☐ 112 Brian Barnes .25 .11 .03
☐ 113 Thomas Howard .25 .11 .03
☐ 114 Mel Hall .25 .11 .03
☐ 115 Robby Thompson .25 .11 .03
☐ 116 Mark Lemke .25 .11 .03
☐ 117 Eddie Taubensee .25 .11 .03
☐ 118 David Hulse .12 .05 .02
☐ 119 Pedro Munoz .28 .13 .04
☐ 120 Ramon Martinez .28 .13 .04
☐ 121 Todd Worrell .25 .11 .03
☐ 122 Joey Cora .25 .11 .03
☐ 123 Moises Alou .28 .13 .04
☐ 124 Franklin Stubbs .25 .11 .03
☐ 125 Pete O'Brien .25 .11 .03
☐ 126 Bob Ayrault .08 .04 .01
☐ 127 Carney Lansford .28 .13 .04
☐ 128 Kal Daniels .25 .11 .03
☐ 129 Joe Grahe .25 .11 .03
☐ 130 Jeff Montgomery .25 .11 .03
☐ 131 Dave Winfield .10 .05 .01
☐ 132 Preston Wilson .40 .18 .05
☐ 133 Steve Wilson .25 .11 .03
☐ 134 Lee Guetterman .25 .11 .03
☐ 135 Mickey Tettleton .28 .13 .04
☐ 136 Jeff King .25 .11 .03
☐ 137 Alan Mills .25 .11 .03
☐ 138 Joe Oliver .25 .11 .03
☐ 139 Gary Gaetti .25 .11 .03
☐ 140 Gary Sheffield .15 .07 .02
☐ 141 Dennis Cook .25 .11 .03
☐ 142 Charlie Hayes .25 .11 .03
☐ 143 Jeff Huson .25 .11 .03
☐ 144 Kent Mercker .25 .11 .03
☐ 145 Eric Young .12 .05 .02
☐ 146 Scott Leius .25 .11 .03
☐ 147 Bryan Hickerson .25 .11 .03
☐ 148 Steve Finley .25 .11 .03
☐ 149 Rheal Cormier .25 .11 .03
☐ 150 Frank Thomas .75 .35 .09
☐ 151 Archi Cianfrocco .25 .11 .03
☐ 152 Rich DeLucia .25 .11 .03
☐ 153 Greg Vaughn .28 .13 .04
☐ 154 Wes Chamberlain .25 .11 .03
☐ 155 Dennis Eckersley .10 .05 .01
☐ 156 Sammy Sosa .25 .11 .03
☐ 157 Gary DiSarcina .25 .11 .03
☐ 158 Kevin Koslofski .25 .11 .03
☐ 159 Doug Linton .10 .05 .01
☐ 160 Lou Whitaker .28 .13 .04
☐ 161 Chad McConnell .20 .09 .03
☐ 162 Joe Hesketh .25 .11 .03
☐ 163 Tim Wakefield .60 .25 .08
☐ 164 Leo Gomez .28 .13 .04
☐ 165 Jose Rijo .28 .13 .04
☐ 166 Tim Scott .25 .11 .03
☐ 167 Steve Olin .25 .11 .03
☐ 168 Kevin Maas .28 .13 .04
☐ 169 Kenny Rogers .25 .11 .03
☐ 170 David Justice .15 .07 .02
☐ 171 Doug Jones .25 .11 .03
☐ 172 Jeff Reboulet .08 .04 .01
☐ 173 Andres Galarraga .25 .11 .03
☐ 174 Randy Velarde .25 .11 .03
☐ 175 Kirk McCaskill .25 .11 .03
☐ 176 Darren Lewis .25 .11 .03
☐ 177 Lenny Harris .25 .11 .03
☐ 178 Jeff Fassero .25 .11 .03
☐ 179 Ken Griffey Jr. .50 .23 .06
☐ 180 Darren Daulton .28 .13 .04
☐ 181 John Jaha .10 .05 .01
☐ 182 Ron Darling .28 .13 .04
☐ 183 Greg Maddux .10 .05 .01
☐ 184 Damion Easley .15 .07 .02
☐ 185 Jack Morris .10 .05 .01
☐ 186 Mike Magnante .25 .11 .03
☐ 187 John Dopson .25 .11 .03
☐ 188 Sid Fernandez .28 .13 .04
☐ 189 Tony Phillips .25 .11 .03
☐ 190 Doug Drabek .28 .13 .04
☐ 191 Sean Lowe .20 .09 .03
☐ 192 Bob Milacki .25 .11 .03
☐ 193 Steve Foster .25 .11 .03
☐ 194 Jerald Clark .25 .11 .03
☐ 195 Pete Harnisch .25 .11 .03
☐ 196 Pat Kelly .28 .13 .04
☐ 197 Jeff Frye .25 .11 .03
☐ 198 Alejandro Pena .25 .11 .03
☐ 199 Junior Ortiz .25 .11 .03
☐ 200 Kirby Puckett .20 .09 .03
☐ 201 Jose Uribe .25 .11 .03
☐ 202 Mike Scioscia .25 .11 .03
☐ 203 Bernard Gilkey .28 .13 .04
☐ 204 Dan Pasqua .25 .11 .03
☐ 205 Gary Carter .28 .13 .04
☐ 206 Henry Cotto .25 .11 .03
☐ 207 Paul Molitor .28 .13 .04
☐ 208 Mike Hartley .25 .11 .03
☐ 209 Jeff Parrett .25 .11 .03
☐ 210 Mark Langston .28 .13 .04
☐ 211 Doug Dascenzo .25 .11 .03
☐ 212 Rick Reed .25 .11 .03
☐ 213 Candy Maldonado .25 .11 .03
☐ 214 Danny Darwin .25 .11 .03
☐ 215 Pat Howell .10 .05 .01
☐ 216 Mark Leiter .25 .11 .03
☐ 217 Kevin Mitchell .28 .13 .04
☐ 218 Ben McDonald .28 .13 .04
☐ 219 Bip Roberts .28 .13 .04
☐ 220 Benny Santiago .28 .13 .04
☐ 221 Carlos Baerga .15 .07 .02
☐ 222 Bernie Williams .28 .13 .04
☐ 223 Roger Pavlik .10 .05 .01
☐ 224 Sid Bream .25 .11 .03
☐ 225 Matt Williams .28 .13 .04
☐ 226 Willie Banks .28 .13 .04
☐ 227 Jeff Bagwell .20 .09 .03
☐ 228 Tom Goodwin .25 .11 .03
☐ 229 Mike Perez .25 .11 .03
☐ 230 Carlton Fisk .10 .05 .01
☐ 231 John Wetteland .25 .11 .03
☐ 232 Tino Martinez .28 .13 .04
☐ 233 Rick Greene .15 .07 .02
☐ 234 Tim McIntosh .25 .11 .03
☐ 235 Mitch Williams .25 .11 .03
☐ 236 Kevin Campbell .25 .11 .03
☐ 237 Jose Vizcaino .25 .11 .03
☐ 238 Chris Donnels .25 .11 .03
☐ 239 Mike Boddicker .25 .11 .03
☐ 240 John Olerud .10 .05 .01
☐ 241 Mike Gardiner .25 .11 .03
☐ 242 Charlie O'Brien .25 .11 .03
☐ 243 Rob Deer .25 .11 .03
☐ 244 Denny Neagle .25 .11 .03
☐ 245 Chris Sabo .28 .13 .04
☐ 246 Gregg Olson .28 .13 .04
☐ 247 Frank Seminara .25 .11 .03
☐ 248 Scott Scudder .25 .11 .03
☐ 249 Tim Burke .25 .11 .03
☐ 250 Chuck Knoblauch .15 .07 .02
☐ 251 Mike Bielecki .25 .11 .03
☐ 252 Xavier Hernandez .25 .11 .03
☐ 253 Jose Guzman .25 .11 .03
☐ 254 Cory Snyder .25 .11 .03
☐ 255 Orel Hershiser .28 .13 .04
☐ 256 Wilfredo Cordero .10 .05 .01
☐ 257 Luis Alicea .25 .11 .03
☐ 258 Mike Schooler .25 .11 .03
☐ 259 Craig Grebeck .25 .11 .03
☐ 260 Duane Ward .25 .11 .03
☐ 261 Bill Wegman .25 .11 .03
☐ 262 Mickey Morandini .25 .11 .03
☐ 263 Vince Horsman .25 .11 .03

Card			
☐ 264 Paul Sorrento	.25	.11	.03
☐ 265 Andre Dawson	.10	.05	.01
☐ 266 Rene Gonzales	.25	.11	.03
☐ 267 Keith Miller	.25	.11	.03
☐ 268 Derek Bell	.28	.13	.04
☐ 269 Todd Steverson	.20	.09	.03
☐ 270 Frank Viola	.28	.13	.04
☐ 271 Wally Whitehurst	.25	.11	.03
☐ 272 Kurt Knudsen	.08	.04	.01
☐ 273 Dan Walters	.25	.11	.03
☐ 274 Rick Sutcliffe	.28	.13	.04
☐ 275 Andy Van Slyke	.28	.13	.04
☐ 276 Paul O'Neill	.28	.13	.04
☐ 277 Mark Whiten	.25	.11	.03
☐ 278 Chris Nabholz	.25	.11	.03
☐ 279 Todd Burns	.25	.11	.03
☐ 280 Tom Glavine	.12	.05	.02
☐ 281 Butch Henry	.25	.11	.03
☐ 282 Shane Mack	.28	.13	.04
☐ 283 Mike Jackson	.25	.11	.03
☐ 284 Henry Rodriguez	.28	.13	.04
☐ 285 Bob Tewksbury	.25	.11	.03
☐ 286 Ron Karkovice	.25	.11	.03
☐ 287 Mike Gallego	.25	.11	.03
☐ 288 Dave Cochrane	.25	.11	.03
☐ 289 Jesse Orosco	.25	.11	.03
☐ 290 Dave Stewart	.28	.13	.04
☐ 291 Tommy Greene	.25	.11	.03
☐ 292 Rey Sanchez	.25	.11	.03
☐ 293 Rob Ducey	.25	.11	.03
☐ 294 Brent Mayne	.25	.11	.03
☐ 295 Dave Stieb	.25	.11	.03
☐ 296 Luis Rivera	.25	.11	.03
☐ 297 Jeff Innis	.25	.11	.03
☐ 298 Scott Livingstone	.25	.11	.03
☐ 299 Bob Patterson	.25	.11	.03
☐ 300 Cal Ripken	.25	.11	.03
☐ 301 Cesar Hernandez	.08	.04	.01
☐ 302 Randy Myers	.25	.11	.03
☐ 303 Brook Jacoby	.25	.11	.03
☐ 304 Melido Perez	.25	.11	.03
☐ 305 Rafael Palmeiro	.28	.13	.04
☐ 306 Damon Berryhill	.25	.11	.03
☐ 307 Dan Serafini	.30	.14	.04
☐ 308 Darryl Kile	.25	.11	.03
☐ 309 J.T. Bruett	.10	.05	.01
☐ 310 Dave Righetti	.25	.11	.03
☐ 311 Jay Howell	.25	.11	.03
☐ 312 Geronimo Pena	.25	.11	.03
☐ 313 Greg Hibbard	.25	.11	.03
☐ 314 Mark Gardner	.25	.11	.03
☐ 315 Edgar Martinez	.28	.13	.04
☐ 316 Dave Nilsson	.10	.05	.01
☐ 317 Kyle Abbott	.25	.11	.03
☐ 318 Willie Wilson	.25	.11	.03
☐ 319 Paul Assenmacher	.25	.11	.03
☐ 320 Tim Fortugno	.25	.11	.03
☐ 321 Rusty Meacham	.25	.11	.03
☐ 322 Pat Borders	.25	.11	.03
☐ 323 Mike Greenwell	.28	.13	.04
☐ 324 Willie Randolph	.28	.13	.04
☐ 325 Bill Gullickson	.25	.11	.03
☐ 326 Gary Varsho	.25	.11	.03
☐ 327 Tim Hulett	.25	.11	.03
☐ 328 Scott Ruskin	.25	.11	.03
☐ 329 Mike Maddux	.25	.11	.03
☐ 330 Danny Tartabull	.28	.13	.04
☐ 331 Kenny Lofton	.20	.09	.03
☐ 332 Geno Petralli	.25	.11	.03
☐ 333 Otis Nixon	.25	.11	.03
☐ 334 Jason Kendall	.25	.11	.03
☐ 335 Mark Portugal	.25	.11	.03
☐ 336 Mike Pagliarulo	.25	.11	.03
☐ 337 Kirt Manwaring	.25	.11	.03
☐ 338 Bob Ojeda	.25	.11	.03
☐ 339 Mark Clark	.25	.11	.03
☐ 340 John Kruk	.28	.13	.04
☐ 341 Mel Rojas	.25	.11	.03
☐ 342 Erik Hanson	.25	.11	.03
☐ 343 Doug Henry	.25	.11	.03
☐ 344 Jack McDowell	.28	.13	.04
☐ 345 Harold Baines	.28	.13	.04
☐ 346 Chuck McElroy	.25	.11	.03
☐ 347 Luis Sojo	.25	.11	.03
☐ 348 Andy Stankiewicz	.28	.13	.04
☐ 349 Hipolito Pichardo	.25	.11	.03
☐ 350 Joe Carter	.12	.05	.02
☐ 351 Ellis Burks	.28	.13	.04
☐ 352 Pete Schourek	.28	.13	.04
☐ 353 Bubby Groom	.08	.04	.01
☐ 354 Jay Bell	.25	.11	.03
☐ 355 Brady Anderson	.28	.13	.04
☐ 356 Freddie Benavides	.25	.11	.03
☐ 357 Phil Stephenson	.25	.11	.03
☐ 358 Kevin Wickander	.25	.11	.03
☐ 359 Mike Stanley	.25	.11	.03
☐ 360 Ivan Rodriguez	.20	.09	.03
☐ 361 Scott Bankhead	.25	.11	.03
☐ 362 Luis Gonzalez	.28	.13	.04
☐ 363 John Smiley	.28	.13	.04
☐ 364 Trevor Wilson	.25	.11	.03
☐ 365 Tom Candiotti	.25	.11	.03
☐ 366 Craig Wilson	.25	.11	.03
☐ 367 Steve Sax	.28	.13	.04
☐ 368 Delino DeShields	.10	.05	.01
☐ 369 Jaime Navarro	.28	.13	.04
☐ 370 Dave Valle	.25	.11	.03
☐ 371 Mariano Duncan	.25	.11	.03
☐ 372 Rod Nichols	.25	.11	.03
☐ 373 Mike Morgan	.25	.11	.03
☐ 374 Julio Valera	.25	.11	.03
☐ 375 Wally Joyner	.28	.13	.04
☐ 376 Tom Henke	.28	.13	.04
☐ 377 Herm Winningham	.25	.11	.03
☐ 378 Orlando Merced	.25	.11	.03
☐ 379 Mike Munoz	.25	.11	.03
☐ 380 Todd Hundley	.25	.11	.03
☐ 381 Mike Flanagan	.25	.11	.03
☐ 382 Tim Belcher	.28	.13	.04
☐ 383 Jerry Browne	.25	.11	.03
☐ 384 Mike Benjamin	.25	.11	.03
☐ 385 Jim Leyritz	.25	.11	.03
☐ 386 Ray Lankford	.10	.05	.01
☐ 387 Devon White	.28	.13	.04
☐ 388 Jeremy Hernandez	.25	.11	.03
☐ 389 Brian Harper	.25	.11	.03
☐ 390 Wade Boggs	.12	.05	.02
☐ 391 Derrick May	.28	.13	.04
☐ 392 Travis Fryman	.20	.09	.03
☐ 393 Ron Gant	.08	.04	.01
☐ 394 Checklist 1-132	.25	.03	.01
☐ 395 Checklist 133-264	.25	.03	.01
☐ 396 Checklist 265-396	.25	.03	.01

1993 Topps Black Gold

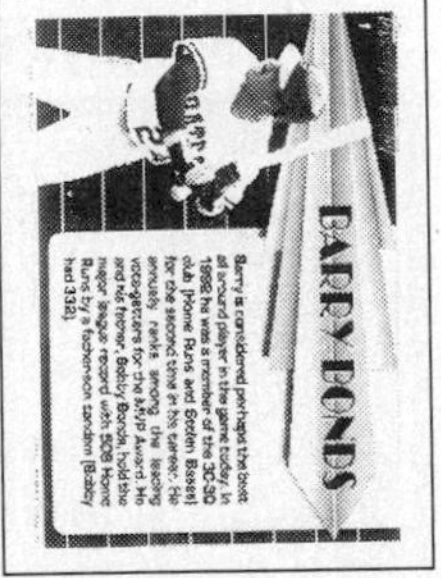

Topps Black Gold cards 1-22 were randomly inserted in series I wax packs while card numbers 23-44 were featured in series II packs. Hobbyists could obtain the set by collecting individual random insert cards or receive 11, 22, or 44 Black Gold cards by mail when they sent in special "You've Just Won" cards, which were randomly inserted in packs. Series I packs featured three different "You've Just Won" cards, entitling the holder to receive Group A (cards 1-11), Group B (cards 12-22), or Groups A and B (Cards 1-22). In a similar fashion, four "You've Just Won" cards were inserted in series II packs and entitled the holder to receive Group C (23-33), Group D (34-44), Groups C and D (23-44), or Groups A-D (1-44). By returning the "You've Just Won" card with 1.50 for postage and handling, the collector received not only the Black Gold cards won but also a special "You've Just Won" card and a congratulatory letter informing the collector that his/her name has been entered into a drawing for one of 500 uncut sheets of all 44 Topps Black Gold cards in a leatherette frame. These standard-size

(2 1/2" by 3 1/2") cards feature different color player photos than either the 1993 Topps regular issue or the Topps Gold issue. The player pictures are cut out and superimposed on a black gloss background. Inside white borders, gold refractory foil edges the top and bottom of the card face. On a black-and-gray pinstripe pattern inside white borders, the horizontal backs have a a second cut out player photo and a player profile on a blue panel. The player's name appears in gold foil lettering on a blue-and-gray geometric shape. The cards are numbered on the back in the upper left corner.

	MT	EX-MT	VG
COMPLETE SET (22)	75.00	34.00	9.50
COMMON PLAYER (1-22)	3.00	1.35	.40
☐ 1 Barry Bonds	7.50	3.40	.95
☐ 2 Will Clark	7.50	3.40	.95
☐ 3 Darren Daulton	3.00	1.35	.40
☐ 4 Andre Dawson	4.50	2.00	.55
☐ 5 Delino DeShields	4.50	2.00	.55
☐ 6 Tom Glavine	6.00	2.70	.75
☐ 7 Marquis Grissom	4.50	2.00	.55
☐ 8 Tony Gwynn	6.00	2.70	.75
☐ 9 Eric Karros	10.00	4.50	1.25
☐ 10 Ray Lankford	4.50	2.00	.55
☐ 11 Barry Larkin	4.50	2.00	.55
☐ 12 Greg Maddux	4.50	2.00	.55
☐ 13 Fred McGriff	6.00	2.70	.75
☐ 14 Joe Oliver	3.00	1.35	.40
☐ 15 Terry Pendleton	4.00	1.80	.50
☐ 16 Bip Roberts	3.00	1.35	.40
☐ 17 Ryne Sandberg	10.00	4.50	1.25
☐ 18 Gary Sheffield	7.00	3.10	.85
☐ 19 Lee Smith	3.50	1.55	.45
☐ 20 Ozzie Smith	5.00	2.30	.60
☐ 21 Andy Van Slyke	4.00	1.80	.50
☐ 22 Larry Walker	5.00	2.30	.60
☐ A0 Winner A 1-11	35.00	16.00	4.40
☐ AB0 Winner A/B 1-22	70.00	32.00	8.75
☐ B0 Winner B 11-22	35.00	16.00	4.40

1987 Toys'R'Us Rookies

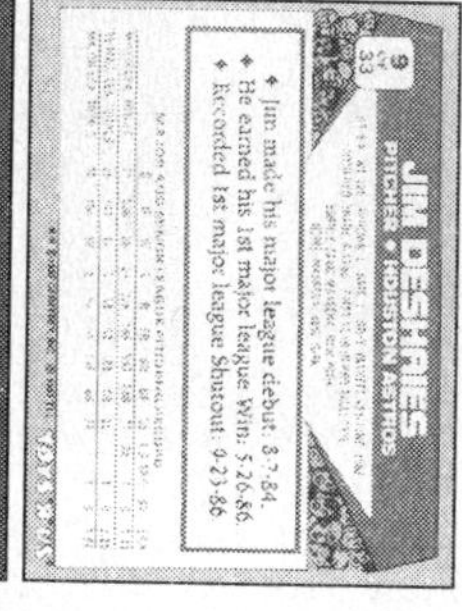

Topps produced this 33-card boxed set for Toys'R'Us stores. The set is subtitled "Baseball Rookies" and features predominantly younger players. The cards measure 2 1/2" by 3 1/2" and feature a high-gloss, full-color photo of the player inside a black border. The card backs are printed in orange and blue on white card stock. The set numbering is in alphabetical order by player's name.

	MT	EX-MT	VG
COMPLETE SET (33)	8.00	3.60	1.00
COMMON PLAYER (1-33)	.10	.05	.01
☐ 1 Andy Allanson	.10	.05	.01
☐ 2 Paul Assenmacher	.15	.07	.02
☐ 3 Scott Bailes	.10	.05	.01
☐ 4 Barry Bonds	1.25	.55	.16
☐ 5 Jose Canseco	1.50	.65	.19
☐ 6 John Cerutti	.10	.05	.01
☐ 7 Will Clark	1.50	.65	.19
☐ 8 Kal Daniels	.25	.11	.03
☐ 9 Jim Deshaies	.10	.05	.01
☐ 10 Mark Eichhorn	.15	.07	.02
☐ 11 Ed Hearn	.10	.05	.01
☐ 12 Pete Incaviglia	.25	.11	.03
☐ 13 Bo Jackson	1.25	.55	.16
☐ 14 Wally Joyner	.60	.25	.08
☐ 15 Charlie Kerfeld	.10	.05	.01
☐ 16 Eric King	.15	.07	.02
☐ 17 John Kruk	.40	.18	.05
☐ 18 Barry Larkin	.75	.35	.09
☐ 19 Mike LaValliere	.10	.05	.01
☐ 20 Greg Mathews	.10	.05	.01
☐ 21 Kevin Mitchell	.75	.35	.09
☐ 22 Dan Plesac	.10	.05	.01
☐ 23 Bruce Ruffin	.10	.05	.01
☐ 24 Ruben Sierra	1.25	.55	.16
☐ 25 Cory Snyder	.20	.09	.03
☐ 26 Kurt Stillwell	.15	.07	.02
☐ 27 Dale Sveum	.10	.05	.01
☐ 28 Danny Tartabull	.75	.35	.09
☐ 29 Andres Thomas	.10	.05	.01
☐ 30 Robby Thompson	.20	.09	.03
☐ 31 Jim Traber	.10	.05	.01
☐ 32 Mitch Williams	.15	.07	.02
☐ 33 Todd Worrell	.20	.09	.03

1988 Toys'R'Us Rookies

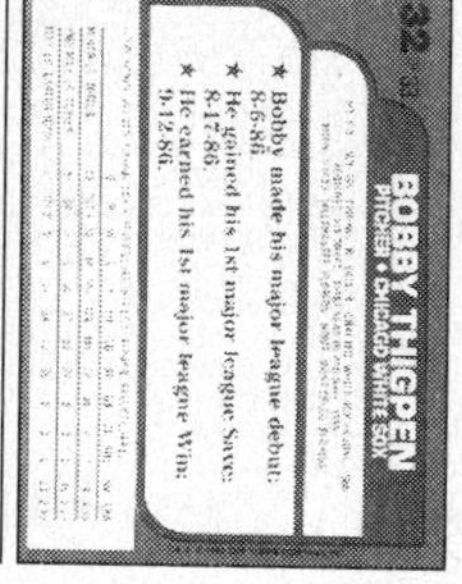

Topps produced this 33-card boxed set for Toys'R'Us stores. The set is subtitled "Baseball Rookies" and features predominantly younger players. The cards measure 2 1/2" by 3 1/2" and feature a high-gloss, full-color photo of the player inside a blue border. The card backs are printed in pink and blue on white card stock. The cards are numbered on the back and the checklist for the set is found on the back panel of the small collector box. The statistics provided on the card backs cover only three lines, Minor League totals, last season, and Major League totals. The set numbering is in alphabetical order by player's name.

	MT	EX-MT	VG
COMPLETE SET (33)	5.00	2.30	.60
COMMON PLAYER (1-33)	.10	.05	.01
☐ 1 Todd Benzinger	.15	.07	.02
☐ 2 Bob Brower	.10	.05	.01
☐ 3 Jerry Browne	.15	.07	.02
☐ 4 DeWayne Buice	.10	.05	.01
☐ 5 Ellis Burks	.45	.20	.06
☐ 6 Ken Caminiti	.25	.11	.03
☐ 7 Casey Candaele	.10	.05	.01
☐ 8 Dave Cone	.60	.25	.08
☐ 9 Kelly Downs	.10	.05	.01
☐ 10 Mike Dunne	.10	.05	.01
☐ 11 Ken Gerhart	.10	.05	.01
☐ 12 Mike Greenwell	.60	.25	.08
☐ 13 Mike Henneman	.20	.09	.03
☐ 14 Sam Horn	.15	.07	.02
☐ 15 Joe Magrane	.15	.07	.02
☐ 16 Fred Manrique	.10	.05	.01
☐ 17 John Marzano	.10	.05	.01
☐ 18 Fred McGriff	1.00	.45	.13
☐ 19 Mark McGwire	1.00	.45	.13
☐ 20 Jeff Musselman	.10	.05	.01
☐ 21 Randy Myers	.25	.11	.03
☐ 22 Matt Nokes	.25	.11	.03
☐ 23 Al Pedrique	.10	.05	.01

	MT	EX-MT	VG
☐ 24 Luis Polonia	.30	.14	.04
☐ 25 Billy Ripken	.15	.07	.02
☐ 26 Benito Santiago	.45	.20	.06
☐ 27 Kevin Seitzer	.20	.09	.03
☐ 28 John Smiley	.30	.14	.04
☐ 29 Mike Stanley	.10	.05	.01
☐ 30 Terry Steinbach	.20	.09	.03
☐ 31 B.J. Surhoff	.15	.07	.02
☐ 32 Bobby Thigpen	.20	.09	.03
☐ 33 Devon White	.25	.11	.03

1989 Toys'R'Us Rookies

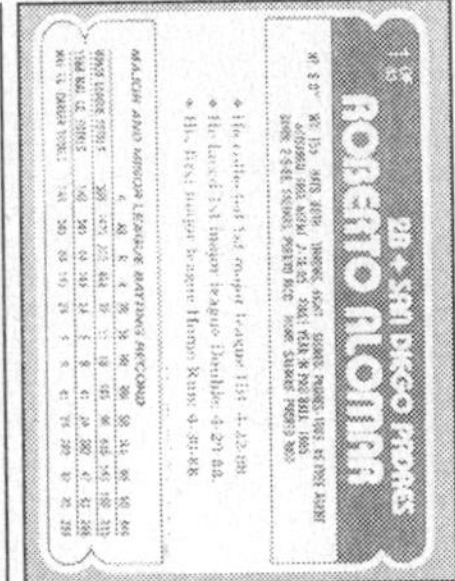

The 1989 Toys'R'Us Rookies set contains 33 standard-size (2 1/2" by 3 1/2") glossy cards. The fronts are yellow and magenta. The horizontally oriented backs are sky blue and red, and feature 1988 and career stats. The cards were distributed through Toys'R'Us stores as a boxed set. The subjects are numbered alphabetically. The set checklist is printed on the back panel of the set's custom box.

	MT	EX-MT	VG
COMPLETE SET (33)	4.50	2.00	.55
COMMON PLAYER (1-33)	.10	.05	.01
☐ 1 Roberto Alomar	1.00	.45	.13
☐ 2 Brady Anderson	.35	.16	.04
☐ 3 Tim Belcher	.20	.09	.03
☐ 4 Damon Berryhill	.15	.07	.02
☐ 5 Jay Buhner	.25	.11	.03
☐ 6 Sherman Corbett	.10	.05	.01
☐ 7 Kevin Elster	.10	.05	.01
☐ 8 Cecil Espy	.10	.05	.01
☐ 9 Dave Gallagher	.10	.05	.01
☐ 10 Ron Gant	.60	.25	.08
☐ 11 Paul Gibson	.10	.05	.01
☐ 12 Mark Grace	.60	.25	.08
☐ 13 Bryan Harvey	.25	.11	.03
☐ 14 Darrin Jackson	.25	.11	.03
☐ 15 Gregg Jefferies	.60	.25	.08
☐ 16 Ron Jones	.10	.05	.01
☐ 17 Ricky Jordan	.15	.07	.02
☐ 18 Roberto Kelly	.35	.16	.04
☐ 19 Al Leiter	.10	.05	.01
☐ 20 Jack McDowell	.40	.18	.05
☐ 21 Melido Perez	.20	.09	.03
☐ 22 Jeff Pico	.10	.05	.01
☐ 23 Jody Reed	.20	.09	.03
☐ 24 Chris Sabo	.30	.14	.04
☐ 25 Nelson Santovenia	.10	.05	.01
☐ 26 Mackey Sasser	.15	.07	.02
☐ 27 Mike Schooler	.10	.05	.01
☐ 28 Gary Sheffield	1.00	.45	.13
☐ 29 Pete Smith	.25	.11	.03
☐ 30 Pete Stanicek	.10	.05	.01
☐ 31 Jeff Treadway	.15	.07	.02
☐ 32 Walt Weiss	.25	.11	.03
☐ 33 Dave West	.15	.07	.02

1990 Toys'R'Us Rookies

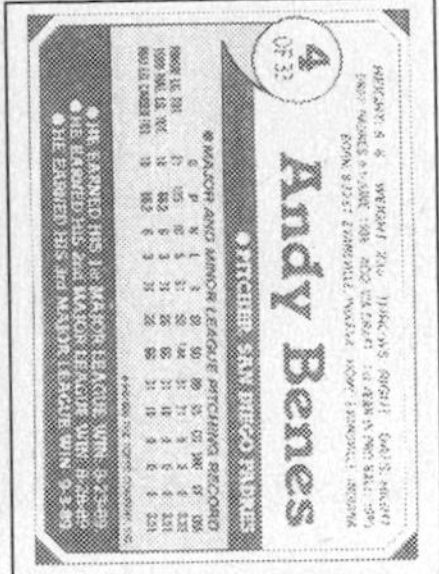

The 1990 Toys'R'Us Rookies set is a 33-card set of young prospects issued by Topps. For the fourth consecutive year Topps issued a rookie set for Toys'R'Us. There are several players in the set which were on Topps cards for the second time in 1990, i.e., not rookies even for the Topps Company. These players included Gregg Jefferies and Gregg Olson. This standard-size (2 1/2" by 3 1/2") card set might be more appropriately called the Young Stars set. The cards are numbered, with the numbering being essentially in alphabetical order by player's name. The set checklist is printed on the back panel of the set's custom box.

	MT	EX-MT	VG
COMPLETE SET (33)	4.50	2.00	.55
COMMON PLAYER (1-33)	.10	.05	.01
☐ 1 Jim Abbott	.50	.23	.06
☐ 2 Eric Anthony	.30	.14	.04
☐ 3 Joey Belle	.40	.18	.05
☐ 4 Andy Benes	.35	.16	.04
☐ 5 Greg Briley	.10	.05	.01
☐ 6 Kevin Brown	.20	.09	.03
☐ 7 Mark Carreon	.10	.05	.01
☐ 8 Mike Devereaux	.20	.09	.03
☐ 9 Junior Felix	.20	.09	.03
☐ 10 Mark Gardner	.10	.05	.01
☐ 11 Bob Geren	.10	.05	.01
☐ 12 Tom Gordon	.15	.07	.02
☐ 13 Ken Griffey Jr.	1.50	.65	.19
☐ 14 Pete Harnisch	.20	.09	.03
☐ 15 Ken Hill	.25	.11	.03
☐ 16 Gregg Jefferies	.35	.16	.04
☐ 17 Derek Lilliquist	.10	.05	.01
☐ 18 Carlos Martinez	.15	.07	.02
☐ 19 Ramon Martinez	.35	.16	.04
☐ 20 Bob Milacki	.10	.05	.01
☐ 21 Gregg Olson	.25	.11	.03
☐ 22 Kenny Rogers	.15	.07	.02
☐ 23 Alex Sanchez	.10	.05	.01
☐ 24 Gary Sheffield	.60	.25	.08
☐ 25 Dwight Smith	.15	.07	.02
☐ 26 Billy Spiers	.10	.05	.01
☐ 27 Greg Vaughn	.25	.11	.03
☐ 28 Robin Ventura	.75	.35	.09
☐ 29 Jerome Walton	.10	.05	.01
☐ 30 Dave West	.10	.05	.01
☐ 31 John Wetteland	.20	.09	.03
☐ 32 Craig Worthington	.10	.05	.01
☐ 33 Todd Zeile	.25	.11	.03

1991 Toys'R'Us Rookies

For the fifth year in a row this 33-card set was produced by Topps for Toys'R'Us, and the sponsor's logo adorns the top of the card front. The cards measure the standard size (2 1/2" by 3 1/2"). The front design features glossy color action player photos with yellow borders on a black card face. The words "Topps 1991 Collectors' Edition" appear in a yellow stripe above the picture. The horizontally oriented

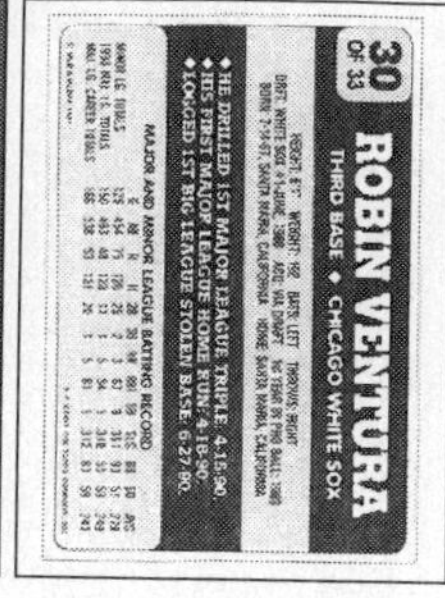

backs are printed in brown and yellow, and present biographical information, career highlights, and statistics. The cards are numbered on the back.

	MT	EX-MT	VG
COMPLETE SET (33)	4.50	2.00	.55
COMMON PLAYER (1-33)	.10	.05	.01
☐ 1 Sandy Alomar Jr.	.15	.07	.02
☐ 2 Kevin Appier	.20	.09	.03
☐ 3 Steve Avery	.60	.25	.08
☐ 4 Carlos Baerga	.60	.25	.08
☐ 5 Alex Cole	.15	.07	.02
☐ 6 Pat Combs	.15	.07	.02
☐ 7 Delino DeShields	.50	.23	.06
☐ 8 Travis Fryman	.75	.35	.09
☐ 9 Marquis Grissom	.50	.23	.06
☐ 10 Mike Harkey	.20	.09	.03
☐ 11 Glenallen Hill	.15	.07	.02
☐ 12 Jeff Huson	.10	.05	.01
☐ 13 Felix Jose	.25	.11	.03
☐ 14 Dave Justice	.60	.25	.08
☐ 15 Dana Kiecker	.10	.05	.01
☐ 16 Kevin Maas	.20	.09	.03
☐ 17 Ben McDonald	.25	.11	.03
☐ 18 Brian McRae	.20	.09	.03
☐ 19 Kent Mercker	.15	.07	.02
☐ 20 Hal Morris	.25	.11	.03
☐ 21 Chris Nabholz	.15	.07	.02
☐ 22 Tim Naehring	.15	.07	.02
☐ 23 Jose Offerman	.20	.09	.03
☐ 24 John Olerud	.50	.23	.06
☐ 25 Scott Radinsky	.15	.07	.02
☐ 26 Bill Sampen	.10	.05	.01
☐ 27 Frank Thomas	1.25	.55	.16
☐ 28 Randy Tomlin	.25	.11	.03
☐ 29 Greg Vaughn	.20	.09	.03
☐ 30 Robin Ventura	.60	.25	.08
☐ 31 Larry Walker	.60	.25	.08
☐ 32 Wally Whitehurst	.10	.05	.01
☐ 33 Todd Zeile	.20	.09	.03

1986 True Value

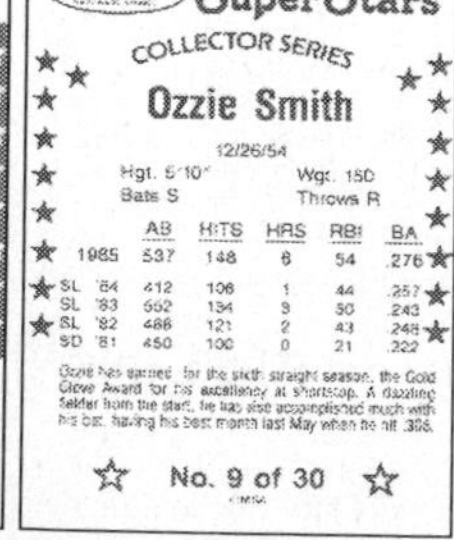

The 1986 True Value set consists of 30 cards, each measuring 2 1/2" by 3 1/2", which were printed as panels of four although one of the cards in the panel only pictures a featured product. The complete panel measures approximately 10 3/8" by 3 1/2". The True Value logo is in the upper left corner of the obverse of each card. Supposedly the cards were distributed to customers purchasing 5.00 or more at the store. Cards are frequently found with perforations intact and still in the closed form where only the top card in the folded panel is visible. The card number appears at the bottom of the reverse. Team logos have been surgically removed (airbrushed) from the photos.

	MT	EX-MT	VG
COMPLETE SET (30)	10.00	4.50	1.25
COMMON PLAYER (1-30)	.15	.07	.02
☐ 1 Pedro Guerrero	.25	.11	.03
☐ 2 Steve Garvey	.35	.16	.04
☐ 3 Eddie Murray	.50	.23	.06
☐ 4 Pete Rose	.75	.35	.09
☐ 5 Don Mattingly	.75	.35	.09
☐ 6 Fernando Valenzuela	.20	.09	.03
☐ 7 Jim Rice	.25	.11	.03
☐ 8 Kirk Gibson	.25	.11	.03
☐ 9 Ozzie Smith	.35	.16	.04
☐ 10 Dale Murphy	.35	.16	.04
☐ 11 Robin Yount	.60	.25	.08
☐ 12 Tom Seaver	.60	.25	.08
☐ 13 Reggie Jackson	.60	.25	.08
☐ 14 Ryne Sandberg	1.00	.45	.13
☐ 15 Bruce Sutter	.15	.07	.02
☐ 16 Gary Carter	.35	.16	.04
☐ 17 George Brett	.60	.25	.08
☐ 18 Rick Sutcliffe	.15	.07	.02
☐ 19 Dave Stieb	.15	.07	.02
☐ 20 Buddy Bell	.15	.07	.02
☐ 21 Alvin Davis	.15	.07	.02
☐ 22 Cal Ripken	1.00	.45	.13
☐ 23 Bill Madlock	.15	.07	.02
☐ 24 Kent Hrbek	.15	.07	.02
☐ 25 Lou Whitaker	.25	.11	.03
☐ 26 Nolan Ryan	1.25	.55	.16
☐ 27 Dwayne Murphy	.15	.07	.02
☐ 28 Mike Schmidt	.75	.35	.09
☐ 29 Andre Dawson	.35	.16	.04
☐ 30 Wade Boggs	.60	.25	.08

1985 Twins 7-Eleven

This 13-card set of Minnesota Twins was produced and distributed by the Twins in conjunction with the 7-Eleven stores and the Fire Marshall's Association. The cards measure approximately 2 1/2" by 3 1/2" and are in full color. Supposedly 20,000 sets of cards were distributed during the promotion which began on June 2nd and lasted throughout the month of July. The card backs have some statistics and a fire safety tip. The set features an early Kirby Puckett card.

	NRMT-MT	EXC	G-VG
COMPLETE SET (13)	9.00	4.00	1.15
COMMON PLAYER (1-13)	.35	.16	.04
☐ 1 Kirby Puckett	5.00	2.30	.60
☐ 2 Frank Viola	1.00	.45	.13
☐ 3 Mickey Hatcher	.35	.16	.04
☐ 4 Kent Hrbek	1.00	.45	.13

☐ 5 John Butcher	.35	.16	.04
☐ 6 Roy Smalley	.45	.20	.06
☐ 7 Tom Brunansky	.60	.25	.08
☐ 8 Ron Davis	.35	.16	.04
☐ 9 Gary Gaetti	.75	.35	.09
☐ 10 Tim Teufel	.45	.20	.06
☐ 11 Mike Smithson	.35	.16	.04
☐ 12 Tim Laudner	.35	.16	.04
☐ NNO Checklist Card	.45	.20	.06

1991 Ultra

This 400-card standard size (2 1/2" by 3 1/2") set marked Fleer's first entry into the high-end premium card market. The set was released in wax packs and features the best players in the majors along with a good mix of young prospects. The cards feature full color action photography on the fronts and three full-color photos on the backs along with 1990 and career statistics. Fleer claimed in their original press release that there would only be 15 percent of Ultra issued as there was of the regular issue. Fleer also issued the sets in their now traditional alphabetical order as well as the teams in alphabetical order. The card numbering is as follows, Atlanta Braves (1-13), Baltimore Orioles (14-26), Boston Red Sox (27-42), California Angels (43-54), Chicago Cubs (55-71), Chicago White Sox (72-86), Cincinnati Reds (87-103), Cleveland Indians (104-119), Detroit Tigers (120-130), Houston Astros (131-142), Kansas City Royals (143-158), Los Angeles Dodgers (159-171), Milwaukee Brewers (172-184), Minnesota Twins (185-196), Montreal Expos (197-210), New York Mets (211-227), New York Yankees (228-242), Oakland Athletics (243-257), Philadelphia Phillies (258-272), Pittsburgh Pirates (273-287), St. Louis Cardinals (288-299), San Diego Padres (300-313), San Francisco Giants (314-331), Seattle Mariners (332-345), Texas Rangers (346-357), Toronto Blue Jays (358-372), Major League Prospects (373-390), Elite Performance (391-396), and Checklists (397-400). The key Rookie Cards in this set are Wes Chamberlain, Eric Karros, Brian McRae, Pedro Munoz, and Phil Plantier.

	MT	EX-MT	VG
COMPLETE SET (400)	25.00	11.50	3.10
COMMON PLAYER (1-400)	.07	.03	.01
☐ 1 Steve Avery	.75	.35	.09
☐ 2 Jeff Blauser	.07	.03	.01
☐ 3 Francisco Cabrera	.07	.03	.01
☐ 4 Ron Gant	.30	.14	.04
☐ 5 Tom Glavine	.50	.23	.06
☐ 6 Tommy Gregg	.07	.03	.01
☐ 7 Dave Justice	1.50	.65	.19
☐ 8 Oddibe McDowell	.07	.03	.01
☐ 9 Greg Olson	.07	.03	.01
☐ 10 Terry Pendleton	.12	.05	.02
☐ 11 Lonnie Smith	.07	.03	.01
☐ 12 John Smoltz	.30	.14	.04
☐ 13 Jeff Treadway	.07	.03	.01
☐ 14 Glenn Davis	.10	.05	.01
☐ 15 Mike Devereaux	.10	.05	.01
☐ 16 Leo Gomez	.60	.25	.08
☐ 17 Chris Hoiles	.25	.11	.03
☐ 18 Dave Johnson	.07	.03	.01
☐ 19 Ben McDonald	.20	.09	.03
☐ 20 Randy Milligan	.07	.03	.01
☐ 21 Gregg Olson	.10	.05	.01
☐ 22 Joe Orsulak	.07	.03	.01
☐ 23 Bill Ripken	.07	.03	.01
☐ 24 Cal Ripken	.75	.35	.09
☐ 25 David Segui	.07	.03	.01
☐ 26 Craig Worthington	.07	.03	.01
☐ 27 Wade Boggs	.30	.14	.04
☐ 28 Tom Bolton	.07	.03	.01
☐ 29 Tom Brunansky	.10	.05	.01
☐ 30 Ellis Burks	.10	.05	.01
☐ 31 Roger Clemens	.60	.25	.08
☐ 32 Mike Greenwell	.12	.05	.02
☐ 33 Greg A. Harris	.07	.03	.01
☐ 34 Daryl Irvine	.07	.03	.01
☐ 35 Mike Marshall UER (1990 in stats is shown as 990)	.07	.03	.01
☐ 36 Tim Naehring	.12	.05	.02
☐ 37 Tony Pena	.07	.03	.01
☐ 38 Phil Plantier	1.25	.55	.16
☐ 39 Carlos Quintana	.07	.03	.01
☐ 40 Jeff Reardon	.12	.05	.02
☐ 41 Jody Reed	.07	.03	.01
☐ 42 Luis Rivera	.07	.03	.01
☐ 43 Jim Abbott	.30	.14	.04
☐ 44 Chuck Finley	.10	.05	.01
☐ 45 Bryan Harvey	.07	.03	.01
☐ 46 Donnie Hill	.07	.03	.01
☐ 47 Jack Howell	.07	.03	.01
☐ 48 Wally Joyner	.10	.05	.01
☐ 49 Mark Langston	.10	.05	.01
☐ 50 Kirk McCaskill	.07	.03	.01
☐ 51 Lance Parrish	.10	.05	.01
☐ 52 Dick Schofield	.07	.03	.01
☐ 53 Lee Stevens	.07	.03	.01
☐ 54 Dave Winfield	.20	.09	.03
☐ 55 George Bell	.10	.05	.01
☐ 56 Damon Berryhill	.07	.03	.01
☐ 57 Mike Bielecki	.07	.03	.01
☐ 58 Andre Dawson	.20	.09	.03
☐ 59 Shawon Dunston	.10	.05	.01
☐ 60 Joe Girardi UER (Bats right, LH hitter shown is Doug Dascenzo)	.07	.03	.01
☐ 61 Mark Grace	.25	.11	.03
☐ 62 Mike Harkey	.10	.05	.01
☐ 63 Les Lancaster	.07	.03	.01
☐ 64 Greg Maddux	.25	.11	.03
☐ 65 Derrick May	.10	.05	.01
☐ 66 Ryne Sandberg	.60	.25	.08
☐ 67 Luis Salazar	.07	.03	.01
☐ 68 Dwight Smith	.07	.03	.01
☐ 69 Hector Villanueva	.07	.03	.01
☐ 70 Jerome Walton	.07	.03	.01
☐ 71 Mitch Williams	.07	.03	.01
☐ 72 Carlton Fisk	.20	.09	.03
☐ 73 Scott Fletcher	.07	.03	.01
☐ 74 Ozzie Guillen	.07	.03	.01
☐ 75 Greg Hibbard	.07	.03	.01
☐ 76 Lance Johnson	.07	.03	.01
☐ 77 Steve Lyons	.07	.03	.01
☐ 78 Jack McDowell	.25	.11	.03
☐ 79 Dan Pasqua	.07	.03	.01
☐ 80 Melido Perez	.10	.05	.01
☐ 81 Tim Raines	.12	.05	.02
☐ 82 Sammy Sosa	.10	.05	.01
☐ 83 Cory Snyder	.07	.03	.01
☐ 84 Bobby Thigpen	.07	.03	.01
☐ 85 Frank Thomas (Card says he is an outfielder)	5.00	2.30	.60
☐ 86 Robin Ventura	.75	.35	.09
☐ 87 Todd Benzinger	.07	.03	.01
☐ 88 Glenn Braggs	.07	.03	.01
☐ 89 Tom Browning UER (Front photo actually Norm Charlton)	.07	.03	.01
☐ 90 Norm Charlton	.10	.05	.01
☐ 91 Eric Davis	.12	.05	.02
☐ 92 Rob Dibble	.10	.05	.01
☐ 93 Bill Doran	.07	.03	.01
☐ 94 Mariano Duncan UER (Right back photo is Billy Hatcher)	.07	.03	.01
☐ 95 Billy Hatcher	.07	.03	.01
☐ 96 Barry Larkin	.20	.09	.03
☐ 97 Randy Myers	.10	.05	.01

98 Hal Morris .10 .05 .01
99 Joe Oliver .07 .03 .01
100 Paul O'Neill .10 .05 .01
101 Jeff Reed .07 .03 .01
(See also 104)
102 Jose Rijo .10 .05 .01
103 Chris Sabo .10 .05 .01
(See also 106)
104 Beau Allred UER .07 .03 .01
(Card number is 101)
105 Sandy Alomar Jr. .10 .05 .01
106 Carlos Baerga UER .50 .23 .06
(Card number is 103)
107 Albert Belle .40 .18 .05
108 Jerry Browne .07 .03 .01
109 Tom Candiotti .07 .03 .01
110 Alex Cole .07 .03 .01
111 John Farrell .07 .03 .01
(See also 114)
112 Felix Fermin .07 .03 .01
113 Brook Jacoby .07 .03 .01
114 Chris James UER .07 .03 .01
(Card number is 111)
115 Doug Jones .07 .03 .01
116 Steve Olin .10 .05 .01
(See also 119)
117 Greg Swindell .10 .05 .01
118 Turner Ward .12 .05 .02
119 Mitch Webster UER .07 .03 .01
(Card number is 116)
120 Dave Bergman .07 .03 .01
121 Cecil Fielder .30 .14 .04
122 Travis Fryman 3.00 1.35 .40
123 Mike Henneman .07 .03 .01
124 Lloyd Moseby .07 .03 .01
125 Dan Petry .07 .03 .01
126 Tony Phillips .07 .03 .01
127 Mark Salas .07 .03 .01
128 Frank Tanana .07 .03 .01
129 Alan Trammell .12 .05 .02
130 Lou Whitaker .12 .05 .02
131 Eric Anthony .12 .05 .02
132 Craig Biggio .12 .05 .02
133 Ken Caminiti .10 .05 .01
134 Casey Candaele .07 .03 .01
135 Andujar Cedeno .30 .14 .04
136 Mark Davidson .07 .03 .01
137 Jim Deshaies .07 .03 .01
138 Mark Portugal .07 .03 .01
139 Rafael Ramirez .07 .03 .01
140 Mike Scott .07 .03 .01
141 Eric Yelding .07 .03 .01
142 Gerald Young .07 .03 .01
143 Kevin Appier .10 .05 .01
144 George Brett .20 .09 .03
145 Jeff Conine .50 .23 .06
146 Jim Eisenreich .07 .03 .01
147 Tom Gordon .10 .05 .01
148 Mark Gubicza .07 .03 .01
149 Bo Jackson .25 .11 .03
150 Brent Mayne .07 .03 .01
151 Mike Macfarlane .07 .03 .01
152 Brian McRae .50 .23 .06
153 Jeff Montgomery .07 .03 .01
154 Bret Saberhagen .10 .05 .01
155 Kevin Seitzer .10 .05 .01
156 Terry Shumpert .07 .03 .01
157 Kurt Stillwell .07 .03 .01
158 Danny Tartabull .12 .05 .02
159 Tim Belcher .10 .05 .01
160 Kal Daniels .07 .03 .01
161 Alfredo Griffin .07 .03 .01
162 Lenny Harris .07 .03 .01
163 Jay Howell .07 .03 .01
164 Ramon Martinez .12 .05 .02
165 Mike Morgan .07 .03 .01
166 Eddie Murray .20 .09 .03
167 Jose Offerman .12 .05 .02
168 Juan Samuel .07 .03 .01
169 Mike Scioscia .07 .03 .01
170 Mike Sharperson .07 .03 .01
171 Darryl Strawberry .30 .14 .04
172 Greg Brock .07 .03 .01
173 Chuck Crim .07 .03 .01
174 Jim Gantner .07 .03 .01
175 Ted Higuera .07 .03 .01
176 Mark Knudson .07 .03 .01
177 Tim McIntosh .07 .03 .01
178 Paul Molitor .12 .05 .02
179 Dan Plesac .07 .03 .01
180 Gary Sheffield .90 .40 .11
181 Bill Spiers .07 .03 .01
182 B.J. Surhoff .07 .03 .01
183 Greg Vaughn .12 .05 .02
184 Robin Yount .25 .11 .03
185 Rick Aguilera .10 .05 .01
186 Greg Gagne .07 .03 .01
187 Dan Gladden .07 .03 .01
188 Brian Harper .07 .03 .01
189 Kent Hrbek .10 .05 .01
190 Gene Larkin .07 .03 .01
191 Shane Mack .10 .05 .01
192 Pedro Munoz .60 .25 .08
193 Al Newman .07 .03 .01
194 Junior Ortiz .07 .03 .01
195 Kirby Puckett .60 .25 .08
196 Kevin Tapani .10 .05 .01
197 Dennis Boyd .07 .03 .01
198 Tim Burke .07 .03 .01
199 Ivan Calderon .07 .03 .01
200 Delino DeShields .40 .18 .05
201 Mike Fitzgerald .07 .03 .01
202 Steve Frey .07 .03 .01
203 Andres Galarraga .07 .03 .01
204 Marquis Grissom .40 .18 .05
205 Dave Martinez .07 .03 .01
206 Dennis Martinez .10 .05 .01
207 Junior Noboa .07 .03 .01
208 Spike Owen .07 .03 .01
209 Scott Ruskin .07 .03 .01
210 Tim Wallach .10 .05 .01
211 Daryl Boston .07 .03 .01
212 Vince Coleman .10 .05 .01
213 David Cone .15 .07 .02
214 Ron Darling .10 .05 .01
215 Kevin Elster .07 .03 .01
216 Sid Fernandez .10 .05 .01
217 John Franco .10 .05 .01
218 Dwight Gooden .12 .05 .02
219 Tom Herr .07 .03 .01
220 Todd Hundley .07 .03 .01
221 Gregg Jefferies .15 .07 .02
222 Howard Johnson .10 .05 .01
223 Dave Magadan .10 .05 .01
224 Kevin McReynolds .10 .05 .01
225 Keith Miller .07 .03 .01
226 Mackey Sasser .07 .03 .01
227 Frank Viola .10 .05 .01
228 Jesse Barfield .07 .03 .01
229 Greg Cadaret .07 .03 .01
230 Alvaro Espinoza .07 .03 .01
231 Bob Geren .07 .03 .01
232 Lee Guetterman .07 .03 .01
233 Mel Hall .07 .03 .01
234 Andy Hawkins UER .07 .03 .01
(Back center photo
is not him)
235 Roberto Kelly .12 .05 .02
236 Tim Leary .07 .03 .01
237 Jim Leyritz .07 .03 .01
238 Kevin Maas .12 .05 .02
239 Don Mattingly .30 .14 .04
240 Hensley Meulens .10 .05 .01
241 Eric Plunk .07 .03 .01
242 Steve Sax .10 .05 .01
243 Todd Burns .07 .03 .01
244 Jose Canseco .50 .23 .06
245 Dennis Eckersley .15 .07 .02
246 Mike Gallego .07 .03 .01
247 Dave Henderson .07 .03 .01
248 Rickey Henderson .30 .14 .04
249 Rick Honeycutt .07 .03 .01
250 Carney Lansford .10 .05 .01
251 Mark McGwire .50 .23 .06
252 Mike Moore .07 .03 .01
253 Terry Steinbach .10 .05 .01
254 Dave Stewart .10 .05 .01
255 Walt Weiss .07 .03 .01
256 Bob Welch .07 .03 .01
257 Curt Young .07 .03 .01
258 Wes Chamberlain .50 .23 .06
259 Pat Combs .07 .03 .01
260 Darren Daulton .10 .05 .01
261 Jose DeJesus .07 .03 .01
262 Len Dykstra .10 .05 .01
263 Charlie Hayes .07 .03 .01
264 Von Hayes .07 .03 .01
265 Ken Howell .07 .03 .01
266 John Kruk .10 .05 .01
267 Roger McDowell .07 .03 .01
268 Mickey Morandini .20 .09 .03
269 Terry Mulholland .07 .03 .01
270 Dale Murphy .10 .05 .01
271 Randy Ready .07 .03 .01
272 Dickie Thon .07 .03 .01
273 Stan Belinda .07 .03 .01

☐ 274 Jay Bell	.10	.05	.01
☐ 275 Barry Bonds	.50	.23	.06
☐ 276 Bobby Bonilla	.20	.09	.03
☐ 277 Doug Drabek	.10	.05	.01
☐ 278 Carlos Garcia	.40	.18	.05
☐ 279 Neal Heaton	.07	.03	.01
☐ 280 Jeff King	.07	.03	.01
☐ 281 Bill Landrum	.07	.03	.01
☐ 282 Mike LaValliere	.07	.03	.01
☐ 283 Jose Lind	.07	.03	.01
☐ 284 Orlando Merced	.40	.18	.05
☐ 285 Gary Redus	.07	.03	.01
☐ 286 Don Slaught	.07	.03	.01
☐ 287 Andy Van Slyke	.15	.07	.02
☐ 288 Jose DeLeon	.07	.03	.01
☐ 289 Pedro Guerrero	.10	.05	.01
☐ 290 Ray Lankford	.75	.35	.09
☐ 291 Joe Magrane	.07	.03	.01
☐ 292 Jose Oquendo	.07	.03	.01
☐ 293 Tom Pagnozzi	.07	.03	.01
☐ 294 Bryn Smith	.07	.03	.01
☐ 295 Lee Smith	.10	.05	.01
☐ 296 Ozzie Smith UER (Born 12-26, 54, should have hyphen)	.20	.09	.03
☐ 297 Milt Thompson	.07	.03	.01
☐ 298 Craig Wilson	.12	.05	.02
☐ 299 Todd Zeile	.12	.05	.02
☐ 300 Shawn Abner	.07	.03	.01
☐ 301 Andy Benes	.15	.07	.02
☐ 302 Paul Faries	.07	.03	.01
☐ 303 Tony Gwynn	.30	.14	.04
☐ 304 Greg W. Harris	.07	.03	.01
☐ 305 Thomas Howard	.07	.03	.01
☐ 306 Bruce Hurst	.10	.05	.01
☐ 307 Craig Lefferts	.07	.03	.01
☐ 308 Fred McGriff	.30	.14	.04
☐ 309 Dennis Rasmussen	.07	.03	.01
☐ 310 Bip Roberts	.10	.05	.01
☐ 311 Benito Santiago	.10	.05	.01
☐ 312 Garry Templeton	.07	.03	.01
☐ 313 Ed Whitson	.07	.03	.01
☐ 314 Dave Anderson	.07	.03	.01
☐ 315 Kevin Bass	.07	.03	.01
☐ 316 Jeff Brantley	.07	.03	.01
☐ 317 John Burkett	.07	.03	.01
☐ 318 Will Clark	.50	.23	.06
☐ 319 Steve Decker	.30	.14	.04
☐ 320 Scott Garrelts	.07	.03	.01
☐ 321 Terry Kennedy	.07	.03	.01
☐ 322 Mark Leonard	.15	.07	.02
☐ 323 Darren Lewis	.20	.09	.03
☐ 324 Greg Litton	.07	.03	.01
☐ 325 Willie McGee	.10	.05	.01
☐ 326 Kevin Mitchell	.10	.05	.01
☐ 327 Don Robinson	.07	.03	.01
☐ 328 Andres Santana	.15	.07	.02
☐ 329 Robby Thompson	.07	.03	.01
☐ 330 Jose Uribe	.07	.03	.01
☐ 331 Matt Williams	.10	.05	.01
☐ 332 Scott Bradley	.07	.03	.01
☐ 333 Henry Cotto	.07	.03	.01
☐ 334 Alvin Davis	.07	.03	.01
☐ 335 Ken Griffey Sr.	.10	.05	.01
☐ 336 Ken Griffey Jr.	1.50	.65	.19
☐ 337 Erik Hanson	.07	.03	.01
☐ 338 Brian Holman	.07	.03	.01
☐ 339 Randy Johnson	.10	.05	.01
☐ 340 Edgar Martinez UER (Listed as playing SS)	.15	.07	.02
☐ 341 Tino Martinez	.20	.09	.03
☐ 342 Pete O'Brien	.07	.03	.01
☐ 343 Harold Reynolds	.07	.03	.01
☐ 344 Dave Valle	.07	.03	.01
☐ 345 Omar Vizquel	.07	.03	.01
☐ 346 Brad Arnsberg	.07	.03	.01
☐ 347 Kevin Brown	.10	.05	.01
☐ 348 Julio Franco	.10	.05	.01
☐ 349 Jeff Huson	.07	.03	.01
☐ 350 Rafael Palmeiro	.15	.07	.02
☐ 351 Geno Petralli	.07	.03	.01
☐ 352 Gary Pettis	.07	.03	.01
☐ 353 Kenny Rogers	.07	.03	.01
☐ 354 Jeff Russell	.07	.03	.01
☐ 355 Nolan Ryan	1.25	.55	.16
☐ 356 Ruben Sierra	.40	.18	.05
☐ 357 Bobby Witt	.07	.03	.01
☐ 358 Roberto Alomar	.75	.35	.09
☐ 359 Pat Borders	.07	.03	.01
☐ 360 Joe Carter UER (Reverse negative on back photo)	.30	.14	.04
☐ 361 Kelly Gruber	.10	.05	.01
☐ 362 Tom Henke	.10	.05	.01
☐ 363 Glenallen Hill	.07	.03	.01
☐ 364 Jimmy Key	.07	.03	.01
☐ 365 Manny Lee	.07	.03	.01
☐ 366 Rance Mulliniks	.07	.03	.01
☐ 367 John Olerud UER (Throwing left on card; back has throws right)	.40	.18	.05
☐ 368 Dave Stieb	.07	.03	.01
☐ 369 Duane Ward	.07	.03	.01
☐ 370 David Wells	.07	.03	.01
☐ 371 Mark Whiten	.15	.07	.02
☐ 372 Mookie Wilson	.07	.03	.01
☐ 373 Willie Banks MLP	.50	.23	.06
☐ 374 Steve Carter MLP	.10	.05	.01
☐ 375 Scott Chiamparino MLP	.10	.05	.01
☐ 376 Steve Chitren MLP	.10	.05	.01
☐ 377 Darrin Fletcher MLP	.10	.05	.01
☐ 378 Rich Garces MLP	.15	.07	.02
☐ 379 Reggie Jefferson MLP	.35	.16	.04
☐ 380 Eric Karros MLP	4.00	1.80	.50
☐ 381 Pat Kelly MLP	.30	.14	.04
☐ 382 Chuck Knoblauch MLP	1.25	.55	.16
☐ 383 Denny Neagle MLP	.30	.14	.04
☐ 384 Dan Opperman MLP	.15	.07	.02
☐ 385 John Ramos MLP	.12	.05	.02
☐ 386 Henry Rodriguez MLP	.50	.23	.06
☐ 387 Maurice Vaughn MLP	.50	.23	.06
☐ 388 Gerald Williams MLP	.50	.23	.06
☐ 389 Mike York MLP	.10	.05	.01
☐ 390 Eddie Zosky MLP	.15	.07	.02
☐ 391 Barry Bonds EP	.15	.07	.02
☐ 392 Cecil Fielder EP	.15	.07	.02
☐ 393 Rickey Henderson EP	.15	.07	.02
☐ 394 Dave Justice EP	.35	.16	.04
☐ 395 Nolan Ryan EP	.50	.23	.06
☐ 396 Bobby Thigpen EP	.07	.03	.01
☐ 397 Checklist Card Gregg Jefferies	.07	.01	.00
☐ 398 Checklist Card Von Hayes	.07	.01	.00
☐ 399 Checklist Card Terry Kennedy	.07	.01	.00
☐ 400 Checklist Card Nolan Ryan	.15	.02	.00

1991 Ultra Gold

This ten-card set presents Fleer's 1991 Ultra Team. The cards measure the standard size (2 1/2" by 3 1/2"). On a gold background that fades as one moves toward the bottom of the card, the front design has a color head shot, with two cut-out action shots below. Player information is given in a dark blue strip at the bottom of the card face. In blue print on white background with gold borders, the back highlights the player's outstanding achievements. The cards are numbered on the back.

	MT	EX-MT	VG
COMPLETE SET (10)	8.00	3.60	1.00
COMMON PLAYER (1-10)	.30	.14	.04
☐ 1 Barry Bonds	1.00	.45	.13
☐ 2 Will Clark	1.00	.45	.13
☐ 3 Doug Drabek	.30	.14	.04
☐ 4 Ken Griffey Jr.	3.00	1.35	.40
☐ 5 Rickey Henderson	.75	.35	.09

	MT	EX-MT	VG
☐ 6 Bo Jackson	.75	.35	.09
☐ 7 Ramon Martinez	.40	.18	.05
☐ 8 Kirby Puckett UER (Boggs won 1988 batting title, so Puckett didn't win consecutive titles)	1.00	.45	.13
☐ 9 Chris Sabo	.30	.14	.04
☐ 10 Ryne Sandberg UER (Johnson and Hornsby didn't hit 40 homers in 1990, Fielder did hit 51 in '90)	1.25	.55	.16

1991 Ultra Update

The 1991 Fleer Ultra Baseball Update set contains 120 cards and 20 team logo stickers. The set includes the year's hottest rookies and important veteran players traded after the original Ultra series was produced. The cards measure the standard size (2 1/2" by 3 1/2"). The front has a color action shot, while the back has a portrait photo and two full-figure action shots. The cards are numbered (with a U prefix) and checklisted below alphabetically within and according to teams for each league as follow: Baltimore Orioles (1-4), Boston Red Sox (5-7), California Angels (8-12), Chicago White Sox (13-18), Cleveland Indians (19-21), Detroit Tigers (22-24), Kansas City Royals (25-29), Milwaukee Brewers (30-33), Minnesota Twins (34-39), New York Yankees (40-44), Oakland Athletics (45-48), Seattle Mariners (49-53), Texas Rangers (54-58), Toronto Blue Jays (59-64), Atlanta Braves (65-69), Chicago Cubs (70-75), Cincinnati Reds (76-78), Houston Astros (79-84), Los Angeles Dodgers (85-89), Montreal Expos (90-93), New York Mets (94-97), Philadelphia Phillies (98-101), Pittsburgh Pirates (102-104), St. Louis Cardinals (105-109), San Diego Padres (110-114), and San Francisco Giants (115-119). The key Rookie Cards in this set are Jeff Bagwell, Juan Guzman, Mike Mussina, and Ivan Rodriguez.

	MT	EX-MT	VG
COMPLETE SET (120)	36.00	16.00	4.50
COMMON PLAYER (1-120)	.10	.05	.01
☐ 1 Dwight Evans	.15	.07	.02
☐ 2 Chito Martinez	.30	.14	.04
☐ 3 Bob Melvin	.10	.05	.01
☐ 4 Mike Mussina	10.00	4.50	1.25
☐ 5 Jack Clark	.15	.07	.02
☐ 6 Dana Kiecker	.10	.05	.01
☐ 7 Steve Lyons	.10	.05	.01
☐ 8 Gary Gaetti	.10	.05	.01
☐ 9 Dave Gallagher	.10	.05	.01
☐ 10 Dave Parker	.15	.07	.02
☐ 11 Luis Polonia	.15	.07	.02
☐ 12 Luis Sojo	.10	.05	.01
☐ 13 Wilson Alvarez	.40	.18	.05
☐ 14 Alex Fernandez	.40	.18	.05
☐ 15 Craig Grebeck	.10	.05	.01
☐ 16 Ron Karkovice	.10	.05	.01
☐ 17 Warren Newson	.20	.09	.03
☐ 18 Scott Radinsky	.10	.05	.01
☐ 19 Glenallen Hill	.10	.05	.01
☐ 20 Charles Nagy	1.50	.65	.19
☐ 21 Mark Whiten	.30	.14	.04
☐ 22 Milt Cuyler	.20	.09	.03
☐ 23 Paul Gibson	.10	.05	.01
☐ 24 Mickey Tettleton	.15	.07	.02
☐ 25 Todd Benzinger	.10	.05	.01
☐ 26 Storm Davis	.10	.05	.01
☐ 27 Kirk Gibson	.15	.07	.02
☐ 28 Bill Pecota	.10	.05	.01
☐ 29 Gary Thurman	.10	.05	.01
☐ 30 Darryl Hamilton	.15	.07	.02
☐ 31 Jaime Navarro	.60	.25	.08
☐ 32 Willie Randolph	.15	.07	.02
☐ 33 Bill Wegman	.10	.05	.01
☐ 34 Randy Bush	.10	.05	.01
☐ 35 Chili Davis	.15	.07	.02
☐ 36 Scott Erickson	.75	.35	.09
☐ 37 Chuck Knoblauch	3.00	1.35	.40
☐ 38 Scott Leius	.25	.11	.03
☐ 39 Jack Morris	.15	.07	.02
☐ 40 John Habyan	.10	.05	.01
☐ 41 Pat Kelly	.40	.18	.05
☐ 42 Matt Nokes	.10	.05	.01
☐ 43 Scott Sanderson	.10	.05	.01
☐ 44 Bernie Williams	1.00	.45	.13
☐ 45 Harold Baines	.15	.07	.02
☐ 46 Brook Jacoby	.10	.05	.01
☐ 47 Earnest Riles	.10	.05	.01
☐ 48 Willie Wilson	.10	.05	.01
☐ 49 Jay Buhner	.15	.07	.02
☐ 50 Rich DeLucia	.10	.05	.01
☐ 51 Mike Jackson	.10	.05	.01
☐ 52 Bill Krueger	.10	.05	.01
☐ 53 Bill Swift	.10	.05	.01
☐ 54 Brian Downing	.10	.05	.01
☐ 55 Juan Gonzalez	10.00	4.50	1.25
☐ 56 Dean Palmer	2.50	1.15	.30
☐ 57 Kevin Reimer	.35	.16	.04
☐ 58 Ivan Rodriguez	5.00	2.30	.60
☐ 59 Tom Candiotti	.10	.05	.01
☐ 60 Juan Guzman	11.00	4.90	1.40
☐ 61 Bob MacDonald	.15	.07	.02
☐ 62 Greg Myers	.10	.05	.01
☐ 63 Ed Sprague	.50	.23	.06
☐ 64 Devon White	.15	.07	.02
☐ 65 Rafael Belliard	.10	.05	.01
☐ 66 Juan Berenguer	.10	.05	.01
☐ 67 Brian Hunter	.90	.40	.11
☐ 68 Kent Mercker	.15	.07	.02
☐ 69 Otis Nixon	.15	.07	.02
☐ 70 Danny Jackson	.10	.05	.01
☐ 71 Chuck McElroy	.15	.07	.02
☐ 72 Gary Scott	.40	.18	.05
☐ 73 Heathcliff Slocumb	.10	.05	.01
☐ 74 Chico Walker	.10	.05	.01
☐ 75 Rick Wilkins	.20	.09	.03
☐ 76 Chris Hammond	.20	.09	.03
☐ 77 Luis Quinones	.10	.05	.01
☐ 78 Herm Winningham	.10	.05	.01
☐ 79 Jeff Bagwell	5.00	2.30	.60
☐ 80 Jim Corsi	.10	.05	.01
☐ 81 Steve Finley	.15	.07	.02
☐ 82 Luis Gonzalez	.75	.35	.09
☐ 83 Pete Harnisch	.15	.07	.02
☐ 84 Darryl Kile	.40	.18	.05
☐ 85 Brett Butler	.15	.07	.02
☐ 86 Gary Carter	.15	.07	.02
☐ 87 Tim Crews	.10	.05	.01
☐ 88 Orel Hershiser	.15	.07	.02
☐ 89 Bob Ojeda	.10	.05	.01
☐ 90 Bret Barberie	.50	.23	.06
☐ 91 Barry Jones	.10	.05	.01
☐ 92 Gilberto Reyes	.10	.05	.01
☐ 93 Larry Walker	1.75	.80	.22
☐ 94 Hubie Brooks	.10	.05	.01
☐ 95 Tim Burke	.10	.05	.01
☐ 96 Rick Cerone	.10	.05	.01
☐ 97 Jeff Innis	.10	.05	.01
☐ 98 Wally Backman	.10	.05	.01
☐ 99 Tommy Greene	.10	.05	.01
☐ 100 Ricky Jordan	.10	.05	.01
☐ 101 Mitch Williams	.10	.05	.01
☐ 102 John Smiley	.15	.07	.02
☐ 103 Randy Tomlin	.60	.25	.08
☐ 104 Gary Varsho	.10	.05	.01
☐ 105 Cris Carpenter	.10	.05	.01
☐ 106 Ken Hill	.15	.07	.02
☐ 107 Felix Jose	.25	.11	.03
☐ 108 Omar Olivares	.40	.18	.05
☐ 109 Gerald Perry	.10	.05	.01
☐ 110 Jerald Clark	.10	.05	.01

☐ 111 Tony Fernandez	.15	.07	.02
☐ 112 Darrin Jackson	.15	.07	.02
☐ 113 Mike Maddux	.10	.05	.01
☐ 114 Tim Teufel	.10	.05	.01
☐ 115 Bud Black	.10	.05	.01
☐ 116 Kelly Downs	.10	.05	.01
☐ 117 Mike Felder	.10	.05	.01
☐ 118 Willie McGee	.15	.07	.02
☐ 119 Trevor Wilson	.10	.05	.01
☐ 120 Checklist 1-120	.15	.02	.00

1992 Ultra

The 1992 Fleer Ultra set consists of two series each with 300 cards. The 1992 Fleer Ultra first series contained 300 cards, including a 21-card Ultra Rookies set. Randomly inserted into the packs were a 25-card Ultra Award Winners subset and a ten-card Tony Gwynn subset (Gwynn autographed more than 2,000 of his cards). The cards measure the standard size (2 1/2" by 3 1/2"). The glossy color action player photos on the fronts are full-bleed except at the bottom where a diagonal gold-foil stripe edges a green marbleized border. The player's name and team appear on the marble-colored area in bars that are color-coded by team. The horizontally oriented backs display an action and close-up cut-out player photo against a grid shaded with a gradated team color. The grid, team-colored bars containing stats and the player's name, biographical information, and the team logo all rest on a green marbleized background. The cards are numbered on the back and checklisted below alphabetically within and according to teams for each league as follows: Baltimore Orioles (1-11), Boston Red Sox (12-23), California Angels (24-31), Chicago White Sox (32-44), Cleveland Indians (45-55), Detroit Tigers (56-65), Kansas City Royals (66-77), Milwaukee Brewers (78-87), Minnesota Twins (88-98), New York Yankees (99-108), Oakland Athletics (109-119), Seattle Mariners (120-130), Texas Rangers (131-142), Toronto Blue Jays (143-156), Atlanta Braves (157-171), Chicago Cubs (172-184), Cincinnati Reds (185-197), Houston Astros (198-208), Los Angeles Dodgers (209-219), Montreal Expos (220-226), New York Mets (227-238), Philadelphia Phillies (239-249), Pittsburgh Pirates (250-262), St. Louis Cardinals (263-273), San Diego Padres (274-283), and San Francisco Giants (284-297). The most noteworthy Rookie Card in the first series is Rey Sanchez. The second series of the 1992 Fleer Ultra baseball set contains 300 cards, including traded players, free agents, and more than 50 Ultra Rookies. The foil packs featured two randomly inserted subsets: a ten-card "Ultra All-Rookie Team" and a 20-card "Ultra All-Star Team". The design is identical to that of the first series, with full-bleed color action player photos on the fronts bordered in marble at the bottom and horizontally oriented backs displaying an action and close-up cut-out player photo against a grid shaded with a gradated team color. The Ultra Rookie cards are identified by a Ultra Rookie gold-foil stamped logo. The cards are checklisted below alphabetically within and according to teams for each league as follows: Baltimore Orioles (301-310), Boston Red Sox (311-320), California Angels (321-331), Chicago White Sox (332-343), Cleveland Indians (344-357), Detroit Tigers (358-368), Kansas City Royals (369-377), Milwaukee Brewers (378-392), Minnesota Twins (393-403), New York Yankees (404-417), Oakland Athletics (418-429), Seattle Mariners (430-436), Texas Rangers (437-447), Toronto Blue Jays (438-454), Atlanta Braves (455-465), Chicago Cubs (466-477), Cincinnati Reds (478-487), Houston Astros (488-498), Los Angeles Dodgers (499-510), Montreal Expos (511-526), New York Mets (527-539), Philadelphia Phillies (540-549), Pittsburgh Pirates (550-561), St. Louis Cardinals (562-574), San Diego Padres (575-585) and San Francisco Giants (586-597). Key Rookie Cards in the second series are Chad Curtis, Pat Listach and Brian Williams. Some cards have been found without the word Fleer on the front.

	MT	EX-MT	VG
COMPLETE SET (600)	70.00	32.00	8.75
COMPLETE SERIES 1 (300)	40.00	18.00	5.00
COMPLETE SERIES 2 (300)	30.00	13.50	3.80
COMMON PLAYER (1-300)	.15	.07	.02
COMMON PLAYER (301-600)	.15	.07	.02
☐ 1 Glenn Davis	.20	.09	.03
☐ 2 Mike Devereaux	.20	.09	.03
☐ 3 Dwight Evans	.20	.09	.03
☐ 4 Leo Gomez	.50	.23	.06
☐ 5 Chris Hoiles	.25	.11	.03
☐ 6 Sam Horn	.15	.07	.02
☐ 7 Chito Martinez	.15	.07	.02
☐ 8 Randy Milligan	.15	.07	.02
☐ 9 Mike Mussina	3.50	1.55	.45
☐ 10 Billy Ripken	.15	.07	.02
☐ 11 Cal Ripken	1.50	.65	.19
☐ 12 Tom Brunansky	.20	.09	.03
☐ 13 Ellis Burks	.20	.09	.03
☐ 14 Jack Clark	.20	.09	.03
☐ 15 Roger Clemens	1.25	.55	.16
☐ 16 Mike Greenwell	.20	.09	.03
☐ 17 Joe Hesketh	.15	.07	.02
☐ 18 Tony Pena	.15	.07	.02
☐ 19 Carlos Quintana	.15	.07	.02
☐ 20 Jeff Reardon	.20	.09	.03
☐ 21 Jody Reed	.15	.07	.02
☐ 22 Luis Rivera	.15	.07	.02
☐ 23 Mo Vaughn	.25	.11	.03
☐ 24 Gary DiSarcina	.15	.07	.02
☐ 25 Chuck Finley	.15	.07	.02
☐ 26 Gary Gaetti	.15	.07	.02
☐ 27 Bryan Harvey	.15	.07	.02
☐ 28 Lance Parrish	.20	.09	.03
☐ 29 Luis Polonia	.20	.09	.03
☐ 30 Dick Schofield	.15	.07	.02
☐ 31 Luis Sojo	.15	.07	.02
☐ 32 Wilson Alvarez	.15	.07	.02
☐ 33 Carlton Fisk	.40	.18	.05
☐ 34 Craig Grebeck	.15	.07	.02
☐ 35 Ozzie Guillen	.15	.07	.02
☐ 36 Greg Hibbard	.15	.07	.02
☐ 37 Charlie Hough	.15	.07	.02
☐ 38 Lance Johnson	.15	.07	.02
☐ 39 Ron Karkovice	.15	.07	.02
☐ 40 Jack McDowell	.25	.11	.03
☐ 41 Donn Pall	.15	.07	.02
☐ 42 Melido Perez	.20	.09	.03
☐ 43 Tim Raines	.20	.09	.03
☐ 44 Frank Thomas	6.00	2.70	.75
☐ 45 Sandy Alomar Jr.	.20	.09	.03
☐ 46 Carlos Baerga	1.00	.45	.13
☐ 47 Albert Belle	.60	.25	.08
☐ 48 Jerry Browne UER (Reversed negative on card back)	.15	.07	.02
☐ 49 Felix Fermin	.15	.07	.02
☐ 50 Reggie Jefferson UER (Born 1968, not 1966)	.40	.18	.05
☐ 51 Mark Lewis	.20	.09	.03
☐ 52 Carlos Martinez	.15	.07	.02
☐ 53 Steve Olin	.15	.07	.02
☐ 54 Jim Thome	.50	.23	.06
☐ 55 Mark Whiten	.15	.07	.02

☐ 56	Dave Bergman	.15	.07	.02
☐ 57	Milt Cuyler	.15	.07	.02
☐ 58	Rob Deer	.20	.09	.03
☐ 59	Cecil Fielder	.60	.25	.08
☐ 60	Travis Fryman	2.00	.90	.25
☐ 61	Scott Livingstone	.40	.18	.05
☐ 62	Tony Phillips	.15	.07	.02
☐ 63	Mickey Tettleton	.20	.09	.03
☐ 64	Alan Trammell	.25	.11	.03
☐ 65	Lou Whitaker	.25	.11	.03
☐ 66	Kevin Appier	.20	.09	.03
☐ 67	Mike Boddicker	.15	.07	.02
☐ 68	George Brett	.50	.23	.06
☐ 69	Jim Eisenreich	.15	.07	.02
☐ 70	Mark Gubicza	.15	.07	.02
☐ 71	David Howard	.15	.07	.02
☐ 72	Joel Johnson	.15	.07	.02
☐ 73	Mike Macfarlane	.15	.07	.02
☐ 74	Brent Mayne	.15	.07	.02
☐ 75	Brian McRae	.20	.09	.03
☐ 76	Jeff Montgomery	.15	.07	.02
☐ 77	Danny Tartabull	.20	.09	.03
☐ 78	Don August	.15	.07	.02
☐ 79	Dante Bichette	.15	.07	.02
☐ 80	Ted Higuera	.15	.07	.02
☐ 81	Paul Molitor	.25	.11	.03
☐ 82	Jaime Navarro	.20	.09	.03
☐ 83	Gary Sheffield	1.50	.65	.19
☐ 84	Bill Spiers	.15	.07	.02
☐ 85	B.J. Surhoff	.15	.07	.02
☐ 86	Greg Vaughn	.20	.09	.03
☐ 87	Robin Yount	.50	.23	.06
☐ 88	Rick Aguilera	.20	.09	.03
☐ 89	Chili Davis	.20	.09	.03
☐ 90	Scott Erickson	.25	.11	.03
☐ 91	Brian Harper	.15	.07	.02
☐ 92	Kent Hrbek	.20	.09	.03
☐ 93	Chuck Knoblauch	1.00	.45	.13
☐ 94	Scott Leius	.15	.07	.02
☐ 95	Shane Mack	.20	.09	.03
☐ 96	Mike Pagliarulo	.15	.07	.02
☐ 97	Kirby Puckett	1.00	.45	.13
☐ 98	Kevin Tapani	.20	.09	.03
☐ 99	Jesse Barfield	.15	.07	.02
☐ 100	Alvaro Espinoza	.15	.07	.02
☐ 101	Mel Hall	.15	.07	.02
☐ 102	Pat Kelly	.20	.09	.03
☐ 103	Roberto Kelly	.20	.09	.03
☐ 104	Kevin Maas	.20	.09	.03
☐ 105	Don Mattingly	.60	.25	.08
☐ 106	Hensley Meulens	.15	.07	.02
☐ 107	Matt Nokes	.15	.07	.02
☐ 108	Steve Sax	.20	.09	.03
☐ 109	Harold Baines	.20	.09	.03
☐ 110	Jose Canseco	1.00	.45	.13
☐ 111	Ron Darling	.20	.09	.03
☐ 112	Mike Gallego	.15	.07	.02
☐ 113	Dave Henderson	.15	.07	.02
☐ 114	Rickey Henderson	.50	.23	.06
☐ 115	Mark McGwire	1.00	.45	.13
☐ 116	Terry Steinbach	.20	.09	.03
☐ 117	Dave Stewart	.20	.09	.03
☐ 118	Todd Van Poppel	.90	.40	.11
☐ 119	Bob Welch	.15	.07	.02
☐ 120	Greg Briley	.15	.07	.02
☐ 121	Jay Buhner	.20	.09	.03
☐ 122	Rick DeLucia	.15	.07	.02
☐ 123	Ken Griffey Jr.	4.00	1.80	.50
☐ 124	Erik Hanson	.15	.07	.02
☐ 125	Randy Johnson	.20	.09	.03
☐ 126	Edgar Martinez	.20	.09	.03
☐ 127	Tino Martinez	.20	.09	.03
☐ 128	Pete O'Brien	.15	.07	.02
☐ 129	Harold Reynolds	.15	.07	.02
☐ 130	Dave Valle	.15	.07	.02
☐ 131	Julio Franco	.20	.09	.03
☐ 132	Juan Gonzalez	2.50	1.15	.30
☐ 133	Jeff Huson (Shows Jose Canseco sliding into second)	.15	.07	.02
☐ 134	Mike Jeffcoat	.15	.07	.02
☐ 135	Terry Mathews	.20	.09	.03
☐ 136	Rafael Palmeiro	.25	.11	.03
☐ 137	Dean Palmer	1.00	.45	.13
☐ 138	Geno Petralli	.15	.07	.02
☐ 139	Ivan Rodriguez	2.00	.90	.25
☐ 140	Jeff Russell	.15	.07	.02
☐ 141	Nolan Ryan	3.00	1.35	.40
☐ 142	Ruben Sierra	.75	.35	.09
☐ 143	Roberto Alomar	1.00	.45	.13
☐ 144	Pat Borders	.15	.07	.02
☐ 145	Joe Carter	.60	.25	.08
☐ 146	Kelly Gruber	.20	.09	.03
☐ 147	Jimmy Key	.15	.07	.02
☐ 148	Manny Lee	.15	.07	.02
☐ 149	Rance Mulliniks	.15	.07	.02
☐ 150	Greg Myers	.15	.07	.02
☐ 151	John Olerud	.50	.23	.06
☐ 152	Dave Stieb	.15	.07	.02
☐ 153	Todd Stottlemyre	.20	.09	.03
☐ 154	Duane Ward	.15	.07	.02
☐ 155	Devon White	.20	.09	.03
☐ 156	Eddie Zosky	.20	.09	.03
☐ 157	Steve Avery	.90	.40	.11
☐ 158	Rafael Belliard	.15	.07	.02
☐ 159	Jeff Blauser	.15	.07	.02
☐ 160	Sid Bream	.15	.07	.02
☐ 161	Ron Gant	.35	.16	.04
☐ 162	Tom Glavine	.60	.25	.08
☐ 163	Brian Hunter	.40	.18	.05
☐ 164	Dave Justice	1.50	.65	.19
☐ 165	Mark Lemke	.15	.07	.02
☐ 166	Greg Olson	.15	.07	.02
☐ 167	Terry Pendleton	.30	.14	.04
☐ 168	Lonnie Smith	.15	.07	.02
☐ 169	John Smoltz	.35	.16	.04
☐ 170	Mike Stanton	.15	.07	.02
☐ 171	Jeff Treadway	.15	.07	.02
☐ 172	Paul Assenmacher	.15	.07	.02
☐ 173	George Bell	.20	.09	.03
☐ 174	Shawon Dunston	.20	.09	.03
☐ 175	Mark Grace	.30	.14	.04
☐ 176	Danny Jackson	.15	.07	.02
☐ 177	Les Lancaster	.15	.07	.02
☐ 178	Greg Maddux	.30	.14	.04
☐ 179	Luis Salazar	.15	.07	.02
☐ 180	Rey Sanchez	.35	.16	.04
☐ 181	Ryne Sandberg	1.25	.55	.16
☐ 182	Jose Vizcaino	.15	.07	.02
☐ 183	Chico Walker	.15	.07	.02
☐ 184	Jerome Walton	.15	.07	.02
☐ 185	Glenn Braggs	.15	.07	.02
☐ 186	Tom Browning	.15	.07	.02
☐ 187	Rob Dibble	.20	.09	.03
☐ 188	Bill Doran	.15	.07	.02
☐ 189	Chris Hammond	.15	.07	.02
☐ 190	Billy Hatcher	.15	.07	.02
☐ 191	Barry Larkin	.35	.16	.04
☐ 192	Hal Morris	.20	.09	.03
☐ 193	Joe Oliver	.15	.07	.02
☐ 194	Paul O'Neill	.20	.09	.03
☐ 195	Jeff Reed	.15	.07	.02
☐ 196	Jose Rijo	.20	.09	.03
☐ 197	Chris Sabo	.20	.09	.03
☐ 198	Jeff Bagwell	1.50	.65	.19
☐ 199	Craig Biggio	.20	.09	.03
☐ 200	Ken Caminiti	.20	.09	.03
☐ 201	Andujar Cedeno	.20	.09	.03
☐ 202	Steve Finley	.20	.09	.03
☐ 203	Luis Gonzalez	.25	.11	.03
☐ 204	Pete Harnisch	.15	.07	.02
☐ 205	Xavier Hernandez	.15	.07	.02
☐ 206	Darryl Kile	.30	.14	.04
☐ 207	Al Osuna	.15	.07	.02
☐ 208	Curt Schilling	.20	.09	.03
☐ 209	Brett Butler	.20	.09	.03
☐ 210	Kal Daniels	.15	.07	.02
☐ 211	Lenny Harris	.15	.07	.02
☐ 212	Stan Javier	.15	.07	.02
☐ 213	Ramon Martinez	.25	.11	.03
☐ 214	Roger McDowell	.15	.07	.02
☐ 215	Jose Offerman	.20	.09	.03
☐ 216	Juan Samuel	.15	.07	.02
☐ 217	Mike Scioscia	.15	.07	.02
☐ 218	Mike Sharperson	.15	.07	.02
☐ 219	Darryl Strawberry	.60	.25	.08
☐ 220	Delino DeShields	.50	.23	.06
☐ 221	Tom Foley	.15	.07	.02
☐ 222	Steve Frey	.15	.07	.02
☐ 223	Dennis Martinez	.20	.09	.03
☐ 224	Spike Owen	.15	.07	.02
☐ 225	Gilberto Reyes	.15	.07	.02
☐ 226	Tim Wallach	.20	.09	.03
☐ 227	Daryl Boston	.15	.07	.02
☐ 228	Tim Burke	.15	.07	.02
☐ 229	Vince Coleman	.20	.09	.03
☐ 230	David Cone	.20	.09	.03
☐ 231	Kevin Elster	.15	.07	.02
☐ 232	Dwight Gooden	.20	.09	.03
☐ 233	Todd Hundley	.15	.07	.02
☐ 234	Jeff Innis	.15	.07	.02
☐ 235	Howard Johnson	.20	.09	.03
☐ 236	Dave Magadan	.20	.09	.03
☐ 237	Mackey Sasser	.15	.07	.02
☐ 238	Anthony Young	.30	.14	.04
☐ 239	Wes Chamberlain	.20	.09	.03

☐ 240 Darren Daulton .20 .09 .03
☐ 241 Len Dykstra .20 .09 .03
☐ 242 Tommy Greene .15 .07 .02
☐ 243 Charlie Hayes .15 .07 .02
☐ 244 Dave Hollins .50 .23 .06
☐ 245 Ricky Jordan .15 .07 .02
☐ 246 John Kruk .20 .09 .03
☐ 247 Mickey Morandini .20 .09 .03
☐ 248 Terry Mulholland .15 .07 .02
☐ 249 Dale Murphy .20 .09 .03
☐ 250 Jay Bell .15 .07 .02
☐ 251 Barry Bonds 1.00 .45 .13
☐ 252 Steve Buechele .15 .07 .02
☐ 253 Doug Drabek .20 .09 .03
☐ 254 Mike LaValliere .15 .07 .02
☐ 255 Jose Lind .15 .07 .02
☐ 256 Lloyd McClendon .15 .07 .02
☐ 257 Orlando Merced .35 .16 .04
☐ 258 Don Slaught .15 .07 .02
☐ 259 John Smiley .20 .09 .03
☐ 260 Zane Smith .15 .07 .02
☐ 261 Randy Tomlin .25 .11 .03
☐ 262 Andy Van Slyke .25 .11 .03
☐ 263 Pedro Guerrero .20 .09 .03
☐ 264 Felix Jose .20 .09 .03
☐ 265 Ray Lankford .75 .35 .09
☐ 266 Omar Olivares .15 .07 .02
☐ 267 Jose Oquendo .15 .07 .02
☐ 268 Tom Pagnozzi .15 .07 .02
☐ 269 Bryn Smith .15 .07 .02
☐ 270 Lee Smith UER .20 .09 .03
(1991 record listed as 61-61)
☐ 271 Ozzie Smith UER .40 .18 .05
(Comma before year of birth on card back)
☐ 272 Milt Thompson .15 .07 .02
☐ 273 Todd Zeile .15 .07 .02
☐ 274 Andy Benes .20 .09 .03
☐ 275 Jerald Clark .15 .07 .02
☐ 276 Tony Fernandez .20 .09 .03
☐ 277 Tony Gwynn .60 .25 .08
☐ 278 Greg W. Harris .15 .07 .02
☐ 279 Thomas Howard .15 .07 .02
☐ 280 Bruce Hurst .20 .09 .03
☐ 281 Mike Maddux .15 .07 .02
☐ 282 Fred McGriff .60 .25 .08
☐ 283 Benito Santiago .20 .09 .03
☐ 284 Kevin Bass .15 .07 .02
☐ 285 Jeff Brantley .15 .07 .02
☐ 286 John Burkett .15 .07 .02
☐ 287 Will Clark 1.00 .45 .13
☐ 288 Royce Clayton .75 .35 .09
☐ 289 Steve Decker .15 .07 .02
☐ 290 Kelly Downs .15 .07 .02
☐ 291 Mike Felder .15 .07 .02
☐ 292 Darren Lewis .20 .09 .03
☐ 293 Kirt Manwaring .15 .07 .02
☐ 294 Willie McGee .20 .09 .03
☐ 295 Robby Thompson .15 .07 .02
☐ 296 Matt Williams .20 .09 .03
☐ 297 Trevor Wilson .15 .07 .02
☐ 298 Checklist 1-100 .15 .02 .00
☐ 299 Checklist 101-200 .15 .02 .00
☐ 300 Checklist 201-300 .15 .02 .00
☐ 301 Brady Anderson .20 .09 .03
☐ 302 Todd Frohwirth .15 .07 .02
☐ 303 Ben McDonald .30 .14 .04
☐ 304 Mark McLemore .15 .07 .02
☐ 305 Jose Mesa .15 .07 .02
☐ 306 Bob Milacki .15 .07 .02
☐ 307 Gregg Olson .20 .09 .03
☐ 308 David Segui .15 .07 .02
☐ 309 Rick Sutcliffe .20 .09 .03
☐ 310 Jeff Tackett .20 .09 .03
☐ 311 Wade Boggs .60 .25 .08
☐ 312 Scott Cooper .50 .23 .06
☐ 313 John Flaherty .25 .11 .03
☐ 314 Wayne Housie .25 .11 .03
☐ 315 Peter Hoy .25 .11 .03
☐ 316 John Marzano .15 .07 .02
☐ 317 Tim Naehring .20 .09 .03
☐ 318 Phil Plantier .60 .25 .08
☐ 319 Frank Viola .20 .09 .03
☐ 320 Matt Young .15 .07 .02
☐ 321 Jim Abbott .40 .18 .05
☐ 322 Hubie Brooks .15 .07 .02
☐ 323 Chad Curtis 1.00 .45 .13
☐ 324 Alvin Davis .15 .07 .02
☐ 325 Junior Felix .15 .07 .02
☐ 326 Von Hayes .15 .07 .02
☐ 327 Mark Langston .20 .09 .03
☐ 328 Scott Lewis .20 .09 .03
☐ 329 Don Robinson .15 .07 .02
☐ 330 Bobby Rose .15 .07 .02
☐ 331 Lee Stevens .15 .07 .02
☐ 332 George Bell .20 .09 .03
☐ 333 Esteban Beltre .30 .14 .04
☐ 334 Joey Cora .15 .07 .02
☐ 335 Alex Fernandez .20 .09 .03
☐ 336 Roberto Hernandez .40 .18 .05
☐ 337 Mike Huff .15 .07 .02
☐ 338 Kirk McCaskill .15 .07 .02
☐ 339 Dan Pasqua .15 .07 .02
☐ 340 Scott Radinsky .15 .07 .02
☐ 341 Steve Sax .20 .09 .03
☐ 342 Bobby Thigpen .15 .07 .02
☐ 343 Robin Ventura 1.00 .45 .13
☐ 344 Jack Armstrong .15 .07 .02
☐ 345 Alex Cole .15 .07 .02
☐ 346 Dennis Cook .15 .07 .02
☐ 347 Glenallen Hill .15 .07 .02
☐ 348 Thomas Howard .15 .07 .02
☐ 349 Brook Jacoby .15 .07 .02
☐ 350 Kenny Lofton 2.50 1.15 .30
☐ 351 Charles Nagy .50 .23 .06
☐ 352 Rod Nichols .15 .07 .02
☐ 353 Junior Ortiz .15 .07 .02
☐ 354 Dave Otto .15 .07 .02
☐ 355 Tony Perezchica .15 .07 .02
☐ 356 Scott Scudder .15 .07 .02
☐ 357 Paul Sorrento .20 .09 .03
☐ 358 Skeeter Barnes .15 .07 .02
☐ 359 Mark Carreon .15 .07 .02
☐ 360 John Doherty .40 .18 .05
☐ 361 Dan Gladden .15 .07 .02
☐ 362 Bill Gullickson .15 .07 .02
☐ 363 Shawn Hare .25 .11 .03
☐ 364 Mike Henneman .15 .07 .02
☐ 365 Chad Kreuter .15 .07 .02
☐ 366 Mark Leiter .15 .07 .02
☐ 367 Mike Munoz .15 .07 .02
☐ 368 Kevin Ritz .15 .07 .02
☐ 369 Mark Davis .15 .07 .02
☐ 370 Tom Gordon .15 .07 .02
☐ 371 Chris Gwynn .15 .07 .02
☐ 372 Gregg Jefferies .20 .09 .03
☐ 373 Wally Joyner .20 .09 .03
☐ 374 Kevin McReynolds .20 .09 .03
☐ 375 Keith Miller .15 .07 .02
☐ 376 Rico Rossy .20 .09 .03
☐ 377 Curtis Wilkerson .15 .07 .02
☐ 378 Ricky Bones .30 .14 .04
☐ 379 Chris Bosio .15 .07 .02
☐ 380 Cal Eldred 2.00 .90 .25
☐ 381 Scott Fletcher .15 .07 .02
☐ 382 Jim Gantner .15 .07 .02
☐ 383 Darryl Hamilton .20 .09 .03
☐ 384 Doug Henry .60 .25 .08
☐ 385 Pat Listach 4.00 1.80 .50
☐ 386 Tim McIntosh .15 .07 .02
☐ 387 Edwin Nunez .15 .07 .02
☐ 388 Dan Plesac .15 .07 .02
☐ 389 Kevin Seitzer .20 .09 .03
☐ 390 Franklin Stubbs .15 .07 .02
☐ 391 William Suero .20 .09 .03
☐ 392 Bill Wegman .15 .07 .02
☐ 393 Willie Banks .50 .23 .06
☐ 394 Jarvis Brown .20 .09 .03
☐ 395 Greg Gagne .15 .07 .02
☐ 396 Mark Guthrie .15 .07 .02
☐ 397 Bill Krueger .15 .07 .02
☐ 398 Pat Mahomes .75 .35 .09
☐ 399 Pedro Munoz .25 .11 .03
☐ 400 John Smiley .20 .09 .03
☐ 401 Gary Wayne .15 .07 .02
☐ 402 Lenny Webster .15 .07 .02
☐ 403 Carl Willis .15 .07 .02
☐ 404 Greg Cadaret .15 .07 .02
☐ 405 Steve Farr .15 .07 .02
☐ 406 Mike Gallego .15 .07 .02
☐ 407 Charlie Hayes .15 .07 .02
☐ 408 Steve Howe .15 .07 .02
☐ 409 Dion James .15 .07 .02
☐ 410 Jeff Johnson .15 .07 .02
☐ 411 Tim Leary .15 .07 .02
☐ 412 Jim Leyritz .15 .07 .02
☐ 413 Melido Perez .20 .09 .03
☐ 414 Scott Sanderson .15 .07 .02
☐ 415 Andy Stankiewicz .40 .18 .05
☐ 416 Mike Stanley .15 .07 .02
☐ 417 Danny Tartabull .25 .11 .03
☐ 418 Lance Blankenship .15 .07 .02
☐ 419 Mike Bordick .30 .14 .04
☐ 420 Scott Brosius .20 .09 .03
☐ 421 Dennis Eckersley .30 .14 .04

☐ 422	Scott Hemond	.15	.07	.02
☐ 423	Carney Lansford	.20	.09	.03
☐ 424	Henry Mercedes	.30	.14	.04
☐ 425	Mike Moore	.15	.07	.02
☐ 426	Gene Nelson	.15	.07	.02
☐ 427	Randy Ready	.15	.07	.02
☐ 428	Bruce Walton	.15	.07	.02
☐ 429	Willie Wilson	.15	.07	.02
☐ 430	Rich Amaral	.20	.09	.03
☐ 431	Dave Cochrane	.15	.07	.02
☐ 432	Henry Cotto	.15	.07	.02
☐ 433	Calvin Jones	.25	.11	.03
☐ 434	Kevin Mitchell	.25	.11	.03
☐ 435	Clay Parker	.15	.07	.02
☐ 436	Omar Vizquel	.15	.07	.02
☐ 437	Floyd Bannister	.15	.07	.02
☐ 438	Kevin Brown	.20	.09	.03
☐ 439	John Cangelosi	.15	.07	.02
☐ 440	Brian Downing	.15	.07	.02
☐ 441	Monty Fariss	.30	.14	.04
☐ 442	Jose Guzman	.15	.07	.02
☐ 443	Donald Harris	.15	.07	.02
☐ 444	Kevin Reimer	.25	.11	.03
☐ 445	Kenny Rogers	.15	.07	.02
☐ 446	Wayne Rosenthal	.20	.09	.03
☐ 447	Dickie Thon	.15	.07	.02
☐ 448	Derek Bell	.60	.25	.08
☐ 449	Juan Guzman	3.50	1.55	.45
☐ 450	Tom Henke	.20	.09	.03
☐ 451	Candy Maldonado	.15	.07	.02
☐ 452	Jack Morris	.25	.11	.03
☐ 453	David Wells	.15	.07	.02
☐ 454	Dave Winfield	.40	.18	.05
☐ 455	Juan Berenguer	.15	.07	.02
☐ 456	Damon Berryhill	.15	.07	.02
☐ 457	Mike Bielecki	.15	.07	.02
☐ 458	Marvin Freeman	.15	.07	.02
☐ 459	Charlie Leibrandt	.15	.07	.02
☐ 460	Kent Mercker	.15	.07	.02
☐ 461	Otis Nixon	.20	.09	.03
☐ 462	Alejandro Pena	.15	.07	.02
☐ 463	Ben Rivera	.25	.11	.03
☐ 464	Deion Sanders	.75	.35	.09
☐ 465	Mark Wohlers	.40	.18	.05
☐ 466	Shawn Boskie	.15	.07	.02
☐ 467	Frank Castillo	.30	.14	.04
☐ 468	Andre Dawson	.40	.18	.05
☐ 469	Joe Girardi	.15	.07	.02
☐ 470	Chuck McElroy	.15	.07	.02
☐ 471	Mike Morgan	.15	.07	.02
☐ 472	Ken Patterson	.15	.07	.02
☐ 473	Bob Scanlan	.15	.07	.02
☐ 474	Gary Scott	.20	.09	.03
☐ 475	Dave Smith	.15	.07	.02
☐ 476	Sammy Sosa	.15	.07	.02
☐ 477	Hector Villanueva	.15	.07	.02
☐ 478	Scott Bankhead	.15	.07	.02
☐ 479	Tim Belcher	.20	.09	.03
☐ 480	Freddie Benavides	.15	.07	.02
☐ 481	Jacob Brumfield	.20	.09	.03
☐ 482	Norm Charlton	.20	.09	.03
☐ 483	Dwayne Henry	.15	.07	.02
☐ 484	Dave Martinez	.15	.07	.02
☐ 485	Bip Roberts	.20	.09	.03
☐ 486	Reggie Sanders	1.50	.65	.19
☐ 487	Greg Swindell	.20	.09	.03
☐ 488	Ryan Bowen	.30	.14	.04
☐ 489	Casey Candaele	.15	.07	.02
☐ 490	Juan Guerrero	.40	.18	.05
☐ 491	Pete Incaviglia	.15	.07	.02
☐ 492	Jeff Juden	.30	.14	.04
☐ 493	Rob Murphy	.15	.07	.02
☐ 494	Mark Portugal	.15	.07	.02
☐ 495	Rafael Ramirez	.15	.07	.02
☐ 496	Scott Servais	.15	.07	.02
☐ 497	Ed Taubensee	.40	.18	.05
☐ 498	Brian Williams	.75	.35	.09
☐ 499	Todd Benzinger	.15	.07	.02
☐ 500	John Candelaria	.15	.07	.02
☐ 501	Tom Candiotti	.15	.07	.02
☐ 502	Tim Crews	.15	.07	.02
☐ 503	Eric Davis	.25	.11	.03
☐ 504	Jim Gott	.15	.07	.02
☐ 505	Dave Hansen	.20	.09	.03
☐ 506	Carlos Hernandez	.15	.07	.02
☐ 507	Orel Hershiser	.25	.11	.03
☐ 508	Eric Karros	3.50	1.55	.45
☐ 509	Bob Ojeda	.15	.07	.02
☐ 510	Steve Wilson	.15	.07	.02
☐ 511	Moises Alou	.40	.18	.05
☐ 512	Bret Barberie	.20	.09	.03
☐ 513	Ivan Calderon	.15	.07	.02
☐ 514	Gary Carter	.20	.09	.03
☐ 515	Archi Cianfrocco	.50	.23	.06
☐ 516	Jeff Fassero	.15	.07	.02
☐ 517	Darrin Fletcher	.15	.07	.02
☐ 518	Marquis Grissom	.50	.23	.06
☐ 519	Chris Haney	.20	.09	.03
☐ 520	Ken Hill	.20	.09	.03
☐ 521	Chris Nabholz	.15	.07	.02
☐ 522	Bill Sampen	.15	.07	.02
☐ 523	John Vander Wal	.40	.18	.05
☐ 524	Dave Wainhouse	.15	.07	.02
☐ 525	Larry Walker	.75	.35	.09
☐ 526	John Wetteland	.15	.07	.02
☐ 527	Bobby Bonilla	.35	.16	.04
☐ 528	Sid Fernandez	.20	.09	.03
☐ 529	John Franco	.20	.09	.03
☐ 530	Dave Gallagher	.15	.07	.02
☐ 531	Paul Gibson	.15	.07	.02
☐ 532	Eddie Murray	.40	.18	.05
☐ 533	Junior Noboa	.15	.07	.02
☐ 534	Charlie O'Brien	.15	.07	.02
☐ 535	Bill Pecota	.15	.07	.02
☐ 536	Willie Randolph	.20	.09	.03
☐ 537	Bret Saberhagen	.25	.11	.03
☐ 538	Dick Schofield	.15	.07	.02
☐ 539	Pete Schourek	.20	.09	.03
☐ 540	Ruben Amaro	.20	.09	.03
☐ 541	Andy Ashby	.25	.11	.03
☐ 542	Kim Batiste	.30	.14	.04
☐ 543	Cliff Brantley	.20	.09	.03
☐ 544	Mariano Duncan	.15	.07	.02
☐ 545	Jeff Grotewold	.20	.09	.03
☐ 546	Barry Jones	.15	.07	.02
☐ 547	Julio Peguero	.20	.09	.03
☐ 548	Curt Schilling	.20	.09	.03
☐ 549	Mitch Williams	.15	.07	.02
☐ 550	Stan Belinda	.15	.07	.02
☐ 551	Scott Bullett	.30	.14	.04
☐ 552	Cecil Espy	.15	.07	.02
☐ 553	Jeff King	.15	.07	.02
☐ 554	Roger Mason	.15	.07	.02
☐ 555	Paul Miller	.30	.14	.04
☐ 556	Denny Neagle	.25	.11	.03
☐ 557	Vicente Palacios	.15	.07	.02
☐ 558	Bob Patterson	.15	.07	.02
☐ 559	Tom Prince	.15	.07	.02
☐ 560	Gary Redus	.15	.07	.02
☐ 561	Gary Varsho	.15	.07	.02
☐ 562	Juan Agosto	.15	.07	.02
☐ 563	Cris Carpenter	.15	.07	.02
☐ 564	Mark Clark	.30	.14	.04
☐ 565	Jose DeLeon	.15	.07	.02
☐ 566	Rich Gedman	.15	.07	.02
☐ 567	Bernard Gilkey	.20	.09	.03
☐ 568	Rex Hudler	.15	.07	.02
☐ 569	Tim Jones	.15	.07	.02
☐ 570	Donovan Osborne	1.25	.55	.16
☐ 571	Mike Perez	.20	.09	.03
☐ 572	Gerald Perry	.15	.07	.02
☐ 573	Bob Tewksbury	.20	.09	.03
☐ 574	Todd Worrell	.15	.07	.02
☐ 575	Dave Eiland	.15	.07	.02
☐ 576	Jeremy Hernandez	.25	.11	.03
☐ 577	Craig Lefferts	.15	.07	.02
☐ 578	Jose Melendez	.20	.09	.03
☐ 579	Randy Myers	.20	.09	.03
☐ 580	Gary Pettis	.15	.07	.02
☐ 581	Rich Rodriguez	.15	.07	.02
☐ 582	Gary Sheffield	1.50	.65	.19
☐ 583	Craig Shipley	.20	.09	.03
☐ 584	Kurt Stillwell	.15	.07	.02
☐ 585	Tim Teufel	.15	.07	.02
☐ 586	Rod Beck	.40	.18	.05
☐ 587	Dave Burba	.15	.07	.02
☐ 588	Craig Colbert	.20	.09	.03
☐ 589	Bryan Hickerson	.20	.09	.03
☐ 590	Mike Jackson	.15	.07	.02
☐ 591	Mark Leonard	.15	.07	.02
☐ 592	Jim McNamara	.25	.11	.03
☐ 593	John Patterson	.40	.18	.05
☐ 594	Dave Righetti	.15	.07	.02
☐ 595	Cory Snyder	.15	.07	.02
☐ 596	Bill Swift	.15	.07	.02
☐ 597	Ted Wood	.30	.14	.04
☐ 598	Checklist 301-400	.15	.02	.00
☐ 599	Checklist 401-500	.15	.02	.00
☐ 600	Checklist 501-600	.15	.02	.00

1992 Ultra All-Rookies

This ten-card standard-size (2 1/2" by 3 1/2") set was randomly inserted in 1992 Fleer Ultra II foil packs. The fronts feature borderless color action player photos except at the bottom where they are edged by a marbleized black wedge. The words "All-Rookie Team" in gold foil lettering appear in a black marbleized inverted triangle at the lower right corner, with the player's name on a color banner. On a black marbleized background, the backs present a color headshot inside an inverted triangle and career summary on a gray marbleized panel. The cards are numbered on the back.

	MT	EX-MT	VG
COMPLETE SET (10)	40.00	18.00	5.00
COMMON PLAYER (1-10)	2.00	.90	.25
☐ 1 Eric Karros	13.00	5.75	1.65
☐ 2 Andy Stankiewicz	2.50	1.15	.30
☐ 3 Gary DiSarcina	2.00	.90	.25
☐ 4 Archi Cianfrocco	3.00	1.35	.40
☐ 5 Jim McNamara	2.00	.90	.25
☐ 6 Chad Curtis	5.00	2.30	.60
☐ 7 Kenny Lofton	9.00	4.00	1.15
☐ 8 Reggie Sanders	6.00	2.70	.75
☐ 9 Pat Mahomes	4.00	1.80	.50
☐ 10 Donovan Osborne	5.00	2.30	.60

1992 Ultra All-Stars

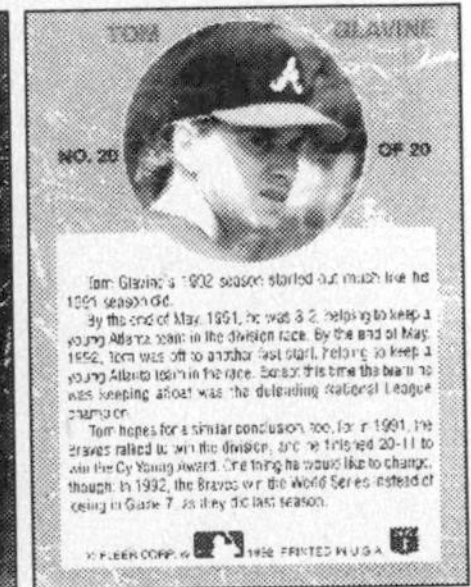

Featuring many of the season's current mega-stars, this 20-card standard-size (2 1/2" by 3 1/2") set was randomly inserted in 1992 Fleer Ultra II foil packs. The front design displays color action player photos enclosed by black marbleized borders. The word "All-Star" and the player's name are printed in gold foil lettering in the bottom border. On a gray marbleized background, the backs carry a color headshot (in a circular format) and a summary of the player's recent performance in on a pastel yellow panel. The cards are numbered on the back.

	MT	EX-MT	VG
COMPLETE SET (20)	75.00	34.00	9.50
COMMON PLAYER (1-20)	2.00	.90	.25
☐ 1 Mark McGwire	6.00	2.70	.75
☐ 2 Roberto Alomar	7.00	3.10	.85
☐ 3 Cal Ripken Jr.	8.00	3.60	1.00
☐ 4 Wade Boggs	4.00	1.80	.50
☐ 5 Mickey Tettleton	2.00	.90	.25
☐ 6 Ken Griffey Jr.	10.00	4.50	1.25
☐ 7 Roberto Kelly	2.00	.90	.25
☐ 8 Kirby Puckett	6.00	2.70	.75
☐ 9 Frank Thomas	15.00	6.75	1.90
☐ 10 Jack McDowell	3.00	1.35	.40
☐ 11 Will Clark	6.00	2.70	.75
☐ 12 Ryne Sandberg	7.00	3.10	.85
☐ 13 Barry Larkin	3.00	1.35	.40
☐ 14 Gary Sheffield	6.00	2.70	.75
☐ 15 Tom Pagnozzi	2.00	.90	.25
☐ 16 Barry Bonds	6.00	2.70	.75
☐ 17 Deion Sanders	5.00	2.30	.60
☐ 18 Darryl Strawberry	4.00	1.80	.50
☐ 19 David Cone	2.50	1.15	.30
☐ 20 Tom Glavine	5.00	2.30	.60

1992 Ultra Award Winners

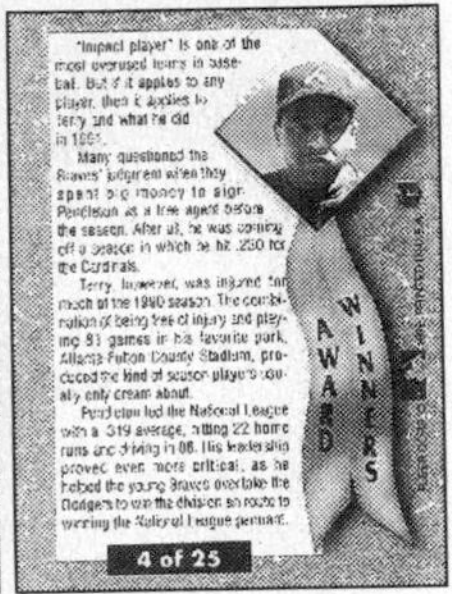

This 25-card set features 18 Gold Glove winners, both Cy Young Award winners, both Rookies of the Year, both league MVP's, and the World Series MVP. The cards measure the standard size (2 1/2" by 3 1/2") and were randomly inserted in 1992 Fleer Ultra I packs. The fronts carry full-bleed color player photos that have a diagonal blue marbleized border at the bottom. The player's name appears in this bottom border, and a diamond-shaped gold foil seal signifying the award the player won is superimposed at the lower right corner. The backs also have blue marbleized borders and carry player profile on a tan marbleized panel. A head shot of the player appears in a diamond at the upper right corner, with the words "Award Winners" on orange ribbons extending below the diamond. The cards are numbered on the back.

	MT	EX-MT	VG
COMPLETE SET (25)	100.00	45.00	12.50
COMMON PLAYER (1-25)	2.50	1.15	.30
☐ 1 Jack Morris	3.00	1.35	.40
☐ 2 Chuck Knoblauch	5.00	2.30	.60
☐ 3 Jeff Bagwell	7.00	3.10	.85
☐ 4 Terry Pendleton	3.50	1.55	.45
☐ 5 Cal Ripken	10.00	4.50	1.25
☐ 6 Roger Clemens	8.00	3.60	1.00
☐ 7 Tom Glavine	6.00	2.70	.75
☐ 8 Tom Pagnozzi	2.50	1.15	.30
☐ 9 Ozzie Smith	4.00	1.80	.50
☐ 10 Andy Van Slyke	3.00	1.35	.40
☐ 11 Barry Bonds	7.00	3.10	.85
☐ 12 Tony Gwynn	5.00	2.30	.60
☐ 13 Matt Williams	3.00	1.35	.40
☐ 14 Will Clark	7.00	3.10	.85
☐ 15 Robin Ventura	7.00	3.10	.85
☐ 16 Mark Langston	2.50	1.15	.30
☐ 17 Tony Pena	2.50	1.15	.30
☐ 18 Devon White	2.50	1.15	.30

☐ 19 Don Mattingly	5.00	2.30	.60
☐ 20 Roberto Alomar	8.00	3.60	1.00
☐ 21A Cal Ripken ERR (Reversed negative on card back)	12.00	5.50	1.50
☐ 21B Cal Ripken COR	12.00	5.50	1.50
☐ 22 Ken Griffey Jr.	12.00	5.50	1.50
☐ 23 Kirby Puckett	7.00	3.10	.85
☐ 24 Greg Maddux	5.00	2.30	.60
☐ 25 Ryne Sandberg	8.00	3.60	1.00

1992 Ultra Tony Gwynn

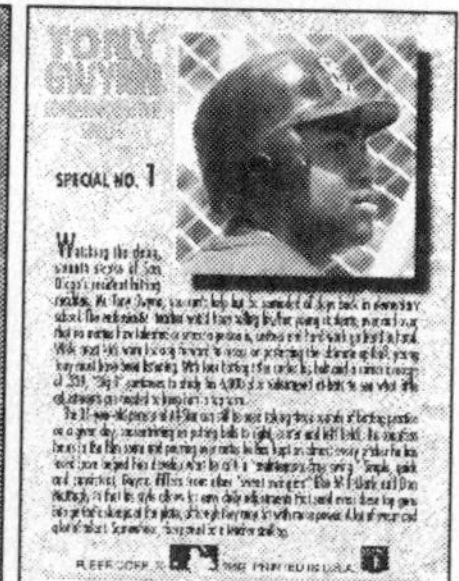

Tony Gwynn served as a spokesperson for Fleer Ultra during 1992 and was the exclusive subject of this 12-card set. The first ten-card standard-size (2 1/2" by 3 1/2") series was randomly inserted in 1992 Fleer Ultra I packs. More than 2,000 of these cards were personaly autographed by Gwynn. The fronts display color posed and action shots of Gwynn framed by green marbled borders. The player's name and the words "Commemorative Series" appear in gold-foil lettering in the bottom border. On a green marbled background, the backs features a color head shot, career summary, and highlights. These insert cards are numbered on the back "No. X of 10." An additional special two-card subset was available through a mail-in offer for ten 1992 Fleer Ultra baseball wrappers plus 1.00 for shipping and handling. This offer was good through October 31st and, according to Fleer, over 100,000 sets were produced. The standard-size (2 1/2" by 3 1/2") cards display action shots of Gwynn framed by green marbled borders. The player's name and the words "Commemorative Series" appear in gold-foil lettering in the bottom border. On a green marbled background, the backs features a color head shot and either a player profile (card number A below but Special No. 1 on the card back) or Gwynn's comments about other players or the game itself (card number B below but Special No. 2 on the card back).

	MT	EX-MT	VG
COMPLETE INSERT SET (10)	25.00	11.50	3.10
COMMON GWYNN (1-10)	2.50	1.15	.30
COMPLETE SEND OFF SET (2)	5.00	2.30	.60
COMMON GWYNN (A/B)	2.50	1.15	.30
☐ 1 Tony Gwynn (Leaping and catching ball at outfield wall)	2.50	1.15	.30
☐ 2 Tony Gwynn (Batting stance, brown Padres' uniform)	2.50	1.15	.30
☐ 3 Tony Gwynn (Awaiting flyball, glove above head)	2.50	1.15	.30
☐ 4 Tony Gwynn (Follow-through on swing)	2.50	1.15	.30
☐ 5 Tony Gwynn (Leading off base; crouching at the knees)	2.50	1.15	.30
☐ 6 Tony Gwynn (Posed with silver bat and Gold Glove trophy)	2.50	1.15	.30
☐ 7 Tony Gwynn (Bunting)	2.50	1.15	.30
☐ 8 Tony Gwynn (Full body shot; swinging)	2.50	1.15	.30
☐ 9 Tony Gwynn (Taking off for first)	2.50	1.15	.30
☐ 10 Tony Gwynn (Batting, following through, sun glasses on)	2.50	1.15	.30
☐ A0 Tony Gwynn (Batting)	2.50	1.15	.30
☐ AU Tony Gwynn (Autographed with certified signature)	200.00	90.00	25.00
☐ B0 Tony Gwynn (Fielding)	2.50	1.15	.30

1988 Upper Deck Samples

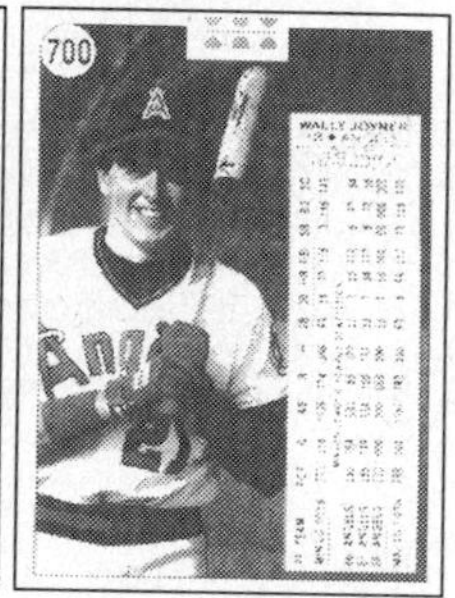

This two-card test issue was given away as samples during the summer of 1988 in anticipation of Upper Deck obtaining licenses from Major League Baseball and the Major League Baseball Players Association. Not many were produced (probably less than 25,000 of each) but almost none were thrown away as they were distributed basically only to those who would hold on to them. There are supposedly versions based on where the hologram is printed but the price below is for the basic variety. These test cards are the same size (2 1/2" by 3 1/2") as the regular issue and are styled similarly. Joyner and Buice were supposedly interested in investing in Upper Deck (conflict of interest prohibited them) and apparently were helpful in getting Upper Deck the necessary licenses. Cards were passed out freely to every dealer at the National Sports Collectors Convention in Atlantic City, New Jersey in August 1988.

	MT	EX-MT	VG
COMPLETE SET (2)	40.00	18.00	5.00
COMMON PLAYER	15.00	6.75	1.90
☐ 1 DeWayne Buice	15.00	6.75	1.90
☐ 700 Wally Joyner	35.00	16.00	4.40

1989 Upper Deck

This attractive 800-card set was introduced in 1989 as an additional fully licensed major card set. The cards feature full color on both the front and the back and are distinguished by the fact that each card has a hologram on the reverse, thus making the cards essentially copy proof. The cards measure standard size, 2 1/2" by 3 1/2". Cards 668-693 feature a "Collector's Choice" (CC) colorful drawing of a player (by artist Vernon Wells) on the card front and a

checklist of that team on the card back. Cards 1-26 are designated "Rookie Stars" by Upper Deck. On many cards "Rookie" and team logos can be found with either a "TM" or (R). Cards with missing or duplicate holograms appear to be relatively common and hence there is little, if any, premium value on these "variations". The more significant variations involving changed photos or changed type are listed below. According to the company, the Murphy and Sheridan cards were corrected very early, after only two percent of the cards had been produced. This means, for example, that out of 1,000,000 Dale Murphy '89 Upper Deck cards produced, there are only 20,000 Murphy error cards. Similarly, the Sheffield was corrected after 15 percent had been printed; Varsho, Gallego, and Schroeder were corrected after 20 percent; and Holton, Manrique, and Winningham were corrected 30 percent of the way through. Collectors should also note that many dealers consider that Upper Deck's "planned" production of 1,000,000 of each player was increased (perhaps even doubled) later in the year due to the explosion in popularity of the Upper Deck cards. The key Rookie Cards in the low number series are Sandy Alomar Jr., Ken Griffey Jr., Felix Jose, Ramon Martinez, Gary Sheffield, and John Smoltz. The high number cards (701-800) were made available three different ways: as part of the 800-card factory set, as a separate boxed set of 100 cards in a custom blue box, and in special high number foil packs. The key Rookie Cards in the high number series are Jim Abbott, Norm Charlton, Junior Felix, Steve Finley, Erik Hanson, Pete Harnisch, Charlie Hayes, Gregg Olson, Jerome Walton, and Todd Zeile.

	MT	EX-MT	VG
COMPLETE SET (800)	140.00	65.00	17.50
COMPLETE FACT.SET (800)	150.00	70.00	19.00
COMPLETE LO SET (700)	130.00	57.50	16.50
COMPLETE HI SET (100)	13.00	5.75	1.65
COMPLETE HI FACT.SET (100)	13.00	5.75	1.65
COMMON PLAYER (1-700)	.10	.05	.01
COMMON PLAYER (701-800)	.10	.05	.01

	MT	EX-MT	VG
☐ 1 Ken Griffey Jr.	55.00	25.00	7.00
☐ 2 Luis Medina	.12	.05	.02
☐ 3 Tony Chance	.12	.05	.02
☐ 4 Dave Otto	.12	.05	.02
☐ 5 Sandy Alomar Jr. UER (Born 6/16/66, should be 6/18/66)	.60	.25	.08
☐ 6 Rolando Roomes	.12	.05	.02
☐ 7 Dave West	.15	.07	.02
☐ 8 Cris Carpenter	.20	.09	.03
☐ 9 Gregg Jefferies	.75	.35	.09
☐ 10 Doug Dascenzo	.12	.05	.02
☐ 11 Ron Jones	.12	.05	.02
☐ 12 Luis De Los Santos	.12	.05	.02
☐ 13A Gary Sheffield ERR (SS upside down on card front)	12.00	5.50	1.50
☐ 13B Gary Sheffield COR	12.00	5.50	1.50
☐ 14 Mike Harkey	.25	.11	.03
☐ 15 Lance Blankenship	.20	.09	.03
☐ 16 William Brennan	.12	.05	.02
☐ 17 John Smoltz	4.00	1.80	.50
☐ 18 Ramon Martinez	2.00	.90	.25
☐ 19 Mark Lemke	.30	.14	.04
☐ 20 Juan Bell	.15	.07	.02
☐ 21 Rey Palacios	.12	.05	.02
☐ 22 Felix Jose	2.00	.90	.25
☐ 23 Van Snider	.12	.05	.02
☐ 24 Dante Bichette	.50	.23	.06
☐ 25 Randy Johnson	1.25	.55	.16
☐ 26 Carlos Quintana	.20	.09	.03
☐ 27 Star Rookie CL	.10	.01	.00
☐ 28 Mike Schooler	.20	.09	.03
☐ 29 Randy St.Claire	.10	.05	.01
☐ 30 Jerald Clark	.35	.16	.04
☐ 31 Kevin Gross	.10	.05	.01
☐ 32 Dan Firova	.10	.05	.01
☐ 33 Jeff Calhoun	.10	.05	.01
☐ 34 Tommy Hinzo	.10	.05	.01
☐ 35 Ricky Jordan	.20	.09	.03
☐ 36 Larry Parrish	.10	.05	.01
☐ 37 Bret Saberhagen UER (Hit total 931, should be 1031)	.12	.05	.02
☐ 38 Mike Smithson	.10	.05	.01
☐ 39 Dave Dravecky	.12	.05	.02
☐ 40 Ed Romero	.10	.05	.01
☐ 41 Jeff Musselman	.10	.05	.01
☐ 42 Ed Hearn	.10	.05	.01
☐ 43 Rance Mulliniks	.10	.05	.01
☐ 44 Jim Eisenreich	.10	.05	.01
☐ 45 Sil Campusano	.10	.05	.01
☐ 46 Mike Krukow	.10	.05	.01
☐ 47 Paul Gibson	.10	.05	.01
☐ 48 Mike LaCoss	.10	.05	.01
☐ 49 Larry Herndon	.10	.05	.01
☐ 50 Scott Garrelts	.10	.05	.01
☐ 51 Dwayne Henry	.10	.05	.01
☐ 52 Jim Acker	.10	.05	.01
☐ 53 Steve Sax	.12	.05	.02
☐ 54 Pete O'Brien	.10	.05	.01
☐ 55 Paul Runge	.10	.05	.01
☐ 56 Rick Rhoden	.10	.05	.01
☐ 57 John Dopson	.10	.05	.01
☐ 58 Casey Candaele UER (No stats for Astros for '88 season)	.10	.05	.01
☐ 59 Dave Righetti	.10	.05	.01
☐ 60 Joe Hesketh	.10	.05	.01
☐ 61 Frank DiPino	.10	.05	.01
☐ 62 Tim Laudner	.10	.05	.01
☐ 63 Jamie Moyer	.10	.05	.01
☐ 64 Fred Toliver	.10	.05	.01
☐ 65 Mitch Webster	.10	.05	.01
☐ 66 John Tudor	.10	.05	.01
☐ 67 John Cangelosi	.10	.05	.01
☐ 68 Mike Devereaux	.60	.25	.08
☐ 69 Brian Fisher	.10	.05	.01
☐ 70 Mike Marshall	.10	.05	.01
☐ 71 Zane Smith	.10	.05	.01
☐ 72A Brian Holton ERR (Photo actually Shawn Hillegas)	1.25	.55	.16
☐ 72B Brian Holton COR	.25	.11	.03
☐ 73 Jose Guzman	.12	.05	.02
☐ 74 Rick Mahler	.10	.05	.01
☐ 75 John Shelby	.10	.05	.01
☐ 76 Jim Deshaies	.10	.05	.01
☐ 77 Bobby Meacham	.10	.05	.01
☐ 78 Bryn Smith	.10	.05	.01
☐ 79 Joaquin Andujar	.10	.05	.01
☐ 80 Richard Dotson	.10	.05	.01
☐ 81 Charlie Lea	.10	.05	.01
☐ 82 Calvin Schiraldi	.10	.05	.01
☐ 83 Les Straker	.10	.05	.01
☐ 84 Les Lancaster	.10	.05	.01
☐ 85 Allan Anderson	.10	.05	.01
☐ 86 Junior Ortiz	.10	.05	.01
☐ 87 Jesse Orosco	.10	.05	.01
☐ 88 Felix Fermin	.10	.05	.01
☐ 89 Dave Anderson	.10	.05	.01
☐ 90 Rafael Belliard UER (Born '61, not '51)	.10	.05	.01
☐ 91 Franklin Stubbs	.10	.05	.01
☐ 92 Cecil Espy	.10	.05	.01
☐ 93 Albert Hall	.10	.05	.01
☐ 94 Tim Leary	.10	.05	.01
☐ 95 Mitch Williams	.12	.05	.02
☐ 96 Tracy Jones	.10	.05	.01
☐ 97 Danny Darwin	.10	.05	.01
☐ 98 Gary Ward	.10	.05	.01
☐ 99 Neal Heaton	.10	.05	.01
☐ 100 Jim Pankovits	.10	.05	.01
☐ 101 Bill Doran	.10	.05	.01
☐ 102 Tim Wallach	.12	.05	.02

□ 103 Joe Magrane	.10	.05	.01
□ 104 Ozzie Virgil	.10	.05	.01
□ 105 Alvin Davis	.10	.05	.01
□ 106 Tom Brookens	.10	.05	.01
□ 107 Shawon Dunston	.12	.05	.02
□ 108 Tracy Woodson	.10	.05	.01
□ 109 Nelson Liriano	.10	.05	.01
□ 110 Devon White UER (Doubles total 46, should be 56)	.12	.05	.02
□ 111 Steve Balboni	.10	.05	.01
□ 112 Buddy Bell	.12	.05	.02
□ 113 German Jimenez	.10	.05	.01
□ 114 Ken Dayley	.10	.05	.01
□ 115 Andres Galarraga	.10	.05	.01
□ 116 Mike Scioscia	.10	.05	.01
□ 117 Gary Pettis	.10	.05	.01
□ 118 Ernie Whitt	.10	.05	.01
□ 119 Bob Boone	.12	.05	.02
□ 120 Ryne Sandberg	1.50	.65	.19
□ 121 Bruce Benedict	.10	.05	.01
□ 122 Hubie Brooks	.10	.05	.01
□ 123 Mike Moore	.10	.05	.01
□ 124 Wallace Johnson	.10	.05	.01
□ 125 Bob Horner	.10	.05	.01
□ 126 Chili Davis	.12	.05	.02
□ 127 Manny Trillo	.10	.05	.01
□ 128 Chet Lemon	.10	.05	.01
□ 129 John Cerutti	.10	.05	.01
□ 130 Orel Hershiser	.12	.05	.02
□ 131 Terry Pendleton	.40	.18	.05
□ 132 Jeff Blauser	.12	.05	.02
□ 133 Mike Fitzgerald	.10	.05	.01
□ 134 Henry Cotto	.10	.05	.01
□ 135 Gerald Young	.10	.05	.01
□ 136 Luis Salazar	.10	.05	.01
□ 137 Alejandro Pena	.10	.05	.01
□ 138 Jack Howell	.10	.05	.01
□ 139 Tony Fernandez	.12	.05	.02
□ 140 Mark Grace	1.50	.65	.19
□ 141 Ken Caminiti	.12	.05	.02
□ 142 Mike Jackson	.10	.05	.01
□ 143 Larry McWilliams	.10	.05	.01
□ 144 Andres Thomas	.10	.05	.01
□ 145 Nolan Ryan (Triple exposure)	4.00	1.80	.50
□ 146 Mike Davis	.10	.05	.01
□ 147 DeWayne Buice	.10	.05	.01
□ 148 Jody Davis	.10	.05	.01
□ 149 Jesse Barfield	.10	.05	.01
□ 150 Matt Nokes	.12	.05	.02
□ 151 Jerry Reuss	.10	.05	.01
□ 152 Rick Cerone	.10	.05	.01
□ 153 Storm Davis	.10	.05	.01
□ 154 Marvell Wynne	.10	.05	.01
□ 155 Will Clark	1.50	.65	.19
□ 156 Luis Aguayo	.10	.05	.01
□ 157 Willie Upshaw	.10	.05	.01
□ 158 Randy Bush	.10	.05	.01
□ 159 Ron Darling	.12	.05	.02
□ 160 Kal Daniels	.12	.05	.02
□ 161 Spike Owen	.10	.05	.01
□ 162 Luis Polonia	.12	.05	.02
□ 163 Kevin Mitchell UER ('88/total HR's 18/52, should be 19/53)	.30	.14	.04
□ 164 Dave Gallagher	.10	.05	.01
□ 165 Benito Santiago	.12	.05	.02
□ 166 Greg Gagne	.10	.05	.01
□ 167 Ken Phelps	.10	.05	.01
□ 168 Sid Fernandez	.12	.05	.02
□ 169 Bo Diaz	.10	.05	.01
□ 170 Cory Snyder	.10	.05	.01
□ 171 Eric Show	.10	.05	.01
□ 172 Robby Thompson	.10	.05	.01
□ 173 Marty Barrett	.10	.05	.01
□ 174 Dave Henderson	.12	.05	.02
□ 175 Ozzie Guillen	.10	.05	.01
□ 176 Barry Lyons	.10	.05	.01
□ 177 Kelvin Torve	.10	.05	.01
□ 178 Don Slaught	.10	.05	.01
□ 179 Steve Lombardozzi	.10	.05	.01
□ 180 Chris Sabo	.60	.25	.08
□ 181 Jose Uribe	.10	.05	.01
□ 182 Shane Mack	.12	.05	.02
□ 183 Ron Karkovice	.10	.05	.01
□ 184 Todd Benzinger	.10	.05	.01
□ 185 Dave Stewart	.12	.05	.02
□ 186 Julio Franco	.12	.05	.02
□ 187 Ron Robinson	.10	.05	.01
□ 188 Wally Backman	.10	.05	.01
□ 189 Randy Velarde	.10	.05	.01
□ 190 Joe Carter	.90	.40	.11
□ 191 Bob Welch	.12	.05	.02
□ 192 Kelly Paris	.10	.05	.01
□ 193 Chris Brown	.10	.05	.01
□ 194 Rick Reuschel	.10	.05	.01
□ 195 Roger Clemens	1.50	.65	.19
□ 196 Dave Concepcion	.12	.05	.02
□ 197 Al Newman	.10	.05	.01
□ 198 Brook Jacoby	.10	.05	.01
□ 199 Mookie Wilson	.12	.05	.02
□ 200 Don Mattingly	.90	.40	.11
□ 201 Dick Schofield	.10	.05	.01
□ 202 Mark Gubicza	.10	.05	.01
□ 203 Gary Gaetti	.10	.05	.01
□ 204 Dan Pasqua	.10	.05	.01
□ 205 Andre Dawson	.50	.23	.06
□ 206 Chris Speier	.10	.05	.01
□ 207 Kent Tekulve	.10	.05	.01
□ 208 Rod Scurry	.10	.05	.01
□ 209 Scott Bailes	.10	.05	.01
□ 210 Rickey Henderson UER (Throws Right)	.90	.40	.11
□ 211 Harold Baines	.12	.05	.02
□ 212 Tony Armas	.10	.05	.01
□ 213 Kent Hrbek	.12	.05	.02
□ 214 Darrin Jackson	.30	.14	.04
□ 215 George Brett	.75	.35	.09
□ 216 Rafael Santana	.10	.05	.01
□ 217 Andy Allanson	.10	.05	.01
□ 218 Brett Butler	.12	.05	.02
□ 219 Steve Jeltz	.10	.05	.01
□ 220 Jay Buhner	.35	.16	.04
□ 221 Bo Jackson	.60	.25	.08
□ 222 Angel Salazar	.10	.05	.01
□ 223 Kirk McCaskill	.10	.05	.01
□ 224 Steve Lyons	.10	.05	.01
□ 225 Bert Blyleven	.12	.05	.02
□ 226 Scott Bradley	.10	.05	.01
□ 227 Bob Melvin	.10	.05	.01
□ 228 Ron Kittle	.10	.05	.01
□ 229 Phil Bradley	.10	.05	.01
□ 230 Tommy John	.12	.05	.02
□ 231 Greg Walker	.10	.05	.01
□ 232 Juan Berenguer	.10	.05	.01
□ 233 Pat Tabler	.10	.05	.01
□ 234 Terry Clark	.10	.05	.01
□ 235 Rafael Palmeiro	.75	.35	.09
□ 236 Paul Zuvella	.10	.05	.01
□ 237 Willie Randolph	.12	.05	.02
□ 238 Bruce Fields	.10	.05	.01
□ 239 Mike Aldrete	.10	.05	.01
□ 240 Lance Parrish	.12	.05	.02
□ 241 Greg Maddux	1.00	.45	.13
□ 242 John Moses	.10	.05	.01
□ 243 Melido Perez	.35	.16	.04
□ 244 Willie Wilson	.10	.05	.01
□ 245 Mark McLemore	.10	.05	.01
□ 246 Von Hayes	.10	.05	.01
□ 247 Matt Williams	.60	.25	.08
□ 248 John Candelaria UER (Listed as Yankee for part of '87, should be Mets)	.10	.05	.01
□ 249 Harold Reynolds	.10	.05	.01
□ 250 Greg Swindell	.12	.05	.02
□ 251 Juan Agosto	.10	.05	.01
□ 252 Mike Felder	.10	.05	.01
□ 253 Vince Coleman	.12	.05	.02
□ 254 Larry Sheets	.10	.05	.01
□ 255 George Bell	.40	.18	.05
□ 256 Terry Steinbach	.12	.05	.02
□ 257 Jack Armstrong	.30	.14	.04
□ 258 Dickie Thon	.10	.05	.01
□ 259 Ray Knight	.12	.05	.02
□ 260 Darryl Strawberry	.90	.40	.11
□ 261 Doug Sisk	.10	.05	.01
□ 262 Alex Trevino	.10	.05	.01
□ 263 Jeffrey Leonard	.10	.05	.01
□ 264 Tom Henke	.12	.05	.02
□ 265 Ozzie Smith	.50	.23	.06
□ 266 Dave Bergman	.10	.05	.01
□ 267 Tony Phillips	.10	.05	.01
□ 268 Mark Davis	.10	.05	.01
□ 269 Kevin Elster	.10	.05	.01
□ 270 Barry Larkin	.60	.25	.08
□ 271 Manny Lee	.10	.05	.01
□ 272 Tom Brunansky	.12	.05	.02
□ 273 Craig Biggio	1.25	.55	.16
□ 274 Jim Gantner	.10	.05	.01
□ 275 Eddie Murray	.50	.23	.06
□ 276 Jeff Reed	.10	.05	.01
□ 277 Tim Teufel	.10	.05	.01
□ 278 Rick Honeycutt	.10	.05	.01
□ 279 Guillermo Hernandez	.10	.05	.01

☐ 280 John Kruk .15 .07 .02
☐ 281 Luis Alicea .15 .07 .02
☐ 282 Jim Clancy .10 .05 .01
☐ 283 Billy Ripken .10 .05 .01
☐ 284 Craig Reynolds .10 .05 .01
☐ 285 Robin Yount .75 .35 .09
☐ 286 Jimmy Jones .10 .05 .01
☐ 287 Ron Oester .10 .05 .01
☐ 288 Terry Leach .10 .05 .01
☐ 289 Dennis Eckersley .35 .16 .04
☐ 290 Alan Trammell .12 .05 .02
☐ 291 Jimmy Key .12 .05 .02
☐ 292 Chris Bosio .10 .05 .01
☐ 293 Jose DeLeon .10 .05 .01
☐ 294 Jim Traber .10 .05 .01
☐ 295 Mike Scott .10 .05 .01
☐ 296 Roger McDowell .10 .05 .01
☐ 297 Garry Templeton .10 .05 .01
☐ 298 Doyle Alexander .10 .05 .01
☐ 299 Nick Esasky .10 .05 .01
☐ 300 Mark McGwire UER 1.50 .65 .19
(Doubles total 52, should be 51)
☐ 301 Darryl Hamilton .40 .18 .05
☐ 302 Dave Smith .10 .05 .01
☐ 303 Rick Sutcliffe .12 .05 .02
☐ 304 Dave Stapleton .10 .05 .01
☐ 305 Alan Ashby .10 .05 .01
☐ 306 Pedro Guerrero .12 .05 .02
☐ 307 Ron Guidry .12 .05 .02
☐ 308 Steve Farr .10 .05 .01
☐ 309 Curt Ford .10 .05 .01
☐ 310 Claudell Washington .10 .05 .01
☐ 311 Tom Prince .10 .05 .01
☐ 312 Chad Kreuter .10 .05 .01
☐ 313 Ken Oberkfell .10 .05 .01
☐ 314 Jerry Browne .10 .05 .01
☐ 315 R.J. Reynolds .10 .05 .01
☐ 316 Scott Bankhead .10 .05 .01
☐ 317 Milt Thompson .10 .05 .01
☐ 318 Mario Diaz .10 .05 .01
☐ 319 Bruce Ruffin .10 .05 .01
☐ 320 Dave Valle .10 .05 .01
☐ 321A Gary Varsho ERR 2.00 .90 .25
(Back photo actually Mike Bielecki bunting)
☐ 321B Gary Varsho COR .10 .05 .01
(In road uniform)
☐ 322 Paul Mirabella .10 .05 .01
☐ 323 Chuck Jackson .10 .05 .01
☐ 324 Drew Hall .10 .05 .01
☐ 325 Don August .10 .05 .01
☐ 326 Israel Sanchez .10 .05 .01
☐ 327 Denny Walling .10 .05 .01
☐ 328 Joel Skinner .10 .05 .01
☐ 329 Danny Tartabull .40 .18 .05
☐ 330 Tony Pena .10 .05 .01
☐ 331 Jim Sundberg .10 .05 .01
☐ 332 Jeff D. Robinson .10 .05 .01
☐ 333 Oddibe McDowell .10 .05 .01
☐ 334 Jose Lind .10 .05 .01
☐ 335 Paul Kilgus .10 .05 .01
☐ 336 Juan Samuel .10 .05 .01
☐ 337 Mike Campbell .10 .05 .01
☐ 338 Mike Maddux .10 .05 .01
☐ 339 Darnell Coles .10 .05 .01
☐ 340 Bob Dernier .10 .05 .01
☐ 341 Rafael Ramirez .10 .05 .01
☐ 342 Scott Sanderson .10 .05 .01
☐ 343 B.J. Surhoff .10 .05 .01
☐ 344 Billy Hatcher .10 .05 .01
☐ 345 Pat Perry .10 .05 .01
☐ 346 Jack Clark .12 .05 .02
☐ 347 Gary Thurman .10 .05 .01
☐ 348 Tim Jones .10 .05 .01
☐ 349 Dave Winfield .75 .35 .09
☐ 350 Frank White .10 .05 .01
☐ 351 Dave Collins .10 .05 .01
☐ 352 Jack Morris .40 .18 .05
☐ 353 Eric Plunk .10 .05 .01
☐ 354 Leon Durham .10 .05 .01
☐ 355 Ivan DeJesus .10 .05 .01
☐ 356 Brian Holman .25 .11 .03
☐ 357A Dale Murphy ERR 50.00 23.00 6.25
(Front has reverse negative)
☐ 357B Dale Murphy COR .40 .18 .05
☐ 358 Mark Portugal .10 .05 .01
☐ 359 Andy McGaffigan .10 .05 .01
☐ 360 Tom Glavine 2.00 .90 .25
☐ 361 Keith Moreland .10 .05 .01
☐ 362 Todd Stottlemyre .30 .14 .04
☐ 363 Dave Leiper .10 .05 .01
☐ 364 Cecil Fielder .90 .40 .11
☐ 365 Carmelo Martinez .10 .05 .01
☐ 366 Dwight Evans .12 .05 .02
☐ 367 Kevin McReynolds .12 .05 .02
☐ 368 Rich Gedman .10 .05 .01
☐ 369 Len Dykstra .12 .05 .02
☐ 370 Jody Reed .10 .05 .01
☐ 371 Jose Canseco UER 1.50 .65 .19
(Strikeout total 391, should be 491)
☐ 372 Rob Murphy .10 .05 .01
☐ 373 Mike Henneman .12 .05 .02
☐ 374 Walt Weiss .12 .05 .02
☐ 375 Rob Dibble .50 .23 .06
☐ 376 Kirby Puckett 1.50 .65 .19
(Mark McGwire in background)
☐ 377 Dennis Martinez .12 .05 .02
☐ 378 Ron Gant 1.75 .80 .22
☐ 379 Brian Harper .12 .05 .02
☐ 380 Nelson Santovenia .10 .05 .01
☐ 381 Lloyd Moseby .10 .05 .01
☐ 382 Lance McCullers .10 .05 .01
☐ 383 Dave Stieb .12 .05 .02
☐ 384 Tony Gwynn .90 .40 .11
☐ 385 Mike Flanagan .10 .05 .01
☐ 386 Bob Ojeda .10 .05 .01
☐ 387 Bruce Hurst .12 .05 .02
☐ 388 Dave Magadan .12 .05 .02
☐ 389 Wade Boggs .75 .35 .09
☐ 390 Gary Carter .12 .05 .02
☐ 391 Frank Tanana .10 .05 .01
☐ 392 Curt Young .10 .05 .01
☐ 393 Jeff Treadway .10 .05 .01
☐ 394 Darrell Evans .12 .05 .02
☐ 395 Glenn Hubbard .10 .05 .01
☐ 396 Chuck Cary .10 .05 .01
☐ 397 Frank Viola .12 .05 .02
☐ 398 Jeff Parrett .10 .05 .01
☐ 399 Terry Blocker .10 .05 .01
☐ 400 Dan Gladden .10 .05 .01
☐ 401 Louie Meadows .10 .05 .01
☐ 402 Tim Raines .12 .05 .02
☐ 403 Joey Meyer .10 .05 .01
☐ 404 Larry Andersen .10 .05 .01
☐ 405 Rex Hudler .10 .05 .01
☐ 406 Mike Schmidt 1.50 .65 .19
☐ 407 John Franco .12 .05 .02
☐ 408 Brady Anderson 1.75 .80 .22
☐ 409 Don Carman .10 .05 .01
☐ 410 Eric Davis .35 .16 .04
☐ 411 Bob Stanley .10 .05 .01
☐ 412 Pete Smith .35 .16 .04
☐ 413 Jim Rice .12 .05 .02
☐ 414 Bruce Sutter .12 .05 .02
☐ 415 Oil Can Boyd .10 .05 .01
☐ 416 Ruben Sierra 1.00 .45 .13
☐ 417 Mike LaValliere .10 .05 .01
☐ 418 Steve Buechele .10 .05 .01
☐ 419 Gary Redus .10 .05 .01
☐ 420 Scott Fletcher .10 .05 .01
☐ 421 Dale Sveum .10 .05 .01
☐ 422 Bob Knepper .10 .05 .01
☐ 423 Luis Rivera .10 .05 .01
☐ 424 Ted Higuera .10 .05 .01
☐ 425 Kevin Bass .10 .05 .01
☐ 426 Ken Gerhart .10 .05 .01
☐ 427 Shane Rawley .10 .05 .01
☐ 428 Paul O'Neill .12 .05 .02
☐ 429 Joe Orsulak .10 .05 .01
☐ 430 Jackie Gutierrez .10 .05 .01
☐ 431 Gerald Perry .10 .05 .01
☐ 432 Mike Greenwell .12 .05 .02
☐ 433 Jerry Royster .10 .05 .01
☐ 434 Ellis Burks .12 .05 .02
☐ 435 Ed Olwine .10 .05 .01
☐ 436 Dave Rucker .10 .05 .01
☐ 437 Charlie Hough .10 .05 .01
☐ 438 Bob Walk .10 .05 .01
☐ 439 Bob Brower .10 .05 .01
☐ 440 Barry Bonds 1.50 .65 .19
☐ 441 Tom Foley .10 .05 .01
☐ 442 Rob Deer .12 .05 .02
☐ 443 Glenn Davis .12 .05 .02
☐ 444 Dave Martinez .12 .05 .02
☐ 445 Bill Wegman .10 .05 .01
☐ 446 Lloyd McClendon .10 .05 .01
☐ 447 Dave Schmidt .10 .05 .01
☐ 448 Darren Daulton .12 .05 .02
☐ 449 Frank Williams .10 .05 .01
☐ 450 Don Aase .10 .05 .01
☐ 451 Lou Whitaker .12 .05 .02
☐ 452 Goose Gossage .12 .05 .02

☐ 453 Ed Whitson .10 .05 .01
☐ 454 Jim Walewander .10 .05 .01
☐ 455 Damon Berryhill .10 .05 .01
☐ 456 Tim Burke .10 .05 .01
☐ 457 Barry Jones .10 .05 .01
☐ 458 Joel Youngblood .10 .05 .01
☐ 459 Floyd Youmans .10 .05 .01
☐ 460 Mark Salas .10 .05 .01
☐ 461 Jeff Russell .10 .05 .01
☐ 462 Darrell Miller .10 .05 .01
☐ 463 Jeff Kunkel .10 .05 .01
☐ 464 Sherman Corbett .10 .05 .01
☐ 465 Curtis Wilkerson .10 .05 .01
☐ 466 Bud Black .10 .05 .01
☐ 467 Cal Ripken 2.00 .90 .25
☐ 468 John Farrell .10 .05 .01
☐ 469 Terry Kennedy .10 .05 .01
☐ 470 Tom Candiotti .10 .05 .01
☐ 471 Roberto Alomar 5.00 2.30 .60
☐ 472 Jeff M. Robinson .10 .05 .01
☐ 473 Vance Law .10 .05 .01
☐ 474 Randy Ready UER .10 .05 .01
(Strikeout total 136, should be 115)
☐ 475 Walt Terrell .10 .05 .01
☐ 476 Kelly Downs .10 .05 .01
☐ 477 Johnny Paredes .10 .05 .01
☐ 478 Shawn Hillegas .10 .05 .01
☐ 479 Bob Brenly .10 .05 .01
☐ 480 Otis Nixon .12 .05 .02
☐ 481 Johnny Ray .10 .05 .01
☐ 482 Geno Petralli .10 .05 .01
☐ 483 Stu Cliburn .10 .05 .01
☐ 484 Pete Incaviglia .10 .05 .01
☐ 485 Brian Downing .10 .05 .01
☐ 486 Jeff Stone .10 .05 .01
☐ 487 Carmen Castillo .10 .05 .01
☐ 488 Tom Niedenfuer .10 .05 .01
☐ 489 Jay Bell .12 .05 .02
☐ 490 Rick Schu .10 .05 .01
☐ 491 Jeff Pico .10 .05 .01
☐ 492 Mark Parent .10 .05 .01
☐ 493 Eric King .10 .05 .01
☐ 494 Al Nipper .10 .05 .01
☐ 495 Andy Hawkins .10 .05 .01
☐ 496 Daryl Boston .10 .05 .01
☐ 497 Ernie Riles .10 .05 .01
☐ 498 Pascual Perez .10 .05 .01
☐ 499 Bill Long UER .10 .05 .01
(Games started total 70, should be 44)
☐ 500 Kirt Manwaring .10 .05 .01
☐ 501 Chuck Crim .10 .05 .01
☐ 502 Candy Maldonado .10 .05 .01
☐ 503 Dennis Lamp .10 .05 .01
☐ 504 Glenn Braggs .10 .05 .01
☐ 505 Joe Price .10 .05 .01
☐ 506 Ken Williams .10 .05 .01
☐ 507 Bill Pecota .10 .05 .01
☐ 508 Rey Quinones .10 .05 .01
☐ 509 Jeff Bittiger .10 .05 .01
☐ 510 Kevin Seitzer .12 .05 .02
☐ 511 Steve Bedrosian .10 .05 .01
☐ 512 Todd Worrell .12 .05 .02
☐ 513 Chris James .10 .05 .01
☐ 514 Jose Oquendo .10 .05 .01
☐ 515 David Palmer .10 .05 .01
☐ 516 John Smiley .12 .05 .02
☐ 517 Dave Clark .10 .05 .01
☐ 518 Mike Dunne .10 .05 .01
☐ 519 Ron Washington .10 .05 .01
☐ 520 Bob Kipper .10 .05 .01
☐ 521 Lee Smith .12 .05 .02
☐ 522 Juan Castillo .10 .05 .01
☐ 523 Don Robinson .10 .05 .01
☐ 524 Kevin Romine .10 .05 .01
☐ 525 Paul Molitor .35 .16 .04
☐ 526 Mark Langston .12 .05 .02
☐ 527 Donnie Hill .10 .05 .01
☐ 528 Larry Owen .10 .05 .01
☐ 529 Jerry Reed .10 .05 .01
☐ 530 Jack McDowell 1.50 .65 .19
☐ 531 Greg Mathews .10 .05 .01
☐ 532 John Russell .10 .05 .01
☐ 533 Dan Quisenberry .12 .05 .02
☐ 534 Greg Gross .10 .05 .01
☐ 535 Danny Cox .10 .05 .01
☐ 536 Terry Francona .10 .05 .01
☐ 537 Andy Van Slyke .30 .14 .04
☐ 538 Mel Hall .10 .05 .01
☐ 539 Jim Gott .10 .05 .01
☐ 540 Doug Jones .12 .05 .02
☐ 541 Craig Lefferts .10 .05 .01
☐ 542 Mike Boddicker .10 .05 .01
☐ 543 Greg Brock .10 .05 .01
☐ 544 Atlee Hammaker .10 .05 .01
☐ 545 Tom Bolton .10 .05 .01
☐ 546 Mike Macfarlane .40 .18 .05
☐ 547 Rich Renteria .10 .05 .01
☐ 548 John Davis .10 .05 .01
☐ 549 Floyd Bannister .10 .05 .01
☐ 550 Mickey Brantley .10 .05 .01
☐ 551 Duane Ward .12 .05 .02
☐ 552 Dan Petry .10 .05 .01
☐ 553 Mickey Tettleton UER .12 .05 .02
(Walks total 175, should be 136)
☐ 554 Rick Leach .10 .05 .01
☐ 555 Mike Witt .10 .05 .01
☐ 556 Sid Bream .10 .05 .01
☐ 557 Bobby Witt .12 .05 .02
☐ 558 Tommy Herr .10 .05 .01
☐ 559 Randy Milligan .10 .05 .01
☐ 560 Jose Cecena .10 .05 .01
☐ 561 Mackey Sasser .10 .05 .01
☐ 562 Carney Lansford .12 .05 .02
☐ 563 Rick Aguilera .12 .05 .02
☐ 564 Ron Hassey .10 .05 .01
☐ 565 Dwight Gooden .35 .16 .04
☐ 566 Paul Assenmacher .10 .05 .01
☐ 567 Neil Allen .10 .05 .01
☐ 568 Jim Morrison .10 .05 .01
☐ 569 Mike Pagliarulo .10 .05 .01
☐ 570 Ted Simmons .12 .05 .02
☐ 571 Mark Thurmond .10 .05 .01
☐ 572 Fred McGriff .90 .40 .11
☐ 573 Wally Joyner .15 .07 .02
☐ 574 Jose Bautista .10 .05 .01
☐ 575 Kelly Gruber .12 .05 .02
☐ 576 Cecilio Guante .10 .05 .01
☐ 577 Mark Davidson .10 .05 .01
☐ 578 Bobby Bonilla UER .60 .25 .08
(Total steals 2 in '87, should be 3)
☐ 579 Mike Stanley .10 .05 .01
☐ 580 Gene Larkin .10 .05 .01
☐ 581 Stan Javier .10 .05 .01
☐ 582 Howard Johnson .12 .05 .02
☐ 583A Mike Gallego ERR 1.25 .55 .16
(Front reversed negative)
☐ 583B Mike Gallego COR .25 .11 .03
☐ 584 David Cone .60 .25 .08
☐ 585 Doug Jennings .10 .05 .01
☐ 586 Charles Hudson .10 .05 .01
☐ 587 Dion James .10 .05 .01
☐ 588 Al Leiter .10 .05 .01
☐ 589 Charlie Puleo .10 .05 .01
☐ 590 Roberto Kelly .60 .25 .08
☐ 591 Thad Bosley .10 .05 .01
☐ 592 Pete Stanicek .10 .05 .01
☐ 593 Pat Borders .60 .25 .08
☐ 594 Bryan Harvey .60 .25 .08
☐ 595 Jeff Ballard .10 .05 .01
☐ 596 Jeff Reardon .12 .05 .02
☐ 597 Doug Drabek .12 .05 .02
☐ 598 Edwin Correa .10 .05 .01
☐ 599 Keith Atherton .10 .05 .01
☐ 600 Dave LaPoint .10 .05 .01
☐ 601 Don Baylor .12 .05 .02
☐ 602 Tom Pagnozzi .10 .05 .01
☐ 603 Tim Flannery .10 .05 .01
☐ 604 Gene Walter .10 .05 .01
☐ 605 Dave Parker .12 .05 .02
☐ 606 Mike Diaz .10 .05 .01
☐ 607 Chris Gwynn .10 .05 .01
☐ 608 Odell Jones .10 .05 .01
☐ 609 Carlton Fisk .50 .23 .06
☐ 610 Jay Howell .10 .05 .01
☐ 611 Tim Crews .10 .05 .01
☐ 612 Keith Hernandez .12 .05 .02
☐ 613 Willie Fraser .10 .05 .01
☐ 614 Jim Eppard .10 .05 .01
☐ 615 Jeff Hamilton .10 .05 .01
☐ 616 Kurt Stillwell .10 .05 .01
☐ 617 Tom Browning .10 .05 .01
☐ 618 Jeff Montgomery .12 .05 .02
☐ 619 Jose Rijo .12 .05 .02
☐ 620 Jamie Quirk .10 .05 .01
☐ 621 Willie McGee .12 .05 .02
☐ 622 Mark Grant UER .10 .05 .01
(Glove on wrong hand)
☐ 623 Bill Swift .12 .05 .02
☐ 624 Orlando Mercado .10 .05 .01
☐ 625 John Costello .10 .05 .01
☐ 626 Jose Gonzalez .10 .05 .01

Card			
☐ 627A Bill Schroeder ERR	1.25	.55	.16
(Back photo actually Ronn Reynolds buckling shin guards)			
☐ 627B Bill Schroeder COR	.25	.11	.03
☐ 628A Fred Manrique ERR	.35	.16	.04
(Back photo actually Ozzie Guillen throwing)			
☐ 628B Fred Manrique COR	.10	.05	.01
(Swinging bat on back)			
☐ 629 Ricky Horton	.10	.05	.01
☐ 630 Dan Plesac	.10	.05	.01
☐ 631 Alfredo Griffin	.10	.05	.01
☐ 632 Chuck Finley	.12	.05	.02
☐ 633 Kirk Gibson	.12	.05	.02
☐ 634 Randy Myers	.12	.05	.02
☐ 635 Greg Minton	.10	.05	.01
☐ 636A Herm Winningham ERR (W1nningham on back)	.35	.16	.04
☐ 636B Herm Winningham COR	.10	.05	.01
☐ 637 Charlie Leibrandt	.10	.05	.01
☐ 638 Tim Birtsas	.10	.05	.01
☐ 639 Bill Buckner	.12	.05	.02
☐ 640 Danny Jackson	.10	.05	.01
☐ 641 Greg Booker	.10	.05	.01
☐ 642 Jim Presley	.10	.05	.01
☐ 643 Gene Nelson	.10	.05	.01
☐ 644 Rod Booker	.10	.05	.01
☐ 645 Dennis Rasmussen	.10	.05	.01
☐ 646 Juan Nieves	.10	.05	.01
☐ 647 Bobby Thigpen	.10	.05	.01
☐ 648 Tim Belcher	.12	.05	.02
☐ 649 Mike Young	.10	.05	.01
☐ 650 Ivan Calderon	.10	.05	.01
☐ 651 Oswaldo Peraza	.10	.05	.01
☐ 652A Pat Sheridan ERR	15.00	6.75	1.90
(No position on front)			
☐ 652B Pat Sheridan COR	.10	.05	.01
☐ 653 Mike Morgan	.12	.05	.02
☐ 654 Mike Heath	.10	.05	.01
☐ 655 Jay Tibbs	.10	.05	.01
☐ 656 Fernando Valenzuela	.12	.05	.02
☐ 657 Lee Mazzilli	.10	.05	.01
☐ 658 AL CY:Frank Viola	.12	.05	.02
☐ 659A AL MVP:Jose Canseco	.50	.23	.06
(Eagle logo in black)			
☐ 659B AL MVP:Jose Canseco	.50	.23	.06
(Eagle logo in blue)			
☐ 660 AL ROY:Walt Weiss	.12	.05	.02
☐ 661 NL CY:Orel Hershiser	.12	.05	.02
☐ 662 NL MVP:Kirk Gibson	.12	.05	.02
☐ 663 NL ROY:Chris Sabo	.20	.09	.03
☐ 664 ALCS MVP:D.Eckersley	.15	.07	.02
☐ 665 NLCS MVP:O.Hershiser	.12	.05	.02
☐ 666 Great WS Moment	.12	.05	.02
(Kirk Gibson's homer)			
☐ 667 WS MVP:Orel Hershiser	.12	.05	.02
☐ 668 Angels Checklist	.10	.05	.01
Wally Joyner			
☐ 669 Astros Checklist	.90	.40	.11
Nolan Ryan			
☐ 670 Athletics Checklist	.40	.18	.05
Jose Canseco			
☐ 671 Blue Jays Checklist	.25	.11	.03
Fred McGriff			
☐ 672 Braves Checklist	.15	.07	.02
Dale Murphy			
☐ 673 Brewers Checklist	.12	.05	.02
Paul Molitor			
☐ 674 Cardinals Checklist	.20	.09	.03
Ozzie Smith			
☐ 675 Cubs Checklist	.40	.18	.05
Ryne Sandberg			
☐ 676 Dodgers Checklist	.10	.05	.01
Kirk Gibson			
☐ 677 Expos Checklist	.10	.05	.01
Andres Galarraga			
☐ 678 Giants Checklist	.40	.18	.05
Will Clark			
☐ 679 Indians Checklist	.10	.05	.01
Cory Snyder			
☐ 680 Mariners Checklist	.10	.05	.01
Alvin Davis			
☐ 681 Mets Checklist	.25	.11	.03
Darryl Strawberry			
☐ 682 Orioles Checklist	.50	.23	.06
Cal Ripken			
☐ 683 Padres Checklist	.25	.11	.03
Tony Gwynn			
☐ 684 Phillies Checklist	.50	.23	.06
Mike Schmidt			
☐ 685 Pirates Checklist	.12	.05	.02
Andy Van Slyke UER (96 Junior Ortiz)			
☐ 686 Rangers Checklist	.25	.11	.03
Ruben Sierra			
☐ 687 Red Sox Checklist	.25	.11	.03
Wade Boggs			
☐ 688 Reds Checklist	.15	.07	.02
Eric Davis			
☐ 689 Royals Checklist	.20	.09	.03
George Brett			
☐ 690 Tigers Checklist	.12	.05	.02
Alan Trammell			
☐ 691 Twins Checklist	.10	.05	.01
Frank Viola			
☐ 692 White Sox Checklist	.10	.05	.01
Harold Baines			
☐ 693 Yankees Checklist	.25	.11	.03
Don Mattingly			
☐ 694 Checklist 1-100	.10	.01	.00
☐ 695 Checklist 101-200	.10	.01	.00
☐ 696 Checklist 201-300	.10	.01	.00
☐ 697 Checklist 301-400	.10	.01	.00
☐ 698 Checklist 401-500 UER	.10	.01	.00
(467 Cal Ripkin Jr.)			
☐ 699 Checklist 501-600 UER	.10	.01	.00
(543 Greg Booker)			
☐ 700 Checklist 601-700	.10	.01	.00
☐ 701 Checklist 701-800	.10	.01	.00
☐ 702 Jesse Barfield	.10	.05	.01
☐ 703 Walt Terrell	.10	.05	.01
☐ 704 Dickie Thon	.10	.05	.01
☐ 705 Al Leiter	.10	.05	.01
☐ 706 Dave LaPoint	.10	.05	.01
☐ 707 Charlie Hayes	.50	.23	.06
☐ 708 Andy Hawkins	.10	.05	.01
☐ 709 Mickey Hatcher	.10	.05	.01
☐ 710 Lance McCullers	.10	.05	.01
☐ 711 Ron Kittle	.10	.05	.01
☐ 712 Bert Blyleven	.12	.05	.02
☐ 713 Rick Dempsey	.10	.05	.01
☐ 714 Ken Williams	.10	.05	.01
☐ 715 Steve Rosenberg	.10	.05	.01
☐ 716 Joe Skalski	.10	.05	.01
☐ 717 Spike Owen	.10	.05	.01
☐ 718 Todd Burns	.10	.05	.01
☐ 719 Kevin Gross	.10	.05	.01
☐ 720 Tommy Herr	.10	.05	.01
☐ 721 Rob Ducey	.10	.05	.01
☐ 722 Gary Green	.10	.05	.01
☐ 723 Gregg Olson	1.50	.65	.19
☐ 724 Greg W. Harris	.25	.11	.03
☐ 725 Craig Worthington	.10	.05	.01
☐ 726 Tom Howard	.40	.18	.05
☐ 727 Dale Mohorcic	.10	.05	.01
☐ 728 Rich Yett	.10	.05	.01
☐ 729 Mel Hall	.10	.05	.01
☐ 730 Floyd Youmans	.10	.05	.01
☐ 731 Lonnie Smith	.10	.05	.01
☐ 732 Wally Backman	.10	.05	.01
☐ 733 Trevor Wilson	.30	.14	.04
☐ 734 Jose Alvarez	.10	.05	.01
☐ 735 Bob Milacki	.20	.09	.03
☐ 736 Tom Gordon	.25	.11	.03
☐ 737 Wally Whitehurst	.12	.05	.02
☐ 738 Mike Aldrete	.10	.05	.01
☐ 739 Keith Miller	.10	.05	.01
☐ 740 Randy Milligan	.10	.05	.01
☐ 741 Jeff Parrett	.10	.05	.01
☐ 742 Steve Finley	.90	.40	.11
☐ 743 Junior Felix	.50	.23	.06
☐ 744 Pete Harnisch	.50	.23	.06
☐ 745 Bill Spiers	.15	.07	.02
☐ 746 Hensley Meulens	.25	.11	.03
☐ 747 Juan Bell	.15	.07	.02
☐ 748 Steve Sax	.12	.05	.02
☐ 749 Phil Bradley	.10	.05	.01
☐ 750 Rey Quinones	.10	.05	.01
☐ 751 Tommy Gregg	.10	.05	.01
☐ 752 Kevin Brown	.50	.23	.06
☐ 753 Derek Lilliquist	.15	.07	.02
☐ 754 Todd Zeile	1.25	.55	.16
☐ 755 Jim Abbott	4.00	1.80	.50
(Triple exposure)			
☐ 756 Ozzie Canseco	.35	.16	.04
☐ 757 Nick Esasky	.10	.05	.01
☐ 758 Mike Moore	.10	.05	.01
☐ 759 Rob Murphy	.10	.05	.01
☐ 760 Rick Mahler	.10	.05	.01
☐ 761 Fred Lynn	.12	.05	.02
☐ 762 Kevin Blankenship	.10	.05	.01
☐ 763 Eddie Murray	.50	.23	.06
☐ 764 Steve Searcy	.10	.05	.01
☐ 765 Jerome Walton	.20	.09	.03
☐ 766 Erik Hanson	.50	.23	.06

	MT	EX-MT	VG
☐ 767 Bob Boone	.12	.05	.02
☐ 768 Edgar Martinez	1.50	.65	.19
☐ 769 Jose DeJesus	.10	.05	.01
☐ 770 Greg Briley	.15	.07	.02
☐ 771 Steve Peters	.10	.05	.01
☐ 772 Rafael Palmeiro	.75	.35	.09
☐ 773 Jack Clark	.12	.05	.02
☐ 774 Nolan Ryan (Throwing football)	4.00	1.80	.50
☐ 775 Lance Parrish	.12	.05	.02
☐ 776 Joe Girardi	.20	.09	.03
☐ 777 Willie Randolph	.12	.05	.02
☐ 778 Mitch Williams	.12	.05	.02
☐ 779 Dennis Cook	.12	.05	.02
☐ 780 Dwight Smith	.20	.09	.03
☐ 781 Lenny Harris	.30	.14	.04
☐ 782 Torey Lovullo	.10	.05	.01
☐ 783 Norm Charlton	.50	.23	.06
☐ 784 Chris Brown	.10	.05	.01
☐ 785 Todd Benzinger	.10	.05	.01
☐ 786 Shane Rawley	.10	.05	.01
☐ 787 Omar Vizquel	.35	.16	.04
☐ 788 LaVel Freeman	.10	.05	.01
☐ 789 Jeffrey Leonard	.10	.05	.01
☐ 790 Eddie Williams	.10	.05	.01
☐ 791 Jamie Moyer	.10	.05	.01
☐ 792 Bruce Hurst UER (Workd Series)	.12	.05	.02
☐ 793 Julio Franco	.12	.05	.02
☐ 794 Claudell Washington	.10	.05	.01
☐ 795 Jody Davis	.10	.05	.01
☐ 796 Oddibe McDowell	.10	.05	.01
☐ 797 Paul Kilgus	.10	.05	.01
☐ 798 Tracy Jones	.10	.05	.01
☐ 799 Steve Wilson	.10	.05	.01
☐ 800 Pete O'Brien	.12	.05	.02

1990 Upper Deck

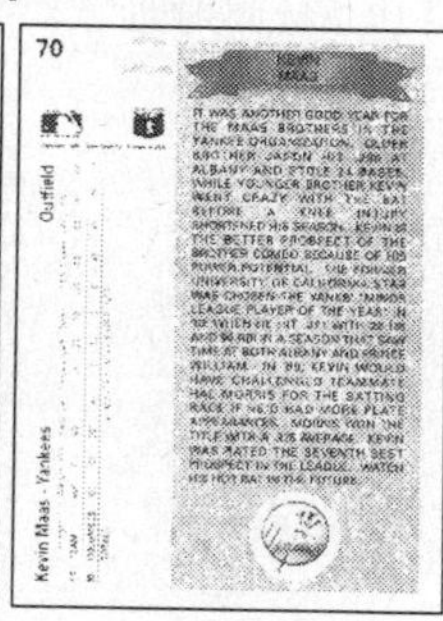

The 1990 Upper Deck set contains 800 standard-size (2 1/2" by 3 1/2") cards issued in two series, low numbers (1-700) and high numbers (701-800). The front and back borders are white, and both sides feature full-color photos. The horizontally oriented backs have recent stats and anti-counterfeiting holograms. Unlike the 1989 Upper Deck set, the team checklist cards are not grouped numerically at the end of the set, but are mixed in with the first 100 cards. The key Rookie Cards in the first series are Juan Gonzalez, Marquis Grissom, Kevin Maas, Ben McDonald, John Olerud, Dean Palmer, and Larry Walker. Cards 101 through 199 have two minor varieties in that the cards either show or omit "Copyright" 1990 Upper Deck Co. Printed in USA below the two licensing logos. Those without are considered minor errors; they were found in the High Number foil packs. The 1990 Upper Deck Extended Set (of high numbers) was issued in July 1990. The cards were in the same style as the first 700 cards of the 1990 Upper Deck set and were issued either as a separate set in its own collectors box, as part of the complete 1-800 factory set, as well as mixed in with the earlier numbered Upper Deck cards in late-season wax packs. The series also contains a Nolan Ryan variation; all cards produced before August 12th only discuss Ryan's sixth no-hitter while the later-issue cards include a stripe honoring Ryan's 300th victory. The key Rookie Cards in the extended or high-number series are Carlos Baerga, Alex Cole, Delino DeShields, Dave Hollins, Dave Justice, and Ray Lankford. Card 702 was originally scheduled to be Mike Witt. A few 702 Witt cards and checklist cards showing 702 Witt escaped into early packs; they are characterized by a black rectangle covering much of the card's back.

	MT	EX-MT	VG
COMPLETE SET (800)	45.00	20.00	5.75
COMPLETE FACT.SET (800)	50.00	23.00	6.25
COMPLETE LO SET (700)	35.00	16.00	4.40
COMPLETE HI SET (100)	10.00	4.50	1.25
COMPLETE HI FACT.SET (100)	10.00	4.50	1.25
COMMON PLAYER (1-700)	.05	.02	.01
COMMON PLAYER (701-800)	.05	.02	.01

	MT	EX-MT	VG
☐ 1 Star Rookie Checklist	.06	.01	.00
☐ 2 Randy Nosek	.05	.02	.01
☐ 3 Tom Drees UER (11th line, hulred, should be hurled)	.05	.02	.01
☐ 4 Curt Young	.05	.02	.01
☐ 5 Devon White TC California Angels	.06	.03	.01
☐ 6 Luis Salazar	.05	.02	.01
☐ 7 Von Hayes TC Philadelphia Phillies	.06	.03	.01
☐ 8 Jose Bautista	.05	.02	.01
☐ 9 Marquis Grissom	2.00	.90	.25
☐ 10 Orel Hershiser TC Los Angeles Dodgers	.06	.03	.01
☐ 11 Rick Aguilera	.08	.04	.01
☐ 12 Benito Santiago TC San Diego Padres	.06	.03	.01
☐ 13 Deion Sanders	1.50	.65	.19
☐ 14 Marvell Wynne	.05	.02	.01
☐ 15 Dave West	.05	.02	.01
☐ 16 Bobby Bonilla TC Pittsburgh Pirates	.10	.05	.01
☐ 17 Sammy Sosa	.30	.14	.04
☐ 18 Steve Sax TC New York Yankees	.06	.03	.01
☐ 19 Jack Howell	.05	.02	.01
☐ 20 Mike Schmidt Special UER (Suprising, should be surprising)	.50	.23	.06
☐ 21 Robin Ventura UER (Samta Maria)	2.50	1.15	.30
☐ 22 Brian Meyer	.05	.02	.01
☐ 23 Blaine Beatty	.05	.02	.01
☐ 24 Ken Griffey Jr. TC Seattle Mariners	.50	.23	.06
☐ 25 Greg Vaughn UER (Association misspelled as assiocation)	.50	.23	.06
☐ 26 Xavier Hernandez	.15	.07	.02
☐ 27 Jason Grimsley	.15	.07	.02
☐ 28 Eric Anthony UER (Ashville, should be Asheville)	.60	.25	.08
☐ 29 Tim Raines TC Montreal Expos UER (Wallach listed before Walker)	.06	.03	.01
☐ 30 David Wells	.08	.04	.01
☐ 31 Hal Morris	.50	.23	.06
☐ 32 Bo Jackson TC Kansas City Royals	.20	.09	.03
☐ 33 Kelly Mann	.05	.02	.01
☐ 34 Nolan Ryan Special	1.00	.45	.13
☐ 35 Scott Service UER (Born Cincinatti on 7/27/67, should be Cincinnati 2/27)	.05	.02	.01
☐ 36 Mark McGwire TC Oakland A's	.20	.09	.03
☐ 37 Tino Martinez	.40	.18	.05
☐ 38 Chili Davis	.08	.04	.01
☐ 39 Scott Sanderson	.05	.02	.01
☐ 40 Kevin Mitchell TC San Francisco Giants	.10	.05	.01
☐ 41 Lou Whitaker TC Detroit Tigers	.06	.03	.01
☐ 42 Scott Coolbaugh UER (Definately)	.05	.02	.01
☐ 43 Jose Cano UER	.05	.02	.01

(Born 9/7/62, should be 3/7/62)			
☐ 44 Jose Vizcaino	.15	.07	.02
☐ 45 Bob Hamelin	.15	.07	.02
☐ 46 Jose Offerman UER	.40	.18	.05
(Posesses)			
☐ 47 Kevin Blankenship	.05	.02	.01
☐ 48 Kirby Puckett TC	.20	.09	.03
Minnesota Twins			
☐ 49 Tommy Greene UER	.25	.11	.03
(Livest, should be liveliest)			
☐ 50 Will Clark Special	.30	.14	.04
UER (Perenial, should be perennial)			
☐ 51 Rob Nelson	.05	.02	.01
☐ 52 Chris Hammond UER	.40	.18	.05
(Chatanooga)			
☐ 53 Joe Carter TC	.15	.07	.02
Cleveland Indians			
☐ 54A Ben McDonald ERR	20.00	9.00	2.50
(No Rookie designation on card front)			
☐ 54B Ben McDonald COR	1.50	.65	.19
☐ 55 Andy Benes UER	.75	.35	.09
(Whichita)			
☐ 56 John Olerud	2.00	.90	.25
☐ 57 Roger Clemens TC	.30	.14	.04
Boston Red Sox			
☐ 58 Tony Armas	.05	.02	.01
☐ 59 George Canale	.05	.02	.01
☐ 60A Mickey Tettleton TC ERR	2.50	1.15	.30
Baltimore Orioles			
(683 Jamie Weston)			
☐ 60B Mickey Tettleton TC COR	.08	.04	.01
Baltimore Orioles			
(683 Mickey Weston)			
☐ 61 Mike Stanton	.30	.14	.04
☐ 62 Dwight Gooden TC	.10	.05	.01
New York Mets			
☐ 63 Kent Mercker UER	.25	.11	.03
(Albuguerque)			
☐ 64 Francisco Cabrera	.20	.09	.03
☐ 65 Steve Avery UER	2.50	1.15	.30
(Born NJ, should be MI, Merker should be Mercker)			
☐ 66 Jose Canseco	.60	.25	.08
☐ 67 Matt Merullo	.05	.02	.01
☐ 68 Vince Coleman TC	.06	.03	.01
St. Louis Cardinals			
UER (Guererro)			
☐ 69 Ron Karkovice	.05	.02	.01
☐ 70 Kevin Maas	.60	.25	.08
☐ 71 Dennis Cook UER	.05	.02	.01
(Shown with righty glove on card back)			
☐ 72 Juan Gonzalez UER	8.00	3.60	1.00
(135 games for Tulsa in '89, should be 133)			
☐ 73 Andre Dawson TC	.10	.05	.01
Chicago Cubs			
☐ 74 Dean Palmer UER	1.75	.80	.22
(Permanent misspelled as perminant)			
☐ 75 Bo Jackson Special	.25	.11	.03
UER (Monsterous, should be monstrous)			
☐ 76 Rob Richie	.05	.02	.01
☐ 77 Bobby Rose UER	.08	.04	.01
(Pickin, should be pick in)			
☐ 78 Brian DuBois UER	.05	.02	.01
(Commiting)			
☐ 79 Ozzie Guillen TC	.06	.03	.01
Chicago White Sox			
☐ 80 Gene Nelson	.05	.02	.01
☐ 81 Bob McClure	.05	.02	.01
☐ 82 Julio Franco TC	.06	.03	.01
Texas Rangers			
☐ 83 Greg Minton	.05	.02	.01
☐ 84 John Smoltz TC UER	.12	.05	.02
Atlanta Braves			
(Oddibe not Odibbe)			
☐ 85 Willie Fraser	.05	.02	.01
☐ 86 Neal Heaton	.05	.02	.01
☐ 87 Kevin Tapani	.90	.40	.11
☐ 88 Mike Scott TC	.06	.03	.01
Houston Astros			
☐ 89A Jim Gott ERR	6.00	2.70	.75
(Photo actually Rick Reed)			
☐ 89B Jim Gott COR	.08	.04	.01
☐ 90 Lance Johnson	.08	.04	.01
☐ 91 Robin Yount TC UER	.10	.05	.01
Milwaukee Brewers			
(Checklist on back has 178 Rob Deer and 176 Mike Felder)			
☐ 92 Jeff Parrett	.05	.02	.01
☐ 93 Julio Machado UER	.05	.02	.01
(Valenzuelan, should be Venezuelan)			
☐ 94 Ron Jones	.05	.02	.01
☐ 95 George Bell TC	.05	.02	.01
Toronto Blue Jays			
☐ 96 Jerry Reuss	.05	.02	.01
☐ 97 Brian Fisher	.05	.02	.01
☐ 98 Kevin Ritz UER	.12	.05	.02
(Amercian)			
☐ 99 Barry Larkin TC	.10	.05	.01
Cincinnati Reds			
☐ 100 Checklist 1-100	.06	.01	.00
☐ 101 Gerald Perry	.05	.02	.01
☐ 102 Kevin Appier	.90	.40	.11
☐ 103 Julio Franco	.08	.04	.01
☐ 104 Craig Biggio	.15	.07	.02
☐ 105 Bo Jackson UER	.30	.14	.04
('89 BA wrong, should be .256)			
☐ 106 Junior Felix	.08	.04	.01
☐ 107 Mike Harkey	.08	.04	.01
☐ 108 Fred McGriff	.40	.18	.05
☐ 109 Rick Sutcliffe	.08	.04	.01
☐ 110 Pete O'Brien	.05	.02	.01
☐ 111 Kelly Gruber	.08	.04	.01
☐ 112 Dwight Evans	.08	.04	.01
☐ 113 Pat Borders	.08	.04	.01
☐ 114 Dwight Gooden	.12	.05	.02
☐ 115 Kevin Batiste	.20	.09	.03
☐ 116 Eric Davis	.12	.05	.02
☐ 117 Kevin Mitchell UER	.15	.07	.02
(Career HR total 99, should be 100)			
☐ 118 Ron Oester	.05	.02	.01
☐ 119 Brett Butler	.08	.04	.01
☐ 120 Danny Jackson	.05	.02	.01
☐ 121 Tommy Gregg	.05	.02	.01
☐ 122 Ken Caminiti	.08	.04	.01
☐ 123 Kevin Brown	.25	.11	.03
☐ 124 George Brett UER	.30	.14	.04
(133 runs, should be 1300)			
☐ 125 Mike Scott	.05	.02	.01
☐ 126 Cory Snyder	.05	.02	.01
☐ 127 George Bell	.08	.04	.01
☐ 128 Mark Grace	.35	.16	.04
☐ 129 Devon White	.08	.04	.01
☐ 130 Tony Fernandez	.08	.04	.01
☐ 131 Don Aase	.05	.02	.01
☐ 132 Rance Mulliniks	.05	.02	.01
☐ 133 Marty Barrett	.05	.02	.01
☐ 134 Nelson Liriano	.05	.02	.01
☐ 135 Mark Carreon	.05	.02	.01
☐ 136 Candy Maldonado	.05	.02	.01
☐ 137 Tim Birtsas	.05	.02	.01
☐ 138 Tom Brookens	.05	.02	.01
☐ 139 John Franco	.08	.04	.01
☐ 140 Mike LaCoss	.05	.02	.01
☐ 141 Jeff Treadway	.05	.02	.01
☐ 142 Pat Tabler	.05	.02	.01
☐ 143 Darrell Evans	.08	.04	.01
☐ 144 Rafael Ramirez	.05	.02	.01
☐ 145 Oddibe McDowell UER	.05	.02	.01
(Misspelled Odibbe)			
☐ 146 Brian Downing	.05	.02	.01
☐ 147 Curt Wilkerson	.05	.02	.01
☐ 148 Ernie Whitt	.05	.02	.01
☐ 149 Bill Schroeder	.05	.02	.01
☐ 150 Domingo Ramos UER	.05	.02	.01
(Says throws right, but shows him throwing lefty)			
☐ 151 Rick Honeycutt	.05	.02	.01
☐ 152 Don Slaught	.05	.02	.01
☐ 153 Mitch Webster	.05	.02	.01
☐ 154 Tony Phillips	.05	.02	.01
☐ 155 Paul Kilgus	.05	.02	.01
☐ 156 Ken Griffey Jr. UER	4.00	1.80	.50
(Simultaniously)			
☐ 157 Gary Sheffield	1.00	.45	.13
☐ 158 Wally Backman	.05	.02	.01
☐ 159 B.J. Surhoff	.05	.02	.01
☐ 160 Louie Meadows	.05	.02	.01
☐ 161 Paul O'Neill	.08	.04	.01
☐ 162 Jeff McKnight	.05	.02	.01
☐ 163 Alvaro Espinoza	.05	.02	.01
☐ 164 Scott Scudder	.05	.02	.01
☐ 165 Jeff Reed	.05	.02	.01

☐ 166 Gregg Jefferies	.25	.11	.03
☐ 167 Barry Larkin	.25	.11	.03
☐ 168 Gary Carter	.08	.04	.01
☐ 169 Robby Thompson	.05	.02	.01
☐ 170 Rolando Roomes	.05	.02	.01
☐ 171 Mark McGwire UER (Total games 427 and hits 479, should be 467 and 427)	.60	.25	.08
☐ 172 Steve Sax	.08	.04	.01
☐ 173 Mark Williamson	.05	.02	.01
☐ 174 Mitch Williams	.08	.04	.01
☐ 175 Brian Holton	.05	.02	.01
☐ 176 Rob Deer	.08	.04	.01
☐ 177 Tim Raines	.08	.04	.01
☐ 178 Mike Felder	.05	.02	.01
☐ 179 Harold Reynolds	.05	.02	.01
☐ 180 Terry Francona	.05	.02	.01
☐ 181 Chris Sabo	.08	.04	.01
☐ 182 Darryl Strawberry	.40	.18	.05
☐ 183 Willie Randolph	.08	.04	.01
☐ 184 Bill Ripken	.05	.02	.01
☐ 185 Mackey Sasser	.05	.02	.01
☐ 186 Todd Benzinger	.05	.02	.01
☐ 187 Kevin Elster	.05	.02	.01
☐ 188 Jose Uribe	.05	.02	.01
☐ 189 Tom Browning	.05	.02	.01
☐ 190 Keith Miller	.05	.02	.01
☐ 191 Don Mattingly	.40	.18	.05
☐ 192 Dave Parker	.08	.04	.01
☐ 193 Roberto Kelly UER (96 RBI, should be 62)	.25	.11	.03
☐ 194 Phil Bradley	.05	.02	.01
☐ 195 Ron Hassey	.05	.02	.01
☐ 196 Gerald Young	.05	.02	.01
☐ 197 Hubie Brooks	.05	.02	.01
☐ 198 Bill Doran	.05	.02	.01
☐ 199 Al Newman	.05	.02	.01
☐ 200 Checklist 101-200	.06	.01	.00
☐ 201 Terry Puhl	.05	.02	.01
☐ 202 Frank DiPino	.05	.02	.01
☐ 203 Jim Clancy	.05	.02	.01
☐ 204 Bob Ojeda	.05	.02	.01
☐ 205 Alex Trevino	.05	.02	.01
☐ 206 Dave Henderson	.05	.02	.01
☐ 207 Henry Cotto	.05	.02	.01
☐ 208 Rafael Belliard UER (Born 1961, not 1951)	.05	.02	.01
☐ 209 Stan Javier	.05	.02	.01
☐ 210 Jerry Reed	.05	.02	.01
☐ 211 Doug Dascenzo	.05	.02	.01
☐ 212 Andres Thomas	.05	.02	.01
☐ 213 Greg Maddux	.40	.18	.05
☐ 214 Mike Schooler	.05	.02	.01
☐ 215 Lonnie Smith	.05	.02	.01
☐ 216 Jose Rijo	.08	.04	.01
☐ 217 Greg Gagne	.05	.02	.01
☐ 218 Jim Gantner	.05	.02	.01
☐ 219 Allan Anderson	.05	.02	.01
☐ 220 Rick Mahler	.05	.02	.01
☐ 221 Jim Deshaies	.05	.02	.01
☐ 222 Keith Hernandez	.08	.04	.01
☐ 223 Vince Coleman	.08	.04	.01
☐ 224 David Cone	.30	.14	.04
☐ 225 Ozzie Smith	.20	.09	.03
☐ 226 Matt Nokes	.05	.02	.01
☐ 227 Barry Bonds	.60	.25	.08
☐ 228 Felix Jose	.35	.16	.04
☐ 229 Dennis Powell	.05	.02	.01
☐ 230 Mike Gallego	.05	.02	.01
☐ 231 Shawon Dunston UER ('89 stats are Andre Dawson's)	.08	.04	.01
☐ 232 Ron Gant	.60	.25	.08
☐ 233 Omar Vizquel	.08	.04	.01
☐ 234 Derek Lilliquist	.05	.02	.01
☐ 235 Erik Hanson	.08	.04	.01
☐ 236 Kirby Puckett UER (824 games, should be 924)	.60	.25	.08
☐ 237 Bill Spiers	.05	.02	.01
☐ 238 Dan Gladden	.05	.02	.01
☐ 239 Bryan Clutterbuck	.05	.02	.01
☐ 240 John Moses	.05	.02	.01
☐ 241 Ron Darling	.08	.04	.01
☐ 242 Joe Magrane	.05	.02	.01
☐ 243 Dave Magadan	.08	.04	.01
☐ 244 Pedro Guerrero UER (Misspelled Guererro)	.08	.04	.01
☐ 245 Glenn Davis	.08	.04	.01
☐ 246 Terry Steinbach	.08	.04	.01
☐ 247 Fred Lynn	.08	.04	.01
☐ 248 Gary Redus	.05	.02	.01
☐ 249 Ken Williams	.05	.02	.01
☐ 250 Sid Bream	.05	.02	.01
☐ 251 Bob Welch UER (2587 career strike-outs, should be 1587)	.08	.04	.01
☐ 252 Bill Buckner	.08	.04	.01
☐ 253 Carney Lansford	.08	.04	.01
☐ 254 Paul Molitor	.15	.07	.02
☐ 255 Jose DeJesus	.05	.02	.01
☐ 256 Orel Hershiser	.08	.04	.01
☐ 257 Tom Brunansky	.08	.04	.01
☐ 258 Mike Davis	.05	.02	.01
☐ 259 Jeff Ballard	.05	.02	.01
☐ 260 Scott Terry	.05	.02	.01
☐ 261 Sid Fernandez	.08	.04	.01
☐ 262 Mike Marshall	.05	.02	.01
☐ 263 Howard Johnson UER (192 SO, should be 592)	.08	.04	.01
☐ 264 Kirk Gibson UER (659 runs, should be 669)	.08	.04	.01
☐ 265 Kevin McReynolds	.08	.04	.01
☐ 266 Cal Ripken	1.00	.45	.13
☐ 267 Ozzie Guillen UER (Career triples 27, should be 29)	.05	.02	.01
☐ 268 Jim Traber	.05	.02	.01
☐ 269 Bobby Thigpen	.05	.02	.01
☐ 270 Joe Orsulak	.05	.02	.01
☐ 271 Bob Boone	.08	.04	.01
☐ 272 Dave Stewart UER (Totals wrong due to omission of '86 stats)	.08	.04	.01
☐ 273 Tim Wallach	.08	.04	.01
☐ 274 Luis Aquino UER (Says throws lefty, but shows him throwing righty)	.05	.02	.01
☐ 275 Mike Moore	.05	.02	.01
☐ 276 Tony Pena	.05	.02	.01
☐ 277 Eddie Murray UER (Several typos in career total stats)	.15	.07	.02
☐ 278 Milt Thompson	.05	.02	.01
☐ 279 Alejandro Pena	.05	.02	.01
☐ 280 Ken Dayley	.05	.02	.01
☐ 281 Carmen Castillo	.05	.02	.01
☐ 282 Tom Henke	.08	.04	.01
☐ 283 Mickey Hatcher	.05	.02	.01
☐ 284 Roy Smith	.05	.02	.01
☐ 285 Manny Lee	.05	.02	.01
☐ 286 Dan Pasqua	.05	.02	.01
☐ 287 Larry Sheets	.05	.02	.01
☐ 288 Garry Templeton	.05	.02	.01
☐ 289 Eddie Williams	.05	.02	.01
☐ 290 Brady Anderson	.20	.09	.03
☐ 291 Spike Owen	.05	.02	.01
☐ 292 Storm Davis	.05	.02	.01
☐ 293 Chris Bosio	.05	.02	.01
☐ 294 Jim Eisenreich	.05	.02	.01
☐ 295 Don August	.05	.02	.01
☐ 296 Jeff Hamilton	.05	.02	.01
☐ 297 Mickey Tettleton	.08	.04	.01
☐ 298 Mike Scioscia	.05	.02	.01
☐ 299 Kevin Hickey	.05	.02	.01
☐ 300 Checklist 201-300	.06	.01	.00
☐ 301 Shawn Abner	.05	.02	.01
☐ 302 Kevin Bass	.05	.02	.01
☐ 303 Bip Roberts	.08	.04	.01
☐ 304 Joe Girardi	.05	.02	.01
☐ 305 Danny Darwin	.05	.02	.01
☐ 306 Mike Heath	.05	.02	.01
☐ 307 Mike Macfarlane	.05	.02	.01
☐ 308 Ed Whitson	.05	.02	.01
☐ 309 Tracy Jones	.05	.02	.01
☐ 310 Scott Fletcher	.05	.02	.01
☐ 311 Darnell Coles	.05	.02	.01
☐ 312 Mike Brumley	.05	.02	.01
☐ 313 Bill Swift	.08	.04	.01
☐ 314 Charlie Hough	.05	.02	.01
☐ 315 Jim Presley	.05	.02	.01
☐ 316 Luis Polonia	.08	.04	.01
☐ 317 Mike Morgan	.05	.02	.01
☐ 318 Lee Guetterman	.05	.02	.01
☐ 319 Jose Oquendo	.05	.02	.01
☐ 320 Wayne Tolleson	.05	.02	.01
☐ 321 Jody Reed	.05	.02	.01
☐ 322 Damon Berryhill	.05	.02	.01
☐ 323 Roger Clemens	.75	.35	.09
☐ 324 Ryne Sandberg	.75	.35	.09
☐ 325 Benito Santiago UER (Misspelled Santago on card back)	.08	.04	.01

☐ 326 Bret Saberhagen UER (1140 hits, should be 1240; 56 CG, should be 52)	.08	.04	.01
☐ 327 Lou Whitaker	.08	.04	.01
☐ 328 Dave Gallagher	.05	.02	.01
☐ 329 Mike Pagliarulo	.05	.02	.01
☐ 330 Doyle Alexander	.05	.02	.01
☐ 331 Jeffrey Leonard	.05	.02	.01
☐ 332 Torey Lovullo	.05	.02	.01
☐ 333 Pete Incaviglia	.05	.02	.01
☐ 334 Rickey Henderson	.40	.18	.05
☐ 335 Rafael Palmeiro	.20	.09	.03
☐ 336 Ken Hill	.40	.18	.05
☐ 337 Dave Winfield UER (1418 RBI, should be 1438)	.30	.14	.04
☐ 338 Alfredo Griffin	.05	.02	.01
☐ 339 Andy Hawkins	.05	.02	.01
☐ 340 Ted Power	.05	.02	.01
☐ 341 Steve Wilson	.05	.02	.01
☐ 342 Jack Clark UER (916 BB, should be 1006; 1142 SO, should be 1130)	.08	.04	.01
☐ 343 Ellis Burks	.08	.04	.01
☐ 344 Tony Gwynn UER (Doubles stats on card back are wrong)	.40	.18	.05
☐ 345 Jerome Walton UER (Total At Bats 476, should be 475)	.08	.04	.01
☐ 346 Roberto Alomar UER (61 doubles, should be 51)	1.25	.55	.16
☐ 347 Carlos Martinez UER (Born 8/11/64, should be 8/11/65)	.05	.02	.01
☐ 348 Chet Lemon	.05	.02	.01
☐ 349 Willie Wilson	.05	.02	.01
☐ 350 Greg Walker	.05	.02	.01
☐ 351 Tom Bolton	.05	.02	.01
☐ 352 German Gonzalez	.05	.02	.01
☐ 353 Harold Baines	.08	.04	.01
☐ 354 Mike Greenwell	.08	.04	.01
☐ 355 Ruben Sierra	.40	.18	.05
☐ 356 Andres Galarraga	.05	.02	.01
☐ 357 Andre Dawson	.20	.09	.03
☐ 358 Jeff Brantley	.05	.02	.01
☐ 359 Mike Bielecki	.05	.02	.01
☐ 360 Ken Oberkfell	.05	.02	.01
☐ 361 Kurt Stillwell	.05	.02	.01
☐ 362 Brian Holman	.05	.02	.01
☐ 363 Kevin Seitzer	.08	.04	.01
☐ 364 Alvin Davis	.05	.02	.01
☐ 365 Tom Gordon	.08	.04	.01
☐ 366 Bobby Bonilla	.25	.11	.03
☐ 367 Carlton Fisk	.15	.07	.02
☐ 368 Steve Carter UER (Charlotesville)	.05	.02	.01
☐ 369 Joel Skinner	.05	.02	.01
☐ 370 John Cangelosi	.05	.02	.01
☐ 371 Cecil Espy	.05	.02	.01
☐ 372 Gary Wayne	.05	.02	.01
☐ 373 Jim Rice	.08	.04	.01
☐ 374 Mike Dyer	.05	.02	.01
☐ 375 Joe Carter	.40	.18	.05
☐ 376 Dwight Smith	.05	.02	.01
☐ 377 John Wetteland	.40	.18	.05
☐ 378 Earnie Riles	.05	.02	.01
☐ 379 Otis Nixon	.08	.04	.01
☐ 380 Vance Law	.05	.02	.01
☐ 381 Dave Bergman	.05	.02	.01
☐ 382 Frank White	.05	.02	.01
☐ 383 Scott Bradley	.05	.02	.01
☐ 384 Israel Sanchez UER (Totals don't include '89 stats)	.05	.02	.01
☐ 385 Gary Pettis	.05	.02	.01
☐ 386 Donn Pall	.05	.02	.01
☐ 387 John Smiley	.08	.04	.01
☐ 388 Tom Candiotti	.05	.02	.01
☐ 389 Junior Ortiz	.05	.02	.01
☐ 390 Steve Lyons	.05	.02	.01
☐ 391 Brian Harper	.08	.04	.01
☐ 392 Fred Manrique	.05	.02	.01
☐ 393 Lee Smith	.08	.04	.01
☐ 394 Jeff Kunkel	.05	.02	.01
☐ 395 Claudell Washington	.05	.02	.01
☐ 396 John Tudor	.05	.02	.01
☐ 397 Terry Kennedy UER (Career totals all wrong)	.05	.02	.01
☐ 398 Lloyd McClendon	.05	.02	.01
☐ 399 Craig Lefferts	.05	.02	.01
☐ 400 Checklist 301-400	.06	.01	.00
☐ 401 Keith Moreland	.05	.02	.01
☐ 402 Rich Gedman	.05	.02	.01
☐ 403 Jeff D. Robinson	.05	.02	.01
☐ 404 Randy Ready	.05	.02	.01
☐ 405 Rick Cerone	.05	.02	.01
☐ 406 Jeff Blauser	.08	.04	.01
☐ 407 Larry Andersen	.05	.02	.01
☐ 408 Joe Boever	.05	.02	.01
☐ 409 Felix Fermin	.05	.02	.01
☐ 410 Glenn Wilson	.05	.02	.01
☐ 411 Rex Hudler	.05	.02	.01
☐ 412 Mark Grant	.05	.02	.01
☐ 413 Dennis Martinez	.08	.04	.01
☐ 414 Darrin Jackson	.08	.04	.01
☐ 415 Mike Aldrete	.05	.02	.01
☐ 416 Roger McDowell	.05	.02	.01
☐ 417 Jeff Reardon	.08	.04	.01
☐ 418 Darren Daulton	.08	.04	.01
☐ 419 Tim Laudner	.05	.02	.01
☐ 420 Don Carman	.05	.02	.01
☐ 421 Lloyd Moseby	.05	.02	.01
☐ 422 Doug Drabek	.08	.04	.01
☐ 423 Lenny Harris UER (Walks 2 in '89, should be 20)	.08	.04	.01
☐ 424 Jose Lind	.05	.02	.01
☐ 425 Dave Johnson (P)	.05	.02	.01
☐ 426 Jerry Browne	.05	.02	.01
☐ 427 Eric Yelding	.05	.02	.01
☐ 428 Brad Komminsk	.05	.02	.01
☐ 429 Jody Davis	.05	.02	.01
☐ 430 Mariano Duncan	.05	.02	.01
☐ 431 Mark Davis	.05	.02	.01
☐ 432 Nelson Santovenia	.05	.02	.01
☐ 433 Bruce Hurst	.08	.04	.01
☐ 434 Jeff Huson	.12	.05	.02
☐ 435 Chris James	.05	.02	.01
☐ 436 Mark Guthrie	.05	.02	.01
☐ 437 Charlie Hayes	.08	.04	.01
☐ 438 Shane Rawley	.05	.02	.01
☐ 439 Dickie Thon	.05	.02	.01
☐ 440 Juan Berenguer	.05	.02	.01
☐ 441 Kevin Romine	.05	.02	.01
☐ 442 Bill Landrum	.05	.02	.01
☐ 443 Todd Frohwirth	.05	.02	.01
☐ 444 Craig Worthington	.05	.02	.01
☐ 445 Fernando Valenzuela	.08	.04	.01
☐ 446 Joey Belle	1.50	.65	.19
☐ 447 Ed Whited UER (Ashville, should be Asheville)	.05	.02	.01
☐ 448 Dave Smith	.05	.02	.01
☐ 449 Dave Clark	.05	.02	.01
☐ 450 Juan Agosto	.05	.02	.01
☐ 451 Dave Valle	.05	.02	.01
☐ 452 Kent Hrbek	.08	.04	.01
☐ 453 Von Hayes	.05	.02	.01
☐ 454 Gary Gaetti	.05	.02	.01
☐ 455 Greg Briley	.05	.02	.01
☐ 456 Glenn Braggs	.05	.02	.01
☐ 457 Kirt Manwaring	.05	.02	.01
☐ 458 Mel Hall	.05	.02	.01
☐ 459 Brook Jacoby	.05	.02	.01
☐ 460 Pat Sheridan	.05	.02	.01
☐ 461 Rob Murphy	.05	.02	.01
☐ 462 Jimmy Key	.08	.04	.01
☐ 463 Nick Esasky	.05	.02	.01
☐ 464 Rob Ducey	.05	.02	.01
☐ 465 Carlos Quintana UER (Internatinoal)	.08	.04	.01
☐ 466 Larry Walker	2.50	1.15	.30
☐ 467 Todd Worrell	.05	.02	.01
☐ 468 Kevin Gross	.05	.02	.01
☐ 469 Terry Pendleton	.15	.07	.02
☐ 470 Dave Martinez	.08	.04	.01
☐ 471 Gene Larkin	.05	.02	.01
☐ 472 Len Dykstra UER ('89 and total runs understated by 10)	.08	.04	.01
☐ 473 Barry Lyons	.05	.02	.01
☐ 474 Terry Mulholland	.08	.04	.01
☐ 475 Chip Hale	.05	.02	.01
☐ 476 Jesse Barfield	.05	.02	.01
☐ 477 Dan Plesac	.05	.02	.01
☐ 478A Scott Garrelts ERR (Photo actually Bill Bathe)	3.50	1.55	.45
☐ 478B Scott Garrelts COR	.08	.04	.01
☐ 479 Dave Righetti	.05	.02	.01
☐ 480 Gus Polidor UER	.05	.02	.01

(Wearing 14 on front,
but 10 on back)
☐ 481 Mookie Wilson .05 .02 .01
☐ 482 Luis Rivera .05 .02 .01
☐ 483 Mike Flanagan .05 .02 .01
☐ 484 Dennis Boyd .05 .02 .01
☐ 485 John Cerutti .05 .02 .01
☐ 486 John Costello .05 .02 .01
☐ 487 Pascual Perez .05 .02 .01
☐ 488 Tommy Herr .05 .02 .01
☐ 489 Tom Foley .05 .02 .01
☐ 490 Curt Ford .05 .02 .01
☐ 491 Steve Lake .05 .02 .01
☐ 492 Tim Teufel .05 .02 .01
☐ 493 Randy Bush .05 .02 .01
☐ 494 Mike Jackson .05 .02 .01
☐ 495 Steve Jeltz .05 .02 .01
☐ 496 Paul Gibson .05 .02 .01
☐ 497 Steve Balboni .05 .02 .01
☐ 498 Bud Black .05 .02 .01
☐ 499 Dale Sveum .05 .02 .01
☐ 500 Checklist 401-500 .06 .01 .00
☐ 501 Tim Jones .05 .02 .01
☐ 502 Mark Portugal .05 .02 .01
☐ 503 Ivan Calderon .05 .02 .01
☐ 504 Rick Rhoden .05 .02 .01
☐ 505 Willie McGee .08 .04 .01
☐ 506 Kirk McCaskill .05 .02 .01
☐ 507 Dave LaPoint .05 .02 .01
☐ 508 Jay Howell .05 .02 .01
☐ 509 Johnny Ray .05 .02 .01
☐ 510 Dave Anderson .05 .02 .01
☐ 511 Chuck Crim .05 .02 .01
☐ 512 Joe Hesketh .05 .02 .01
☐ 513 Dennis Eckersley .20 .09 .03
☐ 514 Greg Brock .05 .02 .01
☐ 515 Tim Burke .05 .02 .01
☐ 516 Frank Tanana .05 .02 .01
☐ 517 Jay Bell .08 .04 .01
☐ 518 Guillermo Hernandez .05 .02 .01
☐ 519 Randy Kramer UER .05 .02 .01
(Codiroli misspelled
as Codoroli)
☐ 520 Charles Hudson .05 .02 .01
☐ 521 Jim Corsi .05 .02 .01
(Word "originally" is
misspelled on back)
☐ 522 Steve Rosenberg .05 .02 .01
☐ 523 Cris Carpenter .05 .02 .01
☐ 524 Matt Winters .05 .02 .01
☐ 525 Melido Perez .08 .04 .01
☐ 526 Chris Gwynn UER .05 .02 .01
(Albeguergue)
☐ 527 Bert Blyleven UER .08 .04 .01
(Games career total is
wrong, should be 644)
☐ 528 Chuck Cary .05 .02 .01
☐ 529 Daryl Boston .05 .02 .01
☐ 530 Dale Mohorcic .05 .02 .01
☐ 531 Geronimo Berroa .05 .02 .01
☐ 532 Edgar Martinez .40 .18 .05
☐ 533 Dale Murphy .15 .07 .02
☐ 534 Jay Buhner .08 .04 .01
☐ 535 John Smoltz UER .50 .23 .06
(HEA Stadium)
☐ 536 Andy Van Slyke .15 .07 .02
☐ 537 Mike Henneman .05 .02 .01
☐ 538 Miguel Garcia .05 .02 .01
☐ 539 Frank Williams .05 .02 .01
☐ 540 R.J. Reynolds .05 .02 .01
☐ 541 Shawn Hillegas .05 .02 .01
☐ 542 Walt Weiss .05 .02 .01
☐ 543 Greg Hibbard .30 .14 .04
☐ 544 Nolan Ryan 1.25 .55 .16
☐ 545 Todd Zeile .30 .14 .04
☐ 546 Hensley Meulens .08 .04 .01
☐ 547 Tim Belcher .08 .04 .01
☐ 548 Mike Witt .05 .02 .01
☐ 549 Greg Cadaret UER .05 .02 .01
(Aquiring, should
be Acquiring)
☐ 550 Franklin Stubbs .05 .02 .01
☐ 551 Tony Castillo .05 .02 .01
☐ 552 Jeff M. Robinson .05 .02 .01
☐ 553 Steve Olin .40 .18 .05
☐ 554 Alan Trammell .08 .04 .01
☐ 555 Wade Boggs 4X .40 .18 .05
(Bo Jackson
in background)
☐ 556 Will Clark .60 .25 .08
☐ 557 Jeff King .08 .04 .01
☐ 558 Mike Fitzgerald .05 .02 .01
☐ 559 Ken Howell .05 .02 .01
☐ 560 Bob Kipper .05 .02 .01
☐ 561 Scott Bankhead .05 .02 .01
☐ 562A Jeff Innis ERR 2.50 1.15 .30
(Photo actually
David West)
☐ 562B Jeff Innis COR .08 .04 .01
☐ 563 Randy Johnson .08 .04 .01
☐ 564 Wally Whitehurst .05 .02 .01
☐ 565 Gene Harris .05 .02 .01
☐ 566 Norm Charlton .08 .04 .01
☐ 567 Robin Yount UER .30 .14 .04
(7602 career hits,
should be 2606)
☐ 568 Joe Oliver UER .12 .05 .02
(Fl.orida)
☐ 569 Mark Parent .05 .02 .01
☐ 570 John Farrell UER .05 .02 .01
(Loss total added wrong)
☐ 571 Tom Glavine .50 .23 .06
☐ 572 Rod Nichols .05 .02 .01
☐ 573 Jack Morris .15 .07 .02
☐ 574 Greg Swindell .08 .04 .01
☐ 575 Steve Searcy .05 .02 .01
☐ 576 Ricky Jordan .05 .02 .01
☐ 577 Matt Williams .15 .07 .02
☐ 578 Mike LaValliere .05 .02 .01
☐ 579 Bryn Smith .05 .02 .01
☐ 580 Bruce Ruffin .05 .02 .01
☐ 581 Randy Myers .08 .04 .01
☐ 582 Rick Wrona .05 .02 .01
☐ 583 Juan Samuel .05 .02 .01
☐ 584 Les Lancaster .05 .02 .01
☐ 585 Jeff Musselman .05 .02 .01
☐ 586 Rob Dibble .08 .04 .01
☐ 587 Eric Show .05 .02 .01
☐ 588 Jesse Orosco .05 .02 .01
☐ 589 Herm Winningham .05 .02 .01
☐ 590 Andy Allanson .05 .02 .01
☐ 591 Dion James .05 .02 .01
☐ 592 Carmelo Martinez .05 .02 .01
☐ 593 Luis Quinones .05 .02 .01
☐ 594 Dennis Rasmussen .05 .02 .01
☐ 595 Rich Yett .05 .02 .01
☐ 596 Bob Walk .05 .02 .01
☐ 597A Andy McGaffigan ERR .35 .16 .04
(Photo actually
Rich Thompson)
☐ 597B Andy McGaffigan COR .08 .04 .01
☐ 598 Billy Hatcher .05 .02 .01
☐ 599 Bob Knepper .05 .02 .01
☐ 600 Checklist 501-600 UER .06 .01 .00
(599 Bob Kneppers)
☐ 601 Joey Cora .05 .02 .01
☐ 602 Steve Finley .12 .05 .02
☐ 603 Kal Daniels UER .05 .02 .01
(12 hits in '87, should
be 123; 335 runs,
should be 235)
☐ 604 Gregg Olson .15 .07 .02
☐ 605 Dave Stieb .08 .04 .01
☐ 606 Kenny Rogers .05 .02 .01
(Shown catching
football)
☐ 607 Zane Smith .05 .02 .01
☐ 608 Bob Geren UER .05 .02 .01
(Origionally)
☐ 609 Chad Kreuter .05 .02 .01
☐ 610 Mike Smithson .05 .02 .01
☐ 611 Jeff Wetherby .05 .02 .01
☐ 612 Gary Mielke .05 .02 .01
☐ 613 Pete Smith .08 .04 .01
☐ 614 Jack Daugherty UER .05 .02 .01
(Born 7/30/60, should
be 7/3/60; origionally)
☐ 615 Lance McCullers .05 .02 .01
☐ 616 Don Robinson .05 .02 .01
☐ 617 Jose Guzman .05 .02 .01
☐ 618 Steve Bedrosian .05 .02 .01
☐ 619 Jamie Moyer .05 .02 .01
☐ 620 Atlee Hammaker .05 .02 .01
☐ 621 Rick Luecken UER .05 .02 .01
(Innings pitched wrong)
☐ 622 Greg W. Harris .05 .02 .01
☐ 623 Pete Harnisch .08 .04 .01
☐ 624 Jerald Clark .08 .04 .01
☐ 625 Jack McDowell .40 .18 .05
☐ 626 Frank Viola .08 .04 .01
☐ 627 Teddy Higuera .05 .02 .01
☐ 628 Marty Pevey .05 .02 .01
☐ 629 Bill Wegman .05 .02 .01
☐ 630 Eric Plunk .05 .02 .01
☐ 631 Drew Hall .05 .02 .01
☐ 632 Doug Jones .08 .04 .01
☐ 633 Geno Petralli .05 .02 .01

☐ 634 Jose Alvarez	.05	.02	.01
☐ 635 Bob Milacki	.05	.02	.01
☐ 636 Bobby Witt	.08	.04	.01
☐ 637 Trevor Wilson	.05	.02	.01
☐ 638 Jeff Russell UER (Shutout stats wrong)	.05	.02	.01
☐ 639 Mike Krukow	.05	.02	.01
☐ 640 Rick Leach	.05	.02	.01
☐ 641 Dave Schmidt	.05	.02	.01
☐ 642 Terry Leach	.05	.02	.01
☐ 643 Calvin Schiraldi	.05	.02	.01
☐ 644 Bob Melvin	.05	.02	.01
☐ 645 Jim Abbott	.40	.18	.05
☐ 646 Jaime Navarro	.60	.25	.08
☐ 647 Mark Langston UER (Several errors in stats totals)	.08	.04	.01
☐ 648 Juan Nieves	.05	.02	.01
☐ 649 Damaso Garcia	.05	.02	.01
☐ 650 Charlie O'Brien	.05	.02	.01
☐ 651 Eric King	.05	.02	.01
☐ 652 Mike Boddicker	.05	.02	.01
☐ 653 Duane Ward	.05	.02	.01
☐ 654 Bob Stanley	.05	.02	.01
☐ 655 Sandy Alomar Jr.	.15	.07	.02
☐ 656 Danny Tartabull UER (395 BB, should be 295)	.20	.09	.03
☐ 657 Randy McCament	.05	.02	.01
☐ 658 Charlie Leibrandt	.05	.02	.01
☐ 659 Dan Quisenberry	.08	.04	.01
☐ 660 Paul Assenmacher	.05	.02	.01
☐ 661 Walt Terrell	.05	.02	.01
☐ 662 Tim Leary	.05	.02	.01
☐ 663 Randy Milligan	.05	.02	.01
☐ 664 Bo Diaz	.05	.02	.01
☐ 665 Mark Lemke UER (Richmond misspelled as Richomond)	.08	.04	.01
☐ 666 Jose Gonzalez	.05	.02	.01
☐ 667 Chuck Finley UER (Born 11/16/62, should be 11/26/62)	.08	.04	.01
☐ 668 John Kruk	.08	.04	.01
☐ 669 Dick Schofield	.05	.02	.01
☐ 670 Tim Crews	.05	.02	.01
☐ 671 John Dopson	.05	.02	.01
☐ 672 John Orton	.12	.05	.02
☐ 673 Eric Hetzel	.05	.02	.01
☐ 674 Lance Parrish	.08	.04	.01
☐ 675 Ramon Martinez	.25	.11	.03
☐ 676 Mark Gubicza	.05	.02	.01
☐ 677 Greg Litton	.05	.02	.01
☐ 678 Greg Mathews	.05	.02	.01
☐ 679 Dave Dravecky	.08	.04	.01
☐ 680 Steve Farr	.05	.02	.01
☐ 681 Mike Devereaux	.08	.04	.01
☐ 682 Ken Griffey Sr.	.08	.04	.01
☐ 683A Mickey Weston ERR (Listed as Jamie on card)	2.50	1.15	.30
☐ 683B Mickey Weston COR (Technically still an error as birthdate is listed as 3/26/81)	.08	.04	.01
☐ 684 Jack Armstrong	.08	.04	.01
☐ 685 Steve Buechele	.05	.02	.01
☐ 686 Bryan Harvey	.08	.04	.01
☐ 687 Lance Blankenship	.05	.02	.01
☐ 688 Dante Bichette	.08	.04	.01
☐ 689 Todd Burns	.05	.02	.01
☐ 690 Dan Petry	.05	.02	.01
☐ 691 Kent Anderson	.05	.02	.01
☐ 692 Todd Stottlemyre	.08	.04	.01
☐ 693 Wally Joyner UER (Several stats errors)	.08	.04	.01
☐ 694 Mike Rochford	.05	.02	.01
☐ 695 Floyd Bannister	.05	.02	.01
☐ 696 Rick Reuschel	.05	.02	.01
☐ 697 Jose DeLeon	.05	.02	.01
☐ 698 Jeff Montgomery	.08	.04	.01
☐ 699 Kelly Downs	.05	.02	.01
☐ 700A Checklist 601-700 ERR (683 Jamie Weston)	2.50	.25	.07
☐ 700B Checklist 601-700 COR (683 Mickey Weston)	.06	.01	.00
☐ 701 Jim Gott	.05	.02	.01
☐ 702 Rookie Threats Delino DeShields Marquis Grissom Larry Walker	1.00	.45	.13
☐ 703 Alejandro Pena	.05	.02	.01
☐ 704 Willie Randolph	.08	.04	.01
☐ 705 Tim Leary	.05	.02	.01
☐ 706 Chuck McElroy	.25	.11	.03
☐ 707 Gerald Perry	.05	.02	.01
☐ 708 Tom Brunansky	.08	.04	.01
☐ 709 John Franco	.08	.04	.01
☐ 710 Mark Davis	.05	.02	.01
☐ 711 Dave Justice	4.00	1.80	.50
☐ 712 Storm Davis	.05	.02	.01
☐ 713 Scott Ruskin	.05	.02	.01
☐ 714 Glenn Braggs	.05	.02	.01
☐ 715 Kevin Bearse	.05	.02	.01
☐ 716 Jose Nunez	.05	.02	.01
☐ 717 Tim Layana	.05	.02	.01
☐ 718 Greg Myers	.05	.02	.01
☐ 719 Pete O'Brien	.05	.02	.01
☐ 720 John Candelaria	.05	.02	.01
☐ 721 Craig Grebeck	.30	.14	.04
☐ 722 Shawn Boskie	.15	.07	.02
☐ 723 Jim Leyritz	.12	.05	.02
☐ 724 Bill Sampen	.05	.02	.01
☐ 725 Scott Radinsky	.30	.14	.04
☐ 726 Todd Hundley	.30	.14	.04
☐ 727 Scott Hemond	.12	.05	.02
☐ 728 Lenny Webster	.12	.05	.02
☐ 729 Jeff Reardon	.08	.04	.01
☐ 730 Mitch Webster	.05	.02	.01
☐ 731 Brian Bohanon	.12	.05	.02
☐ 732 Rick Parker	.05	.02	.01
☐ 733 Terry Shumpert	.05	.02	.01
☐ 734A Ryan's 6th No-Hitter (No stripe on front)	6.00	2.70	.75
☐ 734B Ryan's 6th No-Hitter (stripe added on card front for 300th win)	1.00	.45	.13
☐ 735 John Burkett	.10	.05	.01
☐ 736 Derrick May	.75	.35	.09
☐ 737 Carlos Baerga	3.00	1.35	.40
☐ 738 Greg Smith	.05	.02	.01
☐ 739 Scott Sanderson	.05	.02	.01
☐ 740 Joe Kraemer	.05	.02	.01
☐ 741 Hector Villanueva	.10	.05	.01
☐ 742 Mike Fetters	.15	.07	.02
☐ 743 Mark Gardner	.20	.09	.03
☐ 744 Matt Nokes	.05	.02	.01
☐ 745 Dave Winfield	.30	.14	.04
☐ 746 Delino DeShields	2.00	.90	.25
☐ 747 Dann Howitt	.05	.02	.01
☐ 748 Tony Pena	.05	.02	.01
☐ 749 Oil Can Boyd	.05	.02	.01
☐ 750 Mike Benjamin	.10	.05	.01
☐ 751 Alex Cole	.35	.16	.04
☐ 752 Eric Gunderson	.12	.05	.02
☐ 753 Howard Farmer	.05	.02	.01
☐ 754 Joe Carter	.40	.18	.05
☐ 755 Ray Lankford	2.50	1.15	.30
☐ 756 Sandy Alomar Jr.	.15	.07	.02
☐ 757 Alex Sanchez	.05	.02	.01
☐ 758 Nick Esasky	.05	.02	.01
☐ 759 Stan Belinda	.30	.14	.04
☐ 760 Jim Presley	.05	.02	.01
☐ 761 Gary DiSarcina	.40	.18	.05
☐ 762 Wayne Edwards	.05	.02	.01
☐ 763 Pat Combs	.05	.02	.01
☐ 764 Mickey Pina	.05	.02	.01
☐ 765 Wilson Alvarez	.50	.23	.06
☐ 766 Dave Parker	.08	.04	.01
☐ 767 Mike Blowers	.05	.02	.01
☐ 768 Tony Phillips	.05	.02	.01
☐ 769 Pascual Perez	.05	.02	.01
☐ 770 Gary Pettis	.05	.02	.01
☐ 771 Fred Lynn	.08	.04	.01
☐ 772 Mel Rojas	.20	.09	.03
☐ 773 David Segui	.15	.07	.02
☐ 774 Gary Carter	.08	.04	.01
☐ 775 Rafael Valdez	.12	.05	.02
☐ 776 Glenallen Hill	.08	.04	.01
☐ 777 Keith Hernandez	.08	.04	.01
☐ 778 Billy Hatcher	.05	.02	.01
☐ 779 Marty Clary	.05	.02	.01
☐ 780 Candy Maldonado	.05	.02	.01
☐ 781 Mike Marshall	.05	.02	.01
☐ 782 Billy Joe Robidoux	.05	.02	.01
☐ 783 Mark Langston	.08	.04	.01
☐ 784 Paul Sorrento	.50	.23	.06
☐ 785 Dave Hollins	1.75	.80	.22
☐ 786 Cecil Fielder	.40	.18	.05
☐ 787 Matt Young	.05	.02	.01
☐ 788 Jeff Huson	.05	.02	.01
☐ 789 Lloyd Moseby	.05	.02	.01
☐ 790 Ron Kittle	.05	.02	.01
☐ 791 Hubie Brooks	.05	.02	.01
☐ 792 Craig Lefferts	.05	.02	.01
☐ 793 Kevin Bass	.05	.02	.01
☐ 794 Bryn Smith	.05	.02	.01

	MT	EX-MT	VG
☐ 795 Juan Samuel	.05	.02	.01
☐ 796 Sam Horn	.05	.02	.01
☐ 797 Randy Myers	.08	.04	.01
☐ 798 Chris James	.05	.02	.01
☐ 799 Bill Gullickson	.05	.02	.01
☐ 800 Checklist 701-800	.08	.01	.00

1990 Upper Deck Reggie Jackson Heroes

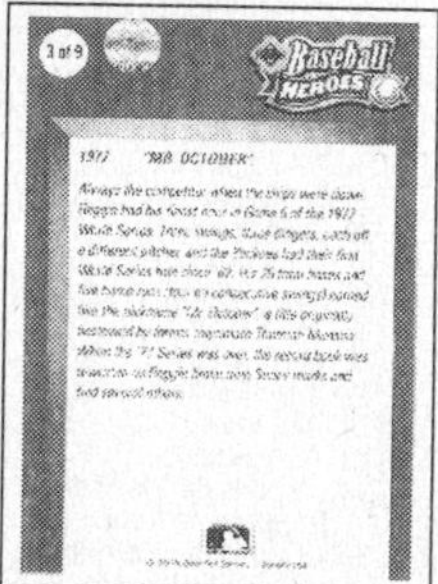

This ten-card subset was issued as an insert in 1990 Upper Deck High Number packs as part of the Upper Deck promotional giveaway of 2,500 officially signed and personally numbered Reggie Jackson cards. These cards were the standard size (2 1/2" by 3 1/2") and cover Reggie's complete major league career. The complete set price refers only to the unautographed card set of ten.

	MT	EX-MT	VG
COMPLETE SET (10)	30.00	13.50	3.80
COMMON REGGIE (1-9)	3.50	1.55	.45
☐ 1 1969 Emerging Superstar	3.50	1.55	.45
☐ 2 1973 An MVP Year	3.50	1.55	.45
☐ 3 1977 Mr. October	3.50	1.55	.45
☐ 4 1978 Jackson vs. Welch	3.50	1.55	.45
☐ 5 1982 Under the Halo	3.50	1.55	.45
☐ 6 1984 500 Homers	3.50	1.55	.45
☐ 7 1986 Moving Up the List	3.50	1.55	.45
☐ 8 1987 A Great Career Ends	3.50	1.55	.45
☐ 9 Baseball Heroes Checklist	3.50	1.55	.45
☐ AU1 Reggie Jackson (Signed and Numbered out of 2500)	400.00	180.00	50.00
☐ NNO Reggie Jackson Header Card	7.00	3.10	.85

1991 Upper Deck

This set marked the third year Upper Deck has issued a 700-card set in January. The cards measure 2 1/2" by 3 1/2". The set features 26 star rookies to lead off the set as well as other special cards featuring multi-players. The set is made on the typical Upper Deck card stock and features full-color photos on both the front and the back. The team checklist (TC) cards in the set feature an attractive Vernon Wells drawing of a featured player for that particular team. A special Michael Jordan card (numbered SP1) was randomly included in packs on a somewhat limited basis; this Jordan card is not included in the set price below. The Hank Aaron hologram card was randomly inserted in the 1991 Upper Deck high number foil packs. The key Rookie Cards in this set include Wes Chamberlain, Wilfredo Cordero, Luis Gonzalez, Chipper Jones, Eric Karros, Brian McRae, Pedro Munoz, Mike Mussina, Phil Plantier, Reggie Sanders, and Todd Van Poppel. This 100-card extended or high-number series was issued by Upper Deck several months after the release of their first series. The extended series features rookie players as well as players who switched teams between seasons. In the extended wax packs were low number cards, special cards featuring Hank Aaron as the next featured player in their baseball heroes series, and a special card honoring the May 1st exploits of Rickey Henderson and Nolan Ryan. For the first time in Upper Deck's three-year history, they did not issue a factory Extended set. The only noteworthy Rookie Card in the high-number series is Jeff Bagwell.

	MT	EX-MT	VG
COMPLETE SET (800)	30.00	13.50	3.80
COMPLETE FACT.SET (800)	33.00	15.00	4.10
COMPLETE LO SET (700)	24.00	11.00	3.00
COMPLETE HI SET (100)	6.00	2.70	.75
COMMON PLAYER (1-700)	.05	.02	.01
COMMON PLAYER (701-800)	.05	.02	.01
☐ 1 Star Rookie Checklist	.06	.01	.00
☐ 2 Phil Plantier	.90	.40	.11
☐ 3 D.J. Dozier	.15	.07	.02
☐ 4 Dave Hansen	.15	.07	.02
☐ 5 Maurice Vaughn	.35	.16	.04
☐ 6 Leo Gomez	.50	.23	.06
☐ 7 Scott Aldred	.15	.07	.02
☐ 8 Scott Chiamparino	.08	.04	.01
☐ 9 Lance Dickson	.15	.07	.02
☐ 10 Sean Berry	.20	.09	.03
☐ 11 Bernie Williams	.40	.18	.05
☐ 12 Brian Barnes UER (Photo either not him or in wrong jersey)	.15	.07	.02
☐ 13 Narciso Elvira	.10	.05	.01
☐ 14 Mike Gardiner	.15	.07	.02
☐ 15 Greg Colbrunn	.40	.18	.05
☐ 16 Bernard Gilkey	.25	.11	.03
☐ 17 Mark Lewis	.20	.09	.03
☐ 18 Mickey Morandini	.20	.09	.03
☐ 19 Charles Nagy	.60	.25	.08
☐ 20 Geronimo Pena	.15	.07	.02
☐ 21 Henry Rodriguez	.35	.16	.04
☐ 22 Scott Cooper	.40	.18	.05
☐ 23 Andujar Cedeno UER (Shown batting left, back says right)	.25	.11	.03
☐ 24 Eric Karros	2.50	1.15	.30
☐ 25 Steve Decker UER (Lewis-Clark State College, not Lewis and Clark)	.25	.11	.03
☐ 26 Kevin Belcher	.10	.05	.01
☐ 27 Jeff Conine	.40	.18	.05
☐ 28 Oakland Athletics TC Dave Stewart	.06	.03	.01
☐ 29 Chicago White Sox TC Carlton Fisk	.10	.05	.01
☐ 30 Texas Rangers TC Rafael Palmeiro	.06	.03	.01
☐ 31 California Angels TC Chuck Finley	.06	.03	.01
☐ 32 Seattle Mariners TC Harold Reynolds	.06	.03	.01

☐ 33 Kansas City Royals TC .06 .03 .01
Bret Saberhagen
☐ 34 Minnesota Twins TC .06 .03 .01
Gary Gaetti
☐ 35 Scott Leius .15 .07 .02
☐ 36 Neal Heaton .05 .02 .01
☐ 37 Terry Lee .08 .04 .01
☐ 38 Gary Redus .05 .02 .01
☐ 39 Barry Jones .05 .02 .01
☐ 40 Chuck Knoblauch 1.00 .45 .13
☐ 41 Larry Andersen .05 .02 .01
☐ 42 Darryl Hamilton .08 .04 .01
☐ 43 Boston Red Sox TC .06 .03 .01
Mike Greenwell
☐ 44 Toronto Blue Jays TC .06 .03 .01
Kelly Gruber
☐ 45 Detroit Tigers TC .06 .03 .01
Jack Morris
☐ 46 Cleveland Indians TC .06 .03 .01
Sandy Alomar Jr.
☐ 47 Baltimore Orioles TC .06 .03 .01
Gregg Olson
☐ 48 Milwaukee Brewers TC .06 .03 .01
Dave Parker
☐ 49 New York Yankees TC .06 .03 .01
Roberto Kelly
☐ 50 Top Prospect Checklist .06 .01 .00
☐ 51 Kyle Abbott .20 .09 .03
☐ 52 Jeff Juden .20 .09 .03
☐ 53 Todd Van Poppel UER 1.00 .45 .13
(Born Arlington and attended John Martin HS, should say Hinsdale and James Martin HS)
☐ 54 Steve Karsay .40 .18 .05
☐ 55 Chipper Jones 1.50 .65 .19
☐ 56 Chris Johnson UER .10 .05 .01
(Called Tim on back)
☐ 57 John Ericks .08 .04 .01
☐ 58 Gary Scott .30 .14 .04
☐ 59 Kiki Jones .05 .02 .01
☐ 60 Wilfredo Cordero 1.00 .45 .13
☐ 61 Royce Clayton .60 .25 .08
☐ 62 Tim Costo .40 .18 .05
☐ 63 Roger Salkeld .30 .14 .04
☐ 64 Brook Fordyce .15 .07 .02
☐ 65 Mike Mussina 2.50 1.15 .30
☐ 66 Dave Staton .40 .18 .05
☐ 67 Mike Lieberthal .35 .16 .04
☐ 68 Kurt Miller .40 .18 .05
☐ 69 Dan Peltier .20 .09 .03
☐ 70 Greg Blosser .30 .14 .04
☐ 71 Reggie Sanders 1.25 .55 .16
☐ 72 Brent Mayne .05 .02 .01
☐ 73 Rico Brogna .25 .11 .03
☐ 74 Willie Banks .40 .18 .05
☐ 75 Len Brutcher .10 .05 .01
☐ 76 Pat Kelly .25 .11 .03
☐ 77 Cincinnati Reds TC .06 .03 .01
Chris Sabo
☐ 78 Los Angeles Dodgers TC .06 .03 .01
Ramon Martinez
☐ 79 San Fran. Giants TC .06 .03 .01
Matt Williams
☐ 80 San Diego Padres TC .12 .05 .02
Roberto Alomar
☐ 81 Houston Astros TC .06 .03 .01
Glenn Davis
☐ 82 Atlanta Braves TC .10 .05 .01
Ron Gant
☐ 83 Fielder's Feat .15 .07 .02
Cecil Fielder
☐ 84 Orlando Merced .35 .16 .04
☐ 85 Domingo Ramos .05 .02 .01
☐ 86 Tom Bolton .05 .02 .01
☐ 87 Andres Santana .10 .05 .01
☐ 88 John Dopson .05 .02 .01
☐ 89 Kenny Williams .05 .02 .01
☐ 90 Marty Barrett .05 .02 .01
☐ 91 Tom Pagnozzi .05 .02 .01
☐ 92 Carmelo Martinez .05 .02 .01
☐ 93 Save Master .05 .02 .01
(Bobby Thigpen)
☐ 94 Pittsburgh Pirates TC .10 .05 .01
Barry Bonds
☐ 95 New York Mets TC .06 .03 .01
Gregg Jefferies
☐ 96 Montreal Expos TC .06 .03 .01
Tim Wallach
☐ 97 Phila. Phillies TC .06 .03 .01
Len Dykstra
☐ 98 St.Louis Cardinals TC .06 .03 .01
Pedro Guerrero
☐ 99 Chicago Cubs TC .09 .04 .01
Mark Grace
☐ 100 Checklist 1-100 .06 .01 .00
☐ 101 Kevin Elster .05 .02 .01
☐ 102 Tom Brookens .05 .02 .01
☐ 103 Mackey Sasser .05 .02 .01
☐ 104 Felix Fermin .05 .02 .01
☐ 105 Kevin McReynolds .08 .04 .01
☐ 106 Dave Stieb .05 .02 .01
☐ 107 Jeffrey Leonard .05 .02 .01
☐ 108 Dave Henderson .05 .02 .01
☐ 109 Sid Bream .05 .02 .01
☐ 110 Henry Cotto .05 .02 .01
☐ 111 Shawon Dunston .08 .04 .01
☐ 112 Mariano Duncan .05 .02 .01
☐ 113 Joe Girardi .05 .02 .01
☐ 114 Billy Hatcher .05 .02 .01
☐ 115 Greg Maddux .15 .07 .02
☐ 116 Jerry Browne .05 .02 .01
☐ 117 Juan Samuel .05 .02 .01
☐ 118 Steve Olin .08 .04 .01
☐ 119 Alfredo Griffin .05 .02 .01
☐ 120 Mitch Webster .05 .02 .01
☐ 121 Joel Skinner .05 .02 .01
☐ 122 Frank Viola .08 .04 .01
☐ 123 Cory Snyder .05 .02 .01
☐ 124 Howard Johnson .08 .04 .01
☐ 125 Carlos Baerga .35 .16 .04
☐ 126 Tony Fernandez .08 .04 .01
☐ 127 Dave Stewart .08 .04 .01
☐ 128 Jay Buhner .08 .04 .01
☐ 129 Mike LaValliere .05 .02 .01
☐ 130 Scott Bradley .05 .02 .01
☐ 131 Tony Phillips .05 .02 .01
☐ 132 Ryne Sandberg .40 .18 .05
☐ 133 Paul O'Neill .08 .04 .01
☐ 134 Mark Grace .15 .07 .02
☐ 135 Chris Sabo .08 .04 .01
☐ 136 Ramon Martinez .10 .05 .01
☐ 137 Brook Jacoby .05 .02 .01
☐ 138 Candy Maldonado .05 .02 .01
☐ 139 Mike Scioscia .05 .02 .01
☐ 140 Chris James .05 .02 .01
☐ 141 Craig Worthington .05 .02 .01
☐ 142 Manny Lee .05 .02 .01
☐ 143 Tim Raines .08 .04 .01
☐ 144 Sandy Alomar Jr. .08 .04 .01
☐ 145 John Olerud .25 .11 .03
☐ 146 Ozzie Canseco .10 .05 .01
(With Jose)
☐ 147 Pat Borders .05 .02 .01
☐ 148 Harold Reynolds .05 .02 .01
☐ 149 Tom Henke .08 .04 .01
☐ 150 R.J. Reynolds .05 .02 .01
☐ 151 Mike Gallego .05 .02 .01
☐ 152 Bobby Bonilla .15 .07 .02
☐ 153 Terry Steinbach .08 .04 .01
☐ 154 Barry Bonds .30 .14 .04
☐ 155 Jose Canseco .35 .16 .04
☐ 156 Gregg Jefferies .08 .04 .01
☐ 157 Matt Williams .08 .04 .01
☐ 158 Craig Biggio .08 .04 .01
☐ 159 Daryl Boston .05 .02 .01
☐ 160 Ricky Jordan .05 .02 .01
☐ 161 Stan Belinda .05 .02 .01
☐ 162 Ozzie Smith .15 .07 .02
☐ 163 Tom Brunansky .08 .04 .01
☐ 164 Todd Zeile .08 .04 .01
☐ 165 Mike Greenwell .08 .04 .01
☐ 166 Kal Daniels .05 .02 .01
☐ 167 Kent Hrbek .08 .04 .01
☐ 168 Franklin Stubbs .05 .02 .01
☐ 169 Dick Schofield .05 .02 .01
☐ 170 Junior Ortiz .05 .02 .01
☐ 171 Hector Villanueva .05 .02 .01
☐ 172 Dennis Eckersley .12 .05 .02
☐ 173 Mitch Williams .05 .02 .01
☐ 174 Mark McGwire .35 .16 .04
☐ 175 Fernando Valenzuela 3X .08 .04 .01
☐ 176 Gary Carter .08 .04 .01
☐ 177 Dave Magadan .08 .04 .01
☐ 178 Robby Thompson .05 .02 .01
☐ 179 Bob Ojeda .05 .02 .01
☐ 180 Ken Caminiti .08 .04 .01
☐ 181 Don Slaught .05 .02 .01
☐ 182 Luis Rivera .05 .02 .01
☐ 183 Jay Bell .08 .04 .01
☐ 184 Jody Reed .05 .02 .01
☐ 185 Wally Backman .05 .02 .01
☐ 186 Dave Martinez .05 .02 .01
☐ 187 Luis Polonia .08 .04 .01
☐ 188 Shane Mack .08 .04 .01
☐ 189 Spike Owen .05 .02 .01

☐ 190 Scott Bailes .05 .02 .01
☐ 191 John Russell .05 .02 .01
☐ 192 Walt Weiss .05 .02 .01
☐ 193 Jose Oquendo .05 .02 .01
☐ 194 Carney Lansford .08 .04 .01
☐ 195 Jeff Huson .05 .02 .01
☐ 196 Keith Miller .05 .02 .01
☐ 197 Eric Yelding .05 .02 .01
☐ 198 Ron Darling .08 .04 .01
☐ 199 John Kruk .08 .04 .01
☐ 200 Checklist 101-200 .06 .01 .00
☐ 201 John Shelby .05 .02 .01
☐ 202 Bob Geren .05 .02 .01
☐ 203 Lance McCullers .05 .02 .01
☐ 204 Alvaro Espinoza .05 .02 .01
☐ 205 Mark Salas .05 .02 .01
☐ 206 Mike Pagliarulo .05 .02 .01
☐ 207 Jose Uribe .05 .02 .01
☐ 208 Jim Deshaies .05 .02 .01
☐ 209 Ron Karkovice .05 .02 .01
☐ 210 Rafael Ramirez .05 .02 .01
☐ 211 Donnie Hill .05 .02 .01
☐ 212 Brian Harper .05 .02 .01
☐ 213 Jack Howell .05 .02 .01
☐ 214 Wes Gardner .05 .02 .01
☐ 215 Tim Burke .05 .02 .01
☐ 216 Doug Jones .05 .02 .01
☐ 217 Hubie Brooks .05 .02 .01
☐ 218 Tom Candiotti .05 .02 .01
☐ 219 Gerald Perry .05 .02 .01
☐ 220 Jose DeLeon .05 .02 .01
☐ 221 Wally Whitehurst .05 .02 .01
☐ 222 Alan Mills .15 .07 .02
☐ 223 Alan Trammell .08 .04 .01
☐ 224 Dwight Gooden .08 .04 .01
☐ 225 Travis Fryman 2.00 .90 .25
☐ 226 Joe Carter .20 .09 .03
☐ 227 Julio Franco .08 .04 .01
☐ 228 Craig Lefferts .05 .02 .01
☐ 229 Gary Pettis .05 .02 .01
☐ 230 Dennis Rasmussen .05 .02 .01
☐ 231A Brian Downing ERR .25 .11 .03
(No position on front)
☐ 231B Brian Downing COR .40 .18 .05
(DH on front)
☐ 232 Carlos Quintana .05 .02 .01
☐ 233 Gary Gaetti .05 .02 .01
☐ 234 Mark Langston .08 .04 .01
☐ 235 Tim Wallach .08 .04 .01
☐ 236 Greg Swindell .08 .04 .01
☐ 237 Eddie Murray .15 .07 .02
☐ 238 Jeff Manto .05 .02 .01
☐ 239 Lenny Harris .05 .02 .01
☐ 240 Jesse Orosco .05 .02 .01
☐ 241 Scott Lusader .05 .02 .01
☐ 242 Sid Fernandez .08 .04 .01
☐ 243 Jim Leyritz .05 .02 .01
☐ 244 Cecil Fielder .20 .09 .03
☐ 245 Darryl Strawberry .20 .09 .03
☐ 246 Frank Thomas UER 4.00 1.80 .50
(Comiskey Park
misspelled Comisky)
☐ 247 Kevin Mitchell .08 .04 .01
☐ 248 Lance Johnson .05 .02 .01
☐ 249 Rick Reuschel .05 .02 .01
☐ 250 Mark Portugal .05 .02 .01
☐ 251 Derek Lilliquist .05 .02 .01
☐ 252 Brian Holman .05 .02 .01
☐ 253 Rafael Valdez UER .05 .02 .01
(Born 4/17/68,
should be 12/17/67)
☐ 254 B.J. Surhoff .05 .02 .01
☐ 255 Tony Gwynn .20 .09 .03
☐ 256 Andy Van Slyke .10 .05 .01
☐ 257 Todd Stottlemyre .08 .04 .01
☐ 258 Jose Lind .05 .02 .01
☐ 259 Greg Myers .05 .02 .01
☐ 260 Jeff Ballard .05 .02 .01
☐ 261 Bobby Thigpen .05 .02 .01
☐ 262 Jimmy Kremers .05 .02 .01
☐ 263 Robin Ventura .40 .18 .05
☐ 264 John Smoltz .20 .09 .03
☐ 265 Sammy Sosa .08 .04 .01
☐ 266 Gary Sheffield .40 .18 .05
☐ 267 Len Dykstra .08 .04 .01
☐ 268 Bill Spiers .05 .02 .01
☐ 269 Charlie Hayes .05 .02 .01
☐ 270 Brett Butler .08 .04 .01
☐ 271 Bip Roberts .08 .04 .01
☐ 272 Rob Deer .08 .04 .01
☐ 273 Fred Lynn .08 .04 .01
☐ 274 Dave Parker .08 .04 .01
☐ 275 Andy Benes .12 .05 .02
☐ 276 Glenallen Hill .05 .02 .01
☐ 277 Steve Howard .10 .05 .01
☐ 278 Doug Drabek .08 .04 .01
☐ 279 Joe Oliver .05 .02 .01
☐ 280 Todd Benzinger .05 .02 .01
☐ 281 Eric King .05 .02 .01
☐ 282 Jim Presley .05 .02 .01
☐ 283 Ken Patterson .05 .02 .01
☐ 284 Jack Daugherty .05 .02 .01
☐ 285 Ivan Calderon .05 .02 .01
☐ 286 Edgar Diaz .05 .02 .01
☐ 287 Kevin Bass .05 .02 .01
☐ 288 Don Carman .05 .02 .01
☐ 289 Greg Brock .05 .02 .01
☐ 290 John Franco .08 .04 .01
☐ 291 Joey Cora .05 .02 .01
☐ 292 Bill Wegman .05 .02 .01
☐ 293 Eric Show .05 .02 .01
☐ 294 Scott Bankhead .05 .02 .01
☐ 295 Garry Templeton .05 .02 .01
☐ 296 Mickey Tettleton .08 .04 .01
☐ 297 Luis Sojo .05 .02 .01
☐ 298 Jose Rijo .08 .04 .01
☐ 299 Dave Johnson .05 .02 .01
☐ 300 Checklist 201-300 .06 .01 .00
☐ 301 Mark Grant .05 .02 .01
☐ 302 Pete Harnisch .08 .04 .01
☐ 303 Greg Olson .05 .02 .01
☐ 304 Anthony Telford .05 .02 .01
☐ 305 Lonnie Smith .05 .02 .01
☐ 306 Chris Hoiles .25 .11 .03
☐ 307 Bryn Smith .05 .02 .01
☐ 308 Mike Devereaux .08 .04 .01
☐ 309A Milt Thompson ERR .25 .11 .03
(Under yr information
has print dot)
☐ 309B Milt Thompson COR .05 .02 .01
(Under yr information
says 86)
☐ 310 Bob Melvin .05 .02 .01
☐ 311 Luis Salazar .05 .02 .01
☐ 312 Ed Whitson .05 .02 .01
☐ 313 Charlie Hough .05 .02 .01
☐ 314 Dave Clark .05 .02 .01
☐ 315 Eric Gunderson .05 .02 .01
☐ 316 Dan Petry .05 .02 .01
☐ 317 Dante Bichette UER .05 .02 .01
(Assists misspelled
as assissts)
☐ 318 Mike Heath .05 .02 .01
☐ 319 Damon Berryhill .05 .02 .01
☐ 320 Walt Terrell .05 .02 .01
☐ 321 Scott Fletcher .05 .02 .01
☐ 322 Dan Plesac .05 .02 .01
☐ 323 Jack McDowell .15 .07 .02
☐ 324 Paul Molitor .10 .05 .01
☐ 325 Ozzie Guillen .05 .02 .01
☐ 326 Gregg Olson .08 .04 .01
☐ 327 Pedro Guerrero .08 .04 .01
☐ 328 Bob Milacki .05 .02 .01
☐ 329 John Tudor UER .05 .02 .01
('90 Cardinals,
should be '90 Dodgers)
☐ 330 Steve Finley UER .08 .04 .01
(Born 3/12/65,
should be 5/12)
☐ 331 Jack Clark .08 .04 .01
☐ 332 Jerome Walton .05 .02 .01
☐ 333 Andy Hawkins .05 .02 .01
☐ 334 Derrick May .08 .04 .01
☐ 335 Roberto Alomar .50 .23 .06
☐ 336 Jack Morris .10 .05 .01
☐ 337 Dave Winfield .15 .07 .02
☐ 338 Steve Searcy .05 .02 .01
☐ 339 Chili Davis .08 .04 .01
☐ 340 Larry Sheets .05 .02 .01
☐ 341 Ted Higuera .05 .02 .01
☐ 342 David Segui .05 .02 .01
☐ 343 Greg Cadaret .05 .02 .01
☐ 344 Robin Yount .15 .07 .02
☐ 345 Nolan Ryan .75 .35 .09
☐ 346 Ray Lankford .35 .16 .04
☐ 347 Cal Ripken .50 .23 .06
☐ 348 Lee Smith .08 .04 .01
☐ 349 Brady Anderson .08 .04 .01
☐ 350 Frank DiPino .05 .02 .01
☐ 351 Hal Morris .08 .04 .01
☐ 352 Deion Sanders .30 .14 .04
☐ 353 Barry Larkin .15 .07 .02
☐ 354 Don Mattingly .20 .09 .03
☐ 355 Eric Davis .08 .04 .01
☐ 356 Jose Offerman .08 .04 .01
☐ 357 Mel Rojas .05 .02 .01

☐ 358 Rudy Seanez .15 .07 .02
☐ 359 Oil Can Boyd .05 .02 .01
☐ 360 Nelson Liriano .05 .02 .01
☐ 361 Ron Gant .20 .09 .03
☐ 362 Howard Farmer .05 .02 .01
☐ 363 David Justice .60 .25 .08
☐ 364 Delino DeShields .25 .11 .03
☐ 365 Steve Avery .40 .18 .05
☐ 366 David Cone .12 .05 .02
☐ 367 Lou Whitaker .08 .04 .01
☐ 368 Von Hayes .05 .02 .01
☐ 369 Frank Tanana .05 .02 .01
☐ 370 Tim Teufel .05 .02 .01
☐ 371 Randy Myers .08 .04 .01
☐ 372 Roberto Kelly .08 .04 .01
☐ 373 Jack Armstrong .05 .02 .01
☐ 374 Kelly Gruber .08 .04 .01
☐ 375 Kevin Maas .10 .05 .01
☐ 376 Randy Johnson .08 .04 .01
☐ 377 David West .05 .02 .01
☐ 378 Brent Knackert .05 .02 .01
☐ 379 Rick Honeycutt .05 .02 .01
☐ 380 Kevin Gross .05 .02 .01
☐ 381 Tom Foley .05 .02 .01
☐ 382 Jeff Blauser .05 .02 .01
☐ 383 Scott Ruskin .05 .02 .01
☐ 384 Andres Thomas .05 .02 .01
☐ 385 Dennis Martinez .08 .04 .01
☐ 386 Mike Henneman .05 .02 .01
☐ 387 Felix Jose .08 .04 .01
☐ 388 Alejandro Pena .05 .02 .01
☐ 389 Chet Lemon .05 .02 .01
☐ 390 Craig Wilson .10 .05 .01
☐ 391 Chuck Crim .05 .02 .01
☐ 392 Mel Hall .05 .02 .01
☐ 393 Mark Knudson .05 .02 .01
☐ 394 Norm Charlton .08 .04 .01
☐ 395 Mike Felder .05 .02 .01
☐ 396 Tim Layana .05 .02 .01
☐ 397 Steve Frey .05 .02 .01
☐ 398 Bill Doran .05 .02 .01
☐ 399 Dion James .05 .02 .01
☐ 400 Checklist 301-400 .06 .01 .00
☐ 401 Ron Hassey .05 .02 .01
☐ 402 Don Robinson .05 .02 .01
☐ 403 Gene Nelson .05 .02 .01
☐ 404 Terry Kennedy .05 .02 .01
☐ 405 Todd Burns .05 .02 .01
☐ 406 Roger McDowell .05 .02 .01
☐ 407 Bob Kipper .05 .02 .01
☐ 408 Darren Daulton .08 .04 .01
☐ 409 Chuck Cary .05 .02 .01
☐ 410 Bruce Ruffin .05 .02 .01
☐ 411 Juan Berenguer .05 .02 .01
☐ 412 Gary Ward .05 .02 .01
☐ 413 Al Newman .05 .02 .01
☐ 414 Danny Jackson .05 .02 .01
☐ 415 Greg Gagne .05 .02 .01
☐ 416 Tom Herr .05 .02 .01
☐ 417 Jeff Parrett .05 .02 .01
☐ 418 Jeff Reardon .08 .04 .01
☐ 419 Mark Lemke .05 .02 .01
☐ 420 Charlie O'Brien .05 .02 .01
☐ 421 Willie Randolph .08 .04 .01
☐ 422 Steve Bedrosian .05 .02 .01
☐ 423 Mike Moore .05 .02 .01
☐ 424 Jeff Brantley .05 .02 .01
☐ 425 Bob Welch .05 .02 .01
☐ 426 Terry Mulholland .05 .02 .01
☐ 427 Willie Blair .05 .02 .01
☐ 428 Darrin Fletcher .05 .02 .01
☐ 429 Mike Witt .05 .02 .01
☐ 430 Joe Boever .05 .02 .01
☐ 431 Tom Gordon .08 .04 .01
☐ 432 Pedro Munoz .50 .23 .06
☐ 433 Kevin Seitzer .08 .04 .01
☐ 434 Kevin Tapani .08 .04 .01
☐ 435 Bret Saberhagen .08 .04 .01
☐ 436 Ellis Burks .08 .04 .01
☐ 437 Chuck Finley .08 .04 .01
☐ 438 Mike Boddicker .05 .02 .01
☐ 439 Francisco Cabrera .05 .02 .01
☐ 440 Todd Hundley .05 .02 .01
☐ 441 Kelly Downs .05 .02 .01
☐ 442 Dann Howitt .05 .02 .01
☐ 443 Scott Garrelts .05 .02 .01
☐ 444 Rickey Henderson 3X .20 .09 .03
☐ 445 Will Clark .30 .14 .04
☐ 446 Ben McDonald .15 .07 .02
☐ 447 Dale Murphy .08 .04 .01
☐ 448 Dave Righetti .05 .02 .01
☐ 449 Dickie Thon .05 .02 .01
☐ 450 Ted Power .05 .02 .01
☐ 451 Scott Coolbaugh .05 .02 .01
☐ 452 Dwight Smith .05 .02 .01
☐ 453 Pete Incaviglia .05 .02 .01
☐ 454 Andre Dawson .15 .07 .02
☐ 455 Ruben Sierra .25 .11 .03
☐ 456 Andres Galarraga .05 .02 .01
☐ 457 Alvin Davis .05 .02 .01
☐ 458 Tony Castillo .05 .02 .01
☐ 459 Pete O'Brien .05 .02 .01
☐ 460 Charlie Leibrandt .05 .02 .01
☐ 461 Vince Coleman .08 .04 .01
☐ 462 Steve Sax .08 .04 .01
☐ 463 Omar Olivares .20 .09 .03
☐ 464 Oscar Azocar .05 .02 .01
☐ 465 Joe Magrane .05 .02 .01
☐ 466 Karl Rhodes .05 .02 .01
☐ 467 Benito Santiago .08 .04 .01
☐ 468 Joe Klink .05 .02 .01
☐ 469 Sil Campusano .05 .02 .01
☐ 470 Mark Parent .05 .02 .01
☐ 471 Shawn Boskie UER .05 .02 .01
(Depleted misspelled
as depleated)
☐ 472 Kevin Brown .08 .04 .01
☐ 473 Rick Sutcliffe .08 .04 .01
☐ 474 Rafael Palmeiro .12 .05 .02
☐ 475 Mike Harkey .08 .04 .01
☐ 476 Jaime Navarro .08 .04 .01
☐ 477 Marquis Grissom UER .25 .11 .03
(DeShields misspelled
as DeSheilds)
☐ 478 Marty Clary .05 .02 .01
☐ 479 Greg Briley .05 .02 .01
☐ 480 Tom Glavine .35 .16 .04
☐ 481 Lee Guetterman .05 .02 .01
☐ 482 Rex Hudler .05 .02 .01
☐ 483 Dave LaPoint .05 .02 .01
☐ 484 Terry Pendleton .10 .05 .01
☐ 485 Jesse Barfield .05 .02 .01
☐ 486 Jose DeJesus .05 .02 .01
☐ 487 Paul Abbott .10 .05 .01
☐ 488 Ken Howell .05 .02 .01
☐ 489 Greg W. Harris .05 .02 .01
☐ 490 Roy Smith .05 .02 .01
☐ 491 Paul Assenmacher .05 .02 .01
☐ 492 Geno Petralli .05 .02 .01
☐ 493 Steve Wilson .05 .02 .01
☐ 494 Kevin Reimer .12 .05 .02
☐ 495 Bill Long .05 .02 .01
☐ 496 Mike Jackson .05 .02 .01
☐ 497 Oddibe McDowell .05 .02 .01
☐ 498 Bill Swift .05 .02 .01
☐ 499 Jeff Treadway .05 .02 .01
☐ 500 Checklist 401-500 .06 .01 .00
☐ 501 Gene Larkin .05 .02 .01
☐ 502 Bob Boone .08 .04 .01
☐ 503 Allan Anderson .05 .02 .01
☐ 504 Luis Aquino .05 .02 .01
☐ 505 Mark Guthrie .05 .02 .01
☐ 506 Joe Orsulak .05 .02 .01
☐ 507 Dana Kiecker .05 .02 .01
☐ 508 Dave Gallagher .05 .02 .01
☐ 509 Greg A. Harris .05 .02 .01
☐ 510 Mark Williamson .05 .02 .01
☐ 511 Casey Candaele .05 .02 .01
☐ 512 Mookie Wilson .05 .02 .01
☐ 513 Dave Smith .05 .02 .01
☐ 514 Chuck Carr .05 .02 .01
☐ 515 Glenn Wilson .05 .02 .01
☐ 516 Mike Fitzgerald .05 .02 .01
☐ 517 Devon White .08 .04 .01
☐ 518 Dave Hollins .20 .09 .03
☐ 519 Mark Eichhorn .05 .02 .01
☐ 520 Otis Nixon .08 .04 .01
☐ 521 Terry Shumpert .05 .02 .01
☐ 522 Scott Erickson .35 .16 .04
☐ 523 Danny Tartabull .08 .04 .01
☐ 524 Orel Hershiser .08 .04 .01
☐ 525 George Brett .15 .07 .02
☐ 526 Greg Vaughn .10 .05 .01
☐ 527 Tim Naehring .12 .05 .02
☐ 528 Curt Schilling .08 .04 .01
☐ 529 Chris Bosio .05 .02 .01
☐ 530 Sam Horn .05 .02 .01
☐ 531 Mike Scott .05 .02 .01
☐ 532 George Bell .08 .04 .01
☐ 533 Eric Anthony .08 .04 .01
☐ 534 Julio Valera .25 .11 .03
☐ 535 Glenn Davis .08 .04 .01
☐ 536 Larry Walker UER .30 .14 .04
(Should have comma
after Expos in text)
☐ 537 Pat Combs .05 .02 .01

☐ 538	Chris Nabholz	.15	.07	.02
☐ 539	Kirk McCaskill	.05	.02	.01
☐ 540	Randy Ready	.05	.02	.01
☐ 541	Mark Gubicza	.05	.02	.01
☐ 542	Rick Aguilera	.08	.04	.01
☐ 543	Brian McRae	.35	.16	.04
☐ 544	Kirby Puckett	.35	.16	.04
☐ 545	Bo Jackson	.20	.09	.03
☐ 546	Wade Boggs	.20	.09	.03
☐ 547	Tim McIntosh	.05	.02	.01
☐ 548	Randy Milligan	.05	.02	.01
☐ 549	Dwight Evans	.08	.04	.01
☐ 550	Billy Ripken	.05	.02	.01
☐ 551	Erik Hanson	.05	.02	.01
☐ 552	Lance Parrish	.08	.04	.01
☐ 553	Tino Martinez	.10	.05	.01
☐ 554	Jim Abbott	.20	.09	.03
☐ 555	Ken Griffey Jr. UER (Second most votes for 1991 All-Star Game)	1.00	.45	.13
☐ 556	Milt Cuyler	.15	.07	.02
☐ 557	Mark Leonard	.10	.05	.01
☐ 558	Jay Howell	.05	.02	.01
☐ 559	Lloyd Moseby	.05	.02	.01
☐ 560	Chris Gwynn	.05	.02	.01
☐ 561	Mark Whiten	.20	.09	.03
☐ 562	Harold Baines	.08	.04	.01
☐ 563	Junior Felix	.05	.02	.01
☐ 564	Darren Lewis	.15	.07	.02
☐ 565	Fred McGriff	.20	.09	.03
☐ 566	Kevin Appier	.08	.04	.01
☐ 567	Luis Gonzalez	.40	.18	.05
☐ 568	Frank White	.05	.02	.01
☐ 569	Juan Agosto	.05	.02	.01
☐ 570	Mike Macfarlane	.05	.02	.01
☐ 571	Bert Blyleven	.08	.04	.01
☐ 572	Ken Griffey Sr.	.25	.11	.03
☐ 573	Lee Stevens	.05	.02	.01
☐ 574	Edgar Martinez	.08	.04	.01
☐ 575	Wally Joyner	.08	.04	.01
☐ 576	Tim Belcher	.08	.04	.01
☐ 577	John Burkett	.05	.02	.01
☐ 578	Mike Morgan	.05	.02	.01
☐ 579	Paul Gibson	.05	.02	.01
☐ 580	Jose Vizcaino	.05	.02	.01
☐ 581	Duane Ward	.05	.02	.01
☐ 582	Scott Sanderson	.05	.02	.01
☐ 583	David Wells	.05	.02	.01
☐ 584	Willie McGee	.08	.04	.01
☐ 585	John Cerutti	.05	.02	.01
☐ 586	Danny Darwin	.05	.02	.01
☐ 587	Kurt Stillwell	.05	.02	.01
☐ 588	Rich Gedman	.05	.02	.01
☐ 589	Mark Davis	.05	.02	.01
☐ 590	Bill Gullickson	.05	.02	.01
☐ 591	Matt Young	.05	.02	.01
☐ 592	Bryan Harvey	.05	.02	.01
☐ 593	Omar Vizquel	.05	.02	.01
☐ 594	Scott Lewis	.15	.07	.02
☐ 595	Dave Valle	.05	.02	.01
☐ 596	Tim Crews	.05	.02	.01
☐ 597	Mike Bielecki	.05	.02	.01
☐ 598	Mike Sharperson	.05	.02	.01
☐ 599	Dave Bergman	.05	.02	.01
☐ 600	Checklist 501-600	.06	.01	.00
☐ 601	Steve Lyons	.05	.02	.01
☐ 602	Bruce Hurst	.08	.04	.01
☐ 603	Donn Pall	.05	.02	.01
☐ 604	Jim Vatcher	.05	.02	.01
☐ 605	Dan Pasqua	.05	.02	.01
☐ 606	Kenny Rogers	.05	.02	.01
☐ 607	Jeff Schulz	.05	.02	.01
☐ 608	Brad Arnsberg	.05	.02	.01
☐ 609	Willie Wilson	.05	.02	.01
☐ 610	Jamie Moyer	.05	.02	.01
☐ 611	Ron Oester	.05	.02	.01
☐ 612	Dennis Cook	.05	.02	.01
☐ 613	Rick Mahler	.05	.02	.01
☐ 614	Bill Landrum	.05	.02	.01
☐ 615	Scott Scudder	.05	.02	.01
☐ 616	Tom Edens	.10	.05	.01
☐ 617	1917 Revisited (White Sox in vintage uniforms)	.10	.05	.01
☐ 618	Jim Gantner	.05	.02	.01
☐ 619	Darrel Akerfelds	.05	.02	.01
☐ 620	Ron Robinson	.05	.02	.01
☐ 621	Scott Radinsky	.05	.02	.01
☐ 622	Pete Smith	.08	.04	.01
☐ 623	Melido Perez	.08	.04	.01
☐ 624	Jerald Clark	.05	.02	.01
☐ 625	Carlos Martinez	.05	.02	.01
☐ 626	Wes Chamberlain	.40	.18	.05
☐ 627	Bobby Witt	.05	.02	.01
☐ 628	Ken Dayley	.05	.02	.01
☐ 629	John Barfield	.05	.02	.01
☐ 630	Bob Tewksbury	.08	.04	.01
☐ 631	Glenn Braggs	.05	.02	.01
☐ 632	Jim Neidlinger	.05	.02	.01
☐ 633	Tom Browning	.05	.02	.01
☐ 634	Kirk Gibson	.08	.04	.01
☐ 635	Rob Dibble	.08	.04	.01
☐ 636A	Stolen Base Leaders (Rickey Henderson and Lou Brock in tuxedos and no date on card)	.25	.11	.03
☐ 636B	Stolen Base Leaders (Dated May 1, 1991 on card front)	.50	.23	.06
☐ 637	Jeff Montgomery	.05	.02	.01
☐ 638	Mike Schooler	.05	.02	.01
☐ 639	Storm Davis	.05	.02	.01
☐ 640	Rich Rodriguez	.10	.05	.01
☐ 641	Phil Bradley	.05	.02	.01
☐ 642	Kent Mercker	.08	.04	.01
☐ 643	Carlton Fisk	.15	.07	.02
☐ 644	Mike Bell	.10	.05	.01
☐ 645	Alex Fernandez	.25	.11	.03
☐ 646	Juan Gonzalez	.90	.40	.11
☐ 647	Ken Hill	.08	.04	.01
☐ 648	Jeff Russell	.05	.02	.01
☐ 649	Chuck Malone	.05	.02	.01
☐ 650	Steve Buechele	.05	.02	.01
☐ 651	Mike Benjamin	.05	.02	.01
☐ 652	Tony Pena	.05	.02	.01
☐ 653	Trevor Wilson	.05	.02	.01
☐ 654	Alex Cole	.05	.02	.01
☐ 655	Roger Clemens	.40	.18	.05
☐ 656	The Bashing Years (Mark McGwire)	.15	.07	.02
☐ 657	Joe Grahe	.30	.14	.04
☐ 658	Jim Eisenreich	.05	.02	.01
☐ 659	Dan Gladden	.05	.02	.01
☐ 660	Steve Farr	.05	.02	.01
☐ 661	Bill Sampen	.05	.02	.01
☐ 662	Dave Rohde	.05	.02	.01
☐ 663	Mark Gardner	.05	.02	.01
☐ 664	Mike Simms	.12	.05	.02
☐ 665	Moises Alou	.50	.23	.06
☐ 666	Mickey Hatcher	.05	.02	.01
☐ 667	Jimmy Key	.05	.02	.01
☐ 668	John Wetteland	.08	.04	.01
☐ 669	John Smiley	.08	.04	.01
☐ 670	Jim Acker	.05	.02	.01
☐ 671	Pascual Perez	.05	.02	.01
☐ 672	Reggie Harris UER (Opportunity misspelled as oppurtinty)	.12	.05	.02
☐ 673	Matt Nokes	.05	.02	.01
☐ 674	Rafael Novoa	.10	.05	.01
☐ 675	Hensley Meulens	.08	.04	.01
☐ 676	Jeff M. Robinson	.05	.02	.01
☐ 677	Ground Breaking (New Comiskey Park; Carlton Fisk and Robin Ventura)	.20	.09	.03
☐ 678	Johnny Ray	.05	.02	.01
☐ 679	Greg Hibbard	.05	.02	.01
☐ 680	Paul Sorrento	.08	.04	.01
☐ 681	Mike Marshall	.05	.02	.01
☐ 682	Jim Clancy	.05	.02	.01
☐ 683	Rob Murphy	.05	.02	.01
☐ 684	Dave Schmidt	.05	.02	.01
☐ 685	Jeff Gray	.05	.02	.01
☐ 686	Mike Hartley	.05	.02	.01
☐ 687	Jeff King	.05	.02	.01
☐ 688	Stan Javier	.05	.02	.01
☐ 689	Bob Walk	.05	.02	.01
☐ 690	Jim Gott	.05	.02	.01
☐ 691	Mike LaCoss	.05	.02	.01
☐ 692	John Farrell	.05	.02	.01
☐ 693	Tim Leary	.05	.02	.01
☐ 694	Mike Walker	.05	.02	.01
☐ 695	Eric Plunk	.05	.02	.01
☐ 696	Mike Fetters	.05	.02	.01
☐ 697	Wayne Edwards	.05	.02	.01
☐ 698	Tim Drummond	.05	.02	.01
☐ 699	Willie Fraser	.05	.02	.01
☐ 700	Checklist 601-700	.06	.01	.00
☐ 701	Mike Heath	.05	.02	.01
☐ 702	Rookie Threats Luis Gonzalez Karl Rhodes Jeff Bagwell	.50	.23	.06
☐ 703	Jose Mesa	.05	.02	.01
☐ 704	Dave Smith	.05	.02	.01

☐ 705 Danny Darwin	.05	.02	.01
☐ 706 Rafael Belliard	.05	.02	.01
☐ 707 Rob Murphy	.05	.02	.01
☐ 708 Terry Pendleton	.10	.05	.01
☐ 709 Mike Pagliarulo	.05	.02	.01
☐ 710 Sid Bream	.05	.02	.01
☐ 711 Junior Felix	.05	.02	.01
☐ 712 Dante Bichette	.05	.02	.01
☐ 713 Kevin Gross	.05	.02	.01
☐ 714 Luis Sojo	.05	.02	.01
☐ 715 Bob Ojeda	.05	.02	.01
☐ 716 Julio Machado	.05	.02	.01
☐ 717 Steve Farr	.05	.02	.01
☐ 718 Franklin Stubbs	.05	.02	.01
☐ 719 Mike Boddicker	.05	.02	.01
☐ 720 Willie Randolph	.08	.04	.01
☐ 721 Willie McGee	.08	.04	.01
☐ 722 Chili Davis	.08	.04	.01
☐ 723 Danny Jackson	.05	.02	.01
☐ 724 Cory Snyder	.05	.02	.01
☐ 725 MVP Lineup Andre Dawson George Bell Ryne Sandberg	.15	.07	.02
☐ 726 Rob Deer	.08	.04	.01
☐ 727 Rich DeLucia	.05	.02	.01
☐ 728 Mike Perez	.20	.09	.03
☐ 729 Mickey Tettleton	.08	.04	.01
☐ 730 Mike Blowers	.05	.02	.01
☐ 731 Gary Gaetti	.05	.02	.01
☐ 732 Brett Butler	.08	.04	.01
☐ 733 Dave Parker	.08	.04	.01
☐ 734 Eddie Zosky	.15	.07	.02
☐ 735 Jack Clark	.08	.04	.01
☐ 736 Jack Morris	.10	.05	.01
☐ 737 Kirk Gibson	.08	.04	.01
☐ 738 Steve Bedrosian	.05	.02	.01
☐ 739 Candy Maldonado	.05	.02	.01
☐ 740 Matt Young	.05	.02	.01
☐ 741 Rich Garces	.12	.05	.02
☐ 742 George Bell	.08	.04	.01
☐ 743 Deion Sanders	.30	.14	.04
☐ 744 Bo Jackson	.20	.09	.03
☐ 745 Luis Mercedes	.40	.18	.05
☐ 746 Reggie Jefferson UER (Throwing left on card; back has throws right)	.30	.14	.04
☐ 747 Pete Incaviglia	.05	.02	.01
☐ 748 Chris Hammond	.10	.05	.01
☐ 749 Mike Stanton	.05	.02	.01
☐ 750 Scott Sanderson	.05	.02	.01
☐ 751 Paul Faries	.05	.02	.01
☐ 752 Al Osuna	.10	.05	.01
☐ 753 Steve Chitren	.10	.05	.01
☐ 754 Tony Fernandez	.08	.04	.01
☐ 755 Jeff Bagwell UER (Strikeout and walk totals reversed)	2.00	.90	.25
☐ 756 Kirk Dressendorfer	.10	.05	.01
☐ 757 Glenn Davis	.08	.04	.01
☐ 758 Gary Carter	.08	.04	.01
☐ 759 Zane Smith	.05	.02	.01
☐ 760 Vance Law	.05	.02	.01
☐ 761 Denis Boucher	.20	.09	.03
☐ 762 Turner Ward	.10	.05	.01
☐ 763 Roberto Alomar	.50	.23	.06
☐ 764 Albert Belle	.30	.14	.04
☐ 765 Joe Carter	.20	.09	.03
☐ 766 Pete Schourek	.20	.09	.03
☐ 767 Heathcliff Slocumb	.05	.02	.01
☐ 768 Vince Coleman	.08	.04	.01
☐ 769 Mitch Williams	.05	.02	.01
☐ 770 Brian Downing	.05	.02	.01
☐ 771 Dana Allison	.12	.05	.02
☐ 772 Pete Harnisch	.08	.04	.01
☐ 773 Tim Raines	.08	.04	.01
☐ 774 Darryl Kile	.20	.09	.03
☐ 775 Fred McGriff	.20	.09	.03
☐ 776 Dwight Evans	.08	.04	.01
☐ 777 Joe Slusarski	.15	.07	.02
☐ 778 Dave Righetti	.05	.02	.01
☐ 779 Jeff Hamilton	.05	.02	.01
☐ 780 Ernest Riles	.05	.02	.01
☐ 781 Ken Dayley	.05	.02	.01
☐ 782 Eric King	.05	.02	.01
☐ 783 Devon White	.08	.04	.01
☐ 784 Beau Allred	.05	.02	.01
☐ 785 Mike Timlin	.15	.07	.02
☐ 786 Ivan Calderon	.05	.02	.01
☐ 787 Hubie Brooks	.05	.02	.01
☐ 788 Juan Agosto	.05	.02	.01
☐ 789 Barry Jones	.05	.02	.01
☐ 790 Wally Backman	.05	.02	.01
☐ 791 Jim Presley	.05	.02	.01
☐ 792 Charlie Hough	.05	.02	.01
☐ 793 Larry Andersen	.05	.02	.01
☐ 794 Steve Finley	.08	.04	.01
☐ 795 Shawn Abner	.05	.02	.01
☐ 796 Jeff M. Robinson	.05	.02	.01
☐ 797 Joe Bitker	.05	.02	.01
☐ 798 Eric Show	.05	.02	.01
☐ 799 Bud Black	.05	.02	.01
☐ 800 Checklist 701-800	.06	.01	.00
☐ HH1 Hank Aaron Hologram	2.50	1.15	.30
☐ SP1 Michael Jordan SP (Shown batting in White Sox uniform)	10.00	4.50	1.25
☐ SP2 Henderson/Ryan (Rickey and Nolan) (Commemorating 5/1/91 record breaking)	4.00	1.80	.50

1991 Upper Deck Hank Aaron Heroes

These standard-size (2 1/2" by 3 1/2") cards were issued in honor of Hall of Famer Hank Aaron and inserted in Upper Deck high number wax packs. The fronts have color player photos superimposed over a circular shot. Inside a red border stripe, a tan background fills in the rest of the card face. The Baseball Heroes logo adorns the card face. The backs have a similar design, except with an extended caption presented on a light gray background. Aaron autographed 2,500 of card number 27, which featured his portrait by noted sports artist Vernon Wells. The cards are numbered on the back in continuation of the Baseball Heroes set.

	MT	EX-MT	VG
COMPLETE SET (10)	8.00	3.60	1.00
COMMON AARON (19-27)	.60	.25	.08
☐ 19 1954: Rookie Year	.60	.25	.08
☐ 20 1957: MVP	.60	.25	.08
☐ 21 1966: Move to Atlanta	.60	.25	.08
☐ 22 1970: 3,000	.60	.25	.08
☐ 23 1974: 715	.60	.25	.08
☐ 24 1975: Return to Milwaukee	.60	.25	.08
☐ 25 1976: 755	.60	.25	.08
☐ 26 1982: Hall of Fame	.60	.25	.08
☐ 27 Checklist 19-27	.60	.25	.08
☐ AU3 Hank Aaron (Signed and Numbered out of 2500)	350.00	160.00	45.00
☐ NNO Title/Header card SP	4.00	1.80	.50

1991 Upper Deck Final Edition

The 1991 Upper Deck Final Edition boxed set contains 100 cards and showcases players who made major contributions during their team's late-season pennant drive. In addition to the late season traded and impact Rookie Cards (22-78), the

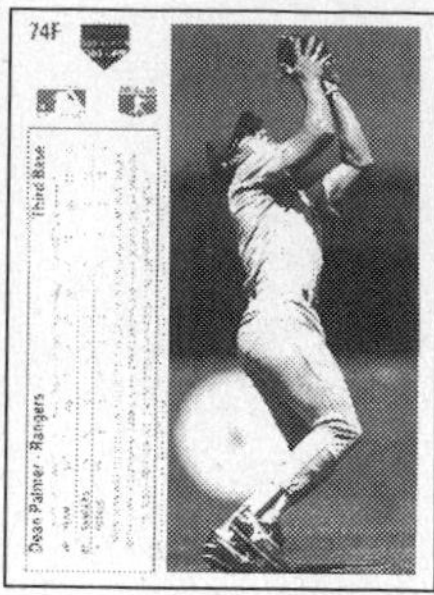

set includes two special subsets: Diamond Skills cards (1-21), depicting the best Minor League prospects, and All-Star cards (80-99). Six assorted hologram cards were issued with each set. The cards measure the standard size (2 1/2" by 3 1/2"). The fronts feature posed or action color player photos on a white card face, with the upper left corner of the picture cut out to provide space for the Upper Deck logo. The pictures are bordered in green on the left, with the player's name in a tan border below the picture. Two-thirds of the back are occupied by another color action photo, with biography, statistics, and career highlights in a horizontally oriented red rectangle to the left of the picture. The cards are numbered on the back with an F suffix. Among the outstanding Rookie Cards in this set are Ryan Klesko, Pedro Martinez, Marc Newfield, Frankie Rodriguez, Ivan Rodriguez, and Dmitri Young.

	MT	EX-MT	VG
COMPLETE SET (100)	14.00	6.25	1.75
COMMON PLAYER (1F-100F)	.05	.02	.01
☐ 1F Diamond Skills Checklist Card (Ryan Klesko and Reggie Sanders)	.40	.12	.04
☐ 2F Pedro Martinez	.90	.40	.11
☐ 3F Lance Dickson	.10	.05	.01
☐ 4F Royce Clayton	.30	.14	.04
☐ 5F Scott Bryant	.15	.07	.02
☐ 6F Dan Wilson	.30	.14	.04
☐ 7F Dmitri Young	1.50	.65	.19
☐ 8F Ryan Klesko	1.50	.65	.19
☐ 9F Tom Goodwin	.15	.07	.02
☐ 10F Rondell White	1.00	.45	.13
☐ 11F Reggie Sanders	.40	.18	.05
☐ 12F Todd Van Poppel	.35	.16	.04
☐ 13F Arthur Rhodes	.75	.35	.09
☐ 14F Eddie Zosky	.08	.04	.01
☐ 15F Gerald Williams	.40	.18	.05
☐ 16F Robert Eenhoorn	.15	.07	.02
☐ 17F Jim Thome	.40	.18	.05
☐ 18F Marc Newfield	.75	.35	.09
☐ 19F Kerwin Moore	.20	.09	.03
☐ 20F Jeff McNeely	.30	.14	.04
☐ 21F Frankie Rodriguez	.75	.35	.09
☐ 22F Andy Mota	.12	.05	.02
☐ 23F Chris Haney	.20	.09	.03
☐ 24F Kenny Lofton	1.75	.80	.22
☐ 25F Dave Nilsson	.60	.25	.08
☐ 26F Derek Bell	.50	.23	.06
☐ 27F Frank Castillo	.25	.11	.03
☐ 28F Candy Maldonado	.05	.02	.01
☐ 29F Chuck McElroy	.05	.02	.01
☐ 30F Chito Martinez	.15	.07	.02
☐ 31F Steve Howe	.05	.02	.01
☐ 32F Freddie Benavides	.05	.02	.01
☐ 33F Scott Kamieniecki	.12	.05	.02
☐ 34F Denny Neagle	.20	.09	.03
☐ 35F Mike Humphreys	.20	.09	.03
☐ 36F Mike Remlinger	.05	.02	.01
☐ 37F Scott Coolbaugh	.05	.02	.01
☐ 38F Darren Lewis	.10	.05	.01
☐ 39F Thomas Howard	.05	.02	.01
☐ 40F John Candelaria	.05	.02	.01
☐ 41F Todd Benzinger	.05	.02	.01
☐ 42F Wilson Alvarez	.10	.05	.01
☐ 43F Patrick Lennon	.20	.09	.03
☐ 44F Rusty Meacham	.15	.07	.02
☐ 45F Ryan Bowen	.20	.09	.03
☐ 46F Rick Wilkins	.12	.05	.02
☐ 47F Ed Sprague	.30	.14	.04
☐ 48F Bob Scanlan	.12	.05	.02
☐ 49F Tom Candiotti	.05	.02	.01
☐ 50F Perfecto (Dennis Martinez)	.08	.04	.01
☐ 51F Oil Can Boyd	.05	.02	.01
☐ 52F Glenallen Hill	.05	.02	.01
☐ 53F Scott Livingstone	.35	.16	.04
☐ 54F Brian Hunter	.40	.18	.05
☐ 55F Ivan Rodriguez	2.00	.90	.25
☐ 56F Keith Mitchell	.30	.14	.04
☐ 57F Roger McDowell	.05	.02	.01
☐ 58F Otis Nixon	.08	.04	.01
☐ 59F Juan Bell	.05	.02	.01
☐ 60F Bill Krueger	.05	.02	.01
☐ 61F Chris Donnels	.15	.07	.02
☐ 62F Tommy Greene	.05	.02	.01
☐ 63F Doug Simons	.05	.02	.01
☐ 64F Andy Ashby	.20	.09	.03
☐ 65F Anthony Young	.25	.11	.03
☐ 66F Kevin Morton	.15	.07	.02
☐ 67F Bret Barberie	.20	.09	.03
☐ 68F Scott Servais	.10	.05	.01
☐ 69F Ron Darling	.08	.04	.01
☐ 70F Tim Burke	.05	.02	.01
☐ 71F Vicente Palacios	.05	.02	.01
☐ 72F Gerald Alexander	.10	.05	.01
☐ 73F Reggie Jefferson	.15	.07	.02
☐ 74F Dean Palmer	.30	.14	.04
☐ 75F Mark Whiten	.12	.05	.02
☐ 76F Randy Tomlin	.40	.18	.05
☐ 77F Mark Wohlers	.35	.16	.04
☐ 78F Brook Jacoby	.05	.02	.01
☐ 79F All-Star Checklist (Ken Griffey Jr. and Ryne Sandberg)	.30	.09	.03
☐ 80F Jack Morris AS	.08	.04	.01
☐ 81F Sandy Alomar Jr. AS	.05	.02	.01
☐ 82F Cecil Fielder AS	.15	.07	.02
☐ 83F Roberto Alomar AS	.25	.11	.03
☐ 84F Wade Boggs AS	.15	.07	.02
☐ 85F Cal Ripken AS	.50	.23	.06
☐ 86F Rickey Henderson AS	.15	.07	.02
☐ 87F Ken Griffey Jr. AS	.50	.23	.06
☐ 88F Dave Henderson AS	.05	.02	.01
☐ 89F Danny Tartabull AS	.08	.04	.01
☐ 90F Tom Glavine AS	.15	.07	.02
☐ 91F Benito Santiago AS	.05	.02	.01
☐ 92F Will Clark AS	.20	.09	.03
☐ 93F Ryne Sandberg AS	.25	.11	.03
☐ 94F Chris Sabo AS	.05	.02	.01
☐ 95F Ozzie Smith AS	.10	.05	.01
☐ 96F Ivan Calderon AS	.05	.02	.01
☐ 97F Tony Gwynn AS	.15	.07	.02
☐ 98F Andre Dawson AS	.10	.05	.01
☐ 99F Bobby Bonilla AS	.08	.04	.01
☐ 100F Checklist 1-100	.08	.01	.00

1991 Upper Deck HOF Heroes

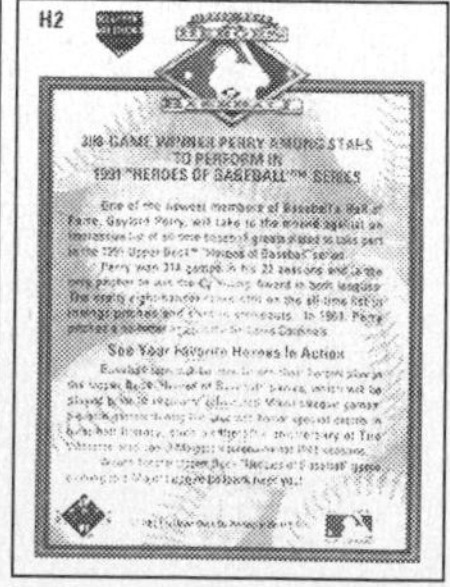

These standard-size (2 1/2" by 3 1/2") cards were (random) insert cards in Upper Deck Baseball Heroes wax packs. On a white card face, the fronts of the first three cards have sepia-toned player photos, with red, gold, and blue border stripes. The player's name appears in a gold border stripe beneath the picture, with the Upper Deck "Heroes of

Baseball" logo in the lower right corner. The backs have a similar design to the fronts, except with a career summary and an advertisement for Upper Deck "Heroes of Baseball" games that will be played prior to regularly scheduled Major League games. The fourth card features a color portrait of the three players by noted sports artist Vernon Wells. The cards are numbered on the back.

	MT	EX-MT	VG
COMPLETE SET (4)	50.00	23.00	6.25
COMMON HOF HEROES (H1-H4)	15.00	6.75	1.90
☐ H1 Harmon Killebrew	15.00	6.75	1.90
☐ H1AU Harmon Killebrew (Signed and Numbered out of 3000)	150.00	70.00	19.00
☐ H2 Gaylord Perry	15.00	6.75	1.90
☐ H2AU Gaylord Perry (Signed and Numbered out of 3000)	150.00	70.00	19.00
☐ H3 Ferguson Jenkins	15.00	6.75	1.90
☐ H3AU Ferguson Jenkins (Signed and Numbered out of 3000)	150.00	70.00	19.00
☐ H4 Header (Drawing of all three players)	15.00	6.75	1.90

1991 Upper Deck Nolan Ryan Heroes

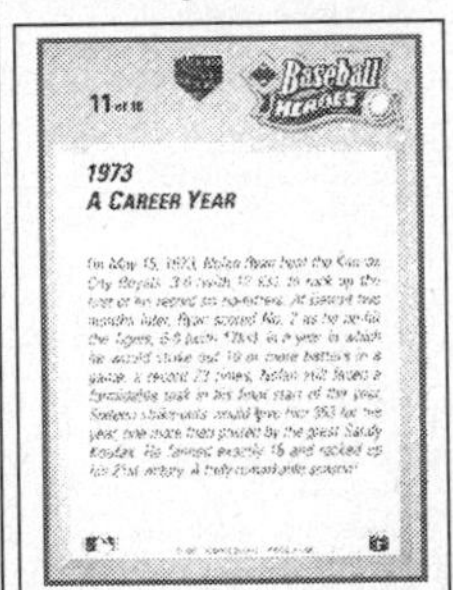

This nine-card standard size, 2 1/2" by 3 1/2", set was included in first series 1991 Upper Deck packs. The set which honors Nolan Ryan and is numbered as a continuation of the Baseball Heroes set which began with Reggie Jackson in 1990. This set honors Ryan's long career and his place in Baseball History. Card number 18 features the artwork of Vernon Wells while the other cards are photos. The complete set price below does not include the signed Ryan card of which only 2500 were made. These Ryan cards were apparently issued on 100-card sheets with the following configuration: ten each of the nine Ryan Baseball Heroes cards, five Michael Jordan cards and five Baseball Heroes header cards. The Baseball Heroes header card is a standard size card which explains the continuation of the Baseball Heroes series on the back while the front just says Baseball Heroes.

	MT	EX-MT	VG
COMPLETE SET (10)	8.00	3.60	1.00
COMMON RYAN (10-18)	.60	.25	.08
☐ 10 1968 Victory 1	.60	.25	.08
☐ 11 1973 A Career Year	.60	.25	.08
☐ 12 1975 Double Milestone	.60	.25	.08
☐ 13 1979 Back Home	.60	.25	.08
☐ 14 1981 All Time Leader	.60	.25	.08
☐ 15 1989 5,000 K's	.60	.25	.08
☐ 16 1990 6th No-Hitter	.60	.25	.08
☐ 17 1990 And Still Counting	.60	.25	.08
☐ 18 Checklist Card (Vernon Wells drawing with 5 poses of Ryan including each team he played for)	.60	.25	.08
☐ AU2 Nolan Ryan (Signed and Numbered out of 2500)	600.00	275.00	75.00
☐ NNO Baseball Heroes SP (Header card)	4.00	1.80	.50

1991 Upper Deck Silver Sluggers

The Upper Deck Silver Slugger set features nine players from each league, representing the nine batting positions on the team. The cards measure the standard size (2 1/2" by 3 1/2"). The fronts have glossy color action player photos, with white borders on three sides and a "Silver Slugger" bat serving as the border on the left side. The player's name appears in a tan stripe below the picture, with the team logo superimposed at the lower right corner. The card back is dominated by another color action photo with career highlights in a horizontally oriented rectangle to the left of the picture. The cards are numbered on the back with an SS prefix.

	MT	EX-MT	VG
COMPLETE SET (18)	20.00	9.00	2.50
COMMON PLAYER (SS1-SS18)	.75	.35	.09
☐ SS1 Julio Franco	.75	.35	.09
☐ SS2 Alan Trammell	.75	.35	.09
☐ SS3 Rickey Henderson	2.50	1.15	.30
☐ SS4 Jose Canseco	3.50	1.55	.45
☐ SS5 Barry Bonds	3.50	1.55	.45
☐ SS6 Eddie Murray	1.25	.55	.16
☐ SS7 Kelly Gruber	.75	.35	.09
☐ SS8 Ryne Sandberg	4.00	1.80	.50
☐ SS9 Darryl Strawberry	2.50	1.15	.30
☐ SS10 Ellis Burks	.75	.35	.09
☐ SS11 Lance Parrish	.75	.35	.09
☐ SS12 Cecil Fielder	2.50	1.15	.30
☐ SS13 Matt Williams	1.00	.45	.13
☐ SS14 Dave Parker	.75	.35	.09
☐ SS15 Bobby Bonilla	1.50	.65	.19
☐ SS16 Don Robinson	.75	.35	.09
☐ SS17 Benito Santiago	.75	.35	.09
☐ SS18 Barry Larkin	1.50	.65	.19

1992 Upper Deck

The 1992 Upper Deck set contains 800 standard-size (2 1/2" by 3 1/2") cards. The set was produced in two series: a low-number series of 700 cards and a high-number series of 100 cards later in the season. Special subsets included in the set are Star Rookies (1-27; SR), Team Checklists (29-40, 86-99; TC), with player portraits by Vernon Wells; Top Prospects (52-77; TP); Bloodlines (79-85), and Diamond Skills (640-650; DS). Moreover, a nine-card Baseball Heroes subset (randomly inserted in packs) focuses on the career

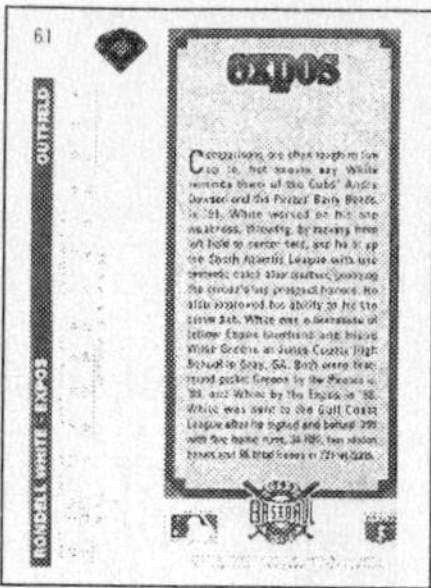

of Ted Williams. He autographed and numbered 2,500 cards, which were randomly inserted in low series foil packs. The cards are numbered on the back. The key Rookie Cards in the low-number series are Shawn Green, Tyler Green, Joey Hamilton, David McCarty, Eduardo Perez, Manny Ramirez, Mark Smith, Joe Vitiello, and Brian Williams. By mailing in 15 1992 low number foil wrappers, a completed order form, and a handling fee, the collector could receive an 8 1/2" by 11" numbered, black and white lithograph picturing Ted Williams in his batting swing. A standard-size Ted Williams hologram card was randomly inserted in 1992 low number foil packs. The front design of the Williams hologram is horizontally oriented and features the artwork of Vernon Wells showing Williams in three different poses. The horizontally oriented back has a full-bleed sepia-tone photo of Williams and career highlights printed in black over the photo. Factory sets feature a unique gold-foil hologram on the card backs (in contrast to the silver hologram on foil pack cards). In addition to traded players and called-up rookies, the extended series features a National League Diamond Skills subset (711-721), a Diamond Debuts subset (771-780), two expansion-team player cards (701 Clemente Nunez and 710 Ryan Turner), and two commemorative cards highlighting Eddie Murray's 400th home run (728) and Rickey Henderson's 1,000th stolen base (782). Randomly inserted into high number foil packs were a 20-card Ted Williams' Best Hitters subset, a three-card hologram subset featuring College Player of the Year winners for 1989 through 1991, a ten-card Baseball Heroes subset highlighting the careers of Joe Morgan and Johnny Bench and featuring 2,500 dual autographed checklist cards. and a special card picturing Tom Selleck and Frank Thomas and commemorating the movie "Mr. Baseball." The fronts features shadow-bordered action color player photos on a white card face. The player's name appears above the photo, with the team name superimposed at the lower right corner. The backs include color action player photos, biography and statistics. The cards are numbered on the back. Key Rookie Cards in the extended include Chad Curtis, Mike Kelly, Pat Listach, Clemente Nunez, and Ryan Turner.

	MT	EX-MT	VG
COMPLETE SET (800)	30.00	13.50	3.80
COMPLETE FACT.SET (800)	48.00	22.00	6.00
COMPLETE LO SET (700)	24.00	11.00	3.00
COMPLETE HI SET (100)	7.00	3.10	.85
COMMON PLAYER (1-700)	.05	.02	.01
COMMON PLAYER (701-800)	.05	.02	.01
☐ 1 Star Rookie Checklist Ryan Klesko Jim Thome	.25	.08	.03
☐ 2 Royce Clayton SR	.20	.09	.03
☐ 3 Brian Jordan SR	.30	.14	.04
☐ 4 Dave Fleming SR	.75	.35	.09
☐ 5 Jim Thome SR	.15	.07	.02
☐ 6 Jeff Juden SR	.08	.04	.01
☐ 7 Roberto Hernandez SR	.15	.07	.02
☐ 8 Kyle Abbott SR	.09	.04	.01
☐ 9 Chris George SR	.06	.03	.01
☐ 10 Rob Maurer SR	.15	.07	.02
☐ 11 Donald Harris SR	.06	.03	.01
☐ 12 Ted Wood SR	.12	.05	.02
☐ 13 Patrick Lennon SR	.06	.03	.01
☐ 14 Willie Banks SR	.09	.04	.01
☐ 15 Roger Salkeld SR UER (Bill was his grand- father, not his father)	.10	.05	.01
☐ 16 Wilfredo Cordero SR	.20	.09	.03
☐ 17 Arthur Rhodes SR	.20	.09	.03
☐ 18 Pedro Martinez SR	.25	.11	.03
☐ 19 Andy Ashby SR	.06	.03	.01
☐ 20 Tom Goodwin SR	.10	.05	.01
☐ 21 Braulio Castillo SR	.20	.09	.03
☐ 22 Todd Van Poppel SR	.25	.11	.03
☐ 23 Brian Williams SR	.35	.16	.04
☐ 24 Ryan Klesko SR	.75	.35	.09
☐ 25 Kenny Lofton SR	.50	.23	.06
☐ 26 Derek Bell SR	.12	.05	.02
☐ 27 Reggie Sanders SR	.30	.14	.04
☐ 28 Dave Winfield's 400th	.10	.05	.01
☐ 29 Atlanta TC Dave Justice	.12	.05	.02
☐ 30 Cincinnati TC Rob Dibble	.06	.03	.01
☐ 31 Houston TC Craig Biggio	.06	.03	.01
☐ 32 Los Angeles TC Eddie Murray	.10	.05	.01
☐ 33 San Diego TC Fred McGriff	.10	.05	.01
☐ 34 San Francisco TC Willie McGee	.06	.03	.01
☐ 35 Chicago Cubs TC Shawon Dunston	.06	.03	.01
☐ 36 Montreal TC Delino DeShields	.09	.04	.01
☐ 37 New York Mets TC Howard Johnson	.06	.03	.01
☐ 38 Philadelphia TC John Kruk	.06	.03	.01
☐ 39 Pittsburgh TC Doug Drabek	.06	.03	.01
☐ 40 St. Louis TC Todd Zeile	.06	.03	.01
☐ 41 Playoff Perfection Steve Avery	.15	.07	.02
☐ 42 Jeremy Hernandez	.12	.05	.02
☐ 43 Doug Henry	.20	.09	.03
☐ 44 Chris Donnels	.05	.02	.01
☐ 45 Mo Sanford	.05	.02	.01
☐ 46 Scott Kamieniecki	.05	.02	.01
☐ 47 Mark Lemke	.05	.02	.01
☐ 48 Steve Farr	.05	.02	.01
☐ 49 Francisco Oliveras	.05	.02	.01
☐ 50 Ced Landrum	.05	.02	.01
☐ 51 Top Prospect Checklist Rondell White Craig Griffey	.20	.06	.02
☐ 52 Eduardo Perez TP	.40	.18	.05
☐ 53 Tom Nevers TP	.10	.05	.01
☐ 54 David Zancanaro TP	.12	.05	.02
☐ 55 Shawn Green TP	.40	.18	.05
☐ 56 Mark Wohlers TP	.10	.05	.01
☐ 57 Dave Nilsson TP	.20	.09	.03
☐ 58 Dmitri Young TP	.40	.18	.05
☐ 59 Ryan Hawblitzel TP	.30	.14	.04
☐ 60 Raul Mondesi TP	.35	.16	.04
☐ 61 Rondell White TP	.25	.11	.03
☐ 62 Steve Hosey TP	.40	.18	.05
☐ 63 Manny Ramirez TP	.75	.35	.09
☐ 64 Marc Newfield TP	.20	.09	.03
☐ 65 Jeromy Burnitz TP	.25	.11	.03
☐ 66 Mark Smith TP	.40	.18	.05
☐ 67 Joey Hamilton TP	.60	.25	.08
☐ 68 Tyler Green TP	.35	.16	.04
☐ 69 Jon Farrell TP	.12	.05	.02
☐ 70 Kurt Miller TP	.10	.05	.01
☐ 71 Jeff Plympton TP	.12	.05	.02
☐ 72 Dan Wilson TP	.06	.03	.01
☐ 73 Joe Vitiello TP	.40	.18	.05
☐ 74 Rico Brogna TP	.10	.05	.01
☐ 75 David McCarty TP	1.00	.45	.13
☐ 76 Bob Wickman TP	.60	.25	.08
☐ 77 Carlos Rodriguez TP	.06	.03	.01
☐ 78 Stay In School Jim Abbott	.10	.05	.01
☐ 79 Ramon Martinez Pedro Martinez	.15	.07	.02
☐ 80 Kevin Mitchell	.10	.05	.01

		Keith Mitchell			
☐	81	Sandy Alomar Jr.	.15	.07	.02
		Roberto Alomar			
☐	82	Cal Ripken	.20	.09	.03
		Billy Ripken			
☐	83	Tony Gwynn	.15	.07	.02
		Chris Gwynn			
☐	84	Dwight Gooden	.20	.09	.03
		Gary Sheffield			
☐	85	Ken Griffey Sr.	.60	.25	.08
		Ken Griffey Jr.			
		Craig Griffey			
☐	86	California TC	.10	.05	.01
		Jim Abbott			
☐	87	Chicago White Sox TC	.35	.16	.04
		Frank Thomas			
☐	88	Kansas City TC	.06	.03	.01
		Danny Tartabull			
☐	89	Minnesota TC	.06	.03	.01
		Scott Erickson			
☐	90	Oakland TC	.10	.05	.01
		Rickey Henderson			
☐	91	Seattle TC	.06	.03	.01
		Edgar Martinez			
☐	92	Texas TC	.25	.11	.03
		Nolan Ryan			
☐	93	Baltimore TC	.06	.03	.01
		Ben McDonald			
☐	94	Boston TC	.06	.03	.01
		Ellis Burks			
☐	95	Cleveland TC	.06	.03	.01
		Greg Swindell			
☐	96	Detroit TC	.10	.05	.01
		Cecil Fielder			
☐	97	Milwaukee TC	.06	.03	.01
		Greg Vaughn			
☐	98	New York Yankees TC	.06	.03	.01
		Kevin Maas			
☐	99	Toronto Checklist	.06	.03	.01
		Dave Stieb			
☐	100	Checklist 1-100	.05	.01	.00
☐	101	Joe Oliver	.05	.02	.01
☐	102	Hector Villanueva	.05	.02	.01
☐	103	Ed Whitson	.05	.02	.01
☐	104	Danny Jackson	.05	.02	.01
☐	105	Chris Hammond	.05	.02	.01
☐	106	Ricky Jordan	.05	.02	.01
☐	107	Kevin Bass	.05	.02	.01
☐	108	Darrin Fletcher	.05	.02	.01
☐	109	Junior Ortiz	.05	.02	.01
☐	110	Tom Bolton	.05	.02	.01
☐	111	Jeff King	.05	.02	.01
☐	112	Dave Magadan	.08	.04	.01
☐	113	Mike LaValliere	.05	.02	.01
☐	114	Hubie Brooks	.05	.02	.01
☐	115	Jay Bell	.05	.02	.01
☐	116	David Wells	.05	.02	.01
☐	117	Jim Leyritz	.05	.02	.01
☐	118	Manuel Lee	.05	.02	.01
☐	119	Alvaro Espinoza	.05	.02	.01
☐	120	B.J. Surhoff	.05	.02	.01
☐	121	Hal Morris	.08	.04	.01
☐	122	Shawon Dunston	.08	.04	.01
☐	123	Chris Sabo	.08	.04	.01
☐	124	Andre Dawson	.12	.05	.02
☐	125	Eric Davis	.08	.04	.01
☐	126	Chili Davis	.08	.04	.01
☐	127	Dale Murphy	.08	.04	.01
☐	128	Kirk McCaskill	.05	.02	.01
☐	129	Terry Mulholland	.05	.02	.01
☐	130	Rick Aguilera	.08	.04	.01
☐	131	Vince Coleman	.08	.04	.01
☐	132	Andy Van Slyke	.08	.04	.01
☐	133	Gregg Jefferies	.08	.04	.01
☐	134	Barry Bonds	.20	.09	.03
☐	135	Dwight Gooden	.08	.04	.01
☐	136	Dave Stieb	.05	.02	.01
☐	137	Albert Belle	.15	.07	.02
☐	138	Teddy Higuera	.05	.02	.01
☐	139	Jesse Barfield	.05	.02	.01
☐	140	Pat Borders	.05	.02	.01
☐	141	Bip Roberts	.08	.04	.01
☐	142	Rob Dibble	.08	.04	.01
☐	143	Mark Grace	.08	.04	.01
☐	144	Barry Larkin	.12	.05	.02
☐	145	Ryne Sandberg	.30	.14	.04
☐	146	Scott Erickson	.10	.05	.01
☐	147	Luis Polonia	.08	.04	.01
☐	148	John Burkett	.05	.02	.01
☐	149	Luis Sojo	.05	.02	.01
☐	150	Dickie Thon	.05	.02	.01
☐	151	Walt Weiss	.05	.02	.01
☐	152	Mike Scioscia	.05	.02	.01
☐	153	Mark McGwire	.25	.11	.03
☐	154	Matt Williams	.08	.04	.01
☐	155	Rickey Henderson	.15	.07	.02
☐	156	Sandy Alomar Jr.	.08	.04	.01
☐	157	Brian McRae	.08	.04	.01
☐	158	Harold Baines	.08	.04	.01
☐	159	Kevin Appier	.08	.04	.01
☐	160	Felix Fermin	.05	.02	.01
☐	161	Leo Gomez	.12	.05	.02
☐	162	Craig Biggio	.08	.04	.01
☐	163	Ben McDonald	.10	.05	.01
☐	164	Randy Johnson	.08	.04	.01
☐	165	Cal Ripken	.35	.16	.04
☐	166	Frank Thomas	1.00	.45	.13
☐	167	Delino DeShields	.12	.05	.02
☐	168	Greg Gagne	.05	.02	.01
☐	169	Ron Karkovice	.05	.02	.01
☐	170	Charlie Leibrandt	.05	.02	.01
☐	171	Dave Righetti	.05	.02	.01
☐	172	Dave Henderson	.05	.02	.01
☐	173	Steve Decker	.05	.02	.01
☐	174	Darryl Strawberry	.15	.07	.02
☐	175	Will Clark	.25	.11	.03
☐	176	Ruben Sierra	.20	.09	.03
☐	177	Ozzie Smith	.12	.05	.02
☐	178	Charles Nagy	.12	.05	.02
☐	179	Gary Pettis	.05	.02	.01
☐	180	Kirk Gibson	.08	.04	.01
☐	181	Randy Milligan	.05	.02	.01
☐	182	Dave Valle	.05	.02	.01
☐	183	Chris Hoiles	.08	.04	.01
☐	184	Tony Phillips	.05	.02	.01
☐	185	Brady Anderson	.08	.04	.01
☐	186	Scott Fletcher	.05	.02	.01
☐	187	Gene Larkin	.05	.02	.01
☐	188	Lance Johnson	.05	.02	.01
☐	189	Greg Olson	.05	.02	.01
☐	190	Melido Perez	.08	.04	.01
☐	191	Lenny Harris	.05	.02	.01
☐	192	Terry Kennedy	.05	.02	.01
☐	193	Mike Gallego	.05	.02	.01
☐	194	Willie McGee	.08	.04	.01
☐	195	Juan Samuel	.05	.02	.01
☐	196	Jeff Huson	.05	.02	.01
		(Shows Jose Canseco sliding into second)			
☐	197	Alex Cole	.05	.02	.01
☐	198	Ron Robinson	.05	.02	.01
☐	199	Joel Skinner	.05	.02	.01
☐	200	Checklist 101-200	.05	.01	.00
☐	201	Kevin Reimer	.08	.04	.01
☐	202	Stan Belinda	.05	.02	.01
☐	203	Pat Tabler	.05	.02	.01
☐	204	Jose Guzman	.05	.02	.01
☐	205	Jose Lind	.05	.02	.01
☐	206	Spike Owen	.05	.02	.01
☐	207	Joe Orsulak	.05	.02	.01
☐	208	Charlie Hayes	.05	.02	.01
☐	209	Mike Devereaux	.08	.04	.01
☐	210	Mike Fitzgerald	.05	.02	.01
☐	211	Willie Randolph	.08	.04	.01
☐	212	Rod Nichols	.05	.02	.01
☐	213	Mike Boddicker	.05	.02	.01
☐	214	Bill Spiers	.05	.02	.01
☐	215	Steve Olin	.05	.02	.01
☐	216	David Howard	.05	.02	.01
☐	217	Gary Varsho	.05	.02	.01
☐	218	Mike Harkey	.08	.04	.01
☐	219	Luis Aquino	.05	.02	.01
☐	220	Chuck McElroy	.05	.02	.01
☐	221	Doug Drabek	.08	.04	.01
☐	222	Dave Winfield	.12	.05	.02
☐	223	Rafael Palmeiro	.08	.04	.01
☐	224	Joe Carter	.15	.07	.02
☐	225	Bobby Bonilla	.12	.05	.02
☐	226	Ivan Calderon	.05	.02	.01
☐	227	Gregg Olson	.08	.04	.01
☐	228	Tim Wallach	.08	.04	.01
☐	229	Terry Pendleton	.10	.05	.01
☐	230	Gilberto Reyes	.05	.02	.01
☐	231	Carlos Baerga	.25	.11	.03
☐	232	Greg Vaughn	.08	.04	.01
☐	233	Bret Saberhagen	.08	.04	.01
☐	234	Gary Sheffield	.35	.16	.04
☐	235	Mark Lewis	.08	.04	.01
☐	236	George Bell	.08	.04	.01
☐	237	Danny Tartabull	.08	.04	.01
☐	238	Willie Wilson	.05	.02	.01
☐	239	Doug Dascenzo	.05	.02	.01
☐	240	Bill Pecota	.05	.02	.01
☐	241	Julio Franco	.08	.04	.01
☐	242	Ed Sprague	.08	.04	.01
☐	243	Juan Gonzalez	.50	.23	.06
☐	244	Chuck Finley	.05	.02	.01

☐ 245 Ivan Rodriguez .50 .23 .06
☐ 246 Len Dykstra .08 .04 .01
☐ 247 Deion Sanders .20 .09 .03
☐ 248 Dwight Evans .08 .04 .01
☐ 249 Larry Walker .20 .09 .03
☐ 250 Billy Ripken .05 .02 .01
☐ 251 Mickey Tettleton .08 .04 .01
☐ 252 Tony Pena .05 .02 .01
☐ 253 Benito Santiago .08 .04 .01
☐ 254 Kirby Puckett .25 .11 .03
☐ 255 Cecil Fielder .15 .07 .02
☐ 256 Howard Johnson .08 .04 .01
☐ 257 Andujar Cedeno .08 .04 .01
☐ 258 Jose Rijo .08 .04 .01
☐ 259 Al Osuna .05 .02 .01
☐ 260 Todd Hundley .05 .02 .01
☐ 261 Orel Hershiser .08 .04 .01
☐ 262 Ray Lankford .20 .09 .03
☐ 263 Robin Ventura .20 .09 .03
☐ 264 Felix Jose .08 .04 .01
☐ 265 Eddie Murray .12 .05 .02
☐ 266 Kevin Mitchell .08 .04 .01
☐ 267 Gary Carter .08 .04 .01
☐ 268 Mike Benjamin .05 .02 .01
☐ 269 Dick Schofield .05 .02 .01
☐ 270 Jose Uribe .05 .02 .01
☐ 271 Pete Incaviglia .05 .02 .01
☐ 272 Tony Fernandez .08 .04 .01
☐ 273 Alan Trammell .08 .04 .01
☐ 274 Tony Gwynn .15 .07 .02
☐ 275 Mike Greenwell .08 .04 .01
☐ 276 Jeff Bagwell .40 .18 .05
☐ 277 Frank Viola .08 .04 .01
☐ 278 Randy Myers .08 .04 .01
☐ 279 Ken Caminiti .08 .04 .01
☐ 280 Bill Doran .05 .02 .01
☐ 281 Dan Pasqua .05 .02 .01
☐ 282 Alfredo Griffin .05 .02 .01
☐ 283 Jose Oquendo .05 .02 .01
☐ 284 Kal Daniels .05 .02 .01
☐ 285 Bobby Thigpen .05 .02 .01
☐ 286 Robby Thompson .05 .02 .01
☐ 287 Mark Eichhorn .05 .02 .01
☐ 288 Mike Felder .05 .02 .01
☐ 289 Dave Gallagher .05 .02 .01
☐ 290 Dave Anderson .05 .02 .01
☐ 291 Mel Hall .05 .02 .01
☐ 292 Jerald Clark .05 .02 .01
☐ 293 Al Newman .05 .02 .01
☐ 294 Rob Deer .08 .04 .01
☐ 295 Matt Nokes .05 .02 .01
☐ 296 Jack Armstrong .05 .02 .01
☐ 297 Jim Deshaies .05 .02 .01
☐ 298 Jeff Innis .05 .02 .01
☐ 299 Jeff Reed .05 .02 .01
☐ 300 Checklist 201-300 .05 .01 .00
☐ 301 Lonnie Smith .05 .02 .01
☐ 302 Jimmy Key .05 .02 .01
☐ 303 Junior Felix .05 .02 .01
☐ 304 Mike Heath .05 .02 .01
☐ 305 Mark Langston .08 .04 .01
☐ 306 Greg W. Harris .05 .02 .01
☐ 307 Brett Butler .08 .04 .01
☐ 308 Luis Rivera .05 .02 .01
☐ 309 Bruce Ruffin .05 .02 .01
☐ 310 Paul Faries .05 .02 .01
☐ 311 Terry Leach .05 .02 .01
☐ 312 Scott Brosius .10 .05 .01
☐ 313 Scott Leius .05 .02 .01
☐ 314 Harold Reynolds .05 .02 .01
☐ 315 Jack Morris .12 .05 .02
☐ 316 David Segui .05 .02 .01
☐ 317 Bill Gullickson .05 .02 .01
☐ 318 Todd Frohwirth .05 .02 .01
☐ 319 Mark Leiter .05 .02 .01
☐ 320 Jeff M. Robinson .05 .02 .01
☐ 321 Gary Gaetti .05 .02 .01
☐ 322 John Smoltz .12 .05 .02
☐ 323 Andy Benes .08 .04 .01
☐ 324 Kelly Gruber .08 .04 .01
☐ 325 Jim Abbott .12 .05 .02
☐ 326 John Kruk .08 .04 .01
☐ 327 Kevin Seitzer .08 .04 .01
☐ 328 Darrin Jackson .08 .04 .01
☐ 329 Kurt Stillwell .05 .02 .01
☐ 330 Mike Maddux .05 .02 .01
☐ 331 Dennis Eckersley .12 .05 .02
☐ 332 Dan Gladden .05 .02 .01
☐ 333 Jose Canseco .25 .11 .03
☐ 334 Kent Hrbek .08 .04 .01
☐ 335 Ken Griffey Sr. .08 .04 .01
☐ 336 Greg Swindell .08 .04 .01
☐ 337 Trevor Wilson .05 .02 .01
☐ 338 Sam Horn .05 .02 .01
☐ 339 Mike Henneman .05 .02 .01
☐ 340 Jerry Browne .05 .02 .01
☐ 341 Glenn Braggs .05 .02 .01
☐ 342 Tom Glavine .15 .07 .02
☐ 343 Wally Joyner .08 .04 .01
☐ 344 Fred McGriff .15 .07 .02
☐ 345 Ron Gant .12 .05 .02
☐ 346 Ramon Martinez .08 .04 .01
☐ 347 Wes Chamberlain .08 .04 .01
☐ 348 Terry Shumpert .05 .02 .01
☐ 349 Tim Teufel .05 .02 .01
☐ 350 Wally Backman .05 .02 .01
☐ 351 Joe Girardi .05 .02 .01
☐ 352 Devon White .08 .04 .01
☐ 353 Greg Maddux .12 .05 .02
☐ 354 Ryan Bowen .08 .04 .01
☐ 355 Roberto Alomar .30 .14 .04
☐ 356 Don Mattingly .15 .07 .02
☐ 357 Pedro Guerrero .08 .04 .01
☐ 358 Steve Sax .08 .04 .01
☐ 359 Joey Cora .05 .02 .01
☐ 360 Jim Gantner .05 .02 .01
☐ 361 Brian Barnes .05 .02 .01
☐ 362 Kevin McReynolds .08 .04 .01
☐ 363 Bret Barberie .05 .02 .01
☐ 364 David Cone .08 .04 .01
☐ 365 Dennis Martinez .08 .04 .01
☐ 366 Brian Hunter .10 .05 .01
☐ 367 Edgar Martinez .08 .04 .01
☐ 368 Steve Finley .08 .04 .01
☐ 369 Greg Briley .05 .02 .01
☐ 370 Jeff Blauser .05 .02 .01
☐ 371 Todd Stottlemyre .08 .04 .01
☐ 372 Luis Gonzalez .08 .04 .01
☐ 373 Rick Wilkins .05 .02 .01
☐ 374 Darryl Kile .08 .04 .01
☐ 375 John Olerud .12 .05 .02
☐ 376 Lee Smith .08 .04 .01
☐ 377 Kevin Maas .08 .04 .01
☐ 378 Dante Bichette .05 .02 .01
☐ 379 Tom Pagnozzi .05 .02 .01
☐ 380 Mike Flanagan .05 .02 .01
☐ 381 Charlie O'Brien .05 .02 .01
☐ 382 Dave Martinez .05 .02 .01
☐ 383 Keith Miller .05 .02 .01
☐ 384 Scott Ruskin .05 .02 .01
☐ 385 Kevin Elster .05 .02 .01
☐ 386 Alvin Davis .05 .02 .01
☐ 387 Casey Candaele .05 .02 .01
☐ 388 Pete O'Brien .05 .02 .01
☐ 389 Jeff Treadway .05 .02 .01
☐ 390 Scott Bradley .05 .02 .01
☐ 391 Mookie Wilson .05 .02 .01
☐ 392 Jimmy Jones .05 .02 .01
☐ 393 Candy Maldonado .05 .02 .01
☐ 394 Eric Yelding .05 .02 .01
☐ 395 Tom Henke .08 .04 .01
☐ 396 Franklin Stubbs .05 .02 .01
☐ 397 Milt Thompson .05 .02 .01
☐ 398 Mark Carreon .05 .02 .01
☐ 399 Randy Velarde .05 .02 .01
☐ 400 Checklist 301-400 .05 .01 .00
☐ 401 Omar Vizquel .05 .02 .01
☐ 402 Joe Boever .05 .02 .01
☐ 403 Bill Krueger .05 .02 .01
☐ 404 Jody Reed .05 .02 .01
☐ 405 Mike Schooler .05 .02 .01
☐ 406 Jason Grimsley .05 .02 .01
☐ 407 Greg Myers .05 .02 .01
☐ 408 Randy Ready .05 .02 .01
☐ 409 Mike Timlin .05 .02 .01
☐ 410 Mitch Williams .05 .02 .01
☐ 411 Garry Templeton .05 .02 .01
☐ 412 Greg Cadaret .05 .02 .01
☐ 413 Donnie Hill .05 .02 .01
☐ 414 Wally Whitehurst .05 .02 .01
☐ 415 Scott Sanderson .05 .02 .01
☐ 416 Thomas Howard .05 .02 .01
☐ 417 Neal Heaton .05 .02 .01
☐ 418 Charlie Hough .05 .02 .01
☐ 419 Jack Howell .05 .02 .01
☐ 420 Greg Hibbard .05 .02 .01
☐ 421 Carlos Quintana .05 .02 .01
☐ 422 Kim Batiste .05 .02 .01
☐ 423 Paul Molitor .08 .04 .01
☐ 424 Ken Griffey Jr. .75 .35 .09
☐ 425 Phil Plantier .20 .09 .03
☐ 426 Denny Neagle .05 .02 .01
☐ 427 Von Hayes .05 .02 .01
☐ 428 Shane Mack .08 .04 .01
☐ 429 Darren Daulton .08 .04 .01
☐ 430 Dwayne Henry .05 .02 .01

☐ 431	Lance Parrish	.08	.04	.01
☐ 432	Mike Humphreys	.08	.04	.01
☐ 433	Tim Burke	.05	.02	.01
☐ 434	Bryan Harvey	.05	.02	.01
☐ 435	Pat Kelly	.08	.04	.01
☐ 436	Ozzie Guillen	.05	.02	.01
☐ 437	Bruce Hurst	.08	.04	.01
☐ 438	Sammy Sosa	.05	.02	.01
☐ 439	Dennis Rasmussen	.05	.02	.01
☐ 440	Ken Patterson	.05	.02	.01
☐ 441	Jay Buhner	.08	.04	.01
☐ 442	Pat Combs	.05	.02	.01
☐ 443	Wade Boggs	.15	.07	.02
☐ 444	George Brett	.12	.05	.02
☐ 445	Mo Vaughn	.08	.04	.01
☐ 446	Chuck Knoblauch	.25	.11	.03
☐ 447	Tom Candiotti	.05	.02	.01
☐ 448	Mark Portugal	.05	.02	.01
☐ 449	Mickey Morandini	.08	.04	.01
☐ 450	Duane Ward	.05	.02	.01
☐ 451	Otis Nixon	.08	.04	.01
☐ 452	Bob Welch	.05	.02	.01
☐ 453	Rusty Meacham	.05	.02	.01
☐ 454	Keith Mitchell	.08	.04	.01
☐ 455	Marquis Grissom	.12	.05	.02
☐ 456	Robin Yount	.12	.05	.02
☐ 457	Harvey Pulliam	.10	.05	.01
☐ 458	Jose DeLeon	.05	.02	.01
☐ 459	Mark Gubicza	.05	.02	.01
☐ 460	Darryl Hamilton	.08	.04	.01
☐ 461	Tom Browning	.05	.02	.01
☐ 462	Monty Fariss	.10	.05	.01
☐ 463	Jerome Walton	.05	.02	.01
☐ 464	Paul O'Neill	.08	.04	.01
☐ 465	Dean Palmer	.12	.05	.02
☐ 466	Travis Fryman	.50	.23	.06
☐ 467	John Smiley	.08	.04	.01
☐ 468	Lloyd Moseby	.05	.02	.01
☐ 469	John Wehner	.05	.02	.01
☐ 470	Skeeter Barnes	.05	.02	.01
☐ 471	Steve Chitren	.05	.02	.01
☐ 472	Kent Mercker	.05	.02	.01
☐ 473	Terry Steinbach	.08	.04	.01
☐ 474	Andres Galarraga	.05	.02	.01
☐ 475	Steve Avery	.20	.09	.03
☐ 476	Tom Gordon	.05	.02	.01
☐ 477	Cal Eldred	.60	.25	.08
☐ 478	Omar Olivares	.05	.02	.01
☐ 479	Julio Machado	.05	.02	.01
☐ 480	Bob Milacki	.05	.02	.01
☐ 481	Les Lancaster	.05	.02	.01
☐ 482	John Candelaria	.05	.02	.01
☐ 483	Brian Downing	.05	.02	.01
☐ 484	Roger McDowell	.05	.02	.01
☐ 485	Scott Scudder	.05	.02	.01
☐ 486	Zane Smith	.05	.02	.01
☐ 487	John Cerutti	.05	.02	.01
☐ 488	Steve Buechele	.05	.02	.01
☐ 489	Paul Gibson	.05	.02	.01
☐ 490	Curtis Wilkerson	.05	.02	.01
☐ 491	Marvin Freeman	.05	.02	.01
☐ 492	Tom Foley	.05	.02	.01
☐ 493	Juan Berenguer	.05	.02	.01
☐ 494	Ernest Riles	.05	.02	.01
☐ 495	Sid Bream	.05	.02	.01
☐ 496	Chuck Crim	.05	.02	.01
☐ 497	Mike Macfarlane	.05	.02	.01
☐ 498	Dale Sveum	.05	.02	.01
☐ 499	Storm Davis	.05	.02	.01
☐ 500	Checklist 401-500	.05	.01	.00
☐ 501	Jeff Reardon	.08	.04	.01
☐ 502	Shawn Abner	.05	.02	.01
☐ 503	Tony Fossas	.05	.02	.01
☐ 504	Cory Snyder	.05	.02	.01
☐ 505	Matt Young	.05	.02	.01
☐ 506	Allan Anderson	.05	.02	.01
☐ 507	Mark Lee	.05	.02	.01
☐ 508	Gene Nelson	.05	.02	.01
☐ 509	Mike Pagliarulo	.05	.02	.01
☐ 510	Rafael Belliard	.05	.02	.01
☐ 511	Jay Howell	.05	.02	.01
☐ 512	Bob Tewksbury	.08	.04	.01
☐ 513	Mike Morgan	.05	.02	.01
☐ 514	John Franco	.08	.04	.01
☐ 515	Kevin Gross	.05	.02	.01
☐ 516	Lou Whitaker	.08	.04	.01
☐ 517	Orlando Merced	.08	.04	.01
☐ 518	Todd Benzinger	.05	.02	.01
☐ 519	Gary Redus	.05	.02	.01
☐ 520	Walt Terrell	.05	.02	.01
☐ 521	Jack Clark	.08	.04	.01
☐ 522	Dave Parker	.08	.04	.01
☐ 523	Tim Naehring	.08	.04	.01
☐ 524	Mark Whiten	.05	.02	.01
☐ 525	Ellis Burks	.08	.04	.01
☐ 526	Frank Castillo	.10	.05	.01
☐ 527	Brian Harper	.05	.02	.01
☐ 528	Brook Jacoby	.05	.02	.01
☐ 529	Rick Sutcliffe	.08	.04	.01
☐ 530	Joe Klink	.05	.02	.01
☐ 531	Terry Bross	.05	.02	.01
☐ 532	Jose Offerman	.08	.04	.01
☐ 533	Todd Zeile	.05	.02	.01
☐ 534	Eric Karros	.75	.35	.09
☐ 535	Anthony Young	.10	.05	.01
☐ 536	Milt Cuyler	.05	.02	.01
☐ 537	Randy Tomlin	.05	.02	.01
☐ 538	Scott Livingstone	.12	.05	.02
☐ 539	Jim Eisenreich	.05	.02	.01
☐ 540	Don Slaught	.05	.02	.01
☐ 541	Scott Cooper	.08	.04	.01
☐ 542	Joe Grahe	.05	.02	.01
☐ 543	Tom Brunansky	.08	.04	.01
☐ 544	Eddie Zosky	.08	.04	.01
☐ 545	Roger Clemens	.30	.14	.04
☐ 546	David Justice	.30	.14	.04
☐ 547	Dave Stewart	.08	.04	.01
☐ 548	David West	.05	.02	.01
☐ 549	Dave Smith	.05	.02	.01
☐ 550	Dan Plesac	.05	.02	.01
☐ 551	Alex Fernandez	.08	.04	.01
☐ 552	Bernard Gilkey	.08	.04	.01
☐ 553	Jack McDowell	.08	.04	.01
☐ 554	Tino Martinez	.08	.04	.01
☐ 555	Bo Jackson	.15	.07	.02
☐ 556	Bernie Williams	.10	.05	.01
☐ 557	Mark Gardner	.05	.02	.01
☐ 558	Glenallen Hill	.05	.02	.01
☐ 559	Oil Can Boyd	.05	.02	.01
☐ 560	Chris James	.05	.02	.01
☐ 561	Scott Servais	.05	.02	.01
☐ 562	Rey Sanchez	.15	.07	.02
☐ 563	Paul McClellan	.05	.02	.01
☐ 564	Andy Mota	.05	.02	.01
☐ 565	Darren Lewis	.08	.04	.01
☐ 566	Jose Melendez	.05	.02	.01
☐ 567	Tommy Greene	.05	.02	.01
☐ 568	Rich Rodriguez	.05	.02	.01
☐ 569	Heathcliff Slocumb	.05	.02	.01
☐ 570	Joe Hesketh	.05	.02	.01
☐ 571	Carlton Fisk	.12	.05	.02
☐ 572	Erik Hanson	.05	.02	.01
☐ 573	Wilson Alvarez	.05	.02	.01
☐ 574	Rheal Cormier	.05	.02	.01
☐ 575	Tim Raines	.08	.04	.01
☐ 576	Bobby Witt	.05	.02	.01
☐ 577	Roberto Kelly	.08	.04	.01
☐ 578	Kevin Brown	.08	.04	.01
☐ 579	Chris Nabholz	.08	.04	.01
☐ 580	Jesse Orosco	.05	.02	.01
☐ 581	Jeff Brantley	.05	.02	.01
☐ 582	Rafael Ramirez	.05	.02	.01
☐ 583	Kelly Downs	.05	.02	.01
☐ 584	Mike Simms	.05	.02	.01
☐ 585	Mike Remlinger	.05	.02	.01
☐ 586	Dave Hollins	.08	.04	.01
☐ 587	Larry Andersen	.05	.02	.01
☐ 588	Mike Gardiner	.05	.02	.01
☐ 589	Craig Lefferts	.05	.02	.01
☐ 590	Paul Assenmacher	.05	.02	.01
☐ 591	Bryn Smith	.05	.02	.01
☐ 592	Donn Pall	.05	.02	.01
☐ 593	Mike Jackson	.05	.02	.01
☐ 594	Scott Radinsky	.05	.02	.01
☐ 595	Brian Holman	.05	.02	.01
☐ 596	Geronimo Pena	.05	.02	.01
☐ 597	Mike Jeffcoat	.05	.02	.01
☐ 598	Carlos Martinez	.05	.02	.01
☐ 599	Geno Petralli	.05	.02	.01
☐ 600	Checklist 501-600	.05	.01	.00
☐ 601	Jerry Don Gleaton	.05	.02	.01
☐ 602	Adam Peterson	.05	.02	.01
☐ 603	Craig Grebeck	.05	.02	.01
☐ 604	Mark Guthrie	.05	.02	.01
☐ 605	Frank Tanana	.05	.02	.01
☐ 606	Hensley Meulens	.05	.02	.01
☐ 607	Mark Davis	.05	.02	.01
☐ 608	Eric Plunk	.05	.02	.01
☐ 609	Mark Williamson	.05	.02	.01
☐ 610	Lee Guetterman	.05	.02	.01
☐ 611	Bobby Rose	.05	.02	.01
☐ 612	Bill Wegman	.05	.02	.01
☐ 613	Mike Hartley	.05	.02	.01
☐ 614	Chris Beasley	.12	.05	.02
☐ 615	Chris Bosio	.05	.02	.01
☐ 616	Henry Cotto	.05	.02	.01

☐ 617 Chico Walker	.05	.02	.01
☐ 618 Russ Swan	.05	.02	.01
☐ 619 Bob Walk	.05	.02	.01
☐ 620 Billy Swift	.05	.02	.01
☐ 621 Warren Newson	.05	.02	.01
☐ 622 Steve Bedrosian	.05	.02	.01
☐ 623 Ricky Bones	.10	.05	.01
☐ 624 Kevin Tapani	.08	.04	.01
☐ 625 Juan Guzman	1.00	.45	.13
☐ 626 Jeff Johnson	.05	.02	.01
☐ 627 Jeff Montgomery	.05	.02	.01
☐ 628 Ken Hill	.08	.04	.01
☐ 629 Gary Thurman	.05	.02	.01
☐ 630 Steve Howe	.05	.02	.01
☐ 631 Jose DeJesus	.05	.02	.01
☐ 632 Kirk Dressendorfer	.05	.02	.01
☐ 633 Jaime Navarro	.08	.04	.01
☐ 634 Lee Stevens	.05	.02	.01
☐ 635 Pete Harnisch	.05	.02	.01
☐ 636 Bill Landrum	.05	.02	.01
☐ 637 Rich DeLucia	.05	.02	.01
☐ 638 Luis Salazar	.05	.02	.01
☐ 639 Rob Murphy	.05	.02	.01
☐ 640 Diamond Skills Checklist	.20	.06	.02
Jose Canseco			
Rickey Henderson			
☐ 641 Roger Clemens DS	.15	.07	.02
☐ 642 Jim Abbott DS	.10	.05	.01
☐ 643 Travis Fryman DS	.30	.14	.04
☐ 644 Jesse Barfield DS	.05	.02	.01
☐ 645 Cal Ripken DS	.20	.09	.03
☐ 646 Wade Boggs DS	.12	.05	.02
☐ 647 Cecil Fielder DS	.12	.05	.02
☐ 648 Rickey Henderson DS	.12	.05	.02
☐ 649 Jose Canseco DS	.15	.07	.02
☐ 650 Ken Griffey Jr. DS	.40	.18	.05
☐ 651 Kenny Rogers	.05	.02	.01
☐ 652 Luis Mercedes	.08	.04	.01
☐ 653 Mike Stanton	.05	.02	.01
☐ 654 Glenn Davis	.08	.04	.01
☐ 655 Nolan Ryan	.50	.23	.06
☐ 656 Reggie Jefferson	.15	.07	.02
☐ 657 Javier Ortiz	.05	.02	.01
☐ 658 Greg A. Harris	.05	.02	.01
☐ 659 Mariano Duncan	.05	.02	.01
☐ 660 Jeff Shaw	.05	.02	.01
☐ 661 Mike Moore	.05	.02	.01
☐ 662 Chris Haney	.05	.02	.01
☐ 663 Joe Slusarski	.05	.02	.01
☐ 664 Wayne Housie	.12	.05	.02
☐ 665 Carlos Garcia	.15	.07	.02
☐ 666 Bob Ojeda	.05	.02	.01
☐ 667 Bryan Hickerson	.12	.05	.02
☐ 668 Tim Belcher	.08	.04	.01
☐ 669 Ron Darling	.08	.04	.01
☐ 670 Rex Hudler	.05	.02	.01
☐ 671 Sid Fernandez	.08	.04	.01
☐ 672 Chito Martinez	.05	.02	.01
☐ 673 Pete Schourek	.05	.02	.01
☐ 674 Armando Reynoso	.12	.05	.02
☐ 675 Mike Mussina	.75	.35	.09
☐ 676 Kevin Morton	.05	.02	.01
☐ 677 Norm Charlton	.08	.04	.01
☐ 678 Danny Darwin	.05	.02	.01
☐ 679 Eric King	.05	.02	.01
☐ 680 Ted Power	.05	.02	.01
☐ 681 Barry Jones	.05	.02	.01
☐ 682 Carney Lansford	.08	.04	.01
☐ 683 Mel Rojas	.05	.02	.01
☐ 684 Rick Honeycutt	.05	.02	.01
☐ 685 Jeff Fassero	.05	.02	.01
☐ 686 Cris Carpenter	.05	.02	.01
☐ 687 Tim Crews	.05	.02	.01
☐ 688 Scott Terry	.05	.02	.01
☐ 689 Chris Gwynn	.05	.02	.01
☐ 690 Gerald Perry	.05	.02	.01
☐ 691 John Barfield	.05	.02	.01
☐ 692 Bob Melvin	.05	.02	.01
☐ 693 Juan Agosto	.05	.02	.01
☐ 694 Alejandro Pena	.05	.02	.01
☐ 695 Jeff Russell	.05	.02	.01
☐ 696 Carmelo Martinez	.05	.02	.01
☐ 697 Bud Black	.05	.02	.01
☐ 698 Dave Otto	.05	.02	.01
☐ 699 Billy Hatcher	.05	.02	.01
☐ 700 Checklist 601-700	.07	.01	.00
☐ 701 Clemente Nunez	.40	.18	.05
☐ 702 Rookie Threats	.30	.14	.04
☐ 703 Mike Morgan	.05	.02	.01
☐ 704 Keith Miller	.05	.02	.01
☐ 705 Kurt Stillwell	.05	.02	.01
☐ 706 Damon Berryhill	.05	.02	.01
☐ 707 Von Hayes	.05	.02	.01
☐ 708 Rick Sutcliffe	.08	.04	.01
☐ 709 Hubie Brooks	.05	.02	.01
☐ 710 Ryan Turner	.50	.23	.06
☐ 711 Diamond Skills Checklist	.15	.07	.02
Barry Bonds			
Andy Van Slyke			
☐ 712 Jose Rijo DS	.06	.03	.01
☐ 713 Tom Glavine DS	.12	.05	.02
☐ 714 Shawon Dunston DS	.06	.03	.01
☐ 715 Andy Van Slyke DS	.09	.04	.01
☐ 716 Ozzie Smith DS	.12	.05	.02
☐ 717 Tony Gwynn DS	.12	.05	.02
☐ 718 Will Clark DS	.20	.09	.03
☐ 719 Marquis Grissom DS	.10	.05	.01
☐ 720 Howard Johnson DS	.06	.03	.01
☐ 721 Barry Bonds DS	.20	.09	.03
☐ 722 Kirk McCaskill	.05	.02	.01
☐ 723 Sammy Sosa	.05	.02	.01
☐ 724 George Bell	.08	.04	.01
☐ 725 Gregg Jefferies	.08	.04	.01
☐ 726 Gary DiSarcina	.05	.02	.01
☐ 727 Mike Bordick	.10	.05	.01
☐ 728 Eddie Murray	.15	.07	.02
400 Home Run Club			
☐ 729 Rene Gonzales	.05	.02	.01
☐ 730 Mike Bielecki	.05	.02	.01
☐ 731 Calvin Jones	.12	.05	.02
☐ 732 Jack Morris	.08	.04	.01
☐ 733 Frank Viola	.08	.04	.01
☐ 734 Dave Winfield	.12	.05	.02
☐ 735 Kevin Mitchell	.08	.04	.01
☐ 736 Bill Swift	.05	.02	.01
☐ 737 Dan Gladden	.05	.02	.01
☐ 738 Mike Jackson	.05	.02	.01
☐ 739 Mark Carreon	.05	.02	.01
☐ 740 Kirt Manwaring	.05	.02	.01
☐ 741 Randy Myers	.08	.04	.01
☐ 742 Kevin McReynolds	.08	.04	.01
☐ 743 Steve Sax	.08	.04	.01
☐ 744 Wally Joyner	.08	.04	.01
☐ 745 Gary Sheffield	.35	.16	.04
☐ 746 Danny Tartabull	.08	.04	.01
☐ 747 Julio Valera	.08	.04	.01
☐ 748 Denny Neagle	.05	.02	.01
☐ 749 Lance Blankenship	.05	.02	.01
☐ 750 Mike Gallego	.05	.02	.01
☐ 751 Bret Saberhagen	.08	.04	.01
☐ 752 Ruben Amaro	.05	.02	.01
☐ 753 Eddie Murray	.12	.05	.02
☐ 754 Kyle Abbott	.08	.04	.01
☐ 755 Bobby Bonilla	.12	.05	.02
☐ 756 Eric Davis	.08	.04	.01
☐ 757 Eddie Taubensee	.15	.07	.02
☐ 758 Andres Galarraga	.05	.02	.01
☐ 759 Pete Incaviglia	.05	.02	.01
☐ 760 Tom Candiotti	.05	.02	.01
☐ 761 Tim Belcher	.08	.04	.01
☐ 762 Ricky Bones	.10	.05	.01
☐ 763 Bip Roberts	.08	.04	.01
☐ 764 Pedro Munoz	.08	.04	.01
☐ 765 Greg Swindell	.08	.04	.01
☐ 766 Kenny Lofton	.40	.18	.05
☐ 767 Gary Carter	.08	.04	.01
☐ 768 Charlie Hayes	.05	.02	.01
☐ 769 Dickie Thon	.05	.02	.01
☐ 770 Diamond Debut	.20	.06	.02
Checklist			
☐ 771 Bret Boone DD	.75	.35	.09
☐ 772 Archi Cianfrocco DD	.20	.09	.03
☐ 773 Mark Clark DD	.12	.05	.02
☐ 774 Chad Curtis DD	.35	.16	.04
☐ 775 Pat Listach DD	1.75	.80	.22
☐ 776 Pat Mahomes DD	.25	.11	.03
☐ 777 Donovan Osborne DD	.40	.18	.05
☐ 778 John Patterson DD	.15	.07	.02
☐ 779 Andy Stankiewicz DD	.20	.09	.03
☐ 780 Turk Wendell DD	.15	.07	.02
☐ 781 Bill Krueger	.05	.02	.01
☐ 782 Rickey Henderson	.15	.07	.02
Grand Theft			
☐ 783 Kevin Seitzer	.08	.04	.01
☐ 784 Dave Martinez	.05	.02	.01
☐ 785 John Smiley	.08	.04	.01
☐ 786 Matt Stairs	.20	.09	.03
☐ 787 Scott Scudder	.05	.02	.01
☐ 788 John Wetteland	.05	.02	.01
☐ 789 Jack Armstrong	.05	.02	.01
☐ 790 Ken Hill	.08	.04	.01
☐ 791 Dick Schofield	.05	.02	.01
☐ 792 Mariano Duncan	.05	.02	.01
☐ 793 Bill Pecota	.05	.02	.01
☐ 794 Mike Kelly	1.00	.45	.13
☐ 795 Willie Randolph	.08	.04	.01

☐ 796 Butch Henry	.05	.02	.01
☐ 797 Carlos Hernandez	.05	.02	.01
☐ 798 Doug Jones	.05	.02	.01
☐ 799 Melido Perez	.08	.04	.01
☐ 800 Checklist 701-800	.07	.01	.00
☐ CP1 David McCarty holo	1.00	.45	.13
☐ CP2 Mike Kelly Holo	1.00	.45	.13
☐ CP3 Ben McDonald Holo	.50	.23	.06
☐ HH2 Ted Williams Hologram (Top left corner says, 91 Upper Deck 92)	6.00	2.70	.75
☐ SP3 Deion Sanders SP (Two-sport card)	10.00	4.50	1.25
☐ SP4 Tom Selleck and Frank Thomas SP (Mr. Baseball)	10.00	4.50	1.25

1992 Upper Deck All-Star FanFest

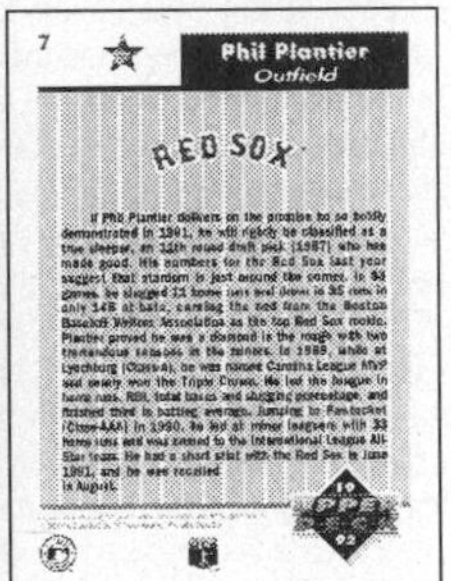

As a title sponsor of the 1992 All-Star FanFest in San Diego, Upper Deck produced this 54-card standard size (2 1/2" by 3 1/2") set to commemorate past, present, and future All-Stars Heroes of Major League Baseball. Sixty sets were packaged in a case, and each case had at least one gold foil set. Cards 1-10 feature 10 Future Heroes that are, in Upper Deck's opinion, sure bets to make an upcoming team; cards 11-44 present active All-Star alumni; and cards 45-54 salute All-Star Heroes of the past with 10 fan favorites. The glossy action color photos on the front are borderless except for a pinstripe-patterned bottom border and an All-Star FanFest insignia superimposed at the lower left corner. The bottom border on the ten Future Heroes cards is navy blue and silver while the bottom border on the All-Star Heroes is silver and white. The player's name is superimposed on the photo in silver and runs vertically down the left edge of the card. The backs display the team name and career and personal information on a gray and white pinstripe panel. The player's name and position appear in a navy bar in the upper right corner. The cards are numbered on the back.

	MT	EX-MT	VG
COMPLETE SET (54)	16.00	7.25	2.00
COMMON PLAYER (1-54)	.15	.07	.02
☐ 1 Steve Avery	.50	.23	.06
☐ 2 Ivan Rodriguez	.75	.35	.09
☐ 3 Jeff Bagwell	.60	.25	.08
☐ 4 Delino DeShields	.35	.16	.04
☐ 5 Royce Clayton	.35	.16	.04
☐ 6 Robin Ventura	.60	.25	.08
☐ 7 Phil Plantier	.35	.16	.04
☐ 8 Ray Lankford	.35	.16	.04
☐ 9 Juan Gonzalez	.75	.35	.09
☐ 10 Frank Thomas	2.00	.90	.25
☐ 11 Roberto Alomar	.60	.25	.08
☐ 12 Sandy Alomar Jr.	.15	.07	.02
☐ 13 Wade Boggs	.40	.18	.05
☐ 14 Barry Bonds	.40	.18	.05
☐ 15 Bobby Bonilla	.30	.14	.04
☐ 16 George Brett	.40	.18	.05
☐ 17 Jose Canseco	.50	.23	.06
☐ 18 Will Clark	.50	.23	.06
☐ 19 Roger Clemens	.60	.25	.08
☐ 20 Eric Davis	.25	.11	.03
☐ 21 Rob Dibble	.15	.07	.02
☐ 22 Cecil Fielder	.35	.16	.04
☐ 23 Dwight Gooden	.25	.11	.03
☐ 24 Ken Griffey Jr.	1.50	.65	.19
☐ 25 Tony Gwynn	.40	.18	.05
☐ 26 Bryan Harvey	.15	.07	.02
☐ 27 Rickey Henderson	.40	.18	.05
☐ 28 Howard Johnson	.25	.11	.03
☐ 29 Wally Joyner	.15	.07	.02
☐ 30 Barry Larkin	.25	.11	.03
☐ 31 Don Mattingly	.50	.23	.06
☐ 32 Mark McGwire	.50	.23	.06
☐ 33 Dale Murphy	.15	.07	.02
☐ 34 Rafael Palmeiro	.25	.11	.03
☐ 35 Kirby Puckett	.60	.25	.08
☐ 36 Cal Ripken	1.00	.45	.13
☐ 37 Nolan Ryan	1.25	.55	.16
☐ 38 Chris Sabo	.15	.07	.02
☐ 39 Ryne Sandberg	1.00	.45	.13
☐ 40 Benito Santiago	.25	.11	.03
☐ 41 Ruben Sierra	.40	.18	.05
☐ 42 Ozzie Smith	.30	.14	.04
☐ 43 Darryl Strawberry	.40	.18	.05
☐ 44 Robin Yount	.40	.18	.05
☐ 45 Rollie Fingers	.25	.11	.03
☐ 46 Reggie Jackson	.50	.23	.06
☐ 47 Billy Williams	.25	.11	.03
☐ 48 Lou Brock	.30	.14	.04
☐ 49 Gaylord Perry	.25	.11	.03
☐ 50 Ted Williams	1.00	.45	.13
☐ 51 Brooks Robinson	.30	.14	.04
☐ 52 Bob Gibson	.30	.14	.04
☐ 53 Bobby Bonds	.15	.07	.02
☐ 54 Robin Roberts	.20	.09	.03

1992 Upper Deck Bench/Morgan Heroes

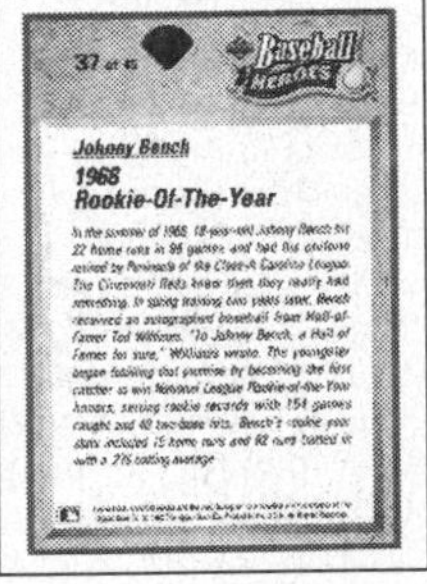

This standard size (2 1/2" by 3 1/2") 10-card set was randomly inserted in 1992 Upper Deck high number packs. Both Bench and Morgan autographed 2,500 of card number 45, which displays a portrait by sports artist Vernon Wells. The fronts feature color photos of Bench (37-39), Morgan (40-42), or both (43-44) at various stages of their baseball careers. These pictures are partially contained within a blue and white bordered circle. The photos rest on a parchment card face trimmed with a brick red and white border. The Upper Deck Baseball Heroes logo appears in the lower right corner. The back design displays career highlights on a gray plaque resting on the same parchment background as on the front. The cards are numbered on the back.

	MT	EX-MT	VG
COMPLETE SET (10)	20.00	9.00	2.50
COMMON BENCH/MORGAN (37-45)	1.50	.65	.19
☐ 37 1968 Rookie-of-the-Year	1.50	.65	.19
☐ 38 1968-77 Ten Straight Gold Gloves	1.50	.65	.19
☐ 39 1970 and 1972 MVP	1.50	.65	.19
☐ 40 1965 Rookie Year	1.50	.65	.19

☐ 41 1975-76 Back-to-Back MVP	1.50	.65	.19
☐ 42 1980-83 The Golden Years	1.50	.65	.19
☐ 43 1972-79 Big Red Machine	1.50	.65	.19
☐ 44 1989 and 1990 Hall of Fame	1.50	.65	.19
☐ 45 Checklist-Heroes 37-45	1.50	.65	.19
☐ AU5 Johnny Bench and Joe Morgan (Signed and Numbered of 2500)	350.00	160.00	45.00
☐ NNO Baseball Heroes SP (Header card)	12.00	5.50	1.50

1992 Upper Deck HOF Heroes

Continuing a popular subset introduced the previous year, Upper Deck produced four new commemorative cards, including three player cards and one portrait card by sports artist Vernon Wells. These cards were randomly inserted in 1992 Upper Deck baseball low number foil packs. Three thousand of each card were personally numbered and autographed by each player. On a white card face, the fronts carry sepia-tone player photos with red, gold, and blue border stripes. The player's name appears in a gold border stripe beneath the picture, with the Upper Deck "Heroes of Baseball" logo in the lower right corner. The backs have a similar design to the fronts except for a career summary and an advertisement for Upper Deck "Heroes of Baseball" games that will be played before regularly scheduled Major League games. The cards are arranged alphabetically and numbered on the back.

	MT	EX-MT	VG
COMPLETE SET (4)	36.00	16.00	4.50
COMMON PLAYER (H5-H8)	6.00	2.70	.75
☐ H5 Vida Blue	6.00	2.70	.75
☐ H5AU Vida Blue (Signed and Numbered out of 3000)	75.00	34.00	9.50
☐ H6 Lou Brock	12.00	5.50	1.50
☐ H6AU Lou Brock (Signed and Numbered out of 3000)	150.00	70.00	19.00
☐ H7 Rollie Fingers	12.00	5.50	1.50
☐ H7AU Rollie Fingers (Signed and Numbered out of 3000)	150.00	70.00	19.00
☐ H8 Header (Portrait of all three players)	12.00	5.50	1.50

1992 Upper Deck Heroes Highlights

To dealers participating in Heroes of Baseball Collectors shows, Upper Deck made available this ten-card insert set,

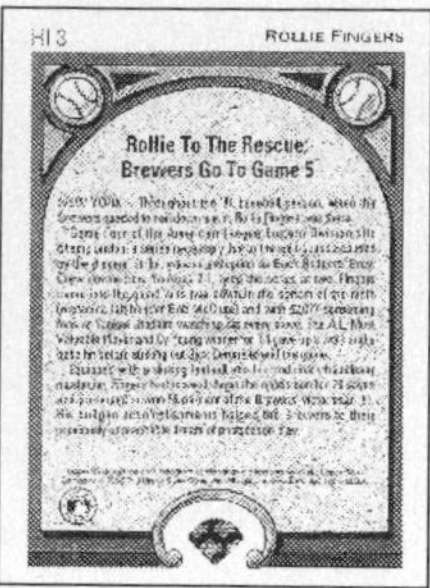

which commemorates one of the greatest moments in the careers of ten of baseball's all-time players. The cards, which measure the standard size (2 1/2" by 3 1/2"), were randomly inserted in high number packs sold at these shows. The fronts feature color player photos with a shadowed strip for a three-dimensional effect. The player's name and the date of the great moment in the hero's career appear with a "Heroes Highlights" logo in a bottom border of varying shades of brown and blue-green. The backs have white borders and display a blue-green and brown bordered monument design accented with baseballs. The major portion of the design is parchment-textured and contains text highlighting a special moment in the player's career. The cards are numbered on the back with an HI prefix. The card numbering follows alphabetical order by player's name.

	MT	EX-MT	VG
COMPLETE SET (10)	50.00	23.00	6.25
COMMON PLAYER (1-10)	3.00	1.35	.40
☐ 1 Bobby Bonds	3.00	1.35	.40
☐ 2 Lou Brock	6.00	2.70	.75
☐ 3 Rollie Fingers	5.00	2.30	.60
☐ 4 Bob Gibson	6.00	2.70	.75
☐ 5 Reggie Jackson	8.00	3.60	1.00
☐ 6 Gaylord Perry	5.00	2.30	.60
☐ 7 Robin Roberts	4.00	1.80	.50
☐ 8 Brooks Robinson	6.00	2.70	.75
☐ 9 Billy Williams	4.00	1.80	.50
☐ 10 Ted Williams	10.00	4.50	1.25

1992 Upper Deck Home Run Heroes

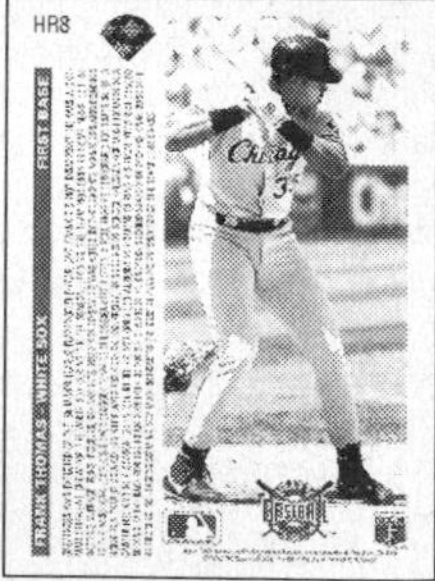

This 26-card subset measures the standard size (2 1/2" by 3 1/2") and was randomly inserted into 1992 Upper Deck baseball jumbo foil packs. The set spotlights the 1991 home run leaders from each of the 26 Major League teams. The fronts display color action player photos with a shadow strip around the picture for a three-dimensional effect. A gold bat icon runs vertically down the left side and contains the words "Homerun Heroes" printed in white. The backs have action photos in color and career highlights on a white background. AL players have their name printed in a red bar while NL players' names are printed in a green bar. The cards are numbered on the back with an HR prefix.

	MT	EX-MT	VG
COMPLETE SET (26)	24.00	11.00	3.00
COMMON PLAYER (1-26)	.50	.23	.06
☐ 1 Jose Canseco	2.00	.90	.25
☐ 2 Cecil Fielder	1.25	.55	.16
☐ 3 Howard Johnson	.50	.23	.06
☐ 4 Cal Ripken	3.00	1.35	.40
☐ 5 Matt Williams	.50	.23	.06
☐ 6 Joe Carter	1.25	.55	.16
☐ 7 Ron Gant	.75	.35	.09
☐ 8 Frank Thomas	5.00	2.30	.60
☐ 9 Andre Dawson	.75	.35	.09
☐ 10 Fred McGriff	1.25	.55	.16
☐ 11 Danny Tartabull	.50	.23	.06
☐ 12 Chili Davis	.50	.23	.06
☐ 13 Albert Belle	1.00	.45	.13
☐ 14 Jack Clark	.50	.23	.06
☐ 15 Paul O'Neill	.50	.23	.06
☐ 16 Darryl Strawberry	1.25	.55	.16
☐ 17 Dave Winfield	.75	.35	.09
☐ 18 Jay Buhner	.50	.23	.06
☐ 19 Juan Gonzalez	3.00	1.35	.40
☐ 20 Greg Vaughan	.50	.23	.06
☐ 21 Barry Bonds	1.50	.65	.19
☐ 22 Matt Nokes	.50	.23	.06
☐ 23 John Kruk	.50	.23	.06
☐ 24 Ivan Calderon	.50	.23	.06
☐ 25 Jeff Bagwell	2.00	.90	.25
☐ 26 Todd Zeile	.50	.23	.06

1992 Upper Deck Scouting Report

Randomly inserted one per high series jumbo pack, this 25-card set features outstanding prospects in baseball. The cards measure the standard size (2 1/2" by 3 1/2"). The fronts carry color action player photos that are full-bleed on the top and right, bordered below by a black stripe with the player's name, and by a black jagged left border that resembles torn paper. The words "Scouting Report" are printed vertically in silver lettering in the left border. The back design features a clipboard with three items held fast by the clamp: 1) a color player photo; 2) a 4" by 6" index card with major league rating in five categories (average, power, speed, fielding, and arm), and an 8 1/2" by 11" piece of paper typed with a player profile. The cards are numbered on the back with an SR prefix. The card numbering follows alphabetical order by player's name.

	MT	EX-MT	VG
COMPLETE SET (25)	27.00	12.00	3.40
COMMON PLAYER (1-25)	.50	.23	.06
☐ 1 Andy Ashby	.50	.23	.06
☐ 2 Willie Banks	1.00	.45	.13
☐ 3 Kim Batiste	.50	.23	.06
☐ 4 Derek Bell	1.00	.45	.13
☐ 5 Archi Cianfrocco	.60	.25	.08
☐ 6 Royce Clayton	1.00	.45	.13
☐ 7 Gary DiSarcina	.50	.23	.06
☐ 8 Dave Fleming	3.00	1.35	.40
☐ 9 Butch Henry	.50	.23	.06
☐ 10 Todd Hundley	.50	.23	.06
☐ 11 Brian Jordan	1.00	.45	.13
☐ 12 Eric Karros	7.00	3.10	.85
☐ 13 Pat Listach	7.00	3.10	.85
☐ 14 Scott Livingstone	.50	.23	.06
☐ 15 Kenny Lofton	4.00	1.80	.50
☐ 16 Pat Mahomes	1.50	.65	.19
☐ 17 Denny Neagle	.50	.23	.06
☐ 18 Dave Nilsson	1.25	.55	.16
☐ 19 Donovan Osborne	2.00	.90	.25
☐ 20 Reggie Sanders	2.50	1.15	.30
☐ 21 Andy Stankiewicz	.60	.25	.08
☐ 22 Jim Thome	1.00	.45	.13
☐ 23 Julio Valera	.50	.23	.06
☐ 24 Mark Wohlers	.75	.35	.09
☐ 25 Anthony Young	.50	.23	.06

1992 Upper Deck Team MVP Holograms

The 54 hologram cards in this standard size (2 1/2" by 3 1/2") set feature the top offensive player and pitcher from each Major League team plus two checklist cards. Only 216,000 number sets were produced, and each set was packaged in a custom-designed box with protective sleeve and included a numbered certificate. To display the set, Upper Deck also made available a custom album through a mail-in offer for 10.00. The horizontally oriented fronts display the players in action and close-up in three-dimensional form. The player's name appears at the bottom in a striped border. In the lower right corner, a baseball image on a black home plate design radiates streaks of light up into the picture. The backs are also horizontally oriented and show the player in action in a full-color picture. A green-bordered pale yellow panel contains a career summary. Cards 1-2 feature the AL and NL MVPs (with checklists) while cards 3-54 are arranged in alphabetical order. The cards are numbered on the back.

	MT	EX-MT	VG
COMPLETE SET (54)	25.00	11.50	3.10
COMMON PLAYER (1-54)	.35	.16	.04
☐ 1 Cal Ripken MVP AL Checklist	.90	.40	.11
☐ 2 Terry Pendleton MVP NL Checklist	.45	.20	.06
☐ 3 Jim Abbott	.45	.20	.06
☐ 4 Roberto Alomar	.75	.35	.09
☐ 5 Kevin Appier	.45	.20	.06
☐ 6 Steve Avery	.75	.35	.09
☐ 7 Jeff Bagwell	.75	.35	.09
☐ 8 Albert Belle	.60	.25	.08
☐ 9 Andy Benes	.45	.20	.06
☐ 10 Wade Boggs	.60	.25	.08
☐ 11 Barry Bonds	.60	.25	.08
☐ 12 George Brett	.60	.25	.08
☐ 13 Ivan Calderon	.35	.16	.04

		MT	EX-MT	VG
☐	14 Jose Canseco	.75	.35	.09
☐	15 Will Clark	.75	.35	.09
☐	16 Roger Clemens	.90	.40	.11
☐	17 David Cone	.45	.20	.06
☐	18 Doug Drabek	.45	.20	.06
☐	19 Dennis Eckersley	.45	.20	.06
☐	20 Scott Erickson	.45	.20	.06
☐	21 Cecil Fielder	.60	.25	.08
☐	22 Ken Griffey Jr.	2.00	.90	.25
☐	23 Bill Gullickson	.35	.16	.04
☐	24 Juan Guzman	1.00	.45	.13
☐	25 Pete Harnisch	.35	.16	.04
☐	26 Howard Johnson	.45	.20	.06
☐	27 Randy Johnson	.35	.16	.04
☐	28 John Kruk	.45	.20	.06
☐	29 Barry Larkin	.60	.25	.08
☐	30 Greg Maddux	.60	.25	.08
☐	31 Dennis Martinez	.45	.20	.06
☐	32 Ramon Martinez	.45	.20	.06
☐	33 Don Mattingly	.60	.25	.08
☐	34 Jack McDowell	.45	.20	.06
☐	35 Fred McGriff	.60	.25	.08
☐	36 Paul Molitor	.60	.25	.08
☐	37 Charles Nagy	.60	.25	.08
☐	38 Gregg Olson	.45	.20	.06
☐	39 Terry Pendleton	.45	.20	.06
☐	40 Luis Polonia	.45	.20	.06
☐	41 Kirby Puckett	.75	.35	.09
☐	42 Dave Righetti	.35	.16	.04
☐	43 Jose Rijo	.35	.16	.04
☐	44 Cal Ripken	1.50	.65	.19
☐	45 Nolan Ryan	2.00	.90	.25
☐	46 Ryne Sandberg	1.25	.55	.16
☐	47 Scott Sanderson	.35	.16	.04
☐	48 Ruben Sierra	.60	.25	.08
☐	49 Lee Smith	.45	.20	.06
☐	50 Ozzie Smith	.60	.25	.08
☐	51 Darryl Strawberry	.60	.25	.08
☐	52 Frank Thomas	3.00	1.35	.40
☐	53 Bill Wegman	.35	.16	.04
☐	54 Mitch Williams	.35	.16	.04

1992 Upper Deck Ted Williams Best

This 20-card set contains Ted Williams' choices of best current and future hitters in the game. The standard size cards (2 1/2" by 3 1/2") were randomly inserted in Upper Deck high number foil packs. The fronts feature full-bleed color action photos with the player's name in a black field separated from the picture by Ted Williams' gold-stamped signature. The back design displays a color close-up of the player in a purple and gold bordered oval on a gray cement-textured background. The upper right corner appears peeled back to reveal the Upper Deck hologram. A Ted Williams' quote about the player is included below the photo. Player's statistics in a purple and gold bordered box round out the card back. The cards are numbered on the back with a T prefix.

	MT	EX-MT	VG
COMPLETE SET (20)	60.00	27.00	7.50
COMMON PLAYER (1-20)	1.50	.65	.19
☐ 1 Wade Boggs	2.50	1.15	.30
☐ 2 Barry Bonds	4.00	1.80	.50
☐ 3 Jose Canseco	4.00	1.80	.50
☐ 4 Will Clark	4.00	1.80	.50
☐ 5 Cecil Fielder	3.00	1.35	.40
☐ 6 Tony Gwynn	3.00	1.35	.40
☐ 7 Rickey Henderson	3.00	1.35	.40
☐ 8 Fred McGriff	3.00	1.35	.40
☐ 9 Kirby Puckett	4.00	1.80	.50
☐ 10 Ruben Sierra	3.00	1.35	.40
☐ 11 Roberto Alomar	4.50	2.00	.55
☐ 12 Jeff Bagwell	4.00	1.80	.50
☐ 13 Albert Belle	2.50	1.15	.30
☐ 14 Juan Gonzalez	6.00	2.70	.75
☐ 15 Ken Griffey Jr.	9.00	4.00	1.15
☐ 16 Chris Hoiles	1.50	.65	.19
☐ 17 David Justice	3.50	1.55	.45
☐ 18 Phil Plantier	2.00	.90	.25
☐ 19 Frank Thomas	12.00	5.50	1.50
☐ 20 Robin Ventura	3.00	1.35	.40

1992 Upper Deck Ted Williams Heroes

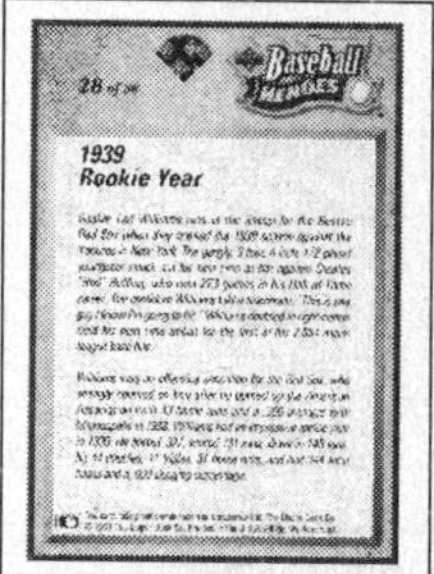

This standard size (2 1/2" by 3 1/2") ten-card set was randomly inserted in 1992 Upper Deck low number foil packs. Williams autographed 2,500 of card 36, which displays his portrait by sports artist Vernon Wells. The fronts features sepia-tone photos of Williams in various stages of his career that are partially contained within a blue and white bordered circle. The photos rest on a parchment card face trimmed with a brick red and white border. The Upper Deck Baseball Heroes logo appears in the lower right corner. The back design displays career highlights on a gray plaque resting on the same parchment background as on the front. The cards are numbered on the back.

	MT	EX-MT	VG
COMPLETE SET (10)	12.00	5.50	1.50
COMMON WILLIAMS (28-36)	.60	.25	.08
☐ 28 1939 Rookie Year	.60	.25	.08
☐ 29 1941 .406	.60	.25	.08
☐ 30 1942 Triple Crown Year	.60	.25	.08
☐ 31 1946 and 1949 MVP	.60	.25	.08
☐ 32 1947 Second Triple Crown	.60	.25	.08
☐ 33 1950s Player of the Decade	.60	.25	.08
☐ 34 1960 500 Home Run Club	.60	.25	.08
☐ 35 1966 Hall of Fame	.60	.25	.08
☐ 36 Baseball Heroes CL	.60	.25	.08
☐ AU4 Ted Williams (Signed and Numbered of 2500)	450.00	200.00	57.50
☐ NNO Baseball Heroes SP (Header card)	8.00	3.60	1.00

1992 Upper Deck Ted Williams Waxboxes

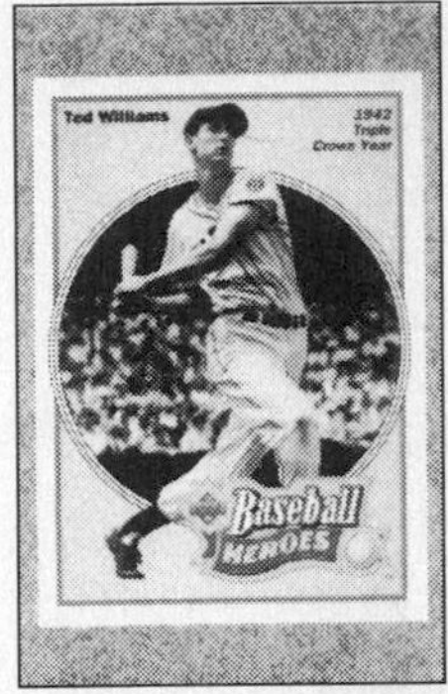

These eight oversized "cards," measuring approximately 5 1/4" by 7 1/4", were featured on the bottom panels of 1992 Upper Deck low series waxboxes. They are identical in design to the Williams Heroes insert cards, displaying color player photos in an oval frame. The backs are blank and they are unnumbered. We have checklisted them below according to the numbering of the Heroes cards.

	MT	EX-MT	VG
COMPLETE SET (8)	3.00	1.35	.40
COMMON PLAYER (28-35)	.50	.23	.06
☐ 28 1939 Rookie Year	.50	.23	.06
☐ 29 1941 .406	.50	.23	.06
☐ 30 1942 Triple Crown Year	.50	.23	.06
☐ 31 1946 and 1949 MVP	.50	.23	.06
☐ 32 1947 Second Triple Crown	.50	.23	.06
☐ 33 1950s Player of the Decade	.50	.23	.06
☐ 34 1960 500 Home Run Club	.50	.23	.06
☐ 35 1966 Hall of Fame	.50	.23	.06

1993 Upper Deck

The first series of the 1993 Upper Deck baseball set consists of 420 cards measuring the standard size (2 1/2" by 3 1/2"). A ten-card hobby-only insert set featured Triple Crown Contenders while a 26-card Walter Iooss Collection was found in retail foil packs only. A ten-card Baseball Heroes insert set pays tribute to Willie Mays. Also a nine-card "Then and Now" hologram set was randomly inserted in foil packs and one card of a 28-card insert set was featured exclusively in each jumbo foil pack. Finally a special card (SP5) was randomly inserted in packs to commemorate the 3,000th hit of Brett and Yount. The front designs features color action player photos bordered in white. The company name is printed along the photo surface of the card top. The player's name appears in script in a color stripe cutting across the bottom of the picture while the team name and his position appear in another color stripe immediately below. The backs have a color close-up photo on the upper portion and biography, statistics, and career higlights on the lower portion. Special subsets featured include Star Rookies (1-29), Community Heroes (30-40), and American League Teammates (41-55). The cards are numbered on the back.

	MT	EX-MT	VG
COMPLETE SET (420)	30.00	13.50	3.80
COMMON PLAYER (1-420)	.06	.03	.01
COMMUNITY HEROES (30-40)	.07	.03	.01
☐ 1 Star Rookie CL Tim Salmon	.25	.08	.03
☐ 2 Mike Piazza SR	.50	.23	.06
☐ 3 Rene Arocha SR	.50	.23	.06
☐ 4 Willie Greene SR	.25	.11	.03
☐ 5 Manny Alexander SR	.15	.07	.02
☐ 6 Dan Wilson SR	.10	.05	.01
☐ 7 Dan Smith SR	.15	.07	.02
☐ 8 Kevin Rogers SR	.15	.07	.02
☐ 9 Kurt Miller SR	2.00	.90	.25
☐ 10 Joe Vitko SR	.30	.14	.04
☐ 11 Tim Costo SR	.15	.07	.02
☐ 12 Alan Embree SR	.40	.18	.05
☐ 13 Jim Tatum SR	.30	.14	.04
☐ 14 Cris Colon SR	.15	.07	.02
☐ 15 Steve Hosey SR	.25	.11	.03
☐ 16 Sterling Hitchcock SR	.50	.23	.06
☐ 17 Dave Mlicki SR	.25	.11	.03
☐ 18 Jessie Hollins SR	.30	.14	.04
☐ 19 Bobby Jones SR	.50	.23	.06
☐ 20 Kurt Miller SR	.10	.05	.01
☐ 21 Melvin Nieves SR	.50	.23	.06
☐ 22 Billy Ashley SR	.40	.18	.05
☐ 23 J.T. Snow SR	.75	.35	.09
☐ 24 Chipper Jones SR	.40	.18	.05
☐ 25 Tim Salmon SR	.40	.18	.05
☐ 26 Tim Pugh SR	.35	.16	.04
☐ 27 David Nied SR	2.00	.90	.25
☐ 28 Mike Trombley SR	.20	.09	.03
☐ 29 Javy Lopez SR	.50	.23	.06
☐ 30 Community Heroes CL Jim Abbott	.12	.04	.01
☐ 31 Jim Abbott CH	.12	.05	.02
☐ 32 Dale Murphy CH	.09	.04	.01
☐ 33 Tony Pena CH	.07	.03	.01
☐ 34 Kirby Puckett CH	.20	.09	.03
☐ 35 Harold Reynolds CH	.07	.03	.01
☐ 36 Cal Ripken CH	.25	.11	.03
☐ 37 Nolan Ryan CH	.30	.14	.04
☐ 38 Ryne Sandberg CH	.20	.09	.03
☐ 39 Dave Stewart CH	.09	.04	.01
☐ 40 Dave Winfield CH	.10	.05	.01
☐ 41 Teammates CL Joe Carter Mark McGwire	.15	.05	.02
☐ 42 Blockbuster Trade Joe Carter Roberto Alomar	.15	.07	.02
☐ 43 Brew Crew Paul Molitor Pat Listach Robin Yount	.25	.11	.03
☐ 44 Iron and Steel Cal Ripken Brady Anderson	.20	.09	.03
☐ 45 Youthful Tribe Albert Belle Sandy Alomar Jr. Jim Thome Carlos Baerga Kenny Lofton	.15	.07	.02
☐ 46 Motown Mashers Cecil Fielder Mickey Tettleton	.12	.05	.02
☐ 47 Yankee Pride Roberto Kelly Don Mattingly	.12	.05	.02
☐ 48 Boston Cy Sox Frank Viola Roger Clemens	.12	.05	.02
☐ 49 Bash Brothers Ruben Sierra Mark McGwire	.15	.07	.02

☐ 50 Twin Titles .12 .05 .02
Kent Hrbek
Kirby Puckett
☐ 51 Southside Sluggers .40 .18 .05
Robin Ventura
Frank Thomas
☐ 52 Latin Stars .35 .16 .04
Juan Gonzalez
Jose Canseco
Ivan Rodriguez
Rafael Palmeiro
☐ 53 Lethal Lefties .07 .03 .01
Mark Langston
Jim Abbott
Chuck Finley
☐ 54 Royal Family .12 .05 .02
Wally Joyner
Gregg Jefferies
George Brett
☐ 55 Pacific Sock Exchange .25 .11 .03
Kevin Mitchell
Ken Griffey Jr.
Jay Buhner
☐ 56 George Brett .15 .07 .02
☐ 57 Scott Cooper .08 .04 .01
☐ 58 Mike Maddux .06 .03 .01
☐ 59 Rusty Meacham .06 .03 .01
☐ 60 Wilfredo Cordero .15 .07 .02
☐ 61 Tim Teufel .06 .03 .01
☐ 62 Jeff Montgomery .06 .03 .01
☐ 63 Scott Livingstone .08 .04 .01
☐ 64 Doug Dascenzo .20 .09 .03
☐ 65 Bret Boone .40 .18 .05
☐ 66 Tim Wakefield .90 .40 .11
☐ 67 Curt Schilling .06 .03 .01
☐ 68 Frank Tanana .06 .03 .01
☐ 69 Len Dykstra .08 .04 .01
☐ 70 Derek Lilliquist .06 .03 .01
☐ 71 Anthony Young .08 .04 .01
☐ 72 Hipolito Pichardo .06 .03 .01
☐ 73 Rod Beck .08 .04 .01
☐ 74 Kent Hrbek .08 .04 .01
☐ 75 Tom Glavine .20 .09 .03
☐ 76 Kevin Brown .08 .04 .01
☐ 77 Chuck Finley .06 .03 .01
☐ 78 Bob Walk .06 .03 .01
☐ 79 Rheal Cormier .06 .03 .01
☐ 80 Rick Sutcliffe .08 .04 .01
☐ 81 Harold Baines .08 .04 .01
☐ 82 Lee Smith .08 .04 .01
☐ 83 Geno Petralli .06 .03 .01
☐ 84 Jose Oquendo .06 .03 .01
☐ 85 Mark Gubicza .06 .03 .01
☐ 86 Mickey Tettleton .08 .04 .01
☐ 87 Bobby Witt .06 .03 .01
☐ 88 Mark Lewis .08 .04 .01
☐ 89 Kevin Appier .08 .04 .01
☐ 90 Mike Stanton .06 .03 .01
☐ 91 Rafael Belliard .06 .03 .01
☐ 92 Kenny Rogers .06 .03 .01
☐ 93 Randy Velarde .06 .03 .01
☐ 94 Luis Sojo .06 .03 .01
☐ 95 Mark Leiter .06 .03 .01
☐ 96 Jody Reed .06 .03 .01
☐ 97 Pete Harnisch .06 .03 .01
☐ 98 Tom Candiotti .06 .03 .01
☐ 99 Mark Portugal .06 .03 .01
☐ 100 Dave Valle .06 .03 .01
☐ 101 Shawon Dunston .08 .04 .01
☐ 102 B.J. Surhoff .06 .03 .01
☐ 103 Jay Bell .06 .03 .01
☐ 104 Sid Bream .06 .03 .01
☐ 105 Checklist 1-105 .11 .03 .01
Frank Thomas
☐ 106 Mike Morgan .06 .03 .01
☐ 107 Bill Doran .06 .03 .01
☐ 108 Lance Blankenship .06 .03 .01
☐ 109 Mark Lemke .06 .03 .01
☐ 110 Brian Harper .06 .03 .01
☐ 111 Brady Anderson .08 .04 .01
☐ 112 Bip Roberts .08 .04 .01
☐ 113 Mitch Williams .06 .03 .01
☐ 114 Craig Biggio .08 .04 .01
☐ 115 Eddie Murray .15 .07 .02
☐ 116 Matt Nokes .06 .03 .01
☐ 117 Lance Parrish .08 .04 .01
☐ 118 Bill Swift .06 .03 .01
☐ 119 Jeff Innis .06 .03 .01
☐ 120 Mike LaValliere .06 .03 .01
☐ 121 Hal Morris .08 .04 .01
☐ 122 Walt Weiss .06 .03 .01
☐ 123 Ivan Rodriguez .30 .14 .04
☐ 124 Andy Van Slyke .08 .04 .01
☐ 125 Roberto Alomar .35 .16 .04
☐ 126 Robby Thompson .06 .03 .01
☐ 127 Sammy Sosa .06 .03 .01
☐ 128 Mark Langston .08 .04 .01
☐ 129 Jerry Browne .06 .03 .01
☐ 130 Chuck McElroy .06 .03 .01
☐ 131 Frank Viola .08 .04 .01
☐ 132 Leo Gomez .08 .04 .01
☐ 133 Ramon Martinez .08 .04 .01
☐ 134 Don Mattingly .20 .09 .03
☐ 135 Roger Clemens .35 .16 .04
☐ 136 Rickey Henderson .20 .09 .03
☐ 137 Darren Daulton .08 .04 .01
☐ 138 Ken Hill .08 .04 .01
☐ 139 Ozzie Guillen .06 .03 .01
☐ 140 Jerald Clark .06 .03 .01
☐ 141 Dave Fleming .30 .14 .04
☐ 142 Delino DeShields .15 .07 .02
☐ 143 Matt Williams .08 .04 .01
☐ 144 Larry Walker .20 .09 .03
☐ 145 Ruben Sierra .25 .11 .03
☐ 146 Ozzie Smith .15 .07 .02
☐ 147 Chris Sabo .08 .04 .01
☐ 148 Carlos Hernandez .08 .04 .01
☐ 149 Pat Borders .06 .03 .01
☐ 150 Orlando Merced .08 .04 .01
☐ 151 Royce Clayton .08 .04 .01
☐ 152 Kurt Stillwell .06 .03 .01
☐ 153 Dave Hollins .08 .04 .01
☐ 154 Mike Greenwell .08 .04 .01
☐ 155 Nolan Ryan .60 .25 .08
☐ 156 Felix Jose .08 .04 .01
☐ 157 Junior Felix .06 .03 .01
☐ 158 Derek Bell .08 .04 .01
☐ 159 Steve Buechele .06 .03 .01
☐ 160 John Burkett .06 .03 .01
☐ 161 Pat Howell .15 .07 .02
☐ 162 Milt Cuyler .06 .03 .01
☐ 163 Terry Pendleton .08 .04 .01
☐ 164 Jack Morris .10 .05 .01
☐ 165 Tony Gwynn .20 .09 .03
☐ 166 Deion Sanders .20 .09 .03
☐ 167 Mike Devereaux .08 .04 .01
☐ 168 Ron Darling .08 .04 .01
☐ 169 Orel Hershiser .08 .04 .01
☐ 170 Mike Jackson .06 .03 .01
☐ 171 Doug Jones .06 .03 .01
☐ 172 Dan Walters .06 .03 .01
☐ 173 Darren Lewis .06 .03 .01
☐ 174 Carlos Baerga .25 .11 .03
☐ 175 Ryne Sandberg .35 .16 .04
☐ 176 Gregg Jefferies .08 .04 .01
☐ 177 John Jaha .08 .04 .01
☐ 178 Luis Polonia .06 .03 .01
☐ 179 Kirt Manwaring .06 .03 .01
☐ 180 Mike Magnante .06 .03 .01
☐ 181 Billy Ripken .06 .03 .01
☐ 182 Mike Moore .06 .03 .01
☐ 183 Eric Anthony .08 .04 .01
☐ 184 Lenny Harris .06 .03 .01
☐ 185 Tony Pena .06 .03 .01
☐ 186 Mike Felder .06 .03 .01
☐ 187 Greg Olson .06 .03 .01
☐ 188 Rene Gonzales .06 .03 .01
☐ 189 Mike Bordick .08 .04 .01
☐ 190 Mel Rojas .06 .03 .01
☐ 191 Todd Frohwirth .06 .03 .01
☐ 192 Darryl Hamilton .08 .04 .01
☐ 193 Mike Fetters .06 .03 .01
☐ 194 Omar Olivares .06 .03 .01
☐ 195 Tony Phillips .06 .03 .01
☐ 196 Paul Sorrento .06 .03 .01
☐ 197 Trevor Wilson .06 .03 .01
☐ 198 Kevin Gross .06 .03 .01
☐ 199 Ron Karkovice .06 .03 .01
☐ 200 Brook Jacoby .06 .03 .01
☐ 201 Mariano Duncan .06 .03 .01
☐ 202 Dennis Cook .06 .03 .01
☐ 203 Daryl Boston .06 .03 .01
☐ 204 Mike Perez .08 .04 .01
☐ 205 Manuel Lee .06 .03 .01
☐ 206 Steve Olin .06 .03 .01
☐ 207 Charlie Hough .06 .03 .01
☐ 208 Scott Scudder .06 .03 .01
☐ 209 Charlie O'Brien .06 .03 .01
☐ 210 Checklist 106-210 .09 .02 .01
Barry Bonds
☐ 211 Jose Vizcaino .06 .03 .01
☐ 212 Scott Leius .06 .03 .01
☐ 213 Kevin Mitchell .08 .04 .01
☐ 214 Brian Barnes .06 .03 .01
☐ 215 Pat Kelly .08 .04 .01
☐ 216 Chris Hammond .06 .03 .01

☐ 217 Rob Deer .08 .04 .01
☐ 218 Cory Snyder .06 .03 .01
☐ 219 Gary Carter .08 .04 .01
☐ 220 Danny Darwin .06 .03 .01
☐ 221 Tom Gordon .06 .03 .01
☐ 222 Gary Sheffield .30 .14 .04
☐ 223 Joe Carter .20 .09 .03
☐ 224 Jay Buhner .08 .04 .01
☐ 225 Jose Offerman .08 .04 .01
☐ 226 Jose Rijo .08 .04 .01
☐ 227 Mark Whiten .08 .04 .01
☐ 228 Randy Milligan .06 .03 .01
☐ 229 Bud Black .06 .03 .01
☐ 230 Gary DiSarcina .08 .04 .01
☐ 231 Steve Finley .06 .03 .01
☐ 232 Dennis Martinez .08 .04 .01
☐ 233 Mike Mussina .50 .23 .06
☐ 234 Joe Oliver .06 .03 .01
☐ 235 Chad Curtis .20 .09 .03
☐ 236 Shane Mack .08 .04 .01
☐ 237 Jaime Navarro .08 .04 .01
☐ 238 Brian McRae .08 .04 .01
☐ 239 Chili Davis .08 .04 .01
☐ 240 Jeff King .06 .03 .01
☐ 241 Dean Palmer .08 .04 .01
☐ 242 Danny Tartabull .08 .04 .01
☐ 243 Charles Nagy .08 .04 .01
☐ 244 Ray Lankford .15 .07 .02
☐ 245 Barry Larkin .15 .07 .02
☐ 246 Steve Avery .25 .11 .03
☐ 247 John Kruk .08 .04 .01
☐ 248 Derrick May .08 .04 .01
☐ 249 Stan Javier .06 .03 .01
☐ 250 Roger McDowell .06 .03 .01
☐ 251 Dan Gladden .06 .03 .01
☐ 252 Wally Joyner .08 .04 .01
☐ 253 Pat Listach .60 .25 .08
☐ 254 Chuck Knoblauch .25 .11 .03
☐ 255 Sandy Alomar Jr. .06 .03 .01
☐ 256 Jeff Bagwell .30 .14 .04
☐ 257 Andy Stankiewicz .08 .04 .01
☐ 258 Darrin Jackson .06 .03 .01
☐ 259 Brett Butler .08 .04 .01
☐ 260 Joe Orsulak .06 .03 .01
☐ 261 Andy Benes .08 .04 .01
☐ 262 Kenny Lofton .30 .14 .04
☐ 263 Robin Ventura .25 .11 .03
☐ 264 Ron Gant .08 .04 .01
☐ 265 Ellis Burks .06 .03 .01
☐ 266 Juan Guzman .50 .23 .06
☐ 267 Wes Chamberlain .06 .03 .01
☐ 268 John Smiley .08 .04 .01
☐ 269 Franklin Stubbs .06 .03 .01
☐ 270 Tom Browning .06 .03 .01
☐ 271 Dennis Eckersley .10 .05 .01
☐ 272 Carlton Fisk .15 .07 .02
☐ 273 Lou Whitaker .08 .04 .01
☐ 274 Phil Plantier .15 .07 .02
☐ 275 Bobby Bonilla .15 .07 .02
☐ 276 Ben McDonald .08 .04 .01
☐ 277 Bob Zupcic .08 .04 .01
☐ 278 Terry Steinbach .08 .04 .01
☐ 279 Terry Mulholland .06 .03 .01
☐ 280 Lance Johnson .06 .03 .01
☐ 281 Willie McGee .08 .04 .01
☐ 282 Bret Saberhagen .08 .04 .01
☐ 283 Randy Myers .06 .03 .01
☐ 284 Randy Tomlin .06 .03 .01
☐ 285 Mickey Morandini .08 .04 .01
☐ 286 Brian Williams .08 .04 .01
☐ 287 Tino Martinez .08 .04 .01
☐ 288 Jose Melendez .06 .03 .01
☐ 289 Jeff Huson .06 .03 .01
☐ 290 Joe Grahe .06 .03 .01
☐ 291 Mel Hall .06 .03 .01
☐ 292 Otis Nixon .06 .03 .01
☐ 293 Todd Hundley .06 .03 .01
☐ 294 Casey Candaele .06 .03 .01
☐ 295 Kevin Seitzer .08 .04 .01
☐ 296 Eddie Taubensee .06 .03 .01
☐ 297 Moises Alou .08 .04 .01
☐ 298 Scott Radinsky .06 .03 .01
☐ 299 Thomas Howard .06 .03 .01
☐ 300 Kyle Abbott .06 .03 .01
☐ 301 Omar Vizquel .06 .03 .01
☐ 302 Keith Miller .06 .03 .01
☐ 303 Rick Aguilera .08 .04 .01
☐ 304 Bruce Hurst .08 .04 .01
☐ 305 Ken Caminiti .08 .04 .01
☐ 306 Mike Pagliarulo .06 .03 .01
☐ 307 Frank Seminara .06 .03 .01
☐ 308 Andre Dawson .15 .07 .02
☐ 309 Jose Lind .06 .03 .01
☐ 310 Joe Boever .06 .03 .01
☐ 311 Jeff Parrett .06 .03 .01
☐ 312 Alan Mills .06 .03 .01
☐ 313 Kevin Tapani .08 .04 .01
☐ 314 Darryl Kile .06 .03 .01
☐ 315 Checklist 211-315 .09 .02 .01
Will Clark
☐ 316 Mike Sharperson .06 .03 .01
☐ 317 John Orton .06 .03 .01
☐ 318 Bob Tewksbury .08 .04 .01
☐ 319 Xavier Hernandez .06 .03 .01
☐ 320 Paul Assenmacher .06 .03 .01
☐ 321 John Franco .06 .03 .01
☐ 322 Mike Timlin .06 .03 .01
☐ 323 Jose Guzman .06 .03 .01
☐ 324 Pedro Martinez .10 .04 .01
☐ 325 Bill Spiers .06 .03 .01
☐ 326 Melido Perez .06 .03 .01
☐ 327 Mike Macfarlane .06 .03 .01
☐ 328 Ricky Bones .06 .03 .01
☐ 329 Scott Bankhead .06 .03 .01
☐ 330 Rich Rodriguez .06 .03 .01
☐ 331 Geronimo Pena .06 .03 .01
☐ 332 Bernie Williams .08 .04 .01
☐ 333 Paul Molitor .08 .04 .01
☐ 334 Carlos Garcia .08 .04 .01
☐ 335 David Cone .08 .04 .01
☐ 336 Randy Johnson .08 .04 .01
☐ 337 Pat Mahomes .08 .04 .01
☐ 338 Erik Hanson .06 .03 .01
☐ 339 Duane Ward .06 .03 .01
☐ 340 Al Martin .10 .04 .01
☐ 341 Pedro Munoz .08 .04 .01
☐ 342 Greg Colbrunn .06 .03 .01
☐ 343 Julio Valera .08 .04 .01
☐ 344 John Olerud .15 .07 .02
☐ 345 George Bell .08 .04 .01
☐ 346 Devon White .08 .04 .01
☐ 347 Donovan Osborne .20 .09 .03
☐ 348 Mark Gardner .06 .03 .01
☐ 349 Zane Smith .06 .03 .01
☐ 350 Wilson Alvarez .06 .03 .01
☐ 351 Kevin Koslofski .06 .03 .01
☐ 352 Roberto Hernandez .06 .03 .01
☐ 353 Glenn Davis .08 .04 .01
☐ 354 Reggie Sanders .20 .09 .03
☐ 355 Ken Griffey Jr. .75 .35 .09
☐ 356 Marquis Grissom .15 .07 .02
☐ 357 Jack McDowell .08 .04 .01
☐ 358 Jimmy Key .06 .03 .01
☐ 359 Stan Belinda .06 .03 .01
☐ 360 Gerald Williams .08 .04 .01
☐ 361 Sid Fernandez .08 .04 .01
☐ 362 Alex Fernandez .08 .04 .01
☐ 363 John Smoltz .15 .07 .02
☐ 364 Travis Fryman .30 .14 .04
☐ 365 Jose Canseco .30 .14 .04
☐ 366 David Justice .30 .14 .04
☐ 367 Pedro Astacio .30 .14 .04
☐ 368 Tim Belcher .08 .04 .01
☐ 369 Steve Sax .08 .04 .01
☐ 370 Gary Gaetti .06 .03 .01
☐ 371 Jeff Frye .06 .03 .01
☐ 372 Bob Wickman .15 .07 .02
☐ 373 Ryan Thompson .30 .14 .04
☐ 374 David Hulse .15 .07 .02
☐ 375 Cal Eldred .30 .14 .04
☐ 376 Ryan Klesko .40 .18 .05
☐ 377 Damion Easley .20 .09 .03
☐ 378 John Kiely .06 .03 .01
☐ 379 Jim Bullinger .08 .04 .01
☐ 380 Brian Bohanon .06 .03 .01
☐ 381 Rod Brewer .20 .09 .03
☐ 382 Fernando Ramsey .15 .07 .02
☐ 383 Sam Militello .25 .11 .03
☐ 384 Arthur Rhodes .15 .07 .02
☐ 385 Eric Karros .50 .23 .06
☐ 386 Rico Brogna .08 .04 .01
☐ 387 John Valentin .20 .09 .03
☐ 388 Kerry Woodson .06 .03 .01
☐ 389 Ben Rivera .08 .04 .01
☐ 390 Matt Whiteside .15 .07 .02
☐ 391 Henry Rodriguez .08 .04 .01
☐ 392 John Wetteland .06 .03 .01
☐ 393 Kent Mercker .06 .03 .01
☐ 394 Bernard Gilkey .08 .04 .01
☐ 395 Doug Henry .06 .03 .01
☐ 396 Mo Vaughn .08 .04 .01
☐ 397 Scott Erickson .08 .04 .01
☐ 398 Bill Gullickson .06 .03 .01
☐ 399 Mark Guthrie .06 .03 .01
☐ 400 Dave Martinez .06 .03 .01
☐ 401 Jeff Kent .12 .05 .02

☐ 402 Chris Hoiles	.08	.04	.01
☐ 403 Mike Henneman	.06	.03	.01
☐ 404 Chris Nabholz	.08	.04	.01
☐ 405 Tom Pagnozzi	.06	.03	.01
☐ 406 Kelly Gruber	.08	.04	.01
☐ 407 Bob Welch	.06	.03	.01
☐ 408 Frank Castillo	.06	.03	.01
☐ 409 John Dopson	.06	.03	.01
☐ 410 Steve Farr	.06	.03	.01
☐ 411 Henry Cotto	.06	.03	.01
☐ 412 Bob Patterson	.06	.03	.01
☐ 413 Todd Stottlemyre	.08	.04	.01
☐ 414 Greg A. Harris	.06	.03	.01
☐ 415 Denny Neagle	.06	.03	.01
☐ 416 Bill Wegman	.06	.03	.01
☐ 417 Willie Wilson	.06	.03	.01
☐ 418 Terry Leach	.06	.03	.01
☐ 419 Willie Randolph	.08	.04	.01
☐ 420 Checklist 316-420 Mark McGwire	.09	.02	.01
☐ SP5 George Brett and Robin Yount (Commemorating 3,000th Hit)	10.00	4.50	1.25

1993 Upper Deck Willie Mays Heroes

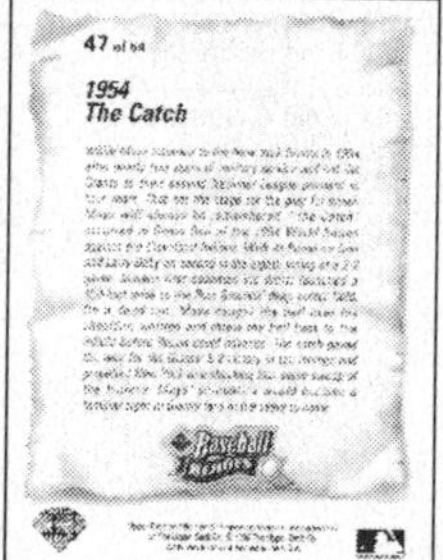

This standard size (2 1/2" by 3 1/2") ten-card set was randomly inserted in 1993 Upper Deck first series foil packs. The fronts feature color photos of Mays at various stages of his career that are partially contained within a black bordered circle. The photos rest on a rough-edged sports page from a newspaper. The Upper Deck Baseball Heroes logo appears in the lower right corner. The back design displays career highlights on a blank newspaper page. The cards are numbered on the back.

	MT	EX-MT	VG
COMPLETE SET (10)	30.00	13.50	3.80
COMMON MAYS (46-54)	3.00	1.35	.40
☐ 46 1951 Rookie-of-the-Year	3.00	1.35	.40
☐ 47 1954 The Catch	3.00	1.35	.40
☐ 48 1956-57 30-30 Club	3.00	1.35	.40
☐ 49 1961 Four-Homer Game	3.00	1.35	.40
☐ 50 1965 Most Valuable Player	3.00	1.35	.40
☐ 51 1969 600-Home Run Club	3.00	1.35	.40
☐ 52 1972 New York Homecoming	3.00	1.35	.40
☐ 53 1979 Hall of Fame	3.00	1.35	.40
☐ 54 Baseball Heroes CL (Portrait by Vernon Wells)	3.00	1.35	.40
☐ NNO Baseball Heroes (Header card)	10.00	4.50	1.25

1993 Upper Deck Then And Now

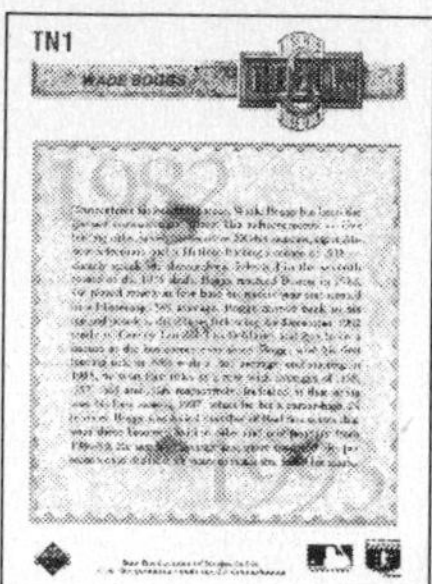

This nine-card, standard-size (2 1/2" by 3 1/2") hologram set highlights nine veteran stars in their rookie year and today, reflecting on how they and the game have changed. The cards were randomly inserted in series I foil packs. The horizontal fronts have a color close-up photo cutout and superimposed at the left corner of a full-bleed hologram portraying the player in an action scene. The skyline of the player's city serves as the background for the holograms. The player's name and the manufacturer's name form a right angle at the upper right corner. At the upper left corner, a "Then and Now" logo which includes the length of the player's career in years rounds out the front. On a sand-colored panel that resembles a postage stamp, the backs present career summary. The cards are numbered on the back with a TN prefix and arranged alphabetically according to player's last name.

	MT	EX-MT	VG
COMPLETE SET (9)	40.00	18.00	5.00
COMMON PLAYER (1-9)	4.00	1.80	.50
☐ 1 Wade Boggs	4.00	1.80	.50
☐ 2 George Brett	5.00	2.30	.60
☐ 3 Rickey Henderson	5.00	2.30	.60
☐ 4 Cal Ripken	8.00	3.60	1.00
☐ 5 Nolan Ryan	10.00	4.50	1.25
☐ 6 Ryne Sandberg	7.00	3.10	.85
☐ 7 Ozzie Smith	4.00	1.80	.50
☐ 8 Darryl Strawberry	4.00	1.80	.50
☐ 9 Dave Winfield	4.00	1.80	.50

1993 Upper Deck Triple Crown

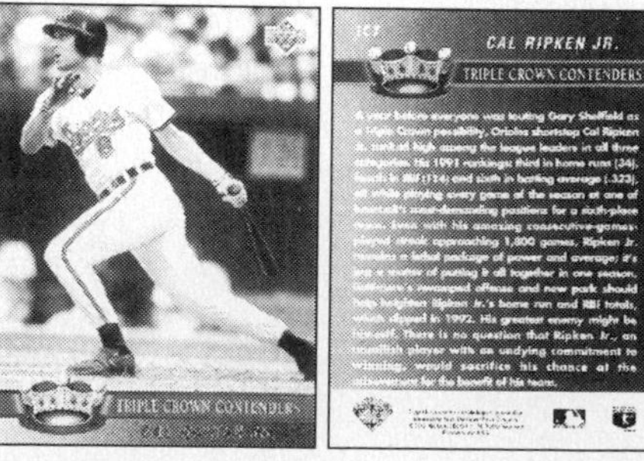

This ten-card, standard-size (2 1/2" by 3 1/2") subset highlights ten players who were selected by Upper Deck as having the best shot at winning Major League Baseball's Triple Crown. The cards were randomly inserted in series I foil packs sold by hobby dealers only. The fronts display glossy full-bleed color player photos. At the bottom, a purple ribbon edged in gold foil carries the words "Triple Crown Contenders," while the player's name appears in gold foil lettering immediately below on a gradated black background. A crown overlays the ribbon at the lower left corner and rounds out the front. On a gradated black background, the backs summarize the player's performance in home runs, RBIs, and batting average. The cards are numbered on the back with a TC prefix and arranged alphabetically by player's last name.

	MT	EX-MT	VG
COMPLETE SET (10)	60.00	27.00	7.50
COMMON PLAYER (1-10)	5.00	2.30	.60
☐ 1 Barry Bonds	8.00	3.60	1.00
☐ 2 Jose Canseco	8.00	3.60	1.00
☐ 3 Will Clark	8.00	3.60	1.00
☐ 4 Ken Griffey Jr.	12.00	5.50	1.50
☐ 5 Fred McGriff	7.00	3.10	.85
☐ 6 Kirby Puckett	8.00	3.60	1.00
☐ 7 Cal Ripken Jr.	10.00	4.50	1.25
☐ 8 Gary Sheffield	7.00	3.10	.85
☐ 9 Frank Thomas	15.00	6.75	1.90
☐ 10 Larry Walker	5.00	2.30	.60

1990 U.S. Playing Cards All-Stars

This 56-card standard size (2 1/2" by 3 1/2") set features members of the 1990 All-Star teams. The set was issued by the United States Playing Card Company and was sold in a blue playing card box just as if it were a playing card deck. The fronts of these rounded-corner cards feature full-color action shots of the players while the backs of the cards have the 1990 Baseball Major League All-Stars design in a white and blue pinstripe pattern, with blue borders. The team logo appears in the lower left corner of each picture. The player's name and position appears in a colored stripe below the pictures; the stripe is aqua on the clubs and spades, and dark red on the hearts and diamonds. Since this set is similar to a playing card set, the set is arranged just like a card deck, therefore the set is checklisted below as if it were a playing card deck. In the checklist below S means Spades, D means Diamonds, C means Clubs, H means Hearts, JK means Joker, and WC means Wild Card. The cards are checklisted below in playing card order by suits and numbers are assigned to Aces (1), Jacks (11), Queens (12), and Kings (13). The jokers and wild cards are unnumbered and listed at the end. Also produced later was a "Silver Set" which came in a black case with the All-Star logo stamped on top in silver. The year "1990" was stamped in the lower left of the All-Star logo, while the year "1991" is stamped in the lower right corner. Inside the case were two silver-bordered decks, one of the 1990 All-Star team and one of the 1991 All-Star team. The production run was stated to be 2,000 sets. The sets also came with a "parchment-type" paper explaining the limited edition silver set within each case.

	MT	EX-MT	VG
COMPLETE SET (56)	5.00	2.30	.60
COMMON PLAYER	.05	.02	.01
☐ 1C Bob Welch	.05	.02	.01
☐ 1D Frank Viola	.05	.02	.01
☐ 1H Ramon Martinez	.15	.07	.02
☐ 1S Roger Clemens	.50	.23	.06
☐ 2C Lance Parrish	.10	.05	.01
☐ 2D Greg Olson	.05	.02	.01
☐ 2H Mike Scioscia	.05	.02	.01
☐ 2S Sandy Alomar Jr.	.10	.05	.01
☐ 3C Bret Saberhagen	.15	.07	.02
☐ 3D Dennis Martinez	.05	.02	.01
☐ 3H Jeff Brantley	.05	.02	.01
☐ 3S Randy Johnson	.10	.05	.01
☐ 4C Gregg Olson	.10	.05	.01
☐ 4D Roberto Alomar	.35	.16	.04
☐ 4H Ryne Sandberg	.50	.23	.06
☐ 4S Steve Sax	.10	.05	.01
☐ 5C Brook Jacoby	.05	.02	.01
☐ 5D Tim Wallach	.05	.02	.01
☐ 5H Chris Sabo	.15	.07	.02
☐ 5S Kelly Gruber	.10	.05	.01
☐ 6C Ozzie Guillen	.05	.02	.01
☐ 6D Barry Larkin	.15	.07	.02
☐ 6H Ozzie Smith	.20	.09	.03
☐ 6S Cal Ripken	.50	.23	.06
☐ 7C Ellis Burks	.15	.07	.02
☐ 7D Neal Heaton	.05	.02	.01
☐ 7H John Franco	.05	.02	.01
☐ 7S Doug Jones	.05	.02	.01
☐ 8C Dennis Eckersley	.15	.07	.02
☐ 8D Dave Smith	.05	.02	.01
☐ 8H Matt Williams	.10	.05	.01
☐ 8S Kirby Puckett	.40	.18	.05
☐ 9C Bobby Thigpen	.05	.02	.01
☐ 9D Len Dysktra	.10	.05	.01
☐ 9H Andre Dawson	.20	.09	.03
☐ 9S Chuck Finley	.05	.02	.01
☐ 10C Dave Stieb	.05	.02	.01
☐ 10D Shawon Dunston	.05	.02	.01
☐ 10H Benito Santiago	.10	.05	.01
☐ 10S Alan Trammell	.10	.05	.01
☐ 11C Wade Boggs	.25	.11	.03
☐ 11D Tony Gwynn	.30	.14	.04
☐ 11H Bobby Bonilla	.20	.09	.03
☐ 11S Ken Griffey Jr.	.75	.35	.09
☐ 12C George Bell	.10	.05	.01
☐ 12D Will Clark	.40	.18	.05
☐ 12H Kevin Mitchell	.15	.07	.02
☐ 12S Dave Parker	.10	.05	.01
☐ 13C Rickey Henderson	.35	.16	.04
☐ 13D Barry Bonds	.30	.14	.04
☐ 13H Darryl Strawberry	.35	.16	.04
☐ 13S Cecil Fielder	.25	.11	.03
☐ JKO Julio Franco (Red)	.10	.05	.01
☐ JKO Jack Armstrong (Black)	.05	.02	.01
☐ WCO Rob Dibble and Randy Myers (Red)	.05	.02	.01
☐ WCO Mark McGwire and Jose Canseco (Black)	.35	.16	.04

1991 U.S. Playing Cards All-Stars

This 56-card standard size (2 1/2" by 3 1/2") set features 1991 All-Star Game players. The set was issued by the United States Playing Card Company and was sold in a red playing card box just as if it were a playing card deck. The fronts of these rounded-corner cards feature full-color action shots of the players while the backs have the 1991 Baseball Major League All-Stars design on a white and red pinstripe pattern, with red borders. The team logo appears at the upper right corner of each picture. The player's name and position appear in a color stripe below the pictures; the stripe is yellow on the spades and clubs, and green on the hearts and diamonds. Since this set is similar to a playing card set, the set is checklisted below as if it were a playing

card deck. In the checklist S means Spades, D means Diamonds, C means Clubs, H means Hearts, JK means Joker, and WC means Wild Card. The cards are checklisted in playing card order by suits and numbers are assigned to Aces (1), Jacks (11), Queens (12), and Kings (13). The jokers and wild cards are unnumbered and listed at the end. Also produced later was a "Silver Set" which came in a black case with the All-Star logo stamped on top in silver. The year "1990" was stamped in the lower left of the All-Star logo, while the year "1991" was stamped in the lower right corner. Inside the case were two silver-bordered decks, one of the 1990 All-Star team and one of the 1991 All-Star team. The production run was stated to be 2,000 sets. The sets also came with a "parchment-type" paper explaining the limited edition silver set within each case.

	MT	EX-MT	VG
COMPLETE SET (56)	5.00	2.30	.60
COMMON PLAYER	.05	.02	.01
☐ 1C Tony Gwynn	.30	.14	.04
☐ 1D Ken Griffey Jr.	.75	.35	.09
☐ 1H Jack Morris	.20	.09	.03
☐ 1S Tom Glavine	.25	.11	.03
☐ 2C Paul O'Neill	.05	.02	.01
☐ 2D Carlton Fisk	.25	.11	.03
☐ 2H Ozzie Guillen	.10	.05	.01
☐ 2S Eddie Murray	.25	.11	.03
☐ 3C John Smiley	.05	.02	.01
☐ 3D Scott Sanderson	.05	.02	.01
☐ 3H Jack McDowell	.15	.07	.02
☐ 3S Pete Harnisch	.10	.05	.01
☐ 4C Howard Johnson	.10	.05	.01
☐ 4D Kirby Puckett	.40	.18	.05
☐ 4H Joe Carter	.25	.11	.03
☐ 4S John Kruk	.15	.07	.02
☐ 5C Mike Morgan	.05	.02	.01
☐ 5D Jeff Reardon	.10	.05	.01
☐ 5H Mark Langston	.10	.05	.01
☐ 5S Tom Browning	.05	.02	.01
☐ 6C Barry Larkin	.15	.07	.02
☐ 6D Rafael Palmeiro	.15	.07	.02
☐ 6H Julio Franco	.10	.05	.01
☐ 6S George Bell	.10	.05	.01
☐ 7C Frank Viola	.10	.05	.01
☐ 7D Bryan Harvey	.10	.05	.01
☐ 7H Rick Aguilera	.10	.05	.01
☐ 7S Dennis Martinez	.08	.04	.01
☐ 8C Juan Samuel	.05	.02	.01
☐ 8D Jimmy Key	.10	.05	.01
☐ 8H Paul Molitor	.15	.07	.02
☐ 8S Brett Butler	.10	.05	.01
☐ 9C Craig Biggio	.10	.05	.01
☐ 9D Harold Baines	.10	.05	.01
☐ 9H Ruben Sierra	.30	.14	.04
☐ 9S Felix Jose	.15	.07	.02
☐ 10C Lee Smith	.10	.05	.01
☐ 10D Dennis Eckersley	.15	.07	.02
☐ 10H Roger Clemens	.50	.23	.06
☐ 10S Rob Dibble	.10	.05	.01
☐ 11C Andre Dawson	.20	.09	.03
☐ 11D Sandy Alomar Jr.	.10	.05	.01
☐ 11H Rickey Henderson	.35	.16	.04
☐ 11S Benito Santiago	.15	.07	.02
☐ 12C Chris Sabo	.15	.07	.02
☐ 12D Cecil Fielder	.25	.11	.03
☐ 12H Roberto Alomar	.35	.16	.04
☐ 12S Ryne Sandberg	.45	.20	.06
☐ 13C Ivan Calderon	.05	.02	.01
☐ 13D Cal Ripken	.50	.23	.06
☐ 13H Dave Henderson	.05	.02	.01
☐ 13S Ozzie Smith	.20	.09	.03
☐ JKO Danny Tartabull (Red)	.15	.07	.02
☐ JKO Bobby Bonilla (Black)	.20	.09	.03
☐ WCO Wade Boggs (Red)	.25	.11	.03
☐ WCO Will Clark (Black)	.40	.18	.05

1992 U.S. Playing Cards Aces

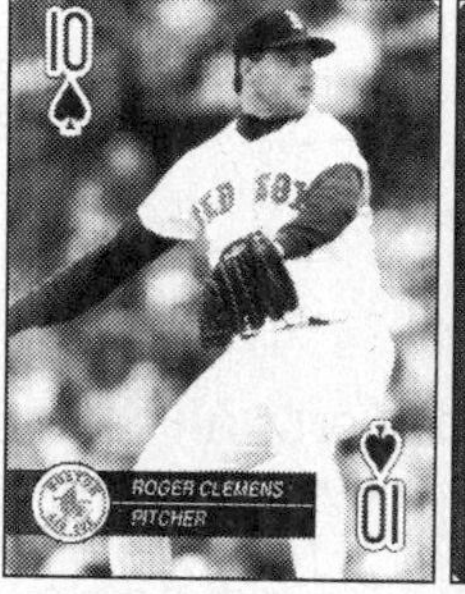

This 54-card standard size (2 1/2" by 3 1/2") set features the top 13 players in four categories according to suits: lowest ERA's (spades), most RBI's (hearts), most home runs (clubs), and highest batting average (diamonds). The set was issued by the United States Playing Card Company. The fronts of these rounded-corner cards feature full-color action shots of the players while the backs have the 1992 Major League Baseball Aces design on a black background. The team logo appears at the lower left corner of each picture. The player's name and position appear in a black stripe that intersects the team logo at the bottom. Since this set is similar to a playing card set, the set is checklisted below as if it were a playing card deck. In the checklist C means Clubs, D means Diamonds, H means Hearts, S means Spades, and JK means Joker. The cards are checklisted in playing card order by suits and numbers are assigned to Aces (1), Jacks (11), Queens (12), and Kings (13). The jokers, Home Run Rummy card, and the title card are unnumbered and listed at the end.

	MT	EX-MT	VG
COMPLETE SET (56)	5.00	2.30	.60
COMMON PLAYER	.05	.02	.01
☐ 1C Jose Canseco	.35	.16	.04
☐ 1D Julio Franco	.08	.04	.01
☐ 1H Cecil Fielder	.15	.07	.02
☐ 1S Dennis Martinez	.08	.04	.01
☐ 2C Chili Davis	.05	.02	.01
☐ 2D Danny Tartabull	.10	.05	.01
☐ 2H Juan Gonzalez	.30	.14	.04
☐ 2S Mike Moore	.05	.02	.01
☐ 3C Mickey Tettleton	.10	.05	.01
☐ 3D Tony Gwynn	.25	.11	.03
☐ 3H Andre Dawson	.15	.07	.02
☐ 3S Nolan Ryan	.60	.25	.08
☐ 4C Danny Tartabull	.12	.05	.02
☐ 4D Frank Thomas	.60	.25	.08
☐ 4H Ron Gant	.12	.05	.02
☐ 4S Jim Abbott	.15	.07	.02
☐ 5C Fred McGriff	.15	.07	.02
☐ 5D Hal Morris	.08	.04	.01
☐ 5H Fred McGriff	.15	.07	.02
☐ 5S Bill Wegman	.05	.02	.01
☐ 6C Andre Dawson	.15	.07	.02
☐ 6D Kirby Puckett	.40	.18	.05
☐ 6H Joe Carter	.15	.07	.02
☐ 6S Mike Morgan	.05	.02	.01

	Card	Player	MT	EX-MT	VG
☐	7C	Frank Thomas	.60	.25	.08
☐	7D	Terry Pendleton	.10	.05	.01
☐	7H	Frank Thomas	.60	.25	.08
☐	7S	Jose DeLeon	.05	.02	.01
☐	8C	Ron Gant	.12	.05	.02
☐	8D	Rafael Palmiero	.10	.05	.01
☐	8H	Cal Ripken UER (Name misspelled Ripkin)	.50	.23	.06
☐	8S	Pete Harnisch	.08	.04	.01
☐	9C	Joe Carter	.15	.07	.02
☐	9D	Cal Ripken UER (Name misspelled Ripkin on front)	.50	.23	.06
☐	9H	Ruben Sierra	.25	.11	.03
☐	9S	Tom Candiotti	.05	.02	.01
☐	10C	Matt Williams	.10	.05	.01
☐	10D	Paul Molitor	.12	.05	.02
☐	10H	Barry Bonds	.30	.14	.04
☐	10S	Roger Clemens	.50	.23	.06
☐	11C	Cal Ripken UER (Name misspelled Ripkin on front)	.50	.23	.06
☐	11D	Ken Griffey Jr.	.60	.25	.08
☐	11H	Will Clark	.35	.16	.04
☐	11S	Tim Belcher	.05	.02	.01
☐	12C	Howard Johnson	.10	.05	.01
☐	12D	Willie Randolph	.05	.02	.01
☐	12H	Howard Johnson	.10	.05	.01
☐	12S	Tom Glavine	.25	.11	.03
☐	13C	Cecil Fielder	.15	.07	.02
☐	13D	Wade Boggs	.20	.09	.03
☐	13H	Jose Canseco	.35	.16	.04
☐	13S	Jose Rijo	.10	.05	.01
☐	JKO	Tom Glavine	.25	.11	.03
☐	JKO	Roger Clemens	.45	.20	.06
☐	XXO	Home Run Rummy Card (Game Instructions)	.10	.05	.01
☐	XXO	Title Card	.05	.02	.01

1992 U.S. Playing Cards Braves

This 56-card standard size (2 1/2" by 3 1/2") set features 1991 Atlanta Braves. The set was issued by the United States Playing Card Company. The fronts of these rounded-corner cards feature full-color posed and action shots of the players while the backs have the team logo on a gray background with navy blue pinstripes. The player's name and position appear in a yellow bar at the bottom of the photo. Since this set is similar to a playing card set, the set is checklisted below as if it were a playing card deck. In the checklist C means Clubs, D means Diamonds, H means Hearts, S means Spades, and JK means Joker. The cards are checklisted in playing card order by suits and numbers are assigned to Aces (1), Jacks (11), Queens (12), and Kings (13). Included in the set are an Atlanta Braves team history card and a 1992 home schedule card. The jokers, home schedule card, and the history card are unnumbered and listed at the end.

	MT	EX-MT	VG
COMPLETE SET (56)	5.00	2.30	.60
COMMON PLAYER	.05	.02	.01

	Card	Player	MT	EX-MT	VG
☐	1C	Terry Pendleton	.15	.07	.02
☐	1D	Steve Avery	.50	.23	.06
☐	1H	Otis Nixon	.08	.04	.01
☐	1S	Tom Glavine	.35	.16	.04
☐	2C	Mark Lemke	.05	.02	.01
☐	2D	Marvin Freeman	.05	.02	.01
☐	2H	Deion Sanders	.50	.23	.06
☐	2S	Jim Clancy	.05	.02	.01
☐	3C	Armando Reynoso	.05	.02	.01
☐	3D	Pete Smith	.20	.09	.03
☐	3H	Mike Stanton	.08	.04	.01
☐	3S	Deion Sanders	.50	.23	.06
☐	4C	Kent Mercker	.10	.05	.01
☐	4D	Mike Heath	.05	.02	.01
☐	4H	Sid Bream	.08	.04	.01
☐	4S	Mark Lemke	.05	.02	.01
☐	5C	Marvin Freeman	.05	.02	.01
☐	5D	Jeff Blauser	.10	.05	.01
☐	5H	Armando Reynoso	.05	.02	.01
☐	5S	Mike Heath	.05	.02	.01
☐	6C	Rico Rossy	.05	.02	.01
☐	6D	Jim Clancy	.05	.02	.01
☐	6H	Brian Hunter	.15	.07	.02
☐	6S	Mike Stanton	.10	.05	.01
☐	7C	Dave Justice	.50	.23	.06
☐	7D	Rico Rossy	.05	.02	.01
☐	7H	Kent Mercker	.10	.05	.01
☐	7S	Sid Bream	.08	.04	.01
☐	8C	Juan Berenguer	.05	.02	.01
☐	8D	John Smoltz	.30	.14	.04
☐	8H	Lonnie Smith	.05	.02	.01
☐	8S	Rafael Belliard	.05	.02	.01
☐	9C	Ron Gant	.35	.16	.04
☐	9D	Charlie Leibrandt	.08	.04	.01
☐	9H	Jeff Treadway	.05	.02	.01
☐	9S	Greg Olson	.05	.02	.01
☐	10C	Otis Nixon	.12	.05	.02
☐	10D	Terry Pendleton	.15	.07	.02
☐	10H	Tom Glavine	.35	.16	.04
☐	10S	Steve Avery	.50	.23	.06
☐	11C	Pete Smith	.20	.09	.03
☐	11D	Brian Hunter	.15	.07	.02
☐	11H	Dave Justice	.50	.23	.06
☐	11S	John Smoltz	.30	.14	.04
☐	12C	Jeff Blauser	.10	.05	.01
☐	12D	Rafael Belliard	.05	.02	.01
☐	12H	Juan Berenguer	.05	.02	.01
☐	12S	Lonnie Smith	.05	.02	.01
☐	13C	Charlie Leibrandt	.08	.04	.01
☐	13D	Greg Olson	.05	.02	.01
☐	13H	Ron Gant	.35	.16	.04
☐	13S	Jeff Treadway	.05	.02	.01
☐	JKO	National League Logo	.05	.02	.01
☐	JKO	National League Logo	.05	.02	.01
☐	XXO	1992 Home Schedule	.05	.02	.01
☐	XXO	Team History	.05	.02	.01

1992 U.S. Playing Cards Cubs

This 56-card standard size (2 1/2" by 3 1/2") set features 1991 Chicago Cubs. The set was issued by the United States Playing Card Company. The fronts of these rounded-corner cards feature full-color posed and action shots of the players while the backs have the team logo on a gray background with red pinstripes. The player's name and position appear in a yellow bar at the bottom of the photo. Since this set is similar to a playing card set, the set is checklisted below as if it were a playing card deck. In the checklist C means Clubs, D means Diamonds, H means Hearts, S means Spades, and JK means Joker. The cards are checklisted in playing card order by suits and numbers are assigned to Aces (1), Jacks (11), Queens (12), and Kings (13). Included in the set are a Chicago Cubs team history card and a 1992 home schedule card. The jokers, home schedule card, and the history card are unnumbered and listed at the end.

	MT	EX-MT	VG
COMPLETE SET (56)	4.50	2.00	.55
COMMON PLAYER	.05	.02	.01
☐ 1C George Bell	.15	.07	.02
☐ 1D Greg Maddux	.45	.20	.06
☐ 1H Andre Dawson	.35	.16	.04
☐ 1S Ryne Sandberg	.60	.25	.08
☐ 2C Gary Scott	.15	.07	.02
☐ 2D Shawn Boskie	.10	.05	.01
☐ 2H Dwight Smith	.08	.04	.01
☐ 2S Frank Castillo	.10	.05	.01
☐ 3C Jose Vizcaino	.10	.05	.01
☐ 3D Ced Landrum	.05	.02	.01
☐ 3H Rick Wilkins	.08	.04	.01
☐ 3S Mike Harkey	.25	.11	.03
☐ 4C Heathcliff Slocumb	.05	.02	.01
☐ 4D Gary Scott	.15	.07	.02
☐ 4H Doug Dascenzo	.05	.02	.01
☐ 4S Dave Smith	.05	.02	.01
☐ 5C Danny Jackson	.05	.02	.01
☐ 5D Ced Landrum	.05	.02	.01
☐ 5H Bob Scanlan	.05	.02	.01
☐ 5S Les Lancaster	.05	.02	.01
☐ 6C Shawn Boskie	.10	.05	.01
☐ 6D Jose Vizcaino	.10	.05	.01
☐ 6H Chico Walker	.05	.02	.01
☐ 6S Hector Villanueva	.08	.04	.01
☐ 7C Luis Salazar	.05	.02	.01
☐ 7D Mike Harkey	.25	.11	.03
☐ 7H Paul Assenmacher	.05	.02	.01
☐ 7S Shawon Dunston	.10	.05	.01
☐ 8C Chuck McElroy	.10	.05	.01
☐ 8D Jerome Walton	.08	.04	.01
☐ 8H Mark Grace	.50	.23	.06
☐ 8S Heathcliff Slocumb	.05	.02	.01
☐ 9C Andre Dawson	.35	.16	.04
☐ 9D George Bell	.15	.07	.02
☐ 9H Ryne Sandberg	.60	.25	.08
☐ 9S Greg Maddux	.50	.23	.06
☐ 10C Dave Smith	.05	.02	.01
☐ 10D Frank Castillo	.10	.05	.01
☐ 10H Danny Jackson	.05	.02	.01
☐ 10S Dwight Smith	.08	.04	.01
☐ 11C Hector Villanueva	.08	.04	.01
☐ 11D Rick Wilkins	.08	.04	.01
☐ 11H Jerome Walton	.08	.04	.01
☐ 11S Bob Scanlan	.08	.04	.01
☐ 12C Doug Dascenzo	.05	.02	.01
☐ 12D Les Lancaster	.05	.02	.01
☐ 12H Chico Walker	.05	.02	.01
☐ 12S Luis Salazar	.05	.02	.01
☐ 13C Shawon Dunston	.10	.05	.01
☐ 13D Paul Assenmacher	.05	.02	.01
☐ 13H Chuck McElroy	.10	.05	.01
☐ 13S Mark Grace	.50	.23	.06
☐ JK0 National League Logo	.05	.02	.01
☐ JK0 National League Logo	.05	.02	.01
☐ XX0 1992 Home Schedule	.05	.02	.01
☐ XX0 Team History	.05	.02	.01

1992 U.S. Playing Cards Red Sox

This 56-card standard size (2 1/2" by 3 1/2") set features 1991 Boston Red Sox. The set was issued by the United States Playing Card Company. The fronts of these rounded-corner cards feature full-color posed and action shots of the players while the backs have the team logo on a gray background with navy blue pinstripes. The player's name and position appear in a blue bar at the bottom of the photo. Since this set is similar to a playing card set, the set is checklisted below as if it were a playing card deck. In the

checklist C means Clubs, D means Diamonds, H means Hearts, S means Spades, and JK means Joker. The cards are checklisted in playing card order by suits and numbers are assigned to Aces (1), Jacks (11), Queens (12), and Kings (13). Included in the set are a Red Sox team history card, and a 1992 home schedule card. The jokers, home schedule card, and the history card are unnumbered and listed at the end.

	MT	EX-MT	VG
COMPLETE SET (56)	4.50	2.00	.55
COMMON PLAYER	.05	.02	.01
☐ 1C Mike Greenwell	.15	.07	.02
☐ 1D Joe Hesketh	.05	.02	.01
☐ 1H Roger Clemens	.60	.25	.08
☐ 1S Wade Boggs	.35	.16	.04
☐ 2C Danny Darwin	.05	.02	.01
☐ 2D Steve Lyons	.05	.02	.01
☐ 2H Matt Young	.05	.02	.01
☐ 2S Tom Bolton	.05	.02	.01
☐ 3C Dan Petry	.05	.02	.01
☐ 3D Dana Kiecker	.05	.02	.01
☐ 3H John Marzano	.05	.02	.01
☐ 3S Mo Vaughn	.25	.11	.03
☐ 4C Dana Kiecker	.05	.02	.01
☐ 4D Tony Fossas	.05	.02	.01
☐ 4H Dennis Lamp	.05	.02	.01
☐ 4S Kevin Morton	.08	.04	.01
☐ 5C Greg A. Harris	.05	.02	.01
☐ 5D Matt Young	.05	.02	.01
☐ 5H Danny Darwin	.05	.02	.01
☐ 5S Steve Lyons	.05	.02	.01
☐ 6C Tony Pena	.10	.05	.01
☐ 6D Luis Rivera	.05	.02	.01
☐ 6H Jeff Reardon	.15	.07	.02
☐ 6S Tom Brunansky	.10	.05	.01
☐ 7C Dan Petry	.05	.02	.01
☐ 7D Tom Bolton	.05	.02	.01
☐ 7H Phil Plantier	.35	.16	.04
☐ 7S Dennis Lamp	.05	.02	.01
☐ 8C Jeff Gray	.05	.02	.01
☐ 8D Kevin Morton	.08	.04	.01
☐ 8H Tony Fossas	.05	.02	.01
☐ 8S Joe Hesketh	.05	.02	.01
☐ 9C Jack Clark	.10	.05	.01
☐ 9D Jody Reed	.08	.04	.01
☐ 9H Carlos Quintana	.05	.02	.01
☐ 9S Ellis Burks	.15	.07	.02
☐ 10C Roger Clemens	.60	.25	.08
☐ 10D Mike Greenwell	.15	.07	.02
☐ 10H Wade Boggs	.35	.16	.04
☐ 10S Jeff Reardon	.15	.07	.02
☐ 11C Luis Rivera	.05	.02	.01
☐ 11D Tom Brunansky	.10	.05	.01
☐ 11H Jack Clark	.10	.05	.01
☐ 11S Tony Pena	.10	.05	.01
☐ 12C John Marzano	.05	.02	.01
☐ 12D Mo Vaughn	.25	.11	.03
☐ 12H Jeff Gray	.05	.02	.01
☐ 12S Phil Plantier	.35	.16	.04
☐ 13C Jody Reed	.08	.04	.01
☐ 13D Ellis Burks	.15	.07	.02
☐ 13H Greg A. Harris	.05	.02	.01
☐ 13S Carlos Quintana	.08	.04	.01
☐ JK0 American League Logo	.05	.02	.01
☐ JK0 American League Logo	.05	.02	.01
☐ XX0 1992 Home Schedule	.05	.02	.01
☐ XX0 Team History	.05	.02	.01

1992 U.S. Playing Cards Tigers

This 56-card standard size (2 1/2" by 3 1/2") set features 1991 Detroit Tigers. The set was issued by the United States Playing Card Company. The fronts of these rounded-corner cards feature full-color posed and action shots of the players while the backs have the team logo on a gray background with navy blue pinstripes. The player's name and position appear in a blue bar at the bottom of the photo. Since this set is similar to a playing card set, the set is checklisted below as if it were a playing card deck. In the checklist C means Clubs, D means Diamonds, H means Hearts, S means Spades, and JK means Joker. The cards are checklisted in playing card order by suits and numbers are assigned to Aces (1), Jacks (11), Queens (12), and Kings (13). Included in the set are a Tigers team history card, and a 1992 home schedule card. The jokers, home schedule card, and the history card are unnumbered and listed at the end.

	MT	EX-MT	VG
COMPLETE SET (56)	4.50	2.00	.55
COMMON PLAYER	.05	.02	.01
☐ 1C Tony Phillips	.10	.05	.01
☐ 1D Bill Gullickson	.08	.04	.01
☐ 1H Cecil Fielder	.35	.16	.04
☐ 1S Frank Tanana	.10	.05	.01
☐ 2C Dan Gakeler	.05	.02	.01
☐ 2D John Cerutti	.05	.02	.01
☐ 2H Andy Allanson	.05	.02	.01
☐ 2S Scott Aldred	.05	.02	.01
☐ 3C Walt Terrell	.05	.02	.01
☐ 3D Steve Searcy	.05	.02	.01
☐ 3H Dave Bergman	.05	.02	.01
☐ 3S Scott Livingstone	.15	.07	.02
☐ 4C David Haas	.10	.05	.01
☐ 4D David Haas	.10	.05	.01
☐ 4H Steve Searcy	.05	.02	.01
☐ 4S John Shelby	.05	.02	.01
☐ 5C Pete Incaviglia	.08	.04	.01
☐ 5D Lloyd Moseby	.05	.02	.01
☐ 5H Dan Gakeler	.05	.02	.01
☐ 5S Rob Deer	.10	.05	.01
☐ 6C Travis Fryman	.60	.25	.08
☐ 6D Scott Livingstone	.15	.07	.02
☐ 6H Jerry Don Gleaton	.05	.02	.01
☐ 6S Milt Cuyler	.08	.04	.01
☐ 7C Scott Aldred	.05	.02	.01
☐ 7D John Shelby	.05	.02	.01
☐ 7H Paul Gibson	.05	.02	.01
☐ 7S Andy Allanson	.05	.02	.01
☐ 8C Skeeter Barnes	.05	.02	.01
☐ 8D Mike Henneman	.10	.05	.01
☐ 8H Alan Trammell	.25	.11	.03
☐ 8S Paul Gibson	.05	.02	.01
☐ 9C Mickey Tettleton	.15	.07	.02
☐ 9D Dave Bergman	.05	.02	.01
☐ 9H Frank Tanana	.10	.05	.01
☐ 9S Lou Whitaker	.25	.11	.03
☐ 10C Cecil Fielder	.35	.16	.04
☐ 10D Tony Phillips	.10	.05	.01
☐ 10H John Cerutti	.05	.02	.01
☐ 10S Bill Gullickson	.08	.04	.01
☐ 11C Rob Deer	.10	.05	.01
☐ 11D Milt Cuyler	.08	.04	.01
☐ 11H Lloyd Moseby	.05	.02	.01
☐ 11S Alan Trammell	.25	.11	.03
☐ 12C Skeeter Barnes	.05	.02	.01
☐ 12D Travis Fryman	.60	.25	.08
☐ 12H Walt Terrell	.05	.02	.01
☐ 12S Jerry Don Gleaton	.05	.02	.01
☐ 13C Pete Incaviglia	.08	.04	.01
☐ 13D Lou Whitaker	.25	.11	.03
☐ 13H Mickey Tettleton	.15	.07	.02
☐ 13S Mike Henneman	.10	.05	.01
☐ JKO American League Logo	.05	.02	.01
☐ JKO American League Logo	.05	.02	.01
☐ XXO 1992 Home Schedule	.05	.02	.01
☐ XXO Team History	.05	.02	.01

1992 U.S. Playing Cards Twins

This 56-card standard size (2 1/2" by 3 1/2") set features 1991 Minnesota Twins. The set was issued by the United States Playing Card Company. The fronts of these rounded-corner cards feature full-color posed and action shots of the players while the backs have the team logo on a gray background with navy blue pinstripes. The player's name and position appear in a blue bar at the bottom of the photo. Since this set is similar to a playing card set, the set is checklisted below as if it were a playing card deck. In the checklist C means Clubs, D means Diamonds, H means Hearts, S means Spades, and JK means Joker. The cards are checklisted in playing card order by suits and numbers are assigned to Aces (1), Jacks (11), Queens (12), and Kings (13). Included in the set are a Twins team history card, and a 1992 home schedule card. The jokers, home schedule card, and the history card are unnumbered and listed at the end.

	MT	EX-MT	VG
COMPLETE SET (56)	4.50	2.00	.55
COMMON PLAYER	.05	.02	.01
☐ 1C Shane Mack	.20	.09	.03
☐ 1D Brian Harper	.08	.04	.01
☐ 1H Kirby Puckett	.60	.25	.08
☐ 1S Scott Erickson	.25	.11	.03
☐ 2C Allan Anderson	.05	.02	.01
☐ 2D Al Newman	.05	.02	.01
☐ 2H Junior Ortiz	.05	.02	.01
☐ 2S Paul Abbott	.08	.04	.01
☐ 3C Al Newman	.05	.02	.01
☐ 3D Allan Anderson	.05	.02	.01
☐ 3H Paul Abbott	.08	.04	.01
☐ 3S David West	.05	.02	.01
☐ 4C Junior Ortiz	.05	.02	.01
☐ 4D David West	.05	.02	.01
☐ 4H Steve Bedrosian	.08	.04	.01
☐ 4S Steve Bedrosian	.08	.04	.01
☐ 5C Mike Pagliarulo	.05	.02	.01
☐ 5D Terry Leach	.05	.02	.01
☐ 5H Pedro Munoz	.20	.09	.03
☐ 5S Mark Guthrie	.05	.02	.01
☐ 6C Terry Leach	.05	.02	.01
☐ 6D Mark Guthrie	.05	.02	.01
☐ 6H Mike Pagliarulo	.05	.02	.01
☐ 6S Pedro Munoz	.20	.09	.03

☐ 7C Scott Leius	.05	.02	.01
☐ 7D Carl Willis	.05	.02	.01
☐ 7H Greg Gagne	.08	.04	.01
☐ 7S Gene Larkin	.05	.02	.01
☐ 8C Rick Aguilera	.10	.05	.01
☐ 8D Dan Gladden	.05	.02	.01
☐ 8H Chuck Knoblauch	.30	.14	.04
☐ 8S Randy Bush	.05	.02	.01
☐ 9C Jack Morris	.20	.09	.03
☐ 9D Kent Hrbek	.15	.07	.02
☐ 9H Kevin Tapani	.15	.07	.02
☐ 9S Chili Davis	.08	.04	.01
☐ 10C Kirby Puckett	.60	.25	.08
☐ 10D Shane Mack	.20	.09	.03
☐ 10H Scott Erickson	.25	.11	.03
☐ 10S Brian Harper	.08	.04	.01
☐ 11C Carl Willis	.05	.02	.01
☐ 11D Gene Larkin	.05	.02	.01
☐ 11H Scott Leius	.05	.02	.01
☐ 11S Greg Gagne	.08	.04	.01
☐ 12C Dan Gladden	.05	.02	.01
☐ 12D Randy Bush	.05	.02	.01
☐ 12H Rick Aguilera	.10	.05	.01
☐ 12S Chuck Knoblauch	.30	.14	.04
☐ 13C Kent Hrbek	.15	.07	.02
☐ 13D Chili Davis	.08	.04	.01
☐ 13H Jack Morris	.20	.09	.03
☐ 13S Kevin Tapani	.15	.07	.02
☐ JKO American League Logo	.05	.02	.01
☐ JKO American League Logo	.05	.02	.01
☐ XXO 1992 Home Schedule	.05	.02	.01
☐ XXO Team History	.05	.02	.01

1989 USPS Legends Stamp Cards

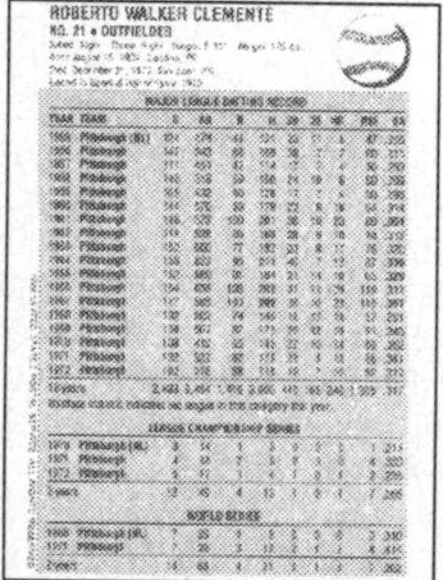

The 1989 USPS Legends Stamp Cards set includes four cards each measuring 2 1/2" by 3 9/16". On the fronts, the cards depict the four baseball-related stamp designs which featured actual players. The outer front borders are white; the inner front borders are orange and purple. The vertically oriented backs are beige and pink. These cards were sold by the U.S. Postal Service as a set (kit) for 7.95 along with the actual stamps, an attractive booklet, and other materials. The first printing of the set was sold out and so a second printing was made. The first printing cards did not have the USPS copyright logo. All the stamps in the set are drawings; for example, the Gehrig stamp was painted by noted sports artist, Bart Forbes. All of the stamps except Gehrig (25 cents) are 20-cent stamps.

	MT	EX-MT	VG
COMPLETE SET (4)	20.00	9.00	2.50
COMMON PLAYER (1-4)	6.00	2.70	.75
☐ 1 Roberto Clemente Issued August 17, 1984	6.00	2.70	.75
☐ 2 Lou Gehrig Issued June 10, 1989	6.00	2.70	.75
☐ 3 Jackie Robinson Issued August 2, 1982	6.00	2.70	.75
☐ 4 Babe Ruth Issued July 6, 1983	7.50	3.40	.95

1983 White Sox True Value

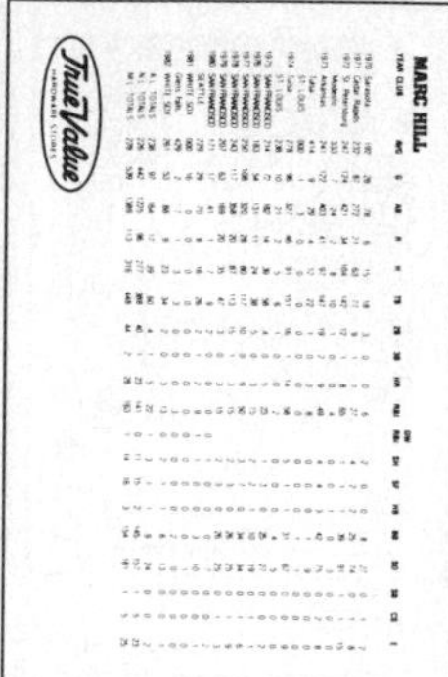

This 23-card set was sponsored by True Value Hardware Stores and features full-color (approximately 2 5/8" by 4 1/4") cards of the Chicago White Sox. Most of the set was intended for distribution two cards per game at selected White Sox Tuesday night home games. The cards are unnumbered except for uniform number given in the lower right corner of the obverse. The card backs contain statistical information in basic black and white. The cards of Harold Baines, Salome Barojas, and Marc Hill were not issued at the park; hence they are more difficult to obtain than the other 20 cards and are marked SP in the checklist below.

	NRMT-MT	EXC	G-VG
COMPLETE SET (23)	35.00	16.00	4.40
COMMON PLAYER (1-23)	.50	.23	.06
☐ 1 Scott Fletcher	.90	.40	.11
☐ 3 Harold Baines SP	10.00	4.50	1.25
☐ 5 Vance Law	.60	.25	.08
☐ 7 Marc Hill SP	5.00	2.30	.60
☐ 10 Tony LaRussa MG	1.00	.45	.13
☐ 11 Rudy Law	.50	.23	.06
☐ 14 Tony Bernazard	.60	.25	.08
☐ 17 Jerry Hairston	.50	.23	.06
☐ 19 Greg Luzinski	1.00	.45	.13
☐ 24 Floyd Bannister	.60	.25	.08
☐ 25 Mike Squires	.50	.23	.06
☐ 30 Salome Barojas SP	5.00	2.30	.60
☐ 31 LaMarr Hoyt	.60	.25	.08
☐ 34 Richard Dotson	.60	.25	.08
☐ 36 Jerry Koosman	.90	.40	.11
☐ 40 Britt Burns	.60	.25	.08
☐ 41 Dick Tidrow	.50	.23	.06
☐ 42 Ron Kittle	1.00	.45	.13
☐ 44 Tom Paciorek	.75	.35	.09
☐ 45 Kevin Hickey	.50	.23	.06
☐ 53 Dennis Lamp	.50	.23	.06
☐ 67 Jim Kern	.50	.23	.06
☐ 72 Carlton Fisk	4.50	2.00	.55

1984 White Sox True Value

This 30-card set features full color (approximately 2 1/2" by 4") cards of the Chicago White Sox. Most of the set was distributed two cards per game at selected White Sox Tuesday home games. Faust and Minoso were not given out although their cards were available through direct (promotional) contact with them. Brennan and Hulett were not released directly since they were sent down to the minors. The cards are unnumbered except for uniform number given in the lower right corner of the obverse; they are arbitrarily listed below in alphabetical order. The card

backs contain statistical information in basic black and white.

	NRMT-MT	EXC	G-VG
COMPLETE SET (30)	30.00	13.50	3.80
COMMON PLAYER (1-30)	.50	.23	.06
☐ 1 Juan Agosto	.50	.23	.06
☐ 2 Luis Aparicio	3.00	1.35	.40
☐ 3 Harold Baines	1.50	.65	.19
☐ 4 Floyd Bannister	.60	.25	.08
☐ 5 Salome Barojas	.50	.23	.06
☐ 6 Tom Brennan SP	4.00	1.80	.50
☐ 7 Britt Burns	.60	.25	.08
☐ 8 Coaching Staff (Blank back)	.60	.25	.08
☐ 9 Julio Cruz	.50	.23	.06
☐ 10 Richard Dotson	.60	.25	.08
☐ 11 Jerry Dybzinski	.50	.23	.06
☐ 12 Nancy Faust ORG (Blank back)	2.50	1.15	.30
☐ 13 Carlton Fisk	4.00	1.80	.50
☐ 14 Scott Fletcher	.60	.25	.08
☐ 15 Jerry Hairston	.50	.23	.06
☐ 16 Marc Hill	.50	.23	.06
☐ 17 LaMarr Hoyt	.60	.25	.08
☐ 18 Tim Hulett SP	4.00	1.80	.50
☐ 19 Ron Kittle	1.00	.45	.13
☐ 20 Tony LaRussa MG	1.00	.45	.13
☐ 21 Rudy Law	.50	.23	.06
☐ 22 Vance Law	.60	.25	.08
☐ 23 Greg Luzinski	1.00	.45	.13
☐ 24 Minnie Minoso	3.50	1.55	.45
☐ 25 Tom Paciorek	.75	.35	.09
☐ 26 Ron Reed	.50	.23	.06
☐ 27 Tom Seaver	4.50	2.00	.55
☐ 28 Dave Stegman	.50	.23	.06
☐ 29 Mike Squires	.50	.23	.06
☐ 30 Greg Walker	.60	.25	.08

1985 White Sox Coke

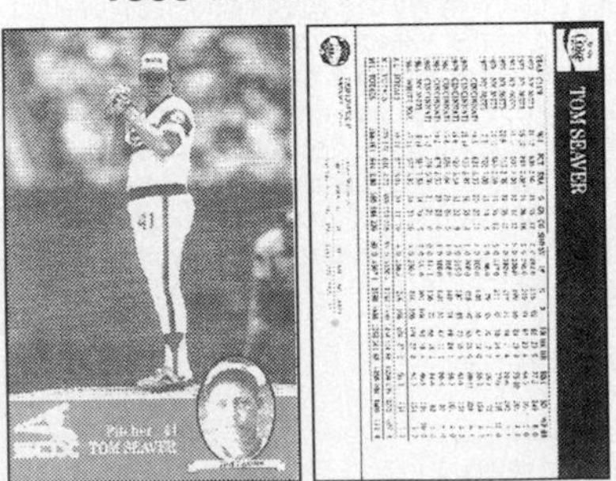

This 30-card set features present and past Chicago White Sox players and personnel. Cards measure approximately 2 5/8" by 4 1/8" and feature a red band at the bottom of the card. Within the red band are the White Sox logo, the player's name, position, uniform number, and a small oval portrait of an all-time White Sox Great at a similar position. The cards were available two at a time at Tuesday night White Sox home games or as a complete set through membership in the Coca-Cola White Sox Fan Club. The cards below are numbered by uniform number; the last three cards are unnumbered.

	NRMT-MT	EXC	G-VG
COMPLETE SET (30)	12.00	5.50	1.50
COMMON PLAYER	.40	.18	.05
☐ 0 Oscar Gamble Zeke Bonura	.40	.18	.05
☐ 1 Scott Fletcher Luke Appling	.60	.25	.08
☐ 3 Harold Baines Bill Melton	.90	.40	.11
☐ 5 Luis Salazar Chico Carrasquel	.40	.18	.05
☐ 7 Marc Hill Sherm Lollar	.40	.18	.05
☐ 8 Daryl Boston Jim Landis	.40	.18	.05
☐ 10 Tony LaRussa MG Al Lopez MG	1.00	.45	.13
☐ 12 Julio Cruz Nellie Fox	.60	.25	.08
☐ 13 Ozzie Guillen Luis Aparicio	2.00	.90	.25
☐ 17 Jerry Hairston Smoky Burgess	.40	.18	.05
☐ 20 Joe DeSa Carlos May	.40	.18	.05
☐ 22 Joel Skinner J.C. Martin	.40	.18	.05
☐ 23 Rudy Law Bill Skowron	.40	.18	.05
☐ 24 Floyd Bannister Red Faber	.50	.23	.06
☐ 29 Greg Walker Dick Allen	.60	.25	.08
☐ 30 Gene Nelson Early Wynn	.60	.25	.08
☐ 32 Tim Hulett Pete Ward	.40	.18	.05
☐ 34 Richard Dotson Ed Walsh	.50	.23	.06
☐ 37 Dan Spillner Thornton Lee	.40	.18	.05
☐ 40 Britt Burns Gary Peters	.40	.18	.05
☐ 41 Tom Seaver Ted Lyons	2.50	1.15	.30
☐ 42 Ron Kittle Minnie Minoso	.60	.25	.08
☐ 43 Bob James Hoyt Wilhelm	.50	.23	.06
☐ 44 Tom Paciorek Eddie Collins	.50	.23	.06
☐ 46 Tim Lollar Billy Pierce	.40	.18	.05
☐ 50 Juan Agosto Wilbur Wood	.40	.18	.05
☐ 72 Carlton Fisk Ray Schalk	2.50	1.15	.30
☐ NNO Comiskey Park	.40	.18	.05
☐ NNO Nancy Faust ORG	.40	.18	.05
☐ NNO Ribbie and Roobarb	.40	.18	.05

1986 White Sox Coke

This colorful 30-card set features a borderless photo on top of a blue-on-white name, position, and uniform number. Card backs provide complete major and minor season-by-season career statistical information. Since the cards are unnumbered, they are numbered below according to uniform number. The cards measure approximately 2 5/8" by 4". The five unnumbered non-player cards are listed at the end of the checklist below.

	MT	EX-MT	VG
COMPLETE SET (30)	14.00	6.25	1.75
COMMON PLAYER	.40	.18	.05
☐ 1 Wayne Tolleson	.40	.18	.05

	MT	EX-MT	VG
☐ 3 Harold Baines	1.00	.45	.13
☐ 7 Marc Hill	.40	.18	.05
☐ 8 Daryl Boston	.40	.18	.05
☐ 12 Julio Cruz	.40	.18	.05
☐ 13 Ozzie Guillen	1.00	.45	.13
☐ 17 Jerry Hairston	.40	.18	.05
☐ 19 Floyd Bannister	.40	.18	.05
☐ 20 Reid Nichols	.40	.18	.05
☐ 22 Joel Skinner	.40	.18	.05
☐ 24 Dave Schmidt	.40	.18	.05
☐ 26 Bobby Bonilla	5.00	2.30	.60
☐ 29 Greg Walker	.50	.23	.06
☐ 30 Gene Nelson	.40	.18	.05
☐ 32 Tim Hulett	.40	.18	.05
☐ 33 Neil Allen	.50	.23	.06
☐ 34 Richard Dotson	.50	.23	.06
☐ 40 Joe Cowley	.40	.18	.05
☐ 41 Tom Seaver	2.00	.90	.25
☐ 42 Ron Kittle	.60	.25	.08
☐ 43 Bob James	.40	.18	.05
☐ 44 John Cangelosi	.40	.18	.05
☐ 50 Juan Agosto	.40	.18	.05
☐ 52 Joel Davis	.40	.18	.05
☐ 72 Carlton Fisk	2.00	.90	.25
☐ NNO Nancy Faust ORG	.40	.18	.05
☐ NNO Ken(Hawk) Harrelson GM	.50	.23	.06
☐ NNO Tony LaRussa MG	.60	.25	.08
☐ NNO Minnie Minoso CO	.50	.23	.06
☐ NNO Ribbie and Roobarb	.40	.18	.05

1987 White Sox Coke

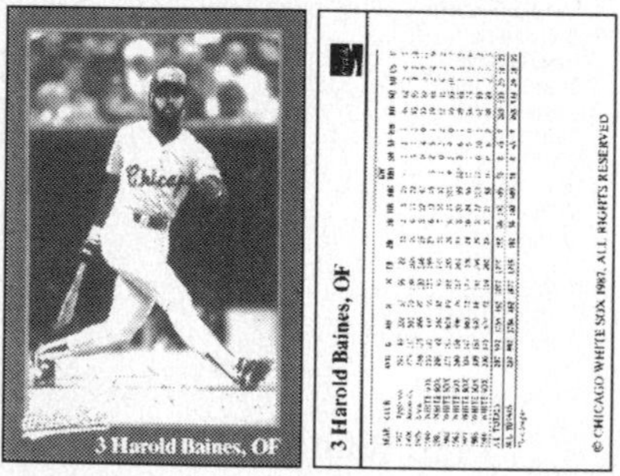

3 Harold Baines, OF
© CHICAGO WHITE SOX 1987. ALL RIGHTS RESERVED

This colorful 30-card set features a card front with a blue-bordered photo and name, position, and uniform number. Card backs provide complete major and minor season-by-season career statistical information. Since the cards are unnumbered, they are numbered below in uniform number order. The cards measure approximately 2 5/8" by 4". The three unnumbered non-player cards are listed at the end. The card set, sponsored by Coca-Cola, is an exclusive for fan club members who join (for 10.00) in 1987.

	MT	EX-MT	VG
COMPLETE SET (30)	10.00	4.50	1.25
COMMON PLAYER (1-30)	.30	.14	.04
☐ 1 Jerry Royster 1	.30	.14	.04
☐ 2 Harold Baines 3	.90	.40	.11
☐ 3 Ron Karkovice 5	.50	.23	.06
☐ 4 Daryl Boston 8	.30	.14	.04
☐ 5 Fred Manrique 10	.30	.14	.04
☐ 6 Steve Lyons 12	.30	.14	.04
☐ 7 Ozzie Guillen 13	.75	.35	.09
☐ 8 Russ Morman 14	.30	.14	.04
☐ 9 Donnie Hill 15	.30	.14	.04
☐ 10 Jim Fregosi MG 16	.40	.18	.05
☐ 11 Jerry Hairston 17	.30	.14	.04
☐ 12 Floyd Bannister 19	.30	.14	.04
☐ 13 Gary Redus 21	.40	.18	.05
☐ 14 Ivan Calderon 22	.75	.35	.09
☐ 15 Ron Hassey 25	.40	.18	.05
☐ 16 Jose DeLeon 26	.30	.14	.04
☐ 17 Greg Walker 29	.40	.18	.05
☐ 18 Tim Hulett 32	.30	.14	.04
☐ 19 Neil Allen 33	.40	.18	.05
☐ 20 Richard Dotson 34	.40	.18	.05
☐ 21 Ray Searage 36	.30	.14	.04
☐ 22 Bobby Thigpen 37	1.00	.45	.13
☐ 23 Jim Winn 40	.30	.14	.04
☐ 24 Bob James 43	.30	.14	.04
☐ 25 Joel McKeon 50	.30	.14	.04
☐ 26 Joel Davis 52	.30	.14	.04
☐ 27 Carlton Fisk 72	1.50	.65	.19
☐ 28 Nancy Faust ORG (Unnumbered)	.30	.14	.04
☐ 29 Minnie Minoso (Unnumbered)	.40	.18	.05
☐ 30 Ribbie and Roobarb (Unnumbered)	.30	.14	.04

1988 White Sox Coke

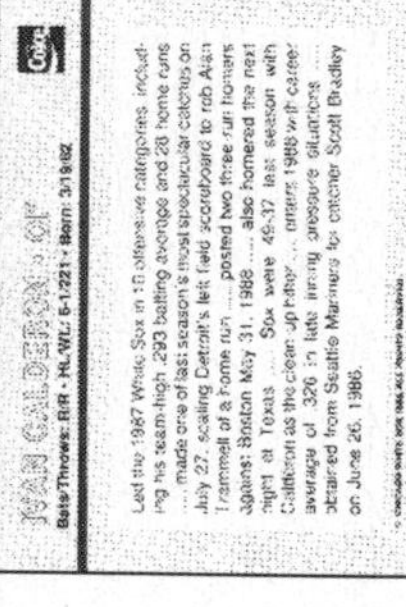

This colorful 30-card set features a card front with a red-bordered photo and name and position. Card backs provide a narrative without any statistical tables. Since the cards are unnumbered, they are numbered below in alphabetical order according to the subject's name or card's title. The cards measure approximately 2 5/8" by 3 1/2". The card set, sponsored by Coca-Cola, was for fan club members who join (for 10.00) in 1988. The cards were also given out at the May 22nd game at Comiskey Park. These cards do not even list the player's uniform number anywhere on the card. Card backs are printed in black and gray on thin white card stock.

	MT	EX-MT	VG
COMPLETE SET (30)	7.00	3.10	.85
COMMON PLAYER (1-30)	.20	.09	.03
☐ 1 Harold Baines	.60	.25	.08
☐ 2 Daryl Boston	.20	.09	.03
☐ 3 Ivan Calderon	.50	.23	.06
☐ 4 Comiskey Park	.20	.09	.03
☐ 5 John Davis	.20	.09	.03
☐ 6 Nancy Faust ORG	.20	.09	.03
☐ 7 Jim Fregosi MG	.30	.14	.04
☐ 8 Carlton Fisk	1.00	.45	.13
☐ 9 Ozzie Guillen	.50	.23	.06
☐ 10 Donnie Hill	.20	.09	.03
☐ 11 Ricky Horton	.30	.14	.04
☐ 12 Lance Johnson	.50	.23	.06

	MT	EX-MT	VG
☐ 13 Dave LaPoint	.30	.14	.04
☐ 14 Bill Long	.20	.09	.03
☐ 15 Steve Lyons	.20	.09	.03
☐ 16 Jack McDowell	2.00	.90	.25
☐ 17 Fred Manrique	.20	.09	.03
☐ 18 Minnie Minoso	.40	.18	.05
☐ 19 Dan Pasqua	.30	.14	.04
☐ 20 John Pawlowski	.20	.09	.03
☐ 21 Melido Perez	.50	.23	.06
☐ 22 Billy Pierce	.30	.14	.04
☐ 23 Jerry Reuss	.30	.14	.04
☐ 24 Gary Redus	.30	.14	.04
☐ 25 Ribbie and Roobarb	.20	.09	.03
☐ 26 Mark Salas	.20	.09	.03
☐ 27 Jose Segura	.30	.14	.04
☐ 28 Bobby Thigpen	.50	.23	.06
☐ 29 Greg Walker	.30	.14	.04
☐ 30 Kenny Williams	.20	.09	.03

1988 White Sox Kodak

This five-card, approximately 8" by 11 1/2" set was issued by Kodak including members of the 1988 Chicago White Sox. The cards are borderless and say "1988 Kodak Collectible Series" on top with the player's photo dominating the middle of the photo. Underneath the photo is a facsimile autograph and on the bottom left of the photo is an advertisment for Kodak and the bottom right of the card the White Sox logo is featured. The backs are blank.

	MT	EX-MT	VG
COMPLETE SET (5)	8.00	3.60	1.00
COMMON PLAYER (1-5)	1.50	.65	.19
☐ 1 Ozzie Guillen	2.00	.90	.25
☐ 2 Carlton Fisk	4.00	1.80	.50
☐ 3 Rick Horton	1.50	.65	.19
☐ 4 Ivan Calderon	2.00	.90	.25
☐ 5 Harold Baines	2.00	.90	.25

1989 White Sox Coke

The 1989 Coke Chicago White Sox set contains 30 cards measuring approximately 2 5/8" by 3 1/2". The players in the set represent the White Sox opening day roster. The fronts are blue. The horizontally oriented backs are gray and white, and feature biographical information. The set was a promotional give-away August 10, 1989 at the Baseball Card Night game against the Oakland A's to the first 15,000 fans. The set includes a special "New Comiskey Park, 1991" card. The complete set was also available with (10.00) membership in the Chi-Sox Fan Club. The cards in the set are numbered on the backs in the lower right corner in very small print.

	MT	EX-MT	VG
COMPLETE SET (30)	7.00	3.10	.85
COMMON PLAYER (1-30)	.20	.09	.03
☐ 1 New Comiskey Park 1991	.30	.14	.04
☐ 2 Comiskey Park	.20	.09	.03
☐ 3 Jeff Torborg MG	.30	.14	.04
☐ 4 Coaching Staff	.30	.14	.04
☐ 5 Harold Baines	.60	.25	.08
☐ 6 Daryl Boston	.20	.09	.03
☐ 7 Ivan Calderon	.50	.23	.06
☐ 8 Carlton Fisk	1.00	.45	.13
☐ 9 Dave Gallagher	.20	.09	.03
☐ 10 Ozzie Guillen	.50	.23	.06
☐ 11 Shawn Hillegas	.20	.09	.03
☐ 12 Barry Jones	.30	.14	.04
☐ 13 Ron Karkovice	.20	.09	.03
☐ 14 Eric King	.20	.09	.03
☐ 15 Ron Kittle	.30	.14	.04
☐ 16 Bill Long	.20	.09	.03
☐ 17 Steve Lyons	.20	.09	.03
☐ 18 Donn Pall	.20	.09	.03
☐ 19 Dan Pasqua	.30	.14	.04
☐ 20 Ken Patterson	.20	.09	.03
☐ 21 Melido Perez	.40	.18	.05
☐ 22 Jerry Reuss	.30	.14	.04
☐ 23 Billy Joe Robidoux	.20	.09	.03
☐ 24 Steve Rosenberg	.20	.09	.03
☐ 25 Jeff Schaefer	.20	.09	.03
☐ 26 Bobby Thigpen	.50	.23	.06
☐ 27 Greg Walker	.30	.14	.04
☐ 28 Eddie Williams	.20	.09	.03
☐ 29 Nancy Faust ORG	.20	.09	.03
☐ 30 Minnie Minoso	.30	.14	.04

1989 White Sox Kodak

For the second consecutive year Kodak in conjunction with the Chicago White Sox issued a set about the White Sox. The 1989 set was marked by a color photo of the active star dominating the upper right half of the card with the bottom half of the card depicting two other famous White Sox players at the same position that the current star played. This six-card, approximately 8" by 11 1/2", set was given away at various games at Comiskey Park.

	MT	EX-MT	VG
COMPLETE SET (6)	8.00	3.60	1.00
COMMON PLAYER (1-6)	1.50	.65	.19
☐ 1 Greg Walker Dick Allen Ted Kluszewski	1.50	.65	.19
☐ 2 Steve Lyons Eddie Collins Nellie Fox	1.50	.65	.19
☐ 3 Carlton Fisk Sherm Lollar Ray Schalk	3.00	1.35	.40
☐ 4 Harold Baines Minnie Minoso Jim Landis	1.50	.65	.19
☐ 5 Bobby Thigpen Gerry Staley Hoyt Wilhelm	1.50	.65	.19
☐ 6 Ozzie Guillen Luke Appling Luis Aparicio	2.50	1.15	.30

1990 White Sox Coke

The 1990 Coca Cola White Sox set contains 30 cards. The set is a beautiful full-color set commemorating the 1990 White Sox who were celebrating the eightieth and last season played in old Comiskey Park. This (approximately) 2 5/8" by 3 1/2" set has a Comiskey Park logo on the front with 1989 statistics and a brief biography on the back. The set is checklisted alphabetically and notated by the uniform number on the front of the card.

	MT	EX-MT	VG
COMPLETE SET (30)	10.00	4.00	1.15
COMMON PLAYER (1-30)	.25	.11	.03
☐ 1 Ivan Calderon 22	.60	.25	.08
☐ 2 Wayne Edwards 45	.35	.16	.04
☐ 3 Carlton Fisk 72	1.00	.45	.13
☐ 4 Scott Fletcher 7	.25	.11	.03
☐ 5 Dave Gallagher 17	.25	.11	.03
☐ 6 Craig Grebeck 14	.45	.20	.06
☐ 7 Ozzie Guillen 13	.60	.25	.08
☐ 8 Greg Hibbard 27	.45	.20	.06
☐ 9 Lance Johnson 1	.45	.20	.06
☐ 10 Barry Jones 50	.35	.16	.04
☐ 11 Ron Karkovice 20	.35	.16	.04
☐ 12 Eric King 36	.35	.16	.04
☐ 13 Ron Kittle 42	.35	.16	.04
☐ 14 Jerry Kutzler 52	.25	.11	.03
☐ 15 Steve Lyons 12	.25	.11	.03
☐ 16 Carlos Martinez 24	.35	.16	.04
☐ 17 Jack McDowell 29	1.00	.45	.13
☐ 18 Donn Pall 30	.25	.11	.03
☐ 19 Dan Pasqua 44	.35	.16	.04
☐ 20 Ken Patterson 34	.25	.11	.03
☐ 21 Melido Perez 33	.45	.20	.06
☐ 22 Scott Radinsky 31	.45	.20	.06
☐ 23 Sammy Sosa 25	.60	.25	.08
☐ 24 Bobby Thigpen 37	.60	.25	.08
☐ 25 Frank Thomas	5.00	2.30	.60
☐ 26 Jeff Torborg MG 10	.35	.16	.04
☐ 27 Robin Ventura 23	2.50	1.15	.30
☐ 28 Rookies: Jerry Kutzler Wayne Edwards Craig Grebeck Scott Radinsky Robin Ventura	.50	.23	.06
☐ 29 Captains: Ozzie Guillen and Carlton Fisk	.50	.23	.06
☐ 30 Coaches: Barry Foote Sammy Ellis Walt Hriniak Terry Bevington Dave LaRoche Joe Nossek Ron Clark	.25	.11	.03

1990 White Sox Kodak

In 1990 Kodak again in conjunction with the Chicago White Sox issued a beautiful six-card set about some key members of the 1990 White Sox. This was slightly reduced in size (from the previous two years) to be approximately 7" by 11" and featured a full-color picture with an advertisement for Kodak on the lower left corner of the front of the card and the White Sox logo in the lower right hand corner. The cards were again borderless and blank-backed.

	MT	EX-MT	VG
COMPLETE SET (6)	8.00	3.60	1.00
COMMON PLAYER (1-6)	1.25	.55	.16
☐ 1 Carlton Fisk	3.00	1.35	.40
☐ 2 Melido Perez	1.50	.65	.19
☐ 3 Ozzie Guillen	1.50	.65	.19
☐ 4 Ron Kittle	1.25	.55	.16
☐ 5 Scott Fletcher	1.25	.55	.16
☐ 6 Comiskey Park	1.25	.55	.16

1991 White Sox Kodak

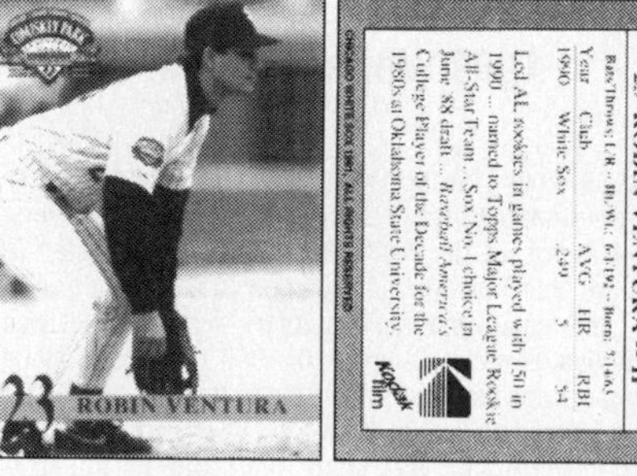

This 28-card set was sponsored by Kodak and measures approximately 2 5/8" by 3 1/2". The front design depicts borderless glossy color action player photos. A Comiskey Park insignia is superimposed at the upper left corner of the picture. The player's name appears in black lettering in a silver stripe toward the card bottom, with a black oversized (uniform) number in the lower left corner. In a horizontal format, the backs are printed in black on white with gray borders, and provide 1990 statistics and highlights. The cards are skip-numbered by uniform number and checklisted below accordingly, with the unnumbered cards listed at the end.

	MT	EX-MT	VG
COMPLETE SET (28)	12.50	5.75	1.55
COMMON PLAYER	.30	.14	.04
☐ 1 Lance Johnson	.50	.23	.06
☐ 5 Matt Merullo	.40	.18	.05
☐ 7 Scott Fletcher	.30	.14	.04
☐ 8 Bo Jackson	2.00	.90	.25
☐ 10 Jeff Torborg MG	.40	.18	.05
☐ 13 Ozzie Guillen	.50	.23	.06
☐ 14 Craig Grebeck	.40	.18	.05
☐ 20 Ron Karkovice	.40	.18	.05
☐ 21 Joey Cora	.30	.14	.04
☐ 22 Donn Pall	.30	.14	.04
☐ 23 Robin Ventura	1.25	.55	.16
☐ 25 Sammy Sosa	.50	.23	.06
☐ 27 Greg Hibbard	.40	.18	.05
☐ 28 Cory Snyder	.50	.23	.06
☐ 29 Jack McDowell	1.00	.45	.13
☐ 30 Tim Raines	.50	.23	.06
☐ 31 Scott Radinsky	.40	.18	.05
☐ 32 Alex Fernandez	.60	.25	.08
☐ 33 Melido Perez	.50	.23	.06
☐ 34 Ken Patterson	.30	.14	.04
☐ 35 Frank Thomas	4.00	1.80	.50
☐ 37 Bobby Thigpen	.50	.23	.06
☐ 44 Dan Pasqua	.40	.18	.05
☐ 45 Wayne Edwards	.30	.14	.04
☐ 49 Charlie Hough	.40	.18	.05
☐ 50 Brian Drahman	.30	.14	.04
☐ 72 Carlton Fisk	1.00	.45	.13
☐ xx No. 1 Draft Choices Jack McDowell Robin Ventura Alex Fernandez Frank Thomas	2.00	.90	.25
☐ xx 1991 Co-Captains Carlton Fisk and Ozzie Guillen	.50	.23	.06
☐ xx 1991 Coaching Staff Walt Hriniak Sammy Ellis Terry Bevington Barry Foote Joe Nossek John Stephenson Dave LaRoche	.40	.18	.05

1992 White Sox Kodak

This 30-card set was sponsored by Kodak and measures slightly larger (2 5/8" by 3 1/2") than standard size. The set was distributed at a White Sox vs. Milwaukee four-game series at Comiskey Park. The fronts display glossy borderless color player photos. All the players are pictured in black attire, in keeping with the "Good Guys Wear Black" team slogan, which is tilted slightly to the left and superimposed at the upper left corner. The player's name appears in a black diagonal stripe that cuts across the bottom of the picture; at the lower right corner, it intersects a diamond bearing his jersey number. The horizontally oriented backs have gray borders and feature biography, statistics (1991 and career), and a White Sox trivia question and answer. The cards are skip-numbered on the front by uniform number and checklisted below accordingly.

	MT	EX-MT	VG
COMPLETE SET (30)	10.00	4.50	1.25
COMMON PLAYER	.30	.14	.04
☐ 0 Waldo the Wolf	.30	.14	.04
☐ 1 Lance Johnson	.40	.18	.05
☐ 5 Matt Merullo	.30	.14	.04
☐ 7 Steve Sax	.50	.23	.06
☐ 12 Mike Huff	.30	.14	.04
☐ 13 Ozzie Guillen	.50	.23	.06
☐ 14 Craig Grebeck	.40	.18	.05
☐ 20 Ron Karkovice	.30	.14	.04
☐ 21 George Bell	.60	.25	.08
☐ 22 Donn Pall	.30	.14	.04
☐ 23 Robin Ventura	1.00	.45	.13
☐ 24 Warren Newson	.30	.14	.04
☐ 25 Kirk McCaskill	.30	.14	.04
☐ 27 Greg Hibbard	.40	.18	.05
☐ 28 Joey Cora	.30	.14	.04
☐ 29 Jack McDowell	.75	.35	.09
☐ 30 Tim Raines	.50	.23	.06
☐ 31 Scott Radinsky	.40	.18	.05
☐ 32 Alex Fernandez	.50	.23	.06
☐ 33 Gene Lamont MG	.30	.14	.04
☐ 34 Terry Leach	.30	.14	.04
☐ 35 Frank Thomas	2.00	.90	.25
☐ 37 Bobby Thigpen	.40	.18	.05
☐ 39 Roberto Hernandez	.50	.23	.06
☐ 40 Wilson Alvarez	.40	.18	.05
☐ 44 Dan Pasqua	.30	.14	.04
☐ 45 Shawn Abner	.30	.14	.04
☐ 49 Charlie Hough	.40	.18	.05
☐ 72 Carlton Fisk	1.00	.45	.13
☐ NNO Coaching Staff Walt Hriniak Doug Mansolino Dave Huppert Mike Squires Terry Bevington Gene Lamont MG Joe Nossek Jackie Brown	.30	.14	.04

1992 Whitehall Legends to Life

This five-card hologram set from the Whitehall Collection, which measures the standard size (2 1/2" by 3 1/2"), features hologram images created from actual photographs on the card fronts. The players are shown in action in front of the scene in the original photo. The pictures are bordered and have striped banners at the corners. The player's name appears in an arch at the top. The words "Whitehall

Collection" and "Limited Edition" are printed at the top and bottom respectively. The back design shows a "color" close-up photo colorized with a special process called Photonix. The picture is displayed on a tan monument-shaped graphic design with antiquated roman pillars partially visible at the top corners. Below the photo are the player's name and a career summary. The cards are unnumbered and checklisted below in alphabetical order.

	MT	EX-MT	VG
COMPLETE SET (5)	15.00	6.75	1.90
COMMON PLAYER (1-5)	2.50	1.15	.30
☐ 1 Ty Cobb	5.00	2.30	.60
☐ 2 Lou Gehrig	5.00	2.30	.60
☐ 3 Babe Ruth	7.50	3.40	.95
☐ 4 Honus Wagner	3.00	1.35	.40
☐ 5 Cy Young	2.50	1.15	.30

1954 Wilson

The cards in this 20-card set measure approximately 2 5/8" by 3 3/4". The 1954 "Wilson Wieners" set contains 20 full color, unnumbered cards. The obverse design of a package of hot dogs appearing to fly through the air is a distinctive feature of this set. Uncut sheets have been seen. Cards are numbered below alphabetically by player's name.

	NRMT	VG-E	GOOD
COMPLETE SET (20)	7500.00	3400.00	950.00
COMMON PLAYER (1-20)	150.00	70.00	19.00
☐ 1 Roy Campanella	750.00	350.00	95.00
☐ 2 Del Ennis	150.00	70.00	19.00
☐ 3 Carl Erskine	175.00	80.00	22.00
☐ 4 Ferris Fain	150.00	70.00	19.00
☐ 5 Bob Feller	600.00	275.00	75.00
☐ 6 Nelson Fox	250.00	115.00	31.00
☐ 7 Johnny Groth	150.00	70.00	19.00
☐ 8 Stan Hack MG	150.00	70.00	19.00
☐ 9 Gil Hodges	400.00	180.00	50.00
☐ 10 Ray Jablonski	150.00	70.00	19.00
☐ 11 Harvey Kuenn	250.00	115.00	31.00
☐ 12 Roy McMillan	150.00	70.00	19.00
☐ 13 Andy Pafko	150.00	70.00	19.00
☐ 14 Paul Richards MG	150.00	70.00	19.00
☐ 15 Hank Sauer	150.00	70.00	19.00
☐ 16 Red Schoendienst	400.00	180.00	50.00
☐ 17 Enos Slaughter	450.00	200.00	57.50
☐ 18 Vern Stephens	150.00	70.00	19.00
☐ 19 Sammy White	150.00	70.00	19.00
☐ 20 Ted Williams	3000.00	1200.00	400.00

1990 Wonder Bread Stars

The 1990 Wonder Bread set was issued in 1990 by MSA (Michael Schechter Associates) in conjunction with Wonder Bread. One card was issued inside each specially marked package of Wonder Bread. Cards were available in grocery

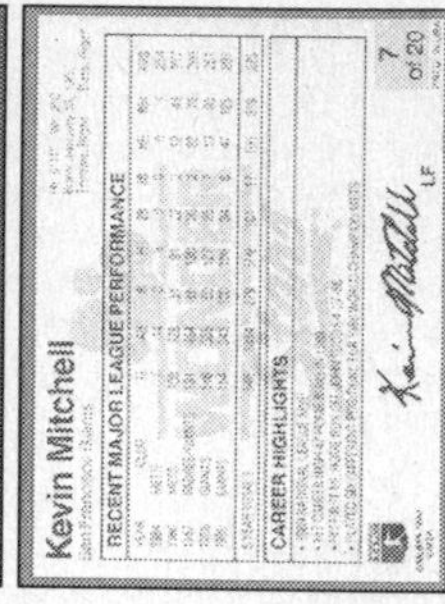

stores through June 15, 1990. The card was sealed in a pouch in the bread wrapper. This standard-size (2 1/2" by 3 1/2") card set was issued without logos like many of the sets produced by MSA. Cards were printed on thin stock and hence were easily creased during bread handling making the set more difficult to put together one card at a time for condition-conscious collectors. Cards are numbered on the back in the lower right corner. Wonder Bread also offered sets in uncut sheet form to collectors mailing in with 3.00 and five proofs of purchase.

	MT	EX-MT	VG
COMPLETE SET (20)	15.00	6.75	1.90
COMMON PLAYER (1-20)	.35	.16	.04
☐ 1 Bo Jackson	1.25	.55	.16
☐ 2 Roger Clemens	1.50	.65	.19
☐ 3 Jim Abbott	.75	.35	.09
☐ 4 Orel Hershiser	.45	.20	.06
☐ 5 Ozzie Smith	.75	.35	.09
☐ 6 Don Mattingly	1.25	.55	.16
☐ 7 Kevin Mitchell	.60	.25	.08
☐ 8 Jerome Walton	.35	.16	.04
☐ 9 Kirby Puckett	1.25	.55	.16
☐ 10 Darryl Strawberry	1.00	.45	.13
☐ 11 Robin Yount	1.00	.45	.13
☐ 12 Tony Gwynn	1.00	.45	.13
☐ 13 Alan Trammell	.50	.23	.06
☐ 14 Jose Canseco	1.50	.65	.19
☐ 15 Greg Swindell	.45	.20	.06
☐ 16 Nolan Ryan	3.00	1.35	.40
☐ 17 Howard Johnson	.45	.20	.06
☐ 18 Ken Griffey Jr.	3.00	1.35	.40
☐ 19 Will Clark	1.25	.55	.16
☐ 20 Ryne Sandberg	1.50	.65	.19

1985 Woolworth's

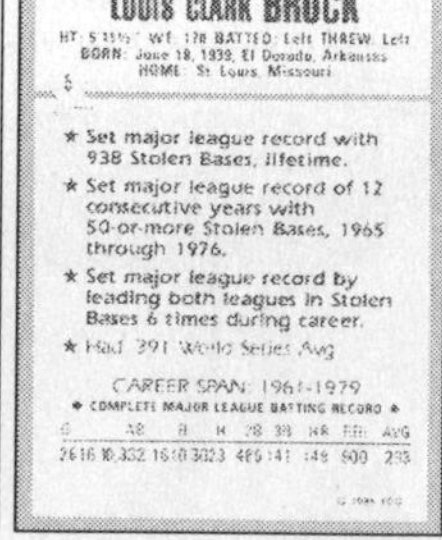

This 44-card set features color as well as black and white cards of All Time Record Holders. The cards are standard size (2 1/2" by 3 1/2") and are printed with blue ink on an orange and white back. The set was produced for Woolworth's by Topps and was packaged in a colorful box which contained a checklist of the cards in the set on the back panel. The numerical order of the cards coincides alphabetically with the player's name.

	NRMT-MT	EXC	G-VG
COMPLETE SET (44)	4.00	1.80	.50
COMMON PLAYER (1-44)	.07	.03	.01
☐ 1 Hank Aaron	.35	.16	.04
☐ 2 Grover C. Alexander	.15	.07	.02
☐ 3 Ernie Banks	.15	.07	.02
☐ 4 Yogi Berra	.25	.11	.03
☐ 5 Lou Brock	.15	.07	.02
☐ 6 Steve Carlton	.15	.07	.02
☐ 7 Jack Chesbro	.07	.03	.01
☐ 8 Ty Cobb	.50	.23	.06
☐ 9 Sam Crawford	.07	.03	.01
☐ 10 Rollie Fingers	.15	.07	.02
☐ 11 Whitey Ford	.15	.07	.02
☐ 12 John Frederick	.07	.03	.01
☐ 13 Frankie Frisch	.10	.05	.01
☐ 14 Lou Gehrig	.50	.23	.06
☐ 15 Jim Gentile	.07	.03	.01
☐ 16 Dwight Gooden	.25	.11	.03
☐ 17 Rickey Henderson	.35	.16	.04
☐ 18 Rogers Hornsby	.15	.07	.02
☐ 19 Frank Howard	.10	.05	.01
☐ 20 Cliff Johnson	.07	.03	.01
☐ 21 Walter Johnson	.25	.11	.03
☐ 22 Hub Leonard	.07	.03	.01
☐ 23 Mickey Mantle	.75	.35	.09
☐ 24 Roger Maris	.25	.11	.03
☐ 25 Christy Mathewson	.25	.11	.03
☐ 26 Willie Mays	.35	.16	.04
☐ 27 Stan Musial	.25	.11	.03
☐ 28 Dan Quisenberry	.07	.03	.01
☐ 29 Frank Robinson	.15	.07	.02
☐ 30 Pete Rose	.30	.14	.04
☐ 31 Babe Ruth	.75	.35	.09
☐ 32 Nolan Ryan	.75	.35	.09
☐ 33 George Sisler	.10	.05	.01
☐ 34 Tris Speaker	.15	.07	.02
☐ 35 Ed Walsh	.10	.05	.01
☐ 36 Lloyd Waner	.10	.05	.01
☐ 37 Earl Webb	.07	.03	.01
☐ 38 Ted Williams	.40	.18	.05
☐ 39 Maury Wills	.07	.03	.01
☐ 40 Hack Wilson	.10	.05	.01
☐ 41 Owen Wilson	.07	.03	.01
☐ 42 Willie Wilson	.07	.03	.01
☐ 43 Rudy York	.07	.03	.01
☐ 44 Cy Young	.25	.11	.03

1986 Woolworth's

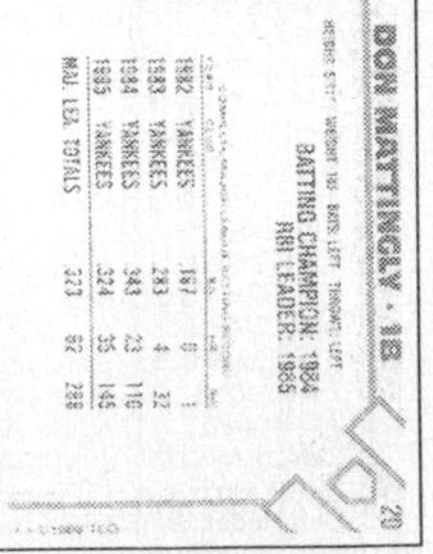

This boxed set of 33 cards was produced by Topps for Woolworth's variety stores. The set features players who hold or have held hitting, home run or RBI titles. Cards are the standard 2 1/2" by 3 1/2" and have a glossy finish. The card fronts are bordered in yellow with the subtitle "Topps Collectors' Series" across the top. The card backs are printed in green and blue ink on white card stock. The custom box gives the set checklist on the back.

	MT	EX-MT	VG
COMPLETE SET (33)	3.50	1.55	.45
COMMON PLAYER (1-33)	.07	.03	.01
☐ 1 Tony Armas	.07	.03	.01
☐ 2 Don Baylor	.10	.05	.01
☐ 3 Wade Boggs	.50	.23	.06
☐ 4 George Brett	.50	.23	.06
☐ 5 Bill Buckner	.07	.03	.01
☐ 6 Rod Carew	.40	.18	.05
☐ 7 Gary Carter	.25	.11	.03
☐ 8 Cecil Cooper	.10	.05	.01
☐ 9 Darrell Evans	.07	.03	.01
☐ 10 Dwight Evans	.10	.05	.01
☐ 11 George Foster	.10	.05	.01
☐ 12 Bob Grich	.07	.03	.01
☐ 13 Tony Gwynn	.50	.23	.06
☐ 14 Keith Hernandez	.15	.07	.02
☐ 15 Reggie Jackson	.50	.23	.06
☐ 16 Dave Kingman	.10	.05	.01
☐ 17 Carney Lansford	.07	.03	.01
☐ 18 Fred Lynn	.10	.05	.01
☐ 19 Bill Madlock	.07	.03	.01
☐ 20 Don Mattingly	.50	.23	.06
☐ 21 Willie McGee	.15	.07	.02
☐ 22 Hal McRae	.10	.05	.01
☐ 23 Dale Murphy	.25	.11	.03
☐ 24 Eddie Murray	.30	.14	.04
☐ 25 Ben Oglivie	.07	.03	.01
☐ 26 Al Oliver	.07	.03	.01
☐ 27 Dave Parker	.10	.05	.01
☐ 28 Jim Rice	.15	.07	.02
☐ 29 Pete Rose	.50	.23	.06
☐ 30 Mike Schmidt	.50	.23	.06
☐ 31 Gorman Thomas	.10	.05	.01
☐ 32 Willie Wilson	.10	.05	.01
☐ 33 Dave Winfield	.35	.16	.04

1987 Woolworth's Highlights

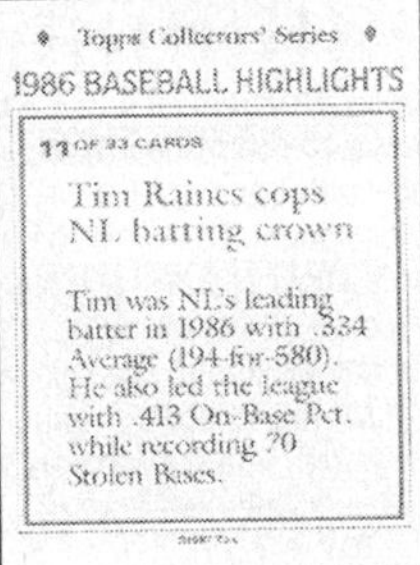

Topps produced this 33-card set for Woolworth's stores. The set is subtitled "Topps Collectors' Series Baseball Highlights" and consists of high gloss card fronts with full-color photos. Cards are the standard 2 1/2" by 3 1/2". The cards show and describe highlights of the previous season. The card backs are printed in gold and purple and are numbered. The set was sold nationally in Woolworth's for a 1.99 suggested retail price.

	MT	EX-MT	VG
COMPLETE SET (33)	3.50	1.55	.45
COMMON PLAYER (1-33)	.07	.03	.01
☐ 1 Steve Carlton	.25	.11	.03
☐ 2 Cecil Cooper	.10	.05	.01
☐ 3 Rickey Henderson	.35	.16	.04
☐ 4 Reggie Jackson	.35	.16	.04
☐ 5 Jim Rice	.15	.07	.02
☐ 6 Don Sutton	.20	.09	.03
☐ 7 Roger Clemens	.50	.23	.06
☐ 8 Mike Schmidt	.50	.23	.06
☐ 9 Jesse Barfield	.15	.07	.02
☐ 10 Wade Boggs	.40	.18	.05
☐ 11 Tim Raines	.15	.07	.02
☐ 12 Jose Canseco	.60	.25	.08
☐ 13 Todd Worrell	.15	.07	.02
☐ 14 Dave Righetti	.10	.05	.01
☐ 15 Don Mattingly	.50	.23	.06
☐ 16 Tony Gwynn	.40	.18	.05
☐ 17 Marty Barrett	.07	.03	.01
☐ 18 Mike Scott	.10	.05	.01

	MT	EX-MT	VG
☐ 19 Bruce Hurst	.10	.05	.01
☐ 20 Calvin Schiraldi	.07	.03	.01
☐ 21 Dwight Evans	.15	.07	.02
☐ 22 Dave Henderson	.07	.03	.01
☐ 23 Len Dykstra	.10	.05	.01
☐ 24 Bob Ojeda	.07	.03	.01
☐ 25 Gary Carter	.20	.09	.03
☐ 26 Ron Darling	.10	.05	.01
☐ 27 Jim Rice	.15	.07	.02
☐ 28 Bruce Hurst	.10	.05	.01
☐ 29 Darryl Strawberry	.45	.20	.06
☐ 30 Ray Knight	.10	.05	.01
☐ 31 Keith Hernandez	.15	.07	.02
☐ 32 Mets Celebration	.07	.03	.01
☐ 33 Ray Knight	.10	.05	.01

1988 Woolworth's Highlights

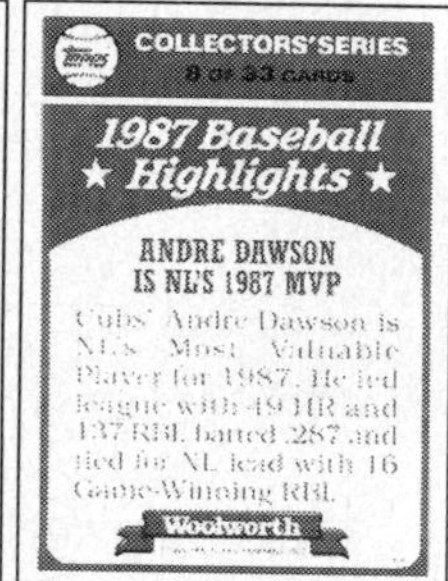

Topps produced this 33-card set for Woolworth's stores. The set is subtitled "Topps Collectors' Series Baseball Highlights" and consists of high gloss card fronts with full-color photos. Cards are the standard 2 1/2" by 3 1/2". The cards show and describe highlights of the previous season. Cards 19-33 commemorate the World Series with highlights and key players of each game in the series. The card backs are printed in red and blue on white card stock and are numbered. The set was sold nationally in Woolworth's for a 1.99 suggested retail price.

	MT	EX-MT	VG
COMPLETE SET (33)	3.50	1.55	.45
COMMON PLAYER (1-33)	.07	.03	.01
☐ 1 Don Baylor	.10	.05	.01
☐ 2 Vince Coleman	.15	.07	.02
☐ 3 Darrell Evans	.07	.03	.01
☐ 4 Don Mattingly	.50	.23	.06
☐ 5 Eddie Murray	.30	.14	.04
☐ 6 Nolan Ryan	.75	.35	.09
☐ 7 Mike Schmidt	.50	.23	.06
☐ 8 Andre Dawson	.25	.11	.03
☐ 9 George Bell	.15	.07	.02
☐ 10 Steve Bedrosian	.07	.03	.01
☐ 11 Roger Clemens	.60	.25	.08
☐ 12 Tony Gwynn	.50	.23	.06
☐ 13 Wade Boggs	.50	.23	.06
☐ 14 Benito Santiago	.20	.09	.03
☐ 15 Mark McGwire UER (Referenced on card back as NL ROY, sic)	.50	.23	.06
☐ 16 Dave Righetti	.10	.05	.01
☐ 17 Jeffrey Leonard	.07	.03	.01
☐ 18 Gary Gaetti	.07	.03	.01
☐ 19 Frank Viola WS1	.10	.05	.01
☐ 20 Dan Gladden WS1	.07	.03	.01
☐ 21 Bert Blyleven WS2	.07	.03	.01
☐ 22 Gary Gaetti WS2	.07	.03	.01
☐ 23 John Tudor WS3	.07	.03	.01
☐ 24 Todd Worrell WS3	.10	.05	.01
☐ 25 Tom Lawless WS4	.07	.03	.01
☐ 26 Willie McGee WS4	.10	.05	.01
☐ 27 Danny Cox WS5	.07	.03	.01
☐ 28 Curt Ford WS5	.07	.03	.01
☐ 29 Don Baylor WS6	.12	.05	.02
☐ 30 Kent Hrbek WS6	.12	.05	.02
☐ 31 Kirby Puckett WS7	.45	.20	.06
☐ 32 Greg Gagne WS7	.07	.03	.01
☐ 33 Frank Viola WS-MVP	.12	.05	.02

1989 Woolworth's Highlights

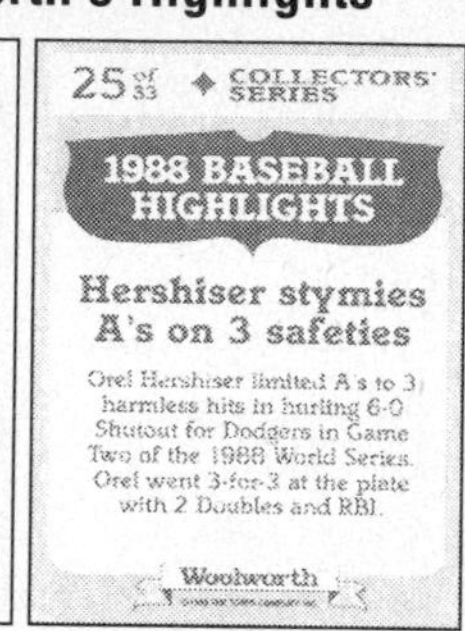

The 1989 Woolworth's Highlights set contains 33 standard-size (2 1/2" by 3 1/2") glossy cards. The fronts have red and white borders. The vertically oriented backs are yellow and red, and describe highlights from the 1988 season including the World Series. The cards were distributed through Woolworth stores as a boxed set.

	MT	EX-MT	VG
COMPLETE SET (33)	3.50	1.55	.45
COMMON PLAYER (1-33)	.07	.03	.01
☐ 1 Jose Canseco	.50	.23	.06
☐ 2 Kirk Gibson	.15	.07	.02
☐ 3 Frank Viola	.12	.05	.02
☐ 4 Orel Hershiser	.15	.07	.02
☐ 5 Walt Weiss	.12	.05	.02
☐ 6 Chris Sabo	.25	.11	.03
☐ 7 George Bell	.10	.05	.01
☐ 8 Wade Boggs	.35	.16	.04
☐ 9 Tom Browning	.10	.05	.01
☐ 10 Gary Carter	.20	.09	.03
☐ 11 Andre Dawson	.25	.11	.03
☐ 12 John Franco	.10	.05	.01
☐ 13 Randy Johnson	.15	.07	.02
☐ 14 Doug Jones	.07	.03	.01
☐ 15 Kevin McReynolds	.10	.05	.01
☐ 16 Gene Nelson	.07	.03	.01
☐ 17 Jeff Reardon	.15	.07	.02
☐ 18 Pat Tabler	.07	.03	.01
☐ 19 Tim Belcher	.10	.05	.01
☐ 20 Dennis Eckersley	.15	.07	.02
☐ 21 Orel Hershiser	.15	.07	.02
☐ 22 Gregg Jefferies	.35	.16	.04
☐ 23 Jose Canseco	.50	.23	.06
☐ 24 Kirk Gibson	.15	.07	.02
☐ 25 Orel Hershiser	.15	.07	.02
☐ 26 Mike Marshall	.10	.05	.01
☐ 27 Mark McGwire	.40	.18	.05
☐ 28 Rick Honeycutt	.07	.03	.01
☐ 29 Tim Belcher	.10	.05	.01
☐ 30 Jay Howell	.07	.03	.01
☐ 31 Mickey Hatcher	.07	.03	.01
☐ 32 Mike Davis	.07	.03	.01
☐ 33 Orel Hershiser	.15	.07	.02

1990 Woolworth Highlights

The 1990 Woolworth set is a 33-card set highlighting some of the more important events of the 1989 season. This set which has standard-size cards, 2 1/2" by 3 1/2", is broken down between major award winners, career highlights, and post-season heroes. The first six cards of the set feature the award winners while the last 11 cards of the set feature post-season heroes.

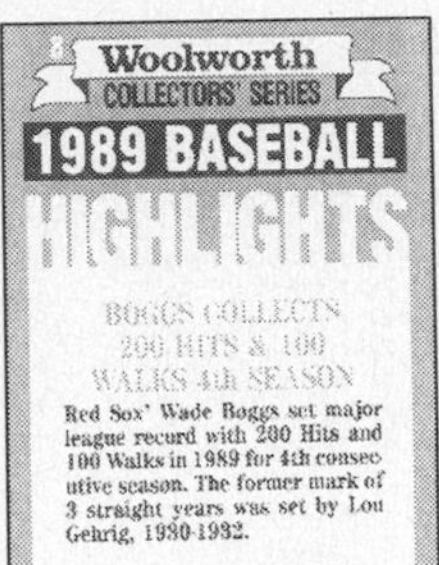

	MT	EX-MT	VG
COMPLETE SET (33)	3.50	1.55	.45
COMMON PLAYER (1-33)	.07	.03	.01
☐ 1 Robin Yount MVP	.40	.18	.05
☐ 2 Kevin Mitchell MVP	.20	.09	.03
☐ 3 Bret Saberhagen CY	.15	.07	.02
☐ 4 Mark Davis CY	.07	.03	.01
☐ 5 Gregg Olson ROY	.15	.07	.02
☐ 6 Jerome Walton ROY	.10	.05	.01
☐ 7 Bert Blyleven	.10	.05	.01
☐ 8 Wade Boggs	.40	.18	.05
☐ 9 George Brett	.40	.18	.05
☐ 10 Vince Coleman	.15	.07	.02
☐ 11 Andre Dawson	.25	.11	.03
☐ 12 Dwight Evans	.10	.05	.01
☐ 13 Carlton Fisk	.25	.11	.03
☐ 14 Rickey Henderson	.40	.18	.05
☐ 15 Dale Murphy	.25	.11	.03
☐ 16 Eddie Murray	.30	.14	.04
☐ 17 Jeff Reardon	.15	.07	.02
☐ 18 Rick Reuschel	.07	.03	.01
☐ 19 Cal Ripken	.50	.23	.06
☐ 20 Nolan Ryan	.75	.35	.09
☐ 21 Ryne Sandberg	.50	.23	.06
☐ 22 Robin Yount	.40	.18	.05
☐ 23 Rickey Henderson	.40	.18	.05
☐ 24 Will Clark	.45	.20	.06
☐ 25 Dave Stewart	.10	.05	.01
☐ 26 Walt Weiss	.10	.05	.01
☐ 27 Mike Moore	.07	.03	.01
☐ 28 Terry Steinbach	.10	.05	.01
☐ 29 Dave Henderson	.07	.03	.01
☐ 30 Matt Williams	.20	.09	.03
☐ 31 Rickey Henderson	.40	.18	.05
☐ 32 Kevin Mitchell	.20	.09	.03
☐ 33 Dave Stewart	.10	.05	.01

1991 Woolworth Highlights

Topps produced this 33-card boxed set for Woolworth stores. The standard size (2 1/2" by 3 1/2") cards feature glossy color player photos on the fronts, with yellow borders on a white card face. The backs are printed in red, black, and white, and commemorate outstanding achievements of the players featured on the cards. The set can be subdivided as follows: MVPs (1-2), Cy Young winners (3-4), ROYs (5-6), '90 highlights in alphabetical order (7-22), playoff MVPs (23-24), and World Series action in chronological order (25-33). The cards are numbered on the back.

	MT	EX-MT	VG
COMPLETE SET (33)	3.50	1.55	.45
COMMON PLAYER (1-33)	.07	.03	.01
☐ 1 Barry Bonds	.35	.16	.04
☐ 2 Rickey Henderson (Bat on shoulder)	.35	.16	.04
☐ 3 Doug Drabek	.15	.07	.02
☐ 4 Bob Welch	.10	.05	.01
☐ 5 Dave Justice	.50	.23	.06
☐ 6 Sandy Alomar Jr.	.10	.05	.01
☐ 7 Bert Blyleven	.10	.05	.01
☐ 8 George Brett	.35	.16	.04
☐ 9 Andre Dawson	.25	.11	.03
☐ 10 Dwight Evans	.10	.05	.01
☐ 11 Alex Fernandez	.15	.07	.02
☐ 12 Carlton Fisk	.25	.11	.03
☐ 13 Kevin Maas	.15	.07	.02
☐ 14 Dale Murphy	.25	.11	.03
☐ 15 Eddie Murray	.30	.14	.04
☐ 16 Dave Parker	.10	.05	.01
☐ 17 Jeff Reardon	.15	.07	.02
☐ 18 Cal Ripken	.50	.23	.06
☐ 19 Nolan Ryan	.60	.25	.08
☐ 20 Ryne Sandberg	.50	.23	.06
☐ 21 Bobby Thigpen	.07	.03	.01
☐ 22 Robin Yount	.35	.16	.04
☐ 23 Rob Dibble and Randy Myers	.10	.05	.01
☐ 24 Dave Stewart	.10	.05	.01
☐ 25 Eric Davis	.20	.09	.03
☐ 26 Rickey Henderson (Running bases)	.35	.16	.04
☐ 27 Billy Hatcher	.07	.03	.01
☐ 28 Joe Oliver	.07	.03	.01
☐ 29 Chris Sabo	.15	.07	.02
☐ 30 Barry Larkin	.20	.09	.03
☐ 31 Jose Rijo (Pitching Game 4)	.10	.05	.01
☐ 32 Reds Celebrate (1990 World Champions)	.10	.05	.01
☐ 33 Jose Rijo World Series MVP	.10	.05	.01

1950-56 W576 Callahan HOF

The cards in this 82-card set measure approximately 1 3/4" by 2 1/2". The 1950-56 Callahan Hall of Fame set was issued over a number of years at the Baseball Hall of Fame museum in Cooperstown, New York. New cards were added to the set each year when new members were inducted into the Hall of Fame. The cards with (2) in the checklist exist with two different biographies. The year of each card's first inclusion in the set is also given in parentheses; those not listed parenthetically below were issued in 1950 as well as in all the succeeding years and are hence the most common. Naturally the supply of cards is directly related to how many years a player was included in the set; cards that were not issued until 1955 are much scarcer than those printed all the years between 1950 and 1956. The catalog designation is W576. One frequently finds "complete" sets in the original box; take care to investigate the year of issue, the set may be complete in the sense of all the cards issued up to a certain year, but not all 82 cards below. For example, a "complete" 1950 set would obviously not include any of the cards marked below with ('52), ('54), or ('55) as none of those cards existed in 1950 since those respective players had not yet been inducted. The complete set price below refers to a set including all 83 cards below. Since the cards are unnumbered, they are numbered below for reference alphabetically by player's name.

	NRMT	VG-E	GOOD
COMPLETE SET (83)	700.00	325.00	90.00
COMMON PLAYER ('50)	3.00	1.35	.40
COMMON PLAYER ('52)	3.50	1.55	.45
COMMON PLAYER ('54)	4.00	1.80	.50
COMMON PLAYER ('55)	6.00	2.70	.75
☐ 1 Grover Alexander	4.00	1.80	.50
☐ 2 Cap Anson	3.00	1.35	.40
☐ 3 Frank Baker '55	6.00	2.70	.75
☐ 4 Edward Barrow '54	4.00	1.80	.50
☐ 5 Chief Bender (2) '54	4.00	1.80	.50
☐ 6 Roger Bresnahan	3.00	1.35	.40
☐ 7 Dan Brouthers	3.00	1.35	.40
☐ 8 Mordecai Brown	3.00	1.35	.40
☐ 9 Morgan Bulkeley	3.00	1.35	.40
☐ 10 Jesse Burkett	3.00	1.35	.40
☐ 11 Alexander Cartwright	3.00	1.35	.40
☐ 12 Henry Chadwick	3.00	1.35	.40
☐ 13 Frank Chance	3.00	1.35	.40
☐ 14 Happy Chandler '52	40.00	18.00	5.00
☐ 15 Jack Chesbro	3.00	1.35	.40
☐ 16 Fred Clarke	3.00	1.35	.40
☐ 17 Ty Cobb	60.00	27.00	7.50
☐ 18A Mickey Cochran ERR (Sic, Cochrane)	6.00	2.70	.75
☐ 18B Mickey Cochrane COR	30.00	13.50	3.80
☐ 19 Eddie Collins (2)	3.00	1.35	.40
☐ 20 Jimmie Collins	3.00	1.35	.40
☐ 21 Charles Comiskey	3.00	1.35	.40
☐ 22 Tom Connolly '54	4.00	1.80	.50
☐ 23 Candy Cummings	3.00	1.35	.40
☐ 24 Dizzy Dean '54	20.00	9.00	2.50
☐ 25 Ed Delahanty	3.00	1.35	.40
☐ 26 Bill Dickey '54 (2)	10.00	4.50	1.25
☐ 27 Joe DiMaggio '55	125.00	57.50	15.50
☐ 28 Hugh Duffy	3.00	1.35	.40
☐ 29 Johnny Evers	3.00	1.35	.40
☐ 30 Buck Ewing	3.00	1.35	.40
☐ 31 Jimmie Foxx	6.00	2.70	.75
☐ 32 Frank Frisch	3.00	1.35	.40
☐ 33 Lou Gehrig	60.00	27.00	7.50
☐ 34 Charles Gehringer	4.00	1.80	.50
☐ 35 Clark Griffith	3.00	1.35	.40
☐ 36 Lefty Grove	4.50	2.00	.55
☐ 37 Gabby Hartnett '55	6.00	2.70	.75
☐ 38 Harry Heilmann '52	3.50	1.55	.45
☐ 39 Rogers Hornsby	6.00	2.70	.75
☐ 40 Carl Hubbell	3.00	1.35	.40
☐ 41 Hughie Jennings	3.00	1.35	.40
☐ 42 Ban Johnson	3.00	1.35	.40
☐ 43 Walter Johnson	10.00	4.50	1.25
☐ 44 Willie Keeler	3.00	1.35	.40
☐ 45 Mike Kelly	3.00	1.35	.40
☐ 46 Bill Klem '54	4.50	2.00	.55
☐ 47 Napoleon Lajoie	4.50	2.00	.55
☐ 48 Kenesaw Landis	3.00	1.35	.40
☐ 49 Ted Lyons '55	6.00	2.70	.75
☐ 50 Connie Mack	3.00	1.35	.40
☐ 51 Rabbit Maranville '54	4.50	2.00	.55
☐ 52 Christy Mathewson	10.00	4.50	1.25
☐ 53 Tommy McCarthy	3.00	1.35	.40
☐ 54 Joe McGinnity	3.00	1.35	.40
☐ 55 John McGraw	3.00	1.35	.40
☐ 56 Kid Nichols	3.00	1.35	.40
☐ 57 Jim O'Rourke	3.00	1.35	.40
☐ 58 Mel Ott	4.00	1.80	.50
☐ 59 Herb Pennock	3.00	1.35	.40
☐ 60 Eddie Plank	3.00	1.35	.40
☐ 61 Charles Radbourne	3.00	1.35	.40
☐ 62 Wilbert Robinson	3.00	1.35	.40
☐ 63 Babe Ruth	100.00	45.00	12.50
☐ 64 Ray Schalk '55	6.00	2.70	.75
☐ 65 Al Simmons '54	4.50	2.00	.55
☐ 66 George Sisler (2)	3.00	1.35	.40
☐ 67 Albert G. Spalding	3.00	1.35	.40
☐ 68 Tris Speaker	4.50	2.00	.55
☐ 69 Bill Terry '54	6.00	2.70	.75
☐ 70 Joe Tinker	3.00	1.35	.40
☐ 71 Pie Traynor	3.00	1.35	.40
☐ 72 Dazzy Vance '55	6.00	2.70	.75
☐ 73 Rube Waddell	3.00	1.35	.40
☐ 74 Hans Wagner	10.00	4.50	1.25
☐ 75 Bobby Wallace '54	6.00	2.70	.75
☐ 76 Ed Walsh	3.00	1.35	.40
☐ 77 Paul Waner '52	5.00	2.30	.60
☐ 78 George Wright	3.00	1.35	.40
☐ 79 Harry Wright '54	4.50	2.00	.55
☐ 80 Cy Young	6.00	2.70	.75
☐ 81 Museum Interior '54 (2)	5.00	2.30	.60
☐ 82 Museum Exterior '54 (2)	5.00	2.30	.60

1955 W605 Robert Gould

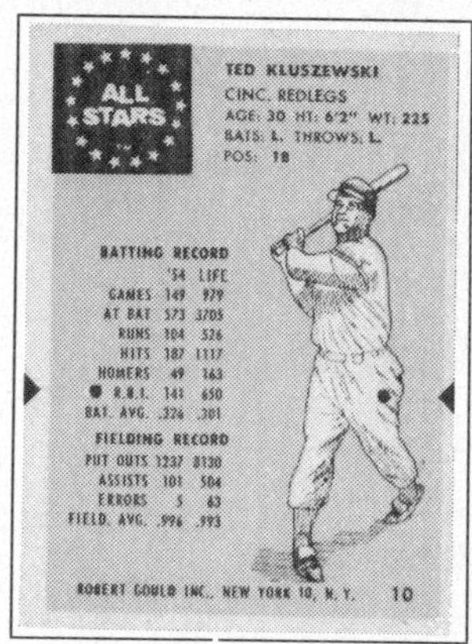

The cards in this 28-card set measure 2 1/2" by 3 1/2". The 1955 Robert F. Gould set of black and white on green cards were toy store cardboard holders for small plastic statues. The statues were attached to the card by a rubber band through two holes on the side of the card. The catalog designation is W605. The cards are numbered in the bottom right corner of the obverse and are blank-backed.

	NRMT	VG-E	GOOD
COMPLETE SET (28)	1500.00	700.00	190.00
COMMON PLAYER (1-28)	30.00	13.50	3.80
☐ 1 Willie Mays	375.00	170.00	47.50
☐ 2 Gus Zernial	30.00	13.50	3.80
☐ 3 Red Schoendienst	90.00	40.00	11.50
☐ 4 Chico Carrasquel	30.00	13.50	3.80
☐ 5 Jim Hegan	30.00	13.50	3.80
☐ 6 Curt Simmons	35.00	16.00	4.40
☐ 7 Bob Porterfield	30.00	13.50	3.80
☐ 8 Jim Busby	30.00	13.50	3.80
☐ 9 Don Mueller	30.00	13.50	3.80
☐ 10 Ted Kluszewski	60.00	27.00	7.50
☐ 11 Ray Boone	30.00	13.50	3.80
☐ 12 Smoky Burgess	35.00	16.00	4.40
☐ 13 Bob Rush	30.00	13.50	3.80
☐ 14 Early Wynn	90.00	40.00	11.50
☐ 15 Bill Bruton	30.00	13.50	3.80
☐ 16 Gus Bell	30.00	13.50	3.80
☐ 17 Jim Finigan	30.00	13.50	3.80
☐ 18 Granny Hamner	30.00	13.50	3.80
☐ 19 Hank Thompson	35.00	16.00	4.40
☐ 20 Joe Coleman	30.00	13.50	3.80
☐ 21 Don Newcombe	50.00	23.00	6.25
☐ 22 Richie Ashburn	75.00	34.00	9.50
☐ 23 Bobby Thomson	40.00	18.00	5.00
☐ 24 Sid Gordon	30.00	13.50	3.80
☐ 25 Gerry Coleman	30.00	13.50	3.80
☐ 26 Ernie Banks	175.00	80.00	22.00
☐ 27 Billy Pierce	40.00	18.00	5.00
☐ 28 Mel Parnell	35.00	16.00	4.40

1989 Yankees Score Nat West

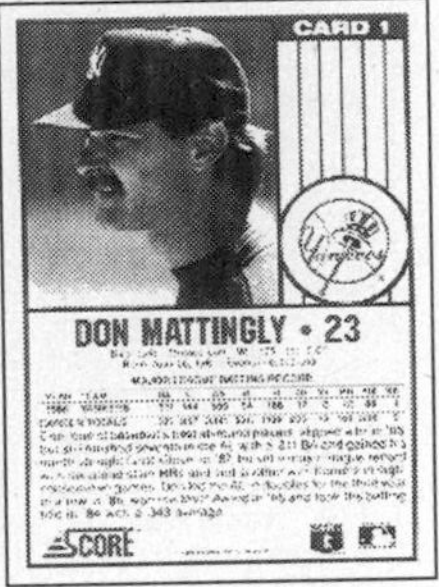

The 1989 Score National Westminster Bank New York Yankees set features 33 standard-size (2 1/2" by 3 1/2") cards. The fronts and backs are navy; the backs have color mug shots, 1988 and career stats. The set was given away at a 1989 Yankees' home game.

	MT	EX-MT	VG
COMPLETE SET (33)	18.00	8.00	2.30
COMMON PLAYER (1-33)	.35	.16	.04
☐ 1 Don Mattingly	2.50	1.15	.30
☐ 2 Steve Sax	.75	.35	.09
☐ 3 Alvaro Espinoza	.35	.16	.04
☐ 4 Luis Polonia	.75	.35	.09
☐ 5 Jesse Barfield	.45	.20	.06
☐ 6 Dave Righetti	.45	.20	.06
☐ 7 Dave Winfield	1.50	.65	.19
☐ 8 John Candelaria	.35	.16	.04
☐ 9 Wayne Tolleson	.35	.16	.04
☐ 10 Ken Phelps	.35	.16	.04
☐ 11 Rafael Santana	.35	.16	.04
☐ 12 Don Slaught	.35	.16	.04
☐ 13 Mike Pagliarulo	.45	.20	.06
☐ 14 Lance McCullers	.35	.16	.04
☐ 15 Dave LaPoint	.35	.16	.04
☐ 16 Dale Mohorcic	.35	.16	.04
☐ 17 Steve Balboni	.35	.16	.04
☐ 18 Roberto Kelly	1.00	.45	.13
☐ 19 Andy Hawkins	.35	.16	.04
☐ 20 Mel Hall	.60	.25	.08
☐ 21 Tom Brookens	.35	.16	.04
☐ 22 Deion Sanders	2.50	1.15	.30
☐ 23 Richard Dotson	.35	.16	.04
☐ 24 Lee Guetterman	.35	.16	.04
☐ 25 Bob Geren	.35	.16	.04
☐ 26 Jimmy Jones	.35	.16	.04
☐ 27 Chuck Cary	.35	.16	.04
☐ 28 Ron Guidry	.60	.25	.08
☐ 29 Hal Morris	1.25	.55	.16
☐ 30 Clay Parker	.35	.16	.04
☐ 31 Dallas Green MG	.35	.16	.04
☐ 32 Thurman Munson MEM	3.00	1.35	.40
☐ 33 Yankees Team Card	.75	.35	.09

1990 Yankees Score Nat West

1990 Score National Westminster Bank Yankees is a 32-card, standard-size (2 1/2" by 3 1/2") set featuring members of the 1990 New York Yankees. This set also has a special Billy Martin memorial card which honored the late Yankee manager who died in a truck accident on 12/25/89.

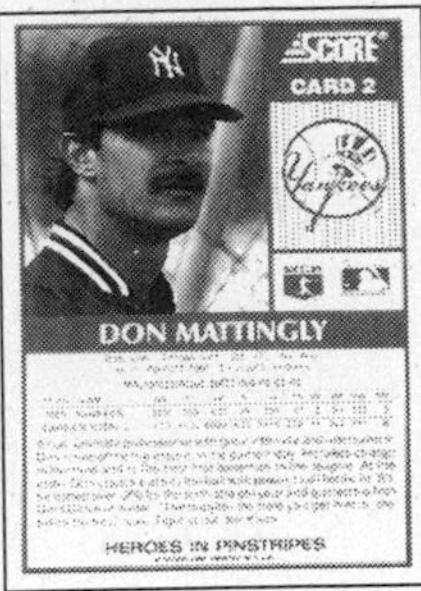

	MT	EX-MT	VG
COMPLETE SET (32)	13.50	6.00	1.70
COMMON PLAYER (1-32)	.35	.16	.04
☐ 1 Stump Merrill MG	.45	.20	.06
☐ 2 Don Mattingly	1.50	.65	.19
☐ 3 Steve Sax	.60	.25	.08
☐ 4 Alvaro Espinoza	.35	.16	.04
☐ 5 Jesse Barfield	.45	.20	.06
☐ 6 Roberto Kelly	.90	.40	.11
☐ 7 Mel Hall	.60	.25	.08
☐ 8 Claudell Washington	.45	.20	.06
☐ 9 Bob Geren	.35	.16	.04
☐ 10 Jim Leyritz	.45	.20	.06
☐ 11 Pascual Perez	.45	.20	.06
☐ 12 Dave LaPoint	.35	.16	.04
☐ 13 Tim Leary	.35	.16	.04
☐ 14 Mike Witt	.35	.16	.04
☐ 15 Chuck Cary	.35	.16	.04
☐ 16 Dave Righetti	.45	.20	.06
☐ 17 Lee Guetterman	.35	.16	.04
☐ 18 Andy Hawkins	.35	.16	.04
☐ 19 Greg Cadaret	.35	.16	.04
☐ 20 Eric Plunk	.35	.16	.04
☐ 21 Jimmy Jones	.35	.16	.04
☐ 22 Deion Sanders	1.50	.65	.19
☐ 23 Jeff D. Robinson	.35	.16	.04
☐ 24 Matt Nokes	.45	.20	.06
☐ 25 Steve Balboni	.35	.16	.04
☐ 26 Wayne Tolleson	.35	.16	.04
☐ 27 Randy Velarde	.35	.16	.04
☐ 28 Rick Cerone	.35	.16	.04
☐ 29 Alan Mills	.60	.25	.08
☐ 30 Billy Martin MEM	.75	.35	.09
☐ 31 Stadium Card	.35	.16	.04
☐ 32 All-Time Yankee Record	.35	.16	.04

1992 Yankee WIZ All-Stars

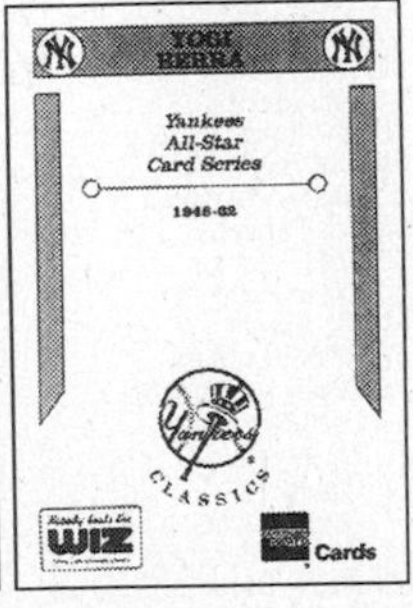

This 86-card set was sponsored by WIZ Home Entertainment Centers and American Express. The set was issued on five 15-card sheets and one 11-card title sheet, all measuring approximately 10" by 9". The perforated sheets yielded cards measuring approximately 2" by 3". The fronts have black-and-white action and posed shots of the players on a white background enhanced with a blue bridge design. The player's name appears in a blue bordered box at the bottom. The team logo in the upper left corner completes the card face. The backs have blue lettering and include the player's name and years with the team. The team and sponsor logos are also on the back. The cards are unnumbered and checklisted below in alphabetical order.

	MT	EX-MT	VG
COMPLETE SET (86)	12.50	5.75	1.55
COMMON PLAYER (1-86)	.15	.07	.02
☐ 1 Luis Arroyo	.15	.07	.02
☐ 2 Hank Bauer	.20	.09	.03
☐ 3 Yogi Berra	.50	.23	.06
☐ 4 Bobby Bonds	.20	.09	.03
☐ 5 Ernie Bonham	.15	.07	.02
☐ 6 Hank Borowy	.15	.07	.02
☐ 7 Jim Bouton	.20	.09	.03
☐ 8 Tommy Byrne	.15	.07	.02
☐ 9 Chris Chambliss	.20	.09	.03
☐ 10 Spud Chandler	.20	.09	.03
☐ 11 Ben Chapman	.15	.07	.02
☐ 12 Jim Coates	.15	.07	.02
☐ 13 Jerry Coleman	.15	.07	.02
☐ 14 Frank Crosetti	.20	.09	.03
☐ 15 Ron Davis	.15	.07	.02
☐ 16 Bucky Dent	.20	.09	.03
☐ 17 Bill Dickey	.30	.14	.04
☐ 18 Joe DiMaggio	1.00	.45	.13
☐ 19 Al Downing	.15	.07	.02
☐ 20 Ryne Duren	.20	.09	.03
☐ 21 Whitey Ford	.40	.18	.05
☐ 22 Lou Gehrig	.90	.40	.11
☐ 23 Lefty Gomez	.30	.14	.04
☐ 24 Joe Gordon	.20	.09	.03
☐ 25 Rich Gossage	.20	.09	.03
☐ 26 Bob Grim	.15	.07	.02
☐ 27 Ron Guidry	.20	.09	.03
☐ 28 Rollie Hemsley	.15	.07	.02
☐ 29 Rickey Henderson	.30	.14	.04
☐ 30 Tommy Henrich	.20	.09	.03
☐ 31 Elston Howard	.20	.09	.03
☐ 32 Catfish Hunter	.30	.14	.04
☐ 33 Reggie Jackson	.45	.20	.06
☐ 34 Tommy John	.20	.09	.03
☐ 35 Billy Johnson	.15	.07	.02
☐ 36 Charlie Keller	.15	.07	.02
☐ 37 Tony Kubek	.20	.09	.03
☐ 38 Johnny Kucks	.15	.07	.02
☐ 39 Tony Lazzeri	.30	.14	.04
☐ 40 Johnny Lindell	.15	.07	.02
☐ 41 Ed Lopat	.20	.09	.03
☐ 42 Sparky Lyle	.20	.09	.03
☐ 43 Mickey Mantle	1.25	.55	.16
☐ 44 Roger Maris	.60	.25	.08
☐ 45 Billy Martin	.40	.18	.05
☐ 46 Don Mattingly	.50	.23	.06
☐ 47 Gil McDougald	.20	.09	.03
☐ 48 George McQuinn	.15	.07	.02
☐ 49 Johnny Mize	.30	.14	.04
☐ 50 Thurman Munson	.30	.14	.04
☐ 51 Bobby Murcer	.20	.09	.03
☐ 52 Johnny Murphy	.15	.07	.02
☐ 53 Graig Nettles	.20	.09	.03
☐ 54 Phil Niekro	.25	.11	.03
☐ 55 Irv Noren	.15	.07	.02
☐ 56 Joe Page	.15	.07	.02
☐ 57 Monte Pearson	.15	.07	.02
☐ 58 Joe Pepitone	.15	.07	.02
☐ 59 Fritz Peterson	.15	.07	.02
☐ 60 Willie Randolph	.20	.09	.03
☐ 61 Vic Raschi	.20	.09	.03
☐ 62 Allie Reynolds	.20	.09	.03
☐ 63 Bobby Richardson	.20	.09	.03
☐ 64 Dave Righetti	.15	.07	.02
☐ 65 Mickey Rivers	.15	.07	.02
☐ 66 Phil Rizzuto	.30	.14	.04
☐ 67 Aaron Robinson	.15	.07	.02
☐ 68 Red Rolfe	.15	.07	.02
☐ 69 Buddy Rosar	.15	.07	.02
☐ 70 Red Ruffing	.30	.14	.04
☐ 71 Marius Russo	.15	.07	.02
☐ 72 Babe Ruth	1.25	.55	.16
☐ 73 Johnny Sain	.20	.09	.03
☐ 74 Scott Sanderson	.15	.07	.02
☐ 75 Steve Sax	.20	.09	.03
☐ 76 George Selkirk	.15	.07	.02
☐ 77 Bobby Shantz	.15	.07	.02
☐ 78 Spec Shea	.15	.07	.02
☐ 79 Bill Skowron	.20	.09	.03
☐ 80 Snuffy Stirnweiss	.15	.07	.02
☐ 81 Mel Stottlemyre	.20	.09	.03
☐ 82 Ralph Terry	.15	.07	.02
☐ 83 Tom Tresh	.15	.07	.02
☐ 84 Bob Turley	.20	.09	.03
☐ 85 Roy White	.15	.07	.02
☐ 86 Dave Winfield	.40	.18	.05

1992 Yankees WIZ HOF

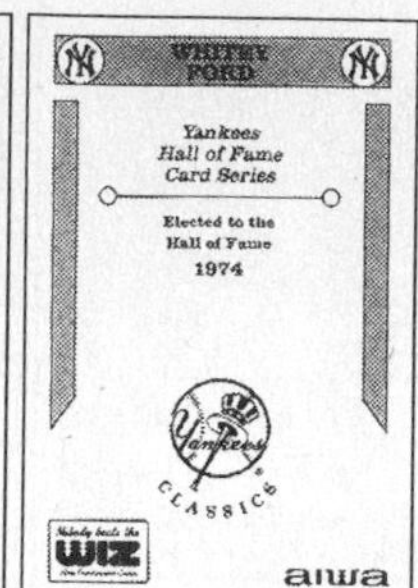

This 35-card set was sponsored by WIZ Home Entertainment Centers and Aiwa. The set was issued on two 15-card sheets and one five-card title sheet, all measuring approximately 10" by 9". The perforated sheets yielded cards measuring approximately 2" by 3". The fronts have black-and-white action and posed shots of the players on a white background enhanced with a blue bridge design. A white banner with the words "Hall of Fame" in the upper left corner completes the card face. The player's name appears in a blue bordered box at the bottom. The backs have blue lettering and include the player's name and the year he was inducted into the Hall of Fame. The team and sponsor logos are also on the back. The cards are unnumbered and checklisted below in alphabetical order.

	MT	EX-MT	VG
COMPLETE SET (35)	5.00	2.30	.60
COMMON PLAYER (1-35)	.15	.07	.02
☐ 1 Home Run Baker	.20	.09	.03
☐ 2 Edward G. Barrow	.15	.07	.02
☐ 3 Yogi Berra	.40	.18	.05
☐ 4 Frank Chance	.20	.09	.03
☐ 5 Jack Chesbro	.20	.09	.03
☐ 6 Earle Combs	.15	.07	.02
☐ 7 Stan Coveleski	.15	.07	.02
☐ 8 Bill Dickey	.30	.14	.04
☐ 9 Joe DiMaggio	1.00	.45	.13
☐ 10 Whitey Ford	.35	.16	.04
☐ 11 Lou Gehrig	.90	.40	.11
☐ 12 Lefty Gomez	.25	.11	.03
☐ 13 Clark C. Griffith	.15	.07	.02
☐ 14 Burleigh Grimes	.15	.07	.02
☐ 15 Bucky Harris	.15	.07	.02
☐ 16 Waite Hoyt	.15	.07	.02
☐ 17 Miller Huggins	.15	.07	.02
☐ 18 Catfish Hunter	.25	.11	.03
☐ 19 Willie Keller	.20	.09	.03
☐ 20 Tony Lazzeri	.30	.14	.04
☐ 21 Larry MacPhail	.25	.11	.03
☐ 22 Mickey Mantle	1.25	.55	.16
☐ 23 Joe McCarthy MG	.20	.09	.03
☐ 24 Johnny Mize	.25	.11	.03
☐ 25 Herb Pennock	.20	.09	.03
☐ 26 Gaylord Perry	.25	.11	.03
☐ 27 Branch Rickey	.20	.09	.03
☐ 28 Red Ruffing	.20	.09	.03
☐ 29 Babe Ruth	1.25	.55	.16
☐ 30 Joe Sewell	.15	.07	.02
☐ 31 Enos Slaughter	.20	.09	.03
☐ 32 Casey Stengel	.30	.14	.04
☐ 33 Dazzy Vance	.15	.07	.02
☐ 34 Paul Waner	.15	.07	.02
☐ 35 George M. Weiss	.20	.09	.03

1992 Yankees WIZ 60s

This 140-card set was sponsored by WIZ Home Entertainment Centers and American Express. The set was

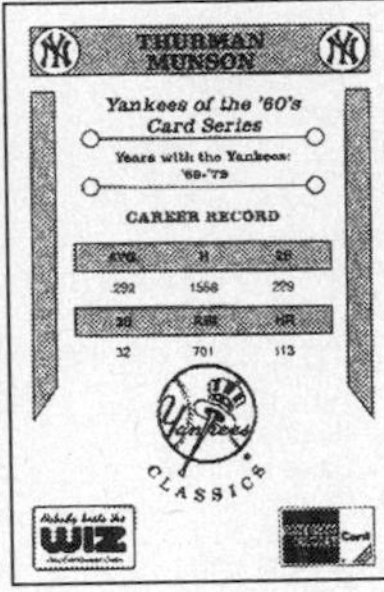

issued on 10" by 9" perforated sheets yielding cards measuring approximately 2" by 3". The fronts have black-and-white action and posed shots of the players on a white background enhanced with a blue bridge design. The player's name appears in a blue bordered box at the bottom. The backs have blue lettering and include the player's name, career record, and number of years with the Yankees. The team and sponsor logos are also on the back. The cards are unnumbered and checklisted below in alphabetical order.

	MT	EX-MT	VG
COMPLETE SET (140)	10.00	4.50	1.25
COMMON PLAYER (1-140)	.15	.07	.02
☐ 1 Jack Aker	.15	.07	.02
☐ 2 Ruben Amaro	.15	.07	.02
☐ 3 Luis Arroyo	.15	.07	.02
☐ 4 Stan Bahnsen	.15	.07	.02
☐ 5 Steve Barber	.15	.07	.02
☐ 6 Ray Barker	.15	.07	.02
☐ 7 Rich Beck	.15	.07	.02
☐ 8 Yogi Berra	.40	.18	.05
☐ 9 Johnny Blanchard	.15	.07	.02
☐ 10 Gil Blanco	.15	.07	.02
☐ 11 Ron Blomberg	.15	.07	.02
☐ 12 Len Boehmer	.15	.07	.02
☐ 13 Jim Bouton	.25	.11	.03
☐ 14 Clete Boyer	.20	.09	.03
☐ 15 Jim Brenneman	.15	.07	.02
☐ 16 Marshall Bridges	.15	.07	.02
☐ 17 Harry Bright	.15	.07	.02
☐ 18 Hal Brown	.15	.07	.02
☐ 19 Billy Bryan	.15	.07	.02
☐ 20 Bill Burbach	.15	.07	.02
☐ 21 Andy Carey	.15	.07	.02
☐ 22 Duke Carmel	.15	.07	.02
☐ 23 Bob Cerv	.15	.07	.02
☐ 24 Horace Clarke	.15	.07	.02
☐ 25 Tex Clevenger	.15	.07	.02
☐ 26 Lu Clinton	.15	.07	.02
☐ 27 Jim Coates	.15	.07	.02
☐ 28 Rocky Colavito	.35	.16	.04
☐ 29 Billy Cowan	.15	.07	.02
☐ 30 Bobby Cox	.25	.11	.03
☐ 31 Jack Cullen	.15	.07	.02
☐ 32 John Cumberland	.15	.07	.02
☐ 33 Bud Daley	.15	.07	.02
☐ 34 Joe DeMaestri	.15	.07	.02
☐ 35 Art Ditmar	.15	.07	.02
☐ 36 Al Downing	.20	.09	.03
☐ 37 Ryne Duren	.20	.09	.03
☐ 38 Doc Edwards	.15	.07	.02
☐ 39 John Ellis	.15	.07	.02
☐ 40 Frank Fernandez	.15	.07	.02
☐ 41 Mike Ferraro	.20	.09	.03
☐ 42 Whitey Ford	.40	.18	.05
☐ 43 Bob Friend	.20	.09	.03
☐ 44 John Gabler	.15	.07	.02
☐ 45 Billy Gardner	.15	.07	.02
☐ 46 Jake Gibbs	.20	.09	.03
☐ 47 Jesse Gonder	.15	.07	.02
☐ 48 Pedro Gonzalez	.15	.07	.02
☐ 49 Eli Grba	.15	.07	.02
☐ 50 Kent Hadley	.15	.07	.02
☐ 51 Bob Hale	.15	.07	.02
☐ 52 Jimmie Hall	.15	.07	.02
☐ 53 Steve Hamilton	.15	.07	.02
☐ 54 Mike Hegan	.20	.09	.03
☐ 55 Bill Henry	.15	.07	.02
☐ 56 Elston Howard	.30	.14	.04
☐ 57 Dick Howser	.20	.09	.03
☐ 58 Ken Hunt	.15	.07	.02
☐ 59 Johnny James	.15	.07	.02
☐ 60 Deron Johnson	.20	.09	.03
☐ 61 Ken Johnson	.15	.07	.02
☐ 62 Elvio Jimenez	.15	.07	.02
☐ 63 Mike Jurewicz	.15	.07	.02
☐ 64 Mike Kekich	.15	.07	.02
☐ 65 John Kennedy	.15	.07	.02
☐ 66 Jerry Kenney	.15	.07	.02
☐ 67 Fred Kipp	.15	.07	.02
☐ 68 Ron Klimkowski	.15	.07	.02
☐ 69 Andy Kosco	.15	.07	.02
☐ 70 Tony Kubek	.30	.14	.04
☐ 71 Bill Kunkel	.15	.07	.02
☐ 72 Phil Linz	.20	.09	.03
☐ 73 Dale Long	.15	.07	.02
☐ 74 Art Lopez	.15	.07	.02
☐ 75 Hector Lopez	.15	.07	.02
☐ 76 Jim Lyttle	.15	.07	.02
☐ 77 Duke Maas	.15	.07	.02
☐ 78 Mickey Mantle	1.25	.55	.16
☐ 79 Roger Maris	.60	.25	.08
☐ 80 Lindy McDaniel	.20	.09	.03
☐ 81 Danny McDevitt	.15	.07	.02
☐ 82 Dave McDonald	.15	.07	.02
☐ 83 Gil McDougald	.20	.09	.03
☐ 84 Tom Metcalf	.15	.07	.02
☐ 85 Bob Meyer	.15	.07	.02
☐ 86 Gene Michael	.20	.09	.03
☐ 87 Pete Mikkelsen	.15	.07	.02
☐ 88 John Miller	.15	.07	.02
☐ 89 Bill Monbouquette	.15	.07	.02
☐ 90 Archie Moore	.15	.07	.02
☐ 91 Ross Moschitto	.15	.07	.02
☐ 92 Thurman Munson	.30	.14	.04
☐ 93 Bobby Murcer	.25	.11	.03
☐ 94 Don Nottebart	.15	.07	.02
☐ 95 Nate Oliver	.15	.07	.02
☐ 96 Joe Pepitone	.20	.09	.03
☐ 97 Cecil Perkins	.15	.07	.02
☐ 98 Fritz Peterson	.15	.07	.02
☐ 99 Jim Pisoni	.15	.07	.02
☐ 100 Pedro Ramos	.15	.07	.02
☐ 101 Jack Reed	.15	.07	.02
☐ 102 Hal Reniff	.15	.07	.02
☐ 103 Roger Repoz	.15	.07	.02
☐ 104 Bobby Richardson	.30	.14	.04
☐ 105 Dale Roberts	.15	.07	.02
☐ 106 Bill Robinson	.20	.09	.03
☐ 107 Ellie Rodriguez	.15	.07	.02
☐ 108 Charlie Sands	.15	.07	.02
☐ 109 Bob Schmidt	.15	.07	.02
☐ 110 Dick Schofield	.15	.07	.02
☐ 111 Billy Shantz	.15	.07	.02
☐ 112 Bobby Shantz	.20	.09	.03
☐ 113 Rollie Sheldon	.15	.07	.02
☐ 114 Tom Shopay	.15	.07	.02
☐ 115 Bill Short	.15	.07	.02
☐ 116 Dick Simpson	.15	.07	.02
☐ 117 Bill Skowron	.20	.09	.03
☐ 118 Charley Smith	.15	.07	.02
☐ 119 Tony Solaita	.15	.07	.02
☐ 120 Bill Stafford	.15	.07	.02
☐ 121 Mel Stottlemyre	.20	.09	.03
☐ 122 Hal Stowe	.15	.07	.02
☐ 123 Fred Talbot	.15	.07	.02
☐ 124 Frank Tepedino	.15	.07	.02
☐ 125 Ralph Terry	.20	.09	.03
☐ 126 Lee Thomas	.20	.09	.03
☐ 127 Bobby Tiefenauer	.15	.07	.02
☐ 128 Bob Tillman	.15	.07	.02
☐ 129 Thad Tillotson	.15	.07	.02
☐ 130 Earl Torgeson	.15	.07	.02
☐ 131 Tom Tresh	.20	.09	.03
☐ 132 Bob Turley	.20	.09	.03
☐ 133 Elmer Valo	.15	.07	.02
☐ 134 Joe Verbanic	.15	.07	.02
☐ 135 Steve Whitaker	.15	.07	.02
☐ 136 Roy White	.20	.09	.03
☐ 137 Stan Williams	.20	.09	.03
☐ 138 Dooley Womack	.15	.07	.02
☐ 139 Ron Woods	.15	.07	.02
☐ 140 John Wyatt	.15	.07	.02

1992 Yankees WIZ 70s

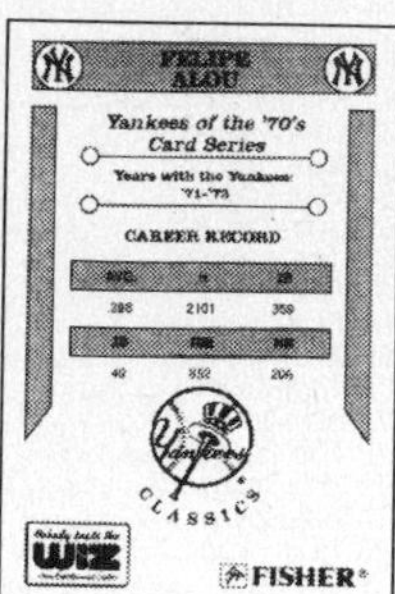

This 172-card set was sponsored by WIZ Home Entertainment Centers and Fisher. The set was issued on 10" by 9" perforated sheets yielding cards measuring approximately 2" by 3". The fronts have black-and-white action and posed shots of the players on a white background enhanced with a blue bridge design. The player's name appears in a blue bordered box at the bottom. The backs have blue lettering and include the player's name, career record, and number of years with the Yankees. The team and sponsor logos are also on the back. The cards are unnumbered and checklisted below in alphabetical order.

	MT	EX-MT	VG
COMPLETE SET (172)	11.00	4.90	1.40
COMMON PLAYER (1-172)	.15	.07	.02
☐ 1 Jack Aker	.15	.07	.02
☐ 2 Doyle Alexander	.20	.09	.03
☐ 3 Bernie Allen	.15	.07	.02
☐ 4 Sandy Alomar	.20	.09	.03
☐ 5 Felipe Alou	.25	.11	.03
☐ 6 Matty Alou	.20	.09	.03
☐ 7 Dell Alston	.15	.07	.02
☐ 8 Rick Anderson	.15	.07	.02
☐ 9 Stan Bahnsen	.15	.07	.02
☐ 10 Frank Baker	.15	.07	.02
☐ 11 Jim Beattie	.15	.07	.02
☐ 12 Fred Beene	.15	.07	.02
☐ 13 Juan Beniquez	.15	.07	.02
☐ 14 Dave Bergman	.15	.07	.02
☐ 15 Juan Bernhardt	.15	.07	.02
☐ 16 Rick Bladt	.15	.07	.02
☐ 17 Paul Blair	.15	.07	.02
☐ 18 Wade Blasingame	.15	.07	.02
☐ 19 Steve Blateric	.15	.07	.02
☐ 20 Curt Blefary	.20	.09	.03
☐ 21 Ron Blomberg	.20	.09	.03
☐ 22 Len Boehmer	.15	.07	.02
☐ 23 Bobby Bonds	.25	.11	.03
☐ 24 Ken Brett	.15	.07	.02
☐ 25 Ed Brinkman	.15	.07	.02
☐ 26 Bobby Brown	.15	.07	.02
☐ 27 Bill Burbach	.15	.07	.02
☐ 28 Ray Burris	.20	.09	.03
☐ 29 Tom Buskey	.15	.07	.02
☐ 30 Johnny Callison	.20	.09	.03
☐ 31 Danny Cater	.15	.07	.02
☐ 32 Chris Chambliss	.20	.09	.03
☐ 33 Horace Clarke	.20	.09	.03
☐ 34 Ken Clay	.15	.07	.02
☐ 35 Al Closter	.15	.07	.02
☐ 36 Rich Coggins	.15	.07	.02
☐ 37 Loyd Colson	.15	.07	.02
☐ 38 Casey Cox	.15	.07	.02
☐ 39 John Cumberland	.15	.07	.02
☐ 40 Ron Davis	.15	.07	.02
☐ 41 Jim Deidel	.15	.07	.02
☐ 42 Rick Dempsey	.20	.09	.03
☐ 43 Bucky Dent	.25	.11	.03
☐ 44 Kerry Dineen	.15	.07	.02
☐ 45 Pat Dobson	.20	.09	.03
☐ 46 Brian Doyle	.15	.07	.02
☐ 47 Rawly Eastwick	.15	.07	.02
☐ 48 Dock Ellis	.15	.07	.02
☐ 49 John Ellis	.15	.07	.02
☐ 50 Ed Figueroa	.15	.07	.02
☐ 51 Oscar Gamble	.20	.09	.03
☐ 52 Damaso Garcia	.15	.07	.02
☐ 53 Rob Gardner	.15	.07	.02
☐ 54 Jake Gibbs	.20	.09	.03
☐ 55 Fernando Gonzalez	.15	.07	.02
☐ 56 Rich Gossage	.25	.11	.03
☐ 57 Larry Gowell	.15	.07	.02
☐ 58 Wayne Granger	.15	.07	.02
☐ 59 Mike Griffin	.15	.07	.02
☐ 60 Ron Guidry	.25	.11	.03
☐ 61 Brad Gulden	.15	.07	.02
☐ 62 Don Gullett	.20	.09	.03
☐ 63 Larry Gura	.20	.09	.03
☐ 64 Roger Hambright	.15	.07	.02
☐ 65 Steve Hamilton	.15	.07	.02
☐ 66 Ron Hansen	.15	.07	.02
☐ 67 Jim Hardin	.15	.07	.02
☐ 68 Jim Ray Hart	.20	.09	.03
☐ 69 Fran Healy	.15	.07	.02
☐ 70 Mike Heath	.15	.07	.02
☐ 71 Mike Hegan	.20	.09	.03
☐ 72 Elrod Hendricks	.15	.07	.02
☐ 73 Ed Herrmann	.15	.07	.02
☐ 74 Rich Hinton	.15	.07	.02
☐ 75 Ken Holtzman	.20	.09	.03
☐ 76 Don Hood	.15	.07	.02
☐ 77 Catfish Hunter	.30	.14	.04
☐ 78 Grant Jackson	.15	.07	.02
☐ 79 Reggie Jackson	.45	.20	.06
☐ 80 Tommy John	.30	.14	.04
☐ 81 Alex Johnson	.20	.09	.03
☐ 82 Cliff Johnson	.20	.09	.03
☐ 83 Jay Johnstone	.20	.09	.03
☐ 84 Darryl Jones	.15	.07	.02
☐ 85 Gary Jones	.15	.07	.02
☐ 86 Jim Kaat	.25	.11	.03
☐ 87 Bob Kammeyer	.15	.07	.02
☐ 88 Mike Kekich	.15	.07	.02
☐ 89 Jerry Kenney	.15	.07	.02
☐ 90 Dave Kingman	.25	.11	.03
☐ 91 Ron Klimkowski	.15	.07	.02
☐ 92 Steve Kline	.15	.07	.02
☐ 93 Mickey Klutts	.15	.07	.02
☐ 94 Hal Lanier	.20	.09	.03
☐ 95 Eddie Leon	.15	.07	.02
☐ 96 Terry Ley	.15	.07	.02
☐ 97 Paul Lindblad	.15	.07	.02
☐ 98 Gene Locklear	.15	.07	.02
☐ 99 Sparky Lyle	.25	.11	.03
☐ 100 Jim Lyttle	.15	.07	.02
☐ 101 Elliott Maddox	.15	.07	.02
☐ 102 Jim Magnuson	.15	.07	.02
☐ 103 Tippy Martinez	.20	.09	.03
☐ 104 Jim Mason	.15	.07	.02
☐ 105 Carlos May	.15	.07	.02
☐ 106 Rudy May	.15	.07	.02
☐ 107 Larry McCall	.15	.07	.02
☐ 108 Mike McCormick	.20	.09	.03
☐ 109 Lindy McDaniel	.20	.09	.03
☐ 110 Sam McDowell	.20	.09	.03
☐ 111 Rich McKinney	.15	.07	.02
☐ 112 George Medich	.15	.07	.02
☐ 113 Andy Messersmith	.20	.09	.03
☐ 114 Gene Michael	.20	.09	.03
☐ 115 Paul Mirabella	.15	.07	.02
☐ 116 Bobby Mitchell	.15	.07	.02
☐ 117 Gerry Moses	.15	.07	.02
☐ 118 Thurman Munson	.30	.14	.04
☐ 119 Bobby Murcer	.25	.11	.03
☐ 120 Larry Murray	.15	.07	.02
☐ 121 Jerry Narron	.15	.07	.02
☐ 122 Graig Nettles	.25	.11	.03
☐ 123 Bob Oliver	.15	.07	.02
☐ 124 Dave Pagan	.15	.07	.02
☐ 125 Gil Patterson	.15	.07	.02
☐ 126 Marty Perez	.15	.07	.02
☐ 127 Fritz Peterson	.15	.07	.02
☐ 128 Lou Piniella	.25	.11	.03
☐ 129 Dave Rajsich	.15	.07	.02
☐ 130 Domingo Ramos	.15	.07	.02
☐ 131 Lenny Randle	.15	.07	.02
☐ 132 Willie Randolph	.20	.09	.03
☐ 133 Dave Righetti	.20	.09	.03
☐ 134 Mickey Rivers	.20	.09	.03
☐ 135 Bruce Robinson	.15	.07	.02
☐ 136 Jim Roland	.15	.07	.02
☐ 137 Celerino Sanchez	.15	.07	.02
☐ 138 Rick Sawyer	.15	.07	.02
☐ 139 George Scott	.20	.09	.03
☐ 140 Duke Sims	.15	.07	.02
☐ 141 Roger Slagle	.15	.07	.02
☐ 142 Jim Spencer	.15	.07	.02
☐ 143 Charlie Spikes	.15	.07	.02

☐ 144 Roy Staiger	.15	.07	.02
☐ 145 Fred Stanley	.15	.07	.02
☐ 146 Bill Sudakis	.15	.07	.02
☐ 147 Ron Swoboda	.20	.09	.03
☐ 148 Frank Tepedino	.15	.07	.02
☐ 149 Stan Thomas	.15	.07	.02
☐ 150 Gary Thomasson	.15	.07	.02
☐ 151 Luis Tiant	.20	.09	.03
☐ 152 Dick Tidrow	.15	.07	.02
☐ 153 Rusty Torres	.15	.07	.02
☐ 154 Mike Torrez	.20	.09	.03
☐ 155 Cesar Tovar	.15	.07	.02
☐ 156 Cecil Upshaw	.15	.07	.02
☐ 157 Otto Velez	.15	.07	.02
☐ 158 Joe Verbanic	.15	.07	.02
☐ 159 Mike Wallace	.15	.07	.02
☐ 160 Danny Walton	.15	.07	.02
☐ 161 Pete Ward	.15	.07	.02
☐ 162 Gary Waslewski	.15	.07	.02
☐ 163 Dennis Werth	.15	.07	.02
☐ 164 Roy White	.20	.09	.03
☐ 165 Terry Whitfield	.15	.07	.02
☐ 166 Walt Williams	.15	.07	.02
☐ 167 Ron Woods	.15	.07	.02
☐ 168 Dick Woodson	.15	.07	.02
☐ 169 Ken Wright	.15	.07	.02
☐ 170 Jimmy Wynn	.20	.09	.03
☐ 171 Jim York	.15	.07	.02
☐ 172 George Zeber	.15	.07	.02

1992 Yankees WIZ 80s

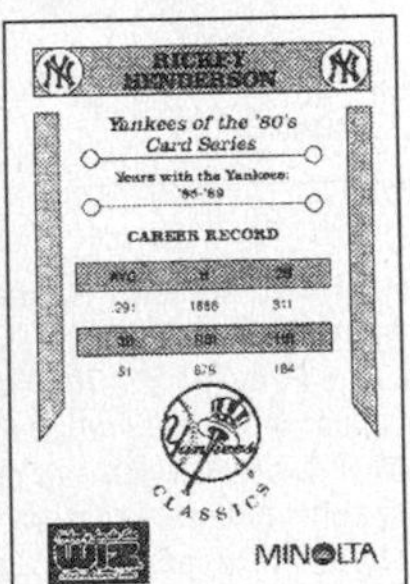

This 206-card set was sponsored by WIZ Home Entertainment Centers and Minolta. The set was issued on 10" by 9" perforated sheets yielding cards measuring approximately 2" by 3". The fronts have black-and-white action and posed shots of the players on a white background enhanced with a blue bridge design. The player's name appears in a blue bordered box at the bottom. The backs have blue lettering and include the player's name, career record, and number of years with the Yankees. The team and sponsor logos are also on the back. The cards are unnumbered and checklisted below in alphabetical order.

	MT	EX-MT	VG
COMPLETE SET (206)	12.50	5.75	1.55
COMMON PLAYER (1-206)	.15	.07	.02
☐ 1 Luis Aguayo	.15	.07	.02
☐ 2 Doyle Alexander	.20	.09	.03
☐ 3 Neil Allen	.20	.09	.03
☐ 4 Mike Armstrong	.15	.07	.02
☐ 5 Brad Arnsberg	.15	.07	.02
☐ 6 Tucker Ashford	.15	.07	.02
☐ 7 Steve Balboni	.20	.09	.03
☐ 8 Jesse Barfield	.20	.09	.03
☐ 9 Don Baylor	.25	.11	.03
☐ 10 Dale Berra	.15	.07	.02
☐ 11 Doug Bird	.15	.07	.02
☐ 12 Paul Blair	.20	.09	.03
☐ 13 Mike Blowers	.15	.07	.02
☐ 14 Juan Bonilla	.15	.07	.02
☐ 15 Rick Bordi	.15	.07	.02
☐ 16 Scott Bradley	.15	.07	.02
☐ 17 Marshall Brant	.15	.07	.02
☐ 18 Tom Brookens	.15	.07	.02
☐ 19 Bob Brower	.15	.07	.02
☐ 20 Bobby Brown	.15	.07	.02
☐ 21 Curt Brown	.15	.07	.02
☐ 22 Jay Buhner	.25	.11	.03
☐ 23 Marty Bystrom	.15	.07	.02
☐ 24 Greg Cadaret	.15	.07	.02
☐ 25 Bert Campaneris	.20	.09	.03
☐ 26 John Candelaria	.20	.09	.03
☐ 27 Chuck Cary	.15	.07	.02
☐ 28 Bill Castro	.15	.07	.02
☐ 29 Rick Cerone	.15	.07	.02
☐ 30 Chris Chambliss	.20	.09	.03
☐ 31 Clay Christiansen	.15	.07	.02
☐ 32 Jack Clark	.20	.09	.03
☐ 33 Pat Clements	.15	.07	.02
☐ 34 Dave Collins	.20	.09	.03
☐ 35 Don Cooper	.15	.07	.02
☐ 36 Henry Cotto	.15	.07	.02
☐ 37 Joe Cowley	.15	.07	.02
☐ 38 Jose Cruz	.20	.09	.03
☐ 39 Bobby Davidson	.15	.07	.02
☐ 40 Ron Davis	.15	.07	.02
☐ 41 Brian Dayett	.15	.07	.02
☐ 42 Ivan DeJesus	.15	.07	.02
☐ 43 Bucky Dent	.20	.09	.03
☐ 44 Jim Deshaies	.15	.07	.02
☐ 45 Orestes Destrade	.30	.14	.04
☐ 46 Brian Dorsett	.15	.07	.02
☐ 47 Richard Dotson	.20	.09	.03
☐ 48 Brian Doyle	.15	.07	.02
☐ 49 Doug Drabek	.30	.14	.04
☐ 50 Mike Easler	.15	.07	.02
☐ 51 Dave Eiland	.15	.07	.02
☐ 52 Roger Erickson	.15	.07	.02
☐ 53 Juan Espino	.15	.07	.02
☐ 54 Alvaro Espinoza	.15	.07	.02
☐ 55 Barry Evans	.15	.07	.02
☐ 56 Ed Figueroa	.15	.07	.02
☐ 57 Pete Filson	.15	.07	.02
☐ 58 Mike Fischlin	.15	.07	.02
☐ 59 Brian Fisher	.15	.07	.02
☐ 60 Tim Foli	.15	.07	.02
☐ 61 Ray Fontenot	.15	.07	.02
☐ 62 Barry Foote	.15	.07	.02
☐ 63 George Frazier	.15	.07	.02
☐ 64 Bill Fulton	.15	.07	.02
☐ 65 Oscar Gamble	.20	.09	.03
☐ 66 Bob Geren	.15	.07	.02
☐ 67 Rich Gossage	.20	.09	.03
☐ 68 Mike Griffin	.15	.07	.02
☐ 69 Ken Griffey	.20	.09	.03
☐ 70 Cecilio Guante	.15	.07	.02
☐ 71 Lee Guetterman	.15	.07	.02
☐ 72 Ron Guidry	.20	.09	.03
☐ 73 Brad Gulden	.15	.07	.02
☐ 74 Don Gullett	.20	.09	.03
☐ 75 Bill Gullickson	.20	.09	.03
☐ 76 Mel Hall	.25	.11	.03
☐ 77 Toby Harrah	.20	.09	.03
☐ 78 Ron Hassey	.20	.09	.03
☐ 79 Andy Hawkins	.20	.09	.03
☐ 80 Rickey Henderson	.35	.16	.04
☐ 81 Leo Hernandez	.15	.07	.02
☐ 82 Butch Hobson	.20	.09	.03
☐ 83 Al Holland	.15	.07	.02
☐ 84 Roger Holt	.15	.07	.02
☐ 85 Jay Howell	.20	.09	.03
☐ 86 Rex Hudler	.20	.09	.03
☐ 87 Charles Hudson	.15	.07	.02
☐ 88 Keith Hughes	.20	.09	.03
☐ 89 Reggie Jackson	.50	.23	.06
☐ 90 Stan Javier	.15	.07	.02
☐ 91 Stan Jefferson	.15	.07	.02
☐ 92 Tommy John	.25	.11	.03
☐ 93 Jimmy Jones	.15	.07	.02
☐ 94 Ruppert Jones	.15	.07	.02
☐ 95 Jim Kaat	.25	.11	.03
☐ 96 Curt Kaufman	.15	.07	.02
☐ 97 Roberto Kelly	.30	.14	.04
☐ 98 Steve Kemp	.20	.09	.03
☐ 99 Matt Keough	.15	.07	.02
☐ 100 Steve Kiefer	.15	.07	.02
☐ 101 Ron Kittle	.20	.09	.03
☐ 102 Dave LaPoint	.15	.07	.02
☐ 103 Marcus Lawton	.15	.07	.02
☐ 104 Joe Lefebvre	.15	.07	.02
☐ 105 Al Leiter	.15	.07	.02
☐ 106 Jim Lewis	.15	.07	.02
☐ 107 Bryan Little	.15	.07	.02
☐ 108 Tim Lollar	.15	.07	.02
☐ 109 Phil Lombardi	.15	.07	.02
☐ 110 Vic Mata	.15	.07	.02

☐ 111	Don Mattingly	.50	.23	.06
☐ 112	Rudy May	.15	.07	.02
☐ 113	John Mayberry	.20	.09	.03
☐ 114	Lee Mazzilli	.20	.09	.03
☐ 115	Lance McCullers	.15	.07	.02
☐ 116	Andy McGaffigan	.15	.07	.02
☐ 117	Lynn McGlothen	.15	.07	.02
☐ 118	Bobby Meacham	.15	.07	.02
☐ 119	Hensley Meulens	.25	.11	.03
☐ 120	Larry Milbourne	.15	.07	.02
☐ 121	Kevin Mmahat	.15	.07	.02
☐ 122	Dale Mohorcic	.15	.07	.02
☐ 123	John Montefusco	.15	.07	.02
☐ 124	Omar Moreno	.15	.07	.02
☐ 125	Mike Morgan	.20	.09	.03
☐ 126	Jeff Moronko	.15	.07	.02
☐ 127	Hal Morris	.25	.11	.03
☐ 128	Jerry Mumphrey	.15	.07	.02
☐ 129	Bobby Murcer	.20	.09	.03
☐ 130	Dale Murray	.15	.07	.02
☐ 131	Gene Nelson	.15	.07	.02
☐ 132	Joe Niekro	.20	.09	.03
☐ 133	Phil Niekro	.30	.14	.04
☐ 134	Scott Nielsen	.15	.07	.02
☐ 135	Otis Nixon	.25	.11	.03
☐ 136	Johnny Oates	.20	.09	.03
☐ 137	Mike O'Berry	.15	.07	.02
☐ 138	Rowland Office	.15	.07	.02
☐ 139	John Pacella	.15	.07	.02
☐ 140	Mike Pagliarulo	.15	.07	.02
☐ 141	Clay Parker	.15	.07	.02
☐ 142	Dan Pasqua	.15	.07	.02
☐ 143	Mike Patterson	.15	.07	.02
☐ 144	Hipolito Pena	.15	.07	.02
☐ 145	Gaylord Perry	.30	.14	.04
☐ 146	Ken Phelps	.15	.07	.02
☐ 147	Lou Piniella	.25	.11	.03
☐ 148	Eric Plunk	.15	.07	.02
☐ 149	Luis Polonia	.30	.14	.04
☐ 150	Alfonso Pulido	.15	.07	.02
☐ 151	Jamie Quirk	.15	.07	.02
☐ 152	Bobby Ramos	.15	.07	.02
☐ 153	Willie Randolph	.20	.09	.03
☐ 154	Dennis Rasmussen	.15	.07	.02
☐ 155	Shane Rawley	.15	.07	.02
☐ 156	Rick Reuschel	.20	.09	.03
☐ 157	Dave Revering	.15	.07	.02
☐ 158	Rick Rhoden	.15	.07	.02
☐ 159	Dave Righetti	.20	.09	.03
☐ 160	Jose Rijo	.20	.09	.03
☐ 161	Andre Robertson	.15	.07	.02
☐ 162	Bruce Robinson	.15	.07	.02
☐ 163	Aurelio Rodriguez	.15	.07	.02
☐ 164	Edwin Rodriguez	.15	.07	.02
☐ 165	Gary Roenicke	.15	.07	.02
☐ 166	Jerry Royster	.15	.07	.02
☐ 167	Lenn Sakata	.15	.07	.02
☐ 168	Mark Salas	.15	.07	.02
☐ 169	Billy Sample	.15	.07	.02
☐ 170	Deion Sanders	.50	.23	.06
☐ 171	Rafael Santana	.15	.07	.02
☐ 172	Steve Sax	.20	.09	.03
☐ 173	Don Schulze	.15	.07	.02
☐ 174	Rodney Scott	.15	.07	.02
☐ 175	Rod Scurry	.15	.07	.02
☐ 176	Dennis Sherrill	.15	.07	.02
☐ 177	Steve Shields	.15	.07	.02
☐ 179	Bob Shirley	.15	.07	.02
☐ 180	Joel Skinner	.15	.07	.02
☐ 181	Don Slaught	.20	.09	.03
☐ 182	Roy Smalley	.15	.07	.02
☐ 183	Keith Smith	.15	.07	.02
☐ 184	Eric Soderholm	.15	.07	.02
☐ 185	Jim Spencer	.15	.07	.02
☐ 186	Fred Stanley	.15	.07	.02
☐ 187	Dave Stegman	.15	.07	.02
☐ 188	Tim Stoddard	.15	.07	.02
☐ 189	Walt Terrell	.20	.09	.03
☐ 190	Bob Tewksbury	.30	.14	.04
☐ 191	Luis Tiant	.20	.09	.03
☐ 192	Wayne Tolleson	.15	.07	.02
☐ 193	Steve Trout	.15	.07	.02
☐ 194	Tom Underwood	.15	.07	.02
☐ 195	Randy Velarde	.15	.07	.02
☐ 196	Gary Ward	.15	.07	.02
☐ 197	Claudell Washington	.20	.09	.03
☐ 198	Bob Watson	.20	.09	.03
☐ 199	Dave Wehrmeister	.15	.07	.02
☐ 200	Dennis Werth	.15	.07	.02
☐ 201	Stefan Wever	.15	.07	.02
☐ 202	Ed Whitson	.15	.07	.02
☐ 203	Ted Wilborn	.15	.07	.02
☐ 204	Dave Winfield	.35	.16	.04
☐ 205	Butch Wynegar	.20	.09	.03
☐ 206	Paul Zuvella	.15	.07	.02

1992 Ziploc

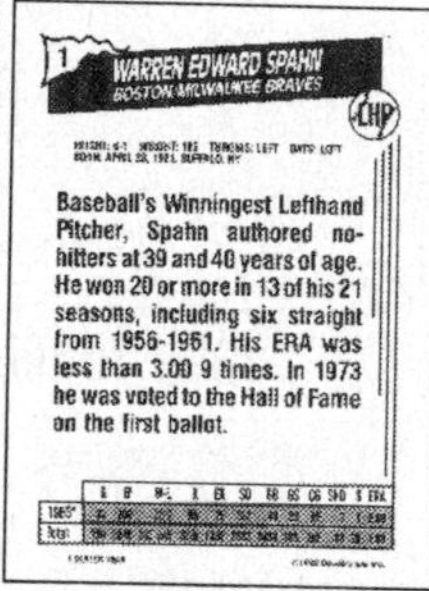

This 11-card set features posed player photos of many of the game's all-time greats. The cards measure the standard size (2 1/2" by 3 1/2"). The Ziploc logo appears diagonally in the upper left corner, while the player's name is printed in black in a bright-yellow stripe accented with red and blue stars at the bottom. The team logo is superimposed over the photo at the upper right. The back design displays the player's full name and team in a slightly diagonal red stripe at the top. A biography, career summary, and statistics are printed in medium blue on a white background. The set was available via a mail-in offer for 50 cents and two UPC's from Ziploc sandwich bags. Individual cards were found one per specially marked package. The cards are numbered on the back.

		MT	EX-MT	VG
COMPLETE SET (11)		7.50	3.40	.95
COMMON PLAYER (1-11)		.50	.23	.06
☐ 1	Warren Spahn	.75	.35	.09
☐ 2	Bob Gibson	.75	.35	.09
☐ 3	Rollie Fingers	.60	.25	.08
☐ 4	Carl Yastrzemski	.90	.40	.11
☐ 5	Brooks Robinson	.75	.35	.09
☐ 6	Pee Wee Reese	.75	.35	.09
☐ 7	Willie McCovey	.75	.35	.09
☐ 8	Willie Mays	1.25	.55	.16
☐ 9	Nellie Fox	.50	.23	.06
☐ 10	Yogi Berra	1.00	.45	.13
☐ 11	Hank Aaron	1.25	.55	.16

Acknowledgments

Each year we refine the process of developing the most accurate and up-to-date information for this book. I believe this year's Price Guide is our best yet. For that, you can thank all of the contributors nationwide (listed below) as well as our staff here in Dallas.

Part of this refining process involves an ever larger number of people and types of expertise on our home team.

For example, our company now boasts a substantial Technical Services team which has made (and is continuing to make) direct and important contributions to this work. Technical Services capably handled numerous technical details and provided able assistance in pricing for this edition of the annual guide. It is very difficult to be "accurate" — one can only do one's best. But this job is especially difficult since we're shooting at a moving target: Prices are fluctuating all the time. Having several full-time pricing experts has definitely proven to be better than just one, and I thank all of them for working together to provide you, our readers, with the most accurate prices possible.

That effort was directed by Technical Services manager Pepper Hastings.He was assisted by Technical Services assistant manager Mary Gregory, coordinator Grant Sandground, Price Guide analysts Theo Chen, Mike Hersh, Dan Hitt, Mary Huston, Rich Klein, Allan Muir, Bob Smith, Dave Sliepka, and Steve Smith. Analyst Tom Layberger played a major part in this year's book, working closely with our computer software development team to streamline the pricing process, allowing us to provide even more timely prices. Also contributing to our Technical Services functions were Peter Tepp and Todd Davis.

The price gathering and analytical talents of this fine group of hobbyists has helped make our Beckett team stronger, while making this guide and its companion monthly Price Guides more widely recognized as the hobby's most reliable and relied upon sources of pricing information.

Granted, the production of any book is a total staff effort. However, I owe special thanks to the members of our Book Team who demonstrated extraordinary contributions to this baseball book.

Scott Layton, assistant manager of Special Projects, served as point man in the demanding area of new set entry and was a key person in the organization of both technological and people resources for the book. He was ably assisted by Jana Threatt and Maria Neubauer, who ensured the proper administration of our contributor price guide surveys and performed various other tasks. Pricing analysts Theo Chen, Rich Klein, Mary Huston, Tom Layberger and Grant Sandground track the baseball card market year round, and their baseline analysis and careful proofreading were key contributions to the accuracy of this annual.

Our computer services team — technological experts Sammy Cantrell, Rich Olivieri and Dan Ferguson — spent months programming, testing and implementing new software to simplify the handling of thousands of prices that must be checked and updated for each edition of this book.

Therese Bellar and Lisa O'Neill contributed new designs and artwork to enhance readability. Airey Baringer spent many late-night hours testing new software, then paginating and typesetting the text layout. Mary Gonzalez-Davis was responsible for many of the card photos you see throughout the book, as well as overseeing paste-up. Production Manager Reed Poole offered his usual fine direction in providing resources and production talent. Tracy Hinton spent tireless hours on the phone attending to the wishes of our dealer advertisers under the direction of advertising manager Jeff Anthony. Once the ad specifications were delivered to our offices, John Marshall used his computer skills to turn raw copy into attractive display advertisements that were carefully proofed by Bruce Felps.

And overseeing it all, Managing Editor of Special Projects, Susan K. Elliott, set up initial schedules and ensured that deadlines were met, while looking for all the fine points to improve our process and presentation throughout the cycle.

This year's volume is the result of a great deal of diligence, hard work, and dedicated effort. It would not have been possible without the expert input and generous amount of time given by our many contributors. Our sincere thanks are extended to each and every one of you.

Those who have worked closely with us on this and many other books have again proven themselves invaluable — Johnny and Sandy Adams, Frank and Vivian Barning *(Baseball Hobby News)*, Chris Benjamin, Sy Berger (Topps), Levi Bleam, Peter Brennan, Card Collectors Co., Cartophilium (Andrew Pywowarczuk), Ira Cetron, Ric Chandgie, Barry Colla, Mike Cramer (Pacific Trading Cards),

MR. MINT

The Buying Machine

THE NO. 1 BUYER

in the hobby invites you to consider the following facts listed below when selling your collectibles

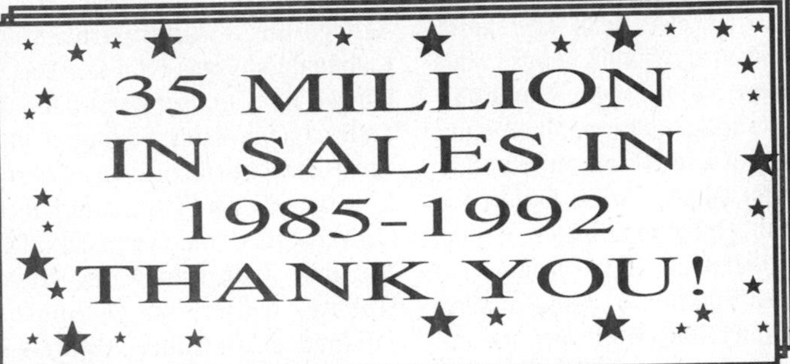

"Featured with an 8-page spread in the July 4th, 1988 issue of Sports Illustrated."

"Appeared nationally on ABC's Good Morning America with Joan Lunden and Joel Siegel."

PRESS CREDENTIALS:

Feature stories in such fine National magazines as Sports Illustrated February 1989, Money Magazine, Forbes Magazine, New York Magazine, Baseball Today, A.C. Delco's In Tune Magazine, Northwest Airlines Magazine, Globe, and in addition, major daily newspapers such as New York Times, New York Post, Star Ledger, Paterson News, Philadelphia Times, New York Daily News, New Jersey's Bergen Record, St. Petersburg Times, L.A. Times, USA Today, Honolulu Advertiser, NBC's Today Show, Topps Magazine, Assets Magazine, Ft. Lauderdale Press, Archie Comics, Japanese (Mono) and mentioned in hundreds of other baseball card related articles across the country.

Has appeared on National Television shows such as Good Morning America, CBS Sports, ESPN, NBC's Game of The Week, ABC Nightline, FNN, CBS News Network, Rod Michaud's Sports Talk, Home Shopping Network, CNBC, Channel 5's Good Day New York, NBC's Sunday A.M., and major radio shows on such stations as The Art Rust Show, WABC, WFAN, WCBS and WNBC affiliates.

ALAN ROSEN

70-I Chestnut Ridge Road, Montvale, NJ 07645

(201) 307-0700 • Fax (201) 307-1653

Bill and Diane Dodge, Doubleheaders (Wayne Varner, Mike Wheat, and Bill Zimpleman), Fleer Corporation (Paul Mullen, Vincent Murray, and Jeff Massien), Steve Freedman, Gervise Ford, Larry and Jeff Fritsch, Tony Galovich (American Card Exchange), Georgia Music and Sports (Dick DeCourcey), Dick Gilkeson, Steve Gold (AU Sports), Bill Goodwin (St. Louis Baseball Cards), Mike and Howard Gordon, George Grauer, John Greenwald, Wayne Grove, Bill Haber, Bill Henderson, Jerry and Etta Hersh, Jay and Mary Kasper, Allan Kaye, David Kohler (SportsCards Plus), Paul Lewicki, Neil Lewis (Leaf), Lew Lipset, Mike Livingston (University Trading Cards), Mark Macrae, Bill Madden, Major League Marketing, Michael McDonald (The Sports Page), Mid-Atlantic Sports Cards (Bill Bossert), Brian Morris, B.A. Murry, Ralph Nozaki, Mike O'Brien, Oldies and Goodies (Nigel Spill), Optigraphics/Score Group, Jack Pollard, Jeff Prillaman, Gavin Riley, Alan Rosen (Mr. Mint), Clifton Rouse, John Rumierz, San Diego Sport Collectibles (Bill Goepner and Nacho Arredondo), Kevin Savage (Sports Gallery), Mike Schechter, Barry Sloate, John E. Spalding, Phil Spector (Scoreboard, Inc.), Sports Collectors Store, Rick Starks (Megacards), Frank Steele, Murvin Sterling, Lee Temanson, Treat (Harold Anderson), Ed Twombly (New England Bullpen), Bill Vizas, Gary Walter, Bill Wesslund (Portland Sports Card Co.), Craig Williamson, Kit Young, and Ted Zanidakis. Of special help on this edition was B.A. Murry, who in early 1991 laid the groundwork for our Technical Services department before becoming our Senior Pricing Consultant.

Many people have provided price input, illustrative material, checklist verifications, errata, and/or background information. We should like to individually thank AbD Cards (Dale Wesolewski), Jerry Adamic, Ben Agave, Michael Albert, Will Allison, David S. Anderson, Dennis Anderson, Ed Anderson, Glenn Anderson, Shane Anderson, Bruce W. Andrews, Tom Antonowicz, Scott Apple, Ric Apter, Jason Arasate, Burl Armstrong, Neil Armstrong (World Series Cards), Bill Aubin (Field of Dreams), Robert August, Chris Austin, Shawn Bailey, Darryl B. Baker, Jeremy Baldwin, Ball Four Cards (Frank and Steve Pemper), Tim Bamford, John Barbier, Joe Barney, Daniel Barry, David M. Bartlett, Bob Bartosz (Baseball Card Shop), Nathan Basford, Ron Beatty, Robert Beaumont, Elvis Begley, Ken Behr, Jeff Belding, Eddie Benton, Carl Berg, Raymond P. Berg, C.D. Bergstrom, Dave Berman, Mark Besser, Beulah Sports (Jeff Blatt), Seth Bienstock, Brian Bigelow, John R. Bigus, Randy Binns, Josh Bird, George Birsic, Benjamin Blake, David Blanchard, Ron Bloede, James L. Boak, Robert Bodis, Bob Boffa, Steve Bohnenblust, Tim Bond (Tim's Cards & Comics), Matt Bosse, Brian W. Bottles, Bottom of the 9th, Michael Bow, Jeff Breitenfield, John Brenner, Bob Bresnahan, John Brigandi, Dan Britton, Philip Bronikowski, Chuck Brooks, D. Bruce Brown, Jenny Brown, Jody Brown, Garry M. Brownfield, David Brundage, Dan Bruner, Celeste Buckhalt, Ed Burkey Jr., Bubba Burnett, Raleigh Burns, Virgil Burns, Ned Busby, Grant Calhoun, California Card Co., Luis Canino, Danny Cariseo, Jim Carr, Patrick Carroll, Sam Carter, Pedro Cartes, Carves Cards, Ed Caston, Ira Cetron, Sandy Chan, Dwight Chapin, Ray Cherry, Bigg Wayne Christian, Richard Cianciotta, Cincinnati Baseball Cards, Chris Clark, Dave Clark, Derrick F. Clark, Marvin C. Clark, James Claugherty, Coin Corner & Hobbie, Collection de Sport AZ (Ronald Villaneuve), G. Collett, Andrew T. Collier, Les Colvin, Charles A. Coon, Curt Cooter, Kimberly Cooter, Steven Cooter, Lou Costanzo (Champion Sports), Tina Cox, Coyne Cards, Taylor Crane (Crane's Cards), James Craven, Chad Cripe, James Critzer, Tom Crook, Brian Cunningham, Paul Curran, Allen Custer, W.F. Cyrus Jr., Jim Dahl, Larry Daigneault, Phillip D'Amato, Dave Dame, Brett Daniel, Roy Datema, Jeffrey J. Daub, Brad Davis, Travis Deaton, Dee's Baseball Cards, Eric Delgadillo, Jonathan Delmas, Tim DelVecchio, Steve Dempski, Drew Dennington, John Derossett, Gilberto Diaz, David Dickens, Joel Dilley, Ken Dinerman (California Cruizers), Joe Dinglasan, Walter D. Dinkfelt, Discount Dorothy, Walter J. Dodds Sr., Richard Dolloff (Dolloff Coin Center), Dan Domino, Mike Donatelli, Peter E. D'Onofrio, Ron Dorsey, Thomas Drye, Richard Duglin (Baseball Cards-n-More), B.M. Dungan, Mike Dunn, Gerald Dupire, Heather A. Eades, Ron Edge, Ken Edick (Home Plate of Utah), John Ehm, Marc Ely, William Ension Jr., Richard Eudaley, Doak Ewing, Matt Fagerlind, Gail Fairbrother, R.J. Faletti, James Feathersmith, John Fedak, Daniel Fellows, Adam Felsenthal, David Festberg, Sam P. Figaro, Anthony Fillizola, Louis Fineberg, Jay Finglass, Anthony Fisher, Michael G. Fisher, Aaron Fong, Fremont Fong, Perry Fong, Craig Frank, Mark Franke, Walter Franklin, Gary Frazier, Guy Frodl, Timothy Fuller, Gary Fullerton, Richard Galasso, R. Gallagher, Stephen Gamblin, David Garza, Gerald R. Gatlin,

David Gaumer, Ricky Gelboim, Willie George, Tim Gerdes, Raymond Gillen, Herbert Gladhill, Pat Gobble, Dick Goddard, Alvin Goldblum, Brian Goldner, Greg Goldstein, Jeff Goldstein, Ron Gomez, Aaron A. Goodwin, Bryan Greaves, David D. Gresham, Dayton Griffith, Kraig Gross, Terry Gutberiet, Travis Ryan Habey, Shawn Hagene, Evan Hahn, Iran Hall Jr., Hall's Nostalgia, Hershell Hanks, Josh Hanman, Joel Hansen, Gregg Hara, Zac Hargis, Jed Hart, Walter Y. Hashimoto, Alex Haugh, Trevor Hawkins, Michael Head, Rick Heckler, Kevin Heimbigner, Joel Hellman, Arthur W. Henkel, Scott Heuer, Matt Hibbett, Austin Hill, Eric Hitchcock, Greg Hlavka, Adam Hochfeld, Irwin Hoffman, Gary L. Holcomb, Bob Hooper, Craig Huckaby, Travis Hummel, Aaron Hunt, Tom Imboden, Chris Imbriaco, Corey Inskip, Vern Isenberg, Robert A. Ivanjack (Kit Young Cards), Paul S. Jastrzembski, Paul Jennen, Donn Jennings Cards, Michael Jessap, Doug Jodts, L.D. Johansen, Don Johnson, Fred Johnson, Justin Johnson, Rob Johnson, Anthony Johnston, Richard A. Jones, Stewart W. Jones, Joe Juhasz, A.A. Julian III, Charles Juliana, Loyd Jungling, Dave Jurgensmeier, John Just, Kurt Kalafsky, Nick Kasemeotes, Frank J. Katen, Jerry I. Katz, Andrew F. Kazmierski, Don Kelemer, Marty Kenton, Rick Keplinger, Kevin's Kards, Michael Keyton, Gene Kieffer, John Kilian, Larry Killian, Jamie King, L. Kirkwood, Steve Klein, Steven Koenigsberg, Kenneth Krieger, Jeff Kroll, K & S Companies, Scott Ku, Thomas Kunnecke, Arthur A. Kusserou, Michael Landolina, Howard Landrum, Jason Lassic, Allan Latawiec, Rocco Lattanzi, Gerald A. Lavelle, Dan Lavin, William Lawrence, Joshua Lawson, Jerry Leahy, Cory Leader, Jonathan Lee, Morley Leeking, Ronald Lenhardt, Carmen Leon, Don Lepore, Irv Lerner, Shawn Leubner, Dr. Ernest J. Lewis, Tim Licitra, David Lloyd, Sue Longaker, Brett Love, Allan H. Lowenberg, Robert Luce, Lummus, Corinne Lyon, Dan Mabey, David Macaray, Jim Macie, Mike MacRoberts, Richard Maddigan, Robert F. Maerten Jr., Joe Magnani, Paul Marchant, Steve Markovic, Bob Marquette, Saul Martinez, Pat Massa, Bill Mastro, Duane Matthes, Dr. William McAvoy, McDag Productions Inc., [illegible] niel, Branson H. McKay, [illegible] Kay, Scott McKevitt, Tony [illegible] McPartland, Mendal Mearkle, [illegible] Ken Melanson, Ari Melber, [illegible] Mendy's Sports Cards, Eric [illegible], Dallin Merrill, Blake Meyer [illegible] ds), Charles L. Meyers, Joe Michalowicz, Lee Milazzo, Jimmy Milburn, D. Allan Miles (D.A.M. Cards of Richmond), Cary Miller, David (Otis) Miller, George Miller, Harold M. Miller, Jason Miller, Wayne Miller, Dick Millerd, Mitchell's Baseball Cards, Craig T. Miyamoto, Perry Miyashita, Jeff Moerssen, Peter Molick, Frank Monzo, Rick Moore, Bob Mosher, Mike Mosier, Matt Mozingo, Joe Mullins, William Munn, Jim Munter, Tony Murello, Mark Murphy, John R. Musacchio, Joseph Nardini, Eduardo Navarro, New York Card Company (David Greenhill), Eric Newport, Jim Newsom (Jim's Cards), Devin Nielsen, Sharon Niemi, David B. Niethamer, William R. Norris Jr., Eugene Nunes, Andy Nunnally, Bud Obermeyer (Baseball Cards, etc.), Mark Obert, Francisco Ochoa, John O'Hara, Keith Olbermann, William Oldfather, Ryan Ollila, Danny Orear, Dick Ornstein, John Ortega, Ron Oser, Luther Owen, Stephen Padwe, Travers Paine, Dave Pappenheim, Robert Parramore, Past Times, Clay Pasternack, James Paul, Rhett Paul, John Pawleska, Mickey Payne, Gary Pecherkiewicz, Michael Perrotta, Jon Peterson (Hit and Run Cards), Tom Pfirrmann, Larry D. Philbrick, Robert Pirro, Steve Pittard, David Pollack, George Pollitt, Seth Poppel, Don Prestia, Coy Priest, Bob Ragonese, Janice P. Rahm, Randy Ramuglia, Richard H. Ranck, Rick Rapa, Robert Ray, Phil Regli, Tom Reid, Fred Reis, H. Glenn Renick, Lonny Renick, John Revell, Dave Ring, Randy Rioux, Vincent Roberto, Jason Roberts, Dee Robinson, Tyler Rodin, Bill Rodman, Steven Rondorf, Michael H. Rosen, Martin Rotunno, Clifton Rouse, R.W. Roy, Jeremy Royels, Ernesto Ruiz, Joseph Rushlow, George Rusnak, Mark Russell, Tom Rutlin, Terry Sack, Joe Sak, Jennifer Salems, Barry Sanders, Everett Sands, Jon Sands, Gary Sawatzki, Fred Scade Jr., Michael Scarborough, Dave Schau (Baseball Cards), Kurt Schell, Joe Schenone, A.J. Schmidt, Sam Schmidt, W. Schoolcraft, Aron Schor, Joseph J. Schuld, Bruce M. Schwartz, Richard [illegible], Charlie Seaver, Chris Seholius, John Selsam, Tom Shanyfelt, Richard Sheldon, Geoff Shmidt, Don Shoaff, Jeff Shoemaker, Mark Shreve, Jerry Simmons, Art Smith, Eric Smith, John E. Smith, Michael Smith, Marshall G. Snedaker, David Snover, Fred M. Snyder, Joe Soldano, Mike Solis, John Spadora, John Spadora Jr., Carl Specht, Dave Spencer, D. Spurgeon, Dennis Srnel, John G. Stanek, Star City Cards, John Starkman, Chris Starks, Scott Steinbruegge, Lenny Steren, Bob Stern, Jim Stiern, Mark Stillwell, Brett Stiltner, Chad Stockwell, William A. Stone, Tim Strandberg (East Texas

Sports Cards), Edward Strauss, Richard Strobino, Mark Sumlin, Danny Summerlin, Superior Sport Card, Brad Sutton, Dr. Richard Swales, Ian Taylor, Lyle Telfer, L.E. Temanson, Sam Tessier, Ron Tetrault, Larry Tharp, Chris Thiemann, The Thirdhand Shoppe, James Thomas, Jim Thompson, Paul B. Thornton, Eric Thorson, Carl Thrower, Jim Thurtell, Tom Tillotson (Highland Sports Cards), Reece Todd, Al Tom, Patrick Tomberlin, Bud Tompkins (Minnesota Connection), Fred Tremiti, Harvey Trevino, Dr. Ralph Triplette, Mike Trotta, Umpire's Choice Inc., Eric Unglaub, Paul Valecce, Valley Cards, Jeff Vanover, Alan Vickroy, Steven Wagman, Brian Wagner, Frank Walls, Rob Walton, Jerry Wasilko, Jay Weaver, John Weaver, Mark Weber, Jordan Weinstein, John and Joe Weisenburger, Richard West, What-A-Card, Justin White, Mike White, Richard Wiercinski, Christopher M. Wiley, Ed Willett, Jeff Williams, Terry Williams, Scott Williard, Mark Willis, Darrell Winfield, Opry Winston, Chris Wohlfarth, D. Woldin, John Wolf Jr., Jay Wolt (Cavalcade of Sports), Carl Womack, John Wood, William L. Wood, Pete Wooten, Paul Yarnold, Ray Yeary, Yesterday's Heroes, Mark Yin, Kevin Yoho, Wes Young, Barry Zabell, Robert Zanze, Dean Zindler, Tom Zmuda (Koinz & Kardz), and Tim Zwick.

Every year we make active solicitations for expert input. We are particularly appreciative of help (however extensive or cursory) provided for this volume. We receive many inquiries, comments and questions regarding material within this book. In fact, each and every one is read and digested. Time constraints, however, prevent us from personally replying. But keep sharing your knowledge. Your letters and input are part of the "big picture" of hobby information we can pass along to readers in our books and magazines. Even though we cannot respond to each letter, you are making significant contributions to the hobby through your interest and comments.

In the years since this guide debuted, Beckett Publications has grown beyond any rational expectation. A great many talented and hard working individuals have been instrumental in this growth and [illegible] whole team is to be congratulated [illegible] her have accomplished. Our [illegible] ns team is lead by Associate [illegible] Backus, Vice Presidents Joe [illegible] Reed III, and Director of [illegible] o. They are ably assisted by [illegible], Therese Bellar, Dianne Boudreaux, Patrick Cunningham, Mary Gregory, Jeff Greer, Tracy Hinton, Teri McGahey, Kirk McKinney, Jeff Anthony, Kaye Ball, Marvin Bang, Wayne Bangs, Airey Baringer, Barbara Barry, Nancy Bassi, Kimberly Bauer, James R. Beane, Louise Bird, Cathryn Black, Terry Bloom, Lisa Borden, Lisa Boyer, Amy Brougher, Anthony Brown, Michael Brunelli, Chris Calandro, Randy Calvert, Emily Camp, Renata Campos, Mary Campana, Sammy Cantrell, Susan Catka, Jud Chappell, Albert Chavez, Theo Chen, Lynne Chinn, Tommy Collins, Belinda Cross, Randy Cummings, Shannon Cunningham, Todd Davis, Gail Docekal, Alejandro Egusquiza, Carrie Ehrhardt, Susan K. Elliott, Danny Evans, Bruce Felps, George Field, Sara Field, Gean Paul Figari, Jeany Finch, Kim Ford, Gayle Gasperin, Loretta Gibbs, Maria L. Gonzalez-Davis, Rosanna Gonzalez-Oleachea, Anita Gonzalez, Jenifer Grellhesl, Julie Grove, Patti Harris, Vivian Harmon, Beth Harwell, Jenny Harwell, Mark Harwell, Pepper Hastings, Joanna Hayden, Chris Hellem, Mike Hersh, Barbara Hinkle, Dan Hitt, E.J. Hradek, Rex Hudson, Mary Huston, Don James, Sara Jenks, Julia Jernigan, Jay Johnson, David Johnson, Fran Keng, Monte King, Sheri Kirk, Amy Kirk, Wendy Kizer, Rudy J. Klancnik, Rich Klein, Frances Knight, Tamera Krause, Tom Layberger, Jane Ann Layton, Scott Layton, Lori Lindsey, Cheryl Lingenfelter, Robert Luke, Louis Marroquin, John Marshall, Kaki Matheson, Lisa McQuilkin Monaghan, Omar Mediano, Edras Mendez, Theresa Merola, Sherry Monday, Robert Montenegro, Glen Morante, Mila Morante, Mike Moss, Randy Mosty, Daniel Moscoso Jr., Allan Muir, Hugh Murphy, Shawn Murphy, Maria Neubauer, Wendy Neumann, Brad Newton, Lisa O'Neill, Rich Olivieri, Stacy Olivieri, Abraham Pacheco, Laura Patterson, Mike Payne, Ronda Pearson, Robert Piekenbrock, Tim Polzer, Julie Polomis, Reed Poole, Roger Randall, Patrick Richard, Yamile Romero, Gary Santaniello, Grant Sandground, Walter Santos, Maggie Seward, Elaine Simmons, Dave Sliepka, Judi Smalling, Bob Smith, Steve Smith, Lynn Smith, Lisa Spaight, Margaret Steele, Cindy Struble, Dan Swanson, Doree Tate, Diane Taylor, Peter Tepp, Jim Tereschuk, Jana Threatt, Valerie Voigt, Steve Wilson, Carol Ann Wurster, and Robert Yearby.

The whole Beckett Publications team has my thanks for jobs well done. Thank you, everyone.

I also thank my family, especially my wife, Patti, and daughters, Christina, Rebecca, and Melissa, for putting up with me again.

CLEVELAND AREA SPORTS COLLECTORS SHOW PRESENTS TWO BIG SHOWS FOR 1993!

16TH ANNUAL CLEVELAND AREA SPORTS COLLECTORS SHOW
APRIL 15-18, 1993
FIFTH ANNUAL SUMMER/FALL CLASSIC
AUGUST 26-29, 1993
Holiday Inn - U.S. Route 82 and Interstate 71, Cleveland (Strongsville), OH
SHOW HOURS (Both Shows): THURSDAY, 5-10; FRIDAY, 12-10; SATURDAY, 10-8; SUNDAY, 10-4
ADMISSION: THURSDAY - $4.00; FRIDAY, SATURDAY & SUNDAY - $2.50
Children 6 years old and under admitted FREE all four days!

AUCTION OF QUALITY MATERIAL: Will be held at both shows on Friday and Saturday evenings from 7-10 • James R. Flory, Auctioneer, Dilgard & Associates, Inc., License #481 62-72-0481

GUESTS: To Be Announced - Watch for our ads in the May and September issues of *Beckett Baseball Card Monthly* and all hobby papers for guest information!

129 DEALER TABLES - ALL SPACE IS SOLD OUT!
Corporate Sponsor: Megacards (Conlon Collection)

HOTEL ACCOMMODATIONS: Please call (216) 238-8800 for direct room reservation service. Rooms are specially blocked for both shows. Single or double occupancy only $59.00 Please specify you are attending the show to get the special rate.

FOR SHOW INFORMATION: Please call (216) 331-7238 (8-11 p. m. EST)
24 hour fax service: (216) 243-4063
Mailing Address: P.O. Box 16754, Cleveland, OH 44116
Shows sponsored by Cleveland Area Sports Collectors Show, Inc.
Mike Roether, Geoff Sindelar, Clayton Pasternack

Beverly Hills BASEBALL CARD SHOP

LARGEST SELECTION AT THE LOWEST PRICES
Baseball • Football • Basketball • Hockey
Sets • Unopened Packs • Boxes • Cases
Rookies • Stars • Autographs

TOP PRICES PAID
NO COLLECTION
TOO LARGE OR
TOO SMALL

"IF WE DON'T HAVE IT, WE'LL DO OUR BEST TO FIND IT"

ROBERTSON
OLYMPIC
PICO
10 FWY
405 FWY

CONVENIENTLY LOCATED OFF THE 405 & 10 FREEWAYS BETWEEN OLYMPIC & PICO BLVD. ON ROBERTSON BLVD.

(310) 278-4263
Beverly Hills Baseball Card Shop
1137 S Robertson Blvd.

WE ONLY SOUND EXPENSIVE!

BUY - SELL - TRADE

ST. LOUIS CARDINALS SPECIALIST

ODDBALL SUPERSTAR SPECIALIST

B. A. MURRY CARDS

BASEBALL - BASKETBALL

709 TAYLOR DRIVE
CARBONDALE, IL 62901

SEND WANT LIST WITH AN SASE
(618) 457-8278

SPORTSNET IL-202

COLLECTORS WORLD

One of the largest selections of
NON-SPORTS • FOOTBALL & BASEBALL
GUM CARDS IN THE COUNTRY

Buying any vending packs, boxes, sports & non-sports wrappers, and wax packs of baseball, football, basketball & non-sports. Buying complete non-sports collections, large or small.

612 Quince Orchard Rd.
Gaithersburg, MD 20878
(301) 840-0520

235 Muddy Branch Rd.
Gaithersburg, MD 20878
(301) 840-9729

Mon.-Sat. 11-8
Sunday 11-5 • Closed Tues.

BASEBALL

WE
SELL - BUY - TRADE

HOCKEY

BOB - JOE

Locker Room

SPORTS CARDS
(617) 770-0362
557 HANCOCK ST.
QUINCY, MA 02170

FOOTBALL

BASKETBALL

CENTER FIELD, INC.

EST. 1978
M-F 1-6
Sat. 10-5

BUY - SELL - TRADE

BASEBALL AND FOOTBALL CARDS

- Over 500,000 in stock!
- Topps 1952 to present, Bowman Football
- SUPER STARS: 1952 - present

Founding Member

Rick & Jo Ann Hamilton
(612) 884-0355

10746 France Ave. So.
Bloomington, MN 55431

BURT BROWN **(505) 292-1149**

Baseball Nostalgia

Baseball & Football Cards
Autographs & Memorabilia

1510-B Wyoming Blvd. NE
Albuquerque, NM 87112

COMIC BOOKS • BASEBALL CARDS PLUS

(212) 831-2273

256 E. 89th St.
New York, NY 10128

SPORTS MEMORABILIA INSURANCE

Cornell & Finkelmeier, Inc.

P.O. Box 210
Wapakoneta, OH 45895
(419) 738-3314

THE NATION'S LARGEST INSURER OF SPORTS MEMORABILIA DEALERS AND COLLECTORS

BASEBALL, FOOTBALL & OTHER SPORTS CARDS
BOUGHT & SOLD

WANT LISTS FILLED

SASE Please

Pat's Coins & Cards

3229 WEST 24th ST.
ERIE, PA 16506

By Appointment Only
9 - 9
DAILY & SUNDAY

(814) 833-0566
OR (814) 838-9703

MAILING LISTS!

Names & Addresses of card collectors responsive to mail offers.
1000 names — $32.95

Smaller and larger lists available.

B&F SPORTS CARDS, DEPT. B84, BOX 1921
WOONSOCKET, RI 02895
(401) 765-0934

Mon.-Sat. • 10-9

Sunday • 1-6

E Gads!
BASEBALL CARDS

4050 NOLENSVILLE RD.
HARDING MALL • SUITE 111
NASHVILLE, TN 37211

ED GADDY
(615) 833-6910

Roanoke Coin Exchange
Towers Mall
Roanoke, VA 24015
703-982-8587

Baseball, Football,
Hockey, Basketball,
Non-Sports Cards
Mon-Sat 10-6

Lynchburg
Roanoke

Lynchburg Coin & Collectibles
218 Wards Road (Hills Plaza)
Lynchburg, VA 24502
804-237-2741

Coins, Stamps,
Gold, Silver
Bought & Sold Daily.

Specializing in
Sports Cards
through the mail

Send Your
Want List

TWO CAPITALS CARD CO.

P.O. Box 920
Williamsburg, VA 23187

Baseball · Football
Basketball · Hockey

All Inquiries
Promptly Answered

(509) 483-6403

BASEBALL CARDS & NORTH

BUY & SELL

KEN JOHNSON
MANANER

E. 34 WELLESLEY
SPOKANE, WA 99207

Hours: Mon. - Sat. 10:30 to 5:30

FOUR CLASSIC RYAN SCORE BASEBALL CARDS

not available in any other Score set

His 300th Win, 5000th Strikeout, 6th and 7th No Hitters

"This set is a must for every serious collector" **Mark Jordan**

This also includes 4 full color commemorative programs entitled "The Life and Times of Nolan Ryan"

ALL FOR $29.95 + 2.95
FOR SHIPPING AND HANDLING
(MasterCard and Visa accepted)

FREE: With each order,
a #7th No-Hit Poster ($8.00 value)

Call toll free 1-800-899-3106

Tarrant Printing, Inc.
P.O. Box 1850
Euless, TX 76039
Attn: Teresa

ALL ORDERS PROCESSED WITHIN 24 HOURS
DEALER & QUANTITY DISCOUNTS AVAILABLE

TEMDEE

Wholesale & Retail

We Carry A Full Line Of:

- **Complete Sets** In Football, Baseball, Hockey, Basketball & Non-Sports Cards.
- **Manufacturers** Include Topps, Fleer, Donruss, Score, Bowman, Leaf, Star, OPC, Upper Deck, Kelloggs, Pro Set Football, Hoops, Sportflics & Others.
- **Supplies** Card Pages (all sizes), Binders (2"&3"), Boxes (100, 400, 500, 600 & 800), Single Card Sleeves, Lucite Holders, Ball & Bat Holders, Plastic Cases and much more!
- **Pennants** All sports and major colleges, plus specials.
- **Autographed Baseballs**
- **Photographs**
- **Porcelain Figurines & Plates** Sports Impressions & Gartlans.
- **Unopened Boxes & Packs**
- **Yearbooks & Price Guides**
- **Souvenirs** Hats, Scarves, Bobble Dolls, Buttons & More.
- **Starting Lineups** For '88 & '89 in Baseball, Football & Basketball.
- **Minor League Sets** Pro Cards, Star Co. & Grand Slam.
- **Want Lists** Filled for all sports. Send for specific wants or needs with an SASE.

WE BUY AND SELL

Temdee

1201 Black Horse Pike
Turnersville, NJ 08012
(609) 228-8645

Store hours: Mon.- Fri. 12 - 8
Sat. 10 - 5 · Sun. 12 - 5

Let us know what your interests are. To get our FREE catolog send 60¢ or large 52¢ self-addressed stamped envelope.

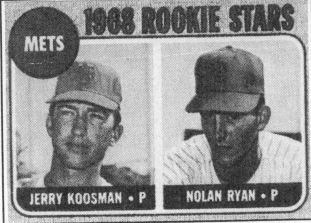

Unopened Boxes • Guaranteed Unopened

Baseball

Wax or Foil Boxes

1993 Topps Series 1 (540 Cards) $24.00
1993 Topps Series 2 (540 Cards) 24.00
1992 Topps (540) 18.00
1991 Topps (540) 16.00
1990 Topps (576) 16.00
1989 Topps (540) 16.00
1988 Topps (540) 16.00
1987 Topps (612) 32.00
1986 Topps (540) 45.00
1991 '53 Topps Archives (432) 90.00
1992 Stadium Club 1 (540) 45.00
1992 Stadium Club 2 (540) 45.00
1992 Stadium Club 3 (540) 45.00
1991 Stadium Club 1 (432) 200.00
1991 Stadium Club 2 (432) 135.00
1993 Action Packed (216) 50.00
1991 Bowman (504) 17.00
1990 Bowman (504) 17.00
1989 Bowman (432) 17.00
1992 Classic Best Minor League (432) 25.00
1993 Donruss Series 1 (540) 35.00
1993 Donruss Series 2 (540) 35.00
1992 Donruss Series 1 (540) 35.00
1992 Donruss Series 2 (540) 30.00
1991 Donruss Series 1 (576) 16.00
1991 Donruss Series 2 (576) 16.00
1990 Donruss (576) 14.00
1989 Donruss (540) 16.00
1988 Donruss (540) 14.00
1987 Donruss (540) 55.00
1985 Donruss (540) 350.00
1982 Donruss (540) 300.00
1992 Donruss Triple Play (540) 20.00
1993 Fleer Series 1 (540) 35.00
1993 Fleer Series 2 (540) 35.00
1992 Fleer (612) 33.00
1991 Fleer (540) 16.00
1989 Fleer (540) 27.00
1987 Fleer (612) 150.00
1992 Fleer Ultra 1 (504) 90.00
1992 Fleer Ultra 2 (504) 50.00
1991 Fleer Ultra (504) 25.00
1992 Leaf Studio (480) 45.00
1991 Leaf Studio (480) 40.00
1992 Leaf Series 1 (540) 40.00
1992 Leaf Series 2 (540) 40.00
1991 Leaf Series 1 (540) 40.00
1991 Leaf Series 2 (540) 40.00
1990 Leaf Series 1 (540) 325.00
1990 Leaf Series 2 (540) 325.00
1991 O-Pee-Chee Premier (252) 30.00
1993 Score (576) 24.00
1992 Score Series 1 (576) 18.00
1992 Score Series 2 (576) 18.00
1991 Score Series 1 (576) 16.00
1991 Score Series 2 (576) 19.00
1990 Score (576) 25.00
1989 Score (612) 16.00
1988 Score (612) 16.00
1993 Score Select (540) 45.00
1993 Score Pinnacle 1 (576) 55.00
1993 Upper Deck LO# (540) 40.00
1992 Upper Deck LO# (540) 30.00
1992 Upper Deck HI# (540) 30.00
1991 Upper Deck LO# (540) 30.00
1991 Upper Deck HI# (540) 30.00
1990 Upper Deck LO# (540) 40.00
1990 Upper Deck HI# (540) 50.00
1989 Upper Deck LO# (540) 160.00
1989 Upper Deck HI# (540) 140.00

Rack-Pack Boxes

1991 Topps (1,080 cards) 28.00
1990 Topps (1,104) 28.00
1989 Topps (1,032) 28.00
1988 Topps (1,032) 28.00
1987 Topps (1,080) 45.00
1986 Topps (1,176) 60.00
1988 Score (1,320) 30.00
1989 Bowman (936) 30.00

Cello Boxes

1989 Donruss (864 cards) 18.00
1988 Donruss (864) 15.00

Topps 500 Count Vending Boxes

1991 ....15.00
1990 ....16.00
1989 ....16.00
1988 ....16.00
1987 ....25.00
1986 ....28.00

Arena Hologram

Frank Thomas (1) 4.00
Ken Griffey Jr. (1) 4.00

Silver Star Hologram

Rickey Henderson (1) 7.00
Nolan Ryan (1) 7.00

Call for prices & availability on any 1993 products that are not listed.
We also carry football, basketball, hockey & non-sports cards. Call for prices.

All prices include shipping
Same day service with VISA or MasterCard
Please provide adequate street address for U.P.S. delivery
U.S. funds only
Alaska and Hawaii add 15% postage
Foreign add 25% postage
All prices subject to change

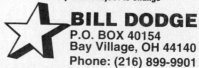

BILL DODGE
P.O. BOX 40154
Bay Village, OH 44140
Phone: (216) 899-9901

Fifteen years of quality mail order service

Complete Baseball Card Sets

Regular Issues

1993 Topps (792 Cards)	$28.00
1992 Topps (792)	25.00
1991 Topps (792)	25.00
1990 Topps (792)	25.00
1989 Topps (792)	25.00
1988 Topps (792)	25.00
Topps Sets 88-93	145.00
1987 Topps (792)	35.00
1986 Topps (792)	45.00
Topps Sets 86-93	220.00
1985 Topps (792)	110.00
1984 Topps (792)	100.00
1991 Topps '53 Archives (330)	95.00
1992 Stadium Club 1 (300)	38.00
1992 Stadium Club 2 (300)	38.00
1992 Stadium Club 3 (300)	38.00
1991 Stadium Club 1 (300)	160.00
1991 Stadium Club 2 (300)	110.00
1992 Stadium Club Skydome (200)	50.00
1993 Action Packed (84)	35.00
1991 Bowman (704)	20.00
1990 Bowman (528)	20.00
1989 Bowman (484)	20.00
All 3 Above Bowman Sets	57.00
1993 Donruss Series 1 (396)	20.00
1993 Donruss Series 2 (396)	20.00
1992 Donruss (784)	30.00
1991 Donruss W/Leaf Promo	30.00
1990 Donruss (716)	17.00
1989 Donruss (660)	22.00
1988 Donruss (660)	24.00
All 7 above Donruss Sets	155.00
1987 Donruss (660)	65.00
1993 Fleer Series 1 (360)	20.00
1993 Fleer Series 2 (360)	20.00
1992 Fleer (720)	45.00
1991 Fleer (720)	20.00
1990 Fleer (660)	17.00
1989 Fleer (660)	23.00
All 6 above Fleer Sets	135.00
1988 Fleer (660)	40.00
1987 Fleer (660)	100.00
1986 Fleer (660)	135.00
1992 Fleer Ultra 1 (300)	50.00
1992 Fleer Ultra 2 (300)	35.00
1991 Fleer Ultra (400)	30.00
1992 Leaf Studio (264)	30.00
1991 Leaf Studio (264)	40.00
1992 Leaf (528)	50.00
1991 Leaf (528)	55.00
1990 Leaf (528)	290.00
1992 O-Pee-Chee Premier (198)	25.00
1991 O-Pee-Chee Premier (132)	25.00
1990 O-Pee-Chee (792)	30.00
1989 O-Pee-Chee (396)	16.00
1988 O-Pee-Chee (396)	16.00
1993 Score (660)	25.00
1992 Score (900)	35.00
1991 Score (900)	25.00
1990 Score (704)	25.00
All 4 Above Score Sets	100.00
1990 Score (714)	35.00
1989 Score (660)	20.00
1988 Score (660)	20.00
1993 Score Select (405)	35.00
1993 Score Pinnacle 1 (310)	40.00
1993 Score Pinnacle 2 (310)	40.00
1992 Score Pinnacle 1 (310)	40.00
1992 Score Pinnacle 2 (310)	30.00
1990 Sportflics (225)	38.00
1989 Sportflics (225)	42.00
1987 Sportflics (200)	32.00
1993 Upper Deck Series 1 (420)	30.00
1993 Upper Deck Series 2 (420)	30.00
1992 Upper Deck (800)	52.00
1991 Upper Deck (800)	40.00
1990 Upper Deck (800)	55.00
1989 Upper Deck (800)	160.00

Traded or Update Issues

1992 Topps (132)	20.00
1991 Topps (132)	15.00
1990 Topps (132)	9.00
1989 Topps (132)	11.00
1988 Topps (132)	36.00
1987 Topps (132)	14.00
1986 Topps (132)	30.00
1985 Topps (132)	35.00
'85 to '92 Topps Traded	160.00
1992 Classic Best Minor League Update (50)	10.00
1991 Donruss Rookies (56)	8.00
1990 Donruss Rookies (56)	9.00
1989 Donruss Rookies (56)	20.00
1988 Donruss Rookies (56)	23.00
1987 Donruss Rookies (56)	25.00
All 5 Above Donruss Sets	80.00
1992 Fleer (132)	Call for Price
1991 Fleer (132)	10.00
1990 Fleer (132)	10.00
1989 Fleer (132)	14.00
1988 Fleer (132)	21.00
1987 Fleer (132)	18.00
1986 Fleer (132)	35.00
1985 Fleer (132)	40.00
All 7 Above Fleer Sets	140.00
1991 Fleer Ultra (120)	40.00
1992 Score (110)	20.00
1991 Score (110)	10.00
1990 Score (110)	22.00
1989 Score (110)	14.00
Above Score Sets '89-'92	60.00
1988 Score (110)	105.00
1992 Score Pinnacle Rookies (30)	15.00
1986 Sportflics Rookies (50)	20.00
1992 Upper Deck (100)	12.00
1991 Upper Deck, Final Edition (100)	20.00
1991 Upper Deck (100)	12.00
1990 Upper Deck (100)	15.00
1989 Upper Deck (100)	17.00

Specialty Sets

1991 Classic Draft Pick (51)	15.00
1987 Donruss Opening Day (272)	20.00
1987 Donruss Highlights (56)	5.00
1992 Fleer Ultra Award Winners (25)	135.00
1987 Fleer Minis (120)	10.00
1986 Fleer Minis (120)	12.00
1991 Leaf Gold Bonus (26)	110.00
1991 Leaf Promo Cards (26)	200.00
1992 Score Pinnacle Team 2000 (80)	55.00
1989 Score Masters (42)	12.00
1991 Topps Micro (792)	15.00
1991 Topps '90 Debut (171)	40.00
1990 Topps '89 Debut (152)	17.00
1990 Topps Bigs (330)	30.00
1988 Topps Bigs (264)	30.00
1989 Topps Sr. League (132)	9.00
1990 Topps Glossy All Stars (22)	6.00
1988 Topps Glossy All Stars (22)	6.00
1986 Topps Supers (60)	8.00
1991 Upper Deck Silver Sluggers (18)	45.00
1992 Upper Deck Home Run Heroes (26)	50.00
1992 Upper Deck All-Star Fan Fest (54)	25.00
1992 Upper Deck Hologram (54)	30.00

BILL DODGE
P.O. BOX 40154
Bay Village, OH 44140
Phone: (216) 899-9901

Fifteen years of quality mail order service

More Exciting Than A Flea-Flicker In Overtime!

Get Your Subscription To *Beckett® Football Card Monthly* Today.

Age
Name *(please print)*
ZIP
Address
Card
City
(please do not send cash)
Payment enclosed via:
Exp.
❑ Check or Money Order *(US funds only)*

Card No.
anteed! All foreign addresses
r for postage (includes G.S.T.).
Cardholder's Signature
iption Customer Service, please
4) 383-5772. Please allow 6 to 8 weeks
Cardholder's Name *(ple*
elivery of first issue.
y, P.O. Box 1915, Marion, OH 43305-1915
Check One Plea

❑ 1 year (1

❑ 2 y

Mail

Beckett® Football Card Monthly

DSB15-0

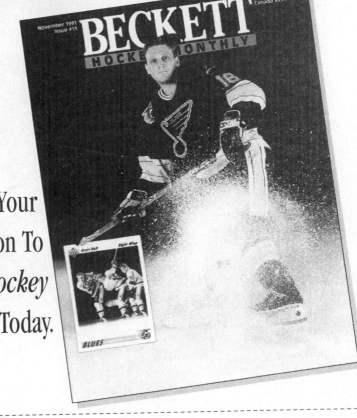